W9-BMZ-346

THE HOME RUN ENCYCLOPEDIA

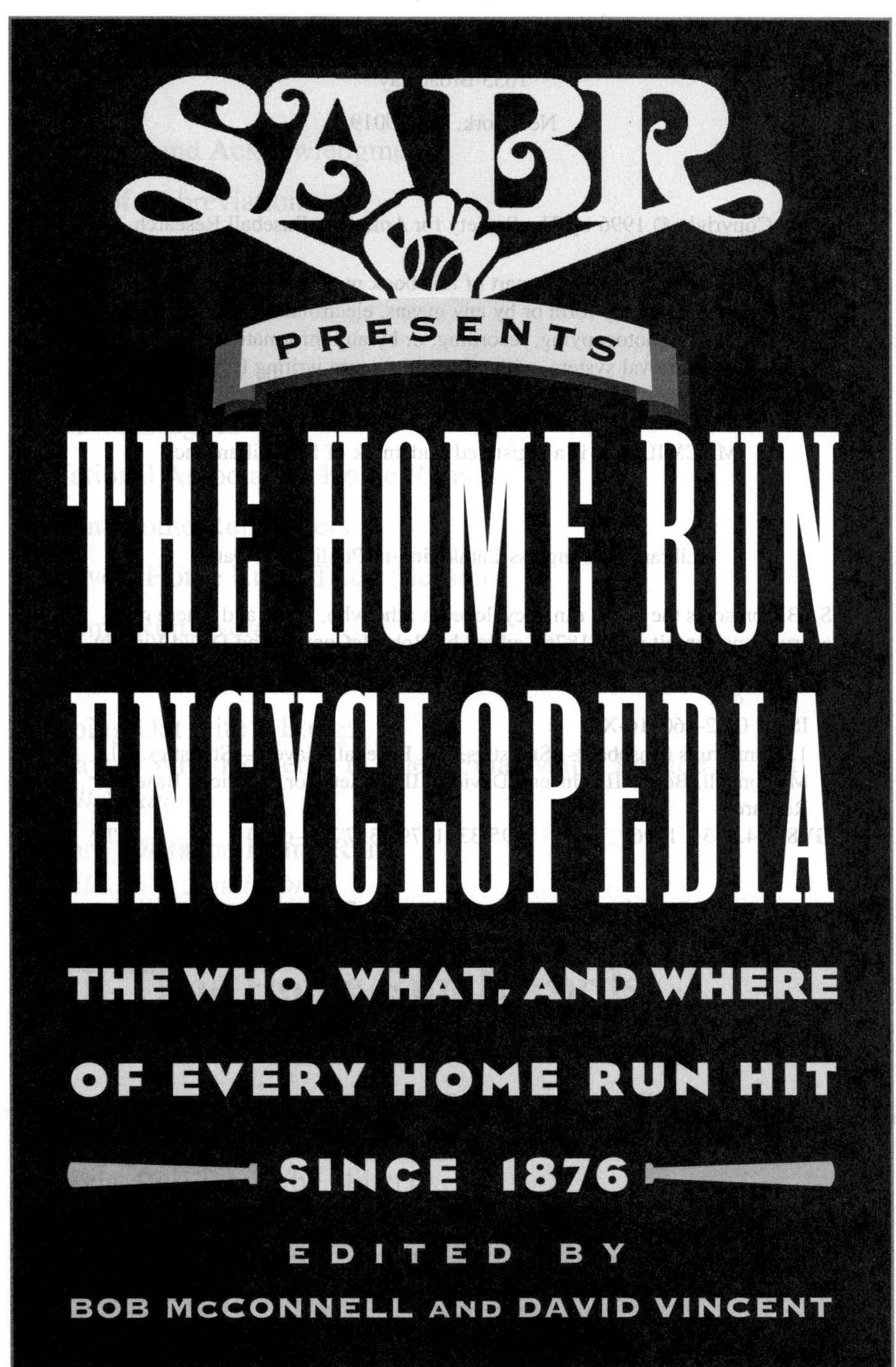

Macmillan • USA

Sources and Acknowledgments

The source material for this book is contained in the Tattersall/McConnell Home Run Log, a computerized database of all homers hit in the majors since the start of the National League in 1876. This database is the property of the Society for American Baseball Research (SABR). The original compilation of homers was created by John C. Tattersall, an early member of SABR. In 1941, Tattersall purchased a large number of baseball scrapbooks from the *Boston Transcript*, a newspaper that was going out of business. Contained in these books was a box score for almost every game in major league history. During the 1950s, Tattersall developed his Home Run Log from these box scores; this log lists each homer by year and team and contains information on the pitcher, inning, and other appropriate data. Tattersall was an expert on many aspects of baseball statistics and he was a primary source of information for the first edition of the Macmillan *Baseball Encyclopedia*.

After Tattersall's death in 1981, Robert C. McConnell, one of the original 16 members of SABR, assumed responsibility for maintaining the Home Run Log. McConnell updated the lists each year and expanded on the information already contained in the log. He also created listings of all homers hit in the World Series, League Championship Series, and All-Star games.

In 1990, the Computerization Committee of SABR started a project to convert the home run lists into an on-line format. James D. Johnston and Arnold Braunstein provided initial leadership for this task and the conversion was done by approximately 30 members of SABR. During the project, David W. Vincent assumed the lead role. Vincent has verified and expanded the information contained in the log and has coordinated efforts to create a complete and accurate history of major league home runs.

Information about all homers since 1984 has been provided by The Baseball Workshop and its president, Gary Gillette. The Baseball Workshop is a baseball research and consulting company founded in 1992 to collect and publish baseball statistics and analysis, which it provides to fans, the media, teams, and professionals such as player agents. A member of the Baseball Workshop team, David W. Smith, has worked closely with the editors to provide the data in an appropriate computer format.

Many homers before 1984 have been verified and had their information expanded through the courtesy of Retrosheet, a nonprofit organization founded by David W. Smith. Retrosheet collects scoresheets for games before 1984 and computerizes them for free distribution to the public.

The editors wish to thank both The Baseball Workshop and Retrosheet for contributing to the Tattersall/McConnell Home Run Log. For more information on these organizations, write to:

The Baseball Workshop
619 Wardsworth Avenue
Philadelphia, PA 19119

Retrosheet
6 Penncross Circle
Newark, DE 19702

Special thanks go to two people without whom this book would not have come into being. The first is our editor at Macmillan, Ken Samelson, whose love of baseball made him a joy to work with. Mark Alvarez, SABR's Director of Publications, spent many hours helping us find the right project and connecting us with the right publisher. Thanks, guys.

All biographical data on the players come from SABR's Biographical Committee and its current chair, Bill Carle. Since the creation of SABR in 1971, this committee has worked hard to create an accurate account of each player's personal information and many of the standard commercial research books on baseball draw from this committee's work.

In addition, the editors would like to thank the scores of SABR members who have contributed to this project through the years as well as the members of the media who have provided ideas for many of the leader lists contained in this book. The final thank you goes to the thousands of major league players who have provided so many thrills through the years by hitting all of these four-baggers.

Team Abbreviations

ALT	Altoona, PA	MIN	Minneapolis, MN
ATL	Atlanta, GA	MON	Montreal, QUE
BAL	Baltimore, MD	NWK	Newark, NJ
BOS	Boston, MA	NY	New York, NY
BRO	Brooklyn, NY	OAK	Oakland, CA
BUF	Buffalo, NY	PHI	Philadelphia, PA
CAL	Anaheim, CA	PIT	Pittsburgh, PA
CHI	Chicago, IL	PRO	Providence, RI
CIN	Cincinnati, OH	RIC	Richmond, VA
CLE	Cleveland, OH	ROC	Rochester, NY
COL	Columbus, OH	SD	San Diego, CA
	(American Association)	SEA	Seattle, WA
	Denver, CO	SF	San Francisco, CA
	(National League)	STL	St. Louis, MO
DET	Detroit, MI	STP	St. Paul, MN
FLO	Miami, FL	SYR	Syracuse, NY
HAR	Hartford, CT	TEX	Arlington, TX
HOU	Houston, TX	TOL	Toledo, OH
IND	Indianapolis, IN	TOR	Toronto, ONT
KC	Kansas City, MO	TRO	Troy, NY
LA	Los Angeles, CA	WAS	Washington, DC
LOU	Louisville, KY	WIL	Wilmington, DE
MIL	Milwaukee, WI	WOR	Worcester, MA

League Abbreviations

AA	American Association
AL	American League
FL	Federal League
NL	National League
PL	Players' League
UA	Union Association

Game Abbreviations

G1	first game of doubleheader
G2	first game of doubleheader

Part One

Introduction

Introduction

A Brief History of the Home Run

John Henry Holder hit the first home run that ever showed up in a published box score. This historic clout came on July 20, 1858, in a game between all-star aggregations from New York and Brooklyn at the Fashion Race Course on Long Island. Holder played for the well-known Brooklyn Excelsiors from 1858 through 1860.

Baseball was strictly an amateur sport during that period. However, professionalism began to creep in during the 1860s. Clubs enticed good players with under-the-table payments. Al Reach, an outstanding player during the period and one of the first professionals, hit about 100 home runs during the 10-year period from 1861 through 1870, with a high of 37 in 1867.

The Cincinnati Red Stockings became the first all-professional team in 1869. With George Wright as their leading hitter, the club went through the entire season undefeated. Wright was credited by various sources with between 49 and 59 home runs for the season.

In spite of the slugging of players such as Reach and Wright, home runs were scarce during those early days, in both amateur and professional ranks.

The National League was founded in 1876. The honor of hitting the first National League homer went to Ross Barnes of the Chicago White Stockings. In the fifth inning of a game at Cincinnati on May 2, 1876, Barnes "made the finest hit of the game, straight down the left field to the carriages for a clean home run," according to one report of the game. Two innings later, Charley Jones of Cincinnati hit the second home run. Barnes had been a star in the earlier National Association, but his best days were over. He hit only one more home run in the National League. On the other hand, Charley Jones became a good home run hitter. He finished his career with 56 homers, an admirable total for the period.

A total of 40 homers were hit in the National League during its first year. The figure dropped to 24 for the second year, with Chicago not hitting any. In 1878, the total decreased again, to 23. After that, there was a slow, but not always steady, increase.

In 1882, the American Association was founded to compete with the National League. The following season, an Association player became the first to reach double digits in homers for a season. Harry Stovey, playing for Philadelphia, hit his 10th home run of the year on August 1. He finished the season with 14 to win the home run crown; runner-up Charley Jones hit 10 that season.

An unusual situation arose during the 1884 season. The Chicago National League club played its home games at Lake Park. The exact dimensions of the playing field are not known, but the distance down the right-field line could not have been more than 215 feet and the fence cut across at a right angle so that the distance to right-center was not too great. In addition, the fence was not very high. In previous years, any ball hit over the fence had been a double; however, in 1884 management decided to spice up the game and declared that balls hit over the fence would be homers. Both right- and left-handed batters on the team became adept at popping balls over the short fence. As a result, Chicago hit 142 home runs—131 at their home park. Four players on the team exceeded 20 home runs, led by Ned Williamson with 27. Williamson's mark was to remain the record for many years. The following year Chicago moved to a new field.

In 1885, the National League added a new playing rule. It stated that any ball hit over a fence at a point less than 210 feet from home plate was a double. A distinctive mark was to be painted on the fence at that point. It is a safe assumption that the Chicago situation of the previous year triggered this rule.

In 1890, Harry Stovey, now playing for Boston in the Players' League, became the first major league player to reach 100 career home runs. He finished his career several years later with a total of 122. Roger Connor exceeded this figure during the 1895 season, and he wound up his career in 1897 with 138. Connor's mark stood until Babe Ruth came along.

The rule regarding balls hit over short fences was revised in 1892. Anything less than 235 feet was now a double.

The pitching position was moved back in 1893 to its current distance of 60 feet 6 inches. Hitting increased, but not as much as might be expected. The league averaged 0.45 home runs per game in 1892; this figure increased to 0.59 in 1893. In 1894, it leaped to 0.79 homers per game and then fell back to 0.61 per game in 1895. There have been a number of wide variations during the history of major league baseball in the homers per game average.

Things remained quiet on the home run front for the next 20 years. John Freeman hit 25 homers for Washington in 1899, but Tommy Leach led the National League in 1902 with six. League-leading totals didn't climb much higher than this for the next 15 years. In 1914, Babe Ruth arrived on the scene.

Ruth tied for the major league lead in home runs in 1918 while alternating between the mound and the outfield. The next year he started to assert himself as a home run slugger. The story was the same every time he hit a homer as a visitor in a ballpark: Ruth hits the longest drive ever seen at the park. By midseason, reporters had dug up the long-forgotten season record of Ned Williamson (27 in 1884). When Ruth tied and then surpassed the record, it was duly noted in the press. Ruth finished the 1919 campaign with 29 home runs. This was 12 percent of all the homers hit in the league that year. Ruth's Boston teammates hit a total of four.

The sudden death home run rule went into effect for the 1920 season. This rule stated that a player would be allowed to circle the bases and score, along with all runners in front of him, if he hit the ball out of the playing field in the last half of the last inning of a game, regardless of the score. Previously in this situation, only enough runners advanced to home plate to allow the team to win the game by one run. In other words, a batter did not get credit for a home run if his run was not needed to win the game.

There are 40 known cases in which a batter "lost" a home run to this rule. They range from Roger Connor on June 17, 1884, through Irish Meusel on April 19, 1918. Among the batters affected are Roger Bresnahan, Joe Tinker, Cy Williams, Frank "Home Run" Baker, and Babe Ruth. It should be emphasized that these hits were never homers according to the rules of the day.

Ruth was sold over the winter of 1919–20 to the New York Yankees. In 1920, his home run production jumped. Babe Ruth and the home run became synonymous. Each Ruth homer was duly noted in the headline of the sports page of almost every small-town newspaper in the country. The Babe finished the year with 54 home runs. This was 15 percent of the league total, an even higher percentage than the previous year, and he outhomered each of the other seven teams. The runner-up for the individual home run title that year was George Sisler with 19. Cy Williams, the National League leader, hit 15. In comparing these records to those of a couple of modern players, Roger Maris hit 4 percent of the league home runs when he set his record in 1961. Cecil Fielder passed the 50 mark in 1990 but hit only 2.8 percent of the league total.

In 1926, the rule regarding balls hit over short fences was revised again. It now required a drive of at least 250 feet to earn a home run.

Ruth continued to hit homers everywhere he went. In 1927, he hit 60. He finally retired in the middle of the 1935 season with a career total of 714 home runs—a figure that people said would never be broken.

Hack Wilson made the first serious run at the Babe's season record. Wilson hit 56 homers in 1930 while playing with the Chicago Cubs. Jimmie Foxx reached the 58 mark in 1932, and Hank Greenberg hit 58 in 1938.

Two new rules went into effect for the 1931 season that had a significant impact on home run hitting. The first rule stated that any fair ball that bounded into the stands or over the fence would be a double. Before this such hits had been home runs. Al Lopez, playing for Brooklyn, was the last beneficiary of the bounding ball rule. He bounced a homer into the left-field bleachers at Brooklyn on September 12, 1930.

The second new rule stated that a fly ball that left the playing field was to be judged fair or foul on the basis of its location at the time it left the playing field. Before passage of this rule, the ball was judged fair or foul on the basis of its location at the time it disappeared from the view of the umpires. In other words, if a ball curved foul after it was well beyond the fence but the umpire could still see it, then it was a foul ball. Tom Winsett of the Boston Red Sox was the first player to cash in on the fair/foul rule. On opening day (April 14, 1931) at Yankee Stadium, Winsett hit a ball that curved foul after leaving the playing field.

This rule had come up before. Prior to the 1920 season, the "where it disappears from view" ruling had been in effect. But at the start of the 1920 season, the rule had been changed to make the judgment on the basis of where the ball left the playing field. However, on June 24, 1920, the American League office announced that the rule (at that time Paragraph 48) would be changed to the "disappears from view" judgment and that this change would apply to both leagues. On at least one occasion in the mid-1920s, umpires spoke out about changing the rule to the "leaving the playing field" version.

Babe Ruth's career was nearly over when the two rules went into effect in 1931. How did they affect his career record? The Babe never hit a bounce homer, thus that rule did not help him. However, Ruth did hit many high, long drives and, no doubt, a number of them were called foul balls.

The next big event in the home run story was World War II. Most of the stars went off to war and surrendered time from their playing careers. In general, home run production dropped off during this period.

When the war ended, the stars returned and a new home run slugger appeared by the name of Ralph Kiner. Kiner was one of the dominant home run hitters in the National League for nine years and has one of the best home run averages of all time.

Another significant event occurred shortly after the end of the war that had a major impact on the home run. In 1947, Jackie Robinson became the first African-American in modern times to play in the major leagues. Although not a great home run hitter himself, Robinson paved the way for others who followed him. Within 10 years players such as Hank Aaron, Willie Mays, Frank Robinson, and Ernie Banks were hitting homers in the majors. All four of these men ended their careers with over 500 home runs.

After 60 years of eight-team leagues, the American League expanded to 10 teams in 1961. The schedule was expanded as well, from 154 to 162 games. The New York Yankees demolished the record for most homers in a season by a team by hitting 240 that year; the old record of 221 was held by the 1947 New York Giants and the 1956 Cincinnati Reds. But the biggest home run news of the year was the assault on Babe Ruth's season record by two members of that Yankee team. Roger Maris and Mickey Mantle made headlines all summer as they raced each other to match the Babe's historic total from 1927. Mantle ended the season in the hospital and Maris hit home run 61 on the last day of the season to set the current record.

In 1968, a special baseball records committee was formed to rule on a number of problems regarding records. One of these issues was sudden death home runs. At that time, there were 37 known cases, and the committee ruled that these batters should be credited retroactively with a home run. Since Ruth was one of the batters involved, this meant that the career homer record changed from 714 to 715. The announcement of this change caused a great uproar and the committee reversed itself in 1969.

Hank Aaron made his major league debut in 1954. Although he never reached 50 in a season, Aaron reached the 40 mark eight times in his career and the 30 mark an additional seven times. On April 8, 1974, Aaron hit his 715th home run to eclipse Babe Ruth's record; Aaron ended with 755 when he retired in 1976.

In the years since 1961, further expansion has offered more players than ever the chance to play in the big leagues. Many home run records have been broken in that time and many more unusual events involving homers have been witnessed by baseball fans. Also, the home run has been combined with other statistics in an attempt to analyze player performance in new ways. One of these pairings is the "30/30 Club," which notes a season in which a player has 30 homers and 30 stolen bases. This list has grown considerably over the last few years; however, the power/speed combination champion might be Jose Canseco, who in 1988 hit 42 home runs and stole 40 bases to become the first and only member of the "40/40 Club."

Minor Leagues

Most major league home run records have been exceeded in the minor leagues, with the exception of career totals.

A number of major leaguers have connected for two homers in an inning; however, no big leaguer has managed to hit three home runs in an inning. The most explosive inning by any slugger in organized baseball was achieved by southpaw swinger Gene "Half Pint" Rye, a stocky five-six, 165-pound player with Waco of the Texas League. He drove three shots over the fences of Katy Park in Waco during the eighth inning of a game on August 6, 1930. Waco scored 18 runs during that inning to swamp Beaumont 22–4.

With Jerry Mallett pitching for Beaumont, Rye led off the eighth inning and gave an indication of things to come when he drove the ball over the right-field fence but foul by a couple of feet. He completed his at bat by driving the ball fair over the left-field fence. Rye came up for the second time in the inning with two men on base. Walter Newman was now pitching for Beaumont. Half Pint blasted a pitch over the right-field fence. The bases were loaded when Rye came up for the third time in the inning. Poor Walt Newman was still pitching. Rye proceeded to hit another ball over the right-field fence to complete his big inning.

Rye hit 26 homers that season. Thus, an incredible 12 percent of his home runs were hit in one inning! He was brought up by the Red Sox the following year. However, he was injured early in the spring and was limited to 17 games with no homers in his short major league career.

Twelve major league players have had four home run games; a minor leaguer doubled this figure. Jay Clarke, playing for Corsicana of the Texas League, hit eight home runs in a game on June 15, 1902. The game had been switched to Ennis, Texas, due to the Sunday blue laws in effect in Corsicana at that time. Not many details are known about the game or the ballpark. In later years, Clarke told reporters that he thought the right-field fence was about 210 feet down the line. For the record, Corsicana defeated Texarkana 51–3 in the game. Clarke hit only three additional homers that season while playing in over 100 games. He hit a total of 22 minor league homers and six during a nine-year major league career.

Four players—Pete Schneider, Lou Frierson, Cecil Dunn, and Dick Lane—have hit five home runs in a minor league game. Schneider performed the feat on May 11, 1923, while playing for Vernon in the Pacific Coast League. Pete had a very interesting game. The details are as follows:

Inn.	*Result*
1	HR (2 RBI)
2	fly out
3	HR (4 RBI)
4	HR (3 RBI)
6	double (hit two feet from top of center-field fence)
7	HR (4 RBI)
	HR (1 RBI)
9	line out to center field

The game was played at Salt Lake City with Vernon winning 35–11. Schneider had previously put in six years in the majors as a pitcher before converting to the outfield.

Cecil Dunn and Lou Frierson were long-time minor leaguers who never made it to the majors. Dunn had his five-homer game on April 29, 1936, while playing for Alexandria of the Evangeline League. Frierson's big day was on May 30, 1934, for Paris of the West Dixie League.

Dick Lane is the last player to hit five homers in a game, connecting on July 3, 1948, while playing for Muskegon of the Central League. Lane hit only 18 home runs during a four-year minor league career and none during a 12-game stretch with the Chicago White Sox in 1949.

Seventy-one players have hit four home runs in a game. This includes Buzz Arlett, who did it twice. Amazingly, Arlett's two big games came within 33 days of each other in 1932.

The most dramatic four-homer game was played on August 31, 1954, at Roswell, New Mexico. Joe Bauman was shooting for the organized baseball season home run record of 69. Going into this Longhorn League game against Sweetwater, Joe needed six homers in his remaining seven games to break the record. His chances did not look too bright. After the fireworks had concluded in this game, Joe's chances looked much better; he now only needed two in the remaining six games. He went on to hit four more and set a record of 72, which still stands.

Bob Seeds of Newark (International League) had one of the greatest two-day batting sprees in the history of the upper-level minor leagues. On May 6, 1938, Bob hit four homers and two singles to knock in 12 runs. The next day, he added three more home runs to his collection. Seeds tore up the International League during the first part of the season. After 59 games, he was batting .335 with 28 homers, 73 runs scored, and 95 RBI. The Yankees, who owned the Newark club, decided that Seeds did not fit into their plans and sold him to the Giants in June.

Of the players with four or more home runs in a game, 32 made the majors, but only 19 of them played as many as 100 major league games. George Kelly, a Hall of Famer, is probably the best-known player on the list. However, Tom Brunansky and Matt Williams are better known to more recent fans. Brunansky is the top major league home run hitter on the list with 271. He is followed by Williams (225) and Jim Lemon (164).

Batting statistics are incomplete for the early years of the minor leagues. Thus, we can't be sure who the season home run record setters were. In 1894, Perry Werden hit 42 homers for Minneapolis of the Western League. Historians accepted that as the record. Werden hit 45 the following year while still with Minneapolis. This record stood until 1923, when Moses Solomon hit 49 for Hutchinson of the Southwestern League. Then Clarence Kraft hit 55 for Fort Worth (Texas League) in 1924, Tony Lazzeri hit 60 for Salt Lake City (Pacific Coast League) in 1925, and Moose Clabaugh hit 62 for Tyler (East Texas League) in 1926. The record then lasted for four years until Joe Hauser connected 63 times for Baltimore (International League) in 1930. Hauser upped the figure to 69 in 1933 with Minneapolis (American Association). Bob Crues tied the record while playing for Amarillo of the West Texas–New Mexico League in 1948. Then Joe Bauman came along, as mentioned above, and set the standard of 72 that still stands.

Nine players have reached the 60-homer mark, with Joe Hauser turning the trick twice.

Players with 60 or More Homers in a Season

Player	*Team*	*League*	*Year*	*HR*
Joe Bauman	Roswell	Longhorn	1954	72
Joe Hauser	Minneapolis	American Association	1933	69
Bob Crues	Amarillo	West Texas–New Mexico	1948	69
Dick Stuart	Lincoln	Western	1956	66
Bob Lennon	Nashville	Southern Association	1954	64
Joe Hauser	Baltimore	International	1930	63
John Clabaugh	Tyler	East Texas	1926	62
Ken Guettler	Shreveport	Texas	1956	62
Tony Lazzeri	Salt Lake City	Pacific Coast	1925	60
Forrest Kennedy	Plainview	Southwestern	1956	60

The career record is held by Hector Espino. With the exception of 32 games with Jacksonville of the International League in 1964, Espino spent his career south of the border. His first two seasons were in the Mexican Center League; then he played 23 years in the Mexican League. The runner-up to Espino is another longtime Mexican League player, Andres Mora. Mora, however, spent some time in U.S. leagues, including parts of four seasons in the majors. Of the top 10 career leaders, eight made the majors. However, of the eight, only Joe Hauser made a respectable showing in the majors.

Minor League Career Leaders

Hector Espino	484
Andres Mora	438
Buzz Arlett	432
Nick Cullop	420
Merv Connors	400
Joe Hauser	399
Bobby Prescott	398
Jack Pierce	395
Jack Graham	384
Nelson Barrera	378

Other Interesting Facts

During a stretch of less than one month during the 1923 season, Bob Ostergaard of Galveston (Texas) hit five home runs. Every one of them was a grand slam.

In the first game of a Western League doubleheader on July 1, 1923, the first four batters of the game for Wichita hit homers. The batters were Lyman Smith, Jocko Conlan, Wes Griffin, and Jim Blakesley.

Bob Crues of Amarillo (West Texas–New Mexico) hit 20 home runs in August 1948. This is the most that any player in organized ball has ever hit in one month.

Ken Myers of Las Vegas (Sunset) hit two grand slams in the third inning of a game on May 2, 1947. Pitcher Ned Klingensmith added a third slam as Las Vegas scored 16 runs in the inning. Las Vegas hit 10 homers in the game to route Ontario 30–5.

Two other players have hit two grand slams in one inning. Armando Flores of Laredo (Gulf Coast) hit two in the eighth inning on June 25, 1952. Lance Junker of Redwood (California) hit two in the ninth inning on June 30, 1983.

The Douglas team of the Arizona-Mexico League hit nine home runs in a game that was called after eight innings due to darkness on August 19, 1958. Each player in the lineup hit one homer.

During the 1952 season, Cordele (Georgia-Florida) hit a home run in their 73rd game. This was the only homer that the team hit during its 139-game season. While the league could be considered a pitcher's league, the other seven teams did manage to hit 185 home runs that year.

There have been three occasions on which teammates each hit two home runs in the same inning. They are Oscar Vitt and Paul Strand of Salt Lake City (Pacific Coast) on May 13, 1923; Roy Peeler and Len Cross of Knoxville (Tri-State) on August 14, 1947; and Alex Ochoa and Brent Miller of Bowie (Eastern) on June 5, 1994.

In the seventh inning of a home game against Omaha on August 9, 1952, Bill Pinckard of Denver (Western) hit a long drive to left field. Left-fielder Dick Cordell made a frantic grab for the ball as he crashed into the fence. The ball bounced out of his glove, hit the wall, rebounded, and caromed off his head over the fence. After a lengthy dispute, the umpires ruled it a home run. This gave Denver a 1–0 victory.

Brothers Kitty and Roy Brashear hit consecutive homers in the first inning for Vernon in a Pacific Coast League game on

August 3, 1910. Neither of the brothers was considered a home run slugger, especially Kitty, who hit only 36 during a long career.

Harry Heslet set a California League record with 51 homers in 1956 while playing for Visalia. He did not hit more than one home run in any game.

Bob Crues holds the organized baseball record for most grand slams in a season with eight. He set the mark in 1948 while playing for Amarillo in the West Texas–New Mexico League.

The Sacramento team of the Pacific Coast League set the season record in organized baseball with 305 home runs in 1974. Playing in makeshift Hughes Stadium, Sacramento hit 250 homers in their home park and their opponents hit 241. This totals 491 homers at the park, where the distance down the left-field line was only 233 feet.

National Association Home Runs

The National Association operated from 1871 through 1875. It was the first organized professional league. Many baseball historians do not consider this a true major league, though many of its players went on to star in its successor, the National League.

Home runs were hit in the league at about the same rate as they were during the early years of the National League—that is to say, not many were hit. The honor of hitting the first National Association homer went to Ezra Sutton of the Cleveland Forest Citys. In a game at Chicago on May 8, 1871, he hit a ball over the center fielder's head in the fourth inning off pitcher George Zettlein. Sutton connected again in the seventh and thus became the first player with a multiple home run game.

The first grand slam homer was hit by Charles Gould of the Boston Red Stockings on September 5, 1871; Zettlein of the Chicago White Stockings was again the victim. This was the only slam hit in 1871.

Career Leaders

Lipman Pike	15
Jim O'Rourke	12
Levi Meyerle	10
George Wright	9
Ned Cuthbert	8
George Hall	8
Cal McVey	8
Joe Start	8
Fred Treacey	7
Tom York	6

Yearly Home Run Leaders

1871		
Levi Meyerle	PHI	4
Lipman Pike	TRO	4
Fred Treacey	CHI	4
John Bass	CLE	3
Ned Cuthbert	PHI	3
Ezra Sutton	CLE	3
1872		
Lipman Pike	BAL	6
Alfred Gedney	TRO	3
1873		
Lipman Pike	BAL	4
Levi Meyerle	PHI	3
George Wright	BOS	3
1874		
Jim O'Rourke	BOS	5
John Clapp	PHI	3
Cal McVey	BOS	3
Jim White	BOS	3
1875		
Jim O'Rourke	BOS	6
George Hall	PHI	4
Joe Start	NY	4

Non–Home Run Hitters

Who was William Holbert? No, not the founder of the National League; that was William A. Hulbert, who was recently elected to the Hall of Fame. William H. Holbert was a National League catcher from 1876 to 1888. His claim to fame is that he is the only major league player to go to bat at least 2,000 times in his career without hitting a home run.

This section is about the homerless Holberts of the baseball world, the non–home run hitters. They can't be called hitless wonders because some of them were good hitters—they hit the ball well, just not far.

Holbert was not an isolated case in the dead-ball era. The infrequent homer hitter has always been around. Several recent players are good examples. Jerry Remy ended his career in 1984, going his last 2,292 at bats without a home run. Duane Kuiper ended his career a year later with a streak of 1,997 homerless at bats. Al Newman hit his only major league home run as an Expo in 1986. He went to the American League the following year and accumulated 1,893 at bats in the junior circuit before retiring after the 1992 season. This is the American League record for most at bats in a career without hitting a home run.

Another recent player is 23-year pitcher Don Sutton. Don completed his big league career with 1,354 at bats and no homers. He is the top pitcher in the non–home run hitter sweepstakes; Tommy Bond doesn't qualify because he played some games at other positions. Sutton could have "improved" his record if he hadn't spent 5½ years in the American League near the end of his career. Obviously, they didn't let him bat in the AL. (By the way, Sutton was not a complete stranger to the home run, since he surrendered 473 of them to batters during his career. This places him fourth on the career list for homers allowed.)

The following table shows the players with the lowest career home run averages, in other words the top non–home run hitters.

The table is broken down into four groups, based on length of service. There are several good hitters in this list, such as Sam Rice, Lloyd Waner, and Richie Ashburn, all of whom compiled career batting averages over .300.

As defined in the next article in this volume, home run average is the average number of home runs that a player would hit in a season with 600 at bats.

Lowest Career Home Run Averages

7,500+ AB	*AB*	*HR*	*HR Ave.*
Larry Bowa	8,418	15	1.069
Don Kessinger	7,651	14	1.098
Stuffy McInnis	7,822	20	1.534
Maury Wills	7,588	20	1.581
Rabbit Maranville	10,078	28	1.667
Fred Tenney	7,595	22	1.738
Monte Ward	7,647	25	1.962
Richie Ashburn	8,365	29	2.080
Lloyd Waner	7,772	28	2.162
Sam Rice	9,269	34	2.201
5,000+ AB	*AB*	*HR*	*HR Ave.*
Eddie Foster	5,652	6	.637
Donie Bush	7,210	9	.749
George McBride	5,526	7	.760
Roy Thomas	5,296	7	.793
Bill Wambsganss	5,236	7	.802
Terry Turner	5,917	8	.811
Wally Gerber	5,096	7	.824
Sparky Adams	5,557	9	.972
Miller Huggins	5,557	9	.972
Johnny Evers	6,137	12	1.173
2,500+ AB	*AB*	*HR*	*HR Ave.*
Duane Kuiper	3,379	1	.178
Dave Force	2,950	1	.203
Emil Verban	2,911	1	.206
Jimmy Slagle	4,994	2	.240
Al Bridwell	4,167	2	.288
Tommy Thevenow	4,164	2	.288
Frank Taveras	4,043	2	.297
Johnny Cooney	3,372	2	.356
Mike Tresh	3,169	2	.379
Bill Bergen	3,028	2	.396
1,000+ AB	*AB*	*HR*	*HR Ave.*
William Holbert	2,335	0	.000
Tom Oliver	1,931	0	.000
Irvin Hall	1,904	0	.000
Pat Deasley	1,466	0	.000
Tommy Bond	1,441	0	.000
Roxy Walters	1,426	0	.000
Paul Cook	1,364	0	.000
Don Sutton	1,354	0	.000
Joe McGinnity	1,297	0	.000
Waite Hoyt	1,287	0	.000

Another way to measure lack of home run performance is by checking what players went through an entire season without hitting a homer. The following table shows the top 10 performances in that category. Note that many of the seasons listed are in more recent times.

Most AB, Season, No Home Runs

Player	*Team*	*Year*	*AB*
Rabbit Maranville	PIT NL	1922	672
Doc Cramer	BOS AL	1938	658
Frank Taveras	PIT NL	1978	654
Marvell Wynne	PIT NL	1984	653
Maury Wills	LA NL	1965	650
Larry Bowa	PHI NL	1971	650
Dave Cash	MON NL	1977	650
Nellie Fox	CHI AL	1952	648
Sparky Adams	CHI NL	1927	647
Tom Oliver	BOS AL	1930	646

Donie Bush had six homerless seasons with at least 500 at bats, including four consecutive years from 1916 through 1919. Ironically, Bush never led the majors in the category of most at bats, no homers. Conversely, Doc Cramer had five homerless seasons with 500+ at bats and each one was good enough to lead the majors. Like Bush, Cramer put together four consecutive seasons, 1936 through 1939. Maury Wills and Ozzie Smith, two switch-hitting shortstops, are the only other players with five homerless seasons with at least 500 at bats.

Bush and Cramer each compiled long at-bat streaks without homers, due to their consecutive years without hitting any home runs. The record in this category belongs to Tommy Thevenow, a National League infielder, who went from September 24, 1926, to the end of his career in 1938 without a four-base blow. This is a streak of 3,347 at bats. He hit two homers early in his career and they were both inside-the-park jobs.

In the American League, Eddie Foster, a third baseman who spent much of his career with the Washington Senators, went from April 20, 1916, to the end of his career without connecting for a four-bagger. His last homer came in Washington's 1916 opener with President Wilson in attendance. It was also an inside-the-park homer. If it hadn't been for that misplayed outfield fly, Foster would have had over 4,000 homerless at bats instead of 3,278.

It looked as if Johnny Cooney was going to go through his entire career without a home run. Johnny started in the majors in 1921 as a pitcher and part-time utility player. After a stint in the minors, he returned to the majors in the early 1930s as a full-time outfielder. As the 1939 season was winding down, Cooney was 38 years old and still homerless. Then on two consecutive days in late September he hit the only roundtrippers of his major league career.

As in the case of most major league records, a minor leaguer has surpassed Thevenow's streak. Albert E. Wright chalked up a run of 4,607 at bats during the late 1930s and early 1940s, mostly while playing in the Pacific Coast League. John O'Neil set an organized baseball record with a streak of 4,635 at bats from June 12, 1942, to the end of his career. His streak included 4,541 at bats in the minors and 94 for the Philadelphia Phillies in 1946.

Most Consecutive At Bats Without a Homer

Player	*AB*	*Homerless Period*
Tommy Thevenow	3,347	9/22/1926 to end of career (1938)
Eddie Foster	3,278	4/20/1916 to end of career (1923)
Al Bridwell	3,246	Start of career (1905) to 4/30/1913
Terry Turner	3,186	7/16/1906 to 6/30/1914
Sparky Adams	3,104	7/26/1925 to 6/30/1931
Jack McCarthy	3,021	6/28/1899 to end of career (1907)
Lee Tannehill	2,701	9/2/1903 to 7/31/1910
Doc Cramer	2,663	9/8/1935 to 5/21/1940
Donie Bush	2,617	8/29/1915 to 8/21/1920
Mike Tresh	2,568	5/19/1940 to 4/20/1948

Fewest Home Runs, Team (Season)

This compilation is divided into four eras. Each will be discussed separately.

Era 1: 1876 Through 1900

The National League is considered by many historians to be the first major league. This period covers the time from the start of the N.L. until the end of the century. Statistics for this period can be misleading. The playing schedule varied from 70 games in 1876, to 60 games in 1877 and 1878, to 84 games from 1879 through 1882, to 98 games in 1883, to 100-plus games for the balance of the century. There were more variations in the dimensions of the parks than in modern times; in addition, most ballparks in the last century were not enclosed in the outfield. Playing rules were still evolving, and a number of the rule changes affected batting performance.

It can be noted from the table below that the Chicago team hit six homers over the three-year period from 1877 through 1879. This was in spite of the fact that the great Cap Anson was in their lineup. Cap was one of the leading home run hitters of the nineteenth century, with 97 roundtrippers.

Several teams in the 1884 Union Association did not play a full schedule, and they are not included in this list.

1	CHI	NL	1877	0
2	STL	NL	1877	1
3	HAR	NL	1876	2
	NY	NL	1876	2
	STL	NL	1876	2
	BOS	NL	1878	2
	MIL	NL	1878	2
	BUF	NL	1879	2
	PIT	AA	1884	2
10	CHI	NL	1878	3
	IND	NL	1878	3
	CHI	NL	1878	3
	BUF	NL	1880	3
	PHI	NL	1883	3

Era 2: 1901 Through 1919

This period starts with the inception of the American League. Many historians regard 1901 as the start of "modern" baseball. Both the American and National leagues used a 154-game schedule during this period with the exception of 1901 through 1903 and 1919. The 1918 season was cut short due to World War I. Teams played from 123 to 129 games during that season.

The famous "Hitless Wonders" Chicago White Sox team of 1906 managed to slug seven homers; this was more than double the output of the 1908 White Sox.

1	CHI	AL	1908	3
2	CHI	AL	1909	4
	WAS	AL	1917	4
	WAS	AL	1918	4
5	PHI	NL	1902	5
	CHI	AL	1907	5
	STL	AL	1918	5
8	CHI	NL	1902	6
9	CHI	AL	1906	7
	CHI	AL	1910	7

Era 3: 1920 Through 1960

Babe Ruth had amazed the baseball world by hitting 29 homers in 1919, and the fans loved it. In 1920, many players started swinging for the fences. However, a few teams were a little slow in putting sluggers into their lineups, as can be noted from the table below. Also affecting this list is the fact that some ballparks had larger outfield areas: Notable among these were the Boston National League park, Braves Field, and the Washington park, Griffith Stadium.

1	PIT	NL	1920	16
	BOS	NL	1926	16
3	BOS	AL	1921	17
4	CIN	NL	1920	18
5	CIN	NL	1921	20
6	CIN	NL	1931	21
7	BOS	AL	1920	22
	WAS	AL	1924	22
	CHI	AL	1945	22
10	BOS	NL	1920	23
	CHI	AL	1944	23

Era 4: 1961 Through the Present

This period starts with the first expansion in the American League, which added two teams for a total of 10 and expanded its schedule to 162 games that year. The National League followed suit a year later. Further expansion of teams has followed regularly since then. Also during this time many teams reduced the distances to the fences in the power alleys, thus providing a more tempting target to batters.

The strike-shortened 1981 season statistics were not considered in this compilation. San Diego hit 32 homers that year, which prorated over a 162-game schedule calculates to 47 home runs.

1	HOU NL	1979	49
2	CAL AL	1975	55
3	TEX AL	1972	56
4	STL NL	1986	58
5	NY NL	1980	61
6	HOU NL	1963	62
7	CAL AL	1976	63
	STL NL	1976	63
9	SD NL	1976	64
10	KC AL	1976	65

Home Run Average

Many people use batting averages to measure a player's ability to produce base hits. Yet, when it comes to other offensive categories, totals are the criteria historically used to measure a player's performance. However, normalizing performance per opportunity allows more equitable comparisons.

With home runs being the most popular of the offensive categories, several methods have been devised to compute home runs averages. Two of the most popular formulas are home runs per 100 at bats and at bats per home run. The difficulty with these and other systems is that the averages do not have real meaning to the fan. When a player hits .300, this registers with a fan; that fan can decide what kind of season the player had.

This is not the case with the home run averages mentioned above. Saying a player hit 7.5 homers per 100 at bats does not immediately register with a fan. The fan must do some mental arithmetic to decide whether or not it is a good performance. The home run average used here is home runs per 600 at bats. In an average season, a full-time player will accumulate about 600 at bats. Thus, the home runs per 600 at bats reports the homer total for a player for a season.

Babe Ruth dominates in both season and career averages. In comparison with his contemporaries, he is even more dominant. During the 15-year period from 1919 to 1933, the Babe's season average never fell below 40.0 and overall for the period it was an amazing 54.86. During that same period, only ten other major leaguers reached the 40.0 mark. They did it 16 times among them. When the Babe set the single-season record of 70.74 in 1920, George Sisler had the second-best average with a figure of 18.07!

Ted Williams's 1953 season does not qualify for the list of top season averages because he did not hit 20 homers that year. However, it is worth mentioning. Williams returned to the Red Sox late in the season after serving as a Marine pilot in Korea. He played in 37 games and hit 13 homers to give him a home run average of 85.71. This is, by far, the highest figure for any player with 10 or more home runs in a season.

In 1995, Mark McGwire played another injury-plagued season. However, when he was in the lineup, he hit homers at the highest pace of any batter in history. McGwire broke Ruth's 75 year old record with 39 home runs in only 317 at bats.

Home Run Average, Season (Minimum 20 HR)

	Player	*Team*	*Year*	*HR*	*HR Ave.*
1	Mark McGwire	OAK AL	1995	39	73.82
2	Babe Ruth	NY AL	1920	54	70.74
3	Babe Ruth	NY AL	1927	60	66.67
4	Babe Ruth	NY AL	1921	59	65.56
5	Mickey Mantle	NY AL	1961	54	63.04
6	Hank Greenberg	DET AL	1938	58	62.59
7	Roger Maris	NY AL	1961	61	62.03
8	Hank Aaron	ATL NL	1973	40	61.22
9	Babe Ruth	NY AL	1928	54	60.45
10	Jimmie Foxx	PHI AL	1932	58	59.49
11	Ralph Kiner	PIT NL	1949	54	59.02
12	Mickey Mantle	NY AL	1956	52	58.54
13	Jeff Bagwell	HOU NL	1994	39	58.50
14	Kevin Mitchell	CIN NL	1994	30	58.06
15	Matt Williams	SF NL	1994	43	57.98
16	Hack Wilson	CHI NL	1930	56	57.44
17	Frank Thomas	CHI AL	1994	38	57.14
18	Hank Aaron	ATL NL	1971	47	56.97
	Babe Ruth	NY AL	1926	47	56.97
20	Jim Gentile	BAL AL	1961	46	56.79

Home Run Average, Career (Minimum 200 HR)

	Player	*HR*	*HR Ave.*
1	Babe Ruth	714	51.01
2	Mark McGwire	277	45.42
3	Ralph Kiner	369	42.54
4	Harmon Killebrew	573	42.20
5	Ted Williams	521	40.57
6	Dave Kingman	442	39.72
7	Mickey Mantle	536	39.69
8	Cecil Fielder	250	39.59
9	Jimmie Foxx	534	39.39
10	Mike Schmidt	548	39.37
11	Fred McGriff	289	38.43
12	Hank Greenberg	331	38.24
13	Jose Canseco	300	38.21
14	Willie McCovey	521	38.14
15	Lou Gehrig	493	36.97
16	Darryl Strawberry	297	36.80
17	Hank Aaron	755	36.64
18	Willie Mays	660	36.39
19	Hank Sauer	288	36.03
20	Eddie Mathews	512	35.98
21	Willie Stargell	475	35.95
22	Rob Deer	226	35.40
23	Frank Howard	382	35.33
24	Kevin Mitchell	220	35.28
25	Frank Robinson	586	35.14

The following players have home run averages high enough to make this career list, but did not meet the 200-homer minimum. They all have at least 100 homers, however.

Player	*HR*	*HR Ave.*
Albert Belle	194	41.00
Ken Phelps	123	39.81
Frank E. Thomas	182	39.51
Ron Kittle	176	39.00

Juan Gonzalez	167	38.70
Jim Gentile	179	36.76
Bo Jackson	141	35.35

The concept of team home run average is slightly different from individual players' home run average. One must think in terms of the average number of homers that each of the nine players in the lineup hit in a season. The team home run average, like that for individual players, gives a better picture of a season's performance. This list adjusts for the 154- versus 162-game schedule and also for the strike-shortened seasons of recent years.

In spite of adjusting for the length of the schedule, all but two of the top 10 home run averages have been achieved since the start of the 162-game schedule. Interestingly, these two are the only National League teams in the top 10.

Home Run Average, Team

	Team	*Year*	*HR*	*HR Ave*
1	NY AL	1961	240	25.90
2	CIN NL	1956	221	25.06
3	CLE AL	1994	167	24.91
4	NY NL	1947	221	24.82
5	CLE AL	1995	207	24.70
6	DET AL	1994	161	24.42
7	MIN AL	1963	225	24.41
8	COL NL	1995	200	24.03
9	DET AL	1987	225	23.90
10	SEA AL	1994	153	23.64

Lost Home Runs

In the history of major league baseball, many players have hit home runs that do not appear as part of their career records. Most of these "non–home runs" were lost to inclement weather, such as rain-outs, and will not be itemized here. However, there have been quite a few four-baggers that have been credited as other events (including nonevents) in the history of these players due to human error. This article details many of the stories of these "lost homers."

This category does not include the sudden death home run from the period before 1920. At that time, when the team batting last won the game after the eighth inning, the rules stated that that team could win by one run only. Thus, a batter was credited only with enough bases on his hit to score the winning run. For example, if a team was down by one run in the bottom of the ninth with runners on first and second and the batter homered, it would take an advance of three bases for the winning run to score. Therefore, the batter received credit for a triple. By the rules of the day, these were never home runs. (There are at least 40 of these hits.)

The first two lost homer stories are about Babe Ruth, and they concern two occurrences of the same feat. In 1930, Ruth hit two balls into the right-center-field stands in Philadelphia's Shibe Park. They hit a loudspeaker horn and bounced back onto the playing field. In both cases, the "homers" were ruled as doubles. The first was on April 15 off Lefty Grove and the second came on September 26 off Cy Perkins.

On April 26, 1931, Lou Gehrig hit a ball into the center-field bleachers at Griffith Stadium in Washington. It came in the first inning with Lyn Lary on first and two men out. However, the ball caromed back to the Senators center fielder, who caught it. Lary, rounding second base, saw the catch and jogged past Yankee manager Joe McCarthy, coaching at third. Lary returned to the dugout without circling the bases. Gehrig was called out for passing Lary and ended the year tied for the AL home run lead with Ruth. This was the last time McCarthy coached at third base.

Harvey Haddix pitched 12 innings of perfect ball against the Braves in Milwaukee on May 26, 1959. In the bottom of the 13th, Felix Mantilla reached first on an error and was sacrificed to second. Hank Aaron was walked intentionally. Joe Adcock then homered; however, after Mantilla scored, Aaron returned to the dugout without completing his trip around the bases and Adcock was called out for passing Aaron. The "homer" was credited as a double.

On August 28, 1960, Ted Kluszewski of the White Sox batted in the eighth inning of a game at Baltimore. The Orioles' Milt Pappas, leading 3–0, delivered a pitch as umpire Ed Hurley called time. Klu hammered a three-run homer, but it was called back by Hurley. Baltilmore won 3–1.

Clete Boyer homered off Cleveland's Jim Perry in Yankee Stadium on September 10, 1961. This was the sixth inning of the second game of a Sunday afternoon doubleheader. The ball hit in the far left-hand corner of the lower level of the grandstand and bounced back onto the playing field. Home-plate umpire Joe Linsalata signaled it a homer and immediately Jimmy Piersall ran out of the visitors' bullpen in left field. Piersall contended that the ball was in play and two umpires agreed with him (Frank Umont at third and Charlie Berry at second). Boyer, already in his home run trot, was tagged out at third base, receiving credit for a double and two runs batted in. The game was protested by the Yankees. (In the first game, Piersall fought with a fan who came onto the field.)

On August 2, 1964, Oriole Brooks Robinson's ball struck the foul pole down the left-field line high above the fence. Umpire John Rice ruled it in play and Robinson was tagged out sliding into third base. After the game Rice admitted that he probably made a mistake.

In the second game of a doubleheader at Fenway Park on August 10, 1965, Brooks Robinson's ball to left field was ruled in play by Lou DiMuro, the second-base umpire, even though it appeared to strike the net above the wall. It came in the third inning with two out and one on and Robinson legged out a triple on the play. He received credit for a homer in the seventh inning of the same game.

On April 21, 1967, Tony Oliva of Minnesota lost a home run because of a base-running blunder. Playing in Detroit in the third inning, Cesar Tovar was the runner at first base. Oliva hit the ball out of the park, but then passed Tovar between first and second. He was credited with a single and one RBI for scoring Tovar.

Oriole Don Buford hit a ball into the right-field seats in Fenway Park in the eighth inning of the game on July 18, 1969. Tony Conigliaro leaped and fell into the stands, but did not have the ball when he came up. The first-base umpire, Bob Stewart, gave no signal. Dave May, running at first, hesitated, then started back to first base. Buford passed him and May was called out while Buford circled the bases. A five-minute argument followed. Earl Weaver argued about Stewart's delayed home run call. Eventually, the correct calls were made: Buford was credited with a run-scoring single, and May with a run scored, even though those events never actually happened on the field. Home-plate umpire Red Flaherty allegedly called May out, which was why he stopped running. The hit came off Ray Jarvis, who was ahead 6–0 at the time. May's run was the only tally of the game for the Orioles.

Leo Cardenas lost a solo home run to an umpire's decision on September 3, 1970. In the eighth inning of a game in Minneapolis, Cardenas hit a ball that appeared to hit the left field foul pole off Kansas City pitcher Wally Bunker. However, the umpires ruled it a foul ball. Both Bill Rigney and Bob Allison were ejected for protesting the call and Cardenas finished his plate appearance with a strikeout.

In the first inning of a game in Anaheim on September 20, 1972, Kansas City pitcher Steve Busby hit a grand slam homer off Lloyd Allen. Unfortunately for Busby, first-base umpire John Rice called time as the play started, which nullified the blast. John Mayberry had already hit a slam in the inning, so the Royals would have been added to the very short list of teams with two grand slams in one inning (this list is included elsewhere in this volume).

On June 10, 1974, Phillie Mike Schmidt hit a towering fly ball in the Astrodome off Claude Osteen. The ball struck a speaker 117 feet off the floor 329 feet from home plate and was still rising when it struck the speaker. Schmidt only got a single out of the shot.

Giant Ed Goodson hit a home run in the third inning on June 19, 1974, off Bob Gibson at St. Louis. It came with Garry Maddox on first and no one out. Goodson passed Maddox between first and second and was credited only with a single and a run batted in.

On July 21, 1975, Cardinal catcher Ted Simmons hit a homer to lead off the fourth inning in San Diego. However, Padres manager John McNamara claimed that his bat was illegal. Home-plate umpire Art Williams agreed with McNamara because there were grooves cut into the fat part of the bat, clearly above the 18-inch area from the handle end of the stick. Williams ruled Simmons out and the bat was confiscated by crew chief Ed Vargo. The game was protested by the Cardinals, but they won 4–0.

In Milwaukee on April 10, 1976, the Brewers' Don Money batted with the bases loaded in the bottom of the ninth. The Brewers were behind the Yankees 9–6. Because of the noise from the packed house, Dave Pagan did not hear that first baseman Chris Chambliss was granted time and delivered a pitch. Money's apparent game-winning grand slam was nullified and he eventually hit a sacrifice fly for the final run of the game. The Brewers protested the outcome to no avail.

Catcher Tim McCarver of the Phillies celebrated the U.S. Bicentennial on July 4, 1976, by hitting a grand slam in the second inning of the first game of a doubleheader at Pittsburgh. The 375-foot homer came off Larry Demery and barely cleared the fence. However, after rounding first base, McCarver passed Garry Maddox, who was returning toward first thinking the ball might be caught. McCarver was called out and received credit for a single and three runs batted in. The Phillies still beat the Pirates 10–5. (Perhaps the most interesting note here is that twice in two years Garry Maddox was passed on the bases by batters! In describing the speed of Maddux, Ralph Kiner once said, "Two-thirds of the earth is covered by water; the other one-third is covered by Garry Maddox.")

Ralph Garr of the White Sox homered off Minnesota's Paul Thormodsgard in Minneapolis on June 24, 1977. It came in the third inning with two men on and no one out. Jim Essian, the runner on first, thought the ball might be caught by the Twins' right fielder, Dan Ford, so he retreated toward first base. Garr was watching the flight of the ball and passed Essian after rounding the bag. He was credited with a single and two runs batted in.

On June 5, 1979, Seattle's Willie Horton hit a towering fly ball in the eighth inning of a game in the Kingdome. The drive, off Detroit's John Hiller, hit a speaker in left field and was ruled a single. Without the interference, it would have been Horton's 300th home run, which came the next day off Jack Morris.

Pittsburgh's Lee Lacy batted in the bottom of the eighth inning of a game on May 14, 1982, as the first batter to face Tom Hume of the Reds. The bases were loaded with no outs and Lacy hit one of Hume's pitches out of the park. However, in the celebration during his run around the bases, Lacy passed Omar Moreno between first and second. He was credited with a single and three runs batted in. Luckily for him, Moreno's run won the game for the Pirates 8–7.

On April 29, 1985, Yankee Bobby Meacham batted in the top of the fourth inning in Texas with two runners on and one out and homered off Frank Tanana. While Meacham was running toward and around first, the runner at first, Willie Randolph, was headed back to the bag to tag up. Neither Randolph nor Meacham expected the ball to leave the yard. They collided just past first base and Meacham was credited with a two-run single. By the way, this was Billy Martin's first day on the job for his third stint as New York manager.

On July 22, 1993, Kirby Puckett of Minnesota hit a ball just to the left of the end of the "baggie" hung over the Metrodome's right-field fence. It was ruled in play, even though replays clearly showed that it was a home run.

Larry Walker of the Rockies hit a ball into the first row of seats at Coors Field on May 5, 1995. However, it rebounded so quickly off a seat back and back onto the field that second base umpire Randy Marsh thought it hit high off the wall. Walker got a double out of what should have been the 100th home run of his career. The hit came off Ismael Valdes of the Dodgers.

At Shea Stadium on August 23, 1995, the Giants led 3–2 with two out in the ninth inning with Chris Jones at bat for the Mets. Jones hit a drive to right field, which appeared to be a game-tying homer off Terry Mulholland. However, first-base umpire Gary Darling ruled the ball foul, even though replays of the hit showed the ball hitting the pole. Mulholland struck out Jones on the next pitch to end the game.

Going Out with a Bang: Players Who Homered in Their Final Major League At Bat

Bill Deane

On September 28, 1960, Ted Williams closed out his career in grand fashion. The legendary slugger came to the plate in the eighth inning for his final big league at bat, against Baltimore's Jack Fisher. On the third pitch, Williams launched a blast into Fenway Park's right-center-field bullpen for his 521st and last home run. It was a storybook finish to a Hall of Fame career.

Williams wasn't the only man to homer in his final at bat, however: No fewer than 34 other players have "gone out with a bang." Most did it in virtual anonymity, with observers neither realizing nor caring that a career was coming to a close. Record books duly note players who homer in their *first* major league appearances, but none has ever listed those who did it in their last, because this feat had never been documented—until now.

Here, for the first time in print, is a list of the 35 perpetrators (among players inactive in 1995) of this unusual feat. It includes a few well-known names and a whole lot of little-known ones. There is a story to go with each name.

The first player to homer in his last at bat isn't included on this list, because his league has not yet been recognized as "major." The National Association, forerunner of the National League, operated from 1871 to 1875 as the first organized professional circuit and, obviously, represented the highest level of baseball in those years. Bill Boyd, third baseman for the Brooklyn Atlantics, was completing his fourth N.A. season on October 9, 1875. In the eighth inning Boyd came to bat against Hartford's Bob "Death to Flying Things" Ferguson at Brooklyn's Union Grounds. With an 11–0 lead, Ferguson had stepped over from third base an inning earlier to mop up for ace Tommy Bond. Boyd connected for a home run (possibly a grand slam, but documentation is lacking) to cap a six-run inning, but Hartford piled on nine runs in the bottom of the frame to pad a 20–7 win. Bill Boyd never again played professional baseball.

Following are details of the 35 instances of a player homering in his final major league at bat, listed chronologically:

1. Buck West, September 18, 1890. In a National League game played "on bad grounds" at Canton, Ohio, Pittsburgh led Cleveland 9–8 going into the bottom of the eighth inning. Outfielder Milton "Buck" West, batting cleanup in his final big league game, came up against Bill Phillips with two on. Buck delivered his third career home run, giving Cleveland the lead, and they held on to win 11–10.

2. Frank O'Connor, August 7, 1893. O'Connor, a 22-year-old Dartmouth College recruit, had joined the Phillies as a pitcher a few days earlier. In one inning of work at Baltimore on this day, O'Connor gave up three walks and two runs, raising his career ERA to 11.25 for three games. His batting record was much more impressive: a 1.000 lifetime batting average and a 2.500 slugging percentage. Having singled in his only previous big league at bat, O'Connor batted against Baltimore's Bill Hawke in the second inning and hit a three-run homer. The Phillies lost anyway, 14–9, and O'Connor never again played in the majors.

3. Hercules Burnett, September 29, 1895. Playing in his sixth and final major league contest, center fielder Burnett had already singled, tripled, stolen a base, and scored two runs when he came up in the seventh inning. Facing Cleveland's Phil Knell, Burnett completed his Herculean performance by drilling a solo home run. His Louisville Colonels (N.L.) won 13–8 in a home game stopped by darkness after eight innings.

4. Ed Scott, August 3, 1901. In one of the most dramatic ends to a career, Scott pitched a 10-inning victory at Milwaukee and hit the game-winning home run over the left-field fence. It came off Bill Reidy with nobody aboard in the top of the tenth, and gave Cleveland an 8–7 win. Ed had hit only one homer in 170 previous big league at bats.

5. Chick Stahl, October 6, 1906. Stahl was completing his 10th season in the majors, having established himself as a star. The outfielder sported a .305 lifetime average and had played for four pennant winners, all in Boston. He was now acting manager of the Red Sox, who were closing their season at home against the New York Highlanders.

New York led by three when Stahl batted in the bottom of the eighth. Stahl was not much of a home run threat, having hit but 35 in 5,068 previous big league at bats; nevertheless, he connected for a two-run shot off Tom Hughes. It wasn't enough, as the Sox lost 5–4.

Less than six months later, Chick Stahl was dead at age 34. Stahl ended his life by drinking three ounces of carbolic acid on March 28, 1907.

6. Del Gainer, September 30, 1922. Gainer had been bouncing between the majors and minors since 1909. Although he had played in 10 big league seasons, he had only 1,607 at bats (and 13 homers) to show for it. With southpaw Percy Jones pitching for the Cubs, the right-handed-hitting

Gainer was elected to start at first base for the Cardinals in game two of this day's doubleheader at Wrigley Field. Del came through with a three-run, first-inning home run to give the Cards a lead they would not relinquish. His heroics were forgotten by the second inning, however; Jones gave way to right-hander Virgil Cheeves, so St. Louis manager Branch Rickey—the prototypical percentages man—replaced Gainer with portside swinger Jack Fournier. Fournier went 0-for-2 but the Cards held on to win 5–3 in a game shortened to five innings by darkness.

Gainer never appeared in another major league box score, but returned to the minors for seven more seasons.

7. Mahlon Higbee, October 1, 1922. Just one day after Gainer's feat, "Hy" Higbee also concluded his career with a homer. The New York Giants were wrapping up their season with a doubleheader at home against the Boston Braves. In game two, Higbee was inserted in right field for his third and final Giants game. In the sixth inning Higbee picked out an Al Yeargin pitch from the gathering darkness and drove it over the fence in deep right-center field for a two-run blast. The game was stopped an inning later with New York victorious, 3–0. Higbee finished his major league career with a .400 average and just the one home run.

Higbee returned to the minors, and he was through with baseball by 1927.

8. Walt Kinney, May 9, 1923. Kinney was a hurler for Connie Mack's Athletics during one of their hapless periods. He had more success during his career as a batter (.280 average) than as a pitcher (11–20 record). On this day, the 29-year-old Kinney was brought into a game at St. Louis, inheriting a 3–0 deficit score in the third inning. He held the Browns at bay until the sixth, when Philadelphia scored three to tie up the game. Contributing to his own cause, Kinney hit an Urban Shocker pitch into the right-field stands for a solo homer. But in the bottom of the frame, Kinney was knocked out of the box during a four-run rally. The A's lost 10–5; ironically, as it turned out, Kinney's homer had made him the pitcher of record—on the losing side!

Kinney was out of organized baseball for four years, put on the "ineligible list" for playing in an outlaw league. He returned to pitch six seasons in the Pacific Coast League before retiring in 1932.

9. Clay Van Alstyne, May 7, 1928. Van Alstyne was appearing in his sixth and final major league game as a pitcher for the Washington Senators, mopping up during a blowout loss against the Browns. The home team trailed 15–1 as the pitcher's spot came due to bat in the bottom of the ninth. Manager Bucky Harris saw no reason to bother with a pinch-hitter, so he let Van Alstyne—a career 1-for-7—bat for himself. Van Alstyne, who had singled earlier in the game and scored the Nats' only run thus far, hit a Lefty Stewart pitch for a home run. Final score: 15–2.

Van Alstyne is one of six pitchers to homer in his final at bat, and one of nine players whose *only* career circuit clout came in his last try. He returned to the minor leagues for five more years.

10. Johnny Schulte, September 20, 1932. Schulte had joined the Braves late in the 1932 season, having been plucked from the stands for a job. Released by the Browns earlier that year, the St. Louis native was watching a Cardinals' home game when Boston catcher Pinky Hargrave broke a leg. Manager Bill McKechnie sent a courier into the stands to fetch Schulte and signed him after the game. It was the second time that year Schulte had been hired out of the Sportsman's Park seats, having joined the Browns when Rick Ferrell broke his hand in a game Johnny was watching.

In Schulte's final big league appearance, he drove a solo home run into the lower-right-field stands at New York's Polo Grounds. It came off the Giants' Fred Fitzsimmons in the ninth inning, but did not prevent a 13–3 New York victory. It was Schulte's 14th major league homer, but his first in four years. He later coached with the Yankees and Red Sox. With the Yankees, he was principally responsible for the signing and development of Hall of Famers Phil Rizzuto, Yogi Berra, and Whitey Ford. Following his coaching career, Schulte scouted for Cleveland before retiring in 1963.

11. Mickey Cochrane, May 25, 1937. When Cochrane hit a game-tying solo home run off the Yankees' Bump Hadley in the third inning, nobody realized it would be the final official at bat of Mickey's career. At 34, the Tigers' catcher-manager was still at the top of his game. The homer had brought his season average over the .300 mark for the ninth time in his 13 big league seasons. Cochrane was regarded as the best all-around catcher in the sport, probably the best of all time.

Two innings later, Cochrane lay prostrate at Yankee Stadium's home plate, his skull fractured in three places. A Hadley fastball had sailed inside, crashing into Cochrane's temple with a sickening sound. He would battle for his life, slipping into and out of consciousness for some 10 days before recuperating. Except for a one-inning stint in a 1938 exhibition game, Mickey Cochrane would never play again. His career had ended not with a bang, but with a thud.

The Tigers were battling the Yankees in the pennant race as the two teams began a crucial series on May 25. "This first game is all-important," said Cochrane. "If we can win it we'll take the series." He had respect for the opposing pitcher that day. "He has everything," Cochrane had once said of Hadley. "A fastball that buzzes by your chin, and a curve that has you breaking your back when you swing at it." When Cochrane poled a Hadley pitch into the right-field stands, the score stood at 1–1. It was the same when Mickey batted two innings later. "I relaxed, thinking it would go by," Cochrane later said about the fateful pitch. "All of a sudden I lost sight of it . . . I think I could have played four or five more years, but there's nothing that can be done about that now." Mickey finished his career with a .320 lifetime average.

Cochrane returned as Tigers' manager in 1938, but without the same fire. He just wasn't able to lead as effectively from the bench as from the field. Mickey made a few brief returns to baseball: as a coach and later general manager with the Athletics in 1950; as a scout with the Yankees in 1955; and as a scout and later vice-president of the Tigers between 1960 and 1962. On July 21, 1947, Cochrane was inducted into the Baseball Hall of

Fame along with former batterymate Lefty Grove, who had debuted in the majors on the same day as Mickey.

12. George Jumonville, May 20, 1941. The infielder's lifetime batting record showed 5-for-40 (.125) with no home runs, hardly better than that of the pitcher, Si Johnson, for whom he was pinch-hitting. His Phillies were losing to the home Cardinals 4–0 as the sixth inning began. With nobody on base, Jumonville connected with a Clyde Shoun pitch for his first and last major league homer, and the Phils went on to win in eleven innings, 6–4. Jumonville played in the minors through 1943 before going into military service.

13. Paul Gillespie, September 29, 1945. In the second game of a doubleheader at Pittsburgh, Gillespie hit a two-run homer off Rip Sewell. It keyed a five-run rally in the fourth frame, two innings before darkness ended the contest with the Cubs victorious, 5–0. Gillespie did appear in a game the following day, but did not come to bat; the catcher also played in the 1945 World Series against Detroit, going 0-for-6, but retained the distinction of homering in his last regular-season at bat. Gillespie had also connected in his first big league at bat, for the Cubs on September 11, 1942; thus, two of his six career four-baggers made history. Gillespie returned to the minor leagues, playing until 1949.

14. Bert Haas, August 26, 1951. Haas knew that he was going to be released outright the following day, allowing him to hook on with Montreal of the International League. The 37-year-old utility player had played in nine big league seasons for five teams, and had accumulated just 21 career home runs in 2,439 at bats. The youngest and most successful of nine ballplaying brothers, Haas had begun his pro career in 1936, and became an All-Star with the Reds before suffering a fractured skull in 1948. He would perform as a minor league player and manager until 1962.

The White Sox sent him up to pinch-hit for pitcher Howie Judson in game two of a Comiskey Park doubleheader against the Yankees. It was the seventh inning, there was a man on base, and lefty Art Schallock was pitching. "I knew [Yankee manager Casey Stengel] thought he could get me out by having Schallock throw me a curveball," Haas recalls. Schallock did, and Haas deposited it out of reach. The Sox lost 8–6 but Haas had ended his big league career in style.

15. Joe Frazier, September 30, 1956. Cobra Joe—nicknamed by Eddie Stanky because of his ability to "strike like a snake" in the pinch—played in nearly 2,000 professional games, but only 217 were in the major leagues. Frazier made his first big league stop with Cleveland in 1947. From there it was back to the bushes, where he won the Texas League's Player of the Year Award in 1953 after topping the loop in runs, doubles, total bases, and batting. Promoted to the Cardinals the following year, Frazier led the major leagues with 20 pinch-hits. From St. Louis he went to Cincinnati, then to Baltimore, where he was wrapping up his big league career on this day.

It was a memorable finish. In a doubleheader at Washington, Frazier blasted out five hits, good for 10 total bases. In the nightcap, Senators' submarine pitcher Ted Abernathy was working on a one-hitter until the eighth, but Frazier doubled in that frame and hit a solo homer in the ninth to spark the Orioles to a 6–3 win. Frazier was released 11 days later, and he returned to the minors in 1957. He quit as a player in 1960, having amassed 1,728 minor league hits, including 144 home runs.

Frazier was far from through with the game, though. He later scouted, coached, and was a successful minor league manager. He made it back to the majors in 1976 as manager of the Mets. He led them to a third-place finish that season but was fired after a slow start in '77.

16. Marv Blaylock, September 28, 1957. Blaylock was in the throes of an 0-for-summer slump: He had not had a hit (in 16 at bats) since June 15, and had not even come to bat since July 27. The Phillies' first baseman had lost his starting job to rookie Ed Bouchee, and was now finishing his career as a pinch-hitter for pitcher Jim Hearn.

Batting against Brooklyn's Rene Valdez in the fifth inning, Blaylock blasted a solo home run. "The ball cleared the scoreboard in right-center field in Connie Mack Stadium, which was a good distance," recalled Blaylock more than 30 years later. The Phils lost 8–4 and Blaylock's contract was sold to Cincinnati after the season. The Reds "wanted me to report to Havana or Seattle," Blaylock said in explaining the end of his career. "I refused."

17. Ron Samford, September 7, 1959. Samford had a connection with the last perpetrator of this feat, Marv Blaylock: The two came up together in the early 1950s as promising youths in the New York Giants' system. Samford, an infielder, went from the Giants to the Tigers to the Senators, with whom he was winding down his career on this day.

It was the second game of a doubleheader at Baltimore. The game went into extra innings tied at one, but Washington erupted for seven runs in the top of the 10th to win 8–1. Capping off the rally, Samford—who had doubled earlier in the game—cracked a three-run homer off Ernie Johnson, who is now a Braves' announcer. It was the second and most recent time someone concluded his career with an extra-inning homer.

Samford appeared in four more games, but did not get another official at bat (he did have one sacrifice bunt). He returned to the minors, playing at the Triple-A level until 1963.

18. Ted Williams, September 28, 1960. So much has been written about Williams's career and his final home run that anything added here will seem superfluous. On the other hand, it would be ridiculous to ignore the story.

Ted Williams set out to become "the greatest hitter who ever lived," and he succeeded. Some players hit more than his 521 home runs, and a few batted higher than his .344 lifetime, but none did both. The left fielder won two Triple Crowns, and his staggering .483 career on-base percentage is the highest in the game's history. Ted's credentials might be even more awesome, including the all-time leaderships in walks, runs, and RBI, had he not lost five prime seasons in military service. He was overwhelmingly elected to the Hall of Fame on his first try in 1966.

Williams had a flair for the dramatic. He homered in his last regular-season at bat for San Diego in 1937, before moving to Minneapolis. He homered on the last pitch of the 1941 All-Star Game to give the A.L. a come-from-behind victory. He homered in his last at bat in 1952, before going off to Korea as a fighter pilot. Then, there was his last at-bat, in 1960.

Williams was 42 years old and ready to hang it up after this, his last scheduled game at Fenway Park, rather than travel to New York for the final three games of the season. It was a cool, gray day, and the air was heavy. Before the game, Williams was honored with gifts, and during it, it was announced that his uniform number would be retired. Everyone there knew how he would try to complete the day.

Against Baltimore starter Steve Barber in the first inning, Williams had walked on four pitches and come around to score on a sacrifice fly. Jack Fisher replaced Barber and held the Red Sox in check until the eighth, by which time the Orioles had built a 4–2 lead. Williams flied deep to center field in the third inning, then hit a long drive to right-center in the fifth. It looked to be gone, but right-fielder Al Pilarcik backed up against the wall and caught it. "I hit the living hell out of that one," Ted said upon his return to the bench. "If that one didn't go out, nothing is going out today."

Williams proved himself a better hitter than prophet in the eighth inning. A standing ovation greeted Ted's appearance, which the fans realized would probably be his last. "I was gunning for the big one," he would say later. "I really wanted that one." With nobody on base, he turned on a 1–1 fastball and sent it toward the right-center-field bullpen. "The ball kept going and going into the jowls of that strong wind," recalled Boston executive Haywood Sullivan, "and it finally made the bullpen." It traveled anywhere from 415 to 450 feet, depending on which account one chooses to believe. The *Boston Traveler* headlined it as the "Most Dramatic Moment in Baseball History."

After the game (which the Sox came from behind to win 5–4), Williams issued the following release: "I am convinced I've quit at the right time. There's nothing more I can do than hit a farewell home run. Goodbye." The statement, along with the home run bat and ball, would wind up in Cooperstown.

Williams returned to baseball in 1969 as manager of the Senators. He led them to the best Washington finish since 1945, earning the A.P.'s "A.L. Manager of the Year" nomination over Billy Martin and Earl Weaver. It was all downhill from there, though, and Williams left after the 1972 season (by which time the club had moved to Texas).

19. Don Gile, September 30, 1962. Gile was playing first base for Boston the day Ted Williams hit his farewell homer, but no one would have dreamed Gile would end his career in similarly dramatic fashion two years later.

Gile, who also caught for the Sox during his four-year career, entered his final day in the big leagues with a lifetime average of .142—more than 200 points lower than Williams's—and all of two home runs. In this season, he had a perfect record: 34 times up, 34 times retired. He broke the slump with a single in the first game of a season-ending doubleheader but, by the last inning of the nightcap, his 1962 record stood at 1-for-40.

Boston's Bill Monbouquette and Washington's Jack Jenkins were engaged in a pitchers' duel. There had been 16 strikeouts and only 12 hits in the game. Going into the bottom of the ninth, the score stood at 1–1, as it had since the third. Boston had one out and a man on first. Extra innings seemed imminent, but Gile stepped to the plate and *boom!* As suddenly as the ball disappeared from the confines of Fenway Park, it was all over: the game, the season, and Don Gile's big league career.

Gile played one more year in the Pacific Coast League before retiring.

20. Ed Hobaugh, September 2, 1963. "Hoby" had been called up from the minors for the third and final time. He had been pitching professionally since 1956, and had won nine of 19 decisions in his previous trials with the hapless Senators. On this day, he was picked to start at Cleveland in the second game of a doubleheader.

Cleveland led 3–2 going into the fourth, when homers by Don Zimmer and Ed Brinkman gave Washington three runs. Jerry Walker then came in to pitch to Hobaugh, a career .111 hitter with nary a home run to his credit. Nevertheless, Hobaugh recalls "a very strong feeling that I was going to hit the ball out of the park." Walker delivered a high fastball, and Hobaugh deposited it over the left-center-field fence.

Hobaugh was knocked out of the box in the bottom of the inning, but the Nats held on to win 8–7. The 29-year-old righty would appear in eight more games, all in relief, and walk in his only plate appearance on September 7. After the season, Hobaugh was traded to the Pittsburgh organization. He pitched for six more years in the minors.

21. Tony Kubek, October 3, 1965. Kubek joined the Yankees in 1957, alternating between third base, second base, left field, and center field. He batted .297, earning selection as A.L. Rookie of the Year.

Kubek became the team's regular shortstop, making the All-Star team three times and helping the Yankees to seven pennants. However, his batting averages started to tumble after 1962, a year in which he was in military service until August. Tony didn't realize it then, but a touch-football injury suffered in the service had literally broken his neck: Three vertebrae in the cervical section of the neck were crushed, imperiling his spinal cord and impairing his reflexes and mobility. The injury was finally diagnosed after the 1965 season, and Kubek was forced to retire at age 29 rather than risk permanent paralysis. He finished with a .266 career average and 57 homers.

Before he quit, Kubek had had one last hurrah. In his final game, at Boston's Fenway Park, he went 3-for-4 with a sacrifice and three RBI. In his last at bat, facing monstrous relief pitcher Dick Radatz in the ninth inning, Tony poled a two-run homer to pad a New York victory. Kubek didn't realize he had homered in his last at bat until 1988, when he and Radatz were chatting near the batting cage at Fenway. "Dick talked about how easily he got Mickey out and the trouble he had with me," recalls Kubek.

Kubek was hired to do color commentary for NBC-TV's *Game of the Week* series starting in 1966. Three years later, he was promoted from the backup-game team to join Curt Gowdy in the national booth. Kubek became known as a bright, outspoken analyst, not afraid to ruffle feathers. He sometimes became embroiled in controversies with those he criticized, most notably George Steinbrenner.

Kubek was with NBC until 1988, also doing telecasts for CBC in Toronto. He later worked Yankees' games for the MSG cable network.

22. John Miller, September 23, 1969. Miller had only two major league home runs, but both made history: one came in his first major league at bat, the other in his last.

Miller made his big league debut with the Yankees on September 11, 1966. The outfielder–first baseman became the first Yankee ever to homer in his initial at bat, but went just 1-for-22 the rest of the year to earn a return trip to the minors. He resurfaced with the Dodgers at age 25 in 1969, but was hitting just .189 with no homers in 24 games. In the first game of a doubleheader at Cincinnati on this day, Miller was sent in to hit for pitcher Al McBean in the eighth. It was to be his last at bat, although he didn't know it at the time.

Miller came through with a solo home run off Jim Merritt, but the Dodgers lost 6–3. Miller technically appeared in one more game: He was announced as a pinch-hitter for Jim Brewer on September 27, but was replaced by lefty Len Gabrielson when the Giants brought in a right-hander.

Miller's contract was sold to Japan's Chunichi Dragons after the season.

23. Ken McMullen, September 14, 1977. Unlike most of the players on this list, McMullen was an accomplished slugger. Despite playing his entire career in pitchers' parks, with the Senators, Dodgers, Angels, Athletics, and Brewers, he hit 156 home runs, reaching double figures seven times in a row. His last circuit clout was unexpected, however.

His final appearance with the Brewers came a week after he tore a nail off one of his fingers. "I didn't expect to hit for another week," recalls McMullen, "but [I] got called to pinch-hit [for Jim Gantner] and was just trying to hit a sacrifice fly to score the run." It was the eighth inning of a game at Seattle, and the Brewers were clinging to a 6–5 lead. Tom House—best remembered as the man who caught Hank Aaron's 715th home run ball in the Braves' bullpen in 1974—was on the mound. "I took a pitch for a strike," says Ken, "and then swung at the next pitch almost one-handed and it went out." Milwaukee won 8–5.

McMullen was released on December 14, then retired. McMullen was aware of his last-at-bat feat. "I've never wanted to brag about it," he says, "but it's the only way to finish a career."

24. Kevin Pasley, October 1, 1978. Pasley had been playing professionally since 1971, had a few cups of coffee with the Dodgers between 1974 and 1977, and was winding up his major league career with the Mariners. Coming into the season finale against Texas, his lifetime totals showed 118 at bats, no home runs.

Pasley doubled and scored in his second trip to the plate against future Hall of Famer Ferguson Jenkins, but the Rangers were lighting up the Kingdome scoreboard. They led 9–2 by the time Pasley came up in the bottom of the seventh. He knocked Jenkins out of the game with his first and last big league homer, a two-run shot. Pasley did come to bat once more, drawing a walk from reliever Paul Mirabella, but the Mariners lost 9–4. Kevin was released after the season, aware he had homered in his last at bat, but not yet aware that it *was* his last at bat.

25. Mike Cubbage, October 3, 1981. Cubbage hit only 34 home runs during his eight-year career, but many were noteworthy ones. Four were grand slams, one each in 1975 (his first major league hit), '76, '77 (when he drove in five runs in one inning), and '78. One was part of a "cycle" performance in 1978. And one was hit off the last pitch he received in the majors in 1981.

Cubbage began his pro career in 1971. He moved up the ladder and made his first big league appearance at age 23 with the 1974 Texas Rangers. Two years later he was dealt to the Twins, developing into a solid third baseman. After an injury-plagued 1980 season, Cubbage signed a lucrative free-agent deal with the New York Mets. He was expected to solve the team's third-base problems, but instead lost his job to rookie Hubie Brooks. By the season's final weekend, Cubbage had accumulated just 79 at bats, with no home runs.

With the Mets down by two runs against the visiting Expos, Cubbage came in to pinch-hit for Doug Flynn in the bottom of the eighth. Facing ace reliever Jeff Reardon, Cubbage cracked a solo home run, but the Mets lost anyway 5–4. Cubbage was released during spring training, 1982, agreeing to a demotion to the minors. He remained with the organization as a minor league manager and major league coach, and served as Met manager for the final seven games of the 1991 season.

26. Joe Rudi, October 3, 1982. Of the perpetrators of this feat, only Ted Williams hit more than the 179 home runs collected by Rudi. And Rudi is the only man to homer in his last at bats in both regular-season and World Series play.

Rudi had three trials with the A's in the late 1960s before he finally stuck with the big club in 1970, batting .309 in 106 games, with help from Oakland batting coach Charlie Lau. Joe would reach his zenith two years later.

In 1972, Rudi led the A.L. in hits and triples, batted .305, and finished second in the league MVP voting. The outfielder made the All-Star team and paced his club to the first of three consecutive world championships. In game two of the World Series, his homer provided the margin of victory in a 2–1 contest, and his spectacular leaping, wall-crashing, backhanded catch—one of the best in Series history—in the bottom of the ninth saved the game for Oakland.

Rudi had another big year in '74, leading the A.L. in doubles and total bases, and again finished second in MVP balloting (he is one of 11 players to twice finish second without ever winning the award). He also won his first of three straight

Gold Glove Awards. His homer won the final game of the World Series.

Rudi stayed with Oakland through 1976, before signing a rich free-agent deal with the Angels. Hampered by injuries, his career spiraled downhill. He went to Boston in 1981, then finished out his career back with Oakland in '82. This set the stage for his farewell homer.

On this date—a year to the day after Mike Cubbage's farewell homer—Oakland was wrapping up its season at Kansas City. Rudi had doubled and scored (on a homer by Dave McKay, also playing his last game) in the second, and the game was tied at three when Joe came to bat in the fourth. Rudi walloped a two-run homer off Larry Gura and was replaced by rookie Kelvin Moore. Rudi watched as the A's held on to win 6–3.

Rudi, bothered by a torn Achilles tendon, retired following the season. He did not realize he had homered in his last at bat, recalling "nothing unusual" about the event.

27. Eddie Miller, September 30, 1984. Despite his stocky build, Miller was known more for stealing bases than hitting home runs. In 331 at bats spread over seven seasons, he had yet to put a positive number in the "HR" column. He spoiled that perfect record on this day.

Ed (his preferred nickname) started out in the Rangers' system, getting his first big league trial with them at age 20 in 1977. That fall, he was sent to the Braves in a four-team swap. In 1981, he was beaten out for a Braves' outfield spot by Rufino Linares—ironically, a future perpetrator of the "out with a bang" feat. Miller was dealt to the Tigers in 1982, and finally wound up with the Padres in '84.

At Atlanta, against his former team, Miller was inserted to replace batting champion Tony Gwynn in the season finale. Going into the ninth inning, the Braves' Pascual Perez held a three-run lead, but Miller led off the frame with his first and only big league four-bagger. The Padres added another run, but fell short, 4–3.

It was the end of the big league trail for Miller, who would finish his career in the Texas League in 1985.

28. Tony Brewer, September 30, 1984. Just hours after Eddie Miller's feat, Brewer duplicated it in Los Angeles. Batting against San Francisco's Mark Calvert in the seventh inning, Brewer drilled a solo shot—the only homer of his big league career—to ice a 7–2 victory.

Brewer began his pro career in the Dodgers' system in 1980, batting .371 in the California League. The outfielder continued to excel in the minors, but didn't make it to "The Show" until August 1984, after he had won the P.C.L. batting crown with a .357 mark. For the Dodgers, Brewer had come to bat just 34 times in two months and, nearing his 27th birthday, realized the club had no serious plans for him. "I knew I wouldn't be back," he recalls. Brewer was especially frustrated that he hadn't gotten to play in front of his family and friends at San Francisco's Candlestick Park a few days earlier, but the season finale would be televised in the Bay Area, so Tony's entourage would at least get to see him on TV on this, his last day in the majors.

Brewer had walked, singled, and driven in a run before he hit his homer. "I often think about it," he says of the farewell blast. "It is my greatest memory of U.S. baseball." Before the 1985 season, Brewer asked the Dodgers to sell his contract to Japan, and they acceded.

29. Willie Aikens, April 27, 1985. When Aikens's mother gave birth to a boy in 1954, 15 days after Willie Mays's historic World Series catch off Vic Wertz, she named him after his uncle, Willie. The doctor who delivered him added the middle name "Mays" (although it was never officially added to the birth certificate), predicting that the newborn would become a "famous ballplayer." Two decades later, the prediction was well on its way to realization, as Willie Mays Aikens became the Angels' number-one pick in the January 1975 free-agent draft.

Aikens got his first shot at the majors in 1977, but didn't stick. After winning the P.C.L. home run crown in '78, Willie was called up to stay.

Aikens helped the Angels win the A.L. West title in 1979, before tearing knee ligaments while sliding late in the season. In December he was traded to the Mets, but the deal was quashed, and he went instead to Kansas City (taking uniform number 24, the one used by Mays). Aikens had 20 homers, 98 RBI, and a .278 average for the Royals, as they made it to the 1980 World Series.

Aikens excelled in the Fall Classic. In game one, on his 26th birthday, Aikens smashed two home runs and drove in four runs, becoming just the third player to collect two round-trippers in his first Series game. In game four he became the first player ever to have two two-homer games in one World Series, leading the Royals to a 5–3 win. All told, Aikens batted .400 in the six-game Series loss, with a triple (his first in the majors), four homers, eight RBI, and a 1.100 slugging percentage.

Aikens helped K.C. to the postseason again in 1981, batted .281 in '82, and reached career highs with 23 homers and a .302 average in '83. Regrettably, those were not the only highs Aikens experienced that year. Convicted of cocaine possession, Willie spent three months in a Fort Worth, Texas, prison and was suspended for the 1984 season. The suspension was lifted on May 15, 1984, by which time Aikens had spent time in rehabilitation and been traded to the Blue Jays.

Aikens played sparingly in 1984, and by early 1985 the writing was on the wall. On April 27, he came to bat for the last time, pinch-hitting at Texas in the ninth inning. Batting for Tony Fernandez against Tommy Boggs, Aikens crashed a dramatic, game-tying, two-run homer, and Toronto went on to win 9–8. Three days later, Aikens was "designated for assignment," winding up in the minor leagues. "There's no doubt in my mind I can still hit," said Aikens. "I don't think it's over yet." But his major league career was.

Aikens batted .311 for the Syracuse Chiefs, but never got the call back to the bigs. He became convinced that he was persona non grata in U.S. baseball. Released by Syracuse, Aikens signed with the Puebla Black Angels of the Mexican League for 1986.

Willie stayed in the Mexican League for five more seasons. Aikens also played in the short-lived Senior Professional Baseball Association in the winter of 1989–90.

On August 17, 1994, he was convicted by a federal jury on four counts of distributing crack cocaine and one count of using a gun in a drug transaction. He was fined $18,000 and sentenced to more than 20 years in prison, without parole.

30. Rufino Linares, October 6, 1985. As a 30-year-old rookie, Linares batted .265 for the Braves in 1981, and he hit .298 in '82. That winter, he suffered a devastating ankle fracture in winter league play, causing him to miss most of the 1983 season. After slipping to .207 for the Braves in '84, he was released, winding up back in the minors. A year later, he was picked up by the Angels.

Linares homered in his first at bat for California on July 20, and in his last on October 6. He came to bat just 43 times for the Angels, but collected three game-winning homers. The last came off Rick Surhoff at Texas.

Going into the eighth inning of the season finale, the Rangers held a one-run lead. Linares, who had already singled twice and scored a run, now connected for a three-run homer. The Angels won 6–4.

Linares returned to the minors for two more seasons.

31. Tim Stoddard, June 18, 1986. The massive (six-foot-seven, 250-pound) reliever pitched in parts of 13 big league seasons, but came to bat only 20 times, due mostly to the American League's designated-hitter rule. He began his career in 1975 with the White Sox and would make stops with the Orioles, Cubs, Padres, Yankees, and Indians before hanging up his spikes in 1990.

It was at San Diego that Stoddard made his last big league plate appearance. Against the Giants' Mike LaCoss, Stoddard slugged a solo home run in the third inning of a 6–3 loss. An inning later, he was removed for a pinch-hitter.

Stoddard appeared in five more games for the Padres in '86, and a total of 123 more contests in the A.L. between 1986 and 1989, without another opportunity to swing the bat.

After the 1989 season, Stoddard competed in the Senior Professional Baseball Association.

32. Chris Jelic, October 3, 1990. Jelic was called up to the Mets late in the 1990 season. Three years earlier, he had been traded there (along with David Cone) by Kansas City. Jelic's home run helped New York to a 6–3 win at Pittsburgh, where he had been a college quarterback. The homer was a bases-empty blast off Doug Bair in the eighth inning, and, although he didn't know it at the time, was Jelic's "first, last, and only hit" in a four-game, 11-at-bat career. "The fact that it was my first hit and in my home town made it special," says Jelic, the only man whose sole big league hit was a last-at-bat homer. He was released by the Mets on November 13, 1990, and spent several more seasons in the minors.

33. Bobby Rose, May 19, 1992. Rose was pinch-hitting for California's Lee Stevens at New York when he connected for the home run. It was a two-run shot off Steve Howe in the eighth inning and gave the Angels a 4–3 lead, but they went on to lose in 10 innings, 5–4. Two days later, Rose was placed on the disabled list; when he came off it, he was back in the minors.

Rose, an infielder who has played every position, began his pro career at age 18 in 1985. He got his first taste of the majors in 1989, after he had led the Texas League with a .359 average. Rose bounced back and forth over the next three seasons, appearing in a total of only 73 big league games. After the 1992 season, his contract was sold to the Japanese Central League.

34. Glenn Braggs, September 10, 1992. Braggs never quite lived up to his promise in the majors after an impressive minor league career. After averaging .255 in parts of five seasons with Milwaukee, Braggs was traded to the Reds in June 1990.

Glenn batted .299 the rest of the season, helping the Reds to the World Series. He appeared in the Fall Classic. Braggs was a reserve outfielder for the Reds in 1991 and '92. After the season, he signed a two-year, $6-million contract to play in Japan.

Braggs's homer came in the second inning at Atlanta, a solo shot off Steve Avery. Glenn left the game in favor of Cesar Hernandez, and the Reds lost 3–2. Braggs left the majors with 70 career homers and a .257 average.

35. Chico Walker, October 3, 1993. Three years to the day after the Mets' Chris Jelic homered in his final at bat, another Met duplicated the feat. For Chico Walker, it was the climax of a long, colorful pro career that included 15 seasons in the minors before he reached the majors to stay after brief trials with the Red Sox, Cubs, and Angels. In 1983, he was Carl Yastrzemski's defensive replacement in the Hall of Famer's final game.

Walker had spent all or part of every year of the 1980s at the Triple-A level. He had had eight stops in the majors, but had only 377 at bats to show for them.

Chico was picked up by the Cubs' organization in 1990 and had one of his best minor league seasons.

He finally stuck in the majors in 1991, a veritable 32-year-old rookie. He appeared in 124 games at six different positions for the Cubs. He had an inside-the-park grand slam on August 28 and a two-homer game on September 15. And he led N.L. pinch-hitters in batting (.406) and on-base percentage (.500).

Walker became a free agent once again, and was promptly re-signed by the Cubs. But, after a slow start in 1992, he was put on waivers and claimed by the Mets.

Over the last five months of the '92 season, Chico appeared in 107 games for the Mets, batted .308, and became a fan favorite. After 17 years in the pros, he had finally reached the promised land.

But it was not to last: Walker slipped to .225 in 1993 and became expendable. In the last inning of the last game of the season, Walker hit a solo homer off Florida's Matt Turner. The next day, he was released. He finished his checkered big league career with 299 hits—the first and last of which were home runs.

Walker had one last chance to return to the majors, joining the San Diego Padres as a "replacement player" in the spring of 1995. He was released on March 30, just days before the players' strike ended.

PLAYERS WHO HIT HOME RUNS IN THEIR FINAL MAJOR LEAGUE AT BATS

(Compiled by Bill Deane, with assistance from Bob McConnell)

No.	*Date*	*DH*	*Player*	*CLUB*	*LG*	*SITE*	*OPP*	*Pitcher*	*Inn*	*OB**
1.	9/18/1890		Buck West	CLE	NL	CAN	PIT	Bill Phillips	8	2
2.	8/7/1893		Frank O'Connor	PHI	NL	BAL	BAL	Bill Hawke	2	2
3.	9/29/1895		Hercules Burnett	LOU	NL	LOU	CLE	Phil Knell	7	0
4.	8/3/1901		Ed Scott	CLE	AL	MIL	MIL	Bill Reidy	10	0
5.	10/6/1906		Chick Stahl	BOS	AL	BOS	NY	Tom Hughes	8	1
6.	9/30/1922	2	Del Gainer	SL	NL	CHI	CHI	Percy Jones	1	2
7.	10/1/1922	2	Mahlon Higbee	NY	NL	NY	BOS	Al Yeargin	6	1
8.	5/9/1923		Walt Kinney	PHI	AL	SL	SL	Urban Shocker	6	0
9.	5/7/1928		Clay Van Alstyne	WAS	AL	WAS	SL	Lefty Stewart	9	0
10.	9/20/1932		Johnny Schulte	BOS	NL	NY	NY	Fred Fitzsimmons	9	0
11.	5/25/1937		Mickey Cochrane	DET	AL	NY	NY	Bump Hadley	3	0[1]
12.	5/20/1941		George Jumonville	PHI	NL	SL	SL	Clyde Shoun	6	0
13.	9/29/1945	2	Paul Gillespie	CHI	NL	PIT	PIT	Rip Sewell	4	1[2]
14.	8/26/1951	2	Bert Haas	CHI	AL	CHI	NY	Art Schallock	7	1[2]
15.	9/30/1956	2	Joe Frazier	BAL	AL	WAS	WAS	Ted Abernathy	9	0[2]
16.	9/28/1957		Marv Blaylock	PHI	NL	PHI	BKN	Rene Valdez	5	0
17.	9/7/1959	2	Ron Samford	WAS	AL	BAL	BAL	Ernie Johnson	10	2[3]
18.	9/28/1960		Ted Williams	BOS	AL	BOS	BAL	Jack Fisher	8	0
19.	9/30/1962	2	Don Gile	BOS	AL	BOS	WAS	Jack Jenkins	9	1
20.	9/2/1963	2	Ed Hobaugh	WAS	AL	CLE	CLE	Jerry Walker	4	0[4]
21.	10/3/1965		Tony Kubek	NY	AL	BOS	BOS	Dick Radatz	9	1
22.	9/23/1969	1	John Miller	LA	NL	CIN	CIN	Jim Merritt	8	0[2]
23.	9/14/1977		Ken McMullen	MIL	AL	SEA	SEA	Tom House	8	1
24.	10/1/1978		Kevin Pasley	SEA	AL	SEA	TEX	Fergie Jenkins		7[1,5]
25.	10/3/1981		Mike Cubbage	NY	NL	NY	MON	Jeff Reardon	8	0
26.	10/3/1982		Joe Rudi	OAK	AL	KC	KC	Larry Gura	4	1
27.	9/30/1984		Eddie Miller	SD	NL	ATL	ATL	Pascual Perez	9	0
28.	9/30/1984		Tony Brewer	LA	NL	LA	SF	Mark Calvert	7	0
29.	4/27/1985		Willie Aikens	TOR	AL	TEX	TEX	Tommy Boggs	9	1
30.	10/6/1985		Rufino Linares	CAL	AL	TEX	TEX	Rick Surhoff	8	2
31.	6/18/1986		Tim Stoddard	SD	NL	SD	SF	Mike LaCoss	3	0[6]
32.	10/3/1990		Chris Jelic	NY	NL	PIT	PIT	Doug Bair	8	0
33.	5/19/1992		Bobby Rose	CAL	AL	NY	NY	Steve Howe	8	1
34.	9/10/1992		Glenn Braggs	CIN	NL	ATL	ATL	Steve Avery	2	0
35.	10/3/1993		Chico Walker	NY	NL	FLA	FLA	Matt Turner	9	0

**Notes: (1) Hit by pitch in subsequent plate appearance. (2) Appeared in one more game, with no plate appearances. (3) Appeared in four more games, with sacrifice hit in only plate appearance. (4) Appeared in eight more games, with walk in only plate appearance. (5) Walked in subsequent plate appearance. (6) Appeared in 128 more games, 1986–89, with no plate appearances.*

***KEY:** DH = game of doubleheader, if applicable; LG = league; OPP = opposing team; Inn = inning; OB = number of men on base. See narrative to decipher club and site abbreviations.*

Players Who Homered in Their Last Postseason At Bats

Nobody has ever finished his career with a postseason home run, but 25 players since 1903 have homered in their last World Series at bats, and another dozen have done it in their last League Championship appearances. Two players homered in their last Divisional Series at bat. The lists follow this narrative. Keep in mind that several of the perpetrators are still active in 1996, thus may return to postseason play and spoil their claims to immortality.

Following are some interesting notes about the postseason parting shots:

- Fred Luderus had hits in each of his last four official World Series at bats in 1915. In two plate appearances after his homer, he drew a walk and was hit by a pitch. Wally Post also was hit by a pitch after his home run (1961), and Len Dykstra walked after his (1993).
- Hall of Famers who homered in their last World Series at

bats are Earle Combs (1932) and Johnny Bench (1976). Pitchers who did it are Bucky Walters (1940) and Mudcat Grant (1965).

- Four players hit pinch-homers in their last World Series at bats: Hank Majeski (for Ray Narleski, 1954); Chuck Essegian (for Hall of Famer Duke Snider, 1959); Jay Johnstone (for Tom Niedenfuer, 1981); and Kirk Gibson (for Alejandro Peña, 1988).
- Seven players who homered in their last World Series at bats later competed in Championship Series play (thus, didn't homer in their last postseason appearances). The players, with the years they appeared in the L.C.S.: Clete Boyer (1969), Mudcat Grant (1971), Joe Rudi (1975), Johnny Bench (1979), Jay Johnstone (1985), Pedro Guerrero (1983, 1985), and Darryl Strawberry (1988). Grant did not bat in the L.C.S.
- Three of the players who homered in their last Fall Classic at bat did it in the same game. In game seven of the 1964 World Series, Phil Linz and brothers Ken and Clete Boyer all connected in their last trips. Linz and Clete homered in the same inning, off Hall of Famer Bob Gibson. Other Hall of Famers to surrender last-at-bat homers are Grover Alexander (1928) and Burleigh Grimes (1932). Grimes's gopher ball was to another Hall of Famer, Earle Combs.
- Jim Mason homered in the only postseason at bat of his career on October 19, 1976. Mason, who had hit just one homer in 217 at bats during the regular season, was the only Yankee player to homer in the '76 World Series.
- Joe Rudi homered not only in his last World Series at bat in 1974, but in his last regular-season at bat eight years later (number 26 in this chapter).
- Two players homered in each of their last *two* World Series at bats. Chuck Essegian connected as a pinch-hitter in games two and six of the 1959 Fall Classic, separated by a walk in game five. Kirk Gibson homered in his last A.L. World Series at bat for Detroit in 1984, then hit perhaps the most dramatic four-bagger of all time in his only National League World Series appearance four years later. The homers came off Goose Gossage and Dennis Eckersley, two of the best relief pitchers in history.
- Six of the 12 players who homered in their final League Championship Series at bat went on to play in that year's World Series: Pat Kelly (1979), Rick Monday (1981), Tom Brunansky (1987), Devon White (1993), Dave Hollins (who, incidentally, walked after his 1993 blast), and Carlos Baerga (1994). Thus, although there are 39 players on these two lists, only 28 homered in their final post-season at bats. All 28 returned to play in the regular season.
- Dave Stewart has given up no fewer than three of the post-season pops. In 1989, with Oakland, he surrendered last-at-bat homers to Toronto's Lloyd Moseby and George Bell in the A.L.C.S. Four years later, now with Toronto, Stewart served up a goodbye-gopher to Len Dykstra.
- Only one of the 39 homers listed here ended a series. It was, of course, the most recent entry: Joe Carter's World Series-winning homer in game six of the 1993 World Series.

Players Who Hit Home Runs in Their Final World Series At Bats (1903–Present)

(Compiled by Bill Deane)

Date	*G#*	*Player*	*CLUB*	*LG*	*SITE*	*OPP*	*Pitcher*	*Inn*	*OB*
10/13/15	5	Fred Luderus	PHI	NL	PHI	BOS	Rube Foster	4	0
10/15/25	7	Roger Peckinpaugh	WAS	AL	PIT	PIT	Ray Kremer	8	0
10/9/28	4	Cedric Durst	NY	AL	SL	SL	Grover Alexander	8	0
10/2/32	4	Earle Combs	NY	AL	CHI	CHI	Burleigh Grimes	9	0
10/7/40	6	Bucky Walters	CIN	NL	CIN	DET	Fred Hutchinson	8	0
10/2/54	4	Hank Majeski	CLE	AL	CLE	NY	Don Liddle	5	2
10/8/59	6	Chuck Essegian	LA	NL	CHI	CHI	Ray Moore	9	0
10/13/60	7	Hal Smith	PIT	NL	PIT	NY	Jim Coates	8	2
10/9/61	5	Wally Post	CIN	NL	CIN	NY	Bud Daley	5	1
10/15/64	7	Ken Boyer	SL	NL	SL	NY	Steve Hamilton	7	0
10/15/64	7	Clete Boyer	NY	AL	SL	SL	Bob Gibson	9	0
10/15/64	7	Phil Linz	NY	AL	SL	SL	Bob Gibson	9	0
10/13/65	6	Mudcat Grant	MIN	AL	MIN	LA	Howie Reed	6	2
10/10/68	7	Mike Shannon	SL	NL	SL	DET	Mickey Lolich	9	0
10/17/74	5	Joe Rudi	OAK	AL	OAK	LA	Mike Marshall	7	0
10/19/76	3	Jim Mason	NY	AL	NY	CIN	Pat Zachry	7	0
10/21/76	4	Johnny Bench	CIN	NL	NY	NY	Dick Tidrow	9	2
10/24/81	4	Jay Johnstone	LA	NL	LA	NY	Ron Davis	6	1
10/28/81	6	Pedro Guerrero	LA	NL	NY	NY	Rudy May	8	0
10/14/84	5	Kurt Bevacqua	SD	NL	DET	DET	Willie Hernandez	8	0
10/27/86	7	Darryl Strawberry	NY	NL	NY	BOS	Al Nipper	8	0
10/15/88	1	Kirk Gibson	LA	NL	LA	OAK	Dennis Eckersley	9	1
10/23/93	6	Lenny Dykstra	PHI	NL	TOR	TOR	Dave Stewart	7	2
10/23/93	6	Joe Carter	TOR	AL	TOR	PHI	Mitch Williams	9	2

Players Who Hit Home Runs in Their Final League Championship Series At Bats

(Compiled by Bill Deane)

Date	*G#*	*Player*	*CLUB*	*LG*	*SITE*	*OPP*	*Pitcher*	*Inn*	*OB*
10/6/79	4	Pat Kelly	BAL	AL	CAL	CAL	John Montague	7	2
10/19/81	5	Rick Monday	LA	NL	MON	MON	Steve Rogers	9	0
10/9/82	4	Mark Brouhard	MIL	AL	MIL	CAL	Dave Goltz	8	1
10/12/87	5	Chet Lemon	DET	AL	DET	MIN	Juan Berenguer	8	0
10/12/87	5	Tom Brunansky	MIN	AL	DET	DET	Mike Henneman	9	0
10/8/89	5	Lloyd Moseby	TOR	AL	TOR	OAK	Dave Stewart	8	0
10/8/89	5	George Bell	TOR	AL	TOR	OAK	Dave Stewart	9	0
10/13/92	6	Lloyd McClendon	PIT	NL	ATL	ATL	Marvin Freeman	6	0
10/12/93	6	Devon White	TOR	AL	CHI	CHI	Scott Radinsky	9	0
10/12/93	6	Warren Newson	CHI	AL	CHI	TOR	Duane Ward	9	0
10/13/93	6	Dave Hollins	PHI	NL	PHI	ATL	Greg Maddux	5	1
10/17/95	6	Carlos Baerga	CLE	AL	SEA	SEA	Randy Johnson	8	0

Players Who Hit Home Runs in Their Final Divisional Series At Bats

(Compiled by Bill Deane)

Date	*G#*	*Player*	*CLUB*	*LG*	*SITE*	*OPP*	*Pitcher*	*Inn*	*OB*
10/3/95	1	Tony Pena	CLE	AL	CLE	BOS	Zane Smith	13	0
10/6/95	3	Mark Lewis	CIN	NL	CIN	LA	Mark Guthrie	6	3

Long-Distance Home Runs

William J. Jenkinson

As long as baseball has been played, observers and participants alike have been fascinated with those rare individuals who have been capable of batting balls farther than others of their time. As long ago as opening day 1883, there is information describing the excitement generated by Hall of Famer Roger Connor, who struck an unusually long home run at the original Polo Grounds in New York. This feat was accomplished at a time before home runs were hit with enough frequency to be considered a regular part of the game. This is dramatized by the fact that Connor's blow was the only home run he would hit that season. And yet, everyone in attendance was apparently moved to awe and admiration by this single event, which resulted in the scoring of a lone run. By looking back, we can confirm the preoccupation with long-distance hitting in the early stages of baseball history. It is even easier to consider modern history to help us understand that nothing has changed in the intervening years in our fascination with long home runs.

The vast popularity of major league baseball's home run–hitting contest before the annual All-Star game is ample evidence that we remain enamored of the players blessed with unique levels of power. Almost predictably, it is not the winners of the formal contest who receive the greatest admiration. Almost every year, it is the man who strikes the ball the farthest during the competition who receives the highest plaudits. Juan Gonzalez and Ken Griffey, Jr., were the most widely discussed participants at Baltimore's 1993 All-Star celebration, though neither player did anything heroic in the game itself. Griffey shared center stage the following year in Pittsburgh with Frank Thomas, as the two men took turns bombarding the upper decks at Three Rivers Stadium. Their displays of pure power were greeted with passionate enthusiasm, though they did not occur in an actual game. Is there a logical explanation for that behavior?

Americans, along with people everywhere, are fascinated with power. It is for that reason that home run hitters have always been and always will be the most popular players. From a functional standpoint, it makes no difference by what margin a ball clears a set home run barrier. Whether it skips across the top of the railing into the first row of bleachers, or completely passes out of the stadium, the batter is awarded four bases—no more, no less. Why then would anyone care how far they go?

We naturally like to quantify any phenomenon that interests us. What is the highest mountain in the world? How old is the oldest person on the planet? How long will it take the next Olympic champion to run the 100-meter sprint? Who is baseball's mightiest batsman and how far can he hit a baseball? The rules of baseball were made and refined by men; they have limitations. The founding fathers decided to reward a powerfully hit ball by allowing the batter to circle the bases for an automatic run. They did not or could not find a way to further reward the batter who hit a ball significantly farther than the established home run distance. However, fans don't need additional inducements to maintain their fascination with "tape measure" home runs. They have always liked them, and always will.

Along with Roger Connor, the longest hitters in the early days of the major leagues during the 19th century included such men as Harry Stovey, Buck Ewing, Jocko Milligan, and Ed Delahanty. Perhaps the mightiest of all the early sluggers was Big Dan Brouthers, who played for several National League teams before the turn of the century. His longest drive was probably struck on May 4, 1884, at old Union Park in Baltimore. Brouthers rocketed a rising line drive that cleared the fence in distant right-center field, and reportedly rolled another two blocks. The distance traveled through the air has been obscured with the passage of time, and herein lies an interesting aspect of this subject. Despite many unsubstantiated claims, none of the early sluggers recorded drives of such length that they could compare with those of the modern era. Years after the fact, Brouthers was credited with a 500-foot home run on the aforementioned date, but it seems highly unlikely that the ball traveled nearly that far. The great Honus Wagner is said to have hit a drive of comparable length at the Polo Grounds, and Sam Crawford was credited with a 473-foot home run in Detroit. These were men of great skill and power, and they unquestionably set the distance standards for their times. A careful analysis indicates, however, that accounts of 450- to 500-foot home runs in those days are almost certainly apocryphal. It was not until Babe Ruth came upon the scene that we can find confirmed accounts of batted balls that can favorably compare with any hit during subsequent generations.

On July 21, 1915, as a rookie with the Boston Red Sox, Ruth struck a prodigious drive that sailed far over the right-field bleachers at Sportsman's Park in St. Louis. The ball cleared the wide breadth of Grand Boulevard and landed on the sidewalk approximately 470 feet from home plate. That was the start of modern long-distance hitting, and it is a testimony to Ruth's uniqueness that he was able to set objective standards of performance that have never been surpassed.

In order to fully understand and appreciate long-distance hitting, a frame of reference should be established. Any drive of over 400 feet is noteworthy. A blow of 450 feet shows exceptional power, as the majority of major league players are unable to hit a ball that far. Anything in the 500-foot range is genuinely historic. For perspective, consider the computerized measuring system implemented by IBM in most major league cities in 1982. By 1995, the sponsorship had changed, but the program had been expanded to include every big league ballpark. During those years, only one drive of 500 feet was confirmed by this system. Cecil Fielder of the Detroit Tigers is credited with powering a ball 502 feet in the air over the left-field bleachers at Milwaukee's County Stadium on September 14, 1991. Such renowned sluggers and extraordinary physical specimens as Jose Canseco and Juan Gonzalez have never come genuinely close to the 500-foot threshold. The best effort on the part of either player was Canseco's famous blast into the fifth level at Toronto's Sky Dome during the 1989 American League playoffs, which was estimated at 484 feet.

It should be noted that those regular references over the years to 500- and 600-foot home runs were born out of scientific ignorance, misinformation, or even deliberate exaggeration. The most common cause for overstatement has been the basic misconception about the flight of a batted ball once it has reached its apex. Seeing great drives land atop distant upper-deck roofs, sportswriters observing the occurrence from a press box would resort to their limited skills in mathematics without any regard for the laws of physics. Perhaps the ball had already flown over 400 feet, whereupon it was interrupted in midflight at a height of 70 feet above field level. Awed by such a demonstration of power, the writers would then describe the event for posterity as a 500-and-some-foot home run. With the guidance of our scientific brethren, we know that once a batted ball has reached its highest point and lost most of its velocity, it falls in a rapidly declining trajectory. The aforementioned fictional home run could have been reported at 550 feet in a prominent newspaper, and re-created at that length by historians for years thereafter, when in fact it traveled about 100 feet less. Hyperbole has always been part of the phenomenon of long-distance home runs, and this factor must also be considered.

Not surprisingly, all of the great true distance hitters have also been the source of the greatest exaggerations. Despite his extraordinary accomplishments, Babe Ruth is not immune. His tremendous blow to right-center field in Detroit on June 8, 1926, has often been reported as traveling over 600 feet. Certainly, this drive was propelled somewhere around 500 feet in the air, which makes it legitimately historic, but proof that it traveled 600 feet cannot be found. When Mickey Mantle cleared the left-center-field bleachers at Griffith Stadium in Washington on April 17, 1953, the entire baseball world was led to believe the ball had traveled 565 feet from home plate to the point where it landed. In truth, that figure derived from the distance from home plate to the place where a neighborhood child retrieved the ball. Since this home run was the only one that ever cleared those bleachers during decades of major league and Negro League competition, it is genuinely deserving of recognition. However, the actual distance in the air was probably about 510 feet. The same process was at work for Mantle on September 10, 1960, in Detroit, where his right-center-field rooftopper was reported to have traveled more than 600 feet. From interviews with the surviving source of the original data, it is readily apparent once again that the ball had bounced several times before it reached the estimated distance. Included among the other great exaggerations in the history of tape measure home runs are Dave Nicholson's Comiskey Park rooftopper on May 6, 1964, and Dave Kingman's Wrigley Field blast on April 14, 1976. In the case of Nicholson, who was a powerful man, as was Kingman, the figure of 573 feet was provided by "White Sox mathematicians." These unidentified individuals based their calculations on the assumption that the ball traveled completely over the left-center-field roof. However, subsequent investigation indicated that the ball landed on the back of the roof before bouncing out into the night. When Kingman launched his wind-aided blow in Chicago, *The New York Times* somehow concluded that it had flown 630 feet. It has been confirmed that the ball struck against the third house beyond Waveland Avenue, which is situated about 530 feet from home plate. Yet again, we have an example of a genuinely epic home run that has been grievously overstated.

One other aspect of misrepresentation should be explored. Again, the vast talents of the Herculean Mickey Mantle have been compromised by individuals who have unwittingly perpetrated a hoax. Let it be emphasized that the mighty Mick was undoubtedly one of baseball's all-time longest hitters. He was an honest, sometimes even self-effacing individual, who was never known to overstate his own accomplishments. It is due to his immense popularity and constant involvement in the tape measure process that he is often thrust into the muddle of misrepresentation. By his own account he hit the longest home run of his career on May 22, 1963, at Yankee Stadium. The ball struck the façade on the right-field roof approximately 370 feet from home plate and 115 feet above field level. Almost everyone in attendance believed that the ball was still rising when it was interrupted in midflight by the roof structure. Based upon that belief, this drive has commonly been estimated at about 620 feet if left unimpeded. However, the reality is that the ball was already on its way down, and those reporting the trajectory were victimized by a common optical illusion. It is a scientific fact that if Mantle, or anyone else, had sufficient strength to hit a ball that was still traveling upward when it met the towering façade, he would also have enough strength to clear that same façade by a distance of at least 100 feet. In order for the ball to be rising at roof level, it would have to have been traveling at a lower angle than that which produces maximum distance. If Mantle had provided the same power or velocity, but had launched the ball at a higher and more efficient angle, it would have passed out of Yankee Stadium at a height of over 200 feet! Mantle hit the façade on two or perhaps three occasions, but never cleared it. By his own admission, during his 18-year career at Yankee Stadium, which included thousands of swing variables, he hit several balls to right field in an optimum manner. If he had the power to clear the roof by over 100 feet, he surely would have cleared it marginally on many occasions.

It may be appropriate to cite another example of this same optical illusion. The enigmatic Dick Allen was also one of baseball's greatest long-distance hitters. On July 6, 1974, he powered a torrid drive that crashed against the roof façade in deep left-center field at Tiger Stadium. This memorable blow was knocked down at a linear distance of approximately 415 feet and an altitude of about 85 feet. Almost all of the players on the field, and everyone in the home-plate area, including the press box, swore that the ball was still ascending when it hit the roof. And, as was the case with Mantle, Allen was one of the few men in the entire history of the game who possessed legitimate 500-foot-plus power. His 1974 blast certainly traveled over 500 feet, but just as certainly it was not rising when it was forced to a sudden stop. Such a batted ball would require literally superhuman velocity, which would render the batsman capable of authoring 700-foot home runs. Allen may have hit some of his sport's longest home runs, but neither he nor anyone else ever hit a baseball nearly that far.

In returning the discussion to Babe Ruth, it can be said that he defies rational analysis. Not only did he set distance records in every major league ballpark (including National League stadiums where he played only infrequently), he also set similar standards in hundreds of other fields, where he made exhibition and barnstorming appearances. Amazingly, many of those records remain unequaled, which is to say that Ruth is a true athletic anachronism. In virtually every other field of endeavor in which physical performance can be measured, there are no Ruthian equivalents. In 1921 alone, which was Ruth's best tape measure season, he hit at least one 500-foot home run in all eight American League cities. There should be no doubt about the authentication of these conclusions. Despite the scarcity of film on Ruth, we can still make definitive evaluations of the approximate landing points of all of his 714 career home runs.

Ruth played during the height of America's newspaper culture, when approximately 10 daily New York papers gave first-hand accounts of each Yankee game. When you consider that the other baseball towns averaged about five comparable publications, it is clear that we can draw upon approximately 15 descriptions of most of the hundreds of four-base blows struck during his career. A suitable example can be identified in Ruth's classic Comiskey Park rooftopper on August 16, 1927. Fifteen writers from New York, Chicago, and other places emphatically stated that Ruth's fifth-inning drive cleared the 52-foot-wide grandstand roof by a considerable margin.

Although other sluggers occasionally reached the rooftops during Comiskey's long lifetime, the only other left-handed batter known to have flown the right-field roof was Detroit's Kirk Gibson in 1985. The magnitude of Ruth's accomplishment can be understood with the knowledge that, because home plate had been moved, the distance to the grandstand for Gibson was 341 feet, while for Ruth it was 365 feet. Similarly, Comiskey's left-field roof was also visited by many batted balls, but only one is confirmed to have cleared it on the fly. That homeric deed was performed by the powerful Jimmie Foxx on June 16, 1936. As Ruth's talents waned in the early 1930s, Foxx began his ascendancy. In 1932, the muscular "Double X" almost equaled Ruth's season record of 60 home runs. Many of them even rivaled the Babe's for distance. It was heresy to suggest that Ruth's accomplishments could be surpassed, but for a few seasons it appeared that Foxx might do just that. One of the greatest quirks in baseball history is that Jimmie Foxx, following immediately in the footsteps of Babe Ruth, was to establish the second-greatest distance legacy in the annals of the game. Foxx never quite measured up to Ruth, but it is remarkable that no one since Foxx has measured up to him. The other great distance hitters of that period were Lou Gehrig and Hank Greenberg, but their optimum drives fell about 50 feet short of those struck by Ruth and Foxx.

The next truly great slugger in the chronology of long-distance hitting was Ted Williams, who arrived on the major league scene in 1939. His slender physique belied his subtle strength and natural ability to generate bat speed. On May 4 of that year, Williams cleared the towering right-field grandstand in Detroit and served notice that he was as powerful as he was refined with a bat in his hands. As late as 1960, Teddy Ballgame was still going strong, when he opened the season in Washington with a 475-foot bolt to right-center field. Coincidentally, that was the same ballpark where Mickey Mantle had supplanted Williams as the game's longest hitter seven years earlier.

During Mantle's rookie season in 1951, he had struck several impressive drives, but it was not until he cleared the left-center-field bleachers at Griffith Stadium two years later that he was crowned as the new King of the Tape Measure. The term tape measure is especially relevant in this instance, since it was popularized on this occasion for the first time.

Mantle was a switch-hitter who was equally powerful from both sides of the plate. As a result, he's the only player in history to establish true tape measure standards in all directions. There were no American League stadiums where Mantle played where he did not hit a home run of at least 450 feet to both the left and right sides of the field. After Ruth and Foxx, Mantle ranks as high as or higher than anyone else who ever tried to hit a baseball to faroff places. The decade of the fifties was particularly blessed with the presence of many great sluggers, who should be mentioned in any discussion of long hitters. The list includes Larry Doby, Joe Adcock, Eddie Mathews, Henry Aaron, Willie Mays, and Frank Robinson. Perhaps the longest hitter of those not previously mentioned was Ralph Kiner, who bombarded all the National League left-field distance plateaus of his time.

When gargantuan Frank Howard hit a mighty home run off Robin Roberts in Philadelphia on September 1, 1958, the next great tape measure home run career was initiated. One of the largest men ever to play major league baseball, at six feet seven inches, 275 pounds, Howard was the absolute epitome of size and strength. His trail of National League home runs was already legendary when he moved to the American League in 1965. Before he retired after the 1973 season, he had performed even more extraordinary feats of long-distance hitting in the junior circuit. It took prodigious strength to reach the upper deck at Washington's Robert F. Kennedy Stadium, but "Hondo" did it 24 times, ranging from the left-field foul pole all the way to straightaway center field.

Dick Allen, too, played in both leagues, thereby providing himself the advantage of leaving his signature on more ballparks than those who only played in one league. Allen walloped 18 home runs over the 75-foot-high left-field grandstand at Philadelphia's Connie Mack Stadium, but his opposite-field drives to right and right-center fields may have been even more impressive. Allen could not hit with the same power in those directions as when he pulled the ball, but he seems to have lost less distance than almost anyone else when hitting to the opposite field. Directly behind Allen in the historic ranking of tape measure hitters were contemporaries Willie Stargell and Willie McCovey. Other great distance hitters from the sixties were Harmon Killebrew, Dick Stuart, and Boog Powell.

Entering the 1970s, Reggie Jackson was already established as one of the best ever. His 1971 All-Star blast off the light tower atop the right-center-field roof at Tiger Stadium ranks as one of the 10 longest drives in major league history. Also ranking among the elite during that decade were Greg Luzinski, Dave Kingman, and George Foster.

Moving into the eighties, Mike Schmidt, Jim Rice, and Darryl Strawberry set the pace at a time when modern technology permitted us to better understand the limitations of the flight of a batted ball. The same home runs that had once been described as 500 footers were now being scientifically calculated in the 450-foot range.

As of 1995, the mantle of baseball's longest hitter can probably best be worn by Cecil Fielder. His regular bombardment of the left-field roof at Tiger Stadium has not been approximated in the 60-year history of that structure. If Bo Jackson had not been forced into early retirement, he might have challenged Fielder for modern supremacy. Others who should be recognized are Jose Canseco, Fred McGriff, Mark McGwire, Ken Griffey, Jr., Frank Thomas, and Andres Galarraga. It is only fair to also mention the great distance sluggers of the old Negro Leagues. That list is topped by the legendary Josh Gibson, and includes George "Mule" Suttles, Norman "Turkey" Stearnes, and John Beckwith. With each passing year, others will join the long list of true tape measure champions. They represent a fraction of those who have applied their ability to the act of hitting a baseball. Fewer than one in a million men are capable of powering a ball 450 feet against major league caliber pitching. It is for that reason that we find their actions so thrilling, and will always want to identify them for special reward and distinction.

Part Two

All-Time Home Run Records

All-Time Home Run Records

Total number of batters hitting homers: 5,863
Total number of pitchers surrendering homers: 5,205

Total Home Runs by Innings & Men On Base

	Men On Base						
Inn	0	1	2	3	Unkn	Totals	
1	8,826	7,678	3,355	573	1	20,433	(11.15%)
2	12,053	4,708	1,643	327	0	18,731	(10.22%)
3	9,397	6,485	2,756	538	0	19,176	(10.46%)
4	13,449	6,479	2,341	440	0	22,709	(12.39%)
5	10,905	6,157	2,620	527	1	20,210	(11.03%)
6	12,643	6,716	2,600	534	2	22,495	(12.27%)
7	11,564	5,960	2,513	489	1	20,527	(11.20%)
8	11,367	6,095	2,457	473	2	20,394	(11.13%)
9	8,703	4,311	1,638	353	1	15,006	(8.19%)
10	1,002	407	183	56	0	1,648	(0.90%)
11	516	229	90	36	0	871	(0.48%)
12	262	105	52	17	0	436	(0.24%)
13	184	68	33	10	0	295	(0.16%)
14	92	27	15	8	0	142	(0.08%)
15	41	15	9	0	0	65	(0.04%)
16	26	8	3	1	0	38	(0.02%)
17	16	3	2	0	0	21	(0.01%)
18	7	3	0	0	0	10	(0.01%)
19	3	3	1	0	0	7	(0.00%)
20	2	1	0	0	0	3	(0.00%)
21	0	1	3	0	0	4	(0.00%)
22	2	1	0	0	0	3	(0.00%)
25	1	0	0	0	0	1	(0.00%)
Unk	1	1	2	0	34	38	(0.02%)
Tot	101,062	55,461	22,316	4,382	42	183,263	
Pct	55.1	30.3	12.2	2.4	0.0		

Total Home Runs hit at Home: 92,709
Total Home Runs hit on Road: 90,554

Home Runs by Day of the Week

Sun	32,923	(18.0%)
Mon	19,370	(10.6%)
Tue	26,370	(14.4%)
Wed	26,225	(14.3%)
Thu	21,147	(11.5%)
Fri	27,289	(14.9%)
Sat	29,939	(16.3%)

Home Runs by Month

Apr	17,918	(9.8%)
May	32,283	(17.6%)
Jun	34,509	(18.8%)
Jul	34,747	(19.0%)
Aug	33,406	(18.2%)
Sep	28,341	(15.4%)
Oct	2,059	(1.1%)

First HR in NL
05/02/1876 Ross Barnes CHI

First HR in AL
04/25/1901 Erve Beck CLE

First HR in extra innings
06/29/1876 Pop Snyder LOU NL (10th Inning)

First HR at night
07/10/1935 Babe Herman CIN NL

First HR by Pinch Hitter
05/14/1892 Tom Daly BRO NL

First HR by Designated Hitter
04/06/1973 Tony Oliva MIN AL

Most Home Runs by Position, (Season)

Pitcher

	Player	Team	Year	HR
1	Wes Ferrell	CLE AL	1931	9
2	Jack Stivetts	STL AA	1890	7
	Wes Ferrell	CLE AL	1933	7
	Bob Lemon	CLE AL	1949	7
	Don Newcombe	BRO NL	1955	7
	Don Drysdale	LA NL	1958	7
	Don Drysdale	LA NL	1965	7
	Earl Wilson	DET AL	1968	7

Catcher

	Player	Team	Year	HR
1	Roy Campanella	BRO NL	1953	40
2	Johnny Bench	CIN NL	1970	38
3	Gabby Hartnett	CHI NL	1930	36
4	Walker Cooper	NY NL	1947	35
	Mike Piazza	LA NL	1993	35

First Baseman

	Player	Team	Year	HR
1	Hank Greenberg	DET AL	1938	58
2	Jimmie Foxx	PHI AL	1932	51
	Johnny Mize	NY NL	1947	51
4	Jimmy Foxx	BOS AL	1938	50
5	Lou Gehrig	NY AL	1934	49
	Lou Gehrig	NY AL	1936	49
	Ted Kluszewski	CIN NL	1954	49

Second Baseman

	Player	Team	Year	HR
1	Rogers Hornsby	STL NL	1922	42
	Dave Johnson	ATL NL	1973	42
3	Ryne Sandberg	CHI NL	1990	40
4	Rogers Hornsby	STL NL	1925	39
	Rogers Hornsby	CHI NL	1929	39

Third Baseman

	Player	Team	Year	HR
1	Mike Schmidt	PHI NL	1980	48
2	Eddie Mathews	MIL NL	1953	47
3	Eddie Mathews	MIL NL	1959	46
4	Mike Schmidt	PHI NL	1979	45
5	Al Rosen	CLE AL	1953	43
	Matt Williams	SF NL	1994	43

Shortstop

	Player	Team	Year	HR
1	Ernie Banks	CHI NL	1958	47
2	Ernie Banks	CHI NL	1959	45
3	Ernie Banks	CHI NL	1955	44
4	Ernie Banks	CHI NL	1960	41
5	Rico Petrocelli	BOS AL	1969	40

Outfielder

	Player	Team	Year	HR
1	Roger Maris	NY AL	1961	61
2	Babe Ruth	NY AL	1927	60
3	Babe Ruth	NY AL	1921	58
4	Hack Wilson	CHI NL	1930	56
5	Babe Ruth	NY AL	1920	54
	Babe Ruth	NY AL	1928	54
	Ralph Kiner	PIT NL	1949	54
	Mickey Mantle	NY AL	1961	54
9	Mickey Mantle	NY AL	1956	52
	Willie Mays	SF NL	1965	52
	George Foster	CIN NL	1977	52
12	Ralph Kiner	PIT NL	1947	51
	Willie Mays	SF NL	1962	51
14	Albert Belle	CLE AL	1995	50
15	Babe Ruth	NY AL	1930	49
	Willie Mays	SF NL	1962	49
	Harmon Killebrew	MIN AL	1964	49
	Frank Robinson	BAL AL	1966	49
	Andre Dawson	CHI NL	1987	49

Designated Hitter

	Player	Team	Year	HR
1	Dave Kingman	OAK AL	1984	35
	Dave Kingman	OAK AL	1986	35
3	Greg Luzinski	CHI AL	1983	32
	Gorman Thomas	SEA AL	1985	32
5	Jim Rice	BOS AL	1977	31
	Rico Carty	TOR AL	1978	31
	Andre Thornton	CLE AL	1982	31
	Jose Canseco	TEX AL	1994	31

Most Home Runs by Position, (Career)

Pitcher

	Player	HR
1	Wes Ferrell	37
2	Bob Lemon	35
	Warren Spahn	35
4	Red Ruffing	34
5	Earl Wilson	33

Catcher

	Player	HR
1	Carlton Fisk	351
2	Johnny Bench	327
3	Yogi Berra	306
4	Gary Carter	298
5	Lance Parrish	295

First Baseman

	Player	HR
1	Lou Gehrig	493
2	Jimmie Foxx	480
3	Willie McCovey	439
4	Eddie Murray	409
5	Norm Cash	367

Second Baseman

	Player	HR
1	Joe Morgan	266
2	Rogers Hornsby	264
3	Joe Gordon	246
4	Ryne Sandberg	240
5	Lou Whitaker	239

Third Baseman

	Player	HR
1	Mike Schmidt	509
2	Eddie Mathews	486
3	Graig Nettles	368
4	Ron Santo	337
5	Ron Cey	312

Shortstop

	Player	HR
1	Cal Ripken	319
2	Ernie Banks	277
3	Vern Stephens	213
4	Alan Trammell	176
5	Joe Cronin	155

Outfielder

	Player	HR
1	Babe Ruth	692
2	Hank Aaron	661
3	Willie Mays	642
4	Ted Williams	514
5	Mickey Mantle	490
6	Frank Robinson	463
7	Reggie Jackson	458
8	Mel Ott	457
9	Andre Dawson	396
10	Duke Snider	400
	Dave Winfield	400
12	Billy Williams	377
13	Rocky Colavito	372
14	Al Kaline	369
15	Joe DiMaggio	360

Designated Hitter

	Player	HR
1	Don Baylor	219
2	Harold Baines	154
3	Hal McRae	145
4	Brian Downing	125
	Andre Thornton	125

Most Home Runs for Current Teams, (Career)

Franchise: Baltimore Orioles

MIL AL 1901

	Player	HR
1	John Anderson	8
2	Wid Conroy	5
3	Bill Friel	4
4	Davy Jones	3
5	Hugh Duffy	2
	Bill Hallman	2

STL AL 1902–53

	Player	HR
1	Ken Williams	185
2	Harlond Clift	170
3	Vern Stephens	113
4	George McQuinn	108
5	Chet Laabs	101

BAL AL 1954–95

	Player	HR
1	Eddie Murray	333
2	Cal Ripken	327
3	Boog Powell	303
4	Brooks Robinson	268
5	Ken Singleton	182

Total

	Player	HR
1	Eddie Murray	333
2	Cal Ripken	327
3	Boog Powell	303
4	Brooks Robinson	268
5	Ken Williams	185

Franchise: Boston Red Sox

BOS AL 1901–95

	Player	HR
1	Ted Williams	521
2	Carl Yastrzemski	452
3	Jim Rice	382

4	Dwight Evans	379
5	Bobby Doerr	223

Franchise: California Angels
LA AL 1961–65

	Player	*HR*
1	Leon Wagner	91
2	Lee Thomas	61
3	Ken Hunt	31
4	Jim Fregosi	30
5	Steve Bilko	28

CAL AL 1966–95

	Player	*HR*
1	Brian Downing	222
2	Bobby Grich	154
3	Don Baylor	141
4	Doug DeCinces	130
5	Chili Davis	128

Total

	Player	*HR*
1	Brian Downing	222
2	Bobby Grich	154
3	Don Baylor	141
4	Doug DeCinces	130
5	Chili Davis	128

Franchise: Chicago White Sox
CHI AL 1901–95

	Player	*HR*
1	Carlton Fisk	214
2	Harold Baines	186
3	Frank Thomas	182
4	Bill Melton	154
5	Ron Kittle	140

Franchise: Cleveland Indians
CLE AL 1901–95

	Player	*HR*
1	Earl Averill	226
2	Hal Trosky	216
3	Larry Doby	215
4	Andre Thornton	214
5	Albert Belle	194

Franchise: Detroit Tigers
DET AL 1901–95

	Player	*HR*
1	Al Kaline	399
2	Norm Cash	373
3	Hank Greenberg	306
4	Willie Horton	262
5	Lou Whitaker	244

Franchise: Kansas City Royals
KC AL 1969–95

	Player	*HR*
1	George Brett	317
2	Amos Otis	193
3	Hal McRae	169
4	Frank White	160
5	John Mayberry	143

Franchise: Milwaukee Brewers
SEA AL 1969

	Player	*HR*
1	Don Mincher	25
2	Wayne Comer	15
3	Greg Goossen	10
4	Tommy Harper	9
5	Mike Hegan	8
	Jerry McNertney	8

MIL AL 1970–95

	Player	*HR*
1	Robin Yount	251
2	Gorman Thomas	208
3	Cecil Cooper	201
4	Ben Oglivie	176
5	Paul Molitor	160

Total

	Player	*HR*
1	Robin Yount	251
2	Gorman Thomas	208
3	Cecil Cooper	201
4	Ben Oglivie	176
5	Paul Molitor	160

Franchise: Minnesota Twins
WAS AL 1901–60

	Player	*HR*
1	Roy Sievers	180
2	Jim Lemon	144
3	Goose Goslin	127
4	Mickey Vernon	121
5	Eddie Yost	101

MIN AL 1961–95

	Player	*HR*
1	Harmon Killebrew	475
2	Kent Hrbek	293
3	Tony Oliva	220
4	Bob Allison	211
5	Kirby Puckett	207

Total

	Player	*HR*
1	Harmon Killebrew	559
2	Kent Hrbek	293
3	Bob Allison	256
4	Tony Oliva	220
5	Kirby Puckett	207

Franchise: New York Yankees
BAL AL 1901–02

	Player	*HR*
1	Jimmy Williams	15
2	Mike Donlin	5
	Roger Bresnahan	5
4	Harry Howell	4
	Cy Seymour	4

NY AL 1903–95

	Player	*HR*
1	Babe Ruth	659
2	Mickey Mantle	536
3	Lou Gehrig	493
4	Joe DiMaggio	361
5	Yogi Berra	358

Total

	Player	*HR*
1	Babe Ruth	659
2	Mickey Mantle	536
3	Lou Gehrig	493
4	Joe DiMaggio	361
5	Yogi Berra	358

Franchise: Oakland Athletics
PHI AL 1901–54

	Player	*HR*
1	Jimmie Foxx	302
2	Bob Johnson	252
3	Al Simmons	209
4	Sam Chapman	174
5	Gus Zernial	118

KC AL 1955–67

	Player	*HR*
1	Norm Siebern	78
2	Bob Cerv	75
3	Gus Zernial	73
4	Hector Lopez	67
5	Ed Charles	65

OAK AL 1968–95

	Player	*HR*
1	Mark McGwire	277
2	Reggie Jackson	268
3	Jose Canseco	231
4	Sal Bando	192
5	Dwayne Murphy	153

Total

	Player	*HR*
1	Jimmie Foxx	302
2	Mark McGwire	277
3	Reggie Jackson	269
4	Bob Johnson	252
5	Jose Canseco	231

Franchise: Seattle Mariners
SEA AL 1977–95

	Player	*HR*
1	Ken Griffey	189
2	Jay Buhner	166
3	Alvin Davis	160
4	Jim Presley	115
5	Ken Phelps	105

Franchise: Texas Rangers
WAS AL 1961–71

	Player	*HR*
1	Frank Howard	237
2	Don Lock	99
3	Jim King	89
4	Ken McMullen	86
5	Mike Epstein	73

TEX AL 1972—95

	Player	*HR*
1	Juan Gonzalez	167
2	Ruben Sierra	153
3	Larry Parrish	149
4	Pete Incaviglia	124
5	Toby Harrah	122

Total

	Player	*HR*
1	Frank Howard	246
2	Juan Gonzalez	167

	Player	HR
3	Ruben Sierra	153
4	Larry Parrish	149
5	Toby Harrah	124
	Pete Incaviglia	124

Franchise: Toronto Blue Jays
TOR AL 1977–95

	Player	HR
1	George Bell	202
2	Jesse Barfield	179
3	Joe Carter	152
4	Lloyd Moseby	149
5	Ernie Whitt	131

Franchise: Atlanta Braves
BOS NL 1876–1952

	Player	HR
1	Wally Berger	199
2	Bob Elliott	101
3	Herman Long	88
	Tommy Holmes	88
5	Earl Torgeson	82

MIL NL 1953–65

	Player	HR
1	Eddie Mathews	452
2	Hank Aaron	398
3	Joe Adcock	239
4	Del Crandall	162
5	Johnny Logan	88

ATL NL 1966–95

	Player	HR
1	Dale Murphy	371
2	Hank Aaron	335
3	Bob Horner	215
4	Dave Justice	154
5	Ron Gant	147

Total

	Player	HR
1	Hank Aaron	733
2	Eddie Mathews	493
3	Dale Murphy	371
4	Joe Adcock	239
5	Bob Horner	215

Franchise: Chicago Cubs
CHI NL 1876–1995

	Player	HR
1	Ernie Banks	512
2	Billy Williams	392
3	Ron Santo	337
4	Ryne Sandberg	245
5	Gabby Hartnett	231

Franchise: Cincinnati Reds
CIN AA 1882–89

	Player	HR
1	John Reilly	59
2	Charles Jones	30
3	Frank Fennelly	28
4	Bid McPhee	27
5	Bug Holliday	19

CIN NL 1890-1995

	Player	HR
1	Johnny Bench	389
2	Frank Robinson	324
3	Tony Perez	287
4	Ted Kluszewski	251
5	George Foster	244

Total

	Player	HR
1	Johnny Bench	389
2	Frank Robinson	324
3	Tony Perez	287
4	Ted Kluszewski	251
5	George Foster	244

Franchise: Colorado Rockies
COL NL 1993–95

	Player	HR
1	Dante Bichette	88
2	Andres Galarraga	84
3	Vinny Castilla	44
4	Larry Walker	36
5	Charlie Hayes	35

Franchise: Florida Marlins
FLO NL 1993–95

	Player	HR
1	Jeff Conine	55
2	Gary Sheffield	53
3	Greg Colbrunn	29
4	Kurt Abbott	26
5	Orestes Destrade	25

Franchise: Houston Astros
HOU NL 1962–95

	Player	HR
1	Jim Wynn	223
2	Glenn Davis	166
3	Cesar Cedeno	163
4	Bob Watson	139
5	Jose Cruz	138

Franchise: Los Angeles Dodgers
BRO AA 1884–89

	Player	HR
1	Germany Smith	16
2	George Pinckney	11
3	Dave Foutz	9
	Pop Corkhill	9
5	Adonis Terry	8
	Joe Visner	8

BRO NL 1890–1957

	Player	HR
1	Duke Snider	316
2	Gil Hodges	298
3	Roy Campanella	242
4	Carl Furillo	174
5	Dolph Camilli	139

LA NL 1958–95

	Player	HR
1	Ron Cey	228
2	Steve Garvey	211
3	Pedro Guerrero	171
4	Willie Davis	154
5	Dusty Baker	144

Total

	Player	HR
1	Duke Snider	389
2	Gil Hodges	361
3	Roy Campanella	242
4	Ron Cey	228
5	Steve Garvey	211

Franchise: Montreal Expos
MON NL 1969–95

	Player	HR
1	Andre Dawson	225
2	Gary Carter	220
3	Tim Wallach	204
4	Bob Bailey	118
5	Andres Galarraga	106

Franchise: New York Mets
NY NL 1962–95

	Player	HR
1	Darryl Strawberry	252
2	Howard Johnson	192
3	Dave Kingman	154
4	Kevin McReynolds	122
5	Ed Kranepool	118

Franchise: Philadelphia Phillies
WOR NL 1880–82

	Player	HR
1	Harry Stovey	13
2	Jackie Hayes	4
3	Hick Carpenter	2
	Lee Richmond	2
	Frank Mountain	2

PHI NL 1883–1995

	Player	HR
1	Mike Schmidt	548
2	Del Ennis	259
3	Chuck Klein	243
4	Greg Luzinski	223
5	Cy Williams	217

Total

	Player	HR
1	Mike Schmidt	548
2	Del Ennis	259
3	Chuck Klein	243
4	Greg Luzinski	223
5	Cy Williams	217

Franchise: Pittsburgh Pirates
PIT AA 1882–86

	Player	HR
1	Ed Swartwood	7
2	Mike Mansell	6
3	Billy Taylor	5
	Tom Brown	5
	Fred Carroll	5

PIT NL 1887–95

	Player	HR
1	Willie Stargell	475
2	Ralph Kiner	301
3	Roberto Clemente	240
4	Barry Bonds	176
5	Dave Parker	166

Total

	Player	HR
1	Willie Stargell	475

	Player	HR
2	Ralph Kiner	301
3	Roberto Clemente	240
4	Barry Bonds	176
5	Dave Parker	166

Franchise: San Diego Padres
SD NL

	Player	HR
1	Nate Colbert	163
2	Dave Winfield	154
3	Tony Gwynn	87
4	Benito Santiago	85
5	Fred McGriff	84

Franchise: San Francisco Giants
TRO NL 1879–82

	Player	HR
1	Roger Connor	9
2	Dan Brouthers	4
	Pete Gillespie	4
4	Buck Ewing	2
5	Frank Hankinson	1
	John Cassidy	1
	Bob Ferguson	1
	Fred Pfeffer	1
	Mickey Welch	1
	Chief Roseman	1
	Tim Keefe	1

NY NL 1883–1957

	Player	HR
1	Mel Ott	511
2	Bobby Thomson	189
3	Willie Mays	187
4	Johnny Mize	157
5	Bill Terry	154

SF NL 1958–95

	Player	HR
1	Willie McCovey	469
2	Willie Mays	459
3	Orlando Cepeda	226
4	Matt Williams	225
5	Bobby Bonds	186

Total

	Player	HR
1	Willie Mays	646
2	Mel Ott	511
3	Willie McCovey	469
4	Orlando Cepeda	226
5	Matt Williams	225

Franchise: St. Louis Cardinals
STL AA 1882–91

	Player	HR
1	Tip O'Neill	47
2	Charlie Comiskey	25
3	Charlie Duffee	19
4	Tommy McCarthy	17
	Jocko Milligan	17

STL NL 1892–95

	Player	HR
1	Stan Musial	475
2	Ken Boyer	255
3	Rogers Hornsby	193
4	Jim Bottomley	181
5	Ted Simmons	172

Total

	Player	HR
1	Stan Musial	475
2	Ken Boyer	255
3	Rogers Hornsby	193
4	Jim Bottomley	181
5	Ted Simmons	172

Most Home Runs, Team (Game)

Date	Team	HR
09/14/1987	TOR AL	10
06/28/1939	NY AL	8
08/30/1953	MIL NL	8
08/18/1956	CIN NL	8
04/30/1961	SF NL	8
08/29/1963	MIN AL	8
07/04/1977	BOS AL	8
07/30/1978	MON NL	8

Most Home Runs, Team (Month)

	Team	Month	HR
1	BAL AL	May 1987	58
2	MIN AL	May 1964	55
	NY NL	Jul 1947	55
4	NY AL	Jul 1940	54
5	BOS AL	Jul 1964	53
	MIN AL	Jul 1963	53
	NY AL	Jun 1961	53

200 or More Home Runs, Team (Season)

	Team	Season	HR
1	NY AL	1961	240
2	MIN AL	1963	225
	DET AL	1987	225
4	NY NL	1947	221
	CIN NL	1956	221
	MIN AL	1964	221
7	MIL AL	1982	216
8	TOR AL	1987	215
9	BAL AL	1985	214
10	BOS AL	1977	213
11	BAL AL	1987	211
12	DET AL	1962	209
	CHI NL	1987	209
	DET AL	1991	209
15	BRO NL	1953	208
16	ATL NL	1966	207
	CLE AL	1995	207
18	ATL NL	1973	206
19	SF NL	1987	205
20	SF NL	1962	204
21	BOS AL	1970	203
	MIL AL	1980	203
23	DET AL	1985	202
24	BRO NL	1955	201
25	COL NL	1995	200

Most Home Runs by Two Teammates (Season)

	Team	Season	HR
1	NY AL	1961	115
	Roger Maris		(61)
	Mickey Mantle		(54)
2	NY AL	1927	107
	Babe Ruth		(60)
	Lou Gehrig		(47)
3	PHI AL	1932	93
	Jimmie Foxx		(58)
	Al Simmons		(35)
	CHI NL	1930	93
	Hack Wilson		(56)
	Gabby Hartnett		(37)
5	NY AL	1931	92
	Lou Gehrig		(46)
	Babe Ruth		(46)
6	DET AL	1938	91
	Hank Greenberg		(58)
	Rudy York		(33)
	SF NL	1965	91
	Willie Mays		(52)
	Willie McCovey		(39)
8	NY AL	1930	90
	Babe Ruth		(49)
	Lou Gehrig		(41)
9	NY AL	1961	89
	Roger Maris		(61)
	Bill Skowron		(28)
10	CIN NL	1955	87
	Ted Kluszewski		(47)
	Wally Post		(40)
	NY NL	1947	87
	Johnny Mize		(51)
	Willard Marshall		(36)

Most Home Runs by Three Teammates (Season)

	Team	Season	HR
1	NY AL	1961	143
	Roger Maris		(61)
	Mickey Mantle		(54)
	Bill Skowron		(28)
2	NY AL	1961	137
	Roger Maris		(61)
	Mickey Mantle		(54)
	Yogi Berra		(22)
3	NY AL	1961	136
	Roger Maris		(61)
	Mickey Mantle		(54)
	Johnny Blanchard		(21)
	NY AL	1961	136
	Roger Maris		(61)
	Mickey Mantle		(54)
	Elston Howard		(21)
5	NY AL	1961	126
	Roger Maris		(61)
	Mickey Mantle		(54)
	Clete Boyer		(11)
6	NY AL	1927	125
	Babe Ruth		(60)
	Lou Gehrig		(47)
	Tony Lazzeri		(18)
7	ATL NL	1973	124
	Dave Johnson		(43)
	Darrell Evans		(41)
	Hank Aaron		(40)
8	NY AL	1961	123
	Roger Maris		(61)
	Mickey Mantle		(54)
	Tony Kubek		(8)
9	NY NL	1947	122
	Johnny Mize		(51)
	Willard Marshall		(36)
	Walker Cooper		(35)
10	NY AL	1961	121

Roger Maris		(61)
Mickey Mantle		(54)
Bob Cerv		(6)

Most Players with 10 or more Home Runs, Team (Season)

	Team	*Year*	*Players*
1	NY NL	1952	9
	SF NL	1958	9
	CLE AL	1962	9
	CIN NL	1965	9
	DET AL	1969	9
	CHI AL	1977	9
	NY AL	1980	9
	TOR AL	1983	9
	BAL AL	1985	9
	BAL AL	1987	9
	TOR AL	1987	9
	SF NL	1987	9
	SEA AL	1988	9

Most Players with 20 or more Home Runs, Team (Season)

	Team	*Year*	*Players*
1	NY AL	1961	6
	MIN AL	1964	6
	MIL NL	1965	6
	DET AL	1986	6
5	NY AL	1938	5
	BOS AL	1940	5
	NY NL	1953	5
	CIN NL	1956	5
	CHI NL	1958	5
	LA AL	1961	5
	NY AL	1962	5
	SF NL	1963	5
	MIL NL	1964	5
	BOS AL	1977	5
	BOS AL	1979	5
	LA NL	1979	5
	CAL AL	1982	5
	MIL AL	1982	5
	BOS AL	1984	5
	MIN AL	1986	5
	DET AL	1987	5
	DET AL	1991	5
	CAL AL	1995	5
	CLE AL	1995	5

Most Players with 30 or more Home Runs, Team (Season)

	Team	*Year*	*Players*
1	LA NL	1977	4
	COL NL	1995	4
3	PHI NL	1929	3
	NY AL	1941	3
	NY NL	1947	3
	BRO NL	1950	3
	BRO NL	1953	3
	CIN NL	1956	3
	WAS AL	1959	3
	MIL NL	1961	3
	MIN AL	1963	3
	SF NL	1963	3
	MIN AL	1964	3
	SF NL	1964	3
	MIL NL	1965	3
	ATL NL	1966	3
	SF NL	1966	3
	CIN NL	1970	3
	ATL NL	1973	3
	BOS AL	1977	3
	MIL AL	1982	3
	CLE AL	1987	3
	MIN AL	1987	3
	DET AL	1992	3
	TEX AL	1993	3

Most Extra Inning Home Runs, Team (Season)

	Team	*Year*	*HR*
1	WAS AL	1962	9
	PIT NL	1966	9
	CLE AL	1967	9
	HOU NL	1992	9
5	NY AL	1941	8
	BOS AL	1951	8
	BOS AL	1959	8
	NY AL	1962	8
	CIN NL	1962	8
	CLE AL	1963	8
	MIN AL	1964	8
	BAL AL	1969	8
	SEA AL	1969	8
	BAL AL	1982	8
	TOR AL	1985	8
	NY AL	1988	8

Most Home Runs Hit by Pitchers, Team (Season)

	Team	*Year*	*HR*
1	CHI NL	1887	16
2	CHI AL	1956	12
3	CLE AL	1949	11
	BRO NL	1955	11
5	NY NL	1934	10
	OAK AL	1969	10

Most Home Runs Hit at Home, Team (Season)

	Team	*Year*	*HR*
1	COL NL	1995	134
2	CLE AL	1970	133
3	CHI NL	1884	131
	NY NL	1947	131
5	CIN NL	1956	128

Most Home Runs Hit on Road, Team (Season)

	Team	*Year*	*HR*
1	NY AL	1961	128
2	MIL AL	1982	127
3	MIL NL	1957	124
4	TOR AL	1987	114
5	MIN AL	1963	113
	MIL AL	1980	113

Back-to-back Home Runs hit twice in same game by same players

Date	
06/14/1889	Paul Hines
IND NL	Jerry Denny
05/26/1930	Goose Goslin
WAS AL	Joe Judge
06/01/1930	Johnny Frederick
BRO NL	Babe Herman
08/13/1932	Bill Terry
NY NL	Mel Ott
05/25/1938	Rudy York
DET AL	Hank Greenberg
07/28/1940	Joe DiMaggio
NY AL	Charlie Keller
05/06/1941	Hank Greenberg
DET AL	Bruce Campbell
04/27/1954	Toby Atwell
PIT NL	Jerry Lynch
04/16/1955	Ernie Banks
CHI NL	Dee Fondy
09/19/1962	Walt Bond
CLE AL	John Romano
07/17/1966	Chuck Hinton
CLE AL	Rocky Colavito
10/03/1972	Don Money
PHI NL	Greg Luzinski
08/06/1992	Gary Sheffield
SD NL	Fred McGriff
08/15/1993	Barry Bonds
SF NL	Matt Williams
08/25/1993	Fred McGriff
ATL NL	Dave Justice
04/19/1994	Mo Vaughn
BOS AL	Tim Naehring
04/24/1994	Julio Franco
CHI AL	Robin Ventura

Most Home Runs by Teammates, Same Game (Career)

	Player	*Times Homering in Same Game*
1	Hank Aaron	75
	Eddie Mathews	
2	Lou Gehrig	73
	Babe Ruth	
3	Willie Mays	68
	Willie McCovey	
4	Gil Hodges	67
	Duke Snider	
5	Ron Santo	64
	Billy Williams	

Most Home Runs Hit as Teenager

	Player	*HR*
1	Tony Conigliaro	24
2	Mel Ott	19
3	Ken Griffey	16
4	Phil Cavarretta	14
5	Mickey Mantle	13
6	Ed Kranepool	12
7	Robin Yount	11
8	Harmon Killebrew	8
9	Cesar Cedeno	7
	Jimmy Sheckard	7

Most Home Runs Hit after Fortieth Birthday

	Player	*HR*
1	Carlton Fisk	72
2	Darrell Evans	60
3	Dave Winfield	59
4	Carl Yastrzemski	49
5	Stan Musial	46
6	Ted Williams	44
7	Hank Aaron	42

8	Graig Nettles	40
9	Hank Sauer	39
10	Willie McCovey	28

Youngest Players to hit Home Run

Player	Age	Date
Tommy Brown	17.257	08/20/1945
Tommy Brown	17.262	08/25/1945
Pat Callahan	17.264	07/06/1884
Pat Callahan	17.268	07/10/1884
Danny Murphy	18.021	09/13/1960

Oldest Players to hit Home Run

Player	Age	Date
Jack Quinn	46.357	06/27/1930
Cap Anson	45.175	10/03/1897
Cap Anson	45.175	10/03/1897
Carlton Fisk	45.102	04/07/1993
Cap Anson	45.069	06/19/1897

Most Home Runs in Each Month, Batter (Season)

	Player	Team	Month	HR
1	Graig Nettles	NY AL	Apr 1974	11
	Mike Schmidt	PHI NL	Apr 1976	11
	Willie Stargell	PIT NL	Apr 1971	11
4	Reggie Jackson	OAK AL	Apr 1974	10
	Dave Kingman	OAK AL	Apr 1984	10
	Mark McGwire	OAK AL	Apr 1992	10
	Tony Perez	CIN NL	Apr 1970	10
	Frank Robinson	BAL AL	Apr 1969	10
	Gary Sheffield	FLO NL	Apr 1994	10
	Matt Williams	SF NL	Apr 1994	10

	Player	Team	Month	HR
1	Mickey Mantle	NY AL	May 1956	16
2	Ken Griffey	SEA AL	May 1994	15
	Frank Howard	WAS AL	May 1968	15
	Harmon Killebrew	WAS AL	May 1959	15
	Mark McGwire	OAK AL	May 1987	15
	Babe Ruth	NY AL	May 1928	15
	Cy Williams	PHI NL	May 1923	15

	Player	Team	Month	HR
1	Pedro Guerrero	LA NL	Jun 1985	15
	Bob Johnson	PHI AL	Jun 1934	15
	Roger Maris	NY AL	Jun 1961	15
	Babe Ruth	NY AL	Jun 1930	15
5	Norm Cash	DET AL	Jun 1961	14
	Reggie Jackson	OAK AL	Jun 1969	14
	Jackie Jensen	BOS AL	Jun 1958	14
	Harmon Killebrew	MIN AL	Jun 1964	14
	Ralph Kiner	PIT NL	Jun 1947	14
	Roger Maris	NY AL	Jun 1960	14
	Ryne Sandberg	CHI NL	Jun 1990	14
	Mike Schmidt	PHI NL	Jun 1977	14

	Player	Team	Month	HR
1	Joe Adcock	MIL NL	Jul 1956	15
	Joe DiMaggio	NY AL	Jul 1937	15
	Hank Greenberg	DET AL	Jul 1938	15
4	Bob Horner	ATL NL	Jul 1980	14
	Chuck Klein	PHI NL	Jul 1929	14
	Mickey Mantle	NY AL	Jul 1958	14
	Mickey Mantle	NY AL	Jul 1961	14
	Babe Ruth	NY AL	Jul 1924	14

	Player	Team	Month	HR
1	Rudy York	DET AL	Aug 1937	18
2	Willie Mays	SF NL	Aug 1965	17
	Rudy York	DET AL	Aug 1943	17
4	Harlond Clift	STL AL	Aug 1938	15
	Andre Dawson	CHI NL	Aug 1987	15
	Jim Gentile	BAL AL	Aug 1961	15
	Babe Ruth	NY AL	Aug 1929	15
	Duke Snider	BRO NL	Aug 1953	15

	Player	Team	Month	HR
1	Albert Belle	CLE AL	Sep 1995	17
	Babe Ruth	NY AL	Sep 1927	17
3	Hank Greenberg	DET AL	Sep 1946	16
	Ralph Kiner	PIT NL	Sep 1949	16
5	Hank Greenberg	DET AL	Sep 1940	15

	Player	Team	Month	HR
1	George Brett	KC AL	Oct 1985	4
	Bug Holliday	CIN NL	Oct 1892	4
	Wally Joyner	CAL AL	Oct 1987	4
	Ron Kittle	CHI AL	Oct 1985	4
	Jocko Milligan	STL AA	Oct 1889	4
	Dave Parker	CIN NL	Oct 1985	4
	Mike Schmidt	PHI NL	Oct 1980	4
	Ned Williamson	CHI NL	Oct 1884	4
	Gus Zernial	CHI AL	Oct 1950	4

Most Hit Before Each Month, Batter (Season)

	Player	Team	Month	HR
1	Graig Nettles	NY AL	May 1974	11
	Mike Schmidt	PHI NL	May 1976	11
	Willie Stargell	PIT NL	May 1971	11
4	Reggie Jackson	OAK AL	May 1974	10
	Dave Kingman	OAK AL	May 1984	10
	Mark McGwire	OAK AL	May 1992	10
	Tony Perez	CIN NL	May 1970	10
	Frank Robinson	BAL AL	May 1969	10
	Gary Sheffield	FLO NL	May 1994	10
	Matt Williams	SF NL	May 1994	10

	Player	Team	Month	HR
1	Ken Griffey	SEA AL	Jun 1994	22
2	Mickey Mantle	NY AL	Jun 1956	20
	Frank Thomas	CHI AL	Jun 1994	20
4	Eric Davis	CIN NL	Jun 1987	19
	Frank Howard	WAS AL	Jun 1968	19
	Mark McGwire	OAK AL	Jun 1987	19
	Babe Ruth	NY AL	Jun 1928	19
	Matt Williams	SF NL	Jun 1994	19

	Player	Team	Month	HR
1	Ken Griffey	SEA AL	Jul 1994	32
2	Babe Ruth	NY AL	Jul 1928	30
	Babe Ruth	NY AL	Jul 1930	30
4	Jimmie Foxx	PHI AL	Jul 1932	29
	Reggie Jackson	OAK AL	Jul 1969	29
	Matt Williams	SF NL	Jul 1994	29
	Frank Thomas	CHI AL	Jul 1994	29

	Player	Team	Month	HR
1	Jimmie Foxx	PHI AL	Aug 1932	41
	Babe Ruth	NY AL	Aug 1928	41
3	Reggie Jackson	OAK AL	Aug 1969	40
	Roger Maris	NY AL	Aug 1961	40
	Matt Williams	SF NL	Aug 1994	40

	Player	Team	Month	HR
1	Roger Maris	NY AL	Sep 1961	51
2	Jimmie Foxx	PHI AL	Sep 1932	48
	Mickey Mantle	NY AL	Sep 1961	48
	Babe Ruth	NY AL	Sep 1921	48
5	Mickey Mantle	NY AL	Sep 1956	47
	Babe Ruth	NY AL	Sep 1928	47

	Player	Team	Month	HR
1	Roger Maris	NY AL	Oct 1961	60
	Babe Ruth	NY AL	Oct 1927	60
3	Jimmie Foxx	PHI AL	Oct 1932	58
	Hank Greenberg	DET AL	Oct 1938	58
	Babe Ruth	NY AL	Oct 1921	58

Two in One Inning, Batter

Player	Team	Date	Inning
Carlos Baerga	CLE AL	04/08/1993	7
Jeff Bagwell	HOU NL	06/24/1994	6
Lou Bierbauer	BRO PL	07/12/1890	3
John Boccabella	MON NL	07/06/1973	6
Ellis Burks	BOS AL	08/27/1990	4
Joe Carter	TOR AL	10/03/1993	2
Ed Cartwright	STL AA	09/23/1890	3
Andre Dawson	MON NL	07/30/1978	3
	MON NL	09/24/1985	5
Joe DiMaggio	NY AL	06/24/1936	5
Sid Gordon	NY NL	07/31/1949	2
Von Hayes	PHI NL	06/11/1985	1
Cliff Johnson	NY AL	06/30/1977	8
Charles Jones	BOS NL	06/10/1880	8
Al Kaline	DET AL	04/17/1955	6
Jeff King	PIT NL	08/08/1995	2
Ray Knight	CIN NL	05/13/1980	5
Hank Leiber	NY NL	08/24/1935	2
Jim Lemon	WAS AL	09/05/1959	3
Bobby Lowe	BOS NL	05/30/1894	3
Lee May	HOU NL	04/29/1974	6
Willie McCovey	SF NL	04/12/1973	4
	SF NL	06/27/1977	6
Dale Murphy	ATL NL	07/27/1989	6
Joe Pepitone	NY AL	05/23/1962	8
Bill Regan	BOS AL	06/16/1928	4
Rick Reichardt	CAL AL	04/30/1966	8
Andy Seminick	PHI NL	06/02/1949	8
Jake Stenzel	PIT NL	06/06/1894	3
Ken Williams	STL AL	08/07/1922	6
Hack Wilson	NY NL	07/01/1925	3

Switch Hitting HRs in One Game, Batter

Player	Team	Date
Luis Alicea	BOS AL	07/28/1995
Roberto Alomar	TOR AL	05/10/1991
	TOR AL	05/03/1995
Alan Ashby	HOU NL	09/27/1982
Carlos Baerga	CLE AL	04/08/1993
Mark Bailey	HOU NL	09/16/1984
Bret Barberie	MON NL	08/02/1991
Kevin Bass	HOU NL	08/03/1987
	HOU NL	09/02/1987
	HOU NL	08/20/1989
Todd Benzinger	SF NL	08/30/1993
Tony Bernazard	CLE AL	07/01/1986
Bobby Bonilla	PIT NL	07/03/1987
	PIT NL	04/06/1988

	NY NL	04/23/1993	
	NY NL	06/10/1993	
	NY NL	05/04/1994	
	NY NL	05/12/1995	
Don Buford	BAL AL	04/09/1970	
Ellis Burton	CHI NL	08/01/1963	
	CHI NL	09/07/1964	G1
Ken Caminiti	HOU NL	07/03/1994	
	SD NL	09/16/1995	
	SD NL	09/17/1995	
	SD NL	09/19/1995	
Chili Davis	SF NL	06/05/1983	
	SF NL	06/27/1987	
	SF NL	09/15/1987	
	CAL AL	07/30/1988	
	CAL AL	07/01/1989	
	CAL AL	09/15/1993	
	CAL AL	05/11/1994	
	CAL AL	07/30/1994	
Augie Galan	CHI NL	06/25/1937	
Ken Henderson	CHI AL	08/29/1975	
Todd Hundley	NY NL	06/18/1994	
Steve Jeltz	PHI NL	06/08/1989	
Howard Johnson	NY NL	08/31/1991	
Chad Kreuter	DET AL	09/07/1993	
Jim Lefebvre	LA NL	05/07/1966	
Mickey Mantle	NY AL	05/13/1955	
	NY AL	08/15/1955	G2
	NY AL	05/18/1956	
	NY AL	07/01/1956	G2
	NY AL	06/12/1957	
	NY AL	07/28/1958	
	NY AL	09/15/1959	
	NY AL	04/26/1961	
	NY AL	05/06/1962	G2
	NY AL	08/12/1964	
Lee Mazzilli	NY NL	09/03/1978	
Larry Milbourne	SEA AL	07/15/1978	
Eddie Murray	BAL AL	08/03/1977	
	BAL AL	08/29/1979	G2
	BAL AL	08/16/1981	
	BAL AL	04/24/1982	
	BAL AL	08/26/1982	
	BAL AL	08/26/1985	
	BAL AL	05/08/1987	
	BAL AL	05/09/1987	
	LA NL	04/18/1990	
	LA NL	06/09/1990	
	CLE AL	04/21/1994	
Wes Parker	LA NL	06/05/1966	G1
Geronimo Pena	STL NL	04/17/1994	
Tim Raines	MON NL	07/16/1988	
	CHI AL	08/31/1993	
Pete Rose	CIN NL	08/30/1966	
	CIN NL	08/02/1967	
Jim Russell	BOS NL	06/07/1948	
	BRO NL	07/26/1950	
Wally Schang	PHI AL	09/08/1916	
Red Schoendienst	STL NL	07/08/1951	G2
Donnie Scott	SEA AL	04/29/1985	
Ruben Sierra	TEX AL	09/13/1986	
	TEX AL	08/27/1988	
	TEX AL	06/08/1989	
	OAK AL	06/07/1994	
Nelson Simmons	DET AL	09/16/1985	
Ted Simmons	STL NL	04/17/1975	
	STL NL	06/11/1979	
	MIL AL	05/02/1982	
Roy Smalley	NY AL	09/05/1982	
	MIN AL	05/30/1986	
Reggie Smith	BOS AL	08/20/1967	G1
	BOS AL	08/11/1968	G2
	BOS AL	07/02/1972	G1
	BOS AL	04/16/1973	
	STL NL	05/04/1975	
	STL NL	05/22/1976	
Dale Sveum	MIL AL	07/17/1987	
	MIL AL	06/12/1988	
Mickey Tettleton	BAL AL	06/13/1988	
	DET AL	05/07/1993	
	TEX AL	04/28/1995	
Tom Tresh	NY AL	09/01/1963	
	NY AL	07/13/1964	
	NY AL	06/06/1965	G2
U.L. Washington	KC AL	09/21/1979	
Devon White	CAL AL	06/23/1987	
	CAL AL	06/29/1990	
	TOR AL	06/01/1992	
Roy White	NY AL	05/07/1970	
	NY AL	08/13/1973	
	NY AL	04/23/1975	
	NY AL	08/18/1976	
	NY AL	06/13/1978	
Mark Whiten	STL NL	09/14/1993	
Bernie Williams	NY AL	06/06/1994	
Maury Wills	LA NL	05/30/1962	G1
Willie Wilson	KC AL	06/15/1979	
Mike Young	BAL AL	08/13/1985	

Players Who Have Hit 30 Home Runs by the All-Star Break

Player	*Team*	*Year*	*HR*
Reggie Jackson	OAK AL	1969	37
Frank Howard	WAS AL	1969	34
Ken Griffey	SEA AL	1994	33
Roger Maris	NY AL	1961	33
Mark McGwire	OAK AL	1987	33
Matt Williams	SF NL	1994	33
Frank Thomas	CHI AL	1994	32
Willie Mays	NY NL	1954	31
Kevin Mitchell	SF NL	1989	31
Mike Schmidt	PHI NL	1979	31
Harmon Killebrew	MIN AL	1964	30
Dave Kingman	NY NL	1976	30
Willie McCovey	SF NL	1969	30
Willie Stargell	PIT NL	1971	30
Willie Stargell	PIT NL	1973	30

40 Home Run Seasons (Alphabetically)

Player	*Team*	*Year*	*HR*
Hank Aaron	MIL NL	1957	44
	MIL NL	1960	40
	MIL NL	1962	45
	MIL NL	1963	44
	ATL NL	1966	44
	ATL NL	1969	44
	ATL NL	1971	47
	ATL NL	1973	40
Dick Allen	PHI NL	1966	40
Tony Armas	BOS AL	1984	43
Ernie Banks	CHI NL	1955	44
	CHI NL	1957	43
	CHI NL	1958	47
	CHI NL	1959	45
	CHI NL	1960	41
Jesse Barfield	TOR AL	1986	40
George Bell	TOR AL	1987	47
Albert Belle	CLE AL	1995	50
Johnny Bench	CIN NL	1970	45
	CIN NL	1972	40
Dante Bichette	COL AL	1995	40
Barry Bonds	SF NL	1993	46
Jay Buhner	SEA AL	1995	40
Jeff Burroughs	ATL NL	1977	41
Roy Campanella	BRO NL	1953	41
Jose Canseco	OAK AL	1988	42
	OAK AL	1991	44
Norm Cash	DET AL	1961	41
Orlando Cepeda	SF NL	1961	46
Rocky Colavito	CLE AL	1958	41
	CLE AL	1959	42
	DET AL	1961	45
Andre Dawson	CHI NL	1987	49
Joe DiMaggio	NY AL	1937	46
Darrell Evans	ATL NL	1973	41
	DET AL	1985	40
Cecil Fielder	DET AL	1990	51
	DET AL	1991	44
George Foster	CIN NL	1977	52
	CIN NL	1978	40
Jimmie Foxx	PHI AL	1932	58
	PHI AL	1933	48
	PHI AL	1934	44
	BOS AL	1936	41
	BOS AL	1938	50
Lou Gehrig	NY AL	1927	47
	NY AL	1930	41
	NY AL	1931	46
	NY AL	1934	49
	NY AL	1936	49
Jim Gentile	BAL AL	1961	46
Juan Gonzalez	TEX AL	1992	43
	TEX AL	1993	46
Hank Greenberg	DET AL	1937	40
	DET AL	1938	58
	DET AL	1940	41
	DET AL	1946	44
Ken Griffey	SEA AL	1993	45
	SEA AL	1994	40
Gil Hodges	BRO NL	1951	40
	BRO NL	1954	42
Rogers Hornsby	STL NL	1922	42
Frank Howard	WAS AL	1968	44
	WAS AL	1969	48
	WAS AL	1970	44
Reggie Jackson	OAK AL	1969	47
	NY AL	1980	41
Dave Johnson	ATL NL	1973	43
Dave Justice	ATL NL	1993	40
Harmon Killebrew	WAS AL	1959	42
	MIN AL	1961	46
	MIN AL	1962	48
	MIN AL	1963	45
	MIN AL	1964	49
	MIN AL	1967	44
	MIN AL	1969	49
	MIN AL	1970	41
Ralph Kiner	PIT NL	1947	51
	PIT NL	1948	40
	PIT NL	1949	54
	PIT NL	1950	47

	PIT NL	1951	42
Dave Kingman	CHI NL	1979	48
Chuck Klein	PHI NL	1929	43
	PHI NL	1930	40
Ted Kluszewski	CIN NL	1953	40
	CIN NL	1954	49
	CIN NL	1955	47
Mickey Mantle	NY AL	1956	52
	NY AL	1958	42
	NY AL	1960	40
	NY AL	1961	54
Roger Maris	NY AL	1961	61
Eddie Mathews	MIL NL	1953	47
	MIL NL	1954	40
	MIL NL	1955	41
	MIL NL	1959	46
Willie Mays	NY NL	1954	41
	NY NL	1955	51
	SF NL	1961	40
	SF NL	1962	49
	SF NL	1964	47
	SF NL	1965	52
Willie McCovey	SF NL	1963	44
	SF NL	1969	45
Mark McGwire	OAK AL	1987	49
	OAK AL	1992	42
Kevin Mitchell	SF NL	1989	47
Johnny Mize	STL NL	1940	43
	NY NL	1947	51
	NY NL	1948	40
Dale Murphy	ATL NL	1987	44
Ben Oglivie	MIL AL	1980	41
Mel Ott	NY NL	1929	42
Tony Perez	CIN NL	1970	40
Rico Petrocelli	BOS AL	1969	40
Wally Post	CIN NL	1955	40
Jim Rice	BOS AL	1978	46
Frank Robinson	BAL AL	1966	49
Al Rosen	CLE AL	1953	43
Babe Ruth	NY AL	1920	54
	NY AL	1921	59
	NY AL	1923	41
	NY AL	1924	46
	NY AL	1926	47
	NY AL	1927	60
	NY AL	1928	54
	NY AL	1929	46
	NY AL	1930	49
	NY AL	1931	46
	NY AL	1932	41
Ryne Sandberg	CHI NL	1990	40
Hank Sauer	CHI NL	1954	41
Mike Schmidt	PHI NL	1979	45
	PHI NL	1980	48
	PHI NL	1983	40
Roy Sievers	WAS AL	1957	42
Duke Snider	BRO NL	1953	42
	BRO NL	1954	40
	BRO NL	1955	42
	BRO NL	1956	43
	BRO NL	1957	40
Willie Stargell	PIT NL	1971	48
	PIT NL	1973	44
Dick Stuart	BOS AL	1963	42
Frank Thomas	CHI AL	1993	41
	CHI AL	1995	40
Gorman Thomas	MIL AL	1979	45
Hal Trosky	CLE AL	1936	42
Billy Williams	CHI NL	1970	42
Cy Williams	PHI NL	1923	41
Matt Williams	SF NL	1994	43
Ted Williams	BOS AL	1949	43
Hack Wilson	CHI NL	1930	56
Carl Yastrzemski	BOS AL	1967	44
	BOS AL	1969	40
	BOS AL	1970	40
Gus Zernial	PHI AL	1953	42

Most Home Runs, Season (40 or more)

	Player	*Team*	*Year*	*HR*
1	Roger Maris	NY AL	1961	61
2	Babe Ruth	NY AL	1927	60
3	Babe Ruth	NY AL	1921	59
4	Jimmie Foxx	PHI AL	1932	58
	Hank Greenberg	DET AL	1938	58
6	Hack Wilson	CHI NL	1930	56
7	Ralph Kiner	PIT NL	1949	54
	Mickey Mantle	NY AL	1961	54
	Babe Ruth	NY AL	1920	54
	Babe Ruth	NY AL	1928	54
11	George Foster	CIN NL	1977	52
	Mickey Mantle	NY AL	1956	52
	Willie Mays	SF NL	1965	52
14	Cecil Fielder	DET AL	1990	51
	Ralph Kiner	PIT NL	1947	51
	Willie Mays	NY NL	1955	51
	Johnny Mize	NY NL	1947	51
18	Albert Belle	CLE AL	1995	50
	Jimmie Foxx	BOS AL	1938	50
20	Andre Dawson	CHI NL	1987	49
	Lou Gehrig	NY AL	1934	49
	Lou Gehrig	NY AL	1936	49
	Harmon Killebrew	MIN AL	1964	49
	Harmon Killebrew	MIN AL	1969	49
	Ted Kluszewski	CIN NL	1954	49
	Willie Mays	SF NL	1962	49
	Mark McGwire	OAK AL	1987	49
	Frank Robinson	BAL AL	1966	49
	Babe Ruth	NY AL	1930	49
30	Jimmie Foxx	PHI AL	1933	48
	Frank Howard	WAS AL	1969	48
	Harmon Killebrew	MIN AL	1962	48
	Dave Kingman	CHI NL	1979	48
	Mike Schmidt	PHI NL	1980	48
	Willie Stargell	PIT NL	1971	48
36	Hank Aaron	ATL NL	1971	47
	Ernie Banks	CHI NL	1958	47
	George Bell	TOR AL	1987	47
	Lou Gehrig	NY AL	1927	47
	Reggie Jackson	OAK AL	1969	47
	Ralph Kiner	PIT NL	1950	47
	Ted Kluszewski	CIN NL	1955	47
	Eddie Mathews	MIL NL	1953	47
	Willie Mays	SF NL	1964	47
	Kevin Mitchell	SF NL	1989	47
	Babe Ruth	NY AL	1926	47
47	Barry Bonds	SF NL	1993	46
	Orlando Cepeda	SF NL	1961	46
	Joe DiMaggio	NY AL	1937	46
	Lou Gehrig	NY AL	1931	46
	Jim Gentile	BAL AL	1961	46
	Juan Gonzalez	TEX AL	1993	46
	Harmon Killebrew	MIN AL	1961	46
	Eddie Mathews	MIL NL	1959	46
	Jim Rice	BOS AL	1978	46
	Babe Ruth	NY AL	1924	46
	Babe Ruth	NY AL	1929	46
	Babe Ruth	NY AL	1931	46
59	Hank Aaron	MIL NL	1962	45
	Ernie Banks	CHI NL	1959	45
	Johnny Bench	CIN NL	1970	45
	Rocky Colavito	DET AL	1961	45
	Ken Griffey	SEA AL	1993	45
	Harmon Killebrew	MIN AL	1963	45
	Willie McCovey	SF NL	1969	45
	Mike Schmidt	PHI NL	1979	45
	Gorman Thomas	MIL AL	1979	45
68	Hank Aaron	MIL NL	1957	44
	Hank Aaron	MIL NL	1963	44
	Hank Aaron	ATL NL	1966	44
	Hank Aaron	ATL NL	1969	44
	Ernie Banks	CHI NL	1955	44
	Jose Canseco	OAK AL	1991	44
	Cecil Fielder	DET AL	1991	44
	Jimmie Foxx	PHI AL	1934	44
	Hank Greenberg	DET AL	1946	44
	Frank Howard	WAS AL	1968	44
	Frank Howard	WAS AL	1970	44
	Harmon Killebrew	MIN AL	1967	44
	Willie McCovey	SF NL	1963	44
	Dale Murphy	ATL NL	1987	44
	Willie Stargell	PIT NL	1973	44
	Carl Yastrzemski	BOS AL	1967	44
84	Tony Armas	BOS AL	1984	43
	Ernie Banks	CHI NL	1957	43
	Juan Gonzalez	TEX AL	1992	43
	Dave Johnson	ATL NL	1973	43
	Chuck Klein	PHI NL	1929	43
	Johnny Mize	STL NL	1940	43
	Al Rosen	CLE AL	1953	43
	Duke Snider	BRO NL	1956	43
	Matt Williams	SF NL	1994	43
	Ted Williams	BOS AL	1949	43
94	Jose Canseco	OAK AL	1988	42
	Rocky Colavito	CLE AL	1959	42
	Gil Hodges	BRO NL	1954	42
	Rogers Hornsby	STL NL	1922	42
	Harmon Killebrew	WAS AL	1959	42
	Ralph Kiner	PIT NL	1951	42
	Mickey Mantle	NY AL	1958	42
	Mark McGwire	OAK AL	1992	42
	Mel Ott	NY NL	1929	42
	Roy Sievers	WAS AL	1957	42
	Duke Snider	BRO NL	1953	42
	Duke Snider	BRO NL	1955	42
	Dick Stuart	BOS AL	1963	42
	Hal Trosky	CLE AL	1936	42
	Billy Williams	CHI NL	1970	42
	Gus Zernial	PHI AL	1953	42
110	Ernie Banks	CHI NL	1960	41
	Jeff Burroughs	ATL NL	1977	41
	Roy Campanella	BRO NL	1953	41
	Norm Cash	DET AL	1961	41
	Rocky Colavito	CLE AL	1958	41
	Darrell Evans	ATL NL	1973	41
	Jimmie Foxx	BOS AL	1936	41
	Lou Gehrig	NY AL	1930	41
	Hank Greenberg	DET AL	1940	41
	Reggie Jackson	NY AL	1980	41
	Harmon Killebrew	MIN AL	1970	41

	Eddie Mathews	MIL NL	1955	41
	Willie Mays	NY NL	1954	41
	Ben Oglivie	MIL AL	1980	41
	Babe Ruth	NY AL	1923	41
	Babe Ruth	NY AL	1932	41
	Hank Sauer	CHI NL	1954	41
	Cy Williams	PHI NL	1923	41
	Frank Thomas	CHI AL	1993	41
129	Hank Aaron	MIL NL	1960	40
	Hank Aaron	ATL NL	1973	40
	Dick Allen	PHI NL	1966	40
	Jesse Barfield	TOR AL	1986	40
	Johnny Bench	CIN NL	1972	40
	Dante Bichette	COL NL	1995	40
	Jay Buhner	SEA AL	1995	40
	Darrell Evans	DET AL	1985	40
	George Foster	CIN NL	1978	40
	Hank Greenberg	DET AL	1937	40
	Ken Griffey	SEA AL	1994	40
	Gil Hodges	BRO NL	1951	40
	Dave Justice	ATL NL	1993	40
	Ralph Kiner	PIT NL	1948	40
	Chuck Klein	PHI NL	1930	40
	Ted Kluszewski	CIN NL	1953	40
	Mickey Mantle	NY AL	1960	40
	Eddie Mathews	MIL NL	1954	40
	Willie Mays	SF NL	1961	40
	Johnny Mize	NY NL	1948	40
	Tony Perez	CIN NL	1970	40
	Rico Petrocelli	BOS AL	1969	40
	Wally Post	CIN NL	1955	40
	Ryne Sandberg	CHI NL	1990	40
	Mike Schmidt	PHI NL	1983	40
	Duke Snider	BRO NL	1954	40
	Duke Snider	BRO NL	1957	40
	Frank Thomas	CHI AL	1995	40
	Carl Yastrzemski	BOS AL	1969	40
	Carl Yastrzemski	BOS AL	1970	40

Most Home Runs by Right-Handed Batter (Season)

	Player	*Team*	*Year*	*HR*
1	Jimmie Foxx	PHI AL	1932	58
	Hank Greenberg	DET AL	1938	58
3	Hack Wilson	CHI NL	1930	56
4	Ralph Kiner	PIT NL	1949	54
5	George Foster	CIN NL	1977	52
	Willie Mays	SF NL	1965	52
7	Cecil Fielder	DET AL	1990	51
	Ralph Kiner	PIT NL	1947	51
	Willie Mays	NY NL	1955	51
10	Albert Belle	CLE AL	1995	50
	Jimmie Foxx	BOS AL	1938	50

Most Home Runs by Left-Handed Batter (Season)

	Player	*Team*	*Year*	*HR*
1	Roger Maris	NY AL	1961	61
2	Babe Ruth	NY AL	1927	60
3	Babe Ruth	NY AL	1921	59
4	Babe Ruth	NY AL	1920	54
	Babe Ruth	NY AL	1928	54
6	Johnny Mize	NY NL	1947	51
7	Lou Gehrig	NY AL	1934	49
	Lou Gehrig	NY AL	1936	49
	Ted Kluszewski	CIN NL	1954	49
	Babe Ruth	NY AL	1930	49

Most Home Runs by Switch Hitter (Season)

	Player	*Team*	*Year*	*HR*
1	Mickey Mantle	NY AL	1961	54
2	Mickey Mantle	NY AL	1956	52
3	Mickey Mantle	NY AL	1958	42
4	Mickey Mantle	NY AL	1960	40
5	Howard Johnson	NY NL	1991	38
6	Mickey Mantle	NY AL	1955	37
7	Howard Johnson	NY NL	1987	36
	Howard Johnson	NY NL	1989	36
9	Ripper Collins	STL NL	1934	35
	Mickey Mantle	NY AL	1964	35
	Ken Singleton	BAL AL	1979	35

Yearly Leaders

Year	*League*	*Player*	*Team*	*HR*
1876	NL	George Hall	PHI	5
1877	NL	Lip Pike	CIN	4
1878	NL	Paul Hines	PRO	4
1879	NL	Charles Jones	BOS	9
1880	NL	Jim O'Rourke	BOS	6
		Harry Stovey	WOR	6
1881	NL	Dan Brouthers	BUF	8
1882	AA	Oscar Walker	STL	7
	NL	George Wood	DET	7
1883	AA	Harry Stovey	PHI	14
	NL	Buck Ewing	NY	10
1884	AA	John Reilly	CIN	11
	NL	Ned Williamson	CHI	27
	UA	Fred Dunlap	STL	13
1885	AA	Harry Stovey	PHI	13
	NL	Abner Dalrymple	CHI	11
1886	AA	Bid McPhee	CIN	8
	NL	Dan Brouthers	DET	11
		Hardy Richardson	DET	11
1887	AA	Tip O'Neill	STL	14
	NL	Billy O'Brien	WAS	19
1888	AA	John Reilly	CIN	13
	NL	Jimmy Ryan	CHI	16
1889	AA	Bug Holliday	CIN	19
		Harry Stovey	PHI	19
	NL	Sam Thompson	PHI	20
1890	AA	Count Campau	STL	9
	NL	Oyster Burns	BRO	13
		Mike Tiernan	NY	13
		Walt Wilmot	CHI	13
	PL	Roger Connor	NY	14
1891	AA	Duke Farrell	BOS	12
	NL	Harry Stovey	BOS	16
		Mike Tiernan	NY	16
1892	NL	Bug Holliday	CIN	13
1893	NL	Ed Delahanty	PHI	19
1894	NL	Hugh Duffy	BOS	18
1895	NL	Sam Thompson	PHI	18
1896	NL	Ed Delahanty	PHI	13
		Bill Joyce	WAS	13
1897	NL	Hugh Duffy	BOS	11
1898	NL	Jimmy Collins	BOS	15
1899	NL	Buck Freeman	WAS	25
1900	NL	Herman Long	BOS	12
1901	AL	Nap Lajoie	PHI	14
	NL	Sam Crawford	CIN	16
1902	AL	Socks Seybold	PHI	16
	NL	Tommy Leach	PIT	6
1903	AL	Buck Freeman	BOS	13
	NL	Jimmy Sheckard	BRO	9
1904	AL	Harry Davis	PHI	10
	NL	Harry Lumley	BRO	9
1905	AL	Harry Davis	PHI	8
	NL	Fred Odwell	CIN	9
1906	AL	Harry Davis	PHI	12
	NL	Tim Jordan	BRO	12
1907	AL	Harry Davis	PHI	8
	NL	Dave Brain	BOS	10
1908	AL	Sam Crawford	DET	7
	NL	Tim Jordan	BRO	12
1909	AL	Ty Cobb	DET	9
	NL	Red Murray	NY	7
1910	AL	Jacob Stahl	BOS	10
	NL	Fred Beck	BOS	10
		Wildfire Schulte	CHI	10
1911	AL	Frank Baker	PHI	11
	NL	Wildfire Schulte	CHI	21
1912	AL	Frank Baker	PHI	10
		Tris Speaker	BOS	10
	NL	Heinie Zimmerman	CHI	14
1913	AL	Frank Baker	PHI	12
	NL	Gavvy Cravath	PHI	19
1914	AL	Frank Baker	PHI	9
	FL	Edward Zwilling	CHI	16
	NL	Gavvy Cravath	PHI	19
1915	AL	Braggo Roth	CHI	7
	FL	Hal Chase	BUF	17
	NL	Gavvy Cravath	PHI	24
1916	AL	Wally Pipp	NY	12
	NL	Dave Robertson	NY	12
		Cy Williams	CHI	12
1917	AL	Wally Pipp	NY	9
	NL	Gavvy Cravath	PHI	12
		Dave Robertson	NY	12
1918	AL	Babe Ruth	BOS	11
		Tilly Walker	PHI	11
	NL	Gavvy Cravath	PHI	8
1919	AL	Babe Ruth	BOS	29
	NL	Gavvy Cravath	PHI	12
1920	AL	Babe Ruth	NY	54
	NL	Cy Williams	PHI	15
1921	AL	Babe Ruth	NY	59
	NL	George Kelly	NY	23
1922	AL	Ken Williams	STL	39
	NL	Rogers Hornsby	STL	42
1923	AL	Babe Ruth	NY	41
	NL	Cy Williams	PHI	41
1924	AL	Babe Ruth	NY	46
	NL	Jack Fournier	BRO	27
1925	AL	Bob Meusel	NY	33
	NL	Rogers Hornsby	STL	39
1926	AL	Babe Ruth	NY	47
	NL	Hack Wilson	CHI	21
1927	AL	Babe Ruth	NY	60
	NL	Cy Williams	PHI	30
		Hack Wilson	CHI	30
1928	AL	Babe Ruth	NY	54
	NL	Jim Bottomley	STL	31
		Hack Wilson	CHI	31
1929	AL	Babe Ruth	NY	46
	NL	Chuck Klein	PHI	43
1930	AL	Babe Ruth	NY	49
	NL	Hack Wilson	CHI	56
1931	AL	Lou Gehrig	NY	46
		Babe Ruth	NY	46
	NL	Chuck Klein	PHI	31
1932	AL	Jimmie Foxx	PHI	58
	NL	Chuck Klein	PHI	38

Year	League	Player	Team	HR
		Mel Ott	NY	38
1933	AL	Jimmie Foxx	PHI	48
	NL	Chuck Klein	PHI	28
1934	AL	Lou Gehrig	NY	49
	NL	Ripper Collins	STL	35
		Mel Ott	NY	35
1935	AL	Jimmie Foxx	PHI	36
		Hank Greenberg	DET	36
	NL	Wally Berger	BOS	34
1936	AL	Lou Gehrig	NY	49
	NL	Mel Ott	NY	33
1937	AL	Joe DiMaggio	NY	46
	NL	Joe Medwick	STL	31
		Mel Ott	NY	31
1938	AL	Hank Greenberg	DET	58
	NL	Mel Ott	NY	36
1939	AL	Jimmie Foxx	BOS	35
	NL	Johnny Mize	STL	28
1940	AL	Hank Greenberg	DET	41
	NL	Johnny Mize	STL	43
1941	AL	Ted Williams	BOS	37
	NL	Dolph Camilli	BRO	34
1942	AL	Ted Williams	BOS	36
	NL	Mel Ott	NY	30
1943	AL	Rudy York	DET	34
	NL	Bill Nicholson	CHI	29
1944	AL	Nick Etten	NY	22
	NL	Bill Nicholson	CHI	33
1945	AL	Vern Stephens	STL	24
	NL	Tommy Holmes	BOS	28
1946	AL	Hank Greenberg	DET	44
	NL	Ralph Kiner	PIT	23
1947	AL	Ted Williams	BOS	32
	NL	Ralph Kiner	PIT	51
		Johnny Mize	NY	51
1948	AL	Joe DiMaggio	NY	39
	NL	Ralph Kiner	PIT	40
		Johnny Mize	NY	40
1949	AL	Ted Williams	BOS	43
	NL	Ralph Kiner	PIT	54
1950	AL	Al Rosen	CLE	37
	NL	Ralph Kiner	PIT	47
1951	AL	Gus Zernial	PHI	33
	NL	Ralph Kiner	PIT	42
1952	AL	Larry Doby	CLE	32
	NL	Ralph Kiner	PIT	37
		Hank Sauer	CHI	37
1953	AL	Al Rosen	CLE	43
	NL	Eddie Mathews	MIL	47
1954	AL	Larry Doby	CLE	32
	NL	Ted Kluszewski	CIN	49
1955	AL	Mickey Mantle	NY	37
	NL	Willie Mays	NY	51
1956	AL	Mickey Mantle	NY	52
	NL	Duke Snider	BRO	43
1957	AL	Roy Sievers	WAS	42
	NL	Hank Aaron	MIL	44
1958	AL	Mickey Mantle	NY	42
	NL	Ernie Banks	CHI	47
1959	AL	Rocky Colavito	CLE	42
		Harmon Killebrew	WAS	42
	NL	Eddie Mathews	MIL	46
1960	AL	Mickey Mantle	NY	40
	NL	Ernie Banks	CHI	41
1961	AL	Roger Maris	NY	61
	NL	Orlando Cepeda	SF	46
1962	AL	Harmon Killebrew	MIN	48
	NL	Willie Mays	SF	49
1963	AL	Harmon Killebrew	MIN	45
	NL	Hank Aaron	MIL	44
		Willie McCovey	SF	44
1964	AL	Harmon Killebrew	MIN	49
	NL	Willie Mays	SF	47
1965	AL	Tony Conigliaro	BOS	32
	NL	Willie Mays	SF	52
1966	AL	Frank Robinson	BAL	49
	NL	Hank Aaron	ATL	44
1967	AL	Harmon Killebrew	MIN	44
		Carl Yastrzemski	BOS	44
	NL	Hank Aaron	ATL	39
1968	AL	Frank Howard	WAS	44
	NL	Willie McCovey	SF	36
1969	AL	Harmon Killebrew	MIN	49
	NL	Willie McCovey	SF	45
1970	AL	Frank Howard	WAS	44
	NL	Johnny Bench	CIN	45
1971	AL	Bill Melton	CHI	33
	NL	Willie Stargell	PIT	48
1972	AL	Dick Allen	CHI	37
	NL	Johnny Bench	CIN	40
1973	AL	Reggie Jackson	OAK	32
	NL	Willie Stargell	PIT	44
1974	AL	Dick Allen	CHI	32
	NL	Mike Schmidt	PHI	36
1975	AL	Reggie Jackson	OAK	36
		George Scott	MIL	36
	NL	Mike Schmidt	PHI	38
1976	AL	Graig Nettles	NY	32
	NL	Mike Schmidt	PHI	38
1977	AL	Jim Rice	BOS	39
	NL	George Foster	CIN	52
1978	AL	Jim Rice	BOS	46
	NL	George Foster	CIN	40
1979	AL	Gorman Thomas	MIL	45
	NL	Dave Kingman	CHI	48
1980	AL	Reggie Jackson	NY	41
		Ben Oglivie	MIL	41
	NL	Mike Schmidt	PHI	48
1981	AL	Tony Armas	OAK	22
		Dwight Evans	BOS	22
		Bobby Grich	CAL	22
		Eddie Murray	BAL	22
	NL	Mike Schmidt	PHI	31
1982	AL	Reggie Jackson	CAL	39
		Gorman Thomas	MIL	39
	NL	Dave Kingman	NY	37
1983	AL	Jim Rice	BOS	39
	NL	Mike Schmidt	PHI	40
1984	AL	Tony Armas	BOS	43
	NL	Dale Murphy	ATL	36
		Mike Schmidt	PHI	36
1985	AL	Darrell Evans	DET	40
	NL	Dale Murphy	ATL	37
1986	AL	Jesse Barfield	TOR	40
	NL	Mike Schmidt	PHI	37
1987	AL	Mark McGwire	OAK	49
	NL	Andre Dawson	CHI	49
1988	AL	Jose Canseco	OAK	42
	NL	Darryl Strawberry	NY	39
1989	AL	Fred McGriff	TOR	36
	NL	Kevin Mitchell	SF	47
1990	AL	Cecil Fielder	DET	51
	NL	Ryne Sandberg	CHI	40
1991	AL	Jose Canseco	OAK	44
		Cecil Fielder	DET	44
	NL	Howard Johnson	NY	38
1992	AL	Juan Gonzalez	TEX	43
	NL	Fred McGriff	SD	35
1993	AL	Juan Gonzalez	TEX	46
	NL	Barry Bonds	SF	46
1994	AL	Ken Griffey	SEA	40
	NL	Matt Williams	SF	43
1995	AL	Albert Belle	CLE	50
	NL	Dante Bichette	COL	40

Most Home Runs without Leading League, Batter (Season)

	Player	*HR*	*Year*	*Leader*
1	Mickey Mantle	54	1961	(Roger Maris 61)
2	Jimmie Foxx	50	1938	(Hank Greenberg 58)
3	Frank Howard	48	1969	(Harmon Killebrew 49)
4	Hank Aaron	47	1971	(Willie Stargell 48)
	George Bell	47	1987	(Mark McGwire 49)
	Lou Gehrig	47	1927	(Babe Ruth 60)
	Reggie Jackson	47	1969	(Harmon Killebrew 49)
	Ted Kluszewski	47	1955	(Willie Mays 51)

Most Home Runs in Two Consecutive Seasons

	Player	*Years*	*HR*
1	Babe Ruth	1927–28	114
2	Babe Ruth	1920–21	113
3	Babe Ruth	1926–27	107
4	Jimmie Foxx	1932–33	106
5	Ralph Kiner	1949–50	101
6	Roger Maris	1960–61	100
	Babe Ruth	1928–29	100
8	Willie Mays	1964–65	99
9	Hank Greenberg	1937–38	98
10	Ted Kluszewski	1954–55	96

Most Home Runs in Three Consecutive Seasons

	Player	*Years*	*HR*
1	Babe Ruth	1926–28	161
2	Babe Ruth	1927–29	160
3	Jimmie Foxx	1932–34	150
4	Babe Ruth	1928–30	149
5	Babe Ruth	1920–22	148
6	Ralph Kiner	1947–49	145
7	Ralph Kiner	1949–51	143
8	Harmon Killebrew	1962–64	142
	Babe Ruth	1919–21	142
10	Ralph Kiner	1948–50	141
	Babe Ruth	1929–31	141

Most Home Runs in Four Consecutive Seasons

	Player	*Years*	*HR*
1	Babe Ruth	1927–30	209
2	Babe Ruth	1926–29	207
3	Babe Ruth	1928–31	195
4	Ralph Kiner	1947–50	192
5	Babe Ruth	1920–23	189
6	Harmon Killebrew	1961–64	188
7	Jimmie Foxx	1932–35	186
	Willie Mays	1962–65	186
	Babe Ruth	1925–28	186
10	Ralph Kiner	1948–51	183

Most Home Runs in Five Consecutive Seasons

	Player	*Years*	*HR*
1	Babe Ruth	1926–30	256
2	Babe Ruth	1927–31	255

3	Babe Ruth	1928–32	236
4	Babe Ruth	1920–24	235
5	Ralph Kiner	1947–51	234
6	Babe Ruth	1924–28	232
	Babe Ruth	1925–29	232
8	Jimmie Foxx	1932–36	227
9	Willie Mays	1961–65	226
10	Willie Mays	1962–66	223

Most Home Runs in Six Consecutive Seasons

	Player	Years	HR
1	Babe Ruth	1926–31	302
2	Babe Ruth	1927–32	296
3	Babe Ruth	1925–30	281
4	Babe Ruth	1924–29	278
5	Babe Ruth	1923–28	273
6	Ralph Kiner	1947–52	271
7	Babe Ruth	1928–33	270
8	Babe Ruth	1919–24	264
9	Jimmie Foxx	1932–37	263
	Willie Mays	1961–66	263

Most Home Runs in Seven Consecutive Seasons

	Player	Years	HR
1	Babe Ruth	1926–32	343
2	Babe Ruth	1927–33	330
3	Babe Ruth	1924–30	327
	Babe Ruth	1925–31	327
5	Babe Ruth	1923–29	319
6	Jimmie Foxx	1932–38	313
	Babe Ruth	1921–27	313
8	Babe Ruth	1922–28	308
9	Babe Ruth	1920–26	307
10	Ralph Kiner	1947–53	306

Most Home Runs in Eight Consecutive Seasons

	Player	Years	HR
1	Babe Ruth	1926–33	377
2	Babe Ruth	1924–31	373
3	Babe Ruth	1923–30	368
	Babe Ruth	1925–32	368
5	Babe Ruth	1920–27	367
	Babe Ruth	1921–28	367
7	Babe Ruth	1922–29	354
8	Babe Ruth	1927–34	352
9	Jimmie Foxx	1932–39	348
10	Jimmie Foxx	1931–38	343

Most Home Runs in Nine Consecutive Seasons

	Player	Years	HR
1	Babe Ruth	1920–28	421
2	Babe Ruth	1923–31	414
	Babe Ruth	1924–32	414
4	Babe Ruth	1921–29	413
5	Babe Ruth	1922–30	403
6	Babe Ruth	1925–33	402
7	Babe Ruth	1926–34	399
8	Babe Ruth	1919–27	396
9	Jimmie Foxx	1932–40	384
10	Jimmie Foxx	1930–38	380

Most Home Runs in Ten Consecutive Seasons

	Player	Years	HR
1	Babe Ruth	1920–29	467
2	Babe Ruth	1921–30	462
3	Babe Ruth	1923–32	455
4	Babe Ruth	1919–28	450
5	Babe Ruth	1922–31	449
6	Babe Ruth	1924–33	448
7	Babe Ruth	1925–34	424
8	Jimmie Foxx	1930–39	415
9	Jimmie Foxx	1931–40	414
10	Jimmie Foxx	1929–38	413

Most Consecutive Seasons with 50 or more Home Runs

	Player	Years	HR
1	Babe Ruth	1920–21	2
	Babe Ruth	1927–28	2

Most Consecutive Seasons with 40 or more Home Runs

	Player	Years	HR
1	Babe Ruth	1926–32	7
2	Ralph Kiner	1947–51	5
	Duke Snider	1953–57	5
4	Ernie Banks	1957–60	4
	Harmon Killebrew	1961–64	4
6	Jimmie Foxx	1932–34	3
	Frank Howard	1968–70	3
	Ted Kluszewski	1953–55	3
	Eddie Mathews	1953–55	3
10	Hank Aaron	1962–63	2
	Rocky Colavito	1958–59	2
	Cecil Fielder	1990–91	2
	George Foster	1977–78	2
	Lou Gehrig	1930–31	2
	Juan Gonzalez	1992–93	2
	Hank Greenberg	1937–38	2
	Ken Griffey	1993–94	2
	Harmon Killebrew	1969–70	2
	Chuck Klein	1929–30	2
	Mickey Mantle	1960–61	2
	Willie Mays	1954–55	2
	Willie Mays	1961–62	2
	Willie Mays	1964–65	2
	Johnny Mize	1947–48	2
	Babe Ruth	1920–21	2
	Babe Ruth	1923–24	2
	Mike Schmidt	1979–80	2
	Carl Yastrzemski	1969–70	2

Most Consecutive Seasons with 30 or more Home Runs

	Player	Years	HR
1	Jimmie Foxx	1929–40	12
2	Lou Gehrig	1929–37	9
	Eddie Mathews	1953–61	9
	Mike Schmidt	1979–87	9
5	Mickey Mantle	1955–62	8
	Babe Ruth	1926–33	8
7	Hank Aaron	1957–63	7
	Ralph Kiner	1947–53	7
	Fred McGriff	1988–94	7
10	Harmon Killebrew	1959–64	6
	Willie Mays	1961–66	6
	Willie McCovey	1965–70	6

Most Consecutive Seasons with 20 or more Home Runs

	Player	Years	HR
1	Hank Aaron	1955–74	20
2	Babe Ruth	1919–34	16
3	Willie Mays	1954–68	15
4	Eddie Mathews	1952–65	14
	Mike Schmidt	1974–87	14
6	Reggie Jackson	1968–80	13
	Willie Stargell	1964–76	13
	Billy Williams	1961–73	13

Most Consecutive Seasons with 10 or more Home Runs

	Player	Years	HR
1	Hank Aaron	1954–76	23
2	Reggie Jackson	1968–87	20
	Al Kaline	1955–74	20
	Carl Yastrzemski	1961–80	20
5	Darrell Evans	1971–89	19
	Eddie Murray	1977–95	19
	Frank Robinson	1956–74	19
8	Andre Dawson	1977–94	18
	Dwight Evans	1973–90	18
	Mickey Mantle	1951–68	18
	Willie Mays	1954–71	18
	Stan Musial	1946–63	18
	Mel Ott	1928–45	18
	Willie Stargell	1963–80	18

Most Consecutive Seasons Hitting a Home Run

	Player	Years	HR
1	Ty Cobb	1905–28	24
2	Hank Aaron	1954–76	23
	Carlton Fisk	1971–93	23
	Rusty Staub	1963–85	23
	Carl Yastrzemski	1961–83	23
6	Al Kaline	1953–74	22
	Willie McCovey	1959–80	22
	Tony Perez	1965–86	22
	Brooks Robinson	1956–77	22
10	Ron Fairly	1958–78	21
	Reggie Jackson	1967–87	21
	Graig Nettles	1968–88	21
	Frank Robinson	1956–76	21
	Babe Ruth	1915–35	21
15	George Brett	1974–93	20
	Bill Buckner	1971–90	20
	Brian Downing	1973–92	20
	Dwight Evans	1972–91	20
	Willie Mays	1954–73	20
	Mel Ott	1927–46	20
	Honus Wagner	1897–16	20
	Robin Yount	1974–93	20

Hitting 30 or More Home Runs for 3 or More Teams

Player	HR	Year	Team
Dick Allen	40	1966	PHI NL
	33	1968	PHI NL
	32	1969	PHI NL
	34	1970	STL NL
	37	1972	CHI AL
	32	1974	CHI AL
Bobby Bonds	32	1969	SF NL
	33	1971	SF NL
	39	1973	SF NL
	32	1975	NY AL
	37	1977	CAL AL
Rocky Colavito	41	1958	CLE AL
	42	1959	CLE AL
	35	1960	DET AL

	45	1961	DET AL
	37	1962	DET AL
	34	1964	KC AL
	30	1966	CLE AL
Darrell Evans	41	1973	ATL NL
	30	1983	SF NL
	40	1985	DET AL
	34	1987	DET AL
Reggie Jackson	47	1969	OAK AL
	32	1971	OAK AL
	32	1973	OAK AL
	36	1975	OAK AL
	32	1977	NY AL
	41	1980	NY AL
	39	1982	CAL AL
Dave Kingman	36	1975	NY NL
	37	1976	NY NL
	48	1979	CHI NL
	37	1982	NY NL
	35	1984	OAK AL
	30	1985	OAK AL
	35	1986	OAK AL
Fred McGriff	34	1988	TOR AL
	36	1989	TOR AL
	35	1990	TOR AL
	31	1991	SD NL
	35	1992	SD NL
	34	1994	ATL NL
Frank Robinson	38	1956	CIN NL
	31	1958	CIN NL
	36	1959	CIN NL
	31	1960	CIN NL
	37	1961	CIN NL
	39	1962	CIN NL
	33	1965	CIN NL
	49	1966	BAL AL
	30	1967	BAL AL
	32	1969	BAL AL
	30	1973	CAL AL

Youngest Players to reach 100

Player	*Age*
Mel Ott	22.132
Tony Conigliaro	22.197
Eddie Mathews	22.292
Johnny Bench	23.161
Hank Aaron	23.191

Most Home Runs by Right-Handed Batter (Career)

	Player	*HR*
1	Hank Aaron	755
2	Willie Mays	660
3	Frank Robinson	586
4	Harmon Killebrew	573
5	Mike Schmidt	548
6	Jimmie Foxx	534
7	Ernie Banks	512
8	Dave Winfield	465
9	Dave Kingman	442
10	Andre Dawson	436
11	Al Kaline	399
12	Dale Murphy	398
13	Johnny Bench	389
14	Dwight Evans	385
15	Frank Howard	382
	Jim Rice	382
17	Orlando Cepeda	379
	Tony Perez	379
19	Carlton Fisk	376
20	Rocky Colavito	374
21	Gil Hodges	370
22	Ralph Kiner	369
23	Joe DiMaggio	361
24	Lee May	354
25	Dick Allen	351

Most Home Runs by Left-Handed Batter (Career)

	Player	*HR*
1	Babe Ruth	714
2	Reggie Jackson	563
3	Willie McCovey	521
	Ted Williams	521
5	Eddie Mathews	512
6	Mel Ott	511
7	Lou Gehrig	493
8	Stan Musial	475
	Willie Stargell	475
10	Carl Yastrzemski	452
11	Billy Williams	426
12	Darrell Evans	414
13	Duke Snider	407
14	Graig Nettles	390
15	Norm Cash	377
16	Johnny Mize	359
17	Yogi Berra	358
18	Dave Parker	339
	Boog Powell	339
20	George Brett	317
21	Fred Lynn	306
22	Harold Baines	301
23	Chuck Klein	300
24	Darryl Strawberry	294
25	Kent Hrbek	293

Most Home Runs by Switch Hitter (Career)

	Player	*HR*
1	Mickey Mantle	536
2	Eddie Murray	479
3	Reggie Smith	314
4	Chili Davis	270
5	Ted Simmons	248
6	Ken Singleton	246
7	Howard Johnson	228
8	Ruben Sierra	220-
9	Mickey Tettleton	218
10	Bobby Bonilla	217
11	Roy Smalley	163
12	Pete Rose	160
	Roy White	160
14	Tom Tresh	153
15	Tim Raines	146
16	Ripper Collins	135
17	Devon White	131
18	Terry Pendleton	125
19	Ken Henderson	122
20	Tony Phillips	121
21	Kevin Bass	118
22	Roy Cullenbine	110
23	Frankie Frisch	105
24	Ken Caminiti	101
25	Augie Galan	100

Most Home Runs Hit at Home (Career)

	Player	*HR*
1	Hank Aaron	385
2	Babe Ruth	347
3	Willie Mays	335
4	Mel Ott	323
5	Frank Robinson	321
6	Jimmie Foxx	299
7	Harmon Killebrew	291
8	Ernie Banks	290
9	Reggie Jackson	280
10	Mickey Mantle	266

Most Home Runs Hit on the Road (Career)

	Player	*HR*
1	Hank Aaron	370
2	Babe Ruth	367
3	Willie Mays	325
4	Reggie Jackson	283
	Mike Schmidt	283
6	Harmon Killebrew	282
7	Eddie Mathews	274
8	Ted Williams	273
9	Mickey Mantle	270
10	Frank Robinson	265

Leaders for Each Decade

1876–1880

	Player	*HR*
1	Charles Jones	23
2	Paul Hines	11
3	Jim O'Rourke	10
4	John O'Rourke	9
5	Lew Brown	6
	Harry Stovey	6
7	George Hall	5
	Lip Pike	5
	Pop Snyder	5
10	Joe Gerhardt	4
	Jack Manning	4
	Deacon White	4
	Tom York	4
	Joe Start	4
	Dan Brouthers	4
	Jack Farrell	4
	Fred Dunlap	4

1881–1890

1	Harry Stovey	95
2	Dan Brouthers	78
3	Roger Connor	77
4	Fred Pfeffer	75
5	Jerry Denny	73
6	Cap Anson	72
7	George Wood	65
	John Reilly	65
9	King Kelly	62
	Ned Williamson	62

1891–1900

1	Ed Delahanty	78
	Hugh Duffy	78
3	Herman Long	75
4	Sam Thompson	71
5	Bill Joyce	69
6	Bobby Lowe	65
7	Mike Tiernan	64

8	Bill Dahlen	62
9	Jack Clements	60
10	Roger Connor	58

1901–1910

1	Harry Davis	68
2	Sam Crawford	55
3	Socks Seybold	51
	Honus Wagner	51
5	Charlie Hickman	49
6	Buck Freeman	48
7	Nap Lajoie	44
	Cy Seymour	44
9	Hobe Ferris	40
10	Tommy Leach	39

1911–1920

1	Gavvy Cravath	117
2	Babe Ruth	103
3	Fred Luderus	83
4	Frank Baker	74
5	Wildfire Schulte	65
6	Cy Williams	64
7	Larry Doyle	60
8	Zach Wheat	58
9	Tilly Walker	56
10	Sherry Magee	55
	Fred Merkle	55
	Vic Saier	55
	Heinie Zimmerman	55

1921–1930

1	Babe Ruth	462
2	Rogers Hornsby	243
3	Hack Wilson	193
4	Cy Williams	187
	Lou Gehrig	187
6	Ken Williams	180
7	Jim Bottomley	161
8	Harry Heilmann	152
9	Al Simmons	151
10	Goose Goslin	145
	Bob Meusel	145

1931–1940

1	Jimmie Foxx	414
2	Lou Gehrig	306
3	Mel Ott	302
4	Hank Greenberg	247
5	Bob Johnson	217
6	Chuck Klein	205
	Hal Trosky	205
8	Wally Berger	204
9	Earl Averill	201
10	Bill Dickey	172

1941–1950

1	Ted Williams	239
2	Ralph Kiner	215
3	Vern Stephens	207
4	Johnny Mize	199
5	Bill Nicholson	189
6	Joe DiMaggio	181
7	Stan Musial	174
8	Joe Gordon	170
9	Bobby Doerr	169
10	Rudy York	156

1951–1960

1	Eddie Mathews	338
2	Mickey Mantle	320
3	Duke Snider	309
4	Gil Hodges	286
5	Willie Mays	279
6	Ernie Banks	269
7	Stan Musial	255
8	Yogi Berra	243
9	Ted Williams	228
10	Ted Kluszewski	219
	Hank Aaron	219

1961–1970

1	Harmon Killebrew	403
2	Hank Aaron	373
3	Willie Mays	349
4	Willie McCovey	326
5	Frank Robinson	310
6	Frank Howard	309
7	Billy Williams	289
8	Norm Cash	275
9	Ron Santo	270
10	Orlando Cepeda	264

1971–1980

1	Reggie Jackson	310
2	Mike Schmidt	283
3	Willie Stargell	276
4	Dave Kingman	270
5	Johnny Bench	269
6	Bobby Bonds	259
7	Lee May	243
8	Graig Nettles	242
9	George Foster	225
10	Greg Luzinski	223
	John Mayberry	223

1981–1990

1	Dale Murphy	299
2	Eddie Murray	268
3	Mike Schmidt	265
4	Andre Dawson	260
5	Darryl Strawberry	252
6	Dwight Evans	251
7	Lance Parrish	225
	Cal Ripken	225
9	Tom Brunansky	224
	Dave Winfield	224

1991–1995

1	Albert Belle	186
2	Barry Bonds	175
	Frank Thomas	175
4	Cecil Fielder	168
5	Fred McGriff	164
6	Juan Gonzalez	162
7	Matt Williams	158
8	Joe Carter	152
9	Ken Griffey	151
10	Rafael Palmeiro	147

Players Who Led Two Major Leagues in Home Runs (Different Seasons)

Player	*Years*		
Sam Crawford	1901 (NL)	1908 (AL)	
Buck Freeman	1899 (NL)	1903 (AL)	
Bug Holliday	1889 (AA)	1892 (NL)	
Fred McGriff	1989 (AL)	1992 (NL)	
Harry Stovey	1880 (NL)	1883 (AA)	1885 (AA)
	1889 (AA)	1891 (NL)	

Most Home Runs (Career) without Winning Season Title

	Player	*HR*
1	Stan Musial	475
2	Dave Winfield	465
3	Billy Williams	426
4	Al Kaline	399
5	Tony Perez	379

100 or More Home Runs for 2 or more teams

Player	*Team HR*	*Team HR*
Hank Aaron	MIL (NL) 398	ATL (NL) 335
Tony Armas	OAK (AL) 111	BOS (AL) 113
Barry Bonds	PIT (NL) 176	SF (NL) 116
Joe Carter	CLE (AL) 151	TOR (AL) 127
Rocky Colavito	CLE (AL) 190	DET (AL) 139
Chili Davis	SF (NL) 101	CAL (AL) 108
Andre Dawson	MON (NL) 225	CHI (NL) 174
Doug DeCinces	BAL (AL) 107	CAL (AL) 130
Darrell Evans	ATL (NL) 131	SF (NL) 142
	DET (AL) 141	
Carlton Fisk	BOS (AL) 162	CHI (AL) 214
Jimmie Foxx	PHI (AL) 302	BOS (AL) 222
Joe Gordon	NY (AL) 153	CLE (AL) 100
Frank Howard	LA (NL) 123	WAS (AL) 237
Reggie Jackson	OAK (AL) 268	NY (AL) 144
	CAL (AL) 123	
Dave Kingman	NY (NL) 154	OAK (AL) 100
Lee May	CIN (NL) 147	BAL (AL) 123
Willie Mays	NY (NL) 201	SF (NL) 459
Johnny Mize	STL (NL) 158	NY (NL) 157
Dave Parker	PIT (NL) 166	CIN (NL) 107
Larry Parrish	MON (NL) 100	TEX (AL) 149
Frank Robinson	CIN (NL) 324	BAL (AL) 179
George Scott	BOS (AL) 154	MIL (AL) 115
Vern Stephens	STL (AL) 113	BOS (AL) 122
Dave Winfield	SD (NL) 154	NY (AL) 205

Most in each League

NL

	Player	*HR*
1	Hank Aaron	733
2	Willie Mays	660
3	Mike Schmidt	548
4	Willie McCovey	521
5	Ernie Banks	512
6	Mel Ott	511
7	Eddie Mathews	503
8	Stan Musial	475
	Willie Stargell	475
10	Andre Dawson	407
	Duke Snider	407

AA

	Player	*HR*
1	Harry Stovey	76
2	John Reilly	59
3	Tip O'Neill	47
4	Jocko Milligan	40
5	Denny Lyons	39

UA

	Player	HR
1	Fred Dunlap	13
2	Ed Crane	12
3	Charlie Levis	5
4	Henry Boyle	4
	Dick Burns	4
	Joe Flynn	4
	Jack Gleason	4
	Emil Gross	4
	Bill Hawes	4
	Tom O'Brien	4
	Dave Rowe	4

PL

	Player	HR
1	Roger Connor	14
2	Hardy Richardson	13
3	Harry Stovey	12
4	George Gore	10
	Billy Shindle	10

AL

	Player	HR
1	Babe Ruth	708
2	Harmon Killebrew	573
3	Reggie Jackson	563
4	Mickey Mantle	536
5	Jimmie Foxx	524
6	Mel Oit	511
7	Eddie Mathews	503
8	Stan Musial	475
	Willie Stargell	475
10	Andre Dawson	407
	Duke Snider	407

FL

	Player	HR
1	Edward Zwilling	29
2	Hal Chase	20
	Benny Kauff	20
4	Jimmy Walsh	19
5	Duke Kenworthy	18

Most Home Runs without a 40 HR Season

	Player	HR
1	Eddie Murray	479
2	Stan Musial	475
3	Dave Winfield	465
4	Al Kaline	399
5	Graig Nettles	390

Most Home Runs by Players with Same Last Name (Career)

	Player	HR
1	Williams	2128
2	Davis	1715
3	Johnson	1611
4	Robinson	1521
5	Smith	1269
6	Jackson	1160
7	Thomas	1022
8	Bell	929
9	Jones	879
10	Evans	850

Most Home Runs Hit on Birthday (Career)

	Player	HR
1	Al Simmons	5
2	Lou Gehrig	4
	Kirk Gibson	4
	Joe Morgan	4
	Lance Parrish	4
	Tony Perez	4
	Duke Snider	4
	Jason Thompson	4
	Gus Zernial	4

Most by Initial Letter of Last Name (Career)

*** A ***

1	Hank Aaron	755
2	Dick Allen	351
3	Joe Adcock	336
4	Bob Allison	256
5	Tony Armas	251

*** B ***

1	Ernie Banks	512
2	Johnny Bench	389
3	Yogi Berra	358
4	Don Baylor	338
5	Bobby Bonds	332

*** C ***

1	Orlando Cepeda	379
2	Norm Cash	377
3	Rocky Colavito	374
4	Jack Clark	340
5	Joe Carter	327

*** D ***

1	Andre Dawson	436
2	Joe DiMaggio	361
3	Brian Downing	275
4	Chili Davis	270
5	Larry Doby	253

*** E ***

1	Darrell Evans	414
2	Dwight Evans	385
3	Del Ennis	288
4	Bob Elliott	170
5	Mike Epstein	130

*** F ***

1	Jimmie Foxx	534
2	Carlton Fisk	376
3	George Foster	348
4	Cecil Fielder	250
5	Ron Fairly	215

*** G ***

1	Lou Gehrig	493
2	Hank Greenberg	331
3	Gary Gaetti	292
4	Steve Garvey	272
5	Kirk Gibson	255

*** H ***

1	Frank Howard	382
2	Gil Hodges	370
3	Willie Horton	325
4	Rogers Hornsby	301
5	Kent Hrbek	293

*** I ***

1	Pete Incaviglia	183
2	Monte Irvin	99
3	Mike Ivie	81
4	Garth Iorg	20
5	Charlie Irwin	16

*** J ***

1	Reggie Jackson	563
2	Bob Johnson	288
3	Deron Johnson	245
4	Howard Johnson	228
5	Jackie Jensen	199

*** K ***

1	Harmon Killebrew	573
2	Dave Kingman	442
3	Al Kaline	399
4	Ralph Kiner	369
5	Chuck Klein	300

*** L ***

1	Greg Luzinski	307
2	Fred Lynn	306
3	Chet Lemon	215
4	Ernie Lombardi	190
5	Tony Lazzeri	178

*** M ***

1	Willie Mays	660
2	Mickey Mantle	536
3	Willie McCovey	521
4	Eddie Mathews	512
5	Eddie Murray	479

*** N ***

1	Graig Nettles	390
2	Bill Nicholson	235
3	Jim Northrup	153
4	Matt Nokes	136
5	Bob Nieman	125

*** O ***

1	Mel Ott	511
2	Ben Oglivie	235
3	Tony Oliva	220
4	Al Oliver	219
5	Amos Otis	193

*** P ***

1	Tony Perez	379
2	Dave Parker	339
	Boog Powell	339
4	Lance Parrish	324
5	Larry Parrish	256

*** Q ***

1	Jamie Quirk	43
2	Joe Quinn	29
	Rey Quinones	29
4	Luis Quinones	19
	Carlos Quintana	19

*** R ***

1	Babe Ruth	714

2	Frank Robinson	586
3	Jim Rice	382
4	Cal Ripken	327
5	Brooks Robinson	268

*** S ***

1	Mike Schmidt	548
2	Willie Stargell	475
3	Duke Snider	407
4	Ron Santo	342
5	Roy Sievers	318

*** T ***

1	Frank Thomas	286
2	Gorman Thomas	268
3	Bobby Thomson	264
4	Andre Thornton	253
5	Joe Torre	252

*** U ***

1	Willie Upshaw	123
2	Del Unser	87
3	Ted Uhlaender	36
4	Billy Urbanski	19
	Jose Uribe	19

*** V ***

1	Mickey Vernon	172
2	Andy Van Slyke	164
3	Greg Vaughn	138
4	Ellis Valentine	123
5	Mo Vaughn	111

*** W ***

1	Ted Williams	521
2	Dave Winfield	465
3	Billy Williams	426
4	Jim Wynn	291
5	Vic Wertz	266

*** Y ***

1	Carl Yastrzemski	452
2	Rudy York	277
3	Robin Yount	251
4	Eddie Yost	139
5	Steve Yeager	102

*** Z ***

1	Gus Zernial	237
2	Richie Zisk	207
3	Don Zimmer	91
4	Todd Zeile	84
5	Al Zarilla	61

State Leaders (Career)

Alabama

1	Hank Aaron	755
2	Willie Mays	660
3	Willie McCovey	521
4	Billy Williams	426
5	Lee May	354

Alaska

1	Randy Kutcher	10
2	Steve Staggs	2

Arizona

1	Hank Leiber	101
2	Jack Howell	84
3	Ron Hassey	71
4	Billy Hatcher	54
5	Solly Hemus	51

Arkansas

1	Brooks Robinson	268
2	Rick Monday	241
3	Kevin McReynolds	211
4	Willie Davis	182
5	Lloyd Moseby	169

California

1	Ted Williams	521
2	Eddie Murray	479
3	Darrell Evans	414
4	Duke Snider	407
5	Graig Nettles	390

Colorado

1	Johnny Frederick	85
2	Johnny Lindell	72
3	Buster Adams	50
4	John Stearns	46
5	Jimmy Welsh	35

Connecticut

1	Dick McAuliffe	197
2	Walt Dropo	152
3	Roger Connor	138
4	Mo Vaughn	111
5	Jim Piersall	104

D.C.

1	Don Money	176
2	Paul Hines	56
3	Milt Thompson	47
4	Lu Blue	44
5	Bump Wills	36

Delaware

1	Randy Bush	96
	Dave May	96
3	Delino DeShields	33
4	Hans Lobert	32
5	Bert Cunningham	9

Florida

1	Andre Dawson	436
2	Boog Powell	339
3	Fred McGriff	289
4	Steve Garvey	272
5	Larry Parrish	256

Georgia

1	Johnny Mize	359
2	Ron Fairly	215
3	Frank Thomas	182
4	Wally Joyner	158
5	Bill Terry	154

Hawaii

1	Mike Lum	90
2	Lenn Sakata	25
3	Joey Meyer	18
4	Mike Huff	9
5	Ron Darling	2

Idaho

1	Harmon Killebrew	573
2	Vance Law	71
3	Bill Salkeld	31
4	Kent Hadley	14
5	Vern Law	11

Illinois

1	Greg Luzinski	307
2	Fred Lynn	306
3	Gary Gaetti	292
4	Ted Kluszewski	279
5	Robin Yount	251

Indiana

1	Gil Hodges	370
2	Chuck Klein	300
3	Cy Williams	251
4	Don Mattingly	222
5	Ron Kittle	176

Iowa

1	Hal Trosky	228
2	Ken Henderson	122
3	Bing Miller	116
4	Denis Menke	101
5	Cap Anson	96

Kansas

1	Bob Horner	218
2	Darren Daulton	123
3	Don Lock	122
4	George Grantham	105
	Daryl Spencer	105

Kentucky

1	Gus Bell	206
2	Jay Buhner	169
3	Pee Wee Reese	126
4	Mike Greenwell	123
5	Don Hurst	115

Louisiana

1	Mel Ott	511
2	Joe Adcock	336
3	Reggie Smith	314
4	Rusty Staub	292
5	Will Clark	205

Maine

1	Del Bissonette	66
2	George Gore	46
3	Freddy Parent	20
4	Sid Farrar	18
5	Harry Lord	14

Maryland

1	Babe Ruth	714
2	Jimmie Foxx	534
3	Al Kaline	399
4	Cal Ripken	327
5	Harold Baines	301

Massachusetts

1	Richie Hebner	203
2	Steve Balboni	181
3	Tony Conigliaro	166

4 Mike Pagliarulo 134
5 Mickey Cochrane 119

Michigan
1 Kirk Gibson 255
John Mayberry 255
3 Ted Simmons 248
4 Bobby Grich 224
5 Bill Freehan 200

Minnesota
1 Dave Winfield 465
2 Kent Hrbek 293
3 Roger Maris 275
4 Paul Molitor 211
5 Rip Repulski 106

Mississippi
1 Dave Parker 339
2 George Scott 271
3 Chet Lemon 215
4 Bill Melton 160
Frank White 160

Missouri
1 Yogi Berra 358
2 Roy Sievers 318
3 Ken Boyer 282
4 Bob Allison 256
5 Darrell Porter 188

Montana
1 John Lowenstein 116
2 Ed Bouchee 61
3 Dave McNally 9
4 Herb Plews 4
5 Johnny Couch 3

Nebraska
1 Jackie Brandt 112
2 Ron Hansen 106
3 Bob Cerv 105
4 Wade Boggs 103
5 Sam Crawford 97

Nevada
1 Marty Cordova 24
2 Jim Nash 4
3 Gordon Rhodes 2
4 Robert Richie 1
Shawn Boskie 1

New Hampshire
1 Phil Plantier 79
2 Red Rolfe 69
3 Bernie Friberg 38
4 Joe Lefebvre 31
5 Arlie Latham 27

New Jersey
1 Goose Goslin 248
2 Joe Medwick 205
3 John Briggs 139
4 Earl Williams 138
5 John Romano 129

New Mexico
1 Ralph Kiner 369
2 Vern Stephens 247
3 Fred Haney 8
4 Chuck Stevens 4
5 Wade Blasingame 3

New York
1 Lou Gehrig 493
2 Carl Yastrzemski 452
3 Rocky Colavito 374
4 Hank Greenberg 331
5 Joe Torre 252

North Carolina
1 Jim Ray Hart 170
2 Enos Slaughter 169
3 Wes Covington 131
4 Smoky Burgess 126
5 Jimmie Hall 121

North Dakota
1 Ken Hunt 33
2 Truck Hannah 5
Lynn Nelson 5

Ohio
1 Mike Schmidt 548
2 Frank Howard 382
3 Jim Wynn 291
4 Sal Bando 242
5 Al Oliver 219

Oklahoma
1 Mickey Mantle 536
2 Willie Stargell 475
3 Johnny Bench 389
4 Joe Carter 327
5 Bob Johnson 288

Oregon
1 Dave Kingman 442
2 Dale Murphy 398
3 Ken Williams 196
4 Greg Brock 110
5 John Jaha 53

Pennsylvania
1 Reggie Jackson 563
2 Stan Musial 475
3 Dick Allen 351
4 Jack Clark 340
5 Lance Parrish 324

Rhode Island
1 Gabby Hartnett 236
2 Davey Lopes 155
3 Hugh Duffy 106
4 Nap Lajoie 82
5 Hobe Ferris 40

South Carolina
1 Jim Rice 382
2 Gorman Thomas 268
3 Larry Doby 253
4 Al Rosen 192
5 Willie Jones 190

South Dakota
1 Dave Collins 32
2 Carroll Hardy 17
3 Terry Francona 16
4 Kermit Wahl 3
5 Rube Fischer 2

Tennessee
1 Vada Pinson 256
2 Leon Wagner 211
3 Bill Madlock 163
4 Jim Hickman 159
5 Ed Bailey 155

Texas
1 Frank Robinson 586
2 Ernie Banks 512
Eddie Mathews 512
4 Norm Cash 377
5 Don Baylor 338

Utah
1 Duke Sims 100
2 Gordon Slade 8
3 Herman Franks 3
Ed Heusser 3
Bobby Mitchell 3

Vermont
1 Carlton Fisk 376
2 Pat Putnam 63
3 Birdie Tebbetts 38
4 Larry Gardner 27
5 Fred Mann 12

Virginia
1 Willie Horton 325
2 Jim Lemon 164
3 George McQuinn 135
4 Willard Marshall 130
5 Granny Hamner 104

Washington
1 Ron Santo 342
2 Ron Cey 316
3 Ryne Sandberg 245
4 Earl Averill 238
5 Earl Torgeson 149

West Virginia
1 George Brett 317
2 Toby Harrah 195
3 Andy Seminick 164
4 Bill Mazeroski 138
5 Gene Freese 115

Wisconsin
1 Al Simmons 307
2 Andy Pafko 213
3 Ken Keltner 163
4 Chet Laabs 117
5 Rick Reichardt 116

Wyoming
1 Mike Devereaux 97
2 Mike Lansing 18
3 Rick Sofield 9
4 Tom Browning 2

Four HR Game

Batter	Team	Date	Inn	Men	Opp	Pitchers
Joe Adcock	MIL NL	07/31/1954	2	0	@BRO	Don Newcombe
	Age	26	5	2		Erv Palica
			7	1		Pete Wojey
			9	0		Johnny Podres
Total RBI from HR = 7						
Rocky Colavito	CLE AL	06/10/1959	3	1	@BAL	Jerry Walker
	Age	25	5	0		Arnie Portocarrero
			6	1		Arnie Portocarrero
			9	0		Ernie Johnson
Total RBI from HR = 6						
Ed Delahanty	PHI NL	07/13/1896	1	1	@CHI	Adonis Terry
	Age	28	5	2		Adonis Terry
			7	0		Adonis Terry
			9	0		Adonis Terry
Total RBI from HR = 7						
Lou Gehrig	NY AL	06/03/1932	1	1	@PHI	George Earnshaw
	Age	28	4	0		George Earnshaw
			5	0		George Earnshaw
			7	0		Roy Mahaffey
Total RBI from HR = 5						
Gil Hodges	BRO NL	08/31/1950	2	1	@BOS	Warren Spahn
	Age	26	3	2		Normie Roy
			6	1		Bob Hall
			8	1		Johnny Antonelli
Total RBI from HR = 9						
Bob Horner	ATL NL	07/06/1986	2	0	@MON	Andy McGaffigan
	Age	28	4	0		Andy McGaffigan
			5	2		Andy McGaffigan
			9	0		Jeff Reardon
Total RBI from HR = 6						
Chuck Klein	PHI NL	07/10/1936	1	2	@PI	Jim Weaver
	Age	31	5	0		Jim Weaver
			7	0		Mace Brown
			10	0		Bill Swift
Total RBI from HR = 6						
Bobby Lowe	BOS NL	05/30/1894 G2	3	0	@CIN	Elton Chamberlin
	Age	25	3	1		Elton Chamberlin
			5	0		Elton Chamberlin
			6	1		Elton Chamberlin
Total RBI from HR = 6						
Willie Mays	SF NL	04/30/1961	1	0	@MIL	Lew Burdette
	Age	29	3	1		Lew Burdette
			6	2		Seth Morehead
			8	1		Don McMahon
Total RBI from HR = 8						
Mike Schmidt	PHI NL	04/17/1976	5	1	@CHI	Rick Reuschel
	Age	26	7	0		Rick Reuschel
			8	2		Mike Garman
			10	1		Paul Reuschel
Total RBI from HR = 8						
Pat Seerey	CHI AL	07/18/1948 G1	4	0	@PHI	Carl Scheib
	Age	25	5	1		Carl Scheib
			6	2		Bob Savage
			11	0		Lou Brissie
Total RBI from HR = 7						
Mark Whiten	STL NL	09/07/1993 G2	1	3	@CIN	Larry Luebbers
	Age	26	6	2		Mike Anderson
			7	2		Mike Anderson
			9	1		Rob Dibble
Total RBI from HR = 12						

Three Home Runs in a Game

Player	*Team*	*Date*
Hank Aaron	MIL NL	06/21/1959
Dick Allen	PHI NL	09/29/1968
Bob Allison	MIN AL	05/17/1963
Cap Anson	CHI NL	08/06/1884
Earl Averill	CLE AL	09/17/1930
Bobby Avila	CLE AL	06/20/1951
Carlos Baerga	CLE AL	06/17/1993
Jeff Bagwell	HOU NL	06/24/1994
Ed Bailey	CIN NL	06/24/1956
Harold Baines	CHI AL	07/07/1982
	CHI AL	09/17/1984
	OAK AL	05/07/1991
Ernie Banks	CHI NL	08/04/1955
	CHI NL	09/14/1957
	CHI NL	05/29/1962
	CHI NL	06/09/1963
Don Baylor	BAL AL	07/02/1975
Jake Beckley	CIN NL	09/26/1897
George Bell	TOR AL	04/04/1988
Gus Bell	CIN NL	07/21/1955
	CIN NL	05/29/1956
Les Bell	BOS NL	06/02/1928
Albert Belle	CLE AL	09/06/1992
	CLE AL	09/19/1995
Johnny Bench	CIN NL	07/26/1970
	CIN NL	05/09/1973
	CIN NL	05/29/1980
Juan Beniquez	BAL AL	06/12/1986
Paul Blair	BAL AL	04/29/1970
Jeff Blauser	ATL NL	07/12/1992
Curt Blefary	BAL AL	06/06/1967
Barry Bonds	SF NL	08/02/1994
Steve Boros	DET AL	08/06/1962
Mickey Brantley	SEA AL	09/14/1987
George Brett	KC AL	07/22/1979
	KC AL	04/20/1983
Dan Brouthers	DET NL	09/10/1886
Tommy Brown	BRO NL	09/18/1950
Tom Brunansky	BOS AL	09/29/1990
Smoky Burgess	CIN NL	07/29/1955
Jeff Burroughs	SEA AL	08/14/1981
Johnny Callison	PHI NL	09/27/1964
	PHI NL	06/06/1965
Roy Campanella	BRO NL	08/26/1950
Jose Canseco	OAK AL	07/03/1988
	TEX AL	06/13/1994
Gary Carter	MON NL	04/20/1977
	NY NL	09/03/1985
Joe Carter	CLE AL	08/29/1986
	CLE AL	05/28/1987
	CLE AL	06/24/1989
	CLE AL	07/19/1989
	TOR AL	08/23/1993
Rico Carty	ATL NL	05/31/1970
Orlando Cepeda	ATL NL	07/26/1970
Bob Cerv	KC AL	08/20/1959
Ben Chapman	NY AL	07/09/1932
Sam Chapman	PHI AL	08/15/1946
Jack Clark	BOS AL	07/31/1991
Roberto Clemente	PIT NL	05/15/1967
	PIT NL	08/13/1969
Ty Cobb	DET AL	05/05/1925
Mickey Cochrane	PHI AL	05/21/1925
Rocky Colavito	DET AL	08/27/1961
	DET AL	07/05/1962
Nate Colbert	SD NL	08/01/1972
Ed Coleman	PHI AL	08/17/1934
Darnell Coles	PIT NL	09/30/1987
	TOR AL	07/05/1994
Roger Connor	NY NL	05/09/1888
Merv Connors	CHI AL	09/17/1938
Cecil Cooper	MIL AL	07/27/1979
Walker Cooper	CIN NL	07/06/1949
Eric Davis	CIN NL	09/10/1986
	CIN NL	05/03/1987
Glenn Davis	HOU NL	09/10/1987
	HOU NL	06/01/1990
Andre Dawson	MON NL	09/24/1985
	CHI NL	08/01/1987
Doug DeCinces	CAL AL	08/03/1982
	CAL AL	08/08/1982
Don Demeter	LA NL	04/21/1959
	PHI NL	09/12/1961
Bill Dickey	NY AL	07/26/1939
Joe DiMaggio	NY AL	06/13/1937

	NY AL	05/23/1948
	NY AL	09/10/1950
Larry Doby	CLE AL	08/02/1950
Bobby Doerr	BOS AL	06/08/1950
Bob Elliott	BOS NL	09/24/1949
Del Ennis	PHI NL	07/23/1955
Mike Epstein	WAS AL	05/16/1969
Darrell Evans	SF NL	06/15/1983
Cecil Fielder	DET AL	05/06/1990
	DET AL	06/06/1990
Dan Ford	BAL AL	07/20/1983
George Foster	CIN NL	07/14/1977
Jack Fournier	BRO NL	07/13/1926
Jimmie Foxx	PHI AL	07/10/1932
	PHI AL	06/08/1933
Bill Freehan	DET AL	08/09/1971
Andres Galarraga	COL NL	06/25/1995
Lou Gehrig	NY AL	06/23/1927
	NY AL	05/04/1929
	NY AL	05/22/1930
Bill Glynn	CLE AL	07/05/1954
Juan Gonzalez	TEX AL	06/07/1992
	TEX AL	08/28/1993
Goose Goslin	WAS AL	06/19/1925
	STL AL	08/19/1930
	STL AL	06/23/1932
Bobby Grich	BAL AL	06/18/1974
Ken Griffey	ATL NL	07/22/1986
George Harper	STL NL	09/20/1928
Ken Harrelson	BOS AL	06/14/1968
Joe Hauser	PHI AL	08/02/1924
Von Hayes	PHI NL	08/29/1989
Guy Hecker	LOU AA	08/15/1886
Dave Henderson	OAK AL	08/03/1991
George Hendrick	CLE AL	06/19/1973
Butch Henline	PHI NL	09/15/1922
Babe Herman	CHI NL	07/20/1933
Gene Hermanski	BRO NL	08/05/1948
Larry Herndon	DET AL	05/18/1982
Jim Hickman	NY NL	09/03/1965
Mike Higgins	PHI AL	06/27/1935
	DET AL	05/20/1940
Rogers Hornsby	CHI NL	04/24/1931
Tony Horton	CLE AL	05/24/1970
Willie Horton	DET AL	06/09/1970
	TEX AL	05/15/1977
Bo Jackson	KC AL	07/17/1990
Reggie Jackson	OAK AL	07/02/1969
	CAL AL	09/18/1986
Brook Jacoby	CLE AL	07/03/1987
Manny Jimenez	KC AL	07/04/1964
Cliff Johnson	NY AL	06/30/1977
Deron Johnson	PHI NL	07/11/1971
Bill Joyce	WAS NL	08/20/1894
Wally Joyner	CAL AL	10/03/1987
Al Kaline	DET AL	04/17/1955
Alex Kampouris	CIN NL	05/09/1937
Charlie Keller	NY AL	07/28/1940
George Kelly	NY NL	09/17/1923
	NY NL	06/14/1924
Ken Keltner	CLE AL	05/25/1939
Harmon Killebrew	MIN AL	09/21/1963
Ralph Kiner	PIT NL	08/16/1947
	PIT NL	09/11/1947
	PIT NL	07/05/1948
	PIT NL	07/18/1951
Jim King	WAS AL	06/08/1964
Dave Kingman	NY NL	06/04/1976
	CHI NL	05/14/1978
	CHI NL	05/17/1979
	CHI NL	07/28/1979
	OAK AL	04/16/1984
Willie Kirkland	CLE AL	07/09/1961
Ted Kluszewski	CIN NL	07/01/1956
Lee Lacy	BAL AL	06/08/1986
Joe Lahoud	BOS AL	06/11/1969
Carney Lansford	CAL AL	09/01/1979
Barry Larkin	CIN NL	06/28/1991
Tony Lazzeri	NY AL	06/08/1927
	NY AL	05/24/1936
Hal Lee	BOS NL	07/06/1934
Hank Leiber	CHI NL	07/04/1939
Jim Lemon	WAS AL	08/31/1956
Don Leppert	WAS AL	04/11/1963
Davey Lopes	LA NL	08/20/1974
Hector Lopez	KC AL	06/26/1958
Mike Lum	ATL NL	07/03/1970
Fred Lynn	BOS AL	06/18/1975
Bill Madlock	DET AL	06/28/1987
Jack Manning	PHI NL	10/09/1884
Mickey Mantle	NY AL	05/13/1955
Willard Marshall	NY NL	07/18/1947
Eddie Mathews	BOS NL	09/27/1952
Gary Matthews	SF NL	09/25/1976
Charlie Maxwell	DET AL	05/03/1959
Lee May	HOU NL	06/21/1973
John Mayberry	KC AL	07/01/1975
	KC AL	06/01/1977
Willie Mays	SF NL	06/29/1961
	SF NL	06/02/1963
Willie McCovey	SF NL	09/22/1963
	SF NL	04/22/1964
	SF NL	09/17/1966
Tommy McCraw	CHI AL	05/24/1967
Tom McCreery	LOU NL	07/12/1897
Clyde McCullough	CHI NL	07/26/1942
Mark McGwire	OAK AL	06/27/1987
	OAK NL	06/11/1995
Ramon Mejias	PIT NL	05/04/1958
Bill Melton	CHI AL	06/24/1969
Randy Milligan	BAL AL	06/09/1990
Kevin Mitchell	SF NL	05/25/1990
George Mitterwald	CHI NL	04/17/1974
Johnny Mize	STL NL	07/13/1938
	STL NL	07/20/1938
	STL NL	05/13/1940
	STL NL	09/08/1940
	NY NL	04/24/1947
	NY AL	09/15/1950
Paul Molitor	MIL AL	05/12/1982
Rick Monday	CHI NL	05/16/1972
Johnny Moore	PHI NL	07/22/1936
Walt Moryn	CHI NL	05/30/1958
Don Mueller	NY NL	09/01/1951
Pat Mullin	DET AL	06/26/1949
Bobby Murcer	NY AL	06/24/1970
	NY AL	07/13/1973
Dale Murphy	ATL NL	05/18/1979
Eddie Murray	BAL AL	08/29/1979
	BAL AL	09/14/1980
	BAL AL	08/26/1985
Stan Musial	STL NL	05/02/1954
	STL NL	07/08/1962
Bill Nicholson	CHI NL	07/23/1944
Paul O'Neill	NY AL	08/31/1995
Ben Oglivie	MIL AL	07/08/1979
	MIL AL	06/20/1982
	MIL AL	05/14/1983
Tony Oliva	MIN AL	07/03/1973
Al Oliver	TEX AL	05/23/1979
	TEX AL	08/17/1980
Gene Oliver	ATL NL	07/30/1966
Mel Ott	NY NL	08/31/1930
Andy Pafko	CHI NL	08/02/1950
Larry Parrish	MON NL	05/29/1977
	MON NL	07/30/1978
	MON NL	04/25/1980
	TEX AL	04/29/1985
Freddie Patek	CAL AL	06/20/1980
Jim Pendleton	MIL NL	08/30/1953
Adolfo Phillips	CHI NL	06/11/1967
Boog Powell	BAL AL	08/10/1963
	BAL AL	06/27/1964
	BAL AL	08/15/1966
Jim Presley	SEA AL	09/01/1986
Tim Raines	CHI AL	04/18/1994
Carl Reynolds	CHI AL	07/02/1930
Dusty Rhodes	NY NL	08/26/1953
	NY NL	07/28/1954
Karl Rhodes	CHI NL	04/04/1994
Jim Rice	BOS AL	08/29/1977
	BOS AL	08/29/1983
Bill Robinson	PIT NL	06/05/1976
Frank Robinson	CIN NL	08/22/1959
Pete Rose	CIN NL	04/29/1978
Al Rosen	CLE AL	04/29/1952
Babe Ruth	NY AL	05/21/1930
	BOS NL	05/25/1935
Reggie Sanders	CIN NL	08/15/1995
Hank Sauer	CHI NL	08/28/1950
	CHI NL	06/11/1952
Mike Schmidt	PHI NL	07/07/1979
	PHI NL	06/14/1987
Pat Seerey	CLE AL	07/13/1945
Andy Seminick	PHI NL	06/02/1949
Art Shamsky	CIN NL	08/12/1966
Frank Shugart	STL NL	05/10/1894
Al Simmons	PHI AL	07/15/1932
Reggie Smith	STL NL	05/22/1976
Duke Snider	BRO NL	05/30/1950
	BRO NL	06/01/1955
Cory Snyder	CLE AL	05/21/1987
	LA NL	04/17/1994
Tony Solaita	KC AL	09/07/1975
Moose Solters	STL AL	07/07/1935
Mike Stanley	NY AL	08/10/1995
Leroy Stanton	CAL AL	07/10/1973
Willie Stargell	PIT NL	06/24/1965
	PIT NL	05/22/1968
	PIT NL	04/10/1971
	PIT NL	04/21/1971
Darryl Strawberry	NY NL	08/05/1985
Dick Stuart	PIT NL	06/30/1960
Dale Sveum	MIL AL	07/17/1987
Jim Tabor	BOS AL	07/04/1939
Danny Tartabull	KC AL	07/06/1991
Bill Terry	NY NL	08/13/1932
Frank Thomas	PIT NL	08/16/1958
Gorman Thomas	SEA AL	04/11/1985
Lee Thomas	LA AL	09/05/1961
Jim Thome	CLE AL	07/22/1994
Hank Thompson	NY NL	06/03/1954
Bob Thurman	CIN NL	08/18/1956
Bob Tillman	ATL NL	07/30/1969

Jim Tobin	BOS NL	05/13/1942
Jeff Treadway	ATL NL	05/26/1990
Tom Tresh	NY AL	06/06/1965
Hal Trosky	CLE AL	05/30/1934
	CLE AL	07/05/1937
John Valentin	BOS AL	06/02/1995
Otto Velez	TOR AL	05/04/1980
Clyde Vollmer	BOS AL	07/26/1951
Tim Wallach	MON NL	05/04/1987
Lee Walls	CHI NL	04/24/1958
Preston Ward	KC AL	09/09/1958
Claudell Washington	CHI AL	07/14/1979
	NY NL	06/22/1980
George Watkins	STL NL	06/24/1931
Wes Westrum	NY NL	06/24/1950
Bill White	STL NL	07/05/1961
Ernie Whitt	TOR AL	09/14/1987
Del Wilber	PHI NL	08/27/1951
Billy Williams	CHI NL	09/10/1968
Cy Williams	PHI NL	05/11/1923
Ken Williams	STL AL	04/22/1922
Ted Williams	BOS AL	07/14/1946
	BOS AL	05/08/1957
	BOS AL	06/13/1957
Ned Williamson	CHI NL	05/30/1884
Hack Wilson	CHI NL	07/26/1930
Dave Winfield	CAL AL	04/13/1991
Jim Wynn	HOU NL	06/15/1967
	LA NL	05/11/1974
Carl Yastrzemski	BOS AL	05/19/1976
Rudy York	DET AL	09/01/1941
Norm Zauchin	BOS AL	05/27/1955
Gus Zernial	CHI AL	10/01/1950

Most Multiple Home Run Games (Career)

	Player	*Games*
1	Babe Ruth	72
2	Willie Mays	63
3	Hank Aaron	62
4	Jimmie Foxx	55
5	Frank Robinson	54
6	Eddie Mathews	49
	Mel Ott	49
8	Harmon Killebrew	46
	Mickey Mantle	46
10	Willie McCovey	44
	Mike Schmidt	44
12	Dave Kingman	43
13	Ernie Banks	42
	Lou Gehrig	42
	Reggie Jackson	42
16	Ralph Kiner	40
17	Andre Dawson	38
18	Stan Musial	37
	Ted Williams	37
20	Willie Stargell	36
21	Joe DiMaggio	35
	Hank Greenberg	35
	Lee May	35
	Jim Rice	35
25	Duke Snider	34

Most Multiple Home Run Games (Season)

	Player	*Year*	*Team*	*Games*
1	Hank Greenberg	1938	DET AL	11
2	Jimmie Foxx	1938	BOS AL	10
	Ralph Kiner	1947	PIT NL	10
4	George Bell	1987	TOR AL	9
	Willie Mays	1955	NY NL	9
6	Albert Belle	1995	CLE AL	8
	Andre Dawson	1987	CHI NL	8
	George Foster	1977	CIN NL	8
	Reggie Jackson	1969	OAK AL	8
	Mickey Mantle	1961	NY AL	8
	Willie Mays	1964	SF NL	8
	Babe Ruth	1927	NY AL	8
	Hack Wilson	1930	CHI NL	8

Homering in All Ballparks (Season)
Ten or more parks in league

Player	*Year*	*Team*	*Parks*
Rocky Colavito	1961	DET AL	10
Mickey Mantle	1961	NY AL	10
Roger Maris	1961	NY AL	10
Ernie Banks	1962	CHI NL	10
Jim Gentile	1962	BAL AL	10
Harmon Killebrew	1962	MIN AL	10
Ramon Mejias	1962	HOU NL	10
Bill Skowron	1962	NY AL	10
Leon Wagner	1962	LA AL	10
Hank Aaron	1963	MIL NL	10
Orlando Cepeda	1963	SF NL	10
Willie McCovey	1963	SF NL	10
Mickey Mantle	1964	NY AL	10
Ron Santo	1964	CHI NL	10
Dick Stuart	1964	BOS AL	10
Billy Williams	1964	CHI NL	10
Jim Ray Hart	1965	SF NL	10
Frank Howard	1965	WAS AL	10
Willie McCovey	1965	SF NL	10
Hank Aaron	1966	ATL NL	10
Dick Allen	1966	PHI NL	10
Norm Cash	1966	DET AL	10
Willie Mays	1966	SF NL	11
Willie Stargell	1966	PIT NL	10
Bob Allison	1967	MIN AL	10
Orlando Cepeda	1967	STL NL	10
Frank Howard	1967	WAS AL	10
Harmon Killebrew	1967	MIN AL	10
Willie McCovey	1967	SF NL	10
Frank Howard	1968	WAS AL	10
Joe Pepitone	1968	NY AL	10
Jim Wynn	1968	HOU NL	10
Carl Yastrzemski	1968	BOS AL	10
Harmon Killebrew	1969	MIN AL	12
Willie McCovey	1970	SF NL	12
Joe Pepitone	1970	CHI NL	12
Tony Perez	1970	CIN NL	12
Willie Stargell	1970	PIT NL	13
Johnny Bench	1972	CIN NL	12
Reggie Jackson	1975	OAK AL	12
George Foster	1977	CIN NL	12
Mike Schmidt	1979	PHI NL	12
Rickey Henderson	1990	OAK AL	14
Matt Williams	1991	SF NL	12
Frank Thomas	1995	CHI AL	14

Most Ballparks Homered In (Career)

	Player	*Parks*
1	Hank Aaron	32
	Roger Connor	32
	Frank Robinson	32
	Rusty Staub	32
	Harry Stovey	32
	Dave Winfield	32
7	Eddie Murray	31
8	Chili Davis	30
	Ron Fairly	30
	Kirk Gibson	30
	Fred McGriff	30
	Al Oliver	30

Most Ballparks Homered In (Season)

	Player	*Year*	*Team*	*Parks*
1	Rickey Henderson	1990	OAK AL	14
	Frank Thomas	1995	CHI AL	14
3	Harold Baines	1995	BAL AL	13
	Albert Belle	1995	CLE AL	13
	Barry Bonds	1993	SF NL	13
	Bobby Bonilla	1995	NY NL	13
	Jose Canseco	1988	OAK AL	13
	Jose Canseco	1991	OAK AL	13
	Joe Carter	1989	CLE AL	13
	Dwight Evans	1986	BOS AL	13
	Cecil Fielder	1990	DET AL	13
	Juan Gonzalez	1991	TEX AL	13
	Lance Parrish	1980	DET AL	13
	Willie Stargell	1970	PIT NL	13
	Gorman Thomas	1979	MIL AL	13
	Gorman Thomas	1980	MIL AL	13
	Gorman Thomas	1982	MIL AL	13
	Matt Williams	1994	SF NL	13
	Dave Winfield	1982	NY AL	13

Ballparks with most Home Runs Hit

	Park	*HR*	*Years*
1	Tiger Stadium, Detroit	10,255	(1912–1995)
2	Wrigley Field, Chicago	9,262	(1914–1995)
3	Yankee Stadium, New York	9,105	(1923–1973, 1976–1995)
4	Fenway Park, Boston	8,714	(1912–1995)
5	Sportsman's Park III, St Louis	8,277	(1909–1965)
6	Shibe Park, Philadelphia	6,960	(1909–1970)
7	Cleveland Stadium	6,664	(1932–1993)
8	Polo Grounds V, New York	6,660	(1911–1957, 1962–1963)
9	Comiskey Park I, Chicago	6,248	(1911–1990)
10	County Stadium, Milwaukee	4,997	(1953–1965, 1970–1995)

Current Ballparks
Oriole Park at Camden Yards, Baltimore
First HR: Paul Sorrento CLE 4/08/1992
Total hit in park: 631

Visitors

1	Dean Palmer	7
2	Albert Belle	6
	Cecil Fielder	6
	Tim Salmon	6
	Danny Tartabull	6
	Mickey Tettleton	6
	Frank Thomas	6

Home

1	Chris Hoiles	44
2	Brady Anderson	34
	Cal Ripken	34
4	Rafael Palmiero	33
5	Harold Baines	30

Total

1	Chris Hoiles	44

2	Brady Anderson	34
	Cal Ripken	34
4	Rafael Palmiero	33
5	Harold Baines	31

Fenway Park, Boston
First HR: Hugh Bradley BOS 4/26/1912
Total hit in park: 8,714

Visitors

1	Babe Ruth	38
	Mickey Mantle	38
3	Harmon Killebrew	37
4	Al Kaline	30
5	Joe DiMaggio	29

Home

1	Ted Williams	248
2	Carl Yastrzemski	237
3	Jim Rice	208
4	Dwight Evans	199
5	Bobby Doerr	145

Total

1	Ted Williams	248
2	Carl Yastrzemski	237
3	Jim Rice	208
4	Dwight Evans	199
5	Bobby Doerr	145

Anaheim Stadium, California
First HR: Rick Reichardt CAL 4/19/1966
Total hit in park: 3,803

Visitors

1	Reggie Jackson	18
2	Harmon Killebrew	17
	Jose Canseco	17
4	Eddie Murray	16
5	Willie Horton	15
	Carlton Fisk	15

Home

1	Brian Downing	113
2	Don Baylor	78
3	Doug DeCinces	73
4	Bobby Grich	72
5	Reggie Jackson	69

Total

1	Brian Downing	114
2	Reggie Jackson	87
3	Don Baylor	84
4	Doug DeCinces	76
5	Bobby Grich	73

Comiskey Park II, Chicago
First HR: Cecil Fielder DET 4/18/1991
Total hit in park: 658

Visitors

1	Cecil Fielder	12
2	Danny Tartabull	9
3	Rob Deer	8
	Albert Belle	8
5	Juan Gonzalez	5
	Ken Griffey	6

Home

1	Frank Thomas	97
2	Robin Ventura	51
3	Tim Raines	23
	George Bell	23
5	Ron Karkovice	22

Total

1	Frank Thomas	97
2	Robin Ventura	51
3	Tim Raines	23
	George Bell	23
5	Ron Karkovice	22

Jacobs Field, Cleveland
First HR: Eric Anthony SEA 4/04/1994
Total hit in park: 290

Visitors

1	Juan Gonzalez	4
2	Tom Brunansky	3
	Jay Buhner	3
	Joe Carter	3
	Frank Thomas	3

Home

1	Albert Belle	46
2	Jim Thome	23
3	Manny Ramirez	21
4	Paul Sorrento	20
5	Eddie Murray	18

Total

1	Albert Belle	46
2	Jim Thome	23
3	Manny Ramirez	21
4	Paul Sorrento	20
5	Eddie Murray	18

Tiger Stadium, Detroit
First HR: Del Pratt STL 5/05/1912
Total hit in park: 10,255

Visitors

1	Babe Ruth	60
2	Ted Williams	55
3	Jimmie Foxx	52
4	Mickey Mantle	42
5	Yogi Berra	37

Home

1	Al Kaline	226
2	Norm Cash	211
3	Hank Greenberg	187
4	Lou Whitaker	146
5	Rudy York	139

Total

1	Al Kaline	226
2	Norm Cash	212
3	Hank Greenberg	187
4	Lou Whitaker	146
5	Rudy York	140

Kauffman Stadium, Kansas City
First HR: John Mayberry KC 4/10/1973
Total hit in park: 2,105

Visitors

1	Don Baylor	17
2	Dave Winfield	14
3	Reggie Jackson	12
	Harold Baines	12
5	Sal Bando	11
	Dwight Evans	11
	Juan Gonzalez	11
	Cal Ripken	11

Home

1	George Brett	136
2	Frank White	75
3	Amos Otis	74
	Hal McRae	74
5	Danny Tartabull	57

Total

1	George Brett	136
2	Frank White	75
3	Amos Otis	74
	Hal McRae	74
5	Danny Tartabull	59

County Stadium, Milwaukee
First HR: Bill Bruton MIL 4/14/1953
Total hit in park: 4,997

Visitors

1	Frank Robinson	35
2	Willie Mays	31
	Reggie Jackson	31
4	Ernie Banks	24
5	Frank Howard	23

Home

1	Eddie Mathews	211
2	Hank Aaron	195
3	Robin Yount	124
4	Joe Adcock	104
5	Gorman Thomas	102

Total

1	Eddie Mathews	211
2	Hank Aaron	195
3	Robin Yount	124
4	Gorman Thomas	108
5	Joe Adcock	104

Hubert H. Humphrey Metrodome, Minnesota
First HR: Dave Engle MIN 4/06/1982
Total hit in park: 2,141

Visitors

1	Eddie Murray	21
2	Lance Parrish	14
3	Joe Carter	14
	Cal Ripken	14
	Danny Tartabull	14

Home

1	Kent Hrbek	156
2	Kirby Puckett	113
3	Gary Gaetti	94
4	Tom Brunansky	78
5	Randy Bush	50

Total

1	Kent Hrbek	156
2	Kirby Puckett	113
3	Gary Gaetti	101
4	Tom Brunansky	82
5	Randy Bush	50

Yankee Stadium, New York
First HR: Babe Ruth NY 4/18/1923
Total hit in park: 9,105

Visitors

1	Goose Goslin	32
2	Mickey Vernon	31
3	Ted Williams	30
4	Al Simmons	27
5	Boog Powell	26

Home

1	Mickey Mantle	266
2	Babe Ruth	259
3	Lou Gehrig	251
4	Yogi Berra	210
5	Joe DiMaggio	148

Total

1	Mickey Mantle	266
2	Babe Ruth	259
3	Lou Gehrig	251
4	Yogi Berra	210
5	Joe DiMaggio	148

Oakland-Alameda County Stadium, Oakland
First HR: Boog Powell BAL 4/17/1968
Total hit in park: 3,630

Visitors

1	Carlton Fisk	18
2	Brian Downing	17
3	Danny Tartabull	16
4	Dwight Evans	14
	Eddie Murray	14
	Larry Parrish	14
	Cal Ripken	14

Home

1	Reggie Jackson	133
2	Mark McGwire	125
3	Jose Canseco	104
4	Sal Bando	90
5	Rickey Henderson	73

Total

1	Reggie Jackson	146
2	Mark McGwire	125
3	Jose Canseco	107
4	Sal Bando	90
5	Rickey Henderson	76

Kingdome, Seattle
First HR: Joe Rudi CAL 4/06/1977
Total hit in park: 2,971

Visitors

1	Brian Downing	19
2	Carlton Fisk	18
3	Dave Winfield	16
4	Dwight Evans	15
5	Tony Armas	14
	Don Baylor	14
	George Bell	14
	Gary Gaetti	14
	Ruben Sierra	14
	Ken Singleton	14
	Roy Smalley	14

Home

1	Ken Griffey	102
2	Alvin Davis	101
3	Jay Buhner	81
4	Ken Phelps	60
5	Jim Presley	58

Total

1	Ken Griffey	102
2	Alvin Davis	101
3	Jay Buhner	81
4	Ken Phelps	60
5	Jim Presley	58

The Ballpark in Arlington, Texas
First HR: Dave Nilsson MIL 4/11/1994
Total hit in park: 284

Visitors

1	Ken Griffey	6
2	Chili Davis	4
	Cecil Fielder	4
	Tim Salmon	4
	Paul Sorrento	4
	Frank Thomas	4
	Bernie Williams	4
	Tino Martinez	2

Home

1	Mickey Tettleton	22
2	Juan Gonzalez	21
3	Will Clark	19
4	Jose Canseco	17
5	Dean Palmer	16

Total

1	Mickey Tettleton	23
2	Juan Gonzalez	21
3	Jose Canseco	20
4	Will Clark	19
5	Dean Palmer	16

SkyDome, Toronto
First HR: Fred McGriff TOR 6/05/1989
Total hit in park: 995

Visitors

1	Jose Canseco	11
	Cecil Fielder	11
3	Paul Sorrento	9
4	Albert Belle	8
5	Rob Deer	7
	Mike Greenwell	7
	Wally Joyner	7
	Cal Ripken	7
	Greg Vaughn	7

Home

1	Joe Carter	96
2	Kelly Gruber	44
3	John Olerud	38
4	Devon White	35
5	Roberto Alomar	30
	Ed Sprague	30

Total

1	Joe Carter	97
2	Kelly Gruber	45
3	John Olerud	38
4	Devon White	36
5	Paul Molitor	32

Atlanta-Fulton County Stadium, Atlanta
First HR: Joe Torre ATL 4/12/1966
Total hit in park: 4,445

Visitors

1	Willie McCovey	32
	Johnny Bench	32
3	Andre Dawson	26
4	Willie Stargell	25
	Mike Schmidt	25

Home

1	Dale Murphy	205
2	Hank Aaron	190
3	Bob Horner	142
4	Dave Justice	83
5	Darrell Evans	76
	Ron Gant	76

Total

1	Dale Murphy	205
2	Hank Aaron	190
3	Bob Horner	142
4	Darrell Evans	86
5	Dave Justice	83

Wrigley Field, Chicago
First HR: Art Wilson CHI FL 4/23/1914
First NL HR: Johnny Beall CIN 4/20/1916
Total hit in park: 9,262

Visitors

1	Willie Mays	54
2	Hank Aaron	50
	Mike Schmidt	50
4	Mel Ott	38
5	Eddie Mathews	36

Home

1	Ernie Banks	290
2	Billy Williams	231
3	Ron Santo	212
4	Ryne Sandberg	143
5	Gabby Hartnett	115

Total

1	Ernie Banks	290
2	Billy Williams	231
3	Ron Santo	212
4	Ryne Sandberg	143
5	Hank Sauer	117

Riverfront Stadium, Cincinnati
First HR: Hank Aaron ATL 6/30/1970
Total hit in park: 3,348

Visitors

1	Mike Schmidt	29
2	Steve Garvey	23
3	Andre Dawson	23
	Dale Murphy	23
5	Cesar Cedeno	21

Home

1	Johnny Bench	154
2	George Foster	128
3	Tony Perez	84
4	Eric Davis	80
5	Joe Morgan	75

Total

1	Johnny Bench	154
2	George Foster	132
3	Tony Perez	88
4	Eric Davis	81
5	Joe Morgan	80

Coors Field, Colorado
First HR: Rico Brogna NY 4/26/1995
Total hit in park: 241
Visitors

1	Matt Williams	5
2	Sammy Sosa	4
3	Bernard Gilkey	3
	Raul Mondesi	3
	Mike Piazza	3
	Phil Plantier	3

Home

1	Dante Bichette	31
2	Larry Walker	24
3	Vinny Castilla	23
4	Andres Galarraga	18
5	Ellis Burks	8

Total

1	Dante Bichette	31
2	Larry Walker	24
3	Vinny Castilla	23
4	Andres Galarraga	18
5	Ellis Burks	8

Joe Robbie Stadium, Florida
First HR: Tim Wallach LA 4/05/1993
Total hit in park: 360
Visitors

1	Sean Berry	5
	Fred McGriff	5
3	Wil Cordero	4
	Darren Daulton	4
	Dave Justice	4
	Jeff Kent	4
	Tom Pagnozzi	4
	Reggie Sanders	4
	Sammy Sosa	4
	Todd Zeile	4

Home

1	Jeff Conine	26
2	Gary Sheffield	23
3	Kurt Abbott	16
4	Greg Colbrunn	15
5	Orestes Destrade	12

Total

1	Jeff Conine	26
2	Gary Sheffield	23
3	Kurt Abbott	16
4	Greg Colbrunn	15
5	Orestes Destrade	12

Astrodome, Houston
First HR: Dick Allen PHI 4/12/1965
Total hit in park: 2,419
Visitors

1	Tony Perez	19
2	Willie McCovey	18
3	Willie Stargell	17
	Johnny Bench	17
5	Mike Schmidt	14
	Andre Dawson	14

Home

1	Jim Wynn	93
2	Glenn Davis	72
3	Cesar Cedeno	64
4	Doug Rader	63
5	Jeff Bagwell	56

Total

1	Jim Wynn	97
2	Glenn Davis	72
3	Cesar Cedeno	66
4	Doug Rader	63
5	Jeff Bagwell	56

Dodger Stadium, Los Angeles
First HR: Wally Post CIN 4/10/1962
Total hit in park: 3,713
Visitors

1	George Foster	23
2	Hank Aaron	22
	Mike Schmidt	22
	Dale Murphy	22
5	Willie Stargell	21

Home

1	Ron Cey	121
2	Steve Garvey	117
3	Dusty Baker	73
4	Pedro Guerrero	72
5	Mike Marshall	70

Total

1	Ron Cey	123
2	Steve Garvey	118
3	Dusty Baker	77
4	Pedro Guerrero	74
5	Mike Marshall	71

Olympic Stadium, Montreal
First HR: Ellis Valentine MON 4/15/1977
Total hit in park: 1,944
Visitors

1	Mike Schmidt	26
2	Barry Bonds	24
3	Darryl Strawberry	20
4	Tony Pena	16
5	Jack Clark	13

Home

1	Gary Carter	98
2	Andre Dawson	95
3	Tim Wallach	81
4	Andres Galarraga	47
	Larry Walker	47

Total

1	Gary Carter	106
2	Andre Dawson	102
3	Tim Wallach	83
4	Andres Galarraga	52
5	Larry Walker	48

Shea Stadium, New York
First HR: Willie Stargell PIT 4/17/1964
Total hit in park: 3,588
Visitors

1	Willie Stargell	26
	Mike Schmidt	26
3	Dick Allen	20
4	Jim Wynn	17
	Dale Murphy	17

Home

1	Darryl Strawberry	123
2	Howard Johnson	90
3	Dave Kingman	73
4	Ed Kranepool	66
5	Kevin McReynolds	64

Total

1	Darryl Strawberry	126
2	Howard Johnson	90
3	Dave Kingman	88
4	Kevin McReynolds	67
5	Ed Kranepool	66

Veterans Stadium, Philadelphia
First HR: Don Money PHI 4/10/1971
Total hit in park: 3,105
Visitors

1	Gary Carter	26
2	Barry Bonds	22
3	Andre Dawson	21
4	Johnny Bench	17
	Dave Parker	17

Home

1	Mike Schmidt	265
2	Greg Luzinski	130
3	Von Hayes	77
4	Darren Daulton	61
5	Juan Samuel	52

Total

1	Mike Schmidt	265
2	Greg Luzinski	130
3	Von Hayes	77
5	Darren Daulton	61
4	Juan Samuel	55

Three Rivers Stadium, Pittsburgh
First HR: Tony Perez CIN 7/16/1970
Total hit in park: 2,873
Visitors

1	Mike Schmidt	25
2	Andre Dawson	23
3	Jack Clark	22
4	Dave Kingman	19
	Darryl Strawberry	19

Home

1	Willie Stargell	147
2	Barry Bonds	83
3	Dave Parker	82
4	Bill Robinson	63
5	Andy Van Slyke	61

Total

1	Willie Stargell	147
2	Dave Parker	88
3	Barry Bonds	85
4	Bill Robinson	64
5	Andy Van Slyke	63

San Diego/Jack Murphy Stadium, San Diego
First HR: Ed Spiezio SD 4/08/1969
Total hit in park: 3,049

Visitors

1	Johnny Bench	24
	Dale Murphy	24
3	Mike Schmidt	22
	Pedro Guerrero	22
5	Dave Parker	19
	Gary Carter	19

Home

1	Nate Colbert	72
2	Dave Winfield	71
3	Carmelo Martinez	50
4	Fred McGriff	46
5	Tony Gwynn	45

Total

1	Nate Colbert	73
2	Dave Winfield	71
3	Carmelo Martinez	52
4	Fred McGriff	49
5	Steve Garvey	46

Candlestick Park, San Francisco
First HR: Leon Wagner STL 4/12/1960
Total hit in park: 4,585

Visitors

1	Willie Stargell	25
	Dale Murphy	25
3	Ron Cey	24
4	Tony Perez	21
5	Dick Allen	19
	Andre Dawson	19
	Eric Davis	19

Home

1	Willie McCovey	231
2	Willie Mays	202
3	Matt Williams	116
4	Bobby Bonds	103
5	Will Clark	93

Total

1	Willie McCovey	236
2	Willie Mays	203
3	Matt Williams	116
4	Bobby Bonds	103
5	Will Clark	93

Busch Stadium II, St. Louis
First HR: Felipe Alou ATL 5/12/1966
Total hit in park: 2,556

Visitors

1	Mike Schmidt	27
2	Willie Stargell	19
3	Andre Dawson	17
4	Hank Aaron	15
	Darryl Strawberry	15

Home

1	Ted Simmons	81
2	George Hendrick	55
3	Ray Lankford	49
4	Lou Brock	48
5	Joe Torre	39

Total

1	Ted Simmons	81
2	George Hendrick	55
3	Ray Lankford	49
4	Lou Brock	48
5	Joe Torre	43

Most Home Runs in Park by Visitor (Season)

	Player	*Park*	*HR*
1	Harry Heilmann	Shibe Park, 1922	10
2	Lou Gehrig	Sportsman's Park III, 1931	9
	Jimmie Foxx	Tiger Stadium, 1932	9
	Stan Spence	Sportsman's Park III, 1943	9
	Joe Adcock	Ebbets Field, 1954	9
	Willie Mays	Ebbets Field, 1955	9

Most in Current Parks, Visitor (Season)

Oriole Park at Camden Yards

	Player	*Year*	*HR*
1	Dean Palmer	1993	6
2	Danny Tartabull	1992	4
	Eddie Murray	1994	4
	Albert Belle	1994	4
5	Mo Vaughn	1995	4

Fenway Park

	Player	*Year*	*HR*
1	Babe Ruth	1927	8
2	Gus Zernial	1955	7
	Vic Wertz	1957	7
	Joe Carter	1987	7
5	Lou Gehrig	1927	6
	Hank Greenberg	1937	6
	Pat Seerey	1944	6
	Mickey Mantle	1961	6
	Harmon Killebrew	1963	6

Anaheim Stadium

	Player	*Year*	*HR*
1	Willie Horton	1968	5
	Matt Nokes	1987	5
	Albert Belle	1991	5
4	Tommie Agee	1966	4
	Curt Blefary	1967	4
	Harmon Killebrew	1968	4
	Frank Howard	1970	4
	Tony Conigliaro	1970	4
	Bill Melton	1970	4
	John Mayberry	1975	4
	Graig Nettles	1977	4
	Ben Oglivie	1980	4
	Gorman Thomas	1980	4
	Tom Brunansky	1984	4
	Gary Ward	1984	4
	Steve Balboni	1984	4
	Eddie Murray	1985	4
	Wade Boggs	1987	4
	Dwight Evans	1987	4
	Fred Lynn	1987	4
	Carlton Fisk	1987	4
	Jay Buhner	1991	4
	Rafael Palmeiro	1994	4

Comiskey Park II

	Player	*Year*	*HR*
1	Cecil Fielder	1994	5
	Albert Belle	1995	5
2	Rob Deer	1991	3
	Cecil Fielder	1991	3
	Danny Tartabull	1991	3
	Carlos Baerga	1991	3
	Rafael Palmeiro	1992	3
	Cecil Fielder	1992	3
	Rob Deer	1992	3
	Danny Tartabull	1993	3
	Dave Henderson	1993	3
	Ken Griffey	1993	3
	Jim Edmonds	1995	3
	Mark McGwire	1995	3

Jacobs Field

	Player	*Year*	*HR*
1	Juan Gonzalez	1994	4
2	Tom Brunansky	1994	3
	Jay Buhner	1995	3
4	Bob Hamelin	1994	2
	Dave Winfield	1994	2
	Mickey Tettleton	1994	2
	Kirk Gibson	1994	2
	Jim Leyritz	1994	2
	Pat Meares	1995	2
	Frank Thomas	1995	2
	Robin Ventura	1995	2
	Joe Carter	1995	2
	Shawn Green	1995	2
	Paul O'Neill	1995	2
	Mike Greenwell	1995	2
	Mo Vaughn	1995	2
	Tino Martinez	1995	2
	John Jaha	1995	2

Tiger Stadium

	Player	*Year*	*HR*
1	Jimmie Foxx	1932	9
2	Jimmie Foxx	1937	7
	Yogi Berra	1951	7
	Gus Zernial	1953	7
	Mickey Mantle	1956	7
	Roger Maris	1958	7
	Gary Geiger	1963	7
	Mark McGwire	1987	7

Royals Stadium

	Player	Year	HR
1	Sal Bando	1973	5
	Juan Gonzalez	1993	5
3	Sal Bando	1976	4
	Willie Horton	1977	4
	Gary Roenicke	1979	4
	Gorman Thomas	1979	4
	Don Baylor	1979	4
	Tom Paciorek	1981	4
	Greg Luzinski	1983	4

County Stadium

	Player	*Year*	*HR*
1	Willie Mays	1961	8
2	Frank Howard	1963	6

	Player	Year	HR
3	Orlando Cepeda	1959	5
	Frank Howard	1960	5
	Frank Thomas	1962	5
	Andre Thornton	1978	5

Hubert H. Humphrey Metrodome

	Player	Year	HR
1	Harold Baines	1984	5
	Darrell Evans	1985	5
	Oddibe McDowell	1987	5
	Joe Carter	1989	5
	Lance Parrish	1991	5
	Jay Buhner	1995	5
	Eddie Murray	1995	5

Yankee Stadium

	Player	Year	HR
1	Joe Kuhel	1940	7
2	Goose Goslin	1926	6
	Al Simmons	1929	6
	Larry Doby	1954	6
	Roy Sievers	1958	6
	Fred Whitfield	1965	6

Oakland-Alameda County Stadium

	Player	Year	HR
1	Ken Harrelson	1968	5
	Harmon Killebrew	1969	5
	Tony Oliva	1969	5
4	Carl Yastrzemski	1970	4
	Bob Oliver	1971	4
	Jeff Burroughs	1973	4
	George Scott	1975	4
	Dan Ford	1976	4
	Bobby Grich	1979	4
	Bobby Grich	1981	4
	Andre Thornton	1982	4
	Tony Armas	1984	4
	Greg Walker	1985	4
	Larry Parrish	1987	4
	Danny Tartabull	1990	4
	Danny Tartabull	1991	4

Kingdome

	Player	Year	HR
1	Dave Kingman	1986	6
	Jose Canseco	1988	6
3	Roy Smalley	1978	5
	John Mayberry	1980	5
	Ben Oglivie	1980	5
	Jesse Barfield	1986	5
	George Bell	1987	5
	Fred McGriff	1989	5

The Ballpark in Arlington

	Player	Year	HR
1	Ken Griffey	1994	5
2	Chili Davis	1994	4
	Bernie Williams	1994	4
4	Paul Sorrento	1995	3
	Cecil Fielder	1995	3
	Mark McGwire	1995	3
	Tim Salmon	1995	3
	Jose Canseco	1995	3

Skydome

	Player	Year	HR
1	Jose Canseco	1991	5
2	Cecil Fielder	1990	4
	Dave Parker	1990	4
	Dave Winfield	1991	4
	Glenallen Hill	1992	4
	Paul Sorrento	1993	4
	Chili Davis	1993	4
	Manny Ramirez	1995	4

Atlanta-Fulton County Stadium

	Player	Year	HR
1	Cito Gaston	1970	6
	Nate Colbert	1972	6
	Joe Morgan	1973	6
	Jack Clark	1978	6
	Kevin Mitchell	1989	6

Wrigley Field

	Player	Year	HR
1	Mike Schmidt	1980	8
2	Johnny Callison	1965	7
	Gene Oliver	1965	7
	Mike Schmidt	1976	7
5	Irish Meusel	1923	6
	George Kelly	1923	6
	George Kelly	1924	6
	Les Bell	1925	6
	Johnny Mize	1947	6
	Ralph Kiner	1947	6
	Gil Hodges	1951	6
	Frank Thomas	1958	6
	Joe Adcock	1960	6
	Tony Perez	1968	6
	Dave Kingman	1976	6

Riverfront Stadium

	Player	Year	HR
1	Mike Schmidt	1974	5
	Willie McCovey	1977	5
	Pedro Guerrero	1985	5
	Glenn Davis	1988	5
	Matt Williams	1993	5

Coors Field

	Player	Year	HR
1	Matt Williams	1995	5
2	Sammy Sosa	1995	4
3	Raul Mondesi	1995	3
	Mike Piazza	1995	3
	Bernard Gilkey	1995	3
	Phil Plantier	1995	3

Joe Robbie Stadium

	Player	Year	HR
1	Dave Justice	1993	4
2	Darren Daulton	1993	3
	Todd Benzinger	1993	3
	Kevin Mitchell	1994	3
	Todd Zeile	1994	3
	Fred McGriff	1994	3
	Tom Pagnozzi	1994	3
	Vinny Castilla	1995	3
	Wil Cordero	1995	3

Astrodome

	Player	Year	HR
1	Dale Murphy	1984	6
	Darryl Strawberry	1991	6
3	Willie Stargell	1966	5
	Johnny Bench	1972	5
	Pedro Guerrero	1985	5

Dodger Stadium

	Player	Year	HR
1	Jim Wynn	1967	6
	Mike Schmidt	1979	6
3	Orlando Cepeda	1970	5
	Nate Colbert	1971	5
	George Foster	1977	5

Olympic Stadium

	Player	Year	HR
1	Willie McCovey	1977	4
	John Stearns	1977	4
	George Foster	1977	4
	Mike Schmidt	1980	4
	Chris Chambliss	1983	4
	Tony Pena	1983	4
	Chili Davis	1984	4
	Leon Durham	1987	4
	Mike Schmidt	1987	4
	Darryl Strawberry	1987	4
	Barry Bonds	1990	4
	Barry Bonds	1994	4
	Mike Piazza	1995	4

Shea Stadium

	Player	Year	HR
1	Dick Allen	1968	7
2	Dave Kingman	1979	6
	Dave Kingman	1980	6
4	Donn Clendenon	1966	5
	Willie Stargell	1966	5
	Wes Parker	1966	5
	Bill Mazeroski	1966	5
	Dick Allen	1967	5
	Dusty Baker	1980	5

Veterans Stadium

	Player	Year	HR
1	Gary Carter	1978	7
2	Dave Parker	1978	6
3	Bob Robertson	1971	5
	Hal Breeden	1973	5
	Andre Dawson	1979	5
	Eric Davis	1987	5

Three Rivers Stadium

	Player	Year	HR
1	Dave Kingman	1975	7
2	Joe Morgan	1976	5
	Jack Clark	1982	5
	Mark Carreon	1995	5
5	Reggie Smith	1977	4
	Gene Tenace	1977	4
	Ellis Valentine	1977	4
	Greg Luzinski	1978	4
	Tony Perez	1978	4
	Jack Clark	1979	4
	Dave Kingman	1982	4
	Andre Dawson	1983	4
	Darryl Strawberry	1985	4
	Mike Schmidt	1986	4
	Eric Davis	1986	4

	Player	Year	HR
	Jim Lindeman	1987	4
	Tim Raines	1987	4
	Rafael Palmeiro	1987	4
	Andres Galarraga	1988	4
	Glenn Davis	1989	4
	Kevin Mitchell	1990	4
	Phil Plantier	1993	4
	Reggie Sanders	1995	4
	Mike Piazza	1995	4

San Diego/Jack Murphy Stadium

	Player	Year	HR
1	Gary Carter	1985	6
2	Hank Aaron	1973	5
	Alan Ashby	1982	5
	Pedro Guerrero	1983	5
	Tom Brunansky	1988	5
	Kevin Mitchell	1991	5
	Mark Parent	1995	5
	Andres Galarraga	1995	5

Candlestick Park

	Player	Year	HR
1	Willie Stargell	1971	6
2	Dale Murphy	1983	5
	Dale Murphy	1985	5
	Eddie Murray	1990	5
	Glenn Davis	1990	5
	Gary Sheffield	1992	5

Busch Stadium II

	Player	Year	HR
1	Mike Schmidt	1987	5
2	Orlando Cepeda	1969	4
	Dave Kingman	1979	4
	Gary Carter	1980	4
	Bobby Bonds	1981	4
	Dave Kingman	1982	4
	Darryl Strawberry	1984	4
	Bobby Bonilla	1994	4

Home Run in First Major League At Bat

Player	Team	Date
Brant Alyea	WAS AL	09/12/1965
Earl Averill	CLE AL	04/16/1929
Benny Ayala	NY NL	08/27/1974
Dan Bankhead	BRO NL	08/26/1947
Cuno Barragan	CHI NL	09/01/1961
Johnny Bates	BOS NL	04/12/1906
Jay Bell	CLE AL	09/29/1986
Gates Brown	DET AL	06/19/1963
Jim Bullinger	CHI NL	06/08/1992
Bert Campaneris	KC AL	07/23/1964
Will Clark	SF NL	04/08/1986
Andre David	MIN AL	06/29/1984
Clise Dudley	BRO NL	04/27/1929
Bill Duggleby	PHI NL	04/21/1898
Dave Eiland	SD NL	04/10/1992
Frank Ernaga	CHI NL	05/24/1957
Junior Felix	TOR AL	05/04/1989
Mike Fitzgerald	NY NL	09/13/1983
Gary Gaetti	MIN AL	09/20/1981
Jay Gainer	COL NL	05/14/1993
Paul Gillespie	CHI NL	09/11/1942
Rusty Greer	TEX AL	05/16/1994
Mike Griffin	BAL AA	04/16/1887
Billy Gumbert	PIT NL	06/19/1890
Joe Harrington	BOS NL	09/10/1895
Gene Hasson	PHI AL	09/09/1937
Garey Ingram	LA NL	05/19/1994
Ricky Jordan	PHI NL	07/17/1988
John Kennedy	WAS AL	09/05/1962
Joe Keough	OAK AL	08/07/1968
Buddy Kerr	NY NL	09/08/1943
Ernie Koy	BRO NL	04/19/1938
Gene Lamont	DET AL	09/02/1970
Les Layton	NY NL	05/21/1948
Bill LeFebvre	BOS AL	06/10/1938
Johnnie LeMaster	SF NL	09/02/1975
Don Leppert	PIT NL	06/18/1961
Whitey Lockman	NY NL	07/05/1945
Mitch Lyden	FLO NL	06/16/1993
Dave Machemer	CAL AL	06/21/1978
Carmelo Martinez	CHI NL	08/22/1983
Dave McKay	MIN AL	08/22/1975
Hack Miller	DET AL	04/23/1944
John Miller	NY AL	09/11/1966
John Montefusco	SF NL	09/03/1974
Wally Moon	STL NL	04/13/1954
Eddie Morgan	STL NL	04/14/1936
Heinie Mueller	PHI NL	04/19/1938
Walter Mueller	PIT NL	05/07/1922
Buster Narum	BAL AL	05/03/1963
Bob Nieman	STL AL	09/13/1951
Jon Nunnally	KC AL	04/29/1995
Jose Offerman	LA NL	08/19/1990
Ace Parker	PHI AL	04/30/1937
Eddie Pellagrini	BOS AL	04/22/1946
Rick Renick	MIN AL	07/11/1968
Bill Roman	DET AL	09/30/1964
Don Rose	CAL AL	05/24/1972
Reggie Sanders	DET AL	09/01/1974
Ed Sanicki	PHI NL	09/14/1949
Gordon Slade	BRO NL	05/24/1930
Jose Sosa	HOU NL	07/30/1975
Terry Steinbach	OAK AL	09/12/1986
Luke Stuart	STL AL	08/08/1921
Chuck Tanner	MIL NL	04/12/1955
Ted Tappe	CIN NL	09/14/1950
George Tebeau	CIN AA	04/16/1887
Bob Tillman	BOS AL	05/19/1962
Sam Vico	DET AL	04/20/1948
Clyde Vollmer	CIN NL	05/31/1942
Tim Wallach	MON NL	09/06/1980
Bill White	NY NL	05/07/1956
Hoyt Wilhelm	NY NL	04/23/1952
Al Woods	TOR AL	04/07/1977

Most Inside-the-Park Home Runs (Game)

	Player	Team	Date	HR
1	Guy Hecker	LOU AA	08/15/1886	3
	Tom McCreery	LOU NL	07/12/1897	3
3	Dick Allen	CHI AL	07/31/1972	2
	Ginger Beaumont	PIT NL	07/16/1903	2
	Beals Becker	PHI NL	06/09/1913	2
	Chief Bender	PHI AL	05/08/1906	2
	Roger Bresnahan	BAL AL	05/30/1902	2
	Roger Bresnahan	NY NL	06/06/1904	2
	Dan Brouthers	BUF NL	08/10/1882	2
	Dan Brouthers	DET NL	09/10/1886	2
	Jesse Burkett	STL NL	08/28/1899	2
	Jesse Burkett	STL NL	07/08/1900	2
	Ken Caminiti	SD NL	09/16/1995	2
	Ben Chapman	NY AL	07/09/1932	2
	Ty Cobb	DET AL	07/15/1909	2
	Monte Cross	PHI AL	04/28/1902	2
	George Cutshaw	BRO NL	08/04/1913	2
	Kiki Cuyler	PIT NL	08/28/1925	2
	Tom Daly	BRO NL	07/08/1894	2
	George Davis	NY NL	07/08/1901	2
	Ed Delahanty	PHI NL	06/01/1893	2
	Ed Delahanty	PHI NL	07/13/1896	2
	Mike Donlin	STL NL	10/05/1900	2
	Larry Doyle	NY NL	09/08/1909	2
	Hugh Duffy	CHI NL	08/09/1889	2
	Hugh Duffy	BOS AA	07/23/1891	2
	Duke Farrell	PIT NL	07/06/1892	2
	Hobe Ferris	BOS AL	05/04/1903	2
	Tom Fisher	BRO NL	08/16/1913	2
	Jack Fournier	CHI AL	08/31/1914	2
	Greg Gagne	MIN AL	10/04/1986	2
	Larry Gardner	BOS AL	07/02/1912	2
	Topsy Hartsel	CHI NL	08/05/1901	2
	Danny Hoffman	PHI AL	05/12/1904	2
	Mike Hornung	BOS NL	06/09/1883	2
	Hal Janvrin	BOS AL	10/04/1913	2
	Willie Keeler	NY AL	08/24/1904	2
	Joe Kelley	BAL NL	08/16/1895	2
	George Kelly	NY NL	04/29/1922	2
	Billy Klusman	BOS NL	07/17/1888	2
	Ed Konetchy	STL NL	08/05/1912	2
	Tommy Leach	PIT NL	05/21/1903	2
	Rabbit Maranville	BOS NL	07/01/1919	2
	Stuffy McInnis	PHI AL	08/14/1912	2
	Bill McKechnie	PIT NL	09/02/1911	2
	Terry Moore	STL NL	08/16/1939	2
	Ben Paschal	NY AL	09/22/1925	2
	Morris Rath	CIN NL	09/20/1920	2
	John Reilly	CIN AA	05/06/1888	2
	Carl Reynolds	CHI AL	07/02/1930	2
	Jimmy Sebring	PIT NL	04/23/1903	2
	Cy Seymour	CIN NL	09/24/1905	2
	Homer Smoot	STL NL	04/25/1902	2
	Sammy Sosa	CHI NL	09/16/1995	2
	Casey Stengel	BRO NL	05/01/1913	2
	Hank Thompson	NY NL	08/16/1950	2
	Heinie Wagner	BOS AL	08/22/1907	2
	Honus Wagner	LOU NL	07/30/1899	2

Most Inside-the-Park Home Runs (Season)

	Player	Team		HR
1	Sam Crawford	CIN NL	1901	12
2	Ty Cobb	DET AL	1909	9
3	Kiki Cuyler	PIT NL	1925	8
	John Reilly	CIN AA	1888	8
	Tris Speaker	BOS AL	1912	8
	Chief Wilson	PIT NL	1911	8
7	Tony Boeckel	BOS NL	1921	7
	George Cutshaw	BRO NL	1913	7
	Jake Daubert	BRO NL	1910	7
	Tommy Leach	PIT NL	1903	7
	Cy Seymour	CIN NL	1905	7

Most Inside-the-Park Home Runs (Career)

	Player	HR
1	Sam Crawford	51
2	Tommy Leach	49
3	Ty Cobb	46
4	Honus Wagner	41

5	Tris Speaker	37
6	Jake Daubert	33
7	Chief Wilson	31
8	Rogers Hornsby	30
	Willie Keeler	30
	Edd Roush	30
11	Max Carey	28
	Ed Konetchy	28
13	Jesse Burkett	27
14	Zach Wheat	25
15	Hal Chase	24
16	Fred Clarke	23
	Earle Combs	23
18	Rabbit Maranville	22
	Danny Murphy	22
20	Ginger Beaumont	21
	Sherry Magee	21
	Sam Rice	21
	Cy Seymour	21
24	George Sisler	20
25	George Cutshaw	19

Pinch Hit Home Run and Another Home Run (Game)

Player	Team	Date
Shane Andrews	SN NL	09/28/1995
Jeff Bagwell	HOU NL	05/10/1992
Steve Balboni	NY AL	05/23/1990
Thad Bosley	CHI NL	08/12/1985
Steve Brye	MIN AL	09/07/1975
Joe Foy	BOS AL	06/09/1967
Jim Gentile	BAL AL	06/30/1960
Kirk Gibson	DET AL	05/28/1994
Goose Goslin	WAS AL	08/24/1933
Jeff Heath	BOS NL	08/27/1949
Tony Horton	CLE AL	07/24/1970
Frank Howard	DET AL	07/26/1973
Jack Howell	CAL AL	05/27/1987
Darrin Jackson	CHI AL	04/06/1994
Joe Lefebvre	SD NL	04/30/1981
Les Mann	STL NL	05/11/1923
John Mayberry	TOR AL	06/26/1978
Don Mincher	MIN AL	04/28/1962
Geno Petralli	TEX AL	09/29/1987
Wally Post	CIN NL	07/02/1960
Del Rice	LA AL	06/18/1961
Mark Ryal	CAL AL	05/13/1987
Roy Sievers	CHI AL	06/21/1961
Marvell Wynne	SD NL	04/13/1986

Pinch Hit HRs, each game (doubleheader)

Player	Team	Date
Hal Breeden	MON NL	07/13/1973
Joe Cronin	BOS AL	06/17/1943

Most Pinch Hit Home Runs (Season)

	Player	Team	Year	HR
1	Johnny Frederick	BRO NL	1932	6
2	Joe Cronin	BOS AL	1943	5
	Gene Freese	PHI NL	1959	5
	Cliff Johnson	HOU NL	1974	5
	Lee Lacy	LA NL	1978	5
	Jerry Lynch	CIN NL	1961	5
	Butch Nieman	BOS NL	1945	5
	Jerry Turner	SD NL	1978	5
9	Johnny Blanchard	NY AL	1961	4
	Hal Breeden	MON NL	1973	4
	Jeff Burroughs	OAK AL	1982	4
	Mark Carreon	NY NL	1989	4
	George Crowe	STL NL	1959	4
	George Crowe	STL NL	1960	4
	Tommy Gregg	ATL NL	1990	4
	Danny Heep	NY NL	1983	4
	Mike Ivie	SF NL	1978	4
	Howard Johnson	COL NL	1994	4
	Ernie Lombardi	NY NL	1946	4
	Jerry Lynch	CIN NL	1963	4
	Candy Maldonado	SF NL	1986	4
	Don Mincher	MIN AL	1964	4
	Rip Repulski	PHI NL	1958	4
	Ernest Riles	SF NL	1990	4
	Carl Sawatski	STL NL	1961	4
	Bill Taylor	NY NL	1955	4
	Bob Thurman	CIN NL	1957	4
	Del Unser	PHI NL	1979	4
	Del Wilber	BOS AL	1953	4
	John Vander Wal	COL NL	1995	4

Most Pinch Hit HRs, Batter (Career)

	Player	HR
1	Cliff Johnson	20
2	Jerry Lynch	18
3	Gates Brown	16
	Smoky Burgess	16
	Willie McCovey	16
6	George Crowe	14
7	Joe Adcock	12
	Bob Cerv	12
	Jose Morales	12
	Graig Nettles	12
11	Jeff Burroughs	11
	Jay Johnstone	11
	Candy Maldonado	11
	Fred Whitfield	11
	Cy Williams	11
16	Jim Dwyer	10
	Mike Lum	10
	Ken McMullen	10
	Don Mincher	10
	Wally Post	10
	Roy Sievers	10
	Champ Summers	10
	Jerry Turner	10
	Gus Zernial	10
25	Mark Carreon	9
	Norm Cash	9
	Gene Freese	9
	John Grubb	9
	Bobby Hofman	9
	Howard Johnson	9
	Bobby Murcer	9
	Ron Northey	9
	Tony Perez	9
	Carl Sawatski	9
	Bill Skowron	9
	Rusty Staub	9
	Vic Wertz	9

Most Pinch Hit Home Runs, Team (Game)

	Team	Date	HR
1	PHI NL	05/30/1925	2
	PHI NL	06/02/1928	2
	STL NL	07/21/1930	2
	CLE AL	05/26/1937	2
	STL NL	05/12/1951	2
	NY NL	08/05/1952	2
	CHI NL	06/09/1954	2
	NY NL	06/20/1954	2
	NY AL	07/23/1955	2
	SF NL	06/04/1958	2
	PHI NL	08/13/1958	2
	NY NL	08/15/1962	2
	LA NL	08/08/1963	2
	NY NL	09/17/1963	2
	CLE AL	08/15/1965	2
	NY NL	08/04/1966	2
	BAL AL	08/26/1966	2
	DET AL	08/11/1968	2
	SEA AL	08/02/1969	2
	MIN AL	07/31/1970	2
	MON NL	07/13/1973	2
	MIN AL	07/28/1974	2
	CHI NL	09/10/1974	2
	LA NL	07/23/1975	2
	CHI NL	08/23/1975	2
	SEA AL	04/27/1979	2
	CHI AL	07/06/1980	2
	LA NL	08/27/1982	2
	MIN AL	05/16/1983	2
	BAL AL	05/05/1984	2
	BAL AL	08/12/1985	2
	TOR AL	06/14/1986	2
	TEX AL	09/01/1986	2
	CAL AL	06/28/1987	2
	SF NL	09/28/1987	2
	NY NL	05/04/1991	2
	COL NL	05/06/1995	2
	CIN NL	06/22/1995	2
	HOU NL	09/28/1995	2

Most Pinch Hit Home Runs, Both Teams (Game)

	Teams	Date	HR
1	STL @ PHI NL	06/02/1928	3
	STL @ BRO NL	07/21/1930	3
	LA @ COL NL	05/06/1995	3

Most Pinch Hit HRs, Team (Season)

	Team	Year	HR
1	CIN NL	1957	12
	NY NL	1983	12
3	PHI NL	1958	11
	SF NL	1977	11
	BAL AL	1982	11
	SF NL	1987	11
	COL NL	1995	11

Extra Inning Pinch Hit Grand Slam

Date	Player	Team	Inning
09/13/1931	Rogers Hornsby	CHI NL	11
07/23/1933	Harvey Hendrick	CHI NL	10
06/06/1946	Frank Secory	CHI NL	12
07/26/1952	Bud Souchock	DET AL	11
09/16/1967	Rick Joseph	PHI NL	11
05/01/1979	Roger Freed	STL NL	11
06/30/1979	Mike Vail	CHI NL	11
06/10/1986	Tim Teufel	NY NL	11
07/26/1988	Mike Fitzgerald	MON NL	11
10/04/1992	Greg Litton	SF NL	13
05/04/1995	Todd Hundley	NY NL	10

Two Grand Slams in Same Game

Player	Team	Date
Tony Cloninger	ATL NL	07/03/1966
Jim Gentile	BAL AL	05/09/1961
Tony Lazzeri	NY AL	05/24/1936
Jim Northrup	DET AL	06/24/1968
Frank Robinson	BAL AL	06/26/1970
Jim Tabor	BOS AL	07/04/1939
Rudy Ventura	CHI AL	09/04/1995
Rudy York	BOS AL	07/27/1946

Most Grand Slams (Season)

	Player	Team	Year	HR
1	Don Mattingly	NY AL	1987	6
2	Ernie Banks	CHI NL	1955	5
	Jim Gentile	BAL AL	1961	5
4	Ray Boone	CLE AL	1953	4
	Vince DiMaggio	PHI NL	1945	4
	Lou Gehrig	NY AL	1934	4
	Sid Gordon	BOS NL	1950	4
	Tommy Henrich	NY AL	1948	4
	Ralph Kiner	PIT NL	1949	4
	Jim Northrup	DET AL	1968	4
	Al Rosen	CLE AL	1951	4
	Babe Ruth	BOS AL	1919	4
	Wildfire Schulte	CHI NL	1911	4
	Rudy York	DET AL	1938	4
15	Hank Aaron	MIL NL	1962	3
	Bob Allison	MIN AL	1961	3
	Wally Berger	BOS NL	1935	3
	Mike Blowers	SEA AL	1993	3
	Mike Blowers	SEA AL	1995	3
	Jim Bottomley	STL NL	1925	3
	Jeff Burroughs	TEX AL	1973	3
	Rod Carew	MIN AL	1976	3
	Del Crandall	MIL NL	1955	3
	Kal Daniels	LA NL	1990	3
	Alvin Davis	SEA AL	1990	3
	Eric Davis	CIN NL	1987	3
	Joe DiMaggio	NY AL	1937	3
	Jimmie Foxx	PHI AL	1932	3
	Jimmie Foxx	PHI AL	1934	3
	Jimmie Foxx	BOS AL	1938	3
	Jimmie Foxx	BOS AL	1940	3
	Gene Freese	PHI NL	1959	3
	Lou Gehrig	NY AL	1931	3
	Dan Gladden	DET AL	1993	3
	Sid Gordon	NY NL	1948	3
	Ken Griffey	SEA AL	1991	3
	Keith Hernandez	STL NL	1977	3
	Willie Horton	DET AL	1969	3
	Kent Hrbek	MIN AL	1985	3
	Reggie Jackson	BAL AL	1976	3
	John Jaha	MIL AL	1995	3
	Bob Johnson	PHI AL	1938	3
	George Kelly	NY NL	1921	3
	Ralph Kiner	PIT NL	1951	3
	Dave Kingman	OAK AL	1984	3
	Chuck Klein	PHI NL	1929	3
	Chuck Klein	PHI NL	1932	3
	Ray Knight	CIN NL	1980	3
	Don Lenhardt	BOS AL	1952	3
	Lee May	CIN NL	1970	3
	Willie McCovey	SF NL	1967	3
	John Milner	NY NL	1976	3
	Eddie Murray	BAL AL	1985	3
	Larry Parrish	TEX AL	1982	3
	Rico Petrocelli	BOS AL	1972	3
	Kirby Puckett	MIN AL	1992	3
	Frank Robinson	CIN NL	1962	3
	Joe Rudi	CAL AL	1978	3
	Joe Rudi	CAL AL	1979	3
	Babe Ruth	NY AL	1929	3
	Chris Sabo	CIN NL	1993	3
	Tris Speaker	CLE AL	1923	3
	Mike Stanley	NY AL	1993	3
	Dick Stuart	BOS AL	1964	3
	Danny Tartabull	KC AL	1988	3
	Gene Tenace	OAK AL	1974	3
	Andre Thornton	CLE AL	1979	3
	Mo Vaughn	BOS AL	1995	3
	Pete Ward	CHI AL	1964	3
	Vic Wertz	BOS AL	1960	3
	Wes Westrum	NY NL	1951	3
	Ted Williams	BOS AL	1955	3
	Carl Yastrzemski	BOS AL	1969	3
	Gus Zernial	PHI AL	1952	3

Most Grand Slams (Career)

	Player	HR
1	Lou Gehrig	23
2	Willie McCovey	18
3	Jimmie Foxx	17
	Eddie Murray	17
	Ted Williams	17
6	Hank Aaron	16
	Dave Kingman	16
	Babe Ruth	16
9	Gil Hodges	14
10	Joe DiMaggio	13
	George Foster	13
	Ralph Kiner	13
13	Ernie Banks	12
	Don Baylor	12
	Rogers Hornsby	12
	Joe Rudi	12
	Rudy York	12
18	Johnny Bench	11
	Gary Carter	11
	Hank Greenberg	11
	Reggie Jackson	11
	Harmon Killebrew	11
	Lee May	11
	Willie Stargell	11
	Dave Winfield	11

Most Home Runs Without Hitting a Grand Slam (Career)

	Player	HR
1	Glenn Davis	190
2	Ron Kittle	176
3	Claudell Washington	164
4	Willie Kirkland	148
5	Hector Lopez	136
	Matt Nokes	136

Most Extra Inning Grand Slams (Career)

	Player	HR
1	Tommy Davis	2
	Ruppert Jones	2
	Roger Maris	2
	Jim Presley	2
	Cookie Rojas	2
	Cy Williams	2

Most Grand Slams, Team (Game)

	Team	Date	HR
1	CHI NL	08/16/1890	2
	BOS NL	05/28/1894	2
	CHI AL	05/01/1901	2
	BRO NL	09/23/1901	2
	BOS NL	08/12/1903	2
	PHI NL	04/28/1921	2
	NY NL	09/05/1924	2
	PIT NL	06/22/1925	2
	STL NL	07/06/1929	2
	PIT NL	05/01/1933	2
	BOS AL	05/13/1934	2
	NY AL	05/24/1936	2
	BOS NL	04/30/1938	2
	NY NL	07/04/1938	2
	BOS AL	07/04/1939	2
	BOS AL	07/27/1946	2
	NY NL	07/13/1951	2
	DET AL	06/11/1954	2
	CIN NL	07/29/1955	2
	BAL AL	04/24/1960	2
	BOS AL	05/10/1960	2
	BAL AL	05/09/1961	2
	MIN AL	07/18/1962	2
	ATL NL	07/03/1966	2
	DET AL	06/24/1968	2
	HOU NL	07/30/1969	2
	SF NL	04/26/1970	2
	BAL AL	06/26/1970	2
	MIL AL	06/17/1973	2
	MIL AL	04/12/1980	2
	PIT NL	09/14/1982	2
	CAL AL	04/27/1983	2
	BOS AL	08/07/1984	2
	LA NL	08/23/1985	2
	CAL AL	07/31/1986	2
	BAL AL	08/06/1986	2
	ATL NL	05/02/1987	2
	CHI NL	06/03/1987	2
	BOS AL	06/10/1987	2
	NY AL	06/29/1987	2
	CLE AL	04/22/1988	2
	CIN NL	04/24/1993	2
	BOS AL	05/02/1995	2
	CHI AL	09/04/1995	2

Most Grand Slams, Both Teams (Game)

	Teams	Date	HR
1	TEX @ BAL AL	08/06/1986	3
	HOU @ CHI NL	06/03/1987	3

Most Grand Slams, Team (Season)

	Teams	Year	HR
1	DET AL	1938	10
	NY AL	1987	10
	MIL AL	1995	10
	SEA AL	1995	10
3	CHI NL	1929	9
	BOS AL	1941	9
	BOS AL	1950	9
	BOS AL	1987	9
	SD NL	1995	9

Two Extra Inning Home Runs (Same Game)

Player	Team	Date
Ralph Garr	ATL NL	05/17/1971

Willie Kirkland	CLE AL	06/14/1963
Art Shamsky	CIN NL	08/12/1966
Vern Stephens	STL AL	09/29/1943
Mike Young	BAL AL	05/28/1987

Most Extra Inning Home Runs (Season)

	Player	*Team*	*Year*	*HR*
1	Charlie Maxwell	DET AL	1960	5
2	Ron Gant	CIN NL	1995	4
	Willie Mays	NY NL	1955	4
4	Bob Aspromonte	HOU NL	1963	3
	Bob Bailey	PIT NL	1966	3
	Ernie Banks	CHI NL	1955	3
	Kevin Bass	HOU NL	1987	3
	Bobby Bonilla	PIT NL	1989	3
	Ken Boyer	STL NL	1958	3
	Jay Buhner	SEA AL	1991	3
	Dolph Camilli	BRO NL	1940	3
	Jack Clark	SF NL	1981	3
	Jack Clark	STL NL	1987	3
	Ron Fairly	MON NL	1973	3
	Joe Ferguson	HOU NL	1977	3
	Joe Ferguson	LA NL	1980	3
	Lou Gehrig	NY AL	1935	3
	Terry Harper	ATL NL	1985	3
	Jeff Heath	CLE AL	1943	3
	Reggie Jackson	OAK AL	1971	3
	Felix Jose	STL NL	1992	3
	Willie Kirkland	CLE AL	1963	3
	Mickey Mantle	NY AL	1959	3
	Dave May	MIL AL	1973	3
	Lee May	CIN NL	1970	3
	Willie Mays	NY NL	1951	3
	Willie Mays	SF NL	1963	3
	Mark McGwire	OAK AL	1987	3
	Eddie Murray	BAL AL	1978	3
	Andy Pafko	BRO NL	1952	3
	Tony Pena	PIT NL	1985	3
	Tony Perez	CIN NL	1973	3
	Frank Robinson	CIN NL	1962	3
	Frank Robinson	BAL AL	1969	3
	Jackie Robinson	BRO NL	1951	3
	Ron Santo	CHI NL	1966	3
	Art Shamsky	CIN NL	1966	3
	Roy Sievers	WAS AL	1957	3
	Willie Stargell	PIT NL	1966	3
	Gene Tenace	OAK AL	1973	3
	Del Unser	WAS AL	1969	3
	Ted Williams	BOS AL	1946	3
	Rudy York	DET AL	1943	3
	Babe Young	NY NL	1941	3
	Jeff Bagwell	HOU NL	1992	3

Most Extra Inning Home Runs (Career)

	Player	*HR*
1	Willie Mays	22
2	Jack Clark	18
3	Frank Robinson	16
	Babe Ruth	16
5	Hank Aaron	14
	Jimmie Foxx	14
	Mickey Mantle	14
8	Ted Williams	13
9	Willie Stargell	12
10	Harmon Killebrew	11
	Stan Musial	11
	Graig Nettles	11
	Lance Parrish	11
14	Dick Allen	10
	Don Baylor	10
	Reggie Jackson	10
	Howard Johnson	10
	Willie McCovey	10
	Eddie Murray	10
	Tony Perez	10
21	Ernie Banks	9
	Yogi Berra	9
	Bobby Bonilla	9
	Mike Schmidt	9
	Billy Williams	9
	Dave Winfield	9

Most Extra Inning Home Runs, Team (Game)

	Team	*Date*	*HR*
1	MIN AL	05/02/1964	4
	MIL NL	06/08/1965	4
3	DET AL	06/19/1935	3
	CLE AL	08/21/1944	3
	BOS AL	04/29/1951	3
	SEA AL	05/16/1969	3
	PIT NL	07/15/1971	3

Most Extra Inning Home Runs, Both Teams (Game)

	Teams	*Date*	*HR*
1	NY @ DET AL	06/19/1935	4
	BOS @ PHI AL	04/29/1951	4
	MIN @ KC AL	05/02/1964	4
	MIL @ CHI NL	06/08/1965	4
	SEA @ BOS AL	05/16/1969	4
	SD @ PIT NL	07/15/1971	4
7	BRO @ PHI NL	07/01/1911	3
	CHI @ STL NL	06/21/1927	3
	BOS @ PHI AL	09/04/1930	3
	CHI @ STL NL	05/26/1941	3
	CLE @ BOS AL	08/21/1944	3
	BRO @ CHI NL	05/17/1949	3
	PHI @ NY NL	07/03/1951	3
	CHI @ STL NL	04/16/1955	3
	DET @ CLE AL	08/14/1956	3
	CHI @ BRO NL	07/19/1957	3
	DET @ WAS AL	08/10/1966	3
	PIT @ CIN NL	08/12/1966	3
	NY @ ATL NL	05/17/1971	3
	SD @ MON NL	05/21/1977	3
	NY @ CHI NL	06/30/1979	3
	SF @ LA NL	09/09/1981	3
	CHI @ OAK AL	06/12/1983	3
	TOR @ BAL AL	08/24/1983	3
	NY @ ATL NL	07/04/1985	3
	HOU @ NY NL	07/03/1986	3
	MON @ STL NL	06/27/1988	3
	OAK @ TOR AL	07/03/1988	3
	SF @ PHI NL	05/15/1989	3

Most Extra Inning Home Runs, Team (Season)

	Team	*Year*	*HR*
1	WAS AL	1962	9
	PIT NL	1966	9
	CLE AL	1967	9
	HOU NL	1992	9
5	NY AL	1941	8
	BOS AL	1951	8
	BOS AL	1959	8
	NY AL	1962	8
	CIN NL	1962	8
	CLE AL	1963	8
	MIN AL	1964	8
	BAL AL	1969	8
	SEA AL	1969	8
	BAL AL	1982	8
	TOR AL	1985	8
	NY AL	1988	8

Home Runs Hit in Inning 15 and Later

Player	*Team*	*Date*	*Inning*
Harold Baines	CHI AL	05/08/1984	25
Rick Dempsey	LA NL	08/23/1989	22
Pedro Munoz	MIN AL	08/31/1993	22
Jack Reed	NY AL	06/24/1962	22
Dick Allen	CHI AL	05/26/1973	21
Larry Doyle	NY NL	07/17/1914	21
Ben Oglivie	MIL AL	05/08/1984	21
Merv Rettenmund	SD NL	05/21/1977	21
Tommy Harper	SEA AL	07/27/1969	20
Joe Lahoud	BOS AL	07/27/1969	20
Ken McMullen	WAS AL	08/09/1967	20
Dave Duncan	KC AL	06/17/1967	19
Andy Etchebarren	BAL AL	06/04/1967	19
Willie Kirkland	CLE AL	06/14/1963	19
Hi Myers	BRO NL	04/30/1919	19
Tim Naehring	BOS AL	04/11/1992	19
Joe Rudi	OAK AL	08/10/1972	19
Joe Wood	CLE AL	05/24/1918	19
Rick Camp	ATL NL	07/04/1985	18
Billy Hatcher	HOU NL	09/02/1986	18
Randy Johnson	ATL NL	09/06/1984	18
George Kelly	NY NL	07/07/1922	18
Jeff King	PIT NL	08/06/1989	18
Don Pavletich	CIN NL	07/19/1966	18
Charley Radbourn	PRO NL	08/17/1882	18
Cesar Tovar	MIN AL	09/06/1969	18
Claudell Washington	NY AL	09/11/1988	18
Art Wilson	PIT NL	06/28/1916	18
Johnny Bench	CIN NL	06/02/1972	17
Roberto Clemente	PIT NL	07/15/1971	17
Monte Cross	PHI AL	07/09/1902	17
Jim Davenport	SF NL	05/13/1966	17
Del Ennis	PHI NL	09/06/1952	17
Jim Finigan	KC AL	05/23/1956	17
Jimmie Foxx	PHI AL	08/14/1929	17
Mule Haas	PHI AL	08/22/1928	17
Tommy Henrich	NY AL	07/20/1941	17
Gene Hermanski	BRO NL	08/23/1950	17
Charlie Keller	NY AL	07/20/1941	17
Dave Kingman	NY NL	06/10/1983	17
Dave May	MIL AL	05/15/1973	17
Joe Medwick	STL NL	07/01/1934	17
Keith Moreland	CHI NL	09/02/1986	17
Len Randle	NY NL	07/09/1977	17
Pete Reiser	BRO NL	09/15/1941	17
Mike Ryan	PHI NL	06/02/1972	17
Roy Sievers	WAS AL	08/03/1957	17
Earl Torgeson	CHI AL	06/04/1959	17
Del Unser	NY NL	04/19/1976	17

Ken Berry	CHI AL	07/25/1967	16
Max Bishop	PHI AL	06/01/1932	16
George Brett	KC AL	05/28/1979	16
Greg Briley	SEA AL	05/05/1991	16
Doug Clarey	STL NL	04/28/1976	16
Bob Coluccio	MIL AL	04/17/1974	16
Wes Covington	PHI NL	09/23/1961	16
Clay Dalrymple	PHI NL	08/18/1964	16
Doug DeCinces	CAL AL	04/08/1982	16
Jimmie Foxx	PHI AL	07/10/1932	16
Adrian Garrett	CAL AL	09/22/1975	16
Steve Garvey	LA NL	09/13/1982	16
Jim Gosger	BOS AL	06/04/1966	16
Tim Harkness	NY NL	09/01/1963	16
Richie Hebner	PIT NL	07/15/1971	16
Stan Javier	OAK AL	07/04/1988	16
Whitey Kurowski	STL NL	09/24/1944	16
Whitey Lockman	SF NL	09/01/1958	16
Kevin Maas	NY AL	05/05/1991	16
Willie Mays	SF NL	07/02/1963	16
Oddibe McDowell	TEX AL	06/11/1986	16
Mark McGwire	OAK AL	07/03/1988	16
Mark McGwire	OAK AL	07/04/1988	16
Kevin Mitchell	SF NL	05/11/1988	16
Jim Northrup	DET AL	08/01/1971	16
Jon Nunnally	KC AL	07/29/1995	16
Tony Oliva	MIN AL	09/06/1969	16
Jorge Orta	CLE AL	05/13/1981	16
Mark Parent	SD NL	09/28/1988	16
Lance Parrish	DET AL	05/16/1978	16
Bill Pecota	NY NL	08/10/1992	16
Greg Pryor	KC AL	08/26/1984	16
Babe Ruth	NY AL	08/15/1931	16
Benito Santiago	SD NL	08/10/1988	16
George Selkirk	NY AL	06/07/1936	16
Joe Torre	ATL NL	08/11/1967	16
Clyde Vollmer	BOS AL	07/28/1951	16
Bud Zipfel	WAS AL	09/12/1962	16
Earl Averill	CLE AL	08/24/1935	15
Gene Baker	CHI NL	06/01/1956	15
Wayne Belardi	DET AL	08/14/1956	15
George Bell	TOR AL	06/22/1990	15
Charlie Bennett	DET NL	06/08/1888	15
Craig Biggio	HOU NL	06/16/1995	15
Ray Boone	DET AL	08/14/1956	15
Rube Bressler	BRO NL	06/21/1929	15
Rod Carew	CAL AL	08/07/1980	15
Danny Cater	CHI AL	06/04/1965	15
Donn Clendenon	NY NL	06/19/1971	15
Rocky Colavito	KC AL	09/29/1964	15
Jim Davenport	SF NL	05/16/1964	15
Chili Davis	SF NL	07/03/1982	15
Duffy Dyer	PIT NL	08/03/1975	15
Del Ennis	PHI NL	07/21/1956	15
Darrell Evans	ATL NL	08/02/1975	15
Mike Ferraro	MIL AL	05/13/1972	15
Carlton Fisk	CHI AL	07/11/1987	15
Ron Gant	ATL NL	07/02/1988	15
Lou Gehrig	NY AL	08/26/1935	15
Marquis Grissom	MON NL	05/07/1991	15
Jim Ray Hart	SF NL	06/20/1965	15
Larry Herndon	SF NL	07/21/1980	15
Chuck Hinton	CLE AL	06/27/1965	15
Brian Hunter	HOU NL	06/16/1995	15
Steve Huntz	SD NL	05/23/1970	15
John Jaha	MIL AL	09/15/1995	15
Bob Johnson	TEX AL	07/11/1983	15
Dave Johnson	BAL AL	05/06/1966	15
Lou Johnson	LA NL	08/19/1965	15
Al Kaline	DET AL	04/24/1963	15
Al Kaline	DET AL	05/08/1965	15
Ron Karkovice	CHI AL	06/12/1993	15
Marty Keough	WAS AL	06/10/1961	15
Dave Kingman	CHI NL	05/14/1978	15
Paul Lehner	PHI AL	04/22/1950	15
Frank Malzone	BOS AL	06/11/1963	15
Willie Mays	SF NL	09/27/1968	15
Mike Miley	CAL AL	08/19/1975	15
Don Mincher	WAS AL	05/15/1971	15
Rick Monday	KC AL	04/29/1967	15
Fred Nicholson	BOS NL	06/16/1921	15
Ron Northey	PHI NL	06/22/1944	15
Jorge Orta	CHI AL	09/19/1972	15
Jose Pagan	SF NL	06/28/1961	15
Jim Pagliaroni	SEA AL	07/19/1969	15
Tony Pena	PIT NL	06/29/1985	15
Roger Repoz	KC AL	09/13/1966	15
Floyd Robinson	CHI AL	06/04/1965	15
Billy Rogell	DET AL	08/15/1931	15
Babe Ruth	NY AL	05/22/1923	15
Babe Ruth	NY AL	07/03/1923	15
Vic Saier	CHI NL	06/17/1915	15
Tim Salmon	CAL AL	09/02/1992	15
Eric Soderholm	MIN AL	05/13/1972	15
Mickey Stanley	DET AL	06/17/1967	15
Vern Stephens	BOS AL	05/30/1951	15
Dick Stuart	BOS AL	06/11/1963	15
Jerry Tabb	OAK AL	09/27/1977	15
Valmy Thomas	NY NL	05/11/1957	15
Robby Thompson	SF NL	05/02/1995	15
Bobby Thomson	NY NL	05/29/1949	15
Billy Williams	CHI NL	08/11/1968	15
Gene Woodling	CLE AL	08/14/1956	15

Most Leadoff Home Runs, (Season)

	Player	*Team*	*Year*	*HR*
1	Bobby Bonds	SF NL	1973	11
2	Rickey Henderson	NY AL	1986	9
3	Barry Bonds	PIT NL	1988	8
	Kal Daniels	CIN NL	1987	8
	Rickey Henderson	OAK AL	1993	8
	Rick Monday	CHI NL	1976	8
7	Brian Downing	CAL AL	1987	7
	Rickey Henderson	NY AL	1985	7
	Davey Lopes	LA NL	1979	7
10	Bert Campaneris	OAK AL	1970	6
	Brian Downing	CAL AL	1982	6
	Tommy Harper	MIL AL	1970	6
	Rickey Henderson	NY AL	1987	6
	Eddie Joost	PHI AL	1948	6
	Davey Lopes	LA NL	1980	6
	Paul Molitor	MIL AL	1991	6
	Rick Monday	CHI NL	1973	6
	Jimmy Ryan	CHI NL	1889	6
	Devon White	TOR AL	1991	6
	Eddie Yost	DET AL	1959	6

Most Leadoff Home Runs (Career)

	Player	*HR*
1	Rickey Henderson	67
2	Bobby Bonds	35
3	Paul Molitor	33
4	Davey Lopes	28
	Eddie Yost	28
6	Devon White	26
7	Brian Downing	25
8	Lou Brock	24
9	Tommy Harper	23
	Lou Whitaker	23
11	Jimmy Ryan	22
12	Tony Phillips	21
13	Felipe Alou	20
	Barry Bonds	20
15	Lenny Dykstra	19
	Eddie Joost	19
	Dick McAuliffe	19
18	Hank Bauer	17
	Dan Gladden	17
	Rick Monday	17
	Pete Rose	17
22	Don Buford	15
23	Frankie Crosetti	14
	Gary Redus	14
	Juan Samuel	14

Home Runs by First Three Batters of Game

Team	Date
SD NL	04/13/1987
	Marvell Wynne
	Tony Gwynn
	John Kruk

Home Runs by First Two Batters of Game

Team	*Date*
BOS AA	06/25/1891
	Tom Brown
	Bill Joyce
PHI AA	08/21/1891
	Jim McTamany
	Henry Larkin
BOS NL	08/06/1937
	Roy Johnson
	Rabbit Warstler
CHI AL	09/02/1937
	Boze Berger
	Mike Kreevich
DET AL	06/22/1939
	Barney McCosky
	Earl Averill
PIT NL	07/06/1945
	Pete Coscarart
	Jim Russell
CIN NL	04/19/1952
	Grady Hatton
	Bobby Adams
NY AL	04/27/1955
	Hank Bauer
	Andy Carey
SF NL	07/06/1958
	Whitey Lockman
	Willie Kirkland
STL NL	08/17/1958
	Curt Flood
	Gene Freese
KC AL	09/18/1958
	Bill Tuttle
	Roger Maris
MIN AL	05/10/1962
	Lenny Green
	Vic Power

SF NL 05/27/1964
Chuck Hiller
Duke Snider
CIN NL 04/07/1969
Pete Rose
Bobby Tolan
CIN NL 08/17/1969
Pete Rose
Bobby Tolan
CIN NL 06/28/1970
Pete Rose
Bobby Tolan
BOS AL 05/01/1971
Luis Aparicio
Reggie Smith
CLE AL 06/19/1971
Graig Nettles
Vada Pinson
BOS AL 06/20/1973
Rick Miller
Reggie Smith
MIL AL 07/29/1975
Don Money
Darrell Porter
BOS AL 06/17/1977
Rick Burleson
Fred Lynn
PIT NL 07/05/1982
Omar Moreno
Johnny Ray
OAK AL 09/09/1983
Rickey Henderson
Mike Davis
KC AL 05/03/1984
Darryl Motley
Pat Sheridan
PHI NL 07/29/1984
Juan Samuel
Von Hayes
BOS AL 09/05/1985
Dwight Evans
Wade Boggs
PHI NL 07/07/1986
Gary Redus
Juan Samuel
MIN AL 07/18/1986
Kirby Puckett
Gary Gaetti
DET AL 08/05/1986
Lou Whitaker
Alan Trammell
CIN NL 06/20/1987
Kal Daniels
Tracy Jones
BAL AL 06/23/1988
Ken Gerhart
Fred Lynn
TOR AL 08/18/1991
Devon White
Roberto Alomar
BAL AL 07/09/1992
Brady Anderson
Mike Devereaux
OAK AL 06/12/1993
Rickey Henderson
Craig Paquette
ATL NL 06/22/1994
Bobby Kelly
Jeff Blauser
CIN NL 08/03/1994
Jacob Brumfield
Bret Boone
BAL AL 06/08/1995
Brady Anderson
Kevin Bass
BOS AL 07/21/1995
Troy O'Leary
John Valentin
CHI NL 09/27/1995
Luis Gonzalez
Jose Hernandez

Leadoff Home Runs by Both Teams (Same Game)

05/29/1884 @ CHI NL
Abner Dalrymple CHI
George Wood DET
05/16/1889 @ CIN AA
Mike Griffin BAL
Bug Holliday CIN
06/25/1891 @ BOS AA
Curt Welch BAL
Tom Brown BOS
09/29/1892 @ CIN NL
Jimmy Ryan CHI
Bug Holliday CIN
06/25/1920 @ NY AL
Harry Hooper BOS
Roger Peckinpaugh NY
06/03/1950 @ PIT NL
Sam Jethroe BOS
Hank Schenz PIT
09/03/1955 @ NY AL
Hank Bauer NY
Eddie Yost WAS
08/15/1980 @ BAL AL
Al Bumbry BAL
Willie Randolph NY
10/02/1983 @ OAK AL
Butch Davis KC
Rickey Henderson OAK
07/27/1985 @ TEX AL
Rickey Henderson NY
Oddibe McDowell TEX
10/01/1985 @ SF NL
Eric Davis CIN
Dan Gladden SF
06/20/1986 @ PHI NL
Jeff Stone PHI
Curt Ford STL
06/05/1994 @ DET AL
Tony Phillips DET
Chuck Knoblauch MIN
08/25/1995 @ COL NL
Trent Hubbard COL
Bernard Gilkey STL
09/08/1995 @ CAL AL
Tony Phillips CAL
Chuck Knoblauch MIN

Most Leadoff HRs, Team (Season)

	Team	*Year*	*HR*
1	SF NL	1973	11
2	CAL AL	1986	10
	NY AL	1986	10
	CIN NL	1987	10
5	CHI NL	1976	9
	PIT NL	1988	9
	CHI NL	1994	9

Most Home Runs by One Batter off One Pitcher (Career)

	Player	*HR*	*Pitcher*
1	Duke Snider	19	off Robin Roberts
2	Willie Mays	18	off Warren Spahn
3	Hank Aaron	17	off Don Drysdale
	Stan Musial	17	off Warren Spahn
	Babe Ruth	17	off Rube Walberg

Most Home Runs Allowed, Pitcher (Game)

	Player	*Team*	*Date*	*HR*
1	Charlie Sweeney	DET NL	06/12/1886	7
2	Larry Benton	CHI NL	05/12/1930	6
	Kid Carsey	LOU NL	08/14/1894	6
	George Caster	BOS AL	09/24/1940	6
	Frank Foreman	CHI NL	07/04/1895	6
	Egyptian Healy	NY NL	05/09/1888	6
	Bill Kerksieck	NY NL	08/13/1939	6
	Tom Lee	PRO NL	06/28/1884	6
	Tom Parrott	STL NL	05/10/1894	6
	Tommy Thomas	NY AL	06/27/1936	6
	Sloppy Thurston	NY NL	08/13/1932	6

Most Allowed, Pitcher (Season)

	Player	*Team*	*Year*	*HR*
1	Bert Blyleven	MIN AL	1986	50
2	Bert Blyleven	MIN AL	1987	46
	Robin Roberts	PHI NL	1956	46
4	Pedro Ramos	WAS AL	1957	43
5	Denny McLain	DET AL	1966	42
6	Phil Niekro	ATL NL	1979	41
	Robin Roberts	PHI NL	1955	41
8	Bill Gullickson	CIN NL	1987	40
	Ferguson Jenkins	TEX AL	1979	40
	Jack Morris	DET AL	1986	40
	Phil Niekro	ATL NL	1970	40
	Orlando Pena	KC AL	1964	40
	Robin Roberts	PHI NL	1957	40
	Ralph Terry	NY AL	1962	40
15	Murry Dickson	STL NL	1948	39
	Catfish Hunter	OAK AL	1973	39
	Jack Morris	DET AL	1987	39
	Jim Perry	MIN AL	1971	39
	Pedro Ramos	MIN AL	1961	39
20	Floyd Bannister	CHI AL	1987	38
	Jim Bunning	DET AL	1963	38
	Lew Burdette	MIL NL	1959	38
	Warren Hacker	CHI NL	1955	38
	Matt Keough	OAK AL	1982	38
	Mickey Lolich	DET AL	1974	38
	Pedro Ramos	WAS AL	1958	38
	Don Sutton	LA NL	1970	38
	Don Sutton	CAL AL	1987	38
	Curt Young	OAK AL	1987	38

Most Home Runs Allowed, Pitcher (Career)

	Player	*HR*
1	Robin Roberts	505
2	Ferguson Jenkins	484
3	Phil Niekro	482
4	Don Sutton	473

5	Frank Tanana	448
6	Warren Spahn	434
7	Bert Blyleven	430
8	Steve Carlton	413
9	Gaylord Perry	399
10	Jim Kaat	394
11	Jack Morris	390
12	Charlie Hough	382
13	Tom Seaver	380
14	Catfish Hunter	374
15	Jim Bunning	372
16	Mickey Lolich	349
17	Luis Tiant	346
18	Dennis Martinez	344
19	Early Wynn	339
20	Doyle Alexander	324
	Dennis Eckersley	324
22	Nolan Ryan	321
23	Juan Marichal	320
24	Pedro Ramos	316
25	Jim Perry	308

Most Home Runs Allowed, Team (Season)

	Team	*Year*	*HR*
1	BAL AL	1987	226
2	KC AL	1964	220
3	CLE AL	1987	219
4	CAL AL	1987	212
5	MIN AL	1987	210
	MIN AL	1995	210
7	MIN AL	1982	208
8	MIN AL	1986	200
9	KC AL	1962	199
	SEA AL	1987	199
	TEX AL	1987	199
12	DET AL	1963	195
13	SEA AL	1977	194
14	NY NL	1962	192
15	BOS AL	1987	190
16	CHI AL	1987	189
17	DET AL	1993	188
18	KC AL	1956	187
19	STL NL	1955	185
	DET AL	1966	185
	ATL NL	1970	185
22	CHI NL	1966	184
23	DET AL	1986	183
24	CLE AL	1993	182
25	MIN AL	1964	181
	COL NL	1993	181

Home Run Surrendered to First Batter Faced in Major Leagues

Player	*Team*	*Date*
Norm Angelini	KC AL	07/22/1972
Ernie Baker	CIN NL	08/18/1905
Dick Baney	SEA AL	07/11/1969
Bill Bevens	NY AL	05/12/1944
Charlie Biggs	CHI AL	09/03/1932
Bert Blyleven	MIN AL	06/05/1970
Dave Boswell	MIN AL	09/18/1964
Roy Branch	SEA AL	09/11/1979
Cal Browning	STL NL	06/12/1960
Chris Bushing	CIN NL	09/03/1993
Bert Conn	PHI NL	09/16/1898
Bobby Coombs	PHI AL	06/08/1933
Jim Davis	CHI NL	04/18/1954
Cal Dorsett	CLE AL	08/19/1940
Tom Drees	CHI AL	09/03/1991
Dave Eiland	NY AL	08/03/1988
Tom Funk	HOU NL	07/24/1986
Bob Gibson	STL NL	04/15/1959
Fred Gladding	DET AL	07/01/1995
Greg Gohr	DET AL	04/07/1993
Gil Heredia	SF NL	09/01/1991
Ken Holtzman	CHI NL	09/04/1965
Ricky Horton	STL NL	04/07/1984
Bob Kaiser	CLE AL	09/03/1971
Bill Kerksieck	PHI NL	06/21/1939
Bill Macdonald	PIT NL	05/06/1950
Mickey Mahler	ATL NL	09/13/1977
John Martina	WAS AL	04/19/1924
Ralph McCabe	CLE AL	09/18/1946
Jack Meyer	PHI NL	04/16/1955
Glenn Mickens	BRO NL	07/19/1953
Gary Mielke	TEX AL	08/19/1987
Charlie Mitchell	BOS AL	08/09/1984
Bobby Moore	SF NL	09/11/1985
Mike Munoz	LA NL	09/06/1989
Rob Murphy	CIN NL	09/13/1985
Dickie Noles	PHI NL	07/05/1979
Chi-chi Olivo	MIL NL	06/05/1961
Pat Osborn	CIN NL	04/13/1974
John Papa	BAL AL	04/11/1961
Tim Pugh	CIN NL	09/01/1992
Spencer Pumpelly	WAS AL	07/11/1925
Tom Qualters	PHI NL	09/13/1953
Ed Rakow	LA NL	04/22/1960
Alberto Reyes	MIL AL	04/27/1995
Kevin Rogers	SF NL	09/04/1992
Henry Schmidt	BRO NL	04/17/1903
Jeff Stember	SF NL	08/05/1980
Harry Sullivan	STL NL	08/11/1909
Jeff Suppan	BOS AL	07/17/1995
John Wasdin	OAK AL	08/24/1995
Bill Webb	PHI NL	05/15/1943
Ted Wieand	CIN NL	09/27/1958

Players with No Position

The following players had either pinch hit (H) or pinch run (R) earlier in the inning. Officially, they hit these homers with no defensive position.

Date		*Player*	*Team*
04/14/1925	(R)	Pat McNulty	CLE AL
06/10/1952	(R)	Al Zarilla	CHI AL
06/06/1953	(R)	Johnny Temple	CIN NL
07/18/1953	(H)	Wayne Belardi	BRO NL
07/29/1953	(R)	Fred Marsh	CHI AL
04/21/1958	(H)	Frank House	KC AL
07/22/1970	(H)	Von Joshua	LA NL
07/04/1971	(H)	Jim Lefebvre	LA NL
07/01/1973	(R)	Dave Kingman	SF NL
05/31/1975	(H)	Cliff Johnson	HOU NL
08/14/1982	(H)	Bill Robinson	PHI NL
07/06/1986	(H)	Jeff Stone	PHI NL
04/08/1993	(H)	Alvaro Espinoza	CLE AL

Career

Batters with 300 Career Homers

H—Member of Hall of Fame
A—Active in 1995

Nbr	Player	Total	Home	Away	Home Pct	NL	AL	Men-On-Base 0	1	2	3	One-Game 2	3	4	RBI/ HR	LO	XIN	IP	PH	DH	Seasons 50+	40+	30+	Pitchers RHP	LHP	Prk
1	*H* Hank Aaron	755	385	370	.510	733	22	400	242	97	16	61	1	0	1.64	0	14	1	3	21	0	8	7	534	221	32
2	*H* Babe Ruth	714	347	367	.486	6	708	348	252	98	16	70	2	0	1.69	0	16	10	1	—	4	7	2	495	219	12
3	*H* Willie Mays	660	335	325	.508	660	0	365	220	67	8	60	2	1	1.57	0	22	8	5	—	2	4	5	451	209	22
4	*H* Frank Robinson	586	321	265	.548	343	243	324	184	71	7	53	1	0	1.59	0	16	0	2	58	0	1	10	392	194	32
5	*H* Harmon Killebrew	573	291	282	.508	0	573	275	225	62	11	45	1	0	1.67	2	11	1	7	21	0	8	2	423	150	18
6	*H* Reggie Jackson	563	280	283	.497	0	563	308	175	69	11	40	2	0	1.61	0	10	4	6	101	0	2	5	384	179	18
7	*H* Mike Schmidt	548	265	283	.484	548	0	291	168	82	7	41	2	1	1.64	1	9	3	2	—	0	3	10	407	141	13
8	*H* Mickey Mantle	536	266	270	.496	0	536	297	163	67	9	45	1	0	1.60	1	14	6	7	—	2	2	5	373	163	16
9	*H* Jimmie Foxx	534	299	235	.560	10	524	255	167	95	17	53	2	0	1.76	0	14	8	3	—	2	3	7	438	96	14
10	*H* Willie McCovey	521	264	257	.507	521	0	281	155	67	18	41	3	0	1.66	0	10	1	16	—	0	2	5	421	100	22
	H Ted Williams	521	248	273	.476	0	521	235	192	77	17	34	3	0	1.76	0	13	1	7	—	0	1	7	457	64	11
12	*H* Ernie Banks	512	290	222	.566	512	0	262	161	77	12	38	4	0	1.69	0	9	4	5	—	0	5	2	372	140	20
	H Eddie Mathews	512	238	274	.465	503	9	270	183	51	8	48	1	0	1.60	0	6	1	2	—	0	4	6	418	94	24
14	*H* Mel Ott	511	323	188	.632	511	0	235	185	84	7	48	1	0	1.73	0	7	2	3	—	0	1	7	400	111	8
15	*H* Lou Gehrig	493	251	242	.509	0	493	230	167	73	23	38	3	1	1.77	0	4	10	0	—	0	5	5	350	143	9
16	*A* Eddie Murray	479	227	252	.474	108	371	231	166	65	17	27	3	0	1.72	0	10	0	2	67	0	0	5	343	136	31
17	*H* Stan Musial	475	252	223	.531	475	0	232	180	54	9	35	2	0	1.66	0	11	9	2	—	0	0	6	320	155	12
	H Willie Stargell	475	221	254	.465	475	0	238	161	65	11	32	4	0	1.68	0	12	3	8	—	0	2	4	372	103	20
19	*A* Dave Winfield	465	218	247	.469	154	311	257	134	63	11	29	1	0	1.63	0	9	1	3	60	0	0	3	284	181	32
20	*H* Carl Yastrzemski	452	237	215	.524	0	452	238	154	53	7	26	1	0	1.62	0	8	3	1	46	0	3	0	374	78	18
21	Dave Kingman	442	217	225	.491	336	106	228	137	61	16	38	5	0	1.69	0	5	1	3	101	0	1	6	289	153	25
22	*A* Andre Dawson	436	205	231	.470	407	29	253	135	41	7	37	2	0	1.55	1	8	3	3	29	0	1	2	302	134	21
23	*H* Billy Williams	426	245	181	.575	392	34	218	158	42	8	31	1	0	1.62	0	9	6	1	33	0	1	4	325	101	29
24	Darrell Evans	414	219	195	.529	273	141	245	115	44	10	23	1	0	1.56	1	7	0	7	50	0	2	2	317	97	27
25	*H* Duke Snider	407	224	183	.550	407	0	218	140	44	5	32	2	0	1.60	0	4	3	7	—	0	5	1	374	33	14
26	*H* Al Kaline	399	226	173	.566	0	399	220	136	40	3	22	1	0	1.56	0	7	2	2	13	0	0	0	271	128	17
27	Dale Murphy	398	217	181	.545	398	0	199	136	58	5	31	1	0	1.67	0	6	1	1	—	0	1	5	278	120	12
28	Graig Nettles	390	216	174	.554	57	333	222	123	41	4	27	0	0	1.56	2	11	0	12	0	0	0	2	281	109	28
29	*H* Johnny Bench	389	195	194	.501	389	0	205	114	59	11	16	3	0	1.68	0	8	1	5	—	0	2	2	263	126	16
30	Dwight Evans	385	203	182	.527	0	385	214	108	57	6	22	0	0	1.62	7	7	1	1	31	0	0	3	272	113	16
31	Frank Howard	382	186	196	.487	123	259	202	133	42	5	26	0	0	1.61	0	5	0	8	11	0	3	2	228	154	24
	Jim Rice	382	208	174	.545	0	382	197	139	38	8	33	2	0	1.63	0	7	0	1	96	0	1	3	275	107	15
33	Orlando Cepeda	379	182	197	.480	358	21	220	102	48	9	22	1	0	1.59	0	5	2	2	21	0	1	4	258	121	26
	Tony Perez	379	182	197	.480	339	40	188	142	43	6	17	0	0	1.65	0	10	0	9	6	0	1	1	250	129	28
35	Norm Cash	377	214	163	.568	0	377	214	122	33	8	25	0	0	1.56	0	3	2	9	0	0	1	4	316	61	18
36	Carlton Fisk	376	188	188	.500	0	376	216	105	50	5	24	0	0	1.59	0	6	1	3	17	0	0	1	257	119	17
37	Rocky Colavito	374	193	181	.516	3	371	192	116	59	7	29	2	1	1.68	0	6	0	1	—	0	3	4	277	97	14
38	Gil Hodges	370	210	160	.568	370	0	196	106	54	14	29	0	1	1.69	0	5	2	0	—	0	2	4	296	74	12
39	*H* Ralph Kiner	369	210	159	.569	351	18	190	121	45	13	36	4	0	1.68	0	6	0	3	—	2	3	2	310	59	14
40	*H* Joe DiMaggio	361	148	213	.410	0	361	170	118	60	13	32	3	0	1.77	0	4	3	1	—	0	1	6	241	120	9
41	*H* Johnny Mize	359	212	147	.591	315	44	175	123	55	6	24	6	0	1.70	0	6	1	7	—	1	2	0	274	85	15
42	*H* Yogi Berra	358	210	148	.587	0	358	169	130	50	9	19	0	0	1.72	0	9	1	8	—	0	0	2	273	85	12
43	Lee May	354	179	175	.506	228	126	194	109	40	11	34	1	0	1.63	0	7	0	0	60	0	0	3	252	102	29
44	Dick Allen	351	183	168	.521	261	90	185	119	39	8	31	1	0	1.63	1	10	7	1	1	0	1	5	213	138	29
45	George Foster	348	184	164	.529	347	1	179	97	59	13	21	1	0	1.73	0	3	0	4	0	1	1	1	215	133	14
46	Ron Santo	342	216	126	.632	337	5	180	112	44	6	26	0	0	1.64	0	8	1	0	0	0	0	4	244	98	22
47	Jack Clark	340	155	185	.456	280	60	182	103	46	9	18	1	0	1.65	0	18	0	4	52	0	0	1	229	111	26
48	Dave Parker	339	170	169	.501	273	66	154	124	53	8	18	0	0	1.75	0	3	2	4	60	0	0	3	237	102	25
	Boog Powell	339	150	189	.442	0	339	160	131	41	7	20	3	0	1.69	0	5	1	3	1	0	0	4	270	69	16
50	Don Baylor	338	156	182	.462	0	338	183	107	36	12	17	1	0	1.64	1	10	1	4	219	0	0	3	223	115	16
51	Joe Adcock	336	137	199	.408	270	66	182	106	38	10	27	0	1	1.63	0	3	7	12	—	0	0	2	237	99	25
52	Bobby Bonds	332	173	159	.521	197	135	188	99	38	7	21	0	0	1.59	35	6	2	2	16	0	0	6	251	81	29
53	*H* Hank Greenberg	331	205	126	.619	25	306	160	109	51	11	35	0	0	1.74	0	4	2	0	—	1	3	2	258	73	12
54	*A* Joe Carter	327	177	150	.541	24	303	179	106	35	7	27	5	0	1.60	2	3	2	0	11	0	0	5	234	93	27
	A Cal Ripken	327	163	164	.498	0	327	184	96	43	4	15	0	0	1.59	0	4	0	0	0	0	0	1	222	105	18
56	Willie Horton	325	153	172	.471	0	325	165	101	50	9	28	2	0	1.70	0	5	2	3	96	0	0	1	207	118	17
57	Gary Carter	324	162	162	.500	324	0	183	96	34	11	26	2	0	1.61	0	3	2	1	—	0	0	2	215	109	13

Nbr	Player	Total	Home	Away	Home Pct	NL	AL	Men-On-Base 0	1	2	3	One-Game 2	3	4	RBI/ HR	LO	XIN	IP	PH	DH	Seasons 50+	40+	30+	Pitchers RHP	LHP	Prk
	A Lance Parrish	324	160	164	.494	35	289	182	104	31	7	22	0	0	1.58	0	11	0	1	18	0	0	2	195	129	26
59	Roy Sievers	318	150	168	.472	44	274	163	99	46	10	27	0	0	1.69	0	8	0	9	—	0	1	1	229	89	21
60	George Brett	317	136	181	.429	0	317	171	107	37	2	15	2	0	1.59	2	7	7	1	51	0	0	1	229	88	18
61	Ron Cey	316	166	150	.525	312	4	175	87	47	7	17	0	0	1.64	0	5	1	1	3	0	0	1	210	106	15
62	Reggie Smith	314	158	156	.503	165	149	181	98	32	3	23	1	0	1.54	4	5	0	2	5	0	0	2	251	63	27
63	Greg Luzinski	307	179	128	.583	223	84	167	100	33	7	23	0	0	1.61	0	4	0	2	83	0	0	4	226	81	25
	H Al Simmons	307	162	145	.528	7	300	144	109	44	10	18	1	0	1.74	0	4	1	1	—	0	0	3	214	93	12
65	Fred Lynn	306	177	129	.578	6	300	159	92	48	7	21	1	0	1.68	1	2	0	4	8	0	0	1	246	60	19
66	*A* Harold Baines	301	148	153	.492	0	301	164	99	28	10	10	3	0	1.61	0	4	0	2	154	0	0	0	243	58	20
	H Rogers Hornsby	301	163	138	.542	298	3	151	92	46	12	20	1	0	1.73	0	3	30	5	—	0	1	2	231	70	9
68	*A* Jose Canseco	300	140	160	.467	0	300	150	104	42	4	21	2	0	1.67	0	4	0	0	86	0	2	4	210	90	18
	H Chuck Klein	300	190	110	.633	300	0	141	106	46	7	27	0	1	1.73	0	4	3	3	—	0	2	2	241	59	91

Batters with 300 Career Homers Legend

Nbr	Ranking
Total	Number of home runs hit overall
Home	Number of home runs hit at home
Away	Number of home runs hit in road games
Home Pct	Percentage of home runs hit at home
NL	Number of home runs hit in National League
AL	Number of home runs hit in American League
Men-On	Home runs with each number of men on base
One-Gm	Games with multiple home runs
RBI/HR	Number of runs batted in per home run
LO	Lead-off home runs (first inning, first batter either team)
XN	Home runs hit in extra innings
IP	Inside-the-Park home runs
PH	Pinch hit home runs
DH	Number of home runs hit as a designated hitter
Seasons	Number of times hit 50, 40, 30 home runs in a season
RHP	Home runs vs right-handed pitcher
LHP	Home runs vs left-handed pitcher
PRK	Number of ballparks homered in

Part Three

Yearly Home Run Totals by Team and League

1876

Tm	Tot	H	A	Consec			1-Inn			One-Game						Men-On-Base				Batters					Totals					Pitchers	
				2	3	4	3	4	5	5	6	7	8	9	10	0	1	2	3	PH	LO	XN	IP	P	1	10	20	30	40	RHP	LHP
NL																															
BOS	9	5	4	0	0	0	0	0	0	0	0	0	0	0	0	6	2	1	0	0	1	0	0	1	5	0	0	0	0	9	0
CHI	8	3	5	0	0	0	0	0	0	0	0	0	0	0	0	4	2	2	0	0	0	0	3	0	6	0	0	0	0	8	0
CIN	4	2	2	0	0	0	0	0	0	0	0	0	0	0	0	3	0	1	0	0	0	0	3	0	1	0	0	0	0	4	0
HAR	2	0	2	0	0	0	0	0	0	0	0	0	0	0	0	1	1	0	0	0	1	0	0	0	2	0	0	0	0	2	0
LOU	6	6	0	0	0	0	0	0	0	0	0	0	0	0	0	2	3	1	0	0	1	1	6	0	5	0	0	0	0	6	0
NY	2	2	0	0	0	0	0	0	0	0	0	0	0	0	0	1	1	0	0	0	0	0	0	0	1	0	0	0	0	2	0
PHI	7	4	3	0	0	0	0	0	0	0	0	0	0	0	0	2	2	3	0	0	0	0	1	0	3	0	0	0	0	7	0
STL	2	1	1	0	0	0	0	0	0	0	0	0	0	0	0	2	0	0	0	0	0	0	0	0	2	0	0	0	0	2	0
NL	40	23	17	0	0	0	0	0	0	0	0	0	0	0	0	21	11	8	0	0	3	1	13	1	25	0	0	0	0	40	0

Home Run Listing Legend (Yearly Team Totals by Hitter)

Tm	Team Abbreviation
Tot	Total home runs by team
H	Home runs hit at the home ballpark
A	Home runs hit away from home
Consec	Number of times home runs were hit by consecutive batters in one inning
1 Inn	Number of times multiple home runs were hit in one inning
One-Gm	Multiple home run games by team
Men-On	Home runs hit with various numbers of men on base
PH	Pinch Hit home runs
LO	Home runs hit by the first batter of the game for the team
XN	Home runs hit in extra innings
IP	Inside-the-Park home runs
P	Home runs hit by pitchers
Totals	
1	Number of batters with 1–9 home runs for season
10	Number of batters with 10–19 home runs for season
20	Number of batters with 20–29 home runs for season
30	Number of batters with 30–39 home runs for season
40	Number of batters with 40 or more home runs for season
RHP	Home runs vs right-handed pitcher
LHP	Home runs vs left-handed pitcher

Yearly Home Run Totals by Team and League (by Hitter)

1876

NL

Tm	Tot	H	A	Consec 2	3	4	1-Inn 3	4	5	One-Game 5	6	7	8	9	10	Men-On-Base 0	1	2	3	Batters PH	LO	XN	IP	P	Totals 1	10	20	30	40	Pitchers RHP	LHP
BOS	9	5	4	0	0	0	0	0	0	0	0	0	0	0	0	6	2	1	0	0	1	0	0	1	5	0	0	0	0	9	0
CHI	8	3	5	0	0	0	0	0	0	0	0	0	0	0	0	4	2	2	0	0	0	0	3	0	6	0	0	0	0	8	0
CIN	4	2	2	0	0	0	0	0	0	0	0	0	0	0	0	3	0	1	0	0	0	0	3	0	1	0	0	0	0	4	0
HAR	2	0	2	0	0	0	0	0	0	0	0	0	0	0	0	1	1	0	0	0	1	0	0	0	2	0	0	0	0	2	0
LOU	6	6	0	0	0	0	0	0	0	0	0	0	0	0	0	2	3	1	0	0	1	1	6	0	5	0	0	0	0	6	0
NY	2	2	0	0	0	0	0	0	0	0	0	0	0	0	0	1	1	0	0	0	0	0	0	0	1	0	0	0	0	2	0
PHI	7	4	3	0	0	0	0	0	0	0	0	0	0	0	0	2	2	3	0	0	0	0	1	0	3	0	0	0	0	7	0
STL	2	1	1	0	0	0	0	0	0	0	0	0	0	0	0	2	0	0	0	0	0	0	0	0	2	0	0	0	0	2	0
NL	40	23	17	0	0	0	0	0	0	0	0	0	0	0	0	21	11	8	0	0	3	1	13	1	25	0	0	0	0	40	0

NL
5 George Hall
4 Charles Jones
2 Multiple Players Tied

1877

NL

Tm	Tot	H	A	Consec 2	3	4	1-Inn 3	4	5	One-Game 5	6	7	8	9	10	Men-On-Base 0	1	2	3	Batters PH	LO	XN	IP	P	Totals 1	10	20	30	40	Pitchers RHP	LHP
BOS	4	0	4	0	0	0	0	0	0	0	0	0	0	0	0	2	1	1	0	0	0	0	1	0	3	0	0	0	0	4	0
CIN	6	4	2	0	0	0	0	0	0	0	0	0	0	0	0	4	1	1	0	0	1	0	1	0	2	0	0	0	0	6	0
HAR	4	2	2	0	0	0	0	0	0	0	0	0	0	0	0	1	1	2	0	0	0	0	1	1	4	0	0	0	0	4	0
LOU	9	7	2	0	0	0	0	0	0	0	0	0	0	0	0	2	3	4	0	0	0	0	2	1	6	0	0	0	0	9	0
STL	1	0	1	0	0	0	0	0	0	0	0	0	0	0	0	0	1	0	0	0	0	0	0	0	1	0	0	0	0	1	0
NL	24	13	11	0	0	0	0	0	0	0	0	0	0	0	0	9	7	8	0	0	1	0	5	2	16	0	0	0	0	24	0

NL
4 Lip Pike
3 Orator Shaffer
2 Charles Jones
2 Pop Snyder
2 Deacon White

1878

NL

Tm	Tot	H	A	Consec 2	3	4	1-Inn 3	4	5	One-Game 5	6	7	8	9	10	Men-On-Base 0	1	2	3	Batters PH	LO	XN	IP	P	Totals 1	10	20	30	40	Pitchers RHP	LHP
BOS	2	1	1	0	0	0	0	0	0	0	0	0	0	0	0	2	0	0	0	0	0	1	0	0	2	0	0	0	0	2	0
CHI	3	2	1	0	0	0	0	0	0	0	0	0	0	0	0	1	1	1	0	0	0	0	0	0	3	0	0	0	0	3	0
CIN	5	4	1	0	0	0	0	0	0	0	0	0	0	0	0	2	3	0	0	0	0	0	0	0	2	0	0	0	0	5	0
IND	3	1	2	0	0	0	0	0	0	0	0	0	0	0	0	1	1	1	0	0	0	0	1	0	2	0	0	0	0	2	1
MIL	2	1	1	0	0	0	0	0	0	0	0	0	0	0	0	1	0	1	0	0	0	0	0	0	2	0	0	0	0	2	0
PRO	8	5	3	0	0	0	0	0	0	0	0	0	0	0	0	2	4	2	0	0	0	0	0	1	5	0	0	0	0	8	0
NL	23	14	9	0	0	0	0	0	0	0	0	0	0	0	0	9	9	5	0	0	0	1	1	1	16	0	0	0	0	22	1

NL
4 Paul Hines
3 Charles Jones
2 Russ McKelvy
2 Cal McVey
1 Multiple Players Tied

1879

NL

Tm	Tot	H	A	Consec 2	3	4	1-Inn 3	4	5	One-Game 5	6	7	8	9	10	Men-On-Base 0	1	2	3	Batters PH	LO	XN	IP	P	Totals 1	10	20	30	40	Pitchers RHP	LHP
BOS	20	11	9	0	0	0	0	0	0	0	0	0	0	0	0	10	8	2	0	0	2	0	1	0	5	0	0	0	0	20	0
BUF	2	1	1	0	0	0	0	0	0	0	0	0	0	0	0	1	1	0	0	0	0	0	0	0	2	0	0	0	0	2	0

				Consec			1-Inn			One-Game						Men-On-Base				Batters					Totals					Pitchers	
Tm	Tot	H	A	2	3	4	3	4	5	5	6	7	8	9	10	0	1	2	3	PH	LO	XN	IP	P	1	10	20	30	40	RHP	LHP
CHI	3	2	1	0	0	0	0	0	0	0	0	0	0	0	0	2	1	0	0	0	0	0	1	0	3	0	0	0	0	1	2
CIN	8	8	0	0	0	0	0	0	0	0	0	0	0	0	0	6	1	1	0	0	1	0	0	0	6	0	0	0	0	8	0
CLE	4	2	2	0	0	0	0	0	0	0	0	0	0	0	0	2	1	1	0	0	0	0	0	0	2	0	0	0	0	3	0
PRO	12	9	3	0	0	0	0	0	0	0	0	0	0	0	0	4	5	3	0	0	0	2	1	2	8	0	0	0	0	12	0
SYR	5	1	4	0	0	0	0	0	0	0	0	0	0	0	0	4	1	0	0	0	1	0	0	1	5	0	0	0	0	5	0
TRO	4	3	1	0	0	0	0	0	0	0	0	0	0	0	0	3	1	0	0	0	0	0	0	0	1	0	0	0	0	4	0
NL	58	37	21	0	0	0	0	0	0	0	0	0	0	0	0	32	19	7	0	0	4	2	3	3	32	0	0	0	0	55	2

NL
9 Charles Jones
6 John O'Rourke
4 Dan Brouthers
3 Charlie Eden
2 Multiple Players Tied

1880

NL

				Consec			1-Inn			One-Game						Men-On-Base				Batters					Totals					Pitchers	
Tm	Tot	H	A	2	3	4	3	4	5	5	6	7	8	9	10	0	1	2	3	PH	LO	XN	IP	P	1	10	20	30	40	RHP	LHP
BOS	20	14	6	0	0	0	0	0	0	0	0	0	0	0	0	10	9	1	0	0	1	0	2	0	6	0	0	0	0	17	2
BUF	3	1	2	0	0	0	0	0	0	0	0	0	0	0	0	1	2	0	0	0	0	0	0	0	3	0	0	0	0	2	0
CHI	4	1	3	0	0	0	0	0	0	0	0	0	0	0	0	1	3	0	0	0	0	0	0	0	3	0	0	0	0	4	0
CIN	7	5	2	0	0	0	0	0	0	0	0	0	0	0	0	6	1	0	0	0	0	0	0	0	5	0	0	0	0	7	0
CLE	7	2	5	0	0	0	0	0	0	0	0	0	0	0	0	1	2	4	0	0	0	0	0	0	4	0	0	0	0	4	3
PRO	8	4	4	0	0	0	0	0	0	0	0	0	0	0	0	4	3	1	0	0	0	0	1	0	4	0	0	0	0	4	4
TRO	5	5	0	0	0	0	0	0	0	0	0	0	0	0	0	1	2	2	0	0	0	0	0	0	2	0	0	0	0	5	0
WOR	8	5	3	0	0	0	0	0	0	0	0	0	0	0	0	4	3	1	0	0	2	0	2	0	3	0	0	0	0	8	0
NL	62	37	25	0	0	0	0	0	0	0	0	0	0	0	0	28	25	9	0	0	3	0	5	0	30	0	0	0	0	51	9

NL
6 Jim O'Rourke
6 Harry Stovey
5 Charles Jones
4 Fred Dunlap
3 Multiple Players Tied

1881

NL

				Consec			1-Inn			One-Game						Men-On-Base				Batters					Totals					Pitchers	
Tm	Tot	H	A	2	3	4	3	4	5	5	6	7	8	9	10	0	1	2	3	PH	LO	XN	IP	P	1	10	20	30	40	RHP	LHP
BOS	5	2	3	0	0	0	0	0	0	0	0	0	0	0	0	4	1	0	0	0	0	0	0	0	4	0	0	0	0	5	0
BUF	12	2	10	1	0	0	0	0	0	0	0	0	0	0	0	9	3	0	0	0	0	0	0	0	4	0	0	0	0	11	1
CHI	12	7	5	1	0	0	0	0	0	0	0	0	0	0	0	4	8	0	0	0	0	0	2	0	8	0	0	0	0	8	4
CLE	7	3	4	0	0	0	0	0	0	0	0	0	0	0	0	6	1	0	0	0	1	0	2	0	4	0	0	0	0	7	0
DET	17	14	3	0	0	0	0	0	0	0	0	0	0	0	0	11	2	4	0	0	1	0	2	0	7	0	0	0	0	17	0
PRO	11	4	7	0	0	0	0	0	0	0	0	0	0	0	0	6	4	1	0	0	0	0	0	0	5	0	0	0	0	10	1
TRO	5	4	1	0	0	0	0	0	0	0	0	0	0	0	0	4	0	0	1	0	0	0	0	0	4	0	0	0	0	3	2
WOR	7	7	0	0	0	0	0	0	0	0	0	0	0	0	0	2	3	1	1	0	1	0	0	0	5	0	0	0	0	7	0
NL	76	43	33	2	0	0	0	0	0	0	0	0	0	0	0	46	22	6	2	0	3	0	6	0	41	0	0	0	0	68	8

NL
8 Dan Brouthers
7 Charlie Bennett
5 Jack Farrell
4 Tom Burns
3 Multiple Players Tied

1882

AA

				Consec			1-Inn			One-Game						Men-On-Base				Batters					Totals					Pitchers	
Tm	Tot	H	A	2	3	4	3	4	5	5	6	7	8	9	10	0	1	2	3	PH	LO	XN	IP	P	1	10	20	30	40	RHP	LHP
BAL	4	2	2	0	0	0	0	0	0	0	0	0	0	0	0	3	1	0	0	0	0	0	1	0	4	0	0	0	0	3	0
CIN	5	0	5	0	0	0	0	0	0	0	0	0	0	0	0	1	2	2	0	0	0	0	0	0	5	0	0	0	0	4	0
LOU	9	0	9	0	0	0	0	0	0	0	0	0	0	0	0	4	4	0	1	0	0	0	0	1	3	0	0	0	0	8	0
PHI	5	3	2	0	0	0	0	0	0	0	0	0	0	0	0	2	2	1	0	0	0	0	0	0	3	0	0	0	0	0	1

Tm	Tot	H	A	Consec 2	3	4	1-Inn 3	4	5	One-Game 5	6	7	8	9	10	Men-On-Base 0	1	2	3	Batters PH	LO	XN	IP	P	Totals 1	10	20	30	40	Pitchers RHP	LHP
PIT	18	12	6	0	0	0	0	0	0	0	0	0	0	0	0	8	4	5	1	0	0	0	2	1	9	0	0	0	0	12	0
STL	11	7	4	0	0	0	0	0	0	0	0	0	0	0	0	5	5	1	0	0	0	0	1	0	4	0	0	0	0	5	0
NL																															
BOS	15	8	7	0	0	0	0	0	0	0	0	0	0	0	0	8	4	3	0	0	0	0	1	4	6	0	0	0	0	14	1
BUF	18	5	13	0	0	0	0	0	0	0	0	0	0	0	0	7	3	6	2	0	1	0	2	0	8	0	0	0	0	16	2
CHI	15	9	6	0	0	0	0	0	0	0	0	0	0	0	0	2	8	4	1	0	0	1	1	1	8	0	0	0	0	14	1
CLE	20	6	14	2	0	0	0	0	0	0	0	0	0	0	0	8	6	1	0	0	0	0	0	2	6	0	0	0	0	15	5
DET	19	14	5	0	0	0	0	0	0	0	0	0	0	0	0	9	7	3	0	0	3	0	3	0	5	0	0	0	0	18	1
PRO	11	6	5	0	0	0	0	0	0	0	0	0	0	0	0	7	4	0	0	0	1	1	1	1	6	0	0	0	0	9	2
TRO	12	7	5	0	0	0	0	0	0	0	0	0	0	0	0	5	3	4	0	0	0	0	0	2	7	0	0	0	0	11	1
WOR	16	9	7	0	0	0	0	0	0	0	0	0	0	0	0	10	5	1	0	0	1	0	2	3	7	0	0	0	0	16	0
AA	52	24	28	0	0	0	0	0	0	0	0	0	0	0	0	23	18	9	2	0	0	0	4	2	28	0	0	0	0	32	1
NL	126	64	62	2	0	0	0	0	0	0	0	0	0	0	0	56	40	22	3	0	6	2	10	13	53	0	0	0	0	113	13
YR	178	88	90	2	0	0	0	0	0	0	0	0	0	0	0	79	58	31	5	0	6	2	14	15	81	0	0	0	0	145	14

	AA		*NL*
7	Oscar Walker	7	George Wood
5	Pete Browning	6	Dan Brouthers
4	Ed Swartwood	6	Mike Muldoon
3	Multiple Players Tied	5	Multiple Players Tied

1883

Tm	Tot	H	A	Consec 2	3	4	1-Inn 3	4	5	One-Game 5	6	7	8	9	10	Men-On-Base 0	1	2	3	Batters PH	LO	XN	IP	P	Totals 1	10	20	30	40	Pitchers RHP	LHP
AA																															
BAL	5	4	1	0	0	0	0	0	0	0	0	0	0	0	0	2	2	1	0	0	1	0	1	1	5	0	0	0	0	5	0
CIN	34	29	5	0	0	0	0	0	0	0	0	0	0	0	0	12	16	6	0	0	1	1	0	0	6	1	0	0	0	29	2
COL	15	5	10	0	0	0	0	0	0	0	0	0	0	0	0	9	4	2	0	0	3	0	1	3	6	0	0	0	0	13	0
LOU	14	4	10	0	0	0	0	0	0	0	0	0	0	0	0	5	5	3	0	0	2	0	1	1	7	0	0	0	0	14	0
NY	6	3	3	0	0	0	0	0	0	0	0	0	0	0	0	3	1	2	0	0	0	0	0	0	3	0	0	0	0	6	0
PHI	20	9	11	0	0	0	0	0	0	0	0	0	0	0	0	7	13	0	0	0	1	0	6	1	6	1	0	0	0	19	1
PIT	13	9	4	0	0	0	0	0	0	0	0	0	0	0	0	7	3	3	0	0	0	0	1	1	6	0	0	0	0	10	1
STL	7	5	2	0	0	0	0	0	0	0	0	0	0	0	0	1	3	3	0	0	0	0	0	0	5	0	0	0	0	7	0
NL																															
BOS	34	21	13	0	0	0	0	0	0	0	0	0	0	0	0	12	13	9	0	0	2	0	4	3	8	0	0	0	0	28	6
BUF	8	3	5	0	0	0	0	0	0	0	0	0	0	0	0	4	1	2	1	0	0	0	1	1	6	0	0	0	0	6	2
CHI	13	11	2	0	0	0	0	0	0	0	0	0	0	0	0	6	5	2	0	0	0	0	0	0	7	0	0	0	0	11	2
CLE	8	0	8	0	0	0	0	0	0	0	0	0	0	0	0	5	3	0	0	0	0	0	0	0	3	0	0	0	0	5	3
DET	13	12	1	0	0	0	0	0	0	0	0	0	0	0	0	8	2	3	0	0	1	0	2	0	5	0	0	0	0	13	0
NY	24	20	4	0	0	0	0	0	0	0	0	0	0	0	0	14	4	2	0	0	4	0	2	7	6	1	0	0	0	23	0
PHI	3	0	3	0	0	0	0	0	0	0	0	0	0	0	0	1	1	1	0	0	0	0	0	0	3	0	0	0	0	3	0
PRO	21	10	11	1	0	0	1	0	0	0	0	0	0	0	0	11	8	2	0	0	0	1	0	3	7	0	0	0	0	18	3
AA	114	68	46	0	0	0	0	0	0	0	0	0	0	0	0	46	47	20	0	0	8	1	10	7	44	2	0	0	0	103	4
NL	124	77	47	1	0	0	1	0	0	0	0	0	0	0	0	61	37	21	1	0	7	1	9	14	45	1	0	0	0	107	16
YR	238	145	93	1	0	0	1	0	0	0	0	0	0	0	0	107	84	41	1	0	15	2	19	21	89	3	0	0	0	210	20

	AA		*NL*
14	Harry Stovey	10	Buck Ewing
10	Charles Jones	8	Jerry Denny
9	John Reilly	8	Mike Hornung
5	Tom Brown	7	Monte Ward
5	Chick Fulmer	6	John Morrill

1884

Tm	Tot	H	A	Consec 2	3	4	1-Inn 3	4	5	One-Game 5	6	7	8	9	10	Men-On-Base 0	1	2	3	Batters PH	LO	XN	IP	P	Totals 1	10	20	30	40	Pitchers RHP	LHP
AA																															
BAL	32	21	11	0	0	0	0	0	0	0	0	0	0	0	0	11	15	6	0	0	2	0	1	1	10	0	0	0	0	18	0
BRO	16	9	7	0	0	0	0	0	0	0	0	0	0	0	0	6	6	4	0	0	0	0	1	0	8	0	0	0	0	10	1
CIN	36	31	5	0	0	0	0	0	0	0	0	0	0	0	0	16	12	8	0	0	0	0	2	1	8	1	0	0	0	26	1
COL	40	23	17	0	0	0	0	0	0	0	0	0	0	0	0	16	13	11	0	0	2	0	0	3	8	0	0	0	0	35	1
IND	20	13	7	0	0	0	0	0	0	0	0	0	0	0	0	7	10	3	0	0	0	0	3	0	7	0	0	0	0	18	0
LOU	17	4	13	0	0	0	0	0	0	0	0	0	0	0	0	8	6	3	0	0	1	0	1	5	6	0	0	0	0	8	0

Tm	Tot	H	A	Consec 2	3	4	1-Inn 3	4	5	One-Game 5	6	7	8	9	10	Men-On-Base 0	1	2	3	Batters PH	LO	XN	IP	P	Totals 1	10	20	30	40	Pitchers RHP	LHP
NY	22	11	11	0	0	0	0	0	0	0	0	0	0	0	0	7	9	6	0	0	0	0	1	4	8	0	0	0	0	15	1
PHI	26	12	14	0	0	0	0	0	0	0	0	0	0	0	0	9	10	7	0	0	2	0	4	0	7	1	0	0	0	18	3
PIT	2	1	1	0	0	0	0	0	0	0	0	0	0	0	0	0	1	1	0	0	0	0	0	1	2	0	0	0	0	0	0
RIC	7	3	4	0	0	0	0	0	0	0	0	0	0	0	0	0	6	1	0	0	0	0	0	0	4	0	0	0	0	4	1
STL	11	6	5	0	0	0	0	0	0	0	0	0	0	0	0	5	6	0	0	0	0	0	2	3	6	0	0	0	0	9	0
TOL	8	3	5	0	0	0	0	0	0	0	0	0	0	0	0	6	2	0	0	0	0	0	0	1	6	0	0	0	0	5	0
WAS	6	3	3	0	0	0	0	0	0	0	0	0	0	0	0	3	2	1	0	0	1	0	0	2	4	0	0	0	0	2	2
NL																															
BOS	36	14	22	2	0	0	0	0	0	1	0	0	0	0	0	19	9	7	0	0	2	0	2	2	10	0	0	0	0	26	0
BUF	39	23	16	0	0	0	0	0	0	0	0	0	0	0	0	19	10	8	0	0	1	0	7	0	6	1	0	0	0	33	1
CHI	142	131	11	4	0	0	0	0	0	3	0	0	0	0	0	54	41	23	3	0	4	0	1	8	9	1	4	0	0	119	10
CLE	16	4	12	0	0	0	0	0	0	0	0	0	0	0	0	9	4	2	1	0	0	0	0	0	8	0	0	0	0	11	2
DET	31	14	17	0	0	0	0	0	0	0	0	0	0	0	0	8	13	6	0	0	3	0	1	1	8	0	0	0	0	27	0
NY	22	8	14	0	0	0	0	0	0	0	0	0	0	0	0	10	6	4	1	0	0	1	3	3	10	0	0	0	0	17	2
PHI	14	1	13	1	0	0	0	0	0	0	0	0	0	0	0	7	5	2	0	0	0	1	4	0	7	0	0	0	0	12	1
PRO	21	4	17	2	0	0	0	0	0	0	1	0	0	0	0	11	6	4	0	0	1	1	2	1	10	0	0	0	0	12	2
UA																															
ALT	2	0	2	0	0	0	0	0	0	0	0	0	0	0	0	2	0	0	0	0	0	0	0	1	2	0	0	0	0	2	0
BAL	17	12	5	0	0	0	0	0	0	0	0	0	0	0	0	5	8	4	0	0	0	0	1	0	7	0	0	0	0	5	4
BOS	19	7	12	0	0	0	0	0	0	0	0	0	0	0	0	6	11	2	0	0	1	0	1	1	4	1	0	0	0	13	1
CHI	10	2	8	1	0	0	0	0	0	0	0	0	0	0	0	6	3	1	0	0	0	0	2	0	6	0	0	0	0	6	2
CIN	26	18	8	0	0	0	0	0	0	0	0	0	0	0	0	16	9	1	0	0	1	0	4	2	14	0	0	0	0	16	1
KC	6	3	3	0	0	0	0	0	0	0	0	0	0	0	0	4	1	1	0	0	0	0	0	1	6	0	0	0	0	5	1
PHI	7	4	3	0	0	0	0	0	0	0	0	0	0	0	0	1	4	2	0	0	0	0	1	0	2	0	0	0	0	4	1
STL	32	12	20	1	0	0	0	0	0	0	0	0	0	0	0	10	16	6	0	0	0	0	1	4	7	1	0	0	0	16	3
WAS	4	4	0	0	0	0	0	0	0	0	0	0	0	0	0	3	0	1	0	0	0	0	0	1	3	0	0	0	0	2	1
WIL	2	1	1	0	0	0	0	0	0	0	0	0	0	0	0	1	0	1	0	0	0	0	0	0	1	0	0	0	0	1	0
AA	243	140	103	0	0	0	0	0	0	0	0	0	0	0	0	94	98	51	0	0	8	0	15	21	84	2	0	0	0	168	10
NL	321	199	122	9	0	0	0	0	0	4	1	0	0	0	0	137	94	56	5	0	11	3	20	15	68	2	4	0	0	257	18
UA	125	63	62	2	0	0	0	0	0	0	0	0	0	0	0	54	52	19	0	0	2	0	10	10	52	2	0	0	0	70	14
YR	689	402	287	11	0	0	0	0	0	4	1	0	0	0	0	285	244	126	5	0	21	3	45	46	204	6	4	0	0	495	42

AA

11 John Reilly
10 Harry Stovey
9 Dave Orr
7 Charles Jones
7 Fred Mann

NL

27 Ned Williamson
25 Fred Pfeffer
22 Abner Dalrymple
21 Cap Anson
14 Dan Brouthers

UA

13 Fred Dunlap
12 Ed Crane
5 Charlie Levis
4 Multiple Players Tied

1885

Tm	Tot	H	A	Consec 2	3	4	1-Inn 3	4	5	One-Game 5	6	7	8	9	10	Men-On-Base 0	1	2	3	Batters PH	LO	XN	IP	P	Totals 1	10	20	30	40	Pitchers RHP	LHP
AA																															
BAL	17	11	6	0	0	0	0	0	0	0	0	0	0	0	0	6	6	5	0	0	0	0	3	2	8	0	0	0	0	14	0
BRO	14	9	5	0	0	0	0	0	0	0	0	0	0	0	0	4	7	3	0	0	0	0	0	2	9	0	0	0	0	9	3
CIN	26	17	9	0	0	0	0	0	0	0	0	0	0	0	0	11	12	3	0	0	0	0	2	0	7	1	0	0	0	19	3
LOU	19	16	3	0	0	0	0	0	0	0	0	0	0	0	0	11	7	1	0	0	1	0	5	1	7	0	0	0	0	18	0
NY	21	10	11	0	0	0	0	0	0	0	0	0	0	0	0	11	9	0	1	0	0	0	7	1	8	0	0	0	0	17	1
PHI	30	18	12	2	0	0	0	0	0	0	0	0	0	0	0	11	11	8	0	0	0	0	4	0	6	1	0	0	0	20	2
PIT	5	3	2	0	0	0	0	0	0	0	0	0	0	0	0	3	0	2	0	0	1	0	1	0	2	0	0	0	0	2	0
STL	17	6	11	0	0	0	0	0	0	0	0	0	0	0	0	7	8	2	0	0	0	0	4	2	8	0	0	0	0	12	0
NL																															
BOS	22	7	15	1	0	0	0	0	0	0	0	0	0	0	0	9	10	3	0	0	0	1	0	0	10	0	0	0	0	20	1
BUF	23	13	10	0	0	0	0	0	0	0	0	0	0	0	0	10	10	3	0	0	2	0	0	2	9	0	0	0	0	19	1
CHI	54	47	7	0	0	0	0	0	0	0	0	0	0	0	0	31	13	10	0	0	4	0	1	4	9	1	0	0	0	48	3
DET	25	13	12	1	0	0	0	0	0	0	0	0	0	0	0	12	8	4	1	0	0	0	2	1	9	0	0	0	0	20	3
NY	16	7	9	0	0	0	0	0	0	0	0	0	0	0	0	9	6	1	0	0	1	0	1	2	5	0	0	0	0	15	0
PHI	20	7	13	0	0	0	0	0	0	0	0	0	0	0	0	8	10	2	0	0	1	1	1	2	8	0	0	0	0	18	2
PRO	6	3	3	0	0	0	0	0	0	0	0	0	0	0	0	6	0	0	0	0	1	0	0	0	4	0	0	0	0	6	0
STL	8	6	2	0	0	0	0	0	0	0	0	0	0	0	0	6	2	0	0	0	1	0	0	0	7	0	0	0	0	8	0
AA	149	90	59	2	0	0	0	0	0	0	0	0	0	0	0	64	60	24	1	0	2	0	26	8	55	2	0	0	0	111	9

Tm	Tot	H	A	Consec			1-Inn			One-Game						Men-On-Base				Batters					Totals					Pitchers	
				2	3	4	3	4	5	5	6	7	8	9	10	0	1	2	3	PH	LO	XN	IP	P	1	10	20	30	40	RHP	LHP
NL	174	103	71	2	0	0	0	0	0	0	0	0	0	0	0	91	59	23	1	0	10	2	5	11	61	1	0	0	0	154	10
YR	323	193	130	4	0	0	0	0	0	0	0	0	0	0	0	155	119	47	2	0	12	2	31	19	116	3	0	0	0	265	19

AA
13 Harry Stovey
10 Frank Fennelly
9 Pete Browning
8 Henry Larkin
6 Dave Orr

NL
11 Abner Dalrymple
9 King Kelly
7 Multiple Players Tied

1886

Tm	Tot	H	A	Consec 2	3	4	1-Inn 3	4	5	One-Game 5	6	7	8	9	10	Men-On-Base 0	1	2	3	PH	LO	XN	IP	P	Totals 1	10	20	30	40	RHP	LHP
AA																															
BAL	8	2	6	0	0	0	0	0	0	0	0	0	0	0	0	3	4	1	0	0	0	0	2	0	7	0	0	0	0	6	2
BRO	16	9	7	0	0	0	0	0	0	0	0	0	0	0	0	3	6	6	1	0	0	1	1	1	8	0	0	0	0	11	2
CIN	45	32	13	1	0	0	0	0	0	0	0	0	0	0	0	16	16	12	1	0	0	0	9	2	11	0	0	0	0	22	11
LOU	20	19	1	0	0	0	0	0	0	0	0	0	0	0	0	10	3	6	1	0	0	1	6	3	9	0	0	0	0	12	5
NY	18	10	8	0	0	0	0	0	0	0	0	0	0	0	0	10	7	1	0	0	1	0	4	1	6	0	0	0	0	12	2
PHI	21	13	8	0	0	0	0	0	0	0	0	0	0	0	0	10	7	3	1	0	1	0	3	0	8	0	0	0	0	15	3
PIT	16	2	14	0	0	0	0	0	0	0	0	0	0	0	0	9	3	3	1	0	0	0	2	1	9	0	0	0	0	6	3
STL	20	13	7	0	0	0	0	0	0	0	0	0	0	0	0	9	6	4	1	0	0	0	5	4	8	0	0	0	0	13	3
NL																															
BOS	24	15	9	0	0	0	0	0	0	0	0	0	0	0	0	9	13	2	0	0	0	0	2	3	9	0	0	0	0	22	1
CHI	53	45	8	2	0	0	0	0	0	0	0	0	0	0	0	25	19	8	1	0	2	0	1	8	11	1	0	0	0	42	7
DET	53	37	16	1	0	0	0	0	0	0	0	1	0	0	0	25	19	9	0	0	2	0	12	2	9	2	0	0	0	45	7
KC	19	9	10	0	0	0	0	0	0	0	0	0	0	0	0	7	9	2	1	0	0	0	0	0	7	0	0	0	0	17	2
NY	21	10	11	0	0	0	0	0	0	0	0	0	0	0	0	6	10	4	1	0	0	0	2	1	8	0	0	0	0	12	9
PHI	26	13	13	0	0	0	0	0	0	0	0	0	0	0	0	14	6	4	2	0	0	0	1	3	9	0	0	0	0	23	3
STL	30	13	17	0	0	0	0	0	0	0	0	0	0	0	0	17	9	4	0	0	1	0	2	1	9	0	0	0	0	21	7
WAS	23	13	10	0	0	0	0	0	0	0	0	0	0	0	0	9	11	2	1	0	0	0	0	0	9	0	0	0	0	20	3
AA	164	100	64	1	0	0	0	0	0	0	0	0	0	0	0	70	52	36	6	0	2	2	32	12	66	0	0	0	0	97	31
NL	249	155	94	3	0	0	0	0	0	0	0	1	0	0	0	112	96	35	6	0	5	0	20	18	71	3	0	0	0	202	39
YR	413	255	158	4	0	0	0	0	0	0	0	1	0	0	0	182	148	71	12	0	7	2	52	30	137	3	0	0	0	299	70

AA
8 Bid McPhee
7 Dave Orr
7 Harry Stovey
6 Multiple Players Tied

NL
11 Dan Brouthers
11 Hardy Richardson
10 Cap Anson
9 Jerry Denny
9 Paul Hines

1887

Tm	Tot	H	A	Consec 2	3	4	1-Inn 3	4	5	One-Game 5	6	7	8	9	10	Men-On-Base 0	1	2	3	PH	LO	XN	IP	P	Totals 1	10	20	30	40	RHP	LHP
AA																															
BAL	31	16	15	0	0	0	0	0	0	0	0	0	0	0	0	13	12	6	0	0	0	0	4	1	6	0	0	0	0	22	7
BRO	25	18	7	1	0	0	0	0	0	0	0	0	0	0	0	8	9	6	1	0	0	0	0	5	14	0	0	0	0	16	5
CIN	37	24	13	0	0	0	0	0	0	0	0	0	0	0	0	16	15	6	0	0	0	0	7	3	9	1	0	0	0	26	10
CLE	14	2	12	0	0	0	0	0	0	0	0	0	0	0	0	0	10	3	1	0	0	0	1	0	6	0	0	0	0	12	1
LOU	27	14	13	0	0	0	0	0	0	0	0	0	0	0	0	12	8	7	0	0	1	0	3	2	9	0	0	0	0	18	5
NY	21	10	11	0	0	0	0	0	0	0	0	0	0	0	0	4	7	10	0	0	0	0	3	2	10	0	0	0	0	16	5
PHI	29	18	11	0	0	0	0	0	0	0	0	0	0	0	0	6	16	7	0	0	2	0	6	4	11	0	0	0	0	22	5
STL	39	26	13	0	0	0	0	0	0	0	0	0	0	0	0	15	14	9	1	0	1	1	6	2	8	1	0	0	0	29	4
NL																															
BOS	53	29	24	2	0	0	0	0	0	0	0	0	0	0	0	28	19	5	1	0	0	1	3	3	10	1	0	0	0	45	7
CHI	78	65	13	0	0	0	0	0	0	0	0	0	0	0	0	37	32	9	0	0	1	0	3	16	13	2	0	0	0	63	14
DET	55	25	30	3	0	0	0	0	0	1	0	0	0	0	0	26	20	8	1	0	4	0	3	3	10	2	0	0	0	46	8
IND	33	19	14	0	0	0	0	0	0	0	0	0	0	0	0	16	11	5	1	0	0	0	1	4	10	1	0	0	0	21	11
NY	48	21	27	1	0	0	0	0	0	0	0	0	0	0	0	24	17	6	1	0	0	0	3	3	8	2	0	0	0	35	13
PHI	47	25	22	0	0	0	0	0	0	0	0	0	0	0	0	21	13	13	0	0	1	0	2	3	15	1	0	0	0	36	9
PIT	20	6	14	0	0	0	0	0	0	0	0	0	0	0	0	8	10	2	0	0	0	1	0	2	10	0	0	0	0	8	8

Tm	Tot	H	A	Consec 2	3	4	1-Inn 3	4	5	One-Game 5	6	7	8	9	10	Men-On-Base 0	1	2	3	Batters PH	LO	XN	IP	P	Totals 1	10	20	30	40	Pitchers RHP	LHP
WAS	47	29	18	1	0	0	0	0	0	1	0	0	0	0	0	22	18	5	2	0	3	0	0	1	10	2	0	0	0	28	18
AA	223	128	95	1	0	0	0	0	0	0	0	0	0	0	0	74	91	54	3	0	4	1	30	19	73	2	0	0	0	161	42
NL	381	219	162	7	0	0	0	0	0	2	0	0	0	0	0	182	140	53	6	0	9	2	15	35	86	11	0	0	0	282	88
YR	604	347	257	8	0	0	0	0	0	2	0	0	0	0	0	256	231	107	9	0	13	3	45	54	159	13	0	0	0	443	130

	AA		*NL*
14	Tip O'Neill	19	Billy O'Brien
10	John Reilly	17	Roger Connor
9	Oyster Burns	16	Fred Pfeffer
8	Multiple Players Tied	14	George Wood
		12	Multiple Players Tied

1888

Tm	Tot	H	A	Consec 2	3	4	1-Inn 3	4	5	One-Game 5	6	7	8	9	10	Men-On-Base 0	1	2	3	Batters PH	LO	XN	IP	P	Totals 1	10	20	30	40	Pitchers RHP	LHP
AA																															
BAL	19	7	12	0	0	0	0	0	0	0	0	0	0	0	0	7	10	2	0	0	1	0	4	2	7	0	0	0	0	14	4
BRO	25	18	7	0	0	0	0	0	0	0	0	0	0	0	0	8	13	4	0	0	0	0	3	5	11	0	0	0	0	20	4
CIN	32	24	8	0	0	0	0	0	0	1	0	0	0	0	0	18	9	5	0	0	0	1	12	0	11	1	0	0	0	25	7
CLE	12	8	4	0	0	0	0	0	0	0	0	0	0	0	0	7	4	1	0	0	0	0	6	1	7	0	0	0	0	7	4
KC	19	15	4	0	0	0	0	0	0	0	0	0	0	0	0	6	6	7	0	0	1	0	2	0	8	0	0	0	0	13	6
LOU	14	1	13	0	0	0	0	0	0	0	0	0	0	0	0	5	6	3	0	0	1	0	0	1	8	0	0	0	0	11	3
PHI	31	20	11	2	0	0	0	0	0	0	0	0	0	0	0	11	15	5	0	0	0	0	3	3	10	0	0	0	0	24	7
STL	36	22	14	1	0	0	0	0	0	0	0	0	0	0	0	17	7	11	1	0	0	0	6	5	13	0	0	0	0	24	9
NL																															
BOS	56	23	33	2	0	0	0	0	0	0	0	0	0	0	0	28	20	7	1	0	3	0	13	1	12	1	0	0	0	45	11
CHI	77	50	27	1	0	0	0	0	0	1	0	0	0	0	0	43	31	3	0	0	5	0	16	5	12	2	0	0	0	62	13
DET	51	24	27	1	0	0	0	0	0	0	0	0	0	0	0	25	15	11	0	0	2	1	12	5	14	0	0	0	0	38	12
IND	34	27	7	1	0	0	0	0	0	0	0	0	0	0	0	22	9	3	0	0	2	1	1	2	9	1	0	0	0	27	7
NY	55	21	34	3	0	0	0	0	0	1	0	1	0	0	0	30	18	7	0	0	1	0	7	5	13	1	0	0	0	35	19
PHI	16	6	10	0	0	0	0	0	0	0	0	0	0	0	0	5	9	2	0	0	0	1	2	1	9	0	0	0	0	10	4
PIT	14	0	14	0	0	0	0	0	0	0	0	0	0	0	0	7	6	1	0	0	0	0	2	1	7	0	0	0	0	9	5
WAS	30	17	13	0	0	0	0	0	0	0	0	0	0	0	0	13	12	3	2	0	0	1	2	1	8	0	0	0	0	25	5
AA	188	115	73	3	0	0	0	0	0	1	0	0	0	0	0	79	70	38	1	0	3	1	36	17	75	1	0	0	0	138	44
NL	333	168	165	8	0	0	0	0	0	2	0	1	0	0	0	173	120	37	3	0	13	4	55	21	84	5	0	0	0	251	76
YR	521	283	238	11	0	0	0	0	0	3	0	1	0	0	0	252	190	75	4	0	16	5	91	38	159	6	0	0	0	389	120

	AA		*NL*
13	John Reilly	16	Jimmy Ryan
9	Harry Stovey	14	Roger Connor
7	Henry Larkin	12	Cap Anson
6	Multiple Players Tied	12	Jerry Denny
		12	Richard Johnston

1889

Tm	Tot	H	A	Consec 2	3	4	1-Inn 3	4	5	One-Game 5	6	7	8	9	10	Men-On-Base 0	1	2	3	Batters PH	LO	XN	IP	P	Totals 1	10	20	30	40	Pitchers RHP	LHP
AA																															
BAL	20	10	10	0	0	0	0	0	0	0	0	0	0	0	0	9	6	5	0	0	1	0	2	1	11	0	0	0	0	17	3
BRO	47	28	19	0	0	0	0	0	0	0	0	0	0	0	0	15	19	10	3	0	0	0	8	6	11	0	0	0	0	38	8
CIN	52	37	15	2	0	0	0	0	0	0	0	0	0	0	0	21	18	12	1	0	3	0	6	2	9	1	0	0	0	43	7
COL	36	13	23	0	0	0	0	0	0	0	0	0	0	0	0	15	9	10	2	0	1	1	1	4	13	0	0	0	0	32	4
KC	18	8	10	1	0	0	0	0	0	0	0	0	0	0	0	6	8	4	0	0	1	0	1	0	6	0	0	0	0	15	3
LOU	22	10	12	0	0	0	0	0	0	0	0	0	0	0	0	6	9	6	1	0	1	0	4	5	8	0	0	0	0	20	1
PHI	43	16	27	1	0	0	0	0	0	0	0	0	0	0	0	23	14	5	1	0	0	0	2	2	7	1	0	0	0	32	6
STL	58	45	13	0	0	0	0	0	0	0	0	0	0	0	0	21	19	17	1	0	3	0	3	3	9	2	0	0	0	40	15
NL																															
BOS	42	24	18	0	0	0	0	0	0	0	0	0	0	0	0	23	15	4	0	0	2	1	3	3	11	0	0	0	0	37	5
CHI	79	54	25	3	0	0	0	0	0	0	0	0	0	0	0	39	23	15	2	0	6	5	12	8	10	3	0	0	0	70	7
CLE	25	8	17	0	0	0	0	0	0	0	0	0	0	0	0	7	13	5	0	0	0	3	4	2	10	0	0	0	0	20	4
IND	62	50	12	2	0	0	0	0	0	0	0	0	0	0	0	23	24	12	3	0	2	3	1	3	10	1	0	0	0	54	8
NY	52	18	34	2	0	0	0	0	0	0	0	0	0	0	0	27	18	4	3	0	2	0	5	2	11	2	0	0	0	40	12
PHI	44	27	17	0	0	0	0	0	0	0	0	0	0	0	0	24	12	6	2	0	2	1	5	0	7	0	1	0	0	37	7

Tm	Tot	H	A	Consec			1-Inn			One-Game						Men-On-Base				Batters					Totals					Pitchers	
				2	3	4	3	4	5	5	6	7	8	9	10	0	1	2	3	PH	LO	XN	IP	P	1	10	20	30	40	RHP	LHP
PIT	42	6	36	1	0	0	0	0	0	0	0	0	0	0	0	18	16	7	1	0	0	1	2	1	12	0	0	0	0	36	6
WAS	25	12	13	0	0	0	0	0	0	0	0	0	0	0	0	14	8	3	0	0	0	0	1	3	10	0	0	0	0	23	1
AA	296	167	129	4	0	0	0	0	0	0	0	0	0	0	0	116	102	69	9	0	10	1	27	23	74	4	0	0	0	237	47
NL	371	199	172	8	0	0	0	0	0	0	0	0	0	0	0	175	129	56	11	0	14	14	33	22	81	6	1	0	0	317	50
YR	667	366	301	12	0	0	0	0	0	0	0	0	0	0	0	291	231	125	20	0	24	15	60	45	155	10	1	0	0	554	97

AA

19 Bug Holliday
19 Harry Stovey
16 Charlie Duffee
12 Jocko Milligan
9 Multiple Players Tied

NL

20 Sam Thompson
18 Jerry Denny
17 Jimmy Ryan
13 Roger Connor
12 Hugh Duffy

1890

Tm	Tot	H	A	Consec			1-Inn			One-Game						Men-On-Base				Batters					Totals					Pitchers	
				2	3	4	3	4	5	5	6	7	8	9	10	0	1	2	3	PH	LO	XN	IP	P	1	10	20	30	40	RHP	LHP
AA																															
BAL	2	1	1	0	0	0	0	0	0	0	0	0	0	0	0	1	1	0	0	0	0	0	0	0	2	0	0	0	0	0	2
BRO	13	4	9	0	0	0	0	0	0	0	0	0	0	0	0	4	6	3	0	0	0	0	0	0	7	0	0	0	0	7	5
COL	16	9	7	0	0	0	0	0	0	0	0	0	0	0	0	4	9	2	1	0	1	0	1	1	10	0	0	0	0	7	2
LOU	15	8	7	0	0	0	0	0	0	0	0	0	0	0	0	6	5	4	0	0	0	0	0	0	7	0	0	0	0	2	10
PHI	24	16	8	0	0	0	0	0	0	0	0	0	0	0	0	10	12	2	0	0	1	1	1	2	9	0	0	0	0	13	4
ROC	31	13	18	1	0	0	0	0	0	0	0	0	0	0	0	16	8	4	3	0	2	1	0	3	10	0	0	0	0	28	2
STL	48	42	6	0	0	0	0	0	0	0	0	0	0	0	0	15	18	10	5	0	1	1	1	8	14	0	0	0	0	29	11
SYR	14	2	12	0	0	0	0	0	0	0	0	0	0	0	0	7	2	3	2	0	0	0	2	1	8	0	0	0	0	6	6
TOL	24	17	7	0	0	0	0	0	0	0	0	0	0	0	0	12	9	3	0	0	2	0	0	1	11	0	0	0	0	10	7
NL																															
BOS	31	20	11	1	0	0	0	0	0	0	0	0	0	0	0	19	8	4	0	0	2	1	7	4	11	0	0	0	0	27	3
BRO	43	27	16	1	0	0	0	0	0	0	0	0	0	0	0	15	19	8	1	0	1	0	5	3	10	1	0	0	0	36	7
CHI	67	55	12	0	0	0	0	0	0	0	0	0	0	0	0	28	20	14	5	0	0	0	4	5	13	1	0	0	0	48	11
CIN	27	19	8	0	0	0	0	0	0	0	0	0	0	0	0	13	10	4	0	0	1	1	6	2	10	0	0	0	0	18	6
CLE	21	16	5	0	0	0	0	0	0	0	0	0	0	0	0	5	10	4	2	0	1	0	1	1	7	0	0	0	0	16	3
NY	25	8	17	0	0	0	0	0	0	0	0	0	0	0	0	13	9	3	0	0	3	1	3	0	5	1	0	0	0	19	2
PHI	23	14	9	1	0	0	0	0	0	0	0	0	0	0	0	6	10	4	3	0	0	0	6	0	8	0	0	0	0	20	3
PIT	20	2	18	0	0	0	0	0	0	0	0	0	0	0	0	10	5	5	0	0	0	0	2	1	11	0	0	0	0	13	5
PL																															
BOS	54	42	12	0	0	0	0	0	0	0	0	0	0	0	0	27	17	9	1	0	2	0	4	3	9	2	0	0	0	45	6
BRO	34	20	14	0	0	0	0	0	0	0	0	0	0	0	0	11	11	12	0	0	1	0	3	1	11	0	0	0	0	18	12
BUF	20	7	13	0	0	0	0	0	0	0	0	0	0	0	0	8	5	7	0	0	0	1	1	1	9	0	0	0	0	11	6
CHI	31	18	13	0	0	0	0	0	0	0	0	0	0	0	0	13	12	6	0	0	1	1	1	2	11	0	0	0	0	28	3
CLE	27	10	17	0	0	0	0	0	0	0	0	0	0	0	0	7	10	9	1	0	0	0	1	0	9	0	0	0	0	20	7
NY	66	35	31	1	1	0	0	0	0	0	0	0	0	0	0	25	28	11	2	0	0	0	10	5	12	2	0	0	0	53	12
PHI	49	20	29	2	0	0	0	0	0	0	0	0	0	0	0	20	16	12	1	0	2	0	10	1	12	1	0	0	0	34	13
PIT	35	21	14	1	0	0	0	0	0	0	0	0	0	0	0	17	10	7	1	0	1	0	8	3	11	0	0	0	0	22	12
AA	187	112	75	1	0	0	0	0	0	0	0	0	0	0	0	75	70	31	11	0	7	3	5	16	78	0	0	0	0	102	49
NL	257	161	96	3	0	0	0	0	0	0	0	0	0	0	0	109	91	46	11	0	8	3	34	16	75	3	0	0	0	197	40
PL	316	173	143	4	1	0	0	0	0	0	0	0	0	0	0	128	109	73	6	0	7	2	38	16	84	5	0	0	0	231	71
YR	760	446	314	8	1	0	0	0	0	0	0	0	0	0	0	312	270	150	28	0	22	8	77	48	237	8	0	0	0	530	160

AA

9 Count Campau
8 Ed Cartwright
7 Denny Lyons
7 Jack Stivetts
6 Multiple Players Tied

NL

13 Oyster Burns
13 Mike Tiernan
13 Walt Wilmot
8 Herman Long
7 Multiple Players Tied

PL

14 Roger Connor
13 Hardy Richardson
12 Harry Stovey
10 George Gore
10 Billy Shindle

1891

Tm	Tot	H	A	Consec			1-Inn			One-Game						Men-On-Base				Batters					Totals					Pitchers	
				2	3	4	3	4	5	5	6	7	8	9	10	0	1	2	3	PH	LO	XN	IP	P	1	10	20	30	40	RHP	LHP
AA																															
BAL	30	13	17	0	0	0	0	0	0	0	0	0	0	0	0	11	7	12	0	0	2	0	4	2	11	0	0	0	0	16	11
BOS	52	37	15	2	0	0	0	0	0	0	0	0	0	0	0	20	21	7	4	0	2	0	4	4	11	1	0	0	0	34	8
CIN	28	21	7	0	0	0	0	0	0	0	0	0	0	0	0	11	14	2	1	0	1	0	2	2	10	0	0	0	0	20	7

Tm	Tot	H	A	Consec 2	3	4	1-Inn 3	4	5	One-Game 5	6	7	8	9	10	Men-On-Base 0	1	2	3	Batters PH	LO	XN	IP	P	Totals 1	10	20	30	40	Pitchers RHP	LHP
COL	20	4	16	0	0	0	0	0	0	0	0	0	0	0	0	7	8	4	1	0	0	0	5	1	6	1	0	0	0	13	4
LOU	17	7	10	0	0	0	0	0	0	0	0	0	0	0	0	8	6	2	1	0	0	0	5	2	12	0	0	0	0	8	2
MIL	13	11	2	0	0	0	0	0	0	0	0	0	0	0	0	2	7	2	0	0	0	0	1	0	8	0	0	0	0	8	1
PHI	55	29	26	3	0	0	0	0	0	0	0	0	0	0	0	30	13	11	1	0	1	0	21	3	9	2	0	0	0	42	8
STL	57	41	16	0	0	0	0	0	0	0	0	0	0	0	0	25	19	11	2	0	1	0	4	7	10	2	0	0	0	49	4
WAS	19	13	6	0	0	0	0	0	0	0	0	0	0	0	0	8	7	3	1	0	0	1	2	4	11	0	0	0	0	16	2
NL																															
BOS	53	34	19	1	0	0	0	0	0	0	0	0	0	0	0	28	17	6	2	0	0	2	4	2	11	1	0	0	0	46	4
BRO	23	11	12	0	0	0	0	0	0	0	0	0	0	0	0	8	7	7	1	0	1	0	6	1	8	0	0	0	0	22	1
CHI	60	39	21	2	0	0	0	0	0	0	0	0	0	0	0	31	18	11	0	0	2	1	2	4	11	1	0	0	0	51	2
CIN	40	19	21	0	0	0	0	0	0	0	0	0	0	0	0	17	15	8	0	0	0	1	3	0	10	0	0	0	0	37	2
CLE	22	4	18	1	0	0	1	0	0	0	0	0	0	0	0	10	7	5	0	0	0	0	2	1	11	0	0	0	0	20	1
NY	46	28	18	2	0	0	0	0	0	0	0	0	0	0	0	23	16	6	1	0	1	0	11	1	8	1	0	0	0	37	4
PHI	21	8	13	0	0	0	0	0	0	0	0	0	0	0	0	9	8	4	0	0	0	0	5	0	6	0	0	0	0	17	0
PIT	29	14	15	1	0	0	0	0	0	0	0	0	0	0	0	11	14	4	0	0	0	0	6	1	11	0	0	0	0	26	3
AA	291	176	115	5	0	0	0	0	0	0	0	0	0	0	0	122	102	54	11	0	7	1	48	25	88	6	0	0	0	206	47
NL	294	157	137	7	0	0	1	0	0	0	0	0	0	0	0	137	102	51	4	0	4	4	39	10	76	3	0	0	0	256	17
YR	585	333	252	12	0	0	1	0	0	0	0	0	0	0	0	259	204	105	15	0	11	5	87	35	164	9	0	0	0	462	64

AA

12 Duke Farrell
11 Denny Lyons
11 Jocko Milligan
10 Multiple Players Tied

NL

16 Harry Stovey
16 Mike Tiernan
11 Walt Wilmot
9 Multiple Players Tied

1892

Tm	Tot	H	A	Consec 2	3	4	1-Inn 3	4	5	One-Game 5	6	7	8	9	10	Men-On-Base 0	1	2	3	Batters PH	LO	XN	IP	P	Totals 1	10	20	30	40	Pitchers RHP	LHP
NL																															
BAL	30	13	17	0	0	0	0	0	0	0	0	0	0	0	0	12	12	5	1	0	0	0	1	1	14	0	0	0	0	25	4
BOS	34	20	14	0	0	0	0	0	0	0	0	0	0	0	0	13	14	4	3	0	2	1	0	5	13	0	0	0	0	27	5
BRO	30	14	16	0	0	0	0	0	0	0	0	0	0	0	0	13	16	1	0	1	1	0	3	2	11	0	0	0	0	25	4
CHI	26	9	17	1	0	0	0	0	0	0	0	0	0	0	0	11	12	3	0	0	2	0	6	4	9	1	0	0	0	22	1
CIN	44	30	14	2	0	0	0	0	0	0	0	0	0	0	0	17	17	6	4	0	2	0	6	3	12	1	0	0	0	33	6
CLE	26	4	22	0	0	0	1	0	0	0	0	0	0	0	0	6	12	7	1	0	0	0	5	1	10	0	0	0	0	15	11
LOU	18	7	11	0	0	0	0	0	0	0	0	0	0	0	0	8	6	4	0	0	0	0	3	1	8	0	0	0	0	10	6
NY	39	26	13	0	0	0	0	0	0	0	0	0	0	0	0	20	13	4	2	0	0	0	7	3	10	0	0	0	0	33	4
PHI	50	34	16	0	0	0	0	0	0	0	0	0	0	0	0	20	21	7	2	0	0	0	5	3	11	1	0	0	0	40	1
PIT	38	32	6	0	0	0	0	0	0	0	0	0	0	0	0	11	18	9	0	0	0	1	13	3	8	1	0	0	0	31	6
STL	45	32	13	0	0	0	0	0	0	0	0	0	0	0	0	26	12	6	1	0	5	1	1	5	13	0	0	0	0	38	0
WAS	37	23	14	1	0	0	0	0	0	0	0	0	0	0	0	20	13	4	0	0	0	0	4	7	11	0	0	0	0	27	1
NL	417	244	173	4	0	0	1	0	0	0	0	0	0	0	0	177	166	60	14	1	12	3	54	38	130	4	0	0	0	326	49

NL

13 Bug Holliday
12 Roger Connor
10 Jake Beckley
10 Jimmy Ryan
9 Sam Thompson

1893

Tm	Tot	H	A	Consec 2	3	4	1-Inn 3	4	5	One-Game 5	6	7	8	9	10	Men-On-Base 0	1	2	3	Batters PH	LO	XN	IP	P	Totals 1	10	20	30	40	Pitchers RHP	LHP
NL																															
BAL	27	16	11	0	0	0	0	0	0	0	0	0	0	0	0	18	7	1	1	0	1	0	9	1	12	0	0	0	0	20	3
BOS	65	48	17	0	0	0	0	0	0	0	0	0	0	0	0	27	21	16	1	0	3	1	4	7	11	2	0	0	0	56	5
BRO	45	24	21	0	0	0	0	0	0	0	0	0	0	0	0	18	18	9	0	0	1	0	3	1	14	0	0	0	0	37	4
CHI	32	20	12	0	0	0	0	0	0	0	0	0	0	0	0	18	9	2	3	0	2	0	3	0	10	0	0	0	0	26	4
CIN	29	19	10	1	0	0	1	0	0	0	0	0	0	0	0	15	9	4	1	0	0	0	7	4	14	0	0	0	0	22	4
CLE	32	10	22	1	0	0	0	0	0	0	0	0	0	0	0	14	8	8	2	0	1	1	9	2	11	0	0	0	0	25	6
LOU	19	3	16	0	0	0	0	0	0	0	0	0	0	0	0	9	10	0	0	0	1	0	0	0	9	0	0	0	0	16	0
NY	61	48	13	0	0	0	0	0	0	0	0	0	0	0	0	23	26	10	2	0	1	1	10	4	9	3	0	0	0	44	16
PHI	80	45	35	1	0	0	0	0	0	0	0	0	0	0	0	33	33	12	2	0	2	2	7	1	9	3	0	0	0	68	8
PIT	37	25	12	1	0	0	0	0	0	0	0	0	0	0	0	13	13	10	1	0	1	0	10	5	12	0	0	0	0	33	1
STL	10	7	3	0	0	0	0	0	0	0	0	0	0	0	0	2	5	2	1	0	0	1	3	2	9	0	0	0	0	8	1

Tm	Tot	H	A	Consec			1-Inn			One-Game						Men-On-Base				Batters					Totals					Pitchers	
				2	3	4	3	4	5	5	6	7	8	9	10	0	1	2	3	PH	LO	XN	IP	P	1	10	20	30	40	RHP	LHP
WAS	23	8	15	1	0	0	0	0	0	0	0	0	0	0	0	11	8	4	0	0	0	1	5	3	8	0	0	0	0	22	0
NL	460	273	187	5	0	0	1	0	0	0	0	0	0	0	0	201	167	78	14	0	13	7	70	30	128	8	0	0	0	377	52

NL

19 Ed Delahanty
17 Jack Clements
14 Bobby Lowe
14 Mike Tiernan
11 Multiple Players Tied

1894

NL

Tm	Tot	H	A	Consec 2	3	4	1-Inn 3	4	5	One-Game 5	6	7	8	9	10	Men-On-Base 0	1	2	3	PH	LO	XN	IP	P	Totals 1	10	20	30	40	RHP	LHP
BAL	33	13	20	0	0	0	0	0	0	0	0	0	0	0	0	14	9	8	2	0	0	0	8	1	10	0	0	0	0	25	4
BOS	103	77	26	5	0	0	1	0	0	2	0	0	0	0	0	45	37	16	5	1	1	0	0	6	9	5	0	0	0	84	12
BRO	42	22	20	2	0	0	0	0	0	0	0	0	0	0	0	13	16	12	1	0	1	0	6	2	11	0	0	0	0	35	5
CHI	65	26	39	0	0	0	0	0	0	0	0	0	0	0	0	19	26	17	3	0	0	0	4	8	10	1	0	0	0	51	4
CIN	61	43	18	2	0	0	0	0	0	1	0	0	0	0	0	25	19	12	5	0	0	2	7	5	11	2	0	0	0	47	11
CLE	37	8	29	1	0	0	0	0	0	0	0	0	0	0	0	15	18	3	1	0	1	0	3	3	12	0	0	0	0	33	3
LOU	42	16	26	2	0	0	0	0	0	0	1	0	0	0	0	19	19	4	0	0	1	0	4	3	12	0	0	0	0	35	3
NY	43	29	14	0	0	0	0	0	0	0	0	0	0	0	0	16	20	3	4	0	0	1	3	8	11	0	0	0	0	35	6
PHI	40	26	14	0	0	0	0	0	0	0	0	0	0	0	0	13	15	10	2	0	1	0	3	0	8	1	0	0	0	34	5
PIT	48	26	22	1	0	0	0	0	0	0	0	1	0	0	0	16	22	10	0	0	0	0	7	1	13	1	0	0	0	37	10
STL	54	30	24	1	1	0	0	0	0	0	1	0	0	0	0	25	19	10	0	0	0	0	11	2	11	1	0	0	0	37	11
WAS	59	35	24	0	0	0	0	0	0	0	0	0	0	0	0	19	30	10	0	0	1	0	11	5	8	2	0	0	0	46	8
NL	627	351	276	14	1	0	1	0	0	3	2	1	0	0	0	239	250	115	23	1	6	3	67	44	126	13	0	0	0	499	82

NL

18 Hugh Duffy
17 Bill Joyce
17 Bobby Lowe
15 Bill Dahlen
13 Multiple Players Tied

1895

NL

Tm	Tot	H	A	Consec 2	3	4	1-Inn 3	4	5	One-Game 5	6	7	8	9	10	Men-On-Base 0	1	2	3	PH	LO	XN	IP	P	Totals 1	10	20	30	40	RHP	LHP
BAL	25	10	15	0	0	0	0	0	0	0	0	0	0	0	0	7	11	7	0	0	0	0	7	2	7	1	0	0	0	19	6
BOS	54	50	4	0	0	0	0	0	0	1	0	0	0	0	0	19	23	8	4	0	0	0	1	1	12	1	0	0	0	50	4
BRO	39	22	17	0	0	0	0	0	0	0	0	0	0	0	0	17	17	3	2	0	1	0	1	2	10	0	0	0	0	31	7
CHI	55	32	23	2	0	0	0	0	0	0	1	0	0	0	0	25	17	11	2	0	1	0	4	3	13	1	0	0	0	40	13
CIN	36	8	28	0	0	0	0	0	0	0	0	0	0	0	0	18	11	5	2	0	1	1	8	4	12	1	0	0	0	26	7
CLE	29	5	24	0	0	0	0	0	0	0	0	0	0	0	0	13	9	3	4	0	2	0	3	0	7	0	0	0	0	24	5
LOU	34	14	20	0	0	0	0	0	0	0	0	0	0	0	0	19	10	5	0	0	0	0	3	1	17	0	0	0	0	24	8
NY	32	14	18	1	0	0	0	0	0	0	0	0	0	0	0	13	12	7	0	0	0	1	3	2	12	0	0	0	0	28	3
PHI	61	42	19	0	0	0	1	0	0	0	0	0	0	0	0	23	22	16	0	0	1	0	1	4	8	3	0	0	0	47	9
PIT	26	9	17	0	0	0	0	0	0	0	0	0	0	0	0	17	8	1	0	0	1	1	2	6	9	0	0	0	0	20	4
STL	38	26	12	1	0	0	1	0	0	0	0	0	0	0	0	17	14	5	2	0	0	0	8	1	12	0	0	0	0	30	4
WAS	55	39	16	0	0	0	0	0	0	0	0	0	0	0	0	26	17	11	1	0	0	0	1	1	8	2	0	0	0	46	7
NL	484	271	213	4	0	0	2	0	0	1	1	0	0	0	0	214	171	82	17	0	7	3	42	27	127	9	0	0	0	385	77

NL

18 Sam Thompson
17 Bill Joyce
13 Jack Clements
11 Ed Delahanty
10 Multiple Players Tied

1896

NL

Tm	Tot	H	A	Consec 2	3	4	1-Inn 3	4	5	One-Game 5	6	7	8	9	10	Men-On-Base 0	1	2	3	PH	LO	XN	IP	P	Totals 1	10	20	30	40	RHP	LHP
BAL	23	8	15	1	0	0	0	0	0	0	0	0	0	0	0	9	7	6	1	0	1	0	5	0	7	0	0	0	0	15	6
BOS	36	23	13	0	0	0	0	0	0	0	0	0	0	0	0	18	13	5	0	0	0	0	1	6	15	0	0	0	0	32	4
BRO	28	13	15	0	0	0	0	0	0	0	0	0	0	0	0	15	3	10	0	0	0	0	1	0	10	0	0	0	0	23	5

Tm	Tot	H	A	Consec 2	Consec 3	Consec 4	1-Inn 3	1-Inn 4	1-Inn 5	One-Game 5	One-Game 6	One-Game 7	One-Game 8	One-Game 9	One-Game 10	Men-On-Base 0	Men-On-Base 1	Men-On-Base 2	Men-On-Base 3	Batters PH	Batters LO	Batters XN	Batters IP	Batters P	Totals 1	Totals 10	Totals 20	Totals 30	Totals 40	Pitchers RHP	Pitchers LHP
CHI	34	19	15	0	0	0	0	0	0	0	0	0	0	0	0	14	11	8	1	0	2	1	3	2	13	0	0	0	0	29	4
CIN	20	6	14	0	0	0	0	0	0	0	0	0	0	0	0	12	8	0	0	0	1	0	5	1	10	0	0	0	0	15	4
CLE	28	9	19	1	0	0	0	0	0	0	0	0	0	0	0	13	9	6	0	0	1	1	1	5	12	0	0	0	0	22	6
LOU	37	24	13	0	0	0	0	0	0	0	0	0	0	0	0	20	9	7	1	0	2	0	5	2	14	0	0	0	0	31	6
NY	40	21	19	0	0	0	0	0	0	0	0	0	0	0	0	12	19	6	3	0	3	1	2	3	11	0	0	0	0	24	15
PHI	49	30	19	0	0	0	0	0	0	0	0	0	0	0	0	14	21	12	2	1	1	1	5	2	12	2	0	0	0	38	9
PIT	27	5	22	0	0	0	0	0	0	0	0	0	0	0	0	10	8	6	3	0	0	0	1	3	10	0	0	0	0	20	6
STL	37	25	12	1	0	0	0	0	0	0	0	0	0	0	0	23	12	2	0	0	0	0	2	1	8	1	0	0	0	30	5
WAS	45	30	15	2	0	0	0	0	0	0	0	0	0	0	0	18	20	7	0	0	1	0	5	2	15	0	0	0	0	34	11
NL	404	213	191	5	0	0	0	0	0	0	0	0	0	0	0	178	140	75	11	1	12	4	36	27	137	3	0	0	0	313	81

NL

13 Ed Delahanty
13 Bill Joyce
12 Sam Thompson
11 Roger Connor
9 Multiple Players Tied

1897

NL

Tm	Tot	H	A	Consec 2	Consec 3	Consec 4	1-Inn 3	1-Inn 4	1-Inn 5	One-Game 5	One-Game 6	One-Game 7	One-Game 8	One-Game 9	One-Game 10	Men-On-Base 0	Men-On-Base 1	Men-On-Base 2	Men-On-Base 3	Batters PH	Batters LO	Batters XN	Batters IP	Batters P	Totals 1	Totals 10	Totals 20	Totals 30	Totals 40	Pitchers RHP	Pitchers LHP
BAL	19	4	15	0	0	0	0	0	0	0	0	0	0	0	0	9	8	2	0	0	0	0	2	1	9	0	0	0	0	17	2
BOS	45	26	19	1	0	0	0	0	0	0	0	0	0	0	0	15	24	4	2	1	0	0	1	5	13	1	0	0	0	39	6
BRO	24	11	13	0	0	0	0	0	0	0	0	0	0	0	0	9	10	5	0	0	2	0	2	1	10	0	0	0	0	18	4
CHI	38	16	22	2	0	0	0	0	0	0	0	0	0	0	0	14	16	7	1	0	2	2	3	0	10	0	0	0	0	29	5
CIN	22	4	18	0	0	0	0	0	0	0	0	0	0	0	0	13	6	3	0	1	0	0	3	0	9	0	0	0	0	17	3
CLE	16	8	8	0	0	0	0	0	0	0	0	0	0	0	0	10	3	1	2	0	0	0	5	0	8	0	0	0	0	10	6
LOU	40	26	14	0	0	0	0	0	0	0	0	0	0	0	0	19	17	3	1	0	1	0	12	4	14	0	0	0	0	29	9
NY	31	16	15	0	0	0	0	0	0	0	0	0	0	0	0	14	13	4	0	0	0	0	2	1	11	1	0	0	0	25	6
PHI	40	17	23	0	0	0	0	0	0	0	0	0	0	0	0	14	17	8	1	0	1	0	1	4	12	0	0	0	0	31	7
PIT	25	10	15	0	0	0	0	0	0	0	0	0	0	0	0	11	7	5	2	0	0	0	4	3	12	0	0	0	0	18	7
STL	31	20	11	0	0	0	0	0	0	0	0	0	0	0	0	12	13	5	1	0	1	0	6	3	11	0	0	0	0	25	4
WAS	36	28	8	1	0	0	0	0	0	0	0	0	0	0	0	14	15	5	2	0	3	1	8	0	10	0	0	0	0	31	4
NL	367	186	181	4	0	0	0	0	0	0	0	0	0	0	0	154	149	52	12	2	10	3	49	22	129	2	0	0	0	289	63

NL

11 Hugh Duffy
10 George Davis
9 Nap Lajoie
8 Jake Beckley
7 Multiple Players Tied

1898

NL

Tm	Tot	H	A	Consec 2	Consec 3	Consec 4	1-Inn 3	1-Inn 4	1-Inn 5	One-Game 5	One-Game 6	One-Game 7	One-Game 8	One-Game 9	One-Game 10	Men-On-Base 0	Men-On-Base 1	Men-On-Base 2	Men-On-Base 3	Batters PH	Batters LO	Batters XN	Batters IP	Batters P	Totals 1	Totals 10	Totals 20	Totals 30	Totals 40	Pitchers RHP	Pitchers LHP
BAL	12	4	8	0	0	0	0	0	0	0	0	0	0	0	0	3	7	1	1	0	0	0	3	0	6	0	0	0	0	10	2
BOS	53	45	8	1	0	0	0	0	0	0	0	0	0	0	0	25	17	8	3	1	0	0	0	5	11	1	0	0	0	43	8
BRO	17	10	7	0	0	0	0	0	0	0	0	0	0	0	0	8	6	2	1	0	1	0	4	0	8	0	0	0	0	16	1
CHI	18	10	8	0	0	0	0	0	0	0	0	0	0	0	0	9	5	4	0	0	1	0	7	0	7	0	0	0	0	14	2
CIN	19	2	17	0	0	0	0	0	0	0	0	0	0	0	0	9	8	2	0	0	1	0	5	1	10	0	0	0	0	13	4
CLE	18	4	14	1	0	0	0	0	0	0	0	0	0	0	0	7	6	5	0	0	0	0	3	2	7	0	0	0	0	14	4
LOU	32	24	8	0	0	0	0	0	0	0	0	0	0	0	0	10	16	5	1	0	1	0	11	1	11	1	0	0	0	20	8
NY	34	18	16	1	0	0	0	0	0	0	0	0	0	0	0	16	10	8	0	0	2	1	0	4	10	1	0	0	0	28	5
PHI	33	13	20	1	0	0	0	0	0	0	0	0	0	0	0	12	14	6	1	0	0	0	1	2	11	0	0	0	0	23	10
PIT	14	6	8	0	0	0	0	0	0	0	0	0	0	0	0	10	2	2	0	0	0	0	1	1	8	0	0	0	0	10	3
STL	13	8	5	0	0	0	0	0	0	0	0	0	0	0	0	6	5	2	0	0	0	0	0	3	9	0	0	0	0	8	4
WAS	36	29	7	0	0	0	0	0	0	0	0	0	0	0	0	12	18	4	2	0	0	0	6	1	13	0	0	0	0	27	8
NL	299	173	126	4	0	0	0	0	0	0	0	0	0	0	0	127	114	49	9	1	6	1	41	20	111	3	0	0	0	226	59

NL

15 Jimmy Collins
10 Bill Joyce
10 Honus Wagner
9 John Anderson
9 Ed McKean

Tm	Tot	H	A	Consec			1-Inn			One-Game						Men-On-Base				Batters					Totals					Pitchers	
				2	3	4	3	4	5	5	6	7	8	9	10	0	1	2	3	PH	LO	XN	IP	P	1	10	20	30	40	RHP	LHP

1899

NL

Tm	Tot	H	A	2	3	4	3	4	5	5	6	7	8	9	10	0	1	2	3	PH	LO	XN	IP	P	1	10	20	30	40	RHP	LHP
BAL	17	4	13	0	0	0	0	0	0	0	0	0	0	0	0	6	9	1	1	0	0	0	1	0	8	0	0	0	0	13	4
BOS	39	32	7	1	0	0	0	0	0	0	0	0	0	0	0	18	12	9	0	0	0	0	1	2	13	0	0	0	0	31	6
BRO	27	13	14	0	0	0	0	0	0	0	0	0	0	0	0	10	9	7	1	0	0	1	5	0	9	0	0	0	0	22	4
CHI	27	14	13	0	0	0	0	0	0	0	0	0	0	0	0	10	12	4	1	0	2	0	3	0	10	0	0	0	0	23	3
CIN	13	2	11	0	0	0	0	0	0	0	0	0	0	0	0	7	2	3	1	0	1	0	3	0	9	0	0	0	0	11	1
CLE	12	3	9	0	0	0	0	0	0	0	0	0	0	0	0	6	4	2	0	0	1	0	1	0	8	0	0	0	0	9	3
LOU	40	23	17	0	0	0	0	0	0	0	1	0	0	0	0	21	12	5	2	0	1	0	12	3	14	0	0	0	0	27	12
NY	23	7	16	0	0	0	0	0	0	0	0	0	0	0	0	9	10	4	0	0	0	0	3	2	10	0	0	0	0	18	4
PHI	31	11	20	0	0	0	0	0	0	0	0	0	0	0	0	13	12	5	1	0	0	0	1	2	11	0	0	0	0	27	4
PIT	27	12	15	0	0	0	0	0	0	0	0	0	0	0	0	14	10	2	1	0	0	0	5	0	10	0	0	0	0	25	1
STL	47	38	9	0	0	0	0	0	0	1	0	0	0	0	0	26	11	9	1	1	1	2	8	4	15	1	0	0	0	33	12
WAS	47	30	17	2	0	0	0	0	0	0	0	0	0	0	0	27	12	6	2	0	0	0	3	1	9	0	1	0	0	39	7
NL	350	189	161	3	0	0	0	0	0	1	1	0	0	0	0	167	115	57	11	1	6	3	46	14	126	1	1	0	0	278	61

NL

25 Buck Freeman
12 Rhoderick Wallace
9 Ed Delahanty
9 Sam Mertes
9 Jimmy Williams

1900

NL

Tm	Tot	H	A	2	3	4	3	4	5	5	6	7	8	9	10	0	1	2	3	PH	LO	XN	IP	P	1	10	20	30	40	RHP	LHP
BOS	48	40	8	0	0	0	0	0	0	0	0	0	0	0	0	26	14	8	0	2	0	2	4	1	12	1	0	0	0	42	6
BRO	26	15	11	0	0	0	0	0	0	0	0	0	0	0	0	7	11	7	1	0	0	0	11	1	9	0	0	0	0	21	5
CHI	33	12	21	1	0	0	0	0	0	0	0	0	0	0	0	22	7	4	0	0	3	0	1	2	9	0	0	0	0	25	8
CIN	33	12	21	0	0	0	0	0	0	0	0	0	0	0	0	18	12	3	0	0	1	1	19	5	14	0	0	0	0	30	3
NY	23	13	10	0	0	0	0	0	0	0	0	0	0	0	0	11	12	0	0	0	1	0	0	1	9	0	0	0	0	21	2
PHI	29	13	16	0	0	0	0	0	0	0	0	0	0	0	0	11	11	7	0	0	0	0	2	1	7	1	0	0	0	25	4
PIT	26	14	12	0	0	0	0	0	0	0	0	0	0	0	0	13	6	7	0	0	1	0	9	2	11	0	0	0	0	19	7
STL	36	23	13	1	0	0	0	0	0	0	0	0	0	0	0	17	14	5	0	1	0	0	10	2	11	1	0	0	0	30	6
NL	254	142	112	2	0	0	0	0	0	0	0	0	0	0	0	125	87	41	1	3	6	3	56	15	82	3	0	0	0	213	41

NL

12 Herman Long
11 Elmer Flick
10 Mike Donlin
9 Charlie Hickman
8 Billy Sullivan

1901

AL

Tm	Tot	H	A	2	3	4	3	4	5	5	6	7	8	9	10	0	1	2	3	PH	LO	XN	IP	P	1	10	20	30	40	RHP	LHP
BAL	24	10	14	1	0	0	0	0	0	0	0	0	0	0	0	12	5	6	1	0	0	0	2	1	9	0	0	0	0	23	1
BOS	37	21	16	0	0	0	0	0	0	0	0	0	0	0	0	11	15	11	0	0	0	0	3	1	7	1	0	0	0	27	10
CHI	32	14	18	0	0	0	0	0	0	0	0	0	0	0	0	15	9	6	2	0	0	1	5	6	14	0	0	0	0	21	11
CLE	12	0	12	0	0	0	0	0	0	0	0	0	0	0	0	8	1	3	0	0	0	1	1	2	7	0	0	0	0	8	4
DET	29	15	14	2	0	0	0	0	0	0	0	0	0	0	0	15	8	4	2	0	0	0	6	1	12	0	0	0	0	23	6
MIL	26	15	11	0	0	0	0	0	0	0	0	0	0	0	0	12	10	4	0	0	0	0	3	1	8	0	0	0	0	22	4
PHI	35	15	20	0	0	0	0	0	0	0	0	0	0	0	0	15	15	3	2	0	0	0	2	1	6	1	0	0	0	28	7
WAS	33	17	16	0	0	0	1	0	0	0	0	0	0	0	0	16	14	3	0	0	0	1	2	1	9	0	0	0	0	18	15

NL

Tm	Tot	H	A	2	3	4	3	4	5	5	6	7	8	9	10	0	1	2	3	PH	LO	XN	IP	P	1	10	20	30	40	RHP	LHP
BOS	28	17	11	0	0	0	0	0	0	0	0	0	0	0	0	17	8	3	0	0	0	1	6	5	13	0	0	0	0	21	7
BRO	32	13	19	0	0	0	0	0	0	0	0	0	0	0	0	15	11	3	3	0	0	0	12	3	9	1	0	0	0	27	5
CHI	18	6	12	0	0	0	0	0	0	0	0	0	0	0	0	9	7	2	0	0	0	0	4	2	6	0	0	0	0	16	2
CIN	38	23	15	2	0	0	0	0	0	0	0	0	0	0	0	22	12	4	0	0	0	2	29	0	10	1	0	0	0	35	3
NY	19	8	11	0	0	0	0	0	0	0	0	0	0	0	0	8	8	2	1	0	0	0	4	1	8	0	0	0	0	17	2
PHI	24	11	13	0	0	0	0	0	0	0	0	0	0	0	0	13	4	7	0	0	1	1	4	2	10	0	0	0	0	20	4
PIT	29	15	14	0	0	0	0	0	0	0	0	0	0	0	0	11	12	5	1	0	1	0	17	4	10	0	0	0	0	22	7

				Consec			1-Inn			One-Game						Men-On-Base				Batters					Totals					Pitchers	
Tm	**Tot**	**H**	**A**	**2**	**3**	**4**	**3**	**4**	**5**	**5**	**6**	**7**	**8**	**9**	**10**	**0**	**1**	**2**	**3**	**PH**	**LO**	**XN**	**IP**	**P**	**1**	**10**	**20**	**30**	**40**	**RHP**	**LHP**
STL	39	21	18	0	0	0	0	0	0	0	0	0	0	0	0	21	15	3	0	0	3	1	18	5	14	1	0	0	0	32	7
AL	228	107	121	3	0	0	1	0	0	0	0	0	0	0	0	104	77	40	7	0	0	3	24	14	72	2	0	0	0	170	58
NL	227	114	113	2	0	0	0	0	0	0	0	0	0	0	0	116	77	29	5	0	5	5	94	22	80	3	0	0	0	190	37
YR	455	221	234	5	0	0	1	0	0	0	0	0	0	0	0	220	154	69	12	0	5	8	118	36	152	5	0	0	0	360	95

	AL		*NL*
14	Nap Lajoie	16	Sam Crawford
12	Buck Freeman	11	Jimmy Sheckard
9	Mike Grady	10	Jesse Burkett
8	Multiple Players Tied	8	Multiple Players Tied

1902

AL																															
BAL	33	16	17	0	0	0	0	0	0	0	0	0	0	0	0	11	15	5	2	0	0	0	7	1	13	0	0	0	0	29	4
BOS	42	21	21	1	0	0	0	0	0	0	0	0	0	0	0	19	16	6	1	0	0	0	10	1	8	1	0	0	0	31	11
CHI	14	5	9	0	0	0	0	0	0	0	0	0	0	0	0	5	4	5	0	0	0	1	1	0	7	0	0	0	0	10	4
CLE	33	15	18	1	1	0	1	0	0	0	0	0	0	0	0	16	11	5	1	0	1	1	1	1	6	1	0	0	0	24	9
DET	22	13	9	0	0	0	0	0	0	0	0	0	0	0	0	12	3	5	2	0	0	1	3	1	12	0	0	0	0	13	9
PHI	38	19	19	0	0	0	0	0	0	0	0	0	0	0	0	15	12	9	2	0	1	1	6	1	9	1	0	0	0	33	5
STL	29	16	13	0	0	0	0	0	0	0	0	0	0	0	0	12	12	4	1	0	1	0	12	1	11	0	0	0	0	22	7
WAS	47	35	12	0	0	0	1	0	0	0	0	0	0	0	0	18	17	12	0	0	2	0	5	1	10	1	0	0	0	37	10
NL																															
BOS	14	13	1	0	0	0	0	0	0	0	0	0	0	0	0	8	5	1	0	0	1	1	0	1	9	0	0	0	0	13	0
BRO	19	9	10	0	0	0	0	0	0	0	0	0	0	0	0	13	3	3	0	0	1	0	6	3	9	0	0	0	0	19	0
CHI	6	1	5	0	0	0	0	0	0	0	0	0	0	0	0	2	2	1	1	0	0	1	1	0	4	0	0	0	0	5	1
CIN	18	11	7	0	0	0	0	0	0	0	0	0	0	0	0	6	8	4	0	0	2	0	14	0	10	0	0	0	0	17	1
NY	6	5	1	0	0	0	0	0	0	0	0	0	0	0	0	4	1	1	0	0	0	0	1	2	3	0	0	0	0	5	0
PHI	5	1	4	0	0	0	0	0	0	0	0	0	0	0	0	2	1	2	0	1	0	0	2	0	3	0	0	0	0	4	1
PIT	18	9	9	0	0	0	0	0	0	0	0	0	0	0	0	8	7	2	1	0	0	1	13	3	9	0	0	0	0	12	6
STL	10	3	7	0	0	0	0	0	0	0	0	0	0	0	0	3	5	1	1	1	0	1	7	1	5	0	0	0	0	9	1
AL	258	140	118	2	1	0	2	0	0	0	0	0	0	0	0	108	90	51	9	0	5	4	45	7	76	4	0	0	0	199	59
NL	96	52	44	0	0	0	0	0	0	0	0	0	0	0	0	46	32	15	3	2	4	4	44	10	52	0	0	0	0	84	10
YR	354	192	162	2	1	0	2	0	0	0	0	0	0	0	0	154	122	66	12	2	9	8	89	17	128	4	0	0	0	283	69

	AL		*NL*
16	Socks Seybold	6	Tommy Leach
11	Bill Bradley	5	Jake Beckley
11	Buck Freeman	4	Tom McCreery
11	Charlie Hickman	4	Jimmy Sheckard
10	Ed Delahanty	3	Multiple Players Tied

1903

AL																															
BOS	48	35	13	0	0	0	0	0	0	0	0	0	0	0	0	17	24	6	1	0	1	1	10	2	11	1	0	0	0	27	21
CHI	14	5	9	0	0	0	0	0	0	0	0	0	0	0	0	10	2	2	0	0	0	1	2	0	6	0	0	0	0	10	4
CLE	31	12	19	0	0	0	0	0	0	0	0	0	0	0	0	15	14	2	0	0	1	1	3	0	7	1	0	0	0	22	9
DET	12	5	7	0	0	0	0	0	0	0	0	0	0	0	0	3	6	3	0	0	0	0	4	1	7	0	0	0	0	11	1
NY	18	10	8	0	0	0	0	0	0	0	0	0	0	0	0	8	9	1	0	0	0	0	2	4	9	0	0	0	0	15	3
PHI	32	17	15	0	0	0	0	0	0	0	0	0	0	0	0	18	8	6	0	0	1	1	5	1	10	0	0	0	0	26	6
STL	12	7	5	0	0	0	0	0	0	0	0	0	0	0	0	6	4	2	0	0	1	1	6	0	7	0	0	0	0	8	4
WAS	17	15	2	0	0	0	0	0	0	0	0	0	0	0	0	10	5	2	0	0	0	0	1	0	8	0	0	0	0	14	3
NL																															
BOS	25	11	14	0	0	0	0	0	0	0	0	0	0	0	0	10	8	3	4	1	0	0	2	1	11	0	0	0	0	22	3
BRO	15	8	7	0	0	0	0	0	0	0	0	0	0	0	0	4	5	5	1	0	0	0	4	1	6	0	0	0	0	14	1
CHI	9	2	7	0	0	0	0	0	0	0	0	0	0	0	0	2	5	2	0	0	0	0	1	0	5	0	0	0	0	7	2
CIN	28	12	16	1	0	0	0	0	0	0	0	0	0	0	0	18	6	4	0	0	1	1	15	0	7	0	0	0	0	24	4
NY	20	9	11	0	0	0	0	0	0	0	0	0	0	0	0	7	6	5	2	0	1	0	4	1	7	0	0	0	0	14	5
PHI	12	9	3	0	0	0	0	0	0	0	0	0	0	0	0	4	4	4	0	0	0	1	3	1	9	0	0	0	0	11	1
PIT	34	17	17	0	0	0	0	0	0	0	0	0	0	0	0	16	12	4	2	1	0	0	20	0	9	0	0	0	0	31	3

Tm	Tot	H	A	Consec			1-Inn			One-Game						Men-On-Base				Batters					Totals					Pitchers	
				2	3	4	3	4	5	5	6	7	8	9	10	0	1	2	3	PH	LO	XN	IP	P	1	10	20	30	40	RHP	LHP
STL	8	7	1	0	0	0	0	0	0	0	0	0	0	0	0	2	4	2	0	0	0	0	3	1	5	0	0	0	0	5	2
AL	184	106	78	0	0	0	0	0	0	0	0	0	0	0	0	87	72	24	1	0	4	5	33	8	65	2	0	0	0	133	51
NL	151	75	76	1	0	0	0	0	0	0	0	0	0	0	0	63	50	29	9	2	2	2	52	5	59	0	0	0	0	128	21
YR	335	181	154	1	0	0	0	0	0	0	0	0	0	0	0	150	122	53	10	2	6	7	85	13	124	2	0	0	0	261	72

AL
13 Buck Freeman
12 Charlie Hickman
9 Hobe Ferris
8 Socks Seybold
7 Multiple Players Tied

NL
9 Jimmy Sheckard
7 Multiple Players Tied

1904

AL

Tm	Tot	H	A	Consec			1-Inn			One-Game						Men-On-Base				Batters					Totals					Pitchers	
				2	3	4	3	4	5	5	6	7	8	9	10	0	1	2	3	PH	LO	XN	IP	P	1	10	20	30	40	RHP	LHP
BOS	26	17	9	0	0	0	0	0	0	0	0	0	0	0	0	14	8	3	1	0	0	0	4	1	8	0	0	0	0	19	7
CHI	14	0	14	0	0	0	0	0	0	0	0	0	0	0	0	10	3	1	0	0	0	1	2	4	10	0	0	0	0	12	2
CLE	27	14	13	1	0	0	0	0	0	0	0	0	0	0	0	11	15	1	0	0	0	0	0	0	8	0	0	0	0	22	5
DET	11	3	8	0	0	0	0	0	0	0	0	0	0	0	0	5	4	2	0	0	0	0	3	2	8	0	0	0	0	10	1
NY	27	22	5	0	0	0	0	0	0	0	0	0	0	0	0	18	7	0	2	0	1	0	15	1	10	0	0	0	0	19	8
PHI	31	19	12	0	0	0	0	0	0	0	0	0	0	0	0	19	7	3	2	0	2	0	9	0	9	1	0	0	0	24	7
STL	10	2	8	0	0	0	0	0	0	0	0	0	0	0	0	1	7	2	0	0	0	1	6	1	6	0	0	0	0	5	5
WAS	10	3	7	0	0	0	0	0	0	0	0	0	0	0	0	7	3	0	0	0	1	0	1	2	7	0	0	0	0	10	0

NL

Tm	Tot	H	A	Consec			1-Inn			One-Game						Men-On-Base				Batters					Totals					Pitchers	
				2	3	4	3	4	5	5	6	7	8	9	10	0	1	2	3	PH	LO	XN	IP	P	1	10	20	30	40	RHP	LHP
BOS	24	13	11	0	0	0	0	0	0	0	0	0	0	0	0	14	6	4	0	0	0	0	3	2	9	0	0	0	0	20	4
BRO	15	3	12	0	0	0	0	0	0	0	0	0	0	0	0	8	5	2	0	0	0	0	5	0	5	0	0	0	0	13	2
CHI	22	6	16	0	0	0	0	0	0	0	0	0	0	0	0	12	4	4	2	0	0	0	3	1	11	0	0	0	0	18	4
CIN	21	12	9	0	0	0	0	0	0	0	0	0	0	0	0	9	8	3	1	0	0	0	13	2	10	0	0	0	0	19	2
NY	31	23	8	0	0	0	0	0	0	0	0	0	0	0	0	17	10	2	2	0	2	1	5	1	13	0	0	0	0	25	5
PHI	23	7	16	0	0	0	0	0	0	0	0	0	0	0	0	12	7	3	1	0	1	2	12	2	9	0	0	0	0	20	3
PIT	15	5	10	0	0	0	0	0	0	0	0	0	0	0	0	8	6	1	0	0	2	0	8	3	7	0	0	0	0	14	1
STL	24	14	10	1	0	0	0	0	0	0	0	0	0	0	0	17	5	1	1	0	0	1	8	1	10	0	0	0	0	20	4
AL	156	80	76	1	0	0	0	0	0	0	0	0	0	0	0	85	54	12	5	0	4	2	40	11	66	1	0	0	0	121	35
NL	175	83	92	1	0	0	0	0	0	0	0	0	0	0	0	97	51	20	7	0	5	4	57	12	74	0	0	0	0	149	25
YR	331	163	168	2	0	0	0	0	0	0	0	0	0	0	0	182	105	32	12	0	9	6	97	23	140	1	0	0	0	270	60

AL
10 Harry Davis
7 Buck Freeman
7 Danny Murphy
6 Multiple Players Tied

NL
9 Harry Lumley
7 Dave Brain
6 Multiple Players Tied

1905

AL

Tm	Tot	H	A	Consec			1-Inn			One-Game						Men-On-Base				Batters					Totals					Pitchers	
				2	3	4	3	4	5	5	6	7	8	9	10	0	1	2	3	PH	LO	XN	IP	P	1	10	20	30	40	RHP	LHP
BOS	29	21	8	0	0	0	0	0	0	0	0	0	0	0	0	13	11	5	0	0	1	0	4	3	9	0	0	0	0	23	5
CHI	11	3	8	0	0	0	0	0	0	0	0	0	0	0	0	6	4	1	0	0	0	0	3	1	8	0	0	0	0	9	2
CLE	18	5	13	0	0	0	0	0	0	0	0	0	0	0	0	13	4	1	0	0	0	0	2	2	9	0	0	0	0	13	5
DET	13	5	8	0	0	0	0	0	0	0	0	0	0	0	0	7	4	1	1	0	0	0	7	0	6	0	0	0	0	9	4
NY	23	15	8	1	0	0	0	0	0	0	0	0	0	0	0	15	2	5	1	0	0	0	17	2	10	0	0	0	0	17	6
PHI	24	12	12	1	0	0	0	0	0	0	0	0	0	0	0	11	12	1	0	0	0	1	5	0	5	0	0	0	0	21	3
STL	16	5	11	0	0	0	0	0	0	0	0	0	0	0	0	7	7	2	0	0	0	0	9	1	7	0	0	0	0	11	5
WAS	22	10	12	1	0	0	0	0	0	0	0	0	0	0	0	13	7	1	1	0	1	1	6	2	12	0	0	0	0	20	2

NL

Tm	Tot	H	A	Consec			1-Inn			One-Game						Men-On-Base				Batters					Totals					Pitchers	
				2	3	4	3	4	5	5	6	7	8	9	10	0	1	2	3	PH	LO	XN	IP	P	1	10	20	30	40	RHP	LHP
BOS	17	14	3	1	0	0	0	0	0	0	0	0	0	0	0	9	4	4	0	0	0	0	0	0	6	0	0	0	0	17	0
BRO	29	16	13	1	0	0	0	0	0	0	0	0	0	0	0	12	11	6	0	0	0	0	8	1	11	0	0	0	0	23	6
CHI	12	7	5	0	0	0	0	0	0	0	0	0	0	0	0	6	3	2	1	0	0	0	4	1	9	0	0	0	0	12	0
CIN	27	12	15	0	0	0	0	0	0	0	0	0	0	0	0	7	16	3	1	0	0	1	18	0	10	0	0	0	0	23	4
NY	39	33	6	1	0	0	0	0	0	0	0	0	0	0	0	19	14	5	1	0	1	0	4	2	10	0	0	0	0	37	2
PHI	16	8	8	0	0	0	0	0	0	0	0	0	0	0	0	10	5	1	0	0	0	1	5	2	8	0	0	0	0	12	4
PIT	22	4	18	0	0	0	0	0	0	0	0	0	0	0	0	11	7	4	0	0	0	1	8	0	8	0	0	0	0	20	2

				Consec			1-Inn			One-Game						Men-On-Base				Batters					Totals					Pitchers	
Tm	Tot	H	A	2	3	4	3	4	5	5	6	7	8	9	10	0	1	2	3	PH	LO	XN	IP	P	1	10	20	30	40	RHP	LHP
STL	20	13	7	0	0	0	0	0	0	0	0	0	0	0	0	12	7	1	0	0	0	0	7	0	10	0	0	0	0	18	2
AL	156	76	80	3	0	0	0	0	0	0	0	0	0	0	0	85	51	17	3	0	2	2	53	11	66	0	0	0	0	123	32
NL	182	107	75	3	0	0	0	0	0	0	0	0	0	0	0	86	67	26	3	0	1	3	54	6	72	0	0	0	0	162	20
YR	338	183	155	6	0	0	0	0	0	0	0	0	0	0	0	171	118	43	6	0	3	5	107	17	138	0	0	0	0	285	52

AL		*NL*	
8	Harry Davis	9	Fred Odwell
7	George Stone	8	Cy Seymour
6	Multiple Players Tied	7	Bill Dahlen
		7	Mike Donlin
		7	Harry Lumley

1906

Tm	Tot	H	A	Consec 2	3	4	1-Inn 3	4	5	One-Game 5	6	7	8	9	10	Men-On-Base 0	1	2	3	PH	LO	XN	IP	P	Totals 1	10	20	30	40	RHP	LHP
AL																															
BOS	13	10	3	0	0	0	0	0	0	0	0	0	0	0	0	8	3	2	0	0	1	0	10	0	9	0	0	0	0	11	2
CHI	7	2	5	0	0	0	0	0	0	0	0	0	0	0	0	4	2	1	0	0	0	0	1	0	5	0	0	0	0	5	2
CLE	12	3	9	0	0	0	0	0	0	0	0	0	0	0	0	6	6	0	0	0	0	1	1	0	7	0	0	0	0	9	3
DET	10	4	6	0	0	0	0	0	0	0	0	0	0	0	0	3	5	2	0	1	0	0	2	0	6	0	0	0	0	7	3
NY	17	14	3	0	0	0	0	0	0	0	0	0	0	0	0	8	6	2	1	0	0	2	10	2	8	0	0	0	0	14	3
PHI	32	21	11	0	0	0	0	0	0	0	0	0	0	0	0	16	11	5	0	0	0	1	8	2	10	1	0	0	0	22	10
STL	20	13	7	1	0	0	0	0	0	0	0	0	0	0	0	9	8	3	0	0	0	0	13	1	7	0	0	0	0	15	5
WAS	26	7	19	0	0	0	0	0	0	0	0	0	0	0	0	11	8	5	2	0	0	2	6	5	13	0	0	0	0	22	4
NL																															
BOS	16	11	5	0	0	0	0	0	0	0	0	0	0	0	0	8	5	2	1	0	0	1	2	1	7	0	0	0	0	15	1
BRO	25	11	14	0	0	0	0	0	0	0	0	0	0	0	0	14	5	6	0	0	2	0	6	0	3	1	0	0	0	17	8
CHI	20	7	13	0	0	0	0	0	0	0	0	0	0	0	0	10	8	2	0	0	0	0	8	0	8	0	0	0	0	10	8
CIN	16	10	6	0	0	0	0	0	0	0	0	0	0	0	0	9	6	1	0	0	0	1	11	1	10	0	0	0	0	15	1
NY	15	9	6	0	0	0	0	0	0	0	0	0	0	0	0	11	2	1	1	0	0	1	3	0	8	0	0	0	0	11	4
PHI	12	2	10	0	0	0	0	0	0	0	0	0	0	0	0	5	5	1	1	0	0	0	6	2	6	0	0	0	0	11	1
PIT	12	4	8	0	0	0	0	0	0	0	0	0	0	0	0	4	5	2	1	0	0	0	9	0	8	0	0	0	0	9	3
STL	10	6	4	0	0	0	0	0	0	0	0	0	0	0	0	7	3	0	0	0	0	0	3	2	7	0	0	0	0	7	3
AL	137	74	63	1	0	0	0	0	0	0	0	0	0	0	0	65	49	20	3	1	1	6	51	10	65	1	0	0	0	105	32
NL	126	60	66	0	0	0	0	0	0	0	0	0	0	0	0	68	39	15	4	0	2	3	48	6	57	1	0	0	0	95	29
YR	263	134	129	1	0	0	0	0	0	0	0	0	0	0	0	133	88	35	7	1	3	9	99	16	122	2	0	0	0	200	61

AL		*NL*	
12	Harry Davis	12	Tim Jordan
9	Charlie Hickman	9	Harry Lumley
6	George Stone	8	Cy Seymour
5	Socks Seybold	7	Frank Schulte
4	Multiple Players Tied	6	Multiple Players Tied

1907

Tm	Tot	H	A	Consec 2	3	4	1-Inn 3	4	5	One-Game 5	6	7	8	9	10	Men-On-Base 0	1	2	3	PH	LO	XN	IP	P	Totals 1	10	20	30	40	RHP	LHP
AL																															
BOS	18	12	6	0	0	0	0	0	0	0	0	0	0	0	0	10	5	3	0	1	1	2	5	2	12	0	0	0	0	13	5
CHI	5	0	5	0	0	0	0	0	0	0	0	0	0	0	0	1	3	1	0	0	0	0	1	1	4	0	0	0	0	2	3
CLE	11	6	5	0	0	0	0	0	0	0	0	0	0	0	0	7	3	0	1	0	2	0	0	0	6	0	0	0	0	9	2
DET	11	3	8	0	0	0	0	0	0	0	0	0	0	0	0	7	4	0	0	0	0	0	4	0	4	0	0	0	0	8	3
NY	15	10	5	0	0	0	0	0	0	0	0	0	0	0	0	9	4	2	0	0	0	0	11	2	7	0	0	0	0	10	5
PHI	22	14	8	0	0	0	0	0	0	0	0	0	0	0	0	12	5	5	0	0	2	0	2	2	8	0	0	0	0	17	5
STL	10	6	4	0	0	0	0	0	0	0	0	0	0	0	0	4	2	4	0	0	0	0	6	2	5	0	0	0	0	7	3
WAS	12	2	10	0	0	0	0	0	0	0	0	0	0	0	0	5	5	2	0	0	1	0	2	3	10	0	0	0	0	8	4
NL																															
BOS	22	14	8	0	0	0	0	0	0	0	0	0	0	0	0	14	7	0	1	0	0	0	0	1	6	1	0	0	0	14	8
BRO	18	9	9	1	0	0	0	0	0	0	0	0	0	0	0	8	3	7	0	0	0	1	6	0	4	0	0	0	0	14	4
CHI	13	2	11	0	0	0	0	0	0	0	0	0	0	0	0	7	2	4	0	0	0	2	5	2	11	0	0	0	0	13	0
CIN	15	3	12	1	0	0	0	0	0	0	0	0	0	0	0	12	3	0	0	0	2	0	10	2	10	0	0	0	0	14	1
NY	23	19	4	0	0	0	0	0	0	0	0	0	0	0	0	9	12	2	0	1	0	0	5	1	10	0	0	0	0	20	3
PHI	12	2	10	0	0	0	0	0	0	0	0	0	0	0	0	3	8	1	0	0	0	1	9	0	6	0	0	0	0	9	3

Tm	Tot	H	A	Consec			1-Inn			One-Game						Men-On-Base				Batters					Totals					Pitchers	
				2	3	4	3	4	5	5	6	7	8	9	10	0	1	2	3	PH	LO	XN	IP	P	1	10	20	30	40	RHP	LHP
PIT	19	7	12	0	0	0	0	0	0	0	0	0	0	0	0	8	8	2	1	0	0	0	9	0	7	0	0	0	0	11	8
STL	18	8	10	0	0	0	0	0	0	0	0	0	0	0	0	10	7	1	0	0	0	0	8	2	8	0	0	0	0	12	6
AL	104	53	51	0	0	0	0	0	0	0	0	0	0	0	0	55	31	17	1	1	6	2	31	12	56	0	0	0	0	74	30
NL	140	64	76	2	0	0	0	0	0	0	0	0	0	0	0	71	50	17	2	1	2	4	52	8	62	1	0	0	0	107	33
YR	244	117	127	2	0	0	0	0	0	0	0	0	0	0	0	126	81	34	3	2	8	6	83	20	118	1	0	0	0	181	63

	AL		*NL*
8	Harry Davis	10	Dave Brain
5	Ty Cobb	9	Harry Lumley
5	Danny Hoffman	7	Red Murray
5	Socks Seybold	6	Honus Wagner
4	Multiple Players Tied	5	George Browne

1908

Tm	Tot	H	A	2	3	4	3	4	5	5	6	7	8	9	10	0	1	2	3	PH	LO	XN	IP	P	1	10	20	30	40	RHP	LHP
AL																															
BOS	14	9	5	0	0	0	0	0	0	0	0	0	0	0	0	6	6	2	0	0	0	0	5	0	9	0	0	0	0	10	4
CHI	3	1	2	0	0	0	0	0	0	0	0	0	0	0	0	0	3	0	0	0	0	0	1	1	3	0	0	0	0	3	0
CLE	18	8	10	0	0	0	0	0	0	0	0	0	0	0	0	4	8	6	0	0	0	0	5	0	9	0	0	0	0	16	2
DET	19	6	13	0	0	0	0	0	0	0	0	0	0	0	0	9	9	0	1	0	0	4	9	1	7	0	0	0	0	14	5
NY	13	11	2	0	0	0	0	0	0	0	0	0	0	0	0	8	4	1	0	0	0	0	9	1	9	0	0	0	0	10	3
PHI	21	11	10	0	0	0	0	0	0	0	0	0	0	0	0	13	3	3	2	0	1	0	2	1	8	0	0	0	0	17	4
STL	20	12	8	0	0	0	0	0	0	0	0	0	0	0	0	15	3	1	1	0	2	0	6	2	11	0	0	0	0	20	0
WAS	8	2	6	0	0	0	0	0	0	0	0	0	0	0	0	4	2	2	0	0	0	0	2	0	7	0	0	0	0	8	0
NL																															
BOS	17	13	4	1	0	0	0	0	0	0	0	0	0	0	0	11	5	1	0	1	0	1	1	0	10	0	0	0	0	14	3
BRO	28	16	12	0	0	0	0	0	0	0	0	0	0	0	0	21	6	1	0	1	0	1	6	0	7	1	0	0	0	21	7
CHI	19	9	10	0	0	0	0	0	0	0	0	0	0	0	0	10	7	0	2	0	0	1	2	0	8	0	0	0	0	14	5
CIN	14	9	5	0	0	0	0	0	0	0	0	0	0	0	0	11	1	1	1	1	0	1	12	0	9	0	0	0	0	10	4
NY	20	10	10	0	0	0	0	0	0	0	0	0	0	0	0	11	3	6	0	1	0	0	7	2	8	0	0	0	0	14	6
PHI	11	0	11	2	0	0	0	0	0	0	0	0	0	0	0	6	4	0	1	0	0	0	6	0	5	0	0	0	0	7	4
PIT	25	12	13	1	0	0	0	0	0	0	0	0	0	0	0	15	9	1	0	0	0	1	12	0	7	1	0	0	0	17	8
STL	17	9	8	0	0	0	0	0	0	0	0	0	0	0	0	11	4	2	0	0	0	0	9	0	7	0	0	0	0	14	3
AL	116	60	56	0	0	0	0	0	0	0	0	0	0	0	0	59	38	15	4	0	3	4	39	6	63	0	0	0	0	98	18
NL	151	78	73	4	0	0	0	0	0	0	0	0	0	0	0	96	39	12	4	4	0	5	55	2	61	2	0	0	0	111	40
YR	267	138	129	4	0	0	0	0	0	0	0	0	0	0	0	155	77	27	8	4	3	9	94	8	124	2	0	0	0	209	58

	AL		*NL*
7	Sam Crawford	12	Tim Jordan
6	Bill Hinchman	10	Honus Wagner
5	Harry Davis	7	Red Murray
5	Harry Niles	6	Mike Donlin
5	George Stone	6	Joe Tinker

1909

Tm	Tot	H	A	2	3	4	3	4	5	5	6	7	8	9	10	0	1	2	3	PH	LO	XN	IP	P	1	10	20	30	40	RHP	LHP
AL																															
BOS	20	18	2	0	0	0	0	0	0	0	0	0	0	0	0	6	9	5	0	0	0	0	9	0	7	0	0	0	0	9	11
CHI	4	1	3	0	0	0	0	0	0	0	0	0	0	0	0	3	0	1	0	0	1	0	0	0	4	0	0	0	0	3	1
CLE	10	2	8	0	0	0	0	0	0	0	0	0	0	0	0	2	5	3	0	0	0	0	0	1	8	0	0	0	0	10	0
DET	19	12	7	1	0	0	0	0	0	0	0	0	0	0	0	5	8	6	0	0	0	0	13	0	6	0	0	0	0	11	8
NY	16	11	5	0	0	0	0	0	0	0	0	0	0	0	0	7	8	1	0	0	0	0	5	1	7	0	0	0	0	15	1
PHI	21	9	12	0	0	0	0	0	0	0	0	0	0	0	0	11	7	2	1	0	0	0	9	1	9	0	0	0	0	19	2
STL	10	4	6	0	0	0	0	0	0	0	0	0	0	0	0	5	4	1	0	0	1	0	5	0	4	0	0	0	0	9	1
WAS	9	5	4	0	0	0	0	0	0	0	0	0	0	0	0	8	1	0	0	0	0	0	5	1	7	0	0	0	0	7	2
NL																															
BOS	14	10	4	0	0	0	0	0	0	0	0	0	0	0	0	6	6	1	1	0	1	0	0	1	7	0	0	0	0	8	6
BRO	16	12	4	1	0	0	0	0	0	0	0	0	0	0	0	8	6	2	0	0	0	0	6	0	8	0	0	0	0	11	5
CHI	20	8	12	0	0	0	0	0	0	0	0	0	0	0	0	11	7	2	0	0	0	1	6	2	11	0	0	0	0	16	4
CIN	22	5	17	1	0	0	0	0	0	0	0	0	0	0	0	14	5	3	0	0	1	0	18	0	9	0	0	0	0	19	3
NY	26	19	7	1	0	0	0	0	0	0	0	0	0	0	0	13	8	4	1	0	2	0	9	3	11	0	0	0	0	18	8

				Consec			1-Inn			One-Game						Men-On-Base				Batters					Totals					Pitchers	
Tm	Tot	H	A	2	3	4	3	4	5	5	6	7	8	9	10	0	1	2	3	PH	LO	XN	IP	P	1	10	20	30	40	RHP	LHP
PHI	12	6	6	0	0	0	0	0	0	0	0	0	0	0	0	6	5	1	0	0	0	0	5	1	8	0	0	0	0	11	1
PIT	25	10	15	0	0	0	0	0	0	0	0	0	0	0	0	15	6	3	1	0	0	0	12	0	8	0	0	0	0	20	5
STL	15	9	6	0	0	0	0	0	0	0	0	0	0	0	0	5	6	3	1	0	0	1	3	0	7	0	0	0	0	11	4
AL	109	62	47	1	0	0	0	0	0	0	0	0	0	0	0	47	42	19	1	0	2	0	46	4	52	0	0	0	0	83	26
NL	150	79	71	3	0	0	0	0	0	0	0	0	0	0	0	78	49	19	4	0	4	2	59	7	69	0	0	0	0	114	36
YR	259	141	118	4	0	0	0	0	0	0	0	0	0	0	0	125	91	38	5	0	6	2	105	11	121	0	0	0	0	197	62

	AL		*NL*
9	Ty Cobb	7	Red Murray
7	Tris Speaker	6	Beals Becker
6	Sam Crawford	6	Larry Doyle
6	Jake Stahl	6	Tommy Leach
5	Danny Murphy	5	Honus Wagner

1910

Tm	Tot	H	A	2	3	4	3	4	5	5	6	7	8	9	10	0	1	2	3	PH	LO	XN	IP	P	1	10	20	30	40	RHP	LHP
AL																															
BOS	43	32	11	1	0	0	0	0	0	0	0	0	0	0	0	18	20	4	1	0	1	0	14	4	14	1	0	0	0	31	12
CHI	7	2	5	0	0	0	0	0	0	0	0	0	0	0	0	0	6	0	1	0	0	0	1	0	6	0	0	0	0	5	2
CLE	9	4	5	0	0	0	0	0	0	0	0	0	0	0	0	2	6	1	0	0	0	0	3	0	6	0	0	0	0	8	1
DET	28	18	10	0	0	0	0	0	0	0	0	0	0	0	0	12	9	6	1	0	0	1	11	3	10	0	0	0	0	16	11
NY	20	13	7	1	0	0	0	0	0	0	0	0	0	0	0	9	6	5	0	0	1	0	9	0	8	0	0	0	0	17	3
PHI	19	9	10	0	0	0	0	0	0	0	0	0	0	0	0	16	1	2	0	0	0	1	8	0	8	0	0	0	0	18	1
STL	12	4	8	0	0	0	0	0	0	0	0	0	0	0	0	7	2	3	0	0	0	0	1	2	8	0	0	0	0	8	4
WAS	9	2	7	0	0	0	0	0	0	0	0	0	0	0	0	4	3	1	1	0	0	0	4	2	6	0	0	0	0	8	1
NL																															
BOS	31	25	6	0	0	0	0	0	0	0	0	0	0	0	0	20	6	3	2	0	0	1	0	2	9	1	0	0	0	27	4
BRO	25	9	16	0	0	0	0	0	0	0	0	0	0	0	0	16	5	4	0	1	0	2	13	0	11	0	0	0	0	16	9
CHI	34	18	16	1	0	0	0	0	0	0	0	0	0	0	0	18	12	4	0	0	1	0	7	1	10	1	0	0	0	25	9
CIN	23	6	17	2	0	0	0	0	0	0	0	0	0	0	0	12	6	4	1	1	2	0	13	0	8	0	0	0	0	21	2
NY	31	20	11	0	0	0	0	0	0	0	0	0	0	0	0	17	8	4	2	2	0	0	4	4	13	0	0	0	0	23	8
PHI	22	12	10	0	0	0	0	0	0	0	0	0	0	0	0	8	7	6	1	0	1	0	0	0	8	0	0	0	0	16	6
PIT	33	17	16	0	0	0	1	0	0	0	0	0	0	0	0	17	8	5	3	0	0	0	15	2	12	0	0	0	0	28	5
STL	15	3	12	0	0	0	0	0	0	0	0	0	0	0	0	9	6	0	0	0	0	0	5	1	7	0	0	0	0	14	1
AL	147	84	63	2	0	0	0	0	0	0	0	0	0	0	0	68	53	22	4	0	2	2	51	11	66	1	0	0	0	111	35
NL	214	110	104	3	0	0	1	0	0	0	0	0	0	0	0	117	58	30	9	4	4	3	57	10	78	2	0	0	0	170	44
YR	361	194	167	5	0	0	1	0	0	0	0	0	0	0	0	185	111	52	13	4	6	5	108	21	144	3	0	0	0	281	79

	AL		*NL*
10	Jake Stahl	10	Fred Beck
8	Ty Cobb	10	Frank Schulte
8	Duffy Lewis	8	Jake Daubert
7	Tris Speaker	8	Larry Doyle
5	Sam Crawford	6	Multiple Players Tied

1911

Tm	Tot	H	A	2	3	4	3	4	5	5	6	7	8	9	10	0	1	2	3	PH	LO	XN	IP	P	1	10	20	30	40	RHP	LHP
AL																															
BOS	35	20	15	0	0	0	0	0	0	0	0	0	0	0	0	18	11	6	0	0	0	0	9	4	13	0	0	0	0	29	6
CHI	20	8	12	0	0	0	0	0	0	0	0	0	0	0	0	10	6	4	0	1	0	0	5	0	9	0	0	0	0	19	1
CLE	20	7	13	0	0	0	0	0	0	0	0	0	0	0	0	10	6	2	2	1	0	1	5	0	10	0	0	0	0	17	3
DET	30	21	9	0	0	0	0	0	0	0	0	0	0	0	0	15	10	4	1	0	0	0	11	3	12	0	0	0	0	14	16
NY	25	14	11	0	0	0	0	0	0	0	0	0	0	0	0	15	8	1	1	0	1	0	6	2	10	0	0	0	0	19	6
PHI	35	11	24	0	0	0	0	0	0	0	0	0	0	0	0	20	9	5	1	0	0	2	9	2	10	1	0	0	0	31	4
STL	17	9	8	0	0	0	0	0	0	0	0	0	0	0	0	10	5	1	1	0	0	1	3	0	7	0	0	0	0	14	3
WAS	16	11	5	1	0	0	0	0	0	0	0	0	0	0	0	9	3	3	1	0	1	0	8	2	7	0	0	0	0	13	3
NL																															
BOS	37	28	9	0	0	0	0	0	0	0	0	0	0	0	0	18	13	5	1	0	2	1	2	2	16	0	0	0	0	28	9
BRO	28	10	18	2	0	0	1	0	0	0	0	0	0	0	0	14	7	6	1	0	0	2	12	1	8	0	0	0	0	27	1
CHI	54	26	28	0	0	0	0	0	0	0	0	0	0	0	0	21	18	9	6	0	0	3	4	0	10	0	1	0	0	39	15
CIN	21	5	16	0	0	0	0	0	0	0	0	0	0	0	0	10	6	1	4	0	0	0	7	0	8	1	0	0	0	18	3
NY	41	25	16	1	0	0	0	0	0	0	0	0	0	0	0	24	13	4	0	1	2	0	5	3	11	2	0	0	0	33	8
PHI	60	48	12	1	0	0	0	0	0	0	0	0	0	0	0	33	23	3	1	0	0	2	3	0	9	2	0	0	0	46	14

				Consec			1-Inn			One-Game						Men-On-Base				Batters					Totals					Pitchers	
Tm	Tot	H	A	2	3	4	3	4	5	5	6	7	8	9	10	0	1	2	3	PH	LO	XN	IP	P	1	10	20	30	40	RHP	LHP
PIT	49	29	20	1	0	0	0	0	0	0	0	0	0	0	0	25	14	8	2	0	0	0	26	1	10	1	0	0	0	42	7
STL	26	11	15	0	0	0	0	0	0	0	0	0	0	0	0	7	12	7	0	0	0	0	6	0	10	0	0	0	0	19	7
AL	198	101	97	1	0	0	0	0	0	0	0	0	0	0	0	107	58	26	7	2	2	4	56	13	78	1	0	0	0	156	42
NL	316	182	134	5	0	0	1	0	0	0	0	0	0	0	0	152	106	43	15	1	4	8	65	7	82	6	1	0	0	252	64
YR	514	283	231	6	0	0	1	0	0	0	0	0	0	0	0	259	164	69	22	3	6	12	121	20	160	7	1	0	0	408	106

AL
11 Frank Baker
8 Ty Cobb
8 Tris Speaker
7 Multiple Players Tied

NL
21 Frank Schulte
16 Fred Luderus
15 Sherry Magee
13 Larry Doyle
12 Multiple Players Tied

1912

				Consec			1-Inn			One-Game						Men-On-Base				Batters					Totals					Pitchers	
Tm	Tot	H	A	2	3	4	3	4	5	5	6	7	8	9	10	0	1	2	3	PH	LO	XN	IP	P	1	10	20	30	40	RHP	LHP
AL																															
BOS	29	10	19	0	0	0	0	0	0	0	0	0	0	0	0	16	5	6	2	0	0	1	16	2	8	1	0	0	0	25	4
CHI	17	11	6	0	0	0	0	0	0	0	0	0	0	0	0	7	9	1	0	0	0	0	3	0	8	0	0	0	0	16	1
CLE	12	4	8	0	0	0	0	0	0	0	0	0	0	0	0	5	5	1	1	0	0	0	3	1	9	0	0	0	0	12	0
DET	19	8	11	0	0	0	0	0	0	0	0	0	0	0	0	5	11	2	1	0	0	0	6	4	8	0	0	0	0	13	6
NY	18	14	4	0	0	0	0	0	0	0	0	0	0	0	0	8	4	6	0	0	1	1	5	1	8	0	0	0	0	15	3
PHI	22	11	11	0	0	0	0	0	0	0	0	0	0	0	0	11	8	3	0	0	0	0	3	0	7	1	0	0	0	16	6
STL	19	6	13	0	0	0	0	0	0	0	0	0	0	0	0	9	6	4	0	0	1	0	8	1	11	0	0	0	0	17	2
WAS	20	13	7	0	0	0	0	0	0	0	0	0	0	0	0	13	3	4	0	0	1	0	9	3	11	0	0	0	0	19	1
NL																															
BOS	35	22	13	0	0	0	0	0	0	0	0	0	0	0	0	18	12	5	0	1	2	0	0	0	12	0	0	0	0	28	7
BRO	32	17	15	1	0	0	0	0	0	0	0	0	0	0	0	17	12	3	0	1	1	0	9	1	12	0	0	0	0	26	6
CHI	42	24	18	1	0	0	0	0	0	0	0	0	0	0	0	24	16	2	0	0	0	3	6	1	8	2	0	0	0	28	14
CIN	21	7	14	0	0	0	0	0	0	0	0	0	0	0	0	9	7	5	0	0	2	0	11	1	11	0	0	0	0	17	4
NY	47	31	16	0	0	0	0	0	0	0	0	0	0	0	0	28	9	8	2	0	0	1	1	0	8	2	0	0	0	38	9
PHI	43	25	18	1	0	0	0	0	0	0	0	0	0	0	0	18	15	9	1	1	0	1	3	3	11	2	0	0	0	37	6
PIT	39	14	25	0	0	0	0	0	0	0	0	0	0	0	0	18	15	4	2	0	1	1	10	1	11	1	0	0	0	25	14
STL	27	14	13	0	0	0	0	0	0	0	0	0	0	0	0	14	8	4	1	0	0	0	9	0	8	0	0	0	0	19	8
AL	156	77	79	0	0	0	0	0	0	0	0	0	0	0	0	74	51	27	4	0	3	2	53	12	70	2	0	0	0	133	23
NL	286	154	132	3	0	0	0	0	0	0	0	0	0	0	0	146	94	40	6	3	6	6	49	7	81	7	0	0	0	218	68
YR	442	231	211	3	0	0	0	0	0	0	0	0	0	0	0	220	145	67	10	3	9	8	102	19	151	9	0	0	0	351	91

AL
10 Frank Baker
10 Tris Speaker
7 Ty Cobb
6 Multiple Players Tied

NL
14 Heinie Zimmerman
12 Frank Schulte
11 Gavvy Cravath
11 Fred Merkle
11 Chief Wilson

1913

				Consec			1-Inn			One-Game						Men-On-Base				Batters					Totals					Pitchers	
Tm	Tot	H	A	2	3	4	3	4	5	5	6	7	8	9	10	0	1	2	3	PH	LO	XN	IP	P	1	10	20	30	40	RHP	LHP
AL																															
BOS	17	3	14	0	0	0	0	0	0	0	0	0	0	0	0	11	4	2	0	0	3	0	6	1	8	0	0	0	0	14	3
CHI	24	5	19	0	0	0	0	0	0	0	0	0	0	0	0	17	7	0	0	0	0	0	5	1	11	0	0	0	0	18	6
CLE	16	4	12	0	0	0	0	0	0	0	0	0	0	0	0	9	3	3	1	0	1	0	4	0	5	0	0	0	0	11	5
DET	24	9	15	0	0	0	0	0	0	0	0	0	0	0	0	10	8	4	2	0	0	0	10	4	10	0	0	0	0	16	8
NY	8	5	3	0	0	0	0	0	0	0	0	0	0	0	0	4	2	0	2	0	0	0	2	0	6	0	0	0	0	6	2
PHI	33	19	14	0	0	0	0	0	0	0	0	0	0	0	0	21	9	3	0	0	0	0	3	1	8	1	0	0	0	25	8
STL	18	13	5	0	0	0	0	0	0	0	0	0	0	0	0	10	5	3	0	1	0	0	2	0	9	0	0	0	0	16	2
WAS	19	9	10	0	0	0	0	0	0	0	0	0	0	0	0	10	4	5	0	1	2	0	8	2	11	0	0	0	0	14	5
NL																															
BOS	32	14	18	0	0	0	0	0	0	0	0	0	0	0	0	10	12	8	2	0	0	0	3	2	12	0	0	0	0	24	8
BRO	39	20	19	0	0	0	0	0	0	0	0	0	0	0	0	18	14	7	0	0	1	1	22	1	11	0	0	0	0	28	11
CHI	59	37	22	1	0	0	0	0	0	0	0	0	0	0	0	25	20	12	2	3	0	0	17	0	13	1	0	0	0	41	18
CIN	27	15	12	0	0	0	0	0	0	0	0	0	0	0	0	8	19	0	0	2	0	0	18	1	11	0	0	0	0	20	7
NY	30	22	8	0	0	0	0	0	0	0	0	0	0	0	0	14	10	5	1	0	0	0	1	0	10	0	0	0	0	24	6
PHI	73	51	22	0	0	0	0	0	0	0	0	0	0	0	0	35	27	11	0	3	1	2	7	1	7	3	0	0	0	64	9
PIT	35	13	22	0	0	0	0	0	0	0	0	0	0	0	0	17	14	4	0	3	1	1	7	1	9	1	0	0	0	28	7

Tm	Tot	H	A	Consec 2	3	4	1-Inn 3	4	5	One-Game 5	6	7	8	9	10	Men-On-Base 0	1	2	3	Batters PH	LO	XN	IP	P	Totals 1	10	20	30	40	Pitchers RHP	LHP
STL	15	8	7	0	0	0	0	0	0	0	0	0	0	0	0	9	4	1	1	0	0	0	7	2	5	0	0	0	0	11	4
AL	159	67	92	0	0	0	0	0	0	0	0	0	0	0	0	92	42	20	5	2	6	0	40	9	68	1	0	0	0	120	39
NL	310	180	130	1	0	0	0	0	0	0	0	0	0	0	0	136	120	48	6	11	3	4	82	8	78	5	0	0	0	240	70
YR	469	247	222	1	0	0	0	0	0	0	0	0	0	0	0	228	162	68	11	13	9	4	122	17	146	6	0	0	0	360	109

AL		*NL*	
12	Frank Baker	19	Gavvy Cravath
9	Sam Crawford	18	Fred Luderus
8	Ping Bodie	14	Vic Saier
7	Joe Jackson	11	Sherry Magee
5	Multiple Players Tied	10	Chief Wilson

1914

Tm	Tot	H	A	Consec 2	3	4	1-Inn 3	4	5	One-Game 5	6	7	8	9	10	Men-On-Base 0	1	2	3	Batters PH	LO	XN	IP	P	Totals 1	10	20	30	40	Pitchers RHP	LHP
AL																															
BOS	18	3	15	0	0	0	0	0	0	0	0	0	0	0	0	8	8	2	0	0	0	0	9	0	10	0	0	0	0	13	5
CHI	19	7	12	0	0	0	0	0	0	0	0	0	0	0	0	13	3	2	1	0	2	1	5	0	8	0	0	0	0	14	5
CLE	10	4	6	0	0	0	0	0	0	0	0	0	0	0	0	3	4	3	0	0	1	0	5	0	7	0	0	0	0	6	4
DET	25	11	14	0	0	0	0	0	0	0	0	0	0	0	0	15	9	1	0	0	0	2	4	2	9	0	0	0	0	17	8
NY	12	8	4	0	0	0	0	0	0	0	0	0	0	0	0	7	4	1	0	0	1	0	1	0	8	0	0	0	0	7	5
PHI	29	17	12	1	0	0	0	0	0	0	0	0	0	0	0	14	11	4	0	0	1	0	3	3	11	0	0	0	0	20	9
STL	17	11	6	0	0	0	0	0	0	0	0	0	0	0	0	9	7	1	0	0	0	1	2	0	5	0	0	0	0	12	5
WAS	18	9	9	0	0	0	0	0	0	0	0	0	0	0	0	12	2	3	1	0	1	1	4	4	10	0	0	0	0	15	3
FL																															
BAL	32	25	7	0	0	0	0	0	0	0	0	0	0	0	0	20	7	5	0	1	1	1	0	2	11	1	0	0	0	27	4
BRO	42	26	16	0	0	0	0	0	0	0	0	0	0	0	0	29	4	7	2	0	1	3	0	3	13	1	0	0	0	37	5
BUF	37	20	17	0	0	0	0	0	0	0	0	0	0	0	0	22	12	3	0	1	2	1	4	1	9	1	0	0	0	32	5
CHI	52	31	21	0	0	0	0	0	0	0	0	0	0	0	0	29	14	8	1	0	0	1	1	3	7	3	0	0	0	47	5
IND	33	14	19	0	0	0	0	0	0	0	0	0	0	0	0	16	10	6	1	1	2	2	6	0	11	0	0	0	0	28	5
KC	39	28	11	1	0	0	0	0	0	0	0	0	0	0	0	19	13	5	2	1	0	0	0	4	14	1	0	0	0	35	4
PIT	34	11	23	0	0	0	0	0	0	0	0	0	0	0	0	19	10	4	1	1	0	1	3	0	12	1	0	0	0	24	9
STL	26	12	14	0	0	0	0	0	0	0	0	0	0	0	0	12	11	3	0	0	0	2	0	2	10	0	0	0	0	21	4
NL																															
BOS	35	19	16	0	0	0	0	0	0	0	0	0	0	0	0	21	7	4	3	0	0	2	12	0	12	0	0	0	0	27	8
BRO	31	17	14	0	0	0	0	0	0	0	0	0	0	0	0	16	11	3	1	1	0	0	12	0	10	0	0	0	0	20	11
CHI	42	22	20	0	0	0	0	0	0	0	0	0	0	0	0	24	8	9	1	1	3	1	9	1	8	1	0	0	0	33	9
CIN	16	4	12	0	0	0	0	0	0	0	0	0	0	0	0	7	8	1	0	1	0	0	9	2	10	0	0	0	0	12	4
NY	30	15	15	0	0	0	0	0	0	0	0	0	0	0	0	15	7	7	1	1	2	1	7	0	9	0	0	0	0	23	7
PHI	62	50	12	1	0	0	0	0	0	0	0	0	0	0	0	36	20	6	0	0	1	2	4	1	6	3	0	0	0	53	9
PIT	18	3	15	0	0	0	0	0	0	0	0	0	0	0	0	9	4	4	1	1	1	1	8	2	14	0	0	0	0	15	3
STL	33	20	13	1	0	0	0	0	0	0	0	0	0	0	0	17	14	2	0	1	0	0	18	0	10	0	0	0	0	26	7
AL	148	70	78	1	0	0	0	0	0	0	0	0	0	0	0	81	48	17	2	0	6	5	33	9	68	0	0	0	0	104	44
FL	295	167	128	1	0	0	0	0	0	0	0	0	0	0	0	166	81	41	7	5	6	11	14	15	87	8	0	0	0	251	41
NL	267	150	117	2	0	0	0	0	0	0	0	0	0	0	0	145	79	36	7	6	7	7	79	6	79	4	0	0	0	209	58
YR	710	387	323	4	0	0	0	0	0	0	0	0	0	0	0	392	208	94	16	11	19	23	126	30	234	12	0	0	0	564	143

AL		*FL*		*NL*	
9	Frank Baker	16	Edward Zwilling	19	Gavvy Cravath
8	Sam Crawford	15	Duke Kenworthy	18	Vic Saier
6	Jack Fournier	12	Steve Evans	15	Sherry Magee
6	Tilly Walker	12	Charlie Hanford	12	Fred Luderus
5	Multiple Players Tied	11	Multiple Players Tied	9	Multiple Players Tied

1915

Tm	Tot	H	A	Consec 2	3	4	1-Inn 3	4	5	One-Game 5	6	7	8	9	10	Men-On-Base 0	1	2	3	Batters PH	LO	XN	IP	P	Totals 1	10	20	30	40	Pitchers RHP	LHP
AL																															
BOS	14	5	9	0	0	0	0	0	0	0	0	0	0	0	0	8	5	1	0	0	0	0	3	6	8	0	0	0	0	11	3
CHI	25	9	16	0	0	0	0	0	0	0	0	0	0	0	0	9	9	6	1	0	0	1	5	0	9	0	0	0	0	16	9
CLE	20	7	13	0	0	0	0	0	0	0	0	0	0	0	0	14	5	1	0	0	0	0	0	0	8	0	0	0	0	15	5
DET	23	11	12	0	0	0	0	0	0	0	0	0	0	0	0	9	12	2	0	0	0	0	4	0	9	0	0	0	0	17	6
NY	31	28	3	0	0	0	0	0	0	0	0	0	0	0	0	21	5	5	0	2	2	0	3	2	10	0	0	0	0	21	10
PHI	16	9	7	0	0	0	0	0	0	0	0	0	0	0	0	8	6	2	0	0	0	0	1	1	10	0	0	0	0	13	3

Tm	Tot	H	A	Consec 2	Consec 3	Consec 4	1-Inn 3	1-Inn 4	1-Inn 5	One-Game 5	One-Game 6	One-Game 7	One-Game 8	One-Game 9	One-Game 10	Men-On-Base 0	Men-On-Base 1	Men-On-Base 2	Men-On-Base 3	Batters PH	Batters LO	Batters XN	Batters IP	Batters P	Totals 1	Totals 10	Totals 20	Totals 30	Totals 40	Pitchers RHP	Pitchers LHP
STL	19	6	13	0	0	0	0	0	0	0	0	0	0	0	0	11	6	2	0	0	0	0	3	1	10	0	0	0	0	15	4
WAS	12	3	9	0	0	0	0	0	0	0	0	0	0	0	0	8	3	1	0	0	0	1	3	3	8	0	0	0	0	9	3
FL																															
BAL	36	29	7	0	0	0	0	0	0	0	0	0	0	0	0	23	8	2	3	1	1	1	0	2	15	0	0	0	0	30	6
BRO	36	20	16	0	0	0	0	0	0	0	0	0	0	0	0	18	16	1	1	0	0	1	1	1	11	1	0	0	0	25	11
BUF	40	21	19	1	0	0	0	0	0	0	0	0	0	0	0	24	11	5	0	1	1	1	1	0	10	1	0	0	0	35	5
CHI	50	21	29	0	0	0	0	0	0	0	0	0	0	0	0	21	22	6	1	1	1	0	2	4	11	1	0	0	0	38	11
KC	28	15	13	0	0	0	0	0	0	0	0	0	0	0	0	16	6	5	1	1	0	0	3	2	11	0	0	0	0	24	4
NWK	17	4	13	0	0	0	0	0	0	0	0	0	0	0	0	8	4	5	0	0	0	1	4	1	9	0	0	0	0	12	5
PIT	20	4	16	0	0	0	0	0	0	0	0	0	0	0	0	13	5	2	0	1	2	0	2	0	7	1	0	0	0	14	6
STL	23	12	11	0	0	0	0	0	0	0	0	0	0	0	0	13	8	2	0	0	1	0	0	1	10	0	0	0	0	17	6
NL																															
BOS	17	3	14	0	0	0	0	0	0	0	0	0	0	0	0	5	8	3	1	0	0	0	3	3	11	0	0	0	0	13	4
BRO	14	9	5	0	0	0	0	0	0	0	0	0	0	0	0	8	4	2	0	0	1	0	8	0	5	0	0	0	0	10	4
CHI	53	31	22	0	0	0	0	0	0	0	0	0	0	0	0	25	25	3	0	1	0	1	9	0	8	3	0	0	0	36	17
CIN	15	6	9	0	0	0	0	0	0	0	0	0	0	0	0	9	4	2	0	0	0	0	11	2	7	0	0	0	0	14	1
NY	24	15	9	0	0	0	0	0	0	0	0	0	0	0	0	6	15	3	0	0	0	0	4	1	10	0	0	0	0	21	3
PHI	58	46	12	2	0	0	0	0	0	0	0	0	0	0	0	36	10	11	1	0	0	2	3	2	8	1	1	0	0	50	8
PIT	24	8	16	0	0	0	0	0	0	0	0	0	0	0	0	10	10	3	1	0	0	0	13	0	8	0	0	0	0	15	9
STL	20	11	9	0	0	0	0	0	0	0	0	0	0	0	0	11	3	4	2	0	1	0	9	0	9	0	0	0	0	12	8
AL	160	78	82	0	0	0	0	0	0	0	0	0	0	0	0	88	51	20	1	2	2	2	22	13	72	0	0	0	0	117	43
FL	250	126	124	1	0	0	0	0	0	0	0	0	0	0	0	136	80	28	6	5	6	4	13	11	84	4	0	0	0	195	54
NL	225	129	96	2	0	0	0	0	0	0	0	0	0	0	0	110	79	31	5	1	2	3	60	8	66	4	1	0	0	171	54
YR	635	333	302	3	0	0	0	0	0	0	0	0	0	0	0	334	210	79	12	8	10	9	95	32	222	8	1	0	0	483	151

AL
7 Braggo Roth
6 Rube Oldring
5 Multiple Players Tied

FL
17 Hal Chase
13 Edward Zwilling
12 Benny Kauff
10 Ed Konetchy
9 Jimmy Walsh

NL
24 Gavvy Cravath
13 Cy Williams
12 Frank Schulte
11 Beals Becker
11 Vic Saier

1916

Tm	Tot	H	A	Consec 2	Consec 3	Consec 4	1-Inn 3	1-Inn 4	1-Inn 5	One-Game 5	One-Game 6	One-Game 7	One-Game 8	One-Game 9	One-Game 10	Men-On-Base 0	Men-On-Base 1	Men-On-Base 2	Men-On-Base 3	Batters PH	Batters LO	Batters XN	Batters IP	Batters P	Totals 1	Totals 10	Totals 20	Totals 30	Totals 40	Pitchers RHP	Pitchers LHP
AL																															
BOS	14	1	13	0	0	0	0	0	0	0	0	0	0	0	0	8	4	2	0	1	0	0	1	2	7	0	0	0	0	7	7
CHI	17	9	8	0	0	0	0	0	0	0	0	0	0	0	0	9	5	2	1	0	0	1	3	0	5	0	0	0	0	11	6
CLE	16	4	12	0	0	0	0	0	0	0	0	0	0	0	0	7	7	1	1	4	1	1	2	1	6	0	0	0	0	13	3
DET	17	7	10	0	0	0	0	0	0	0	0	0	0	0	0	8	7	1	1	0	0	0	5	1	7	0	0	0	0	12	5
NY	35	22	13	0	0	0	0	0	0	0	0	0	0	0	0	14	12	7	2	0	0	0	3	0	8	2	0	0	0	26	9
PHI	19	15	4	1	0	0	0	0	0	0	0	0	0	0	0	9	7	2	1	0	1	0	3	1	9	0	0	0	0	10	9
STL	14	7	7	0	0	0	0	0	0	0	0	0	0	0	0	10	2	2	0	0	0	0	3	0	7	0	0	0	0	10	4
WAS	12	6	6	0	0	0	0	0	0	0	0	0	0	0	0	7	2	2	1	0	1	0	5	1	11	0	0	0	0	9	3
NL																															
BOS	22	6	16	1	0	0	0	0	0	0	0	0	0	0	0	11	7	2	2	0	3	0	11	3	10	0	0	0	0	16	6
BRO	28	19	9	0	0	0	0	0	0	0	0	0	0	0	0	17	7	3	1	0	0	1	13	0	8	0	0	0	0	20	8
CHI	46	34	12	0	0	0	0	0	0	0	0	0	0	0	0	27	13	6	0	1	0	1	5	1	14	1	0	0	0	33	13
CIN	14	4	10	0	0	0	0	0	0	0	0	0	0	0	0	9	3	2	0	0	2	1	9	0	8	0	0	0	0	13	1
NY	42	21	21	0	0	0	0	0	0	0	0	0	0	0	0	25	12	4	1	0	1	2	6	1	9	1	0	0	0	30	12
PHI	42	29	13	0	0	0	0	0	0	0	0	0	0	0	0	22	14	6	0	0	2	2	3	0	8	1	0	0	0	33	9
PIT	20	9	11	0	0	0	0	0	0	0	0	0	0	0	0	12	6	2	0	1	0	2	9	0	9	0	0	0	0	17	3
STL	25	12	13	0	0	0	0	0	0	0	0	0	0	0	0	15	5	4	1	0	0	0	8	1	8	0	0	0	0	21	4
AL	144	71	73	1	0	0	0	0	0	0	0	0	0	0	0	72	46	19	7	5	3	2	25	6	60	2	0	0	0	98	46
NL	239	134	105	1	0	0	0	0	0	0	0	0	0	0	0	138	67	29	5	2	8	9	64	6	74	3	0	0	0	183	56
YR	383	205	178	2	0	0	0	0	0	0	0	0	0	0	0	210	113	48	12	7	11	11	89	12	134	5	0	0	0	281	102

AL
12 Wally Pipp
10 Frank Baker
7 Happy Felsch
7 Wally Schang
5 Multiple Players Tied

NL
12 Dave Robertson
12 Cy Williams
11 Gavvy Cravath
9 Benny Kauff
9 Zach Wheat

1917

				Consec			1-Inn			One-Game						Men-On-Base				Batters					Totals					Pitchers	
Tm	Tot	H	A	2	3	4	3	4	5	5	6	7	8	9	10	0	1	2	3	PH	LO	XN	IP	P	1	10	20	30	40	RHP	LHP
AL																															
BOS	14	3	11	0	0	0	0	0	0	0	0	0	0	0	0	7	4	3	0	0	1	0	1	2	8	0	0	0	0	10	4
CHI	18	7	11	0	0	0	0	0	0	0	0	0	0	0	0	8	6	4	0	0	0	0	2	0	6	0	0	0	0	14	4
CLE	13	5	8	0	0	0	0	0	0	0	0	0	0	0	0	6	4	3	0	0	0	1	3	0	6	0	0	0	0	11	2
DET	25	5	20	0	0	0	0	0	0	0	0	0	0	0	0	8	11	5	1	1	0	0	4	1	8	0	0	0	0	20	5
NY	27	20	7	0	0	0	0	0	0	0	0	0	0	0	0	15	7	5	0	0	0	1	4	2	7	0	0	0	0	19	8
PHI	17	11	6	0	0	0	0	0	0	0	0	0	0	0	0	7	6	2	2	0	0	1	2	0	8	0	0	0	0	14	3
STL	15	7	8	0	0	0	0	0	0	0	0	0	0	0	0	6	9	0	0	2	1	0	2	0	9	0	0	0	0	12	3
WAS	4	1	3	0	0	0	0	0	0	0	0	0	0	0	0	3	0	0	1	0	0	0	1	0	3	0	0	0	0	4	0
NL																															
BOS	22	13	9	0	0	0	0	0	0	0	0	0	0	0	0	14	4	4	0	1	1	0	14	1	12	0	0	0	0	19	3
BRO	25	14	11	0	0	0	0	0	0	0	0	0	0	0	0	13	8	4	0	0	0	1	13	0	10	0	0	0	0	20	5
CHI	17	11	6	0	0	0	0	0	0	0	0	0	0	0	0	6	10	1	0	0	0	0	1	0	5	0	0	0	0	12	5
CIN	26	10	16	0	0	0	0	0	0	0	0	0	0	0	0	11	9	6	0	0	0	1	16	1	12	0	0	0	0	16	10
NY	39	21	18	0	0	0	0	0	0	0	0	0	0	0	0	16	20	2	1	0	1	1	7	0	9	1	0	0	0	29	10
PHI	38	26	12	2	0	0	0	0	0	0	0	0	0	0	0	28	4	6	0	1	1	0	3	2	11	1	0	0	0	30	8
PIT	9	2	7	0	0	0	0	0	0	0	0	0	0	0	0	3	4	2	0	0	0	1	2	0	5	0	0	0	0	8	1
STL	26	15	11	0	0	0	0	0	0	0	0	0	0	0	0	17	6	2	1	1	1	0	13	0	10	0	0	0	0	21	5
AL	133	59	74	0	0	0	0	0	0	0	0	0	0	0	0	60	47	22	4	3	2	3	19	5	55	0	0	0	0	104	29
NL	202	112	90	2	0	0	0	0	0	0	0	0	0	0	0	108	65	27	2	3	4	4	69	4	74	2	0	0	0	155	47
YR	335	171	164	2	0	0	0	0	0	0	0	0	0	0	0	168	112	49	6	6	6	7	88	9	129	2	0	0	0	259	76

	AL		*NL*
9	Wally Pipp	12	Gavvy Cravath
8	Bobby Veach	12	Dave Robertson
7	Ping Bodie	8	Rogers Hornsby
6	Multiple Players Tied	6	Multiple Players Tied

1918

				Consec			1-Inn			One-Game						Men-On-Base				Batters					Totals					Pitchers	
Tm	Tot	H	A	2	3	4	3	4	5	5	6	7	8	9	10	0	1	2	3	PH	LO	XN	IP	P	1	10	20	30	40	RHP	LHP
AL																															
BOS	15	2	13	0	0	0	0	0	0	0	0	0	0	0	0	6	8	1	0	0	0	1	2	2	4	1	0	0	0	12	3
CHI	8	4	4	0	0	0	0	0	0	0	0	0	0	0	0	4	4	0	0	0	0	0	2	0	7	0	0	0	0	7	1
CLE	9	1	8	0	0	0	0	0	0	0	0	0	0	0	0	7	1	1	0	0	0	2	1	0	5	0	0	0	0	6	3
DET	13	2	11	0	0	0	0	0	0	0	0	0	0	0	0	5	7	1	0	0	0	0	4	0	5	0	0	0	0	9	4
NY	20	10	10	0	0	0	0	0	0	0	0	0	0	0	0	11	6	3	0	0	0	0	0	0	9	0	0	0	0	15	5
PHI	22	15	7	2	0	0	0	0	0	0	0	0	0	0	0	14	5	3	0	1	0	0	0	0	4	1	0	0	0	18	4
STL	5	1	4	0	0	0	0	0	0	0	0	0	0	0	0	2	2	1	0	0	0	0	1	2	4	0	0	0	0	3	2
WAS	4	1	3	0	0	0	0	0	0	0	0	0	0	0	0	2	2	0	0	0	0	0	2	2	4	0	0	0	0	3	1
NL																															
BOS	13	5	8	1	0	0	0	0	0	0	0	0	0	0	0	8	4	1	0	0	0	0	5	1	8	0	0	0	0	9	4
BRO	10	4	6	0	0	0	0	0	0	0	0	0	0	0	0	6	2	2	0	0	0	0	4	0	6	0	0	0	0	8	2
CHI	21	9	12	0	0	0	0	0	0	0	0	0	0	0	0	10	6	4	1	0	0	0	4	3	9	0	0	0	0	17	4
CIN	15	9	6	0	0	0	0	0	0	0	0	0	0	0	0	2	8	4	1	0	0	1	12	1	8	0	0	0	0	11	4
NY	13	9	4	0	0	0	0	0	0	0	0	0	0	0	0	6	3	4	0	0	0	2	2	0	7	0	0	0	0	8	5
PHI	25	19	6	0	0	0	0	0	0	0	0	0	0	0	0	8	11	4	2	0	0	1	2	0	6	0	0	0	0	16	9
PIT	15	9	6	0	0	0	0	0	0	0	0	0	0	0	0	10	3	2	0	0	0	0	11	0	7	0	0	0	0	10	5
STL	27	14	13	1	0	0	0	0	0	0	0	0	0	0	0	8	9	8	2	0	0	2	7	2	11	0	0	0	0	22	5
AL	96	36	60	2	0	0	0	0	0	0	0	0	0	0	0	51	35	10	0	1	0	3	12	6	42	2	0	0	0	73	23
NL	139	78	61	2	0	0	0	0	0	0	0	0	0	0	0	58	46	29	6	0	0	6	47	7	62	0	0	0	0	101	38
YR	235	114	121	4	0	0	0	0	0	0	0	0	0	0	0	109	81	39	6	1	0	9	59	13	104	2	0	0	0	174	61

	AL		*NL*
11	Babe Ruth	8	Gavvy Cravath
11	Tilly Walker	6	Walton Cruise
6	Frank Baker	6	Cy Williams
6	George Burns	5	Multiple Players Tied
5	Multiple Players Tied		

1919

				Consec			1-Inn			One-Game						Men-On-Base				Batters					Totals					Pitchers	
Tm	Tot	H	A	2	3	4	3	4	5	5	6	7	8	9	10	0	1	2	3	PH	LO	XN	IP	P	1	10	20	30	40	RHP	LHP
AL																															
BOS	33	10	23	0	0	0	0	0	0	0	0	0	0	0	0	14	13	2	4	0	0	1	2	2	2	0	1	0	0	22	11

				Consec			1-Inn			One-Game						Men-On-Base				Batters					Totals					Pitchers	
Tm	Tot	H	A	2	3	4	3	4	5	5	6	7	8	9	10	0	1	2	3	PH	LO	XN	IP	P	1	10	20	30	40	RHP	LHP
CHI	25	5	20	0	0	0	0	0	0	0	0	0	0	0	0	13	8	3	1	0	0	2	4	0	7	0	0	0	0	18	7
CLE	24	12	12	0	0	0	0	0	0	0	0	0	0	0	0	13	8	3	0	0	0	0	9	1	10	0	0	0	0	19	5
DET	23	10	13	1	0	0	0	0	0	0	0	0	0	0	0	14	6	2	1	0	0	1	1	0	8	0	0	0	0	16	7
NY	45	33	12	1	0	0	0	0	0	1	0	0	0	0	0	21	17	6	1	0	1	0	6	0	8	1	0	0	0	33	12
PHI	35	29	6	0	0	0	0	0	0	0	0	0	0	0	0	23	8	4	0	2	0	0	1	3	11	1	0	0	0	25	10
STL	31	19	12	0	0	0	0	0	0	0	0	0	0	0	0	15	11	5	0	0	0	1	5	1	8	1	0	0	0	21	10
WAS	24	2	22	0	0	0	0	0	0	0	0	0	0	0	0	13	8	2	1	1	0	0	6	4	10	0	0	0	0	17	7

NL

Tm	Tot	H	A	2	3	4	3	4	5	5	6	7	8	9	10	0	1	2	3	PH	LO	XN	IP	P	1	10	20	30	40	RHP	LHP
BOS	24	11	13	1	0	0	0	0	0	0	0	0	0	0	0	15	8	1	0	0	1	1	16	2	14	0	0	0	0	15	9
BRO	25	12	13	0	0	0	0	0	0	0	0	0	0	0	0	10	11	3	1	1	0	1	9	0	8	0	0	0	0	21	4
CHI	21	11	10	0	0	0	0	0	0	0	0	0	0	0	0	9	7	5	0	0	1	0	1	1	10	0	0	0	0	16	5
CIN	20	10	10	0	0	0	0	0	0	0	0	0	0	0	0	9	10	1	0	0	1	1	16	1	10	0	0	0	0	9	11
NY	40	28	12	0	0	0	0	0	0	0	0	0	0	0	0	24	11	5	0	0	1	2	4	2	11	1	0	0	0	29	11
PHI	42	29	13	1	0	0	0	0	0	0	0	0	0	0	0	24	11	6	1	2	0	0	5	0	10	1	0	0	0	38	4
PIT	17	8	9	0	0	0	0	0	0	0	0	0	0	0	0	11	5	1	0	1	1	2	10	0	7	0	0	0	0	15	2
STL	18	9	9	0	0	0	0	0	0	0	0	0	0	0	0	10	4	3	1	1	0	0	7	1	9	0	0	0	0	13	5
AL	240	120	120	2	0	0	0	0	0	1	0	0	0	0	0	126	79	27	8	3	1	5	34	11	64	3	1	0	0	171	69
NL	207	118	89	2	0	0	0	0	0	0	0	0	0	0	0	112	67	25	3	5	5	7	68	7	79	2	0	0	0	156	51
YR	447	238	209	4	0	0	0	0	0	1	0	0	0	0	0	238	146	52	11	8	6	12	102	18	143	5	1	0	0	327	120

AL		*NL*	
29	Babe Ruth	12	Gavvy Cravath
10	Frank Baker	10	Benny Kauff
10	George Sisler	9	Cy Williams
10	Tilly Walker	8	Rogers Hornsby
9	Elmer Smith	7	Larry Doyle

1920

AL

Tm	Tot	H	A	2	3	4	3	4	5	5	6	7	8	9	10	0	1	2	3	PH	LO	XN	IP	P	1	10	20	30	40	RHP	LHP
BOS	22	2	20	0	0	0	0	0	0	0	0	0	0	0	0	17	2	2	1	0	2	1	2	1	7	0	0	0	0	20	2
CHI	37	18	19	0	0	0	0	0	0	0	0	0	0	0	0	24	9	1	3	0	0	1	5	0	7	2	0	0	0	29	8
CLE	35	20	15	0	0	0	0	0	0	0	0	0	0	0	0	17	9	7	2	0	0	0	12	1	9	1	0	0	0	26	9
DET	30	12	18	1	0	0	0	0	0	0	0	0	0	0	0	15	13	2	0	1	0	0	2	0	8	1	0	0	0	21	9
NY	115	71	44	3	0	0	0	0	0	0	0	0	0	0	0	59	36	17	3	0	3	2	8	2	7	3	0	0	1	81	34
PHI	44	35	9	0	0	0	0	0	0	0	0	0	0	0	0	28	13	3	0	0	1	0	2	2	11	1	0	0	0	30	14
STL	50	31	19	1	0	0	0	0	0	0	0	0	0	0	0	28	17	3	2	0	1	1	9	0	6	2	0	0	0	39	11
WAS	36	5	31	0	0	0	0	0	0	0	0	0	0	0	0	20	11	5	0	0	0	1	10	3	13	0	0	0	0	21	15

NL

Tm	Tot	H	A	2	3	4	3	4	5	5	6	7	8	9	10	0	1	2	3	PH	LO	XN	IP	P	1	10	20	30	40	RHP	LHP
BOS	23	5	18	0	0	0	0	0	0	0	0	0	0	0	0	13	4	6	0	0	2	0	6	1	11	0	0	0	0	17	6
BRO	28	17	11	0	0	0	0	0	0	0	0	0	0	0	0	17	6	5	0	0	0	1	3	2	10	0	0	0	0	22	6
CHI	34	19	15	1	0	0	0	0	0	0	0	0	0	0	0	19	10	5	0	0	1	2	7	3	10	1	0	0	0	30	4
CIN	18	5	13	0	0	0	0	0	0	0	0	0	0	0	0	7	9	2	0	0	0	1	12	1	7	0	0	0	0	14	4
NY	46	31	15	1	0	0	0	0	0	0	0	0	0	0	0	24	15	6	1	0	1	1	5	0	9	1	0	0	0	29	17
PHI	64	50	14	1	0	0	0	0	0	0	0	0	0	0	0	39	19	6	0	1	1	0	5	1	11	2	0	0	0	51	13
PIT	16	6	10	0	0	0	0	0	0	0	0	0	0	0	0	6	9	1	0	2	0	0	7	1	8	0	0	0	0	16	0
STL	32	10	22	0	0	0	0	0	0	0	0	0	0	0	0	14	12	6	0	2	0	0	4	1	10	1	0	0	0	19	13
AL	369	194	175	5	0	0	0	0	0	0	0	0	0	0	0	208	110	40	11	1	7	6	50	9	68	10	0	0	1	267	102
NL	261	143	118	3	0	0	0	0	0	0	0	0	0	0	0	139	84	37	1	5	5	5	49	10	76	5	0	0	0	198	63
YR	630	337	293	8	0	0	0	0	0	0	0	0	0	0	0	347	194	77	12	6	12	11	99	19	144	15	0	0	1	465	165

AL		*NL*	
54	Babe Ruth	15	Cy Williams
19	George Sisler	14	Irish Meusel
17	Tilly Walker	11	George Kelly
14	Happy Felsch	10	Austin McHenry
12	Multiple Players Tied	10	Dave Robertson

1921

AL

Tm	Tot	H	A	2	3	4	3	4	5	5	6	7	8	9	10	0	1	2	3	PH	LO	XN	IP	P	1	10	20	30	40	RHP	LHP
BOS	17	3	14	0	0	0	0	0	0	0	0	0	0	0	0	8	6	2	1	0	0	1	3	3	7	0	0	0	0	15	2
CHI	35	12	23	0	0	0	0	0	0	0	0	0	0	0	0	16	13	5	1	0	1	1	3	0	8	1	0	0	0	22	13

				Consec			1-Inn			One-Game						Men-On-Base				Batters					Totals					Pitchers	
Tm	Tot	H	A	2	3	4	3	4	5	5	6	7	8	9	10	0	1	2	3	PH	LO	XN	IP	P	1	10	20	30	40	RHP	LHP
CLE	42	15	27	1	0	0	0	0	0	0	0	0	0	0	0	20	13	7	2	0	0	1	4	2	12	1	0	0	0	34	8
DET	58	19	39	2	0	0	0	0	0	0	0	0	0	0	0	30	14	14	0	0	0	1	6	3	5	3	0	0	0	45	13
NY	134	83	51	4	0	0	0	0	0	0	0	0	0	0	0	60	45	28	1	0	1	2	7	5	14	0	1	0	1	103	31
PHI	82	65	17	1	0	0	0	0	0	0	0	1	0	0	0	50	22	9	1	0	1	2	3	3	7	3	1	0	0	59	23
STL	67	42	25	0	0	0	0	0	0	0	0	0	0	0	0	33	20	13	1	0	1	1	6	2	13	1	1	0	0	53	14
WAS	42	14	28	0	0	0	0	0	0	0	0	0	0	0	0	23	12	6	1	0	1	0	11	0	10	0	0	0	0	34	8
NL																															
BOS	61	18	43	2	0	0	1	0	0	0	0	0	0	0	0	28	22	9	2	1	1	2	22	4	13	2	0	0	0	43	18
BRO	59	32	27	2	0	0	0	0	0	0	0	0	0	0	0	46	8	5	0	0	2	3	6	5	14	2	0	0	0	53	6
CHI	37	23	14	0	0	0	0	0	0	0	0	0	0	0	0	23	6	7	1	0	2	0	1	2	13	0	0	0	0	31	6
CIN	20	5	15	0	0	0	0	0	0	0	0	0	0	0	0	12	6	2	0	1	1	0	7	1	11	0	0	0	0	17	3
NY	75	49	26	3	0	0	0	0	0	1	0	0	0	0	0	34	26	10	5	0	0	2	8	4	13	1	1	0	0	53	22
PHI	88	67	21	1	0	0	0	0	0	1	0	0	0	0	0	49	30	7	2	0	1	1	2	4	15	2	0	0	0	67	21
PIT	37	13	24	1	0	0	0	0	0	0	0	0	0	0	0	16	13	7	1	0	0	2	10	0	8	0	0	0	0	24	13
STL	83	43	40	0	0	0	0	0	0	0	0	0	0	0	0	45	26	10	2	2	7	2	7	0	8	2	1	0	0	61	22
AL	477	253	224	8	0	0	0	0	0	0	0	1	0	0	0	240	145	84	8	0	5	9	43	18	76	9	3	0	1	365	112
NL	460	250	210	9	0	0	1	0	0	2	0	0	0	0	0	253	137	57	13	4	14	12	63	20	95	9	2	0	0	349	111
YR	937	503	434	17	0	0	1	0	0	2	0	1	0	0	0	493	282	141	21	4	19	21	106	38	171	18	5	0	1	714	223

	AL		*NL*
59	Babe Ruth	23	George Kelly
24	Bob Meusel	21	Rogers Hornsby
24	Ken Williams	18	Cy Williams
23	Tilly Walker	17	Austin McHenry
19	Harry Heilmann	16	Jack Fournier

1922

AL

Tm	Tot	H	A	2	3	4	3	4	5	5	6	7	8	9	10	0	1	2	3	PH	LO	XN	IP	P	1	10	20	30	40	RHP	LHP
BOS	45	6	39	0	0	0	0	0	0	0	0	0	0	0	0	27	11	6	1	1	1	2	0	1	11	1	0	0	0	42	3
CHI	45	10	35	1	0	0	0	0	0	0	0	0	0	0	0	29	11	4	1	0	1	3	5	0	6	2	0	0	0	34	11
CLE	32	12	20	1	0	0	0	0	0	0	0	0	0	0	0	16	11	4	1	0	0	0	4	0	8	1	0	0	0	29	3
DET	54	15	39	3	0	0	0	0	0	0	0	0	0	0	0	29	9	14	2	2	1	0	9	1	9	0	1	0	0	47	7
NY	95	53	42	1	0	0	0	0	0	0	0	0	0	0	0	52	22	19	2	0	0	5	4	3	14	1	0	1	0	63	32
PHI	111	80	31	1	1	0	0	0	0	0	0	0	0	0	0	67	32	12	0	1	3	2	2	2	9	2	1	1	0	98	13
STL	98	70	28	2	0	0	1	0	0	0	0	0	0	0	0	50	32	11	5	3	1	1	3	3	9	2	0	1	0	73	25
WAS	45	15	30	0	0	0	0	0	0	0	0	0	0	0	0	22	12	9	2	0	0	1	16	3	14	1	0	0	0	37	8
NL																															
BOS	32	6	26	0	0	0	0	0	0	0	0	0	0	0	0	22	8	1	1	0	0	0	8	0	11	0	0	0	0	25	7
BRO	56	25	31	0	0	0	0	0	0	0	0	0	0	0	0	30	20	6	0	1	1	3	4	6	16	1	0	0	0	50	6
CHI	42	22	20	0	0	0	0	0	0	0	0	0	0	0	0	22	11	7	2	0	1	1	2	2	8	2	0	0	0	29	13
CIN	45	8	37	1	0	0	0	0	0	0	0	0	0	0	0	22	17	6	0	0	1	1	7	0	10	1	0	0	0	34	11
NY	80	47	33	0	0	0	0	0	0	1	0	0	0	0	0	37	30	11	2	1	1	2	11	2	13	2	0	0	0	59	21
PHI	116	95	21	4	0	0	0	0	0	1	0	0	0	0	0	53	38	24	1	4	1	2	2	2	10	4	1	0	0	86	30
PIT	52	22	30	1	0	0	0	0	0	1	0	0	0	0	0	29	18	5	0	0	0	3	10	7	11	2	0	0	0	44	8
STL	107	59	48	0	0	0	0	0	0	0	0	0	0	0	0	62	25	17	3	3	2	0	9	2	13	2	0	0	1	87	20
AL	525	261	264	9	1	0	1	0	0	0	0	0	0	0	0	292	140	79	14	7	7	14	43	13	80	10	2	3	0	423	102
NL	530	284	246	6	0	0	0	0	0	3	0	0	0	0	0	277	167	77	9	9	7	12	53	21	92	14	1	0	1	414	116
YR	1055	545	510	15	1	0	1	0	0	3	0	0	0	0	0	569	307	156	23	16	14	26	96	34	172	24	3	3	1	837	218

	AL		*NL*
39	Ken Williams	42	Rogers Hornsby
37	Tilly Walker	26	Cy Williams
35	Babe Ruth	17	George Kelly
21	Harry Heilmann	17	Cliff Lee
21	Bing Miller	16	Multiple Players Tied

1923

AL

Tm	Tot	H	A	2	3	4	3	4	5	5	6	7	8	9	10	0	1	2	3	PH	LO	XN	IP	P	1	10	20	30	40	RHP	LHP
BOS	34	11	23	1	0	0	0	0	0	0	0	0	0	0	0	15	14	5	0	0	0	1	4	0	5	1	0	0	0	26	8
CHI	42	13	29	1	0	0	0	0	0	0	0	0	0	0	0	23	15	4	0	1	1	1	5	4	11	1	0	0	0	32	10

				Consec			1-Inn			One-Game						Men-On-Base				Batters					Totals					Pitchers	
Tm	Tot	H	A	2	3	4	3	4	5	5	6	7	8	9	10	0	1	2	3	PH	LO	XN	IP	P	1	10	20	30	40	RHP	LHP
CLE	59	22	37	1	0	0	0	0	0	0	0	0	0	0	0	26	19	9	5	2	0	3	8	1	10	2	0	0	0	49	10
DET	41	21	20	1	0	0	0	0	0	0	0	0	0	0	0	24	14	2	1	1	1	0	3	2	11	1	0	0	0	32	9
NY	105	62	43	3	0	0	0	0	0	0	0	0	0	0	0	63	27	12	3	2	3	3	21	3	13	1	0	0	1	73	32
PHI	53	28	25	1	0	0	0	0	0	0	0	0	0	0	0	34	14	5	0	1	0	0	2	1	12	2	0	0	0	39	14
STL	82	50	32	2	0	0	0	0	0	0	0	0	0	0	0	46	22	13	1	2	2	1	3	1	7	2	1	0	0	67	15
WAS	26	7	19	0	0	0	0	0	0	0	0	0	0	0	0	15	8	2	1	1	0	0	7	0	9	0	0	0	0	20	6
NL																															
BOS	32	7	25	1	0	0	0	0	0	0	0	0	0	0	0	15	11	4	2	1	0	3	8	0	8	0	0	0	0	29	3
BRO	62	26	36	1	0	0	0	0	0	0	0	0	0	0	0	29	26	7	0	1	0	0	6	3	13	0	1	0	0	50	12
CHI	90	63	27	2	0	0	0	0	0	0	1	0	0	0	0	44	33	10	3	1	1	2	6	3	11	3	1	0	0	60	30
CIN	45	6	39	1	0	0	0	0	0	0	0	0	0	0	0	23	13	9	0	1	0	3	3	2	12	1	0	0	0	41	4
NY	85	44	41	3	0	0	0	0	0	1	0	0	0	0	0	42	28	14	1	1	0	2	10	1	13	3	0	0	0	67	18
PHI	112	76	36	1	0	0	0	0	0	0	1	0	0	0	0	49	46	16	1	2	0	1	5	3	12	3	0	0	1	76	36
PIT	49	16	33	0	0	0	0	0	0	0	0	0	0	0	0	21	24	4	0	0	0	1	10	1	9	1	0	0	0	36	13
STL	63	22	41	0	0	0	0	0	0	0	0	0	0	0	0	37	12	13	1	2	0	2	5	1	14	1	0	0	0	48	15
AL	442	214	228	10	0	0	0	0	0	0	0	0	0	0	0	246	133	52	11	10	7	9	53	12	78	10	1	0	1	338	104
NL	538	260	278	9	0	0	0	0	0	1	2	0	0	0	0	260	193	77	8	9	1	14	53	14	92	12	2	0	1	407	131
YR	980	474	506	19	0	0	0	0	0	1	2	0	0	0	0	506	326	129	19	19	8	23	106	26	170	22	3	0	2	745	235

	AL		*NL*
41	Babe Ruth	41	Cy Williams
29	Ken Williams	22	Jack Fournier
18	Harry Heilmann	20	Hack Miller
17	Joe Hauser	19	Irish Meusel
17	Tris Speaker	17	Rogers Hornsby

1924

				Consec			1-Inn			One-Game						Men-On-Base				Batters					Totals					Pitchers	
Tm	Tot	H	A	2	3	4	3	4	5	5	6	7	8	9	10	0	1	2	3	PH	LO	XN	IP	P	1	10	20	30	40	RHP	LHP
AL																															
BOS	30	8	22	0	0	0	0	0	0	0	0	0	0	0	0	16	8	4	2	0	0	1	1	0	6	1	0	0	0	21	9
CHI	41	13	28	1	0	0	0	0	0	0	0	0	0	0	0	22	10	6	3	0	1	1	0	2	10	1	0	0	0	35	6
CLE	41	13	28	0	0	0	0	0	0	1	0	0	0	0	0	18	16	6	1	3	2	0	5	2	12	0	0	0	0	27	14
DET	35	17	18	1	0	0	0	0	0	0	0	0	0	0	0	20	11	1	3	1	0	0	1	2	9	1	0	0	0	29	6
NY	98	57	41	3	0	0	0	0	0	0	0	0	0	0	0	51	27	18	2	1	1	3	11	4	13	1	0	0	1	72	26
PHI	63	31	32	1	0	0	0	0	0	0	0	0	0	0	0	30	18	15	0	0	2	2	0	0	9	0	1	0	0	51	12
STL	67	44	23	1	0	0	0	0	0	0	0	0	0	0	0	32	27	7	1	0	0	0	6	4	9	2	0	0	0	45	22
WAS	22	1	21	0	0	0	0	0	0	0	0	0	0	0	0	14	7	1	0	0	0	1	3	1	6	1	0	0	0	13	9
NL																															
BOS	25	9	16	1	0	0	0	0	0	0	0	0	0	0	0	14	10	1	0	2	2	1	8	0	14	0	0	0	0	20	5
BRO	72	26	46	1	0	0	0	0	0	0	0	0	0	0	0	35	28	9	0	0	2	2	4	3	12	1	1	0	0	52	20
CHI	66	33	33	0	0	0	0	0	0	0	0	0	0	0	0	39	18	7	2	1	0	2	3	2	13	2	0	0	0	52	14
CIN	36	3	33	1	0	0	0	0	0	0	0	0	0	0	0	26	7	3	0	0	2	1	5	5	16	0	0	0	0	33	3
NY	95	51	44	1	0	0	0	0	0	1	0	0	0	0	0	51	27	12	5	1	2	2	7	9	11	3	1	0	0	77	18
PHI	94	58	36	4	0	0	1	0	0	0	0	0	0	0	0	52	26	12	4	1	2	2	4	4	14	1	1	0	0	79	15
PIT	44	20	24	0	0	0	0	0	0	0	0	0	0	0	0	21	13	9	1	0	2	1	14	1	11	0	0	0	0	37	7
STL	67	32	35	0	0	0	0	0	0	0	0	0	0	0	0	42	17	7	1	0	2	1	6	0	10	2	1	0	0	54	13
AL	397	184	213	7	0	0	0	0	0	1	0	0	0	0	0	203	124	58	12	5	6	8	27	15	74	7	1	0	1	293	104
NL	499	232	267	8	0	0	1	0	0	1	0	0	0	0	0	280	146	60	13	5	14	12	51	24	101	9	4	0	0	404	95
YR	896	416	480	15	0	0	1	0	0	2	0	0	0	0	0	483	270	118	25	10	20	20	78	39	175	16	5	0	1	697	199

	AL		*NL*
46	Babe Ruth	27	Jack Fournier
27	Joe Hauser	25	Rogers Hornsby
19	William Jacobson	24	Cy Williams
18	Ken Williams	21	George Kelly
13	Ike Boone	16	Multiple Players Tied

1925

				Consec			1-Inn			One-Game						Men-On-Base				Batters					Totals					Pitchers	
Tm	Tot	H	A	2	3	4	3	4	5	5	6	7	8	9	10	0	1	2	3	PH	LO	XN	IP	P	1	10	20	30	40	RHP	LHP
AL																															
BOS	41	10	31	0	0	0	0	0	0	0	0	0	0	0	0	24	12	5	0	1	0	0	1	1	9	1	0	0	0	28	13
CHI	38	13	25	1	0	0	0	0	0	0	0	0	0	0	0	20	10	6	2	0	0	1	3	2	10	0	0	0	0	21	17

				Consec			1-Inn			One-Game						Men-On-Base				Batters					Totals					Pitchers	
Tm	Tot	H	A	2	3	4	3	4	5	5	6	7	8	9	10	0	1	2	3	PH	LO	XN	IP	P	1	10	20	30	40	RHP	LHP
CLE	52	23	29	1	0	0	0	0	0	0	0	0	0	0	0	31	15	6	0	0	1	1	6	5	11	2	0	0	0	35	17
DET	50	18	32	2	0	0	0	0	0	0	0	0	0	0	0	28	15	6	1	1	0	0	4	3	8	2	0	0	0	29	21
NY	110	54	56	3	1	0	1	0	0	1	0	0	0	0	0	64	31	13	2	1	0	3	9	0	8	1	2	1	0	52	58
PHI	76	35	41	2	0	0	0	0	0	1	0	0	0	0	0	41	24	11	0	1	0	2	3	2	12	1	1	0	0	52	24
STL	110	73	37	2	0	0	0	0	0	0	0	0	0	0	0	54	33	19	4	2	3	1	4	4	9	5	1	0	0	79	30
WAS	56	13	43	2	0	0	0	0	0	0	0	0	0	0	0	30	18	6	2	1	0	2	5	3	10	2	0	0	0	36	20
NL																															
BOS	41	15	26	0	0	0	0	0	0	0	0	0	0	0	0	25	14	2	0	0	0	2	16	2	15	0	0	0	0	25	16
BRO	64	25	39	0	0	0	0	0	0	0	0	0	0	0	0	30	18	13	3	1	0	0	1	5	11	1	1	0	0	40	24
CHI	86	57	29	0	0	0	0	0	0	0	0	0	0	0	0	55	19	11	1	1	1	0	3	6	12	2	1	0	0	57	29
CIN	44	11	33	2	0	0	0	0	0	0	0	0	0	0	0	23	17	4	0	0	1	4	10	3	14	0	0	0	0	34	10
NY	114	55	59	1	0	0	0	0	0	1	1	0	0	0	0	55	37	20	2	2	1	3	4	4	10	3	2	0	0	81	33
PHI	100	73	27	3	0	0	1	0	0	0	0	0	0	0	0	48	33	11	8	6	0	1	2	4	15	3	0	0	0	79	21
PIT	78	27	51	2	0	0	0	0	0	0	1	0	0	0	0	41	28	5	4	1	0	1	17	2	10	2	0	0	0	57	21
STL	109	66	43	4	0	0	0	0	0	1	0	0	0	0	0	54	38	13	4	0	4	1	4	2	10	2	1	1	0	83	26
AL	533	239	294	13	1	0	1	0	0	2	0	0	0	0	0	292	158	72	11	7	4	10	35	20	77	14	4	1	0	332	200
NL	636	329	307	12	0	0	1	0	0	2	2	0	0	0	0	331	204	79	22	11	7	12	57	28	97	13	5	1	0	456	180
YR	1169	568	601	25	1	0	2	0	0	4	2	0	0	0	0	623	362	151	33	18	11	22	92	48	174	27	9	2	0	788	380

	AL		*NL*
33	Bob Meusel	39	Rogers Hornsby
25	Babe Ruth	24	Gabby Hartnett
25	Ken Williams	22	Jack Fournier
24	Al Simmons	21	Jim Bottomley
20	Lou Gehrig	21	Irish Meusel

1926

AL

Tm	Tot	H	A	2	3	4	3	4	5	5	6	7	8	9	10	0	1	2	3	PH	LO	XN	IP	P	1	10	20	30	40	RHP	LHP
BOS	32	9	23	1	0	0	0	0	0	0	0	0	0	0	0	20	7	4	1	0	0	2	2	1	9	0	0	0	0	24	8
CHI	32	8	24	1	0	0	0	0	0	0	0	0	0	0	0	16	7	8	1	2	1	1	1	0	9	0	0	0	0	18	14
CLE	27	11	16	1	0	0	0	0	0	0	0	0	0	0	0	8	11	8	0	0	0	2	4	4	10	0	0	0	0	18	9
DET	36	16	20	0	0	0	0	0	0	0	0	0	0	0	0	21	12	2	1	0	0	0	2	1	9	1	0	0	0	26	10
NY	121	58	63	2	0	0	0	0	0	0	0	0	0	0	0	55	44	20	2	0	0	1	10	0	5	3	0	0	1	76	45
PHI	61	34	27	0	0	0	0	0	0	0	0	0	0	0	0	29	25	6	1	2	0	2	1	0	10	1	0	0	0	44	17
STL	72	53	19	2	0	0	0	0	0	1	0	0	0	0	0	36	29	5	2	3	0	0	1	3	14	1	0	0	0	51	21
WAS	43	4	39	0	0	0	0	0	0	0	0	0	0	0	0	22	13	7	1	0	0	1	5	2	12	1	0	0	0	32	11
NL																															
BOS	16	4	12	0	0	0	0	0	0	0	0	0	0	0	0	9	5	2	0	1	0	0	6	1	9	0	0	0	0	12	4
BRO	40	23	17	0	0	0	0	0	0	0	0	0	0	0	0	22	15	3	0	0	1	1	2	0	8	2	0	0	0	29	11
CHI	66	35	31	0	0	0	0	0	0	0	0	0	0	0	0	32	28	4	2	1	0	4	4	2	13	1	1	0	0	51	15
CIN	35	8	27	1	0	0	0	0	0	0	0	0	0	0	0	14	13	6	2	0	0	0	8	0	8	0	0	0	0	27	8
NY	73	45	28	1	0	0	0	0	0	0	0	0	0	0	0	34	23	15	1	1	0	3	7	1	14	1	0	0	0	51	22
PHI	75	46	29	2	0	0	0	0	0	0	0	0	0	0	0	37	16	18	4	1	1	2	1	5	13	2	0	0	0	62	13
PIT	44	18	26	0	0	0	0	0	0	0	0	0	0	0	0	24	12	8	0	0	0	1	10	2	11	0	0	0	0	42	2
STL	90	54	36	3	0	0	0	0	0	0	0	0	0	0	0	43	31	15	1	1	1	2	6	2	9	4	0	0	0	78	12
AL	424	193	231	7	0	0	0	0	0	1	0	0	0	0	0	207	148	60	9	7	1	9	26	11	78	7	0	0	1	289	135
NL	439	233	206	7	0	0	0	0	0	0	0	0	0	0	0	215	143	71	10	5	3	13	44	13	85	10	1	0	0	352	87
YR	863	426	437	14	0	0	0	0	0	1	0	0	0	0	0	422	291	131	19	12	4	22	70	24	163	17	1	0	1	641	222

	AL		*NL*
47	Babe Ruth	21	Hack Wilson
19	Al Simmons	19	Jim Bottomley
18	Tony Lazzeri	18	Cy Williams
17	Goose Goslin	17	Les Bell
17	Ken Williams	16	Billy Southworth

1927

AL

Tm	Tot	H	A	2	3	4	3	4	5	5	6	7	8	9	10	0	1	2	3	PH	LO	XN	IP	P	1	10	20	30	40	RHP	LHP
BOS	28	5	23	0	0	0	0	0	0	0	0	0	0	0	0	20	7	0	1	1	0	1	4	1	12	0	0	0	0	20	8
CHI	36	6	30	0	0	0	0	0	0	0	0	0	0	0	0	21	11	2	2	1	1	1	4	5	13	0	0	0	0	29	7

				Consec			1-Inn			One-Game						Men-On-Base				Batters					Totals					Pitchers	
Tm	Tot	H	A	2	3	4	3	4	5	5	6	7	8	9	10	0	1	2	3	PH	LO	XN	IP	P	1	10	20	30	40	RHP	LHP
CLE	26	10	16	0	0	0	0	0	0	0	0	0	0	0	0	13	10	3	0	1	0	0	4	1	12	0	0	0	0	17	9
DET	51	25	26	1	0	0	0	0	0	0	0	0	0	0	0	23	18	8	2	1	0	1	3	2	8	1	0	0	0	34	17
NY	158	83	75	7	0	0	0	0	0	1	0	0	0	0	0	81	50	21	6	0	3	2	8	3	11	1	0	0	2	115	43
PHI	56	26	30	2	0	0	0	0	0	0	0	0	0	0	0	32	17	6	1	1	0	2	5	4	12	2	0	0	0	43	13
STL	55	42	13	1	0	0	0	0	0	0	0	0	0	0	0	24	23	6	2	0	0	2	1	7	12	1	0	0	0	40	15
WAS	29	10	19	0	0	0	0	0	0	0	0	0	0	0	0	12	13	4	0	0	1	0	6	4	11	1	0	0	0	22	7
NL																															
BOS	37	5	32	1	0	0	0	0	0	0	0	0	0	0	0	21	14	2	0	1	0	1	5	2	12	1	0	0	0	26	11
BRO	39	20	19	0	0	0	0	0	0	0	0	0	0	0	0	19	12	7	1	1	1	0	5	0	10	1	0	0	0	31	8
CHI	74	37	37	1	0	0	0	0	0	0	0	0	0	0	0	40	23	10	1	2	0	3	0	1	9	2	0	1	0	63	11
CIN	29	3	26	0	0	0	0	0	0	0	0	0	0	0	0	15	9	4	1	0	0	0	6	1	12	0	0	0	0	23	6
NY	109	62	47	2	0	0	0	0	0	0	0	0	0	0	0	53	42	10	4	1	2	0	8	0	11	2	2	0	0	82	27
PHI	57	32	25	2	0	0	0	0	0	0	0	0	0	0	0	29	16	8	4	1	0	0	0	3	9	1	0	1	0	50	7
PIT	54	25	29	1	0	0	0	0	0	0	0	0	0	0	0	30	15	8	1	1	0	1	7	2	12	0	0	0	0	44	10
STL	84	55	29	2	0	0	1	0	0	0	0	0	0	0	0	42	27	14	1	1	1	5	3	2	10	3	0	0	0	68	16
AL	439	207	232	11	0	0	0	0	0	1	0	0	0	0	0	226	149	50	14	5	5	9	35	27	91	6	0	0	2	320	119
NL	483	239	244	9	0	0	1	0	0	0	0	0	0	0	0	249	158	63	13	8	4	10	34	11	85	10	2	2	0	387	96
YR	922	446	476	20	0	0	1	0	0	1	0	0	0	0	0	475	307	113	27	13	9	19	69	38	176	16	2	2	2	707	215

AL		*NL*	
60	Babe Ruth	30	Cy Williams
47	Lou Gehrig	30	Hack Wilson
18	Tony Lazzeri	26	Rogers Hornsby
17	Ken Williams	20	Bill Terry
15	Al Simmons	19	Jim Bottomley

1928

				Consec			1-Inn			One-Game						Men-On-Base				Batters					Totals					Pitchers	
Tm	Tot	H	A	2	3	4	3	4	5	5	6	7	8	9	10	0	1	2	3	PH	LO	XN	IP	P	1	10	20	30	40	RHP	LHP
AL																															
BOS	38	10	28	0	0	0	0	0	0	0	0	0	0	0	0	21	11	4	2	0	1	0	4	2	8	1	0	0	0	31	7
CHI	24	11	13	0	0	0	0	0	0	0	0	0	0	0	0	10	9	4	1	2	0	0	2	3	14	0	0	0	0	21	3
CLE	34	10	24	0	0	0	0	0	0	0	0	0	0	0	0	15	12	7	0	1	0	2	2	1	14	0	0	0	0	28	6
DET	62	33	29	2	0	0	0	0	0	0	0	0	0	0	0	35	16	8	3	1	0	0	3	2	10	2	0	0	0	49	13
NY	133	69	64	3	0	0	0	0	0	2	0	0	0	0	0	71	39	19	4	1	0	0	7	3	11	2	1	0	1	96	37
PHI	89	54	35	5	0	0	0	0	0	0	0	0	0	0	0	46	27	13	3	1	1	2	1	2	9	4	0	0	0	73	16
STL	63	51	12	2	0	0	1	0	0	0	0	0	0	0	0	35	22	5	1	2	0	1	2	3	10	3	0	0	0	51	12
WAS	40	16	24	0	0	0	0	0	0	0	0	0	0	0	0	19	16	5	0	1	0	0	8	3	9	1	0	0	0	31	9
NL																															
BOS	52	24	28	0	0	0	0	0	0	0	0	0	0	0	0	28	13	10	1	0	1	1	1	1	10	1	1	0	0	46	6
BRO	66	30	36	1	0	0	0	0	0	0	0	0	0	0	0	32	25	7	2	1	0	3	2	3	8	2	1	0	0	45	21
CHI	92	40	52	1	0	0	0	0	0	0	0	0	0	0	0	54	25	10	3	1	0	0	0	2	12	2	0	1	0	73	19
CIN	32	3	29	0	0	0	0	0	0	0	0	0	0	0	0	19	8	5	0	0	0	2	4	3	12	0	0	0	0	25	7
NY	118	80	38	3	0	0	0	0	0	0	0	0	0	0	0	62	35	17	4	3	2	1	5	1	12	5	0	0	0	83	35
PHI	85	54	31	2	0	0	0	0	0	0	0	0	0	0	0	38	36	11	0	6	0	0	2	1	8	5	0	0	0	68	17
PIT	52	16	36	0	0	0	0	0	0	0	0	0	0	0	0	23	22	5	2	0	0	1	6	1	13	1	0	0	0	36	16
STL	113	62	51	7	0	0	1	0	0	1	0	0	0	0	0	58	37	17	1	4	0	3	0	3	11	2	1	1	0	82	31
AL	483	254	229	12	0	0	1	0	0	2	0	0	0	0	0	252	152	65	14	9	2	5	29	19	85	13	1	0	1	380	103
NL	610	309	301	14	0	0	1	0	0	1	0	0	0	0	0	314	201	82	13	15	3	11	20	15	86	18	3	2	0	458	152
YR	1093	563	530	26	0	0	2	0	0	3	0	0	0	0	0	566	353	147	27	24	5	16	49	34	171	31	4	2	1	838	255

AL		*NL*	
54	Babe Ruth	31	Jim Bottomley
27	Lou Gehrig	31	Hack Wilson
17	Goose Goslin	27	Chick Hafey
16	Joe Hauser	25	Del Bissonette
15	Al Simmons	21	Rogers Hornsby

1929

				Consec			1-Inn			One-Game						Men-On-Base				Batters					Totals					Pitchers	
Tm	Tot	H	A	2	3	4	3	4	5	5	6	7	8	9	10	0	1	2	3	PH	LO	XN	IP	P	1	10	20	30	40	RHP	LHP
AL																															
BOS	28	11	17	0	0	0	0	0	0	0	0	0	0	0	0	20	7	0	1	1	1	0	3	3	13	0	0	0	0	21	7
CHI	37	19	18	0	0	0	0	0	0	0	0	0	0	0	0	20	13	4	0	0	0	0	1	1	11	1	0	0	0	25	12

				Consec			1-Inn			One-Game						Men-On-Base				Batters					Totals					Pitchers	
Tm	Tot	H	A	2	3	4	3	4	5	5	6	7	8	9	10	0	1	2	3	PH	LO	XN	IP	P	1	10	20	30	40	RHP	LHP
CLE	62	27	35	3	0	0	1	0	0	0	0	0	0	0	0	30	17	14	1	2	0	0	4	2	12	2	0	0	0	45	17
DET	110	57	53	3	0	0	0	0	0	0	0	0	0	0	0	49	45	13	3	0	4	1	5	4	10	4	1	0	0	86	24
NY	142	69	73	5	1	0	0	0	0	1	0	0	0	0	0	75	42	19	6	3	1	2	12	1	7	3	0	1	1	85	57
PHI	122	72	50	2	0	0	0	0	0	0	0	0	0	0	0	54	52	15	1	0	1	2	6	3	10	2	0	2	0	98	24
STL	46	22	24	2	0	0	0	0	0	0	0	0	0	0	0	22	20	3	1	1	2	0	3	4	15	0	0	0	0	36	10
WAS	48	10	38	0	0	0	0	0	0	0	0	0	0	0	0	26	11	11	0	1	2	0	6	0	9	1	0	0	0	30	18
NL																															
BOS	33	11	22	0	0	0	0	0	0	0	0	0	0	0	0	15	11	6	1	1	0	0	1	2	10	1	0	0	0	23	10
BRO	99	53	46	1	0	0	1	0	0	0	0	0	0	0	0	51	31	14	3	1	3	2	7	2	11	2	2	0	0	78	21
CHI	139	76	63	2	0	0	2	0	0	1	0	0	0	0	0	68	41	21	9	1	0	0	2	3	11	3	0	2	0	104	35
CIN	34	7	27	0	0	0	0	0	0	0	0	0	0	0	0	16	13	4	1	1	2	0	3	1	12	0	0	0	0	30	4
NY	136	79	57	2	0	0	0	0	0	1	0	0	0	0	0	60	55	19	2	3	6	2	9	2	10	2	1	0	1	86	50
PHI	153	86	67	8	0	0	0	0	0	1	0	0	0	0	0	80	48	18	7	4	1	2	2	1	11	0	0	2	1	97	56
PIT	60	27	33	2	0	0	0	0	0	1	0	0	0	0	0	28	17	12	3	0	0	1	7	7	10	2	0	0	0	50	10
STL	100	48	52	1	0	0	0	0	0	0	0	0	0	0	0	39	41	16	4	0	2	1	6	4	11	1	2	0	0	76	24
AL	595	287	308	15	1	0	1	0	0	1	0	0	0	0	0	296	207	79	13	8	11	5	40	18	87	13	1	3	1	426	169
NL	754	387	367	16	0	0	3	0	0	4	0	0	0	0	0	357	257	110	30	11	14	8	37	22	86	11	5	4	2	544	210
YR	1349	674	675	31	1	0	4	0	0	5	0	0	0	0	0	653	464	189	43	19	25	13	77	40	173	24	6	7	3	970	379

AL		*NL*	
46	Babe Ruth	43	Chuck Klein
35	Lou Gehrig	42	Mel Ott
34	Al Simmons	39	Rogers Hornsby
33	Jimmie Foxx	39	Hack Wilson
25	Dale Alexander	32	Lefty O'Doul

1930

				Consec			1-Inn			One-Game						Men-On-Base				Batters					Totals					Pitchers	
Tm	Tot	H	A	2	3	4	3	4	5	5	6	7	8	9	10	0	1	2	3	PH	LO	XN	IP	P	1	10	20	30	40	RHP	LHP
AL																															
BOS	47	15	32	0	0	0	0	0	0	0	0	0	0	0	0	25	16	6	0	1	0	1	3	1	8	2	0	0	0	39	8
CHI	63	25	38	1	0	0	0	0	0	0	0	0	0	0	0	33	21	9	0	2	2	1	8	1	12	1	1	0	0	49	14
CLE	72	34	38	2	0	0	0	0	0	0	0	0	0	0	0	30	31	9	2	1	1	1	2	1	10	1	1	0	0	54	18
DET	82	45	37	2	0	0	0	0	0	0	0	0	0	0	0	37	33	9	3	0	1	2	3	4	15	1	1	0	0	69	13
NY	152	69	83	2	0	0	0	0	0	2	0	0	0	0	0	70	50	26	6	1	1	3	11	6	11	1	0	0	2	110	42
PHI	125	76	49	4	1	0	1	0	0	3	0	0	0	0	0	59	45	19	2	3	3	4	3	4	11	2	0	2	0	100	25
STL	75	35	40	3	0	0	0	0	0	0	0	0	0	0	0	39	29	7	0	0	1	1	1	2	12	1	0	1	0	65	10
WAS	57	17	40	3	0	0	0	0	0	0	0	0	0	0	0	24	20	12	1	1	1	0	6	1	11	2	0	0	0	40	17
NL																															
BOS	66	29	37	1	0	0	0	0	0	0	0	0	0	0	0	42	16	6	2	1	0	0	4	3	11	0	0	1	0	43	23
BRO	122	73	49	3	0	0	0	0	0	1	0	0	0	0	0	60	38	22	2	2	4	2	4	4	14	2	1	1	0	70	52
CHI	171	96	75	5	0	0	0	0	0	2	1	0	0	0	0	75	67	26	3	2	0	2	4	5	13	2	0	1	1	128	43
CIN	74	20	54	1	0	0	0	0	0	0	0	0	0	0	0	43	24	6	1	2	1	0	1	2	13	3	0	0	0	58	16
NY	143	91	52	5	0	0	0	0	0	1	0	0	0	0	0	76	35	28	4	2	0	1	7	7	11	3	3	0	0	108	35
PHI	126	72	54	3	0	0	0	0	0	2	0	0	0	0	0	66	39	20	1	5	2	1	1	4	9	2	1	0	1	89	37
PIT	86	27	59	2	0	0	0	0	0	0	0	0	0	0	0	50	27	9	0	0	1	2	9	4	11	3	0	0	0	61	25
STL	104	52	52	3	0	0	1	0	0	0	0	0	0	0	0	46	38	19	1	6	2	1	2	0	9	3	1	0	0	76	28
AL	673	316	357	17	1	0	1	0	0	5	0	0	0	0	0	317	245	97	14	9	10	13	37	20	90	11	3	3	2	526	147
NL	892	460	432	23	0	0	1	0	0	6	1	0	0	0	0	458	284	136	14	20	10	9	32	29	91	18	6	3	2	633	259
YR	1565	776	789	40	1	0	2	0	0	11	1	0	0	0	0	775	529	233	28	29	20	22	69	49	181	29	9	6	4	1159	406

AL		*NL*	
49	Babe Ruth	56	Hack Wilson
41	Lou Gehrig	40	Chuck Klein
37	Jimmie Foxx	38	Wally Berger
37	Goose Goslin	37	Gabby Hartnett
36	Al Simmons	35	Babe Herman

1931

				Consec			1-Inn			One-Game						Men-On-Base				Batters					Totals					Pitchers	
Tm	Tot	H	A	2	3	4	3	4	5	5	6	7	8	9	10	0	1	2	3	PH	LO	XN	IP	P	1	10	20	30	40	RHP	LHP
AL																															
BOS	37	11	26	0	0	0	0	0	0	0	0	0	0	0	0	19	16	2	0	1	1	0	0	1	7	1	0	0	0	29	8
CHI	27	11	16	0	0	0	0	0	0	0	0	0	0	0	0	10	12	5	0	2	0	2	1	0	13	0	0	0	0	18	9

				Consec			1-Inn			One-Game						Men-On-Base				Batters					Totals					Pitchers	
Tm	Tot	H	A	2	3	4	3	4	5	5	6	7	8	9	10	0	1	2	3	PH	LO	XN	IP	P	1	10	20	30	40	RHP	LHP
CLE	71	38	33	0	0	0	0	0	0	0	0	0	0	0	0	34	24	12	1	1	0	2	0	9	12	1	0	1	0	52	19
DET	43	19	24	1	0	0	0	0	0	0	0	0	0	0	0	28	10	5	0	0	1	2	1	2	12	1	0	0	0	27	16
NY	155	85	70	4	0	0	0	0	0	1	0	0	0	0	0	70	58	21	6	1	1	2	9	4	9	2	0	0	2	110	45
PHI	118	59	59	0	0	0	0	0	0	1	0	0	0	0	0	64	34	18	2	2	0	2	3	4	12	1	1	1	0	87	31
STL	76	42	34	3	0	0	0	0	0	0	0	0	0	0	0	40	26	10	0	2	3	1	1	2	11	1	1	0	0	52	24
WAS	49	13	36	1	0	0	0	0	0	0	0	0	0	0	0	33	12	4	0	1	1	0	7	1	9	1	0	0	0	32	17
NL																															
BOS	34	16	18	0	0	0	0	0	0	0	0	0	0	0	0	17	10	7	0	1	0	0	1	0	8	1	0	0	0	27	7
BRO	71	44	27	0	0	0	0	0	0	0	0	0	0	0	0	38	22	9	2	1	2	1	0	1	7	3	0	0	0	38	33
CHI	84	40	44	1	0	0	0	0	0	0	0	0	0	0	0	41	23	17	3	4	0	1	1	1	11	3	0	0	0	65	19
CIN	21	6	15	0	0	0	0	0	0	0	0	0	0	0	0	7	9	5	0	0	0	0	0	0	8	0	0	0	0	14	7
NY	101	80	21	2	0	0	0	0	0	0	0	0	0	0	0	56	28	15	2	4	0	0	3	5	12	2	1	0	0	82	19
PHI	81	51	30	1	0	0	0	0	0	0	0	0	0	0	0	41	31	9	0	0	0	1	1	0	9	2	0	1	0	56	25
PIT	41	25	16	1	0	0	0	0	0	0	0	0	0	0	0	22	16	2	1	2	0	1	9	0	11	1	0	0	0	22	19
STL	60	30	30	2	0	0	0	0	0	0	0	0	0	0	0	33	15	11	1	1	2	1	0	0	10	2	0	0	0	43	17
AL	576	278	298	9	0	0	0	0	0	2	0	0	0	0	0	298	192	77	9	10	7	11	22	23	85	8	2	2	2	407	169
NL	493	292	201	7	0	0	0	0	0	0	0	0	0	0	0	255	154	75	9	13	4	5	15	7	76	14	1	1	0	347	146
YR	1069	570	499	16	0	0	0	0	0	2	0	0	0	0	0	553	346	152	18	23	11	16	37	30	161	22	3	3	2	754	315

AL		*NL*	
46	Lou Gehrig	31	Chuck Klein
46	Babe Ruth	29	Mel Ott
32	Earl Averill	19	Wally Berger
30	Jimmie Foxx	18	Buzz Arlett
24	Goose Goslin	18	Babe Herman

1932

				Consec			1-Inn			One-Game						Men-On-Base				Batters					Totals					Pitchers	
Tm	Tot	H	A	2	3	4	3	4	5	5	6	7	8	9	10	0	1	2	3	PH	LO	XN	IP	P	1	10	20	30	40	RHP	LHP
AL																															
BOS	53	18	35	2	0	0	0	0	0	0	0	0	0	0	0	28	17	6	2	0	0	2	0	1	7	2	0	0	0	44	9
CHI	36	10	26	0	0	0	0	0	0	0	0	0	0	0	0	25	10	1	0	0	0	0	1	1	12	0	0	0	0	31	5
CLE	78	36	42	0	0	0	0	0	0	0	0	0	0	0	0	37	28	12	1	0	0	1	2	5	10	1	0	1	0	56	22
DET	80	29	51	2	0	0	0	0	0	0	0	0	0	0	0	43	26	10	1	1	2	1	1	4	12	2	0	0	0	51	29
NY	160	81	79	6	0	0	0	0	0	1	0	1	0	0	0	74	57	23	6	0	5	3	6	4	9	4	0	1	1	112	48
PHI	172	110	62	6	0	0	1	0	0	3	0	0	0	0	0	87	52	25	8	1	2	4	2	5	9	1	1	1	1	138	34
STL	67	47	20	0	0	0	0	0	0	0	0	0	0	0	0	35	23	7	2	1	4	3	2	0	8	3	0	0	0	51	16
WAS	61	21	40	0	0	0	0	0	0	0	0	0	0	0	0	30	21	9	1	2	1	1	3	0	11	1	0	0	0	40	21
NL																															
BOS	63	27	36	0	0	0	0	0	0	0	0	0	0	0	0	35	20	7	1	1	0	0	0	0	11	2	0	0	0	52	11
BRO	110	59	51	2	0	0	1	0	0	0	0	0	0	0	0	56	39	12	3	7	3	1	4	1	7	4	2	0	0	84	26
CHI	69	31	38	0	0	0	0	0	0	0	0	0	0	0	0	34	28	7	0	1	0	3	1	2	14	3	0	0	0	63	6
CIN	47	11	36	0	0	0	0	0	0	0	0	0	0	0	0	32	9	6	0	0	0	0	2	0	8	2	0	0	0	28	19
NY	116	78	38	2	1	0	0	0	0	0	1	0	0	0	0	64	30	19	3	1	0	1	3	3	13	1	1	1	0	87	29
PHI	122	86	36	5	0	0	0	0	0	0	0	0	0	0	0	62	41	14	5	1	2	0	1	0	7	3	1	1	0	88	34
PIT	48	22	26	0	0	0	0	0	0	0	0	0	0	0	0	23	15	9	1	2	0	2	7	0	10	0	0	0	0	25	23
STL	76	37	39	3	0	0	0	0	0	0	0	0	0	0	0	40	28	8	0	1	1	2	2	4	17	1	1	0	0	56	20
AL	707	352	355	16	0	0	1	0	0	4	0	1	0	0	0	359	234	93	21	5	14	15	17	20	78	14	1	3	2	523	184
NL	651	351	300	12	1	0	1	0	0	0	1	0	0	0	0	346	210	82	13	14	6	9	20	10	87	16	5	2	0	483	168
YR	1358	703	655	28	1	0	2	0	0	4	1	1	0	0	0	705	444	175	34	19	20	24	37	30	165	30	6	5	2	1006	352

AL		*NL*	
58	Jimmie Foxx	38	Chuck Klein
41	Babe Ruth	38	Mel Ott
35	Al Simmons	28	Bill Terry
34	Lou Gehrig	24	Don Hurst
32	Earl Averill	23	Hack Wilson

1933

				Consec			1-Inn			One-Game						Men-On-Base				Batters					Totals					Pitchers	
Tm	Tot	H	A	2	3	4	3	4	5	5	6	7	8	9	10	0	1	2	3	PH	LO	XN	IP	P	1	10	20	30	40	RHP	LHP
AL																															
BOS	50	23	27	0	0	0	0	0	0	0	0	0	0	0	0	28	15	7	0	3	1	0	1	3	12	1	0	0	0	40	10
CHI	43	20	23	0	0	0	0	0	0	0	0	0	0	0	0	27	9	6	1	1	2	1	1	1	11	2	0	0	0	33	10

Tm	Tot	H	A	Consec 2	3	4	1-Inn 3	4	5	One-Game 5	6	7	8	9	10	Men-On-Base 0	1	2	3	Batters PH	LO	XN	IP	P	Totals 1	10	20	30	40	Pitchers RHP	LHP
CLE	50	22	28	1	0	0	0	0	0	0	0	0	0	0	0	26	20	4	0	0	0	0	3	9	13	2	0	0	0	35	15
DET	57	27	30	1	0	0	0	0	0	0	0	0	0	0	0	20	28	9	0	0	1	2	0	0	6	3	0	0	0	44	13
NY	144	79	65	4	0	0	0	0	0	1	0	0	0	0	0	63	53	24	4	2	3	1	4	3	7	3	0	2	0	103	41
PHI	139	82	57	3	0	0	1	0	0	0	0	0	0	0	0	80	39	18	2	1	4	4	0	1	7	3	1	0	1	112	27
STL	64	43	21	1	0	0	0	0	0	0	0	0	0	0	0	30	25	9	0	2	0	1	3	0	12	2	0	0	0	43	21
WAS	60	14	46	1	0	0	0	0	0	0	0	0	0	0	0	34	20	5	1	2	1	1	4	1	11	2	0	0	0	48	12
NL																															
BOS	54	27	27	2	0	0	0	0	0	0	0	0	0	0	0	32	10	11	1	1	0	3	1	0	8	0	1	0	0	47	7
BRO	62	33	29	0	0	0	0	0	0	0	0	0	0	0	0	35	19	6	2	2	0	2	2	0	13	0	0	0	0	47	15
CHI	72	40	32	1	0	0	0	0	0	0	0	0	0	0	0	33	23	13	3	2	1	1	1	2	13	2	0	0	0	66	6
CIN	34	5	29	0	0	0	0	0	0	0	0	0	0	0	0	18	8	7	1	3	1	0	0	0	9	1	0	0	0	26	8
NY	82	55	27	1	0	0	0	0	0	0	0	0	0	0	0	47	19	12	4	2	0	2	0	4	13	1	1	0	0	66	16
PHI	60	45	15	2	0	0	0	0	0	0	0	0	0	0	0	32	15	12	1	2	0	2	1	0	7	0	1	0	0	52	8
PIT	39	12	27	0	0	0	0	0	0	0	0	0	0	0	0	25	7	5	2	1	0	0	4	0	9	1	0	0	0	33	6
STL	57	18	39	0	0	0	0	0	0	0	0	0	0	0	0	30	19	8	0	1	0	3	2	3	12	2	0	0	0	49	8
AL	607	310	297	11	0	0	1	0	0	1	0	0	0	0	0	308	209	82	8	11	12	10	16	18	79	18	1	2	1	458	149
NL	460	235	225	6	0	0	0	0	0	0	0	0	0	0	0	252	120	74	14	14	2	13	11	9	84	7	3	0	0	386	74
YR	1067	545	522	17	0	0	1	0	0	1	0	0	0	0	0	560	329	156	22	25	14	23	27	27	163	25	4	2	1	844	223

AL		*NL*	
48	Jimmie Foxx	28	Chuck Klein
34	Babe Ruth	27	Wally Berger
32	Lou Gehrig	23	Mel Ott
21	Bob Johnson	18	Joe Medwick
18	Tony Lazzeri	16	Multiple Players Tied

1934

Tm	Tot	H	A	Consec 2	3	4	1-Inn 3	4	5	One-Game 5	6	7	8	9	10	Men-On-Base 0	1	2	3	Batters PH	LO	XN	IP	P	Totals 1	10	20	30	40	Pitchers RHP	LHP
AL																															
BOS	51	23	28	1	0	0	0	0	0	0	0	0	0	0	0	27	12	9	3	3	0	2	3	6	13	1	0	0	0	48	3
CHI	71	47	24	0	0	0	0	0	0	0	0	0	0	0	0	33	28	5	5	0	0	1	0	1	10	1	1	0	0	64	7
CLE	100	45	55	0	0	0	0	0	0	0	0	0	0	0	0	44	35	17	4	0	2	2	4	4	10	1	0	2	0	88	12
DET	74	28	46	2	0	0	0	0	0	0	0	0	0	0	0	33	32	9	0	0	0	2	1	2	7	2	1	0	0	60	14
NY	135	75	60	3	0	0	2	0	0	1	0	0	0	0	0	68	43	19	5	1	1	3	3	3	8	3	1	0	1	101	34
PHI	144	81	63	6	1	0	1	0	0	0	0	0	0	0	0	86	39	15	4	4	3	2	4	1	8	3	0	1	1	131	13
STL	62	35	27	0	0	0	0	0	0	0	0	0	0	0	0	27	19	14	2	1	2	0	1	0	9	2	0	0	0	47	15
WAS	51	14	37	3	0	0	1	0	0	0	0	0	0	0	0	24	19	6	2	1	0	0	4	1	14	1	0	0	0	44	7
NL																															
BOS	83	36	47	1	0	0	0	0	0	0	0	0	0	0	0	42	29	11	1	0	2	1	0	0	7	1	0	1	0	74	9
BRO	79	42	37	1	0	0	1	0	0	0	0	0	0	0	0	44	22	12	1	2	2	0	2	0	10	2	0	0	0	64	15
CHI	101	53	48	1	0	0	0	0	0	0	0	0	0	0	0	51	35	13	2	3	0	2	0	2	13	1	2	0	0	77	24
CIN	55	17	38	0	0	0	0	0	0	0	0	0	0	0	0	32	15	6	2	1	0	1	0	1	9	2	0	0	0	49	6
NY	126	75	51	0	0	0	0	0	0	0	0	0	0	0	0	61	42	20	3	6	1	1	2	10	14	2	0	1	0	100	26
PHI	56	28	28	5	0	0	0	0	0	0	0	0	0	0	0	31	17	8	0	0	0	1	3	1	9	3	0	0	0	42	14
PIT	52	22	30	0	0	0	0	0	0	0	0	0	0	0	0	32	16	3	1	1	0	2	2	0	5	3	0	0	0	44	8
STL	104	56	48	2	0	0	0	0	0	0	0	0	0	0	0	51	36	15	2	1	1	4	1	4	10	3	0	1	0	86	18
AL	688	348	340	15	1	0	4	0	0	1	0	0	0	0	0	342	227	94	25	10	8	12	20	18	79	14	3	3	2	583	105
NL	656	329	327	10	0	0	1	0	0	0	0	0	0	0	0	344	212	88	12	14	6	12	10	18	77	17	2	3	0	536	120
YR	1344	677	667	25	1	0	5	0	0	1	0	0	0	0	0	686	439	182	37	24	14	24	30	36	156	31	5	6	2	1119	225

AL		*NL*	
49	Lou Gehrig	35	Ripper Collins
44	Jimmie Foxx	35	Mel Ott
35	Hal Trosky	34	Wally Berger
34	Bob Johnson	22	Gabby Hartnett
31	Earl Averill	20	Chuck Klein

1935

Tm	Tot	H	A	Consec 2	3	4	1-Inn 3	4	5	One-Game 5	6	7	8	9	10	Men-On-Base 0	1	2	3	Batters PH	LO	XN	IP	P	Totals 1	10	20	30	40	Pitchers RHP	LHP
AL																															
BOS	69	26	43	0	0	0	0	0	0	0	0	0	0	0	0	41	20	6	2	1	1	1	0	8	15	1	0	0	0	59	10
CHI	74	50	24	1	0	0	0	0	0	1	0	0	0	0	0	35	27	9	3	0	0	1	2	1	9	2	1	0	0	58	16

				Consec			1-Inn			One-Game						Men-On-Base				Batters					Totals					Pitchers	
Tm	Tot	H	A	2	3	4	3	4	5	5	6	7	8	9	10	0	1	2	3	PH	LO	XN	IP	P	1	10	20	30	40	RHP	LHP
CLE	93	53	40	2	0	0	0	0	0	0	0	0	0	0	0	45	28	18	2	1	0	2	2	5	8	3	1	0	0	71	22
DET	106	45	61	2	0	0	0	0	0	0	0	0	0	0	0	57	36	9	4	0	2	3	2	5	8	2	0	1	0	76	30
NY	104	60	44	0	0	0	0	0	0	0	1	0	0	0	0	56	26	16	6	0	0	4	9	4	10	3	0	1	0	80	24
PHI	112	63	49	2	0	0	0	0	0	1	0	0	0	0	0	59	42	9	2	0	1	3	1	2	8	0	2	1	0	96	16
STL	73	36	37	2	0	0	0	0	0	0	0	0	0	0	0	35	26	9	3	0	1	1	2	0	6	4	0	0	0	58	15
WAS	32	5	27	0	0	0	0	0	0	0	0	0	0	0	0	11	14	4	3	0	0	1	1	2	14	0	0	0	0	20	12
NL																															
BOS	75	34	41	1	0	0	0	0	0	0	0	0	0	0	0	40	24	7	4	1	1	1	0	0	15	0	0	1	0	66	9
BRO	59	32	27	0	0	0	0	0	0	0	0	0	0	0	0	32	16	8	3	1	0	2	1	0	11	1	0	0	0	55	4
CHI	88	43	45	0	0	0	0	0	0	0	0	0	0	0	0	52	24	10	2	0	0	3	1	2	12	2	1	0	0	73	15
CIN	73	18	55	1	0	0	0	0	0	0	0	0	0	0	0	39	25	9	0	1	0	1	2	0	12	3	0	0	0	55	18
NY	123	84	39	3	0	0	1	0	0	0	0	0	0	0	0	58	46	18	1	3	1	1	4	6	15	2	1	1	0	105	18
PHI	92	52	40	4	0	0	0	0	0	0	0	0	0	0	0	47	31	13	1	1	1	4	1	3	10	2	1	0	0	70	22
PIT	66	32	34	0	1	0	1	0	0	1	0	0	0	0	0	39	16	7	4	0	0	1	5	0	6	3	0	0	0	48	18
STL	86	39	47	1	0	0	0	0	0	0	0	0	0	0	0	48	24	11	3	0	1	5	4	3	11	0	2	0	0	67	19
AL	663	338	325	9	0	0	0	0	0	2	1	0	0	0	0	339	219	80	25	2	5	16	19	27	78	15	4	3	0	518	145
NL	662	334	328	10	1	0	2	0	0	1	0	0	0	0	0	355	206	83	18	7	4	18	18	14	92	13	5	2	0	539	123
YR	1325	672	653	19	1	0	2	0	0	3	1	0	0	0	0	694	425	163	43	9	9	34	37	41	170	28	9	5	0	1057	268

AL		*NL*	
36	Jimmie Foxx	34	Wally Berger
36	Hank Greenberg	31	Mel Ott
30	Lou Gehrig	25	Dolph Camilli
28	Bob Johnson	23	Ripper Collins
26	Hal Trosky	23	Joe Medwick

1936

AL

Tm	Tot	H	A	2	3	4	3	4	5	5	6	7	8	9	10	0	1	2	3	PH	LO	XN	IP	P	1	10	20	30	40	RHP	LHP
BOS	86	38	48	0	0	0	0	0	0	0	0	0	0	0	0	41	27	17	1	1	2	0	2	7	11	1	0	0	1	76	10
CHI	60	23	37	0	0	0	0	0	0	0	0	0	0	0	0	32	18	9	1	0	0	0	0	1	10	1	0	0	0	56	4
CLE	123	73	50	8	0	0	0	0	0	2	0	0	0	0	0	72	33	16	2	0	0	2	2	2	10	1	1	0	1	89	34
DET	94	51	43	1	0	0	0	0	0	0	0	0	0	0	0	48	25	19	2	0	1	1	2	1	10	3	1	0	0	80	14
NY	182	82	100	8	0	0	2	0	0	3	2	0	0	0	0	100	51	26	5	0	2	2	5	6	10	4	2	0	1	133	49
PHI	72	43	29	0	0	0	0	0	0	0	0	0	0	0	0	37	27	7	1	0	0	2	2	0	6	3	1	0	0	65	7
STL	79	47	32	5	0	0	0	0	0	0	0	0	0	0	0	50	21	7	1	1	0	0	2	1	8	3	1	0	0	72	7
WAS	62	16	46	0	0	0	1	0	0	0	0	0	0	0	0	33	21	8	0	1	1	3	6	1	11	2	0	0	0	48	14
NL																															
BOS	67	26	41	2	0	0	0	0	0	0	0	0	0	0	0	39	17	10	1	1	1	2	0	1	8	1	1	0	0	62	5
BRO	33	15	18	0	0	0	0	0	0	0	0	0	0	0	0	16	12	5	0	0	2	0	1	0	13	0	0	0	0	31	2
CHI	76	34	42	2	0	0	0	0	0	1	1	0	0	0	0	50	16	9	1	3	2	0	0	5	15	1	0	0	0	64	12
CIN	82	20	62	0	0	0	0	0	0	0	0	0	0	0	0	40	31	9	2	4	3	1	3	3	13	3	0	0	0	73	9
NY	97	68	29	4	0	0	0	0	0	0	0	0	0	0	0	53	27	16	1	3	0	2	2	2	14	0	0	1	0	86	11
PHI	103	69	34	4	0	0	0	0	0	1	0	0	0	0	0	47	36	19	1	1	0	2	0	3	12	2	2	0	0	77	26
PIT	60	23	37	2	0	0	0	0	0	0	0	0	0	0	0	23	25	12	0	0	0	0	0	2	11	2	0	0	0	40	20
STL	88	38	50	1	0	0	0	0	0	0	0	0	0	0	0	40	31	14	3	4	1	2	3	1	11	4	0	0	0	74	14
AL	758	373	385	22	0	0	3	0	0	5	2	0	0	0	0	413	223	109	13	3	6	10	21	19	76	18	6	0	3	619	139
NL	606	293	313	15	0	0	0	0	0	2	1	0	0	0	0	308	195	94	9	16	9	9	9	17	97	13	3	1	0	507	99
YR	1364	666	698	37	0	0	3	0	0	7	3	0	0	0	0	721	418	203	22	19	15	19	30	36	173	31	9	1	3	1126	238

AL		*NL*	
49	Lou Gehrig	33	Mel Ott
42	Hal Trosky	28	Dolph Camilli
41	Jimmie Foxx	25	Wally Berger
29	Joe DiMaggio	25	Chuck Klein
28	Earl Averill	19	Johnny Mize

1937

AL

Tm	Tot	H	A	2	3	4	3	4	5	5	6	7	8	9	10	0	1	2	3	PH	LO	XN	IP	P	1	10	20	30	40	RHP	LHP
BOS	100	53	47	3	0	0	0	0	0	0	0	0	0	0	0	50	34	15	1	1	1	0	3	1	8	2	0	1	0	89	11
CHI	67	39	28	3	0	0	1	0	0	0	0	0	0	0	0	38	18	10	1	1	2	1	2	3	12	2	0	0	0	63	4

				Consec			1-Inn			One-Game						Men-On-Base				Batters					Totals					Pitchers	
Tm	Tot	H	A	2	3	4	3	4	5	5	6	7	8	9	10	0	1	2	3	PH	LO	XN	IP	P	1	10	20	30	40	RHP	LHP
CLE	103	48	55	2	0	0	0	0	0	0	0	0	0	0	0	55	27	18	3	3	4	2	3	0	8	0	2	1	0	75	28
DET	150	91	59	3	0	0	0	0	0	0	1	0	0	0	0	72	43	29	6	4	3	4	0	3	10	3	0	1	1	126	24
NY	174	94	80	3	0	0	0	0	0	0	0	0	0	0	0	77	64	27	6	2	2	2	1	0	5	3	1	1	1	131	43
PHI	94	51	43	1	0	0	0	0	0	0	0	0	0	0	0	45	32	15	2	3	4	1	2	2	13	1	2	0	0	85	9
STL	71	39	32	1	0	0	0	0	0	0	0	0	0	0	0	31	22	17	1	2	2	1	0	2	12	1	1	0	0	61	10
WAS	47	14	33	0	0	0	0	0	0	0	0	0	0	0	0	26	18	3	0	0	1	0	7	1	12	1	0	0	0	32	15
NL																															
BOS	63	26	37	2	0	0	0	0	0	0	0	0	0	0	0	39	15	7	2	1	2	4	1	1	10	3	0	0	0	51	12
BRO	37	20	17	0	0	0	0	0	0	0	0	0	0	0	0	21	8	6	2	0	0	2	2	0	10	0	0	0	0	30	7
CHI	96	47	49	0	0	0	1	0	0	0	0	0	0	0	0	50	34	9	3	0	1	1	0	6	12	4	0	0	0	78	18
CIN	73	13	60	0	0	0	0	0	0	0	0	0	0	0	0	34	29	7	3	3	1	0	1	0	11	2	0	0	0	63	10
NY	111	76	35	3	0	0	0	0	0	0	0	0	0	0	0	59	34	16	2	3	3	1	2	4	12	3	0	1	0	74	37
PHI	103	65	38	2	0	0	0	0	0	0	0	0	0	0	0	58	29	13	3	0	2	1	0	1	10	2	1	0	0	74	29
PIT	47	13	34	0	0	0	0	0	0	0	0	0	0	0	0	24	16	6	1	0	1	0	2	0	10	0	0	0	0	26	21
STL	94	52	42	2	0	0	0	0	0	1	0	0	0	0	0	47	30	16	1	0	1	1	1	3	10	1	1	1	0	75	19
AL	806	429	377	16	0	0	1	0	0	0	1	0	0	0	0	394	258	134	20	16	19	11	18	12	80	13	6	4	2	662	144
NL	624	312	312	9	0	0	1	0	0	1	0	0	0	0	0	332	195	80	17	7	11	10	9	15	85	15	2	2	0	471	153
YR	1430	741	689	25	0	0	2	0	0	1	1	0	0	0	0	726	453	214	37	23	30	21	27	27	165	28	8	6	2	1133	297

AL

46 Joe DiMaggio
40 Hank Greenberg
37 Lou Gehrig
36 Jimmie Foxx
35 Rudy York

NL

31 Joe Medwick
31 Mel Ott
27 Dolph Camilli
25 Johnny Mize
18 Augie Galan

1938

Tm	Tot	H	A	2	3	4	3	4	5	5	6	7	8	9	10	0	1	2	3	PH	LO	XN	IP	P	1	10	20	30	40	RHP	LHP
AL																															
BOS	98	67	31	3	0	0	0	0	0	0	0	0	0	0	0	46	26	19	7	0	0	1	1	2	9	1	0	0	1	88	10
CHI	67	24	43	2	0	0	0	0	0	0	0	0	0	0	0	34	22	10	1	2	2	0	2	6	13	1	0	0	0	54	13
CLE	113	54	59	2	0	0	0	0	0	0	0	0	0	0	0	53	43	16	1	0	1	1	2	2	9	3	2	0	0	88	25
DET	137	83	54	7	0	0	0	0	0	0	0	0	0	0	0	67	33	27	10	1	1	1	2	0	7	0	1	1	1	111	26
NY	174	112	62	6	0	0	1	0	0	0	0	0	0	0	0	82	68	21	3	1	1	2	3	7	6	2	4	1	0	140	34
PHI	98	55	43	1	0	0	0	0	0	0	0	0	0	0	0	47	38	8	5	3	2	0	1	1	5	4	0	1	0	86	12
STL	92	52	40	2	0	0	0	0	0	0	0	0	0	0	0	50	32	8	2	2	0	0	0	0	9	2	0	1	0	76	16
WAS	85	33	52	5	0	0	0	0	0	0	0	0	0	0	0	40	29	8	8	2	1	0	6	1	11	1	2	0	0	61	24
NL																															
BOS	54	12	42	0	1	0	1	0	0	0	0	0	0	0	0	36	12	3	3	2	0	0	0	0	9	2	0	0	0	39	15
BRO	61	38	23	0	0	0	0	0	0	0	0	0	0	0	0	31	25	4	1	0	1	0	0	1	11	1	1	0	0	45	16
CHI	65	24	41	1	0	0	0	0	0	0	0	0	0	0	0	38	18	7	2	0	0	1	1	3	11	2	0	0	0	53	12
CIN	110	50	60	4	0	0	1	0	0	0	0	0	0	0	0	63	37	9	1	0	1	4	1	2	7	4	0	1	0	89	21
NY	125	89	36	2	0	0	0	0	0	0	0	0	0	0	0	66	29	25	5	0	2	3	5	2	12	3	0	1	0	84	41
PHI	40	23	17	0	0	0	0	0	0	0	0	0	0	0	0	22	11	7	0	1	1	2	0	1	13	0	0	0	0	32	8
PIT	65	22	43	1	0	0	0	0	0	1	0	0	0	0	0	33	19	11	2	0	2	2	3	1	9	0	1	0	0	38	27
STL	91	58	33	2	0	0	0	0	0	0	0	0	0	0	0	47	27	14	3	0	4	1	1	3	11	0	2	0	0	74	17
AL	864	480	384	28	0	0	1	0	0	0	0	0	0	0	0	419	291	117	37	11	8	5	17	19	69	14	9	4	2	704	160
NL	611	316	295	10	1	0	2	0	0	1	0	0	0	0	0	336	178	80	17	3	11	13	11	13	83	12	4	2	0	454	157
YR	1475	796	679	38	1	0	3	0	0	1	0	0	0	0	0	755	469	197	54	14	19	18	28	32	152	26	13	6	2	1158	317

AL

58 Hank Greenberg
50 Jimmie Foxx
34 Harlond Clift
33 Rudy York
32 Joe DiMaggio

NL

36 Mel Ott
30 Ival Goodman
27 Johnny Mize
24 Dolph Camilli
23 Johnny Rizzo

1939

Tm	Tot	H	A	2	3	4	3	4	5	5	6	7	8	9	10	0	1	2	3	PH	LO	XN	IP	P	1	10	20	30	40	RHP	LHP
AL																															
BOS	124	57	67	4	0	0	0	0	0	0	0	0	0	0	0	62	36	21	5	1	0	2	1	4	6	3	0	2	0	109	15
CHI	64	38	26	0	0	0	0	0	0	0	0	0	0	0	0	24	33	7	0	0	1	0	1	1	7	3	0	0	0	57	7

Tm	Tot	H	A	Consec 2	3	4	1-Inn 3	4	5	One-Game 5	6	7	8	9	10	Men-On-Base 0	1	2	3	Batters PH	LO	XN	IP	P	Totals 1	10	20	30	40	Pitchers RHP	LHP
CLE	85	30	55	3	1	0	1	0	0	0	0	0	0	0	0	51	23	11	0	0	0	2	5	2	12	2	1	0	0	61	24
DET	124	66	58	5	0	0	0	0	0	0	0	0	0	0	0	59	43	14	8	4	1	3	2	3	12	2	1	1	0	111	13
NY	166	84	82	1	0	0	0	0	0	2	0	0	1	0	0	91	45	27	3	1	5	0	5	1	4	4	3	1	0	124	42
PHI	98	45	53	2	0	0	0	0	0	0	0	0	0	0	0	47	37	12	2	1	0	2	0	0	9	2	2	0	0	83	15
STL	91	47	44	0	0	0	0	0	0	0	0	0	0	0	0	48	34	8	1	3	1	0	0	2	13	3	1	0	0	79	12
WAS	44	11	33	1	0	0	0	0	0	0	0	0	0	0	0	16	24	4	0	1	0	0	3	1	12	1	0	0	0	33	11
NL																															
BOS	56	13	43	2	0	0	0	0	0	0	0	0	0	0	0	27	19	8	2	0	0	2	0	1	11	1	0	0	0	46	10
BRO	78	41	37	2	0	0	0	0	0	0	0	0	0	0	0	46	24	6	2	1	1	0	1	2	15	1	1	0	0	57	21
CHI	91	44	47	1	0	0	0	0	0	0	0	0	0	0	0	64	19	6	2	2	2	0	1	5	14	1	1	0	0	80	11
CIN	98	49	49	1	0	0	0	0	0	0	0	0	0	0	0	49	36	10	3	0	1	3	2	1	4	4	1	0	0	87	11
NY	116	84	32	3	2	0	1	0	0	1	0	2	0	0	0	69	32	15	0	3	2	3	1	4	15	4	1	0	0	105	11
PHI	49	18	31	0	0	0	0	0	0	0	0	0	0	0	0	30	16	3	0	2	2	0	1	0	17	0	0	0	0	42	7
PIT	63	24	39	1	0	0	0	0	0	0	0	0	0	0	0	31	23	7	2	1	0	1	0	3	14	2	0	0	0	50	13
STL	98	63	35	1	0	0	0	0	0	0	0	0	0	0	0	50	37	10	1	3	0	0	4	3	8	3	1	0	0	87	11
AL	796	378	418	16	1	0	1	0	0	2	0	0	1	0	0	398	275	104	19	11	8	9	17	14	75	20	8	4	0	657	139
NL	649	336	313	11	2	0	1	0	0	1	0	2	0	0	0	366	206	65	12	12	8	9	10	19	98	16	5	0	0	554	95
YR	1445	714	731	27	3	0	2	0	0	3	0	2	1	0	0	764	481	169	31	23	16	18	27	33	173	36	13	4	0	1211	234

AL		*NL*	
35	Jimmie Foxx	28	Johnny Mize
33	Hank Greenberg	27	Mel Ott
31	Ted Williams	26	Dolph Camilli
30	Joe DiMaggio	24	Hank Leiber
28	Joe Gordon	20	Ernie Lombardi

1940

Tm	Tot	H	A	Consec 2	3	4	1-Inn 3	4	5	One-Game 5	6	7	8	9	10	Men-On-Base 0	1	2	3	Batters PH	LO	XN	IP	P	Totals 1	10	20	30	40	Pitchers RHP	LHP
AL																															
BOS	145	73	72	4	1	0	1	0	0	1	1	0	0	0	0	79	40	19	7	2	0	5	0	3	6	0	4	1	0	114	31
CHI	73	36	37	0	0	0	0	0	0	0	0	0	0	0	0	38	26	8	1	5	1	2	0	1	9	1	1	0	0	61	12
CLE	101	37	64	2	0	0	0	0	0	1	0	0	0	0	0	64	25	9	3	1	2	1	2	2	5	4	1	0	0	66	35
DET	134	82	52	2	0	0	0	0	0	0	0	0	0	0	0	68	48	15	3	4	2	0	2	2	11	2	0	1	1	103	31
NY	155	83	72	5	0	0	0	0	0	2	1	0	0	0	0	79	47	22	7	3	3	2	2	3	7	4	1	2	0	105	50
PHI	105	44	61	1	0	0	0	0	0	0	0	0	0	0	0	55	34	14	2	0	2	0	0	2	11	1	1	1	0	81	24
STL	118	68	50	6	0	0	0	0	0	1	0	0	0	0	0	65	36	12	5	2	0	4	0	3	9	3	2	0	0	90	28
WAS	52	19	33	0	0	0	0	0	0	0	0	0	0	0	0	22	20	8	2	1	0	3	3	1	9	2	0	0	0	41	11
NL																															
BOS	59	25	34	2	0	0	0	0	0	0	0	0	0	0	0	28	17	11	3	0	2	1	0	0	8	2	0	0	0	50	9
BRO	93	40	53	1	0	0	0	0	0	0	0	0	0	0	0	51	26	11	5	1	0	5	0	2	16	2	1	0	0	79	14
CHI	86	40	46	1	0	0	0	0	0	0	0	0	0	0	0	39	27	15	5	3	0	5	0	1	14	1	1	0	0	68	18
CIN	89	47	42	2	0	0	0	0	0	0	0	0	0	0	0	51	23	12	3	0	1	2	2	1	10	4	0	0	0	75	14
NY	91	61	30	2	0	0	0	0	0	1	0	0	0	0	0	52	21	15	3	1	2	1	4	2	12	3	0	0	0	75	16
PHI	75	33	42	2	0	0	0	0	0	0	0	0	0	0	0	39	28	6	2	2	0	2	0	0	10	2	1	0	0	60	15
PIT	76	26	50	2	0	0	0	0	0	0	0	0	0	0	0	40	21	14	1	1	1	0	4	1	11	3	0	0	0	62	14
STL	119	69	50	4	0	0	0	0	0	2	0	1	0	0	0	71	33	13	2	1	0	1	2	2	12	2	0	0	1	85	34
AL	883	442	441	20	1	0	1	0	0	5	2	0	0	0	0	470	276	107	30	18	10	17	9	17	67	17	10	5	1	661	222
NL	688	341	347	16	0	0	0	0	0	3	0	1	0	0	0	371	196	97	24	9	6	17	12	9	93	19	3	0	1	554	134
YR	1571	783	788	36	1	0	1	0	0	8	2	1	0	0	0	841	472	204	54	27	16	34	21	26	160	36	13	5	2	1215	356

AL		*NL*	
41	Hank Greenberg	43	Johnny Mize
36	Jimmie Foxx	25	Bill Nicholson
33	Rudy York	24	Johnny Rizzo
31	Joe DiMaggio	23	Dolph Camilli
31	Bob Johnson	19	Multiple Players Tied

1941

Tm	Tot	H	A	Consec 2	3	4	1-Inn 3	4	5	One-Game 5	6	7	8	9	10	Men-On-Base 0	1	2	3	Batters PH	LO	XN	IP	P	Totals 1	10	20	30	40	Pitchers RHP	LHP
AL																															
BOS	124	70	54	4	0	0	0	0	0	0	0	0	0	0	0	60	40	15	9	3	2	3	0	1	7	4	0	1	0	110	14
CHI	47	17	30	0	0	0	0	0	0	0	0	0	0	0	0	33	9	4	1	1	2	1	0	0	9	2	0	0	0	42	5

Tm	Tot	H	A	Consec			1-Inn			One-Game						Men-On-Base				Batters					Totals					Pitchers	
				2	3	4	3	4	5	5	6	7	8	9	10	0	1	2	3	PH	LO	XN	IP	P	1	10	20	30	40	RHP	LHP
CLE	103	45	58	2	0	0	0	0	0	1	0	0	0	0	0	61	26	16	0	1	0	1	2	4	13	2	2	0	0	75	28
DET	81	50	31	2	0	0	0	0	0	0	0	0	0	0	0	43	23	13	2	1	0	0	2	1	12	2	1	0	0	63	18
NY	151	76	75	4	0	0	0	0	0	1	0	0	0	0	0	74	54	18	5	2	0	8	3	2	10	0	1	3	0	113	38
PHI	85	43	42	0	0	0	0	0	0	0	0	0	0	0	0	40	25	16	4	1	0	3	0	1	7	1	2	0	0	74	11
STL	91	49	42	3	0	0	0	0	0	0	0	0	0	0	0	48	26	15	2	2	1	3	2	1	7	4	0	0	0	76	15
WAS	52	13	39	0	0	0	0	0	0	0	0	0	0	0	0	24	22	4	2	1	0	2	4	0	10	1	0	0	0	43	9
NL																															
BOS	48	17	31	0	0	0	0	0	0	0	0	0	0	0	0	26	13	8	1	2	0	3	2	1	11	1	0	0	0	40	8
BRO	101	55	46	1	0	0	0	0	0	0	0	0	0	0	0	58	25	16	2	2	1	3	1	5	12	2	0	1	0	75	26
CHI	99	37	62	3	1	0	1	0	0	0	0	0	0	0	0	60	19	13	7	1	1	2	0	8	16	1	1	0	0	72	27
CIN	64	27	37	0	0	0	0	0	0	0	0	0	0	0	0	37	15	9	3	1	0	0	0	0	10	3	0	0	0	60	4
NY	95	68	27	0	0	0	0	0	0	0	0	0	0	0	0	42	40	9	4	3	0	4	1	1	13	0	2	0	0	77	18
PHI	64	34	30	0	0	0	0	0	0	0	0	0	0	0	0	40	16	6	2	2	1	1	0	0	9	2	0	0	0	57	7
PIT	56	20	36	0	0	0	0	0	0	0	0	0	0	0	0	26	19	10	1	1	0	1	1	1	8	1	1	0	0	45	11
STL	70	37	33	1	0	0	0	0	0	0	0	0	0	0	0	36	25	8	1	1	0	3	2	2	13	2	0	0	0	55	15
AL	734	363	371	15	0	0	0	0	0	2	0	0	0	0	0	383	225	101	25	12	5	21	13	10	75	16	6	4	0	596	138
NL	597	295	302	5	1	0	1	0	0	0	0	0	0	0	0	325	172	79	21	13	3	17	7	18	92	12	4	1	0	481	116
YR	1331	658	673	20	1	0	1	0	0	2	0	0	0	0	0	708	397	180	46	25	8	38	20	28	167	28	10	5	0	1077	254

AL

37 Ted Williams
33 Charlie Keller
31 Tommy Henrich
30 Joe DiMaggio
27 Rudy York

NL

34 Dolph Camilli
27 Mel Ott
26 Bill Nicholson
25 Babe Young
23 Babe Dahlgren

1942

AL

Tm	Tot	H	A	Consec			1-Inn			One-Game						Men-On-Base				Batters					Totals					Pitchers	
				2	3	4	3	4	5	5	6	7	8	9	10	0	1	2	3	PH	LO	XN	IP	P	1	10	20	30	40	RHP	LHP
BOS	103	54	49	1	0	0	0	0	0	0	0	0	0	0	0	57	39	6	1	0	2	1	2	2	8	3	0	1	0	92	11
CHI	25	6	19	0	0	0	0	0	0	0	0	0	0	0	0	13	9	2	1	1	0	0	0	1	9	0	0	0	0	22	3
CLE	50	20	30	1	0	0	0	0	0	0	0	0	0	0	0	33	14	3	0	0	2	1	0	2	9	2	0	0	0	42	8
DET	76	50	26	1	0	0	0	0	0	0	0	0	0	0	0	48	19	8	1	4	2	2	1	1	12	2	1	0	0	59	17
NY	108	62	46	2	0	0	0	0	0	0	0	0	0	0	0	55	37	11	5	1	3	4	0	1	9	2	2	0	0	81	27
PHI	33	16	17	0	0	0	0	0	0	0	0	0	0	0	0	21	5	6	1	0	0	1	0	0	9	1	0	0	0	30	3
STL	98	55	43	4	0	0	0	0	0	0	0	0	0	0	0	49	30	17	2	2	1	3	1	1	10	3	1	0	0	85	13
WAS	40	13	27	2	0	0	0	0	0	0	0	0	0	0	0	25	12	3	0	0	0	1	2	0	10	0	0	0	0	30	10
NL																															
BOS	68	36	32	0	0	0	0	0	0	1	0	0	0	0	0	39	21	6	2	1	1	4	2	5	12	2	0	0	0	51	17
BRO	62	30	32	1	0	0	0	0	0	0	0	0	0	0	0	29	20	10	3	2	0	2	1	0	9	1	1	0	0	46	16
CHI	75	36	39	2	0	0	0	0	0	0	0	0	0	0	0	46	22	5	2	1	4	1	1	2	13	0	1	0	0	57	18
CIN	66	30	36	1	0	0	0	0	0	0	0	0	0	0	0	41	19	4	2	3	0	2	2	2	13	2	0	0	0	65	1
NY	109	80	29	4	0	0	0	0	0	1	0	0	0	0	0	55	36	14	4	2	0	3	1	3	11	2	1	1	0	80	29
PHI	44	18	26	0	0	0	0	0	0	0	0	0	0	0	0	29	12	2	1	1	1	0	3	1	10	0	0	0	0	37	7
PIT	54	15	39	1	0	0	0	0	0	0	0	0	0	0	0	31	15	7	1	0	0	1	2	2	12	1	0	0	0	39	15
STL	60	31	29	1	0	0	0	0	0	0	0	0	0	0	0	36	17	5	2	0	0	4	1	0	8	2	0	0	0	40	20
AL	533	276	257	11	0	0	0	0	0	0	0	0	0	0	0	301	165	56	11	8	10	13	6	8	76	13	4	1	0	441	92
NL	538	276	262	10	0	0	0	0	0	2	0	0	0	0	0	306	162	53	17	10	6	17	13	15	88	10	3	1	0	415	123
YR	1071	552	519	21	0	0	0	0	0	2	0	0	0	0	0	607	327	109	28	18	16	30	19	23	164	23	7	2	0	856	215

AL

36 Ted Williams
27 Chet Laabs
26 Charlie Keller
21 Joe DiMaggio
21 Rudy York

NL

30 Mel Ott
26 Dolph Camilli
26 Johnny Mize
21 Bill Nicholson
16 Max West

1943

AL

Tm	Tot	H	A	Consec			1-Inn			One-Game						Men-On-Base				Batters					Totals					Pitchers	
				2	3	4	3	4	5	5	6	7	8	9	10	0	1	2	3	PH	LO	XN	IP	P	1	10	20	30	40	RHP	LHP
BOS	57	29	28	2	0	0	0	0	0	0	0	0	0	0	0	30	17	10	0	5	0	2	2	0	11	2	0	0	0	56	1
CHI	33	20	13	1	0	0	0	0	0	0	0	0	0	0	0	24	8	0	1	0	1	0	2	3	15	0	0	0	0	27	6

Tm	Tot	H	A	Consec			1-Inn			One-Game						Men-On-Base				Batters					Totals					Pitchers	
				2	3	4	3	4	5	5	6	7	8	9	10	0	1	2	3	PH	LO	XN	IP	P	1	10	20	30	40	RHP	LHP
CLE	55	16	39	1	0	0	0	0	0	0	0	0	0	0	0	34	14	7	0	0	1	4	1	1	12	1	0	0	0	50	5
DET	77	45	32	0	0	0	0	0	0	0	0	0	0	0	0	42	22	12	1	0	0	3	0	2	10	1	0	1	0	63	14
NY	100	60	40	1	0	0	0	0	0	0	0	0	0	0	0	60	24	15	1	0	1	4	3	2	10	2	0	1	0	85	15
PHI	26	14	12	0	0	0	0	0	0	0	0	0	0	0	0	19	3	3	1	1	1	0	3	0	9	1	0	0	0	21	5
STL	78	49	29	2	0	0	0	0	0	0	0	0	0	0	0	37	30	11	0	2	1	4	0	0	6	3	1	0	0	68	10
WAS	47	9	38	0	0	0	0	0	0	0	0	0	0	0	0	26	17	4	0	0	0	0	3	2	12	1	0	0	0	43	4
NL																															
BOS	39	25	14	0	0	0	0	0	0	0	0	0	0	0	0	16	16	6	1	1	0	3	0	2	9	1	0	0	0	30	9
BRO	39	21	18	1	0	0	0	0	0	0	0	0	0	0	0	19	16	2	2	0	0	1	4	1	11	0	0	0	0	34	5
CHI	52	24	28	1	0	0	0	0	0	0	0	0	0	0	0	22	24	6	0	0	0	2	0	0	8	0	1	0	0	44	8
CIN	43	17	26	0	0	0	0	0	0	0	0	0	0	0	0	26	13	3	1	1	0	1	1	1	10	0	0	0	0	39	4
NY	81	63	18	2	0	0	0	0	0	0	0	0	0	0	0	50	21	10	0	3	3	5	2	1	13	2	0	0	0	64	17
PHI	66	29	37	1	0	0	0	0	0	0	0	0	0	0	0	42	16	7	1	2	0	2	0	2	13	2	0	0	0	55	11
PIT	42	19	23	0	0	0	0	0	0	0	0	0	0	0	0	16	15	8	3	0	0	0	3	0	9	1	0	0	0	30	12
STL	70	33	37	0	0	0	0	0	0	0	0	0	0	0	0	36	30	3	1	1	3	1	3	1	9	3	0	0	0	57	13
AL	473	242	231	7	0	0	0	0	0	0	0	0	0	0	0	272	135	62	4	8	5	17	14	10	85	11	1	2	0	413	60
NL	432	231	201	5	0	0	0	0	0	0	0	0	0	0	0	227	151	45	9	8	6	15	13	8	82	9	1	0	0	353	79
YR	905	473	432	12	0	0	0	0	0	0	0	0	0	0	0	499	286	107	13	16	11	32	27	18	167	20	2	2	0	766	139

	AL		*NL*
34	Rudy York	29	Bill Nicholson
31	Charlie Keller	18	Mel Ott
22	Vern Stephens	16	Ron Northey
18	Jeff Heath	15	Vince DiMaggio
17	Multiple Players Tied	15	Coaker Triplett

1944

AL																															
BOS	69	48	21	1	0	0	0	0	0	0	0	0	0	0	0	41	21	6	1	0	1	1	1	0	7	3	0	0	0	63	6
CHI	23	11	12	0	0	0	0	0	0	0	0	0	0	0	0	11	10	2	0	0	1	1	2	1	8	1	0	0	0	19	4
CLE	70	27	43	1	0	0	0	0	0	0	0	0	0	0	0	46	15	7	2	2	1	5	3	1	7	4	0	0	0	62	8
DET	60	38	22	1	0	0	0	0	0	0	0	0	0	0	0	31	20	6	3	2	0	0	5	5	10	2	0	0	0	55	5
NY	96	58	38	3	0	0	0	0	0	0	0	0	0	0	0	56	27	10	3	2	2	2	2	0	9	2	1	0	0	85	11
PHI	36	18	18	0	0	0	0	0	0	0	0	0	0	0	0	21	11	2	2	1	0	1	1	1	9	1	0	0	0	30	6
STL	72	45	27	0	0	0	0	0	0	0	0	0	0	0	0	34	25	9	4	2	0	1	2	3	12	1	1	0	0	58	14
WAS	33	9	24	0	0	0	0	0	0	0	0	0	0	0	0	22	6	5	0	0	0	0	4	1	7	1	0	0	0	31	2
NL																															
BOS	79	51	28	2	0	0	0	0	0	0	0	0	0	0	0	46	21	12	0	1	1	1	1	2	12	3	0	0	0	60	19
BRO	56	27	29	0	0	0	0	0	0	0	0	0	0	0	0	27	19	9	1	1	1	0	2	1	7	3	0	0	0	46	10
CHI	71	32	39	1	0	0	0	0	0	0	0	0	0	0	0	35	25	8	3	2	0	0	1	1	14	0	0	1	0	58	13
CIN	51	14	37	1	0	0	0	0	0	0	0	0	0	0	0	23	16	10	2	0	0	2	0	2	8	1	1	0	0	48	3
NY	93	75	18	1	0	0	1	0	0	0	0	0	0	0	0	49	33	9	2	2	1	1	4	0	12	2	1	0	0	76	17
PHI	55	20	35	1	0	0	0	0	0	0	0	0	0	0	0	39	13	2	1	1	0	1	0	2	9	1	1	0	0	47	8
PIT	70	23	47	4	0	0	1	0	0	1	0	0	0	0	0	39	18	12	1	8	0	2	2	1	12	2	0	0	0	56	14
STL	100	39	61	1	1	0	1	0	0	0	0	0	0	0	0	46	34	19	1	5	2	1	6	0	5	5	1	0	0	76	24
AL	459	254	205	6	0	0	0	0	0	0	0	0	0	0	0	262	135	47	15	9	5	11	20	12	69	15	2	0	0	403	56
NL	575	281	294	11	1	0	3	0	0	1	0	0	0	0	0	304	179	81	11	20	5	8	16	9	79	17	4	1	0	467	108
YR	1034	535	499	17	1	0	3	0	0	1	0	0	0	0	0	566	314	128	26	29	10	19	36	21	148	32	6	1	0	870	164

	AL		*NL*
22	Nick Etten	33	Bill Nicholson
20	Vern Stephens	26	Mel Ott
18	Johnny Lindell	22	Ron Northey
18	Stan Spence	20	Whitey Kurowski
18	Rudy York	20	Frank McCormick

1945

AL																															
BOS	50	22	28	0	0	0	0	0	0	0	0	0	0	0	0	28	14	8	0	0	3	0	1	2	10	2	0	0	0	43	7
CHI	22	8	14	0	0	0	0	0	0	0	0	0	0	0	0	15	4	2	1	0	0	0	0	1	10	0	0	0	0	19	3

				Consec			1-Inn			One-Game						Men-On-Base				Batters					Totals					Pitchers	
Tm	Tot	H	A	2	3	4	3	4	5	5	6	7	8	9	10	0	1	2	3	PH	LO	XN	IP	P	1	10	20	30	40	RHP	LHP
CLE	65	27	38	2	0	0	0	0	0	1	0	0	0	0	0	30	20	13	2	0	0	1	1	2	9	3	0	0	0	52	13
DET	77	43	34	1	0	0	0	0	0	0	0	0	0	0	0	40	21	13	3	2	1	1	0	5	8	4	0	0	0	69	8
NY	93	65	28	4	0	0	0	0	0	0	0	0	0	0	0	46	31	12	4	4	3	0	0	4	12	4	0	0	0	81	12
PHI	33	16	17	0	0	0	0	0	0	0	0	0	0	0	0	21	10	1	1	0	0	2	0	1	9	0	0	0	0	29	4
STL	63	32	31	1	0	0	0	0	0	0	0	0	0	0	0	32	24	4	3	2	1	2	2	4	14	0	1	0	0	49	14
WAS	27	1	26	0	0	0	0	0	0	0	0	0	0	0	0	16	8	1	2	0	0	1	1	0	12	0	0	0	0	20	7
NL																															
BOS	101	69	32	2	0	0	0	0	0	0	0	0	0	0	0	49	38	13	1	6	0	4	0	4	11	1	2	0	0	87	14
BRO	57	29	28	1	0	0	0	0	0	0	0	0	0	0	0	22	22	10	3	1	0	2	1	2	12	2	0	0	0	44	13
CHI	57	24	33	1	0	0	0	0	0	0	0	0	0	0	0	25	20	8	4	0	0	0	1	2	11	2	0	0	0	51	6
CIN	56	25	31	4	0	0	0	0	0	0	0	0	0	0	0	31	17	7	1	0	0	1	0	4	10	2	0	0	0	51	5
NY	114	83	31	5	0	0	1	0	0	0	0	0	0	0	0	62	37	14	1	4	1	3	3	2	15	3	1	0	0	89	25
PHI	56	23	33	1	0	0	0	0	0	0	0	0	0	0	0	24	21	6	5	4	0	1	0	0	11	1	0	0	0	49	7
PIT	72	31	41	3	0	0	0	0	0	0	0	0	0	0	0	39	16	14	3	1	5	3	2	0	7	3	0	0	0	59	13
STL	64	29	35	1	0	0	0	0	0	0	0	0	0	0	0	39	15	8	2	1	0	2	0	0	9	0	2	0	0	48	16
AL	430	214	216	8	0	0	0	0	0	1	0	0	0	0	0	228	132	54	16	8	8	7	5	19	84	13	1	0	0	362	68
NL	577	313	264	18	0	0	1	0	0	0	0	0	0	0	0	291	186	80	20	17	6	16	7	14	86	14	5	0	0	478	99
YR	1007	527	480	26	0	0	1	0	0	1	0	0	0	0	0	519	318	134	36	25	14	23	12	33	170	27	6	0	0	840	167

	AL		*NL*
24	Vern Stephens	28	Tommy Holmes
18	Roy Cullenbine	25	Chuck Workman
18	Nick Etten	22	Buster Adams
18	Rudy York	21	Whitey Kurowski
15	Jeff Heath	21	Mel Ott

1946

AL

Tm	Tot	H	A	Consec 2	Consec 3	Consec 4	1-Inn 3	1-Inn 4	1-Inn 5	One-Game 5	6	7	8	9	10	Men-On-Base 0	1	2	3	PH	LO	XN	IP	P	Totals 1	10	20	30	40	RHP	LHP
BOS	109	65	44	1	0	0	0	0	0	1	0	0	0	0	0	56	35	12	6	0	1	4	3	0	11	2	0	1	0	100	9
CHI	37	17	20	0	0	0	0	0	0	0	0	0	0	0	0	26	7	4	0	0	1	0	1	0	13	0	0	0	0	30	7
CLE	79	25	54	2	0	0	0	0	0	0	0	0	0	0	0	46	27	5	1	0	0	0	0	1	11	2	1	0	0	65	14
DET	108	75	33	3	0	0	0	0	0	0	0	0	0	0	0	66	27	14	1	0	2	0	0	5	13	2	0	0	1	85	23
NY	136	68	68	4	1	0	0	0	0	0	1	0	0	0	0	71	45	16	4	0	0	2	0	3	9	4	1	1	0	98	38
PHI	40	21	19	1	0	0	0	0	0	0	0	0	0	0	0	26	10	3	1	1	0	0	1	1	11	0	1	0	0	33	7
STL	84	46	38	6	0	0	0	0	0	0	0	0	0	0	0	49	24	9	2	0	1	1	0	0	10	4	0	0	0	64	20
WAS	60	16	44	1	0	0	0	0	0	0	0	0	0	0	0	42	12	5	1	1	5	3	6	0	11	1	0	0	0	44	16
NL																															
BOS	44	14	30	2	0	0	0	0	0	0	0	0	0	0	0	29	10	5	0	3	1	0	2	1	15	0	0	0	0	28	16
BRO	55	19	36	1	0	0	0	0	0	0	0	0	0	0	0	31	16	8	0	2	0	1	4	0	11	2	0	0	0	41	14
CHI	56	24	32	2	0	0	0	0	0	0	0	0	0	0	0	28	21	5	2	3	0	3	4	4	16	0	0	0	0	33	23
CIN	65	37	28	0	1	0	1	0	0	0	0	0	0	0	0	41	21	3	0	1	0	1	2	0	11	2	0	0	0	58	7
NY	121	76	45	5	0	0	1	0	0	1	0	0	0	0	0	66	31	19	5	8	1	3	3	2	14	4	1	0	0	76	45
PHI	80	38	42	1	0	0	0	0	0	0	0	0	0	0	0	43	24	9	4	1	0	3	2	3	9	5	0	0	0	67	13
PIT	60	24	36	1	0	0	0	0	0	0	0	0	0	0	0	30	20	9	1	1	0	2	0	0	12	0	1	0	0	44	16
STL	81	41	40	2	0	0	1	0	0	0	0	0	0	0	0	42	27	11	1	7	0	3	1	0	11	3	0	0	0	45	36
AL	653	333	320	18	1	0	0	0	0	1	1	0	0	0	0	382	187	68	16	2	10	10	11	10	89	15	3	2	1	519	134
NL	562	273	289	14	1	0	3	0	0	1	0	0	0	0	0	310	170	69	13	26	2	16	18	10	99	16	2	0	0	392	170
YR	1215	606	609	32	2	0	3	0	0	2	1	0	0	0	0	692	357	137	29	28	12	26	29	20	188	31	5	2	1	911	304

	AL		*NL*
44	Hank Greenberg	23	Ralph Kiner
38	Ted Williams	22	Johnny Mize
30	Charlie Keller	18	Enos Slaughter
26	Pat Seerey	17	Del Ennis
25	Joe DiMaggio	16	Multiple Players Tied

1947

AL

Tm	Tot	H	A	Consec 2	Consec 3	Consec 4	1-Inn 3	1-Inn 4	1-Inn 5	One-Game 5	6	7	8	9	10	Men-On-Base 0	1	2	3	PH	LO	XN	IP	P	Totals 1	10	20	30	40	RHP	LHP
BOS	103	61	42	3	0	0	0	0	0	0	0	0	0	0	0	43	40	16	4	1	4	1	0	0	9	3	0	1	0	97	6
CHI	53	20	33	0	0	0	0	0	0	0	0	0	0	0	0	32	13	6	2	2	0	1	2	0	11	1	0	0	0	48	5

Tm	Tot	H	A	Consec			1-Inn			One-Game						Men-On-Base				Batters					Totals					Pitchers	
				2	3	4	3	4	5	5	6	7	8	9	10	0	1	2	3	PH	LO	XN	IP	P	1	10	20	30	40	RHP	LHP
CLE	112	52	60	5	0	0	0	0	0	1	0	0	0	0	0	57	38	16	1	1	1	0	0	2	9	4	1	0	0	98	14
DET	103	62	41	1	1	0	0	0	0	1	0	0	0	0	0	62	33	7	1	2	3	1	0	4	11	3	1	0	0	81	22
NY	115	54	61	3	1	0	0	0	0	0	0	0	0	0	0	64	28	19	4	3	1	1	1	3	10	6	1	0	0	92	23
PHI	61	33	28	1	0	0	0	0	0	0	0	0	0	0	0	40	16	3	2	0	0	0	1	1	11	2	0	0	0	54	7
STL	90	52	38	2	0	0	0	0	0	0	0	0	0	0	0	43	33	10	4	2	1	4	4	0	11	2	1	0	0	80	10
WAS	42	10	32	0	0	0	0	0	0	0	0	0	0	0	0	22	16	4	0	1	1	0	0	1	9	1	0	0	0	35	7
NL																															
BOS	85	29	56	4	0	0	0	0	0	0	0	0	0	0	0	44	24	15	2	4	1	0	0	0	11	1	1	0	0	61	24
BRO	83	37	46	1	0	0	0	0	0	0	0	0	0	0	0	36	33	11	3	4	1	1	1	1	13	2	0	0	0	49	34
CHI	71	29	42	1	0	0	1	0	0	0	0	0	0	0	0	39	22	6	4	2	0	2	2	2	13	1	1	0	0	39	32
CIN	95	48	47	2	0	0	1	0	0	1	0	0	0	0	0	50	31	12	2	0	0	0	1	0	11	4	0	0	0	78	17
NY	221	131	90	9	0	0	1	0	0	4	2	0	0	0	0	121	71	25	4	3	1	2	3	6	9	3	1	2	1	161	60
PHI	60	24	36	0	0	0	0	0	0	0	0	0	0	0	0	34	16	8	2	1	1	1	2	2	13	2	0	0	0	45	15
PIT	156	95	61	8	0	0	1	0	0	1	0	1	0	0	0	88	45	17	6	1	1	3	0	3	13	2	1	0	1	141	15
STL	115	45	70	2	0	0	1	0	0	0	0	0	0	0	0	64	31	17	3	2	1	1	2	0	8	4	1	0	0	73	42
AL	679	344	335	15	2	0	0	0	0	2	0	0	0	0	0	363	217	81	18	12	11	8	8	11	81	22	4	1	0	585	94
NL	886	438	448	27	0	0	5	0	0	6	2	1	0	0	0	476	273	111	26	17	6	10	11	14	91	19	5	2	2	647	239
YR	1565	782	783	42	2	0	5	0	0	8	2	1	0	0	0	839	490	192	44	29	17	18	19	25	172	41	9	3	2	1232	333

AL		*NL*	
32	Ted Williams	51	Ralph Kiner
29	Joe Gordon	51	Johnny Mize
27	Jeff Heath	36	Willard Marshall
24	Roy Cullenbine	35	Walker Cooper
21	Rudy York	29	Bobby Thomson

1948

AL

Tm	Tot	H	A	Consec 2	Consec 3	Consec 4	1-Inn 3	1-Inn 4	1-Inn 5	One-Game 5	6	7	8	9	10	MOB 0	1	2	3	PH	LO	XN	IP	P	Totals 1	10	20	30	40	RHP	LHP
BOS	121	60	61	4	2	0	2	0	0	0	0	0	0	0	0	57	39	20	5	0	1	2	0	2	12	1	3	0	0	103	18
CHI	55	21	34	2	0	0	0	0	0	0	0	0	0	0	0	30	17	7	1	0	0	1	0	0	9	1	0	0	0	43	12
CLE	155	77	78	7	0	0	0	0	0	0	0	0	0	0	0	88	51	12	4	0	2	2	1	7	10	4	0	2	0	110	45
DET	78	39	39	2	0	0	0	0	0	0	0	0	0	0	0	45	17	14	2	3	0	0	0	2	11	2	1	0	0	59	19
NY	139	70	69	6	0	0	0	0	0	0	0	0	0	0	0	69	43	20	7	3	0	3	2	2	9	4	1	1	0	101	38
PHI	68	33	35	0	0	0	0	0	0	0	0	0	0	0	0	37	21	6	4	1	6	1	0	2	9	3	0	0	0	54	14
STL	63	29	34	1	0	0	0	0	0	0	0	0	0	0	0	36	20	6	1	0	1	1	0	2	12	2	0	0	0	50	13
WAS	31	11	20	0	0	0	0	0	0	0	0	0	0	0	0	19	9	2	1	0	0	1	4	0	12	0	0	0	0	24	7
NL																															
BOS	95	32	63	2	0	0	0	0	0	0	0	0	0	0	0	50	31	12	2	0	0	0	1	1	10	1	2	0	0	74	21
BRO	91	43	48	1	0	0	0	0	0	0	0	0	0	0	0	47	28	13	3	1	0	1	3	0	14	3	0	0	0	58	33
CHI	87	38	49	0	0	0	0	0	0	0	0	0	0	0	0	52	25	10	0	3	0	0	2	1	16	1	1	0	0	70	17
CIN	104	68	36	2	0	0	0	0	0	0	0	0	0	0	0	65	23	12	4	0	1	2	1	3	11	3	0	1	0	67	37
NY	164	89	75	2	1	0	0	0	0	1	0	0	0	0	0	96	43	20	5	4	1	3	1	0	10	5	0	1	1	119	45
PHI	91	32	59	2	0	0	0	0	0	0	1	0	0	0	0	57	23	11	0	1	1	1	3	2	10	3	0	1	0	73	18
PIT	108	69	39	0	0	0	0	0	0	0	0	0	0	0	0	62	28	14	4	5	1	1	2	5	15	2	0	0	1	96	12
STL	105	47	58	3	0	0	0	1	0	0	0	0	0	0	0	54	38	7	6	1	0	2	1	1	10	3	0	1	0	67	38
AL	710	340	370	22	2	0	2	0	0	0	0	0	0	0	0	381	217	87	25	7	10	11	7	17	84	17	5	3	0	544	166
NL	845	418	427	12	1	0	0	1	0	1	1	0	0	0	0	483	239	99	24	15	4	10	14	13	96	21	3	4	2	624	221
YR	1555	758	797	34	3	0	2	1	0	1	1	0	0	0	0	864	456	186	49	22	14	21	21	30	180	38	8	7	2	1168	387

AL		*NL*	
39	Joe DiMaggio	40	Ralph Kiner
32	Joe Gordon	40	Johnny Mize
31	Ken Keltner	39	Stan Musial
29	Vern Stephens	35	Hank Sauer
27	Bobby Doerr	30	Multiple Players Tied

1949

AL

Tm	Tot	H	A	Consec 2	Consec 3	Consec 4	1-Inn 3	1-Inn 4	1-Inn 5	One-Game 5	6	7	8	9	10	MOB 0	1	2	3	PH	LO	XN	IP	P	Totals 1	10	20	30	40	RHP	LHP
BOS	131	71	60	2	0	0	0	0	0	0	0	0	0	0	0	54	47	26	4	0	1	2	1	0	7	1	0	1	1	106	25
CHI	43	15	28	2	0	0	0	0	0	0	0	0	0	0	0	28	10	5	0	2	0	1	1	0	14	0	0	0	0	26	17

				Consec			1-Inn			One-Game						Men-On-Base				Batters					Totals					Pitchers	
Tm	Tot	H	A	2	3	4	3	4	5	5	6	7	8	9	10	0	1	2	3	PH	LO	XN	IP	P	1	10	20	30	40	RHP	LHP
CLE	112	61	51	4	0	0	1	0	0	0	0	0	0	0	0	61	39	11	1	0	0	3	2	11	13	1	2	0	0	65	47
DET	88	57	31	4	0	0	0	0	0	0	0	0	0	0	0	36	29	16	7	5	0	1	1	1	10	3	1	0	0	67	21
NY	115	72	43	4	0	0	0	0	0	0	1	0	0	0	0	63	32	18	2	2	0	1	3	1	13	2	2	0	0	73	42
PHI	82	42	40	1	0	0	0	0	0	0	0	0	0	0	0	46	22	10	4	1	2	1	1	1	8	1	2	0	0	50	32
STL	117	69	48	4	0	0	0	0	0	0	0	0	0	0	0	60	40	16	1	2	0	1	0	1	8	4	2	0	0	85	32
WAS	81	20	61	1	0	0	0	0	0	0	0	1	0	0	0	44	28	8	1	0	1	2	2	0	11	3	0	0	0	60	21
NL																															
BOS	103	40	63	2	0	0	0	0	0	0	0	0	0	0	0	60	31	10	2	4	0	3	2	2	15	2	0	0	0	65	38
BRO	152	86	66	2	0	0	0	0	0	0	0	0	0	0	0	72	52	22	6	4	4	4	1	0	10	3	3	0	0	105	47
CHI	97	53	44	3	0	0	0	0	0	0	0	0	0	0	0	47	34	14	2	2	1	2	0	2	19	1	1	0	0	61	36
CIN	86	50	36	1	0	0	0	0	0	0	0	0	0	0	0	48	23	11	4	3	2	1	0	1	14	3	0	0	0	50	36
NY	147	94	53	3	1	0	0	0	0	1	0	0	0	0	0	70	50	24	3	1	4	3	2	7	14	3	2	0	0	95	52
PHI	122	61	61	3	0	0	1	0	0	0	1	0	0	0	0	66	36	18	2	3	0	1	0	1	11	2	2	0	0	86	36
PIT	126	77	49	4	0	0	0	0	0	1	1	0	0	0	0	65	44	11	6	1	0	2	0	1	12	1	1	0	1	104	22
STL	102	48	54	2	0	0	1	0	0	0	0	0	0	0	0	51	32	14	5	3	0	0	2	1	13	1	0	1	0	50	52
AL	769	407	362	22	0	0	1	0	0	0	1	1	0	0	0	392	247	110	20	12	4	12	11	15	84	15	9	1	1	532	237
NL	935	509	426	20	1	0	2	0	0	2	2	0	0	0	0	479	302	124	30	21	11	16	7	15	108	16	9	1	1	616	319
YR	1704	916	788	42	1	0	3	0	0	2	3	1	0	0	0	871	549	234	50	33	15	28	18	30	192	31	18	2	2	1148	556

	AL		*NL*
43	Ted Williams	54	Ralph Kiner
39	Vern Stephens	36	Stan Musial
24	Multiple Players Tied	31	Hank Sauer
		27	Bobby Thomson
		26	Sid Gordon

1950

Tm	Tot	H	A	Consec 2	3	4	1-Inn 3	4	5	One-Game 5	6	7	8	9	10	Men-On-Base 0	1	2	3	PH	LO	XN	IP	P	Totals 1	10	20	30	40	RHP	LHP
AL																															
BOS	161	100	61	4	0	0	0	0	0	1	1	1	0	0	0	71	61	20	9	2	2	2	0	1	9	0	2	2	0	115	46
CHI	93	52	41	2	0	0	0	0	0	0	0	0	0	0	0	51	30	11	1	1	1	2	1	0	8	1	2	0	0	57	36
CLE	164	102	62	5	1	0	0	0	0	3	0	0	0	0	0	93	45	20	6	1	0	3	1	9	13	2	2	1	0	91	73
DET	114	60	54	4	0	0	1	0	0	1	0	0	0	0	0	59	35	17	3	1	1	2	2	2	10	2	2	0	0	78	36
NY	159	78	81	5	0	0	0	0	0	0	1	0	0	0	0	80	52	23	4	4	0	1	4	3	12	2	2	1	0	102	57
PHI	100	45	55	1	0	0	0	0	0	0	0	0	0	0	0	56	30	11	3	2	3	1	1	4	14	3	1	0	0	72	28
STL	106	52	54	3	0	0	0	0	0	0	0	0	0	0	0	57	29	15	5	4	2	1	0	1	8	4	1	0	0	64	42
WAS	76	18	58	3	0	0	0	0	0	0	0	0	0	0	0	34	25	15	2	0	3	1	2	2	13	3	0	0	0	49	27
NL																															
BOS	148	59	89	1	0	0	1	0	0	1	0	0	0	0	0	71	54	16	7	2	2	2	0	3	13	2	3	0	0	97	51
BRO	194	110	84	5	0	0	0	0	0	2	0	0	0	0	0	103	65	20	6	2	3	2	2	4	10	4	0	3	0	129	65
CHI	161	79	82	7	0	0	2	0	0	0	0	0	0	0	0	102	33	23	3	2	1	4	0	3	14	3	1	2	0	116	45
CIN	99	52	47	2	0	0	0	0	0	1	0	0	0	0	0	57	30	12	0	4	0	2	1	2	17	1	1	0	0	47	52
NY	133	84	49	3	0	0	0	0	0	0	0	1	0	0	0	83	30	14	6	0	3	1	5	6	10	2	3	0	0	82	51
PHI	125	58	67	1	0	0	0	0	0	0	0	0	0	0	0	62	44	13	6	2	1	4	1	0	4	3	2	1	0	91	34
PIT	138	81	57	6	0	0	1	0	0	1	0	0	0	0	0	81	36	16	5	2	3	4	0	2	17	0	1	0	1	113	25
STL	102	50	52	0	0	0	0	0	0	1	0	0	0	0	0	51	35	14	2	2	2	2	1	1	12	3	1	0	0	61	41
AL	973	507	466	27	1	0	1	0	0	5	2	1	0	0	0	501	307	132	33	15	12	13	11	22	87	17	12	4	0	628	345
NL	1100	573	527	25	0	0	4	0	0	6	0	1	0	0	0	610	327	128	35	16	15	21	10	21	97	18	12	6	1	736	364
YR	2073	1080	993	52	1	0	5	0	0	11	2	2	0	0	0	1111	634	260	68	31	27	34	21	43	184	35	24	10	1	1364	709

	AL		*NL*
37	Al Rosen	47	Ralph Kiner
34	Walt Dropo	36	Andy Pafko
32	Joe DiMaggio	32	Gil Hodges
30	Vern Stephens	32	Hank Sauer
29	Gus Zernial	31	Multiple Players Tied

1951

Tm	Tot	H	A	Consec 2	3	4	1-Inn 3	4	5	One-Game 5	6	7	8	9	10	Men-On-Base 0	1	2	3	PH	LO	XN	IP	P	Totals 1	10	20	30	40	RHP	LHP
AL																															
BOS	127	80	47	2	0	0	0	0	0	2	0	0	0	0	0	51	51	20	5	3	0	8	1	2	10	4	1	1	0	97	30
CHI	86	27	59	0	0	0	0	0	0	0	0	0	0	0	0	43	31	11	1	1	0	4	2	0	9	3	1	0	0	63	23
CLE	140	76	64	5	1	0	1	0	0	0	0	0	0	0	0	77	41	16	6	0	2	3	3	5	11	3	3	0	0	86	54

				Consec			1-Inn			One-Game						Men-On-Base				Batters					Totals					Pitchers	
Tm	Tot	H	A	2	3	4	3	4	5	5	6	7	8	9	10	0	1	2	3	PH	LO	XN	IP	P	1	10	20	30	40	RHP	LHP
DET	104	58	46	2	0	0	1	0	0	1	0	0	0	0	0	64	24	16	0	2	2	1	0	4	11	4	1	0	0	78	26
NY	140	72	68	3	0	0	1	0	0	1	0	0	0	0	0	73	47	17	3	3	1	1	1	6	12	6	1	0	0	92	48
PHI	102	54	48	1	0	0	0	0	0	0	0	0	0	0	0	48	36	14	4	2	3	1	0	3	14	1	0	1	0	76	26
STL	86	41	45	0	0	0	0	0	0	0	0	0	0	0	0	52	27	6	1	4	0	1	1	2	21	1	0	0	0	60	26
WAS	54	13	41	2	0	0	0	0	0	0	0	0	0	0	0	24	19	8	3	1	1	2	1	2	12	1	0	0	0	37	17
NL																															
BOS	130	59	71	3	0	0	0	0	0	0	0	0	0	0	0	73	39	17	1	0	4	1	1	3	9	4	2	0	0	90	40
BRO	184	100	84	5	0	0	1	0	0	1	0	0	0	0	0	100	49	28	7	2	7	5	0	1	8	4	1	1	1	139	45
CHI	103	44	59	2	0	0	0	0	0	1	0	0	0	0	0	54	36	9	4	3	3	1	1	2	16	2	0	1	0	83	20
CIN	88	44	44	1	0	0	0	0	0	0	0	0	0	0	0	50	25	11	2	3	1	4	1	2	16	3	0	0	0	43	45
NY	179	115	64	5	0	0	2	0	0	1	0	0	0	0	0	97	51	24	7	4	0	7	3	2	10	4	3	1	0	115	64
PHI	108	43	65	2	0	0	0	0	0	0	0	0	0	0	0	60	33	11	4	2	1	3	2	1	11	3	1	0	0	68	40
PIT	137	72	65	6	0	0	0	0	0	1	0	0	0	0	0	83	38	12	4	4	1	2	0	3	19	3	0	0	1	122	15
STL	95	43	52	2	0	0	0	0	0	0	0	0	0	0	0	56	26	13	0	2	1	1	2	2	16	1	0	1	0	56	39
AL	839	421	418	15	1	0	3	0	0	4	0	0	0	0	0	432	276	108	23	16	9	21	9	24	100	23	7	2	0	589	250
NL	1024	520	504	26	0	0	3	0	0	4	0	0	0	0	0	573	297	125	29	20	18	24	10	16	105	24	7	4	2	716	308
YR	1863	941	922	41	1	0	6	0	0	8	0	0	0	0	0	1005	573	233	52	36	27	45	19	40	205	47	14	6	2	1305	558

AL		*NL*	
33	Gus Zernial	42	Ralph Kiner
30	Ted Williams	40	Gil Hodges
29	Eddie Robinson	33	Roy Campanella
27	Multiple Players Tied	32	Stan Musial
		32	Bobby Thomson

1952

Tm	Tot	H	A	2	3	4	3	4	5	5	6	7	8	9	10	0	1	2	3	PH	LO	XN	IP	P	1	10	20	30	40	RHP	LHP
AL																															
BOS	113	68	45	2	0	0	0	0	0	0	0	0	0	0	0	55	31	19	8	3	2	7	2	4	18	4	0	0	0	91	22
CHI	80	41	39	1	0	0	1	0	0	0	0	0	0	0	0	39	28	13	0	3	0	3	1	2	10	3	1	0	0	56	24
CLE	148	72	76	3	0	0	0	0	0	0	0	0	0	0	0	77	40	26	5	2	2	3	6	3	16	1	1	2	0	89	59
DET	103	65	38	2	0	0	0	0	0	0	0	0	0	0	0	51	39	9	4	5	2	4	0	1	15	2	1	0	0	74	29
NY	129	64	65	3	0	0	0	0	0	0	0	0	0	0	0	68	42	16	3	2	1	0	1	2	8	4	1	1	0	76	53
PHI	89	55	34	0	0	0	0	0	0	0	0	0	0	0	0	49	28	8	4	6	4	0	0	3	14	0	2	0	0	61	28
STL	82	46	36	0	0	0	0	0	0	0	0	0	0	0	0	48	22	12	0	1	1	1	3	1	15	3	0	0	0	55	27
WAS	50	12	38	0	0	0	0	0	0	0	0	0	0	0	0	28	16	5	1	0	1	1	1	0	7	3	0	0	0	26	24
NL																															
BOS	110	48	62	4	0	0	1	0	0	0	0	0	0	0	0	61	37	10	2	2	2	4	0	2	11	2	2	0	0	71	39
BRO	153	77	76	3	1	0	1	0	0	2	0	0	0	0	0	84	45	16	8	1	4	4	0	3	7	2	2	1	0	127	26
CHI	107	51	56	0	0	0	0	0	0	0	0	0	0	0	0	56	35	14	2	2	0	0	0	2	16	2	0	1	0	82	25
CIN	104	43	61	1	0	0	0	0	0	0	0	0	0	0	0	58	27	13	6	2	3	1	2	3	18	3	0	0	0	84	20
NY	151	103	48	6	0	0	1	0	0	0	0	0	0	0	0	86	48	14	3	3	5	3	2	4	9	8	1	0	0	106	45
PHI	93	42	51	1	0	0	0	0	0	0	0	0	0	0	0	49	28	12	4	4	1	3	2	2	12	3	1	0	0	60	33
PIT	92	45	47	1	1	0	1	0	0	0	0	0	0	0	0	47	33	11	1	2	0	3	0	0	12	1	0	1	0	80	12
STL	97	46	51	0	0	0	0	0	0	0	0	0	0	0	0	44	38	10	5	0	2	1	1	0	9	4	1	0	0	63	34
AL	794	423	371	11	0	0	1	0	0	0	0	0	0	0	0	415	246	108	25	22	13	19	14	16	103	20	6	3	0	528	266
NL	907	455	452	16	2	0	4	0	0	2	0	0	0	0	0	485	291	100	31	16	17	19	7	16	94	25	7	3	0	673	234
YR	1701	878	823	27	2	0	5	0	0	2	0	0	0	0	0	900	537	208	56	38	30	38	21	32	197	45	13	6	0	1201	500

AL		*NL*	
32	Larry Doby	37	Ralph Kiner
31	Luke Easter	37	Hank Sauer
30	Yogi Berra	32	Gil Hodges
29	Walt Dropo	25	Sid Gordon
29	Gus Zernial	25	Eddie Mathews

1953

Tm	Tot	H	A	2	3	4	3	4	5	5	6	7	8	9	10	0	1	2	3	PH	LO	XN	IP	P	1	10	20	30	40	RHP	LHP
AL																															
BOS	101	57	44	1	0	0	0	0	0	0	0	0	0	0	0	62	28	11	0	6	0	2	1	2	11	4	1	0	0	83	18
CHI	74	30	44	1	0	0	0	0	0	0	0	0	0	0	0	35	25	10	4	6	1	1	1	1	13	3	0	0	0	51	23
CLE	160	88	72	5	0	0	1	0	0	0	0	0	0	0	0	84	51	20	5	1	2	2	2	6	17	1	1	0	1	98	62
DET	108	55	53	3	0	0	1	0	0	0	0	0	0	0	0	56	33	16	3	3	0	3	1	3	14	4	1	0	0	83	25

				Consec			1-Inn			One-Game						Men-On-Base				Batters					Totals					Pitchers	
Tm	Tot	H	A	2	3	4	3	4	5	5	6	7	8	9	10	0	1	2	3	PH	LO	XN	IP	P	1	10	20	30	40	RHP	LHP
NY	139	64	75	3	0	0	1	0	0	0	0	0	0	0	0	68	46	23	2	7	1	3	2	1	10	5	2	0	0	87	52
PHI	116	49	67	3	0	0	0	0	0	0	0	0	0	0	0	68	34	13	1	1	3	3	1	0	9	1	1	0	1	87	29
STL	112	58	54	2	1	0	1	0	0	1	0	0	0	0	0	76	23	10	3	3	4	2	0	5	13	5	0	0	0	74	38
WAS	69	10	59	1	0	0	0	0	0	0	0	0	0	0	0	36	21	10	2	2	2	0	0	3	10	3	0	0	0	45	24
NL																															
BRO	208	110	98	4	0	0	0	0	0	1	0	0	0	0	0	100	70	32	6	4	1	3	0	2	9	4	1	1	2	176	32
CHI	137	74	63	4	0	0	0	0	0	0	0	0	0	0	0	82	33	19	3	3	0	4	1	3	15	4	1	0	0	113	24
CIN	166	89	77	8	0	0	0	0	0	0	0	0	0	0	0	89	56	19	2	4	2	1	0	5	12	2	1	1	1	110	56
MIL	156	51	105	8	0	0	0	0	0	0	0	0	1	0	0	87	46	21	2	2	0	3	3	4	10	5	0	0	1	127	29
NY	176	109	67	5	1	0	1	0	0	3	0	0	0	0	0	94	60	16	6	4	2	2	2	2	6	3	5	0	0	134	42
PHI	115	63	52	1	0	0	0	0	0	0	0	0	0	0	0	61	43	10	1	2	2	0	1	2	11	2	2	0	0	69	46
PIT	99	51	48	4	0	0	0	0	0	0	0	0	0	0	0	47	36	12	4	5	6	2	2	3	15	1	0	1	0	74	25
STL	140	65	75	1	0	0	0	0	0	1	0	0	0	0	0	82	36	20	2	4	1	0	0	2	9	3	2	1	0	95	45
AL	879	411	468	19	1	0	4	0	0	1	0	0	0	0	0	485	261	113	20	29	13	16	8	21	97	26	6	0	2	608	271
NL	1197	612	585	35	1	0	1	0	0	5	0	0	1	0	0	642	380	149	26	28	14	15	9	23	87	24	12	4	4	898	299
YR	2076	1023	1053	54	2	0	5	0	0	6	0	0	1	0	0	1127	641	262	46	57	27	31	17	44	184	50	18	4	6	1506	570

AL		*NL*	
43	Al Rosen	47	Eddie Mathews
42	Gus Zernial	42	Duke Snider
29	Larry Doby	41	Roy Campanella
27	Yogi Berra	40	Ted Kluszewski
26	Ray Boone	35	Ralph Kiner

1954

				Consec			1-Inn			One-Game						Men-On-Base				Batters					Totals					Pitchers	
Tm	Tot	H	A	2	3	4	3	4	5	5	6	7	8	9	10	0	1	2	3	PH	LO	XN	IP	P	1	10	20	30	40	RHP	LHP
AL																															
BAL	52	19	33	1	0	0	1	0	0	0	0	0	0	0	0	35	14	2	1	1	0	0	2	3	17	0	0	0	0	39	13
BOS	123	69	54	4	0	0	1	0	0	1	0	0	0	0	0	59	36	24	4	3	2	3	0	2	13	2	2	0	0	95	28
CHI	94	39	55	2	0	0	1	0	0	0	0	0	0	0	0	54	23	13	4	2	2	0	2	2	14	3	0	0	0	67	27
CLE	156	78	78	7	0	0	1	0	0	0	0	0	0	0	0	96	34	22	4	2	3	3	1	3	10	6	1	1	0	109	47
DET	90	44	46	1	0	0	0	0	0	0	1	0	0	0	0	54	23	8	5	5	1	6	0	1	14	1	1	0	0	74	16
NY	133	68	65	8	0	0	1	0	0	0	0	0	0	0	0	75	38	17	3	7	5	2	1	2	12	4	2	0	0	92	41
PHI	94	44	50	1	0	0	0	0	0	0	0	0	0	0	0	59	24	9	2	1	0	0	1	2	13	4	0	0	0	72	22
WAS	81	27	54	1	0	0	0	0	0	0	0	0	0	0	0	48	24	8	1	1	2	1	0	2	11	1	2	0	0	65	16
NL																															
BRO	186	101	85	8	0	0	0	0	0	4	0	0	0	0	0	102	60	21	3	3	2	3	1	0	7	5	0	0	2	161	25
CHI	159	86	73	7	0	0	0	0	0	0	1	0	0	0	0	92	47	16	4	3	2	1	1	6	13	3	1	0	1	132	27
CIN	147	94	53	6	1	0	1	0	0	2	0	0	0	0	0	87	42	17	1	0	1	1	1	5	10	2	1	0	1	105	42
MIL	139	43	96	2	0	0	1	0	0	0	0	1	0	0	0	75	45	16	3	2	2	4	1	2	11	2	2	0	1	111	28
NY	186	120	66	9	1	0	4	0	0	3	2	0	0	0	0	102	61	16	7	10	2	2	5	5	12	3	2	0	1	129	57
PHI	102	47	55	2	0	0	0	0	0	1	0	0	0	0	0	48	33	18	3	2	1	1	1	1	9	4	1	0	0	62	40
PIT	76	22	54	5	0	0	0	0	0	0	0	0	0	0	0	40	23	12	1	4	1	0	0	3	14	1	1	0	0	55	21
STL	119	57	62	3	0	0	0	0	0	1	0	0	0	0	0	61	36	20	2	6	4	2	2	1	9	4	0	1	0	72	47
AL	823	388	435	25	0	0	5	0	0	1	1	0	0	0	0	480	216	103	24	22	15	15	7	17	104	21	8	1	0	613	210
NL	1114	570	544	42	2	0	6	0	0	11	3	1	0	0	0	607	347	136	24	30	15	14	12	23	85	24	8	1	6	827	287
YR	1937	958	979	67	2	0	11	0	0	12	4	1	0	0	0	1087	563	239	48	52	30	29	19	40	189	45	16	2	6	1440	497

AL		*NL*	
32	Larry Doby	49	Ted Kluszewski
29	Ted Williams	42	Gil Hodges
27	Mickey Mantle	41	Willie Mays
25	Jackie Jensen	41	Hank Sauer
24	Multiple Players Tied	40	Multiple Players Tied

1955

				Consec			1-Inn			One-Game						Men-On-Base				Batters					Totals					Pitchers	
Tm	Tot	H	A	2	3	4	3	4	5	5	6	7	8	9	10	0	1	2	3	PH	LO	XN	IP	P	1	10	20	30	40	RHP	LHP
AL																															
BAL	54	15	39	1	0	0	0	0	0	0	0	0	0	0	0	33	14	5	2	3	1	0	1	0	15	1	0	0	0	33	21
BOS	137	84	53	4	0	0	0	0	0	0	0	0	0	0	0	64	45	21	7	0	0	2	0	1	7	2	3	0	0	103	34
CHI	116	54	62	4	0	0	0	0	0	0	0	1	0	0	0	63	35	12	6	3	1	0	0	3	13	6	0	0	0	85	31
CLE	148	84	64	5	0	0	1	0	0	0	0	0	0	0	0	86	46	12	4	4	4	2	0	2	12	3	3	0	0	83	65
DET	130	81	49	2	0	0	0	0	0	1	0	0	0	0	0	64	46	19	1	2	1	2	1	3	11	3	2	0	0	99	31

				Consec			1-Inn			One-Game						Men-On-Base				Batters					Totals					Pitchers	
Tm	Tot	H	A	2	3	4	3	4	5	5	6	7	8	9	10	0	1	2	3	PH	LO	XN	IP	P	1	10	20	30	40	RHP	LHP
KC	121	70	51	2	0	0	0	0	0	1	0	0	0	0	0	74	31	14	2	2	3	2	0	1	9	3	0	1	0	85	36
NY	175	89	86	7	0	0	1	0	0	1	0	0	0	0	0	103	42	28	2	5	7	6	4	4	9	5	2	1	0	130	45
WAS	80	20	60	2	0	0	0	0	0	0	0	0	0	0	0	43	24	11	2	4	2	0	1	1	14	1	1	0	0	61	19
NL																															
BRO	201	119	82	12	0	0	1	0	0	1	1	0	0	0	0	100	70	27	4	0	1	1	0	11	10	3	2	1	1	176	25
CHI	164	80	84	7	1	0	1	0	0	0	1	0	0	0	0	92	56	10	6	2	3	7	1	2	8	6	1	0	1	130	34
CIN	181	102	79	5	0	0	1	0	0	2	0	0	0	0	0	106	54	17	4	6	0	1	0	4	14	0	2	0	2	115	66
MIL	182	75	107	7	0	0	0	0	0	0	0	0	0	0	0	104	58	15	5	5	2	3	0	4	7	4	2	0	1	152	30
NY	169	95	74	4	0	0	0	0	0	2	0	0	0	0	0	99	49	18	3	9	3	7	3	8	14	4	0	0	1	113	56
PHI	132	76	56	5	0	0	0	0	0	0	0	0	0	0	0	78	31	20	3	2	1	1	1	4	13	4	2	0	0	92	40
PIT	91	34	57	1	1	0	1	0	0	0	0	0	0	0	0	57	25	7	2	2	2	1	2	3	15	2	1	0	0	54	37
STL	143	84	59	5	0	0	0	0	0	1	0	0	0	0	0	86	46	8	3	2	0	5	0	2	10	4	1	1	0	84	59
AL	961	497	464	27	0	0	2	0	0	3	0	1	0	0	0	530	283	122	26	23	19	14	7	15	90	24	11	2	0	679	282
NL	1263	665	598	46	2	0	4	0	0	6	2	0	0	0	0	722	389	122	30	28	12	26	7	38	91	27	11	2	6	916	347
YR	2224	1162	1062	73	2	0	6	0	0	9	2	1	0	0	0	1252	672	244	56	51	31	40	14	53	181	51	22	4	6	1595	629

AL

37 Mickey Mantle
30 Gus Zernial
28 Ted Williams
27 Multiple Players Tied

NL

51 Willie Mays
47 Ted Kluszewski
44 Ernie Banks
42 Duke Snider
41 Eddie Mathews

1956

				Consec			1-Inn			One-Game						Men-On-Base				Batters					Totals					Pitchers	
Tm	Tot	H	A	2	3	4	3	4	5	5	6	7	8	9	10	0	1	2	3	PH	LO	XN	IP	P	1	10	20	30	40	RHP	LHP
AL																															
BAL	91	35	56	6	0	0	0	0	0	0	0	0	0	0	0	54	24	11	2	2	1	1	2	2	15	3	1	0	0	66	25
BOS	139	68	71	1	0	0	0	0	0	0	0	0	0	0	0	70	50	18	1	2	1	2	2	2	12	4	2	0	0	105	34
CHI	128	69	59	4	0	0	0	0	0	0	1	0	0	0	0	70	38	20	0	4	0	2	1	12	15	3	2	0	0	83	45
CLE	153	71	82	2	0	0	1	0	0	2	0	0	0	0	0	80	45	22	6	3	3	4	1	6	11	4	1	1	0	114	39
DET	150	75	75	6	1	0	1	0	0	0	0	0	0	0	0	86	46	14	4	4	1	4	1	1	8	3	3	0	0	119	31
KC	112	62	50	3	0	0	0	0	0	0	0	0	0	0	0	65	38	7	2	2	0	3	0	1	14	4	1	0	0	77	35
NY	190	88	102	4	0	0	0	0	0	0	0	0	0	0	0	106	57	22	5	5	6	1	3	6	10	1	2	1	1	134	56
WAS	112	63	49	1	0	0	0	0	0	0	0	0	0	0	0	60	34	16	2	2	3	0	1	0	13	1	2	0	0	81	31
NL																															
BRO	179	102	77	5	1	0	2	0	0	2	0	0	0	0	0	108	54	14	3	2	0	3	4	3	10	2	2	1	1	165	14
CHI	142	78	64	3	0	0	0	0	0	1	0	0	0	0	0	79	44	16	3	1	2	4	2	1	8	4	2	0	0	116	26
CIN	221	128	93	14	1	0	1	0	0	2	0	0	1	0	0	120	64	31	6	9	0	6	0	2	6	3	2	3	0	163	58
MIL	177	77	100	6	1	0	1	0	0	2	0	0	0	0	0	101	55	16	5	6	0	1	1	3	10	2	2	2	0	146	31
NY	145	94	51	5	1	0	0	0	0	0	0	1	0	0	0	96	41	8	0	8	3	0	1	5	14	3	1	1	0	106	39
PHI	121	61	60	2	0	0	0	0	0	0	0	0	0	0	0	73	31	13	4	2	0	4	2	2	10	2	1	1	0	96	25
PIT	110	47	63	5	0	0	0	0	0	0	0	0	0	0	0	58	38	12	2	4	1	1	1	2	12	1	2	0	0	80	30
STL	124	58	66	3	0	0	1	0	0	0	0	0	0	0	0	78	30	12	4	5	0	1	0	2	13	2	2	0	0	75	49
AL	1075	531	544	27	1	0	2	0	0	2	1	0	0	0	0	591	332	130	22	24	15	17	11	30	98	23	14	2	1	779	296
NL	1219	645	574	43	4	0	5	0	0	7	0	1	1	0	0	713	357	122	27	37	6	20	11	20	83	19	14	8	1	947	272
YR	2294	1176	1118	70	5	0	7	0	0	9	1	1	1	0	0	1304	689	252	49	61	21	37	22	50	181	42	28	10	2	1726	568

AL

52 Mickey Mantle
32 Vic Wertz
30 Yogi Berra
29 Roy Sievers
28 Charlie Maxwell

NL

43 Duke Snider
38 Joe Adcock
38 Frank Robinson
37 Eddie Mathews
36 Multiple Players Tied

1957

				Consec			1-Inn			One-Game						Men-On-Base				Batters					Totals					Pitchers	
Tm	Tot	H	A	2	3	4	3	4	5	5	6	7	8	9	10	0	1	2	3	PH	LO	XN	IP	P	1	10	20	30	40	RHP	LHP
AL																															
BAL	87	36	51	0	0	0	0	0	0	0	0	0	0	0	0	53	24	10	0	1	1	2	2	3	15	2	0	0	0	61	26
BOS	153	72	81	5	0	0	0	1	0	0	1	0	0	0	0	85	46	19	3	4	1	3	0	0	8	4	1	1	0	118	35
CHI	106	40	66	4	0	0	0	0	0	0	0	0	0	0	0	63	28	11	4	2	2	2	1	8	12	5	0	0	0	73	33
CLE	140	71	69	4	0	0	0	0	0	0	1	0	0	0	0	77	41	17	5	1	4	1	1	4	15	3	2	0	0	98	42
DET	116	71	45	2	0	0	0	0	0	0	0	0	0	0	0	70	31	15	0	0	3	4	0	8	13	2	2	0	0	97	19
KC	166	91	75	3	0	0	0	0	0	1	0	0	0	0	0	113	41	9	3	6	3	2	0	5	10	5	2	0	0	142	24

				Consec			1-Inn			One-Game						Men-On-Base				Batters					Totals					Pitchers	
Tm	Tot	H	A	2	3	4	3	4	5	5	6	7	8	9	10	0	1	2	3	PH	LO	XN	IP	P	1	10	20	30	40	RHP	LHP
NY	145	60	85	6	0	0	1	0	0	0	0	0	0	0	0	85	43	14	3	3	3	7	0	3	11	3	1	1	0	107	38
WAS	111	60	51	3	0	0	2	0	0	0	0	0	0	0	0	61	42	6	2	4	2	4	0	3	16	1	0	0	1	83	28
NL																															
BRO	147	84	63	3	0	0	0	0	0	2	0	0	0	0	0	82	43	19	3	2	3	7	1	5	13	4	1	0	1	139	8
CHI	147	81	66	5	0	0	0	0	0	0	0	0	0	0	0	88	39	19	1	3	1	3	3	1	13	3	1	0	1	107	40
CIN	187	118	69	11	0	0	1	0	0	0	0	1	0	0	0	111	53	19	4	12	0	6	2	4	7	4	3	1	0	144	43
MIL	199	75	124	5	1	0	0	0	0	2	0	0	0	0	0	119	48	28	4	4	4	7	2	6	16	3	1	1	1	165	34
NY	157	99	58	3	0	0	0	0	0	0	1	0	0	0	0	93	43	19	2	6	2	6	2	4	17	1	1	1	0	121	36
PHI	117	60	57	2	0	0	0	0	0	0	0	0	0	0	0	67	36	13	1	5	0	1	6	3	11	4	1	0	0	86	31
PIT	92	20	72	4	1	0	0	0	0	0	0	0	0	0	0	62	27	3	0	3	4	2	2	0	13	1	1	0	0	70	22
STL	132	64	68	5	0	0	0	0	0	0	0	0	0	0	0	71	49	10	2	4	2	5	1	1	11	1	3	0	0	96	36
AL	1024	501	523	27	0	0	3	1	0	1	2	0	0	0	0	607	296	101	20	21	19	25	4	34	100	25	8	2	1	779	245
NL	1178	601	577	38	2	0	1	0	0	4	1	1	0	0	0	693	338	130	17	39	16	37	19	24	101	21	12	3	3	928	250
YR	2202	1102	1100	65	2	0	4	1	0	5	3	1	0	0	0	1300	634	231	37	60	35	62	23	58	201	46	20	5	4	1707	495

AL		*NL*	
42	Roy Sievers	44	Hank Aaron
38	Ted Williams	43	Ernie Banks
34	Mickey Mantle	40	Duke Snider
28	Vic Wertz	35	Willie Mays
27	Gus Zernial	32	Eddie Mathews

1958

				Consec			1-Inn			One-Game						Men-On-Base				Batters					Totals					Pitchers	
Tm	Tot	H	A	2	3	4	3	4	5	5	6	7	8	9	10	0	1	2	3	PH	LO	XN	IP	P	1	10	20	30	40	RHP	LHP
AL																															
BAL	108	46	62	2	0	0	0	0	0	0	0	0	0	0	0	61	38	7	2	1	1	0	1	9	18	2	0	1	0	93	15
BOS	155	73	82	7	0	0	0	0	0	1	0	0	0	0	0	77	52	21	5	3	4	7	0	0	10	2	2	1	0	132	23
CHI	101	47	54	1	0	0	0	0	0	1	0	0	0	0	0	54	35	9	3	3	0	0	3	1	11	3	1	0	0	74	27
CLE	161	72	89	2	0	0	0	0	0	0	0	0	0	0	0	81	55	22	3	7	5	5	1	1	17	2	1	0	1	124	37
DET	109	59	50	1	0	0	0	0	0	0	0	0	0	0	0	60	28	18	3	7	1	0	0	2	13	3	1	0	0	96	13
KC	138	88	50	5	0	0	0	0	0	1	0	0	0	0	0	79	39	16	4	2	6	7	2	1	13	3	0	1	0	120	18
NY	164	78	86	9	0	0	1	0	0	1	0	0	0	0	0	91	47	26	0	2	4	3	5	6	7	6	1	0	1	130	34
WAS	121	49	72	3	0	0	1	0	0	0	0	0	0	0	0	77	30	12	2	2	4	3	1	1	9	1	1	1	0	100	21
NL																															
CHI	182	101	81	5	0	0	0	0	0	2	0	0	0	0	0	109	54	19	0	8	2	4	2	0	9	1	4	0	1	132	50
CIN	123	71	52	1	0	0	0	0	0	0	0	0	0	0	0	70	36	13	4	7	0	4	1	3	14	4	0	1	0	90	33
LA	172	92	80	3	0	0	0	0	0	1	0	0	0	0	0	101	51	19	1	1	2	2	0	8	16	4	2	0	0	141	31
MIL	167	72	95	7	1	0	1	0	0	1	0	0	0	0	0	104	39	18	6	4	3	1	0	6	11	3	1	2	0	121	46
PHI	124	59	65	4	0	0	0	0	0	0	0	0	0	0	0	59	47	15	3	11	0	2	2	0	13	3	1	0	0	87	37
PIT	134	41	93	0	1	0	1	0	0	0	0	0	0	0	0	76	46	10	2	3	2	4	1	3	14	3	0	1	0	92	42
SF	170	85	85	6	0	0	0	0	0	2	0	0	0	0	0	106	44	18	2	5	2	6	3	1	10	7	2	0	0	130	40
STL	111	62	49	2	0	0	0	0	0	0	0	0	0	0	0	67	33	6	5	3	3	5	1	0	14	4	1	0	0	66	45
AL	1057	512	545	30	0	0	2	0	0	4	0	0	0	0	0	580	324	131	22	27	25	25	13	21	98	22	7	4	2	869	188
NL	1183	583	600	28	2	0	2	0	0	6	0	0	0	0	0	692	350	118	23	42	14	28	10	21	101	29	11	4	1	859	324
YR	2240	1095	1145	58	2	0	4	0	0	10	0	0	0	0	0	1272	674	249	45	69	39	53	23	42	199	51	18	8	3	1728	512

AL		*NL*	
42	Mickey Mantle	47	Ernie Banks
41	Rocky Colavito	35	Frank Thomas
39	Roy Sievers	31	Eddie Mathews
38	Bob Cerv	31	Frank Robinson
35	Jackie Jensen	30	Hank Aaron

1959

				Consec			1-Inn			One-Game						Men-On-Base				Batters					Totals					Pitchers	
Tm	Tot	H	A	2	3	4	3	4	5	5	6	7	8	9	10	0	1	2	3	PH	LO	XN	IP	P	1	10	20	30	40	RHP	LHP
AL																															
BAL	109	53	56	5	0	0	0	0	0	0	0	0	0	0	0	59	37	10	3	1	1	3	2	3	14	2	2	0	0	67	42
BOS	125	62	63	5	1	0	1	0	0	0	1	0	0	0	0	75	29	17	4	3	2	8	0	5	13	5	1	0	0	100	25
CHI	97	44	53	4	0	0	0	0	0	0	0	0	0	0	0	52	33	9	3	5	0	4	2	3	19	1	1	0	0	64	33
CLE	167	84	83	2	0	0	0	0	0	0	1	0	0	0	0	91	45	26	5	4	2	5	2	2	12	2	3	0	1	139	28
DET	160	95	65	2	0	0	0	0	0	0	0	0	0	0	0	88	49	18	5	4	6	1	1	5	14	2	2	1	0	122	38
KC	117	58	59	2	0	0	0	0	0	0	0	0	0	0	0	66	37	10	4	1	0	1	1	4	19	3	1	0	0	95	22
NY	153	63	90	2	0	0	0	0	0	0	0	0	0	0	0	82	58	12	1	5	3	5	1	2	11	5	0	1	0	117	36

				Consec			1-Inn			One-Game						Men-On-Base				Batters					Totals					Pitchers	
Tm	Tot	H	A	2	3	4	3	4	5	5	6	7	8	9	10	0	1	2	3	PH	LO	XN	IP	P	1	10	20	30	40	RHP	LHP
WAS	163	83	80	7	0	0	1	0	0	1	0	0	0	0	0	100	46	13	4	3	6	6	0	1	11	1	1	2	1	138	25
NL																															
CHI	163	87	76	6	0	0	0	0	0	1	0	0	0	0	0	94	45	19	5	6	1	7	2	0	8	7	0	0	1	124	39
CIN	161	101	60	3	0	0	1	0	0	1	0	0	0	0	0	88	51	19	3	6	1	0	0	4	12	4	1	1	0	116	45
LA	148	82	66	4	0	0	0	0	0	0	0	0	0	0	0	90	42	16	0	2	4	2	2	6	12	4	2	0	0	123	25
MIL	177	83	94	7	0	0	0	0	0	1	0	0	0	0	0	102	51	21	3	3	1	2	1	2	12	1	2	1	1	129	48
PHI	113	55	58	1	0	0	0	0	0	0	0	0	0	0	0	59	41	9	4	9	1	1	1	1	11	2	2	0	0	70	43
PIT	112	47	65	1	0	0	0	0	0	0	0	0	0	0	0	60	35	15	2	7	1	4	2	3	16	2	1	0	0	81	31
SF	167	80	87	4	0	0	0	0	0	0	0	0	0	0	0	107	42	16	2	3	2	4	0	2	8	4	2	1	0	129	38
STL	118	64	54	3	0	0	0	0	0	0	0	0	0	0	0	62	43	9	4	5	0	0	3	3	15	3	1	0	0	74	44
AL	1091	542	549	29	1	0	2	0	0	1	2	0	0	0	0	613	334	115	29	26	20	33	9	25	113	21	11	4	2	842	249
NL	1159	599	560	29	0	0	1	0	0	3	0	0	0	0	0	662	350	124	23	41	11	20	11	21	94	27	11	3	2	846	313
YR	2250	1141	1109	58	1	0	3	0	0	4	2	0	0	0	0	1275	684	239	52	67	31	53	20	46	207	48	22	7	4	1688	562

AL
42 Rocky Colavito
42 Harmon Killebrew
33 Jim Lemon
31 Mickey Mantle
31 Charlie Maxwell

NL
46 Eddie Mathews
45 Ernie Banks
39 Hank Aaron
36 Frank Robinson
34 Willie Mays

1960

				Consec			1-Inn			One-Game						Men-On-Base				Batters					Totals					Pitchers	
Tm	Tot	H	A	2	3	4	3	4	5	5	6	7	8	9	10	0	1	2	3	PH	LO	XN	IP	P	1	10	20	30	40	RHP	LHP
AL																															
BAL	123	50	73	1	0	0	0	0	0	2	0	0	0	0	0	69	30	17	7	2	3	2	0	2	12	4	2	0	0	82	41
BOS	124	65	59	1	0	0	0	0	0	0	0	0	0	0	0	59	44	15	6	4	3	1	1	1	18	2	1	0	0	101	23
CHI	112	60	52	4	0	0	0	0	0	0	0	0	0	0	0	64	33	14	1	3	1	3	1	1	10	3	2	0	0	95	17
CLE	127	62	65	2	0	0	1	0	0	0	0	0	0	0	0	56	54	15	2	0	3	5	0	0	11	5	1	0	0	101	26
DET	150	78	72	3	0	0	0	0	0	2	0	0	0	0	0	87	41	19	3	4	4	7	0	2	12	3	1	1	0	121	29
KC	110	58	52	4	0	0	0	0	0	0	0	0	0	0	0	76	18	12	4	3	1	3	1	0	13	4	0	0	0	87	23
NY	193	92	101	13	0	0	0	0	0	2	0	0	0	0	0	115	61	16	1	7	2	6	1	1	10	3	1	1	1	149	44
WAS	147	75	72	3	0	0	1	0	0	0	0	0	0	0	0	79	54	11	3	2	3	4	2	5	13	3	0	2	0	121	26
NL																															
CHI	119	52	67	2	0	0	1	0	0	0	0	0	0	0	0	64	36	17	2	3	0	3	1	4	15	1	1	0	1	92	27
CIN	140	75	65	4	0	0	1	0	0	0	0	0	0	0	0	85	39	10	6	3	2	2	0	1	13	4	1	1	0	100	40
LA	126	89	37	4	0	0	0	0	0	0	0	0	0	0	0	70	37	13	6	6	2	5	2	3	16	3	1	0	0	102	24
MIL	170	90	80	4	0	0	0	0	0	2	0	0	0	0	0	114	39	16	1	4	2	3	1	6	10	3	1	1	1	132	38
PHI	99	54	45	0	0	0	1	0	0	0	0	0	0	0	0	62	26	9	2	4	1	3	2	3	19	2	0	0	0	65	34
PIT	120	51	69	3	0	0	0	0	0	0	0	0	0	0	0	55	42	19	4	5	2	2	3	3	7	5	1	0	0	89	31
SF	130	46	84	3	0	0	1	0	0	1	0	0	0	0	0	69	37	21	3	5	0	1	4	0	11	1	3	0	0	84	46
STL	138	78	60	2	0	0	0	0	0	0	0	0	0	0	0	91	35	11	1	7	2	2	0	0	11	4	0	1	0	93	45
AL	1086	540	546	31	0	0	2	0	0	6	0	0	0	0	0	605	335	119	27	25	20	31	6	12	99	27	8	4	1	857	229
NL	1042	535	507	22	0	0	4	0	0	3	0	0	0	0	0	610	291	116	25	37	11	21	13	20	102	23	8	3	2	757	285
YR	2128	1075	1053	53	0	0	6	0	0	9	0	0	0	0	0	1215	626	235	52	62	31	52	19	32	201	50	16	7	3	1614	514

AL
40 Mickey Mantle
39 Roger Maris
38 Jim Lemon
35 Rocky Colavito
31 Harmon Killebrew

NL
41 Ernie Banks
40 Hank Aaron
39 Eddie Mathews
32 Ken Boyer
31 Frank Robinson

1961

				Consec			1-Inn			One-Game						Men-On-Base				Batters					Totals					Pitchers	
Tm	Tot	H	A	2	3	4	3	4	5	5	6	7	8	9	10	0	1	2	3	PH	LO	XN	IP	P	1	10	20	30	40	RHP	LHP
AL																															
BAL	149	61	88	1	1	0	1	0	0	1	0	0	0	0	0	82	48	14	5	4	3	4	0	5	14	3	0	0	1	117	32
BOS	112	63	49	4	0	0	1	0	0	1	0	0	0	0	0	59	34	14	5	2	2	5	1	4	10	6	0	0	0	83	29
CHI	138	80	58	4	0	0	0	0	0	0	0	0	0	0	0	74	45	12	7	6	1	4	1	5	12	2	3	0	0	117	21
CLE	150	74	76	7	0	0	1	0	0	1	0	0	0	0	0	90	45	12	3	5	0	2	2	1	10	3	3	0	0	108	42
DET	180	90	90	7	1	0	1	0	0	1	0	0	0	0	0	104	52	20	4	5	1	2	1	3	13	4	0	0	2	148	32
KC	90	33	57	3	0	0	0	0	0	0	0	0	0	0	0	43	33	12	2	6	0	2	3	3	20	1	0	0	0	64	26
LA	189	122	67	6	0	0	1	0	0	1	0	0	0	0	0	107	51	25	6	7	2	7	0	3	15	2	5	0	0	145	44
MIN	167	92	75	3	0	0	1	0	0	0	0	0	0	0	0	94	48	17	8	4	1	4	1	5	16	2	1	0	1	141	26

Tm	Tot	H	A	Consec			1-Inn			One-Game						Men-On-Base				Batters					Totals					Pitchers	
				2	3	4	3	4	5	5	6	7	8	9	10	0	1	2	3	PH	LO	XN	IP	P	1	10	20	30	40	RHP	LHP
NY	240	112	128	13	0	0	1	0	0	3	0	1	0	0	0	134	71	31	4	10	1	5	1	0	6	1	4	0	2	187	53
WAS	119	34	85	6	1	0	0	0	0	0	0	0	0	0	0	70	34	11	4	1	2	2	2	3	13	5	0	0	0	90	29
NL																															
CHI	176	102	74	4	0	0	0	0	0	0	0	0	0	0	0	107	52	13	4	2	3	2	2	9	13	2	4	0	0	117	59
CIN	158	70	88	5	0	0	0	0	0	0	0	0	0	0	0	83	55	19	1	8	2	2	0	2	11	2	3	1	0	101	57
LA	157	83	74	4	0	0	0	0	0	2	0	0	0	0	0	92	42	19	4	7	0	5	1	5	11	8	0	0	0	113	44
MIL	188	84	104	4	1	1	1	0	0	2	1	0	0	0	0	114	55	15	4	2	1	2	0	7	9	3	1	3	0	127	61
PHI	103	43	60	2	0	0	0	0	0	1	0	0	0	0	0	58	25	18	2	2	4	3	0	0	14	2	1	0	0	66	37
PIT	128	49	79	3	0	0	1	0	0	1	0	0	0	0	0	74	39	13	2	2	2	0	3	1	8	3	1	1	0	92	36
SF	183	97	86	8	0	0	1	1	0	1	1	0	1	0	0	110	46	22	5	4	3	5	1	4	12	4	0	0	2	126	57
STL	103	54	49	3	0	0	0	0	0	0	0	0	0	0	0	51	34	11	7	6	1	2	1	1	13	2	2	0	0	77	26
AL	1534	761	773	54	3	0	7	0	0	8	0	1	0	0	0	857	461	168	48	50	13	37	12	32	129	29	16	0	6	1200	334
NL	1196	582	614	33	1	1	3	1	0	7	2	0	1	0	0	689	348	130	29	33	16	21	8	29	91	26	12	5	2	819	377
YR	2730	1343	1387	87	4	1	10	1	0	15	2	1	1	0	0	1546	809	298	77	83	29	58	20	61	220	55	28	5	8	2019	711

AL		*NL*	
61	Roger Maris	46	Orlando Cepeda
54	Mickey Mantle	40	Willie Mays
46	Jim Gentile	37	Frank Robinson
46	Harmon Killebrew	35	Joe Adcock
45	Rocky Colavito	35	Dick Stuart

1962

Tm	Tot	H	A	Consec			1-Inn			One-Game						Men-On-Base				Batters					Totals					Pitchers	
AL																															
BAL	156	66	90	4	0	0	0	0	0	0	0	0	0	0	0	95	50	8	3	5	1	4	0	5	14	3	1	1	0	115	41
BOS	146	72	74	4	0	0	0	0	0	0	0	0	0	0	0	89	38	16	3	3	0	3	1	4	7	7	1	0	0	121	25
CHI	92	36	56	2	0	0	0	0	0	0	0	0	0	0	0	53	28	9	2	2	0	1	0	2	13	3	0	0	0	78	14
CLE	180	103	77	8	1	0	1	0	0	0	0	0	0	0	0	99	59	20	2	6	0	4	0	8	10	6	3	0	0	139	41
DET	209	117	92	6	0	0	0	0	0	0	1	0	0	0	0	118	61	27	3	3	3	1	1	2	9	4	2	2	0	165	44
KC	116	64	52	1	1	0	2	0	0	0	0	0	0	0	0	57	42	16	1	2	1	1	3	4	9	5	1	0	0	89	27
LA	137	50	87	2	1	0	0	0	0	3	0	0	0	0	0	80	40	17	0	5	2	4	1	2	14	2	1	1	0	97	40
MIN	185	97	88	8	0	0	1	0	0	0	1	0	0	0	0	87	65	27	6	4	1	3	1	5	8	6	1	0	1	168	17
NY	199	92	107	8	0	0	2	0	0	1	0	0	0	0	0	93	69	31	6	5	3	8	1	0	7	3	3	2	0	140	59
WAS	132	65	67	3	0	0	0	0	0	0	0	0	0	0	0	78	38	14	2	4	1	9	1	2	13	6	0	0	0	98	34
NL																															
CHI	126	71	55	6	0	0	0	0	0	1	1	0	0	0	0	76	31	17	2	4	4	3	2	0	9	1	2	1	0	84	42
CIN	167	95	72	4	0	0	0	0	0	0	0	0	0	0	0	92	49	20	6	9	2	8	3	6	12	3	2	1	0	124	43
HOU	105	44	61	1	0	0	0	0	0	0	0	0	0	0	0	61	31	11	2	0	4	2	1	2	14	3	1	0	0	82	23
LA	140	47	93	3	0	0	0	0	0	0	0	0	0	0	0	75	47	16	2	2	0	1	5	4	14	1	2	1	0	93	47
MIL	181	93	88	8	0	0	0	0	0	1	0	0	0	0	0	94	58	21	8	4	1	3	1	3	11	3	2	0	1	132	49
NY	139	93	46	3	1	0	1	0	0	2	0	0	0	0	0	97	28	12	2	9	5	2	2	0	15	4	0	1	0	109	30
PHI	142	70	72	2	0	0	0	0	0	0	0	0	0	0	0	77	47	14	4	2	1	1	0	3	10	1	4	0	0	102	40
PIT	108	48	60	0	0	0	0	0	0	0	0	0	0	0	0	47	38	18	5	2	0	2	2	2	14	4	1	0	0	84	24
SF	204	109	95	11	0	0	1	0	0	0	0	0	0	0	0	119	61	21	3	6	1	2	0	1	6	4	2	1	1	142	62
STL	137	64	73	3	0	0	1	0	0	0	1	0	0	0	0	77	35	22	3	7	1	2	1	4	12	4	2	0	0	100	37
AL	1552	762	790	46	3	0	6	0	0	4	2	0	0	0	0	849	490	185	28	39	12	38	9	34	104	45	13	6	1	1210	342
NL	1449	734	715	41	1	0	3	0	0	4	2	0	0	0	0	815	425	172	37	45	19	26	17	25	117	28	18	5	2	1052	397
YR	3001	1496	1505	87	4	0	9	0	0	8	4	0	0	0	0	1664	915	357	65	84	31	64	26	59	221	73	31	11	3	2262	739

AL		*NL*	
48	Harmon Killebrew	49	Willie Mays
39	Norm Cash	45	Hank Aaron
37	Rocky Colavito	39	Frank Robinson
37	Leon Wagner	37	Ernie Banks
33	Multiple Players Tied	35	Orlando Cepeda

1963

Tm	Tot	H	A	Consec			1-Inn			One-Game						Men-On-Base				Batters					Totals					Pitchers	
AL																															
BAL	146	72	74	2	0	0	0	0	0	0	0	0	0	0	0	88	46	11	1	2	0	1	0	6	13	4	2	0	0	103	43
BOS	171	95	76	4	0	0	0	0	0	0	0	0	0	0	0	97	53	18	3	1	2	6	1	2	7	4	2	0	1	137	34
CHI	114	63	51	1	0	0	0	0	0	0	0	0	0	0	0	64	34	14	2	0	1	1	1	6	13	3	2	0	0	69	45

Tm	Tot	H	A	Consec 2	3	4	1-Inn 3	4	5	One-Game 5	6	7	8	9	10	Men-On-Base 0	1	2	3	Batters PH	LO	XN	IP	P	Totals 1	10	20	30	40	Pitchers RHP	LHP
CLE	169	88	81	5	0	1	1	0	0	0	1	0	0	0	0	104	44	16	5	8	2	8	0	7	16	6	2	0	0	123	46
DET	148	94	54	2	0	0	0	0	0	0	0	0	0	0	0	99	31	15	3	3	6	3	1	2	9	3	3	0	0	106	42
KC	95	52	43	0	0	0	0	0	0	0	0	0	0	0	0	60	24	9	2	2	1	1	0	3	16	2	0	0	0	55	40
LA	95	24	71	1	0	0	0	0	0	0	0	0	0	0	0	53	29	11	2	2	1	1	1	1	17	0	1	0	0	63	32
MIN	225	112	113	10	0	0	0	0	0	2	0	0	1	0	0	135	64	22	4	4	5	0	2	2	9	4	1	2	1	192	33
NY	188	88	100	4	0	0	1	0	0	0	0	0	0	0	0	107	60	17	4	2	1	2	1	1	6	4	4	0	0	117	71
WAS	138	63	75	3	0	0	0	0	0	0	0	0	0	0	0	87	34	13	4	2	3	4	1	3	14	4	2	0	0	98	40
NL																															
CHI	127	63	64	6	0	0	0	0	0	2	0	0	0	0	0	73	40	12	2	2	1	4	4	1	13	2	2	0	0	95	32
CIN	122	65	57	2	0	0	0	0	0	0	0	0	0	0	0	69	37	13	3	7	1	0	4	0	12	3	2	0	0	85	37
HOU	62	25	37	1	0	0	0	0	0	0	0	0	0	0	0	35	16	8	3	1	2	4	1	0	13	1	0	0	0	45	17
LA	110	42	68	3	0	0	1	0	0	0	0	0	0	0	0	63	35	9	3	6	1	2	1	2	15	2	1	0	0	76	34
MIL	139	68	71	3	0	0	1	0	0	0	0	0	0	0	0	81	38	16	4	1	2	1	0	4	10	4	1	0	1	106	33
NY	96	61	35	1	0	0	0	0	0	0	0	0	0	0	0	53	29	10	4	2	4	4	1	1	15	5	0	0	0	70	26
PHI	126	61	65	2	0	0	1	0	0	0	0	0	0	0	0	69	40	16	1	8	0	3	1	1	11	3	2	0	0	87	39
PIT	108	47	61	4	0	0	0	0	0	0	0	0	0	0	0	65	22	19	2	5	2	2	1	1	7	6	0	0	0	75	33
SF	197	101	96	9	1	0	1	0	0	0	1	0	0	0	0	116	58	21	2	3	3	5	1	2	8	1	2	2	1	139	58
STL	128	79	49	4	0	0	0	0	0	1	0	0	0	0	0	65	49	11	3	4	1	4	3	3	13	2	2	0	0	84	44
AL	1489	751	738	32	0	1	2	0	0	2	1	0	1	0	0	894	419	146	30	26	22	27	8	33	120	34	19	2	2	1063	426
NL	1215	612	603	35	1	0	4	0	0	3	1	0	0	0	0	689	364	135	27	39	17	29	17	15	117	29	12	2	2	862	353
YR	2704	1363	1341	67	1	1	6	0	0	5	2	0	1	0	0	1583	783	281	57	65	39	56	25	48	237	63	31	4	4	1925	779

	AL		*NL*
45	Harmon Killebrew	44	Hank Aaron
42	Dick Stuart	44	Willie McCovey
35	Bob Allison	38	Willie Mays
33	Jimmie Hall	34	Orlando Cepeda
28	Elston Howard	28	Frank Howard

1964

Tm	Tot	H	A	Consec 2	3	4	1-Inn 3	4	5	One-Game 5	6	7	8	9	10	Men-On-Base 0	1	2	3	Batters PH	LO	XN	IP	P	Totals 1	10	20	30	40	Pitchers RHP	LHP
AL																															
BAL	162	79	83	7	0	0	0	0	0	1	0	0	0	0	0	104	47	11	0	2	1	3	0	1	10	3	2	1	0	117	45
BOS	186	100	86	7	0	0	1	0	0	1	0	0	0	0	0	103	59	16	8	4	2	4	0	6	9	5	1	2	0	145	41
CHI	106	43	63	3	0	0	0	0	0	0	0	0	0	0	0	66	20	16	4	5	1	4	1	6	14	2	2	0	0	70	36
CLE	164	84	80	9	0	0	0	0	0	0	0	0	0	0	0	103	44	14	3	4	2	4	2	8	14	6	0	1	0	106	58
DET	157	85	72	6	0	0	0	0	0	0	0	0	0	0	0	101	40	15	1	4	1	3	2	0	7	4	3	0	0	112	45
KC	166	107	59	5	0	0	0	0	0	0	0	0	0	0	0	96	46	21	3	7	1	7	1	3	12	5	1	1	0	124	42
LA	102	32	70	7	0	0	1	0	0	0	0	0	0	0	0	64	27	9	2	2	1	5	1	1	13	3	1	0	0	77	25
MIN	221	115	106	13	0	1	2	0	0	1	2	0	0	0	0	129	65	22	5	7	3	8	3	3	6	2	3	2	1	180	41
NY	162	69	93	5	0	0	0	0	0	0	0	0	0	0	0	84	57	19	2	2	3	2	1	0	5	3	2	1	0	112	50
WAS	125	71	54	2	0	0	0	0	0	0	0	0	0	0	0	71	30	23	1	5	2	2	0	3	14	4	1	0	0	94	31
NL																															
CHI	145	84	61	6	0	0	0	0	0	2	0	0	0	0	0	81	41	20	3	2	3	2	1	2	11	2	1	2	0	94	51
CIN	130	62	68	1	0	0	0	0	0	0	0	0	0	0	0	77	38	12	3	2	1	2	1	2	15	0	3	0	0	88	42
HOU	70	29	41	1	0	0	0	0	0	0	0	0	0	0	0	43	23	2	2	0	2	2	1	1	10	1	1	0	0	45	25
LA	79	26	53	2	0	0	0	0	0	0	0	0	0	0	0	43	27	8	1	0	0	1	1	1	9	3	1	0	0	49	30
MIL	159	89	70	1	0	0	0	0	0	1	0	0	0	0	0	84	52	20	3	2	4	2	2	2	8	2	5	0	0	123	36
NY	103	58	45	2	0	0	0	0	0	1	0	0	0	0	0	53	32	16	2	2	2	0	0	1	12	3	1	0	0	74	29
PHI	130	59	71	2	0	0	2	0	0	0	0	0	0	0	0	62	51	15	2	2	2	4	3	1	15	1	1	1	0	82	48
PIT	121	55	66	3	0	0	1	0	0	0	0	0	0	0	0	62	39	18	2	6	1	1	3	1	7	6	1	0	0	81	40
SF	165	86	79	8	0	0	0	0	0	2	0	0	0	0	0	98	54	11	2	3	2	2	0	0	10	2	0	2	1	116	49
STL	109	59	50	4	1	0	1	0	0	0	0	0	0	0	0	60	33	13	3	2	1	3	2	1	13	2	2	0	0	81	28
AL	1551	785	766	64	0	1	4	0	0	3	2	0	0	0	0	921	435	166	29	42	17	42	11	31	104	37	16	8	1	1137	414
NL	1211	607	604	30	1	0	4	0	0	6	0	0	0	0	0	663	390	135	23	21	18	19	14	12	110	22	16	5	1	833	378
YR	2762	1392	1370	94	1	1	8	0	0	9	2	0	0	0	0	1584	825	301	52	63	35	61	25	43	214	59	32	13	2	1970	792

	AL		*NL*
49	Harmon Killebrew	47	Willie Mays
39	Boog Powell	33	Billy Williams
35	Mickey Mantle	31	Johnny Callison
34	Rocky Colavito	31	Orlando Cepeda
33	Dick Stuart	31	James Hart

1965

				Consec			1-Inn			One-Game						Men-On-Base				Batters					Totals					Pitchers	
Tm	Tot	H	A	2	3	4	3	4	5	5	6	7	8	9	10	0	1	2	3	PH	LO	XN	IP	P	1	10	20	30	40	RHP	LHP
AL																															
BAL	125	62	63	1	1	0	1	0	0	1	0	0	0	0	0	66	45	13	1	4	3	2	1	2	14	2	1	0	0	86	39
BOS	165	94	71	6	0	0	1	0	0	2	0	0	0	0	0	103	41	18	3	4	3	5	2	7	13	2	2	1	0	128	37
CAL	92	36	56	2	0	0	0	0	0	0	0	0	0	0	0	61	27	3	1	1	2	0	0	3	17	4	0	0	0	70	22
CHI	125	45	80	1	0	0	0	0	0	0	0	0	0	0	0	87	28	8	2	2	1	7	0	3	11	8	0	0	0	88	37
CLE	156	90	66	4	0	0	1	0	0	1	0	0	0	0	0	87	43	23	3	9	1	5	0	4	14	1	4	0	0	115	41
DET	162	96	66	3	0	0	0	0	0	0	0	0	0	0	0	84	49	25	4	3	3	4	2	0	8	6	1	1	0	112	50
KC	110	47	63	3	0	0	0	0	0	0	0	0	0	0	0	73	22	14	1	2	0	2	2	2	14	3	1	0	0	83	27
MIN	150	67	83	4	0	0	0	0	0	1	0	0	0	0	0	79	50	19	2	4	2	2	3	3	9	2	4	0	0	122	28
NY	149	77	72	3	0	0	0	0	0	0	0	0	0	0	0	86	47	11	5	3	2	2	4	3	17	4	1	0	0	93	56
WAS	136	62	74	2	0	0	0	0	0	1	0	0	0	0	0	80	36	17	3	8	0	4	0	2	14	5	1	0	0	101	35
NL																															
CHI	134	79	55	4	0	0	0	0	0	1	0	0	0	0	0	69	39	24	2	2	0	2	0	1	12	0	1	2	0	100	34
CIN	183	108	75	8	0	0	1	0	0	0	0	0	0	0	0	97	57	26	3	6	4	3	0	1	4	6	1	2	0	112	71
HOU	97	25	72	1	0	0	0	0	0	0	0	0	0	0	0	59	23	15	0	4	4	0	0	2	14	2	1	0	0	69	28
LA	78	26	52	1	0	0	0	0	0	0	0	0	0	0	0	50	24	4	0	1	0	4	1	7	11	3	0	0	0	46	32
MIL	196	98	98	7	0	0	0	1	0	1	0	0	0	0	0	120	56	17	3	7	6	4	1	2	9	1	3	3	0	151	45
NY	107	50	57	3	0	0	0	0	0	0	0	0	0	0	0	68	28	11	0	4	2	3	0	0	12	5	0	0	0	70	37
PHI	144	77	67	5	0	0	0	0	0	1	1	0	0	0	0	87	46	7	4	2	4	3	3	1	12	2	2	1	0	94	50
PIT	111	37	74	3	0	0	0	0	0	1	0	0	0	0	0	66	26	15	4	4	4	3	1	3	10	4	1	0	0	85	26
SF	159	81	78	6	0	0	0	0	0	2	0	0	0	0	0	87	52	18	2	3	1	3	1	2	11	1	1	1	1	118	41
STL	109	68	41	3	0	0	0	0	0	0	0	0	0	0	0	59	36	12	2	3	4	1	2	5	9	4	1	0	0	70	39
AL	1370	676	694	29	1	0	3	0	0	6	0	0	0	0	0	806	388	151	25	40	17	33	14	29	131	37	15	2	0	998	372
NL	1318	649	669	41	0	0	1	1	0	6	1	0	0	0	0	762	387	149	20	36	29	26	9	24	104	28	11	9	1	915	403
YR	2688	1325	1363	70	1	0	4	1	0	12	1	0	0	0	0	1568	775	300	45	76	46	59	23	53	235	65	26	11	1	1913	775

	AL		*NL*
32	Tony Conigliaro	52	Willie Mays
30	Norm Cash	39	Willie McCovey
29	Willie Horton	34	Billy Williams
28	Leon Wagner	33	Frank Robinson
26	Multiple Players Tied	33	Ron Santo

1966

				Consec			1-Inn			One-Game						Men-On-Base				Batters					Totals					Pitchers	
Tm	Tot	H	A	2	3	4	3	4	5	5	6	7	8	9	10	0	1	2	3	PH	LO	XN	IP	P	1	10	20	30	40	RHP	LHP
AL																															
BAL	175	85	90	10	0	0	0	0	0	2	0	0	0	0	0	104	54	16	1	2	1	2	0	3	11	1	2	1	1	126	49
BOS	145	80	65	2	0	0	0	0	0	0	0	0	0	0	0	85	43	13	4	4	1	5	3	3	11	3	2	0	0	113	32
CAL	122	54	68	1	0	0	1	0	0	0	0	0	0	0	0	63	46	12	1	4	2	1	2	1	10	5	0	0	0	85	37
CHI	87	32	55	2	0	0	0	0	0	0	0	0	0	0	0	50	31	5	1	1	0	1	2	3	12	1	1	0	0	59	28
CLE	155	82	73	3	0	0	0	0	0	1	0	1	0	0	0	99	36	19	1	6	1	3	0	0	13	2	2	1	0	96	59
DET	179	96	83	5	0	0	0	0	0	1	0	0	0	0	0	101	49	23	6	6	6	7	1	4	8	3	3	1	0	120	59
KC	70	18	52	2	0	0	0	0	0	0	0	0	0	0	0	45	16	9	0	3	0	2	2	0	12	1	0	0	0	55	15
MIN	144	93	51	2	1	0	0	0	1	0	1	0	0	0	0	77	48	15	4	6	0	4	1	3	11	2	2	1	0	95	49
NY	162	74	88	1	1	0	1	0	0	1	0	0	0	0	0	104	44	9	5	6	3	4	2	1	12	2	2	1	0	97	65
WAS	126	62	64	7	1	0	1	0	0	0	0	0	0	0	0	64	43	16	3	8	2	3	0	3	12	6	0	0	0	88	38
NL																															
ATL	207	119	88	5	0	0	0	0	0	2	0	0	0	0	0	123	57	22	5	2	5	4	1	6	7	3	1	2	1	159	48
CHI	140	80	60	2	0	0	0	0	0	0	0	0	0	0	0	84	38	17	1	2	2	5	1	1	6	4	1	1	0	108	32
CIN	149	91	58	2	0	0	0	0	0	2	0	0	0	0	0	80	45	22	2	4	0	4	1	1	9	3	3	0	0	106	43
HOU	112	47	65	3	0	0	0	0	0	0	0	0	0	0	0	62	29	18	3	3	3	2	4	3	13	4	0	0	0	69	43
LA	108	43	65	5	0	0	0	0	0	1	0	0	0	0	0	62	32	14	0	1	1	2	2	3	11	4	1	0	0	76	32
NY	98	51	47	4	0	0	0	0	0	0	0	0	0	0	0	54	23	19	2	9	0	2	1	0	15	3	0	0	0	58	40
PHI	117	52	65	1	0	0	0	0	0	0	0	0	0	0	0	67	33	16	1	1	3	3	5	1	10	2	1	0	1	73	44
PIT	158	48	110	4	0	0	1	0	0	0	1	0	0	0	0	84	48	23	3	3	1	9	2	1	8	3	2	1	0	122	36
SF	181	91	90	3	0	0	0	0	0	2	0	0	0	0	0	94	69	14	4	4	1	6	1	5	15	0	1	3	0	137	44
STL	108	48	60	3	0	0	1	0	0	0	0	0	0	0	0	63	33	11	1	3	2	2	1	5	13	6	0	0	0	69	39
AL	1365	676	689	35	3	0	3	0	1	5	1	1	0	0	0	792	410	137	26	46	16	32	13	21	112	26	14	5	1	934	431
NL	1378	670	708	32	0	0	2	0	0	7	1	0	0	0	0	773	407	176	22	32	18	39	19	26	107	32	10	7	2	977	401
YR	2743	1346	1397	67	3	0	5	0	1	12	2	1	0	0	0	1565	817	313	48	78	34	71	32	47	219	58	24	12	3	1911	832

Tm	Tot	H	A	Consec			1-Inn			One-Game						Men-On-Base				Batters					Totals					Pitchers	
				2	3	4	3	4	5	5	6	7	8	9	10	0	1	2	3	PH	LO	XN	IP	P	1	10	20	30	40	RHP	LHP

AL		NL	
49	Frank Robinson	44	Hank Aaron
39	Harmon Killebrew	40	Dick Allen
34	Boog Powell	37	Willie Mays
32	Norm Cash	36	Willie McCovey
31	Joe Pepitone	36	Joe Torre

1967

AL

Tm	Tot	H	A	2	3	4	3	4	5	5	6	7	8	9	10	0	1	2	3	PH	LO	XN	IP	P	1	10	20	30	40	RHP	LHP
BAL	138	64	74	6	0	0	0	1	0	0	0	1	0	0	0	82	39	15	2	7	2	2	0	2	11	3	2	1	0	95	43
BOS	158	90	68	5	0	0	0	0	0	1	0	0	0	0	0	94	40	22	2	1	4	3	1	2	13	4	1	0	1	120	38
CAL	114	56	58	2	0	0	0	0	0	0	0	0	0	0	0	66	36	10	2	3	2	0	2	0	13	2	1	0	0	80	34
CHI	89	38	51	0	0	0	0	0	0	0	0	0	0	0	0	49	28	11	1	2	2	4	0	2	13	3	0	0	0	59	30
CLE	131	76	55	4	0	0	0	0	0	0	0	0	0	0	0	82	37	9	3	5	4	9	2	5	14	5	1	0	0	89	42
DET	152	83	69	3	0	0	0	0	0	0	0	0	0	0	0	101	37	10	4	2	4	2	1	3	10	2	4	0	0	98	54
KC	69	19	50	0	0	0	0	0	0	0	0	0	0	0	0	41	20	7	1	1	2	2	3	4	14	2	0	0	0	47	22
MIN	131	70	61	5	0	0	0	0	0	1	0	0	0	0	0	76	43	11	1	7	2	0	1	3	15	1	1	0	1	104	27
NY	100	60	40	3	0	0	0	0	0	0	0	0	0	0	0	57	35	8	0	4	0	3	2	2	16	3	1	0	0	67	33
WAS	115	57	58	5	0	0	0	0	0	0	0	0	0	0	0	69	25	17	4	6	0	2	1	0	14	2	0	1	0	83	32

NL

Tm	Tot	H	A	2	3	4	3	4	5	5	6	7	8	9	10	0	1	2	3	PH	LO	XN	IP	P	1	10	20	30	40	RHP	LHP
ATL	158	91	67	6	0	0	1	0	0	0	0	1	0	0	0	85	52	16	5	4	5	3	1	0	8	3	2	1	0	121	37
CHI	128	70	58	5	0	0	1	0	0	1	0	1	0	0	0	71	39	16	2	2	0	1	1	0	5	2	2	1	0	90	38
CIN	109	57	52	2	0	0	1	0	0	0	0	0	0	0	0	58	41	9	1	4	2	2	1	1	11	4	1	0	0	81	28
HOU	93	31	62	1	0	0	0	0	0	0	0	0	0	0	0	50	27	16	0	1	2	2	1	3	14	2	0	1	0	67	26
LA	82	36	46	4	0	0	0	0	0	0	0	0	0	0	0	56	20	6	0	3	2	0	1	2	11	3	0	0	0	39	43
NY	83	44	39	0	0	0	1	0	0	0	0	0	0	0	0	49	23	9	2	1	0	5	1	2	12	4	0	0	0	58	25
PHI	103	48	55	2	0	0	0	0	0	0	0	0	0	0	0	62	24	14	3	3	3	4	0	2	13	2	1	0	0	65	38
PIT	91	43	48	3	0	0	0	0	0	0	0	0	0	0	0	53	30	8	0	2	0	1	3	0	11	1	2	0	0	68	23
SF	140	65	75	4	0	0	0	0	0	0	0	0	0	0	0	85	28	22	5	4	1	2	1	1	8	2	2	1	0	106	34
STL	115	53	62	3	0	0	0	0	0	0	0	0	0	0	0	68	31	15	1	1	5	2	3	0	9	3	2	0	0	73	42
AL	1197	613	584	33	0	0	0	1	0	2	0	1	0	0	0	717	340	120	20	38	22	27	13	23	133	27	11	2	2	842	355
NL	1102	538	564	30	0	0	4	0	0	1	0	2	0	0	0	637	315	131	19	25	20	22	13	11	102	26	12	4	0	768	334
YR	2299	1151	1148	63	0	0	4	1	0	3	0	3	0	0	0	1354	655	251	39	63	42	49	26	34	235	53	23	6	2	1610	689

AL		NL	
44	Harmon Killebrew	39	Hank Aaron
44	Carl Yastrzemski	37	Jim Wynn
36	Frank Howard	31	Willie McCovey
30	Frank Robinson	31	Ron Santo
25	Multiple Players Tied	29	Jim Ray Hart

1968

AL

Tm	Tot	H	A	2	3	4	3	4	5	5	6	7	8	9	10	0	1	2	3	PH	LO	XN	IP	P	1	10	20	30	40	RHP	LHP
BAL	133	57	76	4	0	0	1	0	0	0	0	0	0	0	0	84	32	14	3	6	3	6	0	6	13	4	1	0	0	96	37
BOS	125	58	67	1	0	0	0	0	0	0	0	0	0	0	0	64	46	11	4	0	1	2	1	1	10	3	1	1	0	92	33
CAL	83	49	34	1	0	0	0	0	0	0	0	0	0	0	0	53	20	10	0	2	3	3	0	0	12	2	1	0	0	60	23
CHI	71	29	42	0	0	0	0	0	0	0	0	0	0	0	0	38	22	5	6	1	0	1	0	3	17	1	0	0	0	52	19
CLE	75	36	39	0	0	0	0	0	0	0	0	0	0	0	0	47	22	6	0	2	2	4	2	0	12	2	0	0	0	52	23
DET	185	107	78	11	0	0	0	0	0	2	1	0	0	0	0	119	44	17	5	7	2	6	0	7	9	4	3	1	0	132	53
MIN	105	50	55	2	0	0	1	0	0	0	0	0	0	0	0	67	31	7	0	1	2	1	0	3	14	2	1	0	0	78	27
NY	109	55	54	4	0	0	0	0	0	0	0	0	0	0	0	58	39	9	3	1	0	0	1	1	9	5	0	0	0	73	36
OAK	94	38	56	4	0	0	1	0	0	0	0	0	0	0	0	59	25	10	0	4	0	0	2	4	17	0	1	0	0	53	41
WAS	124	53	71	2	0	0	0	0	0	0	0	0	0	0	0	73	32	18	1	6	1	2	0	0	15	1	1	0	1	80	44

NL

Tm	Tot	H	A	2	3	4	3	4	5	5	6	7	8	9	10	0	1	2	3	PH	LO	XN	IP	P	1	10	20	30	40	RHP	LHP
ATL	80	42	38	1	0	0	0	0	0	0	0	0	0	0	0	49	21	10	0	1	2	0	0	3	12	2	1	0	0	58	22
CHI	130	83	47	4	0	0	0	0	0	2	0	0	0	0	0	68	45	14	3	2	0	2	1	2	10	1	1	2	0	97	33
CIN	106	55	51	1	0	0	0	0	0	0	0	0	0	0	0	60	39	7	0	0	1	0	2	5	10	4	1	0	0	78	28
HOU	66	22	44	2	0	0	0	0	0	0	0	0	0	0	0	46	12	7	1	1	3	0	0	2	14	0	1	0	0	43	23
LA	67	24	43	1	0	0	1	0	0	0	0	0	0	0	0	43	14	8	2	2	3	3	0	1	16	1	0	0	0	43	24

				Consec			1-Inn			One-Game						Men-On-Base				Batters					Totals					Pitchers	
Tm	Tot	H	A	2	3	4	3	4	5	5	6	7	8	9	10	0	1	2	3	PH	LO	XN	IP	P	1	10	20	30	40	RHP	LHP
NY	81	49	32	1	0	0	0	0	0	0	0	0	0	0	0	53	19	8	1	4	1	0	0	2	12	4	0	0	0	53	28
PHI	100	52	48	1	0	0	0	0	0	0	0	0	0	0	0	57	29	11	3	5	0	1	0	2	13	1	0	1	0	67	33
PIT	80	33	47	3	0	0	0	0	0	0	0	0	0	0	0	47	26	6	1	4	0	0	3	1	11	2	1	0	0	58	22
SF	108	60	48	0	0	0	0	0	0	0	0	0	0	0	0	60	26	18	4	2	2	2	0	1	9	0	2	1	0	76	32
STL	73	31	42	3	0	0	0	0	0	0	0	0	0	0	0	44	23	5	1	0	1	4	1	3	13	2	0	0	0	52	21
AL	1104	532	572	29	0	0	3	0	0	2	1	0	0	0	0	662	313	107	22	30	14	25	6	25	128	24	9	2	1	768	336
NL	891	451	440	17	0	0	1	0	0	2	0	0	0	0	0	527	254	94	16	21	13	12	7	22	120	17	7	4	0	625	266
YR	1995	983	1012	46	0	0	4	0	0	4	1	0	0	0	0	1189	567	201	38	51	27	37	13	47	248	41	16	6	1	1393	602

	AL		*NL*
44	Frank Howard	36	Willie McCovey
36	Willie Horton	33	Dick Allen
35	Ken Harrelson	32	Ernie Banks
29	Reggie Jackson	30	Billy Williams
25	Multiple Players Tied	29	Hank Aaron

1969

AL

Tm	Tot	H	A	2	3	4	3	4	5	5	6	7	8	9	10	0	1	2	3	PH	LO	XN	IP	P	1	10	20	30	40	RHP	LHP
BAL	175	82	93	7	1	0	1	0	0	0	0	0	0	0	0	98	57	20	0	5	3	8	2	3	10	2	2	2	0	128	47
BOS	197	105	92	5	0	0	0	0	0	1	0	0	0	0	0	118	53	21	5	2	4	6	0	3	12	2	2	0	2	152	45
CAL	88	49	39	0	0	0	0	0	0	1	0	0	0	0	0	55	26	6	1	1	1	2	2	2	13	4	0	0	0	52	36
CHI	112	61	51	2	0	0	0	0	0	2	0	0	0	0	0	69	30	11	2	4	4	3	1	2	15	2	1	0	0	88	24
CLE	119	59	60	2	0	0	0	0	0	0	0	0	0	0	0	66	36	15	2	5	2	2	0	2	16	2	2	0	0	92	27
DET	182	104	78	9	0	0	0	0	0	2	1	0	0	0	0	114	48	15	5	4	5	4	0	0	4	5	4	0	0	116	66
KC	98	39	59	2	0	0	0	0	0	0	0	0	0	0	0	51	32	14	1	3	1	0	3	4	12	5	0	0	0	71	27
MIN	163	79	84	4	0	0	0	0	0	0	0	0	0	0	0	84	50	25	4	5	3	5	1	4	12	3	1	0	1	106	57
NY	94	44	50	1	1	0	1	0	0	0	0	0	0	0	0	58	26	8	2	2	1	3	0	1	13	1	2	0	0	59	35
OAK	148	73	75	3	1	0	1	0	0	0	0	0	0	0	0	81	42	20	5	2	0	3	1	10	17	3	0	1	1	90	58
SEA	125	74	51	1	0	0	1	0	0	0	0	0	0	0	0	73	40	9	3	4	1	8	0	5	20	2	1	0	0	86	39
WAS	148	77	71	4	0	0	0	0	0	1	0	0	0	0	0	82	45	19	2	6	0	5	1	1	10	2	0	1	1	106	42

NL

Tm	Tot	H	A	2	3	4	3	4	5	5	6	7	8	9	10	0	1	2	3	PH	LO	XN	IP	P	1	10	20	30	40	RHP	LHP
ATL	141	77	64	6	0	0	1	0	0	1	0	0	0	0	0	85	37	14	5	2	0	5	1	4	10	4	1	0	1	103	38
CHI	142	84	58	5	0	0	1	0	0	0	0	0	0	0	0	76	45	18	3	4	2	2	1	2	11	1	4	0	0	110	32
CIN	171	97	74	6	0	0	0	0	0	1	0	0	0	0	0	91	52	26	2	1	3	6	1	6	10	2	2	2	0	143	28
HOU	104	47	57	0	0	0	0	0	0	0	0	0	0	0	0	56	34	10	4	1	2	2	2	4	10	4	0	1	0	81	23
LA	97	41	56	3	0	0	0	0	0	0	0	0	0	0	0	61	26	8	2	2	2	2	2	1	9	5	0	0	0	55	42
MON	125	73	52	8	0	0	1	0	0	0	0	0	0	0	0	76	32	15	2	3	1	0	0	3	16	2	2	0	0	98	27
NY	109	56	53	0	0	0	0	0	0	0	0	0	0	0	0	67	24	16	2	1	4	3	0	1	11	4	1	0	0	75	34
PHI	137	75	62	2	0	0	0	0	0	0	0	0	0	0	0	88	33	12	4	0	2	0	0	4	10	4	1	1	0	107	30
PIT	119	40	79	1	0	0	0	0	0	0	0	0	0	0	0	66	39	9	5	4	0	2	2	1	13	2	1	0	0	89	30
SD	99	47	52	0	0	0	0	0	0	0	0	0	0	0	0	58	27	10	4	2	1	1	0	1	12	2	2	0	0	76	23
SF	136	77	59	5	1	0	1	0	0	0	0	0	0	0	0	67	49	16	4	7	5	3	0	4	13	2	0	1	1	110	26
STL	90	41	49	1	0	0	0	0	0	0	0	0	0	0	0	56	21	10	3	2	4	3	0	3	14	5	0	0	0	62	28
AL	1649	846	803	40	3	0	4	0	0	7	1	0	0	0	0	949	485	183	32	43	25	49	11	37	154	33	15	4	5	1146	503
NL	1470	755	715	37	1	0	4	0	0	2	0	0	0	0	0	847	419	164	40	29	26	29	9	34	139	37	14	5	2	1109	361
YR	3119	1601	1518	77	4	0	8	0	0	9	1	0	0	0	0	1796	904	347	72	72	51	78	20	71	293	70	29	9	7	2255	864

	AL		*NL*
49	Harmon Killebrew	45	Willie McCovey
48	Frank Howard	44	Hank Aaron
47	Reggie Jackson	38	Lee May
40	Rico Petrocelli	37	Tony Perez
40	Carl Yastrzemski	33	Jim Wynn

1970

AL

Tm	Tot	H	A	2	3	4	3	4	5	5	6	7	8	9	10	0	1	2	3	PH	LO	XN	IP	P	1	10	20	30	40	RHP	LHP
BAL	179	88	91	10	0	0	0	0	0	1	0	0	0	0	0	94	56	22	7	1	2	5	0	4	10	6	1	1	0	127	52
BOS	203	117	86	11	0	0	0	1	0	0	0	0	0	0	0	117	60	21	5	2	4	1	1	5	12	3	2	1	1	152	51
CAL	114	41	73	3	0	0	0	0	0	1	0	0	0	0	0	66	36	10	2	2	0	1	0	5	11	5	1	0	0	84	30
CHI	123	78	45	1	0	0	0	0	0	0	0	0	0	0	0	77	31	13	2	2	2	1	0	1	15	2	0	1	0	93	30

Tm	Tot	H	A	Consec			1-Inn			One-Game						Men-On-Base				Batters					Totals					Pitchers	
				2	3	4	3	4	5	5	6	7	8	9	10	0	1	2	3	PH	LO	XN	IP	P	1	10	20	30	40	RHP	LHP
CLE	183	133	50	5	1	0	0	0	0	2	1	0	0	0	0	114	43	22	4	9	3	2	0	1	11	4	4	0	0	130	53
DET	148	86	62	6	0	0	1	0	0	0	0	0	0	0	0	88	43	13	4	3	6	2	0	2	12	6	1	0	0	102	46
KC	97	46	51	4	0	0	0	0	0	0	0	0	0	0	0	56	27	13	1	1	0	4	1	1	12	3	1	0	0	66	31
MIL	126	68	58	2	0	0	0	0	0	0	0	0	0	0	0	70	42	11	3	5	6	2	2	3	17	4	0	1	0	79	47
MIN	153	66	87	1	0	0	1	0	0	0	0	0	0	0	0	69	55	23	6	6	1	4	0	3	11	5	1	0	1	102	51
NY	111	60	51	0	0	0	0	0	0	0	0	0	0	0	0	65	32	13	1	5	1	2	0	4	14	0	2	0	0	67	44
OAK	171	83	88	6	0	0	0	0	0	1	0	0	0	0	0	102	45	22	2	8	6	1	2	6	14	4	4	0	0	97	74
WAS	138	72	66	5	0	0	0	0	0	1	0	0	0	0	0	76	42	18	2	5	4	3	0	1	12	2	1	0	1	94	44
NL																															
ATL	160	92	68	5	0	0	0	0	0	0	0	0	0	0	0	68	65	21	6	1	1	3	0	3	9	3	1	2	0	132	28
CHI	179	109	70	4	0	0	1	0	0	1	0	1	0	0	0	88	63	24	4	3	1	1	2	7	14	3	1	1	1	141	38
CIN	191	100	91	10	0	0	1	0	0	3	0	1	0	0	0	106	56	24	5	3	2	4	0	6	10	2	1	1	2	137	54
HOU	129	51	78	5	0	0	0	0	0	1	0	0	0	0	0	68	41	15	5	6	0	2	1	1	10	3	2	0	0	95	34
LA	87	35	52	3	0	0	0	0	0	0	0	0	0	0	0	49	25	11	2	3	1	3	2	1	10	4	0	0	0	53	34
MON	136	77	59	3	0	0	0	0	0	0	0	0	0	0	0	77	43	11	5	6	1	0	2	3	10	3	1	1	0	88	48
NY	120	63	57	3	1	0	2	0	0	1	0	0	0	0	0	70	31	17	2	4	3	5	0	1	11	3	2	0	0	88	32
PHI	101	48	53	5	0	0	0	0	0	0	0	0	0	0	0	52	34	12	3	6	3	3	2	2	12	3	1	0	0	66	35
PIT	130	43	87	8	1	0	0	0	0	0	1	0	0	0	0	77	37	12	4	1	0	4	1	0	9	3	1	1	0	100	30
SD	172	68	104	4	0	0	0	1	0	1	0	0	0	0	0	105	47	17	3	3	1	5	0	4	11	5	2	1	0	130	42
SF	165	84	81	2	0	0	1	0	0	0	0	0	0	0	0	84	47	27	7	4	5	4	2	4	12	1	3	1	0	130	35
STL	113	51	62	2	0	0	0	0	0	0	0	0	0	0	0	65	33	12	3	5	5	2	1	2	7	3	1	1	0	84	29
AL	1746	938	808	54	1	0	2	1	0	6	1	0	0	0	0	994	512	201	39	49	35	28	6	36	151	44	18	4	3	1193	553
NL	1683	821	862	54	2	0	5	1	0	7	1	2	0	0	0	909	522	203	49	45	23	36	13	34	125	36	16	9	3	1244	439
YR	3429	1759	1670	108	3	0	7	2	0	13	2	2	0	0	0	1903	1034	404	88	94	58	64	19	70	276	80	34	13	6	2437	992

	AL		*NL*
44	Frank Howard	45	Johnny Bench
41	Harmon Killebrew	42	Billy Williams
40	Carl Yastrzemski	40	Tony Perez
36	Tony Conigliaro	39	Willie McCovey
35	Boog Powell	38	Multiple Players Tied

1971

Tm	Tot	H	A	Consec			1-Inn			One-Game						Men-On-Base				Batters					Totals					Pitchers	
				2	3	4	3	4	5	5	6	7	8	9	10	0	1	2	3	PH	LO	XN	IP	P	1	10	20	30	40	RHP	LHP
AL																															
BAL	158	78	80	3	0	0	1	0	0	0	0	0	0	0	0	81	50	22	5	1	6	1	1	4	9	4	3	0	0	111	47
BOS	161	88	73	6	0	0	1	0	0	0	0	0	0	0	0	84	52	23	2	4	2	1	0	8	11	4	2	1	0	125	36
CAL	96	39	57	3	0	0	0	0	0	0	0	0	0	0	0	58	30	7	1	3	1	3	1	3	15	2	1	0	0	66	30
CHI	138	60	78	5	0	0	0	0	0	0	0	0	0	0	0	81	34	18	5	3	3	2	1	2	11	5	0	1	0	97	41
CLE	109	62	47	1	0	0	0	0	0	0	0	0	0	0	0	61	29	16	3	3	6	4	0	1	13	3	1	0	0	71	38
DET	179	90	89	6	1	0	0	0	0	0	1	0	0	0	0	113	38	25	3	8	6	4	2	1	9	5	2	1	0	125	54
KC	80	23	57	2	0	0	0	0	0	0	0	0	0	0	0	49	17	13	1	4	3	0	1	2	14	2	0	0	0	59	21
MIL	104	46	58	0	0	0	0	0	0	1	0	0	0	0	0	68	22	13	1	2	2	0	0	2	18	4	1	0	0	78	26
MIN	116	57	59	5	0	0	0	0	0	0	0	0	0	0	0	64	33	17	2	2	0	2	1	0	11	3	2	0	0	69	47
NY	97	39	58	3	0	0	0	0	0	0	0	0	0	0	0	53	32	11	1	3	1	2	2	1	15	2	1	0	0	52	45
OAK	160	84	76	2	0	0	0	0	0	1	0	0	0	0	0	104	40	13	3	2	2	4	1	3	11	5	1	1	0	108	52
WAS	86	34	52	1	0	0	0	0	0	0	0	0	0	0	0	47	29	8	2	7	4	2	1	1	13	1	1	0	0	55	31
NL																															
ATL	153	96	57	4	0	0	1	0	0	1	0	0	0	0	0	91	41	19	2	2	0	7	0	0	8	3	0	1	1	115	38
CHI	128	74	54	2	0	0	0	0	0	0	0	0	0	0	0	66	45	15	2	3	1	3	1	8	15	2	2	0	0	90	38
CIN	138	69	69	4	0	0	0	0	0	0	0	0	0	0	0	89	34	14	1	1	3	1	0	2	9	2	2	1	0	99	39
HOU	71	18	53	1	0	0	0	0	0	0	0	0	0	0	0	37	23	9	2	1	0	1	2	1	12	3	0	0	0	54	17
LA	95	43	52	4	0	0	1	0	0	0	0	0	0	0	0	54	27	13	1	1	1	1	0	0	12	2	1	0	0	59	36
MON	88	50	38	2	0	0	0	0	0	0	0	0	0	0	0	44	27	14	3	2	2	1	0	5	15	4	0	0	0	61	27
NY	98	48	50	4	0	0	0	0	0	0	0	0	0	0	0	65	24	6	3	1	1	4	1	2	12	5	0	0	0	78	20
PHI	123	73	50	5	0	0	0	0	0	0	0	0	0	0	0	69	40	11	3	3	0	3	1	7	15	0	0	2	0	87	36
PIT	154	66	88	9	0	0	1	0	0	2	0	0	0	0	0	85	52	15	2	3	0	4	1	1	13	3	1	0	1	104	50
SD	96	42	54	3	0	0	0	0	0	0	0	0	0	0	0	57	24	13	2	1	0	2	0	0	11	1	1	0	0	74	22
SF	140	71	69	3	0	0	0	0	0	0	0	0	0	0	0	74	44	18	4	7	3	4	2	3	13	4	0	1	0	97	43
STL	95	39	56	3	0	0	0	0	0	0	0	0	0	0	0	49	32	13	1	1	0	1	0	2	14	1	1	0	0	69	26
AL	1484	700	784	37	1	0	2	0	0	2	1	0	0	0	0	863	406	186	29	42	36	25	11	28	150	40	15	4	0	1016	468

				Consec			1-Inn			One-Game						Men-On-Base				Batters					Totals					Pitchers	
Tm	Tot	H	A	2	3	4	3	4	5	5	6	7	8	9	10	0	1	2	3	PH	LO	XN	IP	P	1	10	20	30	40	RHP	LHP
NL	1379	689	690	44	0	0	3	0	0	3	0	0	0	0	0	780	413	160	26	26	11	32	8	31	149	30	8	5	2	987	392
YR	2863	1389	1474	81	1	0	5	0	0	5	1	0	0	0	0	1643	819	346	55	68	47	57	19	59	299	70	23	9	2	2003	860

	AL		*NL*
33	Bill Melton	48	Willie Stargell
32	Norm Cash	47	Hank Aaron
32	Reggie Jackson	39	Lee May
30	Reggie Smith	34	Deron Johnson
28	Multiple Players Tied	33	Multiple Players Tied

1972

AL

Tm	Tot	H	A	Consec 2	3	4	1-Inn 3	4	5	One-Game 5	6	7	8	9	10	Men-On-Base 0	1	2	3	PH	LO	XN	IP	P	Totals 1	10	20	30	40	RHP	LHP
BAL	100	44	56	0	0	0	0	0	0	0	0	0	0	0	0	59	26	11	4	2	0	2	0	5	11	3	1	0	0	69	31
BOS	124	71	53	1	0	0	0	0	0	0	0	0	0	0	0	65	38	17	4	3	4	5	0	4	15	3	2	0	0	92	32
CAL	78	30	48	1	0	0	0	0	0	0	0	0	0	0	0	49	21	8	0	3	0	1	1	3	15	2	0	0	0	47	31
CHI	108	65	43	4	0	0	0	0	0	1	0	0	0	0	0	52	33	19	4	3	2	3	3	0	13	2	0	1	0	75	33
CLE	91	59	32	1	0	0	0	0	0	0	0	0	0	0	0	54	28	8	1	1	1	3	1	4	15	2	0	0	0	52	39
DET	122	68	54	3	1	0	1	0	0	0	0	0	0	0	0	72	36	12	2	1	0	6	0	0	8	6	1	0	0	88	34
KC	78	29	49	3	0	0	0	0	0	0	0	0	0	0	0	41	19	15	3	1	0	1	0	0	7	2	1	0	0	47	31
MIL	88	36	52	3	0	0	0	0	0	0	0	0	0	0	0	51	28	8	1	1	0	1	0	0	14	1	2	0	0	64	24
MIN	93	52	41	2	0	0	1	0	0	0	0	0	0	0	0	51	25	13	4	6	0	1	1	2	12	1	2	0	0	55	38
NY	103	53	50	3	0	0	0	0	0	0	0	0	0	0	0	61	27	13	2	4	1	4	0	1	11	2	0	1	0	73	30
OAK	134	68	66	3	0	0	0	0	0	0	0	0	0	0	0	76	37	20	1	2	2	5	0	3	11	3	2	0	0	90	44
TEX	56	33	23	1	0	0	0	0	0	0	0	0	0	0	0	34	14	8	0	0	1	1	0	0	13	1	0	0	0	42	14

NL

Tm	Tot	H	A	Consec 2	3	4	1-Inn 3	4	5	One-Game 5	6	7	8	9	10	Men-On-Base 0	1	2	3	PH	LO	XN	IP	P	Totals 1	10	20	30	40	RHP	LHP
ATL	144	86	58	4	0	0	1	0	0	1	0	0	0	0	0	86	36	20	2	4	0	4	0	2	11	3	1	1	0	93	51
CHI	133	83	50	5	0	0	0	0	0	2	0	0	0	0	0	67	46	16	4	0	0	2	0	3	12	4	0	1	0	101	32
CIN	124	58	66	1	0	0	0	0	0	0	0	0	0	0	0	74	33	14	3	3	0	2	2	1	12	1	1	0	1	82	42
HOU	134	58	76	1	0	0	0	0	0	1	0	0	0	0	0	78	35	20	1	0	0	5	1	3	7	1	4	0	0	99	35
LA	98	46	52	3	0	0	0	0	0	0	0	0	0	0	0	53	34	11	0	3	1	1	2	1	17	2	0	0	0	62	36
MON	91	50	41	4	0	0	0	0	0	0	0	0	0	0	0	63	20	8	0	0	0	0	0	0	9	5	0	0	0	63	28
NY	105	45	60	2	0	0	0	0	0	0	0	0	0	0	0	63	24	16	2	0	1	2	0	3	16	2	0	0	0	75	30
PHI	98	49	49	5	0	0	0	0	0	0	1	0	0	0	0	58	30	10	0	5	0	1	2	3	18	3	0	0	0	64	34
PIT	110	53	57	0	0	0	0	0	0	0	0	0	0	0	0	54	33	21	2	1	1	2	1	0	7	4	0	1	0	80	30
SD	102	41	61	2	0	0	0	0	0	0	0	0	0	0	0	60	33	6	3	5	0	0	0	1	11	1	0	1	0	85	17
SF	150	86	64	6	0	0	0	0	0	0	0	0	0	0	0	80	46	19	5	2	2	2	1	0	10	4	2	0	0	101	49
STL	70	31	39	1	0	0	0	0	0	0	0	0	0	0	0	41	16	10	3	2	1	4	2	8	16	2	0	0	0	46	24
AL	1175	608	567	25	1	0	2	0	0	1	0	0	0	0	0	665	332	152	26	27	11	33	6	22	145	28	11	2	0	794	381
NL	1359	686	673	34	0	0	1	0	0	4	1	0	0	0	0	777	386	171	25	25	6	25	11	25	146	32	8	4	1	951	408
YR	2534	1294	1240	59	1	0	3	0	0	5	1	0	0	0	0	1442	718	323	51	52	17	58	17	47	291	60	19	6	1	1745	789

	AL		*NL*
37	Dick Allen	40	Johnny Bench
33	Bobby Murcer	38	Nate Colbert
26	Mike Epstein	37	Billy Williams
26	Harmon Killebrew	34	Hank Aaron
25	Multiple Players Tied	33	Willie Stargell

1973

AL

Tm	Tot	H	A	Consec 2	3	4	1-Inn 3	4	5	One-Game 5	6	7	8	9	10	Men-On-Base 0	1	2	3	PH	LO	XN	IP	P	Totals 1	10	20	30	40	RHP	LHP
BAL	119	63	56	4	0	0	0	0	0	0	0	0	0	0	0	62	36	17	4	0	3	2	2	0	13	4	1	0	0	83	36
BOS	147	83	64	4	0	0	0	0	0	0	0	0	0	0	0	80	35	26	6	0	5	4	0	0	7	4	3	0	0	111	36
CAL	93	41	52	3	0	0	0	0	0	0	0	0	0	0	0	46	31	16	0	3	0	4	1	0	14	1	0	1	0	61	32
CHI	111	56	55	2	0	0	0	0	0	0	0	0	0	0	0	65	28	17	1	3	2	2	1	0	11	2	2	0	0	72	39
CLE	158	92	66	6	0	0	0	0	0	2	0	0	0	0	0	97	43	16	2	3	2	1	0	0	8	4	3	0	0	109	49
DET	157	85	72	3	0	0	0	0	0	0	0	0	0	0	0	100	40	14	3	4	5	2	0	0	9	8	0	0	0	97	60
KC	114	54	60	3	0	0	1	0	0	0	0	0	0	0	0	62	35	15	2	1	2	1	2	0	14	0	2	0	0	74	40
MIL	145	73	72	4	0	0	1	0	0	0	0	0	0	0	0	77	44	17	7	3	2	3	3	0	5	5	2	0	0	98	47
MIN	120	56	64	2	1	0	1	0	0	0	0	0	0	0	0	72	31	14	3	1	2	3	0	0	12	5	0	0	0	84	36
NY	131	74	57	1	0	0	0	0	0	0	0	0	0	0	0	72	39	17	3	3	0	2	0	0	11	3	3	0	0	74	57
OAK	147	70	77	6	0	0	1	0	0	0	0	0	0	0	0	81	42	19	5	2	0	4	1	0	11	2	2	1	0	96	51

Tm	Tot	H	A	Consec			1-Inn			One-Game						Men-On-Base				Batters					Totals					Pitchers	
				2	3	4	3	4	5	5	6	7	8	9	10	0	1	2	3	PH	LO	XN	IP	P	1	10	20	30	40	RHP	LHP
TEX	110	47	63	2	0	0	1	0	0	0	0	0	0	0	0	68	29	10	3	2	2	2	1	0	15	2	0	1	0	62	48
NL																															
ATL	206	118	88	4	0	0	1	0	0	2	0	0	0	0	0	116	62	24	4	3	2	3	3	7	10	2	1	0	3	117	89
CHI	117	66	51	2	0	0	1	0	0	0	0	0	0	0	0	63	47	6	1	2	6	2	0	1	11	2	3	0	0	86	31
CIN	137	47	90	3	0	0	0	0	0	0	0	0	0	0	0	73	45	17	2	8	1	6	2	0	14	0	3	0	0	99	38
HOU	134	58	76	2	0	0	0	0	0	1	0	0	0	0	0	81	38	10	5	2	4	1	0	1	8	1	4	0	0	100	34
LA	110	63	47	3	0	0	0	0	0	0	0	0	0	0	0	57	33	19	1	3	0	6	0	0	8	3	1	0	0	73	37
MON	125	63	62	2	0	0	0	0	0	0	0	0	0	0	0	67	38	15	5	9	0	6	0	0	14	2	2	0	0	86	39
NY	85	39	46	0	0	0	0	0	0	0	0	0	0	0	0	48	18	14	5	2	4	0	0	1	11	3	1	0	0	63	22
PHI	134	78	56	2	0	0	0	0	0	0	0	0	0	0	0	76	38	17	3	4	2	1	0	6	10	4	2	0	0	89	45
PIT	154	72	82	9	0	0	0	0	0	1	0	0	0	0	0	90	44	17	3	2	1	6	2	1	8	4	2	0	1	110	44
SD	112	51	61	0	0	0	0	0	0	0	0	0	0	0	0	74	24	14	0	3	2	1	1	3	8	2	2	0	0	76	36
SF	161	85	76	5	0	0	1	0	0	0	0	0	0	0	0	105	39	12	5	4	11	5	3	1	7	4	2	1	0	103	58
STL	75	27	48	1	0	0	0	0	0	0	0	0	0	0	0	37	21	13	4	3	1	2	0	6	12	3	0	0	0	46	29
AL	1552	794	758	40	1	0	5	0	0	2	0	0	0	0	0	882	433	198	39	25	25	30	11	0	130	40	18	3	0	1021	531
NL	1550	767	783	33	0	0	3	0	0	4	0	0	0	0	0	887	447	178	38	45	34	39	11	27	121	30	23	1	4	1048	502
YR	3102	1561	1541	73	1	0	8	0	0	6	0	0	0	0	0	1769	880	376	77	70	59	69	22	27	251	70	41	4	4	2069	1033

	AL		*NL*
32	Reggie Jackson	44	Willie Stargell
30	Jeff Burroughs	43	Dave Johnson
30	Frank Robinson	41	Darrell Evans
29	Sal Bando	40	Hank Aaron
26	Multiple Players Tied	39	Bobby Bonds

1974

Tm	Tot	H	A	Consec			1-Inn			One-Game						Men-On-Base				Batters					Totals					Pitchers	
				2	3	4	3	4	5	5	6	7	8	9	10	0	1	2	3	PH	LO	XN	IP	P	1	10	20	30	40	RHP	LHP
AL																															
BAL	116	48	68	1	0	0	0	0	0	0	0	0	0	0	0	70	35	9	2	1	1	3	1	0	9	6	0	0	0	72	44
BOS	109	58	51	2	0	0	0	0	0	0	0	0	0	0	0	64	31	10	4	1	1	2	0	0	12	5	0	0	0	83	26
CAL	95	46	49	2	0	0	0	0	0	0	0	0	0	0	0	55	31	9	0	2	1	0	0	0	14	2	1	0	0	58	37
CHI	135	66	69	5	0	0	0	0	0	0	1	0	0	0	0	71	48	14	2	1	2	4	2	0	7	3	2	1	0	89	46
CLE	131	72	59	2	0	0	2	0	0	1	0	0	0	0	0	71	41	15	4	0	0	0	1	0	10	4	1	0	0	81	50
DET	131	74	57	1	1	0	1	0	0	1	0	0	0	0	0	72	43	15	1	3	1	2	0	0	15	5	0	0	0	82	49
KC	89	38	51	2	0	0	0	0	0	0	0	0	0	0	0	49	31	6	3	0	0	1	2	0	12	2	1	0	0	52	37
MIL	120	58	62	2	0	0	0	0	0	0	0	0	0	0	0	68	36	9	7	4	7	3	0	0	10	6	0	0	0	77	43
MIN	111	60	51	3	0	0	0	0	0	0	0	0	0	0	0	60	29	18	4	4	3	5	1	0	8	4	1	0	0	66	45
NY	101	42	59	4	0	0	1	0	0	0	1	0	0	0	0	50	40	9	2	1	0	3	0	0	12	3	1	0	0	52	49
OAK	132	69	63	1	0	0	0	0	0	1	0	0	0	0	0	69	41	15	7	1	2	1	0	0	9	0	4	0	0	85	47
TEX	99	43	56	1	0	0	1	0	0	0	0	0	0	0	0	62	26	9	2	0	0	0	0	0	11	1	2	0	0	56	43
NL																															
ATL	120	65	55	4	0	0	0	0	0	0	0	0	0	0	0	70	31	13	6	2	4	2	0	4	9	3	3	0	0	93	27
CHI	110	67	43	3	0	0	0	0	0	0	1	0	0	0	0	64	32	8	6	5	4	2	1	0	12	4	1	0	0	84	26
CIN	135	74	61	3	0	0	0	0	0	0	1	0	0	0	0	67	40	21	7	1	0	3	2	0	10	1	2	1	0	100	35
HOU	110	58	52	0	0	0	0	0	0	0	0	0	0	0	0	59	37	12	2	7	0	2	1	4	8	3	2	0	0	77	33
LA	139	68	71	3	0	0	0	0	0	0	1	0	0	0	0	75	40	22	2	3	3	3	1	1	7	5	1	1	0	104	35
MON	86	50	36	1	0	0	0	0	0	1	0	0	0	0	0	49	22	10	5	3	1	0	1	1	9	4	1	0	0	57	29
NY	96	43	53	1	1	0	1	0	0	0	0	0	0	0	0	53	32	11	0	2	0	1	0	0	11	3	1	0	0	65	31
PHI	95	55	40	0	0	0	0	0	0	0	0	0	0	0	0	40	33	20	2	9	1	0	1	1	13	1	0	1	0	62	33
PIT	114	47	67	1	0	0	0	0	0	0	0	0	0	0	0	55	41	15	3	4	1	3	0	2	6	4	1	0	0	76	38
SD	99	47	52	4	1	0	1	0	0	0	0	0	0	0	0	66	20	11	2	3	2	2	1	0	11	1	2	0	0	63	36
SF	93	50	43	2	0	0	0	0	0	0	0	0	0	0	0	52	25	14	2	1	0	2	1	5	12	2	1	0	0	71	22
STL	83	45	38	2	0	0	0	0	0	0	0	0	0	0	0	41	28	13	1	3	0	2	2	0	9	1	2	0	0	65	18
AL	1369	674	695	26	1	0	5	0	0	3	2	0	0	0	0	761	432	138	38	18	18	24	7	0	129	41	13	1	0	853	516
NL	1280	669	611	24	2	0	2	0	0	1	3	0	0	0	0	691	381	170	38	43	16	22	11	18	117	32	17	3	0	917	363
YR	2649	1343	1306	50	3	0	7	0	0	4	5	0	0	0	0	1452	813	308	76	61	34	46	18	18	246	73	30	4	0	1770	879

	AL		*NL*
32	Dick Allen	36	Mike Schmidt
29	Reggie Jackson	33	Johnny Bench
26	Gene Tenace	32	Jim Wynn
25	Jeff Burroughs	28	Tony Perez
25	Bobby Darwin	26	Cesar Cedeno

1975

AL

Tm	Tot	H	A	Consec			1-Inn			One-Game						Men-On-Base				Batters					Totals					Pitchers	
				2	3	4	3	4	5	5	6	7	8	9	10	0	1	2	3	PH	LO	XN	IP	P	1	10	20	30	40	RHP	LHP
BAL	124	46	78	0	0	0	0	0	0	0	0	0	0	0	0	70	31	20	3	1	4	2	0	0	8	3	2	0	0	94	30
BOS	134	74	60	3	0	0	1	0	0	0	0	0	0	0	0	76	35	20	3	1	4	3	0	0	8	5	2	0	0	99	35
CAL	55	24	31	0	0	0	0	0	0	0	0	0	0	0	0	24	20	9	2	1	0	4	0	0	16	1	0	0	0	37	18
CHI	94	42	52	2	0	0	0	0	0	0	0	0	0	0	0	52	24	15	3	1	2	2	0	0	11	3	0	0	0	64	30
CLE	153	79	74	8	0	0	0	0	0	0	0	0	0	0	0	91	40	18	4	3	1	2	1	0	9	5	2	0	0	96	57
DET	125	65	60	5	0	0	1	0	0	1	0	0	0	0	0	71	37	15	2	2	2	3	2	0	12	3	1	0	0	91	34
KC	118	46	72	4	0	0	0	0	0	1	0	0	0	0	0	74	33	10	1	4	3	3	5	0	11	3	0	1	0	77	41
MIL	146	72	74	6	0	0	0	0	0	1	0	0	0	0	0	88	43	14	1	2	4	0	0	0	10	5	0	1	0	100	46
MIN	121	75	46	3	0	0	0	0	0	0	0	0	0	0	0	71	30	19	1	5	0	1	2	0	11	6	0	0	0	83	38
NY	110	50	60	2	0	0	0	0	0	0	0	0	0	0	0	60	36	14	0	1	4	0	0	0	11	2	1	1	0	77	33
OAK	151	75	76	2	0	0	0	0	0	0	0	0	0	0	0	90	41	16	4	1	0	2	1	0	7	2	3	1	0	115	36
TEX	134	52	82	3	0	0	0	0	0	0	0	0	0	0	0	70	48	11	5	2	4	3	0	0	11	4	2	0	0	90	44

NL

Tm	Tot	H	A	Consec			1-Inn			One-Game						Men-On-Base				Batters					Totals					Pitchers	
				2	3	4	3	4	5	5	6	7	8	9	10	0	1	2	3	PH	LO	XN	IP	P	1	10	20	30	40	RHP	LHP
ATL	107	58	49	1	0	0	0	0	0	0	0	0	0	0	0	63	27	15	2	5	3	1	0	0	9	4	1	0	0	66	41
CHI	95	54	41	2	0	0	0	0	0	0	0	0	0	0	0	59	21	12	3	6	0	0	1	1	14	3	0	0	0	66	29
CIN	124	70	54	3	0	0	0	0	0	0	0	0	0	0	0	61	37	22	4	1	1	6	1	0	10	1	3	0	0	93	31
HOU	84	40	44	2	0	0	0	0	0	0	0	0	0	0	0	37	32	14	1	1	0	1	0	2	8	3	1	0	0	65	19
LA	118	64	54	4	0	0	0	0	0	0	0	0	0	0	0	63	32	19	4	4	0	3	0	1	9	3	1	0	0	95	23
MON	98	53	45	1	0	0	0	0	0	0	0	0	0	0	0	64	23	10	1	3	4	1	1	1	13	4	0	0	0	60	38
NY	101	52	49	1	0	0	0	0	0	0	0	0	0	0	0	58	30	11	2	3	3	2	0	0	11	2	0	1	0	65	36
PHI	125	72	53	6	0	0	1	0	0	1	0	0	0	0	0	77	36	11	1	4	1	2	0	2	14	1	0	2	0	96	29
PIT	138	67	71	5	0	0	0	0	0	0	0	0	0	0	0	76	45	16	1	4	0	2	1	1	8	2	3	0	0	87	51
SD	78	33	45	3	0	0	0	0	0	0	0	0	0	0	0	45	22	9	2	2	0	3	0	0	10	1	1	0	0	54	24
SF	84	36	48	2	0	0	0	0	0	1	0	0	0	0	0	53	20	11	0	3	2	1	1	1	13	3	0	0	0	63	21
STL	81	46	35	2	0	0	0	0	0	0	0	0	0	0	0	46	26	6	3	4	3	2	2	1	14	2	0	0	0	48	33
AL	1465	700	765	38	0	0	2	0	0	3	0	0	0	0	0	837	418	181	29	24	28	25	11	0	125	42	13	4	0	1023	442
NL	1233	645	588	32	0	0	1	0	0	2	0	0	0	0	0	702	351	156	24	40	17	24	7	10	133	29	10	3	0	858	375
YR	2698	1345	1353	70	0	0	3	0	0	5	0	0	0	0	0	1539	769	337	53	64	45	49	18	10	258	71	23	7	0	1881	817

AL		*NL*	
36	Reggie Jackson	38	Mike Schmidt
36	George Scott	36	Dave Kingman
34	John Mayberry	34	Greg Luzinski
32	Bobby Bonds	28	Johnny Bench
29	Multiple Players Tied	25	Multiple Players Tied

1976

AL

Tm	Tot	H	A	Consec			1-Inn			One-Game						Men-On-Base				Batters					Totals					Pitchers	
				2	3	4	3	4	5	5	6	7	8	9	10	0	1	2	3	PH	LO	XN	IP	P	1	10	20	30	40	RHP	LHP
BAL	119	58	61	3	0	0	0	0	0	0	0	0	0	0	0	57	40	16	6	2	3	6	1	0	10	3	2	0	0	84	35
BOS	134	71	63	2	0	0	0	0	0	0	0	0	0	0	0	76	39	18	1	2	3	1	1	0	9	4	2	0	0	96	38
CAL	63	24	39	2	0	0	0	0	0	0	0	0	0	0	0	36	16	8	3	1	2	3	1	0	14	1	0	0	0	54	9
CHI	73	31	42	1	0	0	0	0	0	0	0	0	0	0	0	38	23	11	1	1	1	1	1	0	11	2	0	0	0	55	18
CLE	85	40	45	1	0	0	0	0	0	0	0	0	0	0	0	58	20	5	2	1	0	3	0	0	12	1	1	0	0	57	28
DET	101	51	50	1	0	0	0	0	0	0	0	0	0	0	0	52	35	13	1	5	0	2	1	0	12	4	0	0	0	67	34
KC	65	37	28	1	0	0	1	0	0	0	0	0	0	0	0	36	20	9	0	0	1	1	4	0	12	2	0	0	0	43	22
MIL	88	45	43	2	0	0	0	0	0	0	0	0	0	0	0	55	27	6	0	0	4	1	0	0	14	3	0	0	0	65	23
MIN	81	34	47	3	0	0	0	0	0	0	0	0	0	0	0	33	31	12	5	3	1	3	0	0	9	3	1	0	0	54	27
NY	120	67	53	2	0	0	1	0	0	0	0	0	0	0	0	62	34	21	3	0	0	3	1	0	9	4	0	1	0	71	49
OAK	113	56	57	2	0	0	0	0	0	0	0	0	0	0	0	70	33	10	0	1	1	2	0	0	7	3	2	0	0	82	31
TEX	80	40	40	0	0	0	0	0	0	0	0	0	0	0	0	39	30	10	1	0	0	1	0	0	11	2	1	0	0	62	18

NL

Tm	Tot	H	A	Consec			1-Inn			One-Game						Men-On-Base				Batters					Totals					Pitchers	
				2	3	4	3	4	5	5	6	7	8	9	10	0	1	2	3	PH	LO	XN	IP	P	1	10	20	30	40	RHP	LHP
ATL	82	43	39	1	0	0	0	0	0	0	0	0	0	0	0	37	28	16	1	5	1	0	1	1	15	2	0	0	0	59	23
CHI	105	71	34	1	0	0	0	0	0	0	0	0	0	0	0	65	28	11	1	4	9	5	1	0	10	2	0	1	0	79	26
CIN	141	73	68	7	0	0	2	0	0	0	1	0	0	0	0	76	36	24	5	5	3	2	0	0	9	3	2	0	0	94	47
HOU	66	30	36	1	0	0	0	0	0	0	0	0	0	0	0	37	15	13	1	2	0	1	0	4	9	3	0	0	0	37	29
LA	91	42	49	5	0	0	0	0	0	0	0	1	0	0	0	61	22	7	1	2	2	1	0	1	8	3	1	0	0	68	23
MON	94	45	49	1	0	0	0	0	0	0	0	0	0	0	0	58	26	8	2	5	3	1	2	0	18	1	0	0	0	68	26
NY	102	43	59	2	0	0	0	0	0	0	0	0	0	0	0	53	34	12	3	4	1	2	0	0	16	2	0	1	0	77	25
PHI	110	63	47	1	0	0	0	0	0	0	1	0	0	0	0	52	40	11	7	1	0	2	2	3	12	1	1	1	0	74	36

				Consec			1-Inn			One-Game						Men-On-Base				Batters					Totals					Pitchers	
Tm	Tot	H	A	2	3	4	3	4	5	5	6	7	8	9	10	0	1	2	3	PH	LO	XN	IP	P	1	10	20	30	40	RHP	LHP
PIT	110	54	56	4	0	0	1	0	0	0	0	0	0	0	0	62	39	8	1	3	0	4	0	2	10	2	3	0	0	67	43
SD	64	30	34	1	0	0	0	0	0	0	0	0	0	0	0	31	18	12	3	3	2	0	0	0	13	1	0	0	0	46	18
SF	85	44	41	1	0	0	0	0	0	0	0	0	0	0	0	43	30	10	2	3	2	2	0	0	11	1	2	0	0	52	33
STL	63	27	36	1	0	0	0	0	0	0	0	0	0	0	0	36	19	6	2	3	0	2	4	1	15	1	0	0	0	31	32
AL	1122	554	568	20	0	0	2	0	0	0	0	0	0	0	0	612	348	139	23	16	16	27	10	0	130	32	9	1	0	790	332
NL	1113	565	548	26	0	0	3	0	0	0	2	1	0	0	0	611	335	138	29	40	23	22	10	12	146	22	9	3	0	752	361
YR	2235	1119	1116	46	0	0	5	0	0	0	2	1	0	0	0	1223	683	277	52	56	39	49	20	12	276	54	18	4	0	1542	693

AL		*NL*	
32	Graig Nettles	38	Mike Schmidt
27	Sal Bando	37	Dave Kingman
27	Reggie Jackson	32	Rick Monday
25	Multiple Players Tied	29	George Foster
		27	Joe Morgan

1977

AL

Tm	Tot	H	A	2	3	4	3	4	5	5	6	7	8	9	10	0	1	2	3	PH	LO	XN	IP	P	1	10	20	30	40	RHP	LHP
BAL	148	74	74	5	0	0	0	0	0	0	1	0	0	0	0	83	42	17	6	5	1	5	0	0	12	3	3	0	0	108	40
BOS	213	124	89	14	2	0	2	0	0	4	3	0	1	0	0	123	62	24	4	3	2	2	0	0	6	3	2	3	0	179	34
CAL	131	69	62	1	1	0	1	0	0	0	0	0	0	0	0	69	53	7	2	3	1	3	1	0	15	2	1	1	0	97	34
CHI	192	85	107	6	0	0	0	0	0	1	1	0	0	0	0	108	60	22	2	5	2	3	1	0	8	6	1	2	0	134	58
CLE	100	54	46	2	0	0	1	0	0	0	0	0	0	0	0	58	32	8	2	3	1	3	1	0	13	2	1	0	0	75	25
DET	166	81	85	4	0	0	1	0	0	0	0	0	0	0	0	103	47	14	2	6	0	4	2	0	9	4	2	1	0	96	70
KC	146	56	90	5	0	0	0	0	0	1	0	0	0	0	0	76	51	19	0	3	3	2	1	0	9	2	4	0	0	101	45
MIL	125	49	76	3	0	0	1	0	0	1	0	0	0	0	0	78	41	4	2	4	2	3	1	0	11	1	3	0	0	100	25
MIN	123	61	62	1	0	0	0	0	0	0	0	0	0	0	0	71	34	13	5	4	1	5	0	0	9	5	1	0	0	76	47
NY	184	84	100	6	0	0	0	1	0	3	1	0	0	0	0	99	58	24	3	3	3	2	0	0	11	6	0	2	0	108	76
OAK	117	58	59	3	0	0	0	0	0	0	0	0	0	0	0	72	35	8	2	4	0	1	0	0	13	2	2	0	0	81	36
SEA	133	75	58	5	0	0	0	0	0	0	0	0	0	0	0	78	39	15	1	0	0	1	1	0	12	1	3	0	0	92	41
TEX	135	62	73	6	0	0	1	0	0	1	0	0	0	0	0	85	31	18	1	0	5	6	4	0	12	4	1	0	0	93	42
TOR	100	45	55	3	0	0	1	0	0	0	0	0	0	0	0	67	22	10	1	5	1	2	1	0	10	5	0	0	0	65	35

NL

Tm	Tot	H	A	2	3	4	3	4	5	5	6	7	8	9	10	0	1	2	3	PH	LO	XN	IP	P	1	10	20	30	40	RHP	LHP
ATL	139	97	42	3	0	0	1	0	0	0	0	0	0	0	0	74	46	12	7	8	0	3	0	2	16	1	1	0	1	96	43
CHI	111	69	42	3	1	0	0	0	0	0	1	1	0	0	0	66	28	17	0	2	0	1	0	2	11	4	1	0	0	72	39
CIN	181	83	98	4	0	0	0	0	0	1	0	0	0	0	0	91	55	31	4	3	1	2	2	5	12	3	1	1	1	116	65
HOU	114	40	74	3	0	0	0	0	0	1	0	0	0	0	0	61	37	14	2	3	1	5	1	2	8	5	1	0	0	80	34
LA	191	96	95	6	0	0	1	0	0	1	0	0	0	0	0	105	63	17	6	5	5	3	0	5	11	3	0	4	0	149	42
MON	138	66	72	4	0	0	2	0	0	0	0	0	0	0	0	82	44	11	1	4	0	1	2	2	9	4	1	1	0	95	43
NY	88	46	42	0	0	0	0	0	0	0	0	0	0	0	0	47	31	8	2	4	1	3	0	1	13	4	0	0	0	67	21
PHI	186	101	85	7	1	0	3	0	0	1	1	0	0	0	0	104	56	20	6	2	2	4	1	6	11	5	0	2	0	145	41
PIT	133	64	69	3	0	0	1	0	0	0	0	0	0	0	0	75	40	14	4	3	1	4	2	1	12	3	2	0	0	91	42
SD	120	54	66	0	0	0	0	0	0	0	0	0	0	0	0	60	44	12	4	3	2	4	0	2	13	3	2	0	0	85	35
SF	134	62	72	6	0	0	0	0	0	0	0	0	0	0	0	74	41	14	5	11	4	3	1	3	11	4	1	0	0	89	45
STL	96	41	55	2	0	0	0	0	0	0	0	0	0	0	0	41	35	14	6	1	0	2	3	0	11	2	1	0	0	53	43
AL	2013	977	1036	64	3	0	8	1	0	11	6	0	1	0	0	1170	607	203	33	48	22	42	13	0	150	46	24	9	0	1405	608
NL	1631	819	812	41	2	0	8	0	0	4	2	1	0	0	0	880	520	184	47	49	17	35	12	31	138	41	11	8	2	1138	493
YR	3644	1796	1848	105	5	0	16	1	0	15	8	1	1	0	0	2050	1127	387	80	97	39	77	25	31	288	87	35	17	2	2543	1101

AL		*NL*	
39	Jim Rice	52	George Foster
37	Bobby Bonds	41	Jeff Burroughs
37	Graig Nettles	39	Greg Luzinski
33	George Scott	38	Mike Schmidt
32	Reggie Jackson	33	Steve Garvey

1978

AL

Tm	Tot	H	A	2	3	4	3	4	5	5	6	7	8	9	10	0	1	2	3	PH	LO	XN	IP	P	1	10	20	30	40	RHP	LHP
BAL	154	74	80	5	0	0	0	0	0	0	0	0	0	0	0	97	45	8	4	1	3	3	0	0	9	1	4	0	0	104	50
BOS	172	94	78	5	0	0	0	0	0	0	0	0	0	0	0	89	56	26	1	0	1	3	0	0	6	3	3	0	1	126	46
CAL	108	56	52	3	0	0	1	0	0	0	0	0	0	0	0	62	27	12	7	2	2	2	0	0	15	2	0	1	0	76	32
CHI	106	56	50	4	0	0	0	0	0	1	0	0	0	0	0	62	39	4	1	3	1	0	0	0	16	2	1	0	0	70	36

				Consec			1-Inn			One-Game						Men-On-Base				Batters					Totals					Pitchers	
Tm	Tot	H	A	2	3	4	3	4	5	5	6	7	8	9	10	0	1	2	3	PH	LO	XN	IP	P	1	10	20	30	40	RHP	LHP
CLE	106	50	56	3	0	0	0	0	0	0	0	0	0	0	0	63	26	13	4	0	2	2	0	0	14	2	0	1	0	76	30
DET	129	74	55	2	0	0	0	0	0	0	0	0	0	0	0	71	36	17	5	1	2	4	1	0	8	4	2	0	0	63	66
KC	98	43	55	6	0	0	0	0	0	0	0	0	0	0	0	58	28	10	2	1	0	0	4	0	9	2	1	0	0	66	32
MIL	173	94	79	4	0	0	0	0	0	0	0	0	0	0	0	90	56	22	5	0	2	2	0	0	8	5	0	2	0	133	40
MIN	82	44	38	1	0	0	0	0	0	0	0	0	0	0	0	51	21	8	2	4	2	2	0	0	14	2	0	0	0	48	34
NY	125	68	57	3	0	0	0	0	0	0	0	0	0	0	0	74	31	15	5	3	3	4	1	0	11	2	2	0	0	77	48
OAK	100	52	48	1	0	0	0	0	0	0	0	0	0	0	0	61	31	7	1	5	2	0	0	0	14	4	0	0	0	60	40
SEA	97	58	39	1	0	0	0	0	0	0	0	0	0	0	0	50	27	13	7	4	0	2	1	0	14	2	1	0	0	60	37
TEX	132	62	70	2	0	0	0	0	0	1	0	0	0	0	0	79	36	16	1	2	3	5	1	0	12	3	2	0	0	90	42
TOR	98	50	48	2	0	0	0	0	0	0	0	0	0	0	0	61	27	8	2	2	2	2	0	0	13	0	2	0	0	59	39
NL																															
ATL	123	87	36	4	1	0	1	0	0	0	0	0	0	0	0	69	36	14	4	2	0	1	0	2	13	1	3	0	0	95	28
CHI	72	41	31	2	0	0	0	0	0	0	0	0	0	0	0	35	24	10	3	4	0	2	0	2	15	0	1	0	0	48	24
CIN	136	74	62	4	0	0	1	0	0	0	1	0	0	0	0	72	41	20	3	4	0	4	1	1	11	3	1	0	1	87	49
HOU	70	30	40	1	0	0	0	0	0	0	0	0	0	0	0	45	18	7	0	1	2	2	0	1	14	2	0	0	0	42	28
LA	149	78	71	1	0	0	0	0	0	0	0	0	0	0	0	80	44	21	4	6	4	1	2	0	5	4	3	0	0	113	36
MON	121	46	75	6	0	0	0	1	0	1	0	0	1	0	0	78	29	11	3	2	1	1	0	1	5	3	3	0	0	81	40
NY	86	37	49	0	0	0	0	0	0	0	0	0	0	0	0	49	25	10	2	6	3	1	0	1	11	4	0	0	0	55	31
PHI	133	80	53	2	0	0	0	0	0	0	0	0	0	0	0	73	39	18	3	8	6	2	0	4	9	4	1	1	0	95	38
PIT	115	57	58	2	0	0	1	0	0	1	0	0	0	0	0	49	44	15	7	2	0	3	1	2	10	2	1	1	0	76	39
SD	75	31	44	2	0	0	0	0	0	0	0	0	0	0	0	44	19	11	1	5	1	0	0	0	11	1	1	0	0	48	27
SF	117	47	70	2	0	0	0	0	0	1	0	0	0	0	0	72	32	10	3	8	4	2	0	1	11	4	2	0	0	68	49
STL	79	29	50	1	0	0	0	0	0	0	0	0	0	0	0	46	23	8	2	2	2	1	0	1	11	3	1	0	0	41	38
AL	1680	875	805	42	0	0	1	0	0	2	0	0	0	0	0	968	486	179	47	28	25	31	8	0	163	34	18	4	1	1108	572
NL	1276	637	639	27	1	0	3	1	0	3	1	0	1	0	0	712	374	155	35	50	23	20	4	16	126	31	17	2	1	849	427
YR	2956	1512	1444	69	1	0	4	1	0	5	1	0	1	0	0	1680	860	334	82	78	48	51	12	16	289	65	35	6	2	1957	999

	AL		*NL*
46	Jim Rice	40	George Foster
34	Don Baylor	35	Greg Luzinski
34	Larry Hisle	30	Dave Parker
33	Andy Thornton	29	Reggie Smith
32	Gorman Thomas	28	Multiple Players Tied

1979

Tm	Tot	H	A	Consec 2	3	4	1-Inn 3	4	5	One-Game 5	6	7	8	9	10	Men-On-Base 0	1	2	3	PH	LO	XN	IP	P	1	10	20	30	40	RHP	LHP
AL																															
BAL	181	73	108	4	1	0	2	0	0	1	0	0	0	0	0	114	43	16	8	4	3	2	0	0	9	3	2	1	0	133	48
BOS	194	121	73	8	0	0	1	0	0	1	1	0	0	0	0	97	69	25	3	0	0	1	1	0	10	2	3	2	0	140	54
CAL	164	71	93	5	0	0	2	0	0	1	0	0	0	0	0	83	50	23	8	0	1	0	0	0	7	3	2	2	0	124	40
CHI	127	56	71	4	0	0	1	0	0	0	1	0	0	0	0	75	41	10	1	1	4	1	0	0	15	5	0	0	0	84	43
CLE	138	87	51	4	0	0	0	0	0	1	0	0	0	0	0	72	43	15	8	2	2	0	0	0	9	3	3	0	0	96	42
DET	164	101	63	4	0	0	1	0	0	0	0	0	0	0	0	102	47	12	3	5	1	2	0	0	12	3	3	0	0	92	72
KC	116	53	63	4	0	0	0	0	0	0	0	0	0	0	0	61	38	17	0	1	4	4	7	0	12	3	2	0	0	79	37
MIL	185	91	94	6	0	0	1	0	0	0	1	0	0	0	0	108	56	19	2	2	2	2	2	0	9	1	3	0	1	139	46
MIN	112	67	45	3	0	0	0	0	0	1	0	0	0	0	0	68	34	9	1	0	0	1	2	0	12	2	1	0	0	75	37
NY	150	77	73	5	0	0	0	0	0	1	0	0	0	0	0	74	51	22	3	6	2	3	0	0	12	3	3	0	0	94	56
OAK	108	46	62	3	1	0	0	0	0	1	0	0	0	0	0	69	26	11	2	1	3	0	2	0	11	4	1	0	0	85	23
SEA	132	88	44	1	0	0	0	0	0	0	1	0	0	0	0	69	37	20	6	4	1	0	3	0	9	2	3	0	0	86	46
TEX	140	69	71	2	0	0	0	0	0	1	0	0	0	0	0	88	35	15	2	5	4	2	1	0	11	6	0	0	0	89	51
TOR	95	50	45	2	0	0	0	0	0	0	0	0	0	0	0	57	21	14	3	4	1	2	2	0	11	3	1	0	0	67	28
NL																															
ATL	126	73	53	4	0	0	0	0	0	0	0	0	0	0	0	70	34	20	2	6	0	0	1	0	7	2	2	1	0	96	30
CHI	135	79	56	3	0	0	0	0	0	0	1	0	0	0	0	74	45	11	5	5	2	3	0	1	10	3	0	0	1	87	48
CIN	132	71	61	9	0	0	0	0	0	0	0	0	0	0	0	84	32	12	4	0	1	1	2	2	11	3	1	1	0	81	51
HOU	49	15	34	0	0	0	0	0	0	0	0	0	0	0	0	34	6	9	0	2	4	0	2	4	12	0	0	0	0	33	16
LA	183	106	77	4	0	0	0	0	0	0	0	1	0	0	0	102	52	23	6	0	7	7	2	1	6	3	5	0	0	122	61
MON	143	68	75	2	1	0	0	0	0	2	0	0	0	0	0	85	43	13	2	2	3	5	1	2	12	1	3	1	0	117	26
NY	74	30	44	1	0	0	0	0	0	0	0	0	0	0	0	37	28	9	0	1	1	3	2	0	10	3	0	0	0	47	27
PHI	119	52	67	5	0	0	0	0	0	1	0	0	0	0	0	67	32	17	3	5	3	1	1	2	10	3	0	0	1	92	27
PIT	148	74	74	7	0	0	0	0	0	1	0	0	0	0	0	86	49	9	4	5	2	3	2	3	10	2	2	1	0	83	65
SD	93	36	57	2	1	0	1	0	0	0	0	0	0	0	0	51	30	12	0	1	0	4	0	1	11	0	1	1	0	65	28

				Consec			1-Inn			One-Game						Men-On-Base				Batters					Totals					Pitchers	
Tm	Tot	H	A	2	3	4	3	4	5	5	6	7	8	9	10	0	1	2	3	PH	LO	XN	IP	P	1	10	20	30	40	RHP	LHP
SF	125	53	72	6	0	0	2	0	0	0	0	0	0	0	0	82	30	13	0	5	5	3	2	2	14	2	2	0	0	79	46
STL	100	48	52	1	0	0	0	0	0	0	0	0	0	0	0	56	26	13	5	4	1	3	1	0	13	2	1	0	0	53	47
AL	2006	1050	956	55	2	0	8	0	0	8	4	0	0	0	0	1137	591	228	50	35	28	20	20	0	149	43	27	5	1	1383	623
NL	1427	705	722	44	2	0	3	0	0	4	1	1	0	0	0	828	407	161	31	36	29	33	16	18	126	24	17	5	2	955	472
YR	3433	1755	1678	99	4	0	11	0	0	12	5	1	0	0	0	1965	998	389	81	71	57	53	36	18	275	67	44	10	3	2338	1095

AL

45 Gorman Thomas
39 Fred Lynn
39 Jim Rice
36 Don Baylor
35 Ken Singleton

NL

48 Dave Kingman
45 Mike Schmidt
34 Dave Winfield
33 Bob Horner
32 Willie Stargell

1980

AL

Tm	Tot	H	A	2	3	4	3	4	5	5	6	7	8	9	10	0	1	2	3	PH	LO	XN	IP	P	1	10	20	30	40	RHP	LHP
BAL	156	75	81	6	0	0	0	0	0	0	0	0	0	0	0	88	48	17	3	6	2	5	0	0	9	5	1	1	0	99	57
BOS	162	79	83	2	1	0	1	1	0	1	1	0	0	0	0	91	52	18	1	2	1	4	0	0	10	5	2	0	0	108	54
CAL	106	49	57	2	0	0	0	0	0	0	1	0	0	0	0	53	36	16	1	2	2	2	0	0	15	4	0	0	0	75	31
CHI	91	41	50	3	0	0	0	0	0	0	0	0	0	0	0	59	23	9	0	4	0	1	0	0	12	5	0	0	0	60	31
CLE	89	55	34	3	0	0	0	0	0	1	0	0	0	0	0	44	27	14	4	6	0	2	0	0	12	3	1	0	0	67	22
DET	143	77	66	3	0	0	0	0	0	1	0	0	0	0	0	77	40	22	4	5	1	1	0	0	11	4	2	0	0	77	66
KC	115	47	68	1	0	0	0	0	0	0	0	0	0	0	0	64	35	15	1	1	1	1	6	0	9	3	2	0	0	73	42
MIL	203	90	113	9	0	0	2	0	0	1	0	1	0	0	0	125	55	15	8	0	2	1	4	0	11	2	2	1	1	141	62
MIN	99	51	48	4	0	0	1	0	0	0	0	0	0	0	0	54	33	10	2	4	2	2	2	0	15	2	0	0	0	64	35
NY	189	91	98	3	0	0	0	0	0	2	0	0	0	0	0	103	55	24	7	6	3	6	2	0	10	8	0	0	1	130	59
OAK	137	58	79	2	1	0	1	0	0	0	1	0	0	0	0	76	43	17	1	3	1	2	1	0	8	5	0	1	0	92	45
SEA	104	74	30	1	0	0	0	0	0	0	0	0	0	0	0	57	40	7	0	4	0	5	1	0	15	4	0	0	0	62	42
TEX	124	58	66	2	0	0	0	0	0	0	0	0	0	0	0	68	40	11	5	8	2	3	1	0	7	6	0	0	0	84	40
TOR	126	56	70	3	0	0	0	0	0	0	0	0	0	0	0	70	41	13	2	3	0	3	1	0	12	3	1	1	0	82	44

NL

Tm	Tot	H	A	2	3	4	3	4	5	5	6	7	8	9	10	0	1	2	3	PH	LO	XN	IP	P	1	10	20	30	40	RHP	LHP
ATL	144	84	60	6	0	0	1	0	0	2	0	0	0	0	0	83	41	19	1	6	0	4	0	0	8	3	0	2	0	113	31
CHI	107	54	53	3	0	0	0	0	0	2	0	0	0	0	0	58	30	14	5	3	2	3	0	1	17	2	1	0	0	87	20
CIN	113	66	47	3	1	0	3	0	0	1	0	0	0	0	0	54	38	14	7	4	1	0	0	0	10	3	2	0	0	78	35
HOU	75	26	49	0	0	0	0	0	0	0	0	0	0	0	0	54	17	2	2	4	7	3	0	3	10	5	0	0	0	43	32
LA	148	82	66	3	1	0	0	0	0	0	0	0	0	0	0	91	35	22	0	3	6	6	0	2	12	3	3	0	0	118	30
MON	114	51	63	4	0	0	0	0	0	0	0	0	0	0	0	73	32	7	2	4	3	4	2	0	8	4	1	0	0	87	27
NY	61	35	26	0	0	0	0	0	0	0	0	0	0	0	0	34	18	8	1	4	1	2	2	0	8	2	0	0	0	42	19
PHI	117	64	53	9	0	0	0	0	0	0	0	0	0	0	0	72	34	9	2	0	1	1	2	1	10	2	0	0	1	94	23
PIT	116	63	53	1	0	0	0	0	0	0	0	0	0	0	0	60	46	8	2	2	1	1	1	5	13	4	1	0	0	81	35
SD	67	29	38	0	0	0	0	0	0	0	0	0	0	0	0	35	21	10	1	5	0	1	0	0	12	1	1	0	0	48	19
SF	80	24	56	2	0	0	1	0	0	0	0	0	0	0	0	49	21	7	3	3	1	3	0	1	14	0	2	0	0	55	25
STL	101	41	60	1	0	0	1	0	0	0	0	0	0	0	0	53	29	17	2	1	2	3	1	4	9	1	2	0	0	72	29
AL	1844	901	943	44	2	0	5	1	0	6	3	1	0	0	0	1029	568	208	39	54	17	38	18	0	156	59	11	4	2	1214	630
NL	1243	619	624	32	2	0	6	0	0	5	0	0	0	0	0	716	362	137	28	39	25	31	8	17	131	30	13	2	1	918	325
YR	3087	1520	1567	76	4	0	11	1	0	11	3	1	0	0	0	1745	930	345	67	93	42	69	26	17	287	89	24	6	3	2132	955

AL

41 Reggie Jackson
41 Ben Oglivie
38 Gorman Thomas
35 Tony Armas
32 Eddie Murray

NL

48 Mike Schmidt
35 Bob Horner
33 Dale Murphy
29 Dusty Baker
29 Gary Carter

1981

AL

Tm	Tot	H	A	2	3	4	3	4	5	5	6	7	8	9	10	0	1	2	3	PH	LO	XN	IP	P	1	10	20	30	40	RHP	LHP
BAL	88	49	39	2	0	0	0	0	0	0	0	0	0	0	0	43	28	12	5	2	1	1	0	0	12	2	1	0	0	66	22
BOS	90	52	38	4	0	0	0	0	0	0	1	0	0	0	0	45	28	15	2	1	1	3	0	0	9	2	1	0	0	66	24
CAL	97	48	49	1	0	0	0	0	0	0	0	0	0	0	0	59	23	14	1	0	1	2	0	0	13	2	1	0	0	68	29
CHI	76	31	45	1	0	0	0	0	0	1	0	0	0	0	0	45	21	8	2	1	0	1	1	0	8	2	1	0	0	62	14
CLE	39	19	20	0	0	0	0	0	0	0	0	0	0	0	0	23	13	3	0	2	0	1	0	0	13	0	0	0	0	20	19

				Consec			1-Inn			One-Game						Men-On-Base				Batters					Totals					Pitchers	
Tm	Tot	H	A	2	3	4	3	4	5	5	6	7	8	9	10	0	1	2	3	PH	LO	XN	IP	P	1	10	20	30	40	RHP	LHP
DET	65	43	22	0	0	0	0	0	0	0	0	0	0	0	0	35	22	8	0	1	2	1	0	0	14	1	0	0	0	33	32
KC	61	17	44	3	0	0	0	0	0	0	0	0	0	0	0	36	18	5	2	0	1	1	0	0	11	1	0	0	0	38	23
MIL	96	33	63	2	0	0	0	0	0	0	0	0	0	0	0	48	27	19	2	0	1	1	0	0	10	4	1	0	0	70	26
MIN	47	25	22	1	0	0	0	0	0	0	0	0	0	0	0	25	17	4	1	1	1	3	0	0	15	0	0	0	0	27	20
NY	100	47	53	2	0	0	0	0	0	0	0	0	0	0	0	57	32	10	1	3	0	3	2	0	12	4	0	0	0	62	38
OAK	104	57	47	6	0	0	0	0	0	1	0	0	0	0	0	67	27	9	1	4	3	6	0	0	11	3	1	0	0	59	45
SEA	89	52	37	4	0	0	1	0	0	0	0	0	0	0	0	54	21	12	2	2	0	2	0	0	12	4	0	0	0	55	34
TEX	49	21	28	0	0	0	0	0	0	0	0	0	0	0	0	24	12	12	1	0	0	2	0	0	13	1	0	0	0	31	18
TOR	61	34	27	2	0	0	0	0	0	0	0	0	0	0	0	37	17	7	0	1	1	0	1	0	10	2	0	0	0	31	30
NL																															
ATL	64	37	27	1	0	0	0	0	0	0	0	0	0	0	0	34	16	12	2	2	0	2	0	1	9	2	0	0	0	48	16
CHI	57	41	16	0	0	0	0	0	0	0	0	0	0	0	0	27	21	9	0	5	0	0	0	0	13	2	0	0	0	42	15
CIN	64	26	38	3	0	0	0	0	0	0	0	0	0	0	0	34	18	10	2	1	1	1	1	2	12	0	1	0	0	53	11
HOU	45	16	29	3	0	0	0	0	0	0	0	0	0	0	0	29	12	4	0	2	3	0	0	1	12	1	0	0	0	34	11
LA	82	37	45	0	0	0	0	0	0	0	0	0	0	0	0	51	26	5	0	6	2	3	0	0	9	4	0	0	0	61	21
MON	81	39	42	2	0	0	0	0	0	0	0	0	0	0	0	55	19	5	2	2	1	2	2	1	13	1	1	0	0	63	18
NY	57	30	27	1	0	0	0	0	0	0	0	0	0	0	0	37	11	7	2	2	1	1	0	1	12	0	1	0	0	43	14
PHI	69	41	28	2	0	0	0	0	0	0	0	0	0	0	0	36	17	15	1	2	0	3	0	0	10	0	0	1	0	53	16
PIT	55	29	26	2	0	0	0	0	0	0	0	0	0	0	0	32	15	8	0	5	1	0	0	1	15	1	0	0	0	42	13
SD	32	9	23	0	0	0	0	0	0	0	0	0	0	0	0	17	7	7	1	4	0	0	0	1	11	0	0	0	0	28	4
SF	63	28	35	1	0	0	0	0	0	0	0	0	0	0	0	42	15	4	2	1	1	5	1	1	13	2	0	0	0	50	13
STL	50	22	28	3	0	0	0	0	0	0	0	0	0	0	0	30	14	4	2	0	0	3	1	0	9	1	0	0	0	34	16
AL	1062	528	534	28	0	0	1	0	0	2	1	0	0	0	0	598	306	138	20	18	12	27	4	0	163	28	6	0	0	688	374
NL	719	355	364	18	0	0	0	0	0	0	0	0	0	0	0	424	191	90	14	32	10	20	5	9	138	14	3	1	0	551	168
YR	1781	883	898	46	0	0	1	0	0	2	1	0	0	0	0	1022	497	228	34	50	22	47	9	9	301	42	9	1	0	1239	542

AL		*NL*	
22	Tony Armas	31	Mike Schmidt
22	Dwight Evans	24	Andre Dawson
22	Bobby Grich	22	George Foster
22	Eddie Murray	22	Dave Kingman
21	Multiple Players Tied	18	George Hendrick

1982

Tm	Tot	H	A	2	3	4	3	4	5	5	6	7	8	9	10	0	1	2	3	PH	LO	XN	IP	P	1	10	20	30	40	RHP	LHP
AL																															
BAL	179	87	92	7	0	0	1	0	0	1	0	0	0	0	0	94	48	29	8	11	4	8	0	0	11	2	3	1	0	123	56
BOS	136	67	69	3	0	0	0	0	0	1	0	0	0	0	0	68	45	21	2	2	0	3	1	0	7	3	1	1	0	109	27
CAL	186	99	87	4	0	0	0	0	0	1	0	0	0	0	0	110	57	14	5	1	6	5	0	0	9	1	3	2	0	116	70
CHI	136	51	85	4	0	0	1	0	0	1	0	0	0	0	0	73	44	15	4	2	1	1	0	0	11	5	1	0	0	93	43
CLE	109	49	60	5	0	0	1	0	0	1	0	0	0	0	0	59	38	11	1	2	1	3	0	0	11	1	1	1	0	67	42
DET	177	108	69	4	0	0	0	0	0	2	0	0	0	0	0	99	61	15	2	5	5	5	0	0	10	4	1	1	0	124	53
KC	132	61	71	2	0	0	1	0	0	0	0	0	0	0	0	74	42	13	3	1	1	1	6	0	8	5	2	0	0	78	54
MIL	216	89	127	8	3	0	2	0	0	2	0	0	0	0	0	113	79	22	2	1	3	4	1	0	8	2	2	3	0	142	74
MIN	148	81	67	5	1	0	2	0	0	0	0	0	0	0	0	84	42	17	5	2	0	0	4	0	11	1	4	0	0	98	50
NY	161	73	88	6	0	0	1	0	0	0	0	0	0	0	0	91	41	24	5	3	1	3	1	0	13	3	1	1	0	108	53
OAK	149	71	78	2	0	0	0	0	0	0	0	0	0	0	0	78	59	10	2	4	3	1	0	0	14	3	2	0	0	103	46
SEA	130	78	52	5	0	0	2	0	0	0	0	0	0	0	0	80	36	9	5	1	1	4	1	0	15	3	2	0	0	81	49
TEX	115	43	72	2	0	0	1	0	0	0	0	0	0	0	0	67	32	13	3	2	4	2	1	0	14	5	1	0	0	85	30
TOR	106	62	44	3	0	0	1	0	0	0	0	0	0	0	0	71	27	7	1	4	1	1	1	0	15	3	1	0	0	56	50
NL																															
ATL	146	95	51	5	0	0	0	0	0	0	0	0	0	0	0	83	44	17	2	4	1	5	0	2	11	2	1	2	0	106	40
CHI	102	53	49	1	0	0	0	0	0	0	0	0	0	0	0	50	35	17	0	6	2	0	1	1	9	4	1	0	0	77	25
CIN	82	37	45	3	0	0	0	0	0	0	0	0	0	0	0	50	23	8	1	2	1	1	1	1	13	2	0	0	0	62	20
HOU	74	31	43	1	0	0	0	0	0	0	0	0	0	0	0	40	20	13	1	1	2	1	1	0	14	2	0	0	0	54	20
LA	138	57	81	4	0	0	0	0	0	0	0	0	0	0	0	78	42	16	2	4	1	3	0	2	11	2	2	1	0	108	30
MON	133	59	74	2	0	0	0	0	0	0	0	0	0	0	0	74	39	17	3	4	0	4	0	1	6	1	4	0	0	91	42
NY	97	48	49	1	0	0	0	0	0	0	0	0	0	0	0	45	33	18	1	3	1	2	2	1	15	1	0	1	0	71	26
PHI	112	57	55	4	0	0	0	0	0	0	0	0	0	0	0	58	38	14	2	0	1	3	1	3	12	2	0	1	0	86	26
PIT	134	77	57	5	0	0	0	0	0	0	0	0	0	0	0	77	40	12	5	7	1	2	1	5	15	4	0	1	0	100	34
SD	81	33	48	0	0	0	0	0	0	0	0	0	0	0	0	48	24	9	0	4	0	2	3	3	11	2	1	0	0	62	19
SF	133	55	78	5	1	0	0	0	0	2	0	0	0	0	0	82	34	14	3	6	6	5	0	1	11	4	1	0	0	101	32

Tm	Tot	H	A	Consec 2	3	4	1-Inn 3	4	5	One-Game 5	6	7	8	9	10	Men-On-Base 0	1	2	3	Batters PH	LO	XN	IP	P	Totals 1	10	20	30	40	Pitchers RHP	LHP
STL	67	27	40	0	0	0	0	0	0	0	0	0	0	0	0	39	17	8	3	1	1	2	2	0	10	2	0	0	0	45	22
AL	2080	1019	1061	60	4	0	13	0	0	9	0	0	0	0	0	1161	651	220	48	41	31	41	16	0	157	41	25	10	0	1383	697
NL	1299	629	670	31	1	0	0	0	0	2	0	0	0	0	0	724	389	163	23	42	17	30	12	20	138	28	10	6	0	963	336
YR	3379	1648	1731	91	5	0	13	0	0	11	0	0	0	0	0	1885	1040	383	71	83	48	71	28	20	295	69	35	16	0	2346	1033

	AL		*NL*
39	Reggie Jackson	37	Dave Kingman
39	Gorman Thomas	36	Dale Murphy
37	Dave Winfield	35	Mike Schmidt
34	Ben Oglivie	32	Pedro Guerrero
32	Multiple Players Tied	32	Bob Horner

1983

Tm	Tot	H	A	Consec 2	3	4	1-Inn 3	4	5	One-Game 5	6	7	8	9	10	Men-On-Base 0	1	2	3	Batters PH	LO	XN	IP	P	Totals 1	10	20	30	40	Pitchers RHP	LHP
AL																															
BAL	168	79	89	6	0	0	0	0	0	0	1	0	0	0	0	93	51	16	8	4	3	2	0	0	12	3	1	1	0	104	64
BOS	142	65	77	3	0	0	0	0	0	0	0	0	0	0	0	69	53	18	2	0	0	0	1	0	7	2	1	2	0	106	36
CAL	154	86	68	4	0	0	0	0	0	0	0	0	0	0	0	83	43	20	8	4	1	2	1	0	14	5	1	0	0	92	62
CHI	157	84	73	5	1	0	1	0	0	1	0	0	0	0	0	91	49	16	1	2	0	2	2	0	13	1	2	2	0	106	51
CLE	86	48	38	4	0	0	0	0	0	0	0	0	0	0	0	52	23	8	3	1	1	1	1	0	14	2	0	0	0	55	31
DET	156	83	73	1	0	0	0	0	0	0	0	0	0	0	0	95	42	16	3	3	5	4	2	0	8	4	3	0	0	105	51
KC	109	50	59	3	0	0	0	0	0	0	0	0	0	0	0	65	30	14	0	0	2	0	5	0	11	2	2	0	0	73	36
MIL	132	64	68	3	0	0	0	0	0	1	0	0	0	0	0	74	44	12	2	2	4	2	0	0	10	5	0	1	0	83	49
MIN	141	56	85	5	0	0	1	1	0	2	0	0	0	0	0	83	46	11	1	2	4	2	1	0	8	4	2	0	0	90	51
NY	153	67	86	9	0	0	1	0	0	1	0	0	0	0	0	84	48	17	4	3	2	6	2	0	12	3	2	1	0	96	57
OAK	121	60	61	2	0	0	0	0	0	0	0	0	0	0	0	72	36	9	4	1	2	3	0	0	10	5	0	0	0	82	39
SEA	111	64	47	3	1	0	0	0	0	0	1	0	0	0	0	68	33	9	1	2	2	0	2	0	17	4	0	0	0	68	43
TEX	106	45	61	2	0	0	1	0	0	0	0	0	0	0	0	62	33	11	0	2	2	2	0	0	9	4	1	0	0	68	38
TOR	167	101	66	10	0	0	1	0	0	1	0	0	0	0	0	97	49	18	3	5	2	4	4	0	7	6	3	0	0	107	60
NL																															
ATL	130	66	64	5	0	0	0	0	0	0	0	0	0	0	0	73	41	14	2	4	4	1	0	1	13	1	2	1	0	98	32
CHI	140	71	69	0	0	0	0	0	0	0	0	0	0	0	0	89	34	12	5	4	5	0	1	0	9	4	2	0	0	106	34
CIN	107	52	55	3	0	0	1	0	0	0	0	0	0	0	0	66	28	11	2	5	4	1	2	3	12	5	0	0	0	81	26
HOU	97	26	71	5	0	0	0	0	0	0	0	0	0	0	0	60	25	11	1	4	2	2	1	1	14	2	1	0	0	74	23
LA	146	74	72	1	0	0	1	0	0	0	0	0	0	0	0	87	47	8	4	8	1	3	0	3	15	4	1	1	0	123	23
MON	102	40	62	1	0	0	0	0	0	1	0	0	0	0	0	61	30	6	5	0	0	1	1	1	9	3	0	1	0	76	26
NY	112	63	49	4	0	0	0	0	0	0	0	0	0	0	0	61	33	16	2	12	1	4	1	3	13	1	2	0	0	82	30
PHI	125	61	64	3	0	0	0	0	0	0	0	0	0	0	0	69	35	16	5	4	3	2	0	0	11	3	0	0	1	107	18
PIT	121	60	61	4	0	0	0	0	0	0	0	0	0	0	0	75	33	8	5	5	1	1	0	1	10	6	0	0	0	83	38
SD	93	53	40	1	0	0	0	0	0	0	0	0	0	0	0	48	27	14	4	2	1	3	0	1	12	4	0	0	0	62	31
SF	142	73	69	2	0	0	0	0	0	1	0	0	0	0	0	74	54	12	2	3	1	2	0	2	13	2	2	1	0	92	50
STL	83	38	45	2	0	0	0	0	0	0	0	0	0	0	0	44	29	9	1	4	1	3	1	1	13	2	0	0	0	55	28
AL	1903	952	951	60	2	0	5	1	0	6	2	0	0	0	0	1088	580	195	40	31	30	30	21	0	152	50	18	7	0	1235	668
NL	1398	677	721	31	0	0	2	0	0	2	0	0	0	0	0	807	416	137	38	55	24	23	7	17	144	37	10	4	1	1039	359
YR	3301	1629	1672	91	2	0	7	1	0	8	2	0	0	0	0	1895	996	332	78	86	54	53	28	17	296	87	28	11	1	2274	1027

	AL		*NL*
39	Jim Rice	40	Mike Schmidt
36	Tony Armas	36	Dale Murphy
35	Ron Kittle	32	Andre Dawson
33	Eddie Murray	32	Pedro Guerrero
32	Multiple Players Tied	30	Darrell Evans

1984

Tm	Tot	H	A	Consec 2	3	4	1-Inn 3	4	5	One-Game 5	6	7	8	9	10	Men-On-Base 0	1	2	3	Batters PH	LO	XN	IP	P	Totals 1	10	20	30	40	Pitchers RHP	LHP
AL																															
BAL	160	82	78	3	0	0	0	0	0	0	0	0	0	0	0	87	47	18	8	8	2	2	0	0	13	3	3	0	0	120	40
BOS	181	100	81	7	0	0	0	0	0	1	0	0	0	0	0	99	55	22	5	3	1	5	0	0	7	1	3	1	1	142	39
CAL	150	79	71	9	1	0	1	0	0	0	0	0	0	0	0	82	42	23	3	3	1	3	1	0	10	1	4	0	0	103	47
CHI	172	103	69	3	0	0	0	0	0	1	0	0	0	0	0	93	53	22	4	9	1	2	0	0	10	2	3	1	0	113	59
CLE	123	65	58	3	1	0	0	0	0	1	0	0	0	0	0	73	32	11	7	1	2	2	0	0	9	5	0	1	0	81	42
DET	187	85	102	5	0	0	0	0	0	0	0	0	0	0	0	110	44	28	5	6	4	7	1	0	8	5	2	1	0	127	60

				Consec			1-Inn			One-Game						Men-On-Base				Batters					Totals					Pitchers	
Tm	Tot	H	A	2	3	4	3	4	5	5	6	7	8	9	10	0	1	2	3	PH	LO	XN	IP	P	1	10	20	30	40	RHP	LHP
KC	117	48	69	1	1	0	0	0	0	0	0	0	0	0	0	66	34	12	5	2	2	1	1	0	13	3	1	0	0	68	49
MIL	96	42	54	2	0	0	0	0	0	0	0	0	0	0	0	55	30	10	1	0	1	1	0	0	13	4	0	0	0	64	32
MIN	114	63	51	5	0	0	0	0	0	0	0	0	0	0	0	63	36	13	2	1	1	2	3	0	7	3	1	1	0	71	43
NY	130	62	68	0	2	0	2	0	0	0	0	0	0	0	0	62	49	17	2	2	0	5	2	0	13	2	2	0	0	99	31
OAK	158	77	81	1	0	0	0	0	0	1	0	0	0	0	0	91	48	16	3	3	3	1	1	0	10	3	0	2	0	106	52
SEA	129	68	61	4	0	0	0	0	0	0	0	0	0	0	0	73	34	19	3	1	0	4	1	0	12	4	2	0	0	92	37
TEX	120	55	65	4	0	0	1	0	0	0	0	0	0	0	0	71	33	14	2	2	2	1	1	0	12	2	2	0	0	85	35
TOR	143	59	84	5	1	0	0	0	0	0	0	0	0	0	0	87	46	9	1	6	1	1	2	0	8	6	1	0	0	105	38
NL																															
ATL	111	53	58	3	0	0	0	0	0	0	0	0	0	0	0	67	35	8	1	1	7	3	2	0	15	1	0	1	0	76	35
CHI	136	86	50	5	0	0	0	0	0	0	0	0	0	0	0	73	40	20	3	5	0	2	0	0	9	4	2	0	0	99	37
CIN	106	58	48	1	0	0	1	0	0	0	0	0	0	0	0	58	35	11	2	4	3	3	0	1	13	5	0	0	0	72	34
HOU	79	18	61	2	1	0	0	0	0	0	0	0	0	0	0	49	21	7	2	2	2	1	0	1	16	1	0	0	0	55	24
LA	102	49	53	1	0	0	0	0	0	0	0	0	0	0	0	64	24	12	2	6	0	3	0	3	13	3	1	0	0	70	32
MON	96	45	51	1	0	0	0	0	0	0	0	0	0	0	0	44	38	13	1	1	1	0	0	1	10	2	1	0	0	65	31
NY	107	56	51	1	0	0	0	0	0	0	0	0	0	0	0	60	35	11	1	2	0	1	1	1	11	3	2	0	0	65	42
PHI	147	79	68	3	0	0	0	0	0	0	0	0	0	0	0	87	44	15	1	10	3	0	1	1	12	5	0	1	0	110	37
PIT	98	48	50	2	0	0	0	0	0	0	0	0	0	0	0	65	23	5	5	3	0	4	1	2	9	5	0	0	0	68	30
SD	109	60	49	0	0	0	0	0	0	0	0	0	0	0	0	65	31	11	2	4	1	3	1	6	15	2	2	0	0	76	33
SF	112	55	57	2	0	0	0	0	0	0	0	0	0	0	0	62	34	13	3	2	2	1	1	0	11	2	3	0	0	74	38
STL	75	29	46	1	0	0	0	0	0	0	0	0	0	0	0	35	29	8	3	2	4	4	3	2	14	2	0	0	0	45	30
AL	1980	988	992	52	6	0	4	0	0	4	0	0	0	0	0	1112	583	234	51	47	21	37	13	0	145	44	24	7	1	1376	604
NL	1278	636	642	22	1	0	1	0	0	0	0	0	0	0	0	729	389	134	26	42	23	25	10	18	148	35	11	2	0	875	403
YR	3258	1624	1634	74	7	0	5	0	0	4	0	0	0	0	0	1841	972	368	77	89	44	62	23	18	293	79	35	9	1	2251	1007

AL		*NL*	
43	Tony Armas	36	Dale Murphy
35	Dave Kingman	36	Mike Schmidt
33	Dwayne Murphy	27	Gary Carter
33	Lance Parrish	26	Darryl Strawberry
33	Andy Thornton	25	Ron Cey

1985

AL

Tm	Tot	H	A	2	3	4	3	4	5	5	6	7	8	9	10	0	1	2	3	PH	LO	XN	IP	P	1	10	20	30	40	RHP	LHP
BAL	214	103	111	11	1	0	3	0	0	1	1	1	0	0	0	113	68	26	7	6	2	2	0	0	8	5	3	1	0	136	78
BOS	162	73	89	7	0	0	0	0	0	0	0	0	0	0	0	100	41	16	5	1	5	6	0	0	8	3	3	0	0	114	48
CAL	153	75	78	3	0	0	0	0	0	0	1	0	0	0	0	73	56	18	6	2	2	1	0	0	14	1	4	0	0	109	44
CHI	146	74	72	4	1	0	1	0	0	0	0	0	0	0	0	79	44	20	3	3	1	3	1	0	11	1	3	1	0	107	39
CLE	116	52	64	5	0	0	0	0	0	0	0	0	0	0	0	55	48	9	4	1	2	1	1	0	8	3	2	0	0	74	42
DET	202	108	94	12	0	0	0	0	0	2	0	0	0	0	0	126	55	18	3	5	4	5	1	0	7	4	3	0	1	139	63
KC	154	67	87	3	0	0	1	0	0	2	0	0	0	0	0	93	40	18	3	1	2	3	4	0	10	3	1	2	0	100	54
MIL	101	50	51	2	0	0	0	0	0	0	0	0	0	0	0	54	34	10	3	0	1	2	0	0	9	6	0	0	0	61	40
MIN	141	71	70	2	0	0	0	0	0	0	0	0	0	0	0	83	40	13	5	5	0	1	1	0	10	3	3	0	0	100	41
NY	176	92	84	10	0	0	0	0	0	2	0	0	0	0	0	94	59	20	3	5	7	2	0	0	9	3	3	1	0	114	62
OAK	155	66	89	3	0	0	0	0	0	0	0	0	0	0	0	88	47	18	2	0	0	3	1	0	10	4	2	1	0	101	54
SEA	171	92	79	9	0	0	0	0	0	0	0	1	0	0	0	95	49	24	3	3	2	2	0	0	10	3	2	1	0	119	52
TEX	129	76	53	2	0	0	0	0	0	1	0	0	0	0	0	84	34	10	1	3	2	0	0	0	12	4	1	0	0	96	33
TOR	158	75	83	6	0	0	0	0	0	1	0	0	0	0	0	94	46	15	3	4	2	8	0	0	11	4	2	0	0	102	56
NL																															
ATL	126	65	61	0	0	0	0	0	0	0	0	0	0	0	0	66	43	17	0	4	3	7	1	1	10	2	1	1	0	87	39
CHI	150	98	52	1	0	0	0	0	0	0	0	0	0	0	0	76	48	23	3	8	0	2	0	3	11	4	3	0	0	110	40
CIN	114	49	65	0	0	0	0	0	0	0	0	0	0	0	0	57	33	18	6	4	4	3	0	0	15	0	1	1	0	79	35
HOU	121	47	74	2	0	0	0	0	0	0	0	0	0	0	0	70	34	13	4	5	2	2	1	2	14	3	1	0	0	71	50
LA	129	47	82	3	0	0	0	0	0	0	0	0	0	0	0	82	32	9	6	3	1	2	1	1	10	1	2	1	0	93	36
MON	118	45	73	2	0	0	1	0	0	2	0	0	0	0	0	72	32	10	4	3	2	2	1	3	12	4	2	0	0	74	44
NY	134	58	76	4	0	0	1	0	0	1	0	0	0	0	0	72	42	14	6	4	0	7	0	1	11	2	2	1	0	83	51
PHI	141	72	69	4	1	0	1	0	0	0	1	0	0	0	0	84	32	22	3	4	5	4	3	1	10	4	0	1	0	104	37
PIT	80	39	41	0	0	0	0	0	0	0	0	0	0	0	0	46	20	11	3	2	3	4	1	2	17	3	0	0	0	59	21
SD	109	64	45	2	0	0	0	0	0	0	0	0	0	0	0	66	27	12	4	2	1	2	0	1	9	4	1	0	0	67	42
SF	115	58	57	1	0	0	0	0	0	0	0	0	0	0	0	73	30	11	1	5	4	4	0	4	13	4	0	0	0	83	32

Tm	Tot	H	A	Consec 2	3	4	1-Inn 3	4	5	One-Game 5	6	7	8	9	10	Men-On-Base 0	1	2	3	Batters PH	LO	XN	IP	P	Totals 1	10	20	30	40	Pitchers RHP	LHP
STL	87	36	51	2	0	0	0	0	0	0	0	0	0	0	0	48	20	16	3	4	0	2	2	1	8	3	1	0	0	53	34
AL	2178	1074	1104	79	2	0	5	0	0	9	2	2	0	0	0	1231	661	235	51	39	32	39	9	0	137	47	32	7	1	1472	706
NL	1424	678	746	21	1	0	3	0	0	3	1	0	0	0	0	812	393	176	43	48	25	41	10	20	140	34	14	5	0	963	461
YR	3602	1752	1850	100	3	0	8	0	0	12	3	2	0	0	0	2043	1054	411	94	87	57	80	19	20	277	81	46	12	1	2435	1167

	AL		NL
40	Darrell Evans	37	Dale Murphy
37	Carlton Fisk	34	Dave Parker
36	Steve Balboni	33	Pedro Guerrero
35	Don Mattingly	33	Mike Schmidt
32	Gorman Thomas	32	Gary Carter

1986

Tm	Tot	H	A	Consec 2	3	4	1-Inn 3	4	5	One-Game 5	6	7	8	9	10	Men-On-Base 0	1	2	3	Batters PH	LO	XN	IP	P	Totals 1	10	20	30	40	Pitchers RHP	LHP
AL																															
BAL	169	91	78	3	0	0	0	0	0	1	0	0	0	0	0	93	50	19	7	5	3	2	0	0	10	6	2	0	0	112	57
BOS	144	55	89	6	0	0	0	0	0	0	0	0	0	0	0	78	44	15	7	3	1	3	0	0	10	3	2	1	0	105	39
CAL	167	88	79	4	0	0	1	0	0	0	0	0	0	0	0	99	43	18	7	4	10	4	0	0	9	4	3	0	0	116	51
CHI	121	51	70	3	0	0	0	0	0	0	0	0	0	0	0	69	33	18	1	2	1	0	0	0	14	4	1	0	0	84	37
CLE	157	80	77	6	0	0	3	0	0	1	0	0	0	0	0	87	54	13	3	2	4	1	0	0	7	5	2	0	0	111	46
DET	198	96	102	9	2	0	3	0	0	0	1	0	0	0	0	110	63	19	6	6	3	2	1	0	10	2	6	0	0	144	54
KC	137	60	77	2	1	0	1	0	0	1	0	0	0	0	0	81	40	13	3	2	5	3	2	0	11	2	2	0	0	98	39
MIL	127	63	64	4	0	0	0	0	0	0	0	0	0	0	0	71	38	18	0	0	4	2	0	0	16	1	0	1	0	91	36
MIN	196	116	80	11	0	0	0	0	0	2	0	0	0	0	0	116	55	23	2	5	6	1	3	0	8	2	3	2	0	141	55
NY	188	93	95	6	0	0	0	0	0	0	0	0	0	0	0	118	46	23	1	7	10	1	1	0	12	2	3	1	0	135	53
OAK	163	75	88	9	0	0	3	0	0	0	0	0	0	0	0	103	40	19	1	3	2	3	2	0	11	3	0	2	0	110	53
SEA	158	97	61	4	0	0	0	0	0	0	0	0	0	0	0	89	45	19	5	4	0	3	0	0	9	4	3	0	0	129	29
TEX	184	87	97	11	0	0	1	0	0	0	0	1	0	0	0	121	42	17	4	4	4	4	2	0	9	5	2	1	0	129	55
TOR	181	87	94	5	0	0	0	0	0	0	0	0	0	0	0	105	49	24	3	4	4	6	1	0	9	4	1	1	1	126	55
NL																															
ATL	138	77	61	3	0	0	1	0	0	0	0	0	0	0	0	81	37	16	4	7	2	4	0	1	12	2	2	0	0	101	37
CHI	155	89	66	2	0	0	0	0	0	0	0	0	0	0	0	95	40	19	1	3	0	3	1	3	13	4	3	0	0	115	40
CIN	144	84	60	3	0	0	1	0	0	0	0	0	0	0	0	76	42	23	3	1	4	3	0	1	9	3	2	1	0	99	45
HOU	125	49	76	2	0	0	0	0	0	0	0	0	0	0	0	77	32	11	5	7	3	4	0	0	14	2	1	1	0	81	44
LA	130	57	73	4	0	0	0	0	0	0	0	0	0	0	0	78	34	15	3	5	0	4	1	1	14	3	1	0	0	91	39
MON	110	42	68	5	0	0	0	1	0	0	0	0	0	0	0	70	28	10	2	2	1	4	1	3	16	3	1	0	0	70	40
NY	148	77	71	2	1	0	1	0	0	0	0	0	0	0	0	78	48	18	4	2	6	5	0	2	11	5	2	0	0	94	54
PHI	154	86	68	5	0	0	0	0	0	0	0	0	0	0	0	82	49	21	2	6	3	6	0	2	10	5	0	1	0	105	49
PIT	111	49	62	2	0	0	0	0	0	0	0	0	0	0	0	70	28	11	2	3	5	2	2	1	10	4	1	0	0	82	29
SD	136	80	56	6	0	0	0	0	0	0	0	0	0	0	0	79	39	17	1	8	1	4	0	3	13	3	2	0	0	74	62
SF	114	50	64	2	0	0	0	0	0	0	0	0	0	0	0	64	29	17	4	10	2	4	0	5	16	4	0	0	0	77	37
STL	58	27	31	1	0	0	1	0	0	0	0	0	0	0	0	35	16	6	1	3	1	2	1	2	17	1	0	0	0	32	26
AL	2290	1139	1151	83	3	0	12	0	0	5	1	1	0	0	0	1340	642	258	50	51	57	35	12	0	145	47	30	9	1	1631	659
NL	1523	767	756	37	1	0	4	1	0	0	0	0	0	0	0	885	422	184	32	57	28	45	6	24	155	39	15	3	0	1021	502
YR	3813	1906	1907	120	4	0	16	1	0	5	1	1	0	0	0	2225	1064	442	82	108	85	80	18	24	300	86	45	12	1	2652	1161

	AL		NL
40	Jesse Barfield	37	Mike Schmidt
35	Dave Kingman	31	Glenn Davis
34	Gary Gaetti	31	Dave Parker
33	Jose Canseco	29	Dale Murphy
33	Rob Deer	27	Multiple Players Tied

1987

Tm	Tot	H	A	Consec 2	3	4	1-Inn 3	4	5	One-Game 5	6	7	8	9	10	Men-On-Base 0	1	2	3	Batters PH	LO	XN	IP	P	Totals 1	10	20	30	40	Pitchers RHP	LHP
AL																															
BAL	211	110	101	8	0	0	1	0	0	1	2	0	0	0	0	116	67	26	2	5	5	4	0	0	11	5	2	2	0	143	68
BOS	174	86	88	5	0	0	0	0	0	0	0	0	0	0	0	92	46	27	9	2	5	2	0	0	10	4	2	1	0	125	49
CAL	172	88	84	7	0	0	3	0	0	1	1	0	0	0	0	109	42	17	4	9	8	6	1	0	11	1	3	1	0	120	52
CHI	173	72	101	7	0	0	2	0	0	2	0	0	0	0	0	101	53	18	1	3	6	4	0	0	10	3	4	0	0	97	76
CLE	187	94	93	7	0	0	0	0	0	3	0	0	0	0	0	130	42	11	4	3	1	1	0	0	12	4	0	3	0	143	44

				Consec			1-Inn			One-Game						Men-On-Base				Batters					Totals					Pitchers	
Tm	Tot	H	A	2	3	4	3	4	5	5	6	7	8	9	10	0	1	2	3	PH	LO	XN	IP	P	1	10	20	30	40	RHP	LHP
DET	225	125	100	4	1	0	0	0	0	2	0	0	0	0	0	129	64	28	4	1	4	2	0	0	10	3	3	2	0	156	69
KC	168	73	95	7	0	0	1	0	0	1	0	0	0	0	0	104	43	16	5	3	1	2	1	0	12	2	3	1	0	121	47
MIL	163	72	91	2	0	0	0	0	0	2	0	0	0	0	0	80	52	28	3	2	4	1	0	0	8	4	3	0	0	116	47
MIN	196	106	90	5	0	0	2	0	0	0	0	0	0	0	0	122	49	23	2	2	3	2	2	0	8	3	1	3	0	148	48
NY	196	98	98	8	0	0	0	0	0	2	0	0	0	0	0	111	59	16	10	6	8	2	1	0	12	4	1	2	0	136	60
OAK	199	88	111	3	0	0	0	0	0	2	0	0	0	0	0	115	59	24	1	3	1	4	0	0	9	4	1	1	1	129	70
SEA	161	103	58	4	0	0	0	0	0	1	0	0	0	0	0	86	57	16	2	3	3	2	2	0	9	4	3	0	0	110	51
TEX	194	93	101	4	0	0	0	0	0	1	0	0	0	0	0	117	53	19	5	6	6	4	4	0	10	3	2	2	0	117	77
TOR	215	101	114	8	1	0	0	0	0	3	0	0	0	0	1	126	55	31	3	3	0	4	0	0	9	5	3	0	1	152	63
NL																															
ATL	152	82	70	5	0	0	0	0	0	0	0	0	0	0	0	92	36	21	3	6	5	1	0	2	14	3	1	0	1	104	48
CHI	209	114	95	12	0	0	0	0	0	1	1	0	0	0	0	134	55	14	6	8	5	1	0	1	10	4	2	0	1	167	42
CIN	192	94	98	5	0	0	0	0	0	1	0	1	0	0	0	106	55	24	7	5	10	4	1	2	12	4	3	1	0	137	55
HOU	122	51	71	2	0	0	0	0	0	0	0	0	0	0	0	69	39	11	3	0	1	4	2	1	12	5	1	0	0	77	45
LA	125	52	73	5	0	0	0	0	0	0	0	0	0	0	0	75	38	11	1	4	3	2	1	1	13	2	2	0	0	88	37
MON	120	62	58	1	0	0	0	0	0	0	0	0	0	0	0	72	31	11	6	2	0	4	2	1	10	5	1	0	0	85	35
NY	192	93	99	8	0	0	0	0	0	1	0	0	0	0	0	107	50	28	7	7	3	3	1	1	7	3	2	2	0	117	75
PHI	169	80	89	8	1	0	1	0	0	1	0	0	0	0	0	103	45	19	2	4	3	3	0	1	9	4	2	1	0	119	50
PIT	131	71	60	3	0	0	0	0	0	1	0	0	0	0	0	75	34	20	2	4	6	4	1	4	14	3	2	0	0	71	60
SD	113	60	53	1	1	0	1	0	0	0	0	0	0	0	0	63	32	18	0	1	4	5	2	1	12	3	1	0	0	64	49
SF	205	118	87	6	0	0	0	0	0	2	0	0	0	0	0	129	56	15	5	11	4	6	0	2	13	6	2	1	0	139	66
STL	94	42	52	2	0	0	0	0	0	0	0	0	0	0	0	42	38	11	3	1	0	4	0	3	15	2	0	1	0	56	38
AL	2634	1309	1325	79	2	0	9	0	0	21	3	0	0	0	1	1538	741	300	55	51	55	40	11	0	141	49	31	18	2	1813	821
NL	1824	919	905	58	2	0	2	0	0	7	1	1	0	0	0	1067	509	203	45	53	44	41	10	20	141	44	19	6	2	1224	600
YR	4458	2228	2230	137	4	0	11	0	0	28	4	1	0	0	0	2605	1250	503	100	104	99	81	21	20	282	93	50	24	4	3037	1421

AL		*NL*	
49	Mark McGwire	49	Andre Dawson
47	George Bell	44	Dale Murphy
34	Multiple Players Tied	39	Darryl Strawberry
		37	Eric Davis
		36	Howard Johnson

1988

Tm	Tot	H	A	Consec 2	3	4	1-Inn 3	4	5	One-Game 5	6	7	8	9	10	Men-On-Base 0	1	2	3	PH	LO	XN	IP	P	Totals 1	10	20	30	40	RHP	LHP
AL																															
BAL	137	70	67	4	0	0	1	0	0	0	0	0	0	0	0	82	45	9	1	1	6	0	0	0	10	4	2	0	0	94	43
BOS	124	68	56	3	0	0	0	0	0	0	0	0	0	0	0	55	50	15	4	0	2	2	2	0	10	3	2	0	0	94	30
CAL	124	58	66	2	0	0	0	0	0	1	0	0	0	0	0	69	41	13	1	3	4	3	0	0	7	4	2	0	0	79	45
CHI	132	55	77	3	1	0	1	0	0	1	0	0	0	0	0	85	32	12	3	1	2	3	1	0	11	4	1	0	0	95	37
CLE	134	62	72	3	0	0	0	0	0	0	0	0	0	0	0	86	29	15	4	3	2	1	1	0	13	3	2	0	0	90	44
DET	143	83	60	3	0	0	0	0	0	1	0	0	0	0	0	83	39	16	5	2	1	2	0	0	10	6	1	0	0	100	43
KC	121	55	66	4	0	0	2	0	0	0	0	0	0	0	0	73	34	11	3	0	1	0	4	0	12	1	3	0	0	89	32
MIL	113	60	53	0	0	0	0	0	0	0	0	0	0	0	0	59	36	16	2	0	5	1	1	0	11	4	1	0	0	66	47
MIN	151	76	75	6	0	0	0	0	0	1	0	0	0	0	0	91	47	10	3	2	5	1	2	0	9	4	3	0	0	117	34
NY	148	77	71	7	0	0	1	0	0	1	0	0	0	0	0	72	49	23	4	5	2	8	0	0	11	4	2	0	0	99	49
OAK	156	67	89	5	0	0	0	0	0	0	0	0	0	0	0	76	56	21	3	2	0	5	0	0	12	1	1	1	1	120	36
SEA	148	97	51	5	0	0	0	0	0	2	0	0	0	0	0	85	41	20	2	3	1	3	0	0	8	8	1	0	0	107	41
TEX	112	58	54	3	0	0	0	0	0	0	0	0	0	0	0	76	28	6	2	2	1	2	1	0	11	2	2	0	0	76	36
TOR	158	78	80	6	0	0	0	0	0	1	0	0	0	0	0	99	42	14	3	2	1	2	1	0	8	5	1	1	0	105	53
NL																															
ATL	96	48	48	2	0	0	0	0	0	0	0	0	0	0	0	67	18	11	0	2	1	2	0	0	14	2	1	0	0	55	41
CHI	113	58	55	2	0	0	0	0	0	0	0	0	0	0	0	65	35	10	3	2	0	1	0	2	13	2	1	0	0	76	37
CIN	122	75	47	2	0	0	1	0	0	0	0	0	0	0	0	76	32	13	1	2	4	1	0	1	10	6	1	0	0	91	31
HOU	96	33	63	1	0	0	0	0	0	0	0	0	0	0	0	53	32	7	4	3	0	2	0	1	16	1	0	1	0	64	32
LA	99	49	50	2	0	0	0	0	0	0	0	0	0	0	0	55	34	8	2	3	3	1	1	1	12	1	2	0	0	65	34
MON	107	47	60	1	0	0	0	0	0	0	0	0	0	0	0	64	31	10	2	3	2	7	0	0	10	2	2	0	0	74	33
NY	152	67	85	7	1	0	0	0	0	0	1	0	0	0	0	82	52	15	3	1	1	4	0	1	10	2	2	1	0	86	66
PHI	106	62	44	2	0	0	0	0	0	0	0	0	0	0	0	60	37	8	1	1	6	1	0	2	9	6	0	0	0	70	36
PIT	110	56	54	3	0	0	0	0	0	0	0	0	0	0	0	70	29	11	0	7	9	2	0	0	11	1	3	0	0	76	34
SD	94	56	38	3	0	0	0	0	0	0	0	0	0	0	0	59	27	5	3	4	1	4	2	2	14	3	0	0	0	61	33
SF	113	58	55	3	0	0	0	0	0	1	0	0	0	0	0	65	31	15	2	2	1	2	0	2	15	2	1	0	0	83	30

Tm	Tot	H	A	Consec 2	3	4	1-Inn 3	4	5	One-Game 5	6	7	8	9	10	Men-On-Base 0	1	2	3	Batters PH	LO	XN	IP	P	Totals 1	10	20	30	40	Pitchers RHP	LHP
STL	71	29	42	3	0	0	0	0	0	0	0	0	0	0	0	48	13	10	0	0	0	4	0	1	15	1	1	0	0	44	27
AL	1901	964	937	54	1	0	5	0	0	8	0	0	0	0	0	1091	569	201	40	26	33	33	13	0	143	53	24	2	1	1331	570
NL	1279	638	641	31	1	0	1	0	0	1	1	0	0	0	0	764	371	123	21	30	28	31	3	13	149	29	14	2	0	845	434
YR	3180	1602	1578	85	2	0	6	0	0	9	1	0	0	0	0	1855	940	324	61	56	61	64	16	13	292	82	38	4	1	2176	1004

	AL		*NL*
42	Jose Canseco	39	Darryl Strawberry
34	Fred McGriff	30	Glenn Davis
32	Mark McGwire	29	Will Clark
28	Gary Gaetti	29	Andres Galarraga
28	Eddie Murray	27	Kevin McReynolds

1989

Tm	Tot	H	A	Consec 2	3	4	1-Inn 3	4	5	One-Game 5	6	7	8	9	10	Men-On-Base 0	1	2	3	Batters PH	LO	XN	IP	P	Totals 1	10	20	30	40	Pitchers RHP	LHP
AL																															
BAL	129	61	68	2	0	0	0	0	0	0	0	0	0	0	0	73	33	22	1	2	2	3	0	0	12	3	2	0	0	87	42
BOS	108	52	56	1	0	0	0	0	0	0	0	0	0	0	0	55	35	14	4	3	0	2	1	0	11	2	1	1	0	80	28
CAL	145	73	72	2	0	0	0	0	0	0	0	0	0	0	0	96	33	15	1	1	4	1	0	0	6	6	2	0	0	96	49
CHI	94	36	58	2	0	0	0	0	0	0	0	0	0	0	0	52	25	13	4	1	0	0	0	0	12	5	0	0	0	68	26
CLE	127	56	71	5	0	0	0	0	0	0	1	0	0	0	0	70	46	10	1	4	1	1	1	0	13	3	0	1	0	89	38
DET	116	74	42	3	0	0	0	0	0	1	0	0	0	0	0	71	31	13	1	0	2	2	0	0	16	2	1	0	0	76	40
KC	101	38	63	2	0	0	0	0	0	1	0	0	0	0	0	58	31	10	2	2	2	3	1	0	13	2	0	1	0	74	27
MIL	126	69	57	2	0	0	0	0	0	1	0	0	0	0	0	77	35	11	3	1	3	1	1	0	10	3	2	0	0	87	39
MIN	117	59	58	2	0	0	0	0	0	0	0	0	0	0	0	64	29	20	4	2	1	1	0	0	10	2	1	0	0	83	34
NY	130	64	66	3	0	0	0	0	0	1	0	0	0	0	0	75	41	12	2	3	2	2	0	0	13	3	1	0	0	88	42
OAK	127	65	62	1	0	0	0	0	0	0	0	0	0	0	0	71	41	11	4	1	4	1	0	0	12	2	1	1	0	94	33
SEA	134	68	66	4	0	0	0	0	0	0	0	0	0	0	0	82	32	16	4	3	0	4	2	0	10	4	2	0	0	99	35
TEX	122	75	47	4	0	0	1	0	0	0	0	0	0	0	0	74	34	13	1	3	3	1	0	0	15	2	2	0	0	80	42
TOR	142	64	78	4	0	0	0	0	0	0	0	0	0	0	0	78	41	15	8	3	4	3	1	0	11	5	0	1	0	108	34
NL																															
ATL	128	55	73	0	0	0	1	0	0	0	0	0	0	0	0	83	33	12	0	5	6	0	1	1	16	3	2	0	0	93	35
CHI	124	61	63	3	0	0	0	0	0	0	1	0	0	0	0	80	32	10	2	2	2	2	1	1	15	2	1	1	0	84	40
CIN	128	59	69	3	0	0	0	0	0	0	0	0	0	0	0	68	40	17	3	5	3	3	0	1	16	3	0	1	0	84	44
HOU	97	42	55	1	0	0	0	0	0	0	0	0	0	0	0	58	26	7	6	1	0	3	0	3	14	2	0	1	0	66	31
LA	89	37	52	1	0	0	0	0	0	0	0	0	0	0	0	44	30	11	4	3	1	2	1	0	13	3	1	0	0	61	28
MON	100	55	45	4	0	0	0	0	0	1	0	0	0	0	0	51	37	8	4	4	1	1	0	0	11	2	1	0	0	57	43
NY	147	78	69	3	1	0	1	0	0	0	0	0	0	0	0	97	33	16	1	5	3	3	1	3	15	2	2	1	0	97	50
PHI	123	61	62	1	0	0	1	0	0	0	0	0	0	0	0	63	42	16	2	3	6	2	2	0	15	2	1	0	0	84	39
PIT	95	45	50	2	0	0	0	0	0	0	0	0	0	0	0	63	22	10	0	1	3	4	1	1	15	1	1	0	0	68	27
SD	120	66	54	1	0	0	0	0	0	0	0	0	0	0	0	60	32	23	5	5	1	1	0	2	18	2	1	0	0	88	32
SF	141	63	78	5	0	0	0	0	0	0	0	0	0	0	0	75	44	18	4	2	1	4	0	3	11	2	1	0	1	92	49
STL	73	27	46	1	0	0	0	0	0	0	0	0	0	0	0	39	25	9	0	0	0	0	0	3	11	2	1	0	0	43	30
AL	1718	854	864	37	0	0	1	0	0	4	1	0	0	0	0	996	487	195	40	29	28	25	7	0	164	44	15	5	0	1209	509
NL	1365	649	716	25	1	0	3	0	0	1	1	0	0	0	0	781	396	157	31	36	27	25	7	18	170	26	12	4	1	917	448
YR	3083	1503	1580	62	1	0	4	0	0	5	2	0	0	0	0	1777	883	352	71	65	55	50	14	18	334	70	27	9	1	2126	957

	AL		*NL*
36	Fred McGriff	47	Kevin Mitchell
35	Joe Carter	36	Howard Johnson
33	Mark McGwire	34	Eric Davis
32	Bo Jackson	34	Glenn Davis
30	Nick Esasky	30	Ryne Sandberg

1990

Tm	Tot	H	A	Consec 2	3	4	1-Inn 3	4	5	One-Game 5	6	7	8	9	10	Men-On-Base 0	1	2	3	Batters PH	LO	XN	IP	P	Totals 1	10	20	30	40	Pitchers RHP	LHP
AL																															
BAL	132	74	58	3	0	0	0	0	0	0	0	0	0	0	0	90	21	18	3	4	1	4	1	0	13	4	2	0	0	85	47
BOS	106	61	45	3	0	0	0	0	0	0	0	0	0	0	0	63	27	14	2	1	1	2	2	0	11	3	1	0	0	74	32
CAL	147	89	58	5	0	0	0	0	0	0	1	0	0	0	0	82	41	21	3	2	2	4	1	0	14	5	1	0	0	103	44
CHI	106	41	65	3	0	0	0	0	0	0	0	0	0	0	0	63	26	16	1	1	4	2	1	0	9	5	0	0	0	59	47
CLE	110	52	58	2	1	0	0	0	0	1	0	0	0	0	0	66	29	13	2	3	2	3	0	0	14	4	1	0	0	74	36
DET	172	92	80	4	1	0	1	0	0	1	0	0	0	0	0	93	51	24	4	2	0	1	0	0	13	4	0	0	1	110	62

				Consec			1-Inn			One-Game						Men-On-Base				Batters					Totals					Pitchers	
Tm	Tot	H	A	2	3	4	3	4	5	5	6	7	8	9	10	0	1	2	3	PH	LO	XN	IP	P	1	10	20	30	40	RHP	LHP
KC	100	42	58	2	0	0	0	0	0	0	0	0	0	0	0	57	25	15	3	1	1	2	4	0	12	2	1	0	0	68	32
MIL	128	60	68	1	0	0	0	0	0	0	0	0	0	0	0	72	39	16	1	0	3	0	1	0	8	4	2	0	0	80	48
MIN	100	46	54	2	0	0	0	0	0	0	0	0	0	0	0	52	31	15	2	1	2	3	1	0	11	2	1	0	0	73	27
NY	147	64	83	3	0	0	0	0	0	1	1	0	0	0	0	94	37	16	0	6	6	0	2	0	13	3	2	0	0	99	48
OAK	164	69	95	7	2	0	2	0	0	0	0	1	0	0	0	95	54	11	4	2	5	2	1	0	11	0	2	2	0	115	49
SEA	107	49	58	3	0	0	0	0	0	0	0	0	0	0	0	56	32	13	6	1	0	1	1	0	12	3	1	0	0	69	38
TEX	110	64	46	2	0	0	0	0	0	0	0	0	0	0	0	60	37	10	3	3	0	3	0	0	10	4	1	0	0	78	32
TOR	167	93	74	6	0	0	0	0	0	2	0	0	0	0	0	100	45	18	4	0	1	3	0	0	8	4	1	2	0	110	57
NL																															
ATL	162	85	77	7	0	0	1	0	0	1	0	0	0	0	0	101	36	22	3	7	4	3	0	2	12	3	1	1	0	99	63
CHI	136	75	61	1	0	0	1	0	0	1	0	0	0	0	0	81	39	14	2	1	2	2	0	0	12	2	1	0	1	88	48
CIN	125	70	55	1	1	0	1	0	0	1	0	0	0	0	0	80	31	13	1	1	4	1	0	0	12	2	2	0	0	72	53
HOU	94	35	59	1	0	0	0	0	0	0	0	0	0	0	0	54	26	14	0	4	1	3	1	1	15	2	2	0	0	57	37
LA	129	54	75	4	0	0	0	0	0	0	0	0	0	0	0	73	37	15	4	2	2	5	0	2	13	2	3	0	0	85	44
MON	114	48	66	2	0	0	0	0	0	0	0	0	0	0	0	69	28	14	3	4	1	2	1	1	11	2	2	0	0	73	41
NY	172	86	86	5	0	0	0	0	0	1	0	0	0	0	0	97	49	21	5	4	5	4	1	1	13	4	2	1	0	125	47
PHI	103	47	56	1	0	0	0	0	0	0	0	0	0	0	0	57	35	8	3	4	2	0	1	1	15	3	0	0	0	67	36
PIT	138	59	79	3	0	0	0	0	0	0	0	0	0	0	0	75	43	15	5	3	3	0	0	1	9	3	0	2	0	75	63
SD	123	63	60	2	0	0	1	0	0	0	0	0	0	0	0	69	39	11	4	3	2	4	1	2	15	1	2	0	0	80	43
SF	152	81	71	0	0	0	0	0	0	1	0	0	0	0	0	93	37	19	3	10	1	4	0	1	17	2	0	2	0	94	58
STL	73	43	30	2	0	0	1	0	0	0	0	0	0	0	0	49	21	2	1	2	2	1	0	2	17	2	0	0	0	42	31
AL	1796	896	900	46	4	0	3	0	0	5	2	1	0	0	0	1043	495	220	38	27	28	30	15	0	159	47	16	4	1	1197	599
NL	1521	746	775	29	1	0	5	0	0	5	0	0	0	0	0	898	421	168	34	45	29	29	5	14	161	28	15	6	1	957	564
YR	3317	1642	1675	75	5	0	8	0	0	10	2	1	0	0	0	1941	916	388	72	72	57	59	20	14	320	75	31	10	2	2154	1163

	AL		*NL*
51	Cecil Fielder	40	Ryne Sandberg
39	Mark McGwire	37	Darryl Strawberry
37	Jose Canseco	35	Kevin Mitchell
35	Fred McGriff	33	Barry Bonds
31	Kelly Gruber	33	Matt Williams

1991

AL

Tm	Tot	H	A	2	3	4	3	4	5	5	6	7	8	9	10	0	1	2	3	PH	LO	XN	IP	P	1	10	20	30	40	RHP	LHP
BAL	170	80	90	7	0	0	0	0	0	0	0	0	0	0	0	102	46	17	5	7	1	3	0	0	8	6	1	1	0	123	47
BOS	126	69	57	6	0	0	0	0	0	0	0	0	0	0	0	70	39	12	5	1	2	1	1	0	10	4	1	0	0	87	39
CAL	115	59	56	4	0	0	0	0	0	0	0	0	0	0	0	73	26	13	3	2	2	1	1	0	10	3	2	0	0	86	29
CHI	139	74	65	5	0	0	0	0	0	1	0	0	0	0	0	68	49	16	6	6	1	4	0	0	11	3	1	1	0	93	46
CLE	79	22	57	0	0	0	0	0	0	0	0	0	0	0	0	47	20	11	1	1	1	2	0	0	14	1	1	0	0	58	21
DET	209	109	100	5	0	0	0	0	0	0	0	0	0	0	0	106	70	28	5	5	2	5	1	0	9	2	3	1	1	150	59
KC	117	47	70	2	0	0	0	0	0	0	1	0	0	0	0	65	34	11	7	5	0	3	7	0	14	3	0	1	0	81	36
MIL	116	62	54	0	0	0	0	0	0	1	0	0	0	0	0	64	28	20	4	1	6	3	0	0	11	4	1	0	0	87	29
MIN	140	62	78	2	0	0	1	0	0	0	0	0	0	0	0	68	47	21	4	6	3	2	1	0	10	3	2	0	0	94	46
NY	147	82	65	4	0	0	0	0	0	0	0	0	0	0	0	87	41	18	1	4	1	4	0	0	9	3	3	0	0	88	59
OAK	159	76	83	4	0	0	0	0	0	0	1	0	0	0	0	84	39	29	7	3	5	2	0	0	6	2	3	0	1	119	40
SEA	126	69	57	1	0	0	0	0	0	0	0	0	0	0	0	63	50	9	4	0	1	6	1	0	11	3	2	0	0	85	41
TEX	177	79	98	5	0	0	0	0	0	0	0	0	0	0	0	86	62	27	2	3	5	5	0	0	8	4	4	0	0	114	63
TOR	133	75	58	1	0	0	0	0	0	0	0	0	0	0	0	85	40	8	0	1	6	5	1	0	13	2	1	1	0	87	46
NL																															
ATL	141	83	58	6	0	0	0	0	0	0	0	0	0	0	0	81	42	15	3	3	5	2	1	0	11	3	2	1	0	106	35
CHI	159	93	66	4	0	0	0	0	0	0	0	0	0	0	0	91	42	22	4	7	2	5	2	2	11	3	2	1	0	93	66
CIN	164	104	60	7	1	0	2	0	0	1	0	0	0	0	0	99	48	15	2	6	3	3	0	2	12	5	3	0	0	115	49
HOU	79	27	52	0	0	0	0	0	0	0	0	0	0	0	0	42	26	10	1	3	3	0	1	0	14	3	0	0	0	54	25
LA	108	57	51	3	0	0	0	0	0	0	0	0	0	0	0	57	30	18	3	4	0	3	0	2	12	3	1	0	0	69	39
MON	95	35	60	1	0	0	0	0	0	0	0	0	0	0	0	59	27	8	1	5	2	3	0	0	11	4	0	0	0	55	40
NY	117	57	60	2	0	0	0	0	0	0	0	0	0	0	0	75	27	11	4	8	0	7	0	1	15	2	0	1	0	84	33
PHI	111	61	50	2	0	0	0	0	0	0	0	0	0	0	0	63	29	13	6	2	1	4	0	2	11	4	1	0	0	75	36
PIT	126	61	65	3	0	0	0	0	0	0	0	0	0	0	0	59	47	15	5	6	1	3	1	1	14	4	1	0	0	75	51
SD	121	65	56	0	0	0	0	0	0	1	0	0	0	0	0	68	33	16	4	4	3	5	1	1	13	3	1	1	0	66	55
SF	141	69	72	8	0	0	0	0	0	0	0	0	0	0	0	81	44	14	2	0	1	1	0	1	10	2	2	1	0	97	44

				Consec			1-Inn			One-Game						Men-On-Base				Batters					Totals					Pitchers	
Tm	Tot	H	A	2	3	4	3	4	5	5	6	7	8	9	10	0	1	2	3	PH	LO	XN	IP	P	1	10	20	30	40	RHP	LHP
STL	68	32	36	2	0	0	0	0	0	0	0	0	0	0	0	47	17	4	0	2	1	2	0	0	12	1	0	0	0	49	19
AL	1953	965	988	46	0	0	1	0	0	2	2	0	0	0	0	1068	591	240	54	45	36	46	13	0	144	43	25	5	2	1352	601
NL	1430	744	686	38	1	0	2	0	0	2	0	0	0	0	0	822	412	161	35	50	22	38	6	12	146	37	13	5	0	938	492
YR	3383	1709	1674	84	1	0	3	0	0	4	2	0	0	0	0	1890	1003	401	89	95	58	84	19	12	290	80	38	10	2	2290	1093

	AL		*NL*
44	Jose Canseco	38	Howard Johnson
44	Cecil Fielder	34	Matt Williams
34	Cal Ripken	32	Ron Gant
33	Joe Carter	31	Andre Dawson
32	Frank Thomas	31	Fred McGriff

1992

Tm	Tot	H	A	2	3	4	3	4	5	5	6	7	8	9	10	0	1	2	3	PH	LO	XN	IP	P	1	10	20	30	40	RHP	LHP
AL																															
BAL	148	75	73	6	0	0	2	0	0	2	0	0	0	0	0	92	40	11	5	1	4	1	0	0	8	4	3	0	0	109	39
BOS	84	45	39	1	0	0	0	0	0	0	0	0	0	0	0	51	19	7	7	2	0	1	0	0	14	2	0	0	0	57	27
CAL	88	44	44	1	0	0	0	0	0	0	0	0	0	0	0	51	23	13	1	3	1	2	0	0	15	2	0	0	0	63	25
CHI	110	54	56	4	0	0	0	0	0	0	0	0	0	0	0	65	32	9	4	0	1	1	0	0	11	2	2	0	0	89	21
CLE	127	62	65	3	0	0	0	0	0	0	0	0	0	0	0	76	30	17	4	2	2	4	0	0	11	2	1	1	0	98	29
DET	182	91	91	4	1	0	1	0	0	0	0	0	0	0	0	99	46	32	5	1	4	2	0	0	10	3	1	3	0	123	59
KC	75	24	51	1	0	0	0	0	0	0	0	0	0	0	0	44	22	8	1	0	3	1	4	0	11	3	0	0	0	52	23
MIL	82	35	47	4	0	0	0	0	0	0	0	0	0	0	0	45	24	11	2	0	0	5	0	0	11	1	1	0	0	59	23
MIN	104	56	48	3	0	0	0	1	0	1	0	0	0	0	0	62	25	12	5	1	5	0	0	0	8	5	0	0	0	85	19
NY	163	88	75	4	0	0	0	0	0	0	0	0	0	0	0	94	43	22	4	3	1	1	0	0	11	5	2	0	0	110	53
OAK	142	76	66	5	0	0	1	0	0	0	0	0	0	0	0	80	40	18	4	1	5	1	0	0	11	3	1	0	1	99	43
SEA	149	78	71	2	0	0	0	0	0	0	0	0	0	0	0	87	37	20	5	4	1	1	0	0	12	3	2	0	0	100	49
TEX	159	71	88	7	0	0	1	0	0	0	0	0	0	0	0	88	52	16	3	3	2	3	0	0	9	3	2	0	1	120	39
TOR	163	79	84	4	0	0	0	0	0	0	0	0	0	0	0	83	56	22	2	0	5	2	1	0	9	4	2	1	0	123	40
NL																															
ATL	138	72	66	5	1	0	0	1	0	0	0	0	0	0	0	85	38	13	2	9	2	2	1	1	9	5	2	0	0	85	53
CHI	104	59	45	3	0	0	0	0	0	0	0	0	0	0	0	59	28	14	3	2	2	2	0	2	16	0	2	0	0	80	24
CIN	99	60	39	2	0	0	0	0	0	0	0	0	0	0	0	60	25	12	2	2	0	2	0	2	11	5	0	0	0	58	41
HOU	96	49	47	1	0	0	0	0	0	0	0	0	0	0	0	55	29	10	2	4	3	9	2	1	11	5	0	0	0	60	36
LA	72	26	46	1	0	0	0	0	0	0	0	0	0	0	0	38	23	9	2	8	1	0	0	0	17	0	1	0	0	40	32
MON	102	50	52	3	0	0	0	0	0	0	0	0	0	0	0	62	29	10	1	1	2	2	2	1	16	1	1	0	0	60	42
NY	93	42	51	1	0	0	0	0	0	0	0	0	0	0	0	53	20	17	3	4	3	3	0	1	16	3	0	0	0	69	24
PHI	118	67	51	1	0	0	1	0	0	0	0	0	0	0	0	57	42	14	5	4	2	0	2	0	16	1	2	0	0	66	52
PIT	106	51	55	2	0	0	1	0	0	0	0	0	0	0	0	60	33	9	4	1	3	1	1	0	11	2	0	1	0	71	35
SD	135	87	48	5	0	0	0	0	0	0	0	0	0	0	0	73	43	15	4	2	1	4	0	2	9	3	0	2	0	75	60
SF	105	57	48	0	0	0	0	0	0	0	0	0	0	0	0	62	32	10	1	7	3	4	0	0	15	3	1	0	0	70	35
STL	94	55	39	4	0	0	0	0	0	0	0	0	0	0	0	54	32	5	3	4	3	4	0	2	15	2	1	0	0	59	35
AL	1776	878	898	49	1	0	5	1	0	3	0	0	0	0	0	1017	489	218	52	21	34	25	5	0	151	42	17	5	2	1287	489
NL	1262	675	587	28	1	0	2	1	0	0	0	0	0	0	0	718	374	138	32	48	25	33	8	12	162	30	10	3	0	793	469
YR	3038	1553	1485	77	2	0	7	2	0	3	0	0	0	0	0	1735	863	356	84	69	59	58	13	12	313	72	27	8	2	2080	958

	AL		*NL*
43	Juan Gonzalez	35	Fred McGriff
42	Mark McGwire	34	Barry Bonds
35	Cecil Fielder	33	Gary Sheffield
34	Albert Belle	27	Darren Daulton
34	Joe Carter	27	Dave Hollins

1993

Tm	Tot	H	A	2	3	4	3	4	5	5	6	7	8	9	10	0	1	2	3	PH	LO	XN	IP	P	1	10	20	30	40	RHP	LHP
AL																															
BAL	157	87	70	3	0	0	1	0	0	0	0	0	0	0	0	95	37	22	3	0	2	1	0	0	11	4	3	0	0	110	47
BOS	114	54	60	4	0	0	0	0	0	0	0	0	0	0	0	62	39	11	2	1	2	1	0	0	12	3	1	0	0	73	41
CAL	114	64	50	4	0	0	0	0	0	0	0	0	0	0	0	62	31	19	2	3	0	0	0	0	13	1	1	1	0	90	24
CHI	162	82	80	8	0	0	3	0	0	3	0	0	0	0	0	84	52	19	7	1	6	3	0	0	8	4	2	0	1	109	53
CLE	141	69	72	5	0	0	2	0	0	0	0	0	0	0	0	76	46	16	3	4	0	2	0	0	15	2	1	1	0	102	39

				Consec			1-Inn			One-Game						Men-On-Base				Batters					Totals					Pitchers	
Tm	Tot	H	A	2	3	4	3	4	5	5	6	7	8	9	10	0	1	2	3	PH	LO	XN	IP	P	1	10	20	30	40	RHP	LHP
DET	178	103	75	9	0	0	2	0	0	3	0	0	0	0	0	97	46	27	8	2	2	1	0	0	6	5	1	2	0	127	51
KC	125	50	75	3	0	0	0	0	0	0	0	0	0	0	0	74	39	9	3	0	0	2	1	0	10	6	1	0	0	95	30
MIL	125	53	72	2	0	0	0	0	0	0	0	0	0	0	0	86	25	12	2	0	3	4	0	0	13	2	0	1	0	89	36
MIN	121	56	65	2	0	0	0	0	0	0	1	0	0	0	0	57	40	20	4	2	1	3	0	0	9	3	3	0	0	89	32
NY	178	88	90	7	0	0	1	0	0	1	0	0	0	0	0	109	39	25	5	4	2	3	0	0	9	5	2	1	0	118	60
OAK	158	78	80	3	0	0	0	0	0	0	0	0	0	0	0	88	39	27	4	3	7	3	0	0	13	5	2	0	0	96	62
SEA	161	74	87	3	0	0	0	0	0	0	0	0	0	0	0	92	49	12	8	3	1	0	0	0	14	4	1	0	1	111	50
TEX	181	90	91	7	0	0	0	0	0	1	0	0	0	0	0	89	72	16	4	2	1	4	1	0	13	3	0	2	1	149	32
TOR	159	90	69	7	0	0	0	0	0	2	0	0	0	0	0	98	39	20	2	1	6	0	1	0	9	3	2	1	0	121	38
NL																															
ATL	169	78	91	6	0	0	0	0	0	2	1	0	0	0	0	93	47	25	4	5	1	3	2	0	9	3	0	1	1	122	47
CHI	161	76	85	1	1	0	1	0	0	0	0	0	0	0	0	94	46	19	2	8	4	5	0	0	10	5	0	2	0	116	45
CIN	137	69	68	4	0	0	0	0	0	0	0	0	0	0	0	84	32	16	5	3	1	0	0	2	18	2	2	0	0	94	43
COL	142	77	65	2	0	0	0	0	0	0	0	0	0	0	0	81	39	19	3	4	2	2	0	2	13	2	3	0	0	111	31
FLO	94	44	50	0	0	0	0	0	0	0	0	0	0	0	0	46	34	10	4	0	2	0	0	2	13	3	1	0	0	66	28
HOU	138	62	76	4	0	0	1	0	0	0	0	0	0	0	0	89	33	16	0	2	5	1	2	3	9	5	2	0	0	84	54
LA	130	66	64	2	0	0	0	0	0	0	0	0	0	0	0	82	32	14	2	4	0	3	0	1	13	3	1	1	0	95	35
MON	122	62	60	5	1	0	2	0	0	0	0	0	0	0	0	73	33	15	1	4	2	0	1	0	15	4	1	0	0	82	40
NY	158	75	83	2	0	0	1	0	0	1	0	0	0	0	0	94	43	17	4	2	2	5	1	2	11	3	2	1	0	128	30
PHI	156	80	76	4	0	0	2	0	0	1	1	0	0	0	0	82	49	17	8	2	4	3	0	2	9	5	2	0	0	91	65
PIT	110	64	46	2	0	0	0	0	0	0	0	0	0	0	0	65	33	12	0	7	4	2	3	1	13	4	0	0	0	87	23
SD	153	87	66	5	0	0	1	0	0	2	0	0	0	0	0	84	52	15	2	4	1	3	0	1	15	3	1	1	0	105	48
SF	168	82	86	8	0	0	0	0	0	2	0	0	0	0	0	96	54	17	1	4	1	5	0	1	14	2	0	1	1	113	55
STL	118	59	59	1	0	0	0	0	0	1	0	0	0	0	0	60	35	18	5	4	3	1	0	0	10	4	1	0	0	77	41
AL	2074	1038	1036	67	0	0	9	0	0	10	1	0	0	0	0	1169	593	255	57	26	33	27	3	0	155	50	20	9	3	1479	595
NL	1956	981	975	46	2	0	8	0	0	9	2	0	0	0	0	1123	562	230	41	53	32	33	9	17	172	48	16	7	2	1371	585
YR	4030	2019	2011	113	2	0	17	0	0	19	3	0	0	0	0	2292	1155	485	98	79	65	60	12	17	327	98	36	16	5	2850	1180

AL

46 Juan Gonzalez
45 Ken Griffey
41 Frank Thomas
38 Albert Belle
37 Rafael Palmeiro

NL

46 Barry Bonds
40 Dave Justice
38 Matt Williams
37 Fred McGriff
36 Ron Gant

1994

AL

Tm	Tot	H	A	Consec 2	3	4	1-Inn 3	4	5	One-Game 5	6	7	8	9	10	Men-On-Base 0	1	2	3	PH	LO	XN	IP	P	Totals 1	10	20	30	40	RHP	LHP
BAL	139	75	64	4	0	0	0	0	0	2	1	0	0	0	0	90	37	11	1	0	2	1	0	0	7	6	1	0	0	101	38
BOS	120	68	52	3	0	0	1	0	0	1	1	0	0	0	0	65	44	8	3	1	0	2	0	0	11	4	1	0	0	84	36
CAL	120	74	46	4	0	0	0	0	0	3	0	0	0	0	0	69	38	10	3	2	1	1	0	0	11	2	2	0	0	81	39
CHI	121	62	59	8	0	0	1	0	0	1	0	0	0	0	0	70	28	17	6	1	1	1	0	0	9	4	1	1	0	82	39
CLE	167	87	80	8	0	0	1	0	0	2	1	0	0	0	0	99	45	22	1	3	2	5	0	0	8	6	1	1	0	120	47
DET	161	85	76	7	0	0	2	0	0	1	0	0	0	0	0	88	44	23	6	4	5	4	0	0	8	5	2	0	0	129	32
KC	100	41	59	1	0	0	0	0	0	0	0	0	0	0	0	46	32	18	4	1	0	3	1	0	10	3	1	0	0	75	25
MIL	99	48	51	7	0	0	1	0	0	1	0	0	0	0	0	60	20	17	2	1	0	1	0	0	12	5	0	0	0	70	29
MIN	103	48	55	1	0	0	0	0	0	0	0	0	0	0	0	58	31	11	3	0	4	1	1	0	9	5	1	0	0	70	33
NY	139	63	76	2	1	0	1	0	0	0	0	0	0	0	0	72	48	14	5	5	2	3	0	0	10	5	1	0	0	85	54
OAK	113	51	62	3	0	0	0	0	0	0	0	0	0	0	0	60	39	12	2	3	3	0	0	0	7	5	1	0	0	65	48
SEA	153	63	90	4	0	0	0	0	0	2	0	0	0	0	0	89	42	19	3	5	1	3	1	0	14	2	2	0	1	100	53
TEX	124	63	61	5	0	0	0	0	0	1	0	0	0	0	0	67	40	15	2	1	1	2	1	0	5	5	0	1	0	95	29
TOR	115	63	52	2	0	0	0	0	0	0	1	0	0	0	0	58	42	13	2	1	4	2	1	0	7	4	1	0	0	74	41
NL																															
ATL	137	61	76	6	2	0	2	0	0	1	0	0	0	0	0	79	41	17	0	3	2	3	0	1	14	3	0	1	0	101	36
CHI	109	47	62	2	0	0	1	0	0	1	0	0	0	0	0	74	26	9	0	4	9	2	0	0	10	3	1	0	0	74	35
CIN	124	59	65	6	0	0	1	1	0	3	0	0	0	0	0	69	43	10	2	2	2	7	0	1	12	3	0	1	0	94	30
COL	125	59	66	8	0	0	2	0	0	1	0	0	0	0	0	70	38	12	5	6	1	1	2	1	11	3	1	1	0	88	37
FLO	94	46	48	5	0	0	1	0	0	0	0	0	0	0	0	47	36	9	2	1	1	0	1	0	12	2	1	0	0	64	30
HOU	120	57	63	5	0	0	0	0	0	0	0	0	0	0	0	67	35	15	3	6	1	1	1	0	11	2	0	1	0	81	39
LA	115	47	68	5	0	0	1	0	0	0	0	0	0	0	0	59	38	16	2	4	0	2	1	1	10	2	2	0	0	79	36
MON	108	42	66	4	0	0	1	0	0	1	0	0	0	0	0	61	32	14	1	1	1	4	1	0	6	5	1	0	0	76	32
NY	117	53	64	1	0	0	0	0	0	0	0	0	0	0	0	66	39	9	3	3	0	3	0	0	9	4	1	0	0	81	36

				Consec			1-Inn			One-Game						Men-On-Base				Batters					Totals					Pitchers	
Tm	Tot	H	A	2	3	4	3	4	5	5	6	7	8	9	10	0	1	2	3	PH	LO	XN	IP	P	1	10	20	30	40	RHP	LHP
PHI	80	45	35	1	0	0	0	0	0	0	0	0	0	0	0	42	21	16	1	3	3	0	0	1	17	2	0	0	0	57	23
PIT	80	45	35	2	0	0	0	0	0	0	0	0	0	0	0	47	25	5	3	3	0	1	0	1	13	2	0	0	0	57	23
SD	92	51	41	3	0	0	0	0	0	0	0	0	0	0	0	56	23	9	4	2	0	3	0	0	12	4	0	0	0	64	28
SF	123	56	67	5	0	0	0	0	0	0	0	0	0	0	0	79	34	7	3	3	1	1	2	0	14	0	0	1	1	84	39
STL	108	50	58	3	0	0	0	0	0	1	0	0	0	0	0	59	29	18	2	7	5	2	0	1	9	5	0	0	0	78	30
AL	1774	891	883	59	1	0	7	0	0	14	4	0	0	0	0	991	530	210	43	28	26	29	5	0	128	61	15	3	1	1231	543
NL	1532	718	814	56	2	0	9	1	0	8	0	0	0	0	0	875	460	166	31	48	26	30	8	7	160	40	7	5	1	1078	454
YR	3306	1609	1697	115	3	0	16	1	0	22	4	0	0	0	0	1866	990	376	74	76	52	59	13	7	288	101	22	8	2	2309	997

AL		*NL*	
40	Ken Griffey	43	Matt Williams
38	Frank Thomas	39	Jeff Bagwell
36	Albert Belle	37	Barry Bonds
31	Jose Canseco	34	Fred McGriff
28	Cecil Fielder	31	Andres Galarraga

1995

AL

Tm	Tot	H	A	2	3	4	3	4	5	5	6	7	8	9	10	0	1	2	3	PH	LO	XN	IP	P	1	10	20	30	40	RHP	LHP
BAL	173	90	83	6	1	0	2	1	0	2	1	0	0	0	0	95	53	19	6	2	3	1	0	0	11	5	1	1	0	116	57
BOS	175	70	105	8	0	0	1	0	0	1	0	0	0	0	0	102	46	20	7	2	3	3	1	0	12	4	2	1	0	127	48
CAL	186	90	96	6	0	0	0	0	0	0	0	0	0	0	0	105	48	30	3	1	6	3	2	0	10	1	3	2	0	134	52
CHI	146	59	87	5	1	0	1	0	0	2	0	0	0	0	0	91	33	16	6	2	4	2	0	0	13	4	1	0	1	103	43
CLE	207	99	108	6	0	0	2	0	0	3	1	0	0	0	0	115	58	29	5	1	2	6	1	0	10	2	3	1	1	166	41
DET	159	92	67	11	0	0	1	0	0	0	0	1	0	0	0	99	42	13	5	2	3	1	2	0	9	6	1	1	0	124	35
KC	119	49	70	3	0	0	0	0	0	1	0	0	0	0	0	69	33	15	2	6	3	4	1	0	17	2	0	1	0	85	34
MIL	128	56	72	0	0	0	1	0	0	0	0	0	0	0	0	56	39	23	10	2	1	2	3	0	8	6	1	0	0	104	24
MIN	120	59	61	1	0	0	0	0	0	0	0	0	0	0	0	66	38	14	2	4	3	1	0	0	14	3	2	0	0	86	34
NY	122	69	53	2	0	0	0	0	0	0	0	0	0	0	0	70	32	16	4	2	4	1	0	0	14	2	1	0	0	63	59
OAK	169	80	89	3	0	0	0	0	0	0	0	0	0	0	0	88	62	12	7	5	4	1	2	0	10	4	1	1	0	123	46
SEA	182	101	81	6	0	0	0	0	0	1	0	0	0	0	0	99	41	32	10	2	0	2	1	0	13	1	2	1	1	131	51
TEX	138	81	57	9	0	0	1	0	0	0	0	0	0	0	0	74	40	20	4	2	0	3	1	0	9	3	1	1	0	100	38
TOR	140	73	67	5	0	0	1	0	0	0	0	0	0	0	0	85	37	14	4	1	3	1	1	0	10	6	1	0	0	104	36

NL

Tm	Tot	H	A	2	3	4	3	4	5	5	6	7	8	9	10	0	1	2	3	PH	LO	XN	IP	P	1	10	20	30	40	RHP	LHP
ATL	168	94	74	4	0	0	1	0	0	1	0	0	0	0	0	99	45	22	2	3	2	0	1	3	10	3	4	0	0	132	36
CHI	158	83	75	3	0	0	0	0	0	1	0	0	0	0	0	94	47	15	2	6	4	3	3	1	13	5	0	1	0	119	39
CIN	161	76	85	5	0	0	0	0	0	0	0	0	0	0	0	92	49	19	1	5	4	5	3	2	12	5	2	0	0	115	46
COL	200	134	66	11	1	0	4	0	0	1	0	0	0	0	0	117	58	22	3	11	5	1	0	2	12	1	0	3	1	142	58
FLO	144	68	76	4	0	0	0	0	0	0	0	0	0	0	0	84	35	18	7	0	0	1	4	1	13	4	2	0	0	108	36
HOU	109	41	68	5	0	0	0	0	0	1	0	0	0	0	0	60	28	18	3	9	0	6	0	0	18	0	2	0	0	82	27
LA	140	62	78	5	0	0	1	0	0	2	0	0	0	0	0	68	56	12	4	5	1	2	4	0	13	0	1	2	0	107	33
MON	118	43	75	0	0	0	0	0	0	1	0	0	0	0	0	74	24	15	5	3	6	1	0	1	11	8	0	0	0	93	25
NY	125	63	62	3	0	0	0	0	0	0	0	0	0	0	0	80	31	10	4	5	3	3	3	0	11	3	2	0	0	94	31
PHI	94	51	43	2	0	0	0	0	0	0	0	0	0	0	0	54	27	11	2	7	1	4	1	3	18	4	0	0	0	66	28
PIT	125	69	56	1	1	0	1	1	0	0	0	0	0	0	0	71	38	13	3	5	4	1	1	1	10	6	0	0	0	80	45
SD	116	55	61	4	0	0	0	0	0	1	0	0	0	0	0	65	28	14	9	10	1	3	8	2	14	3	1	0	0	76	40
SF	152	76	76	4	0	0	0	0	0	2	0	0	0	0	0	91	44	15	2	1	4	3	0	2	15	2	2	1	0	114	38
STL	107	54	53	1	0	0	0	0	0	0	0	0	0	0	0	66	30	10	1	4	2	1	0	1	15	1	2	0	0	86	21
AL	2164	1068	1096	71	2	0	10	1	0	10	2	1	0	0	0	1214	602	273	75	34	39	31	15	0	160	49	20	10	3	1566	598
NL	1917	969	948	52	2	0	7	1	0	10	0	0	0	0	0	1115	540	214	48	74	37	34	28	19	185	45	18	7	1	1414	503
YR	4081	2037	2044	123	4	0	17	2	0	20	2	1	0	0	0	2329	1142	487	123	108	76	65	43	19	345	94	38	17	4	2980	1101

AL		*NL*	
50	Albert Belle	40	Dante Bichette
40	Jay Buhner	36	Sammy Sosa
40	Frank Thomas	36	Larry Walker
39	Multiple Players Tied	33	Barry Bonds
		32	Multiple Players Tied

1876

NL

				Consec			1-Inn			One-Game						Men-On-Base				Pitchers					Totals					Batters	
Tm	Tot	H	A	2	3	4	3	4	5	5	6	7	8	9	10	0	1	2	3	PH	LO	XN	IP	P	1	10	20	30	40	RHB	LHB
BOS	7	3	4	0	0	0	0	0	0	0	0	0	0	0	0	4	2	1	0	0	0	1	4	0	4	0	0	0	0	5	2

Home Run Listing Legend (Yearly Team Totals by Pitcher)

Tm Team Abbreviation

Tot Total home runs surrendered by team

H Home runs surrendered in the home ballpark

A Home runs surrendered away from home

Consec Number of times home runs were surrendered to consecutive batters in one inning

1 Inn Number of times multiple home runs were surrendered in one inning

One-Gm Multiple home run games by opponents

Men-On Home runs surrendered with various number of men on base

PH Pinch Hit home runs surrendered

LO Home runs surrendered to the first batter of the game for the opponents

XN Home runs surrendered in extra innings

IP Inside-the-Park home runs surrendered

P Home runs hit by opposing pitchers

Totals

1 Number of pitchers surrendering 1–9 home runs for season

10 Number of pitchers surrendering 10–19 home runs for season

20 Number of pitchers surrendering 20–29 home runs for season

30 Number of pitchers surrendering 30–39 home runs for season

40 Number of pitchers surrendering 40 or more home runs for season

RHB Home runs hit by right-handed batters

LHB Home runs hit by left-handed batters

Yearly Home Run Totals by Team and League (by Pitcher)

1876

Tm	Tot	H	A	Consec 2	3	4	1-Inn 3	4	5	One-Game 5	6	7	8	9	10	Men-On-Base 0	1	2	3	Pitchers PH	LO	XN	IP	P	Totals 1	10	20	30	40	Batters RHB	LHB
NL																															
BOS	7	3	4	0	0	0	0	0	0	0	0	0	0	0	0	4	2	1	0	0	0	1	4	0	4	0	0	0	0	5	2
CHI	6	1	5	0	0	0	0	0	0	0	0	0	0	0	0	4	2	0	0	0	3	0	2	0	1	0	0	0	0	5	1
CIN	9	2	7	0	0	0	0	0	0	0	0	0	0	0	0	4	2	3	0	0	0	0	2	0	4	0	0	0	0	4	4
HAR	2	0	2	0	0	0	0	0	0	0	0	0	0	0	0	2	0	0	0	0	0	0	0	0	1	0	0	0	0	0	2
LOU	3	3	0	0	0	0	0	0	0	0	0	0	0	0	0	2	1	0	0	0	0	0	2	0	1	0	0	0	0	2	1
NY	8	7	1	0	0	0	0	0	0	0	0	0	0	0	0	1	4	3	0	0	0	0	0	0	1	0	0	0	0	6	2
PHI	2	0	2	0	0	0	0	0	0	0	0	0	0	0	0	1	0	1	0	0	0	0	1	1	1	0	0	0	0	1	0
STL	3	1	2	0	0	0	0	0	0	0	0	0	0	0	0	3	0	0	0	0	0	0	2	0	1	0	0	0	0	3	0
NL	40	17	23	0	0	0	0	0	0	0	0	0	0	0	0	21	11	8	0	0	3	1	13	1	14	0	0	0	0	26	12

NL

8 Bobby Mathews
6 Cherokee Fisher
6 Al Spalding
4 Joe Borden
3 Multiple Players Tied

1877

Tm	Tot	H	A	Consec 2	3	4	1-Inn 3	4	5	One-Game 5	6	7	8	9	10	Men-On-Base 0	1	2	3	Pitchers PH	LO	XN	IP	P	Totals 1	10	20	30	40	Batters RHB	LHB
NL																															
BOS	5	1	4	0	0	0	0	0	0	0	0	0	0	0	0	2	1	2	0	0	1	0	0	1	1	0	0	0	0	2	3
CHI	7	4	3	0	0	0	0	0	0	0	0	0	0	0	0	3	2	2	0	0	0	0	2	0	3	0	0	0	0	3	4
CIN	4	1	3	0	0	0	0	0	0	0	0	0	0	0	0	1	2	1	0	0	0	0	0	0	3	0	0	0	0	2	2
HAR	2	1	1	0	0	0	0	0	0	0	0	0	0	0	0	1	1	0	0	0	0	0	1	0	1	0	0	0	0	1	1
LOU	4	3	1	0	0	0	0	0	0	0	0	0	0	0	0	2	1	1	0	0	0	0	2	1	1	0	0	0	0	2	2
STL	2	1	1	0	0	0	0	0	0	0	0	0	0	0	0	0	0	2	0	0	0	0	0	0	1	0	0	0	0	2	0
NL	24	11	13	0	0	0	0	0	0	0	0	0	0	0	0	9	7	8	0	0	1	0	5	2	10	0	0	0	0	12	12

NL

5 Tommy Bond
4 George Bradley
4 Jim Devlin
2 Multiple Players Tied

1878

Tm	Tot	H	A	Consec 2	3	4	1-Inn 3	4	5	One-Game 5	6	7	8	9	10	Men-On-Base 0	1	2	3	Pitchers PH	LO	XN	IP	P	Totals 1	10	20	30	40	Batters RHB	LHB
NL																															
BOS	6	3	3	0	0	0	0	0	0	0	0	0	0	0	0	2	1	3	0	0	0	0	0	1	2	0	0	0	0	4	2
CHI	4	2	2	0	0	0	0	0	0	0	0	0	0	0	0	1	3	0	0	0	0	1	0	0	1	0	0	0	0	4	0
CIN	2	2	0	0	0	0	0	0	0	0	0	0	0	0	0	0	1	1	0	0	0	0	1	0	2	0	0	0	0	1	1
IND	3	0	3	0	0	0	0	0	0	0	0	0	0	0	0	2	1	0	0	0	0	0	0	0	3	0	0	0	0	2	1
MIL	3	0	3	0	0	0	0	0	0	0	0	0	0	0	0	2	1	0	0	0	0	0	0	0	2	0	0	0	0	3	0
PRO	5	2	3	0	0	0	0	0	0	0	0	0	0	0	0	2	2	1	0	0	0	0	0	0	3	0	0	0	0	4	0
NL	23	9	14	0	0	0	0	0	0	0	0	0	0	0	0	9	9	5	0	0	0	1	1	1	13	0	0	0	0	18	4

NL

5 Tommy Bond
4 Terry Larkin
3 Monte Ward
2 Tom Healey
2 Sam Weaver

1879

Tm	Tot	H	A	Consec 2	3	4	1-Inn 3	4	5	One-Game 5	6	7	8	9	10	Men-On-Base 0	1	2	3	Pitchers PH	LO	XN	IP	P	Totals 1	10	20	30	40	Batters RHB	LHB
NL																															
BOS	9	2	7	0	0	0	0	0	0	0	0	0	0	0	0	7	2	0	0	0	2	0	0	1	2	0	0	0	0	7	2

Tm	Tot	H	A	Consec 2	3	4	1-Inn 3	4	5	One-Game 5	6	7	8	9	10	Men-On-Base 0	1	2	3	Pitchers PH	LO	XN	IP	P	Totals 1	10	20	30	40	Batters RHB	LHB
BUF	3	0	3	0	0	0	0	0	0	0	0	0	0	0	0	1	1	1	0	0	1	0	0	0	1	0	0	0	0	1	2
CHI	5	0	5	0	0	0	0	0	0	0	0	0	0	0	0	3	1	1	0	0	0	0	0	1	1	0	0	0	0	3	2
CIN	11	6	5	0	0	0	0	0	0	0	0	0	0	0	0	7	2	2	0	0	1	0	1	1	1	1	0	0	0	5	6
CLE	4	1	3	0	0	0	0	0	0	0	0	0	0	0	0	2	2	0	0	0	0	0	1	0	2	0	0	0	0	3	1
PRO	9	4	5	0	0	0	0	0	0	0	0	0	0	0	0	4	5	0	0	0	0	0	0	0	2	0	0	0	0	4	4
SYR	4	2	2	0	0	0	0	0	0	0	0	0	0	0	0	2	1	1	0	0	0	0	0	0	2	0	0	0	0	4	0
TRO	13	6	7	0	0	0	0	0	0	0	0	0	0	0	0	6	5	2	0	0	0	2	1	0	1	1	0	0	0	7	6
NL	58	21	37	0	0	0	0	0	0	0	0	0	0	0	0	32	19	7	0	0	4	2	3	3	12	2	0	0	0	34	23

NL

12 George Bradley
10 Will White
8 Tommy Bond
5 Terry Larkin
5 Monte Ward

1880

NL

Tm	Tot	H	A	Consec 2	3	4	1-Inn 3	4	5	One-Game 5	6	7	8	9	10	Men-On-Base 0	1	2	3	Pitchers PH	LO	XN	IP	P	Totals 1	10	20	30	40	Batters RHB	LHB
BOS	2	1	1	0	0	0	0	0	0	0	0	0	0	0	0	0	0	2	0	0	0	0	0	0	2	0	0	0	0	1	1
BUF	10	1	9	0	0	0	0	0	0	0	0	0	0	0	0	4	5	1	0	0	0	0	2	0	4	0	0	0	0	7	3
CHI	8	0	8	0	0	0	0	0	0	0	0	0	0	0	0	3	5	0	0	0	1	0	0	0	2	0	0	0	0	6	2
CIN	10	8	2	0	0	0	0	0	0	0	0	0	0	0	0	4	4	2	0	0	0	0	1	0	2	0	0	0	0	8	2
CLE	4	1	3	0	0	0	0	0	0	0	0	0	0	0	0	1	3	0	0	0	0	0	2	0	2	0	0	0	0	2	2
PRO	7	2	5	0	0	0	0	0	0	0	0	0	0	0	0	1	5	1	0	0	0	0	0	0	2	0	0	0	0	4	1
TRO	8	6	2	0	0	0	0	0	0	0	0	0	0	0	0	6	2	0	0	0	2	0	0	0	2	0	0	0	0	6	2
WOR	13	6	7	0	0	0	0	0	0	0	0	0	0	0	0	9	1	3	0	0	0	0	0	0	2	0	0	0	0	11	2
NL	62	25	37	0	0	0	0	0	0	0	0	0	0	0	0	28	25	9	0	0	3	0	5	0	18	0	0	0	0	45	15

NL

9 Will White
7 Lee Richmond
7 Mickey Welch
6 Larry Corcoran
6 Fred Corey

1881

NL

Tm	Tot	H	A	Consec 2	3	4	1-Inn 3	4	5	One-Game 5	6	7	8	9	10	Men-On-Base 0	1	2	3	Pitchers PH	LO	XN	IP	P	Totals 1	10	20	30	40	Batters RHB	LHB
BOS	9	4	5	0	0	0	0	0	0	0	0	0	0	0	0	5	3	1	0	0	0	0	0	0	2	0	0	0	0	7	2
BUF	9	0	9	0	0	0	0	0	0	0	0	0	0	0	0	5	3	1	0	0	0	0	1	0	4	0	0	0	0	6	3
CHI	14	6	8	0	0	0	0	0	0	0	0	0	0	0	0	10	3	0	1	0	0	0	1	0	1	1	0	0	0	9	4
CLE	9	4	5	0	0	0	0	0	0	0	0	0	0	0	0	5	2	2	0	0	1	0	0	0	3	0	0	0	0	6	3
DET	8	4	4	0	0	0	0	0	0	0	0	0	0	0	0	4	3	1	0	0	1	0	1	0	4	0	0	0	0	2	6
PRO	5	2	3	0	0	0	0	0	0	0	0	0	0	0	0	2	2	1	0	0	0	0	1	0	3	0	0	0	0	4	0
TRO	11	9	2	1	0	0	0	0	0	0	0	0	0	0	0	9	2	0	0	0	1	0	0	0	2	0	0	0	0	6	5
WOR	11	4	7	1	0	0	0	0	0	0	0	0	0	0	0	6	4	0	1	0	0	0	2	0	3	0	0	0	0	10	1
NL	76	33	43	2	0	0	0	0	0	0	0	0	0	0	0	46	22	6	2	0	3	0	6	0	22	1	0	0	0	50	24

NL

10 Larry Corcoran
7 Lee Richmond
7 Mickey Welch
6 Jim Whitney
4 Multiple Players Tied

1882

AA

Tm	Tot	H	A	Consec 2	3	4	1-Inn 3	4	5	One-Game 5	6	7	8	9	10	Men-On-Base 0	1	2	3	Pitchers PH	LO	XN	IP	P	Totals 1	10	20	30	40	Batters RHB	LHB
BAL	15	7	8	0	0	0	0	0	0	0	0	0	0	0	0	5	6	3	1	0	0	0	2	1	6	0	0	0	0	6	6
CIN	7	5	2	0	0	0	0	0	0	0	0	0	0	0	0	5	1	0	1	0	0	0	0	1	2	0	0	0	0	6	1
LOU	6	0	6	0	0	0	0	0	0	0	0	0	0	0	0	3	3	0	0	0	0	0	1	0	2	0	0	0	0	2	4
PHI	13	11	2	0	0	0	0	0	0	0	0	0	0	0	0	4	5	4	0	0	0	0	1	0	5	0	0	0	0	9	3

				Consec			1-Inn			One-Game						Men-On-Base				Pitchers					Totals					Batters	
Tm	Tot	H	A	2	3	4	3	4	5	5	6	7	8	9	10	0	1	2	3	PH	LO	XN	IP	P	1	10	20	30	40	RHB	LHB
PIT	4	3	1	0	0	0	0	0	0	0	0	0	0	0	0	3	0	1	0	0	0	0	0	0	2	0	0	0	0	3	1
STL	7	2	5	0	0	0	0	0	0	0	0	0	0	0	0	3	3	1	0	0	0	0	0	0	3	0	0	0	0	5	1
NL																															
BOS	10	7	3	0	0	0	0	0	0	0	0	0	0	0	0	4	4	2	0	0	1	0	0	1	3	0	0	0	0	5	3
BUF	16	7	9	0	0	0	0	0	0	0	0	0	0	0	0	7	6	3	0	0	1	0	1	1	3	0	0	0	0	6	9
CHI	13	8	5	0	0	0	0	0	0	0	0	0	0	0	0	7	4	2	0	0	1	0	1	0	3	0	0	0	0	8	3
CLE	22	7	15	0	0	0	0	0	0	0	0	0	0	0	0	11	7	3	1	0	0	0	0	3	2	1	0	0	0	13	7
DET	19	10	9	1	0	0	0	0	0	0	0	0	0	0	0	9	7	2	1	0	0	1	2	3	2	1	0	0	0	9	7
PRO	12	6	6	0	0	0	0	0	0	0	0	0	0	0	0	8	1	3	0	0	2	0	2	0	2	0	0	0	0	7	4
TRO	13	2	11	0	0	0	0	0	0	0	0	0	0	0	0	5	6	2	0	0	1	1	1	1	3	0	0	0	0	9	4
WOR	21	15	6	1	0	0	0	0	0	0	0	0	0	0	0	5	5	5	1	0	0	0	3	4	3	1	0	0	0	7	8
AA	52	28	24	0	0	0	0	0	0	0	0	0	0	0	0	23	18	9	2	0	0	0	4	2	20	0	0	0	0	31	16
NL	126	62	64	2	0	0	0	0	0	0	0	0	0	0	0	56	40	22	3	0	6	2	10	13	21	3	0	0	0	64	45
YR	178	90	88	2	0	0	0	0	0	0	0	0	0	0	0	79	58	31	5	0	6	2	14	15	41	3	0	0	0	95	61

AA		*NL*	
8	Doc Landis	14	Jim McCormick
6	Sam Weaver	11	Lee Richmond
4	Harry McCormick	10	Stump Wiedman
4	Bill Sweeney	8	George Derby
3	Multiple Players Tied	8	Jim Galvin

1883

				Consec			1-Inn			One-Game						Men-On-Base				Pitchers					Totals					Batters	
Tm	Tot	H	A	2	3	4	3	4	5	5	6	7	8	9	10	0	1	2	3	PH	LO	XN	IP	P	1	10	20	30	40	RHB	LHB
AA																															
BAL	12	6	6	0	0	0	0	0	0	0	0	0	0	0	0	4	4	4	0	0	1	0	0	0	6	0	0	0	0	8	3
CIN	17	14	3	0	0	0	0	0	0	0	0	0	0	0	0	7	8	2	0	0	1	0	1	2	1	1	0	0	0	13	2
COL	16	8	8	0	0	0	0	0	0	0	0	0	0	0	0	5	7	4	0	0	1	0	0	0	3	0	0	0	0	11	1
LOU	7	0	7	0	0	0	0	0	0	0	0	0	0	0	0	3	3	1	0	0	1	0	0	0	2	0	0	0	0	6	1
NY	12	4	8	0	0	0	0	0	0	0	0	0	0	0	0	7	2	2	0	0	0	1	1	2	2	0	0	0	0	9	3
PHI	22	8	14	0	0	0	0	0	0	0	0	0	0	0	0	10	7	5	0	0	2	0	2	3	3	1	0	0	0	13	7
PIT	21	3	18	0	0	0	0	0	0	0	0	0	0	0	0	6	13	2	0	0	1	0	6	0	4	0	0	0	0	17	3
STL	7	3	4	0	0	0	0	0	0	0	0	0	0	0	0	4	3	0	0	0	1	0	0	0	3	0	0	0	0	4	2
NL																															
BOS	11	3	8	0	0	0	0	0	0	0	0	0	0	0	0	9	2	0	0	0	0	0	3	4	2	0	0	0	0	4	7
BUF	12	4	8	0	0	0	0	0	0	0	0	0	0	0	0	4	4	4	0	0	2	0	0	0	2	0	0	0	0	8	4
CHI	21	6	15	0	0	0	0	0	0	0	0	0	0	0	0	10	7	2	0	0	2	0	1	3	1	1	0	0	0	18	3
CLE	7	4	3	0	0	0	0	0	0	0	0	0	0	0	0	4	1	2	0	0	1	0	0	0	3	0	0	0	0	5	2
DET	22	9	13	0	0	0	0	0	0	0	0	0	0	0	0	7	8	6	1	0	1	1	2	1	5	0	0	0	0	17	4
NY	19	15	4	1	0	0	1	0	0	0	0	0	0	0	0	13	4	2	0	0	1	0	0	2	2	1	0	0	0	13	5
PHI	20	1	19	0	0	0	0	0	0	0	0	0	0	0	0	7	7	4	0	0	0	0	3	3	2	1	0	0	0	11	9
PRO	12	5	7	0	0	0	0	0	0	0	0	0	0	0	0	7	4	1	0	0	0	0	0	1	3	0	0	0	0	8	4
AA	114	46	68	0	0	0	0	0	0	0	0	0	0	0	0	46	47	20	0	0	8	1	10	7	24	2	0	0	0	81	22
NL	124	47	77	1	0	0	1	0	0	0	0	0	0	0	0	61	37	21	1	0	7	1	9	14	20	3	0	0	0	84	38
YR	238	93	145	1	0	0	1	0	0	0	0	0	0	0	0	107	84	41	1	0	15	2	19	21	44	5	0	0	0	165	60

AA		*NL*	
16	Will White	17	John Coleman
11	Bobby Mathews	14	Fred Goldsmith
10	Jack Neagle	11	Mickey Welch
8	Frank Mountain	9	Jim Galvin
7	Multiple Players Tied	8	Multiple Players Tied

1884

				Consec			1-Inn			One-Game						Men-On-Base				Pitchers					Totals					Batters	
Tm	Tot	H	A	2	3	4	3	4	5	5	6	7	8	9	10	0	1	2	3	PH	LO	XN	IP	P	1	10	20	30	40	RHB	LHB
AA																															
BAL	16	8	8	0	0	0	0	0	0	0	0	0	0	0	0	7	6	3	0	0	0	0	0	1	3	0	0	0	0	4	8
BRO	20	8	12	0	0	0	0	0	0	0	0	0	0	0	0	10	7	3	0	0	0	0	3	3	2	1	0	0	0	14	4
CIN	27	20	7	0	0	0	0	0	0	0	0	0	0	0	0	14	12	1	0	0	3	0	2	1	2	1	0	0	0	19	7
COL	22	14	8	0	0	0	0	0	0	0	0	0	0	0	0	10	7	5	0	0	1	0	0	0	5	0	0	0	0	13	7
IND	30	15	15	0	0	0	0	0	0	0	0	0	0	0	0	8	12	10	0	0	1	0	0	2	4	0	1	0	0	20	4
LOU	9	2	7	0	0	0	0	0	0	0	0	0	0	0	0	4	4	1	0	0	1	0	0	2	3	0	0	0	0	8	1

				Consec			1-Inn			One-Game						Men-On-Base				Pitchers					Totals					Batters	
Tm	Tot	H	A	2	3	4	3	4	5	5	6	7	8	9	10	0	1	2	3	PH	LO	XN	IP	P	1	10	20	30	40	RHB	LHB
NY	15	4	11	0	0	0	0	0	0	0	0	0	0	0	0	8	3	4	0	0	0	0	1	3	1	1	0	0	0	11	4
PHI	16	4	12	0	0	0	0	0	0	0	0	0	0	0	0	7	5	4	0	0	0	0	2	0	2	1	0	0	0	14	2
PIT	25	4	21	0	0	0	0	0	0	0	0	0	0	0	0	7	11	7	0	0	0	0	2	2	4	1	0	0	0	17	6
RIC	14	8	6	0	0	0	0	0	0	0	0	0	0	0	0	3	9	2	0	0	0	0	1	3	3	0	0	0	0	7	6
STL	16	10	6	0	0	0	0	0	0	0	0	0	0	0	0	5	8	3	0	0	0	0	1	1	5	0	0	0	0	13	2
TOL	12	2	10	0	0	0	0	0	0	0	0	0	0	0	0	6	2	4	0	0	1	0	1	1	3	0	0	0	0	10	0
WAS	21	4	17	0	0	0	0	0	0	0	0	0	0	0	0	5	12	4	0	0	1	0	2	2	3	0	0	0	0	16	2
NL																															
BOS	30	4	26	1	0	0	0	0	0	1	0	0	0	0	0	10	10	8	1	0	1	1	1	0	2	2	0	0	0	18	12
BUF	46	20	26	2	0	0	0	0	0	1	0	0	0	0	0	16	13	9	1	0	0	0	4	4	2	0	2	0	0	34	11
CHI	83	66	17	4	0	0	0	0	0	1	1	0	0	0	0	38	25	11	2	0	5	2	4	4	8	3	0	1	0	46	34
CLE	35	6	29	1	0	0	0	0	0	0	0	0	0	0	0	13	12	3	0	0	1	0	2	1	4	1	0	0	0	23	12
DET	36	16	20	0	0	0	0	0	0	0	0	0	0	0	0	18	4	10	0	0	2	0	5	1	4	1	0	0	0	21	12
NY	28	4	24	1	0	0	0	0	0	0	0	0	0	0	0	14	8	5	0	0	1	0	1	1	3	1	0	0	0	24	3
PHI	37	0	37	0	0	0	0	0	0	1	0	0	0	0	0	13	14	9	1	0	0	0	3	3	6	1	0	0	0	26	8
PRO	26	6	20	0	0	0	0	0	0	0	0	0	0	0	0	15	8	1	0	0	1	0	0	1	2	1	0	0	0	21	5
UA																															
ALT	3	0	3	1	0	0	0	0	0	0	0	0	0	0	0	2	0	1	0	0	0	0	0	0	1	0	0	0	0	3	0
BAL	24	16	8	1	0	0	0	0	0	0	0	0	0	0	0	17	5	2	0	0	1	0	2	4	7	1	0	0	0	18	1
BOS	17	5	12	0	0	0	0	0	0	0	0	0	0	0	0	5	9	3	0	0	0	0	1	1	4	1	0	0	0	9	4
CHI	11	2	9	0	0	0	0	0	0	0	0	0	0	0	0	6	3	2	0	0	0	0	1	0	1	1	0	0	0	5	2
CIN	17	12	5	0	0	0	0	0	0	0	0	0	0	0	0	10	7	0	0	0	1	0	3	0	3	0	0	0	0	13	1
KC	14	6	8	0	0	0	0	0	0	0	0	0	0	0	0	4	4	6	0	0	0	0	0	0	8	0	0	0	0	9	3
MIL	1	1	0	0	0	0	0	0	0	0	0	0	0	0	0	0	1	0	0	0	0	0	0	0	1	0	0	0	0	1	0
PHI	7	1	6	0	0	0	0	0	0	0	0	0	0	0	0	1	6	0	0	0	0	0	0	0	3	0	0	0	0	5	1
PIT	1	1	0	0	0	0	0	0	0	0	0	0	0	0	0	0	1	0	0	0	0	0	0	0	1	0	0	0	0	0	1
STL	9	4	5	0	0	0	0	0	0	0	0	0	0	0	0	3	5	1	0	0	0	0	2	2	5	0	0	0	0	5	3
STP	1	0	1	0	0	0	0	0	0	0	0	0	0	0	0	0	1	0	0	0	0	0	0	0	1	0	0	0	0	1	0
WAS	16	10	6	0	0	0	0	0	0	0	0	0	0	0	0	5	8	3	0	0	0	0	1	2	5	0	0	0	0	12	3
WIL	4	4	0	0	0	0	0	0	0	0	0	0	0	0	0	1	2	1	0	0	0	0	0	1	2	0	0	0	0	3	0
AA	243	103	140	0	0	0	0	0	0	0	0	0	0	0	0	94	98	51	0	0	8	0	15	21	40	5	1	0	0	166	53
NL	321	122	199	9	0	0	0	0	0	4	1	0	0	0	0	137	94	56	5	0	11	3	20	15	31	10	2	1	0	213	97
UA	125	62	63	2	0	0	0	0	0	0	0	0	0	0	0	54	52	19	0	0	2	0	10	10	42	3	0	0	0	84	19
YR	689	287	402	11	0	0	0	0	0	4	1	0	0	0	0	285	244	126	5	0	21	3	45	46	113	18	3	1	0	463	169

AA

20 Larry McKeon
16 Will White
15 Fleury Sullivan
11 Bob Barr
10 Multiple Players Tied

NL

35 Larry Corcoran
23 Jim Galvin
21 Billy Serad
18 Charley Radbourn
16 Jim McCormick

UA

13 Bill Sweeney
11 Hugh Daily
10 Walter Burke
7 George Bradley
7 Dick Burns

1885

				Consec			1-Inn			One-Game						Men-On-Base				Pitchers					Totals					Batters	
Tm	Tot	H	A	2	3	4	3	4	5	5	6	7	8	9	10	0	1	2	3	PH	LO	XN	IP	P	1	10	20	30	40	RHB	LHB
AA																															
BAL	12	2	10	0	0	0	0	0	0	0	0	0	0	0	0	3	6	3	0	0	0	0	1	1	4	0	0	0	0	11	0
BRO	27	14	13	1	0	0	0	0	0	0	0	0	0	0	0	14	11	1	1	0	0	0	3	1	2	1	0	0	0	24	2
CIN	24	17	7	0	0	0	0	0	0	0	0	0	0	0	0	11	8	5	0	0	0	0	4	2	7	0	0	0	0	16	5
LOU	13	4	9	0	0	0	0	0	0	0	0	0	0	0	0	3	9	1	0	0	0	0	2	0	4	0	0	0	0	11	1
NY	36	5	31	1	0	0	0	0	0	0	0	0	0	0	0	16	11	9	0	0	1	0	6	2	6	1	0	0	0	29	3
PHI	11	9	2	0	0	0	0	0	0	0	0	0	0	0	0	6	5	0	0	0	0	0	4	1	6	0	0	0	0	8	0
PIT	14	3	11	0	0	0	0	0	0	0	0	0	0	0	0	5	4	5	0	0	1	0	4	0	6	0	0	0	0	12	2
STL	12	5	7	0	0	0	0	0	0	0	0	0	0	0	0	6	6	0	0	0	0	0	2	1	3	0	0	0	0	10	1
NL																															
BOS	26	5	21	0	0	0	0	0	0	0	0	0	0	0	0	13	9	4	0	0	2	0	0	2	1	2	0	0	0	16	6
BUF	31	13	18	0	0	0	0	0	0	0	0	0	0	0	0	13	13	5	0	0	0	0	1	1	3	1	0	0	0	15	16
CHI	37	27	10	1	0	0	0	0	0	0	0	0	0	0	0	21	13	3	0	0	3	0	1	3	4	0	1	0	0	26	9
DET	18	8	10	0	0	0	0	0	0	0	0	0	0	0	0	11	5	2	0	0	0	0	1	1	4	0	0	0	0	10	6
NY	11	6	5	1	0	0	0	0	0	0	0	0	0	0	0	6	4	1	0	0	2	1	0	0	3	0	0	0	0	7	4
PHI	18	7	11	0	0	0	0	0	0	0	0	0	0	0	0	12	5	1	0	0	1	0	0	3	2	1	0	0	0	14	4
PRO	18	1	17	0	0	0	0	0	0	0	0	0	0	0	0	7	6	5	0	0	1	1	1	1	7	0	0	0	0	13	4

				Consec			1-Inn			One-Game						Men-On-Base				Pitchers					Totals					Batters	
Tm	Tot	H	A	2	3	4	3	4	5	5	6	7	8	9	10	0	1	2	3	PH	LO	XN	IP	P	1	10	20	30	40	RHB	LHB
STL	15	4	11	0	0	0	0	0	0	0	0	0	0	0	0	8	4	2	1	0	1	0	1	0	4	0	0	0	0	6	7
AA	149	59	90	2	0	0	0	0	0	0	0	0	0	0	0	64	60	24	1	0	2	0	26	8	38	2	0	0	0	121	14
NL	174	71	103	2	0	0	0	0	0	0	0	0	0	0	0	91	59	23	1	0	10	2	5	11	28	4	1	0	0	107	56
YR	323	130	193	4	0	0	0	0	0	0	0	0	0	0	0	155	119	47	2	0	12	2	31	19	66	6	1	0	0	228	70

AA

17 Jack Lynch
11 Henry Porter
9 Adonis Terry
9 Will White
8 Dave Foutz

NL

21 John Clarkson
14 Jim Whitney
12 Ed Daily
10 Charlie Buffinton
10 Pete Conway

1886

				Consec			1-Inn			One-Game						Men-On-Base				Pitchers					Totals					Batters	
Tm	Tot	H	A	2	3	4	3	4	5	5	6	7	8	9	10	0	1	2	3	PH	LO	XN	IP	P	1	10	20	30	40	RHB	LHB
AA																															
BAL	25	2	23	0	0	0	0	0	0	0	0	0	0	0	0	9	6	9	1	0	0	0	8	4	4	1	0	0	0	21	2
BRO	17	7	10	0	0	0	0	0	0	0	0	0	0	0	0	3	7	4	3	0	0	0	2	3	4	0	0	0	0	14	3
CIN	25	16	9	0	0	0	0	0	0	0	0	0	0	0	0	11	9	4	1	0	1	1	5	2	5	1	0	0	0	22	2
LOU	16	9	7	0	0	0	0	0	0	0	0	0	0	0	0	11	3	1	1	0	0	0	1	0	4	0	0	0	0	12	4
NY	23	9	14	1	0	0	0	0	0	0	0	0	0	0	0	12	5	6	0	0	0	0	4	0	2	1	0	0	0	17	5
PHI	35	11	24	0	0	0	0	0	0	0	0	0	0	0	0	16	12	7	0	0	1	1	10	2	7	1	0	0	0	29	3
PIT	10	3	7	0	0	0	0	0	0	0	0	0	0	0	0	5	2	3	0	0	0	0	1	0	4	0	0	0	0	8	1
STL	13	7	6	0	0	0	0	0	0	0	0	0	0	0	0	3	8	2	0	0	0	0	1	1	4	0	0	0	0	8	4
NL																															
BOS	33	8	25	0	0	0	0	0	0	0	0	0	0	0	0	16	12	5	0	0	0	0	1	2	1	2	0	0	0	19	14
CHI	49	34	15	0	0	0	0	0	0	0	0	0	0	0	0	25	17	5	2	0	1	0	5	2	2	2	0	0	0	29	15
DET	20	10	10	0	0	0	0	0	0	0	0	0	0	0	0	8	7	5	0	0	0	0	2	2	4	1	0	0	0	16	3
KC	27	4	23	1	0	0	0	0	0	0	0	0	0	0	0	12	13	2	0	0	0	0	2	3	3	1	0	0	0	17	8
NY	23	4	19	0	0	0	0	0	0	0	0	0	0	0	0	7	10	5	1	0	1	0	1	0	2	1	0	0	0	19	2
PHI	29	12	17	0	0	0	0	0	0	0	0	0	0	0	0	15	11	3	0	0	0	0	2	2	4	1	0	0	0	20	6
STL	34	10	24	1	0	0	1	0	0	0	0	1	0	0	0	12	15	5	2	0	3	0	3	3	8	0	0	0	0	18	13
WAS	34	12	22	1	0	0	0	0	0	0	0	0	0	0	0	17	11	5	1	0	0	0	4	4	8	1	0	0	0	22	7
AA	164	64	100	1	0	0	0	0	0	0	0	0	0	0	0	70	52	36	6	0	2	2	32	12	34	4	0	0	0	131	24
NL	249	94	155	3	0	0	1	0	0	0	0	1	0	0	0	112	96	35	6	0	5	0	20	18	32	9	0	0	0	160	68
YR	413	158	255	4	0	0	0	0	0	0	0	1	0	0	0	182	148	71	12	0	7	2	52	30	66	13	0	0	0	291	92

AA

11 Al Atkinson
11 Tony Mullane
10 Matt Kilroy
10 Jack Lynch
8 Multiple Players Tied

NL

19 John Clarkson
18 Jim McCormick
18 Charley Radbourn
13 Mickey Welch
12 Dupee Shaw

1887

				Consec			1-Inn			One-Game						Men-On-Base				Pitchers					Totals					Batters	
Tm	Tot	H	A	2	3	4	3	4	5	5	6	7	8	9	10	0	1	2	3	PH	LO	XN	IP	P	1	10	20	30	40	RHB	LHB
AA																															
BAL	16	6	10	0	0	0	0	0	0	0	0	0	0	0	0	10	6	0	0	0	0	0	2	2	2	0	0	0	0	14	1
BRO	27	14	13	0	0	0	0	0	0	0	0	0	0	0	0	9	12	6	0	0	1	1	5	0	4	1	0	0	0	22	5
CIN	28	16	12	0	0	0	0	0	0	0	0	0	0	0	0	8	16	4	0	0	0	0	2	0	4	1	0	0	0	23	5
CLE	34	7	27	0	0	0	0	0	0	0	0	0	0	0	0	14	9	9	2	0	2	0	7	6	6	1	0	0	0	21	11
LOU	31	15	16	1	0	0	0	0	0	0	0	0	0	0	0	8	16	6	0	0	0	0	3	3	5	0	0	0	0	24	6
NY	39	10	29	0	0	0	0	0	0	0	0	0	0	0	0	14	12	12	1	0	0	0	9	3	8	1	0	0	0	27	7
PHI	29	11	18	0	0	0	0	0	0	0	0	0	0	0	0	7	11	11	0	0	0	0	1	2	7	1	0	0	0	22	5
STL	19	16	3	0	0	0	0	0	0	0	0	0	0	0	0	4	9	6	0	0	1	0	1	3	4	0	0	0	0	14	5
NL																															
BOS	53	17	36	2	0	0	1	0	0	1	0	0	0	0	0	21	23	7	2	0	3	0	3	2	3	1	1	0	0	30	23
CHI	55	44	11	1	0	0	0	0	0	1	0	0	0	0	0	27	19	8	1	0	2	1	0	4	5	1	1	0	0	27	25
DET	52	20	32	1	0	0	0	0	0	0	0	0	0	0	0	32	16	4	0	0	0	0	3	6	6	0	1	0	0	35	16
IND	60	28	32	0	0	0	0	0	0	0	0	0	0	0	0	25	24	11	0	0	1	0	3	8	9	1	1	0	0	39	20
NY	27	8	19	2	0	0	0	0	0	0	0	0	0	0	0	12	7	8	0	0	1	1	2	1	6	1	0	0	0	24	3
PHI	48	22	26	1	0	0	0	0	0	0	0	0	0	0	0	23	20	4	1	0	0	0	2	3	2	3	0	0	0	22	25
PIT	39	4	35	0	0	0	0	0	0	0	0	0	0	0	0	21	13	3	2	0	2	0	1	5	1	3	0	0	0	29	7

				Consec			1-Inn			One-Game						Men-On-Base				Pitchers					Totals					Batters	
Tm	Tot	H	A	2	3	4	3	4	5	5	6	7	8	9	10	0	1	2	3	PH	LO	XN	IP	P	1	10	20	30	40	RHB	LHB
WAS	47	19	28	0	0	0	0	0	0	0	0	0	0	0	0	21	18	8	0	0	0	0	1	6	3	2	0	0	0	34	12
AA	223	95	128	1	0	0	0	0	0	0	0	0	0	0	0	74	91	54	3	0	4	1	30	19	40	5	0	0	0	167	45
NL	381	162	219	7	0	0	1	0	0	2	0	0	0	0	0	182	140	53	6	0	9	2	15	35	35	12	4	0	0	240	131
YR	604	257	347	8	0	0	0	0	0	2	0	0	0	0	0	256	231	107	9	0	13	3	45	54	75	17	4	0	0	407	176

AA

13 Mike Morrison
12 Gus Weyhing
11 Al Mays
11 Tony Mullane
10 Adonis Terry

NL

24 Pretzels Getzien
24 Egyptian Healy
22 Mark Baldwin
20 Kid Madden
19 Multiple Players Tied

1888

AA

Tm	Tot	H	A	2	3	4	3	4	5	5	6	7	8	9	10	0	1	2	3	PH	LO	XN	IP	P	1	10	20	30	40	RHB	LHB
BAL	23	11	12	0	0	0	0	0	0	0	0	0	0	0	0	11	6	6	0	0	0	1	3	1	6	0	0	0	0	22	0
BRO	15	10	5	0	0	0	0	0	0	0	0	0	0	0	0	9	3	3	0	0	1	0	4	2	5	0	0	0	0	12	2
CIN	19	5	14	1	0	0	0	0	0	0	0	0	0	0	0	8	6	4	1	0	0	0	2	0	5	0	0	0	0	17	2
CLE	38	12	26	1	0	0	0	0	0	0	0	0	0	0	0	15	17	6	0	0	0	0	6	6	7	1	0	0	0	31	5
KC	32	10	22	0	0	0	1	0	0	1	0	0	0	0	0	12	13	7	0	0	1	0	8	2	6	1	0	0	0	25	6
LOU	28	4	24	1	0	0	0	0	0	0	0	0	0	0	0	12	8	8	0	0	0	0	9	3	5	1	0	0	0	24	2
PHI	14	8	6	0	0	0	0	0	0	0	0	0	0	0	0	6	5	3	0	0	1	0	2	0	3	0	0	0	0	13	1
STL	19	13	6	0	0	0	0	0	0	0	0	0	0	0	0	6	12	1	0	0	0	0	2	3	5	0	0	0	0	14	3

NL

Tm	Tot	H	A	2	3	4	3	4	5	5	6	7	8	9	10	0	1	2	3	PH	LO	XN	IP	P	1	10	20	30	40	RHB	LHB
BOS	36	16	20	0	0	0	0	0	0	0	0	0	0	0	0	20	12	4	0	0	2	3	3	2	4	1	0	0	0	23	11
CHI	63	44	19	1	0	0	0	0	0	1	0	0	0	0	0	33	22	7	1	0	2	0	10	4	6	2	1	0	0	37	24
DET	44	18	26	2	0	0	0	0	0	1	0	0	0	0	0	22	17	5	0	0	0	0	10	2	4	2	0	0	0	37	7
IND	64	40	24	3	0	0	1	0	0	0	0	1	0	0	0	30	25	9	0	0	3	0	6	5	3	3	1	0	0	36	28
NY	27	9	18	0	0	0	0	0	0	0	0	0	0	0	0	14	9	3	1	0	2	0	4	2	5	1	0	0	0	19	5
PHI	26	12	14	0	0	0	0	0	0	0	0	0	0	0	0	14	8	3	1	0	1	1	3	1	3	1	0	0	0	14	12
PIT	23	1	22	1	0	0	0	0	0	0	0	0	0	0	0	11	9	3	0	0	0	0	12	0	4	0	0	0	0	15	7
WAS	50	25	25	1	0	0	0	0	0	0	0	0	0	0	0	29	18	3	0	0	3	0	7	5	7	1	0	0	0	41	8
AA	188	73	115	3	0	0	1	0	0	1	0	0	0	0	0	79	70	38	1	0	3	1	36	17	42	3	0	0	0	158	21
NL	333	165	168	8	0	0	1	0	0	2	0	1	0	0	0	173	120	37	3	0	13	4	55	21	36	11	2	0	0	222	102
YR	521	238	283	11	0	0	0	0	0	3	0	1	0	0	0	252	190	75	4	0	16	5	91	38	78	14	2	0	0	380	123

AA

16 Henry Porter
14 Jersey Bakely
10 Toad Ramsey
9 Billy Crowell
9 Tony Mullane

NL

23 Lev Shreve
20 Gus Krock
19 Hank O'Day
17 John Clarkson
15 George Van Haltren

1889

AA

Tm	Tot	H	A	2	3	4	3	4	5	5	6	7	8	9	10	0	1	2	3	PH	LO	XN	IP	P	1	10	20	30	40	RHB	LHB
BAL	27	4	23	0	0	0	0	0	0	0	0	0	0	0	0	9	9	9	0	0	2	0	1	1	2	1	0	0	0	24	1
BRO	33	19	14	0	0	0	0	0	0	0	0	0	0	0	0	20	8	5	0	0	1	0	1	1	4	1	0	0	0	25	6
CIN	35	19	16	0	0	0	0	0	0	0	0	0	0	0	0	10	11	10	4	0	1	0	5	6	4	1	0	0	0	25	8
COL	33	11	22	0	0	0	0	0	0	0	0	0	0	0	0	15	10	7	1	0	1	0	2	7	4	1	0	0	0	24	8
KC	51	17	34	2	0	0	0	0	0	0	0	0	0	0	0	17	21	12	1	0	1	0	3	5	5	1	1	0	0	42	7
LOU	43	18	25	1	0	0	0	0	0	0	0	0	0	0	0	14	16	12	1	0	1	0	4	1	6	1	0	0	0	31	11
PHI	35	13	22	0	0	0	0	0	0	0	0	0	0	0	0	15	10	10	0	0	1	0	9	1	6	1	0	0	0	22	11
STL	39	28	11	1	0	0	0	0	0	0	0	0	0	0	0	16	17	4	2	0	2	1	2	1	2	2	0	0	0	24	14

NL

Tm	Tot	H	A	2	3	4	3	4	5	5	6	7	8	9	10	0	1	2	3	PH	LO	XN	IP	P	1	10	20	30	40	RHB	LHB
BOS	41	14	27	0	0	0	0	0	0	0	0	0	0	0	0	20	15	6	0	0	2	0	5	1	3	2	0	0	0	30	8
CHI	71	52	19	3	0	0	1	0	0	0	0	0	0	0	0	34	26	9	2	0	1	6	4	4	1	5	0	0	0	39	27
CLE	36	13	23	1	0	0	0	0	0	0	0	0	0	0	0	16	12	6	2	0	1	3	3	5	3	1	0	0	0	23	13
IND	73	54	19	1	0	0	0	0	0	0	0	0	0	0	0	39	23	11	0	0	4	2	4	6	6	2	1	0	0	45	28
NY	38	15	23	0	0	0	0	0	0	0	0	0	0	0	0	17	15	6	0	0	3	1	6	1	4	2	0	0	0	25	11
PHI	33	12	21	0	0	0	0	0	0	0	0	0	0	0	0	14	14	5	0	0	0	2	3	1	4	1	0	0	0	17	15
PIT	42	2	40	3	0	0	0	0	0	0	0	0	0	0	0	20	12	8	2	0	1	0	1	1	6	2	0	0	0	24	14

				Consec			1-Inn			One-Game						Men-On-Base				Pitchers					Totals					Batters	
Tm	Tot	H	A	2	3	4	3	4	5	5	6	7	8	9	10	0	1	2	3	PH	LO	XN	IP	P	1	10	20	30	40	RHB	LHB
WAS	37	10	27	0	0	0	0	0	0	0	0	0	0	0	0	15	12	5	5	0	2	0	7	3	6	1	0	0	0	23	12
AA	296	129	167	4	0	0	0	0	0	0	0	0	0	0	0	116	102	69	9	0	10	1	27	23	33	9	1	0	0	217	66
NL	371	172	199	8	0	0	1	0	0	0	0	0	0	0	0	175	129	56	11	0	14	14	33	22	33	16	1	0	0	226	128
YR	667	301	366	12	0	0	0	0	0	0	0	0	0	0	0	291	231	125	20	0	24	15	60	45	66	25	2	0	0	443	194

AA

21 Parke Swartzel
18 Elton Chamberlin
16 Bob Caruthers
15 Silver King
15 Gus Weyhing

NL

27 Pretzels Getzien
19 Jim Galvin
16 John Clarkson
16 Ad Gumbert
16 John Tener

1890

AA

Tm	Tot	H	A	Consec 2	3	4	1-Inn 3	4	5	One-Game 5	6	7	8	9	10	Men-On-Base 0	1	2	3	PH	LO	XN	IP	P	Totals 1	10	20	30	40	RHB	LHB
BAL	3	0	3	0	0	0	0	0	0	0	0	0	0	0	0	3	0	0	0	0	1	0	0	0	2	0	0	0	0	2	0
BRO	21	3	18	0	0	0	0	0	0	0	0	0	0	0	0	9	6	5	1	0	1	0	1	3	7	0	0	0	0	11	5
COL	20	8	12	0	0	0	0	0	0	0	0	0	0	0	0	10	8	1	1	0	1	0	1	3	5	0	0	0	0	13	4
LOU	18	8	10	0	0	0	0	0	0	0	0	0	0	0	0	7	8	2	1	0	0	1	0	0	6	0	0	0	0	7	9
PHI	17	6	11	0	0	0	0	0	0	0	0	0	0	0	0	7	2	5	3	0	0	0	0	0	7	0	0	0	0	13	2
ROC	19	4	15	0	0	0	0	0	0	0	0	0	0	0	0	5	9	5	0	0	0	0	1	3	4	0	0	0	0	12	4
STL	38	31	7	0	0	0	0	0	0	0	0	0	0	0	0	16	13	6	3	0	2	1	1	1	5	2	0	0	0	20	7
SYR	28	4	24	0	0	0	0	0	0	0	0	0	0	0	0	8	15	4	1	0	2	0	0	0	8	0	0	0	0	20	6
TOL	23	11	12	1	0	0	0	0	0	0	0	0	0	0	0	10	9	3	1	0	0	1	1	6	2	1	0	0	0	15	2

NL

Tm	Tot	H	A	Consec 2	3	4	1-Inn 3	4	5	One-Game 5	6	7	8	9	10	Men-On-Base 0	1	2	3	PH	LO	XN	IP	P	Totals 1	10	20	30	40	RHB	LHB
BOS	27	11	16	0	0	0	0	0	0	0	0	0	0	0	0	18	6	3	0	0	1	1	2	3	2	1	0	0	0	11	13
BRO	27	9	18	0	0	0	0	0	0	0	0	0	0	0	0	12	8	5	2	0	1	0	1	3	3	1	0	0	0	11	12
CHI	41	29	12	0	0	0	0	0	0	0	0	0	0	0	0	17	16	8	0	0	1	0	5	3	4	0	1	0	0	21	16
CIN	41	25	16	1	0	0	0	0	0	0	0	0	0	0	0	19	16	5	1	0	2	0	4	3	5	1	0	0	0	20	16
CLE	33	8	25	0	0	0	0	0	0	0	0	0	0	0	0	16	8	9	0	0	2	1	5	3	7	1	0	0	0	18	9
NY	14	2	12	0	0	0	0	0	0	0	0	0	0	0	0	5	8	1	0	0	0	0	2	0	4	0	0	0	0	8	4
PHI	22	10	12	0	0	0	0	0	0	0	0	0	0	0	0	9	7	4	2	0	1	1	5	1	4	0	0	0	0	10	8
PIT	52	2	50	2	0	0	0	0	0	0	0	0	0	0	0	13	22	11	6	0	0	0	10	0	13	1	0	0	0	32	16

PL

Tm	Tot	H	A	Consec 2	3	4	1-Inn 3	4	5	One-Game 5	6	7	8	9	10	Men-On-Base 0	1	2	3	PH	LO	XN	IP	P	Totals 1	10	20	30	40	RHB	LHB
BOS	49	38	11	0	0	0	0	0	0	0	0	0	0	0	0	23	15	10	1	0	1	1	3	2	3	2	0	0	0	29	14
BRO	26	7	19	0	0	0	0	0	0	0	0	0	0	0	0	11	13	2	0	0	0	0	3	0	4	1	0	0	0	18	7
BUF	67	20	47	1	0	0	0	0	0	0	0	0	0	0	0	26	18	23	0	0	4	0	11	5	10	2	0	0	0	46	18
CHI	27	12	15	2	0	0	0	0	0	0	0	0	0	0	0	10	9	6	2	0	0	0	4	1	3	1	0	0	0	18	9
CLE	45	15	30	0	0	0	0	0	0	0	0	0	0	0	0	16	17	12	0	0	0	0	5	3	5	2	0	0	0	26	17
NY	37	21	16	1	0	0	0	0	0	0	0	0	0	0	0	15	15	5	2	0	0	0	2	3	4	2	0	0	0	26	10
PHI	33	15	18	0	0	0	0	0	0	0	0	0	0	0	0	17	8	8	0	0	2	0	4	2	2	2	0	0	0	19	12
PIT	32	15	17	0	1	0	1	0	0	0	0	0	0	0	0	10	14	7	1	0	0	1	6	0	4	1	0	0	0	19	12
AA	187	75	112	1	0	0	0	0	0	0	0	0	0	0	0	75	70	31	11	0	7	3	5	16	46	3	0	0	0	113	39
NL	257	96	161	3	0	0	0	0	0	0	0	0	0	0	0	109	91	46	11	0	8	3	34	16	42	5	1	0	0	131	94
PL	316	143	173	4	1	0	1	0	0	0	0	0	0	0	0	128	109	73	6	0	7	2	38	16	35	13	0	0	0	201	99
YR	760	314	446	8	1	0	0	0	0	0	0	0	0	0	0	312	270	150	28	0	22	8	77	48	123	21	1	0	0	445	232

AA

14 Jack Stivetts
13 Fred Smith
10 Toad Ramsey
9 John Keefe
8 Multiple Players Tied

NL

20 Bill Hutchison
14 John Clarkson
14 Tom Lovett
12 Lee Viau
11 Multiple Players Tied

PL

18 Ad Gumbert
15 Henry Gruber
15 George Haddock
14 Matt Kilroy
13 Multiple Players Tied

1891

AA

Tm	Tot	H	A	Consec 2	3	4	1-Inn 3	4	5	One-Game 5	6	7	8	9	10	Men-On-Base 0	1	2	3	PH	LO	XN	IP	P	Totals 1	10	20	30	40	RHB	LHB
BAL	33	8	25	2	0	0	0	0	0	0	0	0	0	0	0	14	11	5	3	0	1	0	7	1	5	1	0	0	0	19	11
BOS	42	22	20	1	0	0	0	0	0	0	0	0	0	0	0	23	13	6	0	0	3	0	1	1	6	1	0	0	0	34	3
CIN	20	9	11	0	0	0	0	0	0	0	0	0	0	0	0	9	5	4	2	0	0	0	2	2	5	1	0	0	0	14	4
COL	29	8	21	0	0	0	0	0	0	0	0	0	0	0	0	9	11	7	2	0	1	0	2	4	8	0	0	0	0	20	8
LOU	32	6	26	1	0	0	0	0	0	0	0	0	0	0	0	14	13	4	1	0	1	0	8	3	6	1	0	0	0	24	8

				Consec			1-Inn			One-Game						Men-On-Base				Pitchers					Totals					Batters	
Tm	Tot	H	A	2	3	4	3	4	5	5	6	7	8	9	10	0	1	2	3	PH	LO	XN	IP	P	1	10	20	30	40	RHB	LHB
MIL	6	5	1	0	0	0	0	0	0	0	0	0	0	0	0	2	3	1	0	0	0	0	2	2	4	0	0	0	0	4	1
PHI	35	9	26	0	0	0	0	0	0	0	0	0	0	0	0	10	18	6	1	0	0	1	8	5	4	2	0	0	0	24	9
STL	50	30	20	1	0	0	0	0	0	0	0	0	0	0	0	24	14	11	1	0	1	0	10	4	6	2	0	0	0	29	17
WAS	44	18	26	0	0	0	0	0	0	0	0	0	0	0	0	17	14	10	1	0	0	0	8	3	7	1	0	0	0	31	9
NL																															
BOS	51	33	18	2	0	0	0	0	0	0	0	0	0	0	0	27	15	8	1	0	1	0	2	3	2	3	0	0	0	30	18
BRO	40	19	21	1	0	0	0	0	0	0	0	0	0	0	0	18	15	7	0	0	2	2	4	1	4	2	0	0	0	25	13
CHI	53	30	23	2	0	0	1	0	0	0	0	0	0	0	0	22	19	11	1	0	0	0	9	0	3	1	1	0	0	34	16
CIN	40	17	23	2	0	0	0	0	0	0	0	0	0	0	0	15	16	9	0	0	0	2	5	2	4	2	0	0	0	26	12
CLE	24	6	18	0	0	0	0	0	0	0	0	0	0	0	0	10	8	5	1	0	0	0	4	2	7	1	0	0	0	14	10
NY	26	14	12	0	0	0	0	0	0	0	0	0	0	0	0	13	10	3	0	0	1	0	6	0	9	0	0	0	0	16	10
PHI	30	9	21	0	0	0	0	0	0	0	0	0	0	0	0	12	13	5	0	0	0	0	4	0	8	1	0	0	0	16	14
PIT	30	9	21	0	0	0	0	0	0	0	0	0	0	0	0	20	6	3	1	0	0	0	5	2	3	1	0	0	0	18	11
AA	291	115	176	5	0	0	0	0	0	0	0	0	0	0	0	122	102	54	11	0	7	1	48	25	51	9	0	0	0	199	70
NL	294	137	157	7	0	0	1	0	0	0	0	0	0	0	0	137	102	51	4	0	4	4	39	10	40	11	1	0	0	179	104
YR	585	252	333	12	0	0	1	0	0	0	0	0	0	0	0	259	204	105	15	0	11	5	87	35	91	20	1	0	0	378	174

	AA		*NL*
17	Kid Carsey	26	Bill Hutchison
15	Jack Stivetts	18	John Clarkson
13	Sadie McMahon	16	Harry Staley
13	Darby O'Brien	15	Tony Mullane
12	Multiple Players Tied	15	Kid Nichols

1892

				Consec			1-Inn			One-Game						Men-On-Base				Pitchers					Totals					Batters	
Tm	Tot	H	A	2	3	4	3	4	5	5	6	7	8	9	10	0	1	2	3	PH	LO	XN	IP	P	1	10	20	30	40	RHB	LHB
NL																															
BAL	51	14	37	1	0	0	0	0	0	0	0	0	0	0	0	19	19	11	2	0	2	0	8	4	10	0	1	0	0	31	20
BOS	41	26	15	0	0	0	0	0	0	0	0	0	0	0	0	21	13	5	2	1	0	1	2	4	1	3	0	0	0	24	13
BRO	26	8	18	0	0	0	0	0	0	0	0	0	0	0	0	10	13	3	0	0	0	1	2	5	4	1	0	0	0	14	11
CHI	35	9	26	0	0	0	0	0	0	0	0	0	0	0	0	18	13	3	1	0	1	0	8	3	3	3	0	0	0	19	12
CIN	39	21	18	0	0	0	0	0	0	0	0	0	0	0	0	17	12	8	2	0	1	0	4	1	6	1	0	0	0	15	21
CLE	28	4	24	0	0	0	0	0	0	0	0	0	0	0	0	14	9	5	0	0	2	0	2	3	6	0	0	0	0	13	14
LOU	26	3	23	0	0	0	0	0	0	0	0	0	0	0	0	10	9	7	0	0	0	0	4	4	8	0	0	0	0	11	14
NY	32	12	20	0	0	0	0	0	0	0	0	0	0	0	0	8	18	4	2	0	0	1	4	1	1	2	0	0	0	16	16
PHI	24	8	16	0	0	0	0	0	0	0	0	0	0	0	0	12	8	2	2	0	2	0	0	3	6	0	0	0	0	13	9
PIT	28	14	14	0	0	0	0	0	0	0	0	0	0	0	0	11	12	5	0	0	1	0	7	2	5	1	0	0	0	13	12
STL	47	32	15	3	0	0	1	0	0	0	0	0	0	0	0	20	22	4	1	0	1	0	4	3	7	2	0	0	0	35	10
WAS	40	22	18	0	0	0	0	0	0	0	0	0	0	0	0	17	18	3	2	0	2	0	9	5	6	1	0	0	0	25	15
NL	417	173	244	4	0	0	1	0	0	0	0	0	0	0	0	177	166	60	14	1	12	3	54	38	63	14	1	0	0	229	167

	NL
21	George Cobb
15	Frank Killen
15	Silver King
15	Kid Nichols
12	Multiple Players Tied

1893

				Consec			1-Inn			One-Game						Men-On-Base				Pitchers					Totals					Batters	
Tm	Tot	H	A	2	3	4	3	4	5	5	6	7	8	9	10	0	1	2	3	PH	LO	XN	IP	P	1	10	20	30	40	RHB	LHB
NL																															
BAL	29	9	20	1	0	0	0	0	0	0	0	0	0	0	0	14	8	6	1	0	1	0	3	4	6	0	0	0	0	18	10
BOS	66	41	25	2	0	0	2	0	0	0	0	0	0	0	0	33	24	7	2	0	0	1	11	5	3	2	1	0	0	42	22
BRO	41	17	24	0	0	0	0	0	0	0	0	0	0	0	0	15	16	8	2	0	1	1	11	2	6	2	0	0	0	19	21
CHI	26	15	11	0	0	0	0	0	0	0	0	0	0	0	0	14	9	3	0	0	0	0	5	3	10	0	0	0	0	16	10
CIN	38	21	17	0	0	0	0	0	0	0	0	0	0	0	0	17	15	5	1	0	1	0	5	0	8	1	0	0	0	22	14
CLE	35	9	26	0	0	0	0	0	0	0	0	0	0	0	0	15	14	6	0	0	2	0	5	3	5	2	0	0	0	18	16
LOU	38	14	24	1	0	0	0	0	0	0	0	0	0	0	0	14	13	9	2	0	0	1	6	3	7	1	0	0	0	19	18
NY	36	19	17	0	0	0	0	0	0	0	0	0	0	0	0	19	12	4	1	0	3	1	5	3	7	1	0	0	0	19	16
PHI	30	13	17	0	0	0	0	0	0	0	0	0	0	0	0	12	10	7	1	0	0	0	3	0	5	1	0	0	0	9	20
PIT	29	8	21	0	0	0	0	0	0	0	0	0	0	0	0	13	11	4	1	0	3	0	5	0	5	1	0	0	0	18	11
STL	38	14	24	0	0	0	0	0	0	0	0	0	0	0	0	18	11	8	1	0	1	1	6	2	5	1	0	0	0	22	16

				Consec			1-Inn			One-Game						Men-On-Base				Pitchers					Totals					Batters	
Tm	Tot	H	A	2	3	4	3	4	5	5	6	7	8	9	10	0	1	2	3	PH	LO	XN	IP	P	1	10	20	30	40	RHB	LHB
WAS	54	7	47	1	0	0	1	0	0	0	0	0	0	0	0	17	24	11	2	0	1	2	5	5	6	2	0	0	0	30	22
NL	460	187	273	5	0	0	3	0	0	0	0	0	0	0	0	201	167	78	14	0	13	7	70	30	73	14	1	0	0	252	196

NL
22 Harry Staley
18 Kid Gleason
17 Frank Dwyer
17 Al Maul
17 Jack Stivetts

1894

NL

Tm	Tot	H	A	2	3	4	3	4	5	5	6	7	8	9	10	0	1	2	3	PH	LO	XN	IP	P	1	10	20	30	40	RHB	LHB
BAL	31	9	22	0	0	0	1	0	0	0	0	0	0	0	0	11	16	4	0	0	1	0	4	3	7	0	0	0	0	23	8
BOS	89	70	19	2	0	0	0	1	0	0	0	1	0	0	0	37	35	15	2	0	1	0	1	4	4	2	2	0	0	58	29
BRO	41	15	26	0	0	0	0	0	0	0	0	0	0	0	0	11	16	13	1	0	1	0	6	0	5	2	0	0	0	23	18
CHI	43	13	30	1	0	0	0	0	0	0	0	0	0	0	0	18	11	9	5	0	1	0	10	4	4	2	0	0	0	30	13
CIN	85	45	40	3	1	0	1	0	0	1	1	0	0	0	0	34	27	20	4	0	0	0	12	8	7	2	1	0	0	42	40
CLE	54	18	36	2	0	0	0	0	0	1	0	0	0	0	0	18	27	8	1	0	0	0	8	2	7	2	0	0	0	31	20
LOU	39	7	32	1	0	0	0	0	0	0	0	0	0	0	0	15	15	9	0	0	0	0	4	2	8	1	0	0	0	23	14
NY	37	21	16	0	0	0	0	0	0	0	0	0	0	0	0	14	16	7	0	0	2	0	2	2	3	2	0	0	0	22	11
PHI	62	31	31	2	0	0	0	0	0	0	1	0	0	0	0	26	25	8	3	0	0	1	1	5	6	2	1	0	0	32	29
PIT	39	11	28	1	0	0	0	0	0	0	0	0	0	0	0	14	19	4	2	0	0	2	6	5	4	2	0	0	0	25	14
STL	48	16	32	0	0	0	0	0	0	1	0	0	0	0	0	20	20	7	1	1	0	0	6	2	4	1	1	0	0	31	15
WAS	59	20	39	2	0	0	0	0	0	0	0	0	0	0	0	21	23	11	4	0	0	0	7	7	8	3	0	0	0	33	25
NL	627	276	351	14	1	0	2	1	0	3	2	1	0	0	0	239	250	115	23	1	6	3	67	44	67	21	5	0	0	373	236

NL
27 Jack Stivetts
26 Frank Dwyer
23 Kid Nichols
22 Kid Carsey
21 Ted Breitenstein

1895

NL

Tm	Tot	H	A	2	3	4	3	4	5	5	6	7	8	9	10	0	1	2	3	PH	LO	XN	IP	P	1	10	20	30	40	RHB	LHB
BAL	31	8	23	0	0	0	0	0	0	0	0	0	0	0	0	15	11	4	1	0	1	0	3	0	5	1	0	0	0	13	18
BOS	56	38	18	1	0	0	0	0	0	0	0	0	0	0	0	32	13	7	4	0	0	1	3	3	3	4	0	0	0	36	18
BRO	41	20	21	0	0	0	1	0	0	0	0	0	0	0	0	19	19	2	1	0	1	0	4	2	3	2	0	0	0	22	17
CHI	38	23	15	0	0	0	0	0	0	0	0	0	0	0	0	22	11	5	0	0	2	1	3	7	5	2	0	0	0	18	20
CIN	39	7	32	2	0	0	0	0	0	0	1	0	0	0	0	19	11	8	1	0	0	1	3	0	3	2	0	0	0	17	20
CLE	33	10	23	1	0	0	0	0	0	0	0	0	0	0	0	18	6	9	0	0	0	0	3	3	5	1	0	0	0	13	19
LOU	40	12	28	0	0	0	0	0	0	0	0	0	0	0	0	17	13	9	1	0	1	0	2	4	9	0	0	0	0	18	21
NY	34	8	26	0	0	0	0	0	0	0	0	0	0	0	0	13	14	7	0	0	0	0	1	1	5	1	0	0	0	17	16
PHI	36	16	20	0	0	0	0	0	0	0	0	0	0	0	0	13	16	3	4	0	0	0	4	1	8	1	0	0	0	14	21
PIT	17	3	14	0	0	0	0	0	0	0	0	0	0	0	0	5	7	5	0	0	0	0	1	2	6	0	0	0	0	9	8
STL	64	35	29	0	0	0	1	0	0	0	0	0	0	0	0	21	31	10	2	0	2	0	6	4	5	3	0	0	0	34	27
WAS	55	33	22	0	0	0	0	0	0	1	0	0	0	0	0	20	19	13	3	0	0	0	9	0	9	2	0	0	0	28	26
NL	484	213	271	4	0	0	2	0	0	1	1	0	0	0	0	214	171	82	17	0	7	3	42	27	66	19	0	0	0	239	231

NL
17 Win Mercer
16 Ted Breitenstein
15 Kid Nichols
15 Jack Stivetts
14 Kid Carsey

1896

NL

Tm	Tot	H	A	2	3	4	3	4	5	5	6	7	8	9	10	0	1	2	3	PH	LO	XN	IP	P	1	10	20	30	40	RHB	LHB
BAL	22	4	18	1	0	0	0	0	0	0	0	0	0	0	0	8	8	6	0	0	0	0	0	0	6	0	0	0	0	11	11
BOS	57	39	18	2	0	0	0	0	0	0	0	0	0	0	0	35	18	3	1	0	2	2	1	5	5	3	0	0	0	31	26

				Consec			1-Inn			One-Game						Men-On-Base				Pitchers					Totals					Batters	
Tm	Tot	H	A	2	3	4	3	4	5	5	6	7	8	9	10	0	1	2	3	PH	LO	XN	IP	P	1	10	20	30	40	RHB	LHB
BRO	39	19	20	1	0	0	0	0	0	0	0	0	0	0	0	20	10	9	0	0	2	0	5	4	6	1	0	0	0	21	13
CHI	30	16	14	0	0	0	0	0	0	0	0	0	0	0	0	14	11	4	1	0	0	0	7	2	5	1	0	0	0	13	15
CIN	27	1	26	0	0	0	0	0	0	0	0	0	0	0	0	8	11	6	2	0	0	1	6	4	6	0	0	0	0	8	17
CLE	27	4	23	0	0	0	0	0	0	0	0	0	0	0	0	12	11	3	1	0	0	0	3	1	5	0	0	0	0	12	13
LOU	48	38	10	0	0	0	0	0	0	0	0	0	0	0	0	22	16	9	1	0	1	0	4	4	9	1	0	0	0	25	20
NY	33	14	19	1	0	0	0	0	0	0	0	0	0	0	0	11	13	6	3	0	1	0	3	1	7	0	0	0	0	14	16
PHI	39	24	15	0	0	0	0	0	0	0	0	0	0	0	0	19	13	6	1	0	3	0	1	4	4	2	0	0	0	13	25
PIT	18	2	16	0	0	0	0	0	0	0	0	0	0	0	0	2	9	7	0	0	0	0	4	1	6	0	0	0	0	11	7
STL	40	18	22	0	0	0	0	0	0	0	0	0	0	0	0	16	13	10	1	1	1	0	2	1	4	2	0	0	0	20	16
WAS	24	12	12	0	0	0	0	0	0	0	0	0	0	0	0	11	7	6	0	0	2	1	0	0	5	1	0	0	0	6	17
NL	404	191	213	5	0	0	0	0	0	0	0	0	0	0	0	178	140	75	11	1	12	4	36	27	68	11	0	0	0	185	196

NL

19 Jack Stivetts
17 Jack Taylor
14 Bill Hill
14 Kid Nichols
13 Jim Sullivan

1897

NL

Tm	Tot	H	A	2	3	4	3	4	5	5	6	7	8	9	10	0	1	2	3	PH	LO	XN	IP	P	1	10	20	30	40	RHB	LHB
BAL	18	7	11	0	0	0	0	0	0	0	0	0	0	0	0	8	7	3	0	0	1	0	3	0	5	0	0	0	0	11	7
BOS	39	26	13	0	0	0	0	0	0	0	0	0	0	0	0	18	15	4	2	1	0	1	1	0	3	2	0	0	0	24	15
BRO	34	19	15	1	0	0	0	0	0	0	0	0	0	0	0	15	14	3	2	0	2	0	1	8	6	0	0	0	0	19	12
CHI	30	15	15	1	0	0	0	0	0	0	0	0	0	0	0	15	10	4	1	0	1	0	6	3	8	0	0	0	0	16	12
CIN	18	3	15	0	0	0	0	0	0	0	0	0	0	0	0	8	4	4	2	0	0	1	4	2	6	0	0	0	0	10	8
CLE	32	11	21	0	0	0	0	0	0	0	0	0	0	0	0	12	17	3	0	0	0	0	5	3	8	0	0	0	0	10	18
LOU	39	23	16	0	0	0	0	0	0	0	0	0	0	0	0	13	17	8	1	0	1	0	7	1	8	1	0	0	0	25	11
NY	26	12	14	1	0	0	0	0	0	0	0	0	0	0	0	12	9	4	1	1	1	0	3	2	5	0	0	0	0	12	13
PHI	28	6	22	1	0	0	0	0	0	0	0	0	0	0	0	11	12	5	0	0	1	1	5	1	3	1	0	0	0	11	17
PIT	22	5	17	0	0	0	0	0	0	0	0	0	0	0	0	8	11	2	1	0	0	0	4	0	6	0	0	0	0	12	9
STL	54	41	13	0	0	0	0	0	0	0	0	0	0	0	0	23	20	10	1	0	1	0	8	1	7	2	0	0	0	20	30
WAS	27	13	14	0	0	0	0	0	0	0	0	0	0	0	0	11	13	2	1	0	2	0	2	1	6	0	0	0	0	12	15
NL	367	181	186	4	0	0	0	0	0	0	0	0	0	0	0	154	149	52	12	2	10	3	49	22	71	6	0	0	0	182	167

NL

16 Red Donahue
13 Fred Klobedanz
12 Al Orth
11 Chick Fraser
11 Ted Lewis

1898

NL

Tm	Tot	H	A	2	3	4	3	4	5	5	6	7	8	9	10	0	1	2	3	PH	LO	XN	IP	P	1	10	20	30	40	RHB	LHB
BAL	17	2	15	0	0	0	0	0	0	0	0	0	0	0	0	7	4	5	1	0	0	0	3	1	4	0	0	0	0	7	9
BOS	37	22	15	0	0	0	0	0	0	0	0	0	0	0	0	17	16	3	1	0	2	0	1	1	5	1	0	0	0	18	18
BRO	34	15	19	0	0	0	0	0	0	0	0	0	0	0	0	20	10	4	0	0	1	1	6	2	3	2	0	0	0	14	18
CHI	17	4	13	0	0	0	0	0	0	0	0	0	0	0	0	7	7	3	0	0	1	0	2	2	6	0	0	0	0	6	10
CIN	16	3	13	0	0	0	0	0	0	0	0	0	0	0	0	6	8	1	1	1	0	0	3	2	5	0	0	0	0	7	9
CLE	26	1	25	1	0	0	0	0	0	0	0	0	0	0	0	12	11	2	1	0	0	0	5	1	6	0	0	0	0	13	13
LOU	33	25	8	0	0	0	0	0	0	0	0	0	0	0	0	13	12	8	0	0	0	0	6	0	7	0	0	0	0	17	14
NY	21	10	11	0	0	0	0	0	0	0	0	0	0	0	0	7	5	6	3	0	1	0	3	3	5	0	0	0	0	13	6
PHI	23	9	14	0	0	0	0	0	0	0	0	0	0	0	0	7	9	5	2	0	1	0	2	0	9	0	0	0	0	9	14
PIT	14	3	11	1	0	0	0	0	0	0	0	0	0	0	0	5	6	3	0	0	0	0	3	1	5	0	0	0	0	6	7
STL	32	15	17	2	0	0	0	0	0	0	0	0	0	0	0	12	14	6	0	0	0	0	4	4	4	2	0	0	0	13	18
WAS	29	17	12	0	0	0	0	0	0	0	0	0	0	0	0	14	12	3	0	0	0	0	3	3	6	1	0	0	0	16	13
NL	299	126	173	4	0	0	0	0	0	0	0	0	0	0	0	127	114	49	9	1	6	1	41	20	65	6	0	0	0	139	149

NL

14 Jack Taylor
13 Fred Klobedanz

Tm	Tot	H	A	Consec			1-Inn			One-Game						Men-On-Base				Pitchers					Totals					Batters	
				2	3	4	3	4	5	5	6	7	8	9	10	0	1	2	3	PH	LO	XN	IP	P	1	10	20	30	40	RHB	LHB

12 Brickyard Kennedy
11 Willie Sudhoff
10 Multiple Players Tied

1899

NL

Tm	Tot	H	A	Consec 2	3	4	1-Inn 3	4	5	One-Game 5	6	7	8	9	10	Men-On-Base 0	1	2	3	PH	LO	XN	IP	P	Totals 1	10	20	30	40	RHB	LHB
BAL	13	2	11	0	0	0	0	0	0	0	0	0	0	0	0	8	4	1	0	0	0	0	2	0	6	0	0	0	0	5	8
BOS	44	33	11	0	0	0	0	0	0	0	0	0	0	0	0	24	13	7	0	0	1	2	1	1	7	2	0	0	0	28	15
BRO	32	18	14	0	0	0	0	0	0	0	0	0	0	0	0	20	8	3	1	0	1	0	5	1	6	1	0	0	0	18	13
CHI	20	14	6	0	0	0	0	0	0	0	0	0	0	0	0	8	10	0	2	0	0	0	5	0	6	0	0	0	0	10	9
CIN	26	7	19	1	0	0	0	0	0	1	0	0	0	0	0	12	7	7	0	0	0	0	1	1	8	0	0	0	0	17	9
CLE	43	5	38	0	0	0	0	0	0	0	0	0	0	0	0	16	15	11	1	0	0	1	13	2	7	1	0	0	0	24	18
LOU	33	17	16	1	0	0	0	0	0	0	0	0	0	0	0	18	10	5	0	1	0	0	5	1	6	1	0	0	0	17	15
NY	19	6	13	0	0	0	0	0	0	0	0	0	0	0	0	6	6	3	4	0	0	0	4	2	6	0	0	0	0	10	9
PHI	17	3	14	0	0	0	0	0	0	0	0	0	0	0	0	7	6	3	1	0	1	0	1	0	5	0	0	0	0	5	10
PIT	27	8	19	0	0	0	0	0	0	0	0	0	0	0	0	17	5	5	0	0	1	0	2	0	9	0	0	0	0	11	15
STL	41	33	8	1	0	0	0	0	0	0	0	0	0	0	0	21	11	7	2	0	1	0	2	3	6	2	0	0	0	15	24
WAS	35	15	20	0	0	0	1	0	0	0	1	0	0	0	0	10	20	5	0	0	1	0	5	3	10	0	0	0	0	18	16
NL	350	161	189	3	0	0	1	0	0	1	1	0	0	0	0	167	115	57	11	1	6	3	46	14	82	7	0	0	0	178	161

NL
15 Jack Powell
11 Brickyard Kennedy
11 Charlie Knepper
11 Kid Nichols
10 Multiple Players Tied

1900

NL

Tm	Tot	H	A	Consec 2	3	4	1-Inn 3	4	5	One-Game 5	6	7	8	9	10	Men-On-Base 0	1	2	3	PH	LO	XN	IP	P	Totals 1	10	20	30	40	RHB	LHB
BOS	59	43	16	0	0	0	0	0	0	0	0	0	0	0	0	37	14	7	1	0	2	0	7	4	2	4	0	0	0	35	23
BRO	30	15	15	0	0	0	0	0	0	0	0	0	0	0	0	15	10	5	0	0	0	0	6	0	7	1	0	0	0	10	19
CHI	21	5	16	0	0	0	0	0	0	0	0	0	0	0	0	9	6	6	0	0	1	0	4	2	6	0	0	0	0	10	11
CIN	28	9	19	0	0	0	0	0	0	0	0	0	0	0	0	11	12	5	0	0	1	1	13	1	5	1	0	0	0	10	17
NY	26	8	18	1	0	0	0	0	0	0	0	0	0	0	0	13	9	4	0	0	0	0	3	2	6	0	0	0	0	11	13
PHI	29	7	22	1	0	0	0	0	0	0	0	0	0	0	0	13	10	6	0	2	1	0	3	3	7	0	0	0	0	12	16
PIT	24	7	17	0	0	0	0	0	0	0	0	0	0	0	0	10	11	3	0	1	0	0	6	0	8	0	0	0	0	16	8
STL	37	18	19	0	0	0	0	0	0	0	0	0	0	0	0	17	15	5	0	0	1	2	14	3	6	1	0	0	0	13	23
NL	254	112	142	2	0	0	0	0	0	0	0	0	0	0	0	125	87	41	1	3	6	3	56	15	47	7	0	0	0	117	130

NL
12 Frank Kitson
11 Bill Dinneen
11 Ted Lewis
11 Kid Nichols
11 Vic Willis

1901

AL

Tm	Tot	H	A	Consec 2	3	4	1-Inn 3	4	5	One-Game 5	6	7	8	9	10	Men-On-Base 0	1	2	3	PH	LO	XN	IP	P	Totals 1	10	20	30	40	RHB	LHB
BAL	21	11	10	0	0	0	1	0	0	0	0	0	0	0	0	8	9	4	0	0	0	0	7	1	5	0	0	0	0	11	10
BOS	33	18	15	0	0	0	0	0	0	0	0	0	0	0	0	18	12	3	0	0	0	0	1	1	7	1	0	0	0	18	14
CHI	27	11	16	1	0	0	0	0	0	0	0	0	0	0	0	8	15	4	0	0	0	1	2	1	6	1	0	0	0	16	11
CLE	22	12	10	0	0	0	0	0	0	0	0	0	0	0	0	8	8	5	1	0	0	0	3	1	9	0	0	0	0	14	7
DET	22	10	12	0	0	0	0	0	0	0	0	0	0	0	0	10	7	3	2	0	0	0	1	4	6	0	0	0	0	17	5
MIL	32	14	18	1	0	0	0	0	0	0	0	0	0	0	0	15	8	8	1	0	0	1	4	1	5	1	0	0	0	18	13
PHI	20	9	11	0	0	0	0	0	0	0	0	0	0	0	0	10	3	7	0	0	0	0	2	0	6	0	0	0	0	9	11
WAS	51	36	15	1	0	0	0	0	0	0	0	0	0	0	0	27	15	6	3	0	0	1	4	5	3	2	0	0	0	38	13

NL

Tm	Tot	H	A	Consec 2	3	4	1-Inn 3	4	5	One-Game 5	6	7	8	9	10	Men-On-Base 0	1	2	3	PH	LO	XN	IP	P	Totals 1	10	20	30	40	RHB	LHB
BOS	29	17	12	0	0	0	0	0	0	0	0	0	0	0	0	17	7	5	0	0	0	1	5	1	4	0	0	0	0	13	16
BRO	18	6	12	0	0	0	0	0	0	0	0	0	0	0	0	10	6	2	0	0	1	0	8	1	8	0	0	0	0	6	12

				Consec			1-Inn			One-Game						Men-On-Base				Pitchers					Totals					Batters	
Tm	Tot	H	A	2	3	4	3	4	5	5	6	7	8	9	10	0	1	2	3	PH	LO	XN	IP	P	1	10	20	30	40	RHB	LHB
CHI	27	10	17	0	0	0	0	0	0	0	0	0	0	0	0	13	8	6	0	0	1	2	10	2	5	0	0	0	0	6	21
CIN	51	34	17	0	0	0	0	0	0	0	0	0	0	0	0	26	14	7	4	0	2	0	34	8	10	2	0	0	0	19	31
NY	24	11	13	0	0	0	0	0	0	0	0	0	0	0	0	6	13	5	0	0	0	0	9	4	9	0	0	0	0	10	13
PHI	19	6	13	0	0	0	0	0	0	0	0	0	0	0	0	15	2	1	1	0	1	0	4	2	5	0	0	0	0	1	17
PIT	20	8	12	1	0	0	0	0	0	0	0	0	0	0	0	6	13	1	0	0	0	2	9	0	7	0	0	0	0	8	12
STL	39	21	18	1	0	0	0	0	0	0	0	0	0	0	0	23	14	2	0	0	0	0	15	4	7	1	0	0	0	18	19
AL	228	121	107	3	0	0	1	0	0	0	0	0	0	0	0	104	77	40	7	0	0	3	24	14	47	5	0	0	0	141	84
NL	227	113	114	2	0	0	0	0	0	0	0	0	0	0	0	116	77	29	5	0	5	5	94	22	55	3	0	0	0	81	141
YR	455	234	221	5	0	0	1	0	0	0	0	0	0	0	0	220	154	69	12	0	5	8	118	36	102	8	0	0	0	222	225

	AL		*NL*
14	Watty Lee	14	Jack Powell
14	Ted Lewis	12	Noodles Hahn
14	Bill Reidy	10	Archie Stimmel
12	Bill Carrick	9	Multiple Players Tied
11	Roy Patterson		

1902

Tm	Tot	H	A	2	3	4	3	4	5	5	6	7	8	9	10	0	1	2	3	PH	LO	XN	IP	P	1	10	20	30	40	RHB	LHB
AL																															
BAL	30	18	12	0	0	0	0	0	0	0	0	0	0	0	0	6	16	8	0	0	1	0	8	0	10	0	0	0	0	10	20
BOS	27	15	12	0	0	0	0	0	0	0	0	0	0	0	0	14	5	6	2	0	1	2	7	0	7	0	0	0	0	11	16
CHI	30	2	28	1	0	0	1	0	0	0	0	0	0	0	0	17	8	4	1	0	1	0	3	0	4	1	0	0	0	21	8
CLE	26	7	19	0	0	0	0	0	0	0	0	0	0	0	0	8	12	5	1	0	2	0	6	1	8	0	0	0	0	18	7
DET	20	8	12	0	0	0	0	0	0	0	0	0	0	0	0	4	12	4	0	0	0	0	3	1	6	0	0	0	0	13	6
PHI	33	15	18	0	0	0	0	0	0	0	0	0	0	0	0	14	10	8	1	0	0	0	6	1	8	0	0	0	0	20	12
STL	36	14	22	0	1	0	1	0	0	0	0	0	0	0	0	17	12	5	2	0	0	1	3	2	5	1	0	0	0	26	10
WAS	56	39	17	1	0	0	0	0	0	0	0	0	0	0	0	28	15	11	2	0	0	1	9	2	1	4	0	0	0	36	19
NL																															
BOS	16	11	5	0	0	0	0	0	0	0	0	0	0	0	0	7	5	3	1	2	0	0	4	2	5	0	0	0	0	9	6
BRO	10	2	8	0	0	0	0	0	0	0	0	0	0	0	0	3	5	2	0	0	0	0	6	0	4	0	0	0	0	4	6
CHI	7	3	4	0	0	0	0	0	0	0	0	0	0	0	0	2	3	1	1	0	0	1	2	1	5	0	0	0	0	4	3
CIN	15	8	7	0	0	0	0	0	0	0	0	0	0	0	0	9	4	2	0	0	1	1	9	1	10	0	0	0	0	6	8
NY	16	6	10	0	0	0	0	0	0	0	0	0	0	0	0	11	3	2	0	0	3	0	6	2	7	0	0	0	0	7	9
PHI	12	6	6	0	0	0	0	0	0	0	0	0	0	0	0	4	4	3	1	0	0	1	6	2	8	0	0	0	0	8	3
PIT	4	2	2	0	0	0	0	0	0	0	0	0	0	0	0	3	0	1	0	0	0	0	2	0	3	0	0	0	0	2	2
STL	16	6	10	0	0	0	0	0	0	0	0	0	0	0	0	7	8	1	0	0	0	1	9	2	7	0	0	0	0	3	12
AL	258	118	140	2	1	0	2	0	0	0	0	0	0	0	0	108	90	51	9	0	5	4	45	7	49	6	0	0	0	155	98
NL	96	44	52	0	0	0	0	0	0	0	0	0	0	0	0	46	32	15	3	2	4	4	44	10	49	0	0	0	0	43	49
YR	354	162	192	2	1	0	2	0	0	0	0	0	0	0	0	154	122	66	12	2	9	8	89	17	98	6	0	0	0	198	147

	AL		*NL*
18	Al Orth	7	Ed Murphy
12	Jack Powell	6	Vic Willis
12	Happy Townsend	4	Multiple Players Tied
11	Multiple Players Tied		

1903

Tm	Tot	H	A	2	3	4	3	4	5	5	6	7	8	9	10	0	1	2	3	PH	LO	XN	IP	P	1	10	20	30	40	RHB	LHB
AL																															
BOS	23	12	11	0	0	0	0	0	0	0	0	0	0	0	0	11	8	4	0	0	0	0	6	1	5	0	0	0	0	12	11
CHI	23	2	21	0	0	0	0	0	0	0	0	0	0	0	0	9	10	3	1	0	0	1	5	1	6	0	0	0	0	11	11
CLE	16	5	11	0	0	0	0	0	0	0	0	0	0	0	0	7	7	2	0	0	0	1	3	0	8	0	0	0	0	10	6
DET	19	6	13	0	0	0	0	0	0	0	0	0	0	0	0	11	6	2	0	0	0	0	3	1	5	0	0	0	0	10	8
NY	19	6	13	0	0	0	0	0	0	0	0	0	0	0	0	11	7	1	0	0	1	0	1	0	6	0	0	0	0	10	9
PHI	20	8	12	0	0	0	0	0	0	0	0	0	0	0	0	7	9	4	0	0	1	1	2	2	6	0	0	0	0	14	6
STL	26	15	11	0	0	0	0	0	0	0	0	0	0	0	0	10	13	3	0	0	0	1	3	0	6	1	0	0	0	20	6
WAS	38	24	14	0	0	0	0	0	0	0	0	0	0	0	0	21	12	5	0	0	2	1	10	3	5	1	0	0	0	28	10
NL																															
BOS	30	19	11	0	0	0	0	0	0	0	0	0	0	0	0	12	11	7	0	0	0	0	6	1	5	1	0	0	0	14	16
BRO	18	9	9	0	0	0	0	0	0	0	0	0	0	0	0	7	7	4	0	1	1	0	8	0	8	0	0	0	0	12	6
CHI	14	7	7	0	0	0	0	0	0	0	0	0	0	0	0	7	4	1	2	1	0	1	2	0	6	0	0	0	0	9	5

				Consec			1-Inn			One-Game						Men-On-Base				Pitchers					Totals					Batters	
Tm	Tot	H	A	2	3	4	3	4	5	5	6	7	8	9	10	0	1	2	3	PH	LO	XN	IP	P	1	10	20	30	40	RHB	LHB
CIN	14	7	7	0	0	0	0	0	0	0	0	0	0	0	0	2	4	7	1	0	0	0	7	0	5	0	0	0	0	5	9
NY	20	10	10	0	0	0	0	0	0	0	0	0	0	0	0	11	7	1	1	0	0	1	5	2	5	0	0	0	0	9	11
PHI	21	6	15	1	0	0	0	0	0	0	0	0	0	0	0	9	7	3	2	0	0	0	6	1	5	0	0	0	0	11	10
PIT	9	5	4	0	0	0	0	0	0	0	0	0	0	0	0	2	4	3	0	0	1	0	4	1	5	0	0	0	0	5	4
STL	25	13	12	0	0	0	0	0	0	0	0	0	0	0	0	13	6	3	3	0	0	0	14	0	7	0	0	0	0	14	11
AL	184	78	106	0	0	0	0	0	0	0	0	0	0	0	0	87	72	24	1	0	4	5	33	8	47	2	0	0	0	115	67
NL	151	76	75	1	0	0	0	0	0	0	0	0	0	0	0	63	50	29	9	2	2	2	52	5	46	1	0	0	0	79	72
YR	335	154	181	1	0	0	0	0	0	0	0	0	0	0	0	150	122	53	10	2	6	7	85	13	93	3	0	0	0	194	139

	AL		*NL*
11	Case Patten	12	Togie Pittinger
11	Jack Powell	8	Clarence Currie
9	Patsy Flaherty	8	Chick Fraser
8	Frank Kitson	7	Mordecai Brown
8	Al Orth	6	Dummy Taylor

1904

AL

Tm	Tot	H	A	2	3	4	3	4	5	5	6	7	8	9	10	0	1	2	3	PH	LO	XN	IP	P	1	10	20	30	40	RHB	LHB
BOS	31	18	13	0	0	0	0	0	0	0	0	0	0	0	0	19	11	0	1	0	1	1	6	5	5	0	0	0	0	18	13
CHI	13	2	11	1	0	0	0	0	0	0	0	0	0	0	0	7	4	2	0	0	1	1	5	0	6	0	0	0	0	8	5
CLE	10	2	8	0	0	0	0	0	0	0	0	0	0	0	0	5	5	0	0	0	0	0	2	0	5	0	0	0	0	6	4
DET	16	4	12	0	0	0	0	0	0	0	0	0	0	0	0	8	5	3	0	0	0	0	4	0	4	0	0	0	0	12	4
NY	29	26	3	0	0	0	0	0	0	0	0	0	0	0	0	19	7	2	1	0	1	0	12	1	5	1	0	0	0	12	17
PHI	13	8	5	0	0	0	0	0	0	0	0	0	0	0	0	8	5	0	0	0	0	0	3	0	6	0	0	0	0	8	5
STL	25	14	11	0	0	0	0	0	0	0	0	0	0	0	0	13	7	3	2	0	1	0	4	2	7	0	0	0	0	15	10
WAS	19	2	17	0	0	0	0	0	0	0	0	0	0	0	0	6	10	2	1	0	0	0	4	3	7	0	0	0	0	14	5

NL

Tm	Tot	H	A	2	3	4	3	4	5	5	6	7	8	9	10	0	1	2	3	PH	LO	XN	IP	P	1	10	20	30	40	RHB	LHB
BOS	25	11	14	1	0	0	0	0	0	0	0	0	0	0	0	17	5	2	1	0	1	1	4	3	6	0	0	0	0	13	12
BRO	27	11	16	0	0	0	0	0	0	0	0	0	0	0	0	14	7	5	1	0	0	1	12	1	3	1	0	0	0	12	14
CHI	16	10	6	0	0	0	0	0	0	0	0	0	0	0	0	8	7	0	1	0	0	0	8	2	7	0	0	0	0	9	5
CIN	13	6	7	0	0	0	0	0	0	0	0	0	0	0	0	7	4	1	1	0	1	0	3	0	7	0	0	0	0	6	7
NY	36	30	6	0	0	0	0	0	0	0	0	0	0	0	0	19	10	6	1	0	0	1	6	1	8	0	0	0	0	20	16
PHI	22	7	15	0	0	0	0	0	0	0	0	0	0	0	0	9	8	4	1	0	0	0	7	3	9	0	0	0	0	10	12
PIT	13	2	11	0	0	0	0	0	0	0	0	0	0	0	0	6	6	0	1	0	1	1	10	0	7	0	0	0	0	9	2
STL	23	15	8	0	0	0	0	0	0	0	0	0	0	0	0	17	4	2	0	0	2	0	7	2	7	0	0	0	0	11	12
AL	156	76	80	1	0	0	0	0	0	0	0	0	0	0	0	85	54	12	5	0	4	2	40	11	45	1	0	0	0	93	63
NL	175	92	83	1	0	0	0	0	0	0	0	0	0	0	0	97	51	20	7	0	5	4	57	12	54	1	0	0	0	90	80
YR	331	168	163	2	0	0	0	0	0	0	0	0	0	0	0	182	105	32	12	0	9	6	97	23	99	2	0	0	0	183	143

	AL		*NL*
15	Jack Powell	10	Jack Cronin
8	Bill Dinneen	8	Joe McGinnity
8	Norwood Gibson	8	Kaiser Wilhelm
8	Willie Sudhoff	8	Hooks Wiltse
7	Multiple Players Tied	7	Multiple Players Tied

1905

AL

Tm	Tot	H	A	2	3	4	3	4	5	5	6	7	8	9	10	0	1	2	3	PH	LO	XN	IP	P	1	10	20	30	40	RHB	LHB
BOS	33	21	12	1	0	0	0	0	0	0	0	0	0	0	0	23	6	2	2	0	0	0	11	3	6	0	0	0	0	21	12
CHI	11	2	9	0	0	0	0	0	0	0	0	0	0	0	0	6	5	0	0	0	0	1	1	0	3	0	0	0	0	10	1
CLE	23	13	10	0	0	0	0	0	0	0	0	0	0	0	0	13	6	3	1	0	1	0	3	3	7	0	0	0	0	18	5
DET	11	5	6	2	0	0	0	0	0	0	0	0	0	0	0	8	1	2	0	0	0	0	4	1	5	0	0	0	0	9	2
NY	26	16	10	0	0	0	0	0	0	0	0	0	0	0	0	5	18	3	0	0	1	0	17	3	10	0	0	0	0	12	14
PHI	21	12	9	0	0	0	0	0	0	0	0	0	0	0	0	14	5	2	0	0	0	1	3	1	6	0	0	0	0	13	8
STL	19	7	12	0	0	0	0	0	0	0	0	0	0	0	0	8	8	3	0	0	0	0	6	0	6	0	0	0	0	11	8
WAS	12	4	8	0	0	0	0	0	0	0	0	0	0	0	0	8	2	2	0	0	0	0	8	0	7	0	0	0	0	6	6

NL

Tm	Tot	H	A	2	3	4	3	4	5	5	6	7	8	9	10	0	1	2	3	PH	LO	XN	IP	P	1	10	20	30	40	RHB	LHB
BOS	36	14	22	1	0	0	0	0	0	0	0	0	0	0	0	19	11	6	0	0	0	1	7	2	7	0	0	0	0	18	17
BRO	24	16	8	0	0	0	0	0	0	0	0	0	0	0	0	11	11	2	0	0	0	2	6	0	6	0	0	0	0	7	17
CHI	14	4	10	0	0	0	0	0	0	0	0	0	0	0	0	6	4	4	0	0	0	0	6	0	7	0	0	0	0	6	7

				Consec			1-Inn			One-Game						Men-On-Base				Pitchers					Totals					Batters	
Tm	**Tot**	**H**	**A**	**2**	**3**	**4**	**3**	**4**	**5**	**5**	**6**	**7**	**8**	**9**	**10**	**0**	**1**	**2**	**3**	**PH**	**LO**	**XN**	**IP**	**P**	**1**	**10**	**20**	**30**	**40**	**RHB**	**LHB**
CIN	22	2	20	0	0	0	0	0	0	0	0	0	0	0	0	9	7	5	1	0	1	0	2	2	8	0	0	0	0	12	9
NY	25	19	6	0	0	0	0	0	0	0	0	0	0	0	0	12	12	1	0	0	0	0	9	0	6	0	0	0	0	14	9
PHI	21	9	12	0	0	0	0	0	0	0	0	0	0	0	0	13	4	4	0	0	0	0	7	0	6	1	0	0	0	9	11
PIT	12	1	11	0	0	0	0	0	0	0	0	0	0	0	0	4	7	1	0	0	0	0	5	0	6	0	0	0	0	5	7
STL	28	10	18	2	0	0	0	0	0	0	0	0	0	0	0	12	11	3	2	0	0	0	12	2	8	1	0	0	0	16	12
AL	156	80	76	3	0	0	0	0	0	0	0	0	0	0	0	85	51	17	3	0	2	2	53	11	50	0	0	0	0	100	56
NL	182	75	107	3	0	0	0	0	0	0	0	0	0	0	0	86	67	26	3	0	1	3	54	6	54	2	0	0	0	87	89
YR	338	155	183	6	0	0	0	0	0	0	0	0	0	0	0	171	118	43	6	0	3	5	107	17	104	2	0	0	0	187	145

AL		*NL*	
9	Norwood Gibson	10	Bill Duggleby
8	Al Orth	10	Jack Taylor
8	Willie Sudhoff	8	Chick Fraser
7	Bill Dinneen	7	Kaiser Wilhelm
7	Jesse Tannehill	7	Vic Willis

1906

AL

Tm	Tot	H	A	2	3	4	3	4	5	5	6	7	8	9	10	0	1	2	3	PH	LO	XN	IP	P	1	10	20	30	40	RHB	LHB
BOS	37	21	16	1	0	0	0	0	0	0	0	0	0	0	0	16	16	4	1	0	0	0	20	2	8	0	0	0	0	26	11
CHI	11	1	10	0	0	0	0	0	0	0	0	0	0	0	0	6	2	2	1	1	0	0	6	2	5	0	0	0	0	8	3
CLE	16	8	8	0	0	0	0	0	0	0	0	0	0	0	0	6	9	1	0	0	0	1	4	0	7	0	0	0	0	10	5
DET	14	5	9	0	0	0	0	0	0	0	0	0	0	0	0	8	2	4	0	0	0	0	7	0	5	0	0	0	0	9	5
NY	21	8	13	0	0	0	0	0	0	0	0	0	0	0	0	10	6	4	1	0	1	0	7	2	7	0	0	0	0	10	11
PHI	9	4	5	0	0	0	0	0	0	0	0	0	0	0	0	5	3	1	0	0	0	2	2	1	5	0	0	0	0	5	4
STL	14	11	3	0	0	0	0	0	0	0	0	0	0	0	0	11	3	0	0	0	0	3	0	3	6	0	0	0	0	12	2
WAS	15	5	10	0	0	0	0	0	0	0	0	0	0	0	0	3	8	4	0	0	0	0	5	0	8	0	0	0	0	8	7

NL

Tm	Tot	H	A	2	3	4	3	4	5	5	6	7	8	9	10	0	1	2	3	PH	LO	XN	IP	P	1	10	20	30	40	RHB	LHB
BOS	24	16	8	0	0	0	0	0	0	0	0	0	0	0	0	14	9	1	0	0	1	1	4	2	7	0	0	0	0	15	8
BRO	15	5	10	0	0	0	0	0	0	0	0	0	0	0	0	7	4	3	1	0	0	0	8	1	6	0	0	0	0	8	7
CHI	12	5	7	0	0	0	0	0	0	0	0	0	0	0	0	7	2	3	0	0	0	0	4	1	7	0	0	0	0	4	7
CIN	14	10	4	0	0	0	0	0	0	0	0	0	0	0	0	7	6	1	0	0	0	0	4	0	9	0	0	0	0	7	6
NY	13	8	5	0	0	0	0	0	0	0	0	0	0	0	0	8	5	0	0	0	0	0	7	1	6	0	0	0	0	9	4
PHI	18	4	14	0	0	0	0	0	0	0	0	0	0	0	0	8	4	4	2	0	1	1	5	0	6	0	0	0	0	5	12
PIT	13	8	5	0	0	0	0	0	0	0	0	0	0	0	0	7	4	2	0	0	0	1	7	0	6	0	0	0	0	6	7
STL	17	10	7	0	0	0	0	0	0	0	0	0	0	0	0	10	5	1	1	0	0	0	9	1	10	0	0	0	0	10	7
AL	137	63	74	1	0	0	0	0	0	0	0	0	0	0	0	65	49	20	3	1	1	6	51	10	51	0	0	0	0	88	48
NL	126	66	60	0	0	0	0	0	0	0	0	0	0	0	0	68	39	15	4	0	2	3	48	6	57	0	0	0	0	64	58
YR	263	129	134	1	0	0	0	0	0	0	0	0	0	0	0	133	88	35	7	1	3	9	99	16	108	0	0	0	0	152	106

AL		*NL*	
9	Jesse Tannehill	7	Irv Young
8	George Winter	5	Gus Dorner
6	Walter Clarkson	5	Bill Duggleby
5	Multiple Players Tied	5	Doc Scanlan
		4	Multiple Players Tied

1907

AL

Tm	Tot	H	A	2	3	4	3	4	5	5	6	7	8	9	10	0	1	2	3	PH	LO	XN	IP	P	1	10	20	30	40	RHB	LHB
BOS	22	11	11	0	0	0	0	0	0	0	0	0	0	0	0	16	1	5	0	0	2	0	9	1	9	0	0	0	0	15	7
CHI	13	4	9	0	0	0	0	0	0	0	0	0	0	0	0	7	5	0	1	0	1	0	3	0	5	0	0	0	0	8	5
CLE	8	5	3	0	0	0	0	0	0	0	0	0	0	0	0	3	3	2	0	0	0	0	2	0	5	0	0	0	0	6	2
DET	8	3	5	0	0	0	0	0	0	0	0	0	0	0	0	5	3	0	0	1	0	0	3	1	5	0	0	0	0	6	2
NY	13	7	6	0	0	0	0	0	0	0	0	0	0	0	0	4	3	6	0	0	2	0	6	2	9	0	0	0	0	5	8
PHI	13	7	6	0	0	0	0	0	0	0	0	0	0	0	0	6	6	1	0	0	0	2	2	2	6	0	0	0	0	5	8
STL	17	11	6	0	0	0	0	0	0	0	0	0	0	0	0	8	7	2	0	0	1	0	1	3	7	0	0	0	0	10	7
WAS	10	3	7	0	0	0	0	0	0	0	0	0	0	0	0	6	3	1	0	0	0	0	5	3	6	0	0	0	0	7	3

NL

Tm	Tot	H	A	2	3	4	3	4	5	5	6	7	8	9	10	0	1	2	3	PH	LO	XN	IP	P	1	10	20	30	40	RHB	LHB
BOS	28	20	8	0	0	0	0	0	0	0	0	0	0	0	0	14	12	2	0	0	0	0	7	2	6	1	0	0	0	22	6
BRO	16	10	6	1	0	0	0	0	0	0	0	0	0	0	0	7	5	3	1	0	0	0	6	2	7	0	0	0	0	12	4
CHI	11	5	6	0	0	0	0	0	0	0	0	0	0	0	0	6	4	1	0	0	0	1	1	1	6	0	0	0	0	5	6

				Consec			1-Inn			One-Game						Men-On-Base				Pitchers					Totals					Batters	
Tm	Tot	H	A	2	3	4	3	4	5	5	6	7	8	9	10	0	1	2	3	PH	LO	XN	IP	P	1	10	20	30	40	RHB	LHB
CIN	16	5	11	1	0	0	0	0	0	0	0	0	0	0	0	9	4	3	0	0	0	1	5	0	6	0	0	0	0	10	6
NY	24	19	5	0	0	0	0	0	0	0	0	0	0	0	0	15	5	3	1	0	1	2	8	3	7	0	0	0	0	13	11
PHI	13	4	9	0	0	0	0	0	0	0	0	0	0	0	0	6	4	3	0	0	0	0	4	0	5	0	0	0	0	4	9
PIT	12	3	9	0	0	0	0	0	0	0	0	0	0	0	0	6	5	1	0	0	0	0	8	0	6	0	0	0	0	7	5
STL	20	10	10	0	0	0	0	0	0	0	0	0	0	0	0	8	11	1	0	1	1	0	13	0	8	0	0	0	0	9	10
AL	104	51	53	0	0	0	0	0	0	0	0	0	0	0	0	55	31	17	1	1	6	2	31	12	52	0	0	0	0	62	42
NL	140	76	64	2	0	0	0	0	0	0	0	0	0	0	0	71	50	17	2	1	2	4	52	8	51	1	0	0	0	82	57
YR	244	127	117	2	0	0	0	0	0	0	0	0	0	0	0	126	81	34	3	2	8	6	83	20	103	1	0	0	0	144	99

	AL		*NL*
8	Bill Dinneen	10	Vive Lindaman
5	Eddie Plank	6	Joe McGinnity
4	Ralph Glaze	6	Stoney McGlynn
4	Cy Morgan	6	Harry McIntire
4	Jack Powell	6	Jake Weimer

1908

AL

				Consec			1-Inn			One-Game						Men-On-Base				Pitchers					Totals					Batters	
Tm	Tot	H	A	2	3	4	3	4	5	5	6	7	8	9	10	0	1	2	3	PH	LO	XN	IP	P	1	10	20	30	40	RHB	LHB
BOS	18	8	10	0	0	0	0	0	0	0	0	0	0	0	0	10	5	2	1	0	0	1	6	1	9	0	0	0	0	7	11
CHI	11	4	7	0	0	0	0	0	0	0	0	0	0	0	0	3	5	1	2	0	0	0	2	0	5	0	0	0	0	8	3
CLE	16	7	9	0	0	0	0	0	0	0	0	0	0	0	0	10	5	1	0	0	1	1	3	1	9	0	0	0	0	7	9
DET	12	6	6	0	0	0	0	0	0	0	0	0	0	0	0	5	3	3	1	0	1	0	7	1	6	0	0	0	0	8	4
NY	26	16	10	0	0	0	0	0	0	0	0	0	0	0	0	9	11	6	0	0	0	0	13	1	7	0	0	0	0	15	11
PHI	10	4	6	0	0	0	0	0	0	0	0	0	0	0	0	7	2	1	0	0	0	2	1	0	8	0	0	0	0	4	6
STL	7	2	5	0	0	0	0	0	0	0	0	0	0	0	0	4	3	0	0	0	0	0	3	1	5	0	0	0	0	5	2
WAS	16	9	7	0	0	0	0	0	0	0	0	0	0	0	0	11	4	1	0	0	1	0	4	1	6	0	0	0	0	10	6

NL

				Consec			1-Inn			One-Game						Men-On-Base				Pitchers					Totals					Batters	
Tm	Tot	H	A	2	3	4	3	4	5	5	6	7	8	9	10	0	1	2	3	PH	LO	XN	IP	P	1	10	20	30	40	RHB	LHB
BOS	29	20	9	1	0	0	0	0	0	0	0	0	0	0	0	20	4	4	1	1	0	1	4	1	8	0	0	0	0	18	11
BRO	17	3	14	0	0	0	0	0	0	0	0	0	0	0	0	10	3	3	1	0	0	1	8	0	5	0	0	0	0	13	4
CHI	20	15	5	0	0	0	0	0	0	0	0	0	0	0	0	12	8	0	0	1	0	0	10	0	8	0	0	0	0	15	5
CIN	19	7	12	0	0	0	0	0	0	0	0	0	0	0	0	15	4	0	0	0	0	0	7	0	8	0	0	0	0	8	11
NY	26	11	15	2	0	0	0	0	0	0	0	0	0	0	0	18	6	1	1	1	0	1	10	0	6	0	0	0	0	17	9
PHI	8	3	5	0	0	0	0	0	0	0	0	0	0	0	0	5	3	0	0	1	0	0	1	0	5	0	0	0	0	3	5
PIT	16	3	13	0	0	0	0	0	0	0	0	0	0	0	0	8	6	2	0	0	0	1	4	1	6	0	0	0	0	7	9
STL	16	11	5	1	0	0	0	0	0	0	0	0	0	0	0	8	5	2	1	0	0	1	11	0	7	0	0	0	0	10	6
AL	116	56	60	0	0	0	0	0	0	0	0	0	0	0	0	59	38	15	4	0	3	4	39	6	55	0	0	0	0	64	52
NL	151	73	78	4	0	0	0	0	0	0	0	0	0	0	0	96	39	12	4	4	0	5	55	2	53	0	0	0	0	91	60
YR	267	129	138	4	0	0	0	0	0	0	0	0	0	0	0	155	77	27	8	4	3	9	94	8	108	0	0	0	0	155	112

	AL		*NL*
7	Cy Morgan	8	Joe McGinnity
6	Jack Chesbro	7	Jake Boultes
6	Joe Lake	7	Vive Lindaman
4	Multiple Players Tied	6	Multiple Players Tied

1909

AL

				Consec			1-Inn			One-Game						Men-On-Base				Pitchers					Totals					Batters	
Tm	Tot	H	A	2	3	4	3	4	5	5	6	7	8	9	10	0	1	2	3	PH	LO	XN	IP	P	1	10	20	30	40	RHB	LHB
BOS	18	13	5	0	0	0	0	0	0	0	0	0	0	0	0	6	8	3	1	0	0	0	3	0	10	0	0	0	0	7	11
CHI	8	3	5	0	0	0	0	0	0	0	0	0	0	0	0	5	2	1	0	0	1	0	2	0	6	0	0	0	0	5	3
CLE	9	1	8	0	0	0	0	0	0	0	0	0	0	0	0	5	1	3	0	0	0	0	5	0	5	0	0	0	0	5	4
DET	16	9	7	0	0	0	0	0	0	0	0	0	0	0	0	7	6	3	0	0	0	0	7	2	7	0	0	0	0	11	5
NY	21	9	12	1	0	0	0	0	0	0	0	0	0	0	0	8	11	2	0	0	1	0	13	0	10	0	0	0	0	11	10
PHI	9	4	5	0	0	0	0	0	0	0	0	0	0	0	0	7	2	0	0	0	0	0	3	1	6	0	0	0	0	5	4
STL	16	6	10	0	0	0	0	0	0	0	0	0	0	0	0	4	7	5	0	0	0	0	8	1	10	0	0	0	0	8	8
WAS	12	2	10	0	0	0	0	0	0	0	0	0	0	0	0	5	5	2	0	0	0	0	5	0	8	0	0	0	0	7	5

NL

				Consec			1-Inn			One-Game						Men-On-Base				Pitchers					Totals					Batters	
Tm	Tot	H	A	2	3	4	3	4	5	5	6	7	8	9	10	0	1	2	3	PH	LO	XN	IP	P	1	10	20	30	40	RHB	LHB
BOS	23	9	14	0	0	0	0	0	0	0	0	0	0	0	0	10	8	3	2	0	0	0	6	1	11	0	0	0	0	18	5
BRO	31	9	22	2	0	0	0	0	0	0	0	0	0	0	0	18	7	5	1	0	0	2	21	1	9	0	0	0	0	19	12
CHI	6	0	6	0	0	0	0	0	0	0	0	0	0	0	0	2	3	1	0	0	0	0	1	0	5	0	0	0	0	3	3
CIN	5	2	3	0	0	0	0	0	0	0	0	0	0	0	0	1	2	2	0	0	0	0	4	0	4	0	0	0	0	3	2

				Consec			1-Inn			One-Game						Men-On-Base				Pitchers					Totals					Batters	
Tm	Tot	H	A	2	3	4	3	4	5	5	6	7	8	9	10	0	1	2	3	PH	LO	XN	IP	P	1	10	20	30	40	RHB	LHB
NY	28	23	5	0	0	0	0	0	0	0	0	0	0	0	0	15	9	3	1	0	2	0	10	0	7	0	0	0	0	16	12
PHI	23	10	13	1	0	0	0	0	0	0	0	0	0	0	0	11	11	1	0	0	1	0	5	3	5	0	0	0	0	10	13
PIT	12	6	6	0	0	0	0	0	0	0	0	0	0	0	0	9	2	1	0	0	1	0	6	0	5	0	0	0	0	7	5
STL	22	12	10	0	0	0	0	0	0	0	0	0	0	0	0	12	7	3	0	0	0	0	6	2	8	0	0	0	0	13	9
AL	109	47	62	1	0	0	0	0	0	0	0	0	0	0	0	47	42	19	1	0	2	0	46	4	62	0	0	0	0	59	50
NL	150	71	79	3	0	0	0	0	0	0	0	0	0	0	0	78	49	19	4	0	4	2	59	7	54	0	0	0	0	89	61
YR	259	118	141	4	0	0	0	0	0	0	0	0	0	0	0	125	91	38	5	0	6	2	105	11	116	0	0	0	0	148	111

	AL		*NL*
6	Charlie Smith	9	Hooks Wiltse
5	Ed Willett	7	Earl Moore
4	Ed Summers	7	Bugs Raymond
4	Cy Young	6	Multiple Players Tied
3	Multiple Players Tied		

1910

AL

Tm	Tot	H	A	2	3	4	3	4	5	5	6	7	8	9	10	0	1	2	3	PH	LO	XN	IP	P	1	10	20	30	40	RHB	LHB
BOS	30	21	9	1	0	0	0	0	0	0	0	0	0	0	0	15	10	3	2	0	0	0	4	0	10	0	0	0	0	21	9
CHI	16	2	14	0	0	0	0	0	0	0	0	0	0	0	0	5	9	2	0	0	1	0	8	0	6	0	0	0	0	13	3
CLE	10	2	8	0	0	0	0	0	0	0	0	0	0	0	0	5	4	1	0	0	0	0	4	0	5	0	0	0	0	6	4
DET	34	21	13	0	0	0	0	0	0	0	0	0	0	0	0	14	13	6	1	0	0	0	10	4	8	0	0	0	0	24	10
NY	16	7	9	0	0	0	0	0	0	0	0	0	0	0	0	10	4	2	0	0	1	0	9	1	8	0	0	0	0	7	9
PHI	8	0	8	0	0	0	0	0	0	0	0	0	0	0	0	4	4	0	0	0	0	0	2	2	3	0	0	0	0	5	3
STL	14	3	11	0	0	0	0	0	0	0	0	0	0	0	0	7	2	5	0	0	0	1	3	2	7	0	0	0	0	9	5
WAS	19	7	12	1	0	0	0	0	0	0	0	0	0	0	0	8	7	3	1	0	0	1	11	2	7	0	0	0	0	8	11

NL

Tm	Tot	H	A	2	3	4	3	4	5	5	6	7	8	9	10	0	1	2	3	PH	LO	XN	IP	P	1	10	20	30	40	RHB	LHB
BOS	36	25	11	0	0	0	0	0	0	0	0	0	0	0	0	19	13	3	1	1	1	0	4	2	10	0	0	0	0	27	9
BRO	17	5	12	0	0	0	0	0	0	0	0	0	0	0	0	9	4	2	2	0	0	0	4	1	7	0	0	0	0	11	6
CHI	18	9	9	0	0	0	0	0	0	0	0	0	0	0	0	11	4	3	0	0	0	1	3	1	9	0	0	0	0	10	8
CIN	27	8	19	0	0	0	0	0	0	0	0	0	0	0	0	15	8	3	1	0	1	0	9	3	9	0	0	0	0	15	12
NY	30	17	13	2	0	0	0	0	0	0	0	0	0	0	0	14	11	4	1	1	0	0	4	0	7	1	0	0	0	12	18
PHI	36	18	18	0	0	0	1	0	0	0	0	0	0	0	0	18	9	7	2	1	1	1	10	1	11	0	0	0	0	20	16
PIT	20	8	12	0	0	0	0	0	0	0	0	0	0	0	0	13	2	3	2	0	1	1	5	2	7	0	0	0	0	11	9
STL	30	14	16	1	0	0	0	0	0	0	0	0	0	0	0	18	7	5	0	1	0	0	18	0	11	0	0	0	0	17	13
AL	147	63	84	2	0	0	0	0	0	0	0	0	0	0	0	68	53	22	4	0	2	2	51	11	54	0	0	0	0	93	54
NL	214	104	110	3	0	0	1	0	0	0	0	0	0	0	0	117	58	30	9	4	4	3	57	10	71	1	0	0	0	123	91
YR	361	167	194	5	0	0	1	0	0	0	0	0	0	0	0	185	111	52	13	4	6	5	108	21	125	1	0	0	0	216	145

	AL		*NL*
9	Sailor Stroud	10	Doc Crandall
8	Bob Groom	9	Cliff Curtis
8	Ed Summers	8	Sam Frock
7	George Mullin	7	Eddie Stack
6	Charles Hall	6	Multiple Players Tied

1911

AL

Tm	Tot	H	A	2	3	4	3	4	5	5	6	7	8	9	10	0	1	2	3	PH	LO	XN	IP	P	1	10	20	30	40	RHB	LHB
BOS	21	15	6	0	0	0	0	0	0	0	0	0	0	0	0	14	4	1	2	0	0	0	4	1	10	0	0	0	0	16	5
CHI	22	13	9	0	0	0	0	0	0	0	0	0	0	0	0	18	2	2	0	0	1	0	6	1	9	0	0	0	0	10	12
CLE	17	4	13	1	0	0	0	0	0	0	0	0	0	0	0	6	8	3	0	0	0	0	7	1	11	0	0	0	0	9	8
DET	28	15	13	0	0	0	0	0	0	0	0	0	0	0	0	15	8	4	1	1	0	1	5	5	9	0	0	0	0	18	10
NY	26	14	12	0	0	0	0	0	0	0	0	0	0	0	0	9	11	6	0	0	0	1	7	0	7	0	0	0	0	13	13
PHI	17	5	12	0	0	0	0	0	0	0	0	0	0	0	0	5	8	3	1	0	0	0	4	2	7	0	0	0	0	9	8
STL	28	10	18	0	0	0	0	0	0	0	0	0	0	0	0	15	7	4	2	0	1	2	13	1	9	0	0	0	0	11	17
WAS	39	21	18	0	0	0	0	0	0	0	0	0	0	0	0	25	10	3	1	1	0	0	10	2	9	0	0	0	0	20	19

NL

Tm	Tot	H	A	2	3	4	3	4	5	5	6	7	8	9	10	0	1	2	3	PH	LO	XN	IP	P	1	10	20	30	40	RHB	LHB
BOS	76	47	29	0	0	0	0	0	0	0	0	0	0	0	0	35	20	15	6	0	1	2	8	1	8	4	0	0	0	42	34
BRO	27	11	16	0	0	0	0	0	0	0	0	0	0	0	0	16	10	1	0	0	1	2	9	0	7	1	0	0	0	16	11
CHI	26	13	13	1	0	0	1	0	0	0	0	0	0	0	0	17	7	1	1	0	0	0	5	1	8	0	0	0	0	12	14
CIN	36	6	30	1	0	0	0	0	0	0	0	0	0	0	0	14	13	7	2	1	0	1	4	1	9	0	0	0	0	17	19
NY	33	13	20	1	0	0	0	0	0	0	0	0	0	0	0	20	11	1	1	0	0	0	7	0	5	1	0	0	0	20	13

Tm	Tot	H	A	Consec 2	3	4	1-Inn 3	4	5	One-Game 5	6	7	8	9	10	Men-On-Base 0	1	2	3	Pitchers PH	LO	XN	IP	P	Totals 1	10	20	30	40	Batters RHB	LHB
PHI	43	26	17	1	0	0	0	0	0	0	0	0	0	0	0	17	15	9	2	0	1	2	6	3	10	1	0	0	0	21	22
PIT	36	6	30	1	0	0	0	0	0	0	0	0	0	0	0	18	14	4	0	0	1	1	10	0	10	0	0	0	0	21	15
STL	39	12	27	0	0	0	0	0	0	0	0	0	0	0	0	15	16	5	3	0	0	0	16	1	6	1	0	0	0	20	19
AL	198	97	101	1	0	0	0	0	0	0	0	0	0	0	0	107	58	26	7	2	2	4	56	13	71	0	0	0	0	106	92
NL	316	134	182	5	0	0	1	0	0	0	0	0	0	0	0	152	106	43	15	1	4	8	65	7	63	8	0	0	0	169	147
YR	514	231	283	6	0	0	1	0	0	0	0	0	0	0	0	259	164	69	22	3	6	12	121	20	134	8	0	0	0	275	239

	AL		*NL*
9	Bob Groom	13	Al Mattern
8	Jack Coombs	12	Nap Rucker
8	Walter Johnson	11	Buster Brown
7	Multiple Players Tied	11	Earl Moore
		11	Lefty Tyler

1912

Tm	Tot	H	A	Consec 2	3	4	1-Inn 3	4	5	One-Game 5	6	7	8	9	10	Men-On-Base 0	1	2	3	Pitchers PH	LO	XN	IP	P	Totals 1	10	20	30	40	Batters RHB	LHB
AL																															
BOS	18	10	8	0	0	0	0	0	0	0	0	0	0	0	0	9	4	5	0	0	1	0	9	1	5	0	0	0	0	6	12
CHI	26	12	14	0	0	0	0	0	0	0	0	0	0	0	0	14	8	4	0	0	0	1	8	5	9	0	0	0	0	13	13
CLE	15	6	9	0	0	0	0	0	0	0	0	0	0	0	0	3	8	4	0	0	0	0	6	1	6	0	0	0	0	6	9
DET	16	6	10	0	0	0	0	0	0	0	0	0	0	0	0	5	6	5	0	0	1	0	7	0	9	0	0	0	0	8	8
NY	28	16	12	0	0	0	0	0	0	0	0	0	0	0	0	18	8	2	0	0	1	0	9	2	7	1	0	0	0	18	10
PHI	12	6	6	0	0	0	0	0	0	0	0	0	0	0	0	5	5	1	1	0	0	0	3	1	7	0	0	0	0	9	3
STL	17	11	6	0	0	0	0	0	0	0	0	0	0	0	0	9	4	3	1	0	0	1	3	1	7	0	0	0	0	5	12
WAS	24	12	12	0	0	0	0	0	0	0	0	0	0	0	0	11	8	3	2	0	0	0	8	1	9	0	0	0	0	6	18
NL																															
BOS	43	27	16	1	0	0	0	0	0	0	0	0	0	0	0	22	16	4	1	0	0	2	3	2	5	2	0	0	0	23	20
BRO	45	20	25	0	0	0	0	0	0	0	0	0	0	0	0	20	19	6	0	0	0	0	13	1	9	1	0	0	0	27	18
CHI	33	19	14	0	0	0	0	0	0	0	0	0	0	0	0	16	10	5	2	0	1	0	6	2	9	0	0	0	0	16	17
CIN	28	2	26	0	0	0	0	0	0	0	0	0	0	0	0	15	8	5	0	0	0	1	4	1	9	0	0	0	0	11	17
NY	35	20	15	0	0	0	0	0	0	0	0	0	0	0	0	15	14	6	0	0	2	1	3	0	8	0	0	0	0	22	13
PHI	43	26	17	1	0	0	0	0	0	0	0	0	0	0	0	26	9	8	0	1	2	1	3	0	11	1	0	0	0	21	22
PIT	28	9	19	1	0	0	0	0	0	0	0	0	0	0	0	17	9	2	0	1	0	1	9	1	8	0	0	0	0	20	8
STL	31	9	22	0	0	0	0	0	0	0	0	0	0	0	0	15	9	4	3	1	1	0	8	0	8	0	0	0	0	14	17
AL	156	79	77	0	0	0	0	0	0	0	0	0	0	0	0	74	51	27	4	0	3	2	53	12	59	1	0	0	0	71	85
NL	286	132	154	3	0	0	0	0	0	0	0	0	0	0	0	146	94	40	6	3	6	6	49	7	67	4	0	0	0	154	132
YR	442	211	231	3	0	0	0	0	0	0	0	0	0	0	0	220	145	67	10	3	9	8	102	19	126	5	0	0	0	225	217

	AL		*NL*
11	Russ Ford	11	Grover Alexander
8	Tom Hughes	11	Hub Perdue
6	Hugh Bedient	10	Ed Donnelly
6	Ed Walsh	10	Eral Yingling
5	Multiple Players Tied	9	Rube Marquard

1913

Tm	Tot	H	A	Consec 2	3	4	1-Inn 3	4	5	One-Game 5	6	7	8	9	10	Men-On-Base 0	1	2	3	Pitchers PH	LO	XN	IP	P	Totals 1	10	20	30	40	Batters RHB	LHB
AL																															
BOS	6	0	6	0	0	0	0	0	0	0	0	0	0	0	0	4	2	0	0	0	0	0	1	0	4	0	0	0	0	5	1
CHI	10	4	6	0	0	0	0	0	0	0	0	0	0	0	0	6	2	1	1	0	0	0	5	0	6	0	0	0	0	6	4
CLE	19	9	10	0	0	0	0	0	0	0	0	0	0	0	0	9	6	4	0	1	0	0	7	0	8	0	0	0	0	7	12
DET	13	5	8	0	0	0	0	0	0	0	0	0	0	0	0	9	2	1	1	1	0	0	0	0	8	0	0	0	0	6	7
NY	31	20	11	0	0	0	0	0	0	0	0	0	0	0	0	17	9	4	1	0	0	0	7	2	10	0	0	0	0	13	18
PHI	24	14	10	0	0	0	0	0	0	0	0	0	0	0	0	14	7	3	0	0	1	0	3	2	8	0	0	0	0	15	9
STL	21	11	10	0	0	0	0	0	0	0	0	0	0	0	0	13	4	4	0	0	2	0	6	2	6	0	0	0	0	8	13
WAS	35	29	6	0	0	0	0	0	0	0	0	0	0	0	0	20	10	3	2	0	3	0	11	3	11	0	0	0	0	15	20
NL																															
BOS	37	12	25	0	0	0	0	0	0	0	0	0	0	0	0	14	14	8	1	2	1	0	10	2	9	1	0	0	0	20	17
BRO	33	14	19	0	0	0	0	0	0	0	0	0	0	0	0	13	12	7	1	2	0	1	14	0	7	1	0	0	0	18	15
CHI	39	20	19	0	0	0	0	0	0	0	0	0	0	0	0	18	15	6	0	1	0	0	10	1	10	1	0	0	0	17	22
CIN	40	13	27	1	0	0	0	0	0	0	0	0	0	0	0	22	12	4	2	1	0	0	13	1	10	0	0	0	0	22	18
NY	38	22	16	0	0	0	0	0	0	0	0	0	0	0	0	19	14	5	0	2	0	1	4	0	6	1	0	0	0	23	15
PHI	40	23	17	0	0	0	0	0	0	0	0	0	0	0	0	18	13	8	1	2	1	1	4	2	10	0	0	0	0	23	17

Tm	Tot	H	A	Consec 2	3	4	1-Inn 3	4	5	One-Game 5	6	7	8	9	10	Men-On-Base 0	1	2	3	Pitchers PH	LO	XN	IP	P	Totals 1	10	20	30	40	Batters RHB	LHB
PIT	26	6	20	0	0	0	0	0	0	0	0	0	0	0	0	5	17	3	1	0	0	0	7	0	7	0	0	0	0	15	11
STL	57	20	37	0	0	0	0	0	0	0	0	0	0	0	0	27	23	7	0	1	1	1	20	2	9	2	0	0	0	32	25
AL	159	92	67	0	0	0	0	0	0	0	0	0	0	0	0	92	42	20	5	2	6	0	40	9	61	0	0	0	0	75	84
NL	310	130	180	1	0	0	0	0	0	0	0	0	0	0	0	136	120	48	6	11	3	4	82	8	68	6	0	0	0	170	140
YR	469	222	247	1	0	0	0	0	0	0	0	0	0	0	0	228	162	68	11	13	9	4	122	17	129	6	0	0	0	245	224

AL		*NL*	
9	Russ Ford	12	Dan Griner
9	Walter Johnson	12	Otto Hess
8	Bob Groom	11	Slim Sallee
6	Multiple Players Tied	10	Multiple Players Tied

1914

Tm	Tot	H	A	Consec 2	3	4	1-Inn 3	4	5	One-Game 5	6	7	8	9	10	Men-On-Base 0	1	2	3	Pitchers PH	LO	XN	IP	P	Totals 1	10	20	30	40	Batters RHB	LHB
AL																															
BOS	18	5	13	0	0	0	0	0	0	0	0	0	0	0	0	9	7	2	0	0	0	0	4	2	9	0	0	0	0	11	7
CHI	15	4	11	0	0	0	0	0	0	0	0	0	0	0	0	10	3	2	0	0	0	2	7	0	4	0	0	0	0	9	6
CLE	10	3	7	0	0	0	0	0	0	0	0	0	0	0	0	6	2	1	1	0	1	0	4	0	4	0	0	0	0	4	6
DET	17	9	8	0	0	0	0	0	0	0	0	0	0	0	0	10	5	1	1	0	1	0	7	2	8	0	0	0	0	9	8
NY	30	24	6	0	0	0	0	0	0	0	0	0	0	0	0	17	8	5	0	0	1	1	1	2	8	0	0	0	0	17	13
PHI	18	12	6	0	0	0	0	0	0	0	0	0	0	0	0	12	6	0	0	0	0	1	0	2	9	0	0	0	0	15	3
STL	20	14	6	1	0	0	0	0	0	0	0	0	0	0	0	6	9	5	0	0	0	0	3	0	7	0	0	0	0	8	12
WAS	20	7	13	0	0	0	0	0	0	0	0	0	0	0	0	11	8	1	0	0	3	1	7	1	7	0	0	0	0	9	11
FL																															
BAL	34	16	18	0	0	0	0	0	0	0	0	0	0	0	0	20	8	4	2	0	0	1	0	4	7	1	0	0	0	16	18
BRO	31	13	18	1	0	0	0	0	0	0	0	0	0	0	0	14	13	3	1	0	0	2	2	1	10	0	0	0	0	11	20
BUF	45	18	27	0	0	0	0	0	0	0	0	0	0	0	0	28	9	6	2	1	0	0	5	3	9	1	0	0	0	25	20
CHI	43	20	23	0	0	0	0	0	0	0	0	0	0	0	0	27	10	5	1	0	3	2	1	2	9	0	0	0	0	19	23
IND	29	8	21	0	0	0	0	0	0	0	0	0	0	0	0	15	10	4	0	0	0	1	1	1	6	0	0	0	0	13	16
KC	37	21	16	0	0	0	0	0	0	0	0	0	0	0	0	18	15	4	0	1	0	2	1	2	8	0	0	0	0	28	9
PIT	38	10	28	0	0	0	0	0	0	0	0	0	0	0	0	24	9	5	0	1	3	2	4	1	7	0	0	0	0	15	23
STL	38	22	16	0	0	0	0	0	0	0	0	0	0	0	0	20	7	10	1	2	0	1	0	1	8	0	0	0	0	16	22
NL																															
BOS	38	17	21	2	0	0	0	0	0	0	0	0	0	0	0	29	8	1	0	0	2	0	9	1	9	0	0	0	0	22	16
BRO	36	17	19	0	0	0	0	0	0	0	0	0	0	0	0	17	11	4	4	1	1	1	18	0	10	0	0	0	0	22	14
CHI	37	20	17	0	0	0	0	0	0	0	0	0	0	0	0	15	15	6	1	3	0	1	8	1	6	1	0	0	0	19	18
CIN	30	5	25	0	0	0	0	0	0	0	0	0	0	0	0	15	7	8	0	0	1	1	8	1	9	0	0	0	0	18	12
NY	47	22	25	0	0	0	0	0	0	0	0	0	0	0	0	29	11	7	0	2	1	0	13	2	6	1	0	0	0	20	27
PHI	26	16	10	0	0	0	0	0	0	0	0	0	0	0	0	9	11	6	0	0	1	1	7	0	6	0	0	0	0	14	12
PIT	27	6	21	0	0	0	0	0	0	0	0	0	0	0	0	16	8	3	0	0	0	2	7	0	8	0	0	0	0	10	17
STL	26	14	12	0	0	0	0	0	0	0	0	0	0	0	0	15	8	1	2	0	1	1	9	1	9	0	0	0	0	12	14
AL	148	78	70	1	0	0	0	0	0	0	0	0	0	0	0	81	48	17	2	0	6	5	33	9	56	0	0	0	0	82	66
FL	295	128	167	1	0	0	0	0	0	0	0	0	0	0	0	166	81	41	7	5	6	11	14	15	64	2	0	0	0	143	151
NL	267	117	150	2	0	0	0	0	0	0	0	0	0	0	0	145	79	36	7	6	7	7	79	6	63	2	0	0	0	137	130
YR	710	323	387	4	0	0	0	0	0	0	0	0	0	0	0	392	208	94	16	11	19	23	126	30	183	4	0	0	0	362	347

AL		*FL*		*NL*	
8	Jack Warhop	11	Russ Ford	16	Christy Mathewson
6	Cy Pieh	10	Kaiser Wilhelm	11	Jimmy Lavender
5	Multiple Players Tied	9	Bob Groom	9	Multiple Players Tied
		9	Elmer Knetzer		
		8	Multiple Players Tied		

1915

Tm	Tot	H	A	Consec 2	3	4	1-Inn 3	4	5	One-Game 5	6	7	8	9	10	Men-On-Base 0	1	2	3	Pitchers PH	LO	XN	IP	P	Totals 1	10	20	30	40	Batters RHB	LHB
AL																															
BOS	18	4	14	0	0	0	0	0	0	0	0	0	0	0	0	8	8	2	0	0	1	0	2	0	8	0	0	0	0	12	6
CHI	14	4	10	0	0	0	0	0	0	0	0	0	0	0	0	10	0	4	0	2	0	0	1	0	5	0	0	0	0	6	8
CLE	18	9	9	0	0	0	0	0	0	0	0	0	0	0	0	10	5	3	0	0	0	0	5	1	11	0	0	0	0	12	6
DET	14	7	7	0	0	0	0	0	0	0	0	0	0	0	0	8	5	1	0	0	0	0	2	3	7	0	0	0	0	8	6
NY	41	32	9	0	0	0	0	0	0	0	0	0	0	0	0	20	18	3	0	0	0	1	5	6	15	0	0	0	0	16	25
PHI	22	17	5	0	0	0	0	0	0	0	0	0	0	0	0	13	5	3	1	0	1	0	1	1	14	0	0	0	0	17	5
STL	21	7	14	0	0	0	0	0	0	0	0	0	0	0	0	15	3	3	0	0	0	1	3	2	9	0	0	0	0	7	14
WAS	12	2	10	0	0	0	0	0	0	0	0	0	0	0	0	4	7	1	0	0	0	0	3	0	6	0	0	0	0	7	5

Tm	Tot	H	A	Consec 2	3	4	1-Inn 3	4	5	One-Game 5	6	7	8	9	10	Men-On-Base 0	1	2	3	Pitchers PH	LO	XN	IP	P	Totals 1	10	20	30	40	Batters RHB	LHB
FL																															
BAL	52	36	16	0	0	0	0	0	0	0	0	0	0	0	0	33	12	5	2	1	1	0	0	4	9	1	0	0	0	32	20
BRO	27	11	16	1	0	0	0	0	0	0	0	0	0	0	0	14	10	2	1	0	0	0	0	1	11	0	0	0	0	9	18
BUF	35	21	14	0	0	0	0	0	0	0	0	0	0	0	0	22	5	6	2	2	2	0	0	2	8	0	0	0	0	22	13
CHI	34	10	24	0	0	0	0	0	0	0	0	0	0	0	0	17	14	2	1	1	0	1	2	1	8	0	0	0	0	17	17
KC	29	19	10	0	0	0	0	0	0	0	0	0	0	0	0	15	10	4	0	0	1	1	1	1	7	0	0	0	0	19	10
NWK	15	2	13	0	0	0	0	0	0	0	0	0	0	0	0	6	5	4	0	1	1	0	3	0	6	0	0	0	0	6	9
PIT	36	10	26	0	0	0	0	0	0	0	0	0	0	0	0	21	11	4	0	0	1	1	6	0	9	0	0	0	0	17	19
STL	22	15	7	0	0	0	0	0	0	0	0	0	0	0	0	8	13	1	0	0	0	1	1	2	8	0	0	0	0	6	16
NL																															
BOS	23	5	18	0	0	0	0	0	0	0	0	0	0	0	0	14	7	2	0	0	0	0	7	0	8	0	0	0	0	12	11
BRO	29	14	15	0	0	0	0	0	0	0	0	0	0	0	0	13	9	5	2	0	1	1	6	1	9	0	0	0	0	11	18
CHI	28	16	12	0	0	0	0	0	0	0	0	0	0	0	0	12	11	5	0	0	0	0	6	3	9	0	0	0	0	13	15
CIN	28	7	21	2	0	0	0	0	0	0	0	0	0	0	0	15	8	5	0	1	0	0	8	1	10	0	0	0	0	11	17
NY	40	20	20	0	0	0	0	0	0	0	0	0	0	0	0	14	15	8	3	0	0	0	10	0	9	0	0	0	0	20	20
PHI	26	18	8	0	0	0	0	0	0	0	0	0	0	0	0	17	9	0	0	0	0	0	7	2	9	0	0	0	0	17	9
PIT	21	6	15	0	0	0	0	0	0	0	0	0	0	0	0	11	8	2	0	0	0	1	9	1	6	0	0	0	0	13	8
STL	30	10	20	0	0	0	0	0	0	0	0	0	0	0	0	14	12	4	0	0	1	1	7	0	8	0	0	0	0	15	15
AL	160	82	78	0	0	0	0	0	0	0	0	0	0	0	0	88	51	20	1	2	2	2	22	13	75	0	0	0	0	85	75
FL	250	124	126	1	0	0	0	0	0	0	0	0	0	0	0	136	80	28	6	5	6	4	13	11	66	1	0	0	0	128	122
NL	225	96	129	2	0	0	0	0	0	0	0	0	0	0	0	110	79	31	5	1	2	3	60	8	68	0	0	0	0	112	113
YR	635	302	333	3	0	0	0	0	0	0	0	0	0	0	0	334	210	79	12	8	10	9	95	32	209	1	0	0	0	325	310

	AL		*FL*		*NL*
7	Raymund Fisher	12	George Suggs	9	Christy Mathewson
7	Jack Warhop	9	Frank Allen	9	Erskine Mayer
6	Ray Caldwell	9	Bill Bailey	8	Rube Marquard
6	Carl Weilman	9	Jack Quinn	8	Jeff Pfeffer
5	Multiple Players Tied	8	Multiple Players Tied	7	Multiple Players Tied

1916

Tm	Tot	H	A	Consec 2	3	4	1-Inn 3	4	5	One-Game 5	6	7	8	9	10	Men-On-Base 0	1	2	3	Pitchers PH	LO	XN	IP	P	Totals 1	10	20	30	40	Batters RHB	LHB
AL																															
BOS	10	1	9	0	0	0	0	0	0	0	0	0	0	0	0	8	1	0	1	1	0	0	2	0	3	0	0	0	0	5	5
CHI	14	5	9	0	0	0	0	0	0	0	0	0	0	0	0	5	5	2	2	0	0	0	0	2	7	0	0	0	0	8	6
CLE	16	9	7	0	0	0	0	0	0	0	0	0	0	0	0	7	4	4	1	0	0	1	3	0	10	0	0	0	0	2	14
DET	12	8	4	0	0	0	0	0	0	0	0	0	0	0	0	7	3	2	0	0	1	0	2	1	6	0	0	0	0	7	5
NY	37	22	15	1	0	0	0	0	0	0	0	0	0	0	0	22	10	3	2	2	1	0	12	1	9	0	0	0	0	16	21
PHI	26	17	9	0	0	0	0	0	0	0	0	0	0	0	0	10	11	4	1	1	1	0	5	0	9	0	0	0	0	13	13
STL	15	10	5	0	0	0	0	0	0	0	0	0	0	0	0	8	4	3	0	1	0	1	1	2	7	0	0	0	0	6	9
WAS	14	1	13	0	0	0	0	0	0	0	0	0	0	0	0	5	8	1	0	0	0	0	0	0	6	0	0	0	0	1	13
NL																															
BOS	24	4	20	0	0	0	0	0	0	0	0	0	0	0	0	17	4	2	1	0	0	1	8	0	8	0	0	0	0	15	9
BRO	24	9	15	0	0	0	0	0	0	0	0	0	0	0	0	17	7	0	0	0	2	1	4	0	8	0	0	0	0	15	9
CHI	32	22	10	0	0	0	0	0	0	0	0	0	0	0	0	14	11	6	1	0	0	2	4	1	8	0	0	0	0	17	15
CIN	35	10	25	0	0	0	0	0	0	0	0	0	0	0	0	18	11	5	1	0	2	1	15	1	9	0	0	0	0	15	20
NY	41	23	18	1	0	0	0	0	0	0	0	0	0	0	0	24	12	5	0	1	2	0	9	1	8	1	0	0	0	22	19
PHI	28	17	11	0	0	0	0	0	0	0	0	0	0	0	0	20	6	1	1	0	1	1	1	1	8	0	0	0	0	14	14
PIT	24	5	19	0	0	0	0	0	0	0	0	0	0	0	0	14	6	3	1	0	0	3	11	0	10	0	0	0	0	9	15
STL	31	15	16	0	0	0	0	0	0	0	0	0	0	0	0	14	10	7	0	1	1	0	12	2	10	0	0	0	0	13	18
AL	144	73	71	1	0	0	0	0	0	0	0	0	0	0	0	72	46	19	7	5	3	2	25	6	57	0	0	0	0	58	86
NL	239	105	134	1	0	0	0	0	0	0	0	0	0	0	0	138	67	29	5	2	8	9	64	6	69	1	0	0	0	120	119
YR	383	178	205	2	0	0	0	0	0	0	0	0	0	0	0	210	113	48	12	7	11	11	89	12	126	1	0	0	0	178	205

	AL		*NL*
8	Allen Russell	11	Pol Perritt
7	Elmer Myers	9	Jeff Tesreau
6	Multiple Players Tied	8	George McConnell
		7	Multiple Players Tied

1917

Tm	Tot	H	A	Consec 2	3	4	1-Inn 3	4	5	One-Game 5	6	7	8	9	10	Men-On-Base 0	1	2	3	Pitchers PH	LO	XN	IP	P	Totals 1	10	20	30	40	Batters RHB	LHB
AL																															
BOS	12	4	8	0	0	0	0	0	0	0	0	0	0	0	0	5	7	0	0	0	0	0	1	0	7	0	0	0	0	6	6

				Consec			1-Inn			One-Game						Men-On-Base				Pitchers					Totals					Batters	
Tm	Tot	H	A	2	3	4	3	4	5	5	6	7	8	9	10	0	1	2	3	PH	LO	XN	IP	P	1	10	20	30	40	RHB	LHB
CHI	10	3	7	0	0	0	0	0	0	0	0	0	0	0	0	3	5	2	0	0	0	0	0	0	7	0	0	0	0	5	5
CLE	17	8	9	0	0	0	0	0	0	0	0	0	0	0	0	10	4	1	2	0	0	0	3	3	7	0	0	0	0	7	10
DET	12	5	7	0	0	0	0	0	0	0	0	0	0	0	0	7	2	3	0	0	0	0	1	1	5	0	0	0	0	4	8
NY	28	24	4	0	0	0	0	0	0	0	0	0	0	0	0	14	10	4	0	1	2	1	6	1	8	0	0	0	0	12	16
PHI	23	17	6	0	0	0	0	0	0	0	0	0	0	0	0	7	11	5	0	0	0	0	2	0	9	0	0	0	0	15	8
STL	19	10	9	0	0	0	0	0	0	0	0	0	0	0	0	7	6	5	1	1	0	1	2	0	10	0	0	0	0	9	10
WAS	12	3	9	0	0	0	0	0	0	0	0	0	0	0	0	7	2	2	1	1	0	1	4	0	6	0	0	0	0	5	7
NL																															
BOS	19	3	16	0	0	0	0	0	0	0	0	0	0	0	0	11	7	0	1	0	1	0	5	1	7	0	0	0	0	10	9
BRO	32	14	18	1	0	0	0	0	0	0	0	0	0	0	0	16	11	4	1	0	1	2	10	0	8	0	0	0	0	17	15
CHI	34	14	20	1	0	0	0	0	0	0	0	0	0	0	0	21	7	6	0	0	0	1	9	1	7	1	0	0	0	19	15
CIN	20	3	17	0	0	0	0	0	0	0	0	0	0	0	0	7	11	2	0	0	0	0	6	1	6	0	0	0	0	9	11
NY	29	17	12	0	0	0	0	0	0	0	0	0	0	0	0	19	6	4	0	0	0	0	10	1	9	0	0	0	0	20	9
PHI	25	20	5	0	0	0	0	0	0	0	0	0	0	0	0	13	7	5	0	0	1	0	3	0	7	0	0	0	0	17	8
PIT	14	4	10	0	0	0	0	0	0	0	0	0	0	0	0	6	6	2	0	3	0	0	8	0	5	0	0	0	0	9	5
STL	29	15	14	0	0	0	0	0	0	0	0	0	0	0	0	15	10	4	0	0	1	1	18	0	10	0	0	0	0	17	12
AL	133	74	59	0	0	0	0	0	0	0	0	0	0	0	0	60	47	22	4	3	2	3	19	5	59	0	0	0	0	63	70
NL	202	90	112	2	0	0	0	0	0	0	0	0	0	0	0	108	65	27	2	3	4	4	69	4	59	1	0	0	0	118	84
YR	335	164	171	2	0	0	0	0	0	0	0	0	0	0	0	168	112	49	6	6	6	7	88	9	118	1	0	0	0	181	154

AL		*NL*	
8	Ray Caldwell	13	Phil Douglas
6	Jim Bagby	7	Jack Coombs
6	Rube Schauer	7	Joe Oeschger
5	Multiple Players Tied	7	Ferdie Schupp
		6	Multiple Players Tied

1918

				Consec			1-Inn			One-Game						Men-On-Base				Pitchers					Totals					Batters	
Tm	Tot	H	A	2	3	4	3	4	5	5	6	7	8	9	10	0	1	2	3	PH	LO	XN	IP	P	1	10	20	30	40	RHB	LHB
AL																															
BOS	9	3	6	0	0	0	0	0	0	0	0	0	0	0	0	3	5	1	0	1	0	0	1	0	6	0	0	0	0	5	4
CHI	9	4	5	1	0	0	0	0	0	0	0	0	0	0	0	6	2	1	0	0	0	0	0	0	6	0	0	0	0	8	1
CLE	9	4	5	0	0	0	0	0	0	0	0	0	0	0	0	4	5	0	0	0	0	0	2	0	4	0	0	0	0	6	3
DET	10	6	4	0	0	0	0	0	0	0	0	0	0	0	0	6	3	1	0	0	0	1	2	1	5	0	0	0	0	2	8
NY	25	22	3	1	0	0	0	0	0	0	0	0	0	0	0	15	7	3	0	0	0	1	1	3	6	0	0	0	0	18	7
PHI	13	8	5	0	0	0	0	0	0	0	0	0	0	0	0	7	5	1	0	0	0	0	3	2	6	0	0	0	0	11	2
STL	11	7	4	0	0	0	0	0	0	0	0	0	0	0	0	5	4	2	0	0	0	0	1	0	7	0	0	0	0	4	7
WAS	10	6	4	0	0	0	0	0	0	0	0	0	0	0	0	5	4	1	0	0	0	1	2	0	6	0	0	0	0	3	7
NL																															
BOS	14	2	12	0	0	0	0	0	0	0	0	0	0	0	0	3	9	2	0	0	0	1	3	1	7	0	0	0	0	8	6
BRO	22	12	10	1	0	0	0	0	0	0	0	0	0	0	0	7	7	6	2	0	0	2	11	2	3	1	0	0	0	12	10
CHI	13	5	8	0	0	0	0	0	0	0	0	0	0	0	0	6	4	3	0	0	0	1	3	1	7	0	0	0	0	11	2
CIN	19	5	14	0	0	0	0	0	0	0	0	0	0	0	0	10	4	4	1	0	0	0	9	1	8	0	0	0	0	9	10
NY	20	13	7	0	0	0	0	0	0	0	0	0	0	0	0	8	6	6	0	0	0	0	7	1	9	0	0	0	0	9	11
PHI	22	13	9	1	0	0	0	0	0	0	0	0	0	0	0	11	6	4	1	0	0	0	3	1	9	0	0	0	0	14	8
PIT	13	4	9	0	0	0	0	0	0	0	0	0	0	0	0	6	6	1	0	0	0	0	6	0	8	0	0	0	0	8	5
STL	16	7	9	0	0	0	0	0	0	0	0	0	0	0	0	7	4	3	2	0	0	2	5	0	6	0	0	0	0	8	8
AL	96	60	36	2	0	0	0	0	0	0	0	0	0	0	0	51	35	10	0	1	0	3	12	6	46	0	0	0	0	57	39
NL	139	61	78	2	0	0	0	0	0	0	0	0	0	0	0	58	46	29	6	0	0	6	47	7	57	1	0	0	0	79	60
YR	235	121	114	4	0	0	0	0	0	0	0	0	0	0	0	109	81	39	6	1	0	9	59	13	103	1	0	0	0	136	99

AL		*NL*	
7	Happy Finneran	10	Jack Coombs
6	George Mogridge	7	Rube Marquard
6	Allen Russell	6	Gene Packard
4	Multiple Players Tied	6	Mike Prendergast
		5	Multiple Players Tied

1919

				Consec			1-Inn			One-Game						Men-On-Base				Pitchers					Totals					Batters	
Tm	Tot	H	A	2	3	4	3	4	5	5	6	7	8	9	10	0	1	2	3	PH	LO	XN	IP	P	1	10	20	30	40	RHB	LHB
AL																															
BOS	16	3	13	0	0	0	0	0	0	0	0	0	0	0	0	7	7	2	0	0	0	0	5	1	9	0	0	0	0	12	4
CHI	24	10	14	0	0	0	0	0	0	0	0	0	0	0	0	15	7	2	0	1	0	0	3	2	7	0	0	0	0	9	15

				Consec			1-Inn			One-Game						Men-On-Base				Pitchers					Totals					Batters	
Tm	Tot	H	A	2	3	4	3	4	5	5	6	7	8	9	10	0	1	2	3	PH	LO	XN	IP	P	1	10	20	30	40	RHB	LHB
CLE	19	4	15	0	0	0	0	0	0	0	0	0	0	0	0	9	5	4	1	0	0	1	1	0	10	0	0	0	0	9	10
DET	35	14	21	0	0	0	0	0	0	0	0	0	0	0	0	18	12	4	1	2	0	0	4	1	7	0	0	0	0	17	18
NY	47	30	17	1	0	0	0	0	0	0	0	0	0	0	0	28	14	2	3	0	0	2	9	1	10	1	0	0	0	19	28
PHI	44	31	13	0	0	0	0	0	0	1	0	0	0	0	0	18	18	7	1	0	1	1	6	4	14	0	0	0	0	28	16
STL	35	23	12	0	0	0	0	0	0	0	0	0	0	0	0	19	9	5	2	0	0	1	3	2	7	1	0	0	0	12	23
WAS	20	5	15	1	0	0	0	0	0	0	0	0	0	0	0	12	7	1	0	0	0	0	3	0	7	0	0	0	0	11	9
NL																															
BOS	29	9	20	0	0	0	0	0	0	0	0	0	0	0	0	13	11	5	0	0	0	3	14	0	9	0	0	0	0	16	13
BRO	21	10	11	0	0	0	0	0	0	0	0	0	0	0	0	11	9	1	0	1	2	2	8	1	7	0	0	0	0	12	9
CHI	14	7	7	0	0	0	0	0	0	0	0	0	0	0	0	9	4	1	0	0	0	0	6	1	6	0	0	0	0	7	7
CIN	21	5	16	2	0	0	0	0	0	0	0	0	0	0	0	12	5	3	1	0	1	0	9	2	7	0	0	0	0	12	9
NY	34	17	17	0	0	0	0	0	0	0	0	0	0	0	0	23	7	3	1	2	0	0	11	1	9	0	0	0	0	20	14
PHI	40	24	16	0	0	0	0	0	0	0	0	0	0	0	0	17	15	8	0	1	0	2	9	2	11	0	0	0	0	23	17
PIT	23	7	16	0	0	0	0	0	0	0	0	0	0	0	0	13	7	2	1	0	0	0	7	0	5	1	0	0	0	16	7
STL	25	10	15	0	0	0	0	0	0	0	0	0	0	0	0	14	9	2	0	1	2	0	4	0	10	0	0	0	0	13	12
AL	240	120	120	2	0	0	0	0	0	1	0	0	0	0	0	126	79	27	8	3	1	5	34	11	71	2	0	0	0	117	123
NL	207	89	118	2	0	0	0	0	0	0	0	0	0	0	0	112	67	25	3	5	5	7	68	7	64	1	0	0	0	119	88
YR	447	209	238	4	0	0	0	0	0	1	0	0	0	0	0	238	146	52	11	8	6	12	102	18	135	3	0	0	0	236	211

	AL		*NL*
10	Bert Gallia	10	Wilbur Cooper
10	Hank Thormahlen	8	Jess Barnes
9	Hooks Dauss	8	Al Demaree
9	Tom Rogers	8	Art Nehf
8	Multiple Players Tied	8	George Smith

1920

Tm	Tot	H	A	Consec 2	3	4	1-Inn 3	4	5	One-Game 5	6	7	8	9	10	Men-On-Base 0	1	2	3	PH	LO	XN	IP	P	Totals 1	10	20	30	40	RHB	LHB
AL																															
BOS	39	14	25	1	0	0	0	0	0	0	0	0	0	0	0	21	16	1	1	0	1	0	4	0	8	0	0	0	0	19	20
CHI	45	10	35	0	0	0	0	0	0	0	0	0	0	0	0	23	15	6	1	0	2	1	7	2	6	1	0	0	0	16	29
CLE	31	10	21	0	0	0	0	0	0	0	0	0	0	0	0	24	5	2	0	0	2	1	5	1	7	0	0	0	0	15	16
DET	46	24	22	0	0	0	0	0	0	0	0	0	0	0	0	23	17	6	0	0	0	1	8	1	9	1	0	0	0	24	22
NY	48	36	12	0	0	0	0	0	0	0	0	0	0	0	0	33	8	4	3	1	1	0	7	1	6	2	0	0	0	27	21
PHI	56	41	15	1	0	0	0	0	0	0	0	0	0	0	0	26	21	7	2	0	0	1	5	0	10	1	0	0	0	25	31
STL	53	33	20	2	0	0	0	0	0	0	0	0	0	0	0	30	12	10	1	0	0	2	4	4	10	2	0	0	0	22	31
WAS	51	7	44	1	0	0	0	0	0	0	0	0	0	0	0	28	16	4	3	0	1	0	10	0	9	2	0	0	0	26	25
NL																															
BOS	39	11	28	2	0	0	0	0	0	0	0	0	0	0	0	24	8	7	0	0	2	1	12	1	9	1	0	0	0	14	25
BRO	25	14	11	0	0	0	0	0	0	0	0	0	0	0	0	13	8	4	0	0	0	1	7	0	8	0	0	0	0	13	12
CHI	37	15	22	0	0	0	0	0	0	0	0	0	0	0	0	21	10	6	0	1	1	1	7	0	10	0	0	0	0	18	19
CIN	26	1	25	0	0	0	0	0	0	0	0	0	0	0	0	13	9	4	0	1	0	1	3	2	6	0	0	0	0	12	14
NY	44	33	11	1	0	0	0	0	0	0	0	0	0	0	0	20	16	8	0	2	0	0	10	2	9	0	0	0	0	22	22
PHI	35	30	5	0	0	0	0	0	0	0	0	0	0	0	0	21	7	6	1	1	0	1	0	3	9	1	0	0	0	23	12
PIT	25	4	21	0	0	0	0	0	0	0	0	0	0	0	0	15	9	1	0	0	1	0	6	0	9	0	0	0	0	16	9
STL	30	10	20	0	0	0	0	0	0	0	0	0	0	0	0	12	17	1	0	0	1	0	4	2	8	0	0	0	0	15	15
AL	369	175	194	5	0	0	0	0	0	0	0	0	0	0	0	208	110	40	11	1	7	6	50	9	65	9	0	0	0	174	195
NL	261	118	143	3	0	0	0	0	0	0	0	0	0	0	0	139	84	37	1	5	5	5	49	10	68	2	0	0	0	133	128
YR	630	293	337	8	0	0	0	0	0	0	0	0	0	0	0	347	194	77	12	6	12	11	99	19	133	11	0	0	0	307	323

	AL		*NL*
15	Lefty Williams	10	Joe Oeschger
14	Scott Perry	10	George Smith
13	Eric Erickson	9	Jess Barnes
13	Carl Mays	9	Jesse Haines
12	Jim Shaw	8	Multiple Players Tied

1921

Tm	Tot	H	A	Consec 2	3	4	1-Inn 3	4	5	One-Game 5	6	7	8	9	10	Men-On-Base 0	1	2	3	PH	LO	XN	IP	P	Totals 1	10	20	30	40	RHB	LHB
AL																															
BOS	53	16	37	0	0	0	0	0	0	0	0	0	0	0	0	27	18	7	1	0	1	3	6	1	5	3	0	0	0	25	28
CHI	52	20	32	2	0	0	0	0	0	0	0	0	0	0	0	26	14	10	2	0	0	0	7	4	9	2	0	0	0	27	25
CLE	43	10	33	1	0	0	0	0	0	0	0	0	0	0	0	26	11	6	0	0	0	0	3	2	6	1	0	0	0	14	29

Tm	Tot	H	A	Consec 2	3	4	1-Inn 3	4	5	One-Game 5	6	7	8	9	10	Men-On-Base 0	1	2	3	Pitchers PH	LO	XN	IP	P	Totals 1	10	20	30	40	Batters RHB	LHB
DET	71	29	42	1	0	0	1	0	0	0	0	1	0	0	0	35	23	11	2	0	1	2	7	3	5	4	0	0	0	42	29
NY	51	34	17	0	0	0	0	0	0	0	0	0	0	0	0	30	13	7	1	0	1	1	7	2	9	2	0	0	0	14	37
PHI	85	59	26	1	0	0	0	0	0	0	0	0	0	0	0	40	27	18	0	0	0	2	7	2	5	3	1	0	0	44	41
STL	71	43	28	2	0	0	0	0	0	0	0	0	0	0	0	33	20	17	1	0	2	1	1	4	7	3	1	0	0	33	38
WAS	51	13	38	1	0	0	0	0	0	0	0	0	0	0	0	23	19	8	1	0	0	0	5	0	6	2	0	0	0	31	20
NL																															
BOS	54	16	38	0	0	0	0	0	0	0	0	0	0	0	0	36	13	2	3	1	4	2	17	4	4	3	0	0	0	28	26
BRO	46	23	23	1	0	0	0	0	0	0	0	0	0	0	0	18	21	7	0	0	1	0	4	1	8	1	0	0	0	26	20
CHI	67	37	30	1	0	0	0	0	0	0	0	0	0	0	0	37	17	10	3	1	2	2	7	4	7	3	0	0	0	31	36
CIN	37	2	35	0	0	0	0	0	0	0	0	0	0	0	0	25	7	3	2	0	3	1	8	1	8	1	0	0	0	21	16
NY	79	48	31	2	0	0	1	0	0	1	0	0	0	0	0	44	26	7	2	1	3	2	8	3	4	4	0	0	0	48	31
PHI	79	49	30	3	0	0	0	0	0	1	0	0	0	0	0	43	20	15	1	0	0	2	6	3	8	3	0	0	0	37	42
PIT	37	10	27	1	0	0	0	0	0	0	0	0	0	0	0	23	9	5	0	0	1	2	4	1	9	0	0	0	0	27	10
STL	61	25	36	1	0	0	0	0	0	0	0	0	0	0	0	27	24	8	2	1	0	1	9	3	9	2	0	0	0	28	33
AL	477	224	253	8	0	0	1	0	0	0	0	1	0	0	0	240	145	84	8	0	5	9	43	18	52	20	2	0	0	230	247
NL	460	210	250	9	0	0	1	0	0	2	0	0	0	0	0	253	137	57	13	4	14	12	63	20	57	17	0	0	0	246	214
YR	937	434	503	17	0	0	1	0	0	2	0	1	0	0	0	493	282	141	21	4	19	21	106	38	109	37	2	0	0	476	461

	AL		*NL*
21	Eddie Rommel	18	Bill Hubbell
21	Urban Shocker	18	Art Nehf
19	Dave Keefe	17	Leon Cadore
16	Slim Harriss	17	Phil Douglas
15	Multiple Players Tied	15	Jesse Haines

1922

Tm	Tot	H	A	Consec 2	3	4	1-Inn 3	4	5	One-Game 5	6	7	8	9	10	Men-On-Base 0	1	2	3	Pitchers PH	LO	XN	IP	P	Totals 1	10	20	30	40	Batters RHB	LHB
AL																															
BOS	48	17	31	1	0	0	0	0	0	0	0	0	0	0	0	32	7	7	2	0	0	1	4	2	8	1	0	0	0	27	21
CHI	57	21	36	0	0	0	0	0	0	0	0	0	0	0	0	32	12	12	1	1	1	3	2	2	11	2	0	0	0	32	25
CLE	58	20	38	0	0	0	0	0	0	0	0	0	0	0	0	26	22	7	3	1	0	2	6	5	14	1	0	0	0	27	31
DET	62	32	30	0	0	0	0	0	0	0	0	0	0	0	0	30	15	14	3	0	2	3	6	0	7	2	0	0	0	39	23
NY	73	48	25	3	0	0	0	0	0	0	0	0	0	0	0	44	21	7	1	0	1	0	8	0	0	5	0	0	0	30	43
PHI	107	82	25	3	0	0	0	0	0	0	0	0	0	0	0	65	25	16	1	3	2	3	4	2	8	2	2	0	0	61	46
STL	71	41	30	1	0	0	0	0	0	0	0	0	0	0	0	37	24	9	1	2	0	2	8	2	5	3	1	0	0	38	33
WAS	49	3	46	1	1	0	2	0	0	0	0	0	0	0	0	26	14	7	2	0	1	0	5	0	7	1	0	0	0	30	19
NL																															
BOS	57	15	42	1	0	0	0	0	0	1	0	0	0	0	0	25	22	8	2	1	2	3	17	1	12	1	0	0	0	32	25
BRO	74	35	39	0	0	0	0	0	0	0	0	0	0	0	0	41	21	11	1	1	2	1	6	1	6	3	0	0	0	42	32
CHI	77	37	40	2	0	0	0	0	0	0	0	0	0	0	0	36	24	17	0	3	1	1	1	1	6	3	0	0	0	47	30
CIN	49	13	36	0	0	0	0	0	0	0	0	0	0	0	0	29	12	7	1	1	0	2	7	2	5	2	0	0	0	28	21
NY	71	38	33	0	0	0	0	0	0	1	0	0	0	0	0	39	23	9	0	1	1	1	8	3	11	2	0	0	0	39	32
PHI	89	60	29	1	0	0	0	0	0	0	0	0	0	0	0	47	30	11	1	0	1	2	4	10	7	4	0	0	0	59	30
PIT	52	16	36	1	0	0	0	0	0	1	0	0	0	0	0	25	19	4	4	0	0	2	5	1	5	3	0	0	0	39	13
STL	61	32	29	1	0	0	0	0	0	0	0	0	0	0	0	35	16	10	0	2	0	0	5	2	6	4	0	0	0	26	35
AL	525	264	261	9	1	0	2	0	0	0	0	0	0	0	0	292	140	79	14	7	7	14	43	13	60	17	3	0	0	284	241
NL	530	246	284	6	0	0	0	0	0	3	0	0	0	0	0	277	167	77	9	9	7	12	53	21	58	22	0	0	0	312	218
YR	1055	510	545	15	1	0	1	0	0	3	0	0	0	0	0	569	307	156	23	16	14	26	96	34	118	39	3	0	0	596	459

	AL		*NL*
22	Urban Shocker	19	Jimmy Ring
21	Eddie Rommel	17	Burleigh Grimes
20	Bob Hasty	16	George Smith
19	Slim Harriss	15	Multiple Players Tied
18	Fred Heimach		

1923

Tm	Tot	H	A	Consec 2	3	4	1-Inn 3	4	5	One-Game 5	6	7	8	9	10	Men-On-Base 0	1	2	3	Pitchers PH	LO	XN	IP	P	Totals 1	10	20	30	40	Batters RHB	LHB
AL																															
BOS	48	15	33	0	0	0	0	0	0	0	0	0	0	0	0	29	12	4	3	1	1	0	7	1	6	1	0	0	0	16	32
CHI	49	24	25	1	0	0	0	0	0	0	0	0	0	0	0	24	16	8	1	1	0	1	0	0	7	1	0	0	0	21	28
CLE	36	16	20	2	0	0	0	0	0	0	0	0	0	0	0	22	9	5	0	2	1	0	3	1	8	0	0	0	0	15	21

				Consec			1-Inn			One-Game						Men-On-Base				Pitchers					Totals					Batters	
Tm	Tot	H	A	2	3	4	3	4	5	5	6	7	8	9	10	0	1	2	3	PH	LO	XN	IP	P	1	10	20	30	40	RHB	LHB
DET	58	31	27	1	0	0	0	0	0	0	0	0	0	0	0	32	20	5	1	1	1	2	7	1	6	3	0	0	0	25	33
NY	68	50	18	4	0	0	0	0	0	0	0	0	0	0	0	42	20	5	1	3	0	2	14	1	5	3	0	0	0	39	29
PHI	68	32	36	2	0	0	0	0	0	0	0	0	0	0	0	34	20	12	2	0	3	1	8	2	6	4	0	0	0	35	33
STL	59	44	15	0	0	0	0	0	0	0	0	0	0	0	0	30	23	5	1	1	0	2	3	3	6	3	0	0	0	20	39
WAS	56	16	40	0	0	0	0	0	0	0	0	0	0	0	0	33	13	8	2	1	1	1	11	3	10	1	0	0	0	34	22
NL																															
BOS	64	26	38	0	0	0	0	0	0	0	0	0	0	0	0	20	27	16	1	0	0	2	27	2	9	2	0	0	0	34	30
BRO	55	27	28	0	0	0	0	0	0	0	0	0	0	0	0	27	22	5	1	1	0	2	4	0	8	2	0	0	0	32	23
CHI	86	57	29	0	0	0	0	0	0	0	0	0	0	0	0	43	33	8	2	2	0	1	2	2	5	4	0	0	0	54	32
CIN	28	4	24	1	0	0	0	0	0	0	0	0	0	0	0	18	6	4	0	0	1	0	4	1	6	1	0	0	0	19	9
NY	82	53	29	2	0	0	0	0	0	0	0	0	0	0	0	47	28	6	1	2	0	3	5	4	6	5	0	0	0	48	34
PHI	100	75	25	3	0	0	0	0	0	0	0	0	0	0	0	44	37	17	2	2	0	2	2	2	6	6	0	0	0	59	41
PIT	53	9	44	1	0	0	0	0	0	1	1	0	0	0	0	27	17	9	0	0	0	1	5	0	10	1	0	0	0	34	19
STL	70	27	43	2	0	0	0	0	0	0	1	0	0	0	0	34	23	12	1	2	0	3	4	3	8	2	0	0	0	28	42
AL	442	228	214	10	0	0	0	0	0	0	0	0	0	0	0	246	133	52	11	10	7	9	53	12	54	16	0	0	0	205	237
NL	538	278	260	9	0	0	0	0	0	1	2	0	0	0	0	260	193	77	8	9	1	14	53	14	58	23	0	0	0	308	230
YR	980	506	474	19	0	0	0	0	0	1	2	0	0	0	0	506	326	129	19	19	8	23	106	26	112	39	0	0	0	513	467

	AL		*NL*
17	Bob Shawkey	17	Vic Aldridge
14	Fred Heimach	17	Grover Alexander
14	Eddie Rommel	16	Whitey Glazner
12	Multiple Players Tied	15	Multiple Players Tied

1924

				Consec			1-Inn			One-Game						Men-On-Base				Pitchers					Totals					Batters	
Tm	Tot	H	A	2	3	4	3	4	5	5	6	7	8	9	10	0	1	2	3	PH	LO	XN	IP	P	1	10	20	30	40	RHB	LHB
AL																															
BOS	43	17	26	0	0	0	0	0	0	0	0	0	0	0	0	16	15	11	1	1	0	2	2	3	9	1	0	0	0	16	27
CHI	52	23	29	2	0	0	0	0	0	0	0	0	0	0	0	32	13	5	2	1	0	2	3	1	9	2	0	0	0	21	31
CLE	43	18	25	0	0	0	0	0	0	0	0	0	0	0	0	19	18	6	0	0	2	0	4	2	12	0	0	0	0	14	29
DET	55	29	26	0	0	0	0	0	0	0	0	0	0	0	0	31	16	8	0	0	0	2	7	4	9	1	0	0	0	24	31
NY	59	46	13	2	0	0	0	0	0	0	0	0	0	0	0	28	23	6	2	0	2	1	7	1	7	2	0	0	0	17	42
PHI	43	24	19	0	0	0	0	0	0	0	0	0	0	0	0	22	9	10	2	1	1	0	0	2	10	0	0	0	0	22	21
STL	68	49	19	2	0	0	0	0	0	1	0	0	0	0	0	36	20	10	2	2	0	1	0	2	8	3	0	0	0	25	43
WAS	34	7	27	1	0	0	0	0	0	0	0	0	0	0	0	19	10	2	3	0	1	0	4	0	8	1	0	0	0	11	23
NL																															
BOS	49	8	41	0	0	0	0	0	0	0	0	0	0	0	0	19	21	7	2	1	0	2	11	4	11	0	0	0	0	30	19
BRO	58	30	28	2	0	0	0	0	0	0	0	0	0	0	0	37	16	4	1	0	1	2	6	2	6	3	0	0	0	31	27
CHI	89	68	21	0	0	0	0	0	0	1	0	0	0	0	0	46	26	16	1	0	6	0	10	3	7	2	1	0	0	55	34
CIN	30	3	27	0	0	0	0	0	0	0	0	0	0	0	0	14	9	6	1	0	1	0	6	0	8	0	0	0	0	14	16
NY	77	40	37	4	0	0	1	0	0	0	0	0	0	0	0	53	14	7	3	1	1	2	3	2	11	3	0	0	0	36	41
PHI	84	64	20	0	0	0	0	0	0	0	0	0	0	0	0	54	18	8	4	1	4	4	3	4	9	3	0	0	0	49	35
PIT	42	17	25	0	0	0	0	0	0	0	0	0	0	0	0	23	14	4	1	1	0	0	3	3	7	1	0	0	0	25	17
STL	70	37	33	2	0	0	0	0	0	0	0	0	0	0	0	34	28	8	0	1	1	2	9	6	11	2	0	0	0	33	37
AL	397	213	184	7	0	0	0	0	0	1	0	0	0	0	0	203	124	58	12	5	6	8	27	15	72	10	0	0	0	150	247
NL	499	267	232	8	0	0	1	0	0	1	0	0	0	0	0	280	146	60	13	5	14	12	51	24	70	14	1	0	0	273	226
YR	896	480	416	15	0	0	1	0	0	2	0	0	0	0	0	483	270	118	25	10	20	20	78	39	142	24	1	0	0	423	473

	AL		*NL*
17	Sloppy Thurston	21	Tony Kaufmann
16	Dave Danforth	17	Vic Keen
13	Herb Pennock	15	Burleigh Grimes
13	Lil Stoner	14	Multiple Players Tied
11	Multiple Players Tied		

1925

				Consec			1-Inn			One-Game						Men-On-Base				Pitchers					Totals					Batters	
Tm	Tot	H	A	2	3	4	3	4	5	5	6	7	8	9	10	0	1	2	3	PH	LO	XN	IP	P	1	10	20	30	40	RHB	LHB
AL																															
BOS	67	28	39	2	0	0	0	0	0	0	0	0	0	0	0	35	23	9	0	1	0	2	4	5	10	2	0	0	0	40	27
CHI	69	32	37	0	0	0	0	0	0	0	0	0	0	0	0	36	23	8	2	1	0	1	3	1	11	2	0	0	0	38	31
CLE	41	19	22	0	0	0	0	0	0	0	0	0	0	0	0	21	11	9	0	4	0	1	2	2	9	1	0	0	0	14	27
DET	70	36	34	1	0	0	0	0	0	0	0	0	0	0	0	40	16	12	2	1	1	0	7	4	9	2	0	0	0	36	34

				Consec			1-Inn			One-Game						Men-On-Base				Pitchers					Totals					Batters	
Tm	Tot	H	A	2	3	4	3	4	5	5	6	7	8	9	10	0	1	2	3	PH	LO	XN	IP	P	1	10	20	30	40	RHB	LHB
NY	78	56	22	2	0	0	0	0	0	0	0	0	0	0	0	47	23	6	2	0	0	3	13	4	5	5	0	0	0	28	50
PHI	60	37	23	2	1	0	1	0	0	0	0	0	0	0	0	36	15	8	1	0	2	0	2	1	5	4	0	0	0	31	29
STL	99	73	26	5	0	0	0	0	0	2	0	0	0	0	0	51	32	16	0	0	1	1	3	1	6	6	0	0	0	35	64
WAS	49	13	36	1	0	0	0	0	0	0	0	0	0	0	0	26	15	4	4	0	0	2	1	2	11	1	0	0	0	23	26
NL																															
BOS	67	14	53	2	0	0	0	0	0	0	0	0	0	0	0	35	22	9	1	1	0	0	16	1	7	2	0	0	0	38	29
BRO	75	41	34	0	0	0	0	0	0	0	0	0	0	0	0	41	20	10	4	2	1	2	6	4	7	3	0	0	0	35	40
CHI	102	63	39	3	0	0	0	0	0	2	0	0	0	0	0	43	37	15	7	1	2	4	4	3	3	5	0	0	0	68	34
CIN	35	5	30	0	0	0	0	0	0	0	0	0	0	0	0	19	11	4	1	1	0	0	5	2	9	0	0	0	0	20	15
NY	73	39	34	3	0	0	1	0	0	0	0	0	0	0	0	39	26	8	0	2	0	1	6	2	7	3	0	0	0	47	26
PHI	117	74	43	3	0	0	0	0	0	0	1	0	0	0	0	68	35	13	1	1	3	3	9	6	4	5	1	0	0	73	44
PIT	81	31	50	1	0	0	0	0	0	0	0	0	0	0	0	42	26	11	2	2	1	1	3	2	5	5	0	0	0	47	34
STL	86	40	46	0	0	0	0	0	0	0	1	0	0	0	0	44	27	9	6	1	0	1	8	8	7	4	0	0	0	49	37
AL	533	294	239	13	1	0	1	0	0	2	0	0	0	0	0	292	158	72	11	7	4	10	35	20	66	23	0	0	0	245	288
NL	636	307	329	12	0	0	1	0	0	2	2	0	0	0	0	331	204	79	22	11	7	12	57	28	49	27	1	0	0	377	259
YR	1169	601	568	25	1	0	2	0	0	4	2	0	0	0	0	623	362	151	33	18	11	22	92	48	115	50	1	0	0	622	547

AL		*NL*	
19	Dave Danforth	23	Clarence Mitchell
18	Joe Bush	19	Hal Carlson
17	Urban Shocker	19	Ray Kremer
14	Multiple Players Tied	18	Johnny Cooney
		18	Wilbur Cooper

1926

				Consec			1-Inn			One-Game						Men-On-Base				Pitchers					Totals					Batters	
Tm	Tot	H	A	2	3	4	3	4	5	5	6	7	8	9	10	0	1	2	3	PH	LO	XN	IP	P	1	10	20	30	40	RHB	LHB
AL																															
BOS	45	16	29	0	0	0	0	0	0	0	0	0	0	0	0	27	11	6	1	0	0	1	3	2	9	1	0	0	0	24	21
CHI	47	19	28	0	0	0	0	0	0	0	0	0	0	0	0	21	16	8	2	0	0	1	5	1	7	2	0	0	0	18	29
CLE	49	19	30	2	0	0	1	0	0	1	0	0	0	0	0	25	19	4	1	1	0	1	5	2	7	1	0	0	0	10	39
DET	58	38	20	1	0	0	0	0	0	0	0	0	0	0	0	19	22	16	1	0	1	2	3	2	10	1	0	0	0	34	24
NY	56	33	23	1	0	0	0	0	0	0	0	0	0	0	0	27	21	7	1	2	0	1	4	2	7	2	0	0	0	15	41
PHI	38	27	11	1	0	0	0	0	0	0	0	0	0	0	0	21	14	3	0	1	0	0	1	0	7	1	0	0	0	18	20
STL	86	64	22	2	0	0	0	0	0	0	0	0	0	0	0	45	30	9	2	1	0	3	1	2	8	4	0	0	0	34	52
WAS	45	15	30	0	0	0	0	0	0	0	0	0	0	0	0	22	15	7	1	2	0	0	4	0	10	1	0	0	0	11	34
NL																															
BOS	46	5	41	1	0	0	0	0	0	0	0	0	0	0	0	24	16	5	1	1	1	1	8	2	7	2	0	0	0	25	21
BRO	50	31	19	1	0	0	0	0	0	0	0	0	0	0	0	23	14	10	3	0	0	1	8	1	7	1	0	0	0	21	29
CHI	39	16	23	0	0	0	0	0	0	0	0	0	0	0	0	14	13	11	1	0	0	1	4	2	7	1	0	0	0	24	15
CIN	40	8	32	0	0	0	0	0	0	0	0	0	0	0	0	20	13	7	0	1	0	3	5	1	7	1	0	0	0	26	14
NY	70	43	27	2	0	0	0	0	0	0	0	0	0	0	0	38	24	7	1	0	0	2	9	4	7	3	0	0	0	32	38
PHI	68	42	26	2	0	0	0	0	0	0	0	0	0	0	0	29	24	13	2	2	1	1	5	1	9	1	0	0	0	34	34
PIT	50	19	31	0	0	0	0	0	0	0	0	0	0	0	0	22	20	7	1	0	0	3	2	0	9	1	0	0	0	29	21
STL	76	42	34	1	0	0	0	0	0	0	0	0	0	0	0	45	19	11	1	1	1	1	3	2	7	4	0	0	0	36	40
AL	424	231	193	7	0	0	1	0	0	1	0	0	0	0	0	207	148	60	9	7	1	9	26	11	65	13	0	0	0	164	260
NL	439	206	233	7	0	0	0	0	0	0	0	0	0	0	0	215	143	71	10	5	3	13	44	13	60	14	0	0	0	227	212
YR	863	437	426	14	0	0	0	0	0	1	0	0	0	0	0	422	291	131	19	12	4	22	70	24	125	27	0	0	0	391	472

AL		*NL*	
15	Urban Shocker	17	Kent Greenfield
14	Tom Zachary	15	Vic Keen
13	Ted Blankenship	15	Bill Sherdel
13	Milt Gaston	14	Jack Knight
13	Walter Johnson	13	Jack Scott

1927

				Consec			1-Inn			One-Game						Men-On-Base				Pitchers					Totals					Batters	
Tm	Tot	H	A	2	3	4	3	4	5	5	6	7	8	9	10	0	1	2	3	PH	LO	XN	IP	P	1	10	20	30	40	RHB	LHB
AL																															
BOS	56	29	27	1	0	0	0	0	0	0	0	0	0	0	0	28	17	10	1	0	1	1	4	3	9	1	0	0	0	19	37
CHI	55	22	33	1	0	0	0	0	0	0	0	0	0	0	0	29	18	6	2	0	1	2	4	4	6	2	0	0	0	19	36
CLE	37	11	26	1	0	0	0	0	0	1	0	0	0	0	0	18	14	4	1	0	0	1	4	3	10	0	0	0	0	16	21
DET	52	28	24	0	0	0	0	0	0	0	0	0	0	0	0	29	12	9	2	0	1	1	3	5	9	1	0	0	0	21	31

				Consec			1-Inn			One-Game						Men-On-Base				Pitchers					Totals					Batters	
Tm	Tot	H	A	2	3	4	3	4	5	5	6	7	8	9	10	0	1	2	3	PH	LO	XN	IP	P	1	10	20	30	40	RHB	LHB
NY	42	30	12	0	0	0	0	0	0	0	0	0	0	0	0	19	19	3	1	1	0	0	11	0	8	1	0	0	0	18	24
PHI	65	36	29	3	0	0	0	0	0	0	0	0	0	0	0	32	27	3	3	1	1	1	2	6	9	2	0	0	0	24	41
STL	79	57	22	4	0	0	0	0	0	0	0	0	0	0	0	46	24	8	1	1	0	1	2	5	8	3	0	0	0	31	48
WAS	53	19	34	1	0	0	0	0	0	0	0	0	0	0	0	25	18	7	3	2	1	2	5	1	10	1	0	0	0	23	30
NL																															
BOS	43	10	33	0	0	0	0	0	0	0	0	0	0	0	0	24	14	5	0	0	0	0	9	0	12	0	0	0	0	23	20
BRO	63	35	28	0	0	0	0	0	0	0	0	0	0	0	0	31	20	10	2	0	0	1	2	2	7	3	0	0	0	33	30
CHI	50	19	31	1	0	0	0	0	0	0	0	0	0	0	0	23	19	4	4	2	1	1	8	1	8	1	0	0	0	20	30
CIN	36	11	25	1	0	0	0	0	0	0	0	0	0	0	0	17	15	3	1	1	0	0	3	1	8	1	0	0	0	15	21
NY	77	49	28	2	0	0	0	0	0	0	0	0	0	0	0	43	22	11	1	0	0	4	8	3	11	3	0	0	0	41	36
PHI	84	46	38	2	0	0	1	0	0	0	0	0	0	0	0	44	28	10	2	2	2	1	2	3	9	3	0	0	0	41	43
PIT	58	23	35	1	0	0	0	0	0	0	0	0	0	0	0	25	22	10	1	3	1	1	1	1	7	3	0	0	0	32	26
STL	72	51	21	2	0	0	0	0	0	0	0	0	0	0	0	42	18	10	2	0	0	2	1	0	10	3	0	0	0	28	44
AL	439	232	207	11	0	0	0	0	0	1	0	0	0	0	0	226	149	50	14	5	5	9	35	27	69	11	0	0	0	171	268
NL	483	244	239	9	0	0	1	0	0	0	0	0	0	0	0	249	158	63	13	8	4	10	34	11	72	17	0	0	0	233	250
YR	922	476	446	20	0	0	1	0	0	1	0	0	0	0	0	475	307	113	27	13	9	19	69	38	141	28	0	0	0	404	518

	AL		*NL*
18	Milt Gaston	17	Bill Sherdel
18	Rube Walberg	16	Vic Aldridge
16	Tommy Thomas	16	Hal Carlson
16	Sloppy Thurston	16	Charlie Root
14	Ted Blankenship	15	Multiple Players Tied

1928

Tm	Tot	H	A	Consec 2	3	4	1-Inn 3	4	5	One-Game 5	6	7	8	9	10	Men-On-Base 0	1	2	3	PH	LO	XN	IP	P	Totals 1	10	20	30	40	RHB	LHB
AL																															
BOS	49	15	34	3	0	0	0	0	0	0	0	0	0	0	0	29	14	6	0	0	0	0	1	0	9	1	0	0	0	15	34
CHI	66	28	38	1	0	0	0	0	0	1	0	0	0	0	0	36	19	9	2	0	0	1	3	2	4	4	0	0	0	27	39
CLE	52	15	37	1	0	0	0	0	0	0	0	0	0	0	0	22	19	8	3	2	0	2	6	2	11	0	0	0	0	16	36
DET	58	26	32	2	0	0	0	0	0	0	0	0	0	0	0	30	21	7	0	3	0	0	5	4	10	1	0	0	0	21	37
NY	59	36	23	0	0	0	0	0	0	0	0	0	0	0	0	28	20	8	3	1	0	1	4	5	9	2	0	0	0	23	36
PHI	66	33	33	2	0	0	1	0	0	0	0	0	0	0	0	35	21	7	3	1	1	0	3	2	7	3	0	0	0	31	35
STL	93	64	29	2	0	0	0	0	0	0	0	0	0	0	0	49	30	12	2	2	0	1	2	3	6	2	2	0	0	37	56
WAS	40	12	28	1	0	0	0	0	0	1	0	0	0	0	0	23	8	8	1	0	1	0	5	1	9	0	0	0	0	12	28
NL																															
BOS	100	62	38	1	0	0	0	0	0	1	0	0	0	0	0	57	33	10	0	0	0	3	1	4	12	3	1	0	0	64	36
BRO	59	25	34	1	0	0	0	0	0	0	0	0	0	0	0	30	18	10	1	2	0	2	2	0	5	3	0	0	0	36	23
CHI	56	18	38	2	0	0	0	0	0	0	0	0	0	0	0	28	22	6	0	3	0	0	4	3	5	3	0	0	0	17	39
CIN	58	17	41	2	0	0	0	0	0	0	0	0	0	0	0	27	20	9	2	1	0	0	2	0	9	2	0	0	0	31	27
NY	77	46	31	2	0	0	1	0	0	0	0	0	0	0	0	43	20	13	1	3	0	2	4	2	9	3	0	0	0	40	37
PHI	108	67	41	2	0	0	1	0	0	0	0	0	0	0	0	53	34	18	3	1	1	2	2	4	6	6	0	0	0	51	57
PIT	66	15	51	2	0	0	0	0	0	0	0	0	0	0	0	34	23	9	0	2	1	2	2	2	7	3	0	0	0	33	33
STL	86	51	35	2	0	0	0	0	0	0	0	0	0	0	0	42	31	7	6	3	1	0	3	0	7	4	0	0	0	44	42
AL	483	229	254	12	0	0	1	0	0	2	0	0	0	0	0	252	152	65	14	9	2	5	29	19	65	13	2	0	0	182	301
NL	610	301	309	14	0	0	2	0	0	1	0	0	0	0	0	314	201	82	13	15	3	11	20	15	60	27	1	0	0	316	294
YR	1093	530	563	26	0	0	2	0	0	3	0	0	0	0	0	566	353	147	27	24	5	16	49	34	125	40	3	0	0	498	595

	AL		*NL*
23	George Blaeholder	24	Joe Genewich
23	Jack Ogden	22	Ed Brandt
19	Rube Walberg	18	Jesse Petty
16	Multiple Players Tied	17	Bill Sherdel
		16	Multiple Players Tied

1929

Tm	Tot	H	A	Consec 2	3	4	1-Inn 3	4	5	One-Game 5	6	7	8	9	10	Men-On-Base 0	1	2	3	PH	LO	XN	IP	P	Totals 1	10	20	30	40	RHB	LHB
AL																															
BOS	78	36	42	3	0	0	0	0	0	0	0	0	0	0	0	36	32	8	2	2	0	0	2	1	7	3	0	0	0	43	35
CHI	84	41	43	0	1	0	1	0	0	1	0	0	0	0	0	47	27	9	1	1	3	1	5	1	5	5	0	0	0	39	45
CLE	56	21	35	1	0	0	0	0	0	0	0	0	0	0	0	29	20	5	2	2	0	1	6	2	10	1	0	0	0	27	29
DET	73	33	40	1	0	0	0	0	0	0	0	0	0	0	0	35	27	10	1	1	2	0	10	4	9	3	0	0	0	33	40

				Consec			1-Inn			One-Game						Men-On-Base				Pitchers					Totals					Batters	
Tm	Tot	H	A	2	3	4	3	4	5	5	6	7	8	9	10	0	1	2	3	PH	LO	XN	IP	P	1	10	20	30	40	RHB	LHB
NY	83	55	28	2	0	0	0	0	0	0	0	0	0	0	0	37	30	15	1	0	3	0	9	5	7	3	0	0	0	44	39
PHI	73	47	26	4	0	0	1	0	0	0	0	0	0	0	0	37	27	5	4	0	0	1	3	1	6	1	1	0	0	44	29
STL	100	58	42	2	0	0	0	0	0	0	0	0	0	0	0	54	31	15	0	0	3	1	1	3	5	4	1	0	0	44	56
WAS	48	17	31	2	0	0	0	0	0	0	0	0	0	0	0	21	13	12	2	2	0	1	4	1	11	1	0	0	0	22	26
NL																															
BOS	103	39	64	1	0	0	0	0	0	0	0	0	0	0	0	47	43	9	4	3	2	2	4	2	9	4	1	0	0	52	51
BRO	92	48	44	2	0	0	0	0	0	0	0	0	0	0	0	50	26	13	3	2	1	0	6	4	9	4	0	0	0	37	55
CHI	77	41	36	0	0	0	0	0	0	0	0	0	0	0	0	34	28	8	7	0	2	1	3	1	6	4	0	0	0	20	57
CIN	61	18	43	1	0	0	0	0	0	0	0	0	0	0	0	22	28	9	2	0	2	1	1	2	8	2	0	0	0	37	24
NY	102	59	43	4	0	0	1	0	0	1	0	0	0	0	0	54	33	14	1	2	2	2	8	5	4	6	0	0	0	66	36
PHI	122	74	48	0	0	0	0	0	0	2	0	0	0	0	0	48	45	25	4	2	2	1	4	4	9	3	2	0	0	56	66
PIT	96	37	59	4	0	0	1	0	0	1	0	0	0	0	0	44	34	14	4	0	2	1	6	0	6	4	1	0	0	41	55
STL	101	51	50	4	0	0	1	0	0	0	0	0	0	0	0	58	20	18	5	2	1	0	5	4	9	4	1	0	0	47	54
AL	595	308	287	15	1	0	2	0	0	1	0	0	0	0	0	296	207	79	13	8	11	5	40	18	60	21	2	0	0	296	299
NL	754	367	387	16	0	0	3	0	0	4	0	0	0	0	0	357	257	110	30	11	14	8	37	22	60	31	5	0	0	356	398
YR	1349	675	674	31	1	0	4	0	0	5	0	0	0	0	0	653	464	189	43	19	25	13	77	40	120	52	7	0	0	652	697

	AL		*NL*
22	General Crowder	24	Ray Benge
22	Rube Walberg	23	Leo Sweetland
19	Ed Wells	21	Jesse Haines
18	George Blaeholder	21	Ray Kremer
18	Sam Gray	20	Bob Smith

1930

AL

Tm	Tot	H	A	Consec 2	3	4	1-Inn 3	4	5	One-Game 5	6	7	8	9	10	Men-On-Base 0	1	2	3	Pitchers PH	LO	XN	IP	P	Totals 1	10	20	30	40	Batters RHB	LHB
BOS	75	31	44	2	0	0	0	0	0	0	0	0	0	0	0	33	27	14	1	1	2	5	3	3	7	2	1	0	0	33	42
CHI	74	42	32	2	0	0	0	0	0	1	0	0	0	0	0	32	26	14	2	0	0	2	2	2	5	4	0	0	0	40	34
CLE	85	46	39	1	1	0	1	0	0	0	0	0	0	0	0	41	27	14	3	1	3	2	5	2	8	3	0	0	0	34	51
DET	86	48	38	3	0	0	0	0	0	1	0	0	0	0	0	45	32	9	0	2	2	0	4	2	11	2	0	0	0	51	35
NY	93	54	39	3	0	0	0	0	0	1	0	0	0	0	0	37	41	14	1	2	0	2	11	0	8	5	0	0	0	50	43
PHI	84	49	35	0	0	0	0	0	0	1	0	0	0	0	0	38	29	15	2	0	2	1	5	1	5	3	1	0	0	32	52
STL	124	72	52	5	0	0	0	0	0	1	0	0	0	0	0	67	43	11	3	2	0	1	5	8	3	5	2	0	0	63	61
WAS	52	15	37	1	0	0	0	0	0	0	0	0	0	0	0	24	20	6	2	1	1	0	2	2	9	1	0	0	0	30	22
NL																															
BOS	117	51	66	1	0	0	0	0	0	0	0	0	0	0	0	57	42	16	2	2	1	1	1	5	5	5	1	0	0	69	48
BRO	115	66	49	5	0	0	0	0	0	0	0	0	0	0	0	65	37	11	2	4	3	1	5	1	4	4	2	0	0	68	47
CHI	111	62	49	4	0	0	1	0	0	2	0	0	0	0	0	63	30	14	4	3	1	1	4	5	4	5	1	0	0	62	49
CIN	75	21	54	4	0	0	1	0	0	1	0	0	0	0	0	31	31	13	0	4	0	1	1	3	6	4	0	0	0	51	24
NY	117	63	54	3	0	0	0	1	0	0	1	0	0	0	0	63	35	17	2	3	1	1	3	2	7	4	1	0	0	65	52
PHI	142	72	70	4	0	0	0	0	0	2	0	0	0	0	0	65	46	31	0	0	0	2	9	5	8	2	3	0	0	75	67
PIT	128	48	80	2	0	0	0	0	0	1	0	0	0	0	0	67	38	20	3	2	2	1	7	7	9	1	3	0	0	79	49
STL	87	49	38	0	0	0	0	0	0	0	0	0	0	0	0	47	25	14	1	2	2	1	2	1	9	4	0	0	0	41	46
AL	673	357	316	17	1	0	1	0	0	5	0	0	0	0	0	317	245	97	14	9	10	13	37	20	56	25	4	0	0	333	340
NL	892	432	460	23	0	0	2	1	0	6	1	0	0	0	0	458	284	136	14	20	10	9	32	29	52	29	11	0	0	510	382
YR	1565	789	776	40	1	0	2	0	0	11	1	0	0	0	0	775	529	233	28	29	20	22	69	49	108	54	15	0	0	843	722

	AL		*NL*
21	Lefty Stewart	29	Ray Kremer
20	George Blaeholder	26	Freddie Fitzsimmons
20	George Earnshaw	25	Bob Smith
20	Hod Lisenbee	24	Leo Sweetland
18	George Uhle	22	Multiple Players Tied

1931

AL

Tm	Tot	H	A	Consec 2	3	4	1-Inn 3	4	5	One-Game 5	6	7	8	9	10	Men-On-Base 0	1	2	3	Pitchers PH	LO	XN	IP	P	Totals 1	10	20	30	40	Batters RHB	LHB
BOS	54	29	25	0	0	0	0	0	0	0	0	0	0	0	0	23	22	8	1	1	2	3	5	3	9	1	0	0	0	27	27
CHI	82	45	37	0	0	0	0	0	0	0	0	0	0	0	0	36	33	12	1	1	2	1	5	4	6	5	0	0	0	43	39
CLE	64	32	32	0	0	0	0	0	0	0	0	0	0	0	0	33	16	15	0	0	1	0	0	1	9	2	0	0	0	20	44
DET	79	43	36	2	0	0	0	0	0	0	0	0	0	0	0	44	22	12	1	2	0	2	2	5	6	2	1	0	0	53	26

Tm	Tot	H	A	Consec 2	3	4	1-Inn 3	4	5	One-Game 5	6	7	8	9	10	Men-On-Base 0	1	2	3	Pitchers PH	LO	XN	IP	P	Totals 1	10	20	30	40	Batters RHB	LHB
NY	67	41	26	1	0	0	0	0	0	0	0	0	0	0	0	34	25	7	1	1	2	1	3	2	10	2	0	0	0	36	31
PHI	73	36	37	3	0	0	1	0	0	1	0	0	0	0	0	43	23	6	1	1	0	1	1	1	6	3	0	0	0	25	48
STL	84	48	36	3	0	0	0	0	0	0	0	0	0	0	0	47	24	11	2	1	0	3	1	5	5	4	1	0	0	36	48
WAS	73	24	49	0	0	0	0	0	0	1	0	0	0	0	0	38	27	6	2	3	0	0	5	2	3	5	0	0	0	31	42
NL																															
BOS	66	24	42	1	0	0	0	0	0	0	0	0	0	0	0	37	21	6	2	1	0	2	1	1	7	3	0	0	0	39	27
BRO	56	24	32	0	0	0	0	0	0	0	0	0	0	0	0	31	18	7	0	1	1	0	3	1	10	1	0	0	0	29	27
CHI	54	22	32	1	0	0	0	0	0	0	0	0	0	0	0	28	18	7	1	1	0	0	2	1	10	1	0	0	0	17	37
CIN	51	4	47	0	0	0	0	0	0	0	0	0	0	0	0	20	22	8	1	2	0	0	4	0	10	1	0	0	0	17	34
NY	71	47	24	1	0	0	0	0	0	0	0	0	0	0	0	43	20	7	1	1	2	2	1	0	10	3	0	0	0	32	39
PHI	75	35	40	3	0	0	0	0	0	0	0	0	0	0	0	35	23	16	1	3	0	0	3	1	7	4	0	0	0	38	37
PIT	55	16	39	0	0	0	0	0	0	0	0	0	0	0	0	26	15	13	1	0	0	0	1	2	8	1	0	0	0	29	26
STL	65	29	36	1	0	0	0	0	0	0	0	0	0	0	0	35	17	11	2	4	1	1	0	1	6	3	0	0	0	31	34
AL	576	298	278	9	0	0	1	0	0	2	0	0	0	0	0	298	192	77	9	10	7	11	22	23	54	24	2	0	0	271	305
NL	493	201	292	7	0	0	0	0	0	0	0	0	0	0	0	255	154	75	9	13	4	5	15	7	68	17	0	0	0	232	261
YR	1069	499	570	16	0	0	0	0	0	2	0	0	0	0	0	553	346	152	18	23	11	16	37	30	122	41	2	0	0	503	566

	AL		*NL*
22	Earl Whitehill	17	Flint Rhem
20	Sam Gray	16	Freddie Fitzsimmons
17	Pat Caraway	15	Jumbo Elliott
17	Lefty Stewart	14	Phil Collins
17	Tommy Thomas	14	Carl Hubbell

1932

Tm	Tot	H	A	Consec 2	3	4	1-Inn 3	4	5	One-Game 5	6	7	8	9	10	Men-On-Base 0	1	2	3	Pitchers PH	LO	XN	IP	P	Totals 1	10	20	30	40	Batters RHB	LHB
AL																															
BOS	79	31	48	2	0	0	0	0	0	1	0	0	0	0	0	38	26	13	2	2	2	2	2	1	13	3	0	0	0	44	35
CHI	88	36	52	3	0	0	1	0	0	1	0	0	0	0	0	40	25	21	2	1	2	3	4	4	16	3	0	0	0	35	53
CLE	70	33	37	0	0	0	0	0	0	0	0	0	0	0	0	39	28	3	0	0	2	4	1	2	6	3	0	0	0	26	44
DET	89	50	39	2	0	0	0	0	0	0	0	0	0	0	0	39	35	11	4	0	1	0	4	3	5	5	0	0	0	59	30
NY	93	44	49	2	0	0	1	0	0	0	0	0	0	0	0	54	26	10	3	1	3	1	0	2	5	4	1	0	0	39	54
PHI	112	80	32	2	0	0	1	0	0	1	0	1	0	0	0	66	33	10	3	0	2	2	2	4	6	3	2	0	0	38	74
STL	103	56	47	4	0	0	0	0	0	0	0	0	0	0	0	46	37	17	3	0	1	2	2	2	5	2	2	0	0	49	54
WAS	73	25	48	1	0	0	0	0	0	1	0	0	0	0	0	37	24	8	4	1	1	1	2	2	7	3	0	0	0	31	42
NL																															
BOS	61	20	41	0	0	0	0	0	0	0	0	0	0	0	0	28	20	10	3	0	1	1	3	2	8	2	0	0	0	38	23
BRO	72	31	41	1	1	0	1	0	0	0	1	0	0	0	0	40	24	7	1	0	2	0	1	0	8	3	0	0	0	28	44
CHI	68	33	35	1	0	0	0	0	0	0	0	0	0	0	0	37	19	10	2	7	0	2	3	0	5	4	0	0	0	28	40
CIN	69	11	58	1	0	0	0	0	0	0	0	0	0	0	0	37	24	7	1	1	1	0	4	0	5	4	0	0	0	32	37
NY	112	71	41	5	0	0	1	0	0	0	0	0	0	0	0	60	34	16	2	3	1	3	4	2	5	3	2	0	0	65	47
PHI	107	71	36	3	0	0	1	0	0	0	0	0	0	0	0	53	35	19	0	1	1	2	0	3	5	5	1	0	0	46	61
PIT	86	24	62	1	0	0	0	0	0	0	0	0	0	0	0	48	30	7	1	2	0	1	3	2	4	5	0	0	0	38	48
STL	76	39	37	0	0	0	0	0	0	0	0	0	0	0	0	43	24	6	3	0	0	0	2	1	6	4	0	0	0	44	32
AL	707	355	352	16	0	0	3	0	0	4	0	1	0	0	0	359	234	93	21	5	14	15	17	20	63	26	5	0	0	321	386
NL	651	300	351	12	1	0	3	0	0	0	1	0	0	0	0	346	210	82	13	14	6	9	20	10	46	30	3	0	0	319	332
YR	1358	655	703	28	1	0	2	0	0	4	1	1	0	0	0	705	444	175	34	19	20	24	37	30	109	56	8	0	0	640	718

	AL		*NL*
28	George Earnshaw	23	Bill Walker
27	Roy Mahaffey	21	Phil Collins
23	Lefty Gomez	20	Carl Hubbell
23	Bump Hadley	19	Freddie Fitzsimmons
22	Lefty Stewart	18	Jim Mooney

1933

Tm	Tot	H	A	Consec 2	3	4	1-Inn 3	4	5	One-Game 5	6	7	8	9	10	Men-On-Base 0	1	2	3	Pitchers PH	LO	XN	IP	P	Totals 1	10	20	30	40	Batters RHB	LHB
AL																															
BOS	75	35	40	2	0	0	0	0	0	0	0	0	0	0	0	39	26	8	2	1	0	0	2	4	7	3	0	0	0	39	36
CHI	85	42	43	1	0	0	0	0	0	1	0	0	0	0	0	40	34	10	1	0	1	3	2	3	10	4	0	0	0	33	52
CLE	60	24	36	1	0	0	0	0	0	0	0	0	0	0	0	27	19	12	2	1	1	0	5	1	8	2	0	0	0	28	32
DET	84	36	48	1	0	0	0	0	0	0	0	0	0	0	0	49	25	10	0	3	3	3	1	1	12	2	0	0	0	46	38

				Consec			1-Inn			One-Game						Men-On-Base				Pitchers					Totals					Batters	
Tm	Tot	H	A	2	3	4	3	4	5	5	6	7	8	9	10	0	1	2	3	PH	LO	XN	IP	P	1	10	20	30	40	RHB	LHB
NY	66	26	40	1	0	0	0	0	0	0	0	0	0	0	0	28	27	11	0	2	2	1	4	0	11	1	0	0	0	38	28
PHI	77	50	27	2	0	0	0	0	0	0	0	0	0	0	0	34	31	11	1	2	0	1	1	4	8	3	0	0	0	40	37
STL	96	68	28	2	0	0	0	0	0	0	0	0	0	0	0	45	35	14	2	1	4	2	1	3	6	3	1	0	0	63	33
WAS	64	16	48	1	0	0	1	0	0	0	0	0	0	0	0	46	12	6	0	1	1	0	0	2	8	2	0	0	0	36	28
NL																															
BOS	54	26	28	1	0	0	0	0	0	0	0	0	0	0	0	36	15	3	0	1	0	3	1	1	6	3	0	0	0	39	15
BRO	51	29	22	1	0	0	0	0	0	0	0	0	0	0	0	25	14	11	1	3	0	0	2	0	8	1	0	0	0	24	27
CHI	51	32	19	0	0	0	0	0	0	0	0	0	0	0	0	33	11	6	1	0	0	1	2	1	6	2	0	0	0	18	33
CIN	47	10	37	1	0	0	0	0	0	0	0	0	0	0	0	25	16	4	2	1	0	1	0	2	8	1	0	0	0	27	20
NY	61	44	17	1	0	0	0	0	0	0	0	0	0	0	0	41	10	10	0	2	1	0	0	1	10	1	0	0	0	32	29
PHI	87	46	41	1	0	0	0	0	0	0	0	0	0	0	0	38	25	16	8	4	1	3	3	2	9	3	0	0	0	43	44
PIT	54	13	41	1	0	0	0	0	0	0	0	0	0	0	0	27	12	14	1	3	0	4	2	1	7	3	0	0	0	27	27
STL	55	25	30	0	0	0	0	0	0	0	0	0	0	0	0	27	17	10	1	0	0	1	1	1	7	2	0	0	0	29	26
AL	607	297	310	11	0	0	1	0	0	1	0	0	0	0	0	308	209	82	8	11	12	10	16	18	70	20	1	0	0	323	284
NL	460	225	235	6	0	0	0	0	0	0	0	0	0	0	0	252	120	74	14	14	2	13	11	9	61	16	0	0	0	239	221
YR	1067	522	545	17	0	0	1	0	0	1	0	0	0	0	0	560	329	156	22	25	14	23	27	27	131	36	1	0	0	562	505

	AL		*NL*
24	George Blaeholder	18	Ed Holley
19	Lefty Stewart	15	Tex Carleton
19	Bob Weiland	14	Freddie Fitzsimmons
18	Sugar Cain	14	Charlie Root
18	Vic Sorrell	13	Red Lucas

1934

				Consec			1-Inn			One-Game						Men-On-Base				Pitchers					Totals					Batters	
Tm	Tot	H	A	2	3	4	3	4	5	5	6	7	8	9	10	0	1	2	3	PH	LO	XN	IP	P	1	10	20	30	40	RHB	LHB
AL																															
BOS	70	24	46	3	0	0	1	0	0	0	0	0	0	0	0	39	21	7	3	2	1	2	1	4	10	3	0	0	0	46	24
CHI	139	82	57	2	0	0	0	0	0	0	0	0	0	0	0	58	47	25	9	3	0	5	1	3	4	6	2	0	0	82	57
CLE	70	34	36	2	0	0	0	0	0	0	0	0	0	0	0	36	28	5	1	2	1	0	5	1	8	2	0	0	0	37	33
DET	86	32	54	1	0	0	1	0	0	0	0	0	0	0	0	40	29	15	2	2	1	0	1	1	5	5	0	0	0	57	29
NY	71	34	37	2	0	0	0	0	0	0	0	0	0	0	0	39	23	7	2	0	1	1	6	2	7	3	0	0	0	36	35
PHI	84	48	36	2	0	0	0	0	0	0	0	0	0	0	0	41	29	11	3	1	2	1	1	1	10	4	0	0	0	39	45
STL	94	60	34	3	1	0	2	0	0	1	0	0	0	0	0	51	29	14	0	0	0	2	2	4	4	5	0	0	0	48	46
WAS	74	26	48	0	0	0	0	0	0	0	0	0	0	0	0	38	21	10	5	0	2	1	3	2	11	2	0	0	0	48	26
NL																															
BOS	78	28	50	2	0	0	0	0	0	0	0	0	0	0	0	41	23	13	1	2	1	3	3	1	8	3	0	0	0	38	40
BRO	81	38	43	1	0	0	0	0	0	0	0	0	0	0	0	34	29	17	1	4	0	1	1	3	10	3	0	0	0	38	43
CHI	80	44	36	3	0	0	1	0	0	0	0	0	0	0	0	43	26	10	1	1	0	0	0	2	6	3	0	0	0	32	48
CIN	61	24	37	0	0	0	0	0	0	0	0	0	0	0	0	32	22	6	1	0	0	2	3	2	10	3	0	0	0	35	26
NY	75	43	32	2	0	0	1	0	0	0	0	0	0	0	0	45	21	7	2	1	1	2	2	0	8	3	0	0	0	41	34
PHI	126	69	57	1	0	0	0	0	0	0	0	0	0	0	0	66	44	13	3	2	4	3	1	6	5	6	0	1	0	58	68
PIT	78	38	40	0	0	0	0	0	0	0	0	0	0	0	0	37	23	16	2	3	0	1	0	1	7	4	0	0	0	46	32
STL	77	43	34	1	0	0	0	0	0	0	0	0	0	0	0	46	24	6	1	1	0	0	0	3	7	4	0	0	0	39	38
AL	688	340	348	15	1	0	4	0	0	1	0	0	0	0	0	342	227	94	25	10	8	12	20	18	59	30	2	0	0	393	295
NL	656	327	329	10	0	0	2	0	0	0	0	0	0	0	0	344	212	88	12	14	6	12	10	18	61	29	0	1	0	327	329
YR	1344	667	677	25	1	0	5	0	0	1	0	0	0	0	0	686	439	182	37	24	14	24	30	36	120	59	2	1	0	720	624

	AL		*NL*
28	George Earnshaw	30	Phil Collins
20	Les Tietje	19	Paul Dean
18	Red Ruffing	17	Huck Betts
17	Jack Knott	17	Carl Hubbell
16	Multiple Players Tied	16	Multiple Players Tied

1935

				Consec			1-Inn			One-Game						Men-On-Base				Pitchers					Totals					Batters	
Tm	Tot	H	A	2	3	4	3	4	5	5	6	7	8	9	10	0	1	2	3	PH	LO	XN	IP	P	1	10	20	30	40	RHB	LHB
AL																															
BOS	67	29	38	1	0	0	0	0	0	1	1	0	0	0	0	33	26	7	1	0	0	1	2	3	8	3	0	0	0	51	16
CHI	105	61	44	0	0	0	0	0	0	0	0	0	0	0	0	59	39	6	1	0	1	4	1	6	8	5	0	0	0	65	40
CLE	68	30	38	0	0	0	0	0	0	0	0	0	0	0	0	39	22	5	2	0	0	0	1	2	9	2	0	0	0	40	28
DET	78	38	40	3	0	0	0	0	0	0	0	0	0	0	0	40	26	12	0	1	0	2	3	2	7	3	1	0	0	50	28

Tm	Tot	H	A	Consec 2	3	4	1-Inn 3	4	5	One-Game 5	6	7	8	9	10	Men-On-Base 0	1	2	3	Pitchers PH	LO	XN	IP	P	Totals 1	10	20	30	40	Batters RHB	LHB
NY	91	51	40	4	0	0	0	0	0	0	0	0	0	0	0	47	29	9	6	0	3	4	4	1	5	4	0	0	0	51	40
PHI	73	39	34	0	0	0	0	0	0	0	0	0	0	0	0	36	19	13	5	0	1	2	2	1	13	2	0	0	0	46	27
STL	92	49	43	1	0	0	0	0	0	1	0	0	0	0	0	43	36	9	4	0	0	2	0	7	7	5	0	0	0	48	44
WAS	89	28	61	0	0	0	0	0	0	0	0	0	0	0	0	42	22	19	6	1	0	1	6	5	10	3	0	0	0	61	28
NL																															
BOS	81	41	40	1	0	0	0	0	0	0	0	0	0	0	0	39	30	10	2	0	1	2	7	2	5	4	0	0	0	40	41
BRO	88	43	45	1	0	0	0	0	0	0	0	0	0	0	0	41	33	12	2	2	1	4	3	0	4	6	0	0	0	34	54
CHI	85	40	45	0	0	0	1	0	0	0	0	0	0	0	0	47	25	10	3	2	0	4	0	0	5	5	0	0	0	39	46
CIN	65	18	47	3	1	0	1	0	0	1	0	0	0	0	0	39	14	11	1	1	0	3	2	4	8	2	0	0	0	35	30
NY	106	66	40	1	0	0	0	0	0	0	0	0	0	0	0	65	27	11	3	1	0	3	3	3	6	2	2	0	0	57	49
PHI	106	68	38	2	0	0	0	0	0	0	0	0	0	0	0	52	35	14	5	1	0	1	0	3	7	4	1	0	0	40	66
PIT	63	25	38	1	0	0	0	0	0	0	0	0	0	0	0	33	22	7	1	0	0	0	1	0	7	2	0	0	0	34	29
STL	68	27	41	1	0	0	0	0	0	0	0	0	0	0	0	39	20	8	1	0	2	1	2	2	9	2	0	0	0	32	36
AL	663	325	338	9	0	0	0	0	0	2	1	0	0	0	0	339	219	80	25	2	5	16	19	27	67	27	1	0	0	412	251
NL	662	328	334	10	1	0	2	0	0	1	0	0	0	0	0	355	206	83	18	7	4	18	18	14	51	27	3	0	0	311	351
YR	1325	653	672	19	1	0	2	0	0	3	1	0	0	0	0	694	425	163	43	9	9	34	37	41	118	54	4	0	0	723	602

AL		*NL*	
22	Tommy Bridges	27	Carl Hubbell
18	Lefty Gomez	20	Jim Bivin
18	Bump Hadley	20	Leroy Parmelee
17	Multiple Players Tied	19	Lon Warneke
		17	Tex Carleton

1936

Tm	Tot	H	A	Consec 2	3	4	1-Inn 3	4	5	One-Game 5	6	7	8	9	10	Men-On-Base 0	1	2	3	Pitchers PH	LO	XN	IP	P	Totals 1	10	20	30	40	Batters RHB	LHB
AL																															
BOS	78	31	47	0	0	0	0	0	0	0	0	0	0	0	0	45	23	9	1	1	1	2	1	1	7	4	0	0	0	45	33
CHI	104	55	49	3	0	0	1	0	0	1	0	0	0	0	0	61	24	17	2	0	3	2	4	1	7	3	1	0	0	55	49
CLE	73	33	40	2	0	0	0	0	0	0	0	0	0	0	0	45	20	6	2	0	0	1	3	4	6	3	1	0	0	33	40
DET	100	58	42	1	0	0	1	0	0	0	0	0	0	0	0	48	34	18	0	1	0	2	1	2	6	4	1	0	0	62	38
NY	84	41	43	3	0	0	1	0	0	1	0	0	0	0	0	54	20	8	2	0	0	2	2	2	5	3	1	0	0	46	38
PHI	131	77	54	7	0	0	2	0	0	1	1	0	0	0	0	70	36	20	5	1	0	1	5	6	12	2	2	0	0	67	64
STL	115	63	52	4	0	0	0	0	0	1	1	0	0	0	0	50	42	22	1	0	2	0	3	2	6	4	1	0	0	77	38
WAS	73	27	46	2	0	0	0	0	0	1	0	0	0	0	0	40	24	9	0	0	0	0	2	1	9	3	0	0	0	36	37
NL																															
BOS	69	23	46	3	0	0	0	0	0	0	0	0	0	0	0	37	22	9	1	2	0	0	0	6	15	0	1	0	0	31	38
BRO	84	46	38	2	0	0	0	0	0	0	0	0	0	0	0	41	30	11	2	2	1	1	4	3	7	4	0	0	0	46	38
CHI	77	41	36	1	0	0	0	0	0	0	0	0	0	0	0	41	22	12	2	3	1	2	0	2	3	5	0	0	0	28	49
CIN	51	21	30	0	0	0	0	0	0	0	0	0	0	0	0	24	19	8	0	1	0	0	0	2	11	1	0	0	0	21	30
NY	75	54	21	3	0	0	0	0	0	1	0	0	0	0	0	43	19	11	2	2	1	1	0	3	5	3	0	0	0	38	37
PHI	87	56	31	4	0	0	0	0	0	0	1	0	0	0	0	37	31	18	1	1	1	2	0	1	9	4	0	0	0	34	53
PIT	74	25	49	0	0	0	0	0	0	0	0	0	0	0	0	43	21	9	1	2	3	1	3	0	8	2	0	0	0	32	42
STL	89	47	42	2	0	0	0	0	0	1	0	0	0	0	0	42	31	16	0	3	2	2	2	0	12	2	1	0	0	34	55
AL	758	385	373	22	0	0	5	0	0	5	2	0	0	0	0	413	223	109	13	3	6	10	21	19	58	26	7	0	0	421	337
NL	606	313	293	15	0	0	0	0	0	2	1	0	0	0	0	308	195	94	9	16	9	9	9	17	70	21	2	0	0	264	342
YR	1364	698	666	37	0	0	3	0	0	7	3	0	0	0	0	721	418	203	22	19	15	19	30	36	128	47	9	0	0	685	679

AL		*NL*	
26	Gordon Rhodes	21	Tiny Chaplin
25	Tommy Thomas	21	Dizzy Dean
22	Red Ruffing	18	Fred Frankhouse
21	Multiple Players Tied	18	Bill Swift
		17	Curt Davis

1937

Tm	Tot	H	A	Consec 2	3	4	1-Inn 3	4	5	One-Game 5	6	7	8	9	10	Men-On-Base 0	1	2	3	Pitchers PH	LO	XN	IP	P	Totals 1	10	20	30	40	Batters RHB	LHB
AL																															
BOS	92	43	49	1	0	0	0	0	0	0	0	0	0	0	0	44	24	20	4	1	2	0	3	0	8	4	0	0	0	68	24
CHI	115	62	53	3	0	0	0	0	0	0	0	0	0	0	0	53	37	18	7	3	4	3	1	0	4	5	1	0	0	64	51
CLE	61	22	39	1	0	0	0	0	0	0	0	0	0	0	0	29	18	10	4	1	3	1	3	1	9	1	0	0	0	36	25
DET	102	58	44	2	0	0	0	0	0	0	0	0	0	0	0	46	43	12	1	3	1	1	3	2	6	5	0	0	0	66	36

				Consec			1-Inn			One-Game						Men-On-Base				Pitchers					Totals					Batters	
Tm	Tot	H	A	2	3	4	3	4	5	5	6	7	8	9	10	0	1	2	3	PH	LO	XN	IP	P	1	10	20	30	40	RHB	LHB
NY	92	41	51	2	0	0	0	0	0	0	0	0	0	0	0	56	24	12	0	2	2	2	1	2	9	3	0	0	0	59	33
PHI	105	47	58	1	0	0	0	0	0	0	0	0	0	0	0	58	31	16	0	4	3	2	2	2	3	5	1	0	0	64	41
STL	143	74	69	1	0	0	0	0	0	0	1	0	0	0	0	64	49	29	1	1	3	0	1	3	13	6	1	0	0	90	53
WAS	96	30	66	5	0	0	1	0	0	0	0	0	0	0	0	44	32	17	3	1	1	2	4	2	7	4	1	0	0	69	27
NL																															
BOS	60	15	45	0	0	0	0	0	0	1	0	0	0	0	0	26	26	6	2	0	0	2	3	4	8	2	0	0	0	37	23
BRO	68	30	38	1	0	0	0	0	0	0	0	0	0	0	0	33	20	13	2	2	0	0	1	3	13	2	0	0	0	34	34
CHI	91	48	43	6	0	0	0	0	0	0	0	0	0	0	0	52	28	10	1	0	3	0	0	0	5	5	0	0	0	41	50
CIN	38	14	24	0	0	0	0	0	0	0	0	0	0	0	0	25	9	3	1	0	1	0	2	0	11	0	0	0	0	17	21
NY	85	56	29	1	0	0	0	0	0	0	0	0	0	0	0	47	30	6	2	0	2	0	0	1	6	4	0	0	0	39	46
PHI	116	70	46	1	0	0	1	0	0	0	0	0	0	0	0	64	28	20	4	1	3	5	0	2	5	4	2	0	0	69	47
PIT	71	28	43	0	0	0	0	0	0	0	0	0	0	0	0	37	19	13	2	0	2	0	2	4	5	5	0	0	0	37	34
STL	95	51	44	0	0	0	0	0	0	0	0	0	0	0	0	48	35	9	3	4	0	3	1	1	9	2	0	1	0	44	51
AL	806	377	429	16	0	0	1	0	0	0	1	0	0	0	0	394	258	134	20	16	19	11	18	12	59	33	4	0	0	516	290
NL	624	312	312	9	0	0	1	0	0	1	0	0	0	0	0	332	195	80	17	7	11	10	9	15	62	24	2	1	0	318	306
YR	1430	689	741	25	0	0	2	0	0	1	1	0	0	0	0	726	453	214	37	23	30	21	27	27	121	57	6	1	0	834	596

AL		*NL*	
25	Wes Ferrell	32	Lon Warneke
25	Jack Knott	24	Wayne LaMaster
23	George Caster	20	Syl Johnson
21	Ted Lyons	19	Slick Castleman
21	Monte Weaver	18	Multiple Players Tied

1938

AL				Consec			1-Inn			One-Game						Men-On-Base				Pitchers					Totals					Batters	
Tm	Tot	H	A	2	3	4	3	4	5	5	6	7	8	9	10	0	1	2	3	PH	LO	XN	IP	P	1	10	20	30	40	RHB	LHB
BOS	102	52	50	3	0	0	0	0	0	0	0	0	0	0	0	49	33	14	6	0	1	0	0	1	11	3	0	0	0	77	25
CHI	101	41	60	4	0	0	0	0	0	0	0	0	0	0	0	52	38	9	2	3	1	1	0	2	4	6	0	0	0	59	42
CLE	100	35	65	2	0	0	0	0	0	0	0	0	0	0	0	49	33	14	4	2	2	0	3	2	4	6	0	0	0	61	39
DET	110	60	50	5	0	0	0	0	0	0	0	0	0	0	0	56	39	12	3	1	1	1	2	3	5	6	0	0	0	76	34
NY	85	43	42	4	0	0	0	0	0	0	0	0	0	0	0	43	25	14	3	3	0	0	2	2	8	3	0	0	0	56	29
PHI	142	64	78	5	0	0	0	0	0	0	0	0	0	0	0	68	45	23	6	1	1	1	1	2	5	2	4	0	0	82	60
STL	132	62	70	3	0	0	1	0	0	0	0	0	0	0	0	54	51	18	9	1	1	1	5	4	12	3	0	1	0	85	47
WAS	92	27	65	2	0	0	0	0	0	0	0	0	0	0	0	48	27	13	4	0	1	1	4	3	6	6	0	0	0	61	31
NL																															
BOS	66	19	47	2	0	0	1	0	0	0	0	0	0	0	0	36	18	11	1	0	2	3	0	1	9	1	1	0	0	41	25
BRO	88	44	44	1	0	0	0	0	0	0	0	0	0	0	0	49	22	12	5	0	3	1	4	2	7	5	0	0	0	44	44
CHI	71	41	30	2	0	0	0	0	0	0	0	0	0	0	0	38	28	3	2	0	2	4	1	2	6	4	0	0	0	42	29
CIN	75	31	44	0	0	0	0	0	0	0	0	0	0	0	0	44	21	9	1	0	1	2	1	3	10	1	1	0	0	40	35
NY	87	58	29	2	1	0	1	0	0	1	0	0	0	0	0	46	27	13	1	0	0	0	1	2	6	4	0	0	0	44	43
PHI	76	35	41	0	0	0	0	0	0	0	0	0	0	0	0	36	22	14	4	2	0	1	2	2	9	2	0	0	0	38	38
PIT	71	22	49	2	0	0	0	0	0	0	0	0	0	0	0	40	19	10	2	0	2	0	1	0	8	2	0	0	0	36	35
STL	77	45	32	1	0	0	0	0	0	0	0	0	0	0	0	47	21	8	1	1	1	2	1	1	10	2	0	0	0	47	30
AL	864	384	480	28	0	0	1	0	0	0	0	0	0	0	0	419	291	117	37	11	8	5	17	19	55	35	4	1	0	557	307
NL	611	295	316	10	1	0	2	0	0	1	0	0	0	0	0	336	178	80	17	3	11	13	11	13	65	21	2	0	0	332	279
YR	1475	679	796	38	1	0	3	0	0	1	0	0	0	0	0	755	469	197	54	14	19	18	28	32	120	56	6	1	0	889	586

AL		*NL*	
30	Bobo Newsom	21	Jim Turner
29	Lynn Nelson	20	Paul Derringer
25	George Caster	19	Cliff Melton
23	Buck Ross	18	Bill Lee
23	Bud Thomas	17	Multiple Players Tied

1939

AL				Consec			1-Inn			One-Game						Men-On-Base				Pitchers					Totals					Batters	
Tm	Tot	H	A	2	3	4	3	4	5	5	6	7	8	9	10	0	1	2	3	PH	LO	XN	IP	P	1	10	20	30	40	RHB	LHB
BOS	77	39	38	2	0	0	0	0	0	0	0	0	0	0	0	36	33	5	3	2	1	0	1	2	10	3	0	0	0	58	19
CHI	99	51	48	1	0	0	0	0	0	1	0	0	0	0	0	49	38	11	1	2	2	2	2	1	5	6	0	0	0	64	35
CLE	75	33	42	2	0	0	0	0	0	0	0	0	0	0	0	41	23	8	3	2	0	0	1	2	8	3	0	0	0	41	34
DET	104	65	39	1	0	0	0	0	0	0	0	0	0	0	0	53	34	15	2	0	2	2	1	3	14	4	0	0	0	61	43

Tm	Tot	H	A	Consec 2	Consec 3	Consec 4	1-Inn 3	1-Inn 4	1-Inn 5	One-Game 5	One-Game 6	One-Game 7	One-Game 8	One-Game 9	One-Game 10	Men-On-Base 0	Men-On-Base 1	Men-On-Base 2	Men-On-Base 3	Pitchers PH	Pitchers LO	Pitchers XN	Pitchers IP	Pitchers P	Totals 1	Totals 10	Totals 20	Totals 30	Totals 40	Batters RHB	Batters LHB
NY	85	48	37	4	0	0	0	0	0	0	0	0	0	0	0	47	29	9	0	1	1	1	3	1	5	5	0	0	0	49	36
PHI	148	83	65	2	1	0	2	0	0	1	0	0	1	0	0	70	52	21	5	1	2	1	3	4	7	5	2	0	0	86	62
STL	133	80	53	3	0	0	0	0	0	0	0	0	0	0	0	57	45	28	3	3	0	1	4	1	8	8	0	0	0	76	57
WAS	75	19	56	1	0	0	1	0	0	0	0	0	0	0	0	45	21	7	2	0	0	2	2	0	6	4	0	0	0	49	26
NL																															
BOS	63	14	49	1	0	0	0	0	0	0	0	0	0	0	0	33	19	8	3	3	1	2	0	0	10	2	0	0	0	40	23
BRO	93	49	44	0	0	0	0	0	0	1	0	0	0	0	0	59	26	8	0	1	3	0	1	1	10	2	1	0	0	59	34
CHI	74	35	39	1	0	0	0	0	0	0	0	0	0	0	0	42	24	7	1	0	1	1	1	3	9	2	0	0	0	40	34
CIN	81	39	42	0	1	0	0	0	1	0	0	1	0	0	0	44	30	7	0	2	0	0	1	3	7	4	0	0	0	47	34
NY	86	58	28	3	0	0	0	0	0	0	0	0	0	0	0	47	28	9	2	1	0	0	1	4	6	4	1	0	0	53	33
PHI	106	47	59	2	1	0	0	1	0	0	0	1	0	0	0	59	34	10	3	2	0	3	1	5	8	6	0	0	0	70	36
PIT	70	28	42	2	0	0	0	0	0	0	0	0	0	0	0	42	23	4	1	1	2	0	4	1	8	3	0	0	0	36	34
STL	76	43	33	2	0	0	1	0	0	0	0	0	0	0	0	40	22	12	2	2	1	3	1	2	6	3	0	0	0	43	33
AL	796	418	378	16	1	0	3	0	0	2	0	0	1	0	0	398	275	104	19	11	8	9	17	14	63	38	2	0	0	484	312
NL	649	313	336	11	2	0	1	1	1	1	0	2	0	0	0	366	206	65	12	12	8	9	10	19	64	26	2	0	0	388	261
YR	1445	731	714	27	3	0	2	0	0	3	0	2	1	0	0	764	481	169	31	23	16	18	27	33	127	64	4	0	0	872	573

AL
27 Lynn Nelson
26 Johnny Marcum
26 Nels Potter
22 Vern Kennedy
19 Bobo Newsom

NL
27 Luke Hamlin
21 Harry Gumbert
19 Hugh Mulcahy
18 Curt Davis
18 Bill Lee

1940

Tm	Tot	H	A	Consec 2	Consec 3	Consec 4	1-Inn 3	1-Inn 4	1-Inn 5	One-Game 5	One-Game 6	One-Game 7	One-Game 8	One-Game 9	One-Game 10	Men-On-Base 0	Men-On-Base 1	Men-On-Base 2	Men-On-Base 3	Pitchers PH	Pitchers LO	Pitchers XN	Pitchers IP	Pitchers P	Totals 1	Totals 10	Totals 20	Totals 30	Totals 40	Batters RHB	Batters LHB
AL																															
BOS	124	64	60	5	0	0	0	0	0	1	0	0	0	0	0	59	43	16	6	2	3	3	1	2	8	5	1	0	0	84	40
CHI	111	65	46	5	0	0	0	0	0	1	1	0	0	0	0	58	39	12	2	1	1	4	1	4	5	5	1	0	0	75	36
CLE	86	27	59	1	0	0	0	0	0	0	0	0	0	0	0	47	24	11	4	2	1	0	2	1	9	4	0	0	0	56	30
DET	102	64	38	1	0	0	0	0	0	1	0	0	0	0	0	49	31	16	6	2	1	1	1	4	10	5	0	0	0	57	45
NY	119	63	56	2	0	0	0	0	0	1	0	0	0	0	0	72	38	7	2	6	0	2	0	2	6	4	2	0	0	61	58
PHI	135	62	73	3	1	0	0	1	0	1	1	0	0	0	0	77	39	15	4	3	1	4	2	1	5	7	1	0	0	96	39
STL	113	68	45	2	0	0	0	0	0	0	0	0	0	0	0	61	28	19	5	1	1	1	1	2	9	3	1	0	0	72	41
WAS	93	28	65	1	0	0	0	0	0	0	0	0	0	0	0	47	34	11	1	1	2	2	1	1	8	2	1	0	0	59	34
NL																															
BOS	83	30	53	3	0	0	0	0	0	1	0	0	0	0	0	47	20	14	2	0	0	1	2	2	11	2	0	0	0	43	40
BRO	101	55	46	4	0	0	0	0	0	1	0	1	0	0	0	58	29	9	5	2	1	4	2	1	9	5	0	0	0	60	41
CHI	74	32	42	1	0	0	0	0	0	0	0	0	0	0	0	48	17	9	0	2	2	2	0	2	6	4	0	0	0	45	29
CIN	73	36	37	1	0	0	0	0	0	0	0	0	0	0	0	40	21	9	3	0	0	2	0	0	6	3	0	0	0	38	35
NY	110	75	35	3	0	0	0	0	0	0	0	0	0	0	0	57	29	19	5	1	1	4	2	0	8	3	1	0	0	66	44
PHI	92	50	42	3	0	0	0	0	0	0	0	0	0	0	0	44	29	13	6	1	0	4	4	2	8	5	0	0	0	59	33
PIT	72	22	50	0	0	0	0	0	0	1	0	0	0	0	0	36	23	12	1	0	0	0	1	1	10	2	0	0	0	33	39
STL	83	47	36	1	0	0	0	0	0	0	0	0	0	0	0	41	28	12	2	3	2	0	1	1	9	4	0	0	0	38	45
AL	883	441	442	20	1	0	0	1	0	5	2	0	0	0	0	470	276	107	30	18	10	17	9	17	60	35	7	0	0	560	323
NL	688	347	341	16	0	0	0	0	0	3	0	1	0	0	0	371	196	97	24	9	6	17	12	9	67	28	1	0	0	382	306
YR	1571	788	783	36	1	0	1	0	0	8	2	1	0	0	0	841	472	204	54	27	16	34	21	26	127	63	8	0	0	942	629

AL
24 Bob Harris
24 Red Ruffing
22 Johnny Rigney
21 Chubby Dean
20 Multiple Players Tied

NL
22 Carl Hubbell
19 Bill Lohrman
19 Bucky Walters
19 Whit Wyatt
17 Multiple Players Tied

1941

Tm	Tot	H	A	Consec 2	Consec 3	Consec 4	1-Inn 3	1-Inn 4	1-Inn 5	One-Game 5	One-Game 6	One-Game 7	One-Game 8	One-Game 9	One-Game 10	Men-On-Base 0	Men-On-Base 1	Men-On-Base 2	Men-On-Base 3	Pitchers PH	Pitchers LO	Pitchers XN	Pitchers IP	Pitchers P	Totals 1	Totals 10	Totals 20	Totals 30	Totals 40	Batters RHB	Batters LHB
AL																															
BOS	88	51	37	2	0	0	0	0	0	0	0	0	0	0	0	46	22	16	4	0	1	1	2	1	11	3	0	0	0	49	39
CHI	89	40	49	2	0	0	0	0	0	0	0	0	0	0	0	47	21	15	6	1	0	5	3	0	7	2	1	0	0	49	40
CLE	71	35	36	0	0	0	0	0	0	0	0	0	0	0	0	30	32	6	3	1	0	2	1	2	8	3	0	0	0	33	38
DET	80	43	37	1	0	0	0	0	0	0	0	0	0	0	0	40	25	11	4	1	1	5	1	1	7	4	0	0	0	45	35

Tm	Tot	H	A	Consec			1-Inn			One-Game						Men-On-Base				Pitchers					Totals					Batters	
				2	3	4	3	4	5	5	6	7	8	9	10	0	1	2	3	PH	LO	XN	IP	P	1	10	20	30	40	RHB	LHB
NY	81	44	37	3	0	0	0	0	0	0	0	0	0	0	0	53	20	8	0	3	1	2	1	0	6	5	0	0	0	46	35
PHI	136	76	60	4	0	0	0	0	0	2	0	0	0	0	0	72	42	19	3	2	2	2	2	3	10	5	1	0	0	75	61
STL	120	63	57	1	0	0	0	0	0	0	0	0	0	0	0	57	43	18	2	3	0	1	1	3	7	5	1	0	0	54	66
WAS	69	19	50	2	0	0	0	0	0	0	0	0	0	0	0	38	20	8	3	1	0	3	2	0	8	3	0	0	0	42	27
NL																															
BOS	75	28	47	0	0	0	0	0	0	0	0	0	0	0	0	44	22	9	0	0	1	0	0	1	9	2	0	0	0	37	38
BRO	81	40	41	2	0	0	0	0	0	0	0	0	0	0	0	42	18	17	4	2	0	2	1	1	12	3	0	0	0	37	44
CHI	60	20	40	0	0	0	0	0	0	0	0	0	0	0	0	35	17	6	2	2	0	4	1	3	8	2	0	0	0	32	28
CIN	61	27	34	0	0	0	0	0	0	0	0	0	0	0	0	31	23	7	0	1	2	2	0	5	8	2	0	0	0	31	30
NY	90	69	21	1	0	0	0	0	0	0	0	0	0	0	0	54	22	11	3	1	0	0	1	1	7	5	0	0	0	48	42
PHI	79	37	42	1	0	0	0	0	0	0	0	0	0	0	0	36	27	9	7	1	0	4	3	5	10	2	0	0	0	36	43
PIT	66	28	38	0	0	0	0	0	0	0	0	0	0	0	0	38	16	9	3	2	0	1	0	1	10	2	0	0	0	31	35
STL	85	53	32	1	1	0	1	0	0	0	0	0	0	0	0	45	27	11	2	4	0	4	1	1	8	4	0	0	0	44	41
AL	734	371	363	15	0	0	0	0	0	2	0	0	0	0	0	383	225	101	25	12	5	21	13	10	64	30	3	0	0	393	341
NL	597	302	295	5	1	0	1	0	0	0	0	0	0	0	0	325	172	79	21	13	3	17	7	18	72	22	0	0	0	296	301
YR	1331	673	658	20	1	0	1	0	0	2	0	0	0	0	0	708	397	180	46	25	8	38	20	28	136	52	3	0	0	689	642

AL

21 Johnny Rigney
20 Elden Auker
20 Jack Knott
18 Multiple Players Tied

NL

19 Lon Warneke
18 Rip Sewell
17 Kirby Higbe
16 Paul Derringer
15 Multiple Players Tied

1942

Tm	Tot	H	A	Consec			1-Inn			One-Game						Men-On-Base				Pitchers					Totals					Batters	
				2	3	4	3	4	5	5	6	7	8	9	10	0	1	2	3	PH	LO	XN	IP	P	1	10	20	30	40	RHB	LHB
AL																															
BOS	65	33	32	0	0	0	0	0	0	0	0	0	0	0	0	37	17	9	2	2	1	3	0	1	8	2	0	0	0	35	30
CHI	74	31	43	5	0	0	0	0	0	0	0	0	0	0	0	48	20	6	0	1	2	2	2	3	7	3	0	0	0	53	21
CLE	61	24	37	2	0	0	0	0	0	0	0	0	0	0	0	36	18	5	2	0	3	0	0	0	12	1	0	0	0	39	22
DET	60	40	20	0	0	0	0	0	0	0	0	0	0	0	0	37	19	3	1	0	0	1	0	1	10	1	0	0	0	24	36
NY	71	39	32	1	0	0	0	0	0	0	0	0	0	0	0	37	27	7	0	2	1	1	0	0	7	4	0	0	0	32	39
PHI	89	42	47	0	0	0	0	0	0	0	0	0	0	0	0	45	30	10	4	2	1	1	1	2	7	4	0	0	0	45	44
STL	63	37	26	1	0	0	0	0	0	0	0	0	0	0	0	39	18	5	1	0	2	3	1	1	10	3	0	0	0	32	31
WAS	50	11	39	2	0	0	0	0	0	0	0	0	0	0	0	22	16	11	1	1	0	2	2	0	13	0	0	0	0	26	24
NL																															
BOS	82	34	48	2	0	0	0	0	0	0	0	0	0	0	0	41	31	8	2	0	0	3	1	4	9	2	1	0	0	30	52
BRO	73	35	38	2	0	0	0	0	0	1	0	0	0	0	0	46	17	7	3	3	0	2	2	0	9	4	0	0	0	35	38
CHI	70	27	43	0	0	0	0	0	0	1	0	0	0	0	0	39	26	4	1	1	0	2	1	5	12	2	0	0	0	39	31
CIN	47	23	24	1	0	0	0	0	0	0	0	0	0	0	0	27	10	9	1	0	1	3	2	1	8	1	0	0	0	18	29
NY	94	67	27	2	0	0	0	0	0	0	0	0	0	0	0	54	28	7	5	4	2	5	2	1	9	4	0	0	0	45	49
PHI	61	31	30	0	0	0	0	0	0	0	0	0	0	0	0	32	20	7	2	0	1	1	1	3	11	1	0	0	0	43	18
PIT	62	21	41	2	0	0	0	0	0	0	0	0	0	0	0	35	20	5	2	0	1	1	2	1	10	1	0	0	0	28	34
STL	49	24	25	1	0	0	0	0	0	0	0	0	0	0	0	32	10	6	1	2	1	0	2	0	8	1	0	0	0	27	22
AL	533	257	276	11	0	0	0	0	0	0	0	0	0	0	0	301	165	56	11	8	10	13	6	8	74	18	0	0	0	286	247
NL	538	262	276	10	0	0	0	0	0	2	0	0	0	0	0	306	162	53	17	10	6	17	13	15	76	16	1	0	0	265	273
YR	1071	519	552	21	0	0	0	0	0	2	0	0	0	0	0	607	327	109	28	18	16	30	19	23	150	34	1	0	0	551	520

AL

19 Jim Bagby
17 Eddie Smith
16 Elden Auker
16 Bill Dietrich
16 Roger Wolff

NL

20 Jim Tobin
17 Kirby Higbe
17 Carl Hubbell
13 Multiple Players Tied

1943

Tm	Tot	H	A	Consec			1-Inn			One-Game						Men-On-Base				Pitchers					Totals					Batters	
				2	3	4	3	4	5	5	6	7	8	9	10	0	1	2	3	PH	LO	XN	IP	P	1	10	20	30	40	RHB	LHB
AL																															
BOS	61	25	36	1	0	0	0	0	0	0	0	0	0	0	0	34	22	4	1	1	1	5	3	1	9	0	1	0	0	34	27
CHI	54	25	29	0	0	0	0	0	0	0	0	0	0	0	0	32	16	5	1	1	0	3	0	0	10	0	0	0	0	32	22
CLE	52	21	31	0	0	0	0	0	0	0	0	0	0	0	0	33	13	6	0	0	0	1	3	0	10	1	0	0	0	26	26
DET	51	26	25	1	0	0	0	0	0	0	0	0	0	0	0	26	18	7	0	1	1	2	1	0	9	1	0	0	0	25	26

Tm	Tot	H	A	Consec 2	3	4	1-Inn 3	4	5	One-Game 5	6	7	8	9	10	Men-On-Base 0	1	2	3	Pitchers PH	LO	XN	IP	P	Totals 1	10	20	30	40	Batters RHB	LHB
NY	60	33	27	1	0	0	0	0	0	0	0	0	0	0	0	33	18	9	0	0	0	2	2	3	7	3	0	0	0	33	27
PHI	73	36	37	2	0	0	0	0	0	0	0	0	0	0	0	45	16	12	0	3	2	1	1	3	10	3	0	0	0	44	29
STL	74	51	23	0	0	0	0	0	0	0	0	0	0	0	0	45	19	9	1	1	0	3	2	1	8	3	0	0	0	32	42
WAS	48	14	34	2	0	0	0	0	0	0	0	0	0	0	0	24	13	10	1	1	1	0	2	2	9	1	0	0	0	34	14
NL																															
BOS	66	34	32	2	0	0	0	0	0	0	0	0	0	0	0	37	20	7	2	2	2	2	0	1	9	4	0	0	0	35	31
BRO	59	30	29	1	0	0	0	0	0	0	0	0	0	0	0	31	19	7	2	1	2	2	2	0	13	0	0	0	0	31	28
CHI	53	19	34	0	0	0	0	0	0	0	0	0	0	0	0	35	15	2	1	3	0	4	1	1	12	1	0	0	0	34	19
CIN	38	16	22	0	0	0	0	0	0	0	0	0	0	0	0	14	17	6	1	0	0	1	0	1	7	0	0	0	0	18	20
NY	80	52	28	0	0	0	0	0	0	0	0	0	0	0	0	41	24	13	2	1	1	2	4	1	15	1	0	0	0	44	36
PHI	59	18	41	2	0	0	0	0	0	0	0	0	0	0	0	34	20	5	0	0	0	1	2	3	15	1	0	0	0	42	17
PIT	44	15	29	0	0	0	0	0	0	0	0	0	0	0	0	21	20	2	1	1	1	2	4	1	8	1	0	0	0	15	29
STL	33	17	16	0	0	0	0	0	0	0	0	0	0	0	0	14	16	3	0	0	0	1	0	0	9	0	0	0	0	20	13
AL	473	231	242	7	0	0	0	0	0	0	0	0	0	0	0	272	135	62	4	8	5	17	14	10	72	12	1	0	0	260	213
NL	432	201	231	5	0	0	0	0	0	0	0	0	0	0	0	227	151	45	9	8	6	15	13	8	88	8	0	0	0	239	193
YR	905	432	473	12	0	0	0	0	0	0	0	0	0	0	0	499	286	107	13	16	11	32	27	18	160	20	1	0	0	499	406

	AL		*NL*
23	Tex Hughson	14	Johnnie Wittig
17	Lum Harris	13	Al Javery
15	Jim Bagby	12	Jim Tobin
15	Early Wynn	11	Nate Andrews
13	Multiple Players Tied	11	Red Barrett

1944

Tm	Tot	H	A	Consec 2	3	4	1-Inn 3	4	5	One-Game 5	6	7	8	9	10	Men-On-Base 0	1	2	3	Pitchers PH	LO	XN	IP	P	Totals 1	10	20	30	40	Batters RHB	LHB
AL																															
BOS	66	34	32	1	0	0	0	0	0	0	0	0	0	0	0	33	24	6	3	1	1	4	3	2	11	2	0	0	0	40	26
CHI	68	24	44	1	0	0	0	0	0	0	0	0	0	0	0	39	21	6	2	1	0	1	2	5	7	3	0	0	0	44	24
CLE	40	16	24	1	0	0	0	0	0	0	0	0	0	0	0	17	11	10	2	2	0	2	4	0	10	0	0	0	0	23	17
DET	39	21	18	0	0	0	0	0	0	0	0	0	0	0	0	17	12	7	3	0	0	0	0	0	8	0	0	0	0	24	15
NY	82	45	37	0	0	0	0	0	0	0	0	0	0	0	0	44	28	8	2	3	2	0	3	2	8	4	0	0	0	32	50
PHI	58	28	30	2	0	0	0	0	0	0	0	0	0	0	0	37	16	3	2	0	2	1	3	0	7	2	0	0	0	36	22
STL	58	24	34	1	0	0	0	0	0	0	0	0	0	0	0	39	13	6	0	2	0	2	1	1	9	2	0	0	0	33	25
WAS	48	13	35	0	0	0	0	0	0	0	0	0	0	0	0	36	10	1	1	0	0	1	4	2	9	0	0	0	0	32	16
NL																															
BOS	80	44	36	1	0	0	0	0	0	0	0	0	0	0	0	39	28	11	2	6	1	1	1	3	7	4	0	0	0	36	44
BRO	75	34	41	1	0	0	0	0	0	0	0	0	0	0	0	37	21	13	4	2	0	1	0	2	17	3	0	0	0	30	45
CHI	75	40	35	3	0	0	0	0	0	0	0	0	0	0	0	47	22	6	0	2	1	1	4	0	12	1	0	0	0	43	32
CIN	60	24	36	0	1	0	1	0	0	0	0	0	0	0	0	38	17	5	0	2	0	0	2	1	5	3	0	0	0	32	28
NY	116	86	30	2	0	0	1	0	0	1	0	0	0	0	0	56	42	16	2	1	2	1	2	2	11	2	0	1	0	63	53
PHI	49	21	28	1	0	0	1	0	0	0	0	0	0	0	0	24	11	13	1	3	1	3	3	0	12	0	0	0	0	31	18
PIT	65	31	34	1	0	0	0	0	0	0	0	0	0	0	0	33	21	9	2	2	0	0	3	1	8	2	0	0	0	26	39
STL	55	14	41	2	0	0	0	0	0	0	0	0	0	0	0	30	17	8	0	2	0	1	1	0	10	1	0	0	0	27	28
AL	459	205	254	6	0	0	0	0	0	0	0	0	0	0	0	262	135	47	15	9	5	11	20	12	69	13	0	0	0	264	195
NL	575	294	281	11	1	0	3	0	0	1	0	0	0	0	0	304	179	81	11	20	5	8	16	9	82	16	0	1	0	288	287
YR	1034	499	535	17	1	0	3	0	0	1	0	0	0	0	0	566	314	128	26	29	10	19	36	21	151	29	0	1	0	552	482

	AL		*NL*
17	Sig Jakucki	31	Bill Voiselle
15	Hank Borowy	18	Harry Feldman
15	Bill Dietrich	18	Jim Tobin
14	Tiny Bonham	15	Rip Sewell
14	Joe Bowman	14	Nate Andrews

1945

Tm	Tot	H	A	Consec 2	3	4	1-Inn 3	4	5	One-Game 5	6	7	8	9	10	Men-On-Base 0	1	2	3	Pitchers PH	LO	XN	IP	P	Totals 1	10	20	30	40	Batters RHB	LHB
AL																															
BOS	58	28	30	2	0	0	0	0	0	0	0	0	0	0	0	25	20	10	3	2	1	1	0	3	13	0	0	0	0	40	18
CHI	63	34	29	2	0	0	0	0	0	0	0	0	0	0	0	36	21	2	4	1	1	1	1	3	9	2	0	0	0	41	22
CLE	39	15	24	1	0	0	0	0	0	0	0	0	0	0	0	28	5	4	2	0	1	0	1	1	10	0	0	0	0	17	22
DET	48	28	20	0	0	0	0	0	0	0	0	0	0	0	0	23	18	6	1	1	1	0	0	1	12	0	0	0	0	25	23

Tm	Tot	H	A	Consec 2	3	4	1-Inn 3	4	5	One-Game 5	6	7	8	9	10	Men-On-Base 0	1	2	3	Pitchers PH	LO	XN	IP	P	Totals 1	10	20	30	40	Batters RHB	LHB
NY	66	51	15	1	0	0	0	0	0	1	0	0	0	0	0	34	19	10	3	1	1	2	0	3	10	3	0	0	0	33	33
PHI	55	21	34	1	0	0	0	0	0	0	0	0	0	0	0	33	15	7	0	0	2	2	1	2	9	1	0	0	0	33	22
STL	59	33	26	0	0	0	0	0	0	0	0	0	0	0	0	23	25	9	2	0	1	1	1	4	7	2	0	0	0	24	35
WAS	42	6	36	1	0	0	0	0	0	0	0	0	0	0	0	26	9	6	1	3	0	0	1	2	8	1	0	0	0	19	23
NL																															
BOS	99	63	36	4	0	0	0	0	0	0	0	0	0	0	0	57	22	16	4	0	5	3	2	3	17	1	1	0	0	51	48
BRO	74	34	40	3	0	0	0	0	0	0	0	0	0	0	0	34	25	13	2	3	0	1	2	1	12	2	0	0	0	43	31
CHI	57	17	40	3	0	0	1	0	0	0	0	0	0	0	0	35	17	4	1	0	0	0	1	0	11	1	0	0	0	34	23
CIN	70	21	49	3	0	0	0	0	0	0	0	0	0	0	0	31	27	10	2	3	0	1	0	4	8	3	0	0	0	28	42
NY	85	47	38	2	0	0	0	0	0	0	0	0	0	0	0	41	29	14	1	1	1	3	1	2	12	3	0	0	0	35	50
PHI	61	28	33	1	0	0	0	0	0	0	0	0	0	0	0	29	26	5	1	1	0	2	1	1	13	2	0	0	0	33	28
PIT	61	25	36	0	0	0	0	0	0	0	0	0	0	0	0	30	19	8	4	4	0	2	0	2	10	1	0	0	0	29	32
STL	70	29	41	2	0	0	0	0	0	0	0	0	0	0	0	34	21	10	5	5	0	4	0	1	11	2	0	0	0	32	38
AL	430	216	214	8	0	0	0	0	0	1	0	0	0	0	0	228	132	54	16	8	8	7	5	19	78	9	0	0	0	232	198
NL	577	264	313	18	0	0	1	0	0	0	0	0	0	0	0	291	186	80	20	17	6	16	7	14	94	15	1	0	0	285	292
YR	1007	480	527	26	0	0	1	0	0	1	0	0	0	0	0	519	318	134	36	25	14	23	12	33	172	24	1	0	0	517	490

	AL		*NL*
13	Jack Kramer	22	Johnny Hutchings
12	Bill Bevens	18	Red Barrett
12	Orval Grove	17	Hank Wyse
12	Bobo Newsom	15	Bill Voiselle
11	Multiple Players Tied	14	Multiple Players Tied

1946

Tm	Tot	H	A	Consec 2	3	4	1-Inn 3	4	5	One-Game 5	6	7	8	9	10	Men-On-Base 0	1	2	3	Pitchers PH	LO	XN	IP	P	Totals 1	10	20	30	40	Batters RHB	LHB
AL																															
BOS	89	44	45	4	0	0	0	0	0	0	0	0	0	0	0	54	22	11	2	1	2	2	2	2	11	4	0	0	0	52	37
CHI	80	46	34	2	0	0	0	0	0	0	0	0	0	0	0	54	21	4	1	0	0	0	1	3	10	3	0	0	0	55	25
CLE	84	36	48	2	0	0	0	0	0	0	0	0	0	0	0	50	23	8	3	0	2	2	2	0	11	3	1	0	0	21	63
DET	97	68	29	1	1	0	1	0	0	0	1	0	0	0	0	54	31	10	2	1	1	2	2	1	10	3	1	0	0	36	61
NY	66	34	32	3	0	0	0	0	0	0	0	0	0	0	0	37	18	9	2	0	0	2	0	1	15	1	0	0	0	42	24
PHI	83	38	45	3	0	0	0	0	0	0	0	0	0	0	0	45	28	9	1	0	2	0	1	1	11	4	0	0	0	46	37
STL	73	29	44	1	0	0	0	0	0	0	0	0	0	0	0	39	22	7	5	0	1	1	0	1	13	1	0	0	0	48	25
WAS	81	25	56	2	0	0	0	0	0	1	0	0	0	0	0	49	22	10	0	0	2	1	3	1	15	1	0	0	0	43	38
NL																															
BOS	76	29	47	2	0	0	0	0	0	1	0	0	0	0	0	39	23	11	3	5	0	3	1	3	16	1	0	0	0	34	42
BRO	58	22	36	0	0	0	0	0	0	0	0	0	0	0	0	37	11	9	1	2	0	1	2	2	14	2	0	0	0	31	27
CHI	58	30	28	2	0	0	0	0	0	0	0	0	0	0	0	33	19	4	2	3	0	1	1	0	14	0	0	0	0	33	25
CIN	70	39	31	0	0	0	0	0	0	0	0	0	0	0	0	40	21	9	0	4	1	4	1	0	9	3	0	0	0	28	42
NY	114	75	39	5	0	0	0	0	0	0	0	0	0	0	0	61	40	12	1	6	1	2	7	3	16	4	0	0	0	57	57
PHI	73	35	38	3	0	0	1	0	0	0	0	0	0	0	0	39	19	12	3	3	0	3	2	1	15	1	0	0	0	39	34
PIT	50	23	27	0	0	0	1	0	0	0	0	0	0	0	0	23	19	8	0	1	0	0	4	1	11	0	0	0	0	28	22
STL	63	36	27	2	1	0	1	0	0	0	0	0	0	0	0	38	18	4	3	2	0	2	0	0	10	2	0	0	0	34	29
AL	653	320	333	18	1	0	1	0	0	1	1	0	0	0	0	382	187	68	16	2	10	10	11	10	96	20	2	0	0	343	310
NL	562	289	273	14	1	0	3	0	0	1	0	0	0	0	0	310	170	69	13	26	2	16	18	10	105	13	0	0	0	284	278
YR	1215	609	606	32	2	0	3	0	0	2	1	0	0	0	0	692	357	137	29	28	12	26	29	20	201	33	2	0	0	627	588

	AL		*NL*
23	Virgil Trucks	16	Mort Cooper
20	Steve Gromek	15	Joe Beggs
18	Mickey Harris	15	Dave Koslo
18	Eddie Lopat	14	Monita Kennedy
16	Dick Fowler	14	Bill Voiselle

1947

Tm	Tot	H	A	Consec 2	3	4	1-Inn 3	4	5	One-Game 5	6	7	8	9	10	Men-On-Base 0	1	2	3	Pitchers PH	LO	XN	IP	P	Totals 1	10	20	30	40	Batters RHB	LHB
AL																															
BOS	84	39	45	3	0	0	1	0	0	0	0	0	0	0	0	42	28	10	4	1	1	2	2	1	9	4	0	0	0	42	42
CHI	76	31	45	1	1	0	1	0	0	1	0	0	0	0	0	43	19	10	4	3	0	1	0	1	11	2	0	0	0	41	35
CLE	94	51	43	1	0	0	0	0	0	0	0	0	0	0	0	54	30	7	3	2	2	0	0	2	9	4	0	0	0	51	43
DET	79	47	32	3	0	0	0	0	0	1	0	0	0	0	0	36	31	10	2	2	1	1	1	0	6	3	0	0	0	33	46

Tm	Tot	H	A	Consec 2	3	4	1-Inn 3	4	5	One-Game 5	6	7	8	9	10	Men-On-Base 0	1	2	3	Pitchers PH	LO	XN	IP	P	Totals 1	10	20	30	40	Batters RHB	LHB
NY	95	49	46	1	0	0	1	0	0	0	0	0	0	0	0	60	29	5	1	2	2	0	1	1	11	3	1	0	0	42	53
PHI	85	41	44	3	0	0	0	0	0	0	0	0	0	0	0	41	30	12	2	1	2	2	0	1	4	5	0	0	0	38	47
STL	103	57	46	2	1	0	1	0	0	0	0	0	0	0	0	55	30	16	2	1	2	2	0	3	6	6	0	0	0	49	54
WAS	63	20	43	1	0	0	1	0	0	0	0	0	0	0	0	32	20	11	0	0	1	0	4	2	10	2	0	0	0	38	25
NL																															
BOS	93	39	54	0	0	0	0	0	0	1	0	0	0	0	0	42	35	15	1	0	0	2	0	1	9	3	0	0	0	47	46
BRO	104	57	47	5	0	0	2	0	0	1	1	0	0	0	0	59	25	15	5	2	0	1	2	3	12	3	1	0	0	70	34
CHI	106	51	55	4	0	0	0	0	0	0	0	0	0	0	0	54	37	10	5	3	0	2	0	0	9	4	0	0	0	72	34
CIN	102	47	55	4	0	0	1	0	0	2	0	0	0	0	0	63	26	12	1	1	1	1	1	3	9	6	0	0	0	61	41
NY	122	75	47	3	0	0	0	0	0	0	0	0	0	0	0	66	36	15	5	4	2	2	4	0	13	1	2	0	0	75	47
PHI	98	43	55	3	0	0	0	0	0	1	0	0	0	0	0	57	30	8	3	3	0	0	2	0	9	3	1	0	0	65	33
PIT	155	87	68	3	0	0	1	0	0	1	0	0	0	0	0	79	49	24	3	1	2	0	2	4	14	3	2	0	0	113	42
STL	106	49	57	5	0	0	2	0	0	0	1	1	0	0	0	56	35	12	3	3	1	2	0	3	5	6	0	0	0	73	33
AL	679	335	344	15	2	0	5	0	0	2	0	0	0	0	0	363	217	81	18	12	11	8	8	11	66	29	1	0	0	334	345
NL	886	448	438	27	0	0	6	0	0	6	2	1	0	0	0	476	273	111	26	17	6	10	11	14	80	29	6	0	0	576	310
YR	1565	783	782	42	2	0	5	0	0	8	2	1	0	0	0	839	490	192	44	29	17	18	19	25	146	58	7	0	0	910	655

AL
23 Allie Reynolds
18 Don Black
17 Multiple Players Tied

NL
24 Larry Jansen
22 Ralph Branca
22 Dave Koslo
22 Schoolboy Rowe
21 Kirby Higbe

1948

Tm	Tot	H	A	Consec 2	3	4	1-Inn 3	4	5	One-Game 5	6	7	8	9	10	Men-On-Base 0	1	2	3	Pitchers PH	LO	XN	IP	P	Totals 1	10	20	30	40	Batters RHB	LHB
AL																															
BOS	83	43	40	2	0	0	0	0	0	0	0	0	0	0	0	37	31	13	2	2	0	2	0	3	8	4	0	0	0	54	29
CHI	89	36	53	5	0	0	0	0	0	0	0	0	0	0	0	46	27	13	3	1	3	2	2	1	13	1	0	0	0	58	31
CLE	82	41	41	3	0	0	0	0	0	0	0	0	0	0	0	42	25	12	3	1	2	2	0	2	10	2	1	0	0	49	33
DET	92	61	31	3	1	0	1	0	0	0	0	0	0	0	0	50	31	10	1	0	0	2	0	3	7	3	0	1	0	53	39
NY	94	54	40	3	0	0	0	0	0	0	0	0	0	0	0	52	30	9	3	2	0	1	1	0	6	4	0	0	0	49	45
PHI	86	47	39	2	1	0	1	0	0	0	0	0	0	0	0	52	23	7	4	0	1	1	1	2	6	4	0	0	0	56	30
STL	103	64	39	2	0	0	0	0	0	0	0	0	0	0	0	63	25	11	4	0	2	1	2	3	10	4	0	0	0	57	46
WAS	81	24	57	2	0	0	0	0	0	0	0	0	0	0	0	39	25	12	5	1	2	0	1	3	10	3	0	0	0	49	32
NL																															
BOS	93	40	53	0	0	0	0	0	0	1	0	0	0	0	0	57	26	7	3	0	0	2	1	1	8	3	0	0	0	58	35
BRO	119	68	51	0	0	0	0	0	0	0	0	0	0	0	0	69	35	11	4	2	2	2	0	1	10	3	1	0	0	61	58
CHI	89	34	55	4	0	0	0	0	0	0	0	0	0	0	0	51	18	17	3	3	0	1	3	1	9	3	0	0	0	53	36
CIN	104	52	52	0	0	0	0	0	0	0	0	0	0	0	0	52	36	13	3	2	0	0	2	1	6	5	1	0	0	69	35
NY	122	82	40	2	0	0	0	0	0	0	0	0	0	0	0	64	37	20	1	4	1	2	4	1	10	3	2	0	0	65	57
PHI	95	44	51	4	0	0	0	1	0	0	0	0	0	0	0	58	24	10	3	2	0	3	2	5	12	4	0	0	0	64	31
PIT	120	64	56	2	0	0	0	0	0	0	1	0	0	0	0	66	36	11	7	2	1	0	0	2	6	6	0	0	0	72	48
STL	103	43	60	0	1	0	1	0	0	0	0	0	0	0	0	66	27	10	0	0	0	0	2	1	8	2	0	1	0	52	51
AL	710	370	340	22	2	0	2	0	0	0	0	0	0	0	0	381	217	87	25	7	10	11	7	17	70	25	1	1	0	425	285
NL	845	427	418	12	1	0	1	1	0	1	1	0	0	0	0	483	239	99	24	15	4	10	14	13	69	29	4	1	0	494	351
YR	1555	797	758	34	3	0	2	1	0	1	1	0	0	0	0	864	456	186	49	22	14	21	21	30	139	54	5	2	0	919	636

AL
32 Fred Hutchinson
20 Bob Feller
19 Phil Marchildon
18 Fred Sanford
18 Early Wynn

NL
39 Murry Dickson
25 Larry Jansen
24 Ralph Branca
21 Ray Poat
21 Herm Wehmeier

1949

Tm	Tot	H	A	Consec 2	3	4	1-Inn 3	4	5	One-Game 5	6	7	8	9	10	Men-On-Base 0	1	2	3	Pitchers PH	LO	XN	IP	P	Totals 1	10	20	30	40	Batters RHB	LHB
AL																															
BOS	82	43	39	2	0	0	0	0	0	0	0	0	0	0	0	41	26	14	1	1	0	1	0	3	11	2	1	0	0	59	23
CHI	108	52	56	6	0	0	0	0	0	0	0	1	0	0	0	56	30	20	2	2	0	4	2	1	8	5	1	0	0	59	49
CLE	82	42	40	1	0	0	0	0	0	0	0	0	0	0	0	44	26	11	1	1	0	0	2	0	8	2	0	0	0	28	54
DET	102	60	42	2	0	0	1	0	0	0	0	0	0	0	0	50	40	12	0	1	2	2	1	1	6	5	0	0	0	53	49

				Consec			1-Inn			One-Game						Men-On-Base				Pitchers					Totals					Batters	
Tm	Tot	H	A	2	3	4	3	4	5	5	6	7	8	9	10	0	1	2	3	PH	LO	XN	IP	P	1	10	20	30	40	RHB	LHB
NY	98	53	45	5	0	0	0	0	0	0	0	0	0	0	0	55	33	6	4	2	1	3	0	4	7	4	0	0	0	45	53
PHI	105	42	63	2	0	0	1	0	0	0	0	0	0	0	0	47	34	19	5	0	0	1	3	0	4	5	1	0	0	58	47
STL	113	56	57	4	0	0	0	0	0	0	1	0	0	0	0	57	34	18	4	4	1	0	3	2	8	6	0	0	0	63	50
WAS	79	14	65	0	0	0	0	0	0	0	0	0	0	0	0	42	24	10	3	1	0	1	0	4	11	3	0	0	0	41	38
NL																															
BOS	110	40	70	1	0	0	0	0	0	0	0	0	0	0	0	62	32	11	5	0	2	0	0	4	6	2	2	0	0	75	35
BRO	132	73	59	4	0	0	0	0	0	1	0	0	0	0	0	66	49	12	5	6	2	4	1	2	6	4	2	0	0	86	46
CHI	104	38	66	5	0	0	1	0	0	0	0	0	0	0	0	50	36	17	1	2	3	2	2	1	10	4	0	0	0	68	36
CIN	124	54	70	3	1	0	1	0	1	0	1	0	0	0	0	71	33	14	6	2	0	3	0	2	9	3	2	0	0	80	44
NY	132	78	54	2	0	0	0	0	0	0	1	0	0	0	0	68	36	21	7	4	1	3	3	2	6	5	0	1	0	82	50
PHI	104	35	69	2	0	0	0	0	0	0	0	0	0	0	0	49	42	11	2	0	1	2	0	2	7	4	0	0	0	71	33
PIT	142	75	67	2	0	0	1	0	0	1	0	0	0	0	0	65	49	26	2	4	1	2	1	2	9	5	1	0	0	101	41
STL	87	33	54	1	0	0	0	0	0	0	0	0	0	0	0	48	25	12	2	3	1	0	0	0	9	3	0	0	0	66	21
AL	769	362	407	22	0	0	2	0	0	0	1	1	0	0	0	392	247	110	20	12	4	12	11	15	63	32	3	0	0	406	363
NL	935	426	509	20	1	0	3	0	1	2	2	0	0	0	0	479	302	124	30	21	11	16	7	15	62	30	7	1	0	629	306
YR	1704	788	916	42	1	0	3	0	0	2	3	1	0	0	0	871	549	234	50	33	15	28	18	30	125	62	10	1	0	1035	669

AL
22 Randy Gumpert
22 Ellis Kinder
20 Lou Brissie
19 Multiple Players Tied

NL
36 Larry Jansen
27 Warren Spahn
25 Preacher Roe
23 Ken Raffensberger
23 Bill Werle

1950

				Consec			1-Inn			One-Game						Men-On-Base				Pitchers					Totals					Batters	
Tm	Tot	H	A	2	3	4	3	4	5	5	6	7	8	9	10	0	1	2	3	PH	LO	XN	IP	P	1	10	20	30	40	RHB	LHB
AL																															
BOS	121	67	54	3	1	0	1	0	0	1	0	0	0	0	0	65	36	18	2	2	3	2	1	4	9	4	1	0	0	68	53
CHI	107	55	52	1	0	0	0	0	0	0	1	0	0	0	0	53	36	17	1	2	0	2	0	2	6	8	0	0	0	76	31
CLE	120	57	63	5	0	0	1	0	0	0	0	0	0	0	0	73	30	11	6	1	2	0	0	1	7	2	3	0	0	77	43
DET	141	73	68	5	0	0	0	0	0	0	1	0	0	0	0	71	51	15	4	3	2	1	2	3	8	2	3	0	0	79	62
NY	118	51	67	2	0	0	0	1	0	2	0	0	0	0	0	63	38	13	4	1	1	1	3	5	7	4	1	0	0	72	46
PHI	138	67	71	6	0	0	0	0	0	0	0	0	0	0	0	70	42	22	4	0	1	4	1	1	6	4	2	0	0	87	51
STL	129	68	61	2	0	0	1	0	0	1	0	1	0	0	0	52	46	22	9	4	2	1	2	1	8	7	0	0	0	68	61
WAS	99	28	71	3	0	0	0	0	0	1	0	0	0	0	0	54	28	14	3	2	1	2	2	5	13	3	0	0	0	60	39
NL																															
BOS	129	45	84	2	0	0	0	0	0	1	0	0	0	0	0	68	42	18	1	2	3	2	1	5	8	1	2	1	0	84	45
BRO	163	96	67	2	0	0	2	0	0	1	0	0	0	0	0	99	35	22	7	5	1	4	3	3	6	5	2	1	0	115	48
CHI	130	63	67	1	0	0	1	0	0	1	0	0	0	0	0	70	52	4	4	2	2	3	1	1	4	6	1	0	0	91	39
CIN	145	81	64	8	0	0	1	0	0	1	0	1	0	0	0	83	45	13	4	1	0	0	2	3	5	4	1	1	0	98	47
NY	140	67	73	2	0	0	1	0	0	1	0	0	0	0	0	76	43	15	6	1	2	1	2	2	5	4	1	1	0	95	45
PHI	122	53	69	1	0	0	0	0	0	0	0	0	0	0	0	76	29	13	4	1	2	2	0	1	5	4	2	0	0	87	35
PIT	152	79	73	5	0	0	0	0	0	0	0	0	0	0	0	68	45	32	7	1	3	6	1	5	9	5	2	0	0	109	43
STL	119	43	76	4	0	0	0	0	0	1	0	0	0	0	0	70	36	11	2	3	2	3	0	1	5	7	0	0	0	83	36
AL	973	466	507	27	1	0	3	1	0	5	2	1	0	0	0	501	307	132	33	15	12	13	11	22	64	34	10	0	0	587	386
NL	1100	527	573	25	0	0	5	0	0	6	0	1	0	0	0	610	327	128	35	16	15	21	10	21	47	36	11	4	0	762	338
YR	2073	993	1080	52	1	0	5	0	0	11	2	2	0	0	0	1111	634	260	68	31	27	34	21	43	111	70	21	4	0	1349	724

AL
29 Art Houtteman
28 Alex Kellner
28 Bob Lemon
23 Multiple Players Tied

NL
34 Ken Raffensberger
34 Preacher Roe
34 Johnny Sain
31 Larry Jansen
29 Robin Roberts

1951

				Consec			1-Inn			One-Game						Men-On-Base				Pitchers					Totals					Batters	
Tm	Tot	H	A	2	3	4	3	4	5	5	6	7	8	9	10	0	1	2	3	PH	LO	XN	IP	P	1	10	20	30	40	RHB	LHB
AL																															
BOS	99	65	34	2	0	0	0	0	0	0	0	0	0	0	0	51	33	14	1	2	1	2	1	2	7	3	1	0	0	68	31
CHI	109	47	62	2	0	0	0	0	0	1	0	0	0	0	0	62	27	17	3	1	2	1	1	5	11	3	1	0	0	66	43
CLE	85	43	42	1	0	0	0	0	0	0	0	0	0	0	0	38	35	10	2	3	0	2	1	1	5	3	1	0	0	35	50
DET	103	60	43	1	0	0	0	0	0	0	0	0	0	0	0	54	33	11	5	2	3	1	0	5	8	4	0	0	0	45	58

Tm	Tot	H	A	Consec 2	3	4	1-Inn 3	4	5	One-Game 5	6	7	8	9	10	Men-On-Base 0	1	2	3	Pitchers PH	LO	XN	IP	P	Totals 1	10	20	30	40	Batters RHB	LHB
NY	92	43	49	3	0	0	1	0	0	0	0	0	0	0	0	47	28	14	3	3	0	1	1	4	8	4	1	0	0	36	56
PHI	109	59	50	0	0	0	0	0	0	1	0	0	0	0	0	63	33	13	0	0	1	4	1	2	3	5	1	0	0	67	42
STL	132	66	66	5	1	0	2	0	0	1	0	0	0	0	0	61	46	18	7	3	0	7	2	4	16	4	0	0	0	61	71
WAS	110	35	75	1	0	0	0	0	0	1	0	0	0	0	0	56	41	11	2	2	2	3	2	1	12	3	0	0	0	47	63
NL																															
BOS	96	38	58	3	0	0	1	0	0	0	0	0	0	0	0	55	23	15	3	0	1	2	0	0	8	2	2	0	0	69	27
BRO	150	81	69	1	0	0	0	0	0	2	0	0	0	0	0	76	58	14	2	2	4	3	1	2	8	4	1	1	0	106	44
CHI	125	59	66	2	0	0	0	0	0	1	0	0	0	0	0	71	29	23	2	3	3	3	1	2	6	5	1	0	0	92	33
CIN	119	46	73	4	0	0	2	0	0	1	0	0	0	0	0	58	36	22	3	5	2	3	1	3	6	4	0	1	0	83	36
NY	148	89	59	6	0	0	0	0	0	0	0	0	0	0	0	91	42	14	1	3	3	4	1	1	3	3	4	0	0	94	54
PHI	110	50	60	2	0	0	0	0	0	0	0	0	0	0	0	69	28	9	4	3	1	5	1	1	8	4	1	0	0	81	29
PIT	157	84	73	5	0	0	0	0	0	0	0	0	0	0	0	81	52	16	8	4	2	1	5	5	11	1	3	1	0	117	40
STL	119	57	62	3	0	0	0	0	0	0	0	0	0	0	0	72	29	12	6	0	2	3	0	2	6	8	0	0	0	83	36
AL	839	418	421	15	1	0	3	0	0	4	0	0	0	0	0	432	276	108	23	16	9	21	9	24	70	29	5	0	0	425	414
NL	1024	504	520	26	0	0	3	0	0	4	0	0	0	0	0	573	297	125	29	20	18	24	10	16	56	31	12	3	0	725	299
YR	1863	922	941	41	1	0	6	0	0	8	0	0	0	0	0	1005	573	233	52	36	27	45	19	40	126	60	17	3	0	1150	713

AL		*NL*	
22	Bob Feller	32	Murry Dickson
22	Dick Starr	30	Ken Raffensberger
21	Ray Scarborough	30	Preacher Roe
20	Multiple Players Tied	27	Sal Maglie
		26	Larry Jansen

1952

Tm	Tot	H	A	Consec 2	3	4	1-Inn 3	4	5	One-Game 5	6	7	8	9	10	Men-On-Base 0	1	2	3	Pitchers PH	LO	XN	IP	P	Totals 1	10	20	30	40	Batters RHB	LHB
AL																															
BOS	107	49	58	2	0	0	0	0	0	0	0	0	0	0	0	58	36	11	2	1	4	3	1	5	12	5	0	0	0	69	38
CHI	86	40	46	1	0	0	0	0	0	0	0	0	0	0	0	41	29	13	3	3	1	4	1	1	10	3	0	0	0	53	33
CLE	94	44	50	0	0	0	0	0	0	0	0	0	0	0	0	49	25	17	3	4	0	3	0	2	6	3	1	0	0	48	46
DET	111	59	52	2	0	0	0	0	0	0	0	0	0	0	0	60	33	13	5	2	2	0	0	3	10	4	1	0	0	62	49
NY	94	48	46	2	0	0	0	0	0	0	0	0	0	0	0	54	22	15	3	2	2	5	3	2	9	4	0	0	0	51	43
PHI	113	60	53	3	0	0	1	0	0	0	0	0	0	0	0	60	36	14	3	0	1	1	5	2	8	2	3	0	0	76	37
STL	111	53	58	1	0	0	0	0	0	0	0	0	0	0	0	54	39	14	4	3	2	2	3	1	11	5	0	0	0	60	51
WAS	78	18	60	0	0	0	0	0	0	0	0	0	0	0	0	39	26	11	2	7	1	1	1	0	13	3	0	0	0	28	50
NL																															
BOS	106	43	63	1	0	0	1	0	0	0	0	0	0	0	0	47	42	13	4	1	2	2	0	4	11	3	0	0	0	59	47
BRO	121	78	43	3	0	0	2	0	0	0	0	0	0	0	0	64	42	11	4	6	2	1	0	2	10	5	0	0	0	76	45
CHI	101	40	61	1	0	0	0	0	0	0	0	0	0	0	0	52	38	7	4	1	3	2	0	1	7	5	0	0	0	61	40
CIN	111	43	68	2	1	0	1	0	0	1	0	0	0	0	0	64	33	10	4	1	1	2	1	1	7	2	2	0	0	70	41
NY	121	74	47	0	1	0	1	0	0	1	0	0	0	0	0	62	39	13	7	0	2	4	1	1	7	7	0	0	0	78	43
PHI	96	43	53	3	0	0	1	0	0	0	0	0	0	0	0	59	23	12	2	2	1	2	1	1	6	4	1	0	0	56	40
PIT	132	72	60	3	0	0	0	0	0	0	0	0	0	0	0	71	42	16	3	4	3	5	3	4	15	2	2	0	0	86	46
STL	119	59	60	3	0	0	0	0	0	0	0	0	0	0	0	66	32	18	3	1	3	1	1	2	11	4	1	0	0	83	36
AL	794	371	423	11	0	0	1	0	0	0	0	0	0	0	0	415	246	108	25	22	13	19	14	16	79	29	5	0	0	447	347
NL	907	452	455	16	2	0	6	0	0	2	0	0	0	0	0	485	291	100	31	16	17	19	7	16	74	32	6	0	0	569	338
YR	1701	823	878	27	2	0	5	0	0	2	0	0	0	0	0	900	537	208	56	38	30	38	21	32	153	61	11	0	0	1016	685

AL		*NL*	
23	Early Wynn	26	Murry Dickson
21	Ted Gray	23	Herm Wehmeier
21	Alex Kellner	22	Howie Pollet
21	Carl Scheib	22	Robin Roberts
21	Bobby Shantz	21	Multiple Players Tied

1953

Tm	Tot	H	A	Consec 2	3	4	1-Inn 3	4	5	One-Game 5	6	7	8	9	10	Men-On-Base 0	1	2	3	Pitchers PH	LO	XN	IP	P	Totals 1	10	20	30	40	Batters RHB	LHB
AL																															
BOS	92	59	33	2	0	0	0	0	0	0	0	0	0	0	0	49	26	14	3	3	1	1	1	0	11	3	0	0	0	53	39
CHI	113	56	57	3	0	0	1	0	0	0	0	0	0	0	0	62	42	7	2	4	3	2	2	1	9	3	1	0	0	68	45
CLE	92	46	46	2	0	0	1	0	0	0	0	0	0	0	0	54	23	14	1	5	1	0	1	1	7	4	0	0	0	47	45
DET	154	99	55	6	0	0	1	0	0	0	0	0	0	0	0	82	46	21	5	4	4	4	0	5	13	4	2	0	0	100	54

Tm	Tot	H	A	Consec 2	3	4	1-Inn 3	4	5	One-Game 5	6	7	8	9	10	Men-On-Base 0	1	2	3	Pitchers PH	LO	XN	IP	P	Totals 1	10	20	30	40	Batters RHB	LHB
NY	94	39	55	0	1	0	1	0	0	1	0	0	0	0	0	56	22	15	1	3	2	2	1	1	10	4	0	0	0	58	36
PHI	121	74	47	3	0	0	0	0	0	0	0	0	0	0	0	66	39	13	3	2	1	1	1	8	7	3	2	0	0	91	30
STL	101	64	37	1	0	0	0	0	0	0	0	0	0	0	0	52	33	12	4	4	1	3	0	1	10	4	0	0	0	64	37
WAS	112	31	81	2	0	0	1	0	0	0	0	0	0	0	0	64	30	17	1	4	0	3	2	4	7	6	0	0	0	63	49
NL																															
BRO	169	82	87	3	1	0	1	0	0	2	0	0	0	0	0	85	55	24	5	3	3	4	1	4	6	4	4	0	0	105	64
CHI	151	69	82	2	0	0	1	0	0	1	0	0	0	0	0	79	56	14	2	2	4	1	4	3	9	4	1	1	0	83	68
CIN	179	98	81	8	0	0	0	0	0	1	0	0	0	0	0	96	60	18	5	3	1	2	0	0	5	4	4	0	0	120	59
MIL	107	44	63	5	0	0	0	0	0	0	0	0	0	0	0	59	35	12	1	3	1	1	0	0	8	3	1	0	0	68	39
NY	146	81	65	5	0	0	0	0	0	0	0	0	0	0	0	75	39	26	6	2	1	3	2	7	8	4	2	0	0	84	62
PHI	138	65	73	4	0	0	0	0	0	0	0	0	0	0	0	83	37	17	1	5	2	0	0	2	4	4	1	1	0	87	51
PIT	168	88	80	4	0	0	0	0	0	0	0	0	1	0	0	90	57	20	1	3	2	3	1	6	7	4	3	0	0	107	61
STL	139	58	81	4	0	0	0	0	0	1	0	0	0	0	0	75	41	18	5	7	0	1	1	1	9	3	1	1	0	94	45
AL	879	468	411	19	1	0	5	0	0	1	0	0	0	0	0	485	261	113	20	29	13	16	8	21	74	31	5	0	0	544	335
NL	1197	585	612	35	1	0	2	0	0	5	0	0	1	0	0	642	380	149	26	28	14	15	9	23	56	30	17	3	0	748	449
YR	2076	1053	1023	54	2	0	5	0	0	6	0	0	1	0	0	1127	641	262	46	57	27	31	17	44	130	61	22	3	0	1292	784

	AL		*NL*
25	Ted Gray	35	Warren Hacker
24	Billy Hoeft	31	Gerry Staley
23	Harry Byrd	30	Robin Roberts
21	Marion Fricano	27	Murry Dickson
20	Billy Pierce	27	Preacher Roe

1954

Tm	Tot	H	A	Consec 2	3	4	1-Inn 3	4	5	One-Game 5	6	7	8	9	10	Men-On-Base 0	1	2	3	Pitchers PH	LO	XN	IP	P	Totals 1	10	20	30	40	Batters RHB	LHB
AL																															
BAL	78	23	55	1	0	0	1	0	0	1	0	0	0	0	0	49	19	8	2	4	3	2	0	0	8	3	0	0	0	47	31
BOS	118	70	48	4	0	0	1	0	0	0	0	0	0	0	0	67	33	14	4	4	3	1	1	2	10	4	0	0	0	81	37
CHI	94	51	43	2	0	0	0	0	0	0	0	0	0	0	0	54	29	11	0	7	1	1	1	1	7	4	0	0	0	54	40
CLE	89	57	32	5	0	0	1	0	0	0	0	0	0	0	0	57	24	8	0	0	3	3	0	1	7	3	1	0	0	48	41
DET	138	80	58	7	0	0	2	0	0	0	0	0	0	0	0	88	32	15	3	1	2	2	1	3	6	2	4	0	0	81	57
NY	86	42	44	0	0	0	0	0	0	0	0	0	0	0	0	47	23	11	5	3	0	5	0	1	7	5	0	0	0	46	40
PHI	141	85	56	5	0	0	0	0	0	0	1	0	0	0	0	74	36	24	7	3	2	1	1	8	11	5	1	0	0	87	54
WAS	79	27	52	1	0	0	0	0	0	0	0	0	0	0	0	44	20	12	3	0	1	0	3	1	9	2	0	0	0	57	22
NL																															
BRO	164	92	72	6	0	0	2	1	0	1	1	1	0	0	0	92	42	23	7	1	2	1	1	4	8	5	1	1	0	108	56
CHI	131	59	72	2	0	0	0	0	0	3	0	0	0	0	0	65	47	17	2	4	1	1	4	1	9	5	1	0	0	91	40
CIN	169	105	64	10	0	0	3	0	0	2	0	0	0	0	0	85	59	19	6	5	4	2	0	3	8	3	4	0	0	99	70
MIL	106	29	77	2	0	0	0	0	0	1	0	0	0	0	0	65	28	13	0	3	0	2	0	0	6	4	1	0	0	64	42
NY	113	67	46	5	0	0	0	0	0	1	0	0	0	0	0	71	29	11	2	3	2	4	4	2	8	2	3	0	0	66	47
PHI	133	60	73	2	0	0	0	0	0	0	0	0	0	0	0	78	46	9	0	5	3	2	2	2	5	4	0	2	0	93	40
PIT	128	42	86	8	0	0	3	0	0	0	1	0	0	0	0	56	50	17	5	0	2	1	1	5	6	5	2	0	0	76	52
STL	170	90	80	7	2	0	4	0	0	3	1	0	0	0	0	95	46	27	2	9	1	1	0	6	9	5	3	0	0	106	64
AL	823	435	388	25	0	0	5	0	0	1	1	0	0	0	0	480	216	103	24	22	15	15	7	17	65	28	6	0	0	501	322
NL	1114	544	570	42	2	0	12	1	0	11	3	1	0	0	0	607	347	136	24	30	15	14	12	23	59	33	15	3	0	703	411
YR	1937	979	958	67	2	0	11	0	0	12	4	1	0	0	0	1087	563	239	48	52	30	29	19	40	124	61	21	3	0	1204	733

	AL		*NL*
26	Steve Gromek	35	Robin Roberts
25	Arnie Portocarrero	31	Murry Dickson
22	Billy Hoeft	31	Carl Erskine
22	George Zuverink	28	Warren Hacker
21	Early Wynn	26	Harvey Haddix

1955

Tm	Tot	H	A	Consec 2	3	4	1-Inn 3	4	5	One-Game 5	6	7	8	9	10	Men-On-Base 0	1	2	3	Pitchers PH	LO	XN	IP	P	Totals 1	10	20	30	40	Batters RHB	LHB
AL																															
BAL	103	42	61	1	0	0	0	0	0	0	0	0	0	0	0	57	30	13	3	3	1	2	1	2	14	2	0	0	0	66	37
BOS	128	79	49	1	0	0	0	0	0	0	0	0	0	0	0	76	35	14	3	1	4	0	0	2	7	4	2	0	0	91	37
CHI	111	47	64	1	0	0	0	0	0	0	0	0	0	0	0	68	28	11	4	0	2	1	1	0	7	6	0	0	0	69	42
CLE	111	58	53	3	0	0	1	0	0	1	0	0	0	0	0	64	28	18	1	3	2	3	1	3	5	6	0	0	0	69	42

Tm	Tot	H	A	Consec 2	3	4	1-Inn 3	4	5	One-Game 5	6	7	8	9	10	Men-On-Base 0	1	2	3	Pitchers PH	LO	XN	IP	P	Totals 1	10	20	30	40	Batters RHB	LHB
DET	126	59	67	5	0	0	0	0	0	1	0	0	0	0	0	73	37	9	7	6	2	3	0	0	12	2	2	0	0	71	55
KC	175	110	65	9	0	0	2	0	0	1	0	1	0	0	0	89	52	31	3	4	2	3	1	3	15	6	3	0	0	125	50
NY	108	44	64	4	0	0	1	0	0	0	0	0	0	0	0	58	40	8	2	4	3	1	1	2	11	3	1	0	0	71	37
WAS	99	25	74	3	0	0	0	0	0	0	0	0	0	0	0	45	33	18	3	2	3	1	2	3	9	4	0	0	0	65	34
NL																															
BRO	168	85	83	6	1	0	3	0	0	0	0	0	0	0	0	91	59	15	3	4	3	5	2	3	8	5	1	1	0	112	56
CHI	153	62	91	6	0	0	1	0	0	1	0	0	0	0	0	86	50	11	6	6	0	4	1	4	7	5	1	1	0	92	61
CIN	161	91	70	5	0	0	0	0	0	0	0	0	0	0	0	94	48	16	3	6	1	3	0	3	8	5	3	0	0	106	55
MIL	138	51	87	4	0	0	2	0	0	2	1	0	0	0	0	76	42	16	4	3	1	3	0	1	7	2	4	0	0	74	64
NY	155	91	64	8	0	0	1	0	0	0	0	0	0	0	0	93	44	17	1	3	3	2	2	3	6	4	3	0	0	105	50
PHI	161	78	83	7	0	0	4	0	0	2	0	0	0	0	0	97	47	13	4	3	2	2	1	6	11	3	2	0	1	86	75
PIT	142	48	94	3	0	0	0	0	0	1	0	0	0	0	0	76	48	14	4	1	0	1	0	9	9	6	1	0	0	79	63
STL	185	92	93	7	1	0	2	0	0	0	1	0	0	0	0	109	51	20	5	2	2	6	1	9	12	3	4	0	0	104	81
AL	961	464	497	27	0	0	4	0	0	3	0	1	0	0	0	530	283	122	26	23	19	14	7	15	80	33	8	0	0	627	334
NL	1263	598	665	46	2	0	13	0	0	6	2	0	0	0	0	722	389	122	30	28	12	26	7	38	68	33	19	2	1	758	505
YR	2224	1062	1162	73	2	0	6	0	0	9	2	1	0	0	0	1252	672	244	56	51	31	40	14	53	148	66	27	2	1	1385	839

AL

26 Steve Gromek
23 Art Ditmar
23 Frank Sullivan
21 Multiple Players Tied

NL

41 Robin Roberts
38 Warren Hacker
35 Don Newcombe
29 Carl Erskine
27 Multiple Players Tied

1956

Tm	Tot	H	A	Consec 2	3	4	1-Inn 3	4	5	One-Game 5	6	7	8	9	10	Men-On-Base 0	1	2	3	Pitchers PH	LO	XN	IP	P	Totals 1	10	20	30	40	Batters RHB	LHB
AL																															
BAL	99	39	60	0	0	0	1	0	0	0	1	0	0	0	0	44	45	8	2	1	0	1	2	5	11	4	0	0	0	58	41
BOS	130	64	66	2	0	0	0	0	0	0	0	0	0	0	0	64	43	20	3	1	2	0	1	7	6	5	2	0	0	82	48
CHI	118	47	71	1	1	0	2	0	0	1	0	0	0	0	0	72	36	7	3	3	3	1	0	1	10	4	2	0	0	80	38
CLE	116	61	55	5	0	0	1	0	0	0	0	0	0	0	0	73	24	16	3	4	2	5	1	1	8	3	1	0	0	72	44
DET	140	77	63	6	0	0	0	0	0	1	0	0	0	0	0	74	43	19	4	3	2	2	1	7	11	1	4	0	0	71	69
KC	187	113	74	5	0	0	0	0	0	0	0	0	0	0	0	100	58	26	3	6	4	3	2	4	12	6	1	1	0	119	68
NY	114	48	66	3	0	0	1	0	0	0	0	0	0	0	0	71	29	12	2	4	1	1	2	2	6	6	0	0	0	71	43
WAS	171	95	76	5	0	0	0	0	0	0	0	0	0	0	0	93	54	22	2	2	1	4	2	3	6	5	2	1	0	122	49
NL																															
BRO	171	89	82	8	0	0	1	0	0	1	0	0	0	0	0	95	56	16	4	7	1	2	0	2	5	4	3	1	0	112	59
CHI	161	77	84	8	1	0	1	0	0	2	0	0	0	0	0	93	45	18	5	7	0	1	2	3	6	5	2	1	0	95	66
CIN	141	75	66	7	0	0	2	0	0	0	0	0	0	0	0	78	53	9	1	4	2	1	2	2	8	4	2	0	0	89	52
MIL	133	53	80	7	0	0	1	0	0	0	0	0	1	0	0	86	32	11	4	4	0	4	0	2	7	3	2	0	0	77	56
NY	144	86	58	3	0	0	0	0	0	0	0	0	0	0	0	86	35	16	7	2	0	3	2	3	9	4	2	0	0	99	45
PHI	172	76	96	5	1	0	1	0	0	1	0	0	0	0	0	98	53	19	2	6	2	4	4	2	9	3	2	0	1	110	62
PIT	142	45	97	2	1	0	0	1	0	1	0	1	0	0	0	90	37	14	1	3	1	3	0	4	14	1	3	0	0	77	65
STL	155	73	82	3	1	0	2	0	0	2	0	0	0	0	0	87	46	19	3	4	0	2	1	2	13	2	3	0	0	86	69
AL	1075	544	531	27	1	0	5	0	0	2	1	0	0	0	0	591	332	130	22	24	15	17	11	30	70	34	12	2	0	675	400
NL	1219	574	645	43	4	0	8	1	0	7	0	1	1	0	0	713	357	122	27	37	6	20	11	20	71	26	19	2	1	745	474
YR	2294	1118	1176	70	5	0	7	0	0	9	1	1	1	0	0	1304	689	252	49	61	21	37	22	50	141	60	31	4	1	1420	874

AL

33 Camilo Pascual
30 Art Ditmar
29 Chuck Stobbs
25 Steve Gromek
24 Multiple Players Tied

NL

46 Robin Roberts
33 Don Newcombe
30 Bob Rush
28 Warren Hacker
27 Tom Poholsky

1957

Tm	Tot	H	A	Consec 2	3	4	1-Inn 3	4	5	One-Game 5	6	7	8	9	10	Men-On-Base 0	1	2	3	Pitchers PH	LO	XN	IP	P	Totals 1	10	20	30	40	Batters RHB	LHB
AL																															
BAL	95	30	65	3	0	0	1	0	0	0	0	0	0	0	0	51	37	6	1	3	2	4	0	3	9	4	0	0	0	62	33
BOS	116	67	49	1	0	0	0	0	0	0	0	0	0	0	0	66	33	14	3	1	3	3	1	2	8	4	1	0	0	84	32
CHI	124	59	65	3	0	0	2	0	0	0	0	0	0	0	0	81	30	11	2	2	1	5	0	5	8	3	2	0	0	88	36
CLE	130	74	56	6	0	0	0	1	0	1	0	0	0	0	0	72	38	18	2	5	0	0	0	4	7	5	0	1	0	89	41

Tm	Tot	H	A	Consec 2	3	4	1-Inn 3	4	5	One-Game 5	6	7	8	9	10	Men-On-Base 0	1	2	3	Pitchers PH	LO	XN	IP	P	Totals 1	10	20	30	40	Batters RHB	LHB
DET	147	86	61	2	0	0	0	0	0	0	0	0	0	0	0	86	38	18	5	5	3	4	1	4	8	2	2	1	0	87	60
KC	153	77	76	6	0	0	0	1	0	0	2	0	0	0	0	95	42	15	1	2	4	4	1	6	12	7	0	0	0	91	62
NY	110	51	59	2	0	0	0	0	0	0	0	0	0	0	0	62	37	9	2	2	1	2	0	1	6	6	0	0	0	68	42
WAS	149	79	70	4	0	0	0	0	0	0	0	0	0	0	0	94	41	10	4	1	5	3	1	9	12	2	2	0	1	93	56
NL																															
BRO	144	88	56	2	2	0	3	0	0	1	0	0	0	0	0	87	36	17	4	6	2	2	1	3	9	5	1	0	0	82	62
CHI	144	68	76	5	0	0	1	0	0	1	0	1	0	0	0	89	39	11	5	4	2	8	3	1	7	6	2	0	0	86	58
CIN	179	101	78	3	0	0	0	0	0	1	0	0	0	0	0	98	54	23	4	5	2	6	3	5	6	4	4	0	0	103	76
MIL	124	51	73	5	0	0	1	0	0	1	1	0	0	0	0	81	35	8	0	1	3	4	1	3	7	2	2	0	0	81	43
NY	150	86	64	7	0	0	0	0	0	0	0	0	0	0	0	90	41	18	1	7	3	6	1	3	12	4	2	0	0	84	66
PHI	139	60	79	6	0	0	0	0	0	0	0	0	0	0	0	74	45	19	1	5	3	2	3	3	6	4	1	0	1	87	52
PIT	158	53	105	7	0	0	1	0	0	0	0	0	0	0	0	91	48	19	0	5	0	5	5	3	12	3	2	0	0	94	64
STL	140	70	70	3	0	0	0	0	0	0	0	0	0	0	0	83	40	15	2	6	1	4	2	3	7	4	2	0	0	69	71
AL	1024	523	501	27	0	0	3	2	0	1	2	0	0	0	0	607	296	101	20	21	19	25	4	34	70	33	7	2	1	662	362
NL	1178	577	601	38	2	0	6	0	0	4	1	1	0	0	0	693	338	130	17	39	16	37	19	24	66	32	16	0	1	686	492
YR	2202	1100	1102	65	2	0	4	1	0	5	3	1	0	0	0	1300	634	231	37	60	35	62	23	58	136	65	23	2	2	1348	854

AL		*NL*	
43	Pedro Ramos	40	Robin Roberts
33	Jim Bunning	29	Hal Jeffcoat
32	Early Wynn	28	Bob Friend
28	Chuck Stobbs	28	Ruben Gomez
24	Tom Brewer	28	Don Newcombe

1958

Tm	Tot	H	A	Consec 2	3	4	1-Inn 3	4	5	One-Game 5	6	7	8	9	10	Men-On-Base 0	1	2	3	Pitchers PH	LO	XN	IP	P	Totals 1	10	20	30	40	Batters RHB	LHB
AL																															
BAL	106	36	70	2	0	0	0	0	0	1	0	0	0	0	0	58	34	13	1	4	4	3	2	3	7	4	1	0	0	75	31
BOS	121	65	56	3	0	0	0	0	0	0	0	0	0	0	0	59	45	14	3	4	4	4	0	1	10	4	2	0	0	86	35
CHI	152	68	84	4	0	0	2	0	0	1	0	0	0	0	0	94	33	22	3	5	5	4	2	5	8	2	3	1	0	102	50
CLE	123	59	64	5	0	0	0	0	0	1	0	0	0	0	0	61	42	19	1	0	1	4	1	4	12	2	2	0	0	84	39
DET	133	79	54	5	0	0	0	0	0	0	0	0	0	0	0	77	36	15	5	3	2	3	0	0	10	2	3	0	0	67	66
KC	150	96	54	5	0	0	0	0	0	0	0	0	0	0	0	75	53	19	3	2	2	3	0	2	12	2	3	0	0	106	44
NY	116	62	54	2	0	0	0	0	0	0	0	0	0	0	0	63	39	13	1	4	3	2	2	1	10	3	1	0	0	81	35
WAS	156	80	76	4	0	0	0	0	0	1	0	0	0	0	0	93	42	16	5	5	4	2	6	5	11	3	2	1	0	108	48
NL																															
CHI	142	72	70	1	0	0	0	0	0	0	0	0	0	0	0	76	44	16	6	4	1	3	0	4	10	4	2	0	0	97	45
CIN	148	86	62	1	0	0	0	0	0	0	0	0	0	0	0	93	41	14	0	5	2	7	0	3	9	3	3	0	0	98	50
LA	173	101	72	7	0	0	1	0	0	3	0	0	0	0	0	107	48	11	7	7	1	3	1	6	10	6	2	0	0	144	29
MIL	125	48	77	6	0	0	0	0	0	1	0	0	0	0	0	78	31	13	3	7	1	4	0	5	8	4	1	0	0	78	47
PHI	148	77	71	2	0	0	0	0	0	0	0	0	0	0	0	83	44	17	4	4	0	2	4	0	11	3	1	1	0	90	58
PIT	123	40	83	3	1	0	1	0	0	0	0	0	0	0	0	65	43	14	1	7	1	1	3	0	10	2	2	0	0	70	53
SF	166	88	78	4	1	0	1	0	0	1	0	0	0	0	0	100	50	15	1	3	4	4	1	0	8	5	2	1	0	113	53
STL	158	88	70	4	0	0	0	0	0	1	0	0	0	0	0	90	49	18	1	5	4	4	1	3	9	6	2	0	0	98	60
AL	1057	545	512	30	0	0	2	0	0	4	0	0	0	0	0	580	324	131	22	27	25	25	13	21	80	22	17	2	0	709	348
NL	1183	600	583	28	2	0	3	0	0	6	0	0	0	0	0	692	350	118	23	42	14	28	10	21	75	33	15	2	0	788	395
YR	2240	1145	1095	58	2	0	4	0	0	10	0	0	0	0	0	1272	674	249	45	69	39	53	23	42	155	55	32	4	0	1497	743

AL		*NL*	
38	Pedro Ramos	31	Johnny Antonelli
33	Billy Pierce	31	Don Newcombe
29	Ralph Terry	30	Robin Roberts
28	Jim Bunning	29	Warren Spahn
27	Early Wynn	28	Harvey Haddix

1959

Tm	Tot	H	A	Consec 2	3	4	1-Inn 3	4	5	One-Game 5	6	7	8	9	10	Men-On-Base 0	1	2	3	Pitchers PH	LO	XN	IP	P	Totals 1	10	20	30	40	Batters RHB	LHB
AL																															
BAL	111	50	61	2	0	0	0	0	0	0	1	0	0	0	0	70	26	12	3	6	2	5	1	1	9	5	0	0	0	73	38
BOS	135	66	69	2	0	0	0	0	0	0	0	0	0	0	0	75	44	12	4	5	3	3	2	5	12	5	1	0	0	102	33
CHI	129	61	68	4	0	0	0	0	0	0	0	0	0	0	0	71	45	9	4	3	0	4	2	5	5	5	2	0	0	87	42

Tm	Tot	H	A	Consec			1-Inn			One-Game						Men-On-Base				Pitchers					Totals					Batters	
				2	3	4	3	4	5	5	6	7	8	9	10	0	1	2	3	PH	LO	XN	IP	P	1	10	20	30	40	RHB	LHB
CLE	148	74	74	5	0	0	1	0	0	0	0	0	0	0	0	88	41	17	2	3	2	3	1	2	9	1	4	0	0	100	48
DET	177	105	72	4	0	0	1	0	0	1	1	0	0	0	0	94	58	19	6	2	2	7	1	4	8	1	3	2	0	122	55
KC	148	80	68	8	0	0	2	0	0	0	0	0	0	0	0	85	47	15	1	0	5	2	0	2	12	2	3	0	0	103	45
NY	120	45	75	0	1	0	1	0	0	0	0	0	0	0	0	62	35	17	6	5	3	5	1	1	9	6	0	0	0	78	42
WAS	123	68	55	4	0	0	0	0	0	0	0	0	0	0	0	68	38	14	3	2	3	4	1	5	8	3	1	1	0	96	27
NL																															
CHI	152	76	76	3	0	0	0	0	0	0	0	0	0	0	0	94	44	12	2	8	1	2	0	5	8	6	2	0	0	99	53
CIN	162	84	78	1	0	0	1	0	0	0	0	0	0	0	0	96	42	19	5	5	2	3	2	4	8	5	3	0	0	79	83
LA	157	90	67	6	0	0	1	0	0	0	0	0	0	0	0	92	44	17	4	6	1	6	1	1	6	4	3	0	0	108	49
MIL	128	64	64	2	0	0	0	0	0	0	0	0	0	0	0	72	37	15	4	5	2	0	0	2	4	4	1	1	0	83	45
PHI	150	66	84	5	0	0	0	0	0	0	0	0	0	0	0	84	50	13	3	5	1	2	5	4	12	4	1	1	0	82	68
PIT	134	53	81	4	0	0	1	0	0	0	0	0	0	0	0	78	47	9	0	3	1	1	1	1	13	1	3	0	0	75	59
SF	139	63	76	4	0	0	0	0	0	2	0	0	0	0	0	72	51	14	2	5	0	5	1	1	8	2	3	0	0	88	51
STL	137	64	73	4	0	0	0	0	0	1	0	0	0	0	0	74	35	25	3	4	3	1	1	3	14	4	2	0	0	85	52
AL	1091	549	542	29	1	0	5	0	0	1	2	0	0	0	0	613	334	115	29	26	20	33	9	25	72	28	14	3	0	761	330
NL	1159	560	599	29	0	0	3	0	0	3	0	0	0	0	0	662	350	124	23	41	11	20	11	21	73	30	18	2	0	699	460
YR	2250	1109	1141	58	1	0	3	0	0	4	2	0	0	0	0	1275	684	239	52	67	31	53	20	46	145	58	32	5	0	1460	790

AL		*NL*	
37	Jim Bunning	38	Lew Burdette
34	Paul Foytack	34	Robin Roberts
30	Pedro Ramos	29	Johnny Antonelli
28	Gary Bell	26	Multiple Players Tied
28	Herb Score		

1960

AL

Tm	Tot	H	A	Consec 2	Consec 3	Consec 4	1-Inn 3	1-Inn 4	1-Inn 5	One-Game 5	6	7	8	9	10	Men-On-Base 0	1	2	3	PH	LO	XN	IP	P	Totals 1	10	20	30	40	RHB	LHB
BAL	117	49	68	3	0	0	0	0	0	0	0	0	0	0	0	62	39	12	4	3	0	4	1	0	4	7	0	0	0	70	47
BOS	127	69	58	3	0	0	1	0	0	0	0	0	0	0	0	74	37	13	3	4	4	1	1	1	9	5	1	0	0	84	43
CHI	127	54	73	6	0	0	0	0	0	0	0	0	0	0	0	74	41	9	3	2	5	2	1	3	8	4	2	0	0	86	41
CLE	161	84	77	7	0	0	0	0	0	2	0	0	0	0	0	97	41	19	4	6	2	7	0	2	9	5	1	1	0	82	79
DET	141	85	56	3	0	0	0	0	0	0	0	0	0	0	0	77	47	13	4	4	1	3	0	1	7	5	2	0	0	87	54
KC	160	79	81	3	0	0	1	0	0	2	0	0	0	0	0	76	62	19	3	1	3	3	1	3	9	4	3	0	0	104	56
NY	123	52	71	2	0	0	0	0	0	0	0	0	0	0	0	74	28	16	5	4	5	5	1	1	9	4	1	0	0	82	41
WAS	130	74	56	4	0	0	0	0	0	2	0	0	0	0	0	71	40	18	1	1	0	6	1	1	10	5	1	0	0	82	48
NL																															
CHI	152	78	74	2	0	0	1	0	0	1	0	0	0	0	0	90	41	18	3	9	0	3	4	2	10	5	2	0	0	85	67
CIN	134	68	66	4	0	0	1	0	0	0	0	0	0	0	0	82	32	15	5	5	2	3	2	1	10	3	1	1	0	78	56
LA	154	97	57	4	0	0	2	0	0	2	0	0	0	0	0	94	42	16	2	5	2	3	1	4	7	2	4	0	0	106	48
MIL	130	56	74	4	0	0	0	0	0	0	0	0	0	0	0	76	36	13	5	4	2	3	0	3	5	4	2	0	0	90	40
PHI	133	74	59	2	0	0	0	0	0	0	0	0	0	0	0	79	39	12	3	1	3	2	1	3	11	3	1	1	0	92	41
PIT	105	36	69	2	0	0	0	0	0	0	0	0	0	0	0	53	38	14	0	5	0	5	2	2	10	3	1	0	0	65	40
SF	107	34	73	2	0	0	0	0	0	0	0	0	0	0	0	62	27	14	4	6	0	1	1	3	10	4	0	0	0	58	49
STL	127	64	63	2	0	0	0	0	0	0	0	0	0	0	0	74	36	14	3	2	2	1	2	2	11	3	2	0	0	83	44
AL	1086	546	540	31	0	0	2	0	0	6	0	0	0	0	0	605	335	119	27	25	20	31	6	12	65	39	11	1	0	677	409
NL	1042	507	535	22	0	0	4	0	0	3	0	0	0	0	0	610	291	116	25	37	11	21	13	20	74	27	13	2	0	657	385
YR	2128	1053	1075	53	0	0	6	0	0	9	0	0	0	0	0	1215	626	235	52	62	31	52	19	32	139	66	24	3	0	1334	794

AL		*NL*	
35	Jim Perry	31	Jay Hook
28	Dick Hall	31	Robin Roberts
27	Bud Daley	27	Don Drysdale
26	Mudcat Grant	27	Glen Hobbie
25	Multiple Players Tied	26	Multiple Players Tied

1961

AL

Tm	Tot	H	A	Consec 2	Consec 3	Consec 4	1-Inn 3	1-Inn 4	1-Inn 5	One-Game 5	6	7	8	9	10	Men-On-Base 0	1	2	3	PH	LO	XN	IP	P	Totals 1	10	20	30	40	RHB	LHB
BAL	109	46	63	2	0	0	1	0	0	0	0	0	0	0	0	56	34	14	5	3	0	5	0	1	6	6	0	0	0	62	47
BOS	167	91	76	8	0	0	1	0	0	0	0	1	0	0	0	98	45	20	4	6	2	2	1	4	8	3	2	1	0	96	71

				Consec			1-Inn			One-Game						Men-On-Base				Pitchers					Totals					Batters	
Tm	Tot	H	A	2	3	4	3	4	5	5	6	7	8	9	10	0	1	2	3	PH	LO	XN	IP	P	1	10	20	30	40	RHB	LHB
CHI	158	55	103	6	0	0	1	0	0	1	0	0	0	0	0	94	47	10	7	6	3	7	1	3	5	7	2	0	0	87	71
CLE	178	98	80	3	1	0	2	0	0	2	0	0	0	0	0	92	62	19	5	5	1	3	1	3	5	2	2	2	0	96	82
DET	170	95	75	9	1	0	3	0	0	1	0	0	0	0	0	96	55	14	5	3	0	5	1	3	12	2	4	0	0	98	72
KC	141	61	80	3	0	0	0	0	0	0	0	0	0	0	0	68	49	18	6	4	2	1	0	1	10	7	1	0	0	79	62
LA	180	126	54	5	0	0	0	0	0	1	0	0	0	0	0	105	47	23	5	7	2	3	0	6	6	7	2	0	0	99	81
MIN	163	89	74	8	1	0	2	0	0	1	0	0	0	0	0	90	43	24	6	7	0	6	2	6	10	2	2	1	0	97	66
NY	137	59	78	6	0	0	0	0	0	0	0	0	0	0	0	82	37	16	2	4	3	3	4	4	6	6	1	0	0	89	48
WAS	131	53	78	4	0	0	1	0	0	2	0	0	0	0	0	76	42	10	3	5	0	2	2	1	10	6	1	0	0	82	49
NL																															
CHI	165	81	84	5	0	0	0	0	0	1	0	0	0	0	0	88	52	17	8	7	2	3	0	6	3	4	4	0	0	113	52
CIN	147	75	72	7	0	1	1	1	1	1	2	0	0	0	0	95	38	13	1	4	1	1	1	4	4	5	2	0	0	83	64
LA	167	109	58	2	1	0	1	0	0	3	0	0	0	0	0	99	48	17	3	4	3	2	0	5	4	2	5	0	0	120	47
MIL	153	72	81	8	0	0	1	0	0	1	0	0	1	0	0	89	44	15	5	4	2	3	2	4	10	2	3	1	0	102	51
PHI	155	77	78	0	0	0	0	0	0	0	0	0	0	0	0	81	52	20	2	3	1	4	5	3	7	4	2	0	0	97	58
PIT	121	54	67	4	0	0	0	0	0	0	0	0	0	0	0	74	31	13	3	4	2	4	0	2	10	6	0	0	0	86	35
SF	152	77	75	5	0	0	1	0	0	1	0	0	0	0	0	83	46	17	6	3	2	3	0	2	5	4	2	1	0	78	74
STL	136	69	67	2	0	0	0	0	0	0	0	0	0	0	0	80	37	18	1	4	3	1	0	3	5	5	2	0	0	78	58
AL	1534	773	761	54	3	0	11	0	0	8	0	1	0	0	0	857	461	168	48	50	13	37	12	32	78	48	17	4	0	885	649
NL	1196	614	582	33	1	1	4	1	1	7	2	0	1	0	0	689	348	130	29	33	16	21	8	29	48	32	20	2	0	757	439
YR	2730	1387	1343	87	4	1	10	1	0	15	2	1	1	0	0	1546	809	298	77	83	29	58	20	61	126	80	37	6	0	1642	1088

AL		*NL*	
39	Pedro Ramos	33	Mike McCormick
33	Gene Conley	31	Lew Burdette
32	Gary Bell	29	Don Drysdale
32	Mudcat Grant	28	John Buzhardt
29	Don Mossi	28	Ray Sadecki

1962

Tm	Tot	H	A	2	3	4	3	4	5	5	6	7	8	9	10	0	1	2	3	PH	LO	XN	IP	P	1	10	20	30	40	RHB	LHB
AL																															
BAL	147	65	82	5	0	0	0	0	0	0	0	0	0	0	0	82	43	19	3	5	3	2	2	6	6	2	2	1	0	88	59
BOS	159	76	83	5	0	0	1	0	0	0	0	0	0	0	0	84	64	10	1	4	0	4	0	4	5	5	3	0	0	100	59
CHI	123	58	65	2	0	0	1	0	0	0	0	0	0	0	0	62	38	21	2	4	1	2	0	2	7	8	0	0	0	74	49
CLE	174	89	85	8	0	0	1	0	0	0	1	0	0	0	0	105	45	19	5	4	1	4	1	4	8	2	5	0	0	97	77
DET	169	91	78	4	0	0	0	0	0	1	0	0	0	0	0	89	58	17	5	6	2	8	1	5	8	4	3	0	0	96	73
KC	199	118	81	7	1	0	3	0	0	2	1	0	0	0	0	114	55	26	4	3	1	4	0	4	9	5	2	1	0	107	92
LA	118	51	67	5	0	0	0	0	0	0	0	0	0	0	0	65	34	16	3	2	0	5	1	2	10	5	0	0	0	79	39
MIN	166	96	70	5	0	0	1	0	0	0	0	0	0	0	0	86	57	21	2	3	3	5	2	2	9	3	2	1	0	109	57
NY	146	67	79	3	2	0	2	0	0	1	0	0	0	0	0	91	39	16	0	6	1	2	2	2	8	1	2	0	1	74	72
WAS	151	79	72	2	0	0	1	0	0	0	0	0	0	0	0	71	57	20	3	2	0	2	0	3	7	5	2	0	0	90	61
NL																															
CHI	159	94	65	4	0	0	1	0	0	0	0	0	0	0	0	77	51	25	6	6	1	3	4	1	11	3	3	0	0	91	68
CIN	149	68	81	2	0	0	1	0	0	1	0	0	0	0	0	87	43	16	3	5	1	3	1	0	6	4	3	0	0	84	65
HOU	113	41	72	4	0	0	1	0	0	0	0	0	0	0	0	70	29	13	1	2	3	4	1	5	12	4	1	0	0	65	48
LA	115	39	76	2	0	0	0	0	0	1	0	0	0	0	0	63	30	16	6	3	1	2	1	0	5	4	2	0	0	84	31
MIL	151	74	77	5	0	0	1	0	0	0	1	0	0	0	0	98	36	15	2	7	3	1	0	1	9	3	3	0	0	105	46
NY	192	120	72	4	0	0	0	0	0	0	1	0	0	0	0	102	60	25	5	4	3	5	4	6	7	6	1	2	0	109	83
PHI	155	66	89	8	1	0	2	0	0	2	0	0	0	0	0	87	46	16	6	6	0	2	1	4	8	6	0	1	0	103	52
PIT	118	56	62	5	0	0	0	0	0	0	0	0	0	0	0	70	39	7	2	3	2	1	4	2	8	3	2	0	0	66	52
SF	148	74	74	4	0	0	0	0	0	0	0	0	0	0	0	73	54	19	2	2	3	3	0	4	6	4	1	1	0	88	60
STL	149	83	66	3	0	0	0	0	0	0	0	0	0	0	0	88	37	20	4	7	2	2	1	2	6	4	3	0	0	87	62
AL	1552	790	762	46	3	0	10	0	0	4	2	0	0	0	0	849	490	185	28	39	12	38	9	34	77	40	21	3	1	914	638
NL	1449	715	734	41	1	0	6	0	0	4	2	0	0	0	0	815	425	172	37	45	19	26	17	25	78	41	19	4	0	882	567
YR	3001	1505	1496	87	4	0	9	0	0	8	4	0	0	0	0	1664	915	357	65	84	31	64	26	59	155	81	40	7	1	1796	1205

AL		*NL*	
40	Ralph Terry	36	Art Mahaffey
31	Jack Kralick	35	Roger Craig
31	Milt Pappas	34	Juan Marichal
31	Ed Rakow	31	Jay Hook
28	Multiple Players Tied	28	Bob Purkey

1963

				Consec			1-Inn			One-Game						Men-On-Base				Pitchers					Totals					Batters	
Tm	Tot	H	A	2	3	4	3	4	5	5	6	7	8	9	10	0	1	2	3	PH	LO	XN	IP	P	1	10	20	30	40	RHB	LHB
AL																															
BAL	137	56	81	1	0	0	0	0	0	0	0	0	0	0	0	94	34	6	3	7	1	1	0	3	7	4	1	1	0	75	62
BOS	152	73	79	4	0	0	0	0	0	1	0	0	0	0	0	88	39	22	3	5	1	3	1	3	8	4	1	1	0	87	65
CHI	100	46	54	2	0	0	1	0	0	0	0	0	0	0	0	62	27	8	3	0	1	2	1	2	11	4	0	0	0	72	28
CLE	176	87	89	2	0	0	1	0	0	1	0	0	0	0	0	97	56	15	8	3	4	2	1	8	6	3	3	1	0	104	72
DET	195	109	86	7	0	0	0	0	0	0	0	0	0	0	0	118	64	12	1	4	4	4	0	3	9	3	2	2	0	110	85
KC	156	87	69	3	0	0	0	0	0	0	0	0	0	0	0	85	45	24	2	0	2	4	1	3	8	6	2	0	0	85	71
LA	120	44	76	2	0	1	0	1	0	0	1	0	0	0	0	76	28	11	5	1	1	2	0	4	11	4	1	0	0	65	55
MIN	162	99	63	5	0	0	0	0	0	0	0	0	0	0	0	105	38	17	2	3	1	5	1	0	10	2	3	1	0	107	55
NY	115	55	60	1	0	0	0	0	0	0	0	0	0	0	0	70	37	7	1	1	4	0	3	3	7	2	2	0	0	69	46
WAS	176	82	94	5	0	0	0	0	0	0	0	0	1	0	0	99	51	24	2	2	3	4	0	4	11	6	2	0	0	104	72
NL																															
CHI	119	70	49	6	0	0	2	0	0	1	0	0	0	0	0	69	28	17	5	6	3	6	1	1	9	4	1	0	0	69	50
CIN	117	46	71	5	0	0	1	0	0	0	0	0	0	0	0	69	38	7	3	3	3	1	1	1	6	5	1	0	0	66	51
HOU	95	34	61	1	0	0	0	0	0	0	0	0	0	0	0	53	28	10	4	2	1	2	1	1	6	6	0	0	0	45	50
LA	111	43	68	2	0	0	0	0	0	0	0	0	0	0	0	64	34	11	2	3	1	1	0	1	11	2	1	0	0	72	39
MIL	149	81	68	1	0	0	0	0	0	0	0	0	0	0	0	90	42	14	3	8	2	3	2	1	6	5	1	1	0	91	58
NY	162	93	69	6	0	0	0	0	0	0	1	0	0	0	0	93	50	15	4	2	4	3	5	3	4	2	5	0	0	95	67
PHI	113	60	53	6	0	0	0	0	0	0	0	0	0	0	0	66	34	12	1	3	1	2	3	1	5	7	0	0	0	69	44
PIT	99	42	57	1	0	0	0	0	0	0	0	0	0	0	0	49	35	14	1	3	0	4	4	3	10	3	1	0	0	53	46
SF	126	64	62	1	0	0	0	0	0	1	0	0	0	0	0	65	44	14	3	7	0	6	0	2	4	5	2	0	0	69	57
STL	124	70	54	6	1	0	1	0	0	1	0	0	0	0	0	71	31	21	1	2	2	1	0	1	9	3	2	0	0	79	45
AL	1489	738	751	32	0	1	2	1	0	2	1	0	1	0	0	894	419	146	30	26	22	27	8	33	88	38	17	6	0	878	611
NL	1215	603	612	35	1	0	4	0	0	3	1	0	0	0	0	689	364	135	27	39	17	29	17	15	70	42	14	1	0	708	507
YR	2704	1341	1363	67	1	1	6	0	0	5	2	0	1	0	0	1583	783	281	57	65	39	56	25	48	158	80	31	7	0	1586	1118

AL

38 Jim Bunning
35 Robin Roberts
33 Phil Regan
32 Dick Stigman
31 Bill Monbouquette

NL

30 Denny Lemaster
28 Roger Craig
27 Juan Marichal
25 Multiple Players Tied

1964

				Consec			1-Inn			One-Game						Men-On-Base				Pitchers					Totals					Batters	
Tm	Tot	H	A	2	3	4	3	4	5	5	6	7	8	9	10	0	1	2	3	PH	LO	XN	IP	P	1	10	20	30	40	RHB	LHB
AL																															
BAL	129	64	65	5	0	0	1	0	0	0	0	0	0	0	0	75	39	11	4	3	4	2	0	1	10	4	1	0	0	73	56
BOS	178	87	91	8	0	0	0	0	0	1	0	0	0	0	0	96	54	24	4	5	0	5	4	4	6	3	2	2	0	96	82
CHI	124	42	82	9	0	0	1	0	0	0	1	0	0	0	0	73	33	18	0	3	1	2	2	2	6	4	2	0	0	84	40
CLE	154	82	72	7	0	0	2	0	0	0	0	0	0	0	0	94	43	16	1	3	1	7	1	2	5	9	0	0	0	87	67
DET	164	89	75	6	0	0	1	0	0	0	0	0	0	0	0	94	47	19	4	4	2	0	0	3	11	3	3	0	0	102	62
KC	220	132	88	10	0	1	1	1	0	0	1	0	0	0	0	142	50	23	5	6	2	8	1	4	8	4	3	1	1	113	107
LA	100	31	69	4	0	0	0	0	0	0	0	0	0	0	0	58	30	8	4	1	0	1	0	3	16	2	0	0	0	60	40
MIN	181	88	93	6	0	0	0	0	0	1	0	0	0	0	0	114	45	21	1	8	4	6	1	3	13	3	2	2	0	125	56
NY	129	56	73	0	0	0	0	0	0	0	0	0	0	0	0	73	40	13	3	5	0	7	2	5	9	3	1	1	0	80	49
WAS	172	95	77	9	0	0	1	0	0	1	0	0	0	0	0	102	54	13	3	4	3	4	0	4	7	6	2	1	0	94	78
NL																															
CHI	144	88	56	5	0	0	1	0	0	1	0	0	0	0	0	80	41	22	1	2	2	6	0	1	12	3	1	1	0	96	48
CIN	112	59	53	4	0	0	0	0	0	0	0	0	0	0	0	62	37	10	3	2	3	0	1	1	6	4	1	0	0	71	41
HOU	105	44	61	1	0	0	1	0	0	0	0	0	0	0	0	58	38	8	1	1	0	1	3	0	12	3	1	0	0	66	39
LA	88	38	50	2	0	0	1	0	0	1	0	0	0	0	0	42	32	14	0	2	1	0	0	1	9	3	1	0	0	51	37
MIL	160	78	82	5	0	0	1	0	0	1	0	0	0	0	0	94	51	13	2	2	3	2	3	3	10	3	3	0	0	97	63
NY	130	61	69	2	1	0	1	0	0	0	0	0	0	0	0	73	41	14	2	4	2	2	1	3	13	3	2	0	0	71	59
PHI	129	61	68	2	0	0	0	0	0	1	0	0	0	0	0	67	41	16	5	1	0	1	1	1	8	3	2	0	0	88	41
PIT	92	31	61	2	0	0	0	0	0	1	0	0	0	0	0	48	32	9	3	2	2	3	3	0	12	4	0	0	0	58	34
SF	118	63	55	2	0	0	0	0	0	0	0	0	0	0	0	62	37	15	4	1	3	3	1	2	9	5	0	0	0	73	45
STL	133	81	52	5	0	0	1	0	0	1	0	0	0	0	0	77	40	14	2	4	2	1	1	0	11	3	2	0	0	92	41
AL	1551	766	785	64	0	1	7	1	0	3	2	0	0	0	0	921	435	166	29	42	17	42	11	31	91	41	16	7	1	914	637
NL	1211	604	607	30	1	0	6	0	0	6	0	0	0	0	0	663	390	135	23	21	18	19	14	12	102	34	13	1	0	763	448
YR	2762	1370	1392	94	1	1	8	0	0	9	2	0	0	0	0	1584	825	301	52	63	35	61	25	43	193	75	29	8	1	1677	1085

	AL		NL
40	Orlando Pena	34	Dick Ellsworth
37	Earl Wilson	27	Denny Lemaster
34	Bill Monbouquette	25	Bob Gibson
32	Jim Bouton	24	Curt Simmons
32	Mudcat Grant	23	Multiple Players Tied

1965

Tm	Tot	H	A	Consec 2	3	4	1-Inn 3	4	5	One-Game 5	6	7	8	9	10	Men-On-Base 0	1	2	3	Pitchers PH	LO	XN	IP	P	Totals 1	10	20	30	40	Batters RHB	LHB
AL																															
BAL	120	71	49	4	0	0	1	0	0	0	0	0	0	0	0	72	34	13	1	4	1	4	0	2	7	4	1	0	0	71	49
BOS	158	88	70	2	0	0	0	0	0	2	0	0	0	0	0	82	52	22	2	6	3	4	2	5	6	3	2	1	0	99	59
CAL	91	35	56	0	0	0	0	0	0	0	0	0	0	0	0	56	27	8	0	3	1	1	1	0	11	4	0	0	0	52	39
CHI	122	51	71	2	0	0	0	0	0	1	0	0	0	0	0	75	36	6	5	5	2	2	1	6	5	7	0	0	0	74	48
CLE	129	58	71	4	0	0	0	0	0	0	0	0	0	0	0	69	36	20	4	1	1	6	0	2	10	3	2	0	0	72	57
DET	137	85	52	5	0	0	0	0	0	1	0	0	0	0	0	82	38	15	2	7	1	2	0	3	10	2	3	0	0	86	51
KC	161	68	93	2	1	0	2	0	0	0	0	0	0	0	0	98	44	15	4	2	1	3	3	3	11	3	3	0	0	74	87
MIN	166	89	77	5	0	0	0	0	0	0	0	0	0	0	0	107	41	15	3	8	1	4	1	1	7	4	2	1	0	110	56
NY	126	63	63	1	0	0	0	0	0	0	0	0	0	0	0	71	38	17	0	1	4	3	3	3	8	4	2	0	0	61	65
WAS	160	86	74	4	0	0	1	0	0	2	0	0	0	0	0	94	42	20	4	3	2	4	3	4	5	7	0	1	0	110	50
NL																															
CHI	154	94	60	5	0	0	0	1	0	1	0	0	0	0	0	88	44	20	2	6	3	6	0	3	8	3	3	0	0	96	58
CIN	136	69	67	3	0	0	0	0	0	1	0	0	0	0	0	77	36	20	3	4	2	2	1	3	7	4	2	0	0	73	63
HOU	123	32	91	6	0	0	0	0	0	1	0	0	0	0	0	77	34	11	1	4	3	4	3	1	11	4	1	0	0	75	48
LA	127	41	86	5	0	0	0	0	0	1	0	0	0	0	0	81	36	8	2	1	3	2	2	0	7	2	1	1	0	88	39
MIL	123	75	48	4	0	0	0	0	0	1	0	0	0	0	0	68	39	10	6	1	6	2	0	1	7	6	1	0	0	66	57
NY	147	81	66	4	0	0	1	0	0	1	0	0	0	0	0	66	58	22	1	4	1	3	1	5	12	5	1	0	0	82	65
PHI	116	55	61	2	0	0	0	0	0	0	0	0	0	0	0	70	30	14	2	4	3	1	1	2	7	5	1	0	0	66	50
PIT	89	38	51	3	0	0	0	0	0	0	0	0	0	0	0	55	24	10	0	1	4	1	0	2	8	2	1	0	0	51	38
SF	137	81	56	5	0	0	1	0	0	0	1	0	0	0	0	79	38	18	2	5	2	3	1	4	6	4	2	0	0	61	76
STL	166	103	63	4	0	0	0	0	0	0	0	0	0	0	0	101	48	16	1	6	2	2	0	3	8	2	3	1	0	96	70
AL	1370	694	676	29	1	0	4	0	0	6	0	0	0	0	0	806	388	151	25	40	17	33	14	29	80	41	15	3	0	809	561
NL	1318	669	649	41	0	0	2	1	0	6	1	0	0	0	0	762	387	149	20	36	29	26	9	24	81	37	16	2	0	754	564
YR	2688	1363	1325	70	1	0	4	1	0	12	1	0	0	0	0	1568	775	300	45	76	46	59	23	53	161	78	31	5	0	1563	1125

	AL		NL
34	Mudcat Grant	34	Bob Gibson
33	Phil Ortega	30	Don Drysdale
32	Bill Monbouquette	28	Larry Jackson
27	Earl Wilson	27	Juan Marichal
25	Multiple Players Tied	26	Multiple Players Tied

1966

Tm	Tot	H	A	Consec 2	3	4	1-Inn 3	4	5	One-Game 5	6	7	8	9	10	Men-On-Base 0	1	2	3	Pitchers PH	LO	XN	IP	P	Totals 1	10	20	30	40	Batters RHB	LHB
AL																															
BAL	127	65	62	3	0	0	1	0	0	2	0	0	0	0	0	73	33	19	2	6	1	2	0	3	7	4	2	0	0	79	48
BOS	164	98	66	5	1	0	2	0	0	1	0	0	0	0	0	82	61	17	4	4	2	5	1	2	12	7	0	0	0	94	70
CAL	136	67	69	3	0	0	0	0	0	0	0	0	0	0	0	76	44	13	3	2	0	2	0	1	12	3	2	0	0	83	53
CHI	101	36	65	3	0	0	1	0	0	0	0	0	0	0	0	63	22	14	2	2	0	5	0	2	6	5	0	0	0	55	46
CLE	129	64	65	4	0	0	0	0	0	1	0	0	0	0	0	74	47	7	1	4	3	4	2	5	8	5	1	0	0	78	51
DET	185	101	84	6	0	0	1	0	0	1	0	1	0	0	0	108	53	21	3	7	1	3	2	3	4	7	1	0	1	112	73
KC	106	27	79	2	1	0	0	0	1	0	1	0	0	0	0	57	37	8	4	6	2	2	2	1	17	2	0	0	0	61	45
MIN	139	83	56	1	0	0	0	0	0	0	0	0	0	0	0	90	36	11	2	6	5	2	0	0	9	3	2	0	0	86	53
NY	124	63	61	4	1	0	1	0	0	0	0	0	0	0	0	70	36	17	1	5	0	3	5	1	6	5	1	0	0	71	53
WAS	154	85	69	4	0	0	0	0	0	0	0	0	0	0	0	99	41	10	4	4	2	4	1	3	11	1	2	1	0	99	55
NL																															
ATL	129	82	47	4	0	0	1	0	0	0	0	0	0	0	0	74	39	15	1	4	2	5	1	3	15	0	3	0	0	70	59
CHI	184	101	83	3	0	0	0	0	0	2	0	0	0	0	0	91	60	29	4	2	1	6	7	4	12	5	3	0	0	128	56
CIN	153	93	60	3	0	0	0	0	0	2	1	0	0	0	0	81	56	14	2	3	3	6	2	2	6	5	1	1	0	93	60
HOU	130	48	82	4	0	0	0	0	0	0	0	0	0	0	0	66	46	17	1	2	0	2	2	1	10	4	2	0	0	72	58
LA	84	36	48	1	0	0	0	0	0	0	0	0	0	0	0	50	22	11	1	1	3	3	2	2	5	2	1	0	0	61	23

Tm	Tot	H	A	Consec 2	3	4	1-Inn 3	4	5	One-Game 5	6	7	8	9	10	Men-On-Base 0	1	2	3	Pitchers PH	LO	XN	IP	P	Totals 1	10	20	30	40	Batters RHB	LHB
NY	166	94	72	1	0	0	0	0	0	0	0	0	0	0	0	96	47	20	3	4	2	3	2	5	10	7	2	0	0	103	63
PHI	137	65	72	5	0	0	0	0	0	1	0	0	0	0	0	84	33	19	1	5	0	3	0	3	10	2	3	0	0	91	46
PIT	125	48	77	4	0	0	1	0	0	1	0	0	0	0	0	63	45	14	3	5	2	6	2	3	6	6	0	0	0	77	48
SF	140	77	63	4	0	0	0	0	0	1	0	0	0	0	0	82	34	20	4	4	3	4	0	3	6	2	2	1	0	92	48
STL	130	64	66	3	0	0	1	0	0	0	0	0	0	0	0	86	25	17	2	2	2	1	1	0	10	4	1	0	0	80	50
AL	1365	689	676	35	3	0	6	0	1	5	1	1	0	0	0	792	410	137	26	46	16	32	13	21	92	42	11	1	1	818	547
NL	1378	708	670	32	0	0	3	0	0	7	1	0	0	0	0	773	407	176	22	32	18	39	19	26	90	37	18	2	0	867	511
YR	2743	1397	1346	67	3	0	5	0	1	12	2	1	0	0	0	1565	817	313	48	78	34	71	32	47	182	79	29	3	1	1685	1058

	AL		*NL*
42	Denny McLain	35	Sammy Ellis
36	Pete Richert	32	Juan Marichal
30	Earl Wilson	29	Tony Cloninger
29	Jim Kaat	28	Dick Ellsworth
29	Phil Ortega	28	Chris Short

1967

AL

Tm	Tot	H	A	Consec 2	3	4	1-Inn 3	4	5	One-Game 5	6	7	8	9	10	Men-On-Base 0	1	2	3	Pitchers PH	LO	XN	IP	P	Totals 1	10	20	30	40	Batters RHB	LHB
BAL	116	49	67	3	0	0	0	0	0	0	0	0	0	0	0	60	42	13	1	8	3	1	1	2	16	4	0	0	0	64	52
BOS	142	88	54	4	0	0	0	1	0	1	0	1	0	0	0	87	44	9	2	3	3	3	1	2	10	4	2	0	0	86	56
CAL	118	59	59	2	0	0	0	0	0	0	0	0	0	0	0	69	35	12	2	1	1	2	1	3	15	4	0	0	0	77	41
CHI	87	38	49	2	0	0	0	0	0	0	0	0	0	0	0	58	20	9	0	3	1	2	0	2	10	4	0	0	0	54	33
CLE	120	69	51	2	0	0	0	0	0	0	0	0	0	0	0	65	43	9	3	5	2	3	0	1	9	2	2	0	0	78	42
DET	151	79	72	5	0	0	0	0	0	0	0	0	0	0	0	96	39	13	3	4	4	2	2	3	10	2	1	2	0	76	75
KC	125	38	87	4	0	0	0	0	0	0	0	0	0	0	0	68	41	13	3	1	0	5	2	5	9	4	1	0	0	74	51
MIN	115	63	52	4	0	0	0	0	0	0	0	0	0	0	0	70	31	14	0	3	2	4	1	1	5	4	2	0	0	63	52
NY	110	47	63	4	0	0	0	0	0	0	0	0	0	0	0	73	21	11	5	5	4	2	3	2	9	2	2	0	0	60	50
WAS	113	54	59	3	0	0	1	0	0	1	0	0	0	0	0	71	24	17	1	5	2	3	2	2	11	5	0	0	0	64	49

NL

Tm	Tot	H	A	Consec 2	3	4	1-Inn 3	4	5	One-Game 5	6	7	8	9	10	Men-On-Base 0	1	2	3	Pitchers PH	LO	XN	IP	P	Totals 1	10	20	30	40	Batters RHB	LHB
ATL	118	74	44	4	0	0	1	0	0	0	0	0	0	0	0	78	25	13	2	4	3	2	1	2	12	3	1	0	0	74	44
CHI	142	90	52	6	0	0	2	0	0	0	0	1	0	0	0	84	43	15	0	5	3	4	0	2	13	4	1	1	0	98	44
CIN	101	66	35	3	0	0	0	0	0	0	0	0	0	0	0	59	31	11	0	0	1	1	0	0	7	4	0	0	0	66	35
HOU	120	32	88	2	0	0	1	0	0	0	0	0	0	0	0	65	33	18	4	3	4	4	3	1	12	4	1	0	0	86	34
LA	93	35	58	3	0	0	0	0	0	0	0	0	0	0	0	62	17	12	2	2	1	4	2	1	11	3	0	0	0	69	24
NY	124	61	63	4	0	0	0	0	0	0	0	1	0	0	0	68	38	16	2	2	2	3	2	0	20	2	1	0	0	77	47
PHI	86	44	42	4	0	0	1	0	0	1	0	0	0	0	0	54	19	12	1	2	1	1	2	1	12	2	0	0	0	59	27
PIT	108	49	59	1	0	0	0	0	0	0	0	0	0	0	0	54	36	13	5	4	1	2	3	1	9	6	0	0	0	73	35
SF	113	59	54	1	0	0	0	0	0	0	0	0	0	0	0	52	46	13	2	0	2	0	0	2	5	2	3	0	0	79	34
STL	97	54	43	2	0	0	0	0	0	0	0	0	0	0	0	61	27	8	1	3	2	1	0	1	8	3	1	0	0	62	35
AL	1197	584	613	33	0	0	1	1	0	2	0	1	0	0	0	717	340	120	20	38	22	27	13	23	104	35	10	2	0	696	501
NL	1102	564	538	30	0	0	5	0	0	1	0	2	0	0	0	637	315	131	19	25	20	22	13	11	109	33	8	1	0	743	359
YR	2299	1148	1151	63	0	0	4	1	0	3	0	3	0	0	0	1354	655	251	39	63	42	49	26	34	213	68	18	3	0	1439	860

	AL		*NL*
35	Denny McLain	30	Ferguson Jenkins
34	Earl Wilson	25	Mike McCormick
24	Luis Tiant	22	Ray Culp
23	Gary Bell	22	Dick Hughes
23	Jim Lonborg	21	Jack Fisher

1968

AL

Tm	Tot	H	A	Consec 2	3	4	1-Inn 3	4	5	One-Game 5	6	7	8	9	10	Men-On-Base 0	1	2	3	Pitchers PH	LO	XN	IP	P	Totals 1	10	20	30	40	Batters RHB	LHB
BAL	101	54	47	4	0	0	1	0	0	1	0	0	0	0	0	59	34	8	0	2	1	1	1	2	10	2	2	0	0	66	35
BOS	115	62	53	2	0	0	0	0	0	0	0	0	0	0	0	78	26	9	2	6	2	3	0	2	9	5	0	0	0	75	40
CAL	131	66	65	5	0	0	1	0	0	0	1	0	0	0	0	73	48	7	3	3	1	0	1	0	10	3	2	0	0	81	50
CHI	97	47	50	3	0	0	0	0	0	0	0	0	0	0	0	66	25	5	1	5	0	5	0	1	8	5	0	0	0	59	38
CLE	98	56	42	2	0	0	0	0	0	0	0	0	0	0	0	59	23	13	3	2	1	1	0	4	5	6	0	0	0	60	38
DET	129	75	54	4	0	0	0	0	0	0	0	0	0	0	0	66	41	17	5	1	3	1	2	2	8	2	2	1	0	69	60
MIN	92	51	41	0	0	0	1	0	0	0	0	0	0	0	0	56	23	12	1	3	0	1	0	4	7	3	1	0	0	58	34
NY	99	50	49	4	0	0	0	0	0	0	0	0	0	0	0	72	18	6	3	4	0	5	1	5	10	2	1	0	0	42	57

Tm	Tot	H	A	Consec 2	3	4	1-Inn 3	4	5	One-Game 5	6	7	8	9	10	Men-On-Base 0	1	2	3	Pitchers PH	LO	XN	IP	P	Totals 1	10	20	30	40	Batters RHB	LHB
OAK	124	58	66	3	0	0	1	0	0	1	0	0	0	0	0	73	33	16	2	2	2	6	0	4	9	2	2	0	0	68	56
WAS	118	53	65	2	0	0	2	0	0	0	0	0	0	0	0	60	42	14	2	2	4	2	1	1	9	5	0	0	0	68	50
NL																															
ATL	87	43	44	3	0	0	0	0	0	0	0	0	0	0	0	53	23	11	0	2	1	2	1	3	9	4	0	0	0	54	33
CHI	138	83	55	1	0	0	0	0	0	0	0	0	0	0	0	78	48	11	1	4	3	1	2	8	11	3	2	0	0	102	36
CIN	114	66	48	1	0	0	0	0	0	1	0	0	0	0	0	66	28	18	2	2	0	4	1	2	13	3	0	0	0	68	46
HOU	68	30	38	2	0	0	1	0	0	0	0	0	0	0	0	44	17	6	1	0	0	1	1	0	5	3	0	0	0	49	19
LA	65	24	41	1	0	0	0	0	0	0	0	0	0	0	0	42	16	5	2	0	0	0	0	1	8	3	0	0	0	44	21
NY	87	50	37	1	0	0	0	0	0	0	0	0	0	0	0	52	30	4	1	3	0	1	1	1	7	4	0	0	0	56	31
PHI	91	46	45	3	0	0	1	0	0	0	0	0	0	0	0	51	29	10	1	2	2	0	0	1	7	2	1	0	0	66	25
PIT	73	30	43	0	0	0	0	0	0	0	0	0	0	0	0	48	17	5	3	1	1	1	0	2	8	4	0	0	0	37	36
SF	86	33	53	4	0	0	0	0	0	1	0	0	0	0	0	48	25	13	0	2	3	2	1	3	6	3	1	0	0	59	27
STL	82	35	47	1	0	0	0	0	0	0	0	0	0	0	0	45	21	11	5	5	3	0	0	1	8	4	0	0	0	54	28
AL	1104	572	532	29	0	0	6	0	0	2	1	0	0	0	0	662	313	107	22	30	14	25	6	25	85	35	10	1	0	646	458
NL	891	440	451	17	0	0	2	0	0	2	0	0	0	0	0	527	254	94	16	21	13	12	7	22	82	33	4	0	0	589	302
YR	1995	1012	983	46	0	0	4	0	0	4	1	0	0	0	0	1189	567	201	38	51	27	37	13	47	167	68	14	1	0	1235	760

AL		*NL*	
31	Denny McLain	26	Bill Hands
29	Catfish Hunter	26	Ferguson Jenkins
24	Dave McNally	25	Chris Short
23	George Brunet	21	Juan Marichal
23	Mickey Lolich	18	Multiple Players Tied

1969

Tm	Tot	H	A	Consec 2	3	4	1-Inn 3	4	5	One-Game 5	6	7	8	9	10	Men-On-Base 0	1	2	3	Pitchers PH	LO	XN	IP	P	Totals 1	10	20	30	40	Batters RHB	LHB
AL																															
BAL	117	51	66	1	0	0	0	0	0	0	0	0	0	0	0	81	23	12	1	4	3	3	1	2	6	3	2	0	0	75	42
BOS	155	78	77	2	0	0	1	0	0	0	0	0	0	0	0	89	41	21	4	4	1	7	0	4	12	4	2	0	0	93	62
CAL	126	65	61	3	0	0	0	0	0	0	0	0	0	0	0	69	37	16	4	1	1	2	0	6	13	4	1	0	0	76	50
CHI	146	80	66	4	0	0	0	0	0	1	0	0	0	0	0	73	47	24	2	6	0	4	1	3	14	3	2	0	0	91	55
CLE	134	60	74	3	0	0	0	0	0	2	0	0	0	0	0	73	44	13	4	6	3	1	0	3	8	4	1	1	0	91	43
DET	128	72	56	2	1	0	1	0	0	0	0	0	0	0	0	75	40	10	3	5	3	3	1	5	8	3	3	0	0	79	49
KC	136	63	73	5	0	0	0	0	0	0	0	0	0	0	0	76	44	15	1	2	3	5	0	2	8	5	1	0	0	69	67
MIN	119	61	58	2	1	0	1	0	0	0	0	0	0	0	0	72	35	11	1	2	1	5	2	2	10	4	1	0	0	79	40
NY	118	48	70	3	0	0	0	0	0	0	0	0	0	0	0	57	40	20	1	5	1	1	3	3	6	5	1	0	0	69	49
OAK	163	70	93	6	1	0	1	0	0	2	1	0	0	0	0	89	54	16	4	5	3	11	0	2	6	6	1	1	0	82	81
SEA	172	93	79	7	0	0	2	0	0	2	0	0	0	0	0	109	47	14	2	2	2	3	3	4	16	4	2	0	0	97	75
WAS	135	62	73	2	0	0	0	0	0	0	0	0	0	0	0	86	33	11	5	1	4	4	0	1	8	5	1	0	0	72	63
NL																															
ATL	144	84	60	5	0	0	0	0	0	0	0	0	0	0	0	83	40	17	4	7	2	1	0	4	8	1	4	0	0	96	48
CHI	118	65	53	0	0	0	0	0	0	0	0	0	0	0	0	67	36	13	2	0	2	3	1	5	8	3	2	0	0	77	41
CIN	149	74	75	4	0	0	0	0	0	0	0	0	0	0	0	89	42	13	5	4	7	4	1	4	9	4	1	1	0	94	55
HOU	111	43	68	4	0	0	0	0	0	0	0	0	0	0	0	64	26	16	5	0	2	2	4	3	8	5	1	0	0	78	33
LA	122	55	67	5	0	0	0	0	0	0	0	0	0	0	0	78	35	8	1	2	3	3	0	1	8	2	2	0	0	76	46
MON	145	87	58	2	0	0	1	0	0	0	0	0	0	0	0	73	48	19	5	2	2	4	0	2	11	5	1	0	0	89	56
NY	119	59	60	3	0	0	1	0	0	0	0	0	0	0	0	81	25	10	3	2	0	1	0	6	7	3	2	0	0	90	29
PHI	134	64	70	4	1	0	1	0	0	2	0	0	0	0	0	77	39	15	3	4	2	2	1	1	9	6	0	0	0	90	44
PIT	96	33	63	3	0	0	2	0	0	0	0	0	0	0	0	49	35	9	3	2	2	2	2	3	12	2	1	0	0	54	42
SD	113	47	66	2	0	0	0	0	0	0	0	0	0	0	0	58	29	21	5	2	2	0	0	2	12	5	0	0	0	73	40
SF	120	61	59	1	0	0	0	0	0	0	0	0	0	0	0	72	35	10	3	1	1	5	0	0	7	3	2	0	0	83	37
STL	99	43	56	4	0	0	0	0	0	0	0	0	0	0	0	56	29	13	1	3	1	2	0	3	10	3	0	0	0	66	33
AL	1649	803	846	40	3	0	6	0	0	7	1	0	0	0	0	949	485	183	32	43	25	49	11	37	115	50	18	2	0	973	676
NL	1470	715	755	37	1	0	5	0	0	2	0	0	0	0	0	847	419	164	40	29	26	29	9	34	109	42	16	1	0	966	504
YR	3119	1518	1601	77	4	0	8	0	0	9	1	0	0	0	0	1796	904	347	72	72	51	78	20	71	224	92	34	3	0	1939	1180

AL		*NL*	
37	Luis Tiant	33	Jim Merritt
34	Catfish Hunter	27	Ferguson Jenkins
29	Wally Bunker	26	Bill Stoneman
29	Marty Pattin	25	Multiple Players Tied
28	Stan Bahnsen		

1970

Tm	Tot	H	A	Consec			1-Inn			One-Game						Men-On-Base				Pitchers					Totals					Batters	
				2	3	4	3	4	5	5	6	7	8	9	10	0	1	2	3	PH	LO	XN	IP	P	1	10	20	30	40	RHB	LHB
AL																															
BAL	139	58	81	2	0	0	0	0	0	1	0	0	0	0	0	85	36	16	2	4	3	4	1	3	7	2	2	1	0	91	48
BOS	156	75	81	5	0	0	0	0	0	0	0	0	0	0	0	88	43	20	5	5	2	2	1	1	10	3	3	0	0	92	64
CAL	154	59	95	5	0	0	1	0	0	1	0	0	0	0	0	85	50	17	2	3	4	3	1	2	7	2	3	1	0	110	44
CHI	164	97	67	5	0	0	0	0	0	2	0	0	0	0	0	91	45	26	2	5	4	2	0	5	9	7	1	0	0	97	67
CLE	163	103	60	6	0	0	0	1	0	1	0	0	0	0	0	92	56	14	1	4	3	4	2	7	8	5	2	0	0	102	61
DET	153	86	67	6	0	0	0	0	0	0	0	0	0	0	0	82	52	13	6	5	2	0	1	2	8	5	2	0	0	87	66
KC	138	48	90	5	0	0	0	0	0	0	0	0	0	0	0	67	44	22	5	6	3	1	0	4	11	5	1	0	0	74	64
MIL	146	72	74	4	0	0	0	0	0	1	0	0	0	0	0	79	40	21	6	6	2	2	0	3	12	0	3	1	0	88	58
MIN	130	53	77	2	0	0	0	0	0	0	0	0	0	0	0	80	34	13	3	2	4	1	0	2	7	4	2	0	0	71	59
NY	130	40	90	9	0	0	2	0	0	0	1	0	0	0	0	81	37	11	1	3	5	3	0	4	11	1	3	0	0	83	47
OAK	134	56	78	2	1	0	1	0	0	0	0	0	0	0	0	83	37	12	2	2	1	4	0	0	10	2	0	2	0	65	69
WAS	139	61	78	3	0	0	0	0	0	0	0	0	0	0	0	81	38	16	4	4	2	2	0	3	10	3	2	0	0	88	51
NL																															
ATL	185	119	66	6	1	0	1	0	0	1	0	1	0	0	0	102	57	22	4	5	3	4	1	8	9	2	3	0	1	127	58
CHI	143	92	51	7	0	0	0	0	0	1	1	0	0	0	0	87	39	14	3	7	0	3	0	4	11	2	1	2	0	98	45
CIN	118	58	60	1	0	0	0	0	0	0	0	0	0	0	0	66	35	14	3	4	5	1	0	3	8	3	2	0	0	81	37
HOU	131	64	67	4	0	0	1	0	0	0	0	0	0	0	0	65	46	16	4	1	1	3	4	2	10	3	1	1	0	89	42
LA	164	82	82	5	0	0	0	1	0	1	0	0	0	0	0	83	57	16	8	7	4	2	1	3	8	3	2	1	0	116	48
MON	162	91	71	8	1	0	2	0	0	1	0	0	0	0	0	84	49	22	7	4	5	4	2	4	10	3	3	0	0	101	61
NY	135	75	60	3	0	0	0	0	0	0	0	0	0	0	0	77	39	14	5	5	0	2	1	0	7	4	2	0	0	93	42
PHI	132	63	69	4	0	0	0	0	0	0	0	0	0	0	0	67	44	21	0	1	0	4	2	3	6	7	0	0	0	91	41
PIT	106	41	65	5	0	0	1	0	0	0	0	0	0	0	0	56	34	14	2	1	0	1	0	2	17	3	0	0	0	76	30
SD	149	56	93	6	0	0	2	0	0	0	0	1	0	0	0	85	43	15	6	4	3	1	1	2	7	5	2	0	0	87	62
SF	156	77	79	5	0	0	1	0	0	3	0	0	0	0	0	86	46	20	4	5	2	8	0	3	8	3	3	0	0	98	58
STL	102	44	58	0	0	0	0	0	0	0	0	0	0	0	0	51	33	15	3	1	0	3	1	0	13	3	1	0	0	62	40
AL	1746	808	938	54	1	0	4	1	0	6	1	0	0	0	0	994	512	201	39	49	35	28	6	36	110	39	24	5	0	1048	698
NL	1683	862	821	54	2	0	8	1	0	7	1	2	0	0	0	909	522	203	49	45	23	36	13	34	114	41	20	4	1	1119	564
YR	3429	1670	1759	108	3	0	7	2	0	13	2	2	0	0	0	1903	1034	404	88	94	58	64	19	70	224	80	44	9	1	2167	1262

	AL		*NL*
34	Mike Cuellar	40	Phil Niekro
33	Lew Krausse	38	Don Sutton
32	Chuck Dobson	31	Larry Dierker
32	Catfish Hunter	30	Ken Holtzman
32	Tom Murphy	30	Ferguson Jenkins

1971

Tm	Tot	H	A	Consec			1-Inn			One-Game						Men-On-Base				Pitchers					Totals					Batters	
				2	3	4	3	4	5	5	6	7	8	9	10	0	1	2	3	PH	LO	XN	IP	P	1	10	20	30	40	RHB	LHB
AL																															
BAL	125	67	58	5	0	0	0	0	0	0	0	0	0	0	0	79	34	11	1	0	1	1	0	7	7	1	2	1	0	69	56
BOS	136	75	61	3	1	0	1	0	0	1	1	0	0	0	0	80	35	20	1	6	5	1	2	2	11	1	3	0	0	93	43
CAL	101	55	46	1	0	0	0	0	0	0	0	0	0	0	0	61	28	11	1	1	1	3	3	0	6	4	1	0	0	66	35
CHI	100	53	47	1	0	0	0	0	0	0	0	0	0	0	0	63	23	13	1	3	5	2	0	1	6	4	1	0	0	62	38
CLE	154	99	55	2	0	0	0	0	0	0	0	0	0	0	0	81	48	21	4	4	4	2	1	4	8	5	2	0	0	81	73
DET	126	70	56	4	0	0	0	0	0	0	0	0	0	0	0	73	29	21	3	5	2	3	1	2	10	4	0	1	0	88	38
KC	84	36	48	2	0	0	0	0	0	0	0	0	0	0	0	53	20	9	2	5	2	1	1	4	12	2	0	0	0	35	49
MIL	130	64	66	5	0	0	0	0	0	0	0	0	0	0	0	74	34	19	3	3	3	1	1	3	7	3	2	0	0	69	61
MIN	139	71	68	4	0	0	0	0	0	0	0	0	0	0	0	71	48	17	3	2	4	4	0	2	8	2	2	1	0	72	67
NY	126	61	65	4	0	0	1	0	0	0	0	0	0	0	0	72	34	17	3	5	4	4	1	0	7	3	3	0	0	56	70
OAK	131	74	57	3	0	0	0	0	0	0	0	0	0	0	0	77	36	13	5	7	2	2	0	3	9	4	2	0	0	77	54
WAS	132	59	73	3	0	0	2	0	0	1	0	0	0	0	0	79	37	14	2	1	3	1	1	0	10	2	1	1	0	67	65
NL																															
ATL	152	90	62	6	0	0	1	0	0	0	0	0	0	0	0	87	50	13	2	1	1	3	1	2	9	3	2	0	0	85	67
CHI	132	70	62	8	0	0	1	0	0	0	0	0	0	0	0	75	41	14	2	4	0	1	0	5	8	2	3	0	0	80	52
CIN	112	51	61	1	0	0	0	0	0	0	0	0	0	0	0	56	39	15	2	1	2	3	1	4	7	6	0	0	0	70	42
HOU	75	27	48	2	0	0	0	0	0	0	0	0	0	0	0	43	23	8	1	1	3	2	0	0	12	2	0	0	0	47	28
LA	110	56	54	5	0	0	0	0	0	0	0	0	0	0	0	72	21	15	2	4	0	2	1	1	9	4	1	0	0	72	38
MON	133	68	65	6	0	0	0	1	0	1	0	0	0	0	0	71	43	15	4	0	0	2	0	4	6	2	3	0	0	79	54
NY	100	50	50	1	0	0	0	0	0	0	0	0	0	0	0	63	26	10	1	4	1	3	1	3	6	5	0	0	0	67	33

				Consec			1-Inn			One-Game						Men-On-Base				Pitchers					Totals					Batters	
Tm	**Tot**	**H**	**A**	**2**	**3**	**4**	**3**	**4**	**5**	**5**	**6**	**7**	**8**	**9**	**10**	**0**	**1**	**2**	**3**	**PH**	**LO**	**XN**	**IP**	**P**	**1**	**10**	**20**	**30**	**40**	**RHB**	**LHB**
PHI	132	80	52	5	0	0	2	0	0	2	0	0	0	0	0	75	37	20	0	1	2	4	1	5	8	3	3	0	0	86	46
PIT	108	48	60	2	0	0	0	0	0	0	0	0	0	0	0	51	42	11	4	2	1	2	1	1	6	5	0	0	0	62	46
SD	93	43	50	1	0	0	0	0	0	0	0	0	0	0	0	56	28	8	1	2	0	6	0	2	10	2	1	0	0	56	37
SF	128	58	70	5	0	0	0	0	0	0	0	0	0	0	0	77	31	16	4	4	0	2	0	3	9	0	3	0	0	78	50
STL	104	49	55	2	0	0	0	0	0	0	0	0	0	0	0	54	32	15	3	2	1	2	2	1	13	2	2	0	0	64	40
AL	1484	784	700	37	1	0	4	0	0	2	1	0	0	0	0	863	406	186	29	42	36	25	11	28	101	35	19	4	0	835	649
NL	1379	690	689	44	0	0	4	1	0	3	0	0	0	0	0	780	413	160	26	26	11	32	8	31	103	36	18	0	0	846	533
YR	2863	1474	1389	81	1	0	5	0	0	5	1	0	0	0	0	1643	819	346	55	68	47	57	19	59	204	71	37	4	0	1681	1182

AL		*NL*	
39	Jim Perry	29	Ferguson Jenkins
36	Mickey Lolich	28	Barry Lersch
31	Denny McLain	27	Bill Hands
30	Mike Cuellar	27	Juan Marichal
29	Multiple Players Tied	27	Phil Niekro

1972

AL

				Consec			1-Inn			One-Game						Men-On-Base				Pitchers					Totals					Batters	
Tm	Tot	H	A	2	3	4	3	4	5	5	6	7	8	9	10	0	1	2	3	PH	LO	XN	IP	P	1	10	20	30	40	RHB	LHB
BAL	85	40	45	2	0	0	0	0	0	0	0	0	0	0	0	49	26	7	3	2	2	2	0	0	6	2	2	0	0	52	33
BOS	101	49	52	0	0	0	0	0	0	0	0	0	0	0	0	49	28	22	2	2	0	2	0	0	10	3	0	0	0	57	44
CAL	90	31	59	1	0	0	1	0	0	0	0	0	0	0	0	52	23	12	3	2	1	1	0	1	8	4	0	0	0	57	33
CHI	94	44	50	0	0	0	0	0	0	0	0	0	0	0	0	56	31	7	0	3	1	5	1	2	10	1	2	0	0	56	38
CLE	123	79	44	4	0	0	0	0	0	0	0	0	0	0	0	79	35	7	2	2	2	4	0	3	9	4	1	0	0	70	53
DET	101	67	34	2	0	0	0	0	0	0	0	0	0	0	0	64	26	9	2	2	1	2	1	3	12	1	2	0	0	54	47
KC	85	28	57	0	0	0	0	0	0	0	0	0	0	0	0	48	25	11	1	2	0	1	0	1	7	4	1	0	0	53	32
MIL	116	45	71	6	0	0	2	0	0	1	0	0	0	0	0	65	27	20	4	2	1	3	2	5	6	5	1	0	0	56	60
MIN	105	54	51	4	0	0	0	0	0	0	0	0	0	0	0	57	33	13	2	4	0	6	2	2	7	3	1	0	0	54	51
NY	87	37	50	3	1	0	1	0	0	0	0	0	0	0	0	43	24	18	2	3	0	0	0	1	9	4	0	0	0	60	27
OAK	96	52	44	2	0	0	0	0	0	0	0	0	0	0	0	53	30	12	1	1	0	6	0	3	9	2	2	0	0	65	31
TEX	92	41	51	1	0	0	0	0	0	0	0	0	0	0	0	50	24	14	4	2	3	1	0	1	11	3	0	0	0	45	47

NL

				Consec			1-Inn			One-Game						Men-On-Base				Pitchers					Totals					Batters	
Tm	Tot	H	A	2	3	4	3	4	5	5	6	7	8	9	10	0	1	2	3	PH	LO	XN	IP	P	1	10	20	30	40	RHB	LHB
ATL	155	88	67	4	0	0	0	0	0	0	0	0	0	0	0	90	44	19	2	2	0	2	0	6	9	7	1	0	0	101	54
CHI	112	63	49	5	0	0	0	0	0	0	1	0	0	0	0	66	33	10	3	2	0	2	0	0	9	3	0	1	0	69	43
CIN	129	59	70	4	0	0	0	0	0	1	0	0	0	0	0	81	28	19	1	2	0	5	0	3	6	7	0	0	0	89	40
HOU	114	56	58	3	0	0	0	0	0	0	0	0	0	0	0	62	31	18	3	3	1	0	4	1	7	6	0	0	0	65	49
LA	83	37	46	1	0	0	0	0	0	0	0	0	0	0	0	41	27	11	4	1	1	1	0	1	7	4	0	0	0	58	25
MON	103	56	47	1	0	0	0	0	0	0	0	0	0	0	0	52	35	14	2	6	1	1	1	1	5	6	0	0	0	58	45
NY	118	56	62	2	0	0	0	0	0	1	0	0	0	0	0	70	33	12	3	2	0	5	1	2	9	3	2	0	0	78	40
PHI	117	57	60	1	0	0	0	0	0	0	0	0	0	0	0	74	25	15	3	0	2	4	1	2	11	5	0	0	0	81	36
PIT	90	34	56	3	0	0	0	0	0	0	0	0	0	0	0	55	27	7	1	1	0	0	2	1	6	5	0	0	0	47	43
SD	121	64	57	6	0	0	0	0	0	1	0	0	0	0	0	67	33	20	1	3	0	2	1	5	7	5	1	0	0	62	59
SF	130	65	65	2	0	0	1	0	0	1	0	0	0	0	0	75	39	14	2	2	1	2	0	2	7	6	1	0	0	93	37
STL	87	38	49	2	0	0	0	0	0	0	0	0	0	0	0	44	31	12	0	1	0	1	1	1	13	2	1	0	0	52	35
AL	1175	567	608	25	1	0	4	0	0	1	0	0	0	0	0	665	332	152	26	27	11	33	6	22	104	36	12	0	0	679	496
NL	1359	673	686	34	0	0	1	0	0	4	1	0	0	0	0	777	386	171	25	25	6	25	11	25	96	59	6	1	0	853	506
YR	2534	1240	1294	59	1	0	3	0	0	5	1	0	0	0	0	1442	718	323	51	52	17	58	17	47	200	95	18	1	0	1532	1002

AL		*NL*	
29	Mickey Lolich	32	Ferguson Jenkins
28	Wilbur Wood	23	Tom Seaver
27	Bill Parsons	22	Phil Niekro
23	Joe Coleman	21	Reggie Cleveland
23	Ken Holtzman	21	Clay Kirby

1973

AL

				Consec			1-Inn			One-Game						Men-On-Base				Pitchers					Totals					Batters	
Tm	Tot	H	A	2	3	4	3	4	5	5	6	7	8	9	10	0	1	2	3	PH	LO	XN	IP	P	1	10	20	30	40	RHB	LHB
BAL	124	60	64	3	0	0	1	0	0	0	0	0	0	0	0	81	32	11	0	1	1	5	0	0	6	5	1	0	0	84	40
BOS	158	83	75	1	0	0	0	0	0	0	0	0	0	0	0	96	36	24	2	4	2	0	2	0	9	1	2	2	0	110	48
CAL	104	49	55	4	0	0	0	0	0	0	0	0	0	0	0	55	31	13	5	3	1	1	1	0	6	2	2	0	0	73	31
CHI	110	58	52	4	0	0	1	0	0	0	0	0	0	0	0	58	32	15	5	2	2	2	1	0	9	2	2	0	0	66	44

				Consec			1-Inn			One-Game						Men-On-Base				Pitchers					Totals					Batters	
Tm	Tot	H	A	2	3	4	3	4	5	5	6	7	8	9	10	0	1	2	3	PH	LO	XN	IP	P	1	10	20	30	40	RHB	LHB
CLE	172	100	72	4	1	0	1	0	0	0	0	0	0	0	0	105	40	22	5	4	3	5	0	0	9	4	0	2	0	100	72
DET	154	71	83	4	0	0	0	0	0	1	0	0	0	0	0	91	47	14	2	1	2	4	1	0	9	0	2	2	0	100	54
KC	114	61	53	0	0	0	1	0	0	0	0	0	0	0	0	58	40	14	2	0	0	2	4	0	9	5	0	0	0	67	47
MIL	119	53	66	5	0	0	1	0	0	0	0	0	0	0	0	65	32	16	6	3	2	5	0	0	8	3	1	1	0	62	57
MIN	115	60	55	2	0	0	1	0	0	1	0	0	0	0	0	60	36	16	3	3	2	1	1	0	6	5	1	0	0	66	49
NY	109	42	67	4	0	0	0	0	0	0	0	0	0	0	0	66	29	11	3	1	2	1	1	0	9	3	2	0	0	64	45
OAK	143	70	73	5	0	0	2	0	0	0	0	0	0	0	0	82	39	20	2	3	3	1	0	0	8	1	2	1	0	91	52
TEX	130	51	79	4	0	0	0	0	0	0	0	0	0	0	0	65	39	22	4	0	5	3	0	0	13	5	0	0	0	86	44
NL																															
ATL	144	87	57	2	0	0	0	0	0	0	0	0	0	0	0	78	45	18	3	6	2	6	1	3	14	3	2	0	0	91	53
CHI	128	72	56	6	0	0	0	0	0	0	0	0	0	0	0	77	34	16	1	3	3	2	0	0	6	4	1	1	0	73	55
CIN	135	67	68	5	0	0	1	0	0	0	0	0	0	0	0	76	45	11	3	2	4	5	0	2	7	3	3	0	0	88	47
HOU	111	53	58	3	0	0	1	0	0	0	0	0	0	0	0	60	33	14	4	3	2	0	0	3	9	4	1	0	0	55	56
LA	129	62	67	5	0	0	1	0	0	2	0	0	0	0	0	78	37	13	1	5	1	7	1	5	8	3	2	0	0	84	45
MON	128	70	58	1	0	0	0	0	0	0	0	0	0	0	0	70	36	19	3	3	2	2	1	5	8	5	1	0	0	69	59
NY	127	61	66	2	0	0	0	0	0	0	0	0	0	0	0	73	32	15	7	6	4	4	2	3	8	5	1	0	0	86	41
PHI	131	80	51	2	0	0	0	0	0	0	0	0	0	0	0	64	47	18	2	2	3	3	0	0	8	4	2	0	0	83	48
PIT	110	42	68	1	0	0	0	0	0	0	0	0	0	0	0	68	28	9	5	2	4	2	0	0	10	5	0	0	0	57	53
SD	157	80	77	1	0	0	1	0	0	2	0	0	0	0	0	87	46	18	6	6	3	3	4	2	5	4	2	1	0	103	54
SF	145	79	66	1	0	0	0	0	0	0	0	0	0	0	0	90	36	17	2	4	3	3	1	3	7	0	5	0	0	80	65
STL	105	30	75	4	0	0	0	0	0	0	0	0	0	0	0	66	28	10	1	3	3	2	1	1	12	5	0	0	0	59	46
AL	1552	758	794	40	1	0	8	0	0	2	0	0	0	0	0	882	433	198	39	25	25	30	11	0	101	36	15	8	0	969	583
NL	1550	783	767	33	0	0	4	0	0	4	0	0	0	0	0	887	447	178	38	45	34	39	11	27	102	45	20	2	0	928	622
YR	3102	1541	1561	73	1	0	8	0	0	6	0	0	0	0	0	1769	880	376	77	70	59	69	22	27	203	81	35	10	0	1897	1205

AL		*NL*	
39	Catfish Hunter	35	Ferguson Jenkins
35	Mickey Lolich	30	Clay Kirby
34	Gaylord Perry	29	Steve Carlton
32	Joe Coleman	27	Fred Norman
32	Luis Tiant	27	Steve Renko

1974

AL																															
BAL	101	46	55	2	0	0	0	0	0	0	0	0	0	0	0	54	38	4	5	1	3	4	0	0	7	3	1	0	0	67	34
BOS	126	66	60	1	0	0	0	0	0	0	0	0	0	0	0	70	40	13	3	0	1	1	1	0	6	2	3	0	0	88	38
CAL	101	47	54	2	0	0	1	0	0	0	0	0	0	0	0	56	29	11	5	3	2	2	0	0	11	3	1	0	0	75	26
CHI	103	43	60	1	0	0	0	0	0	0	0	0	0	0	0	61	27	11	4	2	0	4	0	0	11	2	1	0	0	72	31
CLE	138	92	46	3	1	0	1	1	0	1	2	0	0	0	0	75	47	11	5	5	1	4	0	0	11	6	1	0	0	83	55
DET	148	84	64	4	0	0	1	0	0	0	0	0	0	0	0	72	56	17	3	1	4	2	1	0	6	3	1	2	0	94	54
KC	91	42	49	2	0	0	0	0	0	0	0	0	0	0	0	51	31	4	5	1	1	2	1	0	8	2	1	0	0	63	28
MIL	126	69	57	3	0	0	1	0	0	0	0	0	0	0	0	71	38	15	2	0	1	1	1	0	7	2	3	0	0	78	48
MIN	115	56	59	1	0	0	1	0	0	0	0	0	0	0	0	66	36	12	1	0	1	1	0	0	7	3	1	0	0	86	29
NY	104	50	54	2	0	0	0	0	0	0	0	0	0	0	0	64	25	10	5	1	1	1	1	0	13	1	2	0	0	53	51
OAK	90	43	47	2	0	0	0	0	0	0	0	0	0	0	0	59	22	9	0	2	1	1	0	0	6	3	1	0	0	68	22
TEX	126	57	69	3	0	0	1	0	0	2	0	0	0	0	0	62	43	21	0	2	2	1	2	0	8	3	2	0	0	71	55
NL																															
ATL	97	44	53	2	0	0	0	0	0	0	0	0	0	0	0	58	24	12	3	6	0	2	1	1	8	5	0	0	0	68	29
CHI	122	72	50	1	0	0	1	0	0	0	2	0	0	0	0	63	36	19	4	7	2	0	3	2	9	5	0	0	0	67	55
CIN	126	62	64	4	0	0	0	0	0	1	0	0	0	0	0	70	31	20	5	1	1	3	0	4	9	5	1	0	0	86	40
HOU	84	35	49	1	0	0	0	0	0	0	0	0	0	0	0	47	28	9	0	2	2	2	2	2	10	3	0	0	0	45	39
LA	112	51	61	3	0	0	0	0	0	0	0	0	0	0	0	58	40	10	4	2	0	2	1	2	9	1	3	0	0	72	40
MON	99	49	50	1	0	0	0	0	0	0	0	0	0	0	0	56	25	14	4	6	2	0	2	1	9	3	1	0	0	47	52
NY	99	49	50	2	0	0	0	0	0	0	0	0	0	0	0	53	33	13	0	4	1	4	0	1	9	5	0	0	0	69	30
PHI	111	56	55	2	1	0	1	0	0	0	0	0	0	0	0	61	32	10	8	1	1	3	1	0	11	3	2	0	0	62	49
PIT	93	32	61	2	0	0	0	0	0	0	1	0	0	0	0	45	31	16	1	7	1	1	0	1	11	3	1	0	0	69	24
SD	124	54	70	1	1	0	1	0	0	0	0	0	0	0	0	63	38	20	3	4	5	2	1	0	14	4	0	0	0	81	43
SF	116	61	55	4	0	0	0	0	0	0	0	0	0	0	0	70	31	11	4	1	0	3	0	2	9	5	0	0	0	73	43
STL	97	46	51	1	0	0	0	0	0	0	0	0	0	0	0	47	32	16	2	2	1	0	0	2	10	3	1	0	0	52	45
AL	1369	695	674	26	1	0	6	1	0	3	2	0	0	0	0	761	432	138	38	18	18	24	7	0	101	33	18	2	0	898	471

				Consec			1-Inn			One-Game						Men-On-Base				Pitchers					Totals					Batters	
Tm	**Tot**	**H**	**A**	**2**	**3**	**4**	**3**	**4**	**5**	**5**	**6**	**7**	**8**	**9**	**10**	**0**	**1**	**2**	**3**	**PH**	**LO**	**XN**	**IP**	**P**	**1**	**10**	**20**	**30**	**40**	**RHB**	**LHB**
NL	1280	611	669	24	2	0	3	0	0	1	3	0	0	0	0	691	381	170	38	43	16	22	11	18	118	45	9	0	0	791	489
YR	2649	1306	1343	50	3	0	7	0	0	4	5	0	0	0	0	1452	813	308	76	61	34	46	18	18	219	78	27	2	0	1689	960

AL

38 Mickey Lolich
31 Joe Coleman
27 Multiple Players Tied

NL

24 Bob Gibson
24 Andy Messersmith
23 Don Sutton
22 Don Gullett
22 Jim Lonborg

1975

AL

Tm	Tot	H	A	Consec 2	3	4	1-Inn 3	4	5	One-Game 5	6	7	8	9	10	Men-On-Base 0	1	2	3	PH	LO	XN	IP	P	Totals 1	10	20	30	40	RHB	LHB
BAL	110	45	65	3	0	0	0	0	0	1	0	0	0	0	0	77	24	9	0	1	3	4	0	0	6	2	2	0	0	76	34
BOS	145	81	64	6	0	0	0	0	0	0	0	0	0	0	0	82	42	18	3	1	3	0	1	0	5	3	2	1	0	94	51
CAL	123	52	71	1	0	0	0	0	0	1	0	0	0	0	0	64	42	14	3	3	2	3	2	0	9	5	1	0	0	61	62
CHI	107	54	53	3	0	0	0	0	0	0	0	0	0	0	0	63	31	11	2	4	2	4	2	0	10	2	2	0	0	71	36
CLE	136	85	51	3	0	0	0	0	0	0	0	0	0	0	0	90	32	14	0	1	2	0	0	0	11	5	0	0	0	82	54
DET	137	83	54	5	0	0	1	0	0	0	0	0	0	0	0	69	43	24	1	1	3	2	1	0	7	4	2	0	0	74	63
KC	108	45	63	3	0	0	0	0	0	0	0	0	0	0	0	56	40	11	1	1	2	1	1	0	5	6	0	0	0	60	48
MIL	133	63	70	5	0	0	1	0	0	0	0	0	0	0	0	68	38	22	5	1	2	3	1	0	10	4	1	0	0	73	60
MIN	137	88	49	3	0	0	0	0	0	1	0	0	0	0	0	77	37	19	4	2	4	4	2	0	6	6	1	0	0	91	46
NY	104	56	48	2	0	0	0	0	0	0	0	0	0	0	0	68	20	14	2	2	4	2	0	0	6	1	3	0	0	58	46
OAK	102	43	59	2	0	0	0	0	0	0	0	0	0	0	0	59	32	8	3	6	0	1	1	0	7	4	1	0	0	68	34
TEX	123	70	53	2	0	0	0	0	0	0	0	0	0	0	0	64	37	17	5	1	1	1	0	0	9	5	0	1	0	66	57

NL

Tm	Tot	H	A	Consec 2	3	4	1-Inn 3	4	5	One-Game 5	6	7	8	9	10	Men-On-Base 0	1	2	3	PH	LO	XN	IP	P	Totals 1	10	20	30	40	RHB	LHB
ATL	101	63	38	5	0	0	1	0	0	0	0	0	0	0	0	55	34	10	2	1	1	1	0	3	15	1	1	0	0	63	38
CHI	130	71	59	6	0	0	0	0	0	1	0	0	0	0	0	69	44	16	1	5	3	1	0	1	11	3	2	0	0	66	64
CIN	112	52	60	4	0	0	0	0	0	0	0	0	0	0	0	63	34	13	2	4	1	1	1	0	6	3	2	0	0	69	43
HOU	106	43	63	3	0	0	0	0	0	0	0	0	0	0	0	71	16	16	3	4	2	2	0	2	9	3	1	0	0	60	46
LA	104	52	52	1	0	0	0	0	0	0	0	0	0	0	0	67	26	9	2	3	2	4	1	0	7	3	1	0	0	62	42
MON	102	57	45	1	0	0	0	0	0	0	0	0	0	0	0	60	26	13	3	4	0	4	0	0	8	3	1	0	0	55	47
NY	99	48	51	2	0	0	0	0	0	0	0	0	0	0	0	63	19	15	2	3	3	2	0	1	9	5	0	0	0	75	24
PHI	111	47	64	4	0	0	0	0	0	0	0	0	0	0	0	51	38	21	1	7	3	2	2	0	9	5	1	0	0	67	44
PIT	79	41	38	0	0	0	0	0	0	0	0	0	0	0	0	50	22	7	0	1	0	0	1	0	6	4	0	0	0	58	21
SD	99	38	61	2	0	0	0	0	0	1	0	0	0	0	0	53	33	11	2	4	1	5	0	2	10	4	0	0	0	62	37
SF	92	37	55	1	0	0	0	0	0	0	0	0	0	0	0	46	32	11	3	0	0	0	1	0	9	4	0	0	0	50	42
STL	98	39	59	3	0	0	0	0	0	0	0	0	0	0	0	54	27	14	3	4	1	2	1	1	11	3	1	0	0	59	39
AL	1465	765	700	38	0	0	2	0	0	3	0	0	0	0	0	837	418	181	29	24	28	25	11	0	91	47	15	2	0	874	591
NL	1233	588	645	32	0	0	1	0	0	2	0	0	0	0	0	702	351	156	24	40	17	24	7	10	110	41	10	0	0	746	487
YR	2698	1353	1345	70	0	0	3	0	0	5	0	0	0	0	0	1539	769	337	53	64	45	49	18	10	201	88	25	2	0	1620	1078

AL

37 Ferguson Jenkins
34 Rick Wise
29 Ross Grimsley
28 Gaylord Perry
28 Jim Slaton

NL

29 Phil Niekro
25 Ray Burris
24 Steve Carlton
24 Larry Dierker
24 Steve Stone

1976

AL

Tm	Tot	H	A	Consec 2	3	4	1-Inn 3	4	5	One-Game 5	6	7	8	9	10	Men-On-Base 0	1	2	3	PH	LO	XN	IP	P	Totals 1	10	20	30	40	RHB	LHB
BAL	80	38	42	0	0	0	0	0	0	0	0	0	0	0	0	47	26	5	2	1	0	2	1	0	9	2	1	0	0	53	27
BOS	109	61	48	1	0	0	0	0	0	0	0	0	0	0	0	61	31	16	1	0	0	1	0	0	7	2	2	0	0	72	37
CAL	95	35	60	1	0	0	0	0	0	0	0	0	0	0	0	43	38	12	2	1	2	0	0	0	7	4	1	0	0	62	33
CHI	87	34	53	0	0	0	1	0	0	0	0	0	0	0	0	34	37	12	4	3	0	2	1	0	11	3	0	0	0	51	36
CLE	80	43	37	2	0	0	0	0	0	0	0	0	0	0	0	46	24	10	0	0	1	1	0	0	9	3	0	0	0	47	33
DET	101	62	39	7	0	0	1	0	0	0	0	0	0	0	0	58	27	14	2	0	0	2	1	0	7	5	0	0	0	58	43
KC	83	35	48	1	0	0	0	0	0	0	0	0	0	0	0	48	22	12	1	0	1	1	1	0	9	3	0	0	0	50	33
MIL	99	43	56	2	0	0	0	0	0	0	0	0	0	0	0	55	27	13	4	2	3	8	2	0	9	2	2	0	0	55	44
MIN	89	52	37	0	0	0	0	0	0	0	0	0	0	0	0	47	20	20	2	3	1	0	1	0	8	3	0	0	0	50	39

Tm	Tot	H	A	Consec			1-Inn			One-Game						Men-On-Base				Pitchers					Totals					Batters	
				2	3	4	3	4	5	5	6	7	8	9	10	0	1	2	3	PH	LO	XN	IP	P	1	10	20	30	40	RHB	LHB
NY	97	51	46	2	0	0	0	0	0	0	0	0	0	0	0	54	34	9	0	1	3	1	1	0	8	3	1	0	0	50	47
OAK	96	57	39	1	0	0	0	0	0	0	0	0	0	0	0	54	34	5	3	1	4	3	0	0	6	5	0	0	0	58	38
TEX	106	57	49	3	0	0	1	0	0	0	0	0	0	0	0	65	28	11	2	4	1	6	2	0	9	5	0	0	0	56	50
NL																															
ATL	86	56	30	0	0	0	0	0	0	0	0	0	0	0	0	52	24	8	2	1	4	1	0	3	11	3	0	0	0	52	34
CHI	123	84	39	8	0	0	2	0	0	0	2	1	0	0	0	67	39	14	3	4	1	1	0	2	9	4	1	0	0	69	54
CIN	100	46	54	2	0	0	1	0	0	0	0	0	0	0	0	61	29	8	2	3	1	2	0	0	8	3	1	0	0	73	27
HOU	82	27	55	0	0	0	0	0	0	0	0	0	0	0	0	46	22	10	4	6	0	2	0	0	13	1	0	0	0	55	27
LA	97	48	49	6	0	0	1	0	0	0	0	0	0	0	0	56	17	23	1	7	3	2	0	1	6	3	1	0	0	58	39
MON	89	41	48	2	0	0	0	0	0	0	0	0	0	0	0	40	37	10	2	0	1	2	2	1	14	3	0	0	0	46	43
NY	97	43	54	2	0	0	0	0	0	0	0	0	0	0	0	51	34	7	5	3	4	3	0	2	6	5	0	0	0	65	32
PHI	98	49	49	0	0	0	0	0	0	0	0	0	0	0	0	58	28	11	1	5	2	3	1	0	7	2	1	0	0	57	41
PIT	95	44	51	1	0	0	0	0	0	0	0	0	0	0	0	55	24	12	4	1	0	1	3	1	6	4	1	0	0	73	22
SD	87	38	49	3	0	0	0	0	0	0	0	0	0	0	0	40	26	19	2	4	0	3	3	0	6	5	0	0	0	56	31
SF	68	32	36	0	0	0	0	0	0	0	0	0	0	0	0	37	25	6	0	3	4	1	1	1	10	2	0	0	0	42	26
STL	91	40	51	2	0	0	0	0	0	0	0	0	0	0	0	48	30	10	3	3	3	1	0	1	7	5	0	0	0	54	37
AL	1122	568	554	20	0	0	3	0	0	0	0	0	0	0	0	612	348	139	23	16	16	27	10	0	99	40	7	0	0	662	460
NL	1113	548	565	26	0	0	4	0	0	0	2	1	0	0	0	611	335	138	29	40	23	22	10	12	103	40	5	0	0	700	413
YR	2235	1116	1119	46	0	0	5	0	0	0	2	1	0	0	0	1223	683	277	52	56	39	49	20	12	202	80	12	0	0	1362	873

AL		*NL*	
28	Catfish Hunter	28	Gary Nolan
25	Luis Tiant	22	Ray Burris
24	Frank Tanana	22	John Candelaria
21	Bill Travers	22	Don Sutton
20	Multiple Players Tied	21	Jim Kaat

1977

Tm	Tot	H	A	Consec			1-Inn			One-Game						Men-On-Base				Pitchers					Totals					Batters	
				2	3	4	3	4	5	5	6	7	8	9	10	0	1	2	3	PH	LO	XN	IP	P	1	10	20	30	40	RHB	LHB
AL																															
BAL	124	62	62	2	1	0	2	0	0	1	0	0	0	0	0	72	43	8	1	4	0	4	0	0	7	2	3	0	0	92	32
BOS	158	95	63	4	0	0	1	0	0	1	1	0	0	0	0	92	54	11	1	2	2	0	0	0	5	4	2	1	0	88	70
CAL	136	65	71	4	0	0	0	0	0	0	0	0	0	0	0	91	27	14	4	3	2	4	1	0	12	7	0	0	0	64	72
CHI	136	58	78	5	0	0	1	0	0	0	1	0	0	0	0	68	48	17	3	3	4	2	3	0	10	5	2	0	0	65	71
CLE	136	66	70	6	0	0	1	0	0	0	0	0	0	0	0	84	29	19	4	3	1	5	1	0	7	2	2	1	0	69	67
DET	162	100	62	3	0	0	0	0	0	2	0	0	0	0	0	90	54	15	3	3	2	6	0	0	8	5	2	0	0	93	69
KC	110	50	60	3	0	0	0	0	0	0	1	0	0	0	0	59	38	13	0	2	0	3	0	0	7	4	1	0	0	66	44
MIL	136	54	82	4	0	0	1	0	0	0	1	0	0	0	0	81	40	14	1	3	1	2	0	0	7	3	3	0	0	72	64
MIN	151	79	72	9	0	0	2	0	0	0	0	0	0	0	0	89	47	13	2	4	1	1	0	0	7	4	3	0	0	89	62
NY	139	63	76	12	0	0	1	1	0	3	1	0	0	0	0	91	36	11	1	4	4	0	4	0	6	3	3	0	0	58	81
OAK	145	69	76	3	0	0	0	0	0	0	0	0	0	0	0	86	42	15	2	4	0	8	1	0	11	6	1	0	0	78	67
SEA	194	103	91	4	1	0	2	0	0	2	1	0	0	0	0	100	62	24	8	4	1	2	0	0	10	6	2	1	0	116	78
TEX	134	78	56	1	0	0	0	0	0	0	0	0	0	0	0	88	33	11	2	3	4	1	0	0	11	3	3	0	0	78	56
TOR	152	94	58	4	1	0	0	2	0	2	0	0	1	0	0	79	54	18	1	6	0	4	3	0	10	2	2	1	0	92	60
NL																															
ATL	169	111	58	5	0	0	0	0	0	1	0	0	0	0	0	98	41	24	6	2	1	4	1	4	16	4	2	0	0	106	63
CHI	128	82	46	2	0	0	1	0	0	1	1	0	0	0	0	66	44	14	4	6	2	2	1	4	10	5	1	0	0	84	44
CIN	156	83	73	5	0	0	1	0	0	2	1	0	0	0	0	92	35	24	5	4	5	2	1	2	11	7	1	0	0	94	62
HOU	110	33	77	1	0	0	1	0	0	0	0	0	0	0	0	51	41	17	1	3	0	1	0	6	5	5	1	0	0	68	42
LA	119	65	54	1	0	0	0	0	0	0	0	0	0	0	0	69	33	13	4	4	2	4	0	2	7	4	2	0	0	69	50
MON	135	65	70	2	1	0	2	0	0	0	0	0	0	0	0	61	58	9	7	6	1	7	4	3	8	7	0	0	0	76	59
NY	118	55	63	4	0	0	2	0	0	0	0	0	0	0	0	52	51	13	2	3	0	3	1	2	8	5	0	0	0	73	45
PHI	134	63	71	6	0	0	1	0	0	0	0	0	0	0	0	75	40	17	2	3	2	0	1	3	6	1	4	0	0	94	40
PIT	149	76	73	7	0	0	0	0	0	0	0	0	0	0	0	98	37	11	3	3	2	3	1	1	4	4	3	0	0	100	49
SD	160	70	90	1	1	0	2	0	0	0	0	1	0	0	0	88	51	18	3	6	0	6	1	0	7	5	3	0	0	108	52
SF	114	56	58	1	0	0	0	0	0	0	0	0	0	0	0	56	41	12	5	4	1	2	0	2	5	5	1	0	0	61	53
STL	139	53	86	6	0	0	1	0	0	0	0	0	0	0	0	74	48	12	5	5	1	1	1	2	8	3	2	0	0	101	38
AL	2013	1036	977	64	3	0	11	3	0	11	6	0	1	0	0	1170	607	203	33	48	22	42	13	0	118	56	29	4	0	1120	893
NL	1631	812	819	41	2	0	11	0	0	4	2	1	0	0	0	880	520	184	47	49	17	35	12	31	95	55	20	0	0	1034	597
YR	3644	1848	1796	105	5	0	16	1	0	15	8	1	1	0	0	2050	1127	387	80	97	39	77	25	31	213	111	49	4	0	2154	1490

				Consec			1-Inn			One-Game						Men-On-Base				Pitchers					Totals					Batters	
Tm	Tot	H	A	2	3	4	3	4	5	5	6	7	8	9	10	0	1	2	3	PH	LO	XN	IP	P	1	10	20	30	40	RHB	LHB

AL		*NL*	
33	Jerry Garvin	29	Ray Burris
32	Glenn Abbott	29	John Candelaria
31	Dennis Eckersley	28	Buzz Capra
30	Ferguson Jenkins	28	Fred Norman
29	Catfish Hunter	27	Ed Halicki

1978

AL

Tm	Tot	H	A	Consec 2	3	4	1-Inn 3	4	5	One-Game 5	6	7	8	9	10	Men-On-Base 0	1	2	3	PH	LO	XN	IP	P	Totals 1	10	20	30	40	RHB	LHB
BAL	107	42	65	4	0	0	0	0	0	0	0	0	0	0	0	59	29	16	3	4	1	3	2	0	5	3	2	0	0	68	39
BOS	137	72	65	3	0	0	0	0	0	1	0	0	0	0	0	88	33	13	3	0	1	2	0	0	7	2	2	1	0	68	69
CAL	125	58	67	5	0	0	0	0	0	0	0	0	0	0	0	80	29	15	1	1	3	1	0	0	7	3	2	0	0	73	52
CHI	128	58	70	1	0	0	0	0	0	0	0	0	0	0	0	64	44	14	6	4	2	3	4	0	9	3	2	0	0	63	65
CLE	100	37	63	1	0	0	0	0	0	0	0	0	0	0	0	48	32	14	6	4	0	3	1	0	10	3	1	0	0	63	37
DET	135	78	57	3	0	0	0	0	0	0	0	0	0	0	0	78	36	18	3	0	2	3	0	0	10	3	2	0	0	84	51
KC	108	44	64	2	0	0	0	0	0	0	0	0	0	0	0	60	30	14	4	3	1	2	0	0	8	2	2	0	0	68	40
MIL	109	50	59	6	0	0	1	0	0	0	0	0	0	0	0	67	30	11	1	1	1	2	0	0	8	4	1	0	0	61	48
MIN	102	39	63	3	0	0	0	0	0	0	0	0	0	0	0	53	32	13	4	3	1	3	0	0	11	4	0	0	0	54	48
NY	111	59	52	6	0	0	0	0	0	0	0	0	0	0	0	71	30	9	1	2	3	3	1	0	11	3	1	0	0	61	50
OAK	106	51	55	3	0	0	0	0	0	0	0	0	0	0	0	62	29	13	2	1	2	0	0	0	8	6	0	0	0	52	54
SEA	155	93	62	3	0	0	0	0	0	1	0	0	0	0	0	92	47	11	5	2	1	3	0	0	7	5	3	0	0	84	71
TEX	108	49	59	0	0	0	0	0	0	0	0	0	0	0	0	68	29	8	3	1	4	2	0	0	7	4	1	0	0	59	49
TOR	149	75	74	2	0	0	0	0	0	0	0	0	0	0	0	78	56	10	5	2	3	1	0	0	4	5	3	0	0	104	45
NL																															
ATL	132	89	43	4	0	0	0	1	0	1	0	0	1	0	0	68	36	23	5	4	1	2	0	2	8	7	0	0	0	92	40
CHI	125	76	49	1	1	0	1	0	0	1	0	0	0	0	0	67	38	17	3	8	1	2	1	1	6	6	0	0	0	84	41
CIN	122	61	61	5	0	0	1	0	0	0	0	0	0	0	0	79	26	16	1	3	2	1	0	1	8	4	1	0	0	82	40
HOU	86	29	57	1	0	0	0	0	0	0	0	0	0	0	0	48	24	11	3	3	4	0	0	2	9	3	1	0	0	52	34
LA	107	59	48	1	0	0	0	0	0	0	0	0	0	0	0	67	28	9	3	2	3	1	0	0	6	4	1	0	0	67	40
MON	117	49	68	3	0	0	1	0	0	0	0	0	0	0	0	53	48	12	4	4	1	1	1	1	12	5	0	0	0	74	43
NY	114	60	54	2	0	0	1	0	0	0	1	0	0	0	0	68	29	15	2	6	1	6	0	0	13	2	1	0	0	71	43
PHI	118	70	48	3	0	0	0	0	0	1	0	0	0	0	0	71	30	11	6	4	2	2	0	2	6	4	0	1	0	71	47
PIT	103	61	42	0	0	0	0	0	0	0	0	0	0	0	0	56	35	11	1	5	4	2	0	2	7	4	1	0	0	67	36
SD	74	23	51	2	0	0	0	0	0	0	0	0	0	0	0	36	26	9	3	4	2	0	1	1	11	3	0	0	0	51	23
SF	84	30	54	2	0	0	0	0	0	0	0	0	0	0	0	46	26	10	2	3	1	1	1	1	8	3	1	0	0	55	29
STL	94	32	62	3	0	0	0	0	0	0	0	0	0	0	0	53	28	11	2	4	1	2	0	3	11	3	0	0	0	51	43
AL	1680	805	875	42	0	0	1	0	0	2	0	0	0	0	0	968	486	179	47	28	25	31	8	0	112	50	22	1	0	962	718
NL	1276	639	637	27	1	0	4	1	0	3	1	0	1	0	0	712	374	155	35	50	23	20	4	16	105	48	6	1	0	817	459
YR	2956	1444	1512	69	1	0	4	1	0	5	1	0	1	0	0	1680	860	334	82	78	48	51	12	16	217	98	28	2	0	1779	1177

AL		*NL*	
30	Dennis Eckersley	30	Steve Carlton
28	Jesse Jefferson	29	Don Sutton
27	Dennis Leonard	26	Tom Seaver
27	Jim Slaton	25	John Montefusco
26	Multiple Players Tied	24	Nino Espinosa

1979

AL

Tm	Tot	H	A	Consec 2	3	4	1-Inn 3	4	5	One-Game 5	6	7	8	9	10	Men-On-Base 0	1	2	3	PH	LO	XN	IP	P	Totals 1	10	20	30	40	RHB	LHB
BAL	133	57	76	1	0	0	0	0	0	0	1	0	0	0	0	80	43	9	1	3	3	1	0	0	3	3	2	1	0	80	53
BOS	133	59	74	3	0	0	0	0	0	1	0	0	0	0	0	81	41	7	4	2	2	2	1	0	9	1	3	0	0	65	68
CAL	131	55	76	0	0	0	0	0	0	0	0	0	0	0	0	71	43	15	2	0	0	0	0	0	10	4	1	0	0	60	71
CHI	114	60	54	2	0	0	0	0	0	0	0	0	0	0	0	61	32	15	6	2	4	1	2	0	12	2	2	0	0	80	34
CLE	138	72	66	3	0	0	3	0	0	0	0	0	0	0	0	68	46	20	4	3	1	0	0	0	7	4	2	0	0	71	67
DET	167	74	93	7	0	0	1	0	0	0	3	0	0	0	0	107	41	16	3	4	2	1	1	0	6	11	0	0	0	74	93
KC	165	81	84	4	1	0	2	0	0	1	0	0	0	0	0	92	50	19	4	2	0	2	4	0	7	4	2	1	0	104	61
MIL	162	81	81	6	0	0	1	0	0	1	0	0	0	0	0	92	50	16	4	4	0	1	3	0	6	3	1	2	0	87	75
MIN	128	62	66	5	0	0	1	0	0	1	0	0	0	0	0	77	39	12	0	3	3	3	0	0	6	5	1	0	0	67	61

Tm	Tot	H	A	Consec 2	3	4	1-Inn 3	4	5	One-Game 5	6	7	8	9	10	Men-On-Base 0	1	2	3	Pitchers PH	LO	XN	IP	P	Totals 1	10	20	30	40	Batters RHB	LHB
NY	123	59	64	6	0	0	1	0	0	1	0	0	0	0	0	74	36	12	1	4	1	1	1	0	12	2	2	0	0	69	54
OAK	147	65	82	6	1	0	3	0	0	1	0	0	0	0	0	77	38	27	5	5	1	1	1	0	5	7	1	0	0	85	62
SEA	165	94	71	4	0	0	0	0	0	0	0	0	0	0	0	98	41	22	4	2	5	3	1	0	9	6	2	0	0	84	81
TEX	135	63	72	2	0	0	1	0	0	0	0	0	0	0	0	73	43	15	4	0	4	1	3	0	11	1	1	0	1	81	54
TOR	165	74	91	6	0	0	1	0	0	2	0	0	0	0	0	86	48	23	8	1	2	3	3	0	9	6	2	0	0	99	66
NL																															
ATL	132	80	52	4	0	0	2	0	0	0	0	0	0	0	0	85	40	5	2	4	6	4	1	4	9	4	0	0	1	83	49
CHI	127	72	55	3	0	0	1	0	0	1	0	0	0	0	0	72	40	13	2	2	4	5	2	2	6	5	1	0	0	78	49
CIN	103	53	50	4	0	0	1	0	0	0	0	1	0	0	0	68	25	10	0	2	1	1	3	1	8	5	0	0	0	74	29
HOU	90	31	59	6	1	0	1	0	0	1	0	0	0	0	0	51	26	11	2	4	1	3	1	0	12	3	0	0	0	68	22
LA	101	55	46	2	0	0	0	0	0	0	0	0	0	0	0	53	30	16	2	3	0	2	1	1	9	3	1	0	0	63	38
MON	116	51	65	3	0	0	0	0	0	0	0	0	0	0	0	69	34	11	2	3	4	4	2	3	4	6	1	0	0	76	40
NY	120	58	62	0	0	0	1	0	0	0	0	0	0	0	0	70	36	13	1	5	1	4	2	2	16	1	2	0	0	81	39
PHI	135	72	63	4	1	0	1	0	0	1	1	0	0	0	0	62	50	16	7	2	2	1	1	4	12	1	3	0	0	93	42
PIT	125	77	48	3	0	0	0	0	0	0	0	0	0	0	0	74	34	12	5	3	3	0	1	0	7	4	2	0	0	87	38
SD	108	47	61	3	0	0	1	0	0	1	0	0	0	0	0	55	35	15	3	2	3	3	0	1	8	5	0	0	0	78	30
SF	143	61	82	9	0	0	1	0	0	0	0	0	0	0	0	83	33	24	3	4	1	1	1	0	6	4	1	1	0	117	26
STL	127	65	62	3	0	0	0	0	0	0	0	0	0	0	0	86	24	15	2	2	3	5	1	0	7	4	2	0	0	82	45
AL	2006	956	1050	55	2	0	14	0	0	8	4	0	0	0	0	1137	591	228	50	35	28	20	20	0	112	59	22	4	1	1106	900
NL	1427	722	705	44	2	0	9	0	0	4	1	1	0	0	0	828	407	161	31	36	29	33	16	18	104	45	13	1	1	980	447
YR	3433	1678	1755	99	4	0	11	0	0	12	5	1	0	0	0	1965	998	389	81	71	57	53	36	18	216	104	35	5	2	2086	1347

AL		*NL*	
40	Ferguson Jenkins	41	Phil Niekro
33	Dennis Leonard	30	Bob Knepper
33	Bill Travers	27	Lynn McGlothen
31	Steve Stone	25	John Candelaria
30	Lary Sorensen	25	Steve Carlton

1980

Tm	Tot	H	A	Consec 2	3	4	1-Inn 3	4	5	One-Game 5	6	7	8	9	10	Men-On-Base 0	1	2	3	Pitchers PH	LO	XN	IP	P	Totals 1	10	20	30	40	Batters RHB	LHB
AL																															
BAL	134	81	53	4	0	0	0	0	0	0	0	0	0	0	0	79	36	16	3	4	2	4	2	0	5	3	3	0	0	76	58
BOS	129	74	55	4	0	0	2	0	0	1	1	0	0	0	0	66	39	19	5	3	1	2	1	0	11	4	1	0	0	60	69
CAL	141	76	65	5	0	0	1	0	0	1	0	0	0	0	0	80	48	13	0	5	1	1	0	0	11	6	0	0	0	71	70
CHI	108	37	71	1	0	0	2	0	0	0	0	0	0	0	0	58	36	11	3	4	0	3	2	0	9	4	1	0	0	64	44
CLE	137	66	71	3	1	0	2	0	0	1	1	1	0	0	0	68	42	21	6	4	0	4	1	0	4	7	1	0	0	74	63
DET	152	95	57	3	0	0	0	0	0	1	0	0	0	0	0	81	44	20	7	2	1	3	0	0	7	4	3	0	0	86	66
KC	129	51	78	2	0	0	0	0	0	0	0	0	0	0	0	75	43	11	0	2	0	0	2	0	7	3	1	1	0	77	52
MIL	137	65	72	4	1	0	1	1	0	0	1	0	0	0	0	85	39	10	3	3	4	1	0	0	11	1	3	0	0	85	52
MIN	120	63	57	0	0	0	0	0	0	0	0	0	0	0	0	59	44	15	2	5	1	5	1	0	8	5	1	0	0	66	54
NY	102	47	55	1	0	0	0	0	0	0	0	0	0	0	0	51	40	9	2	5	5	1	3	0	7	5	0	0	0	47	55
OAK	142	57	85	8	0	0	1	0	0	0	0	0	0	0	0	95	30	12	5	6	0	5	1	0	7	1	4	0	0	69	73
SEA	159	99	60	4	0	0	0	0	0	0	0	0	0	0	0	93	45	20	1	2	0	5	3	0	5	4	3	0	0	76	83
TEX	119	57	62	4	0	0	0	0	0	0	0	0	0	0	0	67	36	14	2	4	1	0	0	0	12	3	1	0	0	53	66
TOR	135	75	60	1	0	0	0	0	0	2	0	0	0	0	0	72	46	17	0	5	1	4	2	0	8	7	0	0	0	61	74
NL																															
ATL	131	79	52	2	0	0	1	0	0	1	0	0	0	0	0	74	42	12	3	3	2	2	0	2	5	2	2	1	0	80	51
CHI	109	62	47	4	0	0	1	0	0	0	0	0	0	0	0	72	26	10	1	3	3	3	0	1	5	5	1	0	0	70	39
CIN	113	70	43	4	0	0	0	0	0	0	0	0	0	0	0	68	35	9	1	3	2	1	1	1	7	5	1	0	0	73	40
HOU	69	22	47	2	0	0	0	0	0	0	0	0	0	0	0	40	20	8	1	2	1	2	1	3	9	3	0	0	0	43	26
LA	105	58	47	2	1	0	1	0	0	0	0	0	0	0	0	52	38	11	4	2	5	2	0	1	6	3	2	0	0	60	45
MON	100	40	60	3	1	0	3	0	0	1	0	0	0	0	0	58	26	13	3	3	2	4	0	0	10	4	0	0	0	66	34
NY	140	80	60	3	0	0	1	0	0	2	0	0	0	0	0	81	34	20	5	3	1	4	0	1	8	5	2	0	0	89	51
PHI	87	44	43	2	0	0	0	0	0	0	0	0	0	0	0	51	30	5	1	3	0	4	2	4	12	2	0	0	0	60	27
PIT	110	53	57	5	0	0	0	0	0	0	0	0	0	0	0	69	33	7	1	6	1	4	1	1	7	3	2	0	0	73	37
SD	97	33	64	1	0	0	0	0	0	1	0	0	0	0	0	54	29	14	0	6	2	1	2	1	10	3	0	0	0	65	32
SF	92	41	51	3	0	0	0	0	0	0	0	0	0	0	0	51	26	14	1	1	3	3	0	1	11	4	0	0	0	67	25
STL	90	42	48	1	0	0	0	0	0	0	0	0	0	0	0	46	23	14	7	4	3	1	1	1	17	3	0	0	0	62	28
AL	1844	943	901	44	2	0	9	1	0	6	3	1	0	0	0	1029	568	208	39	54	17	38	18	0	112	57	22	1	0	965	879

Tm	Tot	H	A	Consec 2	3	4	1-Inn 3	4	5	One-Game 5	6	7	8	9	10	Men-On-Base 0	1	2	3	Pitchers PH	LO	XN	IP	P	Totals 1	10	20	30	40	Batters RHB	LHB
NL	1243	624	619	32	2	0	7	0	0	5	0	0	0	0	0	716	362	137	28	39	25	31	8	17	107	42	10	1	0	808	435
YR	3087	1567	1520	76	4	0	11	1	0	11	3	1	0	0	0	1745	930	345	67	93	42	69	26	17	219	99	32	2	0	1773	1314

AL
30 Dennis Leonard
29 Mike Caldwell
29 Rick Langford
27 Multiple Players Tied

NL
30 Phil Niekro
27 Larry McWilliams
24 Lynn McGlothen
24 Tom Seaver
22 Burt Hooton

1981

Tm	Tot	H	A	Consec 2	3	4	1-Inn 3	4	5	One-Game 5	6	7	8	9	10	Men-On-Base 0	1	2	3	Pitchers PH	LO	XN	IP	P	Totals 1	10	20	30	40	Batters RHB	LHB
AL																															
BAL	83	47	36	2	0	0	0	0	0	0	0	0	0	0	0	44	31	6	2	3	2	3	0	0	8	4	0	0	0	54	29
BOS	90	47	43	7	0	0	0	0	0	0	0	0	0	0	0	49	31	10	0	0	1	5	0	0	7	5	0	0	0	60	30
CAL	81	39	42	1	0	0	0	0	0	0	0	0	0	0	0	49	21	9	2	2	1	4	0	0	14	1	0	0	0	52	29
CHI	73	33	40	1	0	0	0	0	0	0	1	0	0	0	0	42	20	7	4	1	0	1	1	0	10	3	0	0	0	45	28
CLE	67	33	34	2	0	0	0	0	0	0	0	0	0	0	0	41	16	9	1	1	1	1	0	0	10	1	0	0	0	40	27
DET	83	44	39	1	0	0	0	0	0	0	0	0	0	0	0	44	27	11	1	2	0	1	0	0	6	5	0	0	0	49	34
KC	75	27	48	4	0	0	1	0	0	0	0	0	0	0	0	43	24	8	0	0	0	1	1	0	7	4	0	0	0	47	28
MIL	72	29	43	0	0	0	0	0	0	0	0	0	0	0	0	37	22	11	2	1	3	0	0	0	7	3	0	0	0	43	29
MIN	79	47	32	2	0	0	0	0	0	0	0	0	0	0	0	45	17	15	2	0	0	3	0	0	10	3	0	0	0	48	31
NY	64	24	40	1	0	0	0	0	0	0	0	0	0	0	0	35	17	12	0	1	0	1	1	0	11	3	0	0	0	45	19
OAK	80	46	34	5	0	0	0	0	0	1	0	0	0	0	0	47	20	12	1	1	1	2	0	0	6	5	0	0	0	47	33
SEA	76	53	23	1	0	0	0	0	0	1	0	0	0	0	0	40	25	9	2	3	0	2	0	0	10	4	0	0	0	49	27
TEX	67	24	43	0	0	0	0	0	0	0	0	0	0	0	0	41	16	9	1	1	1	1	0	0	10	3	0	0	0	30	37
TOR	72	41	31	1	0	0	0	0	0	0	0	0	0	0	0	41	19	10	2	2	2	2	1	0	9	3	0	0	0	42	30
NL																															
ATL	62	41	21	3	0	0	0	0	0	0	0	0	0	0	0	33	19	10	0	2	2	2	0	1	13	1	0	0	0	35	27
CHI	59	38	21	0	0	0	0	0	0	0	0	0	0	0	0	35	12	12	0	4	1	4	0	1	12	1	0	0	0	36	23
CIN	67	41	26	0	0	0	0	0	0	0	0	0	0	0	0	34	22	8	3	4	1	0	0	1	8	3	0	0	0	38	29
HOU	40	9	31	1	0	0	0	0	0	0	0	0	0	0	0	25	11	3	1	1	0	1	1	1	11	0	0	0	0	28	12
LA	54	34	20	2	0	0	0	0	0	0	0	0	0	0	0	34	15	5	0	4	0	4	2	0	10	2	0	0	0	34	20
MON	58	23	35	2	0	0	0	0	0	0	0	0	0	0	0	35	14	7	2	4	1	1	0	0	12	1	0	0	0	32	26
NY	74	38	36	2	0	0	0	0	0	0	0	0	0	0	0	42	23	9	0	4	2	1	0	1	14	2	0	0	0	49	25
PHI	72	39	33	3	0	0	0	0	0	0	0	0	0	0	0	45	15	8	4	2	2	1	0	3	10	2	0	0	0	44	28
PIT	60	29	31	4	0	0	0	0	0	0	0	0	0	0	0	41	14	4	1	2	0	2	1	1	14	1	0	0	0	34	26
SD	64	27	37	1	0	0	0	0	0	0	0	0	0	0	0	37	16	10	1	2	1	2	1	0	11	3	0	0	0	44	20
SF	57	19	38	0	0	0	0	0	0	0	0	0	0	0	0	36	14	5	2	1	0	1	0	0	10	2	0	0	0	38	19
STL	52	26	26	0	0	0	0	0	0	0	0	0	0	0	0	27	16	9	0	2	0	1	0	0	13	1	0	0	0	37	15
AL	1062	534	528	28	0	0	1	0	0	2	1	0	0	0	0	598	306	138	20	18	12	27	4	0	125	47	0	0	0	651	411
NL	719	364	355	18	0	0	0	0	0	0	0	0	0	0	0	424	191	90	14	32	10	20	5	9	138	19	0	0	0	449	270
YR	1781	898	883	46	0	0	1	0	0	2	1	0	0	0	0	1022	497	228	34	50	22	47	9	9	263	66	0	0	0	1100	681

AL
18 Mike Caldwell
18 Geoff Zahn
17 Mike Norris
17 Frank Tanana
15 Dennis Leonard

NL
13 Mario Soto
13 Pat Zachry
11 Multiple Players Tied

1982

Tm	Tot	H	A	Consec 2	3	4	1-Inn 3	4	5	One-Game 5	6	7	8	9	10	Men-On-Base 0	1	2	3	Pitchers PH	LO	XN	IP	P	Totals 1	10	20	30	40	Batters RHB	LHB
AL																															
BAL	147	87	60	5	0	0	1	0	0	0	0	0	0	0	0	91	40	15	1	3	1	1	0	0	8	0	2	2	0	96	51
BOS	155	82	73	5	0	0	2	0	0	1	0	0	0	0	0	86	43	20	6	2	4	2	1	0	4	5	2	1	0	95	60
CAL	124	69	55	3	1	0	1	0	0	0	0	0	0	0	0	69	37	17	1	2	2	3	2	0	10	3	1	0	0	71	53
CHI	99	43	56	1	0	0	0	0	0	0	0	0	0	0	0	58	25	15	1	5	1	2	0	0	11	3	0	0	0	60	39
CLE	122	64	58	4	0	0	0	0	0	0	0	0	0	0	0	66	46	8	2	1	2	6	1	0	11	5	0	0	0	70	52
DET	172	100	72	4	0	0	1	0	0	2	0	0	0	0	0	91	65	10	6	3	2	3	1	0	7	5	1	1	0	91	81
KC	163	64	99	3	1	0	2	0	0	1	0	0	0	0	0	87	56	16	4	7	5	1	2	0	9	3	2	1	0	109	54

Tm	Tot	H	A	Consec			1-Inn			One-Game						Men-On-Base				Pitchers					Totals					Batters	
				2	3	4	3	4	5	5	6	7	8	9	10	0	1	2	3	PH	LO	XN	IP	P	1	10	20	30	40	RHB	LHB
MIL	152	64	88	2	0	0	0	0	0	0	0	0	0	0	0	84	49	13	6	2	3	6	2	0	7	5	1	1	0	99	53
MIN	208	110	98	5	0	0	1	0	0	1	0	0	0	0	0	120	61	21	6	4	1	7	1	0	7	6	2	1	0	126	82
NY	113	55	58	3	1	0	1	0	0	0	0	0	0	0	0	70	32	10	1	4	2	2	3	0	9	5	1	0	0	71	42
OAK	177	83	94	7	1	0	2	0	0	3	0	0	0	0	0	86	67	20	4	2	4	2	0	0	10	4	1	2	0	105	72
SEA	173	104	69	6	0	0	3	0	0	1	0	0	0	0	0	99	49	22	3	4	2	3	1	0	9	3	2	1	0	103	70
TEX	128	66	62	7	0	0	0	0	0	0	0	0	0	0	0	75	41	11	1	1	1	1	0	0	7	4	2	0	0	76	52
TOR	147	70	77	5	0	0	2	0	0	0	0	0	0	0	0	79	40	22	6	1	1	2	2	0	7	3	3	0	0	83	64
NL																															
ATL	126	86	40	1	0	0	0	0	0	0	0	0	0	0	0	67	41	14	4	3	3	4	2	3	12	3	1	0	0	75	51
CHI	125	62	63	3	0	0	0	0	0	0	0	0	0	0	0	70	39	12	4	4	0	2	0	3	10	4	1	0	0	78	47
CIN	105	47	58	1	0	0	0	0	0	0	0	0	0	0	0	63	25	16	1	3	4	1	0	1	8	5	0	0	0	65	40
HOU	87	26	61	5	0	0	0	0	0	1	0	0	0	0	0	52	25	10	0	2	2	4	0	1	7	4	1	0	0	55	32
LA	81	35	46	0	0	0	0	0	0	0	0	0	0	0	0	43	23	12	3	3	1	1	0	2	9	4	0	0	0	50	31
MON	110	65	45	3	1	0	1	0	0	1	0	0	0	0	0	58	33	18	1	5	2	2	1	2	6	3	2	0	0	56	54
NY	119	60	59	3	0	0	0	0	0	0	0	0	0	0	0	66	37	15	1	3	2	4	4	2	10	5	1	0	0	64	55
PHI	86	46	40	1	0	0	0	0	0	0	0	0	0	0	0	48	24	12	2	4	1	1	2	0	11	3	0	0	0	44	42
PIT	118	65	53	2	0	0	0	0	0	0	0	0	0	0	0	60	35	20	3	5	1	3	1	0	12	3	1	0	0	70	48
SD	139	76	63	5	0	0	0	0	0	0	0	0	0	0	0	81	46	11	1	3	0	5	0	2	5	5	2	0	0	92	47
SF	109	54	55	2	0	0	0	0	0	0	0	0	0	0	0	55	39	14	1	2	1	2	1	1	8	5	0	0	0	68	41
STL	94	48	46	5	0	0	0	0	0	0	0	0	0	0	0	61	22	9	2	5	0	1	1	3	11	3	0	0	0	56	38
AL	2080	1061	1019	60	4	0	16	0	0	9	0	0	0	0	0	1161	651	220	48	41	31	41	16	0	116	54	20	10	0	1255	825
NL	1299	670	629	31	1	0	1	0	0	2	0	0	0	0	0	724	389	163	23	42	17	30	12	20	109	47	9	0	0	773	526
YR	3379	1731	1648	91	5	0	13	0	0	11	0	0	0	0	0	1885	1040	383	71	83	48	71	28	20	225	101	29	10	0	2028	1351

	AL		*NL*
38	Matt Keough	26	Doug Bird
37	Jack Morris	26	Don Robinson
33	Rick Langford	25	Bill Gullickson
32	Floyd Bannister	24	Pete Falcone
32	Brad Havens	24	Scott Sanderson

1983

AL

Tm	Tot	H	A	Consec			1-Inn			One-Game						Men-On-Base				Pitchers					Totals					Batters	
				2	3	4	3	4	5	5	6	7	8	9	10	0	1	2	3	PH	LO	XN	IP	P	1	10	20	30	40	RHB	LHB
BAL	130	66	64	7	0	0	1	0	0	1	0	0	0	0	0	77	36	14	3	6	1	4	0	0	6	6	2	0	0	89	41
BOS	158	76	82	2	0	0	0	0	0	1	0	0	0	0	0	93	52	11	2	2	4	2	1	0	4	4	2	1	0	104	54
CAL	130	67	63	3	1	0	2	0	0	0	0	0	0	0	0	73	44	12	1	0	3	3	0	0	10	3	3	0	0	72	58
CHI	128	64	64	4	0	0	1	0	0	0	0	0	0	0	0	74	41	11	2	4	3	3	0	0	6	5	1	0	0	80	48
CLE	120	71	49	4	0	0	0	0	0	0	0	0	0	0	0	61	42	12	5	1	0	0	1	0	10	3	2	0	0	65	55
DET	170	87	83	7	0	0	1	0	0	0	0	0	0	0	0	101	49	14	6	4	4	5	4	0	9	5	0	2	0	79	91
KC	133	66	67	5	0	0	1	0	0	0	0	0	0	0	0	76	42	12	3	3	2	2	3	0	12	4	1	0	0	96	37
MIL	133	57	76	4	0	0	1	0	0	1	0	0	0	0	0	74	40	15	4	2	2	1	3	0	7	4	1	1	0	95	38
MIN	163	91	72	6	0	0	0	0	0	1	1	0	0	0	0	91	48	23	1	0	1	3	1	0	8	4	1	1	0	99	64
NY	116	55	61	1	0	0	0	0	0	0	0	0	0	0	0	57	42	15	2	1	0	0	1	0	10	4	1	0	0	90	26
OAK	135	54	81	3	1	0	1	1	0	0	1	0	0	0	0	74	43	13	5	4	2	1	1	0	13	5	0	0	0	77	58
SEA	145	80	65	6	0	0	0	0	0	1	0	0	0	0	0	85	41	17	2	2	3	2	2	0	8	6	1	0	0	84	61
TEX	97	33	64	3	0	0	0	0	0	0	0	0	0	0	0	63	20	13	1	0	2	1	2	0	10	2	1	0	0	63	34
TOR	145	84	61	5	0	0	1	0	0	1	0	0	0	0	0	89	40	13	3	2	3	3	2	0	8	3	3	0	0	85	60
NL																															
ATL	132	71	61	4	0	0	0	0	0	0	0	0	0	0	0	76	40	13	3	3	3	2	1	2	7	6	1	0	0	83	49
CHI	117	69	48	3	0	0	0	0	0	0	0	0	0	0	0	73	32	6	6	7	1	3	0	4	10	5	0	0	0	63	54
CIN	135	64	71	3	0	0	0	0	0	0	0	0	0	0	0	78	39	15	3	7	1	4	1	2	7	3	2	0	0	71	64
HOU	94	28	66	1	0	0	1	0	0	0	0	0	0	0	0	54	30	7	3	2	1	5	0	0	9	4	0	0	0	59	35
LA	97	49	48	2	0	0	0	0	0	0	0	0	0	0	0	51	27	18	1	2	1	1	2	1	8	3	1	0	0	58	39
MON	120	56	64	4	0	0	0	0	0	1	0	0	0	0	0	69	34	13	4	2	5	2	1	0	9	6	0	0	0	60	60
NY	97	53	44	1	0	0	0	0	0	1	0	0	0	0	0	60	26	8	3	4	1	0	0	0	8	4	0	0	0	55	42
PHI	111	61	50	3	0	0	0	0	0	0	0	0	0	0	0	67	36	6	2	6	1	1	0	0	12	2	1	0	0	73	38
PIT	109	63	46	2	0	0	0	0	0	0	0	0	0	0	0	65	28	12	4	6	2	1	1	1	10	5	0	0	0	68	41
SD	144	82	62	3	0	0	1	0	0	0	0	0	0	0	0	84	47	11	2	4	3	4	0	4	12	1	3	0	0	85	59
SF	127	67	60	3	0	0	0	0	0	0	0	0	0	0	0	70	43	11	3	8	3	0	1	1	9	6	0	0	0	78	49

Tm	Tot	H	A	Consec 2	3	4	1-Inn 3	4	5	One-Game 5	6	7	8	9	10	Men-On-Base 0	1	2	3	Pitchers PH	LO	XN	IP	P	Totals 1	10	20	30	40	Batters RHB	LHB
STL	115	58	57	2	0	0	1	0	0	0	0	0	0	0	0	60	34	17	4	4	2	0	0	2	10	2	2	0	0	70	45
AL	1903	951	952	60	2	0	9	1	0	6	2	0	0	0	0	1088	580	195	40	31	30	30	21	0	121	58	19	5	0	1178	725
NL	1398	721	677	31	0	0	3	0	0	2	0	0	0	0	0	807	416	137	38	55	24	23	7	17	111	47	10	0	0	823	575
YR	3301	1672	1629	91	2	0	7	1	0	8	2	0	0	0	0	1895	996	332	78	86	54	53	28	17	232	105	29	5	0	2001	1300

	AL		*NL*
37	Dan Petry	28	Mario Soto
35	Mike Caldwell	25	Eric Show
34	Frank Viola	23	Joaquin Andujar
32	John Tudor	23	Bob Forsch
30	Jack Morris	23	Eddie Whitson

1984

AL

Tm	Tot	H	A	Consec 2	3	4	1-Inn 3	4	5	One-Game 5	6	7	8	9	10	Men-On-Base 0	1	2	3	Pitchers PH	LO	XN	IP	P	Totals 1	10	20	30	40	Batters RHB	LHB
BAL	137	59	78	4	0	0	1	0	0	0	0	0	0	0	0	73	44	17	3	3	1	4	1	0	10	1	3	0	0	87	50
BOS	141	76	65	2	1	0	1	0	0	0	0	0	0	0	0	73	47	17	4	4	1	3	1	0	7	5	1	0	0	99	42
CAL	143	83	60	2	1	0	1	0	0	0	0	0	0	0	0	82	38	15	8	3	3	1	1	0	7	6	2	0	0	81	62
CHI	155	77	78	7	0	0	0	0	0	0	0	0	0	0	0	103	35	16	1	2	4	5	2	0	10	0	2	2	0	79	76
CLE	141	73	68	2	0	0	0	0	0	1	0	0	0	0	0	74	53	13	1	5	1	1	0	0	11	5	1	0	0	78	63
DET	130	69	61	3	0	0	1	0	0	0	0	0	0	0	0	70	40	16	4	2	1	1	1	0	6	5	2	0	0	55	75
KC	136	59	77	1	0	0	0	0	0	1	0	0	0	0	0	71	50	12	3	2	1	0	3	0	5	6	2	0	0	81	55
MIL	137	68	69	8	0	0	0	0	0	0	0	0	0	0	0	71	46	16	4	2	1	2	0	0	8	5	1	0	0	74	63
MIN	159	77	82	4	0	0	0	0	0	0	0	0	0	0	0	93	45	19	2	8	2	4	2	0	9	5	1	1	0	79	80
NY	120	49	71	5	0	0	0	0	0	0	0	0	0	0	0	63	34	17	6	1	1	4	0	0	12	3	1	0	0	73	47
OAK	155	72	83	7	1	0	2	0	0	0	0	0	0	0	0	92	43	15	5	3	0	3	1	0	10	5	2	0	0	79	76
SEA	138	82	56	2	0	0	0	0	0	0	0	0	0	0	0	82	30	21	5	5	3	4	0	0	5	8	0	0	0	79	59
TEX	148	70	78	3	2	0	2	0	0	1	0	0	0	0	0	89	36	19	4	4	2	1	0	0	7	2	2	1	0	84	64
TOR	140	78	62	2	1	0	2	0	0	1	0	0	0	0	0	76	42	21	1	3	0	4	1	0	7	2	3	0	0	68	72

NL

Tm	Tot	H	A	Consec 2	3	4	1-Inn 3	4	5	One-Game 5	6	7	8	9	10	Men-On-Base 0	1	2	3	Pitchers PH	LO	XN	IP	P	Totals 1	10	20	30	40	Batters RHB	LHB
ATL	122	72	50	2	0	0	1	0	0	0	0	0	0	0	0	78	28	12	4	4	3	0	1	2	8	5	1	0	0	59	63
CHI	99	70	29	2	0	0	0	0	0	0	0	0	0	0	0	65	25	7	2	3	1	0	0	0	13	3	0	0	0	58	41
CIN	128	73	55	1	0	0	0	0	0	0	0	0	0	0	0	63	47	16	2	5	4	2	1	2	11	5	1	0	0	72	56
HOU	91	29	62	3	0	0	0	0	0	0	0	0	0	0	0	53	27	9	2	6	1	2	1	1	9	2	1	0	0	67	24
LA	76	40	36	0	0	0	0	0	0	0	0	0	0	0	0	44	21	10	1	0	0	2	0	1	10	3	0	0	0	51	25
MON	114	56	58	4	0	0	0	0	0	0	0	0	0	0	0	70	33	8	3	2	3	4	3	4	8	4	1	0	0	62	52
NY	104	47	57	1	0	0	0	0	0	0	0	0	0	0	0	55	35	12	2	4	1	1	1	0	12	3	0	0	0	63	41
PHI	101	45	56	1	0	0	0	0	0	0	0	0	0	0	0	59	30	12	0	2	1	2	1	1	10	5	0	0	0	62	39
PIT	102	44	58	2	0	0	0	0	0	0	0	0	0	0	0	62	28	12	0	5	5	3	1	2	7	5	0	0	0	73	29
SD	122	61	61	2	0	0	1	0	0	0	0	0	0	0	0	69	43	8	2	1	2	1	0	2	6	7	0	0	0	69	53
SF	125	63	62	2	1	0	1	0	0	0	0	0	0	0	0	65	38	16	6	6	1	3	0	1	12	1	3	0	0	71	54
STL	94	42	52	2	0	0	0	0	0	0	0	0	0	0	0	46	34	12	2	4	1	5	1	2	11	1	1	0	0	57	37
AL	1980	992	988	52	6	0	10	0	0	4	0	0	0	0	0	1112	583	234	51	47	21	37	13	0	114	58	23	4	0	1096	884
NL	1278	642	636	22	1	0	3	0	0	0	0	0	0	0	0	729	389	134	26	42	23	25	10	18	117	44	8	0	0	764	514
YR	3258	1634	1624	74	7	0	5	0	0	4	0	0	0	0	0	1841	972	368	77	89	44	62	23	18	231	102	31	4	0	1860	1398

	AL		*NL*
35	Mike Smithson	27	Bill Gullickson
31	Lamarr Hoyt	26	Bob Knepper
30	Floyd Bannister	26	Pascual Perez
30	Frank Tanana	26	Mario Soto
28	Frank Viola	25	Mark Davis

1985

AL

Tm	Tot	H	A	Consec 2	3	4	1-Inn 3	4	5	One-Game 5	6	7	8	9	10	Men-On-Base 0	1	2	3	Pitchers PH	LO	XN	IP	P	Totals 1	10	20	30	40	Batters RHB	LHB
BAL	160	87	73	5	0	0	1	0	0	0	0	0	0	0	0	90	48	18	4	3	3	3	0	0	6	4	2	1	0	91	69
BOS	130	64	66	2	0	0	1	0	0	0	0	0	0	0	0	67	51	8	4	2	1	1	0	0	11	2	1	1	0	77	53
CAL	171	93	78	13	0	0	0	0	0	1	0	1	0	0	0	104	46	19	2	3	1	0	1	0	13	1	4	0	0	87	84
CHI	161	83	78	6	0	0	1	0	0	0	0	0	0	0	0	91	48	17	5	3	1	4	0	0	11	2	3	1	0	96	65
CLE	170	76	94	10	0	0	1	0	0	0	0	0	0	0	0	93	53	20	4	3	5	2	1	0	10	7	1	0	0	96	74

Tm	Tot	H	A	Consec 2	3	4	1-Inn 3	4	5	One-Game 5	6	7	8	9	10	Men-On-Base 0	1	2	3	Pitchers PH	LO	XN	IP	P	Totals 1	10	20	30	40	Batters RHB	LHB
DET	141	93	48	4	1	0	2	0	0	1	1	0	0	0	0	89	37	13	2	1	4	7	0	0	7	5	2	0	0	87	54
KC	103	43	60	2	0	0	0	0	0	0	0	0	0	0	0	64	25	11	3	4	1	4	0	0	8	4	0	0	0	54	49
MIL	175	86	89	5	0	0	0	0	0	1	0	0	0	0	0	106	51	17	1	2	5	6	1	0	10	3	3	1	0	97	78
MIN	164	83	81	9	0	0	1	0	0	1	0	0	0	0	0	73	64	22	5	1	2	1	0	0	11	1	4	0	0	85	79
NY	157	67	90	5	0	0	0	0	0	2	0	0	0	0	0	95	46	12	4	5	3	2	1	0	11	2	3	0	0	77	80
OAK	172	71	101	5	0	0	0	0	0	0	1	1	0	0	0	101	48	21	2	1	2	3	2	0	9	7	1	0	0	104	68
SEA	154	78	76	4	0	0	0	0	0	2	0	0	0	0	0	80	50	18	6	3	0	2	2	0	15	3	2	0	0	92	62
TEX	173	102	71	4	0	0	1	0	0	1	0	0	0	0	0	91	47	28	7	4	3	2	0	0	7	8	2	0	0	91	82
TOR	147	78	69	5	1	0	1	0	0	0	0	0	0	0	0	87	47	11	2	4	1	2	1	0	10	2	3	0	0	77	70
NL																															
ATL	134	80	54	3	0	0	0	0	0	1	0	0	0	0	0	69	45	13	7	7	2	4	2	3	9	4	1	0	0	71	63
CHI	156	104	52	5	1	0	1	1	0	2	1	0	0	0	0	85	44	21	6	4	3	3	0	2	13	5	1	0	0	99	57
CIN	131	65	66	2	0	0	0	0	0	0	0	0	0	0	0	75	38	16	2	2	4	1	0	2	10	3	1	1	0	83	48
HOU	119	47	72	1	0	0	0	0	0	0	0	0	0	0	0	72	33	11	3	5	2	5	2	4	10	1	3	0	0	83	36
LA	102	54	48	0	0	0	0	0	0	0	0	0	0	0	0	52	29	20	1	4	0	5	0	1	10	3	0	0	0	77	25
MON	99	45	54	0	0	0	0	0	0	0	0	0	0	0	0	57	25	13	4	4	1	6	0	0	13	3	0	0	0	63	36
NY	111	58	53	2	0	0	0	0	0	0	0	0	0	0	0	71	27	10	3	1	2	5	3	1	10	3	1	0	0	67	44
PHI	115	57	58	2	0	0	1	0	0	0	0	0	0	0	0	62	29	21	3	6	3	3	1	0	9	4	1	0	0	83	32
PIT	107	53	54	0	0	0	0	0	0	0	0	0	0	0	0	54	29	19	5	4	2	2	0	2	14	3	0	0	0	69	38
SD	127	77	50	2	0	0	0	0	0	0	0	0	0	0	0	78	32	15	2	1	1	2	0	0	10	2	2	0	0	74	53
SF	125	67	58	3	0	0	0	0	0	0	0	0	0	0	0	72	39	11	3	6	5	3	1	2	7	7	0	0	0	75	50
STL	98	39	59	1	0	0	0	0	0	0	0	0	0	0	0	65	23	6	4	4	0	2	1	3	7	5	0	0	0	66	32
AL	2178	1104	1074	79	2	0	9	0	0	9	2	2	0	0	0	1231	661	235	51	39	32	39	9	0	139	51	31	4	0	1211	967
NL	1424	746	678	21	1	0	2	1	0	3	1	0	0	0	0	812	393	176	43	48	25	41	10	20	122	43	10	1	0	910	514
YR	3602	1850	1752	100	3	0	8	0	0	12	3	2	0	0	0	2043	1054	411	94	87	57	80	19	20	261	94	41	5	0	2121	1481

AL		*NL*	
34	Danny Darwin	30	Mario Soto
34	Scott McGregor	29	Tom Browning
31	Bruce Hurst	27	Eric Show
30	Floyd Bannister	24	Rick Mahler
29	Multiple Players Tied	23	Multiple Players Tied

1986

Tm	Tot	H	A	Consec 2	3	4	1-Inn 3	4	5	One-Game 5	6	7	8	9	10	Men-On-Base 0	1	2	3	Pitchers PH	LO	XN	IP	P	Totals 1	10	20	30	40	Batters RHB	LHB
AL																															
BAL	177	98	79	3	0	0	0	0	0	1	0	0	0	0	0	102	53	20	2	3	5	2	1	0	8	3	0	3	0	106	71
BOS	167	85	82	7	0	0	1	0	0	0	0	0	0	0	0	100	52	12	3	5	4	2	0	0	8	3	2	1	0	100	67
CAL	153	84	69	6	0	0	0	0	0	0	0	0	0	0	0	82	38	29	4	5	1	3	0	0	12	4	1	1	0	86	67
CHI	143	63	80	7	0	0	1	0	0	0	0	0	0	0	0	84	38	18	3	4	4	1	2	0	11	3	2	0	0	75	68
CLE	167	80	87	7	1	0	2	0	0	1	0	0	0	0	0	99	42	24	2	4	5	2	0	0	11	4	1	1	0	100	67
DET	183	83	100	10	0	0	1	0	0	0	0	0	0	0	0	118	44	16	5	8	9	3	1	0	6	5	1	1	1	112	71
KC	121	46	75	2	0	0	0	0	0	0	0	0	0	0	0	74	31	13	3	0	3	1	1	0	6	6	1	0	0	62	59
MIL	158	79	79	5	0	0	0	1	0	0	1	0	0	0	0	95	45	15	3	2	3	2	1	0	11	2	2	1	0	90	68
MIN	200	107	93	9	1	0	2	0	0	0	0	1	0	0	0	115	56	21	8	3	5	2	1	0	11	4	1	1	1	102	98
NY	175	96	79	5	0	0	0	0	0	0	0	0	0	0	0	102	48	23	2	1	0	1	1	0	11	5	2	0	0	111	64
OAK	166	81	85	5	1	0	2	0	0	1	0	0	0	0	0	95	54	11	6	3	5	2	2	0	11	6	2	0	0	97	69
SEA	171	99	72	5	0	0	1	0	0	0	0	0	0	0	0	101	49	18	3	1	6	5	2	0	11	3	2	1	0	98	73
TEX	145	61	84	5	0	0	2	0	0	0	0	0	0	0	0	83	38	20	4	3	3	4	0	0	7	5	1	1	0	88	57
TOR	164	89	75	7	0	0	4	0	0	2	0	0	0	0	0	90	54	18	2	9	4	5	0	0	11	1	4	0	0	91	73
NL																															
ATL	117	71	46	2	1	0	1	0	0	0	0	0	0	0	0	72	26	16	3	6	1	3	0	1	14	1	1	0	0	68	49
CHI	143	79	64	6	0	0	0	0	0	0	0	0	0	0	0	76	39	26	2	8	4	6	1	2	13	3	2	0	0	84	59
CIN	136	73	63	4	0	0	0	1	0	0	0	0	0	0	0	76	43	12	5	4	0	3	1	3	5	4	2	0	0	86	50
HOU	116	56	60	2	0	0	0	0	0	0	0	0	0	0	0	70	33	13	0	5	1	5	1	0	13	4	0	0	0	74	42
LA	115	46	69	2	0	0	0	0	0	0	0	0	0	0	0	68	35	8	4	6	1	3	0	1	9	5	0	0	0	68	47
MON	119	58	61	3	0	0	1	0	0	0	0	0	0	0	0	57	39	19	4	5	1	5	2	3	11	6	0	0	0	65	54
NY	103	47	56	4	0	0	1	0	0	0	0	0	0	0	0	58	35	10	0	6	1	2	0	0	7	4	1	0	0	64	39
PHI	130	49	81	3	0	0	0	0	0	0	0	0	0	0	0	88	26	14	2	2	6	3	1	3	9	4	2	0	0	69	61
PIT	138	75	63	3	0	0	0	0	0	0	0	0	0	0	0	77	39	16	6	4	4	3	0	3	10	6	1	0	0	88	50
SD	150	78	72	4	0	0	1	0	0	0	0	0	0	0	0	84	38	25	3	3	0	5	0	2	13	3	2	0	0	94	56

Tm	Tot	H	A	Consec 2	3	4	1-Inn 3	4	5	One-Game 5	6	7	8	9	10	Men-On-Base 0	1	2	3	Pitchers PH	LO	XN	IP	P	Totals 1	10	20	30	40	Batters RHB	LHB
SF	121	61	60	1	0	0	0	0	0	0	0	0	0	0	0	71	35	14	1	3	1	6	0	3	11	3	1	0	0	69	52
STL	135	63	72	3	0	0	0	0	0	0	0	0	0	0	0	88	34	11	2	5	8	1	0	3	9	5	1	0	0	85	50
AL	2290	1151	1139	83	3	0	16	1	0	5	1	1	0	0	0	1340	642	258	50	51	57	35	12	0	135	54	22	11	2	1318	972
NL	1523	756	767	37	1	0	4	1	0	0	0	0	0	0	0	885	422	184	32	57	28	45	6	24	124	48	13	0	0	914	609
YR	3813	1907	1906	120	4	0	16	1	0	5	1	1	0	0	0	2225	1064	442	82	108	85	80	18	24	259	102	35	11	2	2232	1581

	AL		*NL*
50	Bert Blyleven	28	Kevin Gross
40	Jack Morris	27	Lamarr Hoyt
37	Frank Viola	26	Tom Browning
35	Scott McGregor	25	Rick Mahler
34	Ken Schrom	24	Multiple Players Tied

1987

AL

Tm	Tot	H	A	Consec 2	3	4	1-Inn 3	4	5	One-Game 5	6	7	8	9	10	Men-On-Base 0	1	2	3	Pitchers PH	LO	XN	IP	P	Totals 1	10	20	30	40	Batters RHB	LHB
BAL	226	125	101	9	1	0	4	0	0	4	0	0	0	0	1	139	54	27	6	4	6	2	0	0	9	5	2	2	0	127	99
BOS	190	75	115	5	0	0	1	0	0	1	0	0	0	0	0	99	57	32	2	4	2	7	0	0	5	6	0	2	0	116	74
CAL	212	116	96	3	0	0	0	0	0	1	1	0	0	0	0	111	71	25	5	1	2	3	0	0	6	4	2	2	0	112	100
CHI	189	90	99	9	0	0	2	0	0	1	2	0	0	0	0	118	45	22	4	7	4	5	1	0	10	3	3	1	0	101	88
CLE	219	118	101	8	0	0	3	0	0	4	0	0	0	0	0	130	51	33	5	3	10	2	0	0	12	4	4	0	0	136	83
DET	180	101	79	2	0	0	0	0	0	1	0	0	0	0	0	108	57	12	3	4	4	4	1	0	6	2	2	2	0	91	89
KC	128	57	71	5	0	0	1	0	0	0	0	0	0	0	0	73	42	11	2	1	5	1	2	0	9	3	2	0	0	78	50
MIL	169	79	90	4	0	0	0	0	0	0	0	0	0	0	0	97	52	18	2	3	1	3	0	0	10	2	2	1	0	98	71
MIN	210	92	118	5	0	0	1	0	0	2	0	0	0	0	0	116	59	28	7	9	2	0	1	0	7	6	2	0	1	85	125
NY	179	88	91	8	1	0	2	0	0	1	0	0	0	0	0	114	45	17	3	2	5	1	0	0	15	4	1	1	0	109	70
OAK	176	75	101	9	0	0	2	0	0	1	0	0	0	0	0	99	54	20	3	3	2	2	4	0	13	5	1	1	0	102	74
SEA	199	115	84	4	0	0	0	0	0	1	0	0	0	0	0	124	52	23	0	2	6	3	0	0	11	2	2	2	0	114	85
TEX	199	111	88	6	0	0	0	0	0	3	0	0	0	0	0	115	57	20	7	4	2	4	1	0	10	6	0	2	0	109	90
TOR	158	83	75	2	0	0	0	0	0	1	0	0	0	0	0	95	45	12	6	4	4	3	1	0	5	5	2	1	0	91	67

NL

Tm	Tot	H	A	Consec 2	3	4	1-Inn 3	4	5	One-Game 5	6	7	8	9	10	Men-On-Base 0	1	2	3	Pitchers PH	LO	XN	IP	P	Totals 1	10	20	30	40	Batters RHB	LHB
ATL	163	88	75	6	1	0	2	0	0	1	0	1	0	0	0	88	50	23	2	6	4	3	2	1	11	5	2	0	0	88	75
CHI	159	90	69	4	0	0	1	0	0	1	0	0	0	0	0	89	52	15	3	1	3	4	0	3	9	3	3	0	0	82	77
CIN	170	97	73	7	0	0	0	0	0	1	0	0	0	0	0	112	41	14	3	4	2	3	3	4	11	1	3	1	0	97	73
HOU	141	46	95	4	0	0	1	0	0	0	1	0	0	0	0	85	34	13	9	6	6	2	0	0	10	2	3	0	0	83	58
LA	130	56	74	2	0	0	0	0	0	0	0	0	0	0	0	70	46	13	1	1	2	1	1	1	8	4	2	0	0	77	53
MON	145	74	71	6	0	0	1	0	0	2	0	0	0	0	0	78	49	16	2	5	3	1	0	3	14	4	1	0	0	78	67
NY	135	63	72	8	0	0	0	0	0	0	0	0	0	0	0	81	36	12	6	8	5	5	0	1	11	5	1	0	0	77	58
PHI	167	78	89	8	0	0	1	0	0	2	0	0	0	0	0	104	39	19	5	6	0	3	1	2	8	4	2	1	0	104	63
PIT	164	84	80	4	0	0	0	0	0	0	0	0	0	0	0	92	42	24	6	5	6	4	2	0	12	4	3	0	0	96	68
SD	175	97	78	5	0	0	1	0	0	0	0	0	0	0	0	105	49	18	3	5	5	2	0	4	11	5	1	1	0	103	72
SF	146	72	74	2	1	0	1	0	0	0	0	0	0	0	0	82	42	19	3	3	6	7	1	1	14	4	2	0	0	77	69
STL	129	60	69	2	0	0	0	0	0	0	0	0	0	0	0	81	29	17	2	3	2	6	0	0	8	6	0	0	0	93	36
AL	2634	1325	1309	79	2	0	16	0	0	21	3	0	0	0	1	1538	741	300	55	51	55	40	11	0	128	57	25	17	1	1469	1165
NL	1824	905	919	58	2	0	8	0	0	7	1	1	0	0	0	1067	509	203	45	53	44	41	10	20	127	47	23	3	0	1055	769
YR	4458	2230	2228	137	4	0	11	0	0	28	4	1	0	0	0	2605	1250	503	100	104	99	81	21	20	255	104	48	20	1	2524	1934

	AL		*NL*
46	Bert Blyleven	36	Eddie Whitson
39	Jack Morris	34	Don Carman
38	Floyd Bannister	33	Bill Gullickson
38	Don Sutton	28	Jamie Moyer
38	Curt Young	28	Ted Power

1988

AL

Tm	Tot	H	A	Consec 2	3	4	1-Inn 3	4	5	One-Game 5	6	7	8	9	10	Men-On-Base 0	1	2	3	Pitchers PH	LO	XN	IP	P	Totals 1	10	20	30	40	Batters RHB	LHB
BAL	153	77	76	5	0	0	0	0	0	0	0	0	0	0	0	78	55	13	7	2	2	2	0	0	13	7	1	0	0	83	70
BOS	143	73	70	4	1	0	2	0	0	1	0	0	0	0	0	81	46	16	0	1	1	2	0	0	8	2	3	0	0	87	56
CAL	135	71	64	6	0	0	0	0	0	1	0	0	0	0	0	80	41	12	2	4	1	2	0	0	12	4	0	1	0	65	70
CHI	138	64	74	5	0	0	1	0	0	1	0	0	0	0	0	77	47	11	3	5	3	2	2	0	13	4	2	0	0	80	58
CLE	120	52	68	2	0	0	1	0	0	0	0	0	0	0	0	62	42	15	1	1	3	2	0	0	9	4	1	0	0	72	48

				Consec			1-Inn			One-Game						Men-On-Base				Pitchers					Totals					Batters	
Tm	Tot	H	A	2	3	4	3	4	5	5	6	7	8	9	10	0	1	2	3	PH	LO	XN	IP	P	1	10	20	30	40	RHB	LHB
DET	150	76	74	5	0	0	0	0	0	1	0	0	0	0	0	82	47	18	3	1	3	5	0	0	8	1	3	1	0	84	66
KC	102	37	65	1	0	0	0	0	0	1	0	0	0	0	0	61	31	7	3	0	2	0	2	0	9	2	2	0	0	71	31
MIL	125	65	60	4	0	0	0	0	0	1	0	0	0	0	0	76	33	16	0	2	2	0	1	0	7	6	1	0	0	74	51
MIN	146	79	67	5	0	0	2	0	0	0	0	0	0	0	0	86	35	23	2	1	3	3	1	0	13	4	2	0	0	74	72
NY	157	75	82	2	0	0	0	0	0	0	0	0	0	0	0	94	47	12	4	1	1	3	1	0	12	4	2	0	0	100	57
OAK	116	47	69	5	0	0	1	0	0	1	0	0	0	0	0	65	34	16	1	2	1	4	3	0	8	2	2	0	0	66	50
SEA	144	81	63	5	0	0	1	0	0	1	0	0	0	0	0	83	45	12	4	4	3	1	0	0	11	3	1	1	0	88	56
TEX	129	67	62	1	0	0	0	0	0	0	0	0	0	0	0	67	41	12	9	1	3	2	0	0	14	3	2	0	0	82	47
TOR	143	73	70	4	0	0	0	0	0	0	0	0	0	0	0	99	25	18	1	1	5	5	3	0	8	5	2	0	0	94	49
NL																															
ATL	108	64	44	0	0	0	0	0	0	0	0	0	0	0	0	62	35	9	2	2	1	1	0	0	12	4	0	0	0	63	45
CHI	115	71	44	4	0	0	0	0	0	0	0	0	0	0	0	63	39	10	3	3	2	5	0	1	13	3	1	0	0	61	54
CIN	121	71	50	3	1	0	1	0	0	0	0	0	0	0	0	65	42	13	1	4	3	3	1	3	15	1	0	1	0	71	50
HOU	123	50	73	4	0	0	0	0	0	0	0	0	0	0	0	76	30	14	3	2	3	3	0	2	10	3	2	0	0	71	52
LA	84	38	46	2	0	0	1	0	0	0	0	0	0	0	0	53	20	9	2	1	3	2	0	0	12	3	0	0	0	44	40
MON	122	62	60	2	0	0	0	0	0	0	1	0	0	0	0	85	26	9	2	2	3	5	0	1	11	4	1	0	0	69	53
NY	78	34	44	3	0	0	0	0	0	0	0	0	0	0	0	47	24	7	0	1	0	3	0	1	8	2	1	0	0	46	32
PHI	118	64	54	4	0	0	1	0	0	0	0	0	0	0	0	72	31	13	2	5	4	1	1	2	13	1	2	0	0	71	47
PIT	108	50	58	2	0	0	0	0	0	0	0	0	0	0	0	64	32	10	2	1	0	1	1	0	12	3	1	0	0	68	40
SD	112	56	56	2	0	0	0	0	0	0	0	0	0	0	0	66	37	9	0	3	1	1	0	1	8	4	1	0	0	71	41
SF	99	42	57	1	0	0	0	0	0	0	0	0	0	0	0	65	22	10	2	3	5	3	0	1	13	5	0	0	0	68	31
STL	91	39	52	4	0	0	0	0	0	1	0	0	0	0	0	46	33	10	2	3	3	3	0	1	13	2	0	0	0	48	43
AL	1901	937	964	54	1	0	8	0	0	8	0	0	0	0	0	1091	569	201	40	26	33	33	13	0	145	51	24	3	0	1120	781
NL	1279	641	638	31	1	0	3	0	0	1	1	0	0	0	0	764	371	123	21	30	28	31	3	13	140	35	9	1	0	751	528
YR	3180	1578	1602	85	2	0	6	0	0	9	1	0	0	0	0	1855	940	324	61	56	61	64	16	13	285	86	33	4	0	1871	1309

AL		*NL*	
33	Willie Fraser	36	Tom Browning
32	Mark Langston	27	Shane Rawley
30	Doyle Alexander	24	Ron Darling
27	Richard Dotson	22	Eric Show
26	Multiple Players Tied	21	Multiple Players Tied

1989

AL

Tm	Tot	H	A	Consec 2	3	4	1-Inn 3	4	5	One-Game 5	6	7	8	9	10	Men-On-Base 0	1	2	3	PH	LO	XN	IP	P	Totals 1	10	20	30	40	RHB	LHB
BAL	134	65	69	1	0	0	0	0	0	0	0	0	0	0	0	69	50	14	1	0	3	0	1	0	9	5	2	0	0	81	53
BOS	131	70	61	3	0	0	0	0	0	0	0	0	0	0	0	77	36	14	4	1	4	3	1	0	10	3	2	0	0	73	58
CAL	113	75	38	3	0	0	0	0	0	0	0	0	0	0	0	72	27	12	2	3	2	3	0	0	8	4	1	0	0	65	48
CHI	144	58	86	2	0	0	0	0	0	0	0	0	0	0	0	89	37	15	3	2	4	3	0	0	12	6	1	0	0	77	67
CLE	107	51	56	1	0	0	0	0	0	0	0	0	0	0	0	69	27	10	1	3	5	1	0	0	11	5	0	0	0	63	44
DET	150	77	73	1	0	0	2	0	0	0	0	0	0	0	0	87	39	18	6	4	0	2	0	0	13	3	3	0	0	83	67
KC	86	26	60	2	0	0	0	0	0	0	0	0	0	0	0	48	23	13	2	1	0	0	0	0	12	4	0	0	0	52	34
MIL	129	54	75	1	0	0	0	0	0	1	0	0	0	0	0	64	44	20	1	4	0	3	0	0	13	4	0	0	0	75	54
MIN	139	69	70	5	0	0	0	0	0	1	0	0	0	0	0	79	42	14	4	4	3	0	1	0	15	4	1	0	0	88	51
NY	150	88	62	2	0	0	0	0	0	2	0	0	0	0	0	85	42	21	2	2	1	3	2	0	16	3	1	0	0	84	66
OAK	103	51	52	3	0	0	0	0	0	0	0	0	0	0	0	65	27	7	4	2	2	3	1	0	8	4	1	0	0	65	38
SEA	114	67	47	7	0	0	0	0	0	0	0	0	0	0	0	62	36	13	3	0	2	1	0	0	16	3	0	0	0	57	57
TEX	119	63	56	5	0	0	0	0	0	0	1	0	0	0	0	70	31	14	4	1	0	2	1	0	11	4	1	0	0	70	49
TOR	99	50	49	1	0	0	0	0	0	0	0	0	0	0	0	60	26	10	3	2	2	1	0	0	12	5	0	0	0	66	33
NL																															
ATL	114	61	53	1	0	0	0	0	0	0	0	0	0	0	0	63	38	8	5	4	2	3	1	0	12	3	1	0	0	72	42
CHI	106	64	42	1	0	0	0	0	0	0	0	0	0	0	0	62	32	10	2	3	2	2	1	0	9	4	0	0	0	53	53
CIN	125	71	54	1	0	0	0	0	0	1	0	0	0	0	0	70	38	15	2	2	2	2	2	2	11	3	0	1	0	77	48
HOU	105	50	55	3	0	0	0	0	0	0	0	0	0	0	0	60	36	7	2	3	3	2	0	0	8	4	1	0	0	52	53
LA	95	46	49	3	0	0	0	0	0	0	0	0	0	0	0	59	21	11	4	6	1	0	0	1	12	2	1	0	0	52	43
MON	120	60	60	4	0	0	1	0	0	0	0	0	0	0	0	75	26	18	1	2	3	4	1	0	14	3	2	0	0	64	56
NY	115	56	59	2	0	0	0	0	0	0	0	0	0	0	0	63	35	16	1	1	1	2	0	3	13	2	2	0	0	64	51
PHI	127	67	60	2	1	0	1	0	0	0	0	0	0	0	0	78	35	10	4	2	2	2	1	3	16	3	1	0	0	79	48
PIT	121	62	59	0	0	0	0	0	0	0	0	0	0	0	0	65	35	17	4	3	2	2	0	1	11	4	2	0	0	78	43
SD	133	82	51	4	0	0	0	0	0	0	0	0	0	0	0	77	41	15	0	5	1	3	0	1	12	4	1	0	0	75	58

				Consec			1-Inn			One-Game						Men-On-Base				Pitchers					Totals					Batters	
Tm	Tot	H	A	2	3	4	3	4	5	5	6	7	8	9	10	0	1	2	3	PH	LO	XN	IP	P	1	10	20	30	40	RHB	LHB
SF	120	61	59	2	0	0	1	0	0	0	0	0	0	0	0	65	31	21	3	2	5	2	1	4	14	4	1	0	0	66	54
STL	84	36	48	2	0	0	1	0	0	0	1	0	0	0	0	44	28	9	3	3	3	1	0	3	13	2	0	0	0	46	38
AL	1718	864	854	37	0	0	2	0	0	4	1	0	0	0	0	996	487	195	40	29	28	25	7	0	166	57	13	0	0	999	719
NL	1365	716	649	25	1	0	4	0	0	1	1	0	0	0	0	781	396	157	31	36	27	25	7	18	145	38	12	1	0	778	587
YR	3083	1580	1503	62	1	0	4	0	0	5	2	0	0	0	0	1777	883	352	71	65	55	50	14	18	311	95	25	1	0	1777	1306

	AL		*NL*
28	Doyle Alexander	31	Tom Browning
28	Charlie Hough	23	Mike Scott
26	Mike Witt	22	Don Robinson
24	Dave Schmidt	22	John Smiley
23	Multiple Players Tied	22	Eddie Whitson

1990

Tm	Tot	H	A	Consec 2	3	4	1-Inn 3	4	5	One-Game 5	6	7	8	9	10	Men-On-Base 0	1	2	3	PH	LO	XN	IP	P	Totals 1	10	20	30	40	RHB	LHB
AL																															
BAL	161	82	79	2	0	0	0	0	0	1	0	0	0	0	0	85	55	19	2	1	2	1	0	0	16	2	1	1	0	89	72
BOS	92	44	48	2	0	0	0	0	0	0	0	0	0	0	0	56	24	9	3	1	3	4	1	0	11	4	0	0	0	53	39
CAL	106	55	51	4	0	0	1	0	0	0	0	0	0	0	0	66	22	17	1	2	3	2	1	0	11	4	0	0	0	71	35
CHI	106	53	53	2	0	0	0	0	0	0	0	0	0	0	0	66	28	10	2	0	1	1	0	0	10	4	1	0	0	65	41
CLE	163	86	77	2	2	0	3	0	0	0	0	1	0	0	0	107	47	9	0	0	2	2	1	0	12	5	2	0	0	108	55
DET	154	75	79	7	0	0	1	0	0	1	0	0	0	0	0	85	46	18	5	2	1	2	0	0	10	2	3	0	0	105	49
KC	116	46	70	3	0	0	0	0	0	1	0	0	0	0	0	63	26	25	2	6	2	0	3	0	19	2	0	0	0	62	54
MIL	121	59	62	4	1	0	1	0	0	1	0	0	0	0	0	71	33	13	4	1	2	3	0	0	12	5	0	0	0	85	36
MIN	134	69	65	3	0	0	0	0	0	0	1	0	0	0	0	72	44	16	2	2	2	1	3	0	11	1	3	0	0	91	43
NY	144	78	66	2	0	0	0	0	0	0	0	0	0	0	0	80	36	22	6	2	1	4	3	0	13	2	2	0	0	98	46
OAK	123	52	71	5	0	0	1	0	0	0	0	0	0	0	0	72	34	16	1	1	1	3	2	0	6	3	2	0	0	68	55
SEA	120	60	60	4	0	0	0	0	0	0	0	0	0	0	0	74	30	15	1	4	2	4	1	0	13	3	1	0	0	81	39
TEX	113	59	54	2	0	0	0	0	0	0	0	0	0	0	0	66	27	16	4	2	3	0	0	0	9	4	1	0	0	74	39
TOR	143	82	61	4	1	0	2	0	0	1	1	0	0	0	0	80	43	15	5	3	3	3	0	0	10	4	2	0	0	97	46
NL																															
ATL	128	70	58	0	0	0	0	0	0	1	0	0	0	0	0	66	38	21	3	4	1	4	0	0	16	3	1	0	0	74	54
CHI	121	73	48	3	0	0	0	0	0	0	0	0	0	0	0	68	38	14	1	4	0	2	0	2	12	6	0	0	0	63	58
CIN	124	73	51	1	0	0	1	0	0	0	0	0	0	0	0	83	28	7	6	4	2	5	0	2	9	5	1	0	0	65	59
HOU	130	47	83	3	1	0	1	0	0	1	0	0	0	0	0	80	34	14	2	3	2	4	0	1	9	1	4	0	0	71	59
LA	137	73	64	2	0	0	1	0	0	0	0	0	0	0	0	79	35	18	5	6	1	1	0	2	15	3	1	0	0	77	60
MON	127	62	65	3	0	0	2	0	0	1	0	0	0	0	0	76	42	7	2	1	5	3	0	2	14	4	0	0	0	57	70
NY	119	52	67	2	0	0	0	0	0	1	0	0	0	0	0	75	27	12	5	3	1	2	2	2	7	4	2	0	0	70	49
PHI	124	67	57	4	0	0	0	0	0	0	0	0	0	0	0	61	42	17	4	2	3	0	1	0	6	9	0	0	0	65	59
PIT	135	63	72	2	0	0	0	0	0	1	0	0	0	0	0	87	35	12	1	2	6	2	1	0	15	5	0	0	0	75	60
SD	147	78	69	3	0	0	1	0	0	0	0	0	0	0	0	96	31	20	0	5	5	4	0	1	9	5	2	0	0	79	68
SF	131	70	61	4	0	0	0	0	0	0	0	0	0	0	0	70	39	19	3	6	2	2	0	1	18	4	0	0	0	64	67
STL	98	47	51	2	0	0	1	0	0	0	0	0	0	0	0	57	32	7	2	5	1	0	1	1	13	4	0	0	0	52	46
AL	1796	900	896	46	4	0	9	0	0	5	2	1	0	0	0	1043	495	220	38	27	28	30	15	0	163	45	18	1	0	1147	649
NL	1521	775	746	29	1	0	7	0	0	5	0	0	0	0	0	898	421	168	34	45	29	29	5	14	143	53	11	0	0	812	709
YR	3317	1675	1642	75	5	0	8	0	0	10	2	1	0	0	0	1941	916	388	72	72	57	59	20	14	306	98	29	1	0	1959	1358

	AL		*NL*
30	Dave Johnson	28	Dennis Rasmussen
27	Scott Sanderson	27	Mike Scott
27	Greg Swindell	24	Tom Browning
26	Multiple Players Tied	22	Ramon Martinez
		21	Multiple Players Tied

1991

Tm	Tot	H	A	Consec 2	3	4	1-Inn 3	4	5	One-Game 5	6	7	8	9	10	Men-On-Base 0	1	2	3	PH	LO	XN	IP	P	Totals 1	10	20	30	40	RHB	LHB
AL																															
BAL	147	72	75	3	0	0	0	0	0	0	0	0	0	0	0	84	38	22	3	2	0	3	1	0	13	6	0	0	0	84	63
BOS	147	76	71	6	0	0	1	0	0	0	0	0	0	0	0	81	45	19	2	8	2	1	0	0	9	6	0	0	0	107	40
CAL	141	74	67	4	0	0	0	0	0	0	0	0	0	0	0	75	48	15	3	3	2	3	1	0	13	2	1	1	0	88	53
CHI	154	79	75	4	0	0	0	0	0	0	0	0	0	0	0	88	41	23	2	3	4	4	1	0	9	5	2	0	0	96	58
CLE	110	41	69	1	0	0	0	0	0	0	0	0	0	0	0	50	37	18	5	0	2	2	0	0	16	1	1	0	0	76	34

				Consec			1-Inn			One-Game						Men-On-Base				Pitchers					Totals					Batters	
Tm	Tot	H	A	2	3	4	3	4	5	5	6	7	8	9	10	0	1	2	3	PH	LO	XN	IP	P	1	10	20	30	40	RHB	LHB
DET	148	89	59	5	0	0	0	0	0	2	1	0	0	0	0	86	39	20	3	1	4	3	2	0	12	3	2	0	0	83	65
KC	105	40	65	3	0	0	0	0	0	0	0	0	0	0	0	54	32	12	7	2	0	3	0	0	5	7	0	0	0	57	48
MIL	147	73	74	3	0	0	1	0	0	0	0	0	0	0	0	84	39	19	5	3	2	7	1	0	11	7	0	0	0	75	72
MIN	139	75	64	4	0	0	0	0	0	0	1	0	0	0	0	81	38	16	4	3	3	2	0	0	9	5	2	0	0	89	50
NY	152	84	68	3	0	0	1	0	0	0	0	0	0	0	0	76	55	15	6	4	4	2	0	0	12	4	2	0	0	78	74
OAK	155	67	88	3	0	0	0	0	0	0	0	0	0	0	0	87	45	19	4	6	3	3	3	0	13	4	2	0	0	98	57
SEA	136	69	67	2	0	0	0	0	0	0	0	0	0	0	0	86	41	7	2	3	6	4	1	0	10	4	0	1	0	91	45
TEX	151	77	74	3	0	0	0	0	0	0	0	0	0	0	0	82	47	18	4	2	2	4	3	0	12	8	0	0	0	99	52
TOR	121	72	49	2	0	0	0	0	0	0	0	0	0	0	0	54	46	17	4	5	2	5	0	0	12	2	2	0	0	74	47
NL																															
ATL	118	73	45	1	0	0	0	0	0	0	0	0	0	0	0	66	35	13	4	4	5	2	2	3	15	3	1	0	0	71	47
CHI	117	75	42	1	0	0	0	0	0	1	0	0	0	0	0	63	37	11	6	7	3	3	0	1	11	5	0	0	0	46	71
CIN	127	77	50	5	0	0	0	0	0	1	0	0	0	0	0	77	38	11	1	1	2	1	1	1	14	0	1	1	0	67	60
HOU	129	44	85	5	1	0	3	0	0	0	0	0	0	0	0	72	37	16	4	2	0	5	0	0	14	4	0	0	0	62	67
LA	96	46	50	0	0	0	0	0	0	0	0	0	0	0	0	63	21	10	2	0	1	2	0	0	7	5	0	0	0	50	46
MON	111	33	78	5	0	0	0	0	0	0	0	0	0	0	0	58	35	16	2	4	2	3	0	2	14	3	0	0	0	58	53
NY	108	55	53	2	0	0	0	0	0	0	0	0	0	0	0	56	40	11	1	5	1	2	1	1	12	3	1	0	0	57	51
PHI	111	53	58	6	0	0	0	0	0	0	0	0	0	0	0	64	31	15	1	4	0	3	0	1	13	4	0	0	0	62	49
PIT	117	55	62	2	0	0	0	0	0	0	0	0	0	0	0	63	39	11	4	8	0	7	0	0	8	6	0	0	0	72	45
SD	139	72	67	3	0	0	0	0	0	0	0	0	0	0	0	87	30	16	6	3	5	4	0	3	10	6	1	0	0	74	65
SF	143	62	81	7	0	0	1	0	0	0	0	0	0	0	0	89	36	17	1	7	1	3	1	0	9	6	1	0	0	75	68
STL	114	41	73	1	0	0	0	0	0	0	0	0	0	0	0	64	33	14	3	5	2	3	1	0	11	5	0	0	0	65	49
AL	1953	988	965	46	0	0	3	0	0	2	2	0	0	0	0	1068	591	240	54	45	36	46	13	0	156	64	14	2	0	1195	758
NL	1430	686	744	38	1	0	4	0	0	2	0	0	0	0	0	822	412	161	35	50	22	38	6	12	138	50	5	1	0	759	671
YR	3383	1674	1709	84	1	0	3	0	0	4	2	0	0	0	0	1890	1003	401	89	95	58	84	19	12	294	114	19	3	0	1954	1429

AL		*NL*	
31	Rich DeLucia	32	Tom Browning
30	Mark Langston	25	Jack Armstrong
26	Frank Tanana	25	Bud Black
25	Bob Welch	25	Frank Viola
24	Multiple Players Tied	23	Andy Benes

1992

				Consec			1-Inn			One-Game						Men-On-Base				Pitchers					Totals					Batters	
Tm	Tot	H	A	2	3	4	3	4	5	5	6	7	8	9	10	0	1	2	3	PH	LO	XN	IP	P	1	10	20	30	40	RHB	LHB
AL																															
BAL	124	69	55	3	1	0	1	0	0	0	0	0	0	0	0	73	34	15	2	1	3	1	0	0	10	2	1	1	0	76	48
BOS	107	46	61	0	0	0	0	0	0	0	0	0	0	0	0	62	33	10	2	0	1	3	0	0	8	6	0	0	0	78	29
CAL	130	60	70	1	0	0	1	0	0	1	0	0	0	0	0	81	31	16	2	0	2	0	2	0	10	5	1	0	0	97	33
CHI	123	62	61	5	0	0	0	0	0	0	0	0	0	0	0	71	34	14	4	0	3	2	1	0	5	4	2	0	0	76	47
CLE	159	94	65	7	0	0	1	0	0	0	0	0	0	0	0	77	54	24	4	2	2	5	0	0	14	4	2	0	0	107	52
DET	155	90	65	8	0	0	0	0	0	0	0	0	0	0	0	92	46	10	7	1	2	2	0	0	9	4	1	1	0	103	52
KC	106	41	65	2	0	0	0	0	0	0	0	0	0	0	0	58	33	13	2	1	0	2	0	0	18	2	0	0	0	61	45
MIL	127	51	76	3	0	0	0	0	0	0	0	0	0	0	0	76	33	14	4	0	2	2	0	0	10	1	3	0	0	80	47
MIN	121	56	65	4	0	0	0	0	0	0	0	0	0	0	0	72	24	21	4	4	4	1	1	0	12	4	0	0	0	76	45
NY	129	70	59	4	0	0	1	1	0	1	0	0	0	0	0	74	33	19	3	5	4	3	0	0	13	4	1	0	0	76	53
OAK	129	73	56	3	0	0	0	0	0	0	0	0	0	0	0	87	29	12	1	1	5	0	0	0	12	3	2	0	0	80	49
SEA	129	63	66	2	0	0	1	0	0	1	0	0	0	0	0	60	41	18	10	3	2	3	1	0	17	4	0	0	0	86	43
TEX	113	63	50	1	0	0	0	0	0	0	0	0	0	0	0	59	28	21	5	1	2	1	0	0	19	3	0	0	0	68	45
TOR	124	60	64	6	0	0	0	0	0	0	0	0	0	0	0	75	36	11	2	2	2	0	0	0	10	2	2	0	0	83	41
NL																															
ATL	89	45	44	2	0	0	0	0	0	0	0	0	0	0	0	53	27	6	3	3	1	3	1	1	13	2	0	0	0	44	45
CHI	107	49	58	2	0	0	1	0	0	0	0	0	0	0	0	59	36	9	3	3	0	5	1	0	13	3	0	0	0	46	61
CIN	109	60	49	2	0	0	0	0	0	0	0	0	0	0	0	62	35	9	3	6	3	2	0	1	13	4	0	0	0	58	51
HOU	114	41	73	4	1	0	1	1	0	0	0	0	0	0	0	63	33	17	1	6	1	0	0	0	12	4	0	0	0	54	60
LA	82	33	49	2	0	0	0	0	0	0	0	0	0	0	0	47	23	10	2	3	2	1	0	2	9	4	0	0	0	32	50
MON	92	48	44	0	0	0	0	0	0	0	0	0	0	0	0	52	24	11	5	3	2	3	0	0	14	4	0	0	0	43	49
NY	98	49	49	1	0	0	0	0	0	0	0	0	0	0	0	59	26	10	3	2	3	1	0	1	15	3	0	0	0	54	44
PHI	113	49	64	3	0	0	0	0	0	0	0	0	0	0	0	64	35	12	2	1	2	0	2	3	16	2	1	0	0	66	47
PIT	101	37	64	3	0	0	0	0	0	0	0	0	0	0	0	51	22	24	4	10	2	8	2	1	14	4	0	0	0	45	56
SD	111	64	47	1	0	0	0	0	0	0	0	0	0	0	0	64	41	5	1	4	4	2	1	0	11	3	1	0	0	47	64
SF	128	60	68	5	0	0	0	0	0	0	0	0	0	0	0	75	37	12	4	6	3	5	0	2	13	3	1	0	0	66	62

				Consec			1-Inn			One-Game						Men-On-Base				Pitchers					Totals					Batters	
Tm	Tot	H	A	2	3	4	3	4	5	5	6	7	8	9	10	0	1	2	3	PH	LO	XN	IP	P	1	10	20	30	40	RHB	LHB
STL	118	52	66	3	0	0	0	0	0	0	0	0	0	0	0	69	35	13	1	1	2	3	1	1	8	5	1	0	0	55	63
AL	1776	898	878	49	1	0	5	1	0	3	0	0	0	0	0	1017	489	218	52	21	34	25	5	0	167	48	15	2	0	1147	629
NL	1262	587	675	28	1	0	2	1	0	0	0	0	0	0	0	718	374	138	32	48	25	33	8	12	151	41	4	0	0	610	652
YR	3038	1485	1553	77	2	0	7	2	0	3	0	0	0	0	0	1735	863	356	84	69	59	58	13	12	318	89	19	2	0	1757	1281

	AL		NL
35	Bill Gullickson	23	Bud Black
32	Ben McDonald	22	Bruce Hurst
29	Dennis Cook	20	Omar Olivares
28	Scott Sanderson	20	Kyle Abbott
28	Bill Wegman	19	Frank Castillo

1993

AL

				Consec			1-Inn			One-Game						Men-On-Base				Pitchers					Totals					Batters	
Tm	Tot	H	A	2	3	4	3	4	5	5	6	7	8	9	10	0	1	2	3	PH	LO	XN	IP	P	1	10	20	30	40	RHB	LHB
BAL	153	81	72	5	0	0	0	0	0	1	0	0	0	0	0	83	45	19	6	6	2	1	1	0	8	5	2	0	0	103	50
BOS	127	53	74	4	0	0	0	0	0	0	0	0	0	0	0	83	33	8	3	0	2	0	1	0	10	4	0	1	0	67	60
CAL	153	84	69	4	0	0	0	0	0	2	0	0	0	0	0	73	46	28	6	0	2	4	0	0	17	2	3	0	0	96	57
CHI	125	70	55	1	0	0	0	0	0	0	0	0	0	0	0	72	35	15	3	2	1	2	0	0	12	3	2	0	0	76	49
CLE	182	83	99	9	0	0	2	0	0	1	0	0	0	0	0	112	45	24	1	1	3	4	0	0	19	4	1	0	0	111	71
DET	188	99	89	6	0	0	0	0	0	0	0	0	0	0	0	100	60	20	8	1	1	2	0	0	14	2	2	1	0	103	85
KC	105	49	56	3	0	0	1	0	0	0	0	0	0	0	0	67	27	8	3	1	5	1	0	0	11	4	1	0	0	53	52
MIL	153	65	88	5	0	0	2	0	0	0	0	0	0	0	0	80	51	20	2	3	2	2	0	0	12	2	2	1	0	89	64
MIN	148	70	78	7	0	0	1	0	0	1	0	0	0	0	0	93	37	15	3	1	4	1	0	0	9	4	2	0	0	77	71
NY	170	85	85	6	0	0	2	0	0	2	0	0	0	0	0	93	50	26	1	2	3	3	0	0	14	3	3	0	0	105	65
OAK	157	78	79	6	0	0	0	0	0	0	1	0	0	0	0	74	51	24	8	3	3	2	0	0	15	4	2	0	0	91	66
SEA	135	66	69	4	0	0	1	0	0	1	0	0	0	0	0	78	36	16	5	2	4	1	0	0	14	3	2	0	0	91	44
TEX	144	72	72	3	0	0	0	0	0	1	0	0	0	0	0	87	34	17	6	3	0	3	0	0	13	5	0	0	0	96	48
TOR	134	81	53	4	0	0	0	0	0	1	0	0	0	0	0	74	43	15	2	1	1	1	1	0	8	3	2	0	0	73	61

NL

Tm	Tot	H	A	2	3	4	3	4	5	5	6	7	8	9	10	0	1	2	3	PH	LO	XN	IP	P	1	10	20	30	40	RHB	LHB
ATL	101	52	49	1	0	0	0	0	0	0	0	0	0	0	0	65	27	7	2	5	1	2	0	1	7	4	1	0	0	65	36
CHI	153	94	59	5	0	0	1	0	0	3	0	0	0	0	0	88	47	14	4	7	3	6	0	0	8	5	2	0	0	75	78
CIN	158	81	77	1	0	0	0	0	0	2	0	0	0	0	0	83	48	23	4	1	0	0	1	2	15	7	0	0	0	86	72
COL	181	107	74	5	0	0	2	0	0	1	1	0	0	0	0	95	58	23	5	3	4	2	3	1	18	5	2	0	0	104	77
FLO	135	72	63	3	0	0	0	0	0	0	0	0	0	0	0	76	42	15	2	5	4	0	2	1	13	2	2	0	0	63	72
HOU	117	56	61	2	0	0	0	0	0	0	0	0	0	0	0	63	40	13	1	1	0	1	0	1	8	3	2	0	0	58	59
LA	103	48	55	1	0	0	0	0	0	0	0	0	0	0	0	60	32	11	0	4	2	4	1	2	8	5	0	0	0	49	54
MON	119	50	69	1	0	0	0	0	0	0	0	0	0	0	0	69	35	8	7	4	3	0	0	0	18	2	1	0	0	56	63
NY	139	72	67	4	0	0	0	0	0	0	0	0	0	0	0	81	39	18	1	1	3	2	0	1	10	6	1	0	0	90	49
PHI	129	57	72	4	1	0	1	0	0	0	0	0	0	0	0	76	30	20	3	2	3	4	1	0	14	3	2	0	0	68	61
PIT	153	67	86	4	1	0	1	0	0	0	0	0	0	0	0	89	40	22	2	6	2	3	0	1	14	4	2	0	0	91	62
SD	148	79	69	3	0	0	1	0	0	0	0	0	0	0	0	94	32	21	1	3	2	6	1	4	16	5	1	0	0	73	75
SF	168	81	87	7	0	0	0	0	0	0	1	0	0	0	0	97	50	16	5	5	3	2	0	2	9	9	0	0	0	85	83
STL	152	59	93	5	0	0	2	0	0	3	0	0	0	0	0	87	42	19	4	6	2	1	0	1	10	7	1	0	0	90	62
AL	2074	1036	1038	67	0	0	9	0	0	10	1	0	0	0	0	1169	593	255	57	26	33	27	3	0	176	48	24	3	0	1231	843
NL	1956	975	981	46	2	0	8	0	0	9	2	0	0	0	0	1123	562	230	41	53	32	33	9	17	168	67	17	0	0	1053	903
YR	4030	2011	2019	113	2	0	17	0	0	19	3	0	0	0	0	2292	1155	485	98	79	65	60	12	17	344	115	41	3	0	2284	1746

	AL		NL
35	Mike Moore	33	Greg Harris
32	Cal Eldred	29	Jack Armstrong
31	Danny Darwin	27	Dennis Martinez
28	Bill Gullickson	26	Frank Tanana
28	Ricky Bones	25	Jose Guzman

1994

AL

Tm	Tot	H	A	2	3	4	3	4	5	5	6	7	8	9	10	0	1	2	3	PH	LO	XN	IP	P	1	10	20	30	40	RHB	LHB
BAL	131	70	61	6	0	0	1	0	0	1	0	0	0	0	0	78	41	11	1	3	2	2	0	0	10	2	2	0	0	86	45
BOS	120	67	53	2	1	0	1	0	0	0	0	0	0	0	0	63	39	13	5	2	3	3	0	0	19	3	0	0	0	73	47
CAL	150	93	57	7	0	0	0	0	0	1	1	0	0	0	0	87	42	16	5	4	2	3	0	0	10	5	1	0	0	88	62
CHI	115	43	72	6	0	0	1	0	0	1	1	0	0	0	0	64	34	17	0	2	1	4	0	0	7	3	2	0	0	61	54
CLE	94	44	50	2	0	0	0	0	0	0	0	0	0	0	0	52	29	11	2	1	0	2	0	0	15	4	0	0	0	52	42

Tm	Tot	H	A	Consec 2	3	4	1-Inn 3	4	5	One-Game 5	6	7	8	9	10	Men-On-Base 0	1	2	3	Pitchers PH	LO	XN	IP	P	Totals 1	10	20	30	40	Batters RHB	LHB
DET	148	76	72	10	0	0	1	0	0	0	0	0	0	0	0	85	43	18	2	0	2	1	0	0	10	4	3	0	0	92	56
KC	95	48	47	2	0	0	0	0	0	1	0	0	0	0	0	48	30	15	2	3	0	2	1	0	10	4	0	0	0	54	41
MIL	127	63	64	2	0	0	1	0	0	1	0	0	0	0	0	73	38	12	4	1	2	2	0	0	8	5	1	0	0	67	60
MIN	153	88	65	6	0	0	0	0	0	2	1	0	0	0	0	86	46	20	1	4	4	1	0	0	7	5	1	1	0	87	66
NY	120	62	58	3	0	0	0	0	0	0	0	0	0	0	0	70	39	9	2	2	2	2	1	0	11	3	2	0	0	77	43
OAK	128	54	74	5	0	0	1	0	0	0	1	0	0	0	0	68	38	18	4	2	0	0	1	0	13	3	2	0	0	59	69
SEA	109	44	65	3	0	0	1	0	0	1	0	0	0	0	0	57	34	12	6	0	2	1	1	0	13	4	0	0	0	67	42
TEX	157	67	90	1	0	0	0	0	0	5	0	0	0	0	0	84	46	22	5	1	2	4	0	0	16	5	1	0	0	72	85
TOR	127	64	63	4	0	0	0	0	0	1	0	0	0	0	0	76	31	16	4	3	4	2	1	0	11	1	3	0	0	71	56
NL																															
ATL	76	37	39	5	0	0	0	1	0	1	0	0	0	0	0	46	18	10	2	2	2	0	0	1	9	4	0	0	0	53	23
CHI	120	71	49	3	1	0	1	0	0	1	0	0	0	0	0	67	38	14	1	8	2	3	2	2	12	5	0	0	0	69	51
CIN	117	65	52	6	0	0	1	0	0	0	0	0	0	0	0	74	33	9	1	3	3	1	1	0	11	5	0	0	0	67	50
COL	120	61	59	4	0	0	0	0	0	1	0	0	0	0	0	62	43	13	2	3	4	1	0	0	14	3	1	0	0	61	59
FLO	120	70	50	10	0	0	0	0	0	1	0	0	0	0	0	68	36	14	2	0	1	0	0	1	15	4	0	0	0	77	43
HOU	102	56	46	2	0	0	0	0	0	0	0	0	0	0	0	59	32	10	1	0	3	1	0	0	7	4	1	0	0	63	39
LA	90	49	41	0	0	0	0	0	0	0	0	0	0	0	0	56	25	9	0	3	0	2	0	2	10	4	0	0	0	38	52
MON	100	47	53	4	0	0	0	0	0	0	0	0	0	0	0	58	32	7	3	3	0	5	1	1	7	6	0	0	0	49	51
NY	117	60	57	5	0	0	1	0	0	0	0	0	0	0	0	60	39	16	2	5	4	3	1	0	14	2	1	0	0	65	52
PHI	98	40	58	1	0	0	0	0	0	0	0	0	0	0	0	61	26	10	1	3	0	0	0	0	13	3	0	0	0	62	36
PIT	117	61	56	3	0	0	2	0	0	1	0	0	0	0	0	69	29	14	5	4	2	3	0	0	13	3	1	0	0	73	44
SD	99	57	42	3	0	0	0	0	0	0	0	0	0	0	0	55	27	12	5	4	0	1	1	0	14	2	1	0	0	64	35
SF	122	74	48	5	0	0	1	0	0	3	0	0	0	0	0	74	31	14	3	6	4	6	0	0	11	5	1	0	0	77	45
STL	134	66	68	5	1	0	3	0	0	0	0	0	0	0	0	66	51	14	3	4	1	4	2	0	10	6	0	0	0	82	52
AL	1774	883	891	59	1	0	7	0	0	14	4	0	0	0	0	991	530	210	43	28	26	29	5	0	160	51	18	1	0	1006	768
NL	1532	814	718	56	2	0	9	1	0	8	0	0	0	0	0	875	460	166	31	48	26	30	8	7	160	56	6	0	0	900	632
YR	3306	1697	1609	115	3	0	16	1	0	22	4	0	0	0	0	1866	990	376	74	76	52	59	13	7	320	107	24	1	0	1906	1400

AL

30 Jim Deshaies
27 Sid Fernandez
27 Mike Moore
26 Dave Stewart
25 Alex Fernandez

NL

25 Pete Smith
22 Greg Harris
21 Steve Cooke
20 Multiple Players Tied

1995

Tm	Tot	H	A	Consec 2	3	4	1-Inn 3	4	5	One-Game 5	6	7	8	9	10	Men-On-Base 0	1	2	3	Pitchers PH	LO	XN	IP	P	Totals 1	10	20	30	40	Batters RHB	LHB
AL																															
BAL	149	84	65	3	0	0	0	0	0	0	0	0	0	0	0	79	50	14	6	3	3	2	0	0	15	4	1	0	0	94	55
BOS	127	63	64	5	0	0	0	0	0	0	0	0	0	0	0	71	30	22	4	3	2	1	1	0	18	3	1	0	0	78	49
CAL	163	88	75	4	1	0	0	1	0	1	1	0	0	0	0	93	41	24	5	1	2	0	2	0	12	4	3	0	0	96	67
CHI	164	73	91	6	0	0	0	0	0	0	1	1	0	0	0	92	49	19	4	4	2	2	1	0	16	5	2	0	0	99	65
CLE	135	60	75	2	0	0	0	0	0	1	0	0	0	0	0	82	34	14	5	1	3	1	0	0	13	3	2	0	0	66	69
DET	170	93	77	5	1	0	1	0	0	2	0	0	0	0	0	99	40	23	8	1	3	6	3	0	11	7	1	0	0	72	98
KC	142	68	74	3	0	0	1	0	0	0	0	0	0	0	0	83	39	16	4	3	3	1	1	0	15	4	1	0	0	73	69
MIL	146	71	75	6	0	0	2	0	0	1	0	0	0	0	0	85	39	19	3	2	4	0	1	0	13	5	1	0	0	86	60
MIN	210	120	90	11	0	0	2	0	0	2	0	0	0	0	0	114	63	26	7	4	3	0	0	0	11	6	2	1	0	116	94
NY	159	76	83	9	0	0	0	0	0	0	0	0	0	0	0	88	46	17	8	2	3	2	3	0	13	4	2	0	0	92	67
OAK	153	75	78	7	0	0	1	0	0	0	0	0	0	0	0	81	42	24	6	2	0	4	1	0	12	6	1	0	0	83	70
SEA	149	73	76	3	0	0	0	0	0	1	0	0	0	0	0	80	40	24	5	3	6	2	0	0	14	6	0	0	0	88	61
TEX	152	73	79	5	0	0	2	0	0	1	0	0	0	0	0	89	40	17	6	4	3	2	2	0	15	3	2	0	0	85	67
TOR	145	79	66	2	0	0	1	0	0	1	0	0	0	0	0	78	49	14	4	1	2	8	0	0	12	6	1	0	0	71	74
NL																															
ATL	107	66	41	1	0	0	0	0	0	1	0	0	0	0	0	58	33	14	2	4	1	4	0	0	14	2	1	0	0	75	32
CHI	162	83	79	7	0	0	1	0	0	3	0	0	0	0	0	107	38	12	5	8	1	3	5	6	11	3	2	1	0	103	59
CIN	131	58	73	4	0	0	0	0	0	0	0	0	0	0	0	80	35	12	4	3	1	2	3	1	14	5	0	0	0	73	58
COL	160	107	53	4	0	0	0	0	0	0	0	0	0	0	0	91	44	22	3	3	2	1	1	1	14	6	0	0	0	95	65
FLO	139	60	79	3	0	0	0	0	0	2	0	0	0	0	0	73	48	15	3	9	3	4	1	0	20	3	1	0	0	86	53
HOU	118	48	70	3	0	0	0	0	0	1	0	0	0	0	0	68	31	15	4	3	3	4	1	1	11	4	1	0	0	63	55
LA	125	48	77	7	0	0	2	0	0	0	0	0	0	0	0	63	39	19	4	5	2	3	4	3	15	5	0	0	0	64	61
MON	128	55	73	7	1	0	2	0	0	0	0	0	0	0	0	73	45	7	3	6	3	1	0	0	16	3	1	0	0	81	47
NY	133	68	65	4	0	0	1	0	0	0	0	0	0	0	0	88	27	17	1	1	5	4	0	0	15	3	2	0	0	79	54

				Consec			1-Inn			One-Game						Men-On-Base				Pitchers					Totals					Batters	
Tm	Tot	H	A	2	3	4	3	4	5	5	6	7	8	9	10	0	1	2	3	PH	LO	XN	IP	P	1	10	20	30	40	RHB	LHB
PHI	134	78	56	1	0	0	0	0	0	2	0	0	0	0	0	67	45	18	4	6	3	1	2	3	17	5	1	0	0	79	55
PIT	130	67	63	2	0	0	0	0	0	0	0	0	0	0	0	80	37	11	2	8	1	1	1	2	11	2	2	0	0	75	55
SD	142	72	70	2	0	0	1	0	0	0	0	0	0	0	0	78	41	19	4	7	2	3	10	1	9	8	0	0	0	94	48
SF	173	78	95	5	1	0	0	1	0	1	0	0	0	0	0	106	40	21	6	7	5	2	0	1	18	4	2	0	0	110	63
STL	135	60	75	2	0	0	0	0	0	0	0	0	0	0	0	83	37	12	3	4	5	1	0	0	10	7	0	0	0	84	51
AL	2164	1096	1068	71	2	0	10	1	0	10	2	1	0	0	0	1214	602	273	75	34	39	31	15	0	190	66	20	1	0	1199	965
NL	1917	948	969	52	2	0	7	1	0	10	0	0	0	0	0	1115	540	214	48	74	37	34	28	19	195	60	13	1	0	1161	756
YR	4081	2044	2037	123	4	0	17	2	0	20	2	1	0	0	0	2329	1142	487	123	108	76	65	43	19	385	126	33	2	0	2360	1721

	AL		*NL*
32	Brad Radke	32	Kevin Foster
27	Kevin Gross	25	Terry Mulholland
26	Kenny Rogers	25	Steve Trachsel
26	Todd Stottlemyre	24	Jose Bautista
26	Ricky Bones	23	David Mlicki

Totals for Current Teams

This chart shows various totals for all 28 current teams. It is broken down by each city in which the franchise has played as well as franchise totals.

				Consec			1-Inn			One-Game						Men-On-Base				Pitchers					Totals					Batters	
Tm	Tot	H	A	2	3	4	3	4	5	5	6	7	8	9	10	0	1	2	3	PH	LO	XN	IP	P	1	10	20	30	40	RHB	LHB
MIL AL	26	15	11	0	0	0	0	0	0	0	0	0	0	0	0	12	10	4	0	0	0	0	3	1	8	0	0	0	0	22	4
STL AL	3014	1740	1274	67	1	0	5	0	0	3	0	0	0	0	0	1579	993	374	68	59	45	50	158	79	496	81	17	3	0	2321	692
BAL AL	5911	2816	3095	175	6	0	27	2	0	19	7	2	0	0	0	3400	1721	635	155	130	94	111	19	68	482	142	68	17	2	4137	1774
Total	8951	4571	4380	242	7	0	32	2	0	22	7	2	0	0	0	4991	2724	1013	223	189	139	161	180	148	986	223	85	20	2	6480	2470
BOS AL	9123	4732	4391	237	7	0	24	6	0	23	11	1	1	0	0	4859	2831	1166	267	124	121	192	200	161	909	200	81	33	10	7081	2041
LA AL	523	228	295	17	1	0	3	0	0	4	0	0	0	0	0	304	147	62	10	16	6	17	3	7	59	7	8	1	0	381	142
CAL AL	3720	1848	1872	93	2	0	14	0	0	9	4	0	0	0	0	2122	1092	424	82	73	69	67	18	17	382	81	40	11	0	2582	1138
Total	4243	2076	2167	110	3	0	17	0	0	13	4	0	0	0	0	2426	1239	486	92	89	75	84	21	24	441	88	48	12	0	2963	1280
CHI AL	6944	3173	3771	160	4	0	21	0	0	21	4	1	0	0	0	3893	2077	804	170	144	91	129	142	122	997	172	52	12	2	5000	1944
CLE AL	8736	4351	4385	239	8	1	40	1	0	34	7	1	0	0	0	4891	2596	1046	203	163	111	184	173	182	1011	194	83	25	5	6222	2514
DET AL	9712	5268	4444	264	11	0	34	3	0	28	7	1	0	0	0	5426	2841	1199	246	205	152	183	205	152	925	230	94	26	9	7010	2701
KC AL	2950	1233	1717	76	2	0	12	0	0	8	1	0	0	0	0	1682	864	343	61	44	42	47	78	7	308	69	31	7	0	2003	947
SEA AL	125	74	51	1	0	0	1	0	0	0	0	0	0	0	0	73	40	9	3	4	1	8	0	5	20	2	1	0	0	86	39
MIL AL	3351	1578	1773	80	3	0	11	0	0	12	1	1	0	0	0	1892	1000	383	76	33	73	48	19	5	285	92	27	11	2	2343	1008
Total	3476	1652	1824	81	3	0	12	0	0	12	1	1	0	0	0	1965	1040	392	79	37	74	56	19	10	305	94	28	11	2	2429	1047
WAS AL	2786	957	1829	48	0	0	10	0	0	1	0	1	0	0	0	1499	896	326	65	42	58	53	242	92	615	50	9	5	2	2106	680
MIN AL	4641	2378	2263	132	3	1	22	3	1	12	5	0	1	0	0	2587	1391	549	114	116	70	79	41	36	371	105	51	11	7	3333	1308
Total	7427	3335	4092	180	3	1	32	3	1	13	5	1	1	0	0	4086	2287	875	179	158	128	132	283	128	986	155	60	16	9	5439	1988
BAL AL	57	26	31	1	0	0	0	0	0	0	0	0	0	0	0	23	20	11	3	0	0	0	9	2	22	0	0	0	0	52	5
NY AL	11157	5728	5429	320	9	0	45	1	0	45	10	2	1	0	0	6007	3438	1440	272	220	167	215	330	154	925	234	98	41	23	7687	3470
Total	11214	5754	5460	321	9	0	45	1	0	45	10	2	1	0	0	6030	3458	1451	275	220	167	215	339	156	947	234	98	41	23	7739	3475
PHI AL	3502	1935	1567	55	3	0	4	0	0	9	0	1	0	0	0	1901	1088	427	86	46	61	62	134	81	506	67	24	12	4	2791	711
KC AL	1480	767	713	33	1	0	2	0	0	3	0	0	0	0	0	888	407	156	29	39	18	35	18	31	175	41	7	3	0	1124	356
OAK AL	3949	1886	2063	95	5	0	15	0	0	8	2	1	0	0	0	2266	1167	434	82	74	66	61	18	26	307	84	40	16	5	2655	1294
Total	8931	4588	4343	183	9	0	26	0	0	20	2	2	0	0	0	5055	2662	1017	197	159	145	158	170	138	988	192	71	31	9	6570	2361
SEA AL	2575	1448	1127	69	1	0	7	0	0	6	2	1	0	0	0	1452	742	304	77	49	14	45	18	0	228	63	32	2	3	1756	819
WAS AL	1387	650	737	40	2	0	1	0	0	3	0	0	0	0	0	797	389	173	28	58	19	38	7	19	144	38	7	2	3	987	400
TEX AL	3030	1467	1563	86	0	0	11	0	0	7	0	1	0	0	0	1753	893	327	57	57	54	61	20	0	262	79	29	8	2	2091	939
Total	4417	2117	2300	126	2	0	14	0	0	10	0	1	0	0	0	2550	1282	500	85	115	73	99	27	19	406	117	36	10	5	3078	1339
TOR AL	2627	1335	1292	84	2	0	13	0	0	10	1	0	0	0	1	1558	742	280	47	50	45	51	20	0	190	74	24	9	2	1784	843

Tm	Tot	H	A	Consec 2	3	4	1-Inn 3	4	5	One-Game 5	6	7	8	9	10	Men-On-Base 0	1	2	3	Pitchers PH	LO	XN	IP	P	Totals 1	10	20	30	40	Batters RHB	LHB
BOS NL	3424	1705	1719	62	1	0	5	0	0	6	0	0	0	0	0	1791	1095	449	88	51	58	69	234	137	784	54	15	3	0	2698	690
MIL NL	2230	998	1232	69	4	1	5	1	0	13	1	1	1	0	0	1299	639	240	51	46	29	36	13	51	134	36	23	13	8	1722	508
ATL NL	4096	2279	1817	116	4	0	20	2	0	14	1	1	0	0	0	2353	1166	497	80	118	68	78	17	50	331	77	37	19	9	2929	1167
Total	9750	4982	4768	247	9	1	35	4	0	33	2	2	1	0	0	5444	2900	1186	219	215	155	183	264	238	1249	167	75	35	17	7349	2365
CHI NL	10051	5544	4507	216	4	0	33	1	0	31	12	3	0	0	0	5489	3065	1238	238	214	154	184	269	260	1305	198	80	27	11	7561	2423
CIN AA	267	194	73	3	0	0	1	0	0	1	0	0	0	0	0	111	100	54	2	0	4	2	38	8	66	6	0	0	0	194	41
CIN NL	8798	4342	4456	224	6	0	37	1	0	24	3	3	1	0	0	4855	2669	1069	205	210	127	174	461	176	1155	185	68	26	9	6414	2360
Total	9065	4536	4529	227	6	0	38	1	0	25	3	3	1	0	0	4966	2769	1123	207	210	131	176	499	184	1221	191	68	26	9	6608	2401
COL NL	467	270	197	21	1	0	6	0	0	2	0	0	0	0	0	268	135	53	11	21	8	4	2	5	36	6	4	4	1	341	126
FLO NL	332	158	174	9	0	0	1	0	0	0	0	0	0	0	0	177	105	37	13	1	3	1	5	3	38	9	4	0	0	238	94
HOU NL	3237	1278	1959	61	1	0	2	0	0	5	0	0	0	0	0	1875	912	379	71	93	68	76	30	58	412	82	28	6	0	2220	1017
BRO AA	143	91	52	1	0	0	0	0	0	0	0	0	0	0	0	44	60	33	5	0	0	1	13	19	61	0	0	0	0	104	23
BRO NL	4336	2273	2063	80	2	0	16	0	0	16	1	0	0	0	0	2232	1395	598	111	62	68	84	304	103	674	78	25	10	8	3401	924
LA NL	4507	2125	2382	117	1	0	13	0	0	7	1	2	0	0	0	2587	1327	504	89	135	63	102	37	74	444	109	47	12	0	3207	1300
Total	8986	4489	4497	198	3	0	29	0	0	23	2	2	0	0	0	4863	2782	1135	205	197	131	187	354	196	1179	187	72	22	8	6712	2247
MON NL	2985	1406	1579	72	2	0	9	2	0	10	0	0	1	0	0	1777	837	299	72	82	41	57	23	32	305	84	32	4	0	2055	930
NY NL	3760	1889	1871	73	6	0	12	0	0	8	1	0	0	0	0	2175	1047	451	87	127	66	99	21	35	414	103	28	12	0	2608	1152
WOR NL	31	21	10	0	0	0	0	0	0	0	0	0	0	0	0	16	11	3	1	0	4	0	4	3	15	0	0	0	0	31	0
PHI NL	9208	5011	4197	209	3	0	21	1	1	14	9	0	0	0	0	4922	2880	1180	226	239	129	163	237	191	1185	212	55	27	7	6723	2453
Total	9239	5032	4207	209	3	0	21	1	1	14	9	0	0	0	0	4938	2891	1183	227	239	133	163	241	194	1200	212	55	27	7	6754	2453
PIT AA	54	27	27	0	0	0	0	0	0	0	0	0	0	0	0	27	11	14	2	0	1	0	6	4	28	0	0	0	0	30	4
PIT NL	7991	3567	4424	189	7	0	26	2	0	17	4	2	0	0	0	4323	2511	954	203	203	108	165	496	171	1154	178	48	13	7	5826	2149
Total	8045	3594	4451	189	7	0	26	2	0	17	4	2	0	0	0	4350	2522	968	205	203	109	165	502	175	1182	178	48	13	7	5856	2153
SD NL	2804	1398	1406	54	3	0	5	1	0	5	0	0	0	0	0	1606	793	333	72	95	29	69	20	40	327	59	28	7	0	1898	906
TRO NL	26	19	7	0	0	0	0	0	0	0	0	0	0	0	0	13	6	6	1	0	0	0	0	2	14	0	0	0	0	23	3
NY NL	5774	3637	2137	128	8	0	24	3	1	27	7	5	0	0	0	3038	1817	763	151	121	90	107	300	207	804	119	40	13	5	4291	1456
SF NL	5253	2599	2654	156	3	0	13	0	1	23	2	0	1	0	0	3054	1513	574	112	167	95	123	29	69	450	96	49	24	10	3684	1569
Total	11053	6255	4798	284	11	0	37	3	2	50	9	5	1	0	0	6105	3336	1343	264	288	185	230	329	278	1268	215	89	37	15	7998	3028
STL AA	304	213	91	1	0	0	0	0	0	0	0	0	0	0	0	120	105	68	11	0	6	2	32	34	85	5	0	0	0	217	46
STL NL	7769	3892	3877	157	3	0	20	1	0	13	2	1	0	0	0	4200	2420	960	189	195	125	171	345	173	1131	184	57	13	2	5393	2350
Total	8073	4105	3968	158	3	0	20	1	0	13	2	1	0	0	0	4320	2525	1028	200	195	131	173	377	207	1216	189	57	13	2	5610	2396

Part Four

Hitter Register

Year	Tm	Lg	Tot	H	A	Men-On				One-Game			LO	XN	IP	PH	RHP	LHP
						0	1	2	3	2	3	4						

Hank Aaron

HENRY LOUIS AARON
B: 02/05/1934
BR HOF

Year	Tm	Lg	Tot	H	A	0	1	2	3	2	3	4	LO	XN	IP	PH	RHP	LHP
1954	MIL	NL	13	1	12	6	7	0	0	0	0	0	0	1	0	0	11	2
1955	MIL	NL	27	14	13	16	9	2	0	2	0	0	0	0	0	0	21	6
1956	MIL	NL	26	15	11	16	6	4	0	1	0	0	0	1	0	0	21	5
1957	MIL	NL	44	18	26	22	11	10	1	2	0	0	0	1	0	0	35	9
1958	MIL	NL	30	10	20	18	7	3	2	3	0	0	0	1	0	0	22	8
1959	MIL	NL	39	20	19	25	11	3	0	5	1	0	0	1	0	0	26	13
1960	MIL	NL	40	21	19	25	10	5	0	3	0	0	0	0	0	0	27	13
1961	MIL	NL	34	19	15	19	11	3	1	4	0	0	0	0	0	0	23	11
1962	MIL	NL	45	18	27	22	15	5	3	6	0	0	0	0	0	1	28	17
1963	MIL	NL	44	19	25	20	18	4	2	1	0	0	0	0	0	0	36	8
1964	MIL	NL	24	11	13	9	8	7	0	1	0	0	0	0	0	0	18	6
1965	MIL	NL	32	19	13	20	9	3	0	3	0	0	0	1	0	0	22	10
1966	ATL	NL	44	21	23	23	14	6	1	5	0	0	0	0	0	1	28	16
1967	ATL	NL	39	23	16	15	17	6	1	3	0	0	0	0	1	0	30	9
1968	ATL	NL	29	17	12	14	11	4	0	2	0	0	0	0	0	0	21	8
1969	ATL	NL	44	21	23	28	10	5	1	3	0	0	0	2	0	0	30	14
1970	ATL	NL	38	23	15	8	23	6	1	3	0	0	0	1	0	0	35	3
1971	ATL	NL	47	31	16	24	19	4	0	6	0	0	0	1	0	0	29	18
1972	ATL	NL	34	19	15	20	9	4	1	3	0	0	0	2	0	0	17	17
1973	ATL	NL	40	24	16	22	10	8	0	4	0	0	0	0	0	1	22	18
1974	ATL	NL	20	11	9	10	5	3	2	1	0	0	0	1	0	0	17	3
1975	MIL	AL	12	4	8	10	1	1	0	0	0	0	0	0	0	0	9	3
1976	MIL	AL	10	6	4	8	1	1	0	0	0	0	0	1	0	0	6	4
Total			755	385	370	400	242	97	16	61	1	0	0	14	1	3	534	221

Rank among batters: 1 • *Top target (17 home runs)*: Don Drysdale • Number of pitchers victimized: 310 • *Total ballparks homered in*: 32 • *First HR*: 04/23/1954 off Vic Raschi • *World Series HR*—3; *LCS HR*—3; *All-Star HR*—2

Home Run Listing Legend (Batters)

Year	Season in which home runs were hit
Tm	Team for which home runs were hit
Lg	League in which home runs were hit
Tot	Total number of home runs
H	Home runs hit at home
A	Home runs hit away from home
Men On	Home runs with each number of men on base
One Gm	Games with multiple home runs
LO	Lead-off home runs (first inning, first batter either team)
XN	Home runs hit in extra innings
IP	Inside-the-Park home runs
PH	Pinch Hit home runs
RHP	Home runs vs right-handed pitcher
LHP	Home runs vs left-handed pitcher

Hank Aaron

HENRY LOUIS AARON
B: 02/05/1934
BR HOF

Year	Tm	Lg	Tot	H	A	Men-On 0	1	2	3	One-Game 2	3	4	LO	XN	IP	PH	RHP	LHP
1954	MIL	NL	13	1	12	6	7	0	0	0	0	0	0	1	0	0	11	2
1955	MIL	NL	27	14	13	16	9	2	0	2	0	0	0	0	0	0	21	6
1956	MIL	NL	26	15	11	16	6	4	0	1	0	0	0	1	0	0	21	5
1957	MIL	NL	44	18	26	22	11	10	1	2	0	0	0	1	0	0	35	9
1958	MIL	NL	30	10	20	18	7	3	2	3	0	0	0	1	0	0	22	8
1959	MIL	NL	39	20	19	25	11	3	0	5	1	0	0	1	0	0	26	13
1960	MIL	NL	40	21	19	25	10	5	0	3	0	0	0	0	0	0	27	13
1961	MIL	NL	34	19	15	19	11	3	1	4	0	0	0	0	0	0	23	11
1962	MIL	NL	45	18	27	22	15	5	3	6	0	0	0	0	0	1	28	17
1963	MIL	NL	44	19	25	20	18	4	2	1	0	0	0	0	0	0	36	8
1964	MIL	NL	24	11	13	9	8	7	0	1	0	0	0	0	0	0	18	6
1965	MIL	NL	32	19	13	20	9	3	0	3	0	0	0	1	0	0	22	10
1966	ATL	NL	44	21	23	23	14	6	1	5	0	0	0	0	0	1	28	16
1967	ATL	NL	39	23	16	15	17	6	1	3	0	0	0	0	1	0	30	9
1968	ATL	NL	29	17	12	14	11	4	0	2	0	0	0	0	0	0	21	8
1969	ATL	NL	44	21	23	28	10	5	1	3	0	0	0	2	0	0	30	14
1970	ATL	NL	38	23	15	8	23	6	1	3	0	0	0	1	0	0	35	3
1971	ATL	NL	47	31	16	24	19	4	0	6	0	0	0	1	0	0	29	18
1972	ATL	NL	34	19	15	20	9	4	1	3	0	0	0	2	0	0	17	17
1973	ATL	NL	40	24	16	22	10	8	0	4	0	0	0	0	0	1	22	18
1974	ATL	NL	20	11	9	10	5	3	2	1	0	0	0	1	0	0	17	3
1975	MIL	AL	12	4	8	10	1	1	0	0	0	0	0	0	0	0	9	3
1976	MIL	AL	10	6	4	8	1	1	0	0	0	0	0	1	0	0	6	4
Total			755	385	370	400	242	97	16	61	1	0	0	14	1	3	534	221

Rank among batters: 1 • *Top target (17 home runs)*: Don Drysdale • *Number of pitchers victimized*: 310 • *Total ballparks homered in*: 32 • *First HR*: 04/23/1954 off Vic Raschi • *World Series HR*—3; *LCS HR*—3; *All-Star HR*—2

Tommie Aaron

TOMMIE LEE AARON
B: 08/05/1939 D: 08/16/1984
BR

Year	Tm	Lg	Tot	H	A	Men-On 0	1	2	3	One-Game 2	3	4	LO	XN	IP	PH	RHP	LHP
1962	MIL	NL	8	7	1	3	3	1	1	0	0	0	0	0	0	1	8	0
1963	MIL	NL	1	0	1	1	0	0	0	0	0	0	0	0	0	0	0	1
1968	ATL	NL	1	0	1	0	1	0	0	0	0	0	0	0	0	0	0	1
1969	ATL	NL	1	1	0	1	0	0	0	0	0	0	0	0	0	0	1	0
1970	ATL	NL	2	1	1	1	1	0	0	0	0	0	0	0	0	0	0	2
Total			13	9	4	6	5	1	1	0	0	0	0	0	0	1	9	4

Rank among batters: 2,248 • *Top target (2 home runs)*: Larry Jackson • *Number of pitchers victimized*: 12 • *Total ballparks homered in*: 6 • *First HR*: 04/26/1962 off Jack Hamilton

Ed Abbaticchio

EDWARD JAMES ABBATICCHIO
B: 04/15/1877 D: 01/06/1957
BR

Year	Tm	Lg	Tot	H	A	Men-On 0	1	2	3	One-Game 2	3	4	LO	XN	IP	PH	RHP	LHP
1903	BOS	NL	1	0	1	0	1	0	0	0	0	0	0	0	1	0	1	0
1904	BOS	NL	3	2	1	1	0	2	0	0	0	0	0	0	1	0	3	0
1905	BOS	NL	3	2	1	1	1	1	0	0	0	0	0	0	0	0	3	0
1907	PIT	NL	2	1	1	1	1	0	0	0	0	0	0	0	1	0	1	1
1908	PIT	NL	1	0	1	0	1	0	0	0	0	0	0	0	0	0	0	1
1909	PIT	NL	1	1	0	1	0	0	0	0	0	0	0	0	1	0	1	0
Total			11	6	5	4	4	3	0	0	0	0	0	0	4	0	9	2

Rank among batters: 2,419 • *Top target (2 home runs)*: Frank Corridon • *Number of pitchers victimized*: 10 • *Total ballparks homered in*: 5 • *First HR*: 06/11/1903 off Bob Rhoads

Charlie Abbey

CHARLES S. ABBEY
B: 10/14/1866 D: 04/27/1926
BL

Year	Tm	Lg	Tot	H	A	Men-On 0	1	2	3	One-Game 2	3	4	LO	XN	IP	PH	RHP	LHP
1894	WAS	NL	7	6	1	0	5	2	0	0	0	0	0	0	3	0	6	1
1895	WAS	NL	8	7	1	4	1	2	1	0	0	0	0	0	1	0	8	0
1896	WAS	NL	1	1	0	0	1	0	0	0	0	0	0	0	0	0	1	0

Year	Tm	Lg	Tot	H	A	Men-On 0	1	2	3	One-Game 2	3	4	LO	XN	IP	PH	RHP	LHP

Charlie Abbey *continued*

Year	Tm	Lg	Tot	H	A	0	1	2	3	2	3	4	LO	XN	IP	PH	RHP	LHP
1897	WAS	NL	3	2	1	1	1	1	0	0	0	0	0	0	2	0	3	0
Total			19	16	3	5	8	5	1	0	0	0	0	0	6	0	18	1

Rank among batters: 1,861 • *Top target (2 home runs)*: Frank Dwyer, Brickyard Kennedy • *Number of pitchers victimized*: 17 • *Total ballparks homered in*: 4 • *First HR*: 05/31/1894 off Frank Killen

Fred Abbott

HARRY FREDERICK ABBOTT
B: 10/22/1874 D: 06/11/1935
BR

Year	Tm	Lg	Tot	H	A	0	1	2	3	2	3	4	LO	XN	IP	PH	RHP	LHP
1903	CLE	AL	1	1	0	1	0	0	0	0	0	0	0	0	0	0	1	0

Rank among batters: 4,707 • *Total ballparks homered in*: 1 • *First HR*: 05/08/1903 off Frank Kitson

Kurt Abbott

KURT THOMAS ABBOTT
B: 06/02/1969
BR

Year	Tm	Lg	Tot	H	A	0	1	2	3	2	3	4	LO	XN	IP	PH	RHP	LHP
1993	OAK	AL	3	0	3	1	2	0	0	0	0	0	0	0	0	1	1	2
1994	FLO	NL	9	4	5	4	3	0	2	0	0	0	0	0	0	0	7	2
1995	FLO	NL	17	12	5	12	2	2	1	0	0	0	0	0	2	0	14	3
Total			29	16	13	17	7	2	3	0	0	0	0	0	2	1	22	7

Rank among batters: 1,465 • *Top target (2 home runs)*: Pete Schourek, Esteban Loaiza • *Number of pitchers victimized*: 27 • *Total ballparks homered in*: 12 • *First HR*: 09/09/1993 off Jack Morris

Cliff Aberson

CLIFFORD ALEXANDER ABERSON
B: 08/28/1921 D: 06/23/1973
BR

Year	Tm	Lg	Tot	H	A	0	1	2	3	2	3	4	LO	XN	IP	PH	RHP	LHP
1947	CHI	NL	4	2	2	1	2	0	1	0	0	0	0	0	0	1	1	3
1948	CHI	NL	1	1	0	1	0	0	0	0	0	0	0	0	0	0	1	0
Total			5	3	2	2	2	0	1	0	0	0	0	0	0	1	2	3

Rank among batters: 3,191 • *Total ballparks homered in*: 3 • *First HR*: 08/17/1947 off Ken Raffensberger

Shawn Abner

SHAWN WESLEY ABNER
B: 06/17/1966
BR

Year	Tm	Lg	Tot	H	A	0	1	2	3	2	3	4	LO	XN	IP	PH	RHP	LHP
1987	SD	NL	2	1	1	0	2	0	0	0	0	0	0	0	0	0	2	0
1988	SD	NL	2	2	0	2	0	0	0	0	0	0	0	0	0	0	1	1
1989	SD	NL	2	1	1	0	0	2	0	0	0	0	0	0	0	0	1	1
1990	SD	NL	1	1	0	0	1	0	0	0	0	0	0	0	0	0	1	0
1991	SD	NL	1	1	0	1	0	0	0	0	0	0	0	0	0	0	0	1
	CAL	AL	2	1	1	1	0	1	0	0	0	0	0	0	0	0	0	2
	Total		3	2	1	2	0	1	0	0	0	0	0	0	0	0	0	3
1992	CHI	AL	1	0	1	1	0	0	0	0	0	0	0	0	0	0	0	1
Total			11	7	4	5	3	3	0	0	0	0	0	0	0	0	5	6

Rank among batters: 2,419 • *Total ballparks homered in*: 6 • *First HR*: 09/15/1987 off John Burkett

Cal Abrams

CALVIN ROSS ABRAMS
B: 03/02/1924
BL

Year	Tm	Lg	Tot	H	A	0	1	2	3	2	3	4	LO	XN	IP	PH	RHP	LHP
1951	BRO	NL	3	1	2	1	2	0	0	0	0	0	1	0	0	0	3	0
1952	CIN	NL	2	1	1	2	0	0	0	0	0	0	1	0	0	0	2	0
1953	PIT	NL	15	9	6	13	1	0	1	1	0	0	5	0	1	0	14	1
1954	BAL	AL	6	2	4	6	0	0	0	0	0	0	0	0	0	0	6	0
1955	BAL	AL	6	1	5	3	3	0	0	0	0	0	0	0	0	2	3	3
Total			32	14	18	25	6	0	1	1	0	0	7	0	1	2	28	4

Rank among batters: 1,360 • *Top target (3 home runs)*: Ruben Gomez • *Number of pitchers victimized*: 25 • *Total ballparks homered in*: 13 • *First HR*: 05/05/1951 off Jim Blackburn

						Men-On				One-Game								
Year	Tm	Lg	Tot	H	A	0	1	2	3	2	3	4	LO	XN	IP	PH	RHP	LHP

Joe Abreu

JOSEPH LAWRENCE ABREU
B: 05/24/1913 D: 03/17/1993
BR

Year	Tm	Lg	Tot	H	A	0	1	2	3	2	3	4	LO	XN	IP	PH	RHP	LHP
1942	CIN	NL	1	0	1	1	0	0	0	0	0	0	0	0	0	0	1	0

Rank among batters: 4,707 • *Total ballparks homered in*: 1 • *First HR*: 04/24/1942 off Nick Strincevich

Bill Abstein

WILLIAM HENRY ABSTEIN
B: 02/02/1883 D: 04/08/1940
BR

Year	Tm	Lg	Tot	H	A	0	1	2	3	2	3	4	LO	XN	IP	PH	RHP	LHP
1909	PIT	NL	1	1	0	0	1	0	0	0	0	0	0	0	0	0	1	0

Rank among batters: 4,707 • *Total ballparks homered in*: 1 • *First HR*: 09/07/1909 off Ed Reulbach

Jerry Adair

KENNETH JERRY ADAIR
B: 12/17/1936 D: 05/31/1987
BR

Year	Tm	Lg	Tot	H	A	0	1	2	3	2	3	4	LO	XN	IP	PH	RHP	LHP
1960	BAL	AL	1	0	1	1	0	0	0	0	0	0	0	0	0	0	1	0
1961	BAL	AL	9	2	7	4	5	0	0	1	0	0	0	0	0	0	6	3
1962	BAL	AL	11	5	6	9	2	0	0	0	0	0	1	0	0	0	7	4
1963	BAL	AL	6	4	2	5	1	0	0	0	0	0	0	0	0	0	3	3
1964	BAL	AL	9	5	4	7	2	0	0	1	0	0	0	0	0	0	7	2
1965	BAL	AL	7	4	3	2	3	2	0	0	0	0	1	0	0	0	4	3
1966	CHI	AL	4	1	3	1	2	1	0	0	0	0	0	1	0	0	3	1
1967	BOS	AL	3	2	1	3	0	0	0	0	0	0	0	0	0	0	3	0
1968	BOS	AL	2	1	1	2	0	0	0	0	0	0	0	0	0	0	1	1
1969	KC	AL	5	1	4	4	0	1	0	0	0	0	0	0	1	0	4	1
Total			57	25	32	38	15	4	0	2	0	0	2	1	1	0	39	18

Rank among batters: 902 • *Top target (3 home runs)*: Jim Kaat • *Number of pitchers victimized*: 50 • *Total ballparks homered in*: 12 • *First HR*: 09/27/1960 off Tom Sturdivant

Babe Adams

CHARLES BENJAMIN ADAMS
B: 05/18/1882 D: 07/27/1968
BL

Year	Tm	Lg	Tot	H	A	0	1	2	3	2	3	4	LO	XN	IP	PH	RHP	LHP
1914	PIT	NL	1	1	0	1	0	0	0	0	0	0	0	0	1	0	0	1
1920	PIT	NL	1	0	1	1	0	0	0	0	0	0	0	0	0	0	1	0
1922	PIT	NL	1	0	1	1	0	0	0	0	0	0	0	0	0	0	1	0
Total			3	1	2	3	0	0	0	0	0	0	0	0	1	0	2	1

Rank among batters: 3,735 • *Total ballparks homered in*: 3 • *First HR*: 08/18/1914 off Rube Marquard

Bert Adams

JOHN BERTRAM ADAMS
B: 06/21/1891 D: 06/24/1940
BB

Year	Tm	Lg	Tot	H	A	0	1	2	3	2	3	4	LO	XN	IP	PH	RHP	LHP
1917	PHI	NL	1	1	0	1	0	0	0	0	0	0	0	0	0	1	0	1
1919	PHI	NL	1	1	0	1	0	0	0	0	0	0	0	0	0	0	1	0
Total			2	2	0	2	0	0	0	0	0	0	0	0	0	1	1	1

Rank among batters: 4,129 • *Total ballparks homered in*: 1 • *First HR*: 05/16/1917 off Wilbur Cooper

Bob Adams

ROBERT MELVIN ADAMS
B: 01/06/1952
BR

Year	Tm	Lg	Tot	H	A	0	1	2	3	2	3	4	LO	XN	IP	PH	RHP	LHP
1977	DET	AL	2	2	0	2	0	0	0	0	0	0	0	0	0	1	0	2

Rank among batters: 4,129 • *Total ballparks homered in*: 1 • *First HR*: 08/09/1977 off Bill Travers

Bobby Adams

ROBERT HENRY ADAMS
B: 12/14/1921
BR

Year	Tm	Lg	Tot	H	A	0	1	2	3	2	3	4	LO	XN	IP	PH	RHP	LHP
1946	CIN	NL	4	2	2	3	0	1	0	0	0	0	0	0	0	0	4	0

Bobby Adams *continued*

Year	Tm	Lg	Tot	H	A	Men-On 0	1	2	3	One-Game 2	3	4	LO	XN	IP	PH	RHP	LHP
1947	CIN	NL	4	2	2	3	0	1	0	0	0	0	0	0	0	0	4	0
1948	CIN	NL	1	1	0	1	0	0	0	0	0	0	0	0	0	0	1	0
1950	CIN	NL	3	0	3	3	0	0	0	0	0	0	0	0	0	0	0	3
1951	CIN	NL	5	3	2	4	1	0	0	0	0	0	1	0	0	0	3	2
1952	CIN	NL	6	1	5	6	0	0	0	0	0	0	1	0	0	0	6	0
1953	CIN	NL	8	4	4	6	2	0	0	0	0	0	1	0	0	0	5	3
1954	CIN	NL	3	0	3	2	1	0	0	0	0	0	1	0	0	0	3	0
1955	CIN	NL	2	1	1	1	1	0	0	0	0	0	0	0	0	1	0	2
1957	CHI	NL	1	1	0	0	1	0	0	0	0	0	0	0	0	0	1	0
Total			37	15	22	29	6	2	0	0	0	0	4	0	0	1	27	10

Rank among batters: 1,252 • *Top target (3 home runs)*: Larry Jansen, Preacher Roe • *Number of pitchers victimized*: 32 • *Total ballparks homered in*: 7 • *First HR*: 06/02/1946 off Les Webber

Buster Adams

ELVIN CLARK ADAMS
B: 06/24/1915 D: 09/01/1990
BR

Year	Tm	Lg	Tot	H	A	Men-On 0	1	2	3	One-Game 2	3	4	LO	XN	IP	PH	RHP	LHP
1943	PHI	NL	4	4	0	2	2	0	0	0	0	0	0	0	0	0	3	1
1944	PHI	NL	17	11	6	12	4	1	0	1	0	0	0	0	0	0	14	3
1945	PHI	NL	2	1	1	2	0	0	0	0	0	0	0	0	0	0	2	0
	STL	NL	20	9	11	12	5	3	0	0	0	0	0	0	0	0	13	7
	Total		22	10	12	14	5	3	0	0	0	0	0	0	0	0	15	7
1946	STL	NL	5	3	2	4	1	0	0	0	0	0	0	0	0	2	0	5
1947	PHI	NL	2	0	2	2	0	0	0	0	0	0	0	0	0	1	2	0
Total			50	28	22	34	12	4	0	1	0	0	0	0	0	3	34	16

Rank among batters: 991 • *Top target (3 home runs)*: Hank Wyse • *Number of pitchers victimized*: 40 • *Total ballparks homered in*: 8 • *First HR*: 06/27/1943 off Freddie Fitzsimmons

Dan Adams

DANIEL LESLIE ADAMS
B: 06/19/1889 D: 10/06/1964
BR

Year	Tm	Lg	Tot	H	A	Men-On 0	1	2	3	One-Game 2	3	4	LO	XN	IP	PH	RHP	LHP
1914	KC	FL	1	1	0	1	0	0	0	0	0	0	0	0	0	0	0	1

Rank among batters: 4,707 • *Total ballparks homered in*: 1 • *First HR*: 07/19/1914 off Ad Brennan

Dick Adams

RICHARD LEROY ADAMS
B: 04/08/1920
BR

Year	Tm	Lg	Tot	H	A	Men-On 0	1	2	3	One-Game 2	3	4	LO	XN	IP	PH	RHP	LHP
1947	PHI	AL	2	2	0	2	0	0	0	0	0	0	0	0	0	0	2	0

Rank among batters: 4,129 • *Total ballparks homered in*: 1 • *First HR*: 05/28/1947 off Dave Ferriss

Glenn Adams

GLENN CHARLES ADAMS
B: 10/04/1947
BL

Year	Tm	Lg	Tot	H	A	Men-On 0	1	2	3	One-Game 2	3	4	LO	XN	IP	PH	RHP	LHP
1975	SF	NL	4	0	4	2	1	1	0	1	0	0	0	0	0	1	4	0
1977	MIN	AL	6	4	2	3	1	1	1	0	0	0	0	0	0	0	6	0
1978	MIN	AL	7	3	4	3	4	0	0	1	0	0	0	0	0	1	7	0
1979	MIN	AL	8	6	2	4	3	1	0	0	0	0	0	0	0	0	8	0
1980	MIN	AL	6	3	3	5	1	0	0	0	0	0	0	0	0	0	6	0
1981	MIN	AL	2	1	1	1	1	0	0	0	0	0	0	0	0	0	2	0
1982	TOR	AL	1	0	1	1	0	0	0	0	0	0	0	0	0	0	1	0
Total			34	17	17	19	11	3	1	2	0	0	0	0	0	2	34	0

Rank among batters: 1,315 • Top target (2 home runs): Doug Bird, Mike Paxton, Steve Baker, Kip Young, Steve Stone, Pete Vuckovich • *Number of pitchers victimized*: 28 • *Total ballparks homered in*: 13 • *First HR*: 05/31/1975 off Steve Rogers

Mike Adams

ROBERT MICHAEL ADAMS
B: 07/24/1948
BR

Year	Tm	Lg	Tot	H	A	Men-On 0	1	2	3	One-Game 2	3	4	LO	XN	IP	PH	RHP	LHP
1973	MIN	AL	3	0	3	2	1	0	0	0	0	0	0	0	0	0	2	1

Rank among batters: 3,735 • *Total ballparks homered in*: 2 • *First HR*: 06/27/1973 off David Clyde

Ricky Adams

RICKY LEE ADAMS
B: 01/21/1959
BR

Year	Tm	Lg	Tot	H	A	Men-On 0	Men-On 1	Men-On 2	Men-On 3	One-Game 2	One-Game 3	One-Game 4	LO	XN	IP	PH	RHP	LHP
1983	CAL	AL	2	1	1	2	0	0	0	0	0	0	0	0	0	0	0	2
1985	SF	NL	2	1	1	1	0	1	0	0	0	0	0	0	0	0	1	1
Total			4	2	2	3	0	1	0	0	0	0	0	0	0	0	1	3

Rank among batters: 3,427 • *Total ballparks homered in*: 4 • *First HR*: 06/08/1983 off Jerry Koosman

Sparky Adams

EARL JOHN ADAMS
B: 08/26/1894 D: 02/24/1989
BR

Year	Tm	Lg	Tot	H	A	Men-On 0	Men-On 1	Men-On 2	Men-On 3	One-Game 2	One-Game 3	One-Game 4	LO	XN	IP	PH	RHP	LHP
1923	CHI	NL	4	2	2	1	3	0	0	0	0	0	0	0	2	0	2	2
1924	CHI	NL	1	0	1	1	0	0	0	0	0	0	0	0	1	0	1	0
1925	CHI	NL	2	2	0	2	0	0	0	0	0	0	1	0	0	0	2	0
1931	STL	NL	1	0	1	1	0	0	0	0	0	0	1	0	0	0	0	1
1933	CIN	NL	1	0	1	1	0	0	0	0	0	0	0	0	0	0	0	1
Total			9	4	5	6	3	0	0	0	0	0	2	0	3	0	5	4

Rank among batters: 2,587 • *Top target (2 home runs)*: Clarence Mitchell • *Number of pitchers victimized*: 8 • *Total ballparks homered in*: 4 • *First HR*: 07/01/1923 off Bill Sherdel

Joe Adcock

JOSEPH WILBUR ADCOCK
B: 10/30/1927
BR

Year	Tm	Lg	Tot	H	A	Men-On 0	Men-On 1	Men-On 2	Men-On 3	One-Game 2	One-Game 3	One-Game 4	LO	XN	IP	PH	RHP	LHP
1950	CIN	NL	8	3	5	3	3	2	0	1	0	0	0	0	0	0	4	4
1951	CIN	NL	10	3	7	5	3	2	0	1	0	0	0	0	1	0	4	6
1952	CIN	NL	13	5	8	6	5	1	1	2	0	0	0	0	1	0	8	5
1953	MIL	NL	18	7	11	11	6	1	0	0	0	0	0	0	2	0	16	2
1954	MIL	NL	23	6	17	10	8	4	1	0	0	1	0	0	0	0	21	2
1955	MIL	NL	15	6	9	9	4	2	0	1	0	0	0	0	0	0	8	7
1956	MIL	NL	38	23	15	21	11	4	2	5	0	0	0	0	1	2	34	4
1957	MIL	NL	12	3	9	7	3	1	1	2	0	0	0	0	1	0	11	1
1958	MIL	NL	19	9	10	12	4	2	1	1	0	0	0	0	0	2	11	8
1959	MIL	NL	25	11	14	15	7	3	0	0	0	0	0	0	0	1	14	11
1960	MIL	NL	25	13	12	16	8	0	1	2	0	0	0	0	0	1	20	5
1961	MIL	NL	35	12	23	16	13	5	1	4	0	0	0	1	0	0	26	9
1962	MIL	NL	29	14	15	13	11	3	2	3	0	0	0	0	1	1	22	7
1963	CLE	AL	13	5	8	6	3	4	0	1	0	0	0	1	0	2	7	6
1964	LA	AL	21	6	15	16	3	2	0	3	0	0	0	1	0	0	16	5
1965	CAL	AL	14	4	10	8	6	0	0	0	0	0	0	0	0	0	8	6
1966	CAL	AL	18	7	11	8	8	2	0	1	0	0	0	0	0	3	7	11
Total			336	137	199	182	106	38	10	27	0	1	0	3	7	12	237	99

Rank among batters: 51 • *Top target (8 home runs)*: Roger Craig • *Number of pitchers victimized*: 189 • *Total ballparks homered in*: 25 • *First HR*: 07/05/1950 off Howie Pollet

Bob Addis

ROBERT GORDON ADDIS
B: 11/06/1925
BL

Year	Tm	Lg	Tot	H	A	Men-On 0	Men-On 1	Men-On 2	Men-On 3	One-Game 2	One-Game 3	One-Game 4	LO	XN	IP	PH	RHP	LHP
1951	BOS	NL	1	1	0	1	0	0	0	0	0	0	0	0	0	0	1	0
1952	CHI	NL	1	0	1	0	0	1	0	0	0	0	0	0	0	1	1	0
Total			2	1	1	1	0	1	0	0	0	0	0	0	0	1	2	0

Rank among batters: 4,129 • *Total ballparks homered in*: 2 • *First HR*: 09/26/1951 off Don Newcombe

Jim Adduci

JAMES DAVID ADDUCI
B: 08/09/1959
BL

Year	Tm	Lg	Tot	H	A	Men-On 0	Men-On 1	Men-On 2	Men-On 3	One-Game 2	One-Game 3	One-Game 4	LO	XN	IP	PH	RHP	LHP
1988	MIL	AL	1	1	0	0	1	0	0	0	0	0	0	0	0	0	1	0

Rank among batters: 4,707 • *Total ballparks homered in*: 1 • *First HR*: 08/14/1988 off Dave Schmidt

Morrie Aderholt

MORRIS WOODROW ADERHOLT
B: 09/13/1915 D: 03/18/1955
BL

Year	Tm	Lg	Tot	H	A	Men-On 0	Men-On 1	Men-On 2	Men-On 3	One-Game 2	One-Game 3	One-Game 4	LO	XN	IP	PH	RHP	LHP
1939	WAS	AL	1	1	0	1	0	0	0	0	0	0	0	0	0	0	1	0

Morrie Aderholt *continued*

Year	Tm	Lg	Tot	H	A	Men-On 0	Men-On 1	Men-On 2	Men-On 3	One-Game 2	One-Game 3	One-Game 4	LO	XN	IP	PH	RHP	LHP
1945	BOS	NL	2	2	0	0	1	1	0	0	0	0	0	0	0	0	2	0
Total			3	3	0	1	1	1	0	0	0	0	0	0	0	0	3	0

Rank among batters: 3,735 • *Total ballparks homered in*: 2 • *First HR*: 09/13/1939 off Jack Knott

Dewey Adkins

JOHN DEWEY ADKINS
B: 05/11/1918
BR

Year	Tm	Lg	Tot	H	A	Men-On 0	Men-On 1	Men-On 2	Men-On 3	One-Game 2	One-Game 3	One-Game 4	LO	XN	IP	PH	RHP	LHP
1949	CHI	NL	1	1	0	1	0	0	0	0	0	0	0	0	0	0	1	0

Rank among batters: 4,707 • *Total ballparks homered in*: 1 • *First HR*: 06/22/1949 off Bob Hall

Dave Adlesh

DAVID GEORGE ADLESH
B: 07/15/1943
BR

Year	Tm	Lg	Tot	H	A	Men-On 0	Men-On 1	Men-On 2	Men-On 3	One-Game 2	One-Game 3	One-Game 4	LO	XN	IP	PH	RHP	LHP
1967	HOU	NL	1	0	1	1	0	0	0	0	0	0	0	0	0	0	1	0

Rank among batters: 4,707 • *Total ballparks homered in*: 1 • *First HR*: 08/05/1967 off John Boozer

Tommie Agee

TOMMIE LEE AGEE
B: 08/09/1942
BR

Year	Tm	Lg	Tot	H	A	Men-On 0	Men-On 1	Men-On 2	Men-On 3	One-Game 2	One-Game 3	One-Game 4	LO	XN	IP	PH	RHP	LHP
1963	CLE	AL	1	1	0	1	0	0	0	0	0	0	0	0	0	0	1	0
1966	CHI	AL	22	12	10	12	8	2	0	0	0	0	0	0	1	0	13	9
1967	CHI	AL	14	5	9	9	4	1	0	0	0	0	1	1	0	0	10	4
1968	NY	NL	5	1	4	4	1	0	0	0	0	0	0	0	0	0	3	2
1969	NY	NL	26	14	12	21	4	1	0	4	0	0	4	1	0	0	17	9
1970	NY	NL	24	13	11	16	5	3	0	3	0	0	3	1	0	0	16	8
1971	NY	NL	14	6	8	10	3	0	1	1	0	0	0	0	0	0	11	3
1972	NY	NL	13	6	7	6	6	0	1	0	0	0	1	2	0	0	9	4
1973	HOU	NL	8	3	5	7	1	0	0	0	0	0	2	0	0	0	8	0
	STL	NL	3	1	2	2	1	0	0	0	0	0	0	0	0	1	0	3
	Total		11	4	7	9	2	0	0	0	0	0	2	0	0	1	8	3
Total			130	62	68	88	33	7	2	8	0	0	11	5	1	1	88	42

Rank among batters: 348 • *Top target (6 home runs)*: Ferguson Jenkins • *Number of pitchers victimized*: 96 • *Total ballparks homered in*: 22 • *First HR*: 09/22/1963 off Art Fowler • *Hit for Cycle*—vs STL: 07/06/1970 • *World Series HR*—1; *LCS HR*—2

Harry Agganis

HARRY AGGANIS
B: 04/20/1929 D: 06/27/1955
BL

Year	Tm	Lg	Tot	H	A	Men-On 0	Men-On 1	Men-On 2	Men-On 3	One-Game 2	One-Game 3	One-Game 4	LO	XN	IP	PH	RHP	LHP
1954	BOS	AL	11	7	4	5	3	2	1	0	0	0	0	0	0	0	9	2

Rank among batters: 2,419 • *Total ballparks homered in*: 3 • *First HR*: 04/18/1954 off Arnie Portocarrero

Sam Agnew

SAMUEL LESTER AGNEW
B: 04/12/1887 D: 07/19/1951
BR

Year	Tm	Lg	Tot	H	A	Men-On 0	Men-On 1	Men-On 2	Men-On 3	One-Game 2	One-Game 3	One-Game 4	LO	XN	IP	PH	RHP	LHP
1913	STL	AL	2	1	1	1	0	1	0	0	0	0	0	0	0	0	2	0

Rank among batters: 4,129 • *Total ballparks homered in*: 2 • *First HR*: 06/11/1913 off Boardwalk Brown

Luis Aguayo

LUIS (MURIEL) AGUAYO
B: 03/13/1959
BR

Year	Tm	Lg	Tot	H	A	Men-On 0	Men-On 1	Men-On 2	Men-On 3	One-Game 2	One-Game 3	One-Game 4	LO	XN	IP	PH	RHP	LHP
1980	PHI	NL	1	0	1	0	1	0	0	0	0	0	0	0	0	0	0	1
1981	PHI	NL	1	0	1	1	0	0	0	0	0	0	0	0	0	0	1	0
1982	PHI	NL	3	2	1	2	0	1	0	0	0	0	0	1	0	0	3	0
1984	PHI	NL	3	1	2	2	1	0	0	0	0	0	0	0	0	1	3	0
1985	PHI	NL	6	4	2	4	2	0	0	2	0	0	0	1	0	0	5	1
1986	PHI	NL	4	3	1	3	1	0	0	0	0	0	0	0	0	1	2	2
1987	PHI	NL	12	5	7	11	1	0	0	2	0	0	0	1	0	1	5	7

Luis Aguayo *continued*

Year	Tm	Lg	Tot	H	A	Men-On 0	1	2	3	One-Game 2	3	4	LO	XN	IP	PH	RHP	LHP
1988	PHI	NL	3	3	0	3	0	0	0	0	0	0	0	0	0	0	1	2
	NY	AL	3	0	3	2	1	0	0	0	0	0	0	0	0	1	1	2
	Total		6	3	3	5	1	0	0	0	0	0	0	0	0	1	2	4
1989	CLE	AL	1	1	0	0	1	0	0	0	0	0	0	0	0	0	1	0
Total			37	19	18	28	8	1	0	4	0	0	0	3	0	4	22	15

Rank among batters: 1,252 • *Top target (2 home runs)*: Tom Browning, Jamie Moyer, Neal Heaton • *Number of pitchers victimized*: 34 • *Total ballparks homered in*: 10 • *First HR*: 05/01/1980 off Pete Falcone

Rick Aguilera

RICHARD WARREN AGUILERA
B: 12/31/1961
BR

Year	Tm	Lg	Tot	H	A	Men-On 0	1	2	3	One-Game 2	3	4	LO	XN	IP	PH	RHP	LHP
1986	NY	NL	2	1	1	1	1	0	0	0	0	0	0	0	0	0	2	0
1987	NY	NL	1	0	1	1	0	0	0	0	0	0	0	0	0	0	1	0
Total			3	1	2	2	1	0	0	0	0	0	0	0	0	0	3	0

Rank among batters: 3,735 • *Total ballparks homered in*: 3 • *First HR*: 06/06/1986 off Jose DeLeon

Willie Aikens

WILLIE MAYS AIKENS
B: 10/14/1954
BL

Year	Tm	Lg	Tot	H	A	Men-On 0	1	2	3	One-Game 2	3	4	LO	XN	IP	PH	RHP	LHP
1979	CAL	AL	21	9	12	8	9	2	2	1	0	0	0	0	0	0	20	1
1980	KC	AL	20	5	15	11	8	1	0	1	0	0	0	0	0	0	14	6
1981	KC	AL	17	4	13	11	5	1	0	0	0	0	0	0	0	0	12	5
1982	KC	AL	17	11	6	10	5	1	1	2	0	0	0	0	0	1	13	4
1983	KC	AL	23	11	12	15	5	3	0	2	0	0	0	0	0	0	22	1
1984	TOR	AL	11	3	8	7	3	1	0	1	0	0	0	0	0	1	10	1
1985	TOR	AL	1	0	1	0	1	0	0	0	0	0	0	0	0	1	1	0
Total			110	43	67	62	36	9	3	7	0	0	0	0	0	3	92	18

Rank among batters: 436 • *Top target (4 home runs)*: Jack Morris • *Number of pitchers victimized*: 88 • *Total ballparks homered in*: 15 • *First HR*: 04/12/1979 off Roger Erickson • *World Series HR*—4

Danny Ainge

DANIEL RAE AINGE
B: 03/17/1959
BR

Year	Tm	Lg	Tot	H	A	Men-On 0	1	2	3	One-Game 2	3	4	LO	XN	IP	PH	RHP	LHP
1979	TOR	AL	2	0	2	2	0	0	0	0	0	0	0	0	0	0	2	0

Rank among batters: 4,129 • *Total ballparks homered in*: 1 • *First HR*: 06/02/1979 off Joe Decker

Eddie Ainsmith

EDWARD WILBUR AINSMITH
B: 02/04/1892 D: 09/06/1981
BR

Year	Tm	Lg	Tot	H	A	Men-On 0	1	2	3	One-Game 2	3	4	LO	XN	IP	PH	RHP	LHP
1913	WAS	AL	2	1	1	1	0	1	0	0	0	0	0	0	1	0	2	0
1919	DET	AL	3	2	1	2	0	1	0	0	0	0	0	0	0	0	2	1
1920	DET	AL	1	1	0	0	1	0	0	0	0	0	0	0	0	0	1	0
1922	STL	NL	13	8	5	8	5	0	0	0	0	0	0	0	0	0	7	6
1923	STL	NL	3	1	2	1	1	1	0	0	0	0	0	0	0	0	2	1
Total			22	13	9	12	7	3	0	0	0	0	0	0	1	0	14	8

Rank among batters: 1,719 • *Top target (2 home runs)*: Percy Jones, Dazzy Vance • *Number of pitchers victimized*: 20 • *Total ballparks homered in*: 7 • *First HR*: 09/09/1913 off Fred Blanding

Bill Akers

WILLIAM G. AKERS
B: 12/25/1904 D: 04/13/1962
BR

Year	Tm	Lg	Tot	H	A	Men-On 0	1	2	3	One-Game 2	3	4	LO	XN	IP	PH	RHP	LHP
1929	DET	AL	1	1	0	1	0	0	0	0	0	0	0	0	0	0	1	0
1930	DET	AL	9	9	0	3	5	1	0	1	0	0	0	0	1	0	8	1
1932	BOS	NL	1	0	1	0	1	0	0	0	0	0	0	0	0	0	1	0
Total			11	10	1	4	6	1	0	1	0	0	0	0	1	0	10	1

Rank among batters: 2,419 • *Total ballparks homered in*: 2 • *First HR*: 09/24/1929 off General Crowder

Gus Alberts

AUGUSTUS PETER ALBERTS
B: 1861 D: 05/07/1912
BR

Year	Tm	Lg	Tot	H	A	Men-On 0	1	2	3	One-Game 2	3	4	LO	XN	IP	PH	RHP	LHP
1888	CLE	AA	1	1	0	1	0	0	0	0	0	0	0	0	1	0	0	0

Rank among batters: 4,707 • *Total ballparks homered in*: 1 • *First HR*: 05/16/1888 off Al Mays

Jack Albright

HAROLD JOHN ALBRIGHT
B: 06/30/1921 D: 07/22/1991
BR

Year	Tm	Lg	Tot	H	A	Men-On 0	1	2	3	One-Game 2	3	4	LO	XN	IP	PH	RHP	LHP
1947	PHI	NL	2	0	2	2	0	0	0	0	0	0	0	0	0	0	2	0

Rank among batters: 4,129 • *Total ballparks homered in*: 2 • *First HR*: 06/28/1947 off Mort Cooper

Santo Alcala

SANTO ALCALA
B: 12/23/1952
BR

Year	Tm	Lg	Tot	H	A	Men-On 0	1	2	3	One-Game 2	3	4	LO	XN	IP	PH	RHP	LHP
1977	MON	NL	1	0	1	1	0	0	0	0	0	0	0	0	0	0	1	0

Rank among batters: 4,707 • *Total ballparks homered in*: 1 • *First HR*: 05/27/1977 off Larry Dierker

Luis Alcaraz

ANGEL LUIS (ACOSTA) ALCARAZ
B: 06/20/1941
BR

Year	Tm	Lg	Tot	H	A	Men-On 0	1	2	3	One-Game 2	3	4	LO	XN	IP	PH	RHP	LHP
1968	LA	NL	2	0	2	1	0	1	0	0	0	0	0	0	0	0	1	1
1969	KC	AL	1	0	1	1	0	0	0	0	0	0	0	0	0	0	0	1
1970	KC	AL	1	1	0	1	0	0	0	0	0	0	0	0	0	0	1	0
Total			4	1	3	3	0	1	0	0	0	0	0	0	0	0	2	2

Rank among batters: 3,427 • *Total ballparks homered in*: 4 • *First HR*: 04/26/1968 off Ray Sadecki

Mike Aldrete

MICHAEL PETER ALDRETE
B: 01/29/1961
BL

Year	Tm	Lg	Tot	H	A	Men-On 0	1	2	3	One-Game 2	3	4	LO	XN	IP	PH	RHP	LHP
1986	SF	NL	2	1	1	2	0	0	0	0	0	0	0	0	0	0	2	0
1987	SF	NL	9	7	2	5	3	1	0	1	0	0	0	0	0	1	9	0
1988	SF	NL	3	3	0	1	2	0	0	0	0	0	0	0	0	0	2	1
1989	MON	NL	1	0	1	1	0	0	0	0	0	0	0	0	0	0	1	0
1990	MON	NL	1	0	1	1	0	0	0	0	0	0	0	0	0	1	1	0
1991	CLE	AL	1	0	1	1	0	0	0	0	0	0	0	0	0	0	1	0
1993	OAK	AL	10	5	5	3	5	1	1	0	0	0	0	0	0	1	8	2
1994	OAK	AL	4	2	2	2	2	0	0	0	0	0	0	0	0	2	4	0
1995	OAK	AL	4	2	2	3	1	0	0	0	0	0	0	0	0	2	4	0
Total			35	20	15	19	13	2	1	1	0	0	0	0	0	7	32	3

Rank among batters: 1,291 • *Top target (2 home runs)*: Mike Scott, Jeff Reardon • *Number of pitchers victimized*: 33 • *Total ballparks homered in*: 16 • *First HR*: 06/08/1986 off John Denny

Vic Aldridge

VICTOR EDDINGTON ALDRIDGE
B: 10/25/1893 D: 04/17/1973
BR

Year	Tm	Lg	Tot	H	A	Men-On 0	1	2	3	One-Game 2	3	4	LO	XN	IP	PH	RHP	LHP
1925	PIT	NL	1	0	1	1	0	0	0	0	0	0	0	0	0	0	1	0
1928	NY	NL	1	1	0	1	0	0	0	0	0	0	0	0	0	0	0	1
Total			2	1	1	2	0	0	0	0	0	0	0	0	0	0	1	1

Rank among batters: 4,129 • *Total ballparks homered in*: 2 • *First HR*: 09/01/1925 off Hal Carlson

Chuck Aleno

CHARLES ALENO
B: 02/19/1917
BR

Year	Tm	Lg	Tot	H	A	Men-On 0	1	2	3	One-Game 2	3	4	LO	XN	IP	PH	RHP	LHP
1941	CIN	NL	1	0	1	1	0	0	0	0	0	0	0	0	0	0	1	0
1944	CIN	NL	1	1	0	1	0	0	0	0	0	0	0	0	0	0	1	0
Total			2	1	1	2	0	0	0	0	0	0	0	0	0	0	2	0

Rank among batters: 4,129 • *Total ballparks homered in*: 2 • *First HR*: 06/06/1941 off Si Johnson

Dale Alexander

DAVID DALE ALEXANDER
B: 04/26/1903 D: 03/02/1979
BR

Year	Tm	Lg	Tot	H	A	Men-On 0	1	2	3	One-Game 2	3	4	LO	XN	IP	PH	RHP	LHP
1929	DET	AL	25	10	15	11	9	5	0	1	0	0	0	0	1	0	21	4
1930	DET	AL	20	10	10	9	8	3	0	1	0	0	0	0	0	0	17	3
1931	DET	AL	3	1	2	3	0	0	0	0	0	0	0	0	0	0	2	1
1932	BOS	AL	8	3	5	3	3	1	1	0	0	0	0	0	0	0	4	4
1933	BOS	AL	5	3	2	2	2	1	0	0	0	0	0	0	0	0	3	2
Total			61	27	34	28	22	10	1	2	0	0	0	0	1	0	47	14

Rank among batters: 844 • *Top target (4 home runs)*: George Blaeholder • *Number of pitchers victimized*: 40 • *Total ballparks homered in*: 8 • *First HR*: 04/21/1929 off Chad Kimsey

Gary Alexander

GARY WAYNE ALEXANDER
B: 03/27/1953
BR

Year	Tm	Lg	Tot	H	A	Men-On 0	1	2	3	One-Game 2	3	4	LO	XN	IP	PH	RHP	LHP
1976	SF	NL	2	1	1	1	1	0	0	0	0	0	0	0	0	0	1	1
1977	SF	NL	5	4	1	2	2	1	0	0	0	0	0	0	0	2	4	1
1978	OAK	AL	10	7	3	6	4	0	0	0	0	0	0	0	0	0	8	2
	CLE	AL	17	8	9	6	6	4	1	0	0	0	0	0	0	0	13	4
	Total		27	15	12	12	10	4	1	0	0	0	0	0	0	0	21	6
1979	CLE	AL	15	11	4	9	5	1	0	0	0	0	0	0	0	1	6	9
1980	CLE	AL	5	3	2	2	2	1	0	0	0	0	0	0	0	2	3	2
1981	PIT	NL	1	0	1	0	1	0	0	0	0	0	0	0	0	0	0	1
Total			55	34	21	26	21	7	1	0	0	0	0	0	0	5	35	20

Rank among batters: 926 • *Top target (3 home runs)*: Jack Billingham, Dick Pole • *Number of pitchers victimized*: 46 • *Total ballparks homered in*: 16 • *First HR*: 09/05/1976 off Dave Tomlin

Grover Alexander

GROVER CLEVELAND ALEXANDER
B: 01/26/1887 D: 11/04/1950
BR HOF

Year	Tm	Lg	Tot	H	A	Men-On 0	1	2	3	One-Game 2	3	4	LO	XN	IP	PH	RHP	LHP
1912	PHI	NL	2	2	0	1	0	1	0	0	0	0	0	0	0	0	2	0
1915	PHI	NL	1	1	0	1	0	0	0	0	0	0	0	0	0	0	1	0
1917	PHI	NL	1	1	0	1	0	0	0	0	0	0	0	0	0	0	1	0
1920	CHI	NL	1	1	0	1	0	0	0	0	0	0	0	1	0	0	1	0
1921	CHI	NL	1	1	0	1	0	0	0	0	0	0	0	0	0	0	1	0
1923	CHI	NL	1	1	0	0	0	1	0	0	0	0	0	0	0	0	1	0
1924	CHI	NL	1	0	1	1	0	0	0	0	0	0	0	0	0	0	1	0
1925	CHI	NL	2	2	0	2	0	0	0	0	0	0	0	0	0	0	0	2
1928	STL	NL	1	0	1	1	0	0	0	0	0	0	0	0	0	0	1	0
Total			11	9	2	9	0	2	0	0	0	0	0	1	0	0	9	2

Rank among batters: 2,419 • *Total ballparks homered in*: 3 • *First HR*: 08/10/1912 off Bert Humphries

Manny Alexander

MANUEL DEJESUS ALEXANDER
B: 03/20/1971
BR

Year	Tm	Lg	Tot	H	A	Men-On 0	1	2	3	One-Game 2	3	4	LO	XN	IP	PH	RHP	LHP
1995	BAL	AL	3	2	1	2	1	0	0	0	0	0	0	0	0	0	1	2

Rank among batters: 3,735 • *Total ballparks homered in*: 2 • *First HR*: 06/06/1995 off Dave Fleming

Walt Alexander

WALTER ERNEST ALEXANDER
B: 03/05/1891 D: 12/29/1978
BR

Year	Tm	Lg	Tot	H	A	Men-On 0	1	2	3	One-Game 2	3	4	LO	XN	IP	PH	RHP	LHP
1915	NY	AL	1	1	0	1	0	0	0	0	0	0	0	0	0	0	1	0

Rank among batters: 4,707 • *Total ballparks homered in*: 1 • *First HR*: 09/24/1915 off Clarence Garrett

Edgardo Alfonzo

EDGARDO ANTONIO ALFONZO
B: 08/11/1973
BR

Year	Tm	Lg	Tot	H	A	Men-On 0	1	2	3	One-Game 2	3	4	LO	XN	IP	PH	RHP	LHP
1995	NY	NL	4	0	4	1	2	1	0	0	0	0	0	0	1	0	2	2

Rank among batters: 3,427 • *Total ballparks homered in*: 3 • *First HR*: 05/06/1995 off Matt Grott

Year	Tm	Lg	Tot	H	A	Men-On 0	1	2	3	One-Game 2	3	4	LO	XN	IP	PH	RHP	LHP

Luis Alicea

LUIS RENE (DEJESUS) ALICEA
B: 07/29/1965
BB

Year	Tm	Lg	Tot	H	A	0	1	2	3	2	3	4	LO	XN	IP	PH	RHP	LHP
1988	STL	NL	1	1	0	1	0	0	0	0	0	0	0	0	0	0	1	0
1992	STL	NL	2	2	0	2	0	0	0	0	0	0	0	0	0	0	2	0
1993	STL	NL	3	2	1	0	1	1	1	0	0	0	0	0	0	0	2	1
1994	STL	NL	5	3	2	3	1	1	0	0	0	0	0	0	0	2	5	0
1995	BOS	AL	6	0	6	4	1	1	0	1	0	0	0	0	0	0	4	2
Total			17	8	9	10	3	3	1	1	0	0	0	0	0	2	14	3

Rank among batters: 1,969 • *Total ballparks homered in*: 7 • *First HR*: 05/08/1988 off Don Sutton • *Switch hit HR in 1 game*—1 time • *LCS HR*—1

Andy Allanson

ANDREW NEAL ALLANSON
B: 12/22/1961
BR

Year	Tm	Lg	Tot	H	A	0	1	2	3	2	3	4	LO	XN	IP	PH	RHP	LHP
1986	CLE	AL	1	0	1	0	1	0	0	0	0	0	0	0	0	0	1	0
1987	CLE	AL	3	2	1	2	1	0	0	0	0	0	0	0	0	0	3	0
1988	CLE	AL	5	4	1	3	0	1	1	0	0	0	0	0	0	0	5	0
1989	CLE	AL	3	1	2	2	1	0	0	0	0	0	0	0	0	0	3	0
1991	DET	AL	1	0	1	0	0	1	0	0	0	0	0	0	0	0	1	0
1995	CAL	AL	3	1	2	2	1	0	0	1	0	0	0	0	0	0	3	0
Total			16	8	8	9	4	2	1	1	0	0	0	0	0	0	16	0

Rank among batters: 2,029 • *Total ballparks homered in*: 7 • *First HR*: 06/23/1986 off Jim Beattie

Bernie Allen

BERNARD KEITH ALLEN
B: 04/16/1939
BL

Year	Tm	Lg	Tot	H	A	0	1	2	3	2	3	4	LO	XN	IP	PH	RHP	LHP
1962	MIN	AL	12	6	6	6	3	3	0	0	0	0	0	0	0	0	11	1
1963	MIN	AL	9	5	4	6	3	0	0	1	0	0	1	0	0	0	9	0
1964	MIN	AL	6	3	3	4	2	0	0	1	0	0	0	0	0	0	6	0
1966	MIN	AL	5	4	1	1	3	1	0	0	0	0	0	0	0	1	4	1
1967	WAS	AL	3	1	2	2	1	0	0	0	0	0	0	0	0	0	3	0
1968	WAS	AL	6	1	5	1	4	1	0	0	0	0	0	0	0	0	5	1
1969	WAS	AL	9	4	5	6	3	0	0	0	0	0	0	0	0	0	9	0
1970	WAS	AL	8	4	4	5	1	2	0	0	0	0	0	0	0	0	8	0
1971	WAS	AL	4	2	2	3	1	0	0	0	0	0	0	0	0	1	4	0
1972	NY	AL	9	3	6	7	2	0	0	0	0	0	0	1	0	0	9	0
1973	MON	NL	2	1	1	1	1	0	0	0	0	0	0	0	0	0	2	0
Total			73	34	39	42	24	7	0	2	0	0	1	1	0	2	70	3

Rank among batters: 715 • *Top target (3 home runs)*: Sonny Siebert, Stan Bahnsen • *Number of pitchers victimized*: 58 • *Total ballparks homered in*: 15 • *First HR*: 04/20/1962 off Jim Donohue

Bob Allen

ROBERT GILMAN ALLEN
B: 07/10/1867 D: 05/04/1943
BR

Year	Tm	Lg	Tot	H	A	0	1	2	3	2	3	4	LO	XN	IP	PH	RHP	LHP
1890	PHI	NL	2	0	2	0	1	0	1	0	0	0	0	0	0	0	1	1
1891	PHI	NL	1	0	1	1	0	0	0	0	0	0	0	0	0	0	1	0
1892	PHI	NL	2	0	2	1	0	1	0	0	0	0	0	0	0	0	1	1
1893	PHI	NL	8	4	4	3	3	1	1	0	0	0	0	0	1	0	6	0
1897	BOS	NL	1	1	0	0	1	0	0	0	0	0	0	0	0	0	0	1
Total			14	5	9	5	5	2	2	0	0	0	0	0	1	0	9	2

Rank among batters: 2,169 • *Total ballparks homered in*: 8 • *First HR*: 07/04/1890 off Frank Foreman

Dick Allen

RICHARD ANTHONY ALLEN
B: 03/08/1942
BR

Year	Tm	Lg	Tot	H	A	0	1	2	3	2	3	4	LO	XN	IP	PH	RHP	LHP
1964	PHI	NL	29	14	15	16	11	2	0	3	0	0	0	2	2	0	18	11
1965	PHI	NL	20	9	11	12	7	0	1	1	0	0	1	0	0	0	14	6
1966	PHI	NL	40	17	23	22	12	6	0	4	0	0	0	2	3	0	15	25
1967	PHI	NL	23	9	14	11	7	5	0	1	0	0	0	1	0	0	15	8

Year	Tm	Lg	Tot	H	A	Men-On 0	1	2	3	One-Game 2	3	4	LO	XN	IP	PH	RHP	LHP

Dick Allen *continued*

Year	Tm	Lg	Tot	H	A	Men-On 0	1	2	3	One-Game 2	3	4	LO	XN	IP	PH	RHP	LHP
1968	PHI	NL	33	17	16	19	9	3	2	6	1	0	0	0	0	0	24	9
1969	PHI	NL	32	21	11	21	8	2	1	2	0	0	0	0	0	0	21	11
1970	STL	NL	34	17	17	14	13	5	2	4	0	0	0	0	0	0	26	8
1971	LA	NL	23	11	12	14	7	2	0	1	0	0	0	1	0	0	13	10
1972	CHI	AL	37	27	10	15	16	6	0	4	0	0	0	1	2	1	22	15
1973	CHI	AL	16	7	9	8	5	3	0	1	0	0	0	1	0	0	9	7
1974	CHI	AL	32	15	17	15	13	3	1	2	0	0	0	1	0	0	18	14
1975	PHI	NL	12	6	6	8	3	1	0	1	0	0	0	0	0	0	7	5
1976	PHI	NL	15	9	6	8	5	1	1	1	0	0	0	1	0	0	8	7
1977	OAK	AL	5	4	1	2	3	0	0	0	0	0	0	0	0	0	3	2
Total			351	183	168	185	119	39	8	31	1	0	1	10	7	1	213	138

Rank among batters: 44 • *Top target (11 home runs)*: Ken Holtzman • *Number of pitchers victimized*: 206 • *Total ballparks homered in*: 29 • *First HR*: 04/17/1964 off Dick Ellsworth • *All-Star HR*—1

Ethan Allen

ETHAN NATHAN ALLEN
B: 01/01/1904 D: 09/15/1993
BR

Year	Tm	Lg	Tot	H	A	Men-On 0	1	2	3	One-Game 2	3	4	LO	XN	IP	PH	RHP	LHP
1927	CIN	NL	2	1	1	1	1	0	0	0	0	0	0	0	1	0	2	0
1928	CIN	NL	1	0	1	0	1	0	0	0	0	0	0	0	0	0	1	0
1929	CIN	NL	6	3	3	3	2	1	0	0	0	0	0	0	1	0	6	0
1930	CIN	NL	3	3	0	3	0	0	0	0	0	0	0	0	0	0	0	3
	NY	NL	7	5	2	5	1	0	1	0	0	0	0	0	0	0	4	3
	Total		10	8	2	8	1	0	1	0	0	0	0	0	0	0	4	6
1931	NY	NL	5	5	0	3	1	0	1	0	0	0	0	0	0	2	4	1
1932	NY	NL	1	0	1	1	0	0	0	0	0	0	0	0	0	0	0	1
1934	PHI	NL	10	4	6	5	3	2	0	0	0	0	0	0	0	0	9	1
1935	PHI	NL	8	6	2	5	3	0	0	0	0	0	1	0	0	0	5	3
1936	PHI	NL	1	1	0	0	0	1	0	0	0	0	0	0	0	0	1	0
	CHI	NL	3	0	3	3	0	0	0	0	0	0	0	0	0	0	3	0
	Total		4	1	3	3	0	1	0	0	0	0	0	0	0	0	4	0
Total			47	28	19	29	12	4	2	0	0	0	1	0	2	2	35	12

Rank among batters: 1,040 • *Top target (4 home runs)*: Watty Clark • *Number of pitchers victimized*: 35 • *Total ballparks homered in*: 7 • *First HR*: 05/06/1927 off Johnny Wertz

Frank Allen

FRANK LEON ALLEN
B: 08/26/1889 D: 07/30/1933
BR

Year	Tm	Lg	Tot	H	A	Men-On 0	1	2	3	One-Game 2	3	4	LO	XN	IP	PH	RHP	LHP
1912	BRO	NL	1	0	1	1	0	0	0	0	0	0	0	0	0	0	1	0
1913	BRO	NL	1	0	1	1	0	0	0	0	0	0	0	0	0	0	1	0
Total			2	0	2	2	0	0	0	0	0	0	0	0	0	0	2	0

Rank among batters: 4,129 • *Total ballparks homered in*: 2 • *First HR*: 05/18/1912 off Laurence Cheney

Hank Allen

HAROLD ANDREW ALLEN
B: 07/23/1940
BR

Year	Tm	Lg	Tot	H	A	Men-On 0	1	2	3	One-Game 2	3	4	LO	XN	IP	PH	RHP	LHP
1966	WAS	AL	1	1	0	0	0	1	0	0	0	0	0	0	0	0	0	1
1967	WAS	AL	3	1	2	2	0	1	0	0	0	0	0	0	0	1	2	1
1968	WAS	AL	1	1	0	0	1	0	0	0	0	0	0	0	0	0	0	1
1969	WAS	AL	1	1	0	1	0	0	0	0	0	0	0	0	0	0	1	0
Total			6	4	2	3	1	2	0	0	0	0	0	0	0	1	3	3

Rank among batters: 2,988 • *Total ballparks homered in*: 3 • *First HR*: 09/23/1966 off Tommy John

Jamie Allen

JAMES BRADLEY ALLEN
B: 05/29/1958
BR

Year	Tm	Lg	Tot	H	A	Men-On 0	1	2	3	One-Game 2	3	4	LO	XN	IP	PH	RHP	LHP
1983	SEA	AL	4	1	3	2	2	0	0	0	0	0	0	0	0	0	1	3

Rank among batters: 3,427 • *Total ballparks homered in*: 4 • *First HR*: 05/08/1983 off Mark Clear

Johnny Allen

JOHN THOMAS ALLEN
B: 09/30/1905 D: 05/29/1959
BR

Year	Tm	Lg	Tot	H	A	Men-On 0	Men-On 1	Men-On 2	Men-On 3	One-Game 2	One-Game 3	One-Game 4	LO	XN	IP	PH	RHP	LHP
1932	NY	AL	1	1	0	0	0	1	0	0	0	0	0	0	0	0	1	0
1935	NY	AL	1	0	1	0	1	0	0	0	0	0	0	0	0	0	1	0
1938	CLE	AL	1	1	0	0	0	1	0	0	0	0	0	0	0	0	0	1
1941	STL	AL	1	0	1	1	0	0	0	0	0	0	0	0	0	0	1	0
Total			4	2	2	1	1	2	0	0	0	0	0	0	0	0	3	1

Rank among batters: 3,427 • *Total ballparks homered in*: 4 • *First HR*: 05/21/1932 off General Crowder

Lloyd Allen

LLOYD CECIL ALLEN
B: 05/08/1950
BR

Year	Tm	Lg	Tot	H	A	Men-On 0	Men-On 1	Men-On 2	Men-On 3	One-Game 2	One-Game 3	One-Game 4	LO	XN	IP	PH	RHP	LHP
1971	CAL	AL	1	1	0	1	0	0	0	0	0	0	0	0	0	0	1	0

Rank among batters: 4,707 • *Total ballparks homered in*: 1 • *First HR*: 07/16/1971 off Dave Boswell

Myron Allen

MYRON SMITH ALLEN
B: 03/22/1854 D: 03/08/1924
BR

Year	Tm	Lg	Tot	H	A	Men-On 0	Men-On 1	Men-On 2	Men-On 3	One-Game 2	One-Game 3	One-Game 4	LO	XN	IP	PH	RHP	LHP
1887	CLE	AA	4	1	3	0	2	2	0	0	0	0	0	0	0	0	1	2

Rank among batters: 3,427 • *Top target (2 home runs)*: Tony Mullane • *Number of pitchers victimized*: 3 • *Total ballparks homered in*: 4 • *First HR*: 04/26/1887 off Peak-A-Boo Veach

Ron Allen

RONALD FREDERICK ALLEN
B: 12/23/1943
BB

Year	Tm	Lg	Tot	H	A	Men-On 0	Men-On 1	Men-On 2	Men-On 3	One-Game 2	One-Game 3	One-Game 4	LO	XN	IP	PH	RHP	LHP
1972	STL	NL	1	0	1	1	0	0	0	0	0	0	0	0	0	0	1	0

Rank among batters: 4,707 • *Total ballparks homered in*: 1 • *First HR*: 08/17/1972 off Mike Corkins

Gary Allenson

GARY MARTIN ALLENSON
B: 02/04/1955
BR

Year	Tm	Lg	Tot	H	A	Men-On 0	Men-On 1	Men-On 2	Men-On 3	One-Game 2	One-Game 3	One-Game 4	LO	XN	IP	PH	RHP	LHP
1979	BOS	AL	3	1	2	2	0	0	1	0	0	0	0	0	0	0	1	2
1981	BOS	AL	5	3	2	2	1	1	1	0	0	0	0	0	0	0	3	2
1982	BOS	AL	6	3	3	4	1	1	0	0	0	0	0	0	0	0	5	1
1983	BOS	AL	3	1	2	0	2	1	0	0	0	0	0	0	0	0	2	1
1984	BOS	AL	2	0	2	1	0	1	0	0	0	0	0	0	0	0	0	2
Total			19	8	11	9	4	4	2	0	0	0	0	0	0	0	11	8

Rank among batters: 1,861 • *Top target (2 home runs)*: Ross Baumgarten, Britt Burns • *Number of pitchers victimized*: 17 • *Total ballparks homered in*: 9 • *First HR*: 04/16/1979 off Rick Wise

Gene Alley

LEONARD EUGENE ALLEY
B: 07/10/1940
BR

Year	Tm	Lg	Tot	H	A	Men-On 0	Men-On 1	Men-On 2	Men-On 3	One-Game 2	One-Game 3	One-Game 4	LO	XN	IP	PH	RHP	LHP
1964	PIT	NL	6	2	4	6	0	0	0	0	0	0	0	0	0	0	1	5
1965	PIT	NL	5	3	2	2	2	1	0	0	0	0	0	0	0	0	3	2
1966	PIT	NL	7	3	4	5	2	0	0	0	0	0	1	0	0	0	5	2
1967	PIT	NL	6	1	5	3	3	0	0	0	0	0	0	0	0	0	5	1
1968	PIT	NL	4	1	3	4	0	0	0	0	0	0	0	0	0	0	1	3
1969	PIT	NL	8	1	7	5	2	1	0	1	0	0	0	1	1	0	7	1
1970	PIT	NL	8	1	7	6	1	0	1	1	0	0	0	0	1	0	5	3
1971	PIT	NL	6	2	4	4	2	0	0	1	0	0	0	0	0	0	5	1
1972	PIT	NL	3	2	1	2	0	1	0	0	0	0	0	0	0	0	3	0
1973	PIT	NL	2	1	1	1	0	1	0	0	0	0	0	0	0	0	2	0
Total			55	17	38	38	12	4	1	3	0	0	1	1	2	0	37	18

Rank among batters: 926 • *Top target (3 home runs)*: Carl Morton • *Number of pitchers victimized*: 46 • *Total ballparks homered in*: 14 • *First HR*: 05/03/1964 off Ernie Broglio

Gair Allie

GAIR ROOSEVELT ALLIE
B: 10/28/1931
BR

Year	Tm	Lg	Tot	H	A	Men-On 0	Men-On 1	Men-On 2	Men-On 3	One-Game 2	One-Game 3	One-Game 4	LO	XN	IP	PH	RHP	LHP
1954	PIT	NL	3	2	1	2	0	1	0	0	0	0	1	0	0	0	1	2

Rank among batters: 3,735 • *Total ballparks homered in*: 2 • *First HR*: 04/22/1954 off Windy McCall

Bob Allietta

ROBERT GEORGE ALLIETTA
B: 05/01/1952
BR

Year	Tm	Lg	Tot	H	A	Men-On 0	Men-On 1	Men-On 2	Men-On 3	One-Game 2	One-Game 3	One-Game 4	LO	XN	IP	PH	RHP	LHP
1975	CAL	AL	1	0	1	1	0	0	0	0	0	0	0	0	0	0	1	0

Rank among batters: 4,707 • *Total ballparks homered in*: 1 • *First HR*: 09/14/1975 off Steve Busby

Bob Allison

WILLIAM ROBERT ALLISON
B: 07/11/1934 D: 04/09/1995
BR

Year	Tm	Lg	Tot	H	A	Men-On 0	Men-On 1	Men-On 2	Men-On 3	One-Game 2	One-Game 3	One-Game 4	LO	XN	IP	PH	RHP	LHP
1959	WAS	AL	30	17	13	22	6	1	1	2	0	0	0	0	0	0	27	3
1960	WAS	AL	15	9	6	10	5	0	0	0	0	0	1	1	0	0	11	4
1961	MIN	AL	29	14	15	13	9	4	3	5	0	0	1	0	0	0	22	7
1962	MIN	AL	29	15	14	11	10	7	1	2	0	0	0	0	0	0	24	5
1963	MIN	AL	35	15	20	20	11	4	0	2	1	0	0	0	0	0	31	4
1964	MIN	AL	32	15	17	23	8	1	0	1	0	0	0	1	0	1	21	11
1965	MIN	AL	23	10	13	12	7	4	0	1	0	0	0	0	0	1	16	7
1966	MIN	AL	8	1	7	5	2	1	0	0	0	0	0	1	0	2	0	8
1967	MIN	AL	24	13	11	12	8	4	0	2	0	0	1	0	0	2	12	12
1968	MIN	AL	22	9	13	14	7	1	0	0	0	0	0	0	0	0	15	7
1969	MIN	AL	8	5	3	5	2	1	0	1	0	0	0	0	0	1	0	8
1970	MIN	AL	1	0	1	0	1	0	0	0	0	0	0	0	0	1	0	1
Total			256	123	133	147	76	28	5	16	1	0	2	3	0	8	179	77

Rank among batters: 98 • *Top target (5 home runs)*: Bill Monbouquette, Earl Wilson, Steve Barber • *Number of pitchers victimized*: 152 • *Total ballparks homered in*: 14 • *First HR*: 04/16/1959 off Herb Moford • *World Series HR*—1

Beau Allred

DALE LEBEAU ALLRED
B: 06/04/1965
BL

Year	Tm	Lg	Tot	H	A	Men-On 0	Men-On 1	Men-On 2	Men-On 3	One-Game 2	One-Game 3	One-Game 4	LO	XN	IP	PH	RHP	LHP
1990	CLE	AL	1	0	1	0	1	0	0	0	0	0	0	0	0	0	1	0
1991	CLE	AL	3	0	3	3	0	0	0	0	0	0	0	0	0	0	3	0
Total			4	0	4	3	1	0	0	0	0	0	0	0	0	0	4	0

Rank among batters: 3,427 • *Total ballparks homered in*: 4 • *First HR*: 06/08/1990 off Roger Clemens

Mel Almada

BALDOMERO MELO (QUIROS) ALMADA
B: 02/07/1913 D: 08/13/1988
BL

Year	Tm	Lg	Tot	H	A	Men-On 0	Men-On 1	Men-On 2	Men-On 3	One-Game 2	One-Game 3	One-Game 4	LO	XN	IP	PH	RHP	LHP
1933	BOS	AL	1	1	0	1	0	0	0	0	0	0	0	0	0	0	0	1
1935	BOS	AL	3	0	3	2	1	0	0	0	0	0	0	0	0	0	3	0
1936	BOS	AL	1	0	1	1	0	0	0	0	0	0	0	0	0	0	1	0
1937	BOS	AL	1	0	1	0	1	0	0	0	0	0	0	0	0	0	1	0
	WAS	AL	4	1	3	2	1	1	0	0	0	0	1	0	0	0	3	1
	Total		5	1	4	2	2	1	0	0	0	0	1	0	0	0	4	1
1938	WAS	AL	1	0	1	1	0	0	0	0	0	0	1	0	1	0	1	0
	STL	AL	3	2	1	2	1	0	0	0	0	0	0	0	0	0	2	1
	Total		4	2	2	3	1	0	0	0	0	0	1	0	1	0	3	1
1939	STL	AL	1	0	1	1	0	0	0	0	0	0	0	0	0	0	1	0
Total			15	4	11	10	4	1	0	0	0	0	2	0	1	0	12	3

Rank among batters: 2,096 • *Top target (2 home runs)*: Bill Dietrich • *Number of pitchers victimized*: 14 • *Total ballparks homered in*: 8 • *First HR*: 09/23/1933 off Herb Pennock

Rafael Almeida

RAFAEL D. ALMEIDA
B: 07/30/1887 D: 03/ /1968
BR

Year	Tm	Lg	Tot	H	A	Men-On 0	Men-On 1	Men-On 2	Men-On 3	One-Game 2	One-Game 3	One-Game 4	LO	XN	IP	PH	RHP	LHP
1913	CIN	NL	3	0	3	1	2	0	0	0	0	0	0	0	1	0	1	2

Rank among batters: 3,735 • *Total ballparks homered in*: 3 • *First HR*: 04/30/1913 off George Pearce

Bill Almon

WILLIAM FRANCIS ALMON
B: 11/21/1952
BR

Year	Tm	Lg	Tot	H	A	Men-On 0	1	2	3	One-Game 2	3	4	LO	XN	IP	PH	RHP	LHP
1976	SD	NL	1	0	1	0	1	0	0	0	0	0	0	0	0	0	1	0
1977	SD	NL	2	1	1	1	0	1	0	0	0	0	0	0	0	0	2	0
1979	SD	NL	1	0	1	1	0	0	0	0	0	0	0	0	0	0	1	0
1981	CHI	AL	4	1	3	2	0	2	0	0	0	0	0	0	0	0	2	2
1982	CHI	AL	4	2	2	4	0	0	0	0	0	0	0	0	0	0	4	0
1983	OAK	AL	4	3	1	2	1	1	0	0	0	0	0	0	0	0	2	2
1984	OAK	AL	7	5	2	6	1	0	0	0	0	0	1	0	0	1	1	6
1985	PIT	NL	6	3	3	1	3	0	2	0	0	0	1	0	0	1	3	3
1986	PIT	NL	7	4	3	4	2	1	0	0	0	0	1	1	1	0	4	3
Total			36	19	17	21	8	5	2	0	0	0	3	1	1	2	20	16

Rank among batters: 1,274 • *Top target (2 home runs)*: Charles Hudson, Joe Hesketh • *Number of pitchers victimized*: 34 • *Total ballparks homered in*: 13 • *First HR*: 09/19/1976 off Bo McLaughlin

Roberto Alomar

ROBERTO (VELAZQUEZ) ALOMAR
B: 02/05/1968
BB

Year	Tm	Lg	Tot	H	A	Men-On 0	1	2	3	One-Game 2	3	4	LO	XN	IP	PH	RHP	LHP
1988	SD	NL	9	5	4	8	1	0	0	0	0	0	0	1	0	0	5	4
1989	SD	NL	7	3	4	5	2	0	0	0	0	0	1	0	0	0	3	4
1990	SD	NL	6	4	2	3	3	0	0	0	0	0	1	0	0	0	3	3
1991	TOR	AL	9	6	3	7	2	0	0	1	0	0	0	1	0	0	5	4
1992	TOR	AL	8	5	3	2	4	2	0	0	0	0	0	0	0	0	3	5
1993	TOR	AL	17	8	9	10	3	3	1	1	0	0	0	0	1	0	13	4
1994	TOR	AL	8	4	4	3	3	2	0	0	0	0	0	0	0	0	4	4
1995	TOR	AL	13	7	6	9	4	0	0	1	0	0	0	0	0	0	11	2
Total			77	42	35	47	22	7	1	3	0	0	2	2	1	0	47	30

Rank among batters: 682 • *Top target (3 home runs)*: Jack McDowell • *Number of pitchers victimized*: 67 • *Total ballparks homered in*: 20 • *First HR*: 04/30/1988 off Bob Kipper • *Switch hit HR in 1 game*—2 times • *LCS HR*—2; *All-Star HR*—1

Sandy Alomar

SANTOS (CONDE) ALOMAR
B: 10/19/1943
BB

Year	Tm	Lg	Tot	H	A	Men-On 0	1	2	3	One-Game 2	3	4	LO	XN	IP	PH	RHP	LHP
1969	CAL	AL	1	1	0	1	0	0	0	0	0	0	1	0	1	0	1	0
1970	CAL	AL	2	1	1	1	1	0	0	0	0	0	0	0	0	0	0	2
1971	CAL	AL	4	1	3	3	1	0	0	0	0	0	1	0	0	0	0	4
1972	CAL	AL	1	0	1	1	0	0	0	0	0	0	0	0	0	0	1	0
1974	NY	AL	1	0	1	0	1	0	0	0	0	0	0	0	0	0	0	1
1975	NY	AL	2	1	1	1	1	0	0	0	0	0	0	0	0	0	1	1
1976	NY	AL	1	0	1	0	1	0	0	0	0	0	0	1	0	0	0	1
1977	TEX	AL	1	0	1	1	0	0	0	0	0	0	0	0	0	0	1	0
Total			13	4	9	8	5	0	0	0	0	0	2	1	1	0	4	9

Rank among batters: 2,248 • *Total ballparks homered in*: 8 • *First HR*: 06/23/1969 off Dick Woodson

Sandy Alomar

SANTOS (VELAZQUEZ) ALOMAR
B: 06/18/1966
BR

Year	Tm	Lg	Tot	H	A	Men-On 0	1	2	3	One-Game 2	3	4	LO	XN	IP	PH	RHP	LHP
1989	SD	NL	1	1	0	0	0	1	0	0	0	0	0	0	0	0	1	0
1990	CLE	AL	9	5	4	8	1	0	0	0	0	0	0	2	0	0	7	2
1992	CLE	AL	2	1	1	0	1	0	1	0	0	0	0	0	0	0	2	0
1993	CLE	AL	6	3	3	4	2	0	0	0	0	0	0	0	0	0	5	1
1994	CLE	AL	14	4	10	10	1	3	0	0	0	0	0	0	0	0	14	0
1995	CLE	AL	10	4	6	4	3	3	0	2	0	0	0	1	0	0	6	4
Total			42	18	24	26	8	7	1	2	0	0	0	3	0	0	35	7

Rank among batters: 1,138 • *Top target (2 home runs)*: Greg Harris, Tim Belcher, Kenny Rogers • *Number of pitchers victimized*: 39 • *Total ballparks homered in*: 16 • *First HR*: 09/30/1989 off Rick Reuschel

Felipe Alou

FELIPE ROJAS ALOU
B: 05/12/1935
BR

Year	Tm	Lg	Tot	H	A	Men-On 0	1	2	3	One-Game 2	3	4	LO	XN	IP	PH	RHP	LHP
1958	SF	NL	4	1	3	2	2	0	0	0	0	0	1	0	0	0	3	1
1959	SF	NL	10	6	4	5	5	0	0	0	0	0	0	0	0	0	7	3

Felipe Alou *continued*

Year	Tm	Lg	Tot	H	A	Men-On 0	1	2	3	One-Game 2	3	4	LO	XN	IP	PH	RHP	LHP
1960	SF	NL	8	3	5	5	0	3	0	0	0	0	0	0	0	0	3	5
1961	SF	NL	18	10	8	11	4	2	1	2	0	0	1	1	0	0	9	9
1962	SF	NL	25	15	10	16	7	2	0	2	0	0	0	0	0	0	17	8
1963	SF	NL	20	8	12	11	7	2	0	0	0	0	1	0	0	0	13	7
1964	MIL	NL	9	4	5	6	2	1	0	0	0	0	0	0	1	0	7	2
1965	MIL	NL	23	11	12	16	4	3	0	3	0	0	5	1	0	2	17	6
1966	ATL	NL	31	19	12	24	6	1	0	6	0	0	5	1	0	0	23	8
1967	ATL	NL	15	11	4	12	2	0	1	0	0	0	5	1	0	1	13	2
1968	ATL	NL	11	4	7	8	3	0	0	1	0	0	2	0	0	0	9	2
1969	ATL	NL	5	2	3	3	2	0	0	0	0	0	0	0	0	0	4	1
1970	OAK	AL	8	3	5	5	1	2	0	0	0	0	0	0	0	0	5	3
1971	NY	AL	8	4	4	3	3	2	0	0	0	0	0	0	0	1	2	6
1972	NY	AL	6	2	4	3	2	1	0	0	0	0	0	0	0	1	0	6
1973	NY	AL	4	2	2	2	2	0	0	0	0	0	0	0	0	0	1	3
	MON	NL	1	0	1	1	0	0	0	0	0	0	0	0	0	0	0	1
	Total		5	2	3	3	2	0	0	0	0	0	0	0	0	0	1	4
Total			206	105	101	133	52	19	2	14	0	0	20	4	1	5	133	73

Rank among batters: 171 • *Top target (7 home runs)*: Sandy Koufax • *Number of pitchers victimized*: 122 • *Total ballparks homered in*: 26 • *First HR*: 06/11/1958 off Vern Law

Jesus Alou

JESUS MARIA ROJAS ALOU
B: 03/24/1942
BR

Year	Tm	Lg	Tot	H	A	Men-On 0	1	2	3	One-Game 2	3	4	LO	XN	IP	PH	RHP	LHP
1964	SF	NL	3	0	3	3	0	0	0	0	0	0	0	0	0	0	1	2
1965	SF	NL	9	5	4	6	3	0	0	0	0	0	0	0	0	0	5	4
1966	SF	NL	1	0	1	1	0	0	0	0	0	0	0	0	0	0	0	1
1967	SF	NL	5	4	1	4	0	1	0	0	0	0	1	0	0	0	2	3
1969	HOU	NL	5	1	4	2	2	1	0	0	0	0	0	0	0	0	1	4
1970	HOU	NL	1	1	0	1	0	0	0	0	0	0	0	0	0	0	1	0
1971	HOU	NL	2	0	2	1	1	0	0	0	0	0	0	0	0	0	2	0
1973	HOU	NL	1	0	1	0	0	1	0	0	0	0	0	0	0	0	1	0
	OAK	AL	1	0	1	0	1	0	0	0	0	0	0	0	0	0	1	0
	Total		2	0	2	0	1	1	0	0	0	0	0	0	0	0	2	0
1974	OAK	AL	2	0	2	2	0	0	0	0	0	0	1	0	0	0	1	1
1978	HOU	NL	2	1	1	1	0	1	0	0	0	0	0	0	0	1	0	2
Total			32	12	20	21	7	4	0	0	0	0	2	0	0	1	15	17

Rank among batters: 1,360 • *Top target (2 home runs)*: Larry Jaster, Ferguson Jenkins, Jerry Koosman • *Number of pitchers victimized*: 29 • *Total ballparks homered in*: 13 • *First HR*: 06/06/1964 off Dennis Bennett

Matty Alou

MATEO ROJAS ALOU
B: 12/22/1938
BL

Year	Tm	Lg	Tot	H	A	Men-On 0	1	2	3	One-Game 2	3	4	LO	XN	IP	PH	RHP	LHP
1961	SF	NL	6	6	0	4	1	1	0	0	0	0	0	0	0	0	6	0
1962	SF	NL	3	1	2	3	0	0	0	0	0	0	0	0	0	0	3	0
1964	SF	NL	1	1	0	1	0	0	0	0	0	0	0	1	0	0	1	0
1965	SF	NL	2	2	0	2	0	0	0	0	0	0	0	0	0	0	2	0
1966	PIT	NL	2	1	1	1	1	0	0	0	0	0	0	0	0	0	2	0
1967	PIT	NL	2	1	1	2	0	0	0	0	0	0	0	0	0	0	2	0
1969	PIT	NL	1	1	0	1	0	0	0	0	0	0	0	0	0	0	1	0
1970	PIT	NL	1	0	1	0	1	0	0	0	0	0	0	0	0	0	1	0
1971	STL	NL	7	3	4	4	1	2	0	0	0	0	0	0	0	0	7	0
1972	STL	NL	3	2	1	2	1	0	0	0	0	0	0	0	0	0	3	0
	OAK	AL	1	1	0	0	1	0	0	0	0	0	0	0	0	0	0	1
	Total		4	3	1	2	2	0	0	0	0	0	0	0	0	0	3	1
1973	NY	AL	2	2	0	1	1	0	0	0	0	0	0	0	0	0	0	2
Total			31	21	10	21	7	3	0	0	0	0	0	1	0	0	28	3

Rank among batters: 1,400 • *Total ballparks homered in*: 12 • *First HR*: 05/15/1961 off Joe Schaffernoth

Moises Alou

MOISES ROJAS ALOU
B: 07/03/1966
BR

Year	Tm	Lg	Tot	H	A	Men-On 0	1	2	3	One-Game 2	3	4	LO	XN	IP	PH	RHP	LHP
1992	MON	NL	9	6	3	3	3	2	1	0	0	0	0	1	0	0	7	2
1993	MON	NL	18	10	8	12	3	3	0	2	0	0	0	0	0	0	13	5

Moises Alou *continued*

Year	Tm	Lg	Tot	H	A	Men-On 0	1	2	3	One-Game 2	3	4	LO	XN	IP	PH	RHP	LHP
1994	MON	NL	22	9	13	13	5	4	0	3	0	0	0	0	0	0	17	5
1995	MON	NL	14	4	10	10	3	1	0	0	0	0	0	0	0	0	9	5
Total			63	29	34	38	14	10	1	5	0	0	0	1	0	0	46	17

Rank among batters: 826 • *Top target (2 home runs)*: Bryan Hickerson, Jeff Brantley, Tim Worrell, Dwight Gooden, Bob Tewksbury, Mark Portugal, Blas Minor, Terry Mulholland, Andy Ashby, John Smiley • *Number of pitchers victimized*: 53 • *Total ballparks homered in*: 13 • *First HR*: 05/27/1992 off Mark Portugal

Whitey Alperman

CHARLES AUGUSTUS ALPERMAN
B: 11/11/1879 D: 12/25/1942
BR

Year	Tm	Lg	Tot	H	A	Men-On 0	1	2	3	One-Game 2	3	4	LO	XN	IP	PH	RHP	LHP
1906	BRO	NL	3	1	2	3	0	0	0	0	0	0	0	0	1	0	3	0
1907	BRO	NL	2	2	0	1	1	0	0	0	0	0	0	0	2	0	2	0
1908	BRO	NL	1	0	1	1	0	0	0	0	0	0	0	0	0	0	1	0
1909	BRO	NL	1	1	0	0	1	0	0	0	0	0	0	0	0	0	1	0
Total			7	4	3	5	2	0	0	0	0	0	0	0	3	0	7	0

Rank among batters: 2,834 • *Top target (2 home runs)*: Togie Pittinger • *Number of pitchers victimized*: 6 • *Total ballparks homered in*: 3 • *First HR*: 07/05/1906 off Togie Pittinger

Dell Alston

WENDELL ALSTON
B: 09/22/1952
BL

Year	Tm	Lg	Tot	H	A	Men-On 0	1	2	3	One-Game 2	3	4	LO	XN	IP	PH	RHP	LHP
1977	NY	AL	1	0	1	1	0	0	0	0	0	0	0	0	0	0	1	0
1978	OAK	AL	1	0	1	1	0	0	0	0	0	0	0	0	0	0	1	0
1979	CLE	AL	1	0	1	1	0	0	0	0	0	0	0	0	0	0	1	0
Total			3	0	3	3	0	0	0	0	0	0	0	0	0	0	3	0

Rank among batters: 3,735 • *Total ballparks homered in*: 2 • *First HR*: 07/13/1977 off Jim Slaton

Tom Alston

THOMAS EDISON ALSTON
B: 01/31/1926 D: 12/30/1993
BL

Year	Tm	Lg	Tot	H	A	Men-On 0	1	2	3	One-Game 2	3	4	LO	XN	IP	PH	RHP	LHP
1954	STL	NL	4	1	3	2	0	2	0	0	0	0	0	0	1	1	2	2

Rank among batters: 3,427 • *Total ballparks homered in*: 3 • *First HR*: 04/17/1954 off Jim Brosnan

Dave Altizer

DAVID TILDEN ALTIZER
B: 11/06/1876 D: 05/14/1964
BL

Year	Tm	Lg	Tot	H	A	Men-On 0	1	2	3	One-Game 2	3	4	LO	XN	IP	PH	RHP	LHP
1906	WAS	AL	1	0	1	1	0	0	0	0	0	0	0	0	1	0	0	1
1907	WAS	AL	2	0	2	0	2	0	0	0	0	0	0	0	0	0	1	1
1909	CHI	AL	1	0	1	1	0	0	0	0	0	0	0	0	0	0	1	0
Total			4	0	4	2	2	0	0	0	0	0	0	0	1	0	2	2

Rank among batters: 3,427 • *Total ballparks homered in*: 3 • *First HR*: 06/02/1906 off Jesse Tannehill

George Altman

GEORGE LEE ALTMAN
B: 03/20/1933
BL

Year	Tm	Lg	Tot	H	A	Men-On 0	1	2	3	One-Game 2	3	4	LO	XN	IP	PH	RHP	LHP
1959	CHI	NL	12	6	6	5	6	1	0	2	0	0	0	0	0	0	11	1
1960	CHI	NL	13	8	5	7	1	5	0	1	0	0	0	1	0	0	12	1
1961	CHI	NL	27	10	17	16	8	3	0	1	0	0	0	0	1	0	18	9
1962	CHI	NL	22	9	13	12	7	3	0	2	0	0	0	1	1	0	14	8
1963	STL	NL	9	6	3	6	2	1	0	0	0	0	0	0	0	0	8	1
1964	NY	NL	9	5	4	5	3	1	0	0	0	0	0	0	0	0	5	4
1965	CHI	NL	4	3	1	3	1	0	0	0	0	0	0	1	0	1	4	0
1966	CHI	NL	5	1	4	4	1	0	0	1	0	0	0	0	0	1	5	0
Total			101	48	53	58	29	14	0	7	0	0	0	3	2	2	77	24

Rank among batters: 491 • *Top target (6 home runs)*: Jack Sanford • *Number of pitchers victimized*: 69 • *Total ballparks homered in*: 12 • *First HR*: 04/29/1959 off Brooks Lawrence • *All-Star HR*—1

Joe Altobelli

JOSEPH SALVATORE ALTOBELLI
B: 05/26/1932
BL

Year	Tm	Lg	Tot	H	A	Men-On 0	Men-On 1	Men-On 2	Men-On 3	One-Game 2	One-Game 3	One-Game 4	LO	XN	IP	PH	RHP	LHP
1955	CLE	AL	2	0	2	2	0	0	0	0	0	0	0	0	0	0	1	1
1961	MIN	AL	3	2	1	2	0	1	0	0	0	0	0	0	0	1	3	0
Total			5	2	3	4	0	1	0	0	0	0	0	0	0	1	4	1

Rank among batters: 3,191 • *Total ballparks homered in*: 3 • *First HR*: 09/24/1955 off Ned Garver

Nick Altrock

NICHOLAS ALTROCK
B: 09/15/1876 D: 01/20/1965
BB

Year	Tm	Lg	Tot	H	A	Men-On 0	Men-On 1	Men-On 2	Men-On 3	One-Game 2	One-Game 3	One-Game 4	LO	XN	IP	PH	RHP	LHP
1904	CHI	AL	1	0	1	1	0	0	0	0	0	0	0	0	0	0	0	1
1918	WAS	AL	1	1	0	1	0	0	0	0	0	0	0	0	1	0	1	0
Total			2	1	1	2	0	0	0	0	0	0	0	0	1	0	1	1

Rank among batters: 4,129 • *Total ballparks homered in*: 2 • *First HR*: 05/26/1904 off Jesse Tannehill

George Alusik

GEORGE JOSEPH ALUSIK
B: 02/11/1935
BR

Year	Tm	Lg	Tot	H	A	Men-On 0	Men-On 1	Men-On 2	Men-On 3	One-Game 2	One-Game 3	One-Game 4	LO	XN	IP	PH	RHP	LHP
1962	KC	AL	11	6	5	4	5	2	0	0	0	0	0	0	0	2	9	2
1963	KC	AL	9	6	3	6	2	0	1	0	0	0	0	0	0	1	5	4
1964	KC	AL	3	2	1	1	2	0	0	0	0	0	0	0	0	1	2	1
Total			23	14	9	11	9	2	1	0	0	0	0	0	0	4	16	7

Rank among batters: 1,686 • *Top target (2 home runs)*: Early Wynn • *Number of pitchers victimized*: 22 • *Total ballparks homered in*: 5 • *First HR*: 06/19/1962 off Ken McBride

Luis Alvarado

LUIS CESAR (MARTINEZ) ALVARADO
B: 01/15/1949
BR

Year	Tm	Lg	Tot	H	A	Men-On 0	Men-On 1	Men-On 2	Men-On 3	One-Game 2	One-Game 3	One-Game 4	LO	XN	IP	PH	RHP	LHP
1970	BOS	AL	1	1	0	0	1	0	0	0	0	0	0	0	0	0	0	1
1972	CHI	AL	4	3	1	3	0	1	0	0	0	0	0	0	1	0	3	1
Total			5	4	1	3	1	1	0	0	0	0	0	0	1	0	3	2

Rank among batters: 3,191 • *Total ballparks homered in*: 3 • *First HR*: 09/30/1970 off Fritz Peterson

Orlando Alvarez

JESUS MANUEL ORLANDO (MONGE) ALVAREZ
B: 02/28/1952
BR

Year	Tm	Lg	Tot	H	A	Men-On 0	Men-On 1	Men-On 2	Men-On 3	One-Game 2	One-Game 3	One-Game 4	LO	XN	IP	PH	RHP	LHP
1976	CAL	AL	2	1	1	1	0	1	0	0	0	0	0	0	0	0	1	1

Rank among batters: 4,129 • *Total ballparks homered in*: 2 • *First HR*: 05/13/1976 off Stan Perzanowski

Max Alvis

ROY MAXWELL ALVIS
B: 02/02/1938
BR

Year	Tm	Lg	Tot	H	A	Men-On 0	Men-On 1	Men-On 2	Men-On 3	One-Game 2	One-Game 3	One-Game 4	LO	XN	IP	PH	RHP	LHP
1963	CLE	AL	22	12	10	15	3	3	1	1	0	0	0	0	0	0	12	10
1964	CLE	AL	18	8	10	11	2	4	1	1	0	0	0	0	1	0	11	7
1965	CLE	AL	21	14	7	12	6	3	0	0	0	0	0	0	0	1	13	8
1966	CLE	AL	17	10	7	12	4	1	0	0	0	0	0	0	0	0	10	7
1967	CLE	AL	21	13	8	12	7	2	0	2	0	0	1	1	1	0	12	9
1968	CLE	AL	8	3	5	5	3	0	0	0	0	0	0	0	0	0	7	1
1969	CLE	AL	1	0	1	1	0	0	0	0	0	0	0	0	0	0	0	1
1970	MIL	AL	3	2	1	2	1	0	0	0	0	0	0	0	0	1	0	3
Total			111	62	49	70	26	13	2	4	0	0	1	1	2	2	65	46

Rank among batters: 434 • *Top target (6 home runs)*: Jim Kaat • *Number of pitchers victimized*: 78 • *Total ballparks homered in*: 13 • *First HR*: 04/09/1963 off Camilo Pascual

Billy Alvord

WILLIAM CHARLES ALVORD
B: 08/ /1863

Year	Tm	Lg	Tot	H	A	Men-On 0	Men-On 1	Men-On 2	Men-On 3	One-Game 2	One-Game 3	One-Game 4	LO	XN	IP	PH	RHP	LHP
1890	TOL	AA	2	0	2	1	0	1	0	0	0	0	0	0	0	0	1	1

Billy Alvord *continued*

Year	Tm	Lg	Tot	H	A	Men-On 0	1	2	3	One-Game 2	3	4	LO	XN	IP	PH	RHP	LHP
1891	CLE	NL	1	0	1	0	1	0	0	0	0	0	0	0	0	0	1	0
Total			3	0	3	1	1	1	0	0	0	0	0	0	0	0	2	1

Rank among batters: 3,735 • *Total ballparks homered in*: 2 • *First HR*: 04/24/1890 off Toad Ramsey

Brant Alyea

GARRABRANT RYERSON ALYEA
B: 12/08/1940
BR

Year	Tm	Lg	Tot	H	A	Men-On 0	1	2	3	One-Game 2	3	4	LO	XN	IP	PH	RHP	LHP
1965	WAS	AL	2	2	0	0	0	2	0	0	0	0	0	0	0	1	0	2
1968	WAS	AL	6	3	3	2	2	2	0	0	0	0	0	0	0	2	2	4
1969	WAS	AL	11	6	5	5	5	1	0	0	0	0	0	1	0	3	5	6
1970	MIN	AL	16	5	11	5	5	4	2	2	0	0	0	0	0	1	11	5
1971	MIN	AL	2	1	1	2	0	0	0	0	0	0	0	0	0	1	0	2
1972	OAK	AL	1	1	0	1	0	0	0	0	0	0	0	0	0	0	0	1
Total			38	18	20	15	12	9	2	2	0	0	0	1	0	8	18	20

Rank among batters: 1,225 • *Top target (3 home runs)*: Wilbur Wood • *Number of pitchers victimized*: 33 • *Total ballparks homered in*: 9 • *First HR*: 09/12/1965 off Rudy May • *Hit HR on first major league pitch*—vs CAL: 09/12/1965

Joey Amalfitano

JOHN JOSEPH AMALFITANO
B: 01/23/1934
BR

Year	Tm	Lg	Tot	H	A	Men-On 0	1	2	3	One-Game 2	3	4	LO	XN	IP	PH	RHP	LHP
1960	SF	NL	1	1	0	0	1	0	0	0	0	0	0	0	0	0	1	0
1961	SF	NL	2	1	1	2	0	0	0	0	0	0	2	0	0	0	2	0
1962	HOU	NL	1	0	1	0	1	0	0	0	0	0	0	0	0	0	1	0
1963	SF	NL	1	1	0	1	0	0	0	0	0	0	0	1	0	0	1	0
1964	CHI	NL	4	2	2	1	2	0	1	0	0	0	0	0	0	0	3	1
Total			9	5	4	4	4	0	1	0	0	0	2	1	0	0	8	1

Rank among batters: 2,587 • *Total ballparks homered in*: 5 • *First HR*: 06/03/1960 off Ernie Broglio

Rich Amaral

RICHARD LOUIS AMARAL
B: 04/01/1962
BR

Year	Tm	Lg	Tot	H	A	Men-On 0	1	2	3	One-Game 2	3	4	LO	XN	IP	PH	RHP	LHP
1992	SEA	AL	1	0	1	0	0	1	0	0	0	0	0	0	0	0	0	1
1993	SEA	AL	1	0	1	1	0	0	0	0	0	0	0	0	0	0	1	0
1994	SEA	AL	4	2	2	3	1	0	0	0	0	0	0	0	0	1	0	4
1995	SEA	AL	2	1	1	1	0	1	0	0	0	0	0	1	0	0	1	1
Total			8	3	5	5	1	2	0	0	0	0	0	1	0	1	2	6

Rank among batters: 2,703 • *Total ballparks homered in*: 6 • *First HR*: 04/26/1992 off Mark Langston

Ruben Amaro

RUBEN (MORA) AMARO
B: 01/06/1936
BR

Year	Tm	Lg	Tot	H	A	Men-On 0	1	2	3	One-Game 2	3	4	LO	XN	IP	PH	RHP	LHP
1961	PHI	NL	1	0	1	1	0	0	0	0	0	0	0	0	0	0	1	0
1963	PHI	NL	2	1	1	2	0	0	0	0	0	0	0	0	0	0	1	1
1964	PHI	NL	4	3	1	2	1	1	0	0	0	0	0	0	0	0	2	2
1967	NY	AL	1	0	1	0	0	1	0	0	0	0	0	0	0	0	0	1
Total			8	4	4	5	1	2	0	0	0	0	0	0	0	0	4	4

Rank among batters: 2,703 • *Total ballparks homered in*: 5 • *First HR*: 09/12/1961 off Phil Ortega

Ruben Amaro

RUBEN AMARO, JR.
B: 02/12/1965
BB

Year	Tm	Lg	Tot	H	A	Men-On 0	1	2	3	One-Game 2	3	4	LO	XN	IP	PH	RHP	LHP
1992	PHI	NL	7	5	2	5	2	0	0	0	0	0	1	0	0	0	5	2
1993	PHI	NL	1	0	1	0	1	0	0	0	0	0	0	0	0	0	0	1
1994	CLE	AL	2	0	2	2	0	0	0	0	0	0	0	0	0	1	1	1

Ruben Amaro *continued*

Year	Tm	Lg	Tot	H	A	Men-On 0	1	2	3	One-Game 2	3	4	LO	XN	IP	PH	RHP	LHP
1995	CLE	AL	1	1	0	0	1	0	0	0	0	0	0	0	0	0	0	1
Total			11	6	5	7	4	0	0	0	0	0	1	0	0	1	6	5

Rank among batters: 2,419 • *Total ballparks homered in*: 6 • *First HR*: 04/08/1992 off Ken Patterson

Red Ames

LEON KESSLING AMES
B: 08/02/1882 D: 10/08/1936
BB

Year	Tm	Lg	Tot	H	A	Men-On 0	1	2	3	One-Game 2	3	4	LO	XN	IP	PH	RHP	LHP
1907	NY	NL	1	1	0	0	1	0	0	0	0	0	0	0	0	0	1	0
1910	NY	NL	1	0	1	1	0	0	0	0	0	0	0	0	0	0	0	1
1914	CIN	NL	1	0	1	0	1	0	0	0	0	0	0	0	0	0	1	0
Total			3	1	2	1	2	0	0	0	0	0	0	0	0	0	2	1

Rank among batters: 3,735 • *Total ballparks homered in*: 3 • *First HR*: 08/21/1907 off Jack Taylor

Sandy Amoros

EDMUNDO (ISASI) AMOROS
B: 01/30/1930 D: 06/27/1992
BL

Year	Tm	Lg	Tot	H	A	Men-On 0	1	2	3	One-Game 2	3	4	LO	XN	IP	PH	RHP	LHP
1954	BRO	NL	9	5	4	5	3	1	0	1	0	0	0	0	0	0	9	0
1955	BRO	NL	10	5	5	7	3	0	0	0	0	0	0	0	0	0	10	0
1956	BRO	NL	16	9	7	6	10	0	0	1	0	0	0	0	1	1	16	0
1957	BRO	NL	7	3	4	4	3	0	0	0	0	0	0	0	0	1	6	1
1960	DET	AL	1	0	1	1	0	0	0	0	0	0	0	0	0	1	1	0
Total			43	22	21	23	19	1	0	2	0	0	0	0	1	3	42	1

Rank among batters: 1,116 • *Top target (4 home runs)*: Murry Dickson, Bob Friend • *Number of pitchers victimized*: 33 • *Total ballparks homered in*: 9 • *First HR*: 07/23/1954 off Vic Raschi • *World Series HR*—1

Alf Anderson

ALFRED WALTON ANDERSON
B: 01/28/1914 D: 06/23/1985
BR

Year	Tm	Lg	Tot	H	A	Men-On 0	1	2	3	One-Game 2	3	4	LO	XN	IP	PH	RHP	LHP
1941	PIT	NL	1	1	0	0	1	0	0	0	0	0	0	0	0	0	0	1

Rank among batters: 4,707 • *Total ballparks homered in*: 1 • *First HR*: 09/14/1941 off Lefty Hoerst

Andy Anderson

ANDY HOLM ANDERSON
B: 11/13/1922 D: 07/18/1982
BR

Year	Tm	Lg	Tot	H	A	Men-On 0	1	2	3	One-Game 2	3	4	LO	XN	IP	PH	RHP	LHP
1948	STL	AL	1	0	1	0	0	0	1	0	0	0	0	0	0	0	1	0
1949	STL	AL	1	0	1	1	0	0	0	0	0	0	0	0	0	0	1	0
Total			2	0	2	1	0	0	1	0	0	0	0	0	0	0	2	0

Rank among batters: 4,129 • *Total ballparks homered in*: 2 • *First HR*: 06/11/1948 off Phil Marchildon

Bob Anderson

ROBERT CARL ANDERSON
B: 09/29/1935
BR

Year	Tm	Lg	Tot	H	A	Men-On 0	1	2	3	One-Game 2	3	4	LO	XN	IP	PH	RHP	LHP
1961	CHI	NL	2	0	2	0	2	0	0	0	0	0	0	0	0	0	1	1

Rank among batters: 4,129 • *Total ballparks homered in*: 2 • *First HR*: 08/09/1961 off Mike McCormick

Brady Anderson

BRADY KEVIN ANDERSON
B: 01/18/1964
BL

Year	Tm	Lg	Tot	H	A	Men-On 0	1	2	3	One-Game 2	3	4	LO	XN	IP	PH	RHP	LHP
1988	BAL	AL	1	1	0	0	1	0	0	0	0	0	0	0	0	0	1	0
1989	BAL	AL	4	2	2	2	1	1	0	0	0	0	0	0	0	0	3	1
1990	BAL	AL	3	1	2	2	1	0	0	0	0	0	0	0	0	0	3	0
1991	BAL	AL	2	1	1	1	1	0	0	0	0	0	0	1	0	0	2	0
1992	BAL	AL	21	15	6	14	5	2	0	1	0	0	4	0	0	0	16	5

Brady Anderson *continued*

Year	Tm	Lg	Tot	H	A	Men-On 0	Men-On 1	Men-On 2	Men-On 3	One-Game 2	One-Game 3	One-Game 4	LO	XN	IP	PH	RHP	LHP
1993	BAL	AL	13	2	11	11	2	0	0	1	0	0	2	0	0	0	11	2
1994	BAL	AL	12	7	5	10	1	1	0	2	0	0	2	0	0	0	11	1
1995	BAL	AL	16	10	6	10	4	1	1	1	0	0	3	0	0	0	13	3
Total			72	39	33	50	16	5	1	5	0	0	11	1	0	0	60	12

Rank among batters: 723 • *Top target (3 home runs)*: Bill Wegman, Scott Erickson, Dave Fleming • *Number of pitchers victimized*: 61 • *Total ballparks homered in*: 13 • *First HR*: 08/06/1988 off Tom Filer

Dave Anderson

DAVID CARTER ANDERSON
B: 08/01/1960
BR

Year	Tm	Lg	Tot	H	A	Men-On 0	Men-On 1	Men-On 2	Men-On 3	One-Game 2	One-Game 3	One-Game 4	LO	XN	IP	PH	RHP	LHP
1983	LA	NL	1	1	0	1	0	0	0	0	0	0	0	0	0	1	1	0
1984	LA	NL	3	2	1	3	0	0	0	0	0	0	0	0	0	0	1	2
1985	LA	NL	4	1	3	3	1	0	0	0	0	0	1	1	0	0	2	2
1986	LA	NL	1	0	1	0	1	0	0	0	0	0	0	0	0	0	1	0
1987	LA	NL	1	0	1	1	0	0	0	0	0	0	1	0	0	0	1	0
1988	LA	NL	2	1	1	2	0	0	0	0	0	0	0	0	0	0	2	0
1989	LA	NL	1	1	0	0	1	0	0	0	0	0	0	0	0	0	1	0
1990	SF	NL	1	1	0	1	0	0	0	0	0	0	0	0	0	1	0	1
1991	SF	NL	2	1	1	0	2	0	0	0	0	0	0	0	0	0	1	1
1992	LA	NL	3	0	3	2	1	0	0	0	0	0	0	0	0	1	1	2
Total			19	8	11	13	6	0	0	0	0	0	2	1	0	3	11	8

Rank among batters: 1,861 • *Total ballparks homered in*: 10 • *First HR*: 09/30/1983 off Scott Garrelts

Dwain Anderson

DWAIN CLEAVEN ANDERSON
B: 11/23/1947
BR

Year	Tm	Lg	Tot	H	A	Men-On 0	Men-On 1	Men-On 2	Men-On 3	One-Game 2	One-Game 3	One-Game 4	LO	XN	IP	PH	RHP	LHP
1972	STL	NL	1	0	1	0	1	0	0	0	0	0	0	1	0	0	1	0

Rank among batters: 4,707 • *Total ballparks homered in*: 1 • *First HR*: 09/08/1972 off Bob Rauch

Ferrell Anderson

FERRELL JACK ANDERSON
B: 01/09/1918 D: 03/12/1978
BR

Year	Tm	Lg	Tot	H	A	Men-On 0	Men-On 1	Men-On 2	Men-On 3	One-Game 2	One-Game 3	One-Game 4	LO	XN	IP	PH	RHP	LHP
1946	BRO	NL	2	1	1	2	0	0	0	0	0	0	0	0	0	0	2	0

Rank among batters: 4,129 • *Total ballparks homered in*: 2 • *First HR*: 04/23/1946 off Mort Cooper

Garret Anderson

GARRET JOSEPH ANDERSON
B: 06/30/1972
BL

Year	Tm	Lg	Tot	H	A	Men-On 0	Men-On 1	Men-On 2	Men-On 3	One-Game 2	One-Game 3	One-Game 4	LO	XN	IP	PH	RHP	LHP
1995	CAL	AL	16	7	9	10	3	3	0	0	0	0	0	0	0	0	11	5

Rank among batters: 2,029 • *Total ballparks homered in*: 7 • *First HR*: 06/13/1995 off Kevin Tapani

George Anderson

GEORGE JENDRUS ANDERSON
B: 09/26/1889 D: 05/28/1962
BL

Year	Tm	Lg	Tot	H	A	Men-On 0	Men-On 1	Men-On 2	Men-On 3	One-Game 2	One-Game 3	One-Game 4	LO	XN	IP	PH	RHP	LHP
1914	BRO	FL	3	2	1	2	1	0	0	0	0	0	0	0	0	0	3	0
1915	BRO	FL	2	2	0	2	0	0	0	0	0	0	0	0	0	0	2	0
Total			5	4	1	4	1	0	0	0	0	0	0	0	0	0	5	0

Rank among batters: 3,191 • *Top target (2 home runs)*: Fred Anderson • *Number of pitchers victimized*: 4 • *Total ballparks homered in*: 2 • *First HR*: 07/01/1914 off Fred Anderson

Goat Anderson

EDWARD JOHN ANDERSON
B: 01/13/1880 D: 03/15/1923
BL

Year	Tm	Lg	Tot	H	A	Men-On 0	Men-On 1	Men-On 2	Men-On 3	One-Game 2	One-Game 3	One-Game 4	LO	XN	IP	PH	RHP	LHP
1907	PIT	NL	1	0	1	1	0	0	0	0	0	0	0	0	0	0	1	0

Rank among batters: 4,707 • *Total ballparks homered in*: 1 • *First HR*: 06/29/1907 off Ed Reulbach

Harry Anderson

HARRY WALTER ANDERSON
B: 09/10/1931
BL

Year	Tm	Lg	Tot	H	A	Men-On 0	1	2	3	One-Game 2	3	4	LO	XN	IP	PH	RHP	LHP
1957	PHI	NL	17	4	13	8	6	2	1	0	0	0	0	0	2	1	16	1
1958	PHI	NL	23	11	12	9	12	2	0	1	0	0	0	1	1	0	20	3
1959	PHI	NL	14	6	8	9	4	1	0	0	0	0	0	0	0	0	12	2
1960	PHI	NL	5	4	1	4	1	0	0	1	0	0	0	0	0	0	5	0
	CIN	NL	1	0	1	1	0	0	0	0	0	0	0	0	0	0	1	0
	Total		6	4	2	5	1	0	0	1	0	0	0	0	0	0	6	0
Total			60	25	35	31	23	5	1	2	0	0	0	1	3	1	54	6

Rank among batters: 863 • *Top target (5 home runs)*: Larry Jackson • *Number of pitchers victimized*: 36 • *Total ballparks homered in*: 9 • *First HR*: 05/03/1957 off Tom Poholsky

Jim Anderson

JAMES LEA ANDERSON
B: 02/23/1957
BR

Year	Tm	Lg	Tot	H	A	Men-On 0	1	2	3	One-Game 2	3	4	LO	XN	IP	PH	RHP	LHP
1979	CAL	AL	3	0	3	3	0	0	0	0	0	0	0	0	0	0	1	2
1980	SEA	AL	8	7	1	7	1	0	0	0	0	0	0	0	0	1	6	2
1981	SEA	AL	2	2	0	2	0	0	0	0	0	0	0	0	0	0	2	0
Total			13	9	4	12	1	0	0	0	0	0	0	0	0	1	9	4

Rank among batters: 2,248 • *Top target (2 home runs)*: Larry Gura • *Number of pitchers victimized*: 12 • *Total ballparks homered in*: 4 • *First HR*: 06/26/1979 off Jon Matlack

John Anderson

JOHN JOSEPH ANDERSON
B: 12/14/1873 D: 07/23/1949
BB

Year	Tm	Lg	Tot	H	A	Men-On 0	1	2	3	One-Game 2	3	4	LO	XN	IP	PH	RHP	LHP
1894	BRO	NL	1	0	1	0	1	0	0	0	0	0	0	0	0	0	1	0
1895	BRO	NL	9	4	5	5	2	1	1	0	0	0	0	0	0	0	7	2
1896	BRO	NL	1	0	1	0	1	0	0	0	0	0	0	0	0	0	1	0
1897	BRO	NL	4	2	2	0	2	2	0	0	0	0	0	0	0	0	3	1
1898	WAS	NL	9	8	1	2	6	1	0	0	0	0	0	0	2	0	8	1
1899	BRO	NL	4	1	3	2	0	2	0	0	0	0	0	0	1	0	4	0
1901	MIL	AL	8	6	2	3	4	1	0	0	0	0	0	0	1	0	6	2
1902	STL	AL	4	3	1	1	2	0	1	0	0	0	0	0	1	0	4	0
1903	STL	AL	2	0	2	1	0	1	0	0	0	0	0	1	0	0	2	0
1904	NY	AL	3	3	0	0	3	0	0	0	0	0	0	0	2	0	2	1
1905	WAS	AL	1	1	0	0	1	0	0	0	0	0	0	0	0	0	0	1
1906	WAS	AL	3	0	3	1	2	0	0	0	0	0	0	0	0	0	3	0
Total			49	28	21	15	24	8	2	0	0	0	0	1	7	0	41	8

Rank among batters: 1,008 • *Top target (2 home runs)*: Jack Stivetts, Jouett Meekin, Jerry Nops, Roscoe Miller, Bert Husting, Cy Young • *Number of pitchers victimized*: 43 • *Total ballparks homered in*: 17 • *First HR*: 09/22/1894 off Chauncey Fisher

Kent Anderson

KENT MCKAY ANDERSON
B: 08/12/1963
BR

Year	Tm	Lg	Tot	H	A	Men-On 0	1	2	3	One-Game 2	3	4	LO	XN	IP	PH	RHP	LHP
1990	CAL	AL	1	1	0	1	0	0	0	0	0	0	0	0	0	0	0	1

Rank among batters: 4,707 • *Total ballparks homered in*: 1 • *First HR*: 06/24/1990 off Frank Tanana

Mike Anderson

MICHAEL ALLEN ANDERSON
B: 06/22/1951
BR

Year	Tm	Lg	Tot	H	A	Men-On 0	1	2	3	One-Game 2	3	4	LO	XN	IP	PH	RHP	LHP
1971	PHI	NL	2	1	1	2	0	0	0	0	0	0	0	0	0	0	2	0
1972	PHI	NL	2	1	1	2	0	0	0	0	0	0	0	0	0	0	2	0
1973	PHI	NL	9	7	2	4	3	2	0	1	0	0	0	0	0	1	1	8
1974	PHI	NL	5	3	2	3	1	1	0	0	0	0	0	0	0	0	2	3
1975	PHI	NL	4	3	1	2	2	0	0	0	0	0	0	0	0	0	3	1
1976	STL	NL	1	0	1	1	0	0	0	0	0	0	0	0	0	0	1	0
1977	STL	NL	4	2	2	2	1	1	0	0	0	0	0	0	0	0	1	3
1979	PHI	NL	1	1	0	1	0	0	0	0	0	0	0	0	0	0	1	0
Total			28	18	10	17	7	4	0	1	0	0	0	0	0	1	13	15

Rank among batters: 1,500 • *Top target (2 home runs)*: Dock Ellis, Steve Renko • *Number of pitchers victimized*: 26 • *Total ballparks homered in*: 9 • *First HR*: 09/24/1971 off Phil Regan

Ed Andrews

GEORGE EDWARD ANDREWS
B: 04/05/1859 D: 08/12/1934
BR

Year	Tm	Lg	Tot	H	A	Men-On 0	Men-On 1	Men-On 2	Men-On 3	One-Game 2	One-Game 3	One-Game 4	LO	XN	IP	PH	RHP	LHP
1886	PHI	NL	2	1	1	1	1	0	0	0	0	0	0	0	0	0	2	0
1887	PHI	NL	4	3	1	3	1	0	0	0	0	0	0	0	0	0	1	2
1888	PHI	NL	3	0	3	0	2	1	0	0	0	0	0	0	0	0	3	0
1890	BRO	PL	3	1	2	2	1	0	0	0	0	0	0	0	1	0	3	0
Total			12	5	7	6	5	1	0	0	0	0	0	0	1	0	9	2

Rank among batters: 2,325 • *Total ballparks homered in*: 7 • *First HR*: 05/24/1886 off Jim McCormick

Jim Andrews

JAMES PRATT ANDREWS
B: 06/05/1865 D: 12/27/1907

Year	Tm	Lg	Tot	H	A	Men-On 0	Men-On 1	Men-On 2	Men-On 3	One-Game 2	One-Game 3	One-Game 4	LO	XN	IP	PH	RHP	LHP
1890	CHI	NL	3	1	2	1	1	1	0	0	0	0	0	0	1	0	3	0

Rank among batters: 3,735 • *Total ballparks homered in*: 3 • *First HR*: 04/22/1890 off Lee Viau

Mike Andrews

MICHAEL JAY ANDREWS
B: 07/09/1943
BR

Year	Tm	Lg	Tot	H	A	Men-On 0	Men-On 1	Men-On 2	Men-On 3	One-Game 2	One-Game 3	One-Game 4	LO	XN	IP	PH	RHP	LHP
1967	BOS	AL	8	2	6	5	1	2	0	0	0	0	1	0	0	0	4	4
1968	BOS	AL	7	5	2	4	2	1	0	0	0	0	1	0	0	0	6	1
1969	BOS	AL	15	9	6	14	0	1	0	0	0	0	1	0	0	0	13	2
1970	BOS	AL	17	10	7	13	2	1	1	0	0	0	4	0	0	0	12	5
1971	CHI	AL	12	5	7	6	3	2	1	0	0	0	0	0	0	0	7	5
1972	CHI	AL	7	5	2	2	3	1	1	0	0	0	0	0	0	0	5	2
Total			66	36	30	44	11	8	3	0	0	0	7	0	0	0	47	19

Rank among batters: 786 • *Top target (3 home runs)*: Pete Richert, Stan Bahnsen • *Number of pitchers victimized*: 60 • *Total ballparks homered in*: 12 • *First HR*: 04/25/1967 off Pete Richert

Rob Andrews

ROBERT PATRICK ANDREWS
B: 12/11/1952
BR

Year	Tm	Lg	Tot	H	A	Men-On 0	Men-On 1	Men-On 2	Men-On 3	One-Game 2	One-Game 3	One-Game 4	LO	XN	IP	PH	RHP	LHP
1978	SF	NL	1	0	1	1	0	0	0	0	0	0	0	0	0	0	0	1
1979	SF	NL	2	0	2	2	0	0	0	1	0	0	0	0	0	0	2	0
Total			3	0	3	3	0	0	0	1	0	0	0	0	0	0	2	1

Rank among batters: 3,735 • *Top target (2 home runs)*: Tom Seaver • *Number of pitchers victimized*: 2 • *Total ballparks homered in*: 2 • *First HR*: 07/17/1978 off Buddy Schultz

Shane Andrews

DARRELL SHANE ANDREWS
B: 08/28/1971
BR

Year	Tm	Lg	Tot	H	A	Men-On 0	Men-On 1	Men-On 2	Men-On 3	One-Game 2	One-Game 3	One-Game 4	LO	XN	IP	PH	RHP	LHP
1995	MON	NL	8	2	6	3	2	2	1	0	0	0	0	0	0	1	6	2

Rank among batters: 2,703 • *Total ballparks homered in*: 6 • *First HR*: 04/27/1995 off Jim Gott

Stan Andrews

STANLEY JOSEPH ANDREWS
B: 04/17/1917 D: 06/10/1995
BR

Year	Tm	Lg	Tot	H	A	Men-On 0	Men-On 1	Men-On 2	Men-On 3	One-Game 2	One-Game 3	One-Game 4	LO	XN	IP	PH	RHP	LHP
1945	PHI	NL	1	1	0	1	0	0	0	0	0	0	0	0	0	0	1	0

Rank among batters: 4,707 • *Total ballparks homered in*: 1 • *First HR*: 08/21/1945 off Joe Bowman

Joaquin Andujar

JOAQUIN ANDUJAR
B: 12/21/1952
BB

Year	Tm	Lg	Tot	H	A	Men-On 0	Men-On 1	Men-On 2	Men-On 3	One-Game 2	One-Game 3	One-Game 4	LO	XN	IP	PH	RHP	LHP
1979	HOU	NL	2	1	1	0	2	0	0	0	0	0	0	0	1	0	1	1
1980	HOU	NL	1	1	0	1	0	0	0	0	0	0	0	0	0	0	1	0

Joaquin Andujar *continued*

Year	Tm	Lg	Tot	H	A	Men-On 0	1	2	3	One-Game 2	3	4	LO	XN	IP	PH	RHP	LHP
1984	STL	NL	2	1	1	1	0	0	1	0	0	0	0	0	0	0	2	0
Total			5	3	2	2	2	0	1	0	0	0	0	0	1	0	4	1

Rank among batters: 3,191 • *Top target (2 home runs)*: Steve Rogers • *Number of pitchers victimized*: 4 • *Total ballparks homered in*: 3 • *First HR*: 08/14/1979 off Bill Lee

Cap Anson

ADRIAN CONSTANTINE ANSON
B: 04/11/1852 D: 04/14/1922
BR HOF

Year	Tm	Lg	Tot	H	A	Men-On 0	1	2	3	One-Game 2	3	4	LO	XN	IP	PH	RHP	LHP
1876	CHI	NL	2	1	1	1	0	1	0	0	0	0	0	0	1	0	2	0
1880	CHI	NL	1	0	1	0	1	0	0	0	0	0	0	0	0	0	1	0
1881	CHI	NL	1	0	1	1	0	0	0	0	0	0	0	0	0	0	1	0
1882	CHI	NL	1	0	1	0	1	0	0	0	0	0	0	0	0	0	1	0
1884	CHI	NL	21	20	1	8	9	1	0	2	1	0	0	0	0	0	17	1
1885	CHI	NL	7	5	2	2	1	4	0	1	0	0	0	0	0	0	7	0
1886	CHI	NL	10	8	2	2	7	1	0	1	0	0	0	0	0	0	9	0
1887	CHI	NL	6	6	0	3	2	1	0	0	0	0	0	0	0	0	5	1
1888	CHI	NL	12	8	4	7	5	0	0	1	0	0	0	0	1	0	11	1
1889	CHI	NL	7	3	4	5	2	0	0	0	0	0	0	1	1	0	7	0
1890	CHI	NL	7	5	2	4	0	3	0	0	0	0	0	0	1	0	6	1
1891	CHI	NL	8	5	3	4	3	1	0	0	0	0	0	0	1	0	7	0
1892	CHI	NL	1	0	1	1	0	0	0	0	0	0	0	0	0	0	1	0
1894	CHI	NL	5	3	2	0	4	0	1	0	0	0	0	0	1	0	3	1
1895	CHI	NL	2	1	1	2	0	0	0	0	0	0	0	0	0	0	1	1
1896	CHI	NL	2	2	0	0	2	0	0	0	0	0	0	0	0	0	2	0
1897	CHI	NL	3	0	3	2	1	0	0	1	0	0	0	0	0	0	3	0
Total			96	67	29	42	38	12	1	6	1	0	0	1	6	0	84	6

Rank among batters: 520 • *Top target (7 home runs)*: Charley Radbourn • *Number of pitchers victimized*: 57 • *Total ballparks homered in*: 28 • *First HR*: 08/26/1876 off George Bradley

Eric Anthony

ERIC TODD ANTHONY
B: 11/08/1967
BL

Year	Tm	Lg	Tot	H	A	Men-On 0	1	2	3	One-Game 2	3	4	LO	XN	IP	PH	RHP	LHP
1989	HOU	NL	4	2	2	3	1	0	0	0	0	0	0	0	0	0	4	0
1990	HOU	NL	10	5	5	7	1	2	0	0	0	0	0	1	0	1	7	3
1991	HOU	NL	1	0	1	1	0	0	0	0	0	0	0	0	0	0	1	0
1992	HOU	NL	19	9	10	8	9	0	2	2	0	0	0	2	0	1	14	5
1993	HOU	NL	15	5	10	7	5	3	0	0	0	0	0	0	0	0	10	5
1994	SEA	AL	10	3	7	7	2	1	0	0	0	0	0	0	0	1	10	0
1995	CIN	NL	5	3	2	4	0	1	0	0	0	0	0	0	0	1	4	1
Total			64	27	37	37	18	7	2	2	0	0	0	3	0	4	50	14

Rank among batters: 815 • *Top target (2 home runs)*: Tommy Greene, Bruce Hurst, Bob Walk • *Number of pitchers victimized*: 61 • *Total ballparks homered in*: 20 • *First HR*: 07/29/1989 off Rick Reuschel

John Antonelli

JOHN LAWRENCE ANTONELLI
B: 07/15/1915 D: 04/18/1990
BR

Year	Tm	Lg	Tot	H	A	Men-On 0	1	2	3	One-Game 2	3	4	LO	XN	IP	PH	RHP	LHP
1945	PHI	NL	1	0	1	1	0	0	0	0	0	0	0	0	0	0	1	0

Rank among batters: 4,707 • *Total ballparks homered in*: 1 • *First HR*: 08/31/1945 off Bill Lee

Johnny Antonelli

JOHN AUGUST ANTONELLI
B: 04/12/1930
BL

Year	Tm	Lg	Tot	H	A	Men-On 0	1	2	3	One-Game 2	3	4	LO	XN	IP	PH	RHP	LHP
1954	NY	NL	2	2	0	1	1	0	0	0	0	0	0	0	0	0	0	2
1955	NY	NL	4	1	3	1	1	2	0	0	0	0	0	0	0	0	4	0
1956	NY	NL	3	3	0	2	1	0	0	0	0	0	0	0	0	0	2	1
1957	NY	NL	3	2	1	1	2	0	0	0	0	0	0	1	0	0	3	0
1958	SF	NL	1	1	0	1	0	0	0	0	0	0	0	0	0	0	1	0

Johnny Antonelli *continued*

Year	Tm	Lg	Tot	H	A	Men-On 0	Men-On 1	Men-On 2	Men-On 3	One-Game 2	One-Game 3	One-Game 4	LO	XN	IP	PH	RHP	LHP
1959	SF	NL	2	0	2	1	1	0	0	0	0	0	0	0	0	0	2	0
Total			15	9	6	7	6	2	0	0	0	0	0	1	0	0	12	3

Rank among batters: 2,096 • *Top target (2 home runs)*: Ray Crone • *Number of pitchers victimized*: 14 • *Total ballparks homered in*: 7 • *First HR*: 05/25/1954 off Joe Page

Bill Antonello

WILLIAM JAMES ANTONELLO
B: 05/19/1927 D: 03/04/1993
BR

Year	Tm	Lg	Tot	H	A	Men-On 0	Men-On 1	Men-On 2	Men-On 3	One-Game 2	One-Game 3	One-Game 4	LO	XN	IP	PH	RHP	LHP
1953	BRO	NL	1	0	1	0	1	0	0	0	0	0	0	0	0	0	0	1

Rank among batters: 4,707 • *Total ballparks homered in*: 1 • *First HR*: 05/17/1953 off Ken Raffensberger

Luis Aparicio

LUIS ERNESTO (MONTIEL) APARICIO
B: 04/29/1934
BR HOF

Year	Tm	Lg	Tot	H	A	Men-On 0	Men-On 1	Men-On 2	Men-On 3	One-Game 2	One-Game 3	One-Game 4	LO	XN	IP	PH	RHP	LHP
1956	CHI	AL	3	1	2	2	1	0	0	0	0	0	0	0	1	0	2	1
1957	CHI	AL	3	2	1	2	0	1	0	1	0	0	1	0	1	0	2	1
1958	CHI	AL	2	1	1	1	1	0	0	0	0	0	0	0	1	0	1	1
1959	CHI	AL	6	2	4	4	1	1	0	0	0	0	0	0	1	0	5	1
1960	CHI	AL	2	2	0	1	0	1	0	0	0	0	0	0	1	0	2	0
1961	CHI	AL	6	4	2	4	2	0	0	0	0	0	0	0	0	0	4	2
1962	CHI	AL	7	4	3	4	3	0	0	0	0	0	0	0	0	0	6	1
1963	BAL	AL	5	2	3	4	0	0	1	0	0	0	0	0	0	0	4	1
1964	BAL	AL	10	5	5	9	1	0	0	0	0	0	0	0	0	0	6	4
1965	BAL	AL	8	4	4	5	3	0	0	0	0	0	0	0	0	0	5	3
1966	BAL	AL	6	3	3	4	2	0	0	0	0	0	1	0	0	0	4	2
1967	BAL	AL	4	1	3	3	1	0	0	0	0	0	1	0	0	0	3	1
1968	CHI	AL	4	1	3	2	2	0	0	0	0	0	0	0	0	0	1	3
1969	CHI	AL	5	3	2	4	1	0	0	0	0	0	0	0	0	0	3	2
1970	CHI	AL	5	4	1	4	1	0	0	0	0	0	0	0	0	0	3	2
1971	BOS	AL	4	1	3	3	0	0	1	0	0	0	1	0	0	0	2	2
1972	BOS	AL	3	1	2	2	1	0	0	0	0	0	0	0	0	0	2	1
Total			83	41	42	58	20	3	2	1	0	0	4	0	5	0	55	28

Rank among batters: 628 • *Top target (3 home runs)*: Paul Foytack • *Number of pitchers victimized*: 73 • *Total ballparks homered in*: 12 • *First HR*: 05/28/1956 off Tom Lasorda

Luke Appling

LUCIUS BENJAMIN APPLING
B: 04/02/1907 D: 01/03/1991
BR HOF

Year	Tm	Lg	Tot	H	A	Men-On 0	Men-On 1	Men-On 2	Men-On 3	One-Game 2	One-Game 3	One-Game 4	LO	XN	IP	PH	RHP	LHP
1931	CHI	AL	1	1	0	0	1	0	0	0	0	0	0	0	0	1	0	1
1932	CHI	AL	3	0	3	2	1	0	0	0	0	0	0	0	0	0	3	0
1933	CHI	AL	6	4	2	6	0	0	0	0	0	0	0	1	0	0	5	1
1934	CHI	AL	2	1	1	2	0	0	0	0	0	0	0	0	0	0	2	0
1935	CHI	AL	1	1	0	1	0	0	0	0	0	0	0	0	0	0	0	1
1936	CHI	AL	6	2	4	3	2	1	0	0	0	0	0	0	0	0	6	0
1937	CHI	AL	4	2	2	4	0	0	0	0	0	0	0	0	0	0	4	0
1941	CHI	AL	1	1	0	1	0	0	0	0	0	0	0	0	0	0	1	0
1942	CHI	AL	3	1	2	2	1	0	0	0	0	0	0	0	0	0	2	1
1943	CHI	AL	3	2	1	3	0	0	0	0	0	0	0	0	0	0	2	1
1945	CHI	AL	1	0	1	1	0	0	0	0	0	0	0	0	0	0	1	0
1946	CHI	AL	1	0	1	0	1	0	0	0	0	0	0	0	0	0	1	0
1947	CHI	AL	8	4	4	7	1	0	0	0	0	0	0	0	0	0	8	0
1949	CHI	AL	5	3	2	3	2	0	0	0	0	0	0	1	1	0	3	2
Total			45	22	23	35	9	1	0	0	0	0	0	2	1	1	38	7

Rank among batters: 1,082 • Top target (2 home runs): Mel Harder, Buck Ross, Marv Breuer, Tiny Bonham, Tommy Bridges, Bill Zuber • *Number of pitchers victimized*: 39 • *Total ballparks homered in*: 8 • *First HR*: 06/20/1931 off Rube Walberg

Jimmy Archer

JAMES PATRICK ARCHER
B: 05/13/1883 D: 03/29/1958
BR

Year	Tm	Lg	Tot	H	A	Men-On 0	Men-On 1	Men-On 2	Men-On 3	One-Game 2	One-Game 3	One-Game 4	LO	XN	IP	PH	RHP	LHP
1909	CHI	NL	1	1	0	1	0	0	0	0	0	0	0	0	0	0	1	0
1910	CHI	NL	2	1	1	1	1	0	0	0	0	0	0	0	1	0	2	0

Jimmy Archer *continued*

Year	Tm	Lg	Tot	H	A	Men-On 0	Men-On 1	Men-On 2	Men-On 3	One-Game 2	One-Game 3	One-Game 4	LO	XN	IP	PH	RHP	LHP
1911	CHI	NL	4	3	1	2	2	0	0	0	0	0	0	1	0	0	3	1
1912	CHI	NL	5	1	4	3	2	0	0	0	0	0	0	0	0	0	3	2
1913	CHI	NL	2	0	2	2	0	0	0	0	0	0	0	0	0	0	1	1
1915	CHI	NL	1	1	0	0	1	0	0	0	0	0	0	0	0	0	0	1
1916	CHI	NL	1	1	0	0	1	0	0	0	0	0	0	0	0	0	0	1
Total			16	8	8	9	7	0	0	0	0	0	0	1	1	0	10	6

Rank among batters: 2,029 • *Top target (2 home runs)*: Earl Moore, Grover Alexander, Rube Marquard • *Number of pitchers victimized*: 13 • *Total ballparks homered in*: 5 • *First HR*: 08/04/1909 off George Ferguson

George Archie

GEORGE ALBERT ARCHIE
B: 04/27/1914
BR

Year	Tm	Lg	Tot	H	A	Men-On 0	Men-On 1	Men-On 2	Men-On 3	One-Game 2	One-Game 3	One-Game 4	LO	XN	IP	PH	RHP	LHP
1941	WAS	AL	3	0	3	1	2	0	0	0	0	0	0	1	0	0	2	1

Rank among batters: 3,735 • *Total ballparks homered in*: 3 • *First HR*: 04/23/1941 off Nels Potter

Jose Arcia

JOSE RAIMUNDO (ORTA) ARCIA
B: 08/22/1943
BR

Year	Tm	Lg	Tot	H	A	Men-On 0	Men-On 1	Men-On 2	Men-On 3	One-Game 2	One-Game 3	One-Game 4	LO	XN	IP	PH	RHP	LHP
1968	CHI	NL	1	1	0	1	0	0	0	0	0	0	0	0	0	0	0	1

Rank among batters: 4,707 • *Total ballparks homered in*: 1 • *First HR*: 07/07/1968 off Bob Veale

Frank Arellanes

FRANK JULIAN ARELLANES
B: 01/28/1882 D: 12/13/1918
BR

Year	Tm	Lg	Tot	H	A	Men-On 0	Men-On 1	Men-On 2	Men-On 3	One-Game 2	One-Game 3	One-Game 4	LO	XN	IP	PH	RHP	LHP
1910	BOS	AL	1	0	1	0	0	1	0	0	0	0	0	0	0	0	0	1

Rank among batters: 4,707 • *Total ballparks homered in*: 1 • *First HR*: 06/16/1910 off Ed Killian

Hank Arft

HENRY IRVEN ARFT
B: 01/28/1922
BL

Year	Tm	Lg	Tot	H	A	Men-On 0	Men-On 1	Men-On 2	Men-On 3	One-Game 2	One-Game 3	One-Game 4	LO	XN	IP	PH	RHP	LHP
1948	STL	AL	5	3	2	2	2	1	0	0	0	0	0	0	0	0	5	0
1950	STL	AL	1	1	0	1	0	0	0	0	0	0	0	0	0	1	1	0
1951	STL	AL	7	5	2	3	3	1	0	0	0	0	0	1	0	2	7	0
Total			13	9	4	6	5	2	0	0	0	0	0	1	0	3	13	0

Rank among batters: 2,248 • *Total ballparks homered in*: 4 • *First HR*: 07/27/1948 off Frank Hiller

Alex Arias

ALEJANDRO ARIAS
B: 11/20/1967
BR

Year	Tm	Lg	Tot	H	A	Men-On 0	Men-On 1	Men-On 2	Men-On 3	One-Game 2	One-Game 3	One-Game 4	LO	XN	IP	PH	RHP	LHP
1993	FLO	NL	2	1	1	2	0	0	0	0	0	0	0	0	0	0	2	0
1995	FLO	NL	3	2	1	2	0	1	0	0	0	0	0	0	1	0	3	0
Total			5	3	2	4	0	1	0	0	0	0	0	0	1	0	5	0

Rank among batters: 3,191 • *Total ballparks homered in*: 2 • *First HR*: 04/20/1993 off Greg Maddux

Buzz Arlett

RUSSELL LORIS ARLETT
B: 01/03/1899 D: 05/16/1964
BB

Year	Tm	Lg	Tot	H	A	Men-On 0	Men-On 1	Men-On 2	Men-On 3	One-Game 2	One-Game 3	One-Game 4	LO	XN	IP	PH	RHP	LHP
1931	PHI	NL	18	10	8	5	13	0	0	1	0	0	0	1	0	0	13	5

Rank among batters: 1,914 • *Top target (2 home runs)*: Bill Sherdel, Pat Malone • *Number of pitchers victimized*: 16 • *Total ballparks homered in*: 6 • *First HR*: 04/15/1931 off Bill Morrell

Marcos Armas

MARCOS RAFAEL (RUIZ) ARMAS
B: 08/05/1969
BR

Year	Tm	Lg	Tot	H	A	Men-On 0	Men-On 1	Men-On 2	Men-On 3	One-Game 2	One-Game 3	One-Game 4	LO	XN	IP	PH	RHP	LHP
1993	OAK	AL	1	1	0	1	0	0	0	0	0	0	0	0	0	0	0	1

Rank among batters: 4,707 • *Total ballparks homered in*: 1 • *First HR*: 05/26/1993 off George Tsamis

Tony Armas

ANTONIO RAFAEL (MACHADO) ARMAS
B: 07/02/1953
BR

Year	Tm	Lg	Tot	H	A	Men-On 0	1	2	3	One-Game 2	3	4	LO	XN	IP	PH	RHP	LHP
1977	OAK	AL	13	7	6	5	7	0	1	0	0	0	0	0	0	0	9	4
1978	OAK	AL	2	0	2	1	1	0	0	0	0	0	0	0	0	0	0	2
1979	OAK	AL	11	4	7	6	3	2	0	1	0	0	0	0	0	0	11	0
1980	OAK	AL	35	17	18	16	12	6	1	3	0	0	0	1	0	0	25	10
1981	OAK	AL	22	13	9	13	7	2	0	2	0	0	0	2	0	0	13	9
1982	OAK	AL	28	14	14	13	13	1	1	1	0	0	0	1	0	0	21	7
1983	BOS	AL	36	17	19	18	12	5	1	6	0	0	0	0	1	0	27	9
1984	BOS	AL	43	21	22	25	14	3	1	2	0	0	0	2	0	0	39	4
1985	BOS	AL	23	11	12	15	6	2	0	1	0	0	0	0	0	0	14	9
1986	BOS	AL	11	5	6	6	2	2	1	1	0	0	0	0	0	0	9	2
1987	CAL	AL	3	1	2	2	0	1	0	0	0	0	0	0	0	0	1	2
1988	CAL	AL	13	5	8	7	4	2	0	1	0	0	0	0	0	1	5	8
1989	CAL	AL	11	5	6	8	1	2	0	0	0	0	0	0	0	0	6	5
Total			251	120	131	135	82	28	6	18	0	0	0	6	1	1	180	71

Rank among batters: 108 • *Top target (5 home runs)*: Scott McGregor • *Number of pitchers victimized*: 173 • *Total ballparks homered in*: 15 • *First HR*: 05/20/1977 off Rick Jones

Ed Armbrister

EDISON ROSANDA ARMBRISTER
B: 07/04/1948
BR

Year	Tm	Lg	Tot	H	A	Men-On 0	1	2	3	One-Game 2	3	4	LO	XN	IP	PH	RHP	LHP
1973	CIN	NL	1	0	1	1	0	0	0	0	0	0	0	0	0	0	0	1
1976	CIN	NL	2	2	0	2	0	0	0	1	0	0	0	0	0	0	0	2
1977	CIN	NL	1	0	1	0	1	0	0	0	0	0	0	0	0	0	0	1
Total			4	2	2	3	1	0	0	1	0	0	0	0	0	0	0	4

Rank among batters: 3,427 • *Top target (2 home runs)*: Brent Strom • *Number of pitchers victimized*: 3 • *Total ballparks homered in*: 3 • *First HR*: 09/05/1973 off Jerry Reuss

Harry Armbruster

HARRY ARMBRUSTER
B: 03/02/1882 D: 12/10/1953
BL

Year	Tm	Lg	Tot	H	A	Men-On 0	1	2	3	One-Game 2	3	4	LO	XN	IP	PH	RHP	LHP
1906	PHI	AL	2	1	1	0	2	0	0	0	0	0	0	0	1	0	2	0

Rank among batters: 4,129 • *Total ballparks homered in*: 2 • *First HR*: 06/23/1906 off Joe Harris

Harry Arndt

HARRY J. ARNDT
B: 02/12/1879 D: 03/25/1921

Year	Tm	Lg	Tot	H	A	Men-On 0	1	2	3	One-Game 2	3	4	LO	XN	IP	PH	RHP	LHP
1902	BAL	AL	2	1	1	0	1	1	0	0	0	0	0	0	0	0	2	0
1905	STL	NL	2	2	0	2	0	0	0	0	0	0	0	0	1	0	2	0
1906	STL	NL	2	1	1	0	2	0	0	0	0	0	0	0	2	0	2	0
Total			6	4	2	2	3	1	0	0	0	0	0	0	3	0	6	0

Rank among batters: 2,988 • *Top target (2 home runs)*: Bill Duggleby • *Number of pitchers victimized*: 5 • *Total ballparks homered in*: 4 • *First HR*: 07/26/1902 off Earl Moore

Chris Arnold

CHRISTOPHER PAUL ARNOLD
B: 11/06/1947
BR

Year	Tm	Lg	Tot	H	A	Men-On 0	1	2	3	One-Game 2	3	4	LO	XN	IP	PH	RHP	LHP
1971	SF	NL	1	0	1	0	1	0	0	0	0	0	0	0	0	0	1	0
1972	SF	NL	1	1	0	1	0	0	0	0	0	0	0	0	0	0	1	0
1973	SF	NL	1	1	0	0	0	0	1	0	0	0	0	0	0	1	0	1
1974	SF	NL	1	1	0	0	1	0	0	0	0	0	0	0	0	0	0	1
Total			4	3	1	1	2	0	1	0	0	0	0	0	0	1	2	2

Rank among batters: 3,427 • *Total ballparks homered in*: 2 • *First HR*: 09/10/1971 off Phil Niekro

Morrie Arnovich

MORRIS ARNOVICH
B: 11/16/1910 D: 07/20/1959
BR

Year	Tm	Lg	Tot	H	A	Men-On 0	1	2	3	One-Game 2	3	4	LO	XN	IP	PH	RHP	LHP
1936	PHI	NL	1	1	0	0	1	0	0	0	0	0	0	0	0	0	1	0

Morrie Arnovich *continued*

Year	Tm	Lg	Tot	H	A	Men-On 0	Men-On 1	Men-On 2	Men-On 3	One-Game 2	One-Game 3	One-Game 4	LO	XN	IP	PH	RHP	LHP
1937	PHI	NL	10	5	5	6	2	2	0	0	0	0	0	1	0	0	4	6
1938	PHI	NL	4	2	2	2	2	0	0	0	0	0	0	0	0	0	4	0
1939	PHI	NL	5	2	3	3	1	1	0	0	0	0	0	0	0	0	4	1
1941	NY	NL	2	1	1	1	1	0	0	0	0	0	0	0	0	0	0	2
Total			22	11	11	12	7	3	0	0	0	0	0	1	0	0	13	9

Rank among batters: 1,719 • *Top target (2 home runs)*: Ed Brandt, Bill Lee, Larry French • *Number of pitchers victimized*: 19 • *Total ballparks homered in*: 8 • *First HR*: 09/27/1936 off Ben Cantwell

Gerry Arrigo

GERALD WILLIAM ARRIGO
B: 06/12/1941
BL

Year	Tm	Lg	Tot	H	A	Men-On 0	Men-On 1	Men-On 2	Men-On 3	One-Game 2	One-Game 3	One-Game 4	LO	XN	IP	PH	RHP	LHP
1965	CIN	NL	1	0	1	0	0	1	0	0	0	0	0	0	0	0	1	0

Rank among batters: 4,707 • *Total ballparks homered in*: 1 • *First HR*: 05/29/1965 off Jack Sanford

Luis Arroyo

LUIS ENRIQUE ARROYO
B: 02/18/1927
BL

Year	Tm	Lg	Tot	H	A	Men-On 0	Men-On 1	Men-On 2	Men-On 3	One-Game 2	One-Game 3	One-Game 4	LO	XN	IP	PH	RHP	LHP
1955	STL	NL	1	0	1	1	0	0	0	0	0	0	0	0	0	0	1	0

Rank among batters: 4,707 • *Total ballparks homered in*: 1 • *First HR*: 08/27/1955 off Murry Dickson

Casper Asbjornson

ROBERT ANTHONY ASBJORNSON
B: 06/19/1909 D: 01/21/1970
BR

Year	Tm	Lg	Tot	H	A	Men-On 0	Men-On 1	Men-On 2	Men-On 3	One-Game 2	One-Game 3	One-Game 4	LO	XN	IP	PH	RHP	LHP
1932	CIN	NL	1	0	1	1	0	0	0	0	0	0	0	0	0	0	1	0

Rank among batters: 4,707 • *Total ballparks homered in*: 1 • *First HR*: 06/19/1932 off Ben Cantwell

Richie Ashburn

DON RICHARD ASHBURN
B: 03/19/1927
BL

Year	Tm	Lg	Tot	H	A	Men-On 0	Men-On 1	Men-On 2	Men-On 3	One-Game 2	One-Game 3	One-Game 4	LO	XN	IP	PH	RHP	LHP
1948	PHI	NL	2	1	1	2	0	0	0	0	0	0	1	0	2	0	0	2
1949	PHI	NL	1	1	0	0	1	0	0	0	0	0	0	0	0	0	1	0
1950	PHI	NL	2	0	2	2	0	0	0	0	0	0	0	0	0	0	1	1
1951	PHI	NL	4	1	3	2	0	2	0	0	0	0	1	0	1	0	4	0
1952	PHI	NL	1	1	0	1	0	0	0	0	0	0	0	0	1	0	1	0
1953	PHI	NL	2	0	2	2	0	0	0	0	0	0	0	0	0	0	1	1
1954	PHI	NL	1	0	1	0	0	1	0	0	0	0	0	0	1	0	1	0
1955	PHI	NL	3	0	3	1	2	0	0	1	0	0	0	0	0	0	1	2
1956	PHI	NL	3	0	3	2	0	1	0	1	0	0	0	0	1	0	1	2
1958	PHI	NL	2	1	1	0	2	0	0	0	0	0	0	0	0	0	2	0
1959	PHI	NL	1	1	0	1	0	0	0	0	0	0	0	0	1	0	1	0
1962	NY	NL	7	6	1	5	2	0	0	1	0	0	1	0	1	0	6	1
Total			29	12	17	18	7	4	0	3	0	0	3	0	8	0	20	9

Rank among batters: 1,465 • *Top target (2 home runs)*: Johnny Antonelli, Don Newcombe • *Number of pitchers victimized*: 27 • *Total ballparks homered in*: 8 • *First HR*: 05/29/1948 off Thornton Lee

Alan Ashby

ALAN DEAN ASHBY
B: 07/08/1951
BB

Year	Tm	Lg	Tot	H	A	Men-On 0	Men-On 1	Men-On 2	Men-On 3	One-Game 2	One-Game 3	One-Game 4	LO	XN	IP	PH	RHP	LHP
1973	CLE	AL	1	0	1	0	1	0	0	0	0	0	0	0	0	0	0	1
1975	CLE	AL	5	1	4	2	2	0	1	0	0	0	0	0	0	0	4	1
1976	CLE	AL	4	1	3	2	1	1	0	0	0	0	0	0	0	0	4	0
1977	TOR	AL	2	1	1	1	0	1	0	0	0	0	0	0	0	0	1	1
1978	TOR	AL	9	6	3	7	1	1	0	0	0	0	0	0	0	0	8	1
1979	HOU	NL	2	1	1	2	0	0	0	0	0	0	0	0	0	0	1	1
1980	HOU	NL	3	1	2	2	1	0	0	0	0	0	0	0	0	0	3	0
1981	HOU	NL	4	3	1	3	1	0	0	0	0	0	0	0	0	0	3	1
1982	HOU	NL	12	5	7	8	2	2	0	2	0	0	0	0	0	0	9	3

						Men-On				One-Game								
Year	**Tm**	**Lg**	**Tot**	**H**	**A**	**0**	**1**	**2**	**3**	**2**	**3**	**4**	**LO**	**XN**	**IP**	**PH**	**RHP**	**LHP**

Alan Ashby *continued*

Year	Tm	Lg	Tot	H	A	0	1	2	3	2	3	4	LO	XN	IP	PH	RHP	LHP
1983	HOU	NL	8	2	6	4	4	0	0	1	0	0	0	0	0	0	7	1
1984	HOU	NL	4	0	4	2	2	0	0	0	0	0	0	1	0	0	2	2
1985	HOU	NL	8	3	5	7	0	0	1	0	0	0	0	0	0	0	6	2
1986	HOU	NL	7	1	6	5	2	0	0	0	0	0	0	0	0	0	5	2
1987	HOU	NL	14	8	6	9	4	0	1	0	0	0	0	0	0	0	14	0
1988	HOU	NL	7	0	7	5	2	0	0	1	0	0	0	1	0	0	7	0
Total			90	33	57	59	23	5	3	4	0	0	0	2	0	0	74	16

Rank among batters: 573 • *Top target (3 home runs)*: Dick Pole, John Montefusco, Mario Soto • *Number of pitchers victimized*: 78 • *Total ballparks homered in*: 20 • *First HR*: 09/29/1973 off Mike Cuellar • *Switch hit HR in 1 game*—1 time • *LCS HR*—2

Tucker Ashford

THOMAS STEVEN ASHFORD
B: 12/04/1954
BR

Year	Tm	Lg	Tot	H	A	0	1	2	3	2	3	4	LO	XN	IP	PH	RHP	LHP
1977	SD	NL	3	2	1	2	1	0	0	0	0	0	0	0	0	0	3	0
1978	SD	NL	3	1	2	2	1	0	0	0	0	0	0	0	0	0	3	0
Total			6	3	3	4	2	0	0	0	0	0	0	0	0	0	6	0

Rank among batters: 2,988 • *Total ballparks homered in*: 4 • *First HR*: 07/05/1977 off Bo McLaughlin

Billy Ashley

BILLY MANUAL ASHLEY
B: 07/11/1970
BR

Year	Tm	Lg	Tot	H	A	0	1	2	3	2	3	4	LO	XN	IP	PH	RHP	LHP
1992	LA	NL	2	2	0	2	0	0	0	0	0	0	0	0	0	0	0	2
1995	LA	NL	8	6	2	5	1	2	0	1	0	0	0	0	0	0	6	2
Total			10	8	2	7	1	2	0	1	0	0	0	0	0	0	6	4

Rank among batters: 2,500 • *Total ballparks homered in*: 2 • *First HR*: 09/10/1992 off Jim Deshaies

Bob Aspromonte

ROBERT THOMAS ASPROMONTE
B: 06/19/1938
BR

Year	Tm	Lg	Tot	H	A	0	1	2	3	2	3	4	LO	XN	IP	PH	RHP	LHP
1960	LA	NL	1	1	0	1	0	0	0	0	0	0	0	0	0	0	1	0
1962	HOU	NL	11	7	4	5	5	1	0	0	0	0	0	0	0	0	7	4
1963	HOU	NL	8	4	4	5	0	1	2	0	0	0	0	3	0	0	6	2
1964	HOU	NL	12	10	2	6	4	0	2	0	0	0	0	0	0	0	9	3
1965	HOU	NL	5	2	3	3	1	1	0	0	0	0	0	0	0	0	4	1
1966	HOU	NL	8	1	7	3	1	2	2	0	0	0	0	0	0	0	6	2
1967	HOU	NL	6	1	5	3	1	2	0	0	0	0	0	0	0	0	2	4
1968	HOU	NL	1	0	1	0	1	0	0	0	0	0	0	0	0	0	1	0
1969	ATL	NL	3	2	1	2	0	1	0	0	0	0	0	0	0	1	2	1
1971	NY	NL	5	2	3	4	0	1	0	1	0	0	0	0	0	0	3	2
Total			60	30	30	32	13	9	6	1	0	0	0	3	0	1	41	19

Rank among batters: 863 • *Top target (3 home runs)*: Tracy Stallard • *Number of pitchers victimized*: 49 • *Total ballparks homered in*: 14 • *First HR*: 05/05/1960 off Lew Burdette

Ken Aspromonte

KENNETH JOSEPH ASPROMONTE
B: 09/22/1931
BR

Year	Tm	Lg	Tot	H	A	0	1	2	3	2	3	4	LO	XN	IP	PH	RHP	LHP
1958	WAS	AL	5	0	5	3	1	1	0	0	0	0	0	1	0	0	5	0
1959	WAS	AL	2	1	1	2	0	0	0	0	0	0	1	0	0	0	1	1
1960	CLE	AL	10	5	5	5	5	0	0	0	0	0	1	1	0	0	5	5
1961	LA	AL	2	2	0	0	2	0	0	0	0	0	0	0	0	0	1	1
Total			19	8	11	10	8	1	0	0	0	0	2	2	0	0	12	7

Rank among batters: 1,861 • *Top target (3 home runs)*: Billy Pierce • *Number of pitchers victimized*: 15 • *Total ballparks homered in*: 7 • *First HR*: 05/09/1958 off Bob Turley

Brian Asselstine

BRIAN HANLY ASSELSTINE
B: 09/23/1953
BL

Year	Tm	Lg	Tot	H	A	0	1	2	3	2	3	4	LO	XN	IP	PH	RHP	LHP
1976	ATL	NL	1	1	0	0	1	0	0	0	0	0	0	0	0	0	1	0

Year	Tm	Lg	Tot	H	A	Men-On 0	Men-On 1	Men-On 2	Men-On 3	One-Game 2	One-Game 3	One-Game 4	LO	XN	IP	PH	RHP	LHP

Brian Asselstine *continued*

Year	Tm	Lg	Tot	H	A	0	1	2	3	2	3	4	LO	XN	IP	PH	RHP	LHP
1977	ATL	NL	4	3	1	3	1	0	0	0	0	0	0	0	0	1	4	0
1978	ATL	NL	2	1	1	2	0	0	0	0	0	0	0	0	0	0	1	1
1980	ATL	NL	3	1	2	2	1	0	0	0	0	0	0	0	0	0	3	0
1981	ATL	NL	2	1	1	0	1	1	0	0	0	0	0	0	0	1	2	0
Total			12	7	5	7	4	1	0	0	0	0	0	0	0	2	11	1

Rank among batters: 2,325 • *Top target (2 home runs)*: John Montefusco, Burt Hooton • *Number of pitchers victimized*: 10 • *Total ballparks homered in*: 5 • *First HR*: 09/26/1976 off Rick Sawyer

Joe Astroth

JOSEPH HENRY ASTROTH
B: 09/01/1922
BR

Year	Tm	Lg	Tot	H	A	0	1	2	3	2	3	4	LO	XN	IP	PH	RHP	LHP
1950	PHI	AL	1	0	1	0	0	0	1	0	0	0	0	0	0	0	1	0
1951	PHI	AL	2	1	1	0	2	0	0	0	0	0	0	0	0	0	2	0
1952	PHI	AL	1	0	1	0	1	0	0	0	0	0	0	0	0	0	0	1
1953	PHI	AL	3	1	2	3	0	0	0	1	0	0	0	0	0	0	1	2
1954	PHI	AL	1	1	0	1	0	0	0	0	0	0	0	0	0	0	1	0
1955	KC	AL	5	4	1	4	0	1	0	0	0	0	0	0	0	0	3	2
Total			13	7	6	8	3	1	1	1	0	0	0	0	0	0	8	5

Rank among batters: 2,248 • *Total ballparks homered in*: 6 • *First HR*: 09/23/1950 off Julio Moreno

Al Atkinson

ALBERT WRIGHT ATKINSON
B: 03/09/1861 D: 06/17/1952
BR

Year	Tm	Lg	Tot	H	A	0	1	2	3	2	3	4	LO	XN	IP	PH	RHP	LHP
1887	PHI	AA	1	1	0	0	1	0	0	0	0	0	0	0	0	0	1	0

Rank among batters: 4,707 • *Total ballparks homered in*: 1 • *First HR*: 06/10/1887 off Dave Foutz

Dick Attreau

RICHARD GILBERT ATTREAU
B: 04/08/1897 D: 07/05/1964
BL

Year	Tm	Lg	Tot	H	A	0	1	2	3	2	3	4	LO	XN	IP	PH	RHP	LHP
1927	PHI	NL	1	0	1	0	1	0	0	0	0	0	0	0	0	0	0	1

Rank among batters: 4,707 • *Total ballparks homered in*: 1 • *First HR*: 07/27/1927 off Bill Sherdel

Toby Atwell

MAURICE DAILEY ATWELL
B: 03/08/1924
BL

Year	Tm	Lg	Tot	H	A	0	1	2	3	2	3	4	LO	XN	IP	PH	RHP	LHP
1952	CHI	NL	2	0	2	1	0	1	0	1	0	0	0	0	0	0	2	0
1953	CHI	NL	1	0	1	1	0	0	0	0	0	0	0	0	0	0	1	0
1954	PIT	NL	3	1	2	1	2	0	0	1	0	0	0	0	0	0	3	0
1955	PIT	NL	1	0	1	1	0	0	0	0	0	0	0	0	0	0	1	0
1956	MIL	NL	2	1	1	0	2	0	0	0	0	0	0	0	0	0	2	0
Total			9	2	7	4	4	1	0	2	0	0	0	0	0	0	9	0

Rank among batters: 2,587 • *Top target (2 home runs)*: Cloyd Boyer, Corky Valentine • *Number of pitchers victimized*: 7 • *Total ballparks homered in*: 5 • *First HR*: 07/04/1952 off Cloyd Boyer

Bill Atwood

WILLIAM FRANKLIN ATWOOD
B: 09/25/1911 D: 09/14/1993
BR

Year	Tm	Lg	Tot	H	A	0	1	2	3	2	3	4	LO	XN	IP	PH	RHP	LHP
1936	PHI	NL	2	0	2	1	1	0	0	0	0	0	0	0	0	1	0	2
1937	PHI	NL	2	1	1	1	0	1	0	0	0	0	0	0	0	0	1	1
1938	PHI	NL	3	2	1	2	1	0	0	0	0	0	0	1	0	0	1	2
Total			7	3	4	4	2	1	0	0	0	0	0	1	0	1	2	5

Rank among batters: 2,834 • *Top target (2 home runs)*: Larry French • *Number of pitchers victimized*: 6 • *Total ballparks homered in*: 5 • *First HR*: 07/01/1936 off Watty Clark

Rich Aude

RICHARD THOMAS AUDE
B: 07/13/1971
BR

Year	Tm	Lg	Tot	H	A	Men-On 0	1	2	3	One-Game 2	3	4	LO	XN	IP	PH	RHP	LHP
1995	PIT	NL	2	1	1	1	1	0	0	0	0	0	0	0	0	1	1	1

Rank among batters: 4,129 • *Total ballparks homered in*: 2 • *First HR*: 05/18/1995 off Todd Williams

Rick Auerbach

FREDERICK STEVEN AUERBACH
B: 02/15/1950
BR

Year	Tm	Lg	Tot	H	A	Men-On 0	1	2	3	One-Game 2	3	4	LO	XN	IP	PH	RHP	LHP
1971	MIL	AL	1	0	1	1	0	0	0	0	0	0	0	0	0	0	1	0
1972	MIL	AL	2	0	2	2	0	0	0	0	0	0	0	0	0	0	2	0
1974	LA	NL	1	0	1	1	0	0	0	0	0	0	0	0	0	0	1	0
1978	CIN	NL	2	1	1	2	0	0	0	0	0	0	0	0	0	0	0	2
1979	CIN	NL	1	1	0	1	0	0	0	0	0	0	0	0	0	0	1	0
1980	CIN	NL	1	0	1	1	0	0	0	0	0	0	0	0	0	1	0	1
1981	SEA	AL	1	1	0	0	1	0	0	0	0	0	0	0	0	0	0	1
Total			9	3	6	8	1	0	0	0	0	0	0	0	0	1	5	4

Rank among batters: 2,587 • *Total ballparks homered in*: 7 • *First HR*: 09/24/1971 off Diego Segui

Elden Auker

ELDEN LEROY AUKER
B: 09/21/1910
BR

Year	Tm	Lg	Tot	H	A	Men-On 0	1	2	3	One-Game 2	3	4	LO	XN	IP	PH	RHP	LHP
1937	DET	AL	3	3	0	1	1	1	0	1	0	0	0	0	0	0	3	0
1939	BOS	AL	2	0	2	1	1	0	0	0	0	0	0	0	0	0	2	0
1940	STL	AL	1	0	1	1	0	0	0	0	0	0	0	0	0	0	1	0
Total			6	3	3	3	2	1	0	1	0	0	0	0	0	0	6	0

Rank among batters: 2,988 • *Top target (2 home runs)*: Nig Lipscomb • *Number of pitchers victimized*: 5 • *Total ballparks homered in*: 4 • *First HR*: 07/16/1937 off Johnny Broaca

Doug Ault

DOUGLAS REAGAN AULT
B: 03/09/1950
BR

Year	Tm	Lg	Tot	H	A	Men-On 0	1	2	3	One-Game 2	3	4	LO	XN	IP	PH	RHP	LHP
1977	TOR	AL	11	7	4	6	2	3	0	1	0	0	0	0	0	1	5	6
1978	TOR	AL	3	2	1	2	1	0	0	0	0	0	0	0	0	0	0	3
1980	TOR	AL	3	0	3	0	3	0	0	0	0	0	0	0	0	1	0	3
Total			17	9	8	8	6	3	0	1	0	0	0	0	0	2	5	12

Rank among batters: 1,969 • *Top target (2 home runs)*: Ken Brett, Vida Blue, Rick Waits, Sid Monge • *Number of pitchers victimized*: 13 • *Total ballparks homered in*: 5 • *First HR*: 04/07/1977 off Ken Brett

Rich Aurilia

RICHARD SANTO AURILIA
B: 09/02/1971
BR

Year	Tm	Lg	Tot	H	A	Men-On 0	1	2	3	One-Game 2	3	4	LO	XN	IP	PH	RHP	LHP
1995	SF	NL	2	0	2	2	0	0	0	0	0	0	0	0	0	0	1	1

Rank among batters: 4,129 • *Total ballparks homered in*: 1 • *First HR*: 09/28/1995 off Lance Painter

Brad Ausmus

BRADLEY DAVID AUSMUS
B: 04/14/1969
BR

Year	Tm	Lg	Tot	H	A	Men-On 0	1	2	3	One-Game 2	3	4	LO	XN	IP	PH	RHP	LHP
1993	SD	NL	5	4	1	3	2	0	0	0	0	0	0	0	0	0	4	1
1994	SD	NL	7	6	1	4	1	2	0	0	0	0	0	1	0	0	6	1
1995	SD	NL	5	2	3	4	1	0	0	0	0	0	0	0	0	0	2	3
Total			17	12	5	11	4	2	0	0	0	0	0	1	0	0	12	5

Rank among batters: 1,969 • *Total ballparks homered in*: 5 • *First HR*: 08/04/1993 off Greg Brummett

Jimmy Austin

JAMES PHILIP AUSTIN
B: 12/08/1879 D: 03/06/1965
BB

Year	Tm	Lg	Tot	H	A	Men-On 0	1	2	3	One-Game 2	3	4	LO	XN	IP	PH	RHP	LHP
1909	NY	AL	1	1	0	1	0	0	0	0	0	0	0	0	1	0	1	0

Year	Tm	Lg	Tot	H	A	Men-On 0	Men-On 1	Men-On 2	Men-On 3	One-Game 2	One-Game 3	One-Game 4	LO	XN	IP	PH	RHP	LHP

Jimmy Austin *continued*

Year	Tm	Lg	Tot	H	A	0	1	2	3	2	3	4	LO	XN	IP	PH	RHP	LHP
1910	NY	AL	2	2	0	0	1	1	0	0	0	0	0	0	2	0	2	0
1911	STL	AL	2	2	0	0	1	1	0	0	0	0	0	0	0	0	1	1
1912	STL	AL	2	0	2	0	1	1	0	0	0	0	0	0	1	0	2	0
1913	STL	AL	2	2	0	1	1	0	0	0	0	0	0	0	0	0	2	0
1915	STL	AL	1	0	1	0	1	0	0	0	0	0	0	0	1	0	1	0
1916	STL	AL	1	0	1	0	1	0	0	0	0	0	0	0	0	0	0	1
1919	STL	AL	1	0	1	0	1	0	0	0	0	0	0	0	1	0	1	0
1920	STL	AL	1	1	0	0	1	0	0	0	0	0	0	0	1	0	1	0
Total			13	8	5	2	8	3	0	0	0	0	0	0	7	0	11	2

Rank among batters: 2,248 • *Total ballparks homered in*: 5 • *First HR*: 07/05/1909 off Chief Bender

Chick Autry

MARTIN GORDON AUTRY
B: 03/05/1903 D: 01/26/1950
BR

Year	Tm	Lg	Tot	H	A	0	1	2	3	2	3	4	LO	XN	IP	PH	RHP	LHP
1928	CLE	AL	1	0	1	0	1	0	0	0	0	0	0	1	0	0	0	1
1929	CHI	AL	1	1	0	1	0	0	0	0	0	0	0	0	0	0	0	1
Total			2	1	1	1	1	0	0	0	0	0	0	1	0	0	0	2

Rank among batters: 4,129 • *Total ballparks homered in*: 2 • *First HR*: 08/19/1928 off Fred Heimach

Earl Averill

HOWARD EARL AVERILL
B: 05/21/1902 D: 08/16/1983
BL HOF

Year	Tm	Lg	Tot	H	A	0	1	2	3	2	3	4	LO	XN	IP	PH	RHP	LHP
1929	CLE	AL	18	10	8	8	6	3	1	2	0	0	0	0	2	0	14	4
1930	CLE	AL	19	13	6	7	8	3	1	1	1	0	0	0	0	0	16	3
1931	CLE	AL	32	20	12	14	13	4	1	5	0	0	0	1	0	0	22	10
1932	CLE	AL	32	16	16	15	12	5	0	4	0	0	0	1	0	0	20	12
1933	CLE	AL	11	6	5	6	4	1	0	0	0	0	0	0	2	0	10	1
1934	CLE	AL	31	17	14	13	11	7	0	2	0	0	0	0	3	0	27	4
1935	CLE	AL	19	12	7	12	4	3	0	1	0	0	0	1	0	0	14	5
1936	CLE	AL	28	19	9	18	7	3	0	2	0	0	0	1	0	0	15	13
1937	CLE	AL	21	15	6	10	7	3	1	0	0	0	0	0	0	0	15	6
1938	CLE	AL	14	8	6	6	4	4	0	0	0	0	0	0	0	0	11	3
1939	CLE	AL	1	1	0	0	0	1	0	0	0	0	0	0	0	0	0	1
	DET	AL	10	7	3	5	4	1	0	1	0	0	0	1	0	0	10	0
	Total		11	8	3	5	4	2	0	1	0	0	0	1	0	0	10	1
1940	DET	AL	2	0	2	1	1	0	0	0	0	0	0	0	0	0	2	0
Total			238	144	94	115	81	38	4	18	1	0	0	5	7	0	176	62

Rank among batters: 131 • *Top target (11 home runs)*: Bump Hadley • *Number of pitchers victimized*: 114 • *Total ballparks homered in*: 9 • *First HR*: 04/16/1929 off Earl Whitehill • *Hit for Cycle*—vs PHI: 08/17/1933 • *Hit HR in first major league AB*—vs DET: 04/16/1929

Earl Averill

EARL DOUGLAS AVERILL
B: 09/09/1931
BR

Year	Tm	Lg	Tot	H	A	0	1	2	3	2	3	4	LO	XN	IP	PH	RHP	LHP
1956	CLE	AL	3	1	2	2	1	0	0	0	0	0	0	0	0	0	2	1
1958	CLE	AL	2	1	1	0	1	1	0	0	0	0	0	0	0	0	2	0
1959	CHI	NL	10	3	7	5	2	1	2	0	0	0	0	2	0	1	8	2
1960	CHI	NL	1	1	0	1	0	0	0	0	0	0	0	0	0	1	0	1
1961	LA	AL	21	16	5	13	5	3	0	1	0	0	0	0	0	0	14	7
1962	LA	AL	4	3	1	3	0	1	0	0	0	0	0	0	0	1	2	2
1963	PHI	NL	3	1	2	3	0	0	0	0	0	0	0	0	0	1	1	2
Total			44	26	18	27	9	6	2	1	0	0	0	2	0	4	29	15

Rank among batters: 1,095 • *Top target (3 home runs)*: Pedro Ramos • *Number of pitchers victimized*: 40 • *Total ballparks homered in*: 13 • *First HR*: 06/04/1956 off Pedro Ramos

Steve Avery

STEVEN THOMAS AVERY
B: 04/14/1970
BL

Year	Tm	Lg	Tot	H	A	0	1	2	3	2	3	4	LO	XN	IP	PH	RHP	LHP
1995	ATL	NL	2	2	0	2	0	0	0	0	0	0	0	0	0	0	2	0

Rank among batters: 4,129 • *Total ballparks homered in*: 1 • *First HR*: 06/05/1995 off Mike Morgan

Year	Tm	Lg	Tot	H	A	Men-On 0	1	2	3	One-Game 2	3	4	LO	XN	IP	PH	RHP	LHP

Bobby Avila

ROBERTO FRANCISCO (GONZALEZ) AVILA
B: 04/02/1924
BR

Year	Tm	Lg	Tot	H	A	Men-On 0	1	2	3	One-Game 2	3	4	LO	XN	IP	PH	RHP	LHP
1950	CLE	AL	1	1	0	1	0	0	0	0	0	0	0	0	0	0	0	1
1951	CLE	AL	10	5	5	7	3	0	0	0	1	0	0	1	1	0	6	4
1952	CLE	AL	7	4	3	6	1	0	0	0	0	0	0	1	0	0	4	3
1953	CLE	AL	8	4	4	6	2	0	0	0	0	0	0	0	1	0	4	4
1954	CLE	AL	15	10	5	11	1	2	1	2	0	0	0	0	0	0	11	4
1955	CLE	AL	13	5	8	8	3	2	0	1	0	0	0	0	0	0	8	5
1956	CLE	AL	10	6	4	4	3	2	1	0	0	0	0	1	1	0	9	1
1957	CLE	AL	5	5	0	2	1	2	0	0	0	0	0	0	0	0	4	1
1958	CLE	AL	5	4	1	3	2	0	0	0	0	0	0	0	0	1	1	4
1959	BOS	AL	3	3	0	2	0	1	0	1	0	0	0	0	0	1	2	1
	MIL	NL	3	2	1	1	1	0	1	0	0	0	1	0	0	0	1	2
	Total		6	5	1	3	1	1	1	1	0	0	1	0	0	1	3	3
Total			80	49	31	51	17	9	3	4	1	0	1	3	3	2	50	30

Rank among batters: 650 • *Top target (6 home runs)*: Billy Pierce • *Number of pitchers victimized*: 61 • *Total ballparks homered in*: 10 • *First HR*: 06/24/1950 off Mickey Harris

Ramon Aviles

RAMON ANTONIO (MIRANDA) AVILES
B: 01/22/1952
BR

Year	Tm	Lg	Tot	H	A	Men-On 0	1	2	3	One-Game 2	3	4	LO	XN	IP	PH	RHP	LHP
1980	PHI	NL	2	1	1	2	0	0	0	0	0	0	0	0	0	0	2	0

Rank among batters: 4,129 • *Total ballparks homered in*: 2 • *First HR*: 05/21/1980 off Mario Soto

Benny Ayala

BENIGNO (FELIX) AYALA
B: 02/07/1951
BR

Year	Tm	Lg	Tot	H	A	Men-On 0	1	2	3	One-Game 2	3	4	LO	XN	IP	PH	RHP	LHP
1974	NY	NL	2	2	0	2	0	0	0	0	0	0	0	0	0	0	1	1
1976	NY	NL	1	0	1	1	0	0	0	0	0	0	0	0	0	1	1	0
1979	BAL	AL	6	5	1	3	3	0	0	1	0	0	0	0	0	0	1	5
1980	BAL	AL	10	6	4	2	6	2	0	0	0	0	0	0	0	2	0	10
1981	BAL	AL	3	1	2	0	2	1	0	0	0	0	0	0	0	1	0	3
1982	BAL	AL	6	3	3	1	3	1	1	0	0	0	0	0	0	2	0	6
1983	BAL	AL	4	4	0	4	0	0	0	0	0	0	0	0	0	0	0	4
1984	BAL	AL	4	1	3	2	1	1	0	0	0	0	0	0	0	2	0	4
1985	CLE	AL	2	0	2	0	2	0	0	0	0	0	0	0	0	0	0	2
Total			38	22	16	15	17	5	1	1	0	0	0	0	0	8	3	35

Rank among batters: 1,225 • *Top target (3 home runs)*: Jon Matlack, Mike Caldwell • *Number of pitchers victimized*: 30 • *Total ballparks homered in*: 14 • *First HR*: 08/27/1974 off Tom Griffin • *Hit HR in first major league AB*—vs HOU: 08/27/1974 • *World Series HR*—1

Joe Azcue

JOSE JOAQUIN (LOPEZ) AZCUE
B: 08/18/1939
BR

Year	Tm	Lg	Tot	H	A	Men-On 0	1	2	3	One-Game 2	3	4	LO	XN	IP	PH	RHP	LHP
1962	KC	AL	2	1	1	1	1	0	0	0	0	0	0	0	0	0	1	1
1963	CLE	AL	14	8	6	10	2	2	0	3	0	0	0	0	0	0	10	4
1964	CLE	AL	4	2	2	2	1	1	0	0	0	0	0	0	0	0	2	2
1965	CLE	AL	2	0	2	0	2	0	0	0	0	0	0	0	0	0	0	2
1966	CLE	AL	9	2	7	5	1	3	0	0	0	0	0	0	0	0	3	6
1967	CLE	AL	11	4	7	7	4	0	0	0	0	0	0	1	0	0	5	6
1968	CLE	AL	4	2	2	3	0	1	0	0	0	0	0	0	0	0	1	3
1969	CLE	AL	1	1	0	1	0	0	0	0	0	0	0	0	0	0	1	0
	CAL	AL	1	1	0	1	0	0	0	0	0	0	0	0	0	0	0	1
	Total		2	2	0	2	0	0	0	0	0	0	0	0	0	0	1	1
1970	CAL	AL	2	0	2	1	1	0	0	0	0	0	0	0	0	0	1	1
Total			50	21	29	31	12	7	0	3	0	0	0	1	0	0	24	26

Rank among batters: 991 • *Top target (3 home runs)*: Dick Stigman, Jim Kaat, George Brunet • *Number of pitchers victimized*: 38 • *Total ballparks homered in*: 10 • *First HR*: 05/21/1962 off Gene Conley

Oscar Azocar

OSCAR GREGORIO (AZOCAR) AZOCAR
B: 02/21/1965
BL

Year	Tm	Lg	Tot	H	A	Men-On 0	1	2	3	One-Game 2	3	4	LO	XN	IP	PH	RHP	LHP
1990	NY	AL	5	3	2	3	2	0	0	0	0	0	0	0	0	0	4	1

Year	Tm	Lg	Tot	H	A	Men-On 0	Men-On 1	Men-On 2	Men-On 3	One-Game 2	One-Game 3	One-Game 4	LO	XN	IP	PH	RHP	LHP

Oscar Azocar *continued*

Rank among batters: 3,191 • *Total ballparks homered in*: 3 • *First HR*: 07/18/1990 off Tom Gordon

Loren Babe

LOREN ROLLAND BABE
B: 01/11/1928 D: 02/14/1984
BL

Year	Tm	Lg	Tot	H	A	0	1	2	3	2	3	4	LO	XN	IP	PH	RHP	LHP
1953	NY	AL	2	2	0	1	1	0	0	0	0	0	0	0	0	0	2	0

Rank among batters: 4,129 • *Total ballparks homered in*: 1 • *First HR*: 04/22/1953 off Hal Brown

Wally Backman

WALTER WAYNE BACKMAN
B: 09/22/1959
BB

Year	Tm	Lg	Tot	H	A	0	1	2	3	2	3	4	LO	XN	IP	PH	RHP	LHP
1982	NY	NL	3	1	2	1	1	1	0	0	0	0	0	0	1	0	3	0
1984	NY	NL	1	0	1	0	1	0	0	0	0	0	0	1	0	0	1	0
1985	NY	NL	1	0	1	0	1	0	0	0	0	0	0	0	0	0	1	0
1986	NY	NL	1	1	0	1	0	0	0	0	0	0	0	0	0	0	1	0
1987	NY	NL	1	0	1	1	0	0	0	0	0	0	0	0	0	0	1	0
1989	MIN	AL	1	0	1	1	0	0	0	0	0	0	0	0	0	0	1	0
1990	PIT	NL	2	0	2	2	0	0	0	0	0	0	0	0	0	0	2	0
Total			10	2	8	6	3	1	0	0	0	0	0	1	1	0	10	0

Rank among batters: 2,500 • *Total ballparks homered in*: 6 • *First HR*: 05/26/1982 off Rick Camp

Fred Baczewski

FREDERIC JOHN BACZEWSKI
B: 05/15/1926 D: 11/14/1976
BL

Year	Tm	Lg	Tot	H	A	0	1	2	3	2	3	4	LO	XN	IP	PH	RHP	LHP
1953	CIN	NL	1	1	0	0	1	0	0	0	0	0	0	0	0	0	1	0

Rank among batters: 4,707 • *Total ballparks homered in*: 1 • *First HR*: 07/12/1953 off Warren Hacker

Red Badgro

MORRIS HIRAM BADGRO
B: 12/01/1902
BL

Year	Tm	Lg	Tot	H	A	0	1	2	3	2	3	4	LO	XN	IP	PH	RHP	LHP
1929	STL	AL	1	1	0	1	0	0	0	0	0	0	0	0	0	0	1	0
1930	STL	AL	1	0	1	1	0	0	0	0	0	0	0	0	0	0	1	0
Total			2	1	1	2	0	0	0	0	0	0	0	0	0	0	2	0

Rank among batters: 4,129 • *Total ballparks homered in*: 2 • *First HR*: 06/25/1929 off Jimmy Zinn

Carlos Baerga

CARLOS OBED (ORTIZ) BAERGA
B: 11/04/1968
BB

Year	Tm	Lg	Tot	H	A	0	1	2	3	2	3	4	LO	XN	IP	PH	RHP	LHP
1990	CLE	AL	7	3	4	4	3	0	0	0	0	0	0	0	0	1	5	2
1991	CLE	AL	11	2	9	6	1	4	0	2	0	0	0	0	0	0	9	2
1992	CLE	AL	20	9	11	10	8	2	0	1	0	0	0	1	0	0	16	4
1993	CLE	AL	21	8	13	11	4	5	1	1	1	0	0	1	0	0	15	6
1994	CLE	AL	19	8	11	9	6	4	0	1	0	0	0	0	0	0	11	8
1995	CLE	AL	15	7	8	7	7	1	0	1	0	0	0	0	1	0	11	4
Total			93	37	56	47	29	16	1	6	1	0	0	2	1	1	67	26

Rank among batters: 545 • *Top target (3 home runs)*: Mike Moore, Kevin Tapani • *Number of pitchers victimized*: 76 • *Total ballparks homered in*: 16 • *First HR*: 04/27/1990 off David West • *2 HR in 1 inning*—vs NY: 04/08/1993 • *Switch hit HR in 1 game*—1 time • *LCS HR*—1

Jose Baez

JOSE ANTONIO BAEZ
B: 12/31/1953
BR

Year	Tm	Lg	Tot	H	A	0	1	2	3	2	3	4	LO	XN	IP	PH	RHP	LHP
1977	SEA	AL	1	1	0	1	0	0	0	0	0	0	0	0	0	0	1	0

Rank among batters: 4,707 • *Total ballparks homered in*: 1 • *First HR*: 06/12/1977 off Pete Vuckovich

Year	Tm	Lg	Tot	H	A	Men-On 0	1	2	3	One-Game 2	3	4	LO	XN	IP	PH	RHP	LHP

Jim Bagby

JAMES CHARLES JACOB, SR. BAGBY
B: 10/05/1889 D: 07/28/1954
BB

Year	Tm	Lg	Tot	H	A	Men-On 0	1	2	3	One-Game 2	3	4	LO	XN	IP	PH	RHP	LHP
1919	CLE	AL	1	0	1	1	0	0	0	0	0	0	0	0	0	0	0	1
1920	CLE	AL	1	1	0	1	0	0	0	0	0	0	0	0	0	0	1	0
Total			2	1	1	2	0	0	0	0	0	0	0	0	0	0	1	1

Rank among batters: 4,129 • *Total ballparks homered in*: 2 • *First HR*: 09/06/1919 off Lefty Williams • *World Series HR*—1

Jim Bagby

JAMES CHARLES JACOB, JR. BAGBY
B: 09/08/1916 D: 09/02/1988
BR

Year	Tm	Lg	Tot	H	A	Men-On 0	1	2	3	One-Game 2	3	4	LO	XN	IP	PH	RHP	LHP
1939	BOS	AL	1	0	1	1	0	0	0	0	0	0	0	0	0	0	1	0
1942	CLE	AL	1	1	0	1	0	0	0	0	0	0	0	0	0	0	1	0
1944	CLE	AL	1	0	1	1	0	0	0	0	0	0	0	1	0	0	1	0
Total			3	1	2	3	0	0	0	0	0	0	0	1	0	0	3	0

Rank among batters: 3,735 • *Total ballparks homered in*: 3 • *First HR*: 04/30/1939 off George Caster

Bill Bagwell

WILLIAM MALLORY BAGWELL
B: 02/24/1896 D: 10/05/1976
BL

Year	Tm	Lg	Tot	H	A	Men-On 0	1	2	3	One-Game 2	3	4	LO	XN	IP	PH	RHP	LHP
1923	BOS	NL	2	0	2	2	0	0	0	0	0	0	0	0	0	1	2	0

Rank among batters: 4,129 • *Total ballparks homered in*: 1 • *First HR*: 04/28/1923 off Jack Scott

Jeff Bagwell

JEFFREY ROBERT BAGWELL
B: 05/27/1968
BR

Year	Tm	Lg	Tot	H	A	Men-On 0	1	2	3	One-Game 2	3	4	LO	XN	IP	PH	RHP	LHP
1991	HOU	NL	15	6	9	5	7	3	0	0	0	0	0	0	0	1	8	7
1992	HOU	NL	18	8	10	11	3	4	0	1	0	0	0	3	0	1	9	9
1993	HOU	NL	20	9	11	13	4	3	0	0	0	0	0	0	0	0	10	10
1994	HOU	NL	39	23	16	22	12	5	0	4	1	0	0	0	0	0	21	18
1995	HOU	NL	21	10	11	13	4	4	0	0	0	0	0	1	0	0	19	2
Total			113	56	57	64	30	19	0	5	1	0	0	4	0	2	67	46

Rank among batters: 421 • *Top target (4 home runs)*: Bryan Hickerson • *Number of pitchers victimized*: 89 • *Total ballparks homered in*: 14 • *First HR*: 04/15/1991 off Kent Mercker • *2 HR in 1 inning*—vs LA: 06/24/1994

Stan Bahnsen

STANLEY RAYMOND BAHNSEN
B: 12/15/1944
BR

Year	Tm	Lg	Tot	H	A	Men-On 0	1	2	3	One-Game 2	3	4	LO	XN	IP	PH	RHP	LHP
1979	MON	NL	1	1	0	0	1	0	0	0	0	0	0	0	0	0	1	0

Rank among batters: 4,707 • *Total ballparks homered in*: 1 • *First HR*: 08/19/1979 off Tony Brizzolara

Bob Bailey

ROBERT SHERWOOD BAILEY
B: 10/13/1942
BR

Year	Tm	Lg	Tot	H	A	Men-On 0	1	2	3	One-Game 2	3	4	LO	XN	IP	PH	RHP	LHP
1963	PIT	NL	12	5	7	7	2	3	0	1	0	0	2	1	0	1	9	3
1964	PIT	NL	11	7	4	8	1	2	0	0	0	0	1	1	0	0	9	2
1965	PIT	NL	11	5	6	8	1	1	1	0	0	0	4	1	1	0	7	4
1966	PIT	NL	13	2	11	9	3	0	1	2	0	0	0	3	0	0	9	4
1967	LA	NL	4	3	1	4	0	0	0	0	0	0	0	0	0	0	2	2
1968	LA	NL	8	3	5	4	2	2	0	0	0	0	0	1	0	0	2	6
1969	MON	NL	9	6	3	3	5	1	0	2	0	0	0	0	0	0	8	1
1970	MON	NL	28	13	15	16	8	3	1	1	0	0	0	0	0	3	13	15
1971	MON	NL	14	4	10	8	1	5	0	0	0	0	0	0	0	0	9	5
1972	MON	NL	16	4	12	13	2	1	0	0	0	0	0	0	0	0	9	7
1973	MON	NL	26	12	14	15	8	1	2	3	0	0	0	1	0	0	16	10
1974	MON	NL	20	12	8	14	4	1	1	1	0	0	0	0	0	0	11	9
1975	MON	NL	5	1	4	3	2	0	0	0	0	0	1	0	0	0	0	5
1976	CIN	NL	6	4	2	2	3	1	0	1	0	0	0	0	0	0	1	5

Bob Bailey *continued*

Year	Tm	Lg	Tot	H	A	Men-On 0	1	2	3	One-Game 2	3	4	LO	XN	IP	PH	RHP	LHP
1977	CIN	NL	2	0	2	1	1	0	0	0	0	0	0	0	0	1	0	2
1978	BOS	AL	4	2	2	3	0	1	0	0	0	0	0	0	0	0	0	4
Total			189	83	106	118	43	22	6	11	0	0	8	8	1	5	105	84

Rank among batters: 204 • *Top target (5 home runs)*: Phil Niekro, Ferguson Jenkins, Steve Carlton • *Number of pitchers victimized*: 120 • *Total ballparks homered in*: 21 • *First HR*: 04/09/1963 off Lew Burdette

Ed Bailey

LONAS EDGAR BAILEY
B: 04/15/1931
BL

Year	Tm	Lg	Tot	H	A	Men-On 0	1	2	3	One-Game 2	3	4	LO	XN	IP	PH	RHP	LHP
1954	CIN	NL	9	5	4	7	2	0	0	0	0	0	0	0	0	0	9	0
1955	CIN	NL	1	1	0	1	0	0	0	0	0	0	0	0	0	0	1	0
1956	CIN	NL	28	16	12	13	8	5	2	1	1	0	0	1	0	2	26	2
1957	CIN	NL	20	12	8	14	5	1	0	0	0	0	0	1	0	1	12	8
1958	CIN	NL	11	7	4	4	6	1	0	1	0	0	0	0	0	1	8	3
1959	CIN	NL	12	8	4	7	5	0	0	1	0	0	0	0	0	0	10	2
1960	CIN	NL	13	9	4	5	7	0	1	0	0	0	0	0	0	0	10	3
1961	SF	NL	13	8	5	11	1	1	0	2	0	0	0	0	0	0	6	7
1962	SF	NL	17	11	6	9	6	1	1	0	0	0	0	1	0	3	14	3
1963	SF	NL	21	11	10	5	12	3	1	2	0	0	0	0	0	1	14	7
1964	MIL	NL	5	3	2	3	1	0	1	0	0	0	0	0	0	0	4	1
1965	CHI	NL	5	4	1	2	0	2	1	1	0	0	0	0	0	0	5	0
Total			155	95	60	81	53	14	7	8	1	0	0	3	0	8	119	36

Rank among batters: 274 • *Top target (5 home runs)*: Robin Roberts • *Number of pitchers victimized*: 100 • *Total ballparks homered in*: 14 • *First HR*: 04/18/1954 off Bob Buhl • *World Series HR*—1

Fred Bailey

FREDERICK MIDDLETON BAILEY
B: 08/16/1895 D: 08/16/1972
BL

Year	Tm	Lg	Tot	H	A	Men-On 0	1	2	3	One-Game 2	3	4	LO	XN	IP	PH	RHP	LHP
1917	BOS	NL	1	1	0	1	0	0	0	0	0	0	0	0	1	1	1	0

Rank among batters: 4,707 • *Total ballparks homered in*: 1 • *First HR*: 07/16/1917 off Burleigh Grimes

Gene Bailey

ARTHUR EUGENE BAILEY
B: 11/25/1893 D: 11/14/1973
BR

Year	Tm	Lg	Tot	H	A	Men-On 0	1	2	3	One-Game 2	3	4	LO	XN	IP	PH	RHP	LHP
1923	BRO	NL	1	0	1	1	0	0	0	0	0	0	0	0	1	0	0	1
1924	BRO	NL	1	0	1	1	0	0	0	0	0	0	0	0	0	0	0	1
Total			2	0	2	2	0	0	0	0	0	0	0	0	1	0	0	2

Rank among batters: 4,129 • *Total ballparks homered in*: 1 • *First HR*: 05/30/1923 off Art Nehf

Mark Bailey

JOHN MARK BAILEY
B: 11/04/1961
BB

Year	Tm	Lg	Tot	H	A	Men-On 0	1	2	3	One-Game 2	3	4	LO	XN	IP	PH	RHP	LHP
1984	HOU	NL	9	7	2	7	2	0	0	2	0	0	0	0	0	0	7	2
1985	HOU	NL	10	4	6	4	3	1	2	0	0	0	0	0	0	0	6	4
1986	HOU	NL	4	1	3	3	1	0	0	0	0	0	0	0	0	0	3	1
1990	SF	NL	1	0	1	0	0	1	0	0	0	0	0	0	0	0	1	0
Total			24	12	12	14	6	2	2	2	0	0	0	0	0	0	17	7

Rank among batters: 1,643 • *Top target (2 home runs)*: Danny Cox, Mike Krukow • *Number of pitchers victimized*: 22 • *Total ballparks homered in*: 9 • *First HR*: 05/09/1984 off Larry Andersen • *Switch hit HR in 1 game*—1 time

Bob Bailor

ROBERT MICHAEL BAILOR
B: 07/10/1951
BR

Year	Tm	Lg	Tot	H	A	Men-On 0	1	2	3	One-Game 2	3	4	LO	XN	IP	PH	RHP	LHP
1977	TOR	AL	5	1	4	3	2	0	0	0	0	0	1	1	0	0	3	2
1978	TOR	AL	1	0	1	1	0	0	0	0	0	0	0	0	0	0	1	0
1979	TOR	AL	1	0	1	1	0	0	0	0	0	0	0	0	0	0	0	1

Bob Bailor *continued*

Year	Tm	Lg	Tot	H	A	Men-On 0	1	2	3	One-Game 2	3	4	LO	XN	IP	PH	RHP	LHP
1980	TOR	AL	1	1	0	0	1	0	0	0	0	0	0	0	0	0	0	1
1983	NY	NL	1	0	1	1	0	0	0	0	0	0	0	0	0	0	0	1
Total			9	2	7	6	3	0	0	0	0	0	1	1	0	0	4	5

Rank among batters: 2,587 • *Total ballparks homered in*: 6 • *First HR*: 04/16/1977 off Steve Stone

Harold Baines

HAROLD DOUGLAS BAINES
B: 03/15/1959
BL

Year	Tm	Lg	Tot	H	A	Men-On 0	1	2	3	One-Game 2	3	4	LO	XN	IP	PH	RHP	LHP
1980	CHI	AL	13	3	10	8	4	1	0	1	0	0	0	0	0	0	12	1
1981	CHI	AL	10	3	7	7	2	1	0	0	0	0	0	0	0	0	10	0
1982	CHI	AL	25	11	14	12	11	0	2	2	1	0	0	0	0	0	17	8
1983	CHI	AL	20	12	8	11	8	0	1	1	0	0	0	1	0	0	17	3
1984	CHI	AL	29	16	13	13	12	3	1	2	1	0	0	1	0	0	19	10
1985	CHI	AL	22	13	9	9	6	6	1	0	0	0	0	1	0	0	16	6
1986	CHI	AL	21	8	13	13	6	2	0	1	0	0	0	0	0	0	18	3
1987	CHI	AL	20	12	8	7	11	2	0	0	0	0	0	0	0	1	14	6
1988	CHI	AL	13	5	8	8	5	0	0	0	0	0	0	0	0	0	11	2
1989	CHI	AL	13	4	9	9	2	2	0	1	0	0	0	0	0	0	10	3
	TEX	AL	3	1	2	1	2	0	0	0	0	0	0	0	0	0	2	1
	Total		16	5	11	10	4	2	0	1	0	0	0	0	0	0	12	4
1990	TEX	AL	13	6	7	11	1	1	0	0	0	0	0	1	0	0	10	3
	OAK	AL	3	3	0	3	0	0	0	0	0	0	0	0	0	0	3	0
	Total		16	9	7	14	1	1	0	0	0	0	0	1	0	0	13	3
1991	OAK	AL	20	11	9	9	6	3	2	0	1	0	0	0	0	1	17	3
1992	OAK	AL	16	10	6	4	8	4	0	0	0	0	0	0	0	0	15	1
1993	BAL	AL	20	12	8	11	7	1	1	0	0	0	0	0	0	0	16	4
1994	BAL	AL	16	11	5	12	4	0	0	1	0	0	0	0	0	0	15	1
1995	BAL	AL	24	7	17	16	4	2	2	1	0	0	0	0	0	0	21	3
Total			301	148	153	164	99	28	10	10	3	0	0	4	0	2	243	58

Rank among batters: 66 • *Top target (5 home runs)*: Charlie Hough, Todd Stottlemyre • *Number of pitchers victimized*: 212 • *Total ballparks homered in*: 20 • *First HR*: 04/19/1980 off Jim Palmer • *World Series HR*—1; *LCS HR*—1

Doug Bair

CHARLES DOUGLAS BAIR
B: 08/22/1949
BR

Year	Tm	Lg	Tot	H	A	Men-On 0	1	2	3	One-Game 2	3	4	LO	XN	IP	PH	RHP	LHP
1981	CIN	NL	1	0	1	0	0	1	0	0	0	0	0	0	0	0	1	0

Rank among batters: 4,707 • *Total ballparks homered in*: 1 • *First HR*: 05/20/1981 off Dick Tidrow

Doug Baird

HOWARD DOUGLAS BAIRD
B: 09/27/1891 D: 06/13/1967
BR

Year	Tm	Lg	Tot	H	A	Men-On 0	1	2	3	One-Game 2	3	4	LO	XN	IP	PH	RHP	LHP
1915	PIT	NL	1	0	1	0	1	0	0	0	0	0	0	0	1	0	0	1
1916	PIT	NL	1	0	1	1	0	0	0	0	0	0	0	0	0	0	1	0
1918	STL	NL	2	1	1	0	1	1	0	0	0	0	0	0	0	0	1	1
1919	PHI	NL	2	1	1	1	1	0	0	0	0	0	0	0	1	0	2	0
Total			6	2	4	2	3	1	0	0	0	0	0	0	2	0	4	2

Rank among batters: 2,988 • *Total ballparks homered in*: 5 • *First HR*: 07/17/1915 off Sherry Smith

Jersey Bakely

EDWARD ENOCH BAKELY
B: 04/17/1864 D: 12/17/1915
BR

Year	Tm	Lg	Tot	H	A	Men-On 0	1	2	3	One-Game 2	3	4	LO	XN	IP	PH	RHP	LHP
1888	CLE	AA	1	1	0	0	1	0	0	0	0	0	0	0	0	0	0	1
1889	CLE	NL	1	1	0	0	1	0	0	0	0	0	0	0	0	0	1	0
Total			2	2	0	0	2	0	0	0	0	0	0	0	0	0	1	1

Rank among batters: 4,129 • *Total ballparks homered in*: 2 • *First HR*: 09/02/1888 off Toad Ramsey

Bill Baker

WILLIAM PRESLEY BAKER
B: 02/22/1911
BR

Year	Tm	Lg	Tot	H	A	Men-On 0	1	2	3	One-Game 2	3	4	LO	XN	IP	PH	RHP	LHP
1943	PIT	NL	1	1	0	0	0	0	1	0	0	0	0	0	0	0	0	1

Year	Tm	Lg	Tot	H	A	Men-On 0	1	2	3	One-Game 2	3	4	LO	XN	IP	PH	RHP	LHP

Bill Baker *continued*

Year	Tm	Lg	Tot	H	A	0	1	2	3	2	3	4	LO	XN	IP	PH	RHP	LHP
1946	PIT	NL	1	1	0	1	0	0	0	0	0	0	0	0	0	0	1	0
Total			2	2	0	1	0	0	1	0	0	0	0	0	0	0	1	1

Rank among batters: 4,129 • *Total ballparks homered in*: 1 • *First HR*: 07/30/1943 off Cliff Melton

Charlie Baker

CHARLES A. BAKER
B: 01/15/1856 D: 01/15/1937

Year	Tm	Lg	Tot	H	A	0	1	2	3	2	3	4	LO	XN	IP	PH	RHP	LHP
1884	CHI	UA	1	0	1	1	0	0	0	0	0	0	0	0	1	0	0	1

Rank among batters: 4,707 • *Total ballparks homered in*: 1 • *First HR*: 08/20/1884 off Dick Burns

Dusty Baker

JOHNNIE B. BAKER
B: 06/15/1949
BR

Year	Tm	Lg	Tot	H	A	0	1	2	3	2	3	4	LO	XN	IP	PH	RHP	LHP
1972	ATL	NL	17	10	7	8	7	2	0	0	0	0	0	1	0	0	11	6
1973	ATL	NL	21	10	11	10	8	3	0	1	0	0	0	0	0	0	9	12
1974	ATL	NL	20	11	9	11	7	2	0	1	0	0	0	1	0	0	16	4
1975	ATL	NL	19	9	10	11	5	3	0	2	0	0	0	0	0	0	9	10
1976	LA	NL	4	3	1	4	0	0	0	0	0	0	0	1	0	0	4	0
1977	LA	NL	30	18	12	14	12	3	1	0	0	0	0	0	0	0	23	7
1978	LA	NL	11	5	6	7	3	0	1	0	0	0	0	0	0	0	11	0
1979	LA	NL	23	14	9	12	7	3	1	1	0	0	0	1	0	0	17	6
1980	LA	NL	29	14	15	15	7	7	0	3	0	0	0	1	0	0	25	4
1981	LA	NL	9	4	5	6	3	0	0	0	0	0	0	1	0	1	8	1
1982	LA	NL	23	7	16	11	9	2	1	2	0	0	0	1	0	0	17	6
1983	LA	NL	15	8	7	5	8	2	0	1	0	0	0	0	0	0	13	2
1984	SF	NL	3	2	1	2	0	1	0	0	0	0	0	0	0	1	3	0
1985	OAK	AL	14	5	9	7	3	4	0	0	0	0	0	0	0	0	9	5
1986	OAK	AL	4	1	3	2	2	0	0	0	0	0	0	0	0	0	2	2
Total			242	121	121	125	81	32	4	11	0	0	0	7	0	2	177	65

Rank among batters: 121 • *Top target (7 home runs)*: Jim Rooker • *Number of pitchers victimized*: 159 • *Total ballparks homered in*: 24 • *First HR*: 05/16/1972 off Jerry Reuss • *World Series HR—2; LCS HR—3*

Floyd Baker

FLOYD WILSON BAKER
B: 10/10/1916
BL

Year	Tm	Lg	Tot	H	A	0	1	2	3	2	3	4	LO	XN	IP	PH	RHP	LHP
1949	CHI	AL	1	1	0	0	1	0	0	0	0	0	0	0	0	0	1	0

Rank among batters: 4,707 • *Total ballparks homered in*: 1 • *First HR*: 05/04/1949 off Sid Hudson

Frank Baker

JOHN FRANKLIN BAKER
B: 03/13/1886 D: 06/28/1963
BL HOF

Year	Tm	Lg	Tot	H	A	0	1	2	3	2	3	4	LO	XN	IP	PH	RHP	LHP
1909	PHI	AL	4	2	2	0	2	1	1	0	0	0	0	0	0	0	4	0
1910	PHI	AL	2	1	1	2	0	0	0	0	0	0	0	0	0	0	2	0
1911	PHI	AL	11	9	2	6	4	1	0	1	0	0	0	0	1	0	10	1
1912	PHI	AL	10	6	4	6	2	2	0	0	0	0	0	0	0	0	9	1
1913	PHI	AL	12	7	5	8	3	1	0	0	0	0	0	0	0	0	8	4
1914	PHI	AL	9	5	4	4	5	0	0	1	0	0	0	0	0	0	7	2
1916	NY	AL	10	6	4	4	3	3	0	0	0	0	0	0	0	0	7	3
1917	NY	AL	6	5	1	2	4	0	0	0	0	0	0	1	1	0	5	1
1918	NY	AL	6	5	1	5	0	1	0	0	0	0	0	0	0	0	4	2
1919	NY	AL	10	8	2	5	5	0	0	1	0	0	0	0	0	0	7	3
1921	NY	AL	9	9	0	2	5	2	0	2	0	0	0	0	0	0	8	1
1922	NY	AL	7	7	0	4	2	1	0	0	0	0	0	0	0	0	7	0
Total			96	70	26	48	35	12	1	5	0	0	0	1	2	0	78	18

Rank among batters: 520 • *Top target (5 home runs)*: Walter Johnson • *Number of pitchers victimized*: 71 • *Total ballparks homered in*: 10 • *First HR*: 04/24/1909 off Frank Arellanes • *Hit for Cycle*—@NY: 07/03/1911 (2) • *World Series HR*—3

Frank Baker

FRANK BAKER
B: 01/11/1944
BL

Year	Tm	Lg	Tot	H	A	0	1	2	3	2	3	4	LO	XN	IP	PH	RHP	LHP
1969	CLE	AL	3	3	0	2	1	0	0	0	0	0	0	0	0	0	3	0

Frank Baker *continued*

Year	Tm	Lg	Tot	H	A	Men-On 0	1	2	3	One-Game 2	3	4	LO	XN	IP	PH	RHP	LHP
1971	CLE	AL	1	1	0	0	0	1	0	0	0	0	0	0	0	0	0	1
Total			4	4	0	2	1	1	0	0	0	0	0	0	0	0	3	1

Rank among batters: 3,427 • *Total ballparks homered in*: 1 • *First HR*: 08/04/1969 off Tom Phoebus

Frank Baker

FRANK WATTS BAKER
B: 10/29/1946
BL

Year	Tm	Lg	Tot	H	A	Men-On 0	1	2	3	One-Game 2	3	4	LO	XN	IP	PH	RHP	LHP
1973	BAL	AL	1	1	0	0	0	0	1	0	0	0	0	0	0	0	1	0

Rank among batters: 4,707 • *Total ballparks homered in*: 1 • *First HR*: 09/28/1973 off Dick Bosman

Gene Baker

EUGENE WALTER BAKER
B: 06/15/1925
BR

Year	Tm	Lg	Tot	H	A	Men-On 0	1	2	3	One-Game 2	3	4	LO	XN	IP	PH	RHP	LHP
1954	CHI	NL	13	6	7	8	3	2	0	0	0	0	0	0	1	0	11	2
1955	CHI	NL	11	6	5	9	1	0	1	0	0	0	0	0	0	0	9	2
1956	CHI	NL	12	9	3	4	4	2	2	0	0	0	0	1	0	0	11	1
1957	CHI	NL	1	0	1	0	1	0	0	0	0	0	0	0	0	0	1	0
	PIT	NL	2	0	2	1	1	0	0	0	0	0	0	0	0	0	2	0
	Total		3	0	3	1	2	0	0	0	0	0	0	0	0	0	3	0
Total			39	21	18	22	10	4	3	0	0	0	0	1	1	0	34	5

Rank among batters: 1,204 • *Top target (3 home runs)*: Don Newcombe • *Number of pitchers victimized*: 32 • *Total ballparks homered in*: 7 • *First HR*: 04/13/1954 off Tom Poholsky

Jack Baker

JACK EDWARD BAKER
B: 05/04/1950
BR

Year	Tm	Lg	Tot	H	A	Men-On 0	1	2	3	One-Game 2	3	4	LO	XN	IP	PH	RHP	LHP
1976	BOS	AL	1	1	0	1	0	0	0	0	0	0	0	0	0	0	0	1

Rank among batters: 4,707 • *Total ballparks homered in*: 1 • *First HR*: 09/23/1976 off Bill Travers

Phil Baker

PHILIP BAKER
B: 09/19/1856 D: 06/04/1940
BL

Year	Tm	Lg	Tot	H	A	Men-On 0	1	2	3	One-Game 2	3	4	LO	XN	IP	PH	RHP	LHP
1883	BAL	AA	1	1	0	1	0	0	0	0	0	0	1	0	0	0	1	0
1884	WAS	UA	1	1	0	1	0	0	0	0	0	0	0	0	0	0	0	1
1886	WAS	NL	1	1	0	0	1	0	0	0	0	0	0	0	0	0	1	0
Total			3	3	0	2	1	0	0	0	0	0	1	0	0	0	2	1

Rank among batters: 3,735 • *Total ballparks homered in*: 3 • *First HR*: 05/09/1883 off Bobby Mathews

John Balaz

JOHN LAWRENCE BALAZ
B: 11/24/1950
BR

Year	Tm	Lg	Tot	H	A	Men-On 0	1	2	3	One-Game 2	3	4	LO	XN	IP	PH	RHP	LHP
1974	CAL	AL	1	0	1	0	1	0	0	0	0	0	0	0	0	0	0	1
1975	CAL	AL	1	1	0	0	1	0	0	0	0	0	0	0	0	0	0	1
Total			2	1	1	0	2	0	0	0	0	0	0	0	0	0	0	2

Rank among batters: 4,129 • *Total ballparks homered in*: 2 • *First HR*: 09/24/1974 off Paul Splittorff

Steve Balboni

STEPHEN CHARLES BALBONI
B: 01/16/1957
BR

Year	Tm	Lg	Tot	H	A	Men-On 0	1	2	3	One-Game 2	3	4	LO	XN	IP	PH	RHP	LHP
1982	NY	AL	2	0	2	1	1	0	0	0	0	0	0	0	0	0	1	1
1983	NY	AL	5	0	5	1	3	0	1	0	0	0	0	0	0	0	2	3
1984	KC	AL	28	10	18	17	6	5	0	3	0	0	0	0	0	0	18	10
1985	KC	AL	36	17	19	21	10	3	2	4	0	0	0	2	0	0	28	8
1986	KC	AL	29	10	19	18	5	6	0	1	0	0	0	0	0	0	17	12

Steve Balboni *continued*

Year	Tm	Lg	Tot	H	A	Men-On 0	1	2	3	One-Game 2	3	4	LO	XN	IP	PH	RHP	LHP
1987	KC	AL	24	8	16	13	8	3	0	1	0	0	0	0	0	2	18	6
1988	KC	AL	2	1	1	1	1	0	0	0	0	0	0	0	0	0	2	0
	SEA	AL	21	14	7	10	5	6	0	0	0	0	0	1	0	0	15	6
	Total		23	15	8	11	6	6	0	0	0	0	0	1	0	0	17	6
1989	NY	AL	17	7	10	7	8	1	1	1	0	0	0	0	0	0	4	13
1990	NY	AL	17	8	9	14	3	0	0	2	0	0	0	0	0	2	3	14
Total			181	75	106	103	50	24	4	12	0	0	0	3	0	4	108	73

Rank among batters: 218 • *Top target (5 home runs)*: Frank Tanana • *Number of pitchers victimized*: 121 • *Total ballparks homered in*: 15 • *First HR*: 05/13/1982 off Tom Underwood

Billy Baldwin

ROBERT HARVEY BALDWIN
B: 06/09/1951
BL

Year	Tm	Lg	Tot	H	A	Men-On 0	1	2	3	One-Game 2	3	4	LO	XN	IP	PH	RHP	LHP
1975	DET	AL	4	2	2	3	0	1	0	0	0	0	0	0	0	0	4	0
1976	NY	NL	1	1	0	1	0	0	0	0	0	0	0	0	0	1	1	0
Total			5	3	2	4	0	1	0	0	0	0	0	0	0	1	5	0

Rank among batters: 3,191 • *Total ballparks homered in*: 4 • *First HR*: 08/05/1975 off Eric Raich

Kid Baldwin

CLARENCE GEOGHAN BALDWIN
B: 11/01/1864 D: 07/10/1897
BR

Year	Tm	Lg	Tot	H	A	Men-On 0	1	2	3	One-Game 2	3	4	LO	XN	IP	PH	RHP	LHP
1885	CIN	AA	1	0	1	1	0	0	0	0	0	0	0	0	0	0	1	0
1886	CIN	AA	3	1	2	2	1	0	0	0	0	0	0	0	2	0	3	0
1887	CIN	AA	1	1	0	0	1	0	0	0	0	0	0	0	0	0	1	0
1888	CIN	AA	1	1	0	1	0	0	0	0	0	0	0	0	0	0	0	1
1889	CIN	AA	1	1	0	0	1	0	0	0	0	0	0	0	0	0	1	0
Total			7	4	3	4	3	0	0	0	0	0	0	0	2	0	6	1

Rank among batters: 2,834 • *Top target (2 home runs)*: Adonis Terry • *Number of pitchers victimized*: 6 • *Total ballparks homered in*: 3 • *First HR*: 06/15/1885 off Adonis Terry

Mark Baldwin

MARCUS ELMORE BALDWIN
B: 10/29/1863 D: 11/10/1929
BR

Year	Tm	Lg	Tot	H	A	Men-On 0	1	2	3	One-Game 2	3	4	LO	XN	IP	PH	RHP	LHP
1887	CHI	NL	4	2	2	2	2	0	0	0	0	0	0	0	0	0	3	1
1888	CHI	NL	1	1	0	1	0	0	0	0	0	0	0	0	0	0	1	0
1889	COL	AA	2	2	0	1	0	1	0	0	0	0	0	0	0	0	1	1
1890	CHI	PL	1	0	1	0	1	0	0	0	0	0	0	0	0	0	1	0
1891	PIT	NL	1	1	0	1	0	0	0	0	0	0	0	0	0	0	1	0
1892	PIT	NL	1	1	0	0	0	1	0	0	0	0	0	0	1	0	1	0
Total			10	7	3	5	3	2	0	0	0	0	0	0	1	0	8	1

Rank among batters: 2,500 • *Total ballparks homered in*: 6 • *First HR*: 06/13/1887 off Egyptian Healy

Reggie Baldwin

REGINALD CONRAD BALDWIN
B: 08/19/1954
BR

Year	Tm	Lg	Tot	H	A	Men-On 0	1	2	3	One-Game 2	3	4	LO	XN	IP	PH	RHP	LHP
1978	HOU	NL	1	1	0	1	0	0	0	0	0	0	0	0	0	0	1	0

Rank among batters: 4,707 • *Total ballparks homered in*: 1 • *First HR*: 06/13/1978 off Jim Bibby

Neal Ball

CORNELIUS BALL
B: 04/22/1881 D: 10/15/1957
BR

Year	Tm	Lg	Tot	H	A	Men-On 0	1	2	3	One-Game 2	3	4	LO	XN	IP	PH	RHP	LHP
1909	CLE	AL	1	1	0	1	0	0	0	0	0	0	0	0	0	0	1	0
1911	CLE	AL	3	0	3	2	1	0	0	0	0	0	0	0	1	0	3	0
Total			4	1	3	3	1	0	0	0	0	0	0	0	1	0	4	0

Rank among batters: 3,427 • *Total ballparks homered in*: 4 • *First HR*: 07/19/1909 off Charlie Chech

Year	Tm	Lg	Tot	H	A	Men-On 0	Men-On 1	Men-On 2	Men-On 3	One-Game 2	One-Game 3	One-Game 4	LO	XN	IP	PH	RHP	LHP

Win Ballou

NOBLE WINFIELD BALLOU
B: 11/30/1897 D: 01/30/1963
BR

Year	Tm	Lg	Tot	H	A	0	1	2	3	2	3	4	LO	XN	IP	PH	RHP	LHP
1926	STL	AL	1	1	0	1	0	0	0	0	0	0	0	0	0	0	1	0

Rank among batters: 4,707 • *Total ballparks homered in*: 1 • *First HR*: 08/07/1926 off Paul Zahniser

Dave Bancroft

DAVID JAMES BANCROFT
B: 04/20/1891 D: 10/09/1972
BB HOF

Year	Tm	Lg	Tot	H	A	0	1	2	3	2	3	4	LO	XN	IP	PH	RHP	LHP
1915	PHI	NL	7	6	1	6	0	1	0	0	0	0	0	1	1	0	5	2
1916	PHI	NL	3	0	3	1	1	1	0	0	0	0	0	0	0	0	3	0
1917	PHI	NL	4	3	1	2	0	2	0	0	0	0	0	0	1	0	3	1
1921	NY	NL	6	5	1	2	2	2	0	0	0	0	0	0	1	0	3	3
1922	NY	NL	4	2	2	2	1	1	0	0	0	0	1	0	2	0	3	1
1923	NY	NL	1	1	0	0	1	0	0	0	0	0	0	0	0	0	1	0
1924	BOS	NL	2	0	2	2	0	0	0	0	0	0	1	0	0	0	1	1
1925	BOS	NL	2	2	0	0	1	1	0	0	0	0	0	0	2	0	1	1
1926	BOS	NL	1	0	1	1	0	0	0	0	0	0	0	0	0	0	1	0
1927	BOS	NL	1	1	0	1	0	0	0	0	0	0	0	0	1	0	1	0
1929	BRO	NL	1	1	0	0	1	0	0	0	0	0	0	0	0	0	0	1
Total			32	21	11	17	7	8	0	0	0	0	2	1	8	0	22	10

Rank among batters: 1,360 • *Top target (2 home runs)*: Pete Schneider, Rube Marquard • *Number of pitchers victimized*: 30 • *Total ballparks homered in*: 7 • *First HR*: 04/29/1915 off Wheezer Dell • *Hit for Cycle*—vs PHI: 06/01/1921 (2)

Chris Bando

CHRISTOPHER MICHAEL BANDO
B: 02/04/1956
BB

Year	Tm	Lg	Tot	H	A	0	1	2	3	2	3	4	LO	XN	IP	PH	RHP	LHP
1982	CLE	AL	3	1	2	0	2	1	0	0	0	0	0	0	0	0	0	3
1983	CLE	AL	4	4	0	1	2	1	0	0	0	0	0	0	0	0	0	4
1984	CLE	AL	12	5	7	7	4	1	0	0	0	0	0	1	0	1	8	4
1986	CLE	AL	2	1	1	1	0	1	0	0	0	0	0	0	0	0	1	1
1987	CLE	AL	5	2	3	3	2	0	0	0	0	0	0	0	0	0	5	0
1988	CLE	AL	1	0	1	0	1	0	0	0	0	0	0	0	0	0	1	0
Total			27	13	14	12	11	4	0	0	0	0	0	1	0	1	15	12

Rank among batters: 1,532 • *Top target (2 home runs)*: Dave Stieb • *Number of pitchers victimized*: 26 • *Total ballparks homered in*: 10 • *First HR*: 07/09/1982 off Floyd Bannister

Sal Bando

SALVATORE LEONARD BANDO
B: 02/13/1944
BR

Year	Tm	Lg	Tot	H	A	0	1	2	3	2	3	4	LO	XN	IP	PH	RHP	LHP
1968	OAK	AL	9	2	7	5	4	0	0	1	0	0	0	0	0	0	4	5
1969	OAK	AL	31	14	17	15	10	4	2	3	0	0	0	1	0	0	19	12
1970	OAK	AL	20	11	9	10	8	2	0	1	0	0	0	1	0	0	10	10
1971	OAK	AL	24	9	15	14	6	2	2	2	0	0	0	1	0	0	12	12
1972	OAK	AL	15	6	9	7	6	1	1	1	0	0	0	0	0	0	8	7
1973	OAK	AL	29	14	15	16	11	2	0	2	0	0	0	0	1	0	21	8
1974	OAK	AL	22	10	12	6	12	3	1	1	0	0	1	0	0	0	14	8
1975	OAK	AL	15	8	7	9	2	3	1	1	0	0	0	0	0	0	13	2
1976	OAK	AL	27	16	11	14	13	0	0	2	0	0	0	0	0	0	20	7
1977	MIL	AL	17	10	7	11	6	0	0	1	0	0	0	0	0	0	12	5
1978	MIL	AL	17	10	7	10	3	4	0	0	0	0	0	1	0	0	12	5
1979	MIL	AL	9	6	3	7	1	1	0	0	0	0	0	0	0	0	5	4
1980	MIL	AL	5	2	3	4	1	0	0	1	0	0	0	0	0	0	4	1
1981	MIL	AL	2	1	1	1	1	0	0	0	0	0	0	0	0	0	0	2
Total			242	119	123	129	84	22	7	16	0	0	1	4	1	0	154	88

Rank among batters: 121 • *Top target (6 home runs)*: Paul Splittorff • *Number of pitchers victimized*: 148 • *Total ballparks homered in*: 15 • *First HR*: 04/13/1968 off Phil Ortega • *LCS HR*—5

Dan Bankhead

DANIEL ROBERT BANKHEAD
B: 05/03/1920 D: 05/02/1976
BR

Year	Tm	Lg	Tot	H	A	0	1	2	3	2	3	4	LO	XN	IP	PH	RHP	LHP
1947	BRO	NL	1	1	0	0	1	0	0	0	0	0	0	0	0	0	0	1

Year	Tm	Lg	Tot	H	A	Men-On 0	Men-On 1	Men-On 2	Men-On 3	One-Game 2	One-Game 3	One-Game 4	LO	XN	IP	PH	RHP	LHP

Dan Bankhead *continued*

Rank among batters: 4,707 • *Total ballparks homered in*: 1 • *First HR*: 08/26/1947 off Fritz Ostermueller • *Hit HR in first major league AB*—vs PIT: 08/26/1947

Ernie Banks

ERNEST BANKS
B: 01/31/1931
BR HOF

Year	Tm	Lg	Tot	H	A	0	1	2	3	2	3	4	LO	XN	IP	PH	RHP	LHP
1953	CHI	NL	2	1	1	2	0	0	0	0	0	0	0	0	0	0	2	0
1954	CHI	NL	19	11	8	9	7	3	0	1	0	0	0	0	0	0	16	3
1955	CHI	NL	44	26	18	24	12	3	5	3	1	0	0	3	1	0	34	10
1956	CHI	NL	28	16	12	13	13	2	0	1	0	0	0	0	1	0	24	4
1957	CHI	NL	43	25	18	25	11	7	0	3	1	0	0	0	1	0	30	13
1958	CHI	NL	47	30	17	23	18	6	0	6	0	0	0	0	1	0	39	8
1959	CHI	NL	45	24	21	21	16	6	2	2	0	0	0	2	0	0	35	10
1960	CHI	NL	41	18	23	21	15	4	1	2	0	0	0	1	0	0	33	8
1961	CHI	NL	29	19	10	15	11	2	1	4	0	0	0	0	0	1	17	12
1962	CHI	NL	37	19	18	22	7	8	0	1	1	0	0	1	0	1	21	16
1963	CHI	NL	18	10	8	10	6	2	0	2	1	0	0	0	0	0	11	7
1964	CHI	NL	23	12	11	13	6	3	1	0	0	0	0	0	0	0	14	9
1965	CHI	NL	28	14	14	16	6	6	0	2	0	0	0	0	0	0	22	6
1966	CHI	NL	15	6	9	6	5	4	0	1	0	0	0	1	0	0	11	4
1967	CHI	NL	23	14	9	11	8	4	0	1	0	0	0	1	0	0	17	6
1968	CHI	NL	32	21	11	17	9	5	1	5	0	0	0	0	0	1	24	8
1969	CHI	NL	23	15	8	8	7	7	1	3	0	0	0	0	0	0	15	8
1970	CHI	NL	12	7	5	4	4	4	0	1	0	0	0	0	0	1	5	7
1971	CHI	NL	3	2	1	2	0	1	0	0	0	0	0	0	0	1	2	1
Total			512	290	222	262	161	77	12	38	4	0	0	9	4	5	372	140

Rank among batters: 12 • *Top target (15 home runs)*: Robin Roberts • *Number of pitchers victimized*: 216 • *Total ballparks homered in*: 20 • *First HR*: 09/20/1953 off Gerry Staley • *All-Star HR*—1

George Banks

GEORGE EDWARD BANKS
B: 09/24/1938 D: 03/01/1985
BR

Year	Tm	Lg	Tot	H	A	0	1	2	3	2	3	4	LO	XN	IP	PH	RHP	LHP
1962	MIN	AL	4	3	1	2	2	0	0	0	0	0	0	0	0	1	4	0
1963	MIN	AL	3	1	2	1	2	0	0	0	0	0	0	0	0	0	2	1
1964	CLE	AL	2	1	1	2	0	0	0	0	0	0	0	0	0	0	1	1
Total			9	5	4	5	4	0	0	0	0	0	0	0	0	1	7	2

Rank among batters: 2,587 • *Total ballparks homered in*: 5 • *First HR*: 05/27/1962 off Ray Herbert

Bill Bankston

WILBORN EVERETT BANKSTON
B: 05/25/1893 D: 02/26/1970
BL

Year	Tm	Lg	Tot	H	A	0	1	2	3	2	3	4	LO	XN	IP	PH	RHP	LHP
1915	PHI	AL	1	1	0	0	1	0	0	0	0	0	0	0	0	0	1	0

Rank among batters: 4,707 • *Total ballparks homered in*: 1 • *First HR*: 09/22/1915 off Jean Dubuc

Alan Bannister

ALAN BANNISTER
B: 09/03/1951
BR

Year	Tm	Lg	Tot	H	A	0	1	2	3	2	3	4	LO	XN	IP	PH	RHP	LHP
1977	CHI	AL	3	1	2	3	0	0	0	0	0	0	0	0	1	0	1	2
1979	CHI	AL	2	1	1	1	1	0	0	0	0	0	0	0	0	0	2	0
1980	CLE	AL	1	1	0	0	1	0	0	0	0	0	0	0	0	0	0	1
1981	CLE	AL	1	1	0	1	0	0	0	0	0	0	0	0	0	0	0	1
1982	CLE	AL	4	2	2	3	1	0	0	0	0	0	1	0	0	0	0	4
1983	CLE	AL	5	2	3	3	1	0	1	0	0	0	0	1	0	1	3	2
1984	TEX	AL	2	0	2	2	0	0	0	0	0	0	0	0	0	0	0	2
1985	TEX	AL	1	0	1	1	0	0	0	0	0	0	0	0	0	0	1	0
Total			19	8	11	14	4	0	1	0	0	0	1	1	1	1	7	12

Rank among batters: 1,861 • *Total ballparks homered in*: 10 • *First HR*: 06/12/1977 off Ross Grimsley

Year	Tm	Lg	Tot	H	A	Men-On 0	Men-On 1	Men-On 2	Men-On 3	One-Game 2	One-Game 3	One-Game 4	LO	XN	IP	PH	RHP	LHP

Jimmy Bannon

JAMES HENRY BANNON
B: 05/05/1871 D: 03/24/1948
BR

Year	Tm	Lg	Tot	H	A	0	1	2	3	2	3	4	LO	XN	IP	PH	RHP	LHP
1894	BOS	NL	13	10	3	2	6	3	2	1	0	0	0	0	0	0	8	4
1895	BOS	NL	6	6	0	1	3	2	0	0	0	0	0	0	0	0	5	1
Total			19	16	3	3	9	5	2	1	0	0	0	0	0	0	13	4

Rank among batters: 1,861 • *Top target (4 home runs)*: Ted Breitenstein • *Number of pitchers victimized*: 13 • *Total ballparks homered in*: 5 • *First HR*: 05/22/1894 off Amos Rusie

Walter Barbare

WALTER LAWRENCE BARBARE
B: 08/11/1891 D: 10/28/1965
BR

Year	Tm	Lg	Tot	H	A	0	1	2	3	2	3	4	LO	XN	IP	PH	RHP	LHP
1919	PIT	NL	1	1	0	0	1	0	0	0	0	0	0	0	1	0	1	0

Rank among batters: 4,707 • *Total ballparks homered in*: 1 • *First HR*: 09/11/1919 off Lee Meadows

Dave Barbee

DAVID MONROE BARBEE
B: 05/07/1905 D: 07/01/1968
BR

Year	Tm	Lg	Tot	H	A	0	1	2	3	2	3	4	LO	XN	IP	PH	RHP	LHP
1926	PHI	AL	1	1	0	1	0	0	0	0	0	0	0	0	0	0	0	1
1932	PIT	NL	5	2	3	3	1	1	0	0	0	0	0	0	0	2	4	1
Total			6	3	3	4	1	1	0	0	0	0	0	0	0	2	4	2

Rank among batters: 2,988 • *Total ballparks homered in*: 5 • *First HR*: 08/17/1926 off Joe Shaute

Steve Barber

STEPHEN DAVID BARBER
B: 02/22/1939
BL

Year	Tm	Lg	Tot	H	A	0	1	2	3	2	3	4	LO	XN	IP	PH	RHP	LHP
1961	BAL	AL	2	1	1	2	0	0	0	0	0	0	0	0	0	0	2	0
1963	BAL	AL	1	0	1	1	0	0	0	0	0	0	0	0	0	0	1	0
1964	BAL	AL	1	0	1	0	1	0	0	0	0	0	0	0	0	0	1	0
1965	BAL	AL	1	0	1	1	0	0	0	0	0	0	0	0	0	0	1	0
Total			5	1	4	4	1	0	0	0	0	0	0	0	0	0	5	0

Rank among batters: 3,191 • *Total ballparks homered in*: 4 • *First HR*: 06/23/1961 off Ron Kline

Turner Barber

TYRUS TURNER BARBER
B: 07/09/1893 D: 10/20/1968
BL

Year	Tm	Lg	Tot	H	A	0	1	2	3	2	3	4	LO	XN	IP	PH	RHP	LHP
1916	WAS	AL	1	0	1	0	1	0	0	0	0	0	0	0	0	0	1	0
1921	CHI	NL	1	0	1	0	0	1	0	0	0	0	0	0	1	0	0	1
Total			2	0	2	0	1	1	0	0	0	0	0	0	1	0	1	1

Rank among batters: 4,129 • *Total ballparks homered in*: 2 • *First HR*: 05/08/1916 off Elmer Myers

Bret Barberie

BRET EDWARD BARBERIE
B: 08/16/1967
BB

Year	Tm	Lg	Tot	H	A	0	1	2	3	2	3	4	LO	XN	IP	PH	RHP	LHP
1991	MON	NL	2	2	0	2	0	0	0	1	0	0	0	0	0	0	1	1
1992	MON	NL	1	0	1	1	0	0	0	0	0	0	0	0	0	0	1	0
1993	FLO	NL	5	2	3	3	1	1	0	0	0	0	0	0	0	0	3	2
1994	FLO	NL	5	2	3	4	0	1	0	0	0	0	0	0	1	0	5	0
1995	BAL	AL	2	1	1	1	0	0	1	0	0	0	0	0	0	0	2	0
Total			15	7	8	11	1	2	1	1	0	0	0	0	1	0	12	3

Rank among batters: 2,096 • *Total ballparks homered in*: 11 • *First HR*: 08/02/1991 off Danny Cox • *Switch hit HR in 1 game*—1 time

George Barclay

GEORGE OLIVER BARCLAY
B: 05/16/1876 D: 04/03/1909

Year	Tm	Lg	Tot	H	A	0	1	2	3	2	3	4	LO	XN	IP	PH	RHP	LHP
1902	STL	NL	3	1	2	1	2	0	0	0	0	0	0	0	1	0	3	0

George Barclay *continued*

Year	Tm	Lg	Tot	H	A	Men-On 0	Men-On 1	Men-On 2	Men-On 3	One-Game 2	One-Game 3	One-Game 4	LO	XN	IP	PH	RHP	LHP
1904	STL	NL	1	1	0	1	0	0	0	0	0	0	0	0	0	0	1	0
Total			4	2	2	2	2	0	0	0	0	0	0	0	1	0	4	0

Rank among batters: 3,427 • *Total ballparks homered in*: 3 • *First HR*: 04/27/1902 off Len Swormstedt

Jesse Barfield

JESSE LEE BARFIELD
B: 10/29/1959
BR

Year	Tm	Lg	Tot	H	A	Men-On 0	Men-On 1	Men-On 2	Men-On 3	One-Game 2	One-Game 3	One-Game 4	LO	XN	IP	PH	RHP	LHP
1981	TOR	AL	2	1	1	1	1	0	0	0	0	0	0	0	0	0	1	1
1982	TOR	AL	18	11	7	11	3	3	1	0	0	0	0	0	0	2	3	15
1983	TOR	AL	27	22	5	16	8	3	0	4	0	0	0	0	0	0	14	13
1984	TOR	AL	14	10	4	9	3	2	0	2	0	0	0	0	0	1	8	6
1985	TOR	AL	27	15	12	16	7	4	0	2	0	0	0	1	0	0	18	9
1986	TOR	AL	40	16	24	27	7	6	0	5	0	0	0	1	0	0	31	9
1987	TOR	AL	28	11	17	20	3	5	0	2	0	0	0	2	0	0	19	9
1988	TOR	AL	18	12	6	13	2	1	2	0	0	0	0	0	0	1	9	9
1989	TOR	AL	5	1	4	2	1	2	0	0	0	0	0	0	0	0	2	3
	NY	AL	18	6	12	9	5	4	0	2	0	0	0	1	0	0	13	5
	Total		23	7	16	11	6	6	0	2	0	0	0	1	0	0	15	8
1990	NY	AL	25	12	13	14	8	3	0	1	0	0	0	0	0	1	12	13
1991	NY	AL	17	11	6	10	5	2	0	2	0	0	0	0	0	1	8	9
1992	NY	AL	2	2	0	1	0	1	0	0	0	0	0	0	0	0	1	1
Total			241	130	111	149	53	36	3	20	0	0	0	5	0	6	139	102

Rank among batters: 125 • *Top target (6 home runs)*: Floyd Bannister • *Number of pitchers victimized*: 156 • *Total ballparks homered in*: 16 • *First HR*: 09/06/1981 off Britt Burns • *LCS HR*—1

Ray Barker

RAYMOND HERRELL BARKER
B: 03/12/1936
BL

Year	Tm	Lg	Tot	H	A	Men-On 0	Men-On 1	Men-On 2	Men-On 3	One-Game 2	One-Game 3	One-Game 4	LO	XN	IP	PH	RHP	LHP
1965	NY	AL	7	6	1	3	2	2	0	0	0	0	0	0	1	3	6	1
1966	NY	AL	3	1	2	1	2	0	0	0	0	0	0	0	0	0	3	0
Total			10	7	3	4	4	2	0	0	0	0	0	0	1	3	9	1

Rank among batters: 2,500 • *Top target (2 home runs)*: Denny McLain • *Number of pitchers victimized*: 9 • *Total ballparks homered in*: 3 • *First HR*: 05/18/1965 off Dave Morehead

Sam Barkley

SAMUEL E. BARKLEY
B: 05/24/1858 D: 04/20/1912
BR

Year	Tm	Lg	Tot	H	A	Men-On 0	Men-On 1	Men-On 2	Men-On 3	One-Game 2	One-Game 3	One-Game 4	LO	XN	IP	PH	RHP	LHP
1884	TOL	AA	1	0	1	1	0	0	0	0	0	0	0	0	0	0	0	0
1885	STL	AA	3	3	0	1	2	0	0	0	0	0	0	0	0	0	2	0
1886	PIT	AA	1	0	1	1	0	0	0	0	0	0	0	0	0	0	1	0
1887	PIT	NL	1	0	1	0	1	0	0	0	0	0	0	0	0	0	0	1
1888	KC	AA	4	2	2	2	1	1	0	0	0	0	0	0	0	0	3	1
Total			10	5	5	5	4	1	0	0	0	0	0	0	0	0	6	1

Rank among batters: 2,500 • *Total ballparks homered in*: 7 • *First HR*: 10/15/1884 off Pete Meegan • *Hit for Cycle*—vs CIN: 06/13/1888

Babe Barna

HERBERT PAUL BARNA
B: 03/02/1915 D: 05/18/1972
BL

Year	Tm	Lg	Tot	H	A	Men-On 0	Men-On 1	Men-On 2	Men-On 3	One-Game 2	One-Game 3	One-Game 4	LO	XN	IP	PH	RHP	LHP
1937	PHI	AL	2	1	1	0	1	1	0	0	0	0	0	0	0	0	2	0
1941	NY	NL	1	1	0	0	1	0	0	0	0	0	0	0	0	0	1	0
1942	NY	NL	6	3	3	1	4	1	0	0	0	0	0	0	0	1	3	3
1943	NY	NL	1	0	1	0	0	1	0	0	0	0	0	0	1	0	1	0
	BOS	AL	2	0	2	1	1	0	0	0	0	0	0	0	0	0	2	0
	Total		3	0	3	1	1	1	0	0	0	0	0	0	1	0	3	0
Total			12	5	7	2	7	3	0	0	0	0	0	0	1	1	9	3

Rank among batters: 2,325 • *Total ballparks homered in*: 6 • *First HR*: 09/30/1937 off Frank Makosky

Charlie Barnabe

CHARLES EDWARD BARNABE
B: 06/12/1900 D: 08/16/1977
BL

Year	Tm	Lg	Tot	H	A	Men-On 0	1	2	3	One-Game 2	3	4	LO	XN	IP	PH	RHP	LHP
1928	CHI	AL	1	1	0	0	0	1	0	0	0	0	0	0	0	1	1	0

Rank among batters: 4,707 • *Total ballparks homered in*: 1 • *First HR*: 05/01/1928 off Josh Billings

Jess Barnes

JESSE LAWRENCE BARNES
B: 08/26/1892 D: 09/09/1961
BL

Year	Tm	Lg	Tot	H	A	Men-On 0	1	2	3	One-Game 2	3	4	LO	XN	IP	PH	RHP	LHP
1925	BOS	NL	1	1	0	0	1	0	0	0	0	0	0	0	1	0	0	1

Rank among batters: 4,707 • *Total ballparks homered in*: 1 • *First HR*: 07/07/1925 off Art Reinhart

Red Barnes

EMILE DEERING BARNES
B: 12/25/1903 D: 07/03/1959
BL

Year	Tm	Lg	Tot	H	A	Men-On 0	1	2	3	One-Game 2	3	4	LO	XN	IP	PH	RHP	LHP
1928	WAS	AL	6	4	2	0	5	1	0	1	0	0	0	0	1	0	4	2
1929	WAS	AL	1	1	0	1	0	0	0	0	0	0	0	0	0	0	1	0
1930	CHI	AL	1	0	1	0	1	0	0	0	0	0	0	0	0	0	1	0
Total			8	5	3	1	6	1	0	1	0	0	0	0	1	0	6	2

Rank among batters: 2,703 • *Top target (2 home runs)*: Eddie Rommel • *Number of pitchers victimized*: 7 • *Total ballparks homered in*: 4 • *First HR*: 06/23/1928 off Rube Walberg

Ross Barnes

ROSCOE CHARLES BARNES
B: 05/08/1850 D: 02/05/1915
BR

Year	Tm	Lg	Tot	H	A	Men-On 0	1	2	3	One-Game 2	3	4	LO	XN	IP	PH	RHP	LHP
1876	CHI	NL	1	0	1	1	0	0	0	0	0	0	0	0	0	0	1	0
1879	CIN	NL	1	1	0	1	0	0	0	0	0	0	0	0	0	0	1	0
Total			2	1	1	2	0	0	0	0	0	0	0	0	0	0	2	0

Rank among batters: 4,129 • *Total ballparks homered in*: 1 • *First HR*: 05/02/1876 off Cherokee Fisher

Skeeter Barnes

WILLIAM HENRY BARNES
B: 03/03/1957
BR

Year	Tm	Lg	Tot	H	A	Men-On 0	1	2	3	One-Game 2	3	4	LO	XN	IP	PH	RHP	LHP
1983	CIN	NL	1	1	0	1	0	0	0	0	0	0	0	0	0	0	1	0
1984	CIN	NL	1	1	0	1	0	0	0	0	0	0	0	1	0	0	1	0
1987	STL	NL	1	0	1	0	0	1	0	0	0	0	0	0	0	0	1	0
1991	DET	AL	5	1	4	4	0	1	0	0	0	0	0	0	0	0	2	3
1992	DET	AL	3	3	0	0	2	1	0	0	0	0	0	0	0	0	0	3
1993	DET	AL	2	2	0	2	0	0	0	0	0	0	0	0	0	0	1	1
1994	DET	AL	1	0	1	0	0	1	0	0	0	0	0	0	0	0	1	0
Total			14	8	6	8	2	4	0	0	0	0	0	1	0	0	7	7

Rank among batters: 2,169 • *Total ballparks homered in*: 7 • *First HR*: 09/25/1983 off Andy Hawkins

Clyde Barnhart

CLYDE LEE BARNHART
B: 12/29/1895 D: 01/21/1980
BR

Year	Tm	Lg	Tot	H	A	Men-On 0	1	2	3	One-Game 2	3	4	LO	XN	IP	PH	RHP	LHP
1921	PIT	NL	3	1	2	2	0	1	0	0	0	0	0	0	2	0	2	1
1922	PIT	NL	1	1	0	1	0	0	0	0	0	0	0	0	0	0	1	0
1923	PIT	NL	9	2	7	4	4	1	0	1	0	0	0	0	1	0	6	3
1924	PIT	NL	3	0	3	1	1	1	0	0	0	0	0	0	0	0	3	0
1925	PIT	NL	4	0	4	3	1	0	0	0	0	0	0	0	0	0	4	0
1927	PIT	NL	3	2	1	1	2	0	0	0	0	0	0	0	1	0	1	2
1928	PIT	NL	4	1	3	3	1	0	0	0	0	0	0	0	0	0	3	1
Total			27	7	20	15	9	3	0	1	0	0	0	0	4	0	20	7

Rank among batters: 1,532 • Top target (2 home runs): Johnny Couch, Grover Alexander, Jimmy Ring, Virgil Barne • *Number of pitchers victimized*: 23 • *Total ballparks homered in*: 8 • *First HR*: 05/29/1921 off Eppa Rixey

Bob Barr

ROBERT MCCLELLAND BARR
B: 12/ /1856 D: 03/11/1930
BR

Year	Tm	Lg	Tot	H	A	Men-On 0	1	2	3	One-Game 2	3	4	LO	XN	IP	PH	RHP	LHP
1884	WAS	AA	2	0	2	1	1	0	0	0	0	0	0	0	0	0	0	1
1890	ROC	AA	2	0	2	1	1	0	0	0	0	0	0	0	0	0	2	0
Total			4	0	4	2	2	0	0	0	0	0	0	0	0	0	2	1

Rank among batters: 3,427 • *Top target (2 home runs)*: Fred Smith • *Number of pitchers victimized*: 3 • *Total ballparks homered in*: 3 • *First HR*: 06/28/1884 off Denny Driscoll

Jim Barr

JAMES LELAND BARR
B: 02/10/1948
BR

Year	Tm	Lg	Tot	H	A	Men-On 0	1	2	3	One-Game 2	3	4	LO	XN	IP	PH	RHP	LHP
1974	SF	NL	1	0	1	1	0	0	0	0	0	0	0	0	0	0	1	0

Rank among batters: 4,707 • *Total ballparks homered in*: 1 • *First HR*: 09/02/1974 off Andy Messersmith

Cuno Barragan

FACUNDO ANTHONY BARRAGAN
B: 06/20/1932
BR

Year	Tm	Lg	Tot	H	A	Men-On 0	1	2	3	One-Game 2	3	4	LO	XN	IP	PH	RHP	LHP
1961	CHI	NL	1	1	0	1	0	0	0	0	0	0	0	0	0	0	0	1

Rank among batters: 4,707 • *Total ballparks homered in*: 1 • *First HR*: 09/01/1961 off Dick LeMay • *Hit HR in first major league AB*—vs SF: 09/01/1961

Bill Barrett

WILLIAM JOSEPH BARRETT
B: 05/28/1900 D: 01/26/1951
BR

Year	Tm	Lg	Tot	H	A	Men-On 0	1	2	3	One-Game 2	3	4	LO	XN	IP	PH	RHP	LHP
1923	CHI	AL	2	0	2	0	2	0	0	0	0	0	0	0	0	0	1	1
1924	CHI	AL	2	1	1	2	0	0	0	0	0	0	0	0	0	0	0	2
1925	CHI	AL	3	1	2	1	0	2	0	0	0	0	0	0	0	0	1	2
1926	CHI	AL	6	2	4	1	2	2	1	0	0	0	0	0	1	1	3	3
1927	CHI	AL	4	0	4	0	3	0	1	0	0	0	0	0	0	0	4	0
1928	CHI	AL	3	1	2	2	0	1	0	0	0	0	0	0	0	0	3	0
1929	BOS	AL	3	1	2	3	0	0	0	0	0	0	0	0	1	0	2	1
Total			23	6	17	9	7	5	2	0	0	0	0	0	2	1	14	9

Rank among batters: 1,686 • *Top target (2 home runs)*: Ed Wells, Eddie Rommel • *Number of pitchers victimized*: 21 • *Total ballparks homered in*: 7 • *First HR*: 09/04/1923 off Bert Cole

Bob Barrett

ROBERT SCHLEY BARRETT
B: 01/27/1899 D: 01/18/1982
BR

Year	Tm	Lg	Tot	H	A	Men-On 0	1	2	3	One-Game 2	3	4	LO	XN	IP	PH	RHP	LHP
1924	CHI	NL	5	1	4	2	3	0	0	0	0	0	0	0	0	0	4	1
1927	BRO	NL	5	2	3	3	1	1	0	0	0	0	0	0	0	0	4	1
Total			10	3	7	5	4	1	0	0	0	0	0	0	0	0	8	2

Rank among batters: 2,500 • *Top target (2 home runs)*: Clarence Mitchell • *Number of pitchers victimized*: 9 • *Total ballparks homered in*: 4 • *First HR*: 07/26/1924 off Clarence Mitchell

Jimmy Barrett

JAMES ERIGENA BARRETT
B: 03/28/1875 D: 10/24/1921
BL

Year	Tm	Lg	Tot	H	A	Men-On 0	1	2	3	One-Game 2	3	4	LO	XN	IP	PH	RHP	LHP
1900	CIN	NL	5	1	4	4	0	1	0	0	0	0	1	0	4	0	5	0
1901	DET	AL	4	1	3	3	0	1	0	0	0	0	0	0	1	0	4	0
1902	DET	AL	4	3	1	2	1	1	0	0	0	0	0	0	0	0	2	2
1903	DET	AL	2	2	0	2	0	0	0	0	0	0	0	0	0	0	2	0
1907	BOS	AL	1	1	0	1	0	0	0	0	0	0	0	1	0	0	0	1
Total			16	8	8	12	1	3	0	0	0	0	1	1	5	0	13	3

Rank among batters: 2,029 • *Top target (3 home runs)*: Clark Griffith • *Number of pitchers victimized*: 14 • *Total ballparks homered in*: 9 • *First HR*: 05/03/1900 off Clark Griffith

Year	Tm	Lg	Tot	H	A	Men-On 0	1	2	3	One-Game 2	3	4	LO	XN	IP	PH	RHP	LHP

Johnny Barrett

JOHN JOSEPH BARRETT
B: 12/18/1915 D: 08/17/1974
BL

Year	Tm	Lg	Tot	H	A	0	1	2	3	2	3	4	LO	XN	IP	PH	RHP	LHP
1943	PIT	NL	1	1	0	1	0	0	0	0	0	0	0	0	1	0	1	0
1944	PIT	NL	7	2	5	2	4	1	0	0	0	0	0	0	0	0	5	2
1945	PIT	NL	15	7	8	10	1	3	1	1	0	0	1	1	1	0	12	3
Total			23	10	13	13	5	4	1	1	0	0	1	1	2	0	18	5

Rank among batters: 1,686 • *Top target (3 home runs)*: Nate Andrews, Hal Gregg • *Number of pitchers victimized*: 18 • *Total ballparks homered in*: 5 • *First HR*: 09/28/1943 off Hal Gregg

Marty Barrett

MARTIN GLENN BARRETT
B: 06/23/1958
BR

Year	Tm	Lg	Tot	H	A	0	1	2	3	2	3	4	LO	XN	IP	PH	RHP	LHP
1984	BOS	AL	3	1	2	2	0	1	0	0	0	0	0	0	0	0	2	1
1985	BOS	AL	5	3	2	3	0	1	1	0	0	0	0	0	0	0	5	0
1986	BOS	AL	4	4	0	1	2	1	0	0	0	0	0	0	0	0	0	4
1987	BOS	AL	3	2	1	1	0	1	1	0	0	0	0	0	0	0	1	2
1988	BOS	AL	1	1	0	0	1	0	0	0	0	0	0	0	0	0	1	0
1989	BOS	AL	1	0	1	1	0	0	0	0	0	0	0	0	0	0	1	0
1991	SD	NL	1	1	0	0	0	1	0	0	0	0	0	0	0	1	0	1
Total			18	12	6	8	3	5	2	0	0	0	0	0	0	1	10	8

Rank among batters: 1,914 • *Total ballparks homered in*: 8 • *First HR*: 05/11/1984 off Larry Gura

Jack Barry

JOHN JOSEPH BARRY
B: 04/26/1887 D: 04/23/1961
BR

Year	Tm	Lg	Tot	H	A	0	1	2	3	2	3	4	LO	XN	IP	PH	RHP	LHP
1909	PHI	AL	1	1	0	1	0	0	0	0	0	0	0	0	0	0	1	0
1910	PHI	AL	3	2	1	3	0	0	0	0	0	0	0	1	0	0	3	0
1911	PHI	AL	1	0	1	1	0	0	0	0	0	0	0	0	0	0	1	0
1913	PHI	AL	3	3	0	2	1	0	0	1	0	0	0	0	0	0	1	2
1917	BOS	AL	2	0	2	2	0	0	0	0	0	0	0	0	0	0	2	0
Total			10	6	4	9	1	0	0	1	0	0	0	1	0	0	8	2

Rank among batters: 2,500 • *Total ballparks homered in*: 4 • *First HR*: 09/08/1909 off Jack Warhop

Shad Barry

JOHN C. BARRY
B: 10/27/1878 D: 11/27/1936
BR

Year	Tm	Lg	Tot	H	A	0	1	2	3	2	3	4	LO	XN	IP	PH	RHP	LHP
1899	WAS	NL	1	1	0	0	1	0	0	0	0	0	0	0	0	0	1	0
1900	BOS	NL	1	0	1	1	0	0	0	0	0	0	0	0	1	0	1	0
1901	PHI	NL	1	0	1	0	0	1	0	0	0	0	0	0	0	0	0	1
1902	PHI	NL	3	1	2	2	1	0	0	0	0	0	0	0	2	0	2	1
1903	PHI	NL	1	0	1	0	1	0	0	0	0	0	0	0	0	0	1	0
1904	CHI	NL	1	0	1	1	0	0	0	0	0	0	0	0	0	0	1	0
1905	CIN	NL	1	1	0	0	1	0	0	0	0	0	0	0	1	0	1	0
1906	CIN	NL	1	1	0	0	0	1	0	0	0	0	0	0	1	0	0	1
Total			10	4	6	4	4	2	0	0	0	0	0	0	5	0	7	3

Rank among batters: 2,500 • *Top target (2 home runs)*: Henry Thielman, Vic Willis • *Number of pitchers victimized*: 8 • *Total ballparks homered in*: 8 • *First HR*: 09/16/1899 off Charlie Knepper

Dick Bartell

RICHARD WILLIAM BARTELL
B: 11/22/1907 D: 08/04/1995
BR

Year	Tm	Lg	Tot	H	A	0	1	2	3	2	3	4	LO	XN	IP	PH	RHP	LHP
1928	PIT	NL	1	0	1	0	0	1	0	0	0	0	0	0	0	0	1	0
1929	PIT	NL	2	2	0	2	0	0	0	0	0	0	0	0	2	0	2	0
1930	PIT	NL	4	0	4	2	2	0	0	0	0	0	0	0	1	0	3	1
1932	PHI	NL	1	1	0	0	1	0	0	0	0	0	0	0	0	0	1	0
1933	PHI	NL	1	1	0	1	0	0	0	0	0	0	0	0	0	0	1	0
1935	NY	NL	14	12	2	10	4	0	0	0	0	0	0	0	0	0	13	1
1936	NY	NL	8	7	1	5	2	1	0	0	0	0	0	1	0	0	7	1
1937	NY	NL	14	12	2	8	4	1	1	1	0	0	3	0	0	0	9	5
1938	NY	NL	9	8	1	4	4	0	1	1	0	0	0	0	0	0	6	3

Year	Tm	Lg	Tot	H	A	Men-On 0	Men-On 1	Men-On 2	Men-On 3	One-Game 2	One-Game 3	One-Game 4	LO	XN	IP	PH	RHP	LHP

Dick Bartell *continued*

Year	Tm	Lg	Tot	H	A	0	1	2	3	2	3	4	LO	XN	IP	PH	RHP	LHP
1939	CHI	NL	3	2	1	2	1	0	0	0	0	0	0	0	0	0	3	0
1940	DET	AL	7	4	3	4	2	1	0	0	0	0	1	0	0	0	5	2
1941	NY	NL	5	5	0	3	2	0	0	0	0	0	0	1	0	0	5	0
1942	NY	NL	5	5	0	3	1	1	0	0	0	0	0	0	0	0	4	1
1943	NY	NL	5	5	0	3	0	2	0	0	0	0	1	0	0	1	2	3
Total			79	64	15	47	23	7	2	2	0	0	5	2	3	1	62	17

Rank among batters: 661 • *Top target (3 home runs)*: George Earnshaw, Paul Derringer, Bob Weiland • *Number of pitchers victimized*: 64 • *Total ballparks homered in*: 10 • *First HR*: 06/09/1928 off Joe Genewich • *World Series HR*—1

Bob Barton

ROBERT WILBUR BARTON
B: 07/30/1941
BR

Year	Tm	Lg	Tot	H	A	0	1	2	3	2	3	4	LO	XN	IP	PH	RHP	LHP
1970	SD	NL	4	0	4	2	2	0	0	0	0	0	0	0	0	0	3	1
1971	SD	NL	5	2	3	2	2	0	1	0	0	0	0	0	0	0	5	0
Total			9	2	7	4	4	0	1	0	0	0	0	0	0	0	8	1

Rank among batters: 2,587 • *Top target (2 home runs)*: Jim McGlothlin • *Number of pitchers victimized*: 8 • *Total ballparks homered in*: 7 • *First HR*: 05/08/1970 off Steve Renko

Vince Barton

VINCENT DAVID BARTON
B: 02/01/1908 D: 09/13/1973
BL

Year	Tm	Lg	Tot	H	A	0	1	2	3	2	3	4	LO	XN	IP	PH	RHP	LHP
1931	CHI	NL	13	7	6	5	5	2	1	1	0	0	0	0	0	0	11	2
1932	CHI	NL	3	1	2	2	1	0	0	0	0	0	0	0	0	0	2	1
Total			16	8	8	7	6	2	1	1	0	0	0	0	0	0	13	3

Rank among batters: 2,029 • *Total ballparks homered in*: 5 • *First HR*: 08/03/1931 off Si Johnson

Monty Basgall

ROMANUS BASGALL
B: 02/08/1922
BR

Year	Tm	Lg	Tot	H	A	0	1	2	3	2	3	4	LO	XN	IP	PH	RHP	LHP
1948	PIT	NL	2	1	1	2	0	0	0	0	0	0	0	0	0	0	2	0
1949	PIT	NL	2	1	1	1	1	0	0	0	0	0	0	0	0	0	1	1
Total			4	2	2	3	1	0	0	0	0	0	0	0	0	0	3	1

Rank among batters: 3,427 • *Total ballparks homered in*: 3 • *First HR*: 04/20/1948 off Russ Meyer

Eddie Basinski

EDWIN FRANK BASINSKI
B: 11/04/1922
BR

Year	Tm	Lg	Tot	H	A	0	1	2	3	2	3	4	LO	XN	IP	PH	RHP	LHP
1947	PIT	NL	4	1	3	3	1	0	0	0	0	0	0	0	0	0	4	0

Rank among batters: 3,427 • *Total ballparks homered in*: 3 • *First HR*: 04/23/1947 off Ken Burkhart

Kevin Bass

KEVIN CHARLES BASS
B: 05/12/1959
BB

Year	Tm	Lg	Tot	H	A	0	1	2	3	2	3	4	LO	XN	IP	PH	RHP	LHP
1983	HOU	NL	2	2	0	1	1	0	0	0	0	0	0	0	0	0	1	1
1984	HOU	NL	2	1	1	2	0	0	0	0	0	0	1	0	0	0	0	2
1985	HOU	NL	16	9	7	8	7	1	0	1	0	0	0	1	0	1	6	10
1986	HOU	NL	20	5	15	15	4	0	1	0	0	0	0	0	0	0	8	12
1987	HOU	NL	19	10	9	9	8	2	0	2	0	0	0	3	0	0	9	10
1988	HOU	NL	14	5	9	7	4	2	1	2	0	0	0	0	0	1	8	6
1989	HOU	NL	5	2	3	3	0	0	2	1	0	0	0	0	0	0	3	2
1990	SF	NL	7	3	4	3	3	1	0	0	0	0	0	0	0	0	2	5
1991	SF	NL	10	5	5	7	1	2	0	1	0	0	0	0	0	0	4	6
1992	SF	NL	7	5	2	4	2	1	0	1	0	0	0	1	0	0	3	4
	NY	NL	2	2	0	2	0	0	0	0	0	0	0	0	0	0	2	0
	Total		9	7	2	6	2	1	0	1	0	0	0	1	0	0	5	4
1993	HOU	NL	3	2	1	1	1	1	0	0	0	0	0	0	0	0	1	2
1994	HOU	NL	6	3	3	3	2	1	0	0	0	0	0	0	0	2	3	3

Kevin Bass *continued*

Year	Tm	Lg	Tot	H	A	Men-On 0	1	2	3	One-Game 2	3	4	LO	XN	IP	PH	RHP	LHP
1995	BAL	AL	5	2	3	3	2	0	0	0	0	0	0	0	0	0	2	3
Total			118	56	62	68	35	11	4	8	0	0	1	5	0	4	52	66

Rank among batters: 396 • *Top target (4 home runs)*: Tom Browning • *Number of pitchers victimized*: 90 • *Total ballparks homered in*: 16 • *First HR*: 04/15/1983 off Steve Rogers • *Switch hit HR in 1 game*—3 times

Norm Bass

NORMAN DELANEY BASS
B: 01/21/1939
BR

Year	Tm	Lg	Tot	H	A	Men-On 0	1	2	3	One-Game 2	3	4	LO	XN	IP	PH	RHP	LHP
1961	KC	AL	1	0	1	1	0	0	0	0	0	0	0	0	0	0	1	0

Rank among batters: 4,707 • *Total ballparks homered in*: 1 • *First HR*: 08/16/1961 off Pedro Ramos

Randy Bass

RANDY WILLIAM BASS
B: 03/13/1954
BL

Year	Tm	Lg	Tot	H	A	Men-On 0	1	2	3	One-Game 2	3	4	LO	XN	IP	PH	RHP	LHP
1980	SD	NL	3	2	1	2	1	0	0	0	0	0	0	0	0	0	3	0
1981	SD	NL	4	1	3	2	1	0	1	0	0	0	0	0	0	0	4	0
1982	SD	NL	1	0	1	0	1	0	0	0	0	0	0	0	0	0	1	0
	TEX	AL	1	0	1	1	0	0	0	0	0	0	0	0	0	0	1	0
	Total		2	0	2	1	1	0	0	0	0	0	0	0	0	0	2	0
Total			9	3	6	5	3	0	1	0	0	0	0	0	0	0	9	0

Rank among batters: 2,587 • *Total ballparks homered in*: 7 • *First HR*: 09/09/1980 off Allen Ripley

Charley Bassett

CHARLES EDWIN BASSETT
B: 02/09/1863 D: 05/28/1942
BR

Year	Tm	Lg	Tot	H	A	Men-On 0	1	2	3	One-Game 2	3	4	LO	XN	IP	PH	RHP	LHP
1886	KC	NL	2	2	0	1	1	0	0	0	0	0	0	0	0	0	2	0
1887	IND	NL	1	0	1	1	0	0	0	0	0	0	0	0	0	0	1	0
1888	IND	NL	2	2	0	0	1	1	0	0	0	0	0	0	0	0	2	0
1889	IND	NL	4	2	2	0	2	1	1	0	0	0	0	0	0	0	4	0
1891	NY	NL	4	4	0	2	1	1	0	0	0	0	0	0	3	0	3	0
1892	LOU	NL	2	0	2	0	2	0	0	0	0	0	0	0	0	0	1	1
Total			15	10	5	4	7	3	1	0	0	0	0	0	3	0	13	1

Rank among batters: 2,096 • *Total ballparks homered in*: 7 • *First HR*: 07/02/1886 off Charlie Ferguson

Johnny Bassler

JOHN LANDIS BASSLER
B: 06/03/1895 D: 06/29/1979
BL

Year	Tm	Lg	Tot	H	A	Men-On 0	1	2	3	One-Game 2	3	4	LO	XN	IP	PH	RHP	LHP
1924	DET	AL	1	0	1	1	0	0	0	0	0	0	0	0	0	0	1	0

Rank among batters: 4,707 • *Total ballparks homered in*: 1 • *First HR*: 07/23/1924 off Bob Shawkey

Charlie Bastian

CHARLES J. BASTIAN
B: 07/04/1860 D: 01/18/1932
BR

Year	Tm	Lg	Tot	H	A	Men-On 0	1	2	3	One-Game 2	3	4	LO	XN	IP	PH	RHP	LHP
1884	WIL	UA	2	1	1	1	0	1	0	0	0	0	0	0	0	0	1	0
	KC	UA	1	0	1	0	1	0	0	0	0	0	0	0	0	0	1	0
	Total		3	1	2	2	0	1	0	0	0	0	0	0	0	0	2	0
1885	PHI	NL	4	3	1	2	1	1	0	1	0	0	0	0	0	0	4	0
1886	PHI	NL	2	2	0	1	0	1	0	0	0	0	0	0	0	0	2	0
1887	PHI	NL	1	1	0	1	0	0	0	0	0	0	0	0	0	0	1	0
1888	PHI	NL	1	0	1	1	0	0	0	0	0	0	0	0	0	0	0	1
Total			11	7	4	7	1	3	0	1	0	0	0	0	0	0	9	1

Rank among batters: 2,419 • *Top target (2 home runs)*: Charlie Buffinton • *Number of pitchers victimized*: 10 • *Total ballparks homered in*: 7 • *First HR*: 08/23/1884 off Charlie Geggus

Emil Batch

EMIL BATCH
B: 01/21/1880 D: 08/23/1926
BR

Year	Tm	Lg	Tot	H	A	Men-On 0	1	2	3	One-Game 2	3	4	LO	XN	IP	PH	RHP	LHP
1904	BRO	NL	2	0	2	1	1	0	0	0	0	0	0	0	0	0	2	0

Year	Tm	Lg	Tot	H	A	Men-On 0	Men-On 1	Men-On 2	Men-On 3	One-Game 2	One-Game 3	One-Game 4	LO	XN	IP	PH	RHP	LHP

Emil Batch *continued*

Year	Tm	Lg	Tot	H	A	0	1	2	3	2	3	4	LO	XN	IP	PH	RHP	LHP
1905	BRO	NL	5	1	4	1	2	2	0	0	0	0	0	0	3	0	4	1
Total			7	1	6	2	3	2	0	0	0	0	0	0	3	0	6	1

Rank among batters: 2,834 • *Top target (2 home runs)*: Jack Taylor • *Number of pitchers victimized*: 6 • *Total ballparks homered in*: 4 • *First HR*: 09/16/1904 off Christy Mathewson

John Bateman

JOHN ALVIN BATEMAN
B: 07/21/1942
BR

Year	Tm	Lg	Tot	H	A	0	1	2	3	2	3	4	LO	XN	IP	PH	RHP	LHP
1963	HOU	NL	10	5	5	5	2	3	0	0	0	0	0	0	1	0	7	3
1964	HOU	NL	5	1	4	4	1	0	0	0	0	0	0	0	0	0	3	2
1965	HOU	NL	7	3	4	5	2	0	0	1	0	0	0	0	0	0	6	1
1966	HOU	NL	17	7	10	10	5	2	0	1	0	0	0	0	0	1	10	7
1967	HOU	NL	2	0	2	0	2	0	0	0	0	0	0	0	0	0	2	0
1968	HOU	NL	4	1	3	3	1	0	0	0	0	0	0	0	0	0	1	3
1969	MON	NL	8	6	2	6	1	1	0	0	0	0	0	0	0	0	6	2
1970	MON	NL	15	11	4	7	4	3	1	0	0	0	0	0	0	0	10	5
1971	MON	NL	10	6	4	7	0	1	2	0	0	0	0	0	0	0	7	3
1972	PHI	NL	3	1	2	2	1	0	0	0	0	0	0	0	0	0	2	1
Total			81	41	40	49	19	10	3	2	0	0	0	0	1	1	54	27

Rank among batters: 645 • *Top target (4 home runs)*: Dick Ellsworth, Gary Gentry • *Number of pitchers victimized*: 63 • *Total ballparks homered in*: 16 • *First HR*: 04/21/1963 off Pete Richert

Bud Bates

HUBERT EDGAR BATES
B: 03/16/1912 D: 04/29/1987
BR

Year	Tm	Lg	Tot	H	A	0	1	2	3	2	3	4	LO	XN	IP	PH	RHP	LHP
1939	PHI	NL	1	1	0	1	0	0	0	0	0	0	0	0	0	0	1	0

Rank among batters: 4,707 • *Total ballparks homered in*: 1 • *First HR*: 09/28/1939 off Hal Schumacher

Jason Bates

JASON CHARLES BATES
B: 01/05/1971
BB

Year	Tm	Lg	Tot	H	A	0	1	2	3	2	3	4	LO	XN	IP	PH	RHP	LHP
1995	COL	NL	8	4	4	5	2	1	0	0	0	0	0	0	0	0	6	2

Rank among batters: 2,703 • *Total ballparks homered in*: 4 • *First HR*: 04/28/1995 off Darryl Kile

Johnny Bates

JOHN WILLIAM BATES
B: 08/21/1882 D: 02/10/1949
BL

Year	Tm	Lg	Tot	H	A	0	1	2	3	2	3	4	LO	XN	IP	PH	RHP	LHP
1906	BOS	NL	6	5	1	3	2	0	1	0	0	0	0	0	0	0	6	0
1907	BOS	NL	2	0	2	1	1	0	0	0	0	0	0	0	0	0	0	2
1908	BOS	NL	1	1	0	1	0	0	0	0	0	0	0	0	0	0	1	0
1909	BOS	NL	1	1	0	0	1	0	0	0	0	0	0	0	0	0	1	0
	PHI	NL	1	1	0	0	1	0	0	0	0	0	0	0	1	0	1	0
	Total		2	2	0	0	2	0	0	0	0	0	0	0	1	0	2	0
1910	PHI	NL	3	3	0	1	1	1	0	0	0	0	0	0	0	0	3	0
1911	CIN	NL	1	1	0	1	0	0	0	0	0	0	0	0	1	0	1	0
1912	CIN	NL	1	0	1	1	0	0	0	0	0	0	0	0	0	0	1	0
1913	CIN	NL	6	4	2	2	4	0	0	0	0	0	0	0	4	2	6	0
1914	CIN	NL	2	0	2	0	2	0	0	0	0	0	0	0	0	1	1	1
	BAL	FL	1	0	1	1	0	0	0	0	0	0	0	0	0	0	1	0
	Total		3	0	3	1	2	0	0	0	0	0	0	0	0	1	2	1
Total			25	16	9	11	12	1	1	0	0	0	0	0	6	3	22	3

Rank among batters: 1,608 • *Top target (2 home runs)*: Laurence Cheney, Ed Reulbach • *Number of pitchers victimized*: 23 • *Total ballparks homered in*: 8 • *First HR*: 04/12/1906 off Harry McIntire • *Hit for Cycle*—@BRO: 04/26/1907 • *Hit HR in first major league AB*—@BRO: 04/12/1906

Ray Bates

RAYMOND BATES
B: 02/08/1890 D: 08/15/1970
BR

Year	Tm	Lg	Tot	H	A	0	1	2	3	2	3	4	LO	XN	IP	PH	RHP	LHP
1917	PHI	AL	2	2	0	1	1	0	0	0	0	0	0	0	0	0	2	0

Rank among batters: 4,129 • *Total ballparks homered in*: 1 • *First HR*: 06/06/1917 off Jim Park

Bill Bathe

WILLIAM DAVID BATHE
B: 10/14/1960
BR

Year	Tm	Lg	Tot	H	A	Men-On 0	1	2	3	One-Game 2	3	4	LO	XN	IP	PH	RHP	LHP
1986	OAK	AL	5	4	1	4	1	0	0	1	0	0	0	0	0	0	2	3
1990	SF	NL	3	1	2	1	2	0	0	0	0	0	0	0	0	2	0	3
Total			8	5	3	5	3	0	0	1	0	0	0	0	0	2	2	6

Rank among batters: 2,703 • *Top target (2 home runs)*: Bill Wegman, Ron Guidry • *Number of pitchers victimized*: 6 • *Total ballparks homered in*: 5 • *First HR*: 05/07/1986 off Bill Wegman • *World Series HR*—1

Kim Batiste

KIMOTHY EMIL BATISTE
B: 03/15/1968
BR

Year	Tm	Lg	Tot	H	A	Men-On 0	1	2	3	One-Game 2	3	4	LO	XN	IP	PH	RHP	LHP
1992	PHI	NL	1	0	1	0	1	0	0	0	0	0	0	0	0	0	1	0
1993	PHI	NL	5	1	4	2	2	0	1	0	0	0	0	0	0	0	1	4
1994	PHI	NL	1	1	0	1	0	0	0	0	0	0	0	0	0	0	1	0
Total			7	2	5	3	3	0	1	0	0	0	0	0	0	0	3	4

Rank among batters: 2,834 • *Total ballparks homered in*: 6 • *First HR*: 04/23/1992 off Frank Castillo

Earl Battey

EARL JESSE BATTEY
B: 01/05/1935
BR

Year	Tm	Lg	Tot	H	A	Men-On 0	1	2	3	One-Game 2	3	4	LO	XN	IP	PH	RHP	LHP
1957	CHI	AL	3	0	3	2	1	0	0	0	0	0	0	0	0	0	1	2
1958	CHI	AL	8	4	4	3	4	1	0	1	0	0	0	0	0	0	7	1
1959	CHI	AL	2	1	1	1	1	0	0	0	0	0	0	0	0	0	1	1
1960	WAS	AL	15	8	7	8	6	0	1	0	0	0	0	0	0	0	10	5
1961	MIN	AL	17	8	9	13	3	1	0	2	0	0	0	0	0	0	16	1
1962	MIN	AL	11	6	5	6	4	1	0	0	0	0	0	1	0	0	10	1
1963	MIN	AL	26	16	10	14	7	5	0	0	0	0	0	0	0	0	23	3
1964	MIN	AL	12	4	8	7	2	2	1	0	0	0	0	0	0	1	11	1
1965	MIN	AL	6	2	4	3	1	2	0	0	0	0	0	0	0	0	5	1
1966	MIN	AL	4	3	1	2	1	1	0	0	0	0	0	0	0	0	2	2
Total			104	52	52	59	30	13	2	3	0	0	0	1	0	1	86	18

Rank among batters: 469 • *Top target (4 home runs)*: Hoyt Wilhelm • *Number of pitchers victimized*: 72 • *Total ballparks homered in*: 12 • *First HR*: 05/26/1957 off Dick Tomanek

Joe Battin

JOSEPH V. BATTIN
B: 11/11/1851 D: 12/10/1937
BR

Year	Tm	Lg	Tot	H	A	Men-On 0	1	2	3	One-Game 2	3	4	LO	XN	IP	PH	RHP	LHP
1877	STL	NL	1	0	1	0	1	0	0	0	0	0	0	0	0	0	1	0
1882	PIT	AA	1	1	0	0	1	0	0	0	0	0	0	0	0	0	1	0
1883	PIT	AA	1	0	1	1	0	0	0	0	0	0	0	0	0	0	1	0
Total			3	1	2	1	2	0	0	0	0	0	0	0	0	0	3	0

Rank among batters: 3,735 • *Total ballparks homered in*: 3 • *First HR*: 05/30/1877 off Jim Devlin

Matt Batts

MATTHEW DANIEL BATTS
B: 10/16/1921
BR

Year	Tm	Lg	Tot	H	A	Men-On 0	1	2	3	One-Game 2	3	4	LO	XN	IP	PH	RHP	LHP
1947	BOS	AL	1	1	0	1	0	0	0	0	0	0	0	0	0	0	1	0
1948	BOS	AL	1	0	1	1	0	0	0	0	0	0	0	0	0	0	1	0
1949	BOS	AL	3	2	1	0	3	0	0	0	0	0	0	0	0	0	2	1
1950	BOS	AL	4	3	1	2	2	0	0	0	0	0	0	0	0	0	2	2
1951	STL	AL	5	1	4	4	1	0	0	0	0	0	0	0	0	0	4	1
1952	DET	AL	3	2	1	2	1	0	0	0	0	0	0	0	0	0	2	1
1953	DET	AL	6	2	4	5	1	0	0	1	0	0	0	0	0	1	3	3
1954	CHI	AL	3	2	1	1	0	2	0	0	0	0	0	0	0	0	3	0
Total			26	13	13	16	8	2	0	1	0	0	0	0	0	1	18	8

Rank among batters: 1,576 • Top target (2 home runs): Virgil Trucks, Joe Dobson, Morrie Martin, Marion Fricano, Ned Garver • *Number of pitchers victimized*: 21 • *Total ballparks homered in*: 7 • *First HR*: 09/11/1947 off Ed Klieman

Hank Bauer

HENRY ALBERT BAUER
B: 07/31/1922
BR

Year	Tm	Lg	Tot	H	A	Men-On 0	Men-On 1	Men-On 2	Men-On 3	One-Game 2	One-Game 3	One-Game 4	LO	XN	IP	PH	RHP	LHP
1948	NY	AL	1	0	1	0	0	1	0	0	0	0	0	0	0	0	1	0
1949	NY	AL	10	2	8	6	3	1	0	1	0	0	0	0	1	0	4	6
1950	NY	AL	13	4	9	7	4	2	0	1	0	0	0	0	1	0	4	9
1951	NY	AL	10	3	7	4	6	0	0	2	0	0	0	0	0	0	3	7
1952	NY	AL	17	6	11	11	4	2	0	1	0	0	1	0	0	0	7	10
1953	NY	AL	10	6	4	5	5	0	0	0	0	0	0	1	1	1	5	5
1954	NY	AL	12	7	5	10	0	2	0	0	0	0	1	0	1	1	5	7
1955	NY	AL	20	11	9	15	5	0	0	1	0	0	5	0	0	0	14	6
1956	NY	AL	26	14	12	16	6	3	1	3	0	0	3	0	2	1	18	8
1957	NY	AL	18	6	12	13	4	0	1	0	0	0	3	1	0	0	10	8
1958	NY	AL	12	6	6	11	1	0	0	1	0	0	4	0	0	0	12	0
1959	NY	AL	9	3	6	5	4	0	0	0	0	0	0	0	0	1	5	4
1960	KC	AL	3	1	2	3	0	0	0	0	0	0	0	0	0	0	0	3
1961	KC	AL	3	1	2	1	2	0	0	0	0	0	0	0	1	0	0	3
Total			164	70	94	107	44	11	2	10	0	0	17	2	7	4	88	76

Rank among batters: 250 • *Top target (7 home runs)*: Alex Kellner, Camilo Pascual • *Number of pitchers victimized*: 84 • *Total ballparks homered in*: 11 • *First HR*: 09/29/1948 off Dick Fowler • *World Series HR*—7

Frank Baumann

FRANK MATT BAUMANN
B: 07/01/1933
BL

Year	Tm	Lg	Tot	H	A	Men-On 0	Men-On 1	Men-On 2	Men-On 3	One-Game 2	One-Game 3	One-Game 4	LO	XN	IP	PH	RHP	LHP
1961	CHI	AL	2	1	1	2	0	0	0	0	0	0	0	0	0	0	2	0

Rank among batters: 4,129 • *Total ballparks homered in*: 2 • *First HR*: 06/27/1961 off Jerry Casale

Paddy Baumann

CHARLES JOHN BAUMANN
B: 12/20/1885 D: 11/20/1969
BR

Year	Tm	Lg	Tot	H	A	Men-On 0	Men-On 1	Men-On 2	Men-On 3	One-Game 2	One-Game 3	One-Game 4	LO	XN	IP	PH	RHP	LHP
1913	DET	AL	1	0	1	0	1	0	0	0	0	0	0	0	1	0	0	1
1915	NY	AL	2	2	0	1	1	0	0	0	0	0	0	0	0	0	1	1
1916	NY	AL	1	1	0	1	0	0	0	0	0	0	0	0	0	0	0	1
Total			4	3	1	2	2	0	0	0	0	0	0	0	1	0	1	3

Rank among batters: 3,427 • *Total ballparks homered in*: 1 • *First HR*: 08/05/1913 off Al Schulz

Frank Baumholtz

FRANK CONRAD BAUMHOLTZ
B: 10/07/1918
BL

Year	Tm	Lg	Tot	H	A	Men-On 0	Men-On 1	Men-On 2	Men-On 3	One-Game 2	One-Game 3	One-Game 4	LO	XN	IP	PH	RHP	LHP
1947	CIN	NL	5	4	1	3	2	0	0	0	0	0	0	0	0	0	5	0
1948	CIN	NL	4	3	1	3	0	0	1	0	0	0	0	0	1	0	3	1
1949	CIN	NL	1	1	0	0	1	0	0	0	0	0	0	0	0	1	1	0
	CHI	NL	1	0	1	0	1	0	0	0	0	0	0	0	0	1	1	0
	Total		2	1	1	0	2	0	0	0	0	0	0	0	0	2	2	0
1951	CHI	NL	2	1	1	2	0	0	0	0	0	0	0	0	0	0	2	0
1952	CHI	NL	4	2	2	1	2	1	0	0	0	0	0	0	0	0	4	0
1953	CHI	NL	3	1	2	3	0	0	0	0	0	0	0	0	0	1	3	0
1954	CHI	NL	4	2	2	4	0	0	0	0	0	0	2	0	0	1	4	0
1955	CHI	NL	1	0	1	0	0	1	0	0	0	0	0	0	0	1	1	0
Total			25	14	11	16	6	2	1	0	0	0	2	0	1	4	24	1

Rank among batters: 1,608 • *Top target (2 home runs)*: Jim Hearn • *Number of pitchers victimized*: 24 • *Total ballparks homered in*: 6 • *First HR*: 04/17/1947 off Johnny Grodzicki

Danny Bautista

DANIEL (ALCANTARA) BAUTISTA
B: 05/24/1972
BR

Year	Tm	Lg	Tot	H	A	Men-On 0	Men-On 1	Men-On 2	Men-On 3	One-Game 2	One-Game 3	One-Game 4	LO	XN	IP	PH	RHP	LHP
1993	DET	AL	1	0	1	1	0	0	0	0	0	0	0	0	0	0	0	1
1994	DET	AL	4	1	3	1	2	1	0	0	0	0	0	0	0	1	2	2
1995	DET	AL	7	3	4	4	3	0	0	0	0	0	0	0	0	0	3	4
Total			12	4	8	6	5	1	0	0	0	0	0	0	0	1	5	7

Rank among batters: 2,325 • *Total ballparks homered in*: 7 • *First HR*: 10/01/1993 off Frank Tanana

Jim Baxes

DIMITRIOS SPEROS BAXES
B: 07/05/1928
BR

Year	Tm	Lg	Tot	H	A	Men-On 0	Men-On 1	Men-On 2	Men-On 3	One-Game 2	One-Game 3	One-Game 4	LO	XN	IP	PH	RHP	LHP
1959	LA	NL	2	2	0	1	0	1	0	0	0	0	0	0	0	0	2	0
	CLE	AL	15	8	7	1	10	4	1	0	0	0	0	0	0	2	11	4
	Total		17	10	7	11	4	2	0	0	0	0	0	1	0	2	13	4
Total			17	10	7	11	4	2	0	0	0	0	0	1	0	2	13	4

Rank among batters: 1,969 • *Total ballparks homered in*: 6 • *First HR*: 04/15/1959 off Bob Gibson

Mike Baxes

MICHAEL BAXES
B: 12/18/1930
BR

Year	Tm	Lg	Tot	H	A	Men-On 0	Men-On 1	Men-On 2	Men-On 3	One-Game 2	One-Game 3	One-Game 4	LO	XN	IP	PH	RHP	LHP
1956	KC	AL	1	0	1	1	0	0	0	0	0	0	0	0	0	0	1	0

Rank among batters: 4,707 • *Total ballparks homered in*: 1 • *First HR*: 06/11/1956 off Hal Griggs

Harry Bay

HARRY ELBERT BAY
B: 01/17/1878 D: 03/20/1952
BL

Year	Tm	Lg	Tot	H	A	Men-On 0	Men-On 1	Men-On 2	Men-On 3	One-Game 2	One-Game 3	One-Game 4	LO	XN	IP	PH	RHP	LHP
1901	CIN	NL	1	1	0	1	0	0	0	0	0	0	0	0	1	0	1	0
1903	CLE	AL	1	0	1	1	0	0	0	0	0	0	1	0	1	0	1	0
1904	CLE	AL	3	1	2	2	1	0	0	0	0	0	0	0	0	0	3	0
Total			5	2	3	4	1	0	0	0	0	0	1	0	2	0	5	0

Rank among batters: 3,191 • *Total ballparks homered in*: 4 • *First HR*: 10/06/1901 off Stan Yerkes

Dick Bayless

HARRY OWEN BAYLESS
B: 09/06/1883 D: 12/16/1920
BL

Year	Tm	Lg	Tot	H	A	Men-On 0	Men-On 1	Men-On 2	Men-On 3	One-Game 2	One-Game 3	One-Game 4	LO	XN	IP	PH	RHP	LHP
1908	CIN	NL	1	0	1	1	0	0	0	0	0	0	0	0	1	0	1	0

Rank among batters: 4,707 • *Total ballparks homered in*: 1 • *First HR*: 09/26/1908 off Christy Mathewson

Don Baylor

DON EDWARD BAYLOR
B: 06/28/1949
BR

Year	Tm	Lg	Tot	H	A	Men-On 0	Men-On 1	Men-On 2	Men-On 3	One-Game 2	One-Game 3	One-Game 4	LO	XN	IP	PH	RHP	LHP
1972	BAL	AL	11	3	8	6	4	1	0	1	0	0	0	0	0	1	7	4
1973	BAL	AL	11	4	7	8	1	2	0	0	0	0	0	0	0	0	6	5
1974	BAL	AL	10	3	7	6	3	1	0	0	0	0	0	1	0	0	5	5
1975	BAL	AL	25	10	15	15	8	2	0	0	1	0	0	0	0	0	19	6
1976	OAK	AL	15	5	10	13	1	1	0	1	0	0	0	1	0	0	8	7
1977	CAL	AL	25	17	8	15	7	2	1	1	0	0	1	1	0	0	22	3
1978	CAL	AL	34	21	13	18	10	4	2	0	0	0	0	1	0	0	22	12
1979	CAL	AL	36	17	19	17	10	7	2	5	0	0	0	0	0	0	22	14
1980	CAL	AL	5	0	5	2	3	0	0	0	0	0	0	0	0	0	4	1
1981	CAL	AL	17	10	7	9	4	4	0	0	0	0	0	0	0	0	12	5
1982	CAL	AL	24	13	11	10	12	1	1	2	0	0	0	2	0	0	16	8
1983	NY	AL	21	10	11	10	8	1	2	0	0	0	0	2	0	1	8	13
1984	NY	AL	27	10	17	14	12	1	0	2	0	0	0	1	1	0	18	9
1985	NY	AL	23	12	11	12	7	2	2	1	0	0	0	0	0	2	12	11
1986	BOS	AL	31	9	22	16	12	2	1	1	0	0	0	1	0	0	26	5
1987	BOS	AL	16	10	6	8	3	4	1	3	0	0	0	0	0	0	10	6
1988	OAK	AL	7	2	5	4	2	1	0	0	0	0	0	0	0	0	6	1
Total			338	156	182	183	107	36	12	17	1	0	1	10	1	4	223	115

Rank among batters: 50 • *Top target (6 home runs)*: Geoff Zahn, Mike Flanagan • *Number of pitchers victimized*: 209 • *Total ballparks homered in*: 16 • *First HR*: 04/29/1972 off Andy Messersmith • *World Series HR—1; LCS HR—3*

Bill Bayne

WILLIAM LEAR BAYNE
B: 04/18/1899 D: 05/22/1981
BL

Year	Tm	Lg	Tot	H	A	Men-On 0	Men-On 1	Men-On 2	Men-On 3	One-Game 2	One-Game 3	One-Game 4	LO	XN	IP	PH	RHP	LHP
1921	STL	AL	1	1	0	0	0	1	0	0	0	0	0	0	0	0	0	1

Rank among batters: 4,707 • *Total ballparks homered in*: 1 • *First HR*: 07/02/1921 off Dickie Kerr

Bob Beall

ROBERT BROOKS BEALL
B: 04/24/1948
BB

Year	Tm	Lg	Tot	H	A	Men-On 0	Men-On 1	Men-On 2	Men-On 3	One-Game 2	One-Game 3	One-Game 4	LO	XN	IP	PH	RHP	LHP
1978	ATL	NL	1	1	0	0	1	0	0	0	0	0	0	0	0	1	1	0

Rank among batters: 4,707 • *Total ballparks homered in*: 1 • *First HR*: 08/26/1978 off Silvio Martinez

Johnny Beall

JOHN WOOLF BEALL
B: 03/12/1882 D: 06/14/1926
BL

Year	Tm	Lg	Tot	H	A	Men-On 0	Men-On 1	Men-On 2	Men-On 3	One-Game 2	One-Game 3	One-Game 4	LO	XN	IP	PH	RHP	LHP
1913	CHI	AL	2	1	1	1	1	0	0	0	0	0	0	0	0	0	2	0
1916	CIN	NL	1	0	1	1	0	0	0	0	0	0	0	0	0	0	1	0
Total			3	1	2	2	1	0	0	0	0	0	0	0	0	0	3	0

Rank among batters: 3,735 • *Total ballparks homered in*: 3 • *First HR*: 06/30/1913 off Carl Zamloch

Belve Bean

BEVERIC BENTON BEAN
B: 04/25/1905 D: 06/01/1988
BR

Year	Tm	Lg	Tot	H	A	Men-On 0	Men-On 1	Men-On 2	Men-On 3	One-Game 2	One-Game 3	One-Game 4	LO	XN	IP	PH	RHP	LHP
1935	WAS	AL	1	0	1	1	0	0	0	0	0	0	0	0	0	0	1	0

Rank among batters: 4,707 • *Total ballparks homered in*: 1 • *First HR*: 06/16/1935 off Ivy Andrews

Bill Bean

WILLIAM DARO BEAN
B: 05/11/1964
BL

Year	Tm	Lg	Tot	H	A	Men-On 0	Men-On 1	Men-On 2	Men-On 3	One-Game 2	One-Game 3	One-Game 4	LO	XN	IP	PH	RHP	LHP
1993	SD	NL	5	4	1	1	2	1	1	0	0	0	0	0	0	0	5	0

Rank among batters: 3,191 • *Total ballparks homered in*: 2 • *First HR*: 07/15/1993 off Larry Andersen

Billy Beane

WILLIAM LAMAR BEANE
B: 03/29/1962
BR

Year	Tm	Lg	Tot	H	A	Men-On 0	Men-On 1	Men-On 2	Men-On 3	One-Game 2	One-Game 3	One-Game 4	LO	XN	IP	PH	RHP	LHP
1986	MIN	AL	3	0	3	1	0	2	0	0	0	0	0	0	0	0	2	1

Rank among batters: 3,735 • *Total ballparks homered in*: 3 • *First HR*: 04/29/1986 off Eddie Whitson

Ollie Beard

OLIVER PERRY BEARD
B: 05/02/1862 D: 05/28/1929
BR

Year	Tm	Lg	Tot	H	A	Men-On 0	Men-On 1	Men-On 2	Men-On 3	One-Game 2	One-Game 3	One-Game 4	LO	XN	IP	PH	RHP	LHP
1889	CIN	AA	1	1	0	0	0	1	0	0	0	0	0	0	0	0	1	0
1890	CIN	NL	3	2	1	0	2	1	0	0	0	0	0	0	1	0	1	2
Total			4	3	1	0	2	2	0	0	0	0	0	0	1	0	2	2

Rank among batters: 3,427 • *Total ballparks homered in*: 2 • *First HR*: 10/08/1889 off Frank Pears

Ted Beard

CRAMER THEODORE BEARD
B: 01/07/1921
BL

Year	Tm	Lg	Tot	H	A	Men-On 0	Men-On 1	Men-On 2	Men-On 3	One-Game 2	One-Game 3	One-Game 4	LO	XN	IP	PH	RHP	LHP
1950	PIT	NL	4	2	2	2	2	0	0	0	0	0	1	0	0	0	3	1
1951	PIT	NL	1	0	1	1	0	0	0	0	0	0	0	0	0	1	1	0
1958	CHI	AL	1	1	0	0	1	0	0	0	0	0	0	0	0	0	1	0
Total			6	3	3	3	3	0	0	0	0	0	1	0	0	1	5	1

Rank among batters: 2,988 • *Total ballparks homered in*: 5 • *First HR*: 04/20/1950 off Howie Pollet

Gene Bearden

HENRY EUGENE BEARDEN
B: 09/05/1920
BL

Year	Tm	Lg	Tot	H	A	Men-On 0	Men-On 1	Men-On 2	Men-On 3	One-Game 2	One-Game 3	One-Game 4	LO	XN	IP	PH	RHP	LHP
1948	CLE	AL	2	1	1	1	0	1	0	0	0	0	0	0	0	0	1	1
1951	DET	AL	2	2	0	1	0	1	0	0	0	0	0	0	0	0	2	0
Total			4	3	1	2	0	2	0	0	0	0	0	0	0	0	3	1

Rank among batters: 3,427 • *Total ballparks homered in*: 3 • *First HR*: 08/05/1948 off Ray Scarborough

Ed Beatin

EBENEZER AMBROSE BEATIN
B: 08/10/1866 D: 05/09/1925
BR

Year	Tm	Lg	Tot	H	A	Men-On 0	Men-On 1	Men-On 2	Men-On 3	One-Game 2	One-Game 3	One-Game 4	LO	XN	IP	PH	RHP	LHP
1888	DET	NL	2	2	0	0	2	0	0	0	0	0	0	0	2	0	1	1
1889	CLE	NL	1	1	0	0	1	0	0	0	0	0	0	0	0	0	1	0
1890	CLE	NL	1	0	1	0	1	0	0	0	0	0	0	0	0	0	1	0
Total			4	3	1	0	4	0	0	0	0	0	0	0	2	0	3	1

Rank among batters: 3,427 • *Total ballparks homered in*: 3 • *First HR*: 07/17/1888 off Kid Madden

Jim Beauchamp

JAMES EDWARD BEAUCHAMP
B: 08/21/1939
BR

Year	Tm	Lg	Tot	H	A	Men-On 0	Men-On 1	Men-On 2	Men-On 3	One-Game 2	One-Game 3	One-Game 4	LO	XN	IP	PH	RHP	LHP
1964	HOU	NL	2	1	1	2	0	0	0	0	0	0	0	0	0	0	0	2
1968	CIN	NL	2	2	0	0	2	0	0	0	0	0	0	0	0	0	0	2
1969	CIN	NL	1	1	0	0	1	0	0	0	0	0	0	0	0	0	0	1
1970	HOU	NL	1	0	1	1	0	0	0	0	0	0	0	0	0	1	0	1
	STL	NL	1	1	0	1	0	0	0	0	0	0	0	0	0	0	0	1
	Total		2	1	1	2	0	0	0	0	0	0	0	0	0	1	0	2
1971	STL	NL	2	1	1	1	1	0	0	0	0	0	0	0	0	0	0	2
1972	NY	NL	5	4	1	3	2	0	0	1	0	0	0	0	0	0	1	4
Total			14	10	4	8	6	0	0	1	0	0	0	0	0	1	1	13

Rank among batters: 2,169 • *Top target (2 home runs)*: Chris Short • *Number of pitchers victimized*: 13 • *Total ballparks homered in*: 7 • *First HR*: 05/03/1964 off Fred Norman

Ginger Beaumont

CLARENCE HOWETH BEAUMONT
B: 07/23/1876 D: 04/10/1956
BL

Year	Tm	Lg	Tot	H	A	Men-On 0	Men-On 1	Men-On 2	Men-On 3	One-Game 2	One-Game 3	One-Game 4	LO	XN	IP	PH	RHP	LHP
1899	PIT	NL	3	2	1	2	1	0	0	0	0	0	0	0	2	0	3	0
1900	PIT	NL	5	4	1	4	0	1	0	0	0	0	1	0	3	0	3	2
1901	PIT	NL	8	5	3	2	4	2	0	0	0	0	0	0	5	0	7	1
1903	PIT	NL	7	6	1	4	1	2	0	1	0	0	0	0	5	0	7	0
1904	PIT	NL	3	2	1	1	1	1	0	0	0	0	0	0	2	0	3	0
1905	PIT	NL	3	2	1	0	1	2	0	0	0	0	0	0	2	0	3	0
1906	PIT	NL	2	0	2	0	1	0	1	0	0	0	0	0	2	0	1	1
1907	BOS	NL	4	2	2	4	0	0	0	0	0	0	0	0	0	0	3	1
1908	BOS	NL	2	2	0	0	2	0	0	0	0	0	0	0	0	0	1	1
1910	CHI	NL	2	1	1	1	1	0	0	0	0	0	0	0	0	0	0	2
Total			39	26	13	18	12	8	1	1	0	0	1	0	21	0	31	8

Rank among batters: 1,204 • *Top target (5 home runs)*: Togie Pittinger • *Number of pitchers victimized*: 29 • *Total ballparks homered in*: 7 • *First HR*: 08/25/1899 off Ted Lewis

Clyde Beck

CLYDE EUGENE BECK
B: 01/06/1900 D: 07/15/1988
BR

Year	Tm	Lg	Tot	H	A	Men-On 0	Men-On 1	Men-On 2	Men-On 3	One-Game 2	One-Game 3	One-Game 4	LO	XN	IP	PH	RHP	LHP
1926	CHI	NL	1	0	1	1	0	0	0	0	0	0	0	0	0	0	0	1
1927	CHI	NL	2	1	1	1	1	0	0	0	0	0	0	0	0	0	2	0
1928	CHI	NL	3	2	1	1	1	0	1	0	0	0	0	0	0	0	3	0
1930	CHI	NL	6	2	4	2	3	1	0	1	0	0	0	0	1	0	4	2
Total			12	5	7	5	5	1	1	1	0	0	0	0	1	0	9	3

Rank among batters: 2,325 • *Top target (2 home runs)*: Jimmy Ring, Larry Benton • *Number of pitchers victimized*: 10 • *Total ballparks homered in*: 6 • *First HR*: 09/26/1926 off Jesse Petty

Erve Beck

ERVIN THOMAS BECK
B: 07/19/1878 D: 12/23/1916
BR

Year	Tm	Lg	Tot	H	A	Men-On 0	Men-On 1	Men-On 2	Men-On 3	One-Game 2	One-Game 3	One-Game 4	LO	XN	IP	PH	RHP	LHP
1901	CLE	AL	6	0	6	3	0	3	0	0	0	0	0	0	0	0	4	2
1902	CIN	NL	1	1	0	0	1	0	0	0	0	0	0	0	1	0	1	0
	DET	AL	2	1	1	1	0	0	1	0	0	0	0	0	0	0	1	1
	Total		3	2	1	1	1	0	1	0	0	0	0	0	1	0	2	1
Total			9	2	7	4	1	3	1	0	0	0	0	0	1	0	6	3

Rank among batters: 2,587 • *Top target (2 home runs)*: Ted Lewis • *Number of pitchers victimized*: 8 • *Total ballparks homered in*: 7 • *First HR*: 04/25/1901 off John Skopec

Fred Beck

FREDERICK THOMAS BECK
B: 11/17/1886 D: 03/12/1962
BL

Year	Tm	Lg	Tot	H	A	Men-On 0	1	2	3	One-Game 2	3	4	LO	XN	IP	PH	RHP	LHP
1909	BOS	NL	2	1	1	2	0	0	0	0	0	0	0	0	0	0	0	2
1910	BOS	NL	10	8	2	6	2	2	0	0	0	0	0	0	0	0	8	2
1911	CIN	NL	2	0	2	1	0	0	1	0	0	0	0	0	0	0	1	1
	PHI	NL	3	2	1	2	1	0	0	0	0	0	0	0	0	0	3	0
	Total		5	2	3	3	1	0	1	0	0	0	0	0	0	0	4	1
1914	CHI	FL	11	8	3	5	3	3	0	0	0	0	0	1	0	0	11	0
1915	CHI	FL	5	1	4	2	2	1	0	0	0	0	0	0	0	0	5	0
Total			33	20	13	18	8	6	1	0	0	0	0	1	0	0	28	5

Rank among batters: 1,336 • Top target (2 home runs): Hooks Wiltse, Earl Moore, Fred Anderson, Thomas Seaton • *Number of pitchers victimized*: 29 • *Total ballparks homered in*: 9 • *First HR*: 07/30/1909 off Slim Sallee

Zinn Beck

ZINN BERTRAM BECK
B: 09/30/1885 D: 03/19/1981
BR

Year	Tm	Lg	Tot	H	A	Men-On 0	1	2	3	One-Game 2	3	4	LO	XN	IP	PH	RHP	LHP
1914	STL	NL	3	3	0	1	2	0	0	0	0	0	0	0	2	0	3	0

Rank among batters: 3,735 • *Total ballparks homered in*: 1 • *First HR*: 05/21/1914 off Art Fromme

Beals Becker

DAVID BEALS BECKER
B: 07/05/1886 D: 08/16/1943
BL

Year	Tm	Lg	Tot	H	A	Men-On 0	1	2	3	One-Game 2	3	4	LO	XN	IP	PH	RHP	LHP
1909	BOS	NL	6	4	2	2	3	0	1	0	0	0	1	0	0	0	5	1
1910	NY	NL	3	1	2	0	2	0	1	0	0	0	0	0	1	2	3	0
1911	NY	NL	1	1	0	1	0	0	0	0	0	0	0	0	0	0	1	0
1912	NY	NL	6	4	2	4	1	1	0	0	0	0	0	0	0	0	5	1
1913	PHI	NL	9	3	6	5	3	1	0	1	0	0	0	0	2	0	9	0
1914	PHI	NL	9	8	1	4	5	0	0	0	0	0	0	0	0	0	8	1
1915	PHI	NL	11	9	2	6	2	3	0	0	0	0	0	0	0	0	11	0
Total			45	30	15	22	16	5	2	1	0	0	1	0	3	2	42	3

Rank among batters: 1,082 • *Top target (3 home runs)*: Laurence Cheney, Art Fromme, Red Ames • *Number of pitchers victimized*: 35 • *Total ballparks homered in*: 8 • *First HR*: 06/23/1909 off Christy Mathewson

Heinz Becker

HEINZ REINHARD BECKER
B: 08/26/1915 D: 11/11/1991
BB

Year	Tm	Lg	Tot	H	A	Men-On 0	1	2	3	One-Game 2	3	4	LO	XN	IP	PH	RHP	LHP
1945	CHI	NL	2	1	1	0	2	0	0	0	0	0	0	0	0	0	2	0

Rank among batters: 4,129 • *Total ballparks homered in*: 2 • *First HR*: 06/10/1945 off Ed Heusser

Joe Becker

JOSEPH EDWARD BECKER
B: 06/25/1908
BR

Year	Tm	Lg	Tot	H	A	Men-On 0	1	2	3	One-Game 2	3	4	LO	XN	IP	PH	RHP	LHP
1936	CLE	AL	1	0	1	1	0	0	0	0	0	0	0	0	0	0	1	0

Rank among batters: 4,707 • *Total ballparks homered in*: 1 • *First HR*: 06/02/1936 off Jim Henry

Rich Becker

RICHARD GODHARD BECKER
B: 02/01/1972
BB

Year	Tm	Lg	Tot	H	A	Men-On 0	1	2	3	One-Game 2	3	4	LO	XN	IP	PH	RHP	LHP
1994	MIN	AL	1	1	0	0	0	1	0	0	0	0	0	0	0	0	1	0
1995	MIN	AL	2	1	1	1	0	1	0	0	0	0	0	0	0	0	2	0
Total			3	2	1	1	0	2	0	0	0	0	0	0	0	0	3	0

Rank among batters: 3,735 • *Total ballparks homered in*: 2 • *First HR*: 04/21/1994 off Mark Clark

Glenn Beckert

GLENN ALFRED BECKERT
B: 10/12/1940
BR

Year	Tm	Lg	Tot	H	A	Men-On 0	1	2	3	One-Game 2	3	4	LO	XN	IP	PH	RHP	LHP
1965	CHI	NL	3	3	0	2	0	1	0	1	0	0	0	0	0	0	1	2
1966	CHI	NL	1	1	0	0	1	0	0	0	0	0	0	0	0	0	1	0

Glenn Beckert *continued*

Year	Tm	Lg	Tot	H	A	Men-On 0	1	2	3	One-Game 2	3	4	LO	XN	IP	PH	RHP	LHP
1967	CHI	NL	5	3	2	3	1	1	0	0	0	0	0	0	1	0	5	0
1968	CHI	NL	4	3	1	3	1	0	0	0	0	0	0	0	0	0	2	2
1969	CHI	NL	1	1	0	1	0	0	0	0	0	0	0	0	0	0	0	1
1970	CHI	NL	3	3	0	3	0	0	0	0	0	0	0	0	0	0	2	1
1971	CHI	NL	2	2	0	1	1	0	0	0	0	0	0	0	0	0	2	0
1972	CHI	NL	3	3	0	3	0	0	0	0	0	0	0	0	0	0	2	1
Total			22	19	3	16	4	2	0	1	0	0	0	0	1	0	15	7

Rank among batters: 1,719 • *Total ballparks homered in*: 4 • *First HR*: 05/09/1965 off Bob Bruce

Jake Beckley

JACOB PETER BECKLEY
B: 08/04/1867 D: 06/25/1918
BL HOF

Year	Tm	Lg	Tot	H	A	Men-On 0	1	2	3	One-Game 2	3	4	LO	XN	IP	PH	RHP	LHP
1889	PIT	NL	9	0	9	5	4	0	0	0	0	0	0	1	1	0	9	0
1890	PIT	PL	9	6	3	3	4	2	0	0	0	0	0	0	1	0	5	4
1891	PIT	NL	4	0	4	2	2	0	0	0	0	0	0	0	1	0	3	1
1892	PIT	NL	10	8	2	2	6	2	0	0	0	0	0	0	2	0	9	1
1893	PIT	NL	5	3	2	2	1	2	0	0	0	0	0	0	0	0	5	0
1894	PIT	NL	7	6	1	2	4	1	0	1	0	0	0	0	0	0	5	1
1895	PIT	NL	5	0	5	2	3	0	0	0	0	0	0	0	0	0	5	0
1896	PIT	NL	3	0	3	2	0	0	1	1	0	0	0	0	0	0	2	0
	NY	NL	6	3	3	3	3	0	0	0	0	0	2	0	0	0	4	2
	Total		9	3	6	5	3	0	1	1	0	0	2	0	0	0	6	2
1897	NY	NL	1	0	1	0	0	1	0	0	0	0	0	0	0	0	1	0
	CIN	NL	7	0	7	4	2	1	0	0	1	0	0	0	0	0	4	1
	Total		8	0	8	4	2	2	0	0	1	0	0	0	0	0	5	1
1898	CIN	NL	4	0	4	2	2	0	0	0	0	0	0	0	1	0	3	1
1899	CIN	NL	3	1	2	2	0	0	1	0	0	0	0	0	0	0	3	0
1900	CIN	NL	2	1	1	0	1	1	0	0	0	0	0	0	1	0	2	0
1901	CIN	NL	3	1	2	2	0	1	0	0	0	0	0	1	2	0	3	0
1902	CIN	NL	5	2	3	2	2	1	0	0	0	0	0	0	4	0	4	1
1903	CIN	NL	2	2	0	1	0	1	0	0	0	0	0	0	2	0	2	0
1904	STL	NL	1	0	1	1	0	0	0	0	0	0	0	0	0	0	1	0
1905	STL	NL	1	1	0	0	1	0	0	0	0	0	0	0	0	0	1	0
Total			87	34	53	37	35	13	2	2	1	0	2	2	15	0	68	12

Rank among batters: 594 • *Top target (5 home runs)*: Jack Stivetts, Willie Sudhoff • *Number of pitchers victimized*: 66 • *Total ballparks homered in*: 18 • *First HR*: 05/06/1889 off Lev Shreve

Julio Becquer

JULIO (VILLEGAS) BECQUER
B: 12/20/1931
BL

Year	Tm	Lg	Tot	H	A	Men-On 0	1	2	3	One-Game 2	3	4	LO	XN	IP	PH	RHP	LHP
1957	WAS	AL	2	2	0	1	1	0	0	0	0	0	0	0	0	0	2	0
1959	WAS	AL	1	0	1	0	0	1	0	0	0	0	0	0	0	1	1	0
1960	WAS	AL	4	2	2	1	3	0	0	0	0	0	0	0	0	0	4	0
1961	MIN	AL	5	3	2	1	3	0	1	0	0	0	0	0	0	3	5	0
Total			12	7	5	3	7	1	1	0	0	0	0	0	0	4	12	0

Rank among batters: 2,325 • *Total ballparks homered in*: 5 • *First HR*: 06/30/1957 off Bob Keegan

Ed Beecher

EDWARD HARRY BEECHER
B: 07/02/1860 D: 09/12/1935
BL

Year	Tm	Lg	Tot	H	A	Men-On 0	1	2	3	One-Game 2	3	4	LO	XN	IP	PH	RHP	LHP
1887	PIT	NL	2	1	1	0	2	0	0	0	0	0	0	0	0	0	1	1
1890	BUF	PL	3	0	3	1	1	1	0	0	0	0	0	0	0	0	3	0
1891	WAS	AA	2	2	0	0	2	0	0	0	0	0	0	1	1	0	1	0
Total			7	3	4	1	5	1	0	0	0	0	0	1	1	0	5	1

Rank among batters: 2,834 • *Total ballparks homered in*: 4 • *First HR*: 06/30/1887 off Charley Radbourn

Ed Begley

EDWARD N. BEGLEY
B: 1863 D: 07/24/1919

Year	Tm	Lg	Tot	H	A	Men-On 0	1	2	3	One-Game 2	3	4	LO	XN	IP	PH	RHP	LHP
1885	NY	AA	1	0	1	1	0	0	0	0	0	0	0	0	0	0	1	0

Rank among batters: 4,707 • *Total ballparks homered in*: 1 • *First HR*: 05/14/1885 off Bill Mountjoy

Year	Tm	Lg	Tot	H	A	Men-On 0	Men-On 1	Men-On 2	Men-On 3	One-Game 2	One-Game 3	One-Game 4	LO	XN	IP	PH	RHP	LHP

Rick Behenna

RICHARD KIPP BEHENNA
B: 03/06/1960
BR

Year	Tm	Lg	Tot	H	A	Men-On 0	Men-On 1	Men-On 2	Men-On 3	One-Game 2	One-Game 3	One-Game 4	LO	XN	IP	PH	RHP	LHP
1983	ATL	NL	1	1	0	1	0	0	0	0	0	0	0	0	0	0	0	1

Rank among batters: 4,707 • *Total ballparks homered in*: 1 • *First HR*: 06/08/1983 off Fernando Valenzuela

Aloysius Bejma

ALOYSIUS FRANK BEJMA
B: 09/12/1907 D: 01/03/1995
BR

Year	Tm	Lg	Tot	H	A	Men-On 0	Men-On 1	Men-On 2	Men-On 3	One-Game 2	One-Game 3	One-Game 4	LO	XN	IP	PH	RHP	LHP
1934	STL	AL	2	1	1	1	0	1	0	0	0	0	0	0	0	0	2	0
1935	STL	AL	2	0	2	0	2	0	0	0	0	0	0	0	0	0	0	2
1936	STL	AL	2	1	1	2	0	0	0	0	0	0	0	0	0	0	1	1
1939	CHI	AL	8	3	5	4	2	2	0	1	0	0	1	0	0	0	8	0
Total			14	5	9	7	4	3	0	1	0	0	1	0	0	0	11	3

Rank among batters: 2,169 • *Top target (2 home runs)*: Vern Kennedy • *Number of pitchers victimized*: 13 • *Total ballparks homered in*: 4 • *First HR*: 05/31/1934 off Luke Hamlin

Mark Belanger

MARK HENRY BELANGER
B: 06/08/1944
BR

Year	Tm	Lg	Tot	H	A	Men-On 0	Men-On 1	Men-On 2	Men-On 3	One-Game 2	One-Game 3	One-Game 4	LO	XN	IP	PH	RHP	LHP
1967	BAL	AL	1	0	1	1	0	0	0	0	0	0	0	0	0	0	1	0
1968	BAL	AL	2	0	2	2	0	0	0	0	0	0	0	0	0	0	2	0
1969	BAL	AL	2	2	0	1	1	0	0	0	0	0	0	0	0	0	2	0
1970	BAL	AL	1	1	0	1	0	0	0	0	0	0	0	0	0	0	0	1
1972	BAL	AL	2	1	1	2	0	0	0	0	0	0	0	0	0	0	0	2
1974	BAL	AL	5	2	3	3	1	1	0	0	0	0	0	0	0	0	3	2
1975	BAL	AL	3	1	2	2	1	0	0	0	0	0	0	0	0	0	1	2
1976	BAL	AL	1	1	0	1	0	0	0	0	0	0	0	0	0	0	1	0
1977	BAL	AL	2	0	2	2	0	0	0	0	0	0	0	0	0	0	1	1
1981	BAL	AL	1	1	0	1	0	0	0	0	0	0	0	0	0	0	0	1
Total			20	9	11	16	3	1	0	0	0	0	0	0	0	0	11	9

Rank among batters: 1,810 • *Total ballparks homered in*: 8 • *First HR*: 05/14/1967 off Mel Stottlemyre • *LCS HR*—1

Wayne Belardi

CARROLL WAYNE BELARDI
B: 09/05/1930 D: 10/21/1993
BL

Year	Tm	Lg	Tot	H	A	Men-On 0	Men-On 1	Men-On 2	Men-On 3	One-Game 2	One-Game 3	One-Game 4	LO	XN	IP	PH	RHP	LHP
1953	BRO	NL	11	3	8	5	3	2	1	0	0	0	0	0	0	1	10	1
1954	DET	AL	11	6	5	9	2	0	0	0	0	0	0	0	0	0	11	0
1956	DET	AL	6	1	5	3	3	0	0	0	0	0	0	1	0	1	5	1
Total			28	10	18	17	8	2	1	0	0	0	0	1	0	2	26	2

Rank among batters: 1,500 • *Top target (2 home runs)*: Marion Fricano, Bob Feller • *Number of pitchers victimized*: 26 • *Total ballparks homered in*: 11 • *First HR*: 05/28/1953 off Hoyt Wilhelm

Tim Belcher

TIMOTHY WAYNE BELCHER
B: 10/19/1961
BR

Year	Tm	Lg	Tot	H	A	Men-On 0	Men-On 1	Men-On 2	Men-On 3	One-Game 2	One-Game 3	One-Game 4	LO	XN	IP	PH	RHP	LHP
1988	LA	NL	1	1	0	1	0	0	0	0	0	0	0	0	0	0	0	1
1992	CIN	NL	1	1	0	1	0	0	0	0	0	0	0	0	0	0	0	1
Total			2	2	0	2	0	0	0	0	0	0	0	0	0	0	0	2

Rank among batters: 4,129 • *Total ballparks homered in*: 2 • *First HR*: 09/11/1988 off Tom Browning

Beau Bell

ROY CHESTER BELL
B: 08/20/1907 D: 09/14/1977
BR

Year	Tm	Lg	Tot	H	A	Men-On 0	Men-On 1	Men-On 2	Men-On 3	One-Game 2	One-Game 3	One-Game 4	LO	XN	IP	PH	RHP	LHP
1935	STL	AL	3	2	1	1	1	0	1	0	0	0	0	0	0	0	3	0
1936	STL	AL	11	7	4	8	3	0	0	0	0	0	0	0	0	0	11	0
1937	STL	AL	14	7	7	5	6	3	0	1	0	0	0	0	0	0	13	1
1938	STL	AL	13	4	9	9	4	0	0	0	0	0	0	0	0	0	12	1
1939	STL	AL	1	1	0	0	1	0	0	0	0	0	0	0	0	0	1	0

Beau Bell *continued*

Year	Tm	Lg	Tot	H	A	Men-On				One-Game			LO	XN	IP	PH	RHP	LHP
						0	1	2	3	2	3	4						
1940	CLE	AL	4	2	2	3	0	1	0	0	0	0	0	0	0	0	2	2
Total			46	23	23	26	15	4	1	1	0	0	0	0	0	0	42	4

Rank among batters: 1,060 • *Top target (4 home runs)*: Wes Ferrell • *Number of pitchers victimized*: 35 • *Total ballparks homered in*: 7 • *First HR*: 04/21/1935 off Vern Kennedy

Buddy Bell

DAVID GUS BELL
B: 08/27/1951
BR

Year	Tm	Lg	Tot	H	A	Men-On				One-Game			LO	XN	IP	PH	RHP	LHP
						0	1	2	3	2	3	4						
1972	CLE	AL	9	7	2	5	3	0	1	0	0	0	1	0	0	0	4	5
1973	CLE	AL	14	8	6	9	4	1	0	1	0	0	2	0	0	0	10	4
1974	CLE	AL	7	4	3	3	2	2	0	0	0	0	0	0	0	0	4	3
1975	CLE	AL	10	6	4	7	1	1	1	1	0	0	0	1	0	0	4	6
1976	CLE	AL	7	3	4	5	1	1	0	0	0	0	0	0	0	0	2	5
1977	CLE	AL	11	3	8	5	3	2	1	0	0	0	0	0	0	0	7	4
1978	CLE	AL	6	3	3	2	3	0	1	0	0	0	0	0	0	0	4	2
1979	TEX	AL	18	9	9	12	4	1	1	1	0	0	0	0	0	0	9	9
1980	TEX	AL	17	8	9	10	7	0	0	4	0	0	0	0	0	0	13	4
1981	TEX	AL	10	2	8	4	1	4	1	1	0	0	0	0	0	0	6	4
1982	TEX	AL	13	3	10	10	3	0	0	2	0	0	0	0	0	0	10	3
1983	TEX	AL	14	8	6	9	5	0	0	0	0	0	0	0	0	0	11	3
1984	TEX	AL	11	6	5	9	1	0	1	0	0	0	0	0	0	0	7	4
1985	TEX	AL	4	2	2	4	0	0	0	0	0	0	0	0	0	0	4	0
	CIN	NL	6	4	2	1	2	3	0	0	0	0	0	0	0	0	5	1
	Total		10	6	4	5	2	3	0	0	0	0	0	0	0	0	9	1
1986	CIN	NL	20	14	6	9	6	5	0	1	0	0	0	1	0	0	12	8
1987	CIN	NL	17	8	9	9	4	4	0	0	0	0	0	2	0	0	10	7
1988	HOU	NL	7	1	6	5	0	1	1	0	0	0	0	0	0	0	5	2
Total			201	99	102	118	50	25	8	11	0	0	3	4	0	0	127	74

Rank among batters: 181 • Top target (3 home runs): Andy Hassler, Luis Tiant, Floyd Bannister, Rick Waits, Dennis Eckersley, Mike Armstrong, Eddie Whitson, Lary Sorensen • *Number of pitchers victimized*: 154 • *Total ballparks homered in*: 27 • *First HR*: 04/22/1972 off Eddie Watt

David Bell

DAVID MICHAEL BELL
B: 09/14/1972
BR

Year	Tm	Lg	Tot	H	A	Men-On				One-Game			LO	XN	IP	PH	RHP	LHP
						0	1	2	3	2	3	4						
1995	STL	NL	2	1	1	0	2	0	0	0	0	0	0	0	0	0	2	0

Rank among batters: 4,129 • *Total ballparks homered in*: 2 • *First HR*: 08/30/1995 off Mark Portugal

Derek Bell

DEREK NATHANIEL BELL
B: 12/11/1968
BR

Year	Tm	Lg	Tot	H	A	Men-On				One-Game			LO	XN	IP	PH	RHP	LHP
						0	1	2	3	2	3	4						
1992	TOR	AL	2	2	0	2	0	0	0	0	0	0	0	0	0	0	1	1
1993	SD	NL	21	12	9	10	9	2	0	1	0	0	0	0	0	0	11	10
1994	SD	NL	14	8	6	7	6	1	0	1	0	0	0	0	0	0	10	4
1995	HOU	NL	8	3	5	5	1	2	0	0	0	0	0	0	0	0	6	2
Total			45	25	20	24	16	5	0	2	0	0	0	0	0	0	28	17

Rank among batters: 1,082 • *Top target (3 home runs)*: John Smoltz • *Number of pitchers victimized*: 40 • *Total ballparks homered in*: 12 • *First HR*: 05/20/1992 off Mark Guthrie

Fern Bell

FERNANDO JEROME LEE BELL
B: 01/21/1913
BR

Year	Tm	Lg	Tot	H	A	Men-On				One-Game			LO	XN	IP	PH	RHP	LHP
						0	1	2	3	2	3	4						
1939	PIT	NL	2	0	2	1	1	0	0	0	0	0	0	0	0	0	2	0

Rank among batters: 4,129 • *Total ballparks homered in*: 2 • *First HR*: 05/27/1939 off Ray Harrell

Gary Bell

GARY BELL
B: 11/17/1936
BR

Year	Tm	Lg	Tot	H	A	Men-On				One-Game			LO	XN	IP	PH	RHP	LHP
						0	1	2	3	2	3	4						
1965	CLE	AL	1	1	0	1	0	0	0	0	0	0	0	0	0	0	1	0

Rank among batters: 4,707 • *Total ballparks homered in*: 1 • *First HR*: 05/23/1965 off Jim Lonborg

Year	Tm	Lg	Tot	H	A	Men-On 0	1	2	3	One-Game 2	3	4	LO	XN	IP	PH	RHP	LHP

George Bell

GEORGE ANTONIO (MATHEY) BELL
B: 10/21/1959
BR

Year	Tm	Lg	Tot	H	A	0	1	2	3	2	3	4	LO	XN	IP	PH	RHP	LHP
1981	TOR	AL	5	3	2	3	2	0	0	0	0	0	0	0	0	0	1	4
1983	TOR	AL	2	1	1	0	2	0	0	0	0	0	0	0	0	0	0	2
1984	TOR	AL	26	12	14	17	8	1	0	0	0	0	0	0	1	1	15	11
1985	TOR	AL	28	10	18	17	6	3	2	0	0	0	0	2	0	0	17	11
1986	TOR	AL	31	15	16	20	6	4	1	2	0	0	0	1	0	0	21	10
1987	TOR	AL	47	19	28	26	14	5	2	9	0	0	0	1	0	0	31	16
1988	TOR	AL	24	9	15	12	9	2	1	0	1	0	0	0	0	0	14	10
1989	TOR	AL	18	8	10	11	6	1	0	0	0	0	0	1	0	0	9	9
1990	TOR	AL	21	11	10	13	4	3	1	3	0	0	0	1	0	0	16	5
1991	CHI	NL	25	9	16	17	4	4	0	1	0	0	0	1	0	2	10	15
1992	CHI	AL	25	16	9	11	8	4	2	1	0	0	0	0	0	0	19	6
1993	CHI	AL	13	7	6	6	4	2	1	1	0	0	0	0	0	0	10	3
Total			265	120	145	153	73	29	10	17	1	0	0	7	1	3	163	102

Rank among batters: 96 • Top target (5 home runs): Scott Bankhead, Bret Saberhagen, Jack Morris, Frank Viola • *Number of pitchers victimized*: 183 • *Total ballparks homered in*: 25 • *First HR*: 05/02/1981 off Scott McGregor • *LCS HR*—1

Gus Bell

DAVID RUSSELL BELL
B: 11/15/1928 D: 05/07/1995
BL

Year	Tm	Lg	Tot	H	A	0	1	2	3	2	3	4	LO	XN	IP	PH	RHP	LHP
1950	PIT	NL	8	6	2	5	3	0	0	2	0	0	0	0	0	0	7	1
1951	PIT	NL	16	4	12	10	5	0	1	0	0	0	0	0	0	1	14	2
1952	PIT	NL	16	3	13	7	5	3	1	1	0	0	0	2	0	0	15	1
1953	CIN	NL	30	15	15	18	7	4	1	3	0	0	0	0	0	0	24	6
1954	CIN	NL	17	15	2	12	4	1	0	2	0	0	0	0	0	0	15	2
1955	CIN	NL	27	16	11	17	7	2	1	1	1	0	0	0	0	0	22	5
1956	CIN	NL	29	20	9	12	12	5	0	3	1	0	0	1	0	0	23	6
1957	CIN	NL	13	7	6	8	3	2	0	0	0	0	0	0	2	0	10	3
1958	CIN	NL	10	8	2	7	1	1	1	1	0	0	0	1	0	0	8	2
1959	CIN	NL	19	8	11	8	6	5	0	2	0	0	0	0	0	1	16	3
1960	CIN	NL	12	9	3	6	6	0	0	0	0	0	0	1	0	1	10	2
1961	CIN	NL	3	2	1	2	1	0	0	0	0	0	0	0	0	1	3	0
1962	NY	NL	1	1	0	1	0	0	0	0	0	0	0	0	0	0	1	0
	MIL	NL	5	3	2	3	0	2	0	0	0	0	0	0	0	0	4	1
	Total		6	4	2	4	0	2	0	0	0	0	0	0	0	0	5	1
Total			206	117	89	116	60	25	5	15	2	0	0	5	2	4	172	34

Rank among batters: 171 • *Top target (8 home runs)*: Robin Roberts • *Number of pitchers victimized*: 117 • *Total ballparks homered in*: 12 • *First HR*: 06/05/1950 off Clint Hartung • *Hit for Cycle*—@PHI: 06/04/1951 • *All-Star HR*—1

Jay Bell

JAY STUART BELL
B: 12/11/1965
BR

Year	Tm	Lg	Tot	H	A	0	1	2	3	2	3	4	LO	XN	IP	PH	RHP	LHP
1986	CLE	AL	1	0	1	1	0	0	0	0	0	0	0	0	0	0	1	0
1987	CLE	AL	2	1	1	0	2	0	0	0	0	0	0	0	0	0	1	1
1988	CLE	AL	2	2	0	1	1	0	0	0	0	0	0	0	0	0	2	0
1989	PIT	NL	2	1	1	2	0	0	0	0	0	0	0	0	1	0	1	1
1990	PIT	NL	7	1	6	4	1	2	0	0	0	0	0	0	0	0	5	2
1991	PIT	NL	16	7	9	11	2	2	1	1	0	0	0	0	1	0	10	6
1992	PIT	NL	9	5	4	6	3	0	0	0	0	0	0	0	0	0	8	1
1993	PIT	NL	9	3	6	9	0	0	0	0	0	0	0	0	0	0	6	3
1994	PIT	NL	9	3	6	7	1	0	1	0	0	0	0	1	0	0	5	4
1995	PIT	NL	13	8	5	8	4	1	0	1	0	0	0	0	0	0	6	7
Total			70	31	39	49	14	5	2	2	0	0	0	1	2	0	45	25

Rank among batters: 742 • *Top target (3 home runs)*: Francisco Oliveras • *Number of pitchers victimized*: 59 • *Total ballparks homered in*: 17 • *First HR*: 09/29/1986 off Bert Blyleven • *Hit HR on first major league pitch*—@MIN: 09/29/1986 • *LCS HR*—3

Juan Bell

JUAN (MATHEY) BELL
B: 03/29/1968
BR

Year	Tm	Lg	Tot	H	A	0	1	2	3	2	3	4	LO	XN	IP	PH	RHP	LHP
1991	BAL	AL	1	0	1	0	1	0	0	0	0	0	0	0	0	0	1	0
1992	PHI	NL	1	1	0	1	0	0	0	0	0	0	0	0	1	0	1	0
1993	MIL	AL	5	2	3	4	1	0	0	0	0	0	0	0	0	0	2	3

Juan Bell *continued*

Year	Tm	Lg	Tot	H	A	Men-On 0	Men-On 1	Men-On 2	Men-On 3	One-Game 2	One-Game 3	One-Game 4	LO	XN	IP	PH	RHP	LHP
1994	MON	NL	2	0	2	1	1	0	0	0	0	0	0	0	0	0	2	0
1995	BOS	AL	1	0	1	1	0	0	0	0	0	0	0	0	0	0	1	0
Total			10	3	7	7	3	0	0	0	0	0	0	0	1	0	7	3

Rank among batters: 2,500 • *Total ballparks homered in*: 8 • *First HR*: 07/29/1991 off Erik Hanson

Kevin Bell

KEVIN ROBERT BELL
B: 07/13/1955
BR

Year	Tm	Lg	Tot	H	A	Men-On 0	Men-On 1	Men-On 2	Men-On 3	One-Game 2	One-Game 3	One-Game 4	LO	XN	IP	PH	RHP	LHP
1976	CHI	AL	5	1	4	2	1	1	1	0	0	0	0	0	1	0	4	1
1977	CHI	AL	1	0	1	1	0	0	0	0	0	0	0	0	0	0	0	1
1978	CHI	AL	2	0	2	1	1	0	0	1	0	0	0	0	0	0	0	2
1979	CHI	AL	4	0	4	2	1	1	0	0	0	0	0	0	0	0	2	2
1980	CHI	AL	1	1	0	0	0	1	0	0	0	0	0	0	0	0	1	0
Total			13	2	11	6	3	3	1	1	0	0	0	0	1	0	7	6

Rank among batters: 2,248 • *Top target (2 home runs)*: Jerry Garvin, Bill Travers • *Number of pitchers victimized*: 11 • *Total ballparks homered in*: 8 • *First HR*: 06/22/1976 off Steve Busby

Les Bell

LESTER ROWLAND BELL
B: 12/14/1901 D: 12/26/1985
BR

Year	Tm	Lg	Tot	H	A	Men-On 0	Men-On 1	Men-On 2	Men-On 3	One-Game 2	One-Game 3	One-Game 4	LO	XN	IP	PH	RHP	LHP
1924	STL	NL	1	1	0	0	1	0	0	0	0	0	0	0	0	0	1	0
1925	STL	NL	11	4	7	4	6	1	0	1	0	0	0	1	0	0	9	2
1926	STL	NL	17	12	5	11	5	1	0	0	0	0	0	0	1	0	15	2
1927	STL	NL	9	6	3	3	3	2	1	0	0	0	0	2	1	0	5	4
1928	BOS	NL	10	7	3	5	1	3	1	0	1	0	0	0	0	0	9	1
1929	BOS	NL	9	4	5	5	1	2	1	0	0	0	0	0	0	1	5	4
1930	CHI	NL	5	4	1	3	0	1	1	0	0	0	0	0	0	0	5	0
1931	CHI	NL	4	2	2	2	2	0	0	0	0	0	0	0	0	0	4	0
Total			66	40	26	33	19	10	4	1	1	0	0	3	2	1	53	13

Rank among batters: 786 • *Top target (4 home runs)*: Grover Alexander • *Number of pitchers victimized*: 48 • *Total ballparks homered in*: 8 • *First HR*: 04/16/1924 off Grover Alexander • *World Series HR—1*

Mike Bell

MICHAEL ALLEN BELL
B: 04/22/1968
BL

Year	Tm	Lg	Tot	H	A	Men-On 0	Men-On 1	Men-On 2	Men-On 3	One-Game 2	One-Game 3	One-Game 4	LO	XN	IP	PH	RHP	LHP
1990	ATL	NL	1	0	1	0	0	1	0	0	0	0	0	0	0	0	1	0
1991	ATL	NL	1	1	0	1	0	0	0	0	0	0	0	0	0	0	1	0
Total			2	1	1	1	0	1	0	0	0	0	0	0	0	0	2	0

Rank among batters: 4,129 • *Total ballparks homered in*: 2 • *First HR*: 10/02/1990 off John Burkett

Zeke Bella

JOHN BELLA
B: 08/23/1930
BR

Year	Tm	Lg	Tot	H	A	Men-On 0	Men-On 1	Men-On 2	Men-On 3	One-Game 2	One-Game 3	One-Game 4	LO	XN	IP	PH	RHP	LHP
1959	KC	AL	1	1	0	0	1	0	0	0	0	0	0	0	0	0	0	1

Rank among batters: 4,707 • *Total ballparks homered in*: 1 • *First HR*: 08/13/1959 off Jack Harshman

Albert Belle

ALBERT JOJUAN BELLE
B: 08/25/1966
BR

Year	Tm	Lg	Tot	H	A	Men-On 0	Men-On 1	Men-On 2	Men-On 3	One-Game 2	One-Game 3	One-Game 4	LO	XN	IP	PH	RHP	LHP
1989	CLE	AL	7	3	4	3	3	0	1	1	0	0	0	0	0	0	4	3
1990	CLE	AL	1	1	0	0	1	0	0	0	0	0	0	0	0	0	0	1
1991	CLE	AL	28	8	20	13	12	3	0	1	0	0	0	0	0	0	20	8
1992	CLE	AL	34	15	19	16	11	6	1	4	1	0	0	0	0	0	26	8
1993	CLE	AL	38	20	18	21	12	5	0	6	0	0	0	1	0	0	26	12
1994	CLE	AL	36	21	15	19	11	5	1	1	0	0	0	1	0	0	27	9
1995	CLE	AL	50	25	25	30	12	6	2	7	1	0	0	2	0	0	42	8
Total			194	93	101	102	62	25	5	20	2	0	0	4	0	0	145	49

Rank among batters: 194 • *Top target (4 home runs)*: Ben McDonald, Jimmy Key, Erik Hanson • *Number of pitchers victimized*: 138 • *Total ballparks homered in*: 17 • *First HR*: 07/19/1989 off Randy St. Claire • *World Series HR—2*; *LCS HR—2*

Rafael Belliard

RAFAEL LEONIDAS (MATIAS) BELLIARD
B: 10/24/1961
BR

Year	Tm	Lg	Tot	H	A	Men-On 0	Men-On 1	Men-On 2	Men-On 3	One-Game 2	One-Game 3	One-Game 4	LO	XN	IP	PH	RHP	LHP
1987	PIT	NL	1	0	1	0	0	1	0	0	0	0	0	0	0	0	1	0

Rank among batters: 4,707 • *Total ballparks homered in*: 1 • *First HR*: 05/05/1987 off Eric Show

Esteban Beltre

ESTEBAN (VALERA) BELTRE
B: 12/26/1967
BR

Year	Tm	Lg	Tot	H	A	Men-On 0	Men-On 1	Men-On 2	Men-On 3	One-Game 2	One-Game 3	One-Game 4	LO	XN	IP	PH	RHP	LHP
1992	CHI	AL	1	1	0	0	1	0	0	0	0	0	0	0	0	0	0	1

Rank among batters: 4,707 • *Total ballparks homered in*: 1 • *First HR*: 08/04/1992 off Bill Krueger

Harry Bemis

HARRY PARKER BEMIS
B: 02/01/1874 D: 05/23/1947
BR

Year	Tm	Lg	Tot	H	A	Men-On 0	Men-On 1	Men-On 2	Men-On 3	One-Game 2	One-Game 3	One-Game 4	LO	XN	IP	PH	RHP	LHP
1902	CLE	AL	1	0	1	0	1	0	0	0	0	0	0	0	0	0	1	0
1903	CLE	AL	1	0	1	1	0	0	0	0	0	0	0	0	0	0	1	0
1906	CLE	AL	2	0	2	1	1	0	0	0	0	0	0	1	0	0	2	0
1910	CLE	AL	1	0	1	1	0	0	0	0	0	0	0	0	0	0	1	0
Total			5	0	5	3	2	0	0	0	0	0	0	1	0	0	5	0

Rank among batters: 3,191 • *Total ballparks homered in*: 3 • *First HR*: 05/29/1902 off Al Orth

Marvin Benard

MARVIN LARRY BENARD
B: 01/20/1971
BL

Year	Tm	Lg	Tot	H	A	Men-On 0	Men-On 1	Men-On 2	Men-On 3	One-Game 2	One-Game 3	One-Game 4	LO	XN	IP	PH	RHP	LHP
1995	SF	NL	1	0	1	0	1	0	0	0	0	0	0	0	0	0	0	1

Rank among batters: 4,707 • *Total ballparks homered in*: 1 • *First HR*: 09/29/1995 off Mike Munoz

Freddie Benavides

ALFREDO BENAVIDES
B: 04/07/1966
BR

Year	Tm	Lg	Tot	H	A	Men-On 0	Men-On 1	Men-On 2	Men-On 3	One-Game 2	One-Game 3	One-Game 4	LO	XN	IP	PH	RHP	LHP
1992	CIN	NL	1	1	0	0	1	0	0	0	0	0	0	0	0	0	0	1
1993	COL	NL	3	3	0	2	0	1	0	0	0	0	0	0	0	0	2	1
Total			4	4	0	2	1	1	0	0	0	0	0	0	0	0	2	2

Rank among batters: 3,427 • *Total ballparks homered in*: 2 • *First HR*: 04/14/1992 off Steve Avery

Johnny Bench

JOHNNY LEE BENCH
B: 12/07/1947
BR HOF

Year	Tm	Lg	Tot	H	A	Men-On 0	Men-On 1	Men-On 2	Men-On 3	One-Game 2	One-Game 3	One-Game 4	LO	XN	IP	PH	RHP	LHP
1967	CIN	NL	1	0	1	0	0	1	0	0	0	0	0	0	0	0	1	0
1968	CIN	NL	15	10	5	6	8	1	0	0	0	0	0	0	0	0	14	1
1969	CIN	NL	26	16	10	16	3	6	1	0	0	0	0	1	0	0	22	4
1970	CIN	NL	45	30	15	18	17	10	0	2	1	0	0	1	0	0	28	17
1971	CIN	NL	27	14	13	17	9	1	0	2	0	0	0	0	0	0	21	6
1972	CIN	NL	40	16	24	23	12	4	1	4	0	0	0	2	1	0	26	14
1973	CIN	NL	25	7	18	11	9	5	0	1	1	0	0	1	0	0	19	6
1974	CIN	NL	33	17	16	14	11	6	2	1	0	0	0	1	0	0	27	6
1975	CIN	NL	28	15	13	13	6	7	2	1	0	0	0	2	0	0	21	7
1976	CIN	NL	16	12	4	8	4	4	0	1	0	0	0	0	0	0	10	6
1977	CIN	NL	31	16	15	17	8	4	2	2	0	0	0	0	0	0	20	11
1978	CIN	NL	23	11	12	15	6	1	1	0	0	0	0	0	0	1	10	13
1979	CIN	NL	22	7	15	15	3	4	0	1	0	0	0	0	0	0	9	13
1980	CIN	NL	24	9	15	14	7	1	2	0	1	0	0	0	0	1	14	10
1981	CIN	NL	8	5	3	4	3	1	0	1	0	0	0	0	0	1	4	4
1982	CIN	NL	13	5	8	10	3	0	0	0	0	0	0	0	0	0	10	3
1983	CIN	NL	12	5	7	4	5	3	0	0	0	0	0	0	0	2	7	5
Total			389	195	194	205	114	59	11	16	3	0	0	8	1	5	263	126

Rank among batters: 29 • *Top target (12 home runs)*: Steve Carlton, Don Sutton • *Number of pitchers victimized*: 217 • *Total ballparks homered in*: 16 • *First HR*: 09/20/1967 off Jim Britton • *World Series HR—5; LCS HR—5; All-Star HR—3*

Chief Bender

CHARLES ALBERT BENDER
B: 05/05/1884 D: 05/22/1954
BR HOF

Year	Tm	Lg	Tot	H	A	Men-On 0	Men-On 1	Men-On 2	Men-On 3	One-Game 2	One-Game 3	One-Game 4	LO	XN	IP	PH	RHP	LHP
1906	PHI	AL	3	0	3	1	0	2	0	1	0	0	0	0	2	0	1	2
1914	PHI	AL	1	1	0	0	1	0	0	0	0	0	0	0	0	0	1	0
1915	BAL	FL	1	0	1	1	0	0	0	0	0	0	0	0	0	0	1	0
1917	PHI	NL	1	1	0	1	0	0	0	0	0	0	0	0	0	0	1	0
Total			6	2	4	3	1	2	0	1	0	0	0	0	2	0	4	2

Rank among batters: 2,988 • *Top target (2 home runs)*: Jesse Tannehill • *Number of pitchers victimized*: 5 • *Total ballparks homered in*: 5 • *First HR*: 05/05/1906 off Bill Hogg

Bruce Benedict

BRUCE EDWIN BENEDICT
B: 08/18/1955
BR

Year	Tm	Lg	Tot	H	A	Men-On 0	Men-On 1	Men-On 2	Men-On 3	One-Game 2	One-Game 3	One-Game 4	LO	XN	IP	PH	RHP	LHP
1980	ATL	NL	2	1	1	2	0	0	0	0	0	0	0	0	0	0	1	1
1981	ATL	NL	5	2	3	2	0	2	1	1	0	0	0	0	0	0	1	4
1982	ATL	NL	3	2	1	0	2	0	1	0	0	0	0	0	0	0	1	2
1983	ATL	NL	2	1	1	2	0	0	0	0	0	0	0	0	0	0	1	1
1984	ATL	NL	4	2	2	4	0	0	0	0	0	0	0	1	0	0	2	2
1987	ATL	NL	1	1	0	0	1	0	0	0	0	0	0	0	0	0	1	0
1989	ATL	NL	1	0	1	1	0	0	0	0	0	0	0	0	0	0	1	0
Total			18	9	9	11	3	2	2	1	0	0	0	1	0	0	8	10

Rank among batters: 1,914 • *Top target (2 home runs)*: Vida Blue • *Number of pitchers victimized*: 17 • *Total ballparks homered in*: 7 • *First HR*: 06/13/1980 off Lynn McGlothen

Andy Benes

ANDREW CHARLES BENES
B: 08/20/1967
BR

Year	Tm	Lg	Tot	H	A	Men-On 0	Men-On 1	Men-On 2	Men-On 3	One-Game 2	One-Game 3	One-Game 4	LO	XN	IP	PH	RHP	LHP
1989	SD	NL	1	1	0	0	1	0	0	0	0	0	0	0	0	0	0	1
1991	SD	NL	1	0	1	1	0	0	0	0	0	0	0	0	0	0	1	0
1992	SD	NL	1	0	1	1	0	0	0	0	0	0	0	0	0	0	0	1
1993	SD	NL	1	0	1	1	0	0	0	0	0	0	0	0	0	0	1	0
Total			4	1	3	3	1	0	0	0	0	0	0	0	0	0	2	2

Rank among batters: 3,427 • *Total ballparks homered in*: 4 • *First HR*: 09/03/1989 off Dennis Cook

Juan Beniquez

JUAN JOSE (TORRES) BENIQUEZ
B: 05/13/1950
BR

Year	Tm	Lg	Tot	H	A	Men-On 0	Men-On 1	Men-On 2	Men-On 3	One-Game 2	One-Game 3	One-Game 4	LO	XN	IP	PH	RHP	LHP
1972	BOS	AL	1	1	0	1	0	0	0	0	0	0	0	0	0	0	1	0
1974	BOS	AL	5	3	2	4	0	0	1	1	0	0	0	1	0	0	3	2
1975	BOS	AL	2	1	1	2	0	0	0	0	0	0	0	0	0	0	2	0
1977	TEX	AL	10	5	5	7	2	1	0	1	0	0	0	0	0	0	7	3
1978	TEX	AL	11	5	6	7	3	1	0	0	0	0	0	1	0	0	5	6
1979	NY	AL	4	0	4	2	1	1	0	0	0	0	0	0	0	0	1	3
1980	SEA	AL	6	5	1	3	3	0	0	0	0	0	0	1	0	0	4	2
1981	CAL	AL	3	2	1	3	0	0	0	0	0	0	0	0	0	0	2	1
1982	CAL	AL	3	1	2	1	1	1	0	0	0	0	0	0	0	0	2	1
1983	CAL	AL	3	1	2	2	0	0	1	0	0	0	0	0	0	0	2	1
1984	CAL	AL	8	5	3	4	3	1	0	1	0	0	0	1	0	0	5	3
1985	CAL	AL	8	6	2	2	5	1	0	0	0	0	0	0	0	1	2	6
1986	BAL	AL	6	4	2	4	2	0	0	0	1	0	0	0	0	0	3	3
1987	KC	AL	3	0	3	2	1	0	0	0	0	0	0	0	0	0	2	1
	TOR	AL	5	2	3	2	0	3	0	0	0	0	0	0	0	1	0	5
	Total		8	2	6	4	1	3	0	0	0	0	0	0	0	1	2	6
1988	TOR	AL	1	1	0	0	1	0	0	0	0	0	0	0	0	0	0	1
Total			79	42	37	46	22	9	2	3	1	0	0	4	0	2	41	38

Rank among batters: 661 • *Top target (3 home runs)*: Frank Tanana • *Number of pitchers victimized*: 70 • *Total ballparks homered in*: 13 • *First HR*: 07/04/1972 off Ray Corbin

Yamil Benitez

YAMIL ANTONIO BENITEZ
B: 10/05/1972
BR

Year	Tm	Lg	Tot	H	A	Men-On 0	Men-On 1	Men-On 2	Men-On 3	One-Game 2	One-Game 3	One-Game 4	LO	XN	IP	PH	RHP	LHP
1995	MON	NL	2	1	1	1	1	0	0	0	0	0	0	0	0	0	0	2

Rank among batters: 4,129 • *Total ballparks homered in*: 2 • *First HR*: 09/18/1995 off Pete Schourek

Mike Benjamin

MICHAEL PAUL BENJAMIN
B: 11/22/1965
BR

Year	Tm	Lg	Tot	H	A	Men-On 0	1	2	3	One-Game 2	3	4	LO	XN	IP	PH	RHP	LHP
1990	SF	NL	2	2	0	2	0	0	0	0	0	0	0	0	0	0	2	0
1991	SF	NL	2	0	2	2	0	0	0	0	0	0	0	0	0	0	1	1
1992	SF	NL	1	0	1	1	0	0	0	0	0	0	0	0	0	0	0	1
1993	SF	NL	4	3	1	0	4	0	0	0	0	0	0	0	0	0	1	3
1994	SF	NL	1	1	0	0	1	0	0	0	0	0	0	0	1	0	1	0
1995	SF	NL	3	1	2	2	1	0	0	0	0	0	0	0	0	0	2	1
Total			13	7	6	7	6	0	0	0	0	0	0	0	1	0	7	6

Rank among batters: 2,248 • *Top target (2 home runs)*: Butch Henry • *Number of pitchers victimized*: 12 • *Total ballparks homered in*: 6 • *First HR*: 08/26/1990 off Jason Grimsley

Stan Benjamin

ALFRED STANLEY BENJAMIN
B: 05/20/1914
BR

Year	Tm	Lg	Tot	H	A	Men-On 0	1	2	3	One-Game 2	3	4	LO	XN	IP	PH	RHP	LHP
1941	PHI	NL	3	2	1	3	0	0	0	0	0	0	0	0	0	0	3	0
1942	PHI	NL	2	1	1	1	1	0	0	0	0	0	1	0	0	0	0	2
Total			5	3	2	4	1	0	0	0	0	0	1	0	0	0	3	2

Rank among batters: 3,191 • *Total ballparks homered in*: 3 • *First HR*: 06/19/1941 off Harry Gumbert

Ike Benners

ISAAC B. BENNERS
B: 06/07/1856 D: 04/18/1932
BL

Year	Tm	Lg	Tot	H	A	Men-On 0	1	2	3	One-Game 2	3	4	LO	XN	IP	PH	RHP	LHP
1884	BRO	AA	1	1	0	0	0	1	0	0	0	0	0	0	0	0	0	1

Rank among batters: 4,707 • *Total ballparks homered in*: 1 • *First HR*: 06/05/1884 off Denny Driscoll

Charlie Bennett

CHARLES WESLEY BENNETT
B: 11/21/1854 D: 02/24/1927
BR

Year	Tm	Lg	Tot	H	A	Men-On 0	1	2	3	One-Game 2	3	4	LO	XN	IP	PH	RHP	LHP
1878	MIL	NL	1	0	1	1	0	0	0	0	0	0	0	0	0	0	1	0
1881	DET	NL	7	6	1	3	0	4	0	0	0	0	0	0	1	0	7	0
1882	DET	NL	5	3	2	3	1	1	0	0	0	0	0	0	1	0	4	1
1883	DET	NL	5	4	1	2	1	2	0	0	0	0	0	0	1	0	5	0
1884	DET	NL	3	3	0	0	2	1	0	0	0	0	0	0	0	0	3	0
1885	DET	NL	5	0	5	3	0	1	1	0	0	0	0	0	0	0	4	0
1886	DET	NL	4	2	2	2	0	2	0	0	0	0	0	0	0	0	4	0
1887	DET	NL	3	0	3	3	0	0	0	0	0	0	0	0	0	0	1	2
1888	DET	NL	5	1	4	3	0	2	0	0	0	0	0	1	1	0	4	1
1889	BOS	NL	4	4	0	3	1	0	0	0	0	0	0	0	0	0	4	0
1890	BOS	NL	3	2	1	1	2	0	0	0	0	0	0	1	0	0	2	1
1891	BOS	NL	5	4	1	3	2	0	0	0	0	0	0	0	0	0	5	0
1892	BOS	NL	1	1	0	1	0	0	0	0	0	0	0	0	0	0	1	0
1893	BOS	NL	4	4	0	2	1	1	0	0	0	0	0	0	0	0	4	0
Total			55	34	21	30	10	14	1	0	0	0	0	2	4	0	49	5

Rank among batters: 926 • *Top target (6 home runs)*: Mickey Welch • *Number of pitchers victimized*: 40 • *Total ballparks homered in*: 15 • *First HR*: 07/25/1878 off Monte Ward • *World Series HR—1*

Dennis Bennett

DENNIS JOHN BENNETT
B: 10/05/1939
BL

Year	Tm	Lg	Tot	H	A	Men-On 0	1	2	3	One-Game 2	3	4	LO	XN	IP	PH	RHP	LHP
1962	PHI	NL	1	0	1	0	1	0	0	0	0	0	0	0	0	0	1	0
1963	PHI	NL	1	0	1	1	0	0	0	0	0	0	0	0	0	0	0	1
1966	BOS	AL	1	1	0	1	0	0	0	0	0	0	0	0	0	0	1	0
1967	BOS	AL	1	0	1	0	0	1	0	0	0	0	0	0	0	0	1	0
Total			4	1	3	2	1	1	0	0	0	0	0	0	0	0	3	1

Rank among batters: 3,427 • *Total ballparks homered in*: 4 • *First HR*: 08/19/1962 off Vern Law

Fred Bennett

JAMES FRED BENNETT
B: 03/15/1902 D: 05/12/1957
BR

Year	Tm	Lg	Tot	H	A	Men-On 0	1	2	3	One-Game 2	3	4	LO	XN	IP	PH	RHP	LHP
1931	PIT	NL	1	0	1	0	1	0	0	0	0	0	0	0	0	0	0	1

Rank among batters: 4,707 • *Total ballparks homered in*: 1 • *First HR*: 06/27/1931 off Jumbo Elliott

Year	Tm	Lg	Tot	H	A	Men-On 0	Men-On 1	Men-On 2	Men-On 3	One-Game 2	One-Game 3	One-Game 4	LO	XN	IP	PH	RHP	LHP

Herschel Bennett

HERSCHEL EMMETT BENNETT
B: 09/21/1896 D: 09/09/1964
BL

Year	Tm	Lg	Tot	H	A	Men-On 0	Men-On 1	Men-On 2	Men-On 3	One-Game 2	One-Game 3	One-Game 4	LO	XN	IP	PH	RHP	LHP
1924	STL	AL	1	1	0	0	1	0	0	0	0	0	0	0	0	0	1	0
1925	STL	AL	2	2	0	1	1	0	0	0	0	0	0	0	0	0	2	0
1926	STL	AL	1	1	0	0	1	0	0	0	0	0	0	0	0	0	1	0
1927	STL	AL	3	3	0	2	1	0	0	0	0	0	0	0	0	0	1	2
Total			7	7	0	3	4	0	0	0	0	0	0	0	0	0	5	2

Rank among batters: 2,834 • *Total ballparks homered in*: 1 • *First HR*: 06/07/1924 off Bob Shawkey

Pug Bennett

JUSTIN TITUS BENNETT
B: 02/20/1874 D: 09/12/1935
BR

Year	Tm	Lg	Tot	H	A	Men-On 0	Men-On 1	Men-On 2	Men-On 3	One-Game 2	One-Game 3	One-Game 4	LO	XN	IP	PH	RHP	LHP
1906	STL	NL	1	1	0	1	0	0	0	0	0	0	0	0	0	0	0	1

Rank among batters: 4,707 • *Total ballparks homered in*: 1 • *First HR*: 07/22/1906 off Irv Young

Vern Benson

VERNON ADAIR BENSON
B: 09/19/1924
BL

Year	Tm	Lg	Tot	H	A	Men-On 0	Men-On 1	Men-On 2	Men-On 3	One-Game 2	One-Game 3	One-Game 4	LO	XN	IP	PH	RHP	LHP
1951	STL	NL	1	1	0	1	0	0	0	0	0	0	0	0	0	0	1	0
1952	STL	NL	2	2	0	1	1	0	0	0	0	0	0	0	0	0	2	0
Total			3	3	0	2	1	0	0	0	0	0	0	0	0	0	3	0

Rank among batters: 3,735 • *Total ballparks homered in*: 1 • *First HR*: 09/18/1951 off Ralph Branca

Jack Bentley

JACK NEEDLES BENTLEY
B: 03/08/1895 D: 10/24/1969
BL

Year	Tm	Lg	Tot	H	A	Men-On 0	Men-On 1	Men-On 2	Men-On 3	One-Game 2	One-Game 3	One-Game 4	LO	XN	IP	PH	RHP	LHP
1923	NY	NL	1	1	0	0	1	0	0	0	0	0	0	0	0	1	1	0
1925	NY	NL	3	2	1	2	0	1	0	0	0	0	0	1	0	1	2	1
1926	PHI	NL	2	1	1	2	0	0	0	0	0	0	0	0	0	0	2	0
1927	NY	NL	1	1	0	1	0	0	0	0	0	0	0	0	0	0	1	0
Total			7	5	2	5	1	1	0	0	0	0	0	1	0	2	6	1

Rank among batters: 2,834 • *Total ballparks homered in*: 4 • *First HR*: 08/26/1923 off Vic Aldridge • *World Series HR*—1

Larry Benton

LAWRENCE JAMES BENTON
B: 11/20/1897 D: 04/03/1953
BR

Year	Tm	Lg	Tot	H	A	Men-On 0	Men-On 1	Men-On 2	Men-On 3	One-Game 2	One-Game 3	One-Game 4	LO	XN	IP	PH	RHP	LHP
1929	NY	NL	1	0	1	0	1	0	0	0	0	0	0	0	0	0	1	0
1930	NY	NL	1	0	1	0	0	1	0	0	0	0	0	0	0	0	1	0
Total			2	0	2	0	1	1	0	0	0	0	0	0	0	0	2	0

Rank among batters: 4,129 • *Total ballparks homered in*: 2 • *First HR*: 04/18/1929 off Ray Benge

Rube Benton

JOHN CLEBON BENTON
B: 06/27/1887 D: 12/12/1937
BR

Year	Tm	Lg	Tot	H	A	Men-On 0	Men-On 1	Men-On 2	Men-On 3	One-Game 2	One-Game 3	One-Game 4	LO	XN	IP	PH	RHP	LHP
1919	NY	NL	1	1	0	0	1	0	0	0	0	0	0	0	0	0	0	1

Rank among batters: 4,707 • *Total ballparks homered in*: 1 • *First HR*: 07/23/1919 off Slim Sallee

Todd Benzinger

TODD ERIC BENZINGER
B: 02/11/1963
BB

Year	Tm	Lg	Tot	H	A	Men-On 0	Men-On 1	Men-On 2	Men-On 3	One-Game 2	One-Game 3	One-Game 4	LO	XN	IP	PH	RHP	LHP
1987	BOS	AL	8	5	3	2	4	1	1	0	0	0	0	0	0	0	6	2
1988	BOS	AL	13	6	7	7	3	3	0	1	0	0	0	1	0	0	12	1
1989	CIN	NL	17	6	11	10	3	2	2	0	0	0	0	0	0	0	11	6
1990	CIN	NL	5	4	1	4	0	1	0	0	0	0	0	0	0	0	3	2
1991	CIN	NL	1	1	0	1	0	0	0	0	0	0	0	0	0	0	0	1
	KC	AL	2	1	1	1	0	0	1	0	0	0	0	0	0	0	2	0
	Total		3	2	1	2	0	0	1	0	0	0	0	0	0	0	2	1

						Men-On				One-Game								
Year	Tm	Lg	Tot	H	A	0	1	2	3	2	3	4	LO	XN	IP	PH	RHP	LHP

Todd Benzinger *continued*

Year	Tm	Lg	Tot	H	A	0	1	2	3	2	3	4	LO	XN	IP	PH	RHP	LHP
1992	LA	NL	4	1	3	1	1	0	2	0	0	0	0	0	0	2	4	0
1993	SF	NL	6	0	6	3	1	2	0	2	0	0	0	0	0	0	4	2
1994	SF	NL	9	5	4	9	0	0	0	1	0	0	0	0	0	2	8	1
1995	SF	NL	1	1	0	1	0	0	0	0	0	0	0	0	0	0	0	1
Total			66	30	36	39	12	9	6	4	0	0	0	1	0	4	50	16

Rank among batters: 786 • *Top target (4 home runs)*: Walt Terrell • *Number of pitchers victimized*: 55 • *Total ballparks homered in*: 19 • *First HR*: 07/01/1987 off Mike Griffin • *Switch hit HR in 1 game*—1 time

Johnny Berardino

JOHN BERARDINO
B: 05/01/1917
BR

Year	Tm	Lg	Tot	H	A	0	1	2	3	2	3	4	LO	XN	IP	PH	RHP	LHP
1939	STL	AL	5	1	4	2	3	0	0	0	0	0	0	0	0	0	4	1
1940	STL	AL	16	8	8	5	6	4	1	1	0	0	0	1	0	0	11	5
1941	STL	AL	5	2	3	3	1	1	0	0	0	0	0	0	0	0	5	0
1942	STL	AL	1	1	0	0	1	0	0	0	0	0	0	0	0	0	1	0
1946	STL	AL	5	2	3	3	1	0	1	0	0	0	0	0	0	0	4	1
1947	STL	AL	1	0	1	1	0	0	0	0	0	0	0	0	0	0	1	0
1948	CLE	AL	2	1	1	1	1	0	0	0	0	0	0	0	0	0	2	0
1950	PIT	NL	1	1	0	1	0	0	0	0	0	0	0	0	0	0	1	0
Total			36	16	20	16	13	5	2	1	0	0	0	1	0	0	29	7

Rank among batters: 1,274 • *Top target (3 home runs)*: Red Ruffing • *Number of pitchers victimized*: 30 • *Total ballparks homered in*: 8 • *First HR*: 06/29/1939 off Thornton Lee

Lou Berberet

LOUIS JOSEPH BERBERET
B: 11/20/1929
BL

Year	Tm	Lg	Tot	H	A	0	1	2	3	2	3	4	LO	XN	IP	PH	RHP	LHP
1956	WAS	AL	4	3	1	2	1	1	0	0	0	0	0	0	0	0	3	1
1957	WAS	AL	7	3	4	3	4	0	0	0	0	0	0	0	0	1	7	0
1958	BOS	AL	2	0	2	1	0	1	0	0	0	0	0	0	0	0	2	0
1959	DET	AL	13	6	7	8	3	2	0	0	0	0	0	0	0	0	11	2
1960	DET	AL	5	2	3	3	0	1	1	0	0	0	0	0	0	0	5	0
Total			31	14	17	17	8	5	1	0	0	0	0	0	0	1	28	3

Rank among batters: 1,400 • *Top target (4 home runs)*: Early Wynn • *Number of pitchers victimized*: 28 • *Total ballparks homered in*: 8 • *First HR*: 05/13/1956 off Frank Sullivan

Moe Berg

MORRIS BERG
B: 03/02/1902 D: 05/29/1972
BR

Year	Tm	Lg	Tot	H	A	0	1	2	3	2	3	4	LO	XN	IP	PH	RHP	LHP
1932	WAS	AL	1	1	0	1	0	0	0	0	0	0	0	0	0	0	0	1
1933	WAS	AL	2	0	2	1	0	1	0	0	0	0	0	0	0	0	2	0
1935	BOS	AL	2	2	0	1	1	0	0	0	0	0	0	0	0	0	2	0
1939	BOS	AL	1	0	1	1	0	0	0	0	0	0	0	0	0	0	1	0
Total			6	3	3	4	1	1	0	0	0	0	0	0	0	0	5	1

Rank among batters: 2,988 • *Total ballparks homered in*: 5 • *First HR*: 04/23/1932 off Bob Weiland

Augie Bergamo

AUGUST SAMUEL BERGAMO
B: 02/14/1917 D: 08/19/1974
BL

Year	Tm	Lg	Tot	H	A	0	1	2	3	2	3	4	LO	XN	IP	PH	RHP	LHP
1944	STL	NL	2	0	2	1	1	0	0	0	0	0	0	0	0	0	2	0
1945	STL	NL	3	0	3	0	2	0	1	1	0	0	0	0	0	0	3	0
Total			5	0	5	1	3	0	1	1	0	0	0	0	0	0	5	0

Rank among batters: 3,191 • *Total ballparks homered in*: 3 • *First HR*: 07/22/1944 off Red Barrett

Bill Bergen

WILLIAM ALOYSIUS BERGEN
B: 06/13/1878 D: 12/19/1943
BR

Year	Tm	Lg	Tot	H	A	0	1	2	3	2	3	4	LO	XN	IP	PH	RHP	LHP
1901	CIN	NL	1	1	0	0	1	0	0	0	0	0	0	0	0	0	1	0

Bill Bergen *continued*

Year	Tm	Lg	Tot	H	A	Men-On 0	Men-On 1	Men-On 2	Men-On 3	One-Game 2	One-Game 3	One-Game 4	LO	XN	IP	PH	RHP	LHP
1909	BRO	NL	1	1	0	0	1	0	0	0	0	0	0	0	0	0	1	0
Total			2	2	0	0	2	0	0	0	0	0	0	0	0	0	2	0

Rank among batters: 4,129 • *Total ballparks homered in*: 2 • *First HR*: 06/03/1901 off Jim Hughes

Marty Bergen

MARTIN BERGEN
B: 10/25/1871 D: 01/19/1900

Year	Tm	Lg	Tot	H	A	Men-On 0	Men-On 1	Men-On 2	Men-On 3	One-Game 2	One-Game 3	One-Game 4	LO	XN	IP	PH	RHP	LHP
1896	BOS	NL	4	3	1	1	2	1	0	0	0	0	0	0	0	0	4	0
1897	BOS	NL	2	1	1	0	2	0	0	0	0	0	0	0	0	0	2	0
1898	BOS	NL	3	3	0	1	1	1	0	0	0	0	0	0	0	0	3	0
1899	BOS	NL	1	1	0	1	0	0	0	0	0	0	0	0	0	0	1	0
Total			10	8	2	3	5	2	0	0	0	0	0	0	0	0	10	0

Rank among batters: 2,500 • *Total ballparks homered in*: 3 • *First HR*: 07/10/1896 off Bill Hart

Boze Berger

LOUIS WILLIAM BERGER
B: 05/13/1910 D: 11/03/1992
BR

Year	Tm	Lg	Tot	H	A	Men-On 0	Men-On 1	Men-On 2	Men-On 3	One-Game 2	One-Game 3	One-Game 4	LO	XN	IP	PH	RHP	LHP
1935	CLE	AL	5	2	3	2	2	1	0	0	0	0	0	0	0	0	5	0
1937	CHI	AL	5	3	2	4	1	0	0	1	0	0	1	0	0	1	4	1
1938	CHI	AL	3	2	1	3	0	0	0	0	0	0	2	0	1	0	3	0
Total			13	7	6	9	3	1	0	1	0	0	3	0	1	1	12	1

Rank among batters: 2,248 • *Top target (2 home runs)*: Johnny Allen, Johnny Marcum, Wes Ferrell • *Number of pitchers victimized*: 10 • *Total ballparks homered in*: 6 • *First HR*: 05/17/1935 off Johnny Allen

Joe Berger

JOSEPH AUGUST BERGER
B: 12/20/1886 D: 03/06/1956
BR

Year	Tm	Lg	Tot	H	A	Men-On 0	Men-On 1	Men-On 2	Men-On 3	One-Game 2	One-Game 3	One-Game 4	LO	XN	IP	PH	RHP	LHP
1913	CHI	AL	2	1	1	2	0	0	0	0	0	0	0	0	0	0	2	0

Rank among batters: 4,129 • *Total ballparks homered in*: 2 • *First HR*: 08/25/1913 off Bob Groom

Tun Berger

JOHN HENRY BERGER
B: 12/06/1867 D: 06/10/1907

Year	Tm	Lg	Tot	H	A	Men-On 0	Men-On 1	Men-On 2	Men-On 3	One-Game 2	One-Game 3	One-Game 4	LO	XN	IP	PH	RHP	LHP
1891	PIT	NL	1	0	1	0	1	0	0	0	0	0	0	0	0	0	1	0

Rank among batters: 4,707 • *Total ballparks homered in*: 1 • *First HR*: 08/11/1891 off John Clarkson

Wally Berger

WALTER ANTONE BERGER
B: 10/10/1905 D: 11/30/1988
BR

Year	Tm	Lg	Tot	H	A	Men-On 0	Men-On 1	Men-On 2	Men-On 3	One-Game 2	One-Game 3	One-Game 4	LO	XN	IP	PH	RHP	LHP
1930	BOS	NL	38	18	20	21	10	6	1	4	0	0	0	0	1	1	24	14
1931	BOS	NL	19	7	12	10	4	5	0	0	0	0	0	0	0	0	16	3
1932	BOS	NL	17	10	7	10	7	0	0	1	0	0	0	0	0	0	13	4
1933	BOS	NL	27	16	11	20	2	4	1	3	0	0	0	2	1	1	24	3
1934	BOS	NL	34	15	19	16	12	6	0	5	0	0	0	1	0	0	31	3
1935	BOS	NL	34	18	16	15	9	7	3	2	0	0	0	1	0	0	30	4
1936	BOS	NL	25	14	11	14	6	4	1	2	0	0	0	2	0	0	23	2
1937	BOS	NL	5	5	0	3	1	1	0	1	0	0	0	0	0	0	3	2
	NY	NL	12	5	7	6	4	2	0	0	0	0	0	0	0	1	8	4
	Total		17	10	7	9	5	3	0	1	0	0	0	0	0	1	11	6
1938	CIN	NL	16	7	9	9	7	0	0	1	0	0	0	0	0	0	15	1
1939	CIN	NL	14	5	9	7	5	1	1	1	0	0	0	0	0	0	12	2
1940	PHI	NL	1	0	1	1	0	0	0	0	0	0	0	0	0	0	0	1
Total			242	120	122	132	67	36	7	20	0	0	0	6	2	3	199	43

Rank among batters: 121 • *Top target (9 home runs)*: Tex Carleton • *Number of pitchers victimized*: 104 • *Total ballparks homered in*: 9 • *First HR*: 04/20/1930 off Watty Clark

Marty Berghammer

MARTIN ANDREW BERGHAMMER
B: 06/18/1888 D: 12/21/1957
BL

Year	Tm	Lg	Tot	H	A	Men-On 0	Men-On 1	Men-On 2	Men-On 3	One-Game 2	One-Game 3	One-Game 4	LO	XN	IP	PH	RHP	LHP
1913	CIN	NL	1	1	0	0	1	0	0	0	0	0	0	0	1	0	1	0

Rank among batters: 4,707 • *Total ballparks homered in*: 1 • *First HR*: 07/29/1913 off Mysterious Walker

Year	Tm	Lg	Tot	H	A	Men-On 0	1	2	3	One-Game 2	3	4	LO	XN	IP	PH	RHP	LHP

Dave Bergman

DAVID BRUCE BERGMAN
B: 06/06/1953
BL

Year	Tm	Lg	Tot	H	A	Men-On 0	1	2	3	One-Game 2	3	4	LO	XN	IP	PH	RHP	LHP
1979	HOU	NL	1	0	1	1	0	0	0	0	0	0	0	0	0	1	1	0
1981	HOU	NL	1	0	1	1	0	0	0	0	0	0	0	0	0	1	1	0
	SF	NL	3	1	2	2	1	0	0	0	0	0	0	1	0	0	3	0
	Total		4	1	3	3	1	0	0	0	0	0	0	1	0	1	4	0
1982	SF	NL	4	2	2	3	1	0	0	0	0	0	0	0	0	0	3	1
1983	SF	NL	6	3	3	3	2	1	0	1	0	0	0	0	0	2	5	1
1984	DET	AL	7	4	3	4	1	2	0	0	0	0	1	2	0	1	7	0
1985	DET	AL	3	2	1	3	0	0	0	0	0	0	0	1	0	0	3	0
1986	DET	AL	1	0	1	0	1	0	0	0	0	0	0	0	0	0	1	0
1987	DET	AL	6	4	2	4	1	1	0	0	0	0	0	0	0	0	6	0
1988	DET	AL	5	4	1	2	3	0	0	0	0	0	0	0	0	0	5	0
1989	DET	AL	7	6	1	7	0	0	0	0	0	0	0	0	0	0	7	0
1990	DET	AL	2	1	1	1	1	0	0	0	0	0	0	0	0	0	2	0
1991	DET	AL	7	2	5	6	1	0	0	1	0	0	0	0	0	0	7	0
1992	DET	AL	1	1	0	1	0	0	0	0	0	0	0	0	0	1	1	0
Total			54	30	24	38	12	4	0	2	0	0	1	4	0	6	52	2

Rank among batters: 938 • *Top target (3 home runs)*: Willie Fraser • *Number of pitchers victimized*: 47 • *Total ballparks homered in*: 19 • *First HR*: 09/26/1979 off Phil Niekro

Tony Bernazard

ANTONIO (GARCIA) BERNAZARD
B: 08/24/1956
BB

Year	Tm	Lg	Tot	H	A	Men-On 0	1	2	3	One-Game 2	3	4	LO	XN	IP	PH	RHP	LHP
1979	MON	NL	1	0	1	0	0	1	0	0	0	0	0	0	0	0	1	0
1980	MON	NL	5	2	3	3	1	1	0	0	0	0	0	0	0	1	5	0
1981	CHI	AL	6	3	3	5	1	0	0	0	0	0	0	0	0	0	5	1
1982	CHI	AL	11	1	10	10	0	1	0	0	0	0	0	0	0	0	9	2
1983	CHI	AL	2	2	0	1	1	0	0	0	0	0	0	0	0	0	1	1
	SEA	AL	6	4	2	4	1	0	1	0	0	0	0	0	0	0	6	0
	Total		8	6	2	5	2	0	1	0	0	0	0	0	0	0	7	1
1984	CLE	AL	2	1	1	1	1	0	0	0	0	0	0	0	0	0	0	2
1985	CLE	AL	11	4	7	9	1	1	0	0	0	0	0	1	0	0	11	0
1986	CLE	AL	17	9	8	12	5	0	0	2	0	0	4	0	0	0	12	5
1987	CLE	AL	11	3	8	9	1	0	1	1	0	0	0	0	0	0	8	3
	OAK	AL	3	0	3	2	0	1	0	0	0	0	0	0	0	0	2	1
	Total		14	3	11	11	1	1	1	1	0	0	0	0	0	0	10	4
Total			75	29	46	56	12	5	2	3	0	0	4	1	0	1	60	15

Rank among batters: 699 • *Top target (3 home runs)*: Mike Moore • *Number of pitchers victimized*: 63 • *Total ballparks homered in*: 18 • *First HR*: 07/21/1979 off Don Sutton • *Switch hit HR in 1 game*—1 time

Juan Bernhardt

JUAN RAMON (CORADIN) BERNHARDT
B: 08/31/1953
BR

Year	Tm	Lg	Tot	H	A	Men-On 0	1	2	3	One-Game 2	3	4	LO	XN	IP	PH	RHP	LHP
1977	SEA	AL	7	6	1	6	0	1	0	0	0	0	0	0	0	0	5	2
1978	SEA	AL	2	2	0	2	0	0	0	0	0	0	0	0	0	0	1	1
Total			9	8	1	8	0	1	0	0	0	0	0	0	0	0	6	3

Rank among batters: 2,587 • *Top target (2 home runs)*: Jim Colborn • *Number of pitchers victimized*: 8 • *Total ballparks homered in*: 2 • *First HR*: 04/10/1977 off Frank Tanana

Carlos Bernier

CARLOS (RODRIGUEZ) BERNIER
B: 01/28/1927 D: 04/06/1989
BR

Year	Tm	Lg	Tot	H	A	Men-On 0	1	2	3	One-Game 2	3	4	LO	XN	IP	PH	RHP	LHP
1953	PIT	NL	3	2	1	3	0	0	0	0	0	0	1	0	1	0	1	2

Rank among batters: 3,735 • *Total ballparks homered in*: 2 • *First HR*: 05/24/1953 off Larry Jansen

Johnny Bero

JOHN GEORGE BERO
B: 12/22/1922 D: 05/11/1985
BL

Year	Tm	Lg	Tot	H	A	Men-On 0	1	2	3	One-Game 2	3	4	LO	XN	IP	PH	RHP	LHP
1951	STL	AL	5	2	3	4	1	0	0	1	0	0	0	0	0	0	4	1

Rank among batters: 3,191 • *Top target (2 home runs)*: Dick Fowler • *Number of pitchers victimized*: 4 • *Total ballparks homered in*: 4 • *First HR*: 05/25/1951 off Hal Newhouser

Dale Berra

DALE ANTHONY BERRA
B: 12/13/1956
BR

Year	Tm	Lg	Tot	H	A	Men-On 0	1	2	3	One-Game 2	3	4	LO	XN	IP	PH	RHP	LHP
1978	PIT	NL	6	4	2	4	1	1	0	0	0	0	0	0	0	0	3	3
1979	PIT	NL	3	1	2	2	1	0	0	0	0	0	0	0	0	0	2	1
1980	PIT	NL	6	3	3	1	3	1	1	0	0	0	0	0	0	0	5	1
1981	PIT	NL	2	1	1	1	0	1	0	0	0	0	0	0	0	0	1	1
1982	PIT	NL	10	4	6	9	1	0	0	0	0	0	0	0	0	0	7	3
1983	PIT	NL	10	5	5	6	3	1	0	1	0	0	0	0	0	0	6	4
1984	PIT	NL	9	7	2	7	1	0	1	0	0	0	0	0	0	0	4	5
1985	NY	AL	1	1	0	1	0	0	0	0	0	0	0	0	0	0	0	1
1986	NY	AL	2	2	0	2	0	0	0	0	0	0	0	1	0	0	0	2
Total			49	28	21	33	10	4	2	1	0	0	0	1	0	0	28	21

Rank among batters: 1,008 • *Top target (3 home runs)*: John Montefusco, Bob Knepper • *Number of pitchers victimized*: 44 • *Total ballparks homered in*: 11 • *First HR*: 08/20/1978 off Tom Dixon

Yogi Berra

LAWRENCE PETER BERRA
B: 05/12/1925
BL HOF

Year	Tm	Lg	Tot	H	A	Men-On 0	1	2	3	One-Game 2	3	4	LO	XN	IP	PH	RHP	LHP
1946	NY	AL	2	2	0	1	1	0	0	0	0	0	0	0	0	0	2	0
1947	NY	AL	11	6	5	5	4	0	2	0	0	0	0	0	1	1	10	1
1948	NY	AL	14	9	5	7	4	3	0	0	0	0	0	1	0	0	13	1
1949	NY	AL	20	14	6	9	6	4	1	1	0	0	0	0	0	1	17	3
1950	NY	AL	28	14	14	11	13	3	1	1	0	0	0	0	0	0	19	9
1951	NY	AL	27	12	15	18	6	2	1	0	0	0	0	1	0	0	15	12
1952	NY	AL	30	18	12	15	12	3	0	5	0	0	0	0	0	0	19	11
1953	NY	AL	27	13	14	10	12	4	1	1	0	0	0	0	0	1	20	7
1954	NY	AL	22	15	7	8	9	4	1	0	0	0	0	1	0	0	15	7
1955	NY	AL	27	20	7	10	10	7	0	3	0	0	0	0	0	1	22	5
1956	NY	AL	30	19	11	16	13	1	0	1	0	0	0	0	0	0	21	9
1957	NY	AL	24	17	7	14	5	5	0	1	0	0	0	2	0	1	16	8
1958	NY	AL	22	13	9	8	9	5	0	1	0	0	0	1	0	0	18	4
1959	NY	AL	19	10	9	8	9	2	0	1	0	0	0	0	0	0	14	5
1960	NY	AL	15	9	6	9	5	0	1	2	0	0	0	1	0	1	15	0
1961	NY	AL	22	12	10	14	6	2	0	2	0	0	0	0	0	1	19	3
1962	NY	AL	10	4	6	5	2	2	1	0	0	0	0	2	0	1	10	0
1963	NY	AL	8	3	5	1	4	3	0	0	0	0	0	0	0	0	8	0
Total			358	210	148	169	130	50	9	19	0	0	0	9	1	8	273	85

Rank among batters: 42 • *Top target (11 home runs)*: Early Wynn • *Number of pitchers victimized*: 168 • *Total ballparks homered in*: 12 • *First HR*: 09/22/1946 off Jesse Flores • *World Series HR*—12; *All-Star HR*—1

Ray Berres

RAYMOND FREDERICK BERRES
B: 08/31/1907
BR

Year	Tm	Lg	Tot	H	A	Men-On 0	1	2	3	One-Game 2	3	4	LO	XN	IP	PH	RHP	LHP
1936	BRO	NL	1	0	1	1	0	0	0	0	0	0	0	0	0	0	1	0
1941	BOS	NL	1	1	0	0	1	0	0	0	0	0	0	0	1	0	0	1
1944	NY	NL	1	1	0	1	0	0	0	0	0	0	0	0	0	0	1	0
Total			3	2	1	2	1	0	0	0	0	0	0	0	1	0	2	1

Rank among batters: 3,735 • *Total ballparks homered in*: 2 • *First HR*: 08/18/1936 off Freddie Fitzsimmons

Geronimo Berroa

GERONIMO EMILIANO LETTA BERROA
B: 03/18/1965
BR

Year	Tm	Lg	Tot	H	A	Men-On 0	1	2	3	One-Game 2	3	4	LO	XN	IP	PH	RHP	LHP
1989	ATL	NL	2	1	1	2	0	0	0	0	0	0	0	0	0	0	0	2
1994	OAK	AL	13	4	9	6	6	1	0	0	0	0	0	0	0	0	7	6
1995	OAK	AL	22	10	12	7	14	0	1	1	0	0	0	0	1	0	19	3
Total			37	15	22	15	20	1	1	1	0	0	0	0	1	0	26	11

Rank among batters: 1,252 • *Top target (2 home runs)*: Scott Kamieniecki, Mike Trombley • *Number of pitchers victimized*: 35 • *Total ballparks homered in*: 12 • *First HR*: 06/07/1989 off Fernando Valenzuela

Charlie Berry

CHARLES JOSEPH BERRY
B: 09/06/1860 D: 02/16/1940
BR

Year	Tm	Lg	Tot	H	A	Men-On 0	1	2	3	One-Game 2	3	4	LO	XN	IP	PH	RHP	LHP
1884	KC	UA	1	1	0	0	1	0	0	0	0	0	0	0	0	0	1	0

Year	Tm	Lg	Tot	H	A	Men-On 0	1	2	3	One-Game 2	3	4	LO	XN	IP	PH	RHP	LHP

Charlie Berry *continued*

Rank among batters: 4,707 • *Total ballparks homered in*: 1 • *First HR*: 06/09/1884 off Hugh Daily

Charlie Berry

CHARLES FRANCIS BERRY
B: 10/18/1902 D: 09/06/1972
BR

Year	Tm	Lg	Tot	H	A	0	1	2	3	2	3	4	LO	XN	IP	PH	RHP	LHP
1928	BOS	AL	1	0	1	1	0	0	0	0	0	0	0	0	0	0	1	0
1929	BOS	AL	1	1	0	1	0	0	0	0	0	0	0	0	0	0	1	0
1930	BOS	AL	6	3	3	5	1	0	0	0	0	0	0	0	0	0	6	0
1931	BOS	AL	6	3	3	3	3	0	0	0	0	0	0	0	0	0	6	0
1932	CHI	AL	4	2	2	3	1	0	0	0	0	0	0	0	0	0	3	1
1933	CHI	AL	2	1	1	0	2	0	0	0	0	0	0	0	0	0	1	1
1935	PHI	AL	3	1	2	2	1	0	0	0	0	0	0	0	0	0	2	1
Total			23	11	12	15	8	0	0	0	0	0	0	0	0	0	20	3

Rank among batters: 1,686 • *Top target (3 home runs)*: Tommy Thomas • *Number of pitchers victimized*: 18 • *Total ballparks homered in*: 7 • *First HR*: 06/13/1928 off Jack Ogden

Claude Berry

CLAUDE ELZY BERRY
B: 02/14/1880 D: 02/01/1974
BR

Year	Tm	Lg	Tot	H	A	0	1	2	3	2	3	4	LO	XN	IP	PH	RHP	LHP
1914	PIT	FL	2	1	1	2	0	0	0	0	0	0	0	0	1	0	1	1
1915	PIT	FL	1	0	1	1	0	0	0	0	0	0	0	0	0	0	1	0
Total			3	1	2	3	0	0	0	0	0	0	0	0	1	0	2	1

Rank among batters: 3,735 • *Total ballparks homered in*: 3 • *First HR*: 06/02/1914 off Harry Moran

Ken Berry

ALLEN KENT BERRY
B: 05/10/1941
BR

Year	Tm	Lg	Tot	H	A	0	1	2	3	2	3	4	LO	XN	IP	PH	RHP	LHP
1964	CHI	AL	1	0	1	0	0	1	0	0	0	0	0	0	0	0	0	1
1965	CHI	AL	12	4	8	11	1	0	0	0	0	0	0	0	0	0	5	7
1966	CHI	AL	8	0	8	8	0	0	0	0	0	0	0	0	0	0	5	3
1967	CHI	AL	7	4	3	5	2	0	0	0	0	0	0	1	0	0	4	3
1968	CHI	AL	7	4	3	6	0	0	1	0	0	0	0	0	0	0	6	1
1969	CHI	AL	4	4	0	2	2	0	0	0	0	0	0	0	0	0	4	0
1970	CHI	AL	7	6	1	4	2	1	0	1	0	0	0	0	0	0	4	3
1971	CAL	AL	3	0	3	3	0	0	0	0	0	0	0	0	0	0	1	2
1972	CAL	AL	5	2	3	4	1	0	0	0	0	0	0	0	0	0	1	4
1973	CAL	AL	3	1	2	0	0	3	0	0	0	0	0	0	0	0	0	3
1974	MIL	AL	1	0	1	1	0	0	0	0	0	0	1	0	0	0	0	1
Total			58	25	33	44	8	5	1	1	0	0	1	1	0	0	30	28

Rank among batters: 886 • *Top target (5 home runs)*: Mickey Lolich • *Number of pitchers victimized*: 47 • *Total ballparks homered in*: 14 • *First HR*: 09/25/1964 off John O'Donoghue

Sean Berry

SEAN ROBERT BERRY
B: 03/22/1966
BR

Year	Tm	Lg	Tot	H	A	0	1	2	3	2	3	4	LO	XN	IP	PH	RHP	LHP
1992	MON	NL	1	0	1	1	0	0	0	0	0	0	0	0	0	0	1	0
1993	MON	NL	14	5	9	10	1	3	0	2	0	0	0	0	1	1	11	3
1994	MON	NL	11	4	7	7	3	1	0	0	0	0	0	1	0	0	5	6
1995	MON	NL	14	5	9	7	4	2	1	1	0	0	0	0	0	1	13	1
Total			40	14	26	25	8	6	1	3	0	0	0	1	1	2	30	10

Rank among batters: 1,181 • *Top target (2 home runs)*: Bobby Ayala, Tom Urbani, Bill VanLandingham • *Number of pitchers victimized*: 37 • *Total ballparks homered in*: 13 • *First HR*: 10/03/1992 off Jim Bullinger

Damon Berryhill

DAMON SCOTT BERRYHILL
B: 12/03/1963
BB

Year	Tm	Lg	Tot	H	A	0	1	2	3	2	3	4	LO	XN	IP	PH	RHP	LHP
1988	CHI	NL	7	5	2	3	2	1	1	1	0	0	0	1	0	0	6	1
1989	CHI	NL	5	2	3	4	1	0	0	0	0	0	0	1	0	0	2	3
1990	CHI	NL	1	1	0	0	0	1	0	0	0	0	0	0	0	0	0	1

Damon Berryhill *continued*

Year	Tm	Lg	Tot	H	A	Men-On 0	1	2	3	One-Game 2	3	4	LO	XN	IP	PH	RHP	LHP
1991	CHI	NL	5	3	2	3	1	1	0	0	0	0	0	0	0	0	5	0
1992	ATL	NL	10	6	4	6	2	2	0	0	0	0	0	0	0	1	9	1
1993	ATL	NL	8	6	2	3	3	2	0	0	0	0	0	1	0	0	6	2
1994	BOS	AL	6	3	3	4	2	0	0	0	0	0	0	0	0	0	4	2
1995	CIN	NL	2	2	0	0	1	1	0	0	0	0	0	0	0	1	2	0
Total			44	28	16	23	12	8	1	1	0	0	0	3	0	2	34	10

Rank among batters: 1,095 • *Top target (2 home runs)*: Pete Harnisch • *Number of pitchers victimized*: 43 • *Total ballparks homered in*: 14 • *First HR*: 06/02/1988 off David Cone • *World Series HR*—1; *LCS HR*—1

Frank Bertaina

FRANK LOUIS BERTAINA
B: 04/14/1944
BL

Year	Tm	Lg	Tot	H	A	Men-On 0	1	2	3	One-Game 2	3	4	LO	XN	IP	PH	RHP	LHP
1969	WAS	AL	1	0	1	0	0	1	0	0	0	0	0	0	0	0	1	0

Rank among batters: 4,707 • *Total ballparks homered in*: 1 • *First HR*: 04/27/1969 off Stan Williams

Dick Bertell

RICHARD GEORGE BERTELL
B: 11/21/1935
BR

Year	Tm	Lg	Tot	H	A	Men-On 0	1	2	3	One-Game 2	3	4	LO	XN	IP	PH	RHP	LHP
1961	CHI	NL	2	1	1	2	0	0	0	0	0	0	0	0	0	0	1	1
1962	CHI	NL	2	2	0	2	0	0	0	0	0	0	0	0	0	1	0	2
1963	CHI	NL	2	1	1	2	0	0	0	0	0	0	0	0	0	0	2	0
1964	CHI	NL	4	3	1	3	0	1	0	0	0	0	0	0	0	0	2	2
Total			10	7	3	9	0	1	0	0	0	0	0	0	0	1	5	5

Rank among batters: 2,500 • *Top target (2 home runs)*: Jim O'Toole • *Number of pitchers victimized*: 9 • *Total ballparks homered in*: 3 • *First HR*: 07/06/1961 off Wilmer Mizell

Reno Bertoia

RENO PETER BERTOIA
B: 01/08/1935
BR

Year	Tm	Lg	Tot	H	A	Men-On 0	1	2	3	One-Game 2	3	4	LO	XN	IP	PH	RHP	LHP
1954	DET	AL	1	1	0	1	0	0	0	0	0	0	0	0	0	0	1	0
1955	DET	AL	1	0	1	0	0	1	0	0	0	0	0	0	0	0	1	0
1956	DET	AL	1	0	1	1	0	0	0	0	0	0	0	0	0	0	1	0
1957	DET	AL	4	2	2	3	1	0	0	0	0	0	0	0	0	0	3	1
1958	DET	AL	6	4	2	3	2	0	1	1	0	0	0	0	0	0	5	1
1959	WAS	AL	8	5	3	5	3	0	0	0	0	0	3	0	0	0	6	2
1960	WAS	AL	4	3	1	1	3	0	0	0	0	0	0	0	1	0	4	0
1961	MIN	AL	1	0	1	0	1	0	0	0	0	0	0	0	0	0	1	0
	DET	AL	1	1	0	1	0	0	0	0	0	0	0	0	0	0	0	1
	Total		2	1	1	1	1	0	0	0	0	0	0	0	0	0	1	1
Total			27	16	11	15	10	1	1	1	0	0	3	0	1	0	22	5

Rank among batters: 1,532 • Top target (2 home runs): Bob Turley, Billy O'Dell, Dick Donovan, Early Wynn, Ike Delock • *Number of pitchers victimized*: 22 • *Total ballparks homered in*: 7 • *First HR*: 07/11/1954 off Bob Chakales

Bob Bescher

ROBERT HENRY BESCHER
B: 02/25/1884 D: 11/29/1942
BB

Year	Tm	Lg	Tot	H	A	Men-On 0	1	2	3	One-Game 2	3	4	LO	XN	IP	PH	RHP	LHP
1909	CIN	NL	1	0	1	1	0	0	0	0	0	0	1	0	1	0	1	0
1910	CIN	NL	4	2	2	4	0	0	0	0	0	0	2	0	3	0	4	0
1911	CIN	NL	1	0	1	1	0	0	0	0	0	0	0	0	0	0	1	0
1912	CIN	NL	4	1	3	3	1	0	0	0	0	0	2	0	3	0	4	0
1913	CIN	NL	1	1	0	1	0	0	0	0	0	0	0	0	1	0	0	1
1914	NY	NL	6	3	3	5	1	0	0	0	0	0	2	0	3	0	4	2
1915	STL	NL	4	3	1	3	0	0	1	0	0	0	1	0	3	0	4	0
1916	STL	NL	6	4	2	2	0	3	1	0	0	0	0	0	2	0	5	1
1917	STL	NL	1	1	0	1	0	0	0	0	0	0	0	0	0	0	1	0
Total			28	15	13	21	2	3	2	0	0	0	8	0	16	0	24	4

Rank among batters: 1,500 • *Top target (3 home runs)*: Erskine Mayer • *Number of pitchers victimized*: 24 • *Total ballparks homered in*: 11 • *First HR*: 07/14/1909 off Bugs Raymond

Larry Bettencourt

LAWRENCE JOSEPH BETTENCOURT
B: 09/22/1905 D: 09/15/1978
BR

Year	Tm	Lg	Tot	H	A	Men-On				One-Game			LO	XN	IP	PH	RHP	LHP
						0	1	2	3	2	3	4						
1928	STL	AL	4	4	0	1	1	1	1	0	0	0	0	0	0	0	3	1
1931	STL	AL	3	2	1	3	0	0	0	0	0	0	0	1	0	0	2	1
1932	STL	AL	1	1	0	1	0	0	0	0	0	0	0	0	0	1	0	1
Total			8	7	1	5	1	1	1	0	0	0	0	1	0	1	5	3

Rank among batters: 2,703 • *Total ballparks homered in*: 2 • *First HR*: 06/08/1928 off Eddie Rommel

Bruno Betzel

CHRISTIAN FREDERICK ALBERT JOHN BETZEL
B: 12/06/1894 D: 02/07/1965
BR

Year	Tm	Lg	Tot	H	A	Men-On				One-Game			LO	XN	IP	PH	RHP	LHP
						0	1	2	3	2	3	4						
1916	STL	NL	1	0	1	1	0	0	0	0	0	0	0	0	0	0	1	0
1917	STL	NL	1	0	1	0	1	0	0	0	0	0	0	0	1	0	0	1
Total			2	0	2	1	1	0	0	0	0	0	0	0	1	0	1	1

Rank among batters: 4,129 • *Total ballparks homered in*: 2 • *First HR*: 06/14/1916 off Jack Coombs

Kurt Bevacqua

KURT ANTHONY BEVACQUA
B: 01/23/1947
BR

Year	Tm	Lg	Tot	H	A	Men-On				One-Game			LO	XN	IP	PH	RHP	LHP
						0	1	2	3	2	3	4						
1971	CLE	AL	3	1	2	2	1	0	0	0	0	0	0	0	0	0	0	3
1972	CLE	AL	1	1	0	1	0	0	0	0	0	0	0	0	0	0	0	1
1973	KC	AL	2	1	1	1	0	0	1	0	0	0	0	0	0	1	1	1
1975	MIL	AL	2	1	1	0	2	0	0	0	0	0	0	0	0	0	2	0
1977	TEX	AL	5	3	2	4	1	0	0	1	0	0	0	0	0	0	2	3
1978	TEX	AL	6	1	5	4	1	1	0	0	0	0	0	0	0	0	2	4
1979	SD	NL	1	0	1	1	0	0	0	0	0	0	0	0	0	0	1	0
1981	PIT	NL	1	1	0	1	0	0	0	0	0	0	0	0	0	1	1	0
1983	SD	NL	2	2	0	0	1	0	1	0	0	0	0	0	0	1	1	1
1984	SD	NL	1	1	0	0	1	0	0	0	0	0	0	0	0	1	0	1
1985	SD	NL	3	2	1	0	1	0	2	0	0	0	0	0	0	0	0	3
Total			27	14	13	14	8	1	4	1	0	0	0	0	0	4	10	17

Rank among batters: 1,532 • *Top target (3 home runs)*: Balor Moore • *Number of pitchers victimized*: 25 • *Total ballparks homered in*: 13 • *First HR*: 08/12/1971 off Wilbur Wood • *World Series HR*—2

Hal Bevan

JOSEPH HAROLD BEVAN
B: 11/15/1930 D: 10/05/1968
BR

Year	Tm	Lg	Tot	H	A	Men-On				One-Game			LO	XN	IP	PH	RHP	LHP
						0	1	2	3	2	3	4						
1961	CIN	NL	1	0	1	1	0	0	0	0	0	0	0	0	0	1	0	1

Rank among batters: 4,707 • *Total ballparks homered in*: 1 • *First HR*: 05/12/1961 off Wilmer Mizell

Bill Bevens

FLOYD CLIFFORD BEVENS
B: 10/21/1916 D: 10/26/1991
BR

Year	Tm	Lg	Tot	H	A	Men-On				One-Game			LO	XN	IP	PH	RHP	LHP
						0	1	2	3	2	3	4						
1945	NY	AL	1	0	1	0	0	1	0	0	0	0	0	0	0	0	1	0
1946	NY	AL	2	1	1	1	1	0	0	0	0	0	0	0	0	0	0	2
Total			3	1	2	1	1	1	0	0	0	0	0	0	0	0	1	2

Rank among batters: 3,735 • *Total ballparks homered in*: 3 • *First HR*: 08/01/1945 off Jim Wilson

Buddy Biancalana

ROLAND AMERICO BIANCALANA
B: 02/02/1960
BB

Year	Tm	Lg	Tot	H	A	Men-On				One-Game			LO	XN	IP	PH	RHP	LHP
						0	1	2	3	2	3	4						
1984	KC	AL	2	0	2	0	2	0	0	0	0	0	0	0	0	1	2	0
1985	KC	AL	1	1	0	0	0	1	0	0	0	0	0	0	0	0	1	0
1986	KC	AL	2	0	2	2	0	0	0	0	0	0	0	0	0	0	2	0
1987	KC	AL	1	1	0	0	0	1	0	0	0	0	0	0	0	0	0	1
Total			6	2	4	2	2	2	0	0	0	0	0	0	0	1	5	1

Rank among batters: 2,988 • *Total ballparks homered in*: 3 • *First HR*: 08/18/1984 off Dave Stewart

Jim Bibby

JAMES BLAIR BIBBY
B: 10/29/1944
BR

Year	Tm	Lg	Tot	H	A	Men-On 0	1	2	3	One-Game 2	3	4	LO	XN	IP	PH	RHP	LHP
1978	PIT	NL	1	1	0	1	0	0	0	0	0	0	0	0	0	0	1	0
1979	PIT	NL	2	1	1	1	1	0	0	0	0	0	0	0	0	0	1	1
1980	PIT	NL	1	1	0	1	0	0	0	0	0	0	0	0	0	0	0	1
1981	PIT	NL	1	1	0	0	1	0	0	0	0	0	0	0	0	0	1	0
Total			5	4	1	3	2	0	0	0	0	0	0	0	0	0	3	2

Rank among batters: 3,191 • *Total ballparks homered in*: 2 • *First HR*: 08/18/1978 off Rick Williams

Dante Bichette

ALPHONSE DANTE BICHETTE
B: 11/18/1963
BR

Year	Tm	Lg	Tot	H	A	Men-On 0	1	2	3	One-Game 2	3	4	LO	XN	IP	PH	RHP	LHP
1989	CAL	AL	3	2	1	2	1	0	0	0	0	0	0	0	0	0	0	3
1990	CAL	AL	15	8	7	9	2	4	0	1	0	0	0	1	0	0	10	5
1991	MIL	AL	15	6	9	8	4	2	1	2	0	0	0	0	0	0	9	6
1992	MIL	AL	5	3	2	3	2	0	0	0	0	0	0	0	0	0	3	2
1993	COL	NL	21	11	10	11	7	3	0	0	0	0	0	2	0	0	17	4
1994	COL	NL	27	15	12	15	5	5	2	4	0	0	0	0	0	1	17	10
1995	COL	NL	40	31	9	17	15	7	1	2	0	0	0	1	0	1	26	14
Total			126	76	50	65	36	21	4	9	0	0	0	4	0	2	82	44

Rank among batters: 360 • *Top target (3 home runs)*: Frank Castillo • *Number of pitchers victimized*: 104 • *Total ballparks homered in*: 27 • *First HR*: 04/09/1989 off Steve Trout • *LCS HR*—1

Lou Bierbauer

LOUIS W. BIERBAUER
B: 09/23/1865 D: 01/31/1926
BL

Year	Tm	Lg	Tot	H	A	Men-On 0	1	2	3	One-Game 2	3	4	LO	XN	IP	PH	RHP	LHP
1886	PHI	AA	2	1	1	0	2	0	0	0	0	0	0	0	1	0	1	0
1887	PHI	AA	1	1	0	0	1	0	0	0	0	0	0	0	0	0	1	0
1889	PHI	AA	7	0	7	3	2	1	1	1	0	0	0	0	0	0	5	1
1890	BRO	PL	7	6	1	4	1	2	0	2	0	0	0	0	0	0	3	2
1891	PIT	NL	1	0	1	0	0	1	0	0	0	0	0	0	0	0	1	0
1892	PIT	NL	8	6	2	5	2	1	0	0	0	0	0	0	4	0	7	1
1893	PIT	NL	4	1	3	0	2	2	0	0	0	0	0	0	0	0	3	0
1894	PIT	NL	3	0	3	0	3	0	0	1	0	0	0	0	0	0	2	1
Total			33	15	18	12	13	7	1	4	0	0	0	0	5	0	21	5

Rank among batters: 1,336 • *Top target (3 home runs)*: Silver King • *Number of pitchers victimized*: 26 • *Total ballparks homered in*: 14 • *First HR*: 06/11/1886 off Al Mays • *2 HR in 1 inning*—vs BUF: 07/12/1890

Carson Bigbee

CARSON LEE BIGBEE
B: 03/31/1895 D: 10/17/1964
BL

Year	Tm	Lg	Tot	H	A	Men-On 0	1	2	3	One-Game 2	3	4	LO	XN	IP	PH	RHP	LHP
1918	PIT	NL	1	1	0	1	0	0	0	0	0	0	0	0	1	0	0	1
1919	PIT	NL	2	1	1	2	0	0	0	0	0	0	0	1	1	0	2	0
1920	PIT	NL	4	2	2	1	2	1	0	0	0	0	0	0	3	0	4	0
1921	PIT	NL	3	2	1	1	2	0	0	0	0	0	0	1	3	0	1	2
1922	PIT	NL	5	1	4	3	2	0	0	0	0	0	0	1	1	0	5	0
1926	PIT	NL	2	0	2	1	1	0	0	0	0	0	0	0	1	0	2	0
Total			17	7	10	9	7	1	0	0	0	0	0	3	10	0	14	3

Rank among batters: 1,969 • *Top target (2 home runs)*: Rube Marquard, Dana Fillingim • *Number of pitchers victimized*: 15 • *Total ballparks homered in*: 7 • *First HR*: 07/15/1918 off Rube Marquard

Lyle Bigbee

LYLE RANDOLPH BIGBEE
B: 08/22/1893 D: 08/05/1942
BL

Year	Tm	Lg	Tot	H	A	Men-On 0	1	2	3	One-Game 2	3	4	LO	XN	IP	PH	RHP	LHP
1920	PHI	AL	1	1	0	0	1	0	0	0	0	0	0	0	0	0	1	0

Rank among batters: 4,707 • *Total ballparks homered in*: 1 • *First HR*: 09/04/1920 off Eric Erickson

Elliott Bigelow

ELLIOTT ALLARDICE BIGELOW
B: 10/13/1897 D: 08/10/1933
BL

Year	Tm	Lg	Tot	H	A	Men-On 0	1	2	3	One-Game 2	3	4	LO	XN	IP	PH	RHP	LHP
1929	BOS	AL	1	0	1	1	0	0	0	0	0	0	0	0	0	0	1	0

Rank among batters: 4,707 • *Total ballparks homered in*: 1 • *First HR*: 05/13/1929 off Grady Adkins

Craig Biggio

CRAIG ALAN BIGGIO
B: 12/14/1965
BR

Year	Tm	Lg	Tot	H	A	Men-On 0	1	2	3	One-Game 2	3	4	LO	XN	IP	PH	RHP	LHP
1988	HOU	NL	3	1	2	3	0	0	0	0	0	0	0	1	0	0	1	2
1989	HOU	NL	13	6	7	8	3	1	1	1	0	0	0	0	0	0	12	1
1990	HOU	NL	4	2	2	3	1	0	0	0	0	0	0	0	0	0	2	2
1991	HOU	NL	4	0	4	3	1	0	0	0	0	0	0	0	0	0	3	1
1992	HOU	NL	6	3	3	5	1	0	0	0	0	0	3	0	0	0	3	3
1993	HOU	NL	21	8	13	17	2	2	0	1	0	0	5	0	0	0	13	8
1994	HOU	NL	6	4	2	4	1	0	1	0	0	0	1	0	0	0	6	0
1995	HOU	NL	22	6	16	13	6	3	0	2	0	0	0	1	0	0	15	7
Total			79	30	49	56	15	6	2	4	0	0	9	2	0	0	55	24

Rank among batters: 661 • Top target (2 home runs): John Wetteland, Rusty Richards, Ben Rivera, John Smoltz, Pedro Astacio, Tom Glavine, Sid Fernandez, Anthony Young • *Number of pitchers victimized*: 71 • *Total ballparks homered in*: 14 • *First HR*: 08/22/1988 off Rich Gossage • *All-Star HR*—1

Larry Biittner

LAWRENCE DAVID BIITTNER
B: 07/27/1945
BL

Year	Tm	Lg	Tot	H	A	Men-On 0	1	2	3	One-Game 2	3	4	LO	XN	IP	PH	RHP	LHP
1972	TEX	AL	3	3	0	3	0	0	0	0	0	0	0	0	0	0	3	0
1973	TEX	AL	1	0	1	0	1	0	0	0	0	0	0	0	0	0	1	0
1975	MON	NL	3	2	1	2	0	1	0	0	0	0	0	0	0	0	3	0
1977	CHI	NL	12	8	4	6	6	0	0	1	0	0	0	0	0	0	12	0
1978	CHI	NL	4	4	0	2	2	0	0	0	0	0	0	0	0	0	3	1
1979	CHI	NL	3	1	2	1	2	0	0	0	0	0	0	0	0	1	2	1
1980	CHI	NL	1	1	0	0	1	0	0	0	0	0	0	0	0	1	1	0
1982	CIN	NL	2	0	2	1	0	1	0	0	0	0	0	0	0	0	2	0
Total			29	19	10	15	12	2	0	1	0	0	0	0	0	2	27	2

Rank among batters: 1,465 • *Top target (2 home runs)*: Eric Rasmussen • *Number of pitchers victimized*: 28 • *Total ballparks homered in*: 10 • *First HR*: 06/30/1972 off Lloyd Allen

Dann Bilardello

DANN JAMES BILARDELLO
B: 05/26/1959
BR

Year	Tm	Lg	Tot	H	A	Men-On 0	1	2	3	One-Game 2	3	4	LO	XN	IP	PH	RHP	LHP
1983	CIN	NL	9	7	2	7	2	0	0	0	0	0	0	0	0	0	7	2
1984	CIN	NL	2	2	0	1	1	0	0	0	0	0	0	0	0	0	1	1
1985	CIN	NL	1	1	0	0	1	0	0	0	0	0	0	0	0	0	1	0
1986	MON	NL	4	1	3	1	2	1	0	0	0	0	0	0	0	0	4	0
1989	PIT	NL	2	1	1	1	1	0	0	0	0	0	0	0	0	0	0	2
Total			18	12	6	10	7	1	0	0	0	0	0	0	0	0	13	5

Rank among batters: 1,914 • *Top target (2 home runs)*: Andy Hawkins • *Number of pitchers victimized*: 17 • *Total ballparks homered in*: 8 • *First HR*: 04/26/1983 off Tom Seaver

Steve Bilko

STEPHEN THOMAS BILKO
B: 11/13/1928 D: 03/07/1978
BR

Year	Tm	Lg	Tot	H	A	Men-On 0	1	2	3	One-Game 2	3	4	LO	XN	IP	PH	RHP	LHP
1951	STL	NL	2	1	1	2	0	0	0	0	0	0	0	0	0	0	2	0
1952	STL	NL	1	0	1	0	1	0	0	0	0	0	0	0	0	0	0	1
1953	STL	NL	21	11	10	13	5	2	1	2	0	0	0	0	0	0	16	5
1954	CHI	NL	4	3	1	1	3	0	0	0	0	0	0	0	0	0	1	3
1958	CIN	NL	4	1	3	2	2	0	0	0	0	0	0	0	0	0	3	1
	LA	NL	7	5	2	3	2	2	0	0	0	0	0	0	0	0	3	4
	Total		11	6	5	5	4	2	0	0	0	0	0	0	0	0	6	5
1960	DET	AL	9	3	6	6	2	1	0	0	0	0	0	0	0	0	3	6
1961	LA	AL	20	11	9	11	5	4	0	0	0	0	0	1	0	1	7	13
1962	LA	AL	8	2	6	6	1	1	0	1	0	0	0	0	0	0	2	6
Total			76	37	39	44	21	10	1	3	0	0	0	1	0	1	37	39

Rank among batters: 695 • *Top target (4 home runs)*: Joe Nuxhall, Don Mossi • *Number of pitchers victimized*: 59 • *Total ballparks homered in*: 21 • *First HR*: 04/22/1951 off Bob Rush

Dick Billings

RICHARD ARLIN BILLINGS
B: 12/04/1942
BR

Year	Tm	Lg	Tot	H	A	Men-On 0	1	2	3	One-Game 2	3	4	LO	XN	IP	PH	RHP	LHP
1968	WAS	AL	1	1	0	0	1	0	0	0	0	0	0	0	0	0	0	1

Dick Billings *continued*

Year	Tm	Lg	Tot	H	A	Men-On 0	1	2	3	One-Game 2	3	4	LO	XN	IP	PH	RHP	LHP
1970	WAS	AL	1	0	1	1	0	0	0	0	0	0	0	0	0	0	0	1
1971	WAS	AL	6	2	4	2	1	2	1	0	0	0	0	0	0	0	5	1
1972	TEX	AL	5	3	2	1	2	2	0	0	0	0	0	0	0	0	4	1
1973	TEX	AL	3	2	1	1	1	1	0	0	0	0	0	0	0	0	2	1
Total			16	8	8	5	5	5	1	0	0	0	0	0	0	0	11	5

Rank among batters: 2,029 • *Top target (2 home runs)*: Mel Stottlemyre • *Number of pitchers victimized*: 15 • *Total ballparks homered in*: 8 • *First HR*: 09/22/1968 off John Hiller

George Binks

GEORGE ALVIN BINKS
B: 07/11/1916
BL

Year	Tm	Lg	Tot	H	A	Men-On 0	1	2	3	One-Game 2	3	4	LO	XN	IP	PH	RHP	LHP
1945	WAS	AL	6	0	6	1	3	1	1	0	0	0	0	0	0	0	5	1
1947	PHI	AL	2	0	2	2	0	0	0	0	0	0	0	0	0	0	2	0
Total			8	0	8	3	3	1	1	0	0	0	0	0	0	0	7	1

Rank among batters: 2,703 • *Total ballparks homered in*: 4 • *First HR*: 05/20/1945 off Stubby Overmire

Jud Birchall

ADONIRAM JUDSON BIRCHALL
B: 1858 D: 12/22/1887

Year	Tm	Lg	Tot	H	A	Men-On 0	1	2	3	One-Game 2	3	4	LO	XN	IP	PH	RHP	LHP
1883	PHI	AA	1	0	1	1	0	0	0	0	0	0	1	0	0	0	1	0

Rank among batters: 4,707 • *Total ballparks homered in*: 1 • *First HR*: 09/13/1883 off Frank Mountain

Frank Bird

FRANK ZEPHRIN BIRD
B: 03/10/1869 D: 05/20/1958
BR

Year	Tm	Lg	Tot	H	A	Men-On 0	1	2	3	One-Game 2	3	4	LO	XN	IP	PH	RHP	LHP
1892	STL	NL	1	0	1	1	0	0	0	0	0	0	0	0	0	0	1	0

Rank among batters: 4,707 • *Total ballparks homered in*: 1 • *First HR*: 04/25/1892 off Elton Chamberlin

Joe Birmingham

JOSEPH LEO BIRMINGHAM
B: 08/06/1884 D: 04/24/1946
BR

Year	Tm	Lg	Tot	H	A	Men-On 0	1	2	3	One-Game 2	3	4	LO	XN	IP	PH	RHP	LHP
1907	CLE	AL	1	0	1	1	0	0	0	0	0	0	0	0	0	0	1	0
1908	CLE	AL	2	1	1	0	2	0	0	0	0	0	0	0	1	0	1	1
1909	CLE	AL	1	0	1	0	0	1	0	0	0	0	0	0	0	0	1	0
1911	CLE	AL	2	1	1	1	0	1	0	0	0	0	0	0	0	0	2	0
1912	CLE	AL	1	0	1	0	1	0	0	0	0	0	0	0	1	0	1	0
Total			7	2	5	2	3	2	0	0	0	0	0	0	2	0	6	1

Rank among batters: 2,834 • *Total ballparks homered in*: 5 • *First HR*: 09/20/1907 off Tex Pruiett

Babe Birrer

WERNER JOSEPH BIRRER
B: 07/04/1928
BR

Year	Tm	Lg	Tot	H	A	Men-On 0	1	2	3	One-Game 2	3	4	LO	XN	IP	PH	RHP	LHP
1955	DET	AL	2	2	0	0	0	2	0	1	0	0	0	0	0	0	1	1

Rank among batters: 4,129 • *Total ballparks homered in*: 1 • *First HR*: 07/19/1955 off George Zuverink

Tim Birtsas

TIMOTHY DEAN BIRTSAS
B: 09/05/1960
BL

Year	Tm	Lg	Tot	H	A	Men-On 0	1	2	3	One-Game 2	3	4	LO	XN	IP	PH	RHP	LHP
1989	CIN	NL	1	1	0	1	0	0	0	0	0	0	0	0	0	0	0	1

Rank among batters: 4,707 • *Total ballparks homered in*: 1 • *First HR*: 07/02/1989 off Sid Fernandez

John Bischoff

JOHN GEORGE BISCHOFF
B: 10/28/1894 D: 12/28/1981
BR

Year	Tm	Lg	Tot	H	A	Men-On 0	1	2	3	One-Game 2	3	4	LO	XN	IP	PH	RHP	LHP
1925	BOS	AL	1	0	1	1	0	0	0	0	0	0	0	0	0	0	0	1

Rank among batters: 4,707 • *Total ballparks homered in*: 1 • *First HR*: 08/22/1925 off Dave Danforth

						Men-On				One-Game								
Year	Tm	Lg	Tot	H	A	0	1	2	3	2	3	4	LO	XN	IP	PH	RHP	LHP

Max Bishop

MAX FREDERICK BISHOP
B: 09/05/1899 D: 02/24/1962
BL

Year	Tm	Lg	Tot	H	A	0	1	2	3	2	3	4	LO	XN	IP	PH	RHP	LHP
1924	PHI	AL	2	1	1	1	1	0	0	0	0	0	1	0	0	0	1	1
1925	PHI	AL	4	1	3	3	1	0	0	0	0	0	0	1	0	0	4	0
1928	PHI	AL	6	2	4	4	2	0	0	0	0	0	0	0	0	0	6	0
1929	PHI	AL	3	2	1	3	0	0	0	0	0	0	1	0	0	0	3	0
1930	PHI	AL	10	7	3	9	1	0	0	1	0	0	3	0	0	0	9	1
1931	PHI	AL	5	1	4	2	2	1	0	0	0	0	0	0	0	0	4	1
1932	PHI	AL	5	3	2	3	2	0	0	0	0	0	2	1	0	0	5	0
1933	PHI	AL	4	2	2	3	0	1	0	0	0	0	2	0	0	0	3	1
1934	BOS	AL	1	0	1	1	0	0	0	0	0	0	0	0	0	0	1	0
1935	BOS	AL	1	0	1	0	1	0	0	0	0	0	0	0	0	0	1	0
Total			41	19	22	29	10	2	0	1	0	0	9	2	0	0	37	4

Rank among batters: 1,163 • *Top target (3 home runs)*: Waite Hoyt, Red Ruffing • *Number of pitchers victimized*: 31 • *Total ballparks homered in*: 7 • *First HR*: 07/10/1924 off Stan Coveleski

Del Bissonette

DELPHIA LOUIS BISSONETTE
B: 09/06/1899 D: 06/09/1972
BL

Year	Tm	Lg	Tot	H	A	0	1	2	3	2	3	4	LO	XN	IP	PH	RHP	LHP
1928	BRO	NL	25	12	13	13	5	6	1	0	0	0	0	2	0	0	15	10
1929	BRO	NL	12	7	5	7	2	3	0	0	0	0	0	0	0	0	9	3
1930	BRO	NL	16	9	7	8	5	1	2	1	0	0	0	1	2	0	10	6
1931	BRO	NL	12	6	6	7	2	3	0	0	0	0	0	1	0	0	6	6
1933	BRO	NL	1	1	0	1	0	0	0	0	0	0	0	0	0	0	1	0
Total			66	35	31	36	14	13	3	1	0	0	0	4	2	0	41	25

Rank among batters: 786 • *Top target (4 home runs)*: Charlie Root, Jesse Haines, Carl Hubbell • *Number of pitchers victimized*: 41 • *Total ballparks homered in*: 7 • *First HR*: 04/13/1928 off Ray Benge

Jeff Bittiger

JEFFREY SCOTT BITTIGER
B: 04/13/1962
BR

Year	Tm	Lg	Tot	H	A	0	1	2	3	2	3	4	LO	XN	IP	PH	RHP	LHP
1986	PHI	NL	1	0	1	1	0	0	0	0	0	0	0	0	0	0	0	1

Rank among batters: 4,707 • *Total ballparks homered in*: 1 • *First HR*: 09/22/1986 off Bob Kipper

George Bjorkman

GEORGE ANTON BJORKMAN
B: 08/26/1956
BR

Year	Tm	Lg	Tot	H	A	0	1	2	3	2	3	4	LO	XN	IP	PH	RHP	LHP
1983	HOU	NL	2	1	1	0	1	1	0	0	0	0	0	0	0	0	2	0

Rank among batters: 4,129 • *Total ballparks homered in*: 2 • *First HR*: 07/13/1983 off Bryn Smith

Bob Black

ROBERT BENJAMIN BLACK
B: 12/10/1862 D: 03/21/1933

Year	Tm	Lg	Tot	H	A	0	1	2	3	2	3	4	LO	XN	IP	PH	RHP	LHP
1884	KC	UA	1	0	1	1	0	0	0	0	0	0	0	0	0	0	1	0

Rank among batters: 4,707 • *Total ballparks homered in*: 1 • *First HR*: 09/22/1884 off Al Atkinson

Ron Blackburn

RONALD HAMILTON BLACKBURN
B: 04/23/1935
BR

Year	Tm	Lg	Tot	H	A	0	1	2	3	2	3	4	LO	XN	IP	PH	RHP	LHP
1959	PIT	NL	1	1	0	1	0	0	0	0	0	0	0	0	0	0	1	0

Rank among batters: 4,707 • *Total ballparks homered in*: 1 • *First HR*: 06/06/1959 off Moe Drabowsky

Lena Blackburne

RUSSELL AUBREY BLACKBURNE
B: 10/23/1886 D: 02/29/1968
BR

Year	Tm	Lg	Tot	H	A	0	1	2	3	2	3	4	LO	XN	IP	PH	RHP	LHP
1914	CHI	AL	1	0	1	1	0	0	0	0	0	0	0	0	1	0	0	1
1918	CIN	NL	1	1	0	0	1	0	0	0	0	0	0	0	1	0	1	0
1919	PHI	NL	2	1	1	1	1	0	0	0	0	0	0	0	1	0	1	1
Total			4	2	2	2	2	0	0	0	0	0	0	0	3	0	2	2

Rank among batters: 3,427 • *Total ballparks homered in*: 4 • *First HR*: 07/08/1914 off Dutch Leonard

Ewell Blackwell

EWELL BLACKWELL
B: 10/23/1922
BR

Year	Tm	Lg	Tot	H	A	Men-On 0	1	2	3	One-Game 2	3	4	LO	XN	IP	PH	RHP	LHP
1951	CIN	NL	1	0	1	1	0	0	0	0	0	0	0	0	0	0	0	1

Rank among batters: 4,707 • *Total ballparks homered in*: 1 • *First HR*: 07/15/1951 off Preacher Roe

Tim Blackwell

TIMOTHY P. BLACKWELL
B: 08/19/1952
BB

Year	Tm	Lg	Tot	H	A	Men-On 0	1	2	3	One-Game 2	3	4	LO	XN	IP	PH	RHP	LHP
1980	CHI	NL	5	4	1	1	2	2	0	0	0	0	0	0	0	0	5	0
1981	CHI	NL	1	1	0	0	1	0	0	0	0	0	0	0	0	0	1	0
Total			6	5	1	1	3	2	0	0	0	0	0	0	0	0	6	0

Rank among batters: 2,988 • *Total ballparks homered in*: 2 • *First HR*: 05/30/1980 off Dan Larson

Ray Blades

FRANCIS RAYMOND BLADES
B: 08/06/1896 D: 05/18/1979
BR

Year	Tm	Lg	Tot	H	A	Men-On 0	1	2	3	One-Game 2	3	4	LO	XN	IP	PH	RHP	LHP
1922	STL	NL	3	1	2	2	0	1	0	0	0	0	0	0	0	0	3	0
1923	STL	NL	5	2	3	3	2	0	0	0	0	0	0	0	0	0	5	0
1924	STL	NL	11	3	8	7	2	2	0	0	0	0	2	0	1	0	7	4
1925	STL	NL	12	7	5	12	0	0	0	1	0	0	2	0	1	0	8	4
1926	STL	NL	8	5	3	5	2	1	0	0	0	0	1	0	0	0	8	0
1927	STL	NL	2	1	1	2	0	0	0	0	0	0	1	0	0	0	2	0
1928	STL	NL	1	0	1	0	0	1	0	0	0	0	0	0	0	1	0	1
1930	STL	NL	4	1	3	3	0	1	0	0	0	0	0	0	0	0	0	4
1931	STL	NL	1	0	1	1	0	0	0	0	0	0	0	0	0	0	0	1
1932	STL	NL	3	2	1	1	1	1	0	0	0	0	0	0	0	0	1	2
Total			50	22	28	36	7	7	0	1	0	0	6	0	2	1	34	16

Rank among batters: 991 • *Top target (4 home runs)*: Elmer Jacobs • *Number of pitchers victimized*: 37 • *Total ballparks homered in*: 7 • *First HR*: 09/01/1922 off Johnny Morrison

Rick Bladt

RICHARD ALAN BLADT
B: 12/09/1946
BR

Year	Tm	Lg	Tot	H	A	Men-On 0	1	2	3	One-Game 2	3	4	LO	XN	IP	PH	RHP	LHP
1975	NY	AL	1	1	0	1	0	0	0	0	0	0	0	0	0	0	0	1

Rank among batters: 4,707 • *Total ballparks homered in*: 1 • *First HR*: 08/23/1975 off Andy Hassler

George Blaeholder

GEORGE FRANKLIN BLAEHOLDER
B: 01/26/1904 D: 12/29/1947
BR

Year	Tm	Lg	Tot	H	A	Men-On 0	1	2	3	One-Game 2	3	4	LO	XN	IP	PH	RHP	LHP
1928	STL	AL	2	1	1	2	0	0	0	0	0	0	0	0	0	0	1	1
1929	STL	AL	1	0	1	0	0	1	0	0	0	0	0	0	1	0	0	1
Total			3	1	2	2	0	1	0	0	0	0	0	0	1	0	1	2

Rank among batters: 3,735 • *Total ballparks homered in*: 2 • *First HR*: 07/08/1928 off Hank Johnson

Buddy Blair

LOUIS NATHAN BLAIR
B: 09/10/1910
BL

Year	Tm	Lg	Tot	H	A	Men-On 0	1	2	3	One-Game 2	3	4	LO	XN	IP	PH	RHP	LHP
1942	PHI	AL	5	2	3	2	1	1	1	0	0	0	0	0	0	0	5	0

Rank among batters: 3,191 • *Total ballparks homered in*: 4 • *First HR*: 04/15/1942 off Joe Dobson

Footsie Blair

CLARENCE VICK BLAIR
B: 07/13/1900 D: 07/01/1982
BL

Year	Tm	Lg	Tot	H	A	Men-On 0	1	2	3	One-Game 2	3	4	LO	XN	IP	PH	RHP	LHP
1929	CHI	NL	1	0	1	1	0	0	0	0	0	0	0	0	0	0	1	0
1930	CHI	NL	6	5	1	3	1	2	0	0	0	0	0	0	2	0	3	3

Footsie Blair *continued*

Year	Tm	Lg	Tot	H	A	Men-On				One-Game			LO	XN	IP	PH	RHP	LHP
						0	1	2	3	2	3	4						
1931	CHI	NL	3	2	1	0	2	1	0	0	0	0	0	0	1	1	3	0
Total			10	7	3	4	3	3	0	0	0	0	0	0	3	1	7	3

Rank among batters: 2,500 • *Total ballparks homered in*: 2 • *First HR*: 07/01/1929 off Jesse Haines

Paul Blair

PAUL L.D. BLAIR
B: 02/01/1944
BR

Year	Tm	Lg	Tot	H	A	Men-On 0	Men-On 1	Men-On 2	Men-On 3	One-Game 2	One-Game 3	One-Game 4	LO	XN	IP	PH	RHP	LHP
1965	BAL	AL	5	1	4	4	1	0	0	0	0	0	2	0	0	0	4	1
1966	BAL	AL	6	3	3	5	1	0	0	0	0	0	0	0	0	0	1	5
1967	BAL	AL	11	3	8	9	1	1	0	0	0	0	1	0	0	1	7	4
1968	BAL	AL	7	3	4	5	0	2	0	0	0	0	0	1	0	0	1	6
1969	BAL	AL	26	11	15	17	7	2	0	3	0	0	0	2	1	0	19	7
1970	BAL	AL	18	8	10	9	7	2	0	2	1	0	0	0	0	0	9	9
1971	BAL	AL	10	4	6	7	2	0	1	0	0	0	1	0	0	0	6	4
1972	BAL	AL	8	5	3	7	0	1	0	0	0	0	0	0	0	0	4	4
1973	BAL	AL	10	4	6	5	2	2	1	1	0	0	0	0	2	0	5	5
1974	BAL	AL	17	7	10	10	5	1	1	0	0	0	1	0	0	0	7	10
1975	BAL	AL	5	4	1	3	0	2	0	0	0	0	0	0	0	0	2	3
1976	BAL	AL	3	1	2	1	2	0	0	0	0	0	0	1	0	0	0	3
1977	NY	AL	4	2	2	0	4	0	0	0	0	0	0	0	0	0	1	3
1978	NY	AL	2	1	1	1	0	1	0	0	0	0	0	1	0	0	1	1
1979	CIN	NL	2	0	2	1	1	0	0	0	0	0	0	0	0	0	0	2
Total			134	57	77	84	33	14	3	6	1	0	5	5	3	1	67	67

Rank among batters: 331 • *Top target (5 home runs)*: Fritz Peterson, Jim Kaat • *Number of pitchers victimized*: 95 • *Total ballparks homered in*: 17 • *First HR*: 04/17/1965 off Bill Monbouquette • *World Series HR*—1; *LCS HR*—2

Walter Blair

WALTER ALLEN BLAIR
B: 10/13/1883 D: 08/20/1948
BR

Year	Tm	Lg	Tot	H	A	Men-On 0	Men-On 1	Men-On 2	Men-On 3	One-Game 2	One-Game 3	One-Game 4	LO	XN	IP	PH	RHP	LHP
1908	NY	AL	1	1	0	0	1	0	0	0	0	0	0	0	0	0	1	0
1915	BUF	FL	2	0	2	2	0	0	0	0	0	0	0	0	0	0	2	0
Total			3	1	2	2	1	0	0	0	0	0	0	0	0	0	3	0

Rank among batters: 3,735 • *Total ballparks homered in*: 2 • *First HR*: 09/07/1908 off Tom Hughes

Harry Blake

HARRY COOPER BLAKE
B: 06/16/1874 D: 10/14/1919
BR

Year	Tm	Lg	Tot	H	A	Men-On 0	Men-On 1	Men-On 2	Men-On 3	One-Game 2	One-Game 3	One-Game 4	LO	XN	IP	PH	RHP	LHP
1894	CLE	NL	1	1	0	1	0	0	0	0	0	0	0	0	1	0	1	0
1895	CLE	NL	3	1	2	2	1	0	0	0	0	0	0	0	0	0	2	1
1896	CLE	NL	1	0	1	0	0	1	0	0	0	0	0	0	0	0	0	1
1897	CLE	NL	1	1	0	0	1	0	0	0	0	0	0	0	0	0	1	0
1899	STL	NL	2	2	0	1	0	1	0	0	0	0	0	0	0	1	0	2
Total			8	5	3	4	2	2	0	0	0	0	0	0	1	1	4	4

Rank among batters: 2,703 • *Top target (2 home runs)*: Cy Seymour • *Number of pitchers victimized*: 7 • *Total ballparks homered in*: 5 • *First HR*: 07/31/1894 off George Hemming

Johnny Blanchard

JOHN EDWIN BLANCHARD
B: 02/26/1933
BL

Year	Tm	Lg	Tot	H	A	Men-On 0	Men-On 1	Men-On 2	Men-On 3	One-Game 2	One-Game 3	One-Game 4	LO	XN	IP	PH	RHP	LHP
1959	NY	AL	2	1	1	2	0	0	0	0	0	0	0	0	0	0	2	0
1960	NY	AL	4	4	0	3	1	0	0	0	0	0	0	0	0	0	3	1
1961	NY	AL	21	14	7	13	5	2	1	3	0	0	0	2	0	4	19	2
1962	NY	AL	13	8	5	7	2	4	0	0	0	0	0	1	0	1	12	1
1963	NY	AL	16	8	8	9	3	2	2	3	0	0	0	0	0	0	15	1
1964	NY	AL	7	5	2	3	3	1	0	0	0	0	0	0	0	1	7	0
1965	NY	AL	1	0	1	1	0	0	0	0	0	0	0	0	0	0	1	0
	KC	AL	2	2	0	2	0	0	0	0	0	0	0	0	0	0	2	0
	MIL	NL	1	0	1	1	0	0	0	0	0	0	0	0	0	1	1	0

Year	Tm	Lg	Tot	H	A	Men-On 0	1	2	3	One-Game 2	3	4	LO	XN	IP	PH	RHP	LHP

Johnny Blanchard *continued*

Year	Tm	Lg	Tot	H	A	0	1	2	3	2	3	4	LO	XN	IP	PH	RHP	LHP
1965	Total		4	2	2	4	0	0	0	0	0	0	0	0	0	1	4	0
Total			67	42	25	41	14	9	3	6	0	0	0	3	0	7	62	5

Rank among batters: 777 • *Top target (5 home runs)*: Milt Pappas • *Number of pitchers victimized*: 48 • *Total ballparks homered in*: 10 • *First HR*: 06/03/1959 off Frank Lary • *World Series HR*—2

Fred Blanding

FREDERICK JAMES BLANDING
B: 02/08/1888 D: 07/16/1950
BR

Year	Tm	Lg	Tot	H	A	0	1	2	3	2	3	4	LO	XN	IP	PH	RHP	LHP
1912	CLE	AL	1	0	1	0	1	0	0	0	0	0	0	0	0	0	1	0

Rank among batters: 4,707 • *Total ballparks homered in*: 1 • *First HR*: 08/27/1912 off Iron Davis

Lance Blankenship

LANCE ROBERT BLANKENSHIP
B: 12/06/1963
BR

Year	Tm	Lg	Tot	H	A	0	1	2	3	2	3	4	LO	XN	IP	PH	RHP	LHP
1989	OAK	AL	1	1	0	1	0	0	0	0	0	0	0	0	0	0	0	1
1991	OAK	AL	3	0	3	2	1	0	0	0	0	0	0	0	0	0	2	1
1992	OAK	AL	3	1	2	3	0	0	0	0	0	0	0	0	0	0	3	0
1993	OAK	AL	2	2	0	1	0	1	0	0	0	0	0	0	0	0	2	0
Total			9	4	5	7	1	1	0	0	0	0	0	0	0	0	7	2

Rank among batters: 2,587 • *Top target (2 home runs)*: Danny Darwin • *Number of pitchers victimized*: 8 • *Total ballparks homered in*: 6 • *First HR*: 04/21/1989 off Chuck Finley

Ted Blankenship

THEODORE BLANKENSHIP
B: 05/10/1901 D: 01/14/1945
BR

Year	Tm	Lg	Tot	H	A	0	1	2	3	2	3	4	LO	XN	IP	PH	RHP	LHP
1923	CHI	AL	3	3	0	2	1	0	0	0	0	0	0	0	0	0	1	2
1924	CHI	AL	1	1	0	1	0	0	0	0	0	0	0	0	0	0	1	0
1925	CHI	AL	2	1	1	0	1	1	0	0	0	0	0	0	0	0	2	0
1927	CHI	AL	3	0	3	2	1	0	0	0	0	0	0	0	0	0	3	0
Total			9	5	4	5	3	1	0	0	0	0	0	0	0	0	7	2

Rank among batters: 2,587 • *Total ballparks homered in*: 4 • *First HR*: 05/18/1923 off Bonnie Hollingsworth

Larvell Blanks

LARVELL BLANKS
B: 01/28/1950
BR

Year	Tm	Lg	Tot	H	A	0	1	2	3	2	3	4	LO	XN	IP	PH	RHP	LHP
1972	ATL	NL	1	0	1	1	0	0	0	0	0	0	0	0	0	0	1	0
1975	ATL	NL	3	1	2	2	1	0	0	0	0	0	0	0	0	0	1	2
1976	CLE	AL	5	4	1	3	2	0	0	0	0	0	0	0	0	0	0	5
1977	CLE	AL	6	5	1	3	2	1	0	1	0	0	0	0	0	1	5	1
1978	CLE	AL	2	1	1	2	0	0	0	0	0	0	0	0	0	0	1	1
1979	TEX	AL	1	1	0	1	0	0	0	0	0	0	0	0	0	0	1	0
1980	ATL	NL	2	2	0	2	0	0	0	0	0	0	0	1	0	0	0	2
Total			20	14	6	14	5	1	0	1	0	0	0	1	0	1	9	11

Rank among batters: 1,810 • *Total ballparks homered in*: 7 • *First HR*: 08/05/1972 off Jack Billingham

Don Blasingame

DON LEE BLASINGAME
B: 03/16/1932
BL

Year	Tm	Lg	Tot	H	A	0	1	2	3	2	3	4	LO	XN	IP	PH	RHP	LHP
1957	STL	NL	8	4	4	3	5	0	0	0	0	0	1	0	0	0	6	2
1958	STL	NL	2	1	1	0	2	0	0	0	0	0	0	0	0	0	1	1
1959	STL	NL	1	0	1	1	0	0	0	0	0	0	0	0	0	0	0	1
1960	SF	NL	2	0	2	0	1	1	0	0	0	0	0	0	1	0	1	1
1961	CIN	NL	1	0	1	1	0	0	0	0	0	0	1	0	0	0	0	1
1962	CIN	NL	2	0	2	2	0	0	0	0	0	0	0	0	0	0	2	0
1963	WAS	AL	2	0	2	2	0	0	0	0	0	0	1	0	0	0	2	0
1964	WAS	AL	1	1	0	1	0	0	0	0	0	0	0	0	0	0	1	0
1965	WAS	AL	1	1	0	1	0	0	0	0	0	0	0	0	0	0	1	0

Don Blasingame *continued*

Year	Tm	Lg	Tot	H	A	Men-On 0	Men-On 1	Men-On 2	Men-On 3	One-Game 2	One-Game 3	One-Game 4	LO	XN	IP	PH	RHP	LHP
1966	WAS	AL	1	0	1	1	0	0	0	0	0	0	0	0	0	0	1	0
Total			21	7	14	12	8	1	0	0	0	0	3	0	1	0	15	6

Rank among batters: 1,768 • *Top target (2 home runs)*: Phil Regan • *Number of pitchers victimized*: 20 • *Total ballparks homered in*: 9 • *First HR*: 05/12/1957 off Red Murff

Wade Blasingame

WADE ALLEN BLASINGAME
B: 11/22/1943
BL

Year	Tm	Lg	Tot	H	A	Men-On 0	Men-On 1	Men-On 2	Men-On 3	One-Game 2	One-Game 3	One-Game 4	LO	XN	IP	PH	RHP	LHP
1964	MIL	NL	1	1	0	0	1	0	0	0	0	0	0	0	0	0	1	0
1965	MIL	NL	1	0	1	1	0	0	0	0	0	0	0	0	0	0	1	0
1971	HOU	NL	1	0	1	1	0	0	0	0	0	0	0	0	0	0	0	1
Total			3	1	2	2	1	0	0	0	0	0	0	0	0	0	2	1

Rank among batters: 3,735 • *Total ballparks homered in*: 3 • *First HR*: 06/26/1964 off Tracy Stallard

Steve Blass

STEPHEN ROBERT BLASS
B: 04/18/1942
BR

Year	Tm	Lg	Tot	H	A	Men-On 0	Men-On 1	Men-On 2	Men-On 3	One-Game 2	One-Game 3	One-Game 4	LO	XN	IP	PH	RHP	LHP
1969	PIT	NL	1	0	1	0	0	1	0	0	0	0	0	0	0	0	0	1

Rank among batters: 4,707 • *Total ballparks homered in*: 1 • *First HR*: 09/05/1969 off Ken Holtzman

Johnny Blatnik

JOHN LOUIS BLATNIK
B: 03/10/1921
BR

Year	Tm	Lg	Tot	H	A	Men-On 0	Men-On 1	Men-On 2	Men-On 3	One-Game 2	One-Game 3	One-Game 4	LO	XN	IP	PH	RHP	LHP
1948	PHI	NL	6	5	1	4	1	1	0	0	0	0	0	0	0	0	4	2

Rank among batters: 2,988 • *Total ballparks homered in*: 2 • *First HR*: 05/23/1948 off Red Munger

Buddy Blattner

ROBERT GARNETT BLATTNER
B: 02/08/1920
BR

Year	Tm	Lg	Tot	H	A	Men-On 0	Men-On 1	Men-On 2	Men-On 3	One-Game 2	One-Game 3	One-Game 4	LO	XN	IP	PH	RHP	LHP
1946	NY	NL	11	7	4	8	2	0	1	1	0	0	1	1	0	0	8	3
1949	PHI	NL	5	1	4	2	2	1	0	0	0	0	0	0	0	1	4	1
Total			16	8	8	10	4	1	1	1	0	0	1	1	0	1	12	4

Rank among batters: 2,029 • *Top target (2 home runs)*: Hank Borowy • *Number of pitchers victimized*: 15 • *Total ballparks homered in*: 6 • *First HR*: 04/28/1946 off Glen Moulder

Jeff Blauser

JEFFREY MICHAEL BLAUSER
B: 11/08/1965
BR

Year	Tm	Lg	Tot	H	A	Men-On 0	Men-On 1	Men-On 2	Men-On 3	One-Game 2	One-Game 3	One-Game 4	LO	XN	IP	PH	RHP	LHP
1987	ATL	NL	2	1	1	1	1	0	0	0	0	0	0	0	0	0	0	2
1988	ATL	NL	2	2	0	2	0	0	0	0	0	0	0	0	0	0	1	1
1989	ATL	NL	12	5	7	11	1	0	0	1	0	0	0	0	0	0	8	4
1990	ATL	NL	8	3	5	5	2	1	0	1	0	0	0	1	0	1	5	3
1991	ATL	NL	11	7	4	7	1	2	1	0	0	0	0	0	0	0	7	4
1992	ATL	NL	14	5	9	8	5	1	0	0	1	0	0	1	1	0	5	9
1993	ATL	NL	15	4	11	9	5	1	0	1	0	0	0	0	0	0	10	5
1994	ATL	NL	6	3	3	3	3	0	0	0	0	0	0	0	0	0	5	1
1995	ATL	NL	12	7	5	9	2	1	0	0	0	0	0	0	0	0	11	1
Total			82	37	45	55	20	6	1	3	1	0	0	2	1	1	52	30

Rank among batters: 637 • *Top target (3 home runs)*: Mark Portugal • *Number of pitchers victimized*: 72 • *Total ballparks homered in*: 15 • *First HR*: 08/16/1987 off Jim Deshaies • *LCS HR*—3

Gary Blaylock

GARY NELSON BLAYLOCK
B: 10/11/1931
BR

Year	Tm	Lg	Tot	H	A	Men-On 0	Men-On 1	Men-On 2	Men-On 3	One-Game 2	One-Game 3	One-Game 4	LO	XN	IP	PH	RHP	LHP
1959	STL	NL	2	2	0	0	2	0	0	0	0	0	0	0	0	0	1	1
Total			2	2	0	0	2	0	0	0	0	0	0	0	0	0	1	1

Rank among batters: 4,129 • *Total ballparks homered in*: 1 • *First HR*: 05/12/1959 off Jim O'Toole

Marv Blaylock

MARVIN EDWARD BLAYLOCK
B: 09/30/1929 D: 10/23/1993
BL

Year	Tm	Lg	Tot	H	A	Men-On 0	Men-On 1	Men-On 2	Men-On 3	One-Game 2	One-Game 3	One-Game 4	LO	XN	IP	PH	RHP	LHP
1955	PHI	NL	3	1	2	3	0	0	0	0	0	0	0	0	0	0	3	0
1956	PHI	NL	10	3	7	7	3	0	0	0	0	0	0	0	0	0	9	1
1957	PHI	NL	2	1	1	1	0	1	0	0	0	0	0	0	0	2	2	0
Total			15	5	10	11	3	1	0	0	0	0	0	0	0	2	14	1

Rank among batters: 2,096 • *Total ballparks homered in*: 6 • *First HR*: 05/04/1955 off Gerry Staley

Curt Blefary

CURTIS LEROY BLEFARY
B: 07/05/1943
BL

Year	Tm	Lg	Tot	H	A	Men-On 0	Men-On 1	Men-On 2	Men-On 3	One-Game 2	One-Game 3	One-Game 4	LO	XN	IP	PH	RHP	LHP
1965	BAL	AL	22	11	11	13	5	3	1	3	0	0	0	0	0	0	19	3
1966	BAL	AL	23	13	10	18	3	2	0	1	0	0	0	0	0	0	20	3
1967	BAL	AL	22	11	11	12	7	1	2	1	1	0	0	0	0	0	19	3
1968	BAL	AL	15	6	9	10	3	2	0	0	0	0	0	0	0	0	14	1
1969	HOU	NL	12	5	7	3	6	3	0	1	0	0	0	0	0	0	10	2
1970	NY	AL	9	7	2	5	3	1	0	0	0	0	0	0	0	2	8	1
1971	NY	AL	1	0	1	1	0	0	0	0	0	0	0	0	1	0	1	0
	OAK	AL	5	2	3	4	0	1	0	0	0	0	0	0	0	1	5	0
	Total		6	2	4	5	0	1	0	0	0	0	0	0	1	1	6	0
1972	SD	NL	3	0	3	3	0	0	0	0	0	0	0	0	0	1	3	0
Total			112	55	57	69	27	13	3	6	1	0	0	0	1	4	99	13

Rank among batters: 429 • *Top target (7 home runs)*: Denny McLain • *Number of pitchers victimized*: 82 • *Total ballparks homered in*: 17 • *First HR*: 04/17/1965 off Bob Heffner

Ned Bligh

EDWIN FORREST BLIGH
B: 06/30/1864 D: 04/18/1892
BR

Year	Tm	Lg	Tot	H	A	Men-On 0	Men-On 1	Men-On 2	Men-On 3	One-Game 2	One-Game 3	One-Game 4	LO	XN	IP	PH	RHP	LHP
1890	LOU	AA	1	0	1	0	0	1	0	0	0	0	0	0	0	0	0	1

Rank among batters: 4,707 • *Total ballparks homered in*: 1 • *First HR*: 09/01/1890 off Cannonball Titcomb

Jack Bliss

JOHN JOSEPH ALBERT BLISS
B: 01/09/1882 D: 10/23/1968
BR

Year	Tm	Lg	Tot	H	A	Men-On 0	Men-On 1	Men-On 2	Men-On 3	One-Game 2	One-Game 3	One-Game 4	LO	XN	IP	PH	RHP	LHP
1908	STL	NL	1	1	0	1	0	0	0	0	0	0	0	0	1	0	1	0
1909	STL	NL	1	0	1	1	0	0	0	0	0	0	0	0	0	0	1	0
1911	STL	NL	1	0	1	0	0	1	0	0	0	0	0	0	0	0	0	1
Total			3	1	2	2	0	1	0	0	0	0	0	0	1	0	2	1

Rank among batters: 3,735 • *Total ballparks homered in*: 3 • *First HR*: 07/19/1908 off Joe McGinnity

Bruno Block

JAMES JOHN BLOCK
B: 03/13/1885 D: 08/06/1937
BR

Year	Tm	Lg	Tot	H	A	Men-On 0	Men-On 1	Men-On 2	Men-On 3	One-Game 2	One-Game 3	One-Game 4	LO	XN	IP	PH	RHP	LHP
1911	CHI	AL	1	0	1	1	0	0	0	0	0	0	0	0	0	0	1	0

Rank among batters: 4,707 • *Total ballparks homered in*: 1 • *First HR*: 06/19/1911 off Ed Willett

Terry Blocker

TERRY FENNELL BLOCKER
B: 08/18/1959
BL

Year	Tm	Lg	Tot	H	A	Men-On 0	Men-On 1	Men-On 2	Men-On 3	One-Game 2	One-Game 3	One-Game 4	LO	XN	IP	PH	RHP	LHP
1988	ATL	NL	2	1	1	1	1	0	0	0	0	0	0	0	0	0	2	0

Rank among batters: 4,129 • *Total ballparks homered in*: 2 • *First HR*: 08/12/1988 off Frank Williams

Ron Blomberg

RONALD MARK BLOMBERG
B: 08/23/1948
BL

Year	Tm	Lg	Tot	H	A	Men-On 0	Men-On 1	Men-On 2	Men-On 3	One-Game 2	One-Game 3	One-Game 4	LO	XN	IP	PH	RHP	LHP
1971	NY	AL	7	2	5	2	3	2	0	2	0	0	0	0	0	0	7	0

Ron Blomberg *continued*

Year	Tm	Lg	Tot	H	A	Men-On 0	Men-On 1	Men-On 2	Men-On 3	One-Game 2	One-Game 3	One-Game 4	LO	XN	IP	PH	RHP	LHP
1972	NY	AL	14	8	6	8	5	1	0	0	0	0	0	0	0	1	14	0
1973	NY	AL	12	7	5	8	1	3	0	1	0	0	0	0	0	1	11	1
1974	NY	AL	10	3	7	3	5	2	0	1	0	0	0	0	0	1	9	1
1975	NY	AL	4	2	2	2	1	1	0	0	0	0	0	0	0	0	4	0
1978	CHI	AL	5	4	1	2	2	0	1	0	0	0	0	0	0	1	5	0
Total			52	26	26	25	17	9	1	4	0	0	0	0	0	4	50	2

Rank among batters: 965 • *Top target (3 home runs)*: Dick Tidrow, Steve Dunning • *Number of pitchers victimized*: 39 • *Total ballparks homered in*: 11 • *First HR*: 06/25/1971 off Pete Broberg

Jimmy Bloodworth

JAMES HENRY BLOODWORTH
B: 07/26/1917
BR

Year	Tm	Lg	Tot	H	A	Men-On 0	Men-On 1	Men-On 2	Men-On 3	One-Game 2	One-Game 3	One-Game 4	LO	XN	IP	PH	RHP	LHP
1939	WAS	AL	4	0	4	1	3	0	0	0	0	0	0	0	0	0	4	0
1940	WAS	AL	11	4	7	3	4	3	1	0	0	0	0	1	0	0	8	3
1941	WAS	AL	7	1	6	2	4	0	1	0	0	0	0	1	0	0	4	3
1942	DET	AL	13	7	6	8	4	1	0	0	0	0	2	1	0	0	9	4
1943	DET	AL	6	4	2	3	2	1	0	0	0	0	0	0	0	0	4	2
1946	DET	AL	5	4	1	3	2	0	0	0	0	0	0	0	0	0	5	0
1947	PIT	NL	7	3	4	3	3	1	0	0	0	0	0	0	0	0	6	1
1949	CIN	NL	9	4	5	6	2	1	0	1	0	0	0	0	0	0	4	5
Total			62	27	35	29	24	7	2	1	0	0	2	3	0	0	44	18

Rank among batters: 835 • *Top target (4 home runs)*: Elden Auker, Thornton Lee • *Number of pitchers victimized*: 49 • *Total ballparks homered in*: 12 • *First HR*: 07/08/1939 off Cotton Pippen

Mike Blowers

MICHAEL ROY BLOWERS
B: 04/24/1965
BR

Year	Tm	Lg	Tot	H	A	Men-On 0	Men-On 1	Men-On 2	Men-On 3	One-Game 2	One-Game 3	One-Game 4	LO	XN	IP	PH	RHP	LHP
1990	NY	AL	5	1	4	3	2	0	0	1	0	0	0	0	0	0	3	2
1991	NY	AL	1	0	1	1	0	0	0	0	0	0	0	0	0	0	0	1
1992	SEA	AL	1	0	1	1	0	0	0	0	0	0	0	0	0	0	1	0
1993	SEA	AL	15	8	7	8	3	1	3	1	0	0	0	0	0	0	5	10
1994	SEA	AL	9	3	6	5	2	2	0	0	0	0	0	1	1	0	4	5
1995	SEA	AL	23	17	6	9	6	5	3	3	0	0	0	0	0	0	16	7
Total			54	29	25	27	13	8	6	5	0	0	0	1	1	0	29	25

Rank among batters: 938 • *Top target (3 home runs)*: Mike Moore, Wilson Alvarez • *Number of pitchers victimized*: 42 • *Total ballparks homered in*: 15 • *First HR*: 04/21/1990 off Charlie Hough • *LCS HR*—1

Lu Blue

LUZERNE ATWELL BLUE
B: 03/05/1897 D: 07/28/1958
BB

Year	Tm	Lg	Tot	H	A	Men-On 0	Men-On 1	Men-On 2	Men-On 3	One-Game 2	One-Game 3	One-Game 4	LO	XN	IP	PH	RHP	LHP
1921	DET	AL	5	0	5	3	1	1	0	0	0	0	0	0	0	0	5	0
1922	DET	AL	6	1	5	4	1	1	0	0	0	0	1	0	1	0	4	2
1923	DET	AL	1	0	1	0	1	0	0	0	0	0	0	0	0	0	1	0
1924	DET	AL	2	2	0	1	1	0	0	0	0	0	0	0	0	0	1	1
1925	DET	AL	3	1	2	0	1	2	0	0	0	0	0	0	2	0	3	0
1926	DET	AL	1	1	0	0	1	0	0	0	0	0	0	0	0	0	0	1
1927	DET	AL	1	0	1	0	1	0	0	0	0	0	0	0	0	0	1	0
1928	STL	AL	14	11	3	10	4	0	0	1	0	0	0	0	0	0	14	0
1929	STL	AL	6	4	2	5	1	0	0	1	0	0	2	0	0	0	5	1
1930	STL	AL	4	2	2	3	1	0	0	0	0	0	1	0	0	0	4	0
1931	CHI	AL	1	0	1	1	0	0	0	0	0	0	0	0	0	0	1	0
Total			44	22	22	27	13	4	0	2	0	0	4	0	3	0	39	5

Rank among batters: 1,095 • *Top target (3 home runs)*: Elam Vangilder, Ted Lyons, Hank Johnson • *Number of pitchers victimized*: 32 • *Total ballparks homered in*: 6 • *First HR*: 06/03/1921 off Slim Harriss

Vida Blue

VIDA ROCHELLE BLUE
B: 07/28/1949
BB

Year	Tm	Lg	Tot	H	A	Men-On 0	Men-On 1	Men-On 2	Men-On 3	One-Game 2	One-Game 3	One-Game 4	LO	XN	IP	PH	RHP	LHP
1970	OAK	AL	1	0	1	0	0	1	0	0	0	0	0	0	0	0	1	0

Year	Tm	Lg	Tot	H	A	Men-On 0	Men-On 1	Men-On 2	Men-On 3	One-Game 2	One-Game 3	One-Game 4	LO	XN	IP	PH	RHP	LHP

Vida Blue *continued*

Year	Tm	Lg	Tot	H	A	0	1	2	3	2	3	4	LO	XN	IP	PH	RHP	LHP
1978	SF	NL	1	1	0	1	0	0	0	0	0	0	0	0	0	0	1	0
1979	SF	NL	1	0	1	1	0	0	0	0	0	0	0	0	0	0	1	0
1986	SF	NL	1	0	1	1	0	0	0	0	0	0	0	0	0	0	1	0
Total			4	1	3	3	0	1	0	0	0	0	0	0	0	0	4	0

Rank among batters: 3,427 • *Total ballparks homered in*: 4 • *First HR*: 09/07/1970 off Jerry Crider

Ossie Bluege

OSWALD LOUIS BLUEGE
B: 10/24/1900 D: 10/14/1985
BR

Year	Tm	Lg	Tot	H	A	0	1	2	3	2	3	4	LO	XN	IP	PH	RHP	LHP
1923	WAS	AL	2	1	1	1	1	0	0	0	0	0	0	0	1	0	2	0
1924	WAS	AL	2	0	2	1	1	0	0	0	0	0	0	0	1	0	1	1
1925	WAS	AL	4	1	3	2	2	0	0	0	0	0	0	0	0	0	4	0
1926	WAS	AL	3	1	2	0	1	2	0	0	0	0	0	0	1	0	2	1
1927	WAS	AL	1	0	1	0	1	0	0	0	0	0	0	0	0	0	0	1
1928	WAS	AL	2	1	1	1	1	0	0	0	0	0	0	0	1	0	2	0
1929	WAS	AL	5	0	5	4	0	1	0	0	0	0	0	0	0	0	2	3
1930	WAS	AL	3	0	3	0	1	2	0	0	0	0	0	0	0	0	3	0
1931	WAS	AL	8	2	6	5	3	0	0	0	0	0	0	0	2	0	6	2
1932	WAS	AL	5	0	5	3	1	1	0	0	0	0	0	0	0	0	2	3
1933	WAS	AL	6	0	6	2	2	2	0	0	0	0	0	0	0	0	5	1
1936	WAS	AL	1	0	1	1	0	0	0	0	0	0	0	0	0	0	1	0
1937	WAS	AL	1	0	1	1	0	0	0	0	0	0	0	0	0	0	0	1
Total			43	6	37	21	14	8	0	0	0	0	0	0	6	0	30	13

Rank among batters: 1,116 • *Top target (3 home runs)*: Charlie Robertson, Milt Gaston • *Number of pitchers victimized*: 33 • *Total ballparks homered in*: 7 • *First HR*: 05/19/1923 off Charlie Robertson

John Boccabella

JOHN DOMINIC BOCCABELLA
B: 06/29/1941
BR

Year	Tm	Lg	Tot	H	A	0	1	2	3	2	3	4	LO	XN	IP	PH	RHP	LHP
1963	CHI	NL	1	0	1	1	0	0	0	0	0	0	0	0	0	0	1	0
1965	CHI	NL	2	0	2	2	0	0	0	1	0	0	0	0	0	0	0	2
1966	CHI	NL	6	4	2	5	1	0	0	0	0	0	0	0	0	0	4	2
1969	MON	NL	1	1	0	1	0	0	0	0	0	0	0	0	0	0	0	1
1970	MON	NL	5	4	1	2	2	1	0	0	0	0	0	0	0	1	2	3
1971	MON	NL	3	1	2	3	0	0	0	0	0	0	0	1	0	0	2	1
1972	MON	NL	1	1	0	1	0	0	0	0	0	0	0	0	0	0	0	1
1973	MON	NL	7	3	4	4	1	1	1	1	0	0	0	0	0	0	4	3
Total			26	14	12	19	4	2	1	2	0	0	0	1	0	1	13	13

Rank among batters: 1,576 • *Top target (2 home runs)*: Warren Spahn, Ray Sadecki, Ron Herbel • *Number of pitchers victimized*: 23 • *Total ballparks homered in*: 9 • *First HR*: 09/12/1963 off Ernie Broglio • *2 HR in 1 inning*—vs HOU: 07/06/1973 (1)

Milt Bocek

MILTON FRANK BOCEK
B: 07/16/1912
BR

Year	Tm	Lg	Tot	H	A	0	1	2	3	2	3	4	LO	XN	IP	PH	RHP	LHP
1933	CHI	AL	1	0	1	1	0	0	0	0	0	0	0	0	0	0	0	1

Rank among batters: 4,707 • *Total ballparks homered in*: 1 • *First HR*: 09/24/1933 off Thornton Lee

Bruce Bochte

BRUCE ANTON BOCHTE
B: 11/12/1950
BL

Year	Tm	Lg	Tot	H	A	0	1	2	3	2	3	4	LO	XN	IP	PH	RHP	LHP
1974	CAL	AL	5	2	3	3	2	0	0	1	0	0	0	0	0	0	5	0
1975	CAL	AL	3	2	1	0	2	1	0	0	0	0	0	0	0	0	2	1
1976	CAL	AL	2	0	2	1	0	1	0	0	0	0	0	0	0	0	2	0
1977	CAL	AL	2	1	1	1	1	0	0	0	0	0	0	0	0	0	0	2
	CLE	AL	5	2	3	3	2	0	0	0	0	0	0	0	0	0	5	0
	Total		7	3	4	4	3	0	0	0	0	0	0	0	0	0	5	2
1978	SEA	AL	11	8	3	9	2	0	0	0	0	0	0	0	0	0	10	1
1979	SEA	AL	16	11	5	2	8	5	1	0	0	0	0	0	0	0	12	4
1980	SEA	AL	13	10	3	9	4	0	0	0	0	0	0	1	0	0	8	5

Bruce Bochte *continued*

Year	Tm	Lg	Tot	H	A	Men-On 0	1	2	3	One-Game 2	3	4	LO	XN	IP	PH	RHP	LHP
1981	SEA	AL	6	4	2	4	1	1	0	0	0	0	0	0	0	0	3	3
1982	SEA	AL	12	7	5	8	4	0	0	0	0	0	0	0	0	0	9	3
1984	OAK	AL	5	1	4	2	2	1	0	0	0	0	0	0	0	1	5	0
1985	OAK	AL	14	6	8	3	8	3	0	0	0	0	0	0	0	0	10	4
1986	OAK	AL	6	3	3	5	1	0	0	0	0	0	0	0	0	0	6	0
Total			100	57	43	50	37	12	1	1	0	0	0	1	0	1	77	23

Rank among batters: 499 • *Top target (5 home runs)*: Paul Splittorff • *Number of pitchers victimized*: 77 • *Total ballparks homered in*: 14 • *First HR*: 07/28/1974 off Bill Hands

Bruce Bochy

BRUCE DOUGLAS BOCHY
B: 04/16/1955
BR

Year	Tm	Lg	Tot	H	A	Men-On 0	1	2	3	One-Game 2	3	4	LO	XN	IP	PH	RHP	LHP
1978	HOU	NL	3	0	3	3	0	0	0	0	0	0	0	0	0	0	0	3
1979	HOU	NL	1	1	0	1	0	0	0	0	0	0	0	0	0	0	1	0
1982	NY	NL	2	1	1	2	0	0	0	0	0	0	0	0	0	0	1	1
1984	SD	NL	4	0	4	2	2	0	0	0	0	0	0	0	0	0	2	2
1985	SD	NL	6	4	2	4	2	0	0	0	0	0	0	1	0	0	2	4
1986	SD	NL	8	6	2	6	1	1	0	0	0	0	0	1	0	2	0	8
1987	SD	NL	2	1	1	0	1	1	0	0	0	0	0	0	0	0	2	0
Total			26	13	13	18	6	2	0	0	0	0	0	2	0	2	8	18

Rank among batters: 1,576 • *Top target (2 home runs)*: Tom Browning, Bob Kipper • *Number of pitchers victimized*: 24 • *Total ballparks homered in*: 11 • *First HR*: 07/20/1978 off Kevin Kobel

Eddie Bockman

JOSEPH EDWARD BOCKMAN
B: 07/26/1920
BR

Year	Tm	Lg	Tot	H	A	Men-On 0	1	2	3	One-Game 2	3	4	LO	XN	IP	PH	RHP	LHP
1947	CLE	AL	1	1	0	1	0	0	0	0	0	0	0	0	0	0	1	0
1948	PIT	NL	4	2	2	1	3	0	0	0	0	0	0	0	0	0	4	0
1949	PIT	NL	6	6	0	4	2	0	0	1	0	0	0	0	0	0	5	1
Total			11	9	2	6	5	0	0	1	0	0	0	0	0	0	10	1

Rank among batters: 2,419 • *Total ballparks homered in*: 4 • *First HR*: 08/23/1947 off Allie Reynolds

Ping Bodie

FRANK STEPHEN BODIE
B: 10/08/1887 D: 12/17/1961
BR

Year	Tm	Lg	Tot	H	A	Men-On 0	1	2	3	One-Game 2	3	4	LO	XN	IP	PH	RHP	LHP
1911	CHI	AL	4	1	3	1	1	2	0	0	0	0	0	0	0	0	4	0
1912	CHI	AL	5	3	2	2	3	0	0	0	0	0	0	0	0	0	5	0
1913	CHI	AL	8	0	8	5	3	0	0	0	0	0	0	0	0	0	8	0
1914	CHI	AL	3	0	3	3	0	0	0	0	0	0	0	0	0	0	3	0
1917	PHI	AL	7	5	2	3	3	0	1	0	0	0	0	0	0	0	5	2
1918	NY	AL	3	3	0	2	1	0	0	0	0	0	0	0	0	0	3	0
1919	NY	AL	6	4	2	1	4	1	0	1	0	0	0	0	1	0	5	1
1920	NY	AL	7	5	2	1	2	2	2	0	0	0	0	0	1	0	5	2
Total			43	21	22	18	17	5	3	1	0	0	0	0	2	0	38	5

Rank among batters: 1,116 • Top target (2 home runs): George Mullin, Boardwalk Brown, Chief Bender, Dave Davenport, George Dumont, Joe Bush, Eric Erickson, Hooks Dauss, Lefty Williams • *Number of pitchers victimized*: 34 • *Total ballparks homered in*: 8 • *First HR*: 06/03/1911 off Eddie Cicotte

Tony Boeckel

NORMAN DOXIE BOECKEL
B: 08/25/1892 D: 02/16/1924
BR

Year	Tm	Lg	Tot	H	A	Men-On 0	1	2	3	One-Game 2	3	4	LO	XN	IP	PH	RHP	LHP
1919	BOS	NL	1	1	0	1	0	0	0	0	0	0	0	0	1	0	1	0
1920	BOS	NL	3	0	3	1	1	1	0	0	0	0	0	0	0	0	3	0
1921	BOS	NL	10	4	6	3	6	0	1	0	0	0	0	1	7	0	5	5
1922	BOS	NL	6	0	6	5	1	0	0	0	0	0	0	0	0	0	4	2
1923	BOS	NL	7	1	6	3	2	2	0	0	0	0	0	0	1	0	7	0
Total			27	6	21	13	10	3	1	0	0	0	0	1	9	0	20	7

Rank among batters: 1,532 • *Top target (3 home runs)*: Bill Hubbell • *Number of pitchers victimized*: 22 • *Total ballparks homered in*: 7 • *First HR*: 06/28/1919 off Jess Barnes

Joe Boehling

JOHN JOSEPH BOEHLING
B: 03/20/1891 D: 09/08/1941
BL

Year	Tm	Lg	Tot	H	A	Men-On 0	Men-On 1	Men-On 2	Men-On 3	One-Game 2	One-Game 3	One-Game 4	LO	XN	IP	PH	RHP	LHP
1915	WAS	AL	1	0	1	0	1	0	0	0	0	0	0	0	0	0	1	0

Rank among batters: 4,707 • *Total ballparks homered in*: 1 • *First HR*: 04/26/1915 off Ray Fisher

Tim Bogar

TIMOTHY PAUL BOGAR
B: 10/28/1966
BR

Year	Tm	Lg	Tot	H	A	Men-On 0	Men-On 1	Men-On 2	Men-On 3	One-Game 2	One-Game 3	One-Game 4	LO	XN	IP	PH	RHP	LHP
1993	NY	NL	3	1	2	2	0	1	0	1	0	0	0	0	1	0	2	1
1994	NY	NL	2	0	2	1	1	0	0	0	0	0	0	0	0	0	0	2
1995	NY	NL	1	0	1	0	0	1	0	0	0	0	0	0	0	0	0	1
Total			6	1	5	3	1	2	0	1	0	0	0	0	1	0	2	4

Rank among batters: 2,988 • *Top target (2 home runs)*: Kent Mercker • *Number of pitchers victimized*: 5 • *Total ballparks homered in*: 4 • *First HR*: 05/30/1993 off Tom Browning

Terry Bogener

TERRY WAYNE BOGENER
B: 09/28/1955
BL

Year	Tm	Lg	Tot	H	A	Men-On 0	Men-On 1	Men-On 2	Men-On 3	One-Game 2	One-Game 3	One-Game 4	LO	XN	IP	PH	RHP	LHP
1982	TEX	AL	1	0	1	1	0	0	0	0	0	0	0	0	0	0	1	0

Rank among batters: 4,707 • *Total ballparks homered in*: 1 • *First HR*: 06/18/1982 off Robert Castillo

Tommy Boggs

THOMAS WINTON BOGGS
B: 10/25/1955
BR

Year	Tm	Lg	Tot	H	A	Men-On 0	Men-On 1	Men-On 2	Men-On 3	One-Game 2	One-Game 3	One-Game 4	LO	XN	IP	PH	RHP	LHP
1978	ATL	NL	1	1	0	1	0	0	0	0	0	0	0	0	0	0	1	0

Rank among batters: 4,707 • *Total ballparks homered in*: 1 • *First HR*: 05/05/1978 off Joe Niekro

Wade Boggs

WADE ANTHONY BOGGS
B: 06/15/1958
BL

Year	Tm	Lg	Tot	H	A	Men-On 0	Men-On 1	Men-On 2	Men-On 3	One-Game 2	One-Game 3	One-Game 4	LO	XN	IP	PH	RHP	LHP
1982	BOS	AL	5	4	1	1	3	1	0	0	0	0	0	1	0	0	5	0
1983	BOS	AL	5	2	3	4	1	0	0	0	0	0	0	0	0	0	4	1
1984	BOS	AL	6	5	1	4	2	0	0	1	0	0	1	0	0	0	4	2
1985	BOS	AL	8	6	2	6	2	0	0	0	0	0	0	0	0	0	6	2
1986	BOS	AL	8	3	5	4	3	0	1	0	0	0	0	0	0	0	5	3
1987	BOS	AL	24	10	14	13	9	1	1	1	0	0	1	0	0	0	17	7
1988	BOS	AL	5	4	1	4	1	0	0	0	0	0	0	0	1	0	3	2
1989	BOS	AL	3	2	1	3	0	0	0	0	0	0	0	0	0	0	3	0
1990	BOS	AL	6	3	3	4	2	0	0	0	0	0	1	0	0	0	5	1
1991	BOS	AL	8	6	2	5	3	0	0	0	0	0	1	0	0	0	6	2
1992	BOS	AL	7	4	3	5	0	1	1	1	0	0	0	0	0	0	6	1
1993	NY	AL	2	1	1	1	0	1	0	0	0	0	0	1	0	0	1	1
1994	NY	AL	11	6	5	8	1	2	0	1	0	0	0	0	0	0	10	1
1995	NY	AL	5	4	1	4	0	1	0	0	0	0	1	0	0	1	4	1
Total			103	60	43	66	27	7	3	4	0	0	5	2	1	1	79	24

Rank among batters: 477 • *Top target (4 home runs)*: Dave Stewart • *Number of pitchers victimized*: 85 • *Total ballparks homered in*: 18 • *First HR*: 06/22/1982 off Dave Tobik • *LCS HR—2; All-Star HR—1*

Sam Bohne

SAMUEL ARTHUR BOHNE
B: 10/22/1896 D: 05/23/1977
BR

Year	Tm	Lg	Tot	H	A	Men-On 0	Men-On 1	Men-On 2	Men-On 3	One-Game 2	One-Game 3	One-Game 4	LO	XN	IP	PH	RHP	LHP
1921	CIN	NL	3	1	2	3	0	0	0	0	0	0	1	0	2	0	3	0
1922	CIN	NL	3	2	1	0	3	0	0	0	0	0	0	0	0	0	2	1
1923	CIN	NL	3	0	3	1	1	1	0	0	0	0	0	0	0	0	3	0
1924	CIN	NL	4	0	4	4	0	0	0	1	0	0	0	0	0	0	4	0
1925	CIN	NL	2	0	2	1	0	1	0	0	0	0	0	1	0	0	1	1
1926	BRO	NL	1	0	1	1	0	0	0	0	0	0	0	0	0	0	1	0
Total			16	3	13	10	4	2	0	1	0	0	1	1	2	0	14	2

Rank among batters: 2,029 • *Top target (4 home runs)*: Tony Kaufmann • *Number of pitchers victimized*: 13 • *Total ballparks homered in*: 5 • *First HR*: 05/28/1921 off Whitey Glazner

Bruce Boisclair

BRUCE ARMAND BOISCLAIR
B: 12/09/1952
BL

Year	Tm	Lg	Tot	H	A	Men-On 0	Men-On 1	Men-On 2	Men-On 3	One-Game 2	One-Game 3	One-Game 4	LO	XN	IP	PH	RHP	LHP
1976	NY	NL	2	2	0	2	0	0	0	0	0	0	0	0	0	1	2	0
1977	NY	NL	4	2	2	0	3	1	0	0	0	0	0	0	0	1	4	0
1978	NY	NL	4	2	2	2	2	0	0	0	0	0	0	0	0	0	4	0
Total			10	6	4	4	5	1	0	0	0	0	0	0	0	2	10	0

Rank among batters: 2,500 • *Total ballparks homered in*: 5 • *First HR*: 08/28/1976 off Rick Rhoden

Bob Boken

ROBERT ANTHONY BOKEN
B: 02/23/1908 D: 10/08/1988
BR

Year	Tm	Lg	Tot	H	A	Men-On 0	Men-On 1	Men-On 2	Men-On 3	One-Game 2	One-Game 3	One-Game 4	LO	XN	IP	PH	RHP	LHP
1933	WAS	AL	3	0	3	2	1	0	0	0	0	0	0	1	0	0	3	0
1934	CHI	AL	3	2	1	1	1	0	1	0	0	0	0	0	0	0	3	0
Total			6	2	4	3	2	0	1	0	0	0	0	1	0	0	6	0

Rank among batters: 2,988 • *Total ballparks homered in*: 4 • *First HR*: 05/07/1933 off Schoolboy Rowe

Joe Boley

JOHN PETER BOLEY
B: 07/19/1896 D: 12/30/1962
BR

Year	Tm	Lg	Tot	H	A	Men-On 0	Men-On 1	Men-On 2	Men-On 3	One-Game 2	One-Game 3	One-Game 4	LO	XN	IP	PH	RHP	LHP
1927	PHI	AL	1	0	1	1	0	0	0	0	0	0	0	0	0	0	1	0
1929	PHI	AL	2	2	0	2	0	0	0	0	0	0	0	0	0	0	2	0
1930	PHI	AL	4	2	2	4	0	0	0	1	0	0	0	0	0	0	3	1
Total			7	4	3	7	0	0	0	1	0	0	0	0	0	0	6	1

Rank among batters: 2,834 • *Top target (2 home runs)*: General Crowder • *Number of pitchers victimized*: 6 • *Total ballparks homered in*: 3 • *First HR*: 07/15/1927 off Tommy Thomas

Jim Bolger

JAMES CYRIL BOLGER
B: 02/23/1932
BR

Year	Tm	Lg	Tot	H	A	Men-On 0	Men-On 1	Men-On 2	Men-On 3	One-Game 2	One-Game 3	One-Game 4	LO	XN	IP	PH	RHP	LHP
1957	CHI	NL	5	3	2	3	1	1	0	0	0	0	0	0	0	1	2	3
1958	CHI	NL	1	1	0	0	0	1	0	0	0	0	0	0	0	1	1	0
Total			6	4	2	3	1	2	0	0	0	0	0	0	0	2	3	3

Rank among batters: 2,988 • *Top target (2 home runs)*: Luis Arroyo • *Number of pitchers victimized*: 5 • *Total ballparks homered in*: 3 • *First HR*: 04/24/1957 off Joe Nuxhall

Frank Bolick

FRANK CHARLES BOLICK
B: 06/28/1966
BB

Year	Tm	Lg	Tot	H	A	Men-On 0	Men-On 1	Men-On 2	Men-On 3	One-Game 2	One-Game 3	One-Game 4	LO	XN	IP	PH	RHP	LHP
1993	MON	NL	4	2	2	1	2	1	0	0	0	0	0	0	0	0	2	2

Rank among batters: 3,427 • *Total ballparks homered in*: 3 • *First HR*: 04/29/1993 off Steve Wilson

Bobby Bolin

BOBBY DONALD BOLIN
B: 01/29/1939
BR

Year	Tm	Lg	Tot	H	A	Men-On 0	Men-On 1	Men-On 2	Men-On 3	One-Game 2	One-Game 3	One-Game 4	LO	XN	IP	PH	RHP	LHP
1963	SF	NL	1	0	1	0	1	0	0	0	0	0	0	0	0	0	0	1
1965	SF	NL	1	0	1	0	1	0	0	0	0	0	0	0	0	0	1	0
1966	SF	NL	2	2	0	1	1	0	0	0	0	0	0	0	0	0	1	1
1969	SF	NL	1	0	1	0	1	0	0	0	0	0	0	0	0	0	1	0
1970	MIL	AL	1	1	0	1	0	0	0	0	0	0	0	0	0	0	1	0
Total			6	3	3	2	4	0	0	0	0	0	0	0	0	0	4	2

Rank among batters: 2,988 • *Total ballparks homered in*: 5 • *First HR*: 09/13/1963 off Joe Gibbon

Frank Bolling

FRANK ELMORE BOLLING
B: 11/16/1931
BR

Year	Tm	Lg	Tot	H	A	Men-On 0	Men-On 1	Men-On 2	Men-On 3	One-Game 2	One-Game 3	One-Game 4	LO	XN	IP	PH	RHP	LHP
1954	DET	AL	6	3	3	5	1	0	0	0	0	0	0	0	0	0	4	2
1956	DET	AL	7	4	3	5	1	1	0	0	0	0	0	0	0	0	6	1
1957	DET	AL	15	9	6	13	2	0	0	1	0	0	2	1	0	0	12	3

Year	Tm	Lg	Tot	H	A	Men-On 0	1	2	3	One-Game 2	3	4	LO	XN	IP	PH	RHP	LHP

Frank Bolling *continued*

Year	Tm	Lg	Tot	H	A	Men-On 0	1	2	3	One-Game 2	3	4	LO	XN	IP	PH	RHP	LHP
1958	DET	AL	14	3	11	9	2	3	0	1	0	0	1	0	0	0	12	2
1959	DET	AL	13	8	5	8	4	1	0	1	0	0	0	0	0	0	11	2
1960	DET	AL	9	3	6	2	2	5	0	0	0	0	0	0	0	0	8	1
1961	MIL	NL	15	6	9	10	4	1	0	0	0	0	0	0	0	0	8	7
1962	MIL	NL	9	4	5	6	3	0	0	0	0	0	0	0	0	0	7	2
1963	MIL	NL	5	2	3	4	1	0	0	0	0	0	0	0	0	0	4	1
1964	MIL	NL	5	1	4	2	3	0	0	1	0	0	0	0	0	0	5	0
1965	MIL	NL	7	4	3	4	2	0	1	0	0	0	0	0	0	0	4	3
1966	ATL	NL	1	0	1	1	0	0	0	0	0	0	0	0	0	0	0	1
Total			106	47	59	69	25	11	1	4	0	0	3	1	0	0	81	25

Rank among batters: 451 • *Top target (4 home runs)*: Pedro Ramos, Arnie Portocarrero, Hal Brown • *Number of pitchers victimized*: 76 • *Total ballparks homered in*: 18 • *First HR*: 04/13/1954 off Don Larsen

Jack Bolling

JOHN EDWARD BOLLING
B: 02/20/1917
BL

Year	Tm	Lg	Tot	H	A	Men-On 0	1	2	3	One-Game 2	3	4	LO	XN	IP	PH	RHP	LHP
1939	PHI	NL	3	0	3	2	1	0	0	0	0	0	0	0	1	0	3	0
1944	BRO	NL	1	1	0	0	1	0	0	0	0	0	0	0	0	0	1	0
Total			4	1	3	2	2	0	0	0	0	0	0	0	1	0	4	0

Rank among batters: 3,427 • *Total ballparks homered in*: 3 • *First HR*: 06/28/1939 off Bill Lohrman

Milt Bolling

MILTON JOSEPH BOLLING
B: 08/09/1930
BR

Year	Tm	Lg	Tot	H	A	Men-On 0	1	2	3	One-Game 2	3	4	LO	XN	IP	PH	RHP	LHP
1952	BOS	AL	1	0	1	1	0	0	0	0	0	0	0	0	0	0	1	0
1953	BOS	AL	5	3	2	5	0	0	0	0	0	0	0	0	0	0	3	2
1954	BOS	AL	6	5	1	2	2	2	0	1	0	0	1	0	0	0	4	2
1956	BOS	AL	3	2	1	3	0	0	0	0	0	0	1	0	0	1	1	2
1957	WAS	AL	4	2	2	3	0	1	0	0	0	0	0	0	0	0	2	2
Total			19	12	7	14	2	3	0	1	0	0	2	0	0	1	11	8

Rank among batters: 1,861 • *Total ballparks homered in*: 7 • *First HR*: 09/16/1952 off Duane Pillette

Don Bollweg

DONALD RAYMOND BOLLWEG
B: 02/12/1921
BL

Year	Tm	Lg	Tot	H	A	Men-On 0	1	2	3	One-Game 2	3	4	LO	XN	IP	PH	RHP	LHP
1953	NY	AL	6	5	1	4	0	2	0	0	0	0	0	0	0	0	5	1
1954	PHI	AL	5	1	4	2	3	0	0	0	0	0	0	0	0	0	4	1
Total			11	6	5	6	3	2	0	0	0	0	0	0	0	0	9	2

Rank among batters: 2,419 • *Total ballparks homered in*: 6 • *First HR*: 05/13/1953 off Mike Garcia

Cliff Bolton

WILLIAM CLIFTON BOLTON
B: 04/10/1907 D: 04/21/1979
BL

Year	Tm	Lg	Tot	H	A	Men-On 0	1	2	3	One-Game 2	3	4	LO	XN	IP	PH	RHP	LHP
1934	WAS	AL	1	0	1	0	0	0	1	0	0	0	0	0	0	1	1	0
1935	WAS	AL	2	0	2	1	1	0	0	0	0	0	0	0	0	0	1	1
1936	WAS	AL	2	1	1	1	0	1	0	0	0	0	0	0	0	0	2	0
1937	DET	AL	1	1	0	0	1	0	0	0	0	0	0	0	0	0	1	0
Total			6	2	4	2	2	1	1	0	0	0	0	0	0	1	5	1

Rank among batters: 2,988 • *Total ballparks homered in*: 5 • *First HR*: 09/10/1934 off Hugo Klaerner

Walt Bond

WALTER FRANKLIN BOND
B: 10/19/1937 D: 09/14/1967
BL

Year	Tm	Lg	Tot	H	A	Men-On 0	1	2	3	One-Game 2	3	4	LO	XN	IP	PH	RHP	LHP
1960	CLE	AL	5	2	3	2	3	0	0	1	0	0	0	0	0	0	5	0
1961	CLE	AL	2	1	1	1	0	0	1	0	0	0	0	0	0	1	2	0
1962	CLE	AL	6	2	4	3	3	0	0	2	0	0	0	0	0	0	6	0

Walt Bond *continued*

Year	Tm	Lg	Tot	H	A	Men-On 0	1	2	3	One-Game 2	3	4	LO	XN	IP	PH	RHP	LHP
1964	HOU	NL	20	8	12	12	7	1	0	1	0	0	0	1	0	0	15	5
1965	HOU	NL	7	1	6	5	2	0	0	0	0	0	0	0	0	0	6	1
1967	MIN	AL	1	0	1	0	1	0	0	0	0	0	0	0	0	1	1	0
Total			41	14	27	23	16	1	1	4	0	0	0	1	0	2	35	6

Rank among batters: 1,163 • *Top target (3 home runs)*: Don Lee, Larry Jackson, Don Drysdale • *Number of pitchers victimized*: 30 • *Total ballparks homered in*: 13 • *First HR*: 04/23/1960 off Bob Trowbridge

Barry Bonds

BARRY LAMAR BONDS
B: 07/24/1964
BL

Year	Tm	Lg	Tot	H	A	Men-On 0	1	2	3	One-Game 2	3	4	LO	XN	IP	PH	RHP	LHP
1986	PIT	NL	16	9	7	12	3	1	0	0	0	0	3	0	0	0	13	3
1987	PIT	NL	25	12	13	15	6	4	0	2	0	0	5	0	1	0	17	8
1988	PIT	NL	24	14	10	19	4	1	0	3	0	0	8	0	0	1	15	9
1989	PIT	NL	19	7	12	14	3	2	0	1	0	0	3	0	0	1	15	4
1990	PIT	NL	33	14	19	19	10	3	1	3	0	0	1	0	0	0	16	17
1991	PIT	NL	25	12	13	8	13	4	0	2	0	0	0	1	0	0	18	7
1992	PIT	NL	34	15	19	16	12	5	1	1	0	0	0	0	0	0	22	12
1993	SF	NL	46	21	25	24	15	6	1	7	0	0	0	2	0	0	32	14
1994	SF	NL	37	15	22	24	11	1	1	4	1	0	0	0	0	0	26	11
1995	SF	NL	33	16	17	19	10	4	0	3	0	0	0	0	0	0	28	5
Total			292	135	157	170	87	31	4	26	1	0	20	3	1	2	202	90

Rank among batters: 72 • *Top target (6 home runs)*: Terry Mulholland, Greg Maddux • *Number of pitchers victimized*: 187 • *Total ballparks homered in*: 15 • *First HR*: 06/04/1986 off Craig McMurtry • *LCS HR*—1

Bobby Bonds

BOBBY LEE BONDS
B: 03/15/1946
BR

Year	Tm	Lg	Tot	H	A	Men-On 0	1	2	3	One-Game 2	3	4	LO	XN	IP	PH	RHP	LHP
1968	SF	NL	9	8	1	4	2	2	1	2	0	0	2	0	0	0	8	1
1969	SF	NL	32	23	9	17	11	4	0	4	0	0	5	0	0	0	30	2
1970	SF	NL	26	14	12	22	3	1	0	2	0	0	5	1	1	0	22	4
1971	SF	NL	33	17	16	17	11	5	0	1	0	0	3	0	0	0	24	9
1972	SF	NL	26	14	12	16	5	5	0	0	0	0	2	2	0	0	19	7
1973	SF	NL	39	19	20	26	8	3	2	2	0	0	11	2	0	1	26	13
1974	SF	NL	21	8	13	12	5	3	1	0	0	0	0	0	0	0	17	4
1975	NY	AL	32	9	23	16	11	5	0	4	0	0	4	0	0	1	21	11
1976	CAL	AL	10	6	4	6	2	1	1	0	0	0	0	0	0	0	8	2
1977	CAL	AL	37	18	19	16	20	1	0	1	0	0	0	1	1	0	26	11
1978	CHI	AL	2	1	1	2	0	0	0	0	0	0	0	0	0	0	1	1
	TEX	AL	29	14	15	15	10	4	0	3	0	0	0	0	0	0	21	8
	Total		31	15	16	17	10	4	0	3	0	0	0	0	0	0	22	9
1979	CLE	AL	25	19	6	12	8	3	2	0	0	0	1	0	0	0	20	5
1980	STL	NL	5	1	4	4	1	0	0	0	0	0	2	0	0	0	4	1
1981	CHI	NL	6	2	4	3	2	1	0	2	0	0	0	0	0	0	4	2
Total			332	173	159	188	99	38	7	21	0	0	35	6	2	2	251	81

Rank among batters: 52 • *Top target (7 home runs)*: Dave Roberts • *Number of pitchers victimized*: 201 • *Total ballparks homered in*: 29 • *First HR*: 06/25/1968 off John Purdin • *All-Star HR*—1

Bobby Bonilla

ROBERTO MARTIN ANTONIO BONILLA
B: 02/23/1963
BB

Year	Tm	Lg	Tot	H	A	Men-On 0	1	2	3	One-Game 2	3	4	LO	XN	IP	PH	RHP	LHP
1986	CHI	AL	2	2	0	0	1	1	0	0	0	0	0	0	0	0	2	0
	PIT	NL	1	0	1	0	1	0	0	0	0	0	0	0	0	1	1	0
	Total		3	2	1	1	1	1	0	0	0	0	0	0	0	1	3	0
1987	PIT	NL	15	7	8	9	2	4	0	2	0	0	0	1	0	0	8	7
1988	PIT	NL	24	9	15	12	8	4	0	1	0	0	0	1	0	0	18	6
1989	PIT	NL	24	13	11	18	5	1	0	1	0	0	0	3	0	0	16	8
1990	PIT	NL	32	13	19	20	6	4	2	3	0	0	0	0	0	0	18	14
1991	PIT	NL	18	9	9	7	9	2	0	1	0	0	0	0	0	0	4	14
1992	NY	NL	19	5	14	10	5	3	1	1	0	0	0	1	0	0	16	3
1993	NY	NL	34	18	16	21	11	2	0	5	0	0	0	2	0	0	24	10
1994	NY	NL	20	8	12	12	7	1	0	2	0	0	0	0	0	0	11	9

Bobby Bonilla *continued*

Year	Tm	Lg	Tot	H	A	Men-On 0	1	2	3	One-Game 2	3	4	LO	XN	IP	PH	RHP	LHP
1995	NY	NL	18	7	11	14	4	0	0	2	0	0	0	1	0	0	14	4
	BAL	AL	10	7	3	3	5	1	1	0	0	0	0	0	0	0	6	4
	Total		28	14	14	17	9	1	1	2	0	0	0	1	0	0	20	8
Total			217	98	119	127	63	23	4	18	0	0	0	9	0	1	138	79

Rank among batters: 157 • *Top target (10 home runs)*: Tom Browning • *Number of pitchers victimized*: 147 • *Total ballparks homered in*: 20 • *First HR*: 05/03/1986 off Phil Niekro • *Switch hit HR in 1 game*—6 times

Juan Bonilla

JUAN GUILLERMO (URANIA) BONILLA
B: 01/12/1956
BR

Year	Tm	Lg	Tot	H	A	Men-On 0	1	2	3	One-Game 2	3	4	LO	XN	IP	PH	RHP	LHP
1981	SD	NL	1	1	0	1	0	0	0	0	0	0	0	0	0	0	1	0
1983	SD	NL	4	3	1	3	1	0	0	0	0	0	0	0	0	0	2	2
1986	BAL	AL	1	0	1	1	0	0	0	0	0	0	1	0	0	0	0	1
1987	NY	AL	1	1	0	1	0	0	0	0	0	0	0	0	0	0	0	1
Total			7	5	2	6	1	0	0	0	0	0	1	0	0	0	3	4

Rank among batters: 2,834 • *Total ballparks homered in*: 4 • *First HR*: 05/17/1981 off Nino Espinosa

Barry Bonnell

ROBERT BARRY BONNELL
B: 10/27/1953
BR

Year	Tm	Lg	Tot	H	A	Men-On 0	1	2	3	One-Game 2	3	4	LO	XN	IP	PH	RHP	LHP
1977	ATL	NL	1	1	0	0	0	0	1	0	0	0	0	0	0	0	1	0
1978	ATL	NL	1	1	0	1	0	0	0	0	0	0	0	0	0	0	1	0
1979	ATL	NL	12	9	3	7	5	0	0	0	0	0	0	0	0	0	10	2
1980	TOR	AL	13	4	9	7	4	1	1	0	0	0	0	0	0	0	8	5
1981	TOR	AL	4	2	2	2	0	2	0	0	0	0	0	0	0	0	1	3
1982	TOR	AL	6	4	2	3	2	1	0	0	0	0	0	0	0	0	1	5
1983	TOR	AL	10	6	4	5	4	0	1	0	0	0	0	1	1	0	4	6
1984	SEA	AL	8	4	4	2	5	1	0	0	0	0	0	1	0	0	4	4
1985	SEA	AL	1	1	0	0	1	0	0	0	0	0	0	0	0	0	1	0
Total			56	32	24	27	21	5	3	0	0	0	0	2	1	0	31	25

Rank among batters: 913 • *Top target (3 home runs)*: Charlie Hough • *Number of pitchers victimized*: 50 • *Total ballparks homered in*: 15 • *First HR*: 06/05/1977 off Randy Moffitt

Frank Bonner

FRANK J. BONNER
B: 08/20/1869 D: 12/31/1905
BR

Year	Tm	Lg	Tot	H	A	Men-On 0	1	2	3	One-Game 2	3	4	LO	XN	IP	PH	RHP	LHP
1895	STL	NL	1	0	1	1	0	0	0	0	0	0	0	0	0	0	1	0
1899	WAS	NL	2	2	0	0	1	1	0	0	0	0	0	0	0	0	2	0
1903	BOS	NL	1	0	1	0	0	0	1	0	0	0	0	0	0	0	1	0
Total			4	2	2	1	1	1	1	0	0	0	0	0	0	0	4	0

Rank among batters: 3,427 • *Total ballparks homered in*: 3 • *First HR*: 06/14/1895 off Brickyard Kennedy

Zeke Bonura

HENRY JOHN BONURA
B: 09/20/1908 D: 03/09/1987
BR

Year	Tm	Lg	Tot	H	A	Men-On 0	1	2	3	One-Game 2	3	4	LO	XN	IP	PH	RHP	LHP
1934	CHI	AL	27	21	6	12	9	5	1	4	0	0	0	1	0	0	25	2
1935	CHI	AL	21	12	9	11	6	4	0	3	0	0	0	0	0	0	19	2
1936	CHI	AL	12	4	8	6	2	4	0	3	0	0	0	0	0	0	12	0
1937	CHI	AL	19	11	8	12	4	2	1	1	0	0	0	0	0	0	16	3
1938	WAS	AL	22	11	11	7	10	3	2	0	0	0	0	0	0	0	14	8
1939	NY	NL	11	5	6	5	4	2	0	1	0	0	0	0	0	1	11	0
1940	WAS	AL	3	1	2	1	1	0	1	0	0	0	0	0	0	0	3	0
	CHI	NL	4	2	2	2	1	1	0	0	0	0	0	0	0	0	1	3
	Total		7	3	4	3	2	1	1	0	0	0	0	0	0	0	4	3
Total			119	67	52	56	37	21	5	12	0	0	0	1	0	1	101	18

Rank among batters: 392 • *Top target (5 home runs)*: Tommy Bridges • *Number of pitchers victimized*: 73 • *Total ballparks homered in*: 13 • *First HR*: 04/18/1934 off Vic Sorrell

Buddy Booker

RICHARD LEE BOOKER
B: 05/28/1942
BL

Year	Tm	Lg	Tot	H	A	Men-On 0	1	2	3	One-Game 2	3	4	LO	XN	IP	PH	RHP	LHP
1966	CLE	AL	2	0	2	1	1	0	0	0	0	0	0	0	0	0	2	0

Rank among batters: 4,129 • *Total ballparks homered in*: 2 • *First HR*: 06/18/1966 off Ron Kline

Al Bool

ALBERT J. BOOL
B: 08/24/1897 D: 09/27/1981
BR

Year	Tm	Lg	Tot	H	A	Men-On 0	1	2	3	One-Game 2	3	4	LO	XN	IP	PH	RHP	LHP
1930	PIT	NL	7	1	6	3	2	2	0	1	0	0	0	0	0	0	2	5

Rank among batters: 2,834 • *Total ballparks homered in*: 5 • *First HR*: 06/05/1930 off Jumbo Elliott

Bob Boone

ROBERT RAYMOND BOONE
B: 11/19/1947
BR

Year	Tm	Lg	Tot	H	A	Men-On 0	1	2	3	One-Game 2	3	4	LO	XN	IP	PH	RHP	LHP
1972	PHI	NL	1	0	1	1	0	0	0	0	0	0	0	0	0	0	1	0
1973	PHI	NL	10	4	6	8	2	0	0	0	0	0	0	0	0	0	9	1
1974	PHI	NL	3	3	0	2	0	1	0	0	0	0	0	0	0	0	2	1
1975	PHI	NL	2	0	2	2	0	0	0	0	0	0	0	0	0	0	2	0
1976	PHI	NL	4	3	1	1	1	1	1	0	0	0	0	0	1	0	3	1
1977	PHI	NL	11	7	4	9	2	0	0	0	0	0	0	0	0	0	9	2
1978	PHI	NL	12	8	4	9	2	1	0	0	0	0	0	0	0	1	9	3
1979	PHI	NL	9	4	5	6	2	1	0	0	0	0	0	0	0	0	7	2
1980	PHI	NL	9	5	4	6	3	0	0	0	0	0	0	0	0	0	9	0
1981	PHI	NL	4	2	2	3	1	0	0	0	0	0	0	0	0	0	4	0
1982	CAL	AL	7	5	2	4	3	0	0	1	0	0	0	0	0	0	4	3
1983	CAL	AL	9	6	3	6	3	0	0	0	0	0	0	0	0	0	5	4
1984	CAL	AL	3	1	2	3	0	0	0	0	0	0	0	1	0	0	3	0
1985	CAL	AL	5	0	5	4	1	0	0	0	0	0	0	0	0	0	4	1
1986	CAL	AL	7	1	6	4	1	1	1	0	0	0	0	0	0	0	5	2
1987	CAL	AL	3	1	2	3	0	0	0	0	0	0	0	0	0	0	3	0
1988	CAL	AL	5	3	2	3	2	0	0	0	0	0	0	0	0	0	4	1
1989	KC	AL	1	1	0	0	0	1	0	0	0	0	0	0	0	0	1	0
Total			105	54	51	74	23	6	2	1	0	0	0	1	1	1	84	21

Rank among batters: 462 • *Top target (4 home runs)*: Bob Forsch, Jack Morris • *Number of pitchers victimized*: 84 • *Total ballparks homered in*: 20 • *First HR*: 09/21/1972 off Jim Bibby • *LCS HR*—2

Bret Boone

BRET ROBERT BOONE
B: 04/06/1969
BR

Year	Tm	Lg	Tot	H	A	Men-On 0	1	2	3	One-Game 2	3	4	LO	XN	IP	PH	RHP	LHP
1992	SEA	AL	4	2	2	2	2	0	0	0	0	0	0	0	0	0	4	0
1993	SEA	AL	12	7	5	6	5	1	0	0	0	0	0	0	0	0	8	4
1994	CIN	NL	12	5	7	7	5	0	0	0	0	0	0	1	0	0	10	2
1995	CIN	NL	15	6	9	10	3	2	0	2	0	0	0	1	0	0	11	4
Total			43	20	23	25	15	3	0	2	0	0	0	2	0	0	33	10

Rank among batters: 1,116 • *Top target (4 home runs)*: Kevin Foster • *Number of pitchers victimized*: 37 • *Total ballparks homered in*: 16 • *First HR*: 08/22/1992 off Mike Gardiner • *LCS HR*—1

Ike Boone

ISAAC MORGAN BOONE
B: 02/17/1897 D: 08/01/1958
BL

Year	Tm	Lg	Tot	H	A	Men-On 0	1	2	3	One-Game 2	3	4	LO	XN	IP	PH	RHP	LHP
1924	BOS	AL	13	4	9	7	4	1	1	0	0	0	0	0	0	0	8	5
1925	BOS	AL	9	4	5	7	1	1	0	0	0	0	0	0	1	0	8	1
1927	CHI	AL	1	0	1	0	1	0	0	0	0	0	0	0	0	1	1	0
1930	BRO	NL	3	3	0	1	2	0	0	0	0	0	0	0	0	0	3	0
Total			26	11	15	15	8	2	1	0	0	0	0	0	1	1	20	6

Rank among batters: 1,576 • Top target (2 home runs): Dave Danforth, Bob Shawkey, Joe Bush, Syl Johnson • *Number of pitchers victimized*: 22 • *Total ballparks homered in*: 5 • *First HR*: 04/24/1924 off Bob Shawkey

Luke Boone

LUTE JOSEPH BOONE
B: 05/06/1890 D: 07/29/1982
BR

Year	Tm	Lg	Tot	H	A	Men-On 0	1	2	3	One-Game 2	3	4	LO	XN	IP	PH	RHP	LHP
1915	NY	AL	5	5	0	2	2	1	0	0	0	0	0	0	1	0	3	2
1916	NY	AL	1	1	0	0	1	0	0	0	0	0	0	0	0	0	0	1
Total			6	6	0	2	3	1	0	0	0	0	0	0	1	0	3	3

Rank among batters: 2,988 • *Total ballparks homered in*: 1 • *First HR*: 04/22/1915 off Jim Shaw

Ray Boone

RAYMOND OTIS BOONE
B: 07/27/1923
BR

Year	Tm	Lg	Tot	H	A	Men-On 0	1	2	3	One-Game 2	3	4	LO	XN	IP	PH	RHP	LHP
1949	CLE	AL	4	1	3	1	3	0	0	1	0	0	0	1	0	0	2	2
1950	CLE	AL	7	6	1	5	0	1	1	0	0	0	0	0	0	0	6	1
1951	CLE	AL	12	5	7	6	5	1	0	1	0	0	0	0	0	0	6	6
1952	CLE	AL	7	4	3	2	2	3	0	0	0	0	0	0	0	0	2	5
1953	CLE	AL	4	2	2	2	0	0	2	0	0	0	1	0	0	0	3	1
	DET	AL	22	8	14	10	6	4	2	1	0	0	0	2	0	0	17	5
	Total		26	10	16	12	6	4	4	1	0	0	1	2	0	0	20	6
1954	DET	AL	20	10	10	13	3	3	1	2	0	0	0	1	0	0	16	4
1955	DET	AL	20	10	10	9	8	3	0	1	0	0	0	0	0	0	11	9
1956	DET	AL	25	16	9	15	7	2	1	2	0	0	0	1	0	0	20	5
1957	DET	AL	12	8	4	5	5	2	0	0	0	0	0	0	0	0	7	5
1958	DET	AL	6	3	3	2	2	1	1	0	0	0	0	0	0	1	4	2
	CHI	AL	7	4	3	4	2	1	0	0	0	0	0	0	0	0	3	4
	Total		13	7	6	6	4	2	1	0	0	0	0	0	0	1	7	6
1959	CHI	AL	1	0	1	1	0	0	0	0	0	0	0	0	0	0	0	1
	KC	AL	2	1	1	1	1	0	0	0	0	0	0	0	0	0	2	0
	MIL	NL	1	0	1	1	0	0	0	0	0	0	0	0	0	0	1	0
	Total		4	1	3	3	1	0	0	0	0	0	0	0	0	0	3	1
1960	BOS	AL	1	0	1	0	1	0	0	0	0	0	0	0	0	0	0	1
Total			151	78	73	77	45	21	8	8	0	0	1	5	0	1	100	51

Rank among batters: 286 • *Top target (5 home runs)*: Arnie Portocarrero, Bob Porterfield • *Number of pitchers victimized*: 90 • *Total ballparks homered in*: 11 • *First HR*: 06/15/1949 off Walt Masterson • *All-Star HR*—1

Frenchy Bordagaray

STANLEY GEORGE BORDAGARAY
B: 01/03/1910
BR

Year	Tm	Lg	Tot	H	A	Men-On 0	1	2	3	One-Game 2	3	4	LO	XN	IP	PH	RHP	LHP
1935	BRO	NL	1	0	1	0	0	1	0	0	0	0	0	0	1	0	1	0
1936	BRO	NL	4	1	3	3	1	0	0	0	0	0	1	0	0	0	4	0
1937	STL	NL	1	0	1	1	0	0	0	0	0	0	0	0	0	0	1	0
1944	BRO	NL	6	2	4	4	2	0	0	0	0	0	1	0	0	0	4	2
1945	BRO	NL	2	1	1	1	1	0	0	0	0	0	0	0	0	1	2	0
Total			14	4	10	9	4	1	0	0	0	0	2	0	1	1	12	2

Rank among batters: 2,169 • *Top target (2 home runs)*: Bill Swift, Rube Fischer • *Number of pitchers victimized*: 12 • *Total ballparks homered in*: 8 • *First HR*: 09/17/1935 off Ed Heusser

Pat Borders

PATRICK LANCE BORDERS
B: 05/14/1963
BR

Year	Tm	Lg	Tot	H	A	Men-On 0	1	2	3	One-Game 2	3	4	LO	XN	IP	PH	RHP	LHP
1988	TOR	AL	5	2	3	4	1	0	0	0	0	0	0	0	0	0	1	4
1989	TOR	AL	3	1	2	2	0	0	1	0	0	0	0	0	0	0	1	2
1990	TOR	AL	15	10	5	8	6	1	0	0	0	0	0	0	0	0	5	10
1991	TOR	AL	5	2	3	1	2	2	0	0	0	0	0	1	0	1	4	1
1992	TOR	AL	13	7	6	10	2	1	0	0	0	0	0	0	0	0	13	0
1993	TOR	AL	9	6	3	5	4	0	0	0	0	0	0	0	0	0	7	2
1994	TOR	AL	3	3	0	3	0	0	0	0	0	0	0	0	0	0	2	1
1995	KC	AL	4	1	3	2	2	0	0	0	0	0	0	0	0	0	2	2
Total			57	32	25	35	17	4	1	0	0	0	0	1	0	1	35	22

Rank among batters: 902 • *Top target (3 home runs)*: Bill Gullickson, Jim Abbott • *Number of pitchers victimized*: 49 • *Total ballparks homered in*: 14 • *First HR*: 04/14/1988 off Al Leiter • *World Series HR*—1; *LCS HR*—1

Mike Bordick

MICHAEL TODD BORDICK
B: 07/21/1965
BR

Year	Tm	Lg	Tot	H	A	Men-On 0	1	2	3	One-Game 2	3	4	LO	XN	IP	PH	RHP	LHP
1992	OAK	AL	3	3	0	2	1	0	0	0	0	0	0	0	0	0	2	1

Year	Tm	Lg	Tot	H	A	Men-On 0	Men-On 1	Men-On 2	Men-On 3	One-Game 2	One-Game 3	One-Game 4	LO	XN	IP	PH	RHP	LHP

Mike Bordick *continued*

Year	Tm	Lg	Tot	H	A	0	1	2	3	2	3	4	LO	XN	IP	PH	RHP	LHP
1993	OAK	AL	3	2	1	1	1	1	0	0	0	0	0	0	0	0	2	1
1994	OAK	AL	2	1	1	2	0	0	0	0	0	0	0	0	0	0	1	1
1995	OAK	AL	8	2	6	5	2	0	1	0	0	0	1	0	0	0	6	2
Total			16	8	8	10	4	1	1	0	0	0	1	0	0	0	11	5

Rank among batters: 2,029 • *Top target (2 home runs)*: Sid Fernandez • *Number of pitchers victimized*: 15 • *Total ballparks homered in*: 6 • *First HR*: 05/10/1992 off Greg Cadaret

Glenn Borgmann

GLENN DENNIS BORGMANN
B: 05/25/1950
BR

Year	Tm	Lg	Tot	H	A	0	1	2	3	2	3	4	LO	XN	IP	PH	RHP	LHP
1972	MIN	AL	3	1	2	2	1	0	0	0	0	0	0	0	0	0	2	1
1974	MIN	AL	3	3	0	3	0	0	0	0	0	0	0	0	0	0	3	0
1975	MIN	AL	2	2	0	2	0	0	0	0	0	0	0	0	0	0	0	2
1976	MIN	AL	1	0	1	1	0	0	0	0	0	0	0	0	0	0	0	1
1977	MIN	AL	2	2	0	1	1	0	0	0	0	0	0	0	0	0	1	1
1978	MIN	AL	3	3	0	2	1	0	0	0	0	0	0	0	0	0	0	3
1980	CHI	AL	2	1	1	0	2	0	0	0	0	0	0	0	0	0	0	2
Total			16	12	4	11	5	0	0	0	0	0	0	0	0	0	6	10

Rank among batters: 2,029 • *Top target (2 home runs)*: Bill Travers • *Number of pitchers victimized*: 15 • *Total ballparks homered in*: 6 • *First HR*: 08/19/1972 off Jim Palmer

Bob Borkowski

ROBERT VILARIAN BORKOWSKI
B: 01/27/1926
BR

Year	Tm	Lg	Tot	H	A	0	1	2	3	2	3	4	LO	XN	IP	PH	RHP	LHP
1950	CHI	NL	4	0	4	4	0	0	0	0	0	0	0	0	0	0	1	3
1952	CIN	NL	4	1	3	2	1	1	0	0	0	0	0	0	1	0	3	1
1953	CIN	NL	7	3	4	4	3	0	0	0	0	0	0	0	0	1	4	3
1954	CIN	NL	1	1	0	1	0	0	0	0	0	0	0	0	0	0	1	0
Total			16	5	11	11	4	1	0	0	0	0	0	0	1	1	9	7

Rank among batters: 2,029 • *Top target (2 home runs)*: Preacher Roe, Carl Erskine • *Number of pitchers victimized*: 14 • *Total ballparks homered in*: 7 • *First HR*: 05/28/1950 off Bill Werle

Steve Boros

STEPHEN BOROS
B: 09/03/1936
BR

Year	Tm	Lg	Tot	H	A	0	1	2	3	2	3	4	LO	XN	IP	PH	RHP	LHP
1961	DET	AL	5	3	2	3	2	0	0	0	0	0	0	0	0	0	2	3
1962	DET	AL	16	6	10	12	2	1	1	0	1	0	0	0	0	0	8	8
1963	CHI	NL	3	0	3	2	1	0	0	0	0	0	0	0	0	0	2	1
1964	CIN	NL	2	1	1	1	1	0	0	0	0	0	0	0	0	0	1	1
Total			26	10	16	18	6	1	1	0	1	0	0	0	0	0	13	13

Rank among batters: 1,576 • Top target (2 home runs): Bud Daley, Ray Moore, Sam McDowell, Frank Baumann • *Number of pitchers victimized*: 22 • *Total ballparks homered in*: 11 • *First HR*: 05/21/1961 off Bud Daley

Babe Borton

WILLIAM BAKER BORTON
B: 08/14/1888 D: 07/29/1954
BL

Year	Tm	Lg	Tot	H	A	0	1	2	3	2	3	4	LO	XN	IP	PH	RHP	LHP
1915	STL	FL	3	3	0	2	1	0	0	0	0	0	0	0	0	0	2	1
1916	STL	AL	1	1	0	0	0	1	0	0	0	0	0	0	0	0	1	0
Total			4	4	0	2	1	1	0	0	0	0	0	0	0	0	3	1

Rank among batters: 3,427 • *Total ballparks homered in*: 2 • *First HR*: 07/26/1915 off Fin Wilson

Don Bosch

DONALD JOHN BOSCH
B: 07/15/1942
BB

Year	Tm	Lg	Tot	H	A	0	1	2	3	2	3	4	LO	XN	IP	PH	RHP	LHP
1968	NY	NL	3	3	0	2	1	0	0	0	0	0	1	0	0	0	2	1
1969	MON	NL	1	0	1	1	0	0	0	0	0	0	0	0	0	0	0	1
Total			4	3	1	3	1	0	0	0	0	0	1	0	0	0	2	2

Rank among batters: 3,427 • *Total ballparks homered in*: 2 • *First HR*: 06/14/1968 off Mike McCormick

Year	Tm	Lg	Tot	H	A	Men-On 0	1	2	3	One-Game 2	3	4	LO	XN	IP	PH	RHP	LHP

Rick Bosetti

RICHARD ALAN BOSETTI
B: 08/05/1953
BR

Year	Tm	Lg	Tot	H	A	0	1	2	3	2	3	4	LO	XN	IP	PH	RHP	LHP
1978	TOR	AL	5	3	2	3	1	0	1	0	0	0	2	0	0	0	5	0
1979	TOR	AL	8	4	4	6	2	0	0	0	0	0	0	0	0	0	4	4
1980	TOR	AL	4	2	2	2	1	1	0	0	0	0	0	0	0	0	3	1
Total			17	9	8	11	4	1	1	0	0	0	2	0	0	0	12	5

Rank among batters: 1,969 • *Top target (2 home runs)*: John Henry Johnson, Ferguson Jenkins • *Number of pitchers victimized*: 15 • *Total ballparks homered in*: 7 • *First HR*: 05/07/1978 off Enrique Romo

Shawn Boskie

SHAWN KEALOHA BOSKIE
B: 03/28/1967
BR

Year	Tm	Lg	Tot	H	A	0	1	2	3	2	3	4	LO	XN	IP	PH	RHP	LHP
1991	CHI	NL	1	0	1	0	1	0	0	0	0	0	0	0	0	0	0	1

Rank among batters: 4,707 • *Total ballparks homered in*: 1 • *First HR*: 04/27/1991 off Norm Charlton

Thad Bosley

THADDIS BOSLEY
B: 09/17/1956
BL

Year	Tm	Lg	Tot	H	A	0	1	2	3	2	3	4	LO	XN	IP	PH	RHP	LHP
1978	CHI	AL	2	1	1	1	1	0	0	0	0	0	1	0	0	0	2	0
1979	CHI	AL	1	1	0	1	0	0	0	0	0	0	0	0	0	0	1	0
1980	CHI	AL	2	2	0	2	0	0	0	0	0	0	0	0	0	0	2	0
1983	CHI	NL	2	1	1	2	0	0	0	0	0	0	1	0	0	1	2	0
1984	CHI	NL	2	0	2	1	0	1	0	0	0	0	0	0	0	1	2	0
1985	CHI	NL	7	4	3	3	3	1	0	1	0	0	0	0	0	3	7	0
1986	CHI	NL	1	0	1	1	0	0	0	0	0	0	0	0	0	1	1	0
1987	KC	AL	1	0	1	1	0	0	0	0	0	0	0	0	0	0	1	0
1989	TEX	AL	1	1	0	0	1	0	0	0	0	0	0	0	0	1	1	0
1990	TEX	AL	1	1	0	0	0	1	0	0	0	0	0	0	0	1	1	0
Total			20	11	9	12	5	3	0	1	0	0	2	0	0	8	20	0

Rank among batters: 1,810 • *Top target (3 home runs)*: Jeff Reardon • *Number of pitchers victimized*: 18 • *Total ballparks homered in*: 10 • *First HR*: 05/29/1978 off Chris Knapp

Harley Boss

ELMER HARLEY BOSS
B: 11/19/1908 D: 05/15/1964
BL

Year	Tm	Lg	Tot	H	A	0	1	2	3	2	3	4	LO	XN	IP	PH	RHP	LHP
1933	CLE	AL	1	0	1	1	0	0	0	0	0	0	0	0	0	0	1	0

Rank among batters: 4,707 • *Total ballparks homered in*: 1 • *First HR*: 05/26/1933 off Hank Johnson

Lyman Bostock

LYMAN WESLEY BOSTOCK
B: 11/22/1950 D: 09/23/1978
BL

Year	Tm	Lg	Tot	H	A	0	1	2	3	2	3	4	LO	XN	IP	PH	RHP	LHP
1976	MIN	AL	4	1	3	3	1	0	0	0	0	0	1	0	0	0	4	0
1977	MIN	AL	14	8	6	7	7	0	0	0	0	0	0	1	0	0	13	1
1978	CAL	AL	5	4	1	4	0	1	0	0	0	0	0	0	0	0	3	2
Total			23	13	10	14	8	1	0	0	0	0	1	1	0	0	20	3

Rank among batters: 1,686 • *Top target (2 home runs)*: Jim Colborn, Jesse Jefferson • *Number of pitchers victimized*: 21 • *Total ballparks homered in*: 10 • *First HR*: 04/18/1976 off Catfish Hunter • *Hit for Cycle—@CHI*: 07/24/1976

Daryl Boston

DARYL LAMONT BOSTON
B: 01/04/1963
BL

Year	Tm	Lg	Tot	H	A	0	1	2	3	2	3	4	LO	XN	IP	PH	RHP	LHP
1985	CHI	AL	3	1	2	2	1	0	0	0	0	0	0	0	0	0	3	0
1986	CHI	AL	5	1	4	3	1	1	0	0	0	0	1	0	0	0	4	1
1987	CHI	AL	10	5	5	8	0	2	0	1	0	0	1	0	0	0	10	0
1988	CHI	AL	15	6	9	10	4	0	1	0	0	0	1	0	0	1	15	0
1989	CHI	AL	5	3	2	2	1	1	1	0	0	0	0	0	0	1	5	0
1990	NY	NL	12	4	8	6	5	1	0	0	0	0	0	0	0	0	12	0

						Men-On				One-Game								
Year	Tm	Lg	Tot	H	A	0	1	2	3	2	3	4	LO	XN	IP	PH	RHP	LHP

Daryl Boston *continued*

Year	Tm	Lg	Tot	H	A	0	1	2	3	2	3	4	LO	XN	IP	PH	RHP	LHP
1991	NY	NL	4	2	2	3	0	0	1	0	0	0	0	0	0	0	3	1
1992	NY	NL	11	5	6	8	2	1	0	0	0	0	2	0	0	3	10	1
1993	COL	NL	14	3	11	10	3	1	0	2	0	0	0	0	0	1	13	1
1994	NY	AL	4	2	2	1	1	2	0	0	0	0	0	0	0	2	4	0
Total			83	32	51	53	18	9	3	3	0	0	5	0	0	8	79	4

Rank among batters: 628 • Top target (2 home runs): Ken Schrom, Mike Loynd, Bert Blyleven, Mike Boddicker, Bob Welch, Charlie Hough, Mike Morgan, Xavier Hernandez, Juan Berenguer, Lee Smith, Bob Walk, Scott Bankhead, Greg Harris, Kevin Gross, Andy Benes • *Number of pitchers victimized*: 68 • *Total ballparks homered in*: 26 • *First HR*: 05/19/1985 off Charlie Hough

Dave Boswell

DAVID WILSON BOSWELL
B: 01/20/1945
BR

Year	Tm	Lg	Tot	H	A	0	1	2	3	2	3	4	LO	XN	IP	PH	RHP	LHP
1967	MIN	AL	1	1	0	1	0	0	0	0	0	0	0	0	0	0	1	0
1968	MIN	AL	1	0	1	1	0	0	0	0	0	0	0	0	0	0	0	1
1969	MIN	AL	2	1	1	2	0	0	0	0	0	0	0	0	0	0	1	1
Total			4	2	2	4	0	0	0	0	0	0	0	0	0	0	2	2

Rank among batters: 3,427 • *Top target (2 home runs)*: Jim Nash • *Number of pitchers victimized*: 3 • *Total ballparks homered in*: 3 • *First HR*: 05/12/1967 off Jim Nash

Ken Boswell

KENNETH GEORGE BOSWELL
B: 02/23/1946
BL

Year	Tm	Lg	Tot	H	A	0	1	2	3	2	3	4	LO	XN	IP	PH	RHP	LHP
1967	NY	NL	1	0	1	1	0	0	0	0	0	0	0	0	0	0	1	0
1968	NY	NL	4	1	3	4	0	0	0	0	0	0	0	0	0	0	3	1
1969	NY	NL	3	2	1	3	0	0	0	0	0	0	0	0	0	0	3	0
1970	NY	NL	5	4	1	4	1	0	0	0	0	0	0	0	0	0	5	0
1971	NY	NL	5	1	4	3	1	0	1	0	0	0	0	0	0	0	3	2
1972	NY	NL	9	1	8	6	0	3	0	0	0	0	0	0	0	0	6	3
1973	NY	NL	2	0	2	2	0	0	0	0	0	0	0	0	0	2	2	0
1974	NY	NL	2	0	2	0	2	0	0	0	0	0	0	0	0	1	2	0
Total			31	9	22	23	4	3	1	0	0	0	0	0	0	3	25	6

Rank among batters: 1,400 • *Top target (3 home runs)*: John Cumberland • *Number of pitchers victimized*: 26 • *Total ballparks homered in*: 11 • *First HR*: 09/30/1967 off Don Drysdale • *LCS HR—2*

John Bottarini

JOHN CHARLES BOTTARINI
B: 09/14/1908 D: 10/08/1976
BR

Year	Tm	Lg	Tot	H	A	0	1	2	3	2	3	4	LO	XN	IP	PH	RHP	LHP
1937	CHI	NL	1	0	1	0	1	0	0	0	0	0	0	0	0	0	1	0

Rank among batters: 4,707 • *Total ballparks homered in*: 1 • *First HR*: 05/04/1937 off Hal Kelleher

Jim Bottomley

JAMES LEROY BOTTOMLEY
B: 04/23/1900 D: 12/11/1959
BL HOF

Year	Tm	Lg	Tot	H	A	0	1	2	3	2	3	4	LO	XN	IP	PH	RHP	LHP
1922	STL	NL	5	0	5	3	2	0	0	0	0	0	0	0	1	0	5	0
1923	STL	NL	8	3	5	5	1	1	1	1	0	0	0	0	1	0	8	0
1924	STL	NL	14	6	8	7	4	2	1	2	0	0	0	0	2	0	12	2
1925	STL	NL	21	16	5	11	4	3	3	1	0	0	0	0	0	0	16	5
1926	STL	NL	19	10	9	7	7	5	0	0	0	0	0	0	1	0	15	4
1927	STL	NL	19	14	5	7	8	4	0	0	0	0	0	1	0	0	17	2
1928	STL	NL	31	14	17	13	10	8	0	4	0	0	0	1	0	0	25	6
1929	STL	NL	29	12	17	10	13	5	1	4	0	0	0	1	0	0	27	2
1930	STL	NL	15	10	5	6	6	3	0	1	0	0	0	1	0	1	9	6
1931	STL	NL	9	2	7	5	3	1	0	0	0	0	0	1	0	0	6	3
1932	STL	NL	11	2	9	8	1	2	0	3	0	0	0	0	0	0	8	3
1933	CIN	NL	13	1	12	6	4	3	0	0	0	0	0	0	0	0	11	2
1934	CIN	NL	11	3	8	6	3	2	0	1	0	0	0	0	0	0	10	1
1935	CIN	NL	1	0	1	0	1	0	0	0	0	0	0	0	0	0	0	1
1936	STL	AL	12	9	3	6	4	2	0	1	0	0	0	0	0	0	12	0

Jim Bottomley *continued*

Year	Tm	Lg	Tot	H	A	Men-On 0	Men-On 1	Men-On 2	Men-On 3	One-Game 2	One-Game 3	One-Game 4	LO	XN	IP	PH	RHP	LHP
1937	STL	AL	1	1	0	0	0	1	0	0	0	0	0	0	0	0	1	0
Total			219	103	116	100	71	42	6	18	0	0	0	5	5	1	182	37

Rank among batters: 152 • *Top target (7 home runs)*: Freddie Fitzsimmons, Charlie Root • *Number of pitchers victimized*: 117 • *Total ballparks homered in*: 12 • *First HR*: 09/10/1922 off Johnny Couch • *Hit for Cycle—@PHI*: 07/15/1927 • *World Series HR*—1

Ed Bouchee

EDWARD FRANCIS BOUCHEE
B: 03/07/1933
BL

Year	Tm	Lg	Tot	H	A	Men-On 0	Men-On 1	Men-On 2	Men-On 3	One-Game 2	One-Game 3	One-Game 4	LO	XN	IP	PH	RHP	LHP
1957	PHI	NL	17	6	11	10	3	4	0	0	0	0	0	0	1	0	13	4
1958	PHI	NL	9	2	7	7	1	0	1	0	0	0	0	0	0	0	5	4
1959	PHI	NL	15	6	9	6	8	0	1	0	0	0	0	1	0	0	10	5
1960	CHI	NL	5	1	4	3	1	1	0	0	0	0	0	0	0	0	4	1
1961	CHI	NL	12	7	5	8	3	1	0	0	0	0	0	0	0	0	9	3
1962	NY	NL	3	3	0	0	1	2	0	0	0	0	0	0	0	2	3	0
Total			61	25	36	34	17	8	2	0	0	0	0	1	1	2	44	17

Rank among batters: 844 • *Top target (3 home runs)*: Lew Burdette, Juan Pizarro, Larry Jackson • *Number of pitchers victimized*: 50 • *Total ballparks homered in*: 10 • *First HR*: 04/20/1957 off Max Surkont

Al Boucher

ALEXANDER FRANCIS BOUCHER
B: 11/13/1881 D: 06/23/1974
BR

Year	Tm	Lg	Tot	H	A	Men-On 0	Men-On 1	Men-On 2	Men-On 3	One-Game 2	One-Game 3	One-Game 4	LO	XN	IP	PH	RHP	LHP
1914	STL	FL	2	2	0	1	1	0	0	0	0	0	0	0	0	0	1	1

Rank among batters: 4,129 • *Total ballparks homered in*: 1 • *First HR*: 05/05/1914 off Kaiser Wilhelm

Lou Boudreau

LOUIS BOUDREAU
B: 07/17/1917
BR HOF

Year	Tm	Lg	Tot	H	A	Men-On 0	Men-On 1	Men-On 2	Men-On 3	One-Game 2	One-Game 3	One-Game 4	LO	XN	IP	PH	RHP	LHP
1940	CLE	AL	9	1	8	6	2	1	0	2	0	0	1	0	0	0	5	4
1941	CLE	AL	10	2	8	5	4	1	0	0	0	0	0	1	0	0	5	5
1942	CLE	AL	2	0	2	2	0	0	0	0	0	0	1	1	0	0	0	2
1943	CLE	AL	3	1	2	2	1	0	0	0	0	0	0	0	0	0	3	0
1944	CLE	AL	3	0	3	1	2	0	0	1	0	0	0	1	0	0	3	0
1945	CLE	AL	3	1	2	0	3	0	0	0	0	0	0	0	0	0	1	2
1946	CLE	AL	6	0	6	2	3	1	0	0	0	0	0	0	0	0	5	1
1947	CLE	AL	4	2	2	3	1	0	0	0	0	0	0	0	0	0	4	0
1948	CLE	AL	18	6	12	12	5	0	1	2	0	0	0	0	0	0	10	8
1949	CLE	AL	4	2	2	2	2	0	0	0	0	0	0	0	0	0	1	3
1950	CLE	AL	1	1	0	1	0	0	0	0	0	0	0	0	0	0	1	0
1951	BOS	AL	5	2	3	3	1	1	0	0	0	0	0	0	0	0	3	2
Total			68	18	50	39	24	4	1	5	0	0	2	3	0	0	41	27

Rank among batters: 767 • *Top target (3 home runs)*: Hal Newhouser • *Number of pitchers victimized*: 53 • *Total ballparks homered in*: 8 • *First HR*: 04/27/1940 off Hal Newhouser • *All-Star HR*—1

Chris Bourjos

CHRISTOPHER BOURJOS
B: 10/16/1954
BR

Year	Tm	Lg	Tot	H	A	Men-On 0	Men-On 1	Men-On 2	Men-On 3	One-Game 2	One-Game 3	One-Game 4	LO	XN	IP	PH	RHP	LHP
1980	SF	NL	1	1	0	0	1	0	0	0	0	0	0	0	0	1	1	0

Rank among batters: 4,707 • *Total ballparks homered in*: 1 • *First HR*: 09/03/1980 off Dick Ruthven

Pat Bourque

PATRICK DANIEL BOURQUE
B: 03/23/1947
BL

Year	Tm	Lg	Tot	H	A	Men-On 0	Men-On 1	Men-On 2	Men-On 3	One-Game 2	One-Game 3	One-Game 4	LO	XN	IP	PH	RHP	LHP
1971	CHI	NL	1	0	1	1	0	0	0	0	0	0	0	0	0	0	1	0
1973	CHI	NL	7	5	2	4	3	0	0	0	0	0	0	0	0	1	7	0
	OAK	AL	2	0	2	2	0	0	0	0	0	0	0	0	0	0	2	0
	Total		9	5	4	6	3	0	0	0	0	0	0	0	0	1	9	0
1974	OAK	AL	1	1	0	1	0	0	0	0	0	0	0	0	0	1	1	0
	MIN	AL	1	1	0	0	0	1	0	0	0	0	0	0	0	0	1	0

Pat Bourque *continued*

Year	Tm	Lg	Tot	H	A	Men-On 0	1	2	3	One-Game 2	3	4	LO	XN	IP	PH	RHP	LHP
1974	Total		2	2	0	1	0	1	0	0	0	0	0	0	0	1	2	0
Total			12	7	5	8	3	1	0	0	0	0	0	0	0	2	12	0

Rank among batters: 2,325 • *Total ballparks homered in*: 7 • *First HR*: 09/18/1971 off Rick Wise

Larry Bowa

LAWRENCE ROBERT BOWA
B: 12/06/1945
BB

Year	Tm	Lg	Tot	H	A	Men-On 0	1	2	3	One-Game 2	3	4	LO	XN	IP	PH	RHP	LHP
1972	PHI	NL	1	1	0	1	0	0	0	0	0	0	0	0	1	0	0	1
1974	PHI	NL	1	0	1	0	1	0	0	0	0	0	0	0	0	0	0	1
1975	PHI	NL	2	1	1	1	1	0	0	0	0	0	0	0	0	0	1	1
1977	PHI	NL	4	3	1	3	0	0	1	0	0	0	0	0	0	0	1	3
1978	PHI	NL	3	1	2	2	1	0	0	0	0	0	0	0	0	0	1	2
1980	PHI	NL	2	1	1	2	0	0	0	0	0	0	0	0	2	0	2	0
1983	CHI	NL	2	1	1	1	0	1	0	0	0	0	0	0	0	0	0	2
Total			15	8	7	10	3	1	1	0	0	0	0	0	3	0	5	10

Rank among batters: 2,096 • *Total ballparks homered in*: 6 • *First HR*: 08/18/1972 off Dave Roberts

Benny Bowcock

BENJAMIN JAMES BOWCOCK
B: 10/28/1879 D: 06/16/1961
BR

Year	Tm	Lg	Tot	H	A	Men-On 0	1	2	3	One-Game 2	3	4	LO	XN	IP	PH	RHP	LHP
1903	STL	AL	1	0	1	0	1	0	0	0	0	0	0	0	0	0	1	0

Rank among batters: 4,707 • *Total ballparks homered in*: 1 • *First HR*: 09/26/1903 off Cy Young

Sam Bowen

SAMUEL THOMAS BOWEN
B: 09/18/1952
BR

Year	Tm	Lg	Tot	H	A	Men-On 0	1	2	3	One-Game 2	3	4	LO	XN	IP	PH	RHP	LHP
1978	BOS	AL	1	0	1	1	0	0	0	0	0	0	0	0	0	0	0	1

Rank among batters: 4,707 • *Total ballparks homered in*: 1 • *First HR*: 07/27/1978 off Jon Matlack

Sam Bowens

SAMUEL EDWARD BOWENS
B: 03/23/1939
BR

Year	Tm	Lg	Tot	H	A	Men-On 0	1	2	3	One-Game 2	3	4	LO	XN	IP	PH	RHP	LHP
1963	BAL	AL	1	1	0	0	1	0	0	0	0	0	0	0	0	0	1	0
1964	BAL	AL	22	13	9	16	3	3	0	2	0	0	0	1	0	0	11	11
1965	BAL	AL	7	3	4	4	3	0	0	0	0	0	0	0	0	0	2	5
1966	BAL	AL	6	3	3	6	0	0	0	0	0	0	0	0	0	0	2	4
1967	BAL	AL	5	2	3	4	1	0	0	0	0	0	0	0	0	3	2	3
1968	WAS	AL	4	3	1	3	1	0	0	0	0	0	0	0	0	1	1	3
Total			45	25	20	33	9	3	0	2	0	0	0	1	0	4	19	26

Rank among batters: 1,082 • *Top target (3 home runs)*: Mudcat Grant, Sam McDowell, Jim Kaat • *Number of pitchers victimized*: 35 • *Total ballparks homered in*: 9 • *First HR*: 09/28/1963 off Phil Regan

Frank Bowerman

FRANK EUGENE BOWERMAN
B: 12/05/1868 D: 11/30/1948
BR

Year	Tm	Lg	Tot	H	A	Men-On 0	1	2	3	One-Game 2	3	4	LO	XN	IP	PH	RHP	LHP
1897	BAL	NL	1	1	0	1	0	0	0	0	0	0	0	0	0	0	1	0
1899	PIT	NL	3	1	2	0	3	0	0	0	0	0	0	0	0	0	2	1
1900	NY	NL	1	0	1	0	1	0	0	0	0	0	0	0	0	0	1	0
1903	NY	NL	1	0	1	1	0	0	0	0	0	0	0	0	0	0	0	1
1904	NY	NL	2	2	0	1	1	0	0	0	0	0	0	0	0	0	1	1
1905	NY	NL	3	2	1	2	0	1	0	0	0	0	0	0	0	0	3	0
1906	NY	NL	1	1	0	0	0	1	0	0	0	0	0	0	0	0	0	1
1908	BOS	NL	1	1	0	1	0	0	0	0	0	0	0	0	0	0	1	0
Total			13	8	5	6	5	2	0	0	0	0	0	0	0	0	9	4

Rank among batters: 2,248 • *Top target (2 home runs)*: Charlie Chech • *Number of pitchers victimized*: 12 • *Total ballparks homered in*: 6 • *First HR*: 07/02/1897 off Silver King

Year	Tm	Lg	Tot	H	A	Men-On 0	Men-On 1	Men-On 2	Men-On 3	One-Game 2	One-Game 3	One-Game 4	LO	XN	IP	PH	RHP	LHP

Steve Bowling

STEPHEN SHADDON BOWLING
B: 06/26/1952
BR

Year	Tm	Lg	Tot	H	A	0	1	2	3	2	3	4	LO	XN	IP	PH	RHP	LHP
1977	TOR	AL	1	1	0	1	0	0	0	0	0	0	0	0	0	0	1	0

Rank among batters: 4,707 • *Total ballparks homered in*: 1 • *First HR*: 08/26/1977 off Rick Langford

Bob Bowman

ROBERT JAMES BOWMAN
B: 10/03/1910 D: 09/04/1972
BR

Year	Tm	Lg	Tot	H	A	0	1	2	3	2	3	4	LO	XN	IP	PH	RHP	LHP
1941	NY	NL	1	1	0	1	0	0	0	0	0	0	0	0	0	0	1	0

Rank among batters: 4,707 • *Total ballparks homered in*: 1 • *First HR*: 06/11/1941 off Tot Pressnell

Bob Bowman

ROBERT LEROY BOWMAN
B: 05/10/1931
BR

Year	Tm	Lg	Tot	H	A	0	1	2	3	2	3	4	LO	XN	IP	PH	RHP	LHP
1956	PHI	NL	1	0	1	1	0	0	0	0	0	0	0	0	0	0	0	1
1957	PHI	NL	6	4	2	4	2	0	0	0	0	0	0	0	0	0	4	2
1958	PHI	NL	8	8	0	4	2	2	0	0	0	0	0	0	0	3	3	5
1959	PHI	NL	2	2	0	2	0	0	0	0	0	0	0	0	0	1	1	1
Total			17	14	3	11	4	2	0	0	0	0	0	0	0	4	8	9

Rank among batters: 1,969 • *Top target (2 home runs)*: Bob Friend, Juan Pizarro • *Number of pitchers victimized*: 15 • *Total ballparks homered in*: 4 • *First HR*: 09/21/1956 off Johnny Antonelli

Ernie Bowman

ERNEST FERRELL BOWMAN
B: 07/28/1935
BR

Year	Tm	Lg	Tot	H	A	0	1	2	3	2	3	4	LO	XN	IP	PH	RHP	LHP
1962	SF	NL	1	0	1	1	0	0	0	0	0	0	0	0	0	0	0	1

Rank among batters: 4,707 • *Total ballparks homered in*: 1 • *First HR*: 08/23/1962 off Al Jackson

Joe Bowman

JOSEPH EMIL BOWMAN
B: 06/17/1910 D: 11/22/1990
BL

Year	Tm	Lg	Tot	H	A	0	1	2	3	2	3	4	LO	XN	IP	PH	RHP	LHP
1935	PHI	NL	1	1	0	1	0	0	0	0	0	0	0	0	0	0	1	0
1940	PIT	NL	1	1	0	0	0	1	0	0	0	0	0	0	0	1	1	0
Total			2	2	0	1	0	1	0	0	0	0	0	0	0	1	2	0

Rank among batters: 4,129 • *Total ballparks homered in*: 2 • *First HR*: 06/23/1935 off Leroy Herrmann

Bob Boyd

ROBERT RICHARD BOYD
B: 10/01/1925
BL

Year	Tm	Lg	Tot	H	A	0	1	2	3	2	3	4	LO	XN	IP	PH	RHP	LHP
1953	CHI	AL	3	1	2	1	1	1	0	0	0	0	1	0	0	0	3	0
1956	BAL	AL	2	1	1	1	1	0	0	0	0	0	0	0	0	0	2	0
1957	BAL	AL	4	1	3	2	2	0	0	0	0	0	0	1	0	0	3	1
1958	BAL	AL	7	3	4	6	1	0	0	0	0	0	0	0	0	0	7	0
1959	BAL	AL	3	1	2	1	2	0	0	0	0	0	0	0	0	0	3	0
Total			19	7	12	11	7	1	0	0	0	0	1	1	0	0	18	1

Rank among batters: 1,861 • *Top target (2 home runs)*: Frank Sullivan, Herb Moford, Jim Bunning • *Number of pitchers victimized*: 16 • *Total ballparks homered in*: 8 • *First HR*: 08/09/1953 off Vic Raschi

Jake Boyd

JACOB HENRY BOYD
B: 01/19/1874 D: 08/12/1932

Year	Tm	Lg	Tot	H	A	0	1	2	3	2	3	4	LO	XN	IP	PH	RHP	LHP
1895	WAS	NL	1	1	0	0	0	1	0	0	0	0	0	0	0	0	1	0

Rank among batters: 4,707 • *Total ballparks homered in*: 1 • *First HR*: 06/01/1895 off Pat Luby

Clete Boyer

CLETIS LEROY BOYER
B: 02/09/1937
BR

Year	Tm	Lg	Tot	H	A	0	1	2	3	2	3	4	LO	XN	IP	PH	RHP	LHP
1956	KC	AL	1	0	1	1	0	0	0	0	0	0	0	0	0	0	1	0

Clete Boyer *continued*

Year	Tm	Lg	Tot	H	A	Men-On 0	1	2	3	One-Game 2	3	4	LO	XN	IP	PH	RHP	LHP
1960	NY	AL	14	5	9	8	5	1	0	0	0	0	0	0	0	0	7	7
1961	NY	AL	11	5	6	6	4	1	0	1	0	0	0	0	0	0	8	3
1962	NY	AL	18	6	12	8	8	1	1	1	0	0	1	0	0	0	12	6
1963	NY	AL	12	6	6	10	1	0	1	0	0	0	0	1	0	0	2	10
1964	NY	AL	8	3	5	3	4	1	0	0	0	0	0	0	0	0	4	4
1965	NY	AL	18	7	11	14	3	0	1	0	0	0	0	0	0	0	5	13
1966	NY	AL	14	5	9	12	2	0	0	0	0	0	0	0	0	0	5	9
1967	ATL	NL	26	10	16	14	9	1	2	1	0	0	0	0	0	0	17	9
1968	ATL	NL	4	2	2	4	0	0	0	1	0	0	0	0	0	0	3	1
1969	ATL	NL	14	7	7	8	5	1	0	2	0	0	0	0	0	0	11	3
1970	ATL	NL	16	8	8	7	7	2	0	2	0	0	0	0	0	0	11	5
1971	ATL	NL	6	5	1	2	2	2	0	1	0	0	0	0	0	1	4	2
Total			162	69	93	97	50	10	5	9	0	0	1	1	0	1	90	72

Rank among batters: 261 • Top target (4 home runs): Hank Aguirre, Dave McNally, Joe Niekro, Jim Bunning • *Number of pitchers victimized*: 110 • *Total ballparks homered in*: 23 • *First HR*: 08/09/1956 off Virgil Trucks • *World Series HR*—2

Ken Boyer

KENTON LLOYD BOYER
B: 05/20/1931 D: 09/07/1982
BR

Year	Tm	Lg	Tot	H	A	Men-On 0	1	2	3	One-Game 2	3	4	LO	XN	IP	PH	RHP	LHP
1955	STL	NL	18	7	11	10	7	1	0	2	0	0	0	1	0	0	7	11
1956	STL	NL	26	12	14	19	4	2	1	3	0	0	0	0	0	0	13	13
1957	STL	NL	19	10	9	15	3	1	0	0	0	0	1	0	0	0	14	5
1958	STL	NL	23	14	9	15	5	1	2	2	0	0	0	3	1	0	11	12
1959	STL	NL	28	14	14	12	13	2	1	0	0	0	0	0	3	0	17	11
1960	STL	NL	32	16	16	21	10	1	0	3	0	0	0	0	0	0	16	16
1961	STL	NL	24	11	13	11	8	4	1	3	0	0	0	1	0	0	20	4
1962	STL	NL	24	10	14	14	7	3	0	1	0	0	0	0	0	0	15	9
1963	STL	NL	24	15	9	8	13	3	0	2	0	0	0	1	0	0	15	9
1964	STL	NL	24	12	12	11	9	2	2	1	0	0	0	0	0	0	19	5
1965	STL	NL	13	9	4	7	4	2	0	0	0	0	0	0	0	0	6	7
1966	NY	NL	14	10	4	7	5	2	0	0	0	0	0	0	0	0	8	6
1967	NY	NL	3	3	0	2	1	0	0	0	0	0	0	0	0	0	2	1
	CHI	AL	4	1	3	3	1	0	0	0	0	0	0	0	0	0	2	2
	Total		7	4	3	5	2	0	0	0	0	0	0	0	0	0	4	3
1968	LA	NL	6	4	2	3	3	0	0	1	0	0	0	0	0	0	2	4
Total			282	148	134	158	93	24	7	18	0	0	1	6	4	0	167	115

Rank among batters: 81 • *Top target (11 home runs)*: Warren Spahn • *Number of pitchers victimized*: 145 • *Total ballparks homered in*: 18 • *First HR*: 04/12/1955 off Paul Minner • *Hit for Cycle*—vs CHI: 09/14/1961 (2); @HOU: 06/16/1964 • *World Series HR*—2; *All-Star HR*—2

Buzz Boyle

RALPH FRANCIS BOYLE
B: 02/09/1908 D: 11/12/1978
BL

Year	Tm	Lg	Tot	H	A	Men-On 0	1	2	3	One-Game 2	3	4	LO	XN	IP	PH	RHP	LHP
1929	BOS	NL	1	0	1	1	0	0	0	0	0	0	0	0	1	0	1	0
1934	BRO	NL	7	3	4	3	3	1	0	0	0	0	0	0	0	0	7	0
1935	BRO	NL	4	2	2	4	0	0	0	0	0	0	0	0	0	0	4	0
Total			12	5	7	8	3	1	0	0	0	0	0	0	1	0	12	0

Rank among batters: 2,325 • *Top target (2 home runs)*: Tex Carleton, Charlie Root, Phil Collins • *Number of pitchers victimized*: 9 • *Total ballparks homered in*: 6 • *First HR*: 09/29/1929 off Ray Moss

Henry Boyle

HENRY J. BOYLE
B: 09/20/1860 D: 05/25/1932

Year	Tm	Lg	Tot	H	A	Men-On 0	1	2	3	One-Game 2	3	4	LO	XN	IP	PH	RHP	LHP
1884	STL	UA	4	0	4	1	2	1	0	0	0	0	0	0	1	0	2	0
1885	STL	NL	1	1	0	0	1	0	0	0	0	0	0	0	0	0	1	0
1886	STL	NL	1	1	0	1	0	0	0	0	0	0	0	0	0	0	1	0
1887	IND	NL	2	1	1	1	1	0	0	0	0	0	0	0	0	0	2	0
1888	IND	NL	1	0	1	1	0	0	0	0	0	0	0	0	0	0	0	1
1889	IND	NL	1	1	0	1	0	0	0	0	0	0	0	0	0	0	1	0
Total			10	4	6	5	4	1	0	0	0	0	0	0	1	0	7	1

Rank among batters: 2,500 • *Total ballparks homered in*: 8 • *First HR*: 07/09/1884 off Jerry Dorsey

Jack Boyle

JOHN ANTHONY BOYLE
B: 03/22/1866 D: 01/07/1913
BR

Year	Tm	Lg	Tot	H	A	Men-On 0	1	2	3	One-Game 2	3	4	LO	XN	IP	PH	RHP	LHP
1887	STL	AA	2	2	0	0	1	1	0	0	0	0	0	0	1	0	1	1
1888	STL	AA	1	1	0	0	0	1	0	0	0	0	0	0	0	0	0	0
1889	STL	AA	3	2	1	2	1	0	0	0	0	0	0	0	0	0	1	2
1890	CHI	PL	1	0	1	1	0	0	0	0	0	0	0	0	0	0	1	0
1891	STL	AA	5	4	1	3	1	1	0	0	0	0	0	0	0	0	3	2
1893	PHI	NL	4	2	2	1	1	2	0	0	0	0	0	0	0	0	4	0
1894	PHI	NL	4	3	1	1	2	1	0	0	0	0	0	0	0	0	3	1
1896	PHI	NL	1	1	0	0	1	0	0	0	0	0	0	0	0	0	1	0
1897	PHI	NL	2	2	0	0	0	1	1	0	0	0	0	0	0	0	2	0
Total			23	17	6	8	7	7	1	0	0	0	0	0	1	0	16	6

Rank among batters: 1,686 • *Top target (2 home runs)*: Sadie McMahon, Frank Foreman, Harry Staley • *Number of pitchers victimized*: 20 • *Total ballparks homered in*: 8 • *First HR*: 08/10/1887 off John Kirby

Gene Brabender

EUGENE MATHEW BRABENDER
B: 08/16/1941
BR

Year	Tm	Lg	Tot	H	A	Men-On 0	1	2	3	One-Game 2	3	4	LO	XN	IP	PH	RHP	LHP
1968	BAL	AL	1	0	1	1	0	0	0	0	0	0	0	0	0	0	1	0
1969	SEA	AL	1	0	1	1	0	0	0	0	0	0	0	0	0	0	1	0
Total			2	0	2	2	0	0	0	0	0	0	0	0	0	0	2	0

Rank among batters: 4,129 • *Total ballparks homered in*: 2 • *First HR*: 05/05/1968 off Dennis Higgins

Gibby Brack

GILBERT HERMAN BRACK
B: 03/29/1908 D: 01/20/1960
BR

Year	Tm	Lg	Tot	H	A	Men-On 0	1	2	3	One-Game 2	3	4	LO	XN	IP	PH	RHP	LHP
1937	BRO	NL	5	3	2	5	0	0	0	0	0	0	0	0	0	0	3	2
1938	BRO	NL	1	0	1	0	1	0	0	0	0	0	0	0	0	0	0	1
	PHI	NL	4	1	3	1	2	1	0	0	0	0	0	0	0	0	2	2
	Total		5	1	4	1	3	1	0	0	0	0	0	0	0	0	2	3
1939	PHI	NL	6	6	0	4	2	0	0	0	0	0	0	0	0	1	6	0
Total			16	10	6	10	5	1	0	0	0	0	0	0	0	1	11	5

Rank among batters: 2,029 • *Top target (2 home runs)*: Max Macon, Paul Derringer • *Number of pitchers victimized*: 14 • *Total ballparks homered in*: 7 • *First HR*: 05/11/1937 off Bob Weiland

Buddy Bradford

CHARLES WILLIAM BRADFORD
B: 07/25/1944
BR

Year	Tm	Lg	Tot	H	A	Men-On 0	1	2	3	One-Game 2	3	4	LO	XN	IP	PH	RHP	LHP
1968	CHI	AL	5	0	5	2	3	0	0	1	0	0	0	1	0	0	2	3
1969	CHI	AL	11	7	4	8	2	1	0	0	0	0	1	0	0	0	8	3
1970	CHI	AL	2	0	2	2	0	0	0	0	0	0	0	0	0	0	2	0
	CLE	AL	7	6	1	3	1	2	1	1	0	0	0	0	0	0	3	4
	Total		9	6	3	5	1	2	1	1	0	0	0	0	0	0	5	4
1971	CIN	NL	2	1	1	0	1	1	0	0	0	0	0	0	0	0	1	1
1972	CHI	AL	2	0	2	0	1	0	1	0	0	0	0	0	0	1	1	1
1973	CHI	AL	8	4	4	7	1	0	0	0	0	0	0	1	0	0	6	2
1974	CHI	AL	5	3	2	4	1	0	0	0	0	0	1	0	0	1	0	5
1975	CHI	AL	2	1	1	0	0	2	0	0	0	0	0	0	0	0	0	2
	STL	NL	4	1	3	1	3	0	0	1	0	0	0	0	0	1	1	3
	Total		6	2	4	1	3	2	0	1	0	0	0	0	0	1	1	5
1976	CHI	AL	4	1	3	3	0	1	0	0	0	0	0	0	0	0	3	1
Total			52	24	28	30	13	7	2	3	0	0	2	2	0	3	27	25

Rank among batters: 965 • *Top target (3 home runs)*: Ken Brett • *Number of pitchers victimized*: 46 • *Total ballparks homered in*: 17 • *First HR*: 04/14/1968 off Mickey Lolich

Bill Bradley

WILLIAM JOSEPH BRADLEY
B: 02/13/1878 D: 03/11/1954
BR

Year	Tm	Lg	Tot	H	A	Men-On 0	1	2	3	One-Game 2	3	4	LO	XN	IP	PH	RHP	LHP
1899	CHI	NL	2	2	0	1	1	0	0	0	0	0	0	0	1	0	2	0
1900	CHI	NL	5	2	3	4	1	0	0	0	0	0	0	0	0	0	4	1

Year	Tm	Lg	Tot	H	A	Men-On				One-Game			LO	XN	IP	PH	RHP	LHP
						0	1	2	3	2	3	4						

Bill Bradley *continued*

Year	Tm	Lg	Tot	H	A	0	1	2	3	2	3	4	LO	XN	IP	PH	RHP	LHP
1901	CLE	AL	1	0	1	0	1	0	0	0	0	0	0	0	0	0	0	1
1902	CLE	AL	11	3	8	6	3	2	0	0	0	0	0	0	0	0	8	3
1903	CLE	AL	6	1	5	4	2	0	0	0	0	0	0	0	1	0	4	2
1904	CLE	AL	6	4	2	3	3	0	0	0	0	0	0	0	0	0	4	2
1906	CLE	AL	2	1	1	1	1	0	0	0	0	0	0	0	0	0	2	0
1908	CLE	AL	1	0	1	0	1	0	0	0	0	0	0	0	0	0	1	0
Total			34	13	21	19	13	2	0	0	0	0	0	0	2	0	25	9

Rank among batters: 1,315 • *Top target (3 home runs)*: Cy Young • *Number of pitchers victimized*: 28 • *Total ballparks homered in*: 9 • *First HR*: 10/03/1899 off Bert Cunningham • *Hit for Cycle*—@WAS: 09/24/1903

George Bradley

GEORGE WASHINGTON BRADLEY
B: 07/13/1852 D: 10/02/1931
BR

Year	Tm	Lg	Tot	H	A	0	1	2	3	2	3	4	LO	XN	IP	PH	RHP	LHP
1881	CLE	NL	2	1	1	2	0	0	0	0	0	0	0	0	1	0	2	0
1883	PHI	AA	1	0	1	0	1	0	0	0	0	0	0	0	0	0	1	0
Total			3	1	2	2	1	0	0	0	0	0	0	0	1	0	3	0

Rank among batters: 3,735 • *Total ballparks homered in*: 3 • *First HR*: 08/20/1881 off Jim Galvin

Hugh Bradley

HUGH FREDERICK BRADLEY
B: 05/23/1885 D: 01/26/1949
BR

Year	Tm	Lg	Tot	H	A	0	1	2	3	2	3	4	LO	XN	IP	PH	RHP	LHP
1911	BOS	AL	1	1	0	0	0	1	0	0	0	0	0	0	0	0	0	1
1912	BOS	AL	1	1	0	0	0	1	0	0	0	0	0	0	0	0	0	1
Total			2	2	0	0	0	2	0	0	0	0	0	0	0	0	0	2

Rank among batters: 4,129 • *Total ballparks homered in*: 2 • *First HR*: 09/25/1911 off Lefty George

Mark Bradley

MARK ALLEN BRADLEY
B: 12/03/1956
BR

Year	Tm	Lg	Tot	H	A	0	1	2	3	2	3	4	LO	XN	IP	PH	RHP	LHP
1983	NY	NL	3	2	1	3	0	0	0	0	0	0	0	0	1	2	0	3

Rank among batters: 3,735 • *Top target (2 home runs)*: Fernando Valenzuela • *Number of pitchers victimized*: 2 • *Total ballparks homered in*: 2 • *First HR*: 06/02/1983 off Fernando Valenzuela

Phil Bradley

PHILIP POOLE BRADLEY
B: 03/11/1959
BR

Year	Tm	Lg	Tot	H	A	0	1	2	3	2	3	4	LO	XN	IP	PH	RHP	LHP
1985	SEA	AL	26	15	11	17	6	2	1	1	0	0	0	1	0	0	17	9
1986	SEA	AL	12	5	7	11	0	1	0	0	0	0	0	0	0	0	10	2
1987	SEA	AL	14	12	2	11	2	1	0	1	0	0	0	0	0	0	3	11
1988	PHI	NL	11	8	3	8	2	1	0	0	0	0	3	0	0	0	7	4
1989	BAL	AL	11	3	8	9	2	0	0	0	0	0	2	0	0	0	3	8
1990	BAL	AL	4	4	0	2	0	1	1	0	0	0	1	0	1	1	2	2
Total			78	47	31	58	12	6	2	2	0	0	6	1	1	1	42	36

Rank among batters: 672 • *Top target (3 home runs)*: Bruce Hurst, Curt Young • *Number of pitchers victimized*: 66 • *Total ballparks homered in*: 18 • *First HR*: 04/11/1985 off Curt Young

Scott Bradley

SCOTT WILLIAM BRADLEY
B: 03/22/1960
BL

Year	Tm	Lg	Tot	H	A	0	1	2	3	2	3	4	LO	XN	IP	PH	RHP	LHP
1986	SEA	AL	5	4	1	2	2	1	0	0	0	0	0	0	0	1	5	0
1987	SEA	AL	5	5	0	2	3	0	0	1	0	0	0	0	0	0	4	1
1988	SEA	AL	4	3	1	2	0	2	0	0	0	0	0	1	0	0	4	0
1989	SEA	AL	3	1	2	1	0	2	0	0	0	0	0	0	0	0	3	0
1990	SEA	AL	1	1	0	0	0	1	0	0	0	0	0	0	0	0	1	0
Total			18	14	4	7	5	6	0	1	0	0	0	1	0	1	17	1

Rank among batters: 1,914 • *Top target (3 home runs)*: Richard Dotson • *Number of pitchers victimized*: 15 • *Total ballparks homered in*: 5 • *First HR*: 07/02/1986 off Scott Bankhead

Tom Bradley

THOMAS WILLIAM BRADLEY
B: 03/16/1947
BR

Year	Tm	Lg	Tot	H	A	Men-On 0	Men-On 1	Men-On 2	Men-On 3	One-Game 2	One-Game 3	One-Game 4	LO	XN	IP	PH	RHP	LHP
1971	CHI	AL	1	1	0	1	0	0	0	0	0	0	0	0	0	0	1	0

Rank among batters: 4,707 • *Total ballparks homered in*: 1 • *First HR*: 07/06/1971 off Diego Segui

Steve Brady

STEPHEN A. BRADY
B: 07/14/1851 D: 11/01/1917

Year	Tm	Lg	Tot	H	A	Men-On 0	Men-On 1	Men-On 2	Men-On 3	One-Game 2	One-Game 3	One-Game 4	LO	XN	IP	PH	RHP	LHP
1884	NY	AA	1	1	0	0	1	0	0	0	0	0	0	0	0	0	0	0
1885	NY	AA	3	1	2	1	2	0	0	0	0	0	0	0	0	0	2	0
Total			4	2	2	1	3	0	0	0	0	0	0	0	0	0	2	0

Rank among batters: 3,427 • *Total ballparks homered in*: 4 • *First HR*: 05/29/1884 off Larry McKeon

Bobby Bragan

ROBERT RANDALL BRAGAN
B: 10/30/1917
BR

Year	Tm	Lg	Tot	H	A	Men-On 0	Men-On 1	Men-On 2	Men-On 3	One-Game 2	One-Game 3	One-Game 4	LO	XN	IP	PH	RHP	LHP
1940	PHI	NL	7	7	0	3	4	0	0	1	0	0	0	1	0	0	6	1
1941	PHI	NL	4	2	2	3	0	0	1	0	0	0	0	0	0	0	3	1
1942	PHI	NL	2	2	0	2	0	0	0	0	0	0	0	0	0	0	2	0
1943	BRO	NL	2	1	1	1	1	0	0	0	0	0	0	0	0	0	2	0
Total			15	12	3	9	5	0	1	1	0	0	0	1	0	0	13	2

Rank among batters: 2,096 • *Top target (2 home runs)*: Bucky Walters, Bill McGee • *Number of pitchers victimized*: 13 • *Total ballparks homered in*: 5 • *First HR*: 06/16/1940 off Bill McGee

Darren Bragg

DARREN WILLIAM BRAGG
B: 09/07/1969
BL

Year	Tm	Lg	Tot	H	A	Men-On 0	Men-On 1	Men-On 2	Men-On 3	One-Game 2	One-Game 3	One-Game 4	LO	XN	IP	PH	RHP	LHP
1995	SEA	AL	3	1	2	2	1	0	0	0	0	0	0	0	0	0	3	0

Rank among batters: 3,735 • *Total ballparks homered in*: 3 • *First HR*: 05/23/1995 off Aaron Sele

Glenn Braggs

GLENN ERICK BRAGGS
B: 10/17/1962
BR

Year	Tm	Lg	Tot	H	A	Men-On 0	Men-On 1	Men-On 2	Men-On 3	One-Game 2	One-Game 3	One-Game 4	LO	XN	IP	PH	RHP	LHP
1986	MIL	AL	4	2	2	3	1	0	0	1	0	0	0	0	0	0	1	3
1987	MIL	AL	13	4	9	10	2	1	0	0	0	0	0	0	0	0	11	2
1988	MIL	AL	10	6	4	5	3	2	0	0	0	0	0	0	0	0	5	5
1989	MIL	AL	15	8	7	9	6	0	0	1	0	0	0	0	0	0	9	6
1990	MIL	AL	3	1	2	3	0	0	0	0	0	0	0	0	0	0	2	1
	CIN	NL	6	4	2	4	2	0	0	0	0	0	0	0	0	0	1	5
	Total		9	5	4	7	2	0	0	0	0	0	0	0	0	0	3	6
1991	CIN	NL	11	8	3	8	2	1	0	1	0	0	0	0	0	2	6	5
1992	CIN	NL	8	4	4	3	3	1	1	0	0	0	0	1	0	1	3	5
Total			70	37	33	45	19	5	1	3	0	0	0	1	0	3	38	32

Rank among batters: 742 • *Top target (4 home runs)*: Steve Avery • *Number of pitchers victimized*: 61 • *Total ballparks homered in*: 18 • *First HR*: 08/02/1986 off Charlie Hough

Dave Brain

DAVID LEONARD BRAIN
B: 01/24/1879 D: 05/25/1959
BR

Year	Tm	Lg	Tot	H	A	Men-On 0	Men-On 1	Men-On 2	Men-On 3	One-Game 2	One-Game 3	One-Game 4	LO	XN	IP	PH	RHP	LHP
1903	STL	NL	1	1	0	0	1	0	0	0	0	0	0	0	0	0	1	0
1904	STL	NL	7	5	2	3	2	1	1	0	0	0	0	0	3	0	6	1
1905	STL	NL	1	1	0	1	0	0	0	0	0	0	0	0	0	0	1	0
	PIT	NL	3	0	3	3	0	0	0	0	0	0	0	0	1	0	3	0
	Total		4	1	3	4	0	0	0	0	0	0	0	0	1	0	4	0
1906	BOS	NL	5	4	1	2	2	1	0	0	0	0	0	1	1	0	5	0
1907	BOS	NL	10	10	0	6	4	0	0	0	0	0	0	0	0	0	7	3
Total			27	21	6	15	9	2	1	0	0	0	0	1	5	0	23	4

Rank among batters: 1,532 • Top target (2 home runs): Tom Fisher, Christy Mathewson, Sam Leever, Deacon Phillippe • *Number of pitchers victimized*: 23 • *Total ballparks homered in*: 5 • *First HR*: 09/27/1903 off Chick Fraser

Fred Brainerd

FREDERICK F. BRAINERD
B: 02/17/1892 D: 04/17/1959
BR

Year	Tm	Lg	Tot	H	A	Men-On 0	1	2	3	One-Game 2	3	4	LO	XN	IP	PH	RHP	LHP
1915	NY	NL	1	0	1	0	1	0	0	0	0	0	0	0	1	0	1	0

Rank among batters: 4,707 • *Total ballparks homered in*: 1 • *First HR*: 08/01/1915 off Bill Doak

Erv Brame

ERVIN BECKHAM BRAME
B: 10/12/1901 D: 11/22/1949
BL

Year	Tm	Lg	Tot	H	A	Men-On 0	1	2	3	One-Game 2	3	4	LO	XN	IP	PH	RHP	LHP
1928	PIT	NL	1	0	1	0	1	0	0	0	0	0	0	0	0	0	1	0
1929	PIT	NL	4	0	4	1	2	1	0	0	0	0	0	0	0	0	4	0
1930	PIT	NL	3	1	2	1	2	0	0	0	0	0	0	0	0	0	3	0
Total			8	1	7	2	5	1	0	0	0	0	0	0	0	0	8	0

Rank among batters: 2,703 • *Top target (2 home runs)*: Red Lucas • *Number of pitchers victimized*: 7 • *Total ballparks homered in*: 5 • *First HR*: 09/22/1928 off Earl Caldwell

Ralph Branca

RALPH THEODORE JOSEPH BRANCA
B: 01/06/1926
BR

Year	Tm	Lg	Tot	H	A	Men-On 0	1	2	3	One-Game 2	3	4	LO	XN	IP	PH	RHP	LHP
1950	BRO	NL	2	0	2	1	1	0	0	0	0	0	0	0	0	0	1	1

Rank among batters: 4,129 • *Total ballparks homered in*: 1 • *First HR*: 06/08/1950 off Cliff Chambers

Al Brancato

ALBERT BRANCATO
B: 05/29/1919
BR

Year	Tm	Lg	Tot	H	A	Men-On 0	1	2	3	One-Game 2	3	4	LO	XN	IP	PH	RHP	LHP
1939	PHI	AL	1	1	0	1	0	0	0	0	0	0	0	0	0	0	1	0
1940	PHI	AL	1	0	1	0	1	0	0	0	0	0	0	0	0	0	0	1
1941	PHI	AL	2	0	2	0	1	1	0	0	0	0	0	0	0	0	1	1
Total			4	1	3	1	2	1	0	0	0	0	0	0	0	0	2	2

Rank among batters: 3,427 • *Total ballparks homered in*: 3 • *First HR*: 09/30/1939 off Joe Haynes

Ron Brand

RONALD GEORGE BRAND
B: 01/13/1940
BR

Year	Tm	Lg	Tot	H	A	Men-On 0	1	2	3	One-Game 2	3	4	LO	XN	IP	PH	RHP	LHP
1963	PIT	NL	1	0	1	1	0	0	0	0	0	0	0	0	0	0	0	1
1965	HOU	NL	2	1	1	0	1	1	0	0	0	0	0	0	0	0	1	1
Total			3	1	2	1	1	1	0	0	0	0	0	0	0	0	1	2

Rank among batters: 3,735 • *Total ballparks homered in*: 3 • *First HR*: 06/20/1963 off Denny Lemaster

Jackie Brandt

JOHN GEORGE BRANDT
B: 04/28/1934
BR

Year	Tm	Lg	Tot	H	A	Men-On 0	1	2	3	One-Game 2	3	4	LO	XN	IP	PH	RHP	LHP
1956	STL	NL	1	1	0	1	0	0	0	0	0	0	0	0	0	0	0	1
	NY	NL	11	8	3	0	9	2	0	0	1	0	0	1	0	1	5	6
	Total		12	9	3	10	2	0	0	1	0	0	1	0	0	1	5	7
1959	SF	NL	12	6	6	7	3	1	1	0	0	0	0	0	0	0	11	1
1960	BAL	AL	15	4	11	11	4	0	0	0	0	0	2	1	0	0	9	6
1961	BAL	AL	16	8	8	11	3	2	0	2	0	0	1	0	0	0	13	3
1962	BAL	AL	19	6	13	13	6	0	0	1	0	0	0	0	0	0	12	7
1963	BAL	AL	15	10	5	6	6	3	0	0	0	0	0	0	0	0	9	6
1964	BAL	AL	13	6	7	4	7	2	0	3	0	0	1	0	0	0	10	3
1965	BAL	AL	8	4	4	6	2	0	0	0	0	0	0	1	0	1	5	3
1966	PHI	NL	1	1	0	1	0	0	0	0	0	0	0	0	0	0	0	1
1967	HOU	NL	1	0	1	0	0	1	0	0	0	0	0	0	0	0	1	0
Total			112	54	58	69	33	9	1	7	0	0	5	2	0	2	75	37

Rank among batters: 429 • *Top target (4 home runs)*: Mudcat Grant • *Number of pitchers victimized*: 89 • *Total ballparks homered in*: 21 • *First HR*: 05/28/1956 off Lou Sleater

Year	Tm	Lg	Tot	H	A	Men-On 0	1	2	3	One-Game 2	3	4	LO	XN	IP	PH	RHP	LHP

Otis Brannan

OTIS OWEN BRANNAN
B: 03/13/1899 D: 06/06/1967
BL

Year	Tm	Lg	Tot	H	A	0	1	2	3	2	3	4	LO	XN	IP	PH	RHP	LHP
1928	STL	AL	10	9	1	4	6	0	0	1	0	0	0	0	0	0	9	1
1929	STL	AL	1	0	1	0	1	0	0	0	0	0	0	0	0	1	1	0
Total			11	9	2	4	7	0	0	1	0	0	0	0	0	1	10	1

Rank among batters: 2,419 • *Top target (2 home runs)*: Jack Russell • *Number of pitchers victimized*: 10 • *Total ballparks homered in*: 3 • *First HR*: 05/17/1928 off Stan Coveleski

Kitty Bransfield

WILLIAM EDWARD BRANSFIELD
B: 01/07/1875 D: 05/01/1947
BR

Year	Tm	Lg	Tot	H	A	0	1	2	3	2	3	4	LO	XN	IP	PH	RHP	LHP
1903	PIT	NL	2	1	1	2	0	0	0	0	0	0	0	0	1	0	2	0
1905	PHI	NL	3	1	2	1	1	1	0	0	0	0	0	0	2	0	1	2
1906	PHI	NL	1	0	1	0	0	0	1	0	0	0	0	0	1	0	1	0
1908	PHI	NL	3	0	3	1	1	0	1	0	0	0	0	0	2	0	1	2
1909	PHI	NL	1	0	1	0	0	1	0	0	0	0	0	0	0	0	0	1
1910	PHI	NL	3	1	2	0	1	2	0	0	0	0	0	0	0	0	2	1
Total			13	3	10	4	3	4	2	0	0	0	0	0	6	0	7	6

Rank among batters: 2,248 • *Top target (2 home runs)*: Hooks Wiltse, Carl Lundgren • *Number of pitchers victimized*: 11 • *Total ballparks homered in*: 7 • *First HR*: 05/27/1903 off Vic Willis

Jeff Branson

JEFFERY GLENN BRANSON
B: 01/26/1967
BL

Year	Tm	Lg	Tot	H	A	0	1	2	3	2	3	4	LO	XN	IP	PH	RHP	LHP
1993	CIN	NL	3	2	1	2	1	0	0	0	0	0	0	0	0	0	2	1
1994	CIN	NL	6	1	5	3	3	0	0	0	0	0	0	0	0	0	5	1
1995	CIN	NL	12	9	3	8	2	2	0	0	0	0	0	0	1	0	12	0
Total			21	12	9	13	6	2	0	0	0	0	0	0	1	0	19	2

Rank among batters: 1,768 • *Top target (2 home runs)*: John Smoltz • *Number of pitchers victimized*: 20 • *Total ballparks homered in*: 7 • *First HR*: 06/12/1993 off John Smoltz

Mickey Brantley

MICHAEL CHARLES BRANTLEY
B: 06/17/1961
BR

Year	Tm	Lg	Tot	H	A	0	1	2	3	2	3	4	LO	XN	IP	PH	RHP	LHP
1986	SEA	AL	3	2	1	2	1	0	0	0	0	0	0	0	0	0	2	1
1987	SEA	AL	14	11	3	7	4	3	0	0	1	0	1	0	1	0	7	7
1988	SEA	AL	15	11	4	9	4	1	1	0	0	0	0	1	0	1	12	3
Total			32	24	8	18	9	4	1	0	1	0	1	1	1	1	21	11

Rank among batters: 1,360 • *Top target (3 home runs)*: Oil Can Boyd • *Number of pitchers victimized*: 28 • *Total ballparks homered in*: 8 • *First HR*: 08/12/1986 off Joaquin Andujar

Kitty Brashear

NORMAN C. BRASHEAR
B: 08/27/1877 D: 12/22/1934
BR

Year	Tm	Lg	Tot	H	A	0	1	2	3	2	3	4	LO	XN	IP	PH	RHP	LHP
1902	STL	NL	1	1	0	0	1	0	0	0	0	0	0	0	1	0	0	1

Rank among batters: 4,707 • *Total ballparks homered in*: 1 • First HR: 05/19/1902 off Doc Newton

Steve Braun

STEPHEN RUSSELL BRAUN
B: 05/08/1948
BL

Year	Tm	Lg	Tot	H	A	0	1	2	3	2	3	4	LO	XN	IP	PH	RHP	LHP
1971	MIN	AL	5	1	4	5	0	0	0	0	0	0	0	0	0	0	2	3
1972	MIN	AL	2	1	1	0	2	0	0	0	0	0	0	0	0	0	1	1
1973	MIN	AL	6	4	2	4	1	1	0	1	0	0	0	0	0	0	5	1
1974	MIN	AL	8	5	3	6	1	1	0	0	0	0	1	2	0	0	8	0
1975	MIN	AL	11	9	2	7	4	0	0	0	0	0	0	0	0	1	10	1
1976	MIN	AL	3	1	2	2	0	1	0	0	0	0	0	0	0	0	3	0
1977	SEA	AL	5	2	3	4	1	0	0	0	0	0	0	0	0	0	4	1
1978	SEA	AL	3	3	0	2	1	0	0	0	0	0	0	0	0	1	3	0
1979	KC	AL	4	2	2	3	1	0	0	0	0	0	0	0	0	0	4	0
1980	TOR	AL	1	0	1	1	0	0	0	0	0	0	0	1	0	0	1	0

Steve Braun *continued*

Year	Tm	Lg	Tot	H	A	Men-On 0	1	2	3	One-Game 2	3	4	LO	XN	IP	PH	RHP	LHP
1983	STL	NL	3	1	2	2	1	0	0	0	0	0	0	0	0	2	3	0
1985	STL	NL	1	0	1	0	1	0	0	0	0	0	0	1	0	1	1	0
Total			52	29	23	36	13	3	0	1	0	0	1	4	0	5	45	7

Rank among batters: 965 • *Top target (3 home runs)*: Catfish Hunter, Ferguson Jenkins • *Number of pitchers victimized*: 44 • *Total ballparks homered in*: 17 • *First HR*: 05/21/1971 off Darold Knowles

Angel Bravo

ANGEL ALFONSO (URDANETA) BRAVO
B: 08/04/1942
BL

Year	Tm	Lg	Tot	H	A	Men-On 0	1	2	3	One-Game 2	3	4	LO	XN	IP	PH	RHP	LHP
1969	CHI	AL	1	1	0	0	1	0	0	0	0	0	0	0	0	0	1	0

Rank among batters: 4,707 • *Total ballparks homered in*: 1 • *First HR*: 09/12/1969 off Lew Krausse

Sid Bream

SIDNEY EUGENE BREAM
B: 08/03/1960
BL

Year	Tm	Lg	Tot	H	A	Men-On 0	1	2	3	One-Game 2	3	4	LO	XN	IP	PH	RHP	LHP
1985	LA	NL	3	2	1	2	1	0	0	0	0	0	0	0	0	0	2	1
	PIT	NL	3	0	3	0	3	0	0	0	0	0	0	0	0	0	3	0
	Total		6	2	4	5	1	0	0	0	0	0	0	0	0	0	5	1
1986	PIT	NL	16	5	11	8	6	2	0	0	0	0	0	1	0	0	14	2
1987	PIT	NL	13	10	3	7	6	0	0	1	0	0	0	0	0	0	5	8
1988	PIT	NL	10	6	4	5	4	1	0	0	0	0	0	1	0	1	7	3
1990	PIT	NL	15	8	7	6	7	2	0	0	0	0	0	0	0	0	13	2
1991	ATL	NL	11	3	8	6	2	1	2	0	0	0	0	0	0	2	11	0
1992	ATL	NL	10	4	6	7	3	0	0	0	0	0	0	0	0	0	9	1
1993	ATL	NL	9	5	4	5	3	0	1	0	0	0	0	0	0	1	9	0
Total			90	43	47	49	32	6	3	1	0	0	0	2	0	4	73	17

Rank among batters: 573 • *Top target (4 home runs)*: Kevin Gross • *Number of pitchers victimized*: 76 • *Total ballparks homered in*: 13 • *First HR*: 04/12/1985 off Mike Krukow • *LCS HR*—3

Jim Breazeale

JAMES LEO BREAZEALE
B: 10/03/1949
BL

Year	Tm	Lg	Tot	H	A	Men-On 0	1	2	3	One-Game 2	3	4	LO	XN	IP	PH	RHP	LHP
1971	ATL	NL	1	1	0	1	0	0	0	0	0	0	0	0	0	0	1	0
1972	ATL	NL	5	4	1	1	2	2	0	0	0	0	0	0	0	3	4	1
1978	CHI	AL	3	2	1	2	1	0	0	1	0	0	0	0	0	0	3	0
Total			9	7	2	4	3	2	0	1	0	0	0	0	0	3	8	1

Rank among batters: 2,587 • *Top target (2 home runs)*: Paul Mitchell • *Number of pitchers victimized*: 8 • *Total ballparks homered in*: 4 • *First HR*: 09/30/1971 off Milt Wilcox

Harry Brecheen

HARRY DAVID BRECHEEN
B: 10/14/1914
BL

Year	Tm	Lg	Tot	H	A	Men-On 0	1	2	3	One-Game 2	3	4	LO	XN	IP	PH	RHP	LHP
1950	STL	NL	1	0	1	1	0	0	0	0	0	0	0	0	0	0	1	0
1951	STL	NL	1	0	1	1	0	0	0	0	0	0	0	0	0	0	1	0
Total			2	0	2	2	0	0	0	0	0	0	0	0	0	0	2	0

Rank among batters: 4,129 • *Total ballparks homered in*: 2 • *First HR*: 09/19/1950 off Johnny Sain

Hal Breeden

HAROLD NOEL BREEDEN
B: 06/28/1944
BR

Year	Tm	Lg	Tot	H	A	Men-On 0	1	2	3	One-Game 2	3	4	LO	XN	IP	PH	RHP	LHP
1971	CHI	NL	1	1	0	1	0	0	0	0	0	0	0	0	0	0	1	0
1972	MON	NL	3	1	2	2	1	0	0	0	0	0	0	0	0	0	1	2
1973	MON	NL	15	4	11	8	5	2	0	1	0	0	0	0	0	4	6	9
1974	MON	NL	2	0	2	1	1	0	0	0	0	0	0	0	0	0	0	2
Total			21	6	15	12	7	2	0	1	0	0	0	0	0	4	8	13

Rank among batters: 1,768 • *Top target (2 home runs)*: Claude Osteen, Steve Carlton, Ken Brett • *Number of pitchers victimized*: 18 • *Total ballparks homered in*: 10 • *First HR*: 04/23/1971 off Charlie Williams

Marv Breeding

MARVIN EUGENE BREEDING
B: 03/08/1934
BR

Year	Tm	Lg	Tot	H	A	Men-On 0	Men-On 1	Men-On 2	Men-On 3	One-Game 2	One-Game 3	One-Game 4	LO	XN	IP	PH	RHP	LHP
1960	BAL	AL	3	2	1	2	1	0	0	0	0	0	1	0	0	0	1	2
1961	BAL	AL	1	1	0	1	0	0	0	0	0	0	0	0	0	0	1	0
1962	BAL	AL	2	1	1	1	0	1	0	0	0	0	0	0	0	0	1	1
1963	WAS	AL	1	1	0	1	0	0	0	0	0	0	1	0	0	0	1	0
Total			7	5	2	5	1	1	0	0	0	0	2	0	0	0	4	3

Rank among batters: 2,834 • *Total ballparks homered in*: 4 • *First HR*: 05/15/1960 off Jerry Casale

Ted Breitenstein

THEODORE P. BREITENSTEIN
B: 06/01/1869 D: 05/03/1935
BL

Year	Tm	Lg	Tot	H	A	Men-On 0	Men-On 1	Men-On 2	Men-On 3	One-Game 2	One-Game 3	One-Game 4	LO	XN	IP	PH	RHP	LHP
1893	STL	NL	1	0	1	0	1	0	0	0	0	0	0	0	0	0	1	0
1899	CIN	NL	1	0	1	1	0	0	0	0	0	0	0	0	0	0	0	0
1900	CIN	NL	2	0	2	2	0	0	0	0	0	0	0	0	0	0	2	0
Total			4	0	4	3	1	0	0	0	0	0	0	0	0	0	3	0

Rank among batters: 3,427 • *Total ballparks homered in*: 3 • *First HR*: 05/30/1893 off Al Maul

Herb Bremer

HERBERT FREDERICK BREMER
B: 10/25/1913 D: 11/28/1979
BR

Year	Tm	Lg	Tot	H	A	Men-On 0	Men-On 1	Men-On 2	Men-On 3	One-Game 2	One-Game 3	One-Game 4	LO	XN	IP	PH	RHP	LHP
1938	STL	NL	2	2	0	2	0	0	0	0	0	0	0	0	0	0	2	0

Rank among batters: 4,129 • *Total ballparks homered in*: 1 • *First HR*: 05/03/1938 off Lou Fette

Bob Brenly

ROBERT EARL BRENLY
B: 02/25/1954
BR

Year	Tm	Lg	Tot	H	A	Men-On 0	Men-On 1	Men-On 2	Men-On 3	One-Game 2	One-Game 3	One-Game 4	LO	XN	IP	PH	RHP	LHP
1981	SF	NL	1	1	0	0	1	0	0	0	0	0	0	0	0	0	0	1
1982	SF	NL	4	1	3	3	1	0	0	1	0	0	0	0	0	0	1	3
1983	SF	NL	7	5	2	3	3	1	0	0	0	0	0	0	0	0	2	5
1984	SF	NL	20	6	14	7	8	4	1	2	0	0	0	1	1	0	17	3
1985	SF	NL	19	9	10	11	7	1	0	1	0	0	0	0	0	0	13	6
1986	SF	NL	16	8	8	9	3	4	0	1	0	0	0	0	0	0	10	6
1987	SF	NL	18	10	8	14	2	1	1	0	0	0	0	1	0	1	11	7
1988	SF	NL	5	2	3	2	2	1	0	1	0	0	0	0	0	0	4	1
1989	TOR	AL	1	0	1	1	0	0	0	0	0	0	0	0	0	0	1	0
Total			91	42	49	50	27	12	2	6	0	0	0	2	1	1	59	32

Rank among batters: 559 • *Top target (3 home runs)*: Rick Mahler, Bill Gullickson • *Number of pitchers victimized*: 72 • *Total ballparks homered in*: 12 • *First HR*: 08/28/1981 off Rod Scurry • *LCS HR*—1

Ad Brennan

ADDISON FOSTER BRENNAN
B: 07/18/1881 D: 01/07/1962
BL

Year	Tm	Lg	Tot	H	A	Men-On 0	Men-On 1	Men-On 2	Men-On 3	One-Game 2	One-Game 3	One-Game 4	LO	XN	IP	PH	RHP	LHP
1912	PHI	NL	1	0	1	0	1	0	0	0	0	0	0	0	0	0	1	0

Rank among batters: 4,707 • *Total ballparks homered in*: 1 • *First HR*: 07/04/1912 off Buster Brown

Roger Bresnahan

ROGER PHILIP BRESNAHAN
B: 06/11/1879 D: 12/04/1944
BR HOF

Year	Tm	Lg	Tot	H	A	Men-On 0	Men-On 1	Men-On 2	Men-On 3	One-Game 2	One-Game 3	One-Game 4	LO	XN	IP	PH	RHP	LHP
1901	BAL	AL	1	0	1	1	0	0	0	0	0	0	0	0	0	0	1	0
1902	BAL	AL	4	2	2	1	2	1	0	1	0	0	0	0	2	0	4	0
	NY	NL	1	1	0	0	0	1	0	0	0	0	0	0	0	0	1	0
	Total		5	3	2	1	2	2	0	1	0	0	0	0	2	0	5	0
1903	NY	NL	4	2	2	0	2	1	1	0	0	0	0	0	2	0	2	1
1904	NY	NL	5	3	2	3	2	0	0	1	0	0	1	0	3	0	4	1
1907	NY	NL	4	3	1	2	2	0	0	0	0	0	0	0	2	0	4	0
1908	NY	NL	1	0	1	1	0	0	0	0	0	0	0	0	0	0	1	0
1911	STL	NL	3	0	3	3	0	0	0	0	0	0	0	0	0	0	1	2

Roger Bresnahan *continued*

Year	Tm	Lg	Tot	H	A	Men-On 0	1	2	3	One-Game 2	3	4	LO	XN	IP	PH	RHP	LHP
1912	STL	NL	1	0	1	0	0	1	0	0	0	0	0	0	0	0	0	1
1913	CHI	NL	1	0	1	0	1	0	0	0	0	0	0	0	0	0	0	1
1915	CHI	NL	1	1	0	0	1	0	0	0	0	0	0	0	0	0	1	0
Total			26	12	14	11	10	4	1	2	0	0	1	0	9	0	19	6

Rank among batters: 1,576 • *Top target (2 home runs)*: Gene Wright, Roscoe Miller, Stoney McGlynn • *Number of pitchers victimized*: 23 • *Total ballparks homered in*: 12 • *First HR*: 07/21/1901 off Bill Reidy

Rube Bressler

RAYMOND BLOOM BRESSLER
B: 10/23/1894 D: 11/07/1966
BR

Year	Tm	Lg	Tot	H	A	Men-On 0	1	2	3	One-Game 2	3	4	LO	XN	IP	PH	RHP	LHP
1915	PHI	AL	1	0	1	1	0	0	0	0	0	0	0	0	0	0	1	0
1919	CIN	NL	2	0	2	2	0	0	0	0	0	0	0	0	2	0	1	1
1921	CIN	NL	1	0	1	1	0	0	0	0	0	0	0	0	1	0	1	0
1924	CIN	NL	4	0	4	3	1	0	0	0	0	0	0	0	1	0	4	0
1925	CIN	NL	4	2	2	2	2	0	0	0	0	0	0	0	2	0	4	0
1926	CIN	NL	1	0	1	0	1	0	0	0	0	0	0	0	0	0	1	0
1927	CIN	NL	3	0	3	0	2	1	0	0	0	0	0	0	1	0	1	2
1928	BRO	NL	4	2	2	3	1	0	0	0	0	0	0	0	0	0	3	1
1929	BRO	NL	9	8	1	7	1	1	0	0	0	0	0	1	1	0	6	3
1930	BRO	NL	3	1	2	1	0	2	0	0	0	0	0	1	0	0	2	1
Total			32	13	19	20	8	4	0	0	0	0	0	2	8	0	24	8

Rank among batters: 1,360 • *Top target (2 home runs)*: Jack Knight, Percy Jones, Joe Genewich • *Number of pitchers victimized*: 29 • *Total ballparks homered in*: 8 • *First HR*: 08/16/1915 off Ray Caldwell

Eddie Bressoud

EDWARD FRANCIS BRESSOUD
B: 05/02/1932
BR

Year	Tm	Lg	Tot	H	A	Men-On 0	1	2	3	One-Game 2	3	4	LO	XN	IP	PH	RHP	LHP
1957	NY	NL	5	4	1	4	1	0	0	0	0	0	0	0	0	0	5	0
1959	SF	NL	9	7	2	8	0	1	0	0	0	0	0	0	0	0	4	5
1960	SF	NL	9	2	7	6	2	1	0	0	0	0	0	0	1	0	6	3
1961	SF	NL	3	2	1	2	0	1	0	0	0	0	0	0	0	0	2	1
1962	BOS	AL	14	7	7	10	2	2	0	1	0	0	0	0	0	0	14	0
1963	BOS	AL	20	14	6	14	4	1	1	4	0	0	0	0	0	0	16	4
1964	BOS	AL	15	9	6	10	4	1	0	0	0	0	0	0	0	0	13	2
1965	BOS	AL	8	5	3	4	2	2	0	0	0	0	0	0	0	1	7	1
1966	NY	NL	10	5	5	4	0	5	1	1	0	0	0	0	0	0	4	6
1967	STL	NL	1	1	0	1	0	0	0	0	0	0	0	0	0	0	1	0
Total			94	56	38	63	15	14	2	6	0	0	0	0	1	1	72	22

Rank among batters: 535 • *Top target (4 home runs)*: Harvey Haddix • *Number of pitchers victimized*: 70 • *Total ballparks homered in*: 22 • *First HR*: 07/05/1957 off Joe Trimble

George Brett

GEORGE HOWARD BRETT
B: 05/15/1953
BL

Year	Tm	Lg	Tot	H	A	Men-On 0	1	2	3	One-Game 2	3	4	LO	XN	IP	PH	RHP	LHP
1974	KC	AL	2	0	2	2	0	0	0	0	0	0	0	0	0	0	2	0
1975	KC	AL	11	2	9	5	5	1	0	0	0	0	0	0	0	0	8	3
1976	KC	AL	7	6	1	4	3	0	0	0	0	0	0	0	1	0	4	3
1977	KC	AL	22	9	13	10	6	6	0	1	0	0	2	0	0	0	16	6
1978	KC	AL	9	4	5	5	3	1	0	0	0	0	0	0	0	0	8	1
1979	KC	AL	23	11	12	11	10	2	0	1	1	0	0	2	0	0	19	4
1980	KC	AL	24	13	11	12	7	4	1	0	0	0	0	1	1	1	16	8
1981	KC	AL	6	2	4	3	1	2	0	0	0	0	0	0	0	0	5	1
1982	KC	AL	21	9	12	14	5	2	0	0	0	0	0	0	1	0	16	5
1983	KC	AL	25	7	18	9	12	4	0	1	1	0	0	0	0	0	19	6
1984	KC	AL	13	6	7	5	5	2	1	0	0	0	0	0	0	0	5	8
1985	KC	AL	30	15	15	17	8	5	0	3	0	0	0	0	2	0	20	10
1986	KC	AL	16	8	8	9	6	1	0	2	0	0	0	0	0	0	11	5
1987	KC	AL	22	14	8	14	7	1	0	1	0	0	0	1	0	0	15	7
1988	KC	AL	24	13	11	12	11	1	0	3	0	0	0	0	1	0	14	10
1989	KC	AL	12	3	9	6	6	0	0	0	0	0	0	0	0	0	10	2
1990	KC	AL	14	3	11	10	2	2	0	0	0	0	0	1	0	0	9	5
1991	KC	AL	10	3	7	6	3	1	0	1	0	0	0	1	0	0	8	2

George Brett *continued*

Year	Tm	Lg	Tot	H	A	Men-On 0	Men-On 1	Men-On 2	Men-On 3	One-Game 2	One-Game 3	One-Game 4	LO	XN	IP	PH	RHP	LHP
1992	KC	AL	7	1	6	5	2	0	0	0	0	0	0	0	1	0	7	0
1993	KC	AL	19	7	12	12	5	2	0	2	0	0	0	1	0	0	17	2
Total			317	136	181	171	107	37	2	15	2	0	2	7	7	1	229	88

Rank among batters: 60 • *Top target (6 home runs)*: Dan Petry • *Number of pitchers victimized*: 211 • *Total ballparks homered in*: 18 • *First HR*: 05/08/1974 off Ferguson Jenkins • *Hit for Cycle*—vs BAL: 05/28/1979; @TOR: 07/25/1990 • *World Series HR*—1; *LCS HR*—9; *All-Star HR*—1

Ken Brett

KENNETH ALVEN BRETT
B: 09/18/1948
BL

Year	Tm	Lg	Tot	H	A	Men-On 0	Men-On 1	Men-On 2	Men-On 3	One-Game 2	One-Game 3	One-Game 4	LO	XN	IP	PH	RHP	LHP
1969	BOS	AL	1	0	1	1	0	0	0	0	0	0	0	0	0	0	0	1
1970	BOS	AL	2	1	1	2	0	0	0	0	0	0	0	0	0	0	2	0
1973	PHI	NL	4	3	1	4	0	0	0	0	0	0	0	0	0	0	3	1
1974	PIT	NL	2	2	0	2	0	0	0	0	0	0	0	0	0	0	1	1
1975	PIT	NL	1	0	1	1	0	0	0	0	0	0	0	0	0	0	1	0
Total			10	6	4	10	0	0	0	0	0	0	0	0	0	0	7	3

Rank among batters: 2,500 • *Total ballparks homered in*: 7 • *First HR*: 09/12/1969 off Mike Kekich

Rod Brewer

RODNEY LEE BREWER
B: 02/24/1966
BL

Year	Tm	Lg	Tot	H	A	Men-On 0	Men-On 1	Men-On 2	Men-On 3	One-Game 2	One-Game 3	One-Game 4	LO	XN	IP	PH	RHP	LHP
1993	STL	NL	2	0	2	2	0	0	0	0	0	0	0	0	0	1	2	0

Rank among batters: 4,129 • *Total ballparks homered in*: 2 • *First HR*: 07/24/1993 off Kent Bottenfield

Tom Brewer

THOMAS AUSTIN BREWER
B: 09/03/1931
BR

Year	Tm	Lg	Tot	H	A	Men-On 0	Men-On 1	Men-On 2	Men-On 3	One-Game 2	One-Game 3	One-Game 4	LO	XN	IP	PH	RHP	LHP
1956	BOS	AL	1	1	0	0	0	1	0	0	0	0	0	0	0	0	1	0
1959	BOS	AL	1	0	1	1	0	0	0	0	0	0	0	0	0	0	1	0
1960	BOS	AL	1	0	1	1	0	0	0	0	0	0	0	0	0	0	1	0
Total			3	1	2	2	0	1	0	0	0	0	0	0	0	0	3	0

Rank among batters: 3,735 • *Total ballparks homered in*: 3 • *First HR*: 05/27/1956 off Connie Grob

Tony Brewer

ANTHONY BRUCE BREWER
B: 11/25/1957
BR

Year	Tm	Lg	Tot	H	A	Men-On 0	Men-On 1	Men-On 2	Men-On 3	One-Game 2	One-Game 3	One-Game 4	LO	XN	IP	PH	RHP	LHP
1984	LA	NL	1	1	0	1	0	0	0	0	0	0	0	0	0	0	1	0

Rank among batters: 4,707 • *Total ballparks homered in*: 1 • *First HR*: 09/30/1984 off Mark Calvert

Fred Brickell

GEORGE FREDERICK BRICKELL
B: 11/09/1906 D: 04/08/1961
BL

Year	Tm	Lg	Tot	H	A	Men-On 0	Men-On 1	Men-On 2	Men-On 3	One-Game 2	One-Game 3	One-Game 4	LO	XN	IP	PH	RHP	LHP
1927	PIT	NL	1	0	1	0	1	0	0	0	0	0	0	0	0	1	1	0
1928	PIT	NL	3	0	3	2	1	0	0	0	0	0	0	0	0	0	3	0
1930	PIT	NL	1	0	1	1	0	0	0	0	0	0	0	0	0	0	1	0
1931	PHI	NL	1	1	0	1	0	0	0	0	0	0	0	0	0	0	0	1
Total			6	1	5	4	2	0	0	0	0	0	0	0	0	1	5	1

Rank among batters: 2,988 • *Total ballparks homered in*: 2 • *First HR*: 07/16/1927 off Art Decatur

Fritz Brickell

FRITZ DARRELL BRICKELL
B: 03/19/1935 D: 10/15/1965
BR

Year	Tm	Lg	Tot	H	A	Men-On 0	Men-On 1	Men-On 2	Men-On 3	One-Game 2	One-Game 3	One-Game 4	LO	XN	IP	PH	RHP	LHP
1959	NY	AL	1	0	1	0	1	0	0	0	0	0	0	0	0	0	1	0

Rank among batters: 4,707 • *Total ballparks homered in*: 1 • *First HR*: 07/25/1959 off Tom Morgan

Year	Tm	Lg	Tot	H	A	Men-On 0	Men-On 1	Men-On 2	Men-On 3	One-Game 2	One-Game 3	One-Game 4	LO	XN	IP	PH	RHP	LHP

Jim Brideweser

JAMES EHRENFELD BRIDEWESER
B: 02/13/1927 D: 08/25/1989
BR

Year	Tm	Lg	Tot	H	A	0	1	2	3	2	3	4	LO	XN	IP	PH	RHP	LHP
1957	BAL	AL	1	1	0	0	0	1	0	0	0	0	0	0	0	0	1	0

Rank among batters: 4,707 • *Total ballparks homered in*: 1 • *First HR*: 05/24/1957 off Frank Sullivan

Marshall Bridges

MARSHALL BRIDGES
B: 06/02/1931 D: 09/03/1990
BB

Year	Tm	Lg	Tot	H	A	0	1	2	3	2	3	4	LO	XN	IP	PH	RHP	LHP
1959	STL	NL	1	0	1	0	1	0	0	0	0	0	0	0	0	0	1	0

Rank among batters: 4,707 • *Total ballparks homered in*: 1 • *First HR*: 06/28/1959 off Orlando Pena

Rocky Bridges

EVERETT LAMAR BRIDGES
B: 08/07/1927
BR

Year	Tm	Lg	Tot	H	A	0	1	2	3	2	3	4	LO	XN	IP	PH	RHP	LHP
1951	BRO	NL	1	0	1	0	1	0	0	0	0	0	0	0	0	0	0	1
1953	CIN	NL	1	0	1	1	0	0	0	0	0	0	0	0	0	0	1	0
1955	CIN	NL	1	0	1	1	0	0	0	0	0	0	0	0	0	0	0	1
1957	WAS	AL	3	1	2	2	1	0	0	0	0	0	0	0	0	0	2	1
1958	WAS	AL	5	3	2	4	1	0	0	0	0	0	0	0	0	0	2	3
1959	DET	AL	3	2	1	1	1	0	1	0	0	0	0	0	0	0	2	1
1961	LA	AL	2	2	0	1	0	1	0	0	0	0	0	0	0	0	2	0
Total			16	8	8	10	4	1	1	0	0	0	0	0	0	0	9	7

Rank among batters: 2,029 • *Total ballparks homered in*: 7 • *First HR*: 06/23/1951 off Bill Werle

Al Bridwell

ALBERT HENRY BRIDWELL
B: 01/04/1884 D: 01/23/1969
BL

Year	Tm	Lg	Tot	H	A	0	1	2	3	2	3	4	LO	XN	IP	PH	RHP	LHP
1913	CHI	NL	1	1	0	0	1	0	0	0	0	0	0	0	0	0	1	0
1914	STL	FL	1	0	1	0	1	0	0	0	0	0	0	0	0	0	1	0
Total			2	1	1	0	2	0	0	0	0	0	0	0	0	0	2	0

Rank among batters: 4,129 • *Total ballparks homered in*: 2 • *First HR*: 04/30/1913 off George Suggs

Bunny Brief

ANTHONY VINCENT BRIEF
B: 07/03/1892 D: 02/10/1963
BR

Year	Tm	Lg	Tot	H	A	0	1	2	3	2	3	4	LO	XN	IP	PH	RHP	LHP
1913	STL	AL	1	1	0	1	0	0	0	0	0	0	0	0	0	0	0	1
1915	CHI	AL	2	1	1	2	0	0	0	0	0	0	0	1	0	0	1	1
1917	PIT	NL	2	0	2	1	1	0	0	0	0	0	0	0	0	0	2	0
Total			5	2	3	4	1	0	0	0	0	0	0	1	0	0	3	2

Rank among batters: 3,191 • *Total ballparks homered in*: 3 • *First HR*: 05/16/1913 off Ray Collins

Buttons Briggs

HERBERT THEODORE BRIGGS
B: 07/08/1875 D: 02/18/1911
BR

Year	Tm	Lg	Tot	H	A	0	1	2	3	2	3	4	LO	XN	IP	PH	RHP	LHP
1904	CHI	NL	1	0	1	1	0	0	0	0	0	0	0	0	0	0	0	1

Rank among batters: 4,707 • *Total ballparks homered in*: 1 • *First HR*: 09/28/1904 off Hooks Wiltse

Charlie Briggs

CHARLES R. BRIGGS
B: 1861

Year	Tm	Lg	Tot	H	A	0	1	2	3	2	3	4	LO	XN	IP	PH	RHP	LHP
1884	CHI	UA	1	1	0	0	1	0	0	0	0	0	0	0	0	0	1	0

Rank among batters: 4,707 • *Total ballparks homered in*: 1 • *First HR*: 05/08/1884 off Sam Weaver

Dan Briggs

DAN LEE BRIGGS
B: 11/18/1952
BL

Year	Tm	Lg	Tot	H	A	0	1	2	3	2	3	4	LO	XN	IP	PH	RHP	LHP
1975	CAL	AL	1	0	1	0	1	0	0	0	0	0	0	0	0	0	1	0

Dan Briggs *continued*

Year	Tm	Lg	Tot	H	A	Men-On 0	1	2	3	One-Game 2	3	4	LO	XN	IP	PH	RHP	LHP
1976	CAL	AL	1	1	0	1	0	0	0	0	0	0	0	0	0	0	1	0
1977	CAL	AL	1	1	0	1	0	0	0	0	0	0	0	0	0	0	1	0
1978	CLE	AL	1	1	0	1	0	0	0	0	0	0	0	0	0	0	0	1
1979	SD	NL	8	5	3	3	4	1	0	0	0	0	0	0	0	0	7	1
Total			12	8	4	6	5	1	0	0	0	0	0	0	0	0	10	2

Rank among batters: 2,325 • *Total ballparks homered in*: 7 • *First HR*: 09/14/1975 off Steve Busby

John Briggs

JOHN EDWARD BRIGGS
B: 03/10/1944
BL

Year	Tm	Lg	Tot	H	A	Men-On 0	1	2	3	One-Game 2	3	4	LO	XN	IP	PH	RHP	LHP
1964	PHI	NL	1	0	1	1	0	0	0	0	0	0	1	0	0	0	1	0
1965	PHI	NL	4	2	2	1	3	0	0	0	0	0	0	1	0	0	4	0
1966	PHI	NL	10	4	6	9	1	0	0	1	0	0	3	1	0	0	9	1
1967	PHI	NL	9	2	7	5	3	1	0	0	0	0	1	0	0	0	7	2
1968	PHI	NL	7	1	6	4	3	0	0	1	0	0	0	0	0	0	7	0
1969	PHI	NL	12	5	7	5	5	1	1	1	0	0	1	0	0	0	10	2
1970	PHI	NL	9	4	5	5	2	2	0	1	0	0	0	1	0	0	7	2
1971	MIL	AL	21	6	15	15	4	2	0	2	0	0	0	0	0	0	17	4
1972	MIL	AL	21	7	14	12	5	3	1	2	0	0	0	0	0	0	18	3
1973	MIL	AL	18	10	8	10	6	2	0	0	0	0	0	0	1	0	14	4
1974	MIL	AL	17	6	11	6	8	2	1	2	0	0	0	0	0	0	12	5
1975	MIL	AL	3	2	1	3	0	0	0	0	0	0	0	0	0	0	3	0
	MIN	AL	7	3	4	5	1	1	0	0	0	0	0	0	0	0	5	2
	Total		10	5	5	8	1	1	0	0	0	0	0	0	0	0	8	2
Total			139	52	87	81	41	14	3	10	0	0	6	3	1	0	114	25

Rank among batters: 311 • Top target (3 home runs): Sammy Ellis, Marty Pattin, Ray Corbin, Stan Bahnsen, Doyle Alexander, Jim Perry • *Number of pitchers victimized*: 100 • *Total ballparks homered in*: 25 • *First HR*: 06/21/1964 off Frank Lary

Harry Bright

HARRY JAMES BRIGHT
B: 09/22/1929
BR

Year	Tm	Lg	Tot	H	A	Men-On 0	1	2	3	One-Game 2	3	4	LO	XN	IP	PH	RHP	LHP
1958	PIT	NL	1	1	0	0	1	0	0	0	0	0	0	0	0	0	0	1
1959	PIT	NL	3	1	2	1	1	1	0	0	0	0	0	1	0	1	0	3
1961	WAS	AL	4	2	2	3	1	0	0	0	0	0	0	0	0	0	0	4
1962	WAS	AL	17	8	9	8	4	5	0	0	0	0	0	1	0	1	13	4
1963	NY	AL	7	4	3	4	3	0	0	0	0	0	0	0	0	0	2	5
Total			32	16	16	16	10	6	0	0	0	0	0	2	0	2	15	17

Rank among batters: 1,360 • Top target (2 home runs): Bud Daley, Bill Monbouquette, Mudcat Grant, Ted Bowsfield, Dick Donovan, Dick Stigman, Hank Aguirre • *Number of pitchers victimized*: 25 • *Total ballparks homered in*: 10 • *First HR*: 08/09/1958 off Alex Kellner

Nelson Briles

NELSON KELLEY BRILES
B: 08/05/1943
BR

Year	Tm	Lg	Tot	H	A	Men-On 0	1	2	3	One-Game 2	3	4	LO	XN	IP	PH	RHP	LHP
1969	STL	NL	1	0	1	1	0	0	0	0	0	0	0	0	0	0	0	1
1971	PIT	NL	1	0	1	1	0	0	0	0	0	0	0	0	0	0	0	1
1973	PIT	NL	1	1	0	1	0	0	0	0	0	0	0	0	0	0	1	0
Total			3	1	2	3	0	0	0	0	0	0	0	0	0	0	1	2

Rank among batters: 3,735 • *Total ballparks homered in*: 3 • *First HR*: 06/21/1969 off Jack DiLauro

Greg Briley

GREGORY BRILEY
B: 05/24/1965
BL

Year	Tm	Lg	Tot	H	A	Men-On 0	1	2	3	One-Game 2	3	4	LO	XN	IP	PH	RHP	LHP
1988	SEA	AL	1	0	1	1	0	0	0	0	0	0	0	0	0	0	1	0
1989	SEA	AL	13	5	8	9	3	1	0	2	0	0	0	0	0	0	12	1
1990	SEA	AL	5	4	1	2	2	1	0	1	0	0	0	0	0	0	5	0
1991	SEA	AL	2	2	0	0	2	0	0	0	0	0	0	1	0	0	2	0
1992	SEA	AL	5	1	4	5	0	0	0	0	0	0	1	0	0	2	5	0
1993	FLO	NL	3	2	1	1	2	0	0	1	0	0	0	0	0	0	2	1
Total			29	14	15	18	9	2	0	4	0	0	1	1	0	2	27	2

Rank among batters: 1,465 • *Top target (2 home runs)*: Eric King, Dave Johnson, Jaime Navarro • *Number of pitchers victimized*: 26 • *Total ballparks homered in*: 12 • *First HR*: 07/09/1988 off Todd Stottlemyre

Jim Brillheart

JAMES BENSON BRILLHEART
B: 09/28/1903 D: 09/02/1972
BR

Year	Tm	Lg	Tot	H	A	Men-On 0	1	2	3	One-Game 2	3	4	LO	XN	IP	PH	RHP	LHP
1931	BOS	AL	1	0	1	0	1	0	0	0	0	0	0	0	0	0	1	0

Rank among batters: 4,707 • *Total ballparks homered in*: 1 • *First HR*: 04/15/1931 off Hank Johnson

Chuck Brinkman

CHARLES ERNEST BRINKMAN
B: 09/16/1944
BR

Year	Tm	Lg	Tot	H	A	Men-On 0	1	2	3	One-Game 2	3	4	LO	XN	IP	PH	RHP	LHP
1973	CHI	AL	1	1	0	0	1	0	0	0	0	0	0	0	0	0	0	1

Rank among batters: 4,707 • *Total ballparks homered in*: 1 • *First HR*: 05/22/1973 off Rudy May

Ed Brinkman

EDWIN ALBERT BRINKMAN
B: 12/08/1941
BR

Year	Tm	Lg	Tot	H	A	Men-On 0	1	2	3	One-Game 2	3	4	LO	XN	IP	PH	RHP	LHP
1963	WAS	AL	7	3	4	4	2	1	0	0	0	0	1	0	0	0	6	1
1964	WAS	AL	8	6	2	5	3	0	0	0	0	0	1	0	0	0	5	3
1965	WAS	AL	5	2	3	0	5	0	0	0	0	0	0	0	0	0	3	2
1966	WAS	AL	7	3	4	4	2	1	0	0	0	0	0	0	0	0	6	1
1967	WAS	AL	1	0	1	1	0	0	0	0	0	0	0	0	0	0	1	0
1969	WAS	AL	2	0	2	1	1	0	0	0	0	0	0	0	0	0	2	0
1970	WAS	AL	1	0	1	1	0	0	0	0	0	0	1	0	0	0	0	1
1971	DET	AL	1	1	0	0	1	0	0	0	0	0	0	0	0	0	1	0
1972	DET	AL	6	4	2	2	2	2	0	0	0	0	0	0	0	0	5	1
1973	DET	AL	7	2	5	6	1	0	0	0	0	0	0	0	0	0	4	3
1974	DET	AL	14	6	8	9	5	0	0	1	0	0	0	0	0	0	5	9
1975	STL	NL	1	0	1	1	0	0	0	0	0	0	0	0	0	0	1	0
Total			60	27	33	34	22	4	0	1	0	0	3	0	0	0	39	21

Rank among batters: 863 • *Top target (3 home runs)*: Diego Segui • *Number of pitchers victimized*: 49 • *Total ballparks homered in*: 12 • *First HR*: 04/24/1963 off Camilo Pascual

Fatty Briody

CHARLES F. BRIODY
B: 08/13/1858 D: 06/22/1903

Year	Tm	Lg	Tot	H	A	Men-On 0	1	2	3	One-Game 2	3	4	LO	XN	IP	PH	RHP	LHP
1884	CLE	NL	1	0	1	1	0	0	0	0	0	0	0	0	0	0	1	0
1885	STL	NL	1	1	0	1	0	0	0	0	0	0	0	0	0	0	1	0
1887	DET	NL	1	1	0	0	1	0	0	0	0	0	0	0	0	0	1	0
Total			3	2	1	2	1	0	0	0	0	0	0	0	0	0	3	0

Rank among batters: 3,735 • *Total ballparks homered in*: 3 • *First HR*: 08/07/1884 off Larry Corcoran

Bernardo Brito

BERNARDO (PEREZ) BRITO
B: 12/04/1963
BR

Year	Tm	Lg	Tot	H	A	Men-On 0	1	2	3	One-Game 2	3	4	LO	XN	IP	PH	RHP	LHP
1993	MIN	AL	4	0	4	1	2	1	0	1	0	0	0	1	0	0	0	4
1995	MIN	AL	1	0	1	1	0	0	0	0	0	0	0	0	0	0	1	0
Total			5	0	5	2	2	1	0	1	0	0	0	1	0	0	1	4

Rank among batters: 3,191 • *Top target (2 home runs)*: Mike Mohler • *Number of pitchers victimized*: 4 • *Total ballparks homered in*: 4 • *First HR*: 07/31/1993 off Chuck Finley

Pete Broberg

PETER SVEN BROBERG
B: 03/02/1950
BR

Year	Tm	Lg	Tot	H	A	Men-On 0	1	2	3	One-Game 2	3	4	LO	XN	IP	PH	RHP	LHP
1971	WAS	AL	1	1	0	1	0	0	0	0	0	0	0	0	0	0	0	1

Rank among batters: 4,707 • *Total ballparks homered in*: 1 • *First HR*: 09/19/1971 off Rogelio Moret

Greg Brock

GREGORY ALLEN BROCK
B: 06/14/1957
BL

Year	Tm	Lg	Tot	H	A	Men-On 0	1	2	3	One-Game 2	3	4	LO	XN	IP	PH	RHP	LHP
1983	LA	NL	20	14	6	11	7	1	1	1	0	0	0	0	0	0	18	2
1984	LA	NL	14	8	6	10	2	2	0	0	0	0	0	1	0	0	8	6

Greg Brock *continued*

Year	Tm	Lg	Tot	H	A	Men-On 0	1	2	3	One-Game 2	3	4	LO	XN	IP	PH	RHP	LHP
1985	LA	NL	21	7	14	9	6	4	2	2	0	0	0	0	0	0	19	2
1986	LA	NL	16	5	11	8	5	2	1	2	0	0	0	0	0	0	16	0
1987	MIL	AL	13	5	8	6	4	3	0	0	0	0	0	0	0	1	10	3
1988	MIL	AL	6	4	2	3	1	2	0	0	0	0	0	0	0	0	5	1
1989	MIL	AL	12	7	5	6	4	2	0	0	0	0	0	0	0	0	10	2
1990	MIL	AL	7	3	4	4	2	1	0	0	0	0	0	0	0	0	5	2
1991	MIL	AL	1	0	1	1	0	0	0	0	0	0	0	0	0	0	0	1
Total			110	53	57	58	31	17	4	5	0	0	0	1	0	1	91	19

Rank among batters: 436 • *Top target (3 home runs)*: Mario Soto, Charles Hudson • *Number of pitchers victimized*: 87 • *Total ballparks homered in*: 23 • *First HR*: 04/10/1983 off Steve Rogers • *LCS HR*—1

Lou Brock

LOUIS CLARK BROCK
B: 06/18/1939
BL HOF

Year	Tm	Lg	Tot	H	A	Men-On 0	1	2	3	One-Game 2	3	4	LO	XN	IP	PH	RHP	LHP
1962	CHI	NL	9	5	4	6	2	0	1	0	0	0	3	0	1	0	8	1
1963	CHI	NL	9	4	5	7	2	0	0	1	0	0	0	0	2	0	9	0
1964	CHI	NL	2	2	0	0	2	0	0	0	0	0	0	0	0	0	2	0
	STL	NL	12	4	8	11	1	0	0	0	0	0	0	1	1	0	9	3
	Total		14	6	8	11	3	0	0	0	0	0	0	1	1	0	11	3
1965	STL	NL	16	10	6	9	5	2	0	0	0	0	1	0	1	0	6	10
1966	STL	NL	15	6	9	11	3	1	0	0	0	0	2	1	0	0	12	3
1967	STL	NL	21	13	8	14	3	4	0	4	0	0	5	0	0	0	15	6
1968	STL	NL	6	2	4	3	2	1	0	0	0	0	1	1	0	0	5	1
1969	STL	NL	12	6	6	10	1	1	0	0	0	0	3	2	0	0	9	3
1970	STL	NL	13	7	6	7	4	2	0	1	0	0	5	0	1	0	11	2
1971	STL	NL	7	3	4	6	1	0	0	0	0	0	0	0	0	0	2	5
1972	STL	NL	3	2	1	2	1	0	0	0	0	0	1	0	0	0	2	1
1973	STL	NL	7	4	3	2	4	1	0	0	0	0	1	0	0	0	4	3
1974	STL	NL	3	1	2	0	2	1	0	0	0	0	0	0	0	0	3	0
1975	STL	NL	3	1	2	3	0	0	0	0	0	0	1	0	0	0	3	0
1976	STL	NL	4	2	2	1	3	0	0	0	0	0	0	0	2	0	2	2
1977	STL	NL	2	0	2	1	1	0	0	0	0	0	0	0	1	0	1	1
1979	STL	NL	5	2	3	4	1	0	0	0	0	0	1	0	0	0	5	0
Total			149	74	75	97	38	13	1	6	0	0	24	5	9	0	108	41

Rank among batters: 289 • *Top target (5 home runs)*: Bill Stoneman • *Number of pitchers victimized*: 107 • *Total ballparks homered in*: 17 • *First HR*: 04/13/1962 off Ray Washburn • *Hit for Cycle*—vs SD: 05/27/1975 • *World Series HR*—4

Steve Brodie

WALTER SCOTT BRODIE
B: 09/11/1868 D: 10/30/1935
BL

Year	Tm	Lg	Tot	H	A	Men-On 0	1	2	3	One-Game 2	3	4	LO	XN	IP	PH	RHP	LHP
1891	BOS	NL	2	2	0	1	1	0	0	0	0	0	0	0	0	0	2	0
1892	STL	NL	4	4	0	4	0	0	0	0	0	0	0	0	1	0	4	0
1893	STL	NL	2	2	0	0	1	0	1	0	0	0	0	0	1	0	1	0
1894	BAL	NL	3	0	3	2	0	1	0	0	0	0	0	0	1	0	3	0
1895	BAL	NL	2	1	1	1	0	1	0	0	0	0	0	0	0	0	2	0
1896	BAL	NL	2	0	2	0	1	1	0	0	0	0	0	0	0	0	2	0
1897	PIT	NL	2	1	1	0	1	0	1	0	0	0	0	0	0	0	2	0
1899	BAL	NL	3	1	2	0	2	1	0	0	0	0	0	0	1	0	2	1
1901	BAL	AL	2	1	1	2	0	0	0	0	0	0	0	0	0	0	2	0
1902	NY	NL	3	2	1	3	0	0	0	0	0	0	0	0	1	0	3	0
Total			25	14	11	13	6	4	2	0	0	0	0	0	5	0	23	1

Rank among batters: 1,608 • *Total ballparks homered in*: 14 • *First HR*: 04/28/1891 off Kid Gleason

Dick Brodowski

RICHARD STANLEY BRODOWSKI
B: 07/26/1932
BR

Year	Tm	Lg	Tot	H	A	Men-On 0	1	2	3	One-Game 2	3	4	LO	XN	IP	PH	RHP	LHP
1952	BOS	AL	1	1	0	1	0	0	0	0	0	0	0	0	0	0	0	1
1955	BOS	AL	1	1	0	0	1	0	0	0	0	0	0	0	0	0	1	0
Total			2	2	0	1	1	0	0	0	0	0	0	0	0	0	1	1

Rank among batters: 4,129 • *Total ballparks homered in*: 1 • *First HR*: 07/11/1952 off Ted Gray

Rico Brogna

RICO JOSEPH BROGNA
B: 04/18/1970
BL

Year	Tm	Lg	Tot	H	A	Men-On 0	1	2	3	One-Game 2	3	4	LO	XN	IP	PH	RHP	LHP
1992	DET	AL	1	1	0	0	1	0	0	0	0	0	0	0	0	0	1	0
1994	NY	NL	7	2	5	3	4	0	0	0	0	0	0	1	0	0	7	0
1995	NY	NL	22	13	9	13	7	1	1	1	0	0	0	0	1	0	20	2
Total			30	16	14	16	12	1	1	1	0	0	0	1	1	0	28	2

Rank among batters: 1,437 • *Top target (2 home runs)*: Mike Williams, Jeff Juden • *Number of pitchers victimized*: 28 • *Total ballparks homered in*: 10 • *First HR*: 08/11/1992 off Melido Perez

Jack Brohamer

JOHN ANTHONY BROHAMER
B: 02/26/1950
BL

Year	Tm	Lg	Tot	H	A	Men-On 0	1	2	3	One-Game 2	3	4	LO	XN	IP	PH	RHP	LHP
1972	CLE	AL	5	5	0	4	1	0	0	1	0	0	0	1	0	0	5	0
1973	CLE	AL	4	3	1	3	1	0	0	0	0	0	0	0	0	0	4	0
1974	CLE	AL	2	2	0	1	1	0	0	0	0	0	0	0	0	0	2	0
1975	CLE	AL	6	1	5	4	1	1	0	0	0	0	0	0	0	1	5	1
1976	CHI	AL	7	3	4	3	3	1	0	0	0	0	0	0	0	0	4	3
1977	CHI	AL	2	0	2	1	0	1	0	0	0	0	0	0	0	0	2	0
1978	BOS	AL	1	0	1	0	1	0	0	0	0	0	0	0	0	0	1	0
1979	BOS	AL	1	0	1	1	0	0	0	0	0	0	0	0	0	0	1	0
1980	BOS	AL	1	1	0	1	0	0	0	0	0	0	0	0	0	0	1	0
	CLE	AL	1	0	1	1	0	0	0	0	0	0	0	0	0	0	1	0
	Total		2	1	1	2	0	0	0	0	0	0	0	0	0	0	2	0
Total			30	15	15	19	8	3	0	1	0	0	0	1	0	1	26	4

Rank among batters: 1,437 • *Top target (4 home runs)*: Bert Blyleven • *Number of pitchers victimized*: 21 • *Total ballparks homered in*: 10 • *First HR*: 06/09/1972 off Bert Blyleven • *Hit for Cycle*—@SEA: 09/24/1977

Herman Bronkie

HERMAN CHARLES BRONKIE
B: 03/30/1885 D: 05/27/1968
BR

Year	Tm	Lg	Tot	H	A	Men-On 0	1	2	3	One-Game 2	3	4	LO	XN	IP	PH	RHP	LHP
1918	STL	NL	1	0	1	0	0	1	0	0	0	0	0	0	0	0	1	0

Rank among batters: 4,707 • *Total ballparks homered in*: 1 • *First HR*: 07/27/1918 off Jack Coombs

Tom Brookens

THOMAS DALE BROOKENS
B: 08/10/1953
BR

Year	Tm	Lg	Tot	H	A	Men-On 0	1	2	3	One-Game 2	3	4	LO	XN	IP	PH	RHP	LHP
1979	DET	AL	4	3	1	2	2	0	0	0	0	0	0	0	0	0	3	1
1980	DET	AL	10	7	3	5	3	2	0	0	0	0	0	0	0	0	4	6
1981	DET	AL	4	3	1	2	0	2	0	0	0	0	0	0	0	0	3	1
1982	DET	AL	9	4	5	5	3	1	0	0	0	0	1	1	0	1	7	2
1983	DET	AL	6	5	1	6	0	0	0	0	0	0	0	0	0	0	2	4
1984	DET	AL	5	4	1	4	1	0	0	0	0	0	0	0	0	0	2	3
1985	DET	AL	7	3	4	6	1	0	0	0	0	0	0	0	0	0	3	4
1986	DET	AL	3	2	1	1	1	1	0	0	0	0	0	0	0	0	1	2
1987	DET	AL	13	6	7	6	4	2	1	0	0	0	0	0	0	0	6	7
1988	DET	AL	5	4	1	3	1	0	1	0	0	0	0	1	0	0	3	2
1989	NY	AL	4	0	4	3	1	0	0	0	0	0	0	0	0	0	0	4
1990	CLE	AL	1	0	1	1	0	0	0	0	0	0	0	0	0	0	0	1
Total			71	41	30	44	17	8	2	0	0	0	1	2	0	1	34	37

Rank among batters: 731 • *Top target (3 home runs)*: Mike Caldwell • *Number of pitchers victimized*: 60 • *Total ballparks homered in*: 13 • *First HR*: 07/24/1979 off Bill Travers

Bobby Brooks

ROBERT BROOKS
B: 11/01/1945 D: 10/11/1994
BR

Year	Tm	Lg	Tot	H	A	Men-On 0	1	2	3	One-Game 2	3	4	LO	XN	IP	PH	RHP	LHP
1969	OAK	AL	3	1	2	2	0	1	0	0	0	0	0	0	0	0	1	2
1970	OAK	AL	2	2	0	1	1	0	0	0	0	0	0	0	0	0	1	1
Total			5	3	2	3	1	1	0	0	0	0	0	0	0	0	2	3

Rank among batters: 3,191 • *Total ballparks homered in*: 3 • *First HR*: 09/14/1969 off Gary Peters

Hubie Brooks

HUBERT BROOKS
B: 09/24/1956
BR

Year	Tm	Lg	Tot	H	A	Men-On 0	1	2	3	One-Game 2	3	4	LO	XN	IP	PH	RHP	LHP
1980	NY	NL	1	0	1	1	0	0	0	0	0	0	0	0	0	0	1	0
1981	NY	NL	4	2	2	3	1	0	0	0	0	0	0	0	0	0	2	2
1982	NY	NL	2	1	1	2	0	0	0	0	0	0	0	0	0	0	2	0
1983	NY	NL	5	4	1	3	0	2	0	0	0	0	0	1	0	0	4	1
1984	NY	NL	16	12	4	13	2	1	0	0	0	0	0	0	0	0	9	7
1985	MON	NL	13	4	9	8	1	2	2	0	0	0	0	0	0	1	9	4
1986	MON	NL	14	3	11	9	3	1	1	0	0	0	0	1	1	0	9	5
1987	MON	NL	14	9	5	10	3	0	1	0	0	0	0	0	0	0	9	5
1988	MON	NL	20	9	11	9	7	3	1	1	0	0	0	1	0	0	13	7
1989	MON	NL	14	7	7	8	4	1	1	0	0	0	0	0	0	0	8	6
1990	LA	NL	20	9	11	12	4	4	0	0	0	0	0	1	0	0	11	9
1991	NY	NL	16	4	12	12	3	0	1	1	0	0	0	1	0	0	11	5
1992	CAL	AL	8	2	6	4	3	1	0	0	0	0	0	0	0	0	7	1
1993	KC	AL	1	0	1	0	1	0	0	0	0	0	0	0	0	0	0	1
1994	KC	AL	1	1	0	0	0	0	1	0	0	0	0	0	0	1	1	0
Total			149	67	82	94	32	15	8	2	0	0	0	5	1	2	96	53

Rank among batters: 289 • *Top target (7 home runs)*: Shane Rawley • *Number of pitchers victimized*: 112 • *Total ballparks homered in*: 20 • *First HR*: 10/04/1980 off Jim Otten

Jerry Brooks

JEROME EDWARD BROOKS
B: 03/23/1967
BR

Year	Tm	Lg	Tot	H	A	Men-On 0	1	2	3	One-Game 2	3	4	LO	XN	IP	PH	RHP	LHP
1993	LA	NL	1	0	1	1	0	0	0	0	0	0	0	0	0	0	1	0

Rank among batters: 4,707 • *Total ballparks homered in*: 1 • *First HR*: 09/17/1993 off Willie Blair

Mandy Brooks

JONATHAN JOSEPH BROOKS
B: 08/18/1897 D: 06/17/1962
BR

Year	Tm	Lg	Tot	H	A	Men-On 0	1	2	3	One-Game 2	3	4	LO	XN	IP	PH	RHP	LHP
1925	CHI	NL	14	10	4	6	4	3	1	2	0	0	0	0	0	0	5	9
1926	CHI	NL	1	1	0	0	1	0	0	0	0	0	0	0	0	0	1	0
Total			15	11	4	6	5	3	1	2	0	0	0	0	0	0	6	9

Rank among batters: 2,096 • Top target (2 home runs): Rube Marquard, Art Decatur, Art Nehf, Jack Bentley • *Number of pitchers victimized*: 11 • *Total ballparks homered in*: 4 • *First HR*: 06/05/1925 off Dazzy Vance

Scott Brosius

SCOTT DAVID BROSIUS
B: 08/15/1966
BR

Year	Tm	Lg	Tot	H	A	Men-On 0	1	2	3	One-Game 2	3	4	LO	XN	IP	PH	RHP	LHP
1991	OAK	AL	2	1	1	2	0	0	0	0	0	0	0	0	0	0	2	0
1992	OAK	AL	4	1	3	2	1	1	0	1	0	0	0	0	0	0	1	3
1993	OAK	AL	6	3	3	2	2	2	0	0	0	0	0	0	0	0	3	3
1994	OAK	AL	14	9	5	9	3	1	1	1	0	0	0	0	0	0	7	7
1995	OAK	AL	17	12	5	11	5	1	0	2	0	0	2	0	0	0	14	3
Total			43	26	17	26	11	5	1	4	0	0	2	0	0	0	27	16

Rank among batters: 1,116 • *Top target (3 home runs)*: Erik Hanson • *Number of pitchers victimized*: 35 • *Total ballparks homered in*: 13 • *First HR*: 08/07/1991 off Brian Holman

Jim Brosnan

JAMES PATRICK BROSNAN
B: 10/24/1929
BR

Year	Tm	Lg	Tot	H	A	Men-On 0	1	2	3	One-Game 2	3	4	LO	XN	IP	PH	RHP	LHP
1960	CIN	NL	1	1	0	1	0	0	0	0	0	0	0	0	0	0	1	0

Rank among batters: 4,707 • *Total ballparks homered in*: 1 • *First HR*: 05/23/1960 off Bob Anderson

Mark Brouhard

MARK STEVEN BROUHARD
B: 05/22/1956
BR

Year	Tm	Lg	Tot	H	A	Men-On 0	1	2	3	One-Game 2	3	4	LO	XN	IP	PH	RHP	LHP
1980	MIL	AL	5	3	2	4	0	1	0	0	0	0	0	0	0	0	4	1
1981	MIL	AL	2	1	1	1	0	1	0	0	0	0	0	0	0	0	1	1

						Men-On				One-Game								
Year	Tm	Lg	Tot	H	A	0	1	2	3	2	3	4	LO	XN	IP	PH	RHP	LHP

Mark Brouhard *continued*

Year	Tm	Lg	Tot	H	A	0	1	2	3	2	3	4	LO	XN	IP	PH	RHP	LHP
1982	MIL	AL	4	2	2	1	3	0	0	0	0	0	0	0	0	0	0	4
1983	MIL	AL	7	4	3	4	2	1	0	0	0	0	0	0	0	1	2	5
1984	MIL	AL	6	5	1	4	1	1	0	0	0	0	0	0	0	0	0	6
1985	MIL	AL	1	1	0	0	1	0	0	0	0	0	0	0	0	0	0	1
Total			25	16	9	14	7	4	0	0	0	0	0	0	0	1	7	18

Rank among batters: 1,608 • *Top target (3 home runs)*: Dave Righetti • *Number of pitchers victimized*: 21 • *Total ballparks homered in*: 6 • *First HR*: 05/25/1980 off Roger Erickson • *LCS HR*—1

Dan Brouthers

DENNIS JOSEPH BROUTHERS
B: 05/08/1858 D: 08/02/1932
BL HOF

Year	Tm	Lg	Tot	H	A	0	1	2	3	2	3	4	LO	XN	IP	PH	RHP	LHP
1879	TRO	NL	4	3	1	3	1	0	0	0	0	0	0	0	0	0	4	0
1881	BUF	NL	8	2	6	6	2	0	0	0	0	0	0	0	0	0	8	0
1882	BUF	NL	6	1	5	3	2	1	0	1	0	0	0	0	2	0	6	0
1883	BUF	NL	3	0	3	2	1	0	0	0	0	0	0	0	1	0	2	1
1884	BUF	NL	14	9	5	5	5	3	0	1	0	0	0	0	3	0	13	0
1885	BUF	NL	7	4	3	3	3	1	0	1	0	0	0	0	0	0	6	1
1886	DET	NL	11	7	4	6	4	1	0	0	1	0	0	0	4	0	8	2
1887	DET	NL	12	6	6	5	5	2	0	1	0	0	0	0	0	0	10	2
1888	DET	NL	9	5	4	5	2	2	0	0	0	0	1	0	1	0	6	3
1889	BOS	NL	7	3	4	3	2	2	0	0	0	0	0	0	0	0	5	2
1890	BOS	PL	1	0	1	0	1	0	0	0	0	0	0	0	1	0	1	0
1891	BOS	AA	5	3	2	1	1	3	0	0	0	0	0	0	0	0	4	0
1892	BRO	NL	5	2	3	2	2	1	0	1	0	0	0	0	1	0	4	0
1893	BRO	NL	2	0	2	0	2	0	0	0	0	0	0	0	0	0	1	0
1894	BAL	NL	9	5	4	4	3	2	0	0	0	0	0	0	0	0	6	1
1895	LOU	NL	2	0	2	1	1	0	0	1	0	0	0	0	0	0	2	0
1896	PHI	NL	1	0	1	0	1	0	0	0	0	0	0	0	0	0	1	0
Total			106	50	56	49	38	18	0	6	1	0	1	0	13	0	87	12

Rank among batters: 451 • *Top target (7 home runs)*: Jim McCormick • *Number of pitchers victimized*: 59 • *Total ballparks homered in*: 28 • *First HR*: 07/19/1879 off Will White

Bob Brower

ROBERT RICHARD BROWER
B: 01/10/1960
BR

Year	Tm	Lg	Tot	H	A	0	1	2	3	2	3	4	LO	XN	IP	PH	RHP	LHP
1987	TEX	AL	14	7	7	8	5	0	1	2	0	0	4	0	1	0	6	8
1988	TEX	AL	1	1	0	0	0	0	1	0	0	0	0	0	0	0	1	0
1989	NY	AL	2	0	2	2	0	0	0	0	0	0	0	0	0	0	1	1
Total			17	8	9	10	5	0	2	2	0	0	4	0	1	0	8	9

Rank among batters: 1,969 • *Top target (2 home runs)*: Steve Carlton • *Number of pitchers victimized*: 16 • *Total ballparks homered in*: 7 • *First HR*: 04/28/1987 off Dennis Rasmussen

Frank Brower

FRANK WILLARD BROWER
B: 03/26/1893 D: 11/20/1960
BL

Year	Tm	Lg	Tot	H	A	0	1	2	3	2	3	4	LO	XN	IP	PH	RHP	LHP
1920	WAS	AL	1	0	1	1	0	0	0	0	0	0	0	0	0	0	1	0
1921	WAS	AL	1	1	0	1	0	0	0	0	0	0	0	0	0	0	1	0
1922	WAS	AL	9	3	6	3	2	3	1	1	0	0	0	0	2	0	9	0
1923	CLE	AL	16	6	10	8	6	2	0	2	0	0	0	0	2	0	15	1
1924	CLE	AL	3	1	2	2	1	0	0	0	0	0	1	0	0	0	2	1
Total			30	11	19	15	9	5	1	3	0	0	1	0	4	0	28	2

Rank among batters: 1,437 • *Top target (4 home runs)*: Waite Hoyt • *Number of pitchers victimized*: 23 • *Total ballparks homered in*: 8 • *First HR*: 09/09/1920 off Allen Sothoron

Boardwalk Brown

CARROLL WILLIAM BROWN
B: 02/20/1887 D: 02/08/1977
BR

Year	Tm	Lg	Tot	H	A	0	1	2	3	2	3	4	LO	XN	IP	PH	RHP	LHP
1913	PHI	AL	1	1	0	1	0	0	0	0	0	0	0	0	0	0	0	1

Rank among batters: 4,707 • *Total ballparks homered in*: 1 • *First HR*: 08/02/1913 off Earl Hamilton

Year	Tm	Lg	Tot	H	A	Men-On 0	1	2	3	One-Game 2	3	4	LO	XN	IP	PH	RHP	LHP

Bobby Brown

ROBERT WILLIAM BROWN
B: 10/25/1924
BL

Year	Tm	Lg	Tot	H	A	0	1	2	3	2	3	4	LO	XN	IP	PH	RHP	LHP
1947	NY	AL	1	1	0	1	0	0	0	0	0	0	0	0	0	0	1	0
1948	NY	AL	3	3	0	1	2	0	0	0	0	0	0	0	0	0	3	0
1949	NY	AL	6	6	0	3	2	1	0	0	0	0	0	0	1	0	5	1
1950	NY	AL	4	2	2	3	1	0	0	0	0	0	0	0	0	0	4	0
1951	NY	AL	6	3	3	2	2	2	0	0	0	0	0	0	0	0	5	1
1952	NY	AL	1	1	0	1	0	0	0	0	0	0	0	0	0	0	1	0
1954	NY	AL	1	1	0	0	1	0	0	0	0	0	0	0	0	0	1	0
Total			22	17	5	11	8	3	0	0	0	0	0	0	1	0	20	2

Rank among batters: 1,719 • Top target (2 home runs): Karl Drews, Joe Coleman, Cliff Fannin, Early Wynn, Mickey Harris • *Number of pitchers victimized*: 17 • *Total ballparks homered in*: 3 • *First HR*: 09/16/1947 off Fred Sanford

Bobby Brown

ROGERS LEE BROWN
B: 05/25/1954
BB

Year	Tm	Lg	Tot	H	A	0	1	2	3	2	3	4	LO	XN	IP	PH	RHP	LHP
1980	NY	AL	14	9	5	10	3	1	0	0	0	0	0	0	0	0	12	2
1982	SEA	AL	4	1	3	2	2	0	0	0	0	0	0	0	0	0	2	2
1983	SD	NL	5	4	1	1	1	2	1	0	0	0	0	1	0	0	4	1
1984	SD	NL	3	1	2	1	2	0	0	0	0	0	0	0	0	0	3	0
Total			26	15	11	14	8	3	1	0	0	0	0	1	0	0	21	5

Rank among batters: 1,576 • *Top target (2 home runs)*: Dave Tobik, Don Aase, Tom Hume • *Number of pitchers victimized*: 23 • *Total ballparks homered in*: 11 • *First HR*: 05/21/1980 off Dave Tobik

Buster Brown

CHARLES EDWARD BROWN
B: 08/31/1881 D: 02/09/1914
BR

Year	Tm	Lg	Tot	H	A	0	1	2	3	2	3	4	LO	XN	IP	PH	RHP	LHP
1906	STL	NL	1	0	1	1	0	0	0	0	0	0	0	0	0	0	1	0
1910	BOS	NL	1	0	1	1	0	0	0	0	0	0	0	0	0	0	1	0
1911	BOS	NL	1	1	0	1	0	0	0	0	0	0	0	0	0	0	1	0
Total			3	1	2	3	0	0	0	0	0	0	0	0	0	0	3	0

Rank among batters: 3,735 • *Total ballparks homered in*: 3 • *First HR*: 06/16/1906 off Dummy Taylor

Chris Brown

JOHN CHRISTOPHER BROWN
B: 08/15/1961
BR

Year	Tm	Lg	Tot	H	A	0	1	2	3	2	3	4	LO	XN	IP	PH	RHP	LHP
1984	SF	NL	1	0	1	1	0	0	0	0	0	0	0	0	0	0	1	0
1985	SF	NL	16	5	11	10	3	2	1	1	0	0	0	1	0	0	11	5
1986	SF	NL	7	3	4	5	2	0	0	0	0	0	0	0	0	0	4	3
1987	SF	NL	6	2	4	2	4	0	0	0	0	0	0	0	0	0	6	0
	SD	NL	6	3	3	3	2	1	0	0	0	0	0	0	0	0	1	5
	Total		12	5	7	5	6	1	0	0	0	0	0	0	0	0	7	5
1988	SD	NL	2	1	1	2	0	0	0	0	0	0	0	0	0	0	1	1
Total			38	14	24	23	11	3	1	1	0	0	0	1	0	0	24	14

Rank among batters: 1,225 • *Top target (3 home runs)*: Bob Knepper • *Number of pitchers victimized*: 32 • *Total ballparks homered in*: 11 • *First HR*: 09/19/1984 off Eric Show

Clint Brown

CLINTON HAROLD BROWN
B: 07/08/1903 D: 12/31/1955
BL

Year	Tm	Lg	Tot	H	A	0	1	2	3	2	3	4	LO	XN	IP	PH	RHP	LHP
1932	CLE	AL	2	1	1	0	1	1	0	0	0	0	0	0	0	0	2	0

Rank among batters: 4,129 • *Total ballparks homered in*: 2 • *First HR*: 06/19/1932 off Bob Kline

Darrell Brown

DARRELL WAYNE BROWN
B: 10/29/1955
BB

Year	Tm	Lg	Tot	H	A	0	1	2	3	2	3	4	LO	XN	IP	PH	RHP	LHP
1984	MIN	AL	1	1	0	1	0	0	0	0	0	0	1	0	0	0	0	1

Rank among batters: 4,707 • *Total ballparks homered in*: 1 • *First HR*: 04/18/1984 off Geoff Zahn

Dick Brown

RICHARD ERNEST BROWN
B: 01/17/1935 D: 04/12/1970
BR

Year	Tm	Lg	Tot	H	A	Men-On 0	Men-On 1	Men-On 2	Men-On 3	One-Game 2	One-Game 3	One-Game 4	LO	XN	IP	PH	RHP	LHP
1957	CLE	AL	4	2	2	3	1	0	0	0	0	0	0	0	0	0	3	1
1958	CLE	AL	7	1	6	4	2	1	0	0	0	0	0	0	1	0	2	5
1959	CLE	AL	5	1	4	3	2	0	0	0	0	0	0	0	0	0	4	1
1960	CHI	AL	3	1	2	1	2	0	0	0	0	0	0	0	0	0	2	1
1961	DET	AL	16	7	9	12	3	0	1	0	0	0	0	0	0	0	15	1
1962	DET	AL	12	8	4	7	5	0	0	1	0	0	0	0	0	0	11	1
1963	BAL	AL	2	2	0	1	1	0	0	0	0	0	0	0	0	1	0	2
1964	BAL	AL	8	4	4	5	3	0	0	2	0	0	0	0	0	0	4	4
1965	BAL	AL	5	2	3	3	1	1	0	0	0	0	0	0	0	0	3	2
Total			62	28	34	39	20	2	1	3	0	0	0	0	1	1	44	18

Rank among batters: 835 • Top target (2 home runs): Jim Bunning, Bob Smith, Whitey Ford, Bob Shaw, Mike Fornieles, Eli Grba • *Number of pitchers victimized*: 56 • *Total ballparks homered in*: 11 • *First HR*: 07/12/1957 off Connie Johnson

Drummond Brown

DRUMMOND NICOL BROWN
B: 01/31/1885 D: 01/27/1927
BR

Year	Tm	Lg	Tot	H	A	Men-On 0	Men-On 1	Men-On 2	Men-On 3	One-Game 2	One-Game 3	One-Game 4	LO	XN	IP	PH	RHP	LHP
1913	BOS	NL	1	0	1	1	0	0	0	0	0	0	0	0	0	0	0	1
1915	KC	FL	1	1	0	0	0	1	0	0	0	0	0	0	0	0	1	0
Total			2	1	1	1	0	1	0	0	0	0	0	0	0	0	1	1

Rank among batters: 4,129 • *Total ballparks homered in*: 2 • *First HR*: 06/25/1913 off Rube Marquard

Eddie Brown

EDWARD WILLIAM BROWN
B: 07/17/1891 D: 09/10/1956
BR

Year	Tm	Lg	Tot	H	A	Men-On 0	Men-On 1	Men-On 2	Men-On 3	One-Game 2	One-Game 3	One-Game 4	LO	XN	IP	PH	RHP	LHP
1924	BRO	NL	5	1	4	4	1	0	0	1	0	0	0	0	0	0	2	3
1925	BRO	NL	5	4	1	3	1	0	1	0	0	0	0	0	0	0	2	3
1926	BOS	NL	2	1	1	1	0	1	0	0	0	0	0	0	2	0	2	0
1927	BOS	NL	2	0	2	0	2	0	0	0	0	0	0	0	0	0	0	2
1928	BOS	NL	2	0	2	0	1	1	0	0	0	0	0	0	1	0	2	0
Total			16	6	10	8	5	2	1	1	0	0	0	0	3	0	8	8

Rank among batters: 2,029 • *Top target (2 home runs)*: Hal Carlson • *Number of pitchers victimized*: 15 • *Total ballparks homered in*: 8 • *First HR*: 06/28/1924 off Clarence Mitchell

Gates Brown

WILLIAM JAMES BROWN
B: 05/02/1939
BL

Year	Tm	Lg	Tot	H	A	Men-On 0	Men-On 1	Men-On 2	Men-On 3	One-Game 2	One-Game 3	One-Game 4	LO	XN	IP	PH	RHP	LHP
1963	DET	AL	2	0	2	1	1	0	0	0	0	0	0	0	0	1	2	0
1964	DET	AL	15	9	6	9	4	2	0	1	0	0	0	0	0	1	12	3
1965	DET	AL	10	5	5	5	0	4	1	0	0	0	0	0	0	1	10	0
1966	DET	AL	7	4	3	4	2	1	0	0	0	0	0	0	0	2	6	1
1967	DET	AL	2	0	2	1	1	0	0	0	0	0	0	0	0	0	0	2
1968	DET	AL	6	5	1	5	0	1	0	0	0	0	0	1	0	3	6	0
1969	DET	AL	1	1	0	1	0	0	0	0	0	0	0	0	0	0	1	0
1970	DET	AL	3	1	2	3	0	0	0	0	0	0	0	0	0	1	3	0
1971	DET	AL	11	4	7	7	2	2	0	0	0	0	0	0	0	2	10	1
1972	DET	AL	10	7	3	9	1	0	0	0	0	0	0	1	0	1	9	1
1973	DET	AL	12	9	3	5	3	4	0	0	0	0	0	1	0	0	12	0
1974	DET	AL	4	4	0	1	3	0	0	0	0	0	0	0	0	3	4	0
1975	DET	AL	1	1	0	1	0	0	0	0	0	0	0	0	0	1	1	0
Total			84	50	34	52	17	14	1	1	0	0	0	3	0	16	76	8

Rank among batters: 617 • *Top target (4 home runs)*: Jim Palmer • *Number of pitchers victimized*: 65 • *Total ballparks homered in*: 10 • *First HR*: 06/19/1963 off Bob Heffner • *Hit HR in first major league AB*—@BOS: 06/19/1963

Hal Brown

HECTOR HAROLD BROWN
B: 12/11/1924
BR

Year	Tm	Lg	Tot	H	A	Men-On 0	Men-On 1	Men-On 2	Men-On 3	One-Game 2	One-Game 3	One-Game 4	LO	XN	IP	PH	RHP	LHP
1952	CHI	AL	1	1	0	0	0	1	0	0	0	0	0	0	0	0	0	1

Hal Brown *continued*

Year	Tm	Lg	Tot	H	A	Men-On 0	Men-On 1	Men-On 2	Men-On 3	One-Game 2	One-Game 3	One-Game 4	LO	XN	IP	PH	RHP	LHP
1953	BOS	AL	1	0	1	0	1	0	0	0	0	0	0	0	0	0	1	0
Total			2	1	1	0	1	1	0	0	0	0	0	0	0	0	1	1

Rank among batters: 4,129 • *Total ballparks homered in*: 2 • *First HR*: 08/30/1952 off Mickey Harris

Ike Brown

ISAAC BROWN
B: 04/13/1942
BR

Year	Tm	Lg	Tot	H	A	Men-On 0	Men-On 1	Men-On 2	Men-On 3	One-Game 2	One-Game 3	One-Game 4	LO	XN	IP	PH	RHP	LHP
1969	DET	AL	5	3	2	4	1	0	0	0	0	0	0	0	0	0	1	4
1970	DET	AL	4	3	1	2	1	1	0	1	0	0	0	0	0	0	0	4
1971	DET	AL	8	6	2	5	1	2	0	0	0	0	1	0	0	2	2	6
1972	DET	AL	2	1	1	1	1	0	0	0	0	0	0	0	0	0	0	2
1973	DET	AL	1	0	1	0	1	0	0	0	0	0	0	0	0	0	0	1
Total			20	13	7	12	5	3	0	1	0	0	1	0	0	2	3	17

Rank among batters: 1,810 • *Top target (3 home runs)*: Jim Kaat • *Number of pitchers victimized*: 14 • *Total ballparks homered in*: 5 • *First HR*: 06/17/1969 off Mike Kekich

Jarvis Brown

JARVIS ARDEL BROWN
B: 03/26/1967
BR

Year	Tm	Lg	Tot	H	A	Men-On 0	Men-On 1	Men-On 2	Men-On 3	One-Game 2	One-Game 3	One-Game 4	LO	XN	IP	PH	RHP	LHP
1994	ATL	NL	1	0	1	1	0	0	0	0	0	0	0	1	0	0	1	0

Rank among batters: 4,707 • *Total ballparks homered in*: 1 • *First HR*: 05/30/1994 off Rod Beck

Jim Brown

JAMES W.H. BROWN
B: 12/12/1860 D: 04/06/1908

Year	Tm	Lg	Tot	H	A	Men-On 0	Men-On 1	Men-On 2	Men-On 3	One-Game 2	One-Game 3	One-Game 4	LO	XN	IP	PH	RHP	LHP
1884	ALT	UA	1	0	1	1	0	0	0	0	0	0	0	0	0	0	1	0

Rank among batters: 4,707 • *Total ballparks homered in*: 1 • *First HR*: 04/24/1884 off Perry Werden

Jim Brown

JAMES DONALDSON BROWN
B: 03/31/1897
BR

Year	Tm	Lg	Tot	H	A	Men-On 0	Men-On 1	Men-On 2	Men-On 3	One-Game 2	One-Game 3	One-Game 4	LO	XN	IP	PH	RHP	LHP
1916	PHI	AL	1	1	0	1	0	0	0	0	0	0	0	0	0	0	1	0

Rank among batters: 4,707 • *Total ballparks homered in*: 1 • *First HR*: 09/08/1916 off Allen Russell

Jimmy Brown

JAMES ROBERTSON BROWN
B: 04/25/1910 D: 12/29/1977
BB

Year	Tm	Lg	Tot	H	A	Men-On 0	Men-On 1	Men-On 2	Men-On 3	One-Game 2	One-Game 3	One-Game 4	LO	XN	IP	PH	RHP	LHP
1937	STL	NL	2	0	2	2	0	0	0	0	0	0	0	0	0	0	1	1
1939	STL	NL	3	2	1	2	1	0	0	0	0	0	0	0	1	0	3	0
1941	STL	NL	3	2	1	2	1	0	0	0	0	0	0	1	0	0	1	2
1942	STL	NL	1	1	0	1	0	0	0	0	0	0	0	0	0	0	1	0
Total			9	5	4	7	2	0	0	0	0	0	0	1	1	0	6	3

Rank among batters: 2,587 • *Top target (2 home runs)*: Hugh Mulcahy, Rip Sewell • *Number of pitchers victimized*: 7 • *Total ballparks homered in*: 4 • *First HR*: 05/08/1937 off Al Smith

Larry Brown

LARRY LESLIE BROWN
B: 03/01/1940
BR

Year	Tm	Lg	Tot	H	A	Men-On 0	Men-On 1	Men-On 2	Men-On 3	One-Game 2	One-Game 3	One-Game 4	LO	XN	IP	PH	RHP	LHP
1963	CLE	AL	5	4	1	3	1	1	0	0	0	0	0	0	0	0	4	1
1964	CLE	AL	12	5	7	9	2	1	0	1	0	0	0	0	0	0	6	6
1965	CLE	AL	8	8	0	5	3	0	0	0	0	0	1	1	0	0	3	5
1966	CLE	AL	3	3	0	2	1	0	0	0	0	0	0	0	0	0	2	1
1967	CLE	AL	7	5	2	6	1	0	0	0	0	0	0	0	0	0	3	4
1968	CLE	AL	6	5	1	5	1	0	0	0	0	0	0	0	1	0	5	1
1969	CLE	AL	4	0	4	4	0	0	0	0	0	0	0	0	0	0	3	1
1971	OAK	AL	1	1	0	0	1	0	0	0	0	0	0	0	0	0	0	1

						Men-On				One-Game								
Year	Tm	Lg	Tot	H	A	0	1	2	3	2	3	4	LO	XN	IP	PH	RHP	LHP

Larry Brown *continued*

Year	Tm	Lg	Tot	H	A	0	1	2	3	2	3	4	LO	XN	IP	PH	RHP	LHP
1973	BAL	AL	1	0	1	0	1	0	0	0	0	0	0	0	0	0	1	0
Total			47	31	16	34	11	2	0	1	0	0	1	1	1	0	27	20

Rank among batters: 1,040 • *Top target (3 home runs)*: Mickey Lolich • *Number of pitchers victimized*: 37 • *Total ballparks homered in*: 9 • *First HR*: 07/31/1963 off Paul Foytack

Lew Brown

LEWIS J. BROWN
B: 02/01/1858 D: 01/16/1889
BR

Year	Tm	Lg	Tot	H	A	0	1	2	3	2	3	4	LO	XN	IP	PH	RHP	LHP
1876	BOS	NL	2	0	2	0	1	1	0	0	0	0	0	0	0	0	2	0
1877	BOS	NL	1	0	1	1	0	0	0	0	0	0	0	0	0	0	1	0
1878	PRO	NL	1	0	1	0	1	0	0	0	0	0	0	0	0	0	1	0
1879	PRO	NL	2	2	0	2	0	0	0	0	0	0	0	0	0	0	2	0
1881	DET	NL	3	2	1	2	1	0	0	0	0	0	0	0	0	0	3	0
1884	BOS	UA	1	0	1	1	0	0	0	0	0	0	0	0	0	0	1	0
Total			10	4	6	6	3	1	0	0	0	0	0	0	0	0	10	0

Rank among batters: 2,500 • *Top target (3 home runs)*: Tommy Bond • *Number of pitchers victimized*: 7 • *Total ballparks homered in*: 7 • *First HR*: 07/20/1876 off Bobby Mathews

Lloyd Brown

LLOYD ANDREW BROWN
B: 12/25/1904 D: 01/14/1974
BL

Year	Tm	Lg	Tot	H	A	0	1	2	3	2	3	4	LO	XN	IP	PH	RHP	LHP
1930	WAS	AL	1	1	0	0	0	1	0	0	0	0	0	0	1	0	1	0
1933	BOS	AL	2	0	2	1	0	1	0	0	0	0	0	0	0	0	2	0
1936	CLE	AL	1	1	0	1	0	0	0	0	0	0	0	0	0	0	1	0
Total			4	2	2	2	0	2	0	0	0	0	0	0	1	0	4	0

Rank among batters: 3,427 • *Total ballparks homered in*: 4 • *First HR*: 09/01/1930 off Ed Durham

Mike Brown

MICHAEL CHARLES BROWN
B: 12/29/1959
BR

Year	Tm	Lg	Tot	H	A	0	1	2	3	2	3	4	LO	XN	IP	PH	RHP	LHP
1983	CAL	AL	3	3	0	2	1	0	0	0	0	0	0	0	0	0	3	0
1984	CAL	AL	7	3	4	5	2	0	0	2	0	0	0	0	0	0	3	4
1985	CAL	AL	4	1	3	1	3	0	0	0	0	0	0	0	0	0	0	4
	PIT	NL	5	3	2	3	1	1	0	0	0	0	0	0	0	0	4	1
	Total		9	4	5	4	4	1	0	0	0	0	0	0	0	0	4	5
1986	PIT	NL	4	1	3	1	1	2	0	0	0	0	0	0	0	0	3	1
Total			23	11	12	12	8	3	0	2	0	0	0	0	0	0	13	10

Rank among batters: 1,686 • *Top target (2 home runs)*: Bruce Hurst • *Number of pitchers victimized*: 22 • *Total ballparks homered in*: 11 • *First HR*: 07/22/1983 off Milt Wilcox

Mordecai Brown

MORDECAI PETER CENTENNIAL BROWN
B: 10/19/1876 D: 02/14/1948
BB HOF

Year	Tm	Lg	Tot	H	A	0	1	2	3	2	3	4	LO	XN	IP	PH	RHP	LHP
1905	CHI	NL	1	1	0	0	1	0	0	0	0	0	0	0	0	0	1	0
1907	CHI	NL	1	0	1	0	0	1	0	0	0	0	0	0	0	0	1	0
Total			2	1	1	0	1	1	0	0	0	0	0	0	0	0	2	0

Rank among batters: 4,129 • *Total ballparks homered in*: 2 • *First HR*: 10/08/1905 off Art Hoelskoetter

Ollie Brown

OLLIE LEE BROWN
B: 02/11/1944
BR

Year	Tm	Lg	Tot	H	A	0	1	2	3	2	3	4	LO	XN	IP	PH	RHP	LHP
1966	SF	NL	7	5	2	4	2	1	0	0	0	0	0	0	0	0	6	1
1967	SF	NL	13	6	7	9	3	1	0	0	0	0	0	0	0	0	11	2
1969	SD	NL	20	7	13	14	3	2	1	0	0	0	0	0	0	0	12	8
1970	SD	NL	23	11	12	13	5	5	0	1	0	0	0	1	0	0	17	6
1971	SD	NL	9	3	6	5	3	1	0	0	0	0	0	0	0	0	9	0
1972	OAK	AL	1	0	1	0	1	0	0	0	0	0	0	0	0	0	1	0

Ollie Brown *continued*

Year	Tm	Lg	Tot	H	A	Men-On 0	1	2	3	One-Game 2	3	4	LO	XN	IP	PH	RHP	LHP
1972	MIL	AL	3	1	2	1	1	1	0	0	0	0	0	0	0	0	1	2
	Total		4	1	3	1	2	1	0	0	0	0	0	0	0	0	2	2
1973	MIL	AL	7	3	4	6	1	0	0	0	0	0	0	0	0	0	1	6
1974	HOU	NL	3	2	1	2	1	0	0	0	0	0	0	0	0	1	1	2
	PHI	NL	4	4	0	2	2	0	0	0	0	0	0	0	0	2	2	2
	Total		7	6	1	4	3	0	0	0	0	0	0	0	0	3	3	4
1975	PHI	NL	6	4	2	4	1	1	0	0	0	0	0	0	0	1	2	4
1976	PHI	NL	5	4	1	2	2	0	1	0	0	0	0	0	0	1	2	3
1977	PHI	NL	1	1	0	0	0	1	0	0	0	0	0	1	0	0	1	0
Total			102	51	51	62	25	13	2	1	0	0	0	2	0	5	66	36

Rank among batters: 483 • *Top target (4 home runs)*: Milt Pappas, Woodie Fryman, Phil Niekro • *Number of pitchers victimized*: 76 • *Total ballparks homered in*: 19 • *First HR*: 04/27/1966 off Milt Pappas

Oscar Brown

OSCAR LEE BROWN
B: 02/08/1946
BR

Year	Tm	Lg	Tot	H	A	Men-On 0	1	2	3	One-Game 2	3	4	LO	XN	IP	PH	RHP	LHP
1970	ATL	NL	1	0	1	0	1	0	0	0	0	0	0	0	0	0	0	1
1972	ATL	NL	3	3	0	1	1	1	0	0	0	0	0	0	0	0	2	1
Total			4	3	1	1	2	1	0	0	0	0	0	0	0	0	2	2

Rank among batters: 3,427 • *Total ballparks homered in*: 2 • *First HR*: 09/10/1970 off Dave Roberts

Tom Brown

THOMAS TARLTON BROWN
B: 09/21/1860 D: 10/25/1927
BL

Year	Tm	Lg	Tot	H	A	Men-On 0	1	2	3	One-Game 2	3	4	LO	XN	IP	PH	RHP	LHP
1882	BAL	AA	1	0	1	0	1	0	0	0	0	0	0	0	1	0	1	0
1883	COL	AA	5	1	4	3	1	1	0	1	0	0	3	0	0	0	3	0
1884	COL	AA	5	1	4	3	0	2	0	0	0	0	2	0	0	0	4	0
1885	PIT	AA	4	3	1	2	0	2	0	0	0	0	1	0	0	0	2	0
1886	PIT	AA	1	1	0	1	0	0	0	0	0	0	0	0	0	0	0	0
1887	IND	NL	2	1	1	1	1	0	0	0	0	0	0	0	0	0	1	1
1888	BOS	NL	9	5	4	2	4	2	1	0	0	0	0	0	4	0	8	1
1889	BOS	NL	2	1	1	2	0	0	0	0	0	0	0	0	2	0	2	0
1890	BOS	PL	4	1	3	4	0	0	0	1	0	0	2	0	1	0	4	0
1891	BOS	AA	5	3	2	3	2	0	0	0	0	0	2	0	1	0	4	0
1892	LOU	NL	2	1	1	1	0	1	0	0	0	0	0	0	0	0	0	2
1893	LOU	NL	5	1	4	3	2	0	0	0	0	0	1	0	0	0	4	0
1894	LOU	NL	9	6	3	5	2	2	0	1	0	0	1	0	1	0	8	1
1895	STL	NL	1	0	1	1	0	0	0	0	0	0	0	0	0	0	1	0
	WAS	NL	2	2	0	0	2	0	0	0	0	0	0	0	0	0	1	0
	Total		3	2	1	1	2	0	0	0	0	0	0	0	0	0	2	0
1896	WAS	NL	2	2	0	1	0	1	0	0	0	0	1	0	0	0	2	0
1897	WAS	NL	5	4	1	2	1	2	0	0	0	0	0	0	1	0	5	0
Total			64	33	31	34	16	13	1	3	0	0	13	0	11	0	49	5

Rank among batters: 815 • *Top target (3 home runs)*: Jack Stivetts, Kid Carsey • *Number of pitchers victimized*: 53 • *Total ballparks homered in*: 25 • *First HR*: 09/21/1882 off Bill Sweeney

Tom Brown

THOMAS WILLIAM BROWN
B: 12/12/1940
BB

Year	Tm	Lg	Tot	H	A	Men-On 0	1	2	3	One-Game 2	3	4	LO	XN	IP	PH	RHP	LHP
1963	WAS	AL	1	1	0	1	0	0	0	0	0	0	0	0	0	0	1	0

Rank among batters: 4,707 • *Total ballparks homered in*: 1 • *First HR*: 09/09/1963 off Phil Regan

Tommy Brown

THOMAS MICHAEL BROWN
B: 12/06/1927
BR

Year	Tm	Lg	Tot	H	A	Men-On 0	1	2	3	One-Game 2	3	4	LO	XN	IP	PH	RHP	LHP
1945	BRO	NL	2	2	0	2	0	0	0	0	0	0	0	0	0	0	0	2
1948	BRO	NL	2	1	1	2	0	0	0	0	0	0	0	0	0	0	2	0
1949	BRO	NL	3	1	2	0	3	0	0	0	0	0	0	0	0	0	0	3

Tommy Brown *continued*

Year	Tm	Lg	Tot	H	A	Men-On 0	1	2	3	One-Game 2	3	4	LO	XN	IP	PH	RHP	LHP
1950	BRO	NL	8	7	1	4	4	0	0	0	1	0	0	0	0	2	6	2
1951	PHI	NL	10	6	4	6	2	1	1	0	0	0	0	1	0	1	2	8
1952	PHI	NL	1	1	0	1	0	0	0	0	0	0	0	0	0	1	0	1
	CHI	NL	3	0	3	2	1	0	0	0	0	0	0	0	0	0	2	1
	Total		4	1	3	3	1	0	0	0	0	0	0	0	0	1	2	2
1953	CHI	NL	2	2	0	0	0	2	0	0	0	0	0	0	0	1	1	1
Total			31	20	11	17	10	3	1	0	1	0	0	1	0	5	13	18

Rank among batters: 1,400 • *Top target (3 home runs)*: Monk Dubiel, Preacher Roe • *Number of pitchers victimized*: 26 • *Total ballparks homered in*: 8 • *First HR*: 08/20/1945 off Preacher Roe

Willard Brown

WILLARD BROWN
B: 1866 D: 12/20/1897
BR

Year	Tm	Lg	Tot	H	A	Men-On 0	1	2	3	One-Game 2	3	4	LO	XN	IP	PH	RHP	LHP
1889	NY	NL	1	1	0	1	0	0	0	0	0	0	0	0	1	0	1	0
1890	NY	PL	4	3	1	1	2	0	1	1	0	0	0	0	1	0	2	2
1893	LOU	NL	1	0	1	1	0	0	0	0	0	0	0	0	0	0	0	0
Total			6	4	2	3	2	0	1	1	0	0	0	0	2	0	3	2

Rank among batters: 2,988 • *Top target (2 home runs)*: Phil Knell • *Number of pitchers victimized*: 5 • *Total ballparks homered in*: 4 • *First HR*: 08/03/1889 off Ben Sanders • *World Series HR*—1

Willard Brown

WILLARD JESSIE BROWN
B: 06/26/1915
BR

Year	Tm	Lg	Tot	H	A	Men-On 0	1	2	3	One-Game 2	3	4	LO	XN	IP	PH	RHP	LHP
1947	STL	AL	1	1	0	0	1	0	0	0	0	0	0	0	1	1	0	1

Rank among batters: 4,707 • *Total ballparks homered in*: 1 • *First HR*: 08/13/1947 off Hal Newhouser

Byron Browne

BYRON ELLIS BROWNE
B: 12/27/1942
BR

Year	Tm	Lg	Tot	H	A	Men-On 0	1	2	3	One-Game 2	3	4	LO	XN	IP	PH	RHP	LHP
1966	CHI	NL	16	7	9	6	5	5	0	1	0	0	0	0	0	0	11	5
1969	STL	NL	1	0	1	1	0	0	0	0	0	0	0	0	0	0	1	0
1970	PHI	NL	10	5	5	7	2	0	1	0	0	0	0	0	0	0	5	5
1971	PHI	NL	3	2	1	2	1	0	0	0	0	0	0	0	0	1	0	3
Total			30	14	16	16	8	5	1	1	0	0	0	0	0	1	17	13

Rank among batters: 1,437 • Top target (2 home runs): Juan Marichal, Larry Jaster, Chris Short, Larry Dierker, Claude Osteen • *Number of pitchers victimized*: 25 • *Total ballparks homered in*: 12 • *First HR*: 04/19/1966 off Frank Linzy

Earl Browne

EARL JAMES BROWNE
B: 03/05/1911 D: 01/12/1993
BL

Year	Tm	Lg	Tot	H	A	Men-On 0	1	2	3	One-Game 2	3	4	LO	XN	IP	PH	RHP	LHP
1937	PHI	NL	6	2	4	1	2	3	0	0	0	0	0	0	0	0	5	1

Rank among batters: 2,988 • *Total ballparks homered in*: 5 • *First HR*: 05/25/1937 off Bill Lee

George Browne

GEORGE EDWARD BROWNE
B: 01/12/1876 D: 12/09/1920
BL

Year	Tm	Lg	Tot	H	A	Men-On 0	1	2	3	One-Game 2	3	4	LO	XN	IP	PH	RHP	LHP
1903	NY	NL	3	3	0	3	0	0	0	0	0	0	1	0	0	0	3	0
1904	NY	NL	4	3	1	1	2	1	0	0	0	0	0	0	0	0	4	0
1905	NY	NL	4	3	1	0	4	0	0	0	0	0	0	0	1	0	4	0
1907	NY	NL	5	4	1	1	4	0	0	0	0	0	0	0	0	0	5	0
1908	BOS	NL	1	0	1	1	0	0	0	0	0	0	0	0	0	0	0	1
1909	WAS	AL	1	1	0	1	0	0	0	0	0	0	0	0	0	0	1	0
Total			18	14	4	7	10	1	0	0	0	0	1	0	1	0	17	1

Rank among batters: 1,914 • *Top target (2 home runs)*: Mike Lynch, Bob Ewing • *Number of pitchers victimized*: 16 • *Total ballparks homered in*: 6 • *First HR*: 04/17/1903 off Henry Schmidt

Jerry Browne

JEROME AUSTIN BROWNE
B: 02/13/1966
BB

						Men-On				One-Game								
Year	**Tm**	**Lg**	**Tot**	**H**	**A**	**0**	**1**	**2**	**3**	**2**	**3**	**4**	**LO**	**XN**	**IP**	**PH**	**RHP**	**LHP**
1987	TEX	AL	1	1	0	1	0	0	0	0	0	0	1	0	0	0	0	1
1988	TEX	AL	1	1	0	1	0	0	0	0	0	0	0	0	0	0	1	0
1989	CLE	AL	5	1	4	4	0	1	0	0	0	0	1	0	0	0	3	2
1990	CLE	AL	6	2	4	4	1	1	0	0	0	0	1	0	0	0	6	0
1991	CLE	AL	1	1	0	0	1	0	0	0	0	0	0	0	0	1	1	0
1992	OAK	AL	3	1	2	1	2	0	0	0	0	0	0	0	0	0	3	0
1993	OAK	AL	2	1	1	2	0	0	0	0	0	0	0	0	0	0	1	1
1994	FLO	NL	3	0	3	3	0	0	0	0	0	0	1	0	0	0	1	2
1995	FLO	NL	1	0	1	1	0	0	0	0	0	0	0	0	0	0	1	0
Total			23	8	15	17	4	2	0	0	0	0	4	0	0	1	17	6

Rank among batters: 1,686 • *Total ballparks homered in*: 12 • *First HR*: 08/19/1987 off Bud Black

Pidge Browne

PRENTICE ALMONT BROWNE
B: 03/21/1929
BL

						Men-On				One-Game								
Year	**Tm**	**Lg**	**Tot**	**H**	**A**	**0**	**1**	**2**	**3**	**2**	**3**	**4**	**LO**	**XN**	**IP**	**PH**	**RHP**	**LHP**
1962	HOU	NL	1	0	1	1	0	0	0	0	0	0	0	0	0	0	1	0

Rank among batters: 4,707 • *Total ballparks homered in*: 1 • *First HR*: 05/06/1962 off Cecil Butler

Pete Browning

LOUIS ROGERS BROWNING
B: 06/17/1861 D: 09/10/1905
BR

						Men-On				One-Game								
Year	**Tm**	**Lg**	**Tot**	**H**	**A**	**0**	**1**	**2**	**3**	**2**	**3**	**4**	**LO**	**XN**	**IP**	**PH**	**RHP**	**LHP**
1882	LOU	AA	5	0	5	2	2	0	1	1	0	0	0	0	0	0	5	0
1883	LOU	AA	4	0	4	2	1	1	0	0	0	0	1	0	1	0	4	0
1884	LOU	AA	4	2	2	3	1	0	0	0	0	0	1	0	1	0	0	1
1885	LOU	AA	9	6	3	7	2	0	0	0	0	0	1	0	2	0	8	0
1886	LOU	AA	2	2	0	2	0	0	0	0	0	0	0	0	0	0	1	1
1887	LOU	AA	4	1	3	2	1	1	0	0	0	0	0	0	2	0	4	0
1888	LOU	AA	3	0	3	1	1	1	0	0	0	0	0	0	0	0	2	1
1889	LOU	AA	2	1	1	1	0	1	0	0	0	0	0	0	1	0	2	0
1890	CLE	PL	5	1	4	2	2	1	0	0	0	0	0	0	0	0	4	1
1891	PIT	NL	4	3	1	3	1	0	0	0	0	0	0	0	1	0	4	0
1892	CIN	NL	3	2	1	1	1	1	0	0	0	0	0	0	0	0	2	0
1893	LOU	NL	1	0	1	0	1	0	0	0	0	0	0	0	0	0	1	0
Total			46	18	28	26	13	6	1	1	0	0	3	0	8	0	37	3

Rank among batters: 1,060 • *Top target (5 home runs)*: Jack Lynch • *Number of pitchers victimized*: 34 • *Total ballparks homered in*: 19 • *First HR*: 05/16/1882 off Sam Weaver • *Hit for Cycle*—vs NY: 08/08/1886; @PHI: 06/07/1889

Tom Browning

THOMAS LEO BROWNING
B: 04/28/1960
BL

						Men-On				One-Game								
Year	**Tm**	**Lg**	**Tot**	**H**	**A**	**0**	**1**	**2**	**3**	**2**	**3**	**4**	**LO**	**XN**	**IP**	**PH**	**RHP**	**LHP**
1991	CIN	NL	1	0	1	1	0	0	0	0	0	0	0	0	0	0	1	0
1993	CIN	NL	1	1	0	0	1	0	0	0	0	0	0	0	0	0	1	0
Total			2	1	1	1	1	0	0	0	0	0	0	0	0	0	2	0

Rank among batters: 4,129 • *Total ballparks homered in*: 2 • *First HR*: 10/04/1991 off Jose Melendez

Wilber Brubaker

WILBER LEE BRUBAKER
B: 11/07/1910 D: 12/02/1978
BR

						Men-On				One-Game								
Year	**Tm**	**Lg**	**Tot**	**H**	**A**	**0**	**1**	**2**	**3**	**2**	**3**	**4**	**LO**	**XN**	**IP**	**PH**	**RHP**	**LHP**
1936	PIT	NL	6	3	3	1	1	4	0	0	0	0	0	0	0	0	4	2
1937	PIT	NL	6	2	4	3	2	1	0	0	0	0	0	0	0	0	3	3
1938	PIT	NL	3	2	1	0	3	0	0	0	0	0	0	0	0	0	2	1
1939	PIT	NL	7	1	6	4	2	1	0	0	0	0	0	0	0	0	6	1
Total			22	8	14	8	8	6	0	0	0	0	0	0	0	0	15	7

Rank among batters: 1,719 • *Top target (2 home runs)*: Wayne LaMaster, Bill Lee, Bucky Walters • *Number of pitchers victimized*: 19 • *Total ballparks homered in*: 8 • *First HR*: 04/30/1936 off Orville Jorgens

Earle Brucker

EARLE FRANCIS BRUCKER, SR.
B: 05/06/1901 D: 05/08/1981
BR

						Men-On				One-Game								
Year	**Tm**	**Lg**	**Tot**	**H**	**A**	**0**	**1**	**2**	**3**	**2**	**3**	**4**	**LO**	**XN**	**IP**	**PH**	**RHP**	**LHP**
1937	PHI	AL	6	3	3	4	2	0	0	0	0	0	0	0	0	0	5	1

Year	Tm	Lg	Tot	H	A	Men-On				One-Game			LO	XN	IP	PH	RHP	LHP
						0	1	2	3	2	3	4						

Earle Brucker *continued*

Year	Tm	Lg	Tot	H	A	0	1	2	3	2	3	4	LO	XN	IP	PH	RHP	LHP
1938	PHI	AL	3	1	2	2	1	0	0	0	0	0	0	0	0	0	2	1
1939	PHI	AL	3	0	3	0	1	1	1	0	0	0	0	0	0	0	3	0
Total			12	4	8	6	4	1	1	0	0	0	0	0	0	0	10	2

Rank among batters: 2,325 • *Top target (2 home runs)*: Ed Linke, Monte Pearson • *Number of pitchers victimized*: 10 • *Total ballparks homered in*: 5 • *First HR*: 08/03/1937 off Tommy Bridges

Frank Bruggy

FRANK LEO BRUGGY
B: 05/04/1891 D: 04/05/1959
BR

Year	Tm	Lg	Tot	H	A	0	1	2	3	2	3	4	LO	XN	IP	PH	RHP	LHP
1921	PHI	NL	5	3	2	4	0	1	0	0	0	0	0	0	1	0	5	0
1923	PHI	AL	1	0	1	1	0	0	0	0	0	0	0	0	1	0	1	0
Total			6	3	3	5	0	1	0	0	0	0	0	0	2	0	6	0

Rank among batters: 2,988 • *Total ballparks homered in*: 3 • *First HR*: 04/16/1921 off Fred Toney

Jacob Brumfield

JACOB DONNELL BRUMFIELD
B: 05/27/1965
BR

Year	Tm	Lg	Tot	H	A	0	1	2	3	2	3	4	LO	XN	IP	PH	RHP	LHP
1993	CIN	NL	6	1	5	5	1	0	0	0	0	0	0	0	0	0	4	2
1994	CIN	NL	4	3	1	2	2	0	0	0	0	0	1	0	0	0	1	3
1995	PIT	NL	4	4	0	3	1	0	0	0	0	0	0	0	0	0	3	1
Total			14	8	6	10	4	0	0	0	0	0	1	0	0	0	8	6

Rank among batters: 2,169 • *Total ballparks homered in*: 6 • *First HR*: 07/02/1993 off Tim Wakefield

Mike Brumley

TONY MIKE BRUMLEY
B: 07/10/1938
BL

Year	Tm	Lg	Tot	H	A	0	1	2	3	2	3	4	LO	XN	IP	PH	RHP	LHP
1964	WAS	AL	2	0	2	0	0	2	0	0	0	0	0	0	0	0	2	0
1965	WAS	AL	3	2	1	1	2	0	0	1	0	0	0	0	0	0	3	0
Total			5	2	3	1	2	2	0	1	0	0	0	0	0	0	5	0

Rank among batters: 3,191 • *Total ballparks homered in*: 4 • *First HR*: 07/04/1964 off Dave Wickersham

Mike Brumley

ANTHONY MICHAEL BRUMLEY
B: 04/09/1963
BB

Year	Tm	Lg	Tot	H	A	0	1	2	3	2	3	4	LO	XN	IP	PH	RHP	LHP
1987	CHI	NL	1	0	1	0	1	0	0	0	0	0	0	0	0	0	1	0
1989	DET	AL	1	1	0	0	1	0	0	0	0	0	0	0	0	0	0	1
1995	HOU	NL	1	0	1	1	0	0	0	0	0	0	0	1	0	1	1	0
Total			3	1	2	1	2	0	0	0	0	0	0	1	0	1	2	1

Rank among batters: 3,735 • *Total ballparks homered in*: 3 • *First HR*: 06/23/1987 off Ron Darling

Glenn Brummer

GLENN EDWARD BRUMMER
B: 11/23/1954
BR

Year	Tm	Lg	Tot	H	A	0	1	2	3	2	3	4	LO	XN	IP	PH	RHP	LHP
1984	STL	NL	1	0	1	1	0	0	0	0	0	0	0	0	0	0	1	0

Rank among batters: 4,707 • *Total ballparks homered in*: 1 • *First HR*: 04/18/1984 off Scott Sanderson

Tom Brunansky

THOMAS ANDREW BRUNANSKY
B: 08/20/1960
BR

Year	Tm	Lg	Tot	H	A	0	1	2	3	2	3	4	LO	XN	IP	PH	RHP	LHP
1981	CAL	AL	3	1	2	1	2	0	0	1	0	0	0	0	0	0	1	2
1982	MIN	AL	20	10	10	12	5	2	1	1	0	0	0	0	2	0	11	9
1983	MIN	AL	28	8	20	16	9	2	1	4	0	0	0	0	1	0	18	10
1984	MIN	AL	32	14	18	22	7	3	0	1	0	0	0	0	0	0	17	15
1985	MIN	AL	27	12	15	15	10	2	0	1	0	0	0	0	0	1	22	5
1986	MIN	AL	23	15	8	12	11	0	0	3	0	0	0	0	0	0	12	11
1987	MIN	AL	32	19	13	20	9	2	1	1	0	0	0	0	0	0	22	10
1988	MIN	AL	1	0	1	1	0	0	0	0	0	0	0	0	0	0	1	0

Year	Tm	Lg	Tot	H	A	Men-On 0	Men-On 1	Men-On 2	Men-On 3	One-Game 2	One-Game 3	One-Game 4	LO	XN	IP	PH	RHP	LHP

Tom Brunansky *continued*

Year	Tm	Lg	Tot	H	A	Men-On 0	Men-On 1	Men-On 2	Men-On 3	One-Game 2	One-Game 3	One-Game 4	LO	XN	IP	PH	RHP	LHP
1988	STL	NL	22	7	15	15	5	2	0	1	0	0	0	2	0	0	18	4
	Total		23	7	16	16	5	2	0	1	0	0	0	2	0	0	19	4
1989	STL	NL	20	4	16	8	10	2	0	1	0	0	0	0	0	0	9	11
1990	STL	NL	1	0	1	1	0	0	0	0	0	0	0	0	0	0	1	0
	BOS	AL	15	13	2	6	5	4	0	1	1	0	0	0	0	0	9	6
	Total		16	13	3	7	5	4	0	1	1	0	0	0	0	0	10	6
1991	BOS	AL	16	10	6	6	6	3	1	0	0	0	0	0	0	0	11	5
1992	BOS	AL	15	10	5	9	2	2	2	1	0	0	0	0	0	0	9	6
1993	MIL	AL	6	2	4	3	3	0	0	0	0	0	0	1	0	0	4	2
1994	BOS	AL	10	4	6	3	4	2	1	1	0	0	0	0	0	0	9	1
Total			271	129	142	150	88	26	7	17	1	0	0	3	3	1	174	97

Rank among batters: 88 • *Top target (7 home runs)*: Floyd Bannister • *Number of pitchers victimized*: 189 • *Total ballparks homered in*: 27 • *First HR*: 04/11/1981 off Floyd Bannister • *LCS HR—2*

George Brunet

GEORGE STUART BRUNET
B: 06/08/1935 D: 10/25/1991
BR

Year	Tm	Lg	Tot	H	A	Men-On 0	Men-On 1	Men-On 2	Men-On 3	One-Game 2	One-Game 3	One-Game 4	LO	XN	IP	PH	RHP	LHP
1966	CAL	AL	1	0	1	1	0	0	0	0	0	0	0	0	0	0	1	0
1969	SEA	AL	1	1	0	1	0	0	0	0	0	0	0	0	0	0	0	1
1970	WAS	AL	1	1	0	0	0	1	0	0	0	0	0	0	0	0	1	0
Total			3	2	1	2	0	1	0	0	0	0	0	0	0	0	2	1

Rank among batters: 3,735 • *Total ballparks homered in*: 2 • *First HR*: 05/20/1966 off Phil Ortega

Bill Bruton

WILLIAM HARON BRUTON
B: 12/22/1925
BL

Year	Tm	Lg	Tot	H	A	Men-On 0	Men-On 1	Men-On 2	Men-On 3	One-Game 2	One-Game 3	One-Game 4	LO	XN	IP	PH	RHP	LHP
1953	MIL	NL	1	1	0	1	0	0	0	0	0	0	0	1	0	0	1	0
1954	MIL	NL	4	1	3	2	2	0	0	0	0	0	2	0	1	0	4	0
1955	MIL	NL	9	1	8	4	4	1	0	0	0	0	2	1	0	0	9	0
1956	MIL	NL	8	1	7	6	0	1	1	0	0	0	0	0	0	0	8	0
1957	MIL	NL	5	3	2	4	1	0	0	1	0	0	2	0	0	0	5	0
1958	MIL	NL	3	0	3	3	0	0	0	0	0	0	2	0	0	0	3	0
1959	MIL	NL	6	1	5	6	0	0	0	0	0	0	0	1	0	0	6	0
1960	MIL	NL	12	7	5	9	0	3	0	0	0	0	2	0	1	0	9	3
1961	DET	AL	17	9	8	10	4	3	0	1	0	0	0	1	0	0	15	2
1962	DET	AL	16	7	9	6	5	4	1	0	0	0	0	0	0	0	15	1
1963	DET	AL	8	4	4	7	0	1	0	0	0	0	1	0	0	0	7	1
1964	DET	AL	5	4	1	4	1	0	0	0	0	0	1	0	0	0	5	0
Total			94	39	55	62	17	13	2	2	0	0	12	4	2	0	87	7

Rank among batters: 535 • *Top target (5 home runs)*: Robin Roberts • *Number of pitchers victimized*: 66 • *Total ballparks homered in*: 20 • *First HR*: 04/14/1953 off Gerry Staley • *World Series HR—1*

Billy Bryan

WILLIAM RONALD BRYAN
B: 12/04/1938
BL

Year	Tm	Lg	Tot	H	A	Men-On 0	Men-On 1	Men-On 2	Men-On 3	One-Game 2	One-Game 3	One-Game 4	LO	XN	IP	PH	RHP	LHP
1961	KC	AL	1	0	1	1	0	0	0	0	0	0	0	0	0	0	1	0
1962	KC	AL	2	1	1	1	0	1	0	0	0	0	0	0	0	0	2	0
1963	KC	AL	3	2	1	2	1	0	0	0	0	0	0	0	0	0	3	0
1964	KC	AL	13	7	6	7	5	1	0	1	0	0	0	1	0	2	13	0
1965	KC	AL	14	6	8	7	5	2	0	0	0	0	0	1	0	0	14	0
1966	NY	AL	4	3	1	4	0	0	0	0	0	0	0	1	0	2	4	0
1967	NY	AL	1	1	0	1	0	0	0	0	0	0	0	0	0	0	1	0
1968	WAS	AL	3	1	2	1	0	2	0	0	0	0	0	0	0	0	1	2
Total			41	21	20	24	11	6	0	1	0	0	0	3	0	4	39	2

Rank among batters: 1,163 • *Top target (3 home runs)*: Ralph Terry • *Number of pitchers victimized*: 33 • *Total ballparks homered in*: 12 • *First HR*: 09/17/1961 off Hector Maestri

Clay Bryant

CLAIBORNE HENRY BRYANT
B: 11/26/1911
BR

Year	Tm	Lg	Tot	H	A	Men-On 0	Men-On 1	Men-On 2	Men-On 3	One-Game 2	One-Game 3	One-Game 4	LO	XN	IP	PH	RHP	LHP
1935	CHI	NL	1	0	1	1	0	0	0	0	0	0	0	0	0	0	1	0

Clay Bryant *continued*

Year	Tm	Lg	Tot	H	A	Men-On 0	Men-On 1	Men-On 2	Men-On 3	One-Game 2	One-Game 3	One-Game 4	LO	XN	IP	PH	RHP	LHP
1937	CHI	NL	1	0	1	0	0	0	1	0	0	0	0	1	0	0	1	0
1938	CHI	NL	3	1	2	3	0	0	0	0	0	0	0	0	1	0	3	0
Total			5	1	4	4	0	0	1	0	0	0	0	1	1	0	5	0

Rank among batters: 3,191 • *Total ballparks homered in*: 5 • *First HR*: 06/13/1935 off Orville Jorgens

Don Bryant

DONALD RAY BRYANT
B: 07/13/1941
BR

Year	Tm	Lg	Tot	H	A	Men-On 0	Men-On 1	Men-On 2	Men-On 3	One-Game 2	One-Game 3	One-Game 4	LO	XN	IP	PH	RHP	LHP
1969	HOU	NL	1	1	0	0	1	0	0	0	0	0	0	0	0	0	1	0

Rank among batters: 4,707 • *Total ballparks homered in*: 1 • *First HR*: 05/03/1969 off Bobby Bolin

Ralph Bryant

RALPH WENDELL BRYANT
B: 05/20/1961
BL

Year	Tm	Lg	Tot	H	A	Men-On 0	Men-On 1	Men-On 2	Men-On 3	One-Game 2	One-Game 3	One-Game 4	LO	XN	IP	PH	RHP	LHP
1986	LA	NL	6	1	5	4	1	1	0	0	0	0	0	0	0	2	6	0
1987	LA	NL	2	0	2	1	1	0	0	0	0	0	0	0	0	1	2	0
Total			8	1	7	5	2	1	0	0	0	0	0	0	0	3	8	0

Rank among batters: 2,703 • *Total ballparks homered in*: 7 • *First HR*: 09/01/1986 off Jeff Reardon

Steve Brye

STEPHEN ROBERT BRYE
B: 02/04/1949
BR

Year	Tm	Lg	Tot	H	A	Men-On 0	Men-On 1	Men-On 2	Men-On 3	One-Game 2	One-Game 3	One-Game 4	LO	XN	IP	PH	RHP	LHP
1971	MIN	AL	3	3	0	2	0	1	0	0	0	0	0	0	0	0	2	1
1973	MIN	AL	6	3	3	3	1	2	0	0	0	0	0	0	0	0	2	4
1974	MIN	AL	2	0	2	1	0	1	0	0	0	0	1	0	0	0	0	2
1975	MIN	AL	9	5	4	5	2	2	0	1	0	0	0	0	1	1	4	5
1976	MIN	AL	2	1	1	0	1	1	0	0	0	0	0	0	0	0	1	1
1977	MIL	AL	7	2	5	5	2	0	0	1	0	0	0	0	0	0	3	4
1978	PIT	NL	1	0	1	1	0	0	0	0	0	0	0	0	0	0	0	1
Total			30	14	16	17	6	7	0	2	0	0	1	0	1	1	12	18

Rank among batters: 1,437 • *Top target (2 home runs)*: Mickey Lolich, Dave Roberts, Rudy May • *Number of pitchers victimized*: 27 • *Total ballparks homered in*: 7 • *First HR*: 09/03/1971 off Vida Blue

Johnny Bucha

JOHN GEORGE BUCHA
B: 01/22/1925
BR

Year	Tm	Lg	Tot	H	A	Men-On 0	Men-On 1	Men-On 2	Men-On 3	One-Game 2	One-Game 3	One-Game 4	LO	XN	IP	PH	RHP	LHP
1953	DET	AL	1	0	1	1	0	0	0	0	0	0	0	0	0	0	1	0

Rank among batters: 4,707 • *Total ballparks homered in*: 1 • *First HR*: 09/09/1953 off Harry Byrd

Jerry Buchek

GERALD PETER BUCHEK
B: 05/09/1942
BR

Year	Tm	Lg	Tot	H	A	Men-On 0	Men-On 1	Men-On 2	Men-On 3	One-Game 2	One-Game 3	One-Game 4	LO	XN	IP	PH	RHP	LHP
1965	STL	NL	3	1	2	2	1	0	0	0	0	0	0	0	0	0	3	0
1966	STL	NL	4	2	2	1	3	0	0	0	0	0	0	0	0	0	1	3
1967	NY	NL	14	6	8	9	2	3	0	2	0	0	0	1	0	1	9	5
1968	NY	NL	1	1	0	0	0	1	0	0	0	0	0	0	0	0	0	1
Total			22	10	12	12	6	4	0	2	0	0	0	1	0	1	13	9

Rank among batters: 1,719 • Top target (2 home runs): Woodie Fryman, Dick Kelley, Dick Calmus, Mike McCormick • *Number of pitchers victimized*: 18 • *Total ballparks homered in*: 8 • *First HR*: 07/04/1965 off Gary Kroll

Jim Bucher

JAMES QUINTER BUCHER
B: 03/11/1911
BL

Year	Tm	Lg	Tot	H	A	Men-On 0	Men-On 1	Men-On 2	Men-On 3	One-Game 2	One-Game 3	One-Game 4	LO	XN	IP	PH	RHP	LHP
1935	BRO	NL	7	5	2	2	3	2	0	0	0	0	0	1	0	0	6	1
1936	BRO	NL	2	1	1	0	2	0	0	0	0	0	0	0	0	0	2	0
1937	BRO	NL	4	1	3	2	1	0	1	0	0	0	0	0	0	0	3	1

Jim Bucher *continued*

Year	Tm	Lg	Tot	H	A	Men-On 0	1	2	3	One-Game 2	3	4	LO	XN	IP	PH	RHP	LHP
1944	BOS	AL	4	1	3	1	2	0	1	1	0	0	1	0	0	0	3	1
Total			17	8	9	5	8	2	2	1	0	0	1	1	0	0	14	3

Rank among batters: 1,969 • *Top target (2 home runs)*: Charlie Root • *Number of pitchers victimized*: 16 • *Total ballparks homered in*: 7 • *First HR*: 06/02/1935 off Jim Bivin

Garland Buckeye

GARLAND MAIERS BUCKEYE
B: 10/16/1897 D: 11/14/1975
BB

Year	Tm	Lg	Tot	H	A	Men-On 0	1	2	3	One-Game 2	3	4	LO	XN	IP	PH	RHP	LHP
1925	CLE	AL	3	0	3	1	1	1	0	1	0	0	0	0	0	0	2	1
1926	CLE	AL	2	2	0	1	0	1	0	0	0	0	0	0	0	0	2	0
Total			5	2	3	2	1	2	0	1	0	0	0	0	0	0	4	1

Rank among batters: 3,191 • *Total ballparks homered in*: 3 • *First HR*: 07/30/1925 off Paul Zahniser

Dick Buckley

RICHARD D. BUCKLEY
B: 09/21/1858 D: 12/12/1929

Year	Tm	Lg	Tot	H	A	Men-On 0	1	2	3	One-Game 2	3	4	LO	XN	IP	PH	RHP	LHP
1888	IND	NL	5	4	1	5	0	0	0	0	0	0	0	0	0	0	3	2
1889	IND	NL	8	8	0	4	2	2	0	1	0	0	0	0	0	0	6	2
1890	NY	NL	2	0	2	2	0	0	0	0	0	0	0	0	0	0	0	1
1891	NY	NL	4	3	1	3	1	0	0	0	0	0	0	0	1	0	3	0
1892	STL	NL	5	3	2	3	1	1	0	0	0	0	0	0	0	0	4	0
1894	STL	NL	1	1	0	1	0	0	0	0	0	0	0	0	1	0	1	0
	PHI	NL	1	1	0	1	0	0	0	0	0	0	0	0	0	0	1	0
	Total		2	2	0	2	0	0	0	0	0	0	0	0	1	0	2	0
Total			26	20	6	19	4	3	0	1	0	0	0	0	2	0	18	5

Rank among batters: 1,576 • *Top target (4 home runs)*: Mickey Welch • *Number of pitchers victimized*: 19 • *Total ballparks homered in*: 9 • *First HR*: 05/04/1888 off Dad Clarke

Bill Buckner

WILLIAM JOSEPH BUCKNER
B: 12/14/1949
BL

Year	Tm	Lg	Tot	H	A	Men-On 0	1	2	3	One-Game 2	3	4	LO	XN	IP	PH	RHP	LHP
1971	LA	NL	5	2	3	1	2	1	1	0	0	0	0	0	0	0	4	1
1972	LA	NL	5	1	4	2	2	1	0	0	0	0	0	0	0	0	5	0
1973	LA	NL	8	4	4	5	3	0	0	0	0	0	0	0	0	0	7	1
1974	LA	NL	7	3	4	4	2	1	0	0	0	0	0	1	0	0	7	0
1975	LA	NL	6	3	3	4	2	0	0	0	0	0	0	0	0	0	5	1
1976	LA	NL	7	4	3	6	1	0	0	0	0	0	0	0	0	0	5	2
1977	CHI	NL	11	7	4	5	2	4	0	2	0	0	0	0	0	0	8	3
1978	CHI	NL	5	3	2	2	2	1	0	0	0	0	0	0	0	0	3	2
1979	CHI	NL	14	8	6	10	2	1	1	1	0	0	0	0	0	0	9	5
1980	CHI	NL	10	3	7	5	5	0	0	0	0	0	0	0	0	0	9	1
1981	CHI	NL	10	7	3	7	1	2	0	1	0	0	0	0	0	0	7	3
1982	CHI	NL	15	9	6	8	6	1	0	1	0	0	0	0	0	0	13	2
1983	CHI	NL	16	6	10	13	2	1	0	1	0	0	0	0	0	0	14	2
1984	BOS	AL	11	6	5	6	3	0	2	1	0	0	0	0	0	0	6	5
1985	BOS	AL	16	6	10	5	6	4	1	0	0	0	0	0	0	0	12	4
1986	BOS	AL	18	8	10	11	6	1	0	2	0	0	0	0	0	0	14	4
1987	BOS	AL	2	0	2	0	1	1	0	0	0	0	0	0	0	0	2	0
	CAL	AL	3	2	1	2	0	1	0	0	0	0	0	0	0	0	3	0
	Total		5	2	3	2	1	2	0	0	0	0	0	0	0	0	5	0
1988	KC	AL	3	0	3	3	0	0	0	1	0	0	0	0	0	0	3	0
1989	KC	AL	1	0	1	1	0	0	0	0	0	0	0	0	0	0	1	0
1990	BOS	AL	1	1	0	1	0	0	0	0	0	0	0	0	1	0	1	0
Total			174	83	91	101	48	20	5	10	0	0	0	1	1	0	138	36

Rank among batters: 230 • *Top target (5 home runs)*: Bruce Kison • *Number of pitchers victimized*: 127 • *Total ballparks homered in*: 27 • *First HR*: 04/06/1971 off Don Wilson • *World Series HR*—1

Don Buddin

DONALD THOMAS BUDDIN
B: 05/05/1934
BR

Year	Tm	Lg	Tot	H	A	Men-On 0	1	2	3	One-Game 2	3	4	LO	XN	IP	PH	RHP	LHP
1956	BOS	AL	5	2	3	3	1	1	0	0	0	0	0	0	0	0	5	0

Don Buddin *continued*

Year	Tm	Lg	Tot	H	A	Men-On 0	1	2	3	One-Game 2	3	4	LO	XN	IP	PH	RHP	LHP
1958	BOS	AL	12	5	7	8	2	2	0	0	0	0	0	0	0	0	9	3
1959	BOS	AL	10	7	3	7	0	2	1	0	0	0	0	2	0	0	7	3
1960	BOS	AL	6	2	4	6	0	0	0	0	0	0	1	0	0	0	5	1
1961	BOS	AL	6	6	0	4	2	0	0	1	0	0	0	0	0	0	5	1
1962	HOU	NL	2	1	1	0	0	1	1	0	0	0	0	1	0	0	2	0
Total			41	23	18	28	5	6	2	1	0	0	1	3	0	0	33	8

Rank among batters: 1,163 • *Top target (4 home runs)*: Billy Pierce • *Number of pitchers victimized*: 27 • *Total ballparks homered in*: 10 • *First HR*: 05/15/1956 off Paul Foytack

Mike Budnick

MICHAEL JOE BUDNICK
B: 09/15/1919
BR

Year	Tm	Lg	Tot	H	A	Men-On 0	1	2	3	One-Game 2	3	4	LO	XN	IP	PH	RHP	LHP
1946	NY	NL	1	1	0	1	0	0	0	0	0	0	0	0	0	0	1	0

Rank among batters: 4,707 • *Total ballparks homered in*: 1 • *First HR*: 07/06/1946 off Al Jurisich

Steve Buechele

STEVEN BERNARD BUECHELE
B: 09/26/1961
BR

Year	Tm	Lg	Tot	H	A	Men-On 0	1	2	3	One-Game 2	3	4	LO	XN	IP	PH	RHP	LHP
1985	TEX	AL	6	5	1	3	3	0	0	0	0	0	0	0	0	0	3	3
1986	TEX	AL	18	6	12	15	1	2	0	0	0	0	0	0	0	1	13	5
1987	TEX	AL	13	6	7	10	3	0	0	1	0	0	0	0	0	0	5	8
1988	TEX	AL	16	8	8	12	3	1	0	1	0	0	0	1	0	0	11	5
1989	TEX	AL	16	7	9	12	3	1	0	0	0	0	0	0	0	0	10	6
1990	TEX	AL	7	5	2	3	3	0	1	0	0	0	0	0	0	0	3	4
1991	TEX	AL	18	7	11	9	6	3	0	0	0	0	0	0	0	0	12	6
	PIT	NL	4	2	2	1	3	0	0	0	0	0	0	0	0	0	1	3
	Total		22	9	13	10	9	3	0	0	0	0	0	0	0	0	13	9
1992	PIT	NL	8	3	5	5	3	0	0	0	0	0	0	0	0	0	4	4
	CHI	NL	1	1	0	1	0	0	0	0	0	0	0	0	0	0	0	1
	Total		9	4	5	6	3	0	0	0	0	0	0	0	0	0	4	5
1993	CHI	NL	15	8	7	10	4	1	0	0	0	0	0	0	0	0	10	5
1994	CHI	NL	14	7	7	7	6	1	0	0	0	0	0	0	0	0	12	2
1995	CHI	NL	1	0	1	1	0	0	0	0	0	0	0	0	0	0	0	1
Total			137	65	72	89	38	9	1	2	0	0	0	1	0	1	84	53

Rank among batters: 319 • *Top target (4 home runs)*: Kirk McCaskill, John Cerutti, Bud Black • *Number of pitchers victimized*: 113 • *Total ballparks homered in*: 26 • *First HR*: 08/09/1985 off Mike Flanagan

Fritz Buelow

FREDERICK WILLIAM ALEXANDER BUELOW
B: 02/13/1876 D: 12/27/1933
BR

Year	Tm	Lg	Tot	H	A	Men-On 0	1	2	3	One-Game 2	3	4	LO	XN	IP	PH	RHP	LHP
1901	DET	AL	2	2	0	2	0	0	0	0	0	0	0	0	0	0	1	1
1902	DET	AL	2	1	1	0	1	1	0	0	0	0	0	0	1	0	2	0
1903	DET	AL	1	0	1	0	0	1	0	0	0	0	0	0	0	0	1	0
1905	CLE	AL	1	0	1	0	1	0	0	0	0	0	0	0	0	0	1	0
Total			6	3	3	2	2	2	0	0	0	0	0	0	1	0	5	1

Rank among batters: 2,988 • *Total ballparks homered in*: 4 • *First HR*: 06/05/1901 off Wiley Piatt

Charlie Buffinton

CHARLES G. BUFFINTON
B: 06/14/1861 D: 09/23/1907
BR

Year	Tm	Lg	Tot	H	A	Men-On 0	1	2	3	One-Game 2	3	4	LO	XN	IP	PH	RHP	LHP
1883	BOS	NL	1	0	1	0	0	1	0	0	0	0	0	0	0	0	1	0
1884	BOS	NL	1	0	1	0	0	1	0	0	0	0	0	0	0	0	0	0
1885	BOS	NL	1	0	1	0	1	0	0	0	0	0	0	0	0	0	1	0
1886	BOS	NL	1	1	0	0	1	0	0	0	0	0	0	0	0	0	1	0
1887	PHI	NL	1	0	1	0	1	0	0	0	0	0	0	0	0	0	1	0
1890	PHI	PL	1	1	0	0	0	1	0	0	0	0	0	0	1	0	1	0
1891	BOS	AA	1	1	0	1	0	0	0	0	0	0	0	0	0	0	1	0
Total			7	3	4	1	3	3	0	0	0	0	0	0	1	0	6	0

Rank among batters: 2,834 • *Total ballparks homered in*: 6 • *First HR*: 07/10/1883 off Stump Wiedman

Damon Buford

DAMON JACKSON BUFORD
B: 06/12/1970
BR

Year	Tm	Lg	Tot	H	A	Men-On 0	1	2	3	One-Game 2	3	4	LO	XN	IP	PH	RHP	LHP
1993	BAL	AL	2	0	2	2	0	0	0	0	0	0	0	0	0	0	2	0
1995	NY	NL	4	2	2	3	1	0	0	1	0	0	2	0	0	0	2	2
Total			6	2	4	5	1	0	0	1	0	0	2	0	0	0	4	2

Rank among batters: 2,988 • *Top target (2 home runs)*: Mike Hampton • *Number of pitchers victimized*: 5 • *Total ballparks homered in*: 4 • *First HR*: 05/06/1993 off Scott Brow

Don Buford

DONALD ALVIN BUFORD
B: 02/02/1937
BB

Year	Tm	Lg	Tot	H	A	Men-On 0	1	2	3	One-Game 2	3	4	LO	XN	IP	PH	RHP	LHP
1964	CHI	AL	4	2	2	1	1	2	0	0	0	0	0	0	0	0	4	0
1965	CHI	AL	10	5	5	7	3	0	0	0	0	0	1	2	0	0	9	1
1966	CHI	AL	8	2	6	2	6	0	0	0	0	0	0	0	1	0	6	2
1967	CHI	AL	4	1	3	3	0	0	1	0	0	0	1	1	0	0	4	0
1968	BAL	AL	15	6	9	12	2	0	1	0	0	0	3	0	0	2	13	2
1969	BAL	AL	11	3	8	10	0	1	0	0	0	0	3	0	0	0	10	1
1970	BAL	AL	17	10	7	11	3	2	1	1	0	0	2	0	0	0	15	2
1971	BAL	AL	19	9	10	13	4	2	0	1	0	0	5	0	0	0	17	2
1972	BAL	AL	5	3	2	4	1	0	0	0	0	0	0	0	0	1	3	2
Total			93	41	52	63	20	7	3	2	0	0	15	3	1	3	81	12

Rank among batters: 545 • *Top target (5 home runs)*: Joe Coleman, Bert Blyleven • *Number of pitchers victimized*: 65 • *Total ballparks homered in*: 12 • *First HR*: 05/31/1964 off Ed Rakow • *Switch hit HR in 1 game*—1 time • *World Series HR*—4; *LCS HR*—1

Jay Buhner

JAY CAMPBELL BUHNER
B: 08/13/1964
BR

Year	Tm	Lg	Tot	H	A	Men-On 0	1	2	3	One-Game 2	3	4	LO	XN	IP	PH	RHP	LHP
1988	NY	AL	3	1	2	1	1	0	1	0	0	0	0	0	0	0	2	1
	SEA	AL	10	7	3	0	6	3	1	0	0	0	0	0	0	0	7	3
	Total		13	8	5	7	4	1	1	0	0	0	0	0	0	0	9	4
1989	SEA	AL	9	7	2	4	4	1	0	0	0	0	0	0	0	0	7	2
1990	SEA	AL	7	2	5	2	3	1	1	0	0	0	0	0	0	0	3	4
1991	SEA	AL	27	14	13	15	10	2	0	2	0	0	0	3	0	0	18	9
1992	SEA	AL	25	9	16	14	7	3	1	2	0	0	0	1	0	1	15	10
1993	SEA	AL	27	13	14	14	11	1	1	2	0	0	0	0	0	1	19	8
1994	SEA	AL	21	8	13	11	8	2	0	1	0	0	0	0	0	0	13	8
1995	SEA	AL	40	21	19	20	9	9	2	5	0	0	0	0	0	0	32	8
Total			169	82	87	87	56	20	6	12	0	0	0	4	0	2	116	53

Rank among batters: 238 • *Top target (4 home runs)*: Dave Stewart • *Number of pitchers victimized*: 132 • *Total ballparks homered in*: 17 • *First HR*: 06/01/1988 off Curt Young • *Hit for Cycle*—vs OAK: 06/23/1993 • *LCS HR*—4

Scott Bullett

SCOTT DOUGLAS BULLETT
B: 12/25/1968
BB

Year	Tm	Lg	Tot	H	A	Men-On 0	1	2	3	One-Game 2	3	4	LO	XN	IP	PH	RHP	LHP
1995	CHI	NL	3	2	1	1	1	1	0	0	0	0	0	0	0	1	3	0

Rank among batters: 3,735 • *Total ballparks homered in*: 2 • *First HR*: 05/05/1995 off Jon Lieber

Bud Bulling

TERRY CHARLES BULLING
B: 12/15/1952
BR

Year	Tm	Lg	Tot	H	A	Men-On 0	1	2	3	One-Game 2	3	4	LO	XN	IP	PH	RHP	LHP
1981	SEA	AL	2	2	0	1	0	1	0	0	0	0	0	0	0	0	1	1
1982	SEA	AL	1	1	0	1	0	0	0	0	0	0	0	0	0	0	1	0
Total			3	3	0	2	0	1	0	0	0	0	0	0	0	0	2	1

Rank among batters: 3,735 • *Total ballparks homered in*: 1 • *First HR*: 08/22/1981 off Bobby Ojeda

Jim Bullinger

JAMES ERIC BULLINGER
B: 08/21/1965
BR

Year	Tm	Lg	Tot	H	A	Men-On 0	1	2	3	One-Game 2	3	4	LO	XN	IP	PH	RHP	LHP
1992	CHI	NL	1	0	1	1	0	0	0	0	0	0	0	0	0	0	0	1

Rank among batters: 4,707 • *Total ballparks homered in*: 1 • *First HR*: 06/08/1992 off Rheal Cormier • *Hit HR on first major league pitch*—@STL: 06/08/1992 (1)

Year	Tm	Lg	Tot	H	A	Men-On 0	1	2	3	One-Game 2	3	4	LO	XN	IP	PH	RHP	LHP

Eric Bullock

ERIC GERALD BULLOCK
B: 02/16/1960
BL

Year	Tm	Lg	Tot	H	A	Men-On 0	1	2	3	One-Game 2	3	4	LO	XN	IP	PH	RHP	LHP
1991	MON	NL	1	1	0	0	0	1	0	0	0	0	0	0	0	0	1	0

Rank among batters: 4,707 • *Total ballparks homered in*: 1 • *First HR*: 07/12/1991 off Mike Hartley

Al Bumbry

ALONZA BENJAMIN BUMBRY
B: 04/21/1947
BL

Year	Tm	Lg	Tot	H	A	Men-On 0	1	2	3	One-Game 2	3	4	LO	XN	IP	PH	RHP	LHP
1973	BAL	AL	7	2	5	6	1	0	0	0	0	0	1	0	0	0	7	0
1974	BAL	AL	1	1	0	0	1	0	0	0	0	0	0	0	1	0	1	0
1975	BAL	AL	2	0	2	0	0	2	0	0	0	0	0	0	0	0	2	0
1976	BAL	AL	9	6	3	8	1	0	0	0	0	0	2	0	1	0	9	0
1977	BAL	AL	4	3	1	2	2	0	0	0	0	0	0	0	0	0	2	2
1978	BAL	AL	2	0	2	2	0	0	0	0	0	0	0	0	0	0	2	0
1979	BAL	AL	7	2	5	5	2	0	0	0	0	0	3	0	0	0	6	1
1980	BAL	AL	9	6	3	6	3	0	0	0	0	0	2	0	0	0	7	2
1981	BAL	AL	1	1	0	0	1	0	0	0	0	0	0	0	0	0	1	0
1982	BAL	AL	5	4	1	4	1	0	0	0	0	0	3	0	0	0	4	1
1983	BAL	AL	3	2	1	2	1	0	0	0	0	0	1	0	0	0	3	0
1984	BAL	AL	3	0	3	2	1	0	0	0	0	0	1	0	0	0	3	0
1985	SD	NL	1	0	1	1	0	0	0	0	0	0	0	0	0	1	1	0
Total			54	27	27	38	14	2	0	0	0	0	13	0	2	1	48	6

Rank among batters: 938 • *Top target (5 home runs)*: Catfish Hunter • *Number of pitchers victimized*: 45 • *Total ballparks homered in*: 14 • *First HR*: 05/09/1973 off Catfish Hunter

Jim Bunning

JAMES PAUL DAVID BUNNING
B: 10/23/1931
BR

Year	Tm	Lg	Tot	H	A	Men-On 0	1	2	3	One-Game 2	3	4	LO	XN	IP	PH	RHP	LHP
1957	DET	AL	1	0	1	1	0	0	0	0	0	0	0	0	0	0	1	0
1959	DET	AL	1	0	1	0	0	1	0	0	0	0	0	0	0	0	0	1
1962	DET	AL	1	0	1	1	0	0	0	0	0	0	0	0	0	0	1	0
1965	PHI	NL	1	0	1	1	0	0	0	0	0	0	0	0	0	0	0	1
1967	PHI	NL	2	0	2	2	0	0	0	0	0	0	0	0	0	0	2	0
1971	PHI	NL	1	0	1	1	0	0	0	0	0	0	0	0	0	0	0	1
Total			7	0	7	6	0	1	0	0	0	0	0	0	0	0	4	3

Rank among batters: 2,834 • *Total ballparks homered in*: 7 • *First HR*: 09/11/1957 off Camilo Pascual

Al Burch

ALBERT WILLIAM BURCH
B: 10/07/1883 D: 10/05/1926
BL

Year	Tm	Lg	Tot	H	A	Men-On 0	1	2	3	One-Game 2	3	4	LO	XN	IP	PH	RHP	LHP
1908	BRO	NL	2	1	1	2	0	0	0	0	0	0	0	0	0	0	2	0
1909	BRO	NL	1	1	0	0	1	0	0	0	0	0	0	0	0	0	1	0
1910	BRO	NL	1	0	1	1	0	0	0	0	0	0	0	0	0	0	1	0
Total			4	2	2	3	1	0	0	0	0	0	0	0	0	0	4	0

Rank among batters: 3,427 • *Total ballparks homered in*: 3 • *First HR*: 07/01/1908 off Joe McGinnity

Ernie Burch

EARNEST W. BURCH
B: 1856
BL

Year	Tm	Lg	Tot	H	A	Men-On 0	1	2	3	One-Game 2	3	4	LO	XN	IP	PH	RHP	LHP
1886	BRO	AA	2	2	0	0	1	0	1	0	0	0	0	0	0	0	1	0
1887	BRO	AA	2	2	0	0	1	1	0	0	0	0	0	0	0	0	0	0
Total			4	4	0	0	2	1	1	0	0	0	0	0	0	0	1	0

Rank among batters: 3,427 • *Total ballparks homered in*: 1 • *First HR*: 05/19/1886 off Jumbo McGinnis

Bob Burda

EDWARD ROBERT BURDA
B: 07/16/1938
BL

Year	Tm	Lg	Tot	H	A	Men-On 0	1	2	3	One-Game 2	3	4	LO	XN	IP	PH	RHP	LHP
1969	SF	NL	6	3	3	1	1	3	1	0	0	0	0	0	0	3	4	2
1970	MIL	AL	4	1	3	2	2	0	0	0	0	0	0	0	0	0	4	0
1971	STL	NL	1	0	1	1	0	0	0	0	0	0	0	0	0	1	1	0

Year	Tm	Lg	Tot	H	A	Men-On				One-Game			LO	XN	IP	PH	RHP	LHP
						0	1	2	3	2	3	4						

Bob Burda *continued*

Year	Tm	Lg	Tot	H	A	0	1	2	3	2	3	4	LO	XN	IP	PH	RHP	LHP
1972	BOS	AL	2	1	1	1	0	1	0	0	0	0	0	0	0	0	2	0
Total			13	5	8	5	3	4	1	0	0	0	0	0	0	4	11	2

Rank among batters: 2,248 • *Total ballparks homered in*: 10 • *First HR*: 05/09/1969 off Phil Regan

Lew Burdette

SELVA LEWIS BURDETTE
B: 11/22/1926
BR

Year	Tm	Lg	Tot	H	A	0	1	2	3	2	3	4	LO	XN	IP	PH	RHP	LHP
1957	MIL	NL	2	0	2	1	0	1	0	1	0	0	0	0	0	0	0	2
1958	MIL	NL	3	0	3	1	1	0	1	1	0	0	0	0	0	0	1	2
1960	MIL	NL	2	1	1	2	0	0	0	0	0	0	0	1	0	0	2	0
1961	MIL	NL	3	0	3	3	0	0	0	0	0	0	0	0	0	0	2	1
1964	CHI	NL	2	1	1	2	0	0	0	0	0	0	0	0	0	0	1	1
Total			12	2	10	9	1	1	1	2	0	0	0	1	0	0	6	6

Rank among batters: 2,325 • *Top target (2 home runs)*: Joe Nuxhall, Sandy Koufax • *Number of pitchers victimized*: 10 • *Total ballparks homered in*: 5 • *First HR*: 08/13/1957 off Joe Nuxhall • *World Series HR—*1

Jack Burdock

JOHN JOSEPH BURDOCK
B: 04/ /1852 D: 11/27/1931
BR

Year	Tm	Lg	Tot	H	A	0	1	2	3	2	3	4	LO	XN	IP	PH	RHP	LHP
1880	BOS	NL	2	2	0	1	1	0	0	0	0	0	1	0	0	0	2	0
1881	BOS	NL	1	0	1	1	0	0	0	0	0	0	0	0	0	0	1	0
1883	BOS	NL	5	3	2	3	2	0	0	0	0	0	0	0	0	0	5	0
1884	BOS	NL	6	4	2	3	2	1	0	1	0	0	0	0	0	0	3	0
1888	BRO	AA	1	1	0	1	0	0	0	0	0	0	0	0	0	0	1	0
Total			15	10	5	9	5	1	0	1	0	0	1	0	0	0	12	0

Rank among batters: 2,096 • *Top target (3 home runs)*: Fred Goldsmith • *Number of pitchers victimized*: 9 • *Total ballparks homered in*: 6 • *First HR*: 06/01/1880 off Fred Goldsmith

Smoky Burgess

FORREST HARRILL BURGESS
B: 02/06/1927 D: 09/15/1991
BL

Year	Tm	Lg	Tot	H	A	0	1	2	3	2	3	4	LO	XN	IP	PH	RHP	LHP
1949	CHI	NL	1	1	0	0	1	0	0	0	0	0	0	0	0	1	1	0
1951	CHI	NL	2	1	1	1	0	1	0	0	0	0	0	0	0	0	2	0
1952	PHI	NL	6	3	3	2	4	0	0	0	0	0	0	0	0	0	6	0
1953	PHI	NL	4	1	3	4	0	0	0	0	0	0	0	0	0	0	2	2
1954	PHI	NL	4	3	1	1	2	1	0	0	0	0	0	0	0	1	4	0
1955	PHI	NL	1	0	1	1	0	0	0	0	0	0	0	0	0	0	1	0
	CIN	NL	20	16	4	10	6	2	2	2	1	0	0	0	0	0	17	3
	Total		21	16	5	11	6	2	2	2	1	0	0	0	0	0	18	3
1956	CIN	NL	12	5	7	6	4	2	0	0	0	0	0	1	0	2	7	5
1957	CIN	NL	14	12	2	10	3	1	0	1	0	0	0	0	0	1	12	2
1958	CIN	NL	6	2	4	2	2	2	0	0	0	0	0	1	0	3	6	0
1959	PIT	NL	11	6	5	5	2	4	0	2	0	0	0	0	0	2	8	3
1960	PIT	NL	7	5	2	5	2	0	0	0	0	0	0	0	0	1	7	0
1961	PIT	NL	12	3	9	5	5	2	0	3	0	0	0	0	0	0	12	0
1962	PIT	NL	13	4	9	6	3	4	0	3	0	0	0	1	0	0	10	3
1963	PIT	NL	6	3	3	4	2	0	0	0	0	0	0	0	0	0	5	1
1964	PIT	NL	2	1	1	0	0	2	0	0	0	0	0	0	0	0	2	0
	CHI	AL	1	0	1	1	0	0	0	0	0	0	0	0	0	1	1	0
	Total		3	1	2	1	0	2	0	0	0	0	0	0	0	1	3	0
1965	CHI	AL	2	0	2	1	1	0	0	0	0	0	0	0	0	2	0	2
1967	CHI	AL	2	1	1	0	2	0	0	0	0	0	0	0	0	2	1	1
Total			126	67	59	64	39	21	2	11	1	0	0	3	0	16	104	22

Rank among batters: 360 • *Top target (5 home runs)*: Bob Buhl, Robin Roberts, Larry Jackson • *Number of pitchers victimized*: 91 • *Total ballparks homered in*: 16 • *First HR*: 05/17/1949 off Ralph Branca

Tom Burgess

THOMAS ROLAND BURGESS
B: 09/01/1927
BL

Year	Tm	Lg	Tot	H	A	0	1	2	3	2	3	4	LO	XN	IP	PH	RHP	LHP
1962	LA	AL	2	1	1	1	0	1	0	0	0	0	0	0	0	1	2	0

Rank among batters: 4,129 • *Total ballparks homered in*: 2 • *First HR*: 05/13/1962 off John Buzhardt

Year	Tm	Lg	Tot	H	A	Men-On 0	Men-On 1	Men-On 2	Men-On 3	One-Game 2	One-Game 3	One-Game 4	LO	XN	IP	PH	RHP	LHP

Bill Burgo

WILLIAM ROSS BURGO
B: 11/05/1919 D: 10/19/1988
BR

Year	Tm	Lg	Tot	H	A	Men-On 0	Men-On 1	Men-On 2	Men-On 3	One-Game 2	One-Game 3	One-Game 4	LO	XN	IP	PH	RHP	LHP
1943	PHI	AL	1	1	0	1	0	0	0	0	0	0	0	0	0	0	1	0
1944	PHI	AL	1	1	0	1	0	0	0	0	0	0	0	0	0	0	1	0
Total			2	2	0	2	0	0	0	0	0	0	0	0	0	0	2	0

Rank among batters: 4,129 • *Total ballparks homered in*: 1 • *First HR*: 09/28/1943 off Charlie Fuchs

Eddie Burke

EDWARD D. BURKE
B: 10/06/1866 D: 11/26/1907
BL

Year	Tm	Lg	Tot	H	A	Men-On 0	Men-On 1	Men-On 2	Men-On 3	One-Game 2	One-Game 3	One-Game 4	LO	XN	IP	PH	RHP	LHP
1890	PHI	NL	4	3	1	2	2	0	0	0	0	0	0	0	2	0	4	0
	PIT	NL	1	0	1	0	0	1	0	0	0	0	0	0	0	0	1	0
	Total		5	3	2	2	3	0	0	0	0	0	0	0	2	0	5	0
1891	MIL	AA	2	1	1	0	0	1	0	0	0	0	0	0	0	0	1	0
1892	NY	NL	6	3	3	3	3	0	0	0	0	0	0	0	2	0	5	0
1893	NY	NL	9	8	1	2	4	2	1	0	0	0	0	0	3	0	6	2
1894	NY	NL	4	4	0	2	1	0	1	0	0	0	0	0	0	0	3	1
1895	NY	NL	1	1	0	1	0	0	0	0	0	0	0	0	0	0	1	0
	CIN	NL	1	0	1	0	0	0	1	0	0	0	0	0	0	0	1	0
	Total		2	1	1	1	0	0	1	0	0	0	0	0	0	0	2	0
1896	CIN	NL	1	0	1	1	0	0	0	0	0	0	1	0	0	0	0	1
1897	CIN	NL	1	1	0	1	0	0	0	0	0	0	0	0	1	0	0	1
Total			30	21	9	12	11	3	3	0	0	0	1	0	8	0	22	5

Rank among batters: 1,437 • *Top target (3 home runs)*: Kirtley Baker, Jack Stivetts • *Number of pitchers victimized*: 23 • *Total ballparks homered in*: 11 • *First HR*: 06/20/1890 off Kirtley Baker

Glenn Burke

GLENN LAWRENCE BURKE
B: 11/16/1952 D: 05/30/1995
BR

Year	Tm	Lg	Tot	H	A	Men-On 0	Men-On 1	Men-On 2	Men-On 3	One-Game 2	One-Game 3	One-Game 4	LO	XN	IP	PH	RHP	LHP
1977	LA	NL	1	1	0	1	0	0	0	0	0	0	0	0	0	0	1	0
1978	OAK	AL	1	1	0	1	0	0	0	0	0	0	0	0	0	0	0	1
Total			2	2	0	2	0	0	0	0	0	0	0	0	0	0	1	1

Rank among batters: 4,129 • *Total ballparks homered in*: 2 • *First HR*: 10/02/1977 off J.R. Richard

Jimmy Burke

JAMES TIMOTHY BURKE
B: 10/12/1874 D: 03/26/1942
BR

Year	Tm	Lg	Tot	H	A	Men-On 0	Men-On 1	Men-On 2	Men-On 3	One-Game 2	One-Game 3	One-Game 4	LO	XN	IP	PH	RHP	LHP
1905	STL	NL	1	1	0	0	1	0	0	0	0	0	0	0	1	0	1	0

Rank among batters: 4,707 • *Total ballparks homered in*: 1 • *First HR*: 06/08/1905 off Bill Duggleby

Leo Burke

LEO PATRICK BURKE
B: 05/06/1934
BR

Year	Tm	Lg	Tot	H	A	Men-On 0	Men-On 1	Men-On 2	Men-On 3	One-Game 2	One-Game 3	One-Game 4	LO	XN	IP	PH	RHP	LHP
1958	BAL	AL	1	0	1	1	0	0	0	0	0	0	0	0	0	0	1	0
1962	LA	AL	4	1	3	1	1	2	0	0	0	0	0	0	0	0	2	2
1963	STL	NL	1	1	0	1	0	0	0	0	0	0	0	0	0	1	0	1
	CHI	NL	2	1	1	0	1	1	0	0	0	0	0	0	0	1	1	1
	Total		3	2	1	1	1	1	0	0	0	0	0	0	0	2	1	2
1964	CHI	NL	1	1	0	0	0	1	0	0	0	0	0	0	0	1	1	0
Total			9	4	5	3	2	4	0	0	0	0	0	0	0	3	5	4

Rank among batters: 2,587 • *Total ballparks homered in*: 7 • *First HR*: 09/28/1958 off Zach Monroe

Jesse Burkett

JESSE CAIL BURKETT
B: 12/04/1868 D: 05/27/1953
BL HOF

Year	Tm	Lg	Tot	H	A	Men-On 0	Men-On 1	Men-On 2	Men-On 3	One-Game 2	One-Game 3	One-Game 4	LO	XN	IP	PH	RHP	LHP
1890	NY	NL	4	0	4	3	0	1	0	0	0	0	0	0	1	0	4	0
1892	CLE	NL	6	1	5	1	4	1	0	0	0	0	0	0	0	0	2	4
1893	CLE	NL	6	1	5	4	1	0	1	1	0	0	0	0	1	0	5	0
1894	CLE	NL	8	3	5	1	5	2	0	1	0	0	0	0	0	0	7	1
1895	CLE	NL	5	1	4	3	2	0	0	0	0	0	2	0	2	0	5	0

Jesse Burkett *continued*

Year	Tm	Lg	Tot	H	A	Men-On 0	1	2	3	One-Game 2	3	4	LO	XN	IP	PH	RHP	LHP
1896	CLE	NL	6	1	5	5	1	0	0	0	0	0	1	1	0	0	3	3
1897	CLE	NL	2	2	0	2	0	0	0	0	0	0	0	0	1	0	2	0
1899	STL	NL	7	7	0	4	1	2	0	3	0	0	0	0	2	0	7	0
1900	STL	NL	7	4	3	2	4	1	0	1	0	0	0	0	4	0	6	1
1901	STL	NL	10	4	6	6	3	1	0	0	0	0	3	0	6	0	8	2
1902	STL	AL	5	2	3	3	2	0	0	0	0	0	1	0	4	0	3	2
1903	STL	AL	3	3	0	1	2	0	0	0	0	0	1	0	3	0	1	2
1904	STL	AL	2	1	1	1	1	0	0	0	0	0	0	0	2	0	1	1
1905	BOS	AL	4	3	1	3	1	0	0	0	0	0	1	0	1	0	4	0
Total			75	33	42	39	27	8	1	6	0	0	9	1	27	0	58	16

Rank among batters: 699 • *Top target (5 home runs)*: Gus Weyhing • *Number of pitchers victimized*: 56 • *Total ballparks homered in*: 23 • *First HR*: 06/23/1890 off Bill Hutchison

Ken Burkhart

KENNETH WILLIAM BURKHART
B: 11/18/1916
BR

Year	Tm	Lg	Tot	H	A	Men-On 0	1	2	3	One-Game 2	3	4	LO	XN	IP	PH	RHP	LHP
1948	CIN	NL	1	0	1	1	0	0	0	0	0	0	0	0	0	0	1	0

Rank among batters: 4,707 • *Total ballparks homered in*: 1 • *First HR*: 09/16/1948 off Ralph Branca

Ellis Burks

ELLIS RENA BURKS
B: 09/11/1964
BR

Year	Tm	Lg	Tot	H	A	Men-On 0	1	2	3	One-Game 2	3	4	LO	XN	IP	PH	RHP	LHP
1987	BOS	AL	20	11	9	12	5	1	2	1	0	0	4	0	0	0	16	4
1988	BOS	AL	18	8	10	8	5	3	2	1	0	0	1	0	0	0	13	5
1989	BOS	AL	12	6	6	6	3	2	1	1	0	0	0	0	0	0	10	2
1990	BOS	AL	21	10	11	12	5	4	0	2	0	0	0	0	0	1	16	5
1991	BOS	AL	14	8	6	10	2	2	0	1	0	0	1	0	0	0	9	5
1992	BOS	AL	8	4	4	5	2	0	1	0	0	0	0	0	0	0	5	3
1993	CHI	AL	17	7	10	11	2	2	2	1	0	0	0	1	0	0	9	8
1994	COL	NL	13	7	6	11	2	0	0	0	0	0	0	1	1	0	9	4
1995	COL	NL	14	8	6	10	2	2	0	2	0	0	1	0	0	1	9	5
Total			137	69	68	85	28	16	8	9	0	0	7	2	1	2	96	41

Rank among batters: 319 • *Top target (3 home runs)*: Erik Hanson • *Number of pitchers victimized*: 116 • *Total ballparks homered in*: 27 • *First HR*: 05/10/1987 off Don Sutton • *2 HR in 1 inning—*@CLE: 08/27/1990 • *LCS HR—*1

Rick Burleson

RICHARD PAUL BURLESON
B: 04/29/1951
BR

Year	Tm	Lg	Tot	H	A	Men-On 0	1	2	3	One-Game 2	3	4	LO	XN	IP	PH	RHP	LHP
1974	BOS	AL	4	3	1	2	1	1	0	0	0	0	0	0	0	0	4	0
1975	BOS	AL	6	3	3	4	1	1	0	0	0	0	0	0	0	0	4	2
1976	BOS	AL	7	3	4	5	1	1	0	0	0	0	1	0	0	0	5	2
1977	BOS	AL	3	2	1	2	1	0	0	0	0	0	2	0	0	0	3	0
1978	BOS	AL	5	3	2	4	1	0	0	0	0	0	1	0	0	0	4	1
1979	BOS	AL	5	4	1	4	0	0	1	0	0	0	0	0	1	0	3	2
1980	BOS	AL	8	3	5	6	1	1	0	0	0	0	1	0	0	0	3	5
1981	CAL	AL	5	2	3	4	0	1	0	0	0	0	0	0	0	0	3	2
1986	CAL	AL	5	2	3	5	0	0	0	0	0	0	3	0	0	0	1	4
1987	BAL	AL	2	2	0	2	0	0	0	0	0	0	0	0	0	0	2	0
Total			50	27	23	38	6	5	1	0	0	0	8	0	1	0	32	18

Rank among batters: 991 • *Top target (5 home runs)*: Doyle Alexander • *Number of pitchers victimized*: 41 • *Total ballparks homered in*: 15 • *First HR*: 05/05/1974 off Lloyd Allen

Hercules Burnett

HERCULES H. BURNETT
B: 08/13/1869 D: 10/04/1936
BR

Year	Tm	Lg	Tot	H	A	Men-On 0	1	2	3	One-Game 2	3	4	LO	XN	IP	PH	RHP	LHP
1895	LOU	NL	2	1	1	2	0	0	0	0	0	0	0	0	0	0	1	1

Rank among batters: 4,129 • *Total ballparks homered in*: 2 • *First HR*: 09/20/1895 off Frank Dwyer

Johnny Burnett

JOHN HENDERSON BURNETT
B: 11/01/1904 D: 08/13/1959
BL

Year	Tm	Lg	Tot	H	A	Men-On 0	Men-On 1	Men-On 2	Men-On 3	One-Game 2	One-Game 3	One-Game 4	LO	XN	IP	PH	RHP	LHP
1931	CLE	AL	1	1	0	0	1	0	0	0	0	0	0	0	0	0	1	0
1932	CLE	AL	4	3	1	3	1	0	0	0	0	0	0	0	1	0	4	0
1933	CLE	AL	1	1	0	0	1	0	0	0	0	0	0	0	0	0	1	0
1934	CLE	AL	3	1	2	2	1	0	0	0	0	0	0	1	0	0	3	0
Total			9	6	3	5	4	0	0	0	0	0	0	1	1	0	9	0

Rank among batters: 2,587 • *Top target (2 home runs)*: Ed Durham • *Number of pitchers victimized*: 8 • *Total ballparks homered in*: 5 • *First HR*: 05/14/1931 off Sam Jones

Jeromy Burnitz

JEROMY NEAL BURNITZ
B: 04/15/1969
BL

Year	Tm	Lg	Tot	H	A	Men-On 0	Men-On 1	Men-On 2	Men-On 3	One-Game 2	One-Game 3	One-Game 4	LO	XN	IP	PH	RHP	LHP
1993	NY	NL	13	6	7	7	4	1	1	0	0	0	0	0	0	0	12	1
1994	NY	NL	3	2	1	2	1	0	0	0	0	0	0	0	0	0	3	0
Total			16	8	8	9	5	1	1	0	0	0	0	0	0	0	15	1

Rank among batters: 2,029 • *Top target (2 home runs)*: Charlie Hough, Pete Harnisch • *Number of pitchers victimized*: 14 • *Total ballparks homered in*: 8 • *First HR*: 06/29/1993 off Ryan Bowen

Dick Burns

RICHARD SIMON BURNS
B: 12/26/1863 D: 11/16/1937
BL

Year	Tm	Lg	Tot	H	A	Men-On 0	Men-On 1	Men-On 2	Men-On 3	One-Game 2	One-Game 3	One-Game 4	LO	XN	IP	PH	RHP	LHP
1884	CIN	UA	4	3	1	1	3	0	0	0	0	0	0	0	1	0	3	0

Rank among batters: 3,427 • *Total ballparks homered in*: 2 • *First HR*: 05/17/1884 off Tommy Bond

George Burns

GEORGE JOSEPH BURNS
B: 11/24/1889 D: 08/15/1966
BR

Year	Tm	Lg	Tot	H	A	Men-On 0	Men-On 1	Men-On 2	Men-On 3	One-Game 2	One-Game 3	One-Game 4	LO	XN	IP	PH	RHP	LHP
1913	NY	NL	2	1	1	2	0	0	0	0	0	0	0	0	0	0	1	1
1914	NY	NL	3	1	2	0	0	2	1	0	0	0	0	0	1	0	3	0
1915	NY	NL	3	2	1	1	1	1	0	0	0	0	0	0	0	0	2	1
1916	NY	NL	5	3	2	1	4	0	0	1	0	0	1	1	0	0	4	1
1917	NY	NL	5	3	2	4	1	0	0	0	0	0	1	1	2	0	3	2
1918	NY	NL	4	4	0	3	1	0	0	0	0	0	0	0	1	0	2	2
1919	NY	NL	2	2	0	2	0	0	0	0	0	0	1	0	1	0	1	1
1920	NY	NL	6	4	2	4	2	0	0	0	0	0	1	0	0	0	5	1
1921	NY	NL	4	3	1	3	1	0	0	0	0	0	0	0	2	0	2	2
1922	CIN	NL	1	0	1	1	0	0	0	0	0	0	1	0	1	0	0	1
1923	CIN	NL	3	0	3	3	0	0	0	0	0	0	0	1	0	0	3	0
1924	CIN	NL	2	0	2	2	0	0	0	0	0	0	1	0	0	0	2	0
1925	PHI	NL	1	0	1	0	1	0	0	0	0	0	0	0	0	0	1	0
Total			41	23	18	26	11	3	1	1	0	0	6	3	8	0	29	12

Rank among batters: 1,163 • Top target (2 home runs): Gene Dale, Earl Moseley, Babe Adams, Wilbur Cooper, Hugh McQuillan • *Number of pitchers victimized*: 36 • *Total ballparks homered in*: 8 • *First HR*: 07/22/1913 off Babe Adams • *Hit for Cycle*—vs PIT: 09/17/1920

George Burns

GEORGE HENRY BURNS
B: 01/31/1893 D: 01/07/1978
BR

Year	Tm	Lg	Tot	H	A	Men-On 0	Men-On 1	Men-On 2	Men-On 3	One-Game 2	One-Game 3	One-Game 4	LO	XN	IP	PH	RHP	LHP
1914	DET	AL	5	2	3	4	1	0	0	0	0	0	0	0	0	0	3	2
1915	DET	AL	5	3	2	1	3	1	0	0	0	0	0	0	1	0	3	2
1916	DET	AL	4	0	4	3	0	0	1	0	0	0	0	0	1	0	3	1
1917	DET	AL	1	1	0	0	1	0	0	0	0	0	0	0	0	0	0	1
1918	PHI	AL	6	5	1	3	2	1	0	1	0	0	0	0	0	0	4	2
1919	PHI	AL	8	6	2	7	0	1	0	0	0	0	0	0	0	0	4	4
1920	PHI	AL	1	1	0	1	0	0	0	0	0	0	0	0	0	0	1	0
1922	BOS	AL	12	2	10	7	3	2	0	2	0	0	0	1	0	0	10	2
1923	BOS	AL	7	2	5	3	3	1	0	0	0	0	0	0	0	0	4	3
1924	CLE	AL	4	0	4	1	3	0	0	1	0	0	0	0	1	0	3	1
1925	CLE	AL	6	3	3	5	1	0	0	0	0	0	0	0	0	0	2	4

George Burns *continued*

Year	Tm	Lg	Tot	H	A	Men-On 0	Men-On 1	Men-On 2	Men-On 3	One-Game 2	One-Game 3	One-Game 4	LO	XN	IP	PH	RHP	LHP
1926	CLE	AL	4	1	3	1	3	0	0	0	0	0	0	0	0	0	3	1
1927	CLE	AL	3	3	0	2	1	0	0	0	0	0	0	0	1	0	3	0
1928	CLE	AL	5	1	4	1	2	2	0	1	0	0	0	0	0	1	5	0
1929	PHI	AL	1	1	0	0	1	0	0	0	0	0	0	0	0	0	1	0
Total			72	31	41	39	24	8	1	5	0	0	0	1	4	1	49	23

Rank among batters: 723 • Top target (3 home runs): Red Faber, Hooks Dauss, Fred Heimach, Eddie Rommel, Lil Stoner • *Number of pitchers victimized*: 52 • *Total ballparks homered in*: 9 • *First HR*: 05/15/1914 off Ray Caldwell

Jack Burns

JOHN IRVING BURNS
B: 08/31/1907 D: 04/18/1975
BL

Year	Tm	Lg	Tot	H	A	Men-On 0	Men-On 1	Men-On 2	Men-On 3	One-Game 2	One-Game 3	One-Game 4	LO	XN	IP	PH	RHP	LHP
1931	STL	AL	4	2	2	2	2	0	0	0	0	0	0	0	0	0	4	0
1932	STL	AL	11	7	4	6	3	1	1	0	0	0	0	0	1	0	7	4
1933	STL	AL	7	6	1	2	4	1	0	1	0	0	0	0	0	0	6	1
1934	STL	AL	13	5	8	5	4	4	0	0	0	0	0	0	0	0	11	2
1935	STL	AL	5	0	5	3	2	0	0	0	0	0	0	0	0	0	5	0
1936	DET	AL	4	4	0	2	0	2	0	0	0	0	1	0	0	0	4	0
Total			44	24	20	20	15	8	1	1	0	0	1	0	1	0	37	7

Rank among batters: 1,095 • *Top target (3 home runs)*: Vic Sorrell, Willis Hudlin • *Number of pitchers victimized*: 31 • *Total ballparks homered in*: 6 • *First HR*: 06/11/1931 off Lew Krausse

Jim Burns

JAMES M. BURNS

Year	Tm	Lg	Tot	H	A	Men-On 0	Men-On 1	Men-On 2	Men-On 3	One-Game 2	One-Game 3	One-Game 4	LO	XN	IP	PH	RHP	LHP
1889	KC	AA	5	2	3	2	2	1	0	0	0	0	0	0	0	0	3	2

Rank among batters: 3,191 • *Total ballparks homered in*: 4 • *First HR*: 04/20/1889 off Toad Ramsey

Joe Burns

JOSEPH JAMES BURNS
B: 06/17/1916 D: 06/24/1974
BR

Year	Tm	Lg	Tot	H	A	Men-On 0	Men-On 1	Men-On 2	Men-On 3	One-Game 2	One-Game 3	One-Game 4	LO	XN	IP	PH	RHP	LHP
1943	BOS	NL	1	0	1	1	0	0	0	0	0	0	0	0	0	0	1	0
1944	PHI	AL	1	0	1	1	0	0	0	0	0	0	0	0	0	0	1	0
Total			2	0	2	2	0	0	0	0	0	0	0	0	0	0	2	0

Rank among batters: 4,129 • *Total ballparks homered in*: 2 • *First HR*: 04/27/1943 off Bill Lohrman

Oyster Burns

THOMAS P. BURNS
B: 09/06/1864 D: 11/11/1928
BR

Year	Tm	Lg	Tot	H	A	Men-On 0	Men-On 1	Men-On 2	Men-On 3	One-Game 2	One-Game 3	One-Game 4	LO	XN	IP	PH	RHP	LHP
1884	BAL	AA	6	3	3	1	3	2	0	1	0	0	0	0	0	0	4	0
1885	BAL	AA	5	3	2	1	1	3	0	0	0	0	0	0	1	0	4	0
1887	BAL	AA	9	4	5	5	2	2	0	0	0	0	0	0	1	0	5	3
1888	BAL	AA	4	1	3	1	3	0	0	0	0	0	0	0	2	0	3	1
	BRO	AA	2	2	0	1	1	0	0	0	0	0	0	0	0	0	2	0
	Total		6	3	3	2	4	0	0	0	0	0	0	0	2	0	5	1
1889	BRO	AA	5	3	2	1	2	2	0	0	0	0	0	0	0	0	5	0
1890	BRO	NL	13	9	4	4	5	3	1	0	0	0	0	0	2	0	9	4
1891	BRO	NL	4	2	2	1	2	0	1	0	0	0	0	0	2	0	4	0
1892	BRO	NL	4	2	2	1	3	0	0	0	0	0	0	0	0	0	3	1
1893	BRO	NL	7	3	4	3	3	1	0	0	0	0	0	0	0	0	6	1
1894	BRO	NL	5	3	2	2	3	0	0	0	0	0	0	0	1	0	4	1
1895	NY	NL	1	0	1	0	1	0	0	0	0	0	0	0	0	0	1	0
Total			65	35	30	21	29	13	2	1	0	0	0	0	9	0	50	10

Rank among batters: 799 • *Top target (4 home runs)*: Gus Weyhing, Jesse Duryea • *Number of pitchers victimized*: 52 • *Total ballparks homered in*: 19 • *First HR*: 08/21/1884 off Ed Dugan • *Hit for Cycle*—vs PIT: 08/01/1890 (2) • *World Series HR*—3

Tom Burns

THOMAS EVERETT BURNS
B: 03/30/1857 D: 03/19/1902
BR

Year	Tm	Lg	Tot	H	A	Men-On 0	Men-On 1	Men-On 2	Men-On 3	One-Game 2	One-Game 3	One-Game 4	LO	XN	IP	PH	RHP	LHP
1881	CHI	NL	4	2	2	1	3	0	0	0	0	0	0	0	0	0	2	2
1883	CHI	NL	2	2	0	0	1	1	0	0	0	0	0	0	0	0	1	1

Tom Burns *continued*

Year	Tm	Lg	Tot	H	A	Men-On				One-Game			LO	XN	IP	PH	RHP	LHP
						0	1	2	3	2	3	4						
1884	CHI	NL	7	7	0	4	1	0	0	1	0	0	0	0	0	0	5	1
1885	CHI	NL	7	6	1	3	3	1	0	2	0	0	0	0	0	0	6	0
1886	CHI	NL	3	3	0	0	3	0	0	0	0	0	0	0	0	0	2	1
1887	CHI	NL	3	1	2	1	1	1	0	0	0	0	0	0	1	0	3	0
1888	CHI	NL	3	2	1	2	0	1	0	0	0	0	0	0	0	0	1	2
1889	CHI	NL	4	4	0	2	1	1	0	0	0	0	0	0	0	0	3	1
1890	CHI	NL	5	4	1	1	3	0	1	0	0	0	0	0	0	0	3	0
1891	CHI	NL	1	1	0	1	0	0	0	0	0	0	0	0	0	0	1	0
Total			39	32	7	15	16	5	1	3	0	0	0	0	1	0	27	8

Rank among batters: 1,204 • *Top target (4 home runs)*: Pretzels Getzien • *Number of pitchers victimized*: 28 • *Total ballparks homered in*: 10 • *First HR*: 05/06/1881 off Jim McCormick

Buster Burrell

FRANK ANDREW BURRELL
B: 12/22/1866 D: 05/08/1962
BR

Year	Tm	Lg	Tot	H	A	0	1	2	3	2	3	4	LO	XN	IP	PH	RHP	LHP
1895	BRO	NL	1	1	0	0	1	0	0	0	0	0	0	0	0	0	1	0
1897	BRO	NL	2	0	2	0	1	1	0	0	0	0	0	0	0	0	2	0
Total			3	1	2	0	2	1	0	0	0	0	0	0	0	0	3	0

Rank among batters: 3,735 • *Total ballparks homered in*: 3 • *First HR*: 06/14/1895 off Harry Staley

Larry Burright

LARRY ALLEN BURRIGHT
B: 07/10/1937
BR

Year	Tm	Lg	Tot	H	A	0	1	2	3	2	3	4	LO	XN	IP	PH	RHP	LHP
1962	LA	NL	4	1	3	0	2	2	0	0	0	0	0	0	1	0	3	1

Rank among batters: 3,427 • *Total ballparks homered in*: 4 • *First HR*: 05/10/1962 off Bob Bruce

Paul Burris

PAUL ROBERT BURRIS
B: 07/21/1923
BR

Year	Tm	Lg	Tot	H	A	0	1	2	3	2	3	4	LO	XN	IP	PH	RHP	LHP
1952	BOS	NL	2	0	2	1	1	0	0	0	0	0	0	0	0	0	1	1

Rank among batters: 4,129 • *Total ballparks homered in*: 2 • *First HR*: 05/30/1952 off Carl Erskine

Ray Burris

BERTRAM RAY BURRIS
B: 08/22/1950
BR

Year	Tm	Lg	Tot	H	A	0	1	2	3	2	3	4	LO	XN	IP	PH	RHP	LHP
1977	CHI	NL	1	0	1	1	0	0	0	0	0	0	0	0	0	0	1	0

Rank among batters: 4,707 • *Total ballparks homered in*: 1 • *First HR*: 05/20/1977 off Buzz Capra

Jeff Burroughs

JEFFREY ALAN BURROUGHS
B: 03/07/1951
BR

Year	Tm	Lg	Tot	H	A	0	1	2	3	2	3	4	LO	XN	IP	PH	RHP	LHP
1971	WAS	AL	5	1	4	3	1	1	0	0	0	0	0	0	0	1	1	4
1972	TEX	AL	1	1	0	0	1	0	0	0	0	0	0	0	0	0	1	0
1973	TEX	AL	30	10	20	21	6	0	3	2	0	0	0	0	0	0	22	8
1974	TEX	AL	25	8	17	16	5	2	2	1	0	0	0	0	0	0	12	13
1975	TEX	AL	29	11	18	17	11	1	0	1	0	0	0	0	0	0	19	10
1976	TEX	AL	18	12	6	7	6	5	0	1	0	0	0	0	0	0	14	4
1977	ATL	NL	41	27	14	16	18	5	2	1	0	0	0	0	0	0	26	15
1978	ATL	NL	23	19	4	10	12	1	0	1	0	0	0	0	0	0	17	6
1979	ATL	NL	11	3	8	6	2	2	1	1	0	0	0	0	0	0	9	2
1980	ATL	NL	13	8	5	5	5	3	0	0	0	0	0	0	0	3	9	4
1981	SEA	AL	10	5	5	5	2	2	1	0	1	0	0	0	0	0	8	2
1982	OAK	AL	16	6	10	10	4	1	1	0	0	0	0	0	0	4	11	5
1983	OAK	AL	10	3	7	3	5	2	0	0	0	0	0	0	0	0	4	6
1984	OAK	AL	2	1	1	2	0	0	0	0	0	0	0	0	0	1	1	1
1985	TOR	AL	6	4	2	4	1	1	0	0	0	0	0	0	0	2	0	6
Total			240	119	121	125	79	26	10	8	1	0	0	0	0	11	154	86

Rank among batters: 128 • *Top target (6 home runs)*: Larry Christenson, Don Sutton • *Number of pitchers victimized*: 163 • *Total ballparks homered in*: 28 • *First HR*: 08/02/1971 off Ron Perranoski

Dick Burrus

MAURICE LENNON BURRUS
B: 01/29/1898 D: 02/02/1972
BL

Year	Tm	Lg	Tot	H	A	Men-On 0	1	2	3	One-Game 2	3	4	LO	XN	IP	PH	RHP	LHP
1925	BOS	NL	5	2	3	1	4	0	0	0	0	0	0	0	2	0	3	2
1926	BOS	NL	3	0	3	3	0	0	0	0	0	0	0	0	0	0	1	2
1928	BOS	NL	3	0	3	3	0	0	0	0	0	0	0	0	0	0	3	0
Total			11	2	9	7	4	0	0	0	0	0	0	0	2	0	7	4

Rank among batters: 2,419 • *Total ballparks homered in*: 6 • *First HR*: 05/02/1925 off Hal Carlson

Ellis Burton

ELLIS NARRINGTON BURTON
B: 08/12/1936
BB

Year	Tm	Lg	Tot	H	A	Men-On 0	1	2	3	One-Game 2	3	4	LO	XN	IP	PH	RHP	LHP
1958	STL	NL	2	1	1	1	1	0	0	0	0	0	1	0	0	0	1	1
1963	CLE	AL	1	0	1	1	0	0	0	0	0	0	0	0	0	0	1	0
	CHI	NL	12	4	8	8	2	1	1	1	0	0	1	0	0	0	7	5
	Total		13	4	9	9	2	1	1	1	0	0	1	0	0	0	8	5
1964	CHI	NL	2	2	0	1	0	1	0	1	0	0	0	0	0	0	1	1
Total			17	7	10	11	3	2	1	2	0	0	2	0	0	0	10	7

Rank among batters: 1,969 • *Top target (2 home runs)*: Hank Fischer • *Number of pitchers victimized*: 16 • *Total ballparks homered in*: 9 • *First HR*: 09/21/1958 off Ramon Monzant • *Switch hit HR in 1 game*—2 times

Jim Busby

JAMES FRANKLIN BUSBY
B: 01/08/1927
BR

Year	Tm	Lg	Tot	H	A	Men-On 0	1	2	3	One-Game 2	3	4	LO	XN	IP	PH	RHP	LHP
1951	CHI	AL	5	2	3	2	2	1	0	0	0	0	0	1	0	0	3	2
1952	WAS	AL	2	0	2	1	1	0	0	0	0	0	0	0	0	0	1	1
1953	WAS	AL	6	0	6	2	2	2	0	1	0	0	0	0	0	0	4	2
1954	WAS	AL	7	1	6	4	3	0	0	0	0	0	0	0	0	0	5	2
1955	WAS	AL	6	0	6	6	0	0	0	1	0	0	0	0	0	0	5	1
	CHI	AL	1	0	1	0	0	1	0	0	0	0	0	0	0	0	1	0
	Total		7	0	7	6	0	1	0	1	0	0	0	0	0	0	6	1
1956	CLE	AL	12	3	9	4	4	2	2	0	0	0	0	0	0	0	10	2
1957	CLE	AL	2	0	2	1	0	1	0	0	0	0	1	0	0	0	2	0
	BAL	AL	3	3	0	3	0	0	0	0	0	0	0	0	1	0	3	0
	Total		5	3	2	4	0	1	0	0	0	0	1	0	1	0	5	0
1958	BAL	AL	3	2	1	0	1	1	1	0	0	0	0	0	0	0	1	2
1959	BOS	AL	1	1	0	1	0	0	0	0	0	0	1	0	0	0	1	0
Total			48	12	36	24	13	8	3	2	0	0	2	1	1	0	36	12

Rank among batters: 1,024 • Top target (2 home runs): Allie Reynolds, Mel Parnell, Ted Gray, Cloyd Boyer, Johnny Kucks, Troy Herriage, Jack Crimian, Arnie Portocarrero, Billy Hoeft, Billy Pierce, Ned Garver • *Number of pitchers victimized*: 37 • *Total ballparks homered in*: 10 • *First HR*: 06/05/1951 off Mel Parnell

Mike Busch

MICHAEL ANTHONY BUSCH
B: 07/07/1968
BR

Year	Tm	Lg	Tot	H	A	Men-On 0	1	2	3	One-Game 2	3	4	LO	XN	IP	PH	RHP	LHP
1995	LA	NL	3	0	3	1	1	1	0	0	0	0	0	0	1	1	2	1

Rank among batters: 3,735 • *Total ballparks homered in*: 2 • *First HR*: 09/09/1995 off Jason Christiansen

Donie Bush

OWEN JOSEPH BUSH
B: 10/08/1887 D: 03/28/1972
BB

Year	Tm	Lg	Tot	H	A	Men-On 0	1	2	3	One-Game 2	3	4	LO	XN	IP	PH	RHP	LHP
1910	DET	AL	3	0	3	1	1	0	1	0	0	0	0	0	1	0	1	2
1911	DET	AL	1	0	1	1	0	0	0	0	0	0	0	0	1	0	0	1
1912	DET	AL	2	1	1	0	2	0	0	0	0	0	0	0	1	0	0	2
1913	DET	AL	1	0	1	0	0	1	0	0	0	0	0	0	1	0	1	0
1915	DET	AL	1	1	0	0	1	0	0	0	0	0	0	0	1	0	1	0
1920	DET	AL	1	0	1	0	1	0	0	0	0	0	0	0	0	0	1	0
Total			9	2	7	2	5	1	1	0	0	0	0	0	5	0	4	5

Rank among batters: 2,587 • *Total ballparks homered in*: 6 • *First HR*: 05/17/1910 off Ray Collins

Joe Bush

LESLIE AMBROSE BUSH
B: 11/27/1892 D: 11/01/1974
BR

Year	Tm	Lg	Tot	H	A	Men-On 0	Men-On 1	Men-On 2	Men-On 3	One-Game 2	One-Game 3	One-Game 4	LO	XN	IP	PH	RHP	LHP
1914	PHI	AL	1	1	0	0	1	0	0	0	0	0	0	0	0	0	1	0
1923	NY	AL	2	2	0	1	1	0	0	0	0	0	0	0	0	0	0	2
1924	NY	AL	1	0	1	1	0	0	0	0	0	0	0	0	0	1	0	1
1925	STL	AL	2	1	1	1	1	0	0	0	0	0	0	0	0	0	1	1
1926	PIT	NL	1	0	1	0	1	0	0	0	0	0	0	0	0	0	1	0
Total			7	4	3	3	4	0	0	0	0	0	0	0	0	1	3	4

Rank among batters: 2,834 • *Total ballparks homered in*: 4 • *First HR*: 05/06/1914 off Hugh Bedient

Randy Bush

ROBERT RANDALL BUSH
B: 10/05/1958
BL

Year	Tm	Lg	Tot	H	A	Men-On 0	Men-On 1	Men-On 2	Men-On 3	One-Game 2	One-Game 3	One-Game 4	LO	XN	IP	PH	RHP	LHP
1982	MIN	AL	4	2	2	2	2	0	0	1	0	0	0	0	0	0	4	0
1983	MIN	AL	11	4	7	7	4	0	0	1	0	0	0	0	0	0	11	0
1984	MIN	AL	11	8	3	6	3	1	1	0	0	0	0	0	1	1	11	0
1985	MIN	AL	10	5	5	6	2	1	1	0	0	0	0	0	0	1	10	0
1986	MIN	AL	7	6	1	3	2	2	0	0	0	0	0	0	0	2	7	0
1987	MIN	AL	11	3	8	7	3	1	0	0	0	0	0	0	0	0	11	0
1988	MIN	AL	14	10	4	7	5	2	0	0	0	0	0	0	0	0	14	0
1989	MIN	AL	14	6	8	7	5	2	0	1	0	0	0	0	0	0	14	0
1990	MIN	AL	6	4	2	2	3	1	0	0	0	0	0	1	0	0	6	0
1991	MIN	AL	6	2	4	4	1	1	0	1	0	0	0	0	0	2	6	0
1992	MIN	AL	2	0	2	2	0	0	0	0	0	0	0	0	0	0	2	0
Total			96	50	46	53	30	11	2	4	0	0	0	1	1	6	96	0

Rank among batters: 520 • *Top target (4 home runs)*: Jack Morris • *Number of pitchers victimized*: 77 • *Total ballparks homered in*: 14 • *First HR*: 09/06/1982 off Charlie Hough

Doc Bushong

ALBERT JOHN BUSHONG
B: 09/15/1856 D: 08/19/1908
BR

Year	Tm	Lg	Tot	H	A	Men-On 0	Men-On 1	Men-On 2	Men-On 3	One-Game 2	One-Game 3	One-Game 4	LO	XN	IP	PH	RHP	LHP
1882	WOR	NL	1	0	1	0	1	0	0	0	0	0	0	0	0	0	1	0
1886	STL	AA	1	0	1	0	0	1	0	0	0	0	0	0	0	0	0	1
Total			2	0	2	0	1	1	0	0	0	0	0	0	0	0	1	1

Rank among batters: 4,129 • *Total ballparks homered in*: 2 • *First HR*: 06/22/1882 off Larry Corcoran

Ray Busse

RAYMOND EDWARD BUSSE
B: 09/25/1948
BR

Year	Tm	Lg	Tot	H	A	Men-On 0	Men-On 1	Men-On 2	Men-On 3	One-Game 2	One-Game 3	One-Game 4	LO	XN	IP	PH	RHP	LHP
1973	STL	NL	2	1	1	2	0	0	0	0	0	0	0	0	0	0	1	1

Rank among batters: 4,129 • *Total ballparks homered in*: 2 • *First HR*: 04/14/1973 off Rick Reuschel

Hank Butcher

HENRY JOSEPH BUTCHER
B: 07/12/1886 D: 12/28/1979
BR

Year	Tm	Lg	Tot	H	A	Men-On 0	Men-On 1	Men-On 2	Men-On 3	One-Game 2	One-Game 3	One-Game 4	LO	XN	IP	PH	RHP	LHP
1911	CLE	AL	1	1	0	1	0	0	0	0	0	0	0	0	0	0	0	1
1912	CLE	AL	1	0	1	0	1	0	0	0	0	0	0	0	0	0	1	0
Total			2	1	1	1	1	0	0	0	0	0	0	0	0	0	1	1

Rank among batters: 4,129 • *Total ballparks homered in*: 2 • *First HR*: 09/04/1911 off George Mogridge

Max Butcher

ALBERT MAXWELL BUTCHER
B: 09/21/1910 D: 09/15/1957
BR

Year	Tm	Lg	Tot	H	A	Men-On 0	Men-On 1	Men-On 2	Men-On 3	One-Game 2	One-Game 3	One-Game 4	LO	XN	IP	PH	RHP	LHP
1938	BRO	NL	1	1	0	0	1	0	0	0	0	0	0	0	0	0	1	0

Rank among batters: 4,707 • *Total ballparks homered in*: 1 • *First HR*: 04/28/1938 off Bucky Walters

Year	Tm	Lg	Tot	H	A	Men-On 0	1	2	3	One-Game 2	3	4	LO	XN	IP	PH	RHP	LHP

Sal Butera

SALVATORE PHILIP BUTERA
B: 09/25/1952
BR

Year	Tm	Lg	Tot	H	A	0	1	2	3	2	3	4	LO	XN	IP	PH	RHP	LHP
1985	MON	NL	3	0	3	1	2	0	0	0	0	0	0	0	0	0	1	2
1986	CIN	NL	2	0	2	1	0	1	0	0	0	0	0	0	0	0	2	0
1987	CIN	NL	1	0	1	0	1	0	0	0	0	0	0	0	0	0	1	0
	MIN	AL	1	1	0	1	0	0	0	0	0	0	0	0	0	0	1	0
	Total		2	1	1	1	1	0	0	0	0	0	0	0	0	0	2	0
1988	TOR	AL	1	1	0	0	1	0	0	0	0	0	0	0	0	0	0	1
Total			8	2	6	3	4	1	0	0	0	0	0	0	0	0	5	3

Rank among batters: 2,703 • *Total ballparks homered in*: 7 • *First HR*: 08/14/1985 off Ray Fontenot

Art Butler

ARTHUR EDWARD BUTLER
B: 12/19/1887 D: 10/07/1984
BR

Year	Tm	Lg	Tot	H	A	0	1	2	3	2	3	4	LO	XN	IP	PH	RHP	LHP
1912	PIT	NL	1	1	0	1	0	0	0	0	0	0	0	0	0	0	1	0
1914	STL	NL	1	0	1	1	0	0	0	0	0	0	0	0	0	0	0	1
1915	STL	NL	1	1	0	1	0	0	0	0	0	0	0	0	1	0	1	0
Total			3	2	1	3	0	0	0	0	0	0	0	0	1	0	2	1

Rank among batters: 3,735 • *Total ballparks homered in*: 3 • *First HR*: 09/25/1912 off Rube Geyer

Brett Butler

BRETT MORGAN BUTLER
B: 06/15/1957
BL

Year	Tm	Lg	Tot	H	A	0	1	2	3	2	3	4	LO	XN	IP	PH	RHP	LHP
1983	ATL	NL	5	4	1	5	0	0	0	0	0	0	3	0	0	0	5	0
1984	CLE	AL	3	1	2	2	0	0	1	0	0	0	0	0	0	0	3	0
1985	CLE	AL	5	1	4	2	2	1	0	1	0	0	0	0	0	0	4	1
1986	CLE	AL	4	0	4	4	0	0	0	0	0	0	0	0	0	0	3	1
1987	CLE	AL	9	4	5	7	2	0	0	0	0	0	1	0	0	0	7	2
1988	SF	NL	6	1	5	5	1	0	0	0	0	0	1	0	0	0	5	1
1989	SF	NL	4	2	2	4	0	0	0	0	0	0	1	1	0	0	3	1
1990	SF	NL	3	3	0	2	1	0	0	0	0	0	1	0	0	0	2	1
1991	LA	NL	2	2	0	1	0	1	0	0	0	0	0	0	0	0	2	0
1992	LA	NL	3	1	2	2	1	0	0	0	0	0	1	0	0	0	2	1
1993	LA	NL	1	0	1	1	0	0	0	0	0	0	0	0	0	0	1	0
1994	LA	NL	8	2	6	7	1	0	0	0	0	0	0	0	0	0	7	1
1995	NY	NL	1	0	1	1	0	0	0	0	0	0	0	0	0	0	0	1
Total			54	21	33	43	8	2	1	1	0	0	8	1	0	0	44	10

Rank among batters: 938 • Top target (2 home runs): Phil Niekro, Ray Burris, Charlie Leibrandt, Doug Drabek • *Number of pitchers victimized*: 50 • *Total ballparks homered in*: 21 • *First HR*: 06/27/1983 off Mario Soto

Johnny Butler

JOHN STEPHEN BUTLER
B: 03/20/1893 D: 04/29/1967
BR

Year	Tm	Lg	Tot	H	A	0	1	2	3	2	3	4	LO	XN	IP	PH	RHP	LHP
1926	BRO	NL	1	0	1	1	0	0	0	0	0	0	0	0	0	0	0	1
1927	BRO	NL	2	2	0	1	0	1	0	0	0	0	0	0	1	0	2	0
Total			3	2	1	2	0	1	0	0	0	0	0	0	1	0	2	1

Rank among batters: 3,735 • *Total ballparks homered in*: 2 • *First HR*: 07/13/1926 off Bill Sherdel

Samuel Byrd

SAMUEL DEWEY BYRD
B: 10/15/1907 D: 05/11/1981
BR

Year	Tm	Lg	Tot	H	A	0	1	2	3	2	3	4	LO	XN	IP	PH	RHP	LHP
1929	NY	AL	5	2	3	2	3	0	0	0	0	0	0	0	1	0	2	3
1930	NY	AL	6	2	4	2	2	2	0	0	0	0	0	0	1	0	2	4
1931	NY	AL	3	1	2	1	2	0	0	0	0	0	0	0	0	0	3	0
1932	NY	AL	8	1	7	4	3	1	0	2	0	0	1	0	0	0	5	3
1933	NY	AL	2	1	1	1	1	0	0	0	0	0	1	0	0	1	0	2
1934	NY	AL	3	0	3	1	1	1	0	0	0	0	0	0	0	0	2	1
1935	CIN	NL	9	5	4	6	2	1	0	0	0	0	0	0	0	0	7	2
1936	CIN	NL	2	1	1	1	0	0	1	0	0	0	0	0	0	1	2	0
Total			38	13	25	18	14	5	1	2	0	0	2	0	2	2	23	15

Rank among batters: 1,225 • *Top target (3 home runs)*: Rube Walberg, George Earnshaw • *Number of pitchers victimized*: 29 • *Total ballparks homered in*: 12 • *First HR*: 06/09/1929 off Rip Collins

Year	Tm	Lg	Tot	H	A	Men-On				One-Game			LO	XN	IP	PH	RHP	LHP
						0	1	2	3	2	3	4						

Bobby Byrne

ROBERT MATTHEW BYRNE
B: 12/31/1884 D: 12/31/1964
BR

Year	Tm	Lg	Tot	H	A	0	1	2	3	2	3	4	LO	XN	IP	PH	RHP	LHP
1909	STL	NL	1	1	0	0	1	0	0	0	0	0	0	0	1	0	0	1
1910	PIT	NL	2	1	1	1	1	0	0	0	0	0	0	0	1	0	1	1
1911	PIT	NL	2	1	1	1	1	0	0	0	0	0	0	0	1	0	2	0
1912	PIT	NL	3	2	1	2	1	0	0	0	0	0	1	0	1	0	2	1
1913	PIT	NL	1	0	1	1	0	0	0	0	0	0	1	0	0	0	1	0
	PHI	NL	1	1	0	0	1	0	0	0	0	0	0	0	0	0	1	0
	Total		2	1	1	1	1	0	0	0	0	0	1	0	0	0	2	0
Total			10	6	4	5	5	0	0	0	0	0	2	0	4	0	7	3

Rank among batters: 2,500 • *Total ballparks homered in*: 5 • *First HR*: 08/15/1909 off Nap Rucker

Tommy Byrne

THOMAS JOSEPH BYRNE
B: 12/31/1919
BL

Year	Tm	Lg	Tot	H	A	0	1	2	3	2	3	4	LO	XN	IP	PH	RHP	LHP
1948	NY	AL	1	0	1	0	1	0	0	0	0	0	0	0	1	0	1	0
1950	NY	AL	2	1	1	1	0	1	0	0	0	0	0	0	0	0	2	0
1951	NY	AL	1	0	1	0	0	1	0	0	0	0	0	0	0	0	1	0
	STL	AL	1	0	1	0	0	0	1	0	0	0	0	0	0	0	1	0
	Total		2	0	2	0	0	1	1	0	0	0	0	0	0	0	2	0
1952	STL	AL	1	0	1	1	0	0	0	0	0	0	0	0	0	0	1	0
1953	CHI	AL	1	0	1	0	0	0	1	0	0	0	0	0	0	1	1	0
1955	NY	AL	1	1	0	1	0	0	0	0	0	0	0	0	0	0	1	0
1956	NY	AL	3	2	1	3	0	0	0	0	0	0	0	0	0	0	3	0
1957	NY	AL	3	1	2	1	0	2	0	0	0	0	0	1	0	1	2	1
Total			14	5	9	7	1	4	2	0	0	0	0	1	1	2	13	1

Rank among batters: 2,169 • *Top target (2 home runs)*: Frank Lary • *Number of pitchers victimized*: 13 • *Total ballparks homered in*: 7 • *First HR*: 07/11/1948 off Walt Masterson

Milt Byrnes

MILTON JOHN BYRNES
B: 11/15/1916 D: 02/01/1979
BL

Year	Tm	Lg	Tot	H	A	0	1	2	3	2	3	4	LO	XN	IP	PH	RHP	LHP
1943	STL	AL	4	3	1	1	3	0	0	0	0	0	0	0	0	1	3	1
1944	STL	AL	4	2	2	1	2	1	0	0	0	0	0	0	1	0	4	0
1945	STL	AL	8	4	4	4	3	1	0	0	0	0	0	1	0	1	7	1
Total			16	9	7	6	8	2	0	0	0	0	0	1	1	2	14	2

Rank among batters: 2,029 • *Total ballparks homered in*: 5 • *First HR*: 06/27/1943 off Hal White

Putsy Caballero

RALPH JOSEPH CABALLERO
B: 11/05/1927
BR

Year	Tm	Lg	Tot	H	A	0	1	2	3	2	3	4	LO	XN	IP	PH	RHP	LHP
1951	PHI	NL	1	0	1	1	0	0	0	0	0	0	0	0	0	0	1	0

Rank among batters: 4,707 • *Total ballparks homered in*: 1 • *First HR*: 08/11/1951 off George Spencer

Enos Cabell

ENOS MILTON CABELL
B: 10/08/1949
BR

Year	Tm	Lg	Tot	H	A	0	1	2	3	2	3	4	LO	XN	IP	PH	RHP	LHP
1973	BAL	AL	1	1	0	1	0	0	0	0	0	0	0	0	0	0	0	1
1974	BAL	AL	3	0	3	2	1	0	0	0	0	0	0	0	0	0	2	1
1975	HOU	NL	2	1	1	1	1	0	0	0	0	0	0	0	0	0	1	1
1976	HOU	NL	2	1	1	2	0	0	0	0	0	0	0	0	0	0	1	1
1977	HOU	NL	16	7	9	11	4	1	0	1	0	0	0	0	0	0	10	6
1978	HOU	NL	7	2	5	6	1	0	0	0	0	0	0	1	0	0	6	1
1979	HOU	NL	6	1	5	5	0	1	0	0	0	0	0	0	0	0	3	3
1980	HOU	NL	2	0	2	2	0	0	0	0	0	0	0	0	0	0	1	1
1981	SF	NL	2	0	2	1	1	0	0	0	0	0	1	0	0	0	1	1
1982	DET	AL	2	2	0	2	0	0	0	0	0	0	0	0	0	0	0	2
1983	DET	AL	5	1	4	3	1	1	0	0	0	0	0	0	0	0	2	3
1984	HOU	NL	8	2	6	6	2	0	0	0	0	0	0	0	0	1	4	4
1985	HOU	NL	2	1	1	1	1	0	0	0	0	0	0	0	0	0	1	1

Year	Tm	Lg	Tot	H	A	Men-On 0	Men-On 1	Men-On 2	Men-On 3	One-Game 2	One-Game 3	One-Game 4	LO	XN	IP	PH	RHP	LHP

Enos Cabell *continued*

Year	Tm	Lg	Tot	H	A	0	1	2	3	2	3	4	LO	XN	IP	PH	RHP	LHP
1986	LA	NL	2	2	0	1	0	0	1	0	0	0	0	0	0	0	0	2
Total			60	21	39	44	12	3	1	1	0	0	1	1	0	1	32	28

Rank among batters: 863 • Top target (2 home runs): Steve Carlton, Ed Halicki, Paul Moskau, Pete Falcone • *Number of pitchers victimized*: 56 • *Total ballparks homered in*: 18 • *First HR*: 07/06/1973 off Vida Blue

Francisco Cabrera

FRANCISCO (PAULINO) CABRERA
B: 10/10/1966
BR

Year	Tm	Lg	Tot	H	A	0	1	2	3	2	3	4	LO	XN	IP	PH	RHP	LHP
1990	ATL	NL	7	4	3	4	2	1	0	0	0	0	0	0	0	1	1	6
1991	ATL	NL	4	2	2	2	1	1	0	1	0	0	0	0	0	0	3	1
1992	ATL	NL	2	0	2	1	1	0	0	0	0	0	0	0	0	2	0	2
1993	ATL	NL	4	1	3	3	0	0	1	0	0	0	0	0	0	1	0	4
Total			17	7	10	10	4	2	1	1	0	0	0	0	0	4	4	13

Rank among batters: 1,969 • *Top target (2 home runs)*: Dennis Rasmussen, Greg Swindell • *Number of pitchers victimized*: 15 • *Total ballparks homered in*: 7 • *First HR*: 05/21/1990 off Bryn Smith

Edgar Caceres

EDGAR F. CACERES
B: 06/06/1964
BB

Year	Tm	Lg	Tot	H	A	0	1	2	3	2	3	4	LO	XN	IP	PH	RHP	LHP
1995	KC	AL	1	0	1	0	0	1	0	0	0	0	0	0	0	0	0	1

Rank among batters: 4,707 • *Total ballparks homered in*: 1 • *First HR*: 08/04/1995 off Eddie Guardado

Leon Cadore

LEON JOSEPH CADORE
B: 11/20/1890 D: 03/16/1958
BR

Year	Tm	Lg	Tot	H	A	0	1	2	3	2	3	4	LO	XN	IP	PH	RHP	LHP
1920	BRO	NL	2	1	1	1	1	0	0	0	0	0	0	0	0	0	2	0
1921	BRO	NL	1	1	0	1	0	0	0	0	0	0	0	0	0	0	1	0
1922	BRO	NL	2	1	1	2	0	0	0	0	0	0	0	1	0	0	2	0
Total			5	3	2	4	1	0	0	0	0	0	0	1	0	0	5	0

Rank among batters: 3,191 • *Total ballparks homered in*: 3 • *First HR*: 08/30/1920 off Ferdie Schupp

Hick Cady

FORREST LEROY CADY
B: 01/26/1886 D: 03/03/1946
BR

Year	Tm	Lg	Tot	H	A	0	1	2	3	2	3	4	LO	XN	IP	PH	RHP	LHP
1919	PHI	NL	1	1	0	0	0	1	0	0	0	0	0	0	0	0	1	0

Rank among batters: 4,707 • *Total ballparks homered in*: 1 • *First HR*: 06/25/1919 off Jack Scott

Joe Caffie

JOSEPH CLIFFORD CAFFIE
B: 02/14/1931
BL

Year	Tm	Lg	Tot	H	A	0	1	2	3	2	3	4	LO	XN	IP	PH	RHP	LHP
1957	CLE	AL	3	1	2	2	1	0	0	0	0	0	1	0	0	0	3	0

Rank among batters: 3,735 • *Total ballparks homered in*: 3 • *First HR*: 08/24/1957 off Tom Sturdivant

Wayne Cage

WAYNE LEVELL CAGE
B: 11/23/1951
BL

Year	Tm	Lg	Tot	H	A	0	1	2	3	2	3	4	LO	XN	IP	PH	RHP	LHP
1978	CLE	AL	4	3	1	3	1	0	0	0	0	0	0	0	0	0	4	0
1979	CLE	AL	1	0	1	1	0	0	0	0	0	0	0	0	0	0	1	0
Total			5	3	2	4	1	0	0	0	0	0	0	0	0	0	5	0

Rank among batters: 3,191 • *Total ballparks homered in*: 3 • *First HR*: 05/07/1978 off Don Aase

John Cahill

JOHN PATRICK FRANCIS CAHILL
B: 04/30/1865 D: 10/31/1901
BR

Year	Tm	Lg	Tot	H	A	0	1	2	3	2	3	4	LO	XN	IP	PH	RHP	LHP
1886	STL	NL	1	1	0	1	0	0	0	0	0	0	0	0	0	0	1	0

Rank among batters: 4,707 • *Total ballparks homered in*: 1 • *First HR*: 07/01/1886 off Bob Barr

Year	Tm	Lg	Tot	H	A	Men-On				One-Game			LO	XN	IP	PH	RHP	LHP
						0	1	2	3	2	3	4						

Tom Cahill

THOMAS H. CAHILL
B: 10/ /1868 D: 12/25/1894

Year	Tm	Lg	Tot	H	A	0	1	2	3	2	3	4	LO	XN	IP	PH	RHP	LHP
1891	LOU	AA	3	2	1	1	1	1	0	0	0	0	0	0	0	0	2	0

Rank among batters: 3,735 • *Total ballparks homered in*: 2 • *First HR*: 05/27/1891 off Will Callahan

Les Cain

LESLIE CAIN
B: 01/13/1948
BL

Year	Tm	Lg	Tot	H	A	0	1	2	3	2	3	4	LO	XN	IP	PH	RHP	LHP
1970	DET	AL	1	1	0	1	0	0	0	0	0	0	0	0	0	0	0	1
1971	DET	AL	1	1	0	1	0	0	0	0	0	0	0	0	0	0	1	0
Total			2	2	0	2	0	0	0	0	0	0	0	0	0	0	1	1

Rank among batters: 4,129 • *Total ballparks homered in*: 1 • *First HR*: 06/30/1970 off Fritz Peterson

Ivan Calderon

IVAN (PEREZ) CALDERON
B: 03/19/1962
BR

Year	Tm	Lg	Tot	H	A	0	1	2	3	2	3	4	LO	XN	IP	PH	RHP	LHP
1984	SEA	AL	1	0	1	1	0	0	0	0	0	0	0	0	0	0	0	1
1985	SEA	AL	8	6	2	6	0	2	0	0	0	0	0	0	0	1	5	3
1986	SEA	AL	2	1	1	1	1	0	0	0	0	0	0	0	0	0	2	0
1987	CHI	AL	28	15	13	19	5	4	0	3	0	0	0	1	0	0	15	13
1988	CHI	AL	14	6	8	8	4	2	0	0	0	0	0	0	1	0	9	5
1989	CHI	AL	14	2	12	5	6	2	1	0	0	0	0	0	0	0	10	4
1990	CHI	AL	14	6	8	5	6	3	0	0	0	0	0	0	0	0	8	6
1991	MON	NL	19	7	12	12	6	1	0	2	0	0	0	1	0	1	8	11
1992	MON	NL	3	2	1	1	2	0	0	0	0	0	0	0	0	0	3	0
1993	BOS	AL	1	0	1	1	0	0	0	0	0	0	0	0	0	0	1	0
Total			104	45	59	59	30	14	1	5	0	0	0	2	1	2	61	43

Rank among batters: 469 • Top target (3 home runs): Dennis Rasmussen, Doyle Alexander, Frank Tanana • *Number of pitchers victimized*: 85 • *Total ballparks homered in*: 24 • *First HR*: 08/14/1984 off Dennis Rasmussen

Sam Calderone

SAMUEL FRANCIS CALDERONE
B: 02/06/1926
BR

Year	Tm	Lg	Tot	H	A	0	1	2	3	2	3	4	LO	XN	IP	PH	RHP	LHP
1950	NY	NL	1	1	0	1	0	0	0	0	0	0	0	0	1	0	1	0

Rank among batters: 4,707 • *Total ballparks homered in*: 1 • *First HR*: 08/17/1950 off Erv Palica

Earl Caldwell

EARL WELTON CALDWELL
B: 04/09/1905 D: 09/15/1981
BR

Year	Tm	Lg	Tot	H	A	0	1	2	3	2	3	4	LO	XN	IP	PH	RHP	LHP
1936	STL	AL	1	0	1	0	1	0	0	0	0	0	0	0	0	0	1	0

Rank among batters: 4,707 • *Total ballparks homered in*: 1 • *First HR*: 06/06/1936 off Harry Kelley

Ray Caldwell

RAYMOND BENJAMIN CALDWELL
B: 04/26/1888 D: 08/17/1967
BL

Year	Tm	Lg	Tot	H	A	0	1	2	3	2	3	4	LO	XN	IP	PH	RHP	LHP
1915	NY	AL	4	3	1	2	0	2	0	0	0	0	0	0	0	2	2	2
1917	NY	AL	2	1	1	1	1	0	0	0	0	0	0	0	1	0	2	0
1918	NY	AL	1	0	1	0	1	0	0	0	0	0	0	0	0	0	1	0
1921	CLE	AL	1	0	1	0	1	0	0	0	0	0	0	0	0	0	1	0
Total			8	4	4	3	3	2	0	0	0	0	0	0	1	2	6	2

Rank among batters: 2,703 • *Total ballparks homered in*: 3 • *First HR*: 04/19/1915 off Herb Pennock

Leo Callahan

LEO DAVID CALLAHAN
B: 08/09/1890 D: 05/02/1982
BL

Year	Tm	Lg	Tot	H	A	0	1	2	3	2	3	4	LO	XN	IP	PH	RHP	LHP
1919	PHI	NL	1	1	0	1	0	0	0	0	0	0	0	0	0	0	1	0
Total			1	1	0	1	0	0	0	0	0	0	0	0	0	0	1	0

Rank among batters: 4,707 • *Total ballparks homered in*: 1 • *First HR*: 07/05/1919 off Jean Dubuc

Nixey Callahan

JAMES JOSEPH CALLAHAN
B: 03/18/1874 D: 10/04/1934
BR

Year	Tm	Lg	Tot	H	A	Men-On 0	Men-On 1	Men-On 2	Men-On 3	One-Game 2	One-Game 3	One-Game 4	LO	XN	IP	PH	RHP	LHP
1897	CHI	NL	3	1	2	1	2	0	0	0	0	0	0	0	1	0	3	0
1901	CHI	AL	1	1	0	0	0	1	0	0	0	0	0	0	0	0	1	0
1903	CHI	AL	2	1	1	1	0	1	0	0	0	0	0	0	0	0	1	1
1905	CHI	AL	1	0	1	0	1	0	0	0	0	0	0	0	0	0	0	1
1911	CHI	AL	3	2	1	1	2	0	0	0	0	0	0	0	1	0	3	0
1912	CHI	AL	1	1	0	1	0	0	0	0	0	0	0	0	0	0	1	0
Total			11	6	5	4	5	2	0	0	0	0	0	0	2	0	9	2

Rank among batters: 2,419 • *Total ballparks homered in*: 8 • *First HR*: 08/08/1897 off Jack Powell

Pat Callahan

PATRICK HENRY CALLAHAN
B: 10/15/1866 D: 02/04/1940

Year	Tm	Lg	Tot	H	A	Men-On 0	Men-On 1	Men-On 2	Men-On 3	One-Game 2	One-Game 3	One-Game 4	LO	XN	IP	PH	RHP	LHP
1884	IND	AA	2	2	0	1	1	0	0	0	0	0	0	0	1	0	2	0

Rank among batters: 4,129 • *Total ballparks homered in*: 2 • *First HR*: 07/06/1884 off John Hamill

Will Callahan

WILLIAM T. CALLAHAN
B: 1869 D: 12/20/1917

Year	Tm	Lg	Tot	H	A	Men-On 0	Men-On 1	Men-On 2	Men-On 3	One-Game 2	One-Game 3	One-Game 4	LO	XN	IP	PH	RHP	LHP
1890	ROC	AA	1	1	0	1	0	0	0	0	0	0	0	1	0	0	1	0

Rank among batters: 4,707 • *Total ballparks homered in*: 1 • *First HR*: 05/24/1890 off Fred Smith

Johnny Callison

JOHN WESLEY CALLISON
B: 03/12/1939
BL

Year	Tm	Lg	Tot	H	A	Men-On 0	Men-On 1	Men-On 2	Men-On 3	One-Game 2	One-Game 3	One-Game 4	LO	XN	IP	PH	RHP	LHP
1958	CHI	AL	1	1	0	1	0	0	0	0	0	0	0	0	1	0	1	0
1959	CHI	AL	3	0	3	1	1	0	1	0	0	0	0	0	0	0	3	0
1960	PHI	NL	9	4	5	5	3	1	0	0	0	0	0	0	0	1	9	0
1961	PHI	NL	9	4	5	5	1	3	0	0	0	0	1	0	0	0	8	1
1962	PHI	NL	23	10	13	14	5	4	0	0	0	0	0	0	0	1	20	3
1963	PHI	NL	26	12	14	14	8	4	0	3	0	0	0	2	1	0	18	8
1964	PHI	NL	31	13	18	13	15	2	1	1	1	0	0	0	0	0	18	13
1965	PHI	NL	32	15	17	18	10	3	1	1	1	0	0	1	2	0	22	10
1966	PHI	NL	11	4	7	9	1	1	0	1	0	0	0	0	0	0	9	2
1967	PHI	NL	14	8	6	10	3	1	0	1	0	0	0	0	0	0	10	4
1968	PHI	NL	14	7	7	9	4	1	0	0	0	0	0	0	0	2	10	4
1969	PHI	NL	16	9	7	12	3	1	0	1	0	0	0	0	0	0	14	2
1970	CHI	NL	19	12	7	8	10	1	0	0	0	0	0	0	0	0	15	4
1971	CHI	NL	8	3	5	4	2	1	1	0	0	0	0	0	0	0	6	2
1972	NY	AL	9	7	2	7	0	1	1	0	0	0	0	0	0	0	8	1
1973	NY	AL	1	1	0	1	0	0	0	0	0	0	0	0	0	0	1	0
Total			226	110	116	131	66	24	5	8	2	0	1	3	4	4	172	54

Rank among batters: 143 • *Top target (7 home runs)*: Juan Marichal • *Number of pitchers victimized*: 142 • *Total ballparks homered in*: 24 • *First HR*: 09/14/1958 off Russ Kemmerer • *Hit for Cycle*—@PIT: 06/27/1963 • *All-Star HR*—1

Jack Calvo

JACINTO (GONZALEZ) CALVO
B: 06/11/1894 D: 06/15/1965
BL

Year	Tm	Lg	Tot	H	A	Men-On 0	Men-On 1	Men-On 2	Men-On 3	One-Game 2	One-Game 3	One-Game 4	LO	XN	IP	PH	RHP	LHP
1913	WAS	AL	1	1	0	1	0	0	0	0	0	0	0	0	1	0	1	0

Rank among batters: 4,707 • *Total ballparks homered in*: 1 • *First HR*: 06/05/1913 off Roy Mitchell

Hank Camelli

HENRY RICHARD CAMELLI
B: 12/12/1914
BR

Year	Tm	Lg	Tot	H	A	Men-On 0	Men-On 1	Men-On 2	Men-On 3	One-Game 2	One-Game 3	One-Game 4	LO	XN	IP	PH	RHP	LHP
1944	PIT	NL	1	0	1	0	1	0	0	0	0	0	0	0	0	0	1	0
1947	BOS	NL	1	0	1	0	0	1	0	0	0	0	0	0	0	0	0	1
Total			2	0	2	0	1	1	0	0	0	0	0	0	0	0	1	1

Rank among batters: 4,129 • *Total ballparks homered in*: 2 • *First HR*: 09/10/1944 off Bucky Walters

Mike Cameron

MICHAEL TERRANCE CAMERON
B: 01/08/1973
BR

Year	Tm	Lg	Tot	H	A	Men-On 0	Men-On 1	Men-On 2	Men-On 3	One-Game 2	One-Game 3	One-Game 4	LO	XN	IP	PH	RHP	LHP
1995	CHI	AL	1	0	1	1	0	0	0	0	0	0	0	0	0	0	0	1

Rank among batters: 4,707 • *Total ballparks homered in*: 1 • *First HR*: 09/27/1995 off Jason Jacome

Dolph Camilli

ADOLPH LOUIS CAMILLI
B: 04/23/1907
BL

Year	Tm	Lg	Tot	H	A	Men-On 0	Men-On 1	Men-On 2	Men-On 3	One-Game 2	One-Game 3	One-Game 4	LO	XN	IP	PH	RHP	LHP
1933	CHI	NL	2	2	0	1	1	0	0	0	0	0	0	0	0	0	2	0
1934	CHI	NL	4	4	0	3	1	0	0	0	0	0	0	0	0	0	2	2
	PHI	NL	12	6	6	7	3	2	0	1	0	0	0	0	0	0	12	0
	Total		16	10	6	10	4	2	0	1	0	0	0	0	0	0	14	2
1935	PHI	NL	25	15	10	15	6	4	0	3	0	0	0	1	0	0	21	4
1936	PHI	NL	28	24	4	15	7	6	0	4	0	0	0	0	0	0	18	10
1937	PHI	NL	27	16	11	17	7	1	2	3	0	0	0	0	0	0	19	8
1938	BRO	NL	24	15	9	12	10	1	1	2	0	0	0	0	0	0	20	4
1939	BRO	NL	26	14	12	12	12	2	0	1	0	0	0	0	0	0	21	5
1940	BRO	NL	23	12	11	12	8	3	0	1	0	0	0	3	0	0	18	5
1941	BRO	NL	34	19	15	22	7	5	0	2	0	0	0	0	0	0	24	10
1942	BRO	NL	26	15	11	10	9	5	2	2	0	0	0	2	0	0	22	4
1943	BRO	NL	6	2	4	3	3	0	0	1	0	0	0	0	0	0	5	1
1945	BOS	AL	2	0	2	0	2	0	0	0	0	0	0	0	0	0	2	0
Total			239	144	95	129	76	29	5	20	0	0	0	6	0	0	186	53

Rank among batters: 130 • *Top target (12 home runs)*: Lon Warneke • *Number of pitchers victimized*: 114 • *Total ballparks homered in*: 10 • *First HR*: 09/10/1933 off Jack Berly

Doug Camilli

DOUGLAS JOSEPH CAMILLI
B: 09/22/1936
BR

Year	Tm	Lg	Tot	H	A	Men-On 0	Men-On 1	Men-On 2	Men-On 3	One-Game 2	One-Game 3	One-Game 4	LO	XN	IP	PH	RHP	LHP
1960	LA	NL	1	1	0	1	0	0	0	0	0	0	0	0	0	0	1	0
1961	LA	NL	3	2	1	2	1	0	0	0	0	0	0	0	0	0	2	1
1962	LA	NL	4	1	3	2	2	0	0	0	0	0	0	0	1	0	2	2
1963	LA	NL	3	1	2	1	2	0	0	0	0	0	0	0	0	0	1	2
1965	WAS	AL	3	2	1	3	0	0	0	0	0	0	0	0	0	0	2	1
1966	WAS	AL	2	2	0	2	0	0	0	0	0	0	0	0	0	0	1	1
1967	WAS	AL	2	2	0	2	0	0	0	0	0	0	0	0	0	0	1	1
Total			18	11	7	13	5	0	0	0	0	0	0	0	1	0	10	8

Rank among batters: 1,914 • *Top target (2 home runs)*: Al Jackson • *Number of pitchers victimized*: 17 • *Total ballparks homered in*: 8 • *First HR*: 09/30/1960 off Glen Hobbie

Ken Caminiti

KENNETH GENE CAMINITI
B: 04/21/1963
BB

Year	Tm	Lg	Tot	H	A	Men-On 0	Men-On 1	Men-On 2	Men-On 3	One-Game 2	One-Game 3	One-Game 4	LO	XN	IP	PH	RHP	LHP
1987	HOU	NL	3	2	1	2	1	0	0	0	0	0	0	0	0	0	1	2
1988	HOU	NL	1	0	1	0	1	0	0	0	0	0	0	0	0	0	0	1
1989	HOU	NL	10	3	7	7	2	1	0	0	0	0	0	0	0	0	6	4
1990	HOU	NL	4	2	2	2	2	0	0	0	0	0	0	0	0	0	2	2
1991	HOU	NL	13	9	4	4	6	2	1	0	0	0	0	0	1	0	4	9
1992	HOU	NL	13	7	6	7	4	2	0	0	0	0	0	0	1	0	7	6
1993	HOU	NL	13	5	8	8	3	2	0	1	0	0	0	1	1	0	8	5
1994	HOU	NL	18	6	12	11	5	2	0	1	0	0	0	0	1	0	13	5
1995	SD	NL	26	16	10	12	10	3	1	4	0	0	0	0	3	0	16	10
Total			101	50	51	53	34	12	2	6	0	0	0	1	7	0	57	44

Rank among batters: 491 • Top target (3 home runs): Trevor Wilson, Orel Hershiser, Andy Benes, Ismael Valdes • *Number of pitchers victimized*: 82 • *Total ballparks homered in*: 14 • *First HR*: 07/16/1987 off Kevin Gross • *Switch hit HR in 1 game*—4 times

Howie Camnitz

SAMUEL HOWARD CAMNITZ
B: 08/22/1881 D: 03/02/1960
BR

Year	Tm	Lg	Tot	H	A	Men-On 0	Men-On 1	Men-On 2	Men-On 3	One-Game 2	One-Game 3	One-Game 4	LO	XN	IP	PH	RHP	LHP
1910	PIT	NL	1	1	0	1	0	0	0	0	0	0	0	0	1	0	1	0

Rank among batters: 4,707 • *Total ballparks homered in*: 1 • *First HR*: 08/22/1910 off Eddie Stack

Lew Camp

LLEWELLYN ROBERT CAMP
B: 02/22/1868 D: 10/01/1948
BL

Year	Tm	Lg	Tot	H	A	Men-On 0	1	2	3	One-Game 2	3	4	LO	XN	IP	PH	RHP	LHP
1892	STL	NL	2	1	1	1	0	1	0	0	0	0	0	0	0	0	2	0
1893	CHI	NL	2	2	0	1	1	0	0	0	0	0	0	0	0	0	2	0
Total			4	3	1	2	1	1	0	0	0	0	0	0	0	0	4	0

Rank among batters: 3,427 • *Total ballparks homered in*: 4 • *First HR*: 09/08/1892 off Jack Stivetts

Rick Camp

RICK LAMAR CAMP
B: 06/10/1953
BR

Year	Tm	Lg	Tot	H	A	Men-On 0	1	2	3	One-Game 2	3	4	LO	XN	IP	PH	RHP	LHP
1985	ATL	NL	1	1	0	1	0	0	0	0	0	0	0	1	0	0	0	1

Rank among batters: 4,707 • *Total ballparks homered in*: 1 • *First HR*: 07/04/1985 off Tom Gorman

Roy Campanella

ROY CAMPANELLA
B: 11/19/1921 D: 06/26/1993
BR HOF

Year	Tm	Lg	Tot	H	A	Men-On 0	1	2	3	One-Game 2	3	4	LO	XN	IP	PH	RHP	LHP
1948	BRO	NL	9	5	4	4	4	1	0	1	0	0	0	0	0	0	6	3
1949	BRO	NL	22	15	7	10	10	2	0	2	0	0	0	1	0	1	12	10
1950	BRO	NL	31	18	13	16	11	2	2	1	1	0	0	0	0	0	16	15
1951	BRO	NL	33	21	12	12	12	7	2	5	0	0	0	1	0	1	22	11
1952	BRO	NL	22	7	15	10	7	3	2	1	0	0	0	0	0	0	17	5
1953	BRO	NL	41	22	19	15	14	12	0	5	0	0	0	0	0	1	31	10
1954	BRO	NL	19	9	10	12	6	1	0	1	0	0	0	1	0	0	16	3
1955	BRO	NL	32	21	11	17	10	5	0	2	0	0	0	0	0	0	28	4
1956	BRO	NL	20	12	8	9	7	4	0	1	0	0	0	0	0	0	19	1
1957	BRO	NL	13	10	3	7	2	4	0	2	0	0	0	0	0	0	11	2
Total			242	140	102	112	83	41	6	21	1	0	0	3	0	3	178	64

Rank among batters: 121 • *Top target (13 home runs)*: Robin Roberts • *Number of pitchers victimized*: 108 • *Total ballparks homered in*: 9 • *First HR*: 07/04/1948 off Ray Poat • *World Series HR*—4

Bert Campaneris

DAGOBERTO (BLANCO) CAMPANERIS
B: 03/09/1942
BR

Year	Tm	Lg	Tot	H	A	Men-On 0	1	2	3	One-Game 2	3	4	LO	XN	IP	PH	RHP	LHP
1964	KC	AL	4	1	3	3	1	0	0	1	0	0	1	0	0	0	2	2
1965	KC	AL	6	2	4	3	2	1	0	0	0	0	0	0	2	0	3	3
1966	KC	AL	5	1	4	3	2	0	0	0	0	0	0	0	1	0	4	1
1967	KC	AL	3	0	3	3	0	0	0	0	0	0	2	0	0	0	3	0
1968	OAK	AL	4	3	1	3	1	0	0	0	0	0	0	0	0	0	4	0
1969	OAK	AL	2	2	0	1	1	0	0	0	0	0	0	0	0	0	1	1
1970	OAK	AL	22	10	12	14	5	3	0	1	0	0	6	0	0	0	13	9
1971	OAK	AL	5	3	2	3	1	1	0	1	0	0	2	0	0	0	3	2
1972	OAK	AL	8	2	6	5	3	0	0	0	0	0	2	1	0	0	5	3
1973	OAK	AL	4	2	2	3	1	0	0	0	0	0	0	0	0	0	4	0
1974	OAK	AL	2	1	1	2	0	0	0	0	0	0	0	0	0	0	1	1
1975	OAK	AL	4	1	3	4	0	0	0	0	0	0	0	0	0	0	3	1
1976	OAK	AL	1	0	1	1	0	0	0	0	0	0	0	0	0	0	1	0
1977	TEX	AL	5	0	5	5	0	0	0	0	0	0	0	1	0	0	4	1
1978	TEX	AL	1	0	1	1	0	0	0	0	0	0	0	0	0	0	1	0
1980	CAL	AL	2	0	2	0	1	1	0	0	0	0	0	0	0	0	2	0
1981	CAL	AL	1	0	1	1	0	0	0	0	0	0	0	0	0	0	0	1
Total			79	28	51	55	18	6	0	3	0	0	13	2	3	0	54	25

Rank among batters: 661 • *Top target (4 home runs)*: Sam McDowell • *Number of pitchers victimized*: 62 • *Total ballparks homered in*: 15 • *First HR*: 07/23/1964 off Jim Kaat • *Hit HR on first major league pitch*—@MIN: 07/23/1964 • *World Series HR*—1; *LCS HR*—2

Jim Campanis

JAMES ALEXANDER CAMPANIS
B: 02/09/1944
BR

Year	Tm	Lg	Tot	H	A	Men-On 0	1	2	3	One-Game 2	3	4	LO	XN	IP	PH	RHP	LHP
1967	LA	NL	2	1	1	2	0	0	0	0	0	0	0	0	0	2	0	2
1970	KC	AL	2	2	0	2	0	0	0	0	0	0	0	0	0	0	2	0
Total			4	3	1	4	0	0	0	0	0	0	0	0	0	2	2	2

Rank among batters: 3,427 • *Total ballparks homered in*: 3 • *First HR*: 05/13/1967 off Bob Hendley

Count Campau

CHARLES COLUMBUS CAMPAU
B: 10/17/1863 D: 04/03/1938
BL

Year	Tm	Lg	Tot	H	A	Men-On 0	Men-On 1	Men-On 2	Men-On 3	One-Game 2	One-Game 3	One-Game 4	LO	XN	IP	PH	RHP	LHP
1888	DET	NL	1	1	0	1	0	0	0	0	0	0	0	0	1	0	0	1
1890	STL	AA	9	7	2	4	3	0	2	1	0	0	0	0	0	0	4	5
Total			10	8	2	5	3	0	2	1	0	0	0	0	1	0	4	6

Rank among batters: 2,500 • *Top target (2 home runs)*: Cannonball Titcomb, John Keefe • *Number of pitchers victimized*: 8 • *Total ballparks homered in*: 3 • *First HR*: 07/24/1888 off Ed Morris

Bruce Campbell

BRUCE DOUGLAS CAMPBELL
B: 10/20/1909 D: 06/17/1995
BL

Year	Tm	Lg	Tot	H	A	Men-On 0	Men-On 1	Men-On 2	Men-On 3	One-Game 2	One-Game 3	One-Game 4	LO	XN	IP	PH	RHP	LHP
1931	CHI	AL	2	0	2	1	1	0	0	0	0	0	0	1	0	0	1	1
1932	STL	AL	14	11	3	7	6	1	0	0	0	0	0	0	1	0	12	2
1933	STL	AL	16	12	4	8	7	1	0	0	0	0	0	1	0	0	12	4
1934	STL	AL	9	4	5	6	0	2	1	0	0	0	0	0	0	0	9	0
1935	CLE	AL	7	5	2	4	1	1	1	0	0	0	0	1	1	0	6	1
1936	CLE	AL	6	5	1	3	3	0	0	0	0	0	0	0	0	0	4	2
1937	CLE	AL	4	1	3	2	1	1	0	0	0	0	0	0	0	1	3	1
1938	CLE	AL	12	5	7	5	5	2	0	1	0	0	0	0	1	0	12	0
1939	CLE	AL	8	4	4	3	2	3	0	1	0	0	0	0	1	0	6	2
1940	DET	AL	8	2	6	6	1	1	0	0	0	0	0	0	1	1	7	1
1941	DET	AL	15	8	7	7	5	3	0	3	0	0	0	0	0	0	12	3
1942	WAS	AL	5	2	3	4	0	1	0	0	0	0	0	0	0	0	4	1
Total			106	59	47	56	32	16	2	5	0	0	0	3	5	2	88	18

Rank among batters: 451 • *Top target (5 home runs)*: Mel Harder, Elden Auker • *Number of pitchers victimized*: 67 • *Total ballparks homered in*: 9 • *First HR*: 09/26/1931 off Bob Cooney • *World Series HR*—1

Dave Campbell

DAVID WILSON CAMPBELL
B: 01/14/1942
BR

Year	Tm	Lg	Tot	H	A	Men-On 0	Men-On 1	Men-On 2	Men-On 3	One-Game 2	One-Game 3	One-Game 4	LO	XN	IP	PH	RHP	LHP
1968	DET	AL	1	1	0	0	1	0	0	0	0	0	0	0	0	0	0	1
1970	SD	NL	12	5	7	12	0	0	0	0	0	0	1	0	0	0	9	3
1971	SD	NL	7	4	3	6	0	1	0	1	0	0	0	0	0	0	3	4
Total			20	10	10	18	1	1	0	1	0	0	1	0	0	0	12	8

Rank among batters: 1,810 • *Top target (2 home runs)*: Don Sutton, George Stone • *Number of pitchers victimized*: 18 • *Total ballparks homered in*: 8 • *First HR*: 08/07/1968 off Mike Paul

Gilly Campbell

WILLIAM GILTHORPE CAMPBELL
B: 02/13/1908 D: 02/21/1973
BL

Year	Tm	Lg	Tot	H	A	Men-On 0	Men-On 1	Men-On 2	Men-On 3	One-Game 2	One-Game 3	One-Game 4	LO	XN	IP	PH	RHP	LHP
1933	CHI	NL	1	1	0	1	0	0	0	0	0	0	0	0	0	0	1	0
1935	CIN	NL	3	0	3	2	1	0	0	0	0	0	0	0	0	0	3	0
1936	CIN	NL	1	0	1	0	1	0	0	0	0	0	0	0	0	0	1	0
Total			5	1	4	3	2	0	0	0	0	0	0	0	0	0	5	0

Rank among batters: 3,191 • *Total ballparks homered in*: 4 • *First HR*: 09/16/1933 off Bill Shores

Jim Campbell

JAMES ROBERT CAMPBELL
B: 06/24/1937
BR

Year	Tm	Lg	Tot	H	A	Men-On 0	Men-On 1	Men-On 2	Men-On 3	One-Game 2	One-Game 3	One-Game 4	LO	XN	IP	PH	RHP	LHP
1962	HOU	NL	3	0	3	2	1	0	0	0	0	0	0	0	0	0	2	1
1963	HOU	NL	4	1	3	2	0	1	1	0	0	0	0	1	0	0	3	1
Total			7	1	6	4	1	1	1	0	0	0	0	1	0	0	5	2

Rank among batters: 2,834 • *Total ballparks homered in*: 6 • *First HR*: 08/21/1962 off Jack Hamilton

Paul Campbell

PAUL MCLAUGHLIN CAMPBELL
B: 09/01/1917
BL

Year	Tm	Lg	Tot	H	A	Men-On 0	Men-On 1	Men-On 2	Men-On 3	One-Game 2	One-Game 3	One-Game 4	LO	XN	IP	PH	RHP	LHP
1948	DET	AL	1	1	0	0	0	1	0	0	0	0	0	0	0	0	1	0

Paul Campbell *continued*

Year	Tm	Lg	Tot	H	A	Men-On 0	1	2	3	One-Game 2	3	4	LO	XN	IP	PH	RHP	LHP
1949	DET	AL	3	1	2	1	0	1	1	0	0	0	0	0	0	2	3	0
Total			4	2	2	1	0	2	1	0	0	0	0	0	0	2	4	0

Rank among batters: 3,427 • *Total ballparks homered in*: 3 • *First HR*: 06/26/1948 off Allie Reynolds

Ron Campbell

RONALD THOMAS CAMPBELL
B: 04/05/1940
BR

Year	Tm	Lg	Tot	H	A	Men-On 0	1	2	3	One-Game 2	3	4	LO	XN	IP	PH	RHP	LHP
1964	CHI	NL	1	0	1	1	0	0	0	0	0	0	0	0	0	0	0	1

Rank among batters: 4,707 • *Total ballparks homered in*: 1 • *First HR*: 09/06/1964 off Ray Sadecki

Soup Campbell

CLARENCE CAMPBELL
B: 03/07/1915
BL

Year	Tm	Lg	Tot	H	A	Men-On 0	1	2	3	One-Game 2	3	4	LO	XN	IP	PH	RHP	LHP
1941	CLE	AL	3	1	2	1	1	1	0	0	0	0	0	0	0	1	3	0

Rank among batters: 3,735 • *Total ballparks homered in*: 2 • *First HR*: 05/14/1941 off Red Ruffing

Vin Campbell

ARTHUR VINCENT CAMPBELL
B: 01/30/1888 D: 11/16/1969
BL

Year	Tm	Lg	Tot	H	A	Men-On 0	1	2	3	One-Game 2	3	4	LO	XN	IP	PH	RHP	LHP
1910	PIT	NL	4	3	1	3	1	0	0	0	0	0	0	0	3	0	4	0
1912	BOS	NL	3	3	0	2	1	0	0	0	0	0	1	0	0	0	3	0
1914	IND	FL	7	3	4	6	0	1	0	0	0	0	2	1	1	0	7	0
1915	NWK	FL	1	0	1	0	0	1	0	0	0	0	0	0	0	0	1	0
Total			15	9	6	11	2	2	0	0	0	0	3	1	4	0	15	0

Rank among batters: 2,096 • *Top target (2 home runs)*: Cy Barger • *Number of pitchers victimized*: 14 • *Total ballparks homered in*: 6 • *First HR*: 06/08/1910 off Al Mattern

Sil Campusano

SILVESTRE (DIAZ) CAMPUSANO
B: 12/31/1965
BR

Year	Tm	Lg	Tot	H	A	Men-On 0	1	2	3	One-Game 2	3	4	LO	XN	IP	PH	RHP	LHP
1988	TOR	AL	2	1	1	2	0	0	0	0	0	0	0	0	0	0	0	2
1990	PHI	NL	2	2	0	1	1	0	0	0	0	0	0	0	0	0	1	1
1991	PHI	NL	1	0	1	1	0	0	0	0	0	0	0	0	0	1	1	0
Total			5	3	2	4	1	0	0	0	0	0	0	0	0	1	2	3

Rank among batters: 3,191 • *Total ballparks homered in*: 4 • *First HR*: 04/14/1988 off Al Leiter

George Canale

GEORGE ANTHONY CANALE
B: 08/11/1965
BL

Year	Tm	Lg	Tot	H	A	Men-On 0	1	2	3	One-Game 2	3	4	LO	XN	IP	PH	RHP	LHP
1989	MIL	AL	1	0	1	0	1	0	0	0	0	0	0	0	0	0	1	0
1991	MIL	AL	3	1	2	2	1	0	0	0	0	0	0	0	0	0	3	0
Total			4	1	3	2	2	0	0	0	0	0	0	0	0	0	4	0

Rank among batters: 3,427 • *Total ballparks homered in*: 4 • *First HR*: 09/06/1989 off Dan Petry

Willie Canate

EMISAEL WILLIAM (LIBRADA) CANATE
B: 12/11/1971
BR

Year	Tm	Lg	Tot	H	A	Men-On 0	1	2	3	One-Game 2	3	4	LO	XN	IP	PH	RHP	LHP
1993	TOR	AL	1	1	0	1	0	0	0	0	0	0	0	0	0	0	1	0

Rank among batters: 4,707 • *Total ballparks homered in*: 1 • *First HR*: 07/18/1993 off Hipolito Pichardo

Jim Canavan

JAMES EDWARD CANAVAN
B: 11/26/1866 D: 05/27/1949
BR

Year	Tm	Lg	Tot	H	A	Men-On 0	1	2	3	One-Game 2	3	4	LO	XN	IP	PH	RHP	LHP
1891	CIN	AA	7	4	3	4	2	1	0	0	0	0	0	0	1	0	7	0

Jim Canavan *continued*

Year	Tm	Lg	Tot	H	A	Men-On				One-Game			LO	XN	IP	PH	RHP	LHP
						0	1	2	3	2	3	4						
1891	MIL	AA	3	2	1	0	1	2	0	0	0	0	0	0	1	0	3	0
	Total		10	6	4	5	4	1	0	0	0	0	0	0	2	0	10	0
1893	CIN	NL	5	4	1	4	1	0	0	0	0	0	0	0	2	0	4	1
1894	CIN	NL	13	8	5	10	2	1	0	1	0	0	0	0	2	0	8	5
1897	BRO	NL	2	0	2	0	1	1	0	0	0	0	0	0	0	0	1	1
Total			30	18	12	19	8	3	0	1	0	0	0	0	6	0	23	7

Rank among batters: 1,437 • *Top target (3 home runs)*: Ted Breitenstein • *Number of pitchers victimized*: 24 • *Total ballparks homered in*: 11 • *First HR*: 04/13/1891 off Joe Neale

Casey Candaele

CASEY TODD CANDAELE
B: 01/12/1961
BB

Year	Tm	Lg	Tot	H	A	Men-On				One-Game			LO	XN	IP	PH	RHP	LHP
						0	1	2	3	2	3	4						
1987	MON	NL	1	1	0	1	0	0	0	0	0	0	0	0	0	0	1	0
1990	HOU	NL	3	1	2	2	1	0	0	0	0	0	0	0	0	1	1	2
1991	HOU	NL	4	1	3	3	1	0	0	0	0	0	0	0	0	0	3	1
1992	HOU	NL	1	1	0	1	0	0	0	0	0	0	0	0	0	0	0	1
1993	HOU	NL	1	0	1	1	0	0	0	0	0	0	0	0	0	0	0	1
Total			10	4	6	8	2	0	0	0	0	0	0	0	0	1	5	5

Rank among batters: 2,500 • *Top target (2 home runs)*: Fernando Valenzuela • *Number of pitchers victimized*: 9 • *Total ballparks homered in*: 6 • *First HR*: 07/19/1987 off Rick Mahler

John Candelaria

JOHN ROBERT CANDELARIA
B: 11/06/1953
BL

Year	Tm	Lg	Tot	H	A	Men-On				One-Game			LO	XN	IP	PH	RHP	LHP
						0	1	2	3	2	3	4						
1984	PIT	NL	1	1	0	0	1	0	0	0	0	0	0	0	0	0	0	1

Rank among batters: 4,707 • *Total ballparks homered in*: 1 • *First HR*: 07/19/1984 off Tim Lollar

Milo Candini

MILO CAIN CANDINI
B: 08/03/1917
BR

Year	Tm	Lg	Tot	H	A	Men-On				One-Game			LO	XN	IP	PH	RHP	LHP
						0	1	2	3	2	3	4						
1943	WAS	AL	1	0	1	1	0	0	0	0	0	0	0	0	1	0	1	0

Rank among batters: 4,707 • *Total ballparks homered in*: 1 • *First HR*: 06/23/1943 off Bill Zuber

John Cangelosi

JOHN ANTHONY CANGELOSI
B: 03/10/1963
BB

Year	Tm	Lg	Tot	H	A	Men-On				One-Game			LO	XN	IP	PH	RHP	LHP
						0	1	2	3	2	3	4						
1986	CHI	AL	2	1	1	1	1	0	0	0	0	0	0	0	0	0	0	2
1987	PIT	NL	4	2	2	3	0	1	0	0	0	0	1	0	0	1	0	4
1992	TEX	AL	1	0	1	0	1	0	0	0	0	0	0	0	0	0	0	1
1995	HOU	NL	2	2	0	1	0	1	0	0	0	0	0	0	0	0	0	2
Total			9	5	4	5	2	2	0	0	0	0	1	0	0	1	0	9

Rank among batters: 2,587 • *Total ballparks homered in*: 7 • *First HR*: 04/09/1986 off Ray Searage

Chris Cannizzaro

CHRISTOPHER JOHN CANNIZZARO
B: 05/03/1938
BR

Year	Tm	Lg	Tot	H	A	Men-On				One-Game			LO	XN	IP	PH	RHP	LHP
						0	1	2	3	2	3	4						
1968	PIT	NL	1	1	0	0	1	0	0	0	0	0	0	0	0	0	0	1
1969	SD	NL	4	3	1	3	1	0	0	0	0	0	0	0	0	0	3	1
1970	SD	NL	5	3	2	4	1	0	0	0	0	0	0	0	0	0	2	3
1971	SD	NL	1	0	1	1	0	0	0	0	0	0	0	0	0	0	1	0
	CHI	NL	5	4	1	4	1	0	0	0	0	0	0	0	0	0	3	2
	Total		6	4	2	5	1	0	0	0	0	0	0	0	0	0	4	2
1972	LA	NL	2	0	2	1	1	0	0	0	0	0	0	0	0	0	1	1
Total			18	11	7	13	5	0	0	0	0	0	0	0	0	0	10	8

Rank among batters: 1,914 • *Top target (2 home runs)*: Jim Merritt • *Number of pitchers victimized*: 17 • *Total ballparks homered in*: 7 • *First HR*: 08/17/1968 off Mike Kekich

Joe Cannon

JOSEPH JEROME CANNON
B: 07/13/1953
BL

Year	Tm	Lg	Tot	H	A	Men-On 0	1	2	3	One-Game 2	3	4	LO	XN	IP	PH	RHP	LHP
1979	TOR	AL	1	0	1	1	0	0	0	0	0	0	0	0	0	0	1	0

Rank among batters: 4,707 • *Total ballparks homered in*: 1 • *First HR*: 07/05/1979 off Kip Young

Jose Canseco

JOSE (CAPAS) CANSECO
B: 07/02/1964
BR

Year	Tm	Lg	Tot	H	A	Men-On 0	1	2	3	One-Game 2	3	4	LO	XN	IP	PH	RHP	LHP
1985	OAK	AL	5	4	1	4	1	0	0	1	0	0	0	0	0	0	4	1
1986	OAK	AL	33	14	19	11	16	6	0	1	0	0	0	0	0	0	25	8
1987	OAK	AL	31	16	15	19	6	6	0	4	0	0	0	0	0	0	16	15
1988	OAK	AL	42	16	26	16	21	5	0	1	1	0	0	1	0	0	32	10
1989	OAK	AL	17	8	9	8	7	2	0	1	0	0	0	0	0	0	10	7
1990	OAK	AL	37	18	19	19	13	4	1	7	0	0	0	0	0	0	25	12
1991	OAK	AL	44	16	28	24	10	8	2	2	0	0	0	1	0	0	36	8
1992	OAK	AL	22	12	10	14	6	1	1	1	0	0	0	0	0	0	15	7
	TEX	AL	4	3	1	1	2	1	0	0	0	0	0	0	0	0	4	0
	Total		26	15	11	15	8	2	1	1	0	0	0	0	0	0	19	7
1993	TEX	AL	10	6	4	4	5	1	0	0	0	0	0	0	0	0	7	3
1994	TEX	AL	31	17	14	17	11	3	0	3	1	0	0	1	0	0	24	7
1995	BOS	AL	24	10	14	13	6	5	0	0	0	0	0	1	0	0	12	12
Total			300	140	160	150	104	42	4	21	2	0	0	4	0	0	210	90

Rank among batters: 68 • *Top target (8 home runs)*: Todd Stottlemyre • *Number of pitchers victimized*: 180 • *Total ballparks homered in*: 18 • *First HR*: 09/09/1985 off Jeff Russell • *World Series HR*—3; *LCS HR*—4

Nick Capra

NICK LEE CAPRA
B: 03/08/1958
BR

Year	Tm	Lg	Tot	H	A	Men-On 0	1	2	3	One-Game 2	3	4	LO	XN	IP	PH	RHP	LHP
1982	TEX	AL	1	0	1	1	0	0	0	0	0	0	0	0	0	0	1	0

Rank among batters: 4,707 • *Total ballparks homered in*: 1 • *First HR*: 09/22/1982 off Steve Baker

Ramon Caraballo

RAMON (SANCHEZ) CARABALLO
B: 05/23/1969
BB

Year	Tm	Lg	Tot	H	A	Men-On 0	1	2	3	One-Game 2	3	4	LO	XN	IP	PH	RHP	LHP
1995	STL	NL	2	0	2	2	0	0	0	0	0	0	0	0	0	1	2	0

Rank among batters: 4,129 • *Total ballparks homered in*: 1 • *First HR*: 06/29/1995 off Kevin Foster

Bernie Carbo

BERNARDO CARBO
B: 08/05/1947
BL

Year	Tm	Lg	Tot	H	A	Men-On 0	1	2	3	One-Game 2	3	4	LO	XN	IP	PH	RHP	LHP
1970	CIN	NL	21	6	15	15	2	4	0	1	0	0	0	0	0	1	20	1
1971	CIN	NL	5	1	4	4	1	0	0	0	0	0	0	0	0	0	4	1
1972	STL	NL	7	4	3	5	1	1	0	0	0	0	0	0	0	0	6	1
1973	STL	NL	8	2	6	7	1	0	0	0	0	0	0	0	0	0	6	2
1974	BOS	AL	12	8	4	5	5	1	1	0	0	0	0	0	0	0	12	0
1975	BOS	AL	15	11	4	9	2	3	1	3	0	0	4	0	0	0	15	0
1976	BOS	AL	2	1	1	0	1	1	0	0	0	0	0	0	0	0	2	0
	MIL	AL	3	1	2	1	2	0	0	0	0	0	0	0	0	0	2	1
	Total		5	2	3	1	3	1	0	0	0	0	0	0	0	0	4	1
1977	BOS	AL	15	10	5	11	3	0	1	1	0	0	0	1	0	3	14	1
1978	BOS	AL	1	1	0	1	0	0	0	0	0	0	0	0	0	0	1	0
	CLE	AL	4	1	3	3	1	0	0	0	0	0	0	0	0	0	4	0
	Total		5	2	3	4	1	0	0	0	0	0	0	0	0	0	5	0
1979	STL	NL	3	2	1	1	1	1	0	0	0	0	0	0	0	1	3	0
Total			96	48	48	62	20	11	3	5	0	0	4	1	0	5	89	7

Rank among batters: 520 • Top target (4 home runs): Lerrin LaGrow, Nelson Briles, Ferguson Jenkins • *Number of pitchers victimized*: 70 • *Total ballparks homered in*: 26 • *First HR*: 04/06/1970 off Joe Sparma • *World Series HR*—2

Jose Cardenal

JOSE ROSARIO DOMEC CARDENAL
B: 10/07/1943
BR

Year	Tm	Lg	Tot	H	A	Men-On 0	1	2	3	One-Game 2	3	4	LO	XN	IP	PH	RHP	LHP
1965	CAL	AL	11	5	6	5	3	3	0	0	0	0	2	0	0	0	7	4

Jose Cardenal *continued*

Year	Tm	Lg	Tot	H	A	Men-On 0	1	2	3	One-Game 2	3	4	LO	XN	IP	PH	RHP	LHP
1966	CAL	AL	16	9	7	11	3	2	0	0	0	0	1	0	1	1	12	4
1967	CAL	AL	6	3	3	5	1	0	0	0	0	0	2	0	1	0	5	1
1968	CLE	AL	7	1	6	5	2	0	0	1	0	0	1	1	1	0	3	4
1969	CLE	AL	11	5	6	8	2	0	1	0	0	0	2	1	0	0	9	2
1970	STL	NL	10	5	5	6	4	0	0	0	0	0	0	1	0	2	7	3
1971	STL	NL	7	4	3	3	2	2	0	0	0	0	0	0	0	0	4	3
	MIL	AL	3	0	3	1	0	1	1	0	0	0	0	0	0	0	3	0
	Total		10	4	6	4	2	3	1	0	0	0	0	0	0	0	7	3
1972	CHI	NL	17	11	6	9	8	0	0	2	0	0	0	0	0	0	10	7
1973	CHI	NL	11	4	7	8	3	0	0	0	0	0	0	0	0	0	8	3
1974	CHI	NL	13	9	4	7	4	2	0	0	0	0	0	0	0	0	10	3
1975	CHI	NL	9	4	5	8	1	0	0	1	0	0	0	0	0	0	5	4
1976	CHI	NL	8	7	1	5	3	0	0	0	0	0	0	0	0	0	6	2
1977	CHI	NL	3	3	0	2	0	1	0	0	0	0	0	0	0	0	1	2
1978	PHI	NL	4	1	3	2	2	0	0	0	0	0	0	0	0	1	2	2
1979	NY	NL	2	0	2	2	0	0	0	0	0	0	0	0	0	0	1	1
Total			138	71	67	87	38	11	2	4	0	0	8	3	3	4	93	45

Rank among batters: 314 • *Top target (4 home runs)*: Al Downing, Jim Lonborg • *Number of pitchers victimized*: 103 • *Total ballparks homered in*: 25 • *First HR*: 04/14/1965 off Whitey Ford

Leo Cardenas

LEONARDO LAZARO (ALFONSO) CARDENAS
B: 12/17/1938
BR

Year	Tm	Lg	Tot	H	A	Men-On 0	1	2	3	One-Game 2	3	4	LO	XN	IP	PH	RHP	LHP
1960	CIN	NL	1	0	1	0	1	0	0	0	0	0	0	0	0	0	1	0
1961	CIN	NL	5	1	4	2	2	1	0	0	0	0	0	0	0	0	3	2
1962	CIN	NL	10	6	4	7	3	0	0	0	0	0	1	0	0	0	9	1
1963	CIN	NL	7	3	4	4	1	2	0	0	0	0	0	0	1	0	6	1
1964	CIN	NL	9	3	6	4	4	0	1	0	0	0	0	0	0	0	8	1
1965	CIN	NL	11	7	4	10	1	0	0	1	0	0	0	1	0	0	6	5
1966	CIN	NL	20	11	9	12	5	3	0	3	0	0	0	0	0	0	16	4
1967	CIN	NL	2	2	0	1	1	0	0	0	0	0	0	0	0	0	2	0
1968	CIN	NL	7	2	5	5	2	0	0	0	0	0	0	0	1	0	5	2
1969	MIN	AL	10	3	7	7	2	1	0	0	0	0	0	0	0	0	10	0
1970	MIN	AL	11	5	6	4	5	1	1	0	0	0	0	0	0	0	8	3
1971	MIN	AL	18	11	7	13	3	2	0	0	0	0	0	0	0	0	10	8
1972	CAL	AL	6	3	3	5	0	1	0	0	0	0	0	0	1	0	3	3
1975	TEX	AL	1	0	1	0	1	0	0	0	0	0	0	0	0	0	1	0
Total			118	57	61	74	31	11	2	4	0	0	1	1	3	0	88	30

Rank among batters: 396 • *Top target (6 home runs)*: Juan Marichal • *Number of pitchers victimized*: 91 • *Total ballparks homered in*: 27 • *First HR*: 07/28/1960 off Roger Craig

Don Cardwell

DONALD EUGENE CARDWELL
B: 12/07/1935
BR

Year	Tm	Lg	Tot	H	A	Men-On 0	1	2	3	One-Game 2	3	4	LO	XN	IP	PH	RHP	LHP
1957	PHI	NL	1	1	0	0	1	0	0	0	0	0	0	0	0	0	1	0
1959	PHI	NL	1	0	1	0	1	0	0	0	0	0	0	0	0	0	1	0
1960	PHI	NL	2	2	0	1	1	0	0	0	0	0	0	0	0	0	2	0
	CHI	NL	3	1	2	2	1	0	0	1	0	0	0	0	0	0	2	1
	Total		5	3	2	3	2	0	0	1	0	0	0	0	0	0	4	1
1961	CHI	NL	3	2	1	2	1	0	0	0	0	0	0	0	0	0	2	1
1965	PIT	NL	2	1	1	1	0	1	0	0	0	0	0	0	0	0	1	1
1967	NY	NL	1	0	1	0	1	0	0	0	0	0	0	0	0	0	1	0
1968	NY	NL	1	1	0	0	1	0	0	0	0	0	0	0	0	0	1	0
1969	NY	NL	1	1	0	0	0	1	0	0	0	0	0	0	0	0	1	0
Total			15	9	6	6	7	2	0	1	0	0	0	0	0	0	12	3

Rank among batters: 2,096 • *Total ballparks homered in*: 6 • *First HR*: 08/31/1957 off Bob Friend

Rod Carew

RODNEY CLINE CAREW
B: 10/01/1945
BL HOF

Year	Tm	Lg	Tot	H	A	Men-On 0	1	2	3	One-Game 2	3	4	LO	XN	IP	PH	RHP	LHP
1967	MIN	AL	8	1	7	5	2	1	0	0	0	0	0	0	0	0	8	0
1968	MIN	AL	1	1	0	1	0	0	0	0	0	0	1	0	0	0	1	0
1969	MIN	AL	8	4	4	1	7	0	0	1	0	0	0	0	1	0	5	3

Rod Carew *continued*

Year	Tm	Lg	Tot	H	A	Men-On 0	1	2	3	One-Game 2	3	4	LO	XN	IP	PH	RHP	LHP
1970	MIN	AL	4	0	4	1	2	1	0	0	0	0	0	0	0	0	1	3
1971	MIN	AL	2	1	1	1	1	0	0	0	0	0	0	0	0	0	1	1
1973	MIN	AL	6	3	3	4	1	1	0	0	0	0	1	0	0	0	4	2
1974	MIN	AL	3	2	1	3	0	0	0	0	0	0	0	1	0	1	3	0
1975	MIN	AL	14	10	4	9	4	1	0	1	0	0	0	0	0	0	10	4
1976	MIN	AL	9	4	5	1	4	1	3	0	0	0	0	0	0	1	8	1
1977	MIN	AL	14	8	6	8	4	1	1	1	0	0	0	0	0	0	12	2
1978	MIN	AL	5	1	4	4	1	0	0	0	0	0	0	0	0	0	4	1
1979	CAL	AL	3	1	2	1	2	0	0	0	0	0	0	0	0	0	2	1
1980	CAL	AL	3	2	1	0	2	1	0	0	0	0	0	1	0	0	2	1
1981	CAL	AL	2	0	2	2	0	0	0	0	0	0	0	0	0	0	2	0
1982	CAL	AL	3	1	2	2	0	1	0	0	0	0	0	0	0	1	2	1
1983	CAL	AL	2	1	1	0	1	0	1	0	0	0	0	0	0	0	1	1
1984	CAL	AL	3	3	0	1	2	0	0	0	0	0	0	0	0	0	3	0
1985	CAL	AL	2	1	1	1	1	0	0	0	0	0	0	0	0	0	2	0
Total			92	44	48	45	34	8	5	3	0	0	2	2	1	3	71	21

Rank among batters: 554 • *Top target (7 home runs)*: Catfish Hunter • *Number of pitchers victimized*: 65 • *Total ballparks homered in*: 17 • *First HR*: 04/21/1967 off Denny McLain • *Hit for Cycle*—@KC: 05/20/1970

Andy Carey

ANDREW ARTHUR CAREY
B: 10/18/1931
BR

Year	Tm	Lg	Tot	H	A	Men-On 0	1	2	3	One-Game 2	3	4	LO	XN	IP	PH	RHP	LHP
1953	NY	AL	4	1	3	2	1	1	0	0	0	0	0	0	0	0	2	2
1954	NY	AL	8	3	5	3	4	1	0	0	0	0	0	0	0	0	5	3
1955	NY	AL	7	2	5	4	2	1	0	0	0	0	0	0	0	0	4	3
1956	NY	AL	7	1	6	3	3	1	0	0	0	0	0	0	0	0	4	3
1957	NY	AL	6	2	4	1	5	0	0	1	0	0	0	0	0	0	4	2
1958	NY	AL	12	4	8	8	3	1	0	3	0	0	0	0	0	0	9	3
1959	NY	AL	3	1	2	3	0	0	0	0	0	0	0	0	0	0	3	0
1960	KC	AL	12	10	2	7	3	2	0	0	0	0	0	0	0	1	10	2
1961	KC	AL	3	1	2	1	2	0	0	0	0	0	0	0	0	0	3	0
1962	LA	NL	2	1	1	2	0	0	0	0	0	0	0	0	0	0	1	1
Total			64	26	38	34	23	7	0	4	0	0	0	0	0	1	45	19

Rank among batters: 815 • *Top target (3 home runs)*: Don Mossi, Frank Sullivan, Dick Donovan • *Number of pitchers victimized*: 52 • *Total ballparks homered in*: 10 • *First HR*: 04/25/1953 off Al Sima

Max Carey

MAX GEORGE CAREY
B: 01/11/1890 D: 05/30/1976
BB HOF

Year	Tm	Lg	Tot	H	A	Men-On 0	1	2	3	One-Game 2	3	4	LO	XN	IP	PH	RHP	LHP
1911	PIT	NL	5	5	0	5	0	0	0	0	0	0	0	0	5	0	4	1
1912	PIT	NL	5	0	5	3	1	0	1	0	0	0	0	1	2	0	3	2
1913	PIT	NL	5	1	4	2	1	2	0	1	0	0	0	0	2	0	5	0
1914	PIT	NL	1	1	0	1	0	0	0	0	0	0	0	0	1	0	1	0
1915	PIT	NL	3	2	1	2	1	0	0	0	0	0	0	0	2	0	1	2
1916	PIT	NL	7	3	4	4	3	0	0	0	0	0	0	1	3	0	6	1
1917	PIT	NL	1	0	1	0	1	0	0	0	0	0	0	0	1	0	1	0
1918	PIT	NL	3	0	3	2	0	1	0	0	0	0	0	0	2	0	2	1
1920	PIT	NL	1	0	1	0	1	0	0	0	0	0	0	0	1	0	1	0
1921	PIT	NL	7	2	5	4	3	0	0	0	0	0	0	0	2	0	2	5
1922	PIT	NL	10	5	5	6	4	0	0	2	0	0	0	0	2	0	6	4
1923	PIT	NL	6	5	1	2	4	0	0	0	0	0	0	0	1	0	2	4
1924	PIT	NL	8	2	6	3	3	2	0	1	0	0	0	0	1	0	3	5
1925	PIT	NL	5	3	2	3	1	1	0	0	0	0	0	0	2	0	1	4
1927	BRO	NL	1	0	1	0	0	0	1	0	0	0	0	0	1	0	0	1
1928	BRO	NL	2	0	2	0	2	0	0	0	0	0	0	0	0	0	1	1
Total			70	29	41	37	25	6	2	4	0	0	0	2	28	0	39	31

Rank among batters: 742 • *Top target (5 home runs)*: Art Nehf • *Number of pitchers victimized*: 53 • *Total ballparks homered in*: 12 • *First HR*: 06/07/1911 off Louis Drucke • *Hit for Cycle*—vs BRO: 06/20/1925

Scoops Carey

GEORGE C. CAREY
B: 12/04/1870 D: 12/17/1916
BR

Year	Tm	Lg	Tot	H	A	Men-On 0	1	2	3	One-Game 2	3	4	LO	XN	IP	PH	RHP	LHP
1895	BAL	NL	1	0	1	0	0	1	0	0	0	0	0	0	0	0	0	1

Rank among batters: 4,707 • *Total ballparks homered in*: 1 • *First HR*: 08/01/1895 off Patrick Dolan

Year	Tm	Lg	Tot	H	A	Men-On 0	1	2	3	One-Game 2	3	4	LO	XN	IP	PH	RHP	LHP

Tom Carey

THOMAS JOHN CAREY
B: 1849 D: 02/13/1899
BR

Year	Tm	Lg	Tot	H	A	Men-On 0	1	2	3	One-Game 2	3	4	LO	XN	IP	PH	RHP	LHP
1877	HAR	NL	1	0	1	0	0	1	0	0	0	0	0	0	0	0	1	0

Rank among batters: 4,707 • *Total ballparks homered in*: 1 • *First HR*: 07/12/1877 off Candy Cummings

Tom Carey

THOMAS FRANCIS ALOYSIUS CAREY
B: 10/11/1906 D: 02/21/1970
BR

Year	Tm	Lg	Tot	H	A	Men-On 0	1	2	3	One-Game 2	3	4	LO	XN	IP	PH	RHP	LHP
1936	STL	AL	1	1	0	1	0	0	0	0	0	0	0	0	0	0	1	0
1937	STL	AL	1	0	1	1	0	0	0	0	0	0	0	0	0	0	1	0
Total			2	1	1	2	0	0	0	0	0	0	0	0	0	0	2	0

Rank among batters: 4,129 • *Total ballparks homered in*: 2 • *First HR*: 08/02/1936 off Hod Lisenbee

Fred Carisch

FREDERICK BEHLMER CARISCH
B: 11/14/1881 D: 04/19/1977
BR

Year	Tm	Lg	Tot	H	A	Men-On 0	1	2	3	One-Game 2	3	4	LO	XN	IP	PH	RHP	LHP
1903	PIT	NL	1	1	0	0	1	0	0	0	0	0	0	0	1	0	1	0

Rank among batters: 4,707 • *Total ballparks homered in*: 1 • *First HR*: 09/21/1903 off Oscar Jones

Tex Carleton

JAMES OTTO CARLETON
B: 08/19/1906 D: 01/11/1977
BB

Year	Tm	Lg	Tot	H	A	Men-On 0	1	2	3	One-Game 2	3	4	LO	XN	IP	PH	RHP	LHP
1932	STL	NL	1	0	1	0	0	1	0	0	0	0	0	0	0	0	1	0
1933	STL	NL	1	0	1	1	0	0	0	0	0	0	0	0	0	0	1	0
1934	STL	NL	1	1	0	0	0	1	0	0	0	0	0	0	0	0	1	0
1936	CHI	NL	3	2	1	0	1	2	0	0	0	0	0	0	0	0	3	0
Total			6	3	3	1	1	4	0	0	0	0	0	0	0	0	6	0

Rank among batters: 2,988 • *Total ballparks homered in*: 4 • *First HR*: 08/09/1932 off Ed Holley

Jim Carlin

JAMES ARTHUR CARLIN
B: 02/23/1918
BR

Year	Tm	Lg	Tot	H	A	Men-On 0	1	2	3	One-Game 2	3	4	LO	XN	IP	PH	RHP	LHP
1941	PHI	NL	1	0	1	0	1	0	0	0	0	0	0	0	0	0	1	0

Rank among batters: 4,707 • *Total ballparks homered in*: 1 • *First HR*: 08/02/1941 off Howie Krist

Hal Carlson

HAROLD GUST CARLSON
B: 05/17/1892 D: 05/28/1930
BR

Year	Tm	Lg	Tot	H	A	Men-On 0	1	2	3	One-Game 2	3	4	LO	XN	IP	PH	RHP	LHP
1922	PIT	NL	1	0	1	0	1	0	0	0	0	0	0	0	0	0	1	0
1924	PHI	NL	2	1	1	0	2	0	0	0	0	0	0	0	0	0	0	2
1925	PHI	NL	2	1	1	2	0	0	0	0	0	0	0	0	0	1	1	1
Total			5	2	3	2	3	0	0	0	0	0	0	0	0	1	2	3

Rank among batters: 3,191 • *Total ballparks homered in*: 2 • *First HR*: 08/10/1922 off Jimmy Ring

Steve Carlton

STEVEN NORMAN CARLTON
B: 12/22/1944
BL HOF

Year	Tm	Lg	Tot	H	A	Men-On 0	1	2	3	One-Game 2	3	4	LO	XN	IP	PH	RHP	LHP
1968	STL	NL	2	0	2	2	0	0	0	0	0	0	0	0	0	0	2	0
1969	STL	NL	1	0	1	0	0	1	0	0	0	0	0	0	0	0	1	0
1972	PHI	NL	1	0	1	1	0	0	0	0	0	0	0	0	0	0	1	0
1973	PHI	NL	2	1	1	1	1	0	0	0	0	0	0	0	0	0	1	1
1977	PHI	NL	3	1	2	2	1	0	0	0	0	0	0	0	0	0	3	0
1982	PHI	NL	2	1	1	1	0	1	0	0	0	0	0	0	0	0	2	0
1984	PHI	NL	1	0	1	0	0	0	1	0	0	0	0	0	0	0	0	1
1986	SF	NL	1	0	1	0	0	1	0	0	0	0	0	0	0	0	0	1
Total			13	3	10	7	2	3	1	0	0	0	0	0	0	0	10	3

Rank among batters: 2,248 • *Top target (2 home runs)*: Don Wilson • *Number of pitchers victimized*: 12 • *Total ballparks homered in*: 9 • *First HR*: 06/13/1968 off Ken Johnson • *LCS HR*—1

Cleo Carlyle

HIRAM CLEO CARLYLE
B: 09/07/1902 D: 11/12/1967
BL

Year	Tm	Lg	Tot	H	A	Men-On 0	1	2	3	One-Game 2	3	4	LO	XN	IP	PH	RHP	LHP
1927	BOS	AL	1	0	1	1	0	0	0	0	0	0	0	0	0	0	1	0

Rank among batters: 4,707 • *Total ballparks homered in*: 1 • *First HR*: 07/15/1927 off Elam Vangilder

Roy Carlyle

ROY EDWARD CARLYLE
B: 12/10/1900 D: 11/22/1956
BL

Year	Tm	Lg	Tot	H	A	Men-On 0	1	2	3	One-Game 2	3	4	LO	XN	IP	PH	RHP	LHP
1925	BOS	AL	7	1	6	3	3	1	0	0	0	0	0	0	0	1	5	2
1926	BOS	AL	2	2	0	2	0	0	0	0	0	0	0	0	0	0	2	0
Total			9	3	6	5	3	1	0	0	0	0	0	0	0	1	7	2

Rank among batters: 2,587 • *Total ballparks homered in*: 6 • *First HR*: 05/16/1925 off Dixie Davis • *Hit for Cycle*—@CHI: 07/21/1925 (1)

Duke Carmel

LEON JAMES CARMEL
B: 04/23/1937
BL

Year	Tm	Lg	Tot	H	A	Men-On 0	1	2	3	One-Game 2	3	4	LO	XN	IP	PH	RHP	LHP
1963	STL	NL	1	1	0	1	0	0	0	0	0	0	0	0	0	1	1	0
	NY	NL	3	2	1	0	2	0	1	0	0	0	0	0	0	0	2	1
	Total		4	3	1	3	0	1	0	0	0	0	0	0	0	1	3	1
Total			4	3	1	3	0	1	0	0	0	0	0	0	0	1	3	1

Rank among batters: 3,427 • *Total ballparks homered in*: 3 • *First HR*: 04/16/1963 off Roy Face

Eddie Carnett

EDWIN ELLIOTT CARNETT
B: 10/21/1916
BL

Year	Tm	Lg	Tot	H	A	Men-On 0	1	2	3	One-Game 2	3	4	LO	XN	IP	PH	RHP	LHP
1944	CHI	AL	1	1	0	0	0	1	0	0	0	0	0	0	0	0	1	0

Rank among batters: 4,707 • *Total ballparks homered in*: 1 • *First HR*: 07/22/1944 off Monk Dubiel

John Carney

JOHN JOSEPH CARNEY
B: 11/10/1866 D: 10/19/1925
BR

Year	Tm	Lg	Tot	H	A	Men-On 0	1	2	3	One-Game 2	3	4	LO	XN	IP	PH	RHP	LHP
1889	WAS	NL	1	0	1	1	0	0	0	0	0	0	0	0	0	0	1	0
1891	CIN	AA	3	3	0	0	2	0	1	0	0	0	0	0	0	0	2	1
	MIL	AA	3	3	0	0	2	1	0	0	0	0	0	0	0	0	1	0
	Total		6	6	0	0	4	1	1	0	0	0	0	0	0	0	3	1
Total			7	6	1	1	4	1	1	0	0	0	0	0	0	0	4	1

Rank among batters: 2,834 • *Top target (2 home runs)*: Jack Easton • *Number of pitchers victimized*: 6 • *Total ballparks homered in*: 4 • *First HR*: 04/30/1889 off Mickey Welch

Pat Carney

PATRICK JOSEPH CARNEY
B: 08/07/1876 D: 01/09/1953
BL

Year	Tm	Lg	Tot	H	A	Men-On 0	1	2	3	One-Game 2	3	4	LO	XN	IP	PH	RHP	LHP
1902	BOS	NL	2	2	0	1	1	0	0	1	0	0	0	0	0	0	2	0
1903	BOS	NL	1	0	1	1	0	0	0	0	0	0	0	0	0	0	1	0
Total			3	2	1	2	1	0	0	1	0	0	0	0	0	0	3	0

Rank among batters: 3,735 • *Top target (2 home runs)*: Frank Kitson • *Number of pitchers victimized*: 2 • *Total ballparks homered in*: 2 • *First HR*: 05/01/1902 off Frank Kitson

Hick Carpenter

WARREN WILLIAM CARPENTER
B: 08/16/1855 D: 04/18/1937
BR

Year	Tm	Lg	Tot	H	A	Men-On 0	1	2	3	One-Game 2	3	4	LO	XN	IP	PH	RHP	LHP
1881	WOR	NL	2	2	0	0	2	0	0	0	0	0	0	0	0	0	1	1
1882	CIN	AA	1	0	1	0	0	1	0	0	0	0	0	0	0	0	1	0
1883	CIN	AA	3	3	0	1	1	1	0	0	0	0	1	0	0	0	3	0
1884	CIN	AA	4	4	0	1	2	1	0	1	0	0	0	0	0	0	2	0
1885	CIN	AA	2	2	0	1	0	1	0	0	0	0	0	0	0	0	1	1

Hick Carpenter *continued*

Year	Tm	Lg	Tot	H	A	Men-On 0	1	2	3	One-Game 2	3	4	LO	XN	IP	PH	RHP	LHP
1886	CIN	AA	2	2	0	1	0	1	0	0	0	0	0	0	0	0	0	1
1887	CIN	AA	1	1	0	1	0	0	0	0	0	0	0	0	0	0	0	1
1888	CIN	AA	3	3	0	2	0	1	0	0	0	0	0	0	0	0	0	3
Total			18	17	1	7	5	6	0	1	0	0	1	0	0	0	8	6

Rank among batters: 1,914 • *Top target (2 home runs)*: Ed Trumbull, Toad Ramsey • *Number of pitchers victimized*: 16 • *Total ballparks homered in*: 4 • *First HR*: 09/23/1881 off Tony Mullane

Charlie Carr

CHARLES CARBITT CARR
B: 12/27/1876 D: 11/25/1932
BR

Year	Tm	Lg	Tot	H	A	Men-On 0	1	2	3	One-Game 2	3	4	LO	XN	IP	PH	RHP	LHP
1903	DET	AL	2	1	1	0	1	1	0	0	0	0	0	0	1	0	2	0
1905	CLE	AL	1	1	0	1	0	0	0	0	0	0	0	0	0	0	0	1
1914	IND	FL	3	1	2	2	1	0	0	0	0	0	0	0	0	0	3	0
Total			6	3	3	3	2	1	0	0	0	0	0	0	1	0	5	1

Rank among batters: 2,988 • *Total ballparks homered in*: 6 • *First HR*: 06/09/1903 off Cy Young

Chuck Carr

CHARLES LEE GLENN CARR
B: 08/10/1967
BB

Year	Tm	Lg	Tot	H	A	Men-On 0	1	2	3	One-Game 2	3	4	LO	XN	IP	PH	RHP	LHP
1993	FLO	NL	4	3	1	2	1	0	1	0	0	0	1	0	0	0	2	2
1994	FLO	NL	2	1	1	0	2	0	0	0	0	0	0	0	0	0	1	1
1995	FLO	NL	2	1	1	2	0	0	0	0	0	0	0	0	0	0	0	2
Total			8	5	3	4	3	0	1	0	0	0	1	0	0	0	3	5

Rank among batters: 2,703 • *Total ballparks homered in*: 4 • *First HR*: 05/12/1993 off Chris Nabholz

Alex Carrasquel

ALEJANDRO ELOY (APARICIO) CARRASQUEL
B: 07/24/1912 D: 08/19/1969
BR

Year	Tm	Lg	Tot	H	A	Men-On 0	1	2	3	One-Game 2	3	4	LO	XN	IP	PH	RHP	LHP
1939	WAS	AL	1	1	0	1	0	0	0	0	0	0	0	0	0	0	1	0

Rank among batters: 4,707 • *Total ballparks homered in*: 1 • *First HR*: 05/30/1939 off Nels Potter

Chico Carrasquel

ALFONSO (COLON) CARRASQUEL
B: 01/23/1926
BR

Year	Tm	Lg	Tot	H	A	Men-On 0	1	2	3	One-Game 2	3	4	LO	XN	IP	PH	RHP	LHP
1950	CHI	AL	4	1	3	3	1	0	0	0	0	0	1	0	0	0	1	3
1951	CHI	AL	2	0	2	1	0	1	0	0	0	0	0	0	0	0	1	1
1952	CHI	AL	1	0	1	1	0	0	0	0	0	0	0	0	0	0	1	0
1953	CHI	AL	2	1	1	1	0	0	1	0	0	0	0	0	0	0	0	2
1954	CHI	AL	12	3	9	9	2	1	0	0	0	0	2	0	0	0	8	4
1955	CHI	AL	11	6	5	9	0	2	0	0	0	0	0	0	0	0	7	4
1956	CLE	AL	7	3	4	5	1	0	1	1	0	0	0	0	0	0	5	2
1957	CLE	AL	8	5	3	3	3	0	2	0	0	0	0	0	0	0	6	2
1958	CLE	AL	2	0	2	1	1	0	0	0	0	0	0	0	0	0	1	1
	KC	AL	2	2	0	2	0	0	0	0	0	0	2	0	0	0	2	0
	Total		4	2	2	3	1	0	0	0	0	0	2	0	0	0	3	1
1959	BAL	AL	4	3	1	2	2	0	0	0	0	0	0	1	0	0	3	1
Total			55	24	31	37	10	4	4	1	0	0	5	1	0	0	35	20

Rank among batters: 926 • Top target (3 home runs): Alex Kellner, Lou Kretlow, Morrie Martin, Tom Brewer • *Number of pitchers victimized*: 42 • *Total ballparks homered in*: 9 • *First HR*: 05/05/1950 off Joe Dobson

Cam Carreon

CAMILO CARREON
B: 08/06/1937 D: 09/02/1987
BR

Year	Tm	Lg	Tot	H	A	Men-On 0	1	2	3	One-Game 2	3	4	LO	XN	IP	PH	RHP	LHP
1961	CHI	AL	4	0	4	4	0	0	0	0	0	0	0	0	0	0	3	1
1962	CHI	AL	4	1	3	3	0	1	0	0	0	0	0	0	0	0	4	0
1963	CHI	AL	2	1	1	1	1	0	0	0	0	0	0	0	0	0	0	2

Year	Tm	Lg	Tot	H	A	Men-On 0	1	2	3	One-Game 2	3	4	LO	XN	IP	PH	RHP	LHP

Cam Carreon *continued*

Year	Tm	Lg	Tot	H	A	0	1	2	3	2	3	4	LO	XN	IP	PH	RHP	LHP
1965	CLE	AL	1	0	1	0	1	0	0	0	0	0	0	0	0	0	1	0
Total			11	2	9	8	2	1	0	0	0	0	0	0	0	0	8	3

Rank among batters: 2,419 • *Top target (2 home runs)*: Mike McCormick • *Number of pitchers victimized*: 10 • *Total ballparks homered in*: 5 • *First HR*: 05/01/1961 off Chuck Stobbs

Mark Carreon

MARK STEVEN CARREON
B: 07/19/1963
BR

Year	Tm	Lg	Tot	H	A	0	1	2	3	2	3	4	LO	XN	IP	PH	RHP	LHP
1988	NY	NL	1	0	1	1	0	0	0	0	0	0	0	0	0	0	0	1
1989	NY	NL	6	4	2	6	0	0	0	0	0	0	0	0	0	4	1	5
1990	NY	NL	10	1	9	6	4	0	0	1	0	0	1	0	0	1	3	7
1991	NY	NL	4	3	1	4	0	0	0	0	0	0	0	0	0	3	1	3
1992	DET	AL	10	5	5	5	3	2	0	0	0	0	0	0	0	0	8	2
1993	SF	NL	7	2	5	2	5	0	0	0	0	0	0	0	0	1	1	6
1994	SF	NL	3	2	1	0	2	1	0	0	0	0	0	0	0	0	2	1
1995	SF	NL	17	7	10	11	6	0	0	1	0	0	0	0	0	0	14	3
Total			58	24	34	35	20	3	0	2	0	0	1	0	0	9	30	28

Rank among batters: 886 • Top target (2 home runs): Neal Heaton, John Smiley, Dave Otto, Esteban Loaiza • *Number of pitchers victimized*: 54 • *Total ballparks homered in*: 19 • *First HR*: 09/27/1988 off Don Carman

Bill Carrigan

WILLIAM FRANCIS CARRIGAN
B: 10/22/1883 D: 07/08/1969
BR

Year	Tm	Lg	Tot	H	A	0	1	2	3	2	3	4	LO	XN	IP	PH	RHP	LHP
1909	BOS	AL	1	1	0	0	1	0	0	0	0	0	0	0	0	0	1	0
1910	BOS	AL	3	3	0	1	2	0	0	0	0	0	0	0	0	0	1	2
1911	BOS	AL	1	0	1	0	1	0	0	0	0	0	0	0	0	0	1	0
1914	BOS	AL	1	0	1	0	0	1	0	0	0	0	0	0	0	0	0	1
Total			6	4	2	1	4	1	0	0	0	0	0	0	0	0	3	3

Rank among batters: 2,988 • *Total ballparks homered in*: 3 • *First HR*: 10/02/1909 off Joe Lake

Clay Carroll

CLAY PALMER CARROLL
B: 05/02/1941
BR

Year	Tm	Lg	Tot	H	A	0	1	2	3	2	3	4	LO	XN	IP	PH	RHP	LHP
1969	CIN	NL	1	0	1	1	0	0	0	0	0	0	0	1	0	0	1	0

Rank among batters: 4,707 • *Total ballparks homered in*: 1 • *First HR*: 05/30/1969 off Bob Gibson

Cliff Carroll

SAMUEL CLIFFORD CARROLL
B: 10/18/1859 D: 06/12/1923
BB

Year	Tm	Lg	Tot	H	A	0	1	2	3	2	3	4	LO	XN	IP	PH	RHP	LHP
1883	PRO	NL	1	1	0	1	0	0	0	0	0	0	0	0	0	0	1	0
1884	PRO	NL	3	0	3	2	0	1	0	1	0	0	0	0	0	0	1	0
1885	PRO	NL	1	0	1	1	0	0	0	0	0	0	0	0	0	0	1	0
1886	WAS	NL	2	0	2	1	1	0	0	1	0	0	0	0	0	0	2	0
1887	WAS	NL	4	3	1	2	2	0	0	0	0	0	1	0	0	0	1	2
1890	CHI	NL	7	5	2	3	3	1	0	0	0	0	0	0	0	0	2	3
1891	CHI	NL	7	2	5	3	2	2	0	0	0	0	0	0	0	0	6	0
1892	STL	NL	4	3	1	2	1	1	0	0	0	0	1	0	0	0	3	0
1893	BOS	NL	2	1	1	1	0	1	0	0	0	0	0	0	0	0	2	0
Total			31	15	16	16	9	6	0	2	0	0	2	0	0	0	19	4

Rank among batters: 1,400 • Top target (2 home runs): Tom Lee, Jocko Flynn, Kid Nichols, Kid Gleason • *Number of pitchers victimized*: 27 • *Total ballparks homered in*: 12 • *First HR*: 09/22/1883 off Hugh Daily

Fred Carroll

FREDERICK HERBERT CARROLL
B: 07/02/1864 D: 11/07/1904
BR

Year	Tm	Lg	Tot	H	A	0	1	2	3	2	3	4	LO	XN	IP	PH	RHP	LHP
1884	COL	AA	6	3	3	3	1	2	0	0	0	0	0	0	0	0	4	1
1886	PIT	AA	5	0	5	2	1	2	0	0	0	0	0	0	1	0	2	2
1887	PIT	NL	6	5	1	4	1	1	0	0	0	0	0	0	0	0	2	2

Fred Carroll *continued*

Year	Tm	Lg	Tot	H	A	Men-On 0	1	2	3	One-Game 2	3	4	LO	XN	IP	PH	RHP	LHP
1888	PIT	NL	2	0	2	1	1	0	0	0	0	0	0	0	0	0	2	0
1889	PIT	NL	2	0	2	0	2	0	0	1	0	0	0	0	0	0	2	0
1890	PIT	PL	2	2	0	0	1	1	0	0	0	0	0	0	0	0	1	1
1891	PIT	NL	4	3	1	2	2	0	0	0	0	0	0	0	2	0	4	0
Total			27	13	14	12	9	6	0	1	0	0	0	0	3	0	17	6

Rank among batters: 1,532 • *Top target (3 home runs)*: Pretzels Getzien • *Number of pitchers victimized*: 22 • *Total ballparks homered in*: 12 • *First HR*: 05/03/1884 off Will White • *Hit for Cycle*—vs DET: 05/02/1887

Kid Carsey

WILFRED CARSEY
B: 10/22/1870 D: 03/29/1960
BL

Year	Tm	Lg	Tot	H	A	Men-On 0	1	2	3	One-Game 2	3	4	LO	XN	IP	PH	RHP	LHP
1892	PHI	NL	1	1	0	1	0	0	0	0	0	0	0	0	0	0	1	0
1898	STL	NL	1	0	1	0	0	1	0	0	0	0	0	0	0	0	0	1
Total			2	1	1	1	0	1	0	0	0	0	0	0	0	0	1	1

Rank among batters: 4,129 • *Total ballparks homered in*: 2 • *First HR*: 07/16/1892 off Ben Sanders

Arnold Carter

ARNOLD LEE CARTER
B: 03/14/1918 D: 04/12/1989
BL

Year	Tm	Lg	Tot	H	A	Men-On 0	1	2	3	One-Game 2	3	4	LO	XN	IP	PH	RHP	LHP
1944	CIN	NL	2	0	2	1	1	0	0	0	0	0	0	0	0	0	2	0

Rank among batters: 4,129 • *Total ballparks homered in*: 2 • *First HR*: 07/25/1944 off Ben Cardoni

Blackie Carter

OTIS LEONARD CARTER
B: 09/30/1902 D: 09/10/1976
BR

Year	Tm	Lg	Tot	H	A	Men-On 0	1	2	3	One-Game 2	3	4	LO	XN	IP	PH	RHP	LHP
1926	NY	NL	1	1	0	1	0	0	0	0	0	0	0	0	0	0	1	0

Rank among batters: 4,707 • *Total ballparks homered in*: 1 • *First HR*: 09/25/1926 off Vic Keen

Gary Carter

GARY EDMUND CARTER
B: 04/08/1954
BR

Year	Tm	Lg	Tot	H	A	Men-On 0	1	2	3	One-Game 2	3	4	LO	XN	IP	PH	RHP	LHP
1974	MON	NL	1	1	0	1	0	0	0	0	0	0	0	0	0	0	0	1
1975	MON	NL	17	9	8	7	8	2	0	1	0	0	0	0	0	0	10	7
1976	MON	NL	6	5	1	4	1	1	0	0	0	0	0	0	0	0	5	1
1977	MON	NL	31	22	9	24	5	2	0	4	1	0	0	0	0	0	19	12
1978	MON	NL	20	7	13	13	3	3	1	2	0	0	0	0	0	0	14	6
1979	MON	NL	22	12	10	13	6	2	1	2	0	0	0	0	1	0	18	4
1980	MON	NL	29	12	17	17	9	1	2	3	0	0	0	0	1	0	20	9
1981	MON	NL	16	7	9	9	5	1	1	1	0	0	0	1	0	0	13	3
1982	MON	NL	29	16	13	12	13	4	0	3	0	0	0	0	0	0	18	11
1983	MON	NL	17	6	11	8	8	0	1	2	0	0	0	0	0	0	14	3
1984	MON	NL	27	14	13	15	9	2	1	0	0	0	0	0	0	0	20	7
1985	NY	NL	32	12	20	18	9	3	2	2	1	0	0	2	0	0	19	13
1986	NY	NL	24	13	11	10	7	6	1	3	0	0	0	0	0	0	14	10
1987	NY	NL	20	9	11	10	6	3	1	2	0	0	0	0	0	0	13	7
1988	NY	NL	11	5	6	7	2	2	0	1	0	0	0	0	0	0	6	5
1989	NY	NL	2	1	1	1	0	1	0	0	0	0	0	0	0	0	0	2
1990	SF	NL	9	6	3	7	1	1	0	0	0	0	0	0	0	1	6	3
1991	LA	NL	6	3	3	5	1	0	0	0	0	0	0	0	0	0	3	3
1992	MON	NL	5	2	3	2	3	0	0	0	0	0	0	0	0	0	3	2
Total			324	162	162	183	96	34	11	26	2	0	0	3	2	1	215	109

Rank among batters: 57 • *Top target (11 home runs)*: Steve Carlton • *Number of pitchers victimized*: 205 • *Total ballparks homered in*: 13 • *First HR*: 09/28/1974 off Steve Carlton • *World Series HR*—2; *LCS HR*—2; *All-Star HR*—3

Joe Carter

JOSEPH CHRIS CARTER
B: 03/07/1960
BR

Year	Tm	Lg	Tot	H	A	Men-On 0	1	2	3	One-Game 2	3	4	LO	XN	IP	PH	RHP	LHP
1984	CLE	AL	13	9	4	9	2	1	1	3	0	0	2	0	0	0	5	8
1985	CLE	AL	15	5	10	10	5	0	0	1	0	0	0	0	1	0	10	5

Joe Carter *continued*

Year	Tm	Lg	Tot	H	A	Men-On 0	1	2	3	One-Game 2	3	4	LO	XN	IP	PH	RHP	LHP
1986	CLE	AL	29	14	15	15	10	2	2	2	1	0	0	0	0	0	22	7
1987	CLE	AL	32	9	23	21	6	5	0	3	1	0	0	0	0	0	25	7
1988	CLE	AL	27	16	11	16	6	4	1	4	0	0	0	0	0	0	20	7
1989	CLE	AL	35	16	19	20	13	2	0	4	2	0	0	0	1	0	27	8
1990	SD	NL	24	12	12	10	10	2	2	0	0	0	0	2	0	0	17	7
1991	TOR	AL	33	23	10	19	12	2	0	4	0	0	0	0	0	0	23	10
1992	TOR	AL	34	21	13	14	14	6	0	1	0	0	0	0	0	0	27	7
1993	TOR	AL	33	21	12	19	9	4	1	1	1	0	0	0	0	0	23	10
1994	TOR	AL	27	18	9	10	13	4	0	0	0	0	0	1	0	0	18	9
1995	TOR	AL	25	13	12	16	6	3	0	4	0	0	0	0	0	0	17	8
Total			327	177	150	179	106	35	7	27	5	0	2	3	2	0	234	93

Rank among batters: 54 • *Top target (7 home runs)*: Mike Moore • *Number of pitchers victimized*: 215 • *Total ballparks homered in*: 27 • *First HR*: 06/28/1984 off Frank Tanana • *2 HR in 1 inning*—@BAL: 10/03/1993 • *World Series HR*—4; *LCS HR*—2

Steve Carter

STEVEN JEROME CARTER
B: 12/03/1964
BL

Year	Tm	Lg	Tot	H	A	Men-On 0	1	2	3	One-Game 2	3	4	LO	XN	IP	PH	RHP	LHP
1989	PIT	NL	1	1	0	0	0	1	0	0	0	0	0	0	0	0	1	0

Rank among batters: 4,707 • *Total ballparks homered in*: 1 • *First HR*: 04/30/1989 off Don Robinson

Ed Cartwright

EDWARD CHARLES CARTWRIGHT
B: 10/06/1859 D: 09/03/1933
BR

Year	Tm	Lg	Tot	H	A	Men-On 0	1	2	3	One-Game 2	3	4	LO	XN	IP	PH	RHP	LHP
1890	STL	AA	8	8	0	1	2	4	1	1	0	0	0	0	0	0	2	2
1894	WAS	NL	12	6	6	4	6	2	0	0	0	0	0	0	2	0	9	1
1895	WAS	NL	3	2	1	1	2	0	0	0	0	0	0	0	0	0	1	1
1896	WAS	NL	1	1	0	0	1	0	0	0	0	0	0	0	0	0	0	1
Total			24	17	7	6	11	6	1	1	0	0	0	0	2	0	12	5

Rank among batters: 1,643 • *Top target (2 home runs)*: Ed Green • *Number of pitchers victimized*: 23 • *Total ballparks homered in*: 8 • *First HR*: 07/10/1890 off Mike Morrison • *2 HR in 1 inning*—vs PHI: 09/23/1890 • *Hit for Cycle*—vs BOS: 09/30/1895 (1)

Rico Carty

RICARDO ADOLFO JACOBO CARTY
B: 09/01/1939
BR

Year	Tm	Lg	Tot	H	A	Men-On 0	1	2	3	One-Game 2	3	4	LO	XN	IP	PH	RHP	LHP
1964	MIL	NL	22	17	5	12	7	3	0	2	0	0	3	0	0	0	15	7
1965	MIL	NL	10	6	4	8	2	0	0	0	0	0	0	0	0	0	9	1
1966	ATL	NL	15	8	7	10	3	2	0	0	0	0	0	0	0	0	13	2
1967	ATL	NL	15	12	3	6	2	7	0	1	0	0	0	0	0	0	12	3
1969	ATL	NL	16	13	3	10	4	2	0	2	0	0	0	0	0	1	10	6
1970	ATL	NL	25	19	6	12	8	4	1	1	1	0	0	1	0	0	20	5
1972	ATL	NL	6	4	2	4	1	1	0	0	0	0	0	0	0	0	5	1
1973	TEX	AL	3	2	1	0	2	1	0	0	0	0	0	0	0	0	1	2
	CHI	NL	1	0	1	0	1	0	0	0	0	0	0	0	0	0	1	0
	OAK	AL	1	1	0	1	0	0	0	0	0	0	0	0	0	1	1	0
	Total		5	3	2	1	3	1	0	0	0	0	0	0	0	1	3	2
1974	CLE	AL	1	1	0	0	1	0	0	0	0	0	0	0	0	0	1	0
1975	CLE	AL	18	11	7	11	6	1	0	0	0	0	0	0	0	0	9	9
1976	CLE	AL	13	6	7	9	4	0	0	2	0	0	0	0	0	0	9	4
1977	CLE	AL	15	10	5	6	7	2	0	1	0	0	0	0	0	0	12	3
1978	TOR	AL	20	10	10	10	7	2	1	1	0	0	0	0	0	0	12	8
	OAK	AL	11	4	7	6	5	0	0	0	0	0	0	0	0	0	7	4
	Total		31	14	17	16	12	2	1	1	0	0	0	0	0	0	19	12
1979	TOR	AL	12	8	4	8	3	0	1	0	0	0	0	0	0	2	6	6
Total			204	132	72	113	63	25	3	10	1	0	3	1	0	4	143	61

Rank among batters: 176 • Top target (4 home runs): Bobby Bolin, Ferguson Jenkins, Dock Ellis, Dennis Leonard • *Number of pitchers victimized*: 143 • *Total ballparks homered in*: 28 • *First HR*: 05/12/1964 off Al Jackson

Bob Caruthers

ROBERT LEE CARUTHERS
B: 01/05/1864 D: 08/05/1911
BL

Year	Tm	Lg	Tot	H	A	Men-On 0	1	2	3	One-Game 2	3	4	LO	XN	IP	PH	RHP	LHP
1884	STL	AA	2	1	1	0	2	0	0	0	0	0	0	0	0	0	1	0
1885	STL	AA	1	0	1	0	1	0	0	0	0	0	0	0	0	0	1	0
1886	STL	AA	4	4	0	2	2	0	0	1	0	0	0	0	0	0	3	0

Bob Caruthers *continued*

Year	Tm	Lg	Tot	H	A	Men-On 0	1	2	3	One-Game 2	3	4	LO	XN	IP	PH	RHP	LHP
1887	STL	AA	8	5	3	4	3	0	1	1	0	0	0	0	3	0	7	0
1888	BRO	AA	5	3	2	0	4	1	0	1	0	0	0	0	1	0	5	0
1889	BRO	AA	2	2	0	1	1	0	0	0	0	0	0	0	0	0	2	0
1890	BRO	NL	1	0	1	1	0	0	0	0	0	0	0	0	0	0	1	0
1891	BRO	NL	2	1	1	0	1	1	0	0	0	0	0	0	0	0	2	0
1892	STL	NL	3	1	2	2	1	0	0	0	0	0	0	0	0	0	2	0
1893	CIN	NL	1	0	1	0	1	0	0	0	0	0	0	0	0	0	1	0
Total			29	17	12	10	16	2	1	3	0	0	0	0	4	0	24	0

Rank among batters: 1,465 • *Top target (5 home runs)*: Henry Porter • *Number of pitchers victimized*: 19 • *Total ballparks homered in*: 15 • *First HR*: 09/23/1884 off Jim Conway

Jerry Casale

JERRY JOSEPH CASALE
B: 09/27/1933
BR

Year	Tm	Lg	Tot	H	A	Men-On 0	1	2	3	One-Game 2	3	4	LO	XN	IP	PH	RHP	LHP
1959	BOS	AL	3	2	1	2	0	1	0	0	0	0	0	0	0	0	3	0
1961	LA	AL	1	1	0	0	1	0	0	0	0	0	0	0	0	0	1	0
Total			4	3	1	2	1	1	0	0	0	0	0	0	0	0	4	0

Rank among batters: 3,427 • *Total ballparks homered in*: 3 • *First HR*: 04/15/1959 off Russ Kemmerer

Paul Casanova

PAULINO (ORTIZ) CASANOVA
B: 12/21/1941
BR

Year	Tm	Lg	Tot	H	A	Men-On 0	1	2	3	One-Game 2	3	4	LO	XN	IP	PH	RHP	LHP
1966	WAS	AL	13	8	5	7	5	1	0	1	0	0	0	1	0	0	12	1
1967	WAS	AL	9	4	5	5	1	2	1	0	0	0	0	0	0	0	5	4
1968	WAS	AL	4	0	4	2	1	1	0	0	0	0	0	0	0	0	2	2
1969	WAS	AL	4	3	1	1	3	0	0	0	0	0	0	0	0	1	1	3
1970	WAS	AL	6	4	2	5	1	0	0	0	0	0	0	0	0	0	4	2
1971	WAS	AL	5	4	1	2	3	0	0	0	0	0	0	0	0	0	3	2
1972	ATL	NL	2	2	0	2	0	0	0	0	0	0	0	0	0	0	0	2
1973	ATL	NL	7	1	6	4	3	0	0	0	0	0	0	0	1	1	3	4
Total			50	26	24	28	17	4	1	1	0	0	0	1	1	2	30	20

Rank among batters: 991 • *Top target (3 home runs)*: Mickey Lolich • *Number of pitchers victimized*: 45 • *Total ballparks homered in*: 15 • *First HR*: 05/08/1966 off Fred Talbot

George Case

GEORGE WASHINGTON CASE
B: 11/11/1915 D: 01/23/1989
BR

Year	Tm	Lg	Tot	H	A	Men-On 0	1	2	3	One-Game 2	3	4	LO	XN	IP	PH	RHP	LHP
1938	WAS	AL	2	0	2	2	0	0	0	0	0	0	0	0	0	0	1	1
1939	WAS	AL	2	1	1	1	1	0	0	0	0	0	0	0	1	0	2	0
1940	WAS	AL	5	1	4	1	3	1	0	0	0	0	0	0	0	0	5	0
1941	WAS	AL	2	0	2	0	2	0	0	0	0	0	0	0	0	0	2	0
1942	WAS	AL	5	0	5	5	0	0	0	0	0	0	0	1	0	0	4	1
1943	WAS	AL	1	0	1	1	0	0	0	0	0	0	0	0	0	0	1	0
1944	WAS	AL	2	0	2	2	0	0	0	0	0	0	0	0	0	0	2	0
1945	WAS	AL	1	0	1	1	0	0	0	0	0	0	0	1	0	0	1	0
1946	CLE	AL	1	0	1	1	0	0	0	0	0	0	0	0	0	0	1	0
Total			21	2	19	14	6	1	0	0	0	0	0	2	1	0	19	2

Rank among batters: 1,768 • *Top target (2 home runs)*: Vern Kennedy • *Number of pitchers victimized*: 20 • *Total ballparks homered in*: 7 • *First HR*: 06/17/1938 off Jake Wade

Bob Casey

ORRIN ROBINSON CASEY
B: 01/26/1859 D: 11/28/1936

Year	Tm	Lg	Tot	H	A	Men-On 0	1	2	3	One-Game 2	3	4	LO	XN	IP	PH	RHP	LHP
1882	DET	NL	1	1	0	0	1	0	0	0	0	0	0	0	0	0	1	0

Rank among batters: 4,707 • *Total ballparks homered in*: 1 • *First HR*: 07/25/1882 off Jim Galvin

Dan Casey

DANIEL MAURICE CASEY
B: 11/20/1862 D: 02/08/1943
BR

Year	Tm	Lg	Tot	H	A	Men-On 0	1	2	3	One-Game 2	3	4	LO	XN	IP	PH	RHP	LHP
1887	PHI	NL	1	1	0	0	1	0	0	0	0	0	0	0	1	0	1	0

Rank among batters: 4,707 • *Total ballparks homered in*: 1 • *First HR*: 06/03/1887 off Dick Conway

Dennis Casey

DENNIS PATRICK CASEY
B: 03/30/1858 D: 01/19/1909
BL

Year	Tm	Lg	Tot	H	A	Men-On 0	1	2	3	One-Game 2	3	4	LO	XN	IP	PH	RHP	LHP
1884	BAL	AA	3	2	1	0	2	1	0	0	0	0	0	0	0	0	2	0
1885	BAL	AA	3	1	2	1	1	1	0	0	0	0	0	0	0	0	3	0
Total			6	3	3	1	3	2	0	0	0	0	0	0	0	0	5	0

Rank among batters: 2,988 • *Top target (2 home runs)*: Will White • *Number of pitchers victimized*: 5 • *Total ballparks homered in*: 2 • *First HR*: 08/22/1884 off Fleury Sullivan

Doc Casey

JAMES PATRICK CASEY
B: 03/15/1870 D: 12/31/1936
BB

Year	Tm	Lg	Tot	H	A	Men-On 0	1	2	3	One-Game 2	3	4	LO	XN	IP	PH	RHP	LHP
1899	BRO	NL	1	0	1	0	1	0	0	0	0	0	0	0	0	0	1	0
1901	DET	AL	2	0	2	2	0	0	0	0	0	0	0	0	0	0	1	1
1902	DET	AL	3	1	2	2	0	1	0	0	0	0	0	0	1	0	2	1
1903	CHI	NL	1	0	1	0	1	0	0	0	0	0	0	0	0	0	0	1
1904	CHI	NL	1	0	1	0	1	0	0	0	0	0	0	0	0	0	1	0
1905	CHI	NL	1	0	1	0	1	0	0	0	0	0	0	0	1	0	1	0
Total			9	1	8	4	4	1	0	0	0	0	0	0	2	0	6	3

Rank among batters: 2,587 • *Total ballparks homered in*: 8 • *First HR*: 07/26/1899 off Walt Woods

Dave Cash

DAVID CASH
B: 06/11/1948
BR

Year	Tm	Lg	Tot	H	A	Men-On 0	1	2	3	One-Game 2	3	4	LO	XN	IP	PH	RHP	LHP
1970	PIT	NL	1	1	0	1	0	0	0	0	0	0	0	0	0	0	1	0
1971	PIT	NL	2	2	0	1	1	0	0	0	0	0	0	0	0	0	1	1
1972	PIT	NL	3	1	2	2	0	1	0	0	0	0	0	0	0	0	1	2
1973	PIT	NL	2	0	2	1	0	1	0	0	0	0	0	0	0	0	2	0
1974	PHI	NL	2	0	2	2	0	0	0	0	0	0	1	0	0	0	0	2
1975	PHI	NL	4	3	1	3	1	0	0	0	0	0	1	0	0	0	2	2
1976	PHI	NL	1	1	0	1	0	0	0	0	0	0	0	0	1	0	1	0
1978	MON	NL	3	1	2	2	0	1	0	0	0	0	1	0	0	0	0	3
1979	MON	NL	2	1	1	1	0	0	1	0	0	0	0	1	0	0	2	0
1980	SD	NL	1	0	1	1	0	0	0	0	0	0	0	0	0	0	0	1
Total			21	10	11	15	2	3	1	0	0	0	3	1	1	0	10	11

Rank among batters: 1,768 • *Top target (2 home runs)*: Fred Norman, Don Sutton • *Number of pitchers victimized*: 19 • *Total ballparks homered in*: 8 • *First HR*: 07/19/1970 off Jim McGlothlin

Norm Cash

NORMAN DALTON CASH
B: 11/10/1934 D: 10/12/1986
BL

Year	Tm	Lg	Tot	H	A	Men-On 0	1	2	3	One-Game 2	3	4	LO	XN	IP	PH	RHP	LHP
1959	CHI	AL	4	3	1	1	2	1	0	0	0	0	0	0	0	1	4	0
1960	DET	AL	18	13	5	12	5	0	1	0	0	0	0	0	0	3	17	1
1961	DET	AL	41	21	20	22	14	3	2	3	0	0	0	0	1	0	36	5
1962	DET	AL	39	25	14	24	11	4	0	4	0	0	0	0	0	0	33	6
1963	DET	AL	26	19	7	15	6	4	1	1	0	0	0	0	0	0	22	4
1964	DET	AL	23	14	9	12	9	2	0	2	0	0	0	0	0	0	21	2
1965	DET	AL	30	17	13	16	9	5	0	1	0	0	0	1	1	0	22	8
1966	DET	AL	32	18	14	18	10	3	1	1	0	0	0	2	0	1	19	13
1967	DET	AL	22	10	12	13	8	0	1	1	0	0	0	0	0	0	19	3
1968	DET	AL	25	19	6	16	6	3	0	3	0	0	0	0	0	1	21	4
1969	DET	AL	22	11	11	11	9	2	0	1	0	0	0	0	0	1	18	4
1970	DET	AL	15	7	8	5	8	2	0	1	0	0	0	0	0	1	13	2
1971	DET	AL	32	14	18	16	10	4	2	5	0	0	0	0	0	0	24	8
1972	DET	AL	22	11	11	15	4	3	0	1	0	0	0	0	0	0	21	1
1973	DET	AL	19	8	11	13	6	0	0	1	0	0	0	0	0	1	19	0
1974	DET	AL	7	4	3	5	2	0	0	0	0	0	0	0	0	0	7	0
Total			377	214	163	214	119	36	8	25	0	0	0	3	2	9	316	61

Rank among batters: 35 • *Top target (9 home runs)*: Bill Monbouquette • *Number of pitchers victimized*: 207 • *Total ballparks homered in*: 18 • *First HR*: 04/12/1959 off Frank Lary • *World Series HR*—1; *LCS HR*—1

Year	Tm	Lg	Tot	H	A	Men-On 0	Men-On 1	Men-On 2	Men-On 3	One-Game 2	One-Game 3	One-Game 4	LO	XN	IP	PH	RHP	LHP

Carl Cashion

JAY CARL CASHION
B: 06/06/1891 D: 11/17/1935
BL

Year	Tm	Lg	Tot	H	A	0	1	2	3	2	3	4	LO	XN	IP	PH	RHP	LHP
1912	WAS	AL	2	2	0	2	0	0	0	0	0	0	0	0	1	0	2	0

Rank among batters: 4,129 • *Total ballparks homered in*: 1 • *First HR*: 05/04/1912 off Hugh Bedient

Ed Caskin

EDWARD JAMES CASKIN
B: 12/30/1851 D: 10/09/1924
BR

Year	Tm	Lg	Tot	H	A	0	1	2	3	2	3	4	LO	XN	IP	PH	RHP	LHP
1883	NY	NL	1	1	0	1	0	0	0	0	0	0	0	0	0	0	1	0
1884	NY	NL	1	0	1	0	0	1	0	0	0	0	0	0	0	0	1	0
Total			2	1	1	1	0	1	0	0	0	0	0	0	0	0	2	0

Rank among batters: 4,129 • *Total ballparks homered in*: 2 • *First HR*: 09/04/1883 off Jim Whitney

Joe Cassidy

JOSEPH PHILLIP CASSIDY
B: 02/08/1883 D: 03/25/1906
BR

Year	Tm	Lg	Tot	H	A	0	1	2	3	2	3	4	LO	XN	IP	PH	RHP	LHP
1904	WAS	AL	1	0	1	1	0	0	0	0	0	0	0	0	1	0	1	0
1905	WAS	AL	1	0	1	1	0	0	0	0	0	0	1	0	0	0	0	1
Total			2	0	2	2	0	0	0	0	0	0	1	0	1	0	1	1

Rank among batters: 4,129 • *Total ballparks homered in*: 2 • *First HR*: 06/01/1904 off Jack Chesbro

John Cassidy

JOHN P. CASSIDY
B: 1855 D: 07/03/1891
BR

Year	Tm	Lg	Tot	H	A	0	1	2	3	2	3	4	LO	XN	IP	PH	RHP	LHP
1881	TRO	NL	1	1	0	1	0	0	0	0	0	0	0	0	0	0	1	0
1884	BRO	AA	2	2	0	0	1	1	0	0	0	0	0	0	0	0	1	0
1885	BRO	AA	1	0	1	0	1	0	0	0	0	0	0	0	0	0	0	0
Total			4	3	1	1	2	1	0	0	0	0	0	0	0	0	2	0

Rank among batters: 3,427 • *Total ballparks homered in*: 3 • *First HR*: 07/25/1881 off Monte Ward

Pete Cassidy

PETER FRANCIS CASSIDY
B: 04/08/1873 D: 07/09/1929
BR

Year	Tm	Lg	Tot	H	A	0	1	2	3	2	3	4	LO	XN	IP	PH	RHP	LHP
1899	WAS	NL	3	3	0	1	1	0	1	0	0	0	0	0	2	0	3	0

Rank among batters: 3,735 • *Total ballparks homered in*: 1 • *First HR*: 04/28/1899 off Bill Carrick

Pedro Castellano

PEDRO ORLANDO (ARRIETA) CASTELLANO
B: 03/11/1970
BR

Year	Tm	Lg	Tot	H	A	0	1	2	3	2	3	4	LO	XN	IP	PH	RHP	LHP
1993	COL	NL	3	1	2	2	1	0	0	0	0	0	0	0	0	0	3	0

Rank among batters: 3,735 • *Total ballparks homered in*: 3 • *First HR*: 07/27/1993 off John Smoltz

Pete Castiglione

PETER PAUL CASTIGLIONE
B: 02/13/1921
BR

Year	Tm	Lg	Tot	H	A	0	1	2	3	2	3	4	LO	XN	IP	PH	RHP	LHP
1949	PIT	NL	6	4	2	2	3	1	0	0	0	0	0	0	0	0	5	1
1950	PIT	NL	3	1	2	3	0	0	0	0	0	0	1	1	0	1	2	1
1951	PIT	NL	7	2	5	4	3	0	0	1	0	0	1	0	0	0	7	0
1952	PIT	NL	4	2	2	4	0	0	0	0	0	0	0	0	0	0	3	1
1953	PIT	NL	4	2	2	3	1	0	0	1	0	0	0	0	0	0	3	1
Total			24	11	13	16	7	1	0	2	0	0	2	1	0	1	20	4

Rank among batters: 1,643 • *Top target (3 home runs)*: Don Newcombe • *Number of pitchers victimized*: 17 • *Total ballparks homered in*: 6 • *First HR*: 05/25/1949 off Rex Barney

Year	Tm	Lg	Tot	H	A	Men-On 0	Men-On 1	Men-On 2	Men-On 3	One-Game 2	One-Game 3	One-Game 4	LO	XN	IP	PH	RHP	LHP

Vinny Castilla

VINICIO (SORIA) CASTILLA
B: 07/04/1967
BR

Year	Tm	Lg	Tot	H	A	0	1	2	3	2	3	4	LO	XN	IP	PH	RHP	LHP
1993	COL	NL	9	5	4	6	3	0	0	1	0	0	0	0	0	0	6	3
1994	COL	NL	3	1	2	2	1	0	0	0	0	0	0	0	0	0	3	0
1995	COL	NL	32	23	9	24	8	0	0	6	0	0	0	0	0	0	20	12
Total			44	29	15	32	12	0	0	7	0	0	0	0	0	0	29	15

Rank among batters: 1,095 • Top target (2 home runs): Tim Pugh, Kevin Jarvis, Paul Wagner, Hector Carrasco, Jason Isringhausen, Butch Henry, Turk Wendell • *Number of pitchers victimized*: 37 • *Total ballparks homered in*: 11 • *First HR*: 04/27/1993 off Dan Plesac • *LCS HR*—3

Braulio Castillo

BRAULIO ROBINSON MEDRANO CASTILLO
B: 05/13/1968
BR

Year	Tm	Lg	Tot	H	A	0	1	2	3	2	3	4	LO	XN	IP	PH	RHP	LHP
1992	PHI	NL	2	1	1	1	0	1	0	0	0	0	0	0	0	0	1	1

Rank among batters: 4,129 • *Total ballparks homered in*: 2 • *First HR*: 09/14/1992 off Brian Barnes

Carmen Castillo

MONTE CARMELO CASTILLO
B: 06/08/1958
BR

Year	Tm	Lg	Tot	H	A	0	1	2	3	2	3	4	LO	XN	IP	PH	RHP	LHP
1982	CLE	AL	2	2	0	1	1	0	0	0	0	0	0	0	0	0	2	0
1983	CLE	AL	1	1	0	1	0	0	0	0	0	0	0	0	0	0	0	1
1984	CLE	AL	10	7	3	6	3	0	1	0	0	0	0	0	0	0	3	7
1985	CLE	AL	11	4	7	7	2	2	0	1	0	0	0	0	0	0	2	9
1986	CLE	AL	8	4	4	2	6	0	0	0	0	0	0	0	0	0	3	5
1987	CLE	AL	11	8	3	9	1	1	0	0	0	0	0	0	0	1	4	7
1988	CLE	AL	4	2	2	3	1	0	0	0	0	0	0	0	0	0	2	2
1989	MIN	AL	8	2	6	5	2	0	1	2	0	0	0	0	0	1	0	8
Total			55	30	25	34	16	3	2	3	0	0	0	0	0	2	16	39

Rank among batters: 926 • *Top target (3 home runs)*: Mike Mason, Roger Clemens • *Number of pitchers victimized*: 42 • *Total ballparks homered in*: 14 • *First HR*: 07/28/1982 off Bill Castro

Juan Castillo

JUAN (BRAYAS) CASTILLO
B: 01/25/1962
BB

Year	Tm	Lg	Tot	H	A	0	1	2	3	2	3	4	LO	XN	IP	PH	RHP	LHP
1987	MIL	AL	3	3	0	2	1	0	0	0	0	0	1	0	0	0	2	1

Rank among batters: 3,735 • *Total ballparks homered in*: 1 • *First HR*: 04/26/1987 off Mike Flanagan

Manny Castillo

ESTEBAN MANUEL ANTONIO (CABRERA) CASTILLO
B: 04/01/1957
BB

Year	Tm	Lg	Tot	H	A	0	1	2	3	2	3	4	LO	XN	IP	PH	RHP	LHP
1982	SEA	AL	3	3	0	3	0	0	0	0	0	0	0	0	0	0	3	0

Rank among batters: 3,735 • *Total ballparks homered in*: 1 • *First HR*: 08/26/1982 off Jack Morris

Marty Castillo

MARTIN HORACE CASTILLO
B: 01/16/1957
BR

Year	Tm	Lg	Tot	H	A	0	1	2	3	2	3	4	LO	XN	IP	PH	RHP	LHP
1983	DET	AL	2	0	2	1	1	0	0	0	0	0	0	0	0	0	1	1
1984	DET	AL	4	2	2	4	0	0	0	0	0	0	0	0	0	0	3	1
1985	DET	AL	2	2	0	2	0	0	0	0	0	0	0	0	0	0	1	1
Total			8	4	4	7	1	0	0	0	0	0	0	0	0	0	5	3

Rank among batters: 2,703 • *Total ballparks homered in*: 4 • *First HR*: 06/28/1983 off Jim Slaton • *World Series HR*—1

John Castino

JOHN ANTHONY CASTINO
B: 10/23/1954
BR

Year	Tm	Lg	Tot	H	A	0	1	2	3	2	3	4	LO	XN	IP	PH	RHP	LHP
1979	MIN	AL	5	4	1	3	2	0	0	0	0	0	0	0	1	0	1	4
1980	MIN	AL	13	7	6	10	3	0	0	0	0	0	1	0	0	0	7	6

John Castino *continued*

Year	Tm	Lg	Tot	H	A	Men-On 0	1	2	3	One-Game 2	3	4	LO	XN	IP	PH	RHP	LHP
1981	MIN	AL	6	3	3	3	3	0	0	0	0	0	0	0	0	0	5	1
1982	MIN	AL	6	2	4	5	1	0	0	0	0	0	0	0	0	0	5	1
1983	MIN	AL	11	4	7	8	1	2	0	0	0	0	0	0	0	0	8	3
Total			41	20	21	29	10	2	0	0	0	0	1	0	1	0	26	15

Rank among batters: 1,163 • *Top target (2 home runs)*: Rich Gale, Gaylord Perry • *Number of pitchers victimized*: 39 • *Total ballparks homered in*: 12 • *First HR*: 05/15/1979 off Sparky Lyle

Vince Castino

VINCENT CHARLES CASTINO
B: 10/11/1917 D: 03/06/1967
BR

Year	Tm	Lg	Tot	H	A	Men-On 0	1	2	3	One-Game 2	3	4	LO	XN	IP	PH	RHP	LHP
1943	CHI	AL	2	1	1	1	0	0	1	0	0	0	0	0	0	0	1	1

Rank among batters: 4,129 • *Total ballparks homered in*: 2 • *First HR*: 07/23/1943 off Dick Newsome

Foster Castleman

FOSTER EPHRAIM CASTLEMAN
B: 01/01/1931
BR

Year	Tm	Lg	Tot	H	A	Men-On 0	1	2	3	One-Game 2	3	4	LO	XN	IP	PH	RHP	LHP
1955	NY	NL	2	2	0	2	0	0	0	0	0	0	0	0	0	0	1	1
1956	NY	NL	14	8	6	10	2	2	0	1	0	0	1	0	0	1	8	6
1957	NY	NL	1	0	1	1	0	0	0	0	0	0	0	0	0	1	1	0
1958	BAL	AL	3	0	3	1	1	1	0	0	0	0	0	0	0	0	3	0
Total			20	10	10	14	3	3	0	1	0	0	1	0	0	2	13	7

Rank among batters: 1,810 • *Top target (2 home runs)*: Sam Jones, Don Kaiser • *Number of pitchers victimized*: 18 • *Total ballparks homered in*: 7 • *First HR*: 05/04/1955 off Sam Jones

Slick Castleman

CLYDELL CASTLEMAN
B: 09/08/1913
BR

Year	Tm	Lg	Tot	H	A	Men-On 0	1	2	3	One-Game 2	3	4	LO	XN	IP	PH	RHP	LHP
1935	NY	NL	1	0	1	0	0	1	0	0	0	0	0	0	0	0	0	1
1936	NY	NL	1	1	0	0	1	0	0	0	0	0	0	0	0	0	0	1
Total			2	1	1	0	1	1	0	0	0	0	0	0	0	0	0	2

Rank among batters: 4,129 • *Total ballparks homered in*: 2 • *First HR*: 07/04/1935 off Ed Brandt

Louis Castro

LUIS MANUEL CASTRO
B: 1877 BR

Year	Tm	Lg	Tot	H	A	Men-On 0	1	2	3	One-Game 2	3	4	LO	XN	IP	PH	RHP	LHP
1902	PHI	AL	1	1	0	1	0	0	0	0	0	0	0	0	0	0	1	0

Rank among batters: 4,707 • *Total ballparks homered in*: 1 • *First HR*: 05/30/1902 off Jack Powell

Danny Cater

DANNY ANDERSON CATER
B: 02/25/1940
BR

Year	Tm	Lg	Tot	H	A	Men-On 0	1	2	3	One-Game 2	3	4	LO	XN	IP	PH	RHP	LHP
1964	PHI	NL	1	0	1	0	1	0	0	0	0	0	0	0	0	0	0	1
1965	CHI	AL	14	5	9	9	3	2	0	0	0	0	0	2	0	0	11	3
1966	KC	AL	7	1	6	3	0	4	0	0	0	0	0	0	0	0	4	3
1967	KC	AL	4	1	3	2	2	0	0	0	0	0	0	0	0	0	2	2
1968	OAK	AL	6	2	4	3	2	1	0	0	0	0	0	0	0	0	2	4
1969	OAK	AL	10	5	5	6	2	1	1	0	0	0	0	0	0	0	6	4
1970	NY	AL	6	3	3	0	5	1	0	0	0	0	0	0	0	0	4	2
1971	NY	AL	4	0	4	3	0	1	0	0	0	0	0	0	0	0	2	2
1972	BOS	AL	8	6	2	5	2	1	0	0	0	0	0	0	0	0	5	3
1973	BOS	AL	1	1	0	0	0	1	0	0	0	0	0	0	0	0	1	0
1974	BOS	AL	5	0	5	4	1	0	0	0	0	0	0	0	0	0	2	3
Total			66	24	42	35	18	12	1	0	0	0	0	2	0	0	39	27

Rank among batters: 786 • *Top target (3 home runs)*: Dave Boswell, Jim Kaat, Mickey Lolich • *Number of pitchers victimized*: 54 • *Total ballparks homered in*: 12 • *First HR*: 06/18/1964 off Dick Ellsworth

Year	Tm	Lg	Tot	H	A	Men-On 0	1	2	3	One-Game 2	3	4	LO	XN	IP	PH	RHP	LHP

Ted Cather

THEODORE PHYSICK CATHER
B: 05/20/1889 D: 04/09/1945
BR

Year	Tm	Lg	Tot	H	A	0	1	2	3	2	3	4	LO	XN	IP	PH	RHP	LHP
1915	BOS	NL	2	0	2	0	2	0	0	0	0	0	0	0	0	0	0	2

Rank among batters: 4,129 • *Top target (2 home runs)*: Rube Marquard • *Number of pitchers victimized*: 1 • *Total ballparks homered in*: 1 • *First HR*: 04/29/1915 off Rube Marquard

Tom Catterson

THOMAS HENRY CATTERSON
B: 08/25/1884 D: 02/05/1920
BL

Year	Tm	Lg	Tot	H	A	0	1	2	3	2	3	4	LO	XN	IP	PH	RHP	LHP
1908	BRO	NL	1	1	0	1	0	0	0	0	0	0	0	1	0	0	1	0

Rank among batters: 4,707 • *Total ballparks homered in*: 1 • *First HR*: 09/22/1908 off Nick Maddox

Wayne Causey

JAMES WAYNE CAUSEY
B: 12/26/1936
BL

Year	Tm	Lg	Tot	H	A	0	1	2	3	2	3	4	LO	XN	IP	PH	RHP	LHP
1955	BAL	AL	1	1	0	1	0	0	0	0	0	0	0	0	0	0	1	0
1956	BAL	AL	1	1	0	1	0	0	0	0	0	0	0	0	0	1	1	0
1961	KC	AL	8	3	5	4	3	0	1	0	0	0	0	0	0	0	7	1
1962	KC	AL	4	4	0	2	2	0	0	0	0	0	0	0	0	0	4	0
1963	KC	AL	8	4	4	7	1	0	0	1	0	0	1	0	0	0	7	1
1964	KC	AL	8	4	4	5	1	2	0	0	0	0	0	0	0	0	7	1
1965	KC	AL	3	3	0	3	0	0	0	0	0	0	0	0	0	0	3	0
1967	CHI	AL	1	0	1	0	0	1	0	0	0	0	0	0	0	0	1	0
1968	ATL	NL	1	1	0	1	0	0	0	0	0	0	0	0	0	0	1	0
Total			35	21	14	24	7	3	1	1	0	0	1	0	0	1	32	3

Rank among batters: 1,291 • *Top target (2 home runs)*: Bennie Daniels, Milt Pappas • *Number of pitchers victimized*: 33 • *Total ballparks homered in*: 8 • *First HR*: 06/17/1955 off Steve Gromek

Phil Cavarretta

PHILIP JOSEPH CAVARRETTA
B: 07/19/1916
BL

Year	Tm	Lg	Tot	H	A	0	1	2	3	2	3	4	LO	XN	IP	PH	RHP	LHP
1934	CHI	NL	1	1	0	1	0	0	0	0	0	0	0	0	0	0	1	0
1935	CHI	NL	8	4	4	8	0	0	0	0	0	0	0	1	0	0	8	0
1936	CHI	NL	9	5	4	7	1	0	1	1	0	0	0	0	0	0	7	2
1937	CHI	NL	6	2	4	5	1	0	0	0	0	0	0	0	0	0	5	1
1938	CHI	NL	1	0	1	0	1	0	0	0	0	0	0	0	0	0	1	0
1940	CHI	NL	2	0	2	1	1	0	0	0	0	0	0	0	0	0	2	0
1941	CHI	NL	6	2	4	5	1	0	0	0	0	0	0	0	0	0	6	0
1942	CHI	NL	3	2	1	2	1	0	0	0	0	0	0	0	0	0	3	0
1943	CHI	NL	8	6	2	4	3	1	0	0	0	0	0	1	0	0	6	2
1944	CHI	NL	5	1	4	1	3	1	0	0	0	0	0	0	0	0	4	1
1945	CHI	NL	6	2	4	2	3	0	1	0	0	0	0	0	0	0	6	0
1946	CHI	NL	8	3	5	4	3	1	0	0	0	0	0	0	0	0	6	2
1947	CHI	NL	2	0	2	1	1	0	0	0	0	0	0	0	1	0	1	1
1948	CHI	NL	3	0	3	2	1	0	0	0	0	0	0	0	0	0	3	0
1949	CHI	NL	8	2	6	6	2	0	0	0	0	0	0	0	0	0	8	0
1950	CHI	NL	10	4	6	8	0	2	0	0	0	0	0	0	0	1	6	4
1951	CHI	NL	6	2	4	3	2	0	1	0	0	0	0	0	0	1	6	0
1952	CHI	NL	1	1	0	0	1	0	0	0	0	0	0	0	0	1	1	0
1954	CHI	AL	3	3	0	1	1	0	1	0	0	0	0	0	0	1	3	0
Total			96	40	56	61	26	5	4	1	0	0	0	2	1	4	83	13

Rank among batters: 520 • *Top target (5 home runs)*: Hal Schumacher • *Number of pitchers victimized*: 79 • *Total ballparks homered in*: 10 • *First HR*: 09/25/1934 off Whitey Wistert • *World Series HR*—1

Ike Caveney

JAMES CHRISTOPHER CAVENEY
B: 12/10/1894 D: 07/06/1949
BR

Year	Tm	Lg	Tot	H	A	0	1	2	3	2	3	4	LO	XN	IP	PH	RHP	LHP
1922	CIN	NL	3	0	3	1	2	0	0	0	0	0	0	0	0	0	2	1
1923	CIN	NL	4	1	3	0	2	2	0	0	0	0	0	0	1	0	3	1
1924	CIN	NL	4	0	4	3	0	1	0	0	0	0	0	0	0	0	4	0

Ike Caveney *continued*

Year	Tm	Lg	Tot	H	A	Men-On 0	1	2	3	One-Game 2	3	4	LO	XN	IP	PH	RHP	LHP
1925	CIN	NL	2	1	1	0	1	1	0	0	0	0	0	0	1	0	2	0
Total			13	2	11	4	5	4	0	0	0	0	0	0	2	0	11	2

Rank among batters: 2,248 • *Top target (2 home runs)*: Tony Kaufmann • *Number of pitchers victimized*: 12 • *Total ballparks homered in*: 6 • *First HR*: 06/02/1922 off Percy Jones

Andujar Cedeno

ANDUJAR (DONASTORG) CEDENO
B: 08/21/1969
BR

Year	Tm	Lg	Tot	H	A	Men-On 0	1	2	3	One-Game 2	3	4	LO	XN	IP	PH	RHP	LHP
1991	HOU	NL	9	4	5	5	3	1	0	0	0	0	0	0	0	0	9	0
1992	HOU	NL	2	2	0	2	0	0	0	0	0	0	0	0	0	0	2	0
1993	HOU	NL	11	6	5	8	3	0	0	0	0	0	0	0	0	0	7	4
1994	HOU	NL	9	5	4	6	2	1	0	0	0	0	0	0	0	1	6	3
1995	SD	NL	6	3	3	2	2	2	0	1	0	0	0	0	0	0	4	2
Total			37	20	17	23	10	4	0	1	0	0	0	0	0	1	28	9

Rank among batters: 1,252 • *Top target (3 home runs)*: Andy Benes, Zane Smith • *Number of pitchers victimized*: 29 • *Total ballparks homered in*: 8 • *First HR*: 08/02/1991 off Jim Gott • *Hit for Cycle*—vs STL: 08/25/1992

Cesar Cedeno

CESAR (ENCARNACION) CEDENO
B: 02/25/1951
BR

Year	Tm	Lg	Tot	H	A	Men-On 0	1	2	3	One-Game 2	3	4	LO	XN	IP	PH	RHP	LHP
1970	HOU	NL	7	2	5	3	3	1	0	0	0	0	0	0	0	0	5	2
1971	HOU	NL	10	4	6	2	6	1	1	0	0	0	0	0	2	0	8	2
1972	HOU	NL	22	10	12	15	6	1	0	0	0	0	0	0	1	0	15	7
1973	HOU	NL	25	9	16	13	9	2	1	2	0	0	0	0	0	0	18	7
1974	HOU	NL	26	12	14	14	6	5	1	2	0	0	0	0	0	0	22	4
1975	HOU	NL	13	6	7	7	4	2	0	2	0	0	0	1	0	0	9	4
1976	HOU	NL	18	8	10	9	6	3	0	0	0	0	0	1	0	0	11	7
1977	HOU	NL	14	5	9	9	4	1	0	2	0	0	1	0	0	0	7	7
1978	HOU	NL	7	3	4	6	1	0	0	0	0	0	0	0	0	0	4	3
1979	HOU	NL	6	2	4	3	0	3	0	0	0	0	0	0	0	0	5	1
1980	HOU	NL	10	2	8	6	3	0	1	0	0	0	0	1	0	0	5	5
1981	HOU	NL	5	1	4	3	1	1	0	0	0	0	0	0	0	0	3	2
1982	CIN	NL	8	6	2	5	2	1	0	1	0	0	0	0	0	0	4	4
1983	CIN	NL	9	7	2	5	4	0	0	0	0	0	0	0	0	2	4	5
1984	CIN	NL	10	5	5	4	6	0	0	1	0	0	0	0	0	1	3	7
1985	CIN	NL	3	2	1	1	1	1	0	0	0	0	0	1	0	0	1	2
	STL	NL	6	3	3	3	2	0	1	0	0	0	0	1	0	1	3	3
	Total		9	5	4	4	3	1	1	0	0	0	0	2	0	1	4	5
Total			199	87	112	108	64	22	5	10	0	0	1	5	3	4	127	72

Rank among batters: 187 • *Top target (5 home runs)*: Jack Billingham, Tom Seaver • *Number of pitchers victimized*: 131 • *Total ballparks homered in*: 13 • *First HR*: 07/06/1970 off Claude Osteen • *Hit for Cycle*—vs CIN: 08/02/1972; @STL: 08/09/1976 • *All-Star HR*—1

Domingo Cedeno

DOMINGO ANTONIO (DONASTORG) CEDENO
B: 11/04/1968
BB

Year	Tm	Lg	Tot	H	A	Men-On 0	1	2	3	One-Game 2	3	4	LO	XN	IP	PH	RHP	LHP
1995	TOR	AL	4	1	3	1	0	3	0	0	0	0	0	0	0	0	2	2

Rank among batters: 3,427 • *Total ballparks homered in*: 3 • *First HR*: 05/17/1995 off Kevin Gross

Orlando Cepeda

ORLANDO MANUEL (PENNE) CEPEDA
B: 09/17/1937
BR

Year	Tm	Lg	Tot	H	A	Men-On 0	1	2	3	One-Game 2	3	4	LO	XN	IP	PH	RHP	LHP
1958	SF	NL	25	13	12	16	4	5	0	2	0	0	0	1	1	0	19	6
1959	SF	NL	27	13	14	16	8	3	0	3	0	0	0	1	0	0	22	5
1960	SF	NL	24	10	14	13	10	1	0	0	0	0	0	1	0	0	15	9
1961	SF	NL	46	24	22	25	11	8	2	1	0	0	0	1	0	0	29	17
1962	SF	NL	35	18	17	22	10	3	0	4	0	0	0	0	0	0	21	14
1963	SF	NL	34	13	21	26	2	6	0	2	0	0	0	0	0	1	22	12
1964	SF	NL	31	19	12	15	12	3	1	2	0	0	0	0	0	0	22	9
1965	SF	NL	1	1	0	0	1	0	0	0	0	0	0	0	0	1	0	1

Orlando Cepeda *continued*

Year	Tm	Lg	Tot	H	A	Men-On 0	1	2	3	One-Game 2	3	4	LO	XN	IP	PH	RHP	LHP
1966	SF	NL	3	1	2	0	2	0	1	0	0	0	0	0	0	0	2	1
	STL	NL	17	8	9	14	2	1	0	1	0	0	0	0	0	0	10	7
	Total		20	9	11	14	4	1	1	1	0	0	0	0	0	0	12	8
1967	STL	NL	25	8	17	13	9	3	0	2	0	0	0	0	1	0	14	11
1968	STL	NL	16	9	7	9	5	2	0	0	0	0	0	0	0	0	9	7
1969	ATL	NL	22	10	12	13	4	4	1	0	0	0	0	0	0	0	20	2
1970	ATL	NL	34	14	20	15	13	4	2	2	1	0	0	0	0	0	30	4
1971	ATL	NL	14	9	5	9	3	1	1	1	0	0	0	1	0	0	8	6
1972	ATL	NL	4	1	3	3	0	1	0	1	0	0	0	0	0	0	1	3
1973	BOS	AL	20	11	9	10	6	3	1	1	0	0	0	0	0	0	14	6
1974	KC	AL	1	0	1	1	0	0	0	0	0	0	0	0	0	0	0	1
Total			379	182	197	220	102	48	9	22	1	0	0	5	2	2	258	121

Rank among batters: 33 • *Top target (10 home runs)*: Warren Spahn, Lew Burdette • *Number of pitchers victimized*: 187 • *Total ballparks homered in*: 26 • *First HR*: 04/15/1958 off Don Bessent • *World Series HR—2; LCS HR—1*

Rick Cerone

RICHARD ALDO CERONE
B: 05/19/1954
BR

Year	Tm	Lg	Tot	H	A	Men-On 0	1	2	3	One-Game 2	3	4	LO	XN	IP	PH	RHP	LHP
1977	TOR	AL	1	0	1	1	0	0	0	0	0	0	0	0	0	0	1	0
1978	TOR	AL	3	2	1	2	1	0	0	0	0	0	0	0	0	0	1	2
1979	TOR	AL	7	3	4	2	3	2	0	0	0	0	0	0	0	0	3	4
1980	NY	AL	14	7	7	5	4	4	1	1	0	0	0	1	1	0	11	3
1981	NY	AL	2	2	0	1	1	0	0	0	0	0	0	0	0	0	1	1
1982	NY	AL	5	1	4	3	1	1	0	0	0	0	0	0	0	0	3	2
1983	NY	AL	2	0	2	1	0	1	0	0	0	0	0	0	0	0	2	0
1984	NY	AL	2	0	2	0	1	1	0	0	0	0	0	0	0	0	1	1
1985	ATL	NL	3	3	0	1	1	1	0	0	0	0	0	0	0	0	2	1
1986	MIL	AL	4	3	1	4	0	0	0	0	0	0	0	0	0	0	3	1
1987	NY	AL	4	1	3	3	1	0	0	0	0	0	0	0	0	0	3	1
1988	BOS	AL	3	3	0	1	2	0	0	0	0	0	0	0	0	0	2	1
1989	BOS	AL	4	2	2	1	3	0	0	0	0	0	0	0	0	0	2	2
1990	NY	AL	2	1	1	1	1	0	0	0	0	0	0	0	0	0	1	1
1991	NY	NL	2	1	1	2	0	0	0	0	0	0	0	0	0	0	2	0
1992	MON	NL	1	1	0	1	0	0	0	0	0	0	0	0	0	0	0	1
Total			59	30	29	29	19	10	1	1	0	0	0	1	1	0	38	21

Rank among batters: 873 • Top target (2 home runs): John Verhoeven, Steve Trout, Larry Gura, Mike Smithson, Nolan Ryan • *Number of pitchers victimized*: 54 • *Total ballparks homered in*: 17 • *First HR*: 08/17/1977 off Nelson Briles • *World Series HR—1; LCS HR—2*

Bob Cerv

ROBERT HENRY CERV
B: 05/05/1926
BR

Year	Tm	Lg	Tot	H	A	Men-On 0	1	2	3	One-Game 2	3	4	LO	XN	IP	PH	RHP	LHP
1952	NY	AL	1	0	1	0	0	1	0	0	0	0	0	0	0	0	0	1
1954	NY	AL	5	1	4	2	2	1	0	1	0	0	1	0	0	1	3	2
1955	NY	AL	3	1	2	3	0	0	0	0	0	0	1	0	0	2	2	1
1956	NY	AL	3	1	2	1	1	0	1	0	0	0	0	0	0	0	1	2
1957	KC	AL	11	7	4	8	3	0	0	0	0	0	0	0	0	3	11	0
1958	KC	AL	38	21	17	20	13	5	0	4	0	0	0	0	1	1	31	7
1959	KC	AL	20	14	6	9	7	3	1	1	1	0	0	0	1	0	18	2
1960	KC	AL	6	2	4	6	0	0	0	1	0	0	0	0	0	0	3	3
	NY	AL	8	3	5	5	1	2	0	0	0	0	0	1	0	2	7	1
	Total		14	5	9	11	1	2	0	1	0	0	0	1	0	2	10	4
1961	LA	AL	2	1	1	1	1	0	0	0	0	0	0	0	0	0	1	1
	NY	AL	6	2	4	3	2	0	1	0	0	0	0	0	0	3	2	4
	Total		8	3	5	4	3	0	1	0	0	0	0	0	0	3	3	5
1962	HOU	NL	2	0	2	1	1	0	0	1	0	0	0	0	0	0	1	1
Total			105	53	52	59	31	12	3	8	1	0	2	1	2	12	80	25

Rank among batters: 462 • *Top target (5 home runs)*: Paul Foytack • *Number of pitchers victimized*: 65 • *Total ballparks homered in*: 12 • *First HR*: 05/18/1952 off Bob Cain • *World Series HR—1*

Ron Cey

RONALD CHARLES CEY
B: 02/15/1948
BR

Year	Tm	Lg	Tot	H	A	Men-On 0	1	2	3	One-Game 2	3	4	LO	XN	IP	PH	RHP	LHP
1972	LA	NL	1	1	0	0	1	0	0	0	0	0	0	0	0	0	0	1

Year	Tm	Lg	Tot	H	A	Men-On 0	Men-On 1	Men-On 2	Men-On 3	One-Game 2	One-Game 3	One-Game 4	LO	XN	IP	PH	RHP	LHP

Ron Cey *continued*

Year	Tm	Lg	Tot	H	A	0	1	2	3	2	3	4	LO	XN	IP	PH	RHP	LHP
1973	LA	NL	15	6	9	7	2	6	0	0	0	0	0	1	0	0	9	6
1974	LA	NL	18	8	10	6	6	6	0	2	0	0	0	0	0	0	13	5
1975	LA	NL	25	18	7	13	6	5	1	2	0	0	0	1	0	0	20	5
1976	LA	NL	23	12	11	16	5	1	1	1	0	0	0	0	0	0	17	6
1977	LA	NL	30	14	16	13	13	2	2	2	0	0	0	2	0	0	20	10
1978	LA	NL	23	10	13	16	3	4	0	2	0	0	0	0	0	0	13	10
1979	LA	NL	28	17	11	13	9	5	1	1	0	0	0	0	0	0	16	12
1980	LA	NL	28	16	12	18	7	3	0	0	0	0	0	0	0	0	22	6
1981	LA	NL	13	9	4	5	7	1	0	1	0	0	0	0	0	0	12	1
1982	LA	NL	24	10	14	16	5	3	0	0	0	0	0	0	0	0	15	9
1983	CHI	NL	24	11	13	16	7	1	0	2	0	0	0	0	1	0	14	10
1984	CHI	NL	25	12	13	11	8	5	1	1	0	0	0	0	0	0	15	10
1985	CHI	NL	22	15	7	10	6	5	1	2	0	0	0	1	0	0	15	7
1986	CHI	NL	13	4	9	12	1	0	0	1	0	0	0	0	0	1	8	5
1987	OAK	AL	4	3	1	3	1	0	0	0	0	0	0	0	0	0	1	3
Total			316	166	150	175	87	47	7	17	0	0	0	5	1	1	210	106

Rank among batters: 61 • *Top target (8 home runs)*: Tom Seaver • *Number of pitchers victimized*: 184 • *Total ballparks homered in*: 15 • *First HR*: 09/26/1972 off Mike Caldwell • *World Series HR*—3; *LCS HR*—4

Elio Chacon

ELIO (RODRIGUEZ) CHACON
B: 10/26/1936 D: 04/24/1992
BR

Year	Tm	Lg	Tot	H	A	0	1	2	3	2	3	4	LO	XN	IP	PH	RHP	LHP
1961	CIN	NL	2	1	1	2	0	0	0	0	0	0	0	0	0	0	0	2
1962	NY	NL	2	1	1	1	1	0	0	0	0	0	1	0	0	0	1	1
Total			4	2	2	3	1	0	0	0	0	0	1	0	0	0	1	3

Rank among batters: 3,427 • *Total ballparks homered in*: 4 • *First HR*: 08/09/1961 off Don Ferrarese

Chet Chadbourne

CHESTER JAMES CHADBOURNE
B: 10/28/1884 D: 06/21/1943
BL

Year	Tm	Lg	Tot	H	A	0	1	2	3	2	3	4	LO	XN	IP	PH	RHP	LHP
1914	KC	FL	1	1	0	1	0	0	0	0	0	0	0	0	0	0	1	0
1915	KC	FL	1	0	1	0	0	1	0	0	0	0	0	0	0	0	1	0
Total			2	1	1	1	0	1	0	0	0	0	0	0	0	0	2	0

Rank among batters: 4,129 • *Total ballparks homered in*: 2 • *First HR*: 06/04/1914 off Max Fiske

Bob Chakales

ROBERT EDWARD CHAKALES
B: 08/10/1927
BR

Year	Tm	Lg	Tot	H	A	0	1	2	3	2	3	4	LO	XN	IP	PH	RHP	LHP
1951	CLE	AL	1	0	1	1	0	0	0	0	0	0	0	0	0	0	0	1

Rank among batters: 4,707 • *Total ballparks homered in*: 1 • *First HR*: 05/13/1951 off Bob Cain

Dave Chalk

DAVID LEE CHALK
B: 08/30/1950
BR

Year	Tm	Lg	Tot	H	A	0	1	2	3	2	3	4	LO	XN	IP	PH	RHP	LHP
1974	CAL	AL	5	1	4	3	2	0	0	0	0	0	0	0	0	0	1	4
1975	CAL	AL	3	1	2	1	2	0	0	0	0	0	0	0	0	0	1	2
1977	CAL	AL	3	2	1	2	1	0	0	0	0	0	0	0	0	0	1	2
1978	CAL	AL	1	0	1	0	1	0	0	0	0	0	0	0	0	0	1	0
1979	OAK	AL	2	0	2	1	0	1	0	0	0	0	0	0	0	0	1	1
1980	KC	AL	1	1	0	1	0	0	0	0	0	0	0	0	0	0	0	1
Total			15	5	10	8	6	1	0	0	0	0	0	0	0	0	5	10

Rank among batters: 2,096 • *Top target (2 home runs)*: Jim Colborn • *Number of pitchers victimized*: 14 • *Total ballparks homered in*: 8 • *First HR*: 04/30/1974 off Lance Clemons

Joe Chamberlain

JOSEPH JEREMIAH CHAMBERLAIN
B: 05/10/1910 D: 01/28/1983
BR

Year	Tm	Lg	Tot	H	A	0	1	2	3	2	3	4	LO	XN	IP	PH	RHP	LHP
1934	CHI	AL	2	1	1	1	1	0	0	0	0	0	0	0	0	0	2	0

Rank among batters: 4,129 • *Total ballparks homered in*: 2 • *First HR*: 04/30/1934 off Belve Bean

Wes Chamberlain

WESLEY POLK CHAMBERLAIN
B: 04/13/1966
BR

Year	Tm	Lg	Tot	H	A	Men-On 0	Men-On 1	Men-On 2	Men-On 3	One-Game 2	One-Game 3	One-Game 4	LO	XN	IP	PH	RHP	LHP
1990	PHI	NL	2	0	2	1	1	0	0	0	0	0	0	0	0	0	1	1
1991	PHI	NL	13	9	4	2	7	4	0	1	0	0	0	0	0	0	6	7
1992	PHI	NL	9	3	6	6	1	1	1	0	0	0	0	0	0	0	6	3
1993	PHI	NL	12	5	7	7	4	1	0	1	0	0	0	0	0	0	3	9
1994	PHI	NL	2	0	2	2	0	0	0	0	0	0	0	0	0	0	1	1
	BOS	AL	4	3	1	1	2	0	1	0	0	0	0	0	0	0	3	1
	Total		6	3	3	3	2	0	1	0	0	0	0	0	0	0	4	2
1995	BOS	AL	1	1	0	1	0	0	0	0	0	0	0	0	0	1	1	0
Total			43	21	22	20	15	6	2	2	0	0	0	0	0	1	21	22

Rank among batters: 1,116 • Top target (2 home runs): Greg Harris, John Smiley, Shawn Boskie, Ken Hill, Greg Hibbard, Andy Ashby • *Number of pitchers victimized*: 37 • *Total ballparks homered in*: 12 • *First HR*: 09/19/1990 off Joe Magrane

Elton Chamberlin

ELTON P. CHAMBERLIN
B: 11/05/1867 D: 09/22/1929
BR

Year	Tm	Lg	Tot	H	A	Men-On 0	Men-On 1	Men-On 2	Men-On 3	One-Game 2	One-Game 3	One-Game 4	LO	XN	IP	PH	RHP	LHP
1887	LOU	AA	1	0	1	0	0	1	0	0	0	0	0	0	0	0	1	0
1888	STL	AA	1	1	0	0	0	1	0	0	0	0	0	0	0	0	1	0
1889	STL	AA	2	2	0	0	0	2	0	0	0	0	0	0	0	0	1	1
1891	PHI	AA	2	1	1	0	1	1	0	0	0	0	0	0	0	0	0	2
1892	CIN	NL	2	1	1	1	0	0	1	0	0	0	0	0	1	0	1	1
1894	CIN	NL	1	1	0	1	0	0	0	0	0	0	0	0	0	0	1	0
Total			9	6	3	2	1	5	1	0	0	0	0	0	1	0	5	4

Rank among batters: 2,587 • *Total ballparks homered in*: 6 • *First HR*: 10/06/1887 off Nat Hudson

Al Chambers

ALBERT EUGENE CHAMBERS
B: 03/24/1961
BL

Year	Tm	Lg	Tot	H	A	Men-On 0	Men-On 1	Men-On 2	Men-On 3	One-Game 2	One-Game 3	One-Game 4	LO	XN	IP	PH	RHP	LHP
1983	SEA	AL	1	1	0	1	0	0	0	0	0	0	0	0	0	0	1	0
1984	SEA	AL	1	0	1	1	0	0	0	0	0	0	0	0	0	0	1	0
Total			2	1	1	2	0	0	0	0	0	0	0	0	0	0	2	0

Rank among batters: 4,129 • *Total ballparks homered in*: 2 • *First HR*: 09/09/1983 off Mike Smithson

Cliff Chambers

CLIFFORD DAY CHAMBERS
B: 01/10/1922
BL

Year	Tm	Lg	Tot	H	A	Men-On 0	Men-On 1	Men-On 2	Men-On 3	One-Game 2	One-Game 3	One-Game 4	LO	XN	IP	PH	RHP	LHP
1950	PIT	NL	2	2	0	1	0	1	0	0	0	0	0	0	0	0	2	0
1951	PIT	NL	1	0	1	1	0	0	0	0	0	0	0	0	0	0	1	0
Total			3	2	1	2	0	1	0	0	0	0	0	0	0	0	3	0

Rank among batters: 3,735 • *Total ballparks homered in*: 2 • *First HR*: 06/08/1950 off Ralph Branca

Chris Chambliss

CARROLL CHRISTOPHER CHAMBLISS
B: 12/26/1948
BL

Year	Tm	Lg	Tot	H	A	Men-On 0	Men-On 1	Men-On 2	Men-On 3	One-Game 2	One-Game 3	One-Game 4	LO	XN	IP	PH	RHP	LHP
1971	CLE	AL	9	5	4	5	2	2	0	0	0	0	0	0	0	0	7	2
1972	CLE	AL	6	3	3	5	0	1	0	0	0	0	0	1	0	0	5	1
1973	CLE	AL	11	8	3	6	4	0	1	1	0	0	0	0	0	0	8	3
1974	NY	AL	6	4	2	5	0	1	0	0	0	0	0	0	0	0	3	3
1975	NY	AL	9	4	5	5	4	0	0	1	0	0	0	0	0	0	7	2
1976	NY	AL	17	10	7	9	3	4	1	0	0	0	0	0	0	0	4	13
1977	NY	AL	17	11	6	7	5	5	0	1	0	0	0	0	0	1	9	8
1978	NY	AL	12	6	6	8	2	1	1	1	0	0	0	1	0	0	8	4
1979	NY	AL	18	10	8	9	6	3	0	2	0	0	0	0	0	0	12	6
1980	ATL	NL	18	12	6	12	3	3	0	0	0	0	0	0	0	0	15	3
1981	ATL	NL	8	2	6	2	4	2	0	0	0	0	0	1	0	0	7	1
1982	ATL	NL	20	11	9	15	2	2	1	0	0	0	0	2	0	2	19	1
1983	ATL	NL	20	9	11	13	5	1	1	3	0	0	0	0	0	0	18	2
1984	ATL	NL	9	6	3	7	2	0	0	0	0	0	0	0	0	0	9	0

Chris Chambliss *continued*

Year	Tm	Lg	Tot	H	A	Men-On 0	Men-On 1	Men-On 2	Men-On 3	One-Game 2	One-Game 3	One-Game 4	LO	XN	IP	PH	RHP	LHP
1985	ATL	NL	3	1	2	2	1	0	0	0	0	0	0	0	0	1	3	0
1986	ATL	NL	2	2	0	0	1	1	0	0	0	0	0	0	0	1	2	0
Total			185	104	81	110	44	26	5	9	0	0	0	5	0	5	136	49

Rank among batters: 209 • *Top target (5 home runs)*: Joe Niekro • *Number of pitchers victimized*: 140 • *Total ballparks homered in*: 26 • *First HR*: 06/06/1971 off Tom Hall • *World Series HR*—1; *LCS HR*—2

Bill Champion

BUFORD BILLY CHAMPION
B: 09/18/1947
BR

Year	Tm	Lg	Tot	H	A	Men-On 0	Men-On 1	Men-On 2	Men-On 3	One-Game 2	One-Game 3	One-Game 4	LO	XN	IP	PH	RHP	LHP
1972	PHI	NL	1	0	1	1	0	0	0	0	0	0	0	0	0	0	1	0

Rank among batters: 4,707 • *Total ballparks homered in*: 1 • *First HR*: 04/30/1972 off Mike Corkins

Mike Champion

ROBERT MICHAEL CHAMPION
B: 02/10/1955
BR

Year	Tm	Lg	Tot	H	A	Men-On 0	Men-On 1	Men-On 2	Men-On 3	One-Game 2	One-Game 3	One-Game 4	LO	XN	IP	PH	RHP	LHP
1976	SD	NL	1	1	0	0	1	0	0	0	0	0	0	0	0	0	0	1
1977	SD	NL	1	0	1	1	0	0	0	0	0	0	0	0	0	0	1	0
Total			2	1	1	1	1	0	0	0	0	0	0	0	0	0	1	1

Rank among batters: 4,129 • *Total ballparks homered in*: 2 • *First HR*: 09/29/1976 off Fred Norman

Bob Chance

ROBERT CHANCE
B: 09/10/1940
BL

Year	Tm	Lg	Tot	H	A	Men-On 0	Men-On 1	Men-On 2	Men-On 3	One-Game 2	One-Game 3	One-Game 4	LO	XN	IP	PH	RHP	LHP
1963	CLE	AL	2	0	2	2	0	0	0	0	0	0	0	0	0	0	2	0
1964	CLE	AL	14	10	4	6	7	1	0	2	0	0	0	0	0	2	7	7
1965	WAS	AL	4	2	2	2	2	0	0	0	0	0	0	0	0	0	4	0
1966	WAS	AL	1	0	1	0	0	0	1	0	0	0	0	0	0	1	1	0
1967	WAS	AL	3	1	2	1	1	1	0	0	0	0	0	0	0	2	3	0
Total			24	13	11	11	10	2	1	2	0	0	0	0	0	5	17	7

Rank among batters: 1,643 • *Top target (2 home runs)*: Dick Stigman, Steve Barber, Ralph Terry • *Number of pitchers victimized*: 21 • *Total ballparks homered in*: 9 • *First HR*: 09/09/1963 off Jim Perry

Frank Chance

FRANK LEROY CHANCE
B: 09/09/1877 D: 09/15/1924
BR HOF

Year	Tm	Lg	Tot	H	A	Men-On 0	Men-On 1	Men-On 2	Men-On 3	One-Game 2	One-Game 3	One-Game 4	LO	XN	IP	PH	RHP	LHP
1898	CHI	NL	1	0	1	1	0	0	0	0	0	0	0	0	1	0	0	0
1899	CHI	NL	1	0	1	0	1	0	0	0	0	0	0	0	0	0	1	0
1902	CHI	NL	1	0	1	0	0	0	1	0	0	0	0	1	0	0	0	1
1903	CHI	NL	2	0	2	0	1	1	0	0	0	0	0	0	0	0	2	0
1904	CHI	NL	6	3	3	5	0	1	0	0	0	0	0	0	2	0	5	1
1905	CHI	NL	2	2	0	2	0	0	0	0	0	0	0	0	1	0	2	0
1906	CHI	NL	3	0	3	2	1	0	0	0	0	0	0	0	1	0	2	1
1907	CHI	NL	1	0	1	1	0	0	0	0	0	0	0	0	0	0	1	0
1908	CHI	NL	2	1	1	1	1	0	0	0	0	0	0	0	1	0	1	1
1911	CHI	NL	1	0	1	0	1	0	0	0	0	0	0	0	0	0	1	0
Total			20	6	14	12	5	2	1	0	0	0	0	1	6	0	15	4

Rank among batters: 1,810 • *Top target (3 home runs)*: Ned Garvin • *Number of pitchers victimized*: 16 • *Total ballparks homered in*: 9 • *First HR*: 07/13/1898 off Cy Swaim

Spud Chandler

SPURGEON FERDINAND CHANDLER
B: 09/12/1907 D: 01/09/1990
BR

Year	Tm	Lg	Tot	H	A	Men-On 0	Men-On 1	Men-On 2	Men-On 3	One-Game 2	One-Game 3	One-Game 4	LO	XN	IP	PH	RHP	LHP
1938	NY	AL	3	0	3	3	0	0	0	0	0	0	0	0	0	0	2	1
1940	NY	AL	2	0	2	1	0	0	1	1	0	0	0	0	0	0	1	1
1943	NY	AL	2	1	1	1	0	1	0	0	0	0	0	0	1	0	2	0

Year	Tm	Lg	Tot	H	A	Men-On 0	Men-On 1	Men-On 2	Men-On 3	One-Game 2	One-Game 3	One-Game 4	LO	XN	IP	PH	RHP	LHP

Spud Chandler *continued*

Year	Tm	Lg	Tot	H	A	Men-On 0	Men-On 1	Men-On 2	Men-On 3	One-Game 2	One-Game 3	One-Game 4	LO	XN	IP	PH	RHP	LHP
1947	NY	AL	2	1	1	1	0	1	0	0	0	0	0	0	0	0	2	0
Total			9	2	7	6	0	2	1	1	0	0	0	0	1	0	7	2

Rank among batters: 2,587 • *Top target (2 home runs)*: Lum Harris • *Number of pitchers victimized*: 8 • *Total ballparks homered in*: 5 • *First HR*: 05/21/1938 off Thornton Lee

Darrel Chaney

DARREL LEE CHANEY
B: 03/09/1948
BB

Year	Tm	Lg	Tot	H	A	Men-On 0	Men-On 1	Men-On 2	Men-On 3	One-Game 2	One-Game 3	One-Game 4	LO	XN	IP	PH	RHP	LHP
1970	CIN	NL	1	0	1	1	0	0	0	0	0	0	0	0	0	0	1	0
1972	CIN	NL	2	2	0	1	1	0	0	0	0	0	0	0	0	0	2	0
1974	CIN	NL	2	1	1	1	0	0	1	0	0	0	0	0	0	0	1	1
1975	CIN	NL	2	1	1	1	0	1	0	0	0	0	0	0	0	0	2	0
1976	ATL	NL	1	0	1	0	1	0	0	0	0	0	0	0	0	0	1	0
1977	ATL	NL	3	3	0	3	0	0	0	0	0	0	0	0	0	1	3	0
1978	ATL	NL	3	3	0	1	1	1	0	0	0	0	0	0	0	0	2	1
Total			14	10	4	8	3	2	1	0	0	0	0	0	0	1	12	2

Rank among batters: 2,169 • *Total ballparks homered in*: 4 • *First HR*: 09/07/1970 off Juan Marichal

Tiny Chaplin

JAMES BAILEY CHAPLIN
B: 07/13/1905 D: 03/25/1939
BR

Year	Tm	Lg	Tot	H	A	Men-On 0	Men-On 1	Men-On 2	Men-On 3	One-Game 2	One-Game 3	One-Game 4	LO	XN	IP	PH	RHP	LHP
1930	NY	NL	1	0	1	0	0	1	0	0	0	0	0	0	0	0	1	0

Rank among batters: 4,707 • *Total ballparks homered in*: 1 • *First HR*: 07/02/1930 off Pat Malone

Ben Chapman

WILLIAM BENJAMIN CHAPMAN
B: 12/25/1908 D: 07/07/1993
BR

Year	Tm	Lg	Tot	H	A	Men-On 0	Men-On 1	Men-On 2	Men-On 3	One-Game 2	One-Game 3	One-Game 4	LO	XN	IP	PH	RHP	LHP
1930	NY	AL	10	3	7	2	8	0	0	0	0	0	0	0	3	0	8	2
1931	NY	AL	17	9	8	10	3	4	0	1	0	0	0	0	0	0	9	8
1932	NY	AL	10	7	3	2	4	4	0	0	1	0	0	0	3	0	4	6
1933	NY	AL	9	4	5	3	4	2	0	0	0	0	0	0	1	0	9	0
1934	NY	AL	5	3	2	3	1	1	0	0	0	0	0	1	1	0	4	1
1935	NY	AL	8	5	3	3	4	1	0	0	0	0	0	1	4	0	6	2
1936	NY	AL	1	0	1	0	0	1	0	0	0	0	0	0	0	0	1	0
	WAS	AL	4	1	3	1	3	0	0	0	0	0	1	0	1	0	3	1
	Total		5	1	4	1	3	1	0	0	0	0	1	0	1	0	4	1
1937	BOS	AL	7	5	2	2	1	3	1	0	0	0	0	0	1	0	6	1
1938	BOS	AL	6	3	3	4	1	1	0	0	0	0	0	0	0	0	6	0
1939	CLE	AL	6	1	5	4	1	1	0	1	0	0	0	0	1	0	2	4
1940	CLE	AL	4	0	4	4	0	0	0	0	0	0	1	0	0	0	3	1
1941	WAS	AL	1	1	0	0	1	0	0	0	0	0	0	0	0	0	1	0
	CHI	AL	2	0	2	1	0	0	1	0	0	0	0	0	0	0	2	0
	Total		3	1	2	1	1	0	1	0	0	0	0	0	0	0	3	0
Total			90	42	48	39	31	18	2	2	1	0	2	2	15	0	64	26

Rank among batters: 573 • *Top target (6 home runs)*: Tommy Bridges • *Number of pitchers victimized*: 61 • *Total ballparks homered in*: 9 • *First HR*: 05/07/1930 off Pete Appleton

Calvin Chapman

CALVIN LOUIS CHAPMAN
B: 12/20/1910 D: 04/01/1983
BL

Year	Tm	Lg	Tot	H	A	Men-On 0	Men-On 1	Men-On 2	Men-On 3	One-Game 2	One-Game 3	One-Game 4	LO	XN	IP	PH	RHP	LHP
1936	CIN	NL	1	0	1	0	1	0	0	0	0	0	0	0	1	1	1	0

Rank among batters: 4,707 • *Total ballparks homered in*: 1 • *First HR*: 04/22/1936 off Leroy Parmelee

Glenn Chapman

GLENN JUSTICE CHAPMAN
B: 01/21/1906 D: 11/05/1988
BR

Year	Tm	Lg	Tot	H	A	Men-On 0	Men-On 1	Men-On 2	Men-On 3	One-Game 2	One-Game 3	One-Game 4	LO	XN	IP	PH	RHP	LHP
1934	BRO	NL	1	0	1	0	1	0	0	0	0	0	0	0	0	0	1	0

Rank among batters: 4,707 • *Total ballparks homered in*: 1 • *First HR*: 08/21/1934 off Hal Smith

Harry Chapman

HARRY E. CHAPMAN
B: 10/26/1887 D: 10/21/1918
BR

Year	Tm	Lg	Tot	H	A	Men-On 0	Men-On 1	Men-On 2	Men-On 3	One-Game 2	One-Game 3	One-Game 4	LO	XN	IP	PH	RHP	LHP
1915	STL	FL	1	0	1	1	0	0	0	0	0	0	0	0	0	0	1	0

Rank among batters: 4,707 • *Total ballparks homered in*: 1 • *First HR*: 08/06/1915 off George Suggs

Kelvin Chapman

KELVIN KEITH CHAPMAN
B: 06/02/1956
BR

Year	Tm	Lg	Tot	H	A	Men-On 0	Men-On 1	Men-On 2	Men-On 3	One-Game 2	One-Game 3	One-Game 4	LO	XN	IP	PH	RHP	LHP
1984	NY	NL	3	1	2	1	0	1	1	0	0	0	0	0	0	0	0	3

Rank among batters: 3,735 • *Total ballparks homered in*: 3 • *First HR*: 08/03/1984 off John Candelaria

Ray Chapman

RAYMOND JOHNSON CHAPMAN
B: 01/15/1891 D: 08/17/1920
BR

Year	Tm	Lg	Tot	H	A	Men-On 0	Men-On 1	Men-On 2	Men-On 3	One-Game 2	One-Game 3	One-Game 4	LO	XN	IP	PH	RHP	LHP
1913	CLE	AL	3	1	2	2	0	1	0	0	0	0	0	0	1	0	1	2
1914	CLE	AL	2	0	2	1	1	0	0	0	0	0	0	0	0	0	1	1
1915	CLE	AL	3	2	1	1	1	1	0	0	0	0	0	0	0	0	1	2
1917	CLE	AL	2	2	0	0	1	1	0	0	0	0	0	0	1	0	2	0
1918	CLE	AL	1	0	1	1	0	0	0	0	0	0	0	1	0	0	1	0
1919	CLE	AL	3	2	1	1	1	1	0	0	0	0	0	0	2	0	3	0
1920	CLE	AL	3	1	2	2	0	1	0	0	0	0	0	0	2	0	2	1
Total			17	8	9	8	4	5	0	0	0	0	0	1	6	0	11	6

Rank among batters: 1,969 • *Top target (2 home runs)*: Carl Weilman • *Number of pitchers victimized*: 16 • *Total ballparks homered in*: 6 • *First HR*: 08/09/1913 off Joe Boehling

Sam Chapman

SAMUEL BLAKE CHAPMAN
B: 04/11/1916
BR

Year	Tm	Lg	Tot	H	A	Men-On 0	Men-On 1	Men-On 2	Men-On 3	One-Game 2	One-Game 3	One-Game 4	LO	XN	IP	PH	RHP	LHP
1938	PHI	AL	17	10	7	9	6	1	1	0	0	0	0	0	0	0	14	3
1939	PHI	AL	15	7	8	7	7	1	0	1	0	0	0	0	0	0	13	2
1940	PHI	AL	23	10	13	16	3	2	2	2	0	0	0	0	0	0	17	6
1941	PHI	AL	25	13	12	13	8	3	1	2	0	0	0	1	0	0	21	4
1946	PHI	AL	20	12	8	13	5	2	0	1	1	0	0	0	0	0	17	3
1947	PHI	AL	14	12	2	10	3	0	1	0	0	0	0	0	0	0	13	1
1948	PHI	AL	13	5	8	3	6	2	2	0	0	0	0	0	0	0	11	2
1949	PHI	AL	24	10	14	15	7	1	1	3	0	0	0	0	0	0	13	11
1950	PHI	AL	23	11	12	9	12	1	1	0	0	0	0	0	1	0	17	6
1951	CLE	AL	6	3	3	4	1	1	0	0	0	0	0	0	0	0	3	3
Total			180	93	87	99	58	14	9	9	1	0	0	1	1	0	139	41

Rank among batters: 220 • *Top target (6 home runs)*: Joe Dobson • *Number of pitchers victimized*: 115 • *Total ballparks homered in*: 9 • *First HR*: 05/30/1938 off Monte Weaver • *Hit for Cycle*—@STL: 05/05/1939

Harry Chappas

HARRY PERRY CHAPPAS
B: 10/26/1957
BB

Year	Tm	Lg	Tot	H	A	Men-On 0	Men-On 1	Men-On 2	Men-On 3	One-Game 2	One-Game 3	One-Game 4	LO	XN	IP	PH	RHP	LHP
1979	CHI	AL	1	0	1	1	0	0	0	0	0	0	0	0	0	0	0	1

Rank among batters: 4,707 • *Total ballparks homered in*: 1 • *First HR*: 08/20/1979 off Bill Travers

Bill Chappelle

WILLIAM HOGAN CHAPPELLE
B: 03/22/1884 D: 12/31/1944
BR

Year	Tm	Lg	Tot	H	A	Men-On 0	Men-On 1	Men-On 2	Men-On 3	One-Game 2	One-Game 3	One-Game 4	LO	XN	IP	PH	RHP	LHP
1909	BOS	NL	1	1	0	0	1	0	0	0	0	0	0	0	0	0	1	0

Rank among batters: 4,707 • *Total ballparks homered in*: 1 • *First HR*: 04/19/1909 off George Bell

Joe Charboneau

JOSEPH CHARBONEAU
B: 06/17/1955
BR

Year	Tm	Lg	Tot	H	A	Men-On 0	Men-On 1	Men-On 2	Men-On 3	One-Game 2	One-Game 3	One-Game 4	LO	XN	IP	PH	RHP	LHP
1980	CLE	AL	23	13	10	8	9	5	1	1	0	0	0	1	0	1	15	8

Year	Tm	Lg	Tot	H	A	Men-On 0	1	2	3	One-Game 2	3	4	LO	XN	IP	PH	RHP	LHP

Joe Charboneau *continued*

Year	Tm	Lg	Tot	H	A	0	1	2	3	2	3	4	LO	XN	IP	PH	RHP	LHP
1981	CLE	AL	4	0	4	2	1	1	0	0	0	0	0	0	0	0	2	2
1982	CLE	AL	2	0	2	2	0	0	0	0	0	0	0	0	0	1	0	2
Total			29	13	16	12	10	6	1	1	0	0	0	1	0	2	17	12

Rank among batters: 1,465 • Top target (2 home runs): Fernando Arroyo, Mike Flanagan, Ross Baumgarten, Floyd Bannister • *Number of pitchers victimized*: 25 • *Total ballparks homered in*: 9 • *First HR*: 04/11/1980 off Dave Frost

Chappy Charles

RAYMOND CHARLES
B: 03/25/1881 D: 08/04/1959
BR

Year	Tm	Lg	Tot	H	A	0	1	2	3	2	3	4	LO	XN	IP	PH	RHP	LHP
1908	STL	NL	1	0	1	1	0	0	0	0	0	0	0	0	0	0	1	0

Rank among batters: 4,707 • *Total ballparks homered in*: 1 • *First HR*: 06/24/1908 off Ed Reulbach

Ed Charles

EDWIN DOUGLAS CHARLES
B: 04/29/1933
BR

Year	Tm	Lg	Tot	H	A	0	1	2	3	2	3	4	LO	XN	IP	PH	RHP	LHP
1962	KC	AL	17	10	7	10	3	3	1	1	0	0	0	0	1	0	14	3
1963	KC	AL	15	11	4	10	3	2	0	1	0	0	0	0	0	0	7	8
1964	KC	AL	16	13	3	12	2	2	0	0	0	0	0	0	0	0	9	7
1965	KC	AL	8	2	6	5	2	1	0	0	0	0	0	1	0	0	6	2
1966	KC	AL	9	3	6	7	2	0	0	0	0	0	0	0	0	0	8	1
1967	NY	NL	3	2	1	3	0	0	0	0	0	0	0	0	0	0	3	0
1968	NY	NL	15	10	5	9	6	0	0	2	0	0	0	0	0	3	5	10
1969	NY	NL	3	2	1	1	0	2	0	0	0	0	0	0	0	0	1	2
Total			86	53	33	57	18	10	1	4	0	0	0	1	1	3	53	33

Rank among batters: 602 • *Top target (3 home runs)*: Ken Holtzman • *Number of pitchers victimized*: 67 • *Total ballparks homered in*: 15 • *First HR*: 04/22/1962 off Ray Herbert

Mike Chartak

MICHAEL GEORGE CHARTAK
B: 04/28/1916 D: 07/25/1967
BL

Year	Tm	Lg	Tot	H	A	0	1	2	3	2	3	4	LO	XN	IP	PH	RHP	LHP
1942	WAS	AL	1	0	1	1	0	0	0	0	0	0	0	0	0	0	1	0
	STL	AL	9	4	5	0	6	1	2	0	1	0	0	0	0	1	8	1
	Total		10	4	6	7	1	2	0	1	0	0	0	0	0	1	9	1
1943	STL	AL	10	7	3	6	4	0	0	0	0	0	0	0	0	0	9	1
1944	STL	AL	1	1	0	0	0	1	0	0	0	0	0	0	0	1	1	0
Total			21	12	9	13	5	3	0	1	0	0	0	0	0	2	19	2

Rank among batters: 1,768 • *Top target (3 home runs)*: Tex Hughson • *Number of pitchers victimized*: 17 • *Total ballparks homered in*: 6 • *First HR*: 05/30/1942 off Spud Chandler

Hal Chase

HAROLD HOMER CHASE
B: 02/13/1883 D: 05/18/1947
BR

Year	Tm	Lg	Tot	H	A	0	1	2	3	2	3	4	LO	XN	IP	PH	RHP	LHP
1905	NY	AL	3	2	1	2	1	0	0	0	0	0	0	0	2	0	2	1
1907	NY	AL	2	2	0	1	1	0	0	0	0	0	0	0	2	0	1	1
1908	NY	AL	1	1	0	1	0	0	0	0	0	0	0	0	1	0	1	0
1909	NY	AL	4	1	3	2	2	0	0	0	0	0	0	0	2	0	4	0
1910	NY	AL	3	2	1	1	1	1	0	0	0	0	0	0	3	0	3	0
1911	NY	AL	3	3	0	0	2	1	0	0	0	0	0	0	2	0	2	1
1912	NY	AL	4	3	1	1	2	1	0	0	0	0	0	0	3	0	4	0
1913	CHI	AL	2	1	1	2	0	0	0	0	0	0	0	0	2	0	0	2
1914	BUF	FL	3	3	0	1	1	1	0	0	0	0	0	0	0	0	3	0
1915	BUF	FL	17	10	7	6	9	2	0	2	0	0	0	0	0	0	15	2
1916	CIN	NL	4	1	3	2	0	2	0	0	0	0	0	1	2	0	4	0
1917	CIN	NL	4	1	3	1	1	2	0	0	0	0	0	0	2	0	2	2
1918	CIN	NL	2	2	0	0	2	0	0	0	0	0	0	0	2	0	1	1
1919	NY	NL	5	5	0	3	2	0	0	0	0	0	0	0	1	0	3	2
Total			57	37	20	23	24	10	0	2	0	0	0	1	24	0	45	12

Rank among batters: 902 • Top target (2 home runs): Addie Joss, Frank Smith, Nick Cullop, Chief Johnson, Mike Prendergast, Dick Rudolph • *Number of pitchers victimized*: 51 • *Total ballparks homered in*: 16 • *First HR*: 05/14/1905 off Nick Altrock

Ken Chase

KENDALL FAY CHASE
B: 10/06/1913 D: 01/16/1985
BL

Year	Tm	Lg	Tot	H	A	Men-On 0	Men-On 1	Men-On 2	Men-On 3	One-Game 2	One-Game 3	One-Game 4	LO	XN	IP	PH	RHP	LHP
1940	WAS	AL	1	0	1	0	1	0	0	0	0	0	0	0	0	0	1	0

Rank among batters: 4,707 • *Total ballparks homered in*: 1 • *First HR*: 07/31/1940 off Bill Trotter

Buster Chatham

CHARLES L. CHATHAM
B: 12/25/1901 D: 12/15/1975
BR

Year	Tm	Lg	Tot	H	A	Men-On 0	Men-On 1	Men-On 2	Men-On 3	One-Game 2	One-Game 3	One-Game 4	LO	XN	IP	PH	RHP	LHP
1930	BOS	NL	5	2	3	4	1	0	0	0	0	0	0	0	0	0	2	3
1931	BOS	NL	1	1	0	0	1	0	0	0	0	0	0	0	0	0	0	1
Total			6	3	3	4	2	0	0	0	0	0	0	0	0	0	2	4

Rank among batters: 2,988 • *Total ballparks homered in*: 4 • *First HR*: 06/17/1930 off Jakie May

Ossie Chavarria

OSVALDO (QUIJANO) CHAVARRIA
B: 08/05/1940
BR

Year	Tm	Lg	Tot	H	A	Men-On 0	Men-On 1	Men-On 2	Men-On 3	One-Game 2	One-Game 3	One-Game 4	LO	XN	IP	PH	RHP	LHP
1966	KC	AL	2	0	2	2	0	0	0	0	0	0	0	0	0	1	1	1

Rank among batters: 4,129 • *Total ballparks homered in*: 2 • *First HR*: 07/01/1966 off Johnny Podres

Virgil Cheeves

VIRGIL EARL CHEEVES
B: 02/12/1901 D: 05/05/1979
BR

Year	Tm	Lg	Tot	H	A	Men-On 0	Men-On 1	Men-On 2	Men-On 3	One-Game 2	One-Game 3	One-Game 4	LO	XN	IP	PH	RHP	LHP
1922	CHI	NL	1	0	1	1	0	0	0	0	0	0	0	0	0	0	0	1

Rank among batters: 4,707 • *Total ballparks homered in*: 1 • *First HR*: 07/29/1922 off Philip Weinert

Laurence Cheney

LAURENCE RUSSELL CHENEY
B: 05/02/1886 D: 01/06/1969
BR

Year	Tm	Lg	Tot	H	A	Men-On 0	Men-On 1	Men-On 2	Men-On 3	One-Game 2	One-Game 3	One-Game 4	LO	XN	IP	PH	RHP	LHP
1912	CHI	NL	1	0	1	1	0	0	0	0	0	0	0	0	0	0	1	0

Rank among batters: 4,707 • *Total ballparks homered in*: 1 • *First HR*: 09/13/1912 off Ed Donnelly

Jack Chesbro

JOHN DWIGHT CHESBRO
B: 06/05/1874 D: 11/06/1931
BR HOF

Year	Tm	Lg	Tot	H	A	Men-On 0	Men-On 1	Men-On 2	Men-On 3	One-Game 2	One-Game 3	One-Game 4	LO	XN	IP	PH	RHP	LHP
1901	PIT	NL	1	0	1	0	1	0	0	0	0	0	0	0	0	0	1	0
1903	NY	AL	2	2	0	1	1	0	0	0	0	0	0	0	0	0	2	0
1904	NY	AL	1	1	0	1	0	0	0	0	0	0	0	0	1	0	1	0
1906	NY	AL	1	0	1	1	0	0	0	0	0	0	0	0	0	0	1	0
Total			5	3	2	3	2	0	0	0	0	0	0	0	1	0	5	0

Rank among batters: 3,191 • *Total ballparks homered in*: 3 • *First HR*: 09/02/1901 off Kid Nichols

Bob Chesnes

ROBERT VINCENT CHESNES
B: 05/06/1921 D: 05/23/1979
BB

Year	Tm	Lg	Tot	H	A	Men-On 0	Men-On 1	Men-On 2	Men-On 3	One-Game 2	One-Game 3	One-Game 4	LO	XN	IP	PH	RHP	LHP
1948	PIT	NL	1	0	1	1	0	0	0	0	0	0	0	0	0	0	1	0
1949	PIT	NL	1	0	1	1	0	0	0	0	0	0	0	0	0	0	1	0
Total			2	0	2	2	0	0	0	0	0	0	0	0	0	0	2	0

Rank among batters: 4,129 • *Total ballparks homered in*: 2 • *First HR*: 09/20/1948 off Robin Roberts

Cupid Childs

CLARENCE ALGERNON CHILDS
B: 08/08/1867 D: 11/08/1912
BL

Year	Tm	Lg	Tot	H	A	Men-On 0	Men-On 1	Men-On 2	Men-On 3	One-Game 2	One-Game 3	One-Game 4	LO	XN	IP	PH	RHP	LHP
1890	SYR	AA	2	0	2	1	0	0	1	0	0	0	0	0	1	0	1	1
1891	CLE	NL	2	1	1	1	0	1	0	0	0	0	0	0	1	0	2	0
1892	CLE	NL	3	0	3	0	3	0	0	0	0	0	0	0	0	0	2	1
1893	CLE	NL	3	0	3	2	1	0	0	0	0	0	1	0	2	0	2	1

Cupid Childs *continued*

Year	Tm	Lg	Tot	H	A	Men-On 0	1	2	3	One-Game 2	3	4	LO	XN	IP	PH	RHP	LHP
1894	CLE	NL	2	1	1	1	1	0	0	0	0	0	1	0	0	0	2	0
1895	CLE	NL	4	0	4	1	1	1	1	0	0	0	0	0	0	0	3	1
1896	CLE	NL	1	0	1	0	0	1	0	0	0	0	0	0	1	0	1	0
1897	CLE	NL	1	1	0	0	0	0	1	0	0	0	0	0	1	0	1	0
1898	CLE	NL	1	0	1	1	0	0	0	0	0	0	0	0	0	0	1	0
1899	STL	NL	1	1	0	1	0	0	0	0	0	0	0	0	0	0	1	0
Total			20	4	16	8	6	3	3	0	0	0	2	0	6	0	16	4

Rank among batters: 1,810 • *Top target (2 home runs)*: Silver King • *Number of pitchers victimized*: 19 • *Total ballparks homered in*: 13 • *First HR*: 04/19/1890 off Jack Lynch

Pearce Chiles

PEARCE NUGET CHILES
B: 05/28/1867
BR

Year	Tm	Lg	Tot	H	A	Men-On 0	1	2	3	One-Game 2	3	4	LO	XN	IP	PH	RHP	LHP
1899	PHI	NL	2	1	1	0	1	1	0	0	0	0	0	0	0	0	2	0
1900	PHI	NL	1	1	0	1	0	0	0	0	0	0	0	0	0	0	1	0
Total			3	2	1	1	1	1	0	0	0	0	0	0	0	0	3	0

Rank among batters: 3,735 • *Total ballparks homered in*: 2 • *First HR*: 08/25/1899 off Nig Cuppy

Rich Chiles

RICHARD FRANCIS CHILES
B: 11/22/1949
BL

Year	Tm	Lg	Tot	H	A	Men-On 0	1	2	3	One-Game 2	3	4	LO	XN	IP	PH	RHP	LHP
1971	HOU	NL	2	0	2	2	0	0	0	0	0	0	0	0	0	0	2	0
1977	MIN	AL	3	1	2	2	1	0	0	0	0	0	0	0	0	1	3	0
1978	MIN	AL	1	0	1	1	0	0	0	0	0	0	0	0	0	0	1	0
Total			6	1	5	5	1	0	0	0	0	0	0	0	0	1	6	0

Rank among batters: 2,988 • *Total ballparks homered in*: 6 • *First HR*: 08/12/1971 off Ron Reed

Lou Chiozza

LOUIS PEO CHIOZZA
B: 05/17/1910 D: 02/28/1971
BL

Year	Tm	Lg	Tot	H	A	Men-On 0	1	2	3	One-Game 2	3	4	LO	XN	IP	PH	RHP	LHP
1935	PHI	NL	3	0	3	1	0	2	0	0	0	0	0	0	1	0	2	1
1936	PHI	NL	1	1	0	0	1	0	0	0	0	0	0	0	0	0	1	0
1937	NY	NL	4	4	0	3	1	0	0	0	0	0	0	0	0	0	3	1
1938	NY	NL	3	3	0	2	0	1	0	0	0	0	1	0	0	0	2	1
1939	NY	NL	3	2	1	3	0	0	0	0	0	0	0	0	0	0	2	1
Total			14	10	4	9	2	3	0	0	0	0	1	0	1	0	10	4

Rank among batters: 2,169 • *Top target (2 home runs)*: Fred Frankhouse • *Number of pitchers victimized*: 13 • *Total ballparks homered in*: 5 • *First HR*: 05/19/1935 off Lon Warneke

Harry Chiti

HARRY CHITI
B: 11/16/1932
BR

Year	Tm	Lg	Tot	H	A	Men-On 0	1	2	3	One-Game 2	3	4	LO	XN	IP	PH	RHP	LHP
1952	CHI	NL	5	2	3	3	0	2	0	0	0	0	0	0	0	0	3	2
1955	CHI	NL	11	2	9	6	4	1	0	1	0	0	0	0	0	0	9	2
1956	CHI	NL	4	2	2	3	1	0	0	0	0	0	0	0	0	0	2	2
1958	KC	AL	9	6	3	6	1	1	1	0	0	0	0	0	0	0	9	0
1959	KC	AL	5	3	2	4	0	1	0	0	0	0	0	0	0	0	5	0
1960	KC	AL	5	4	1	3	2	0	0	0	0	0	0	0	0	0	3	2
	DET	AL	2	2	0	2	0	0	0	0	0	0	0	0	0	0	2	0
	Total		7	6	1	5	2	0	0	0	0	0	0	0	0	0	5	2
Total			41	21	20	27	8	5	1	1	0	0	0	0	0	0	33	8

Rank among batters: 1,163 • *Top target (3 home runs)*: Joe Nuxhall • *Number of pitchers victimized*: 32 • *Total ballparks homered in*: 13 • *First HR*: 04/29/1952 off Curt Simmons

Felix Chouinard

FELIX GEORGE CHOUINARD
B: 10/05/1887 D: 04/28/1955
BR

Year	Tm	Lg	Tot	H	A	Men-On 0	1	2	3	One-Game 2	3	4	LO	XN	IP	PH	RHP	LHP
1914	PIT	FL	1	0	1	1	0	0	0	0	0	0	0	0	0	0	0	1

Rank among batters: 4,707 • *Total ballparks homered in*: 1 • *First HR*: 06/16/1914 off Doc Watson

Neil Chrisley

BARBRA O'NEIL CHRISLEY
B: 12/16/1931
BL

Year	Tm	Lg	Tot	H	A	Men-On 0	1	2	3	One-Game 2	3	4	LO	XN	IP	PH	RHP	LHP
1958	WAS	AL	5	3	2	3	2	0	0	0	0	0	0	0	0	1	4	1
1959	DET	AL	6	5	1	4	2	0	0	0	0	0	0	0	0	0	6	0
1960	DET	AL	5	3	2	3	1	1	0	1	0	0	0	0	0	0	5	0
Total			16	11	5	10	5	1	0	1	0	0	0	0	0	1	15	1

Rank among batters: 2,029 • *Top target (3 home runs)*: Johnny Kucks • *Number of pitchers victimized*: 14 • *Total ballparks homered in*: 5 • *First HR*: 05/09/1958 off Bob Turley

Lloyd Christenbury

LLOYD REID CHRISTENBURY
B: 10/19/1893 D: 12/13/1944
BL

Year	Tm	Lg	Tot	H	A	Men-On 0	1	2	3	One-Game 2	3	4	LO	XN	IP	PH	RHP	LHP
1921	BOS	NL	3	0	3	3	0	0	0	0	0	0	0	0	1	0	3	0
1922	BOS	NL	1	1	0	1	0	0	0	0	0	0	0	0	1	0	1	0
Total			4	1	3	4	0	0	0	0	0	0	0	0	2	0	4	0

Rank among batters: 3,427 • *Total ballparks homered in*: 3 • *First HR*: 07/24/1921 off Leon Cadore

John Christensen

JOHN LAWRENCE CHRISTENSEN
B: 09/15/1960
BR

Year	Tm	Lg	Tot	H	A	Men-On 0	1	2	3	One-Game 2	3	4	LO	XN	IP	PH	RHP	LHP
1985	NY	NL	3	1	2	1	2	0	0	0	0	0	0	1	0	1	0	3
1987	SEA	AL	2	2	0	1	1	0	0	0	0	0	0	0	0	0	0	2
Total			5	3	2	2	3	0	0	0	0	0	0	1	0	1	0	5

Rank among batters: 3,191 • *Total ballparks homered in*: 3 • *First HR*: 06/10/1985 off Don Carman

Larry Christenson

LARRY RICHARD CHRISTENSON
B: 11/10/1953
BR

Year	Tm	Lg	Tot	H	A	Men-On 0	1	2	3	One-Game 2	3	4	LO	XN	IP	PH	RHP	LHP
1975	PHI	NL	2	1	1	0	2	0	0	0	0	0	0	0	0	0	2	0
1976	PHI	NL	2	0	2	2	0	0	0	1	0	0	0	0	0	0	0	2
1977	PHI	NL	3	1	2	1	0	1	1	0	0	0	0	0	0	0	2	1
1978	PHI	NL	1	1	0	0	1	0	0	0	0	0	0	0	0	0	1	0
1979	PHI	NL	1	0	1	1	0	0	0	0	0	0	0	0	0	0	0	1
1980	PHI	NL	1	0	1	0	0	1	0	0	0	0	0	0	0	0	1	0
1982	PHI	NL	1	0	1	0	1	0	0	0	0	0	0	0	0	0	1	0
Total			11	3	8	4	4	2	1	1	0	0	0	0	0	0	7	4

Rank among batters: 2,419 • *Top target (2 home runs)*: Mickey Lolich, Joe Niekro • *Number of pitchers victimized*: 9 • *Total ballparks homered in*: 7 • *First HR*: 05/16/1975 off Buzz Capra

Bob Christian

ROBERT CHARLES CHRISTIAN
B: 10/17/1945 D: 02/20/1974
BR

Year	Tm	Lg	Tot	H	A	Men-On 0	1	2	3	One-Game 2	3	4	LO	XN	IP	PH	RHP	LHP
1969	CHI	AL	3	2	1	1	1	1	0	0	0	0	0	0	0	0	3	0
1970	CHI	AL	1	1	0	0	1	0	0	0	0	0	0	0	0	1	1	0
Total			4	3	1	1	2	1	0	0	0	0	0	0	0	1	4	0

Rank among batters: 3,427 • *Total ballparks homered in*: 2 • *First HR*: 06/14/1969 off Jim Palmer

Mark Christman

MARQUETTE JOSEPH CHRISTMAN
B: 10/21/1913 D: 10/09/1976
BR

Year	Tm	Lg	Tot	H	A	Men-On 0	1	2	3	One-Game 2	3	4	LO	XN	IP	PH	RHP	LHP
1938	DET	AL	1	1	0	1	0	0	0	0	0	0	0	0	1	0	1	0
1943	STL	AL	2	1	1	2	0	0	0	0	0	0	0	0	0	0	1	1
1944	STL	AL	6	2	4	3	1	1	1	0	0	0	0	0	0	0	5	1
1945	STL	AL	4	4	0	2	2	0	0	0	0	0	0	0	0	0	3	1
1946	STL	AL	1	0	1	1	0	0	0	0	0	0	0	0	0	0	0	1
1947	WAS	AL	1	0	1	0	1	0	0	0	0	0	0	0	0	0	1	0
1948	WAS	AL	1	0	1	1	0	0	0	0	0	0	0	0	0	0	1	0

Year	Tm	Lg	Tot	H	A	Men-On 0	Men-On 1	Men-On 2	Men-On 3	One-Game 2	One-Game 3	One-Game 4	LO	XN	IP	PH	RHP	LHP

Mark Christman *continued*

Year	Tm	Lg	Tot	H	A	0	1	2	3	2	3	4	LO	XN	IP	PH	RHP	LHP
1949	WAS	AL	3	0	3	1	2	0	0	0	0	0	0	0	0	0	1	2
Total			19	8	11	11	6	1	1	0	0	0	0	0	1	0	13	6

Rank among batters: 1,861 • *Top target (2 home runs)*: Bill LeFebvre • *Number of pitchers victimized*: 18 • *Total ballparks homered in*: 6 • *First HR*: 09/27/1938 off Jim Walkup

Steve Christmas

STEPHEN RANDALL CHRISTMAS
B: 12/09/1957
BL

Year	Tm	Lg	Tot	H	A	0	1	2	3	2	3	4	LO	XN	IP	PH	RHP	LHP
1984	CHI	AL	1	0	1	0	0	1	0	0	0	0	0	0	0	1	1	0

Rank among batters: 4,707 • *Total ballparks homered in*: 1 • *First HR*: 09/19/1984 off Mike Smithson

Joe Christopher

JOSEPH O'NEAL CHRISTOPHER
B: 12/13/1935
BR

Year	Tm	Lg	Tot	H	A	0	1	2	3	2	3	4	LO	XN	IP	PH	RHP	LHP
1960	PIT	NL	1	1	0	0	0	1	0	0	0	0	0	0	0	0	0	1
1962	NY	NL	6	5	1	4	2	0	0	0	0	0	1	0	0	0	4	2
1963	NY	NL	1	1	0	1	0	0	0	0	0	0	0	0	0	0	1	0
1964	NY	NL	16	9	7	10	4	1	1	1	0	0	0	0	0	0	12	4
1965	NY	NL	5	5	0	3	1	1	0	0	0	0	0	0	0	0	1	4
Total			29	21	8	18	7	3	1	1	0	0	1	0	0	0	18	11

Rank among batters: 1,465 • *Top target (2 home runs)*: Gaylord Perry, Dennis Bennett, Tony Cloninger • *Number of pitchers victimized*: 26 • *Total ballparks homered in*: 8 • *First HR*: 08/07/1960 off Billy O'Dell

Russ Christopher

RUSSELL ORMAND CHRISTOPHER
B: 09/12/1917 D: 12/05/1954
BR

Year	Tm	Lg	Tot	H	A	0	1	2	3	2	3	4	LO	XN	IP	PH	RHP	LHP
1944	PHI	AL	1	0	1	1	0	0	0	0	0	0	0	0	0	0	1	0
1945	PHI	AL	1	1	0	1	0	0	0	0	0	0	0	0	0	0	1	0
Total			2	1	1	2	0	0	0	0	0	0	0	0	0	0	2	0

Rank among batters: 4,129 • *Total ballparks homered in*: 2 • *First HR*: 09/02/1944 off Pinky Woods

Bubba Church

EMORY NICHOLAS CHURCH
B: 09/12/1924
BR

Year	Tm	Lg	Tot	H	A	0	1	2	3	2	3	4	LO	XN	IP	PH	RHP	LHP
1951	PHI	NL	1	1	0	0	1	0	0	0	0	0	0	0	0	0	0	1
1952	CIN	NL	1	0	1	1	0	0	0	0	0	0	0	0	0	0	1	0
1953	CHI	NL	1	0	1	1	0	0	0	0	0	0	0	0	0	0	1	0
Total			3	1	2	2	1	0	0	0	0	0	0	0	0	0	2	1

Rank among batters: 3,735 • *Total ballparks homered in*: 2 • *First HR*: 07/08/1951 off Preacher Roe

Archi Cianfrocco

ANGELO DOMINIC CIANFROCCO
B: 10/06/1966
BR

Year	Tm	Lg	Tot	H	A	0	1	2	3	2	3	4	LO	XN	IP	PH	RHP	LHP
1992	MON	NL	6	3	3	3	2	1	0	0	0	0	0	0	0	0	2	4
1993	MON	NL	1	0	1	1	0	0	0	0	0	0	0	0	0	0	1	0
	SD	NL	11	6	5	6	3	2	0	0	0	0	0	0	0	0	9	2
	Total		12	6	6	7	3	2	0	0	0	0	0	0	0	0	10	2
1994	SD	NL	4	3	1	2	1	1	0	0	0	0	0	0	0	0	4	0
1995	SD	NL	5	1	4	1	0	3	1	0	0	0	0	0	0	3	5	0
Total			27	13	14	13	6	7	1	0	0	0	0	0	0	3	21	6

Rank among batters: 1,532 • *Total ballparks homered in*: 12 • *First HR*: 05/09/1992 off Bud Black

Ted Cieslak

THADDEUS WALTER CIESLAK
B: 11/22/1916
BR

Year	Tm	Lg	Tot	H	A	0	1	2	3	2	3	4	LO	XN	IP	PH	RHP	LHP
1944	PHI	NL	2	0	2	2	0	0	0	0	0	0	0	0	0	0	2	0

Rank among batters: 4,129 • *Total ballparks homered in*: 2 • *First HR*: 05/12/1944 off Paul Derringer

Gino Cimoli

GINO NICHOLAS CIMOLI
B: 12/18/1929
BR

Year	Tm	Lg	Tot	H	A	Men-On 0	1	2	3	One-Game 2	3	4	LO	XN	IP	PH	RHP	LHP
1957	BRO	NL	10	5	5	6	3	1	0	0	0	0	0	2	1	0	10	0
1958	LA	NL	9	5	4	7	2	0	0	0	0	0	0	0	0	0	6	3
1959	STL	NL	8	5	3	4	3	1	0	0	0	0	0	0	0	0	5	3
1961	MIL	NL	3	3	0	3	0	0	0	0	0	0	0	0	0	0	1	2
1962	KC	AL	10	7	3	6	2	2	0	0	0	0	0	0	0	0	6	4
1963	KC	AL	4	1	3	3	1	0	0	0	0	0	0	0	0	0	3	1
Total			44	26	18	29	11	4	0	0	0	0	0	2	1	0	31	13

Rank among batters: 1,095 • Top target (2 home runs): Robin Roberts, Bob Friend, Johnny Antonelli, Hank Aguirre • *Number of pitchers victimized*: 40 • *Total ballparks homered in*: 13 • *First HR*: 04/16/1957 off Robin Roberts

Jeff Cirillo

JEFFREY HOWARD CIRILLO
B: 09/23/1969
BR

Year	Tm	Lg	Tot	H	A	Men-On 0	1	2	3	One-Game 2	3	4	LO	XN	IP	PH	RHP	LHP
1994	MIL	AL	3	1	2	2	0	1	0	0	0	0	0	1	0	0	3	0
1995	MIL	AL	9	6	3	7	1	1	0	1	0	0	0	0	0	0	7	2
Total			12	7	5	9	1	2	0	1	0	0	0	1	0	0	10	2

Rank among batters: 2,325 • *Top target (2 home runs)*: Rusty Meacham • *Number of pitchers victimized*: 11 • *Total ballparks homered in*: 5 • *First HR*: 07/15/1994 off Dave Stevens

Bill Cissell

CHALMER WILLIAM CISSELL
B: 01/03/1904 D: 03/15/1949
BR

Year	Tm	Lg	Tot	H	A	Men-On 0	1	2	3	One-Game 2	3	4	LO	XN	IP	PH	RHP	LHP
1928	CHI	AL	1	0	1	0	1	0	0	0	0	0	0	0	0	0	1	0
1929	CHI	AL	5	4	1	4	1	0	0	0	0	0	0	0	0	0	4	1
1930	CHI	AL	2	0	2	1	0	1	0	0	0	0	1	0	0	0	1	1
1931	CHI	AL	1	1	0	1	0	0	0	0	0	0	0	0	0	0	1	0
1932	CHI	AL	1	0	1	1	0	0	0	0	0	0	0	0	0	0	1	0
	CLE	AL	6	1	5	2	1	3	0	0	0	0	0	0	0	0	5	1
	Total		7	1	6	3	1	3	0	0	0	0	0	0	0	0	6	1
1933	CLE	AL	6	4	2	3	3	0	0	0	0	0	0	0	0	0	3	3
1934	BOS	AL	4	3	1	2	1	0	1	0	0	0	0	0	0	0	3	1
1937	PHI	AL	1	1	0	1	0	0	0	0	0	0	0	0	0	0	1	0
1938	NY	NL	2	1	1	1	0	1	0	0	0	0	0	0	0	0	1	1
Total			29	15	14	16	7	5	1	0	0	0	1	0	0	0	21	8

Rank among batters: 1,465 • *Top target (4 home runs)*: George Uhle • *Number of pitchers victimized*: 22 • *Total ballparks homered in*: 9 • *First HR*: 07/14/1928 off Ed Morris

Bill Clancy

WILLIAM EDWARD CLANCY
B: 04/12/1879 D: 02/10/1948
BL

Year	Tm	Lg	Tot	H	A	Men-On 0	1	2	3	One-Game 2	3	4	LO	XN	IP	PH	RHP	LHP
1905	PIT	NL	2	0	2	0	1	1	0	0	0	0	0	0	1	0	2	0

Rank among batters: 4,129 • *Total ballparks homered in*: 2 • *First HR*: 05/14/1905 off Mal Eason

Bud Clancy

JOHN WILLIAM CLANCY
B: 09/15/1900 D: 09/26/1968
BL

Year	Tm	Lg	Tot	H	A	Men-On 0	1	2	3	One-Game 2	3	4	LO	XN	IP	PH	RHP	LHP
1927	CHI	AL	3	1	2	2	0	0	1	0	0	0	0	0	2	0	1	2
1928	CHI	AL	2	0	2	2	0	0	0	0	0	0	0	0	1	0	2	0
1929	CHI	AL	3	2	1	1	1	1	0	0	0	0	0	0	0	0	3	0
1930	CHI	AL	3	0	3	1	2	0	0	1	0	0	0	0	0	0	2	1
1934	PHI	NL	1	1	0	0	1	0	0	0	0	0	0	0	0	0	0	1
Total			12	4	8	6	4	1	1	1	0	0	0	0	3	0	8	4

Rank among batters: 2,325 • *Top target (2 home runs)*: Sam Gray, Hank Johnson • *Number of pitchers victimized*: 10 • *Total ballparks homered in*: 5 • *First HR*: 06/07/1927 off Waite Hoyt

John Clapp

JOHN EDGAR CLAPP
B: 07/17/1851 D: 12/18/1904
BR

Year	Tm	Lg	Tot	H	A	Men-On 0	1	2	3	One-Game 2	3	4	LO	XN	IP	PH	RHP	LHP
1879	BUF	NL	1	1	0	0	1	0	0	0	0	0	0	0	0	0	1	0

						Men-On				One-Game								
Year	**Tm**	**Lg**	**Tot**	**H**	**A**	**0**	**1**	**2**	**3**	**2**	**3**	**4**	**LO**	**XN**	**IP**	**PH**	**RHP**	**LHP**

John Clapp *continued*

Year	Tm	Lg	Tot	H	A	Men-On 0	1	2	3	One-Game 2	3	4	LO	XN	IP	PH	RHP	LHP
1880	CIN	NL	1	1	0	0	1	0	0	0	0	0	0	0	0	0	1	0
Total			2	2	0	0	2	0	0	0	0	0	0	0	0	0	2	0

Rank among batters: 4,129 • *Total ballparks homered in*: 2 • *First HR*: 07/05/1879 off Jim McCormick

Doug Clarey

DOUGLAS WILLIAM CLAREY
B: 04/20/1954
BR

Year	Tm	Lg	Tot	H	A	Men-On 0	1	2	3	One-Game 2	3	4	LO	XN	IP	PH	RHP	LHP
1976	STL	NL	1	0	1	0	1	0	0	0	0	0	0	1	0	1	0	1

Rank among batters: 4,707 • *Total ballparks homered in*: 1 • *First HR*: 04/28/1976 off Mike Caldwell

Allie Clark

ALFRED ALOYSIUS CLARK
B: 06/16/1923
BR

Year	Tm	Lg	Tot	H	A	Men-On 0	1	2	3	One-Game 2	3	4	LO	XN	IP	PH	RHP	LHP
1947	NY	AL	1	0	1	1	0	0	0	0	0	0	0	0	0	0	1	0
1948	CLE	AL	9	7	2	6	2	1	0	0	0	0	0	0	0	0	1	8
1949	CLE	AL	1	0	1	1	0	0	0	0	0	0	0	0	0	0	0	1
1950	CLE	AL	6	2	4	4	1	1	0	0	0	0	0	0	0	0	1	5
1951	CLE	AL	1	1	0	1	0	0	0	0	0	0	0	0	0	0	0	1
	PHI	AL	4	2	2	2	2	0	0	0	0	0	0	0	0	0	2	2
	Total		5	3	2	3	2	0	0	0	0	0	0	0	0	0	2	3
1952	PHI	AL	7	4	3	5	2	0	0	0	0	0	0	0	0	3	5	2
1953	PHI	AL	3	0	3	0	2	1	0	0	0	0	0	0	0	0	2	1
Total			32	16	16	20	9	3	0	0	0	0	0	0	0	3	12	20

Rank among batters: 1,360 • Top target (2 home runs): Milton Haefner, Eddie Lopat, Bill Wight, Mickey Harris, Tommy Byrne, Early Wynn • *Number of pitchers victimized*: 26 • *Total ballparks homered in*: 8 • *First HR*: 08/06/1947 off Bill McCahan

Bob Clark

ROBERT H. CLARK
B: 05/18/1863 D: 08/21/1919
BR

Year	Tm	Lg	Tot	H	A	Men-On 0	1	2	3	One-Game 2	3	4	LO	XN	IP	PH	RHP	LHP
1888	BRO	AA	1	1	0	0	1	0	0	0	0	0	0	0	1	0	1	0

Rank among batters: 4,707 • *Total ballparks homered in*: 1 • *First HR*: 09/16/1888 off Gus Weyhing

Bob Clark

ROBERT CALE CLARK
B: 06/13/1955
BR

Year	Tm	Lg	Tot	H	A	Men-On 0	1	2	3	One-Game 2	3	4	LO	XN	IP	PH	RHP	LHP
1979	CAL	AL	1	0	1	0	1	0	0	0	0	0	0	0	0	0	1	0
1980	CAL	AL	5	2	3	3	1	1	0	0	0	0	0	0	0	0	3	2
1981	CAL	AL	4	4	0	1	3	0	0	0	0	0	0	0	0	0	1	3
1982	CAL	AL	2	1	1	1	1	0	0	0	0	0	0	0	0	0	0	2
1983	CAL	AL	5	1	4	3	1	1	0	0	0	0	0	0	0	0	1	4
1984	MIL	AL	2	1	1	1	1	0	0	0	0	0	0	0	0	0	0	2
Total			19	9	10	9	8	2	0	0	0	0	0	0	0	0	6	13

Rank among batters: 1,861 • *Top target (2 home runs)*: Dan Schatzeder, Sammy Stewart, Bruce Hurst • *Number of pitchers victimized*: 16 • *Total ballparks homered in*: 9 • *First HR*: 08/25/1979 off Craig Kusick

Danny Clark

DANIEL CURREN CLARK
B: 01/18/1894 D: 05/23/1937
BL

Year	Tm	Lg	Tot	H	A	Men-On 0	1	2	3	One-Game 2	3	4	LO	XN	IP	PH	RHP	LHP
1922	DET	AL	3	0	3	2	0	1	0	0	0	0	0	0	0	1	3	0
1924	BOS	AL	2	0	2	1	0	0	1	0	0	0	0	0	0	0	2	0
Total			5	0	5	3	0	1	1	0	0	0	0	0	0	1	5	0

Rank among batters: 3,191 • *Total ballparks homered in*: 5 • *First HR*: 05/13/1922 off Bob Shawkey

Dave Clark

DAVID EARL CLARK
B: 09/03/1962
BL

Year	Tm	Lg	Tot	H	A	Men-On 0	1	2	3	One-Game 2	3	4	LO	XN	IP	PH	RHP	LHP
1986	CLE	AL	3	1	2	2	1	0	0	0	0	0	0	0	0	0	3	0

Dave Clark *continued*

Year	Tm	Lg	Tot	H	A	Men-On 0	Men-On 1	Men-On 2	Men-On 3	One-Game 2	One-Game 3	One-Game 4	LO	XN	IP	PH	RHP	LHP
1987	CLE	AL	3	1	2	0	2	1	0	0	0	0	0	0	0	0	3	0
1988	CLE	AL	3	2	1	3	0	0	0	0	0	0	0	0	0	0	3	0
1989	CLE	AL	8	4	4	6	1	1	0	0	0	0	0	0	0	2	8	0
1990	CHI	NL	5	3	2	4	1	0	0	0	0	0	1	0	0	0	5	0
1992	PIT	NL	2	2	0	1	0	1	0	0	0	0	0	0	0	0	2	0
1993	PIT	NL	11	8	3	5	6	0	0	0	0	0	0	0	0	2	9	2
1994	PIT	NL	10	7	3	3	5	2	0	1	0	0	0	0	0	1	10	0
1995	PIT	NL	4	2	2	2	1	1	0	0	0	0	0	0	0	1	3	1
Total			49	30	19	26	17	6	0	1	0	0	1	0	0	6	46	3

Rank among batters: 1,008 • Top target (2 home runs): Tim Belcher, Oil Can Boyd, Tommy Greene, Kevin Gross, Dwight Gooden, Jose Rijo, Omar Olivares, Pedro Martinez • *Number of pitchers victimized*: 41 • *Total ballparks homered in*: 17 • *First HR*: 09/25/1986 off Kirk McCaskill

Earl Clark

BAILEY EARL CLARK
B: 11/06/1907 D: 01/16/1938
BR

Year	Tm	Lg	Tot	H	A	Men-On 0	Men-On 1	Men-On 2	Men-On 3	One-Game 2	One-Game 3	One-Game 4	LO	XN	IP	PH	RHP	LHP
1929	BOS	NL	1	1	0	0	1	0	0	0	0	0	0	0	0	0	0	1
1930	BOS	NL	3	1	2	3	0	0	0	0	0	0	0	0	0	0	2	1
Total			4	2	2	3	1	0	0	0	0	0	0	0	0	0	2	2

Rank among batters: 3,427 • *Total ballparks homered in*: 3 • *First HR*: 05/18/1929 off Bill Walker

Jack Clark

JACK ANTHONY CLARK
B: 11/10/1955
BR

Year	Tm	Lg	Tot	H	A	Men-On 0	Men-On 1	Men-On 2	Men-On 3	One-Game 2	One-Game 3	One-Game 4	LO	XN	IP	PH	RHP	LHP
1976	SF	NL	2	2	0	2	0	0	0	0	0	0	0	0	0	0	2	0
1977	SF	NL	13	7	6	9	2	1	1	0	0	0	0	2	0	3	5	8
1978	SF	NL	25	10	15	13	7	4	1	1	0	0	0	0	0	1	12	13
1979	SF	NL	26	10	16	17	6	3	0	1	0	0	0	1	0	0	18	8
1980	SF	NL	22	8	14	12	6	3	1	1	0	0	0	1	0	0	18	4
1981	SF	NL	17	7	10	14	2	1	0	1	0	0	0	3	0	0	14	3
1982	SF	NL	27	9	18	16	5	5	1	3	0	0	0	2	0	0	20	7
1983	SF	NL	20	11	9	10	9	0	1	1	0	0	0	1	0	0	12	8
1984	SF	NL	11	4	7	6	5	0	0	1	0	0	0	0	0	0	7	4
1985	STL	NL	22	8	14	11	6	5	0	0	0	0	0	0	0	0	13	9
1986	STL	NL	9	4	5	7	2	0	0	0	0	0	0	1	0	0	3	6
1987	STL	NL	35	17	18	15	15	4	1	6	0	0	0	3	0	0	25	10
1988	NY	AL	27	13	14	11	12	4	0	0	0	0	0	2	0	0	17	10
1989	SD	NL	26	11	15	8	9	8	1	2	0	0	0	0	0	0	22	4
1990	SD	NL	25	16	9	16	4	5	0	0	0	0	0	1	0	0	16	9
1991	BOS	AL	28	18	10	13	11	2	2	0	1	0	0	1	0	0	22	6
1992	BOS	AL	5	0	5	2	2	1	0	1	0	0	0	0	0	0	3	2
Total			340	155	185	182	103	46	9	18	1	0	0	18	0	4	229	111

Rank among batters: 47 • *Top target (7 home runs)*: Don Robinson • *Number of pitchers victimized*: 231 • *Total ballparks homered in*: 26 • *First HR*: 09/11/1976 off Jack Billingham • *LCS HR*—1

Jerald Clark

JERALD DWAYNE CLARK
B: 08/10/1963
BR

Year	Tm	Lg	Tot	H	A	Men-On 0	Men-On 1	Men-On 2	Men-On 3	One-Game 2	One-Game 3	One-Game 4	LO	XN	IP	PH	RHP	LHP
1989	SD	NL	1	1	0	1	0	0	0	0	0	0	0	0	0	0	1	0
1990	SD	NL	5	2	3	2	3	0	0	1	0	0	0	0	0	0	3	2
1991	SD	NL	10	8	2	4	5	1	0	0	0	0	0	0	0	0	6	4
1992	SD	NL	12	9	3	5	5	1	1	0	0	0	0	0	0	0	6	6
1993	COL	NL	13	8	5	6	3	4	0	0	0	0	0	0	0	0	11	2
1995	MIN	AL	3	1	2	3	0	0	0	0	0	0	0	0	0	1	2	1
Total			44	29	15	21	16	6	1	1	0	0	0	0	0	1	29	15

Rank among batters: 1,095 • *Top target (2 home runs)*: Bobby Ojeda, Greg Maddux, Bud Black • *Number of pitchers victimized*: 41 • *Total ballparks homered in*: 12 • *First HR*: 09/29/1989 off Ernie Camacho

Mel Clark

MELVIN EARL CLARK
B: 07/07/1926
BR

Year	Tm	Lg	Tot	H	A	Men-On 0	Men-On 1	Men-On 2	Men-On 3	One-Game 2	One-Game 3	One-Game 4	LO	XN	IP	PH	RHP	LHP
1951	PHI	NL	1	0	1	1	0	0	0	0	0	0	0	0	0	0	0	1

						Men-On				One-Game								
Year	Tm	Lg	Tot	H	A	0	1	2	3	2	3	4	LO	XN	IP	PH	RHP	LHP

Mel Clark *continued*

Year	Tm	Lg	Tot	H	A	0	1	2	3	2	3	4	LO	XN	IP	PH	RHP	LHP
1952	PHI	NL	1	0	1	0	0	0	1	0	0	0	0	0	0	0	0	1
1954	PHI	NL	1	0	1	1	0	0	0	0	0	0	0	0	0	0	0	1
Total			3	0	3	2	0	0	1	0	0	0	0	0	0	0	0	3

Rank among batters: 3,735 • *Top target (2 home runs)*: Howie Pollet • *Number of pitchers victimized*: 2 • *Total ballparks homered in*: 2 • *First HR*: 09/12/1951 off Howie Pollet

Phil Clark

PHILLIP BENJAMIN CLARK
B: 05/06/1968
BR

Year	Tm	Lg	Tot	H	A	0	1	2	3	2	3	4	LO	XN	IP	PH	RHP	LHP
1992	DET	AL	1	0	1	0	1	0	0	0	0	0	0	0	0	0	0	1
1993	SD	NL	9	6	3	7	1	1	0	0	0	0	0	0	0	1	5	4
1994	SD	NL	5	4	1	2	2	1	0	0	0	0	0	0	0	0	2	3
1995	SD	NL	2	1	1	2	0	0	0	0	0	0	0	1	0	1	1	1
Total			17	11	6	11	4	2	0	0	0	0	0	1	0	2	8	9

Rank among batters: 1,969 • *Top target (2 home runs)*: Todd Burns, Steve Cooke • *Number of pitchers victimized*: 15 • *Total ballparks homered in*: 6 • *First HR*: 05/30/1992 off Bill Krueger

Ron Clark

RONALD BRUCE CLARK
B: 01/14/1943
BR

Year	Tm	Lg	Tot	H	A	0	1	2	3	2	3	4	LO	XN	IP	PH	RHP	LHP
1967	MIN	AL	2	2	0	1	1	0	0	0	0	0	0	0	0	0	1	1
1968	MIN	AL	1	1	0	1	0	0	0	0	0	0	0	0	0	0	0	1
1972	MIL	AL	2	1	1	2	0	0	0	0	0	0	0	0	0	0	2	0
Total			5	4	1	4	1	0	0	0	0	0	0	0	0	0	3	2

Rank among batters: 3,191 • *Total ballparks homered in*: 3 • *First HR*: 05/05/1967 off Billy Rohr

Spider Clark

OWEN F. CLARK
B: 09/16/1867 D: 02/08/1892

Year	Tm	Lg	Tot	H	A	0	1	2	3	2	3	4	LO	XN	IP	PH	RHP	LHP
1889	WAS	NL	3	1	2	3	0	0	0	0	0	0	0	0	0	0	3	0
1890	BUF	PL	2	1	1	2	0	0	0	0	0	0	0	0	0	0	1	1
Total			5	2	3	5	0	0	0	0	0	0	0	0	0	0	4	1

Rank among batters: 3,191 • *Top target (2 home runs)*: Ad Gumbert • *Number of pitchers victimized*: 4 • *Total ballparks homered in*: 4 • *First HR*: 07/04/1889 off Ad Gumbert

Tony Clark

ANTHONY CHRISTOPHER CLARK
B: 06/15/1972
BB

Year	Tm	Lg	Tot	H	A	0	1	2	3	2	3	4	LO	XN	IP	PH	RHP	LHP
1995	DET	AL	3	0	3	1	2	0	0	0	0	0	0	0	0	0	2	1

Rank among batters: 3,735 • *Total ballparks homered in*: 2 • *First HR*: 09/08/1995 off Jeff Ware

Watty Clark

WILLIAM WATSON CLARK
B: 05/16/1902 D: 03/04/1972
BL

Year	Tm	Lg	Tot	H	A	0	1	2	3	2	3	4	LO	XN	IP	PH	RHP	LHP
1930	BRO	NL	1	1	0	0	0	1	0	0	0	0	0	0	0	0	1	0

Rank among batters: 4,707 • *Total ballparks homered in*: 1 • *First HR*: 06/07/1930 off Lynn Nelson

Will Clark

WILLIAM NUSCHLER CLARK
B: 03/13/1964
BL

Year	Tm	Lg	Tot	H	A	0	1	2	3	2	3	4	LO	XN	IP	PH	RHP	LHP
1986	SF	NL	11	7	4	7	4	0	0	1	0	0	0	1	0	1	9	2
1987	SF	NL	35	22	13	20	13	2	0	4	0	0	0	2	0	0	28	7
1988	SF	NL	29	14	15	14	9	6	0	0	0	0	0	1	0	0	22	7
1989	SF	NL	23	9	14	10	7	5	1	0	0	0	0	2	0	0	15	8
1990	SF	NL	19	8	11	10	6	3	0	2	0	0	0	0	0	0	10	9
1991	SF	NL	29	17	12	11	13	3	2	2	0	0	0	0	0	0	21	8
1992	SF	NL	16	11	5	8	8	0	0	0	0	0	0	0	0	1	14	2
1993	SF	NL	14	5	9	8	5	1	0	1	0	0	0	1	0	0	13	1

Will Clark *continued*

Year	Tm	Lg	Tot	H	A	Men-On 0	Men-On 1	Men-On 2	Men-On 3	One-Game 2	One-Game 3	One-Game 4	LO	XN	IP	PH	RHP	LHP
1994	TEX	AL	13	9	4	7	4	2	0	0	0	0	0	0	0	0	12	1
1995	TEX	AL	16	10	6	10	4	2	0	0	0	0	0	0	0	0	12	4
Total			205	112	93	105	73	24	3	10	0	0	0	7	0	2	156	49

Rank among batters: 173 • *Top target (6 home runs)*: Nolan Ryan • *Number of pitchers victimized*: 139 • *Total ballparks homered in*: 20 • *First HR*: 04/08/1986 off Nolan Ryan • *Hit HR in first major league AB—@HOU*: 04/08/1986 • *LCS HR*—3; *All-Star HR*—1

Willie Clark

WILLIAM OTIS CLARK
B: 08/16/1872 D: 11/13/1932
BL

Year	Tm	Lg	Tot	H	A	Men-On 0	Men-On 1	Men-On 2	Men-On 3	One-Game 2	One-Game 3	One-Game 4	LO	XN	IP	PH	RHP	LHP
1897	NY	NL	1	0	1	0	1	0	0	0	0	0	0	0	0	0	0	1
1898	PIT	NL	1	0	1	1	0	0	0	0	0	0	0	0	0	0	1	0
Total			2	0	2	1	1	0	0	0	0	0	0	0	0	0	1	1

Rank among batters: 4,129 • *Total ballparks homered in*: 2 • *First HR*: 05/07/1897 off Harley Payne

Boileryard Clarke

WILLIAM JONES CLARKE
B: 10/18/1868 D: 07/29/1959
BR

Year	Tm	Lg	Tot	H	A	Men-On 0	Men-On 1	Men-On 2	Men-On 3	One-Game 2	One-Game 3	One-Game 4	LO	XN	IP	PH	RHP	LHP
1893	BAL	NL	1	1	0	1	0	0	0	0	0	0	0	0	1	0	1	0
1894	BAL	NL	1	0	1	0	0	1	0	0	0	0	0	0	0	0	1	0
1896	BAL	NL	2	0	2	2	0	0	0	0	0	0	0	0	0	0	2	0
1897	BAL	NL	1	0	1	0	1	0	0	0	0	0	0	0	0	0	1	0
1899	BOS	NL	2	1	1	1	1	0	0	0	0	0	0	0	0	0	2	0
1900	BOS	NL	1	1	0	1	0	0	0	0	0	0	0	0	0	0	1	0
1901	WAS	AL	3	2	1	1	2	0	0	0	0	0	0	0	0	0	1	2
1902	WAS	AL	6	5	1	1	2	3	0	0	0	0	0	0	0	0	6	0
1903	WAS	AL	2	2	0	1	1	0	0	0	0	0	0	0	0	0	2	0
1905	NY	NL	1	0	1	1	0	0	0	0	0	0	0	0	0	0	0	1
Total			20	12	8	9	7	4	0	0	0	0	0	0	1	0	17	3

Rank among batters: 1,810 • *Top target (2 home runs)*: Clark Griffith • *Number of pitchers victimized*: 19 • *Total ballparks homered in*: 9 • *First HR*: 07/19/1893 off Ed Crane • *World Series HR*—1

Dad Clarke

WILLIAM H. CLARKE
B: 01/07/1865 D: 06/03/1911
BB

Year	Tm	Lg	Tot	H	A	Men-On 0	Men-On 1	Men-On 2	Men-On 3	One-Game 2	One-Game 3	One-Game 4	LO	XN	IP	PH	RHP	LHP
1888	CHI	NL	1	0	1	0	1	0	0	0	0	0	0	0	0	0	1	0

Rank among batters: 4,707 • *Total ballparks homered in*: 1 • *First HR*: 04/23/1888 off Lev Shreve

Fred Clarke

FRED CLIFFORD CLARKE
B: 10/03/1872 D: 08/14/1960
BL HOF

Year	Tm	Lg	Tot	H	A	Men-On 0	Men-On 1	Men-On 2	Men-On 3	One-Game 2	One-Game 3	One-Game 4	LO	XN	IP	PH	RHP	LHP
1894	LOU	NL	7	3	4	2	5	0	0	0	0	0	0	0	1	0	5	2
1895	LOU	NL	4	2	2	3	1	0	0	0	0	0	0	0	1	0	3	1
1896	LOU	NL	9	5	4	5	3	1	0	0	0	0	2	0	1	0	8	1
1897	LOU	NL	6	4	2	4	1	1	0	0	0	0	1	0	1	0	4	2
1898	LOU	NL	3	2	1	1	2	0	0	0	0	0	1	0	0	0	3	0
1899	LOU	NL	5	5	0	1	3	1	0	0	0	0	0	0	1	0	3	2
1900	PIT	NL	3	2	1	1	1	1	0	0	0	0	0	0	2	0	3	0
1901	PIT	NL	6	3	3	5	1	0	0	0	0	0	1	0	3	0	4	2
1902	PIT	NL	2	2	0	2	0	0	0	0	0	0	0	0	2	0	2	0
1903	PIT	NL	5	3	2	2	3	0	0	0	0	0	0	0	3	1	4	1
1905	PIT	NL	2	0	2	2	0	0	0	0	0	0	0	0	0	0	2	0
1906	PIT	NL	1	0	1	0	1	0	0	0	0	0	0	0	1	0	1	0
1907	PIT	NL	2	1	1	0	0	2	0	0	0	0	0	0	2	0	0	2
1908	PIT	NL	2	0	2	1	1	0	0	0	0	0	0	0	1	0	1	1
1909	PIT	NL	3	1	2	1	0	2	0	0	0	0	0	0	1	0	3	0
1910	PIT	NL	2	1	1	2	0	0	0	0	0	0	0	0	1	0	2	0
1911	PIT	NL	5	4	1	2	3	0	0	0	0	0	0	0	2	0	5	0
Total			67	38	29	34	25	8	0	0	0	0	5	0	23	1	53	14

Rank among batters: 777 • *Top target (5 home runs)*: Jack Taylor • *Number of pitchers victimized*: 54 • *Total ballparks homered in*: 14 • *First HR*: 07/04/1894 off Bert Inks • *Hit for Cycle*—vs CIN: 07/23/1901; vs CIN: 05/07/1903 • *World Series HR*—2

Year	Tm	Lg	Tot	H	A	Men-On 0	1	2	3	One-Game 2	3	4	LO	XN	IP	PH	RHP	LHP

Horace Clarke

HORACE MEREDITH CLARKE
B: 06/02/1940
BB

Year	Tm	Lg	Tot	H	A	0	1	2	3	2	3	4	LO	XN	IP	PH	RHP	LHP
1965	NY	AL	1	1	0	0	0	0	1	0	0	0	0	0	0	0	1	0
1966	NY	AL	6	2	4	4	1	0	1	0	0	0	1	1	0	0	4	2
1967	NY	AL	3	2	1	0	2	1	0	0	0	0	0	0	0	0	3	0
1968	NY	AL	2	0	2	1	1	0	0	0	0	0	0	0	0	0	1	1
1969	NY	AL	4	1	3	3	0	1	0	0	0	0	1	0	0	0	0	4
1970	NY	AL	4	2	2	3	1	0	0	0	0	0	1	0	0	0	1	3
1971	NY	AL	2	0	2	2	0	0	0	0	0	0	0	0	0	0	0	2
1972	NY	AL	3	2	1	2	0	1	0	0	0	0	1	0	0	0	2	1
1973	NY	AL	2	0	2	2	0	0	0	0	0	0	0	1	0	0	0	2
Total			27	10	17	17	5	3	2	0	0	0	4	2	0	0	12	15

Rank among batters: 1,532 • Top target (2 home runs): Catfish Hunter, Jim Merritt, Barry Moore, Dave McNally, John Hiller • *Number of pitchers victimized*: 22 • *Total ballparks homered in*: 11 • *First HR*: 09/21/1965 off Floyd Weaver

Josh Clarke

JOSHUA BALDWIN CLARKE
B: 03/08/1879 D: 07/02/1962
BL

Year	Tm	Lg	Tot	H	A	0	1	2	3	2	3	4	LO	XN	IP	PH	RHP	LHP
1905	STL	NL	3	2	1	3	0	0	0	0	0	0	0	0	2	0	3	0
1908	CLE	AL	1	0	1	1	0	0	0	0	0	0	0	0	0	0	1	0
1911	BOS	NL	1	1	0	1	0	0	0	0	0	0	1	0	0	0	1	0
Total			5	3	2	5	0	0	0	0	0	0	1	0	2	0	5	0

Rank among batters: 3,191 • *Total ballparks homered in*: 4 • *First HR*: 05/09/1905 off Joe McGinnity

Nig Clarke

JAY JUSTIN CLARKE
B: 12/15/1882 D: 06/15/1949
BL

Year	Tm	Lg	Tot	H	A	0	1	2	3	2	3	4	LO	XN	IP	PH	RHP	LHP
1905	DET	AL	1	0	1	1	0	0	0	0	0	0	0	0	1	0	1	0
1906	CLE	AL	1	1	0	0	1	0	0	0	0	0	0	0	0	0	1	0
1907	CLE	AL	3	2	1	2	1	0	0	0	0	0	0	0	0	0	3	0
1908	CLE	AL	1	1	0	0	1	0	0	0	0	0	0	0	0	0	1	0
Total			6	4	2	3	3	0	0	0	0	0	0	0	1	0	6	0

Rank among batters: 2,988 • *Total ballparks homered in*: 3 • *First HR*: 08/03/1905 off Andy Coakley

Stu Clarke

WILLIAM STUART CLARKE
B: 01/24/1906 D: 08/26/1985
BR

Year	Tm	Lg	Tot	H	A	0	1	2	3	2	3	4	LO	XN	IP	PH	RHP	LHP
1929	PIT	NL	2	1	1	1	1	0	0	0	0	0	0	0	0	0	1	1

Rank among batters: 4,129 • *Total ballparks homered in*: 2 • *First HR*: 07/13/1929 off Sam Dailey

Tommy Clarke

THOMAS ALOYSIUS CLARKE
B: 05/09/1888 D: 08/14/1945
BR

Year	Tm	Lg	Tot	H	A	0	1	2	3	2	3	4	LO	XN	IP	PH	RHP	LHP
1910	CIN	NL	1	0	1	0	0	1	0	0	0	0	0	0	0	0	1	0
1911	CIN	NL	1	0	1	1	0	0	0	0	0	0	0	0	0	0	1	0
1913	CIN	NL	1	0	1	1	0	0	0	0	0	0	0	0	0	0	1	0
1914	CIN	NL	2	0	2	2	0	0	0	0	0	0	0	0	2	0	2	0
1917	CIN	NL	1	0	1	1	0	0	0	0	0	0	0	0	0	0	0	1
Total			6	0	6	5	0	1	0	0	0	0	0	0	2	0	5	1

Rank among batters: 2,988 • *Total ballparks homered in*: 5 • *First HR*: 09/23/1910 off Sam Frock

Dad Clarkson

ARTHUR HAMILTON CLARKSON
B: 08/31/1866 D: 02/05/1911
BR

Year	Tm	Lg	Tot	H	A	0	1	2	3	2	3	4	LO	XN	IP	PH	RHP	LHP
1895	BAL	NL	1	0	1	0	1	0	0	0	0	0	0	0	0	0	1	0

Rank among batters: 4,707 • *Total ballparks homered in*: 1 • *First HR*: 07/14/1895 off Clark Griffith

John Clarkson

JOHN GIBSON CLARKSON
B: 07/01/1861 D: 02/04/1909
BR HOF

Year	Tm	Lg	Tot	H	A	Men-On 0	1	2	3	One-Game 2	3	4	LO	XN	IP	PH	RHP	LHP
1884	CHI	NL	3	3	0	0	3	0	0	1	0	0	0	0	0	0	1	2
1885	CHI	NL	4	3	1	3	1	0	0	0	0	0	0	0	0	0	4	0
1886	CHI	NL	3	3	0	3	0	0	0	0	0	0	0	0	0	0	2	1
1887	CHI	NL	6	5	1	4	2	0	0	1	0	0	0	0	0	0	6	0
1888	BOS	NL	1	0	1	0	1	0	0	0	0	0	0	0	0	0	1	0
1889	BOS	NL	2	0	2	2	0	0	0	0	0	0	0	0	0	0	2	0
1890	BOS	NL	2	0	2	1	1	0	0	0	0	0	0	0	2	0	2	0
1892	BOS	NL	1	0	1	1	0	0	0	0	0	0	0	0	0	0	0	1
1893	CLE	NL	1	1	0	1	0	0	0	0	0	0	0	1	1	0	1	0
1894	CLE	NL	1	0	1	0	0	1	0	0	0	0	0	0	0	0	1	0
Total			24	15	9	15	8	1	0	2	0	0	0	1	3	0	20	4

Rank among batters: 1,643 • *Top target (5 home runs)*: Pretzels Getzien • *Number of pitchers victimized*: 18 • *Total ballparks homered in*: 8 • *First HR*: 10/04/1884 off Mickey Welch • *World Series HR*—1

Ellis Clary

ELLIS CLARY
B: 09/11/1916
BR

Year	Tm	Lg	Tot	H	A	Men-On 0	1	2	3	One-Game 2	3	4	LO	XN	IP	PH	RHP	LHP
1945	STL	AL	1	0	1	1	0	0	0	0	0	0	0	0	0	0	0	1

Rank among batters: 4,707 • *Total ballparks homered in*: 1 • *First HR*: 04/20/1945 off Eddie Lopat

Dain Clay

DAIN ELMER CLAY
B: 07/10/1919 D: 08/28/1994
BR

Year	Tm	Lg	Tot	H	A	Men-On 0	1	2	3	One-Game 2	3	4	LO	XN	IP	PH	RHP	LHP
1945	CIN	NL	1	1	0	0	0	0	1	0	0	0	0	0	0	0	0	1
1946	CIN	NL	2	1	1	1	1	0	0	0	0	0	0	0	0	0	1	1
Total			3	2	1	1	1	0	1	0	0	0	0	0	0	0	1	2

Rank among batters: 3,735 • *Total ballparks homered in*: 2 • *First HR*: 04/17/1945 off Fritz Ostermueller

Royce Clayton

ROYCE SPENCER CLAYTON
B: 01/02/1970
BR

Year	Tm	Lg	Tot	H	A	Men-On 0	1	2	3	One-Game 2	3	4	LO	XN	IP	PH	RHP	LHP
1992	SF	NL	4	3	1	3	1	0	0	0	0	0	0	0	0	0	4	0
1993	SF	NL	6	5	1	5	0	1	0	0	0	0	0	0	0	0	4	2
1994	SF	NL	3	1	2	1	2	0	0	0	0	0	0	0	0	0	1	2
1995	SF	NL	5	2	3	4	1	0	0	0	0	0	0	0	0	0	1	4
Total			18	11	7	13	4	1	0	0	0	0	0	0	0	0	10	8

Rank among batters: 1,914 • *Top target (2 home runs)*: Dave Telgheder, Steve Avery • *Number of pitchers victimized*: 16 • *Total ballparks homered in*: 6 • *First HR*: 05/08/1992 off Mark Gardner

Doug Clemens

DOUGLAS HORACE CLEMENS
B: 06/09/1939
BL

Year	Tm	Lg	Tot	H	A	Men-On 0	1	2	3	One-Game 2	3	4	LO	XN	IP	PH	RHP	LHP
1962	STL	NL	1	1	0	0	1	0	0	0	0	0	0	0	0	0	1	0
1963	STL	NL	1	0	1	0	1	0	0	0	0	0	0	0	0	0	1	0
1964	STL	NL	1	1	0	0	1	0	0	0	0	0	0	0	0	0	1	0
	CHI	NL	2	0	2	1	0	1	0	0	0	0	0	0	0	0	2	0
	Total		3	1	2	1	1	1	0	0	0	0	0	0	0	0	3	0
1965	CHI	NL	4	1	3	2	1	1	0	0	0	0	0	0	0	0	3	1
1966	PHI	NL	1	0	1	0	0	1	0	0	0	0	0	0	0	0	1	0
1968	PHI	NL	2	1	1	0	1	1	0	0	0	0	0	0	0	1	1	1
Total			12	4	8	3	5	4	0	0	0	0	0	0	0	1	10	2

Rank among batters: 2,325 • *Total ballparks homered in*: 7 • *First HR*: 06/30/1962 off Vern Law

Roberto Clemente

ROBERTO (WALKER) CLEMENTE
B: 08/18/1934 D: 12/31/1972
BR HOF

Year	Tm	Lg	Tot	H	A	Men-On 0	1	2	3	One-Game 2	3	4	LO	XN	IP	PH	RHP	LHP
1955	PIT	NL	5	3	2	4	1	0	0	0	0	0	2	0	1	0	2	3

Year	Tm	Lg	Tot	H	A	Men-On 0	Men-On 1	Men-On 2	Men-On 3	One-Game 2	One-Game 3	One-Game 4	LO	XN	IP	PH	RHP	LHP

Roberto Clemente *continued*

Year	Tm	Lg	Tot	H	A	0	1	2	3	2	3	4	LO	XN	IP	PH	RHP	LHP
1956	PIT	NL	7	4	3	3	2	1	1	0	0	0	0	0	1	0	6	1
1957	PIT	NL	4	2	2	4	0	0	0	0	0	0	1	0	1	0	1	3
1958	PIT	NL	6	1	5	1	3	2	0	1	0	0	0	0	1	0	4	2
1959	PIT	NL	4	1	3	4	0	0	0	0	0	0	0	0	1	0	3	1
1960	PIT	NL	16	5	11	7	6	2	1	0	0	0	0	0	0	0	10	6
1961	PIT	NL	23	10	13	16	5	1	1	2	0	0	0	0	1	0	14	9
1962	PIT	NL	10	6	4	3	2	3	2	0	0	0	0	0	0	0	8	2
1963	PIT	NL	17	5	12	10	4	2	1	0	0	0	0	0	0	0	11	6
1964	PIT	NL	12	4	8	6	5	1	0	0	0	0	0	0	0	0	5	7
1965	PIT	NL	10	5	5	8	2	0	0	0	0	0	0	0	0	1	6	4
1966	PIT	NL	29	16	13	16	6	7	0	1	0	0	0	1	1	0	20	9
1967	PIT	NL	23	9	14	15	6	2	0	2	1	0	0	1	0	0	19	4
1968	PIT	NL	18	6	12	10	8	0	0	2	0	0	0	0	2	0	15	3
1969	PIT	NL	19	5	14	6	9	3	1	0	1	0	0	0	0	0	14	5
1970	PIT	NL	14	6	8	10	3	1	0	2	0	0	0	0	0	0	8	6
1971	PIT	NL	13	7	6	5	7	1	0	0	0	0	0	1	1	1	4	9
1972	PIT	NL	10	6	4	2	6	2	0	1	0	0	0	0	0	0	9	1
Total			240	101	139	130	75	28	7	11	2	0	3	3	10	2	159	81

Rank among batters: 128 • *Top target (6 home runs)*: Sandy Koufax, Ferguson Jenkins • *Number of pitchers victimized*: 141 • *Total ballparks homered in*: 19 • *First HR*: 04/18/1955 off Don Liddle • *World Series HR—2; LCS HR—1; All-Star HR—1*

Jack Clements

JOHN J. CLEMENTS
B: 07/24/1864 D: 05/23/1941
BL

Year	Tm	Lg	Tot	H	A	0	1	2	3	2	3	4	LO	XN	IP	PH	RHP	LHP
1884	PHI	UA	3	3	0	0	2	1	0	0	0	0	0	0	1	0	1	0
1885	PHI	NL	1	0	1	1	0	0	0	0	0	0	0	0	0	0	1	0
1887	PHI	NL	1	0	1	0	0	1	0	0	0	0	0	0	0	0	1	0
1888	PHI	NL	1	0	1	1	0	0	0	0	0	0	0	1	0	0	0	1
1889	PHI	NL	4	3	1	2	2	0	0	0	0	0	0	0	0	0	3	1
1890	PHI	NL	7	3	4	3	2	2	0	0	0	0	0	0	1	0	5	2
1891	PHI	NL	4	4	0	1	2	1	0	0	0	0	0	0	0	0	3	0
1892	PHI	NL	8	7	1	4	3	1	0	1	0	0	0	0	1	0	7	0
1893	PHI	NL	17	12	5	5	6	5	1	1	0	0	0	1	0	0	13	3
1894	PHI	NL	3	3	0	2	1	0	0	0	0	0	0	0	0	0	2	1
1895	PHI	NL	13	10	3	7	3	3	0	1	0	0	0	0	0	0	13	0
1896	PHI	NL	5	3	2	2	2	1	0	0	0	0	0	0	0	1	4	1
1897	PHI	NL	6	1	5	2	3	1	0	1	0	0	0	0	0	0	6	0
1898	STL	NL	3	1	2	2	1	0	0	0	0	0	0	0	0	0	1	1
1900	BOS	NL	1	1	0	1	0	0	0	0	0	0	0	0	0	0	1	0
Total			77	51	26	33	27	16	1	4	0	0	0	2	3	1	60	10

Rank among batters: 682 • *Top target (4 home runs)*: Jouett Meekin • *Number of pitchers victimized*: 59 • *Total ballparks homered in*: 20 • *First HR*: 06/09/1884 off Bill Wise

Lance Clemons

LANCE LEVIS CLEMONS
B: 07/06/1947
BL

Year	Tm	Lg	Tot	H	A	0	1	2	3	2	3	4	LO	XN	IP	PH	RHP	LHP
1971	KC	AL	1	0	1	1	0	0	0	0	0	0	0	0	0	0	1	0

Rank among batters: 4,707 • *Total ballparks homered in*: 1 • *First HR*: 08/31/1971 off Ken Sanders

Verne Clemons

VERNE JAMES CLEMONS
B: 09/08/1891 D: 05/05/1959
BR

Year	Tm	Lg	Tot	H	A	0	1	2	3	2	3	4	LO	XN	IP	PH	RHP	LHP
1919	STL	NL	2	0	2	1	1	0	0	0	0	0	0	0	0	0	2	0
1920	STL	NL	1	0	1	1	0	0	0	0	0	0	0	0	0	0	1	0
1921	STL	NL	2	1	1	0	1	1	0	0	0	0	0	0	0	0	1	1
Total			5	1	4	2	2	1	0	0	0	0	0	0	0	0	4	1

Rank among batters: 3,191 • *Total ballparks homered in*: 4 • *First HR*: 05/24/1919 off Jess Barnes

Donn Clendenon

DONN ALVIN CLENDENON
B: 07/15/1935
BR

Year	Tm	Lg	Tot	H	A	0	1	2	3	2	3	4	LO	XN	IP	PH	RHP	LHP
1962	PIT	NL	7	3	4	5	0	1	1	0	0	0	0	0	0	0	4	3

Donn Clendenon *continued*

Year	Tm	Lg	Tot	H	A	Men-On 0	Men-On 1	Men-On 2	Men-On 3	One-Game 2	One-Game 3	One-Game 4	LO	XN	IP	PH	RHP	LHP
1963	PIT	NL	15	8	7	12	2	1	0	1	0	0	0	0	0	0	8	7
1964	PIT	NL	12	3	9	6	6	0	0	0	0	0	0	0	1	1	8	4
1965	PIT	NL	14	5	9	9	3	2	0	1	0	0	0	0	0	0	8	6
1966	PIT	NL	28	3	25	14	10	4	0	2	0	0	0	1	0	0	21	7
1967	PIT	NL	13	8	5	5	6	2	0	0	0	0	0	0	1	1	10	3
1968	PIT	NL	17	5	12	10	6	1	0	0	0	0	0	0	1	0	8	9
1969	MON	NL	4	4	0	2	1	1	0	0	0	0	0	0	0	0	4	0
	NY	NL	12	4	8	5	5	2	0	2	0	0	0	1	0	0	6	6
	Total		16	8	8	7	6	3	0	2	0	0	0	1	0	0	10	6
1970	NY	NL	22	10	12	9	5	8	0	1	0	0	0	0	0	1	11	11
1971	NY	NL	11	5	6	7	3	1	0	1	0	0	0	2	0	0	7	4
1972	STL	NL	4	0	4	3	1	0	0	0	0	0	0	0	0	0	2	2
Total			159	58	101	87	48	23	1	8	0	0	0	4	3	3	97	62

Rank among batters: 268 • *Top target (6 home runs)*: Ken Holtzman • *Number of pitchers victimized*: 107 • *Total ballparks homered in*: 19 • *First HR*: 05/01/1962 off Billy O'Dell • *World Series HR*—3

Elmer Cleveland

ELMER ELLSWORTH CLEVELAND
B: 09/15/1862 D: 10/08/1913
BR

Year	Tm	Lg	Tot	H	A	Men-On 0	Men-On 1	Men-On 2	Men-On 3	One-Game 2	One-Game 3	One-Game 4	LO	XN	IP	PH	RHP	LHP
1888	NY	NL	2	0	2	2	0	0	0	0	0	0	0	0	1	0	2	0
	PIT	NL	2	0	2	0	2	0	0	0	1	0	0	0	0	0	2	0
	Total		4	0	4	4	0	0	0	1	0	0	0	0	1	0	4	0
Total			4	0	4	4	0	0	0	1	0	0	0	0	1	0	4	0

Rank among batters: 3,427 • *Top target (3 home runs)*: Mark Baldwin • *Number of pitchers victimized*: 2 • *Total ballparks homered in*: 2 • *First HR*: 05/12/1888 off Mark Baldwin

Stan Cliburn

STANLEY GENE CLIBURN
B: 12/19/1956
BR

Year	Tm	Lg	Tot	H	A	Men-On 0	Men-On 1	Men-On 2	Men-On 3	One-Game 2	One-Game 3	One-Game 4	LO	XN	IP	PH	RHP	LHP
1980	CAL	AL	2	0	2	1	1	0	0	0	0	0	0	0	0	0	0	2

Rank among batters: 4,129 • *Total ballparks homered in*: 2 • *First HR*: 07/25/1980 off Ross Grimsley

Harlond Clift

HARLOND BENTON CLIFT
B: 08/12/1912 D: 04/27/1992
BR

Year	Tm	Lg	Tot	H	A	Men-On 0	Men-On 1	Men-On 2	Men-On 3	One-Game 2	One-Game 3	One-Game 4	LO	XN	IP	PH	RHP	LHP
1934	STL	AL	14	8	6	7	4	2	1	1	0	0	2	0	1	0	10	4
1935	STL	AL	11	4	7	5	4	2	0	0	0	0	0	0	0	0	8	3
1936	STL	AL	20	12	8	13	5	2	0	1	0	0	0	0	2	0	16	4
1937	STL	AL	29	14	15	8	11	10	0	2	0	0	0	0	0	0	26	3
1938	STL	AL	34	20	14	17	14	2	1	5	0	0	0	0	0	1	26	8
1939	STL	AL	15	6	9	7	6	2	0	0	0	0	0	0	0	0	13	2
1940	STL	AL	20	12	8	15	2	1	2	0	0	0	0	0	0	0	15	5
1941	STL	AL	17	8	9	8	8	0	1	2	0	0	0	0	1	0	15	2
1942	STL	AL	7	3	4	5	1	1	0	0	0	0	0	0	1	0	7	0
1943	STL	AL	3	1	2	2	0	1	0	0	0	0	0	0	0	0	2	1
1945	WAS	AL	8	0	8	6	1	0	1	1	0	0	0	0	0	0	5	3
Total			178	88	90	93	56	23	6	12	0	0	2	0	5	1	143	35

Rank among batters: 225 • *Top target (7 home runs)*: Red Ruffing, Buck Ross • *Number of pitchers victimized*: 96 • *Total ballparks homered in*: 9 • *First HR*: 05/09/1934 off Russ Van Atta

Monk Cline

JOHN P. CLINE
B: 03/03/1858 D: 09/23/1916
BL

Year	Tm	Lg	Tot	H	A	Men-On 0	Men-On 1	Men-On 2	Men-On 3	One-Game 2	One-Game 3	One-Game 4	LO	XN	IP	PH	RHP	LHP
1884	LOU	AA	2	0	2	1	1	0	0	0	0	0	0	0	0	0	1	0

Rank among batters: 4,129 • *Total ballparks homered in*: 2 • *First HR*: 08/14/1884 off Gus Shallix

Ty Cline

TYRONE ALEXANDER CLINE
B: 06/15/1939
BL

Year	Tm	Lg	Tot	H	A	Men-On 0	Men-On 1	Men-On 2	Men-On 3	One-Game 2	One-Game 3	One-Game 4	LO	XN	IP	PH	RHP	LHP
1962	CLE	AL	2	2	0	1	1	0	0	0	0	0	0	0	0	0	2	0

Year	Tm	Lg	Tot	H	A	Men-On 0	Men-On 1	Men-On 2	Men-On 3	One-Game 2	One-Game 3	One-Game 4	LO	XN	IP	PH	RHP	LHP

Ty Cline *continued*

Year	Tm	Lg	Tot	H	A	0	1	2	3	2	3	4	LO	XN	IP	PH	RHP	LHP
1964	MIL	NL	1	0	1	0	1	0	0	0	0	0	0	0	0	1	1	0
1968	SF	NL	1	0	1	0	0	1	0	0	0	0	0	0	0	0	1	0
1969	MON	NL	2	1	1	2	0	0	0	0	0	0	1	0	0	0	2	0
Total			6	3	3	3	2	1	0	0	0	0	1	0	0	1	6	0

Rank among batters: 2,988 • *Total ballparks homered in*: 4 • *First HR*: 04/27/1962 off Georges Maranda

Gene Clines

EUGENE ANTHONY CLINES
B: 10/06/1946
BR

Year	Tm	Lg	Tot	H	A	0	1	2	3	2	3	4	LO	XN	IP	PH	RHP	LHP
1971	PIT	NL	1	0	1	0	0	1	0	0	0	0	0	0	0	0	1	0
1973	PIT	NL	1	0	1	0	0	1	0	0	0	0	0	0	0	0	1	0
1977	CHI	NL	3	3	0	0	3	0	0	0	0	0	0	0	0	1	2	1
Total			5	3	2	0	3	2	0	0	0	0	0	0	0	1	4	1

Rank among batters: 3,191 • *Total ballparks homered in*: 2 • *First HR*: 07/29/1971 off Pete Mikkelsen • *LCS HR*—1

Billy Clingman

WILLIAM FREDERICK CLINGMAN
B: 11/21/1869 D: 05/14/1958
BB

Year	Tm	Lg	Tot	H	A	0	1	2	3	2	3	4	LO	XN	IP	PH	RHP	LHP
1896	LOU	NL	2	1	1	2	0	0	0	0	0	0	0	0	0	0	2	0
1897	LOU	NL	2	0	2	2	0	0	0	0	0	0	0	0	0	0	1	1
1899	LOU	NL	2	1	1	0	1	1	0	0	0	0	0	0	0	0	1	1
1901	WAS	AL	2	0	2	0	2	0	0	0	0	0	0	0	0	0	1	1
Total			8	2	6	4	3	1	0	0	0	0	0	0	0	0	5	3

Rank among batters: 2,703 • *Total ballparks homered in*: 7 • *First HR*: 05/23/1896 off George Hemming

Jim Clinton

JAMES LAWRENCE CLINTON
B: 08/10/1850 D: 09/03/1921
BR

Year	Tm	Lg	Tot	H	A	0	1	2	3	2	3	4	LO	XN	IP	PH	RHP	LHP
1884	BAL	AA	4	2	2	2	2	0	0	0	0	0	1	0	1	0	3	0

Rank among batters: 3,427 • *Total ballparks homered in*: 3 • *First HR*: 05/22/1884 off Adonis Terry

Lou Clinton

LUCIEAN LOUIS CLINTON
B: 10/13/1937
BR

Year	Tm	Lg	Tot	H	A	0	1	2	3	2	3	4	LO	XN	IP	PH	RHP	LHP
1960	BOS	AL	6	3	3	3	2	1	0	0	0	0	0	0	0	0	4	2
1962	BOS	AL	18	7	11	7	7	2	2	2	0	0	0	0	0	0	12	6
1963	BOS	AL	22	10	12	11	8	2	1	1	0	0	0	1	0	0	13	9
1964	BOS	AL	3	1	2	2	1	0	0	0	0	0	0	0	0	0	3	0
	LA	AL	9	4	5	6	3	0	0	0	0	0	0	2	0	0	7	2
	Total		12	5	7	8	4	0	0	0	0	0	0	2	0	0	10	2
1965	CAL	AL	1	1	0	1	0	0	0	0	0	0	0	0	0	0	0	1
	CLE	AL	1	0	1	1	0	0	0	0	0	0	0	0	0	1	0	1
	Total		2	1	1	2	0	0	0	0	0	0	0	0	0	1	0	2
1966	NY	AL	5	1	4	3	1	1	0	0	0	0	0	0	0	0	3	2
Total			65	27	38	34	22	6	3	3	0	0	0	3	0	1	42	23

Rank among batters: 799 • *Top target (7 home runs)*: Jim Kaat • *Number of pitchers victimized*: 49 • *Total ballparks homered in*: 11 • *First HR*: 04/24/1960 off Camilo Pascual • *Hit for Cycle*—@KC: 07/13/1962

Tony Cloninger

TONY LEE CLONINGER
B: 08/13/1940
BR

Year	Tm	Lg	Tot	H	A	0	1	2	3	2	3	4	LO	XN	IP	PH	RHP	LHP
1965	MIL	NL	1	0	1	0	1	0	0	0	0	0	0	0	0	0	0	1
1966	ATL	NL	5	3	2	1	1	1	2	2	0	0	0	0	0	0	4	1
1968	CIN	NL	2	2	0	0	2	0	0	0	0	0	0	0	0	0	0	2
1969	CIN	NL	1	1	0	1	0	0	0	0	0	0	0	0	0	0	1	0
1970	CIN	NL	2	2	0	2	0	0	0	0	0	0	0	0	0	0	2	0
Total			11	8	3	4	4	1	2	2	0	0	0	0	0	0	7	4

Rank among batters: 2,419 • *Total ballparks homered in*: 5 • *First HR*: 09/11/1965 off Al Jackson

Otis Clymer

OTIS EDGAR CLYMER
B: 01/27/1876 D: 02/27/1926
BB

Year	Tm	Lg	Tot	H	A	Men-On 0	1	2	3	One-Game 2	3	4	LO	XN	IP	PH	RHP	LHP
1907	WAS	AL	1	0	1	1	0	0	0	0	0	0	1	0	0	0	1	0
1908	WAS	AL	1	0	1	0	1	0	0	0	0	0	0	0	1	0	1	0
Total			2	0	2	1	1	0	0	0	0	0	1	0	1	0	2	0

Rank among batters: 4,129 • *Total ballparks homered in*: 2 • *First HR*: 07/04/1907 off Ralph Glaze • *Hit for Cycle*—@NY: 10/02/1908

Gil Coan

GILBERT FITZGERALD COAN
B: 05/18/1922
BL

Year	Tm	Lg	Tot	H	A	Men-On 0	1	2	3	One-Game 2	3	4	LO	XN	IP	PH	RHP	LHP
1946	WAS	AL	3	2	1	2	1	0	0	0	0	0	1	0	2	0	2	1
1948	WAS	AL	7	4	3	4	2	1	0	0	0	0	0	0	1	0	5	2
1949	WAS	AL	3	1	2	1	2	0	0	0	0	0	0	1	0	0	3	0
1950	WAS	AL	7	3	4	4	1	0	2	0	0	0	0	0	0	0	7	0
1951	WAS	AL	9	3	6	4	2	3	0	1	0	0	0	1	0	0	6	3
1952	WAS	AL	5	2	3	3	1	1	0	0	0	0	0	0	0	0	5	0
1953	WAS	AL	2	0	2	1	0	1	0	0	0	0	0	0	0	0	2	0
1954	BAL	AL	2	2	0	2	0	0	0	0	0	0	0	0	1	0	2	0
1955	BAL	AL	1	1	0	1	0	0	0	0	0	0	0	0	0	1	1	0
Total			39	18	21	22	9	6	2	1	0	0	1	2	4	1	33	6

Rank among batters: 1,204 • *Top target (3 home runs)*: Vic Raschi • *Number of pitchers victimized*: 28 • *Total ballparks homered in*: 9 • *First HR*: 06/30/1946 off Earl Johnson

George Cobb

GEORGE WOODWORTH COBB
B: 09/25/1865 D: 08/19/1926

Year	Tm	Lg	Tot	H	A	Men-On 0	1	2	3	One-Game 2	3	4	LO	XN	IP	PH	RHP	LHP
1892	BAL	NL	1	1	0	0	0	1	0	0	0	0	0	0	0	0	1	0

Rank among batters: 4,707 • *Total ballparks homered in*: 1 • *First HR*: 06/06/1892 off Pat Luby

Ty Cobb

TYRUS RAYMOND COBB
B: 12/18/1886 D: 07/17/1961
BL HOF

Year	Tm	Lg	Tot	H	A	Men-On 0	1	2	3	One-Game 2	3	4	LO	XN	IP	PH	RHP	LHP
1905	DET	AL	1	0	1	0	0	1	0	0	0	0	0	0	1	0	1	0
1906	DET	AL	1	0	1	0	1	0	0	0	0	0	0	0	0	0	1	0
1907	DET	AL	5	1	4	2	3	0	0	0	0	0	0	0	2	0	3	2
1908	DET	AL	4	0	4	0	4	0	0	0	0	0	0	1	4	0	3	1
1909	DET	AL	9	6	3	2	4	3	0	1	0	0	0	0	9	0	5	4
1910	DET	AL	8	4	4	4	2	2	0	0	0	0	0	1	6	0	5	2
1911	DET	AL	8	5	3	2	3	2	1	0	0	0	0	0	4	0	4	4
1912	DET	AL	7	1	6	1	5	1	0	1	0	0	0	0	1	0	5	2
1913	DET	AL	4	0	4	2	1	0	1	0	0	0	0	0	2	0	3	1
1914	DET	AL	2	1	1	1	1	0	0	0	0	0	0	0	2	0	1	1
1915	DET	AL	3	1	2	1	2	0	0	0	0	0	0	0	1	0	2	1
1916	DET	AL	5	2	3	0	4	1	0	1	0	0	0	0	3	0	5	0
1917	DET	AL	6	1	5	0	4	1	1	0	0	0	0	0	3	0	5	1
1918	DET	AL	3	0	3	0	3	0	0	0	0	0	0	0	2	0	3	0
1919	DET	AL	1	0	1	0	1	0	0	0	0	0	0	0	0	0	1	0
1920	DET	AL	2	0	2	0	2	0	0	0	0	0	0	0	0	0	1	1
1921	DET	AL	12	5	7	7	3	2	0	0	0	0	0	1	4	0	10	2
1922	DET	AL	4	1	3	1	0	3	0	0	0	0	0	0	1	0	4	0
1923	DET	AL	6	2	4	3	2	1	0	0	0	0	0	0	1	0	5	1
1924	DET	AL	4	0	4	1	3	0	0	0	0	0	0	0	0	0	4	0
1925	DET	AL	12	2	10	5	4	2	1	1	1	0	0	0	0	0	8	4
1926	DET	AL	4	0	4	3	1	0	0	1	0	0	0	0	0	0	3	1
1927	PHI	AL	5	2	3	1	4	0	0	0	0	0	0	0	0	0	4	1
1928	PHI	AL	1	1	0	0	1	0	0	0	0	0	0	0	0	0	1	0
Total			117	35	82	36	58	19	4	5	1	0	0	3	46	0	87	29

Rank among batters: 402 • *Top target (5 home runs)*: Urban Shocker • *Number of pitchers victimized*: 86 • *Total ballparks homered in*: 17 • *First HR*: 09/23/1905 off Cy Falkenberg

Dave Cochrane

DAVID CARTER COCHRANE
B: 01/31/1963
BB

Year	Tm	Lg	Tot	H	A	Men-On 0	1	2	3	One-Game 2	3	4	LO	XN	IP	PH	RHP	LHP
1986	CHI	AL	1	1	0	0	1	0	0	0	0	0	0	0	0	0	1	0

Year	Tm	Lg	Tot	H	A	Men-On 0	1	2	3	One-Game 2	3	4	LO	XN	IP	PH	RHP	LHP

Dave Cochrane *continued*

Year	Tm	Lg	Tot	H	A	Men-On 0	1	2	3	One-Game 2	3	4	LO	XN	IP	PH	RHP	LHP
1989	SEA	AL	3	3	0	3	0	0	0	0	0	0	0	0	0	0	3	0
1991	SEA	AL	2	1	1	0	2	0	0	0	0	0	0	0	0	0	2	0
1992	SEA	AL	2	0	2	1	1	0	0	0	0	0	0	0	0	0	1	1
Total			8	5	3	4	4	0	0	0	0	0	0	0	0	0	7	1

Rank among batters: 2,703 • *Total ballparks homered in*: 5 • *First HR*: 09/15/1986 off Rafael Lugo

Mickey Cochrane

GORDON STANLEY COCHRANE
B: 04/06/1903 D: 06/28/1962
BL HOF

Year	Tm	Lg	Tot	H	A	Men-On 0	1	2	3	One-Game 2	3	4	LO	XN	IP	PH	RHP	LHP
1925	PHI	AL	6	1	5	5	1	0	0	0	1	0	0	0	0	0	6	0
1926	PHI	AL	8	5	3	3	3	2	0	0	0	0	0	0	1	0	8	0
1927	PHI	AL	12	6	6	7	3	2	0	0	0	0	0	1	2	0	10	2
1928	PHI	AL	10	6	4	6	3	1	0	0	0	0	0	0	0	0	10	0
1929	PHI	AL	7	6	1	2	5	0	0	0	0	0	0	0	0	0	6	1
1930	PHI	AL	10	6	4	2	7	1	0	0	0	0	0	1	0	0	8	2
1931	PHI	AL	17	9	8	8	7	2	0	1	0	0	0	0	0	0	16	1
1932	PHI	AL	23	12	11	11	9	2	1	1	0	0	0	0	0	1	20	3
1933	PHI	AL	15	8	7	12	3	0	0	2	0	0	0	0	0	0	13	2
1934	DET	AL	2	0	2	1	1	0	0	0	0	0	0	0	0	0	2	0
1935	DET	AL	5	1	4	4	1	0	0	0	0	0	0	0	0	0	4	1
1936	DET	AL	2	0	2	1	0	0	1	0	0	0	0	0	1	0	2	0
1937	DET	AL	2	1	1	2	0	0	0	0	0	0	0	0	0	0	2	0
Total			119	61	58	64	43	10	2	4	1	0	0	2	4	1	107	12

Rank among batters: 392 • *Top target (6 home runs)*: Willis Hudlin • *Number of pitchers victimized*: 65 • *Total ballparks homered in*: 9 • *First HR*: 05/06/1925 off Sam Jones • *Hit for Cycle—*@WAS: 07/22/1932; @NY: 08/02/1933 • *World Series HR—*2

Jack Coffey

JOHN FRANCIS COFFEY
B: 01/28/1887 D: 02/14/1966
BR

Year	Tm	Lg	Tot	H	A	Men-On 0	1	2	3	One-Game 2	3	4	LO	XN	IP	PH	RHP	LHP
1918	BOS	AL	1	1	0	1	0	0	0	0	0	0	0	0	1	0	1	0

Rank among batters: 4,707 • *Total ballparks homered in*: 1 • *First HR*: 08/21/1918 off Allen Sothoron

Frank Coggins

FRANKLIN COGGINS
B: 05/22/1944
BB

Year	Tm	Lg	Tot	H	A	Men-On 0	1	2	3	One-Game 2	3	4	LO	XN	IP	PH	RHP	LHP
1967	WAS	AL	1	0	1	1	0	0	0	0	0	0	0	0	0	0	1	0

Rank among batters: 4,707 • *Total ballparks homered in*: 1 • *First HR*: 09/15/1967 off Dave Wickersham

Rich Coggins

RICHARD ALLEN COGGINS
B: 12/07/1950
BL

Year	Tm	Lg	Tot	H	A	Men-On 0	1	2	3	One-Game 2	3	4	LO	XN	IP	PH	RHP	LHP
1973	BAL	AL	7	3	4	6	1	0	0	0	0	0	0	0	0	0	7	0
1974	BAL	AL	4	0	4	2	2	0	0	0	0	0	0	0	0	0	4	0
1975	NY	AL	1	1	0	0	1	0	0	0	0	0	0	0	0	0	1	0
Total			12	4	8	8	4	0	0	0	0	0	0	0	0	0	12	0

Rank among batters: 2,325 • *Top target (2 home runs)*: Catfish Hunter • *Number of pitchers victimized*: 11 • *Total ballparks homered in*: 9 • *First HR*: 05/09/1973 off Catfish Hunter

Ed Cogswell

EDWARD COGSWELL
B: 02/25/1854 D: 07/27/1888
BR

Year	Tm	Lg	Tot	H	A	Men-On 0	1	2	3	One-Game 2	3	4	LO	XN	IP	PH	RHP	LHP
1879	BOS	NL	1	1	0	1	0	0	0	0	0	0	0	0	0	0	1	0

Rank among batters: 4,707 • *Total ballparks homered in*: 1 • *First HR*: 09/10/1879 off Terry Larkin

Andy Cohen

ANDREW HOWARD COHEN
B: 10/25/1904 D: 10/29/1988
BR

Year	Tm	Lg	Tot	H	A	Men-On 0	1	2	3	One-Game 2	3	4	LO	XN	IP	PH	RHP	LHP
1928	NY	NL	9	9	0	7	1	1	0	0	0	0	0	0	0	0	6	3

Year	Tm	Lg	Tot	H	A	Men-On 0	Men-On 1	Men-On 2	Men-On 3	One-Game 2	One-Game 3	One-Game 4	LO	XN	IP	PH	RHP	LHP

Andy Cohen *continued*

Year	Tm	Lg	Tot	H	A	0	1	2	3	2	3	4	LO	XN	IP	PH	RHP	LHP
1929	NY	NL	5	4	1	1	3	1	0	0	0	0	0	0	0	0	3	2
Total			14	13	1	8	4	2	0	0	0	0	0	0	0	0	9	5

Rank among batters: 2,169 • *Top target (2 home runs)*: Russ Miller, Bill Sherdel • *Number of pitchers victimized*: 12 • *Total ballparks homered in*: 2 • *First HR*: 04/15/1928 off Russ Miller

Jimmie Coker

JIMMIE GOODWIN COKER
B: 03/28/1936 D: 10/29/1991
BR

Year	Tm	Lg	Tot	H	A	0	1	2	3	2	3	4	LO	XN	IP	PH	RHP	LHP
1960	PHI	NL	6	2	4	3	1	1	1	0	0	0	0	0	0	1	4	2
1961	PHI	NL	1	0	1	0	0	1	0	0	0	0	0	0	0	0	1	0
1964	CIN	NL	1	1	0	1	0	0	0	0	0	0	0	0	0	0	1	0
1965	CIN	NL	2	1	1	2	0	0	0	0	0	0	0	1	0	0	1	1
1966	CIN	NL	4	2	2	3	0	0	1	0	0	0	0	0	0	0	1	3
1967	CIN	NL	2	2	0	2	0	0	0	0	0	0	0	0	0	0	1	1
Total			16	8	8	11	1	2	2	0	0	0	0	1	0	1	9	7

Rank among batters: 2,029 • *Top target (2 home runs)*: Chris Short • *Number of pitchers victimized*: 15 • *Total ballparks homered in*: 7 • *First HR*: 04/21/1960 off Fred Green

Rocky Colavito

ROCCO DOMENICO COLAVITO
B: 08/10/1933
BR

Year	Tm	Lg	Tot	H	A	0	1	2	3	2	3	4	LO	XN	IP	PH	RHP	LHP
1956	CLE	AL	21	12	9	10	8	2	1	0	0	0	0	1	0	0	11	10
1957	CLE	AL	25	12	13	13	8	3	1	2	0	0	0	0	0	0	17	8
1958	CLE	AL	41	20	21	20	14	5	2	4	0	0	0	0	0	0	33	8
1959	CLE	AL	42	20	22	21	13	7	1	4	0	1	0	0	0	0	30	12
1960	DET	AL	35	17	18	16	13	6	0	5	0	0	0	1	0	0	27	8
1961	DET	AL	45	18	27	22	14	9	0	3	1	0	0	0	0	0	35	10
1962	DET	AL	37	19	18	17	12	7	1	3	1	0	0	1	0	0	30	7
1963	DET	AL	22	13	9	15	4	3	0	1	0	0	0	0	0	0	16	6
1964	KC	AL	34	22	12	18	12	4	0	2	0	0	0	1	0	0	28	6
1965	CLE	AL	26	16	10	14	6	6	0	0	0	0	0	0	0	0	22	4
1966	CLE	AL	30	16	14	20	6	3	1	4	0	0	0	0	0	1	21	9
1967	CLE	AL	5	2	3	3	1	1	0	0	0	0	0	1	0	0	1	4
	CHI	AL	3	2	1	0	2	1	0	0	0	0	0	1	0	0	2	1
	Total		8	4	4	3	3	2	0	0	0	0	0	2	0	0	3	5
1968	LA	NL	3	0	3	0	2	1	0	1	0	0	0	0	0	0	3	0
	NY	AL	5	4	1	3	1	1	0	0	0	0	0	0	0	0	1	4
	Total		8	4	4	3	3	2	0	1	0	0	0	0	0	0	4	4
Total			374	193	181	192	116	59	7	29	2	1	0	6	0	1	277	97

Rank among batters: 37 • *Top target (13 home runs)*: Ralph Terry • *Number of pitchers victimized*: 181 • *Total ballparks homered in*: 14 • *First HR*: 04/25/1956 off Bobby Shantz • *All-Star HR*—3

Mike Colbern

MICHAEL MALLOY COLBERN
B: 04/19/1955
BR

Year	Tm	Lg	Tot	H	A	0	1	2	3	2	3	4	LO	XN	IP	PH	RHP	LHP
1978	CHI	AL	2	1	1	2	0	0	0	0	0	0	0	0	0	0	0	2

Rank among batters: 4,129 • *Total ballparks homered in*: 2 • *First HR*: 09/11/1978 off Geoff Zahn

Craig Colbert

CRAIG CHARLES COLBERT
B: 02/13/1965
BR

Year	Tm	Lg	Tot	H	A	0	1	2	3	2	3	4	LO	XN	IP	PH	RHP	LHP
1992	SF	NL	1	0	1	0	1	0	0	0	0	0	0	0	0	0	0	1
1993	SF	NL	1	1	0	0	1	0	0	0	0	0	0	0	0	0	1	0
Total			2	1	1	0	2	0	0	0	0	0	0	0	0	0	1	1

Rank among batters: 4,129 • *Total ballparks homered in*: 2 • *First HR*: 09/21/1992 off Jim Deshaies

Nate Colbert

NATHAN COLBERT
B: 04/09/1946
BR

Year	Tm	Lg	Tot	H	A	0	1	2	3	2	3	4	LO	XN	IP	PH	RHP	LHP
1969	SD	NL	24	11	13	14	4	5	1	2	0	0	0	0	0	0	21	3

Nate Colbert *continued*

Year	Tm	Lg	Tot	H	A	Men-On 0	1	2	3	One-Game 2	3	4	LO	XN	IP	PH	RHP	LHP
1970	SD	NL	38	16	22	22	12	4	0	5	0	0	0	2	0	0	28	10
1971	SD	NL	27	13	14	14	8	4	1	2	0	0	0	1	0	0	22	5
1972	SD	NL	38	16	22	21	13	2	2	2	1	0	0	0	0	0	28	10
1973	SD	NL	22	10	12	12	7	3	0	2	0	0	0	0	0	0	14	8
1974	SD	NL	14	6	8	10	3	0	1	0	0	0	0	0	0	0	6	8
1975	DET	AL	4	2	2	1	1	1	1	0	0	0	0	0	0	0	4	0
	MON	NL	4	2	2	2	1	1	0	0	0	0	0	0	0	2	0	4
	Total		8	4	4	3	2	2	1	0	0	0	0	0	0	2	4	4
1976	MON	NL	2	1	1	1	0	1	0	0	0	0	0	0	0	0	2	0
Total			173	77	96	97	49	21	6	13	1	0	0	3	0	2	125	48

Rank among batters: 231 • *Top target (7 home runs)*: Don Sutton • *Number of pitchers victimized*: 98 • *Total ballparks homered in*: 15 • *First HR*: 04/24/1969 off Jack Billingham

Greg Colbrunn

GREGORY JOSEPH COLBRUNN
B: 07/26/1969
BR

Year	Tm	Lg	Tot	H	A	Men-On 0	1	2	3	One-Game 2	3	4	LO	XN	IP	PH	RHP	LHP
1992	MON	NL	2	1	1	2	0	0	0	0	0	0	0	0	0	0	1	1
1993	MON	NL	4	2	2	1	2	1	0	0	0	0	0	0	0	1	0	4
1994	FLO	NL	6	3	3	2	2	2	0	0	0	0	0	0	0	0	4	2
1995	FLO	NL	23	12	11	13	6	3	1	2	0	0	0	1	0	0	20	3
Total			35	18	17	18	10	6	1	2	0	0	0	1	0	1	25	10

Rank among batters: 1,291 • *Top target (2 home runs)*: Steve Cooke • *Number of pitchers victimized*: 34 • *Total ballparks homered in*: 11 • *First HR*: 07/22/1992 off Rod Beck

Alex Cole

ALEXANDER COLE
B: 08/17/1965
BL

Year	Tm	Lg	Tot	H	A	Men-On 0	1	2	3	One-Game 2	3	4	LO	XN	IP	PH	RHP	LHP
1994	MIN	AL	4	2	2	3	1	0	0	0	0	0	1	1	0	0	4	0
1995	MIN	AL	1	0	1	0	0	1	0	0	0	0	0	0	0	0	1	0
Total			5	2	3	3	1	1	0	0	0	0	1	1	0	0	5	0

Rank among batters: 3,191 • *Total ballparks homered in*: 3 • *First HR*: 04/24/1994 off Juan Guzman

Bert Cole

ALBERT GEORGE COLE
B: 07/01/1896 D: 05/30/1975
BL

Year	Tm	Lg	Tot	H	A	Men-On 0	1	2	3	One-Game 2	3	4	LO	XN	IP	PH	RHP	LHP
1923	DET	AL	1	0	1	1	0	0	0	0	0	0	0	0	0	0	1	0

Rank among batters: 4,707 • *Total ballparks homered in*: 1 • *First HR*: 06/29/1923 off Elam Vangilder

Dave Cole

DAVID BRUCE COLE
B: 08/29/1930
BR

Year	Tm	Lg	Tot	H	A	Men-On 0	1	2	3	One-Game 2	3	4	LO	XN	IP	PH	RHP	LHP
1951	BOS	NL	1	1	0	1	0	0	0	0	0	0	0	0	0	0	0	1
1953	MIL	NL	1	1	0	1	0	0	0	0	0	0	0	0	0	0	1	0
1954	CHI	NL	1	1	0	0	1	0	0	0	0	0	0	0	0	0	1	0
Total			3	3	0	2	1	0	0	0	0	0	0	0	0	0	2	1

Rank among batters: 3,735 • *Total ballparks homered in*: 3 • *First HR*: 09/09/1951 off Niles Jordan

Dick Cole

RICHARD ROY COLE
B: 05/06/1926
BR

Year	Tm	Lg	Tot	H	A	Men-On 0	1	2	3	One-Game 2	3	4	LO	XN	IP	PH	RHP	LHP
1951	PIT	NL	1	1	0	1	0	0	0	0	0	0	0	0	0	0	0	1
1954	PIT	NL	1	0	1	1	0	0	0	0	0	0	0	0	0	0	1	0
Total			2	1	1	2	0	0	0	0	0	0	0	0	0	0	1	1

Rank among batters: 4,129 • *Total ballparks homered in*: 2 • *First HR*: 09/19/1951 off Chet Nichols

Year	Tm	Lg	Tot	H	A	Men-On 0	1	2	3	One-Game 2	3	4	LO	XN	IP	PH	RHP	LHP

Bob Coleman

ROBERT HUNTER COLEMAN
B: 09/26/1890 D: 07/16/1959
BR

Year	Tm	Lg	Tot	H	A	Men-On 0	1	2	3	One-Game 2	3	4	LO	XN	IP	PH	RHP	LHP
1914	PIT	NL	1	0	1	0	0	1	0	0	0	0	0	0	0	0	1	0

Rank among batters: 4,707 • *Total ballparks homered in*: 1 • *First HR*: 09/18/1914 off Rube Marshall

Choo Choo Coleman

CLARENCE COLEMAN
B: 08/25/1937
BL

Year	Tm	Lg	Tot	H	A	Men-On 0	1	2	3	One-Game 2	3	4	LO	XN	IP	PH	RHP	LHP
1962	NY	NL	6	6	0	3	3	0	0	0	0	0	0	0	0	2	5	1
1963	NY	NL	3	3	0	2	1	0	0	0	0	0	0	0	0	0	2	1
Total			9	9	0	5	4	0	0	0	0	0	0	0	0	2	7	2

Rank among batters: 2,587 • *Total ballparks homered in*: 1 • *First HR*: 08/03/1962 off Jim Brosnan

Ed Coleman

PARKE EDWARD COLEMAN
B: 12/01/1901 D: 08/05/1964
BL

Year	Tm	Lg	Tot	H	A	Men-On 0	1	2	3	One-Game 2	3	4	LO	XN	IP	PH	RHP	LHP
1932	PHI	AL	1	1	0	0	0	1	0	0	0	0	0	0	0	0	1	0
1933	PHI	AL	6	5	1	4	2	0	0	0	0	0	0	1	0	1	5	1
1934	PHI	AL	14	10	4	5	7	2	0	1	1	0	0	0	0	1	14	0
1935	STL	AL	17	10	7	9	5	2	1	1	0	0	0	0	0	0	16	1
1936	STL	AL	2	0	2	1	1	0	0	0	0	0	0	0	0	0	2	0
Total			40	26	14	19	15	5	1	2	1	0	0	1	0	2	38	2

Rank among batters: 1,181 • *Top target (4 home runs)*: George Earnshaw, Monte Pearson • *Number of pitchers victimized*: 26 • *Total ballparks homered in*: 7 • *First HR*: 05/30/1932 off Firpo Marberry

Gordy Coleman

GORDON CALVIN COLEMAN
B: 07/05/1934 D: 03/12/1994
BL

Year	Tm	Lg	Tot	H	A	Men-On 0	1	2	3	One-Game 2	3	4	LO	XN	IP	PH	RHP	LHP
1960	CIN	NL	6	3	3	4	1	1	0	0	0	0	0	0	0	0	6	0
1961	CIN	NL	26	12	14	14	10	2	0	3	0	0	0	1	0	0	19	7
1962	CIN	NL	28	16	12	14	13	1	0	1	0	0	0	1	0	0	27	1
1963	CIN	NL	14	9	5	10	3	0	1	1	0	0	0	0	0	2	14	0
1964	CIN	NL	5	2	3	5	0	0	0	0	0	0	0	0	0	0	4	1
1965	CIN	NL	14	8	6	7	5	1	1	1	0	0	0	0	0	0	14	0
1966	CIN	NL	5	3	2	2	1	2	0	0	0	0	0	0	0	1	5	0
Total			98	53	45	56	33	7	2	6	0	0	0	2	0	3	89	9

Rank among batters: 506 • *Top target (6 home runs)*: Don Drysdale • *Number of pitchers victimized*: 60 • *Total ballparks homered in*: 12 • *First HR*: 07/24/1960 off Ernie Broglio • *World Series HR*—1

Jerry Coleman

GERALD FRANCIS COLEMAN
B: 09/14/1924
BR

Year	Tm	Lg	Tot	H	A	Men-On 0	1	2	3	One-Game 2	3	4	LO	XN	IP	PH	RHP	LHP
1949	NY	AL	2	1	1	0	1	1	0	0	0	0	0	0	0	0	0	2
1950	NY	AL	6	3	3	3	1	2	0	0	0	0	0	0	0	0	2	4
1951	NY	AL	3	2	1	2	0	1	0	0	0	0	0	0	0	0	0	3
1954	NY	AL	3	1	2	2	0	1	0	0	0	0	0	0	0	0	1	2
1957	NY	AL	2	0	2	2	0	0	0	0	0	0	0	0	0	0	1	1
Total			16	7	9	9	2	5	0	0	0	0	0	0	0	0	4	12

Rank among batters: 2,029 • *Top target (3 home runs)*: Alex Kellner • *Number of pitchers victimized*: 13 • *Total ballparks homered in*: 5 • *First HR*: 04/26/1949 off Alex Kellner

Joe Coleman

JOSEPH PATRICK COLEMAN
B: 07/30/1922
BR

Year	Tm	Lg	Tot	H	A	Men-On 0	1	2	3	One-Game 2	3	4	LO	XN	IP	PH	RHP	LHP
1949	PHI	AL	1	0	1	0	1	0	0	0	0	0	0	0	0	0	0	1
1950	PHI	AL	1	0	1	1	0	0	0	0	0	0	0	0	0	0	0	1
1954	BAL	AL	2	1	1	1	1	0	0	0	0	0	0	0	0	0	1	1
Total			4	1	3	2	2	0	0	0	0	0	0	0	0	0	1	3

Rank among batters: 3,427 • *Total ballparks homered in*: 4 • *First HR*: 08/23/1949 off Milton Haefner

John Coleman

JOHN FRANCIS COLEMAN
B: 03/06/1863 D: 05/31/1922
BL

Year	Tm	Lg	Tot	H	A	Men-On 0	1	2	3	One-Game 2	3	4	LO	XN	IP	PH	RHP	LHP
1884	PHI	AA	2	1	1	1	1	0	0	0	0	0	0	0	1	0	2	0
1885	PHI	AA	3	2	1	0	1	2	0	0	0	0	0	0	1	0	3	0
1887	PIT	NL	2	0	2	1	1	0	0	0	0	0	0	0	0	0	0	2
Total			7	3	4	2	3	2	0	0	0	0	0	0	2	0	5	2

Rank among batters: 2,834 • *Top target (2 home runs)*: Kid Madden • *Number of pitchers victimized*: 6 • *Total ballparks homered in*: 4 • *First HR*: 09/14/1884 off Ed Dundon

Ray Coleman

RAYMOND LEROY COLEMAN
B: 06/04/1922
BL

Year	Tm	Lg	Tot	H	A	Men-On 0	1	2	3	One-Game 2	3	4	LO	XN	IP	PH	RHP	LHP
1947	STL	AL	2	2	0	0	2	0	0	0	0	0	0	0	0	0	2	0
1950	STL	AL	8	4	4	6	0	2	0	0	0	0	0	0	0	0	8	0
1951	STL	AL	5	4	1	3	1	1	0	0	0	0	0	0	0	1	3	2
	CHI	AL	3	2	1	2	0	1	0	0	0	0	0	0	0	0	3	0
	Total		8	6	2	5	1	2	0	0	0	0	0	0	0	1	6	2
1952	CHI	AL	2	1	1	2	0	0	0	0	0	0	0	0	0	0	1	1
Total			20	13	7	13	3	4	0	0	0	0	0	0	0	1	17	3

Rank among batters: 1,810 • *Top target (3 home runs)*: Bob Lemon • *Number of pitchers victimized*: 16 • *Total ballparks homered in*: 5 • *First HR*: 05/01/1947 off Lou Knerr

Vince Coleman

VINCENT MAURICE COLEMAN
B: 09/22/1961
BB

Year	Tm	Lg	Tot	H	A	Men-On 0	1	2	3	One-Game 2	3	4	LO	XN	IP	PH	RHP	LHP
1985	STL	NL	1	1	0	1	0	0	0	0	0	0	0	0	1	0	1	0
1987	STL	NL	3	3	0	2	1	0	0	0	0	0	0	0	0	0	0	3
1988	STL	NL	3	2	1	2	0	1	0	0	0	0	0	0	0	0	1	2
1989	STL	NL	2	1	1	2	0	0	0	0	0	0	0	0	0	0	0	2
1990	STL	NL	6	5	1	5	1	0	0	0	0	0	2	1	0	0	1	5
1991	NY	NL	1	0	1	1	0	0	0	0	0	0	0	0	0	0	0	1
1992	NY	NL	2	2	0	0	1	1	0	0	0	0	0	0	0	0	1	1
1993	NY	NL	2	2	0	2	0	0	0	0	0	0	2	0	0	0	1	1
1994	KC	AL	2	1	1	2	0	0	0	0	0	0	0	0	0	0	0	2
1995	KC	AL	4	2	2	2	2	0	0	0	0	0	0	0	0	0	1	3
	SEA	AL	1	1	0	0	0	0	1	0	0	0	0	0	0	0	1	0
	Total		5	3	2	2	2	0	1	0	0	0	0	0	0	0	2	3
Total			27	20	7	19	5	2	1	0	0	0	4	1	1	0	7	20

Rank among batters: 1,532 • *Top target (3 home runs)*: Jim Deshaies • *Number of pitchers victimized*: 23 • *Total ballparks homered in*: 10 • *First HR*: 05/21/1985 off Len Barker • *LCS HR*—1

Cad Coles

CADWALLADER COLES
B: 01/17/1886 D: 06/30/1942
BL

Year	Tm	Lg	Tot	H	A	Men-On 0	1	2	3	One-Game 2	3	4	LO	XN	IP	PH	RHP	LHP
1914	KC	FL	1	0	1	0	1	0	0	0	0	0	0	0	0	0	1	0

Rank among batters: 4,707 • *Total ballparks homered in*: 1 • *First HR*: 05/21/1914 off Ed Lafitte

Darnell Coles

DARNELL COLES
B: 06/02/1962
BR

Year	Tm	Lg	Tot	H	A	Men-On 0	1	2	3	One-Game 2	3	4	LO	XN	IP	PH	RHP	LHP
1983	SEA	AL	1	0	1	1	0	0	0	0	0	0	0	0	0	0	1	0
1985	SEA	AL	1	0	1	1	0	0	0	0	0	0	0	0	0	0	0	1
1986	DET	AL	20	12	8	12	6	1	1	1	0	0	0	0	0	0	17	3
1987	DET	AL	4	3	1	2	2	0	0	0	0	0	0	0	0	0	2	2
	PIT	NL	6	5	1	2	2	1	1	0	1	0	0	0	0	0	0	6
	Total		10	8	2	4	4	1	1	0	1	0	0	0	0	0	2	8
1988	PIT	NL	5	1	4	4	0	1	0	1	0	0	0	0	0	0	1	4
	SEA	AL	10	9	1	7	2	1	0	0	0	0	0	0	0	0	5	5
	Total		15	10	5	11	2	2	0	1	0	0	0	0	0	0	6	9
1989	SEA	AL	10	4	6	5	3	1	1	1	0	0	0	1	0	0	8	2

Darnell Coles *continued*

Year	Tm	Lg	Tot	H	A	Men-On 0	Men-On 1	Men-On 2	Men-On 3	One-Game 2	One-Game 3	One-Game 4	LO	XN	IP	PH	RHP	LHP
1990	SEA	AL	2	2	0	0	2	0	0	0	0	0	0	0	0	0	1	1
	DET	AL	1	1	0	1	0	0	0	0	0	0	0	0	0	0	1	0
	Total		3	3	0	1	2	0	0	0	0	0	0	0	0	0	2	1
1992	CIN	NL	3	1	2	2	0	1	0	0	0	0	0	0	0	0	2	1
1993	TOR	AL	4	3	1	1	1	2	0	0	0	0	0	0	0	1	4	0
1994	TOR	AL	4	1	3	2	2	0	0	0	1	0	0	0	0	0	1	3
1995	STL	NL	3	3	0	1	0	2	0	0	0	0	0	1	0	0	1	2
Total			74	45	29	41	20	10	3	3	2	0	0	2	0	1	44	30

Rank among batters: 707 • *Top target (3 home runs)*: Jamie Moyer, Mike Moore • *Number of pitchers victimized*: 63 • *Total ballparks homered in*: 18 • *First HR*: 09/05/1983 off Keith Creel

Chris Coletta

CHRISTOPHER MICHAEL COLETTA
B: 08/02/1944
BL

Year	Tm	Lg	Tot	H	A	Men-On 0	Men-On 1	Men-On 2	Men-On 3	One-Game 2	One-Game 3	One-Game 4	LO	XN	IP	PH	RHP	LHP
1972	CAL	AL	1	0	1	1	0	0	0	0	0	0	0	0	0	0	1	0

Rank among batters: 4,707 • *Total ballparks homered in*: 1 • *First HR*: 09/24/1972 off Jim Perry

Bill Collins

WILLIAM SHIRLEY COLLINS
B: 03/27/1882 D: 06/26/1961
BB

Year	Tm	Lg	Tot	H	A	Men-On 0	Men-On 1	Men-On 2	Men-On 3	One-Game 2	One-Game 3	One-Game 4	LO	XN	IP	PH	RHP	LHP
1910	BOS	NL	3	2	1	0	2	0	1	0	0	0	0	0	0	0	3	0

Rank among batters: 3,735 • *Total ballparks homered in*: 2 • *First HR*: 05/02/1910 off Lew Moren • *Hit for Cycle*—vs PHI: 10/06/1910

Bob Collins

ROBERT JOSEPH COLLINS
B: 09/18/1909 D: 04/19/1969
BR

Year	Tm	Lg	Tot	H	A	Men-On 0	Men-On 1	Men-On 2	Men-On 3	One-Game 2	One-Game 3	One-Game 4	LO	XN	IP	PH	RHP	LHP
1940	CHI	NL	1	1	0	1	0	0	0	0	0	0	0	0	0	0	1	0

Rank among batters: 4,707 • *Total ballparks homered in*: 1 • *First HR*: 06/04/1940 off Syl Johnson

Dave Collins

DAVID S. COLLINS
B: 10/20/1952
BB

Year	Tm	Lg	Tot	H	A	Men-On 0	Men-On 1	Men-On 2	Men-On 3	One-Game 2	One-Game 3	One-Game 4	LO	XN	IP	PH	RHP	LHP
1975	CAL	AL	3	1	2	0	2	1	0	0	0	0	0	0	0	0	2	1
1976	CAL	AL	4	1	3	3	1	0	0	0	0	0	2	0	1	0	4	0
1977	SEA	AL	5	2	3	3	2	0	0	0	0	0	0	0	0	0	3	2
1979	CIN	NL	3	0	3	1	2	0	0	0	0	0	0	0	1	0	2	1
1980	CIN	NL	3	3	0	2	1	0	0	0	0	0	1	0	0	0	3	0
1981	CIN	NL	3	1	2	3	0	0	0	0	0	0	1	0	0	0	3	0
1982	NY	AL	3	2	1	2	1	0	0	0	0	0	0	0	1	0	3	0
1983	TOR	AL	1	0	1	1	0	0	0	0	0	0	0	0	0	0	1	0
1984	TOR	AL	2	2	0	1	0	1	0	0	0	0	0	0	0	0	2	0
1985	OAK	AL	4	1	3	3	0	0	1	0	0	0	0	0	0	0	3	1
1986	DET	AL	1	0	1	0	1	0	0	0	0	0	0	0	0	0	0	1
Total			32	13	19	19	10	2	1	0	0	0	4	0	3	0	26	6

Rank among batters: 1,360 • *Top target (2 home runs)*: Jim Hughes, Francisco Barrios, Tommy Boggs • *Number of pitchers victimized*: 29 • *Total ballparks homered in*: 17 • *First HR*: 07/20/1975 off Don Hood

Eddie Collins

EDWARD TROWBRIDGE, SR. COLLINS
B: 05/02/1887 D: 03/25/1951
BL HOF

Year	Tm	Lg	Tot	H	A	Men-On 0	Men-On 1	Men-On 2	Men-On 3	One-Game 2	One-Game 3	One-Game 4	LO	XN	IP	PH	RHP	LHP
1908	PHI	AL	1	1	0	1	0	0	0	0	0	0	0	0	0	0	1	0
1909	PHI	AL	3	2	1	2	1	0	0	0	0	0	0	0	3	0	3	0
1910	PHI	AL	3	1	2	2	0	1	0	0	0	0	0	0	2	0	3	0
1911	PHI	AL	3	0	3	2	0	1	0	0	0	0	0	0	2	0	3	0
1913	PHI	AL	3	2	1	1	2	0	0	0	0	0	0	0	0	0	3	0
1914	PHI	AL	2	2	0	1	0	1	0	0	0	0	0	0	0	0	2	0
1915	CHI	AL	4	1	3	2	2	0	0	0	0	0	0	0	3	0	3	1

Year	Tm	Lg	Tot	H	A	Men-On 0	1	2	3	One-Game 2	3	4	LO	XN	IP	PH	RHP	LHP

Eddie Collins *continued*

Year	Tm	Lg	Tot	H	A	Men-On 0	1	2	3	One-Game 2	3	4	LO	XN	IP	PH	RHP	LHP
1918	CHI	AL	2	1	1	1	1	0	0	0	0	0	0	0	1	0	2	0
1919	CHI	AL	4	1	3	1	0	2	1	0	0	0	0	1	3	0	3	1
1920	CHI	AL	3	2	1	3	0	0	0	0	0	0	0	0	1	0	3	0
1921	CHI	AL	2	0	2	0	1	1	0	0	0	0	0	0	1	0	1	1
1922	CHI	AL	1	0	1	0	1	0	0	0	0	0	0	0	0	0	1	0
1923	CHI	AL	5	0	5	3	0	2	0	0	0	0	0	0	1	0	4	1
1924	CHI	AL	6	2	4	2	3	1	0	0	0	0	0	0	0	0	6	0
1925	CHI	AL	3	1	2	0	2	1	0	0	0	0	0	0	0	0	1	2
1926	CHI	AL	1	0	1	0	1	0	0	0	0	0	0	0	0	0	1	0
1927	PHI	AL	1	0	1	1	0	0	0	0	0	0	0	0	0	0	1	0
Total			47	16	31	22	14	10	1	0	0	0	0	1	17	0	41	6

Rank among batters: 1,040 • *Top target (3 home runs)*: Hooks Dauss, Urban Shocker, Bob Shawkey • *Number of pitchers victimized*: 36 • *Total ballparks homered in*: 11 • *First HR*: 08/21/1908 off Jack Ryan

Hub Collins

HUBERT B. COLLINS
B: 04/15/1864 D: 05/21/1892
BR

Year	Tm	Lg	Tot	H	A	Men-On 0	1	2	3	One-Game 2	3	4	LO	XN	IP	PH	RHP	LHP
1887	LOU	AA	1	0	1	1	0	0	0	0	0	0	0	0	0	0	0	0
1888	LOU	AA	2	0	2	1	1	0	0	0	0	0	0	0	0	0	2	0
1889	BRO	AA	2	2	0	0	1	1	0	0	0	0	0	0	0	0	0	2
1890	BRO	NL	3	2	1	1	1	1	0	0	0	0	1	0	0	0	3	0
1891	BRO	NL	3	0	3	1	1	1	0	0	0	0	1	0	1	0	2	1
Total			11	4	7	4	4	3	0	0	0	0	2	0	1	0	7	3

Rank among batters: 2,419 • *Top target (2 home runs)*: Jesse Duryea • *Number of pitchers victimized*: 10 • *Total ballparks homered in*: 7 • *First HR*: 09/08/1887 off Al Mays • *World Series HR*—1

Jimmy Collins

JAMES JOSEPH COLLINS
B: 01/16/1870 D: 03/06/1943
BR HOF

Year	Tm	Lg	Tot	H	A	Men-On 0	1	2	3	One-Game 2	3	4	LO	XN	IP	PH	RHP	LHP
1895	BOS	NL	1	1	0	1	0	0	0	0	0	0	0	0	0	0	1	0
	LOU	NL	6	3	3	3	2	1	0	0	0	0	0	0	0	0	3	2
	Total		7	4	3	4	2	1	0	0	0	0	0	0	0	0	4	2
1896	BOS	NL	1	0	1	1	0	0	0	0	0	0	0	0	0	0	1	0
1897	BOS	NL	6	2	4	2	2	2	0	0	0	0	0	0	0	0	5	1
1898	BOS	NL	15	12	3	7	4	3	1	1	0	0	0	0	0	0	13	2
1899	BOS	NL	5	5	0	2	2	1	0	1	0	0	0	0	0	0	2	3
1900	BOS	NL	6	5	1	2	3	1	0	1	0	0	0	0	1	0	4	2
1901	BOS	AL	6	4	2	3	1	2	0	1	0	0	0	0	1	0	3	3
1902	BOS	AL	6	4	2	2	2	1	1	0	0	0	0	0	3	0	4	2
1903	BOS	AL	5	4	1	3	2	0	0	0	0	0	0	0	0	0	4	1
1904	BOS	AL	3	3	0	1	2	0	0	1	0	0	0	0	0	0	3	0
1905	BOS	AL	4	3	1	2	2	0	0	0	0	0	0	0	1	0	3	0
1906	BOS	AL	1	1	0	1	0	0	0	0	0	0	0	0	1	0	1	0
Total			65	47	18	30	22	11	2	5	0	0	0	0	7	0	47	16

Rank among batters: 799 • *Top target (3 home runs)*: Win Mercer • *Number of pitchers victimized*: 48 • *Total ballparks homered in*: 12 • *First HR*: 05/03/1895 off Win Mercer

Joe Collins

JOSEPH EDWARD COLLINS
B: 12/03/1922 D: 08/30/1989
BL

Year	Tm	Lg	Tot	H	A	Men-On 0	1	2	3	One-Game 2	3	4	LO	XN	IP	PH	RHP	LHP
1950	NY	AL	8	5	3	5	3	0	0	1	0	0	0	0	0	0	7	1
1951	NY	AL	9	4	5	2	5	1	1	0	0	0	0	0	0	0	9	0
1952	NY	AL	18	13	5	9	5	4	0	3	0	0	0	0	1	0	15	3
1953	NY	AL	17	7	10	13	4	0	0	2	0	0	0	0	0	0	16	1
1954	NY	AL	12	7	5	7	4	1	0	0	0	0	0	0	0	2	12	0
1955	NY	AL	13	8	5	10	2	1	0	2	0	0	0	1	1	0	13	0
1956	NY	AL	7	5	2	4	2	1	0	0	0	0	0	0	0	2	6	1
1957	NY	AL	2	1	1	1	1	0	0	0	0	0	0	0	0	0	2	0
Total			86	50	36	51	26	8	1	8	0	0	0	1	2	4	80	6

Rank among batters: 602 • *Top target (7 home runs)*: Early Wynn, Bob Lemon • *Number of pitchers victimized*: 53 • *Total ballparks homered in*: 9 • *First HR*: 04/27/1950 off Ellis Kinder • *World Series HR*—4

Kevin Collins

KEVIN MICHAEL COLLINS
B: 08/04/1946
BL

Year	Tm	Lg	Tot	H	A	Men-On 0	1	2	3	One-Game 2	3	4	LO	XN	IP	PH	RHP	LHP
1968	NY	NL	1	0	1	0	0	1	0	0	0	0	0	0	0	0	1	0
1969	NY	NL	1	0	1	0	1	0	0	0	0	0	0	0	0	0	1	0
	MON	NL	2	2	0	1	0	1	0	0	0	0	0	0	0	1	2	0
	Total		3	2	1	1	1	1	0	0	0	0	0	0	0	1	3	0
1970	DET	AL	1	1	0	0	0	1	0	0	0	0	0	0	0	1	1	0
1971	DET	AL	1	1	0	0	1	0	0	0	0	0	0	0	0	1	1	0
Total			6	4	2	1	2	3	0	0	0	0	0	0	0	3	6	0

Rank among batters: 2,988 • *Total ballparks homered in*: 4 • *First HR*: 08/06/1968 off Dave Giusti

Pat Collins

THARON PATRICK COLLINS
B: 09/13/1896 D: 05/20/1960
BR

Year	Tm	Lg	Tot	H	A	Men-On 0	1	2	3	One-Game 2	3	4	LO	XN	IP	PH	RHP	LHP
1921	STL	AL	1	0	1	1	0	0	0	0	0	0	0	0	0	0	1	0
1922	STL	AL	8	6	2	7	0	1	0	0	0	0	0	0	1	2	4	4
1923	STL	AL	3	1	2	2	0	1	0	0	0	0	0	0	0	2	2	1
1924	STL	AL	1	1	0	0	0	0	1	0	0	0	0	0	0	0	1	0
1926	NY	AL	7	3	4	5	2	0	0	0	0	0	0	0	0	0	7	0
1927	NY	AL	7	4	3	5	1	0	1	0	0	0	0	0	0	0	6	1
1928	NY	AL	6	2	4	3	3	0	0	0	0	0	0	0	0	0	4	2
Total			33	17	16	23	6	2	2	0	0	0	0	0	1	4	25	8

Rank among batters: 1,336 • *Top target (3 home runs)*: Sloppy Thurston • *Number of pitchers victimized*: 29 • *Total ballparks homered in*: 7 • *First HR*: 06/23/1921 off Hooks Dauss

Phil Collins

PHILIP EUGENE COLLINS
B: 08/27/1901 D: 08/14/1948
BR

Year	Tm	Lg	Tot	H	A	Men-On 0	1	2	3	One-Game 2	3	4	LO	XN	IP	PH	RHP	LHP
1929	PHI	NL	1	0	1	0	0	0	1	0	0	0	0	0	0	0	1	0
1930	PHI	NL	3	3	0	1	2	0	0	1	0	0	0	0	0	0	1	2
Total			4	3	1	1	2	0	1	1	0	0	0	0	0	0	2	2

Rank among batters: 3,427 • *Total ballparks homered in*: 2 • *First HR*: 06/23/1929 off Art Delaney

Ray Collins

RAYMOND WILLISTON COLLINS
B: 02/11/1887 D: 01/09/1970
BL

Year	Tm	Lg	Tot	H	A	Men-On 0	1	2	3	One-Game 2	3	4	LO	XN	IP	PH	RHP	LHP
1913	BOS	AL	1	0	1	1	0	0	0	0	0	0	0	0	0	0	0	1

Rank among batters: 4,707 • *Total ballparks homered in*: 1 • *First HR*: 07/09/1913 off Walt Leverenz

Rip Collins

HARRY WARREN COLLINS
B: 02/26/1896 D: 05/27/1968
BB

Year	Tm	Lg	Tot	H	A	Men-On 0	1	2	3	One-Game 2	3	4	LO	XN	IP	PH	RHP	LHP
1929	STL	AL	1	0	1	1	0	0	0	0	0	0	0	0	0	0	1	0

Rank among batters: 4,707 • *Total ballparks homered in*: 1 • *First HR*: 08/09/1929 off Ted Lyons

Ripper Collins

JAMES ANTHONY COLLINS
B: 03/30/1904 D: 04/15/1970
BB

Year	Tm	Lg	Tot	H	A	Men-On 0	1	2	3	One-Game 2	3	4	LO	XN	IP	PH	RHP	LHP
1931	STL	NL	4	2	2	3	0	1	0	0	0	0	0	0	0	1	3	1
1932	STL	NL	21	11	10	9	11	1	0	1	0	0	0	1	0	1	19	2
1933	STL	NL	10	1	9	7	3	0	0	0	0	0	0	1	1	0	10	0
1934	STL	NL	35	22	13	13	15	7	0	2	0	0	0	1	0	0	31	4
1935	STL	NL	23	7	16	9	6	7	1	2	0	0	0	1	0	0	20	3
1936	STL	NL	13	9	4	8	4	0	1	2	0	0	0	1	0	1	13	0
1937	CHI	NL	16	4	12	7	7	2	0	0	0	0	0	0	0	0	15	1
1938	CHI	NL	13	3	10	10	3	0	0	1	0	0	0	0	0	0	12	1
Total			135	59	76	66	49	18	2	8	0	0	0	5	1	3	123	12

Rank among batters: 326 • *Top target (5 home runs)*: Si Johnson, Guy Bush, Lon Warneke, Bill Swift • *Number of pitchers victimized*: 75 • *Total ballparks homered in*: 8 • *First HR*: 05/09/1931 off Ray Kremer

Shano Collins

JOHN FRANCIS COLLINS
B: 12/04/1885 D: 09/10/1955
BR

Year	Tm	Lg	Tot	H	A	Men-On 0	Men-On 1	Men-On 2	Men-On 3	One-Game 2	One-Game 3	One-Game 4	LO	XN	IP	PH	RHP	LHP
1910	CHI	AL	1	0	1	0	1	0	0	0	0	0	0	0	0	0	1	0
1911	CHI	AL	4	2	2	3	0	1	0	0	0	0	0	0	2	0	4	0
1912	CHI	AL	2	2	0	2	0	0	0	0	0	0	0	0	1	0	2	0
1913	CHI	AL	1	1	0	1	0	0	0	0	0	0	0	0	0	0	1	0
1914	CHI	AL	3	3	0	2	1	0	0	0	0	0	0	0	1	0	3	0
1915	CHI	AL	2	1	1	2	0	0	0	0	0	0	0	0	0	0	1	1
1917	CHI	AL	1	0	1	1	0	0	0	0	0	0	0	0	0	0	1	0
1918	CHI	AL	1	0	1	0	1	0	0	0	0	0	0	0	0	0	1	0
1919	CHI	AL	1	0	1	1	0	0	0	0	0	0	0	0	0	0	0	1
1920	CHI	AL	1	0	1	1	0	0	0	0	0	0	0	0	0	0	0	1
1921	BOS	AL	4	0	4	3	0	0	1	1	0	0	0	0	1	0	3	1
1922	BOS	AL	1	0	1	0	1	0	0	0	0	0	0	0	0	0	1	0
Total			22	9	13	16	4	1	1	1	0	0	0	0	5	0	18	4

Rank among batters: 1,719 • *Top target (2 home runs)*: Eddie Rommel • *Number of pitchers victimized*: 21 • *Total ballparks homered in*: 8 • *First HR*: 06/30/1910 off Sailor Stroud

Zip Collins

JOHN EDGAR COLLINS
B: 03/02/1892 D: 12/19/1983
BL

Year	Tm	Lg	Tot	H	A	Men-On 0	Men-On 1	Men-On 2	Men-On 3	One-Game 2	One-Game 3	One-Game 4	LO	XN	IP	PH	RHP	LHP
1915	PIT	NL	1	1	0	0	0	1	0	0	0	0	0	0	1	0	0	1
1916	BOS	NL	1	0	1	0	1	0	0	0	0	0	0	0	1	0	1	0
Total			2	1	1	0	1	1	0	0	0	0	0	0	2	0	1	1

Rank among batters: 4,129 • *Total ballparks homered in*: 2 • *First HR*: 07/27/1915 off Rube Marquard

Jackie Collum

JACK DEAN COLLUM
B: 06/21/1927
BL

Year	Tm	Lg	Tot	H	A	Men-On 0	Men-On 1	Men-On 2	Men-On 3	One-Game 2	One-Game 3	One-Game 4	LO	XN	IP	PH	RHP	LHP
1954	CIN	NL	1	0	1	0	0	1	0	0	0	0	0	0	0	0	1	0

Rank among batters: 4,707 • *Total ballparks homered in*: 1 • *First HR*: 09/11/1954 off Ruben Gomez

Frank Colman

FRANK LLOYD COLMAN
B: 03/02/1918 D: 02/19/1983
BL

Year	Tm	Lg	Tot	H	A	Men-On 0	Men-On 1	Men-On 2	Men-On 3	One-Game 2	One-Game 3	One-Game 4	LO	XN	IP	PH	RHP	LHP
1942	PIT	NL	1	1	0	1	0	0	0	0	0	0	0	0	1	0	1	0
1944	PIT	NL	6	4	2	3	1	2	0	1	0	0	0	0	0	1	6	0
1945	PIT	NL	4	0	4	2	0	2	0	0	0	0	0	0	0	1	2	2
1946	PIT	NL	1	1	0	1	0	0	0	0	0	0	0	0	0	0	1	0
	NY	AL	1	1	0	0	1	0	0	0	0	0	0	0	0	0	1	0
	Total		2	2	0	1	1	0	0	0	0	0	0	0	0	0	2	0
1947	NY	AL	2	1	1	1	0	1	0	0	0	0	0	0	0	2	2	0
Total			15	8	7	8	2	5	0	1	0	0	0	0	1	4	13	2

Rank among batters: 2,096 • *Total ballparks homered in*: 7 • *First HR*: 09/19/1942 off Bucky Walters

Bob Coluccio

ROBERT PASQUALI COLUCCIO
B: 10/02/1951
BR

Year	Tm	Lg	Tot	H	A	Men-On 0	Men-On 1	Men-On 2	Men-On 3	One-Game 2	One-Game 3	One-Game 4	LO	XN	IP	PH	RHP	LHP
1973	MIL	AL	15	7	8	9	2	3	1	0	0	0	1	0	1	0	10	5
1974	MIL	AL	6	4	2	5	1	0	0	0	0	0	0	1	0	0	3	3
1975	MIL	AL	1	0	1	1	0	0	0	0	0	0	0	0	0	0	1	0
	CHI	AL	4	2	2	2	2	0	0	0	0	0	0	0	0	0	0	4
	Total		5	2	3	3	2	0	0	0	0	0	0	0	0	0	1	4
Total			26	13	13	17	5	3	1	0	0	0	1	1	1	0	14	12

Rank among batters: 1,576 • *Top target (2 home runs)*: Dick Bosman, Mickey Lolich, Doc Medich • *Number of pitchers victimized*: 23 • *Total ballparks homered in*: 10 • *First HR*: 04/23/1973 off Doc Medich

Earle Combs

EARLE BRYAN COMBS
B: 05/14/1899 D: 07/21/1976
BL HOF

Year	Tm	Lg	Tot	H	A	Men-On 0	Men-On 1	Men-On 2	Men-On 3	One-Game 2	One-Game 3	One-Game 4	LO	XN	IP	PH	RHP	LHP
1925	NY	AL	3	2	1	1	2	0	0	0	0	0	0	0	1	0	1	2

Year	Tm	Lg	Tot	H	A	Men-On				One-Game			LO	XN	IP	PH	RHP	LHP
						0	1	2	3	2	3	4						

Earle Combs *continued*

Year	Tm	Lg	Tot	H	A	0	1	2	3	2	3	4	LO	XN	IP	PH	RHP	LHP
1926	NY	AL	8	6	2	5	1	2	0	0	0	0	0	0	3	0	6	2
1927	NY	AL	6	5	1	5	1	0	0	0	0	0	3	0	2	0	6	0
1928	NY	AL	7	4	3	4	2	0	1	0	0	0	0	0	4	0	6	1
1929	NY	AL	3	3	0	1	2	0	0	0	0	0	1	0	2	0	2	1
1930	NY	AL	7	5	2	4	1	2	0	0	0	0	1	0	4	0	6	1
1931	NY	AL	5	4	1	4	1	0	0	0	0	0	1	0	2	0	5	0
1932	NY	AL	9	5	4	8	0	1	0	0	0	0	4	0	1	0	9	0
1933	NY	AL	5	2	3	3	0	2	0	0	0	0	0	0	3	0	5	0
1934	NY	AL	2	1	1	1	1	0	0	0	0	0	0	0	0	0	2	0
1935	NY	AL	3	1	2	1	0	1	1	0	0	0	0	0	1	0	3	0
Total			58	38	20	37	11	8	2	0	0	0	10	0	23	0	51	7

Rank among batters: 886 • *Top target (4 home runs)*: Ted Lyons • *Number of pitchers victimized*: 47 • *Total ballparks homered in*: 9 • *First HR*: 05/26/1925 off Ted Wingfield • *World Series HR*—1

Merl Combs

MERRILL RUSSELL COMBS
B: 12/11/1919 D: 07/08/1981
BL

Year	Tm	Lg	Tot	H	A	0	1	2	3	2	3	4	LO	XN	IP	PH	RHP	LHP
1947	BOS	AL	1	1	0	0	0	1	0	0	0	0	0	0	0	0	1	0
1952	CLE	AL	1	0	1	1	0	0	0	0	0	0	0	0	0	0	0	1
Total			2	1	1	1	0	1	0	0	0	0	0	0	0	0	1	1

Rank among batters: 4,129 • *Total ballparks homered in*: 2 • *First HR*: 09/12/1947 off Bob Lemon

Wayne Comer

HARRY WAYNE COMER
B: 02/03/1944
BR

Year	Tm	Lg	Tot	H	A	0	1	2	3	2	3	4	LO	XN	IP	PH	RHP	LHP
1968	DET	AL	1	1	0	1	0	0	0	0	0	0	0	0	0	1	1	0
1969	SEA	AL	15	7	8	10	4	1	0	1	0	0	0	2	0	0	10	5
Total			16	8	8	11	4	1	0	1	0	0	0	2	0	1	11	5

Rank among batters: 2,029 • *Top target (2 home runs)*: Rollie Fingers • *Number of pitchers victimized*: 15 • *Total ballparks homered in*: 8 • *First HR*: 08/11/1968 off Jim Lonborg

Charlie Comiskey

CHARLES ALBERT COMISKEY
B: 08/15/1859 D: 10/26/1931
BR HOF

Year	Tm	Lg	Tot	H	A	0	1	2	3	2	3	4	LO	XN	IP	PH	RHP	LHP
1882	STL	AA	1	1	0	0	1	0	0	0	0	0	0	0	0	0	0	0
1883	STL	AA	2	1	1	1	1	0	0	0	0	0	0	0	0	0	2	0
1884	STL	AA	2	2	0	1	1	0	0	0	0	0	0	0	2	0	1	0
1885	STL	AA	2	0	2	2	0	0	0	0	0	0	0	0	2	0	1	0
1886	STL	AA	3	2	1	2	1	0	0	0	0	0	0	0	1	0	2	1
1887	STL	AA	4	3	1	2	0	2	0	0	0	0	0	1	0	0	3	0
1888	STL	AA	6	2	4	3	0	3	0	0	0	0	0	0	2	0	3	3
1889	STL	AA	3	2	1	0	2	1	0	0	0	0	0	0	1	0	1	1
1891	STL	AA	2	1	1	0	1	1	0	0	0	0	0	0	1	0	2	0
1892	CIN	NL	3	3	0	0	1	1	1	0	0	0	0	0	0	0	0	1
Total			28	17	11	11	8	8	1	0	0	0	0	1	9	0	15	3

Rank among batters: 1,500 • *Top target (3 home runs)*: Tony Mullane • *Number of pitchers victimized*: 24 • *Total ballparks homered in*: 7 • *First HR*: 05/04/1882 off John Reccius

Jim Command

JAMES DALTON COMMAND
B: 10/15/1928
BL

Year	Tm	Lg	Tot	H	A	0	1	2	3	2	3	4	LO	XN	IP	PH	RHP	LHP
1954	PHI	NL	1	0	1	0	0	0	1	0	0	0	0	0	0	0	1	0

Rank among batters: 4,707 • *Total ballparks homered in*: 1 • *First HR*: 07/11/1954 off Carl Erskine

Adam Comorosky

ADAM ANTHONY COMOROSKY
B: 12/09/1905 D: 03/02/1951
BR

Year	Tm	Lg	Tot	H	A	0	1	2	3	2	3	4	LO	XN	IP	PH	RHP	LHP
1928	PIT	NL	2	1	1	0	2	0	0	0	0	0	0	0	2	0	0	2

Adam Comorosky *continued*

Year	Tm	Lg	Tot	H	A	Men-On 0	Men-On 1	Men-On 2	Men-On 3	One-Game 2	One-Game 3	One-Game 4	LO	XN	IP	PH	RHP	LHP
1929	PIT	NL	6	4	2	3	1	1	1	0	0	0	0	0	3	0	4	2
1930	PIT	NL	12	6	6	8	3	1	0	0	0	0	0	0	2	0	6	6
1931	PIT	NL	1	1	0	0	1	0	0	0	0	0	0	0	1	1	0	1
1932	PIT	NL	4	1	3	3	0	1	0	1	0	0	0	0	1	0	0	4
1933	PIT	NL	1	0	1	1	0	0	0	0	0	0	0	0	0	0	1	0
1935	CIN	NL	2	0	2	0	1	1	0	0	0	0	0	0	0	0	1	1
Total			28	13	15	15	8	4	1	1	0	0	0	0	9	1	12	16

Rank among batters: 1,500 • *Top target (3 home runs)*: Bill Sherdel, Carl Hubbell • *Number of pitchers victimized*: 20 • *Total ballparks homered in*: 6 • *First HR*: 09/04/1928 off Art Nehf

Mike Compton

MICHAEL LYNN COMPTON
B: 08/15/1944
BR

Year	Tm	Lg	Tot	H	A	Men-On 0	Men-On 1	Men-On 2	Men-On 3	One-Game 2	One-Game 3	One-Game 4	LO	XN	IP	PH	RHP	LHP
1970	PHI	NL	1	1	0	0	1	0	0	0	0	0	0	0	0	0	0	1

Rank among batters: 4,707 • *Total ballparks homered in*: 1 • *First HR*: 05/05/1970 off Danny Coombs

Pete Compton

ANNA SEBASTIAN COMPTON
B: 09/28/1889 D: 02/03/1978
BL

Year	Tm	Lg	Tot	H	A	Men-On 0	Men-On 1	Men-On 2	Men-On 3	One-Game 2	One-Game 3	One-Game 4	LO	XN	IP	PH	RHP	LHP
1912	STL	AL	2	1	1	1	1	0	0	0	0	0	0	0	1	0	2	0
1913	STL	AL	2	2	0	2	0	0	0	0	0	0	0	0	0	1	2	0
1915	BOS	NL	1	1	0	0	1	0	0	0	0	0	0	0	1	0	1	0
Total			5	4	1	3	2	0	0	0	0	0	0	0	2	1	5	0

Rank among batters: 3,191 • *Total ballparks homered in*: 3 • *First HR*: 08/15/1912 off Hugh Bedient

Clint Conatser

CLINTON ASTOR CONATSER
B: 07/24/1921
BR

Year	Tm	Lg	Tot	H	A	Men-On 0	Men-On 1	Men-On 2	Men-On 3	One-Game 2	One-Game 3	One-Game 4	LO	XN	IP	PH	RHP	LHP
1948	BOS	NL	3	1	2	1	2	0	0	0	0	0	0	0	0	0	2	1
1949	BOS	NL	3	1	2	3	0	0	0	0	0	0	0	0	0	0	1	2
Total			6	2	4	4	2	0	0	0	0	0	0	0	0	0	3	3

Rank among batters: 2,988 • *Total ballparks homered in*: 4 • *First HR*: 07/27/1948 off Fritz Ostermueller

Dave Concepcion

DAVID ISMAEL (BENITEZ) CONCEPCION
B: 06/17/1948
BR

Year	Tm	Lg	Tot	H	A	Men-On 0	Men-On 1	Men-On 2	Men-On 3	One-Game 2	One-Game 3	One-Game 4	LO	XN	IP	PH	RHP	LHP
1970	CIN	NL	1	0	1	1	0	0	0	0	0	0	0	0	0	0	1	0
1971	CIN	NL	1	0	1	1	0	0	0	0	0	0	0	0	0	0	1	0
1972	CIN	NL	2	1	1	2	0	0	0	0	0	0	0	0	0	0	1	1
1973	CIN	NL	8	1	7	5	2	1	0	0	0	0	0	0	0	0	6	2
1974	CIN	NL	14	10	4	4	3	6	1	0	0	0	0	0	0	0	10	4
1975	CIN	NL	5	2	3	5	0	0	0	0	0	0	0	0	0	0	3	2
1976	CIN	NL	9	4	5	5	4	0	0	1	0	0	0	1	0	0	5	4
1977	CIN	NL	8	5	3	3	4	0	1	0	0	0	0	0	0	0	6	2
1978	CIN	NL	6	3	3	4	2	0	0	0	0	0	0	0	0	0	1	5
1979	CIN	NL	16	10	6	6	6	2	2	0	0	0	0	0	0	0	10	6
1980	CIN	NL	5	4	1	2	3	0	0	0	0	0	0	0	0	0	2	3
1981	CIN	NL	5	4	1	3	1	1	0	2	0	0	0	0	0	0	3	2
1982	CIN	NL	5	3	2	1	1	3	0	0	0	0	0	0	0	0	2	3
1983	CIN	NL	1	0	1	0	0	0	1	0	0	0	0	0	0	0	1	0
1984	CIN	NL	4	3	1	3	0	1	0	0	0	0	0	0	0	0	1	3
1985	CIN	NL	7	1	6	4	2	0	1	0	0	0	0	0	0	0	3	4
1986	CIN	NL	3	0	3	3	0	0	0	1	0	0	0	0	0	0	2	1
1987	CIN	NL	1	1	0	1	0	0	0	0	0	0	0	0	0	0	0	1
Total			101	52	49	53	28	14	6	4	0	0	0	1	0	0	58	43

Rank among batters: 491 • *Top target (5 home runs)*: Phil Niekro • *Number of pitchers victimized*: 80 • *Total ballparks homered in*: 13 • *First HR*: 04/21/1970 off Phil Niekro • *World Series HR*—1; *LCS HR*—1; *All-Star HR*—1

Year	Tm	Lg	Tot	H	A	Men-On 0	1	2	3	One-Game 2	3	4	LO	XN	IP	PH	RHP	LHP

Onix Concepcion

ONIX CARDONA (CARDONA) CONCEPCION
B: 10/05/1957
BR

Year	Tm	Lg	Tot	H	A	0	1	2	3	2	3	4	LO	XN	IP	PH	RHP	LHP
1984	KC	AL	1	1	0	1	0	0	0	0	0	0	1	0	0	0	0	1
1985	KC	AL	2	1	1	1	1	0	0	0	0	0	0	0	0	0	2	0
Total			3	2	1	2	1	0	0	0	0	0	1	0	0	0	2	1

Rank among batters: 3,735 • *Total ballparks homered in*: 2 • *First HR*: 04/03/1984 off Ron Guidry

Bunk Congalton

WILLIAM MILLAR CONGALTON
B: 01/24/1875 D: 08/16/1937
BL

Year	Tm	Lg	Tot	H	A	0	1	2	3	2	3	4	LO	XN	IP	PH	RHP	LHP
1902	CHI	NL	1	0	1	0	0	1	0	0	0	0	0	0	0	0	1	0
1906	CLE	AL	3	1	2	2	1	0	0	0	0	0	0	0	0	0	3	0
1907	BOS	AL	2	2	0	0	1	1	0	0	0	0	0	0	0	0	2	0
Total			6	3	3	2	2	2	0	0	0	0	0	0	0	0	6	0

Rank among batters: 2,988 • *Total ballparks homered in*: 5 • *First HR*: 06/03/1902 off Dummy Taylor

Billy Conigliaro

WILLIAM MICHAEL CONIGLIARO
B: 08/15/1947
BR

Year	Tm	Lg	Tot	H	A	0	1	2	3	2	3	4	LO	XN	IP	PH	RHP	LHP
1969	BOS	AL	4	3	1	3	1	0	0	1	0	0	0	0	0	0	3	1
1970	BOS	AL	18	14	4	13	2	3	0	1	0	0	0	1	0	0	15	3
1971	BOS	AL	11	5	6	6	1	4	0	0	0	0	0	0	0	0	8	3
1972	MIL	AL	7	2	5	4	3	0	0	1	0	0	0	0	0	0	4	3
Total			40	24	16	26	7	7	0	3	0	0	0	1	0	0	30	10

Rank among batters: 1,181 • *Top target (3 home runs)*: Mickey Lolich • *Number of pitchers victimized*: 33 • *Total ballparks homered in*: 10 • *First HR*: 04/16/1969 off Dave Leonhard

Tony Conigliaro

ANTHONY RICHARD CONIGLIARO
B: 01/07/1945 D: 02/24/1990
BR

Year	Tm	Lg	Tot	H	A	0	1	2	3	2	3	4	LO	XN	IP	PH	RHP	LHP
1964	BOS	AL	24	13	11	13	8	2	1	1	0	0	0	1	0	1	16	8
1965	BOS	AL	32	23	9	18	10	2	2	3	0	0	0	0	1	0	25	7
1966	BOS	AL	28	15	13	12	13	3	0	0	0	0	0	0	0	0	20	8
1967	BOS	AL	20	8	12	9	7	4	0	0	0	0	0	1	0	0	17	3
1969	BOS	AL	20	9	11	13	3	4	0	1	0	0	0	1	0	0	15	5
1970	BOS	AL	36	18	18	17	15	2	2	4	0	0	0	0	0	0	23	13
1971	CAL	AL	4	2	2	2	2	0	0	0	0	0	0	0	0	0	2	2
1975	BOS	AL	2	1	1	2	0	0	0	0	0	0	0	0	0	0	0	2
Total			166	89	77	86	58	17	5	9	0	0	0	3	1	1	118	48

Rank among batters: 245 • *Top target (5 home runs)*: Sonny Siebert, Joe Horlen • *Number of pitchers victimized*: 103 • *Total ballparks homered in*: 14 • *First HR*: 04/17/1964 off Joe Horlen

Jeff Conine

JEFFREY GUY CONINE
B: 06/27/1966
BR

Year	Tm	Lg	Tot	H	A	0	1	2	3	2	3	4	LO	XN	IP	PH	RHP	LHP
1993	FLO	NL	12	5	7	3	3	4	2	0	0	0	0	0	0	0	7	5
1994	FLO	NL	18	8	10	10	6	2	0	1	0	0	0	0	0	0	12	6
1995	FLO	NL	25	13	12	14	6	5	0	2	0	0	0	0	0	0	16	9
Total			55	26	29	27	15	11	2	3	0	0	0	0	0	0	35	20

Rank among batters: 926 • *Top target (3 home runs)*: Pete Schourek • *Number of pitchers victimized*: 49 • *Total ballparks homered in*: 13 • *First HR*: 05/01/1993 off David Nied • *All-Star HR*—1

Gene Conley

DONALD EUGENE CONLEY
B: 11/10/1930
BR

Year	Tm	Lg	Tot	H	A	0	1	2	3	2	3	4	LO	XN	IP	PH	RHP	LHP
1958	MIL	NL	1	1	0	1	0	0	0	0	0	0	0	0	0	0	1	0
1960	PHI	NL	1	0	1	0	0	1	0	0	0	0	0	1	0	0	1	0
1961	BOS	AL	2	1	1	1	1	0	0	0	0	0	0	0	0	0	2	0

Gene Conley *continued*

Year	Tm	Lg	Tot	H	A	Men-On 0	1	2	3	One-Game 2	3	4	LO	XN	IP	PH	RHP	LHP
1962	BOS	AL	1	1	0	0	1	0	0	0	0	0	0	0	0	0	1	0
Total			5	3	2	2	2	1	0	0	0	0	0	1	0	0	5	0

Rank among batters: 3,191 • *Total ballparks homered in*: 3 • *First HR*: 07/26/1958 off Dick Drott

Fritz Connally

FRITZIE LEE CONNALLY
B: 05/19/1958
BR

Year	Tm	Lg	Tot	H	A	Men-On 0	1	2	3	One-Game 2	3	4	LO	XN	IP	PH	RHP	LHP
1985	BAL	AL	3	0	3	1	0	0	2	0	0	0	0	0	0	0	2	1

Rank among batters: 3,735 • *Total ballparks homered in*: 3 • *First HR*: 04/19/1985 off Doyle Alexander

Sarge Connally

GEORGE WALTER CONNALLY
B: 08/31/1898 D: 01/27/1978
BR

Year	Tm	Lg	Tot	H	A	Men-On 0	1	2	3	One-Game 2	3	4	LO	XN	IP	PH	RHP	LHP
1932	CLE	AL	1	0	1	1	0	0	0	0	0	0	0	0	0	0	1	0

Rank among batters: 4,707 • *Total ballparks homered in*: 1 • *First HR*: 07/24/1932 off Pete Daglia

Frank Connaughton

FRANK HENRY CONNAUGHTON
B: 01/01/1869 D: 12/01/1942
BR

Year	Tm	Lg	Tot	H	A	Men-On 0	1	2	3	One-Game 2	3	4	LO	XN	IP	PH	RHP	LHP
1894	BOS	NL	2	2	0	0	1	1	0	0	0	0	0	0	0	0	2	0
1896	NY	NL	2	0	2	0	1	1	0	0	0	0	0	0	0	0	0	1
Total			4	2	2	0	2	2	0	0	0	0	0	0	0	0	2	1

Rank among batters: 3,427 • *Total ballparks homered in*: 3 • *First HR*: 08/14/1894 off Ad Gumbert

Joe Connolly

JOSEPH ALOYSIUS CONNOLLY
B: 02/12/1888 D: 09/01/1943
BL

Year	Tm	Lg	Tot	H	A	Men-On 0	1	2	3	One-Game 2	3	4	LO	XN	IP	PH	RHP	LHP
1913	BOS	NL	5	5	0	2	2	0	1	0	0	0	0	0	0	0	5	0
1914	BOS	NL	9	6	3	7	1	1	0	0	0	0	0	0	1	0	9	0
Total			14	11	3	9	3	1	1	0	0	0	0	0	1	0	14	0

Rank among batters: 2,169 • *Top target (2 home runs)*: Chief Johnson • *Number of pitchers victimized*: 13 • *Total ballparks homered in*: 5 • *First HR*: 05/15/1913 off Chief Johnson

Joe Connolly

JOSEPH GEORGE CONNOLLY
B: 06/04/1896 D: 03/30/1960
BR

Year	Tm	Lg	Tot	H	A	Men-On 0	1	2	3	One-Game 2	3	4	LO	XN	IP	PH	RHP	LHP
1923	CLE	AL	3	0	3	1	1	0	1	0	0	0	0	0	0	1	1	2

Rank among batters: 3,735 • *Total ballparks homered in*: 3 • *First HR*: 06/06/1923 off George Murray

Jim Connor

JAMES MATTHEW CONNOR
B: 05/11/1863 D: 09/03/1950
BR

Year	Tm	Lg	Tot	H	A	Men-On 0	1	2	3	One-Game 2	3	4	LO	XN	IP	PH	RHP	LHP
1897	CHI	NL	3	3	0	1	1	1	0	0	0	0	0	0	1	0	1	1

Rank among batters: 3,735 • *Total ballparks homered in*: 1 • *First HR*: 05/22/1897 off Cy Swaim

Joe Connor

JOSEPH FRANCIS CONNOR
B: 12/08/1874 D: 11/08/1957
BR

Year	Tm	Lg	Tot	H	A	Men-On 0	1	2	3	One-Game 2	3	4	LO	XN	IP	PH	RHP	LHP
1901	MIL	AL	1	1	0	1	0	0	0	0	0	0	0	0	0	0	1	0

Rank among batters: 4,707 • *Total ballparks homered in*: 1 • *First HR*: 07/01/1901 off Bill Hart

Roger Connor

ROGER CONNOR
B: 07/01/1857 D: 01/04/1931
BL HOF

Year	Tm	Lg	Tot	H	A	Men-On 0	Men-On 1	Men-On 2	Men-On 3	One-Game 2	One-Game 3	One-Game 4	LO	XN	IP	PH	RHP	LHP
1880	TRO	NL	3	3	0	0	2	1	0	1	0	0	0	0	0	0	3	0
1881	TRO	NL	2	1	1	1	0	0	1	0	0	0	0	0	0	0	1	1
1882	TRO	NL	4	2	2	1	2	1	0	0	0	0	0	0	0	0	4	0
1883	NY	NL	1	1	0	1	0	0	0	0	0	0	0	0	0	0	0	0
1884	NY	NL	4	0	4	3	1	0	0	1	0	0	0	0	1	0	4	0
1885	NY	NL	1	1	0	0	0	1	0	0	0	0	0	0	0	0	0	0
1886	NY	NL	7	4	3	1	5	1	0	1	0	0	0	0	0	0	6	1
1887	NY	NL	17	7	10	9	3	4	1	1	0	0	0	0	1	0	13	4
1888	NY	NL	14	3	11	9	3	2	0	1	1	0	0	0	1	0	11	3
1889	NY	NL	13	4	9	9	3	1	0	1	0	0	0	0	0	0	10	3
1890	NY	PL	14	6	8	5	7	2	0	0	0	0	0	0	2	0	10	4
1891	NY	NL	7	6	1	1	5	1	0	0	0	0	0	0	1	0	7	0
1892	PHI	NL	12	10	2	5	5	2	0	1	0	0	0	0	0	0	9	0
1893	NY	NL	11	8	3	3	4	4	0	1	0	0	0	0	1	0	7	4
1894	NY	NL	1	0	1	1	0	0	0	0	0	0	0	0	0	0	1	0
	STL	NL	7	3	4	2	2	3	0	0	0	0	0	0	1	0	5	1
	Total		8	3	5	3	2	3	0	0	0	0	0	0	1	0	6	1
1895	STL	NL	8	5	3	4	3	1	0	1	0	0	0	0	2	0	8	0
1896	STL	NL	11	9	2	9	2	0	0	0	0	0	0	0	1	0	10	1
1897	STL	NL	1	1	0	1	0	0	0	0	0	0	0	0	0	0	1	0
Total			138	74	64	65	47	24	2	9	1	0	0	0	11	0	107	22

Rank among batters: 314 • *Top target (6 home runs)*: Egyptian Healy • *Number of pitchers victimized*: 79 • *Total ballparks homered in*: 32 • *First HR*: 05/24/1880 off Tommy Bond • *Hit for Cycle*—@BUF: 07/21/1890

Chuck Connors

KEVIN JOSEPH ALOYSIUS CONNORS
B: 04/10/1921 D: 11/10/1992
BL

Year	Tm	Lg	Tot	H	A	Men-On 0	Men-On 1	Men-On 2	Men-On 3	One-Game 2	One-Game 3	One-Game 4	LO	XN	IP	PH	RHP	LHP
1951	CHI	NL	2	0	2	0	1	1	0	0	0	0	0	0	0	0	1	1

Rank among batters: 4,129 • *Total ballparks homered in*: 1 • *First HR*: 07/18/1951 off Dave Koslo

Merv Connors

MERVYN JAMES CONNORS
B: 01/23/1914
BR

Year	Tm	Lg	Tot	H	A	Men-On 0	Men-On 1	Men-On 2	Men-On 3	One-Game 2	One-Game 3	One-Game 4	LO	XN	IP	PH	RHP	LHP
1937	CHI	AL	2	0	2	1	1	0	0	0	0	0	0	0	0	0	2	0
1938	CHI	AL	6	5	1	3	2	1	0	0	1	0	0	0	0	1	5	1
Total			8	5	3	4	3	1	0	0	1	0	0	0	0	1	7	1

Rank among batters: 2,703 • *Top target (3 home runs)*: Jim Reninger • *Number of pitchers victimized*: 6 • *Total ballparks homered in*: 3 • *First HR*: 09/09/1937 off Bill Trotter

Bill Conroy

WILLIAM GORDON CONROY
B: 02/26/1915
BR

Year	Tm	Lg	Tot	H	A	Men-On 0	Men-On 1	Men-On 2	Men-On 3	One-Game 2	One-Game 3	One-Game 4	LO	XN	IP	PH	RHP	LHP
1942	BOS	AL	4	4	0	3	1	0	0	0	0	0	0	0	0	0	4	0
1943	BOS	AL	1	0	1	1	0	0	0	0	0	0	0	0	0	0	1	0
Total			5	4	1	4	1	0	0	0	0	0	0	0	0	0	5	0

Rank among batters: 3,191 • *Total ballparks homered in*: 2 • *First HR*: 04/20/1942 off Jack Wilson

Wid Conroy

WILLIAM EDWARD CONROY
B: 04/05/1877 D: 12/06/1959
BR

Year	Tm	Lg	Tot	H	A	Men-On 0	Men-On 1	Men-On 2	Men-On 3	One-Game 2	One-Game 3	One-Game 4	LO	XN	IP	PH	RHP	LHP
1901	MIL	AL	5	3	2	1	3	1	0	0	0	0	0	0	0	0	4	1
1902	PIT	NL	1	1	0	0	0	0	1	0	0	0	0	0	1	0	1	0
1903	NY	AL	1	0	1	0	1	0	0	0	0	0	0	0	1	0	1	0
1904	NY	AL	1	1	0	0	1	0	0	0	0	0	0	0	1	0	1	0
1905	NY	AL	2	2	0	2	0	0	0	0	0	0	0	0	2	0	2	0
1906	NY	AL	4	3	1	2	1	1	0	0	0	0	0	0	3	0	4	0
1907	NY	AL	3	1	2	2	0	1	0	0	0	0	0	0	3	0	2	1

Wid Conroy *continued*

Year	Tm	Lg	Tot	H	A	Men-On 0	Men-On 1	Men-On 2	Men-On 3	One-Game 2	One-Game 3	One-Game 4	LO	XN	IP	PH	RHP	LHP
1908	NY	AL	1	1	0	1	0	0	0	0	0	0	0	0	0	0	0	1
1909	WAS	AL	1	1	0	1	0	0	0	0	0	0	0	0	0	0	1	0
1910	WAS	AL	1	0	1	0	1	0	0	0	0	0	0	0	0	0	1	0
1911	WAS	AL	2	0	2	1	1	0	0	0	0	0	0	0	1	0	2	0
Total			22	13	9	10	8	3	1	0	0	0	0	0	12	0	19	3

Rank among batters: 1,719 • *Total ballparks homered in*: 9 • *First HR*: 04/28/1901 off Emil Frisk

Billy Consolo

WILLIAM ANGELO CONSOLO
B: 08/18/1934
BR

Year	Tm	Lg	Tot	H	A	Men-On 0	Men-On 1	Men-On 2	Men-On 3	One-Game 2	One-Game 3	One-Game 4	LO	XN	IP	PH	RHP	LHP
1953	BOS	AL	1	1	0	0	1	0	0	0	0	0	0	0	0	0	1	0
1954	BOS	AL	1	1	0	1	0	0	0	0	0	0	0	0	0	0	1	0
1957	BOS	AL	4	2	2	2	2	0	0	0	0	0	0	0	0	0	4	0
1960	WAS	AL	3	2	1	3	0	0	0	0	0	0	0	0	0	0	3	0
Total			9	6	3	6	3	0	0	0	0	0	0	0	0	0	9	0

Rank among batters: 2,587 • *Total ballparks homered in*: 4 • *First HR*: 08/01/1953 off Steve Gromek

Jack Conway

JACK CLEMENTS CONWAY
B: 07/30/1919
BR

Year	Tm	Lg	Tot	H	A	Men-On 0	Men-On 1	Men-On 2	Men-On 3	One-Game 2	One-Game 3	One-Game 4	LO	XN	IP	PH	RHP	LHP
1948	NY	NL	1	1	0	1	0	0	0	0	0	0	0	0	0	0	1	0

Rank among batters: 4,707 • *Total ballparks homered in*: 1 • *First HR*: 07/11/1948 off Willie Ramsdell

Pete Conway

PETER J. CONWAY
B: 10/30/1866 D: 01/13/1903
BR

Year	Tm	Lg	Tot	H	A	Men-On 0	Men-On 1	Men-On 2	Men-On 3	One-Game 2	One-Game 3	One-Game 4	LO	XN	IP	PH	RHP	LHP
1885	BUF	NL	1	1	0	0	1	0	0	0	0	0	0	0	0	0	1	0
1886	KC	NL	1	1	0	0	1	0	0	0	0	0	0	0	0	0	1	0
	DET	NL	2	2	0	2	0	0	0	0	0	0	0	0	1	0	2	0
	Total		3	3	0	2	1	0	0	0	0	0	0	0	1	0	3	0
1887	DET	NL	1	1	0	1	0	0	0	0	0	0	0	0	0	0	1	0
1888	DET	NL	3	2	1	0	3	0	0	0	0	0	0	0	0	0	2	0
1889	PIT	NL	1	1	0	1	0	0	0	0	0	0	0	0	0	0	0	1
Total			9	8	1	4	5	0	0	0	0	0	0	0	1	0	7	1

Rank among batters: 2,587 • *Top target (2 home runs)*: Tim Keefe • *Number of pitchers victimized*: 8 • *Total ballparks homered in*: 5 • *First HR*: 09/19/1885 off Charlie Ferguson

Herb Conyers

HERBERT LEROY CONYERS
B: 01/08/1921 D: 09/16/1964
BL

Year	Tm	Lg	Tot	H	A	Men-On 0	Men-On 1	Men-On 2	Men-On 3	One-Game 2	One-Game 3	One-Game 4	LO	XN	IP	PH	RHP	LHP
1950	CLE	AL	1	0	1	1	0	0	0	0	0	0	0	0	0	0	1	0

Rank among batters: 4,707 • *Total ballparks homered in*: 1 • *First HR*: 10/01/1950 off Marlin Stuart

Dale Coogan

DALE ROGER COOGAN
B: 08/14/1930 D: 03/08/1989
BL

Year	Tm	Lg	Tot	H	A	Men-On 0	Men-On 1	Men-On 2	Men-On 3	One-Game 2	One-Game 3	One-Game 4	LO	XN	IP	PH	RHP	LHP
1950	PIT	NL	1	0	1	0	0	1	0	0	0	0	0	0	0	0	1	0

Rank among batters: 4,707 • *Total ballparks homered in*: 1 • *First HR*: 06/24/1950 off Ralph Branca

Cliff Cook

RAYMOND CLIFFORD COOK
B: 08/20/1936
BR

Year	Tm	Lg	Tot	H	A	Men-On 0	Men-On 1	Men-On 2	Men-On 3	One-Game 2	One-Game 3	One-Game 4	LO	XN	IP	PH	RHP	LHP
1960	CIN	NL	3	2	1	2	1	0	0	0	0	0	0	0	0	0	2	1
1962	NY	NL	2	0	2	2	0	0	0	0	0	0	0	0	0	0	2	0
1963	NY	NL	2	1	1	1	1	0	0	0	0	0	0	0	0	0	0	2
Total			7	3	4	5	2	0	0	0	0	0	0	0	0	0	4	3

Rank among batters: 2,834 • *Total ballparks homered in*: 6 • *First HR*: 08/06/1960 off Ernie Broglio

BORDERS®

- Returns must be accompanied by receipt
- Returns must be completed within 30 days
- Merchandise must be in salable condition
- Opened videos, discs, and cassettes may be exchanged for replacement copies of the original item only
- Periodicals and newspapers may not be returned

BORDERS®

Borders Books, Music & Cafe
Bowie, Maryland
(301) 352-5560

1319   174/0003/01 000543   SALE

ITEM   TX RETAIL DISC SPEC   EXTND

HOME RUN ENCY WHO WHAT WHEN

1 IR 5015703 1   4.99   4.99

SUBTOTAL   4.99

5.000%   TAX1   .25

1 Item   AMOUNT DUE   5.24

CASH   5.24

CHANGE DUE   .00

02/16/98   12:22 PM

All returns must be accompanied by a receipt and must be returned within 30 days. Open compact discs, cassettes and videos are not returnable unless defective. Newspapers and magazines are not returnable. Thank you!

Dennis Cook

DENNIS BRYAN COOK
B: 10/04/1962
BL

Year	Tm	Lg	Tot	H	A	Men-On 0	Men-On 1	Men-On 2	Men-On 3	One-Game 2	One-Game 3	One-Game 4	LO	XN	IP	PH	RHP	LHP
1990	PHI	NL	1	0	1	0	0	1	0	0	0	0	0	0	0	0	0	1

Rank among batters: 4,707 • *Total ballparks homered in*: 1 • *First HR*: 05/19/1990 off Fernando Valenzuela

Doc Cook

LUTHER ALMUS COOK
B: 06/24/1886 D: 06/30/1973
BL

Year	Tm	Lg	Tot	H	A	Men-On 0	Men-On 1	Men-On 2	Men-On 3	One-Game 2	One-Game 3	One-Game 4	LO	XN	IP	PH	RHP	LHP
1914	NY	AL	1	0	1	0	0	1	0	0	0	0	0	0	0	0	1	0
1915	NY	AL	2	2	0	1	0	1	0	0	0	0	0	0	0	0	0	2
Total			3	2	1	1	0	2	0	0	0	0	0	0	0	0	1	2

Rank among batters: 3,735 • *Total ballparks homered in*: 2 • *First HR*: 06/13/1914 off Roy Mitchell

Dusty Cooke

ALLEN LINDSEY COOKE
B: 06/23/1907 D: 11/21/1987
BL

Year	Tm	Lg	Tot	H	A	Men-On 0	Men-On 1	Men-On 2	Men-On 3	One-Game 2	One-Game 3	One-Game 4	LO	XN	IP	PH	RHP	LHP
1930	NY	AL	6	5	1	3	2	1	0	0	0	0	0	1	2	0	6	0
1931	NY	AL	1	1	0	1	0	0	0	0	0	0	0	0	1	0	1	0
1933	BOS	AL	5	3	2	2	2	1	0	0	0	0	0	0	0	0	4	1
1934	BOS	AL	1	0	1	0	0	1	0	0	0	0	0	0	0	0	1	0
1935	BOS	AL	3	0	3	3	0	0	0	0	0	0	0	0	0	0	3	0
1936	BOS	AL	6	1	5	4	1	1	0	0	0	0	2	0	0	1	6	0
1938	CIN	NL	2	1	1	1	0	1	0	0	0	0	0	0	0	0	1	1
Total			24	11	13	14	5	5	0	0	0	0	2	1	3	1	22	2

Rank among batters: 1,643 • *Top target (2 home runs)*: Eddie Rommel, Johnny Marcum, Tommy Thomas • *Number of pitchers victimized*: 21 • *Total ballparks homered in*: 8 • *First HR*: 05/25/1930 off Roy Mahaffey

Scott Coolbaugh

SCOTT ROBERT COOLBAUGH
B: 06/13/1966
BR

Year	Tm	Lg	Tot	H	A	Men-On 0	Men-On 1	Men-On 2	Men-On 3	One-Game 2	One-Game 3	One-Game 4	LO	XN	IP	PH	RHP	LHP
1989	TEX	AL	2	1	1	1	0	1	0	0	0	0	0	0	0	0	2	0
1990	TEX	AL	2	1	1	2	0	0	0	0	0	0	0	0	0	0	2	0
1991	SD	NL	2	1	1	1	1	0	0	0	0	0	0	1	0	0	2	0
1994	STL	NL	2	2	0	1	1	0	0	0	0	0	0	0	0	1	0	2
Total			8	5	3	5	2	1	0	0	0	0	0	1	0	1	6	2

Rank among batters: 2,703 • *Total ballparks homered in*: 6 • *First HR*: 09/10/1989 off Jose Bautista

Duff Cooley

DUFF GORDAN COOLEY
B: 03/14/1873 D: 08/09/1937
BL

Year	Tm	Lg	Tot	H	A	Men-On 0	Men-On 1	Men-On 2	Men-On 3	One-Game 2	One-Game 3	One-Game 4	LO	XN	IP	PH	RHP	LHP
1894	STL	NL	1	1	0	0	1	0	0	0	0	0	0	0	0	0	1	0
1895	STL	NL	7	5	2	2	1	3	1	0	0	0	0	0	3	0	5	1
1896	PHI	NL	2	1	1	1	1	0	0	0	0	0	1	0	0	0	2	0
1897	PHI	NL	4	3	1	2	2	0	0	0	0	0	1	0	0	0	2	2
1898	PHI	NL	4	1	3	2	2	0	0	0	0	0	0	0	1	0	2	2
1899	PHI	NL	1	1	0	1	0	0	0	0	0	0	0	0	0	0	1	0
1903	BOS	NL	1	1	0	0	0	0	1	0	0	0	0	0	0	0	1	0
1904	BOS	NL	5	2	3	2	2	1	0	0	0	0	0	0	0	0	4	1
1905	DET	AL	1	1	0	1	0	0	0	0	0	0	0	0	1	0	1	0
Total			26	16	10	11	9	4	2	0	0	0	2	0	5	0	19	6

Rank among batters: 1,576 • *Top target (2 home runs)*: Kid Nichols, Frank Dwyer • *Number of pitchers victimized*: 24 • *Total ballparks homered in*: 8 • *First HR*: 06/28/1894 off Kid Nichols • *Hit for Cycle*—vs PHI: 06/20/1904 (2)

Jack Coombs

JOHN WESLEY COOMBS
B: 11/18/1882 D: 04/15/1957
BB

Year	Tm	Lg	Tot	H	A	Men-On 0	Men-On 1	Men-On 2	Men-On 3	One-Game 2	One-Game 3	One-Game 4	LO	XN	IP	PH	RHP	LHP
1907	PHI	AL	1	1	0	1	0	0	0	0	0	0	0	0	0	0	0	1
1908	PHI	AL	1	1	0	1	0	0	0	0	0	0	0	0	0	0	1	0

Jack Coombs *continued*

Year	Tm	Lg	Tot	H	A	Men-On 0	1	2	3	One-Game 2	3	4	LO	XN	IP	PH	RHP	LHP
1911	PHI	AL	2	0	2	1	1	0	0	0	0	0	0	2	0	0	2	0
Total			4	2	2	3	1	0	0	0	0	0	0	2	0	0	3	1

Rank among batters: 3,427 • *Total ballparks homered in*: 3 • *First HR*: 06/22/1907 off Case Patten

Ron Coomer

RONALD BRYAN COOMER
B: 11/18/1966
BR

Year	Tm	Lg	Tot	H	A	Men-On 0	1	2	3	One-Game 2	3	4	LO	XN	IP	PH	RHP	LHP
1995	MIN	AL	5	2	3	2	3	0	0	0	0	0	0	0	0	0	2	3

Rank among batters: 3,191 • *Total ballparks homered in*: 4 • *First HR*: 08/16/1995 off Randy Johnson

Jimmy Cooney

JAMES JOSEPH COONEY
B: 07/09/1865 D: 07/01/1903
BB

Year	Tm	Lg	Tot	H	A	Men-On 0	1	2	3	One-Game 2	3	4	LO	XN	IP	PH	RHP	LHP
1890	CHI	NL	4	3	1	2	1	1	0	0	0	0	0	0	1	0	1	3

Rank among batters: 3,427 • *Top target (2 home runs)*: Tony Mullane • *Number of pitchers victimized*: 3 • *Total ballparks homered in*: 2 • *First HR*: 07/23/1890 off Jesse Burkett

Jimmy Cooney

JAMES EDWARD COONEY
B: 08/24/1894 D: 08/07/1991
BR

Year	Tm	Lg	Tot	H	A	Men-On 0	1	2	3	One-Game 2	3	4	LO	XN	IP	PH	RHP	LHP
1924	STL	NL	1	0	1	1	0	0	0	0	0	0	0	0	0	0	0	1
1926	CHI	NL	1	0	1	0	0	1	0	0	0	0	0	0	0	0	1	0
Total			2	0	2	1	0	1	0	0	0	0	0	0	0	0	1	1

Rank among batters: 4,129 • *Total ballparks homered in*: 1 • *First HR*: 06/17/1924 off Jack Bentley

Johnny Cooney

JOHN WALTER COONEY
B: 03/18/1901 D: 07/08/1986
BR

Year	Tm	Lg	Tot	H	A	Men-On 0	1	2	3	One-Game 2	3	4	LO	XN	IP	PH	RHP	LHP
1939	BOS	NL	2	0	2	0	2	0	0	0	0	0	0	0	0	0	2	0

Rank among batters: 4,129 • *Total ballparks homered in*: 1 • *First HR*: 09/24/1939 off Harry Gumbert

Cecil Cooper

CECIL CELESTER COOPER
B: 12/20/1949
BL

Year	Tm	Lg	Tot	H	A	Men-On 0	1	2	3	One-Game 2	3	4	LO	XN	IP	PH	RHP	LHP
1973	BOS	AL	3	3	0	3	0	0	0	0	0	0	0	0	0	0	3	0
1974	BOS	AL	8	5	3	3	3	2	0	0	0	0	0	1	0	0	8	0
1975	BOS	AL	14	6	8	13	1	0	0	0	0	0	0	1	0	1	14	0
1976	BOS	AL	15	9	6	7	7	1	0	0	0	0	2	0	0	0	13	2
1977	MIL	AL	20	9	11	13	6	0	1	0	0	0	0	0	1	0	17	3
1978	MIL	AL	13	5	8	11	1	0	1	1	0	0	0	0	0	0	11	2
1979	MIL	AL	24	13	11	12	10	2	0	3	1	0	0	0	0	0	23	1
1980	MIL	AL	25	12	13	13	10	1	1	2	0	0	0	0	0	0	20	5
1981	MIL	AL	12	5	7	6	4	2	0	1	0	0	0	0	0	0	8	4
1982	MIL	AL	32	12	20	16	13	2	1	3	0	0	0	0	0	0	24	8
1983	MIL	AL	30	14	16	10	20	0	0	2	0	0	0	0	0	0	23	7
1984	MIL	AL	11	3	8	6	3	2	0	0	0	0	0	0	0	0	10	1
1985	MIL	AL	16	6	10	8	5	2	1	0	0	0	0	0	0	0	10	6
1986	MIL	AL	12	6	6	5	4	3	0	1	0	0	0	0	0	0	9	3
1987	MIL	AL	6	4	2	3	2	1	0	0	0	0	0	0	0	0	5	1
Total			241	112	129	129	89	18	5	13	1	0	2	2	1	1	198	43

Rank among batters: 125 • *Top target (6 home runs)*: Catfish Hunter • *Number of pitchers victimized*: 151 • *Total ballparks homered in*: 15 • *First HR*: 09/07/1973 off Bob Miller • *World Series HR*—1

Claude Cooper

CLAUDE WILLIAM COOPER
B: 04/01/1892 D: 01/21/1974
BL

Year	Tm	Lg	Tot	H	A	Men-On 0	1	2	3	One-Game 2	3	4	LO	XN	IP	PH	RHP	LHP
1914	BRO	FL	2	2	0	2	0	0	0	0	0	0	1	0	0	0	1	1

Claude Cooper *continued*

Year	Tm	Lg	Tot	H	A	Men-On 0	1	2	3	One-Game 2	3	4	LO	XN	IP	PH	RHP	LHP
1915	BRO	FL	2	0	2	0	2	0	0	0	0	0	0	0	0	0	1	1
Total			4	2	2	2	2	0	0	0	0	0	1	0	0	0	2	2

Rank among batters: 3,427 • *Total ballparks homered in*: 3 • *First HR*: 07/11/1914 off Mysterious Walker

Mort Cooper

MORTON CECIL COOPER
B: 03/02/1913 D: 11/17/1958
BR

Year	Tm	Lg	Tot	H	A	Men-On 0	1	2	3	One-Game 2	3	4	LO	XN	IP	PH	RHP	LHP
1939	STL	NL	2	1	1	1	1	0	0	0	0	0	0	0	0	0	1	1
1943	STL	NL	1	0	1	1	0	0	0	0	0	0	0	0	0	0	1	0
1945	BOS	NL	1	0	1	1	0	0	0	0	0	0	0	0	0	0	1	0
1946	BOS	NL	1	0	1	1	0	0	0	0	0	0	0	0	0	0	0	1
1947	NY	NL	1	0	1	1	0	0	0	0	0	0	0	0	0	0	1	0
Total			6	1	5	5	1	0	0	0	0	0	0	0	0	0	4	2

Rank among batters: 2,988 • *Total ballparks homered in*: 6 • *First HR*: 07/04/1939 off Earl Whitehill

Scott Cooper

SCOTT KENDRICK COOPER
B: 10/13/1967
BL

Year	Tm	Lg	Tot	H	A	Men-On 0	1	2	3	One-Game 2	3	4	LO	XN	IP	PH	RHP	LHP
1992	BOS	AL	5	2	3	5	0	0	0	0	0	0	0	0	0	0	4	1
1993	BOS	AL	9	3	6	5	2	2	0	0	0	0	0	0	0	0	7	2
1994	BOS	AL	13	9	4	9	3	0	1	1	0	0	0	0	0	0	11	2
1995	STL	NL	3	1	2	3	0	0	0	0	0	0	0	0	0	0	3	0
Total			30	15	15	22	5	2	1	1	0	0	0	0	0	0	25	5

Rank among batters: 1,437 • *Top target (2 home runs)*: Bill Gullickson, Phil Leftwich • *Number of pitchers victimized*: 28 • *Total ballparks homered in*: 12 • *First HR*: 09/04/1992 off Dave Stewart • *Hit for Cycle—@KC*: 04/12/1994

Walker Cooper

WILLIAM WALKER COOPER
B: 01/08/1915 D: 04/11/1991
BR

Year	Tm	Lg	Tot	H	A	Men-On 0	1	2	3	One-Game 2	3	4	LO	XN	IP	PH	RHP	LHP
1941	STL	NL	1	0	1	1	0	0	0	0	0	0	0	0	0	0	1	0
1942	STL	NL	7	3	4	5	2	0	0	0	0	0	0	0	0	0	3	4
1943	STL	NL	9	3	6	3	4	1	1	0	0	0	0	0	0	0	6	3
1944	STL	NL	13	7	6	7	6	0	0	0	0	0	0	0	1	2	8	5
1946	NY	NL	8	1	7	2	2	3	1	0	0	0	0	0	0	1	5	3
1947	NY	NL	35	12	23	16	12	6	1	3	0	0	0	0	0	0	27	8
1948	NY	NL	16	7	9	8	2	4	2	0	0	0	0	1	0	0	10	6
1949	NY	NL	4	1	3	0	3	1	0	0	0	0	0	0	0	0	1	3
	CIN	NL	16	10	6	9	2	4	1	1	1	0	0	1	0	0	10	6
	Total		20	11	9	9	5	5	1	1	1	0	0	1	0	0	11	9
1950	BOS	NL	14	4	10	8	3	2	1	1	0	0	0	0	0	0	8	6
1951	BOS	NL	18	7	11	13	2	3	0	1	0	0	0	0	0	0	11	7
1952	BOS	NL	10	5	5	3	5	2	0	0	0	0	0	0	0	1	7	3
1953	MIL	NL	3	0	3	1	0	2	0	0	0	0	0	0	0	0	2	1
1954	CHI	NL	7	5	2	3	2	0	2	0	0	0	0	0	0	0	4	3
1955	CHI	NL	7	4	3	5	2	0	0	0	0	0	0	0	0	0	5	2
1956	STL	NL	2	0	2	2	0	0	0	0	0	0	0	0	0	1	1	1
1957	STL	NL	3	2	1	2	1	0	0	0	0	0	0	0	0	1	3	0
Total			173	71	102	88	48	28	9	6	1	0	0	2	1	6	112	61

Rank among batters: 231 • *Top target (5 home runs)*: George Spencer • *Number of pitchers victimized*: 106 • *Total ballparks homered in*: 8 • *First HR*: 08/27/1941 off Jumbo Brown

Wilbur Cooper

ARLEY WILBUR COOPER
B: 02/24/1892 D: 08/07/1973
BR

Year	Tm	Lg	Tot	H	A	Men-On 0	1	2	3	One-Game 2	3	4	LO	XN	IP	PH	RHP	LHP
1922	PIT	NL	4	1	3	2	2	0	0	0	0	0	0	0	1	0	4	0
1925	CHI	NL	2	1	1	1	0	1	0	0	0	0	0	0	0	0	2	0
Total			6	2	4	3	2	1	0	0	0	0	0	0	1	0	6	0

Rank among batters: 2,988 • *Total ballparks homered in*: 4 • *First HR*: 06/27/1922 off Virgil Cheeves

Joey Cora

JOSE MANUEL (AMARO) CORA
B: 05/14/1965
BB

Year	Tm	Lg	Tot	H	A	Men-On 0	1	2	3	One-Game 2	3	4	LO	XN	IP	PH	RHP	LHP
1993	CHI	AL	2	0	2	1	1	0	0	0	0	0	0	0	0	0	2	0
1994	CHI	AL	2	2	0	1	1	0	0	0	0	0	0	0	0	0	2	0
1995	SEA	AL	3	1	2	2	1	0	0	0	0	0	0	0	0	0	3	0
Total			7	3	4	4	3	0	0	0	0	0	0	0	0	0	7	0

Rank among batters: 2,834 • *Total ballparks homered in*: 6 • *First HR*: 06/02/1993 off Mike Moore • *LCS HR*—1

Gene Corbett

EUGENE LOUIS CORBETT
B: 10/25/1913
BL

Year	Tm	Lg	Tot	H	A	Men-On 0	1	2	3	One-Game 2	3	4	LO	XN	IP	PH	RHP	LHP
1938	PHI	NL	2	2	0	1	1	0	0	0	0	0	0	0	0	0	2	0

Rank among batters: 4,129 • *Total ballparks homered in*: 1 • *First HR*: 05/16/1938 off Hal Schumacher

Claude Corbitt

CLAUDE ELLIOTT CORBITT
B: 07/21/1915 D: 05/01/1978
BR

Year	Tm	Lg	Tot	H	A	Men-On 0	1	2	3	One-Game 2	3	4	LO	XN	IP	PH	RHP	LHP
1946	CIN	NL	1	0	1	1	0	0	0	0	0	0	0	0	1	0	0	1

Rank among batters: 4,707 • *Total ballparks homered in*: 1 • *First HR*: 09/13/1946 off Johnny Gee

Larry Corcoran

LAWRENCE J. CORCORAN
B: 08/10/1859 D: 10/14/1891
BL

Year	Tm	Lg	Tot	H	A	Men-On 0	1	2	3	One-Game 2	3	4	LO	XN	IP	PH	RHP	LHP
1882	CHI	NL	1	1	0	0	0	0	1	0	0	0	0	0	0	0	0	1
1884	CHI	NL	1	1	0	0	0	0	0	0	0	0	0	0	0	0	1	0
Total			2	2	0	0	0	0	1	0	0	0	0	0	0	0	1	1

Rank among batters: 4,129 • *Total ballparks homered in*: 2 • *First HR*: 06/20/1882 off J Richmond

Tim Corcoran

TIMOTHY MICHAEL CORCORAN
B: 03/19/1953
BL

Year	Tm	Lg	Tot	H	A	Men-On 0	1	2	3	One-Game 2	3	4	LO	XN	IP	PH	RHP	LHP
1977	DET	AL	3	1	2	1	1	1	0	0	0	0	0	0	0	1	2	1
1978	DET	AL	1	1	0	0	0	0	1	0	0	0	0	0	0	0	0	1
1980	DET	AL	3	3	0	2	0	1	0	0	0	0	0	0	0	0	2	1
1984	PHI	NL	5	2	3	3	2	0	0	0	0	0	0	0	0	0	5	0
Total			12	7	5	6	3	2	1	0	0	0	0	0	0	1	9	3

Rank among batters: 2,325 • *Total ballparks homered in*: 6 • *First HR*: 05/20/1977 off Dave Hamilton

Tommy Corcoran

THOMAS WILLIAM CORCORAN
B: 01/04/1869 D: 06/25/1960
BR

Year	Tm	Lg	Tot	H	A	Men-On 0	1	2	3	One-Game 2	3	4	LO	XN	IP	PH	RHP	LHP
1890	PIT	PL	1	1	0	0	1	0	0	0	0	0	0	0	0	0	1	0
1891	PHI	AA	7	4	3	4	1	1	1	0	0	0	0	0	3	0	6	1
1892	BRO	NL	1	1	0	0	1	0	0	0	0	0	0	0	0	0	1	0
1893	BRO	NL	2	2	0	1	0	1	0	0	0	0	0	0	0	0	2	0
1894	BRO	NL	5	2	3	2	2	1	0	0	0	0	0	0	1	0	4	1
1895	BRO	NL	2	1	1	2	0	0	0	0	0	0	0	0	0	0	1	1
1896	BRO	NL	3	3	0	1	0	2	0	0	0	0	0	0	0	0	3	0
1897	CIN	NL	3	0	3	1	2	0	0	0	0	0	0	0	1	0	3	0
1898	CIN	NL	2	0	2	1	1	0	0	0	0	0	0	0	0	0	1	1
1900	CIN	NL	1	1	0	1	0	0	0	0	0	0	0	0	1	0	1	0
1903	CIN	NL	2	2	0	2	0	0	0	0	0	0	0	0	2	0	2	0
1904	CIN	NL	2	0	2	0	2	0	0	0	0	0	0	0	0	0	1	1
1905	CIN	NL	2	1	1	1	0	0	1	0	0	0	0	0	1	0	2	0
1906	CIN	NL	1	0	1	0	1	0	0	0	0	0	0	0	1	0	1	0
Total			34	18	16	16	11	5	2	0	0	0	0	0	10	0	29	5

Rank among batters: 1,315 • *Top target (3 home runs)*: Jack Stivetts, Chick Fraser • *Number of pitchers victimized*: 29 • *Total ballparks homered in*: 15 • *First HR*: 07/28/1890 off Hank O'Day

Wil Cordero

WILFREDO (NIEVA) CORDERO
B: 10/03/1971
BR

Year	Tm	Lg	Tot	H	A	Men-On 0	1	2	3	One-Game 2	3	4	LO	XN	IP	PH	RHP	LHP
1992	MON	NL	2	1	1	1	0	1	0	0	0	0	0	0	0	0	2	0
1993	MON	NL	10	8	2	4	5	1	0	0	0	0	0	0	0	0	9	1
1994	MON	NL	15	5	10	9	5	0	1	0	0	0	0	0	0	0	10	5
1995	MON	NL	10	2	8	6	4	0	0	1	0	0	0	0	0	0	7	3
Total			37	16	21	20	14	2	1	1	0	0	0	0	0	0	28	9

Rank among batters: 1,252 • *Top target (3 home runs)*: Andy Benes, John Burkett • *Number of pitchers victimized*: 30 • *Total ballparks homered in*: 11 • *First HR*: 09/18/1992 off Mark Dewey

Marty Cordova

MARTIN KEEVIN CORDOVA
B: 07/10/1969
BR

Year	Tm	Lg	Tot	H	A	Men-On 0	1	2	3	One-Game 2	3	4	LO	XN	IP	PH	RHP	LHP
1995	MIN	AL	24	16	8	11	11	2	0	0	0	0	0	0	0	0	21	3

Rank among batters: 1,643 • *Top target (2 home runs)*: Carlos Reyes • *Number of pitchers victimized*: 23 • *Total ballparks homered in*: 8 • *First HR*: 05/03/1995 off Tom Gordon

Fred Corey

FREDERICK HARRISON COREY
B: 1857 D: 11/27/1912
BR

Year	Tm	Lg	Tot	H	A	Men-On 0	1	2	3	One-Game 2	3	4	LO	XN	IP	PH	RHP	LHP
1883	PHI	AA	1	0	1	1	0	0	0	0	0	0	0	0	0	0	1	0
1884	PHI	AA	5	4	1	1	2	2	0	0	0	0	0	0	2	0	4	1
1885	PHI	AA	1	1	0	0	1	0	0	0	0	0	0	0	1	0	1	0
Total			7	5	2	2	3	2	0	0	0	0	0	0	3	0	6	1

Rank among batters: 2,834 • *Total ballparks homered in*: 3 • *First HR*: 09/18/1883 off Will White

Mark Corey

MARK MUNDELL COREY
B: 11/03/1955
BR

Year	Tm	Lg	Tot	H	A	Men-On 0	1	2	3	One-Game 2	3	4	LO	XN	IP	PH	RHP	LHP
1980	BAL	AL	1	1	0	0	1	0	0	0	0	0	0	0	0	0	0	1

Rank among batters: 4,707 • *Total ballparks homered in*: 1 • *First HR*: 07/14/1980 off Paul Splittorff

Pop Corkhill

JOHN STEWART CORKHILL
B: 04/11/1858 D: 04/04/1921
BL

Year	Tm	Lg	Tot	H	A	Men-On 0	1	2	3	One-Game 2	3	4	LO	XN	IP	PH	RHP	LHP
1883	CIN	AA	2	1	1	1	0	1	0	0	0	0	0	0	0	0	2	0
1884	CIN	AA	4	4	0	2	1	1	0	0	0	0	0	0	0	0	2	1
1885	CIN	AA	1	1	0	0	1	0	0	0	0	0	0	0	0	0	1	0
1886	CIN	AA	5	3	2	1	3	1	0	0	0	0	0	0	0	0	3	0
1887	CIN	AA	5	2	3	1	4	0	0	0	0	0	0	0	1	0	2	3
1888	CIN	AA	1	1	0	0	1	0	0	0	0	0	0	0	1	0	1	0
	BRO	AA	1	1	0	1	0	0	0	0	0	0	0	0	0	0	0	0
	Total		2	2	0	1	1	0	0	0	0	0	0	0	1	0	1	0
1889	BRO	AA	8	4	4	2	3	3	0	1	0	0	0	0	2	0	8	0
1890	BRO	NL	1	0	1	0	1	0	0	0	0	0	0	0	0	0	1	0
1891	PIT	NL	3	1	2	1	1	1	0	0	0	0	0	0	1	0	2	1
Total			31	18	13	9	15	7	0	1	0	0	0	0	5	0	22	5

Rank among batters: 1,400 • Top target (2 home runs): Bobby Mathews, Toad Ramsey, Henry Porter, Silver King, Scott Stratton • *Number of pitchers victimized*: 26 • *Total ballparks homered in*: 11 • *First HR*: 05/31/1883 off Bobby Mathews • *World Series HR*—1

Mike Corkins

MICHAEL PATRICK CORKINS
B: 05/25/1946
BR

Year	Tm	Lg	Tot	H	A	Men-On 0	1	2	3	One-Game 2	3	4	LO	XN	IP	PH	RHP	LHP
1970	SD	NL	1	0	1	0	0	0	1	0	0	0	0	0	0	0	0	1
1972	SD	NL	1	1	0	1	0	0	0	0	0	0	0	0	0	0	1	0
1973	SD	NL	3	1	2	2	1	0	0	0	0	0	0	0	0	0	3	0
Total			5	2	3	3	1	0	1	0	0	0	0	0	0	0	4	1

Rank among batters: 3,191 • *Total ballparks homered in*: 4 • *First HR*: 09/04/1970 off Jim Merritt

Year	Tm	Lg	Tot	H	A	Men-On				One-Game			LO	XN	IP	PH	RHP	LHP
						0	1	2	3	2	3	4						

Pat Corrales

PATRICK CORRALES
B: 03/20/1941
BR

Year	Tm	Lg	Tot	H	A	0	1	2	3	2	3	4	LO	XN	IP	PH	RHP	LHP
1965	PHI	NL	2	1	1	1	1	0	0	0	0	0	0	0	0	0	0	2
1969	CIN	NL	1	0	1	1	0	0	0	0	0	0	0	0	0	0	1	0
1970	CIN	NL	1	0	1	0	1	0	0	0	0	0	0	0	0	0	0	1
Total			4	1	3	2	2	0	0	0	0	0	0	0	0	0	1	3

Rank among batters: 3,427 • *Total ballparks homered in*: 4 • *First HR*: 06/16/1965 off Denny Lemaster

Vic Correll

VICTOR CROSBY CORRELL
B: 02/05/1946
BR

Year	Tm	Lg	Tot	H	A	0	1	2	3	2	3	4	LO	XN	IP	PH	RHP	LHP
1974	ATL	NL	4	3	1	2	0	1	1	0	0	0	0	0	0	0	1	3
1975	ATL	NL	11	6	5	4	4	2	1	1	0	0	0	0	0	0	5	6
1976	ATL	NL	5	2	3	2	3	0	0	0	0	0	0	0	0	0	2	3
1977	ATL	NL	7	5	2	3	3	1	0	0	0	0	0	1	0	1	4	3
1978	CIN	NL	1	0	1	0	1	0	0	0	0	0	0	0	0	0	0	1
1979	CIN	NL	1	1	0	0	1	0	0	0	0	0	0	0	0	0	1	0
Total			29	17	12	11	12	4	2	1	0	0	0	1	0	1	13	16

Rank among batters: 1,465 • *Top target (3 home runs)*: Pete Falcone • *Number of pitchers victimized*: 26 • *Total ballparks homered in*: 10 • *First HR*: 07/31/1974 off Randy Moffitt

Red Corriden

JOHN MICHAEL, SR. CORRIDEN
B: 09/04/1887 D: 09/28/1959
BR

Year	Tm	Lg	Tot	H	A	0	1	2	3	2	3	4	LO	XN	IP	PH	RHP	LHP
1910	STL	AL	1	1	0	1	0	0	0	0	0	0	0	0	0	0	1	0
1913	CHI	NL	2	2	0	0	1	1	0	0	0	0	0	0	0	0	0	2
1914	CHI	NL	3	0	3	3	0	0	0	0	0	0	0	0	1	1	2	1
Total			6	3	3	4	1	1	0	0	0	0	0	0	1	1	3	3

Rank among batters: 2,988 • *Total ballparks homered in*: 4 • *First HR*: 09/20/1910 off Eddie Cicotte

Frank Corridon

FRANK J. CORRIDON
B: 11/25/1880 D: 02/21/1941
BR

Year	Tm	Lg	Tot	H	A	0	1	2	3	2	3	4	LO	XN	IP	PH	RHP	LHP
1905	PHI	NL	1	1	0	1	0	0	0	0	0	0	0	0	1	0	1	0

Rank among batters: 4,707 • *Total ballparks homered in*: 1 • *First HR*: 05/16/1905 off Jack Taylor

Al Corwin

ELMER NATHAN CORWIN
B: 12/03/1926
BR

Year	Tm	Lg	Tot	H	A	0	1	2	3	2	3	4	LO	XN	IP	PH	RHP	LHP
1953	NY	NL	2	2	0	2	0	0	0	0	0	0	0	0	0	0	1	1

Rank among batters: 4,129 • *Total ballparks homered in*: 1 • *First HR*: 07/07/1953 off Kent Peterson

Joe Coscarart

JOSEPH MARVIN COSCARART
B: 11/18/1909 D: 04/05/1993
BR

Year	Tm	Lg	Tot	H	A	0	1	2	3	2	3	4	LO	XN	IP	PH	RHP	LHP
1935	BOS	NL	1	1	0	1	0	0	0	0	0	0	0	0	0	0	1	0
1936	BOS	NL	2	1	1	2	0	0	0	0	0	0	0	0	0	0	1	1
Total			3	2	1	3	0	0	0	0	0	0	0	0	0	0	2	1

Rank among batters: 3,735 • *Total ballparks homered in*: 2 • *First HR*: 06/22/1935 off Charlie Root

Pete Coscarart

PETER JOSEPH COSCARART
B: 06/16/1913
BR

Year	Tm	Lg	Tot	H	A	0	1	2	3	2	3	4	LO	XN	IP	PH	RHP	LHP
1939	BRO	NL	4	3	1	1	3	0	0	0	0	0	0	0	1	0	3	1
1940	BRO	NL	9	1	8	6	1	2	0	0	0	0	0	0	0	0	9	0

Pete Coscarart *continued*

Year	Tm	Lg	Tot	H	A	Men-On 0	1	2	3	One-Game 2	3	4	LO	XN	IP	PH	RHP	LHP
1942	PIT	NL	3	0	3	1	1	1	0	0	0	0	0	0	0	0	2	1
1944	PIT	NL	4	0	4	2	1	1	0	0	0	0	0	0	0	0	3	1
1945	PIT	NL	8	1	7	4	3	0	1	0	0	0	2	0	0	0	7	1
Total			28	5	23	14	9	4	1	0	0	0	2	0	1	0	24	4

Rank among batters: 1,500 • *Top target (2 home runs)*: Jim Turner, Joe Bowman • *Number of pitchers victimized*: 26 • *Total ballparks homered in*: 8 • *First HR*: 06/06/1939 off Joe Bowman

Tim Costo

TIMOTHY ROGER COSTO
B: 02/16/1969
BR

Year	Tm	Lg	Tot	H	A	Men-On 0	1	2	3	One-Game 2	3	4	LO	XN	IP	PH	RHP	LHP
1993	CIN	NL	3	0	3	2	1	0	0	0	0	0	0	0	0	0	1	2

Rank among batters: 3,735 • *Total ballparks homered in*: 2 • *First HR*: 08/24/1993 off Frank Tanana

Hooks Cotter

HARVEY LOUIS COTTER
B: 05/22/1900 D: 08/06/1955
BL

Year	Tm	Lg	Tot	H	A	Men-On 0	1	2	3	One-Game 2	3	4	LO	XN	IP	PH	RHP	LHP
1924	CHI	NL	4	1	3	3	0	1	0	0	0	0	0	0	0	0	3	1

Rank among batters: 3,427 • *Total ballparks homered in*: 3 • *First HR*: 07/10/1924 off Bill Doak

Chuck Cottier

CHARLES KEITH COTTIER
B: 01/18/1936
BR

Year	Tm	Lg	Tot	H	A	Men-On 0	1	2	3	One-Game 2	3	4	LO	XN	IP	PH	RHP	LHP
1960	MIL	NL	3	1	2	2	1	0	0	0	0	0	0	0	0	0	2	1
1961	WAS	AL	2	0	2	1	1	0	0	0	0	0	0	0	0	0	2	0
1962	WAS	AL	6	4	2	2	4	0	0	0	0	0	0	1	0	0	3	3
1963	WAS	AL	5	3	2	4	0	1	0	1	0	0	0	0	0	0	2	3
1964	WAS	AL	3	2	1	2	0	1	0	0	0	0	0	0	0	0	1	2
Total			19	10	9	11	6	2	0	1	0	0	0	1	0	0	10	9

Rank among batters: 1,861 • *Top target (2 home runs)*: Whitey Ford, Jack Kralick • *Number of pitchers victimized*: 17 • *Total ballparks homered in*: 9 • *First HR*: 07/09/1960 off Don Newcombe

Henry Cotto

HENRY COTTO
B: 01/05/1961
BR

Year	Tm	Lg	Tot	H	A	Men-On 0	1	2	3	One-Game 2	3	4	LO	XN	IP	PH	RHP	LHP
1985	NY	AL	1	0	1	0	1	0	0	0	0	0	0	0	0	0	1	0
1986	NY	AL	1	0	1	0	1	0	0	0	0	0	0	0	0	0	1	0
1987	NY	AL	5	5	0	3	2	0	0	0	0	0	1	0	0	0	3	2
1988	SEA	AL	8	5	3	4	4	0	0	0	0	0	1	0	0	0	4	4
1989	SEA	AL	9	5	4	5	3	1	0	1	0	0	0	0	0	1	4	5
1990	SEA	AL	4	2	2	2	2	0	0	0	0	0	0	0	0	0	2	2
1991	SEA	AL	6	2	4	2	3	1	0	0	0	0	1	0	1	0	2	4
1992	SEA	AL	5	2	3	3	1	1	0	0	0	0	0	0	0	1	1	4
1993	SEA	AL	2	0	2	2	0	0	0	0	0	0	0	0	0	0	1	1
	FLO	NL	3	1	2	1	2	0	0	0	0	0	1	0	0	0	2	1
	Total		5	1	4	3	2	0	0	0	0	0	1	0	0	0	3	2
Total			44	22	22	22	19	3	0	1	0	0	4	0	1	2	21	23

Rank among batters: 1,095 • *Top target (2 home runs)*: Curt Young, Oil Can Boyd, Jeff Ballard • *Number of pitchers victimized*: 41 • *Total ballparks homered in*: 15 • *First HR*: 10/06/1985 off Bill Caudill

Johnny Couch

JOHN DANIEL COUCH
B: 03/31/1891 D: 12/08/1975
BL

Year	Tm	Lg	Tot	H	A	Men-On 0	1	2	3	One-Game 2	3	4	LO	XN	IP	PH	RHP	LHP
1924	PHI	NL	2	1	1	1	1	0	0	0	0	0	0	0	0	0	2	0
1925	PHI	NL	1	1	0	1	0	0	0	0	0	0	0	0	0	0	1	0
Total			3	2	1	2	1	0	0	0	0	0	0	0	0	0	3	0

Rank among batters: 3,735 • *Total ballparks homered in*: 2 • *First HR*: 05/03/1924 off Art Decatur

Year	Tm	Lg	Tot	H	A	Men-On 0	1	2	3	One-Game 2	3	4	LO	XN	IP	PH	RHP	LHP

Bill Coughlin

WILLIAM PAUL COUGHLIN
B: 07/12/1878 D: 05/07/1943
BR

Year	Tm	Lg	Tot	H	A	0	1	2	3	2	3	4	LO	XN	IP	PH	RHP	LHP
1901	WAS	AL	6	2	4	3	3	0	0	0	0	0	0	1	2	0	3	3
1902	WAS	AL	6	4	2	1	2	3	0	0	0	0	0	0	2	0	3	3
1903	WAS	AL	1	0	1	1	0	0	0	0	0	0	0	0	0	0	1	0
1906	DET	AL	2	1	1	1	0	1	0	0	0	0	0	0	0	0	2	0
Total			15	7	8	6	5	4	0	0	0	0	0	1	4	0	9	6

Rank among batters: 2,096 • *Top target (3 home runs)*: George Winter • *Number of pitchers victimized*: 11 • *Total ballparks homered in*: 8 • *First HR*: 05/02/1901 off Harry Howell

Bob Coulson

ROBERT JACKSON COULSON
B: 06/17/1887 D: 09/11/1953
BR

Year	Tm	Lg	Tot	H	A	0	1	2	3	2	3	4	LO	XN	IP	PH	RHP	LHP
1910	BRO	NL	1	1	0	0	0	1	0	0	0	0	0	0	1	0	0	1

Rank among batters: 4,707 • *Total ballparks homered in*: 1 • *First HR*: 09/30/1910 off Ad Brennan

Fritz Coumbe

FREDERICK NICHOLAS COUMBE
B: 12/13/1889 D: 03/21/1978
BL

Year	Tm	Lg	Tot	H	A	0	1	2	3	2	3	4	LO	XN	IP	PH	RHP	LHP
1920	CIN	NL	1	0	1	0	1	0	0	0	0	0	0	0	0	0	1	0

Rank among batters: 4,707 • *Total ballparks homered in*: 1 • *First HR*: 09/19/1920 off Jess Barnes

Clint Courtney

CLINTON DAWSON COURTNEY
B: 03/16/1927 D: 06/16/1975
BL

Year	Tm	Lg	Tot	H	A	0	1	2	3	2	3	4	LO	XN	IP	PH	RHP	LHP
1952	STL	AL	5	3	2	1	3	1	0	0	0	0	0	0	0	0	5	0
1953	STL	AL	4	2	2	4	0	0	0	0	0	0	0	0	0	0	4	0
1954	BAL	AL	4	1	3	2	1	1	0	0	0	0	0	0	0	0	4	0
1955	CHI	AL	1	0	1	0	1	0	0	0	0	0	0	0	0	0	1	0
	WAS	AL	2	0	2	0	2	0	0	0	0	0	0	0	0	0	2	0
	Total		3	0	3	0	3	0	0	0	0	0	0	0	0	0	3	0
1956	WAS	AL	5	1	4	3	1	1	0	0	0	0	0	0	0	1	4	1
1957	WAS	AL	6	2	4	3	2	1	0	1	0	0	0	0	0	1	6	0
1958	WAS	AL	8	2	6	2	5	0	1	0	0	0	0	0	0	0	6	2
1959	WAS	AL	2	0	2	2	0	0	0	0	0	0	0	0	0	1	2	0
1960	BAL	AL	1	0	1	0	1	0	0	0	0	0	0	0	0	0	1	0
Total			38	11	27	17	16	4	1	1	0	0	0	0	0	3	35	3

Rank among batters: 1,225 • *Top target (3 home runs)*: Duke Maas • *Number of pitchers victimized*: 31 • *Total ballparks homered in*: 9 • *First HR*: 05/06/1952 off Bob Hooper

Ernie Courtney

EDWARD ERNEST COURTNEY
B: 01/20/1875 D: 02/29/1920
BL

Year	Tm	Lg	Tot	H	A	0	1	2	3	2	3	4	LO	XN	IP	PH	RHP	LHP
1903	NY	AL	1	1	0	0	1	0	0	0	0	0	0	0	0	0	1	0
1905	PHI	NL	2	0	2	2	0	0	0	0	0	0	0	1	0	0	2	0
1907	PHI	NL	2	0	2	2	0	0	0	0	0	0	0	1	1	0	2	0
Total			5	1	4	4	1	0	0	0	0	0	0	2	1	0	5	0

Rank among batters: 3,191 • *Total ballparks homered in*: 4 • *First HR*: 06/01/1903 off Tom Hughes

Harry Courtney

HENRY SEYMOUR COURTNEY
B: 11/19/1898 D: 12/11/1954
BL

Year	Tm	Lg	Tot	H	A	0	1	2	3	2	3	4	LO	XN	IP	PH	RHP	LHP
1920	WAS	AL	1	0	1	1	0	0	0	0	0	0	0	0	0	0	1	0

Rank among batters: 4,707 • *Total ballparks homered in*: 1 • *First HR*: 09/25/1920 off Bob Shawkey

Stan Coveleski

STANLEY ANTHONY COVELESKI
B: 07/13/1889 D: 03/20/1984
BR HOF

Year	Tm	Lg	Tot	H	A	0	1	2	3	2	3	4	LO	XN	IP	PH	RHP	LHP
1916	CLE	AL	1	0	1	0	0	1	0	0	0	0	0	1	0	0	1	0

Rank among batters: 4,707 • *Total ballparks homered in*: 1 • *First HR*: 05/30/1916 off Dave Davenport

Sam Covington

CLARENCE OTTO COVINGTON
B: 12/17/1892 D: 01/04/1963
BL

Year	Tm	Lg	Tot	H	A	Men-On 0	Men-On 1	Men-On 2	Men-On 3	One-Game 2	One-Game 3	One-Game 4	LO	XN	IP	PH	RHP	LHP
1917	BOS	NL	1	0	1	1	0	0	0	0	0	0	0	0	0	0	1	0

Rank among batters: 4,707 • *Total ballparks homered in*: 1 • *First HR*: 10/03/1917 off Jack Coombs

Wes Covington

JOHN WESLEY COVINGTON
B: 03/27/1932
BL

Year	Tm	Lg	Tot	H	A	Men-On 0	Men-On 1	Men-On 2	Men-On 3	One-Game 2	One-Game 3	One-Game 4	LO	XN	IP	PH	RHP	LHP
1956	MIL	NL	2	0	2	0	1	1	0	0	0	0	0	0	0	1	2	0
1957	MIL	NL	21	8	13	13	3	4	1	2	0	0	0	0	1	0	19	2
1958	MIL	NL	24	11	13	14	6	4	0	2	0	0	0	0	0	0	23	1
1959	MIL	NL	7	5	2	2	3	2	0	0	0	0	0	0	0	0	6	1
1960	MIL	NL	10	6	4	8	0	2	0	0	0	0	0	0	0	2	9	1
1961	CHI	AL	4	2	2	1	2	0	1	0	0	0	0	0	0	0	4	0
	KC	AL	1	1	0	1	0	0	0	0	0	0	0	0	0	1	0	1
	PHI	NL	7	3	4	5	1	1	0	2	0	0	0	2	0	0	6	1
	Total		12	6	6	7	3	1	1	2	0	0	0	2	0	1	10	2
1962	PHI	NL	9	3	6	5	3	1	0	1	0	0	0	0	0	0	8	1
1963	PHI	NL	17	10	7	8	7	2	0	0	0	0	0	0	0	2	16	1
1964	PHI	NL	13	5	8	5	5	3	0	1	0	0	0	1	0	0	13	0
1965	PHI	NL	15	7	8	11	4	0	0	0	0	0	0	0	0	0	15	0
1966	LA	NL	1	0	1	0	1	0	0	0	0	0	0	0	0	1	1	0
Total			131	61	70	73	36	20	2	8	0	0	0	3	1	7	122	9

Rank among batters: 342 • *Top target (6 home runs)*: Don Drysdale • *Number of pitchers victimized*: 84 • *Total ballparks homered in*: 17 • *First HR*: 04/20/1956 off Tom Poholsky

Billy Cowan

BILLY ROLLAND COWAN
B: 08/28/1938
BR

Year	Tm	Lg	Tot	H	A	Men-On 0	Men-On 1	Men-On 2	Men-On 3	One-Game 2	One-Game 3	One-Game 4	LO	XN	IP	PH	RHP	LHP
1963	CHI	NL	1	0	1	0	1	0	0	0	0	0	0	0	0	0	0	1
1964	CHI	NL	19	12	7	13	5	1	0	0	0	0	1	0	0	0	13	6
1965	NY	NL	3	2	1	3	0	0	0	0	0	0	1	0	0	0	1	2
1967	PHI	NL	3	1	2	2	0	1	0	0	0	0	0	0	0	0	0	3
1969	NY	AL	1	0	1	0	1	0	0	0	0	0	0	0	0	1	0	1
	CAL	AL	4	3	1	3	1	0	0	0	0	0	0	1	0	1	1	3
	Total		5	3	2	3	2	0	0	0	0	0	0	1	0	2	1	4
1970	CAL	AL	5	3	2	2	2	1	0	0	0	0	0	0	0	1	1	4
1971	CAL	AL	4	3	1	2	1	1	0	0	0	0	0	0	0	0	1	3
Total			40	24	16	25	11	4	0	0	0	0	2	1	0	3	17	23

Rank among batters: 1,181 • Top target (2 home runs): Don Nottebart, Wade Blasingame, Larry Jaster, Mike Paul • *Number of pitchers victimized*: 36 • *Total ballparks homered in*: 14 • *First HR*: 09/18/1963 off Joe Gibbon

Al Cowens

ALFRED EDWARD COWENS
B: 10/25/1951
BR

Year	Tm	Lg	Tot	H	A	Men-On 0	Men-On 1	Men-On 2	Men-On 3	One-Game 2	One-Game 3	One-Game 4	LO	XN	IP	PH	RHP	LHP
1974	KC	AL	1	1	0	1	0	0	0	0	0	0	0	0	0	0	0	1
1975	KC	AL	4	2	2	0	3	1	0	0	0	0	0	0	0	1	2	2
1976	KC	AL	3	2	1	3	0	0	0	0	0	0	0	0	1	0	3	0
1977	KC	AL	23	11	12	11	10	2	0	1	0	0	0	2	0	0	16	7
1978	KC	AL	5	1	4	3	1	0	1	0	0	0	0	0	0	0	1	4
1979	KC	AL	9	3	6	5	4	0	0	0	0	0	0	0	0	0	6	3
1980	CAL	AL	1	0	1	0	0	1	0	0	0	0	0	0	0	1	0	1
	DET	AL	5	2	3	4	1	0	0	0	0	0	0	0	0	0	3	2
	Total		6	2	4	4	1	1	0	0	0	0	0	0	0	1	3	3
1981	DET	AL	1	1	0	0	1	0	0	0	0	0	0	0	0	0	0	1
1982	SEA	AL	20	13	7	11	7	2	0	0	0	0	0	0	0	0	16	4
1983	SEA	AL	7	2	5	4	3	0	0	1	0	0	0	0	0	0	3	4
1984	SEA	AL	15	7	8	10	2	3	0	0	0	0	0	1	0	0	9	6
1985	SEA	AL	14	8	6	9	2	3	0	0	0	0	0	0	0	1	9	5
Total			108	53	55	61	34	12	1	2	0	0	0	3	1	3	68	40

Rank among batters: 443 • *Top target (3 home runs)*: Mike Caldwell, Lary Sorensen, Dennis Martinez • *Number of pitchers victimized*: 90 • *Total ballparks homered in*: 15 • *First HR*: 07/17/1974 off Rogelio Moret • *LCS HR*—1

Year	Tm	Lg	Tot	H	A	Men-On 0	1	2	3	One-Game 2	3	4	LO	XN	IP	PH	RHP	LHP

Billy Cox

WILLIAM RICHARD COX
B: 08/29/1919 D: 03/30/1978
BR

Year	Tm	Lg	Tot	H	A	Men-On 0	1	2	3	One-Game 2	3	4	LO	XN	IP	PH	RHP	LHP
1946	PIT	NL	2	1	1	1	0	1	0	0	0	0	0	0	0	0	2	0
1947	PIT	NL	15	11	4	8	6	0	1	2	0	0	1	1	0	0	15	0
1948	BRO	NL	3	2	1	2	1	0	0	0	0	0	0	0	0	0	3	0
1949	BRO	NL	8	8	0	6	1	1	0	1	0	0	0	0	0	0	7	1
1950	BRO	NL	8	6	2	7	1	0	0	0	0	0	1	0	0	0	6	2
1951	BRO	NL	9	5	4	8	0	0	1	0	0	0	0	0	0	0	7	2
1952	BRO	NL	6	1	5	6	0	0	0	0	0	0	2	0	0	0	4	2
1953	BRO	NL	10	4	6	5	1	3	1	1	0	0	0	0	0	1	4	6
1954	BRO	NL	2	1	1	2	0	0	0	0	0	0	0	0	0	0	1	1
1955	BAL	AL	3	1	2	3	0	0	0	0	0	0	0	0	0	0	3	0
Total			66	40	26	48	10	5	3	4	0	0	4	1	0	1	52	14

Rank among batters: 786 • *Top target (3 home runs)*: Roger Bowman • *Number of pitchers victimized*: 57 • *Total ballparks homered in*: 8 • *First HR*: 06/16/1946 off Andy Karl • *World Series HR*—1

Bobby Cox

ROBERT JOSEPH COX
B: 05/21/1941
BR

Year	Tm	Lg	Tot	H	A	Men-On 0	1	2	3	One-Game 2	3	4	LO	XN	IP	PH	RHP	LHP
1968	NY	AL	7	3	4	6	1	0	0	0	0	0	0	0	1	0	4	3
1969	NY	AL	2	0	2	1	1	0	0	0	0	0	0	0	0	0	0	2
Total			9	3	6	7	2	0	0	0	0	0	0	0	1	0	4	5

Rank among batters: 2,587 • *Top target (2 home runs)*: Gary Peters • *Number of pitchers victimized*: 8 • *Total ballparks homered in*: 6 • *First HR*: 05/26/1968 off Gary Peters

Dick Cox

ELMER JOSEPH COX
B: 09/30/1897 D: 06/01/1966
BR

Year	Tm	Lg	Tot	H	A	Men-On 0	1	2	3	One-Game 2	3	4	LO	XN	IP	PH	RHP	LHP
1925	BRO	NL	7	2	5	4	2	1	0	0	0	0	0	0	0	0	5	2
1926	BRO	NL	1	1	0	1	0	0	0	0	0	0	1	0	0	0	0	1
Total			8	3	5	5	2	1	0	0	0	0	1	0	0	0	5	3

Rank among batters: 2,703 • *Total ballparks homered in*: 4 • *First HR*: 06/19/1925 off Lee Meadows

Jim Cox

JAMES CHARLES COX
B: 05/28/1950
BR

Year	Tm	Lg	Tot	H	A	Men-On 0	1	2	3	One-Game 2	3	4	LO	XN	IP	PH	RHP	LHP
1974	MON	NL	2	1	1	1	1	0	0	0	0	0	0	0	0	0	1	1
1975	MON	NL	1	1	0	1	0	0	0	0	0	0	0	0	0	0	1	0
Total			3	2	1	2	1	0	0	0	0	0	0	0	0	0	2	1

Rank among batters: 3,735 • *Total ballparks homered in*: 2 • *First HR*: 04/18/1974 off Ray Sadecki

Larry Cox

LARRY EUGENE COX
B: 09/11/1947 D: 02/17/1990
BR

Year	Tm	Lg	Tot	H	A	Men-On 0	1	2	3	One-Game 2	3	4	LO	XN	IP	PH	RHP	LHP
1977	SEA	AL	2	2	0	1	1	0	0	0	0	0	0	0	0	0	2	0
1978	CHI	NL	2	0	2	0	1	1	0	0	0	0	0	0	0	0	1	1
1979	SEA	AL	4	4	0	2	2	0	0	0	0	0	0	0	0	0	1	3
1980	SEA	AL	4	1	3	2	1	1	0	0	0	0	0	0	0	0	1	3
Total			12	7	5	5	5	2	0	0	0	0	0	0	0	0	5	7

Rank among batters: 2,325 • *Total ballparks homered in*: 6 • *First HR*: 07/23/1977 off Mike Norris

Ted Cox

WILLIAM TED COX
B: 01/24/1955
BR

Year	Tm	Lg	Tot	H	A	Men-On 0	1	2	3	One-Game 2	3	4	LO	XN	IP	PH	RHP	LHP
1977	BOS	AL	1	0	1	1	0	0	0	0	0	0	0	0	0	0	1	0
1978	CLE	AL	1	0	1	1	0	0	0	0	0	0	0	1	0	0	1	0
1979	CLE	AL	4	2	2	2	1	1	0	0	0	0	0	0	0	0	4	0
1980	SEA	AL	2	1	1	1	0	1	0	0	0	0	0	0	0	0	1	1

Ted Cox *continued*

Year	Tm	Lg	Tot	H	A	Men-On 0	1	2	3	One-Game 2	3	4	LO	XN	IP	PH	RHP	LHP
1981	TOR	AL	2	2	0	2	0	0	0	0	0	0	0	0	0	0	1	1
Total			10	5	5	7	1	2	0	0	0	0	0	1	0	0	8	2

Rank among batters: 2,500 • *Total ballparks homered in*: 8 • *First HR*: 09/24/1977 off Milt Wilcox

Estel Crabtree

ESTEL CRAYTON CRABTREE
B: 08/19/1903 D: 01/04/1967
BL

Year	Tm	Lg	Tot	H	A	Men-On 0	1	2	3	One-Game 2	3	4	LO	XN	IP	PH	RHP	LHP
1931	CIN	NL	4	1	3	1	3	0	0	0	0	0	0	0	0	0	4	0
1932	CIN	NL	2	0	2	2	0	0	0	0	0	0	0	0	0	0	2	0
1941	STL	NL	5	4	1	3	1	1	0	0	0	0	0	0	0	1	4	1
1943	CIN	NL	2	2	0	0	2	0	0	0	0	0	0	0	0	0	2	0
Total			13	7	6	6	6	1	0	0	0	0	0	0	0	1	12	1

Rank among batters: 2,248 • *Total ballparks homered in*: 6 • *First HR*: 05/31/1931 off Allyn Stout

Harry Craft

HARRY FRANCIS CRAFT
B: 04/19/1915 D: 08/03/1995
BR

Year	Tm	Lg	Tot	H	A	Men-On 0	1	2	3	One-Game 2	3	4	LO	XN	IP	PH	RHP	LHP
1938	CIN	NL	15	4	11	8	5	1	1	1	0	0	0	0	0	0	13	2
1939	CIN	NL	13	6	7	8	3	2	0	0	0	0	0	1	1	0	12	1
1940	CIN	NL	6	4	2	3	1	2	0	0	0	0	0	0	0	0	5	1
1941	CIN	NL	10	3	7	4	3	2	1	1	0	0	0	0	0	0	8	2
Total			44	17	27	23	12	7	2	2	0	0	0	1	1	0	38	6

Rank among batters: 1,095 • *Top target (3 home runs)*: Lon Warneke, Max Butcher • *Number of pitchers victimized*: 34 • *Total ballparks homered in*: 9 • *First HR*: 05/07/1938 off Max Butcher • *Hit for Cycle*—vs BRO: 06/08/1940

Rod Craig

RODNEY PAUL CRAIG
B: 01/12/1958
BB

Year	Tm	Lg	Tot	H	A	Men-On 0	1	2	3	One-Game 2	3	4	LO	XN	IP	PH	RHP	LHP
1980	SEA	AL	3	2	1	1	2	0	0	0	0	0	0	0	0	0	2	1

Rank among batters: 3,735 • *Total ballparks homered in*: 2 • *First HR*: 04/11/1980 off Tom Buskey

Doc Cramer

ROGER MAXWELL CRAMER
B: 07/22/1905 D: 09/09/1990
BL

Year	Tm	Lg	Tot	H	A	Men-On 0	1	2	3	One-Game 2	3	4	LO	XN	IP	PH	RHP	LHP
1931	PHI	AL	2	0	2	1	1	0	0	0	0	0	0	0	0	0	2	0
1932	PHI	AL	3	3	0	2	1	0	0	0	0	0	0	0	1	0	3	0
1933	PHI	AL	8	6	2	4	4	0	0	0	0	0	0	0	0	0	8	0
1934	PHI	AL	6	3	3	5	1	0	0	1	0	0	1	0	0	0	6	0
1935	PHI	AL	3	2	1	3	0	0	0	0	0	0	0	0	0	0	3	0
1940	BOS	AL	1	0	1	1	0	0	0	0	0	0	0	0	0	0	1	0
1941	WAS	AL	2	2	0	1	0	0	1	0	0	0	0	0	2	0	1	1
1943	DET	AL	1	0	1	1	0	0	0	0	0	0	0	0	0	0	1	0
1944	DET	AL	2	1	1	1	1	0	0	0	0	0	0	0	2	0	2	0
1945	DET	AL	6	1	5	4	1	1	0	0	0	0	0	0	0	0	6	0
1946	DET	AL	1	0	1	0	1	0	0	0	0	0	0	0	0	0	1	0
1947	DET	AL	2	0	2	1	1	0	0	0	0	0	0	0	0	0	2	0
Total			37	18	19	24	11	1	1	1	0	0	1	0	5	0	36	1

Rank among batters: 1,252 • *Top target (2 home runs)*: Monte Weaver, Al Gettel • *Number of pitchers victimized*: 35 • *Total ballparks homered in*: 8 • *First HR*: 08/16/1931 off Sarge Connally • *Hit for Cycle*—@NY: 06/10/1934

Del Crandall

DELMAR WESLEY CRANDALL
B: 03/05/1930
BR

Year	Tm	Lg	Tot	H	A	Men-On 0	1	2	3	One-Game 2	3	4	LO	XN	IP	PH	RHP	LHP
1949	BOS	NL	4	1	3	3	1	0	0	0	0	0	0	0	0	0	2	2
1950	BOS	NL	4	0	4	1	2	1	0	0	0	0	0	0	0	0	2	2
1953	MIL	NL	15	9	6	12	2	1	0	0	0	0	0	0	0	0	13	2
1954	MIL	NL	21	8	13	11	5	5	0	1	0	0	0	1	0	0	14	7

Year	Tm	Lg	Tot	H	A	Men-On 0	Men-On 1	Men-On 2	Men-On 3	One-Game 2	One-Game 3	One-Game 4	LO	XN	IP	PH	RHP	LHP

Del Crandall *continued*

Year	Tm	Lg	Tot	H	A	0	1	2	3	2	3	4	LO	XN	IP	PH	RHP	LHP
1955	MIL	NL	26	15	11	18	4	1	3	2	0	0	0	1	0	1	23	3
1956	MIL	NL	16	6	10	10	5	1	0	1	0	0	0	0	0	0	13	3
1957	MIL	NL	15	7	8	11	4	0	0	0	0	0	0	0	0	0	11	4
1958	MIL	NL	18	6	12	11	5	2	0	2	0	0	0	0	0	1	11	7
1959	MIL	NL	21	6	15	12	5	3	1	0	0	0	0	0	0	0	17	4
1960	MIL	NL	19	9	10	16	3	0	0	2	0	0	0	1	0	0	12	7
1962	MIL	NL	8	5	3	6	1	1	0	0	0	0	0	1	0	0	6	2
1963	MIL	NL	3	2	1	2	1	0	0	0	0	0	0	0	0	0	1	2
1964	SF	NL	3	3	0	2	1	0	0	0	0	0	0	0	0	0	3	0
1965	PIT	NL	2	0	2	2	0	0	0	0	0	0	0	1	0	0	2	0
1966	CLE	AL	4	1	3	4	0	0	0	0	0	0	0	0	0	0	1	3
Total			179	78	101	121	39	15	4	8	0	0	0	5	0	2	131	48

Rank among batters: 221 • Top target (5 home runs): Johnny Klippstein, Harvey Haddix, Mike McCormick, Robin Roberts, Don Drysdale • *Number of pitchers victimized*: 105 • *Total ballparks homered in*: 16 • *First HR*: 07/02/1949 off Blix Donnelly • *World Series HR*—2; *All-Star HR*—1

Doc Crandall

JAMES OTIS CRANDALL
B: 10/08/1887 D: 08/17/1951
BR

Year	Tm	Lg	Tot	H	A	0	1	2	3	2	3	4	LO	XN	IP	PH	RHP	LHP
1908	NY	NL	2	1	1	1	0	1	0	0	0	0	0	0	0	0	1	1
1909	NY	NL	1	0	1	0	0	1	0	0	0	0	0	0	0	0	0	1
1910	NY	NL	1	1	0	0	1	0	0	0	0	0	0	0	0	0	0	1
1911	NY	NL	2	0	2	1	1	0	0	0	0	0	0	0	0	0	1	1
1914	STL	FL	2	1	1	2	0	0	0	0	0	0	0	0	0	0	2	0
1915	STL	FL	1	0	1	0	1	0	0	0	0	0	0	0	0	0	1	0
Total			9	3	6	4	3	2	0	0	0	0	0	0	0	0	5	4

Rank among batters: 2,587 • *Top target (2 home runs)*: Howie Camnitz • *Number of pitchers victimized*: 8 • *Total ballparks homered in*: 6 • *First HR*: 04/30/1908 off Patsy Flaherty

Ed Crane

EDWARD NICHOLAS CRANE
B: 05/27/1862 D: 09/19/1896
BR

Year	Tm	Lg	Tot	H	A	0	1	2	3	2	3	4	LO	XN	IP	PH	RHP	LHP
1884	BOS	UA	12	5	7	5	6	1	0	2	0	0	1	0	1	0	9	1
1885	BUF	NL	2	2	0	2	0	0	0	0	0	0	0	0	0	0	2	0
1888	NY	NL	1	1	0	0	1	0	0	0	0	0	0	0	0	0	1	0
1889	NY	NL	2	1	1	2	0	0	0	0	0	0	0	0	0	0	2	0
1891	CIN	AA	1	1	0	0	1	0	0	0	0	0	0	0	0	0	1	0
Total			18	10	8	9	8	1	0	2	0	0	1	0	1	0	15	1

Rank among batters: 1,914 • *Top target (2 home runs)*: Abner Powell, Henry Boyle, Charlie Sweeney • *Number of pitchers victimized*: 15 • *Total ballparks homered in*: 10 • *First HR*: 04/19/1884 off Sam Weaver • *World Series HR*—1

Sam Crane

SAMUEL NEWHALL CRANE
B: 01/02/1854 D: 06/26/1925
BR

Year	Tm	Lg	Tot	H	A	0	1	2	3	2	3	4	LO	XN	IP	PH	RHP	LHP
1884	CIN	UA	1	0	1	0	0	1	0	0	0	0	0	0	0	0	1	0
1885	DET	NL	1	1	0	1	0	0	0	0	0	0	0	0	0	0	1	0
1886	DET	NL	1	1	0	0	1	0	0	0	0	0	0	0	0	0	1	0
Total			3	2	1	1	1	1	0	0	0	0	0	0	0	0	3	0

Rank among batters: 3,735 • *Top target (2 home runs)*: Charlie Sweeney • *Number of pitchers victimized*: 2 • *Total ballparks homered in*: 2 • *First HR*: 08/14/1884 off Bernard McLaughlin

Gavvy Cravath

CLIFFORD CARLTON CRAVATH
B: 03/23/1881 D: 05/23/1963
BR

Year	Tm	Lg	Tot	H	A	0	1	2	3	2	3	4	LO	XN	IP	PH	RHP	LHP
1908	BOS	AL	1	1	0	1	0	0	0	0	0	0	0	0	0	0	1	0
1909	CHI	AL	1	0	1	1	0	0	0	0	0	0	0	0	0	0	1	0
1912	PHI	NL	11	6	5	5	5	1	0	2	0	0	0	1	0	1	10	1
1913	PHI	NL	19	14	5	7	9	3	0	1	0	0	0	1	1	2	17	2
1914	PHI	NL	19	19	0	11	4	4	0	2	0	0	0	2	0	0	15	4

Gavvy Cravath *continued*

Year	Tm	Lg	Tot	H	A	Men-On 0	1	2	3	One-Game 2	3	4	LO	XN	IP	PH	RHP	LHP
1915	PHI	NL	24	19	5	14	3	6	1	0	0	0	0	0	1	0	19	5
1916	PHI	NL	11	8	3	3	6	2	0	1	0	0	0	0	0	0	8	3
1917	PHI	NL	12	8	4	10	1	1	0	0	0	0	0	0	0	0	8	4
1918	PHI	NL	8	8	0	3	4	1	0	0	0	0	0	1	0	0	5	3
1919	PHI	NL	12	10	2	8	3	1	0	0	0	0	0	0	0	2	10	2
1920	PHI	NL	1	0	1	0	0	1	0	0	0	0	0	0	0	1	0	1
Total			119	93	26	63	35	20	1	6	0	0	0	5	2	6	94	25

Rank among batters: 392 • *Top target (7 home runs)*: Jimmy Lavender • *Number of pitchers victimized*: 70 • *Total ballparks homered in*: 14 • *First HR*: 05/29/1908 off Eli Cates

Glenn Crawford

GLENN MARTIN CRAWFORD
B: 12/02/1913 D: 01/02/1972
BL

Year	Tm	Lg	Tot	H	A	Men-On 0	1	2	3	One-Game 2	3	4	LO	XN	IP	PH	RHP	LHP
1945	PHI	NL	2	0	2	0	1	1	0	0	0	0	0	0	0	0	2	0

Rank among batters: 4,129 • *Total ballparks homered in*: 1 • *First HR*: 06/15/1945 off Andy Hansen

Pat Crawford

CLIFFORD RANKIN CRAWFORD
B: 01/28/1902 D: 01/25/1994
BL

Year	Tm	Lg	Tot	H	A	Men-On 0	1	2	3	One-Game 2	3	4	LO	XN	IP	PH	RHP	LHP
1929	NY	NL	3	2	1	1	0	1	1	0	0	0	0	0	0	3	3	0
1930	NY	NL	3	2	1	1	2	0	0	0	0	0	0	0	1	0	3	0
	CIN	NL	3	1	2	2	1	0	0	0	0	0	0	0	1	0	2	1
	Total		6	3	3	3	3	0	0	0	0	0	0	0	2	0	5	1
Total			9	5	4	4	3	1	1	0	0	0	0	0	2	3	8	1

Rank among batters: 2,587 • *Total ballparks homered in*: 5 • *First HR*: 04/27/1929 off Bob Smith

Sam Crawford

SAMUEL EARL CRAWFORD
B: 04/18/1880 D: 06/15/1968
BL HOF

Year	Tm	Lg	Tot	H	A	Men-On 0	1	2	3	One-Game 2	3	4	LO	XN	IP	PH	RHP	LHP
1899	CIN	NL	1	0	1	0	1	0	0	0	0	0	0	0	0	0	1	0
1900	CIN	NL	7	3	4	4	3	0	0	0	0	0	0	1	6	0	7	0
1901	CIN	NL	16	9	7	8	6	2	0	0	0	0	0	0	12	0	13	3
1902	CIN	NL	3	0	3	2	1	0	0	0	0	0	0	0	3	0	3	0
1903	DET	AL	4	1	3	0	4	0	0	0	0	0	0	0	2	0	4	0
1904	DET	AL	2	0	2	0	1	1	0	0	0	0	0	0	2	0	2	0
1905	DET	AL	6	2	4	3	2	0	1	0	0	0	0	0	4	0	3	3
1906	DET	AL	2	1	1	1	1	0	0	0	0	0	0	0	1	0	2	0
1907	DET	AL	4	0	4	3	1	0	0	0	0	0	0	0	1	0	4	0
1908	DET	AL	7	2	5	4	3	0	0	0	0	0	0	2	2	0	5	2
1909	DET	AL	6	3	3	2	2	2	0	0	0	0	0	0	4	0	4	2
1910	DET	AL	5	4	1	3	1	1	0	0	0	0	0	0	2	0	3	2
1911	DET	AL	7	4	3	2	5	0	0	0	0	0	0	0	3	0	4	3
1912	DET	AL	4	2	2	2	1	1	0	0	0	0	0	0	2	0	3	1
1913	DET	AL	9	5	4	3	3	2	1	0	0	0	0	0	6	0	5	4
1914	DET	AL	8	3	5	5	2	1	0	0	0	0	0	2	1	0	5	3
1915	DET	AL	4	2	2	2	2	0	0	0	0	0	0	0	0	0	4	0
1917	DET	AL	2	0	2	1	0	1	0	0	0	0	0	0	0	1	2	0
Total			97	41	56	45	39	11	2	0	0	0	0	5	51	1	74	23

Rank among batters: 515 • *Top target (3 home runs)*: Ed Murphy • *Number of pitchers victimized*: 78 • *Total ballparks homered in*: 23 • *First HR*: 09/21/1899 off Red Donahue • *World Series HR*—1

Willie Crawford

WILLIE MURPHY CRAWFORD
B: 09/07/1946
BL

Year	Tm	Lg	Tot	H	A	Men-On 0	1	2	3	One-Game 2	3	4	LO	XN	IP	PH	RHP	LHP
1968	LA	NL	4	1	3	4	0	0	0	0	0	0	1	0	0	0	4	0
1969	LA	NL	11	9	2	8	2	1	0	0	0	0	1	0	0	0	11	0
1970	LA	NL	8	2	6	4	3	1	0	0	0	0	0	0	0	0	8	0
1971	LA	NL	9	3	6	7	2	0	0	0	0	0	0	0	0	0	8	1
1972	LA	NL	8	4	4	5	2	1	0	0	0	0	0	0	0	0	8	0

Year	Tm	Lg	Tot	H	A	Men-On 0	Men-On 1	Men-On 2	Men-On 3	One-Game 2	One-Game 3	One-Game 4	LO	XN	IP	PH	RHP	LHP

Willie Crawford *continued*

Year	Tm	Lg	Tot	H	A	0	1	2	3	2	3	4	LO	XN	IP	PH	RHP	LHP
1973	LA	NL	14	12	2	7	4	2	1	1	0	0	0	0	0	0	13	1
1974	LA	NL	11	5	6	6	4	1	0	1	0	0	0	0	1	0	8	3
1975	LA	NL	9	6	3	1	7	1	0	0	0	0	0	0	0	1	9	0
1976	STL	NL	9	4	5	6	1	1	1	0	0	0	0	0	0	0	6	3
1977	HOU	NL	2	1	1	1	0	1	0	0	0	0	0	0	0	0	2	0
	OAK	AL	1	1	0	0	0	1	0	0	0	0	0	0	0	1	1	0
	Total		3	2	1	1	0	2	0	0	0	0	0	0	0	1	3	0
Total			86	48	38	49	25	10	2	2	0	0	2	0	1	2	78	8

Rank among batters: 602 • *Top target (4 home runs)*: Clay Kirby • *Number of pitchers victimized*: 68 • *Total ballparks homered in*: 14 • *First HR*: 09/03/1968 off Dick Hall • *World Series HR*—1

George Creamer

GEORGE W. CREAMER
B: 1855 D: 06/27/1886
BR

Year	Tm	Lg	Tot	H	A	0	1	2	3	2	3	4	LO	XN	IP	PH	RHP	LHP
1882	WOR	NL	1	1	0	0	1	0	0	0	0	0	0	0	0	0	1	0

Rank among batters: 4,707 • *Total ballparks homered in*: 1 • *First HR*: 08/05/1882 off George Derby

Birdie Cree

WILLIAM FRANKLIN CREE
B: 10/23/1882 D: 11/08/1942
BR

Year	Tm	Lg	Tot	H	A	0	1	2	3	2	3	4	LO	XN	IP	PH	RHP	LHP
1909	NY	AL	2	1	1	1	1	0	0	0	0	0	0	0	1	0	2	0
1910	NY	AL	4	3	1	1	2	1	0	0	0	0	0	0	3	0	3	1
1911	NY	AL	4	2	2	4	0	0	0	0	0	0	0	0	2	0	2	2
1913	NY	AL	1	0	1	0	0	0	1	0	0	0	0	0	1	0	0	1
Total			11	6	5	6	3	1	1	0	0	0	0	0	7	0	7	4

Rank among batters: 2,419 • *Top target (2 home runs)*: Jim Scott • *Number of pitchers victimized*: 10 • *Total ballparks homered in*: 5 • *First HR*: 06/24/1909 off Cy Morgan

Creepy Crespi

FRANK ANGELO JOSEPH CRESPI
B: 02/16/1918 D: 03/01/1990
BR

Year	Tm	Lg	Tot	H	A	0	1	2	3	2	3	4	LO	XN	IP	PH	RHP	LHP
1941	STL	NL	4	1	3	3	1	0	0	0	0	0	0	0	0	0	2	2

Rank among batters: 3,427 • *Total ballparks homered in*: 4 • *First HR*: 04/18/1941 off Charlie Root

Lou Criger

LOUIS CRIGER
B: 02/03/1872 D: 05/14/1934
BR

Year	Tm	Lg	Tot	H	A	0	1	2	3	2	3	4	LO	XN	IP	PH	RHP	LHP
1898	CLE	NL	1	0	1	0	1	0	0	0	0	0	0	0	0	0	0	1
1899	STL	NL	2	2	0	1	0	1	0	0	0	0	0	0	0	0	2	0
1900	STL	NL	2	2	0	2	0	0	0	0	0	0	0	0	0	0	2	0
1903	BOS	AL	3	2	1	2	0	1	0	0	0	0	0	0	1	0	2	1
1904	BOS	AL	2	2	0	1	1	0	0	0	0	0	0	0	0	0	2	0
1905	BOS	AL	1	1	0	1	0	0	0	0	0	0	0	0	0	0	0	1
Total			11	9	2	7	2	2	0	0	0	0	0	0	1	0	8	3

Rank among batters: 2,419 • *Top target (2 home runs)*: Ted Lewis, Nick Altrock • *Number of pitchers victimized*: 9 • *Total ballparks homered in*: 4 • *First HR*: 09/08/1898 off Nick Altrock

Dave Criscione

DAVID GERALD CRISCIONE
B: 09/02/1951
BR

Year	Tm	Lg	Tot	H	A	0	1	2	3	2	3	4	LO	XN	IP	PH	RHP	LHP
1977	BAL	AL	1	1	0	1	0	0	0	0	0	0	0	1	0	0	1	0

Rank among batters: 4,707 • *Total ballparks homered in*: 1 • *First HR*: 07/25/1977 off Sam Hinds

Tony Criscola

ANTHONY PAUL CRISCOLA
B: 07/09/1915
BL

Year	Tm	Lg	Tot	H	A	0	1	2	3	2	3	4	LO	XN	IP	PH	RHP	LHP
1942	STL	AL	1	0	1	1	0	0	0	0	0	0	0	0	0	0	1	0

Rank among batters: 4,707 • *Total ballparks homered in*: 1 • *First HR*: 06/11/1942 off Mace Brown

Year	Tm	Lg	Tot	H	A	Men-On 0	1	2	3	One-Game 2	3	4	LO	XN	IP	PH	RHP	LHP

Dode Criss

DODE CRISS
B: 03/12/1885 D: 09/08/1955
BL

Year	Tm	Lg	Tot	H	A	0	1	2	3	2	3	4	LO	XN	IP	PH	RHP	LHP
1910	STL	AL	1	1	0	0	0	1	0	0	0	0	0	0	0	0	1	0
1911	STL	AL	2	2	0	0	2	0	0	0	0	0	0	0	0	0	2	0
Total			3	3	0	0	2	1	0	0	0	0	0	0	0	0	3	0

Rank among batters: 3,735 • *Total ballparks homered in*: 1 • *First HR*: 08/10/1910 off Rube Manning

Hughie Critz

HUGH MELVILLE CRITZ
B: 09/17/1900 D: 01/10/1980
BR

Year	Tm	Lg	Tot	H	A	0	1	2	3	2	3	4	LO	XN	IP	PH	RHP	LHP
1924	CIN	NL	3	0	3	3	0	0	0	0	0	0	1	0	1	0	3	0
1925	CIN	NL	2	1	1	1	1	0	0	0	0	0	1	0	2	0	1	1
1926	CIN	NL	3	1	2	1	2	0	0	0	0	0	0	0	2	0	3	0
1927	CIN	NL	4	0	4	1	2	1	0	1	0	0	0	0	1	0	4	0
1928	CIN	NL	5	1	4	5	0	0	0	0	0	0	0	1	2	0	3	2
1929	CIN	NL	1	0	1	1	0	0	0	0	0	0	0	0	0	0	1	0
1930	NY	NL	4	4	0	1	3	0	0	0	0	0	0	0	0	0	3	1
1931	NY	NL	4	3	1	3	0	1	0	0	0	0	0	0	0	0	3	1
1932	NY	NL	2	2	0	2	0	0	0	0	0	0	0	0	0	0	2	0
1933	NY	NL	2	2	0	0	2	0	0	0	0	0	0	0	0	0	1	1
1934	NY	NL	6	6	0	3	3	0	0	0	0	0	0	0	0	0	4	2
1935	NY	NL	2	2	0	1	1	0	0	1	0	0	0	0	1	0	2	0
Total			38	22	16	22	14	2	0	2	0	0	2	1	9	0	30	8

Rank among batters: 1,225 • *Top target (3 home runs)*: Freddie Fitzsimmons, Dizzy Dean • *Number of pitchers victimized*: 30 • *Total ballparks homered in*: 8 • *First HR*: 06/10/1924 off Whitey Glazner

Fred Crolius

FRED JOSEPH CROLIUS
B: 12/16/1876 D: 08/25/1960

Year	Tm	Lg	Tot	H	A	0	1	2	3	2	3	4	LO	XN	IP	PH	RHP	LHP
1901	BOS	NL	1	0	1	0	1	0	0	0	0	0	0	0	0	0	0	1

Rank among batters: 4,707 • *Total ballparks homered in*: 1 • *First HR*: 06/12/1901 off Noodles Hahn

Warren Cromartie

WARREN LIVINGSTON CROMARTIE
B: 09/29/1953
BL

Year	Tm	Lg	Tot	H	A	0	1	2	3	2	3	4	LO	XN	IP	PH	RHP	LHP
1977	MON	NL	5	3	2	2	3	0	0	0	0	0	0	0	0	0	5	0
1978	MON	NL	10	5	5	7	1	1	1	0	0	0	0	0	0	0	7	3
1979	MON	NL	8	3	5	8	0	0	0	0	0	0	2	1	0	0	6	2
1980	MON	NL	14	7	7	10	4	0	0	1	0	0	0	1	0	0	14	0
1981	MON	NL	6	4	2	3	3	0	0	0	0	0	0	0	0	0	5	1
1982	MON	NL	14	4	10	10	4	0	0	1	0	0	0	0	0	0	12	2
1983	MON	NL	3	0	3	2	1	0	0	0	0	0	0	0	0	0	3	0
1991	KC	AL	1	0	1	0	1	0	0	0	0	0	0	0	0	1	1	0
Total			61	26	35	42	17	1	1	2	0	0	2	2	0	1	53	8

Rank among batters: 844 • *Top target (3 home runs)*: Craig Swan, Mike Krukow • *Number of pitchers victimized*: 46 • *Total ballparks homered in*: 11 • *First HR*: 07/02/1977 off Nino Espinosa

Tripp Cromer

ROY BUNYAN CROMER
B: 11/21/1967
BR

Year	Tm	Lg	Tot	H	A	0	1	2	3	2	3	4	LO	XN	IP	PH	RHP	LHP
1995	STL	NL	5	2	3	5	0	0	0	0	0	0	0	0	0	0	3	2

Rank among batters: 3,191 • *Total ballparks homered in*: 3 • *First HR*: 05/20/1995 off Mark Leiter

Joe Cronin

JOSEPH EDWARD CRONIN
B: 10/12/1906 D: 09/07/1984
BR HOF

Year	Tm	Lg	Tot	H	A	0	1	2	3	2	3	4	LO	XN	IP	PH	RHP	LHP
1929	WAS	AL	8	0	8	3	3	2	0	0	0	0	0	0	0	0	6	2
1930	WAS	AL	13	2	11	5	6	2	0	1	0	0	0	0	1	0	7	6
1931	WAS	AL	12	3	9	7	4	1	0	0	0	0	0	0	1	0	7	5
1932	WAS	AL	6	2	4	3	3	0	0	0	0	0	0	0	0	0	1	5

Joe Cronin *continued*

Year	Tm	Lg	Tot	H	A	Men-On 0	1	2	3	One-Game 2	3	4	LO	XN	IP	PH	RHP	LHP
1933	WAS	AL	5	1	4	3	2	0	0	0	0	0	0	0	0	0	3	2
1934	WAS	AL	7	4	3	1	4	2	0	0	0	0	0	0	1	0	7	0
1935	BOS	AL	9	6	3	4	3	1	1	0	0	0	0	0	0	0	8	1
1936	BOS	AL	2	1	1	1	0	1	0	0	0	0	0	0	0	0	2	0
1937	BOS	AL	18	11	7	9	8	1	0	1	0	0	0	0	1	0	16	2
1938	BOS	AL	17	12	5	8	5	3	1	1	0	0	0	0	0	0	17	0
1939	BOS	AL	19	12	7	10	6	3	0	1	0	0	0	0	0	0	17	2
1940	BOS	AL	24	14	10	10	12	2	0	2	0	0	0	0	0	0	19	5
1941	BOS	AL	16	9	7	10	2	2	2	0	0	0	0	0	0	0	13	3
1942	BOS	AL	4	2	2	2	1	1	0	0	0	0	0	0	0	0	3	1
1943	BOS	AL	5	3	2	0	1	4	0	0	0	0	0	0	0	5	5	0
1944	BOS	AL	5	4	1	2	3	0	0	0	0	0	0	0	0	0	4	1
Total			170	86	84	78	63	25	4	6	0	0	0	0	4	5	135	35

Rank among batters: 235 • *Top target (6 home runs)*: George Caster • *Number of pitchers victimized*: 103 • *Total ballparks homered in*: 8 • *First HR*: 05/24/1929 off George Earnshaw • *Hit for Cycle*—@BOS: 09/02/1929 (1); @DET: 08/02/1940

Jack Crooks

JOHN CHARLES CROOKS
B: 11/09/1866 D: 01/29/1918
BR

Year	Tm	Lg	Tot	H	A	Men-On 0	1	2	3	One-Game 2	3	4	LO	XN	IP	PH	RHP	LHP
1890	COL	AA	1	1	0	0	0	0	1	0	0	0	0	0	0	0	0	0
1892	STL	NL	7	7	0	6	1	0	0	0	0	0	4	0	0	0	5	0
1893	STL	NL	1	1	0	0	0	1	0	0	0	0	0	0	1	0	1	0
1895	WAS	NL	6	5	1	1	3	2	0	1	0	0	0	0	0	0	3	3
1896	WAS	NL	3	3	0	1	1	1	0	0	0	0	0	0	0	0	3	0
	LOU	NL	2	1	1	1	1	0	0	0	0	0	0	0	0	0	2	0
	Total		5	4	1	2	2	1	0	0	0	0	0	0	0	0	5	0
1898	STL	NL	1	1	0	1	0	0	0	0	0	0	0	0	0	0	1	0
Total			21	19	2	10	6	4	1	1	0	0	4	0	1	0	15	3

Rank among batters: 1,768 • *Top target (2 home runs)*: Amos Rusie, Cy Young • *Number of pitchers victimized*: 19 • *Total ballparks homered in*: 6 • *First HR*: 10/01/1890 off Charlie Stecher

George Crosby

GEORGE WASHINGTON CROSBY
D: 01/09/1913

Year	Tm	Lg	Tot	H	A	Men-On 0	1	2	3	One-Game 2	3	4	LO	XN	IP	PH	RHP	LHP
1884	CHI	NL	1	1	0	0	0	1	0	0	0	0	0	0	0	0	0	1

Rank among batters: 4,707 • *Total ballparks homered in*: 1 • *First HR*: 05/30/1884 off Dupee Shaw

Frankie Crosetti

FRANK PETER JOSEPH CROSETTI
B: 10/04/1910
BR

Year	Tm	Lg	Tot	H	A	Men-On 0	1	2	3	One-Game 2	3	4	LO	XN	IP	PH	RHP	LHP
1932	NY	AL	5	2	3	1	1	3	0	0	0	0	0	0	1	0	2	3
1933	NY	AL	9	3	6	6	2	1	0	1	0	0	0	0	0	0	4	5
1934	NY	AL	11	7	4	6	4	1	0	0	0	0	1	0	1	0	7	4
1935	NY	AL	8	3	5	6	0	1	1	0	0	0	0	0	0	0	7	1
1936	NY	AL	15	5	10	11	1	3	0	2	0	0	2	0	1	0	10	5
1937	NY	AL	11	3	8	8	2	1	0	1	0	0	2	0	0	1	5	6
1938	NY	AL	9	5	4	6	3	0	0	0	0	0	1	0	0	0	8	1
1939	NY	AL	10	3	7	8	1	1	0	0	0	0	5	0	0	0	8	2
1940	NY	AL	4	1	3	4	0	0	0	0	0	0	1	0	0	0	3	1
1941	NY	AL	1	0	1	0	0	0	1	0	0	0	0	0	0	0	1	0
1942	NY	AL	4	3	1	4	0	0	0	0	0	0	2	0	0	0	3	1
1943	NY	AL	2	1	1	1	1	0	0	0	0	0	0	0	1	0	2	0
1944	NY	AL	5	4	1	3	1	0	1	0	0	0	0	0	0	0	5	0
1945	NY	AL	4	4	0	2	0	2	0	0	0	0	0	0	0	2	2	2
Total			98	44	54	66	16	13	3	4	0	0	14	0	4	3	67	31

Rank among batters: 506 • *Top target (4 home runs)*: Chief Hogsett • *Number of pitchers victimized*: 69 • *Total ballparks homered in*: 8 • *First HR*: 07/04/1932 off Lloyd Brown • *World Series HR*—1

Amos Cross

AMOS C. CROSS
B: 1861 D: 07/16/1888

Year	Tm	Lg	Tot	H	A	Men-On 0	1	2	3	One-Game 2	3	4	LO	XN	IP	PH	RHP	LHP
1886	LOU	AA	1	1	0	0	0	1	0	0	0	0	0	0	1	0	1	0

Rank among batters: 4,707 • *Total ballparks homered in*: 1 • *First HR*: 07/12/1886 off Abner Powell

Lave Cross

LAFAYETTE NAPOLEON CROSS
B: 05/12/1866 D: 09/06/1927
BR

Year	Tm	Lg	Tot	H	A	Men-On 0	1	2	3	One-Game 2	3	4	LO	XN	IP	PH	RHP	LHP
1890	PHI	PL	3	1	2	0	2	1	0	0	0	0	0	0	1	0	1	2
1891	PHI	AA	5	3	2	3	1	1	0	0	0	0	0	0	3	0	4	0
1892	PHI	NL	4	0	4	2	1	0	1	0	0	0	0	0	1	0	3	0
1893	PHI	NL	4	2	2	1	3	0	0	0	0	0	0	0	0	0	3	1
1894	PHI	NL	7	5	2	1	3	2	1	0	0	0	0	0	1	0	5	2
1895	PHI	NL	2	0	2	1	1	0	0	0	0	0	0	0	0	0	1	1
1896	PHI	NL	1	0	1	0	0	0	1	0	0	0	0	0	0	0	1	0
1897	PHI	NL	3	2	1	1	1	1	0	0	0	0	0	0	0	0	3	0
1898	STL	NL	3	2	1	1	2	0	0	0	0	0	0	0	0	0	2	1
1899	CLE	NL	1	1	0	0	1	0	0	0	0	0	0	0	0	0	1	0
	STL	NL	4	3	1	1	1	1	1	0	0	0	0	0	0	0	1	3
	Total		5	4	1	1	2	1	1	0	0	0	0	0	0	0	2	3
1900	BRO	NL	4	1	3	1	1	2	0	0	0	0	0	0	2	0	4	0
1901	PHI	AL	2	1	1	1	1	0	0	0	0	0	0	0	0	0	2	0
1903	PHI	AL	2	1	1	0	2	0	0	0	0	0	0	0	0	0	2	0
1904	PHI	AL	1	1	0	0	1	0	0	0	0	0	0	0	0	0	1	0
1906	WAS	AL	1	1	0	0	0	1	0	0	0	0	0	0	0	0	1	0
Total			47	24	23	13	21	9	4	0	0	0	0	0	8	0	35	10

Rank among batters: 1,040 • *Top target (2 home runs)*: Jack Stivetts, Ted Breitenstein, Cy Young • *Number of pitchers victimized*: 44 • *Total ballparks homered in*: 24 • *First HR*: 05/28/1890 off Lady Baldwin • *Hit for Cycle—@BRO*: 04/24/1894

Monte Cross

MONTFORD MONTGOMERY CROSS
B: 08/31/1869 D: 06/21/1934
BR

Year	Tm	Lg	Tot	H	A	Men-On 0	1	2	3	One-Game 2	3	4	LO	XN	IP	PH	RHP	LHP
1894	PIT	NL	2	2	0	0	0	2	0	0	0	0	0	0	1	0	2	0
1895	PIT	NL	3	1	2	3	0	0	0	0	0	0	0	0	0	0	2	1
1896	STL	NL	6	2	4	3	3	0	0	0	0	0	0	0	0	0	3	1
1897	STL	NL	4	4	0	2	2	0	0	0	0	0	0	0	0	0	3	1
1898	PHI	NL	1	1	0	0	0	1	0	0	0	0	0	0	0	0	1	0
1899	PHI	NL	3	1	2	1	1	1	0	1	0	0	0	0	0	0	3	0
1900	PHI	NL	3	1	2	1	0	2	0	0	0	0	0	0	0	0	3	0
1901	PHI	NL	1	0	1	1	0	0	0	0	0	0	0	0	1	0	1	0
1902	PHI	AL	3	0	3	1	0	2	0	1	0	0	0	1	3	0	3	0
1903	PHI	AL	3	1	2	2	0	1	0	0	0	0	0	0	0	0	3	0
1904	PHI	AL	1	0	1	1	0	0	0	0	0	0	0	0	1	0	1	0
1906	PHI	AL	1	1	0	0	0	1	0	0	0	0	0	0	0	0	0	1
Total			31	14	17	15	6	10	0	2	0	0	0	1	6	0	25	4

Rank among batters: 1,400 • *Top target (3 home runs)*: Al Orth • *Number of pitchers victimized*: 23 • *Total ballparks homered in*: 11 • *First HR*: 09/25/1894 off Brickyard Kennedy

Joe Crotty

JOSEPH P. CROTTY
B: 12/24/1860 D: 06/22/1926
BR

Year	Tm	Lg	Tot	H	A	Men-On 0	1	2	3	One-Game 2	3	4	LO	XN	IP	PH	RHP	LHP
1884	CIN	UA	1	1	0	1	0	0	0	0	0	0	0	0	0	0	1	0

Rank among batters: 4,707 • *Total ballparks homered in*: 1 • *First HR*: 10/15/1884 off Al Atkinson

Jack Crouch

JACK ALBERT CROUCH
B: 06/12/1903 D: 08/25/1972
BR

Year	Tm	Lg	Tot	H	A	Men-On 0	1	2	3	One-Game 2	3	4	LO	XN	IP	PH	RHP	LHP
1933	STL	AL	1	0	1	0	0	1	0	0	0	0	0	0	0	0	1	0

Rank among batters: 4,707 • *Total ballparks homered in*: 1 • *First HR*: 06/08/1933 off Clint Brown

Frank Croucher

FRANK DONALD CROUCHER
B: 07/23/1914 D: 05/21/1980
BR

Year	Tm	Lg	Tot	H	A	Men-On 0	1	2	3	One-Game 2	3	4	LO	XN	IP	PH	RHP	LHP
1939	DET	AL	5	2	3	3	1	0	1	1	0	0	0	0	0	0	4	1
1941	DET	AL	2	1	1	2	0	0	0	0	0	0	0	0	0	0	0	2
Total			7	3	4	5	1	0	1	1	0	0	0	0	0	0	4	3

Rank among batters: 2,834 • *Top target (2 home runs)*: Jimmie DeShong • *Number of pitchers victimized*: 6 • *Total ballparks homered in*: 5 • *First HR*: 06/10/1939 off Jimmie DeShong

Buck Crouse

CLYDE ELSWORTH CROUSE
B: 01/06/1897 D: 10/23/1983
BL

Year	Tm	Lg	Tot	H	A	Men-On 0	1	2	3	One-Game 2	3	4	LO	XN	IP	PH	RHP	LHP
1923	CHI	AL	1	0	1	0	1	0	0	0	0	0	0	0	0	0	1	0
1924	CHI	AL	1	0	1	0	1	0	0	0	0	0	0	0	0	0	1	0
1925	CHI	AL	2	0	2	0	1	1	0	1	0	0	0	0	1	0	2	0
1928	CHI	AL	2	1	1	1	1	0	0	0	0	0	0	0	0	0	2	0
1929	CHI	AL	2	0	2	1	1	0	0	0	0	0	0	0	0	0	2	0
Total			8	1	7	2	5	1	0	1	0	0	0	0	1	0	8	0

Rank among batters: 2,703 • *Top target (2 home runs)*: Joe Bush • *Number of pitchers victimized*: 7 • *Total ballparks homered in*: 4 • *First HR*: 09/30/1923 off Rasty Wright

George Crowe

GEORGE DANIEL CROWE
B: 03/22/1921
BL

Year	Tm	Lg	Tot	H	A	Men-On 0	1	2	3	One-Game 2	3	4	LO	XN	IP	PH	RHP	LHP
1952	BOS	NL	4	2	2	3	1	0	0	0	0	0	0	1	0	1	4	0
1953	MIL	NL	2	0	2	1	1	0	0	0	0	0	0	0	0	1	2	0
1955	MIL	NL	15	4	11	9	5	1	0	2	0	0	0	0	0	1	14	1
1956	CIN	NL	10	6	4	5	4	1	0	1	0	0	0	0	0	3	7	3
1957	CIN	NL	31	19	12	18	9	4	0	3	0	0	0	0	0	0	29	2
1958	CIN	NL	7	5	2	2	3	2	0	0	0	0	0	0	0	0	7	0
1959	STL	NL	8	5	3	3	3	1	1	0	0	0	0	0	0	4	8	0
1960	STL	NL	4	3	1	1	3	0	0	0	0	0	0	0	0	4	4	0
Total			81	44	37	42	29	9	1	6	0	0	0	1	0	14	75	6

Rank among batters: 645 • *Top target (6 home runs)*: Lew Burdette • *Number of pitchers victimized*: 53 • *Total ballparks homered in*: 10 • *First HR*: 05/14/1952 off Woody Main

Bill Crowley

WILLIAM MICHAEL CROWLEY
B: 04/08/1857 D: 07/14/1891
BR

Year	Tm	Lg	Tot	H	A	Men-On 0	1	2	3	One-Game 2	3	4	LO	XN	IP	PH	RHP	LHP
1877	LOU	NL	1	1	0	0	1	0	0	0	0	0	0	0	0	0	1	0
1884	BOS	NL	6	3	3	1	2	2	0	0	0	0	0	0	0	0	5	0
1885	BUF	NL	1	0	1	0	0	1	0	0	0	0	0	0	0	0	1	0
Total			8	4	4	1	3	3	0	0	0	0	0	0	0	0	7	0

Rank among batters: 2,703 • *Top target (2 home runs)*: Charley Radbourn • *Number of pitchers victimized*: 7 • *Total ballparks homered in*: 6 • *First HR*: 08/04/1877 off George Bradley

Terry Crowley

TERRENCE MICHAEL CROWLEY
B: 02/16/1947
BL

Year	Tm	Lg	Tot	H	A	Men-On 0	1	2	3	One-Game 2	3	4	LO	XN	IP	PH	RHP	LHP
1970	BAL	AL	5	2	3	1	2	2	0	0	0	0	0	1	0	0	5	0
1972	BAL	AL	11	4	7	7	2	1	1	0	0	0	0	0	0	0	11	0
1973	BAL	AL	3	2	1	2	1	0	0	0	0	0	0	0	0	0	3	0
1974	CIN	NL	1	0	1	0	1	0	0	0	0	0	0	0	0	0	1	0
1975	CIN	NL	1	0	1	0	0	1	0	0	0	0	0	0	0	0	1	0
1977	BAL	AL	1	1	0	0	0	0	1	0	0	0	0	0	0	1	1	0
1979	BAL	AL	1	0	1	1	0	0	0	0	0	0	0	0	0	1	1	0
1980	BAL	AL	12	8	4	6	2	3	1	1	0	0	0	1	0	1	12	0
1981	BAL	AL	4	4	0	1	0	3	0	1	0	0	0	0	0	0	4	0
1982	BAL	AL	3	2	1	1	1	0	1	0	0	0	0	0	0	2	3	0
Total			42	23	19	19	9	10	4	2	0	0	0	2	0	5	42	0

Rank among batters: 1,138 • *Top target (3 home runs)*: Rick Langford • *Number of pitchers victimized*: 38 • *Total ballparks homered in*: 13 • *First HR*: 05/01/1970 off Dave Boswell

Walton Cruise

WALTON EDWIN CRUISE
B: 05/06/1890 D: 01/09/1975
BL

Year	Tm	Lg	Tot	H	A	Men-On 0	1	2	3	One-Game 2	3	4	LO	XN	IP	PH	RHP	LHP
1914	STL	NL	4	4	0	3	1	0	0	0	0	0	0	0	3	1	4	0
1917	STL	NL	5	3	2	4	1	0	0	0	0	0	0	0	2	0	5	0
1918	STL	NL	6	3	3	2	3	1	0	0	0	0	0	0	0	0	5	1
1919	BOS	NL	1	1	0	1	0	0	0	0	0	0	0	0	1	0	1	0
1920	BOS	NL	1	0	1	1	0	0	0	0	0	0	0	0	0	0	1	0

Year	Tm	Lg	Tot	H	A	Men-On				One-Game			LO	XN	IP	PH	RHP	LHP
						0	1	2	3	2	3	4						

Walton Cruise *continued*

Year	Tm	Lg	Tot	H	A	0	1	2	3	2	3	4	LO	XN	IP	PH	RHP	LHP
1921	BOS	NL	8	1	7	1	5	2	0	1	0	0	0	0	0	0	7	1
1922	BOS	NL	4	1	3	4	0	0	0	0	0	0	0	0	0	0	4	0
1924	BOS	NL	1	0	1	0	1	0	0	0	0	0	0	0	0	1	1	0
Total			30	13	17	16	11	3	0	1	0	0	0	0	6	2	28	2

Rank among batters: 1,437 • *Top target (3 home runs)*: Jess Barnes, Leon Cadore • *Number of pitchers victimized*: 25 • *Total ballparks homered in*: 8 • *First HR*: 04/19/1914 off Laurence Cheney

Hector Cruz

HECTOR LOUIS (DILAN) CRUZ
B: 04/02/1953
BR

Year	Tm	Lg	Tot	H	A	0	1	2	3	2	3	4	LO	XN	IP	PH	RHP	LHP
1976	STL	NL	13	9	4	6	6	1	0	0	0	0	0	0	1	0	4	9
1977	STL	NL	6	4	2	2	3	1	0	0	0	0	0	0	0	0	2	4
1978	CHI	NL	2	0	2	2	0	0	0	1	0	0	0	0	0	0	1	1
	SF	NL	6	4	2	5	1	0	0	0	0	0	0	0	0	1	3	3
	Total		8	4	4	7	1	0	0	1	0	0	0	0	0	1	4	4
1979	CIN	NL	4	3	1	2	2	0	0	0	0	0	0	0	1	0	4	0
1980	CIN	NL	1	1	0	0	0	1	0	0	0	0	0	0	0	0	0	1
1981	CHI	NL	7	4	3	5	1	1	0	0	0	0	0	0	0	1	5	2
Total			39	25	14	22	13	4	0	1	0	0	0	0	2	2	19	20

Rank among batters: 1,204 • *Top target (3 home runs)*: Tom Underwood • *Number of pitchers victimized*: 34 • *Total ballparks homered in*: 11 • *First HR*: 04/13/1976 off Jerry Reuss

Henry Cruz

HENRY ACOSTA CRUZ
B: 02/27/1952
BL

Year	Tm	Lg	Tot	H	A	0	1	2	3	2	3	4	LO	XN	IP	PH	RHP	LHP
1976	LA	NL	4	1	3	1	2	1	0	1	0	0	0	0	0	0	4	0
1977	CHI	AL	2	1	1	1	1	0	0	0	0	0	0	0	0	0	2	0
1978	CHI	AL	2	1	1	2	0	0	0	0	0	0	0	0	0	0	2	0
Total			8	3	5	4	3	1	0	1	0	0	0	0	0	0	8	0

Rank among batters: 2,703 • *Total ballparks homered in*: 4 • *First HR*: 04/25/1976 off Ken Crosby

Jose Cruz

JOSE (DILAN) CRUZ
B: 08/08/1947
BL

Year	Tm	Lg	Tot	H	A	0	1	2	3	2	3	4	LO	XN	IP	PH	RHP	LHP
1971	STL	NL	9	4	5	4	5	0	0	0	0	0	0	0	0	0	7	2
1972	STL	NL	2	0	2	2	0	0	0	0	0	0	0	0	0	0	2	0
1973	STL	NL	10	5	5	4	5	1	0	0	0	0	0	1	0	1	9	1
1974	STL	NL	5	3	2	2	1	2	0	0	0	0	0	0	1	1	5	0
1975	HOU	NL	9	3	6	3	2	4	0	1	0	0	0	0	0	0	9	0
1976	HOU	NL	4	1	3	3	0	1	0	0	0	0	0	0	0	0	3	1
1977	HOU	NL	17	8	9	10	7	0	0	2	0	0	0	2	0	0	16	1
1978	HOU	NL	10	7	3	4	6	0	0	0	0	0	0	1	0	0	7	3
1979	HOU	NL	9	2	7	4	3	2	0	0	0	0	0	0	0	0	5	4
1980	HOU	NL	11	4	7	7	2	1	1	1	0	0	0	2	0	0	4	7
1981	HOU	NL	13	3	10	6	5	2	0	0	0	0	0	0	0	0	11	2
1982	HOU	NL	9	3	6	3	5	1	0	0	0	0	0	0	0	0	5	4
1983	HOU	NL	14	3	11	8	2	3	1	1	0	0	0	0	0	0	12	2
1984	HOU	NL	12	0	12	7	1	3	1	1	0	0	0	0	0	0	8	4
1985	HOU	NL	9	1	8	5	2	2	0	0	0	0	0	0	0	0	4	5
1986	HOU	NL	10	5	5	4	4	2	0	1	0	0	0	0	0	0	8	2
1987	HOU	NL	11	6	5	9	1	1	0	1	0	0	0	1	0	0	7	4
1988	NY	AL	1	1	0	0	0	0	1	0	0	0	0	0	0	1	1	0
Total			165	59	106	85	51	25	4	8	0	0	0	7	1	3	123	42

Rank among batters: 249 • *Top target (5 home runs)*: Burt Hooton • *Number of pitchers victimized*: 134 • *Total ballparks homered in*: 14 • *First HR*: 07/02/1971 off Steve Stone

Julio Cruz

JULIO LOUIS CRUZ
B: 12/02/1954
BB

Year	Tm	Lg	Tot	H	A	0	1	2	3	2	3	4	LO	XN	IP	PH	RHP	LHP
1977	SEA	AL	1	0	1	1	0	0	0	0	0	0	0	0	0	0	0	1

Julio Cruz *continued*

Year	Tm	Lg	Tot	H	A	Men-On 0	Men-On 1	Men-On 2	Men-On 3	One-Game 2	One-Game 3	One-Game 4	LO	XN	IP	PH	RHP	LHP
1978	SEA	AL	1	1	0	0	1	0	0	0	0	0	0	0	1	0	1	0
1979	SEA	AL	1	1	0	1	0	0	0	0	0	0	1	0	0	0	1	0
1980	SEA	AL	2	1	1	2	0	0	0	0	0	0	0	1	0	0	0	2
1981	SEA	AL	2	1	1	1	0	1	0	0	0	0	0	0	0	0	0	2
1982	SEA	AL	8	8	0	6	1	1	0	0	0	0	1	0	1	0	1	7
1983	SEA	AL	2	1	1	2	0	0	0	0	0	0	0	0	0	0	0	2
	CHI	AL	1	0	1	0	1	0	0	0	0	0	0	0	0	0	0	1
	Total		3	1	2	2	1	0	0	0	0	0	0	0	0	0	0	3
1984	CHI	AL	5	1	4	1	3	0	1	0	0	0	0	0	0	0	3	2
Total			23	14	9	14	6	2	1	0	0	0	2	1	2	0	6	17

Rank among batters: 1,686 • *Top target (2 home runs)*: Frank Tanana, Jerry Koosman • *Number of pitchers victimized*: 21 • *Total ballparks homered in*: 9 • *First HR*: 07/08/1977 off Bill Butler

Todd Cruz

TODD RUBEN CRUZ
B: 11/23/1955
BR

Year	Tm	Lg	Tot	H	A	Men-On 0	Men-On 1	Men-On 2	Men-On 3	One-Game 2	One-Game 3	One-Game 4	LO	XN	IP	PH	RHP	LHP
1979	KC	AL	2	0	2	1	1	0	0	0	0	0	0	0	0	0	1	1
1980	CAL	AL	1	0	1	0	1	0	0	0	0	0	0	0	0	0	1	0
	CHI	AL	2	1	1	2	0	0	0	0	0	0	0	0	0	0	1	1
	Total		3	1	2	2	1	0	0	0	0	0	0	0	0	0	2	1
1982	SEA	AL	16	8	8	12	2	1	1	0	0	0	0	2	0	0	11	5
1983	SEA	AL	7	6	1	3	3	1	0	1	0	0	0	0	0	0	5	2
	BAL	AL	3	0	3	1	0	2	0	0	0	0	0	0	0	0	3	0
	Total		10	6	4	4	3	3	0	1	0	0	0	0	0	0	8	2
1984	BAL	AL	3	0	3	1	2	0	0	0	0	0	0	0	0	1	1	2
Total			34	15	19	20	9	4	1	1	0	0	0	2	0	1	23	11

Rank among batters: 1,315 • *Top target (2 home runs)*: Warren Brusstar, Jack Morris • *Number of pitchers victimized*: 32 • *Total ballparks homered in*: 15 • *First HR*: 05/27/1979 off Jerry Koosman

Mike Cubbage

MICHAEL LEE CUBBAGE
B: 07/21/1950
BL

Year	Tm	Lg	Tot	H	A	Men-On 0	Men-On 1	Men-On 2	Men-On 3	One-Game 2	One-Game 3	One-Game 4	LO	XN	IP	PH	RHP	LHP
1975	TEX	AL	4	2	2	1	1	1	1	0	0	0	0	0	0	0	3	1
1976	MIN	AL	3	1	2	1	1	0	1	0	0	0	0	0	0	0	2	1
1977	MIN	AL	9	6	3	5	2	1	1	0	0	0	0	0	0	0	9	0
1978	MIN	AL	7	5	2	3	3	0	1	0	0	0	0	0	0	1	7	0
1979	MIN	AL	2	0	2	1	1	0	0	0	0	0	0	0	0	0	2	0
1980	MIN	AL	8	3	5	2	5	1	0	0	0	0	0	0	1	0	7	1
1981	NY	NL	1	1	0	1	0	0	0	0	0	0	0	0	0	1	1	0
Total			34	18	16	14	13	3	4	0	0	0	0	0	1	2	31	3

Rank among batters: 1,315 • *Top target (2 home runs)*: Dennis Eckersley, Glenn Abbott, Mike Parrott • *Number of pitchers victimized*: 31 • *Total ballparks homered in*: 10 • *First HR*: 06/20/1975 off Bill Singer • *Hit for Cycle*—vs TOR: 07/27/1978

Al Cuccinello

ALFRED EDWARD CUCCINELLO
B: 11/26/1914
BR

Year	Tm	Lg	Tot	H	A	Men-On 0	Men-On 1	Men-On 2	Men-On 3	One-Game 2	One-Game 3	One-Game 4	LO	XN	IP	PH	RHP	LHP
1935	NY	NL	4	4	0	0	4	0	0	0	0	0	0	0	0	0	4	0

Rank among batters: 3,427 • *Top target (2 home runs)*: Van Mungo • *Number of pitchers victimized*: 3 • *Total ballparks homered in*: 1 • *First HR*: 05/30/1935 off Van Mungo

Tony Cuccinello

ANTHONY FRANCIS CUCCINELLO
B: 11/08/1907 D: 09/21/1995
BR

Year	Tm	Lg	Tot	H	A	Men-On 0	Men-On 1	Men-On 2	Men-On 3	One-Game 2	One-Game 3	One-Game 4	LO	XN	IP	PH	RHP	LHP
1930	CIN	NL	10	2	8	4	5	1	0	1	0	0	0	0	0	0	7	3
1931	CIN	NL	2	0	2	1	0	1	0	0	0	0	0	0	0	0	0	2
1932	BRO	NL	12	4	8	6	6	0	0	0	0	0	0	0	2	0	7	5
1933	BRO	NL	9	3	6	4	3	1	1	0	0	0	0	0	1	0	8	1
1934	BRO	NL	14	4	10	8	4	2	0	0	0	0	0	0	0	0	10	4
1935	BRO	NL	8	4	4	6	2	0	0	0	0	0	0	0	0	0	8	0

Tony Cuccinello *continued*

Year	Tm	Lg	Tot	H	A	Men-On 0	1	2	3	One-Game 2	3	4	LO	XN	IP	PH	RHP	LHP
1936	BOS	NL	7	5	2	3	2	2	0	0	0	0	0	0	0	0	7	0
1937	BOS	NL	11	4	7	5	1	5	0	1	0	0	0	1	0	0	6	5
1938	BOS	NL	9	0	9	6	3	0	0	1	0	0	0	0	0	0	5	4
1939	BOS	NL	2	1	1	1	0	1	0	0	0	0	0	0	0	0	2	0
1940	NY	NL	5	3	2	2	1	2	0	0	0	0	0	0	0	0	4	1
1942	BOS	NL	1	0	1	1	0	0	0	0	0	0	0	0	0	0	0	1
1943	CHI	AL	2	1	1	2	0	0	0	0	0	0	0	0	0	0	2	0
1945	CHI	AL	2	2	0	1	0	1	0	0	0	0	0	0	0	0	1	1
Total			94	33	61	50	27	16	1	3	0	0	0	1	3	0	67	27

Rank among batters: 535 • *Top target (4 home runs)*: Charlie Root, Hal Schumacher, Carl Hubbell • *Number of pitchers victimized*: 62 • *Total ballparks homered in*: 10 • *First HR*: 06/13/1930 off Dolf Luque

Mike Cuellar

MIGUEL ANGEL (SANTANA) CUELLAR
B: 05/08/1937
BL

Year	Tm	Lg	Tot	H	A	Men-On 0	1	2	3	One-Game 2	3	4	LO	XN	IP	PH	RHP	LHP
1966	HOU	NL	1	0	1	1	0	0	0	0	0	0	0	0	0	0	1	0
1968	HOU	NL	1	0	1	1	0	0	0	0	0	0	0	0	0	0	1	0
1970	BAL	AL	2	0	2	0	2	0	0	0	0	0	0	0	0	0	2	0
1971	BAL	AL	1	0	1	0	1	0	0	0	0	0	0	0	0	0	1	0
1972	BAL	AL	2	1	1	1	1	0	0	0	0	0	0	0	0	0	2	0
Total			7	1	6	3	4	0	0	0	0	0	0	0	0	0	7	0

Rank among batters: 2,834 • *Total ballparks homered in*: 6 • *First HR*: 09/28/1966 off Sammy Ellis • *LCS HR*—1

Manuel Cueto

MANUEL (MELO) CUETO
B: 02/08/1892 D: 06/29/1942
BR

Year	Tm	Lg	Tot	H	A	Men-On 0	1	2	3	One-Game 2	3	4	LO	XN	IP	PH	RHP	LHP
1917	CIN	NL	1	1	0	0	0	1	0	0	0	0	0	0	1	0	1	0

Rank among batters: 4,707 • *Total ballparks homered in*: 1 • *First HR*: 04/23/1917 off Claude Hendrix

Leon Culberson

DELBERT LEON CULBERSON
B: 08/06/1919 D: 09/17/1989
BR

Year	Tm	Lg	Tot	H	A	Men-On 0	1	2	3	One-Game 2	3	4	LO	XN	IP	PH	RHP	LHP
1943	BOS	AL	3	0	3	2	1	0	0	0	0	0	0	0	1	0	3	0
1944	BOS	AL	2	1	1	1	1	0	0	0	0	0	0	0	0	0	2	0
1945	BOS	AL	6	2	4	4	1	1	0	0	0	0	0	0	1	0	5	1
1946	BOS	AL	3	3	0	2	0	0	1	0	0	0	1	1	0	0	3	0
Total			14	6	8	9	3	1	1	0	0	0	1	1	2	0	13	1

Rank among batters: 2,169 • *Top target (2 home runs)*: Bobo Newsom • *Number of pitchers victimized*: 13 • *Total ballparks homered in*: 5 • *First HR*: 05/23/1943 off Tommy Bridges • *Hit for Cycle—*@CLE: 07/03/1943 • *World Series HR*—1

Tim Cullen

TIMOTHY LEO CULLEN
B: 02/16/1942
BR

Year	Tm	Lg	Tot	H	A	Men-On 0	1	2	3	One-Game 2	3	4	LO	XN	IP	PH	RHP	LHP
1967	WAS	AL	2	2	0	1	0	1	0	0	0	0	0	0	0	0	1	1
1968	CHI	AL	2	1	1	0	2	0	0	0	0	0	0	0	0	0	2	0
	WAS	AL	1	1	0	1	0	0	0	0	0	0	0	0	0	0	1	0
	Total		3	2	1	1	2	0	0	0	0	0	0	0	0	0	3	0
1969	WAS	AL	1	1	0	0	1	0	0	0	0	0	0	0	0	0	0	1
1970	WAS	AL	1	1	0	1	0	0	0	0	0	0	0	0	0	0	0	1
1971	WAS	AL	2	0	2	0	2	0	0	0	0	0	0	0	0	0	0	2
Total			9	6	3	3	5	1	0	0	0	0	0	0	0	0	4	5

Rank among batters: 2,587 • *Total ballparks homered in*: 5 • *First HR*: 07/13/1967 off Joe Sparma

Roy Cullenbine

ROY JOSEPH CULLENBINE
B: 10/18/1913 D: 05/28/1991
BB

Year	Tm	Lg	Tot	H	A	Men-On 0	1	2	3	One-Game 2	3	4	LO	XN	IP	PH	RHP	LHP
1939	DET	AL	6	2	4	4	0	2	0	1	0	0	0	0	0	1	6	0

Roy Cullenbine *continued*

Year	Tm	Lg	Tot	H	A	Men-On 0	Men-On 1	Men-On 2	Men-On 3	One-Game 2	One-Game 3	One-Game 4	LO	XN	IP	PH	RHP	LHP
1940	BRO	NL	1	1	0	0	0	1	0	0	0	0	0	0	0	0	0	1
	STL	AL	7	4	3	5	0	0	2	0	0	0	0	0	0	0	5	2
	Total		8	5	3	5	0	1	2	0	0	0	0	0	0	0	5	3
1941	STL	AL	9	4	5	4	3	1	1	0	0	0	0	0	0	0	6	3
1942	STL	AL	2	2	0	0	1	1	0	0	0	0	0	0	0	0	2	0
	WAS	AL	2	0	2	0	2	0	0	0	0	0	0	0	0	0	2	0
	NY	AL	2	2	0	1	0	1	0	0	0	0	0	0	0	0	1	1
	Total		6	4	2	1	3	2	0	0	0	0	0	0	0	0	5	1
1943	CLE	AL	8	4	4	6	1	1	0	0	0	0	0	0	0	0	6	2
1944	CLE	AL	16	9	7	13	0	3	0	1	0	0	0	0	1	0	16	0
1945	DET	AL	18	11	7	9	5	4	0	0	0	0	0	0	0	0	15	3
1946	DET	AL	15	12	3	8	5	2	0	2	0	0	0	0	0	0	13	2
1947	DET	AL	24	15	9	11	12	1	0	2	0	0	0	0	0	0	21	3
Total			110	66	44	61	29	17	3	6	0	0	0	0	1	1	93	17

Rank among batters: 436 • *Top target (4 home runs)*: Tiny Bonham, Roger Wolff • *Number of pitchers victimized*: 71 • *Total ballparks homered in*: 10 • *First HR*: 07/03/1939 off Bob Feller

Dick Culler

RICHARD BROADUS CULLER
B: 01/15/1915 D: 06/16/1964
BR

Year	Tm	Lg	Tot	H	A	Men-On 0	Men-On 1	Men-On 2	Men-On 3	One-Game 2	One-Game 3	One-Game 4	LO	XN	IP	PH	RHP	LHP
1945	BOS	NL	2	1	1	1	1	0	0	0	0	0	0	0	0	0	1	1

Rank among batters: 4,129 • *Total ballparks homered in*: 2 • *First HR*: 06/19/1945 off Slim Emmerich

Nick Cullop

HENRY NICHOLAS CULLOP
B: 10/16/1900 D: 12/01/1978
BR

Year	Tm	Lg	Tot	H	A	Men-On 0	Men-On 1	Men-On 2	Men-On 3	One-Game 2	One-Game 3	One-Game 4	LO	XN	IP	PH	RHP	LHP
1927	CLE	AL	1	1	0	0	1	0	0	0	0	0	0	0	0	1	1	0
1929	BRO	NL	1	1	0	1	0	0	0	0	0	0	0	0	0	0	1	0
1930	CIN	NL	1	0	1	0	1	0	0	0	0	0	0	0	0	0	1	0
1931	CIN	NL	8	4	4	2	3	3	0	0	0	0	0	0	0	0	3	5
Total			11	6	5	3	5	3	0	0	0	0	0	0	0	1	6	5

Rank among batters: 2,419 • *Top target (2 home runs)*: Bill Hallahan • *Number of pitchers victimized*: 10 • *Total ballparks homered in*: 8 • *First HR*: 07/08/1927 off Bump Hadley

Ray Culp

RAYMOND LEONARD CULP
B: 08/06/1941
BR

Year	Tm	Lg	Tot	H	A	Men-On 0	Men-On 1	Men-On 2	Men-On 3	One-Game 2	One-Game 3	One-Game 4	LO	XN	IP	PH	RHP	LHP
1969	BOS	AL	1	1	0	1	0	0	0	0	0	0	0	0	0	0	1	0

Rank among batters: 4,707 • *Total ballparks homered in*: 1 • *First HR*: 08/09/1969 off Pedro Borbon

Jack Cummings

JOHN WILLIAM CUMMINGS
B: 04/01/1904 D: 10/05/1962
BR

Year	Tm	Lg	Tot	H	A	Men-On 0	Men-On 1	Men-On 2	Men-On 3	One-Game 2	One-Game 3	One-Game 4	LO	XN	IP	PH	RHP	LHP
1927	NY	NL	2	1	1	1	1	0	0	0	0	0	0	0	0	0	2	0
1928	NY	NL	2	1	1	1	0	0	1	0	0	0	0	0	0	2	1	1
Total			4	2	2	2	1	0	1	0	0	0	0	0	0	2	3	1

Rank among batters: 3,427 • *Total ballparks homered in*: 3 • *First HR*: 06/08/1927 off Vic Aldridge

Midre Cummings

MIDRE ALMERIC CUMMINGS
B: 10/14/1971
BB

Year	Tm	Lg	Tot	H	A	Men-On 0	Men-On 1	Men-On 2	Men-On 3	One-Game 2	One-Game 3	One-Game 4	LO	XN	IP	PH	RHP	LHP
1994	PIT	NL	1	1	0	0	1	0	0	0	0	0	0	0	0	0	1	0
1995	PIT	NL	2	1	1	2	0	0	0	0	0	0	0	0	0	0	1	1
Total			3	2	1	2	1	0	0	0	0	0	0	0	0	0	2	1

Rank among batters: 3,735 • *Total ballparks homered in*: 2 • *First HR*: 07/31/1994 off Juan Castillo

Year	Tm	Lg	Tot	H	A	Men-On				One-Game			LO	XN	IP	PH	RHP	LHP
						0	1	2	3	2	3	4						

Bert Cunningham

ELLSWORTH ELMER CUNNINGHAM
B: 11/25/1865 D: 05/14/1952
BR

Year	Tm	Lg	Tot	H	A	0	1	2	3	2	3	4	LO	XN	IP	PH	RHP	LHP
1888	BAL	AA	1	1	0	1	0	0	0	0	0	0	0	0	0	0	1	0
1891	BAL	AA	1	1	0	0	0	1	0	0	0	0	0	0	0	0	1	0
1896	LOU	NL	2	1	1	1	0	1	0	0	0	0	0	0	0	0	2	0
1897	LOU	NL	2	2	0	1	1	0	0	0	0	0	0	0	1	0	1	1
1898	LOU	NL	1	1	0	1	0	0	0	0	0	0	0	0	0	0	1	0
1899	LOU	NL	2	1	1	0	0	0	2	0	0	0	0	0	0	0	2	0
Total			9	7	2	4	1	2	2	0	0	0	0	0	1	0	8	1

Rank among batters: 2,587 • *Total ballparks homered in*: 5 • *First HR*: 07/27/1888 off Silver King

Bill Cunningham

WILLIAM JOHN CUNNINGHAM
B: 06/09/1888 D: 02/21/1946
BR

Year	Tm	Lg	Tot	H	A	0	1	2	3	2	3	4	LO	XN	IP	PH	RHP	LHP
1911	WAS	AL	3	2	1	1	0	2	0	0	0	0	0	0	1	0	3	0
1912	WAS	AL	1	1	0	1	0	0	0	0	0	0	0	0	0	0	1	0
Total			4	3	1	2	0	2	0	0	0	0	0	0	1	0	4	0

Rank among batters: 3,427 • *Total ballparks homered in*: 2 • *First HR*: 05/10/1911 off Jim Scott

Bill Cunningham

WILLIAM ALOYSIUS CUNNINGHAM
B: 07/30/1895 D: 09/26/1953
BR

Year	Tm	Lg	Tot	H	A	0	1	2	3	2	3	4	LO	XN	IP	PH	RHP	LHP
1921	NY	NL	1	1	0	0	0	1	0	0	0	0	0	0	0	0	0	1
1922	NY	NL	2	2	0	0	1	1	0	0	0	0	0	0	1	0	2	0
1923	NY	NL	5	3	2	5	0	0	0	0	0	0	0	0	0	0	3	2
1924	BOS	NL	1	0	1	1	0	0	0	0	0	0	0	0	0	0	1	0
Total			9	6	3	6	1	2	0	0	0	0	0	0	1	0	6	3

Rank among batters: 2,587 • *Top target (2 home runs)*: Wilbur Cooper • *Number of pitchers victimized*: 8 • *Total ballparks homered in*: 3 • *First HR*: 07/23/1921 off Fritz Coumbe

George Cunningham

GEORGE HAROLD CUNNINGHAM
B: 07/13/1894 D: 03/10/1972
BR

Year	Tm	Lg	Tot	H	A	0	1	2	3	2	3	4	LO	XN	IP	PH	RHP	LHP
1917	DET	AL	1	1	0	1	0	0	0	0	0	0	0	0	0	0	1	0

Rank among batters: 4,707 • *Total ballparks homered in*: 1 • *First HR*: 09/12/1917 off Jim Bagby

Joe Cunningham

JOSEPH ROBERT CUNNINGHAM
B: 08/27/1931
BL

Year	Tm	Lg	Tot	H	A	0	1	2	3	2	3	4	LO	XN	IP	PH	RHP	LHP
1954	STL	NL	11	6	5	5	2	4	0	1	0	0	0	0	0	0	8	3
1957	STL	NL	9	7	2	3	5	0	1	0	0	0	0	2	0	3	8	1
1958	STL	NL	12	8	4	4	7	1	0	1	0	0	0	0	0	0	10	2
1959	STL	NL	7	2	5	7	0	0	0	0	0	0	0	0	0	0	7	0
1960	STL	NL	6	3	3	6	0	0	0	0	0	0	0	0	0	0	5	1
1961	STL	NL	7	5	2	4	1	2	0	0	0	0	0	0	0	0	5	2
1962	CHI	AL	8	4	4	5	3	0	0	0	0	0	0	0	0	0	5	3
1963	CHI	AL	1	0	1	0	1	0	0	0	0	0	0	0	0	0	1	0
1965	WAS	AL	3	1	2	0	1	2	0	0	0	0	0	1	0	1	3	0
Total			64	36	28	34	20	9	1	2	0	0	0	3	0	4	52	12

Rank among batters: 815 • Top target (3 home runs): Brooks Lawrence, Jack Sanford, Don Newcombe, Don Drysdale • *Number of pitchers victimized*: 51 • *Total ballparks homered in*: 13 • *First HR*: 06/30/1954 off Art Fowler

Nig Cuppy

GEORGE JOSEPH CUPPY
B: 07/03/1869 D: 07/27/1922
BR

Year	Tm	Lg	Tot	H	A	0	1	2	3	2	3	4	LO	XN	IP	PH	RHP	LHP
1896	CLE	NL	1	0	1	0	0	1	0	0	0	0	0	0	0	0	1	0

Rank among batters: 4,707 • *Total ballparks homered in*: 1 • *First HR*: 07/30/1896 off Bill Kissinger

Year	Tm	Lg	Tot	H	A	Men-On 0	Men-On 1	Men-On 2	Men-On 3	One-Game 2	One-Game 3	One-Game 4	LO	XN	IP	PH	RHP	LHP

Tony Curry

GEORGE ANTHONY CURRY
B: 12/22/1938
BL

Year	Tm	Lg	Tot	H	A	0	1	2	3	2	3	4	LO	XN	IP	PH	RHP	LHP
1960	PHI	NL	6	2	4	3	3	0	0	1	0	0	0	0	1	0	6	0

Rank among batters: 2,988 • *Top target (2 home runs)*: Jay Hook • *Number of pitchers victimized*: 5 • *Total ballparks homered in*: 3 • *First HR*: 05/14/1960 off Jay Hook

Chad Curtis

CHAD DAVID CURTIS
B: 11/06/1968
BR

Year	Tm	Lg	Tot	H	A	0	1	2	3	2	3	4	LO	XN	IP	PH	RHP	LHP
1992	CAL	AL	10	5	5	6	2	2	0	1	0	0	1	0	0	0	4	6
1993	CAL	AL	6	3	3	6	0	0	0	0	0	0	0	0	0	0	4	2
1994	CAL	AL	11	8	3	6	5	0	0	1	0	0	0	0	0	0	9	2
1995	DET	AL	21	11	10	16	5	0	0	1	0	0	3	0	0	0	16	5
Total			48	27	21	34	12	2	0	3	0	0	4	0	0	0	33	15

Rank among batters: 1,024 • *Top target (3 home runs)*: Mike Mussina • *Number of pitchers victimized*: 42 • *Total ballparks homered in*: 13 • *First HR*: 05/09/1992 off Todd Stottlemyre

Jack Curtis

JACK PATRICK CURTIS
B: 01/11/1937
BL

Year	Tm	Lg	Tot	H	A	0	1	2	3	2	3	4	LO	XN	IP	PH	RHP	LHP
1961	CHI	NL	2	1	1	2	0	0	0	0	0	0	0	0	0	0	1	1

Rank among batters: 4,129 • *Total ballparks homered in*: 2 • *First HR*: 08/02/1961 off Bob Hendley

Jim Curtiss

ERVIN DUANE CURTISS
B: 12/27/1861 D: 02/14/1945
BL

Year	Tm	Lg	Tot	H	A	0	1	2	3	2	3	4	LO	XN	IP	PH	RHP	LHP
1891	CIN	NL	1	0	1	0	0	1	0	0	0	0	0	0	0	0	1	0

Rank among batters: 4,707 • *Total ballparks homered in*: 1 • *First HR*: 07/22/1891 off Bill Hutchison

Guy Curtright

GUY PAXTON CURTRIGHT
B: 10/18/1912
BR

Year	Tm	Lg	Tot	H	A	0	1	2	3	2	3	4	LO	XN	IP	PH	RHP	LHP
1943	CHI	AL	3	2	1	1	2	0	0	0	0	0	0	0	0	0	3	0
1944	CHI	AL	2	1	1	0	2	0	0	0	0	0	0	0	1	0	1	1
1945	CHI	AL	4	2	2	4	0	0	0	0	0	0	0	0	0	0	4	0
Total			9	5	4	5	4	0	0	0	0	0	0	0	1	0	8	1

Rank among batters: 2,587 • *Top target (2 home runs)*: Jack Salveson • *Number of pitchers victimized*: 8 • *Total ballparks homered in*: 4 • *First HR*: 06/27/1943 off Jack Salveson

Jack Cusick

JOHN PETER CUSICK
B: 06/12/1928 D: 11/17/1989
BR

Year	Tm	Lg	Tot	H	A	0	1	2	3	2	3	4	LO	XN	IP	PH	RHP	LHP
1951	CHI	NL	2	1	1	1	0	0	1	0	0	0	0	0	1	0	1	1

Rank among batters: 4,129 • *Total ballparks homered in*: 2 • *First HR*: 05/13/1951 off Murry Dickson

George Cutshaw

GEORGE WILLIAM CUTSHAW
B: 07/27/1887 D: 08/22/1973
BR

Year	Tm	Lg	Tot	H	A	0	1	2	3	2	3	4	LO	XN	IP	PH	RHP	LHP
1913	BRO	NL	7	2	5	3	2	2	0	1	0	0	0	0	7	0	4	3
1914	BRO	NL	2	2	0	0	0	1	1	0	0	0	0	0	2	0	1	1
1916	BRO	NL	2	2	0	1	0	1	0	0	0	0	0	1	1	0	2	0
1917	BRO	NL	4	2	2	2	2	0	0	0	0	0	0	0	3	0	4	0
1918	PIT	NL	5	3	2	2	2	1	0	0	0	0	0	0	3	0	4	1
1919	PIT	NL	3	0	3	2	1	0	0	0	0	0	0	0	2	0	3	0

George Cutshaw *continued*

Year	Tm	Lg	Tot	H	A	Men-On 0	1	2	3	One-Game 2	3	4	LO	XN	IP	PH	RHP	LHP
1922	DET	AL	2	1	1	2	0	0	0	0	0	0	0	0	1	0	2	0
Total			25	12	13	12	7	5	1	1	0	0	0	1	19	0	20	5

Rank among batters: 1,608 • *Top target (3 home runs)*: Slim Sallee • *Number of pitchers victimized*: 21 • *Total ballparks homered in*: 9 • *First HR*: 05/16/1913 off Slim Sallee

Kiki Cuyler

HAZEN SHIRLEY CUYLER
B: 08/30/1898 D: 02/11/1950
BR HOF

Year	Tm	Lg	Tot	H	A	Men-On 0	1	2	3	One-Game 2	3	4	LO	XN	IP	PH	RHP	LHP
1924	PIT	NL	9	7	2	1	4	4	0	0	0	0	0	0	5	0	8	1
1925	PIT	NL	18	7	11	10	7	0	1	3	0	0	0	0	8	0	13	5
1926	PIT	NL	8	3	5	6	1	1	0	0	0	0	0	0	2	0	7	1
1927	PIT	NL	3	2	1	2	1	0	0	0	0	0	0	0	0	0	3	0
1928	CHI	NL	17	8	9	9	6	2	0	1	0	0	0	0	0	0	13	4
1929	CHI	NL	15	8	7	6	6	2	1	0	0	0	0	0	0	0	11	4
1930	CHI	NL	13	8	5	1	6	6	0	1	0	0	0	1	0	0	10	3
1931	CHI	NL	9	5	4	3	4	2	0	0	0	0	0	0	0	0	6	3
1932	CHI	NL	10	5	5	4	4	2	0	0	0	0	0	2	0	0	9	1
1933	CHI	NL	5	2	3	3	1	1	0	0	0	0	0	0	0	0	4	1
1934	CHI	NL	6	5	1	4	2	0	0	0	0	0	0	0	0	0	3	3
1935	CHI	NL	4	1	3	3	1	0	0	0	0	0	0	0	1	0	4	0
	CIN	NL	2	1	1	1	1	0	0	0	0	0	0	0	0	0	1	1
	Total		6	2	4	4	2	0	0	0	0	0	0	0	1	0	5	1
1936	CIN	NL	7	4	3	4	2	1	0	0	0	0	2	0	1	0	6	1
1938	BRO	NL	2	2	0	2	0	0	0	0	0	0	1	0	0	0	2	0
Total			128	68	60	59	46	21	2	5	0	0	3	3	17	0	100	28

Rank among batters: 356 • *Top target (7 home runs)*: Dazzy Vance • *Number of pitchers victimized*: 82 • *Total ballparks homered in*: 8 • *First HR*: 06/16/1924 off Jess Barnes • *Hit for Cycle*—vs PHI: 06/04/1925 • *World Series HR*—2

Milt Cuyler

MILTON CUYLER
B: 10/07/1968
BB

Year	Tm	Lg	Tot	H	A	Men-On 0	1	2	3	One-Game 2	3	4	LO	XN	IP	PH	RHP	LHP
1991	DET	AL	3	1	2	2	0	0	1	0	0	0	0	0	0	0	3	0
1992	DET	AL	3	1	2	1	0	1	1	0	0	0	0	0	0	0	1	2
1994	DET	AL	1	1	0	0	1	0	0	0	0	0	0	0	0	0	1	0
Total			7	3	4	3	1	1	2	0	0	0	0	0	0	0	5	2

Rank among batters: 2,834 • *Total ballparks homered in*: 5 • *First HR*: 05/19/1991 off Jack Morris

John D'Acquisto

JOHN FRANCIS D'ACQUISTO
B: 12/24/1951
BR

Year	Tm	Lg	Tot	H	A	Men-On 0	1	2	3	One-Game 2	3	4	LO	XN	IP	PH	RHP	LHP
1974	SF	NL	1	1	0	0	1	0	0	0	0	0	0	0	0	0	1	0

Rank among batters: 4,707 • *Total ballparks homered in*: 1 • *First HR*: 06/07/1974 off Larry Demery

Paul Dade

LONNIE PAUL DADE
B: 12/07/1951
BR

Year	Tm	Lg	Tot	H	A	Men-On 0	1	2	3	One-Game 2	3	4	LO	XN	IP	PH	RHP	LHP
1977	CLE	AL	3	1	2	2	1	0	0	0	0	0	0	0	0	0	2	1
1978	CLE	AL	3	1	2	2	0	0	1	0	0	0	1	0	0	0	2	1
1979	CLE	AL	3	1	2	2	1	0	0	0	0	0	0	0	0	0	2	1
	SD	NL	1	0	1	1	0	0	0	0	0	0	0	0	0	0	1	0
	Total		4	1	3	3	1	0	0	0	0	0	0	0	0	0	3	1
Total			10	3	7	7	2	0	1	0	0	0	1	0	0	0	7	3

Rank among batters: 2,500 • *Total ballparks homered in*: 7 • *First HR*: 06/22/1977 off Pete Vuckovich

Bill Dahlen

WILLIAM FREDERICK DAHLEN
B: 01/05/1870 D: 12/05/1950
BR

Year	Tm	Lg	Tot	H	A	Men-On 0	1	2	3	One-Game 2	3	4	LO	XN	IP	PH	RHP	LHP
1891	CHI	NL	9	4	5	5	4	0	0	0	0	0	0	0	0	0	7	1

Bill Dahlen *continued*

Year	Tm	Lg	Tot	H	A	Men-On 0	1	2	3	One-Game 2	3	4	LO	XN	IP	PH	RHP	LHP
1892	CHI	NL	5	3	2	0	4	1	0	0	0	0	0	0	1	0	4	0
1893	CHI	NL	5	2	3	4	1	0	0	0	0	0	0	0	0	0	5	0
1894	CHI	NL	15	6	9	7	5	3	0	1	0	0	0	0	0	0	11	0
1895	CHI	NL	7	6	1	4	1	2	0	1	0	0	0	0	0	0	4	2
1896	CHI	NL	9	3	6	4	2	3	0	0	0	0	0	0	0	0	9	0
1897	CHI	NL	6	1	5	4	2	0	0	0	0	0	0	0	0	0	4	1
1898	CHI	NL	1	1	0	0	1	0	0	0	0	0	0	0	1	0	1	0
1899	BRO	NL	4	3	1	1	0	3	0	0	0	0	0	0	0	0	3	1
1900	BRO	NL	1	1	0	0	1	0	0	0	0	0	0	0	0	0	0	1
1901	BRO	NL	4	1	3	3	0	1	0	0	0	0	0	0	0	0	4	0
1902	BRO	NL	2	0	2	0	1	1	0	0	0	0	0	0	1	0	2	0
1903	BRO	NL	1	1	0	0	1	0	0	0	0	0	0	0	0	0	1	0
1904	NY	NL	2	1	1	1	0	0	1	0	0	0	0	0	1	0	1	1
1905	NY	NL	7	6	1	3	4	0	0	1	0	0	0	0	1	0	7	0
1906	NY	NL	1	0	1	1	0	0	0	0	0	0	0	0	0	0	0	1
1908	BOS	NL	3	3	0	2	1	0	0	0	0	0	0	0	0	0	2	1
1909	BOS	NL	2	2	0	1	0	1	0	0	0	0	0	0	0	0	1	1
Total			84	44	40	40	28	15	1	3	0	0	0	0	5	0	66	9

Rank among batters: 617 • *Top target (5 home runs)*: Kid Nichols • *Number of pitchers victimized*: 65 • *Total ballparks homered in*: 18 • *First HR*: 04/28/1891 off Jesse Duryea

Babe Dahlgren

ELLSWORTH TENNEY DAHLGREN
B: 06/15/1912
BR

Year	Tm	Lg	Tot	H	A	Men-On 0	1	2	3	One-Game 2	3	4	LO	XN	IP	PH	RHP	LHP
1935	BOS	AL	9	4	5	4	5	0	0	1	0	0	0	0	0	0	7	2
1936	BOS	AL	1	0	1	0	1	0	0	0	0	0	0	0	0	0	1	0
1939	NY	AL	15	2	13	4	7	3	1	3	0	0	0	0	2	0	11	4
1940	NY	AL	12	7	5	6	2	4	0	2	0	0	0	0	0	0	7	5
1941	BOS	NL	7	2	5	3	2	2	0	0	0	0	0	2	0	0	7	0
	CHI	NL	16	13	3	14	2	0	0	1	0	0	0	0	0	0	10	6
	Total		23	15	8	17	4	2	0	1	0	0	0	2	0	0	17	6
1943	PHI	NL	5	1	4	3	2	0	0	0	0	0	0	1	0	0	3	2
1944	PIT	NL	12	1	11	9	2	1	0	1	0	0	0	0	1	0	8	4
1945	PIT	NL	5	1	4	1	3	1	0	0	0	0	0	1	0	0	1	4
Total			82	31	51	44	26	11	1	8	0	0	0	4	3	0	55	27

Rank among batters: 637 • *Top target (4 home runs)*: Nels Potter • *Number of pitchers victimized*: 65 • *Total ballparks homered in*: 14 • *First HR*: 05/10/1935 off George Earnshaw • *World Series HR*—1

Bill Dailey

WILLIAM GARLAND DAILEY
B: 03/13/1935
BR

Year	Tm	Lg	Tot	H	A	Men-On 0	1	2	3	One-Game 2	3	4	LO	XN	IP	PH	RHP	LHP
1963	MIN	AL	1	0	1	0	0	1	0	0	0	0	0	0	0	0	1	0

Rank among batters: 4,707 • *Total ballparks homered in*: 1 • *First HR*: 08/07/1963 off Julio Navarro

Con Daily

CORNELIUS F. DAILY
B: 09/11/1864 D: 06/14/1928
BL

Year	Tm	Lg	Tot	H	A	Men-On 0	1	2	3	One-Game 2	3	4	LO	XN	IP	PH	RHP	LHP
1893	BRO	NL	1	0	1	1	0	0	0	0	0	0	0	0	0	0	1	0
1895	BRO	NL	1	1	0	1	0	0	0	0	0	0	0	0	0	0	1	0
Total			2	1	1	2	0	0	0	0	0	0	0	0	0	0	2	0

Rank among batters: 4,129 • *Total ballparks homered in*: 2 • *First HR*: 07/05/1893 off Cy Young

Ed Daily

EDWARD M. DAILY
B: 09/07/1862 D: 10/21/1891
BR

Year	Tm	Lg	Tot	H	A	Men-On 0	1	2	3	One-Game 2	3	4	LO	XN	IP	PH	RHP	LHP
1885	PHI	NL	1	1	0	0	0	1	0	0	0	0	0	0	0	0	1	0
1886	PHI	NL	4	1	3	3	0	0	1	0	0	0	0	0	1	0	3	1
1887	PHI	NL	1	1	0	0	0	1	0	0	0	0	0	0	0	0	1	0
	WAS	NL	2	2	0	0	1	1	0	0	0	0	0	0	0	0	2	0
	Total		3	3	0	0	1	2	0	0	0	0	0	0	0	0	3	0

Ed Daily *continued*

Year	Tm	Lg	Tot	H	A	Men-On 0	1	2	3	One-Game 2	3	4	LO	XN	IP	PH	RHP	LHP
1888	WAS	NL	7	5	2	4	2	0	1	0	0	0	0	0	0	0	7	0
1889	COL	AA	3	1	2	1	0	2	0	0	0	0	0	0	0	0	3	0
1890	BRO	AA	1	0	1	0	1	0	0	0	0	0	0	0	0	0	1	0
Total			19	11	8	8	4	5	2	0	0	0	0	0	1	0	18	1

Rank among batters: 1,861 • *Top target (3 home runs)*: John Clarkson • *Number of pitchers victimized*: 14 • *Total ballparks homered in*: 10 • *First HR*: 05/06/1885 off Jim McCormick

Mark Dalesandro

MARK ANTHONY DALESANDRO
B: 05/14/1968
BR

Year	Tm	Lg	Tot	H	A	Men-On 0	1	2	3	One-Game 2	3	4	LO	XN	IP	PH	RHP	LHP
1994	CAL	AL	1	1	0	1	0	0	0	0	0	0	0	0	0	0	0	1

Rank among batters: 4,707 • *Total ballparks homered in*: 1 • *First HR*: 07/24/1994 off Jim Abbott

Bill Daley

WILLIAM DALEY
B: 06/27/1868 D: 05/04/1922

Year	Tm	Lg	Tot	H	A	Men-On 0	1	2	3	One-Game 2	3	4	LO	XN	IP	PH	RHP	LHP
1890	BOS	PL	2	2	0	1	0	1	0	0	0	0	0	0	0	0	2	0

Rank among batters: 4,129 • *Total ballparks homered in*: 1 • *First HR*: 04/29/1890 off Hank O'Day

John Daley

JOHN FRANCIS DALEY
B: 05/25/1887 D: 08/31/1988
BR

Year	Tm	Lg	Tot	H	A	Men-On 0	1	2	3	One-Game 2	3	4	LO	XN	IP	PH	RHP	LHP
1912	STL	AL	1	0	1	1	0	0	0	0	0	0	0	0	1	0	1	0

Rank among batters: 4,707 • *Total ballparks homered in*: 1 • *First HR*: 08/15/1912 off Hugh Bedient

Jud Daley

JUDSON LAWRENCE DALEY
B: 03/14/1884 D: 01/26/1967
BL

Year	Tm	Lg	Tot	H	A	Men-On 0	1	2	3	One-Game 2	3	4	LO	XN	IP	PH	RHP	LHP
1912	BRO	NL	1	1	0	1	0	0	0	0	0	0	0	0	0	0	1	0

Rank among batters: 4,707 • *Total ballparks homered in*: 1 • *First HR*: 06/19/1912 off Cliff Curtis

Pete Daley

PETER HARVEY DALEY
B: 01/14/1930
BR

Year	Tm	Lg	Tot	H	A	Men-On 0	1	2	3	One-Game 2	3	4	LO	XN	IP	PH	RHP	LHP
1956	BOS	AL	5	2	3	3	1	0	1	0	0	0	0	0	0	0	4	1
1957	BOS	AL	3	1	2	1	2	0	0	0	0	0	0	1	0	0	2	1
1958	BOS	AL	2	1	1	1	0	1	0	0	0	0	0	0	0	0	1	1
1959	BOS	AL	1	1	0	1	0	0	0	0	0	0	0	0	0	0	1	0
1960	KC	AL	5	3	2	1	2	2	0	0	0	0	0	1	0	1	4	1
1961	WAS	AL	2	0	2	1	1	0	0	0	0	0	0	0	0	0	2	0
Total			18	8	10	8	6	3	1	0	0	0	0	2	0	1	14	4

Rank among batters: 1,914 • *Total ballparks homered in*: 5 • *First HR*: 04/21/1956 off Jim Konstanty

Dom Dallessandro

NICHOLAS DOMINIC DALLESSANDRO
B: 10/03/1913 D: 04/29/1988
BL

Year	Tm	Lg	Tot	H	A	Men-On 0	1	2	3	One-Game 2	3	4	LO	XN	IP	PH	RHP	LHP
1940	CHI	NL	1	1	0	0	0	1	0	0	0	0	0	0	0	0	1	0
1941	CHI	NL	6	0	6	3	0	1	2	0	0	0	0	0	0	0	4	2
1942	CHI	NL	4	1	3	3	0	0	1	1	0	0	0	0	0	1	2	2
1943	CHI	NL	1	0	1	1	0	0	0	0	0	0	0	0	0	0	1	0
1944	CHI	NL	8	4	4	3	3	2	0	0	0	0	0	0	0	0	8	0
1946	CHI	NL	1	1	0	0	1	0	0	0	0	0	0	0	0	0	1	0
1947	CHI	NL	1	1	0	1	0	0	0	0	0	0	0	0	0	0	1	0
Total			22	8	14	11	4	4	3	1	0	0	0	0	0	1	18	4

Rank among batters: 1,719 • Top target (2 home runs): Jim Tobin, Carl Hubbell, Frank Seward, Curt Davis • *Number of pitchers victimized*: 18 • *Total ballparks homered in*: 6 • *First HR*: 08/24/1940 off Curt Davis

Abner Dalrymple

ABNER FRANK DALRYMPLE
B: 09/09/1857 D: 01/25/1939
BL

Year	Tm	Lg	Tot	H	A	Men-On 0	1	2	3	One-Game 2	3	4	LO	XN	IP	PH	RHP	LHP
1881	CHI	NL	1	1	0	0	1	0	0	0	0	0	0	0	0	0	1	0
1882	CHI	NL	1	1	0	1	0	0	0	0	0	0	0	0	0	0	1	0
1883	CHI	NL	2	1	1	2	0	0	0	0	0	0	0	0	0	0	2	0
1884	CHI	NL	22	18	4	8	7	4	0	1	0	0	4	0	1	0	19	1
1885	CHI	NL	11	10	1	8	3	0	0	0	0	0	3	0	0	0	10	1
1886	CHI	NL	3	1	2	2	1	0	0	0	0	0	1	0	0	0	1	0
1887	PIT	NL	2	0	2	2	0	0	0	1	0	0	0	1	0	0	2	0
1891	MIL	AA	1	1	0	0	0	0	0	0	0	0	0	0	0	0	0	0
Total			43	33	10	23	12	4	0	2	0	0	8	1	1	0	36	2

Rank among batters: 1,116 • *Top target (6 home runs)*: Jim Whitney • *Number of pitchers victimized*: 24 • *Total ballparks homered in*: 10 • *First HR*: 07/02/1881 off Tim Keefe • *Hit for Cycle*—vs WAS: 09/12/1891 • *World Series HR*—1

Clay Dalrymple

CLAYTON ERROL DALRYMPLE
B: 12/03/1936
BL

Year	Tm	Lg	Tot	H	A	Men-On 0	1	2	3	One-Game 2	3	4	LO	XN	IP	PH	RHP	LHP
1960	PHI	NL	4	2	2	1	2	1	0	0	0	0	0	0	0	0	3	1
1961	PHI	NL	5	2	3	2	0	3	0	0	0	0	0	0	0	0	4	1
1962	PHI	NL	11	4	7	8	3	0	0	0	0	0	0	0	0	0	11	0
1963	PHI	NL	10	4	6	7	2	1	0	0	0	0	0	0	0	0	9	1
1964	PHI	NL	6	3	3	3	3	0	0	0	0	0	0	1	0	0	6	0
1965	PHI	NL	4	3	1	3	1	0	0	0	0	0	0	0	0	0	3	1
1966	PHI	NL	4	2	2	2	2	0	0	0	0	0	0	0	0	0	3	1
1967	PHI	NL	3	1	2	3	0	0	0	0	0	0	0	0	0	0	3	0
1968	PHI	NL	3	2	1	1	2	0	0	0	0	0	0	0	0	0	3	0
1969	BAL	AL	3	1	2	2	1	0	0	0	0	0	0	0	0	0	3	0
1970	BAL	AL	1	1	0	1	0	0	0	0	0	0	0	0	0	0	1	0
1971	BAL	AL	1	1	0	1	0	0	0	0	0	0	0	0	0	0	1	0
Total			55	26	29	34	16	5	0	0	0	0	0	1	0	0	50	5

Rank among batters: 926 • *Top target (3 home runs)*: John Tsitouris, Ernie Broglio, Juan Marichal • *Number of pitchers victimized*: 47 • *Total ballparks homered in*: 13 • *First HR*: 05/30/1960 off Joe Nuxhall

Jack Dalton

TALBOT PERCY DALTON
B: 07/03/1885
BR

Year	Tm	Lg	Tot	H	A	Men-On 0	1	2	3	One-Game 2	3	4	LO	XN	IP	PH	RHP	LHP
1910	BRO	NL	1	1	0	1	0	0	0	0	0	0	0	0	0	0	1	0
1914	BRO	NL	1	0	1	1	0	0	0	0	0	0	0	0	0	0	0	1
1915	BUF	FL	2	2	0	1	0	1	0	0	0	0	0	0	1	0	1	1
Total			4	3	1	3	0	1	0	0	0	0	0	0	1	0	2	2

Rank among batters: 3,427 • *Total ballparks homered in*: 3 • *First HR*: 09/13/1910 off Jack Rowan

Tom Daly

THOMAS PETER DALY
B: 02/07/1866 D: 10/29/1938
BB

Year	Tm	Lg	Tot	H	A	Men-On 0	1	2	3	One-Game 2	3	4	LO	XN	IP	PH	RHP	LHP
1887	CHI	NL	2	0	2	1	1	0	0	1	0	0	0	0	0	0	0	2
1889	WAS	NL	1	0	1	0	1	0	0	0	0	0	0	0	0	0	1	0
1890	BRO	NL	5	2	3	2	2	1	0	0	0	0	0	0	0	0	5	0
1891	BRO	NL	2	2	0	1	1	0	0	0	0	0	0	0	0	0	2	0
1892	BRO	NL	4	1	3	3	1	0	0	0	0	0	0	0	0	1	4	0
1893	BRO	NL	8	4	4	4	1	3	0	0	0	0	0	0	2	0	7	0
1894	BRO	NL	8	5	3	2	4	2	0	1	0	0	1	0	2	0	6	1
1895	BRO	NL	2	2	0	1	1	0	0	0	0	0	0	0	0	0	2	0
1896	BRO	NL	3	1	2	2	0	1	0	0	0	0	0	0	0	0	1	2
1899	BRO	NL	5	1	4	3	1	1	0	0	0	0	0	0	1	0	3	2
1900	BRO	NL	4	2	2	1	2	1	0	0	0	0	0	0	0	0	3	1
1901	BRO	NL	3	0	3	1	2	0	0	0	0	0	0	0	0	0	2	1
1902	CHI	AL	1	0	1	0	0	1	0	0	0	0	0	0	0	0	1	0
1903	CIN	NL	1	0	1	1	0	0	0	0	0	0	0	0	0	0	1	0
Total			49	20	29	22	17	10	0	2	0	0	1	0	5	1	38	9

Rank among batters: 1,008 • *Top target (3 home runs)*: Ted Breitenstein, Vic Willis • *Number of pitchers victimized*: 38 • *Total ballparks homered in*: 16 • *First HR*: 05/20/1887 off Dan Casey

Year	Tm	Lg	Tot	H	A	Men-On 0	1	2	3	One-Game 2	3	4	LO	XN	IP	PH	RHP	LHP

Johnny Damon

JOHNNY DAVID DAMON
B: 11/05/1973
BL

Year	Tm	Lg	Tot	H	A	Men-On 0	1	2	3	One-Game 2	3	4	LO	XN	IP	PH	RHP	LHP
1995	KC	AL	3	1	2	3	0	0	0	0	0	0	1	0	0	0	3	0

Rank among batters: 3,735 • *Total ballparks homered in*: 3 • *First HR*: 08/31/1995 off Mike Fetters

Bennie Daniels

BENNIE DANIELS
B: 06/17/1932
BL

Year	Tm	Lg	Tot	H	A	Men-On 0	1	2	3	One-Game 2	3	4	LO	XN	IP	PH	RHP	LHP
1959	PIT	NL	1	0	1	0	1	0	0	0	0	0	0	0	0	0	1	0
1961	WAS	AL	2	0	2	2	0	0	0	0	0	0	0	0	0	0	1	1
1962	WAS	AL	1	0	1	1	0	0	0	0	0	0	0	0	0	0	1	0
1964	WAS	AL	1	1	0	0	1	0	0	0	0	0	0	0	0	0	1	0
Total			5	1	4	3	2	0	0	0	0	0	0	0	0	0	4	1

Rank among batters: 3,191 • *Total ballparks homered in*: 5 • *First HR*: 07/28/1959 off Larry Sherry

Bert Daniels

BERNARD ELMER DANIELS
B: 10/31/1882 D: 06/06/1958
BR

Year	Tm	Lg	Tot	H	A	Men-On 0	1	2	3	One-Game 2	3	4	LO	XN	IP	PH	RHP	LHP
1910	NY	AL	1	1	0	1	0	0	0	0	0	0	1	0	1	0	1	0
1911	NY	AL	2	2	0	1	1	0	0	0	0	0	1	0	0	0	1	1
1912	NY	AL	2	2	0	1	0	1	0	0	0	0	1	0	1	0	2	0
Total			5	5	0	3	1	1	0	0	0	0	3	0	2	0	4	1

Rank among batters: 3,191 • *Top target (2 home runs)*: Jim Scott • *Number of pitchers victimized*: 4 • *Total ballparks homered in*: 1 • *First HR*: 07/08/1910 off Jim Scott • *Hit for Cycle*—vs CHI: 07/25/1912

Jack Daniels

HAROLD JACK DANIELS
B: 12/21/1927
BL

Year	Tm	Lg	Tot	H	A	Men-On 0	1	2	3	One-Game 2	3	4	LO	XN	IP	PH	RHP	LHP
1952	BOS	NL	2	2	0	0	2	0	0	0	0	0	0	0	0	0	2	0

Rank among batters: 4,129 • *Total ballparks homered in*: 1 • *First HR*: 07/27/1952 off Cal Hogue

Kal Daniels

KALVOSKI DANIELS
B: 08/20/1963
BL

Year	Tm	Lg	Tot	H	A	Men-On 0	1	2	3	One-Game 2	3	4	LO	XN	IP	PH	RHP	LHP
1986	CIN	NL	6	3	3	4	2	0	0	1	0	0	1	1	0	0	6	0
1987	CIN	NL	26	13	13	21	5	0	0	2	0	0	8	0	0	0	25	1
1988	CIN	NL	18	12	6	14	2	2	0	3	0	0	0	0	0	0	15	3
1989	CIN	NL	2	1	1	2	0	0	0	0	0	0	1	0	0	0	1	1
	LA	NL	2	1	1	1	1	0	0	0	0	0	0	0	0	0	2	0
	Total		4	2	2	3	1	0	0	0	0	0	1	0	0	0	3	1
1990	LA	NL	27	12	15	11	8	5	3	3	0	0	0	2	0	0	21	6
1991	LA	NL	17	12	5	6	6	4	1	0	0	0	0	1	0	0	12	5
1992	LA	NL	2	1	1	1	1	0	0	0	0	0	0	0	0	0	1	1
	CHI	NL	4	2	2	2	1	0	1	0	0	0	0	0	0	0	4	0
	Total		6	3	3	3	2	0	1	0	0	0	0	0	0	0	5	1
Total			104	57	47	62	26	11	5	9	0	0	10	4	0	0	87	17

Rank among batters: 469 • *Top target (4 home runs)*: Orel Hershiser, Mike Scott • *Number of pitchers victimized*: 77 • *Total ballparks homered in*: 12 • *First HR*: 04/13/1986 off Rich Gossage

Law Daniels

LAWRENCE LONG DANIELS
B: 07/14/1862 D: 01/07/1929
BR

Year	Tm	Lg	Tot	H	A	Men-On 0	1	2	3	One-Game 2	3	4	LO	XN	IP	PH	RHP	LHP
1888	KC	AA	2	2	0	0	1	1	0	0	0	0	0	0	1	0	1	1

Rank among batters: 4,129 • *Total ballparks homered in*: 1 • *First HR*: 04/25/1888 off Toad Ramsey

Harry Danning

HARRY DANNING
B: 09/06/1911
BR

Year	Tm	Lg	Tot	H	A	Men-On 0	1	2	3	One-Game 2	3	4	LO	XN	IP	PH	RHP	LHP
1934	NY	NL	1	0	1	1	0	0	0	0	0	0	0	0	0	0	1	0

Harry Danning *continued*

Year	Tm	Lg	Tot	H	A	Men-On 0	1	2	3	One-Game 2	3	4	LO	XN	IP	PH	RHP	LHP
1935	NY	NL	2	0	2	0	2	0	0	0	0	0	0	0	0	0	1	1
1937	NY	NL	8	7	1	4	3	1	0	0	0	0	0	0	0	1	5	3
1938	NY	NL	9	8	1	6	0	2	1	1	0	0	0	1	0	0	7	2
1939	NY	NL	16	12	4	13	3	0	0	0	0	0	0	0	0	0	14	2
1940	NY	NL	13	9	4	4	6	3	0	2	0	0	0	0	1	0	12	1
1941	NY	NL	7	6	1	2	4	0	1	0	0	0	0	0	0	0	5	2
1942	NY	NL	1	1	0	1	0	0	0	0	0	0	0	0	0	0	1	0
Total			57	43	14	31	18	6	2	3	0	0	0	1	1	1	46	11

Rank among batters: 902 • *Top target (3 home runs)*: Hugh Mulcahy, Lon Warneke, Kirby Higbe • *Number of pitchers victimized*: 45 • *Total ballparks homered in*: 7 • *First HR*: 08/23/1934 off Paul Dean • *Hit for Cycle*—vs PIT: 06/15/1940

Cliff Dapper

CLIFFORD ROLAND DAPPER
B: 01/02/1920
BR

Year	Tm	Lg	Tot	H	A	Men-On 0	1	2	3	One-Game 2	3	4	LO	XN	IP	PH	RHP	LHP
1942	BRO	NL	1	0	1	1	0	0	0	0	0	0	0	0	0	0	1	0

Rank among batters: 4,707 • *Total ballparks homered in*: 1 • *First HR*: 04/26/1942 off Isaac Pearson

Al Dark

ALVIN RALPH DARK
B: 01/07/1922
BR

Year	Tm	Lg	Tot	H	A	Men-On 0	1	2	3	One-Game 2	3	4	LO	XN	IP	PH	RHP	LHP
1948	BOS	NL	3	1	2	2	1	0	0	0	0	0	0	0	0	0	3	0
1949	BOS	NL	3	0	3	2	1	0	0	0	0	0	0	0	1	0	1	2
1950	NY	NL	16	11	5	13	2	1	0	2	0	0	0	1	0	0	5	11
1951	NY	NL	14	10	4	10	1	1	2	1	0	0	0	0	1	0	4	10
1952	NY	NL	14	13	1	7	7	0	0	0	0	0	0	0	0	0	8	6
1953	NY	NL	23	16	7	11	10	2	0	0	0	0	0	0	0	0	16	7
1954	NY	NL	20	15	5	14	4	1	1	1	0	0	0	0	1	0	15	5
1955	NY	NL	9	8	1	3	4	2	0	0	0	0	0	0	0	0	6	3
1956	NY	NL	2	2	0	2	0	0	0	0	0	0	0	0	0	0	1	1
	STL	NL	4	1	3	3	1	0	0	0	0	0	0	0	0	0	1	3
	Total		6	3	3	5	1	0	0	0	0	0	0	0	0	0	2	4
1957	STL	NL	4	1	3	4	0	0	0	0	0	0	0	0	0	0	4	0
1958	STL	NL	1	0	1	1	0	0	0	0	0	0	0	0	0	0	0	1
	CHI	NL	3	0	3	3	0	0	0	0	0	0	0	0	0	0	1	2
	Total		4	0	4	4	0	0	0	0	0	0	0	0	0	0	1	3
1959	CHI	NL	6	5	1	3	1	1	1	0	0	0	0	1	0	0	2	4
1960	PHI	NL	3	1	2	2	1	0	0	0	0	0	0	1	0	0	1	2
	MIL	NL	1	0	1	1	0	0	0	0	0	0	0	0	0	0	1	0
	Total		4	1	3	3	1	0	0	0	0	0	0	1	0	0	2	2
Total			126	84	42	81	33	8	4	4	0	0	0	3	3	0	69	57

Rank among batters: 360 • *Top target (7 home runs)*: Preacher Roe • *Number of pitchers victimized*: 68 • *Total ballparks homered in*: 11 • *First HR*: 06/25/1948 off Elmer Singleton • *World Series HR*—1

Dell Darling

CONRAD DARLING
B: 12/21/1861 D: 11/20/1904
BR

Year	Tm	Lg	Tot	H	A	Men-On 0	1	2	3	One-Game 2	3	4	LO	XN	IP	PH	RHP	LHP
1887	CHI	NL	3	3	0	3	0	0	0	0	0	0	0	0	0	0	1	1
1888	CHI	NL	2	1	1	2	0	0	0	0	0	0	0	0	1	0	2	0
1890	CHI	PL	2	1	1	0	1	1	0	0	0	0	0	0	0	0	2	0
Total			7	5	2	5	1	1	0	0	0	0	0	0	1	0	5	1

Rank among batters: 2,834 • *Total ballparks homered in*: 4 • *First HR*: 05/11/1887 off Larry Corcoran

Ron Darling

RONALD MAURICE DARLING
B: 08/19/1960
BR

Year	Tm	Lg	Tot	H	A	Men-On 0	1	2	3	One-Game 2	3	4	LO	XN	IP	PH	RHP	LHP
1989	NY	NL	2	1	1	1	0	1	0	0	0	0	0	0	0	0	1	1

Rank among batters: 4,129 • *Total ballparks homered in*: 2 • *First HR*: 06/24/1989 off Floyd Youmans

Bobby Darwin

ARTHUR BOBBY LEE DARWIN
B: 02/16/1943
BR

Year	Tm	Lg	Tot	H	A	Men-On 0	Men-On 1	Men-On 2	Men-On 3	One-Game 2	One-Game 3	One-Game 4	LO	XN	IP	PH	RHP	LHP
1971	LA	NL	1	1	0	0	0	1	0	0	0	0	0	0	0	1	0	1
1972	MIN	AL	22	11	11	9	7	5	1	1	0	0	0	0	0	0	15	7
1973	MIN	AL	18	7	11	7	8	2	1	1	0	0	0	1	0	0	13	5
1974	MIN	AL	25	14	11	12	7	5	1	4	0	0	0	0	0	0	13	12
1975	MIN	AL	5	2	3	3	2	0	0	0	0	0	0	0	0	0	4	1
	MIL	AL	8	2	6	3	4	1	0	0	0	0	0	0	0	2	5	3
	Total		13	4	9	6	6	1	0	0	0	0	0	0	0	2	9	4
1976	MIL	AL	1	0	1	0	1	0	0	0	0	0	0	0	0	0	1	0
	BOS	AL	3	1	2	1	0	1	1	0	0	0	0	0	0	1	0	3
	Total		4	1	3	1	1	1	1	0	0	0	0	0	0	1	1	3
Total			83	38	45	35	29	15	4	6	0	0	0	1	0	4	51	32

Rank among batters: 628 • *Top target (3 home runs)*: Fritz Peterson, Paul Lindblad, Catfish Hunter • *Number of pitchers victimized*: 61 • *Total ballparks homered in*: 13 • *First HR*: 07/07/1971 off Juan Pizarro

Danny Darwin

DANIEL WAYNE DARWIN
B: 10/25/1955
BR

Year	Tm	Lg	Tot	H	A	Men-On 0	Men-On 1	Men-On 2	Men-On 3	One-Game 2	One-Game 3	One-Game 4	LO	XN	IP	PH	RHP	LHP
1988	HOU	NL	1	0	1	1	0	0	0	0	0	0	0	0	0	0	0	1

Rank among batters: 4,707 • *Total ballparks homered in*: 1 • *First HR*: 09/15/1988 off Norm Charlton

Doug Dascenzo

DOUGLAS CRAIG DASCENZO
B: 06/30/1964
BB

Year	Tm	Lg	Tot	H	A	Men-On 0	Men-On 1	Men-On 2	Men-On 3	One-Game 2	One-Game 3	One-Game 4	LO	XN	IP	PH	RHP	LHP
1989	CHI	NL	1	0	1	0	1	0	0	0	0	0	0	0	0	0	1	0
1990	CHI	NL	1	1	0	0	1	0	0	0	0	0	0	0	0	0	0	1
1991	CHI	NL	1	0	1	1	0	0	0	0	0	0	0	0	0	0	1	0
1993	TEX	AL	2	0	2	2	0	0	0	0	0	0	0	0	0	0	2	0
Total			5	1	4	3	2	0	0	0	0	0	0	0	0	0	4	1

Rank among batters: 3,191 • *Total ballparks homered in*: 5 • *First HR*: 09/07/1989 off Ken Howell

Jake Daubert

JACOB ELLSWORTH DAUBERT
B: 04/17/1884 D: 10/09/1924
BL

Year	Tm	Lg	Tot	H	A	Men-On 0	Men-On 1	Men-On 2	Men-On 3	One-Game 2	One-Game 3	One-Game 4	LO	XN	IP	PH	RHP	LHP
1910	BRO	NL	8	4	4	5	1	2	0	0	0	0	0	2	7	0	5	3
1911	BRO	NL	5	3	2	1	3	1	0	0	0	0	0	0	3	0	5	0
1912	BRO	NL	3	2	1	1	2	0	0	0	0	0	0	0	2	0	3	0
1913	BRO	NL	2	2	0	1	1	0	0	0	0	0	0	0	2	0	2	0
1914	BRO	NL	6	2	4	3	3	0	0	0	0	0	0	0	3	0	5	1
1915	BRO	NL	2	1	1	1	1	0	0	0	0	0	0	0	2	0	1	1
1916	BRO	NL	3	3	0	3	0	0	0	0	0	0	0	0	3	0	2	1
1917	BRO	NL	2	0	2	1	1	0	0	0	0	0	0	0	1	0	2	0
1918	BRO	NL	2	1	1	2	0	0	0	0	0	0	0	0	2	0	2	0
1919	CIN	NL	2	2	0	2	0	0	0	0	0	0	0	0	2	0	0	2
1920	CIN	NL	4	1	3	2	1	1	0	0	0	0	0	1	2	0	3	1
1921	CIN	NL	2	1	1	0	1	1	0	0	0	0	0	0	2	0	2	0
1922	CIN	NL	12	4	8	6	4	2	0	0	0	0	0	0	2	0	12	0
1923	CIN	NL	2	0	2	0	2	0	0	0	0	0	0	0	0	0	2	0
1924	CIN	NL	1	0	1	1	0	0	0	0	0	0	0	0	0	0	0	1
Total			56	26	30	29	20	7	0	0	0	0	0	3	33	0	46	10

Rank among batters: 913 • *Top target (4 home runs)*: Burleigh Grimes • *Number of pitchers victimized*: 48 • *Total ballparks homered in*: 9 • *First HR*: 05/25/1910 off Slim Sallee

Rich Dauer

RICHARD FREMONT DAUER
B: 07/27/1952
BR

Year	Tm	Lg	Tot	H	A	Men-On 0	Men-On 1	Men-On 2	Men-On 3	One-Game 2	One-Game 3	One-Game 4	LO	XN	IP	PH	RHP	LHP
1977	BAL	AL	5	2	3	5	0	0	0	0	0	0	0	0	0	0	2	3
1978	BAL	AL	6	3	3	6	0	0	0	0	0	0	0	0	0	0	3	3
1979	BAL	AL	9	1	8	6	3	0	0	0	0	0	0	0	0	0	5	4

Year	Tm	Lg	Tot	H	A	Men-On 0	Men-On 1	Men-On 2	Men-On 3	One-Game 2	One-Game 3	One-Game 4	LO	XN	IP	PH	RHP	LHP

Rich Dauer *continued*

Year	Tm	Lg	Tot	H	A	0	1	2	3	2	3	4	LO	XN	IP	PH	RHP	LHP
1980	BAL	AL	2	1	1	2	0	0	0	0	0	0	0	0	0	0	2	0
1981	BAL	AL	4	0	4	1	2	1	0	1	0	0	0	0	0	0	3	1
1982	BAL	AL	8	4	4	2	5	1	0	0	0	0	0	1	0	0	4	4
1983	BAL	AL	5	2	3	3	2	0	0	0	0	0	0	0	0	0	3	2
1984	BAL	AL	2	1	1	1	0	1	0	0	0	0	0	0	0	0	2	0
1985	BAL	AL	2	1	1	2	0	0	0	0	0	0	0	0	0	0	0	2
Total			43	15	28	28	12	3	0	1	0	0	0	1	0	0	24	19

Rank among batters: 1,116 • Top target (2 home runs): Jerry Garvin, Rick Waits, Jerry Augustine, Britt Burns • *Number of pitchers victimized*: 39 • *Total ballparks homered in*: 14 • *First HR*: 06/09/1977 off Bill Lee • *World Series HR*—1

Jack Daugherty

JOHN MICHAEL DAUGHERTY
B: 07/03/1960
BB

Year	Tm	Lg	Tot	H	A	0	1	2	3	2	3	4	LO	XN	IP	PH	RHP	LHP
1989	TEX	AL	1	1	0	1	0	0	0	0	0	0	0	0	0	0	0	1
1990	TEX	AL	6	5	1	2	4	0	0	1	0	0	0	0	0	0	6	0
1991	TEX	AL	1	0	1	1	0	0	0	0	0	0	0	0	0	0	1	0
1993	CIN	NL	2	2	0	1	0	1	0	0	0	0	0	0	0	0	2	0
Total			10	8	2	5	4	1	0	1	0	0	0	0	0	0	9	1

Rank among batters: 2,500 • *Total ballparks homered in*: 4 • *First HR*: 08/11/1989 off Frank Tanana

Darren Daulton

DARREN ARTHUR DAULTON
B: 01/03/1962
BL

Year	Tm	Lg	Tot	H	A	0	1	2	3	2	3	4	LO	XN	IP	PH	RHP	LHP
1985	PHI	NL	4	0	4	3	0	1	0	1	0	0	0	0	0	0	4	0
1986	PHI	NL	8	4	4	4	2	2	0	0	0	0	0	0	0	0	8	0
1987	PHI	NL	3	1	2	2	0	1	0	0	0	0	0	1	0	0	3	0
1988	PHI	NL	1	0	1	1	0	0	0	0	0	0	0	0	0	0	1	0
1989	PHI	NL	8	2	6	2	4	2	0	0	0	0	0	0	0	0	7	1
1990	PHI	NL	12	5	7	7	5	0	0	0	0	0	0	0	0	0	11	1
1991	PHI	NL	12	8	4	10	1	0	1	2	0	0	0	0	0	0	10	2
1992	PHI	NL	27	17	10	10	12	3	2	1	0	0	0	0	0	0	16	11
1993	PHI	NL	24	10	14	11	7	4	2	4	0	0	0	0	0	0	16	8
1994	PHI	NL	15	7	8	7	4	4	0	0	0	0	0	0	0	0	11	4
1995	PHI	NL	9	7	2	3	5	1	0	1	0	0	0	0	0	0	7	2
Total			123	61	62	60	40	18	5	9	0	0	0	1	0	0	94	29

Rank among batters: 372 • *Top target (4 home runs)*: David Cone, Jack Armstrong • *Number of pitchers victimized*: 92 • *Total ballparks homered in*: 14 • *First HR*: 08/13/1985 off Rick Aguilera • *World Series HR*—1; *LCS HR*—1

Hooks Dauss

GEORGE AUGUST DAUSS
B: 09/22/1889 D: 07/27/1963
BR

Year	Tm	Lg	Tot	H	A	0	1	2	3	2	3	4	LO	XN	IP	PH	RHP	LHP
1914	DET	AL	1	1	0	1	0	0	0	0	0	0	0	0	0	0	1	0
1916	DET	AL	1	1	0	0	1	0	0	0	0	0	0	0	0	0	1	0
1921	DET	AL	1	0	1	1	0	0	0	0	0	0	0	0	0	0	1	0
1922	DET	AL	1	0	1	1	0	0	0	0	0	0	0	0	0	0	1	0
1925	DET	AL	1	1	0	1	0	0	0	0	0	0	0	0	0	0	0	1
1926	DET	AL	1	1	0	1	0	0	0	0	0	0	0	0	0	0	1	0
Total			6	4	2	5	1	0	0	0	0	0	0	0	0	0	5	1

Rank among batters: 2,988 • *Total ballparks homered in*: 3 • *First HR*: 08/04/1914 off Jack Warhop

Vic Davalillo

VICTOR JOSE (ROMERO) DAVALILLO
B: 07/31/1936
BL

Year	Tm	Lg	Tot	H	A	0	1	2	3	2	3	4	LO	XN	IP	PH	RHP	LHP
1963	CLE	AL	7	2	5	1	6	0	0	0	0	0	0	0	0	0	4	3
1964	CLE	AL	6	2	4	4	2	0	0	0	0	0	0	0	1	0	4	2
1965	CLE	AL	5	1	4	3	1	1	0	1	0	0	0	0	0	0	5	0
1966	CLE	AL	3	1	2	2	1	0	0	0	0	0	0	0	0	1	2	1
1967	CLE	AL	2	1	1	1	1	0	0	0	0	0	0	0	0	0	2	0
1968	CLE	AL	2	1	1	1	0	1	0	0	0	0	0	0	0	0	2	0

Vic Davalillo *continued*

Year	Tm	Lg	Tot	H	A	Men-On 0	1	2	3	One-Game 2	3	4	LO	XN	IP	PH	RHP	LHP
1968	CAL	AL	1	1	0	1	0	0	0	0	0	0	1	0	0	0	1	0
	Total		3	2	1	2	0	1	0	0	0	0	1	0	0	0	3	0
1969	STL	NL	2	2	0	0	0	1	1	0	0	0	0	0	0	1	1	1
1970	STL	NL	1	0	1	0	1	0	0	0	0	0	0	0	0	1	1	0
1971	PIT	NL	1	1	0	1	0	0	0	0	0	0	0	0	0	0	1	0
1972	PIT	NL	4	2	2	2	2	0	0	0	0	0	0	1	0	0	3	1
1973	PIT	NL	1	0	1	1	0	0	0	0	0	0	0	0	0	1	1	0
1978	LA	NL	1	0	1	1	0	0	0	0	0	0	0	0	0	1	1	0
Total			36	14	22	18	14	3	1	1	0	0	1	1	1	5	28	8

Rank among batters: 1,274 • Top target (2 home runs): Jim Bouton, Gary Peters, Phil Ortega, Earl Wilson • *Number of pitchers victimized*: 32 • *Total ballparks homered in*: 16 • *First HR*: 04/14/1963 off Jim Bunning

Jerry DaVanon

FRANK GERALD DAVANON
B: 08/21/1945
BR

Year	Tm	Lg	Tot	H	A	Men-On 0	1	2	3	One-Game 2	3	4	LO	XN	IP	PH	RHP	LHP
1969	STL	NL	1	0	1	0	0	1	0	0	0	0	0	0	0	0	1	0
1975	HOU	NL	1	1	0	0	0	1	0	0	0	0	0	0	0	0	1	0
1976	HOU	NL	1	0	1	0	0	1	0	0	0	0	0	0	0	0	0	1
Total			3	1	2	0	0	3	0	0	0	0	0	0	0	0	2	1

Rank among batters: 3,735 • *Total ballparks homered in*: 3 • *First HR*: 09/26/1969 off Mike Wegener

Dave Davenport

DAVID W. DAVENPORT
B: 02/20/1890 D: 10/16/1954
BR

Year	Tm	Lg	Tot	H	A	Men-On 0	1	2	3	One-Game 2	3	4	LO	XN	IP	PH	RHP	LHP
1918	STL	AL	1	0	1	1	0	0	0	0	0	0	0	0	0	0	0	1

Rank among batters: 4,707 • *Total ballparks homered in*: 1 • *First HR*: 07/23/1918 off George Mogridge

Jim Davenport

JAMES HOUSTON DAVENPORT
B: 08/17/1933
BR

Year	Tm	Lg	Tot	H	A	Men-On 0	1	2	3	One-Game 2	3	4	LO	XN	IP	PH	RHP	LHP
1958	SF	NL	12	6	6	9	1	2	0	2	0	0	0	0	1	0	10	2
1959	SF	NL	6	3	3	5	1	0	0	1	0	0	1	1	0	0	6	0
1960	SF	NL	6	1	5	5	0	1	0	1	0	0	0	0	0	0	4	2
1961	SF	NL	12	3	9	7	3	2	0	0	0	0	0	0	1	0	9	3
1962	SF	NL	14	7	7	11	1	1	1	0	0	0	0	0	0	0	9	5
1963	SF	NL	4	2	2	1	2	1	0	0	0	0	1	0	0	0	3	1
1964	SF	NL	2	1	1	1	1	0	0	0	0	0	0	1	0	0	2	0
1965	SF	NL	4	1	3	2	0	2	0	0	0	0	0	0	0	0	3	1
1966	SF	NL	9	3	6	6	2	0	1	0	0	0	0	1	0	1	5	4
1967	SF	NL	5	1	4	4	1	0	0	1	0	0	0	0	0	0	5	0
1968	SF	NL	1	0	1	0	0	0	1	0	0	0	0	0	0	0	0	1
1969	SF	NL	2	1	1	2	0	0	0	0	0	0	0	0	0	0	2	0
Total			77	29	48	53	12	9	3	5	0	0	2	3	2	1	58	19

Rank among batters: 682 • *Top target (4 home runs)*: Roger Craig, Sandy Koufax • *Number of pitchers victimized*: 55 • *Total ballparks homered in*: 15 • *First HR*: 04/30/1958 off Bob Miller

Andre David

ANDRE ANTER DAVID
B: 05/18/1958
BL

Year	Tm	Lg	Tot	H	A	Men-On 0	1	2	3	One-Game 2	3	4	LO	XN	IP	PH	RHP	LHP
1984	MIN	AL	1	0	1	0	1	0	0	0	0	0	0	0	0	0	1	0

Rank among batters: 4,707 • *Total ballparks homered in*: 1 • *First HR*: 06/29/1984 off Jack Morris • *Hit HR in first major league AB*—@DET: 06/29/1984 (1)

Bill Davidson

WILLIAM SIMPSON DAVIDSON
B: 05/10/1887 D: 05/23/1954
BR

Year	Tm	Lg	Tot	H	A	Men-On 0	1	2	3	One-Game 2	3	4	LO	XN	IP	PH	RHP	LHP
1911	BRO	NL	1	0	1	0	0	1	0	0	0	0	0	0	0	0	1	0

Rank among batters: 4,707 • *Total ballparks homered in*: 1 • *First HR*: 08/12/1911 off Orlie Weaver

Mark Davidson

JOHN MARK DAVIDSON
B: 02/15/1961
BR

Year	Tm	Lg	Tot	H	A	Men-On 0	1	2	3	One-Game 2	3	4	LO	XN	IP	PH	RHP	LHP
1987	MIN	AL	1	0	1	1	0	0	0	0	0	0	0	0	0	0	1	0
1988	MIN	AL	1	0	1	1	0	0	0	0	0	0	0	0	0	0	0	1
1989	HOU	NL	1	0	1	0	1	0	0	0	0	0	0	0	0	0	0	1
1990	HOU	NL	1	0	1	1	0	0	0	0	0	0	0	0	0	0	0	1
1991	HOU	NL	2	1	1	1	1	0	0	0	0	0	0	0	0	0	1	1
Total			6	1	5	4	2	0	0	0	0	0	0	0	0	0	2	4

Rank among batters: 2,988 • *Total ballparks homered in*: 6 • *First HR*: 05/08/1987 off Tim Stoddard

Alfonzo Davis

ALFONZO DEFORD DAVIS
B: 02/04/1875 D: 02/07/1919
BL

Year	Tm	Lg	Tot	H	A	Men-On 0	1	2	3	One-Game 2	3	4	LO	XN	IP	PH	RHP	LHP
1901	PIT	NL	2	0	2	1	0	1	0	0	0	0	0	0	2	0	1	1
1907	CIN	NL	1	0	1	1	0	0	0	0	0	0	0	0	1	0	1	0
Total			3	0	3	2	0	1	0	0	0	0	0	0	3	0	2	1

Rank among batters: 3,735 • *Total ballparks homered in*: 3 • *First HR*: 07/27/1901 off Willie Sudhoff

Alvin Davis

ALVIN GLENN DAVIS
B: 09/09/1960
BL

Year	Tm	Lg	Tot	H	A	Men-On 0	1	2	3	One-Game 2	3	4	LO	XN	IP	PH	RHP	LHP
1984	SEA	AL	27	15	12	10	8	7	2	0	0	0	0	1	0	0	22	5
1985	SEA	AL	18	11	7	11	4	3	0	0	0	0	0	0	0	0	14	4
1986	SEA	AL	18	14	4	13	3	1	1	1	0	0	0	0	0	0	18	0
1987	SEA	AL	29	18	11	12	14	2	1	2	0	0	0	0	0	0	24	5
1988	SEA	AL	18	12	6	12	4	1	1	0	0	0	0	0	0	1	15	3
1989	SEA	AL	21	13	8	12	5	3	1	0	0	0	0	1	0	0	16	5
1990	SEA	AL	17	12	5	11	3	0	3	0	0	0	0	0	0	0	11	6
1991	SEA	AL	12	6	6	2	9	1	0	0	0	0	0	0	0	0	8	4
Total			160	101	59	83	50	18	9	3	0	0	0	2	0	1	128	32

Rank among batters: 263 • *Top target (7 home runs)*: Mike Smithson • *Number of pitchers victimized*: 118 • *Total ballparks homered in*: 13 • *First HR*: 04/11/1984 off Dennis Eckersley

Bill Davis

ARTHUR WILLARD DAVIS
B: 06/06/1942
BL

Year	Tm	Lg	Tot	H	A	Men-On 0	1	2	3	One-Game 2	3	4	LO	XN	IP	PH	RHP	LHP
1966	CLE	AL	1	1	0	0	1	0	0	0	0	0	0	1	0	1	1	0

Rank among batters: 4,707 • *Total ballparks homered in*: 1 • *First HR*: 09/09/1966 off Jack Sanford

Bob Davis

ROBERT JOHN EUGENE DAVIS
B: 03/01/1952
BR

Year	Tm	Lg	Tot	H	A	Men-On 0	1	2	3	One-Game 2	3	4	LO	XN	IP	PH	RHP	LHP
1977	SD	NL	1	0	1	1	0	0	0	0	0	0	0	0	0	0	0	1
1979	TOR	AL	1	0	1	1	0	0	0	0	0	0	0	0	0	0	1	0
1980	TOR	AL	4	4	0	3	1	0	0	0	0	0	0	0	0	1	1	3
Total			6	4	2	5	1	0	0	0	0	0	0	0	0	1	2	4

Rank among batters: 2,988 • *Total ballparks homered in*: 3 • *First HR*: 05/15/1977 off Steve Carlton

Brock Davis

BRYSHEAR BENNETT DAVIS
B: 10/19/1943
BL

Year	Tm	Lg	Tot	H	A	Men-On 0	1	2	3	One-Game 2	3	4	LO	XN	IP	PH	RHP	LHP
1963	HOU	NL	1	0	1	1	0	0	0	0	0	0	0	0	0	0	1	0

Rank among batters: 4,707 • *Total ballparks homered in*: 1 • *First HR*: 06/14/1963 off Jack Sanford

Butch Davis

WALLACE MCARTHUR DAVIS
B: 06/19/1958
BR

Year	Tm	Lg	Tot	H	A	Men-On 0	1	2	3	One-Game 2	3	4	LO	XN	IP	PH	RHP	LHP
1983	KC	AL	2	0	2	2	0	0	0	0	0	0	1	0	0	0	2	0

Butch Davis *continued*

Year	Tm	Lg	Tot	H	A	Men-On 0	Men-On 1	Men-On 2	Men-On 3	One-Game 2	One-Game 3	One-Game 4	LO	XN	IP	PH	RHP	LHP
1984	KC	AL	2	1	1	2	0	0	0	0	0	0	0	0	0	0	0	2
1993	TEX	AL	3	0	3	2	1	0	0	0	0	0	0	0	1	0	1	2
Total			7	1	6	6	1	0	0	0	0	0	1	0	1	0	3	4

Rank among batters: 2,834 • *Top target (2 home runs)*: Ron Guidry • *Number of pitchers victimized*: 6 • *Total ballparks homered in*: 6 • *First HR*: 09/11/1983 off Jay Pettibone

Chili Davis

CHARLES THEODORE DAVIS
B: 01/17/1960
BB

Year	Tm	Lg	Tot	H	A	Men-On 0	Men-On 1	Men-On 2	Men-On 3	One-Game 2	One-Game 3	One-Game 4	LO	XN	IP	PH	RHP	LHP
1982	SF	NL	19	6	13	12	5	1	1	0	0	0	5	1	0	1	16	3
1983	SF	NL	11	7	4	3	8	0	0	2	0	0	0	0	0	0	4	7
1984	SF	NL	21	7	14	13	4	3	1	2	0	0	1	0	0	1	19	2
1985	SF	NL	13	7	6	7	5	1	0	1	0	0	0	1	0	0	12	1
1986	SF	NL	13	7	6	7	5	1	0	1	0	0	0	0	0	1	8	5
1987	SF	NL	24	9	15	12	8	4	0	2	0	0	0	1	0	1	10	14
1988	CAL	AL	21	11	10	10	8	3	0	2	0	0	0	2	0	0	13	8
1989	CAL	AL	22	6	16	12	3	7	0	2	0	0	0	0	0	0	14	8
1990	CAL	AL	12	10	2	3	6	3	0	1	0	0	0	0	0	0	8	4
1991	MIN	AL	29	14	15	15	9	5	0	3	0	0	0	0	0	0	18	11
1992	MIN	AL	12	6	6	8	4	0	0	1	0	0	0	0	0	1	8	4
1993	CAL	AL	27	13	14	10	11	5	1	3	0	0	0	0	0	0	19	8
1994	CAL	AL	26	14	12	14	8	2	2	3	0	0	0	1	0	0	19	7
1995	CAL	AL	20	11	9	6	6	7	1	0	0	0	0	0	1	0	14	6
Total			270	128	142	132	90	42	6	23	0	0	6	6	1	5	182	88

Rank among batters: 90 • *Top target (5 home runs)*: Andy Hawkins, Bill Gullickson • *Number of pitchers victimized*: 188 • *Total ballparks homered in*: 30 • *First HR*: 04/10/1982 off Mario Soto • *Switch hit HR in 1 game*—8 times • *World Series HR*—2

Crash Davis

LAWRENCE COLUMBUS DAVIS
B: 07/14/1919
BR

Year	Tm	Lg	Tot	H	A	Men-On 0	Men-On 1	Men-On 2	Men-On 3	One-Game 2	One-Game 3	One-Game 4	LO	XN	IP	PH	RHP	LHP
1942	PHI	AL	2	1	1	1	1	0	0	0	0	0	0	0	0	0	2	0

Rank among batters: 4,129 • *Total ballparks homered in*: 2 • *First HR*: 05/30/1942 off Yank Terry

Curt Davis

CURTIS BENTON DAVIS
B: 09/07/1903 D: 10/13/1965
BR

Year	Tm	Lg	Tot	H	A	Men-On 0	Men-On 1	Men-On 2	Men-On 3	One-Game 2	One-Game 3	One-Game 4	LO	XN	IP	PH	RHP	LHP
1934	PHI	NL	1	1	0	1	0	0	0	0	0	0	0	0	1	0	0	1
1935	PHI	NL	1	0	1	1	0	0	0	0	0	0	0	1	0	0	0	1
1937	CHI	NL	1	1	0	0	0	1	0	0	0	0	0	0	0	0	1	0
1938	STL	NL	3	0	3	1	1	0	1	0	0	0	0	0	0	0	1	2
1939	STL	NL	1	1	0	1	0	0	0	0	0	0	0	0	0	0	1	0
1940	BRO	NL	1	0	1	0	1	0	0	0	0	0	0	0	0	0	1	0
1941	BRO	NL	2	2	0	1	0	1	0	0	0	0	0	0	0	0	1	1
1945	BRO	NL	1	1	0	0	1	0	0	0	0	0	0	0	0	0	1	0
Total			11	6	5	5	3	2	1	0	0	0	0	1	1	0	6	5

Rank among batters: 2,419 • *Total ballparks homered in*: 7 • *First HR*: 07/17/1934 off Tony Freitas

Dick Davis

RICHARD EARL DAVIS
B: 09/25/1953
BR

Year	Tm	Lg	Tot	H	A	Men-On 0	Men-On 1	Men-On 2	Men-On 3	One-Game 2	One-Game 3	One-Game 4	LO	XN	IP	PH	RHP	LHP
1978	MIL	AL	5	3	2	3	1	0	1	0	0	0	0	0	0	0	5	0
1979	MIL	AL	12	4	8	6	3	2	1	0	0	0	0	0	0	1	9	3
1980	MIL	AL	4	1	3	3	1	0	0	0	0	0	0	0	0	0	3	1
1981	PHI	NL	2	1	1	1	1	0	0	0	0	0	0	0	0	0	1	1
1982	PHI	NL	2	1	1	1	1	0	0	0	0	0	0	0	0	0	0	2
	PIT	NL	2	1	1	0	1	1	0	0	0	0	0	0	0	0	0	2
	Total		4	2	2	1	2	1	0	0	0	0	0	0	0	0	0	4
Total			27	11	16	14	8	3	2	0	0	0	0	0	0	1	18	9

Rank among batters: 1,532 • *Total ballparks homered in*: 13 • *First HR*: 04/16/1978 off Joe Kerrigan

Eric Davis

ERIC KEITH DAVIS
B: 05/29/1962
BR

Year	Tm	Lg	Tot	H	A	Men-On 0	1	2	3	One-Game 2	3	4	LO	XN	IP	PH	RHP	LHP
1984	CIN	NL	10	3	7	3	5	2	0	1	0	0	0	0	0	0	5	5
1985	CIN	NL	8	1	7	7	1	0	0	0	0	0	2	0	0	1	3	5
1986	CIN	NL	27	12	15	14	8	4	1	2	1	0	1	0	0	0	16	11
1987	CIN	NL	37	17	20	22	6	6	3	1	1	0	0	1	1	0	20	17
1988	CIN	NL	26	14	12	12	13	1	0	2	0	0	0	0	0	0	19	7
1989	CIN	NL	34	15	19	13	15	6	0	3	0	0	0	1	0	1	24	10
1990	CIN	NL	24	13	11	14	7	2	1	1	0	0	0	0	0	0	16	8
1991	CIN	NL	11	5	6	6	4	1	0	1	0	0	0	0	0	0	8	3
1992	LA	NL	5	1	4	4	0	1	0	0	0	0	0	0	0	0	1	4
1993	LA	NL	14	7	7	11	1	1	1	0	0	0	0	0	0	0	11	3
	DET	AL	6	3	3	2	2	2	0	1	0	0	0	0	0	0	5	1
	Total		20	10	10	13	3	3	1	1	0	0	0	0	0	0	16	4
1994	DET	AL	3	3	0	1	2	0	0	0	0	0	0	0	0	0	3	0
Total			205	94	111	109	64	26	6	12	2	0	3	2	1	2	131	74

Rank among batters: 173 • *Top target (6 home runs)*: Jim Deshaies • *Number of pitchers victimized*: 130 • *Total ballparks homered in*: 15 • *First HR*: 07/03/1984 off Jerry Koosman • *Hit for Cycle*—vs SD: 06/02/1989 • *World Series HR*—1

George Davis

GEORGE STACEY DAVIS
B: 08/23/1870 D: 10/17/1940
BB

Year	Tm	Lg	Tot	H	A	Men-On 0	1	2	3	One-Game 2	3	4	LO	XN	IP	PH	RHP	LHP
1890	CLE	NL	6	3	3	3	2	0	1	0	0	0	0	0	1	0	4	0
1891	CLE	NL	3	0	3	2	1	0	0	0	0	0	0	0	0	0	3	0
1892	CLE	NL	5	1	4	1	2	2	0	0	0	0	0	0	3	0	3	2
1893	NY	NL	11	7	4	3	5	3	0	0	0	0	0	0	1	0	8	3
1894	NY	NL	8	5	3	3	5	0	0	0	0	0	0	0	1	0	6	1
1895	NY	NL	5	1	4	3	2	0	0	0	0	0	0	0	0	0	4	0
1896	NY	NL	5	4	1	2	0	1	2	0	0	0	0	0	1	0	3	2
1897	NY	NL	10	5	5	5	5	0	0	0	0	0	0	0	1	0	8	2
1898	NY	NL	2	2	0	1	0	1	0	0	0	0	0	0	0	0	1	1
1899	NY	NL	1	0	1	1	0	0	0	0	0	0	0	0	0	0	0	1
1900	NY	NL	3	2	1	0	3	0	0	0	0	0	0	0	0	0	3	0
1901	NY	NL	7	2	5	3	3	1	0	1	0	0	0	0	3	0	7	0
1902	CHI	AL	3	2	1	2	0	1	0	0	0	0	0	0	0	0	2	1
1904	CHI	AL	1	0	1	1	0	0	0	0	0	0	0	0	0	0	1	0
1905	CHI	AL	1	0	1	1	0	0	0	0	0	0	0	0	0	0	1	0
1907	CHI	AL	1	0	1	0	1	0	0	0	0	0	0	0	0	0	1	0
Total			72	34	38	31	29	9	3	1	0	0	0	0	11	0	55	12

Rank among batters: 723 • *Top target (4 home runs)*: Jack Taylor • *Number of pitchers victimized*: 54 • *Total ballparks homered in*: 22 • *First HR*: 05/30/1890 off Tom Vickery

Glenn Davis

GLENN EARLE DAVIS
B: 03/28/1961
BR

Year	Tm	Lg	Tot	H	A	Men-On 0	1	2	3	One-Game 2	3	4	LO	XN	IP	PH	RHP	LHP
1984	HOU	NL	2	1	1	2	0	0	0	0	0	0	0	0	0	0	2	0
1985	HOU	NL	20	8	12	13	6	1	0	1	0	0	0	0	1	0	8	12
1986	HOU	NL	31	17	14	16	11	4	0	2	0	0	0	1	0	0	19	12
1987	HOU	NL	27	12	15	16	8	3	0	0	1	0	0	0	0	0	17	10
1988	HOU	NL	30	15	15	10	16	4	0	1	0	0	0	0	0	0	23	7
1989	HOU	NL	34	15	19	21	11	2	0	2	0	0	0	1	0	0	20	14
1990	HOU	NL	22	4	18	12	5	5	0	2	1	0	0	0	0	0	11	11
1991	BAL	AL	10	3	7	7	2	1	0	0	0	0	0	0	0	1	5	5
1992	BAL	AL	13	5	8	7	6	0	0	1	0	0	0	1	0	1	9	4
1993	BAL	AL	1	1	0	1	0	0	0	0	0	0	0	0	0	0	1	0
Total			190	81	109	105	65	20	0	9	2	0	0	3	1	2	115	75

Rank among batters: 201 • *Top target (6 home runs)*: Tom Browning, Dennis Martinez • *Number of pitchers victimized*: 119 • *Total ballparks homered in*: 22 • *First HR*: 09/06/1984 off Scott Garrelts • *LCS HR*—1

Harry Davis

HARRY H DAVIS
B: 07/19/1873 D: 08/11/1947
BR

Year	Tm	Lg	Tot	H	A	Men-On 0	1	2	3	One-Game 2	3	4	LO	XN	IP	PH	RHP	LHP
1896	NY	NL	2	1	1	0	2	0	0	0	0	0	0	0	0	0	0	2
1897	PIT	NL	2	0	2	2	0	0	0	0	0	0	0	0	0	0	2	0

Harry Davis *continued*

Year	Tm	Lg	Tot	H	A	Men-On 0	1	2	3	One-Game 2	3	4	LO	XN	IP	PH	RHP	LHP
1898	PIT	NL	1	0	1	1	0	0	0	0	0	0	0	0	0	0	1	0
	LOU	NL	1	1	0	1	0	0	0	0	0	0	0	0	1	0	0	1
	Total		2	1	1	2	0	0	0	0	0	0	0	0	1	0	1	1
1901	PHI	AL	8	4	4	5	3	0	0	0	0	0	0	0	1	0	6	2
1902	PHI	AL	6	4	2	2	2	1	1	0	0	0	0	0	1	0	5	1
1903	PHI	AL	6	4	2	4	1	1	0	0	0	0	0	0	3	0	6	0
1904	PHI	AL	10	8	2	4	4	1	1	1	0	0	0	0	1	0	9	1
1905	PHI	AL	8	4	4	4	4	0	0	0	0	0	0	1	1	0	6	2
1906	PHI	AL	12	10	2	5	5	2	0	1	0	0	0	1	0	0	8	4
1907	PHI	AL	8	7	1	6	0	2	0	0	0	0	0	0	0	0	7	1
1908	PHI	AL	5	2	3	4	0	1	0	0	0	0	0	0	0	0	4	1
1909	PHI	AL	4	0	4	2	2	0	0	0	0	0	0	0	1	0	3	1
1910	PHI	AL	1	0	1	1	0	0	0	0	0	0	0	0	0	0	1	0
1911	PHI	AL	1	0	1	0	1	0	0	0	0	0	0	0	0	0	1	0
Total			75	45	30	41	24	8	2	2	0	0	0	2	9	0	59	16

Rank among batters: 699 • *Top target (4 home runs)*: Jack Powell • *Number of pitchers victimized*: 54 • *Total ballparks homered in*: 14 • *First HR*: 05/04/1896 off Fritz Clausen • *Hit for Cycle*—@BOS: 07/10/1901

Harry Davis

HARRY ALBERT DAVIS
B: 03/07/1908
BL

Year	Tm	Lg	Tot	H	A	Men-On 0	1	2	3	One-Game 2	3	4	LO	XN	IP	PH	RHP	LHP
1932	DET	AL	4	0	4	2	1	1	0	1	0	0	1	0	0	0	3	1
1937	STL	AL	3	3	0	3	0	0	0	0	0	0	1	0	0	0	2	1
Total			7	3	4	5	1	1	0	1	0	0	2	0	0	0	5	2

Rank among batters: 2,834 • *Top target (2 home runs)*: Danny MacFayden • *Number of pitchers victimized*: 6 • *Total ballparks homered in*: 3 • *First HR*: 06/27/1932 off Vic Frasier

Jacke Davis

JACKE SYLVESTER DAVIS
B: 03/05/1936
BR

Year	Tm	Lg	Tot	H	A	Men-On 0	1	2	3	One-Game 2	3	4	LO	XN	IP	PH	RHP	LHP
1962	PHI	NL	1	1	0	0	0	1	0	0	0	0	0	0	0	1	0	1

Rank among batters: 4,707 • *Total ballparks homered in*: 1 • *First HR*: 06/04/1962 off Sandy Koufax

Jody Davis

JODY RICHARD DAVIS
B: 11/12/1956
BR

Year	Tm	Lg	Tot	H	A	Men-On 0	1	2	3	One-Game 2	3	4	LO	XN	IP	PH	RHP	LHP
1981	CHI	NL	4	4	0	2	1	1	0	0	0	0	0	0	0	0	2	2
1982	CHI	NL	12	6	6	5	4	3	0	1	0	0	0	0	0	0	10	2
1983	CHI	NL	24	15	9	14	5	3	2	2	0	0	0	0	0	0	19	5
1984	CHI	NL	19	13	6	7	9	2	1	1	0	0	0	0	0	1	13	6
1985	CHI	NL	17	10	7	11	5	1	0	1	0	0	0	0	0	0	12	5
1986	CHI	NL	21	14	7	10	6	4	1	2	0	0	0	0	0	0	18	3
1987	CHI	NL	19	7	12	15	3	0	1	1	0	0	0	0	0	0	14	5
1988	CHI	NL	6	3	3	5	1	0	0	1	0	0	0	0	0	0	5	1
	ATL	NL	1	0	1	0	0	1	0	0	0	0	0	0	0	0	0	1
	Total		7	3	4	5	1	1	0	1	0	0	0	0	0	0	5	2
1989	ATL	NL	4	1	3	2	2	0	0	0	0	0	0	0	0	0	3	1
Total			127	73	54	71	36	15	5	9	0	0	0	0	0	1	96	31

Rank among batters: 358 • *Top target (4 home runs)*: Ron Darling, Bryn Smith • *Number of pitchers victimized*: 95 • *Total ballparks homered in*: 12 • *First HR*: 06/11/1981 off Al Holland • *LCS HR*—2

Jumbo Davis

JAMES J. DAVIS
B: 09/05/1861 D: 02/14/1921
BL

Year	Tm	Lg	Tot	H	A	Men-On 0	1	2	3	One-Game 2	3	4	LO	XN	IP	PH	RHP	LHP
1886	BAL	AA	1	1	0	0	1	0	0	0	0	0	0	0	0	0	1	0
1887	BAL	AA	8	5	3	2	5	1	0	0	0	0	0	0	0	0	6	2
1888	KC	AA	3	3	0	2	1	0	0	0	0	0	0	0	0	0	3	0
1890	BRO	AA	2	0	2	1	0	1	0	0	0	0	0	0	0	0	2	0
Total			14	9	5	5	7	2	0	0	0	0	0	0	0	0	11	2

Rank among batters: 2,169 • *Top target (2 home runs)*: Ed Seward, Bob Caruthers • *Number of pitchers victimized*: 12 • *Total ballparks homered in*: 7 • *First HR*: 09/17/1886 off Dave Foutz • *Hit for Cycle*—@LOU: 07/18/1890

Year	Tm	Lg	Tot	H	A	Men-On 0	Men-On 1	Men-On 2	Men-On 3	One-Game 2	One-Game 3	One-Game 4	LO	XN	IP	PH	RHP	LHP

Kiddo Davis

GEORGE WILLIS DAVIS
B: 02/12/1902 D: 03/04/1983
BR

Year	Tm	Lg	Tot	H	A	0	1	2	3	2	3	4	LO	XN	IP	PH	RHP	LHP
1932	PHI	NL	5	5	0	3	1	1	0	0	0	0	1	0	0	0	3	2
1933	NY	NL	7	5	2	5	1	1	0	0	0	0	0	0	0	0	6	1
1934	STL	NL	1	0	1	1	0	0	0	0	0	0	0	0	0	0	1	0
	PHI	NL	3	2	1	3	0	0	0	0	0	0	0	0	1	0	3	0
	Total		4	2	2	4	0	0	0	0	0	0	0	0	1	0	4	0
1935	NY	NL	2	1	1	1	1	0	0	0	0	0	0	0	0	2	0	2
1937	CIN	NL	1	0	1	1	0	0	0	0	0	0	0	0	0	0	1	0
Total			19	13	6	14	3	2	0	0	0	0	1	0	1	2	14	5

Rank among batters: 1,861 • *Top target (2 home runs)*: Fred Heimach, Syl Johnson, Bob Smith • *Number of pitchers victimized*: 16 • *Total ballparks homered in*: 5 • *First HR*: 04/29/1932 off Fred Heimach

Mark Davis

MARK WILLIAM DAVIS
B: 10/19/1960
BL

Year	Tm	Lg	Tot	H	A	0	1	2	3	2	3	4	LO	XN	IP	PH	RHP	LHP
1988	SD	NL	1	1	0	0	1	0	0	0	0	0	0	0	0	0	1	0

Rank among batters: 4,707 • *Total ballparks homered in*: 1 • *First HR*: 06/13/1988 off Don Robinson

Mike Davis

MICHAEL DWAYNE DAVIS
B: 06/11/1959
BL

Year	Tm	Lg	Tot	H	A	0	1	2	3	2	3	4	LO	XN	IP	PH	RHP	LHP
1980	OAK	AL	1	1	0	0	1	0	0	0	0	0	0	0	0	0	1	0
1982	OAK	AL	1	1	0	0	1	0	0	0	0	0	0	0	0	0	1	0
1983	OAK	AL	8	3	5	4	3	1	0	0	0	0	0	0	0	1	6	2
1984	OAK	AL	9	4	5	5	2	2	0	0	0	0	0	0	0	0	8	1
1985	OAK	AL	24	12	12	15	7	2	0	2	0	0	0	0	0	0	16	8
1986	OAK	AL	19	11	8	15	3	1	0	3	0	0	0	1	0	1	15	4
1987	OAK	AL	22	9	13	14	7	1	0	0	0	0	0	0	0	0	16	6
1988	LA	NL	2	1	1	0	2	0	0	0	0	0	0	0	0	1	2	0
1989	LA	NL	5	2	3	4	1	0	0	0	0	0	0	0	0	0	5	0
Total			91	44	47	57	27	7	0	5	0	0	0	1	0	3	70	21

Rank among batters: 559 • *Top target (3 home runs)*: Dave Stieb, Mark Eichhorn, Mike Witt • *Number of pitchers victimized*: 77 • *Total ballparks homered in*: 18 • *First HR*: 06/07/1980 off Mike Torrez • *World Series HR*—1

Ron Davis

RONALD EVERETTE DAVIS
B: 10/21/1941 D: 09/05/1992
BR

Year	Tm	Lg	Tot	H	A	0	1	2	3	2	3	4	LO	XN	IP	PH	RHP	LHP
1966	HOU	NL	2	0	2	2	0	0	0	0	0	0	0	0	0	0	2	0
1967	HOU	NL	7	3	4	5	1	1	0	0	0	0	2	0	0	0	5	2
1968	HOU	NL	1	1	0	1	0	0	0	0	0	0	1	0	0	0	0	1
Total			10	4	6	8	1	1	0	0	0	0	3	0	0	0	7	3

Rank among batters: 2,500 • *Top target (2 home runs)*: Mike McCormick • *Number of pitchers victimized*: 9 • *Total ballparks homered in*: 6 • *First HR*: 08/13/1966 off Juan Marichal

Russ Davis

RUSSELL STUART DAVIS
B: 09/13/1969
BR

Year	Tm	Lg	Tot	H	A	0	1	2	3	2	3	4	LO	XN	IP	PH	RHP	LHP
1995	NY	AL	2	2	0	1	0	1	0	0	0	0	0	0	0	0	0	2

Rank among batters: 4,129 • *Total ballparks homered in*: 1 • *First HR*: 06/28/1995 off Dave Wells

Spud Davis

VIRGIL LAWRENCE DAVIS
B: 12/20/1904 D: 08/14/1984
BR

Year	Tm	Lg	Tot	H	A	0	1	2	3	2	3	4	LO	XN	IP	PH	RHP	LHP
1928	PHI	NL	3	3	0	0	2	1	0	0	0	0	0	0	0	0	3	0
1929	PHI	NL	7	4	3	4	1	1	1	0	0	0	0	0	0	2	4	3
1930	PHI	NL	14	4	10	7	3	4	0	2	0	0	0	0	0	0	11	3
1931	PHI	NL	4	3	1	1	1	2	0	0	0	0	0	0	1	0	2	2
1932	PHI	NL	14	11	3	8	5	1	0	1	0	0	0	0	0	0	12	2

						Men-On				One-Game								
Year	Tm	Lg	Tot	H	A	0	1	2	3	2	3	4	LO	XN	IP	PH	RHP	LHP

Spud Davis *continued*

Year	Tm	Lg	Tot	H	A	0	1	2	3	2	3	4	LO	XN	IP	PH	RHP	LHP
1933	PHI	NL	9	6	3	7	1	0	1	1	0	0	0	1	0	0	8	1
1934	STL	NL	9	4	5	6	2	1	0	0	0	0	0	0	0	0	5	4
1935	STL	NL	1	1	0	0	1	0	0	0	0	0	0	0	0	0	1	0
1936	STL	NL	4	1	3	2	1	1	0	0	0	0	0	0	0	0	4	0
1937	CIN	NL	3	0	3	1	2	0	0	0	0	0	0	0	0	1	2	1
1938	PHI	NL	2	2	0	2	0	0	0	0	0	0	0	1	0	0	2	0
1940	PIT	NL	5	0	5	4	0	1	0	1	0	0	0	0	0	0	5	0
1944	PIT	NL	2	1	1	1	1	0	0	0	0	0	0	0	0	1	2	0
Total			77	40	37	43	20	12	2	5	0	0	0	2	1	4	61	16

Rank among batters: 682 • *Top target (4 home runs)*: Guy Bush, Ben Cantwell • *Number of pitchers victimized*: 55 • *Total ballparks homered in*: 8 • *First HR*: 06/08/1928 off Sheriff Blake

Tod Davis

THOMAS OSCAR DAVIS
B: 07/24/1924 D: 12/31/1978
BR

Year	Tm	Lg	Tot	H	A	0	1	2	3	2	3	4	LO	XN	IP	PH	RHP	LHP
1949	PHI	AL	1	1	0	1	0	0	0	0	0	0	0	0	0	0	1	0

Rank among batters: 4,707 • *Total ballparks homered in*: 1 • *First HR*: 09/05/1949 off Vic Raschi

Tommy Davis

HERMAN THOMAS DAVIS
B: 03/21/1939
BR

Year	Tm	Lg	Tot	H	A	0	1	2	3	2	3	4	LO	XN	IP	PH	RHP	LHP
1960	LA	NL	11	9	2	7	2	1	1	1	0	0	0	1	0	0	10	1
1961	LA	NL	15	8	7	8	5	1	1	0	0	0	0	2	0	0	7	8
1962	LA	NL	27	14	13	11	10	5	1	1	0	0	0	0	0	0	17	10
1963	LA	NL	16	5	11	6	9	1	0	0	0	0	0	1	0	0	9	7
1964	LA	NL	14	3	11	10	3	1	0	1	0	0	0	0	0	0	10	4
1966	LA	NL	3	2	1	1	1	1	0	0	0	0	0	0	0	0	1	2
1967	NY	NL	16	9	7	9	5	1	1	2	0	0	0	1	0	0	10	6
1968	CHI	AL	8	4	4	4	3	1	0	0	0	0	0	0	0	0	4	4
1969	SEA	AL	6	3	3	4	2	0	0	0	0	0	0	0	0	0	3	3
	HOU	NL	1	0	1	0	1	0	0	0	0	0	0	0	0	0	1	0
	Total		7	3	4	4	3	0	0	0	0	0	0	0	0	0	4	3
1970	HOU	NL	3	1	2	1	2	0	0	0	0	0	0	0	0	0	2	1
	OAK	AL	1	0	1	1	0	0	0	0	0	0	0	0	0	0	0	1
	CHI	NL	2	0	2	0	1	1	0	0	0	0	0	0	0	0	2	0
	Total		6	1	5	2	3	1	0	0	0	0	0	0	0	0	4	2
1971	OAK	AL	3	1	2	1	2	0	0	0	0	0	0	0	0	0	2	1
1973	BAL	AL	7	5	2	6	0	1	0	0	0	0	0	0	0	0	6	1
1974	BAL	AL	11	8	3	4	7	0	0	1	0	0	0	1	0	0	6	5
1975	BAL	AL	6	2	4	2	2	0	2	0	0	0	0	1	0	0	5	1
1976	CAL	AL	3	2	1	1	2	0	0	0	0	0	0	0	0	0	3	0
Total			153	76	77	76	57	14	6	6	0	0	0	7	0	0	98	55

Rank among batters: 280 • Top target (4 home runs): Jim Brewer, Dick Ellsworth, Bob Gibson, Denny Lemaster, Mickey Lolich • *Number of pitchers victimized*: 106 • *Total ballparks homered in*: 25 • *First HR*: 07/10/1960 off Bob Duliba

Willie Davis

WILLIAM HENRY DAVIS
B: 04/15/1940
BL

Year	Tm	Lg	Tot	H	A	0	1	2	3	2	3	4	LO	XN	IP	PH	RHP	LHP
1960	LA	NL	2	1	1	1	0	1	0	0	0	0	0	0	0	0	2	0
1961	LA	NL	12	3	9	7	2	3	0	1	0	0	0	0	0	0	11	1
1962	LA	NL	21	4	17	12	6	2	1	1	0	0	0	0	2	0	17	4
1963	LA	NL	9	3	6	4	3	2	0	1	0	0	1	0	0	0	7	2
1964	LA	NL	12	5	7	5	6	0	1	0	0	0	0	0	1	0	8	4
1965	LA	NL	10	5	5	5	5	0	0	1	0	0	0	0	0	0	9	1
1966	LA	NL	11	5	6	8	2	1	0	0	0	0	0	0	0	0	10	1
1967	LA	NL	6	2	4	4	2	0	0	0	0	0	0	0	0	0	3	3
1968	LA	NL	7	4	3	4	3	0	0	0	0	0	2	0	0	0	5	2
1969	LA	NL	11	0	11	8	2	1	0	1	0	0	0	1	1	0	10	1
1970	LA	NL	8	4	4	4	1	2	1	0	0	0	0	0	1	0	5	3
1971	LA	NL	10	3	7	8	2	0	0	0	0	0	0	0	0	0	9	1
1972	LA	NL	19	7	12	9	7	3	0	1	0	0	0	0	1	0	16	3
1973	LA	NL	16	11	5	6	9	1	0	2	0	0	0	2	0	0	15	1

Willie Davis *continued*

Year	Tm	Lg	Tot	H	A	Men-On 0	1	2	3	One-Game 2	3	4	LO	XN	IP	PH	RHP	LHP
1974	MON	NL	12	7	5	4	4	3	1	1	0	0	0	0	1	0	9	3
1975	TEX	AL	5	1	4	2	3	0	0	0	0	0	0	1	0	0	5	0
	STL	NL	6	3	3	4	1	1	0	0	0	0	0	0	0	0	6	0
	Total		11	4	7	6	4	1	0	0	0	0	0	1	0	0	11	0
1976	SD	NL	5	2	3	2	1	2	0	0	0	0	0	0	0	0	5	0
Total			182	70	112	97	59	22	4	9	0	0	3	4	7	0	152	30

Rank among batters: 216 • *Top target (7 home runs)*: Juan Marichal • *Number of pitchers victimized*: 113 • *Total ballparks homered in*: 23 • *First HR*: 09/13/1960 off Art Mahaffey • *All-Star HR*—1

Andre Dawson

ANDRE NOLAN DAWSON
B: 07/10/1954
BR

Year	Tm	Lg	Tot	H	A	Men-On 0	1	2	3	One-Game 2	3	4	LO	XN	IP	PH	RHP	LHP
1977	MON	NL	19	7	12	10	7	2	0	1	0	0	0	0	0	0	13	6
1978	MON	NL	25	12	13	17	7	1	0	1	0	0	0	1	0	1	19	6
1979	MON	NL	25	13	12	15	9	1	0	3	0	0	1	1	0	0	21	4
1980	MON	NL	17	7	10	10	6	1	0	1	0	0	0	0	0	0	9	8
1981	MON	NL	24	9	15	20	3	0	1	3	0	0	0	0	1	0	18	6
1982	MON	NL	23	9	14	18	4	1	0	2	0	0	0	1	0	0	19	4
1983	MON	NL	32	10	22	20	11	1	0	3	0	0	0	1	1	0	26	6
1984	MON	NL	17	6	11	6	9	2	0	1	0	0	0	0	0	0	10	7
1985	MON	NL	23	11	12	9	9	4	1	1	1	0	0	0	0	0	13	10
1986	MON	NL	20	11	9	14	4	2	0	1	0	0	0	0	0	0	9	11
1987	CHI	NL	49	27	22	26	15	6	2	7	1	0	0	1	0	0	40	9
1988	CHI	NL	24	12	12	16	7	1	0	3	0	0	0	0	0	0	20	4
1989	CHI	NL	21	6	15	12	5	4	0	3	0	0	0	1	1	0	13	8
1990	CHI	NL	27	14	13	16	9	2	0	2	0	0	0	1	0	0	19	8
1991	CHI	NL	31	22	9	12	11	6	2	2	0	0	0	1	0	2	16	15
1992	CHI	NL	22	13	9	13	7	2	0	0	0	0	0	0	0	0	15	7
1993	BOS	AL	13	8	5	7	5	1	0	0	0	0	0	0	0	0	6	7
1994	BOS	AL	16	7	9	8	6	2	0	2	0	0	0	0	0	0	12	4
1995	FLO	NL	8	1	7	4	1	2	1	1	0	0	0	0	0	0	4	4
Total			436	205	231	253	135	41	7	37	2	0	1	8	3	3	302	134

Rank among batters: 22 • *Top target (7 home runs)*: Bob Knepper • *Number of pitchers victimized*: 268 • *Total ballparks homered in*: 21 • *First HR*: 05/18/1977 off Buzz Capra • *2 HR in 1 inning*—@ATL: 07/30/1978; @CHI: 09/24/1985 • *Hit for Cycle*—vs SF: 04/29/1987 • *All-Star HR*—1

Boots Day

CHARLES FREDERICK DAY
B: 08/31/1947
BL

Year	Tm	Lg	Tot	H	A	Men-On 0	1	2	3	One-Game 2	3	4	LO	XN	IP	PH	RHP	LHP
1971	MON	NL	4	3	1	1	2	1	0	0	0	0	1	0	0	0	4	0
1973	MON	NL	4	3	1	3	1	0	0	0	0	0	0	1	0	1	4	0
Total			8	6	2	4	3	1	0	0	0	0	1	1	0	1	8	0

Rank among batters: 2,703 • *Total ballparks homered in*: 3 • *First HR*: 05/11/1971 off Reggie Cleveland

Brian Dayett

BRIAN KELLY DAYETT
B: 01/22/1957
BR

Year	Tm	Lg	Tot	H	A	Men-On 0	1	2	3	One-Game 2	3	4	LO	XN	IP	PH	RHP	LHP
1984	NY	AL	4	2	2	0	3	1	0	0	0	0	0	0	0	0	1	3
1985	CHI	NL	1	1	0	0	0	0	1	0	0	0	0	0	0	1	0	1
1986	CHI	NL	4	3	1	3	1	0	0	0	0	0	0	0	0	0	3	1
1987	CHI	NL	5	1	4	2	2	0	1	1	0	0	0	0	0	0	0	5
Total			14	7	7	5	6	1	2	1	0	0	0	0	0	1	4	10

Rank among batters: 2,169 • *Top target (3 home runs)*: Bob Knepper • *Number of pitchers victimized*: 12 • *Total ballparks homered in*: 8 • *First HR*: 06/22/1984 off Mike Flanagan

Mike de la Hoz

MIGUEL ANGEL (PILOTO) DE LA HOZ
B: 10/02/1938
BR

Year	Tm	Lg	Tot	H	A	Men-On 0	1	2	3	One-Game 2	3	4	LO	XN	IP	PH	RHP	LHP
1960	CLE	AL	6	4	2	5	0	1	0	0	0	0	0	0	0	0	6	0
1961	CLE	AL	3	2	1	1	1	1	0	0	0	0	0	0	0	0	2	1
1963	CLE	AL	5	4	1	0	3	1	1	0	0	0	0	0	0	1	3	2

Mike de la Hoz *continued*

Year	Tm	Lg	Tot	H	A	Men-On 0	1	2	3	One-Game 2	3	4	LO	XN	IP	PH	RHP	LHP
1964	MIL	NL	4	3	1	4	0	0	0	0	0	0	0	0	0	0	1	3
1965	MIL	NL	2	1	1	2	0	0	0	0	0	0	0	0	0	1	2	0
1966	ATL	NL	2	0	2	1	1	0	0	0	0	0	0	0	0	0	1	1
1967	ATL	NL	3	1	2	2	1	0	0	0	0	0	0	0	0	2	1	2
Total			25	15	10	15	6	3	1	0	0	0	0	0	0	4	16	9

Rank among batters: 1,608 • *Top target (2 home runs)*: Jim O'Toole, Dave Giusti • *Number of pitchers victimized*: 23 • *Total ballparks homered in*: 10 • *First HR*: 07/23/1960 off Tom Brewer

Charlie Deal

CHARLES ALBERT DEAL
B: 10/30/1891 D: 09/16/1979
BR

Year	Tm	Lg	Tot	H	A	Men-On 0	1	2	3	One-Game 2	3	4	LO	XN	IP	PH	RHP	LHP
1915	STL	FL	1	0	1	1	0	0	0	0	0	0	0	0	0	0	1	0
1918	CHI	NL	2	0	2	1	1	0	0	0	0	0	0	0	0	0	2	0
1919	CHI	NL	2	1	1	0	2	0	0	0	0	0	0	0	0	0	1	1
1920	CHI	NL	3	3	0	2	1	0	0	0	0	0	0	0	0	0	3	0
1921	CHI	NL	3	1	2	1	0	2	0	0	0	0	0	0	0	0	3	0
Total			11	5	6	5	4	2	0	0	0	0	0	0	0	0	10	1

Rank among batters: 2,419 • *Total ballparks homered in*: 4 • *First HR*: 06/25/1915 off Snipe Conley

Cot Deal

ELLIS FERGUSON DEAL
B: 01/23/1923
BB

Year	Tm	Lg	Tot	H	A	Men-On 0	1	2	3	One-Game 2	3	4	LO	XN	IP	PH	RHP	LHP
1954	STL	NL	1	0	1	1	0	0	0	0	0	0	0	0	0	0	1	0

Rank among batters: 4,707 • *Total ballparks homered in*: 1 • *First HR*: 05/09/1954 off Bud Podbielan

Pat Dealy

PATRICK E. DEALY
D: 12/17/1924
BR

Year	Tm	Lg	Tot	H	A	Men-On 0	1	2	3	One-Game 2	3	4	LO	XN	IP	PH	RHP	LHP
1885	BOS	NL	1	1	0	0	1	0	0	0	0	0	0	0	0	0	1	0
1887	WAS	NL	1	1	0	0	0	0	1	0	0	0	0	0	0	0	0	1
Total			2	2	0	0	1	0	1	0	0	0	0	0	0	0	1	1

Rank among batters: 4,129 • *Total ballparks homered in*: 2 • *First HR*: 06/10/1885 off Charlie Ferguson

Chubby Dean

ALFRED LOVELL DEAN
B: 08/24/1916 D: 12/21/1970
BL

Year	Tm	Lg	Tot	H	A	Men-On 0	1	2	3	One-Game 2	3	4	LO	XN	IP	PH	RHP	LHP
1936	PHI	AL	1	1	0	1	0	0	0	0	0	0	0	0	0	0	1	0
1937	PHI	AL	2	2	0	1	0	1	0	0	0	0	0	0	0	0	2	0
Total			3	3	0	2	0	1	0	0	0	0	0	0	0	0	3	0

Rank among batters: 3,735 • *Total ballparks homered in*: 1 • *First HR*: 08/23/1936 off Pete Appleton

Dizzy Dean

JAY HANNA DEAN
B: 01/16/1910 D: 07/17/1974
BR HOF

Year	Tm	Lg	Tot	H	A	Men-On 0	1	2	3	One-Game 2	3	4	LO	XN	IP	PH	RHP	LHP
1932	STL	NL	2	1	1	1	0	1	0	0	0	0	0	0	0	0	0	2
1933	STL	NL	1	0	1	1	0	0	0	0	0	0	0	0	0	0	1	0
1934	STL	NL	2	0	2	2	0	0	0	0	0	0	0	1	0	0	2	0
1935	STL	NL	2	1	1	1	0	1	0	0	0	0	0	1	0	0	1	1
1937	STL	NL	1	0	1	0	0	1	0	0	0	0	0	0	0	0	0	1
Total			8	2	6	5	0	3	0	0	0	0	0	2	0	0	4	4

Rank among batters: 2,703 • *Top target (3 home runs)*: Ed Brandt • *Number of pitchers victimized*: 6 • *Total ballparks homered in*: 6 • *First HR*: 07/31/1932 off Ed Brandt

Tommy Dean

TOMMY DOUGLAS DEAN
B: 08/30/1945
BR

Year	Tm	Lg	Tot	H	A	Men-On 0	1	2	3	One-Game 2	3	4	LO	XN	IP	PH	RHP	LHP
1969	SD	NL	2	1	1	2	0	0	0	0	0	0	1	0	0	0	2	0

Year	Tm	Lg	Tot	H	A	Men-On				One-Game			LO	XN	IP	PH	RHP	LHP
						0	1	2	3	2	3	4						

Tommy Dean *continued*

Year	Tm	Lg	Tot	H	A	0	1	2	3	2	3	4	LO	XN	IP	PH	RHP	LHP
1970	SD	NL	2	0	2	2	0	0	0	0	0	0	0	0	0	0	2	0
Total			4	1	3	4	0	0	0	0	0	0	1	0	0	0	4	0

Rank among batters: 3,427 • *Top target (2 home runs)*: Phil Niekro • *Number of pitchers victimized*: 3 • *Total ballparks homered in*: 3 • *First HR*: 04/27/1969 off George Culver

Wayland Dean

WAYLAND OGDEN DEAN
B: 06/20/1902 D: 04/10/1930
BB

Year	Tm	Lg	Tot	H	A	0	1	2	3	2	3	4	LO	XN	IP	PH	RHP	LHP
1924	NY	NL	2	1	1	2	0	0	0	0	0	0	0	0	1	0	2	0
1925	NY	NL	1	0	1	1	0	0	0	0	0	0	0	0	0	0	1	0
1926	PHI	NL	3	2	1	2	0	1	0	0	0	0	0	0	0	0	3	0
Total			6	3	3	5	0	1	0	0	0	0	0	0	1	0	6	0

Rank among batters: 2,988 • *Top target (2 home runs)*: Jesse Haines • *Number of pitchers victimized*: 5 • *Total ballparks homered in*: 4 • *First HR*: 06/18/1924 off Jesse Haines

Hank DeBerry

JOHN HERMAN DEBERRY
B: 12/29/1894 D: 09/10/1951
BR

Year	Tm	Lg	Tot	H	A	0	1	2	3	2	3	4	LO	XN	IP	PH	RHP	LHP
1922	BRO	NL	3	0	3	1	2	0	0	0	0	0	0	0	0	0	3	0
1923	BRO	NL	1	1	0	0	1	0	0	0	0	0	0	0	0	0	1	0
1924	BRO	NL	3	0	3	1	1	1	0	0	0	0	0	1	0	0	1	2
1925	BRO	NL	2	0	2	2	0	0	0	0	0	0	0	0	0	0	1	1
1927	BRO	NL	1	0	1	0	1	0	0	0	0	0	0	0	0	0	1	0
1929	BRO	NL	1	0	1	0	0	1	0	0	0	0	0	0	0	0	1	0
Total			11	1	10	4	5	2	0	0	0	0	0	1	0	0	8	3

Rank among batters: 2,419 • *Top target (2 home runs)*: Art Nehf • *Number of pitchers victimized*: 10 • *Total ballparks homered in*: 5 • *First HR*: 05/25/1922 off Jesse Winters

Doug DeCinces

DOUGLAS VERNON DECINCES
B: 08/29/1950
BR

Year	Tm	Lg	Tot	H	A	0	1	2	3	2	3	4	LO	XN	IP	PH	RHP	LHP
1975	BAL	AL	4	3	1	2	2	0	0	0	0	0	0	0	0	0	3	1
1976	BAL	AL	11	5	6	6	2	2	1	0	0	0	0	0	0	0	9	2
1977	BAL	AL	19	11	8	12	6	1	0	1	0	0	0	0	0	0	15	4
1978	BAL	AL	28	14	14	16	11	0	1	3	0	0	0	0	0	0	20	8
1979	BAL	AL	16	10	6	11	4	0	1	1	0	0	0	0	0	0	13	3
1980	BAL	AL	16	7	9	8	7	1	0	0	0	0	0	1	0	0	5	11
1981	BAL	AL	13	10	3	3	6	2	2	3	0	0	0	0	0	0	11	2
1982	CAL	AL	30	17	13	20	8	2	0	3	2	0	0	2	0	0	17	13
1983	CAL	AL	18	10	8	11	6	1	0	2	0	0	0	1	0	0	12	6
1984	CAL	AL	20	10	10	11	5	4	0	1	0	0	0	1	0	0	11	9
1985	CAL	AL	20	12	8	7	8	5	0	1	0	0	0	0	0	0	14	6
1986	CAL	AL	26	14	12	14	9	3	0	2	0	0	0	1	0	0	17	9
1987	CAL	AL	16	10	6	10	3	2	1	0	0	0	0	0	0	0	9	7
Total			237	133	104	131	77	23	6	17	2	0	0	6	0	0	156	81

Rank among batters: 132 • *Top target (6 home runs)*: Mike Moore • *Number of pitchers victimized*: 162 • *Total ballparks homered in*: 15 • *First HR*: 05/04/1975 off Tom Buskey • *World Series HR*—1; *LCS HR*—1

Earle Decker

EARLE HARRY DECKER
B: 06/ /1865
BR

Year	Tm	Lg	Tot	H	A	0	1	2	3	2	3	4	LO	XN	IP	PH	RHP	LHP
1890	PIT	NL	5	0	5	3	1	1	0	0	0	0	0	0	0	0	2	2

Rank among batters: 3,191 • *Total ballparks homered in*: 4 • *First HR*: 07/18/1890 off Tom Lovett

George Decker

GEORGE A. DECKER
B: 06/01/1869 D: 06/07/1909
BL

Year	Tm	Lg	Tot	H	A	0	1	2	3	2	3	4	LO	XN	IP	PH	RHP	LHP
1892	CHI	NL	1	0	1	1	0	0	0	0	0	0	0	0	0	0	0	0

George Decker *continued*

Year	Tm	Lg	Tot	H	A	Men-On 0	Men-On 1	Men-On 2	Men-On 3	One-Game 2	One-Game 3	One-Game 4	LO	XN	IP	PH	RHP	LHP
1893	CHI	NL	2	2	0	1	1	0	0	0	0	0	0	0	0	0	1	1
1894	CHI	NL	8	5	3	2	3	3	0	1	0	0	0	0	1	0	7	1
1895	CHI	NL	2	1	1	2	0	0	0	0	0	0	0	0	0	0	2	0
1896	CHI	NL	5	3	2	2	1	2	0	0	0	0	0	0	0	0	5	0
1897	CHI	NL	5	2	3	2	1	2	0	0	0	0	1	1	1	0	4	1
1898	STL	NL	1	1	0	0	1	0	0	0	0	0	0	0	0	0	1	0
1899	LOU	NL	1	0	1	1	0	0	0	0	0	0	0	0	0	0	1	0
Total			25	14	11	11	7	7	0	1	0	0	1	1	2	0	21	3

Rank among batters: 1,608 • *Top target (3 home runs)*: Ed Stein, George Hemming • *Number of pitchers victimized*: 19 • *Total ballparks homered in*: 11 • *First HR*: 09/29/1892 off Mike Sullivan

Joe Decker

GEORGE HENRY DECKER
B: 06/16/1947
BR

Year	Tm	Lg	Tot	H	A	Men-On 0	Men-On 1	Men-On 2	Men-On 3	One-Game 2	One-Game 3	One-Game 4	LO	XN	IP	PH	RHP	LHP
1970	CHI	NL	1	0	1	1	0	0	0	0	0	0	0	0	0	0	1	0

Rank among batters: 4,707 • *Total ballparks homered in*: 1 • *First HR*: 05/01/1970 off Phil Niekro

Steve Decker

STEVEN MICHAEL DECKER
B: 10/25/1965
BR

Year	Tm	Lg	Tot	H	A	Men-On 0	Men-On 1	Men-On 2	Men-On 3	One-Game 2	One-Game 3	One-Game 4	LO	XN	IP	PH	RHP	LHP
1990	SF	NL	3	1	2	3	0	0	0	0	0	0	0	0	0	0	2	1
1991	SF	NL	5	4	1	3	1	1	0	0	0	0	0	0	0	0	2	3
1995	FLO	NL	3	2	1	2	1	0	0	0	0	0	0	0	0	0	2	1
Total			11	7	4	8	2	1	0	0	0	0	0	0	0	0	6	5

Rank among batters: 2,419 • *Total ballparks homered in*: 6 • *First HR*: 09/19/1990 off Tom Glavine

Rob Deer

ROBERT GEORGE DEER
B: 09/29/1960
BR

Year	Tm	Lg	Tot	H	A	Men-On 0	Men-On 1	Men-On 2	Men-On 3	One-Game 2	One-Game 3	One-Game 4	LO	XN	IP	PH	RHP	LHP
1984	SF	NL	3	2	1	3	0	0	0	0	0	0	0	0	0	0	2	1
1985	SF	NL	8	5	3	5	2	1	0	0	0	0	0	0	0	3	2	6
1986	MIL	AL	33	19	14	15	14	4	0	3	0	0	0	1	0	0	22	11
1987	MIL	AL	28	11	17	14	7	5	2	4	0	0	0	0	0	0	20	8
1988	MIL	AL	23	12	11	11	7	4	1	1	0	0	0	1	0	0	15	8
1989	MIL	AL	26	15	11	15	8	2	1	3	0	0	0	1	0	0	18	8
1990	MIL	AL	27	11	16	13	11	3	0	1	0	0	0	0	0	0	12	15
1991	DET	AL	25	12	13	11	10	3	1	2	0	0	0	1	0	0	16	9
1992	DET	AL	32	13	19	22	6	4	0	5	0	0	0	1	0	0	18	14
1993	DET	AL	14	9	5	10	1	3	0	1	0	0	0	0	0	1	8	6
	BOS	AL	7	3	4	4	3	0	0	1	0	0	0	1	0	0	4	3
	Total		21	12	9	14	4	3	0	2	0	0	0	1	0	1	12	9
Total			226	112	114	123	69	29	5	21	0	0	0	6	0	4	137	89

Rank among batters: 143 • *Top target (6 home runs)*: Tom Candiotti, Mike Moore • *Number of pitchers victimized*: 155 • *Total ballparks homered in*: 20 • *First HR*: 09/09/1984 off Rick Camp

Charlie Dees

CHARLES HENRY DEES
B: 06/24/1935
BL

Year	Tm	Lg	Tot	H	A	Men-On 0	Men-On 1	Men-On 2	Men-On 3	One-Game 2	One-Game 3	One-Game 4	LO	XN	IP	PH	RHP	LHP
1963	LA	AL	3	2	1	1	1	1	0	0	0	0	0	0	0	0	3	0

Rank among batters: 3,735 • *Total ballparks homered in*: 2 • *First HR*: 05/31/1963 off Milt Pappas

Arturo DeFreitas

ARTURO MARCELINO (SIMON) DEFREITAS
B: 04/26/1953
BR

Year	Tm	Lg	Tot	H	A	Men-On 0	Men-On 1	Men-On 2	Men-On 3	One-Game 2	One-Game 3	One-Game 4	LO	XN	IP	PH	RHP	LHP
1978	CIN	NL	1	0	1	1	0	0	0	0	0	0	0	0	0	0	0	1

Rank among batters: 4,707 • *Total ballparks homered in*: 1 • *First HR*: 09/22/1978 off Mickey Mahler

Ivan DeJesus

IVAN (ALVAREZ) DEJESUS
B: 01/09/1953
BR

Year	Tm	Lg	Tot	H	A	Men-On 0	Men-On 1	Men-On 2	Men-On 3	One-Game 2	One-Game 3	One-Game 4	LO	XN	IP	PH	RHP	LHP
1977	CHI	NL	3	2	1	0	1	2	0	0	0	0	0	0	0	0	2	1
1978	CHI	NL	3	1	2	3	0	0	0	0	0	0	0	0	0	0	2	1
1979	CHI	NL	5	4	1	4	0	1	0	0	0	0	2	0	0	0	5	0
1980	CHI	NL	3	3	0	2	1	0	0	0	0	0	1	0	0	0	1	2
1982	PHI	NL	3	1	2	2	0	1	0	0	0	0	0	0	0	0	2	1
1983	PHI	NL	4	2	2	2	2	0	0	0	0	0	0	0	0	0	4	0
Total			21	13	8	13	4	4	0	0	0	0	3	0	0	0	16	5

Rank among batters: 1,768 • *Top target (3 home runs)*: Bob Forsch • *Number of pitchers victimized*: 18 • *Total ballparks homered in*: 6 • *First HR*: 04/10/1977 off Jon Matlack • *Hit for Cycle*—vs STL: 04/22/1980

Bobby Del Greco

ROBERT GEORGE DEL GRECO
B: 04/07/1933
BR

Year	Tm	Lg	Tot	H	A	Men-On 0	Men-On 1	Men-On 2	Men-On 3	One-Game 2	One-Game 3	One-Game 4	LO	XN	IP	PH	RHP	LHP
1952	PIT	NL	1	1	0	1	0	0	0	0	0	0	0	0	0	0	1	0
1956	PIT	NL	2	2	0	1	1	0	0	1	0	0	0	0	0	0	0	2
	STL	NL	5	0	5	5	0	0	0	0	0	0	0	0	0	0	0	5
	Total		7	2	5	6	1	0	0	1	0	0	0	0	0	0	0	7
1960	PHI	NL	10	7	3	9	1	0	0	0	0	0	1	0	0	1	5	5
1961	PHI	NL	2	0	2	2	0	0	0	0	0	0	1	0	0	0	0	2
	KC	AL	5	2	3	2	3	0	0	0	0	0	0	0	0	0	3	2
	Total		7	2	5	4	3	0	0	0	0	0	1	0	0	0	3	4
1962	KC	AL	9	5	4	5	2	2	0	0	0	0	1	0	0	0	7	2
1963	KC	AL	8	2	6	6	1	1	0	0	0	0	0	0	0	1	2	6
Total			42	19	23	31	8	3	0	1	0	0	3	0	0	2	18	24

Rank among batters: 1,138 • *Top target (4 home runs)*: Harvey Haddix • *Number of pitchers victimized*: 35 • *Total ballparks homered in*: 15 • *First HR*: 06/09/1952 off Jim Wilson

Ed Delahanty

EDWARD JAMES DELAHANTY
B: 10/30/1867 D: 07/02/1903
BR HOF

Year	Tm	Lg	Tot	H	A	Men-On 0	Men-On 1	Men-On 2	Men-On 3	One-Game 2	One-Game 3	One-Game 4	LO	XN	IP	PH	RHP	LHP
1888	PHI	NL	1	1	0	0	1	0	0	0	0	0	0	0	1	0	1	0
1890	CLE	PL	3	2	1	2	1	0	0	0	0	0	0	0	0	0	2	1
1891	PHI	NL	5	2	3	2	3	0	0	0	0	0	0	0	2	0	5	0
1892	PHI	NL	6	4	2	2	4	0	0	0	0	0	0	0	2	0	4	1
1893	PHI	NL	19	10	9	8	9	2	0	1	0	0	0	0	4	0	15	3
1894	PHI	NL	4	2	2	0	2	2	0	0	0	0	0	0	0	0	4	0
1895	PHI	NL	11	8	3	3	5	3	0	0	0	0	0	0	0	0	9	2
1896	PHI	NL	13	5	8	4	5	3	1	2	0	1	0	0	2	0	9	4
1897	PHI	NL	5	2	3	2	1	2	0	0	0	0	0	0	0	0	4	1
1898	PHI	NL	4	1	3	2	2	0	0	0	0	0	0	0	0	0	3	1
1899	PHI	NL	9	4	5	4	4	1	0	0	0	0	0	0	0	0	9	0
1900	PHI	NL	2	0	2	2	0	0	0	0	0	0	0	0	1	0	1	1
1901	PHI	NL	8	5	3	4	2	2	0	0	0	0	0	0	0	0	6	2
1902	WAS	AL	10	9	1	4	5	1	0	0	0	0	0	0	1	0	10	0
1903	WAS	AL	1	0	1	1	0	0	0	0	0	0	0	0	0	0	1	0
Total			101	55	46	40	44	16	1	3	0	1	0	0	13	0	83	16

Rank among batters: 491 • *Top target (6 home runs)*: Jouett Meekin • *Number of pitchers victimized*: 63 • *Total ballparks homered in*: 19 • *First HR*: 06/13/1888 off Jerry Denny

Frank Delahanty

FRANK GEORGE DELAHANTY
B: 01/29/1883 D: 07/22/1966
BR

Year	Tm	Lg	Tot	H	A	Men-On 0	Men-On 1	Men-On 2	Men-On 3	One-Game 2	One-Game 3	One-Game 4	LO	XN	IP	PH	RHP	LHP
1906	NY	AL	2	2	0	0	1	1	0	1	0	0	0	0	0	0	2	0
1914	BUF	FL	2	1	1	2	0	0	0	0	0	0	0	0	0	0	2	0
	PIT	FL	1	1	0	1	0	0	0	0	0	0	0	1	0	0	0	1
	Total		3	2	1	3	0	0	0	0	0	0	0	1	0	0	2	1
Total			5	4	1	3	1	1	0	1	0	0	0	1	0	0	4	1

Rank among batters: 3,191 • *Total ballparks homered in*: 4 • *First HR*: 08/31/1906 off Tom Hughes

Year	Tm	Lg	Tot	H	A	Men-On				One-Game			LO	XN	IP	PH	RHP	LHP
						0	1	2	3	2	3	4						

Jim Delahanty

JAMES CHRISTOPHER DELAHANTY
B: 06/20/1879 D: 10/17/1953
BR

Year	Tm	Lg	Tot	H	A	0	1	2	3	2	3	4	LO	XN	IP	PH	RHP	LHP
1904	BOS	NL	3	1	2	2	1	0	0	0	0	0	0	0	1	0	3	0
1905	BOS	NL	5	5	0	2	2	1	0	0	0	0	0	0	0	0	5	0
1906	CIN	NL	1	1	0	0	1	0	0	0	0	0	0	0	1	0	1	0
1907	WAS	AL	2	1	1	2	0	0	0	0	0	0	0	0	0	0	1	1
1908	WAS	AL	1	0	1	1	0	0	0	0	0	0	0	0	0	0	1	0
1909	WAS	AL	1	0	1	1	0	0	0	0	0	0	0	0	1	0	1	0
1910	DET	AL	3	2	1	1	1	1	0	0	0	0	0	0	0	0	3	0
1911	DET	AL	3	3	0	2	0	1	0	0	0	0	0	0	0	0	2	1
Total			19	13	6	11	5	3	0	0	0	0	0	0	3	0	17	2

Rank among batters: 1,861 • *Top target (2 home runs)*: Oscar Jones, Tom Walker • *Number of pitchers victimized*: 17 • *Total ballparks homered in*: 6 • *First HR*: 06/28/1904 off Oscar Jones

Joe Delahanty

JOSEPH NICHOLAS DELAHANTY
B: 10/18/1875 D: 01/09/1936
BR

Year	Tm	Lg	Tot	H	A	0	1	2	3	2	3	4	LO	XN	IP	PH	RHP	LHP
1907	STL	NL	1	1	0	1	0	0	0	0	0	0	0	0	1	0	1	0
1908	STL	NL	1	1	0	1	0	0	0	0	0	0	0	0	1	0	1	0
1909	STL	NL	2	0	2	0	1	0	1	0	0	0	0	0	0	0	2	0
Total			4	2	2	2	1	0	1	0	0	0	0	0	2	0	4	0

Rank among batters: 3,427 • *Total ballparks homered in*: 3 • *First HR*: 10/01/1907 off Sam Frock

Bill DeLancey

WILLIAM PINKNEY DELANCEY
B: 11/28/1911 D: 11/28/1946
BL

Year	Tm	Lg	Tot	H	A	0	1	2	3	2	3	4	LO	XN	IP	PH	RHP	LHP
1934	STL	NL	13	7	6	8	3	2	0	0	0	0	0	0	0	1	12	1
1935	STL	NL	6	3	3	4	1	1	0	0	0	0	0	0	0	0	5	1
Total			19	10	9	12	4	3	0	0	0	0	0	0	0	1	17	2

Rank among batters: 1,861 • *Top target (2 home runs)*: Si Johnson • *Number of pitchers victimized*: 18 • *Total ballparks homered in*: 6 • *First HR*: 05/30/1934 off Si Johnson • *World Series HR*—1

Art Delaney

ARTHUR DEWEY DELANEY
B: 01/05/1897 D: 05/02/1970
BR

Year	Tm	Lg	Tot	H	A	0	1	2	3	2	3	4	LO	XN	IP	PH	RHP	LHP
1929	BOS	NL	1	0	1	0	1	0	0	0	0	0	0	0	0	0	1	0

Rank among batters: 4,707 • *Total ballparks homered in*: 1 • *First HR*: 04/30/1929 off Luther Roy

Bill Delaney

WILLIAM L. DELANEY
B: 03/05/1863 D: 03/01/1942
BR

Year	Tm	Lg	Tot	H	A	0	1	2	3	2	3	4	LO	XN	IP	PH	RHP	LHP
1890	CLE	NL	1	1	0	0	1	0	0	0	0	0	0	0	0	0	1	0

Rank among batters: 4,707 • *Total ballparks homered in*: 1 • *First HR*: 09/18/1890 off Bill Phillips

Carlos Delgado

CARLOS JUAN (HERNANDEZ) DELGADO
B: 06/25/1972
BL

Year	Tm	Lg	Tot	H	A	0	1	2	3	2	3	4	LO	XN	IP	PH	RHP	LHP
1994	TOR	AL	9	5	4	3	2	4	0	1	0	0	0	0	0	0	6	3
1995	TOR	AL	3	2	1	2	1	0	0	0	0	0	0	0	0	1	2	1
Total			12	7	5	5	3	4	0	1	0	0	0	0	0	1	8	4

Rank among batters: 2,325 • *Total ballparks homered in*: 4 • *First HR*: 04/04/1994 off Dennis Cook

Eddie Delker

EDWARD ALBERTS DELKER
B: 04/17/1907
BR

Year	Tm	Lg	Tot	H	A	0	1	2	3	2	3	4	LO	XN	IP	PH	RHP	LHP
1932	PHI	NL	1	1	0	0	1	0	0	0	0	0	0	0	0	0	1	0

Rank among batters: 4,707 • *Total ballparks homered in*: 1 • *First HR*: 06/14/1932 off Jack Ogden

Year	Tm	Lg	Tot	H	A	Men-On 0	Men-On 1	Men-On 2	Men-On 3	One-Game 2	One-Game 3	One-Game 4	LO	XN	IP	PH	RHP	LHP

Ike Delock

IVAN MARTIN DELOCK
B: 11/11/1929
BR

Year	Tm	Lg	Tot	H	A	0	1	2	3	2	3	4	LO	XN	IP	PH	RHP	LHP
1959	BOS	AL	1	1	0	1	0	0	0	0	0	0	0	0	0	0	1	0

Rank among batters: 4,707 • *Total ballparks homered in*: 1 • *First HR*: 06/10/1959 off Paul Foytack

Jim Delsing

JAMES HENRY DELSING
B: 11/13/1925
BL

Year	Tm	Lg	Tot	H	A	0	1	2	3	2	3	4	LO	XN	IP	PH	RHP	LHP
1949	NY	AL	1	1	0	0	1	0	0	0	0	0	0	0	0	0	1	0
1951	STL	AL	8	4	4	6	2	0	0	0	0	0	0	0	0	0	7	1
1952	STL	AL	1	0	1	1	0	0	0	0	0	0	0	0	0	1	1	0
	DET	AL	3	1	2	3	0	0	0	0	0	0	0	0	0	0	2	1
	Total		4	1	3	4	0	0	0	0	0	0	0	0	0	1	3	1
1953	DET	AL	11	8	3	7	3	0	1	2	0	0	0	0	0	0	9	2
1954	DET	AL	6	3	3	3	3	0	0	0	0	0	0	2	0	1	6	0
1955	DET	AL	10	8	2	4	6	0	0	0	0	0	0	0	0	0	10	0
Total			40	25	15	24	15	0	1	2	0	0	0	2	0	2	36	4

Rank among batters: 1,181 • *Top target (4 home runs)*: Joe Coleman • *Number of pitchers victimized*: 30 • *Total ballparks homered in*: 7 • *First HR*: 09/28/1949 off Joe Coleman

Joe DeMaestri

JOSEPH PAUL DEMAESTRI
B: 12/09/1928
BR

Year	Tm	Lg	Tot	H	A	0	1	2	3	2	3	4	LO	XN	IP	PH	RHP	LHP
1951	CHI	AL	1	0	1	0	1	0	0	0	0	0	0	0	0	0	1	0
1952	STL	AL	1	1	0	0	0	1	0	0	0	0	0	0	0	0	0	1
1953	PHI	AL	6	3	3	5	1	0	0	0	0	0	1	0	0	0	5	1
1954	PHI	AL	8	6	2	8	0	0	0	1	0	0	0	0	0	0	6	2
1955	KC	AL	6	4	2	5	1	0	0	0	0	0	1	1	0	0	5	1
1956	KC	AL	6	4	2	5	1	0	0	0	0	0	0	0	0	0	1	5
1957	KC	AL	9	5	4	6	3	0	0	0	0	0	1	0	0	0	8	1
1958	KC	AL	6	5	1	5	1	0	0	0	0	0	0	0	0	0	4	2
1959	KC	AL	6	4	2	6	0	0	0	0	0	0	0	0	0	0	4	2
Total			49	32	17	40	8	1	0	1	0	0	3	1	0	0	34	15

Rank among batters: 1,008 • *Top target (4 home runs)*: Don Larsen • *Number of pitchers victimized*: 34 • *Total ballparks homered in*: 10 • *First HR*: 09/30/1951 off Ned Garver

Frank Demaree

JOSEPH FRANKLIN DEMAREE
B: 06/10/1910 D: 08/30/1958
BR

Year	Tm	Lg	Tot	H	A	0	1	2	3	2	3	4	LO	XN	IP	PH	RHP	LHP
1933	CHI	NL	6	2	4	3	1	2	0	0	0	0	0	0	0	0	5	1
1935	CHI	NL	2	1	1	2	0	0	0	0	0	0	0	0	0	0	2	0
1936	CHI	NL	16	7	9	11	3	2	0	3	0	0	0	0	0	0	14	2
1937	CHI	NL	17	10	7	7	8	1	1	0	0	0	0	0	0	0	11	6
1938	CHI	NL	8	2	6	5	3	0	0	1	0	0	0	1	0	0	4	4
1939	NY	NL	11	9	2	5	5	1	0	1	0	0	0	1	0	0	10	1
1940	NY	NL	7	4	3	5	0	2	0	0	0	0	0	1	0	0	5	2
1941	BOS	NL	2	0	2	1	0	1	0	0	0	0	0	0	0	0	1	1
1942	BOS	NL	3	2	1	1	1	1	0	0	0	0	0	0	0	0	0	3
Total			72	37	35	40	21	10	1	5	0	0	0	3	0	0	52	20

Rank among batters: 723 • *Top target (4 home runs)*: Lon Warneke • *Number of pitchers victimized*: 55 • *Total ballparks homered in*: 8 • *First HR*: 06/15/1933 off Hal Smith • *World Series HR—3*

John DeMerit

JOHN STEPHEN DEMERIT
B: 01/08/1936
BR

Year	Tm	Lg	Tot	H	A	0	1	2	3	2	3	4	LO	XN	IP	PH	RHP	LHP
1961	MIL	NL	2	0	2	1	1	0	0	0	0	0	1	0	0	0	1	1
1962	NY	NL	1	1	0	1	0	0	0	0	0	0	0	0	0	0	0	1
Total			3	1	2	2	1	0	0	0	0	0	1	0	0	0	1	2

Rank among batters: 3,735 • *Total ballparks homered in*: 3 • *First HR*: 04/26/1961 off Larry Jackson

Don Demeter

DONALD LEE DEMETER
B: 06/25/1935
BR

Year	Tm	Lg	Tot	H	A	Men-On 0	1	2	3	One-Game 2	3	4	LO	XN	IP	PH	RHP	LHP
1956	BRO	NL	1	1	0	1	0	0	0	0	0	0	0	0	0	0	0	1
1958	LA	NL	5	2	3	2	3	0	0	0	0	0	0	0	0	0	3	2
1959	LA	NL	18	11	7	8	9	1	0	1	1	0	0	1	1	0	13	5
1960	LA	NL	9	8	1	6	2	1	0	1	0	0	0	0	0	1	8	1
1961	LA	NL	1	1	0	1	0	0	0	0	0	0	0	0	0	0	1	0
	PHI	NL	20	7	13	10	5	4	1	0	1	0	0	0	0	0	10	10
	Total		21	8	13	11	5	4	1	0	1	0	0	0	0	0	11	10
1962	PHI	NL	29	10	19	14	11	2	2	3	0	0	0	0	0	0	17	12
1963	PHI	NL	22	6	16	11	8	3	0	3	0	0	0	1	0	1	12	10
1964	DET	AL	22	10	12	15	4	3	0	2	0	0	0	1	0	1	11	11
1965	DET	AL	16	9	7	9	5	1	1	1	0	0	0	0	0	0	12	4
1966	DET	AL	5	3	2	2	2	1	0	0	0	0	0	0	0	0	3	2
	BOS	AL	9	6	3	7	2	0	0	0	0	0	0	0	0	0	8	1
	Total		14	9	5	9	4	1	0	0	0	0	0	0	0	0	11	3
1967	BOS	AL	1	1	0	0	0	1	0	0	0	0	0	0	0	0	1	0
	CLE	AL	5	4	1	4	1	0	0	1	0	0	0	0	0	1	1	4
	Total		6	5	1	4	1	1	0	1	0	0	0	0	0	1	2	4
Total			163	79	84	90	52	17	4	12	2	0	0	3	1	4	100	63

Rank among batters: 257 • Top target (4 home runs): Jay Hook, Lew Burdette, Harvey Haddix, Bob Buhl, Ray Sadecki, Robin Roberts • *Number of pitchers victimized*: 109 • *Total ballparks homered in*: 22 • *First HR*: 09/19/1956 off Don Liddle

Ray Demmitt

CHARLES RAYMOND DEMMITT
B: 02/02/1884 D: 02/19/1956
BL

Year	Tm	Lg	Tot	H	A	Men-On 0	1	2	3	One-Game 2	3	4	LO	XN	IP	PH	RHP	LHP
1909	NY	AL	4	4	0	2	2	0	0	0	0	0	0	0	0	0	4	0
1914	CHI	AL	2	1	1	1	0	0	1	0	0	0	0	0	0	0	2	0
1918	STL	AL	1	0	1	1	0	0	0	0	0	0	0	0	0	0	1	0
1919	STL	AL	1	1	0	1	0	0	0	0	0	0	0	0	0	0	1	0
Total			8	6	2	5	2	0	1	0	0	0	0	0	0	0	8	0

Rank among batters: 2,703 • *Total ballparks homered in*: 4 • *First HR*: 06/15/1909 off Frank Smith

Gene DeMontreville

EUGENE NAPOLEON DEMONTREVILLE
B: 03/26/1874 D: 02/18/1935
BR

Year	Tm	Lg	Tot	H	A	Men-On 0	1	2	3	One-Game 2	3	4	LO	XN	IP	PH	RHP	LHP
1896	WAS	NL	8	5	3	3	4	1	0	0	0	0	0	0	0	0	6	2
1897	WAS	NL	3	3	0	1	2	0	0	0	0	0	0	0	1	0	3	0
1899	BAL	NL	1	0	1	0	1	0	0	0	0	0	0	0	0	0	0	1
1901	BOS	NL	5	3	2	3	1	1	0	0	0	0	0	0	1	0	3	2
Total			17	11	6	7	8	2	0	0	0	0	0	0	2	0	12	5

Rank among batters: 1,969 • *Top target (2 home runs)*: Bill Hart, Kid Nichols • *Number of pitchers victimized*: 15 • *Total ballparks homered in*: 6 • *First HR*: 05/18/1896 off Bill Hill

Rick Dempsey

JOHN RIKARD DEMPSEY
B: 09/13/1949
BR

Year	Tm	Lg	Tot	H	A	Men-On 0	1	2	3	One-Game 2	3	4	LO	XN	IP	PH	RHP	LHP
1974	NY	AL	2	1	1	1	0	1	0	0	0	0	0	0	0	0	0	2
1975	NY	AL	1	0	1	1	0	0	0	0	0	0	0	0	0	0	0	1
1977	BAL	AL	3	1	2	2	0	1	0	0	0	0	0	0	0	0	3	0
1978	BAL	AL	6	4	2	5	1	0	0	0	0	0	0	0	0	0	3	3
1979	BAL	AL	6	1	5	4	0	1	1	0	0	0	0	0	0	0	5	1
1980	BAL	AL	9	5	4	5	3	1	0	1	0	0	0	0	0	0	3	6
1981	BAL	AL	6	4	2	5	1	0	0	0	0	0	0	0	0	0	2	4
1982	BAL	AL	5	2	3	3	2	0	0	0	0	0	0	0	0	0	3	2
1983	BAL	AL	4	3	1	3	1	0	0	0	0	0	0	0	0	0	2	2
1984	BAL	AL	11	6	5	7	4	0	0	1	0	0	0	0	0	0	6	5
1985	BAL	AL	12	4	8	4	7	1	0	1	0	0	0	0	0	1	5	7
1986	BAL	AL	13	7	6	10	1	1	1	1	0	0	0	0	0	0	7	6
1987	CLE	AL	1	1	0	1	0	0	0	0	0	0	0	0	0	0	0	1
1988	LA	NL	7	3	4	4	3	0	0	0	0	0	0	0	0	0	2	5
1989	LA	NL	4	2	2	3	0	1	0	0	0	0	0	2	0	0	3	1

						Men-On				One-Game								
Year	Tm	Lg	Tot	H	A	0	1	2	3	2	3	4	LO	XN	IP	PH	RHP	LHP

Rick Dempsey *continued*

Year	Tm	Lg	Tot	H	A	0	1	2	3	2	3	4	LO	XN	IP	PH	RHP	LHP
1990	LA	NL	2	2	0	2	0	0	0	1	0	0	0	0	0	0	0	2
1991	MIL	AL	4	2	2	0	3	1	0	0	0	0	0	0	0	0	1	3
Total			96	48	48	60	26	8	2	5	0	0	0	2	0	1	45	51

Rank among batters: 520 • *Top target (3 home runs)*: Luis Tiant, Frank Tanana, Neal Heaton • *Number of pitchers victimized*: 79 • *Total ballparks homered in*: 22 • *First HR*: 05/12/1974 off Kevin Kobel • *World Series HR*—1

Otto Denning

OTTO GEORGE DENNING
B: 12/28/1912 D: 05/25/1992
BR

Year	Tm	Lg	Tot	H	A	0	1	2	3	2	3	4	LO	XN	IP	PH	RHP	LHP
1942	CLE	AL	1	0	1	1	0	0	0	0	0	0	0	0	0	0	1	0

Rank among batters: 4,707 • *Total ballparks homered in*: 1 • *First HR*: 05/04/1942 off Dick Newsome

Jerry Denny

JEREMIAH DENNIS DENNY
B: 03/16/1859 D: 08/16/1927
BR

Year	Tm	Lg	Tot	H	A	0	1	2	3	2	3	4	LO	XN	IP	PH	RHP	LHP
1881	PRO	NL	1	1	0	1	0	0	0	0	0	0	0	0	0	0	0	1
1882	PRO	NL	2	2	0	0	2	0	0	0	0	0	0	0	0	0	2	0
1883	PRO	NL	8	4	4	5	2	1	0	0	0	0	0	0	0	0	8	0
1884	PRO	NL	6	3	3	1	3	2	0	0	0	0	0	0	0	0	3	2
1885	PRO	NL	3	2	1	3	0	0	0	0	0	0	0	0	0	0	3	0
1886	STL	NL	9	2	7	4	1	4	0	1	0	0	0	0	2	0	4	4
1887	IND	NL	11	9	2	4	5	2	0	0	0	0	0	0	1	0	8	3
1888	IND	NL	12	12	0	7	4	1	0	3	0	0	0	1	0	0	12	0
1889	IND	NL	18	16	2	8	7	2	1	2	0	0	0	2	0	0	14	4
1890	NY	NL	3	0	3	2	1	0	0	0	0	0	0	0	0	0	1	1
1893	LOU	NL	1	1	0	0	1	0	0	0	0	0	0	0	0	0	1	0
Total			74	52	22	35	26	12	1	6	0	0	0	3	3	0	56	14

Rank among batters: 707 • Top target (4 home runs): Jim McCormick, Mickey Welch, Charley Radbourn, John Clarkson • *Number of pitchers victimized*: 46 • *Total ballparks homered in*: 17 • *First HR*: 08/27/1881 off J Richmond • *World Series HR*—1

Bucky Dent

RUSSELL EARL DENT
B: 11/25/1951
BR

Year	Tm	Lg	Tot	H	A	0	1	2	3	2	3	4	LO	XN	IP	PH	RHP	LHP
1974	CHI	AL	5	2	3	2	3	0	0	0	0	0	0	0	0	0	3	2
1975	CHI	AL	3	0	3	1	0	2	0	0	0	0	0	0	0	0	2	1
1976	CHI	AL	2	1	1	0	1	1	0	0	0	0	0	0	0	0	1	1
1977	NY	AL	8	3	5	3	2	2	1	1	0	0	0	0	0	0	2	6
1978	NY	AL	5	0	5	2	2	1	0	0	0	0	0	0	0	0	3	2
1979	NY	AL	2	0	2	1	1	0	0	0	0	0	0	0	0	0	1	1
1980	NY	AL	5	2	3	3	2	0	0	0	0	0	0	0	1	0	4	1
1981	NY	AL	7	3	4	2	4	1	0	0	0	0	0	0	0	0	3	4
1982	TEX	AL	1	0	1	0	1	0	0	0	0	0	0	0	0	0	1	0
1983	TEX	AL	2	0	2	2	0	0	0	0	0	0	0	0	0	0	0	2
Total			40	11	29	16	16	7	1	1	0	0	0	0	1	0	20	20

Rank among batters: 1,181 • Top target (2 home runs): Jim Colborn, Dennis Eckersley, Ferguson Jenkins • *Number of pitchers victimized*: 37 • *Total ballparks homered in*: 12 • *First HR*: 05/05/1974 off Jim Slaton

Sam Dente

SAMUEL JOSEPH DENTE
B: 04/26/1922
BR

Year	Tm	Lg	Tot	H	A	0	1	2	3	2	3	4	LO	XN	IP	PH	RHP	LHP
1949	WAS	AL	1	0	1	0	1	0	0	0	0	0	0	0	0	0	1	0
1950	WAS	AL	2	0	2	1	1	0	0	0	0	0	0	0	0	0	1	1
1954	CLE	AL	1	0	1	1	0	0	0	0	0	0	0	0	0	0	0	1
Total			4	0	4	2	2	0	0	0	0	0	0	0	0	0	2	2

Rank among batters: 3,427 • *Total ballparks homered in*: 4 • *First HR*: 06/01/1949 off Red Embree

Bob Dernier

ROBERT EUGENE DERNIER
B: 01/05/1957
BR

Year	Tm	Lg	Tot	H	A	0	1	2	3	2	3	4	LO	XN	IP	PH	RHP	LHP
1982	PHI	NL	4	3	1	3	1	0	0	0	0	0	1	0	0	0	0	4

Year	Tm	Lg	Tot	H	A	Men-On 0	Men-On 1	Men-On 2	Men-On 3	One-Game 2	One-Game 3	One-Game 4	LO	XN	IP	PH	RHP	LHP

Bob Dernier *continued*

Year	Tm	Lg	Tot	H	A	0	1	2	3	2	3	4	LO	XN	IP	PH	RHP	LHP
1983	PHI	NL	1	0	1	1	0	0	0	0	0	0	1	0	0	0	1	0
1984	CHI	NL	3	2	1	3	0	0	0	0	0	0	0	0	0	0	3	0
1985	CHI	NL	1	1	0	1	0	0	0	0	0	0	0	0	0	0	1	0
1986	CHI	NL	4	2	2	2	1	1	0	0	0	0	0	0	0	0	2	2
1987	CHI	NL	8	4	4	7	1	0	0	0	0	0	3	0	0	1	1	7
1988	PHI	NL	1	0	1	1	0	0	0	0	0	0	1	0	0	0	0	1
1989	PHI	NL	1	1	0	0	0	1	0	0	0	0	0	1	1	0	0	1
Total			23	13	10	18	3	2	0	0	0	0	6	1	1	1	8	15

Rank among batters: 1,686 • *Top target (3 home runs)*: Don Carman • *Number of pitchers victimized*: 20 • *Total ballparks homered in*: 8 • *First HR*: 05/15/1982 off Dan Schatzeder • *LCS HR*—1

Claud Derrick

CLAUD LESTER DERRICK
B: 06/11/1886 D: 07/15/1974
BR

Year	Tm	Lg	Tot	H	A	0	1	2	3	2	3	4	LO	XN	IP	PH	RHP	LHP
1913	NY	AL	1	0	1	1	0	0	0	0	0	0	0	0	0	0	1	0

Rank among batters: 4,707 • *Total ballparks homered in*: 1 • *First HR*: 05/10/1913 off Hooks Dauss

Paul Derringer

SAMUEL PAUL DERRINGER
B: 10/17/1906 D: 11/17/1987
BR

Year	Tm	Lg	Tot	H	A	0	1	2	3	2	3	4	LO	XN	IP	PH	RHP	LHP
1938	CIN	NL	2	0	2	1	1	0	0	0	0	0	0	0	0	0	2	0

Rank among batters: 4,129 • *Total ballparks homered in*: 2 • *First HR*: 07/26/1938 off Jim Turner

Russ Derry

ALVA RUSSELL DERRY
B: 10/07/1916
BL

Year	Tm	Lg	Tot	H	A	0	1	2	3	2	3	4	LO	XN	IP	PH	RHP	LHP
1944	NY	AL	4	3	1	3	0	0	1	0	0	0	0	0	0	1	4	0
1945	NY	AL	13	8	5	6	5	0	2	2	0	0	0	0	0	2	13	0
Total			17	11	6	9	5	0	3	2	0	0	0	0	0	3	17	0

Rank among batters: 1,969 • *Top target (2 home runs)*: Rex Cecil, Sig Jakucki • *Number of pitchers victimized*: 15 • *Total ballparks homered in*: 4 • *First HR*: 07/20/1944 off George Caster

Joe DeSa

JOSEPH DESA
B: 07/27/1959 D: 12/20/1986
BL

Year	Tm	Lg	Tot	H	A	0	1	2	3	2	3	4	LO	XN	IP	PH	RHP	LHP
1985	CHI	AL	2	1	1	1	0	0	1	0	0	0	0	0	0	1	2	0

Rank among batters: 4,129 • *Total ballparks homered in*: 2 • *First HR*: 08/11/1985 off Ray Burris

Gene Desautels

EUGENE ABRAHAM DESAUTELS
B: 06/13/1907 D: 11/05/1994
BR

Year	Tm	Lg	Tot	H	A	0	1	2	3	2	3	4	LO	XN	IP	PH	RHP	LHP
1938	BOS	AL	2	1	1	2	0	0	0	0	0	0	0	0	1	0	2	0
1941	CLE	AL	1	0	1	1	0	0	0	0	0	0	0	0	0	0	1	0
Total			3	1	2	3	0	0	0	0	0	0	0	0	1	0	3	0

Rank among batters: 3,735 • *Total ballparks homered in*: 3 • *First HR*: 04/26/1938 off Pete Appleton

Delino DeShields

DELINO LAMONT DESHIELDS
B: 01/15/1969
BL

Year	Tm	Lg	Tot	H	A	0	1	2	3	2	3	4	LO	XN	IP	PH	RHP	LHP
1990	MON	NL	4	3	1	4	0	0	0	0	0	0	1	0	0	0	2	2
1991	MON	NL	10	3	7	7	3	0	0	0	0	0	2	0	0	0	7	3
1992	MON	NL	7	1	6	5	0	2	0	1	0	0	1	0	1	0	5	2
1993	MON	NL	2	2	0	2	0	0	0	0	0	0	0	0	0	0	0	2
1994	LA	NL	2	1	1	0	1	1	0	0	0	0	0	0	0	0	2	0
1995	LA	NL	8	2	6	6	1	0	1	0	0	0	1	0	0	0	6	2
Total			33	12	21	24	5	3	1	1	0	0	5	0	1	0	22	11

Rank among batters: 1,336 • *Top target (2 home runs)*: Curt Schilling • *Number of pitchers victimized*: 32 • *Total ballparks homered in*: 10 • *First HR*: 05/07/1990 off Scott Garrelts

Orestes Destrade

ORESTES (CUCUAS) DESTRADE
B: 05/08/1962
BB

Year	Tm	Lg	Tot	H	A	Men-On 0	1	2	3	One-Game 2	3	4	LO	XN	IP	PH	RHP	LHP
1988	PIT	NL	1	1	0	0	1	0	0	0	0	0	0	0	0	1	1	0
1993	FLO	NL	20	9	11	10	8	2	0	2	0	0	0	0	0	0	14	6
1994	FLO	NL	5	3	2	5	0	0	0	0	0	0	0	0	0	0	3	2
Total			26	13	13	15	9	2	0	2	0	0	0	0	0	1	18	8

Rank among batters: 1,576 • *Top target (2 home runs)*: Jose Guzman, John Burkett, Greg Hibbard • *Number of pitchers victimized*: 23 • *Total ballparks homered in*: 9 • *First HR*: 09/11/1988 off Steve Bedrosian

Bob Detherage

ROBERT WAYNE DETHERAGE
B: 09/20/1954
BR

Year	Tm	Lg	Tot	H	A	Men-On 0	1	2	3	One-Game 2	3	4	LO	XN	IP	PH	RHP	LHP
1980	KC	AL	1	0	1	0	0	1	0	0	0	0	0	0	0	0	1	0

Rank among batters: 4,707 • *Total ballparks homered in*: 1 • *First HR*: 05/07/1980 off Randy Scarbery

Mike Devereaux

MICHAEL DEVEREAUX
B: 04/10/1963
BR

Year	Tm	Lg	Tot	H	A	Men-On 0	1	2	3	One-Game 2	3	4	LO	XN	IP	PH	RHP	LHP
1989	BAL	AL	8	4	4	3	3	2	0	0	0	0	0	1	0	0	5	3
1990	BAL	AL	12	6	6	7	3	1	1	0	0	0	0	0	0	0	5	7
1991	BAL	AL	19	10	9	13	4	2	0	1	0	0	1	0	0	0	13	6
1992	BAL	AL	24	14	10	15	7	0	2	2	0	0	0	0	0	0	15	9
1993	BAL	AL	14	8	6	6	6	2	0	0	0	0	0	0	0	0	9	5
1994	BAL	AL	9	5	4	8	0	1	0	1	0	0	0	0	0	0	7	2
1995	CHI	AL	10	4	6	5	4	1	0	1	0	0	0	0	0	0	5	5
	ATL	NL	1	1	0	0	1	0	0	0	0	0	0	0	0	0	1	0
	Total		11	5	6	5	5	1	0	1	0	0	0	0	0	0	6	5
Total			97	52	45	57	28	9	3	5	0	0	1	1	0	0	60	37

Rank among batters: 515 • *Top target (3 home runs)*: Chuck Finley • *Number of pitchers victimized*: 83 • *Total ballparks homered in*: 18 • *First HR*: 04/21/1989 off Allan Anderson • *LCS HR*—0

Art Devlin

ARTHUR MCARTHUR DEVLIN
B: 10/16/1879 D: 09/18/1948
BR

Year	Tm	Lg	Tot	H	A	Men-On 0	1	2	3	One-Game 2	3	4	LO	XN	IP	PH	RHP	LHP
1904	NY	NL	1	1	0	0	0	0	1	0	0	0	0	0	1	0	1	0
1905	NY	NL	2	2	0	1	1	0	0	0	0	0	0	0	0	0	2	0
1906	NY	NL	2	0	2	2	0	0	0	0	0	0	0	0	1	0	2	0
1907	NY	NL	1	1	0	1	0	0	0	0	0	0	0	0	1	0	1	0
1908	NY	NL	2	1	1	2	0	0	0	0	0	0	0	0	0	0	0	2
1910	NY	NL	2	1	1	1	1	0	0	0	0	0	0	0	0	0	1	1
Total			10	6	4	7	2	0	1	0	0	0	0	0	3	0	7	3

Rank among batters: 2,500 • *Total ballparks homered in*: 4 • *First HR*: 04/22/1904 off John Brackenridge

Jim Devlin

JAMES ALEXANDER DEVLIN
B: 1849 D: 10/10/1883
BR

Year	Tm	Lg	Tot	H	A	Men-On 0	1	2	3	One-Game 2	3	4	LO	XN	IP	PH	RHP	LHP
1877	LOU	NL	1	0	1	0	1	0	0	0	0	0	0	0	0	0	1	0

Rank among batters: 4,707 • *Total ballparks homered in*: 1 • *First HR*: 06/30/1877 off Tommy Bond

Josh Devore

JOSHUA D. DEVORE
B: 11/13/1887 D: 10/06/1954
BL

Year	Tm	Lg	Tot	H	A	Men-On 0	1	2	3	One-Game 2	3	4	LO	XN	IP	PH	RHP	LHP
1910	NY	NL	2	2	0	2	0	0	0	0	0	0	0	0	0	0	2	0
1911	NY	NL	3	3	0	3	0	0	0	1	0	0	2	0	1	0	2	1
1912	NY	NL	2	2	0	1	0	1	0	0	0	0	0	0	0	0	2	0
1913	CIN	NL	3	2	1	1	2	0	0	0	0	0	0	0	2	0	2	1
1914	BOS	NL	1	0	1	1	0	0	0	0	0	0	0	0	1	0	0	1
Total			11	9	2	8	2	1	0	1	0	0	2	0	4	0	8	3

Rank among batters: 2,419 • *Total ballparks homered in*: 4 • *First HR*: 07/01/1910 off Doc Scanlan

Year	Tm	Lg	Tot	H	A	Men-On 0	1	2	3	One-Game 2	3	4	LO	XN	IP	PH	RHP	LHP

Al DeVormer

ALBERT E. DEVORMER
B: 08/19/1891 D: 08/29/1966
BR

Year	Tm	Lg	Tot	H	A	0	1	2	3	2	3	4	LO	XN	IP	PH	RHP	LHP
1927	NY	NL	2	2	0	0	2	0	0	0	0	0	0	0	0	0	2	0

Rank among batters: 4,129 • *Total ballparks homered in*: 1 • *First HR*: 05/21/1927 off Carmen Hill

Jeff DeWillis

JEFFREY ALLEN DEWILLIS
B: 04/13/1965
BR

Year	Tm	Lg	Tot	H	A	0	1	2	3	2	3	4	LO	XN	IP	PH	RHP	LHP
1987	TOR	AL	1	0	1	0	1	0	0	0	0	0	0	0	0	0	0	1

Rank among batters: 4,707 • *Total ballparks homered in*: 1 • *First HR*: 04/25/1987 off Floyd Bannister

Charlie Dexter

CHARLES DANA DEXTER
B: 06/15/1876 D: 06/09/1934
BR

Year	Tm	Lg	Tot	H	A	0	1	2	3	2	3	4	LO	XN	IP	PH	RHP	LHP
1896	LOU	NL	3	2	1	1	1	1	0	0	0	0	0	0	0	0	3	0
1897	LOU	NL	2	1	1	0	2	0	0	0	0	0	0	0	1	0	2	0
1898	LOU	NL	1	1	0	0	1	0	0	0	0	0	0	0	0	0	1	0
1899	LOU	NL	1	1	0	0	1	0	0	0	0	0	0	0	1	0	1	0
1900	CHI	NL	2	1	1	0	1	1	0	0	0	0	0	0	0	0	2	0
1901	CHI	NL	1	0	1	0	0	1	0	0	0	0	0	0	0	0	1	0
1902	CHI	NL	2	1	1	2	0	0	0	0	0	0	0	0	1	0	2	0
	BOS	NL	1	1	0	1	0	0	0	0	0	0	1	0	0	0	1	0
	Total		3	2	1	3	0	0	0	0	0	0	1	0	1	0	3	0
1903	BOS	NL	3	2	1	1	1	1	0	0	0	0	0	0	0	0	2	1
Total			16	10	6	5	7	4	0	0	0	0	1	0	3	0	15	1

Rank among batters: 2,029 • *Total ballparks homered in*: 5 • *First HR*: 05/23/1896 off George Hemming

Alex Diaz

ALEXIS DIAZ
B: 10/05/1968
BB

Year	Tm	Lg	Tot	H	A	0	1	2	3	2	3	4	LO	XN	IP	PH	RHP	LHP
1994	MIL	AL	1	0	1	0	0	1	0	0	0	0	0	0	0	0	1	0
1995	SEA	AL	3	3	0	1	0	2	0	0	0	0	0	0	0	1	2	1
Total			4	3	1	1	0	3	0	0	0	0	0	0	0	1	3	1

Rank among batters: 3,427 • *Total ballparks homered in*: 2 • *First HR*: 06/22/1994 off Ben McDonald

Bo Diaz

BAUDILIO JOSE (SEIJAS) DIAZ
B: 03/23/1953 D: 11/23/1990
BR

Year	Tm	Lg	Tot	H	A	0	1	2	3	2	3	4	LO	XN	IP	PH	RHP	LHP
1978	CLE	AL	2	1	1	2	0	0	0	0	0	0	0	0	0	0	1	1
1980	CLE	AL	3	2	1	2	0	0	1	0	0	0	0	0	0	0	2	1
1981	CLE	AL	7	5	2	3	3	1	0	0	0	0	0	0	0	0	1	6
1982	PHI	NL	18	11	7	10	6	2	0	2	0	0	0	1	0	0	16	2
1983	PHI	NL	15	9	6	8	4	2	1	1	0	0	0	1	0	0	13	2
1984	PHI	NL	1	1	0	0	1	0	0	0	0	0	0	0	0	0	1	0
1985	PHI	NL	2	2	0	1	1	0	0	1	0	0	0	0	0	0	2	0
	CIN	NL	3	2	1	3	0	0	0	0	0	0	0	0	0	0	3	0
	Total		5	4	1	4	1	0	0	1	0	0	0	0	0	0	5	0
1986	CIN	NL	10	8	2	8	1	1	0	0	0	0	0	1	0	0	7	3
1987	CIN	NL	15	8	7	5	7	2	1	1	0	0	0	0	0	0	11	4
1988	CIN	NL	10	5	5	7	2	1	0	0	0	0	0	0	0	0	6	4
1989	CIN	NL	1	1	0	0	1	0	0	0	0	0	0	0	0	0	1	0
Total			87	55	32	49	26	9	3	5	0	0	0	3	0	0	64	23

Rank among batters: 594 • *Top target (3 home runs)*: Bill Gullickson • *Number of pitchers victimized*: 72 • *Total ballparks homered in*: 15 • *First HR*: 07/30/1978 off John Henry Johnson

Mario Diaz

MARIO RAFAEL (TORRES) DIAZ
B: 01/10/1962
BR

Year	Tm	Lg	Tot	H	A	0	1	2	3	2	3	4	LO	XN	IP	PH	RHP	LHP
1989	SEA	AL	1	0	1	0	1	0	0	0	0	0	0	0	0	0	1	0

Mario Diaz *continued*

Year	Tm	Lg	Tot	H	A	Men-On 0	Men-On 1	Men-On 2	Men-On 3	One-Game 2	One-Game 3	One-Game 4	LO	XN	IP	PH	RHP	LHP
1991	TEX	AL	1	1	0	1	0	0	0	0	0	0	0	0	0	0	1	0
1993	TEX	AL	2	1	1	2	0	0	0	0	0	0	0	0	0	0	1	1
1995	FLO	NL	1	0	1	1	0	0	0	0	0	0	0	0	0	0	1	0
Total			5	2	3	4	1	0	0	0	0	0	0	0	0	0	4	1

Rank among batters: 3,191 • *Total ballparks homered in*: 4 • *First HR*: 04/09/1989 off Mike Witt

Mike Diaz

MICHAEL ANTHONY DIAZ
B: 04/15/1960
BR

Year	Tm	Lg	Tot	H	A	Men-On 0	Men-On 1	Men-On 2	Men-On 3	One-Game 2	One-Game 3	One-Game 4	LO	XN	IP	PH	RHP	LHP
1986	PIT	NL	12	6	6	8	2	2	0	1	0	0	0	0	0	1	3	9
1987	PIT	NL	16	9	7	13	0	3	0	1	0	0	0	0	0	2	2	14
1988	CHI	AL	3	3	0	3	0	0	0	0	0	0	0	0	0	0	1	2
Total			31	18	13	24	2	5	0	2	0	0	0	0	0	3	6	25

Rank among batters: 1,400 • *Top target (4 home runs)*: John Tudor • *Number of pitchers victimized*: 25 • *Total ballparks homered in*: 11 • *First HR*: 06/08/1986 off Sid Fernandez

Leo Dickerman

LEO LOUIS DICKERMAN
B: 10/31/1896 D: 04/30/1982
BR

Year	Tm	Lg	Tot	H	A	Men-On 0	Men-On 1	Men-On 2	Men-On 3	One-Game 2	One-Game 3	One-Game 4	LO	XN	IP	PH	RHP	LHP
1923	BRO	NL	2	0	2	2	0	0	0	0	0	0	0	0	0	0	1	1

Rank among batters: 4,129 • *Total ballparks homered in*: 2 • *First HR*: 06/28/1923 off Jimmy Ring

Buttercup Dickerson

LEWIS PESSANO DICKERSON
B: 10/11/1858 D: 07/23/1920
BL

Year	Tm	Lg	Tot	H	A	Men-On 0	Men-On 1	Men-On 2	Men-On 3	One-Game 2	One-Game 3	One-Game 4	LO	XN	IP	PH	RHP	LHP
1879	CIN	NL	2	2	0	1	1	0	0	0	0	0	0	0	0	0	2	0
1881	WOR	NL	1	1	0	1	0	0	0	0	0	0	1	0	0	0	1	0
1884	LOU	AA	1	0	1	1	0	0	0	0	0	0	0	0	0	0	0	0
Total			4	3	1	3	1	0	0	0	0	0	1	0	0	0	2	0

Rank among batters: 3,427 • *Total ballparks homered in*: 3 • *First HR*: 07/19/1879 off George Bradley

Bill Dickey

WILLIAM MALCOLM DICKEY
B: 06/06/1907 D: 11/12/1993
BL HOF

Year	Tm	Lg	Tot	H	A	Men-On 0	Men-On 1	Men-On 2	Men-On 3	One-Game 2	One-Game 3	One-Game 4	LO	XN	IP	PH	RHP	LHP
1929	NY	AL	10	5	5	7	2	1	0	1	0	0	0	0	1	0	9	1
1930	NY	AL	5	3	2	3	0	2	0	0	0	0	0	0	1	1	5	0
1931	NY	AL	6	4	2	3	0	2	1	1	0	0	0	0	0	0	6	0
1932	NY	AL	15	7	8	7	5	1	2	1	0	0	0	1	0	0	13	2
1933	NY	AL	14	9	5	2	10	1	1	0	0	0	0	0	0	0	11	3
1934	NY	AL	12	6	6	7	4	1	0	1	0	0	0	0	0	1	8	4
1935	NY	AL	14	11	3	9	3	2	0	1	0	0	0	0	0	0	10	4
1936	NY	AL	22	14	8	16	1	5	0	1	0	0	0	0	0	0	17	5
1937	NY	AL	29	21	8	12	11	4	2	3	0	0	0	1	0	0	25	4
1938	NY	AL	27	23	4	14	8	4	1	3	0	0	0	0	0	0	22	5
1939	NY	AL	24	19	5	16	7	1	0	2	1	0	0	0	0	0	21	3
1940	NY	AL	9	5	4	3	2	3	1	0	0	0	0	0	0	0	6	3
1941	NY	AL	7	5	2	2	3	2	0	0	0	0	0	0	0	0	6	1
1942	NY	AL	2	1	1	1	1	0	0	0	0	0	0	0	0	0	1	1
1943	NY	AL	4	2	2	1	3	0	0	0	0	0	0	0	0	0	4	0
1946	NY	AL	2	0	2	1	1	0	0	0		0	0	0	0	0	2	0
Total			202	135	67	104	61	29	8	14	1	0	0	2	2	2	166	36

Rank among batters: 178 • *Top target (9 home runs)*: George Blaeholder • *Number of pitchers victimized*: 98 • *Total ballparks homered in*: 10 • *First HR*: 05/07/1929 off General Crowder • *World Series HR*—5

George Dickey

GEORGE WILLARD DICKEY
B: 07/10/1915 D: 07/16/1976
BB

Year	Tm	Lg	Tot	H	A	Men-On 0	Men-On 1	Men-On 2	Men-On 3	One-Game 2	One-Game 3	One-Game 4	LO	XN	IP	PH	RHP	LHP
1941	CHI	AL	2	0	2	1	0	1	0	0	0	0	0	0	0	1	2	0
1942	CHI	AL	1	0	1	0	1	0	0	0	0	0	0	0	0	1	1	0

George Dickey *continued*

Year	Tm	Lg	Tot	H	A	Men-On 0	Men-On 1	Men-On 2	Men-On 3	One-Game 2	One-Game 3	One-Game 4	LO	XN	IP	PH	RHP	LHP
1947	CHI	AL	1	1	0	1	0	0	0	0	0	0	0	0	0	0	1	0
Total			4	1	3	2	1	1	0	0	0	0	0	0	0	2	4	0

Rank among batters: 3,427 • *Top target (2 home runs)*: Marv Breuer • *Number of pitchers victimized*: 3 • *Total ballparks homered in*: 3 • *First HR*: 06/19/1941 off Marv Breuer

Emerson Dickman

GEORGE EMERSON DICKMAN
B: 11/12/1914 D: 04/27/1981
BR

Year	Tm	Lg	Tot	H	A	Men-On 0	Men-On 1	Men-On 2	Men-On 3	One-Game 2	One-Game 3	One-Game 4	LO	XN	IP	PH	RHP	LHP
1938	BOS	AL	1	0	1	0	1	0	0	0	0	0	0	0	0	0	0	1

Rank among batters: 4,707 • *Total ballparks homered in*: 1 • *First HR*: 07/02/1938 off Chubby Dean

Johnny Dickshot

JOHN OSCAR DICKSHOT
B: 01/24/1910
BR

Year	Tm	Lg	Tot	H	A	Men-On 0	Men-On 1	Men-On 2	Men-On 3	One-Game 2	One-Game 3	One-Game 4	LO	XN	IP	PH	RHP	LHP
1937	PIT	NL	3	0	3	2	1	0	0	0	0	0	0	0	0	0	1	2
1945	CHI	AL	4	1	3	4	0	0	0	0	0	0	0	0	0	0	4	0
Total			7	1	6	6	1	0	0	0	0	0	0	0	0	0	5	2

Rank among batters: 2,834 • *Total ballparks homered in*: 7 • *First HR*: 04/27/1937 off Bob Weiland

Murry Dickson

MURRY MONROE DICKSON
B: 08/21/1916 D: 09/21/1989
BR

Year	Tm	Lg	Tot	H	A	Men-On 0	Men-On 1	Men-On 2	Men-On 3	One-Game 2	One-Game 3	One-Game 4	LO	XN	IP	PH	RHP	LHP
1951	PIT	NL	1	1	0	1	0	0	0	0	0	0	0	0	0	0	1	0
1955	PHI	NL	1	0	1	1	0	0	0	0	0	0	0	0	0	0	1	0
1958	KC	AL	1	1	0	1	0	0	0	0	0	0	0	1	0	0	1	0
Total			3	2	1	3	0	0	0	0	0	0	0	1	0	0	3	0

Rank among batters: 3,735 • *Total ballparks homered in*: 3 • *First HR*: 04/17/1951 off Tom Poholsky

Chuck Diering

CHARLES EDWARD ALLEN DIERING
B: 02/05/1923
BR

Year	Tm	Lg	Tot	H	A	Men-On 0	Men-On 1	Men-On 2	Men-On 3	One-Game 2	One-Game 3	One-Game 4	LO	XN	IP	PH	RHP	LHP
1947	STL	NL	2	1	1	0	1	1	0	0	0	0	0	0	0	0	1	1
1949	STL	NL	3	1	2	1	2	0	0	0	0	0	0	0	0	0	1	2
1950	STL	NL	3	1	2	2	0	1	0	1	0	0	0	0	0	0	1	2
1954	BAL	AL	2	1	1	1	1	0	0	0	0	0	0	0	0	0	2	0
1955	BAL	AL	3	1	2	3	0	0	0	0	0	0	0	0	0	0	1	2
1956	BAL	AL	1	1	0	1	0	0	0	0	0	0	0	0	1	0	1	0
Total			14	6	8	8	4	2	0	1	0	0	0	0	1	0	7	7

Rank among batters: 2,169 • *Top target (2 home runs)*: Ken Heintzelman • *Number of pitchers victimized*: 13 • *Total ballparks homered in*: 9 • *First HR*: 04/23/1947 off Ken Heintzelman

Larry Dierker

LAWRENCE EDWARD DIERKER
B: 09/22/1946
BR

Year	Tm	Lg	Tot	H	A	Men-On 0	Men-On 1	Men-On 2	Men-On 3	One-Game 2	One-Game 3	One-Game 4	LO	XN	IP	PH	RHP	LHP
1965	HOU	NL	1	0	1	1	0	0	0	0	0	0	0	0	0	0	1	0
1966	HOU	NL	1	0	1	1	0	0	0	0	0	0	0	0	0	0	1	0
1969	HOU	NL	1	0	1	0	1	0	0	0	0	0	0	0	0	0	1	0
1976	HOU	NL	1	1	0	1	0	0	0	0	0	0	0	0	0	0	1	0
Total			4	1	3	3	1	0	0	0	0	0	0	0	0	0	4	0

Rank among batters: 3,427 • *Total ballparks homered in*: 4 • *First HR*: 08/03/1965 off Bob Purkey

Bill Dietrich

WILLIAM JOHN DIETRICH
B: 03/29/1910 D: 06/20/1978
BR

Year	Tm	Lg	Tot	H	A	Men-On 0	Men-On 1	Men-On 2	Men-On 3	One-Game 2	One-Game 3	One-Game 4	LO	XN	IP	PH	RHP	LHP
1934	PHI	AL	1	1	0	1	0	0	0	0	0	0	0	0	0	0	1	0
1939	CHI	AL	1	1	0	0	1	0	0	0	0	0	0	0	0	0	1	0
1940	CHI	AL	1	1	0	1	0	0	0	0	0	0	0	0	0	0	1	0

Bill Dietrich *continued*

Year	Tm	Lg	Tot	H	A	Men-On 0	1	2	3	One-Game 2	3	4	LO	XN	IP	PH	RHP	LHP
1943	CHI	AL	1	1	0	1	0	0	0	0	0	0	0	0	0	0	0	1
1944	CHI	AL	1	1	0	1	0	0	0	0	0	0	0	0	0	0	1	0
Total			5	5	0	4	1	0	0	0	0	0	0	0	0	0	4	1

Rank among batters: 3,191 • *Total ballparks homered in*: 2 • *First HR*: 05/12/1934 off Firpo Marberry

Dick Dietz

RICHARD ALLEN DIETZ
B: 09/18/1941
BR

Year	Tm	Lg	Tot	H	A	Men-On 0	1	2	3	One-Game 2	3	4	LO	XN	IP	PH	RHP	LHP
1967	SF	NL	4	1	3	1	0	3	0	0	0	0	0	0	0	1	2	2
1968	SF	NL	6	1	5	5	1	0	0	0	0	0	0	0	0	1	5	1
1969	SF	NL	11	5	6	5	6	0	0	0	0	0	0	0	0	0	6	5
1970	SF	NL	22	13	9	7	6	7	2	0	0	0	0	0	0	0	13	9
1971	SF	NL	19	11	8	8	7	3	1	0	0	0	0	1	0	2	12	7
1972	LA	NL	1	0	1	1	0	0	0	0	0	0	0	0	0	0	0	1
1973	ATL	NL	3	1	2	1	2	0	0	0	0	0	0	0	0	0	1	2
Total			66	32	34	28	22	13	3	0	0	0	0	1	0	4	39	27

Rank among batters: 786 • Top target (3 home runs): Bill Hands, George Stone, Jim Merritt, Pat Jarvis • *Number of pitchers victimized*: 51 • *Total ballparks homered in*: 13 • *First HR*: 06/01/1967 off Pete Mikkelsen • *All-Star HR*—1

Don Dillard

DAVID DONALD DILLARD
B: 01/08/1937
BL

Year	Tm	Lg	Tot	H	A	Men-On 0	1	2	3	One-Game 2	3	4	LO	XN	IP	PH	RHP	LHP
1961	CLE	AL	7	3	4	6	1	0	0	0	0	0	0	0	0	2	7	0
1962	CLE	AL	5	5	0	4	0	0	1	0	0	0	0	1	0	0	4	1
1963	MIL	NL	1	0	1	1	0	0	0	0	0	0	0	0	0	1	1	0
1965	MIL	NL	1	0	1	0	1	0	0	0	0	0	0	0	0	1	1	0
Total			14	8	6	11	2	0	1	0	0	0	0	1	0	4	13	1

Rank among batters: 2,169 • *Total ballparks homered in*: 7 • *First HR*: 05/02/1961 off Early Wynn

Steve Dillard

STEPHEN BRADLEY DILLARD
B: 02/08/1951
BR

Year	Tm	Lg	Tot	H	A	Men-On 0	1	2	3	One-Game 2	3	4	LO	XN	IP	PH	RHP	LHP
1976	BOS	AL	1	0	1	0	0	1	0	0	0	0	0	0	0	0	0	1
1977	BOS	AL	1	1	0	1	0	0	0	0	0	0	0	0	0	0	0	1
1979	CHI	NL	5	4	1	3	2	0	0	1	0	0	0	0	0	0	2	3
1980	CHI	NL	4	1	3	3	1	0	0	0	0	0	0	0	0	0	3	1
1981	CHI	NL	2	2	0	1	1	0	0	0	0	0	0	0	0	0	1	1
Total			13	8	5	8	4	1	0	1	0	0	0	0	0	0	6	7

Rank among batters: 2,248 • *Top target (2 home runs)*: John Candelaria • *Number of pitchers victimized*: 12 • *Total ballparks homered in*: 7 • *First HR*: 09/19/1976 off Dave Roberts

Bob Dillinger

ROBERT BERNARD DILLINGER
B: 09/17/1918
BR

Year	Tm	Lg	Tot	H	A	Men-On 0	1	2	3	One-Game 2	3	4	LO	XN	IP	PH	RHP	LHP
1947	STL	AL	3	1	2	3	0	0	0	0	0	0	1	0	0	0	2	1
1948	STL	AL	2	1	1	2	0	0	0	0	0	0	1	1	0	0	1	1
1949	STL	AL	1	1	0	0	1	0	0	0	0	0	0	0	0	0	0	1
1950	PHI	AL	3	2	1	2	1	0	0	0	0	0	1	0	0	0	2	1
	PIT	NL	1	1	0	1	0	0	0	0	0	0	0	1	0	0	0	1
	Total		4	3	1	3	1	0	0	0	0	0	1	1	0	0	2	2
Total			10	6	4	8	2	0	0	0	0	0	3	2	0	0	5	5

Rank among batters: 2,500 • *Total ballparks homered in*: 5 • *First HR*: 05/11/1947 off Red Embree

Pop Dillon

FRANK EDWARD DILLON
B: 10/17/1873 D: 09/12/1931
BL

Year	Tm	Lg	Tot	H	A	Men-On 0	1	2	3	One-Game 2	3	4	LO	XN	IP	PH	RHP	LHP
1901	DET	AL	1	0	1	0	1	0	0	0	0	0	0	0	0	0	1	0

Rank among batters: 4,707 • *Total ballparks homered in*: 1 • *First HR*: 04/29/1901 off Roy Patterson

Miguel Dilone

MIGUEL ANGEL (REYES) DILONE
B: 11/01/1954
BB

Year	Tm	Lg	Tot	H	A	Men-On 0	1	2	3	One-Game 2	3	4	LO	XN	IP	PH	RHP	LHP
1978	OAK	AL	1	1	0	1	0	0	0	0	0	0	1	0	0	0	0	1
1979	OAK	AL	1	1	0	1	0	0	0	0	0	0	0	0	0	0	0	1
1982	CLE	AL	3	2	1	2	1	0	0	0	0	0	0	0	0	0	3	0
1984	MON	NL	1	1	0	0	1	0	0	0	0	0	0	0	0	0	0	1
Total			6	5	1	4	2	0	0	0	0	0	1	0	0	0	3	3

Rank among batters: 2,988 • *Total ballparks homered in*: 4 • *First HR*: 06/04/1978 off Don Gullett

Dom DiMaggio

DOMINIC PAUL DIMAGGIO
B: 02/12/1917
BR

Year	Tm	Lg	Tot	H	A	Men-On 0	1	2	3	One-Game 2	3	4	LO	XN	IP	PH	RHP	LHP
1940	BOS	AL	8	6	2	6	0	2	0	0	0	0	0	0	0	0	6	2
1941	BOS	AL	8	3	5	5	1	0	2	0	0	0	1	0	0	0	5	3
1942	BOS	AL	14	7	7	8	6	0	0	0	0	0	2	0	1	0	11	3
1946	BOS	AL	7	4	3	3	3	1	0	0	0	0	0	0	1	0	7	0
1947	BOS	AL	8	4	4	5	2	0	1	0	0	0	1	0	0	0	8	0
1948	BOS	AL	9	5	4	7	1	0	1	0	0	0	1	0	0	0	8	1
1949	BOS	AL	8	4	4	4	2	2	0	0	0	0	1	0	0	0	8	0
1950	BOS	AL	7	5	2	4	3	0	0	0	0	0	1	0	0	0	5	2
1951	BOS	AL	12	9	3	5	6	1	0	0	0	0	0	1	1	0	10	2
1952	BOS	AL	6	4	2	4	1	0	1	0	0	0	2	1	0	1	4	2
Total			87	51	36	51	25	6	5	0	0	0	9	2	3	1	72	15

Rank among batters: 594 • *Top target (4 home runs)*: Steve Gromek • *Number of pitchers victimized*: 63 • *Total ballparks homered in*: 9 • *First HR*: 07/14/1940 off Bob Harris

Joe DiMaggio

JOSEPH PAUL DIMAGGIO
B: 11/25/1914
BR HOF

Year	Tm	Lg	Tot	H	A	Men-On 0	1	2	3	One-Game 2	3	4	LO	XN	IP	PH	RHP	LHP
1936	NY	AL	29	8	21	14	13	2	0	3	0	0	0	0	1	0	21	8
1937	NY	AL	46	19	27	23	13	7	3	4	1	0	0	0	0	0	34	12
1938	NY	AL	32	15	17	11	14	7	0	2	0	0	0	1	1	0	23	9
1939	NY	AL	30	12	18	14	8	7	1	4	0	0	0	0	1	0	17	13
1940	NY	AL	31	16	15	9	14	6	2	3	0	0	0	0	0	1	19	12
1941	NY	AL	30	16	14	19	7	3	1	2	0	0	0	2	0	0	21	9
1942	NY	AL	21	8	13	9	10	2	0	2	0	0	0	0	0	0	17	4
1946	NY	AL	25	8	17	11	10	3	1	2	0	0	0	0	0	0	17	8
1947	NY	AL	20	9	11	11	2	6	1	1	0	0	0	0	0	0	14	6
1948	NY	AL	39	15	24	18	11	8	2	5	1	0	0	1	0	0	26	13
1949	NY	AL	14	5	9	7	3	3	1	2	0	0	0	0	0	0	6	8
1950	NY	AL	32	9	23	19	9	3	1	1	1	0	0	0	0	0	19	13
1951	NY	AL	12	8	4	5	4	3	0	1	0	0	0	0	0	0	7	5
Total			361	148	213	170	118	60	13	32	3	0	0	4	3	1	241	120

Rank among batters: 40 • *Top target (11 home runs)*: Bob Feller • *Number of pitchers victimized*: 165 • *Total ballparks homered in*: 9 • *First HR*: 05/10/1936 off George Turbeville • *2 HR in 1 inning*—@CHI: 06/24/1936 • *Hit for Cycle*—vs WAS: 07/09/1937; @CHI: 05/20/1948 • *World Series HR*—8; *All-Star HR*—1

Vince DiMaggio

VINCENT PAUL DIMAGGIO
B: 09/06/1912 D: 10/03/1986
BR

Year	Tm	Lg	Tot	H	A	Men-On 0	1	2	3	One-Game 2	3	4	LO	XN	IP	PH	RHP	LHP
1937	BOS	NL	13	7	6	9	3	1	0	1	0	0	0	0	0	0	10	3
1938	BOS	NL	14	3	11	10	3	1	0	0	0	0	0	0	0	0	10	4
1940	PIT	NL	19	6	13	13	3	3	0	2	0	0	0	0	1	0	15	4
1941	PIT	NL	21	8	13	9	5	6	1	0	0	0	0	0	0	0	16	5
1942	PIT	NL	15	3	12	6	5	4	0	2	0	0	0	0	0	0	9	6
1943	PIT	NL	15	9	6	6	4	4	1	2	0	0	0	0	1	0	12	3
1944	PIT	NL	9	3	6	3	4	2	0	0	0	0	0	1	0	2	8	1
1945	PHI	NL	19	9	10	6	8	1	4	2	0	0	0	1	0	1	16	3
Total			125	48	77	62	35	22	6	9	0	0	0	2	2	3	96	29

Rank among batters: 366 • *Top target (5 home runs)*: Jake Mooty • *Number of pitchers victimized*: 80 • *Total ballparks homered in*: 9 • *First HR*: 04/30/1937 off Hugh Mulcahy • *All-Star HR*—1

Vance Dinges

VANCE GEORGE DINGES
B: 05/29/1915 D: 10/04/1990
BL

Year	Tm	Lg	Tot	H	A	Men-On 0	Men-On 1	Men-On 2	Men-On 3	One-Game 2	One-Game 3	One-Game 4	LO	XN	IP	PH	RHP	LHP
1945	PHI	NL	1	0	1	1	0	0	0	0	0	0	0	0	0	0	1	0
1946	PHI	NL	1	0	1	1	0	0	0	0	0	0	0	0	1	1	1	0
Total			2	0	2	2	0	0	0	0	0	0	0	0	1	1	2	0

Rank among batters: 4,129 • *Total ballparks homered in*: 2 • *First HR*: 04/24/1945 off Andy Hansen

Bill Dinneen

WILLIAM HENRY DINNEEN
B: 04/05/1876 D: 01/13/1955
BR

Year	Tm	Lg	Tot	H	A	Men-On 0	Men-On 1	Men-On 2	Men-On 3	One-Game 2	One-Game 3	One-Game 4	LO	XN	IP	PH	RHP	LHP
1901	BOS	NL	1	0	1	1	0	0	0	0	0	0	0	0	1	0	0	1

Rank among batters: 4,707 • *Total ballparks homered in*: 1 • *First HR*: 09/26/1901 off Noodles Hahn

Gary Disarcina

GARY THOMAS DISARCINA
B: 11/19/1967
BR

Year	Tm	Lg	Tot	H	A	Men-On 0	Men-On 1	Men-On 2	Men-On 3	One-Game 2	One-Game 3	One-Game 4	LO	XN	IP	PH	RHP	LHP
1992	CAL	AL	3	2	1	1	2	0	0	0	0	0	0	0	0	0	3	0
1993	CAL	AL	3	2	1	1	1	1	0	0	0	0	0	0	0	0	3	0
1994	CAL	AL	3	2	1	2	1	0	0	0	0	0	0	0	0	0	1	2
1995	CAL	AL	5	1	4	5	0	0	0	0	0	0	0	0	0	0	3	2
Total			14	7	7	9	4	1	0	0	0	0	0	0	0	0	10	4

Rank among batters: 2,169 • *Top target (2 home runs)*: Dave Wells • *Number of pitchers victimized*: 13 • *Total ballparks homered in*: 8 • *First HR*: 06/03/1992 off Bob Milacki

Benny Distefano

BENITO JAMES DISTEFANO
B: 01/23/1962
BL

Year	Tm	Lg	Tot	H	A	Men-On 0	Men-On 1	Men-On 2	Men-On 3	One-Game 2	One-Game 3	One-Game 4	LO	XN	IP	PH	RHP	LHP
1984	PIT	NL	3	0	3	1	1	0	1	0	0	0	0	1	0	1	3	0
1986	PIT	NL	1	0	1	1	0	0	0	0	0	0	0	0	0	1	1	0
1988	PIT	NL	1	0	1	0	0	1	0	0	0	0	0	0	0	1	1	0
1989	PIT	NL	2	2	0	2	0	0	0	0	0	0	0	0	0	0	2	0
Total			7	2	5	4	1	1	1	0	0	0	0	1	0	3	7	0

Rank among batters: 2,834 • *Top target (2 home runs)*: Jose DeLeon • *Number of pitchers victimized*: 6 • *Total ballparks homered in*: 5 • *First HR*: 06/08/1984 off Larry Andersen

Art Ditmar

ARTHUR JOHN DITMAR
B: 04/03/1929
BR

Year	Tm	Lg	Tot	H	A	Men-On 0	Men-On 1	Men-On 2	Men-On 3	One-Game 2	One-Game 3	One-Game 4	LO	XN	IP	PH	RHP	LHP
1956	KC	AL	1	1	0	1	0	0	0	0	0	0	0	0	0	0	1	0
1959	NY	AL	1	0	1	1	0	0	0	0	0	0	0	0	0	0	1	0
Total			2	1	1	2	0	0	0	0	0	0	0	0	0	0	2	0

Rank among batters: 4,129 • *Total ballparks homered in*: 2 • *First HR*: 09/11/1956 off Tom Morgan

Jack Dittmer

JOHN DOUGLAS DITTMER
B: 01/10/1928
BL

Year	Tm	Lg	Tot	H	A	Men-On 0	Men-On 1	Men-On 2	Men-On 3	One-Game 2	One-Game 3	One-Game 4	LO	XN	IP	PH	RHP	LHP
1952	BOS	NL	7	5	2	1	4	2	0	0	0	0	0	1	0	0	5	2
1953	MIL	NL	9	0	9	4	1	4	0	0	0	0	0	0	0	0	6	3
1954	MIL	NL	6	3	3	3	2	1	0	0	0	0	0	1	0	0	6	0
1955	MIL	NL	1	1	0	0	1	0	0	0	0	0	0	0	0	0	1	0
1956	MIL	NL	1	0	1	1	0	0	0	0	0	0	0	0	0	0	1	0
Total			24	9	15	9	8	7	0	0	0	0	0	2	0	0	19	5

Rank among batters: 1,643 • *Top target (3 home runs)*: Frank Smith • *Number of pitchers victimized*: 21 • *Total ballparks homered in*: 8 • *First HR*: 07/02/1952 off Monita Kennedy

Leo Dixon

LEO MOSES DIXON
B: 09/04/1894 D: 04/11/1984
BR

Year	Tm	Lg	Tot	H	A	Men-On 0	Men-On 1	Men-On 2	Men-On 3	One-Game 2	One-Game 3	One-Game 4	LO	XN	IP	PH	RHP	LHP
1925	STL	AL	1	0	1	1	0	0	0	0	0	0	0	0	0	0	1	0

Rank among batters: 4,707 • *Total ballparks homered in*: 1 • *First HR*: 06/06/1925 off Sam Jones

Bill Doak

WILLIAM LEOPOLD DOAK
B: 01/28/1891 D: 11/26/1954
BR

Year	Tm	Lg	Tot	H	A	Men-On 0	Men-On 1	Men-On 2	Men-On 3	One-Game 2	One-Game 3	One-Game 4	LO	XN	IP	PH	RHP	LHP
1924	BRO	NL	1	1	0	1	0	0	0	0	0	0	0	0	0	0	1	0

Rank among batters: 4,707 • *Total ballparks homered in*: 1 • *First HR*: 08/30/1924 off Hugh McQuillan

Dan Dobbek

DANIEL JOHN DOBBEK
B: 12/06/1934
BL

Year	Tm	Lg	Tot	H	A	Men-On 0	Men-On 1	Men-On 2	Men-On 3	One-Game 2	One-Game 3	One-Game 4	LO	XN	IP	PH	RHP	LHP
1959	WAS	AL	1	1	0	1	0	0	0	0	0	0	0	0	0	0	0	1
1960	WAS	AL	10	1	9	8	1	1	0	1	0	0	0	0	0	0	10	0
1961	MIN	AL	4	3	1	2	1	0	1	1	0	0	0	0	0	0	4	0
Total			15	5	10	11	2	1	1	2	0	0	0	0	0	0	14	1

Rank among batters: 2,096 • *Top target (2 home runs)*: Ken Johnson, Jerry Walker, Don Larsen • *Number of pitchers victimized*: 12 • *Total ballparks homered in*: 7 • *First HR*: 09/20/1959 off Billy O'Dell

John Dobbs

JOHN GORDON DOBBS
B: 06/03/1876 D: 09/09/1934
BL

Year	Tm	Lg	Tot	H	A	Men-On 0	Men-On 1	Men-On 2	Men-On 3	One-Game 2	One-Game 3	One-Game 4	LO	XN	IP	PH	RHP	LHP
1901	CIN	NL	2	2	0	2	0	0	0	0	0	0	0	0	2	0	2	0
1902	CIN	NL	1	1	0	1	0	0	0	0	0	0	1	0	1	0	1	0
1903	BRO	NL	2	0	2	0	1	1	0	0	0	0	0	0	1	0	2	0
1905	BRO	NL	2	2	0	2	0	0	0	0	0	0	0	0	1	0	2	0
Total			7	5	2	5	1	1	0	0	0	0	1	0	5	0	7	0

Rank among batters: 2,834 • *Total ballparks homered in*: 4 • *First HR*: 07/14/1901 off Frank Kitson

Joe Dobson

JOSEPH GORDON DOBSON
B: 01/20/1917 D: 06/23/1994
BR

Year	Tm	Lg	Tot	H	A	Men-On 0	Men-On 1	Men-On 2	Men-On 3	One-Game 2	One-Game 3	One-Game 4	LO	XN	IP	PH	RHP	LHP
1941	BOS	AL	1	0	1	1	0	0	0	0	0	0	0	0	0	0	1	0
1948	BOS	AL	1	0	1	0	1	0	0	0	0	0	0	0	0	0	1	0
Total			2	0	2	1	1	0	0	0	0	0	0	0	0	0	2	0

Rank among batters: 4,129 • *Total ballparks homered in*: 2 • *First HR*: 06/02/1941 off Bobo Newsom

Larry Doby

LAWRENCE EUGENE DOBY
B: 12/13/1924
BL

Year	Tm	Lg	Tot	H	A	Men-On 0	Men-On 1	Men-On 2	Men-On 3	One-Game 2	One-Game 3	One-Game 4	LO	XN	IP	PH	RHP	LHP
1948	CLE	AL	14	4	10	5	7	1	1	0	0	0	0	0	0	0	13	1
1949	CLE	AL	24	9	15	12	8	4	0	1	0	0	0	0	1	0	14	10
1950	CLE	AL	25	16	9	9	12	2	2	2	1	0	0	1	0	0	20	5
1951	CLE	AL	20	8	12	13	5	2	0	2	0	0	0	0	0	0	16	4
1952	CLE	AL	32	15	17	16	13	3	0	0	0	0	0	1	2	0	19	13
1953	CLE	AL	29	13	16	15	11	2	1	3	0	0	0	0	0	0	23	6
1954	CLE	AL	32	16	16	13	12	7	0	1	0	0	0	1	0	0	26	6
1955	CLE	AL	26	16	10	20	2	4	0	4	0	0	0	1	0	0	17	9
1956	CHI	AL	24	15	9	10	9	5	0	1	0	0	0	0	0	0	16	8
1957	CHI	AL	14	3	11	6	5	2	1	2	0	0	0	0	0	0	9	5
1958	CLE	AL	13	6	7	5	5	3	0	1	0	0	0	1	0	1	13	0
Total			253	121	132	124	89	35	5	17	1	0	0	5	3	1	186	67

Rank among batters: 103 • *Top target (8 home runs)*: Virgil Trucks • *Number of pitchers victimized*: 112 • *Total ballparks homered in*: 10 • *First HR*: 04/23/1948 off Fred Hutchinson • *Hit for Cycle*—@BOS: 06/04/1952 • *World Series HR*—1; *All-Star HR*—1

Tom Dodd

THOMAS MARION DODD
B: 08/15/1958
BR

Year	Tm	Lg	Tot	H	A	Men-On 0	1	2	3	One-Game 2	3	4	LO	XN	IP	PH	RHP	LHP
1986	BAL	AL	1	0	1	0	1	0	0	0	0	0	0	0	0	0	0	1

Rank among batters: 4,707 • *Total ballparks homered in*: 1 • *First HR*: 08/01/1986 off Jimmy Key

John Dodge

JOHN LEWIS DODGE
B: 04/27/1889 D: 06/19/1916
BR

Year	Tm	Lg	Tot	H	A	Men-On 0	1	2	3	One-Game 2	3	4	LO	XN	IP	PH	RHP	LHP
1913	CIN	NL	4	3	1	1	3	0	0	0	0	0	0	0	3	0	3	1

Rank among batters: 3,427 • *Total ballparks homered in*: 2 • *First HR*: 06/27/1913 off Charlie Smith

Pat Dodson

PATRICK NEAL DODSON
B: 10/11/1959
BL

Year	Tm	Lg	Tot	H	A	Men-On 0	1	2	3	One-Game 2	3	4	LO	XN	IP	PH	RHP	LHP
1986	BOS	AL	1	0	1	1	0	0	0	0	0	0	0	0	0	1	1	0
1987	BOS	AL	2	1	1	1	0	1	0	0	0	0	0	0	0	0	1	1
1988	BOS	AL	1	0	1	1	0	0	0	0	0	0	0	0	0	0	1	0
Total			4	1	3	3	0	1	0	0	0	0	0	0	0	1	3	1

Rank among batters: 3,427 • *Total ballparks homered in*: 3 • *First HR*: 09/14/1986 off Tim Stoddard

Bobby Doerr

ROBERT PERSHING DOERR
B: 04/07/1918
BR HOF

Year	Tm	Lg	Tot	H	A	Men-On 0	1	2	3	One-Game 2	3	4	LO	XN	IP	PH	RHP	LHP
1937	BOS	AL	2	2	0	1	1	0	0	0	0	0	0	0	0	0	2	0
1938	BOS	AL	5	5	0	0	3	1	1	0	0	0	0	0	0	0	4	1
1939	BOS	AL	12	7	5	8	1	2	1	1	0	0	0	0	0	0	9	3
1940	BOS	AL	22	16	6	12	6	3	1	1	0	0	0	1	0	0	17	5
1941	BOS	AL	16	11	5	7	7	1	1	2	0	0	0	0	0	0	16	0
1942	BOS	AL	15	8	7	9	6	0	0	1	0	0	0	1	1	0	15	0
1943	BOS	AL	16	9	7	9	5	2	0	0	0	0	0	0	1	0	16	0
1944	BOS	AL	15	11	4	8	3	4	0	0	0	0	0	1	0	0	14	1
1946	BOS	AL	18	13	5	6	9	2	1	2	0	0	0	0	0	0	13	5
1947	BOS	AL	17	12	5	6	7	3	1	1	0	0	0	0	0	0	17	0
1948	BOS	AL	27	19	8	14	9	3	1	1	0	0	0	1	0	0	22	5
1949	BOS	AL	18	9	9	8	4	6	0	1	0	0	0	0	0	0	12	6
1950	BOS	AL	27	18	9	17	7	2	1	2	1	0	0	1	0	0	23	4
1951	BOS	AL	13	5	8	4	6	3	0	1	0	0	0	0	0	0	9	4
Total			223	145	78	109	74	32	8	13	1	0	0	5	2	0	189	34

Rank among batters: 147 • *Top target (9 home runs)*: Bob Feller • *Number of pitchers victimized*: 123 • *Total ballparks homered in*: 8 • *First HR*: 04/25/1937 off Pat Malone • *Hit for Cycle*—vs STL: 05/17/1944 (2); vs CHI: 05/13/1947 • *World Series HR*—1; *All-Star HR*—1

Ed Doheny

EDWIN RICHARD DOHENY
B: 11/24/1873 D: 12/29/1916
BL

Year	Tm	Lg	Tot	H	A	Men-On 0	1	2	3	One-Game 2	3	4	LO	XN	IP	PH	RHP	LHP
1898	NY	NL	2	1	1	0	1	1	0	0	0	0	0	0	0	0	2	0
1902	PIT	NL	1	1	0	0	1	0	0	0	0	0	0	0	0	0	1	0
Total			3	2	1	0	2	1	0	0	0	0	0	0	0	0	3	0

Rank among batters: 3,735 • *Total ballparks homered in*: 3 • *First HR*: 08/28/1898 off Nixey Callahan

John Doherty

JOHN MICHAEL DOHERTY
B: 08/22/1951
BL

Year	Tm	Lg	Tot	H	A	Men-On 0	1	2	3	One-Game 2	3	4	LO	XN	IP	PH	RHP	LHP
1974	CAL	AL	3	0	3	3	0	0	0	0	0	0	0	0	0	0	3	0
1975	CAL	AL	1	0	1	0	0	1	0	0	0	0	0	0	0	0	1	0
Total			4	0	4	3	0	1	0	0	0	0	0	0	0	0	4	0

Rank among batters: 3,427 • *Total ballparks homered in*: 4 • *First HR*: 08/24/1974 off Pat Dobson

Year	Tm	Lg	Tot	H	A	Men-On 0	Men-On 1	Men-On 2	Men-On 3	One-Game 2	One-Game 3	One-Game 4	LO	XN	IP	PH	RHP	LHP

Biddy Dolan

LEON MARK DOLAN
B: 07/09/1881 D: 07/15/1950
BR

Year	Tm	Lg	Tot	H	A	0	1	2	3	2	3	4	LO	XN	IP	PH	RHP	LHP
1914	IND	FL	1	0	1	0	0	1	0	0	0	0	0	0	0	0	1	0

Rank among batters: 4,707 • *Total ballparks homered in*: 1 • *First HR*: 04/16/1914 off Bob Groom

Cozy Dolan

ALBERT JAMES DOLAN
B: 12/23/1889 D: 12/10/1958
BR

Year	Tm	Lg	Tot	H	A	0	1	2	3	2	3	4	LO	XN	IP	PH	RHP	LHP
1914	STL	NL	4	2	2	3	1	0	0	0	0	0	0	0	2	0	4	0
1915	STL	NL	2	0	2	2	0	0	0	0	0	0	0	0	0	0	2	0
Total			6	2	4	5	1	0	0	0	0	0	0	0	2	0	6	0

Rank among batters: 2,988 • *Total ballparks homered in*: 4 • *First HR*: 05/31/1914 off Zip Zabel

Joe Dolan

JOSEPH DOLAN
B: 02/24/1873 D: 03/24/1938

Year	Tm	Lg	Tot	H	A	0	1	2	3	2	3	4	LO	XN	IP	PH	RHP	LHP
1896	LOU	NL	3	1	2	1	0	2	0	0	0	0	0	0	0	0	3	0
1899	PHI	NL	1	0	1	1	0	0	0	0	0	0	0	0	0	0	1	0
1900	PHI	NL	1	0	1	1	0	0	0	0	0	0	0	0	0	0	0	1
1901	PHI	AL	1	1	0	0	1	0	0	0	0	0	0	0	0	0	1	0
Total			6	2	4	3	1	2	0	0	0	0	0	0	0	0	5	1

Rank among batters: 2,988 • *Total ballparks homered in*: 4 • *First HR*: 08/27/1896 off Brickyard Kennedy

John Dolan

JOHN DOLAN
B: 09/12/1867 D: 05/08/1948

Year	Tm	Lg	Tot	H	A	0	1	2	3	2	3	4	LO	XN	IP	PH	RHP	LHP
1891	COL	AA	1	0	1	1	0	0	0	0	0	0	0	0	0	0	1	0
1893	STL	NL	1	1	0	0	0	1	0	0	0	0	0	0	0	0	1	0
Total			2	1	1	1	0	1	0	0	0	0	0	0	0	0	2	0

Rank among batters: 4,129 • *Total ballparks homered in*: 2 • *First HR*: 06/29/1891 off Joe Neale

Patrick Dolan

PATRICK HENRY DOLAN
B: 12/03/1872 D: 03/29/1907
BL

Year	Tm	Lg	Tot	H	A	0	1	2	3	2	3	4	LO	XN	IP	PH	RHP	LHP
1902	BRO	NL	1	0	1	1	0	0	0	0	0	0	0	0	0	0	1	0
1904	CIN	NL	6	5	1	2	3	1	0	0	0	0	0	0	6	0	6	0
1905	BOS	NL	3	2	1	1	1	1	0	1	0	0	0	0	0	0	3	0
Total			10	7	3	4	4	2	0	1	0	0	0	0	6	0	10	0

Rank among batters: 2,500 • *Total ballparks homered in*: 5 • *First HR*: 06/19/1902 off Bill Duggleby

Tom Dolan

THOMAS J. DOLAN
B: 01/10/1859 D: 01/16/1913
BR

Year	Tm	Lg	Tot	H	A	0	1	2	3	2	3	4	LO	XN	IP	PH	RHP	LHP
1883	STL	AA	1	1	0	0	0	1	0	0	0	0	0	0	0	0	1	0

Rank among batters: 4,707 • *Total ballparks homered in*: 1 • *First HR*: 09/26/1883 off Jack Neagle

Frank Doljack

FRANK JOSEPH DOLJACK
B: 10/05/1907 D: 01/23/1948
BR

Year	Tm	Lg	Tot	H	A	0	1	2	3	2	3	4	LO	XN	IP	PH	RHP	LHP
1930	DET	AL	3	3	0	0	2	1	0	0	0	0	0	0	0	0	1	2
1931	DET	AL	4	2	2	2	1	1	0	0	0	0	0	0	0	0	2	2
1932	DET	AL	1	1	0	0	1	0	0	0	0	0	0	0	0	0	0	1
1934	DET	AL	1	0	1	1	0	0	0	0	0	0	0	0	0	0	1	0
Total			9	6	3	3	4	2	0	0	0	0	0	0	0	0	4	5

Rank among batters: 2,587 • *Top target (3 home runs)*: Lefty Stewart • *Number of pitchers victimized*: 6 • *Total ballparks homered in*: 4 • *First HR*: 09/07/1930 off Lefty Stewart

Jiggs Donahue

JOHN AUGUSTUS DONAHUE
B: 07/13/1879 D: 07/19/1913
BL

Year	Tm	Lg	Tot	H	A	Men-On 0	Men-On 1	Men-On 2	Men-On 3	One-Game 2	One-Game 3	One-Game 4	LO	XN	IP	PH	RHP	LHP
1902	STL	AL	1	0	1	0	1	0	0	0	0	0	0	0	0	0	1	0
1904	CHI	AL	1	0	1	0	1	0	0	0	0	0	0	0	1	0	1	0
1905	CHI	AL	1	0	1	0	0	1	0	0	0	0	0	0	0	0	1	0
1906	CHI	AL	1	1	0	1	0	0	0	0	0	0	0	0	0	0	1	0
Total			4	1	3	1	2	1	0	0	0	0	0	0	1	0	4	0

Rank among batters: 3,427 • *Total ballparks homered in*: 4 • *First HR*: 06/05/1902 off Tom Hughes

Jim Donahue

JAMES AUGUSTUS DONAHUE
B: 01/08/1862 D: 04/19/1935
BR

Year	Tm	Lg	Tot	H	A	Men-On 0	Men-On 1	Men-On 2	Men-On 3	One-Game 2	One-Game 3	One-Game 4	LO	XN	IP	PH	RHP	LHP
1887	NY	AA	1	0	1	0	1	0	0	0	0	0	0	0	0	0	0	1
1888	KC	AA	1	1	0	0	0	1	0	0	0	0	0	0	0	0	1	0
Total			2	1	1	0	1	1	0	0	0	0	0	0	0	0	1	1

Rank among batters: 4,129 • *Total ballparks homered in*: 2 • *First HR*: 09/21/1887 off Matt Kilroy

Pat Donahue

PATRICK WILLIAM DONAHUE
B: 11/03/1884 D: 01/31/1966
BR

Year	Tm	Lg	Tot	H	A	Men-On 0	Men-On 1	Men-On 2	Men-On 3	One-Game 2	One-Game 3	One-Game 4	LO	XN	IP	PH	RHP	LHP
1908	BOS	AL	1	1	0	1	0	0	0	0	0	0	0	0	0	0	0	1
1909	BOS	AL	2	2	0	0	2	0	0	0	0	0	0	0	1	0	1	1
Total			3	3	0	1	2	0	0	0	0	0	0	0	1	0	1	2

Rank among batters: 3,735 • *Total ballparks homered in*: 1 • *First HR*: 09/04/1908 off Gus Salve

Red Donahue

FRANCIS ROSTELL DONAHUE
B: 01/23/1873 D: 08/25/1913
BR

Year	Tm	Lg	Tot	H	A	Men-On 0	Men-On 1	Men-On 2	Men-On 3	One-Game 2	One-Game 3	One-Game 4	LO	XN	IP	PH	RHP	LHP
1897	STL	NL	1	0	1	1	0	0	0	0	0	0	0	0	1	0	1	0

Rank among batters: 4,707 • *Total ballparks homered in*: 1 • *First HR*: 08/02/1897 off Clark Griffith

Tim Donahue

TIMOTHY CORNELIUS DONAHUE
B: 06/08/1870 D: 06/12/1902
BL

Year	Tm	Lg	Tot	H	A	Men-On 0	Men-On 1	Men-On 2	Men-On 3	One-Game 2	One-Game 3	One-Game 4	LO	XN	IP	PH	RHP	LHP
1895	CHI	NL	2	2	0	0	2	0	0	0	0	0	0	0	0	0	1	1

Rank among batters: 4,129 • *Total ballparks homered in*: 1 • *First HR*: 07/04/1895 off Frank Foreman

Atley Donald

RICHARD ATLEY DONALD
B: 08/19/1910 D: 10/19/1992
BL

Year	Tm	Lg	Tot	H	A	Men-On 0	Men-On 1	Men-On 2	Men-On 3	One-Game 2	One-Game 3	One-Game 4	LO	XN	IP	PH	RHP	LHP
1945	NY	AL	1	1	0	1	0	0	0	0	0	0	0	0	0	0	1	0

Rank among batters: 4,707 • *Total ballparks homered in*: 1 • *First HR*: 04/29/1945 off Roger Wolff

John Donaldson

JOHN DAVID DONALDSON
B: 05/05/1943
BL

Year	Tm	Lg	Tot	H	A	Men-On 0	Men-On 1	Men-On 2	Men-On 3	One-Game 2	One-Game 3	One-Game 4	LO	XN	IP	PH	RHP	LHP
1968	OAK	AL	2	1	1	2	0	0	0	0	0	0	0	0	0	0	2	0
1969	SEA	AL	1	0	1	1	0	0	0	0	0	0	0	0	0	0	1	0
1970	OAK	AL	1	0	1	0	0	1	0	0	0	0	0	0	0	1	1	0
Total			4	1	3	3	0	1	0	0	0	0	0	0	0	1	4	0

Rank among batters: 3,427 • *Total ballparks homered in*: 3 • *First HR*: 06/11/1968 off Sonny Siebert

Len Dondero

LEONARD PETER DONDERO
B: 09/12/1903
BR

Year	Tm	Lg	Tot	H	A	Men-On 0	Men-On 1	Men-On 2	Men-On 3	One-Game 2	One-Game 3	One-Game 4	LO	XN	IP	PH	RHP	LHP
1929	STL	AL	1	0	1	0	0	1	0	0	0	0	0	0	1	0	1	0

Rank among batters: 4,707 • *Total ballparks homered in*: 1 • *First HR*: 07/28/1929 off Hank Johnson

Mike Donlin

MICHAEL JOSEPH DONLIN
B: 05/30/1878 D: 09/24/1933
BL

						Men-On				One-Game								
Year	Tm	Lg	Tot	H	A	0	1	2	3	2	3	4	LO	XN	IP	PH	RHP	LHP
1899	STL	NL	6	5	1	4	2	0	0	0	0	0	1	0	2	0	5	0
1900	STL	NL	10	6	4	6	3	1	0	1	0	0	0	0	4	1	7	3
1901	BAL	AL	5	3	2	2	2	1	0	0	0	0	0	0	0	0	5	0
1903	CIN	NL	7	4	3	5	2	0	0	0	0	0	0	0	4	0	7	0
1904	CIN	NL	1	1	0	0	1	0	0	0	0	0	0	0	1	0	1	0
	NY	NL	2	2	0	1	1	0	0	0	0	0	1	0	0	0	1	1
	Total		3	3	0	1	2	0	0	0	0	0	1	0	1	0	2	1
1905	NY	NL	7	7	0	5	1	1	0	0	0	0	1	0	1	0	7	0
1906	NY	NL	1	1	0	0	1	0	0	0	0	0	0	0	1	0	1	0
1908	NY	NL	6	2	4	0	3	3	0	0	0	0	0	0	4	0	4	2
1911	NY	NL	1	1	0	1	0	0	0	0	0	0	0	0	0	1	1	0
	BOS	NL	2	1	1	1	1	0	0	0	0	0	0	0	0	0	1	1
	Total		3	2	1	2	1	0	0	0	0	0	0	0	0	1	2	1
1912	PIT	NL	2	0	2	0	2	0	0	0	0	0	0	0	0	0	2	0
1914	NY	NL	1	0	1	0	0	1	0	0	0	0	0	0	0	1	1	0
Total			51	33	18	25	19	7	0	1	0	0	3	0	17	3	43	7

Rank among batters: 979 • *Top target (3 home runs)*: Ed Scott, Chick Fraser • *Number of pitchers victimized*: 41 • *Total ballparks homered in*: 12 • *First HR*: 08/26/1899 off Bill Bernhard

Jim Donnelly

JAMES B. DONNELLY
B: 07/19/1865 D: 03/15/1915
BR

						Men-On				One-Game								
Year	Tm	Lg	Tot	H	A	0	1	2	3	2	3	4	LO	XN	IP	PH	RHP	LHP
1885	DET	NL	1	1	0	0	1	0	0	0	0	0	0	0	0	0	1	0
1887	WAS	NL	1	0	1	0	0	1	0	0	0	0	0	0	0	0	0	1
Total			2	1	1	0	1	1	0	0	0	0	0	0	0	0	1	1

Rank among batters: 4,129 • *Total ballparks homered in*: 1 • *First HR*: 07/16/1885 off Hugh Daily

Chris Donnels

CHRIS BARTON DONNELS
B: 04/21/1966
BL

						Men-On				One-Game								
Year	Tm	Lg	Tot	H	A	0	1	2	3	2	3	4	LO	XN	IP	PH	RHP	LHP
1993	HOU	NL	2	0	2	0	1	1	0	0	0	0	0	0	0	0	2	0
1994	HOU	NL	3	2	1	3	0	0	0	0	0	0	0	0	0	1	2	1
1995	BOS	AL	2	0	2	2	0	0	0	0	0	0	0	0	0	0	1	1
Total			7	2	5	5	1	1	0	0	0	0	0	0	0	1	5	2

Rank among batters: 2,834 • *Total ballparks homered in*: 6 • *First HR*: 09/12/1993 off Ben Rivera

Pete Donohue

PETER JOSEPH DONOHUE
B: 11/05/1900 D: 02/23/1988
BR

						Men-On				One-Game								
Year	Tm	Lg	Tot	H	A	0	1	2	3	2	3	4	LO	XN	IP	PH	RHP	LHP
1921	CIN	NL	1	0	1	1	0	0	0	0	0	0	0	0	0	0	1	0
1923	CIN	NL	1	0	1	0	1	0	0	0	0	0	0	0	0	0	0	1
1924	CIN	NL	1	0	1	1	0	0	0	0	0	0	0	0	0	0	1	0
1925	CIN	NL	1	0	1	0	1	0	0	0	0	0	0	0	0	0	1	0
1928	CIN	NL	1	0	1	0	1	0	0	0	0	0	0	0	0	0	1	0
1930	NY	NL	1	1	0	0	1	0	0	0	0	0	0	0	0	0	1	0
Total			6	1	5	2	4	0	0	0	0	0	0	0	0	0	5	1

Rank among batters: 2,988 • *Total ballparks homered in*: 3 • *First HR*: 08/19/1921 off Jess Barnes

Tom Donohue

THOMAS JAMES DONOHUE
B: 11/15/1952
BR

						Men-On				One-Game								
Year	Tm	Lg	Tot	H	A	0	1	2	3	2	3	4	LO	XN	IP	PH	RHP	LHP
1979	CAL	AL	3	3	0	2	1	0	0	0	0	0	0	0	0	0	2	1
1980	CAL	AL	2	1	1	1	1	0	0	0	0	0	0	0	0	0	0	2
Total			5	4	1	3	2	0	0	0	0	0	0	0	0	0	2	3

Rank among batters: 3,191 • *Total ballparks homered in*: 2 • *First HR*: 06/06/1979 off Jesse Jefferson

Bill Donovan

WILLIAM EDWARD DONOVAN
B: 10/13/1876 D: 12/09/1923
BB

						Men-On				One-Game								
Year	Tm	Lg	Tot	H	A	0	1	2	3	2	3	4	LO	XN	IP	PH	RHP	LHP
1898	WAS	NL	2	1	1	1	1	0	0	0	0	0	0	0	1	0	2	0

Bill Donovan *continued*

Year	Tm	Lg	Tot	H	A	Men-On 0	1	2	3	One-Game 2	3	4	LO	XN	IP	PH	RHP	LHP
1901	BRO	NL	2	2	0	0	2	0	0	0	0	0	0	0	2	0	1	1
1902	BRO	NL	1	1	0	1	0	0	0	0	0	0	0	0	1	0	1	0
1904	DET	AL	1	1	0	0	1	0	0	0	0	0	0	0	1	0	1	0
1911	DET	AL	1	0	1	1	0	0	0	0	0	0	0	0	1	0	0	1
Total			7	5	2	3	4	0	0	0	0	0	0	0	6	0	5	2

Rank among batters: 2,834 • *Total ballparks homered in*: 5 • *First HR*: 06/14/1898 off Doc McJames

Dick Donovan

RICHARD EDWARD DONOVAN
B: 12/07/1927
BL

Year	Tm	Lg	Tot	H	A	Men-On 0	1	2	3	One-Game 2	3	4	LO	XN	IP	PH	RHP	LHP
1955	CHI	AL	1	0	1	1	0	0	0	0	0	0	0	0	0	0	1	0
1956	CHI	AL	3	2	1	1	1	1	0	0	0	0	0	0	0	0	3	0
1957	CHI	AL	3	0	3	3	0	0	0	0	0	0	0	0	0	0	0	3
1959	CHI	AL	1	0	1	0	1	0	0	0	0	0	0	0	0	0	1	0
1961	WAS	AL	1	0	1	1	0	0	0	0	0	0	0	0	0	0	0	1
1962	CLE	AL	4	4	0	4	0	0	0	2	0	0	0	0	0	0	4	0
1963	CLE	AL	1	1	0	1	0	0	0	0	0	0	0	0	0	0	1	0
1964	CLE	AL	1	0	1	1	0	0	0	0	0	0	0	0	0	0	1	0
Total			15	7	8	12	2	1	0	2	0	0	0	0	0	0	11	4

Rank among batters: 2,096 • *Top target (3 home runs)*: Paul Foytack • *Number of pitchers victimized*: 12 • *Total ballparks homered in*: 6 • *First HR*: 07/03/1955 off Bob Lemon

Patsy Donovan

PATRICK JOSEPH DONOVAN
B: 03/16/1865 D: 12/25/1953
BL

Year	Tm	Lg	Tot	H	A	Men-On 0	1	2	3	One-Game 2	3	4	LO	XN	IP	PH	RHP	LHP
1891	LOU	AA	2	0	2	1	1	0	0	0	0	0	0	0	1	0	2	0
1892	PIT	NL	2	2	0	0	2	0	0	0	0	0	0	0	1	0	1	0
1893	PIT	NL	2	2	0	0	2	0	0	0	0	0	0	0	1	0	2	0
1894	PIT	NL	4	3	1	2	2	0	0	0	0	0	0	0	2	0	4	0
1895	PIT	NL	1	1	0	1	0	0	0	0	0	0	1	0	0	0	1	0
1896	PIT	NL	3	0	3	0	2	0	1	0	0	0	0	0	0	0	3	0
1899	PIT	NL	1	1	0	0	1	0	0	0	0	0	0	0	0	0	1	0
1901	STL	NL	1	1	0	0	1	0	0	0	0	0	0	0	1	0	1	0
Total			16	10	6	4	11	0	1	0	0	0	1	0	6	0	15	0

Rank among batters: 2,029 • *Total ballparks homered in*: 6 • *First HR*: 05/11/1891 off Elton Chamberlin

Red Dooin

CHARLES SEBASTIAN DOOIN
B: 06/12/1879 D: 05/12/1952
BR

Year	Tm	Lg	Tot	H	A	Men-On 0	1	2	3	One-Game 2	3	4	LO	XN	IP	PH	RHP	LHP
1904	PHI	NL	6	2	4	4	1	0	1	0	0	0	0	1	4	0	5	1
1909	PHI	NL	2	1	1	1	1	0	0	0	0	0	0	0	1	0	2	0
1911	PHI	NL	1	1	0	1	0	0	0	0	0	0	0	0	0	0	1	0
1914	PHI	NL	1	0	1	0	1	0	0	0	0	0	0	0	1	0	1	0
Total			10	4	6	6	3	0	1	0	0	0	0	1	6	0	9	1

Rank among batters: 2,500 • *Total ballparks homered in*: 6 • *First HR*: 05/07/1904 off Sam Leever

Mickey Doolan

MICHAEL JOSEPH DOOLAN
B: 05/07/1880 D: 11/01/1951
BR

Year	Tm	Lg	Tot	H	A	Men-On 0	1	2	3	One-Game 2	3	4	LO	XN	IP	PH	RHP	LHP
1905	PHI	NL	1	1	0	1	0	0	0	0	0	0	0	0	0	0	0	1
1906	PHI	NL	1	0	1	0	1	0	0	0	0	0	0	0	0	0	1	0
1907	PHI	NL	1	0	1	0	0	1	0	0	0	0	0	0	1	0	1	0
1908	PHI	NL	2	0	2	1	1	0	0	0	0	0	0	0	1	0	1	1
1909	PHI	NL	1	0	1	1	0	0	0	0	0	0	0	0	0	0	1	0
1910	PHI	NL	2	0	2	0	2	0	0	0	0	0	0	0	0	0	0	2
1911	PHI	NL	1	0	1	1	0	0	0	0	0	0	0	0	0	0	1	0
1912	PHI	NL	1	0	1	0	1	0	0	0	0	0	0	0	0	0	1	0
1913	PHI	NL	1	1	0	1	0	0	0	0	0	0	0	0	0	0	1	0
1914	BAL	FL	1	0	1	1	0	0	0	0	0	0	0	0	0	0	1	0

Year	Tm	Lg	Tot	H	A	Men-On 0	Men-On 1	Men-On 2	Men-On 3	One-Game 2	One-Game 3	One-Game 4	LO	XN	IP	PH	RHP	LHP

Mickey Doolan *continued*

Year	Tm	Lg	Tot	H	A	0	1	2	3	2	3	4	LO	XN	IP	PH	RHP	LHP
1915	BAL	FL	2	1	1	1	1	0	0	0	0	0	0	0	0	0	2	0
1916	NY	NL	1	0	1	1	0	0	0	0	0	0	0	0	0	0	1	0
Total			15	3	12	8	6	1	0	0	0	0	0	0	2	0	11	4

Rank among batters: 2,096 • *Top target (2 home runs)*: Howie Camnitz • *Number of pitchers victimized*: 14 • *Total ballparks homered in*: 10 • *First HR*: 05/24/1905 off Jake Weimer

Bill Doran

WILLIAM DONALD DORAN
B: 05/28/1958
BB

Year	Tm	Lg	Tot	H	A	0	1	2	3	2	3	4	LO	XN	IP	PH	RHP	LHP
1983	HOU	NL	8	1	7	4	3	1	0	0	0	0	1	1	0	0	5	3
1984	HOU	NL	4	2	2	4	0	0	0	0	0	0	1	0	0	0	2	2
1985	HOU	NL	14	5	9	9	3	2	0	0	0	0	2	0	0	0	9	5
1986	HOU	NL	6	3	3	6	0	0	0	0	0	0	3	1	0	0	3	3
1987	HOU	NL	16	7	9	9	6	1	0	2	0	0	1	0	2	0	9	7
1988	HOU	NL	7	2	5	4	2	0	1	0	0	0	0	0	0	0	5	2
1989	HOU	NL	8	3	5	4	3	0	1	0	0	0	0	1	0	0	4	4
1990	HOU	NL	6	3	3	3	2	1	0	0	0	0	0	0	0	0	4	2
	CIN	NL	1	1	0	1	0	0	0	0	0	0	1	0	0	0	1	0
	Total		7	4	3	4	2	1	0	0	0	0	1	0	0	0	5	2
1991	CIN	NL	6	3	3	5	1	0	0	0	0	0	1	1	0	0	4	2
1992	CIN	NL	8	6	2	4	3	0	1	0	0	0	0	0	0	0	6	2
Total			84	36	48	53	23	5	3	2	0	0	10	4	2	0	52	32

Rank among batters: 617 • *Top target (3 home runs)*: Rick Rhoden, Tom Browning, Eric Show • *Number of pitchers victimized*: 72 • *Total ballparks homered in*: 11 • *First HR*: 04/10/1983 off John Candelaria • *LCS HR*—1

Mike Dorgan

MICHAEL CORNELIUS DORGAN
B: 10/02/1853 D: 04/26/1909
BR

Year	Tm	Lg	Tot	H	A	0	1	2	3	2	3	4	LO	XN	IP	PH	RHP	LHP
1879	SYR	NL	1	0	1	1	0	0	0	0	0	0	1	0	0	0	1	0
1884	NY	NL	1	0	1	0	0	0	0	0	0	0	0	0	0	0	1	0
1886	NY	NL	2	1	1	1	0	0	1	0	0	0	0	0	1	0	1	1
Total			4	1	3	2	0	0	1	0	0	0	1	0	1	0	3	1

Rank among batters: 3,427 • *Total ballparks homered in*: 4 • *First HR*: 08/14/1879 off Tommy Bond

Brian Dorsett

BRIAN RICHARD DORSETT
B: 04/09/1961
BR

Year	Tm	Lg	Tot	H	A	0	1	2	3	2	3	4	LO	XN	IP	PH	RHP	LHP
1987	CLE	AL	1	1	0	0	1	0	0	0	0	0	0	0	0	0	1	0
1993	CIN	NL	2	2	0	0	2	0	0	0	0	0	0	0	0	0	1	1
1994	CIN	NL	5	2	3	2	2	0	1	0	0	0	0	1	0	0	4	1
Total			8	5	3	2	5	0	1	0	0	0	0	1	0	0	6	2

Rank among batters: 2,703 • *Total ballparks homered in*: 5 • *First HR*: 09/27/1987 off Don Sutton

Dutch Dotterer

HENRY JOHN DOTTERER
B: 11/11/1931
BR

Year	Tm	Lg	Tot	H	A	0	1	2	3	2	3	4	LO	XN	IP	PH	RHP	LHP
1958	CIN	NL	1	1	0	1	0	0	0	0	0	0	0	0	0	0	0	1
1959	CIN	NL	2	1	1	1	1	0	0	0	0	0	0	0	0	0	0	2
1960	CIN	NL	2	0	2	1	0	0	1	0	0	0	0	0	0	0	0	2
Total			5	2	3	3	1	0	1	0	0	0	0	0	0	0	0	5

Rank among batters: 3,191 • *Top target (2 home runs)*: Johnny Podres • *Number of pitchers victimized*: 4 • *Total ballparks homered in*: 2 • *First HR*: 09/16/1958 off Johnny Podres

Patsy Dougherty

PATRICK HENRY DOUGHERTY
B: 10/27/1876 D: 04/30/1940
BL

Year	Tm	Lg	Tot	H	A	0	1	2	3	2	3	4	LO	XN	IP	PH	RHP	LHP
1903	BOS	AL	4	3	1	1	2	1	0	0	0	0	1	0	1	0	3	1

						Men-On				One-Game								
Year	**Tm**	**Lg**	**Tot**	**H**	**A**	**0**	**1**	**2**	**3**	**2**	**3**	**4**	**LO**	**XN**	**IP**	**PH**	**RHP**	**LHP**

Patsy Dougherty *continued*

Year	Tm	Lg	Tot	H	A	0	1	2	3	2	3	4	LO	XN	IP	PH	RHP	LHP
1904	NY	AL	6	6	0	5	1	0	0	0	0	0	1	0	4	0	5	1
1905	NY	AL	3	3	0	2	1	0	0	0	0	0	0	0	3	0	2	1
1906	CHI	AL	1	0	1	1	0	0	0	0	0	0	0	0	0	0	1	0
1907	CHI	AL	1	0	1	1	0	0	0	0	0	0	0	0	0	0	0	1
1909	CHI	AL	1	1	0	0	0	1	0	0	0	0	0	0	0	0	0	1
1910	CHI	AL	1	0	1	0	1	0	0	0	0	0	0	0	1	0	1	0
Total			17	13	4	10	5	2	0	0	0	0	2	0	9	0	12	5

Rank among batters: 1,969 • *Top target (2 home runs)*: Willie Sudhoff, Barney Pelty, Jesse Tannehill • *Number of pitchers victimized*: 14 • *Total ballparks homered in*: 5 • *First HR*: 04/28/1903 off Watty Lee • *Hit for Cycle*—vs NY: 07/29/1903 • *World Series HR*—2

Phil Douglas

PHILLIP BROOKS DOUGLAS
B: 06/17/1890 D: 08/01/1952
BR

Year	Tm	Lg	Tot	H	A	0	1	2	3	2	3	4	LO	XN	IP	PH	RHP	LHP
1921	NY	NL	1	1	0	1	0	0	0	0	0	0	0	0	0	0	0	1
1922	NY	NL	1	1	0	0	0	1	0	0	0	0	0	0	0	0	0	1
Total			2	2	0	1	0	1	0	0	0	0	0	0	0	0	0	2

Rank among batters: 4,129 • *Total ballparks homered in*: 1 • *First HR*: 07/09/1921 off Hippo Vaughn

Klondike Douglass

WILLIAM BINGHAM DOUGLASS
B: 05/10/1872 D: 12/13/1953
BL

Year	Tm	Lg	Tot	H	A	0	1	2	3	2	3	4	LO	XN	IP	PH	RHP	LHP
1896	STL	NL	1	1	0	1	0	0	0	0	0	0	0	0	0	0	1	0
1897	STL	NL	6	2	4	4	2	0	0	0	0	0	1	0	2	0	5	0
1898	PHI	NL	2	0	2	1	1	0	0	0	0	0	0	0	0	0	1	1
1903	PHI	NL	1	1	0	1	0	0	0	0	0	0	0	0	1	0	1	0
Total			10	4	6	7	3	0	0	0	0	0	1	0	3	0	8	1

Rank among batters: 2,500 • *Top target (3 home runs)*: Zeke Wilson • *Number of pitchers victimized*: 8 • *Total ballparks homered in*: 5 • *First HR*: 05/07/1896 off Jouett Meekin

Taylor Douthit

TAYLOR LEE DOUTHIT
B: 04/22/1901 D: 05/28/1986
BR

Year	Tm	Lg	Tot	H	A	0	1	2	3	2	3	4	LO	XN	IP	PH	RHP	LHP
1925	STL	NL	1	0	1	0	1	0	0	0	0	0	0	0	0	0	0	1
1926	STL	NL	3	1	2	2	1	0	0	0	0	0	0	0	1	0	3	0
1927	STL	NL	5	2	3	4	0	1	0	0	0	0	0	0	0	0	4	1
1928	STL	NL	3	1	2	1	2	0	0	0	0	0	0	0	0	0	1	2
1929	STL	NL	9	3	6	8	0	0	1	0	0	0	2	0	1	0	7	2
1930	STL	NL	7	4	3	4	1	2	0	0	0	0	2	0	0	0	4	3
1931	STL	NL	1	1	0	0	1	0	0	0	0	0	0	0	0	0	1	0
Total			29	12	17	19	6	3	1	0	0	0	4	0	2	0	20	9

Rank among batters: 1,465 • *Top target (2 home runs)*: Freddie Fitzsimmons, Ed Brandt • *Number of pitchers victimized*: 27 • *Total ballparks homered in*: 5 • *First HR*: 04/18/1925 off Percy Jones • *World Series HR*—1

Tommy Dowd

THOMAS JEFFERSON DOWD
B: 04/20/1869 D: 07/02/1933
BR

Year	Tm	Lg	Tot	H	A	0	1	2	3	2	3	4	LO	XN	IP	PH	RHP	LHP
1891	WAS	AA	1	1	0	0	0	1	0	0	0	0	0	0	0	0	1	0
1892	WAS	NL	1	1	0	0	0	1	0	0	0	0	0	0	0	0	1	0
1893	STL	NL	1	1	0	1	0	0	0	0	0	0	0	0	0	0	1	0
1894	STL	NL	4	3	1	3	1	0	0	0	0	0	0	0	2	0	1	2
1895	STL	NL	7	5	2	3	4	0	0	0	0	0	0	0	0	0	5	1
1896	STL	NL	5	3	2	1	4	0	0	0	0	0	0	0	0	0	5	0
1899	CLE	NL	2	1	1	1	1	0	0	0	0	0	1	0	0	0	1	1
1901	BOS	AL	3	2	1	2	0	1	0	0	0	0	0	0	0	0	3	0
Total			24	17	7	11	10	3	0	0	0	0	1	0	2	0	18	4

Rank among batters: 1,643 • *Top target (2 home runs)*: Elton Chamberlin, Cy Young, Zeke Wilson • *Number of pitchers victimized*: 21 • *Total ballparks homered in*: 6 • *First HR*: 06/24/1891 off Elton Chamberlin • *Hit for Cycle*—vs LOU: 08/16/1895

Pete Dowling

HENRY PETER DOWLING
D: 06/30/1905

Year	Tm	Lg	Tot	H	A	Men-On 0	1	2	3	One-Game 2	3	4	LO	XN	IP	PH	RHP	LHP
1901	CLE	AL	1	0	1	1	0	0	0	0	0	0	0	0	0	0	1	0

Rank among batters: 4,707 • *Total ballparks homered in*: 1 • *First HR*: 06/21/1901 off Ted Lewis

Tom Downey

THOMAS EDWARD DOWNEY
B: 01/01/1884 D: 08/03/1961
BR

Year	Tm	Lg	Tot	H	A	Men-On 0	1	2	3	One-Game 2	3	4	LO	XN	IP	PH	RHP	LHP
1909	CIN	NL	1	0	1	0	1	0	0	0	0	0	0	0	1	0	1	0
1910	CIN	NL	2	0	2	2	0	0	0	0	0	0	0	0	0	0	1	1
1912	PHI	NL	1	0	1	0	0	1	0	0	0	0	0	0	0	0	1	0
1914	BUF	FL	2	1	1	2	0	0	0	0	0	0	0	0	0	0	1	1
1915	BUF	FL	1	0	1	1	0	0	0	0	0	0	1	0	0	0	0	1
Total			7	1	6	5	1	1	0	0	0	0	1	0	1	0	4	3

Rank among batters: 2,834 • *Top target (2 home runs)*: Christy Mathewson • *Number of pitchers victimized*: 6 • *Total ballparks homered in*: 6 • *First HR*: 07/13/1909 off Red Ames

Al Downing

ALPHONSO ERWIN DOWNING
B: 06/28/1941
BR

Year	Tm	Lg	Tot	H	A	Men-On 0	1	2	3	One-Game 2	3	4	LO	XN	IP	PH	RHP	LHP
1965	NY	AL	1	0	1	0	0	1	0	0	0	0	0	0	0	0	1	0
1967	NY	AL	1	1	0	1	0	0	0	0	0	0	0	0	0	0	1	0
Total			2	1	1	1	0	1	0	0	0	0	0	0	0	0	2	0

Rank among batters: 4,129 • *Top target (2 home runs)*: Denny McLain • *Number of pitchers victimized*: 1 • *Total ballparks homered in*: 2 • *First HR*: 08/08/1965 off Denny McLain

Brian Downing

BRIAN JAY DOWNING
B: 10/09/1950
BR

Year	Tm	Lg	Tot	H	A	Men-On 0	1	2	3	One-Game 2	3	4	LO	XN	IP	PH	RHP	LHP
1973	CHI	AL	2	1	1	2	0	0	0	0	0	0	0	0	1	0	0	2
1974	CHI	AL	10	6	4	5	1	4	0	0	0	0	0	0	0	0	2	8
1975	CHI	AL	7	5	2	4	3	0	0	0	0	0	0	1	0	0	6	1
1976	CHI	AL	3	0	3	3	0	0	0	0	0	0	0	0	0	0	3	0
1977	CHI	AL	4	1	3	1	3	0	0	0	0	0	0	0	0	0	2	2
1978	CAL	AL	7	2	5	4	1	2	0	0	0	0	0	0	0	0	4	3
1979	CAL	AL	12	3	9	7	2	3	0	0	0	0	0	0	0	0	10	2
1980	CAL	AL	2	2	0	1	1	0	0	0	0	0	0	0	0	0	0	2
1981	CAL	AL	9	6	3	4	2	2	1	0	0	0	1	0	0	0	7	2
1982	CAL	AL	28	15	13	20	4	2	2	2	0	0	6	0	0	0	19	9
1983	CAL	AL	19	10	9	9	8	2	0	0	0	0	1	0	0	0	9	10
1984	CAL	AL	23	9	14	12	5	5	1	2	0	0	0	0	0	0	16	7
1985	CAL	AL	20	10	10	8	9	3	0	0	0	0	2	0	0	0	12	8
1986	CAL	AL	20	13	7	7	8	3	2	2	0	0	0	2	0	0	13	7
1987	CAL	AL	29	11	18	22	7	0	0	1	0	0	7	0	0	0	18	11
1988	CAL	AL	25	11	14	18	6	1	0	1	0	0	0	1	0	0	17	8
1989	CAL	AL	14	10	4	11	3	0	0	0	0	0	1	0	0	0	6	8
1990	CAL	AL	14	11	3	7	4	3	0	1	0	0	1	0	0	0	9	5
1991	TEX	AL	17	8	9	13	2	1	1	1	0	0	5	0	0	0	8	9
1992	TEX	AL	10	4	6	6	3	1	0	0	0	0	1	0	0	0	7	3
Total			275	138	137	164	72	32	7	10	0	0	25	4	1	0	168	107

Rank among batters: 85 • Top target (4 home runs): Jerry Koosman, Frank Tanana, Dave Stewart, Roger Clemens, Mark Langston, Bill Krueger • *Number of pitchers victimized*: 194 • *Total ballparks homered in*: 16 • *First HR*: 08/11/1973 off Mickey Lolich • *LCS HR*—1

Red Downs

JEROME WILLIS DOWNS
B: 08/22/1883 D: 10/19/1939
BR

Year	Tm	Lg	Tot	H	A	Men-On 0	1	2	3	One-Game 2	3	4	LO	XN	IP	PH	RHP	LHP
1907	DET	AL	1	1	0	1	0	0	0	0	0	0	0	0	1	0	1	0
1908	DET	AL	1	0	1	0	1	0	0	0	0	0	0	0	1	0	1	0
1912	CHI	NL	1	0	1	0	0	1	0	0	0	0	0	0	0	0	1	0
Total			3	1	2	1	1	1	0	0	0	0	0	0	2	0	3	0

Rank among batters: 3,735 • *Total ballparks homered in*: 3 • *First HR*: 08/19/1907 off Cy Young

Brian Doyle

BRIAN REED DOYLE
B: 01/26/1955
BL

						Men-On				One-Game								
Year	Tm	Lg	Tot	H	A	0	1	2	3	2	3	4	LO	XN	IP	PH	RHP	LHP
1980	NY	AL	1	1	0	1	0	0	0	0	0	0	0	0	0	0	1	0

Rank among batters: 4,707 • *Total ballparks homered in*: 1 • *First HR*: 06/29/1980 off Len Barker

Carl Doyle

WILLIAM CARL DOYLE
B: 07/30/1912 D: 09/04/1951
BR

						Men-On				One-Game								
Year	Tm	Lg	Tot	H	A	0	1	2	3	2	3	4	LO	XN	IP	PH	RHP	LHP
1940	STL	NL	1	1	0	1	0	0	0	0	0	0	0	0	0	0	1	0

Rank among batters: 4,707 • *Total ballparks homered in*: 1 • *First HR*: 08/25/1940 off Manny Salvo

Denny Doyle

ROBERT DENNIS DOYLE
B: 01/17/1944
BL

						Men-On				One-Game								
Year	Tm	Lg	Tot	H	A	0	1	2	3	2	3	4	LO	XN	IP	PH	RHP	LHP
1970	PHI	NL	2	0	2	2	0	0	0	0	0	0	0	0	1	0	2	0
1971	PHI	NL	3	2	1	1	2	0	0	0	0	0	0	0	1	0	3	0
1972	PHI	NL	1	0	1	1	0	0	0	0	0	0	0	0	0	0	1	0
1973	PHI	NL	3	3	0	2	0	1	0	0	0	0	0	0	0	0	3	0
1974	CAL	AL	1	0	1	1	0	0	0	0	0	0	0	0	0	0	0	1
1975	BOS	AL	4	1	3	0	3	1	0	0	0	0	0	0	0	0	4	0
1977	BOS	AL	2	2	0	0	0	2	0	0	0	0	0	0	0	0	2	0
Total			16	8	8	7	5	4	0	0	0	0	0	0	2	0	15	1

Rank among batters: 2,029 • *Top target (2 home runs)*: Gary Nolan • *Number of pitchers victimized*: 15 • *Total ballparks homered in*: 10 • *First HR*: 06/03/1970 off Gary Nolan

Jack Doyle

JOHN JOSEPH DOYLE
B: 10/25/1869 D: 12/31/1958
BR

						Men-On				One-Game								
Year	Tm	Lg	Tot	H	A	0	1	2	3	2	3	4	LO	XN	IP	PH	RHP	LHP
1890	COL	AA	2	2	0	0	2	0	0	0	0	0	0	0	1	0	0	1
1892	CLE	NL	1	1	0	0	1	0	0	0	0	0	0	0	0	0	1	0
	NY	NL	5	3	2	4	1	0	0	0	0	0	0	0	2	0	4	0
	Total		6	4	2	4	2	0	0	0	0	0	0	0	2	0	5	0
1893	NY	NL	1	1	0	0	1	0	0	0	0	0	0	0	0	0	0	1
1894	NY	NL	3	1	2	1	1	1	0	0	0	0	0	0	0	0	3	0
1895	NY	NL	1	0	1	0	0	1	0	0	0	0	0	0	1	0	1	0
1896	BAL	NL	1	0	1	0	1	0	0	0	0	0	0	0	0	0	0	1
1897	BAL	NL	2	0	2	1	1	0	0	0	0	0	0	0	0	0	2	0
1898	WAS	NL	2	2	0	1	0	1	0	0	0	0	0	0	0	0	1	1
	NY	NL	1	0	1	1	0	0	0	0	0	0	0	0	0	0	1	0
	Total		3	2	1	2	0	1	0	0	0	0	0	0	0	0	2	1
1899	NY	NL	3	0	3	0	2	1	0	0	0	0	0	0	1	0	3	0
1900	NY	NL	1	0	1	1	0	0	0	0	0	0	0	0	0	0	1	0
1902	WAS	AL	1	1	0	0	1	0	0	0	0	0	0	0	0	0	1	0
1904	PHI	NL	1	0	1	0	0	1	0	0	0	0	0	0	1	0	1	0
Total			25	11	14	9	11	5	0	0	0	0	0	0	6	0	19	4

Rank among batters: 1,608 • *Top target (2 home runs)*: Ben Sanders, Cy Seymour, Bill Dinneen • *Number of pitchers victimized*: 22 • *Total ballparks homered in*: 12 • *First HR*: 07/09/1890 off Will Callahan

Jess Doyle

JESSE HERBERT DOYLE
B: 04/14/1898 D: 04/15/1961
BR

						Men-On				One-Game								
Year	Tm	Lg	Tot	H	A	0	1	2	3	2	3	4	LO	XN	IP	PH	RHP	LHP
1925	DET	AL	2	0	2	1	1	0	0	1	0	0	0	0	0	0	0	2

Rank among batters: 4,129 • *Top target (2 home runs)*: Ben Shields • *Number of pitchers victimized*: 1 • *Total ballparks homered in*: 1 • *First HR*: 09/28/1925 off Ben Shields

Jim Doyle

JAMES FRANCIS DOYLE
B: 12/25/1881 D: 02/01/1912
BR

						Men-On				One-Game								
Year	Tm	Lg	Tot	H	A	0	1	2	3	2	3	4	LO	XN	IP	PH	RHP	LHP
1911	CHI	NL	5	1	4	2	2	1	0	0	0	0	0	1	0	0	4	1

Rank among batters: 3,191 • *Total ballparks homered in*: 4 • *First HR*: 05/22/1911 off Grover Alexander

Larry Doyle

LAWRENCE JOSEPH DOYLE
B: 07/31/1886 D: 03/01/1974
BL

Year	Tm	Lg	Tot	H	A	Men-On 0	1	2	3	One-Game 2	3	4	LO	XN	IP	PH	RHP	LHP
1909	NY	NL	6	5	1	3	2	1	0	1	0	0	1	0	5	0	4	2
1910	NY	NL	8	5	3	4	1	3	0	0	0	0	0	0	1	0	7	1
1911	NY	NL	13	5	8	8	4	1	0	0	0	0	0	0	3	0	11	2
1912	NY	NL	10	5	5	5	2	3	0	0	0	0	0	1	1	0	10	0
1913	NY	NL	5	3	2	2	1	1	1	0	0	0	0	0	0	0	4	1
1914	NY	NL	5	2	3	1	2	2	0	0	0	0	0	1	2	0	5	0
1915	NY	NL	4	2	2	1	2	1	0	0	0	0	0	0	1	0	4	0
1916	NY	NL	2	1	1	2	0	0	0	0	0	0	0	0	0	0	1	1
	CHI	NL	1	1	0	1	0	0	0	0	0	0	0	0	0	0	1	0
	Total		3	2	1	3	0	0	0	0	0	0	0	0	0	0	2	1
1917	CHI	NL	6	2	4	2	4	0	0	0	0	0	0	0	0	0	6	0
1918	NY	NL	3	1	2	0	1	2	0	0	0	0	0	1	0	0	2	1
1919	NY	NL	7	2	5	6	0	1	0	0	0	0	0	1	0	0	6	1
1920	NY	NL	4	3	1	1	2	1	0	0	0	0	0	0	0	0	2	2
Total			74	37	37	36	21	16	1	1	0	0	1	4	13	0	63	11

Rank among batters: 707 • Top target (3 home runs): Howie Camnitz, Hub Perdue, Babe Adams, Bill Doak • *Number of pitchers victimized*: 56 • *Total ballparks homered in*: 12 • *First HR*: 06/24/1909 off Jake Boultes • *World Series HR*—1

Doug Drabek

DOUGLAS DEAN DRABEK
B: 07/25/1962
BR

Year	Tm	Lg	Tot	H	A	Men-On 0	1	2	3	One-Game 2	3	4	LO	XN	IP	PH	RHP	LHP
1990	PIT	NL	1	0	1	0	1	0	0	0	0	0	0	0	0	0	1	0
1993	HOU	NL	1	1	0	1	0	0	0	0	0	0	0	0	0	0	1	0
Total			2	1	1	1	1	0	0	0	0	0	0	0	0	0	2	0

Rank among batters: 4,129 • *Total ballparks homered in*: 2 • *First HR*: 04/24/1990 off Scott Garrelts

Moe Drabowsky

MYRON WALTER DRABOWSKY
B: 07/21/1935
BR

Year	Tm	Lg	Tot	H	A	Men-On 0	1	2	3	One-Game 2	3	4	LO	XN	IP	PH	RHP	LHP
1957	CHI	NL	1	1	0	1	0	0	0	0	0	0	0	0	0	0	1	0
1963	KC	AL	2	2	0	2	0	0	0	0	0	0	0	0	0	0	1	1
Total			3	3	0	3	0	0	0	0	0	0	0	0	0	0	2	1

Rank among batters: 3,735 • *Total ballparks homered in*: 2 • *First HR*: 09/17/1957 off Jack Sanford

Delos Drake

DELOS DANIEL DRAKE
B: 12/03/1886 D: 10/03/1965
BR

Year	Tm	Lg	Tot	H	A	Men-On 0	1	2	3	One-Game 2	3	4	LO	XN	IP	PH	RHP	LHP
1911	DET	AL	1	1	0	1	0	0	0	0	0	0	0	0	0	0	0	1
1914	STL	FL	3	0	3	1	1	1	0	0	0	0	0	1	0	0	2	1
1915	STL	FL	1	0	1	0	1	0	0	0	0	0	0	0	0	0	0	1
Total			5	1	4	2	2	1	0	0	0	0	0	1	0	0	2	3

Rank among batters: 3,191 • *Total ballparks homered in*: 3 • *First HR*: 07/07/1911 off Dolly Gray

Solly Drake

SOLOMON LOUIS DRAKE
B: 10/23/1930
BB

Year	Tm	Lg	Tot	H	A	Men-On 0	1	2	3	One-Game 2	3	4	LO	XN	IP	PH	RHP	LHP
1956	CHI	NL	2	2	0	1	0	1	0	0	0	0	0	0	0	0	2	0

Rank among batters: 4,129 • *Total ballparks homered in*: 1 • *First HR*: 04/22/1956 off Joe Black

Dave Dravecky

DAVID FRANCIS DRAVECKY
B: 02/14/1956
BR

Year	Tm	Lg	Tot	H	A	Men-On 0	1	2	3	One-Game 2	3	4	LO	XN	IP	PH	RHP	LHP
1986	SD	NL	1	1	0	1	0	0	0	0	0	0	0	0	0	0	0	1

Rank among batters: 4,707 • *Total ballparks homered in*: 1 • *First HR*: 04/16/1986 off Dennis Powell

Bill Dreesen

WILLIAM RICHARD DREESEN
B: 07/26/1904 D: 11/09/1971
BL

Year	Tm	Lg	Tot	H	A	Men-On 0	Men-On 1	Men-On 2	Men-On 3	One-Game 2	One-Game 3	One-Game 4	LO	XN	IP	PH	RHP	LHP
1931	BOS	NL	1	0	1	1	0	0	0	0	0	0	0	0	0	0	1	0

Rank among batters: 4,707 • *Total ballparks homered in*: 1 • *First HR*: 06/12/1931 off Burleigh Grimes

Chuck Dressen

CHARLES WALTER DRESSEN
B: 09/20/1898 D: 08/10/1966
BR

Year	Tm	Lg	Tot	H	A	Men-On 0	Men-On 1	Men-On 2	Men-On 3	One-Game 2	One-Game 3	One-Game 4	LO	XN	IP	PH	RHP	LHP
1925	CIN	NL	3	0	3	3	0	0	0	0	0	0	0	0	0	0	3	0
1926	CIN	NL	4	1	3	2	1	0	1	0	0	0	0	0	1	0	3	1
1927	CIN	NL	2	0	2	2	0	0	0	0	0	0	0	0	0	0	2	0
1928	CIN	NL	1	0	1	1	0	0	0	0	0	0	0	0	0	0	1	0
1929	CIN	NL	1	0	1	0	1	0	0	0	0	0	0	0	0	0	1	0
Total			11	1	10	8	2	0	1	0	0	0	0	0	1	0	10	1

Rank among batters: 2,419 • *Top target (2 home runs)*: Joe Genewich • *Number of pitchers victimized*: 10 • *Total ballparks homered in*: 5 • *First HR*: 05/22/1925 off Art Decatur

Dan Driessen

DANIEL DRIESSEN
B: 07/29/1951
BL

Year	Tm	Lg	Tot	H	A	Men-On 0	Men-On 1	Men-On 2	Men-On 3	One-Game 2	One-Game 3	One-Game 4	LO	XN	IP	PH	RHP	LHP
1973	CIN	NL	4	3	1	3	1	0	0	0	0	0	0	0	0	0	4	0
1974	CIN	NL	7	4	3	5	2	0	0	0	0	0	0	0	0	0	6	1
1975	CIN	NL	7	5	2	4	0	3	0	0	0	0	0	1	0	0	7	0
1976	CIN	NL	7	3	4	4	1	2	0	0	0	0	0	0	0	2	7	0
1977	CIN	NL	17	10	7	9	4	4	0	1	0	0	0	1	1	0	13	4
1978	CIN	NL	16	10	6	9	5	2	0	0	0	0	0	2	0	0	14	2
1979	CIN	NL	18	12	6	13	2	3	0	0	0	0	0	1	0	0	11	7
1980	CIN	NL	14	11	3	7	7	0	0	0	0	0	0	0	0	0	11	3
1981	CIN	NL	7	2	5	4	1	2	0	0	0	0	0	0	0	0	6	1
1982	CIN	NL	17	7	10	11	5	0	1	2	0	0	0	0	1	0	15	2
1983	CIN	NL	12	3	9	7	4	1	0	0	0	0	0	0	0	1	10	2
1984	CIN	NL	7	3	4	4	3	0	0	0	0	0	0	0	0	0	6	1
	MON	NL	9	8	1	4	3	2	0	1	0	0	0	0	0	0	9	0
	Total		16	11	5	8	6	2	0	1	0	0	0	0	0	0	15	1
1985	MON	NL	6	2	4	5	1	0	0	0	0	0	0	0	0	0	5	1
	SF	NL	3	2	1	3	0	0	0	0	0	0	0	0	0	0	3	0
	Total		9	4	5	8	1	0	0	0	0	0	0	0	0	0	8	1
1986	HOU	NL	1	1	0	1	0	0	0	0	0	0	0	0	0	1	1	0
1987	STL	NL	1	0	1	0	1	0	0	0	0	0	0	0	0	0	1	0
Total			153	86	67	93	40	19	1	4	0	0	0	5	2	4	129	24

Rank among batters: 280 • *Top target (4 home runs)*: Don Sutton • *Number of pitchers victimized*: 119 • *Total ballparks homered in*: 12 • *First HR*: 07/26/1973 off Ron Schueler • *World Series HR*—1

Lew Drill

LEWIS L. DRILL
B: 05/09/1877 D: 07/04/1969
BR

Year	Tm	Lg	Tot	H	A	Men-On 0	Men-On 1	Men-On 2	Men-On 3	One-Game 2	One-Game 3	One-Game 4	LO	XN	IP	PH	RHP	LHP
1902	WAS	AL	1	1	0	0	1	0	0	0	0	0	0	0	0	0	1	0
1904	WAS	AL	1	1	0	1	0	0	0	0	0	0	0	0	0	0	1	0
Total			2	2	0	1	1	0	0	0	0	0	0	0	0	0	2	0

Rank among batters: 4,129 • *Total ballparks homered in*: 2 • *First HR*: 04/24/1902 off Cy Young

Denny Driscoll

JOHN F. DRISCOLL
B: 11/19/1855 D: 07/11/1886
BL

Year	Tm	Lg	Tot	H	A	Men-On 0	Men-On 1	Men-On 2	Men-On 3	One-Game 2	One-Game 3	One-Game 4	LO	XN	IP	PH	RHP	LHP
1882	PIT	AA	1	1	0	1	0	0	0	0	0	0	0	0	0	0	1	0

Rank among batters: 4,707 • *Total ballparks homered in*: 1 • *First HR*: 08/14/1882 off Henry Myers

Jim Driscoll

JAMES BERNARD DRISCOLL
B: 05/14/1944
BL

Year	Tm	Lg	Tot	H	A	Men-On 0	Men-On 1	Men-On 2	Men-On 3	One-Game 2	One-Game 3	One-Game 4	LO	XN	IP	PH	RHP	LHP
1970	OAK	AL	1	1	0	1	0	0	0	0	0	0	0	0	0	0	0	1

Year	Tm	Lg	Tot	H	A	Men-On 0	Men-On 1	Men-On 2	Men-On 3	One-Game 2	One-Game 3	One-Game 4	LO	XN	IP	PH	RHP	LHP

Jim Driscoll *continued*

Rank among batters: 4,707 • *Total ballparks homered in*: 1 • *First HR*: 09/29/1970 off Al Downing

Walt Dropo

WALTER DROPO
B: 01/30/1923
BR

Year	Tm	Lg	Tot	H	A	Men-On 0	Men-On 1	Men-On 2	Men-On 3	One-Game 2	One-Game 3	One-Game 4	LO	XN	IP	PH	RHP	LHP
1950	BOS	AL	34	24	10	13	15	4	2	4	0	0	0	0	0	0	20	14
1951	BOS	AL	11	10	1	4	4	3	0	1	0	0	0	0	0	0	10	1
1952	BOS	AL	6	5	1	3	1	1	1	0	0	0	0	0	0	0	5	1
	DET	AL	23	11	12	13	8	2	0	3	0	0	0	0	0	0	14	9
	Total		29	16	13	16	9	3	1	3	0	0	0	0	0	0	19	10
1953	DET	AL	13	5	8	2	5	6	0	0	0	0	0	0	0	0	9	4
1954	DET	AL	4	1	3	3	1	0	0	0	0	0	0	0	0	1	2	2
1955	CHI	AL	19	10	9	11	5	1	2	1	0	0	0	0	0	0	13	6
1956	CHI	AL	8	6	2	6	1	1	0	0	0	0	0	0	0	0	4	4
1957	CHI	AL	13	7	6	5	5	1	2	0	0	0	0	0	0	2	6	7
1958	CHI	AL	2	2	0	1	0	1	0	0	0	0	0	0	0	0	1	1
	CIN	NL	7	4	3	5	2	0	0	0	0	0	0	0	0	1	4	3
	Total		9	6	3	6	2	1	0	0	0	0	0	0	0	1	5	4
1959	CIN	NL	1	1	0	1	0	0	0	0	0	0	0	0	0	0	1	0
	BAL	AL	6	4	2	4	2	0	0	1	0	0	0	0	0	0	0	6
	Total		7	5	2	5	2	0	0	1	0	0	0	0	0	0	1	6
1960	BAL	AL	4	1	3	2	2	0	0	0	0	0	0	0	0	0	0	4
1961	BAL	AL	1	0	1	1	0	0	0	0	0	0	0	0	0	0	0	1
Total			152	91	61	74	51	20	7	10	0	0	0	0	0	4	89	63

Rank among batters: 284 • *Top target (5 home runs)*: Whitey Ford • *Number of pitchers victimized*: 102 • *Total ballparks homered in*: 12 • *First HR*: 05/03/1950 off Bob Feller

Louis Drucke

LOUIS FRANK DRUCKE
B: 12/03/1888 D: 09/22/1955
BR

Year	Tm	Lg	Tot	H	A	Men-On 0	Men-On 1	Men-On 2	Men-On 3	One-Game 2	One-Game 3	One-Game 4	LO	XN	IP	PH	RHP	LHP
1910	NY	NL	1	1	0	1	0	0	0	0	0	0	0	0	0	0	1	0

Rank among batters: 4,707 • *Total ballparks homered in*: 1 • *First HR*: 09/27/1910 off Art Fromme

Don Drysdale

DONALD SCOTT DRYSDALE
B: 07/23/1936 D: 07/03/1993
BR HOF

Year	Tm	Lg	Tot	H	A	Men-On 0	Men-On 1	Men-On 2	Men-On 3	One-Game 2	One-Game 3	One-Game 4	LO	XN	IP	PH	RHP	LHP
1956	BRO	NL	1	1	0	1	0	0	0	0	0	0	0	0	0	0	1	0
1957	BRO	NL	2	2	0	2	0	0	0	0	0	0	0	0	0	0	2	0
1958	LA	NL	7	5	2	5	1	1	0	1	0	0	0	0	0	0	3	4
1959	LA	NL	4	3	1	2	2	0	0	0	0	0	0	0	0	0	4	0
1961	LA	NL	5	3	2	4	0	0	1	0	0	0	0	0	0	0	3	2
1964	LA	NL	1	0	1	1	0	0	0	0	0	0	0	0	0	0	1	0
1965	LA	NL	7	2	5	6	1	0	0	0	0	0	0	0	0	0	2	5
1966	LA	NL	2	1	1	2	0	0	0	0	0	0	0	0	0	0	2	0
Total			29	17	12	23	4	1	1	1	0	0	0	0	0	0	18	11

Rank among batters: 1,465 • *Top target (2 home runs)*: Juan Pizarro, Warren Spahn, Robin Roberts • *Number of pitchers victimized*: 26 • *Total ballparks homered in*: 9 • *First HR*: 09/09/1956 off Max Surkont

Monk Dubiel

WALTER JOHN DUBIEL
B: 02/12/1918 D: 10/23/1969
BR

Year	Tm	Lg	Tot	H	A	Men-On 0	Men-On 1	Men-On 2	Men-On 3	One-Game 2	One-Game 3	One-Game 4	LO	XN	IP	PH	RHP	LHP
1945	NY	AL	1	0	1	0	1	0	0	0	0	0	0	0	0	0	1	0

Rank among batters: 4,707 • *Total ballparks homered in*: 1 • *First HR*: 05/20/1945 off Bob Muncrief

Jean Dubuc

JEAN JOSEPH OCTAVE DUBUC
B: 09/15/1888 D: 08/28/1958
BR

Year	Tm	Lg	Tot	H	A	Men-On 0	Men-On 1	Men-On 2	Men-On 3	One-Game 2	One-Game 3	One-Game 4	LO	XN	IP	PH	RHP	LHP
1912	DET	AL	1	1	0	0	1	0	0	0	0	0	0	0	0	0	1	0
1913	DET	AL	2	1	1	2	0	0	0	0	0	0	0	0	0	0	2	0

Jean Dubuc *continued*

Year	Tm	Lg	Tot	H	A	Men-On 0	1	2	3	One-Game 2	3	4	LO	XN	IP	PH	RHP	LHP
1914	DET	AL	1	0	1	1	0	0	0	0	0	0	0	0	0	0	1	0
Total			4	2	2	3	1	0	0	0	0	0	0	0	0	0	4	0

Rank among batters: 3,427 • *Total ballparks homered in*: 3 • *First HR*: 08/07/1912 off Iron Davis

Rob Ducey

ROBERT THOMAS DUCEY
B: 05/24/1965
BL

Year	Tm	Lg	Tot	H	A	Men-On 0	1	2	3	One-Game 2	3	4	LO	XN	IP	PH	RHP	LHP
1987	TOR	AL	1	1	0	0	0	1	0	0	0	0	0	0	0	0	0	1
1991	TOR	AL	1	0	1	1	0	0	0	0	0	0	0	1	0	0	0	1
1993	TEX	AL	2	2	0	2	0	0	0	0	0	0	0	0	0	0	2	0
Total			4	3	1	3	0	1	0	0	0	0	0	1	0	0	2	2

Rank among batters: 3,427 • *Total ballparks homered in*: 3 • *First HR*: 09/14/1987 off Mike Kinnunen

Clise Dudley

ELZIE CLISE DUDLEY
B: 08/08/1903 D: 01/12/1989
BL

Year	Tm	Lg	Tot	H	A	Men-On 0	1	2	3	One-Game 2	3	4	LO	XN	IP	PH	RHP	LHP
1929	BRO	NL	2	1	1	2	0	0	0	0	0	0	0	0	0	0	2	0
1932	PHI	NL	1	1	0	1	0	0	0	0	0	0	0	0	0	1	1	0
Total			3	2	1	3	0	0	0	0	0	0	0	0	0	1	3	0

Rank among batters: 3,735 • *Total ballparks homered in*: 3 • *First HR*: 04/27/1929 off Claude Willoughby • *Hit HR on first major league pitch*—vs PHI: 04/27/1929

Jim Duffalo

JAMES FRANCIS DUFFALO
B: 11/25/1935
BR

Year	Tm	Lg	Tot	H	A	Men-On 0	1	2	3	One-Game 2	3	4	LO	XN	IP	PH	RHP	LHP
1961	SF	NL	1	1	0	0	0	1	0	0	0	0	0	0	0	0	0	1

Rank among batters: 4,707 • *Total ballparks homered in*: 1 • *First HR*: 09/13/1961 off Ken Lehman

Charlie Duffee

CHARLES EDWARD DUFFEE
B: 01/27/1866 D: 12/24/1894
BR

Year	Tm	Lg	Tot	H	A	Men-On 0	1	2	3	One-Game 2	3	4	LO	XN	IP	PH	RHP	LHP
1889	STL	AA	16	10	6	4	6	5	1	1	0	0	0	0	2	0	11	4
1890	STL	AA	3	3	0	1	1	1	0	0	0	0	0	1	0	0	2	0
1891	COL	AA	10	1	9	4	5	1	0	0	0	0	0	0	1	0	5	2
1892	WAS	NL	6	4	2	4	2	0	0	0	0	0	0	0	0	0	4	1
Total			35	18	17	13	14	7	1	1	0	0	0	1	3	0	22	6

Rank among batters: 1,291 • *Top target (3 home runs)*: Scott Stratton • *Number of pitchers victimized*: 30 • *Total ballparks homered in*: 9 • *First HR*: 04/18/1889 off Mike Smith

Frank Duffy

FRANK THOMAS DUFFY
B: 10/14/1946
BR

Year	Tm	Lg	Tot	H	A	Men-On 0	1	2	3	One-Game 2	3	4	LO	XN	IP	PH	RHP	LHP
1972	CLE	AL	3	1	2	2	1	0	0	0	0	0	0	0	0	0	2	1
1973	CLE	AL	8	5	3	5	2	1	0	2	0	0	0	0	0	0	5	3
1974	CLE	AL	8	5	3	5	1	2	0	0	0	0	0	0	0	0	5	3
1975	CLE	AL	1	0	1	0	1	0	0	0	0	0	0	0	0	0	1	0
1976	CLE	AL	2	1	1	1	1	0	0	0	0	0	0	0	0	0	2	0
1977	CLE	AL	4	2	2	4	0	0	0	1	0	0	0	0	0	0	0	4
Total			26	14	12	17	6	3	0	3	0	0	0	0	0	0	15	11

Rank among batters: 1,576 • *Top target (3 home runs)*: Dave McNally • *Number of pitchers victimized*: 21 • *Total ballparks homered in*: 10 • *First HR*: 07/29/1972 off Jim Palmer

Hugh Duffy

HUGH DUFFY
B: 11/26/1866 D: 10/19/1954
BR HOF

Year	Tm	Lg	Tot	H	A	Men-On 0	1	2	3	One-Game 2	3	4	LO	XN	IP	PH	RHP	LHP
1888	CHI	NL	7	5	2	3	4	0	0	0	0	0	0	0	4	0	4	3
1889	CHI	NL	12	9	3	7	4	1	0	1	0	0	0	1	5	0	11	1

Hugh Duffy *continued*

Year	Tm	Lg	Tot	H	A	Men-On				One-Game			LO	XN	IP	PH	RHP	LHP
						0	1	2	3	2	3	4						
1890	CHI	PL	7	4	3	3	2	2	0	0	0	0	1	1	0	0	6	1
1891	BOS	AA	9	6	3	2	5	1	1	2	0	0	0	0	2	0	7	2
1892	BOS	NL	5	3	2	2	2	0	1	0	0	0	0	0	0	0	4	1
1893	BOS	NL	6	6	0	2	3	1	0	0	0	0	0	0	0	0	6	0
1894	BOS	NL	18	14	4	10	5	3	0	1	0	0	0	0	0	0	17	1
1895	BOS	NL	9	7	2	4	3	1	1	0	0	0	0	0	1	0	8	1
1896	BOS	NL	5	5	0	0	3	2	0	1	0	0	0	0	0	0	5	0
1897	BOS	NL	11	8	3	3	7	0	1	3	0	0	0	0	0	0	10	1
1898	BOS	NL	8	7	1	4	1	2	1	0	0	0	0	0	0	0	6	1
1899	BOS	NL	5	5	0	2	2	1	0	0	0	0	0	0	0	0	5	0
1900	BOS	NL	2	2	0	2	0	0	0	0	0	0	0	0	0	0	2	0
1901	MIL	AL	2	1	1	2	0	0	0	0	0	0	0	0	0	0	1	1
Total			106	82	24	46	41	14	5	8	0	0	1	2	12	0	92	11

Rank among batters: 451 • *Top target (5 home runs)*: Kid Carsey • *Number of pitchers victimized*: 67 • *Total ballparks homered in*: 22 • *First HR*: 07/11/1888 off Hank O'Day • *World Series HR*—1

Joe Dugan

JOSEPH ANTHONY DUGAN
B: 05/12/1897 D: 07/07/1982
BR

Year	Tm	Lg	Tot	H	A	Men-On				One-Game			LO	XN	IP	PH	RHP	LHP
						0	1	2	3	2	3	4						
1918	PHI	AL	3	2	1	2	0	1	0	0	0	0	0	0	0	0	3	0
1919	PHI	AL	1	1	0	1	0	0	0	0	0	0	0	0	0	0	1	0
1920	PHI	AL	3	3	0	1	2	0	0	0	0	0	0	0	0	0	1	2
1921	PHI	AL	10	7	3	8	0	2	0	0	0	0	0	0	0	0	8	2
1922	BOS	AL	3	0	3	1	1	1	0	0	0	0	0	0	0	0	3	0
	NY	AL	3	2	1	1	0	2	0	0	0	0	0	0	0	0	1	2
	Total		6	2	4	2	1	3	0	0	0	0	0	0	0	0	4	2
1923	NY	AL	7	4	3	4	3	0	0	0	0	0	0	0	2	0	5	2
1924	NY	AL	3	3	0	0	2	1	0	0	0	0	0	0	1	0	1	2
1926	NY	AL	1	1	0	0	1	0	0	0	0	0	0	0	0	0	0	1
1927	NY	AL	2	1	1	0	0	2	0	0	0	0	0	0	0	0	2	0
1928	NY	AL	6	3	3	3	1	1	1	1	0	0	0	0	1	0	4	2
Total			42	27	15	21	10	10	1	1	0	0	0	0	4	0	29	13

Rank among batters: 1,138 • *Top target (4 home runs)*: Rube Walberg • *Number of pitchers victimized*: 32 • *Total ballparks homered in*: 8 • *First HR*: 07/12/1918 off Allen Sothoron • *World Series HR*—1

Gus Dugas

AUGUSTIN JOSEPH DUGAS
B: 03/24/1907
BL

Year	Tm	Lg	Tot	H	A	Men-On				One-Game			LO	XN	IP	PH	RHP	LHP
						0	1	2	3	2	3	4						
1932	PIT	NL	3	0	3	3	0	0	0	0	0	0	0	0	0	0	2	1

Rank among batters: 3,735 • *Total ballparks homered in*: 2 • *First HR*: 07/30/1932 off Snipe Hansen

Oscar Dugey

OSCAR JOSEPH DUGEY
B: 10/25/1887 D: 01/01/1966
BR

Year	Tm	Lg	Tot	H	A	Men-On				One-Game			LO	XN	IP	PH	RHP	LHP
						0	1	2	3	2	3	4						
1914	BOS	NL	1	0	1	0	1	0	0	0	0	0	0	1	1	0	1	0

Rank among batters: 4,707 • *Total ballparks homered in*: 1 • *First HR*: 07/13/1914 off Dan Griner

Bill Duggleby

WILLIAM JAMES DUGGLEBY
B: 03/16/1874 D: 08/30/1944

Year	Tm	Lg	Tot	H	A	Men-On				One-Game			LO	XN	IP	PH	RHP	LHP
						0	1	2	3	2	3	4						
1898	PHI	NL	1	1	0	0	0	0	1	0	0	0	0	0	0	0	0	1
1904	PHI	NL	2	0	2	1	1	0	0	0	0	0	0	0	1	0	2	0
1905	PHI	NL	1	1	0	1	0	0	0	0	0	0	0	0	0	0	1	0
1906	PHI	NL	2	0	2	1	1	0	0	0	0	0	0	0	0	0	2	0
Total			6	2	4	3	2	0	1	0	0	0	0	0	1	0	5	1

Rank among batters: 2,988 • *Total ballparks homered in*: 4 • *First HR*: 04/21/1898 off Cy Seymour • *Hit HR in first major league AB*—vs NY: 04/21/1898

Tom Dunbar

THOMAS JEROME DUNBAR
B: 11/24/1959
BL

Year	Tm	Lg	Tot	H	A	Men-On				One-Game			LO	XN	IP	PH	RHP	LHP
						0	1	2	3	2	3	4						
1984	TEX	AL	2	1	1	1	0	1	0	0	0	0	0	0	0	0	2	0

Tom Dunbar *continued*

Year	Tm	Lg	Tot	H	A	Men-On				One-Game			LO	XN	IP	PH	RHP	LHP
						0	1	2	3	2	3	4						
1985	TEX	AL	1	0	1	1	0	0	0	0	0	0	0	0	0	0	1	0
Total			3	1	2	2	0	1	0	0	0	0	0	0	0	0	3	0

Rank among batters: 3,735 • *Total ballparks homered in*: 3 • *First HR*: 07/17/1984 off Phil Niekro

Dave Duncan

DAVID EDWIN DUNCAN
B: 09/26/1945
BR

Year	Tm	Lg	Tot	H	A	0	1	2	3	2	3	4	LO	XN	IP	PH	RHP	LHP
1964	KC	AL	1	1	0	0	1	0	0	0	0	0	0	0	0	0	0	1
1967	KC	AL	5	2	3	2	2	1	0	0	0	0	0	1	0	0	5	0
1968	OAK	AL	7	1	6	5	2	0	0	0	0	0	0	0	0	0	3	4
1969	OAK	AL	3	1	2	0	1	2	0	0	0	0	0	1	0	0	2	1
1970	OAK	AL	10	9	1	4	3	3	0	0	0	0	0	0	1	0	5	5
1971	OAK	AL	15	10	5	12	3	0	0	1	0	0	0	0	0	0	10	5
1972	OAK	AL	19	15	4	12	4	3	0	1	0	0	0	1	0	0	13	6
1973	CLE	AL	17	10	7	11	2	4	0	1	0	0	0	0	0	0	12	5
1974	CLE	AL	16	12	4	11	3	2	0	1	0	0	0	0	0	0	10	6
1975	BAL	AL	12	3	9	3	6	3	0	2	0	0	0	0	0	0	8	4
1976	BAL	AL	4	2	2	2	2	0	0	0	0	0	0	0	0	0	4	0
Total			109	66	43	62	29	18	0	6	0	0	0	3	1	0	72	37

Rank among batters: 441 • *Top target (4 home runs)*: Sonny Siebert, Fritz Peterson • *Number of pitchers victimized*: 80 • *Total ballparks homered in*: 13 • *First HR*: 09/25/1964 off Juan Pizarro

Jim Duncan

JAMES WILLIAM DUNCAN
B: 07/01/1871 D: 10/16/1901
BR

Year	Tm	Lg	Tot	H	A	0	1	2	3	2	3	4	LO	XN	IP	PH	RHP	LHP
1899	CLE	NL	2	0	2	1	1	0	0	0	0	0	0	0	0	0	2	0

Rank among batters: 4,129 • *Total ballparks homered in*: 2 • *First HR*: 09/18/1899 off Bill Magee

Mariano Duncan

MARIANO (NOLASCO) DUNCAN
B: 03/13/1963
BB

Year	Tm	Lg	Tot	H	A	0	1	2	3	2	3	4	LO	XN	IP	PH	RHP	LHP
1985	LA	NL	6	1	5	3	1	1	1	0	0	0	0	0	0	0	2	4
1986	LA	NL	8	2	6	6	1	1	0	0	0	0	0	1	1	0	4	4
1987	LA	NL	6	3	3	5	1	0	0	0	0	0	0	0	0	0	2	4
1989	CIN	NL	3	2	1	2	1	0	0	0	0	0	1	1	0	0	1	2
1990	CIN	NL	10	5	5	6	3	1	0	0	0	0	0	0	0	0	6	4
1991	CIN	NL	12	10	2	8	4	0	0	2	0	0	0	0	0	0	7	5
1992	PHI	NL	8	3	5	4	1	3	0	1	0	0	0	0	0	0	4	4
1993	PHI	NL	11	5	6	8	1	0	2	0	0	0	0	0	0	1	5	6
1994	PHI	NL	8	6	2	0	3	5	0	0	0	0	0	0	0	0	4	4
1995	PHI	NL	3	1	2	2	1	0	0	0	0	0	0	0	0	0	2	1
	CIN	NL	3	2	1	0	2	1	0	0	0	0	0	0	0	0	2	1
	Total		6	3	3	2	3	1	0	0	0	0	0	0	0	0	4	2
Total			78	40	38	44	19	12	3	3	0	0	1	2	1	1	39	39

Rank among batters: 672 • Top target (2 home runs): Bob Kipper, Tom Browning, Paul McClellan, Bruce Hurst, Bryan Hickerson, Armando Reynoso, Donovan Osborne • *Number of pitchers victimized*: 71 • *Total ballparks homered in*: 14 • *First HR*: 04/15/1985 off Joe Niekro • *LCS HR*—1

Pat Duncan

LOUIS BAIRD DUNCAN
B: 10/06/1893 D: 07/17/1960
BR

Year	Tm	Lg	Tot	H	A	0	1	2	3	2	3	4	LO	XN	IP	PH	RHP	LHP
1919	CIN	NL	2	2	0	1	1	0	0	0	0	0	0	0	2	0	1	1
1920	CIN	NL	2	1	1	1	1	0	0	0	0	0	0	0	2	0	2	0
1921	CIN	NL	2	2	0	1	1	0	0	0	0	0	0	0	1	0	2	0
1922	CIN	NL	8	1	7	4	2	2	0	1	0	0	0	0	0	0	6	2
1923	CIN	NL	7	1	6	4	1	2	0	0	0	0	0	0	0	0	7	0
1924	CIN	NL	2	1	1	0	2	0	0	0	0	0	0	0	1	0	2	0
Total			23	8	15	11	8	4	0	1	0	0	0	0	6	0	20	3

Rank among batters: 1,686 • *Top target (2 home runs)*: Tony Kaufmann • *Number of pitchers victimized*: 22 • *Total ballparks homered in*: 7 • *First HR*: 09/15/1919 off Rube Benton

Taylor Duncan

TAYLOR MCDOWELL DUNCAN
B: 05/12/1953
BR

Year	Tm	Lg	Tot	H	A	Men-On 0	1	2	3	One-Game 2	3	4	LO	XN	IP	PH	RHP	LHP
1977	STL	NL	1	0	1	1	0	0	0	0	0	0	0	0	0	0	1	0
1978	OAK	AL	2	1	1	0	1	1	0	0	0	0	0	0	0	0	0	2
Total			3	1	2	1	1	1	0	0	0	0	0	0	0	0	1	2

Rank among batters: 3,735 • *Total ballparks homered in*: 3 • *First HR*: 09/23/1977 off Roy Lee Jackson

Vern Duncan

VERNON VAN DUKE DUNCAN
B: 01/06/1890 D: 06/01/1954
BL

Year	Tm	Lg	Tot	H	A	Men-On 0	1	2	3	One-Game 2	3	4	LO	XN	IP	PH	RHP	LHP
1914	BAL	FL	2	1	1	0	1	1	0	0	0	0	0	0	0	0	2	0
1915	BAL	FL	2	2	0	2	0	0	0	0	0	0	0	0	0	0	2	0
Total			4	3	1	2	1	1	0	0	0	0	0	0	0	0	4	0

Rank among batters: 3,427 • *Total ballparks homered in*: 2 • *First HR*: 05/06/1914 off Mordecai Brown

Sam Dungan

SAMUEL MORRISON DUNGAN
B: 07/29/1866 D: 03/16/1939
BR

Year	Tm	Lg	Tot	H	A	Men-On 0	1	2	3	One-Game 2	3	4	LO	XN	IP	PH	RHP	LHP
1893	CHI	NL	2	0	2	1	1	0	0	0	0	0	0	0	0	0	2	0
1901	WAS	AL	1	0	1	0	1	0	0	0	0	0	0	0	0	0	1	0
Total			3	0	3	1	2	0	0	0	0	0	0	0	0	0	3	0

Rank among batters: 3,735 • *Total ballparks homered in*: 2 • *First HR*: 04/28/1893 off Elton Chamberlin

Bill Dunlap

WILLIAM JAMES DUNLAP
B: 05/01/1909 D: 11/29/1980
BR

Year	Tm	Lg	Tot	H	A	Men-On 0	1	2	3	One-Game 2	3	4	LO	XN	IP	PH	RHP	LHP
1929	BOS	NL	1	0	1	0	1	0	0	0	0	0	0	0	0	0	0	1

Rank among batters: 4,707 • *Total ballparks homered in*: 1 • *First HR*: 09/25/1929 off Bill Walker

Fred Dunlap

FREDERICK C. DUNLAP
B: 05/21/1859 D: 12/01/1902
BR

Year	Tm	Lg	Tot	H	A	Men-On 0	1	2	3	One-Game 2	3	4	LO	XN	IP	PH	RHP	LHP
1880	CLE	NL	4	1	3	1	2	1	0	0	0	0	0	0	0	0	3	1
1881	CLE	NL	3	1	2	2	1	0	0	0	0	0	1	0	0	0	3	0
1883	CLE	NL	4	0	4	1	3	0	0	0	0	0	0	0	0	0	2	2
1884	STL	UA	13	6	7	2	8	3	0	1	0	0	0	0	0	0	6	3
1885	STL	NL	2	1	1	2	0	0	0	0	0	0	1	0	0	0	2	0
1886	STL	NL	3	1	2	3	0	0	0	0	0	0	0	0	0	0	2	1
	DET	NL	4	2	2	2	2	0	0	0	0	0	0	0	1	0	3	1
	Total		7	3	4	5	2	0	0	0	0	0	0	0	1	0	5	2
1887	DET	NL	5	1	4	3	2	0	0	0	0	0	1	0	2	0	5	0
1888	PIT	NL	1	0	1	0	1	0	0	0	0	0	0	0	0	0	1	0
1889	PIT	NL	2	0	2	1	1	0	0	0	0	0	0	0	0	0	2	0
Total			41	13	28	17	20	4	0	1	0	0	3	0	3	0	29	8

Rank among batters: 1,163 • *Top target (4 home runs)*: Dick Burns • *Number of pitchers victimized*: 31 • *Total ballparks homered in*: 16 • *First HR*: 05/15/1880 off Blondie Purcell • *Hit for Cycle*—vs NY: 05/24/1886

Grant Dunlap

GRANT LESTER DUNLAP
B: 12/20/1923
BR

Year	Tm	Lg	Tot	H	A	Men-On 0	1	2	3	One-Game 2	3	4	LO	XN	IP	PH	RHP	LHP
1953	STL	NL	1	0	1	1	0	0	0	0	0	0	0	0	0	1	0	1

Rank among batters: 4,707 • *Total ballparks homered in*: 1 • *First HR*: 05/10/1953 off Ken Raffensberger

Jack Dunleavy

JOHN FRANCIS DUNLEAVY
B: 09/14/1879 D: 04/11/1944

Year	Tm	Lg	Tot	H	A	Men-On 0	1	2	3	One-Game 2	3	4	LO	XN	IP	PH	RHP	LHP
1904	STL	NL	1	0	1	1	0	0	0	0	0	0	0	0	1	0	0	1

Jack Dunleavy *continued*

Year	Tm	Lg	Tot	H	A	Men-On 0	Men-On 1	Men-On 2	Men-On 3	One-Game 2	One-Game 3	One-Game 4	LO	XN	IP	PH	RHP	LHP
1905	STL	NL	1	0	1	1	0	0	0	0	0	0	0	0	0	0	1	0
Total			2	0	2	2	0	0	0	0	0	0	0	0	1	0	1	1

Rank among batters: 4,129 • *Total ballparks homered in*: 2 • *First HR*: 10/06/1904 off Patsy Flaherty

Jack Dunn

JOHN JOSEPH DUNN
B: 10/06/1872 D: 10/22/1928
BR

Year	Tm	Lg	Tot	H	A	Men-On 0	Men-On 1	Men-On 2	Men-On 3	One-Game 2	One-Game 3	One-Game 4	LO	XN	IP	PH	RHP	LHP
1904	NY	NL	1	1	0	1	0	0	0	0	0	0	0	0	0	0	1	0

Rank among batters: 4,707 • *Total ballparks homered in*: 1 • *First HR*: 09/05/1904 off Kaiser Wilhelm

Ron Dunn

RONALD RAY DUNN
B: 01/24/1950
BR

Year	Tm	Lg	Tot	H	A	Men-On 0	Men-On 1	Men-On 2	Men-On 3	One-Game 2	One-Game 3	One-Game 4	LO	XN	IP	PH	RHP	LHP
1974	CHI	NL	2	0	2	1	1	0	0	0	0	0	0	1	0	0	2	0
1975	CHI	NL	1	1	0	1	0	0	0	0	0	0	0	0	0	0	1	0
Total			3	1	2	2	1	0	0	0	0	0	0	1	0	0	3	0

Rank among batters: 3,735 • *Total ballparks homered in*: 3 • *First HR*: 09/11/1974 off Tom Walker

Steve Dunning

STEVEN JOHN DUNNING
B: 05/15/1949
BR

Year	Tm	Lg	Tot	H	A	Men-On 0	Men-On 1	Men-On 2	Men-On 3	One-Game 2	One-Game 3	One-Game 4	LO	XN	IP	PH	RHP	LHP
1971	CLE	AL	1	1	0	0	0	0	1	0	0	0	0	0	0	0	1	0
1972	CLE	AL	3	2	1	2	1	0	0	0	0	0	0	0	0	0	2	1
Total			4	3	1	2	1	0	1	0	0	0	0	0	0	0	3	1

Rank among batters: 3,427 • *Total ballparks homered in*: 2 • *First HR*: 05/11/1971 off Diego Segui

Shawon Dunston

SHAWON DONNELL DUNSTON
B: 03/21/1963
BR

Year	Tm	Lg	Tot	H	A	Men-On 0	Men-On 1	Men-On 2	Men-On 3	One-Game 2	One-Game 3	One-Game 4	LO	XN	IP	PH	RHP	LHP
1985	CHI	NL	4	3	1	3	1	0	0	0	0	0	0	0	0	0	3	1
1986	CHI	NL	17	10	7	11	3	3	0	0	0	0	0	1	0	0	11	6
1987	CHI	NL	5	3	2	3	1	1	0	0	0	0	0	0	0	0	4	1
1988	CHI	NL	9	5	4	5	3	1	0	0	0	0	0	0	0	0	5	4
1989	CHI	NL	9	3	6	5	2	1	1	1	0	0	0	0	0	0	8	1
1990	CHI	NL	17	7	10	8	7	1	1	2	0	0	0	0	0	0	8	9
1991	CHI	NL	12	7	5	9	3	0	0	0	0	0	0	0	0	0	7	5
1994	CHI	NL	11	2	9	9	1	1	0	1	0	0	3	0	0	1	5	6
1995	CHI	NL	14	8	6	8	2	4	0	0	0	0	0	0	0	0	9	5
Total			98	48	50	61	23	12	2	4	0	0	3	1	0	1	60	38

Rank among batters: 506 • *Top target (4 home runs)*: Ron Darling • *Number of pitchers victimized*: 74 • *Total ballparks homered in*: 13 • *First HR*: 05/04/1985 off Greg Booker

Don Durham

DONALD GARY DURHAM
B: 03/21/1949
BR

Year	Tm	Lg	Tot	H	A	Men-On 0	Men-On 1	Men-On 2	Men-On 3	One-Game 2	One-Game 3	One-Game 4	LO	XN	IP	PH	RHP	LHP
1972	STL	NL	2	1	1	1	0	1	0	0	0	0	0	0	0	0	1	1

Rank among batters: 4,129 • *Total ballparks homered in*: 2 • *First HR*: 08/04/1972 off Ken Reynolds

Joe Durham

JOSEPH VANN DURHAM
B: 07/31/1931
BR

Year	Tm	Lg	Tot	H	A	Men-On 0	Men-On 1	Men-On 2	Men-On 3	One-Game 2	One-Game 3	One-Game 4	LO	XN	IP	PH	RHP	LHP
1954	BAL	AL	1	1	0	1	0	0	0	0	0	0	0	0	0	0	0	1
1957	BAL	AL	4	3	1	0	2	2	0	0	0	0	0	0	0	0	0	4
Total			5	4	1	1	2	2	0	0	0	0	0	0	0	0	0	5

Rank among batters: 3,191 • *Top target (2 home runs)*: Jack Harshman • *Number of pitchers victimized*: 4 • *Total ballparks homered in*: 2 • *First HR*: 09/12/1954 off Al Sima

Leon Durham

LEON DURHAM
B: 07/31/1957
BL

Year	Tm	Lg	Tot	H	A	Men-On 0	1	2	3	One-Game 2	3	4	LO	XN	IP	PH	RHP	LHP
1980	STL	NL	8	3	5	3	3	1	1	1	0	0	0	0	0	0	8	0
1981	CHI	NL	10	8	2	3	6	1	0	1	0	0	0	0	0	0	9	1
1982	CHI	NL	22	9	13	7	14	1	0	2	0	0	0	0	1	1	17	5
1983	CHI	NL	12	9	3	6	3	2	1	0	0	0	0	0	0	0	10	2
1984	CHI	NL	23	19	4	8	10	5	0	2	0	0	0	0	0	0	21	2
1985	CHI	NL	21	15	6	12	4	4	1	2	0	0	0	0	0	0	17	4
1986	CHI	NL	20	13	7	10	9	1	0	0	0	0	0	1	0	0	17	3
1987	CHI	NL	27	16	11	19	7	1	0	3	0	0	0	0	0	0	25	2
1988	CHI	NL	3	0	3	2	1	0	0	0	0	0	0	0	0	0	3	0
	CIN	NL	1	1	0	1	0	0	0	0	0	0	0	0	0	0	1	0
	Total		4	1	3	3	1	0	0	0	0	0	0	0	0	0	4	0
Total			147	93	54	71	57	16	3	11	0	0	0	1	1	1	128	19

Rank among batters: 299 • *Top target (6 home runs)*: Pascual Perez • *Number of pitchers victimized*: 99 • *Total ballparks homered in*: 12 • *First HR*: 06/29/1980 off Lynn McGlothen • *LCS HR*—2

Ray Durham

RAY DURHAM
B: 11/30/1971
BB

Year	Tm	Lg	Tot	H	A	Men-On 0	1	2	3	One-Game 2	3	4	LO	XN	IP	PH	RHP	LHP
1995	CHI	AL	7	1	6	4	1	1	1	0	0	0	0	0	0	0	4	3

Rank among batters: 2,834 • *Total ballparks homered in*: 7 • *First HR*: 05/28/1995 off Dave Wells

Leo Durocher

LEO ERNEST DUROCHER
B: 07/27/1905 D: 10/07/1991
BR HOF

Year	Tm	Lg	Tot	H	A	Men-On 0	1	2	3	One-Game 2	3	4	LO	XN	IP	PH	RHP	LHP
1930	CIN	NL	3	0	3	3	0	0	0	0	0	0	0	0	0	0	2	1
1931	CIN	NL	1	0	1	0	1	0	0	0	0	0	0	0	0	0	1	0
1932	CIN	NL	1	0	1	1	0	0	0	0	0	0	0	0	0	0	0	1
1933	CIN	NL	1	0	1	1	0	0	0	0	0	0	0	0	0	0	0	1
	STL	NL	2	1	1	1	1	0	0	0	0	0	0	0	0	0	1	1
	Total		3	1	2	2	1	0	0	0	0	0	0	0	0	0	1	2
1934	STL	NL	3	3	0	1	1	0	1	0	0	0	0	0	1	0	3	0
1935	STL	NL	8	6	2	6	0	1	1	1	0	0	0	2	1	0	7	1
1936	STL	NL	1	1	0	0	0	1	0	0	0	0	0	0	0	0	1	0
1937	STL	NL	1	0	1	1	0	0	0	0	0	0	0	0	0	0	1	0
1938	BRO	NL	1	1	0	0	1	0	0	0	0	0	0	0	0	0	1	0
1939	BRO	NL	1	0	1	0	1	0	0	0	0	0	0	0	0	0	1	0
1940	BRO	NL	1	1	0	1	0	0	0	0	0	0	0	0	0	0	1	0
Total			24	13	11	15	5	2	2	1	0	0	0	2	2	0	19	5

Rank among batters: 1,643 • *Top target (2 home runs)*: Snipe Hansen, Leo Mangum, Slick Castleman • *Number of pitchers victimized*: 21 • *Total ballparks homered in*: 6 • *First HR*: 07/12/1930 off Ray Benge

Red Durrett

ELMER CABLE DURRETT
B: 02/03/1921 D: 01/17/1992
BL

Year	Tm	Lg	Tot	H	A	Men-On 0	1	2	3	One-Game 2	3	4	LO	XN	IP	PH	RHP	LHP
1944	BRO	NL	1	1	0	1	0	0	0	0	0	0	0	0	0	0	1	0

Rank among batters: 4,707 • *Total ballparks homered in*: 1 • *First HR*: 09/14/1944 off Ira Hutchinson

Cedric Durst

CEDRIC MONTGOMERY DURST
B: 08/23/1896 D: 02/16/1971
BL

Year	Tm	Lg	Tot	H	A	Men-On 0	1	2	3	One-Game 2	3	4	LO	XN	IP	PH	RHP	LHP
1923	STL	AL	5	3	2	3	2	0	0	1	0	0	0	0	0	0	5	0
1926	STL	AL	3	2	1	1	2	0	0	0	0	0	0	0	0	1	2	1
1928	NY	AL	2	2	0	2	0	0	0	0	0	0	0	0	0	0	2	0
1929	NY	AL	4	4	0	2	1	1	0	0	0	0	0	0	1	2	4	0
1930	BOS	AL	1	0	1	1	0	0	0	0	0	0	0	0	0	0	1	0
Total			15	11	4	9	5	1	0	1	0	0	0	0	1	3	14	1

Rank among batters: 2,096 • *Top target (2 home runs)*: Stan Coveleski, Bump Hadley • *Number of pitchers victimized*: 13 • *Total ballparks homered in*: 3 • *First HR*: 04/20/1923 off Herman Pillette • *World Series HR*—1

Year	Tm	Lg	Tot	H	A	Men-On				One-Game			LO	XN	IP	PH	RHP	LHP
						0	1	2	3	2	3	4						

Jesse Duryea

JAMES NEWTON DURYEA
B: 09/07/1859 D: 08/19/1942
BR

Year	Tm	Lg	Tot	H	A	0	1	2	3	2	3	4	LO	XN	IP	PH	RHP	LHP
1890	CIN	NL	1	1	0	1	0	0	0	0	0	0	0	0	1	0	0	1

Rank among batters: 4,707 • *Total ballparks homered in*: 1 • *First HR*: 06/14/1890 off Ed Beatin

Erv Dusak

ERVIN FRANK DUSAK
B: 07/29/1920 D: 11/06/1994
BR

Year	Tm	Lg	Tot	H	A	0	1	2	3	2	3	4	LO	XN	IP	PH	RHP	LHP
1946	STL	NL	9	6	3	2	4	3	0	1	0	0	0	1	0	3	3	6
1947	STL	NL	6	3	3	4	1	1	0	0	0	0	0	0	0	0	3	3
1948	STL	NL	6	2	4	4	2	0	0	0	0	0	0	0	0	0	3	3
1951	STL	NL	1	0	1	1	0	0	0	0	0	0	0	0	0	0	0	1
	PIT	NL	1	0	1	0	1	0	0	0	0	0	0	0	0	0	1	0
	Total		2	0	2	1	1	0	0	0	0	0	0	0	0	0	1	1
1952	PIT	NL	1	0	1	0	0	1	0	0	0	0	0	0	0	1	1	0
Total			24	11	13	11	8	5	0	1	0	0	0	1	0	4	11	13

Rank among batters: 1,643 • *Top target (3 home runs)*: Ken Raffensberger • *Number of pitchers victimized*: 20 • *Total ballparks homered in*: 7 • *First HR*: 06/15/1946 off Monita Kennedy

Frank Dwyer

JOHN FRANCIS DWYER
B: 03/25/1868 D: 02/04/1943
BR

Year	Tm	Lg	Tot	H	A	0	1	2	3	2	3	4	LO	XN	IP	PH	RHP	LHP
1889	CHI	NL	1	1	0	0	1	0	0	0	0	0	0	0	0	0	1	0
1893	CIN	NL	1	0	1	0	0	1	0	0	0	0	0	0	0	0	1	0
1894	CIN	NL	2	2	0	1	1	0	0	0	0	0	0	0	0	0	1	1
1895	CIN	NL	1	0	1	0	1	0	0	0	0	0	0	0	1	0	0	1
Total			5	3	2	1	3	1	0	0	0	0	0	0	1	0	3	2

Rank among batters: 3,191 • *Total ballparks homered in*: 4 • *First HR*: 08/16/1889 off George Haddock

Jim Dwyer

JAMES EDWARD DWYER
B: 06/03/1950
BL

Year	Tm	Lg	Tot	H	A	0	1	2	3	2	3	4	LO	XN	IP	PH	RHP	LHP
1974	STL	NL	2	1	1	2	0	0	0	0	0	0	0	0	0	0	2	0
1975	MON	NL	3	3	0	2	1	0	0	0	0	0	0	0	1	0	3	0
1978	STL	NL	1	0	1	1	0	0	0	0	0	0	0	0	0	0	1	0
	SF	NL	5	3	2	3	2	0	0	0	0	0	0	0	0	0	4	1
	Total		6	3	3	4	2	0	0	0	0	0	0	0	0	0	5	1
1979	BOS	AL	2	2	0	1	1	0	0	0	0	0	0	0	0	0	2	0
1980	BOS	AL	9	1	8	7	1	1	0	2	0	0	0	0	0	0	8	1
1981	BAL	AL	3	3	0	3	0	0	0	0	0	0	0	0	0	0	3	0
1982	BAL	AL	6	4	2	5	0	1	0	0	0	0	0	0	0	2	6	0
1983	BAL	AL	8	3	5	6	0	2	0	0	0	0	0	0	0	1	8	0
1984	BAL	AL	2	1	1	2	0	0	0	0	0	0	0	0	0	1	2	0
1985	BAL	AL	7	1	6	3	3	1	0	1	0	0	0	0	0	0	7	0
1986	BAL	AL	8	5	3	5	0	2	1	0	0	0	0	0	0	3	8	0
1987	BAL	AL	15	3	12	8	6	1	0	0	0	0	1	0	0	2	14	1
1988	MIN	AL	2	2	0	1	0	0	1	0	0	0	0	0	0	1	2	0
1989	MIN	AL	3	2	1	1	0	1	1	0	0	0	0	0	0	0	3	0
1990	MIN	AL	1	0	1	1	0	0	0	0	0	0	0	0	0	0	1	0
Total			77	34	43	51	14	9	3	3	0	0	1	0	1	10	74	3

Rank among batters: 682 • *Top target (3 home runs)*: Joe Cowley, Mike Smithson • *Number of pitchers victimized*: 64 • *Total ballparks homered in*: 21 • *First HR*: 06/24/1974 off Larry Demery • *World Series HR*—1

Jerry Dybzinski

JEROME MATHEW DYBZINSKI
B: 07/07/1955
BR

Year	Tm	Lg	Tot	H	A	0	1	2	3	2	3	4	LO	XN	IP	PH	RHP	LHP
1980	CLE	AL	1	1	0	1	0	0	0	0	0	0	0	0	0	0	1	0
1983	CHI	AL	1	0	1	1	0	0	0	0	0	0	0	0	0	0	1	0
1984	CHI	AL	1	1	0	1	0	0	0	0	0	0	0	0	0	0	0	1
Total			3	2	1	3	0	0	0	0	0	0	0	0	0	0	2	1

Rank among batters: 3,735 • *Total ballparks homered in*: 3 • *First HR*: 04/26/1980 off Jim Kern

Year	Tm	Lg	Tot	H	A	Men-On 0	Men-On 1	Men-On 2	Men-On 3	One-Game 2	One-Game 3	One-Game 4	LO	XN	IP	PH	RHP	LHP

Jim Dyck

JAMES ROBERT DYCK
B: 02/03/1922
BR

Year	Tm	Lg	Tot	H	A	0	1	2	3	2	3	4	LO	XN	IP	PH	RHP	LHP
1952	STL	AL	15	9	6	7	5	3	0	3	0	0	0	1	1	0	5	10
1953	STL	AL	9	7	2	7	1	1	0	2	0	0	0	0	0	0	4	5
1955	BAL	AL	2	2	0	1	0	0	1	0	0	0	0	0	0	0	0	2
Total			26	18	8	15	6	4	1	5	0	0	0	1	1	0	9	17

Rank among batters: 1,576 • Top target (2 home runs): Bobby Shantz, Eddie Lopat, Johnny Sain, Chuck Stobbs, Sid Hudson, Ellis Kinder • *Number of pitchers victimized*: 20 • *Total ballparks homered in*: 7 • *First HR*: 05/02/1952 off Bill Henry

Duffy Dyer

DON ROBERT DYER
B: 08/15/1945
BR

Year	Tm	Lg	Tot	H	A	0	1	2	3	2	3	4	LO	XN	IP	PH	RHP	LHP
1969	NY	NL	3	2	1	0	1	2	0	0	0	0	0	0	0	1	2	1
1970	NY	NL	2	0	2	1	1	0	0	0	0	0	0	1	0	0	2	0
1971	NY	NL	2	0	2	2	0	0	0	0	0	0	0	0	0	0	1	1
1972	NY	NL	8	3	5	3	2	3	0	0	0	0	0	0	0	0	5	3
1973	NY	NL	1	0	1	1	0	0	0	0	0	0	0	0	0	0	1	0
1975	PIT	NL	3	3	0	2	1	0	0	0	0	0	0	1	0	1	2	1
1976	PIT	NL	3	2	1	2	1	0	0	0	0	0	0	0	0	0	3	0
1977	PIT	NL	3	2	1	3	0	0	0	0	0	0	0	0	0	0	1	2
1979	MON	NL	1	0	1	1	0	0	0	0	0	0	0	0	0	0	1	0
1980	DET	AL	4	2	2	1	3	0	0	0	0	0	0	0	0	0	0	4
Total			30	14	16	16	9	5	0	0	0	0	0	2	0	2	18	12

Rank among batters: 1,437 • *Top target (2 home runs)*: Bob Apodaca • *Number of pitchers victimized*: 29 • *Total ballparks homered in*: 11 • *First HR*: 04/08/1969 off Don Shaw

Eddie Dyer

EDWIN HAWLEY DYER
B: 10/11/1900 D: 04/20/1964
BL

Year	Tm	Lg	Tot	H	A	0	1	2	3	2	3	4	LO	XN	IP	PH	RHP	LHP
1923	STL	NL	2	0	2	1	1	0	0	0	0	0	0	0	0	0	2	0

Rank among batters: 4,129 • *Total ballparks homered in*: 1 • *First HR*: 05/08/1923 off Bill Hubbell

Jimmy Dygert

JAMES HENRY DYGERT
B: 07/05/1884 D: 02/08/1936
BR

Year	Tm	Lg	Tot	H	A	0	1	2	3	2	3	4	LO	XN	IP	PH	RHP	LHP
1906	PHI	AL	1	1	0	1	0	0	0	0	0	0	0	0	0	0	0	1

Rank among batters: 4,707 • *Total ballparks homered in*: 1 • *First HR*: 05/25/1906 off Beany Jacobson

Jimmy Dykes

JAMES JOSEPH DYKES
B: 11/10/1896 D: 06/15/1976
BR

Year	Tm	Lg	Tot	H	A	0	1	2	3	2	3	4	LO	XN	IP	PH	RHP	LHP
1920	PHI	AL	8	7	1	7	1	0	0	1	0	0	1	0	0	0	7	1
1921	PHI	AL	16	14	2	9	6	1	0	2	0	0	0	0	1	0	14	2
1922	PHI	AL	12	10	2	10	1	1	0	0	0	0	1	0	1	0	10	2
1923	PHI	AL	4	4	0	2	1	1	0	0	0	0	0	0	0	0	2	2
1924	PHI	AL	3	1	2	1	2	0	0	0	0	0	0	0	0	0	0	3
1925	PHI	AL	5	3	2	1	1	3	0	0	0	0	0	0	0	0	2	3
1926	PHI	AL	1	0	1	1	0	0	0	0	0	0	0	0	0	0	1	0
1927	PHI	AL	3	2	1	3	0	0	0	0	0	0	0	1	1	0	3	0
1928	PHI	AL	5	3	2	2	2	1	0	0	0	0	1	0	0	0	3	2
1929	PHI	AL	13	9	4	5	7	1	0	0	0	0	0	0	1	0	12	1
1930	PHI	AL	6	4	2	5	1	0	0	0	0	0	0	0	0	0	4	2
1931	PHI	AL	3	1	2	3	0	0	0	0	0	0	0	0	0	0	2	1
1932	PHI	AL	7	6	1	3	1	2	1	1	0	0	0	0	0	0	5	2
1933	CHI	AL	1	0	1	1	0	0	0	0	0	0	0	0	0	0	1	0
1934	CHI	AL	7	6	1	3	3	0	1	0	0	0	0	0	0	0	5	2
1935	CHI	AL	4	1	3	2	2	0	0	1	0	0	0	1	0	0	4	0
1936	CHI	AL	7	2	5	5	2	0	0	0	0	0	0	0	0	0	7	0
1937	CHI	AL	1	1	0	1	0	0	0	0	0	0	0	0	0	0	1	0
1938	CHI	AL	2	1	1	1	0	1	0	0	0	0	0	0	0	0	1	1
Total			108	75	33	65	30	11	2	5	0	0	3	2	4	0	84	24

Rank among batters: 443 • *Top target (4 home runs)*: Bob Shawkey, Lefty Stewart, George Blaeholder • *Number of pitchers victimized*: 71 • *Total ballparks homered in*: 10 • *First HR*: 05/12/1920 off Urban Shocker • *World Series HR*—1

Lenny Dykstra

LEONARD KYLE DYKSTRA
B: 02/10/1963
BL

Year	Tm	Lg	Tot	H	A	Men-On 0	1	2	3	One-Game 2	3	4	LO	XN	IP	PH	RHP	LHP
1985	NY	NL	1	0	1	0	1	0	0	0	0	0	0	0	0	0	1	0
1986	NY	NL	8	4	4	6	1	1	0	0	0	0	3	0	0	0	8	0
1987	NY	NL	10	7	3	6	3	0	1	1	0	0	3	0	0	0	9	1
1988	NY	NL	8	3	5	5	2	1	0	0	0	0	1	0	0	0	7	1
1989	NY	NL	3	2	1	2	1	0	0	0	0	0	1	0	0	0	3	0
	PHI	NL	4	3	1	2	2	0	0	0	0	0	0	0	0	0	4	0
	Total		7	5	2	4	3	0	0	0	0	0	1	0	0	0	7	0
1990	PHI	NL	9	6	3	8	1	0	0	0	0	0	2	0	1	0	8	1
1991	PHI	NL	3	3	0	2	1	0	0	0	0	0	1	0	0	0	1	2
1992	PHI	NL	6	5	1	4	1	1	0	0	0	0	1	0	0	0	2	4
1993	PHI	NL	19	12	7	14	4	1	0	1	0	0	4	0	0	0	18	1
1994	PHI	NL	5	3	2	3	2	0	0	0	0	0	3	0	0	0	4	1
1995	PHI	NL	2	2	0	2	0	0	0	0	0	0	0	0	0	0	1	1
Total			78	50	28	54	19	4	1	2	0	0	19	0	1	0	66	12

Rank among batters: 672 • *Top target (4 home runs)*: Dennis Martinez • *Number of pitchers victimized*: 65 • *Total ballparks homered in*: 12 • *First HR*: 05/03/1985 off Mario Soto • *World Series HR*—6; *LCS HR*—4

Bill Eagan

WILLIAM EAGAN
B: 06/01/1869 D: 02/14/1905

Year	Tm	Lg	Tot	H	A	Men-On 0	1	2	3	One-Game 2	3	4	LO	XN	IP	PH	RHP	LHP
1891	STL	AA	4	1	3	2	1	1	0	0	0	0	0	0	0	0	3	0

Rank among batters: 3,427 • *Total ballparks homered in*: 4 • *First HR*: 05/14/1891 off Bert Cunningham

Howard Earl

HOWARD J. EARL
B: 02/25/1867 D: 12/23/1916

Year	Tm	Lg	Tot	H	A	Men-On 0	1	2	3	One-Game 2	3	4	LO	XN	IP	PH	RHP	LHP
1890	CHI	NL	7	7	0	0	3	2	2	1	0	0	0	0	0	0	4	2
1891	MIL	AA	1	1	0	1	0	0	0	0	0	0	0	0	0	0	1	0
Total			8	8	0	1	3	2	2	1	0	0	0	0	0	0	5	2

Rank among batters: 2,703 • *Top target (2 home runs)*: Lee Viau, Ed Beatin • *Number of pitchers victimized*: 6 • *Total ballparks homered in*: 2 • *First HR*: 05/08/1890 off Lee Viau

Billy Earle

WILLIAM MOFFAT EARLE
B: 11/10/1867 D: 05/30/1946
BR

Year	Tm	Lg	Tot	H	A	Men-On 0	1	2	3	One-Game 2	3	4	LO	XN	IP	PH	RHP	LHP
1889	CIN	AA	4	2	2	1	1	2	0	0	0	0	0	0	0	0	4	0
1893	PIT	NL	2	2	0	1	1	0	0	1	0	0	0	0	1	0	2	0
Total			6	4	2	2	2	2	0	1	0	0	0	0	1	0	6	0

Rank among batters: 2,988 • *Top target (2 home runs)*: Dan Daub • *Number of pitchers victimized*: 5 • *Total ballparks homered in*: 4 • *First HR*: 05/26/1889 off Red Ehret

Jake Early

JACOB WILLARD EARLY
B: 05/19/1915 D: 05/31/1985
BL

Year	Tm	Lg	Tot	H	A	Men-On 0	1	2	3	One-Game 2	3	4	LO	XN	IP	PH	RHP	LHP
1940	WAS	AL	5	2	3	4	1	0	0	0	0	0	0	1	0	0	5	0
1941	WAS	AL	10	3	7	6	2	2	0	0	0	0	0	0	0	1	10	0
1942	WAS	AL	3	1	2	2	1	0	0	0	0	0	0	0	0	0	3	0
1943	WAS	AL	5	1	4	1	3	1	0	0	0	0	0	0	0	0	5	0
1946	WAS	AL	4	2	2	3	0	1	0	0	0	0	0	0	0	0	4	0
1947	STL	AL	3	3	0	3	0	0	0	0	0	0	0	0	0	0	3	0
1948	WAS	AL	1	0	1	0	1	0	0	0	0	0	0	0	0	0	1	0
1949	WAS	AL	1	1	0	1	0	0	0	0	0	0	0	0	0	0	1	0
Total			32	13	19	20	8	4	0	0	0	0	0	1	0	1	32	0

Rank among batters: 1,360 • *Top target (3 home runs)*: Jack Knott, Jim Bagby • *Number of pitchers victimized*: 25 • *Total ballparks homered in*: 8 • *First HR*: 06/15/1940 off Bobo Newsom

George Earnshaw

GEORGE LIVINGSTON EARNSHAW
B: 02/15/1900 D: 12/01/1976
BR

Year	Tm	Lg	Tot	H	A	Men-On 0	1	2	3	One-Game 2	3	4	LO	XN	IP	PH	RHP	LHP
1929	PHI	AL	1	1	0	0	1	0	0	0	0	0	0	0	0	0	0	1

Year	Tm	Lg	Tot	H	A	Men-On 0	1	2	3	One-Game 2	3	4	LO	XN	IP	PH	RHP	LHP

George Earnshaw *continued*

Year	Tm	Lg	Tot	H	A	0	1	2	3	2	3	4	LO	XN	IP	PH	RHP	LHP
1931	PHI	AL	2	2	0	2	0	0	0	0	0	0	0	0	0	0	2	0
Total			3	3	0	2	1	0	0	0	0	0	0	0	0	0	2	1

Rank among batters: 3,735 • *Total ballparks homered in*: 1 • *First HR*: 06/01/1929 off Earl Whitehill

Mike Easler

MICHAEL ANTHONY EASLER
B: 11/29/1950
BL

Year	Tm	Lg	Tot	H	A	0	1	2	3	2	3	4	LO	XN	IP	PH	RHP	LHP
1977	PIT	NL	1	1	0	1	0	0	0	0	0	0	0	0	0	0	1	0
1979	PIT	NL	2	1	1	1	1	0	0	0	0	0	0	1	0	2	2	0
1980	PIT	NL	21	9	12	14	4	3	0	2	0	0	0	0	0	2	20	1
1981	PIT	NL	7	4	3	5	1	1	0	1	0	0	0	0	0	0	7	0
1982	PIT	NL	15	9	6	7	7	0	1	0	0	0	0	0	0	0	13	2
1983	PIT	NL	10	2	8	5	2	1	2	0	0	0	0	0	0	1	10	0
1984	BOS	AL	27	16	11	16	9	2	0	1	0	0	0	1	0	0	20	7
1985	BOS	AL	16	4	12	10	3	1	2	1	0	0	0	0	0	1	14	2
1986	NY	AL	14	6	8	9	4	1	0	0	0	0	0	0	0	0	13	1
1987	PHI	NL	1	1	0	1	0	0	0	0	0	0	0	0	0	0	1	0
	NY	AL	4	2	2	2	1	1	0	0	0	0	0	0	0	1	4	0
	Total		5	3	2	3	1	1	0	0	0	0	0	0	0	1	5	0
Total			118	55	63	71	32	10	5	5	0	0	0	2	0	7	105	13

Rank among batters: 396 • *Top target (5 home runs)*: Ray Burris, Scott Sanderson • *Number of pitchers victimized*: 87 • *Total ballparks homered in*: 25 • *First HR*: 10/02/1977 off Ray Burris • *Hit for Cycle—@CIN*: 06/12/1980

Damion Easley

JACINTO DAMION EASLEY
B: 11/11/1969
BR

Year	Tm	Lg	Tot	H	A	0	1	2	3	2	3	4	LO	XN	IP	PH	RHP	LHP
1992	CAL	AL	1	1	0	0	0	1	0	0	0	0	0	0	0	1	1	0
1993	CAL	AL	2	0	2	1	0	1	0	0	0	0	0	0	0	0	1	1
1994	CAL	AL	6	4	2	3	3	0	0	1	0	0	0	0	0	0	3	3
1995	CAL	AL	4	1	3	1	2	1	0	0	0	0	0	0	0	0	2	2
Total			13	6	7	5	5	3	0	1	0	0	0	0	0	1	7	6

Rank among batters: 2,248 • *Top target (2 home runs)*: Wilson Alvarez • *Number of pitchers victimized*: 12 • *Total ballparks homered in*: 7 • *First HR*: 09/20/1992 off Rick Aguilera

Hugh East

GORDON HUGH EAST
B: 07/07/1919 D: 11/02/1981
BR

Year	Tm	Lg	Tot	H	A	0	1	2	3	2	3	4	LO	XN	IP	PH	RHP	LHP
1942	NY	NL	1	0	1	0	1	0	0	0	0	0	0	0	0	0	1	0

Rank among batters: 4,707 • *Total ballparks homered in*: 1 • *First HR*: 05/01/1942 off Jake Mooty

Luke Easter

LUSCIOUS LUKE EASTER
B: 08/04/1915 D: 03/29/1979
BL

Year	Tm	Lg	Tot	H	A	0	1	2	3	2	3	4	LO	XN	IP	PH	RHP	LHP
1950	CLE	AL	28	21	7	11	13	4	0	5	0	0	0	0	0	0	12	16
1951	CLE	AL	27	19	8	13	10	3	1	3	0	0	0	1	0	0	18	9
1952	CLE	AL	31	17	14	15	8	6	2	2	0	0	0	0	0	0	18	13
1953	CLE	AL	7	3	4	4	2	1	0	1	0	0	0	0	0	0	3	4
Total			93	60	33	43	33	14	3	11	0	0	0	1	0	0	51	42

Rank among batters: 545 • *Top target (5 home runs)*: Alex Kellner, Bob Cain • *Number of pitchers victimized*: 57 • *Total ballparks homered in*: 8 • *First HR*: 05/06/1950 off Allie Reynolds

Henry Easterday

HENRY P. EASTERDAY
B: 09/16/1864 D: 03/30/1895
BR

Year	Tm	Lg	Tot	H	A	0	1	2	3	2	3	4	LO	XN	IP	PH	RHP	LHP
1888	KC	AA	3	1	2	1	2	0	0	0	0	0	0	0	1	0	2	1
1889	COL	AA	4	0	4	3	0	1	0	0	0	0	0	0	0	0	3	1
1890	COL	AA	1	0	1	0	1	0	0	0	0	0	0	0	0	0	1	0

Henry Easterday *continued*

Year	Tm	Lg	Tot	H	A	Men-On 0	1	2	3	One-Game 2	3	4	LO	XN	IP	PH	RHP	LHP
1890	PHI	AA	1	0	1	1	0	0	0	0	0	0	0	0	0	0	1	0
	Total		2	0	2	1	1	0	0	0	0	0	0	0	0	0	2	0
Total			9	1	8	5	3	1	0	0	0	0	0	0	1	0	7	2

Rank among batters: 2,587 • *Total ballparks homered in*: 7 • *First HR*: 07/04/1888 off Billy Crowell

Paul Easterling

PAUL EASTERLING
B: 09/28/1905 D: 03/15/1993
BR

Year	Tm	Lg	Tot	H	A	Men-On 0	1	2	3	One-Game 2	3	4	LO	XN	IP	PH	RHP	LHP
1928	DET	AL	3	0	3	3	0	0	0	0	0	0	0	0	0	0	3	0
1930	DET	AL	1	1	0	0	1	0	0	0	0	0	0	0	0	0	0	1
Total			4	1	3	3	1	0	0	0	0	0	0	0	0	0	3	1

Rank among batters: 3,427 • *Total ballparks homered in*: 2 • *First HR*: 04/18/1928 off Dick Coffman

Ted Easterly

THEODORE HARRISON EASTERLY
B: 04/20/1885 D: 07/06/1951
BL

Year	Tm	Lg	Tot	H	A	Men-On 0	1	2	3	One-Game 2	3	4	LO	XN	IP	PH	RHP	LHP
1909	CLE	AL	1	0	1	1	0	0	0	0	0	0	0	0	0	0	1	0
1911	CLE	AL	1	1	0	1	0	0	0	0	0	0	0	0	0	1	1	0
1912	CLE	AL	2	1	1	2	0	0	0	0	0	0	0	0	0	0	2	0
1914	KC	FL	1	0	1	1	0	0	0	0	0	0	0	0	0	0	1	0
1915	KC	FL	3	0	3	2	1	0	0	0	0	0	0	0	2	0	3	0
Total			8	2	6	7	1	0	0	0	0	0	0	0	2	1	8	0

Rank among batters: 2,703 • *Total ballparks homered in*: 6 • *First HR*: 09/27/1909 off Jack Coombs

Roy Easterwood

ROY CHARLES EASTERWOOD
B: 01/12/1915 D: 08/24/1984
BR

Year	Tm	Lg	Tot	H	A	Men-On 0	1	2	3	One-Game 2	3	4	LO	XN	IP	PH	RHP	LHP
1944	CHI	NL	1	1	0	1	0	0	0	0	0	0	0	0	0	0	0	1

Rank among batters: 4,707 • *Total ballparks homered in*: 1 • *First HR*: 04/23/1944 off Max Lanier

Zeb Eaton

ZEBULON VANCE EATON
B: 02/02/1920 D: 12/17/1989
BR

Year	Tm	Lg	Tot	H	A	Men-On 0	1	2	3	One-Game 2	3	4	LO	XN	IP	PH	RHP	LHP
1945	DET	AL	2	1	1	0	1	0	1	0	0	0	0	0	0	2	2	0

Rank among batters: 4,129 • *Total ballparks homered in*: 2 • *First HR*: 07/15/1945 off Hank Borowy

Eddie Eayrs

EDWIN EAYRS
B: 11/10/1890 D: 11/30/1969
BL

Year	Tm	Lg	Tot	H	A	Men-On 0	1	2	3	One-Game 2	3	4	LO	XN	IP	PH	RHP	LHP
1920	BOS	NL	1	0	1	0	0	1	0	0	0	0	0	0	0	0	1	0

Rank among batters: 4,707 • *Total ballparks homered in*: 1 • *First HR*: 05/28/1920 off Jeff Pfeffer

Hi Ebright

HIRAM C. EBRIGHT
B: 06/12/1859 D: 10/24/1916
BR

Year	Tm	Lg	Tot	H	A	Men-On 0	1	2	3	One-Game 2	3	4	LO	XN	IP	PH	RHP	LHP
1889	WAS	NL	1	0	1	0	1	0	0	0	0	0	0	0	0	0	1	0

Rank among batters: 4,707 • *Total ballparks homered in*: 1 • *First HR*: 04/30/1889 off Mickey Welch

Dennis Eckersley

DENNIS LEE ECKERSLEY
B: 10/03/1954
BR

Year	Tm	Lg	Tot	H	A	Men-On 0	1	2	3	One-Game 2	3	4	LO	XN	IP	PH	RHP	LHP
1985	CHI	NL	1	1	0	1	0	0	0	0	0	0	0	0	0	0	0	1

Dennis Eckersley *continued*

Year	Tm	Lg	Tot	H	A	Men-On 0	1	2	3	One-Game 2	3	4	LO	XN	IP	PH	RHP	LHP
1986	CHI	NL	2	2	0	0	2	0	0	0	0	0	0	0	0	0	2	0
Total			3	3	0	1	2	0	0	0	0	0	0	0	0	0	2	1

Rank among batters: 3,735 • *Total ballparks homered in*: 1 • *First HR*: 09/07/1985 off Tom Browning

Ox Eckhardt

OSCAR GEORGE ECKHARDT
B: 12/23/1901 D: 04/22/1951
BL

Year	Tm	Lg	Tot	H	A	Men-On 0	1	2	3	One-Game 2	3	4	LO	XN	IP	PH	RHP	LHP
1936	BRO	NL	1	0	1	0	1	0	0	0	0	0	0	0	0	0	1	0

Rank among batters: 4,707 • *Total ballparks homered in*: 1 • *First HR*: 04/15/1936 off Harry Gumbert

Charlie Eden

CHARLES M. EDEN
B: 01/18/1855 D: 09/17/1920
BL

Year	Tm	Lg	Tot	H	A	Men-On 0	1	2	3	One-Game 2	3	4	LO	XN	IP	PH	RHP	LHP
1879	CLE	NL	3	2	1	1	1	1	0	0	0	0	0	0	0	0	2	0
1884	PIT	AA	1	0	1	0	1	0	0	0	0	0	0	0	0	0	0	0
Total			4	2	2	1	2	1	0	0	0	0	0	0	0	0	2	0

Rank among batters: 3,427 • *Total ballparks homered in*: 3 • *First HR*: 05/22/1879 off Pat McManus

Dave Edler

DAVID DELMER EDLER
B: 08/05/1956
BR

Year	Tm	Lg	Tot	H	A	Men-On 0	1	2	3	One-Game 2	3	4	LO	XN	IP	PH	RHP	LHP
1980	SEA	AL	3	3	0	2	1	0	0	0	0	0	0	0	0	0	1	2
1982	SEA	AL	2	2	0	1	0	0	1	1	0	0	0	0	0	0	0	2
1983	SEA	AL	1	0	1	1	0	0	0	0	0	0	0	0	0	0	1	0
Total			6	5	1	4	1	0	1	1	0	0	0	0	0	0	2	4

Rank among batters: 2,988 • *Total ballparks homered in*: 2 • *First HR*: 09/14/1980 off Bob McClure

Jim Edmonds

JAMES PATRICK EDMONDS
B: 06/27/1970
BL

Year	Tm	Lg	Tot	H	A	Men-On 0	1	2	3	One-Game 2	3	4	LO	XN	IP	PH	RHP	LHP
1994	CAL	AL	5	3	2	3	2	0	0	0	0	0	0	0	0	0	3	2
1995	CAL	AL	33	16	17	17	12	4	0	3	0	0	0	0	0	0	26	7
Total			38	19	19	20	14	4	0	3	0	0	0	0	0	0	29	9

Rank among batters: 1,225 • *Top target (2 home runs)*: Kevin Tapani, Scott Erickson, Kenny Rogers • *Number of pitchers victimized*: 35 • *Total ballparks homered in*: 10 • *First HR*: 05/11/1994 off Rick Helling

Bruce Edwards

CHARLES BRUCE EDWARDS
B: 07/15/1923 D: 04/25/1975
BR

Year	Tm	Lg	Tot	H	A	Men-On 0	1	2	3	One-Game 2	3	4	LO	XN	IP	PH	RHP	LHP
1946	BRO	NL	1	1	0	1	0	0	0	0	0	0	0	0	0	0	1	0
1947	BRO	NL	9	4	5	2	3	3	1	0	0	0	0	0	0	0	4	5
1948	BRO	NL	8	4	4	5	3	0	0	0	0	0	0	0	0	0	2	6
1949	BRO	NL	8	5	3	4	3	0	1	0	0	0	0	0	0	0	5	3
1950	BRO	NL	8	4	4	6	2	0	0	0	0	0	0	0	0	0	4	4
1951	BRO	NL	1	0	1	0	0	1	0	0	0	0	0	0	0	1	0	1
	CHI	NL	3	2	1	0	2	1	0	0	0	0	0	0	0	0	3	0
	Total		4	2	2	0	2	2	0	0	0	0	0	0	0	1	3	1
1952	CHI	NL	1	0	1	1	0	0	0	0	0	0	0	0	0	0	1	0
Total			39	20	19	19	13	5	2	0	0	0	0	0	0	1	20	19

Rank among batters: 1,204 • *Top target (3 home runs)*: Warren Spahn • *Number of pitchers victimized*: 31 • *Total ballparks homered in*: 8 • *First HR*: 09/08/1946 off Mike Budnick

Dave Edwards

DAVID LEONARD EDWARDS
B: 02/24/1954
BR

Year	Tm	Lg	Tot	H	A	Men-On 0	1	2	3	One-Game 2	3	4	LO	XN	IP	PH	RHP	LHP
1978	MIN	AL	1	1	0	1	0	0	0	0	0	0	0	0	0	0	0	1

Year	Tm	Lg	Tot	H	A	Men-On				One-Game			LO	XN	IP	PH	RHP	LHP
						0	1	2	3	2	3	4						

Dave Edwards *continued*

Year	Tm	Lg	Tot	H	A	0	1	2	3	2	3	4	LO	XN	IP	PH	RHP	LHP
1979	MIN	AL	8	5	3	5	1	1	1	1	0	0	0	0	0	0	4	4
1980	MIN	AL	2	1	1	0	2	0	0	0	0	0	0	0	0	1	0	2
1981	SD	NL	2	1	1	2	0	0	0	0	0	0	0	0	0	0	0	2
1982	SD	NL	1	0	1	1	0	0	0	0	0	0	0	0	0	1	0	1
Total			14	8	6	9	3	1	1	1	0	0	0	0	0	2	4	10

Rank among batters: 2,169 • *Total ballparks homered in*: 8 • *First HR*: 09/23/1978 off Paul Splittorff

Doc Edwards

HOWARD RODNEY EDWARDS
B: 12/10/1936
BR

Year	Tm	Lg	Tot	H	A	0	1	2	3	2	3	4	LO	XN	IP	PH	RHP	LHP
1962	CLE	AL	3	2	1	3	0	0	0	0	0	0	0	1	0	0	3	0
1963	KC	AL	6	4	2	5	0	1	0	0	0	0	0	0	0	0	3	3
1964	KC	AL	5	2	3	4	0	1	0	0	0	0	0	1	0	0	2	3
1965	NY	AL	1	0	1	1	0	0	0	0	0	0	0	0	0	0	0	1
Total			15	8	7	13	0	2	0	0	0	0	0	2	0	0	8	7

Rank among batters: 2,096 • *Top target (2 home runs)*: Al Downing • *Number of pitchers victimized*: 14 • *Total ballparks homered in*: 7 • *First HR*: 07/04/1962 off Terry Fox

Hank Edwards

HENRY ALBERT EDWARDS
B: 01/29/1919 D: 06/22/1988
BL

Year	Tm	Lg	Tot	H	A	0	1	2	3	2	3	4	LO	XN	IP	PH	RHP	LHP
1941	CLE	AL	1	0	1	1	0	0	0	0	0	0	0	0	0	0	1	0
1943	CLE	AL	3	0	3	1	2	0	0	0	0	0	0	0	0	0	2	1
1946	CLE	AL	10	5	5	5	5	0	0	0	0	0	0	0	0	0	10	0
1947	CLE	AL	15	6	9	6	8	1	0	0	0	0	0	0	0	0	15	0
1948	CLE	AL	3	1	2	3	0	0	0	0	0	0	0	0	1	0	3	0
1949	CLE	AL	1	0	1	1	0	0	0	0	0	0	0	0	0	0	1	0
	CHI	NL	7	3	4	3	3	1	0	1	0	0	0	1	0	0	7	0
	Total		8	3	5	4	3	1	0	1	0	0	0	1	0	0	8	0
1950	CHI	NL	2	2	0	2	0	0	0	0	0	0	0	0	0	0	2	0
1951	CIN	NL	3	2	1	3	0	0	0	0	0	0	0	0	0	0	2	1
1952	CIN	NL	6	4	2	3	2	1	0	0	0	0	0	0	0	1	6	0
Total			51	23	28	28	20	3	0	1	0	0	0	1	1	1	49	2

Rank among batters: 979 • *Top target (3 home runs)*: Dick Fowler, Virgil Trucks • *Number of pitchers victimized*: 38 • *Total ballparks homered in*: 13 • *First HR*: 09/28/1941 off Bob Muncrief

Johnny Edwards

JOHN ALBAN EDWARDS
B: 06/10/1938
BL

Year	Tm	Lg	Tot	H	A	0	1	2	3	2	3	4	LO	XN	IP	PH	RHP	LHP
1961	CIN	NL	2	0	2	2	0	0	0	0	0	0	0	0	0	0	2	0
1962	CIN	NL	8	5	3	2	4	1	1	0	0	0	0	0	0	0	4	4
1963	CIN	NL	11	7	4	6	2	2	1	0	0	0	0	0	0	0	8	3
1964	CIN	NL	7	3	4	4	2	0	1	0	0	0	0	0	0	0	4	3
1965	CIN	NL	17	12	5	12	3	2	0	0	0	0	0	0	0	1	15	2
1966	CIN	NL	6	5	1	3	1	2	0	0	0	0	0	0	0	0	6	0
1967	CIN	NL	2	1	1	0	1	1	0	0	0	0	0	0	0	1	2	0
1968	STL	NL	3	1	2	1	2	0	0	0	0	0	0	0	0	0	2	1
1969	HOU	NL	6	2	4	5	1	0	0	0	0	0	0	0	0	0	6	0
1970	HOU	NL	7	1	6	2	3	2	0	0	0	0	0	0	0	1	5	2
1971	HOU	NL	1	0	1	0	0	1	0	0	0	0	0	0	0	0	1	0
1972	HOU	NL	5	1	4	4	0	1	0	0	0	0	0	1	0	0	4	1
1973	HOU	NL	5	2	3	4	0	1	0	0	0	0	0	0	0	0	5	0
1974	HOU	NL	1	0	1	0	1	0	0	0	0	0	0	0	0	0	1	0
Total			81	40	41	45	20	13	3	0	0	0	0	1	0	3	65	16

Rank among batters: 645 • *Top target (4 home runs)*: Milt Pappas • *Number of pitchers victimized*: 55 • *Total ballparks homered in*: 16 • *First HR*: 06/28/1961 off Glen Hobbie

Marshall Edwards

MARSHALL LYNN EDWARDS
B: 08/27/1952
BL

Year	Tm	Lg	Tot	H	A	0	1	2	3	2	3	4	LO	XN	IP	PH	RHP	LHP
1982	MIL	AL	2	1	1	2	0	0	0	0	0	0	0	0	0	0	2	0

Marshall Edwards *continued*

Rank among batters: 4,129 • *Total ballparks homered in*: 2 • *First HR*: 05/12/1982 off Dennis Leonard

Mike Edwards

MICHAEL LEWIS EDWARDS
B: 08/27/1952
BR

Year	Tm	Lg	Tot	H	A	Men-On 0	Men-On 1	Men-On 2	Men-On 3	One-Game 2	One-Game 3	One-Game 4	LO	XN	IP	PH	RHP	LHP
1978	OAK	AL	1	1	0	1	0	0	0	0	0	0	0	0	0	0	1	0
1979	OAK	AL	1	1	0	1	0	0	0	0	0	0	1	0	0	0	1	0
Total			2	2	0	2	0	0	0	0	0	0	1	0	0	0	2	0

Rank among batters: 4,129 • *Total ballparks homered in*: 1 • *First HR*: 07/19/1978 off Jim Slaton

Dick Egan

RICHARD JOSEPH EGAN
B: 06/23/1884 D: 07/07/1947
BR

Year	Tm	Lg	Tot	H	A	Men-On 0	Men-On 1	Men-On 2	Men-On 3	One-Game 2	One-Game 3	One-Game 4	LO	XN	IP	PH	RHP	LHP
1909	CIN	NL	2	0	2	1	0	1	0	0	0	0	0	0	2	0	1	1
1911	CIN	NL	1	0	1	0	0	0	1	0	0	0	0	0	0	0	1	0
1914	BRO	NL	1	0	1	1	0	0	0	0	0	0	0	0	0	1	1	0
Total			4	0	4	2	0	1	1	0	0	0	0	0	2	1	3	1

Rank among batters: 3,427 • *Total ballparks homered in*: 3 • *First HR*: 07/12/1909 off Jim Pastorius

Tom Egan

THOMAS PATRICK EGAN
B: 06/09/1946
BR

Year	Tm	Lg	Tot	H	A	Men-On 0	Men-On 1	Men-On 2	Men-On 3	One-Game 2	One-Game 3	One-Game 4	LO	XN	IP	PH	RHP	LHP
1968	CAL	AL	1	1	0	1	0	0	0	0	0	0	0	0	0	0	0	1
1969	CAL	AL	5	3	2	2	2	1	0	0	0	0	0	0	0	0	5	0
1970	CAL	AL	4	1	3	1	2	1	0	0	0	0	0	0	0	0	2	2
1971	CHI	AL	10	3	7	4	5	1	0	0	0	0	0	0	0	1	4	6
1972	CHI	AL	2	1	1	1	1	0	0	0	0	0	0	0	0	0	1	1
Total			22	9	13	9	10	3	0	0	0	0	0	0	0	1	12	10

Rank among batters: 1,719 • *Top target (2 home runs)*: Catfish Hunter, Mike Kekich • *Number of pitchers victimized*: 20 • *Total ballparks homered in*: 9 • *First HR*: 09/29/1968 off Wilbur Wood

Red Ehret

PHILIP SYDNEY EHRET
B: 08/31/1868 D: 07/28/1940
BR

Year	Tm	Lg	Tot	H	A	Men-On 0	Men-On 1	Men-On 2	Men-On 3	One-Game 2	One-Game 3	One-Game 4	LO	XN	IP	PH	RHP	LHP
1889	LOU	AA	1	1	0	0	0	1	0	0	0	0	0	0	0	0	1	0
1893	PIT	NL	1	0	1	0	0	1	0	0	0	0	0	0	1	0	1	0
1895	STL	NL	1	1	0	1	0	0	0	0	0	0	0	0	0	0	1	0
1896	CIN	NL	1	0	1	0	1	0	0	0	0	0	0	0	0	0	1	0
Total			4	2	2	1	1	2	0	0	0	0	0	0	1	0	4	0

Rank among batters: 3,427 • *Total ballparks homered in*: 4 • *First HR*: 05/18/1889 off Hank Gastright

Rube Ehrhardt

WELTON CLAUDE EHRHARDT
B: 11/20/1894 D: 04/27/1980
BR

Year	Tm	Lg	Tot	H	A	Men-On 0	Men-On 1	Men-On 2	Men-On 3	One-Game 2	One-Game 3	One-Game 4	LO	XN	IP	PH	RHP	LHP
1925	BRO	NL	1	0	1	1	0	0	0	0	0	0	0	0	0	0	1	0

Rank among batters: 4,707 • *Total ballparks homered in*: 1 • *First HR*: 10/01/1925 off Jimmy Ring

Dave Eiland

DAVID WILLIAM EILAND
B: 07/05/1966
BR

Year	Tm	Lg	Tot	H	A	Men-On 0	Men-On 1	Men-On 2	Men-On 3	One-Game 2	One-Game 3	One-Game 4	LO	XN	IP	PH	RHP	LHP
1992	SD	NL	1	1	0	0	1	0	0	0	0	0	0	0	0	0	0	1

Rank among batters: 4,707 • *Total ballparks homered in*: 1 • *First HR*: 04/10/1992 off Bobby Ojeda • *Hit HR in first major league AB*—vs LA: 04/10/1992

Jim Eisenreich

JAMES MICHAEL EISENREICH
B: 04/18/1959
BL

Year	Tm	Lg	Tot	H	A	Men-On 0	Men-On 1	Men-On 2	Men-On 3	One-Game 2	One-Game 3	One-Game 4	LO	XN	IP	PH	RHP	LHP
1982	MIN	AL	2	1	1	2	0	0	0	0	0	0	0	0	0	0	2	0

Jim Eisenreich *continued*

Year	Tm	Lg	Tot	H	A	Men-On 0	1	2	3	One-Game 2	3	4	LO	XN	IP	PH	RHP	LHP
1987	KC	AL	4	3	1	2	0	2	0	0	0	0	0	0	0	1	4	0
1988	KC	AL	1	0	1	0	1	0	0	0	0	0	0	0	0	0	1	0
1989	KC	AL	9	4	5	4	2	2	1	0	0	0	0	0	0	1	7	2
1990	KC	AL	5	2	3	3	2	0	0	0	0	0	0	0	0	0	4	1
1991	KC	AL	2	2	0	1	0	1	0	0	0	0	0	0	0	0	1	1
1992	KC	AL	2	1	1	1	1	0	0	0	0	0	0	0	0	0	2	0
1993	PHI	NL	7	3	4	3	3	0	1	0	0	0	0	0	0	0	6	1
1994	PHI	NL	4	3	1	1	2	1	0	0	0	0	0	0	0	1	4	0
1995	PHI	NL	10	5	5	9	0	0	1	0	0	0	0	0	1	1	10	0
Total			46	24	22	26	11	6	3	0	0	0	0	0	1	4	41	5

Rank among batters: 1,060 • *Top target (2 home runs)*: Dave Stewart, Pedro Astacio, Tom Candiotti • *Number of pitchers victimized*: 43 • *Total ballparks homered in*: 15 • *First HR*: 04/15/1982 off Rick Langford • *World Series HR*—1

Kid Elberfeld

NORMAN ARTHUR ELBERFELD
B: 04/13/1875 D: 01/13/1944
BR

Year	Tm	Lg	Tot	H	A	Men-On 0	1	2	3	One-Game 2	3	4	LO	XN	IP	PH	RHP	LHP
1901	DET	AL	3	2	1	3	0	0	0	0	0	0	0	0	0	0	3	0
1902	DET	AL	1	1	0	1	0	0	0	0	0	0	0	0	0	0	0	1
1904	NY	AL	2	2	0	1	1	0	0	0	0	0	0	0	1	0	2	0
1906	NY	AL	2	2	0	1	1	0	0	0	0	0	0	0	2	0	1	1
1910	WAS	AL	2	1	1	0	0	1	1	0	0	0	0	0	2	0	1	1
Total			10	8	2	6	2	1	1	0	0	0	0	0	5	0	7	3

Rank among batters: 2,500 • *Top target (2 home runs)*: Bill Bernhard • *Number of pitchers victimized*: 9 • *Total ballparks homered in*: 5 • *First HR*: 04/29/1901 off Roy Patterson

Lee Elia

LEE CONSTANTINE ELIA
B: 07/16/1937
BR

Year	Tm	Lg	Tot	H	A	Men-On 0	1	2	3	One-Game 2	3	4	LO	XN	IP	PH	RHP	LHP
1966	CHI	AL	3	1	2	2	1	0	0	0	0	0	0	0	0	0	3	0

Rank among batters: 3,735 • *Total ballparks homered in*: 3 • *First HR*: 06/06/1966 off Jack Sanford

Roy Ellam

ROY ELLAM
B: 02/08/1886 D: 10/28/1948
BR

Year	Tm	Lg	Tot	H	A	Men-On 0	1	2	3	One-Game 2	3	4	LO	XN	IP	PH	RHP	LHP
1909	CIN	NL	1	1	0	0	1	0	0	0	0	0	0	0	1	0	1	0

Rank among batters: 4,707 • *Total ballparks homered in*: 1 • *First HR*: 09/29/1909 off Harry McIntire

Hod Eller

HORACE OWEN ELLER
B: 07/05/1894 D: 07/18/1961
BR

Year	Tm	Lg	Tot	H	A	Men-On 0	1	2	3	One-Game 2	3	4	LO	XN	IP	PH	RHP	LHP
1919	CIN	NL	1	0	1	0	0	1	0	0	0	0	0	0	0	0	1	0

Rank among batters: 4,707 • *Total ballparks homered in*: 1 • *First HR*: 08/15/1919 off Jess Barnes

Frank Ellerbe

FRANCIS ROGERS ELLERBE
B: 12/25/1895 D: 07/08/1988
BR

Year	Tm	Lg	Tot	H	A	Men-On 0	1	2	3	One-Game 2	3	4	LO	XN	IP	PH	RHP	LHP
1921	STL	AL	2	0	2	1	1	0	0	0	0	0	0	0	0	0	2	0
1922	STL	AL	1	0	1	1	0	0	0	0	0	0	0	0	0	0	1	0
1924	CLE	AL	1	0	1	0	0	0	1	0	0	0	0	0	0	1	0	1
Total			4	0	4	2	1	0	1	0	0	0	0	0	0	1	3	1

Rank among batters: 3,427 • *Total ballparks homered in*: 4 • *First HR*: 06/13/1921 off Slim Harriss

Larry Elliot

LAWRENCE LEE ELLIOT
B: 03/05/1938
BL

Year	Tm	Lg	Tot	H	A	Men-On 0	1	2	3	One-Game 2	3	4	LO	XN	IP	PH	RHP	LHP
1962	PIT	NL	1	0	1	0	1	0	0	0	0	0	0	0	0	1	1	0

Larry Elliot *continued*

Year	Tm	Lg	Tot	H	A	Men-On 0	Men-On 1	Men-On 2	Men-On 3	One-Game 2	One-Game 3	One-Game 4	LO	XN	IP	PH	RHP	LHP
1964	NY	NL	9	4	5	6	1	2	0	0	0	0	0	0	0	1	9	0
1966	NY	NL	5	3	2	5	0	0	0	0	0	0	0	0	0	0	4	1
Total			15	7	8	11	2	2	0	0	0	0	0	0	0	2	14	1

Rank among batters: 2,096 • *Top target (2 home runs)*: Turk Farrell • *Number of pitchers victimized*: 14 • *Total ballparks homered in*: 7 • *First HR*: 05/03/1962 off Jack Sanford

Allen Elliott

ALLEN CLIFFORD ELLIOTT
B: 12/25/1897 D: 05/06/1979
BL

Year	Tm	Lg	Tot	H	A	Men-On 0	Men-On 1	Men-On 2	Men-On 3	One-Game 2	One-Game 3	One-Game 4	LO	XN	IP	PH	RHP	LHP
1923	CHI	NL	2	0	2	1	0	1	0	0	0	0	0	0	0	0	2	0

Rank among batters: 4,129 • *Total ballparks homered in*: 2 • *First HR*: 07/15/1923 off Rosy Ryan

Bob Elliott

ROBERT IRVING ELLIOTT
B: 11/26/1916 D: 05/04/1966
BR

Year	Tm	Lg	Tot	H	A	Men-On 0	Men-On 1	Men-On 2	Men-On 3	One-Game 2	One-Game 3	One-Game 4	LO	XN	IP	PH	RHP	LHP
1939	PIT	NL	3	2	1	0	3	0	0	0	0	0	0	0	0	0	1	2
1940	PIT	NL	5	1	4	5	0	0	0	0	0	0	0	0	0	0	4	1
1941	PIT	NL	3	0	3	1	1	1	0	0	0	0	0	0	0	0	3	0
1942	PIT	NL	9	2	7	4	3	2	0	2	0	0	0	1	0	0	5	4
1943	PIT	NL	7	1	6	3	4	0	0	0	0	0	0	0	0	0	5	2
1944	PIT	NL	10	4	6	7	0	3	0	2	0	0	0	0	1	0	8	2
1945	PIT	NL	8	5	3	2	3	2	1	0	0	0	0	0	0	0	8	0
1946	PIT	NL	5	0	5	2	2	1	0	1	0	0	0	0	0	0	4	1
1947	BOS	NL	22	7	15	8	8	5	1	1	0	0	0	0	0	0	17	5
1948	BOS	NL	23	9	14	12	4	7	0	1	0	0	0	0	0	0	18	5
1949	BOS	NL	17	2	15	9	5	3	0	1	1	0	0	1	1	0	10	7
1950	BOS	NL	24	11	13	9	11	3	1	0	0	0	0	0	0	1	15	9
1951	BOS	NL	15	5	10	7	8	0	0	2	0	0	0	0	0	0	13	2
1952	NY	NL	10	7	3	10	0	0	0	1	0	0	0	1	0	1	7	3
1953	STL	AL	5	5	0	0	2	2	1	0	0	0	0	0	0	0	3	2
	CHI	AL	4	1	3	3	1	0	0	0	0	0	0	0	0	1	1	3
	Total		9	6	3	3	3	2	1	0	0	0	0	0	0	1	4	5
Total			170	62	108	82	55	29	4	11	1	0	0	3	2	3	122	48

Rank among batters: 235 • *Top target (7 home runs)*: Larry Jansen, Ken Raffensberger • *Number of pitchers victimized*: 113 • *Total ballparks homered in*: 11 • *First HR*: 09/02/1939 off Clyde Shoun • *Hit for Cycle*—vs BRO: 07/15/1945 (2) • *World Series HR*—2; *All-Star HR*—1

Claude Elliott

CLAUDE JUDSON ELLIOTT
B: 11/17/1879 D: 06/21/1923
BR

Year	Tm	Lg	Tot	H	A	Men-On 0	Men-On 1	Men-On 2	Men-On 3	One-Game 2	One-Game 3	One-Game 4	LO	XN	IP	PH	RHP	LHP
1904	CIN	NL	1	0	1	1	0	0	0	0	0	0	0	0	0	0	1	0

Rank among batters: 4,707 • *Total ballparks homered in*: 1 • *First HR*: 06/08/1904 off Vic Willis

Harry Elliott

HARRY LEWIS ELLIOTT
B: 10/30/1923
BR

Year	Tm	Lg	Tot	H	A	Men-On 0	Men-On 1	Men-On 2	Men-On 3	One-Game 2	One-Game 3	One-Game 4	LO	XN	IP	PH	RHP	LHP
1953	STL	NL	1	0	1	1	0	0	0	0	0	0	0	0	0	0	0	1
1955	STL	NL	1	1	0	0	0	1	0	0	0	0	0	0	0	0	0	1
Total			2	1	1	1	0	1	0	0	0	0	0	0	0	0	0	2

Rank among batters: 4,129 • *Total ballparks homered in*: 2 • *First HR*: 09/01/1953 off Preacher Roe

Jumbo Elliott

JAMES THOMAS ELLIOTT
B: 10/22/1900 D: 01/07/1970
BR

Year	Tm	Lg	Tot	H	A	Men-On 0	Men-On 1	Men-On 2	Men-On 3	One-Game 2	One-Game 3	One-Game 4	LO	XN	IP	PH	RHP	LHP
1928	BRO	NL	3	1	2	2	1	0	0	0	0	0	0	0	0	0	3	0
1930	BRO	NL	1	1	0	1	0	0	0	0	0	0	0	0	0	0	1	0
Total			4	2	2	3	1	0	0	0	0	0	0	0	0	0	4	0

Rank among batters: 3,427 • *Total ballparks homered in*: 2 • *First HR*: 04/19/1928 off Jimmy Ring

Year	Tm	Lg	Tot	H	A	Men-On				One-Game			LO	XN	IP	PH	RHP	LHP
						0	1	2	3	2	3	4						

Randy Elliott

RANDY LEE ELLIOTT
B: 06/05/1951
BR

Year	Tm	Lg	Tot	H	A	0	1	2	3	2	3	4	LO	XN	IP	PH	RHP	LHP
1974	SD	NL	1	0	1	1	0	0	0	0	0	0	0	0	0	0	0	1
1977	SF	NL	7	3	4	3	3	0	1	0	0	0	0	0	0	3	1	6
Total			8	3	5	4	3	0	1	0	0	0	0	0	0	3	1	7

Rank among batters: 2,703 • *Total ballparks homered in*: 5 • *First HR*: 09/10/1974 off Don Gullett

Rowdy Elliott

HAROLD B. ELLIOTT
B: 07/08/1890 D: 02/12/1934
BR

Year	Tm	Lg	Tot	H	A	0	1	2	3	2	3	4	LO	XN	IP	PH	RHP	LHP
1920	BRO	NL	1	1	0	0	1	0	0	0	0	0	0	0	0	0	1	0

Rank among batters: 4,707 • *Total ballparks homered in*: 1 • *First HR*: 08/03/1920 off Jesse Haines

John Ellis

JOHN CHARLES ELLIS
B: 08/21/1948
BR

Year	Tm	Lg	Tot	H	A	0	1	2	3	2	3	4	LO	XN	IP	PH	RHP	LHP
1969	NY	AL	1	1	0	1	0	0	0	0	0	0	0	0	0	0	1	0
1970	NY	AL	7	2	5	4	0	3	0	0	0	0	0	0	0	0	3	4
1971	NY	AL	3	1	2	1	1	1	0	0	0	0	0	0	0	0	1	2
1972	NY	AL	5	3	2	1	3	1	0	0	0	0	0	0	0	0	2	3
1973	CLE	AL	14	7	7	6	6	2	0	0	0	0	0	1	0	1	6	8
1974	CLE	AL	10	6	4	4	3	2	1	0	0	0	0	0	0	0	4	6
1975	CLE	AL	7	1	6	4	2	1	0	0	0	0	0	0	0	0	2	5
1976	TEX	AL	1	0	1	1	0	0	0	0	0	0	0	0	0	0	0	1
1977	TEX	AL	4	1	3	4	0	0	0	1	0	0	0	0	0	0	0	4
1978	TEX	AL	3	1	2	1	1	1	0	0	0	0	0	0	0	0	2	1
1979	TEX	AL	12	4	8	4	5	3	0	2	0	0	0	0	0	0	5	7
1980	TEX	AL	1	0	1	0	0	1	0	0	0	0	0	0	0	0	0	1
1981	TEX	AL	1	0	1	1	0	0	0	0	0	0	0	0	0	0	0	1
Total			69	27	42	32	21	15	1	3	0	0	0	1	0	1	26	43

Rank among batters: 756 • *Top target (5 home runs)*: Larry Gura • *Number of pitchers victimized*: 54 • *Total ballparks homered in*: 12 • *First HR*: 05/17/1969 off Bob Priddy

Rube Ellis

GEORGE WILLIAM ELLIS
B: 11/17/1885 D: 03/13/1938
BL

Year	Tm	Lg	Tot	H	A	0	1	2	3	2	3	4	LO	XN	IP	PH	RHP	LHP
1909	STL	NL	3	2	1	2	0	1	0	0	0	0	0	0	0	0	2	1
1910	STL	NL	4	1	3	1	3	0	0	0	0	0	0	0	0	0	4	0
1911	STL	NL	2	0	2	0	2	0	0	0	0	0	0	0	0	0	2	0
1912	STL	NL	4	3	1	2	0	1	1	1	0	0	0	0	0	0	4	0
Total			13	6	7	5	5	2	1	1	0	0	0	0	0	0	12	1

Rank among batters: 2,248 • *Top target (2 home runs)*: Doc Crandall, Earl Moore • *Number of pitchers victimized*: 11 • *Total ballparks homered in*: 5 • *First HR*: 07/17/1909 off Hooks Wiltse

Babe Ellison

HERBERT SPENCER ELLISON
B: 11/15/1895 D: 08/11/1955
BR

Year	Tm	Lg	Tot	H	A	0	1	2	3	2	3	4	LO	XN	IP	PH	RHP	LHP
1917	DET	AL	1	0	1	1	0	0	0	0	0	0	0	0	0	0	1	0

Rank among batters: 4,707 • *Total ballparks homered in*: 1 • *First HR*: 09/29/1917 off Rube Schauer

Kevin Elster

KEVIN DANIEL ELSTER
B: 08/03/1964
BR

Year	Tm	Lg	Tot	H	A	0	1	2	3	2	3	4	LO	XN	IP	PH	RHP	LHP
1988	NY	NL	9	6	3	3	6	0	0	1	0	0	0	1	0	0	6	3
1989	NY	NL	10	5	5	6	3	1	0	0	0	0	0	0	0	0	8	2
1990	NY	NL	9	2	7	6	2	1	0	0	0	0	0	0	1	0	7	2
1991	NY	NL	6	3	3	4	0	2	0	0	0	0	0	0	0	0	5	1

Kevin Elster *continued*

Year	Tm	Lg	Tot	H	A	Men-On 0	1	2	3	One-Game 2	3	4	LO	XN	IP	PH	RHP	LHP
1995	PHI	NL	1	1	0	1	0	0	0	0	0	0	0	0	0	0	1	0
Total			35	17	18	20	11	4	0	1	0	0	0	1	1	0	27	8

Rank among batters: 1,291 • Top target (2 home runs): Tim Leary, John Smiley, Barry Jones, Doug Drabek • *Number of pitchers victimized*: 31 • *Total ballparks homered in*: 12 • *First HR*: 04/04/1988 off Dennis Martinez

Bones Ely

WILLIAM FREDERICK ELY
B: 06/07/1863 D: 01/10/1952
BR

Year	Tm	Lg	Tot	H	A	Men-On 0	1	2	3	One-Game 2	3	4	LO	XN	IP	PH	RHP	LHP
1894	STL	NL	12	7	5	6	3	3	0	0	0	0	0	0	2	0	8	3
1895	STL	NL	1	1	0	1	0	0	0	0	0	0	0	0	0	0	0	0
1896	PIT	NL	3	1	2	1	1	1	0	0	0	0	0	0	0	0	2	1
1897	PIT	NL	2	1	1	0	0	1	1	0	0	0	0	0	1	0	1	1
1898	PIT	NL	2	0	2	1	1	0	0	1	0	0	0	0	0	0	1	1
1899	PIT	NL	3	2	1	2	1	0	0	0	0	0	0	0	0	0	3	0
1902	WAS	AL	1	1	0	1	0	0	0	0	0	0	0	0	0	0	1	0
Total			24	13	11	12	6	5	1	1	0	0	0	0	3	0	16	6

Rank among batters: 1,643 • Top target (2 home runs): George Hodson, Bert Abbey, Fred Klobedanz, Vic Willis • *Number of pitchers victimized*: 20 • *Total ballparks homered in*: 8 • *First HR*: 04/23/1894 off Red Ehret

Angelo Encarnacion

ANGELO BENJAMIN ENCARNACION
B: 04/18/1973
BR

Year	Tm	Lg	Tot	H	A	Men-On 0	1	2	3	One-Game 2	3	4	LO	XN	IP	PH	RHP	LHP
1995	PIT	NL	2	2	0	1	1	0	0	0	0	0	0	0	1	0	0	2

Rank among batters: 4,129 • *Total ballparks homered in*: 1 • *First HR*: 08/19/1995 off Christophe Hammond

Steve Engel

STEVEN MICHAEL ENGEL
B: 12/31/1961
BR

Year	Tm	Lg	Tot	H	A	Men-On 0	1	2	3	One-Game 2	3	4	LO	XN	IP	PH	RHP	LHP
1985	CHI	NL	1	0	1	0	0	1	0	0	0	0	0	0	0	0	0	1

Rank among batters: 4,707 • *Total ballparks homered in*: 1 • *First HR*: 08/26/1985 off Bob Knepper

Clyde Engle

ARTHUR CLYDE ENGLE
B: 03/19/1884 D: 12/26/1939
BR

Year	Tm	Lg	Tot	H	A	Men-On 0	1	2	3	One-Game 2	3	4	LO	XN	IP	PH	RHP	LHP
1909	NY	AL	3	3	0	0	2	1	0	0	0	0	0	0	0	0	2	1
1910	BOS	AL	2	1	1	0	2	0	0	0	0	0	0	0	1	0	1	1
1911	BOS	AL	2	1	1	2	0	0	0	0	0	0	0	0	0	0	2	0
1913	BOS	AL	2	1	1	1	1	0	0	0	0	0	0	0	0	0	2	0
1915	BUF	FL	3	0	3	2	1	0	0	0	0	0	0	0	0	0	3	0
Total			12	6	6	5	6	1	0	0	0	0	0	0	1	0	10	2

Rank among batters: 2,325 • *Total ballparks homered in*: 8 • *First HR*: 04/22/1909 off Charlie Smith

Dave Engle

RALPH DAVID ENGLE
B: 11/30/1956
BR

Year	Tm	Lg	Tot	H	A	Men-On 0	1	2	3	One-Game 2	3	4	LO	XN	IP	PH	RHP	LHP
1981	MIN	AL	5	2	3	4	1	0	0	0	0	0	0	0	0	0	2	3
1982	MIN	AL	4	2	2	2	2	0	0	0	0	0	0	0	0	0	2	2
1983	MIN	AL	8	4	4	8	0	0	0	0	0	0	0	0	0	1	5	3
1984	MIN	AL	4	4	0	2	2	0	0	0	0	0	0	0	0	0	3	1
1985	MIN	AL	7	3	4	5	1	1	0	0	0	0	0	0	1	0	0	7
1987	MON	NL	1	1	0	1	0	0	0	0	0	0	0	0	0	1	0	1
1989	MIL	AL	2	1	1	2	0	0	0	0	0	0	0	0	0	0	0	2
Total			31	17	14	24	6	1	0	0	0	0	0	0	1	2	12	19

Rank among batters: 1,400 • *Top target (3 home runs)*: Britt Burns, Frank Tanana • *Number of pitchers victimized*: 26 • *Total ballparks homered in*: 13 • *First HR*: 09/11/1981 off Britt Burns

Year	Tm	Lg	Tot	H	A	Men-On				One-Game								
						0	1	2	3	2	3	4	LO	XN	IP	PH	RHP	LHP

Charlie English

CHARLES DEWIE ENGLISH
B: 04/08/1910
BR

Year	Tm	Lg	Tot	H	A	0	1	2	3	2	3	4	LO	XN	IP	PH	RHP	LHP
1932	CHI	AL	1	0	1	0	1	0	0	0	0	0	0	0	0	0	0	1

Rank among batters: 4,707 • *Total ballparks homered in*: 1 • *First HR*: 09/21/1932 off Chief Hogsett

Gil English

GILBERT RAYMOND ENGLISH
B: 07/02/1909
BR

Year	Tm	Lg	Tot	H	A	0	1	2	3	2	3	4	LO	XN	IP	PH	RHP	LHP
1932	NY	NL	2	2	0	1	1	0	0	0	0	0	0	0	0	0	1	1
1937	DET	AL	1	0	1	1	0	0	0	0	0	0	0	0	0	0	1	0
	BOS	NL	2	1	1	1	1	0	0	0	0	0	0	0	0	0	1	1
	Total		3	1	2	2	1	0	0	0	0	0	0	0	0	0	2	1
1938	BOS	NL	2	0	2	0	1	1	0	0	0	0	0	0	0	0	2	0
1944	BRO	NL	1	1	0	0	0	1	0	0	0	0	0	0	0	0	0	1
Total			8	4	4	3	3	2	0	0	0	0	0	0	0	0	5	3

Rank among batters: 2,703 • *Total ballparks homered in*: 5 • *First HR*: 07/31/1932 off Larry Benton

Woody English

ELWOOD GEORGE ENGLISH
B: 03/02/1907
BR

Year	Tm	Lg	Tot	H	A	0	1	2	3	2	3	4	LO	XN	IP	PH	RHP	LHP
1927	CHI	NL	1	0	1	1	0	0	0	0	0	0	0	0	0	0	1	0
1928	CHI	NL	2	0	2	1	0	1	0	0	0	0	0	0	0	0	1	1
1929	CHI	NL	1	0	1	1	0	0	0	0	0	0	0	0	0	0	1	0
1930	CHI	NL	14	7	7	9	5	0	0	1	0	0	0	0	0	0	10	4
1931	CHI	NL	2	0	2	2	0	0	0	0	0	0	0	0	0	0	0	2
1932	CHI	NL	3	2	1	3	0	0	0	0	0	0	0	0	0	0	2	1
1933	CHI	NL	3	1	2	2	0	1	0	0	0	0	0	0	0	0	3	0
1934	CHI	NL	3	1	2	1	2	0	0	0	0	0	0	0	0	0	3	0
1935	CHI	NL	2	1	1	2	0	0	0	0	0	0	0	0	0	0	2	0
1937	BRO	NL	1	1	0	1	0	0	0	0	0	0	0	0	0	0	1	0
Total			32	13	19	23	7	2	0	1	0	0	0	0	0	0	24	8

Rank among batters: 1,360 • *Top target (3 home runs)*: Carl Hubbell • *Number of pitchers victimized*: 27 • *Total ballparks homered in*: 8 • *First HR*: 07/19/1927 off Fay Thomas

Del Ennis

DELMER ENNIS
B: 06/08/1925
BR

Year	Tm	Lg	Tot	H	A	0	1	2	3	2	3	4	LO	XN	IP	PH	RHP	LHP
1946	PHI	NL	17	9	8	9	6	2	0	1	0	0	0	0	0	0	14	3
1947	PHI	NL	12	4	8	7	3	2	0	0	0	0	0	1	1	0	9	3
1948	PHI	NL	30	8	22	16	10	4	0	1	0	0	0	1	0	1	25	5
1949	PHI	NL	25	13	12	9	14	2	0	0	0	0	0	1	0	0	15	10
1950	PHI	NL	31	16	15	13	14	2	2	1	0	0	0	0	0	0	20	11
1951	PHI	NL	15	8	7	8	5	2	0	0	0	0	0	0	0	1	11	4
1952	PHI	NL	20	10	10	11	8	0	1	1	0	0	0	1	0	0	14	6
1953	PHI	NL	29	20	9	11	14	4	0	3	0	0	0	0	0	0	21	8
1954	PHI	NL	25	12	13	9	6	9	1	1	0	0	0	0	0	0	17	8
1955	PHI	NL	29	18	11	12	9	8	0	0	1	0	0	0	0	0	19	10
1956	PHI	NL	26	15	11	13	10	2	1	0	0	0	0	1	0	0	21	5
1957	STL	NL	24	11	13	10	11	3	0	1	0	0	0	1	0	0	18	6
1958	STL	NL	3	1	2	1	1	0	1	0	0	0	0	0	0	0	1	2
1959	CHI	AL	2	1	1	1	1	0	0	0	0	0	0	0	0	0	1	1
Total			288	146	142	130	112	40	6	9	1	0	0	6	1	2	206	82

Rank among batters: 77 • *Top target (9 home runs)*: Carl Erskine • *Number of pitchers victimized*: 152 • *Total ballparks homered in*: 12 • *First HR*: 05/05/1946 off Claude Passeau

Jewel Ens

JEWEL WINKLEMEYER ENS
B: 08/24/1889 D: 01/17/1950
BR

Year	Tm	Lg	Tot	H	A	0	1	2	3	2	3	4	LO	XN	IP	PH	RHP	LHP
1925	PIT	NL	1	0	1	0	1	0	0	0	0	0	0	0	0	0	0	1

Rank among batters: 4,707 • *Total ballparks homered in*: 1 • *First HR*: 04/15/1925 off Wilbur Cooper

Hal Epps

HAROLD FRANKLIN EPPS
B: 03/26/1914
BL

Year	Tm	Lg	Tot	H	A	Men-On 0	1	2	3	One-Game 2	3	4	LO	XN	IP	PH	RHP	LHP
1938	STL	NL	1	0	1	1	0	0	0	0	0	0	1	0	0	0	1	0

Rank among batters: 4,707 • *Total ballparks homered in*: 1 • *First HR*: 09/16/1938 off Luke Hamlin

Mike Epstein

MICHAEL PETER EPSTEIN
B: 04/04/1943
BL

Year	Tm	Lg	Tot	H	A	Men-On 0	1	2	3	One-Game 2	3	4	LO	XN	IP	PH	RHP	LHP
1967	WAS	AL	9	3	6	5	2	1	1	2	0	0	0	0	1	0	8	1
1968	WAS	AL	13	8	5	8	3	2	0	0	0	0	0	0	0	1	10	3
1969	WAS	AL	30	15	15	15	7	7	1	0	1	0	0	0	0	0	24	6
1970	WAS	AL	20	8	12	12	6	1	1	2	0	0	0	1	0	0	15	5
1971	WAS	AL	1	1	0	0	1	0	0	0	0	0	0	0	0	0	1	0
	OAK	AL	18	14	4	12	4	2	0	2	0	0	0	0	0	0	14	4
	Total		19	15	4	12	5	2	0	2	0	0	0	0	0	0	15	4
1972	OAK	AL	26	12	14	16	6	4	0	2	0	0	0	0	0	0	22	4
1973	TEX	AL	1	0	1	1	0	0	0	0	0	0	0	0	0	0	1	0
	CAL	AL	8	4	4	4	3	1	0	0	0	0	0	1	0	1	7	1
	Total		9	4	5	5	3	1	0	0	0	0	0	1	0	1	8	1
1974	CAL	AL	4	2	2	3	0	1	0	0	0	0	0	0	0	0	3	1
Total			130	67	63	76	32	19	3	8	1	0	0	2	1	2	105	25

Rank among batters: 348 • *Top target (7 home runs)*: Tom Murphy • *Number of pitchers victimized*: 86 • *Total ballparks homered in*: 14 • *First HR*: 06/05/1967 off Thad Tillotson • *LCS HR*—1

Eric Erickson

ERIC GEORGE ADOLPH ERICKSON
B: 03/13/1895 D: 05/19/1965
BR

Year	Tm	Lg	Tot	H	A	Men-On 0	1	2	3	One-Game 2	3	4	LO	XN	IP	PH	RHP	LHP
1920	WAS	AL	1	0	1	0	1	0	0	0	0	0	0	0	0	0	1	0

Rank among batters: 4,707 • *Total ballparks homered in*: 1 • *First HR*: 09/21/1920 off John Glaiser

Hank Erickson

HENRY NELS ERICKSON
B: 11/11/1907 D: 12/13/1964
BR

Year	Tm	Lg	Tot	H	A	Men-On 0	1	2	3	One-Game 2	3	4	LO	XN	IP	PH	RHP	LHP
1935	CIN	NL	1	0	1	1	0	0	0	0	0	0	0	0	0	0	1	0

Rank among batters: 4,707 • *Total ballparks homered in*: 1 • *First HR*: 04/17/1935 off Guy Bush

Paul Erickson

PAUL WALFORD ERICKSON
B: 12/14/1915
BR

Year	Tm	Lg	Tot	H	A	Men-On 0	1	2	3	One-Game 2	3	4	LO	XN	IP	PH	RHP	LHP
1941	CHI	NL	1	0	1	1	0	0	0	0	0	0	0	0	0	0	1	0
1944	CHI	NL	1	1	0	1	0	0	0	0	0	0	0	0	0	0	1	0
1947	CHI	NL	1	1	0	1	0	0	0	0	0	0	0	0	0	0	1	0
Total			3	2	1	3	0	0	0	0	0	0	0	0	0	0	3	0

Rank among batters: 3,735 • *Total ballparks homered in*: 2 • *First HR*: 08/17/1941 off Bucky Walters

Frank Ernaga

FRANK JOHN ERNAGA
B: 08/22/1930
BR

Year	Tm	Lg	Tot	H	A	Men-On 0	1	2	3	One-Game 2	3	4	LO	XN	IP	PH	RHP	LHP
1957	CHI	NL	2	2	0	2	0	0	0	0	0	0	0	0	0	0	0	2

Rank among batters: 4,129 • *Total ballparks homered in*: 1 • *First HR*: 05/24/1957 off Warren Spahn • *Hit HR in first major league AB*—vs MIL: 05/24/1957

Carl Erskine

CARL DANIEL ERSKINE
B: 12/13/1926
BR

Year	Tm	Lg	Tot	H	A	Men-On 0	1	2	3	One-Game 2	3	4	LO	XN	IP	PH	RHP	LHP
1955	BRO	NL	1	1	0	1	0	0	0	0	0	0	0	0	0	0	1	0

Rank among batters: 4,707 • *Total ballparks homered in*: 1 • *First HR*: 06/10/1955 off Sam Jones

Tex Erwin

ROSS EMIL ERWIN
B: 12/22/1885 D: 04/05/1953
BL

Year	Tm	Lg	Tot	H	A	Men-On 0	1	2	3	One-Game 2	3	4	LO	XN	IP	PH	RHP	LHP
1910	BRO	NL	1	0	1	1	0	0	0	0	0	0	0	0	0	0	1	0
1911	BRO	NL	7	2	5	5	1	0	1	0	0	0	0	1	2	0	7	0
1912	BRO	NL	2	0	2	2	0	0	0	0	0	0	0	0	0	1	2	0
1914	CIN	NL	1	1	0	0	1	0	0	0	0	0	0	0	1	0	1	0
Total			11	3	8	8	2	0	1	0	0	0	0	1	3	1	11	0

Rank among batters: 2,419 • *Total ballparks homered in*: 7 • *First HR*: 04/15/1910 off Lew Moren

Nick Esasky

NICHOLAS ANDREW ESASKY
B: 02/24/1960
BR

Year	Tm	Lg	Tot	H	A	Men-On 0	1	2	3	One-Game 2	3	4	LO	XN	IP	PH	RHP	LHP
1983	CIN	NL	12	5	7	7	3	1	1	0	0	0	0	0	1	0	10	2
1984	CIN	NL	10	5	5	5	3	1	1	0	0	0	0	0	0	0	4	6
1985	CIN	NL	21	7	14	11	6	3	1	0	0	0	0	2	0	0	14	7
1986	CIN	NL	12	9	3	4	7	1	0	0	0	0	0	0	0	0	7	5
1987	CIN	NL	22	10	12	10	7	4	1	2	0	0	0	0	0	0	16	6
1988	CIN	NL	15	7	8	10	2	2	1	0	0	0	0	0	0	0	12	3
1989	BOS	AL	30	15	15	9	14	6	1	0	0	0	0	0	0	0	19	11
Total			122	58	64	56	42	18	6	2	0	0	0	2	1	0	82	40

Rank among batters: 377 • *Top target (4 home runs)*: Bob Welch • *Number of pitchers victimized*: 98 • *Total ballparks homered in*: 21 • *First HR*: 07/01/1983 off Phil Niekro

Jimmy Esmond

JAMES J. ESMOND
B: 08/08/1889 D: 06/26/1948
BR

Year	Tm	Lg	Tot	H	A	Men-On 0	1	2	3	One-Game 2	3	4	LO	XN	IP	PH	RHP	LHP
1911	CIN	NL	1	1	0	1	0	0	0	0	0	0	0	0	1	0	0	1
1912	CIN	NL	1	1	0	0	0	1	0	0	0	0	0	0	1	0	1	0
1914	IND	FL	2	2	0	0	1	1	0	0	0	0	0	0	1	0	2	0
1915	NWK	FL	4	0	4	1	1	2	0	0	0	0	0	0	0	0	2	2
Total			8	4	4	2	2	4	0	0	0	0	0	0	3	0	5	3

Rank among batters: 2,703 • *Top target (2 home runs)*: Al Schulz • *Number of pitchers victimized*: 7 • *Total ballparks homered in*: 5 • *First HR*: 06/10/1911 off Rube Marquard

Duke Esper

CHARLES H. ESPER
B: 07/28/1868 D: 08/31/1910

Year	Tm	Lg	Tot	H	A	Men-On 0	1	2	3	One-Game 2	3	4	LO	XN	IP	PH	RHP	LHP
1892	PHI	NL	1	1	0	0	1	0	0	0	0	0	0	0	0	0	0	0
1894	WAS	NL	1	1	0	1	0	0	0	0	0	0	0	0	0	0	1	0
Total			2	2	0	1	1	0	0	0	0	0	0	0	0	0	1	0

Rank among batters: 4,129 • *Total ballparks homered in*: 2 • *First HR*: 06/06/1892 off Jack Easton

Juan Espino

JUAN (REYES) ESPINO
B: 03/16/1956
BR

Year	Tm	Lg	Tot	H	A	Men-On 0	1	2	3	One-Game 2	3	4	LO	XN	IP	PH	RHP	LHP
1983	NY	AL	1	0	1	1	0	0	0	0	0	0	0	0	0	0	1	0

Rank among batters: 4,707 • *Total ballparks homered in*: 1 • *First HR*: 09/07/1983 off Jaime Cocanower

Alvaro Espinoza

ALVARO ALBERTO (RAMIREZ) ESPINOZA
B: 02/19/1962
BR

Year	Tm	Lg	Tot	H	A	Men-On 0	1	2	3	One-Game 2	3	4	LO	XN	IP	PH	RHP	LHP
1990	NY	AL	2	0	2	2	0	0	0	0	0	0	0	0	1	0	2	0
1991	NY	AL	5	2	3	4	1	0	0	0	0	0	0	0	0	0	4	1
1993	CLE	AL	4	3	1	3	0	1	0	0	0	0	0	0	0	0	2	2
1994	CLE	AL	1	1	0	1	0	0	0	0	0	0	0	0	0	0	0	1
1995	CLE	AL	2	0	2	1	1	0	0	0	0	0	0	0	0	0	1	1
Total			14	6	8	11	2	1	0	0	0	0	0	0	1	0	9	5

Rank among batters: 2,169 • *Total ballparks homered in*: 9 • *First HR*: 06/05/1990 off John Dopson

Sammy Esposito

SAMUEL ESPOSITO
B: 12/15/1931
BR

Year	Tm	Lg	Tot	H	A	Men-On 0	Men-On 1	Men-On 2	Men-On 3	One-Game 2	One-Game 3	One-Game 4	LO	XN	IP	PH	RHP	LHP
1956	CHI	AL	3	2	1	2	1	0	0	0	0	0	0	0	0	0	2	1
1957	CHI	AL	2	1	1	2	0	0	0	0	0	0	0	0	0	0	0	2
1959	CHI	AL	1	0	1	1	0	0	0	0	0	0	0	0	0	0	0	1
1960	CHI	AL	1	1	0	1	0	0	0	0	0	0	0	0	0	0	1	0
1961	CHI	AL	1	0	1	1	0	0	0	0	0	0	0	0	0	0	1	0
Total			8	4	4	7	1	0	0	0	0	0	0	0	0	0	4	4

Rank among batters: 2,703 • *Total ballparks homered in*: 4 • *First HR*: 08/01/1956 off Chuck Stobbs

Cecil Espy

CECIL EDWARD ESPY
B: 01/20/1963
BB

Year	Tm	Lg	Tot	H	A	Men-On 0	Men-On 1	Men-On 2	Men-On 3	One-Game 2	One-Game 3	One-Game 4	LO	XN	IP	PH	RHP	LHP
1988	TEX	AL	2	2	0	0	2	0	0	0	0	0	0	0	0	0	1	1
1989	TEX	AL	3	2	1	3	0	0	0	0	0	0	2	0	0	0	0	3
1991	PIT	NL	1	1	0	0	0	1	0	0	0	0	0	0	0	0	1	0
1992	PIT	NL	1	0	1	0	1	0	0	0	0	0	0	0	0	0	0	1
Total			7	5	2	3	3	1	0	0	0	0	2	0	0	0	2	5

Rank among batters: 2,834 • *Total ballparks homered in*: 4 • *First HR*: 06/11/1988 off Rick Honeycutt

Chuck Essegian

CHARLES ABRAHAM ESSEGIAN
B: 08/09/1931
BR

Year	Tm	Lg	Tot	H	A	Men-On 0	Men-On 1	Men-On 2	Men-On 3	One-Game 2	One-Game 3	One-Game 4	LO	XN	IP	PH	RHP	LHP
1958	PHI	NL	5	4	1	2	3	0	0	0	0	0	0	0	0	0	3	2
1959	LA	NL	1	0	1	0	1	0	0	0	0	0	0	0	0	0	0	1
1960	LA	NL	3	3	0	3	0	0	0	0	0	0	0	1	0	1	2	1
1961	CLE	AL	12	9	3	6	4	2	0	3	0	0	0	1	0	1	4	8
1962	CLE	AL	21	15	6	13	4	4	0	1	0	0	0	0	0	1	11	10
1963	KC	AL	5	2	3	2	2	1	0	0	0	0	0	0	0	0	4	1
Total			47	33	14	26	14	7	0	4	0	0	0	2	0	3	24	23

Rank among batters: 1,040 • *Top target (3 home runs)*: Don Mossi, Whitey Ford, Claude Osteen • *Number of pitchers victimized*: 36 • *Total ballparks homered in*: 12 • *First HR*: 05/06/1958 off Sandy Koufax • *World Series HR*—2

Jim Essian

JAMES SARKIS ESSIAN
B: 01/02/1951
BR

Year	Tm	Lg	Tot	H	A	Men-On 0	Men-On 1	Men-On 2	Men-On 3	One-Game 2	One-Game 3	One-Game 4	LO	XN	IP	PH	RHP	LHP
1977	CHI	AL	10	6	4	7	3	0	0	0	0	0	0	0	0	0	7	3
1978	OAK	AL	3	1	2	1	2	0	0	0	0	0	0	0	0	0	2	1
1979	OAK	AL	8	6	2	5	1	1	1	0	0	0	0	0	1	0	4	4
1980	OAK	AL	5	4	1	3	2	0	0	0	0	0	0	0	0	0	1	4
1982	SEA	AL	3	2	1	1	2	0	0	0	0	0	0	0	0	0	0	3
1983	CLE	AL	2	1	1	0	2	0	0	0	0	0	0	0	0	0	1	1
1984	OAK	AL	2	2	0	2	0	0	0	0	0	0	0	0	0	0	1	1
Total			33	22	11	19	12	1	1	0	0	0	0	0	1	0	16	17

Rank among batters: 1,336 • *Top target (3 home runs)*: Paul Thormodsgard • *Number of pitchers victimized*: 31 • *Total ballparks homered in*: 10 • *First HR*: 04/13/1977 off Ferguson Jenkins

Bobby Estalella

ROBERTO (VENTOZA) ESTALELLA
B: 04/25/1911 D: 01/06/1991
BR

Year	Tm	Lg	Tot	H	A	Men-On 0	Men-On 1	Men-On 2	Men-On 3	One-Game 2	One-Game 3	One-Game 4	LO	XN	IP	PH	RHP	LHP
1935	WAS	AL	2	1	1	0	1	1	0	0	0	0	0	0	0	0	1	1
1939	WAS	AL	8	2	6	2	6	0	0	1	0	0	0	0	1	0	4	4
1942	WAS	AL	8	4	4	4	3	1	0	0	0	0	0	0	1	0	4	4
1943	PHI	AL	11	5	6	7	2	2	0	0	0	0	0	0	1	0	9	2
1944	PHI	AL	7	4	3	3	2	2	0	0	0	0	0	1	0	0	6	1
1945	PHI	AL	7	5	2	3	4	0	0	1	0	0	0	0	0	0	7	0
Total			43	21	22	19	18	6	0	2	0	0	0	1	3	0	31	12

Rank among batters: 1,116 • *Top target (3 home runs)*: Orval Grove • *Number of pitchers victimized*: 38 • *Total ballparks homered in*: 9 • *First HR*: 09/21/1935 off Carl Doyle

Dude Esterbrook

THOMAS JOHN ESTERBROOK
B: 06/09/1857 D: 04/30/1901
BR

Year	Tm	Lg	Tot	H	A	Men-On 0	1	2	3	One-Game 2	3	4	LO	XN	IP	PH	RHP	LHP
1884	NY	AA	1	1	0	1	0	0	0	0	0	0	0	0	0	0	1	0
1885	NY	NL	2	1	1	2	0	0	0	0	0	0	0	0	1	0	2	0
1886	NY	NL	3	2	1	2	0	1	0	0	0	0	0	0	0	0	1	2
Total			6	4	2	5	0	1	0	0	0	0	0	0	1	0	4	2

Rank among batters: 2,988 • *Total ballparks homered in*: 4 • *First HR*: 06/03/1884 off Will White

Chuck Estrada

CHARLES LEONARD ESTRADA
B: 02/15/1938
BR

Year	Tm	Lg	Tot	H	A	Men-On 0	1	2	3	One-Game 2	3	4	LO	XN	IP	PH	RHP	LHP
1962	BAL	AL	1	1	0	0	1	0	0	0	0	0	0	0	0	0	1	0

Rank among batters: 4,707 • *Total ballparks homered in*: 1 • *First HR*: 09/13/1962 off Jack Jenkins

Andy Etchebarren

ANDREW AUGUSTE ETCHEBARREN
B: 06/20/1943
BR

Year	Tm	Lg	Tot	H	A	Men-On 0	1	2	3	One-Game 2	3	4	LO	XN	IP	PH	RHP	LHP
1965	BAL	AL	1	0	1	0	0	1	0	0	0	0	0	0	1	0	1	0
1966	BAL	AL	11	3	8	8	3	0	0	0	0	0	0	0	0	0	7	4
1967	BAL	AL	7	4	3	4	1	2	0	0	0	0	0	1	0	0	6	1
1968	BAL	AL	5	3	2	4	1	0	0	0	0	0	0	1	0	0	3	2
1969	BAL	AL	3	2	1	3	0	0	0	0	0	0	0	0	0	0	2	1
1970	BAL	AL	4	3	1	3	1	0	0	0	0	0	0	0	0	0	4	0
1971	BAL	AL	9	5	4	5	2	2	0	0	0	0	0	0	0	0	2	7
1972	BAL	AL	2	2	0	1	0	1	0	0	0	0	0	0	0	0	0	2
1973	BAL	AL	2	2	0	1	1	0	0	0	0	0	0	0	0	0	0	2
1974	BAL	AL	2	1	1	2	0	0	0	0	0	0	0	0	0	0	0	2
1975	CAL	AL	3	1	2	2	0	1	0	0	0	0	0	0	0	0	2	1
Total			49	26	23	33	9	7	0	0	0	0	0	2	1	0	27	22

Rank among batters: 1,008 • *Top target (4 home runs)*: Mickey Lolich • *Number of pitchers victimized*: 44 • *Total ballparks homered in*: 10 • *First HR*: 09/06/1965 off Bill Stafford • *LCS HR*—1

Buck Etchison

CLARENCE HAMPTON ETCHISON
B: 01/27/1915 D: 01/24/1980
BL

Year	Tm	Lg	Tot	H	A	Men-On 0	1	2	3	One-Game 2	3	4	LO	XN	IP	PH	RHP	LHP
1944	BOS	NL	8	5	3	5	2	1	0	0	0	0	0	0	0	0	7	1

Rank among batters: 2,703 • *Total ballparks homered in*: 4 • *First HR*: 06/18/1944 off Frank Seward

Bobby Etheridge

BOBBY LAMAR ETHERIDGE
B: 11/25/1942
BR

Year	Tm	Lg	Tot	H	A	Men-On 0	1	2	3	One-Game 2	3	4	LO	XN	IP	PH	RHP	LHP
1967	SF	NL	1	1	0	1	0	0	0	0	0	0	0	0	0	0	1	0
1969	SF	NL	1	1	0	1	0	0	0	0	0	0	0	0	0	0	1	0
Total			2	2	0	2	0	0	0	0	0	0	0	0	0	0	2	0

Rank among batters: 4,129 • *Total ballparks homered in*: 1 • *First HR*: 07/28/1967 off Larry Jackson

Nick Etten

NICHOLAS RAYMOND THOMAS ETTEN
B: 09/19/1913 D: 10/18/1990
BL

Year	Tm	Lg	Tot	H	A	Men-On 0	1	2	3	One-Game 2	3	4	LO	XN	IP	PH	RHP	LHP
1939	PHI	AL	3	0	3	2	1	0	0	0	0	0	0	0	0	0	3	0
1941	PHI	NL	14	7	7	6	4	4	0	0	0	0	0	0	0	0	13	1
1942	PHI	NL	8	2	6	7	0	1	0	0	0	0	0	0	0	0	8	0
1943	NY	AL	14	6	8	11	1	2	0	1	0	0	0	0	0	0	14	0
1944	NY	AL	22	15	7	11	9	2	0	1	0	0	0	1	0	0	21	1
1945	NY	AL	18	12	6	10	5	2	1	0	0	0	0	0	0	0	14	4
1946	NY	AL	9	6	3	5	2	1	1	1	0	0	0	0	0	0	7	2
1947	PHI	NL	1	1	0	0	1	0	0	0	0	0	0	0	0	0	1	0
Total			89	49	40	52	23	12	2	3	0	0	0	1	0	0	81	8

Rank among batters: 584 • *Top target (4 home runs)*: Bob Muncrief • *Number of pitchers victimized*: 61 • *Total ballparks homered in*: 11 • *First HR*: 04/25/1939 off Bump Hadley

Year	Tm	Lg	Tot	H	A	Men-On				One-Game			LO	XN	IP	PH	RHP	LHP
						0	1	2	3	2	3	4						

Tony Eusebio

RAUL ANTONIO BARE EUSEBIO
B: 04/27/1967
BR

Year	Tm	Lg	Tot	H	A	0	1	2	3	2	3	4	LO	XN	IP	PH	RHP	LHP
1994	HOU	NL	5	1	4	0	4	1	0	1	0	0	0	1	0	1	2	3
1995	HOU	NL	6	5	1	2	2	0	2	0	0	0	0	1	0	1	5	1
Total			11	6	5	2	6	1	2	1	0	0	0	2	0	2	7	4

Rank among batters: 2,419 • *Total ballparks homered in*: 5 • *First HR*: 04/13/1994 off Christophe Hammond

Frank Eustace

FRANK JOHN EUSTACE
B: 11/07/1873 D: 10/20/1932

Year	Tm	Lg	Tot	H	A	0	1	2	3	2	3	4	LO	XN	IP	PH	RHP	LHP
1896	LOU	NL	1	1	0	1	0	0	0	0	0	0	0	0	1	0	0	1

Rank among batters: 4,707 • *Total ballparks homered in*: 1 • *First HR*: 04/17/1896 off Walter Thornton

Al Evans

ALFRED HUBERT EVANS
B: 09/28/1916 D: 04/06/1979
BR

Year	Tm	Lg	Tot	H	A	0	1	2	3	2	3	4	LO	XN	IP	PH	RHP	LHP
1941	WAS	AL	1	0	1	1	0	0	0	0	0	0	0	0	0	0	1	0
1945	WAS	AL	2	0	2	0	2	0	0	0	0	0	0	0	0	0	2	0
1946	WAS	AL	2	0	2	1	1	0	0	0	0	0	0	0	0	0	1	1
1947	WAS	AL	2	1	1	1	1	0	0	0	0	0	0	0	0	0	1	1
1948	WAS	AL	2	1	1	2	0	0	0	0	0	0	0	0	1	0	2	0
1949	WAS	AL	2	0	2	1	1	0	0	0	0	0	0	1	0	0	2	0
1950	WAS	AL	2	0	2	0	0	2	0	0	0	0	0	0	0	0	1	1
Total			13	2	11	6	5	2	0	0	0	0	0	1	1	0	10	3

Rank among batters: 2,248 • *Total ballparks homered in*: 7 • *First HR*: 07/06/1941 off Dick Newsome

Barry Evans

BARRY STEVEN EVANS
B: 11/30/1955
BR

Year	Tm	Lg	Tot	H	A	0	1	2	3	2	3	4	LO	XN	IP	PH	RHP	LHP
1979	SD	NL	1	0	1	1	0	0	0	0	0	0	0	1	0	0	1	0
1980	SD	NL	1	0	1	0	0	0	1	0	0	0	0	0	0	0	1	0
Total			2	0	2	1	0	0	1	0	0	0	0	1	0	0	2	0

Rank among batters: 4,129 • *Total ballparks homered in*: 2 • *First HR*: 05/19/1979 off J.R. Richard

Darrell Evans

DARRELL WAYNE EVANS
B: 05/26/1947
BL

Year	Tm	Lg	Tot	H	A	0	1	2	3	2	3	4	LO	XN	IP	PH	RHP	LHP
1971	ATL	NL	12	8	4	8	3	1	0	1	0	0	0	1	0	0	12	0
1972	ATL	NL	19	12	7	12	3	3	1	0	0	0	0	1	0	0	15	4
1973	ATL	NL	41	24	17	22	15	3	1	3	0	0	0	1	0	0	24	17
1974	ATL	NL	25	14	11	13	9	2	1	0	0	0	0	0	0	0	20	5
1975	ATL	NL	22	12	10	13	7	2	0	1	0	0	0	1	0	0	16	6
1976	ATL	NL	1	1	0	0	0	1	0	0	0	0	0	0	0	0	0	1
	SF	NL	10	3	7	5	3	1	1	1	0	0	0	0	0	0	8	2
	Total		11	4	7	5	3	2	1	1	0	0	0	0	0	0	8	3
1977	SF	NL	17	12	5	7	7	3	0	1	0	0	0	0	0	2	13	4
1978	SF	NL	20	7	13	11	8	1	0	3	0	0	0	0	0	0	12	8
1979	SF	NL	17	8	9	12	5	0	0	0	0	0	0	0	0	1	9	8
1980	SF	NL	20	8	12	14	5	0	1	0	0	0	1	0	0	1	15	5
1981	SF	NL	12	6	6	8	2	2	0	0	0	0	0	0	0	0	10	2
1982	SF	NL	16	8	8	11	3	2	0	0	0	0	0	0	0	1	13	3
1983	SF	NL	30	16	14	15	11	4	0	3	1	0	0	0	0	0	24	6
1984	DET	AL	16	6	10	9	2	5	0	0	0	0	0	0	0	0	15	1
1985	DET	AL	40	21	19	24	11	3	2	4	0	0	0	2	0	0	31	9
1986	DET	AL	29	15	14	19	6	2	2	3	0	0	0	0	0	2	20	9
1987	DET	AL	34	19	15	18	10	5	1	1	0	0	0	1	0	0	29	5
1988	DET	AL	22	14	8	15	4	3	0	0	0	0	0	0	0	0	22	0
1989	ATL	NL	11	5	6	9	1	1	0	2	0	0	0	0	0	0	9	2
Total			414	219	195	245	115	44	10	23	1	0	1	7	0	7	317	97

Rank among batters: 24 • *Top target (8 home runs)*: Tom Seaver • *Number of pitchers victimized*: 261 • *Total ballparks homered in*: 27 • *First HR*: 05/29/1971 off Bob Gibson

Dwight Evans

DWIGHT MICHAEL EVANS
B: 11/03/1951
BR

						Men-On				One-Game								
Year	Tm	Lg	Tot	H	A	0	1	2	3	2	3	4	LO	XN	IP	PH	RHP	LHP
1972	BOS	AL	1	1	0	1	0	0	0	0	0	0	0	0	0	0	1	0
1973	BOS	AL	10	6	4	7	2	1	0	0	0	0	0	0	0	0	3	7
1974	BOS	AL	10	7	3	4	2	4	0	0	0	0	0	0	0	0	5	5
1975	BOS	AL	13	8	5	9	3	0	1	1	0	0	0	0	0	0	8	5
1976	BOS	AL	17	9	8	10	4	3	0	0	0	0	0	0	0	0	13	4
1977	BOS	AL	14	9	5	8	4	2	0	0	0	0	0	0	0	0	12	2
1978	BOS	AL	24	13	11	16	7	1	0	2	0	0	0	1	0	0	18	6
1979	BOS	AL	21	12	9	13	6	2	0	1	0	0	0	0	0	0	14	7
1980	BOS	AL	18	11	7	10	6	2	0	1	0	0	0	0	0	0	13	5
1981	BOS	AL	22	15	7	9	10	3	0	1	0	0	1	0	0	0	15	7
1982	BOS	AL	32	19	13	18	10	4	0	2	0	0	0	0	0	0	25	7
1983	BOS	AL	22	12	10	14	4	4	0	2	0	0	0	0	0	0	15	7
1984	BOS	AL	32	15	17	15	7	9	1	3	0	0	0	1	0	0	25	7
1985	BOS	AL	29	14	15	19	9	1	0	1	0	0	5	2	0	0	17	12
1986	BOS	AL	26	8	18	14	8	4	0	2	0	0	1	0	0	0	20	6
1987	BOS	AL	34	14	20	18	6	9	1	4	0	0	0	0	0	0	22	12
1988	BOS	AL	21	11	10	7	14	0	0	1	0	0	0	0	1	0	15	6
1989	BOS	AL	20	8	12	12	3	3	2	0	0	0	0	1	0	0	16	4
1990	BOS	AL	13	7	6	7	3	3	0	1	0	0	0	2	0	0	10	3
1991	BAL	AL	6	4	2	3	0	2	1	0	0	0	0	0	0	1	5	1
Total			385	203	182	214	108	57	6	22	0	0	7	7	1	1	272	113

Rank among batters: 30 • *Top target (7 home runs)*: Steve McCatty • *Number of pitchers victimized*: 247 • *Total ballparks homered in*: 16 • *First HR*: 09/20/1972 off Eddie Watt • *Hit for Cycle*—vs SEA: 06/28/1984 • *World Series HR*—3; *LCS HR*—1

Jake Evans

URIAH L. P. EVANS
B: 09/ /1856 D: 01/16/1907

Year	Tm	Lg	Tot	H	A	0	1	2	3	2	3	4	LO	XN	IP	PH	RHP	LHP
1884	CLE	NL	1	0	1	1	0	0	0	0	0	0	0	0	0	0	0	0

Rank among batters: 4,707 • *Total ballparks homered in*: 1 • *First HR*: 06/05/1884 off Frank Meinke

Joe Evans

JOSEPH PATTON EVANS
B: 05/15/1895 D: 08/09/1953
BR

Year	Tm	Lg	Tot	H	A	0	1	2	3	2	3	4	LO	XN	IP	PH	RHP	LHP
1917	CLE	AL	2	1	1	0	2	0	0	0	0	0	0	0	0	0	1	1
1918	CLE	AL	1	1	0	0	0	1	0	0	0	0	0	0	1	0	1	0
Total			3	2	1	0	2	1	0	0	0	0	0	0	1	0	2	1

Rank among batters: 3,735 • *Total ballparks homered in*: 2 • *First HR*: 05/17/1917 off Herb Pennock

Steve Evans

LOUIS RICHARD EVANS
B: 02/17/1885 D: 12/28/1943
BL

Year	Tm	Lg	Tot	H	A	0	1	2	3	2	3	4	LO	XN	IP	PH	RHP	LHP
1909	STL	NL	2	1	1	1	0	1	0	0	0	0	0	0	0	0	2	0
1910	STL	NL	2	1	1	1	1	0	0	0	0	0	0	0	1	0	2	0
1911	STL	NL	5	3	2	1	3	1	0	1	0	0	0	0	0	0	5	0
1912	STL	NL	6	5	1	4	2	0	0	0	0	0	0	0	2	0	5	1
1913	STL	NL	1	0	1	0	1	0	0	0	0	0	0	0	1	0	1	0
1914	BRO	FL	12	8	4	9	1	1	1	0	0	0	0	1	0	0	12	0
1915	BRO	FL	3	2	1	2	1	0	0	0	0	0	0	0	0	0	3	0
	BAL	FL	1	1	0	1	0	0	0	0	0	0	0	0	0	0	1	0
	Total		4	3	1	3	1	0	0	0	0	0	0	0	0	0	4	0
Total			32	21	11	19	9	3	1	1	0	0	0	1	4	0	31	1

Rank among batters: 1,360 • *Top target (4 home runs)*: Howie Camnitz • *Number of pitchers victimized*: 27 • *Total ballparks homered in*: 8 • *First HR*: 05/17/1909 off Gus Dorner

Carl Everett

CARL EDWARD EVERETT
B: 06/03/1970
BB

Year	Tm	Lg	Tot	H	A	0	1	2	3	2	3	4	LO	XN	IP	PH	RHP	LHP
1994	FLO	NL	2	2	0	1	1	0	0	0	0	0	0	0	0	0	1	1

Carl Everett *continued*

Year	Tm	Lg	Tot	H	A	Men-On 0	1	2	3	One-Game 2	3	4	LO	XN	IP	PH	RHP	LHP
1995	NY	NL	12	9	3	8	2	1	1	1	0	0	0	0	0	0	8	4
Total			14	11	3	9	3	1	1	1	0	0	0	0	0	0	9	5

Rank among batters: 2,169 • *Top target (2 home runs)*: Allen Watson, Jamie Brewington • *Number of pitchers victimized*: 12 • *Total ballparks homered in*: 4 • *First HR*: 05/22/1994 off Allen Watson

Bill Everitt

WILLIAM LEE EVERITT
B: 12/13/1868 D: 01/19/1938
BL

Year	Tm	Lg	Tot	H	A	Men-On 0	1	2	3	One-Game 2	3	4	LO	XN	IP	PH	RHP	LHP
1895	CHI	NL	3	3	0	2	0	1	0	0	0	0	0	0	0	0	1	2
1896	CHI	NL	2	2	0	2	0	0	0	0	0	0	2	0	0	0	2	0
1897	CHI	NL	5	3	2	3	0	2	0	1	0	0	1	1	0	0	3	0
1899	CHI	NL	1	1	0	0	0	0	1	0	0	0	0	0	0	0	0	0
Total			11	9	2	7	0	3	1	1	0	0	3	1	0	0	6	2

Rank among batters: 2,419 • *Top target (2 home runs)*: Frank Foreman, Mike Sullivan • *Number of pitchers victimized*: 9 • *Total ballparks homered in*: 2 • *First HR*: 07/04/1895 off Tom Parrott

Hoot Evers

WALTER ARTHUR EVERS
B: 02/08/1921 D: 01/25/1991
BR

Year	Tm	Lg	Tot	H	A	Men-On 0	1	2	3	One-Game 2	3	4	LO	XN	IP	PH	RHP	LHP
1946	DET	AL	4	4	0	4	0	0	0	1	0	0	0	0	0	0	3	1
1947	DET	AL	10	5	5	6	3	1	0	0	0	0	0	0	0	0	4	6
1948	DET	AL	10	3	7	6	2	1	1	0	0	0	0	0	0	0	4	6
1949	DET	AL	7	7	0	2	3	2	0	0	0	0	0	0	0	1	4	3
1950	DET	AL	21	10	11	10	9	2	0	1	0	0	0	1	1	0	14	7
1951	DET	AL	11	6	5	7	1	3	0	0	0	0	0	0	0	0	6	5
1952	BOS	AL	14	10	4	7	5	1	1	0	0	0	0	0	0	0	11	3
1953	BOS	AL	11	3	8	6	4	1	0	0	0	0	0	0	0	0	8	3
1954	NY	NL	1	1	0	0	0	1	0	0	0	0	0	0	0	1	1	0
1955	BAL	AL	6	1	5	2	2	2	0	0	0	0	0	0	0	0	3	3
	CLE	AL	2	2	0	0	1	1	0	0	0	0	0	0	0	1	0	2
	Total		8	3	5	2	3	3	0	0	0	0	0	0	0	1	3	5
1956	BAL	AL	1	0	1	1	0	0	0	0	0	0	0	0	0	0	1	0
Total			98	52	46	51	30	15	2	2	0	0	0	1	1	3	59	39

Rank among batters: 506 • *Top target (7 home runs)*: Eddie Lopat • *Number of pitchers victimized*: 66 • *Total ballparks homered in*: 11 • *First HR*: 08/15/1946 off Eddie Lopat • *Hit for Cycle*—vs CLE: 09/07/1950 • *All-Star HR*—1

Johnny Evers

JOHN JOSEPH EVERS
B: 07/21/1881 D: 03/28/1947
BL HOF

Year	Tm	Lg	Tot	H	A	Men-On 0	1	2	3	One-Game 2	3	4	LO	XN	IP	PH	RHP	LHP
1905	CHI	NL	1	0	1	1	0	0	0	0	0	0	0	0	0	0	1	0
1906	CHI	NL	1	1	0	0	1	0	0	0	0	0	0	0	1	0	0	1
1907	CHI	NL	2	0	2	1	0	1	0	0	0	0	0	0	2	0	2	0
1909	CHI	NL	1	0	1	1	0	0	0	0	0	0	0	0	0	0	1	0
1912	CHI	NL	1	1	0	1	0	0	0	0	0	0	0	0	1	0	1	0
1913	CHI	NL	3	1	2	1	1	1	0	0	0	0	0	0	2	0	3	0
1914	BOS	NL	1	0	1	1	0	0	0	0	0	0	0	0	1	0	1	0
1915	BOS	NL	1	0	1	0	1	0	0	0	0	0	0	0	0	0	1	0
1917	PHI	NL	1	0	1	0	0	1	0	0	0	0	0	0	0	0	1	0
Total			12	3	9	6	3	3	0	0	0	0	0	0	7	0	11	1

Rank among batters: 2,325 • *Total ballparks homered in*: 6 • *First HR*: 07/21/1905 off Chick Fraser

Bob Ewing

GEORGE LEMUEL EWING
B: 04/24/1873 D: 06/20/1947
BR

Year	Tm	Lg	Tot	H	A	Men-On 0	1	2	3	One-Game 2	3	4	LO	XN	IP	PH	RHP	LHP
1904	CIN	NL	1	1	0	0	0	1	0	0	0	0	0	0	1	0	1	0
1906	CIN	NL	1	1	0	1	0	0	0	0	0	0	0	0	1	0	1	0
1907	CIN	NL	1	1	0	0	1	0	0	0	0	0	0	0	1	0	1	0
Total			3	3	0	1	1	1	0	0	0	0	0	0	3	0	3	0

Rank among batters: 3,735 • *Total ballparks homered in*: 1 • *First HR*: 08/21/1904 off Jack Sutthoff

Year	Tm	Lg	Tot	H	A	Men-On 0	1	2	3	One-Game 2	3	4	LO	XN	IP	PH	RHP	LHP

Buck Ewing

WILLIAM EWING
B: 10/17/1859 D: 10/20/1906
BR HOF

Year	Tm	Lg	Tot	H	A	Men-On 0	1	2	3	One-Game 2	3	4	LO	XN	IP	PH	RHP	LHP
1882	TRO	NL	2	2	0	0	0	2	0	0	0	0	0	0	0	0	2	0
1883	NY	NL	10	8	2	6	1	0	0	3	0	0	4	0	1	0	10	0
1884	NY	NL	3	1	2	0	2	1	0	0	0	0	0	1	0	0	3	0
1885	NY	NL	6	1	5	4	2	0	0	1	0	0	0	0	0	0	6	0
1886	NY	NL	4	1	3	1	2	1	0	0	0	0	0	0	0	0	2	2
1887	NY	NL	6	3	3	3	3	0	0	1	0	0	0	0	0	0	4	2
1888	NY	NL	6	3	3	3	2	1	0	0	0	0	0	0	2	0	4	2
1889	NY	NL	4	1	3	1	2	0	1	0	0	0	0	0	0	0	4	0
1890	NY	PL	8	5	3	3	3	2	0	1	0	0	0	0	2	0	8	0
1892	NY	NL	8	4	4	3	4	1	0	0	0	0	0	0	1	0	7	1
1893	CLE	NL	6	1	5	1	3	2	0	1	0	0	0	0	1	0	6	0
1894	CLE	NL	2	0	2	2	0	0	0	0	0	0	0	0	0	0	2	0
1895	CIN	NL	5	2	3	3	2	0	0	0	0	0	0	0	1	0	4	0
1896	CIN	NL	1	0	1	1	0	0	0	0	0	0	0	0	0	0	1	0
Total			71	32	39	31	26	10	1	7	0	0	4	1	8	0	63	7

Rank among batters: 731 • *Top target (5 home runs)*: Fred Goldsmith, Charlie Buffinton • *Number of pitchers victimized*: 45 • *Total ballparks homered in*: 27 • *First HR*: 06/10/1882 off Blondie Purcell • *World Series HR*—1

John Ewing

JOHN EWING
B: 06/01/1863 D: 04/23/1895

Year	Tm	Lg	Tot	H	A	Men-On 0	1	2	3	One-Game 2	3	4	LO	XN	IP	PH	RHP	LHP
1890	NY	PL	2	2	0	0	2	0	0	0	0	0	0	0	0	0	2	0

Rank among batters: 4,129 • *Total ballparks homered in*: 1 • *First HR*: 07/09/1890 off Alex Ferson

Sam Ewing

SAMUEL JAMES EWING
B: 04/09/1949
BL

Year	Tm	Lg	Tot	H	A	Men-On 0	1	2	3	One-Game 2	3	4	LO	XN	IP	PH	RHP	LHP
1977	TOR	AL	4	2	2	2	2	0	0	0	0	0	0	0	0	0	4	0
1978	TOR	AL	2	1	1	1	1	0	0	0	0	0	0	0	0	1	1	1
Total			6	3	3	3	3	0	0	0	0	0	0	0	0	1	5	1

Rank among batters: 2,988 • *Total ballparks homered in*: 3 • *First HR*: 06/18/1977 off Jim Palmer

Jay Faatz

JAYSON S. FAATZ
B: 10/24/1860 D: 04/10/1923
BR

Year	Tm	Lg	Tot	H	A	Men-On 0	1	2	3	One-Game 2	3	4	LO	XN	IP	PH	RHP	LHP
1889	CLE	NL	2	0	2	1	0	1	0	0	0	0	0	0	0	0	2	0
1890	BUF	PL	1	0	1	0	0	1	0	0	0	0	0	0	0	0	1	0
Total			3	0	3	1	0	2	0	0	0	0	0	0	0	0	3	0

Rank among batters: 3,735 • *Total ballparks homered in*: 3 • *First HR*: 07/26/1889 off Harry Staley

Red Faber

URBAN CHARLES FABER
B: 09/06/1888 D: 09/25/1976
BB HOF

Year	Tm	Lg	Tot	H	A	Men-On 0	1	2	3	One-Game 2	3	4	LO	XN	IP	PH	RHP	LHP
1923	CHI	AL	1	0	1	1	0	0	0	0	0	0	0	0	0	0	0	1
1928	CHI	AL	1	0	1	1	0	0	0	0	0	0	0	0	0	0	1	0
1929	CHI	AL	1	0	1	0	1	0	0	0	0	0	0	0	0	0	0	1
Total			3	0	3	2	1	0	0	0	0	0	0	0	0	0	1	2

Rank among batters: 3,735 • *Total ballparks homered in*: 2 • *First HR*: 06/06/1923 off Herb Pennock

Jorge Fabregas

JORGE FABREGAS
B: 03/13/1970
BL

Year	Tm	Lg	Tot	H	A	Men-On 0	1	2	3	One-Game 2	3	4	LO	XN	IP	PH	RHP	LHP
1995	CAL	AL	1	1	0	1	0	0	0	0	0	0	0	0	0	0	1	0

Rank among batters: 4,707 • *Total ballparks homered in*: 1 • *First HR*: 06/18/1995 off Jason Bere

Bunny Fabrique

ALBERT LAVERNE FABRIQUE
B: 12/23/1887 D: 01/10/1960
BB

Year	Tm	Lg	Tot	H	A	Men-On 0	1	2	3	One-Game 2	3	4	LO	XN	IP	PH	RHP	LHP
1917	BRO	NL	1	0	1	1	0	0	0	0	0	0	0	0	0	0	1	0

Rank among batters: 4,707 • *Total ballparks homered in*: 1 • *First HR*: 05/02/1917 off Ferdie Schupp

Lenny Faedo

LEONARDO LAGO FAEDO
B: 05/13/1960
BR

Year	Tm	Lg	Tot	H	A	Men-On 0	1	2	3	One-Game 2	3	4	LO	XN	IP	PH	RHP	LHP
1982	MIN	AL	3	2	1	1	2	0	0	0	0	0	0	0	0	0	1	2
1983	MIN	AL	1	0	1	0	0	1	0	0	0	0	0	0	0	0	1	0
1984	MIN	AL	1	1	0	1	0	0	0	0	0	0	0	0	0	0	0	1
Total			5	3	2	2	2	1	0	0	0	0	0	0	0	0	2	3

Rank among batters: 3,191 • *Total ballparks homered in*: 3 • *First HR*: 07/19/1982 off Jerry Augustine

Bill Fahey

WILLIAM ROGER FAHEY
B: 06/14/1950
BL

Year	Tm	Lg	Tot	H	A	Men-On 0	1	2	3	One-Game 2	3	4	LO	XN	IP	PH	RHP	LHP
1972	TEX	AL	1	1	0	0	1	0	0	0	0	0	0	0	0	0	1	0
1976	TEX	AL	1	0	1	0	1	0	0	0	0	0	0	0	0	0	1	0
1979	SD	NL	3	3	0	2	1	0	0	0	0	0	0	0	0	0	3	0
1980	SD	NL	1	0	1	1	0	0	0	0	0	0	0	0	0	0	1	0
1981	DET	AL	1	1	0	0	1	0	0	0	0	0	0	0	0	0	0	1
Total			7	5	2	3	4	0	0	0	0	0	0	0	0	0	6	1

Rank among batters: 2,834 • *Total ballparks homered in*: 5 • *First HR*: 09/04/1972 off Roger Nelson

Ferris Fain

FERRIS ROY FAIN
B: 05/29/1921
BL

Year	Tm	Lg	Tot	H	A	Men-On 0	1	2	3	One-Game 2	3	4	LO	XN	IP	PH	RHP	LHP
1947	PHI	AL	7	1	6	3	3	0	1	0	0	0	0	0	1	0	6	1
1948	PHI	AL	7	1	6	4	2	1	0	0	0	0	0	0	0	0	5	2
1949	PHI	AL	3	1	2	0	1	1	1	0	0	0	0	0	0	0	0	3
1950	PHI	AL	10	7	3	7	1	2	0	0	0	0	0	0	0	0	8	2
1951	PHI	AL	6	2	4	3	1	2	0	0	0	0	0	0	0	0	4	2
1952	PHI	AL	2	1	1	1	1	0	0	0	0	0	0	0	0	0	2	0
1953	CHI	AL	6	3	3	4	0	2	0	0	0	0	0	0	0	0	3	3
1954	CHI	AL	5	2	3	3	1	0	1	0	0	0	0	0	1	0	4	1
1955	DET	AL	2	1	1	0	2	0	0	0	0	0	0	0	0	0	2	0
Total			48	19	29	25	12	8	3	0	0	0	0	0	2	0	34	14

Rank among batters: 1,024 • Top target (2 home runs): Steve Gromek, Cliff Fannin, Fred Sanford, Allie Reynolds, Art Houtteman • *Number of pitchers victimized*: 43 • *Total ballparks homered in*: 8 • *First HR*: 06/02/1947 off Cliff Fannin

Jim Fairey

JAMES BURKE FAIREY
B: 09/22/1944
BL

Year	Tm	Lg	Tot	H	A	Men-On 0	1	2	3	One-Game 2	3	4	LO	XN	IP	PH	RHP	LHP
1968	LA	NL	1	0	1	1	0	0	0	0	0	0	0	1	0	1	1	0
1969	MON	NL	1	1	0	0	0	1	0	0	0	0	0	0	0	0	1	0
1970	MON	NL	3	2	1	2	0	1	0	0	0	0	0	0	0	1	3	0
1971	MON	NL	1	1	0	0	1	0	0	0	0	0	0	0	0	0	1	0
1972	MON	NL	1	1	0	1	0	0	0	0	0	0	0	0	0	0	1	0
Total			7	5	2	4	1	2	0	0	0	0	0	1	0	2	7	0

Rank among batters: 2,834 • *Top target (2 home runs)*: Tom Seaver • *Number of pitchers victimized*: 6 • *Total ballparks homered in*: 3 • *First HR*: 06/20/1968 off Roy Face

Ron Fairly

RONALD RAY FAIRLY
B: 07/12/1938
BL

Year	Tm	Lg	Tot	H	A	Men-On 0	1	2	3	One-Game 2	3	4	LO	XN	IP	PH	RHP	LHP
1958	LA	NL	2	0	2	2	0	0	0	0	0	0	0	0	0	0	2	0
1959	LA	NL	4	3	1	4	0	0	0	0	0	0	1	0	0	0	4	0

Ron Fairly *continued*

Year	Tm	Lg	Tot	H	A	Men-On 0	1	2	3	One-Game 2	3	4	LO	XN	IP	PH	RHP	LHP
1960	LA	NL	1	1	0	1	0	0	0	0	0	0	0	0	0	0	1	0
1961	LA	NL	10	5	5	7	0	3	0	0	0	0	0	0	0	1	10	0
1962	LA	NL	14	2	12	7	5	2	0	0	0	0	0	0	0	0	9	5
1963	LA	NL	12	3	9	7	4	0	1	1	0	0	0	0	0	0	11	1
1964	LA	NL	10	4	6	4	4	2	0	1	0	0	0	0	0	0	8	2
1965	LA	NL	9	3	6	5	3	1	0	0	0	0	0	1	1	0	4	5
1966	LA	NL	14	5	9	6	7	1	0	1	0	0	0	0	0	0	12	2
1967	LA	NL	10	4	6	5	4	1	0	0	0	0	0	0	0	0	6	4
1968	LA	NL	4	1	3	3	0	0	1	0	0	0	0	0	0	0	4	0
1969	MON	NL	12	9	3	7	3	2	0	1	0	0	0	0	0	0	9	3
1970	MON	NL	15	10	5	7	4	2	2	1	0	0	0	0	0	0	11	4
1971	MON	NL	13	9	4	5	7	1	0	0	0	0	0	0	0	0	10	3
1972	MON	NL	17	11	6	11	4	2	0	0	0	0	0	0	0	0	16	1
1973	MON	NL	17	13	4	13	4	0	0	2	0	0	0	3	0	0	17	0
1974	MON	NL	12	6	6	6	3	1	2	0	0	0	0	0	0	0	9	3
1975	STL	NL	7	7	0	4	2	0	1	0	0	0	0	0	0	0	6	1
1976	OAK	AL	3	2	1	3	0	0	0	0	0	0	0	0	0	0	3	0
1977	TOR	AL	19	10	9	14	4	1	0	0	0	0	0	0	0	0	13	6
1978	CAL	AL	10	4	6	5	5	0	0	0	0	0	0	0	0	0	10	0
Total			215	112	103	126	63	19	7	7	0	0	1	4	1	1	175	40

Rank among batters: 158 • *Top target (5 home runs)*: Ken Holtzman • *Number of pitchers victimized*: 151 • *Total ballparks homered in*: 30 • *First HR*: 09/12/1958 off Ron Kline • *World Series HR*—2

Pete Falcone

PETER FALCONE
B: 10/01/1953
BL

Year	Tm	Lg	Tot	H	A	Men-On 0	1	2	3	One-Game 2	3	4	LO	XN	IP	PH	RHP	LHP
1981	NY	NL	1	0	1	1	0	0	0	0	0	0	0	0	0	0	0	1

Rank among batters: 4,707 • *Total ballparks homered in*: 1 • *First HR*: 09/29/1981 off Mark Davis

Bibb Falk

BIBB AUGUST FALK
B: 01/27/1899 D: 06/08/1989
BL

Year	Tm	Lg	Tot	H	A	Men-On 0	1	2	3	One-Game 2	3	4	LO	XN	IP	PH	RHP	LHP
1921	CHI	AL	5	3	2	2	2	0	1	0	0	0	0	1	0	0	4	1
1922	CHI	AL	12	3	9	8	3	0	1	1	0	0	0	0	1	0	10	2
1923	CHI	AL	5	1	4	3	1	1	0	0	0	0	0	0	0	1	5	0
1924	CHI	AL	6	2	4	2	3	0	1	1	0	0	0	1	0	0	6	0
1925	CHI	AL	4	0	4	2	1	1	0	0	0	0	0	0	0	0	3	1
1926	CHI	AL	8	1	7	3	3	2	0	0	0	0	0	1	0	0	3	5
1927	CHI	AL	9	2	7	6	3	0	0	0	0	0	0	1	0	0	6	3
1928	CHI	AL	1	0	1	0	0	1	0	0	0	0	0	0	0	0	1	0
1929	CLE	AL	14	8	6	7	4	3	0	0	0	0	0	0	0	0	12	2
1930	CLE	AL	4	1	3	3	1	0	0	0	0	0	0	0	0	1	4	0
1931	CLE	AL	2	2	0	2	0	0	0	0	0	0	0	0	0	1	2	0
Total			70	23	47	38	21	8	3	2	0	0	0	4	1	3	56	14

Rank among batters: 742 • *Top target (6 home runs)*: Elam Vangilder • *Number of pitchers victimized*: 49 • *Total ballparks homered in*: 9 • *First HR*: 05/01/1921 off Stan Coveleski

Cy Falkenberg

FREDERICK PETER FALKENBERG
B: 12/17/1880 D: 04/14/1961
BR

Year	Tm	Lg	Tot	H	A	Men-On 0	1	2	3	One-Game 2	3	4	LO	XN	IP	PH	RHP	LHP
1906	WAS	AL	1	1	0	0	0	0	1	0	0	0	0	0	1	0	1	0

Rank among batters: 4,707 • *Total ballparks homered in*: 1 • *First HR*: 07/18/1906 off Frank Owen

George Fallon

GEORGE DECATUR FALLON
B: 07/08/1914 D: 10/25/1994
BR

Year	Tm	Lg	Tot	H	A	Men-On 0	1	2	3	One-Game 2	3	4	LO	XN	IP	PH	RHP	LHP
1944	STL	NL	1	0	1	1	0	0	0	0	0	0	0	0	0	0	1	0

Rank among batters: 4,707 • *Total ballparks homered in*: 1 • *First HR*: 09/22/1944 off Nate Andrews

Carmen Fanzone

CARMEN DONALD FANZONE
B: 08/30/1943
BR

Year	Tm	Lg	Tot	H	A	Men-On 0	Men-On 1	Men-On 2	Men-On 3	One-Game 2	One-Game 3	One-Game 4	LO	XN	IP	PH	RHP	LHP
1971	CHI	NL	2	1	1	2	0	0	0	0	0	0	0	0	0	1	2	0
1972	CHI	NL	8	4	4	5	1	2	0	1	0	0	0	0	0	0	5	3
1973	CHI	NL	6	2	4	3	3	0	0	0	0	0	0	0	0	0	3	3
1974	CHI	NL	4	3	1	1	2	0	1	0	0	0	0	0	0	2	2	2
Total			20	10	10	11	6	2	1	1	0	0	0	0	0	3	12	8

Rank among batters: 1,810 • *Top target (2 home runs)*: Ken Forsch, Ken Brett • *Number of pitchers victimized*: 18 • *Total ballparks homered in*: 7 • *First HR*: 09/08/1971 off Steve Blass

Monty Fariss

MONTY TED FARISS
B: 10/13/1967
BR

Year	Tm	Lg	Tot	H	A	Men-On 0	Men-On 1	Men-On 2	Men-On 3	One-Game 2	One-Game 3	One-Game 4	LO	XN	IP	PH	RHP	LHP
1991	TEX	AL	1	1	0	1	0	0	0	0	0	0	0	0	0	0	0	1
1992	TEX	AL	3	0	3	1	2	0	0	0	0	0	0	1	0	0	1	2
Total			4	1	3	2	2	0	0	0	0	0	0	1	0	0	1	3

Rank among batters: 3,427 • *Total ballparks homered in*: 3 • *First HR*: 09/30/1991 off Bill Krueger

Bob Farley

ROBERT JACOB FARLEY
B: 11/15/1937
BL

Year	Tm	Lg	Tot	H	A	Men-On 0	Men-On 1	Men-On 2	Men-On 3	One-Game 2	One-Game 3	One-Game 4	LO	XN	IP	PH	RHP	LHP
1962	CHI	AL	1	0	1	0	1	0	0	0	0	0	0	0	0	0	1	0
	DET	AL	1	0	1	0	1	0	0	0	0	0	0	0	0	0	1	0
	Total		2	0	2	1	1	0	0	0	0	0	0	0	0	0	2	0
Total			2	0	2	1	1	0	0	0	0	0	0	0	0	0	2	0

Rank among batters: 4,129 • *Total ballparks homered in*: 2 • *First HR*: 05/31/1962 off Paul Foytack

Sid Farrar

SIDNEY DOUGLAS FARRAR
B: 08/10/1859 D: 05/07/1935

Year	Tm	Lg	Tot	H	A	Men-On 0	Men-On 1	Men-On 2	Men-On 3	One-Game 2	One-Game 3	One-Game 4	LO	XN	IP	PH	RHP	LHP
1884	PHI	NL	1	0	1	1	0	0	0	0	0	0	0	0	1	0	1	0
1885	PHI	NL	3	0	3	1	2	0	0	0	0	0	0	0	1	0	3	0
1886	PHI	NL	5	2	3	2	2	0	1	0	0	0	0	0	0	0	5	0
1887	PHI	NL	4	1	3	1	1	2	0	0	0	0	0	0	0	0	2	2
1888	PHI	NL	1	0	1	0	1	0	0	0	0	0	0	0	0	0	1	0
1889	PHI	NL	3	1	2	3	0	0	0	0	0	0	0	0	1	0	2	1
1890	PHI	PL	1	0	1	1	0	0	0	0	0	0	0	0	0	0	1	0
Total			18	4	14	9	6	2	1	0	0	0	0	0	3	0	15	3

Rank among batters: 1,914 • *Top target (2 home runs)*: Henry Boyle, Mark Baldwin, Charley Radbourn • *Number of pitchers victimized*: 15 • *Total ballparks homered in*: 8 • *First HR*: 09/16/1884 off Jim Galvin

Doc Farrell

EDWARD STEPHEN FARRELL
B: 12/26/1901 D: 12/20/1966
BR

Year	Tm	Lg	Tot	H	A	Men-On 0	Men-On 1	Men-On 2	Men-On 3	One-Game 2	One-Game 3	One-Game 4	LO	XN	IP	PH	RHP	LHP
1926	NY	NL	2	2	0	0	0	1	1	0	0	0	0	0	0	0	1	1
1927	NY	NL	3	3	0	1	1	1	0	0	0	0	0	0	0	0	3	0
	BOS	NL	1	0	1	0	1	0	0	0	0	0	0	0	0	0	0	1
	Total		4	3	1	1	2	1	0	0	0	0	0	0	0	0	3	1
1928	BOS	NL	3	0	3	1	1	1	0	0	0	0	0	0	0	0	3	0
1930	CHI	NL	1	0	1	0	1	0	0	0	0	0	0	0	0	0	1	0
Total			10	5	5	2	4	3	1	0	0	0	0	0	0	0	8	2

Rank among batters: 2,500 • *Total ballparks homered in*: 3 • *First HR*: 05/25/1926 off Jess Barnes

Duke Farrell

CHARLES ANDREW FARRELL
B: 08/31/1866 D: 02/15/1925
BB

Year	Tm	Lg	Tot	H	A	Men-On 0	Men-On 1	Men-On 2	Men-On 3	One-Game 2	One-Game 3	One-Game 4	LO	XN	IP	PH	RHP	LHP
1888	CHI	NL	3	1	2	1	2	0	0	0	0	0	1	0	0	0	3	0
1889	CHI	NL	11	8	3	3	5	3	0	0	0	0	0	0	4	0	11	0
1890	CHI	PL	2	1	1	1	1	0	0	0	0	0	0	0	0	0	2	0

Duke Farrell *continued*

Year	Tm	Lg	Tot	H	A	Men-On 0	1	2	3	One-Game 2	3	4	LO	XN	IP	PH	RHP	LHP
1891	BOS	AA	12	7	5	3	6	2	1	1	0	0	0	0	0	0	7	4
1892	PIT	NL	8	8	0	2	4	2	0	1	0	0	0	1	3	0	3	5
1893	WAS	NL	4	2	2	1	1	2	0	0	0	0	0	1	0	0	4	0
1894	NY	NL	4	2	2	0	2	0	2	0	0	0	0	0	0	0	3	0
1895	NY	NL	1	1	0	1	0	0	0	0	0	0	0	1	0	0	1	0
1896	NY	NL	1	0	1	0	1	0	0	0	0	0	0	0	0	0	1	0
	WAS	NL	1	1	0	0	1	0	0	0	0	0	0	0	1	0	1	0
	Total		2	1	1	0	2	0	0	0	0	0	0	0	1	0	2	0
1898	WAS	NL	1	1	0	1	0	0	0	0	0	0	0	0	1	0	1	0
1899	BRO	NL	2	1	1	0	2	0	0	0	0	0	0	1	0	0	2	0
1901	BRO	NL	1	0	1	1	0	0	0	0	0	0	0	0	0	0	1	0
Total			51	33	18	14	25	9	3	2	0	0	1	4	9	0	40	8

Rank among batters: 979 • Top target (3 home runs): Mickey Welch, Jack Stivetts, Kid Gleason, Harry Staley • *Number of pitchers victimized*: 38 • *Total ballparks homered in*: 16 • *First HR*: 04/23/1888 off Lev Shreve

Jack Farrell

JOHN A. FARRELL
B: 07/05/1857 D: 02/10/1914
BR

Year	Tm	Lg	Tot	H	A	Men-On 0	1	2	3	One-Game 2	3	4	LO	XN	IP	PH	RHP	LHP
1879	SYR	NL	1	0	1	1	0	0	0	0	0	0	0	0	0	0	1	0
1880	PRO	NL	3	2	1	2	1	0	0	0	0	0	0	0	1	0	1	2
1881	PRO	NL	5	2	3	2	2	1	0	0	0	0	0	0	0	0	5	0
1882	PRO	NL	2	2	0	1	1	0	0	0	0	0	0	0	0	0	1	1
1883	PRO	NL	3	1	2	2	1	0	0	0	0	0	0	1	0	0	2	1
1884	PRO	NL	1	0	1	1	0	0	0	0	0	0	0	0	1	0	1	0
1885	PRO	NL	1	1	0	1	0	0	0	0	0	0	0	0	0	0	1	0
1886	WAS	NL	2	0	2	0	1	1	0	0	0	0	0	0	0	0	2	0
1888	BAL	AA	4	1	3	1	2	1	0	0	0	0	0	0	2	0	3	1
1889	BAL	AA	1	0	1	0	1	0	0	0	0	0	0	0	0	0	1	0
Total			23	9	14	11	9	3	0	0	0	0	0	1	4	0	18	5

Rank among batters: 1,686 • *Top target (2 home runs)*: Lee Richmond, Edward Nolan, Larry Corcoran • *Number of pitchers victimized*: 20 • *Total ballparks homered in*: 12 • *First HR*: 08/20/1879 off Bobby Mathews

Joe Farrell

JOSEPH F. FARRELL
B: 1857 D: 04/18/1893
BR

Year	Tm	Lg	Tot	H	A	Men-On 0	1	2	3	One-Game 2	3	4	LO	XN	IP	PH	RHP	LHP
1882	DET	NL	1	0	1	0	1	0	0	0	0	0	0	0	0	0	1	0
1884	DET	NL	3	1	2	1	2	0	0	0	0	0	0	0	0	0	3	0
1886	BAL	AA	1	0	1	0	1	0	0	0	0	0	0	0	0	0	0	1
Total			5	1	4	1	4	0	0	0	0	0	0	0	0	0	4	1

Rank among batters: 3,191 • *Total ballparks homered in*: 5 • *First HR*: 07/14/1882 off Larry Corcoran

John Farrell

JOHN SEBASTIAN FARRELL
B: 12/04/1876 D: 05/14/1921
BR

Year	Tm	Lg	Tot	H	A	Men-On 0	1	2	3	One-Game 2	3	4	LO	XN	IP	PH	RHP	LHP
1901	WAS	AL	3	0	3	2	1	0	0	0	0	0	0	0	0	0	1	2
1903	STL	NL	1	1	0	0	1	0	0	0	0	0	0	0	1	0	1	0
Total			4	1	3	2	2	0	0	0	0	0	0	0	1	0	2	2

Rank among batters: 3,427 • *Total ballparks homered in*: 4 • *First HR*: 07/12/1901 off Jerry Nops

Turk Farrell

RICHARD JOSEPH FARRELL
B: 04/08/1934 D: 06/10/1977
BR

Year	Tm	Lg	Tot	H	A	Men-On 0	1	2	3	One-Game 2	3	4	LO	XN	IP	PH	RHP	LHP
1957	PHI	NL	1	1	0	1	0	0	0	0	0	0	0	0	0	0	1	0
1962	HOU	NL	2	2	0	2	0	0	0	0	0	0	0	0	0	0	2	0
1966	HOU	NL	1	1	0	0	0	1	0	0	0	0	0	0	0	0	1	0
Total			4	4	0	3	0	1	0	0	0	0	0	0	0	0	4	0

Rank among batters: 3,427 • *Total ballparks homered in*: 3 • *First HR*: 06/02/1957 off Don Newcombe

Ernie Fazio

ERNEST JOSEPH FAZIO
B: 01/25/1942
BR

Year	Tm	Lg	Tot	H	A	Men-On 0	1	2	3	One-Game 2	3	4	LO	XN	IP	PH	RHP	LHP
1963	HOU	NL	2	1	1	2	0	0	0	0	0	0	0	0	0	0	0	2

Rank among batters: 4,129 • *Total ballparks homered in*: 2 • *First HR*: 07/06/1963 off Denny Lemaster

Mike Felder

MICHAEL OTIS FELDER
B: 11/18/1961
BB

Year	Tm	Lg	Tot	H	A	Men-On 0	1	2	3	One-Game 2	3	4	LO	XN	IP	PH	RHP	LHP
1986	MIL	AL	1	1	0	0	1	0	0	0	0	0	0	0	0	0	1	0
1987	MIL	AL	2	1	1	1	1	0	0	0	0	0	0	0	0	0	2	0
1989	MIL	AL	3	1	2	2	1	0	0	0	0	0	1	0	1	0	3	0
1990	MIL	AL	3	1	2	3	0	0	0	0	0	0	1	0	0	0	0	3
1992	SF	NL	4	1	3	2	1	1	0	0	0	0	2	1	0	0	3	1
1993	SEA	AL	1	0	1	0	1	0	0	0	0	0	0	0	0	0	1	0
Total			14	5	9	8	5	1	0	0	0	0	4	1	1	0	10	4

Rank among batters: 2,169 • *Total ballparks homered in*: 9 • *First HR*: 06/18/1986 off Jim Clancy

Harry Feldman

HARRY FELDMAN
B: 11/10/1919 D: 03/16/1962
BR

Year	Tm	Lg	Tot	H	A	Men-On 0	1	2	3	One-Game 2	3	4	LO	XN	IP	PH	RHP	LHP
1942	NY	NL	1	0	1	1	0	0	0	0	0	0	0	0	0	0	1	0
1945	NY	NL	1	1	0	1	0	0	0	0	0	0	0	0	0	0	1	0
Total			2	1	1	2	0	0	0	0	0	0	0	0	0	0	2	0

Rank among batters: 4,129 • *Total ballparks homered in*: 2 • *First HR*: 05/01/1942 off Jake Mooty

Gus Felix

AUGUST GUENTHER FELIX
B: 05/24/1895 D: 05/12/1960
BR

Year	Tm	Lg	Tot	H	A	Men-On 0	1	2	3	One-Game 2	3	4	LO	XN	IP	PH	RHP	LHP
1923	BOS	NL	6	2	4	3	3	0	0	0	0	0	0	0	3	0	5	1
1924	BOS	NL	1	1	0	1	0	0	0	0	0	0	1	0	1	0	0	1
1925	BOS	NL	2	0	2	1	1	0	0	0	0	0	0	0	0	0	2	0
1926	BRO	NL	3	2	1	2	1	0	0	0	0	0	0	0	0	0	3	0
Total			12	5	7	7	5	0	0	0	0	0	1	0	4	0	10	2

Rank among batters: 2,325 • *Total ballparks homered in*: 5 • *First HR*: 04/21/1923 off Bill Hubbell

Junior Felix

JUNIOR FRANCISCO (SANCHEZ) FELIX
B: 10/03/1967
BB

Year	Tm	Lg	Tot	H	A	Men-On 0	1	2	3	One-Game 2	3	4	LO	XN	IP	PH	RHP	LHP
1989	TOR	AL	9	4	5	4	4	0	1	0	0	0	0	1	1	0	7	2
1990	TOR	AL	15	7	8	9	4	2	0	0	0	0	0	0	0	0	6	9
1991	CAL	AL	2	2	0	2	0	0	0	0	0	0	0	1	0	0	2	0
1992	CAL	AL	9	5	4	7	0	2	0	0	0	0	0	0	0	0	6	3
1993	FLO	NL	7	3	4	2	2	2	1	0	0	0	0	0	0	0	3	4
1994	DET	AL	13	4	9	7	4	2	0	0	0	0	0	0	0	0	10	3
Total			55	25	30	31	14	8	2	0	0	0	0	2	1	0	34	21

Rank among batters: 926 • Top target (2 home runs): Curt Young, Randy Johnson, Jeff Shaw, Bruce Ruffin • *Number of pitchers victimized*: 51 • *Total ballparks homered in*: 17 • *First HR*: 05/04/1989 off Kirk McCaskill • *Hit HR on first major league pitch—vs CAL*: 05/04/1989

Bob Feller

ROBERT WILLIAM ANDREW FELLER
B: 11/03/1918
BR HOF

Year	Tm	Lg	Tot	H	A	Men-On 0	1	2	3	One-Game 2	3	4	LO	XN	IP	PH	RHP	LHP
1940	CLE	AL	2	0	2	2	0	0	0	0	0	0	0	0	0	0	1	1
1941	CLE	AL	1	1	0	0	0	1	0	0	0	0	0	0	0	0	1	0
1949	CLE	AL	2	1	1	2	0	0	0	0	0	0	0	0	0	0	0	2
1950	CLE	AL	2	1	1	1	0	1	0	0	0	0	0	0	0	0	1	1
1952	CLE	AL	1	1	0	0	1	0	0	0	0	0	0	0	0	0	1	0
Total			8	4	4	5	1	2	0	0	0	0	0	0	0	0	4	4

Rank among batters: 2,703 • *Total ballparks homered in*: 4 • *First HR*: 05/24/1940 off Elden Auker

Year	Tm	Lg	Tot	H	A	Men-On 0	1	2	3	One-Game 2	3	4	LO	XN	IP	PH	RHP	LHP

Happy Felsch

OSCAR EMIL FELSCH
B: 08/22/1891 D: 08/17/1964
BR

Year	Tm	Lg	Tot	H	A	Men-On 0	1	2	3	One-Game 2	3	4	LO	XN	IP	PH	RHP	LHP
1915	CHI	AL	3	2	1	1	1	0	1	0	0	0	0	0	0	0	2	1
1916	CHI	AL	7	5	2	3	3	0	1	0	0	0	0	1	1	0	4	3
1917	CHI	AL	6	3	3	2	2	2	0	0	0	0	0	0	0	0	6	0
1918	CHI	AL	1	1	0	1	0	0	0	0	0	0	0	0	0	0	0	1
1919	CHI	AL	7	1	6	2	4	1	0	0	0	0	0	0	0	0	6	1
1920	CHI	AL	14	6	8	8	5	0	1	0	0	0	0	1	1	0	11	3
Total			38	18	20	17	15	3	3	0	0	0	0	2	2	0	29	9

Rank among batters: 1,225 • *Top target (3 home runs)*: Allen Russell, Joe Bush • *Number of pitchers victimized*: 32 • *Total ballparks homered in*: 7 • *First HR*: 06/18/1915 off Joe Bush • *World Series HR*—1

John Felske

JOHN FREDERICK FELSKE
B: 05/30/1942
BR

Year	Tm	Lg	Tot	H	A	Men-On 0	1	2	3	One-Game 2	3	4	LO	XN	IP	PH	RHP	LHP
1972	MIL	AL	1	1	0	0	1	0	0	0	0	0	0	0	0	0	1	0

Rank among batters: 4,707 • *Total ballparks homered in*: 1 • *First HR*: 06/01/1972 off Lindy McDaniel

Frank Fennelly

FRANCIS JOHN FENNELLY
B: 02/18/1860 D: 08/04/1920
BR

Year	Tm	Lg	Tot	H	A	Men-On 0	1	2	3	One-Game 2	3	4	LO	XN	IP	PH	RHP	LHP
1884	WAS	AA	2	1	1	1	0	1	0	0	0	0	1	0	0	0	2	0
	CIN	AA	2	2	0	0	1	1	0	0	0	0	0	0	0	0	2	0
	Total		4	3	1	2	1	1	0	0	0	0	1	0	0	0	4	0
1885	CIN	AA	10	6	4	3	6	1	0	1	0	0	0	0	0	0	6	1
1886	CIN	AA	6	4	2	3	2	1	0	0	0	0	0	0	2	0	3	1
1887	CIN	AA	8	6	2	3	3	2	0	0	0	0	0	0	3	0	5	2
1888	CIN	AA	2	1	1	1	1	0	0	0	0	0	0	0	0	0	2	0
	PHI	AA	1	0	1	0	1	0	0	0	0	0	0	0	1	0	1	0
	Total		3	1	2	1	2	0	0	0	0	0	0	0	1	0	3	0
1889	PHI	AA	1	1	0	0	1	0	0	0	0	0	0	0	0	0	0	1
1890	BRO	AA	2	1	1	2	0	0	0	0	0	0	0	0	0	0	1	1
Total			34	22	12	14	15	5	0	1	0	0	1	0	6	0	22	6

Rank among batters: 1,315 • *Top target (3 home runs)*: Jack Lynch • *Number of pitchers victimized*: 26 • *Total ballparks homered in*: 12 • *First HR*: 05/12/1884 off Jack Lynch

Bob Ferguson

ROBERT VAVASOUR FERGUSON
B: 01/31/1845 D: 05/03/1894
BB

Year	Tm	Lg	Tot	H	A	Men-On 0	1	2	3	One-Game 2	3	4	LO	XN	IP	PH	RHP	LHP
1881	TRO	NL	1	1	0	1	0	0	0	0	0	0	0	0	0	0	1	0

Rank among batters: 4,707 • *Total ballparks homered in*: 1 • *First HR*: 09/16/1881 off Edward Nolan

Charlie Ferguson

CHARLES J. FERGUSON
B: 04/17/1863 D: 04/29/1888
BB

Year	Tm	Lg	Tot	H	A	Men-On 0	1	2	3	One-Game 2	3	4	LO	XN	IP	PH	RHP	LHP
1885	PHI	NL	1	1	0	0	1	0	0	0	0	0	0	0	0	0	1	0
1886	PHI	NL	2	2	0	1	0	1	0	0	0	0	0	0	0	0	2	0
1887	PHI	NL	3	3	0	1	2	0	0	0	0	0	0	0	1	0	3	0
Total			6	6	0	2	3	1	0	0	0	0	0	0	1	0	6	0

Rank among batters: 2,988 • *Top target (2 home runs)*: Bill Stemmeyer • *Number of pitchers victimized*: 5 • *Total ballparks homered in*: 2 • *First HR*: 05/19/1885 off Larry Corcoran

George Ferguson

GEORGE CECIL FERGUSON
B: 08/19/1886 D: 09/05/1943
BR

Year	Tm	Lg	Tot	H	A	Men-On 0	1	2	3	One-Game 2	3	4	LO	XN	IP	PH	RHP	LHP
1910	BOS	NL	1	1	0	0	0	0	1	0	0	0	0	0	0	0	1	0

Rank among batters: 4,707 • *Total ballparks homered in*: 1 • *First HR*: 09/22/1910 off Jack Rowan

Joe Ferguson

JOSEPH VANCE FERGUSON
B: 09/19/1946
BR

Year	Tm	Lg	Tot	H	A	Men-On 0	1	2	3	One-Game 2	3	4	LO	XN	IP	PH	RHP	LHP
1971	LA	NL	2	0	2	2	0	0	0	0	0	0	0	0	0	0	0	2
1972	LA	NL	1	1	0	0	1	0	0	0	0	0	0	0	0	0	0	1
1973	LA	NL	25	13	12	14	8	3	0	2	0	0	0	1	0	1	15	10
1974	LA	NL	16	10	6	8	7	1	0	2	0	0	0	1	0	0	11	5
1975	LA	NL	5	3	2	4	1	0	0	1	0	0	0	0	0	0	4	1
1976	LA	NL	6	1	5	3	2	1	0	0	0	0	0	0	0	0	3	3
	STL	NL	4	1	3	3	0	0	1	0	0	0	0	0	0	1	3	1
	Total		10	2	8	6	2	1	1	0	0	0	0	0	0	1	6	4
1977	HOU	NL	16	6	10	11	3	2	0	1	0	0	0	3	0	0	12	4
1978	HOU	NL	7	2	5	3	3	1	0	0	0	0	0	0	0	0	4	3
	LA	NL	7	4	3	3	1	3	0	0	0	0	0	0	0	0	5	2
	Total		14	6	8	6	4	4	0	0	0	0	0	0	0	0	9	5
1979	LA	NL	20	16	4	13	4	2	1	2	0	0	0	0	1	0	12	8
1980	LA	NL	9	8	1	6	2	1	0	1	0	0	0	3	0	1	7	2
1981	CAL	AL	1	1	0	1	0	0	0	0	0	0	0	0	0	0	0	1
1982	CAL	AL	3	1	2	3	0	0	0	0	0	0	0	0	0	0	0	3
Total			122	67	55	74	32	14	2	9	0	0	0	8	1	3	76	46

Rank among batters: 377 • Top target (3 home runs): Steve Carlton, Phil Niekro, Elias Sosa, Ken Forsch • *Number of pitchers victimized*: 94 • *Total ballparks homered in*: 16 • *First HR*: 07/18/1971 off Luke Walker • *World Series HR*—1

Felix Fermin

FELIX JOSE (MINAYA) FERMIN
B: 10/09/1963
BR

Year	Tm	Lg	Tot	H	A	Men-On 0	1	2	3	One-Game 2	3	4	LO	XN	IP	PH	RHP	LHP
1990	CLE	AL	1	1	0	1	0	0	0	0	0	0	0	0	0	0	1	0
1993	CLE	AL	2	0	2	1	1	0	0	0	0	0	0	0	0	0	1	1
1994	SEA	AL	1	0	1	1	0	0	0	0	0	0	0	0	0	0	1	0
Total			4	1	3	3	1	0	0	0	0	0	0	0	0	0	3	1

Rank among batters: 3,427 • *Total ballparks homered in*: 4 • *First HR*: 04/22/1990 off Donn Pall

Chico Fernandez

HUMBERTO (PEREZ) FERNANDEZ
B: 03/02/1932
BR

Year	Tm	Lg	Tot	H	A	Men-On 0	1	2	3	One-Game 2	3	4	LO	XN	IP	PH	RHP	LHP
1956	BRO	NL	1	1	0	0	0	0	1	0	0	0	0	0	0	0	0	1
1957	PHI	NL	5	4	1	3	1	1	0	0	0	0	0	0	1	0	4	1
1958	PHI	NL	6	4	2	2	3	1	0	0	0	0	0	0	0	0	5	1
1960	DET	AL	4	1	3	3	1	0	0	0	0	0	0	0	0	0	3	1
1961	DET	AL	3	3	0	3	0	0	0	0	0	0	0	0	0	0	2	1
1962	DET	AL	20	13	7	13	5	2	0	0	0	0	0	0	0	0	15	5
1963	NY	NL	1	0	1	0	1	0	0	0	0	0	0	0	0	0	0	1
Total			40	26	14	24	11	4	1	0	0	0	0	0	1	0	29	11

Rank among batters: 1,181 • *Top target (2 home runs)*: Milt Pappas, Eddie Fisher, Jim Kaat • *Number of pitchers victimized*: 37 • *Total ballparks homered in*: 13 • *First HR*: 08/04/1956 off Don Liddle

Frank Fernandez

FRANK FERNANDEZ
B: 04/16/1943
BR

Year	Tm	Lg	Tot	H	A	Men-On 0	1	2	3	One-Game 2	3	4	LO	XN	IP	PH	RHP	LHP
1967	NY	AL	1	1	0	1	0	0	0	0	0	0	0	0	0	0	1	0
1968	NY	AL	7	5	2	3	1	2	1	0	0	0	0	0	0	0	0	7
1969	NY	AL	12	6	6	6	4	1	1	1	0	0	0	1	0	0	6	6
1970	OAK	AL	15	8	7	9	3	2	1	0	0	0	0	0	0	3	5	10
1971	CHI	NL	4	2	2	4	0	0	0	0	0	0	0	0	0	0	2	2
Total			39	22	17	23	8	5	3	1	0	0	0	1	0	3	14	25

Rank among batters: 1,204 • *Top target (3 home runs)*: Dick Ellsworth • *Number of pitchers victimized*: 32 • *Total ballparks homered in*: 14 • *First HR*: 10/01/1967 off Catfish Hunter

Nanny Fernandez

FROILAN FERNANDEZ
B: 10/25/1918
BR

Year	Tm	Lg	Tot	H	A	Men-On 0	1	2	3	One-Game 2	3	4	LO	XN	IP	PH	RHP	LHP
1942	BOS	NL	6	4	2	4	2	0	0	0	0	0	0	1	0	0	5	1

Nanny Fernandez *continued*

Year	Tm	Lg	Tot	H	A	Men-On 0	1	2	3	One-Game 2	3	4	LO	XN	IP	PH	RHP	LHP
1946	BOS	NL	2	1	1	1	1	0	0	0	0	0	0	0	0	1	1	1
1947	BOS	NL	2	2	0	2	0	0	0	0	0	0	0	0	0	0	1	1
1950	PIT	NL	6	6	0	3	1	2	0	1	0	0	0	0	0	0	2	4
Total			16	13	3	10	4	2	0	1	0	0	0	1	0	1	9	7

Rank among batters: 2,029 • *Top target (3 home runs)*: Al Brazle • *Number of pitchers victimized*: 14 • *Total ballparks homered in*: 4 • *First HR*: 04/17/1942 off Hal Schumacher

Sid Fernandez

CHARLES SIDNEY FERNANDEZ
B: 10/12/1962
BL

Year	Tm	Lg	Tot	H	A	Men-On 0	1	2	3	One-Game 2	3	4	LO	XN	IP	PH	RHP	LHP
1989	NY	NL	1	0	1	1	0	0	0	0	0	0	0	0	0	0	1	0

Rank among batters: 4,707 • *Total ballparks homered in*: 1 • *First HR*: 09/21/1989 off Dan Quisenberry

Tony Fernandez

OCTAVIO ANTONIO (CASTRO) FERNANDEZ
B: 06/30/1962
BB

Year	Tm	Lg	Tot	H	A	Men-On 0	1	2	3	One-Game 2	3	4	LO	XN	IP	PH	RHP	LHP
1984	TOR	AL	3	1	2	2	1	0	0	0	0	0	0	0	1	0	3	0
1985	TOR	AL	2	1	1	0	1	1	0	0	0	0	0	0	0	0	2	0
1986	TOR	AL	10	4	6	5	5	0	0	0	0	0	2	0	0	0	5	5
1987	TOR	AL	5	1	4	5	0	0	0	0	0	0	0	0	0	0	3	2
1988	TOR	AL	5	3	2	4	1	0	0	0	0	0	1	1	0	0	2	3
1989	TOR	AL	11	2	9	6	3	1	1	1	0	0	1	0	0	0	9	2
1990	TOR	AL	4	2	2	1	1	1	1	0	0	0	1	0	0	0	3	1
1991	SD	NL	4	1	3	3	0	1	0	0	0	0	0	0	0	0	2	2
1992	SD	NL	4	3	1	3	0	1	0	0	0	0	1	0	0	0	3	1
1993	NY	NL	1	0	1	1	0	0	0	0	0	0	0	0	0	0	1	0
	TOR	AL	4	1	3	2	0	2	0	0	0	0	0	0	0	0	4	0
	Total		5	1	4	3	0	2	0	0	0	0	0	0	0	0	5	0
1994	CIN	NL	8	3	5	4	1	3	0	0	0	0	0	0	0	1	5	3
1995	NY	AL	5	3	2	3	1	1	0	0	0	0	1	0	0	0	3	2
Total			66	25	41	39	14	11	2	1	0	0	7	1	1	1	45	21

Rank among batters: 786 • *Top target (3 home runs)*: Kirk McCaskill • *Number of pitchers victimized*: 63 • *Total ballparks homered in*: 21 • *First HR*: 07/19/1984 off Roy Thomas • *Hit for Cycle*—vs OAK: 09/03/1995

Al Ferrara

ALFRED JOHN FERRARA
B: 12/22/1939
BR

Year	Tm	Lg	Tot	H	A	Men-On 0	1	2	3	One-Game 2	3	4	LO	XN	IP	PH	RHP	LHP
1963	LA	NL	1	0	1	1	0	0	0	0	0	0	0	0	0	0	1	0
1965	LA	NL	1	1	0	0	0	1	0	0	0	0	0	0	0	1	0	1
1966	LA	NL	5	0	5	4	0	1	0	1	0	0	0	1	1	0	2	3
1967	LA	NL	16	9	7	12	3	1	0	1	0	0	0	0	0	0	6	10
1969	SD	NL	14	7	7	7	4	2	1	1	0	0	0	0	0	0	10	4
1970	SD	NL	13	3	10	7	5	1	0	1	0	0	0	0	0	2	12	1
1971	CIN	NL	1	0	1	0	1	0	0	0	0	0	0	0	0	1	0	1
Total			51	20	31	31	13	6	1	4	0	0	0	1	1	4	31	20

Rank among batters: 979 • *Top target (3 home runs)*: Bob Hendley • *Number of pitchers victimized*: 42 • *Total ballparks homered in*: 11 • *First HR*: 08/08/1963 off Bob Buhl

Don Ferrarese

DONALD HUGH FERRARESE
B: 06/19/1929
BR

Year	Tm	Lg	Tot	H	A	Men-On 0	1	2	3	One-Game 2	3	4	LO	XN	IP	PH	RHP	LHP
1962	STL	NL	1	0	1	0	1	0	0	0	0	0	0	0	0	0	1	0

Rank among batters: 4,707 • *Total ballparks homered in*: 1 • *First HR*: 06/22/1962 off Jim Owens

Mike Ferraro

MICHAEL DENNIS FERRARO
B: 08/18/1944
BR

Year	Tm	Lg	Tot	H	A	Men-On 0	1	2	3	One-Game 2	3	4	LO	XN	IP	PH	RHP	LHP
1972	MIL	AL	2	1	1	1	1	0	0	0	0	0	0	1	0	0	1	1

Year	Tm	Lg	Tot	H	A	Men-On 0	Men-On 1	Men-On 2	Men-On 3	One-Game 2	One-Game 3	One-Game 4	LO	XN	IP	PH	RHP	LHP

Mike Ferraro *continued*

Rank among batters: 4,129 • *Total ballparks homered in*: 2 • *First HR*: 05/13/1972 off Dave LaRoche

Rick Ferrell

RICHARD BENJAMIN FERRELL
B: 10/12/1905 D: 07/27/1995
BR HOF

Year	Tm	Lg	Tot	H	A	0	1	2	3	2	3	4	LO	XN	IP	PH	RHP	LHP
1930	STL	AL	1	1	0	0	1	0	0	0	0	0	0	0	0	0	1	0
1931	STL	AL	3	1	2	2	1	0	0	0	0	0	0	0	0	0	0	3
1932	STL	AL	2	2	0	2	0	0	0	0	0	0	0	0	0	0	1	1
1933	STL	AL	1	1	0	1	0	0	0	0	0	0	0	0	0	0	0	1
	BOS	AL	3	2	1	1	1	1	0	0	0	0	0	0	0	0	2	1
	Total		4	3	1	2	1	1	0	0	0	0	0	0	0	0	2	2
1934	BOS	AL	1	0	1	1	0	0	0	0	0	0	0	0	0	0	1	0
1935	BOS	AL	3	2	1	3	0	0	0	0	0	0	0	0	0	0	2	1
1936	BOS	AL	8	3	5	8	0	0	0	0	0	0	0	0	1	0	8	0
1937	BOS	AL	1	0	1	1	0	0	0	0	0	0	0	0	0	0	1	0
	WAS	AL	1	0	1	0	1	0	0	0	0	0	0	0	0	0	1	0
	Total		2	0	2	1	1	0	0	0	0	0	0	0	0	0	2	0
1938	WAS	AL	1	1	0	0	1	0	0	0	0	0	0	0	1	0	1	0
1941	STL	AL	2	0	2	2	0	0	0	0	0	0	0	0	0	0	2	0
1945	WAS	AL	1	0	1	1	0	0	0	0	0	0	0	0	0	0	1	0
Total			28	13	15	22	5	1	0	0	0	0	0	0	2	0	21	7

Rank among batters: 1,500 • *Top target (3 home runs)*: Lefty Gomez • *Number of pitchers victimized*: 26 • *Total ballparks homered in*: 7 • *First HR*: 06/14/1930 off Firpo Marberry

Wes Ferrell

WESLEY CHEEK FERRELL
B: 02/02/1908 D: 12/09/1976
BR

Year	Tm	Lg	Tot	H	A	0	1	2	3	2	3	4	LO	XN	IP	PH	RHP	LHP
1929	CLE	AL	1	1	0	0	1	0	0	0	0	0	0	0	0	0	1	0
1931	CLE	AL	9	4	5	4	3	2	0	1	0	0	0	0	0	0	8	1
1932	CLE	AL	2	0	2	1	1	0	0	0	0	0	0	0	0	0	2	0
1933	CLE	AL	7	3	4	4	3	0	0	0	0	0	0	0	0	0	7	0
1934	BOS	AL	4	2	2	3	0	1	0	2	0	0	0	1	0	0	4	0
1935	BOS	AL	7	3	4	4	1	2	0	1	0	0	0	0	0	1	7	0
1936	BOS	AL	5	3	2	1	3	0	1	1	0	0	0	0	1	0	4	1
1937	BOS	AL	1	1	0	0	1	0	0	0	0	0	0	0	0	0	1	0
1938	WAS	AL	1	0	1	1	0	0	0	0	0	0	0	0	0	0	1	0
1941	BOS	NL	1	0	1	1	0	0	0	0	0	0	0	0	0	0	1	0
Total			38	17	21	19	13	5	1	5	0	0	0	1	1	1	36	2

Rank among batters: 1,225 • *Top target (5 home runs)*: Tommy Bridges • *Number of pitchers victimized*: 26 • *Total ballparks homered in*: 8 • *First HR*: 07/10/1929 off Bump Hadley

Hobe Ferris

ALBERT SAYLES FERRIS
B: 12/07/1877 D: 03/18/1938
BR

Year	Tm	Lg	Tot	H	A	0	1	2	3	2	3	4	LO	XN	IP	PH	RHP	LHP
1901	BOS	AL	2	2	0	0	2	0	0	0	0	0	0	0	1	0	1	1
1902	BOS	AL	8	2	6	5	2	1	0	0	0	0	0	0	1	0	8	0
1903	BOS	AL	9	8	1	4	3	1	1	1	0	0	0	0	6	0	4	5
1904	BOS	AL	3	2	1	2	0	1	0	0	0	0	0	0	0	0	1	2
1905	BOS	AL	6	4	2	4	1	1	0	0	0	0	0	0	1	0	6	0
1906	BOS	AL	2	2	0	0	1	1	0	0	0	0	0	0	2	0	1	1
1907	BOS	AL	4	1	3	1	1	2	0	0	0	0	0	0	1	0	2	2
1908	STL	AL	2	2	0	0	1	0	1	0	0	0	0	0	0	0	2	0
1909	STL	AL	4	0	4	2	2	0	0	0	0	0	0	0	1	0	3	1
Total			40	23	17	18	13	7	2	1	0	0	0	0	13	0	28	12

Rank among batters: 1,181 • Top target (2 home runs): Bill Carrick, Case Patten, Roy Patterson, Jack Powell, Otto Hess, Al Orth, Cy Morgan • *Number of pitchers victimized*: 33 • *Total ballparks homered in*: 10 • *First HR*: 06/11/1901 off Bill Reidy

Dave Ferriss

DAVID MEADOW FERRISS
B: 12/05/1921
BL

Year	Tm	Lg	Tot	H	A	0	1	2	3	2	3	4	LO	XN	IP	PH	RHP	LHP
1945	BOS	AL	1	0	1	0	1	0	0	0	0	0	0	0	0	0	1	0

Rank among batters: 4,707 • *Total ballparks homered in*: 1 • *First HR*: 06/29/1945 off Johnny Humphries

Year	Tm	Lg	Tot	H	A	Men-On 0	1	2	3	One-Game 2	3	4	LO	XN	IP	PH	RHP	LHP

Chick Fewster

WILSON LLOYD FEWSTER
B: 11/10/1895 D: 04/16/1945
BR

Year	Tm	Lg	Tot	H	A	0	1	2	3	2	3	4	LO	XN	IP	PH	RHP	LHP
1919	NY	AL	1	1	0	1	0	0	0	0	0	0	0	0	0	0	1	0
1921	NY	AL	1	1	0	1	0	0	0	0	0	0	0	0	0	0	1	0
1922	NY	AL	1	1	0	0	0	0	1	0	0	0	0	0	1	0	0	1
1925	CLE	AL	1	0	1	1	0	0	0	0	0	0	0	0	0	0	1	0
1926	BRO	NL	2	0	2	1	1	0	0	0	0	0	0	0	0	0	2	0
Total			6	3	3	4	1	0	1	0	0	0	0	0	1	0	5	1

Rank among batters: 2,988 • *Total ballparks homered in*: 2 • *First HR*: 08/01/1919 off Bernie Boland • *World Series HR*—1

Jim Field

JAMES C. FIELD
B: 04/24/1863 D: 05/13/1953

Year	Tm	Lg	Tot	H	A	0	1	2	3	2	3	4	LO	XN	IP	PH	RHP	LHP
1883	COL	AA	1	1	0	0	1	0	0	0	0	0	0	0	0	0	1	0
1884	COL	AA	4	2	2	1	2	1	0	0	0	0	0	0	0	0	3	1
1885	PIT	AA	1	0	1	1	0	0	0	0	0	0	0	0	1	0	0	0
1890	ROC	AA	4	3	1	1	1	1	1	0	0	0	0	0	0	0	3	0
Total			10	6	4	3	4	2	1	0	0	0	0	0	1	0	7	0

Rank among batters: 2,500 • *Total ballparks homered in*: 6 • *First HR*: 09/19/1883 off Jack Neagle

Cecil Fielder

CECIL GRANT FIELDER
B: 09/21/1963
BR

Year	Tm	Lg	Tot	H	A	0	1	2	3	2	3	4	LO	XN	IP	PH	RHP	LHP
1985	TOR	AL	4	2	2	3	1	0	0	0	0	0	0	0	0	0	0	4
1986	TOR	AL	4	0	4	1	2	1	0	0	0	0	0	0	0	0	4	0
1987	TOR	AL	14	10	4	11	3	0	0	0	0	0	0	1	0	1	1	13
1988	TOR	AL	9	6	3	7	2	0	0	2	0	0	0	0	0	0	0	9
1990	DET	AL	51	25	26	26	19	4	2	3	2	0	0	0	0	0	26	25
1991	DET	AL	44	27	17	18	17	8	1	5	0	0	0	0	0	0	31	13
1992	DET	AL	35	18	17	14	13	6	2	4	0	0	0	0	0	0	26	9
1993	DET	AL	30	20	10	17	6	6	1	5	0	0	0	0	0	0	22	8
1994	DET	AL	28	12	16	15	7	5	1	3	0	0	0	1	0	0	22	6
1995	DET	AL	31	16	15	13	14	3	1	3	0	0	0	0	1	0	25	6
Total			250	136	114	125	84	33	8	25	2	0	0	2	1	1	157	93

Rank among batters: 111 • *Top target (7 home runs)*: Pat Hentgen • *Number of pitchers victimized*: 154 • *Total ballparks homered in*: 18 • *First HR*: 08/21/1985 off Neal Heaton

Bruce Fields

BRUCE ALAN FIELDS
B: 10/06/1960
BL

Year	Tm	Lg	Tot	H	A	0	1	2	3	2	3	4	LO	XN	IP	PH	RHP	LHP
1988	SEA	AL	1	0	1	1	0	0	0	0	0	0	0	0	0	1	1	0

Rank among batters: 4,707 • *Total ballparks homered in*: 1 • *First HR*: 07/25/1988 off John Davis

Jocko Fields

JOHN JOSEPH FIELDS
B: 10/20/1864 D: 10/14/1950
BR

Year	Tm	Lg	Tot	H	A	0	1	2	3	2	3	4	LO	XN	IP	PH	RHP	LHP
1888	PIT	NL	1	0	1	1	0	0	0	0	0	0	0	0	0	0	1	0
1889	PIT	NL	2	0	2	1	1	0	0	0	0	0	0	0	0	0	1	1
1890	PIT	PL	9	3	6	6	1	1	1	2	0	0	0	0	2	0	7	1
Total			12	3	9	8	2	1	1	2	0	0	0	0	2	0	9	2

Rank among batters: 2,325 • *Top target (2 home runs)*: Ed Crane, Frank Dwyer, George Haddock • *Number of pitchers victimized*: 9 • *Total ballparks homered in*: 8 • *First HR*: 09/05/1888 off Bill Burdick

Jack Fifield

JOHN PROCTOR FIFIELD
B: 10/05/1871 D: 11/27/1939
BR

Year	Tm	Lg	Tot	H	A	0	1	2	3	2	3	4	LO	XN	IP	PH	RHP	LHP
1897	PHI	NL	2	0	2	2	0	0	0	0	0	0	0	0	0	0	2	0

Rank among batters: 4,129 • *Total ballparks homered in*: 2 • *First HR*: 05/28/1897 off Roger Denzer

Jesus Figueroa

JESUS MARIA (FIGUEROA) FIGUEROA
B: 02/20/1957
BL

Year	Tm	Lg	Tot	H	A	Men-On 0	1	2	3	One-Game 2	3	4	LO	XN	IP	PH	RHP	LHP
1980	CHI	NL	1	1	0	1	0	0	0	0	0	0	0	0	0	0	1	0

Rank among batters: 4,707 • *Total ballparks homered in*: 1 • *First HR*: 08/07/1980 off Eddie Solomon

Steve Filipowicz

STEPHEN CHARLES FILIPOWICZ
B: 06/28/1921 D: 02/21/1975
BR

Year	Tm	Lg	Tot	H	A	Men-On 0	1	2	3	One-Game 2	3	4	LO	XN	IP	PH	RHP	LHP
1945	NY	NL	2	1	1	1	1	0	0	0	0	0	0	0	0	0	2	0

Rank among batters: 4,129 • *Total ballparks homered in*: 2 • *First HR*: 04/21/1945 off Ben Chapman

Dana Fillingim

DANA FILLINGIM
B: 11/06/1893 D: 02/03/1961
BL

Year	Tm	Lg	Tot	H	A	Men-On 0	1	2	3	One-Game 2	3	4	LO	XN	IP	PH	RHP	LHP
1921	BOS	NL	2	0	2	1	1	0	0	0	0	0	0	0	0	0	2	0

Rank among batters: 4,129 • *Total ballparks homered in*: 2 • *First HR*: 04/24/1921 off Leon Cadore

Jack Fimple

JOHN JOSEPH FIMPLE
B: 02/10/1959
BR

Year	Tm	Lg	Tot	H	A	Men-On 0	1	2	3	One-Game 2	3	4	LO	XN	IP	PH	RHP	LHP
1983	LA	NL	2	0	2	2	0	0	0	0	0	0	0	0	0	0	2	0

Rank among batters: 4,129 • *Total ballparks homered in*: 1 • *First HR*: 08/09/1983 off Mario Soto

Rollie Fingers

ROLAND GLEN FINGERS
B: 08/25/1946
BR HOF

Year	Tm	Lg	Tot	H	A	Men-On 0	1	2	3	One-Game 2	3	4	LO	XN	IP	PH	RHP	LHP
1970	OAK	AL	1	0	1	1	0	0	0	0	0	0	0	0	0	0	1	0
1972	OAK	AL	1	0	1	0	1	0	0	0	0	0	0	0	0	0	1	0
Total			2	0	2	1	1	0	0	0	0	0	0	0	0	0	2	0

Rank among batters: 4,129 • *Total ballparks homered in*: 2 • *First HR*: 09/16/1970 off John Gelnar

Jim Finigan

JAMES LEROY FINIGAN
B: 08/19/1928 D: 05/16/1981
BR

Year	Tm	Lg	Tot	H	A	Men-On 0	1	2	3	One-Game 2	3	4	LO	XN	IP	PH	RHP	LHP
1954	PHI	AL	7	4	3	5	2	0	0	0	0	0	0	0	0	0	7	0
1955	KC	AL	9	5	4	3	3	3	0	0	0	0	0	0	0	0	8	1
1956	KC	AL	2	2	0	2	0	0	0	0	0	0	0	1	0	0	2	0
1959	BAL	AL	1	1	0	1	0	0	0	0	0	0	0	0	0	0	0	1
Total			19	12	7	11	5	3	0	0	0	0	0	1	0	0	17	2

Rank among batters: 1,861 • *Top target (2 home runs)*: Tom Brewer, Ned Garver • *Number of pitchers victimized*: 17 • *Total ballparks homered in*: 6 • *First HR*: 05/18/1954 off Steve Gromek

Bob Finley

ROBERT EDWARD FINLEY
B: 11/25/1915 D: 01/02/1986
BR

Year	Tm	Lg	Tot	H	A	Men-On 0	1	2	3	One-Game 2	3	4	LO	XN	IP	PH	RHP	LHP
1943	PHI	NL	1	1	0	1	0	0	0	0	0	0	0	0	0	0	0	1
1944	PHI	NL	1	0	1	1	0	0	0	0	0	0	0	0	0	1	0	1
Total			2	1	1	2	0	0	0	0	0	0	0	0	0	1	0	2

Rank among batters: 4,129 • *Total ballparks homered in*: 2 • *First HR*: 07/05/1943 off Ernie White

Steve Finley

STEVEN ALLEN FINLEY
B: 03/12/1965
BL

Year	Tm	Lg	Tot	H	A	Men-On 0	1	2	3	One-Game 2	3	4	LO	XN	IP	PH	RHP	LHP
1989	BAL	AL	2	0	2	0	0	1	1	0	0	0	0	0	0	0	1	1

						Men-On				One-Game								
Year	Tm	Lg	Tot	H	A	0	1	2	3	2	3	4	LO	XN	IP	PH	RHP	LHP

Steve Finley *continued*

Year	Tm	Lg	Tot	H	A	0	1	2	3	2	3	4	LO	XN	IP	PH	RHP	LHP
1990	BAL	AL	3	1	2	3	0	0	0	0	0	0	0	0	0	0	2	1
1991	HOU	NL	8	0	8	5	2	1	0	0	0	0	3	0	0	0	7	1
1992	HOU	NL	5	5	0	5	0	0	0	0	0	0	0	0	0	0	4	1
1993	HOU	NL	8	1	7	6	2	0	0	0	0	0	0	0	1	0	6	2
1994	HOU	NL	11	4	7	7	3	0	1	0	0	0	0	0	0	0	10	1
1995	SD	NL	10	4	6	7	3	0	0	0	0	0	0	0	0	0	7	3
Total			47	15	32	33	10	2	2	0	0	0	3	0	1	0	37	10

Rank among batters: 1,040 • *Top target (2 home runs)*: Mike Morgan, Vicente Palacios, Paul Wagner • *Number of pitchers victimized*: 44 • *Total ballparks homered in*: 18 • *First HR*: 04/25/1989 off Willie Fraser

Neal Finn

CORNELIUS FRANCIS FINN
B: 01/24/1904 D: 07/07/1933
BR

Year	Tm	Lg	Tot	H	A	0	1	2	3	2	3	4	LO	XN	IP	PH	RHP	LHP
1930	BRO	NL	3	1	2	2	1	0	0	0	0	0	0	0	0	0	0	3

Rank among batters: 3,735 • *Total ballparks homered in*: 2 • *First HR*: 07/04/1930 off Bill Walker

Hal Finney

HAROLD WILSON FINNEY
B: 07/30/1905 D: 12/20/1991
BR

Year	Tm	Lg	Tot	H	A	0	1	2	3	2	3	4	LO	XN	IP	PH	RHP	LHP
1933	PIT	NL	1	0	1	0	0	1	0	0	0	0	0	0	0	1	1	0

Rank among batters: 4,707 • *Total ballparks homered in*: 1 • *First HR*: 08/26/1933 off Dolf Luque

Lou Finney

LOUIS KLOPSCHE FINNEY
B: 08/13/1910 D: 04/22/1966
BL

Year	Tm	Lg	Tot	H	A	0	1	2	3	2	3	4	LO	XN	IP	PH	RHP	LHP
1933	PHI	AL	3	1	2	2	0	1	0	0	0	0	1	0	0	0	3	0
1934	PHI	AL	1	0	1	1	0	0	0	0	0	0	0	0	0	0	1	0
1936	PHI	AL	1	0	1	1	0	0	0	0	0	0	0	0	1	0	1	0
1937	PHI	AL	1	0	1	0	1	0	0	0	0	0	0	0	1	0	1	0
1938	PHI	AL	10	2	8	5	5	0	0	0	0	0	0	0	1	1	10	0
1939	BOS	AL	1	0	1	0	1	0	0	0	0	0	0	0	0	1	1	0
1940	BOS	AL	5	2	3	3	1	0	1	0	0	0	0	0	0	0	4	1
1941	BOS	AL	4	2	2	1	3	0	0	0	0	0	0	0	0	0	4	0
1942	BOS	AL	3	1	2	3	0	0	0	0	0	0	0	0	0	0	3	0
1945	STL	AL	2	0	2	1	0	0	1	0	0	0	0	0	1	0	2	0
Total			31	8	23	17	11	1	2	0	0	0	1	0	4	2	30	1

Rank among batters: 1,400 • *Top target (3 home runs)*: Red Ruffing • *Number of pitchers victimized*: 25 • *Total ballparks homered in*: 8 • *First HR*: 04/15/1933 off George Pipgras

Mike Fiore

MICHAEL GARY JOSEPH FIORE
B: 10/11/1944
BL

Year	Tm	Lg	Tot	H	A	0	1	2	3	2	3	4	LO	XN	IP	PH	RHP	LHP
1969	KC	AL	12	5	7	10	1	1	0	0	0	0	0	0	0	0	12	0
1971	BOS	AL	1	1	0	0	1	0	0	0	0	0	0	0	0	1	1	0
Total			13	6	7	10	2	1	0	0	0	0	0	0	0	1	13	0

Rank among batters: 2,248 • *Top target (2 home runs)*: Ray Culp, Blue Moon Odom • *Number of pitchers victimized*: 11 • *Total ballparks homered in*: 7 • *First HR*: 04/13/1969 off Johnny Odom

Bill Fischer

WILLIAM CHARLES FISCHER
B: 10/11/1930
BR

Year	Tm	Lg	Tot	H	A	0	1	2	3	2	3	4	LO	XN	IP	PH	RHP	LHP
1960	WAS	AL	1	0	1	1	0	0	0	0	0	0	0	0	0	0	0	1

Rank among batters: 4,707 • *Total ballparks homered in*: 1 • *First HR*: 06/26/1960 off Hank Aguirre

Rube Fischer

REUBEN WALTER FISCHER
B: 09/19/1916
BR

Year	Tm	Lg	Tot	H	A	0	1	2	3	2	3	4	LO	XN	IP	PH	RHP	LHP
1943	NY	NL	1	1	0	0	1	0	0	0	0	0	0	0	0	0	1	0

Rube Fischer *continued*

Year	Tm	Lg	Tot	H	A	Men-On 0	Men-On 1	Men-On 2	Men-On 3	One-Game 2	One-Game 3	One-Game 4	LO	XN	IP	PH	RHP	LHP
1945	NY	NL	1	1	0	1	0	0	0	0	0	0	0	0	0	0	1	0
Total			2	2	0	1	1	0	0	0	0	0	0	0	0	0	2	0

Rank among batters: 4,129 • *Total ballparks homered in*: 1 • *First HR*: 07/10/1943 off Ed Hanyzewski

William Fischer

WILLIAM CHARLES FISCHER
B: 03/02/1891 D: 09/04/1945
BL

Year	Tm	Lg	Tot	H	A	Men-On 0	Men-On 1	Men-On 2	Men-On 3	One-Game 2	One-Game 3	One-Game 4	LO	XN	IP	PH	RHP	LHP
1913	BRO	NL	1	1	0	0	0	1	0	0	0	0	0	0	0	0	1	0
1915	CHI	FL	4	0	4	1	2	1	0	1	0	0	0	0	0	0	3	1
1916	CHI	NL	1	1	0	1	0	0	0	0	0	0	0	0	0	0	1	0
	PIT	NL	1	0	1	1	0	0	0	0	0	0	0	0	0	0	1	0
	Total		2	1	1	2	0	0	0	0	0	0	0	0	0	0	2	0
1917	PIT	NL	3	0	3	2	1	0	0	1	0	0	0	1	1	0	3	0
Total			10	2	8	5	3	2	0	2	0	0	0	1	1	0	9	1

Rank among batters: 2,500 • *Top target (2 home runs)*: Joe Oeschger • *Number of pitchers victimized*: 9 • *Total ballparks homered in*: 5 • *First HR*: 08/16/1913 off Rube Geyer

Mike Fischlin

MICHAEL THOMAS FISCHLIN
B: 09/13/1955
BR

Year	Tm	Lg	Tot	H	A	Men-On 0	Men-On 1	Men-On 2	Men-On 3	One-Game 2	One-Game 3	One-Game 4	LO	XN	IP	PH	RHP	LHP
1983	CLE	AL	2	2	0	1	0	0	1	0	0	0	0	0	0	0	0	2
1984	CLE	AL	1	0	1	1	0	0	0	0	0	0	0	0	0	0	0	1
Total			3	2	1	2	0	0	1	0	0	0	0	0	0	0	0	3

Rank among batters: 3,735 • *Total ballparks homered in*: 2 • *First HR*: 09/09/1983 off John Tudor

John Fishel

JOHN ALAN FISHEL
B: 11/08/1962
BR

Year	Tm	Lg	Tot	H	A	Men-On 0	Men-On 1	Men-On 2	Men-On 3	One-Game 2	One-Game 3	One-Game 4	LO	XN	IP	PH	RHP	LHP
1988	HOU	NL	1	1	0	1	0	0	0	0	0	0	0	0	0	1	0	1

Rank among batters: 4,707 • *Total ballparks homered in*: 1 • *First HR*: 09/03/1988 off Steve Peters

Brian Fisher

BRIAN KEVIN FISHER
B: 03/18/1962
BR

Year	Tm	Lg	Tot	H	A	Men-On 0	Men-On 1	Men-On 2	Men-On 3	One-Game 2	One-Game 3	One-Game 4	LO	XN	IP	PH	RHP	LHP
1987	PIT	NL	2	1	1	0	0	2	0	0	0	0	0	0	0	0	1	1

Rank among batters: 4,129 • *Total ballparks homered in*: 2 • *First HR*: 05/24/1987 off Tom Browning

Chauncey Fisher

CHAUNCEY BURR FISHER
B: 01/08/1872 D: 04/27/1939
BR

Year	Tm	Lg	Tot	H	A	Men-On 0	Men-On 1	Men-On 2	Men-On 3	One-Game 2	One-Game 3	One-Game 4	LO	XN	IP	PH	RHP	LHP
1894	CIN	NL	1	1	0	0	0	1	0	0	0	0	0	0	0	0	1	0

Rank among batters: 4,707 • *Total ballparks homered in*: 1 • *First HR*: 09/09/1894 off Otis Stocksdale

Jack Fisher

JOHN HOWARD FISHER
B: 03/04/1939
BR

Year	Tm	Lg	Tot	H	A	Men-On 0	Men-On 1	Men-On 2	Men-On 3	One-Game 2	One-Game 3	One-Game 4	LO	XN	IP	PH	RHP	LHP
1960	BAL	AL	1	0	1	1	0	0	0	0	0	0	0	0	0	0	1	0

Rank among batters: 4,707 • *Total ballparks homered in*: 1 • *First HR*: 08/07/1960 off Bobby Locke

Ray Fisher

RAY LYLE FISHER
B: 10/04/1887 D: 11/03/1982
BR

Year	Tm	Lg	Tot	H	A	Men-On 0	Men-On 1	Men-On 2	Men-On 3	One-Game 2	One-Game 3	One-Game 4	LO	XN	IP	PH	RHP	LHP
1911	NY	AL	1	0	1	0	1	0	0	0	0	0	0	0	0	0	1	0

Year	Tm	Lg	Tot	H	A	Men-On				One-Game			LO	XN	IP	PH	RHP	LHP
						0	1	2	3	2	3	4						

Ray Fisher *continued*

Year	Tm	Lg	Tot	H	A	0	1	2	3	2	3	4	LO	XN	IP	PH	RHP	LHP
1917	NY	AL	1	1	0	1	0	0	0	0	0	0	0	0	0	0	1	0
Total			2	1	1	1	1	0	0	0	0	0	0	0	0	0	2	0

Rank among batters: 4,129 • *Total ballparks homered in*: 2 • *First HR*: 05/10/1911 off George Mullin

Showboat Fisher

GEORGE ALOYS FISHER
B: 01/16/1899 D: 05/15/1994
BL

Year	Tm	Lg	Tot	H	A	0	1	2	3	2	3	4	LO	XN	IP	PH	RHP	LHP
1930	STL	NL	8	4	4	4	3	1	0	0	0	0	0	0	1	1	7	1

Rank among batters: 2,703 • *Total ballparks homered in*: 5 • *First HR*: 04/23/1930 off Charlie Root

Tom Fisher

THOMAS CHALMERS FISHER
B: 11/01/1880 D: 09/03/1972
BR

Year	Tm	Lg	Tot	H	A	0	1	2	3	2	3	4	LO	XN	IP	PH	RHP	LHP
1904	BOS	NL	2	1	1	1	1	0	0	0	0	0	0	0	0	0	1	1

Rank among batters: 4,129 • *Total ballparks homered in*: 2 • *First HR*: 08/25/1904 off Jack Dunleavy

Tom Fisher

ROBERT TAYLOR FISHER
B: 11/03/1886 D: 08/04/1963
BR

Year	Tm	Lg	Tot	H	A	0	1	2	3	2	3	4	LO	XN	IP	PH	RHP	LHP
1913	BRO	NL	4	2	2	3	1	0	0	1	0	0	0	0	3	0	4	0
1915	CHI	NL	5	1	4	2	3	0	0	0	0	0	0	0	1	0	3	2
1918	STL	NL	2	1	1	2	0	0	0	0	0	0	0	0	0	0	2	0
Total			11	4	7	7	4	0	0	1	0	0	0	0	4	0	9	2

Rank among batters: 2,419 • *Total ballparks homered in*: 6 • *First HR*: 04/10/1913 off George Chalmers

Carlton Fisk

CARLTON ERNEST FISK
B: 12/26/1947
BR

Year	Tm	Lg	Tot	H	A	0	1	2	3	2	3	4	LO	XN	IP	PH	RHP	LHP
1971	BOS	AL	2	0	2	1	1	0	0	0	0	0	0	0	0	0	0	2
1972	BOS	AL	22	13	9	14	6	2	0	0	0	0	0	1	0	0	14	8
1973	BOS	AL	26	16	10	13	6	6	1	3	0	0	0	0	0	0	21	5
1974	BOS	AL	11	5	6	9	2	0	0	1	0	0	0	0	0	0	8	3
1975	BOS	AL	10	6	4	4	4	2	0	1	0	0	0	0	0	0	6	4
1976	BOS	AL	17	10	7	11	5	1	0	0	0	0	0	0	0	0	15	2
1977	BOS	AL	26	15	11	10	10	5	1	5	0	0	0	0	0	0	23	3
1978	BOS	AL	20	8	12	10	5	5	0	0	0	0	0	0	0	0	15	5
1979	BOS	AL	10	5	5	7	1	2	0	1	0	0	0	0	0	0	8	2
1980	BOS	AL	18	12	6	12	6	0	0	0	0	0	0	1	0	0	9	9
1981	CHI	AL	7	4	3	3	2	1	1	1	0	0	0	0	0	0	5	2
1982	CHI	AL	14	7	7	5	5	4	0	1	0	0	0	0	0	0	9	5
1983	CHI	AL	26	17	9	19	6	1	0	1	0	0	0	0	1	0	18	8
1984	CHI	AL	21	11	10	18	3	0	0	1	0	0	0	0	0	1	12	9
1985	CHI	AL	37	20	17	18	13	5	1	3	0	0	0	0	0	0	28	9
1986	CHI	AL	14	5	9	7	3	4	0	0	0	0	0	0	0	1	9	5
1987	CHI	AL	23	5	18	13	7	3	0	2	0	0	0	2	0	0	14	9
1988	CHI	AL	19	9	10	13	5	1	0	2	0	0	0	1	0	0	9	10
1989	CHI	AL	13	4	9	7	3	3	0	0	0	0	0	0	0	0	9	4
1990	CHI	AL	18	5	13	14	2	2	0	0	0	0	0	0	0	0	9	9
1991	CHI	AL	18	9	9	5	9	3	1	2	0	0	0	1	0	1	13	5
1992	CHI	AL	3	2	1	2	1	0	0	0	0	0	0	0	0	0	3	0
1993	CHI	AL	1	0	1	1	0	0	0	0	0	0	0	0	0	0	0	1
Total			376	188	188	216	105	50	5	24	0	0	0	6	1	3	257	119

Rank among batters: 36 • *Top target (7 home runs)*: Jim Palmer • *Number of pitchers victimized*: 247 • *Total ballparks homered in*: 17 • *First HR*: 09/12/1971 off Les Cain • *Hit for Cycle*—vs KC: 05/16/1984 • *World Series HR*—2

Wes Fisler

WESTON DICKSON FISLER
B: 07/05/1841 D: 12/25/1922

Year	Tm	Lg	Tot	H	A	0	1	2	3	2	3	4	LO	XN	IP	PH	RHP	LHP
1876	PHI	NL	1	1	0	1	0	0	0	0	0	0	0	0	0	0	1	0

Year	Tm	Lg	Tot	H	A	Men-On 0	1	2	3	One-Game 2	3	4	LO	XN	IP	PH	RHP	LHP

Wes Fisler *continued*

Rank among batters: 4,707 • *Total ballparks homered in*: 1 • *First HR*: 06/15/1876 off Cherokee Fisher

Ed Fitz Gerald

EDWARD RAYMOND FITZ GERALD
B: 05/21/1924
BR

Year	Tm	Lg	Tot	H	A	Men-On 0	1	2	3	One-Game 2	3	4	LO	XN	IP	PH	RHP	LHP
1948	PIT	NL	1	1	0	0	0	1	0	0	0	0	0	0	0	0	1	0
1949	PIT	NL	2	1	1	1	1	0	0	0	0	0	0	0	0	0	2	0
1952	PIT	NL	1	1	0	1	0	0	0	0	0	0	0	0	0	1	1	0
1953	WAS	AL	3	0	3	2	1	0	0	0	0	0	0	0	0	0	2	1
1954	WAS	AL	4	1	3	3	1	0	0	0	0	0	0	0	0	0	4	0
1955	WAS	AL	4	0	4	2	1	1	0	1	0	0	0	0	1	0	3	1
1956	WAS	AL	2	2	0	2	0	0	0	0	0	0	0	0	0	0	1	1
1957	WAS	AL	1	0	1	1	0	0	0	0	0	0	0	0	0	0	0	1
1959	CLE	AL	1	1	0	1	0	0	0	0	0	0	0	0	0	0	1	0
Total			19	7	12	13	4	2	0	1	0	0	0	0	1	1	15	4

Rank among batters: 1,861 • *Top target (2 home runs)*: Art Ditmar • *Number of pitchers victimized*: 18 • *Total ballparks homered in*: 10 • *First HR*: 07/20/1948 off Al Lakeman

John Fitzgerald

JOHN FITZGERALD

Year	Tm	Lg	Tot	H	A	Men-On 0	1	2	3	One-Game 2	3	4	LO	XN	IP	PH	RHP	LHP
1891	LOU	AA	1	1	0	1	0	0	0	0	0	0	0	0	0	0	0	0

Rank among batters: 4,707 • *Total ballparks homered in*: 1 • *First HR*: 09/18/1891 off Ed Cassian

Mike Fitzgerald

MICHAEL ROY FITZGERALD
B: 07/13/1960
BR

Year	Tm	Lg	Tot	H	A	Men-On 0	1	2	3	One-Game 2	3	4	LO	XN	IP	PH	RHP	LHP
1983	NY	NL	1	0	1	1	0	0	0	0	0	0	0	0	0	0	1	0
1984	NY	NL	2	2	0	1	1	0	0	0	0	0	0	0	0	0	0	2
1985	MON	NL	5	3	2	5	0	0	0	1	0	0	0	1	0	0	5	0
1986	MON	NL	6	1	5	4	2	0	0	0	0	0	0	0	0	0	5	1
1987	MON	NL	3	1	2	2	0	0	1	0	0	0	0	0	0	0	1	2
1988	MON	NL	5	3	2	1	3	0	1	0	0	0	0	1	0	1	5	0
1989	MON	NL	7	3	4	3	2	1	1	2	0	0	0	0	0	0	5	2
1990	MON	NL	9	2	7	5	4	0	0	0	0	0	0	0	0	0	4	5
1991	MON	NL	4	1	3	1	2	1	0	0	0	0	0	0	0	1	1	3
1992	CAL	AL	6	3	3	5	1	0	0	0	0	0	0	0	0	0	3	3
Total			48	19	29	28	15	2	3	3	0	0	0	2	0	2	30	18

Rank among batters: 1,024 • Top target (2 home runs): Mike Bielecki, Sid Fernandez, Danny Jackson, Scott Scudder, Dennis Cook • *Number of pitchers victimized*: 43 • *Total ballparks homered in*: 13 • *First HR*: 09/13/1983 off Tony Ghelfi • *Hit HR in first major league AB—@PHI*: 09/13/1983

Ed Fitzpatrick

EDWARD HENRY FITZPATRICK
B: 12/09/1889 D: 10/23/1965
BR

Year	Tm	Lg	Tot	H	A	Men-On 0	1	2	3	One-Game 2	3	4	LO	XN	IP	PH	RHP	LHP
1916	BOS	NL	1	0	1	0	1	0	0	0	0	0	0	0	0	0	0	1

Rank among batters: 4,707 • *Total ballparks homered in*: 1 • *First HR*: 05/08/1916 off Emilio Palmero

Freddie Fitzsimmons

FREDERICK LANDIS FITZSIMMONS
B: 07/26/1901 D: 11/18/1979
BR

Year	Tm	Lg	Tot	H	A	Men-On 0	1	2	3	One-Game 2	3	4	LO	XN	IP	PH	RHP	LHP
1930	NY	NL	2	2	0	1	1	0	0	0	0	0	0	0	0	0	2	0
1931	NY	NL	4	4	0	2	1	0	1	0	0	0	0	0	0	0	3	1
1932	NY	NL	2	2	0	1	1	0	0	0	0	0	0	0	0	0	1	1
1933	NY	NL	2	2	0	2	0	0	0	0	0	0	0	0	0	0	2	0
1934	NY	NL	2	2	0	2	0	0	0	0	0	0	0	0	0	0	2	0
1937	NY	NL	1	1	0	1	0	0	0	0	0	0	0	0	0	0	1	0

Freddie Fitzsimmons *continued*

Year	Tm	Lg	Tot	H	A	Men-On				One-Game			LO	XN	IP	PH	RHP	LHP
						0	1	2	3	2	3	4						
1939	BRO	NL	1	0	1	1	0	0	0	0	0	0	0	0	0	0	0	1
Total			14	13	1	10	3	0	1	0	0	0	0	0	0	0	11	3

Rank among batters: 2,169 • *Top target (2 home runs)*: Erv Brame • *Number of pitchers victimized*: 13 • *Total ballparks homered in*: 1 • *First HR*: 07/26/1930 off Leon Chagnon

Max Flack

MAX JOHN FLACK
B: 02/05/1890 D: 07/31/1975
BL

Year	Tm	Lg	Tot	H	A	Men-On 0	Men-On 1	Men-On 2	Men-On 3	One-Game 2	One-Game 3	One-Game 4	LO	XN	IP	PH	RHP	LHP
1914	CHI	FL	2	2	0	1	1	0	0	0	0	0	0	0	0	0	2	0
1915	CHI	FL	3	2	1	1	1	1	0	0	0	0	0	0	1	0	2	1
1916	CHI	NL	3	3	0	1	2	0	0	0	0	0	0	0	0	0	2	1
1918	CHI	NL	4	1	3	1	1	1	1	0	0	0	0	0	1	0	3	1
1919	CHI	NL	6	3	3	3	1	2	0	0	0	0	1	0	0	0	6	0
1920	CHI	NL	4	0	4	3	1	0	0	0	0	0	1	0	3	0	3	1
1921	CHI	NL	6	5	1	4	1	1	0	0	0	0	2	0	0	0	5	1
1922	STL	NL	2	1	1	2	0	0	0	0	0	0	1	0	0	0	1	1
1923	STL	NL	3	1	2	2	0	1	0	0	0	0	0	0	0	0	2	1
1924	STL	NL	2	2	0	1	0	1	0	0	0	0	0	1	0	0	2	0
Total			35	20	15	19	8	7	1	0	0	0	5	1	5	0	28	7

Rank among batters: 1,291 • *Top target (3 home runs)*: Hugh McQuillan • *Number of pitchers victimized*: 29 • *Total ballparks homered in*: 9 • *First HR*: 04/30/1914 off Kaiser Wilhelm

Wally Flager

WALTER LEONARD FLAGER
B: 11/03/1921 D: 12/16/1990
BL

Year	Tm	Lg	Tot	H	A	Men-On 0	Men-On 1	Men-On 2	Men-On 3	One-Game 2	One-Game 3	One-Game 4	LO	XN	IP	PH	RHP	LHP
1945	PHI	NL	2	0	2	2	0	0	0	0	0	0	0	0	0	0	1	1

Rank among batters: 4,129 • *Total ballparks homered in*: 1 • *First HR*: 06/13/1945 off Mort Cooper

Ira Flagstead

IRA JAMES FLAGSTEAD
B: 09/22/1893 D: 03/13/1940
BR

Year	Tm	Lg	Tot	H	A	Men-On 0	Men-On 1	Men-On 2	Men-On 3	One-Game 2	One-Game 3	One-Game 4	LO	XN	IP	PH	RHP	LHP
1919	DET	AL	5	3	2	4	1	0	0	0	0	0	0	0	0	0	3	2
1920	DET	AL	3	0	3	1	2	0	0	1	0	0	0	0	0	0	2	1
1922	DET	AL	3	2	1	1	1	1	0	0	0	0	0	0	1	1	2	1
1923	BOS	AL	8	1	7	4	3	1	0	0	0	0	0	0	1	0	7	1
1924	BOS	AL	5	1	4	3	0	2	0	0	0	0	0	0	0	0	4	1
1925	BOS	AL	6	1	5	4	1	1	0	0	0	0	0	0	0	0	1	5
1926	BOS	AL	3	1	2	2	1	0	0	0	0	0	0	1	0	0	2	1
1927	BOS	AL	4	1	3	2	2	0	0	0	0	0	0	0	0	1	0	4
1928	BOS	AL	1	0	1	1	0	0	0	0	0	0	1	0	0	0	0	1
1930	PIT	NL	2	1	1	2	0	0	0	0	0	0	0	0	0	0	1	1
Total			40	11	29	24	11	5	0	1	0	0	1	1	2	2	22	18

Rank among batters: 1,181 • *Top target (3 home runs)*: Eddie Rommel, Rube Walberg • *Number of pitchers victimized*: 32 • *Total ballparks homered in*: 10 • *First HR*: 05/13/1919 off Fritz Coumbe

John Flaherty

JOHN TIMOTHY FLAHERTY
B: 10/21/1967
BR

Year	Tm	Lg	Tot	H	A	Men-On 0	Men-On 1	Men-On 2	Men-On 3	One-Game 2	One-Game 3	One-Game 4	LO	XN	IP	PH	RHP	LHP
1995	DET	AL	11	6	5	9	2	0	0	2	0	0	0	0	0	0	11	0

Rank among batters: 2,419 • *Top target (2 home runs)*: Ricky Bones • *Number of pitchers victimized*: 10 • *Total ballparks homered in*: 5 • *First HR*: 05/20/1995 off Pat Hentgen

Patsy Flaherty

PATRICK JOSEPH FLAHERTY
B: 06/29/1876 D: 01/23/1968
BL

Year	Tm	Lg	Tot	H	A	Men-On 0	Men-On 1	Men-On 2	Men-On 3	One-Game 2	One-Game 3	One-Game 4	LO	XN	IP	PH	RHP	LHP
1904	PIT	NL	2	0	2	1	1	0	0	0	0	0	0	0	0	0	2	0
1907	BOS	NL	2	0	2	1	0	0	1	0	0	0	0	0	0	0	1	1

Patsy Flaherty *continued*

Year	Tm	Lg	Tot	H	A	Men-On 0	Men-On 1	Men-On 2	Men-On 3	One-Game 2	One-Game 3	One-Game 4	LO	XN	IP	PH	RHP	LHP
1911	BOS	NL	2	2	0	0	1	1	0	0	0	0	0	0	0	0	2	0
Total			6	2	4	2	2	1	1	0	0	0	0	0	0	0	5	1

Rank among batters: 2,988 • *Total ballparks homered in*: 4 • *First HR*: 08/11/1904 off Vic Willis

Ed Flanagan

EDWARD J. FLANAGAN
B: 09/15/1861 D: 11/10/1926

Year	Tm	Lg	Tot	H	A	Men-On 0	Men-On 1	Men-On 2	Men-On 3	One-Game 2	One-Game 3	One-Game 4	LO	XN	IP	PH	RHP	LHP
1887	PHI	AA	1	1	0	0	0	1	0	0	0	0	0	0	0	0	0	1

Rank among batters: 4,707 • *Total ballparks homered in*: 1 • *First HR*: 04/23/1887 off Ed Cushman

Tim Flannery

TIMOTHY EARL FLANNERY
B: 09/29/1957
BL

Year	Tm	Lg	Tot	H	A	Men-On 0	Men-On 1	Men-On 2	Men-On 3	One-Game 2	One-Game 3	One-Game 4	LO	XN	IP	PH	RHP	LHP
1983	SD	NL	3	1	2	2	0	0	1	0	0	0	0	0	0	0	3	0
1984	SD	NL	2	2	0	2	0	0	0	0	0	0	0	0	0	0	2	0
1985	SD	NL	1	1	0	0	0	1	0	0	0	0	0	0	0	0	1	0
1986	SD	NL	3	1	2	2	1	0	0	0	0	0	0	0	0	0	2	1
Total			9	5	4	6	1	1	1	0	0	0	0	0	0	0	8	1

Rank among batters: 2,587 • *Total ballparks homered in*: 4 • *First HR*: 04/26/1983 off Chuck Rainey

Les Fleming

LESLIE HARVEY FLEMING
B: 08/07/1915 D: 03/05/1980
BL

Year	Tm	Lg	Tot	H	A	Men-On 0	Men-On 1	Men-On 2	Men-On 3	One-Game 2	One-Game 3	One-Game 4	LO	XN	IP	PH	RHP	LHP
1942	CLE	AL	14	6	8	7	5	2	0	0	0	0	0	0	0	0	12	2
1945	CLE	AL	3	1	2	2	1	0	0	0	0	0	0	0	0	0	3	0
1946	CLE	AL	8	2	6	4	4	0	0	0	0	0	0	0	0	0	7	1
1947	CLE	AL	4	1	3	2	1	1	0	1	0	0	0	0	0	0	4	0
Total			29	10	19	15	11	3	0	1	0	0	0	0	0	0	26	3

Rank among batters: 1,465 • *Top target (2 home runs)*: Dizzy Trout, Vic Raschi • *Number of pitchers victimized*: 27 • *Total ballparks homered in*: 9 • *First HR*: 04/14/1942 off Roy Henshaw

Art Fletcher

ARTHUR FLETCHER
B: 01/05/1885 D: 02/06/1950
BR

Year	Tm	Lg	Tot	H	A	Men-On 0	Men-On 1	Men-On 2	Men-On 3	One-Game 2	One-Game 3	One-Game 4	LO	XN	IP	PH	RHP	LHP
1911	NY	NL	1	1	0	1	0	0	0	0	0	0	0	0	0	0	1	0
1912	NY	NL	1	1	0	0	1	0	0	0	0	0	0	0	0	0	1	0
1913	NY	NL	4	3	1	1	2	1	0	0	0	0	0	0	0	0	4	0
1914	NY	NL	2	1	1	1	1	0	0	0	0	0	0	0	0	0	1	1
1915	NY	NL	3	3	0	0	3	0	0	0	0	0	0	0	0	0	3	0
1916	NY	NL	3	1	2	1	2	0	0	0	0	0	0	0	0	0	1	2
1917	NY	NL	4	0	4	1	2	1	0	0	0	0	0	0	1	0	3	1
1919	NY	NL	3	2	1	3	0	0	0	0	0	0	0	0	0	0	2	1
1920	PHI	NL	4	3	1	2	1	1	0	0	0	0	0	0	1	0	3	1
1922	PHI	NL	7	6	1	4	1	2	0	1	0	0	0	1	0	0	5	2
Total			32	21	11	14	13	5	0	1	0	0	0	1	2	0	24	8

Rank among batters: 1,360 • *Top target (2 home runs)*: Sherry Smith, Bill Doak • *Number of pitchers victimized*: 30 • *Total ballparks homered in*: 6 • *First HR*: 07/10/1911 off Lew Richie

Darrin Fletcher

DARRIN GLEN FLETCHER
B: 10/03/1966
BL

Year	Tm	Lg	Tot	H	A	Men-On 0	Men-On 1	Men-On 2	Men-On 3	One-Game 2	One-Game 3	One-Game 4	LO	XN	IP	PH	RHP	LHP
1989	LA	NL	1	1	0	1	0	0	0	0	0	0	0	0	0	1	1	0
1991	PHI	NL	1	1	0	0	0	1	0	0	0	0	0	0	0	0	1	0
1992	MON	NL	2	0	2	1	1	0	0	0	0	0	0	0	0	0	2	0
1993	MON	NL	9	5	4	6	2	1	0	0	0	0	0	0	0	1	7	2
1994	MON	NL	10	4	6	5	3	2	0	2	0	0	0	0	0	0	8	2
1995	MON	NL	11	3	8	8	1	2	0	0	0	0	0	1	0	0	10	1
Total			34	14	20	21	7	6	0	2	0	0	0	1	0	2	29	5

Rank among batters: 1,315 • Top target (2 home runs): Bob Walk, Jose Rijo, Mark Gardner, Doug Drabek, Mark Portugal • *Number of pitchers victimized*: 29 • *Total ballparks homered in*: 12 • *First HR*: 09/23/1989 off Calvin Schiraldi

Year	Tm	Lg	Tot	H	A	Men-On 0	Men-On 1	Men-On 2	Men-On 3	One-Game 2	One-Game 3	One-Game 4	LO	XN	IP	PH	RHP	LHP

Elbie Fletcher

ELBURT PRESTON FLETCHER
B: 03/18/1916 D: 03/09/1994
BL

Year	Tm	Lg	Tot	H	A	0	1	2	3	2	3	4	LO	XN	IP	PH	RHP	LHP
1935	BOS	NL	1	0	1	1	0	0	0	0	0	0	0	0	0	0	1	0
1937	BOS	NL	1	0	1	0	0	0	1	0	0	0	0	0	1	0	1	0
1938	BOS	NL	6	1	5	6	0	0	0	0	0	0	0	0	0	0	5	1
1939	PIT	NL	12	4	8	5	4	1	2	0	0	0	0	0	0	0	9	3
1940	PIT	NL	16	8	8	9	4	2	1	1	0	0	0	0	0	0	13	3
1941	PIT	NL	11	6	5	5	5	1	0	1	0	0	0	1	1	0	9	2
1942	PIT	NL	7	2	5	6	0	0	1	0	0	0	0	0	0	0	6	1
1943	PIT	NL	9	4	5	4	3	2	0	0	0	0	0	0	0	0	6	3
1946	PIT	NL	4	2	2	1	1	2	0	0	0	0	0	0	0	0	2	2
1947	PIT	NL	1	0	1	1	0	0	0	0	0	0	0	0	0	0	1	0
1949	BOS	NL	11	6	5	4	5	2	0	0	0	0	0	0	0	0	8	3
Total			79	33	46	42	22	10	5	2	0	0	0	1	2	0	61	18

Rank among batters: 661 • *Top target (4 home runs)*: Carl Hubbell • *Number of pitchers victimized*: 53 • *Total ballparks homered in*: 8 • *First HR*: 09/09/1935 off Tex Carleton

Scott Fletcher

SCOTT BRIAN FLETCHER
B: 07/30/1958
BR

Year	Tm	Lg	Tot	H	A	0	1	2	3	2	3	4	LO	XN	IP	PH	RHP	LHP
1983	CHI	AL	3	1	2	3	0	0	0	0	0	0	0	0	0	0	1	2
1984	CHI	AL	3	2	1	2	1	0	0	0	0	0	0	0	0	0	2	1
1985	CHI	AL	2	0	2	2	0	0	0	0	0	0	0	0	0	0	0	2
1986	TEX	AL	3	2	1	2	1	0	0	0	0	0	0	0	0	0	1	2
1987	TEX	AL	5	4	1	4	1	0	0	0	0	0	0	0	0	0	2	3
1989	CHI	AL	1	0	1	1	0	0	0	0	0	0	0	0	0	0	1	0
1990	CHI	AL	4	1	3	1	1	2	0	0	0	0	0	0	0	0	3	1
1991	CHI	AL	1	0	1	0	1	0	0	0	0	0	0	0	0	0	1	0
1992	MIL	AL	3	2	1	1	0	2	0	0	0	0	0	0	0	0	3	0
1993	BOS	AL	5	2	3	4	1	0	0	0	0	0	2	0	0	0	2	3
1994	BOS	AL	3	2	1	3	0	0	0	0	0	0	0	1	0	0	2	1
1995	DET	AL	1	1	0	0	1	0	0	0	0	0	0	0	0	0	0	1
Total			34	17	17	23	7	4	0	0	0	0	2	1	0	0	18	16

Rank among batters: 1,315 • Top target (2 home runs): Frank Viola, Frank Tanana, Dan Petry, Scott Sanderson • *Number of pitchers victimized*: 30 • *Total ballparks homered in*: 14 • *First HR*: 06/26/1983 off Len Whitehouse

Elmer Flick

ELMER HARRISON FLICK
B: 01/11/1876 D: 01/09/1971
BL HOF

Year	Tm	Lg	Tot	H	A	0	1	2	3	2	3	4	LO	XN	IP	PH	RHP	LHP
1898	PHI	NL	8	4	4	4	1	3	0	0	0	0	0	0	0	0	7	1
1899	PHI	NL	2	0	2	0	1	0	1	0	0	0	0	0	1	0	2	0
1900	PHI	NL	11	4	7	3	7	1	0	2	0	0	0	0	1	0	10	1
1901	PHI	NL	8	3	5	4	2	2	0	0	0	0	0	1	2	0	7	1
1902	CLE	AL	2	1	1	1	1	0	0	0	0	0	0	0	1	0	2	0
1903	CLE	AL	2	2	0	1	1	0	0	0	0	0	0	0	0	0	2	0
1904	CLE	AL	6	3	3	4	2	0	0	0	0	0	0	0	0	0	6	0
1905	CLE	AL	4	0	4	2	1	1	0	0	0	0	0	0	0	0	3	1
1906	CLE	AL	1	0	1	1	0	0	0	0	0	0	0	0	0	0	0	1
1907	CLE	AL	3	1	2	2	1	0	0	0	0	0	2	0	0	0	2	1
1910	CLE	AL	1	0	1	1	0	0	0	0	0	0	0	0	0	0	1	0
Total			48	18	30	23	17	7	1	2	0	0	2	1	5	0	42	6

Rank among batters: 1,024 • *Top target (4 home runs)*: Frank Kitson • *Number of pitchers victimized*: 34 • *Total ballparks homered in*: 16 • *First HR*: 06/01/1898 off Red Ehret

Silver Flint

FRANK SYLVESTER FLINT
B: 08/03/1855 D: 01/14/1892
BR

Year	Tm	Lg	Tot	H	A	0	1	2	3	2	3	4	LO	XN	IP	PH	RHP	LHP
1879	CHI	NL	1	0	1	0	1	0	0	0	0	0	0	0	0	0	1	0
1881	CHI	NL	1	1	0	0	1	0	0	0	0	0	0	0	0	0	0	1
1882	CHI	NL	4	3	1	0	2	2	0	1	0	0	0	0	0	0	4	0
1884	CHI	NL	9	9	0	3	4	2	0	0	0	0	0	0	0	0	9	0
1885	CHI	NL	1	1	0	1	0	0	0	0	0	0	0	0	0	0	1	0
1886	CHI	NL	1	1	0	1	0	0	0	0	0	0	0	0	0	0	1	0
1887	CHI	NL	3	3	0	1	2	0	0	0	0	0	0	0	0	0	2	1

Silver Flint *continued*

Year	Tm	Lg	Tot	H	A	Men-On 0	Men-On 1	Men-On 2	Men-On 3	One-Game 2	One-Game 3	One-Game 4	LO	XN	IP	PH	RHP	LHP
1889	CHI	NL	1	1	0	1	0	0	0	0	0	0	0	0	0	0	1	0
Total			21	19	2	7	10	4	0	1	0	0	0	0	0	0	19	2

Rank among batters: 1,768 • Top target (2 home runs): Dave Rowe, Jim Galvin, Charley Radbourn, Charlie Ferguson, Charlie Buffinton • *Number of pitchers victimized*: 16 • *Total ballparks homered in*: 4 • *First HR*: 06/05/1879 off Monte Ward

Curt Flood

CURTIS CHARLES FLOOD
B: 01/18/1938
BR

Year	Tm	Lg	Tot	H	A	Men-On 0	Men-On 1	Men-On 2	Men-On 3	One-Game 2	One-Game 3	One-Game 4	LO	XN	IP	PH	RHP	LHP
1957	CIN	NL	1	1	0	1	0	0	0	0	0	0	0	0	0	0	1	0
1958	STL	NL	10	1	9	8	2	0	0	0	0	0	1	2	0	0	5	5
1959	STL	NL	7	4	3	3	2	2	0	0	0	0	0	0	0	0	3	4
1960	STL	NL	8	3	5	6	0	2	0	1	0	0	0	0	0	0	3	5
1961	STL	NL	2	0	2	2	0	0	0	0	0	0	0	0	0	0	1	1
1962	STL	NL	12	6	6	7	5	0	0	0	0	0	0	0	0	0	9	3
1963	STL	NL	5	1	4	4	0	1	0	0	0	0	1	0	0	0	3	2
1964	STL	NL	5	4	1	4	1	0	0	0	0	0	1	0	0	0	4	1
1965	STL	NL	11	6	5	6	3	2	0	1	0	0	2	0	0	0	8	3
1966	STL	NL	10	6	4	5	2	2	1	0	0	0	0	1	0	0	5	5
1967	STL	NL	5	2	3	3	1	1	0	0	0	0	0	0	0	0	1	4
1968	STL	NL	5	2	3	3	2	0	0	1	0	0	0	0	0	0	4	1
1969	STL	NL	4	1	3	4	0	0	0	0	0	0	0	0	0	0	1	3
Total			85	37	48	56	18	10	1	3	0	0	5	3	0	0	48	37

Rank among batters: 612 • *Top target (4 home runs)*: Juan Marichal, Chris Short • *Number of pitchers victimized*: 60 • *Total ballparks homered in*: 16 • *First HR*: 09/25/1957 off Moe Drabowsky

Tim Flood

TIMOTHY A. FLOOD
B: 03/13/1877 D: 06/15/1929
BR

Year	Tm	Lg	Tot	H	A	Men-On 0	Men-On 1	Men-On 2	Men-On 3	One-Game 2	One-Game 3	One-Game 4	LO	XN	IP	PH	RHP	LHP
1902	BRO	NL	3	2	1	0	2	1	0	0	0	0	0	0	0	0	3	0

Rank among batters: 3,735 • *Total ballparks homered in*: 2 • *First HR*: 04/24/1902 off Solly Salisbury

Kevin Flora

KEVIN SCOT FLORA
B: 06/10/1969
BR

Year	Tm	Lg	Tot	H	A	Men-On 0	Men-On 1	Men-On 2	Men-On 3	One-Game 2	One-Game 3	One-Game 4	LO	XN	IP	PH	RHP	LHP
1995	PHI	NL	2	2	0	0	2	0	0	0	0	0	0	0	0	0	2	0

Rank among batters: 4,129 • *Total ballparks homered in*: 1 • *First HR*: 08/18/1995 off Jose Bautista

Paul Florence

PAUL ROBERT FLORENCE
B: 04/22/1900 D: 05/28/1986
BB

Year	Tm	Lg	Tot	H	A	Men-On 0	Men-On 1	Men-On 2	Men-On 3	One-Game 2	One-Game 3	One-Game 4	LO	XN	IP	PH	RHP	LHP
1926	NY	NL	2	2	0	1	1	0	0	0	0	0	0	0	1	0	2	0

Rank among batters: 4,129 • *Total ballparks homered in*: 1 • *First HR*: 05/26/1926 off Bob McGraw

Gil Flores

GILBERTO (GARCIA) FLORES
B: 10/27/1952
BR

Year	Tm	Lg	Tot	H	A	Men-On 0	Men-On 1	Men-On 2	Men-On 3	One-Game 2	One-Game 3	One-Game 4	LO	XN	IP	PH	RHP	LHP
1977	CAL	AL	1	1	0	0	1	0	0	0	0	0	0	0	0	0	1	0
1979	NY	NL	1	0	1	1	0	0	0	0	0	0	0	0	1	0	1	0
Total			2	1	1	1	1	0	0	0	0	0	0	0	1	0	2	0

Rank among batters: 4,129 • *Total ballparks homered in*: 2 • *First HR*: 07/03/1977 off Mike Norris

Jake Flowers

D'ARCY RAYMOND FLOWERS
B: 03/16/1902 D: 12/27/1962
BR

Year	Tm	Lg	Tot	H	A	Men-On 0	Men-On 1	Men-On 2	Men-On 3	One-Game 2	One-Game 3	One-Game 4	LO	XN	IP	PH	RHP	LHP
1926	STL	NL	3	2	1	1	1	1	0	0	0	0	0	0	0	1	3	0
1927	BRO	NL	2	2	0	1	1	0	0	0	0	0	0	0	0	0	1	1
1928	BRO	NL	2	0	2	2	0	0	0	0	0	0	0	1	0	0	0	2

Jake Flowers *continued*

Year	Tm	Lg	Tot	H	A	Men-On 0	1	2	3	One-Game 2	3	4	LO	XN	IP	PH	RHP	LHP
1929	BRO	NL	1	1	0	0	1	0	0	0	0	0	0	0	0	0	1	0
1930	BRO	NL	2	1	1	1	0	1	0	0	0	0	0	0	0	0	1	1
1931	STL	NL	2	2	0	1	1	0	0	0	0	0	1	0	0	0	2	0
1932	STL	NL	2	2	0	2	0	0	0	0	0	0	1	0	0	0	1	1
1933	BRO	NL	2	1	1	1	0	1	0	0	0	0	0	0	0	0	2	0
Total			16	11	5	9	4	3	0	0	0	0	2	1	0	1	11	5

Rank among batters: 2,029 • *Total ballparks homered in*: 5 • *First HR*: 05/23/1926 off Hal Carlson

Cliff Floyd

CORNELIUS CLIFFORD FLOYD
B: 12/05/1972
BL

Year	Tm	Lg	Tot	H	A	Men-On 0	1	2	3	One-Game 2	3	4	LO	XN	IP	PH	RHP	LHP
1993	MON	NL	1	0	1	0	1	0	0	0	0	0	0	0	0	0	1	0
1994	MON	NL	4	2	2	3	0	1	0	0	0	0	0	0	0	0	4	0
1995	MON	NL	1	1	0	0	0	1	0	0	0	0	0	0	0	0	1	0
Total			6	3	3	3	1	2	0	0	0	0	0	0	0	0	6	0

Rank among batters: 2,988 • *Total ballparks homered in*: 4 • *First HR*: 09/26/1993 off Dave Telgheder

Carney Flynn

CORNELIUS FRANCIS XAVIER FLYNN
B: 01/23/1875 D: 02/10/1947
BL

Year	Tm	Lg	Tot	H	A	Men-On 0	1	2	3	One-Game 2	3	4	LO	XN	IP	PH	RHP	LHP
1896	NY	NL	1	0	1	0	1	0	0	0	0	0	0	0	0	0	1	0

Rank among batters: 4,707 • *Total ballparks homered in*: 1 • *First HR*: 04/30/1896 off Jack Taylor

Doug Flynn

ROBERT DOUGLAS FLYNN
B: 04/18/1951
BR

Year	Tm	Lg	Tot	H	A	Men-On 0	1	2	3	One-Game 2	3	4	LO	XN	IP	PH	RHP	LHP
1975	CIN	NL	1	1	0	0	0	1	0	0	0	0	0	0	0	0	0	1
1976	CIN	NL	1	0	1	0	1	0	0	0	0	0	0	0	0	0	1	0
1979	NY	NL	4	3	1	1	1	2	0	0	0	0	0	0	1	0	2	2
1981	NY	NL	1	1	0	1	0	0	0	0	0	0	0	0	0	0	1	0
Total			7	5	2	2	2	3	0	0	0	0	0	0	1	0	4	3

Rank among batters: 2,834 • *Total ballparks homered in*: 4 • *First HR*: 05/21/1975 off Tom Hall

Jocko Flynn

JOHN A. FLYNN
B: 06/30/1864 D: 12/30/1907

Year	Tm	Lg	Tot	H	A	Men-On 0	1	2	3	One-Game 2	3	4	LO	XN	IP	PH	RHP	LHP
1886	CHI	NL	4	3	1	3	1	0	0	0	0	0	0	0	0	0	2	2

Rank among batters: 3,427 • *Total ballparks homered in*: 2 • *First HR*: 05/19/1886 off Dupee Shaw

Joe Flynn

JOSEPH FLYNN

Year	Tm	Lg	Tot	H	A	Men-On 0	1	2	3	One-Game 2	3	4	LO	XN	IP	PH	RHP	LHP
1884	PHI	UA	4	1	3	1	2	1	0	0	0	0	0	0	0	0	3	1

Rank among batters: 3,427 • *Top target (2 home runs)*: Hugh Daily • *Number of pitchers victimized*: 3 • *Total ballparks homered in*: 4 • *First HR*: 05/09/1884 off Hugh Daily

John Flynn

JOHN ANTHONY FLYNN
B: 09/07/1883 D: 03/23/1935
BR

Year	Tm	Lg	Tot	H	A	Men-On 0	1	2	3	One-Game 2	3	4	LO	XN	IP	PH	RHP	LHP
1910	PIT	NL	6	4	2	2	0	4	0	0	0	0	0	0	0	0	5	1

Rank among batters: 2,988 • *Total ballparks homered in*: 3 • *First HR*: 04/28/1910 off Fred Beebe

Jim Fogarty

JAMES G. FOGARTY
B: 02/12/1864 D: 05/20/1891
BR

Year	Tm	Lg	Tot	H	A	Men-On 0	1	2	3	One-Game 2	3	4	LO	XN	IP	PH	RHP	LHP
1884	PHI	NL	1	0	1	0	1	0	0	0	0	0	0	1	0	0	1	0
1886	PHI	NL	3	1	2	2	0	1	0	0	0	0	0	0	0	0	3	0
1887	PHI	NL	8	4	4	3	2	3	0	0	0	0	0	0	0	0	5	2

Year	Tm	Lg	Tot	H	A	Men-On 0	Men-On 1	Men-On 2	Men-On 3	One-Game 2	One-Game 3	One-Game 4	LO	XN	IP	PH	RHP	LHP

Jim Fogarty *continued*

Year	Tm	Lg	Tot	H	A	0	1	2	3	2	3	4	LO	XN	IP	PH	RHP	LHP
1888	PHI	NL	1	0	1	1	0	0	0	0	0	0	0	0	0	0	0	0
1889	PHI	NL	3	0	3	2	1	0	0	0	0	0	0	0	0	0	3	0
1890	PHI	PL	4	1	3	2	2	0	0	0	0	0	0	0	0	0	2	1
Total			20	6	14	10	6	4	0	0	0	0	0	1	0	0	14	3

Rank among batters: 1,810 • *Top target (2 home runs)*: Jim Whitney, Frank Gilmore, Mark Baldwin • *Number of pitchers victimized*: 17 • *Total ballparks homered in*: 14 • *First HR*: 07/03/1884 off Larry Corcoran

Hank Foiles

HENRY LEE FOILES
B: 06/10/1929
BR

Year	Tm	Lg	Tot	H	A	0	1	2	3	2	3	4	LO	XN	IP	PH	RHP	LHP
1955	CLE	AL	1	1	0	0	1	0	0	0	0	0	0	0	0	1	0	1
1956	PIT	NL	7	3	4	4	2	1	0	0	0	0	0	0	0	0	7	0
1957	PIT	NL	9	2	7	7	2	0	0	0	0	0	0	0	0	0	5	4
1958	PIT	NL	8	2	6	3	3	2	0	0	0	0	0	0	0	0	3	5
1959	PIT	NL	3	1	2	3	0	0	0	0	0	0	0	0	0	0	3	0
1960	CLE	AL	1	1	0	1	0	0	0	0	0	0	0	0	0	0	1	0
1961	BAL	AL	6	1	5	4	2	0	0	1	0	0	0	1	0	0	5	1
1962	CIN	NL	7	5	2	3	1	2	1	0	0	0	0	0	0	1	4	3
1963	LA	AL	4	2	2	2	2	0	0	0	0	0	0	0	0	1	1	3
Total			46	18	28	27	13	5	1	1	0	0	0	1	0	3	29	17

Rank among batters: 1,060 • *Top target (2 home runs)*: Willard Schmidt, Johnny Podres • *Number of pitchers victimized*: 44 • *Total ballparks homered in*: 14 • *First HR*: 09/18/1955 off Bob Miller

Curry Foley

CHARLES JOSEPH FOLEY
B: 01/14/1856 D: 10/20/1898

Year	Tm	Lg	Tot	H	A	0	1	2	3	2	3	4	LO	XN	IP	PH	RHP	LHP
1880	BOS	NL	2	2	0	0	1	1	0	0	0	0	0	0	0	0	2	0
1881	BUF	NL	1	0	1	1	0	0	0	0	0	0	0	0	0	0	1	0
1882	BUF	NL	3	1	2	0	1	0	2	0	0	0	0	0	0	0	2	1
Total			6	3	3	1	2	1	2	0	0	0	0	0	0	0	5	1

Rank among batters: 2,988 • *Top target (2 home runs)*: George Bradley • *Number of pitchers victimized*: 5 • *Total ballparks homered in*: 5 • *First HR*: 05/04/1880 off Monte Ward • *Hit for Cycle*—vs CLE: 05/25/1882

Marv Foley

MARVIS EDWIN FOLEY
B: 08/29/1953
BL

Year	Tm	Lg	Tot	H	A	0	1	2	3	2	3	4	LO	XN	IP	PH	RHP	LHP
1979	CHI	AL	2	1	1	2	0	0	0	0	0	0	0	0	0	0	2	0
1980	CHI	AL	4	1	3	3	1	0	0	0	0	0	0	1	0	1	3	1
1984	TEX	AL	6	4	2	3	3	0	0	0	0	0	0	0	0	0	6	0
Total			12	6	6	8	4	0	0	0	0	0	0	1	0	1	11	1

Rank among batters: 2,325 • *Total ballparks homered in*: 6 • *First HR*: 04/14/1979 off Catfish Hunter

Tom Foley

THOMAS MICHAEL FOLEY
B: 09/09/1959
BL

Year	Tm	Lg	Tot	H	A	0	1	2	3	2	3	4	LO	XN	IP	PH	RHP	LHP
1984	CIN	NL	5	2	3	2	3	0	0	0	0	0	0	0	0	1	5	0
1985	PHI	NL	3	2	1	1	1	1	0	0	0	0	0	0	0	0	3	0
1986	MON	NL	1	1	0	1	0	0	0	0	0	0	0	0	0	0	1	0
1987	MON	NL	5	3	2	3	0	2	0	0	0	0	0	0	0	0	5	0
1988	MON	NL	5	3	2	4	1	0	0	1	0	0	0	0	0	0	5	0
1989	MON	NL	7	4	3	3	2	2	0	0	0	0	0	0	0	1	7	0
1993	PIT	NL	3	1	2	1	2	0	0	0	0	0	0	0	0	1	3	0
1994	PIT	NL	3	2	1	3	0	0	0	0	0	0	0	0	0	0	2	1
Total			32	18	14	18	9	5	0	1	0	0	0	0	0	3	31	1

Rank among batters: 1,360 • *Top target (2 home runs)*: Ron Darling • *Number of pitchers victimized*: 31 • *Total ballparks homered in*: 11 • *First HR*: 04/29/1984 off Jeff Robinson

Tim Foli

TIMOTHY JOHN FOLI
B: 12/06/1950
BR

Year	Tm	Lg	Tot	H	A	0	1	2	3	2	3	4	LO	XN	IP	PH	RHP	LHP
1972	MON	NL	2	1	1	1	1	0	0	0	0	0	0	0	0	0	1	1

Tim Foli *continued*

Year	Tm	Lg	Tot	H	A	Men-On 0	1	2	3	One-Game 2	3	4	LO	XN	IP	PH	RHP	LHP
1973	MON	NL	2	2	0	1	1	0	0	0	0	0	0	0	0	0	2	0
1975	MON	NL	1	1	0	1	0	0	0	0	0	0	0	0	0	0	1	0
1976	MON	NL	6	2	4	3	3	0	0	0	0	0	0	0	0	0	4	2
1977	SF	NL	4	2	2	3	1	0	0	1	0	0	0	0	0	0	2	2
1978	NY	NL	1	0	1	1	0	0	0	0	0	0	0	0	0	0	1	0
1979	PIT	NL	1	0	1	1	0	0	0	0	0	0	0	0	0	0	1	0
1980	PIT	NL	3	2	1	3	0	0	0	0	0	0	0	0	0	0	2	1
1982	CAL	AL	3	1	2	3	0	0	0	0	0	0	0	0	0	0	2	1
1983	CAL	AL	2	1	1	1	0	1	0	0	0	0	0	0	0	0	1	1
Total			25	12	13	18	6	1	0	1	0	0	0	0	0	0	17	8

Rank among batters: 1,608 • *Top target (2 home runs)*: Nino Espinosa • *Number of pitchers victimized*: 24 • *Total ballparks homered in*: 12 • *First HR*: 06/30/1972 off Jon Matlack • *Hit for Cycle*—@CHI: 04/21/1976

Dee Fondy

DEE VIRGIL FONDY
B: 10/13/1924
BL

Year	Tm	Lg	Tot	H	A	Men-On 0	1	2	3	One-Game 2	3	4	LO	XN	IP	PH	RHP	LHP
1951	CHI	NL	3	3	0	2	1	0	0	1	0	0	1	0	0	0	3	0
1952	CHI	NL	10	3	7	6	2	1	1	0	0	0	0	0	0	0	9	1
1953	CHI	NL	18	9	9	10	6	2	0	1	0	0	0	1	1	0	17	1
1954	CHI	NL	9	4	5	6	1	2	0	0	0	0	0	0	0	0	8	1
1955	CHI	NL	17	10	7	8	8	1	0	2	0	0	1	1	0	0	14	3
1956	CHI	NL	9	5	4	7	2	0	0	0	0	0	0	2	0	0	9	0
1957	PIT	NL	2	1	1	2	0	0	0	0	0	0	0	0	0	1	2	0
1958	CIN	NL	1	1	0	0	0	1	0	0	0	0	0	0	0	0	0	1
Total			69	36	33	41	20	7	1	4	0	0	2	4	1	1	62	7

Rank among batters: 756 • *Top target (4 home runs)*: Don Newcombe • *Number of pitchers victimized*: 52 • *Total ballparks homered in*: 9 • *First HR*: 05/16/1951 off Dan Bankhead

Lew Fonseca

LEWIS ALBERT FONSECA
B: 01/21/1899 D: 11/26/1989
BR

Year	Tm	Lg	Tot	H	A	Men-On 0	1	2	3	One-Game 2	3	4	LO	XN	IP	PH	RHP	LHP
1921	CIN	NL	1	0	1	1	0	0	0	0	0	0	0	0	0	0	0	1
1922	CIN	NL	4	0	4	3	0	1	0	0	0	0	0	0	1	0	3	1
1923	CIN	NL	3	0	3	2	1	0	0	0	0	0	0	0	0	0	3	0
1925	PHI	NL	7	4	3	2	3	1	1	0	0	0	0	0	0	0	3	4
1927	CLE	AL	2	1	1	1	1	0	0	0	0	0	0	0	2	0	1	1
1928	CLE	AL	3	0	3	2	1	0	0	0	0	0	0	0	0	0	1	2
1929	CLE	AL	6	1	5	3	1	2	0	1	0	0	0	0	0	0	4	2
1931	CLE	AL	1	0	1	0	1	0	0	0	0	0	0	0	0	0	1	0
	CHI	AL	2	1	1	1	0	1	0	0	0	0	0	1	0	0	0	2
	Total		3	1	2	1	1	1	0	0	0	0	0	1	0	0	1	2
1933	CHI	AL	2	0	2	0	0	2	0	0	0	0	0	0	0	0	2	0
Total			31	7	24	15	8	7	1	1	0	0	0	1	3	0	18	13

Rank among batters: 1,400 • *Top target (2 home runs)*: Johnny Cooney, Rube Walberg, Lefty Grove • *Number of pitchers victimized*: 28 • *Total ballparks homered in*: 13 • *First HR*: 04/23/1921 off Earl Hamilton

Barry Foote

BARRY CLIFTON FOOTE
B: 02/16/1952
BR

Year	Tm	Lg	Tot	H	A	Men-On 0	1	2	3	One-Game 2	3	4	LO	XN	IP	PH	RHP	LHP
1974	MON	NL	11	8	3	9	1	1	0	0	0	0	0	0	0	0	6	5
1975	MON	NL	7	2	5	4	2	1	0	0	0	0	0	0	0	0	1	6
1976	MON	NL	7	4	3	5	2	0	0	0	0	0	0	0	1	0	3	4
1977	MON	NL	2	1	1	1	1	0	0	0	0	0	0	0	0	0	2	0
	PHI	NL	1	0	1	0	1	0	0	0	0	0	0	0	0	0	1	0
	Total		3	1	2	1	2	0	0	0	0	0	0	0	0	0	3	0
1978	PHI	NL	1	0	1	0	1	0	0	0	0	0	0	1	0	0	0	1
1979	CHI	NL	16	10	6	8	6	0	2	1	0	0	0	0	0	0	12	4
1980	CHI	NL	6	4	2	4	0	1	1	1	0	0	0	0	0	0	5	1
1981	NY	AL	6	1	5	6	0	0	0	0	0	0	0	0	0	0	3	3
Total			57	30	27	37	14	3	3	2	0	0	0	1	1	0	33	24

Rank among batters: 902 • *Top target (3 home runs)*: Jack Curtis • *Number of pitchers victimized*: 49 • *Total ballparks homered in*: 17 • *First HR*: 04/17/1974 off George Stone

Davy Force

DAVID W. FORCE
B: 07/27/1849 D: 06/21/1918
BR

Year	Tm	Lg	Tot	H	A	Men-On 0	1	2	3	One-Game 2	3	4	LO	XN	IP	PH	RHP	LHP
1882	BUF	NL	1	0	1	0	0	1	0	0	0	0	0	0	0	0	1	0

Rank among batters: 4,707 • *Total ballparks homered in*: 1 • *First HR*: 05/18/1882 off Fred Goldsmith

Curt Ford

CURTIS GLENN FORD
B: 10/11/1960
BL

Year	Tm	Lg	Tot	H	A	Men-On 0	1	2	3	One-Game 2	3	4	LO	XN	IP	PH	RHP	LHP
1986	STL	NL	2	0	2	1	1	0	0	0	0	0	1	0	0	0	2	0
1987	STL	NL	3	1	2	2	1	0	0	1	0	0	0	0	0	0	3	0
1988	STL	NL	1	0	1	1	0	0	0	0	0	0	0	0	0	0	1	0
1989	PHI	NL	1	0	1	1	0	0	0	0	0	0	0	0	0	0	1	0
Total			7	1	6	5	2	0	0	1	0	0	1	0	0	0	7	0

Rank among batters: 2,834 • *Top target (2 home runs)*: Jeff Fischer • *Number of pitchers victimized*: 6 • *Total ballparks homered in*: 5 • *First HR*: 06/20/1986 off Charles Hudson

Dan Ford

DARNELL GLENN FORD
B: 05/19/1952
BR

Year	Tm	Lg	Tot	H	A	Men-On 0	1	2	3	One-Game 2	3	4	LO	XN	IP	PH	RHP	LHP
1975	MIN	AL	15	8	7	11	3	1	0	2	0	0	0	0	1	0	11	4
1976	MIN	AL	20	8	12	9	9	2	0	1	0	0	0	1	0	1	13	7
1977	MIN	AL	11	8	3	8	3	0	0	0	0	0	0	0	0	0	2	9
1978	MIN	AL	11	6	5	5	4	2	0	1	0	0	0	0	0	0	3	8
1979	CAL	AL	21	11	10	10	10	0	1	2	0	0	0	0	0	0	14	7
1980	CAL	AL	7	4	3	5	2	0	0	0	0	0	0	0	0	0	3	4
1981	CAL	AL	15	9	6	11	2	2	0	0	0	0	0	0	0	0	11	4
1982	BAL	AL	10	5	5	5	2	2	1	0	0	0	0	0	0	1	3	7
1983	BAL	AL	9	3	6	7	2	0	0	0	1	0	1	0	0	0	5	4
1984	BAL	AL	1	0	1	1	0	0	0	0	0	0	0	0	0	0	1	0
1985	BAL	AL	1	0	1	1	0	0	0	0	0	0	0	0	0	0	0	1
Total			121	62	59	73	37	9	2	6	1	0	1	1	1	2	66	55

Rank among batters: 382 • Top target (3 home runs): Stan Bahnsen, Jesse Jefferson, Paul Splittorff, Mike Norris, Jim Palmer, Dan Spillner, Bob Lacey • *Number of pitchers victimized*: 88 • *Total ballparks homered in*: 14 • *First HR*: 06/10/1975 off Dennis Eckersley • *Hit for Cycle*—vs SEA: 08/10/1979 • *World Series HR*—1; *LCS HR*—2

Hod Ford

HORACE HILLS FORD
B: 07/23/1897 D: 01/29/1977
BR

Year	Tm	Lg	Tot	H	A	Men-On 0	1	2	3	One-Game 2	3	4	LO	XN	IP	PH	RHP	LHP
1920	BOS	NL	1	0	1	1	0	0	0	0	0	0	0	0	0	0	1	0
1921	BOS	NL	2	0	2	1	1	0	0	0	0	0	0	0	0	0	2	0
1922	BOS	NL	2	1	1	1	1	0	0	0	0	0	0	0	1	0	2	0
1923	BOS	NL	2	0	2	0	1	0	1	0	0	0	0	0	0	0	2	0
1924	PHI	NL	3	2	1	2	0	1	0	0	0	0	0	0	0	0	2	1
1925	BRO	NL	1	0	1	0	0	1	0	0	0	0	0	0	0	0	1	0
1927	CIN	NL	1	0	1	1	0	0	0	0	0	0	0	0	0	0	0	1
1929	CIN	NL	3	1	2	1	2	0	0	0	0	0	0	0	1	0	3	0
1930	CIN	NL	1	0	1	1	0	0	0	0	0	0	0	0	0	0	1	0
Total			16	4	12	8	5	2	1	0	0	0	0	0	2	0	14	2

Rank among batters: 2,029 • *Top target (3 home runs)*: Dazzy Vance • *Number of pitchers victimized*: 12 • *Total ballparks homered in*: 7 • *First HR*: 09/25/1920 off Red Causey

Russ Ford

RUSSELL WILLIAM FORD
B: 04/25/1883 D: 01/24/1960
BR

Year	Tm	Lg	Tot	H	A	Men-On 0	1	2	3	One-Game 2	3	4	LO	XN	IP	PH	RHP	LHP
1912	NY	AL	1	1	0	1	0	0	0	0	0	0	0	0	0	0	1	0

Rank among batters: 4,707 • *Total ballparks homered in*: 1 • *First HR*: 07/23/1912 off Joe Benz

Ted Ford

THEODORE HENRY FORD
B: 02/07/1947
BR

Year	Tm	Lg	Tot	H	A	Men-On 0	1	2	3	One-Game 2	3	4	LO	XN	IP	PH	RHP	LHP
1970	CLE	AL	1	0	1	1	0	0	0	0	0	0	0	0	0	0	0	1

Ted Ford *continued*

Year	Tm	Lg	Tot	H	A	Men-On 0	1	2	3	One-Game 2	3	4	LO	XN	IP	PH	RHP	LHP
1971	CLE	AL	2	0	2	1	0	1	0	0	0	0	1	1	0	0	2	0
1972	TEX	AL	14	6	8	10	2	2	0	0	0	0	0	0	0	0	9	5
Total			17	6	11	12	2	3	0	0	0	0	1	1	0	0	11	6

Rank among batters: 1,969 • *Top target (2 home runs)*: Ron Klimkowski, Wilbur Wood • *Number of pitchers victimized*: 15 • *Total ballparks homered in*: 8 • *First HR*: 04/14/1970 off Mickey Lolich

Whitey Ford

EDWARD CHARLES FORD
B: 10/21/1926
BL HOF

Year	Tm	Lg	Tot	H	A	Men-On 0	1	2	3	One-Game 2	3	4	LO	XN	IP	PH	RHP	LHP
1955	NY	AL	1	1	0	1	0	0	0	0	0	0	0	0	0	0	1	0
1959	NY	AL	1	0	1	1	0	0	0	0	0	0	0	0	0	0	0	1
1963	NY	AL	1	1	0	1	0	0	0	0	0	0	0	0	0	0	1	0
Total			3	2	1	3	0	0	0	0	0	0	0	0	0	0	2	1

Rank among batters: 3,735 • *Total ballparks homered in*: 2 • *First HR*: 07/29/1955 off Vic Raschi

Frank Foreman

FRANCIS ISAIAH FOREMAN
B: 05/01/1863 D: 11/19/1957
BL

Year	Tm	Lg	Tot	H	A	Men-On 0	1	2	3	One-Game 2	3	4	LO	XN	IP	PH	RHP	LHP
1889	BAL	AA	1	0	1	1	0	0	0	0	0	0	0	0	0	0	1	0
1890	CIN	NL	1	1	0	0	1	0	0	0	0	0	0	0	0	0	0	0
1891	WAS	AA	4	4	0	3	1	0	0	0	0	0	0	0	0	0	3	1
1892	WAS	NL	1	1	0	1	0	0	0	0	0	0	0	0	0	0	1	0
1895	CIN	NL	2	0	2	2	0	0	0	1	0	0	0	0	0	0	2	0
Total			9	6	3	7	2	0	0	1	0	0	0	0	0	0	7	1

Rank among batters: 2,587 • *Top target (2 home runs)*: Bill Hutchison • *Number of pitchers victimized*: 8 • *Total ballparks homered in*: 3 • *First HR*: 07/05/1889 off Jesse Duryea

Mike Fornieles

JOSE MIGUEL (TORRES) FORNIELES
B: 01/18/1932
BR

Year	Tm	Lg	Tot	H	A	Men-On 0	1	2	3	One-Game 2	3	4	LO	XN	IP	PH	RHP	LHP
1961	BOS	AL	1	1	0	0	1	0	0	0	0	0	0	0	0	0	1	0

Rank among batters: 4,707 • *Total ballparks homered in*: 1 • *First HR*: 09/08/1961 off Paul Foytack

Bob Forsch

ROBERT HERBERT FORSCH
B: 01/13/1950
BR

Year	Tm	Lg	Tot	H	A	Men-On 0	1	2	3	One-Game 2	3	4	LO	XN	IP	PH	RHP	LHP
1975	STL	NL	1	1	0	0	1	0	0	0	0	0	0	0	0	0	0	1
1976	STL	NL	1	0	1	1	0	0	0	0	0	0	0	0	0	0	0	1
1978	STL	NL	1	1	0	0	1	0	0	0	0	0	0	0	0	0	0	1
1980	STL	NL	3	1	2	2	0	1	0	0	0	0	0	0	0	0	0	3
1983	STL	NL	1	1	0	1	0	0	0	0	0	0	0	0	0	0	0	1
1985	STL	NL	1	1	0	1	0	0	0	0	0	0	0	0	0	0	1	0
1986	STL	NL	2	2	0	0	0	1	1	0	0	0	0	0	0	0	2	0
1987	STL	NL	2	0	2	2	0	0	0	0	0	0	0	0	0	0	2	0
Total			12	7	5	7	2	2	1	0	0	0	0	0	0	0	5	7

Rank among batters: 2,325 • *Total ballparks homered in*: 6 • *First HR*: 08/08/1975 off Rich Folkers

Tom Forster

THOMAS W. FORSTER
B: 05/01/1859 D: 07/17/1946
BR

Year	Tm	Lg	Tot	H	A	Men-On 0	1	2	3	One-Game 2	3	4	LO	XN	IP	PH	RHP	LHP
1886	NY	AA	1	0	1	1	0	0	0	0	0	0	0	0	1	0	0	1

Rank among batters: 4,707 • *Total ballparks homered in*: 1 • *First HR*: 06/08/1886 off Matt Kilroy

Ray Fosse

RAYMOND EARL FOSSE
B: 04/04/1947
BR

Year	Tm	Lg	Tot	H	A	Men-On 0	1	2	3	One-Game 2	3	4	LO	XN	IP	PH	RHP	LHP
1969	CLE	AL	2	1	1	1	0	1	0	0	0	0	0	0	0	0	1	1
1970	CLE	AL	18	12	6	11	2	4	1	1	0	0	0	0	0	0	11	7
1971	CLE	AL	12	7	5	3	3	5	1	0	0	0	0	1	0	0	6	6

Ray Fosse *continued*

Year	Tm	Lg	Tot	H	A	Men-On 0	1	2	3	One-Game 2	3	4	LO	XN	IP	PH	RHP	LHP
1972	CLE	AL	10	5	5	8	2	0	0	1	0	0	0	0	0	0	5	5
1973	OAK	AL	7	3	4	5	2	0	0	0	0	0	0	0	0	0	6	1
1974	OAK	AL	4	1	3	2	2	0	0	0	0	0	0	0	0	0	2	2
1976	CLE	AL	2	1	1	2	0	0	0	0	0	0	0	0	0	0	1	1
1977	CLE	AL	6	2	4	5	1	0	0	0	0	0	0	0	0	0	4	2
Total			61	32	29	37	12	10	2	2	0	0	0	1	0	0	36	25

Rank among batters: 844 • *Top target (3 home runs)*: Mike Cuellar • *Number of pitchers victimized*: 52 • *Total ballparks homered in*: 11 • *First HR*: 05/22/1969 off Dave Wickersham • *World Series HR*—1; *LCS HR*—1

Eddie Foster

EDWARD CUNNINGHAM FOSTER
B: 02/13/1887 D: 01/15/1937
BR

Year	Tm	Lg	Tot	H	A	Men-On 0	1	2	3	One-Game 2	3	4	LO	XN	IP	PH	RHP	LHP
1912	WAS	AL	2	2	0	0	1	1	0	0	0	0	0	0	1	0	2	0
1913	WAS	AL	1	0	1	0	0	1	0	0	0	0	0	0	0	0	1	0
1914	WAS	AL	2	1	1	1	0	1	0	0	0	0	0	0	0	0	2	0
1916	WAS	AL	1	1	0	1	0	0	0	0	0	0	0	0	1	0	0	1
Total			6	4	2	2	1	3	0	0	0	0	0	0	2	0	5	1

Rank among batters: 2,988 • *Top target (2 home runs)*: Jean Dubuc • *Number of pitchers victimized*: 5 • *Total ballparks homered in*: 3 • *First HR*: 04/27/1912 off Ray Caldwell

Elmer Foster

ELMER ELLSWORTH FOSTER
B: 08/15/1861 D: 07/22/1946
BR

Year	Tm	Lg	Tot	H	A	Men-On 0	1	2	3	One-Game 2	3	4	LO	XN	IP	PH	RHP	LHP
1890	CHI	NL	5	5	0	2	0	2	1	1	0	0	0	0	0	0	4	1
1891	CHI	NL	1	0	1	1	0	0	0	0	0	0	0	0	0	0	1	0
Total			6	5	1	3	0	2	1	1	0	0	0	0	0	0	5	1

Rank among batters: 2,988 • *Top target (2 home runs)*: John Dolan • *Number of pitchers victimized*: 5 • *Total ballparks homered in*: 2 • *First HR*: 09/05/1890 off John Dolan

George Foster

GEORGE ARTHUR FOSTER
B: 12/01/1948
BR

Year	Tm	Lg	Tot	H	A	Men-On 0	1	2	3	One-Game 2	3	4	LO	XN	IP	PH	RHP	LHP
1970	SF	NL	1	1	0	1	0	0	0	0	0	0	0	0	0	1	1	0
1971	SF	NL	3	1	2	3	0	0	0	0	0	0	0	0	0	1	2	1
	CIN	NL	10	8	2	6	1	2	1	0	0	0	0	0	0	0	7	3
	Total		13	9	4	9	1	2	1	0	0	0	0	0	0	1	9	4
1972	CIN	NL	2	1	1	1	0	0	1	0	0	0	0	0	0	0	0	2
1973	CIN	NL	4	0	4	3	0	1	0	1	0	0	0	0	0	0	0	4
1974	CIN	NL	7	3	4	2	3	2	0	0	0	0	0	0	0	0	4	3
1975	CIN	NL	23	15	8	11	8	3	1	2	0	0	0	1	0	1	14	9
1976	CIN	NL	29	13	16	15	5	8	1	3	0	0	0	0	0	0	19	10
1977	CIN	NL	52	21	31	26	16	10	0	7	1	0	0	0	0	0	32	20
1978	CIN	NL	40	25	15	22	9	7	2	2	0	0	0	1	0	0	24	16
1979	CIN	NL	30	20	10	18	9	2	1	2	0	0	0	0	0	0	19	11
1980	CIN	NL	25	14	11	10	9	5	1	1	0	0	0	0	0	0	16	9
1981	CIN	NL	22	8	14	7	9	5	1	0	0	0	0	0	0	0	19	3
1982	NY	NL	13	7	6	5	7	1	0	0	0	0	0	0	0	0	9	4
1983	NY	NL	28	17	11	13	7	6	2	1	0	0	0	1	0	1	16	12
1984	NY	NL	24	11	13	16	6	2	0	0	0	0	0	0	0	0	14	10
1985	NY	NL	21	9	12	11	6	3	1	0	0	0	0	0	0	0	12	9
1986	NY	NL	13	9	4	8	2	2	1	2	0	0	0	0	0	0	6	7
	CHI	AL	1	1	0	1	0	0	0	0	0	0	0	0	0	0	1	0
	Total		14	10	4	9	2	2	1	2	0	0	0	0	0	0	7	7
Total			348	184	164	179	97	59	13	21	1	0	0	3	0	4	215	133

Rank among batters: 45 • *Top target (6 home runs)*: Larry McWilliams, Bob Welch • *Number of pitchers victimized*: 198 • *Total ballparks homered in*: 14 • *First HR*: 09/25/1970 off Pat Dobson • *LCS HR*—3; *All-Star HR*—1

Kevin Foster

KEVIN CHRISTOPHER FOSTER
B: 01/13/1969
BR

Year	Tm	Lg	Tot	H	A	Men-On 0	1	2	3	One-Game 2	3	4	LO	XN	IP	PH	RHP	LHP
1995	CHI	NL	1	0	1	1	0	0	0	0	0	0	0	0	0	0	1	0

Rank among batters: 4,707 • *Total ballparks homered in*: 1 • *First HR*: 05/23/1995 off Marvin Freeman

Leo Foster

LEONARD NORRIS FOSTER
B: 02/02/1951
BR

Year	Tm	Lg	Tot	H	A	Men-On 0	Men-On 1	Men-On 2	Men-On 3	One-Game 2	One-Game 3	One-Game 4	LO	XN	IP	PH	RHP	LHP
1974	ATL	NL	1	0	1	1	0	0	0	0	0	0	0	0	0	0	0	1
1976	NY	NL	1	0	1	0	1	0	0	0	0	0	0	0	0	0	1	0
Total			2	0	2	1	1	0	0	0	0	0	0	0	0	0	1	1

Rank among batters: 4,129 • *Total ballparks homered in*: 2 • *First HR*: 05/01/1974 off Jack Curtis

Pop Foster

CLARENCE FRANCIS FOSTER
B: 04/08/1878 D: 04/16/1944
BR

Year	Tm	Lg	Tot	H	A	Men-On 0	Men-On 1	Men-On 2	Men-On 3	One-Game 2	One-Game 3	One-Game 4	LO	XN	IP	PH	RHP	LHP
1899	NY	NL	3	2	1	0	2	1	0	0	0	0	0	0	0	0	2	1
1901	WAS	AL	6	4	2	3	1	2	0	0	0	0	0	0	0	0	3	3
	CHI	AL	1	1	0	1	0	0	0	0	0	0	0	0	0	0	1	0
	Total		7	5	2	4	1	2	0	0	0	0	0	0	0	0	4	3
Total			10	7	3	4	3	3	0	0	0	0	0	0	0	0	6	4

Rank among batters: 2,500 • *Top target (2 home runs)*: Deacon Phillippe • *Number of pitchers victimized*: 9 • *Total ballparks homered in*: 6 • *First HR*: 06/04/1899 off Deacon Phillippe

Roy Foster

ROY FOSTER
B: 07/29/1945
BR

Year	Tm	Lg	Tot	H	A	Men-On 0	Men-On 1	Men-On 2	Men-On 3	One-Game 2	One-Game 3	One-Game 4	LO	XN	IP	PH	RHP	LHP
1970	CLE	AL	23	19	4	13	6	4	0	2	0	0	0	1	0	0	14	9
1971	CLE	AL	18	11	7	11	4	2	1	1	0	0	0	1	0	1	7	11
1972	CLE	AL	4	1	3	1	3	0	0	0	0	0	0	0	0	0	1	3
Total			45	31	14	25	13	6	1	3	0	0	0	2	0	1	22	23

Rank among batters: 1,082 • *Top target (3 home runs)*: Dave McNally, Joe Coleman • *Number of pitchers victimized*: 35 • *Total ballparks homered in*: 8 • *First HR*: 04/07/1970 off Dave McNally

Rube Foster

GEORGE FOSTER
B: 01/05/1888 D: 03/01/1976
BR

Year	Tm	Lg	Tot	H	A	Men-On 0	Men-On 1	Men-On 2	Men-On 3	One-Game 2	One-Game 3	One-Game 4	LO	XN	IP	PH	RHP	LHP
1915	BOS	AL	1	0	1	1	0	0	0	0	0	0	0	0	0	0	0	1

Rank among batters: 4,707 • *Total ballparks homered in*: 1 • *First HR*: 07/10/1915 off Pug Cavet

Bob Fothergill

ROBERT ROY FOTHERGILL
B: 08/16/1897 D: 03/20/1938
BR

Year	Tm	Lg	Tot	H	A	Men-On 0	Men-On 1	Men-On 2	Men-On 3	One-Game 2	One-Game 3	One-Game 4	LO	XN	IP	PH	RHP	LHP
1923	DET	AL	1	1	0	1	0	0	0	0	0	0	0	0	0	0	0	1
1925	DET	AL	2	1	1	2	0	0	0	0	0	0	0	0	0	0	0	2
1926	DET	AL	3	2	1	2	1	0	0	0	0	0	0	0	0	0	2	1
1927	DET	AL	9	5	4	5	3	1	0	0	0	0	0	0	1	0	5	4
1928	DET	AL	3	2	1	2	0	1	0	0	0	0	0	0	0	0	2	1
1929	DET	AL	6	4	2	5	1	0	0	1	0	0	0	0	1	0	5	1
1930	DET	AL	2	1	1	1	0	0	1	0	0	0	0	0	0	0	0	2
1931	CHI	AL	3	1	2	0	3	0	0	0	0	0	0	0	0	0	1	2
1932	CHI	AL	7	2	5	2	4	1	0	0	0	0	0	0	0	0	5	2
Total			36	19	17	20	12	3	1	1	0	0	0	0	2	0	20	16

Rank among batters: 1,274 • *Top target (4 home runs)*: Lefty Grove • *Number of pitchers victimized*: 25 • *Total ballparks homered in*: 7 • *First HR*: 08/16/1923 off Fred Heimach • *Hit for Cycle*—vs BOS: 09/26/1926 (1)

Jack Fournier

JOHN FRANK FOURNIER
B: 09/28/1889 D: 09/05/1973
BL

Year	Tm	Lg	Tot	H	A	Men-On 0	Men-On 1	Men-On 2	Men-On 3	One-Game 2	One-Game 3	One-Game 4	LO	XN	IP	PH	RHP	LHP
1913	CHI	AL	1	0	1	1	0	0	0	0	0	0	0	0	0	0	0	1
1914	CHI	AL	6	0	6	3	2	1	0	1	0	0	0	1	2	0	5	1
1915	CHI	AL	5	2	3	1	2	2	0	0	0	0	0	0	1	0	4	1
1916	CHI	AL	3	0	3	1	1	1	0	0	0	0	0	0	1	0	3	0
1920	STL	NL	3	0	3	1	0	2	0	0	0	0	0	0	1	0	1	2
1921	STL	NL	16	8	8	8	8	0	0	1	0	0	0	0	1	0	13	3

Jack Fournier *continued*

Year	Tm	Lg	Tot	H	A	Men-On 0	Men-On 1	Men-On 2	Men-On 3	One-Game 2	One-Game 3	One-Game 4	LO	XN	IP	PH	RHP	LHP
1922	STL	NL	10	7	3	4	3	2	1	0	0	0	0	0	1	2	10	0
1923	BRO	NL	22	11	11	10	10	2	0	0	0	0	0	0	1	0	18	4
1924	BRO	NL	27	10	17	14	9	4	0	5	0	0	0	0	1	0	18	9
1925	BRO	NL	22	9	13	9	9	4	0	1	0	0	0	0	0	0	16	6
1926	BRO	NL	11	5	6	5	6	0	0	0	1	0	0	0	1	0	8	3
1927	BOS	NL	10	0	10	5	5	0	0	0	0	0	0	0	0	0	6	4
Total			136	52	84	62	55	18	1	8	1	0	0	1	10	2	102	34

Rank among batters: 322 • *Top target (8 home runs)*: Jimmy Ring • *Number of pitchers victimized*: 77 • *Total ballparks homered in*: 13 • *First HR*: 08/07/1913 off Joe Engel

Dave Foutz

DAVID LUTHER FOUTZ
B: 09/07/1856 D: 03/05/1897
BR

Year	Tm	Lg	Tot	H	A	Men-On 0	Men-On 1	Men-On 2	Men-On 3	One-Game 2	One-Game 3	One-Game 4	LO	XN	IP	PH	RHP	LHP
1886	STL	AA	3	2	1	1	2	0	0	0	0	0	0	0	2	0	3	0
1887	STL	AA	4	4	0	0	3	1	0	1	0	0	0	0	0	0	3	0
1888	BRO	AA	3	1	2	1	1	1	0	0	0	0	0	0	0	0	2	1
1889	BRO	AA	6	3	3	1	2	1	2	0	0	0	0	0	1	0	3	2
1890	BRO	NL	5	4	1	2	2	1	0	0	0	0	0	0	1	0	4	1
1891	BRO	NL	2	1	1	0	1	1	0	0	0	0	0	0	2	0	1	1
1892	BRO	NL	1	0	1	0	1	0	0	0	0	0	0	0	0	0	1	0
1893	BRO	NL	7	5	2	3	4	0	0	0	0	0	0	0	0	0	6	0
Total			31	20	11	8	16	5	2	1	0	0	0	0	6	0	23	4

Rank among batters: 1,400 • *Top target (3 home runs)*: Jack Lynch • *Number of pitchers victimized*: 27 • *Total ballparks homered in*: 10 • *First HR*: 08/05/1886 off Jack Lynch • *World Series HR*—1

Frank Foutz

FRANK HAYES FOUTZ
B: 04/08/1877 D: 12/25/1961
BR

Year	Tm	Lg	Tot	H	A	Men-On 0	Men-On 1	Men-On 2	Men-On 3	One-Game 2	One-Game 3	One-Game 4	LO	XN	IP	PH	RHP	LHP
1901	BAL	AL	2	0	2	1	0	1	0	0	0	0	0	0	1	0	1	1

Rank among batters: 4,129 • *Total ballparks homered in*: 1 • *First HR*: 04/30/1901 off Watty Lee

Boob Fowler

JOSEPH CHESTER FOWLER
B: 11/11/1900 D: 10/08/1988
BL

Year	Tm	Lg	Tot	H	A	Men-On 0	Men-On 1	Men-On 2	Men-On 3	One-Game 2	One-Game 3	One-Game 4	LO	XN	IP	PH	RHP	LHP
1923	CIN	NL	1	1	0	0	0	1	0	0	0	0	0	0	1	0	1	0

Rank among batters: 4,707 • *Total ballparks homered in*: 1 • *First HR*: 09/24/1923 off Rosy Ryan

Dick Fowler

RICHARD JOHN FOWLER
B: 03/30/1921 D: 05/22/1972
BR

Year	Tm	Lg	Tot	H	A	Men-On 0	Men-On 1	Men-On 2	Men-On 3	One-Game 2	One-Game 3	One-Game 4	LO	XN	IP	PH	RHP	LHP
1948	PHI	AL	1	0	1	1	0	0	0	0	0	0	0	0	0	0	1	0

Rank among batters: 4,707 • *Total ballparks homered in*: 1 • *First HR*: 08/08/1948 off Blackie Schwamb

Eric Fox

ERIC HOLLIS FOX
B: 08/15/1963
BB

Year	Tm	Lg	Tot	H	A	Men-On 0	Men-On 1	Men-On 2	Men-On 3	One-Game 2	One-Game 3	One-Game 4	LO	XN	IP	PH	RHP	LHP
1992	OAK	AL	3	0	3	2	0	1	0	0	0	0	0	0	0	0	3	0
1993	OAK	AL	1	1	0	0	0	0	1	0	0	0	0	0	0	0	0	1
1994	OAK	AL	1	0	1	1	0	0	0	0	0	0	0	0	0	0	0	1
Total			5	1	4	3	0	1	1	0	0	0	0	0	0	0	3	2

Rank among batters: 3,191 • *Total ballparks homered in*: 5 • *First HR*: 07/11/1992 off Juan Guzman

Howie Fox

HOWARD FRANCIS FOX
B: 03/01/1921 D: 10/09/1955
BR

Year	Tm	Lg	Tot	H	A	Men-On 0	Men-On 1	Men-On 2	Men-On 3	One-Game 2	One-Game 3	One-Game 4	LO	XN	IP	PH	RHP	LHP
1950	CIN	NL	1	0	1	0	0	1	0	0	0	0	0	0	0	0	0	1

Year	Tm	Lg	Tot	H	A	Men-On 0	1	2	3	One-Game 2	3	4	LO	XN	IP	PH	RHP	LHP

Howie Fox *continued*

Year	Tm	Lg	Tot	H	A	Men-On 0	1	2	3	One-Game 2	3	4	LO	XN	IP	PH	RHP	LHP
1951	CIN	NL	1	1	0	1	0	0	0	0	0	0	0	0	0	0	0	1
Total			2	1	1	1	0	1	0	0	0	0	0	0	0	0	0	2

Rank among batters: 4,129 • *Total ballparks homered in*: 2 • *First HR*: 06/28/1950 off Bill Werle

Nellie Fox

JACOB NELSON FOX
B: 12/25/1927 D: 12/01/1975
BL

Year	Tm	Lg	Tot	H	A	Men-On 0	1	2	3	One-Game 2	3	4	LO	XN	IP	PH	RHP	LHP
1951	CHI	AL	4	0	4	2	2	0	0	0	0	0	0	1	2	0	4	0
1953	CHI	AL	3	0	3	0	3	0	0	0	0	0	0	0	0	0	3	0
1954	CHI	AL	2	0	2	1	1	0	0	0	0	0	0	0	0	0	2	0
1955	CHI	AL	6	2	4	5	0	1	0	1	0	0	0	0	0	0	5	1
1956	CHI	AL	4	0	4	4	0	0	0	0	0	0	0	0	0	0	2	2
1957	CHI	AL	6	0	6	5	1	0	0	0	0	0	0	1	0	0	5	1
1959	CHI	AL	2	0	2	0	1	1	0	0	0	0	0	1	0	0	1	1
1960	CHI	AL	2	1	1	1	1	0	0	0	0	0	0	1	0	0	2	0
1961	CHI	AL	2	1	1	2	0	0	0	0	0	0	0	0	1	0	2	0
1962	CHI	AL	2	1	1	2	0	0	0	0	0	0	0	0	0	0	2	0
1963	CHI	AL	2	0	2	1	1	0	0	0	0	0	0	0	0	0	2	0
Total			35	5	30	23	10	2	0	1	0	0	0	4	3	0	30	5

Rank among batters: 1,291 • *Top target (3 home runs)*: Pedro Ramos • *Number of pitchers victimized*: 30 • *Total ballparks homered in*: 10 • *First HR*: 05/15/1951 off Ray Scarborough

Paddy Fox

GEORGE B. FOX
B: 12/01/1868 D: 05/08/1914

Year	Tm	Lg	Tot	H	A	Men-On 0	1	2	3	One-Game 2	3	4	LO	XN	IP	PH	RHP	LHP
1899	PIT	NL	1	0	1	1	0	0	0	0	0	0	0	0	1	0	1	0

Rank among batters: 4,707 • *Total ballparks homered in*: 1 • *First HR*: 09/05/1899 off Nixey Callahan

Pete Fox

ERVIN FOX
B: 03/08/1909 D: 07/05/1966
BR

Year	Tm	Lg	Tot	H	A	Men-On 0	1	2	3	One-Game 2	3	4	LO	XN	IP	PH	RHP	LHP
1933	DET	AL	7	2	5	3	3	1	0	0	0	0	0	1	0	0	6	1
1934	DET	AL	2	2	0	0	2	0	0	0	0	0	0	0	0	0	2	0
1935	DET	AL	15	7	8	7	4	2	2	0	0	0	1	1	0	0	10	5
1936	DET	AL	4	2	2	3	1	0	0	0	0	0	0	0	0	0	3	1
1937	DET	AL	12	6	6	11	0	1	0	0	0	0	2	0	0	0	9	3
1938	DET	AL	7	1	6	3	2	1	1	0	0	0	0	0	0	0	4	3
1939	DET	AL	7	3	4	5	0	0	2	0	0	0	0	0	1	0	5	2
1940	DET	AL	5	2	3	3	2	0	0	0	0	0	0	0	0	0	4	1
1942	BOS	AL	3	0	3	3	0	0	0	0	0	0	0	0	0	0	2	1
1943	BOS	AL	2	2	0	1	0	1	0	0	0	0	0	0	0	0	2	0
1944	BOS	AL	1	0	1	1	0	0	0	0	0	0	0	0	0	0	1	0
Total			65	27	38	40	14	6	5	0	0	0	3	2	1	0	48	17

Rank among batters: 799 • *Top target (5 home runs)*: Red Ruffing • *Number of pitchers victimized*: 51 • *Total ballparks homered in*: 7 • *First HR*: 04/17/1933 off Vic Frasier

Bill Foxen

WILLIAM ALOYSIUS FOXEN
B: 05/31/1884 D: 04/17/1937
BL

Year	Tm	Lg	Tot	H	A	Men-On 0	1	2	3	One-Game 2	3	4	LO	XN	IP	PH	RHP	LHP
1909	PHI	NL	1	1	0	0	1	0	0	0	0	0	0	0	0	0	1	0

Rank among batters: 4,707 • *Total ballparks homered in*: 1 • *First HR*: 04/24/1909 off Vive Lindaman

Jimmie Foxx

JAMES EMORY FOXX
B: 10/22/1907 D: 07/21/1967
BR HOF

Year	Tm	Lg	Tot	H	A	Men-On 0	1	2	3	One-Game 2	3	4	LO	XN	IP	PH	RHP	LHP
1927	PHI	AL	3	3	0	2	0	1	0	0	0	0	0	0	0	0	2	1
1928	PHI	AL	13	7	6	7	3	3	0	0	0	0	0	1	1	1	9	4

Jimmie Foxx *continued*

						Men-On				One-Game								
Year	**Tm**	**Lg**	**Tot**	**H**	**A**	**0**	**1**	**2**	**3**	**2**	**3**	**4**	**LO**	**XN**	**IP**	**PH**	**RHP**	**LHP**
1929	PHI	AL	33	18	15	12	17	4	0	3	0	0	0	1	1	0	27	6
1930	PHI	AL	37	22	15	12	16	8	1	3	0	0	0	0	1	0	31	6
1931	PHI	AL	30	17	13	13	12	4	1	1	0	0	0	0	3	1	20	10
1932	PHI	AL	58	32	26	34	10	11	3	4	1	0	0	2	1	0	45	13
1933	PHI	AL	48	31	17	22	16	9	1	6	1	0	0	2	0	0	38	10
1934	PHI	AL	44	22	22	26	10	5	3	7	0	0	0	0	1	0	40	4
1935	PHI	AL	36	17	19	16	16	4	0	6	0	0	0	2	0	0	29	7
1936	BOS	AL	41	21	20	17	14	10	0	4	0	0	0	0	0	0	33	8
1937	BOS	AL	36	18	18	17	12	7	0	3	0	0	0	0	0	0	32	4
1938	BOS	AL	50	35	15	24	12	11	3	10	0	0	0	1	0	0	43	7
1939	BOS	AL	35	17	18	22	9	4	0	4	0	0	0	1	0	0	31	4
1940	BOS	AL	36	19	17	16	10	7	3	2	0	0	0	2	0	0	28	8
1941	BOS	AL	19	12	7	9	4	5	1	0	0	0	0	2	0	0	16	3
1942	BOS	AL	5	4	1	2	3	0	0	0	0	0	0	0	0	0	4	1
	CHI	NL	3	1	2	1	1	1	0	0	0	0	0	0	0	0	3	0
	Total		8	5	3	3	4	1	0	0	0	0	0	0	0	0	7	1
1945	PHI	NL	7	3	4	3	2	1	1	0	0	0	0	0	0	1	7	0
Total			534	299	235	255	167	95	17	53	2	0	0	14	8	3	438	96

Rank among batters: 9 • *Top target (16 home runs)*: General Crowder, Tommy Bridges, Red Ruffing • *Number of pitchers victimized*: 173 • *Total ballparks homered in*: 14 • *First HR*: 05/31/1927 off Urban Shocker • *Hit for Cycle*—@CLE: 08/14/1933 • *World Series HR*—4; *All-Star HR*—1

Joe Foy

JOSEPH ANTHONY FOY
B: 02/21/1943 D: 10/12/1989
BR

Year	Tm	Lg	Tot	H	A	0	1	2	3	2	3	4	LO	XN	IP	PH	RHP	LHP
1966	BOS	AL	15	10	5	10	3	1	1	1	0	0	0	2	1	0	12	3
1967	BOS	AL	16	9	7	10	2	2	2	1	0	0	0	0	0	1	12	4
1968	BOS	AL	10	7	3	2	6	0	2	1	0	0	0	0	0	0	7	3
1969	KC	AL	11	5	6	4	7	0	0	0	0	0	0	0	0	0	9	2
1970	NY	NL	6	2	4	4	2	0	0	1	0	0	0	2	0	0	5	1
Total			58	33	25	30	20	3	5	4	0	0	0	4	1	1	45	13

Rank among batters: 886 • *Top target (3 home runs)*: Luis Tiant, Joe Horlen • *Number of pitchers victimized*: 50 • *Total ballparks homered in*: 14 • *First HR*: 06/03/1966 off Al Downing

Paul Foytack

PAUL EUGENE FOYTACK
B: 11/16/1930
BR

Year	Tm	Lg	Tot	H	A	0	1	2	3	2	3	4	LO	XN	IP	PH	RHP	LHP
1961	DET	AL	1	1	0	1	0	0	0	0	0	0	0	0	0	0	1	0

Rank among batters: 4,707 • *Total ballparks homered in*: 1 • *First HR*: 06/27/1961 off Don Larsen

Earl Francis

EARL COLEMAN FRANCIS
B: 07/14/1935
BR

Year	Tm	Lg	Tot	H	A	0	1	2	3	2	3	4	LO	XN	IP	PH	RHP	LHP
1962	PIT	NL	1	1	0	0	0	1	0	0	0	0	0	0	0	0	1	0

Rank among batters: 4,707 • *Total ballparks homered in*: 1 • *First HR*: 09/14/1962 off Bobby Bolin

Julio Franco

JULIO CESAR FRANCO
B: 08/23/1958
BR

Year	Tm	Lg	Tot	H	A	0	1	2	3	2	3	4	LO	XN	IP	PH	RHP	LHP
1983	CLE	AL	8	6	2	5	1	2	0	0	0	0	0	0	1	0	6	2
1984	CLE	AL	3	1	2	1	1	0	1	0	0	0	0	0	0	0	0	3
1985	CLE	AL	6	3	3	2	3	0	1	0	0	0	0	0	0	0	2	4
1986	CLE	AL	10	4	6	6	3	1	0	0	0	0	0	0	0	0	4	6
1987	CLE	AL	8	5	3	4	3	1	0	0	0	0	0	0	0	0	4	4
1988	CLE	AL	10	3	7	8	1	1	0	0	0	0	2	0	0	0	5	5
1989	TEX	AL	13	9	4	8	2	3	0	0	0	0	0	1	0	0	8	5
1990	TEX	AL	11	4	7	2	7	1	1	1	0	0	0	0	0	0	8	3
1991	TEX	AL	15	7	8	8	6	1	0	0	0	0	0	0	0	0	7	8

						Men-On				One-Game								
Year	Tm	Lg	Tot	H	A	0	1	2	3	2	3	4	LO	XN	IP	PH	RHP	LHP

Julio Franco *continued*

Year	Tm	Lg	Tot	H	A	0	1	2	3	2	3	4	LO	XN	IP	PH	RHP	LHP
1992	TEX	AL	2	2	0	1	0	1	0	0	0	0	0	0	0	0	1	1
1993	TEX	AL	14	6	8	8	4	0	2	0	0	0	0	0	0	0	11	3
1994	CHI	AL	20	10	10	12	5	3	0	2	0	0	0	1	0	0	13	7
Total			120	60	60	65	36	14	5	3	0	0	2	2	1	0	69	51

Rank among batters: 388 • Top target (3 home runs): Floyd Bannister, Oil Can Boyd, Dave Stewart, Mark Langston, Mike Gardiner • *Number of pitchers victimized*: 99 • *Total ballparks homered in*: 19 • *First HR*: 04/09/1983 off Tippy Martinez

Terry Francona

TERRY JON FRANCONA
B: 04/22/1959
BL

Year	Tm	Lg	Tot	H	A	0	1	2	3	2	3	4	LO	XN	IP	PH	RHP	LHP
1981	MON	NL	1	1	0	1	0	0	0	0	0	0	0	0	0	0	1	0
1983	MON	NL	3	1	2	2	1	0	0	0	0	0	0	0	0	0	3	0
1984	MON	NL	1	1	0	1	0	0	0	0	0	0	0	0	0	0	1	0
1985	MON	NL	2	0	2	2	0	0	0	0	0	0	0	0	0	0	2	0
1986	CHI	NL	2	0	2	2	0	0	0	0	0	0	0	0	0	0	2	0
1987	CIN	NL	3	2	1	2	1	0	0	0	0	0	0	0	0	0	3	0
1988	CLE	AL	1	1	0	1	0	0	0	0	0	0	0	0	0	0	1	0
1989	MIL	AL	3	1	2	2	1	0	0	0	0	0	0	0	0	0	3	0
Total			16	7	9	13	3	0	0	0	0	0	0	0	0	0	16	0

Rank among batters: 2,029 • *Total ballparks homered in*: 11 • *First HR*: 09/16/1981 off Bruce Sutter

Tito Francona

JOHN PATSY FRANCONA
B: 11/04/1933
BL

Year	Tm	Lg	Tot	H	A	0	1	2	3	2	3	4	LO	XN	IP	PH	RHP	LHP
1956	BAL	AL	9	2	7	5	2	1	1	0	0	0	0	0	0	1	9	0
1957	BAL	AL	7	4	3	5	1	1	0	1	0	0	0	0	0	0	7	0
1958	CHI	AL	1	1	0	0	0	1	0	0	0	0	0	0	0	0	1	0
1959	CLE	AL	20	13	7	9	7	4	0	2	0	0	0	2	0	2	17	3
1960	CLE	AL	17	8	9	9	8	0	0	0	0	0	0	0	0	0	15	2
1961	CLE	AL	16	9	7	9	4	3	0	0	0	0	0	0	1	0	12	4
1962	CLE	AL	14	4	10	7	7	0	0	0	0	0	0	0	0	0	14	0
1963	CLE	AL	10	7	3	9	1	0	0	0	0	0	0	2	0	1	9	1
1964	CLE	AL	8	5	3	6	2	0	0	0	0	0	0	0	0	0	7	1
1965	STL	NL	5	3	2	3	1	1	0	0	0	0	0	0	0	0	5	0
1966	STL	NL	4	3	1	4	0	0	0	0	0	0	0	0	0	1	4	0
1967	ATL	NL	6	2	4	3	3	0	0	0	0	0	0	0	0	0	5	1
1968	ATL	NL	2	1	1	2	0	0	0	0	0	0	0	0	0	0	2	0
1969	ATL	NL	2	0	2	1	1	0	0	0	0	0	0	1	0	0	2	0
	OAK	AL	3	2	1	3	0	0	0	0	0	0	0	0	0	1	3	0
	Total		5	2	3	4	1	0	0	0	0	0	0	1	0	1	5	0
1970	OAK	AL	1	0	1	1	0	0	0	0	0	0	0	0	0	1	1	0
Total			125	64	61	76	37	11	1	3	0	0	0	5	1	7	113	12

Rank among batters: 366 • *Top target (5 home runs)*: Jim Bunning • *Number of pitchers victimized*: 87 • *Total ballparks homered in*: 21 • *First HR*: 04/18/1956 off Bob Porterfield

Charlie Frank

CHARLES FRANK
B: 05/30/1870 D: 05/24/1922

Year	Tm	Lg	Tot	H	A	0	1	2	3	2	3	4	LO	XN	IP	PH	RHP	LHP
1893	STL	NL	1	1	0	0	1	0	0	0	0	0	0	1	0	0	1	0
1894	STL	NL	4	4	0	2	2	0	0	0	0	0	0	0	1	0	2	1
Total			5	5	0	2	3	0	0	0	0	0	0	1	1	0	3	1

Rank among batters: 3,191 • *Total ballparks homered in*: 1 • *First HR*: 09/23/1893 off Amos Rusie

Fred Frankhouse

FREDERICK MELOY FRANKHOUSE
B: 04/09/1904 D: 08/17/1989
BR

Year	Tm	Lg	Tot	H	A	0	1	2	3	2	3	4	LO	XN	IP	PH	RHP	LHP
1929	STL	NL	1	1	0	0	0	1	0	0	0	0	0	0	0	0	0	1

Rank among batters: 4,707 • *Total ballparks homered in*: 1 • *First HR*: 07/28/1929 off Frank Henry

Year	Tm	Lg	Tot	H	A	Men-On 0	1	2	3	One-Game 2	3	4	LO	XN	IP	PH	RHP	LHP

Moe Franklin

MURRAY ASHER FRANKLIN
B: 04/01/1914 D: 03/16/1978
BR

Year	Tm	Lg	Tot	H	A	0	1	2	3	2	3	4	LO	XN	IP	PH	RHP	LHP
1942	DET	AL	2	2	0	0	2	0	0	0	0	0	0	0	0	0	0	2

Rank among batters: 4,129 • *Total ballparks homered in*: 1 • *First HR*: 05/29/1942 off Al Smith

Herman Franks

HERMAN LOUIS FRANKS
B: 01/04/1914
BL

Year	Tm	Lg	Tot	H	A	0	1	2	3	2	3	4	LO	XN	IP	PH	RHP	LHP
1940	BRO	NL	1	1	0	0	0	1	0	0	0	0	0	0	0	0	1	0
1941	BRO	NL	1	0	1	0	0	1	0	0	0	0	0	0	0	1	1	0
1948	PHI	AL	1	0	1	0	1	0	0	0	0	0	0	0	0	0	1	0
Total			3	1	2	0	1	2	0	0	0	0	0	0	0	1	3	0

Rank among batters: 3,735 • *Total ballparks homered in*: 3 • *First HR*: 04/23/1940 off Nick Strincevich

Chick Fraser

CHARLES CARROLTON FRASER
B: 03/17/1871 D: 05/08/1940
BR

Year	Tm	Lg	Tot	H	A	0	1	2	3	2	3	4	LO	XN	IP	PH	RHP	LHP
1897	LOU	NL	2	1	1	1	0	0	1	0	0	0	0	0	0	0	2	0
1903	PHI	NL	1	1	0	1	0	0	0	0	0	0	0	1	0	0	1	0
Total			3	2	1	2	0	0	1	0	0	0	0	1	0	0	3	0

Rank among batters: 3,735 • *Total ballparks homered in*: 3 • *First HR*: 07/13/1897 off Al Orth

Joe Frazier

JOSEPH FILMORE FRAZIER
B: 10/06/1922
BL

Year	Tm	Lg	Tot	H	A	0	1	2	3	2	3	4	LO	XN	IP	PH	RHP	LHP
1954	STL	NL	3	2	1	0	2	1	0	0	0	0	0	0	0	3	3	0
1955	STL	NL	4	1	3	2	1	1	0	0	0	0	0	0	0	1	4	0
1956	STL	NL	1	1	0	0	1	0	0	0	0	0	0	0	0	0	1	0
	CIN	NL	1	0	1	1	0	0	0	0	0	0	0	0	0	0	1	0
	BAL	AL	1	0	1	1	0	0	0	0	0	0	0	0	0	0	1	0
	Total		3	1	2	2	1	0	0	0	0	0	0	0	0	0	3	0
Total			10	4	6	4	4	2	0	0	0	0	0	0	0	4	10	0

Rank among batters: 2,500 • *Top target (2 home runs)*: Bob Rush • *Number of pitchers victimized*: 9 • *Total ballparks homered in*: 5 • *First HR*: 05/05/1954 off Robin Roberts

Lou Frazier

ARTHUR LOUIS FRAZIER
B: 01/26/1965
BB

Year	Tm	Lg	Tot	H	A	0	1	2	3	2	3	4	LO	XN	IP	PH	RHP	LHP
1993	MON	NL	1	1	0	1	0	0	0	0	0	0	0	0	0	0	0	1

Rank among batters: 4,707 • *Total ballparks homered in*: 1 • *First HR*: 05/26/1993 off Joe Magrane

Johnny Frederick

JOHN HENRY FREDERICK
B: 01/26/1902 D: 06/18/1977
BL

Year	Tm	Lg	Tot	H	A	0	1	2	3	2	3	4	LO	XN	IP	PH	RHP	LHP
1929	BRO	NL	24	14	10	13	9	2	0	0	0	0	3	1	0	1	21	3
1930	BRO	NL	17	10	7	9	6	2	0	1	0	0	4	0	0	0	6	11
1931	BRO	NL	17	11	6	8	5	3	1	1	0	0	2	0	0	0	9	8
1932	BRO	NL	16	8	8	7	8	1	0	0	0	0	1	0	0	6	13	3
1933	BRO	NL	7	5	2	4	3	0	0	0	0	0	0	0	0	0	6	1
1934	BRO	NL	4	4	0	3	0	1	0	0	0	0	0	0	0	1	4	0
Total			85	52	33	44	31	9	1	2	0	0	10	1	0	8	59	26

Rank among batters: 612 • *Top target (5 home runs)*: Phil Collins • *Number of pitchers victimized*: 52 • *Total ballparks homered in*: 8 • *First HR*: 05/16/1929 off Claude Willoughby

Roger Freed

ROGER VERNON FREED
B: 06/02/1946
BR

Year	Tm	Lg	Tot	H	A	0	1	2	3	2	3	4	LO	XN	IP	PH	RHP	LHP
1971	PHI	NL	6	4	2	3	1	1	1	0	0	0	0	0	0	0	5	1

Roger Freed *continued*

						Men-On				One-Game								
Year	Tm	Lg	Tot	H	A	0	1	2	3	2	3	4	LO	XN	IP	PH	RHP	LHP
1972	PHI	NL	6	1	5	3	2	1	0	0	0	0	0	0	0	1	1	5
1974	CIN	NL	1	0	1	0	0	1	0	0	0	0	0	0	0	1	0	1
1977	STL	NL	5	2	3	1	3	1	0	0	0	0	0	0	0	1	2	3
1978	STL	NL	2	0	2	0	2	0	0	0	0	0	0	0	0	0	0	2
1979	STL	NL	2	1	1	1	0	0	1	0	0	0	0	1	0	2	1	1
Total			22	8	14	8	8	4	2	0	0	0	0	1	0	5	9	13

Rank among batters: 1,719 • *Top target (3 home runs)*: George Stone • *Number of pitchers victimized*: 20 • *Total ballparks homered in*: 11 • *First HR*: 04/11/1971 off Howie Reed

Bill Freehan

WILLIAM ASHLEY FREEHAN
B: 11/29/1941
BR

						Men-On				One-Game								
Year	Tm	Lg	Tot	H	A	0	1	2	3	2	3	4	LO	XN	IP	PH	RHP	LHP
1963	DET	AL	9	3	6	4	5	0	0	2	0	0	0	0	0	0	8	1
1964	DET	AL	18	9	9	15	1	2	0	1	0	0	0	0	0	0	12	6
1965	DET	AL	10	7	3	4	5	0	1	1	0	0	0	0	0	0	7	3
1966	DET	AL	12	6	6	9	2	1	0	0	0	0	0	0	0	0	6	6
1967	DET	AL	20	8	12	15	1	4	0	0	0	0	0	0	0	0	11	9
1968	DET	AL	25	14	11	15	6	4	0	4	0	0	0	2	0	0	18	7
1969	DET	AL	16	7	9	11	4	0	1	1	0	0	0	0	0	0	12	4
1970	DET	AL	16	10	6	13	3	0	0	1	0	0	0	0	0	0	9	7
1971	DET	AL	21	8	13	15	4	2	0	1	1	0	0	1	0	0	13	8
1972	DET	AL	10	6	4	4	4	0	2	0	0	0	0	1	0	0	4	6
1973	DET	AL	6	4	2	5	1	0	0	0	0	0	0	0	0	0	2	4
1974	DET	AL	18	10	8	12	2	3	1	1	0	0	0	0	0	0	11	7
1975	DET	AL	14	6	8	10	1	3	0	1	0	0	0	0	0	0	10	4
1976	DET	AL	5	2	3	4	0	1	0	0	0	0	0	0	0	0	2	3
Total			200	100	100	136	39	20	5	13	1	0	0	4	0	0	125	75

Rank among batters: 183 • *Top target (5 home runs)*: Mudcat Grant, George Brunet, Luis Tiant • *Number of pitchers victimized*: 125 • *Total ballparks homered in*: 14 • *First HR*: 05/05/1963 off Dick Hall • *LCS HR*—1; *All-Star HR*—1

Buck Freeman

JOHN FRANK FREEMAN
B: 10/30/1871 D: 06/25/1949
BL

						Men-On				One-Game								
Year	Tm	Lg	Tot	H	A	0	1	2	3	2	3	4	LO	XN	IP	PH	RHP	LHP
1898	WAS	NL	3	3	0	1	2	0	0	1	0	0	0	0	0	0	3	0
1899	WAS	NL	25	16	9	13	7	4	1	0	0	0	0	0	1	0	19	5
1900	BOS	NL	6	4	2	2	3	1	0	0	0	0	0	0	0	1	5	1
1901	BOS	AL	12	5	7	1	6	5	0	2	0	0	0	0	1	0	8	4
1902	BOS	AL	11	7	4	3	5	3	0	0	0	0	0	0	3	0	8	3
1903	BOS	AL	13	7	6	3	8	2	0	1	0	0	0	1	1	0	9	4
1904	BOS	AL	7	3	4	4	3	0	0	0	0	0	0	0	1	0	5	2
1905	BOS	AL	3	1	2	1	1	1	0	0	0	0	0	0	0	0	3	0
1906	BOS	AL	1	0	1	1	0	0	0	0	0	0	0	0	0	0	0	1
1907	BOS	AL	1	0	1	0	1	0	0	0	0	0	0	1	0	0	1	0
Total			82	46	36	29	36	16	1	4	0	0	0	2	7	1	61	20

Rank among batters: 637 • *Top target (4 home runs)*: Walt Woods, Al Orth • *Number of pitchers victimized*: 58 • *Total ballparks homered in*: 16 • *First HR*: 09/14/1898 off Nig Cuppy • *Hit for Cycle*—@CLE: 06/21/1903

Hersh Freeman

HERSHELL BASKIN FREEMAN
B: 07/01/1928
BR

						Men-On				One-Game								
Year	Tm	Lg	Tot	H	A	0	1	2	3	2	3	4	LO	XN	IP	PH	RHP	LHP
1955	CIN	NL	1	1	0	0	0	1	0	0	0	0	0	0	0	0	1	0

Rank among batters: 4,707 • *Total ballparks homered in*: 1 • *First HR*: 08/07/1955 off Paul Giel

Jerry Freeman

FRANK ELLSWORTH FREEMAN
B: 12/26/1879 D: 09/30/1952
BL

						Men-On				One-Game								
Year	Tm	Lg	Tot	H	A	0	1	2	3	2	3	4	LO	XN	IP	PH	RHP	LHP
1908	WAS	AL	1	1	0	1	0	0	0	0	0	0	0	0	0	0	1	0

Rank among batters: 4,707 • *Total ballparks homered in*: 1 • *First HR*: 04/25/1908 off Cy Morgan

Year	Tm	Lg	Tot	H	A	Men-On 0	Men-On 1	Men-On 2	Men-On 3	One-Game 2	One-Game 3	One-Game 4	LO	XN	IP	PH	RHP	LHP

Marvin Freeman

MARVIN FREEMAN
B: 04/10/1963
BR

Year	Tm	Lg	Tot	H	A	0	1	2	3	2	3	4	LO	XN	IP	PH	RHP	LHP
1994	COL	NL	1	0	1	1	0	0	0	0	0	0	0	0	0	0	1	0
1995	COL	NL	1	1	0	0	0	1	0	0	0	0	0	0	0	0	1	0
Total			2	1	1	1	0	1	0	0	0	0	0	0	0	0	2	0

Rank among batters: 4,129 • *Total ballparks homered in*: 2 • *First HR*: 06/18/1994 off Ramon Martinez

Gene Freese

EUGENE LEWIS FREESE
B: 01/08/1934
BR

Year	Tm	Lg	Tot	H	A	0	1	2	3	2	3	4	LO	XN	IP	PH	RHP	LHP
1955	PIT	NL	14	2	12	11	2	0	1	1	0	0	0	0	0	0	8	6
1956	PIT	NL	3	0	3	0	3	0	0	0	0	0	0	0	0	0	2	1
1957	PIT	NL	6	2	4	3	3	0	0	0	0	0	2	0	0	0	5	1
1958	PIT	NL	1	0	1	1	0	0	0	0	0	0	0	1	0	1	1	0
	STL	NL	6	3	3	5	1	0	0	0	0	0	1	0	0	0	3	3
	Total		7	3	4	6	1	0	0	0	0	0	1	1	0	1	4	3
1959	PHI	NL	23	12	11	14	4	2	3	0	0	0	0	0	0	5	12	11
1960	CHI	AL	17	10	7	8	3	6	0	0	0	0	0	0	0	0	14	3
1961	CIN	NL	26	13	13	13	8	5	0	3	0	0	0	0	0	0	16	10
1963	CIN	NL	6	4	2	3	2	1	0	0	0	0	0	0	0	0	4	2
1964	PIT	NL	9	3	6	3	4	2	0	0	0	0	0	0	0	3	2	7
1965	CHI	AL	1	0	1	1	0	0	0	0	0	0	0	0	0	0	0	1
1966	CHI	AL	3	1	2	1	2	0	0	0	0	0	0	0	0	0	1	2
Total			115	50	65	63	32	16	4	4	0	0	3	1	0	9	68	47

Rank among batters: 415 • *Top target (6 home runs)*: Lew Burdette • *Number of pitchers victimized*: 83 • *Total ballparks homered in*: 18 • *First HR*: 05/04/1955 off Lew Burdette

George Freese

GEORGE WALTER FREESE
B: 09/12/1926
BR

Year	Tm	Lg	Tot	H	A	0	1	2	3	2	3	4	LO	XN	IP	PH	RHP	LHP
1955	PIT	NL	3	3	0	1	1	0	1	0	0	0	0	0	1	0	3	0

Rank among batters: 3,735 • *Total ballparks homered in*: 1 • *First HR*: 04/30/1955 off Art Fowler

Jim Fregosi

JAMES LOUIS FREGOSI
B: 04/04/1942
BR

Year	Tm	Lg	Tot	H	A	0	1	2	3	2	3	4	LO	XN	IP	PH	RHP	LHP
1962	LA	AL	3	2	1	0	1	2	0	0	0	0	0	0	1	0	1	2
1963	LA	AL	9	3	6	6	2	1	0	0	0	0	0	1	1	0	8	1
1964	LA	AL	18	7	11	6	8	4	0	1	0	0	0	1	0	1	14	4
1965	CAL	AL	15	5	10	12	3	0	0	1	0	0	0	0	0	0	12	3
1966	CAL	AL	13	4	9	6	5	1	1	0	0	0	0	0	0	0	9	4
1967	CAL	AL	9	6	3	6	2	1	0	0	0	0	0	0	0	0	8	1
1968	CAL	AL	9	6	3	5	3	1	0	0	0	0	0	1	0	0	7	2
1969	CAL	AL	12	5	7	6	6	0	0	0	0	0	0	0	0	0	9	3
1970	CAL	AL	22	10	12	17	4	1	0	3	0	0	0	0	0	0	16	6
1971	CAL	AL	5	1	4	3	1	1	0	0	0	0	0	1	0	1	4	1
1972	NY	NL	5	4	1	1	1	3	0	0	0	0	0	0	0	0	5	0
1973	TEX	AL	6	4	2	5	1	0	0	0	0	0	0	0	0	0	2	4
1974	TEX	AL	12	8	4	8	2	2	0	1	0	0	0	0	0	0	6	6
1975	TEX	AL	7	2	5	0	5	2	0	0	0	0	0	1	0	0	2	5
1976	TEX	AL	2	1	1	1	1	0	0	0	0	0	0	0	0	0	0	2
1977	TEX	AL	1	0	1	1	0	0	0	0	0	0	0	0	0	0	0	1
	PIT	NL	3	0	3	2	1	0	0	0	0	0	0	1	0	0	1	2
	Total		4	0	4	3	1	0	0	0	0	0	0	1	0	0	1	3
Total			151	68	83	85	46	19	1	6	0	0	0	6	2	2	104	47

Rank among batters: 286 • Top target (4 home runs): Dave Wickersham, Dave Morehead, Mickey Lolich, Sonny Siebert, Jim Kaat • *Number of pitchers victimized*: 106 • *Total ballparks homered in*: 20 • *First HR*: 09/10/1962 off Dick Stigman • *Hit for Cycle*—vs NY: 07/28/1964; vs BOS: 05/20/1968

Howard Freigau

HOWARD EARL FREIGAU
B: 08/01/1902 D: 07/18/1932
BR

Year	Tm	Lg	Tot	H	A	0	1	2	3	2	3	4	LO	XN	IP	PH	RHP	LHP
1923	STL	NL	1	0	1	1	0	0	0	0	0	0	0	0	0	0	0	1

Howard Freigau *continued*

Year	Tm	Lg	Tot	H	A	Men-On 0	1	2	3	One-Game 2	3	4	LO	XN	IP	PH	RHP	LHP
1924	STL	NL	2	0	2	2	0	0	0	0	0	0	0	0	0	0	2	0
1925	CHI	NL	8	7	1	4	2	2	0	0	0	0	0	0	0	0	5	3
1926	CHI	NL	3	2	1	2	1	0	0	0	0	0	0	0	0	0	2	1
1928	BOS	NL	1	1	0	1	0	0	0	0	0	0	0	0	0	0	1	0
Total			15	10	5	10	3	2	0	0	0	0	0	0	0	0	10	5

Rank among batters: 2,096 • *Total ballparks homered in*: 4 • *First HR*: 08/31/1923 off Wilbur Cooper

Jim French

RICHARD JAMES FRENCH
B: 08/13/1941
BL

Year	Tm	Lg	Tot	H	A	Men-On 0	1	2	3	One-Game 2	3	4	LO	XN	IP	PH	RHP	LHP
1965	WAS	AL	1	0	1	1	0	0	0	0	0	0	0	0	0	0	1	0
1968	WAS	AL	1	1	0	1	0	0	0	0	0	0	0	0	0	0	1	0
1969	WAS	AL	2	1	1	1	1	0	0	0	0	0	0	0	0	0	2	0
1970	WAS	AL	1	0	1	1	0	0	0	0	0	0	0	0	0	0	1	0
Total			5	2	3	4	1	0	0	0	0	0	0	0	0	0	5	0

Rank among batters: 3,191 • *Total ballparks homered in*: 4 • *First HR*: 09/21/1965 off Jim Dickson

Larry French

LAWRENCE HERBERT FRENCH
B: 11/01/1907 D: 02/09/1987
BB

Year	Tm	Lg	Tot	H	A	Men-On 0	1	2	3	One-Game 2	3	4	LO	XN	IP	PH	RHP	LHP
1939	CHI	NL	1	1	0	0	1	0	0	0	0	0	0	0	0	0	1	0

Rank among batters: 4,707 • *Total ballparks homered in*: 1 • *First HR*: 09/06/1939 off Curt Davis

Walt French

WALTER EDWARD FRENCH
B: 07/12/1899 D: 05/13/1984
BL

Year	Tm	Lg	Tot	H	A	Men-On 0	1	2	3	One-Game 2	3	4	LO	XN	IP	PH	RHP	LHP
1926	PHI	AL	1	1	0	0	1	0	0	0	0	0	0	0	0	0	1	0
1929	PHI	AL	1	0	1	1	0	0	0	0	0	0	0	0	1	0	1	0
Total			2	1	1	1	1	0	0	0	0	0	0	0	1	0	2	0

Rank among batters: 4,129 • *Total ballparks homered in*: 2 • *First HR*: 05/25/1926 off Alex Ferguson

Lonny Frey

LINUS REINHARD FREY
B: 08/23/1910
BL

Year	Tm	Lg	Tot	H	A	Men-On 0	1	2	3	One-Game 2	3	4	LO	XN	IP	PH	RHP	LHP
1934	BRO	NL	8	3	5	3	3	2	0	0	0	0	0	0	0	0	8	0
1935	BRO	NL	11	7	4	4	3	3	1	0	0	0	0	0	0	0	11	0
1936	BRO	NL	4	1	3	2	2	0	0	0	0	0	0	0	0	0	4	0
1938	CIN	NL	4	2	2	1	2	1	0	0	0	0	0	0	0	0	3	1
1939	CIN	NL	11	4	7	7	3	1	0	0	0	0	0	0	1	0	10	1
1940	CIN	NL	8	5	3	6	2	0	0	1	0	0	0	0	1	0	6	2
1941	CIN	NL	6	1	5	4	1	1	0	0	0	0	0	0	0	0	6	0
1942	CIN	NL	2	0	2	1	1	0	0	0	0	0	0	0	0	0	2	0
1943	CIN	NL	2	0	2	1	1	0	0	0	0	0	0	0	0	0	2	0
1946	CIN	NL	3	3	0	3	0	0	0	0	0	0	0	0	1	0	3	0
1948	NY	NL	1	1	0	1	0	0	0	0	0	0	0	0	0	0	0	1
Total			60	27	33	33	18	8	1	1	0	0	0	0	3	0	55	5

Rank among batters: 863 • *Top target (3 home runs)*: Bill Swift, Larry French, Luke Hamlin • *Number of pitchers victimized*: 46 • *Total ballparks homered in*: 9 • *First HR*: 05/06/1934 off Bill Swift

Pepe Frias

JESUS MARIA (ANDUJAR) FRIAS
B: 07/14/1948
BR

Year	Tm	Lg	Tot	H	A	Men-On 0	1	2	3	One-Game 2	3	4	LO	XN	IP	PH	RHP	LHP
1979	ATL	NL	1	0	1	1	0	0	0	0	0	0	0	0	0	0	0	1

Rank among batters: 4,707 • *Total ballparks homered in*: 1 • *First HR*: 05/02/1979 off John Candelaria

Bernie Friberg

BERNARD ALBERT FRIBERG
B: 08/18/1899 D: 12/08/1958
BR

Year	Tm	Lg	Tot	H	A	Men-On 0	1	2	3	One-Game 2	3	4	LO	XN	IP	PH	RHP	LHP
1923	CHI	NL	12	7	5	6	5	0	1	1	0	0	0	1	2	0	8	4
1924	CHI	NL	5	4	1	0	2	3	0	0	0	0	0	0	1	0	3	2
1925	CHI	NL	1	0	1	1	0	0	0	0	0	0	0	0	0	0	1	0
	PHI	NL	5	3	2	5	0	0	0	0	0	0	0	0	1	0	3	2
	Total		6	3	3	6	0	0	0	0	0	0	0	0	1	0	4	2
1926	PHI	NL	1	0	1	1	0	0	0	0	0	0	0	0	0	0	1	0
1927	PHI	NL	1	1	0	1	0	0	0	0	0	0	0	0	0	0	1	0
1928	PHI	NL	1	0	1	1	0	0	0	0	0	0	0	0	1	0	0	1
1929	PHI	NL	7	7	0	5	2	0	0	0	0	0	0	1	0	0	4	3
1930	PHI	NL	4	4	0	3	1	0	0	0	0	0	0	0	0	1	2	2
1931	PHI	NL	1	0	1	1	0	0	0	0	0	0	0	0	0	0	0	1
Total			38	26	12	24	10	3	1	1	0	0	0	2	5	1	23	15

Rank among batters: 1,225 • *Top target (3 home runs)*: Frank Henry, Clarence Mitchell • *Number of pitchers victimized*: 32 • *Total ballparks homered in*: 7 • *First HR*: 04/20/1923 off Whitey Glazner

Jim Fridley

JAMES RILEY FRIDLEY
B: 09/06/1924
BR

Year	Tm	Lg	Tot	H	A	Men-On 0	1	2	3	One-Game 2	3	4	LO	XN	IP	PH	RHP	LHP
1952	CLE	AL	4	2	2	3	1	0	0	0	0	0	1	0	0	0	2	2
1954	BAL	AL	4	1	3	2	1	1	0	0	0	0	0	0	0	0	2	2
Total			8	3	5	5	2	1	0	0	0	0	1	0	0	0	4	4

Rank among batters: 2,703 • *Top target (2 home runs)*: Eddie Lopat • *Number of pitchers victimized*: 7 • *Total ballparks homered in*: 6 • *First HR*: 04/16/1952 off Joe Dobson

Bill Friel

WILLIAM EDWARD FRIEL
B: 04/01/1876 D: 12/24/1959
BL

Year	Tm	Lg	Tot	H	A	Men-On 0	1	2	3	One-Game 2	3	4	LO	XN	IP	PH	RHP	LHP
1901	MIL	AL	4	3	1	2	2	0	0	0	0	0	0	0	0	0	4	0
1902	STL	AL	2	0	2	1	1	0	0	0	0	0	0	0	1	0	1	1
Total			6	3	3	3	3	0	0	0	0	0	0	0	1	0	5	1

Rank among batters: 2,988 • *Total ballparks homered in*: 4 • *First HR*: 06/04/1901 off Nig Cuppy

Pat Friel

PATRICK HENRY FRIEL
B: 06/11/1860 D: 01/15/1924
BB

Year	Tm	Lg	Tot	H	A	Men-On 0	1	2	3	One-Game 2	3	4	LO	XN	IP	PH	RHP	LHP
1890	SYR	AA	3	1	2	1	0	1	1	0	0	0	0	0	0	0	1	2
Total			3	1	2	1	0	1	1	0	0	0	0	0	0	0	1	2

Rank among batters: 3,735 • *Top target (2 home runs)*: Toad Ramsey • *Number of pitchers victimized*: 2 • *Total ballparks homered in*: 3 • *First HR*: 08/05/1890 off Toad Ramsey

Bob Friend

ROBERT BARTMESS FRIEND
B: 11/24/1930
BR

Year	Tm	Lg	Tot	H	A	Men-On 0	1	2	3	One-Game 2	3	4	LO	XN	IP	PH	RHP	LHP
1954	PIT	NL	1	0	1	1	0	0	0	0	0	0	0	0	0	0	1	0
1956	PIT	NL	1	0	1	1	0	0	0	0	0	0	0	0	0	0	1	0
Total			2	0	2	2	0	0	0	0	0	0	0	0	0	0	2	0

Rank among batters: 4,129 • *Total ballparks homered in*: 2 • *First HR*: 09/25/1954 off Russ Meyer

Danny Friend

DANIEL SEBASTIAN FRIEND
B: 04/18/1873 D: 06/01/1942

Year	Tm	Lg	Tot	H	A	Men-On 0	1	2	3	One-Game 2	3	4	LO	XN	IP	PH	RHP	LHP
1896	CHI	NL	1	0	1	1	0	0	0	0	0	0	0	0	0	0	1	0

Rank among batters: 4,707 • *Total ballparks homered in*: 1 • *First HR*: 04/18/1896 off Gus Weyhing

Owen Friend

OWEN LACEY FRIEND
B: 03/21/1927
BR

Year	Tm	Lg	Tot	H	A	Men-On 0	1	2	3	One-Game 2	3	4	LO	XN	IP	PH	RHP	LHP
1950	STL	AL	8	5	3	1	5	2	0	1	0	0	0	0	0	0	1	7
1953	DET	AL	3	3	0	1	1	1	0	0	0	0	0	0	0	0	3	0
	CLE	AL	2	1	1	0	1	1	0	0	0	0	0	0	0	0	2	0
	Total		5	4	1	1	2	2	0	0	0	0	0	0	0	0	5	0
Total			13	9	4	2	7	4	0	1	0	0	0	0	0	0	6	7

Rank among batters: 2,248 • *Top target (2 home runs)*: Bobby Shantz • *Number of pitchers victimized*: 12 • *Total ballparks homered in*: 5 • *First HR*: 05/23/1950 off Carl Scheib

Frankie Frisch

FRANK FRANCIS FRISCH
B: 09/09/1898 D: 03/12/1973
BB HOF

Year	Tm	Lg	Tot	H	A	Men-On 0	1	2	3	One-Game 2	3	4	LO	XN	IP	PH	RHP	LHP
1919	NY	NL	2	0	2	0	1	1	0	0	0	0	0	0	1	0	2	0
1920	NY	NL	4	2	2	2	1	1	0	0	0	0	0	0	1	0	4	0
1921	NY	NL	8	6	2	2	4	2	0	0	0	0	0	0	2	0	7	1
1922	NY	NL	5	2	3	2	2	1	0	0	0	0	0	0	0	0	3	2
1923	NY	NL	12	8	4	3	6	3	0	0	0	0	0	0	1	0	8	4
1924	NY	NL	7	5	2	4	2	1	0	0	0	0	0	0	1	0	5	2
1925	NY	NL	11	10	1	5	3	3	0	0	0	0	0	0	1	0	6	5
1926	NY	NL	5	3	2	4	1	0	0	0	0	0	0	1	0	0	3	2
1927	STL	NL	10	8	2	8	1	1	0	1	0	0	0	0	0	0	7	3
1928	STL	NL	10	6	4	4	5	1	0	0	0	0	0	0	0	0	8	2
1929	STL	NL	5	3	2	4	1	0	0	0	0	0	0	0	1	0	1	4
1930	STL	NL	10	5	5	3	5	2	0	1	0	0	0	0	0	0	8	2
1931	STL	NL	4	1	3	1	2	1	0	0	0	0	0	0	0	0	4	0
1932	STL	NL	3	3	0	3	0	0	0	1	0	0	0	0	0	0	1	2
1933	STL	NL	4	1	3	1	1	2	0	0	0	0	0	0	0	0	4	0
1934	STL	NL	3	2	1	1	2	0	0	0	0	0	0	0	0	0	2	1
1935	STL	NL	1	1	0	0	1	0	0	0	0	0	0	0	0	0	1	0
1936	STL	NL	1	1	0	0	1	0	0	0	0	0	0	0	0	0	1	0
Total			105	67	38	47	39	19	0	3	0	0	0	1	8	0	75	30

Rank among batters: 462 • *Top target (4 home runs)*: Freddie Fitzsimmons • *Number of pitchers victimized*: 79 • *Total ballparks homered in*: 8 • *First HR*: 09/11/1919 off Grover Alexander • *All-Star HR*—2

Emil Frisk

JOHN EMIL FRISK
B: 10/15/1874 D: 01/27/1922
BL

Year	Tm	Lg	Tot	H	A	Men-On 0	1	2	3	One-Game 2	3	4	LO	XN	IP	PH	RHP	LHP
1901	DET	AL	1	1	0	0	1	0	0	0	0	0	0	0	1	0	0	1
1905	STL	AL	3	2	1	2	1	0	0	0	0	0	0	0	1	0	3	0
Total			4	3	1	2	2	0	0	0	0	0	0	0	2	0	3	1

Rank among batters: 3,427 • *Total ballparks homered in*: 3 • *First HR*: 05/25/1901 off Watty Lee

Harry Fritz

HARRY KOCH FRITZ
B: 09/30/1890 D: 11/04/1974
BR

Year	Tm	Lg	Tot	H	A	Men-On 0	1	2	3	One-Game 2	3	4	LO	XN	IP	PH	RHP	LHP
1915	CHI	FL	3	0	3	1	1	1	0	1	0	0	0	0	0	0	3	0

Rank among batters: 3,735 • *Top target (2 home runs)*: Hugh Bedient • *Number of pitchers victimized*: 2 • *Total ballparks homered in*: 2 • *First HR*: 05/03/1915 off Hugh Bedient

Doug Frobel

DOUGLAS STEVEN FROBEL
B: 06/06/1959
BL

Year	Tm	Lg	Tot	H	A	Men-On 0	1	2	3	One-Game 2	3	4	LO	XN	IP	PH	RHP	LHP
1982	PIT	NL	2	2	0	1	1	0	0	0	0	0	0	0	0	0	2	0
1983	PIT	NL	3	3	0	3	0	0	0	0	0	0	0	0	0	0	3	0
1984	PIT	NL	12	6	6	8	3	0	1	1	0	0	0	0	0	0	12	0
1985	MON	NL	1	0	1	0	1	0	0	0	0	0	0	0	0	1	1	0
1987	CLE	AL	2	2	0	1	1	0	0	0	0	0	0	0	0	1	2	0
Total			20	13	7	13	6	0	1	1	0	0	0	0	0	2	20	0

Rank among batters: 1,810 • *Total ballparks homered in*: 7 • *First HR*: 10/01/1982 off Charlie Lea

Year	Tm	Lg	Tot	H	A	Men-On 0	Men-On 1	Men-On 2	Men-On 3	One-Game 2	One-Game 3	One-Game 4	LO	XN	IP	PH	RHP	LHP

Charlie Frye

CHARLES ANDREW FRYE
B: 07/17/1914 D: 05/25/1945
BR

Year	Tm	Lg	Tot	H	A	0	1	2	3	2	3	4	LO	XN	IP	PH	RHP	LHP
1940	PHI	NL	1	0	1	0	1	0	0	0	0	0	0	1	0	1	0	1

Rank among batters: 4,707 • *Total ballparks homered in*: 1 • *First HR*: 08/21/1940 off Ken Raffensberger

Jeff Frye

JEFFREY DUSTIN FRYE
B: 08/31/1966
BR

Year	Tm	Lg	Tot	H	A	0	1	2	3	2	3	4	LO	XN	IP	PH	RHP	LHP
1992	TEX	AL	1	0	1	1	0	0	0	0	0	0	1	0	0	0	0	1
1995	TEX	AL	4	2	2	2	1	1	0	0	0	0	0	0	0	0	1	3
Total			5	2	3	3	1	1	0	0	0	0	1	0	0	0	1	4

Rank among batters: 3,191 • *Total ballparks homered in*: 4 • *First HR*: 07/24/1992 off Arthur Lee Rhodes

Travis Fryman

DAVID TRAVIS FRYMAN
B: 03/25/1969
BR

Year	Tm	Lg	Tot	H	A	0	1	2	3	2	3	4	LO	XN	IP	PH	RHP	LHP
1990	DET	AL	9	5	4	6	2	1	0	0	0	0	0	0	0	0	4	5
1991	DET	AL	21	8	13	11	7	3	0	0	0	0	0	0	0	0	17	4
1992	DET	AL	20	9	11	13	6	1	0	2	0	0	0	0	0	0	13	7
1993	DET	AL	22	13	9	9	10	3	0	2	0	0	0	0	0	0	13	9
1994	DET	AL	18	10	8	10	7	0	1	0	0	0	0	0	0	0	11	7
1995	DET	AL	15	9	6	11	0	2	2	1	0	0	0	1	0	0	14	1
Total			105	54	51	60	32	10	3	5	0	0	0	1	0	0	72	33

Rank among batters: 462 • *Top target (4 home runs)*: Randy Johnson • *Number of pitchers victimized*: 86 • *Total ballparks homered in*: 15 • *First HR*: 07/08/1990 off Jeff Montgomery • *Hit for Cycle*—vs NY: 07/28/1993

Woodie Fryman

WOODROW THOMPSON FRYMAN
B: 04/15/1940
BR

Year	Tm	Lg	Tot	H	A	0	1	2	3	2	3	4	LO	XN	IP	PH	RHP	LHP
1969	PHI	NL	1	0	1	1	0	0	0	0	0	0	0	0	0	0	0	1
1972	PHI	NL	1	1	0	0	1	0	0	0	0	0	0	0	0	0	1	0
Total			2	1	1	1	1	0	0	0	0	0	0	0	0	0	1	1

Rank among batters: 4,129 • *Total ballparks homered in*: 2 • *First HR*: 08/14/1969 off George Stone

Tito Fuentes

RIGOBERTO (PEAT) FUENTES
B: 01/04/1944
BB

Year	Tm	Lg	Tot	H	A	0	1	2	3	2	3	4	LO	XN	IP	PH	RHP	LHP
1966	SF	NL	9	4	5	5	4	0	0	1	0	0	1	1	0	0	6	3
1967	SF	NL	5	1	4	3	1	1	0	0	0	0	0	0	0	0	4	1
1969	SF	NL	1	1	0	1	0	0	0	0	0	0	0	0	0	0	0	1
1970	SF	NL	2	0	2	1	0	1	0	0	0	0	0	0	0	0	1	1
1971	SF	NL	4	1	3	2	2	0	0	0	0	0	0	0	1	0	2	2
1972	SF	NL	7	4	3	1	4	1	1	0	0	0	0	0	0	0	1	6
1973	SF	NL	6	6	0	5	0	1	0	0	0	0	0	1	1	0	1	5
1975	SD	NL	4	3	1	2	2	0	0	0	0	0	0	1	0	0	0	4
1976	SD	NL	2	2	0	1	1	0	0	0	0	0	0	0	0	0	0	2
1977	DET	AL	5	5	0	1	4	0	0	0	0	0	0	0	0	0	1	4
Total			45	27	18	22	18	4	1	1	0	0	1	3	2	0	16	29

Rank among batters: 1,082 • *Top target (2 home runs)*: George Stone, Woodie Fryman, Ray Sadecki • *Number of pitchers victimized*: 42 • *Total ballparks homered in*: 12 • *First HR*: 05/07/1966 off Curt Simmons • *LCS HR*—1

Jim Fuller

JAMES HARDY FULLER
B: 11/28/1950
BR

Year	Tm	Lg	Tot	H	A	0	1	2	3	2	3	4	LO	XN	IP	PH	RHP	LHP
1973	BAL	AL	2	2	0	1	1	0	0	1	0	0	0	0	0	0	2	0
1974	BAL	AL	7	1	6	4	3	0	0	1	0	0	0	0	0	0	4	3
1977	HOU	NL	2	0	2	0	2	0	0	1	0	0	0	0	0	0	1	1
Total			11	3	8	5	6	0	0	3	0	0	0	0	0	0	7	4

Rank among batters: 2,419 • *Top target (2 home runs)*: Ken Sanders, Woodie Fryman • *Number of pitchers victimized*: 9 • *Total ballparks homered in*: 7 • *First HR*: 09/25/1973 off Jim Perry

Year	Tm	Lg	Tot	H	A	Men-On 0	1	2	3	One-Game 2	3	4	LO	XN	IP	PH	RHP	LHP

Shorty Fuller

WILLIAM BENJAMIN FULLER
B: 10/10/1867 D: 04/11/1904
BR

Year	Tm	Lg	Tot	H	A	0	1	2	3	2	3	4	LO	XN	IP	PH	RHP	LHP
1890	STL	AA	1	1	0	1	0	0	0	0	0	0	1	0	0	0	0	1
1891	STL	AA	2	1	1	2	0	0	0	0	0	0	0	0	0	0	2	0
1892	NY	NL	1	1	0	1	0	0	0	0	0	0	0	0	0	0	1	0
1894	NY	NL	2	2	0	0	2	0	0	0	0	0	0	0	0	0	2	0
Total			6	5	1	4	2	0	0	0	0	0	1	0	0	0	5	1

Rank among batters: 2,988 • *Total ballparks homered in*: 3 • *First HR*: 08/06/1890 off Dan Casey

Vern Fuller

VERNON GORDON FULLER
B: 03/01/1944
BR

Year	Tm	Lg	Tot	H	A	0	1	2	3	2	3	4	LO	XN	IP	PH	RHP	LHP
1966	CLE	AL	2	1	1	2	0	0	0	0	0	0	0	0	0	0	1	1
1967	CLE	AL	7	5	2	5	2	0	0	0	0	0	0	0	0	0	5	2
1969	CLE	AL	4	1	3	2	1	1	0	0	0	0	0	0	0	0	2	2
1970	CLE	AL	1	0	1	1	0	0	0	0	0	0	0	0	0	0	0	1
Total			14	7	7	10	3	1	0	0	0	0	0	0	0	0	8	6

Rank among batters: 2,169 • *Total ballparks homered in*: 6 • *First HR*: 09/21/1966 off Jim Kaat

Chick Fullis

CHARLES PHILIP FULLIS
B: 02/27/1904 D: 03/28/1946
BR

Year	Tm	Lg	Tot	H	A	0	1	2	3	2	3	4	LO	XN	IP	PH	RHP	LHP
1929	NY	NL	7	7	0	6	1	0	0	0	0	0	2	0	1	0	4	3
1931	NY	NL	3	2	1	1	2	0	0	0	0	0	0	0	2	0	3	0
1932	NY	NL	1	1	0	0	1	0	0	0	0	0	0	0	0	0	0	1
1933	PHI	NL	1	1	0	0	0	1	0	0	0	0	0	0	0	0	1	0
Total			12	11	1	7	4	1	0	0	0	0	2	0	3	0	8	4

Rank among batters: 2,325 • *Total ballparks homered in*: 3 • *First HR*: 05/06/1929 off Clarence Mitchell

Chick Fulmer

CHARLES JOHN FULMER
B: 02/12/1851 D: 02/15/1940
BR

Year	Tm	Lg	Tot	H	A	0	1	2	3	2	3	4	LO	XN	IP	PH	RHP	LHP
1876	LOU	NL	1	1	0	0	1	0	0	0	0	0	0	0	1	0	1	0
1883	CIN	AA	5	4	1	4	1	0	0	0	0	0	0	1	0	0	4	0
Total			6	5	1	4	2	0	0	0	0	0	0	1	1	0	5	0

Rank among batters: 2,988 • *Total ballparks homered in*: 3 • *First HR*: 08/01/1876 off Al Spalding

Chris Fulmer

CHRISTOPHER FULMER
B: 07/04/1858 D: 11/09/1931
BR

Year	Tm	Lg	Tot	H	A	0	1	2	3	2	3	4	LO	XN	IP	PH	RHP	LHP
1886	BAL	AA	1	0	1	1	0	0	0	0	0	0	0	0	0	0	0	1

Rank among batters: 4,707 • *Total ballparks homered in*: 1 • *First HR*: 07/17/1886 off Ed Morris

Dave Fultz

DAVID LEWIS FULTZ
B: 05/29/1875 D: 10/29/1959
BR

Year	Tm	Lg	Tot	H	A	0	1	2	3	2	3	4	LO	XN	IP	PH	RHP	LHP
1902	PHI	AL	1	1	0	0	0	1	0	0	0	0	0	0	1	0	1	0
1904	NY	AL	2	2	0	1	0	0	1	0	0	0	0	0	1	0	1	1
Total			3	3	0	1	0	1	1	0	0	0	0	0	2	0	2	1

Rank among batters: 3,735 • *Total ballparks homered in*: 2 • *First HR*: 06/02/1902 off Jack Powell

Mark Funderburk

MARK CLIFFORD FUNDERBURK
B: 05/16/1957
BR

Year	Tm	Lg	Tot	H	A	0	1	2	3	2	3	4	LO	XN	IP	PH	RHP	LHP
1985	MIN	AL	2	0	2	1	1	0	0	0	0	0	0	0	0	0	1	1

Year	Tm	Lg	Tot	H	A	Men-On				One-Game			LO	XN	IP	PH	RHP	LHP
						0	1	2	3	2	3	4						

Mark Funderburk *continued*

Rank among batters: 4,129 • *Total ballparks homered in*: 2 • *First HR*: 09/13/1985 off Curt Wardle

Liz Funk

ELIAS CALVIN FUNK
B: 10/28/1904 D: 01/16/1968
BL

Year	Tm	Lg	Tot	H	A	0	1	2	3	2	3	4	LO	XN	IP	PH	RHP	LHP
1930	DET	AL	4	3	1	1	2	0	1	0	0	0	0	0	0	0	4	0
1932	CHI	AL	2	0	2	2	0	0	0	0	0	0	0	0	0	0	2	0
Total			6	3	3	3	2	0	1	0	0	0	0	0	0	0	6	0

Rank among batters: 2,988 • *Total ballparks homered in*: 3 • *First HR*: 05/27/1930 off Chad Kimsey

Carl Furillo

CARL ANTHONY FURILLO
B: 03/08/1922 D: 01/21/1989
BR

Year	Tm	Lg	Tot	H	A	0	1	2	3	2	3	4	LO	XN	IP	PH	RHP	LHP
1946	BRO	NL	3	0	3	1	2	0	0	0	0	0	0	0	1	0	1	2
1947	BRO	NL	8	6	2	2	3	2	1	0	0	0	0	0	0	1	2	6
1948	BRO	NL	4	0	4	3	1	0	0	0	0	0	0	0	0	0	3	1
1949	BRO	NL	18	10	8	9	5	3	1	0	0	0	0	1	1	0	13	5
1950	BRO	NL	18	11	7	9	7	2	0	1	0	0	0	0	1	0	11	7
1951	BRO	NL	16	12	4	12	2	2	0	1	0	0	5	1	0	0	10	6
1952	BRO	NL	8	3	5	2	3	1	2	0	0	0	0	0	0	0	6	2
1953	BRO	NL	21	9	12	9	9	3	0	0	0	0	0	1	0	0	20	1
1954	BRO	NL	19	12	7	7	9	2	1	1	0	0	0	0	0	0	17	2
1955	BRO	NL	26	17	9	11	10	4	1	2	0	0	0	1	0	0	23	3
1956	BRO	NL	21	12	9	14	5	1	1	2	0	0	0	2	0	0	20	1
1957	BRO	NL	12	7	5	7	2	2	1	0	0	0	0	0	0	0	12	0
1958	LA	NL	18	11	7	6	9	3	0	0	0	0	0	0	0	0	14	4
Total			192	110	82	92	67	25	8	7	0	0	5	6	3	1	152	40

Rank among batters: 198 • *Top target (6 home runs)*: Ruben Gomez, Robin Roberts • *Number of pitchers victimized*: 110 • *Total ballparks homered in*: 12 • *First HR*: 04/24/1946 off Si Johnson • *World Series HR—2*

Eddie Fusselback

EDWARD L. FUSSELBACK
B: 07/04/1858 D: 04/14/1926
BR

Year	Tm	Lg	Tot	H	A	0	1	2	3	2	3	4	LO	XN	IP	PH	RHP	LHP
1884	BAL	UA	1	0	1	1	0	0	0	0	0	0	0	0	1	0	0	1

Rank among batters: 4,707 • *Total ballparks homered in*: 1 • *First HR*: 05/08/1884 off Dick Burns

Fred Fussell

FREDERICK MORRIS FUSSELL
B: 10/07/1895 D: 10/23/1966
BL

Year	Tm	Lg	Tot	H	A	0	1	2	3	2	3	4	LO	XN	IP	PH	RHP	LHP
1929	PIT	NL	2	0	2	1	1	0	0	0	0	0	0	0	0	0	2	0

Rank among batters: 4,129 • *Total ballparks homered in*: 2 • *First HR*: 07/07/1929 off Doug McWeeny

Les Fusselman

LESTER LEROY FUSSELMAN
B: 03/07/1921 D: 05/21/1970
BR

Year	Tm	Lg	Tot	H	A	0	1	2	3	2	3	4	LO	XN	IP	PH	RHP	LHP
1952	STL	NL	1	1	0	1	0	0	0	0	0	0	0	0	0	0	0	1

Rank among batters: 4,707 • *Total ballparks homered in*: 1 • *First HR*: 05/09/1952 off Ken Raffensberger

Len Gabrielson

LEONARD GARY GABRIELSON
B: 02/14/1940
BL

Year	Tm	Lg	Tot	H	A	0	1	2	3	2	3	4	LO	XN	IP	PH	RHP	LHP
1963	MIL	NL	3	2	1	1	1	1	0	0	0	0	0	0	0	0	3	0
1964	CHI	NL	5	3	2	2	2	1	0	0	0	0	0	0	0	1	4	1
1965	CHI	NL	3	1	2	2	1	0	0	0	0	0	0	0	0	1	3	0
	SF	NL	4	2	2	2	2	0	0	0	0	0	0	0	0	0	3	1
	Total		7	3	4	4	3	0	0	0	0	0	0	0	0	1	6	1

Year	Tm	Lg	Tot	H	A	Men-On 0	1	2	3	One-Game 2	3	4	LO	XN	IP	PH	RHP	LHP

Len Gabrielson *continued*

Year	Tm	Lg	Tot	H	A	0	1	2	3	2	3	4	LO	XN	IP	PH	RHP	LHP
1966	SF	NL	4	2	2	3	1	0	0	0	0	0	0	0	0	0	4	0
1967	LA	NL	7	3	4	3	3	1	0	0	0	0	0	0	0	0	7	0
1968	LA	NL	10	3	7	7	2	1	0	0	0	0	0	0	0	0	9	1
1969	LA	NL	1	1	0	1	0	0	0	0	0	0	0	0	0	1	1	0
Total			37	17	20	21	12	4	0	0	0	0	0	0	0	3	34	3

Rank among batters: 1,252 • *Top target (2 home runs)*: Jack Fisher, Ray Culp • *Number of pitchers victimized*: 35 • *Total ballparks homered in*: 11 • *First HR*: 04/13/1963 off Galen Cisco

Gary Gaetti

GARY JOSEPH GAETTI
B: 08/19/1958
BR

Year	Tm	Lg	Tot	H	A	0	1	2	3	2	3	4	LO	XN	IP	PH	RHP	LHP
1981	MIN	AL	2	1	1	1	1	0	0	0	0	0	0	0	0	0	2	0
1982	MIN	AL	25	15	10	13	7	3	2	1	0	0	0	0	0	0	10	15
1983	MIN	AL	21	7	14	9	11	1	0	0	0	0	0	0	0	0	15	6
1984	MIN	AL	5	2	3	0	2	3	0	0	0	0	0	0	0	0	3	2
1985	MIN	AL	20	10	10	12	6	1	1	1	0	0	0	1	0	0	14	6
1986	MIN	AL	34	16	18	18	10	5	1	5	0	0	0	1	0	0	23	11
1987	MIN	AL	31	18	13	19	6	6	0	0	0	0	0	0	1	0	24	7
1988	MIN	AL	28	9	19	16	7	4	1	2	0	0	0	0	0	1	20	8
1989	MIN	AL	19	10	9	7	7	5	0	3	0	0	0	0	0	0	14	5
1990	MIN	AL	16	7	9	7	4	4	1	1	0	0	0	1	0	0	11	5
1991	CAL	AL	18	12	6	13	1	4	0	0	0	0	0	0	0	0	12	6
1992	CAL	AL	12	8	4	7	3	2	0	1	0	0	0	0	0	1	7	5
1993	KC	AL	14	6	8	8	4	1	1	0	0	0	0	0	0	0	7	7
1994	KC	AL	12	5	7	5	2	5	0	2	0	0	0	0	0	0	7	5
1995	KC	AL	35	16	19	17	11	6	1	3	0	0	0	1	0	1	26	9
Total			292	142	150	152	82	50	8	19	0	0	0	4	1	3	195	97

Rank among batters: 72 • *Top target (7 home runs)*: Floyd Bannister • *Number of pitchers victimized*: 208 • *Total ballparks homered in*: 20 • *First HR*: 09/20/1981 off Charlie Hough • *Hit HR in first major league AB*—@TEX: 09/20/1981 • *World Series HR*—1; *LCS HR*—2

Fabian Gaffke

FABIAN SEBASTIAN GAFFKE
B: 08/05/1913 D: 02/08/1992
BR

Year	Tm	Lg	Tot	H	A	0	1	2	3	2	3	4	LO	XN	IP	PH	RHP	LHP
1936	BOS	AL	1	0	1	0	1	0	0	0	0	0	0	0	0	0	1	0
1937	BOS	AL	6	2	4	3	2	1	0	0	0	0	0	0	0	0	6	0
Total			7	2	5	3	3	1	0	0	0	0	0	0	0	0	7	0

Rank among batters: 2,834 • *Total ballparks homered in*: 3 • *First HR*: 09/12/1936 off Tommy Thomas

Phil Gagliano

PHILIP JOSEPH GAGLIANO
B: 12/27/1941
BR

Year	Tm	Lg	Tot	H	A	0	1	2	3	2	3	4	LO	XN	IP	PH	RHP	LHP
1964	STL	NL	1	1	0	0	1	0	0	0	0	0	0	0	0	0	1	0
1965	STL	NL	8	5	3	2	4	2	0	0	0	0	1	0	1	1	5	3
1966	STL	NL	2	0	2	1	1	0	0	0	0	0	0	0	0	0	1	1
1967	STL	NL	2	2	0	2	0	0	0	0	0	0	0	0	0	0	2	0
1969	STL	NL	1	0	1	1	0	0	0	0	0	0	0	0	0	0	1	0
Total			14	8	6	6	6	2	0	0	0	0	1	0	1	1	10	4

Rank among batters: 2,169 • *Top target (2 home runs)*: Juan Marichal • *Number of pitchers victimized*: 13 • *Total ballparks homered in*: 8 • *First HR*: 06/20/1964 off Jim Duffalo

Greg Gagne

GREGORY CHRISTOPHER GAGNE
B: 11/12/1961
BR

Year	Tm	Lg	Tot	H	A	0	1	2	3	2	3	4	LO	XN	IP	PH	RHP	LHP
1985	MIN	AL	2	0	2	2	0	0	0	0	0	0	0	0	0	0	1	1
1986	MIN	AL	12	10	2	8	3	1	0	2	0	0	0	0	2	0	6	6
1987	MIN	AL	10	7	3	8	2	0	0	1	0	0	0	0	1	0	10	0
1988	MIN	AL	14	5	9	8	5	0	1	0	0	0	0	0	0	0	12	2
1989	MIN	AL	9	5	4	7	1	1	0	0	0	0	0	0	0	0	4	5
1990	MIN	AL	7	3	4	4	3	0	0	0	0	0	0	0	0	0	4	3

Greg Gagne *continued*

Year	Tm	Lg	Tot	H	A	Men-On 0	1	2	3	One-Game 2	3	4	LO	XN	IP	PH	RHP	LHP
1991	MIN	AL	8	3	5	5	1	2	0	0	0	0	1	0	0	0	6	2
1992	MIN	AL	7	1	6	2	3	2	0	0	0	0	0	0	0	0	6	1
1993	KC	AL	10	3	7	5	3	1	1	0	0	0	0	0	0	0	9	1
1994	KC	AL	7	2	5	1	4	2	0	0	0	0	0	0	1	0	6	1
1995	KC	AL	6	2	4	4	2	0	0	0	0	0	0	0	0	0	5	1
Total			92	41	51	54	27	9	2	3	0	0	1	0	4	0	69	23

Rank among batters: 554 • *Top target (5 home runs)*: Dave Stewart • *Number of pitchers victimized*: 73 • *Total ballparks homered in*: 16 • *First HR*: 06/13/1985 off Frank Tanana • *World Series HR—2; LCS HR—2*

Del Gainer

DELLOS CLINTON GAINER
B: 11/10/1886 D: 01/29/1947
BR

Year	Tm	Lg	Tot	H	A	Men-On 0	1	2	3	One-Game 2	3	4	LO	XN	IP	PH	RHP	LHP
1911	DET	AL	2	2	0	1	1	0	0	0	0	0	0	0	1	0	1	1
1913	DET	AL	2	1	1	1	1	0	0	0	0	0	0	0	0	0	0	2
1914	BOS	AL	2	1	1	0	2	0	0	0	0	0	0	0	0	0	0	2
1915	BOS	AL	1	0	1	1	0	0	0	0	0	0	0	0	0	0	0	1
1916	BOS	AL	3	0	3	2	0	1	0	1	0	0	0	0	0	0	0	3
1917	BOS	AL	2	0	2	0	2	0	0	0	0	0	0	0	0	0	0	2
1922	STL	NL	2	0	2	0	0	2	0	0	0	0	0	0	0	0	0	2
Total			14	4	10	5	6	3	0	1	0	0	0	0	1	0	1	13

Rank among batters: 2,169 • *Top target (3 home runs)*: Harry Coveleski • *Number of pitchers victimized*: 10 • *Total ballparks homered in*: 8 • *First HR*: 05/18/1911 off Eddie Plank

Jay Gainer

JOHNATHAN KEITH GAINER
B: 10/08/1966
BL

Year	Tm	Lg	Tot	H	A	Men-On 0	1	2	3	One-Game 2	3	4	LO	XN	IP	PH	RHP	LHP
1993	COL	NL	3	1	2	2	0	0	1	0	0	0	0	0	0	2	3	0

Rank among batters: 3,735 • *Total ballparks homered in*: 3 • *First HR*: 05/14/1993 off Tim Pugh • *Hit HR on first major league pitch*—@CIN: 05/14/1993

Joe Gaines

ARNESTA JOE GAINES
B: 11/22/1936
BR

Year	Tm	Lg	Tot	H	A	Men-On 0	1	2	3	One-Game 2	3	4	LO	XN	IP	PH	RHP	LHP
1962	CIN	NL	1	1	0	0	1	0	0	0	0	0	0	0	0	1	0	1
1963	BAL	AL	6	4	2	4	1	1	0	0	0	0	0	0	0	0	2	4
1964	BAL	AL	1	0	1	1	0	0	0	0	0	0	0	0	0	1	0	1
	HOU	NL	7	2	5	4	2	1	0	0	0	0	0	0	1	0	4	3
	Total		8	2	6	5	2	1	0	0	0	0	0	0	1	1	4	4
1965	HOU	NL	6	2	4	3	2	1	0	0	0	0	0	0	0	3	2	4
Total			21	9	12	12	6	3	0	0	0	0	0	0	1	5	8	13

Rank among batters: 1,768 • *Top target (2 home runs)*: Juan Pizarro • *Number of pitchers victimized*: 20 • *Total ballparks homered in*: 14 • *First HR*: 06/08/1962 off Dennis Bennett

Ty Gainey

TELMANCH GAINEY
B: 12/25/1960
BL

Year	Tm	Lg	Tot	H	A	Men-On 0	1	2	3	One-Game 2	3	4	LO	XN	IP	PH	RHP	LHP
1986	HOU	NL	1	0	1	1	0	0	0	0	0	0	0	0	0	1	1	0

Rank among batters: 4,707 • *Total ballparks homered in*: 1 • *First HR*: 09/10/1986 off Orel Hershiser

Augie Galan

AUGUST JOHN GALAN
B: 05/25/1912 D: 12/28/1993
BB

Year	Tm	Lg	Tot	H	A	Men-On 0	1	2	3	One-Game 2	3	4	LO	XN	IP	PH	RHP	LHP
1934	CHI	NL	5	2	3	3	1	1	0	0	0	0	0	0	0	2	5	0
1935	CHI	NL	12	7	5	8	1	2	1	2	0	0	0	1	0	0	11	1
1936	CHI	NL	8	2	6	5	2	1	0	0	0	0	2	0	0	0	4	4
1937	CHI	NL	18	7	11	10	7	1	0	1	0	0	1	0	0	0	12	6
1938	CHI	NL	6	3	3	2	1	2	1	0	0	0	0	0	0	0	6	0

Augie Galan *continued*

Year	Tm	Lg	Tot	H	A	Men-On 0	Men-On 1	Men-On 2	Men-On 3	One-Game 2	One-Game 3	One-Game 4	LO	XN	IP	PH	RHP	LHP
1939	CHI	NL	6	3	3	2	2	1	1	0	0	0	0	0	0	0	6	0
1940	CHI	NL	3	0	3	1	1	1	0	0	0	0	0	0	0	0	2	1
1941	CHI	NL	1	0	1	0	1	0	0	0	0	0	0	0	0	0	0	1
1943	BRO	NL	9	6	3	5	2	1	1	0	0	0	0	0	2	0	9	0
1944	BRO	NL	12	8	4	6	5	1	0	0	0	0	0	0	1	0	11	1
1945	BRO	NL	9	3	6	3	5	1	0	0	0	0	0	0	0	0	8	1
1946	BRO	NL	3	1	2	2	1	0	0	0	0	0	0	0	0	0	3	0
1947	CIN	NL	6	3	3	2	2	1	1	0	0	0	0	0	0	0	5	1
1948	CIN	NL	2	2	0	0	0	2	0	0	0	0	0	0	0	0	2	0
Total			100	47	53	49	31	15	5	3	0	0	3	1	3	2	84	16

Rank among batters: 499 • *Top target (5 home runs)*: Bucky Walters • *Number of pitchers victimized*: 72 • *Total ballparks homered in*: 9 • *First HR*: 05/19/1934 off Phil Collins • *Switch hit HR in 1 game*—1 time • *All-Star HR*—1

Andres Galarraga

ANDRES JOSE GALARRAGA
B: 06/18/1961
BR

Year	Tm	Lg	Tot	H	A	Men-On 0	Men-On 1	Men-On 2	Men-On 3	One-Game 2	One-Game 3	One-Game 4	LO	XN	IP	PH	RHP	LHP
1985	MON	NL	2	0	2	2	0	0	0	0	0	0	0	0	0	0	2	0
1986	MON	NL	10	4	6	6	3	1	0	0	0	0	0	0	0	0	6	4
1987	MON	NL	13	7	6	7	6	0	0	0	0	0	0	1	0	0	6	7
1988	MON	NL	29	14	15	17	9	3	0	2	0	0	0	1	0	1	19	10
1989	MON	NL	23	13	10	8	13	1	1	0	0	0	0	0	0	0	12	11
1990	MON	NL	20	6	14	10	5	4	1	1	0	0	0	0	1	0	11	9
1991	MON	NL	9	3	6	6	2	1	0	0	0	0	0	0	0	0	3	6
1992	STL	NL	10	4	6	6	3	0	1	0	0	0	0	0	0	0	4	6
1993	COL	NL	22	13	9	12	8	2	0	0	0	0	0	0	0	0	16	6
1994	COL	NL	31	16	15	14	11	4	2	4	0	0	0	0	0	0	19	12
1995	COL	NL	31	18	13	13	13	3	2	2	1	0	0	0	0	0	21	10
Total			200	98	102	101	73	19	7	9	1	0	0	2	1	1	119	81

Rank among batters: 183 • Top target (4 home runs): Craig Lefferts, Sid Fernandez, Zane Smith, Doug Drabek • *Number of pitchers victimized*: 145 • *Total ballparks homered in*: 15 • *First HR*: 09/21/1985 off Kurt Kepshire

Milt Galatzer

MILTON GALATZER
B: 05/04/1907 D: 01/29/1976
BL

Year	Tm	Lg	Tot	H	A	Men-On 0	Men-On 1	Men-On 2	Men-On 3	One-Game 2	One-Game 3	One-Game 4	LO	XN	IP	PH	RHP	LHP
1933	CLE	AL	1	1	0	1	0	0	0	0	0	0	0	0	0	0	1	0

Rank among batters: 4,707 • *Total ballparks homered in*: 1 • *First HR*: 06/27/1933 off Tommy Thomas

Rich Gale

RICHARD BLACKWELL GALE
B: 01/19/1954
BR

Year	Tm	Lg	Tot	H	A	Men-On 0	Men-On 1	Men-On 2	Men-On 3	One-Game 2	One-Game 3	One-Game 4	LO	XN	IP	PH	RHP	LHP
1982	SF	NL	1	0	1	0	1	0	0	0	0	0	0	0	0	0	1	0
1983	CIN	NL	1	1	0	0	1	0	0	0	0	0	0	0	0	0	0	1
Total			2	1	1	0	2	0	0	0	0	0	0	0	0	0	1	1

Rank among batters: 4,129 • *Total ballparks homered in*: 2 • *First HR*: 06/05/1982 off Doug Bird

Al Gallagher

ALAN MITCHELL EDWARD GEORGE PATRICK GALLAGHER
B: 10/19/1945
BR

Year	Tm	Lg	Tot	H	A	Men-On 0	Men-On 1	Men-On 2	Men-On 3	One-Game 2	One-Game 3	One-Game 4	LO	XN	IP	PH	RHP	LHP
1970	SF	NL	4	3	1	2	2	0	0	0	0	0	0	1	0	1	3	1
1971	SF	NL	5	2	3	2	3	0	0	0	0	0	0	0	1	0	4	1
1972	SF	NL	2	1	1	1	1	0	0	0	0	0	0	0	0	0	2	0
Total			11	6	5	5	6	0	0	0	0	0	0	1	1	1	9	2

Rank among batters: 2,419 • *Total ballparks homered in*: 6 • *First HR*: 06/07/1970 off Ken Holtzman

Bob Gallagher

ROBERT COLLINS GALLAGHER
B: 07/07/1948
BL

Year	Tm	Lg	Tot	H	A	Men-On 0	Men-On 1	Men-On 2	Men-On 3	One-Game 2	One-Game 3	One-Game 4	LO	XN	IP	PH	RHP	LHP
1973	HOU	NL	2	1	1	2	0	0	0	0	0	0	0	0	0	1	2	0

Bob Gallagher *continued*

Rank among batters: 4,129 • *Total ballparks homered in*: 2 • *First HR*: 05/22/1973 off Ed Sprague

Dave Gallagher

DAVID THOMAS GALLAGHER
B: 09/20/1960
BR

Year	Tm	Lg	Tot	H	A	Men-On 0	1	2	3	One-Game 2	3	4	LO	XN	IP	PH	RHP	LHP
1988	CHI	AL	5	1	4	4	1	0	0	1	0	0	1	1	0	0	4	1
1989	CHI	AL	1	1	0	0	0	1	0	0	0	0	0	0	0	0	1	0
1991	CAL	AL	1	0	1	1	0	0	0	0	0	0	0	0	0	0	1	0
1992	NY	NL	1	1	0	1	0	0	0	0	0	0	0	0	0	0	1	0
1993	NY	NL	6	1	5	4	1	0	1	0	0	0	0	0	0	0	2	4
1994	ATL	NL	2	1	1	1	1	0	0	0	0	0	0	0	0	0	1	1
1995	PHI	NL	1	1	0	1	0	0	0	0	0	0	1	0	0	0	1	0
Total			17	6	11	12	3	1	1	1	0	0	2	1	0	0	11	6

Rank among batters: 1,969 • *Total ballparks homered in*: 12 • *First HR*: 05/15/1988 off Mark Eichhorn

Joe Gallagher

JOSEPH EMMETT GALLAGHER
B: 03/07/1914
BR

Year	Tm	Lg	Tot	H	A	Men-On 0	1	2	3	One-Game 2	3	4	LO	XN	IP	PH	RHP	LHP
1939	NY	AL	2	0	2	1	0	1	0	0	0	0	0	0	1	0	0	2
	STL	AL	9	8	1	0	5	3	1	0	1	0	0	0	0	1	7	2
	Total		11	8	3	6	3	2	0	1	0	0	0	0	1	1	7	4
1940	STL	AL	2	1	1	0	1	1	0	0	0	0	0	0	0	0	2	0
	BRO	NL	3	0	3	1	1	1	0	0	0	0	0	0	0	0	0	3
	Total		5	1	4	1	2	2	0	0	0	0	0	0	0	0	2	3
Total			16	9	7	7	5	4	0	1	0	0	0	0	1	1	9	7

Rank among batters: 2,029 • Top target (2 home runs): Harry Eisenstat, Bud Thomas, Schoolboy Rowe, Buck Ross • *Number of pitchers victimized*: 12 • *Total ballparks homered in*: 6 • *First HR*: 04/21/1939 off Joe Krakauskas

Mike Gallego

MICHAEL ANTHONY GALLEGO
B: 10/31/1960
BR

Year	Tm	Lg	Tot	H	A	Men-On 0	1	2	3	One-Game 2	3	4	LO	XN	IP	PH	RHP	LHP
1985	OAK	AL	1	0	1	1	0	0	0	0	0	0	0	0	0	0	1	0
1987	OAK	AL	2	0	2	1	1	0	0	0	0	0	0	0	0	0	0	2
1988	OAK	AL	2	2	0	2	0	0	0	0	0	0	0	0	0	0	1	1
1989	OAK	AL	3	2	1	2	1	0	0	0	0	0	0	0	0	0	3	0
1990	OAK	AL	3	1	2	2	1	0	0	0	0	0	0	0	0	0	2	1
1991	OAK	AL	12	6	6	8	3	0	1	0	0	0	0	0	0	0	7	5
1992	NY	AL	3	1	2	3	0	0	0	0	0	0	1	0	0	0	3	0
1993	NY	AL	10	5	5	7	2	1	0	1	0	0	0	0	0	0	5	5
1994	NY	AL	6	2	4	3	3	0	0	1	0	0	0	0	0	0	3	3
Total			42	19	23	29	11	1	1	2	0	0	1	0	0	0	25	17

Rank among batters: 1,138 • *Top target (4 home runs)*: Chuck Finley • *Number of pitchers victimized*: 37 • *Total ballparks homered in*: 14 • *First HR*: 09/22/1985 off Joel Davis

Bert Gallia

MELVIN ALLYS GALLIA
B: 10/14/1891 D: 03/19/1976
BR

Year	Tm	Lg	Tot	H	A	Men-On 0	1	2	3	One-Game 2	3	4	LO	XN	IP	PH	RHP	LHP
1919	STL	AL	1	1	0	1	0	0	0	0	0	0	0	0	0	0	0	1

Rank among batters: 4,707 • *Total ballparks homered in*: 1 • *First HR*: 08/27/1919 off Lefty Williams

Chick Galloway

CLARENCE EDWARD GALLOWAY
B: 08/04/1896 D: 11/07/1969
BR

Year	Tm	Lg	Tot	H	A	Men-On 0	1	2	3	One-Game 2	3	4	LO	XN	IP	PH	RHP	LHP
1921	PHI	AL	3	2	1	1	1	1	0	0	0	0	0	0	0	0	1	2
1922	PHI	AL	6	6	0	3	3	0	0	0	0	0	0	1	0	0	6	0
1923	PHI	AL	2	2	0	0	1	1	0	0	0	0	0	0	0	0	0	2
1924	PHI	AL	2	1	1	2	0	0	0	0	0	0	0	0	0	0	2	0
1925	PHI	AL	3	1	2	1	2	0	0	0	0	0	0	0	0	0	0	3

Chick Galloway *continued*

Year	Tm	Lg	Tot	H	A	Men-On 0	Men-On 1	Men-On 2	Men-On 3	One-Game 2	One-Game 3	One-Game 4	LO	XN	IP	PH	RHP	LHP
1928	DET	AL	1	0	1	1	0	0	0	0	0	0	0	0	1	0	0	1
Total			17	12	5	8	7	2	0	0	0	0	0	1	1	0	9	8

Rank among batters: 1,969 • *Top target (2 home runs)*: Benn Karr • *Number of pitchers victimized*: 16 • *Total ballparks homered in*: 4 • *First HR*: 05/24/1921 off Jim Middleton

Jim Galvin

JAMES FRANCIS GALVIN
B: 12/25/1856 D: 03/07/1902
BR HOF

Year	Tm	Lg	Tot	H	A	Men-On 0	Men-On 1	Men-On 2	Men-On 3	One-Game 2	One-Game 3	One-Game 4	LO	XN	IP	PH	RHP	LHP
1883	BUF	NL	1	1	0	1	0	0	0	0	0	0	0	0	0	0	1	0
1885	BUF	NL	1	0	1	0	1	0	0	0	0	0	0	0	0	0	1	0
1887	PIT	NL	2	0	2	1	1	0	0	0	0	0	0	0	0	0	2	0
1888	PIT	NL	1	0	1	1	0	0	0	0	0	0	0	0	0	0	0	1
Total			5	1	4	3	2	0	0	0	0	0	0	0	0	0	4	1

Rank among batters: 3,191 • *Total ballparks homered in*: 4 • *First HR*: 07/31/1883 off Charlie Sweeney

Oscar Gamble

OSCAR CHARLES GAMBLE
B: 12/20/1949
BL

Year	Tm	Lg	Tot	H	A	Men-On 0	Men-On 1	Men-On 2	Men-On 3	One-Game 2	One-Game 3	One-Game 4	LO	XN	IP	PH	RHP	LHP
1969	CHI	NL	1	0	1	1	0	0	0	0	0	0	0	0	0	0	1	0
1970	PHI	NL	1	0	1	1	0	0	0	0	0	0	0	0	0	0	1	0
1971	PHI	NL	6	2	4	6	0	0	0	0	0	0	0	0	0	0	6	0
1972	PHI	NL	1	1	0	1	0	0	0	0	0	0	0	0	0	1	1	0
1973	CLE	AL	20	13	7	16	3	1	0	3	0	0	0	0	0	0	20	0
1974	CLE	AL	19	7	12	12	5	2	0	1	0	0	0	0	0	0	15	4
1975	CLE	AL	15	10	5	9	3	3	0	0	0	0	0	1	0	0	15	0
1976	NY	AL	17	15	2	7	4	5	1	1	0	0	0	0	0	0	16	1
1977	CHI	AL	31	14	17	20	7	4	0	2	0	0	0	1	0	3	30	1
1978	SD	NL	7	2	5	5	2	0	0	0	0	0	0	0	0	0	5	2
1979	TEX	AL	8	5	3	3	3	2	0	0	0	0	0	0	0	1	8	0
	NY	AL	11	6	5	5	4	1	1	1	0	0	0	1	0	1	8	3
	Total		19	11	8	8	7	3	1	1	0	0	0	1	0	2	16	3
1980	NY	AL	14	8	6	6	6	2	0	0	0	0	0	0	0	1	14	0
1981	NY	AL	10	6	4	6	4	0	0	1	0	0	0	0	0	0	10	0
1982	NY	AL	18	11	7	10	7	1	0	0	0	0	0	0	0	0	15	3
1983	NY	AL	7	5	2	2	4	1	0	0	0	0	0	0	0	0	6	1
1984	NY	AL	10	5	5	2	7	1	0	0	0	0	0	0	0	1	10	0
1985	CHI	AL	4	2	2	2	2	0	0	0	0	0	0	0	0	0	4	0
Total			200	112	88	114	61	23	2	9	0	0	0	3	0	8	185	15

Rank among batters: 183 • *Top target (5 home runs)*: Jim Slaton, Dennis Martinez • *Number of pitchers victimized*: 134 • *Total ballparks homered in*: 25 • *First HR*: 09/16/1969 off Jerry Robertson • *LCS HR*—2

Chick Gandil

ARNOLD GANDIL
B: 01/19/1887 D: 12/13/1970
BR

Year	Tm	Lg	Tot	H	A	Men-On 0	Men-On 1	Men-On 2	Men-On 3	One-Game 2	One-Game 3	One-Game 4	LO	XN	IP	PH	RHP	LHP
1910	CHI	AL	2	1	1	0	2	0	0	0	0	0	0	0	0	0	1	1
1912	WAS	AL	2	0	2	2	0	0	0	0	0	0	0	0	0	0	2	0
1913	WAS	AL	1	0	1	1	0	0	0	0	0	0	0	0	0	0	0	1
1914	WAS	AL	3	1	2	2	0	1	0	0	0	0	0	1	1	0	3	0
1915	WAS	AL	2	1	1	0	1	1	0	0	0	0	0	0	1	0	2	0
1919	CHI	AL	1	1	0	0	1	0	0	0	0	0	0	0	0	0	1	0
Total			11	4	7	5	4	2	0	0	0	0	0	1	2	0	9	2

Rank among batters: 2,419 • *Total ballparks homered in*: 6 • *First HR*: 06/28/1910 off George Mullin

Bob Ganley

ROBERT STEPHEN GANLEY
B: 04/23/1875 D: 10/09/1945
BL

Year	Tm	Lg	Tot	H	A	Men-On 0	Men-On 1	Men-On 2	Men-On 3	One-Game 2	One-Game 3	One-Game 4	LO	XN	IP	PH	RHP	LHP
1907	WAS	AL	1	0	1	0	1	0	0	0	0	0	0	0	1	0	1	0
1908	WAS	AL	1	0	1	0	1	0	0	0	0	0	0	0	0	0	1	0
Total			2	0	2	0	2	0	0	0	0	0	0	0	1	0	2	0

Rank among batters: 4,129 • *Total ballparks homered in*: 2 • *First HR*: 07/01/1907 off Bobby Keefe

Ron Gant

RONALD EDWIN GANT
B: 03/02/1965
BR

Year	Tm	Lg	Tot	H	A	Men-On 0	1	2	3	One-Game 2	3	4	LO	XN	IP	PH	RHP	LHP
1987	ATL	NL	2	1	1	1	1	0	0	0	0	0	0	0	0	0	2	0
1988	ATL	NL	19	7	12	14	4	1	0	0	0	0	1	1	0	0	10	9
1989	ATL	NL	9	5	4	9	0	0	0	0	0	0	3	0	0	0	8	1
1990	ATL	NL	32	18	14	22	8	2	0	3	0	0	2	0	0	0	22	10
1991	ATL	NL	32	18	14	18	10	4	0	0	0	0	3	0	1	0	22	10
1992	ATL	NL	17	10	7	13	1	3	0	0	0	0	0	0	0	0	13	4
1993	ATL	NL	36	17	19	22	6	7	1	3	0	0	0	2	0	0	28	8
1995	CIN	NL	29	12	17	15	8	5	1	4	0	0	0	4	0	0	22	7
Total			176	88	88	114	38	22	2	10	0	0	9	7	1	0	127	49

Rank among batters: 227 • *Top target (5 home runs)*: Jack Armstrong • *Number of pitchers victimized*: 119 • *Total ballparks homered in*: 15 • *First HR*: 09/24/1987 off Nolan Ryan • *LCS HR*—4

Joe Gantenbein

JOSEPH STEPHEN GANTENBEIN
B: 08/25/1916
BL

Year	Tm	Lg	Tot	H	A	Men-On 0	1	2	3	One-Game 2	3	4	LO	XN	IP	PH	RHP	LHP
1939	PHI	AL	4	2	2	1	3	0	0	0	0	0	0	0	0	0	4	0
1940	PHI	AL	4	1	3	1	3	0	0	0	0	0	1	0	0	0	3	1
Total			8	3	5	2	6	0	0	0	0	0	1	0	0	0	7	1

Rank among batters: 2,703 • *Total ballparks homered in*: 5 • *First HR*: 05/06/1939 off Johnny Marcum

Jim Gantner

JAMES ELMER GANTNER
B: 01/05/1953
BL

Year	Tm	Lg	Tot	H	A	Men-On 0	1	2	3	One-Game 2	3	4	LO	XN	IP	PH	RHP	LHP
1977	MIL	AL	1	0	1	1	0	0	0	0	0	0	0	0	0	0	1	0
1978	MIL	AL	1	0	1	0	1	0	0	0	0	0	0	0	0	0	1	0
1979	MIL	AL	2	0	2	1	1	0	0	0	0	0	0	0	0	0	2	0
1980	MIL	AL	4	1	3	2	0	1	1	0	0	0	0	0	1	0	4	0
1981	MIL	AL	2	0	2	2	0	0	0	0	0	0	1	0	0	0	2	0
1982	MIL	AL	4	2	2	4	0	0	0	0	0	0	0	0	0	0	4	0
1983	MIL	AL	11	5	6	5	4	2	0	0	0	0	1	0	0	0	9	2
1984	MIL	AL	3	0	3	1	2	0	0	0	0	0	0	0	0	0	3	0
1985	MIL	AL	5	4	1	3	2	0	0	0	0	0	0	0	0	0	5	0
1986	MIL	AL	7	4	3	6	0	1	0	0	0	0	0	0	0	0	7	0
1987	MIL	AL	4	0	4	1	3	0	0	0	0	0	0	0	0	0	4	0
1991	MIL	AL	2	1	1	2	0	0	0	0	0	0	0	0	0	0	2	0
1992	MIL	AL	1	1	0	1	0	0	0	0	0	0	0	1	0	0	1	0
Total			47	18	29	29	13	4	1	0	0	0	2	1	1	0	45	2

Rank among batters: 1,040 • Top target (2 home runs): Fernando Arroyo, Tom Waddell, Doug Drabek, Don Schulze, Bert Blyleven • *Number of pitchers victimized*: 42 • *Total ballparks homered in*: 14 • *First HR*: 09/25/1977 off Ron Schueler

Babe Ganzel

FOSTER PIRIE GANZEL
B: 05/22/1901 D: 02/06/1978
BR

Year	Tm	Lg	Tot	H	A	Men-On 0	1	2	3	One-Game 2	3	4	LO	XN	IP	PH	RHP	LHP
1927	WAS	AL	1	0	1	0	1	0	0	0	0	0	0	0	1	0	0	1

Rank among batters: 4,707 • *Total ballparks homered in*: 1 • *First HR*: 09/29/1927 off Dutch Ruether

Charlie Ganzel

CHARLES WILLIAM GANZEL
B: 06/18/1862 D: 04/07/1914
BR

Year	Tm	Lg	Tot	H	A	Men-On 0	1	2	3	One-Game 2	3	4	LO	XN	IP	PH	RHP	LHP
1886	DET	NL	1	1	0	0	1	0	0	0	0	0	0	0	0	0	1	0
1888	DET	NL	1	1	0	1	0	0	0	0	0	0	0	0	1	0	1	0
1889	BOS	NL	1	1	0	1	0	0	0	0	0	0	0	0	1	0	0	1
1891	BOS	NL	1	1	0	1	0	0	0	0	0	0	0	0	0	0	1	0
1893	BOS	NL	1	1	0	1	0	0	0	0	0	0	0	0	0	0	1	0
1894	BOS	NL	3	1	2	1	2	0	0	0	0	0	0	0	0	0	2	1
1895	BOS	NL	1	1	0	1	0	0	0	0	0	0	0	0	0	0	1	0
1896	BOS	NL	1	1	0	1	0	0	0	0	0	0	0	0	0	0	1	0
Total			10	8	2	7	3	0	0	0	0	0	0	0	2	0	8	1

Rank among batters: 2,500 • *Top target (2 home runs)*: Clark Griffith • *Number of pitchers victimized*: 9 • *Total ballparks homered in*: 6 • *First HR*: 08/13/1886 off Jim Whitney

John Ganzel

JOHN HENRY GANZEL
B: 04/07/1874 D: 01/14/1959
BR

Year	Tm	Lg	Tot	H	A	Men-On 0	1	2	3	One-Game 2	3	4	LO	XN	IP	PH	RHP	LHP
1900	CHI	NL	4	1	3	4	0	0	0	0	0	0	0	0	0	0	4	0
1901	NY	NL	2	0	2	0	1	0	1	0	0	0	0	0	1	0	2	0
1903	NY	AL	3	0	3	1	1	1	0	0	0	0	0	0	1	0	2	1
1904	NY	AL	6	4	2	4	1	0	1	0	0	0	0	0	1	0	2	4
1907	CIN	NL	2	0	2	2	0	0	0	0	0	0	0	0	0	0	2	0
1908	CIN	NL	1	1	0	0	0	0	1	0	0	0	0	0	1	0	0	1
Total			18	6	12	11	3	1	3	0	0	0	0	0	4	0	12	6

Rank among batters: 1,914 • *Top target (2 home runs)*: Joe McGinnity • *Number of pitchers victimized*: 17 • *Total ballparks homered in*: 12 • *First HR*: 07/20/1900 off Ted Lewis

Joe Garagiola

JOSEPH HENRY GARAGIOLA
B: 02/12/1926
BL HOF

Year	Tm	Lg	Tot	H	A	Men-On 0	1	2	3	One-Game 2	3	4	LO	XN	IP	PH	RHP	LHP
1946	STL	NL	3	1	2	2	0	1	0	0	0	0	0	0	0	0	3	0
1947	STL	NL	5	3	2	4	0	1	0	0	0	0	0	0	0	0	5	0
1948	STL	NL	2	0	2	0	0	1	1	0	0	0	0	0	0	0	2	0
1949	STL	NL	3	2	1	1	1	1	0	0	0	0	0	0	0	0	2	1
1950	STL	NL	2	0	2	0	0	1	1	0	0	0	0	0	0	0	2	0
1951	STL	NL	2	1	1	2	0	0	0	0	0	0	0	0	0	0	1	1
	PIT	NL	9	4	5	5	2	2	0	0	0	0	0	0	0	0	9	0
	Total		11	5	6	7	2	2	0	0	0	0	0	0	0	0	10	1
1952	PIT	NL	8	4	4	5	1	2	0	0	0	0	0	0	0	1	7	1
1953	PIT	NL	2	0	2	1	1	0	0	0	0	0	0	0	0	0	2	0
	CHI	NL	1	0	1	1	0	0	0	0	0	0	0	0	0	0	1	0
	Total		3	0	3	2	1	0	0	0	0	0	0	0	0	0	3	0
1954	CHI	NL	5	3	2	3	2	0	0	0	0	0	0	0	0	1	5	0
Total			42	18	24	24	7	9	2	0	0	0	0	0	0	2	39	3

Rank among batters: 1,138 • *Top target (3 home runs)*: Bucky Walters • *Number of pitchers victimized*: 35 • *Total ballparks homered in*: 8 • *First HR*: 08/09/1946 off Bucky Walters

Mike Garbark

NATHANIEL MICHAEL GARBARK
B: 02/02/1916 D: 08/31/1994
BR

Year	Tm	Lg	Tot	H	A	Men-On 0	1	2	3	One-Game 2	3	4	LO	XN	IP	PH	RHP	LHP
1944	NY	AL	1	0	1	1	0	0	0	0	0	0	0	0	0	0	1	0
1945	NY	AL	1	1	0	0	1	0	0	0	0	0	0	0	0	0	1	0
Total			2	1	1	1	1	0	0	0	0	0	0	0	0	0	2	0

Rank among batters: 4,129 • *Total ballparks homered in*: 2 • *First HR*: 06/25/1944 off Joe Berry

Barbaro Garbey

BARBARO (GARBEY) GARBEY
B: 12/04/1956
BR

Year	Tm	Lg	Tot	H	A	Men-On 0	1	2	3	One-Game 2	3	4	LO	XN	IP	PH	RHP	LHP
1984	DET	AL	5	2	3	3	2	0	0	0	0	0	0	0	0	0	0	5
1985	DET	AL	6	4	2	6	0	0	0	0	0	0	0	1	0	1	2	4
Total			11	6	5	9	2	0	0	0	0	0	0	1	0	1	2	9

Rank among batters: 2,419 • *Top target (2 home runs)*: Frank Viola • *Number of pitchers victimized*: 10 • *Total ballparks homered in*: 4 • *First HR*: 05/18/1984 off Bill Krueger

Carlos Garcia

CARLOS JESUS (GUERRERO) GARCIA
B: 10/15/1967
BR

Year	Tm	Lg	Tot	H	A	Men-On 0	1	2	3	One-Game 2	3	4	LO	XN	IP	PH	RHP	LHP
1993	PIT	NL	12	7	5	10	2	0	0	1	0	0	3	0	1	0	8	4
1994	PIT	NL	6	4	2	5	1	0	0	0	0	0	0	0	0	0	3	3
1995	PIT	NL	6	4	2	4	1	1	0	0	0	0	0	0	0	0	5	1
Total			24	15	9	19	4	1	0	1	0	0	3	0	1	0	16	8

Rank among batters: 1,643 • *Top target (2 home runs)*: Mike Harkey • *Number of pitchers victimized*: 23 • *Total ballparks homered in*: 6 • *First HR*: 04/16/1993 off Orel Hershiser

Damaso Garcia

DAMASO DOMINGO (SANCHEZ) GARCIA
B: 02/07/1957
BR

Year	Tm	Lg	Tot	H	A	Men-On 0	Men-On 1	Men-On 2	Men-On 3	One-Game 2	One-Game 3	One-Game 4	LO	XN	IP	PH	RHP	LHP
1980	TOR	AL	4	2	2	2	2	0	0	0	0	0	0	0	0	0	3	1
1981	TOR	AL	1	1	0	0	1	0	0	0	0	0	0	0	0	0	1	0
1982	TOR	AL	5	3	2	4	1	0	0	0	0	0	1	0	0	0	5	0
1983	TOR	AL	3	1	2	2	1	0	0	0	0	0	2	0	0	0	2	1
1984	TOR	AL	5	2	3	4	1	0	0	1	0	0	1	0	0	0	2	3
1985	TOR	AL	8	4	4	6	2	0	0	0	0	0	2	1	0	0	6	2
1986	TOR	AL	6	3	3	3	2	1	0	0	0	0	1	0	0	0	4	2
1988	ATL	NL	1	0	1	0	1	0	0	0	0	0	0	0	0	0	1	0
1989	MON	NL	3	3	0	2	1	0	0	0	0	0	0	0	0	1	0	3
Total			36	19	17	23	12	1	0	1	0	0	7	1	0	1	24	12

Rank among batters: 1,274 • *Top target (2 home runs)*: Dave Rozema, Tommy John, Dennis Leonard • *Number of pitchers victimized*: 33 • *Total ballparks homered in*: 12 • *First HR*: 05/10/1980 off Rick Langford

Kiko Garcia

ALFONSO RAFAEL GARCIA
B: 10/14/1953
BR

Year	Tm	Lg	Tot	H	A	Men-On 0	Men-On 1	Men-On 2	Men-On 3	One-Game 2	One-Game 3	One-Game 4	LO	XN	IP	PH	RHP	LHP
1976	BAL	AL	1	0	1	1	0	0	0	0	0	0	0	0	0	0	0	1
1977	BAL	AL	2	0	2	2	0	0	0	0	0	0	0	0	0	0	2	0
1979	BAL	AL	5	3	2	1	3	1	0	0	0	0	0	0	0	0	4	1
1980	BAL	AL	1	1	0	0	1	0	0	0	0	0	0	0	0	0	1	0
1982	HOU	NL	1	0	1	1	0	0	0	0	0	0	0	0	0	0	0	1
1983	PHI	NL	2	1	1	2	0	0	0	0	0	0	0	0	0	0	1	1
Total			12	5	7	7	4	1	0	0	0	0	0	0	0	0	8	4

Rank among batters: 2,325 • *Top target (2 home runs)*: Ferguson Jenkins, Mike Torrez • *Number of pitchers victimized*: 10 • *Total ballparks homered in*: 8 • *First HR*: 09/22/1976 off Grant Jackson

Leo Garcia

LEONARDO ANTONIO (PERALTA) GARCIA
B: 11/06/1962
BL

Year	Tm	Lg	Tot	H	A	Men-On 0	Men-On 1	Men-On 2	Men-On 3	One-Game 2	One-Game 3	One-Game 4	LO	XN	IP	PH	RHP	LHP
1987	CIN	NL	1	0	1	1	0	0	0	0	0	0	0	0	0	0	1	0

Rank among batters: 4,707 • *Total ballparks homered in*: 1 • *First HR*: 09/15/1987 off Joe Boever

Mike Garcia

EDWARD MIGUEL GARCIA
B: 11/17/1923 D: 01/13/1986
BR

Year	Tm	Lg	Tot	H	A	Men-On 0	Men-On 1	Men-On 2	Men-On 3	One-Game 2	One-Game 3	One-Game 4	LO	XN	IP	PH	RHP	LHP
1949	CLE	AL	1	1	0	1	0	0	0	0	0	0	0	0	0	0	1	0
1951	CLE	AL	1	1	0	0	0	1	0	0	0	0	0	0	0	0	1	0
Total			2	2	0	1	0	1	0	0	0	0	0	0	0	0	2	0

Rank among batters: 4,129 • *Total ballparks homered in*: 1 • *First HR*: 08/29/1949 off Joe Dobson

Pedro Garcia

PEDRO MODESTO (DELFI) GARCIA
B: 04/17/1950
BR

Year	Tm	Lg	Tot	H	A	Men-On 0	Men-On 1	Men-On 2	Men-On 3	One-Game 2	One-Game 3	One-Game 4	LO	XN	IP	PH	RHP	LHP
1973	MIL	AL	15	5	10	10	4	1	0	0	0	0	0	0	0	0	13	2
1974	MIL	AL	12	8	4	7	5	0	0	0	0	0	0	0	0	0	6	6
1975	MIL	AL	6	5	1	3	2	1	0	0	0	0	0	0	0	0	0	6
1976	MIL	AL	1	0	1	1	0	0	0	0	0	0	0	0	0	0	1	0
	DET	AL	3	1	2	2	1	0	0	0	0	0	0	0	0	0	1	2
	Total		4	1	3	3	1	0	0	0	0	0	0	0	0	0	2	2
Total			37	19	18	23	12	2	0	0	0	0	0	0	0	0	21	16

Rank among batters: 1,252 • *Top target (3 home runs)*: Mike Cuellar, Bill Lee • *Number of pitchers victimized*: 30 • *Total ballparks homered in*: 10 • *First HR*: 04/07/1973 off Mike Cuellar

Danny Gardella

DANIEL LEWIS GARDELLA
B: 02/26/1920
BL

Year	Tm	Lg	Tot	H	A	Men-On 0	Men-On 1	Men-On 2	Men-On 3	One-Game 2	One-Game 3	One-Game 4	LO	XN	IP	PH	RHP	LHP
1944	NY	NL	6	5	1	3	3	0	0	0	0	0	0	0	0	1	6	0

Danny Gardella *continued*

Year	Tm	Lg	Tot	H	A	Men-On				One-Game			LO	XN	IP	PH	RHP	LHP
						0	1	2	3	2	3	4						
1945	NY	NL	18	12	6	7	9	2	0	3	0	0	0	1	0	1	15	3
Total			24	17	7	10	12	2	0	3	0	0	0	1	0	2	21	3

Rank among batters: 1,643 • Top target (2 home runs): Ira Hutchinson, Hod Lisenbee, Max Butcher, Ken Gables • *Number of pitchers victimized*: 20 • *Total ballparks homered in*: 5 • *First HR*: 05/26/1944 off Bucky Walters

Ron Gardenhire

RONALD CLYDE GARDENHIRE
B: 10/24/1957
BR

Year	Tm	Lg	Tot	H	A	Men-On				One-Game			LO	XN	IP	PH	RHP	LHP
						0	1	2	3	2	3	4						
1982	NY	NL	3	1	2	2	1	0	0	0	0	0	0	1	0	0	2	1
1984	NY	NL	1	1	0	1	0	0	0	0	0	0	0	0	0	0	0	1
Total			4	2	2	3	1	0	0	0	0	0	0	1	0	0	2	2

Rank among batters: 3,427 • *Total ballparks homered in*: 3 • *First HR*: 06/29/1982 off Ray Burris

Billy Gardner

WILLIAM FREDERICK GARDNER
B: 07/19/1927
BR

Year	Tm	Lg	Tot	H	A	Men-On				One-Game			LO	XN	IP	PH	RHP	LHP
						0	1	2	3	2	3	4						
1954	NY	NL	1	1	0	0	0	1	0	0	0	0	0	0	0	0	1	0
1955	NY	NL	3	1	2	2	1	0	0	0	0	0	0	0	0	0	2	1
1956	BAL	AL	11	2	9	6	4	1	0	1	0	0	0	0	0	0	7	4
1957	BAL	AL	6	1	5	3	3	0	0	1	0	0	1	0	0	0	4	2
1958	BAL	AL	3	1	2	2	1	0	0	0	0	0	1	0	0	0	3	0
1959	BAL	AL	6	2	4	4	1	1	0	0	0	0	0	1	0	0	4	2
1960	WAS	AL	9	6	3	5	3	0	1	0	0	0	1	0	0	0	8	1
1961	MIN	AL	1	1	0	0	0	1	0	0	0	0	0	0	0	0	1	0
	NY	AL	1	0	1	1	0	0	0	0	0	0	0	0	0	0	0	1
	Total		2	1	1	1	0	1	0	0	0	0	0	0	0	0	1	1
Total			41	15	26	23	13	4	1	2	0	0	3	1	0	0	30	11

Rank among batters: 1,163 • *Top target (3 home runs)*: Russ Kemmerer • *Number of pitchers victimized*: 35 • *Total ballparks homered in*: 13 • *First HR*: 05/28/1954 off Ben Wade

Earle Gardner

EARLE MCCLURKIN GARDNER
B: 01/24/1884 D: 03/02/1943
BR

Year	Tm	Lg	Tot	H	A	Men-On				One-Game			LO	XN	IP	PH	RHP	LHP
						0	1	2	3	2	3	4						
1910	NY	AL	1	0	1	1	0	0	0	0	0	0	0	0	0	0	1	0
Total			1	0	1	1	0	0	0	0	0	0	0	0	0	0	1	0

Rank among batters: 4,707 • *Total ballparks homered in*: 1 • *First HR*: 09/10/1910 off Charlie Smith

Franklin Gardner

FRANKLIN WASHINGTON GARDNER
B: 06/09/1859 D: 08/01/1914

Year	Tm	Lg	Tot	H	A	Men-On				One-Game			LO	XN	IP	PH	RHP	LHP
						0	1	2	3	2	3	4						
1883	BAL	AA	1	1	0	0	1	0	0	0	0	0	0	0	0	0	1	0
1884	BAL	AA	2	2	0	1	1	0	0	0	0	0	0	0	0	0	1	0
1887	IND	NL	1	0	1	0	1	0	0	0	0	0	0	0	0	0	0	1
Total			4	3	1	1	3	0	0	0	0	0	0	0	0	0	2	1

Rank among batters: 3,427 • *Total ballparks homered in*: 2 • *First HR*: 09/01/1883 off Will White

Jeff Gardner

JEFFREY SCOTT GARDNER
B: 02/04/1964
BL

Year	Tm	Lg	Tot	H	A	Men-On				One-Game			LO	XN	IP	PH	RHP	LHP
						0	1	2	3	2	3	4						
1993	SD	NL	1	1	0	1	0	0	0	0	0	0	1	0	0	0	1	0

Rank among batters: 4,707 • *Total ballparks homered in*: 1 • *First HR*: 07/20/1993 off Dave Telgheder

Jim Gardner

JAMES ANDERSON GARDNER
B: 10/04/1874 D: 04/24/1905

Year	Tm	Lg	Tot	H	A	Men-On				One-Game			LO	XN	IP	PH	RHP	LHP
						0	1	2	3	2	3	4						
1897	PIT	NL	1	1	0	1	0	0	0	0	0	0	0	0	0	0	0	1

Year	Tm	Lg	Tot	H	A	Men-On 0	1	2	3	One-Game 2	3	4	LO	XN	IP	PH	RHP	LHP

Jim Gardner *continued*

Rank among batters: 4,707 • *Total ballparks homered in*: 1 • *First HR*: 05/27/1897 off Harley Payne

Larry Gardner

WILLIAM LAWRENCE GARDNER
B: 05/13/1886 D: 03/11/1976
BL

Year	Tm	Lg	Tot	H	A	0	1	2	3	2	3	4	LO	XN	IP	PH	RHP	LHP
1910	BOS	AL	2	2	0	2	0	0	0	0	0	0	0	0	1	0	1	1
1911	BOS	AL	4	3	1	2	1	1	0	0	0	0	0	0	3	0	4	0
1912	BOS	AL	3	2	1	3	0	0	0	1	0	0	0	0	2	0	3	0
1914	BOS	AL	3	1	2	3	0	0	0	0	0	0	0	0	2	0	3	0
1915	BOS	AL	1	1	0	1	0	0	0	0	0	0	0	0	0	0	1	0
1916	BOS	AL	2	0	2	1	1	0	0	0	0	0	0	0	0	0	0	2
1917	BOS	AL	1	1	0	0	1	0	0	0	0	0	0	0	1	0	0	1
1918	PHI	AL	1	1	0	1	0	0	0	0	0	0	0	0	0	0	1	0
1919	CLE	AL	2	1	1	0	2	0	0	0	0	0	0	0	1	0	1	1
1920	CLE	AL	3	3	0	2	1	0	0	0	0	0	0	0	2	0	2	1
1921	CLE	AL	3	1	2	1	1	1	0	0	0	0	0	1	1	0	2	1
1922	CLE	AL	2	2	0	1	0	1	0	0	0	0	0	0	0	0	1	1
Total			27	18	9	17	7	3	0	1	0	0	0	1	13	0	19	8

Rank among batters: 1,532 • *Top target (2 home runs)*: Lew Brockett, Russ Ford, Hooks Dauss • *Number of pitchers victimized*: 24 • *Total ballparks homered in*: 9 • *First HR*: 05/30/1910 off Harry Krause • *World Series HR*—3

Ray Gardner

RAYMOND VINCENT GARDNER
B: 10/25/1901 D: 05/03/1968
BR

Year	Tm	Lg	Tot	H	A	0	1	2	3	2	3	4	LO	XN	IP	PH	RHP	LHP
1929	CLE	AL	1	0	1	0	1	0	0	0	0	0	0	0	0	0	0	1

Rank among batters: 4,707 • *Total ballparks homered in*: 1 • *First HR*: 06/29/1929 off Emil Yde

Art Garibaldi

ARTHUR EDWARD GARIBALDI
B: 08/20/1907 D: 10/19/1967
BR

Year	Tm	Lg	Tot	H	A	0	1	2	3	2	3	4	LO	XN	IP	PH	RHP	LHP
1936	STL	NL	1	0	1	0	1	0	0	0	0	0	0	0	1	0	1	0

Rank among batters: 4,707 • *Total ballparks homered in*: 1 • *First HR*: 09/12/1936 off Fred Frankhouse

Debs Garms

DEBS C. GARMS
B: 06/26/1908 D: 12/16/1984
BL

Year	Tm	Lg	Tot	H	A	0	1	2	3	2	3	4	LO	XN	IP	PH	RHP	LHP
1932	STL	AL	1	1	0	1	0	0	0	0	0	0	1	0	0	0	1	0
1933	STL	AL	4	3	1	2	1	1	0	0	0	0	0	0	1	0	4	0
1937	BOS	NL	2	0	2	2	0	0	0	0	0	0	1	0	0	0	2	0
1939	BOS	NL	2	0	2	1	1	0	0	0	0	0	0	0	0	0	2	0
1940	PIT	NL	5	1	4	0	4	1	0	0	0	0	0	0	1	0	4	1
1941	PIT	NL	3	1	2	1	2	0	0	0	0	0	0	0	0	1	3	0
Total			17	6	11	7	8	2	0	0	0	0	2	0	2	1	16	1

Rank among batters: 1,969 • *Total ballparks homered in*: 7 • *First HR*: 09/03/1932 off Charlie Biggs

Phil Garner

PHILIP MASON GARNER
B: 04/30/1949
BR

Year	Tm	Lg	Tot	H	A	0	1	2	3	2	3	4	LO	XN	IP	PH	RHP	LHP
1975	OAK	AL	6	3	3	5	1	0	0	0	0	0	0	0	0	0	4	2
1976	OAK	AL	8	6	2	4	1	3	0	0	0	0	0	0	0	0	6	2
1977	PIT	NL	17	9	8	11	4	2	0	0	0	0	1	0	0	0	7	10
1978	PIT	NL	10	4	6	3	4	1	2	0	0	0	0	0	0	0	6	4
1979	PIT	NL	11	6	5	7	3	1	0	0	0	0	0	1	0	0	6	5
1980	PIT	NL	5	3	2	3	2	0	0	1	0	0	0	0	0	0	2	3
1981	PIT	NL	1	0	1	0	1	0	0	0	0	0	0	0	0	0	1	0
1982	HOU	NL	13	6	7	4	4	5	0	0	0	0	0	0	0	0	11	2
1983	HOU	NL	14	4	10	9	3	2	0	0	0	0	0	0	0	0	9	5

Phil Garner *continued*

Year	Tm	Lg	Tot	H	A	Men-On 0	1	2	3	One-Game 2	3	4	LO	XN	IP	PH	RHP	LHP
1984	HOU	NL	4	1	3	3	1	0	0	0	0	0	0	0	0	0	2	2
1985	HOU	NL	6	2	4	4	2	0	0	0	0	0	0	1	0	0	5	1
1986	HOU	NL	9	2	7	6	1	1	1	1	0	0	0	1	0	1	3	6
1987	HOU	NL	3	0	3	2	1	0	0	0	0	0	0	0	0	0	1	2
	LA	NL	2	0	2	1	1	0	0	0	0	0	0	0	0	0	0	2
	Total		5	0	5	3	2	0	0	0	0	0	0	0	0	0	1	4
Total			109	46	63	62	29	15	3	2	0	0	1	3	0	1	63	46

Rank among batters: 441 • *Top target (4 home runs)*: Steve Carlton • *Number of pitchers victimized*: 94 • *Total ballparks homered in*: 18 • *First HR*: 05/25/1975 off Jim Kern • *LCS HR*—1

Ralph Garr

RALPH ALLEN GARR
B: 12/12/1945
BL

Year	Tm	Lg	Tot	H	A	Men-On 0	1	2	3	One-Game 2	3	4	LO	XN	IP	PH	RHP	LHP
1971	ATL	NL	9	9	0	6	2	1	0	1	0	0	0	2	0	0	9	0
1972	ATL	NL	12	9	3	7	4	1	0	0	0	0	0	0	0	0	10	2
1973	ATL	NL	11	3	8	7	3	0	1	0	0	0	2	0	1	0	8	3
1974	ATL	NL	11	6	5	8	1	2	0	1	0	0	4	0	0	0	10	1
1975	ATL	NL	6	5	1	4	0	2	0	0	0	0	3	0	0	0	5	1
1976	CHI	AL	4	0	4	2	2	0	0	0	0	0	0	0	0	0	4	0
1977	CHI	AL	10	2	8	6	2	2	0	0	0	0	2	0	0	0	9	1
1978	CHI	AL	3	2	1	2	1	0	0	0	0	0	0	0	0	0	3	0
1979	CHI	AL	9	3	6	2	7	0	0	0	0	0	0	0	0	0	9	0
Total			75	39	36	44	22	8	1	2	0	0	11	2	1	0	67	8

Rank among batters: 699 • *Top target (3 home runs)*: Don Wilson, Rick Wise, Ferguson Jenkins • *Number of pitchers victimized*: 62 • *Total ballparks homered in*: 21 • *First HR*: 04/25/1971 off Clay Kirby

Scott Garrelts

SCOTT WILLIAM GARRELTS
B: 10/30/1961
BR

Year	Tm	Lg	Tot	H	A	Men-On 0	1	2	3	One-Game 2	3	4	LO	XN	IP	PH	RHP	LHP
1986	SF	NL	1	0	1	0	0	1	0	0	0	0	0	0	0	0	1	0

Rank among batters: 4,707 • *Total ballparks homered in*: 1 • *First HR*: 09/05/1986 off Bert Roberge

Adrian Garrett

HENRY ADRIAN GARRETT
B: 01/03/1943
BL

Year	Tm	Lg	Tot	H	A	Men-On 0	1	2	3	One-Game 2	3	4	LO	XN	IP	PH	RHP	LHP
1971	OAK	AL	1	0	1	0	1	0	0	0	0	0	0	0	0	0	1	0
1973	CHI	NL	3	2	1	2	1	0	0	0	0	0	0	0	0	1	3	0
1975	CHI	NL	1	0	1	0	0	1	0	0	0	0	0	0	0	0	1	0
	CAL	AL	6	4	2	4	1	1	0	0	0	0	0	1	0	1	6	0
	Total		7	4	3	4	1	2	0	0	0	0	0	1	0	1	7	0
Total			11	6	5	6	3	2	0	0	0	0	0	1	0	2	11	0

Rank among batters: 2,419 • *Total ballparks homered in*: 6 • *First HR*: 09/19/1971 off Bill Parsons

Wayne Garrett

RONALD WAYNE GARRETT
B: 12/03/1947
BL

Year	Tm	Lg	Tot	H	A	Men-On 0	1	2	3	One-Game 2	3	4	LO	XN	IP	PH	RHP	LHP
1969	NY	NL	1	1	0	1	0	0	0	0	0	0	0	0	0	0	1	0
1970	NY	NL	12	8	4	6	4	2	0	1	0	0	0	1	0	0	12	0
1971	NY	NL	1	1	0	1	0	0	0	0	0	0	0	0	0	0	1	0
1972	NY	NL	2	0	2	2	0	0	0	0	0	0	0	0	0	0	2	0
1973	NY	NL	16	7	9	10	2	4	0	0	0	0	3	0	0	0	13	3
1974	NY	NL	13	6	7	7	2	4	0	0	0	0	0	0	0	0	8	5
1975	NY	NL	6	4	2	3	1	2	0	0	0	0	1	0	0	2	5	1
1976	NY	NL	4	2	2	3	1	0	0	0	0	0	0	0	0	0	4	0
	MON	NL	2	1	1	0	1	0	1	0	0	0	0	0	0	0	2	0
	Total		6	3	3	3	2	0	1	0	0	0	0	0	0	0	6	0
1977	MON	NL	2	2	0	1	1	0	0	0	0	0	0	1	0	1	2	0
1978	MON	NL	1	0	1	1	0	0	0	0	0	0	0	0	0	0	1	0

Wayne Garrett *continued*

Year	Tm	Lg	Tot	H	A	Men-On 0	Men-On 1	Men-On 2	Men-On 3	One-Game 2	One-Game 3	One-Game 4	LO	XN	IP	PH	RHP	LHP
1978	STL	NL	1	1	0	0	0	0	1	0	0	0	0	0	0	1	1	0
	Total		2	1	1	1	0	0	1	0	0	0	0	0	0	1	2	0
Total			61	33	28	35	12	12	2	1	0	0	4	2	0	4	52	9

Rank among batters: 844 • *Top target (3 home runs)*: Steve Arlin, Steve Renko • *Number of pitchers victimized*: 50 • *Total ballparks homered in*: 12 • *First HR*: 05/06/1969 off Gary Nolan • *World Series HR*—2; *LCS HR*—1

Gil Garrido

GIL GONZALO GARRIDO
B: 06/26/1941
BR

Year	Tm	Lg	Tot	H	A	Men-On 0	Men-On 1	Men-On 2	Men-On 3	One-Game 2	One-Game 3	One-Game 4	LO	XN	IP	PH	RHP	LHP
1970	ATL	NL	1	1	0	0	1	0	0	0	0	0	0	0	0	0	0	1

Rank among batters: 4,707 • *Total ballparks homered in*: 1 • *First HR*: 05/27/1970 off Denny Lemaster

Ford Garrison

ROBERT FORD GARRISON
B: 08/29/1915
BR

Year	Tm	Lg	Tot	H	A	Men-On 0	Men-On 1	Men-On 2	Men-On 3	One-Game 2	One-Game 3	One-Game 4	LO	XN	IP	PH	RHP	LHP
1943	BOS	AL	1	1	0	0	1	0	0	0	0	0	0	0	0	0	1	0
1944	PHI	AL	4	3	1	3	1	0	0	0	0	0	0	0	0	0	2	2
1945	PHI	AL	1	0	1	0	0	1	0	0	0	0	0	0	0	0	1	0
Total			6	4	2	3	2	1	0	0	0	0	0	0	0	0	4	2

Rank among batters: 2,988 • *Total ballparks homered in*: 3 • *First HR*: 09/23/1943 off Mel Harder

Ned Garver

NED FRANKLIN GARVER
B: 12/25/1925
BR

Year	Tm	Lg	Tot	H	A	Men-On 0	Men-On 1	Men-On 2	Men-On 3	One-Game 2	One-Game 3	One-Game 4	LO	XN	IP	PH	RHP	LHP
1948	STL	AL	1	0	1	1	0	0	0	0	0	0	0	0	0	0	0	1
1950	STL	AL	1	0	1	1	0	0	0	0	0	0	0	0	0	0	0	1
1951	STL	AL	1	1	0	1	0	0	0	0	0	0	0	0	0	0	1	0
1953	DET	AL	1	1	0	0	1	0	0	0	0	0	0	0	0	0	1	0
1955	DET	AL	1	0	1	1	0	0	0	0	0	0	0	0	0	0	1	0
1959	KC	AL	2	1	1	1	1	0	0	0	0	0	0	0	0	0	1	1
Total			7	3	4	5	2	0	0	0	0	0	0	0	0	0	4	3

Rank among batters: 2,834 • *Total ballparks homered in*: 5 • *First HR*: 07/18/1948 off Mickey Harris

Steve Garvey

STEVEN PATRICK GARVEY
B: 12/22/1948
BR

Year	Tm	Lg	Tot	H	A	Men-On 0	Men-On 1	Men-On 2	Men-On 3	One-Game 2	One-Game 3	One-Game 4	LO	XN	IP	PH	RHP	LHP
1970	LA	NL	1	1	0	1	0	0	0	0	0	0	0	0	0	0	1	0
1971	LA	NL	7	5	2	4	2	1	0	0	0	0	0	0	0	0	1	6
1972	LA	NL	9	5	4	5	4	0	0	0	0	0	0	0	0	0	6	3
1973	LA	NL	8	6	2	3	1	4	0	1	0	0	0	0	0	0	3	5
1974	LA	NL	21	8	13	13	4	4	0	2	0	0	0	0	0	0	14	7
1975	LA	NL	18	9	9	7	7	4	0	1	0	0	0	0	0	0	13	5
1976	LA	NL	13	6	7	8	4	1	0	0	0	0	0	0	0	0	9	4
1977	LA	NL	33	16	17	20	7	4	2	3	0	0	0	0	0	0	26	7
1978	LA	NL	21	15	6	9	8	3	1	2	0	0	0	0	0	0	14	7
1979	LA	NL	28	20	8	16	8	3	1	1	0	0	0	1	0	0	21	7
1980	LA	NL	26	16	10	13	8	5	0	1	0	0	0	1	0	0	21	5
1981	LA	NL	10	5	5	4	5	1	0	1	0	0	0	1	0	0	6	4
1982	LA	NL	16	5	11	10	3	3	0	0	0	0	0	1	0	0	14	2
1983	SD	NL	14	8	6	10	3	0	1	0	0	0	0	0	0	0	7	7
1984	SD	NL	8	5	3	5	3	0	0	0	0	0	0	0	0	0	5	3
1985	SD	NL	17	10	7	12	3	2	0	1	0	0	0	0	0	0	8	9
1986	SD	NL	21	11	10	12	7	2	0	0	0	0	0	0	0	0	9	12
1987	SD	NL	1	0	1	0	0	1	0	0	0	0	0	0	0	0	0	1
Total			272	151	121	152	77	38	5	13	0	0	0	4	0	0	178	94

Rank among batters: 87 • *Top target (5 home runs)*: Don Gullett, Jerry Koosman, Tom Seaver • *Number of pitchers victimized*: 174 • *Total ballparks homered in*: 13 • *First HR*: 07/21/1970 off Carl Morton • *World Series HR*—1; *LCS HR*—10; *All-Star HR*—2

Rod Gaspar

RODNEY EARL GASPAR
B: 04/03/1946
BB

Year	Tm	Lg	Tot	H	A	Men-On 0	Men-On 1	Men-On 2	Men-On 3	One-Game 2	One-Game 3	One-Game 4	LO	XN	IP	PH	RHP	LHP
1969	NY	NL	1	1	0	1	0	0	0	0	0	0	0	0	0	0	0	1

Rank among batters: 4,707 • *Total ballparks homered in*: 1 • *First HR*: 05/30/1969 off Mike McCormick

Alex Gaston

ALEXANDER NATHANIEL GASTON
B: 03/12/1893 D: 02/08/1976
BR

Year	Tm	Lg	Tot	H	A	Men-On 0	Men-On 1	Men-On 2	Men-On 3	One-Game 2	One-Game 3	One-Game 4	LO	XN	IP	PH	RHP	LHP
1923	NY	NL	1	0	1	0	0	1	0	0	0	0	0	0	0	0	1	0
1929	BOS	AL	2	0	2	1	1	0	0	0	0	0	0	0	0	0	1	1
Total			3	0	3	1	1	1	0	0	0	0	0	0	0	0	2	1

Rank among batters: 3,735 • *Total ballparks homered in*: 3 • *First HR*: 10/06/1923 off Dazzy Vance

Cito Gaston

CLARENCE EDWIN GASTON
B: 03/17/1944
BR

Year	Tm	Lg	Tot	H	A	Men-On 0	Men-On 1	Men-On 2	Men-On 3	One-Game 2	One-Game 3	One-Game 4	LO	XN	IP	PH	RHP	LHP
1969	SD	NL	2	1	1	0	2	0	0	0	0	0	0	0	0	0	2	0
1970	SD	NL	29	12	17	17	8	4	0	0	0	0	0	0	0	0	21	8
1971	SD	NL	17	7	10	10	3	4	0	1	0	0	0	0	0	0	10	7
1972	SD	NL	7	2	5	3	3	0	1	0	0	0	0	0	0	1	5	2
1973	SD	NL	16	6	10	10	2	4	0	0	0	0	0	0	0	0	8	8
1974	SD	NL	6	3	3	3	2	1	0	0	0	0	0	0	0	2	3	3
1975	ATL	NL	6	2	4	4	1	1	0	0	0	0	0	0	0	1	0	6
1976	ATL	NL	4	3	1	1	2	1	0	1	0	0	0	0	0	1	1	3
1977	ATL	NL	3	3	0	0	2	1	0	0	0	0	0	0	0	2	0	3
1978	ATL	NL	1	0	1	0	1	0	0	0	0	0	0	0	0	0	0	1
Total			91	39	52	48	26	16	1	2	0	0	0	0	0	7	50	41

Rank among batters: 559 • *Top target (5 home runs)*: Pat Jarvis • *Number of pitchers victimized*: 58 • *Total ballparks homered in*: 14 • *First HR*: 08/03/1969 off Dick Selma

Milt Gaston

NATHANIEL MILTON GASTON
B: 01/27/1896
BR

Year	Tm	Lg	Tot	H	A	Men-On 0	Men-On 1	Men-On 2	Men-On 3	One-Game 2	One-Game 3	One-Game 4	LO	XN	IP	PH	RHP	LHP
1925	STL	AL	1	0	1	1	0	0	0	0	0	0	0	0	0	0	1	0
1926	STL	AL	1	1	0	1	0	0	0	0	0	0	0	0	0	0	1	0
1927	STL	AL	3	3	0	0	3	0	0	0	0	0	0	0	0	0	1	2
1929	BOS	AL	1	0	1	1	0	0	0	0	0	0	0	0	0	0	0	1
Total			6	4	2	3	3	0	0	0	0	0	0	0	0	0	3	3

Rank among batters: 2,988 • *Total ballparks homered in*: 3 • *First HR*: 09/10/1925 off Red Faber

Brent Gates

BRENT ROBERT GATES
B: 03/14/1970
BB

Year	Tm	Lg	Tot	H	A	Men-On 0	Men-On 1	Men-On 2	Men-On 3	One-Game 2	One-Game 3	One-Game 4	LO	XN	IP	PH	RHP	LHP
1993	OAK	AL	7	4	3	2	5	0	0	0	0	0	0	0	0	0	5	2
1994	OAK	AL	2	0	2	2	0	0	0	0	0	0	0	0	0	0	2	0
1995	OAK	AL	5	3	2	4	1	0	0	0	0	0	0	0	0	0	4	1
Total			14	7	7	8	6	0	0	0	0	0	0	0	0	0	11	3

Rank among batters: 2,169 • *Top target (2 home runs)*: Pat Mahomes • *Number of pitchers victimized*: 13 • *Total ballparks homered in*: 7 • *First HR*: 05/19/1993 off Tom Gordon

Frank Gatins

FRANK ANTHONY GATINS
B: 03/06/1871 D: 11/08/1911

Year	Tm	Lg	Tot	H	A	Men-On 0	Men-On 1	Men-On 2	Men-On 3	One-Game 2	One-Game 3	One-Game 4	LO	XN	IP	PH	RHP	LHP
1901	BRO	NL	1	0	1	0	1	0	0	0	0	0	0	0	0	0	1	0

Rank among batters: 4,707 • *Total ballparks homered in*: 1 • *First HR*: 07/09/1901 off Ed Murphy

Gary Gearhart

LLOYD WILLIAM GEARHART
B: 08/10/1923
BR

Year	Tm	Lg	Tot	H	A	Men-On 0	Men-On 1	Men-On 2	Men-On 3	One-Game 2	One-Game 3	One-Game 4	LO	XN	IP	PH	RHP	LHP
1947	NY	NL	6	1	5	4	2	0	0	0	0	0	0	1	0	2	5	1

Year	Tm	Lg	Tot	H	A	Men-On				One-Game			LO	XN	IP	PH	RHP	LHP
						0	1	2	3	2	3	4						

Gary Gearhart *continued*

Rank among batters: 2,988 • *Total ballparks homered in*: 4 • *First HR*: 05/31/1947 off Art Herring

Huck Geary

EUGENE FRANCIS JOSEPH GEARY
B: 01/22/1917 D: 01/27/1981
BL

Year	Tm	Lg	Tot	H	A	Men-On 0	1	2	3	One-Game 2	3	4	LO	XN	IP	PH	RHP	LHP
1943	PIT	NL	1	1	0	0	0	0	1	0	0	0	0	0	0	0	1	0

Rank among batters: 4,707 • *Total ballparks homered in*: 1 • *First HR*: 06/06/1943 off Bobby Coombs

Joe Gedeon

ELMER JOSEPH GEDEON
B: 12/05/1893 D: 05/19/1941
BR

Year	Tm	Lg	Tot	H	A	Men-On 0	1	2	3	One-Game 2	3	4	LO	XN	IP	PH	RHP	LHP
1918	STL	AL	1	0	1	0	1	0	0	0	0	0	0	0	0	0	0	1

Rank among batters: 4,707 • *Total ballparks homered in*: 1 • *First HR*: 04/23/1918 off Fritz Coumbe

Rich Gedman

RICHARD LEO GEDMAN
B: 09/26/1959
BL

Year	Tm	Lg	Tot	H	A	Men-On 0	1	2	3	One-Game 2	3	4	LO	XN	IP	PH	RHP	LHP
1981	BOS	AL	5	3	2	4	1	0	0	0	0	0	0	0	0	0	5	0
1982	BOS	AL	4	1	3	1	1	2	0	0	0	0	0	0	0	0	4	0
1983	BOS	AL	2	0	2	1	0	1	0	0	0	0	0	0	0	0	2	0
1984	BOS	AL	24	16	8	17	5	2	0	2	0	0	0	0	0	2	23	1
1985	BOS	AL	18	9	9	13	1	3	1	1	0	0	0	0	0	0	16	2
1986	BOS	AL	16	2	14	10	2	2	2	0	0	0	0	1	0	1	11	5
1987	BOS	AL	1	1	0	1	0	0	0	0	0	0	0	0	0	0	0	1
1988	BOS	AL	9	5	4	4	4	1	0	0	0	0	0	0	0	0	9	0
1989	BOS	AL	4	2	2	3	1	0	0	0	0	0	0	0	0	0	3	1
1990	HOU	NL	1	0	1	0	1	0	0	0	0	0	0	0	0	0	1	0
1991	STL	NL	3	1	2	2	1	0	0	0	0	0	0	0	0	0	3	0
1992	STL	NL	1	1	0	1	0	0	0	0	0	0	0	0	0	0	1	0
Total			88	41	47	57	17	11	3	3	0	0	0	1	0	3	78	10

Rank among batters: 590 • *Top target (3 home runs)*: John Butcher • *Number of pitchers victimized*: 74 • *Total ballparks homered in*: 18 • *First HR*: 05/26/1981 off Wayne Garland • *Hit for Cycle*—vs TOR: 09/18/1985 • *World Series HR*—1; *LCS HR*—2

Lou Gehrig

HENRY LOUIS GEHRIG
B: 06/19/1903 D: 06/02/1941
BL HOF

Year	Tm	Lg	Tot	H	A	Men-On 0	1	2	3	One-Game 2	3	4	LO	XN	IP	PH	RHP	LHP
1923	NY	AL	1	0	1	0	1	0	0	0	0	0	0	0	0	0	1	0
1925	NY	AL	20	11	9	14	4	1	1	1	0	0	0	0	1	0	12	8
1926	NY	AL	16	4	12	6	8	2	0	1	0	0	0	0	2	0	12	4
1927	NY	AL	47	24	23	23	14	8	2	4	1	0	0	0	1	0	33	14
1928	NY	AL	27	12	15	12	8	6	1	3	0	0	0	0	1	0	19	8
1929	NY	AL	35	21	14	21	10	2	2	2	1	0	0	0	1	0	23	12
1930	NY	AL	41	14	27	16	14	9	2	4	1	0	0	1	0	0	28	13
1931	NY	AL	46	24	22	17	20	6	3	3	0	0	0	0	0	0	33	13
1932	NY	AL	34	12	22	13	14	5	2	2	0	1	0	0	0	0	24	10
1933	NY	AL	32	17	15	12	13	7	0	1	0	0	0	0	0	0	19	13
1934	NY	AL	49	30	19	25	14	6	4	7	0	0	0	0	1	0	37	12
1935	NY	AL	30	15	15	14	10	4	2	3	0	0	0	3	1	0	24	6
1936	NY	AL	49	27	22	29	11	7	2	4	0	0	0	0	1	0	36	13
1937	NY	AL	37	24	13	12	15	9	1	3	0	0	0	0	0	0	24	13
1938	NY	AL	29	16	13	16	11	1	1	0	0	0	0	0	1	0	25	4
Total			493	251	242	230	167	73	23	38	3	1	0	4	10	0	350	143

Rank among batters: 15 • *Top target (14 home runs)*: Lloyd Brown, Earl Whitehill • *Number of pitchers victimized*: 166 • *Total ballparks homered in*: 10 • *First HR*: 09/27/1923 off Bill Piercy • *Hit for Cycle*—vs CHI: 06/25/1934; vs STL: 08/01/1937 • *World Series HR*—10; *All-Star HR*—2

Henry Gehring

HENRY GEHRING
B: 01/24/1881 D: 04/18/1912
BR

Year	Tm	Lg	Tot	H	A	Men-On 0	1	2	3	One-Game 2	3	4	LO	XN	IP	PH	RHP	LHP
1907	WAS	AL	1	0	1	0	1	0	0	0	0	0	0	0	1	0	0	1

Rank among batters: 4,707 • *Total ballparks homered in*: 1 • *First HR*: 09/13/1907 off Tex Neuer

Year	Tm	Lg	Tot	H	A	Men-On				One-Game			LO	XN	IP	PH	RHP	LHP
						0	1	2	3	2	3	4						

Charlie Gehringer

CHARLES LEONARD GEHRINGER
B: 05/11/1903 D: 01/21/1993
BL HOF

Year	Tm	Lg	Tot	H	A	0	1	2	3	2	3	4	LO	XN	IP	PH	RHP	LHP
1926	DET	AL	1	0	1	0	1	0	0	0	0	0	0	0	0	0	1	0
1927	DET	AL	4	1	3	2	0	1	1	0	0	0	0	0	1	0	2	2
1928	DET	AL	6	4	2	4	1	1	0	1	0	0	0	0	1	0	5	1
1929	DET	AL	13	7	6	4	8	1	0	0	0	0	0	0	1	0	9	4
1930	DET	AL	16	7	9	8	7	0	1	1	0	0	0	2	1	0	13	3
1931	DET	AL	4	0	4	2	1	1	0	0	0	0	0	0	0	0	3	1
1932	DET	AL	19	6	13	9	7	3	0	1	0	0	0	0	0	0	14	5
1933	DET	AL	12	8	4	3	8	1	0	0	0	0	0	0	0	0	10	2
1934	DET	AL	11	2	9	5	5	1	0	1	0	0	0	1	0	0	10	1
1935	DET	AL	19	11	8	13	5	1	0	0	0	0	0	1	1	0	17	2
1936	DET	AL	15	7	8	9	5	1	0	0	0	0	0	0	0	0	14	1
1937	DET	AL	14	10	4	5	7	2	0	1	0	0	0	0	0	0	13	1
1938	DET	AL	20	12	8	8	6	6	0	1	0	0	0	1	0	0	18	2
1939	DET	AL	16	9	7	5	9	1	1	1	0	0	0	0	1	1	16	0
1940	DET	AL	10	5	5	6	3	1	0	0	0	0	0	0	0	0	8	2
1941	DET	AL	3	2	1	2	1	0	0	0	0	0	0	0	0	0	3	0
1942	DET	AL	1	1	0	0	1	0	0	0	0	0	0	0	0	1	1	0
Total			184	92	92	85	75	21	3	7	0	0	0	5	6	2	157	27

Rank among batters: 210 • *Top target (10 home runs)*: Red Ruffing • *Number of pitchers victimized*: 99 • *Total ballparks homered in*: 9 • *First HR*: 07/15/1926 off Urban Shocker • *Hit for Cycle*—vs STL: 05/27/1939 • *World Series HR*—1

Phil Geier

PHILIP LOUIS GEIER
B: 11/03/1876 D: 09/25/1967
BL

Year	Tm	Lg	Tot	H	A	0	1	2	3	2	3	4	LO	XN	IP	PH	RHP	LHP
1897	PHI	NL	1	1	0	0	1	0	0	0	0	0	0	0	0	0	1	0
1904	BOS	NL	1	0	1	0	1	0	0	0	0	0	0	0	0	0	1	0
Total			2	1	1	0	2	0	0	0	0	0	0	0	0	0	2	0

Rank among batters: 4,129 • *Total ballparks homered in*: 2 • *First HR*: 09/04/1897 off Zeke Wilson

Gary Geiger

GARY MERLE GEIGER
B: 04/04/1937
BL

Year	Tm	Lg	Tot	H	A	0	1	2	3	2	3	4	LO	XN	IP	PH	RHP	LHP
1958	CLE	AL	1	1	0	1	0	0	0	0	0	0	0	0	0	0	1	0
1959	BOS	AL	11	5	6	6	3	2	0	1	0	0	0	1	0	1	9	2
1960	BOS	AL	9	5	4	4	3	2	0	0	0	0	0	0	0	0	9	0
1961	BOS	AL	18	9	9	7	8	2	1	1	0	0	0	0	1	0	18	0
1962	BOS	AL	16	7	9	10	6	0	0	1	0	0	0	0	0	1	13	3
1963	BOS	AL	16	5	11	12	4	0	0	2	0	0	1	0	0	0	14	2
1965	BOS	AL	1	1	0	1	0	0	0	0	0	0	0	0	0	0	1	0
1966	ATL	NL	4	4	0	4	0	0	0	0	0	0	0	0	0	1	4	0
1967	ATL	NL	1	1	0	1	0	0	0	0	0	0	0	0	0	0	1	0
Total			77	38	39	46	24	6	1	5	0	0	1	1	1	3	70	7

Rank among batters: 682 • *Top target (5 home runs)*: Mudcat Grant • *Number of pitchers victimized*: 53 • *Total ballparks homered in*: 10 • *First HR*: 07/23/1958 off Pedro Ramos

William Geiss

WILLIAM J. GEISS
B: 07/15/1858 D: 09/18/1924

Year	Tm	Lg	Tot	H	A	0	1	2	3	2	3	4	LO	XN	IP	PH	RHP	LHP
1884	DET	NL	2	1	1	1	1	0	0	0	0	0	0	0	0	0	1	0

Rank among batters: 4,129 • *Total ballparks homered in*: 2 • *First HR*: 05/30/1884 off George Crosby

Charlie Gelbert

CHARLES MAGNUS GELBERT
B: 01/26/1906 D: 01/13/1967
BR

Year	Tm	Lg	Tot	H	A	0	1	2	3	2	3	4	LO	XN	IP	PH	RHP	LHP
1929	STL	NL	3	1	2	3	0	0	0	0	0	0	0	0	2	0	3	0
1930	STL	NL	3	2	1	0	2	0	1	0	0	0	0	0	0	0	2	1
1931	STL	NL	1	1	0	0	1	0	0	0	0	0	0	0	0	0	1	0
1932	STL	NL	1	0	1	1	0	0	0	0	0	0	0	0	1	0	0	1
1935	STL	NL	2	2	0	1	1	0	0	0	0	0	0	0	0	0	2	0
1936	STL	NL	3	1	2	2	1	0	0	0	0	0	0	0	0	0	2	1

Charlie Gelbert *continued*

Year	Tm	Lg	Tot	H	A	Men-On 0	1	2	3	One-Game 2	3	4	LO	XN	IP	PH	RHP	LHP
1937	CIN	NL	1	0	1	1	0	0	0	0	0	0	0	0	0	0	1	0
1939	WAS	AL	3	1	2	1	1	1	0	0	0	0	0	0	0	0	1	2
Total			17	8	9	9	6	1	1	0	0	0	0	0	3	0	12	5

Rank among batters: 1,969 • *Top target (2 home runs)*: Guy Bush • *Number of pitchers victimized*: 16 • *Total ballparks homered in*: 7 • *First HR*: 06/18/1929 off Guy Bush

Frank Genins

C. FRANK GENINS
B: 11/02/1866 D: 09/30/1922

Year	Tm	Lg	Tot	H	A	Men-On 0	1	2	3	One-Game 2	3	4	LO	XN	IP	PH	RHP	LHP
1895	PIT	NL	2	1	1	1	1	0	0	0	0	0	0	0	0	0	2	0

Rank among batters: 4,129 • *Total ballparks homered in*: 2 • *First HR*: 07/10/1895 off Ad Gumbert

Jim Gentile

JAMES EDWARD GENTILE
B: 06/03/1934
BL

Year	Tm	Lg	Tot	H	A	Men-On 0	1	2	3	One-Game 2	3	4	LO	XN	IP	PH	RHP	LHP
1957	BRO	NL	1	1	0	1	0	0	0	0	0	0	0	0	0	0	1	0
1960	BAL	AL	21	10	11	10	3	7	1	3	0	0	0	0	0	1	18	3
1961	BAL	AL	46	16	30	16	19	6	5	7	0	0	0	1	0	1	38	8
1962	BAL	AL	33	10	23	15	14	4	0	3	0	0	0	2	0	0	24	9
1963	BAL	AL	24	11	13	21	2	1	0	1	0	0	0	1	0	0	20	4
1964	KC	AL	28	18	10	16	8	4	0	5	0	0	0	1	0	0	21	7
1965	KC	AL	10	4	6	7	1	2	0	1	0	0	0	0	0	0	9	1
	HOU	NL	7	0	7	4	2	1	0	1	0	0	0	0	0	1	6	1
	Total		17	4	13	11	3	3	0	2	0	0	0	0	0	1	15	2
1966	HOU	NL	7	4	3	5	2	0	0	0	0	0	0	1	0	0	6	1
	CLE	AL	2	2	0	1	1	0	0	0	0	0	0	0	0	1	1	1
	Total		9	6	3	6	3	0	0	0	0	0	0	1	0	1	7	2
Total			179	76	103	96	52	25	6	21	0	0	0	6	0	4	144	35

Rank among batters: 221 • *Top target (8 home runs)*: Pedro Ramos • *Number of pitchers victimized*: 102 • *Total ballparks homered in*: 21 • *First HR*: 09/22/1957 off Robin Roberts

Bill George

WILLIAM M. GEORGE
B: 01/27/1865 D: 08/23/1916
BR

Year	Tm	Lg	Tot	H	A	Men-On 0	1	2	3	One-Game 2	3	4	LO	XN	IP	PH	RHP	LHP
1888	NY	NL	1	0	1	0	1	0	0	0	0	0	0	0	0	0	1	0

Rank among batters: 4,707 • *Total ballparks homered in*: 1 • *First HR*: 07/12/1888 off Lev Shreve • *World Series HR*—1

Wally Gerber

WALTER GERBER
B: 08/18/1891 D: 06/19/1951
BR

Year	Tm	Lg	Tot	H	A	Men-On 0	1	2	3	One-Game 2	3	4	LO	XN	IP	PH	RHP	LHP
1919	STL	AL	1	0	1	1	0	0	0	0	0	0	0	0	1	0	0	1
1920	STL	AL	2	0	2	0	2	0	0	0	0	0	0	0	1	0	1	1
1921	STL	AL	2	2	0	0	1	1	0	0	0	0	0	0	1	0	0	2
1922	STL	AL	1	0	1	1	0	0	0	0	0	0	0	0	0	0	1	0
1923	STL	AL	1	0	1	1	0	0	0	0	0	0	0	0	0	0	1	0
Total			7	2	5	3	3	1	0	0	0	0	0	0	3	0	3	4

Rank among batters: 2,834 • *Top target (2 home runs)*: Dutch Leonard • *Number of pitchers victimized*: 6 • *Total ballparks homered in*: 4 • *First HR*: 06/23/1919 off Dutch Leonard

Bob Geren

ROBERT PETER GEREN
B: 09/22/1961
BR

Year	Tm	Lg	Tot	H	A	Men-On 0	1	2	3	One-Game 2	3	4	LO	XN	IP	PH	RHP	LHP
1989	NY	AL	9	4	5	4	5	0	0	0	0	0	0	0	0	0	7	2
1990	NY	AL	8	4	4	4	2	2	0	0	0	0	0	0	0	0	4	4
1991	NY	AL	2	1	1	1	0	1	0	0	0	0	0	0	0	0	0	2
1993	SD	NL	3	1	2	3	0	0	0	0	0	0	0	0	0	0	0	3
Total			22	10	12	12	7	3	0	0	0	0	0	0	0	0	11	11

Rank among batters: 1,719 • *Total ballparks homered in*: 11 • *First HR*: 05/20/1989 off Mike Dunne

Joe Gerhardt

JOHN JOSEPH GERHARDT
B: 02/14/1855 D: 03/11/1922
BR

Year	Tm	Lg	Tot	H	A	Men-On 0	1	2	3	One-Game 2	3	4	LO	XN	IP	PH	RHP	LHP
1876	LOU	NL	2	2	0	1	1	0	0	0	0	0	1	0	2	0	2	0
1877	LOU	NL	1	1	0	1	0	0	0	0	0	0	0	0	1	0	1	0
1879	CIN	NL	1	1	0	1	0	0	0	0	0	0	0	0	0	0	1	0
1890	BRO	AA	2	1	1	0	1	1	0	0	0	0	0	0	0	0	1	1
	STL	AA	1	1	0	1	0	0	0	0	0	0	0	0	0	0	1	0
	Total		3	2	1	1	1	1	0	0	0	0	0	0	0	0	2	1
Total			7	6	1	4	2	1	0	0	0	0	1	0	3	0	6	1

Rank among batters: 2,834 • *Total ballparks homered in*: 5 • *First HR*: 05/18/1876 off Cherokee Fisher

Ken Gerhart

HAROLD KENNETH GERHART
B: 05/19/1961
BR

Year	Tm	Lg	Tot	H	A	Men-On 0	1	2	3	One-Game 2	3	4	LO	XN	IP	PH	RHP	LHP
1986	BAL	AL	1	1	0	1	0	0	0	0	0	0	0	0	0	0	0	1
1987	BAL	AL	14	5	9	10	3	1	0	2	0	0	2	0	0	0	10	4
1988	BAL	AL	9	5	4	7	2	0	0	0	0	0	1	0	0	0	4	5
Total			24	11	13	18	5	1	0	2	0	0	3	0	0	0	14	10

Rank among batters: 1,643 • *Top target (3 home runs)*: Charlie Hough • *Number of pitchers victimized*: 21 • *Total ballparks homered in*: 9 • *First HR*: 09/19/1986 off Teddy Higuera

Al Gerheauser

ALBERT GERHEAUSER
B: 06/24/1917 D: 05/28/1972
BL

Year	Tm	Lg	Tot	H	A	Men-On 0	1	2	3	One-Game 2	3	4	LO	XN	IP	PH	RHP	LHP
1944	PHI	NL	1	0	1	1	0	0	0	0	0	0	0	0	0	0	1	0

Rank among batters: 4,707 • *Total ballparks homered in*: 1 • *First HR*: 07/04/1944 off Rip Sewell

Les German

LESTER STANLEY GERMAN
B: 06/01/1869 D: 06/10/1934
BR

Year	Tm	Lg	Tot	H	A	Men-On 0	1	2	3	One-Game 2	3	4	LO	XN	IP	PH	RHP	LHP
1895	NY	NL	2	0	2	0	2	0	0	0	0	0	0	0	0	0	2	0
1896	WAS	NL	1	1	0	0	1	0	0	0	0	0	0	0	0	0	1	0
Total			3	1	2	0	3	0	0	0	0	0	0	0	0	0	3	0

Rank among batters: 3,735 • *Total ballparks homered in*: 2 • *First HR*: 09/21/1895 off Jim Sullivan

Dick Gernert

RICHARD EDWARD GERNERT
B: 09/28/1928
BR

Year	Tm	Lg	Tot	H	A	Men-On 0	1	2	3	One-Game 2	3	4	LO	XN	IP	PH	RHP	LHP
1952	BOS	AL	19	8	11	6	10	3	0	1	0	0	0	2	0	0	15	4
1953	BOS	AL	21	16	5	12	6	3	0	2	0	0	0	0	0	0	17	4
1956	BOS	AL	16	11	5	7	7	2	0	1	0	0	0	0	0	0	8	8
1957	BOS	AL	14	9	5	5	6	3	0	1	0	0	0	0	0	0	8	6
1958	BOS	AL	20	15	5	10	8	2	0	1	0	0	0	2	0	0	14	6
1959	BOS	AL	11	7	4	6	3	2	0	0	0	0	0	1	0	0	8	3
1960	DET	AL	1	0	1	1	0	0	0	0	0	0	0	0	0	0	1	0
1961	DET	AL	1	1	0	1	0	0	0	0	0	0	0	1	0	1	1	0
Total			103	67	36	48	40	15	0	6	0	0	0	6	0	1	72	31

Rank among batters: 477 • *Top target (4 home runs)*: Chuck Stobbs, Billy Pierce, Billy Loes • *Number of pitchers victimized*: 66 • *Total ballparks homered in*: 10 • *First HR*: 06/15/1952 off Chuck Stobbs

Cesar Geronimo

CESAR FRANCISCO (ZORRILLA) GERONIMO
B: 03/11/1948
BL

Year	Tm	Lg	Tot	H	A	Men-On 0	1	2	3	One-Game 2	3	4	LO	XN	IP	PH	RHP	LHP
1971	HOU	NL	1	0	1	0	1	0	0	0	0	0	0	0	0	0	1	0
1972	CIN	NL	4	2	2	4	0	0	0	0	0	0	0	0	1	0	4	0
1973	CIN	NL	4	3	1	3	1	0	0	0	0	0	0	1	0	0	4	0
1974	CIN	NL	7	2	5	6	0	0	1	0	0	0	0	0	0	0	7	0
1975	CIN	NL	6	3	3	2	2	2	0	0	0	0	0	0	1	0	6	0

Cesar Geronimo *continued*

Year	Tm	Lg	Tot	H	A	Men-On 0	1	2	3	One-Game 2	3	4	LO	XN	IP	PH	RHP	LHP
1976	CIN	NL	2	1	1	2	0	0	0	0	0	0	0	0	0	0	1	1
1977	CIN	NL	10	4	6	4	3	3	0	0	0	0	0	0	0	0	5	5
1978	CIN	NL	5	2	3	4	1	0	0	0	0	0	0	0	0	0	5	0
1979	CIN	NL	4	4	0	4	0	0	0	0	0	0	0	0	0	0	4	0
1980	CIN	NL	2	2	0	2	0	0	0	0	0	0	0	0	0	0	2	0
1981	KC	AL	2	0	2	0	2	0	0	0	0	0	0	0	0	0	2	0
1982	KC	AL	4	3	1	4	0	0	0	0	0	0	1	0	0	0	4	0
Total			51	26	25	35	10	5	1	0	0	0	1	1	2	0	45	6

Rank among batters: 979 • *Top target (3 home runs)*: Lynn McGlothen • *Number of pitchers victimized*: 44 • *Total ballparks homered in*: 15 • *First HR*: 09/07/1971 off Ron Reed • *World Series HR*—2; *LCS HR*—1

Doc Gessler

HARRY HOMER GESSLER
B: 12/23/1880 D: 12/25/1924
BL

Year	Tm	Lg	Tot	H	A	Men-On 0	1	2	3	One-Game 2	3	4	LO	XN	IP	PH	RHP	LHP
1904	BRO	NL	2	1	1	2	0	0	0	0	0	0	0	0	1	0	2	0
1905	BRO	NL	3	2	1	1	2	0	0	0	0	0	0	0	1	0	2	1
1908	BOS	AL	3	1	2	1	2	0	0	0	0	0	0	0	1	0	1	2
1910	WAS	AL	2	1	1	2	0	0	0	0	0	0	0	0	2	0	2	0
1911	WAS	AL	4	4	0	1	2	0	1	0	0	0	0	0	2	0	3	1
Total			14	9	5	7	6	0	1	0	0	0	0	0	7	0	10	4

Rank among batters: 2,169 • *Total ballparks homered in*: 7 • *First HR*: 07/20/1904 off Bob Ewing

Tom Gettinger

LEWIS THOMAS LEYTON GETTINGER
B: 12/11/1868 D: 07/26/1943
BL

Year	Tm	Lg	Tot	H	A	Men-On 0	1	2	3	One-Game 2	3	4	LO	XN	IP	PH	RHP	LHP
1889	STL	AA	1	1	0	0	1	0	0	0	0	0	0	0	0	0	0	1
1890	STL	AA	3	3	0	0	2	0	1	1	0	0	0	0	0	0	3	0
1895	LOU	NL	2	1	1	1	0	1	0	0	0	0	0	0	0	0	1	1
Total			6	5	1	1	3	1	1	1	0	0	0	0	0	0	4	2

Rank among batters: 2,988 • *Top target (2 home runs)*: Hank Gastright • *Number of pitchers victimized*: 5 • *Total ballparks homered in*: 3 • *First HR*: 10/02/1889 off John Sowders

Jake Gettman

JACOB JOHN GETTMAN
B: 10/25/1876 D: 10/04/1956
BB

Year	Tm	Lg	Tot	H	A	Men-On 0	1	2	3	One-Game 2	3	4	LO	XN	IP	PH	RHP	LHP
1897	WAS	NL	3	3	0	0	2	0	1	0	0	0	0	0	2	0	3	0
1898	WAS	NL	5	4	1	3	1	1	0	0	0	0	0	0	1	0	3	2
Total			8	7	1	3	3	1	1	0	0	0	0	0	3	0	6	2

Rank among batters: 2,703 • *Total ballparks homered in*: 2 • *First HR*: 09/07/1897 off Bill Magee

Gus Getz

GUSTAVE GETZ
B: 08/03/1889 D: 05/28/1969
BR

Year	Tm	Lg	Tot	H	A	Men-On 0	1	2	3	One-Game 2	3	4	LO	XN	IP	PH	RHP	LHP
1915	BRO	NL	2	1	1	2	0	0	0	0	0	0	0	0	1	0	2	0

Rank among batters: 4,129 • *Total ballparks homered in*: 2 • *First HR*: 09/28/1915 off George Chalmers

Pretzels Getzien

CHARLES H. GETZIEN
B: 02/14/1864 D: 06/19/1932
BR

Year	Tm	Lg	Tot	H	A	Men-On 0	1	2	3	One-Game 2	3	4	LO	XN	IP	PH	RHP	LHP
1887	DET	NL	1	0	1	1	0	0	0	0	0	0	0	0	0	0	1	0
1888	DET	NL	1	1	0	0	1	0	0	0	0	0	0	0	0	0	1	0
1889	IND	NL	2	1	1	1	1	0	0	0	0	0	0	0	0	0	2	0
1890	BOS	NL	2	2	0	1	0	1	0	0	0	0	0	0	0	0	2	0
1891	BOS	NL	1	0	1	0	1	0	0	0	0	0	0	0	0	0	1	0
1892	STL	NL	1	0	1	1	0	0	0	0	0	0	0	0	0	0	1	0
Total			8	4	4	4	3	1	0	0	0	0	0	0	0	0	8	0

Rank among batters: 2,703 • *Top target (2 home runs)*: Henry Gruber • *Number of pitchers victimized*: 7 • *Total ballparks homered in*: 6 • *First HR*: 05/19/1887 off Charlie Ferguson

Year	Tm	Lg	Tot	H	A	Men-On 0	1	2	3	One-Game 2	3	4	LO	XN	IP	PH	RHP	LHP

Patsy Gharrity

EDWARD PATRICK GHARRITY
B: 03/13/1892 D: 10/10/1966
BR

Year	Tm	Lg	Tot	H	A	0	1	2	3	2	3	4	LO	XN	IP	PH	RHP	LHP
1919	WAS	AL	2	0	2	1	1	0	0	1	0	0	0	0	1	0	2	0
1920	WAS	AL	3	0	3	2	1	0	0	0	0	0	0	0	0	0	1	2
1921	WAS	AL	7	1	6	2	3	2	0	0	0	0	0	0	1	0	6	1
1922	WAS	AL	5	1	4	2	2	1	0	0	0	0	0	0	2	0	4	1
1923	WAS	AL	3	2	1	2	0	0	1	0	0	0	0	0	1	1	2	1
Total			20	4	16	9	7	3	1	1	0	0	0	0	5	1	15	5

Rank among batters: 1,810 • *Top target (2 home runs)*: Herb Pennock, Curt Fullerton • *Number of pitchers victimized*: 18 • *Total ballparks homered in*: 6 • *First HR*: 06/23/1919 off Carl Mays

Jason Giambi

JASON GILBERT GIAMBI
B: 01/08/1971
BL

Year	Tm	Lg	Tot	H	A	0	1	2	3	2	3	4	LO	XN	IP	PH	RHP	LHP
1995	OAK	AL	6	3	3	5	1	0	0	0	0	0	0	0	0	0	5	1

Rank among batters: 2,988 • *Total ballparks homered in*: 2 • *First HR*: 07/08/1995 off David Cone

John Gibbons

JOHN MICHAEL GIBBONS
B: 06/08/1962
BR

Year	Tm	Lg	Tot	H	A	0	1	2	3	2	3	4	LO	XN	IP	PH	RHP	LHP
1986	NY	NL	1	1	0	1	0	0	0	0	0	0	0	0	0	0	1	0

Rank among batters: 4,707 • *Total ballparks homered in*: 1 • *First HR*: 09/20/1986 off Michael Jackson

Jake Gibbs

JERRY DEAN GIBBS
B: 11/07/1938
BL

Year	Tm	Lg	Tot	H	A	0	1	2	3	2	3	4	LO	XN	IP	PH	RHP	LHP
1965	NY	AL	2	1	1	1	1	0	0	0	0	0	0	0	0	0	2	0
1966	NY	AL	3	3	0	1	2	0	0	0	0	0	0	0	0	0	3	0
1967	NY	AL	4	4	0	2	2	0	0	0	0	0	0	0	0	1	3	1
1968	NY	AL	3	1	2	1	2	0	0	0	0	0	0	0	0	0	3	0
1970	NY	AL	8	6	2	6	1	1	0	1	0	0	0	1	0	0	8	0
1971	NY	AL	5	4	1	2	2	1	0	0	0	0	0	0	0	0	5	0
Total			25	19	6	13	10	2	0	1	0	0	0	1	0	1	24	1

Rank among batters: 1,608 • Top target (2 home runs): Wes Stock, Gerald Janeski, Dick Bosman, Ray Culp • *Number of pitchers victimized*: 21 • *Total ballparks homered in*: 6 • *First HR*: 08/15/1965 off Wes Stock

Bob Gibson

ROBERT GIBSON
B: 11/09/1935
BR HOF

Year	Tm	Lg	Tot	H	A	0	1	2	3	2	3	4	LO	XN	IP	PH	RHP	LHP
1961	STL	NL	1	0	1	0	1	0	0	0	0	0	0	0	0	0	0	1
1962	STL	NL	2	0	2	2	0	0	0	0	0	0	0	0	0	0	2	0
1963	STL	NL	3	3	0	1	1	1	0	0	0	0	0	0	0	0	2	1
1965	STL	NL	5	2	3	2	1	1	1	0	0	0	0	0	0	0	4	1
1966	STL	NL	1	0	1	1	0	0	0	0	0	0	0	0	1	0	1	0
1969	STL	NL	1	0	1	1	0	0	0	0	0	0	0	0	0	0	0	1
1970	STL	NL	2	1	1	2	0	0	0	0	0	0	0	0	0	0	1	1
1971	STL	NL	2	0	2	1	1	0	0	0	0	0	0	0	0	0	0	2
1972	STL	NL	5	3	2	3	0	2	0	0	0	0	0	0	0	0	2	3
1973	STL	NL	2	2	0	1	0	0	1	0	0	0	0	0	0	0	2	0
Total			24	11	13	14	4	4	2	0	0	0	0	0	1	0	14	10

Rank among batters: 1,643 • *Total ballparks homered in*: 13 • *First HR*: 07/05/1961 off Johnny Podres • *World Series HR*—2

Frank Gibson

FRANK GILBERT GIBSON
B: 09/27/1890 D: 04/27/1961
BB

Year	Tm	Lg	Tot	H	A	0	1	2	3	2	3	4	LO	XN	IP	PH	RHP	LHP
1921	BOS	NL	2	1	1	2	0	0	0	0	0	0	0	0	1	0	2	0
1922	BOS	NL	3	0	3	2	1	0	0	0	0	0	0	0	0	0	3	0

Frank Gibson *continued*

Year	Tm	Lg	Tot	H	A	Men-On				One-Game			LO	XN	IP	PH	RHP	LHP
						0	1	2	3	2	3	4						
1924	BOS	NL	1	0	1	1	0	0	0	0	0	0	0	0	0	0	1	0
1925	BOS	NL	2	0	2	2	0	0	0	0	0	0	0	0	0	0	2	0
Total			8	1	7	7	1	0	0	0	0	0	0	0	1	0	8	0

Rank among batters: 2,703 • *Top target (2 home runs)*: Huck Betts • *Number of pitchers victimized*: 7 • *Total ballparks homered in*: 6 • *First HR*: 06/23/1921 off Fred Toney

George Gibson

GEORGE C. GIBSON
B: 07/22/1880 D: 01/25/1967
BR

Year	Tm	Lg	Tot	H	A	Men-On				One-Game			LO	XN	IP	PH	RHP	LHP
						0	1	2	3	2	3	4						
1905	PIT	NL	2	0	2	2	0	0	0	0	0	0	0	1	1	0	2	0
1907	PIT	NL	3	3	0	1	2	0	0	0	0	0	0	0	2	0	3	0
1908	PIT	NL	2	0	2	2	0	0	0	0	0	0	0	0	0	0	2	0
1909	PIT	NL	2	1	1	2	0	0	0	0	0	0	0	0	1	0	2	0
1910	PIT	NL	3	0	3	2	1	0	0	0	0	0	0	0	0	0	3	0
1912	PIT	NL	2	0	2	2	0	0	0	0	0	0	0	0	0	0	1	1
1915	PIT	NL	1	0	1	1	0	0	0	0	0	0	0	0	0	0	1	0
Total			15	4	11	12	3	0	0	0	0	0	0	1	4	0	14	1

Rank among batters: 2,096 • *Total ballparks homered in*: 6 • *First HR*: 07/18/1905 off Christy Mathewson

Kirk Gibson

KIRK HAROLD GIBSON
B: 05/28/1957
BL

Year	Tm	Lg	Tot	H	A	Men-On				One-Game			LO	XN	IP	PH	RHP	LHP
						0	1	2	3	2	3	4						
1979	DET	AL	1	0	1	1	0	0	0	0	0	0	0	0	0	0	1	0
1980	DET	AL	9	3	6	8	1	0	0	0	0	0	0	0	0	0	7	2
1981	DET	AL	9	4	5	3	5	1	0	0	0	0	1	0	0	0	5	4
1982	DET	AL	8	4	4	3	4	1	0	0	0	0	0	1	0	0	6	2
1983	DET	AL	15	5	10	12	3	0	0	0	0	0	0	1	1	0	14	1
1984	DET	AL	27	11	16	16	6	5	0	2	0	0	0	0	0	0	18	9
1985	DET	AL	29	18	11	21	5	3	0	1	0	0	0	0	1	0	22	7
1986	DET	AL	28	15	13	9	14	5	0	5	0	0	0	2	0	0	21	7
1987	DET	AL	24	14	10	14	6	4	0	0	0	0	0	0	0	0	20	4
1988	LA	NL	25	14	11	15	8	2	0	1	0	0	0	1	0	0	14	11
1989	LA	NL	9	4	5	6	3	0	0	0	0	0	1	0	1	0	5	4
1990	LA	NL	8	2	6	3	3	2	0	1	0	0	0	0	0	0	5	3
1991	KC	AL	16	4	12	8	5	2	1	1	0	0	0	0	0	0	14	2
1992	PIT	NL	2	0	2	1	0	0	1	0	0	0	1	0	0	0	2	0
1993	DET	AL	13	5	8	10	2	0	1	1	0	0	0	0	0	0	13	0
1994	DET	AL	23	9	14	11	5	6	1	3	0	0	0	1	0	2	21	2
1995	DET	AL	9	7	2	5	3	1	0	1	0	0	0	0	0	1	8	1
Total			255	119	136	146	73	32	4	16	0	0	3	6	3	3	196	59

Rank among batters: 101 • *Top target (5 home runs)*: Kirk McCaskill • *Number of pitchers victimized*: 185 • *Total ballparks homered in*: 30 • *First HR*: 09/25/1979 off Steve Stone • *World Series HR—3; LCS HR—4*

Russ Gibson

JOHN RUSSELL GIBSON
B: 05/06/1939
BR

Year	Tm	Lg	Tot	H	A	Men-On				One-Game			LO	XN	IP	PH	RHP	LHP
						0	1	2	3	2	3	4						
1967	BOS	AL	1	1	0	0	1	0	0	0	0	0	0	0	0	0	1	0
1968	BOS	AL	3	1	2	3	0	0	0	0	0	0	0	0	0	0	1	2
1969	BOS	AL	3	0	3	1	1	1	0	0	0	0	0	0	0	1	1	2
1971	SF	NL	1	1	0	0	0	1	0	0	0	0	0	0	0	0	1	0
Total			8	3	5	4	2	2	0	0	0	0	0	0	0	1	4	4

Rank among batters: 2,703 • *Total ballparks homered in*: 7 • *First HR*: 06/12/1967 off Joe Verbanic

Norm Gigon

NORMAN PHILLIP GIGON
B: 05/12/1938
BR

Year	Tm	Lg	Tot	H	A	Men-On				One-Game			LO	XN	IP	PH	RHP	LHP
						0	1	2	3	2	3	4						
1967	CHI	NL	1	1	0	0	0	1	0	0	0	0	0	0	0	0	0	1

Rank among batters: 4,707 • *Total ballparks homered in*: 1 • *First HR*: 04/23/1967 off Juan Pizarro

Benji Gil

ROMAR BENJAMIN (AGUILAR) GIL
B: 10/06/1972
BR

Year	Tm	Lg	Tot	H	A	Men-On 0	1	2	3	One-Game 2	3	4	LO	XN	IP	PH	RHP	LHP
1995	TEX	AL	9	5	4	6	1	1	1	0	0	0	0	0	0	0	9	0

Rank among batters: 2,587 • *Total ballparks homered in*: 4 • *First HR*: 05/03/1995 off Chris Bosio

Gus Gil

TOMAS GUSTAVO (GUILLEN) GIL
B: 04/19/1939
BR

Year	Tm	Lg	Tot	H	A	Men-On 0	1	2	3	One-Game 2	3	4	LO	XN	IP	PH	RHP	LHP
1970	MIL	AL	1	0	1	1	0	0	0	0	0	0	0	0	0	0	0	1

Rank among batters: 4,707 • *Total ballparks homered in*: 1 • *First HR*: 08/05/1970 off Jim Magnuson

Billy Gilbert

WILLIAM OLIVER GILBERT
B: 06/21/1876 D: 08/08/1927
BR

Year	Tm	Lg	Tot	H	A	Men-On 0	1	2	3	One-Game 2	3	4	LO	XN	IP	PH	RHP	LHP
1902	BAL	AL	2	0	2	2	0	0	0	0	0	0	0	0	1	0	2	0
1903	NY	NL	1	0	1	0	1	0	0	0	0	0	0	0	1	0	1	0
1904	NY	NL	1	1	0	0	1	0	0	0	0	0	0	0	0	0	1	0
1906	NY	NL	1	0	1	1	0	0	0	0	0	0	0	0	0	0	1	0
Total			5	1	4	3	2	0	0	0	0	0	0	0	2	0	5	0

Rank among batters: 3,191 • *Total ballparks homered in*: 5 • *First HR*: 09/02/1902 off Addie Joss

Buddy Gilbert

DREW EDWARD GILBERT
B: 07/26/1935
BL

Year	Tm	Lg	Tot	H	A	Men-On 0	1	2	3	One-Game 2	3	4	LO	XN	IP	PH	RHP	LHP
1959	CIN	NL	2	2	0	2	0	0	0	0	0	0	0	0	0	0	2	0

Rank among batters: 4,129 • *Total ballparks homered in*: 1 • *First HR*: 09/26/1959 off Jim Umbricht

Charlie Gilbert

CHARLES MADER GILBERT
B: 07/08/1919 D: 08/13/1983
BL

Year	Tm	Lg	Tot	H	A	Men-On 0	1	2	3	One-Game 2	3	4	LO	XN	IP	PH	RHP	LHP
1940	BRO	NL	2	2	0	0	2	0	0	1	0	0	0	0	0	0	2	0
1946	PHI	NL	1	0	1	1	0	0	0	0	0	0	0	0	0	0	1	0
1947	PHI	NL	2	1	1	0	2	0	0	0	0	0	0	0	0	0	2	0
Total			5	3	2	1	4	0	0	1	0	0	0	0	0	0	5	0

Rank among batters: 3,191 • *Total ballparks homered in*: 4 • *First HR*: 04/23/1940 off Nick Strincevich

Larry Gilbert

LAWRENCE WILLIAM GILBERT
B: 12/03/1891 D: 02/17/1965
BL

Year	Tm	Lg	Tot	H	A	Men-On 0	1	2	3	One-Game 2	3	4	LO	XN	IP	PH	RHP	LHP
1914	BOS	NL	5	5	0	3	1	1	0	0	0	0	0	0	0	0	4	1

Rank among batters: 3,191 • *Total ballparks homered in*: 1 • *First HR*: 06/06/1914 off Phil Douglas

Pete Gilbert

PETER GILBERT
B: 09/06/1867 D: 01/01/1912

Year	Tm	Lg	Tot	H	A	Men-On 0	1	2	3	One-Game 2	3	4	LO	XN	IP	PH	RHP	LHP
1890	BAL	AA	1	0	1	0	1	0	0	0	0	0	0	0	0	0	0	1
1891	BAL	AA	3	1	2	1	2	0	0	0	0	0	0	0	0	0	1	2
1894	LOU	NL	1	1	0	0	1	0	0	0	0	0	0	0	1	0	1	0
Total			5	2	3	1	4	0	0	0	0	0	0	0	1	0	2	3

Rank among batters: 3,191 • *Total ballparks homered in*: 4 • *First HR*: 09/20/1890 off Frank Knauss

Tookie Gilbert

HAROLD JOSEPH GILBERT
B: 04/04/1929 D: 06/23/1967
BL

Year	Tm	Lg	Tot	H	A	Men-On 0	1	2	3	One-Game 2	3	4	LO	XN	IP	PH	RHP	LHP
1950	NY	NL	4	3	1	1	2	1	0	0	0	0	0	0	0	0	1	3

Tookie Gilbert *continued*

Year	Tm	Lg	Tot	H	A	Men-On 0	1	2	3	One-Game 2	3	4	LO	XN	IP	PH	RHP	LHP
1953	NY	NL	3	0	3	2	0	1	0	0	0	0	0	0	0	0	3	0
Total			7	3	4	3	2	2	0	0	0	0	0	0	0	0	4	3

Rank among batters: 2,834 • *Top target (2 home runs)*: Howie Pollet • *Number of pitchers victimized*: 6 • *Total ballparks homered in*: 5 • *First HR*: 05/05/1950 off Mel Queen

Wally Gilbert

WALTER JOHN GILBERT
B: 12/19/1900 D: 09/07/1958
BR

Year	Tm	Lg	Tot	H	A	Men-On 0	1	2	3	One-Game 2	3	4	LO	XN	IP	PH	RHP	LHP
1929	BRO	NL	3	1	2	0	3	0	0	0	0	0	0	0	0	0	3	0
1930	BRO	NL	3	0	3	2	1	0	0	0	0	0	0	0	1	0	2	1
1932	CIN	NL	1	0	1	1	0	0	0	0	0	0	0	0	0	0	0	1
Total			7	1	6	3	4	0	0	0	0	0	0	0	1	0	5	2

Rank among batters: 2,834 • *Total ballparks homered in*: 5 • *First HR*: 05/17/1929 off Luther Roy

Rod Gilbreath

RODNEY JOE GILBREATH
B: 09/24/1952
BR

Year	Tm	Lg	Tot	H	A	Men-On 0	1	2	3	One-Game 2	3	4	LO	XN	IP	PH	RHP	LHP
1975	ATL	NL	2	0	2	2	0	0	0	0	0	0	0	0	0	1	0	2
1976	ATL	NL	1	0	1	1	0	0	0	0	0	0	0	0	0	0	0	1
1977	ATL	NL	8	6	2	3	1	3	1	0	0	0	0	0	0	0	4	4
1978	ATL	NL	3	1	2	2	0	0	1	0	0	0	0	0	0	0	1	2
Total			14	7	7	8	1	3	2	0	0	0	0	0	0	1	5	9

Rank among batters: 2,169 • *Top target (2 home runs)*: Dave Roberts, Jim Kaat • *Number of pitchers victimized*: 12 • *Total ballparks homered in*: 6 • *First HR*: 06/08/1975 off Tom Hall

Don Gile

DONALD LOREN GILE
B: 04/19/1935
BR

Year	Tm	Lg	Tot	H	A	Men-On 0	1	2	3	One-Game 2	3	4	LO	XN	IP	PH	RHP	LHP
1960	BOS	AL	1	1	0	1	0	0	0	0	0	0	0	0	0	0	1	0
1961	BOS	AL	1	1	0	1	0	0	0	0	0	0	0	0	0	0	0	1
1962	BOS	AL	1	1	0	0	1	0	0	0	0	0	0	0	0	0	1	0
Total			3	3	0	2	1	0	0	0	0	0	0	0	0	0	2	1

Rank among batters: 3,735 • *Total ballparks homered in*: 1 • *First HR*: 09/27/1960 off Gordon Jones

Brian Giles

BRIAN JEFFREY GILES
B: 04/27/1960
BR

Year	Tm	Lg	Tot	H	A	Men-On 0	1	2	3	One-Game 2	3	4	LO	XN	IP	PH	RHP	LHP
1982	NY	NL	3	0	3	3	0	0	0	0	0	0	0	1	0	0	3	0
1983	NY	NL	2	1	1	1	1	0	0	0	0	0	0	0	0	0	2	0
1985	MIL	AL	1	1	0	1	0	0	0	0	0	0	0	0	0	0	1	0
1990	SEA	AL	4	2	2	2	0	1	1	1	0	0	0	0	0	0	1	3
Total			10	4	6	7	1	1	1	1	0	0	0	1	0	0	7	3

Rank among batters: 2,500 • *Total ballparks homered in*: 7 • *First HR*: 08/20/1982 off Pascual Perez

Brian Giles

BRIAN STEPHEN GILES
B: 01/21/1971
BL

Year	Tm	Lg	Tot	H	A	Men-On 0	1	2	3	One-Game 2	3	4	LO	XN	IP	PH	RHP	LHP
1995	CLE	AL	1	0	1	0	1	0	0	0	0	0	0	0	0	1	1	0

Rank among batters: 4,707 • *Total ballparks homered in*: 1 • *First HR*: 09/24/1995 off Jeff Montgomery

Frank Gilhooley

FRANK PATRICK GILHOOLEY
B: 06/10/1892 D: 07/11/1959
BL

Year	Tm	Lg	Tot	H	A	Men-On 0	1	2	3	One-Game 2	3	4	LO	XN	IP	PH	RHP	LHP
1916	NY	AL	1	1	0	0	0	0	1	0	0	0	0	0	1	0	1	0

Year	Tm	Lg	Tot	H	A	Men-On				One-Game			LO	XN	IP	PH	RHP	LHP
						0	1	2	3	2	3	4						

Frank Gilhooley *continued*

Year	Tm	Lg	Tot	H	A	0	1	2	3	2	3	4	LO	XN	IP	PH	RHP	LHP
1918	NY	AL	1	0	1	0	0	1	0	0	0	0	0	0	0	0	1	0
Total			2	1	1	0	0	1	1	0	0	0	0	0	1	0	2	0

Rank among batters: 4,129 • *Total ballparks homered in*: 2 • *First HR*: 05/31/1916 off Joe Bush

Bernard Gilkey

OTIS BERNARD GILKEY
B: 09/24/1966
BR

Year	Tm	Lg	Tot	H	A	0	1	2	3	2	3	4	LO	XN	IP	PH	RHP	LHP
1990	STL	NL	1	0	1	1	0	0	0	0	0	0	0	0	0	0	1	0
1991	STL	NL	5	2	3	5	0	0	0	1	0	0	0	0	0	0	3	2
1992	STL	NL	7	3	4	2	3	2	0	0	0	0	0	1	0	0	5	2
1993	STL	NL	16	7	9	10	5	1	0	0	0	0	3	0	0	0	12	4
1994	STL	NL	6	0	6	2	1	3	0	0	0	0	0	0	0	1	4	2
1995	STL	NL	17	5	12	13	4	0	0	0	0	0	1	0	0	0	15	2
Total			52	17	35	33	13	6	0	1	0	0	4	1	0	1	40	12

Rank among batters: 965 • *Top target (2 home runs)*: Shawn Boskie, Kent Bottenfield, Scott Sanders • *Number of pitchers victimized*: 49 • *Total ballparks homered in*: 14 • *First HR*: 10/01/1990 off Howard Farmer

Bob Gilks

ROBERT JAMES GILKS
B: 07/02/1864 D: 08/21/1944
BR

Year	Tm	Lg	Tot	H	A	0	1	2	3	2	3	4	LO	XN	IP	PH	RHP	LHP
1888	CLE	AA	1	1	0	0	0	1	0	0	0	0	0	0	1	0	1	0

Rank among batters: 4,707 • *Total ballparks homered in*: 1 • *First HR*: 06/06/1888 off Guy Hecker

Johnny Gill

JOHN WESLEY GILL
B: 03/27/1905 D: 12/26/1984
BL

Year	Tm	Lg	Tot	H	A	0	1	2	3	2	3	4	LO	XN	IP	PH	RHP	LHP
1927	CLE	AL	1	0	1	1	0	0	0	0	0	0	0	0	0	0	1	0
1934	WAS	AL	2	0	2	1	1	0	0	0	0	0	0	0	0	0	2	0
1936	CHI	NL	7	4	3	4	2	1	0	0	0	0	0	0	0	2	7	0
Total			10	4	6	6	3	1	0	0	0	0	0	0	0	2	10	0

Rank among batters: 2,500 • *Total ballparks homered in*: 6 • *First HR*: 09/10/1927 off Del Lundgren

Carden Gillenwater

CARDEN EDISON GILLENWATER
B: 05/13/1918
BR

Year	Tm	Lg	Tot	H	A	0	1	2	3	2	3	4	LO	XN	IP	PH	RHP	LHP
1945	BOS	NL	7	5	2	4	2	1	0	0	0	0	0	0	0	0	6	1
1946	BOS	NL	1	1	0	1	0	0	0	0	0	0	0	0	0	0	1	0
1948	WAS	AL	3	1	2	2	1	0	0	0	0	0	0	1	0	0	1	2
Total			11	7	4	7	3	1	0	0	0	0	0	1	0	0	8	3

Rank among batters: 2,419 • *Total ballparks homered in*: 6 • *First HR*: 04/18/1945 off Van Mungo

Paul Gillespie

PAUL ALLEN GILLESPIE
B: 09/18/1920 D: 08/11/1970
BL

Year	Tm	Lg	Tot	H	A	0	1	2	3	2	3	4	LO	XN	IP	PH	RHP	LHP
1942	CHI	NL	2	0	2	1	1	0	0	0	0	0	0	0	0	0	2	0
1944	CHI	NL	1	0	1	0	1	0	0	0	0	0	0	0	0	0	1	0
1945	CHI	NL	3	0	3	0	2	0	1	1	0	0	0	0	0	0	3	0
Total			6	0	6	1	4	0	1	1	0	0	0	0	0	0	6	0

Rank among batters: 2,988 • *Total ballparks homered in*: 4 • *First HR*: 09/11/1942 off Harry Feldman • *Hit HR in first major league AB*—@NY: 09/11/1942

Pete Gillespie

PETER PATRICK GILLESPIE
B: 11/30/1851 D: 05/05/1910
BL

Year	Tm	Lg	Tot	H	A	0	1	2	3	2	3	4	LO	XN	IP	PH	RHP	LHP
1880	TRO	NL	2	2	0	1	0	1	0	0	0	0	0	0	0	0	2	0

Year	Tm	Lg	Tot	H	A	Men-On 0	1	2	3	One-Game 2	3	4	LO	XN	IP	PH	RHP	LHP

Pete Gillespie *continued*

Year	Tm	Lg	Tot	H	A	Men-On 0	1	2	3	One-Game 2	3	4	LO	XN	IP	PH	RHP	LHP
1882	TRO	NL	2	1	1	1	0	1	0	0	0	0	0	0	0	0	2	0
1883	NY	NL	1	0	1	0	0	1	0	0	0	0	0	0	0	0	1	0
1884	NY	NL	2	0	2	1	1	0	0	0	0	0	0	0	0	0	0	0
1887	NY	NL	3	2	1	2	1	0	0	0	0	0	0	0	0	0	3	0
Total			10	5	5	5	2	3	0	0	0	0	0	0	0	0	8	0

Rank among batters: 2,500 • *Top target (2 home runs)*: Jim Galvin • *Number of pitchers victimized*: 9 • *Total ballparks homered in*: 6 • *First HR*: 05/29/1880 off Jim Galvin

Jim Gilliam

JAMES WILLIAM GILLIAM
B: 10/17/1928 D: 10/08/1978
BB

Year	Tm	Lg	Tot	H	A	Men-On 0	1	2	3	One-Game 2	3	4	LO	XN	IP	PH	RHP	LHP
1953	BRO	NL	6	4	2	3	1	2	0	0	0	0	0	0	0	0	5	1
1954	BRO	NL	13	4	9	9	3	1	0	1	0	0	2	0	0	0	9	4
1955	BRO	NL	7	3	4	5	2	0	0	0	0	0	1	0	0	0	6	1
1956	BRO	NL	6	2	4	5	1	0	0	0	0	0	0	0	1	0	5	1
1957	BRO	NL	2	0	2	1	1	0	0	0	0	0	1	0	0	0	1	1
1958	LA	NL	2	1	1	2	0	0	0	0	0	0	1	0	0	0	0	2
1959	LA	NL	3	3	0	3	0	0	0	0	0	0	2	0	0	0	2	1
1960	LA	NL	5	5	0	4	1	0	0	0	0	0	2	0	0	0	2	3
1961	LA	NL	4	1	3	2	2	0	0	0	0	0	0	0	0	0	1	3
1962	LA	NL	4	1	3	3	1	0	0	0	0	0	0	0	0	0	4	0
1963	LA	NL	6	2	4	4	0	2	0	0	0	0	0	0	1	0	2	4
1964	LA	NL	2	0	2	0	2	0	0	0	0	0	0	0	0	0	1	1
1965	LA	NL	4	1	3	3	1	0	0	0	0	0	0	0	0	0	2	2
1966	LA	NL	1	0	1	0	1	0	0	0	0	0	0	0	0	0	1	0
Total			65	27	38	44	16	5	0	1	0	0	9	0	2	0	41	24

Rank among batters: 799 • *Top target (5 home runs)*: Johnny Antonelli • *Number of pitchers victimized*: 47 • *Total ballparks homered in*: 13 • *First HR*: 05/31/1953 off Johnny Hetki • *World Series HR—2; All-Star HR—1*

Barney Gilligan

ANDREW BERNARD GILLIGAN
B: 01/03/1856 D: 04/01/1934
BR

Year	Tm	Lg	Tot	H	A	Men-On 0	1	2	3	One-Game 2	3	4	LO	XN	IP	PH	RHP	LHP
1880	CLE	NL	1	0	1	0	0	1	0	0	0	0	0	0	0	0	1	0
1884	PRO	NL	1	0	1	0	1	0	0	0	0	0	0	0	0	0	1	0
1887	WAS	NL	1	0	1	1	0	0	0	0	0	0	0	0	0	0	1	0
Total			3	0	3	1	1	1	0	0	0	0	0	0	0	0	3	0

Rank among batters: 3,735 • *Total ballparks homered in*: 3 • *First HR*: 05/14/1880 off Will White

Grover Gilmore

ERNEST GROVER GILMORE
B: 11/01/1888 D: 11/25/1919
BL

Year	Tm	Lg	Tot	H	A	Men-On 0	1	2	3	One-Game 2	3	4	LO	XN	IP	PH	RHP	LHP
1914	KC	FL	1	1	0	1	0	0	0	0	0	0	0	0	0	0	0	1
1915	KC	FL	1	0	1	1	0	0	0	0	0	0	0	0	0	0	1	0
Total			2	1	1	2	0	0	0	0	0	0	0	0	0	0	1	1

Rank among batters: 4,129 • *Total ballparks homered in*: 2 • *First HR*: 08/13/1914 off Bill Bailey

Joe Ginsberg

MYRON NATHAN GINSBERG
B: 10/11/1926
BL

Year	Tm	Lg	Tot	H	A	Men-On 0	1	2	3	One-Game 2	3	4	LO	XN	IP	PH	RHP	LHP
1951	DET	AL	8	7	1	5	2	1	0	0	0	0	0	0	0	0	7	1
1952	DET	AL	6	5	1	3	1	2	0	0	0	0	0	1	0	0	6	0
1956	KC	AL	1	0	1	0	1	0	0	0	0	0	0	0	0	0	1	0
1957	BAL	AL	1	0	1	1	0	0	0	0	0	0	0	0	0	0	1	0
1958	BAL	AL	3	0	3	1	2	0	0	0	0	0	0	0	0	0	3	0
1959	BAL	AL	1	0	1	0	1	0	0	0	0	0	0	0	0	0	1	0
Total			20	12	8	10	7	3	0	0	0	0	0	1	0	0	19	1

Rank among batters: 1,810 • *Top target (3 home runs)*: Bob Chakales • *Number of pitchers victimized*: 17 • *Total ballparks homered in*: 5 • *First HR*: 04/23/1951 off Don Johnson

						Men-On				One-Game								
Year	Tm	Lg	Tot	H	A	0	1	2	3	2	3	4	LO	XN	IP	PH	RHP	LHP

Al Gionfriddo

ALBERT FRANCIS GIONFRIDDO
B: 03/08/1922
BL

Year	Tm	Lg	Tot	H	A	0	1	2	3	2	3	4	LO	XN	IP	PH	RHP	LHP
1945	PIT	NL	2	2	0	1	1	0	0	0	0	0	0	0	1	0	2	0

Rank among batters: 4,129 • *Total ballparks homered in*: 1 • *First HR*: 05/30/1945 off Leroy Pfund

Tommy Giordano

THOMAS ARTHUR GIORDANO
B: 10/09/1925
BR

Year	Tm	Lg	Tot	H	A	0	1	2	3	2	3	4	LO	XN	IP	PH	RHP	LHP
1953	PHI	AL	2	2	0	1	1	0	0	0	0	0	0	0	0	0	2	0

Rank among batters: 4,129 • *Total ballparks homered in*: 1 • *First HR*: 09/11/1953 off Virgil Trucks

Joe Girardi

JOSEPH ELLIOTT GIRARDI
B: 10/14/1964
BR

Year	Tm	Lg	Tot	H	A	0	1	2	3	2	3	4	LO	XN	IP	PH	RHP	LHP
1989	CHI	NL	1	0	1	1	0	0	0	0	0	0	0	0	0	0	1	0
1990	CHI	NL	1	1	0	0	1	0	0	0	0	0	0	0	0	0	0	1
1992	CHI	NL	1	1	0	1	0	0	0	0	0	0	0	0	0	0	1	0
1993	COL	NL	3	2	1	3	0	0	0	0	0	0	0	0	0	0	2	1
1994	COL	NL	4	1	3	1	3	0	0	0	0	0	0	0	0	0	3	1
1995	COL	NL	8	6	2	4	2	2	0	0	0	0	0	0	0	1	7	1
Total			18	11	7	10	6	2	0	0	0	0	0	0	0	1	14	4

Rank among batters: 1,914 • *Top target (2 home runs)*: Steve Avery • *Number of pitchers victimized*: 17 • *Total ballparks homered in*: 8 • *First HR*: 06/29/1989 off Jeff Brantley

Dave Giusti

DAVID JOHN GIUSTI
B: 11/27/1939
BR

Year	Tm	Lg	Tot	H	A	0	1	2	3	2	3	4	LO	XN	IP	PH	RHP	LHP
1965	HOU	NL	1	0	1	0	1	0	0	0	0	0	0	0	0	0	1	0
1967	HOU	NL	3	1	2	1	2	0	0	0	0	0	0	0	0	0	2	1
Total			4	1	3	1	3	0	0	0	0	0	0	0	0	0	3	1

Rank among batters: 3,427 • *Total ballparks homered in*: 3 • *First HR*: 06/11/1965 off Ray Culp

Dan Gladden

CLINTON DANIEL GLADDEN
B: 07/07/1957
BR

Year	Tm	Lg	Tot	H	A	0	1	2	3	2	3	4	LO	XN	IP	PH	RHP	LHP
1983	SF	NL	1	1	0	0	1	0	0	0	0	0	0	0	0	0	1	0
1984	SF	NL	4	4	0	3	1	0	0	0	0	0	1	0	0	0	2	2
1985	SF	NL	7	6	1	6	0	1	0	0	0	0	4	0	0	0	6	1
1986	SF	NL	4	1	3	2	0	1	1	0	0	0	0	0	0	0	4	0
1987	MIN	AL	8	4	4	6	1	1	0	0	0	0	2	1	0	0	6	2
1988	MIN	AL	11	8	3	9	2	0	0	1	0	0	5	0	0	0	5	6
1989	MIN	AL	8	1	7	6	1	0	1	0	0	0	1	0	0	0	5	3
1990	MIN	AL	5	2	3	3	1	1	0	0	0	0	2	0	0	0	3	2
1991	MIN	AL	6	3	3	4	1	1	0	0	0	0	2	0	0	0	5	1
1992	DET	AL	7	3	4	2	2	3	0	0	0	0	0	0	0	0	3	4
1993	DET	AL	13	11	2	5	4	1	3	1	0	0	0	0	0	0	5	8
Total			74	44	30	46	14	9	5	2	0	0	17	1	0	0	45	29

Rank among batters: 707 • *Top target (3 home runs)*: Mark Langston • *Number of pitchers victimized*: 65 • *Total ballparks homered in*: 19 • *First HR*: 09/09/1983 off Joe Niekro • *World Series HR*—1

Buck Gladman

JOHN H. GLADMAN
B: 1864

Year	Tm	Lg	Tot	H	A	0	1	2	3	2	3	4	LO	XN	IP	PH	RHP	LHP
1884	WAS	AA	1	1	0	1	0	0	0	0	0	0	0	0	0	0	0	1
1886	WAS	NL	1	1	0	0	0	1	0	0	0	0	0	0	0	0	1	0
Total			2	2	0	1	0	1	0	0	0	0	0	0	0	0	1	1

Rank among batters: 4,129 • *Total ballparks homered in*: 2 • *First HR*: 06/04/1884 off Ed Morris

Year	Tm	Lg	Tot	H	A	Men-On 0	Men-On 1	Men-On 2	Men-On 3	One-Game 2	One-Game 3	One-Game 4	LO	XN	IP	PH	RHP	LHP

Roland Gladu

ROLAND EDOUARD GLADU
B: 05/10/1911 D: 07/26/1994
BL

Year	Tm	Lg	Tot	H	A	Men-On 0	Men-On 1	Men-On 2	Men-On 3	One-Game 2	One-Game 3	One-Game 4	LO	XN	IP	PH	RHP	LHP
1944	BOS	NL	1	0	1	1	0	0	0	0	0	0	0	0	0	0	0	1

Rank among batters: 4,707 • *Total ballparks homered in*: 1 • *First HR*: 05/03/1944 off Fritz Ostermueller

Jack Glasscock

JOHN WESLEY GLASSCOCK
B: 07/22/1859 D: 02/24/1947
BR

Year	Tm	Lg	Tot	H	A	Men-On 0	Men-On 1	Men-On 2	Men-On 3	One-Game 2	One-Game 3	One-Game 4	LO	XN	IP	PH	RHP	LHP
1882	CLE	NL	4	2	2	1	3	0	0	0	0	0	0	0	0	0	4	0
1884	CLE	NL	1	0	1	1	0	0	0	0	0	0	0	0	0	0	1	0
	CIN	UA	2	1	1	1	1	0	0	0	0	0	1	0	0	0	2	0
	Total		3	1	2	2	1	0	0	0	0	0	1	0	0	0	3	0
1885	STL	NL	1	0	1	0	1	0	0	0	0	0	0	0	0	0	1	0
1886	STL	NL	3	2	1	3	0	0	0	0	0	0	1	0	0	0	3	0
1888	IND	NL	1	0	1	1	0	0	0	0	0	0	0	0	0	0	1	0
1889	IND	NL	7	6	1	2	2	2	1	0	0	0	0	0	0	0	5	2
1890	NY	NL	1	1	0	0	0	1	0	0	0	0	0	0	0	0	1	0
1892	STL	NL	3	3	0	0	2	1	0	0	0	0	0	1	0	0	2	0
1893	STL	NL	1	1	0	0	1	0	0	0	0	0	0	0	1	0	0	1
	PIT	NL	1	1	0	0	1	0	0	0	0	0	0	0	1	0	1	0
	Total		2	2	0	0	2	0	0	0	0	0	0	0	2	0	1	1
1894	PIT	NL	1	1	0	0	1	0	0	0	0	0	0	0	0	0	1	0
1895	LOU	NL	1	1	0	0	0	1	0	0	0	0	0	0	0	0	1	0
Total			27	19	8	9	12	5	1	0	0	0	2	1	2	0	23	3

Rank among batters: 1,532 • *Top target (2 home runs)*: John Clarkson, Mickey Welch • *Number of pitchers victimized*: 25 • *Total ballparks homered in*: 17 • *First HR*: 05/01/1882 off George Derby • *Hit for Cycle*—vs NY: 08/08/1889

Tommy Glaviano

THOMAS GIATANO GLAVIANO
B: 10/26/1923
BR

Year	Tm	Lg	Tot	H	A	Men-On 0	Men-On 1	Men-On 2	Men-On 3	One-Game 2	One-Game 3	One-Game 4	LO	XN	IP	PH	RHP	LHP
1949	STL	NL	6	3	3	3	1	1	1	0	0	0	0	0	0	1	3	3
1950	STL	NL	11	5	6	9	1	1	0	1	0	0	1	0	0	0	6	5
1951	STL	NL	1	0	1	1	0	0	0	0	0	0	0	0	0	0	0	1
1952	STL	NL	3	1	2	1	2	0	0	0	0	0	0	0	0	0	3	0
1953	PHI	NL	3	0	3	2	1	0	0	1	0	0	0	0	0	0	1	2
Total			24	9	15	16	5	2	1	2	0	0	1	0	0	1	13	11

Rank among batters: 1,643 • *Top target (2 home runs)*: Joe Hatten, Preacher Roe, Ken Raffensberger • *Number of pitchers victimized*: 21 • *Total ballparks homered in*: 8 • *First HR*: 05/09/1949 off Bud Podbielan

Tom Glavine

THOMAS MICHAEL GLAVINE
B: 03/25/1966
BL

Year	Tm	Lg	Tot	H	A	Men-On 0	Men-On 1	Men-On 2	Men-On 3	One-Game 2	One-Game 3	One-Game 4	LO	XN	IP	PH	RHP	LHP
1995	ATL	NL	1	1	0	1	0	0	0	0	0	0	0	0	0	0	0	1

Rank among batters: 4,707 • *Total ballparks homered in*: 1 • *First HR*: 08/10/1995 off John Smiley

Ralph Glaze

DANIEL RALPH GLAZE
B: 03/13/1882 D: 10/31/1968
BR

Year	Tm	Lg	Tot	H	A	Men-On 0	Men-On 1	Men-On 2	Men-On 3	One-Game 2	One-Game 3	One-Game 4	LO	XN	IP	PH	RHP	LHP
1907	BOS	AL	1	1	0	1	0	0	0	0	0	0	0	0	0	0	1	0

Rank among batters: 4,707 • *Total ballparks homered in*: 1 • *First HR*: 08/06/1907 off Harry Howell

Whitey Glazner

CHARLES FRANKLIN GLAZNER
B: 09/17/1893 D: 06/06/1989
BR

Year	Tm	Lg	Tot	H	A	Men-On 0	Men-On 1	Men-On 2	Men-On 3	One-Game 2	One-Game 3	One-Game 4	LO	XN	IP	PH	RHP	LHP
1922	PIT	NL	1	0	1	0	0	1	0	0	0	0	0	0	0	0	1	0
1923	PIT	NL	1	0	1	1	0	0	0	0	0	0	0	0	0	0	1	0
Total			2	0	2	1	0	1	0	0	0	0	0	0	0	0	2	0

Rank among batters: 4,129 • *Total ballparks homered in*: 2 • *First HR*: 08/07/1922 off Bill Hubbell

Bill Gleason

WILLIAM G. GLEASON
B: 11/12/1858 D: 07/21/1932
BR

Year	Tm	Lg	Tot	H	A	Men-On 0	Men-On 1	Men-On 2	Men-On 3	One-Game 2	One-Game 3	One-Game 4	LO	XN	IP	PH	RHP	LHP
1882	STL	AA	1	1	0	1	0	0	0	0	0	0	0	0	0	0	1	0
1883	STL	AA	2	1	1	0	1	1	0	0	0	0	0	0	0	0	2	0
1884	STL	AA	1	0	1	1	0	0	0	0	0	0	0	0	0	0	1	0
1885	STL	AA	3	0	3	1	2	0	0	0	0	0	0	0	0	0	3	0
Total			7	2	5	3	3	1	0	0	0	0	0	0	0	0	7	0

Rank among batters: 2,834 • *Total ballparks homered in*: 5 • *First HR*: 08/12/1882 off Will White

Harry Gleason

HARRY GILBERT GLEASON
B: 03/28/1875 D: 10/21/1961
BR

Year	Tm	Lg	Tot	H	A	Men-On 0	Men-On 1	Men-On 2	Men-On 3	One-Game 2	One-Game 3	One-Game 4	LO	XN	IP	PH	RHP	LHP
1902	BOS	AL	2	1	1	1	1	0	0	0	0	0	0	0	1	0	1	1
1905	STL	AL	1	0	1	0	0	1	0	0	0	0	0	0	1	0	1	0
Total			3	1	2	1	1	1	0	0	0	0	0	0	2	0	2	1

Rank among batters: 3,735 • *Total ballparks homered in*: 2 • *First HR*: 05/16/1902 off Snake Wiltse

Jack Gleason

JOHN DAY GLEASON
B: 07/14/1854 D: 09/04/1944
BR

Year	Tm	Lg	Tot	H	A	Men-On 0	Men-On 1	Men-On 2	Men-On 3	One-Game 2	One-Game 3	One-Game 4	LO	XN	IP	PH	RHP	LHP
1882	STL	AA	2	0	2	1	1	0	0	0	0	0	0	0	0	0	1	0
1883	LOU	AA	2	0	2	1	0	0	0	0	0	0	1	0	0	0	2	0
1884	STL	UA	4	3	1	1	1	2	0	0	0	0	0	0	0	0	0	0
1886	PHI	AA	1	1	0	1	0	0	0	0	0	0	0	0	0	0	0	1
Total			9	4	5	4	2	2	0	0	0	0	1	0	0	0	3	1

Rank among batters: 2,587 • *Top target (2 home runs)*: John Murphy • *Number of pitchers victimized*: 8 • *Total ballparks homered in*: 6 • *First HR*: 05/23/1882 off Ed Halbriter

Kid Gleason

WILLIAM J. GLEASON
B: 10/26/1866 D: 01/02/1933
BB

Year	Tm	Lg	Tot	H	A	Men-On 0	Men-On 1	Men-On 2	Men-On 3	One-Game 2	One-Game 3	One-Game 4	LO	XN	IP	PH	RHP	LHP
1892	STL	NL	3	3	0	2	1	0	0	0	0	0	0	0	0	0	3	0
1896	NY	NL	4	1	3	1	1	2	0	0	0	0	1	0	0	0	4	0
1897	NY	NL	1	1	0	0	1	0	0	0	0	0	0	0	0	0	1	0
1900	NY	NL	1	1	0	0	1	0	0	0	0	0	0	0	0	0	1	0
1901	DET	AL	3	1	2	0	3	0	0	0	0	0	0	0	2	0	3	0
1902	DET	AL	1	0	1	1	0	0	0	0	0	0	0	0	1	0	1	0
1903	PHI	NL	1	1	0	0	0	1	0	0	0	0	0	0	1	0	1	0
1905	PHI	NL	1	1	0	1	0	0	0	0	0	0	0	0	1	0	1	0
Total			15	9	6	5	7	3	0	0	0	0	1	0	5	0	15	0

Rank among batters: 2,096 • *Top target (2 home runs)*: John Malarkey • *Number of pitchers victimized*: 14 • *Total ballparks homered in*: 11 • *First HR*: 05/07/1892 off Dave Foutz

Jim Gleeson

JAMES JOSEPH GLEESON
B: 03/05/1912
BB

Year	Tm	Lg	Tot	H	A	Men-On 0	Men-On 1	Men-On 2	Men-On 3	One-Game 2	One-Game 3	One-Game 4	LO	XN	IP	PH	RHP	LHP
1936	CLE	AL	4	1	3	3	0	1	0	0	0	0	0	0	0	0	3	1
1939	CHI	NL	4	0	4	4	0	0	0	0	0	0	0	0	0	0	2	2
1940	CHI	NL	5	2	3	2	2	0	1	0	0	0	0	0	0	0	4	1
1941	CIN	NL	3	1	2	2	1	0	0	0	0	0	0	0	0	1	3	0
Total			16	4	12	11	3	1	1	0	0	0	0	0	0	1	12	4

Rank among batters: 2,029 • *Top target (2 home runs)*: Bucky Walters • *Number of pitchers victimized*: 15 • *Total ballparks homered in*: 7 • *First HR*: 05/06/1936 off George Turbeville

Bob Glenalvin

ROBERT J. GLENALVIN
B: 01/17/1867 D: 03/24/1944

Year	Tm	Lg	Tot	H	A	Men-On 0	Men-On 1	Men-On 2	Men-On 3	One-Game 2	One-Game 3	One-Game 4	LO	XN	IP	PH	RHP	LHP
1890	CHI	NL	4	4	0	2	1	1	0	0	0	0	0	0	1	0	3	1

Rank among batters: 3,427 • *Top target (2 home runs)*: Pretzels Getzien • *Number of pitchers victimized*: 3 • *Total ballparks homered in*: 1 • *First HR*: 08/01/1890 off Pretzels Getzien

Ed Glenn

EDWARD C. GLENN
B: 09/19/1860 D: 02/10/1892
BR

Year	Tm	Lg	Tot	H	A	Men-On 0	1	2	3	One-Game 2	3	4	LO	XN	IP	PH	RHP	LHP
1884	RIC	AA	1	0	1	0	1	0	0	0	0	0	0	0	0	0	1	0

Rank among batters: 4,707 • *Total ballparks homered in*: 1 • *First HR*: 09/09/1884 off Will White

Joe Glenn

JOSEPH CHARLES GLENN
B: 11/19/1908 D: 05/06/1985
BR

Year	Tm	Lg	Tot	H	A	Men-On 0	1	2	3	One-Game 2	3	4	LO	XN	IP	PH	RHP	LHP
1936	NY	AL	1	1	0	1	0	0	0	0	0	0	0	0	1	0	0	1
1939	STL	AL	4	1	3	3	1	0	0	1	0	0	0	0	0	0	3	1
Total			5	2	3	4	1	0	0	1	0	0	0	0	1	0	3	2

Rank among batters: 3,191 • *Top target (2 home runs)*: Joe Heving • *Number of pitchers victimized*: 4 • *Total ballparks homered in*: 3 • *First HR*: 05/31/1936 off Lefty Grove

Al Glossop

ALBAN GLOSSOP
B: 07/23/1915 D: 07/02/1991
BB

Year	Tm	Lg	Tot	H	A	Men-On 0	1	2	3	One-Game 2	3	4	LO	XN	IP	PH	RHP	LHP
1939	NY	NL	1	1	0	0	0	1	0	0	0	0	0	0	0	0	1	0
1940	NY	NL	4	3	1	3	0	1	0	0	0	0	0	0	0	1	4	0
	BOS	NL	3	1	2	3	0	0	0	0	0	0	1	0	0	0	3	0
	Total		7	4	3	6	0	1	0	0	0	0	1	0	0	1	7	0
1942	PHI	NL	4	1	3	2	1	0	1	0	0	0	0	0	0	0	3	1
1943	BRO	NL	3	3	0	0	3	0	0	0	0	0	0	0	0	0	1	2
Total			15	9	6	8	4	2	1	0	0	0	1	0	0	1	12	3

Rank among batters: 2,096 • *Top target (2 home runs)*: Mort Cooper • *Number of pitchers victimized*: 14 • *Total ballparks homered in*: 5 • *First HR*: 09/26/1939 off Hugh Casey

Bill Glynn

WILLIAM VINCENT GLYNN
B: 07/30/1925
BL

Year	Tm	Lg	Tot	H	A	Men-On 0	1	2	3	One-Game 2	3	4	LO	XN	IP	PH	RHP	LHP
1952	CLE	AL	2	0	2	2	0	0	0	0	0	0	0	1	0	0	2	0
1953	CLE	AL	3	2	1	0	2	1	0	0	0	0	0	0	0	0	2	1
1954	CLE	AL	5	1	4	3	1	0	1	0	1	0	1	0	0	0	4	1
Total			10	3	7	5	3	1	1	0	1	0	1	1	0	0	8	2

Rank among batters: 2,500 • *Total ballparks homered in*: 4 • *First HR*: 07/19/1952 off Sid Hudson

Ed Goebel

EDWIN GOEBEL
B: 09/01/1899 D: 08/12/1959
BR

Year	Tm	Lg	Tot	H	A	Men-On 0	1	2	3	One-Game 2	3	4	LO	XN	IP	PH	RHP	LHP
1922	WAS	AL	1	1	0	1	0	0	0	0	0	0	0	0	1	0	0	1

Rank among batters: 4,707 • *Total ballparks homered in*: 1 • *First HR*: 06/23/1922 off Fred Heimach

Jerry Goff

JERRY LEROY GOFF
B: 04/12/1964
BL

Year	Tm	Lg	Tot	H	A	Men-On 0	1	2	3	One-Game 2	3	4	LO	XN	IP	PH	RHP	LHP
1990	MON	NL	3	0	3	3	0	0	0	0	0	0	0	0	0	1	3	0
1993	PIT	NL	2	2	0	2	0	0	0	0	0	0	0	0	0	0	2	0
1995	HOU	NL	1	1	0	1	0	0	0	0	0	0	0	0	0	0	1	0
Total			6	3	3	6	0	0	0	0	0	0	0	0	0	1	6	0

Rank among batters: 2,988 • *Total ballparks homered in*: 4 • *First HR*: 06/26/1990 off Lester Lancaster

Jonah Goldman

JONAH JOHN GOLDMAN
B: 08/29/1906 D: 08/17/1980
BR

Year	Tm	Lg	Tot	H	A	Men-On 0	1	2	3	One-Game 2	3	4	LO	XN	IP	PH	RHP	LHP
1930	CLE	AL	1	0	1	1	0	0	0	0	0	0	0	0	0	0	1	0

Rank among batters: 4,707 • *Total ballparks homered in*: 1 • *First HR*: 05/05/1930 off Milt Gaston

Gordon Goldsberry

GORDON FREDERICK GOLDSBERRY
B: 08/30/1927
BL

Year	Tm	Lg	Tot	H	A	Men-On 0	1	2	3	One-Game 2	3	4	LO	XN	IP	PH	RHP	LHP
1949	CHI	AL	1	1	0	0	1	0	0	0	0	0	0	0	0	0	1	0
1950	CHI	AL	2	0	2	1	1	0	0	0	0	0	0	0	0	1	2	0
1952	STL	AL	3	2	1	3	0	0	0	0	0	0	0	0	0	0	1	2
Total			6	3	3	4	2	0	0	0	0	0	0	0	0	1	4	2

Rank among batters: 2,988 • *Total ballparks homered in*: 4 • *First HR*: 05/15/1949 off Steve Gromek

Fred Goldsmith

FRED ERNEST GOLDSMITH
B: 05/15/1856 D: 03/28/1939
BR

Year	Tm	Lg	Tot	H	A	Men-On 0	1	2	3	One-Game 2	3	4	LO	XN	IP	PH	RHP	LHP
1883	CHI	NL	1	1	0	0	1	0	0	0	0	0	0	0	0	0	0	1
1884	CHI	NL	2	0	2	2	0	0	0	1	0	0	0	0	0	0	2	0
Total			3	1	2	2	1	0	0	1	0	0	0	0	0	0	2	1

Rank among batters: 3,735 • *Top target (2 home runs)*: Billy Serad • *Number of pitchers victimized*: 2 • *Total ballparks homered in*: 2 • *First HR*: 05/26/1883 off J Richmond

Purnal Goldy

PURNAL WILLIAM GOLDY
B: 11/28/1937
BR

Year	Tm	Lg	Tot	H	A	Men-On 0	1	2	3	One-Game 2	3	4	LO	XN	IP	PH	RHP	LHP
1962	DET	AL	3	3	0	1	1	1	0	1	0	0	0	0	0	0	3	0

Rank among batters: 3,735 • *Top target (2 home runs)*: Don Schwall • *Number of pitchers victimized*: 2 • *Total ballparks homered in*: 1 • *First HR*: 06/17/1962 off Don Schwall

Mike Goliat

MIKE MITCHELL GOLIAT
B: 11/05/1925
BR

Year	Tm	Lg	Tot	H	A	Men-On 0	1	2	3	One-Game 2	3	4	LO	XN	IP	PH	RHP	LHP
1949	PHI	NL	3	2	1	2	0	1	0	0	0	0	0	0	0	0	3	0
1950	PHI	NL	13	9	4	6	5	2	0	1	0	0	0	1	0	0	11	2
1951	PHI	NL	4	1	3	3	0	1	0	0	0	0	0	0	0	0	3	1
Total			20	12	8	11	5	4	0	1	0	0	0	1	0	0	17	3

Rank among batters: 1,810 • *Top target (2 home runs)*: Herm Wehmeier, Larry Jansen, Junior Walsh • *Number of pitchers victimized*: 17 • *Total ballparks homered in*: 7 • *First HR*: 08/21/1949 off Larry Jansen

Chris Gomez

CHRISTOPHER CORY GOMEZ
B: 06/16/1971
BR

Year	Tm	Lg	Tot	H	A	Men-On 0	1	2	3	One-Game 2	3	4	LO	XN	IP	PH	RHP	LHP
1994	DET	AL	8	5	3	5	1	2	0	1	0	0	0	0	0	0	7	1
1995	DET	AL	11	5	6	10	1	0	0	0	0	0	0	0	1	0	8	3
Total			19	10	9	15	2	2	0	1	0	0	0	0	1	0	15	4

Rank among batters: 1,861 • *Top target (3 home runs)*: Chris Bosio • *Number of pitchers victimized*: 16 • *Total ballparks homered in*: 8 • *First HR*: 05/07/1994 off Chris Bosio

Leo Gomez

LEONARDO (VELEZ) GOMEZ
B: 03/02/1966
BR

Year	Tm	Lg	Tot	H	A	Men-On 0	1	2	3	One-Game 2	3	4	LO	XN	IP	PH	RHP	LHP
1991	BAL	AL	16	7	9	9	5	2	0	0	0	0	0	1	0	0	10	6
1992	BAL	AL	17	6	11	9	3	4	1	0	0	0	0	0	0	0	14	3
1993	BAL	AL	10	7	3	7	2	1	0	0	0	0	0	0	0	0	8	2
1994	BAL	AL	15	11	4	11	3	1	0	2	0	0	0	0	0	0	10	5
1995	BAL	AL	4	3	1	3	0	1	0	0	0	0	0	0	0	0	2	2
Total			62	34	28	39	13	9	1	2	0	0	0	1	0	0	44	18

Rank among batters: 835 • Top target (2 home runs): Wayne Rosenthal, Donn Pall, Chuck Finley, Kevin Appier, John Dopson • *Number of pitchers victimized*: 57 • *Total ballparks homered in*: 13 • *First HR*: 06/09/1991 off Todd Stottlemyre

Ruben Gomez

RUBEN (COLON) GOMEZ
B: 07/13/1927
BR

Year	Tm	Lg	Tot	H	A	Men-On 0	1	2	3	One-Game 2	3	4	LO	XN	IP	PH	RHP	LHP
1954	NY	NL	2	1	1	1	1	0	0	0	0	0	0	0	0	0	0	2

Ruben Gomez *continued*

Year	Tm	Lg	Tot	H	A	Men-On 0	1	2	3	One-Game 2	3	4	LO	XN	IP	PH	RHP	LHP
1957	NY	NL	1	0	1	1	0	0	0	0	0	0	0	0	0	0	1	0
Total			3	1	2	2	1	0	0	0	0	0	0	0	0	0	1	2

Rank among batters: 3,735 • *Total ballparks homered in*: 3 • *First HR*: 07/30/1954 off Fred Baczewski

Jesse Gonder

JESSE LEMAR GONDER
B: 01/20/1936
BL

Year	Tm	Lg	Tot	H	A	Men-On 0	1	2	3	One-Game 2	3	4	LO	XN	IP	PH	RHP	LHP
1960	NY	AL	1	1	0	1	0	0	0	0	0	0	0	0	0	1	1	0
1963	CIN	NL	3	2	1	2	1	0	0	0	0	0	0	0	0	2	3	0
	NY	NL	3	3	0	1	1	1	0	1	0	0	0	0	0	0	3	0
	Total		6	5	1	3	2	1	0	1	0	0	0	0	0	2	6	0
1964	NY	NL	7	2	5	3	3	1	0	0	0	0	0	0	0	0	7	0
1965	NY	NL	4	0	4	4	0	0	0	0	0	0	0	0	0	0	4	0
	MIL	NL	1	0	1	1	0	0	0	0	0	0	0	0	0	1	1	0
	Total		5	0	5	5	0	0	0	0	0	0	0	0	0	1	5	0
1966	PIT	NL	7	2	5	4	2	1	0	0	0	0	0	0	0	1	7	0
Total			26	10	16	16	7	3	0	1	0	0	0	0	0	5	26	0

Rank among batters: 1,576 • *Top target (3 home runs)*: Don Drysdale, Bob Gibson • *Number of pitchers victimized*: 18 • *Total ballparks homered in*: 10 • *First HR*: 09/30/1960 off Bill Monbouquette

Rene Gonzales

RENE ADRIAN GONZALES
B: 09/03/1960
BR

Year	Tm	Lg	Tot	H	A	Men-On 0	1	2	3	One-Game 2	3	4	LO	XN	IP	PH	RHP	LHP
1987	BAL	AL	1	1	0	1	0	0	0	0	0	0	0	0	0	0	1	0
1988	BAL	AL	2	1	1	2	0	0	0	0	0	0	0	0	0	0	1	1
1989	BAL	AL	1	0	1	1	0	0	0	0	0	0	0	0	0	0	1	0
1990	BAL	AL	1	1	0	1	0	0	0	0	0	0	0	0	0	0	1	0
1991	TOR	AL	1	1	0	1	0	0	0	0	0	0	0	0	0	0	1	0
1992	CAL	AL	7	6	1	3	3	1	0	0	0	0	0	0	0	0	4	3
1993	CAL	AL	2	1	1	0	1	1	0	0	0	0	0	0	0	0	1	1
1994	CLE	AL	1	0	1	1	0	0	0	0	0	0	0	0	0	0	1	0
1995	CAL	AL	1	0	1	0	1	0	0	0	0	0	0	0	0	0	0	1
Total			17	11	6	10	5	2	0	0	0	0	0	0	0	0	11	6

Rank among batters: 1,969 • *Top target (2 home runs)*: Dave Stewart • *Number of pitchers victimized*: 16 • *Total ballparks homered in*: 8 • *First HR*: 05/02/1987 off Jose DeLeon

Alex Gonzalez

ALEXANDER SCOTT GONZALEZ
B: 04/08/1973
BR

Year	Tm	Lg	Tot	H	A	Men-On 0	1	2	3	One-Game 2	3	4	LO	XN	IP	PH	RHP	LHP
1995	TOR	AL	10	8	2	7	3	0	0	2	0	0	1	0	0	0	7	3

Rank among batters: 2,500 • *Top target (2 home runs)*: Jim Pittsley • *Number of pitchers victimized*: 9 • *Total ballparks homered in*: 3 • *First HR*: 05/23/1995 off Jim Pittsley

Denny Gonzalez

DENIO MARIANO (MANZUETA) GONZALEZ
B: 07/22/1963
BR

Year	Tm	Lg	Tot	H	A	Men-On 0	1	2	3	One-Game 2	3	4	LO	XN	IP	PH	RHP	LHP
1985	PIT	NL	4	3	1	3	1	0	0	0	0	0	1	0	0	0	2	2

Rank among batters: 3,427 • *Total ballparks homered in*: 2 • *First HR*: 08/13/1985 off Joaquin Andujar

Fernando Gonzalez

JOSE FERNANDO (QUINONES) GONZALEZ
B: 06/19/1950
BR

Year	Tm	Lg	Tot	H	A	Men-On 0	1	2	3	One-Game 2	3	4	LO	XN	IP	PH	RHP	LHP
1973	PIT	NL	1	1	0	1	0	0	0	0	0	0	0	0	0	0	0	1
1974	NY	AL	1	0	1	1	0	0	0	0	0	0	0	0	0	0	0	1
1977	PIT	NL	4	2	2	1	1	2	0	0	0	0	0	0	0	1	2	2
1978	SD	NL	2	0	2	0	1	1	0	1	0	0	0	0	0	0	0	2
1979	SD	NL	9	4	5	5	2	2	0	0	0	0	0	0	0	0	7	2
Total			17	7	10	8	4	5	0	1	0	0	0	0	0	1	9	8

Rank among batters: 1,969 • *Top target (3 home runs)*: Dave Roberts • *Number of pitchers victimized*: 15 • *Total ballparks homered in*: 8 • *First HR*: 05/27/1973 off Dave Roberts

						Men-On				One-Game								
Year	**Tm**	**Lg**	**Tot**	**H**	**A**	**0**	**1**	**2**	**3**	**2**	**3**	**4**	**LO**	**XN**	**IP**	**PH**	**RHP**	**LHP**

Jose Gonzalez

JOSE RAFAEL (GUTIERREZ) GONZALEZ
B: 11/23/1964
BR

Year	Tm	Lg	Tot	H	A	0	1	2	3	2	3	4	LO	XN	IP	PH	RHP	LHP
1986	LA	NL	2	1	1	2	0	0	0	0	0	0	0	0	0	0	0	2
1989	LA	NL	3	2	1	2	1	0	0	0	0	0	0	0	0	0	1	2
1990	LA	NL	2	2	0	2	0	0	0	0	0	0	0	1	0	0	2	0
1991	PIT	NL	1	1	0	0	1	0	0	0	0	0	0	0	0	0	1	0
	CLE	AL	1	0	1	0	0	1	0	0	0	0	0	0	0	0	1	0
	Total		2	1	1	0	1	1	0	0	0	0	0	0	0	0	2	0
Total			9	6	3	6	2	1	0	0	0	0	0	1	0	0	5	4

Rank among batters: 2,587 • *Total ballparks homered in*: 5 • *First HR*: 09/10/1986 off Jim Deshaies

Juan Gonzalez

JUAN ALBERTO (VAZQUEZ) GONZALEZ
B: 10/20/1969
BR

Year	Tm	Lg	Tot	H	A	0	1	2	3	2	3	4	LO	XN	IP	PH	RHP	LHP
1989	TEX	AL	1	1	0	0	1	0	0	0	0	0	0	0	0	0	1	0
1990	TEX	AL	4	3	1	3	1	0	0	0	0	0	0	1	0	0	3	1
1991	TEX	AL	27	7	20	8	15	3	1	1	0	0	0	2	0	0	18	9
1992	TEX	AL	43	19	24	27	11	5	0	6	1	0	0	1	0	1	36	7
1993	TEX	AL	46	24	22	18	24	3	1	4	1	0	0	1	0	0	37	9
1994	TEX	AL	19	6	13	6	8	4	1	1	0	0	0	1	0	0	14	5
1995	TEX	AL	27	15	12	10	13	3	1	1	0	0	0	0	0	0	18	9
Total			167	75	92	72	73	18	4	13	2	0	0	6	0	1	127	40

Rank among batters: 242 • *Top target (5 home runs)*: Mike Mussina • *Number of pitchers victimized*: 118 • *Total ballparks homered in*: 17 • *First HR*: 09/18/1989 off Scott Bankhead

Julio Gonzalez

JULIO CESAR (HERNANDEZ) GONZALEZ
B: 12/25/1952
BR

Year	Tm	Lg	Tot	H	A	0	1	2	3	2	3	4	LO	XN	IP	PH	RHP	LHP
1977	HOU	NL	1	0	1	0	1	0	0	0	0	0	0	0	0	0	1	0
1978	HOU	NL	1	0	1	1	0	0	0	0	0	0	0	0	0	0	1	0
1981	STL	NL	1	1	0	0	1	0	0	0	0	0	0	1	0	0	1	0
1982	STL	NL	1	0	1	1	0	0	0	0	0	0	0	1	0	0	0	1
Total			4	1	3	2	2	0	0	0	0	0	0	2	0	0	3	1

Rank among batters: 3,427 • *Total ballparks homered in*: 4 • *First HR*: 06/07/1977 off Jim Lonborg

Luis Gonzalez

LUIS EMILIO GONZALEZ
B: 09/03/1967
BL

Year	Tm	Lg	Tot	H	A	0	1	2	3	2	3	4	LO	XN	IP	PH	RHP	LHP
1991	HOU	NL	13	4	9	8	2	3	0	1	0	0	0	0	0	0	12	1
1992	HOU	NL	10	4	6	6	2	2	0	0	0	0	0	1	0	1	9	1
1993	HOU	NL	15	8	7	9	5	1	0	1	0	0	0	0	0	0	12	3
1994	HOU	NL	8	3	5	5	0	3	0	0	0	0	0	0	0	0	7	1
1995	HOU	NL	6	1	5	3	2	1	0	0	0	0	0	0	0	0	4	2
	CHI	NL	7	5	2	4	2	1	0	0	0	0	1	0	0	0	5	2
	Total		13	6	7	7	4	2	0	0	0	0	1	0	0	0	9	4
Total			59	25	34	35	13	11	0	2	0	0	1	1	0	1	49	10

Rank among batters: 873 • *Top target (4 home runs)*: Chris Hammond • *Number of pitchers victimized*: 48 • *Total ballparks homered in*: 14 • *First HR*: 05/01/1991 off Greg Maddux

Mike Gonzalez

MIGUEL ANGEL (CORDERO) GONZALEZ
B: 09/24/1890 D: 02/19/1977
BR

Year	Tm	Lg	Tot	H	A	0	1	2	3	2	3	4	LO	XN	IP	PH	RHP	LHP
1917	STL	NL	1	1	0	0	1	0	0	0	0	0	0	0	1	1	0	1
1918	STL	NL	3	2	1	2	1	0	0	0	0	0	0	1	2	0	3	0
1924	STL	NL	3	1	2	3	0	0	0	0	0	0	0	0	0	0	3	0
1925	CHI	NL	3	2	1	2	1	0	0	0	0	0	0	0	1	0	2	1
1926	CHI	NL	1	0	1	1	0	0	0	0	0	0	0	0	0	0	1	0
1927	CHI	NL	1	0	1	1	0	0	0	0	0	0	0	1	0	0	1	0
1928	CHI	NL	1	0	1	1	0	0	0	0	0	0	0	0	0	0	1	0
Total			13	6	7	10	3	0	0	0	0	0	0	2	4	1	11	2

Year	Tm	Lg	Tot	H	A	Men-On 0	Men-On 1	Men-On 2	Men-On 3	One-Game 2	One-Game 3	One-Game 4	LO	XN	IP	PH	RHP	LHP

Mike Gonzalez *continued*

Rank among batters: 2,248 • *Top target (2 home runs)*: Jesse Haines • *Number of pitchers victimized*: 12 • *Total ballparks homered in*: 7 • *First HR*: 04/25/1917 off Wilbur Cooper

Pedro Gonzalez

PEDRO (OLIVARES) GONZALEZ
B: 12/12/1937
BR

Year	Tm	Lg	Tot	H	A	Men-On 0	Men-On 1	Men-On 2	Men-On 3	One-Game 2	One-Game 3	One-Game 4	LO	XN	IP	PH	RHP	LHP
1965	CLE	AL	5	4	1	3	1	1	0	0	0	0	0	0	0	0	3	2
1966	CLE	AL	2	0	2	1	1	0	0	0	0	0	0	0	0	0	2	0
1967	CLE	AL	1	0	1	1	0	0	0	0	0	0	0	0	0	0	1	0
Total			8	4	4	5	2	1	0	0	0	0	0	0	0	0	6	2

Rank among batters: 2,703 • *Total ballparks homered in*: 5 • *First HR*: 06/04/1965 off Hank Aguirre

Tony Gonzalez

ANDRES ANTONIO (GONZALEZ) GONZALEZ
B: 08/28/1936
BL

Year	Tm	Lg	Tot	H	A	Men-On 0	Men-On 1	Men-On 2	Men-On 3	One-Game 2	One-Game 3	One-Game 4	LO	XN	IP	PH	RHP	LHP
1960	CIN	NL	3	3	0	2	1	0	0	0	0	0	0	0	0	0	3	0
	PHI	NL	6	3	3	1	3	3	0	0	0	0	0	0	0	0	5	1
	Total		9	6	3	5	4	0	0	0	0	0	0	1	0	0	8	1
1961	PHI	NL	12	5	7	8	4	0	0	0	0	0	0	1	0	1	12	0
1962	PHI	NL	20	12	8	10	7	3	0	0	0	0	0	0	0	0	15	5
1963	PHI	NL	4	3	1	3	1	0	0	0	0	0	0	0	0	0	4	0
1964	PHI	NL	4	2	2	2	1	1	0	0	0	0	0	0	0	0	4	0
1965	PHI	NL	13	9	4	10	3	0	0	0	0	0	2	0	1	0	13	0
1966	PHI	NL	6	3	3	3	2	1	0	0	0	0	0	0	0	0	6	0
1967	PHI	NL	9	4	5	7	1	0	1	0	0	0	1	0	0	1	9	0
1968	PHI	NL	3	1	2	2	1	0	0	0	0	0	0	1	0	0	2	1
1969	SD	NL	2	0	2	1	1	0	0	0	0	0	0	0	0	0	2	0
	ATL	NL	10	7	3	4	4	1	1	1	0	0	0	0	0	0	9	1
	Total		12	7	5	5	5	1	1	1	0	0	0	0	0	0	11	1
1970	ATL	NL	7	5	2	2	2	3	0	0	0	0	0	0	0	0	6	1
	CAL	AL	1	1	0	0	1	0	0	0	0	0	0	0	0	0	1	0
	Total		8	6	2	2	3	3	0	0	0	0	0	0	0	0	7	1
1971	CAL	AL	3	0	3	2	1	0	0	0	0	0	0	0	0	0	3	0
Total			103	58	45	59	33	9	2	1	0	0	3	3	1	2	94	9

Rank among batters: 477 • *Top target (4 home runs)*: Larry Jackson • *Number of pitchers victimized*: 79 • *Total ballparks homered in*: 19 • *First HR*: 04/12/1960 off Robin Roberts • *LCS HR*—1

Johnny Gooch

JOHN BEVERLEY GOOCH
B: 11/09/1897 D: 03/15/1975
BB

Year	Tm	Lg	Tot	H	A	Men-On 0	Men-On 1	Men-On 2	Men-On 3	One-Game 2	One-Game 3	One-Game 4	LO	XN	IP	PH	RHP	LHP
1922	PIT	NL	1	0	1	1	0	0	0	0	0	0	0	0	0	0	1	0
1923	PIT	NL	1	0	1	0	1	0	0	0	0	0	0	0	1	0	1	0
1926	PIT	NL	1	0	1	0	1	0	0	0	0	0	0	0	0	0	1	0
1927	PIT	NL	2	0	2	0	0	2	0	0	0	0	0	0	0	0	2	0
1930	CIN	NL	2	0	2	1	1	0	0	0	0	0	0	0	0	0	2	0
Total			7	0	7	2	3	2	0	0	0	0	0	0	1	0	7	0

Rank among batters: 2,834 • *Total ballparks homered in*: 5 • *First HR*: 06/07/1922 off Lee Meadows

Lee Gooch

LEE CURRIN GOOCH
B: 02/23/1890 D: 05/18/1966
BR

Year	Tm	Lg	Tot	H	A	Men-On 0	Men-On 1	Men-On 2	Men-On 3	One-Game 2	One-Game 3	One-Game 4	LO	XN	IP	PH	RHP	LHP
1917	PHI	AL	1	0	1	0	0	0	1	0	0	0	0	0	1	0	1	0

Rank among batters: 4,707 • *Total ballparks homered in*: 1 • *First HR*: 06/17/1917 off Guy Morton

Wilbur Good

WILBUR DAVID GOOD
B: 09/28/1885 D: 12/30/1963
BL

Year	Tm	Lg	Tot	H	A	Men-On 0	Men-On 1	Men-On 2	Men-On 3	One-Game 2	One-Game 3	One-Game 4	LO	XN	IP	PH	RHP	LHP
1908	CLE	AL	1	0	1	1	0	0	0	0	0	0	0	0	0	0	1	0
1911	CHI	NL	2	1	1	1	1	0	0	0	0	0	0	1	0	0	2	0

Wilbur Good *continued*

Year	Tm	Lg	Tot	H	A	Men-On 0	Men-On 1	Men-On 2	Men-On 3	One-Game 2	One-Game 3	One-Game 4	LO	XN	IP	PH	RHP	LHP
1913	CHI	NL	1	1	0	1	0	0	0	0	0	0	0	0	0	1	1	0
1914	CHI	NL	2	2	0	0	1	1	0	0	0	0	0	0	1	0	2	0
1915	CHI	NL	2	2	0	1	1	0	0	0	0	0	0	0	0	1	2	0
1916	PHI	NL	1	1	0	1	0	0	0	0	0	0	0	0	0	0	1	0
Total			9	7	2	5	3	1	0	0	0	0	0	1	1	2	9	0

Rank among batters: 2,587 • *Total ballparks homered in*: 4 • *First HR*: 08/31/1908 off Ed Summers

Dwight Gooden

DWIGHT EUGENE GOODEN
B: 11/16/1964
BR

Year	Tm	Lg	Tot	H	A	Men-On 0	Men-On 1	Men-On 2	Men-On 3	One-Game 2	One-Game 3	One-Game 4	LO	XN	IP	PH	RHP	LHP
1985	NY	NL	1	1	0	0	0	1	0	0	0	0	0	0	0	0	1	0
1988	NY	NL	1	1	0	0	1	0	0	0	0	0	0	0	0	0	1	0
1990	NY	NL	1	1	0	1	0	0	0	0	0	0	0	0	0	0	1	0
1991	NY	NL	1	0	1	1	0	0	0	0	0	0	0	0	0	0	1	0
1992	NY	NL	1	0	1	0	1	0	0	0	0	0	0	0	0	0	0	1
1993	NY	NL	2	1	1	2	0	0	0	0	0	0	0	0	0	0	2	0
Total			7	4	3	4	2	1	0	0	0	0	0	0	0	0	6	1

Rank among batters: 2,834 • *Total ballparks homered in*: 4 • *First HR*: 09/21/1985 off Rick Rhoden

Billy Goodman

WILLIAM DALE GOODMAN
B: 03/22/1926 D: 10/01/1984
BL

Year	Tm	Lg	Tot	H	A	Men-On 0	Men-On 1	Men-On 2	Men-On 3	One-Game 2	One-Game 3	One-Game 4	LO	XN	IP	PH	RHP	LHP
1948	BOS	AL	1	0	1	0	0	0	1	0	0	0	0	0	0	0	1	0
1950	BOS	AL	4	1	3	1	2	0	1	0	0	0	0	0	0	0	2	2
1952	BOS	AL	4	3	1	3	0	1	0	0	0	0	0	0	0	1	4	0
1953	BOS	AL	2	1	1	2	0	0	0	0	0	0	0	1	0	0	2	0
1954	BOS	AL	1	0	1	0	1	0	0	0	0	0	0	0	0	0	0	1
1956	BOS	AL	2	0	2	0	2	0	0	0	0	0	0	0	0	0	2	0
1957	BAL	AL	3	1	2	1	2	0	0	0	0	0	0	0	0	0	3	0
1959	CHI	AL	1	0	1	0	1	0	0	0	0	0	0	0	0	0	1	0
1961	CHI	AL	1	1	0	0	1	0	0	0	0	0	0	0	0	1	1	0
Total			19	7	12	7	9	1	2	0	0	0	0	1	0	2	16	3

Rank among batters: 1,861 • *Total ballparks homered in*: 8 • *First HR*: 07/29/1948 off Virgil Trucks

Ival Goodman

IVAL RICHARD GOODMAN
B: 07/23/1908 D: 11/25/1984
BL

Year	Tm	Lg	Tot	H	A	Men-On 0	Men-On 1	Men-On 2	Men-On 3	One-Game 2	One-Game 3	One-Game 4	LO	XN	IP	PH	RHP	LHP
1935	CIN	NL	12	1	11	8	2	2	0	0	0	0	0	0	1	0	10	2
1936	CIN	NL	17	3	14	8	7	2	0	1	0	0	0	0	1	0	16	1
1937	CIN	NL	12	3	9	4	8	0	0	0	0	0	0	0	1	1	10	2
1938	CIN	NL	30	17	13	17	10	3	0	3	0	0	0	2	1	0	23	7
1939	CIN	NL	7	5	2	2	3	2	0	0	0	0	0	0	0	0	5	2
1940	CIN	NL	12	5	7	7	4	0	1	0	0	0	0	1	0	0	9	3
1941	CIN	NL	1	0	1	0	1	0	0	0	0	0	0	0	0	0	1	0
1943	CHI	NL	3	0	3	2	0	1	0	0	0	0	0	0	0	0	2	1
1944	CHI	NL	1	0	1	0	0	1	0	0	0	0	0	0	0	0	1	0
Total			95	34	61	48	35	11	1	4	0	0	0	3	4	1	77	18

Rank among batters: 529 • *Top target (6 home runs)*: Joe Bowman, Carl Hubbell • *Number of pitchers victimized*: 56 • *Total ballparks homered in*: 9 • *First HR*: 04/21/1935 off Charlie Root

Jake Goodman

JACOB GOODMAN
B: 09/14/1853 D: 03/09/1890

Year	Tm	Lg	Tot	H	A	Men-On 0	Men-On 1	Men-On 2	Men-On 3	One-Game 2	One-Game 3	One-Game 4	LO	XN	IP	PH	RHP	LHP
1878	MIL	NL	1	1	0	0	0	1	0	0	0	0	0	0	0	0	1	0

Rank among batters: 4,707 • *Total ballparks homered in*: 1 • *First HR*: 06/25/1878 off Harry Wheeler

Ed Goodson

JAMES EDWARD GOODSON
B: 01/25/1948
BL

Year	Tm	Lg	Tot	H	A	Men-On 0	Men-On 1	Men-On 2	Men-On 3	One-Game 2	One-Game 3	One-Game 4	LO	XN	IP	PH	RHP	LHP
1972	SF	NL	6	3	3	3	2	1	0	0	0	0	0	0	0	0	5	1
1973	SF	NL	12	8	4	6	4	1	1	2	0	0	0	0	0	1	9	3
1974	SF	NL	6	4	2	2	3	1	0	0	0	0	0	1	0	0	5	1

Ed Goodson *continued*

Year	Tm	Lg	Tot	H	A	Men-On 0	1	2	3	One-Game 2	3	4	LO	XN	IP	PH	RHP	LHP
1975	SF	NL	1	1	0	1	0	0	0	0	0	0	0	0	0	0	1	0
	ATL	NL	1	0	1	1	0	0	0	0	0	0	0	0	0	0	1	0
	Total		2	1	1	2	0	0	0	0	0	0	0	0	0	0	2	0
1976	LA	NL	3	0	3	0	1	2	0	0	0	0	0	0	0	2	3	0
1977	LA	NL	1	0	1	1	0	0	0	0	0	0	0	0	0	1	1	0
Total			30	16	14	14	10	5	1	2	0	0	0	1	0	4	25	5

Rank among batters: 1,437 • *Top target (2 home runs)*: Jim Crawford, Ron Schueler, Gary Nolan • *Number of pitchers victimized*: 27 • *Total ballparks homered in*: 10 • *First HR*: 05/21/1972 off Ron Schueler

Curtis Goodwin

CURTIS LAMAR GOODWIN
B: 09/30/1972
BL

Year	Tm	Lg	Tot	H	A	Men-On 0	1	2	3	One-Game 2	3	4	LO	XN	IP	PH	RHP	LHP
1995	BAL	AL	1	0	1	0	1	0	0	0	0	0	0	0	0	0	0	1
Total			1	0	1	0	1	0	0	0	0	0	0	0	0	0	0	1

Rank among batters: 4,707 • *Total ballparks homered in*: 1 • *First HR*: 07/01/1995 off Al Leiter

Danny Goodwin

DANNY KAY GOODWIN
B: 09/02/1953
BL

Year	Tm	Lg	Tot	H	A	Men-On 0	1	2	3	One-Game 2	3	4	LO	XN	IP	PH	RHP	LHP
1977	CAL	AL	1	1	0	0	1	0	0	0	0	0	0	0	0	0	1	0
1978	CAL	AL	2	1	1	1	1	0	0	0	0	0	0	0	0	0	2	0
1979	MIN	AL	5	2	3	4	1	0	0	0	0	0	0	0	0	0	5	0
1980	MIN	AL	1	1	0	1	0	0	0	0	0	0	0	0	0	0	1	0
1981	MIN	AL	2	1	1	1	0	1	0	0	0	0	0	0	0	0	1	1
1982	OAK	AL	2	0	2	0	2	0	0	0	0	0	0	0	0	0	2	0
Total			13	6	7	7	5	1	0	0	0	0	0	0	0	0	12	1

Rank among batters: 2,248 • *Top target (2 home runs)*: Ferguson Jenkins • *Number of pitchers victimized*: 12 • *Total ballparks homered in*: 6 • *First HR*: 07/29/1977 off Ferguson Jenkins

Pep Goodwin

CLAIRE VERNON GOODWIN
B: 12/19/1891 D: 02/15/1972
BL

Year	Tm	Lg	Tot	H	A	Men-On 0	1	2	3	One-Game 2	3	4	LO	XN	IP	PH	RHP	LHP
1914	KC	FL	1	0	1	0	0	1	0	0	0	0	0	0	0	0	1	0

Rank among batters: 4,707 • *Total ballparks homered in*: 1 • *First HR*: 07/28/1914 off Elmer Knetzer

Tom Goodwin

THOMAS JONES GOODWIN
B: 07/27/1968
BL

Year	Tm	Lg	Tot	H	A	Men-On 0	1	2	3	One-Game 2	3	4	LO	XN	IP	PH	RHP	LHP
1995	KC	AL	4	2	2	3	1	0	0	0	0	0	0	0	0	0	4	0

Rank among batters: 3,427 • *Top target (2 home runs)*: Todd Stottlemyre • *Number of pitchers victimized*: 3 • *Total ballparks homered in*: 3 • *First HR*: 06/16/1995 off Todd Stottlemyre

Greg Goossen

GREGORY BRYANT GOOSSEN
B: 12/14/1945
BR

Year	Tm	Lg	Tot	H	A	Men-On 0	1	2	3	One-Game 2	3	4	LO	XN	IP	PH	RHP	LHP
1965	NY	NL	1	0	1	1	0	0	0	0	0	0	0	0	0	0	0	1
1966	NY	NL	1	0	1	0	0	1	0	0	0	0	0	0	0	0	1	0
1969	SEA	AL	10	10	0	6	4	0	0	2	0	0	0	0	0	1	5	5
1970	MIL	AL	1	1	0	1	0	0	0	0	0	0	0	0	0	0	0	1
Total			13	11	2	8	4	1	0	2	0	0	0	0	0	1	6	7

Rank among batters: 2,248 • *Top target (2 home runs)*: Casey Cox, Bill Butler • *Number of pitchers victimized*: 11 • *Total ballparks homered in*: 4 • *First HR*: 09/25/1965 off Bo Belinsky

Glen Gorbous

GLEN EDWARD GORBOUS
B: 07/08/1930 D: 06/12/1990
BL

Year	Tm	Lg	Tot	H	A	Men-On 0	1	2	3	One-Game 2	3	4	LO	XN	IP	PH	RHP	LHP
1955	PHI	NL	4	2	2	3	0	1	0	0	0	0	0	0	0	1	4	0

Rank among batters: 3,427 • *Total ballparks homered in*: 3 • *First HR*: 05/22/1955 off Carl Erskine

Joe Gordon

JOSEPH LOWELL GORDON
B: 02/18/1915 D: 04/14/1978
BR

Year	Tm	Lg	Tot	H	A	Men-On 0	Men-On 1	Men-On 2	Men-On 3	One-Game 2	One-Game 3	One-Game 4	LO	XN	IP	PH	RHP	LHP
1938	NY	AL	25	13	12	7	14	4	0	3	0	0	0	1	1	1	15	10
1939	NY	AL	28	11	17	16	4	7	1	4	0	0	0	0	0	0	19	9
1940	NY	AL	30	15	15	24	5	1	0	2	0	0	2	1	0	0	24	6
1941	NY	AL	24	8	16	15	6	3	0	2	0	0	0	1	0	0	18	6
1942	NY	AL	18	7	11	6	8	2	2	1	0	0	0	0	0	0	14	4
1943	NY	AL	17	11	6	10	5	1	1	0	0	0	0	2	0	0	10	7
1946	NY	AL	11	4	7	6	4	1	0	1	0	0	0	0	0	0	8	3
1947	CLE	AL	29	12	17	13	9	6	1	5	0	0	0	0	0	0	23	6
1948	CLE	AL	32	17	15	14	16	2	0	2	0	0	0	0	0	0	21	11
1949	CLE	AL	20	11	9	13	6	0	1	2	0	0	0	0	0	0	14	6
1950	CLE	AL	19	10	9	14	4	1	0	0	0	0	0	0	0	0	6	13
Total			253	119	134	138	81	28	6	22	0	0	2	5	1	1	172	81

Rank among batters: 103 • *Top target (9 home runs)*: Hal Newhouser • *Number of pitchers victimized*: 126 • *Total ballparks homered in*: 9 • *First HR*: 04/26/1938 off Eddie Smith • *Hit for Cycle*—@BOS: 09/08/1940 • *World Series HR*—4

Sid Gordon

SIDNEY GORDON
B: 08/13/1917 D: 06/17/1975
BR

Year	Tm	Lg	Tot	H	A	Men-On 0	Men-On 1	Men-On 2	Men-On 3	One-Game 2	One-Game 3	One-Game 4	LO	XN	IP	PH	RHP	LHP
1943	NY	NL	9	4	5	3	5	1	0	0	0	0	0	0	0	0	8	1
1946	NY	NL	5	2	3	4	0	1	0	0	0	0	0	0	0	1	3	2
1947	NY	NL	13	8	5	9	3	1	0	1	0	0	0	0	0	1	9	4
1948	NY	NL	30	16	14	14	12	1	3	5	0	0	0	1	0	0	24	6
1949	NY	NL	26	12	14	14	9	3	0	2	0	0	0	0	0	0	16	10
1950	BOS	NL	27	5	22	14	8	1	4	3	0	0	0	1	0	0	20	7
1951	BOS	NL	29	10	19	20	6	3	0	1	0	0	0	1	0	0	20	9
1952	BOS	NL	25	12	13	12	11	2	0	1	0	0	0	1	0	0	13	12
1953	MIL	NL	19	5	14	12	4	3	0	1	0	0	0	0	0	0	15	4
1954	PIT	NL	12	4	8	5	4	3	0	1	0	0	0	0	0	2	8	4
1955	NY	NL	7	4	3	3	2	2	0	0	0	0	0	0	0	0	4	3
Total			202	82	120	110	64	21	7	15	0	0	0	4	0	4	140	62

Rank among batters: 178 • *Top target (9 home runs)*: Preacher Roe • *Number of pitchers victimized*: 111 • *Total ballparks homered in*: 9 • *First HR*: 04/27/1943 off Jim Tobin • *2 HR in 1 inning*—@CIN: 07/31/1949 (2)

George Gore

GEORGE F. GORE
B: 05/03/1857 D: 09/16/1933
BL

Year	Tm	Lg	Tot	H	A	Men-On 0	Men-On 1	Men-On 2	Men-On 3	One-Game 2	One-Game 3	One-Game 4	LO	XN	IP	PH	RHP	LHP
1880	CHI	NL	2	1	1	1	1	0	0	0	0	0	0	0	0	0	2	0
1881	CHI	NL	1	1	0	1	0	0	0	0	0	0	0	0	1	0	1	0
1882	CHI	NL	3	2	1	0	2	1	0	0	0	0	0	1	1	0	3	0
1883	CHI	NL	2	2	0	2	0	0	0	0	0	0	0	0	0	0	2	0
1884	CHI	NL	5	5	0	2	3	0	0	1	0	0	0	0	0	0	4	0
1885	CHI	NL	5	4	1	4	1	0	0	1	0	0	1	0	1	0	5	0
1886	CHI	NL	6	5	1	3	2	1	0	0	0	0	1	0	0	0	6	0
1887	NY	NL	1	0	1	0	0	1	0	0	0	0	0	0	0	0	1	0
1888	NY	NL	2	0	2	1	1	0	0	0	0	0	0	0	1	0	1	1
1889	NY	NL	7	2	5	5	1	0	1	1	0	0	2	0	1	0	5	2
1890	NY	PL	10	6	4	7	0	3	0	0	0	0	0	0	0	0	9	1
1891	NY	NL	2	1	1	0	1	0	1	0	0	0	0	0	0	0	1	1
Total			46	29	17	26	12	6	2	3	0	0	4	1	5	0	40	5

Rank among batters: 1,060 • *Top target (3 home runs)*: Hugh Daily, Henry Boyle • *Number of pitchers victimized*: 33 • *Total ballparks homered in*: 16 • *First HR*: 05/04/1880 off Will White • *World Series HR*—1

Bob Gorinski

ROBERT JOHN GORINSKI
B: 01/07/1952
BR

Year	Tm	Lg	Tot	H	A	Men-On 0	Men-On 1	Men-On 2	Men-On 3	One-Game 2	One-Game 3	One-Game 4	LO	XN	IP	PH	RHP	LHP
1977	MIN	AL	3	1	2	0	2	1	0	0	0	0	0	0	0	0	0	3

Rank among batters: 3,735 • *Total ballparks homered in*: 3 • *First HR*: 06/27/1977 off Jerry Augustine

Year	Tm	Lg	Tot	H	A	Men-On 0	1	2	3	One-Game 2	3	4	LO	XN	IP	PH	RHP	LHP

Hank Gornicki

HENRY FRANK GORNICKI
B: 01/14/1911
BR

Year	Tm	Lg	Tot	H	A	0	1	2	3	2	3	4	LO	XN	IP	PH	RHP	LHP
1942	PIT	NL	1	1	0	0	1	0	0	0	0	0	0	0	0	0	1	0

Rank among batters: 4,707 • *Total ballparks homered in*: 1 • *First HR*: 08/27/1942 off Jim Tobin

Johnny Gorsica

JOHN JOSEPH PERRY GORSICA
B: 03/29/1915
BR

Year	Tm	Lg	Tot	H	A	0	1	2	3	2	3	4	LO	XN	IP	PH	RHP	LHP
1940	DET	AL	1	1	0	0	0	1	0	0	0	0	0	0	0	0	1	0

Rank among batters: 4,707 • *Total ballparks homered in*: 1 • *First HR*: 08/03/1940 off Alex Mustaikis

Johnny Goryl

JOHN ALBERT GORYL
B: 10/21/1933
BR

Year	Tm	Lg	Tot	H	A	0	1	2	3	2	3	4	LO	XN	IP	PH	RHP	LHP
1958	CHI	NL	4	3	1	4	0	0	0	0	0	0	0	0	0	0	3	1
1959	CHI	NL	1	0	1	0	1	0	0	0	0	0	0	0	0	1	1	0
1962	MIN	AL	2	0	2	2	0	0	0	1	0	0	0	0	0	0	2	0
1963	MIN	AL	9	2	7	6	3	0	0	0	0	0	1	0	0	0	8	1
Total			16	5	11	12	4	0	0	1	0	0	1	0	0	1	14	2

Rank among batters: 2,029 • *Top target (2 home runs)*: Gary Bell, Phil Regan • *Number of pitchers victimized*: 14 • *Total ballparks homered in*: 10 • *First HR*: 04/17/1958 off Lindy McDaniel

Jim Gosger

JAMES CHARLES GOSGER
B: 11/06/1942
BL

Year	Tm	Lg	Tot	H	A	0	1	2	3	2	3	4	LO	XN	IP	PH	RHP	LHP
1965	BOS	AL	9	4	5	8	0	1	0	0	0	0	2	0	1	0	7	2
1966	BOS	AL	5	2	3	2	2	1	0	1	0	0	0	1	0	0	5	0
	KC	AL	5	0	5	4	1	0	0	0	0	0	0	0	0	0	4	1
	Total		10	2	8	6	3	1	0	1	0	0	0	1	0	0	9	1
1967	KC	AL	5	2	3	4	1	0	0	0	0	0	0	0	0	0	5	0
1969	SEA	AL	1	1	0	1	0	0	0	0	0	0	0	0	0	0	1	0
1970	MON	NL	5	4	1	1	3	1	0	0	0	0	0	0	0	0	5	0
Total			30	13	17	20	7	3	0	1	0	0	2	1	1	0	27	3

Rank among batters: 1,437 • *Top target (2 home runs)*: Denny McLain • *Number of pitchers victimized*: 29 • *Total ballparks homered in*: 9 • *First HR*: 07/09/1965 off Buster Narum

Goose Goslin

LEON ALLEN GOSLIN
B: 10/16/1900 D: 05/15/1971
BL HOF

Year	Tm	Lg	Tot	H	A	0	1	2	3	2	3	4	LO	XN	IP	PH	RHP	LHP
1921	WAS	AL	1	1	0	0	0	1	0	0	0	0	0	0	0	0	1	0
1922	WAS	AL	3	1	2	1	2	0	0	0	0	0	0	0	1	0	3	0
1923	WAS	AL	9	1	8	6	3	0	0	0	0	0	0	0	1	0	6	3
1924	WAS	AL	12	1	11	8	4	0	0	1	0	0	0	1	1	0	9	3
1925	WAS	AL	18	6	12	11	6	1	0	1	1	0	0	1	1	0	11	7
1926	WAS	AL	17	0	17	9	7	1	0	2	0	0	0	0	1	0	13	4
1927	WAS	AL	13	7	6	5	6	2	0	0	0	0	0	0	2	0	11	2
1928	WAS	AL	17	4	13	10	4	3	0	0	0	0	0	0	0	1	14	3
1929	WAS	AL	18	3	15	10	6	2	0	0	0	0	0	0	0	0	13	5
1930	WAS	AL	7	3	4	2	2	3	0	1	0	0	0	0	0	0	5	2
	STL	AL	30	14	16	11	13	6	0	3	1	0	0	0	0	0	28	2
	Total		37	17	20	13	15	9	0	4	1	0	0	0	0	0	33	4
1931	STL	AL	24	15	9	11	9	4	0	1	0	0	0	0	0	0	18	6
1932	STL	AL	17	12	5	7	6	3	1	0	1	0	0	1	0	0	16	1
1933	WAS	AL	10	4	6	5	5	0	0	1	0	0	0	0	1	1	9	1
1934	DET	AL	13	4	9	6	5	2	0	0	0	0	0	0	0	0	12	1
1935	DET	AL	9	1	8	5	3	1	0	0	0	0	0	0	0	0	9	0
1936	DET	AL	24	12	12	12	8	3	1	1	0	0	0	0	1	0	22	2
1937	DET	AL	4	3	1	1	2	0	1	0	0	0	0	0	0	2	4	0

Goose Goslin *continued*

Year	Tm	Lg	Tot	H	A	Men-On 0	1	2	3	One-Game 2	3	4	LO	XN	IP	PH	RHP	LHP
1938	WAS	AL	2	0	2	1	1	0	0	0	0	0	0	0	0	1	2	0
Total			248	92	156	121	92	32	3	11	3	0	0	3	9	5	206	42

Rank among batters: 112 • *Top target (8 home runs)*: Urban Shocker • *Number of pitchers victimized*: 123 • *Total ballparks homered in*: 8 • *First HR*: 09/21/1921 off Red Faber • *Hit for Cycle—*@NY: 08/28/1924 • *World Series HR*—7

Howie Goss

HOWARD WAYNE GOSS
B: 11/01/1934
BR

Year	Tm	Lg	Tot	H	A	Men-On 0	1	2	3	One-Game 2	3	4	LO	XN	IP	PH	RHP	LHP
1962	PIT	NL	2	0	2	0	2	0	0	0	0	0	0	0	0	0	1	1
1963	HOU	NL	9	3	6	5	2	2	0	1	0	0	0	0	0	0	7	2
Total			11	3	8	5	4	2	0	1	0	0	0	0	0	0	8	3

Rank among batters: 2,419 • *Top target (2 home runs)*: Ernie Broglio • *Number of pitchers victimized*: 10 • *Total ballparks homered in*: 6 • *First HR*: 04/29/1962 off Johnny Podres

Julio Gotay

JULIO ENRIQUE (SANCHEZ) GOTAY
B: 06/09/1939
BR

Year	Tm	Lg	Tot	H	A	Men-On 0	1	2	3	One-Game 2	3	4	LO	XN	IP	PH	RHP	LHP
1962	STL	NL	2	0	2	2	0	0	0	0	0	0	0	0	0	0	1	1
1965	CAL	AL	1	0	1	1	0	0	0	0	0	0	0	0	0	1	0	1
1967	HOU	NL	2	0	2	1	1	0	0	0	0	0	0	0	0	0	1	1
1968	HOU	NL	1	0	1	1	0	0	0	0	0	0	0	0	0	1	0	1
Total			6	0	6	5	1	0	0	0	0	0	0	0	0	2	2	4

Rank among batters: 2,988 • *Total ballparks homered in*: 5 • *First HR*: 07/14/1962 off Bob Shaw

Jim Gott

JAMES WILLIAM GOTT
B: 08/03/1959
BR

Year	Tm	Lg	Tot	H	A	Men-On 0	1	2	3	One-Game 2	3	4	LO	XN	IP	PH	RHP	LHP
1985	SF	NL	3	2	1	3	0	0	0	1	0	0	0	0	0	0	3	0
1987	SF	NL	1	0	1	0	1	0	0	0	0	0	0	0	0	0	1	0
Total			4	2	2	3	1	0	0	1	0	0	0	0	0	0	4	0

Rank among batters: 3,427 • *Top target (2 home runs)*: Bob Forsch • *Number of pitchers victimized*: 3 • *Total ballparks homered in*: 3 • *First HR*: 05/12/1985 off Bob Forsch

Hank Gowdy

HENRY MORGAN GOWDY
B: 08/24/1889 D: 08/01/1966
BR

Year	Tm	Lg	Tot	H	A	Men-On 0	1	2	3	One-Game 2	3	4	LO	XN	IP	PH	RHP	LHP
1912	BOS	NL	3	1	2	3	0	0	0	0	0	0	0	0	0	1	2	1
1914	BOS	NL	3	1	2	3	0	0	0	0	0	0	0	0	0	0	2	1
1915	BOS	NL	2	1	1	1	0	0	1	0	0	0	0	0	0	0	0	2
1916	BOS	NL	1	0	1	0	1	0	0	0	0	0	0	0	0	0	1	0
1919	BOS	NL	1	1	0	1	0	0	0	0	0	0	0	0	1	0	1	0
1921	BOS	NL	2	0	2	1	0	0	1	0	0	0	0	0	0	0	0	2
1922	BOS	NL	1	0	1	0	0	0	1	0	0	0	0	0	0	0	0	1
1923	NY	NL	1	0	1	1	0	0	0	0	0	0	0	0	0	0	1	0
1924	NY	NL	4	4	0	2	0	2	0	0	0	0	0	0	0	0	3	1
1925	NY	NL	3	0	3	1	2	0	0	0	0	0	0	0	0	0	1	2
Total			21	8	13	13	3	2	3	0	0	0	0	0	1	1	11	10

Rank among batters: 1,768 • Top target (2 home runs): Slim Sallee, Percy Jones, Wilbur Cooper, Grover Alexander • *Number of pitchers victimized*: 17 • *Total ballparks homered in*: 10 • *First HR*: 06/12/1912 off Slim Sallee • *World Series HR*—1

Billy Grabarkewitz

BILLY CORDELL GRABARKEWITZ
B: 01/18/1946
BR

Year	Tm	Lg	Tot	H	A	Men-On 0	1	2	3	One-Game 2	3	4	LO	XN	IP	PH	RHP	LHP
1970	LA	NL	17	8	9	9	6	2	0	1	0	0	1	1	1	0	11	6
1972	LA	NL	4	3	1	1	2	1	0	0	0	0	0	0	0	1	3	1
1973	CAL	AL	3	1	2	2	1	0	0	0	0	0	0	0	0	0	1	2
	PHI	NL	2	2	0	2	0	0	0	0	0	0	1	0	0	0	0	2
	Total		5	3	2	4	1	0	0	0	0	0	1	0	0	0	1	4

Year	Tm	Lg	Tot	H	A	Men-On 0	Men-On 1	Men-On 2	Men-On 3	One-Game 2	One-Game 3	One-Game 4	LO	XN	IP	PH	RHP	LHP

Billy Grabarkewitz *continued*

Year	Tm	Lg	Tot	H	A	0	1	2	3	2	3	4	LO	XN	IP	PH	RHP	LHP
1974	PHI	NL	1	0	1	1	0	0	0	0	0	0	0	0	0	1	1	0
	CHI	NL	1	1	0	1	0	0	0	0	0	0	0	0	0	0	1	0
	Total		2	1	1	2	0	0	0	0	0	0	0	0	0	1	2	0
Total			28	15	13	16	9	3	0	1	0	0	2	1	1	2	17	11

Rank among batters: 1,500 • *Top target (2 home runs)*: Juan Marichal, Woodie Fryman • *Number of pitchers victimized*: 26 • *Total ballparks homered in*: 12 • *First HR*: 04/12/1970 off Gary Ross

Johnny Grabowski

JOHN PATRICK GRABOWSKI
B: 01/07/1900 D: 05/23/1946
BR

Year	Tm	Lg	Tot	H	A	0	1	2	3	2	3	4	LO	XN	IP	PH	RHP	LHP
1926	CHI	AL	1	1	0	0	0	1	0	0	0	0	0	0	0	1	0	1
1928	NY	AL	1	1	0	0	0	1	0	0	0	0	0	0	0	0	0	1
1931	DET	AL	1	1	0	1	0	0	0	0	0	0	0	0	0	0	1	0
Total			3	3	0	1	0	2	0	0	0	0	0	0	0	1	1	2

Rank among batters: 3,735 • *Total ballparks homered in*: 3 • *First HR*: 04/20/1926 off Joe Shaute

Earl Grace

ROBERT EARL GRACE
B: 02/24/1907 D: 12/22/1980
BL

Year	Tm	Lg	Tot	H	A	0	1	2	3	2	3	4	LO	XN	IP	PH	RHP	LHP
1929	CHI	NL	2	1	1	1	0	1	0	0	0	0	0	0	0	0	2	0
1931	PIT	NL	1	0	1	0	1	0	0	0	0	0	0	0	0	0	1	0
1932	PIT	NL	8	6	2	5	1	2	0	0	0	0	0	0	0	0	4	4
1933	PIT	NL	3	1	2	2	0	0	1	0	0	0	0	0	0	0	3	0
1934	PIT	NL	4	2	2	4	0	0	0	0	0	0	0	0	0	0	4	0
1935	PIT	NL	3	1	2	1	1	0	1	0	0	0	0	0	1	0	3	0
1936	PHI	NL	4	4	0	1	1	2	0	0	0	0	0	0	0	0	4	0
1937	PHI	NL	6	5	1	3	3	0	0	0	0	0	0	0	0	0	6	0
Total			31	20	11	17	7	5	2	0	0	0	0	0	1	0	27	4

Rank among batters: 1,400 • *Top target (2 home runs)*: Freddie Fitzsimmons, Dizzy Dean • *Number of pitchers victimized*: 29 • *Total ballparks homered in*: 5 • *First HR*: 05/04/1929 off Claude Willoughby

Joe Grace

JOSEPH LAVERNE GRACE
B: 01/05/1914 D: 09/18/1969
BL

Year	Tm	Lg	Tot	H	A	0	1	2	3	2	3	4	LO	XN	IP	PH	RHP	LHP
1939	STL	AL	3	2	1	2	1	0	0	0	0	0	0	0	0	0	3	0
1940	STL	AL	5	2	3	2	3	0	0	1	0	0	0	0	0	1	5	0
1941	STL	AL	6	4	2	1	4	1	0	0	0	0	0	0	0	0	6	0
1946	STL	AL	1	1	0	1	0	0	0	0	0	0	0	0	0	0	1	0
	WAS	AL	2	1	1	2	0	0	0	0	0	0	1	0	0	0	2	0
	Total		3	2	1	3	0	0	0	0	0	0	1	0	0	0	3	0
1947	WAS	AL	3	1	2	2	1	0	0	0	0	0	1	0	0	0	3	0
Total			20	11	9	10	9	1	0	1	0	0	2	0	0	1	20	0

Rank among batters: 1,810 • *Top target (2 home runs)*: Dutch Leonard, Bob Feller • *Number of pitchers victimized*: 18 • *Total ballparks homered in*: 6 • *First HR*: 08/12/1939 off Slick Coffman

Mark Grace

MARK EUGENE GRACE
B: 06/28/1964
BL

Year	Tm	Lg	Tot	H	A	0	1	2	3	2	3	4	LO	XN	IP	PH	RHP	LHP
1988	CHI	NL	7	0	7	3	3	1	0	0	0	0	0	0	0	0	4	3
1989	CHI	NL	13	8	5	6	6	1	0	1	0	0	0	0	0	0	9	4
1990	CHI	NL	9	4	5	9	0	0	0	0	0	0	0	0	0	0	6	3
1991	CHI	NL	8	5	3	6	1	1	0	1	0	0	0	1	0	0	6	2
1992	CHI	NL	9	5	4	6	2	1	0	0	0	0	0	0	0	0	6	3
1993	CHI	NL	14	5	9	8	4	2	0	0	0	0	0	0	0	0	8	6
1994	CHI	NL	6	5	1	5	0	1	0	0	0	0	0	1	0	0	5	1
1995	CHI	NL	16	4	12	10	6	0	0	0	0	0	0	1	0	0	13	3
Total			82	36	46	53	22	7	0	2	0	0	0	3	0	0	57	25

Rank among batters: 637 • *Top target (5 home runs)*: John Smoltz • *Number of pitchers victimized*: 68 • *Total ballparks homered in*: 14 • *First HR*: 05/04/1988 off Keith Comstock • *Hit for Cycle*—vs SD: 05/09/1993 • *LCS HR*—1

Mike Grady

MICHAEL WILLIAM GRADY
B: 12/23/1869 D: 12/03/1943
BR

Year	Tm	Lg	Tot	H	A	Men-On 0	1	2	3	One-Game 2	3	4	LO	XN	IP	PH	RHP	LHP
1895	PHI	NL	1	0	1	1	0	0	0	0	0	0	0	0	0	0	1	0
1896	PHI	NL	1	1	0	0	0	1	0	0	0	0	0	0	0	0	1	0
1897	STL	NL	7	5	2	3	2	2	0	0	0	0	0	0	0	0	5	2
1898	NY	NL	3	0	3	2	1	0	0	0	0	0	0	0	0	0	2	1
1899	NY	NL	2	0	2	2	0	0	0	0	0	0	0	0	0	0	1	1
1901	WAS	AL	9	6	3	6	2	1	0	0	0	0	0	0	0	0	6	3
1904	STL	NL	5	3	2	3	2	0	0	0	0	0	0	0	1	0	4	1
1905	STL	NL	4	2	2	2	2	0	0	0	0	0	0	0	0	0	2	2
1906	STL	NL	3	3	0	3	0	0	0	0	0	0	0	0	1	0	2	1
Total			35	20	15	22	9	4	0	0	0	0	0	0	2	0	24	11

Rank among batters: 1,291 • *Top target (3 home runs)*: Hooks Wiltse • *Number of pitchers victimized*: 28 • *Total ballparks homered in*: 10 • *First HR*: 08/03/1895 off Jack Stivetts

Charlie Graham

CHARLES HENRY GRAHAM
B: 04/25/1878 D: 08/29/1948
BR

Year	Tm	Lg	Tot	H	A	Men-On 0	1	2	3	One-Game 2	3	4	LO	XN	IP	PH	RHP	LHP
1906	BOS	AL	1	1	0	1	0	0	0	0	0	0	0	0	1	0	1	0

Rank among batters: 4,707 • *Total ballparks homered in*: 1 • *First HR*: 05/16/1906 off Bob Rhoads

Dan Graham

DANIEL JAY GRAHAM
B: 07/19/1954
BL

Year	Tm	Lg	Tot	H	A	Men-On 0	1	2	3	One-Game 2	3	4	LO	XN	IP	PH	RHP	LHP
1980	BAL	AL	15	7	8	10	1	3	1	1	0	0	0	0	0	0	12	3
1981	BAL	AL	2	1	1	2	0	0	0	0	0	0	0	0	0	0	2	0
Total			17	8	9	12	1	3	1	1	0	0	0	0	0	0	14	3

Rank among batters: 1,969 • *Top target (2 home runs)*: Brian Kingman, Mike Torrez, Ferguson Jenkins • *Number of pitchers victimized*: 14 • *Total ballparks homered in*: 7 • *First HR*: 05/10/1980 off Lary Sorensen

Jack Graham

JOHN BERNARD GRAHAM
B: 12/24/1916
BL

Year	Tm	Lg	Tot	H	A	Men-On 0	1	2	3	One-Game 2	3	4	LO	XN	IP	PH	RHP	LHP
1946	NY	NL	14	9	5	5	5	4	0	1	0	0	0	0	1	1	10	4
1949	STL	AL	24	18	6	15	7	2	0	2	0	0	0	1	0	0	22	2
Total			38	27	11	20	12	6	0	3	0	0	0	1	1	1	32	6

Rank among batters: 1,225 • *Top target (3 home runs)*: Virgil Trucks • *Number of pitchers victimized*: 34 • *Total ballparks homered in*: 9 • *First HR*: 05/09/1946 off Preacher Roe

Oscar Graham

OSCAR M. GRAHAM
B: 07/20/1878 D: 10/15/1931
BL

Year	Tm	Lg	Tot	H	A	Men-On 0	1	2	3	One-Game 2	3	4	LO	XN	IP	PH	RHP	LHP
1907	WAS	AL	1	0	1	1	0	0	0	0	0	0	0	0	0	0	0	1

Rank among batters: 4,707 • *Total ballparks homered in*: 1 • *First HR*: 04/22/1907 off Eddie Plank

Peaches Graham

GEORGE FREDERICK GRAHAM
B: 03/23/1877 D: 07/25/1939
BR

Year	Tm	Lg	Tot	H	A	Men-On 0	1	2	3	One-Game 2	3	4	LO	XN	IP	PH	RHP	LHP
1912	PHI	NL	1	1	0	1	0	0	0	0	0	0	0	0	0	0	0	1

Rank among batters: 4,707 • *Total ballparks homered in*: 1 • *First HR*: 04/24/1912 off Rube Marquard

Skinny Graham

KYLE GRAHAM
B: 08/14/1899 D: 12/01/1973
BR

Year	Tm	Lg	Tot	H	A	Men-On 0	1	2	3	One-Game 2	3	4	LO	XN	IP	PH	RHP	LHP
1929	DET	AL	1	0	1	1	0	0	0	0	0	0	0	0	0	0	1	0

Rank among batters: 4,707 • *Total ballparks homered in*: 1 • *First HR*: 09/10/1929 off George Pipgras

Alex Grammas

ALEXANDER PETER GRAMMAS
B: 04/03/1926
BR

Year	Tm	Lg	Tot	H	A	Men-On 0	Men-On 1	Men-On 2	Men-On 3	One-Game 2	One-Game 3	One-Game 4	LO	XN	IP	PH	RHP	LHP
1954	STL	NL	2	2	0	1	1	0	0	0	0	0	0	0	0	0	0	2
1955	STL	NL	3	1	2	3	0	0	0	0	0	0	0	0	0	0	0	3
1959	STL	NL	3	1	2	3	0	0	0	0	0	0	0	0	0	0	0	3
1960	STL	NL	4	2	2	2	2	0	0	0	0	0	0	0	0	1	1	3
Total			12	6	6	9	3	0	0	0	0	0	0	0	0	1	1	11

Rank among batters: 2,325 • *Top target (2 home runs)*: Harvey Haddix • *Number of pitchers victimized*: 11 • *Total ballparks homered in*: 4 • *First HR*: 09/03/1954 off Paul Minner

Jack Graney

JOHN GLADSTONE GRANEY
B: 06/10/1886 D: 04/20/1978
BL

Year	Tm	Lg	Tot	H	A	Men-On 0	Men-On 1	Men-On 2	Men-On 3	One-Game 2	One-Game 3	One-Game 4	LO	XN	IP	PH	RHP	LHP
1910	CLE	AL	1	1	0	0	0	1	0	0	0	0	0	0	0	0	1	0
1911	CLE	AL	1	0	1	1	0	0	0	0	0	0	0	0	0	0	1	0
1913	CLE	AL	3	0	3	2	0	1	0	0	0	0	0	0	0	0	2	1
1914	CLE	AL	1	0	1	1	0	0	0	0	0	0	1	0	1	0	1	0
1915	CLE	AL	1	0	1	1	0	0	0	0	0	0	0	0	0	0	1	0
1916	CLE	AL	5	0	5	1	4	0	0	1	0	0	1	0	1	0	4	1
1917	CLE	AL	3	1	2	2	0	1	0	0	0	0	0	0	2	0	3	0
1919	CLE	AL	1	0	1	1	0	0	0	0	0	0	0	0	0	0	1	0
1921	CLE	AL	2	0	2	1	0	0	1	1	0	0	0	0	0	0	2	0
Total			18	2	16	10	4	3	1	2	0	0	2	0	4	0	16	2

Rank among batters: 1,914 • *Top target (4 home runs)*: Ray Caldwell • *Number of pitchers victimized*: 14 • *Total ballparks homered in*: 5 • *First HR*: 07/02/1910 off George Mullin

Wayne Granger

WAYNE ALLAN GRANGER
B: 03/15/1944
BR

Year	Tm	Lg	Tot	H	A	Men-On 0	Men-On 1	Men-On 2	Men-On 3	One-Game 2	One-Game 3	One-Game 4	LO	XN	IP	PH	RHP	LHP
1971	CIN	NL	1	1	0	1	0	0	0	0	0	0	0	0	0	0	0	1

Rank among batters: 4,707 • *Total ballparks homered in*: 1 • *First HR*: 07/09/1971 off Ray Sadecki

Eddie Grant

EDWARD LESLIE GRANT
B: 05/21/1883 D: 10/05/1918
BL

Year	Tm	Lg	Tot	H	A	Men-On 0	Men-On 1	Men-On 2	Men-On 3	One-Game 2	One-Game 3	One-Game 4	LO	XN	IP	PH	RHP	LHP
1909	PHI	NL	1	0	1	1	0	0	0	0	0	0	0	0	1	0	1	0
1910	PHI	NL	1	1	0	0	1	0	0	0	0	0	0	0	0	0	1	0
1911	CIN	NL	1	1	0	0	0	0	1	0	0	0	0	0	1	0	1	0
1912	CIN	NL	2	1	1	0	1	1	0	0	0	0	0	0	1	0	1	1
Total			5	3	2	1	2	1	1	0	0	0	0	0	3	0	4	1

Rank among batters: 3,191 • *Total ballparks homered in*: 5 • *First HR*: 07/29/1909 off Deacon Phillippe

Mudcat Grant

JAMES TIMOTHY GRANT
B: 08/13/1935
BR

Year	Tm	Lg	Tot	H	A	Men-On 0	Men-On 1	Men-On 2	Men-On 3	One-Game 2	One-Game 3	One-Game 4	LO	XN	IP	PH	RHP	LHP
1959	CLE	AL	1	0	1	0	0	1	0	0	0	0	0	0	0	0	1	0
1961	CLE	AL	1	0	1	1	0	0	0	0	0	0	0	0	0	0	0	1
1963	CLE	AL	1	1	0	1	0	0	0	0	0	0	0	0	0	0	1	0
1964	CLE	AL	2	1	1	1	1	0	0	0	0	0	0	0	0	0	0	2
1968	LA	NL	1	1	0	0	1	0	0	0	0	0	0	0	0	0	1	0
Total			6	3	3	3	2	1	0	0	0	0	0	0	0	0	3	3

Rank among batters: 2,988 • *Total ballparks homered in*: 4 • *First HR*: 07/04/1959 off Dave Sisler • *World Series HR*—1

Jimmy Grant

JAMES CHARLES GRANT
B: 10/06/1918 D: 07/08/1970
BL

Year	Tm	Lg	Tot	H	A	Men-On 0	Men-On 1	Men-On 2	Men-On 3	One-Game 2	One-Game 3	One-Game 4	LO	XN	IP	PH	RHP	LHP
1943	CHI	AL	4	4	0	3	1	0	0	0	0	0	0	0	1	0	4	0

Jimmy Grant *continued*

Year	Tm	Lg	Tot	H	A	Men-On 0	1	2	3	One-Game 2	3	4	LO	XN	IP	PH	RHP	LHP
1944	CLE	AL	1	1	0	1	0	0	0	0	0	0	0	0	0	0	1	0
Total			5	5	0	4	1	0	0	0	0	0	0	0	1	0	5	0

Rank among batters: 3,191 • *Total ballparks homered in*: 2 • *First HR*: 05/16/1943 off Dick Newsome

George Grantham

GEORGE FARLEY GRANTHAM
B: 05/20/1900 D: 03/16/1954
BL

Year	Tm	Lg	Tot	H	A	Men-On 0	1	2	3	One-Game 2	3	4	LO	XN	IP	PH	RHP	LHP
1923	CHI	NL	8	2	6	5	3	0	0	0	0	0	0	0	0	0	6	2
1924	CHI	NL	12	5	7	7	1	3	1	1	0	0	0	0	0	0	10	2
1925	PIT	NL	8	3	5	4	2	1	1	1	0	0	0	0	0	0	8	0
1926	PIT	NL	8	2	6	5	0	3	0	1	0	0	0	0	1	0	8	0
1927	PIT	NL	8	2	6	5	2	1	0	0	0	0	0	0	2	0	7	1
1928	PIT	NL	10	4	6	5	4	1	0	1	0	0	0	0	0	0	8	2
1929	PIT	NL	12	4	8	3	0	7	2	2	0	0	0	0	0	0	8	4
1930	PIT	NL	18	3	15	9	7	2	0	1	0	0	0	1	1	0	13	5
1931	PIT	NL	10	5	5	7	3	0	0	0	0	0	0	0	1	0	6	4
1932	CIN	NL	6	1	5	4	1	1	0	0	0	0	0	0	0	0	3	3
1933	CIN	NL	4	0	4	3	0	1	0	0	0	0	1	0	0	1	3	1
1934	NY	NL	1	1	0	1	0	0	0	0	0	0	0	0	0	1	1	0
Total			105	32	73	58	23	20	4	7	0	0	1	1	5	2	81	24

Rank among batters: 462 • *Top target (5 home runs)*: Bill Walker • *Number of pitchers victimized*: 68 • *Total ballparks homered in*: 8 • *First HR*: 05/09/1923 off Claude Jonnard

Mickey Grasso

NEWTON MICHAEL GRASSO
B: 05/10/1920 D: 10/15/1975
BR

Year	Tm	Lg	Tot	H	A	Men-On 0	1	2	3	One-Game 2	3	4	LO	XN	IP	PH	RHP	LHP
1950	WAS	AL	1	0	1	1	0	0	0	0	0	0	0	0	0	0	0	1
1951	WAS	AL	1	0	1	0	0	1	0	0	0	0	0	0	0	0	0	1
1953	WAS	AL	2	1	1	2	0	0	0	0	0	0	0	0	0	0	1	1
1954	CLE	AL	1	1	0	1	0	0	0	0	0	0	0	0	0	0	0	1
Total			5	2	3	4	0	1	0	0	0	0	0	0	0	0	1	4

Rank among batters: 3,191 • *Top target (2 home runs)*: Bobby Shantz • *Number of pitchers victimized*: 4 • *Total ballparks homered in*: 3 • *First HR*: 07/09/1950 off Alex Kellner

Dick Gray

RICHARD BENJAMIN GRAY
B: 07/11/1931
BR

Year	Tm	Lg	Tot	H	A	Men-On 0	1	2	3	One-Game 2	3	4	LO	XN	IP	PH	RHP	LHP
1958	LA	NL	9	4	5	6	3	0	0	0	0	0	0	0	0	0	8	1
1959	LA	NL	2	0	2	2	0	0	0	0	0	0	1	0	0	0	1	1
	STL	NL	1	0	1	1	0	0	0	0	0	0	0	0	0	0	1	0
	Total		3	0	3	3	0	0	0	0	0	0	1	0	0	0	2	1
Total			12	4	8	9	3	0	0	0	0	0	1	0	0	0	10	2

Rank among batters: 2,325 • *Total ballparks homered in*: 5 • *First HR*: 04/16/1958 off Ramon Monzant

Gary Gray

GARY GEORGE GRAY
B: 09/21/1952
BR

Year	Tm	Lg	Tot	H	A	Men-On 0	1	2	3	One-Game 2	3	4	LO	XN	IP	PH	RHP	LHP
1978	TEX	AL	2	2	0	1	1	0	0	0	0	0	0	0	0	1	1	1
1980	CLE	AL	2	1	1	1	1	0	0	0	0	0	0	0	0	1	1	1
1981	SEA	AL	13	9	4	5	6	2	0	3	0	0	0	0	0	2	6	7
1982	SEA	AL	7	5	2	5	1	1	0	0	0	0	0	0	0	1	3	4
Total			24	17	7	12	9	3	0	3	0	0	0	0	0	5	11	13

Rank among batters: 1,643 • *Top target (2 home runs)*: Jack Morris, John Tudor • *Number of pitchers victimized*: 22 • *Total ballparks homered in*: 9 • *First HR*: 07/23/1978 off Andy Replogle

Lorenzo Gray

LORENZO GRAY
B: 03/04/1958
BR

Year	Tm	Lg	Tot	H	A	Men-On 0	1	2	3	One-Game 2	3	4	LO	XN	IP	PH	RHP	LHP
1983	CHI	AL	1	1	0	1	0	0	0	0	0	0	0	0	0	0	1	0

Lorenzo Gray *continued*

Rank among batters: 4,707 • *Total ballparks homered in*: 1 • *First HR*: 05/24/1983 off Doug Bird

Reddy Gray

JAMES D. GRAY

Year	Tm	Lg	Tot	H	A	Men-On 0	1	2	3	One-Game 2	3	4	LO	XN	IP	PH	RHP	LHP
1890	PIT	PL	1	1	0	0	0	1	0	0	0	0	0	0	1	0	0	1

Rank among batters: 4,707 • *Total ballparks homered in*: 1 • *First HR*: 06/18/1890 off Lady Baldwin

Sam Gray

SAMUEL DAVID GRAY
B: 10/15/1897 D: 04/16/1953
BR

Year	Tm	Lg	Tot	H	A	Men-On 0	1	2	3	One-Game 2	3	4	LO	XN	IP	PH	RHP	LHP
1928	STL	AL	1	0	1	1	0	0	0	0	0	0	0	0	0	0	0	1
1931	STL	AL	1	0	1	1	0	0	0	0	0	0	0	0	0	0	0	1
Total			2	0	2	2	0	0	0	0	0	0	0	0	0	0	0	2

Rank among batters: 4,129 • *Total ballparks homered in*: 1 • *First HR*: 09/08/1928 off Earl Whitehill

Eli Grba

ELI GRBA
B: 08/09/1934
BR

Year	Tm	Lg	Tot	H	A	Men-On 0	1	2	3	One-Game 2	3	4	LO	XN	IP	PH	RHP	LHP
1960	NY	AL	1	1	0	1	0	0	0	0	0	0	0	0	0	0	1	0
1961	LA	AL	2	1	1	1	1	0	0	0	0	0	0	0	0	0	2	0
1962	LA	AL	1	0	1	1	0	0	0	0	0	0	0	0	0	0	1	0
Total			4	2	2	3	1	0	0	0	0	0	0	0	0	0	4	0

Rank among batters: 3,427 • *Total ballparks homered in*: 4 • *First HR*: 08/23/1960 off Early Wynn

Craig Grebeck

CRAIG ALLEN GREBECK
B: 12/29/1964
BR

Year	Tm	Lg	Tot	H	A	Men-On 0	1	2	3	One-Game 2	3	4	LO	XN	IP	PH	RHP	LHP
1990	CHI	AL	1	1	0	0	0	1	0	0	0	0	0	0	0	0	1	0
1991	CHI	AL	6	3	3	4	1	0	1	0	0	0	0	0	0	1	1	5
1992	CHI	AL	3	2	1	1	2	0	0	0	0	0	0	0	0	0	3	0
1993	CHI	AL	1	0	1	1	0	0	0	0	0	0	0	0	0	0	1	0
1995	CHI	AL	1	0	1	1	0	0	0	0	0	0	0	0	0	0	0	1
Total			12	6	6	7	3	1	1	0	0	0	0	0	0	1	6	6

Rank among batters: 2,325 • *Top target (2 home runs)*: Kenny Rogers, Dave Wells • *Number of pitchers victimized*: 10 • *Total ballparks homered in*: 7 • *First HR*: 08/10/1990 off Nolan Ryan

Danny Green

EDWARD GREEN
B: 11/06/1876 D: 11/09/1914
BL

Year	Tm	Lg	Tot	H	A	Men-On 0	1	2	3	One-Game 2	3	4	LO	XN	IP	PH	RHP	LHP
1898	CHI	NL	4	4	0	2	2	0	0	0	0	0	0	0	2	0	2	1
1899	CHI	NL	6	2	4	3	3	0	0	0	0	0	0	0	0	0	5	1
1900	CHI	NL	5	1	4	3	2	0	0	0	0	0	0	0	1	0	4	1
1901	CHI	NL	6	2	4	3	3	0	0	0	0	0	0	0	0	0	6	0
1903	CHI	AL	6	2	4	4	2	0	0	0	0	0	0	1	0	0	5	1
1904	CHI	AL	2	0	2	1	0	1	0	0	0	0	0	0	0	0	2	0
Total			29	11	18	16	12	1	0	0	0	0	0	1	3	0	24	4

Rank among batters: 1,465 • *Top target (3 home runs)*: Kid Nichols, Frank Kitson, Jack Powell • *Number of pitchers victimized*: 20 • *Total ballparks homered in*: 11 • *First HR*: 09/01/1898 off Kit McKenna

David Green

DAVID ALEJANDRO (CASAYA) GREEN
B: 12/04/1960
BR

Year	Tm	Lg	Tot	H	A	Men-On 0	1	2	3	One-Game 2	3	4	LO	XN	IP	PH	RHP	LHP
1982	STL	NL	2	0	2	2	0	0	0	0	0	0	0	0	0	0	0	2
1983	STL	NL	8	5	3	4	4	0	0	0	0	0	0	1	0	0	3	5
1984	STL	NL	15	5	10	8	6	1	0	1	0	0	0	0	1	0	10	5

David Green *continued*

Year	Tm	Lg	Tot	H	A	Men-On 0	1	2	3	One-Game 2	3	4	LO	XN	IP	PH	RHP	LHP
1985	SF	NL	5	3	2	4	1	0	0	0	0	0	0	1	0	0	4	1
1987	STL	NL	1	1	0	1	0	0	0	0	0	0	0	0	0	0	0	1
Total			31	14	17	19	11	1	0	1	0	0	0	2	1	0	17	14

Rank among batters: 1,400 • *Top target (2 home runs)*: Pete Falcone, Larry McWilliams • *Number of pitchers victimized*: 29 • *Total ballparks homered in*: 8 • *First HR*: 08/15/1982 off Randy Niemann

Dick Green

RICHARD LARRY GREEN
B: 04/21/1941
BR

Year	Tm	Lg	Tot	H	A	Men-On 0	1	2	3	One-Game 2	3	4	LO	XN	IP	PH	RHP	LHP
1963	KC	AL	1	0	1	0	1	0	0	0	0	0	0	0	0	0	1	0
1964	KC	AL	11	9	2	8	3	0	0	0	0	0	0	0	0	0	9	2
1965	KC	AL	15	7	8	9	3	2	1	2	0	0	0	0	0	0	10	5
1966	KC	AL	9	2	7	4	2	3	0	0	0	0	0	0	0	0	7	2
1967	KC	AL	5	1	4	2	0	2	1	0	0	0	0	0	0	0	2	3
1968	OAK	AL	6	3	3	3	1	2	0	0	0	0	0	0	0	0	5	1
1969	OAK	AL	12	4	8	6	4	2	0	0	0	0	0	0	0	0	7	5
1970	OAK	AL	4	2	2	2	0	2	0	0	0	0	0	0	0	0	2	2
1971	OAK	AL	12	7	5	7	2	2	1	1	0	0	0	0	0	0	6	6
1973	OAK	AL	3	1	2	0	1	1	1	0	0	0	0	0	0	0	1	2
1974	OAK	AL	2	2	0	1	1	0	0	0	0	0	0	0	0	0	2	0
Total			80	38	42	42	18	16	4	3	0	0	0	0	0	0	52	28

Rank among batters: 650 • *Top target (4 home runs)*: Gary Peters • *Number of pitchers victimized*: 69 • *Total ballparks homered in*: 13 • *First HR*: 09/25/1963 off Jack Lamabe

Fred Green

FRED ALLEN GREEN
B: 09/14/1933
BR

Year	Tm	Lg	Tot	H	A	Men-On 0	1	2	3	One-Game 2	3	4	LO	XN	IP	PH	RHP	LHP
1960	PIT	NL	2	2	0	2	0	0	0	0	0	0	0	0	0	0	2	0

Rank among batters: 4,129 • *Total ballparks homered in*: 1 • *First HR*: 04/21/1960 off Hank Mason

Gene Green

GENE LEROY GREEN
B: 06/26/1933 D: 05/23/1981
BR

Year	Tm	Lg	Tot	H	A	Men-On 0	1	2	3	One-Game 2	3	4	LO	XN	IP	PH	RHP	LHP
1958	STL	NL	13	8	5	7	4	1	1	0	0	0	0	0	0	0	4	9
1959	STL	NL	1	1	0	1	0	0	0	0	0	0	0	0	0	0	0	1
1961	WAS	AL	18	6	12	8	8	1	1	1	0	0	0	0	0	1	9	9
1962	CLE	AL	11	5	6	6	5	0	0	1	0	0	0	0	0	3	3	8
1963	CLE	AL	2	0	2	2	0	0	0	0	0	0	0	0	0	1	0	2
	CIN	NL	1	1	0	1	0	0	0	0	0	0	0	0	0	0	0	1
	Total		3	1	2	3	0	0	0	0	0	0	0	0	0	1	0	3
Total			46	21	25	25	17	2	2	2	0	0	0	0	0	5	16	30

Rank among batters: 1,060 • *Top target (3 home runs)*: Johnny Podres • *Number of pitchers victimized*: 39 • *Total ballparks homered in*: 15 • *First HR*: 04/26/1958 off Danny McDevitt

Lenny Green

LEONARD CHARLES GREEN
B: 01/06/1933
BL

Year	Tm	Lg	Tot	H	A	Men-On 0	1	2	3	One-Game 2	3	4	LO	XN	IP	PH	RHP	LHP
1957	BAL	AL	1	1	0	1	0	0	0	0	0	0	0	0	0	0	1	0
1959	BAL	AL	1	0	1	0	1	0	0	0	0	0	0	0	1	0	1	0
	WAS	AL	2	1	1	0	1	1	0	0	0	0	0	0	0	0	2	0
	Total		3	1	2	0	2	1	0	0	0	0	0	0	1	0	3	0
1960	WAS	AL	5	2	3	5	0	0	0	0	0	0	0	1	1	1	5	0
1961	MIN	AL	9	3	6	7	2	0	0	1	0	0	1	0	0	0	6	3
1962	MIN	AL	14	8	6	6	7	1	0	0	0	0	1	0	0	0	14	0
1963	MIN	AL	4	2	2	3	1	0	0	0	0	0	1	0	0	1	4	0
1964	LA	AL	2	0	2	2	0	0	0	0	0	0	0	0	0	0	2	0
1965	BOS	AL	7	1	6	7	0	0	0	2	0	0	1	0	0	0	6	1

Lenny Green *continued*

Year	Tm	Lg	Tot	H	A	Men-On 0	1	2	3	One-Game 2	3	4	LO	XN	IP	PH	RHP	LHP
1966	BOS	AL	1	0	1	1	0	0	0	0	0	0	0	0	0	1	1	0
1967	DET	AL	1	1	0	1	0	0	0	0	0	0	0	0	0	0	1	0
Total			47	19	28	33	12	2	0	3	0	0	4	1	2	3	43	4

Rank among batters: 1,040 • Top target (2 home runs): Jim Donohue, Jim Perry, Joe McClain, Turk Lown, Gordon Jones, Ike Delock, Ralph Terry • *Number of pitchers victimized*: 40 • *Total ballparks homered in*: 12 • *First HR*: 09/18/1957 off Jim Wilson

Pumpsie Green

ELIJAH JERRY GREEN
B: 10/27/1933
BB

Year	Tm	Lg	Tot	H	A	Men-On 0	1	2	3	One-Game 2	3	4	LO	XN	IP	PH	RHP	LHP
1959	BOS	AL	1	1	0	1	0	0	0	0	0	0	0	0	0	0	1	0
1960	BOS	AL	3	2	1	1	1	0	1	0	0	0	1	0	1	1	3	0
1961	BOS	AL	6	2	4	5	1	0	0	1	0	0	0	1	0	1	3	3
1962	BOS	AL	2	1	1	1	1	0	0	0	0	0	0	0	0	0	2	0
1963	NY	NL	1	1	0	0	1	0	0	0	0	0	0	0	0	0	1	0
Total			13	7	6	8	4	0	1	1	0	0	1	1	1	2	10	3

Rank among batters: 2,248 • *Top target (2 home runs)*: Eli Grba • *Number of pitchers victimized*: 12 • *Total ballparks homered in*: 6 • *First HR*: 09/07/1959 off Bob Turley

Shawn Green

SHAWN DAVID GREEN
B: 11/10/1972
BL

Year	Tm	Lg	Tot	H	A	Men-On 0	1	2	3	One-Game 2	3	4	LO	XN	IP	PH	RHP	LHP
1995	TOR	AL	15	5	10	9	4	2	0	0	0	0	0	0	0	0	15	0

Rank among batters: 2,096 • *Total ballparks homered in*: 8 • *First HR*: 05/14/1995 off Cal Eldred

Tyler Green

TYLER SCOTT GREEN
B: 02/18/1970
BR

Year	Tm	Lg	Tot	H	A	Men-On 0	1	2	3	One-Game 2	3	4	LO	XN	IP	PH	RHP	LHP
1995	PHI	NL	1	1	0	0	0	1	0	0	0	0	0	0	0	0	0	1

Rank among batters: 4,707 • *Total ballparks homered in*: 1 • *First HR*: 08/23/1995 off Glenn Dishman

Hank Greenberg

HENRY BENJAMIN GREENBERG
B: 01/01/1911 D: 09/04/1986
BR HOF

Year	Tm	Lg	Tot	H	A	Men-On 0	1	2	3	One-Game 2	3	4	LO	XN	IP	PH	RHP	LHP
1933	DET	AL	12	9	3	1	10	1	0	1	0	0	0	0	0	0	9	3
1934	DET	AL	26	15	11	11	11	4	0	2	0	0	0	0	1	0	19	7
1935	DET	AL	36	18	18	16	16	2	2	4	0	0	0	1	0	0	24	12
1936	DET	AL	1	0	1	0	1	0	0	0	0	0	0	0	0	0	1	0
1937	DET	AL	40	25	15	15	13	10	2	5	0	0	0	1	0	0	30	10
1938	DET	AL	58	39	19	34	11	11	2	11	0	0	0	0	1	0	49	9
1939	DET	AL	33	16	17	16	11	5	1	3	0	0	0	2	0	0	29	4
1940	DET	AL	41	27	14	19	17	3	2	1	0	0	0	0	0	0	28	13
1941	DET	AL	2	2	0	1	1	0	0	1	0	0	0	0	0	0	2	0
1945	DET	AL	13	7	6	6	4	2	1	0	0	0	0	0	0	0	11	2
1946	DET	AL	44	29	15	25	11	8	0	4	0	0	0	0	0	0	34	10
1947	PIT	NL	25	18	7	16	3	5	1	3	0	0	0	0	0	0	22	3
Total			331	205	126	160	109	51	11	35	0	0	0	4	2	0	258	73

Rank among batters: 53 • *Top target (9 home runs)*: Lefty Grove • *Number of pitchers victimized*: 156 • *Total ballparks homered in*: 12 • *First HR*: 05/06/1933 off Earl Whitehill • *World Series HR*—5

Al Greene

ALTAR ALFONSE GREENE
B: 11/09/1954
BL

Year	Tm	Lg	Tot	H	A	Men-On 0	1	2	3	One-Game 2	3	4	LO	XN	IP	PH	RHP	LHP
1979	DET	AL	3	2	1	2	1	0	0	0	0	0	0	0	0	1	3	0

Rank among batters: 3,735 • *Total ballparks homered in*: 2 • *First HR*: 07/25/1979 off Jim Slaton

Tommy Greene

IRA THOMAS GREENE
B: 04/06/1967
BR

Year	Tm	Lg	Tot	H	A	Men-On 0	Men-On 1	Men-On 2	Men-On 3	One-Game 2	One-Game 3	One-Game 4	LO	XN	IP	PH	RHP	LHP
1991	PHI	NL	2	2	0	2	0	0	0	0	0	0	0	0	0	0	0	2
1993	PHI	NL	2	0	2	0	2	0	0	0	0	0	0	0	0	0	0	2
Total			4	2	2	2	2	0	0	0	0	0	0	0	0	0	0	4

Rank among batters: 3,427 • *Total ballparks homered in*: 3 • *First HR*: 06/17/1991 off Steve Avery

Willie Greene

WILLIE LOUIS GREENE
B: 09/23/1971
BL

Year	Tm	Lg	Tot	H	A	Men-On 0	Men-On 1	Men-On 2	Men-On 3	One-Game 2	One-Game 3	One-Game 4	LO	XN	IP	PH	RHP	LHP
1992	CIN	NL	2	2	0	1	1	0	0	0	0	0	0	0	0	0	2	0
1993	CIN	NL	2	2	0	2	0	0	0	0	0	0	0	0	0	0	1	1
Total			4	4	0	3	1	0	0	0	0	0	0	0	0	0	3	1

Rank among batters: 3,427 • *Total ballparks homered in*: 1 • *First HR*: 10/01/1992 off Kevin Gross

Jim Greengrass

JAMES RAYMOND GREENGRASS
B: 10/24/1927
BR

Year	Tm	Lg	Tot	H	A	Men-On 0	Men-On 1	Men-On 2	Men-On 3	One-Game 2	One-Game 3	One-Game 4	LO	XN	IP	PH	RHP	LHP
1952	CIN	NL	5	0	5	0	2	2	1	0	0	0	0	0	0	0	5	0
1953	CIN	NL	20	14	6	8	6	6	0	0	0	0	0	0	0	0	10	10
1954	CIN	NL	27	17	10	12	8	6	1	2	0	0	0	0	0	0	16	11
1955	PHI	NL	12	9	3	10	2	0	0	0	0	0	0	0	0	0	7	5
1956	PHI	NL	5	3	2	4	0	1	0	0	0	0	0	0	0	0	4	1
Total			69	43	26	34	18	15	2	2	0	0	0	0	0	0	42	27

Rank among batters: 756 • *Top target (4 home runs)*: Warren Hacker • *Number of pitchers victimized*: 50 • *Total ballparks homered in*: 8 • *First HR*: 09/14/1952 off Johnny Rutherford

Mike Greenwell

MICHAEL LEWIS GREENWELL
B: 07/18/1963
BL

Year	Tm	Lg	Tot	H	A	Men-On 0	Men-On 1	Men-On 2	Men-On 3	One-Game 2	One-Game 3	One-Game 4	LO	XN	IP	PH	RHP	LHP
1985	BOS	AL	4	1	3	2	2	0	0	0	0	0	0	2	0	0	2	2
1987	BOS	AL	19	8	11	9	6	4	0	0	0	0	0	0	0	1	18	1
1988	BOS	AL	22	12	10	7	8	6	1	2	0	0	0	0	0	0	18	4
1989	BOS	AL	14	6	8	10	4	0	0	1	0	0	0	0	1	1	12	2
1990	BOS	AL	14	6	8	9	4	0	1	1	0	0	0	0	1	0	11	3
1991	BOS	AL	9	5	4	5	3	1	0	0	0	0	0	0	0	0	5	4
1992	BOS	AL	2	0	2	0	2	0	0	0	0	0	0	0	0	0	2	0
1993	BOS	AL	13	6	7	4	7	2	0	0	0	0	0	0	0	0	8	5
1994	BOS	AL	11	10	1	6	4	1	0	0	0	0	0	0	0	0	6	5
1995	BOS	AL	15	6	9	9	4	2	0	1	0	0	0	0	0	0	10	5
Total			123	60	63	61	44	16	2	5	0	0	0	2	2	2	92	31

Rank among batters: 372 • *Top target (4 home runs)*: Jose Bautista • *Number of pitchers victimized*: 98 • *Total ballparks homered in*: 17 • *First HR*: 09/25/1985 off John Cerutti • *Hit for Cycle*—vs BAL: 09/14/1988 • *LCS HR*—1

Bill Greenwood

WILLIAM F. GREENWOOD
B: 1857 D: 05/02/1902
BB

Year	Tm	Lg	Tot	H	A	Men-On 0	Men-On 1	Men-On 2	Men-On 3	One-Game 2	One-Game 3	One-Game 4	LO	XN	IP	PH	RHP	LHP
1884	BRO	AA	3	2	1	1	2	0	0	0	0	0	0	0	0	0	2	0
1889	COL	AA	3	0	3	0	3	0	0	0	0	0	0	0	0	0	3	0
1890	ROC	AA	2	0	2	1	0	1	0	0	0	0	0	0	0	0	2	0
Total			8	2	6	2	5	1	0	0	0	0	0	0	0	0	7	0

Rank among batters: 2,703 • *Top target (2 home runs)*: Jack Stivetts • *Number of pitchers victimized*: 7 • *Total ballparks homered in*: 4 • *First HR*: 05/14/1884 off Bob Emslie

Ed Greer

EDWARD C. GREER
B: 1865 D: 02/04/1890
BR

Year	Tm	Lg	Tot	H	A	Men-On 0	Men-On 1	Men-On 2	Men-On 3	One-Game 2	One-Game 3	One-Game 4	LO	XN	IP	PH	RHP	LHP
1886	PHI	AA	1	1	0	1	0	0	0	0	0	0	0	0	1	0	0	1
1887	BRO	AA	2	1	1	0	1	1	0	0	0	0	0	0	0	0	1	1
Total			3	2	1	1	1	1	0	0	0	0	0	0	1	0	1	2

Ed Greer *continued*

Rank among batters: 3,735 • *Total ballparks homered in*: 2 • *First HR*: 08/25/1886 off Matt Kilroy

Rusty Greer

THURMAN CLYDE GREER
B: 01/21/1969
BL

Year	Tm	Lg	Tot	H	A	Men-On 0	Men-On 1	Men-On 2	Men-On 3	One-Game 2	One-Game 3	One-Game 4	LO	XN	IP	PH	RHP	LHP
1994	TEX	AL	10	3	7	5	4	1	0	1	0	0	0	0	1	0	7	3
1995	TEX	AL	13	7	6	5	4	3	1	0	0	0	0	1	0	2	11	2
Total			23	10	13	10	8	4	1	1	0	0	0	1	1	2	18	5

Rank among batters: 1,686 • *Top target (2 home runs)*: Pat Hentgen • *Number of pitchers victimized*: 22 • *Total ballparks homered in*: 10 • *First HR*: 05/16/1994 off Carlos Reyes • *Hit HR in first major league AB*—@OAK: 05/16/1994

Hal Gregg

HAROLD DANA GREGG
B: 07/11/1921 D: 05/13/1991
BR

Year	Tm	Lg	Tot	H	A	Men-On 0	Men-On 1	Men-On 2	Men-On 3	One-Game 2	One-Game 3	One-Game 4	LO	XN	IP	PH	RHP	LHP
1945	BRO	NL	1	0	1	1	0	0	0	0	0	0	0	0	0	0	1	0
1948	PIT	NL	1	1	0	1	0	0	0	0	0	0	0	0	0	0	0	1
Total			2	1	1	2	0	0	0	0	0	0	0	0	0	0	1	1

Rank among batters: 4,129 • *Total ballparks homered in*: 2 • *First HR*: 06/17/1945 off Mort Cooper

Tommy Gregg

WILLIAM THOMAS GREGG
B: 07/29/1963
BL

Year	Tm	Lg	Tot	H	A	Men-On 0	Men-On 1	Men-On 2	Men-On 3	One-Game 2	One-Game 3	One-Game 4	LO	XN	IP	PH	RHP	LHP
1988	PIT	NL	1	0	1	1	0	0	0	0	0	0	0	0	0	0	1	0
1989	ATL	NL	6	2	4	3	3	0	0	0	0	0	0	0	0	2	6	0
1990	ATL	NL	5	2	3	2	0	3	0	0	0	0	0	0	0	4	5	0
1991	ATL	NL	1	1	0	0	1	0	0	0	0	0	0	0	0	0	1	0
1992	ATL	NL	1	1	0	1	0	0	0	0	0	0	0	1	0	0	1	0
1995	FLO	NL	6	2	4	4	1	0	1	0	0	0	0	0	0	0	6	0
Total			20	8	12	11	5	3	1	0	0	0	0	1	0	6	20	0

Rank among batters: 1,810 • *Total ballparks homered in*: 12 • *First HR*: 07/05/1988 off Jimmy Jones

Ed Gremminger

LORENZO EDWARD GREMMINGER
B: 03/30/1874 D: 05/26/1942
BR

Year	Tm	Lg	Tot	H	A	Men-On 0	Men-On 1	Men-On 2	Men-On 3	One-Game 2	One-Game 3	One-Game 4	LO	XN	IP	PH	RHP	LHP
1902	BOS	NL	1	1	0	1	0	0	0	0	0	0	0	0	0	0	1	0
1903	BOS	NL	5	2	3	3	2	0	0	0	0	0	0	0	0	0	4	1
1904	DET	AL	1	1	0	1	0	0	0	0	0	0	0	0	0	0	1	0
Total			7	4	3	5	2	0	0	0	0	0	0	0	0	0	6	1

Rank among batters: 2,834 • *Total ballparks homered in*: 4 • *First HR*: 06/03/1902 off Ed Murphy

Buddy Gremp

LEWIS EDWARD GREMP
B: 08/05/1919
BR

Year	Tm	Lg	Tot	H	A	Men-On 0	Men-On 1	Men-On 2	Men-On 3	One-Game 2	One-Game 3	One-Game 4	LO	XN	IP	PH	RHP	LHP
1942	BOS	NL	3	1	2	2	1	0	0	0	0	0	0	1	0	0	3	0

Rank among batters: 3,735 • *Total ballparks homered in*: 2 • *First HR*: 04/30/1942 off Claude Passeau

Bill Grey

WILLIAM TOBIN GREY
B: 04/05/1871 D: 12/08/1932

Year	Tm	Lg	Tot	H	A	Men-On 0	Men-On 1	Men-On 2	Men-On 3	One-Game 2	One-Game 3	One-Game 4	LO	XN	IP	PH	RHP	LHP
1895	CIN	NL	1	1	0	0	0	1	0	0	0	0	0	0	0	0	1	0

Rank among batters: 4,707 • *Total ballparks homered in*: 1 • *First HR*: 08/18/1895 off Nig Cuppy

Bobby Grich

ROBERT ANTHONY GRICH
B: 01/15/1949
BR

Year	Tm	Lg	Tot	H	A	Men-On 0	Men-On 1	Men-On 2	Men-On 3	One-Game 2	One-Game 3	One-Game 4	LO	XN	IP	PH	RHP	LHP
1971	BAL	AL	1	0	1	0	0	1	0	0	0	0	0	0	0	0	1	0

Bobby Grich *continued*

Year	Tm	Lg	Tot	H	A	Men-On				One-Game			LO	XN	IP	PH	RHP	LHP
						0	1	2	3	2	3	4						
1972	BAL	AL	12	6	6	8	2	1	1	0	0	0	0	1	0	0	9	3
1973	BAL	AL	12	7	5	8	3	0	1	2	0	0	0	0	0	0	6	6
1974	BAL	AL	19	11	8	12	5	2	0	0	1	0	0	0	0	0	13	6
1975	BAL	AL	13	5	8	9	2	2	0	1	0	0	0	0	0	0	7	6
1976	BAL	AL	13	8	5	6	6	1	0	0	0	0	0	2	0	0	12	1
1977	CAL	AL	7	4	3	5	2	0	0	0	0	0	0	1	0	0	4	3
1978	CAL	AL	6	4	2	4	1	1	0	0	0	0	1	0	0	0	3	3
1979	CAL	AL	30	15	15	15	9	6	0	4	0	0	0	0	0	0	23	7
1980	CAL	AL	14	5	9	7	5	1	1	1	0	0	0	1	0	0	12	2
1981	CAL	AL	22	7	15	15	4	3	0	3	0	0	0	2	0	0	17	5
1982	CAL	AL	19	8	11	11	6	2	0	0	0	0	0	0	0	0	12	7
1983	CAL	AL	16	8	8	8	5	2	1	1	0	0	0	0	0	0	9	7
1984	CAL	AL	18	9	9	11	6	1	0	0	0	0	0	0	0	0	11	7
1985	CAL	AL	13	7	6	9	2	1	1	0	0	0	0	0	0	0	8	5
1986	CAL	AL	9	5	4	7	0	2	0	0	0	0	1	0	0	1	3	6
Total			224	109	115	135	58	26	5	12	1	0	2	7	0	1	150	74

Rank among batters: 146 • *Top target (4 home runs)*: Luis Tiant, Tom Underwood • *Number of pitchers victimized*: 164 • *Total ballparks homered in*: 15 • *First HR*: 09/22/1971 off Stan Bahnsen • *LCS HR—3*

Tom Grieve

THOMAS ALAN GRIEVE
B: 03/04/1948
BR

Year	Tm	Lg	Tot	H	A	Men-On 0	Men-On 1	Men-On 2	Men-On 3	One-Game 2	One-Game 3	One-Game 4	LO	XN	IP	PH	RHP	LHP
1970	WAS	AL	3	2	1	1	2	0	0	0	0	0	0	0	0	0	0	3
1972	TEX	AL	3	3	0	3	0	0	0	0	0	0	0	1	0	0	3	0
1973	TEX	AL	7	5	2	3	2	2	0	0	0	0	0	0	0	0	1	6
1974	TEX	AL	9	1	8	6	3	0	0	1	0	0	0	0	0	0	4	5
1975	TEX	AL	14	5	9	7	6	1	0	0	0	0	0	1	0	0	5	9
1976	TEX	AL	20	11	9	10	10	0	0	1	0	0	0	1	0	0	15	5
1977	TEX	AL	7	4	3	4	2	0	1	0	0	0	0	0	0	0	4	3
1978	NY	NL	2	0	2	2	0	0	0	0	0	0	0	0	0	0	0	2
Total			65	31	34	36	25	3	1	2	0	0	0	3	0	0	32	33

Rank among batters: 799 • *Top target (3 home runs)*: Ross Grimsley • *Number of pitchers victimized*: 58 • *Total ballparks homered in*: 15 • *First HR*: 07/09/1970 off Rick Austin

Ken Griffey

GEORGE KENNETH GRIFFEY, SR.
B: 04/10/1950
BL

Year	Tm	Lg	Tot	H	A	Men-On 0	Men-On 1	Men-On 2	Men-On 3	One-Game 2	One-Game 3	One-Game 4	LO	XN	IP	PH	RHP	LHP
1973	CIN	NL	3	2	1	0	2	1	0	0	0	0	0	0	0	0	3	0
1974	CIN	NL	2	2	0	1	1	0	0	0	0	0	0	0	1	0	2	0
1975	CIN	NL	4	1	3	3	1	0	0	0	0	0	0	1	0	0	4	0
1976	CIN	NL	6	2	4	2	3	0	1	0	0	0	0	0	0	0	5	1
1977	CIN	NL	12	4	8	4	6	2	0	0	0	0	0	0	0	0	9	3
1978	CIN	NL	10	7	3	2	6	2	0	1	0	0	0	0	0	0	7	3
1979	CIN	NL	8	3	5	7	1	0	0	0	0	0	1	0	0	0	7	1
1980	CIN	NL	13	9	4	5	5	3	0	0	0	0	0	0	0	0	11	2
1981	CIN	NL	2	0	2	1	1	0	0	0	0	0	0	0	1	0	2	0
1982	NY	AL	12	8	4	7	4	1	0	0	0	0	0	0	0	0	9	3
1983	NY	AL	11	8	3	6	3	1	1	2	0	0	0	0	0	0	6	5
1984	NY	AL	7	5	2	3	1	3	0	0	0	0	0	0	0	0	6	1
1985	NY	AL	10	6	4	4	2	3	1	1	0	0	0	0	0	1	8	2
1986	NY	AL	9	5	4	8	1	0	0	0	0	0	0	0	0	2	9	0
	ATL	NL	12	9	3	9	2	0	1	0	1	0	0	0	0	0	9	3
	Total		21	14	7	17	3	0	1	0	1	0	0	0	0	2	18	3
1987	ATL	NL	14	8	6	13	0	1	0	0	0	0	0	0	0	0	12	2
1988	ATL	NL	2	2	0	1	1	0	0	0	0	0	0	0	0	0	1	1
	CIN	NL	2	1	1	1	1	0	0	0	0	0	0	0	0	0	2	0
	Total		4	3	1	2	2	0	0	0	0	0	0	0	0	0	3	1
1989	CIN	NL	8	2	6	4	2	2	0	1	0	0	0	0	0	1	8	0
1990	CIN	NL	1	1	0	1	0	0	0	0	0	0	0	0	0	0	1	0
	SEA	AL	3	1	2	1	1	1	0	0	0	0	0	0	0	0	3	0
	Total		4	2	2	2	1	1	0	0	0	0	0	0	0	0	4	0
1991	SEA	AL	1	1	0	1	0	0	0	0	0	0	0	0	0	0	1	0
Total			152	87	65	84	44	20	4	5	1	0	1	1	2	4	125	27

Ken Griffey *continued*

Rank among batters: 284 • *Top target (6 home runs)*: Don Sutton • *Number of pitchers victimized*: 116 • *Total ballparks homered in*: 23 • *First HR*: 09/09/1973 off Roric Harrison • *All-Star HR*—1

Ken Griffey

GEORGE KENNETH GRIFFEY, JR.
B: 11/21/1969
BL

Year	Tm	Lg	Tot	H	A	Men-On 0	Men-On 1	Men-On 2	Men-On 3	One-Game 2	One-Game 3	One-Game 4	LO	XN	IP	PH	RHP	LHP
1989	SEA	AL	16	10	6	12	3	1	0	2	0	0	0	0	1	1	14	2
1990	SEA	AL	22	8	14	13	6	3	0	1	0	0	0	0	1	1	17	5
1991	SEA	AL	22	16	6	11	7	1	3	0	0	0	0	1	0	0	17	5
1992	SEA	AL	27	16	11	10	12	4	1	2	0	0	0	0	0	0	15	12
1993	SEA	AL	45	21	24	29	13	2	1	5	0	0	0	0	0	0	33	12
1994	SEA	AL	40	18	22	23	10	5	2	4	0	0	0	2	0	0	24	16
1995	SEA	AL	17	13	4	11	4	1	1	0	0	0	0	0	0	0	14	3
Total			189	102	87	109	55	17	8	14	0	0	0	3	2	2	134	55

Rank among batters: 204 • *Top target (5 home runs)*: Dave Stewart, Tom Gordon • *Number of pitchers victimized*: 131 • *Total ballparks homered in*: 16 • *First HR*: 04/10/1989 off Eric King • *LCS HR*—6; *All-Star HR*—1

Alfredo Griffin

ALFREDO CLAUDINO GRIFFIN
B: 10/06/1957
BB

Year	Tm	Lg	Tot	H	A	Men-On 0	Men-On 1	Men-On 2	Men-On 3	One-Game 2	One-Game 3	One-Game 4	LO	XN	IP	PH	RHP	LHP
1979	TOR	AL	2	2	0	1	1	0	0	0	0	0	1	0	1	0	2	0
1980	TOR	AL	2	1	1	2	0	0	0	0	0	0	0	0	0	0	1	1
1982	TOR	AL	1	0	1	1	0	0	0	0	0	0	0	0	0	0	1	0
1983	TOR	AL	4	2	2	2	1	1	0	0	0	0	0	0	0	0	3	1
1984	TOR	AL	4	1	3	3	1	0	0	0	0	0	0	0	0	0	3	1
1985	OAK	AL	2	0	2	0	1	1	0	0	0	0	0	0	0	0	1	1
1986	OAK	AL	4	1	3	3	1	0	0	0	0	0	0	0	0	0	4	0
1987	OAK	AL	3	2	1	0	3	0	0	0	0	0	0	0	0	0	2	1
1988	LA	NL	1	0	1	1	0	0	0	0	0	0	0	0	0	0	1	0
1990	LA	NL	1	0	1	1	0	0	0	0	0	0	0	0	0	0	0	1
Total			24	9	15	14	8	2	0	0	0	0	1	0	1	0	18	6

Rank among batters: 1,643 • *Top target (2 home runs)*: Rick Langford, Bert Blyleven • *Number of pitchers victimized*: 22 • *Total ballparks homered in*: 13 • *First HR*: 08/28/1979 off Rick Langford

Doug Griffin

DOUGLAS LEE GRIFFIN
B: 06/04/1947
BR

Year	Tm	Lg	Tot	H	A	Men-On 0	Men-On 1	Men-On 2	Men-On 3	One-Game 2	One-Game 3	One-Game 4	LO	XN	IP	PH	RHP	LHP
1971	BOS	AL	3	3	0	2	1	0	0	0	0	0	0	0	0	0	1	2
1972	BOS	AL	2	2	0	2	0	0	0	0	0	0	0	0	0	0	1	1
1973	BOS	AL	1	0	1	1	0	0	0	0	0	0	0	0	0	0	0	1
1975	BOS	AL	1	0	1	1	0	0	0	0	0	0	0	0	0	0	1	0
Total			7	5	2	6	1	0	0	0	0	0	0	0	0	0	3	4

Rank among batters: 2,834 • *Total ballparks homered in*: 3 • *First HR*: 06/28/1971 off Jackie Brown

Mike Griffin

MICHAEL JOSEPH GRIFFIN
B: 03/20/1865 D: 04/10/1908
BL

Year	Tm	Lg	Tot	H	A	Men-On 0	Men-On 1	Men-On 2	Men-On 3	One-Game 2	One-Game 3	One-Game 4	LO	XN	IP	PH	RHP	LHP
1887	BAL	AA	3	2	1	0	2	1	0	0	0	0	0	0	1	0	3	0
1889	BAL	AA	4	1	3	1	3	0	0	0	0	0	1	0	0	0	4	0
1890	PHI	PL	6	3	3	3	3	0	0	0	0	0	2	0	3	0	5	1
1891	BRO	NL	3	3	0	2	1	0	0	0	0	0	0	0	0	0	3	0
1892	BRO	NL	3	3	0	0	3	0	0	0	0	0	0	0	1	0	3	0
1893	BRO	NL	6	2	4	2	2	2	0	0	0	0	1	0	0	0	4	2
1894	BRO	NL	5	3	2	1	2	2	0	0	0	0	0	0	1	0	4	1
1895	BRO	NL	4	1	3	1	3	0	0	0	0	0	1	0	0	0	2	2
1896	BRO	NL	4	0	4	4	0	0	0	0	0	0	0	0	0	0	3	1
1897	BRO	NL	2	1	1	2	0	0	0	0	0	0	2	0	0	0	1	1
1898	BRO	NL	2	1	1	2	0	0	0	0	0	0	1	0	1	0	2	0
Total			42	20	22	18	19	5	0	0	0	0	8	0	7	0	34	8

Rank among batters: 1,138 • Top target (3 home runs): Amos Rusie, Jack Stivetts, Kid Nichols, Ted Breitenstein • *Number of pitchers victimized*: 33 • *Total ballparks homered in*: 18 • *First HR*: 04/16/1887 off Ed Seward • *Hit HR in first major league AB*—vs PHI: 04/16/1887

Pug Griffin

FRANCIS ARTHUR GRIFFIN
B: 04/24/1896 D: 10/12/1951
BR

Year	Tm	Lg	Tot	H	A	Men-On 0	1	2	3	One-Game 2	3	4	LO	XN	IP	PH	RHP	LHP
1917	PHI	AL	1	1	0	1	0	0	0	0	0	0	0	0	0	0	1	0

Rank among batters: 4,707 • *Total ballparks homered in*: 1 • *First HR*: 09/12/1917 off Ray Caldwell

Sandy Griffin

TOBIAS CHARLES GRIFFIN
B: 07/19/1858 D: 06/05/1926
BR

Year	Tm	Lg	Tot	H	A	Men-On 0	1	2	3	One-Game 2	3	4	LO	XN	IP	PH	RHP	LHP
1890	ROC	AA	5	2	3	3	1	1	0	0	0	0	1	0	0	0	5	0

Rank among batters: 3,191 • *Total ballparks homered in*: 3 • *First HR*: 06/09/1890 off Sadie McMahon

Tom Griffin

THOMAS JAMES GRIFFIN
B: 02/22/1948
BR

Year	Tm	Lg	Tot	H	A	Men-On 0	1	2	3	One-Game 2	3	4	LO	XN	IP	PH	RHP	LHP
1969	HOU	NL	2	0	2	1	1	0	0	0	0	0	0	0	1	0	2	0
1972	HOU	NL	1	0	1	1	0	0	0	0	0	0	0	0	0	0	1	0
1973	HOU	NL	1	1	0	1	0	0	0	0	0	0	0	0	0	0	0	1
1974	HOU	NL	2	2	0	1	1	0	0	0	0	0	0	0	0	0	2	0
1977	SD	NL	2	0	2	2	0	0	0	0	0	0	0	0	0	0	0	2
1980	SF	NL	1	0	1	1	0	0	0	0	0	0	0	0	0	0	0	1
1981	SF	NL	1	0	1	1	0	0	0	0	0	0	0	0	0	0	0	1
Total			10	3	7	8	2	0	0	0	0	0	0	0	1	0	5	5

Rank among batters: 2,500 • *Total ballparks homered in*: 6 • *First HR*: 05/30/1969 off Bob Moose

Bert Griffith

BARTHOLOMEW JOSEPH GRIFFITH
B: 03/30/1896 D: 05/05/1973
BR

Year	Tm	Lg	Tot	H	A	Men-On 0	1	2	3	One-Game 2	3	4	LO	XN	IP	PH	RHP	LHP
1922	BRO	NL	2	1	1	2	0	0	0	0	0	0	0	0	0	0	1	1
1923	BRO	NL	2	1	1	2	0	0	0	0	0	0	0	0	0	0	1	1
Total			4	2	2	4	0	0	0	0	0	0	0	0	0	0	2	2

Rank among batters: 3,427 • *Top target (2 home runs)*: Bill Sherdel • *Number of pitchers victimized*: 3 • *Total ballparks homered in*: 2 • *First HR*: 07/08/1922 off Bill Sherdel

Clark Griffith

CLARK CALVIN GRIFFITH
B: 11/20/1869 D: 10/27/1955
BR HOF

Year	Tm	Lg	Tot	H	A	Men-On 0	1	2	3	One-Game 2	3	4	LO	XN	IP	PH	RHP	LHP
1891	STL	AA	1	1	0	0	0	0	1	0	0	0	0	0	0	0	1	0
	BOS	AA	1	1	0	0	1	0	0	0	0	0	0	0	0	0	0	1
	Total		2	2	0	0	1	0	1	0	0	0	0	0	0	0	1	1
1895	CHI	NL	1	1	0	0	1	0	0	0	0	0	0	0	0	0	1	0
1896	CHI	NL	1	1	0	0	1	0	0	0	0	0	0	0	0	0	0	1
1900	CHI	NL	1	1	0	1	0	0	0	0	0	0	0	0	0	0	0	1
1901	CHI	AL	2	0	2	0	2	0	0	0	0	0	0	0	0	0	1	1
1903	NY	AL	1	1	0	0	1	0	0	0	0	0	0	0	0	0	1	0
Total			8	6	2	1	6	0	1	0	0	0	0	0	0	0	4	4

Rank among batters: 2,703 • *Total ballparks homered in*: 5 • *First HR*: 06/27/1891 off John Dolan

Derrell Griffith

ROBERT DERRELL GRIFFITH
B: 12/12/1943
BL

Year	Tm	Lg	Tot	H	A	Men-On 0	1	2	3	One-Game 2	3	4	LO	XN	IP	PH	RHP	LHP
1964	LA	NL	4	1	3	3	0	1	0	0	0	0	0	0	0	0	2	2
1965	LA	NL	1	0	1	1	0	0	0	0	0	0	0	0	0	0	1	0
Total			5	1	4	4	0	1	0	0	0	0	0	0	0	0	3	2

Rank among batters: 3,191 • *Total ballparks homered in*: 5 • *First HR*: 06/17/1964 off Denny Lemaster

Tommy Griffith

THOMAS HERMAN GRIFFITH
B: 10/26/1889 D: 04/13/1967
BL

Year	Tm	Lg	Tot	H	A	Men-On 0	Men-On 1	Men-On 2	Men-On 3	One-Game 2	One-Game 3	One-Game 4	LO	XN	IP	PH	RHP	LHP
1913	BOS	NL	1	1	0	0	1	0	0	0	0	0	0	0	0	0	1	0
1915	CIN	NL	4	2	2	2	1	1	0	0	0	0	0	0	2	0	4	0
1916	CIN	NL	2	2	0	1	1	0	0	0	0	0	0	0	2	0	2	0
1917	CIN	NL	1	0	1	1	0	0	0	0	0	0	0	0	0	0	1	0
1918	CIN	NL	2	1	1	0	2	0	0	0	0	0	0	0	2	0	2	0
1919	BRO	NL	6	4	2	1	4	0	1	0	0	0	0	0	3	0	6	0
1920	BRO	NL	2	2	0	1	0	1	0	0	0	0	0	0	0	0	2	0
1921	BRO	NL	12	8	4	10	1	1	0	0	0	0	0	0	0	0	12	0
1922	BRO	NL	4	3	1	1	1	2	0	0	0	0	0	0	0	0	4	0
1923	BRO	NL	8	3	5	2	4	2	0	0	0	0	0	0	0	0	8	0
1924	BRO	NL	3	1	2	2	1	0	0	0	0	0	0	0	1	0	3	0
1925	CHI	NL	7	2	5	4	2	1	0	0	0	0	0	0	0	1	6	1
Total			52	29	23	25	18	8	1	0	0	0	0	0	10	1	51	1

Rank among batters: 965 • *Top target (3 home runs)*: Jess Barnes, Jeff Pfeffer • *Number of pitchers victimized*: 41 • *Total ballparks homered in*: 10 • *First HR*: 08/23/1913 off Pol Perritt

Art Griggs

ARTHUR CARLE GRIGGS
B: 12/10/1883 D: 12/19/1938
BR

Year	Tm	Lg	Tot	H	A	Men-On 0	Men-On 1	Men-On 2	Men-On 3	One-Game 2	One-Game 3	One-Game 4	LO	XN	IP	PH	RHP	LHP
1910	STL	AL	2	1	1	2	0	0	0	0	0	0	0	0	0	0	1	1
1911	CLE	AL	1	1	0	1	0	0	0	0	0	0	0	0	0	0	0	1
1914	BRO	FL	1	1	0	0	0	1	0	0	0	0	0	0	0	0	1	0
1915	BRO	FL	1	1	0	1	0	0	0	0	0	0	0	0	0	0	1	0
Total			5	4	1	4	0	1	0	0	0	0	0	0	0	0	3	2

Rank among batters: 3,191 • *Total ballparks homered in*: 4 • *First HR*: 08/14/1910 off Charles Hall

Denver Grigsby

DENVER CLARENCE GRIGSBY
B: 03/25/1901 D: 11/10/1973
BL

Year	Tm	Lg	Tot	H	A	Men-On 0	Men-On 1	Men-On 2	Men-On 3	One-Game 2	One-Game 3	One-Game 4	LO	XN	IP	PH	RHP	LHP
1924	CHI	NL	3	2	1	3	0	0	0	0	0	0	0	0	0	0	3	0

Rank among batters: 3,735 • *Total ballparks homered in*: 2 • *First HR*: 06/25/1924 off Lee Meadows

Bob Grim

ROBERT ANTON GRIM
B: 03/08/1930
BR

Year	Tm	Lg	Tot	H	A	Men-On 0	Men-On 1	Men-On 2	Men-On 3	One-Game 2	One-Game 3	One-Game 4	LO	XN	IP	PH	RHP	LHP
1954	NY	AL	1	0	1	0	1	0	0	0	0	0	0	0	0	0	0	1
1957	NY	AL	1	1	0	0	0	1	0	0	0	0	0	0	0	0	1	0
1959	KC	AL	1	0	1	0	0	0	1	0	0	0	0	0	0	0	1	0
Total			3	1	2	0	1	1	1	0	0	0	0	0	0	0	2	1

Rank among batters: 3,735 • *Total ballparks homered in*: 2 • *First HR*: 06/18/1954 off Morrie Martin

John Grim

JOHN HELM GRIM
B: 08/09/1867 D: 07/28/1961
BR

Year	Tm	Lg	Tot	H	A	Men-On 0	Men-On 1	Men-On 2	Men-On 3	One-Game 2	One-Game 3	One-Game 4	LO	XN	IP	PH	RHP	LHP
1890	ROC	AA	2	0	2	1	1	0	0	0	0	0	0	0	0	0	2	0
1891	MIL	AA	1	1	0	0	1	0	0	0	0	0	0	0	0	0	1	0
1892	LOU	NL	1	1	0	0	1	0	0	0	0	0	0	0	0	0	1	0
1893	LOU	NL	3	0	3	1	2	0	0	0	0	0	0	0	0	0	2	0
1894	LOU	NL	7	2	5	3	4	0	0	1	0	0	0	0	0	0	5	0
1896	BRO	NL	2	0	2	1	0	1	0	0	0	0	0	0	0	0	2	0
Total			16	4	12	6	9	1	0	1	0	0	0	0	0	0	13	0

Rank among batters: 2,029 • *Top target (3 home runs)*: Kid Carsey • *Number of pitchers victimized*: 12 • *Total ballparks homered in*: 10 • *First HR*: 08/07/1890 off Fred Smith

Burleigh Grimes

BURLEIGH ARLAND GRIMES
B: 08/18/1893 D: 12/06/1985
BR HOF

Year	Tm	Lg	Tot	H	A	Men-On 0	Men-On 1	Men-On 2	Men-On 3	One-Game 2	One-Game 3	One-Game 4	LO	XN	IP	PH	RHP	LHP
1921	BRO	NL	1	0	1	1	0	0	0	0	0	0	0	0	0	0	0	1

Burleigh Grimes *continued*

Year	Tm	Lg	Tot	H	A	Men-On 0	Men-On 1	Men-On 2	Men-On 3	One-Game 2	One-Game 3	One-Game 4	LO	XN	IP	PH	RHP	LHP
1925	BRO	NL	1	0	1	1	0	0	0	0	0	0	0	0	0	0	1	0
Total			2	0	2	2	0	0	0	0	0	0	0	0	0	0	1	1

Rank among batters: 4,129 • *Total ballparks homered in*: 2 • *First HR*: 07/06/1921 off Rube Benton

Oscar Grimes

OSCAR RAY, JR. GRIMES
B: 04/13/1915 D: 05/19/1993
BR

Year	Tm	Lg	Tot	H	A	Men-On 0	Men-On 1	Men-On 2	Men-On 3	One-Game 2	One-Game 3	One-Game 4	LO	XN	IP	PH	RHP	LHP
1939	CLE	AL	4	2	2	2	0	2	0	0	0	0	0	1	0	0	3	1
1941	CLE	AL	4	1	3	3	1	0	0	0	0	0	0	0	0	0	4	0
1944	NY	AL	5	2	3	3	0	2	0	0	0	0	0	0	0	0	3	2
1945	NY	AL	4	2	2	2	1	1	0	0	0	0	0	0	0	0	4	0
1946	PHI	AL	1	1	0	0	1	0	0	0	0	0	0	0	0	0	1	0
Total			18	8	10	10	3	5	0	0	0	0	0	1	0	0	15	3

Rank among batters: 1,914 • *Top target (2 home runs)*: Vern Kennedy, Rex Cecil • *Number of pitchers victimized*: 16 • *Total ballparks homered in*: 8 • *First HR*: 09/03/1939 off Vern Kennedy

Ray Grimes

OSCAR RAY, SR. GRIMES
B: 09/11/1893 D: 05/25/1953
BR

Year	Tm	Lg	Tot	H	A	Men-On 0	Men-On 1	Men-On 2	Men-On 3	One-Game 2	One-Game 3	One-Game 4	LO	XN	IP	PH	RHP	LHP
1921	CHI	NL	6	4	2	5	1	0	0	0	0	0	0	0	0	0	4	2
1922	CHI	NL	14	9	5	10	2	2	0	0	0	0	0	1	1	0	13	1
1923	CHI	NL	2	2	0	1	1	0	0	0	0	0	0	0	0	0	1	1
1924	CHI	NL	5	4	1	3	2	0	0	0	0	0	0	0	0	0	4	1
Total			27	19	8	19	6	2	0	0	0	0	0	1	1	0	22	5

Rank among batters: 1,532 • *Top target (2 home runs)*: Burleigh Grimes, Sherry Smith, Huck Betts • *Number of pitchers victimized*: 24 • *Total ballparks homered in*: 5 • *First HR*: 05/13/1921 off Bill Hubbell

Charlie Grimm

CHARLES JOHN GRIMM
B: 08/28/1898 D: 11/15/1983
BL

Year	Tm	Lg	Tot	H	A	Men-On 0	Men-On 1	Men-On 2	Men-On 3	One-Game 2	One-Game 3	One-Game 4	LO	XN	IP	PH	RHP	LHP
1920	PIT	NL	2	0	2	2	0	0	0	0	0	0	0	0	0	0	2	0
1921	PIT	NL	7	2	5	3	2	2	0	0	0	0	0	0	2	0	7	0
1923	PIT	NL	7	1	6	2	5	0	0	0	0	0	0	0	0	0	5	2
1924	PIT	NL	2	1	1	1	1	0	0	0	0	0	0	0	1	0	2	0
1925	CHI	NL	10	7	3	8	2	0	0	1	0	0	0	0	0	0	9	1
1926	CHI	NL	8	5	3	5	3	0	0	0	0	0	0	0	0	0	6	2
1927	CHI	NL	2	2	0	0	1	1	0	0	0	0	0	0	0	0	2	0
1928	CHI	NL	5	1	4	4	1	0	0	0	0	0	0	0	0	0	4	1
1929	CHI	NL	10	5	5	5	3	0	2	1	0	0	0	0	0	0	7	3
1930	CHI	NL	6	4	2	3	1	1	1	0	0	0	0	0	0	0	4	2
1931	CHI	NL	4	3	1	4	0	0	0	0	0	0	0	0	0	0	4	0
1932	CHI	NL	7	6	1	3	4	0	0	0	0	0	0	0	0	0	7	0
1933	CHI	NL	3	2	1	3	0	0	0	0	0	0	0	0	0	0	3	0
1934	CHI	NL	5	2	3	1	1	3	0	0	0	0	0	0	0	0	3	2
1936	CHI	NL	1	0	1	1	0	0	0	0	0	0	0	0	0	1	1	0
Total			79	41	38	45	24	7	3	2	0	0	0	0	3	1	66	13

Rank among batters: 661 • *Top target (4 home runs)*: Grover Alexander, Dolf Luque • *Number of pitchers victimized*: 58 • *Total ballparks homered in*: 7 • *First HR*: 06/29/1920 off Claude Hendrix • *World Series HR*—1

Moose Grimshaw

MYRON FREDERICK GRIMSHAW
B: 11/30/1875 D: 12/11/1936
BB

Year	Tm	Lg	Tot	H	A	Men-On 0	Men-On 1	Men-On 2	Men-On 3	One-Game 2	One-Game 3	One-Game 4	LO	XN	IP	PH	RHP	LHP
1905	BOS	AL	4	3	1	0	3	1	0	0	0	0	0	0	1	0	2	2

Rank among batters: 3,427 • *Total ballparks homered in*: 2 • *First HR*: 05/06/1905 off Clark Griffith

Marquis Grissom

MARQUIS DEON GRISSOM
B: 04/17/1967
BR

Year	Tm	Lg	Tot	H	A	Men-On 0	Men-On 1	Men-On 2	Men-On 3	One-Game 2	One-Game 3	One-Game 4	LO	XN	IP	PH	RHP	LHP
1989	MON	NL	1	0	1	1	0	0	0	0	0	0	0	0	0	0	1	0

Year	Tm	Lg	Tot	H	A	Men-On 0	Men-On 1	Men-On 2	Men-On 3	One-Game 2	One-Game 3	One-Game 4	LO	XN	IP	PH	RHP	LHP

Marquis Grissom *continued*

Year	Tm	Lg	Tot	H	A	Men-On 0	Men-On 1	Men-On 2	Men-On 3	One-Game 2	One-Game 3	One-Game 4	LO	XN	IP	PH	RHP	LHP
1990	MON	NL	3	2	1	2	0	1	0	0	0	0	0	1	0	0	1	2
1991	MON	NL	6	3	3	3	0	2	1	0	0	0	0	1	0	0	3	3
1992	MON	NL	14	8	6	10	4	0	0	0	0	0	1	0	0	0	8	6
1993	MON	NL	19	9	10	11	5	3	0	0	0	0	1	0	0	0	12	7
1994	MON	NL	11	4	7	9	2	0	0	0	0	0	1	1	1	0	7	4
1995	ATL	NL	12	5	7	8	3	1	0	0	0	0	2	0	0	0	8	4
Total			66	31	35	44	14	7	1	0	0	0	5	3	1	0	40	26

Rank among batters: 786 • *Top target (5 home runs)*: Greg Swindell • *Number of pitchers victimized*: 55 • *Total ballparks homered in*: 15 • *First HR*: 09/11/1989 off Greg Maddux • *LCS HR*—3; *All-Star HR*—1

Dick Groat

RICHARD MORROW GROAT
B: 11/04/1930
BR

Year	Tm	Lg	Tot	H	A	Men-On 0	Men-On 1	Men-On 2	Men-On 3	One-Game 2	One-Game 3	One-Game 4	LO	XN	IP	PH	RHP	LHP
1952	PIT	NL	1	0	1	1	0	0	0	0	0	0	0	0	0	0	1	0
1955	PIT	NL	4	1	3	3	1	0	0	0	0	0	0	0	0	0	3	1
1957	PIT	NL	7	0	7	6	1	0	0	0	0	0	0	0	0	0	7	0
1958	PIT	NL	3	0	3	3	0	0	0	0	0	0	0	0	0	0	2	1
1959	PIT	NL	5	0	5	3	0	1	1	0	0	0	0	0	0	0	5	0
1960	PIT	NL	2	1	1	2	0	0	0	0	0	0	0	0	1	0	1	1
1961	PIT	NL	6	2	4	5	1	0	0	0	0	0	0	0	0	0	4	2
1962	PIT	NL	2	1	1	1	1	0	0	0	0	0	0	0	0	0	1	1
1963	STL	NL	6	4	2	5	1	0	0	0	0	0	0	0	0	0	4	2
1964	STL	NL	1	0	1	1	0	0	0	0	0	0	0	0	0	0	0	1
1966	PHI	NL	2	1	1	1	1	0	0	0	0	0	0	0	0	0	2	0
Total			39	10	29	31	6	1	1	0	0	0	0	0	1	0	30	9

Rank among batters: 1,204 • Top target (2 home runs): Ruben Gomez, Jack Sanford, Jim Hearn, Robin Roberts, Lew Burdette, Jim Owens • *Number of pitchers victimized*: 33 • *Total ballparks homered in*: 11 • *First HR*: 08/01/1952 off Jim Hearn

Heinie Groh

HENRY KNIGHT GROH
B: 09/18/1889 D: 08/22/1968
BR

Year	Tm	Lg	Tot	H	A	Men-On 0	Men-On 1	Men-On 2	Men-On 3	One-Game 2	One-Game 3	One-Game 4	LO	XN	IP	PH	RHP	LHP
1913	CIN	NL	3	2	1	0	3	0	0	0	0	0	0	0	2	0	2	1
1914	CIN	NL	2	1	1	1	0	1	0	0	0	0	0	0	1	0	1	1
1915	CIN	NL	3	0	3	0	2	1	0	0	0	0	0	0	3	0	2	1
1916	CIN	NL	2	0	2	2	0	0	0	0	0	0	2	0	1	0	2	0
1917	CIN	NL	1	1	0	1	0	0	0	0	0	0	0	0	1	0	1	0
1918	CIN	NL	1	0	1	1	0	0	0	0	0	0	0	0	0	0	0	1
1919	CIN	NL	5	1	4	1	4	0	0	0	0	0	0	1	3	0	2	3
1922	NY	NL	3	2	1	1	1	1	0	0	0	0	0	0	2	0	2	1
1923	NY	NL	4	2	2	2	2	0	0	0	0	0	0	0	1	0	3	1
1924	NY	NL	2	2	0	1	1	0	0	0	0	0	0	0	0	0	1	1
Total			26	11	15	10	13	3	0	0	0	0	2	1	14	0	16	10

Rank among batters: 1,576 • *Top target (2 home runs)*: Art Nehf • *Number of pitchers victimized*: 25 • *Total ballparks homered in*: 9 • *First HR*: 07/28/1913 off Frank Allen • *Hit for Cycle*—@CHI: 07/05/1915 (2)

Emil Gross

EMIL MICHAEL GROSS
B: 03/04/1858 D: 08/24/1921
BR

Year	Tm	Lg	Tot	H	A	Men-On 0	Men-On 1	Men-On 2	Men-On 3	One-Game 2	One-Game 3	One-Game 4	LO	XN	IP	PH	RHP	LHP
1880	PRO	NL	1	0	1	0	1	0	0	0	0	0	0	0	0	0	1	0
1881	PRO	NL	1	0	1	0	1	0	0	0	0	0	0	0	0	0	1	0
1883	PHI	NL	1	0	1	0	1	0	0	0	0	0	0	0	0	0	1	0
1884	CHI	UA	4	0	4	2	1	1	0	0	0	0	0	0	0	0	3	0
Total			7	0	7	2	4	1	0	0	0	0	0	0	0	0	6	0

Rank among batters: 2,834 • *Total ballparks homered in*: 6 • *First HR*: 09/01/1880 off Stump Wiedman

Greg Gross

GREGORY EUGENE GROSS
B: 08/01/1952
BL

Year	Tm	Lg	Tot	H	A	Men-On 0	Men-On 1	Men-On 2	Men-On 3	One-Game 2	One-Game 3	One-Game 4	LO	XN	IP	PH	RHP	LHP
1977	CHI	NL	5	3	2	2	2	1	0	0	0	0	0	0	0	0	4	1

Year	Tm	Lg	Tot	H	A	Men-On 0	1	2	3	One-Game 2	3	4	LO	XN	IP	PH	RHP	LHP

Greg Gross *continued*

Year	Tm	Lg	Tot	H	A	0	1	2	3	2	3	4	LO	XN	IP	PH	RHP	LHP
1978	CHI	NL	1	0	1	0	0	1	0	0	0	0	0	0	0	0	1	0
1987	PHI	NL	1	0	1	0	1	0	0	0	0	0	0	0	0	0	1	0
Total			7	3	4	2	3	2	0	0	0	0	0	0	0	0	6	1

Rank among batters: 2,834 • *Total ballparks homered in*: 3 • *First HR*: 07/06/1977 off Don Stanhouse

Kevin Gross

KEVIN FRANK GROSS
B: 06/08/1961
BR

Year	Tm	Lg	Tot	H	A	0	1	2	3	2	3	4	LO	XN	IP	PH	RHP	LHP
1985	PHI	NL	1	1	0	0	1	0	0	0	0	0	0	0	0	0	1	0
1986	PHI	NL	1	1	0	0	0	1	0	0	0	0	0	0	0	0	1	0
1987	PHI	NL	1	0	1	1	0	0	0	0	0	0	0	0	0	0	0	1
1990	MON	NL	1	0	1	1	0	0	0	0	0	0	0	0	0	0	0	1
1993	LA	NL	1	0	1	0	1	0	0	0	0	0	0	0	0	0	1	0
1994	LA	NL	1	1	0	0	0	1	0	0	0	0	0	0	0	0	1	0
Total			6	3	3	2	2	2	0	0	0	0	0	0	0	0	4	2

Rank among batters: 2,988 • *Total ballparks homered in*: 4 • *First HR*: 08/25/1985 off Jim Gott

Wayne Gross

WAYNE DALE GROSS
B: 01/14/1952
BL

Year	Tm	Lg	Tot	H	A	0	1	2	3	2	3	4	LO	XN	IP	PH	RHP	LHP
1977	OAK	AL	22	12	10	12	9	1	0	2	0	0	0	0	0	0	17	5
1978	OAK	AL	7	4	3	5	2	0	0	0	0	0	0	0	0	0	6	1
1979	OAK	AL	14	3	11	8	3	2	1	1	0	0	0	0	0	1	12	2
1980	OAK	AL	14	3	11	8	2	4	0	2	0	0	0	0	0	1	14	0
1981	OAK	AL	10	3	7	7	2	1	0	0	0	0	0	0	0	1	10	0
1982	OAK	AL	9	3	6	5	3	1	0	0	0	0	0	0	0	0	9	0
1983	OAK	AL	12	4	8	9	3	0	0	1	0	0	0	1	0	0	11	1
1984	BAL	AL	22	12	10	12	7	1	2	1	0	0	0	0	0	0	22	0
1985	BAL	AL	11	9	2	9	0	2	0	2	0	0	0	0	0	1	10	1
Total			121	53	68	75	31	12	3	9	0	0	0	1	0	4	111	10

Rank among batters: 382 • *Top target (4 home runs)*: Lamarr Hoyt • *Number of pitchers victimized*: 94 • *Total ballparks homered in*: 15 • *First HR*: 04/10/1977 off Pete Redfern • *LCS HR—1*

Jerry Grote

GERALD WAYNE GROTE
B: 10/06/1942
BR

Year	Tm	Lg	Tot	H	A	0	1	2	3	2	3	4	LO	XN	IP	PH	RHP	LHP
1964	HOU	NL	3	1	2	2	1	0	0	0	0	0	0	1	0	0	3	0
1966	NY	NL	3	1	2	1	1	1	0	0	0	0	0	0	0	0	3	0
1967	NY	NL	4	3	1	1	3	0	0	0	0	0	0	0	0	0	2	2
1968	NY	NL	3	1	2	2	1	0	0	0	0	0	0	0	0	0	1	2
1969	NY	NL	6	4	2	3	2	1	0	0	0	0	0	1	0	0	5	1
1970	NY	NL	2	1	1	1	1	0	0	0	0	0	0	0	0	0	2	0
1971	NY	NL	2	1	1	2	0	0	0	0	0	0	0	1	0	0	2	0
1972	NY	NL	3	0	3	2	0	1	0	1	0	0	0	0	0	0	1	2
1973	NY	NL	1	0	1	0	0	0	1	0	0	0	0	0	0	0	1	0
1974	NY	NL	5	3	2	2	2	1	0	0	0	0	0	0	0	0	2	3
1975	NY	NL	2	1	1	1	1	0	0	0	0	0	0	0	0	1	1	1
1976	NY	NL	4	1	3	3	1	0	0	0	0	0	0	0	0	0	3	1
1981	KC	AL	1	1	0	0	0	0	1	0	0	0	0	0	0	0	1	0
Total			39	18	21	20	13	4	2	1	0	0	0	3	0	1	27	12

Rank among batters: 1,204 • *Top target (2 home runs)*: Bob Buhl, Don Sutton • *Number of pitchers victimized*: 37 • *Total ballparks homered in*: 11 • *First HR*: 06/26/1964 off Lew Burdette

Jeff Grotewold

JEFFREY SCOTT GROTEWOLD
B: 12/08/1965
BL

Year	Tm	Lg	Tot	H	A	0	1	2	3	2	3	4	LO	XN	IP	PH	RHP	LHP
1992	PHI	NL	3	0	3	2	1	0	0	0	0	0	0	0	0	3	2	1
1995	KC	AL	1	0	1	0	0	1	0	0	0	0	0	0	0	0	1	0
Total			4	0	4	2	1	1	0	0	0	0	0	0	0	3	3	1

Jeff Grotewold *continued*

Rank among batters: 3,427 • *Total ballparks homered in*: 2 • *First HR*: 07/06/1992 off Bud Black

Johnny Groth

JOHN THOMAS GROTH
B: 07/23/1926
BR

Year	Tm	Lg	Tot	H	A	Men-On 0	Men-On 1	Men-On 2	Men-On 3	One-Game 2	One-Game 3	One-Game 4	LO	XN	IP	PH	RHP	LHP
1948	DET	AL	1	1	0	0	1	0	0	0	0	0	0	0	0	0	1	0
1949	DET	AL	11	9	2	3	3	3	2	2	0	0	0	0	1	0	9	2
1950	DET	AL	12	5	7	5	5	1	1	0	0	0	0	0	0	0	8	4
1951	DET	AL	3	1	2	2	1	0	0	0	0	0	0	0	0	0	2	1
1952	DET	AL	4	3	1	2	1	1	0	0	0	0	1	0	0	0	3	1
1953	STL	AL	10	3	7	7	2	1	0	0	0	0	3	0	0	0	5	5
1954	CHI	AL	7	2	5	3	3	1	0	0	0	0	0	0	0	0	3	4
1955	CHI	AL	2	0	2	1	1	0	0	1	0	0	0	0	0	0	2	0
	WAS	AL	2	2	0	2	0	0	0	0	0	0	0	0	0	0	2	0
	Total		4	2	2	3	1	0	0	1	0	0	0	0	0	0	4	0
1956	KC	AL	5	1	4	2	3	0	0	1	0	0	0	1	0	0	3	2
1958	DET	AL	2	0	2	1	1	0	0	0	0	0	0	0	0	0	2	0
1959	DET	AL	1	1	0	0	1	0	0	0	0	0	0	0	0	1	0	1
Total			60	28	32	28	22	7	3	4	0	0	4	1	1	1	40	20

Rank among batters: 863 • *Top target (3 home runs)*: Early Wynn, Alex Kellner, Marion Fricano • *Number of pitchers victimized*: 45 • *Total ballparks homered in*: 10 • *First HR*: 09/28/1948 off Fred Sanford

Lefty Grove

ROBERT MOSES GROVE
B: 03/06/1900 D: 05/22/1975
BL HOF

Year	Tm	Lg	Tot	H	A	Men-On 0	Men-On 1	Men-On 2	Men-On 3	One-Game 2	One-Game 3	One-Game 4	LO	XN	IP	PH	RHP	LHP
1927	PHI	AL	2	2	0	2	0	0	0	0	0	0	0	0	0	0	2	0
1928	PHI	AL	1	0	1	1	0	0	0	0	0	0	0	0	0	0	1	0
1929	PHI	AL	1	1	0	0	0	1	0	0	0	0	0	0	0	0	1	0
1930	PHI	AL	2	2	0	1	0	1	0	0	0	0	0	0	0	0	2	0
1932	PHI	AL	4	2	2	2	1	1	0	0	0	0	0	1	0	0	3	1
1933	PHI	AL	1	1	0	1	0	0	0	0	0	0	0	0	0	0	1	0
1934	BOS	AL	1	0	1	0	0	1	0	0	0	0	0	0	0	0	1	0
1935	BOS	AL	1	0	1	0	0	0	1	0	0	0	0	0	0	0	1	0
1939	BOS	AL	1	1	0	1	0	0	0	0	0	0	0	0	0	0	1	0
1940	BOS	AL	1	0	1	1	0	0	0	0	0	0	0	0	0	0	1	0
Total			15	9	6	9	1	4	1	0	0	0	0	1	0	0	14	1

Rank among batters: 2,096 • *Top target (2 home runs)*: Dick Coffman, George Blaeholder • *Number of pitchers victimized*: 13 • *Total ballparks homered in*: 6 • *First HR*: 07/30/1927 off Sarge Connally

Orval Grove

ORVAL LEROY GROVE
B: 08/29/1919 D: 04/20/1992
BR

Year	Tm	Lg	Tot	H	A	Men-On 0	Men-On 1	Men-On 2	Men-On 3	One-Game 2	One-Game 3	One-Game 4	LO	XN	IP	PH	RHP	LHP
1942	CHI	AL	1	0	1	1	0	0	0	0	0	0	0	0	0	0	1	0

Rank among batters: 4,707 • *Total ballparks homered in*: 1 • *First HR*: 05/02/1942 off Roger Wolff

John Grubb

JOHN RAYMOND GRUBB
B: 08/04/1948
BL

Year	Tm	Lg	Tot	H	A	Men-On 0	Men-On 1	Men-On 2	Men-On 3	One-Game 2	One-Game 3	One-Game 4	LO	XN	IP	PH	RHP	LHP
1973	SD	NL	8	6	2	6	1	1	0	0	0	0	0	0	0	0	8	0
1974	SD	NL	8	3	5	5	1	2	0	0	0	0	0	0	0	0	5	3
1975	SD	NL	4	1	3	2	2	0	0	0	0	0	0	1	0	0	3	1
1976	SD	NL	5	2	3	3	2	0	0	1	0	0	2	0	0	0	5	0
1977	CLE	AL	2	1	1	1	0	0	1	0	0	0	0	0	0	0	1	1
1978	CLE	AL	14	6	8	7	5	2	0	0	0	0	0	0	0	0	12	2
	TEX	AL	1	1	0	1	0	0	0	0	0	0	0	0	0	1	1	0
	Total		15	7	8	8	5	2	0	0	0	0	0	0	0	1	13	2
1979	TEX	AL	10	4	6	5	5	0	0	0	0	0	1	0	0	0	10	0
1980	TEX	AL	9	6	3	4	4	1	0	0	0	0	0	0	0	1	9	0
1981	TEX	AL	3	1	2	2	1	0	0	0	0	0	0	0	0	0	3	0
1982	TEX	AL	3	2	1	2	1	0	0	0	0	0	0	0	0	0	2	1

John Grubb *continued*

Year	Tm	Lg	Tot	H	A	Men-On 0	Men-On 1	Men-On 2	Men-On 3	One-Game 2	One-Game 3	One-Game 4	LO	XN	IP	PH	RHP	LHP
1983	DET	AL	4	3	1	3	1	0	0	0	0	0	0	0	0	1	4	0
1984	DET	AL	8	1	7	8	0	0	0	1	0	0	0	0	0	3	8	0
1985	DET	AL	5	4	1	2	1	2	0	0	0	0	0	0	0	1	5	0
1986	DET	AL	13	8	5	9	1	2	1	1	0	0	0	0	0	1	13	0
1987	DET	AL	2	2	0	2	0	0	0	0	0	0	0	0	0	1	2	0
Total			99	51	48	62	25	10	2	3	0	0	3	1	0	9	91	8

Rank among batters: 503 • *Top target (5 home runs)*: Dennis Leonard • *Number of pitchers victimized*: 80 • *Total ballparks homered in*: 23 • *First HR*: 05/06/1973 off Bob Moose

Frank Grube

FRANKLIN THOMAS GRUBE
B: 01/07/1905 D: 07/02/1945
BR

Year	Tm	Lg	Tot	H	A	Men-On 0	Men-On 1	Men-On 2	Men-On 3	One-Game 2	One-Game 3	One-Game 4	LO	XN	IP	PH	RHP	LHP
1931	CHI	AL	1	0	1	0	1	0	0	0	0	0	0	0	1	0	1	0

Rank among batters: 4,707 • *Total ballparks homered in*: 1 • *First HR*: 09/12/1931 off Ivy Andrews

Henry Gruber

HENRY JOHN GRUBER
B: 12/14/1863 D: 09/26/1932
BR

Year	Tm	Lg	Tot	H	A	Men-On 0	Men-On 1	Men-On 2	Men-On 3	One-Game 2	One-Game 3	One-Game 4	LO	XN	IP	PH	RHP	LHP
1891	CLE	NL	1	0	1	0	0	1	0	0	0	0	0	0	0	0	1	0

Rank among batters: 4,707 • *Total ballparks homered in*: 1 • *First HR*: 05/08/1891 off Ed Stein

Kelly Gruber

KELLY WAYNE GRUBER
B: 02/26/1962
BR

Year	Tm	Lg	Tot	H	A	Men-On 0	Men-On 1	Men-On 2	Men-On 3	One-Game 2	One-Game 3	One-Game 4	LO	XN	IP	PH	RHP	LHP
1984	TOR	AL	1	0	1	0	1	0	0	0	0	0	0	0	0	1	1	0
1986	TOR	AL	5	4	1	2	2	1	0	0	0	0	0	0	1	0	3	2
1987	TOR	AL	12	5	7	10	2	0	0	1	0	0	0	0	0	0	8	4
1988	TOR	AL	16	5	11	11	2	3	0	1	0	0	0	0	1	0	15	1
1989	TOR	AL	18	8	10	11	5	2	0	0	0	0	0	0	0	1	12	6
1990	TOR	AL	31	23	8	14	11	5	1	4	0	0	0	0	0	0	24	7
1991	TOR	AL	20	8	12	12	7	1	0	0	0	0	0	0	0	0	12	8
1992	TOR	AL	11	7	4	5	4	1	1	1	0	0	0	0	0	0	8	3
1993	CAL	AL	3	1	2	2	0	1	0	0	0	0	0	0	0	0	2	1
Total			117	61	56	67	34	14	2	7	0	0	0	0	2	2	85	32

Rank among batters: 402 • *Top target (3 home runs)*: Cecilio Guante, Greg Swindell • *Number of pitchers victimized*: 94 • *Total ballparks homered in*: 16 • *First HR*: 09/25/1984 off Al Nipper • *Hit for Cycle*—vs KC: 04/16/1989 • *World Series HR*—1; *LCS HR*—1

Mark Grudzielanek

MARK JAMES GRUDZIELANEK
B: 06/30/1970
BR

Year	Tm	Lg	Tot	H	A	Men-On 0	Men-On 1	Men-On 2	Men-On 3	One-Game 2	One-Game 3	One-Game 4	LO	XN	IP	PH	RHP	LHP
1995	MON	NL	1	1	0	1	0	0	0	0	0	0	0	0	0	0	1	0

Rank among batters: 4,707 • *Total ballparks homered in*: 1 • *First HR*: 05/16/1995 off Kevin Jarvis

Marv Gudat

MARVIN JOHN GUDAT
B: 08/27/1905 D: 03/01/1954
BL

Year	Tm	Lg	Tot	H	A	Men-On 0	Men-On 1	Men-On 2	Men-On 3	One-Game 2	One-Game 3	One-Game 4	LO	XN	IP	PH	RHP	LHP
1932	CHI	NL	1	0	1	0	0	1	0	0	0	0	0	0	0	1	1	0

Rank among batters: 4,707 • *Total ballparks homered in*: 1 • *First HR*: 06/20/1932 off Ed Holley

Mike Guerra

FERMIN (ROMERO) GUERRA
B: 10/11/1912 D: 10/09/1992
BR

Year	Tm	Lg	Tot	H	A	Men-On 0	Men-On 1	Men-On 2	Men-On 3	One-Game 2	One-Game 3	One-Game 4	LO	XN	IP	PH	RHP	LHP
1944	WAS	AL	1	1	0	0	1	0	0	0	0	0	0	0	0	0	1	0
1945	WAS	AL	1	0	1	0	1	0	0	0	0	0	0	0	0	0	1	0
1948	PHI	AL	1	0	1	1	0	0	0	0	0	0	0	0	0	0	1	0

Mike Guerra *continued*

Year	Tm	Lg	Tot	H	A	Men-On 0	1	2	3	One-Game 2	3	4	LO	XN	IP	PH	RHP	LHP
1949	PHI	AL	3	2	1	2	1	0	0	0	0	0	0	0	0	0	2	1
1950	PHI	AL	2	2	0	0	0	2	0	0	0	0	0	0	0	0	2	0
1951	WAS	AL	1	0	1	0	0	1	0	0	0	0	0	0	0	0	1	0
Total			9	5	4	3	3	3	0	0	0	0	0	0	0	0	8	1

Rank among batters: 2,587 • *Total ballparks homered in*: 5 • *First HR*: 05/15/1944 off Mel Harder

Juan Guerrero

JUAN ANTONIO (DE LA CRUZ) GUERRERO
B: 02/01/1967
BR

Year	Tm	Lg	Tot	H	A	Men-On 0	1	2	3	One-Game 2	3	4	LO	XN	IP	PH	RHP	LHP
1992	HOU	NL	1	1	0	1	0	0	0	0	0	0	0	1	0	0	1	0

Rank among batters: 4,707 • *Total ballparks homered in*: 1 • *First HR*: 07/21/1992 off Roger Mason

Mario Guerrero

MARIO MIGUEL (ABUD) GUERRERO
B: 09/28/1949
BR

Year	Tm	Lg	Tot	H	A	Men-On 0	1	2	3	One-Game 2	3	4	LO	XN	IP	PH	RHP	LHP
1976	CAL	AL	1	0	1	1	0	0	0	0	0	0	0	0	0	0	1	0
1977	CAL	AL	1	0	1	1	0	0	0	0	0	0	0	0	0	0	1	0
1978	OAK	AL	3	1	2	0	2	1	0	0	0	0	0	0	0	0	1	2
1980	OAK	AL	2	1	1	2	0	0	0	0	0	0	0	0	0	0	1	1
Total			7	2	5	4	2	1	0	0	0	0	0	0	0	0	4	3

Rank among batters: 2,834 • *Total ballparks homered in*: 6 • *First HR*: 08/19/1976 off Ray Bare

Pedro Guerrero

PEDRO GUERRERO
B: 06/29/1956
BR

Year	Tm	Lg	Tot	H	A	Men-On 0	1	2	3	One-Game 2	3	4	LO	XN	IP	PH	RHP	LHP
1979	LA	NL	2	0	2	1	1	0	0	0	0	0	0	0	0	0	0	2
1980	LA	NL	7	3	4	3	2	2	0	0	0	0	0	1	0	1	3	4
1981	LA	NL	12	5	7	7	4	1	0	1	0	0	0	0	0	0	9	3
1982	LA	NL	32	15	17	17	12	3	0	1	0	0	0	1	0	0	26	6
1983	LA	NL	32	13	19	18	11	2	1	2	0	0	0	0	0	0	25	7
1984	LA	NL	16	7	9	9	5	2	0	1	0	0	0	0	0	0	13	3
1985	LA	NL	33	13	20	21	7	4	1	1	0	0	0	1	0	0	24	9
1986	LA	NL	5	1	4	3	1	1	0	0	0	0	0	0	0	1	3	2
1987	LA	NL	27	12	15	16	7	4	0	2	0	0	0	0	0	0	20	7
1988	LA	NL	5	3	2	3	2	0	0	0	0	0	0	0	0	0	3	2
	STL	NL	5	2	3	3	1	1	0	0	0	0	0	0	0	0	4	1
	Total		10	5	5	6	3	1	0	0	0	0	0	0	0	0	7	3
1989	STL	NL	17	3	14	7	6	4	0	0	0	0	0	0	0	0	9	8
1990	STL	NL	13	8	5	7	4	1	1	1	0	0	0	0	0	0	9	4
1991	STL	NL	8	4	4	4	3	1	0	1	0	0	0	0	0	0	8	0
1992	STL	NL	1	1	0	1	0	0	0	0	0	0	0	0	0	0	0	1
Total			215	90	125	120	66	26	3	10	0	0	0	3	0	2	156	59

Rank among batters: 158 • *Top target (6 home runs)*: Eddie Whitson • *Number of pitchers victimized*: 146 • *Total ballparks homered in*: 12 • *First HR*: 09/22/1979 off Bob Owchinko • *World Series HR—2; LCS HR—2*

Ozzie Guillen

OSWALDO JOSE (BARRIOS) GUILLEN
B: 01/20/1964
BL

Year	Tm	Lg	Tot	H	A	Men-On 0	1	2	3	One-Game 2	3	4	LO	XN	IP	PH	RHP	LHP
1985	CHI	AL	1	1	0	1	0	0	0	0	0	0	0	0	0	0	1	0
1986	CHI	AL	2	1	1	2	0	0	0	0	0	0	0	0	0	0	1	1
1987	CHI	AL	2	2	0	0	2	0	0	0	0	0	0	0	0	0	2	0
1989	CHI	AL	1	0	1	1	0	0	0	0	0	0	0	0	0	0	1	0
1990	CHI	AL	1	1	0	1	0	0	0	0	0	0	0	0	0	0	1	0
1991	CHI	AL	3	1	2	0	1	1	1	0	0	0	0	0	0	0	2	1
1993	CHI	AL	4	3	1	0	4	0	0	0	0	0	0	0	0	0	4	0
1994	CHI	AL	1	0	1	0	0	1	0	0	0	0	0	0	0	0	0	1
1995	CHI	AL	1	1	0	1	0	0	0	0	0	0	0	0	0	0	1	0
Total			16	10	6	6	7	2	1	0	0	0	0	0	0	0	13	3

Rank among batters: 2,029 • *Total ballparks homered in*: 6 • *First HR*: 08/14/1985 off Eddie Whitson

Year	Tm	Lg	Tot	H	A	Men-On 0	Men-On 1	Men-On 2	Men-On 3	One-Game 2	One-Game 3	One-Game 4	LO	XN	IP	PH	RHP	LHP

Brad Gulden

BRADLEY LEE GULDEN
B: 06/10/1956
BL

Year	Tm	Lg	Tot	H	A	Men-On 0	Men-On 1	Men-On 2	Men-On 3	One-Game 2	One-Game 3	One-Game 4	LO	XN	IP	PH	RHP	LHP
1980	NY	AL	1	1	0	0	1	0	0	0	0	0	0	0	0	0	1	0
1984	CIN	NL	4	2	2	2	1	1	0	0	0	0	0	1	0	0	4	0
Total			5	3	2	2	2	1	0	0	0	0	0	1	0	0	5	0

Rank among batters: 3,191 • *Total ballparks homered in*: 4 • *First HR*: 10/04/1980 off Aurelio Lopez

Ted Gullic

THEODORE JASPER GULLIC
B: 01/02/1907
BR

Year	Tm	Lg	Tot	H	A	Men-On 0	Men-On 1	Men-On 2	Men-On 3	One-Game 2	One-Game 3	One-Game 4	LO	XN	IP	PH	RHP	LHP
1930	STL	AL	4	2	2	3	1	0	0	0	0	0	0	1	0	0	2	2
1933	STL	AL	5	1	4	3	2	0	0	0	0	0	0	0	0	1	4	1
Total			9	3	6	6	3	0	0	0	0	0	0	1	0	1	6	3

Rank among batters: 2,587 • *Top target (2 home runs)*: Frank Henry • *Number of pitchers victimized*: 8 • *Total ballparks homered in*: 5 • *First HR*: 04/15/1930 off George Uhle

Bill Gullickson

WILLIAM LEE GULLICKSON
B: 02/20/1959
BR

Year	Tm	Lg	Tot	H	A	Men-On 0	Men-On 1	Men-On 2	Men-On 3	One-Game 2	One-Game 3	One-Game 4	LO	XN	IP	PH	RHP	LHP
1983	MON	NL	1	1	0	1	0	0	0	0	0	0	0	0	0	0	1	0
1987	CIN	NL	1	0	1	1	0	0	0	0	0	0	0	0	0	0	1	0
1990	HOU	NL	1	0	1	1	0	0	0	0	0	0	0	0	0	0	1	0
Total			3	1	2	3	0	0	0	0	0	0	0	0	0	0	3	0

Rank among batters: 3,735 • *Total ballparks homered in*: 3 • *First HR*: 09/20/1983 off Bob Forsch

Glenn Gulliver

GLENN JAMES GULLIVER
B: 10/15/1954
BL

Year	Tm	Lg	Tot	H	A	Men-On 0	Men-On 1	Men-On 2	Men-On 3	One-Game 2	One-Game 3	One-Game 4	LO	XN	IP	PH	RHP	LHP
1982	BAL	AL	1	1	0	1	0	0	0	0	0	0	0	0	0	0	1	0

Rank among batters: 4,707 • *Total ballparks homered in*: 1 • *First HR*: 10/03/1982 off Don Sutton

Ad Gumbert

ADDISON COURTNEY GUMBERT
B: 10/10/1868 D: 04/23/1925
BR

Year	Tm	Lg	Tot	H	A	Men-On 0	Men-On 1	Men-On 2	Men-On 3	One-Game 2	One-Game 3	One-Game 4	LO	XN	IP	PH	RHP	LHP
1889	CHI	NL	7	4	3	2	1	3	1	0	0	0	0	1	0	0	6	1
1890	BOS	PL	3	3	0	1	1	1	0	0	0	0	0	0	0	0	3	0
1892	CHI	NL	1	1	0	1	0	0	0	0	0	0	0	0	0	0	1	0
1894	PIT	NL	1	0	1	0	0	1	0	0	0	0	0	0	0	0	1	0
1895	BRO	NL	2	2	0	1	1	0	0	0	0	0	0	0	0	0	2	0
1896	PHI	NL	1	0	1	0	1	0	0	0	0	0	0	0	0	0	1	0
Total			15	10	5	5	4	5	1	0	0	0	0	1	0	0	14	1

Rank among batters: 2,096 • *Top target (2 home runs)*: Pretzels Getzien • *Number of pitchers victimized*: 14 • *Total ballparks homered in*: 7 • *First HR*: 05/02/1889 off Bill Burdick

Billy Gumbert

WILLIAM SKEEN GUMBERT
B: 08/08/1865 D: 04/13/1946
BR

Year	Tm	Lg	Tot	H	A	Men-On 0	Men-On 1	Men-On 2	Men-On 3	One-Game 2	One-Game 3	One-Game 4	LO	XN	IP	PH	RHP	LHP
1890	PIT	NL	1	1	0	0	0	1	0	0	0	0	0	0	1	0	1	0

Rank among batters: 4,707 • *Total ballparks homered in*: 1 • *First HR*: 06/19/1890 off Jack Wadsworth • *Hit HR in first major league AB*—vs CLE: 06/19/1890 (1)

Harry Gumbert

HARRY EDWARD GUMBERT
B: 11/05/1909 D: 01/04/1995
BR

Year	Tm	Lg	Tot	H	A	Men-On 0	Men-On 1	Men-On 2	Men-On 3	One-Game 2	One-Game 3	One-Game 4	LO	XN	IP	PH	RHP	LHP
1937	NY	NL	1	1	0	1	0	0	0	0	0	0	0	0	0	0	1	0

Year	Tm	Lg	Tot	H	A	Men-On 0	Men-On 1	Men-On 2	Men-On 3	One-Game 2	One-Game 3	One-Game 4	LO	XN	IP	PH	RHP	LHP

Harry Gumbert *continued*

Year	Tm	Lg	Tot	H	A	0	1	2	3	2	3	4	LO	XN	IP	PH	RHP	LHP
1940	NY	NL	1	1	0	0	1	0	0	0	0	0	0	0	0	0	1	0
1941	STL	NL	2	2	0	0	2	0	0	0	0	0	0	0	0	0	2	0
1948	CIN	NL	1	1	0	1	0	0	0	0	0	0	0	1	0	0	1	0
Total			5	5	0	2	3	0	0	0	0	0	0	1	0	0	5	0

Rank among batters: 3,191 • *Total ballparks homered in*: 3 • *First HR*: 06/07/1937 off Joe Bowman

Tom Gunning

THOMAS FRANCIS GUNNING
B: 03/04/1862 D: 03/17/1931
BR

Year	Tm	Lg	Tot	H	A	0	1	2	3	2	3	4	LO	XN	IP	PH	RHP	LHP
1887	PHI	NL	1	0	1	0	1	0	0	0	0	0	0	0	0	0	1	0
1889	PHI	AA	1	0	1	1	0	0	0	0	0	0	0	0	0	0	1	0
Total			2	0	2	1	1	0	0	0	0	0	0	0	0	0	2	0

Rank among batters: 4,129 • *Total ballparks homered in*: 2 • *First HR*: 06/22/1887 off John Clarkson

Frankie Gustine

FRANK WILLIAM GUSTINE
B: 02/20/1920 D: 04/01/1991
BR

Year	Tm	Lg	Tot	H	A	0	1	2	3	2	3	4	LO	XN	IP	PH	RHP	LHP
1940	PIT	NL	1	1	0	0	0	1	0	0	0	0	0	0	0	0	1	0
1941	PIT	NL	1	0	1	1	0	0	0	0	0	0	0	0	0	0	1	0
1942	PIT	NL	2	1	1	0	2	0	0	0	0	0	0	0	1	0	2	0
1944	PIT	NL	2	0	2	1	1	0	0	0	0	0	0	0	0	0	2	0
1945	PIT	NL	2	0	2	2	0	0	0	0	0	0	1	0	0	0	2	0
1946	PIT	NL	8	3	5	7	1	0	0	1	0	0	0	0	0	0	4	4
1947	PIT	NL	9	6	3	6	3	0	0	0	0	0	0	0	0	0	7	2
1948	PIT	NL	9	6	3	6	3	0	0	0	0	0	0	1	0	0	7	2
1949	CHI	NL	4	1	3	3	1	0	0	0	0	0	0	0	0	0	2	2
Total			38	18	20	26	11	1	0	1	0	0	1	1	1	0	28	10

Rank among batters: 1,225 • *Top target (3 home runs)*: Larry Jansen • *Number of pitchers victimized*: 32 • *Total ballparks homered in*: 8 • *First HR*: 05/06/1940 off George Barnicle

Jackie Gutierrez

JOAQUIN FERNANDO (HERNANDEZ) GUTIERREZ
B: 06/27/1960
BR

Year	Tm	Lg	Tot	H	A	0	1	2	3	2	3	4	LO	XN	IP	PH	RHP	LHP
1984	BOS	AL	2	2	0	2	0	0	0	0	0	0	0	0	0	0	1	1
1985	BOS	AL	2	0	2	1	1	0	0	0	0	0	0	0	0	0	2	0
Total			4	2	2	3	1	0	0	0	0	0	0	0	0	0	3	1

Rank among batters: 3,427 • *Total ballparks homered in*: 3 • *First HR*: 04/22/1984 off Jeff Bettendorf

Ricky Gutierrez

RICARDO GUTIERREZ
B: 05/23/1970
BR

Year	Tm	Lg	Tot	H	A	0	1	2	3	2	3	4	LO	XN	IP	PH	RHP	LHP
1993	SD	NL	5	5	0	3	2	0	0	0	0	0	0	0	0	0	2	3
1994	SD	NL	1	1	0	1	0	0	0	0	0	0	0	0	0	0	0	1
Total			6	6	0	4	2	0	0	0	0	0	0	0	0	0	2	4

Rank among batters: 2,988 • *Total ballparks homered in*: 1 • *First HR*: 06/10/1993 off Ramon Martinez

Don Gutteridge

DONALD JOSEPH GUTTERIDGE
B: 06/19/1912
BR

Year	Tm	Lg	Tot	H	A	0	1	2	3	2	3	4	LO	XN	IP	PH	RHP	LHP
1936	STL	NL	3	0	3	0	3	0	0	1	0	0	0	0	1	0	3	0
1937	STL	NL	7	5	2	4	3	0	0	0	0	0	0	0	1	0	6	1
1938	STL	NL	9	5	4	5	1	3	0	0	0	0	1	0	1	0	7	2
1939	STL	NL	7	5	2	3	3	1	0	0	0	0	0	0	0	0	7	0
1940	STL	NL	3	3	0	2	0	1	0	0	0	0	0	0	0	0	3	0
1942	STL	AL	1	1	0	1	0	0	0	0	0	0	1	0	0	0	1	0
1943	STL	AL	1	1	0	1	0	0	0	0	0	0	1	0	0	0	1	0

Year	Tm	Lg	Tot	H	A	Men-On 0	1	2	3	One-Game 2	3	4	LO	XN	IP	PH	RHP	LHP

Don Gutteridge *continued*

Year	Tm	Lg	Tot	H	A	0	1	2	3	2	3	4	LO	XN	IP	PH	RHP	LHP
1944	STL	AL	3	2	1	2	1	0	0	0	0	0	0	1	1	0	1	2
1945	STL	AL	2	0	2	1	1	0	0	0	0	0	1	0	0	0	2	0
1946	BOS	AL	1	0	1	0	1	0	0	0	0	0	0	0	0	0	1	0
1947	BOS	AL	2	0	2	1	1	0	0	0	0	0	0	0	0	0	2	0
Total			39	22	17	20	14	5	0	1	0	0	4	1	4	0	34	5

Rank among batters: 1,204 • Top target (2 home runs): Jim Turner, Max Butcher, Ira Hutchinson, Hugh Mulcahy, Bucky Walters, Bill Lee • *Number of pitchers victimized*: 33 • *Total ballparks homered in*: 10 • *First HR*: 09/11/1936 off Max Butcher

Doug Gwosdz

DOUG WAYNE GWOSDZ
B: 06/20/1960
BR

Year	Tm	Lg	Tot	H	A	0	1	2	3	2	3	4	LO	XN	IP	PH	RHP	LHP
1983	SD	NL	1	1	0	0	0	1	0	0	0	0	0	0	0	0	1	0

Rank among batters: 4,707 • *Total ballparks homered in*: 1 • *First HR*: 08/21/1983 off Bill Gullickson

Chris Gwynn

CHRISTOPHER KARLTON GWYNN
B: 10/13/1964
BL

Year	Tm	Lg	Tot	H	A	0	1	2	3	2	3	4	LO	XN	IP	PH	RHP	LHP
1990	LA	NL	5	0	5	3	1	0	1	1	0	0	0	0	0	1	5	0
1991	LA	NL	5	3	2	2	1	2	0	0	0	0	0	0	0	2	5	0
1992	KC	AL	1	0	1	0	1	0	0	0	0	0	0	0	0	0	0	1
1993	KC	AL	1	0	1	1	0	0	0	0	0	0	0	0	0	0	1	0
1994	LA	NL	3	0	3	2	1	0	0	0	0	0	0	0	0	2	3	0
1995	LA	NL	1	1	0	0	1	0	0	0	0	0	0	0	0	1	1	0
Total			16	4	12	8	5	2	1	1	0	0	0	0	0	6	15	1

Rank among batters: 2,029 • *Top target (2 home runs)*: David Cone • *Number of pitchers victimized*: 15 • *Total ballparks homered in*: 9 • *First HR*: 06/08/1990 off Greg Harris

Tony Gwynn

ANTHONY KEITH GWYNN
B: 05/09/1960
BL

Year	Tm	Lg	Tot	H	A	0	1	2	3	2	3	4	LO	XN	IP	PH	RHP	LHP
1982	SD	NL	1	0	1	1	0	0	0	0	0	0	0	0	0	0	1	0
1983	SD	NL	1	0	1	0	0	1	0	0	0	0	0	0	0	0	1	0
1984	SD	NL	5	3	2	3	0	2	0	0	0	0	0	0	0	0	4	1
1985	SD	NL	6	3	3	3	3	0	0	0	0	0	0	1	0	0	4	2
1986	SD	NL	14	8	6	8	3	3	0	1	0	0	0	0	0	0	7	7
1987	SD	NL	7	5	2	7	0	0	0	0	0	0	0	0	0	0	4	3
1988	SD	NL	7	3	4	5	0	2	0	0	0	0	0	0	2	0	7	0
1989	SD	NL	4	3	1	3	0	1	0	0	0	0	0	0	0	0	4	0
1990	SD	NL	4	2	2	3	1	0	0	0	0	0	0	0	0	0	1	3
1991	SD	NL	4	1	3	2	2	0	0	0	0	0	0	1	0	0	2	2
1992	SD	NL	6	4	2	2	3	1	0	0	0	0	0	0	0	0	3	3
1993	SD	NL	7	4	3	4	3	0	0	0	0	0	0	0	0	0	4	3
1994	SD	NL	12	4	8	9	2	1	0	0	0	0	0	1	0	0	10	2
1995	SD	NL	9	5	4	3	4	1	1	0	0	0	0	0	1	0	7	2
Total			87	45	42	53	21	12	1	1	0	0	0	3	3	0	59	28

Rank among batters: 594 • *Top target (4 home runs)*: Tom Browning • *Number of pitchers victimized*: 74 • *Total ballparks homered in*: 13 • *First HR*: 08/22/1982 off Bill Campbell

Bert Haas

BERTHOLD JOHN HAAS
B: 02/08/1914
BR

Year	Tm	Lg	Tot	H	A	0	1	2	3	2	3	4	LO	XN	IP	PH	RHP	LHP
1942	CIN	NL	6	3	3	4	2	0	0	0	0	0	0	1	1	0	6	0
1943	CIN	NL	4	1	3	2	2	0	0	0	0	0	0	0	0	0	4	0
1946	CIN	NL	3	3	0	2	1	0	0	0	0	0	0	0	0	0	3	0
1947	CIN	NL	3	2	1	2	0	1	0	0	0	0	0	0	0	0	2	1
1948	PHI	NL	4	1	3	4	0	0	0	0	0	0	0	0	0	0	4	0
1949	NY	NL	1	1	0	0	1	0	0	0	0	0	0	0	0	0	1	0
1951	CHI	AL	1	1	0	0	1	0	0	0	0	0	0	0	0	1	0	1
Total			22	12	10	14	7	1	0	0	0	0	0	1	1	1	20	2

Year	Tm	Lg	Tot	H	A	Men-On 0	1	2	3	One-Game 2	3	4	LO	XN	IP	PH	RHP	LHP

Bert Haas *continued*

Rank among batters: 1,719 • *Top target (2 home runs)*: Si Johnson, Claude Passeau • *Number of pitchers victimized*: 20 • *Total ballparks homered in*: 6 • *First HR*: 04/25/1942 off Claude Passeau

Eddie Haas

GEORGE EDWIN HAAS
B: 05/26/1935
BL

1960	MIL	NL	1	0	1	1	0	0	0	0	0	0	0	0	0	1	1	0

Rank among batters: 4,707 • *Total ballparks homered in*: 1 • *First HR*: 07/22/1960 off Don Elston

Mule Haas

GEORGE WILLIAM HAAS
B: 10/15/1903 D: 06/30/1974
BL

1928	PHI	AL	6	2	4	4	2	0	0	1	0	0	0	1	0	0	5	1
1929	PHI	AL	16	11	5	11	4	1	0	0	0	0	0	1	2	0	11	5
1930	PHI	AL	2	2	0	1	1	0	0	0	0	0	0	0	0	0	2	0
1931	PHI	AL	8	5	3	6	1	1	0	0	0	0	0	1	0	0	4	4
1932	PHI	AL	6	5	1	2	2	0	2	0	0	0	0	0	0	0	5	1
1933	CHI	AL	1	0	1	0	1	0	0	0	0	0	0	0	0	0	1	0
1934	CHI	AL	2	0	2	1	1	0	0	0	0	0	0	0	0	0	2	0
1935	CHI	AL	2	2	0	2	0	0	0	0	0	0	0	0	0	0	2	0
Total			43	27	16	27	12	2	2	1	0	0	0	3	2	0	32	11

Rank among batters: 1,116 • *Top target (5 home runs)*: George Blaeholder • *Number of pitchers victimized*: 30 • *Total ballparks homered in*: 7 • *First HR*: 07/19/1928 off George Blaeholder • *World Series HR*—2

Stan Hack

STANLEY CAMFIELD HACK
B: 12/06/1909 D: 12/15/1979
BL

1932	CHI	NL	2	0	2	2	0	0	0	0	0	0	0	0	1	0	2	0
1933	CHI	NL	1	1	0	1	0	0	0	0	0	0	1	0	0	0	1	0
1934	CHI	NL	1	0	1	1	0	0	0	0	0	0	0	0	0	0	1	0
1935	CHI	NL	4	2	2	3	1	0	0	0	0	0	0	0	0	0	3	1
1936	CHI	NL	6	3	3	3	2	1	0	0	0	0	0	0	0	0	6	0
1937	CHI	NL	2	1	1	1	1	0	0	0	0	0	0	0	0	0	1	1
1938	CHI	NL	4	1	3	1	2	1	0	0	0	0	0	0	0	0	3	1
1939	CHI	NL	8	3	5	7	1	0	0	0	0	0	2	0	0	0	8	0
1940	CHI	NL	8	0	8	6	1	1	0	2	0	0	0	0	0	0	8	0
1941	CHI	NL	7	1	6	5	2	0	0	1	0	0	0	0	0	0	7	0
1942	CHI	NL	6	3	3	5	1	0	0	0	0	0	3	0	0	0	5	1
1943	CHI	NL	3	0	3	2	0	1	0	0	0	0	0	0	0	0	3	0
1944	CHI	NL	3	1	2	3	0	0	0	0	0	0	0	0	0	0	3	0
1945	CHI	NL	2	0	2	2	0	0	0	0	0	0	0	0	0	0	2	0
Total			57	16	41	42	11	4	0	3	0	0	6	0	1	0	53	4

Rank among batters: 902 • *Top target (3 home runs)*: Hal Schumacher, Carl Hubbell • *Number of pitchers victimized*: 41 • *Total ballparks homered in*: 9 • *First HR*: 05/03/1932 off Bill Swift

Mert Hackett

MORTIMER MARTIN HACKETT
B: 11/11/1859 D: 02/22/1938
BR

1883	BOS	NL	2	2	0	1	1	0	0	0	0	0	0	0	0	0	2	0
1884	BOS	NL	1	0	1	1	0	0	0	0	0	0	0	0	0	0	1	0
1886	KC	NL	3	1	2	2	1	0	0	0	0	0	0	0	0	0	2	1
1887	IND	NL	2	1	1	2	0	0	0	0	0	0	0	0	0	0	2	0
Total			8	4	4	6	2	0	0	0	0	0	0	0	0	0	7	1

Rank among batters: 2,703 • *Total ballparks homered in*: 6 • *First HR*: 08/14/1883 off Art Hagan

Walter Hackett

WALTER HENRY HACKETT
B: 08/15/1857 D: 10/02/1920

1884	BOS	UA	1	0	1	0	1	0	0	0	0	0	0	0	0	0	1	0

Rank among batters: 4,707 • *Total ballparks homered in*: 1 • *First HR*: 08/09/1884 off Abner Powell

Harvey Haddix

HARVEY HADDIX
B: 09/18/1925 D: 01/08/1994
BL

Year	Tm	Lg	Tot	H	A	Men-On 0	1	2	3	One-Game 2	3	4	LO	XN	IP	PH	RHP	LHP
1953	STL	NL	1	1	0	0	0	1	0	0	0	0	0	0	0	0	1	0
1955	STL	NL	1	1	0	0	1	0	0	0	0	0	0	0	0	0	1	0
1958	CIN	NL	1	1	0	1	0	0	0	0	0	0	0	0	0	0	1	0
1962	PIT	NL	1	1	0	0	0	1	0	0	0	0	0	0	0	0	1	0
Total			4	4	0	1	1	2	0	0	0	0	0	0	0	0	4	0

Rank among batters: 3,427 • *Total ballparks homered in*: 3 • *First HR*: 06/23/1953 off Frank Hiller

George Haddock

GEORGE SILAS HADDOCK
B: 12/25/1866 D: 04/18/1926
BR

Year	Tm	Lg	Tot	H	A	Men-On 0	1	2	3	One-Game 2	3	4	LO	XN	IP	PH	RHP	LHP
1889	WAS	NL	2	2	0	1	1	0	0	0	0	0	0	0	0	0	2	0
1891	BOS	AA	3	3	0	2	0	0	1	0	0	0	0	0	0	0	2	0
1893	BRO	NL	1	0	1	1	0	0	0	0	0	0	0	0	0	0	0	1
Total			6	5	1	4	1	0	1	0	0	0	0	0	0	0	4	1

Rank among batters: 2,988 • *Top target (2 home runs)*: Frank Dwyer • *Number of pitchers victimized*: 5 • *Total ballparks homered in*: 3 • *First HR*: 05/18/1889 off Frank Dwyer

Kent Hadley

KENT WILLIAM HADLEY
B: 12/17/1934
BL

Year	Tm	Lg	Tot	H	A	Men-On 0	1	2	3	One-Game 2	3	4	LO	XN	IP	PH	RHP	LHP
1959	KC	AL	10	1	9	3	7	0	0	1	0	0	0	0	0	0	10	0
1960	NY	AL	4	1	3	2	2	0	0	1	0	0	0	0	0	1	4	0
Total			14	2	12	5	9	0	0	2	0	0	0	0	0	1	14	0

Rank among batters: 2,169 • *Top target (4 home runs)*: Paul Foytack • *Number of pitchers victimized*: 10 • *Total ballparks homered in*: 7 • *First HR*: 04/15/1959 off Claude Raymond

Bud Hafey

DANIEL ALBERT HAFEY
B: 08/06/1912 D: 07/27/1986
BR

Year	Tm	Lg	Tot	H	A	Men-On 0	1	2	3	One-Game 2	3	4	LO	XN	IP	PH	RHP	LHP
1935	PIT	NL	6	3	3	6	0	0	0	0	0	0	0	0	1	0	2	4
1936	PIT	NL	4	1	3	1	3	0	0	0	0	0	0	0	0	0	1	3
Total			10	4	6	7	3	0	0	0	0	0	0	0	1	0	3	7

Rank among batters: 2,500 • *Top target (2 home runs)*: Roy Henshaw, Al Hollingsworth • *Number of pitchers victimized*: 8 • *Total ballparks homered in*: 5 • *First HR*: 08/06/1935 off Roy Henshaw

Chick Hafey

CHARLES JAMES HAFEY
B: 02/12/1903 D: 07/02/1973
BR HOF

Year	Tm	Lg	Tot	H	A	Men-On 0	1	2	3	One-Game 2	3	4	LO	XN	IP	PH	RHP	LHP
1924	STL	NL	2	1	1	1	1	0	0	0	0	0	0	0	0	0	1	1
1925	STL	NL	5	1	4	1	3	1	0	0	0	0	0	0	1	0	4	1
1926	STL	NL	4	3	1	2	2	0	0	0	0	0	0	1	0	0	3	1
1927	STL	NL	18	11	7	9	7	2	0	1	0	0	0	1	1	1	13	5
1928	STL	NL	27	15	12	16	6	5	0	1	0	0	0	1	0	0	16	11
1929	STL	NL	29	15	14	8	14	6	1	1	0	0	0	0	0	0	22	7
1930	STL	NL	26	12	14	12	8	6	0	1	0	0	0	0	0	0	21	5
1931	STL	NL	16	10	6	7	2	6	1	1	0	0	0	0	0	0	10	6
1932	CIN	NL	2	1	1	1	0	1	0	0	0	0	0	0	0	0	2	0
1933	CIN	NL	7	2	5	3	2	1	1	0	0	0	0	0	0	0	6	1
1934	CIN	NL	18	9	9	11	6	1	0	2	0	0	0	1	0	0	15	3
1935	CIN	NL	1	0	1	1	0	0	0	0	0	0	0	0	0	0	1	0
1937	CIN	NL	9	3	6	4	4	0	1	0	0	0	0	0	0	0	7	2
Total			164	83	81	76	55	29	4	7	0	0	0	4	2	1	121	43

Rank among batters: 250 • *Top target (8 home runs)*: Bob Smith • *Number of pitchers victimized*: 90 • *Total ballparks homered in*: 8 • *First HR*: 08/30/1924 off Guy Bush • *Hit for Cycle*—vs PHI: 08/21/1930

Tom Hafey

THOMAS FRANCIS HAFEY
B: 07/12/1913
BR

Year	Tm	Lg	Tot	H	A	Men-On 0	1	2	3	One-Game 2	3	4	LO	XN	IP	PH	RHP	LHP
1939	NY	NL	6	4	2	3	1	2	0	0	0	0	0	0	0	0	6	0

Year	Tm	Lg	Tot	H	A	Men-On 0	Men-On 1	Men-On 2	Men-On 3	One-Game 2	One-Game 3	One-Game 4	LO	XN	IP	PH	RHP	LHP

Tom Hafey *continued*

Rank among batters: 2,988 • *Total ballparks homered in*: 3 • *First HR*: 07/21/1939 off Jim Tobin

Bill Hague

WILLIAM L. HAGUE
B: 1852 BR

Year	Tm	Lg	Tot	H	A	0	1	2	3	2	3	4	LO	XN	IP	PH	RHP	LHP
1876	LOU	NL	1	1	0	0	1	0	0	0	0	0	0	0	1	0	1	0
1877	LOU	NL	1	1	0	0	0	1	0	0	0	0	0	0	0	0	1	0
Total			2	2	0	0	1	1	0	0	0	0	0	0	1	0	2	0

Rank among batters: 4,129 • *Total ballparks homered in*: 1 • *First HR*: 05/18/1876 off Dave Pierson

Joe Hague

JOE CLARENCE HAGUE
B: 04/25/1944 D: 11/05/1994
BL

Year	Tm	Lg	Tot	H	A	0	1	2	3	2	3	4	LO	XN	IP	PH	RHP	LHP
1968	STL	NL	1	0	1	1	0	0	0	0	0	0	0	0	0	0	1	0
1969	STL	NL	2	2	0	0	2	0	0	0	0	0	0	0	0	0	2	0
1970	STL	NL	14	7	7	9	3	2	0	1	0	0	0	0	0	1	11	3
1971	STL	NL	16	6	10	8	3	4	1	2	0	0	0	1	0	0	16	0
1972	STL	NL	3	1	2	2	1	0	0	0	0	0	0	0	0	0	2	1
	CIN	NL	4	1	3	2	1	1	0	0	0	0	0	0	0	0	4	0
	Total		7	2	5	4	2	1	0	0	0	0	0	0	0	0	6	1
Total			40	17	23	22	10	7	1	3	0	0	0	1	0	1	36	4

Rank among batters: 1,181 • *Top target (3 home runs)*: Steve Renko, Gary Gentry • *Number of pitchers victimized*: 32 • *Total ballparks homered in*: 12 • *First HR*: 09/20/1968 off Bill Singer

Don Hahn

DONALD ANTONE HAHN
B: 11/16/1948
BR

Year	Tm	Lg	Tot	H	A	0	1	2	3	2	3	4	LO	XN	IP	PH	RHP	LHP
1971	NY	NL	1	0	1	1	0	0	0	0	0	0	0	0	1	0	0	1
1973	NY	NL	2	1	1	1	0	1	0	0	0	0	1	0	0	0	1	1
1974	NY	NL	4	1	3	2	1	1	0	0	0	0	0	0	0	0	0	4
Total			7	2	5	4	1	2	0	0	0	0	1	0	1	0	1	6

Rank among batters: 2,834 • *Top target (2 home runs)*: Fred Norman • *Number of pitchers victimized*: 6 • *Total ballparks homered in*: 6 • *First HR*: 09/05/1971 off Woodie Fryman

Ed Hahn

WILLIAM EDGAR HAHN
B: 08/27/1875 D: 11/29/1941
BL

Year	Tm	Lg	Tot	H	A	0	1	2	3	2	3	4	LO	XN	IP	PH	RHP	LHP
1909	CHI	AL	1	0	1	1	0	0	0	0	0	0	1	0	0	0	1	0

Rank among batters: 4,707 • *Total ballparks homered in*: 1 • *First HR*: 06/15/1909 off Rube Manning

Noodles Hahn

FRANK GEORGE HAHN
B: 04/29/1879 D: 02/06/1960
BL

Year	Tm	Lg	Tot	H	A	0	1	2	3	2	3	4	LO	XN	IP	PH	RHP	LHP
1900	CIN	NL	2	1	1	0	1	1	0	0	0	0	0	0	1	0	2	0

Rank among batters: 4,129 • *Total ballparks homered in*: 2 • *First HR*: 06/16/1900 off Jack Powell

Jesse Haines

JESSE JOSEPH HAINES
B: 07/22/1893 D: 08/05/1978
BR HOF

Year	Tm	Lg	Tot	H	A	0	1	2	3	2	3	4	LO	XN	IP	PH	RHP	LHP
1920	STL	NL	1	0	1	0	1	0	0	0	0	0	0	0	0	0	1	0
1929	STL	NL	1	0	1	1	0	0	0	0	0	0	0	0	0	0	1	0
1932	STL	NL	1	0	1	1	0	0	0	0	0	0	0	0	0	0	1	0
Total			3	0	3	2	1	0	0	0	0	0	0	0	0	0	3	0

Rank among batters: 3,735 • *Total ballparks homered in*: 2 • *First HR*: 08/11/1920 off Lee Meadows • *World Series HR*—1

Jerry Hairston

JERRY WAYNE HAIRSTON
B: 02/16/1952
BB

Year	Tm	Lg	Tot	H	A	Men-On 0	1	2	3	One-Game 2	3	4	LO	XN	IP	PH	RHP	LHP
1977	PIT	NL	2	0	2	1	1	0	0	0	0	0	0	0	0	1	0	2
1981	CHI	AL	1	1	0	0	0	0	1	0	0	0	0	0	0	0	1	0
1982	CHI	AL	5	2	3	3	2	0	0	0	0	0	0	0	0	2	4	1
1983	CHI	AL	5	3	2	2	2	1	0	0	0	0	0	0	0	1	5	0
1984	CHI	AL	5	3	2	3	2	0	0	0	0	0	0	0	0	2	4	1
1985	CHI	AL	2	0	2	2	0	0	0	0	0	0	0	0	0	0	1	1
1986	CHI	AL	5	3	2	3	1	1	0	0	0	0	0	0	0	0	3	2
1987	CHI	AL	5	2	3	1	2	2	0	0	0	0	0	0	0	2	3	2
Total			30	14	16	15	10	4	1	0	0	0	0	0	0	8	21	9

Rank among batters: 1,437 • *Top target (3 home runs)*: Dan Petry • *Number of pitchers victimized*: 26 • *Total ballparks homered in*: 14 • *First HR*: 07/03/1977 off Tug McGraw

Bob Hale

ROBERT HOUSTON HALE
B: 11/07/1933
BL

Year	Tm	Lg	Tot	H	A	Men-On 0	1	2	3	One-Game 2	3	4	LO	XN	IP	PH	RHP	LHP
1956	BAL	AL	1	1	0	1	0	0	0	0	0	0	0	0	0	0	1	0
1961	NY	AL	1	1	0	1	0	0	0	0	0	0	0	0	0	0	1	0
Total			2	2	0	2	0	0	0	0	0	0	0	0	0	0	2	0

Rank among batters: 4,129 • *Total ballparks homered in*: 2 • *First HR*: 07/21/1956 off Bob Lemon

Chip Hale

WALTER WILLIAM HALE
B: 12/02/1964
BL

Year	Tm	Lg	Tot	H	A	Men-On 0	1	2	3	One-Game 2	3	4	LO	XN	IP	PH	RHP	LHP
1993	MIN	AL	3	1	2	2	1	0	0	0	0	0	0	0	0	0	3	0
1994	MIN	AL	1	0	1	0	1	0	0	0	0	0	0	0	0	0	0	1
1995	MIN	AL	2	0	2	2	0	0	0	0	0	0	0	1	0	1	2	0
Total			6	1	5	4	2	0	0	0	0	0	0	1	0	1	5	1

Rank among batters: 2,988 • *Total ballparks homered in*: 5 • *First HR*: 06/19/1993 off Scott Kamieniecki

John Hale

JOHN STEVEN HALE
B: 08/05/1953
BL

Year	Tm	Lg	Tot	H	A	Men-On 0	1	2	3	One-Game 2	3	4	LO	XN	IP	PH	RHP	LHP
1975	LA	NL	6	3	3	4	2	0	0	0	0	0	0	1	0	0	6	0
1977	LA	NL	2	1	1	2	0	0	0	0	0	0	0	0	0	1	2	0
1978	SEA	AL	4	2	2	1	0	2	1	0	0	0	0	0	0	0	3	1
1979	SEA	AL	2	2	0	1	1	0	0	0	0	0	0	0	0	0	2	0
Total			14	8	6	8	3	2	1	0	0	0	0	1	0	1	13	1

Rank among batters: 2,169 • *Total ballparks homered in*: 8 • *First HR*: 07/05/1975 off Ed Halicki

Odell Hale

ARVEL ODELL HALE
B: 08/10/1908 D: 06/09/1980
BR

Year	Tm	Lg	Tot	H	A	Men-On 0	1	2	3	One-Game 2	3	4	LO	XN	IP	PH	RHP	LHP
1931	CLE	AL	1	1	0	1	0	0	0	0	0	0	0	0	0	0	0	1
1933	CLE	AL	10	0	10	4	5	1	0	1	0	0	0	0	0	0	6	4
1934	CLE	AL	13	4	9	5	5	2	1	2	0	0	0	1	1	0	13	0
1935	CLE	AL	16	9	7	7	5	4	0	0	0	0	0	0	1	0	13	3
1936	CLE	AL	14	5	9	10	3	0	1	0	0	0	0	0	0	0	10	4
1937	CLE	AL	6	1	5	2	2	2	0	0	0	0	0	0	0	0	4	2
1938	CLE	AL	8	2	6	5	3	0	0	0	0	0	0	0	0	0	5	3
1939	CLE	AL	4	1	3	2	1	1	0	0	0	0	0	0	1	0	3	1
1941	BOS	AL	1	0	1	1	0	0	0	0	0	0	0	0	0	1	0	1
Total			73	23	50	37	24	10	2	3	0	0	0	1	3	1	54	19

Rank among batters: 715 • *Top target (4 home runs)*: Bobo Newsom, Chief Hogsett • *Number of pitchers victimized*: 48 • *Total ballparks homered in*: 9 • *First HR*: 08/09/1931 off Chief Hogsett • *Hit for Cycle*—@WAS: 07/12/1938

Sammy Hale

SAMUEL DOUGLAS HALE
B: 09/10/1896 D: 09/06/1974
BR

Year	Tm	Lg	Tot	H	A	Men-On 0	1	2	3	One-Game 2	3	4	LO	XN	IP	PH	RHP	LHP
1920	DET	AL	1	0	1	1	0	0	0	0	0	0	0	0	0	1	1	0

Sammy Hale *continued*

Year	Tm	Lg	Tot	H	A	Men-On 0	1	2	3	One-Game 2	3	4	LO	XN	IP	PH	RHP	LHP
1923	PHI	AL	3	3	0	1	1	1	0	0	0	0	0	0	0	0	3	0
1924	PHI	AL	2	0	2	1	1	0	0	0	0	0	1	0	0	0	1	1
1925	PHI	AL	8	5	3	4	2	2	0	0	0	0	0	0	2	0	3	5
1926	PHI	AL	4	1	3	1	1	1	1	0	0	0	0	0	0	0	2	2
1927	PHI	AL	5	2	3	2	2	1	0	0	0	0	0	0	0	0	3	2
1928	PHI	AL	4	3	1	1	1	1	1	0	0	0	0	0	0	0	3	1
1929	PHI	AL	1	0	1	0	1	0	0	0	0	0	0	0	1	0	1	0
1930	STL	AL	2	0	2	1	1	0	0	0	0	0	0	0	0	0	2	0
Total			30	14	16	12	10	6	2	0	0	0	1	0	3	1	19	11

Rank among batters: 1,437 • *Top target (3 home runs)*: Lil Stoner, Earl Whitehill • *Number of pitchers victimized*: 22 • *Total ballparks homered in*: 7 • *First HR*: 07/11/1920 off Carl Mays

Ed Halicki

EDWARD LOUIS HALICKI
B: 10/04/1950
BR

Year	Tm	Lg	Tot	H	A	Men-On 0	1	2	3	One-Game 2	3	4	LO	XN	IP	PH	RHP	LHP
1974	SF	NL	1	0	1	1	0	0	0	0	0	0	0	0	0	0	0	1
1977	SF	NL	2	0	2	2	0	0	0	0	0	0	0	0	0	0	2	0
Total			3	0	3	3	0	0	0	0	0	0	0	0	0	0	2	1

Rank among batters: 3,735 • *Total ballparks homered in*: 2 • *First HR*: 09/28/1974 off Fred Norman

Albert Hall

ALBERT HALL
B: 03/07/1958
BB

Year	Tm	Lg	Tot	H	A	Men-On 0	1	2	3	One-Game 2	3	4	LO	XN	IP	PH	RHP	LHP
1984	ATL	NL	1	0	1	1	0	0	0	0	0	0	1	0	0	0	0	1
1987	ATL	NL	3	3	0	3	0	0	0	0	0	0	1	0	0	0	2	1
1988	ATL	NL	1	1	0	1	0	0	0	0	0	0	0	0	0	0	1	0
Total			5	4	1	5	0	0	0	0	0	0	2	0	0	0	3	2

Rank among batters: 3,191 • *Total ballparks homered in*: 2 • *First HR*: 08/22/1984 off Larry McWilliams • *Hit for Cycle*—vs HOU: 09/23/1987

Bill Hall

WILLIAM LEMUEL HALL
B: 07/30/1928 D: 01/01/1986
BL

Year	Tm	Lg	Tot	H	A	Men-On 0	1	2	3	One-Game 2	3	4	LO	XN	IP	PH	RHP	LHP
1958	PIT	NL	1	0	1	1	0	0	0	0	0	0	0	0	0	0	1	0

Rank among batters: 4,707 • *Total ballparks homered in*: 1 • *First HR*: 07/13/1958 off Jim Brosnan

Bob Hall

ROBERT PRILL HALL
B: 12/20/1878 D: 12/01/1950

Year	Tm	Lg	Tot	H	A	Men-On 0	1	2	3	One-Game 2	3	4	LO	XN	IP	PH	RHP	LHP
1905	BRO	NL	2	1	1	1	1	0	0	0	0	0	0	0	0	0	2	0

Rank among batters: 4,129 • *Total ballparks homered in*: 2 • *First HR*: 07/07/1905 off Dummy Taylor

Bob Hall

ROBERT LEWIS HALL
B: 12/22/1923 D: 03/12/1983
BR

Year	Tm	Lg	Tot	H	A	Men-On 0	1	2	3	One-Game 2	3	4	LO	XN	IP	PH	RHP	LHP
1953	PIT	NL	1	1	0	1	0	0	0	0	0	0	0	0	0	0	0	1

Rank among batters: 4,707 • *Total ballparks homered in*: 1 • *First HR*: 06/09/1953 off Harvey Haddix

Charles Hall

CHARLES LOUIS HALL
B: 07/27/1885 D: 12/06/1943
BL

Year	Tm	Lg	Tot	H	A	Men-On 0	1	2	3	One-Game 2	3	4	LO	XN	IP	PH	RHP	LHP
1911	BOS	AL	1	1	0	0	0	1	0	0	0	0	0	0	0	0	1	0
1912	BOS	AL	1	0	1	1	0	0	0	0	0	0	0	0	1	0	1	0
Total			2	1	1	1	0	1	0	0	0	0	0	0	1	0	2	0

Rank among batters: 4,129 • *Total ballparks homered in*: 2 • *First HR*: 08/04/1911 off George Mullin

Dick Hall

RICHARD WALLACE HALL
B: 09/27/1930
BR

Year	Tm	Lg	Tot	H	A	Men-On 0	1	2	3	One-Game 2	3	4	LO	XN	IP	PH	RHP	LHP
1954	PIT	NL	2	0	2	1	1	0	0	0	0	0	0	0	0	0	1	1
1955	PIT	NL	1	1	0	1	0	0	0	0	0	0	0	0	0	0	0	1
1963	BAL	AL	1	0	1	1	0	0	0	0	0	0	0	0	0	0	1	0
Total			4	1	3	3	1	0	0	0	0	0	0	0	0	0	2	2

Rank among batters: 3,427 • *Total ballparks homered in*: 4 • *First HR*: 06/04/1954 off Ernie Johnson

George Hall

GEORGE WILLIAM HALL
B: 03/29/1849 D: 06/11/1923
BL

Year	Tm	Lg	Tot	H	A	Men-On 0	1	2	3	One-Game 2	3	4	LO	XN	IP	PH	RHP	LHP
1876	PHI	NL	5	3	2	1	1	3	0	1	0	0	0	0	0	0	5	0

Rank among batters: 3,191 • *Top target (3 home runs)*: Cherokee Fisher • *Number of pitchers victimized*: 3 • *Total ballparks homered in*: 3 • *First HR*: 05/13/1876 off Joe Borden

Jimmie Hall

JIMMIE RANDOLPH HALL
B: 03/07/1938
BL

Year	Tm	Lg	Tot	H	A	Men-On 0	1	2	3	One-Game 2	3	4	LO	XN	IP	PH	RHP	LHP
1963	MIN	AL	33	13	20	14	16	3	0	2	0	0	0	0	1	1	32	1
1964	MIN	AL	25	15	10	15	8	2	0	0	0	0	0	2	0	0	24	1
1965	MIN	AL	20	9	11	11	8	1	0	2	0	0	0	0	1	1	19	1
1966	MIN	AL	20	16	4	13	5	1	1	4	0	0	0	1	0	0	19	1
1967	CAL	AL	16	8	8	8	7	1	0	1	0	0	0	0	0	1	16	0
1968	CAL	AL	1	1	0	1	0	0	0	0	0	0	0	0	0	0	1	0
	CLE	AL	1	0	1	1	0	0	0	0	0	0	0	0	0	0	1	0
	Total		2	1	1	2	0	0	0	0	0	0	0	0	0	0	2	0
1969	NY	AL	3	0	3	2	1	0	0	0	0	0	0	0	0	0	3	0
1970	ATL	NL	2	2	0	1	1	0	0	0	0	0	0	0	0	1	2	0
Total			121	64	57	66	46	8	1	9	0	0	0	3	2	4	117	4

Rank among batters: 382 • *Top target (4 home runs)*: Robin Roberts, Gary Bell • *Number of pitchers victimized*: 73 • *Total ballparks homered in*: 13 • *First HR*: 05/19/1963 off Pedro Ramos

Joe Hall

JOSEPH GEROY HALL
B: 03/06/1966
BR

Year	Tm	Lg	Tot	H	A	Men-On 0	1	2	3	One-Game 2	3	4	LO	XN	IP	PH	RHP	LHP
1994	CHI	AL	1	1	0	0	1	0	0	0	0	0	0	0	0	0	1	0

Rank among batters: 4,707 • *Total ballparks homered in*: 1 • *First HR*: 04/12/1994 off Scott Kamieniecki

Mel Hall

MELVIN HALL
B: 09/16/1960
BL

Year	Tm	Lg	Tot	H	A	Men-On 0	1	2	3	One-Game 2	3	4	LO	XN	IP	PH	RHP	LHP
1981	CHI	NL	1	1	0	0	1	0	0	0	0	0	0	0	0	1	1	0
1983	CHI	NL	17	6	11	13	3	0	1	4	0	0	2	0	0	1	17	0
1984	CHI	NL	4	3	1	3	1	0	0	0	0	0	0	0	0	0	4	0
	CLE	AL	7	4	3	4	2	1	0	0	0	0	0	1	0	0	7	0
	Total		11	7	4	7	3	1	0	0	0	0	0	1	0	0	11	0
1986	CLE	AL	18	8	10	9	7	2	0	2	0	0	0	0	0	1	18	0
1987	CLE	AL	18	8	10	13	4	1	0	1	0	0	0	0	0	0	17	1
1988	CLE	AL	6	3	3	4	0	2	0	0	0	0	0	0	1	0	5	1
1989	NY	AL	17	11	6	11	4	1	1	1	0	0	0	0	0	0	16	1
1990	NY	AL	12	3	9	7	4	1	0	0	0	0	0	0	0	1	11	1
1991	NY	AL	19	13	6	8	8	3	0	1	0	0	0	1	0	0	14	5
1992	NY	AL	15	7	8	11	4	0	0	1	0	0	0	0	0	0	13	2
Total			134	67	67	83	38	11	2	10	0	0	2	2	1	4	123	11

Rank among batters: 331 • *Top target (4 home runs)*: Mike Witt, Jack Morris • *Number of pitchers victimized*: 104 • *Total ballparks homered in*: 23 • *First HR*: 09/13/1981 off Scott Sanderson

Bill Hallahan

WILLIAM ANTHONY HALLAHAN
B: 08/04/1902 D: 07/08/1981
BR

Year	Tm	Lg	Tot	H	A	Men-On 0	1	2	3	One-Game 2	3	4	LO	XN	IP	PH	RHP	LHP
1935	STL	NL	1	0	1	1	0	0	0	0	0	0	0	0	0	0	1	0

Bill Hallahan *continued*

Year	Tm	Lg	Tot	H	A	Men-On 0	1	2	3	One-Game 2	3	4	LO	XN	IP	PH	RHP	LHP
1936	CIN	NL	1	0	1	1	0	0	0	0	0	0	0	0	0	0	1	0
Total			2	0	2	2	0	0	0	0	0	0	0	0	0	0	2	0

Rank among batters: 4,129 • *Total ballparks homered in*: 1 • *First HR*: 08/14/1935 off Slick Castleman

Tom Haller

THOMAS FRANK HALLER
B: 06/23/1937
BL

Year	Tm	Lg	Tot	H	A	Men-On 0	1	2	3	One-Game 2	3	4	LO	XN	IP	PH	RHP	LHP
1961	SF	NL	2	2	0	2	0	0	0	0	0	0	0	0	0	0	1	1
1962	SF	NL	18	7	11	8	7	3	0	1	0	0	0	0	0	0	14	4
1963	SF	NL	14	11	3	11	2	0	1	1	0	0	0	0	0	1	10	4
1964	SF	NL	16	12	4	12	2	2	0	1	0	0	0	0	0	0	14	2
1965	SF	NL	16	9	7	10	5	1	0	1	0	0	0	1	0	0	14	2
1966	SF	NL	27	14	13	15	10	2	0	2	0	0	0	1	0	0	24	3
1967	SF	NL	14	8	6	12	2	0	0	1	0	0	0	1	0	0	14	0
1968	LA	NL	4	1	3	3	0	1	0	0	0	0	0	0	0	0	3	1
1969	LA	NL	6	3	3	4	1	1	0	0	0	0	0	0	0	0	3	3
1970	LA	NL	10	3	7	4	3	2	1	0	0	0	0	1	0	2	10	0
1971	LA	NL	5	3	2	1	2	2	0	0	0	0	0	0	0	0	4	1
1972	DET	AL	2	1	1	0	1	1	0	0	0	0	0	0	0	0	2	0
Total			134	74	60	82	35	15	2	7	0	0	0	4	0	3	113	21

Rank among batters: 331 • *Top target (5 home runs)*: Hank Fischer, Don Drysdale • *Number of pitchers victimized*: 84 • *Total ballparks homered in*: 18 • *First HR*: 04/12/1961 off Vern Law • *World Series HR*—1

Jack Hallett

JACK PRICE HALLETT
B: 11/13/1914 D: 06/11/1982
BR

Year	Tm	Lg	Tot	H	A	Men-On 0	1	2	3	One-Game 2	3	4	LO	XN	IP	PH	RHP	LHP
1942	PIT	NL	1	0	1	1	0	0	0	0	0	0	0	0	0	0	1	0

Rank among batters: 4,707 • *Total ballparks homered in*: 1 • *First HR*: 09/12/1942 off Al Javery

Jocko Halligan

WILLIAM E. HALLIGAN
B: 12/08/1868 D: 02/13/1945
BL

Year	Tm	Lg	Tot	H	A	Men-On 0	1	2	3	One-Game 2	3	4	LO	XN	IP	PH	RHP	LHP
1890	BUF	PL	3	2	1	1	2	0	0	0	0	0	0	0	0	0	2	0
1891	CIN	NL	3	2	1	1	2	0	0	0	0	0	0	0	1	0	3	0
1892	CIN	NL	2	1	1	1	1	0	0	0	0	0	0	0	0	0	2	0
	BAL	NL	2	1	1	2	0	0	0	0	0	0	0	0	0	0	2	0
	Total		4	2	2	3	1	0	0	0	0	0	0	0	0	0	4	0
Total			10	6	4	5	5	0	0	0	0	0	0	0	1	0	9	0

Rank among batters: 2,500 • *Top target (2 home runs)*: Bob Caruthers • *Number of pitchers victimized*: 9 • *Total ballparks homered in*: 7 • *First HR*: 05/19/1890 off Hank O'Day

Jimmy Hallinan

JAMES H. HALLINAN
B: 05/27/1849 D: 10/28/1879
BL

Year	Tm	Lg	Tot	H	A	Men-On 0	1	2	3	One-Game 2	3	4	LO	XN	IP	PH	RHP	LHP
1876	NY	NL	2	2	0	1	1	0	0	0	0	0	0	0	0	0	2	0

Rank among batters: 4,129 • *Total ballparks homered in*: 1 • *First HR*: 06/15/1876 off Al Spalding

Bill Hallman

WILLIAM WILSON HALLMAN
B: 03/31/1867 D: 09/11/1920
BR

Year	Tm	Lg	Tot	H	A	Men-On 0	1	2	3	One-Game 2	3	4	LO	XN	IP	PH	RHP	LHP
1889	PHI	NL	2	1	1	2	0	0	0	0	0	0	0	0	0	0	1	1
1890	PHI	PL	1	0	1	0	1	0	0	0	0	0	0	0	0	0	1	0
1891	PHI	AA	6	6	0	4	1	1	0	0	0	0	0	0	5	0	6	0
1892	PHI	NL	2	1	1	0	1	1	0	0	0	0	0	0	0	0	2	0
1893	PHI	NL	5	1	4	4	1	0	0	1	0	0	0	0	0	0	5	0
1895	PHI	NL	1	0	1	0	0	1	0	0	0	0	0	0	0	0	0	1
1896	PHI	NL	2	2	0	0	1	1	0	0	0	0	0	0	0	0	2	0

Bill Hallman *continued*

Year	Tm	Lg	Tot	H	A	Men-On 0	1	2	3	One-Game 2	3	4	LO	XN	IP	PH	RHP	LHP
1898	BRO	NL	2	2	0	2	0	0	0	0	0	0	0	0	0	0	2	0
Total			21	13	8	12	5	4	0	1	0	0	0	0	5	0	19	2

Rank among batters: 1,768 • *Top target (2 home runs)*: Les German • *Number of pitchers victimized*: 20 • *Total ballparks homered in*: 12 • *First HR*: 09/09/1889 off Ed Morris

Bill Hallman

WILLIAM HARRY HALLMAN
B: 03/15/1876 D: 04/23/1950
BL

Year	Tm	Lg	Tot	H	A	Men-On 0	1	2	3	One-Game 2	3	4	LO	XN	IP	PH	RHP	LHP
1901	MIL	AL	2	0	2	1	0	1	0	0	0	0	0	0	1	0	2	0
1906	PIT	NL	1	0	1	1	0	0	0	0	0	0	0	0	0	0	1	0
Total			3	0	3	2	0	1	0	0	0	0	0	0	1	0	3	0

Rank among batters: 3,735 • *Total ballparks homered in*: 3 • *First HR*: 06/12/1901 off Bill Bernhard

Al Halt

ALVA WILLIAM HALT
B: 11/23/1890 D: 01/22/1973
BR

Year	Tm	Lg	Tot	H	A	Men-On 0	1	2	3	One-Game 2	3	4	LO	XN	IP	PH	RHP	LHP
1914	BRO	FL	3	2	1	2	0	1	0	0	0	0	0	0	0	0	3	0
1915	BRO	FL	3	3	0	3	0	0	0	0	0	0	0	0	0	0	1	2
Total			6	5	1	5	0	1	0	0	0	0	0	0	0	0	4	2

Rank among batters: 2,988 • *Total ballparks homered in*: 2 • *First HR*: 07/17/1914 off Howie Camnitz

Charlie Hamburg

CHARLES H. HAMBURG
B: 11/22/1863 D: 05/18/1931

Year	Tm	Lg	Tot	H	A	Men-On 0	1	2	3	One-Game 2	3	4	LO	XN	IP	PH	RHP	LHP
1890	LOU	AA	3	1	2	3	0	0	0	0	0	0	0	0	0	0	0	3

Rank among batters: 3,735 • *Total ballparks homered in*: 3 • *First HR*: 05/01/1890 off Toad Ramsey

Bob Hamelin

ROBERT JAMES HAMELIN
B: 11/29/1967
BL

Year	Tm	Lg	Tot	H	A	Men-On 0	1	2	3	One-Game 2	3	4	LO	XN	IP	PH	RHP	LHP
1993	KC	AL	2	1	1	2	0	0	0	0	0	0	0	0	0	0	2	0
1994	KC	AL	24	13	11	11	9	4	0	1	0	0	0	1	0	0	24	0
1995	KC	AL	7	3	4	5	1	1	0	0	0	0	0	1	0	1	3	4
Total			33	17	16	18	10	5	0	1	0	0	0	2	0	1	29	4

Rank among batters: 1,336 • *Top target (3 home runs)*: Todd Van Poppel • *Number of pitchers victimized*: 30 • *Total ballparks homered in*: 10 • *First HR*: 09/21/1993 off Kelly Downs

Billy Hamilton

WILLIAM ROBERT HAMILTON
B: 02/16/1866 D: 12/16/1940
BL HOF

Year	Tm	Lg	Tot	H	A	Men-On 0	1	2	3	One-Game 2	3	4	LO	XN	IP	PH	RHP	LHP
1889	KC	AA	3	1	2	1	2	0	0	0	0	0	0	0	0	0	3	0
1890	PHI	NL	2	1	1	1	1	0	0	0	0	0	0	0	1	0	2	0
1891	PHI	NL	2	0	2	1	0	1	0	0	0	0	0	0	1	0	1	0
1892	PHI	NL	3	2	1	1	1	0	1	0	0	0	0	0	1	0	3	0
1893	PHI	NL	5	3	2	3	2	0	0	1	0	0	2	1	0	0	5	0
1894	PHI	NL	4	3	1	1	2	1	0	0	0	0	1	0	2	0	3	0
1895	PHI	NL	7	5	2	4	1	2	0	0	0	0	1	0	1	0	5	0
1896	BOS	NL	3	2	1	3	0	0	0	0	0	0	0	0	0	0	3	0
1897	BOS	NL	3	0	3	3	0	0	0	0	0	0	0	0	0	0	3	0
1898	BOS	NL	3	3	0	1	2	0	0	0	0	0	0	0	0	0	3	0
1899	BOS	NL	1	0	1	0	1	0	0	0	0	0	0	0	0	0	1	0
1900	BOS	NL	1	1	0	1	0	0	0	0	0	0	0	0	0	0	1	0
1901	BOS	NL	3	3	0	3	0	0	0	0	0	0	0	1	0	0	3	0
Total			40	24	16	23	12	4	1	1	0	0	4	2	6	0	35	0

Rank among batters: 1,181 • Top target (3 home runs): Elton Chamberlin, Al Maul, Ed Stein, Bill Hutchison • *Number of pitchers victimized*: 30 • *Total ballparks homered in*: 16 • *First HR*: 05/03/1889 off Elton Chamberlin

Darryl Hamilton

DARRYL QUINN HAMILTON
B: 12/03/1964
BL

Year	Tm	Lg	Tot	H	A	Men-On 0	1	2	3	One-Game 2	3	4	LO	XN	IP	PH	RHP	LHP
1988	MIL	AL	1	1	0	1	0	0	0	0	0	0	0	0	0	0	1	0
1990	MIL	AL	1	1	0	0	0	0	1	0	0	0	0	0	0	0	1	0
1991	MIL	AL	1	0	1	0	1	0	0	0	0	0	0	0	0	0	1	0
1992	MIL	AL	5	1	4	3	1	1	0	0	0	0	0	0	0	0	5	0
1993	MIL	AL	9	5	4	9	0	0	0	0	0	0	2	0	0	0	8	1
1994	MIL	AL	1	0	1	1	0	0	0	0	0	0	0	0	0	0	1	0
1995	MIL	AL	5	3	2	2	2	0	1	0	0	0	0	0	0	0	5	0
Total			23	11	12	16	4	1	2	0	0	0	2	0	0	0	22	1

Rank among batters: 1,686 • *Top target (2 home runs)*: Bobby Thigpen, Mike Moore • *Number of pitchers victimized*: 21 • *Total ballparks homered in*: 10 • *First HR*: 07/19/1988 off Bret Saberhagen

Jack Hamilton

JACK EDWIN HAMILTON
B: 12/25/1938
BR

Year	Tm	Lg	Tot	H	A	Men-On 0	1	2	3	One-Game 2	3	4	LO	XN	IP	PH	RHP	LHP
1967	NY	NL	1	1	0	0	0	0	1	0	0	0	0	0	0	0	0	1

Rank among batters: 4,707 • *Total ballparks homered in*: 1 • *First HR*: 05/20/1967 off Al Jackson

Jeff Hamilton

JEFFREY ROBERT HAMILTON
B: 03/19/1964
BR

Year	Tm	Lg	Tot	H	A	Men-On 0	1	2	3	One-Game 2	3	4	LO	XN	IP	PH	RHP	LHP
1986	LA	NL	5	2	3	5	0	0	0	0	0	0	0	1	0	0	4	1
1988	LA	NL	6	4	2	2	4	0	0	0	0	0	0	0	0	0	3	3
1989	LA	NL	12	8	4	9	2	0	1	1	0	0	0	0	0	0	10	2
1991	LA	NL	1	1	0	0	0	1	0	0	0	0	0	0	0	0	1	0
Total			24	15	9	16	6	1	1	1	0	0	0	1	0	0	18	6

Rank among batters: 1,643 • *Top target (2 home runs)*: Kevin Gross • *Number of pitchers victimized*: 23 • *Total ballparks homered in*: 8 • *First HR*: 07/24/1986 off Cecilio Guante

Ken Hamlin

KENNETH LEE HAMLIN
B: 05/18/1935
BR

Year	Tm	Lg	Tot	H	A	Men-On 0	1	2	3	One-Game 2	3	4	LO	XN	IP	PH	RHP	LHP
1960	KC	AL	2	1	1	2	0	0	0	0	0	0	0	1	0	0	2	0
1961	LA	AL	1	1	0	1	0	0	0	0	0	0	0	1	0	0	0	1
1962	WAS	AL	3	2	1	2	0	0	1	0	0	0	0	0	0	0	2	1
1965	WAS	AL	4	1	3	3	0	1	0	1	0	0	0	0	0	0	1	3
1966	WAS	AL	1	1	0	1	0	0	0	0	0	0	0	0	0	0	0	1
Total			11	6	5	9	0	1	1	1	0	0	0	2	0	0	5	6

Rank among batters: 2,419 • *Top target (3 home runs)*: Barry Latman • *Number of pitchers victimized*: 9 • *Total ballparks homered in*: 6 • *First HR*: 04/23/1960 off Barry Latman

Luke Hamlin

LUKE DANIEL HAMLIN
B: 07/03/1904 D: 02/18/1978
BL

Year	Tm	Lg	Tot	H	A	Men-On 0	1	2	3	One-Game 2	3	4	LO	XN	IP	PH	RHP	LHP
1939	BRO	NL	1	0	1	1	0	0	0	0	0	0	0	0	0	0	1	0

Rank among batters: 4,707 • *Total ballparks homered in*: 1 • *First HR*: 09/21/1939 off Bill McGee

Chris Hammond

CHRISTOPHER ANDREW HAMMOND
B: 01/21/1966
BL

Year	Tm	Lg	Tot	H	A	Men-On 0	1	2	3	One-Game 2	3	4	LO	XN	IP	PH	RHP	LHP
1992	CIN	NL	1	1	0	0	1	0	0	0	0	0	0	0	0	0	1	0
1993	FLO	NL	2	0	2	2	0	0	0	0	0	0	0	0	0	0	2	0
1995	FLO	NL	1	1	0	0	0	0	1	0	0	0	0	0	0	0	1	0
Total			4	2	2	2	1	0	1	0	0	0	0	0	0	0	4	0

Rank among batters: 3,427 • *Total ballparks homered in*: 4 • *First HR*: 06/17/1992 off John Burkett

Steve Hammond

STEVEN BENJAMIN HAMMOND
B: 05/09/1957
BL

Year	Tm	Lg	Tot	H	A	Men-On 0	1	2	3	One-Game 2	3	4	LO	XN	IP	PH	RHP	LHP
1982	KC	AL	1	0	1	0	1	0	0	0	0	0	0	0	0	0	1	0

Rank among batters: 4,707 • *Total ballparks homered in*: 1 • *First HR*: 07/20/1982 off Dave Stieb

Jeffrey Hammonds

JEFFREY BRYAN HAMMONDS
B: 03/05/1971
BR

Year	Tm	Lg	Tot	H	A	Men-On 0	1	2	3	One-Game 2	3	4	LO	XN	IP	PH	RHP	LHP
1993	BAL	AL	3	2	1	1	1	1	0	0	0	0	0	0	0	0	1	2
1994	BAL	AL	8	6	2	7	1	0	0	1	0	0	0	0	0	0	6	2
1995	BAL	AL	4	2	2	1	2	1	0	0	0	0	0	0	0	0	4	0
Total			15	10	5	9	4	2	0	1	0	0	0	0	0	0	11	4

Rank among batters: 2,096 • *Total ballparks homered in*: 5 • *First HR*: 06/26/1993 off Neal Heaton

Granny Hamner

GRANVILLE WILBUR HAMNER
B: 04/26/1927 D: 09/12/1993
BR

Year	Tm	Lg	Tot	H	A	Men-On 0	1	2	3	One-Game 2	3	4	LO	XN	IP	PH	RHP	LHP
1948	PHI	NL	3	1	2	1	1	1	0	0	0	0	0	0	0	0	2	1
1949	PHI	NL	6	1	5	4	1	1	0	0	0	0	0	0	0	0	5	1
1950	PHI	NL	11	6	5	4	5	2	0	0	0	0	0	1	0	0	6	5
1951	PHI	NL	9	7	2	3	3	2	1	0	0	0	0	0	0	0	5	4
1952	PHI	NL	17	9	8	9	3	4	1	0	0	0	1	1	0	0	9	8
1953	PHI	NL	21	14	7	9	10	1	1	1	0	0	0	0	0	0	11	10
1954	PHI	NL	13	4	9	4	6	3	0	0	0	0	0	0	0	0	7	6
1955	PHI	NL	5	3	2	4	1	0	0	0	0	0	0	0	0	0	3	2
1956	PHI	NL	4	1	3	2	1	1	0	0	0	0	0	0	0	0	4	0
1957	PHI	NL	10	5	5	7	3	0	0	0	0	0	0	0	1	0	4	6
1958	PHI	NL	2	0	2	1	1	0	0	0	0	0	0	0	0	0	1	1
1959	PHI	NL	2	2	0	1	1	0	0	0	0	0	0	0	0	0	0	2
	CLE	AL	1	0	1	1	0	0	0	0	0	0	0	0	0	0	1	0
	Total		3	2	1	2	1	0	0	0	0	0	0	0	0	0	1	2
Total			104	53	51	50	36	15	3	1	0	0	1	2	1	0	58	46

Rank among batters: 469 • *Top target (4 home runs)*: Wilmer Mizell, Joe Nuxhall • *Number of pitchers victimized*: 72 • *Total ballparks homered in*: 10 • *First HR*: 08/28/1948 off Tiny Bonham

Ralph Hamner

RALPH CONANT HAMNER
B: 09/12/1916
BR

Year	Tm	Lg	Tot	H	A	Men-On 0	1	2	3	One-Game 2	3	4	LO	XN	IP	PH	RHP	LHP
1948	CHI	NL	1	0	1	0	1	0	0	0	0	0	0	0	0	0	1	0

Rank among batters: 4,707 • *Total ballparks homered in*: 1 • *First HR*: 06/24/1948 off Andy Hansen

Ike Hampton

ISAAC BERNARD HAMPTON
B: 08/22/1951
BB

Year	Tm	Lg	Tot	H	A	Men-On 0	1	2	3	One-Game 2	3	4	LO	XN	IP	PH	RHP	LHP
1977	CAL	AL	3	0	3	2	1	0	0	0	0	0	0	0	0	1	0	3
1978	CAL	AL	1	0	1	1	0	0	0	0	0	0	0	0	0	0	0	1
Total			4	0	4	3	1	0	0	0	0	0	0	0	0	1	0	4

Rank among batters: 3,427 • *Total ballparks homered in*: 3 • *First HR*: 04/30/1977 off Mike Flanagan

Ray Hamrick

RAYMOND BERNARD HAMRICK
B: 08/01/1921
BR

Year	Tm	Lg	Tot	H	A	Men-On 0	1	2	3	One-Game 2	3	4	LO	XN	IP	PH	RHP	LHP
1944	PHI	NL	1	0	1	0	0	1	0	0	0	0	0	0	0	0	1	0

Rank among batters: 4,707 • *Total ballparks homered in*: 1 • *First HR*: 06/11/1944 off Harry Feldman

Garry Hancock

RONALD GARRY HANCOCK
B: 01/23/1954
BL

Year	Tm	Lg	Tot	H	A	Men-On 0	1	2	3	One-Game 2	3	4	LO	XN	IP	PH	RHP	LHP
1980	BOS	AL	4	4	0	2	1	1	0	0	0	0	0	0	0	0	4	0

Garry Hancock *continued*

Year	Tm	Lg	Tot	H	A	Men-On 0	1	2	3	One-Game 2	3	4	LO	XN	IP	PH	RHP	LHP
1983	OAK	AL	8	3	5	5	3	0	0	0	0	0	0	0	0	0	8	0
Total			12	7	5	7	4	1	0	0	0	0	0	0	0	0	12	0

Rank among batters: 2,325 • *Total ballparks homered in*: 5 • *First HR*: 09/07/1980 off Manny Sarmiento

Lee Handley

LEE ELMER HANDLEY
B: 07/13/1913 D: 04/08/1970
BR

Year	Tm	Lg	Tot	H	A	Men-On 0	1	2	3	One-Game 2	3	4	LO	XN	IP	PH	RHP	LHP
1936	CIN	NL	2	0	2	1	1	0	0	0	0	0	0	0	0	0	1	1
1937	PIT	NL	3	1	2	2	1	0	0	0	0	0	0	0	0	0	0	3
1938	PIT	NL	6	0	6	5	0	1	0	0	0	0	2	0	0	0	4	2
1939	PIT	NL	1	0	1	0	1	0	0	0	0	0	0	0	0	0	1	0
1940	PIT	NL	1	0	1	1	0	0	0	0	0	0	1	0	0	0	0	1
1945	PIT	NL	1	0	1	1	0	0	0	0	0	0	1	0	0	0	1	0
1946	PIT	NL	1	0	1	1	0	0	0	0	0	0	0	1	0	0	1	0
Total			15	1	14	11	3	1	0	0	0	0	4	1	0	0	8	7

Rank among batters: 2,096 • *Top target (2 home runs)*: Carl Hubbell • *Number of pitchers victimized*: 14 • *Total ballparks homered in*: 8 • *First HR*: 05/13/1936 off Curt Davis

Harry Hanebrink

HARRY ALOYSIUS HANEBRINK
B: 11/12/1927
BL

Year	Tm	Lg	Tot	H	A	Men-On 0	1	2	3	One-Game 2	3	4	LO	XN	IP	PH	RHP	LHP
1953	MIL	NL	1	0	1	0	1	0	0	0	0	0	0	0	0	1	1	0
1958	MIL	NL	4	1	3	3	1	0	0	0	0	0	0	0	0	1	4	0
1959	PHI	NL	1	0	1	0	1	0	0	0	0	0	0	0	0	1	1	0
Total			6	1	5	3	3	0	0	0	0	0	0	0	0	3	6	0

Rank among batters: 2,988 • *Top target (2 home runs)*: Robin Roberts • *Number of pitchers victimized*: 5 • *Total ballparks homered in*: 5 • *First HR*: 06/06/1953 off Robin Roberts

Fred Haney

FRED GIRARD HANEY
B: 04/25/1898 D: 11/09/1977
BR

Year	Tm	Lg	Tot	H	A	Men-On 0	1	2	3	One-Game 2	3	4	LO	XN	IP	PH	RHP	LHP
1923	DET	AL	4	2	2	2	1	0	1	0	0	0	1	0	2	0	4	0
1924	DET	AL	1	1	0	1	0	0	0	0	0	0	0	0	0	0	1	0
1927	BOS	AL	3	0	3	3	0	0	0	0	0	0	0	0	0	0	1	2
Total			8	3	5	6	1	0	1	0	0	0	1	0	2	0	6	2

Rank among batters: 2,703 • *Total ballparks homered in*: 3 • *First HR*: 06/18/1923 off Carl Mays

Larry Haney

WALLACE LARRY HANEY
B: 11/19/1942
BR

Year	Tm	Lg	Tot	H	A	Men-On 0	1	2	3	One-Game 2	3	4	LO	XN	IP	PH	RHP	LHP
1966	BAL	AL	1	1	0	0	1	0	0	0	0	0	0	0	0	0	0	1
1967	BAL	AL	3	1	2	3	0	0	0	0	0	0	0	0	0	0	1	2
1968	BAL	AL	1	0	1	1	0	0	0	0	0	0	0	0	0	0	1	0
1969	SEA	AL	2	1	1	2	0	0	0	0	0	0	0	0	0	0	2	0
	OAK	AL	2	0	2	1	1	0	0	0	0	0	0	0	0	0	0	2
	Total		4	1	3	3	1	0	0	0	0	0	0	0	0	0	2	2
1974	OAK	AL	2	1	1	2	0	0	0	0	0	0	0	0	0	0	0	2
1975	OAK	AL	1	0	1	0	1	0	0	0	0	0	0	0	0	0	1	0
Total			12	4	8	9	3	0	0	0	0	0	0	0	0	0	5	7

Rank among batters: 2,325 • *Top target (2 home runs)*: Jim Merritt • *Number of pitchers victimized*: 11 • *Total ballparks homered in*: 9 • *First HR*: 07/27/1966 off John O'Donoghue

Todd Haney

TODD MICHAEL HANEY
B: 07/30/1965
BR

Year	Tm	Lg	Tot	H	A	Men-On 0	1	2	3	One-Game 2	3	4	LO	XN	IP	PH	RHP	LHP
1994	CHI	NL	1	0	1	1	0	0	0	0	0	0	0	0	0	0	1	0
1995	CHI	NL	2	1	1	2	0	0	0	0	0	0	0	0	0	0	1	1
Total			3	1	2	3	0	0	0	0	0	0	0	0	0	0	2	1

Rank among batters: 3,735 • *Total ballparks homered in*: 3 • *First HR*: 07/28/1994 off Mark Dewey

Charlie Hanford

CHARLES JOSEPH HANFORD
B: 06/03/1881 D: 07/19/1963
BR

Year	Tm	Lg	Tot	H	A	Men-On 0	1	2	3	One-Game 2	3	4	LO	XN	IP	PH	RHP	LHP
1914	BUF	FL	12	7	5	8	3	1	0	0	0	0	2	0	2	0	10	2

Rank among batters: 2,325 • *Total ballparks homered in*: 5 • *First HR*: 05/06/1914 off Claude Hendrix

Jay Hankins

JAY NELSON HANKINS
B: 11/07/1935
BL

Year	Tm	Lg	Tot	H	A	Men-On 0	1	2	3	One-Game 2	3	4	LO	XN	IP	PH	RHP	LHP
1961	KC	AL	3	2	1	3	0	0	0	0	0	0	0	0	0	0	2	1
1963	KC	AL	1	0	1	1	0	0	0	0	0	0	0	0	0	0	1	0
Total			4	2	2	4	0	0	0	0	0	0	0	0	0	0	3	1

Rank among batters: 3,427 • *Total ballparks homered in*: 3 • *First HR*: 04/27/1961 off Early Wynn

Frank Hankinson

FRANK EDWARD HANKINSON
B: 04/29/1856 D: 04/05/1911
BR

Year	Tm	Lg	Tot	H	A	Men-On 0	1	2	3	One-Game 2	3	4	LO	XN	IP	PH	RHP	LHP
1878	CHI	NL	1	1	0	0	0	1	0	0	0	0	0	0	0	0	1	0
1880	CLE	NL	1	1	0	0	0	1	0	0	0	0	0	0	0	0	0	1
1881	TRO	NL	1	1	0	1	0	0	0	0	0	0	0	0	0	0	0	1
1883	NY	NL	2	1	1	2	0	0	0	0	0	0	0	0	0	0	2	0
1884	NY	NL	2	2	0	0	1	1	0	0	0	0	0	0	0	0	2	0
1885	NY	AA	2	1	1	1	1	0	0	0	0	0	0	0	1	0	2	0
1886	NY	AA	2	1	1	1	1	0	0	0	0	0	0	0	0	0	2	0
1887	NY	AA	1	0	1	0	0	1	0	0	0	0	0	0	0	0	1	0
1888	KC	AA	1	1	0	0	0	1	0	0	0	0	0	0	0	0	0	1
Total			13	9	4	5	3	5	0	0	0	0	0	0	1	0	10	3

Rank among batters: 2,248 • *Top target (2 home runs)*: Lee Richmond, Henry Porter • *Number of pitchers victimized*: 11 • *Total ballparks homered in*: 10 • *First HR*: 06/27/1878 off Tommy Bond

Ned Hanlon

EDWARD HUGH HANLON
B: 08/22/1857 D: 04/14/1937
BL

Year	Tm	Lg	Tot	H	A	Men-On 0	1	2	3	One-Game 2	3	4	LO	XN	IP	PH	RHP	LHP
1881	DET	NL	2	2	0	2	0	0	0	0	0	0	0	0	0	0	2	0
1882	DET	NL	5	4	1	2	1	2	0	0	0	0	0	0	1	0	5	0
1883	DET	NL	1	1	0	0	1	0	0	0	0	0	0	0	0	0	1	0
1884	DET	NL	5	3	2	0	2	2	0	0	0	0	0	0	1	0	5	0
1885	DET	NL	1	1	0	0	1	0	0	0	0	0	0	0	0	0	1	0
1886	DET	NL	4	4	0	1	1	2	0	0	0	0	0	0	0	0	4	0
1887	DET	NL	4	2	2	1	2	0	1	0	0	0	0	0	0	0	3	0
1888	DET	NL	5	3	2	4	0	1	0	0	0	0	0	0	1	0	3	2
1889	PIT	NL	2	0	2	0	0	1	1	0	0	0	0	0	1	0	1	1
1890	PIT	PL	1	1	0	1	0	0	0	0	0	0	1	0	0	0	0	1
Total			30	21	9	11	8	8	2	0	0	0	1	0	4	0	25	4

Rank among batters: 1,437 • *Top target (3 home runs)*: Mark Baldwin • *Number of pitchers victimized*: 22 • *Total ballparks homered in*: 8 • *First HR*: 07/29/1881 off Jack Lynch

Preston Hanna

PRESTON LEE HANNA
B: 09/10/1954
BR

Year	Tm	Lg	Tot	H	A	Men-On 0	1	2	3	One-Game 2	3	4	LO	XN	IP	PH	RHP	LHP
1978	ATL	NL	1	1	0	1	0	0	0	0	0	0	0	0	0	0	1	0

Rank among batters: 4,707 • *Total ballparks homered in*: 1 • *First HR*: 06/13/1978 off Silvio Martinez

Truck Hannah

JAMES HARRISON HANNAH
B: 06/05/1889 D: 04/27/1982
BR

Year	Tm	Lg	Tot	H	A	Men-On 0	1	2	3	One-Game 2	3	4	LO	XN	IP	PH	RHP	LHP
1918	NY	AL	2	0	2	1	1	0	0	0	0	0	0	0	0	0	1	1

Truck Hannah *continued*

Year	Tm	Lg	Tot	H	A	Men-On 0	1	2	3	One-Game 2	3	4	LO	XN	IP	PH	RHP	LHP
1919	NY	AL	1	1	0	0	1	0	0	0	0	0	0	0	0	0	0	1
1920	NY	AL	2	1	1	2	0	0	0	0	0	0	0	0	0	0	2	0
Total			5	2	3	3	2	0	0	0	0	0	0	0	0	0	3	2

Rank among batters: 3,191 • *Total ballparks homered in*: 2 • *First HR*: 05/07/1918 off Elmer Myers

Jack Hannifin

JOHN JOSEPH HANNIFIN
B: 02/25/1883 D: 10/27/1945
BR

Year	Tm	Lg	Tot	H	A	Men-On 0	1	2	3	One-Game 2	3	4	LO	XN	IP	PH	RHP	LHP
1907	NY	NL	1	1	0	0	0	1	0	0	0	0	0	0	0	0	1	0
1908	BOS	NL	2	1	1	1	1	0	0	0	0	0	0	0	1	1	2	0
Total			3	2	1	1	1	1	0	0	0	0	0	0	1	1	3	0

Rank among batters: 3,735 • *Total ballparks homered in*: 2 • *First HR*: 07/11/1907 off Del Mason

Bob Hansen

ROBERT JOSEPH HANSEN
B: 05/26/1948
BL

Year	Tm	Lg	Tot	H	A	Men-On 0	1	2	3	One-Game 2	3	4	LO	XN	IP	PH	RHP	LHP
1974	MIL	AL	2	0	2	2	0	0	0	0	0	0	0	0	0	2	2	0

Rank among batters: 4,129 • *Total ballparks homered in*: 2 • *First HR*: 08/10/1974 off Marty Pattin

Dave Hansen

DAVID ANDREW HANSEN
B: 11/24/1968
BL

Year	Tm	Lg	Tot	H	A	Men-On 0	1	2	3	One-Game 2	3	4	LO	XN	IP	PH	RHP	LHP
1991	LA	NL	1	0	1	0	0	1	0	0	0	0	0	0	0	1	1	0
1992	LA	NL	6	1	5	5	1	0	0	0	0	0	0	0	0	1	6	0
1993	LA	NL	4	2	2	1	2	0	1	0	0	0	0	0	0	2	4	0
1995	LA	NL	1	0	1	0	1	0	0	0	0	0	0	0	0	0	1	0
Total			12	3	9	6	4	1	1	0	0	0	0	0	0	4	12	0

Rank among batters: 2,325 • *Total ballparks homered in*: 8 • *First HR*: 07/20/1991 off Wally Whitehurst

Ron Hansen

RONALD LAVERN HANSEN
B: 04/05/1938
BR

Year	Tm	Lg	Tot	H	A	Men-On 0	1	2	3	One-Game 2	3	4	LO	XN	IP	PH	RHP	LHP
1960	BAL	AL	22	8	14	15	5	2	0	0	0	0	0	1	0	0	12	10
1961	BAL	AL	12	4	8	7	4	1	0	0	0	0	0	1	0	0	10	2
1962	BAL	AL	3	2	1	1	2	0	0	0	0	0	0	0	0	0	2	1
1963	CHI	AL	13	8	5	6	6	1	0	0	0	0	0	0	0	0	7	6
1964	CHI	AL	20	9	11	14	3	3	0	1	0	0	0	1	1	0	11	9
1965	CHI	AL	11	5	6	8	3	0	0	0	0	0	0	0	0	0	8	3
1967	CHI	AL	8	3	5	4	2	2	0	1	0	0	0	0	0	0	6	2
1968	WAS	AL	8	1	7	5	2	0	1	0	0	0	0	0	0	0	6	2
	CHI	AL	1	0	1	0	1	0	0	0	0	0	0	0	0	0	0	1
	Total		9	1	8	5	3	0	1	0	0	0	0	0	0	0	6	3
1969	CHI	AL	2	1	1	1	0	1	0	0	0	0	0	0	0	0	0	2
1970	NY	AL	4	1	3	3	1	0	0	0	0	0	0	0	0	2	2	2
1971	NY	AL	2	0	2	1	1	0	0	0	0	0	0	0	0	0	0	2
Total			106	42	64	65	30	10	1	2	0	0	0	3	1	2	64	42

Rank among batters: 451 • *Top target (4 home runs)*: Bill Monbouquette • *Number of pitchers victimized*: 82 • *Total ballparks homered in*: 14 • *First HR*: 05/03/1960 off Billy Pierce

Bill Harbidge

WILLIAM ARTHUR HARBIDGE
B: 03/29/1855 D: 03/17/1924
BL

Year	Tm	Lg	Tot	H	A	Men-On 0	1	2	3	One-Game 2	3	4	LO	XN	IP	PH	RHP	LHP
1884	CIN	UA	2	2	0	2	0	0	0	0	0	0	0	0	1	0	2	0

Rank among batters: 4,129 • *Top target (2 home runs)*: Hugh Daily • *Number of pitchers victimized*: 1 • *Total ballparks homered in*: 1 • *First HR*: 04/29/1884 off Hugh Daily

Mel Harder

MELVIN LEROY HARDER
B: 10/15/1909
BR

Year	Tm	Lg	Tot	H	A	Men-On 0	Men-On 1	Men-On 2	Men-On 3	One-Game 2	One-Game 3	One-Game 4	LO	XN	IP	PH	RHP	LHP
1933	CLE	AL	1	1	0	1	0	0	0	0	0	0	0	0	0	0	1	0
1935	CLE	AL	2	0	2	2	0	0	0	1	0	0	0	0	0	0	2	0
1939	CLE	AL	1	0	1	1	0	0	0	0	0	0	0	0	0	0	0	1
Total			4	1	3	4	0	0	0	1	0	0	0	0	0	0	3	1

Rank among batters: 3,427 • *Top target (2 home runs)*: Ray Phelps • *Number of pitchers victimized*: 3 • *Total ballparks homered in*: 3 • *First HR*: 05/11/1933 off Ivy Andrews

Lewis Hardie

LEWIS W. HARDIE
B: 08/24/1864 D: 03/05/1929

Year	Tm	Lg	Tot	H	A	Men-On 0	Men-On 1	Men-On 2	Men-On 3	One-Game 2	One-Game 3	One-Game 4	LO	XN	IP	PH	RHP	LHP
1890	BOS	NL	3	1	2	2	1	0	0	0	0	0	0	0	1	0	3	0

Rank among batters: 3,735 • *Total ballparks homered in*: 3 • *First HR*: 09/04/1890 off Kid Gleason

Jim Hardin

JAMES WARREN HARDIN
B: 08/06/1943 D: 03/09/1991
BR

Year	Tm	Lg	Tot	H	A	Men-On 0	Men-On 1	Men-On 2	Men-On 3	One-Game 2	One-Game 3	One-Game 4	LO	XN	IP	PH	RHP	LHP
1969	BAL	AL	2	2	0	1	0	1	0	0	0	0	0	0	0	0	2	0
1972	ATL	NL	1	0	1	1	0	0	0	0	0	0	0	0	0	0	0	1
Total			3	2	1	2	0	1	0	0	0	0	0	0	0	0	2	1

Rank among batters: 3,735 • *Total ballparks homered in*: 2 • *First HR*: 05/10/1969 off Moe Drabowsky

Carroll Hardy

CARROLL WILLIAM HARDY
B: 05/18/1933
BR

Year	Tm	Lg	Tot	H	A	Men-On 0	Men-On 1	Men-On 2	Men-On 3	One-Game 2	One-Game 3	One-Game 4	LO	XN	IP	PH	RHP	LHP
1958	CLE	AL	1	1	0	0	0	1	0	0	0	0	0	1	0	1	0	1
1960	BOS	AL	2	0	2	1	1	0	0	0	0	0	0	0	0	0	2	0
1961	BOS	AL	3	0	3	2	0	0	1	0	0	0	0	0	0	0	3	0
1962	BOS	AL	8	6	2	3	4	0	1	1	0	0	0	1	0	0	8	0
1964	HOU	NL	2	0	2	0	2	0	0	0	0	0	0	0	0	0	1	1
1967	MIN	AL	1	1	0	0	1	0	0	0	0	0	0	0	0	1	0	1
Total			17	8	9	6	8	1	2	1	0	0	0	2	0	2	14	3

Rank among batters: 1,969 • *Top target (2 home runs)*: Ken McBride • *Number of pitchers victimized*: 16 • *Total ballparks homered in*: 8 • *First HR*: 05/18/1958 off Billy Pierce

Steve Hargan

STEVEN LOWELL HARGAN
B: 09/08/1942
BR

Year	Tm	Lg	Tot	H	A	Men-On 0	Men-On 1	Men-On 2	Men-On 3	One-Game 2	One-Game 3	One-Game 4	LO	XN	IP	PH	RHP	LHP
1967	CLE	AL	1	1	0	0	1	0	0	0	0	0	0	0	0	0	1	0

Rank among batters: 4,707 • *Total ballparks homered in*: 1 • *First HR*: 06/19/1967 off Chuck Dobson

Bubbles Hargrave

EUGENE FRANKLIN HARGRAVE
B: 07/15/1892 D: 02/23/1969
BR

Year	Tm	Lg	Tot	H	A	Men-On 0	Men-On 1	Men-On 2	Men-On 3	One-Game 2	One-Game 3	One-Game 4	LO	XN	IP	PH	RHP	LHP
1921	CIN	NL	1	0	1	0	1	0	0	0	0	0	0	0	0	0	0	1
1922	CIN	NL	7	0	7	5	2	0	0	0	0	0	0	0	0	0	3	4
1923	CIN	NL	10	2	8	7	2	1	0	1	0	0	0	1	0	1	9	1
1924	CIN	NL	3	0	3	2	1	0	0	0	0	0	0	0	0	0	3	0
1925	CIN	NL	2	0	2	1	1	0	0	0	0	0	0	0	0	0	2	0
1926	CIN	NL	6	0	6	3	2	1	0	1	0	0	0	0	0	0	4	2
Total			29	2	27	18	9	2	0	2	0	0	0	1	0	1	21	8

Rank among batters: 1,465 • Top target (2 home runs): Dutch Ruether, Art Nehf, Mule Watson, Tony Kaufmann • *Number of pitchers victimized*: 25 • *Total ballparks homered in*: 7 • *First HR*: 05/10/1921 off Dutch Ruether

Pinky Hargrave

WILLIAM MCKINLEY HARGRAVE
B: 01/31/1896 D: 10/03/1942
BB

Year	Tm	Lg	Tot	H	A	Men-On 0	Men-On 1	Men-On 2	Men-On 3	One-Game 2	One-Game 3	One-Game 4	LO	XN	IP	PH	RHP	LHP
1925	STL	AL	8	6	2	2	2	3	1	1	0	0	0	0	0	0	7	1
1926	STL	AL	7	4	3	3	2	2	0	1	0	0	0	0	0	0	6	1

Pinky Hargrave *continued*

Year	Tm	Lg	Tot	H	A	Men-On 0	1	2	3	One-Game 2	3	4	LO	XN	IP	PH	RHP	LHP
1928	DET	AL	10	2	8	5	4	1	0	1	0	0	0	0	0	1	9	1
1929	DET	AL	3	1	2	0	1	2	0	0	0	0	0	0	0	0	3	0
1930	DET	AL	5	0	5	3	2	0	0	0	0	0	0	0	0	0	5	0
	WAS	AL	1	0	1	1	0	0	0	0	0	0	0	0	0	0	1	0
	Total		6	0	6	4	2	0	0	0	0	0	0	0	0	0	6	0
1931	WAS	AL	1	0	1	0	0	1	0	0	0	0	0	0	0	1	1	0
1932	BOS	NL	4	1	3	0	3	1	0	0	0	0	0	0	0	0	4	0
Total			39	14	25	14	14	10	1	3	0	0	0	0	0	2	36	3

Rank among batters: 1,204 • Top target (3 home runs): Ted Blankenship, George Uhle, Waite Hoyt, George Earnshaw • *Number of pitchers victimized*: 27 • *Total ballparks homered in*: 10 • *First HR*: 06/27/1925 off Ownie Carroll

Charlie Hargreaves

CHARLES RUSSELL HARGREAVES
B: 12/14/1896 D: 05/09/1979
BR

Year	Tm	Lg	Tot	H	A	Men-On 0	1	2	3	One-Game 2	3	4	LO	XN	IP	PH	RHP	LHP
1926	BRO	NL	2	2	0	1	1	0	0	0	0	0	0	0	0	0	1	1
1928	PIT	NL	1	0	1	0	0	0	1	0	0	0	0	0	0	0	0	1
1929	PIT	NL	1	0	1	0	1	0	0	0	0	0	0	0	0	0	0	1
Total			4	2	2	1	2	0	1	0	0	0	0	0	0	0	1	3

Rank among batters: 3,427 • *Total ballparks homered in*: 2 • *First HR*: 06/02/1926 off Larry Benton

Mike Hargrove

DUDLEY MICHAEL HARGROVE
B: 10/26/1949
BL

Year	Tm	Lg	Tot	H	A	Men-On 0	1	2	3	One-Game 2	3	4	LO	XN	IP	PH	RHP	LHP
1974	TEX	AL	4	1	3	3	1	0	0	0	0	0	0	0	0	0	4	0
1975	TEX	AL	11	4	7	9	2	0	0	0	0	0	0	0	0	0	9	2
1976	TEX	AL	7	4	3	2	2	3	0	0	0	0	0	0	0	0	7	0
1977	TEX	AL	18	11	7	13	3	2	0	0	0	0	5	1	0	0	14	4
1978	TEX	AL	7	4	3	5	2	0	0	0	0	0	3	0	0	0	4	3
1979	CLE	AL	10	5	5	5	5	0	0	1	0	0	0	0	0	0	8	2
1980	CLE	AL	11	6	5	8	1	2	0	1	0	0	0	0	0	0	7	4
1981	CLE	AL	2	2	0	0	2	0	0	0	0	0	0	0	0	0	2	0
1982	CLE	AL	4	0	4	3	1	0	0	0	0	0	0	0	0	0	3	1
1983	CLE	AL	3	0	3	3	0	0	0	0	0	0	0	0	0	0	3	0
1984	CLE	AL	2	1	1	0	0	1	1	0	0	0	0	0	0	0	2	0
1985	CLE	AL	1	0	1	0	1	0	0	0	0	0	0	0	0	0	1	0
Total			80	38	42	51	20	8	1	2	0	0	8	1	0	0	64	16

Rank among batters: 650 • Top target (3 home runs): Dennis Eckersley, Steve McCatty, Rick Honeycutt, Dennis Leonard • *Number of pitchers victimized*: 62 • *Total ballparks homered in*: 13 • *First HR*: 04/28/1974 off Doc Medich

John Harkins

JOHN JOSEPH HARKINS
B: 04/12/1859 D: 11/20/1940
BR

Year	Tm	Lg	Tot	H	A	Men-On 0	1	2	3	One-Game 2	3	4	LO	XN	IP	PH	RHP	LHP
1885	BRO	AA	1	0	1	0	1	0	0	0	0	0	0	0	0	0	1	0
1886	BRO	AA	1	1	0	1	0	0	0	0	0	0	0	0	0	0	1	0
Total			2	1	1	1	1	0	0	0	0	0	0	0	0	0	2	0

Rank among batters: 4,129 • *Total ballparks homered in*: 2 • *First HR*: 08/13/1885 off Bobby Mathews

Tim Harkness

THOMAS WILLIAM HARKNESS
B: 12/23/1937
BL

Year	Tm	Lg	Tot	H	A	Men-On 0	1	2	3	One-Game 2	3	4	LO	XN	IP	PH	RHP	LHP
1962	LA	NL	2	0	2	1	1	0	0	0	0	0	0	0	0	0	1	1
1963	NY	NL	10	6	4	4	5	0	1	1	0	0	0	2	0	0	8	2
1964	NY	NL	2	1	1	0	1	1	0	0	0	0	0	0	0	0	2	0
Total			14	7	7	5	7	1	1	1	0	0	0	2	0	0	11	3

Rank among batters: 2,169 • *Total ballparks homered in*: 5 • *First HR*: 04/17/1962 off Mike McCormick

Dick Harley

RICHARD JOSEPH HARLEY
B: 09/25/1872 D: 04/03/1952
BL

Year	Tm	Lg	Tot	H	A	Men-On 0	1	2	3	One-Game 2	3	4	LO	XN	IP	PH	RHP	LHP
1897	STL	NL	3	2	1	0	1	2	0	0	0	0	0	0	0	0	3	0

						Men-On				One-Game								
Year	Tm	Lg	Tot	H	A	0	1	2	3	2	3	4	LO	XN	IP	PH	RHP	LHP

Dick Harley *continued*

Year	Tm	Lg	Tot	H	A	0	1	2	3	2	3	4	LO	XN	IP	PH	RHP	LHP
1899	CLE	NL	1	0	1	0	0	1	0	0	0	0	0	0	0	0	1	0
1901	CIN	NL	4	2	2	2	2	0	0	0	0	0	0	1	4	0	4	0
1902	DET	AL	2	2	0	1	1	0	0	0	0	0	0	0	0	0	2	0
Total			10	6	4	3	4	3	0	0	0	0	0	1	4	0	10	0

Rank among batters: 2,500 • *Total ballparks homered in*: 6 • *First HR*: 07/16/1897 off Jack Taylor

Larry Harlow

LARRY DUANE HARLOW
B: 11/13/1951
BL

Year	Tm	Lg	Tot	H	A	0	1	2	3	2	3	4	LO	XN	IP	PH	RHP	LHP
1978	BAL	AL	8	5	3	5	3	0	0	0	0	0	2	0	0	0	8	0
1980	CAL	AL	4	1	3	1	1	2	0	0	0	0	1	0	0	0	4	0
Total			12	6	6	6	4	2	0	0	0	0	3	0	0	0	12	0

Rank among batters: 2,325 • *Top target (2 home runs)*: Steve Baker • *Number of pitchers victimized*: 11 • *Total ballparks homered in*: 7 • *First HR*: 04/16/1978 off Moose Haas

Bob Harmon

ROBERT GREEN HARMON
B: 10/15/1887 D: 11/27/1961
BB

Year	Tm	Lg	Tot	H	A	0	1	2	3	2	3	4	LO	XN	IP	PH	RHP	LHP
1914	PIT	NL	1	0	1	0	0	1	0	0	0	0	0	0	0	0	1	0

Rank among batters: 4,707 • *Total ballparks homered in*: 1 • *First HR*: 07/05/1914 off Bert Humphries

Chuck Harmon

CHARLES BYRON HARMON
B: 04/23/1924
BR

Year	Tm	Lg	Tot	H	A	0	1	2	3	2	3	4	LO	XN	IP	PH	RHP	LHP
1954	CIN	NL	2	1	1	2	0	0	0	0	0	0	0	0	0	0	1	1
1955	CIN	NL	5	1	4	3	1	1	0	0	0	0	0	0	0	0	1	4
Total			7	2	5	5	1	1	0	0	0	0	0	0	0	0	2	5

Rank among batters: 2,834 • *Total ballparks homered in*: 4 • *First HR*: 07/10/1954 off Warren Spahn

Terry Harmon

TERRY WALTER HARMON
B: 04/12/1944
BR

Year	Tm	Lg	Tot	H	A	0	1	2	3	2	3	4	LO	XN	IP	PH	RHP	LHP
1972	PHI	NL	2	0	2	2	0	0	0	0	0	0	0	0	1	0	1	1
1977	PHI	NL	2	0	2	1	1	0	0	0	0	0	0	0	0	0	2	0
Total			4	0	4	3	1	0	0	0	0	0	0	0	1	0	3	1

Rank among batters: 3,427 • *Total ballparks homered in*: 4 • *First HR*: 08/30/1972 off Jerry Reuss

Brian Harper

BRIAN DAVID HARPER
B: 10/16/1959
BR

Year	Tm	Lg	Tot	H	A	0	1	2	3	2	3	4	LO	XN	IP	PH	RHP	LHP
1982	PIT	NL	2	0	2	1	0	1	0	0	0	0	0	0	0	1	0	2
1983	PIT	NL	7	5	2	5	2	0	0	0	0	0	0	0	0	1	0	7
1984	PIT	NL	2	1	1	1	1	0	0	0	0	0	0	0	0	1	0	2
1988	MIN	AL	3	0	3	3	0	0	0	0	0	0	0	0	0	0	2	1
1989	MIN	AL	8	4	4	4	3	1	0	0	0	0	0	0	0	0	5	3
1990	MIN	AL	6	1	5	4	1	0	1	0	0	0	0	0	0	0	2	4
1991	MIN	AL	10	4	6	1	6	3	0	0	0	0	0	0	0	0	8	2
1992	MIN	AL	9	3	6	7	1	0	1	0	0	0	0	0	0	0	8	1
1993	MIN	AL	12	6	6	9	2	1	0	0	0	0	0	0	0	1	7	5
1994	MIL	AL	4	2	2	2	1	1	0	0	0	0	0	0	0	0	3	1
Total			63	26	37	37	17	7	2	0	0	0	0	0	0	4	35	28

Rank among batters: 826 • *Top target (3 home runs)*: Dan Plesac • *Number of pitchers victimized*: 56 • *Total ballparks homered in*: 20 • *First HR*: 08/30/1982 off Dave Dravecky

George Harper

GEORGE WASHINGTON HARPER
B: 06/24/1892 D: 08/18/1978
BL

Year	Tm	Lg	Tot	H	A	0	1	2	3	2	3	4	LO	XN	IP	PH	RHP	LHP
1922	CIN	NL	2	0	2	1	1	0	0	0	0	0	0	0	0	0	2	0

George Harper *continued*

Year	Tm	Lg	Tot	H	A	Men-On 0	1	2	3	One-Game 2	3	4	LO	XN	IP	PH	RHP	LHP
1923	CIN	NL	3	0	3	3	0	0	0	0	0	0	0	0	0	0	3	0
1924	PHI	NL	16	13	3	9	3	2	2	0	0	0	0	1	2	0	16	0
1925	PHI	NL	18	12	6	7	7	3	1	0	0	0	0	0	1	1	17	1
1926	PHI	NL	7	3	4	4	1	2	0	1	0	0	0	0	0	0	7	0
1927	NY	NL	16	9	7	8	7	0	1	2	0	0	0	0	1	0	14	2
1928	NY	NL	2	2	0	2	0	0	0	0	0	0	0	0	0	0	2	0
	STL	NL	17	11	6	11	5	1	0	0	1	0	0	1	0	2	14	3
	Total		19	13	6	13	5	1	0	0	1	0	0	1	0	2	16	3
1929	BOS	NL	10	2	8	4	3	3	0	0	0	0	0	0	0	0	7	3
Total			91	52	39	49	27	11	4	3	1	0	0	2	4	3	82	9

Rank among batters: 559 • *Top target (5 home runs)*: Rube Ehrhardt • *Number of pitchers victimized*: 52 • *Total ballparks homered in*: 7 • *First HR*: 06/30/1922 off George Stueland

Jack Harper

CHARLES WILLIAM HARPER
B: 04/02/1878 D: 09/30/1950
BR

Year	Tm	Lg	Tot	H	A	Men-On 0	1	2	3	One-Game 2	3	4	LO	XN	IP	PH	RHP	LHP
1901	STL	NL	1	0	1	1	0	0	0	0	0	0	0	0	0	0	1	0

Rank among batters: 4,707 • *Total ballparks homered in*: 1 • *First HR*: 05/08/1901 off Amos Rusie

Terry Harper

TERRY JOE HARPER
B: 08/19/1955
BR

Year	Tm	Lg	Tot	H	A	Men-On 0	1	2	3	One-Game 2	3	4	LO	XN	IP	PH	RHP	LHP
1981	ATL	NL	2	2	0	2	0	0	0	0	0	0	0	0	0	1	0	2
1982	ATL	NL	2	0	2	2	0	0	0	0	0	0	0	0	0	0	0	2
1983	ATL	NL	3	2	1	1	0	2	0	0	0	0	0	0	0	0	1	2
1985	ATL	NL	17	9	8	8	5	4	0	1	0	0	0	3	0	1	9	8
1986	ATL	NL	8	3	5	5	2	0	1	0	0	0	0	1	0	1	6	2
1987	DET	AL	3	2	1	2	1	0	0	0	0	0	0	0	0	0	0	3
	PIT	NL	1	0	1	1	0	0	0	0	0	0	0	0	0	0	0	1
	Total		4	2	2	3	1	0	0	0	0	0	0	0	0	0	0	4
Total			36	18	18	21	8	6	1	1	0	0	0	4	0	3	16	20

Rank among batters: 1,274 • Top target (2 home runs): Tim Lollar, Steve Howe, Tom Gorman, Kent Tekulve, Kevin Gross, John Candelaria • *Number of pitchers victimized*: 30 • *Total ballparks homered in*: 12 • *First HR*: 05/24/1981 off Jack Curtis

Tommy Harper

TOMMY HARPER
B: 10/14/1940
BR

Year	Tm	Lg	Tot	H	A	Men-On 0	1	2	3	One-Game 2	3	4	LO	XN	IP	PH	RHP	LHP
1963	CIN	NL	10	4	6	6	4	0	0	1	0	0	0	0	1	0	1	9
1964	CIN	NL	4	2	2	1	3	0	0	0	0	0	0	0	0	0	0	4
1965	CIN	NL	18	11	7	9	7	2	0	0	0	0	4	0	0	0	10	8
1966	CIN	NL	5	3	2	4	1	0	0	0	0	0	0	0	0	0	2	3
1967	CIN	NL	7	3	4	7	0	0	0	0	0	0	1	0	0	0	6	1
1968	CLE	AL	6	3	3	3	2	1	0	0	0	0	0	0	0	1	2	4
1969	SEA	AL	9	7	2	5	3	1	0	0	0	0	0	2	0	0	8	1
1970	MIL	AL	31	18	13	17	12	2	0	2	0	0	6	0	1	0	24	7
1971	MIL	AL	14	7	7	8	4	2	0	1	0	0	2	0	0	0	10	4
1972	BOS	AL	14	8	6	10	1	3	0	1	0	0	4	1	0	0	10	4
1973	BOS	AL	17	9	8	9	3	3	2	0	0	0	4	0	0	0	14	3
1974	BOS	AL	5	2	3	4	1	0	0	0	0	0	1	0	0	0	4	1
1975	CAL	AL	3	0	3	2	1	0	0	1	0	0	0	0	0	0	1	2
	OAK	AL	2	1	1	2	0	0	0	0	0	0	0	0	0	1	2	0
	Total		5	1	4	4	1	0	0	1	0	0	0	0	0	1	3	2
1976	BAL	AL	1	0	1	1	0	0	0	0	0	0	1	0	0	0	0	1
Total			146	78	68	88	42	14	2	6	0	0	23	3	2	2	94	52

Rank among batters: 302 • *Top target (4 home runs)*: Ray Sadecki, Tom Murphy • *Number of pitchers victimized*: 109 • *Total ballparks homered in*: 25 • *First HR*: 06/11/1963 off Ken MacKenzie

Toby Harrah

COLBERT DALE HARRAH
B: 10/26/1948
BR

Year	Tm	Lg	Tot	H	A	Men-On 0	1	2	3	One-Game 2	3	4	LO	XN	IP	PH	RHP	LHP
1971	WAS	AL	2	0	2	1	1	0	0	0	0	0	0	0	0	0	2	0

Toby Harrah *continued*

Year	Tm	Lg	Tot	H	A	Men-On 0	1	2	3	One-Game 2	3	4	LO	XN	IP	PH	RHP	LHP
1972	TEX	AL	1	0	1	1	0	0	0	0	0	0	0	0	0	0	1	0
1973	TEX	AL	10	6	4	8	1	1	0	0	0	0	0	0	0	0	4	6
1974	TEX	AL	21	11	10	14	6	1	0	2	0	0	0	0	0	0	10	11
1975	TEX	AL	20	8	12	6	12	1	1	0	0	0	0	0	0	0	15	5
1976	TEX	AL	15	4	11	8	5	1	1	2	0	0	0	0	0	0	12	3
1977	TEX	AL	27	13	14	15	5	7	0	2	0	0	0	1	2	0	21	6
1978	TEX	AL	12	6	6	4	3	5	0	2	0	0	0	0	0	0	8	4
1979	CLE	AL	20	15	5	11	7	1	1	2	0	0	0	0	0	0	14	6
1980	CLE	AL	11	7	4	7	1	2	1	0	0	0	0	0	0	0	8	3
1981	CLE	AL	5	3	2	3	2	0	0	1	0	0	0	0	0	0	2	3
1982	CLE	AL	25	17	8	22	3	0	0	0	0	0	0	1	0	0	17	8
1983	CLE	AL	9	7	2	8	1	0	0	1	0	0	1	0	0	0	5	4
1984	NY	AL	1	0	1	1	0	0	0	0	0	0	0	0	0	0	1	0
1985	TEX	AL	9	5	4	4	5	0	0	0	0	0	0	0	0	0	4	5
1986	TEX	AL	7	3	4	6	0	0	1	0	0	0	0	0	0	0	5	2
Total			195	105	90	119	52	19	5	12	0	0	1	2	2	0	129	66

Rank among batters: 193 • *Top target (5 home runs)*: Bert Blyleven • *Number of pitchers victimized*: 140 • *Total ballparks homered in*: 14 • *First HR*: 06/13/1971 off Jim Maloney

Billy Harrell

WILLIAM HARRELL
B: 07/18/1928
BR

Year	Tm	Lg	Tot	H	A	Men-On 0	1	2	3	One-Game 2	3	4	LO	XN	IP	PH	RHP	LHP
1957	CLE	AL	1	1	0	1	0	0	0	0	0	0	0	0	0	0	1	0
1958	CLE	AL	7	5	2	5	2	0	0	0	0	0	2	1	0	0	7	0
Total			8	6	2	6	2	0	0	0	0	0	2	1	0	0	8	0

Rank among batters: 2,703 • *Total ballparks homered in*: 3 • *First HR*: 09/21/1957 off Jim McDonald

Bud Harrelson

DERREL MCKINLEY HARRELSON
B: 06/06/1944
BB

Year	Tm	Lg	Tot	H	A	Men-On 0	1	2	3	One-Game 2	3	4	LO	XN	IP	PH	RHP	LHP
1967	NY	NL	1	0	1	1	0	0	0	0	0	0	0	0	1	0	0	1
1970	NY	NL	1	1	0	1	0	0	0	0	0	0	0	0	0	0	0	1
1972	NY	NL	1	0	1	1	0	0	0	0	0	0	0	0	0	0	0	1
1974	NY	NL	1	0	1	0	1	0	0	0	0	0	0	0	0	0	0	1
1976	NY	NL	1	0	1	1	0	0	0	0	0	0	0	0	0	0	0	1
1977	NY	NL	1	0	1	1	0	0	0	0	0	0	0	0	0	0	0	1
1980	TEX	AL	1	1	0	0	1	0	0	0	0	0	0	0	0	0	0	1
Total			7	2	5	5	2	0	0	0	0	0	0	0	1	0	0	7

Rank among batters: 2,834 • *Total ballparks homered in*: 7 • *First HR*: 08/17/1967 off Juan Pizarro

Ken Harrelson

KENNETH SMITH HARRELSON
B: 09/04/1941
BR

Year	Tm	Lg	Tot	H	A	Men-On 0	1	2	3	One-Game 2	3	4	LO	XN	IP	PH	RHP	LHP
1963	KC	AL	6	3	3	2	4	0	0	0	0	0	0	0	0	0	3	3
1964	KC	AL	7	7	0	4	2	1	0	2	0	0	0	0	0	1	3	4
1965	KC	AL	23	8	15	15	5	3	0	0	0	0	0	0	0	0	15	8
1966	KC	AL	5	3	2	3	2	0	0	0	0	0	0	0	0	0	4	1
	WAS	AL	7	5	2	4	2	1	0	0	0	0	0	1	0	1	5	2
	Total		12	8	4	7	4	1	0	0	0	0	0	1	0	1	9	3
1967	WAS	AL	3	1	2	3	0	0	0	0	0	0	0	0	0	0	1	2
	KC	AL	6	1	5	4	1	1	0	0	0	0	0	0	0	0	3	3
	BOS	AL	3	2	1	3	0	0	0	0	0	0	0	0	0	0	1	2
	Total		12	4	8	10	1	1	0	0	0	0	0	0	0	0	5	7
1968	BOS	AL	35	19	16	15	12	7	1	1	1	0	0	1	0	0	29	6
1969	BOS	AL	3	2	1	1	2	0	0	1	0	0	0	0	0	0	3	0
	CLE	AL	27	13	14	12	12	2	1	1	0	0	0	0	0	0	20	7
	Total		30	15	15	13	14	2	1	2	0	0	0	0	0	0	23	7
1970	CLE	AL	1	0	1	1	0	0	0	0	0	0	0	0	0	0	0	1
1971	CLE	AL	5	2	3	2	2	1	0	0	0	0	0	0	0	1	5	0
Total			131	66	65	69	44	16	2	5	1	0	0	2	0	3	92	39

Rank among batters: 342 • *Top target (7 home runs)*: Luis Tiant • *Number of pitchers victimized*: 86 • *Total ballparks homered in*: 12 • *First HR*: 06/12/1963 off Bill Pleis

Jerry Harrington

JEREMIAH PETER HARRINGTON
B: 08/12/1869 D: 04/16/1913
BR

Year	Tm	Lg	Tot	H	A	Men-On 0	1	2	3	One-Game 2	3	4	LO	XN	IP	PH	RHP	LHP
1890	CIN	NL	1	1	0	0	0	1	0	0	0	0	0	0	0	0	0	1
1891	CIN	NL	2	1	1	0	0	2	0	0	0	0	0	1	0	0	2	0
Total			3	2	1	0	0	3	0	0	0	0	0	1	0	0	2	1

Rank among batters: 3,735 • *Total ballparks homered in*: 2 • *First HR*: 08/04/1890 off Phenomenal Smith

Joe Harrington

JOSEPH C. HARRINGTON
B: 12/21/1869 D: 09/13/1933
BR

Year	Tm	Lg	Tot	H	A	Men-On 0	1	2	3	One-Game 2	3	4	LO	XN	IP	PH	RHP	LHP
1895	BOS	NL	2	2	0	1	1	0	0	0	0	0	0	0	0	0	2	0
1896	BOS	NL	1	0	1	0	1	0	0	0	0	0	0	0	0	0	0	1
Total			3	2	1	1	2	0	0	0	0	0	0	0	0	0	2	1

Rank among batters: 3,735 • *Total ballparks homered in*: 2 • *First HR*: 09/10/1895 off Bill Kissinger • *Hit HR in first major league AB*—vs STL: 09/10/1895

Anthony Harris

ANTHONY SPENCER HARRIS
B: 08/12/1900 D: 07/03/1982
BL

Year	Tm	Lg	Tot	H	A	Men-On 0	1	2	3	One-Game 2	3	4	LO	XN	IP	PH	RHP	LHP
1925	CHI	AL	1	0	1	0	0	0	1	0	0	0	0	0	0	0	1	0
1926	CHI	AL	2	0	2	2	0	0	0	0	0	0	0	0	0	0	2	0
Total			3	0	3	2	0	0	1	0	0	0	0	0	0	0	3	0

Rank among batters: 3,735 • *Total ballparks homered in*: 3 • *First HR*: 07/28/1925 off Curly Ogden

Bucky Harris

STANLEY RAYMOND HARRIS
B: 11/08/1896 D: 11/08/1977
BR HOF

Year	Tm	Lg	Tot	H	A	Men-On 0	1	2	3	One-Game 2	3	4	LO	XN	IP	PH	RHP	LHP
1920	WAS	AL	1	0	1	1	0	0	0	0	0	0	0	0	0	0	0	1
1922	WAS	AL	2	1	1	2	0	0	0	0	0	0	0	0	1	0	0	2
1923	WAS	AL	2	1	1	2	0	0	0	0	0	0	0	0	1	0	2	0
1924	WAS	AL	1	0	1	0	0	1	0	0	0	0	0	0	0	0	1	0
1925	WAS	AL	1	0	1	0	0	1	0	0	0	0	0	0	0	0	1	0
1926	WAS	AL	1	1	0	1	0	0	0	0	0	0	0	0	1	0	0	1
1927	WAS	AL	1	1	0	0	1	0	0	0	0	0	0	0	1	0	1	0
Total			9	4	5	6	1	2	0	0	0	0	0	0	4	0	5	4

Rank among batters: 2,587 • *Top target (2 home runs)*: Eddie Rommel • *Number of pitchers victimized*: 8 • *Total ballparks homered in*: 4 • *First HR*: 06/01/1920 off Hank Thormahlen • *World Series HR*—2

Dave Harris

DAVID STANLEY HARRIS
B: 07/14/1900 D: 09/18/1973
BR

Year	Tm	Lg	Tot	H	A	Men-On 0	1	2	3	One-Game 2	3	4	LO	XN	IP	PH	RHP	LHP
1925	BOS	NL	5	2	3	4	1	0	0	0	0	0	0	2	2	0	2	3
1930	CHI	AL	5	1	4	4	1	0	0	0	0	0	0	0	0	2	3	2
	WAS	AL	4	1	3	1	2	0	1	0	0	0	0	0	0	0	2	2
	Total		9	2	7	5	3	0	1	0	0	0	0	0	0	2	5	4
1931	WAS	AL	5	2	3	4	1	0	0	0	0	0	0	0	0	0	2	3
1932	WAS	AL	6	5	1	4	2	0	0	0	0	0	0	0	0	1	3	3
1933	WAS	AL	5	3	2	3	1	1	0	1	0	0	0	0	0	0	2	3
1934	WAS	AL	2	1	1	2	0	0	0	0	0	0	0	0	0	0	1	1
Total			32	15	17	22	8	1	1	1	0	0	0	2	2	3	15	17

Rank among batters: 1,360 • *Top target (3 home runs)*: Lefty Gomez • *Number of pitchers victimized*: 28 • *Total ballparks homered in*: 12 • *First HR*: 04/18/1925 off Ray Pierce

Donald Harris

DONALD HARRIS
B: 11/12/1967
BR

Year	Tm	Lg	Tot	H	A	Men-On 0	1	2	3	One-Game 2	3	4	LO	XN	IP	PH	RHP	LHP
1991	TEX	AL	1	0	1	0	1	0	0	0	0	0	0	0	0	0	1	0
1993	TEX	AL	1	1	0	1	0	0	0	0	0	0	0	0	0	0	1	0
Total			2	1	1	1	1	0	0	0	0	0	0	0	0	0	2	0

Rank among batters: 4,129 • *Total ballparks homered in*: 2 • *First HR*: 09/29/1991 off Bruce Walton

Gail Harris

BOYD GAIL HARRIS
B: 10/15/1931
BL

Year	Tm	Lg	Tot	H	A	Men-On 0	1	2	3	One-Game 2	3	4	LO	XN	IP	PH	RHP	LHP
1955	NY	NL	12	7	5	8	3	1	0	1	0	0	0	1	0	0	9	3
1956	NY	NL	1	1	0	1	0	0	0	0	0	0	0	0	0	0	0	1
1957	NY	NL	9	5	4	6	1	2	0	1	0	0	0	0	0	0	6	3
1958	DET	AL	20	13	7	8	8	4	0	1	0	0	0	0	0	1	17	3
1959	DET	AL	9	4	5	6	2	1	0	0	0	0	0	0	0	1	4	5
Total			51	30	21	29	14	8	0	3	0	0	0	1	0	2	36	15

Rank among batters: 979 • *Top target (2 home runs)*: Jackie Collum, Robin Roberts, Pedro Ramos • *Number of pitchers victimized*: 48 • *Total ballparks homered in*: 13 • *First HR*: 06/08/1955 off Lew Burdette

Joe Harris

JOSEPH HARRIS
B: 05/30/1891 D: 12/10/1959
BR

Year	Tm	Lg	Tot	H	A	Men-On 0	1	2	3	One-Game 2	3	4	LO	XN	IP	PH	RHP	LHP
1919	CLE	AL	1	0	1	1	0	0	0	0	0	0	0	0	0	0	1	0
1922	BOS	AL	6	3	3	4	2	0	0	0	0	0	0	0	0	0	6	0
1923	BOS	AL	13	8	5	7	5	1	0	0	0	0	0	1	2	0	9	4
1924	BOS	AL	3	1	2	1	1	1	0	0	0	0	0	0	0	0	2	1
1925	BOS	AL	1	0	1	1	0	0	0	0	0	0	0	0	0	0	0	1
	WAS	AL	12	2	10	6	4	2	0	2	0	0	0	1	0	0	9	3
	Total		13	2	11	7	4	2	0	2	0	0	0	1	0	0	9	4
1926	WAS	AL	5	0	5	3	1	1	0	1	0	0	0	1	0	0	2	3
1927	PIT	NL	5	2	3	4	0	1	0	0	0	0	0	0	1	0	4	1
1928	BRO	NL	1	0	1	1	0	0	0	0	0	0	0	0	0	0	0	1
Total			47	16	31	28	13	6	0	3	0	0	0	3	3	0	33	14

Rank among batters: 1,040 • *Top target (3 home runs)*: Paul Zahniser • *Number of pitchers victimized*: 38 • *Total ballparks homered in*: 12 • *First HR*: 09/10/1919 off Carl Mays • *World Series HR*—3

John Harris

JOHN THOMAS HARRIS
B: 09/13/1954
BL

Year	Tm	Lg	Tot	H	A	Men-On 0	1	2	3	One-Game 2	3	4	LO	XN	IP	PH	RHP	LHP
1980	CAL	AL	2	2	0	1	1	0	0	0	0	0	0	0	0	0	2	0
1981	CAL	AL	3	1	2	3	0	0	0	0	0	0	0	0	0	0	3	0
Total			5	3	2	4	1	0	0	0	0	0	0	0	0	0	5	0

Rank among batters: 3,191 • *Total ballparks homered in*: 3 • *First HR*: 09/13/1980 off John Butcher

Lenny Harris

LEONARD ANTHONY HARRIS
B: 10/28/1964
BL

Year	Tm	Lg	Tot	H	A	Men-On 0	1	2	3	One-Game 2	3	4	LO	XN	IP	PH	RHP	LHP
1989	CIN	NL	2	0	2	0	1	1	0	0	0	0	0	0	0	0	2	0
	LA	NL	1	1	0	0	0	1	0	0	0	0	0	0	0	0	1	0
	Total		3	1	2	0	2	1	0	0	0	0	0	0	0	0	3	0
1990	LA	NL	2	0	2	2	0	0	0	0	0	0	1	0	0	0	2	0
1991	LA	NL	3	1	2	0	2	0	1	0	0	0	0	0	0	0	2	1
1993	LA	NL	2	0	2	2	0	0	0	0	0	0	0	0	0	0	2	0
1995	CIN	NL	2	0	2	2	0	0	0	0	0	0	0	0	0	0	1	1
Total			12	2	10	6	4	1	1	0	0	0	1	0	0	0	10	2

Rank among batters: 2,325 • *Total ballparks homered in*: 7 • *First HR*: 06/09/1989 off Orel Hershiser

Lum Harris

CHALMER LUMAN HARRIS
B: 01/17/1915
BR

Year	Tm	Lg	Tot	H	A	Men-On 0	1	2	3	One-Game 2	3	4	LO	XN	IP	PH	RHP	LHP
1946	PHI	AL	1	0	1	0	0	1	0	0	0	0	0	0	0	0	0	1

Rank among batters: 4,707 • *Total ballparks homered in*: 1 • *First HR*: 06/22/1946 off Frank Papish

Ned Harris

ROBERT NED HARRIS
B: 07/09/1916 D: 12/18/1976
BL

Year	Tm	Lg	Tot	H	A	Men-On 0	1	2	3	One-Game 2	3	4	LO	XN	IP	PH	RHP	LHP
1941	DET	AL	1	0	1	1	0	0	0	0	0	0	0	0	1	0	1	0

Ned Harris *continued*

Year	Tm	Lg	Tot	H	A	Men-On 0	Men-On 1	Men-On 2	Men-On 3	One-Game 2	One-Game 3	One-Game 4	LO	XN	IP	PH	RHP	LHP
1942	DET	AL	9	5	4	7	1	1	0	0	0	0	0	1	0	2	9	0
1943	DET	AL	6	5	1	4	2	0	0	0	0	0	0	0	0	0	6	0
Total			16	10	6	12	3	1	0	0	0	0	0	1	1	2	16	0

Rank among batters: 2,029 • *Top target (3 home runs)*: Ted Lyons • *Number of pitchers victimized*: 12 • *Total ballparks homered in*: 6 • *First HR*: 05/11/1941 off Ted Lyons

Vic Harris

VICTOR LANIER HARRIS
B: 03/27/1950
BB

Year	Tm	Lg	Tot	H	A	Men-On 0	Men-On 1	Men-On 2	Men-On 3	One-Game 2	One-Game 3	One-Game 4	LO	XN	IP	PH	RHP	LHP
1973	TEX	AL	8	3	5	6	2	0	0	0	0	0	0	0	1	0	7	1
1976	STL	NL	1	0	1	1	0	0	0	0	0	0	0	0	0	0	0	1
1977	SF	NL	2	0	2	2	0	0	0	0	0	0	0	0	0	0	1	1
1978	SF	NL	1	0	1	1	0	0	0	0	0	0	0	1	0	0	1	0
1980	MIL	AL	1	0	1	1	0	0	0	0	0	0	0	0	0	0	1	0
Total			13	3	10	11	2	0	0	0	0	0	0	1	1	0	10	3

Rank among batters: 2,248 • *Total ballparks homered in*: 9 • *First HR*: 05/11/1973 off Vida Blue

Chuck Harrison

CHARLES WILLIAM HARRISON
B: 04/25/1941
BR

Year	Tm	Lg	Tot	H	A	Men-On 0	Men-On 1	Men-On 2	Men-On 3	One-Game 2	One-Game 3	One-Game 4	LO	XN	IP	PH	RHP	LHP
1965	HOU	NL	1	1	0	0	0	1	0	0	0	0	0	0	0	0	0	1
1966	HOU	NL	9	4	5	3	2	3	1	0	0	0	0	0	0	0	5	4
1967	HOU	NL	2	1	1	2	0	0	0	0	0	0	0	0	0	0	1	1
1969	KC	AL	3	0	3	2	1	0	0	0	0	0	0	0	0	1	1	2
1971	KC	AL	2	0	2	0	1	1	0	0	0	0	0	0	0	1	0	2
Total			17	6	11	7	4	5	1	0	0	0	0	0	0	2	7	10

Rank among batters: 1,969 • *Total ballparks homered in*: 10 • *First HR*: 09/26/1965 off Billy McCool

Roric Harrison

RORIC EDWARD HARRISON
B: 09/20/1946
BR

Year	Tm	Lg	Tot	H	A	Men-On 0	Men-On 1	Men-On 2	Men-On 3	One-Game 2	One-Game 3	One-Game 4	LO	XN	IP	PH	RHP	LHP
1972	BAL	AL	1	0	1	1	0	0	0	0	0	0	0	0	0	0	1	0
1973	ATL	NL	2	1	1	1	0	1	0	0	0	0	0	0	0	0	2	0
1974	ATL	NL	3	2	1	2	1	0	0	0	0	0	0	0	0	0	3	0
Total			6	3	3	4	1	1	0	0	0	0	0	0	0	0	6	0

Rank among batters: 2,988 • *Total ballparks homered in*: 4 • *First HR*: 10/03/1972 off Ray Lamb

Slim Harriss

WILLIAM JENNINGS BRYAN HARRISS
B: 12/11/1896 D: 09/19/1963
BR

Year	Tm	Lg	Tot	H	A	Men-On 0	Men-On 1	Men-On 2	Men-On 3	One-Game 2	One-Game 3	One-Game 4	LO	XN	IP	PH	RHP	LHP
1925	PHI	AL	1	1	0	0	1	0	0	0	0	0	0	0	0	0	1	0
Total			1	1	0	0	1	0	0	0	0	0	0	0	0	0	1	0

Rank among batters: 4,707 • *Total ballparks homered in*: 1 • *First HR*: 05/28/1925 off Walter Johnson

Jack Harshman

JOHN ELVIN HARSHMAN
B: 07/12/1927
BL

Year	Tm	Lg	Tot	H	A	Men-On 0	Men-On 1	Men-On 2	Men-On 3	One-Game 2	One-Game 3	One-Game 4	LO	XN	IP	PH	RHP	LHP
1950	NY	NL	2	2	0	1	0	1	0	0	0	0	0	0	0	0	2	0
1954	CHI	AL	2	0	2	2	0	0	0	0	0	0	0	0	0	0	2	0
1955	CHI	AL	2	0	2	1	1	0	0	0	0	0	0	0	0	0	1	1
1956	CHI	AL	6	3	3	1	2	3	0	0	0	0	0	0	0	0	5	1
1957	CHI	AL	2	2	0	1	1	0	0	0	0	0	0	0	0	0	2	0
1958	BAL	AL	6	5	1	4	1	1	0	2	0	0	0	0	0	0	6	0
1959	BAL	AL	1	1	0	1	0	0	0	0	0	0	0	0	0	0	1	0
Total			21	13	8	11	5	5	0	2	0	0	0	0	0	0	19	2

Rank among batters: 1,768 • *Top target (2 home runs)*: Pedro Ramos • *Number of pitchers victimized*: 20 • *Total ballparks homered in*: 9 • *First HR*: 04/19/1950 off Johnny Sain

Bill Hart

WILLIAM FRANKLIN HART
B: 07/19/1865 D: 09/19/1936

Year	Tm	Lg	Tot	H	A	Men-On 0	Men-On 1	Men-On 2	Men-On 3	One-Game 2	One-Game 3	One-Game 4	LO	XN	IP	PH	RHP	LHP
1892	BRO	NL	2	1	1	1	1	0	0	0	0	0	0	0	0	0	1	1
1897	STL	NL	2	1	1	1	1	0	0	0	0	0	0	0	1	0	2	0
Total			4	2	2	2	2	0	0	0	0	0	0	0	1	0	3	1

Rank among batters: 3,427 • *Total ballparks homered in*: 4 • *First HR*: 06/03/1892 off Alex Jones

Bill Hart

WILLIAM WOODROW HART
B: 03/04/1913 D: 07/29/1968
BR

Year	Tm	Lg	Tot	H	A	Men-On 0	Men-On 1	Men-On 2	Men-On 3	One-Game 2	One-Game 3	One-Game 4	LO	XN	IP	PH	RHP	LHP
1945	BRO	NL	3	2	1	1	0	2	0	0	0	0	0	0	0	0	2	1

Rank among batters: 3,735 • *Total ballparks homered in*: 2 • *First HR*: 05/11/1945 off Ted Wilks

Billy Hart

ROBERT LEE HART
B: 05/16/1866 D: 05/14/1944

Year	Tm	Lg	Tot	H	A	Men-On 0	Men-On 1	Men-On 2	Men-On 3	One-Game 2	One-Game 3	One-Game 4	LO	XN	IP	PH	RHP	LHP
1890	STL	AA	1	1	0	0	0	1	0	0	0	0	0	0	0	0	1	0

Rank among batters: 4,707 • *Total ballparks homered in*: 1 • *First HR*: 08/20/1890 off Bob Barr

Jim Ray Hart

JAMES RAY HART
B: 10/30/1941
BR

Year	Tm	Lg	Tot	H	A	Men-On 0	Men-On 1	Men-On 2	Men-On 3	One-Game 2	One-Game 3	One-Game 4	LO	XN	IP	PH	RHP	LHP
1964	SF	NL	31	12	19	20	11	0	0	2	0	0	0	0	0	0	19	12
1965	SF	NL	23	9	14	10	10	2	1	1	0	0	0	1	1	0	17	6
1966	SF	NL	33	15	18	18	11	3	1	1	0	0	0	0	0	1	27	6
1967	SF	NL	29	13	16	16	7	6	0	3	0	0	0	0	0	0	25	4
1968	SF	NL	23	14	9	10	7	5	1	3	0	0	0	0	0	1	16	7
1969	SF	NL	3	1	2	0	3	0	0	0	0	0	0	0	0	2	2	1
1970	SF	NL	8	1	7	3	3	2	0	1	0	0	0	0	0	0	8	0
1971	SF	NL	2	1	1	1	1	0	0	0	0	0	0	0	0	2	2	0
1972	SF	NL	5	3	2	4	0	1	0	0	0	0	0	0	0	0	3	2
1973	NY	AL	13	3	10	6	4	3	0	1	0	0	0	0	0	1	4	9
Total			170	72	98	88	57	22	3	12	0	0	0	1	1	7	123	47

Rank among batters: 235 • *Top target (6 home runs)*: Jim Bunning • *Number of pitchers victimized*: 106 • *Total ballparks homered in*: 24 • *First HR*: 04/14/1964 off Warren Spahn • *Hit for Cycle*—@ATL: 07/08/1970

Mike Hart

MICHAEL LAWRENCE HART
B: 02/17/1958
BL

Year	Tm	Lg	Tot	H	A	Men-On 0	Men-On 1	Men-On 2	Men-On 3	One-Game 2	One-Game 3	One-Game 4	LO	XN	IP	PH	RHP	LHP
1987	BAL	AL	4	2	2	2	2	0	0	0	0	0	0	0	0	0	3	1

Rank among batters: 3,427 • *Total ballparks homered in*: 3 • *First HR*: 08/23/1987 off Bill Wilkinson

Grover Hartley

GROVER ALLEN HARTLEY
B: 07/02/1888 D: 10/19/1964
BR

Year	Tm	Lg	Tot	H	A	Men-On 0	Men-On 1	Men-On 2	Men-On 3	One-Game 2	One-Game 3	One-Game 4	LO	XN	IP	PH	RHP	LHP
1914	STL	FL	1	0	1	0	1	0	0	0	0	0	0	0	0	0	1	0
1915	STL	FL	1	0	1	1	0	0	0	0	0	0	0	0	0	0	1	0
1927	BOS	AL	1	0	1	1	0	0	0	0	0	0	0	0	0	0	0	1
Total			3	0	3	2	1	0	0	0	0	0	0	0	0	0	2	1

Rank among batters: 3,735 • *Total ballparks homered in*: 3 • *First HR*: 05/25/1914 off Jack Quinn

Fred Hartman

FREDERICK ORRIN HARTMAN
B: 04/25/1868 D: 11/11/1938
BR

Year	Tm	Lg	Tot	H	A	Men-On 0	Men-On 1	Men-On 2	Men-On 3	One-Game 2	One-Game 3	One-Game 4	LO	XN	IP	PH	RHP	LHP
1894	PIT	NL	2	1	1	1	1	0	0	0	0	0	0	0	0	0	2	0
1897	STL	NL	2	2	0	0	1	1	0	0	0	0	0	0	0	0	1	0
1898	NY	NL	2	1	1	0	2	0	0	0	0	0	0	0	0	0	1	1
1899	NY	NL	1	1	0	1	0	0	0	0	0	0	0	0	0	0	1	0

Year	Tm	Lg	Tot	H	A	Men-On 0	Men-On 1	Men-On 2	Men-On 3	One-Game 2	One-Game 3	One-Game 4	LO	XN	IP	PH	RHP	LHP

Fred Hartman *continued*

Year	Tm	Lg	Tot	H	A	0	1	2	3	2	3	4	LO	XN	IP	PH	RHP	LHP
1901	CHI	AL	3	1	2	1	1	1	0	0	0	0	0	1	1	0	1	2
Total			10	6	4	3	5	2	0	0	0	0	0	1	1	0	6	3

Rank among batters: 2,500 • *Total ballparks homered in*: 7 • *First HR*: 07/27/1894 off Nig Cuppy

Gabby Hartnett

CHARLES LEO HARTNETT
B: 12/20/1900 D: 12/20/1972
BR HOF

Year	Tm	Lg	Tot	H	A	0	1	2	3	2	3	4	LO	XN	IP	PH	RHP	LHP
1923	CHI	NL	8	7	1	4	0	4	0	1	0	0	0	1	0	0	6	2
1924	CHI	NL	16	12	4	8	8	0	0	2	0	0	0	1	0	0	13	3
1925	CHI	NL	24	16	8	18	3	3	0	2	0	0	0	0	0	0	17	7
1926	CHI	NL	8	3	5	4	3	0	1	1	0	0	0	0	1	0	6	2
1927	CHI	NL	10	4	6	5	4	1	0	0	0	0	0	1	0	0	9	1
1928	CHI	NL	14	6	8	9	2	3	0	0	0	0	0	0	0	0	10	4
1929	CHI	NL	1	0	1	0	0	1	0	0	0	0	0	0	0	1	0	1
1930	CHI	NL	37	17	20	16	16	4	1	5	0	0	0	1	0	1	30	7
1931	CHI	NL	8	2	6	2	5	1	0	0	0	0	0	0	0	0	5	3
1932	CHI	NL	12	1	11	7	5	0	0	0	0	0	0	0	0	0	10	2
1933	CHI	NL	16	10	6	7	6	2	1	1	0	0	0	0	0	0	14	2
1934	CHI	NL	22	8	14	10	8	4	0	1	0	0	0	1	0	0	13	9
1935	CHI	NL	13	7	6	5	5	2	1	0	0	0	0	0	0	0	9	4
1936	CHI	NL	7	4	3	7	0	0	0	0	0	0	0	0	0	0	5	2
1937	CHI	NL	12	11	1	6	6	0	0	1	0	0	0	0	0	0	12	0
1938	CHI	NL	10	4	6	4	3	2	1	0	0	0	0	0	0	0	9	1
1939	CHI	NL	12	3	9	10	2	0	0	0	0	0	0	0	1	1	8	4
1940	CHI	NL	1	0	1	0	1	0	0	0	0	0	0	0	0	0	0	1
1941	NY	NL	5	4	1	4	1	0	0	0	0	0	0	0	0	1	4	1
Total			236	119	117	126	78	27	5	14	0	0	0	5	2	4	180	56

Rank among batters: 134 • *Top target (7 home runs)*: Freddie Fitzsimmons • *Number of pitchers victimized*: 134 • *Total ballparks homered in*: 8 • *First HR*: 04/20/1923 off Earl Hamilton • *World Series HR*—2

Topsy Hartsel

TULLY FREDERICK HARTSEL
B: 06/26/1874 D: 10/14/1944
BL

Year	Tm	Lg	Tot	H	A	0	1	2	3	2	3	4	LO	XN	IP	PH	RHP	LHP
1899	LOU	NL	1	0	1	0	1	0	0	0	0	0	0	0	0	0	1	0
1900	CIN	NL	2	1	1	2	0	0	0	0	0	0	0	0	1	0	1	1
1901	CHI	NL	7	3	4	4	3	0	0	1	0	0	0	0	3	0	7	0
1902	PHI	AL	5	3	2	2	3	0	0	0	0	0	1	0	0	0	5	0
1903	PHI	AL	5	4	1	3	2	0	0	0	0	0	1	0	0	0	4	1
1904	PHI	AL	2	1	1	2	0	0	0	0	0	0	1	0	0	0	2	0
1906	PHI	AL	1	1	0	0	1	0	0	0	0	0	0	0	1	0	1	0
1907	PHI	AL	3	3	0	2	0	1	0	0	0	0	2	0	0	0	2	1
1908	PHI	AL	4	3	1	3	1	0	0	0	0	0	1	0	0	0	3	1
1909	PHI	AL	1	0	1	1	0	0	0	0	0	0	0	0	0	0	1	0
Total			31	19	12	19	11	1	0	1	0	0	6	0	5	0	27	4

Rank among batters: 1,400 • *Top target (3 home runs)*: Jack Powell • *Number of pitchers victimized*: 25 • *Total ballparks homered in*: 10 • *First HR*: 06/04/1899 off Bill Carrick

Roy Hartsfield

ROY THOMAS HARTSFIELD
B: 10/25/1925
BR

Year	Tm	Lg	Tot	H	A	0	1	2	3	2	3	4	LO	XN	IP	PH	RHP	LHP
1950	BOS	NL	7	4	3	7	0	0	0	0	0	0	1	0	0	0	4	3
1951	BOS	NL	6	0	6	2	4	0	0	0	0	0	1	0	1	0	5	1
Total			13	4	9	9	4	0	0	0	0	0	2	0	1	0	9	4

Rank among batters: 2,248 • *Top target (2 home runs)*: Bubba Church • *Number of pitchers victimized*: 12 • *Total ballparks homered in*: 5 • *First HR*: 06/23/1950 off Red Munger

Clint Hartung

CLINTON CLARENCE HARTUNG
B: 08/10/1922
BR

Year	Tm	Lg	Tot	H	A	0	1	2	3	2	3	4	LO	XN	IP	PH	RHP	LHP
1947	NY	NL	4	3	1	3	1	0	0	0	0	0	0	0	0	0	3	1

Clint Hartung *continued*

Year	Tm	Lg	Tot	H	A	Men-On 0	1	2	3	One-Game 2	3	4	LO	XN	IP	PH	RHP	LHP
1949	NY	NL	4	2	2	2	1	1	0	0	0	0	0	0	0	0	3	1
1950	NY	NL	3	2	1	3	0	0	0	0	0	0	0	0	0	0	1	2
1952	NY	NL	3	3	0	2	1	0	0	0	0	0	0	0	0	1	3	0
Total			14	10	4	10	3	1	0	0	0	0	0	0	0	1	10	4

Rank among batters: 2,169 • *Top target (2 home runs)*: Warren Spahn • *Number of pitchers victimized*: 13 • *Total ballparks homered in*: 4 • *First HR*: 06/02/1947 off Bucky Walters

Roy Hartzell

ROY ALLEN HARTZELL
B: 07/06/1881 D: 11/06/1961
BL

Year	Tm	Lg	Tot	H	A	Men-On 0	1	2	3	One-Game 2	3	4	LO	XN	IP	PH	RHP	LHP
1908	STL	AL	2	2	0	2	0	0	0	0	0	0	0	0	0	0	2	0
1910	STL	AL	2	0	2	0	1	1	0	0	0	0	0	0	1	0	1	1
1911	NY	AL	3	0	3	2	0	0	1	1	0	0	0	0	1	0	3	0
1912	NY	AL	1	1	0	1	0	0	0	0	0	0	0	0	0	0	1	0
1914	NY	AL	1	1	0	1	0	0	0	0	0	0	0	0	0	0	1	0
1915	NY	AL	3	3	0	1	2	0	0	0	0	0	0	0	0	0	3	0
Total			12	7	5	7	3	1	1	1	0	0	0	0	2	0	11	1

Rank among batters: 2,325 • *Top target (2 home runs)*: Carl Cashion • *Number of pitchers victimized*: 11 • *Total ballparks homered in*: 7 • *First HR*: 07/31/1908 off Chief Bender

Erwin Harvey

ERVIN KING HARVEY
B: 01/05/1879 D: 06/03/1954
BL

Year	Tm	Lg	Tot	H	A	Men-On 0	1	2	3	One-Game 2	3	4	LO	XN	IP	PH	RHP	LHP
1901	CLE	AL	1	0	1	1	0	0	0	0	0	0	0	0	0	0	0	1

Rank among batters: 4,707 • *Total ballparks homered in*: 1 • *First HR*: 09/21/1901 off Case Patten

Bill Haselman

WILLIAM JOSEPH HASELMAN
B: 05/25/1966
BR

Year	Tm	Lg	Tot	H	A	Men-On 0	1	2	3	One-Game 2	3	4	LO	XN	IP	PH	RHP	LHP
1993	SEA	AL	5	3	2	4	1	0	0	0	0	0	0	0	0	1	4	1
1994	SEA	AL	1	1	0	1	0	0	0	0	0	0	0	0	0	0	1	0
1995	BOS	AL	5	3	2	2	2	0	1	0	0	0	0	1	0	0	5	0
Total			11	7	4	7	3	0	1	0	0	0	0	1	0	1	10	1

Rank among batters: 2,419 • *Top target (2 home runs)*: Alex Fernandez • *Number of pitchers victimized*: 10 • *Total ballparks homered in*: 6 • *First HR*: 05/08/1993 off Jim Deshaies

Mickey Haslin

MICHAEL JOSEPH HASLIN
B: 08/31/1910
BR

Year	Tm	Lg	Tot	H	A	Men-On 0	1	2	3	One-Game 2	3	4	LO	XN	IP	PH	RHP	LHP
1934	PHI	NL	1	1	0	1	0	0	0	0	0	0	0	0	0	0	1	0
1935	PHI	NL	3	2	1	1	1	1	0	0	0	0	0	0	0	0	1	2
1936	BOS	NL	2	0	2	2	0	0	0	1	0	0	0	0	0	0	2	0
1938	NY	NL	3	3	0	3	0	0	0	1	0	0	0	0	0	0	3	0
Total			9	6	3	7	1	1	0	2	0	0	0	0	0	0	7	2

Rank among batters: 2,587 • *Top target (2 home runs)*: Paul Derringer • *Number of pitchers victimized*: 8 • *Total ballparks homered in*: 3 • *First HR*: 06/10/1934 off Dolf Luque

Bill Hassamaer

WILLIAM LOUIS HASSAMAER
B: 07/26/1864 D: 05/29/1910

Year	Tm	Lg	Tot	H	A	Men-On 0	1	2	3	One-Game 2	3	4	LO	XN	IP	PH	RHP	LHP
1894	WAS	NL	4	3	1	3	1	0	0	0	0	0	0	0	2	0	3	0
1895	WAS	NL	1	1	0	0	1	0	0	0	0	0	0	0	0	0	1	0
1896	LOU	NL	2	2	0	2	0	0	0	0	0	0	0	0	1	0	2	0
Total			7	6	1	5	2	0	0	0	0	0	0	0	3	0	6	0

Rank among batters: 2,834 • *Total ballparks homered in*: 3 • *First HR*: 06/13/1894 off Kid Gleason • *Hit for Cycle*—vs STL: 06/13/1894

Year	Tm	Lg	Tot	H	A	Men-On 0	1	2	3	One-Game 2	3	4	LO	XN	IP	PH	RHP	LHP

Buddy Hassett

JOHN ALOYSIUS HASSETT
B: 09/05/1911
BL

Year	Tm	Lg	Tot	H	A	0	1	2	3	2	3	4	LO	XN	IP	PH	RHP	LHP
1936	BRO	NL	3	2	1	2	0	1	0	0	0	0	0	0	1	0	3	0
1937	BRO	NL	1	0	1	1	0	0	0	0	0	0	0	1	0	0	1	0
1939	BOS	NL	2	0	2	1	1	0	0	0	0	0	0	0	0	0	2	0
1941	BOS	NL	1	0	1	0	1	0	0	0	0	0	0	0	0	0	1	0
1942	NY	AL	5	5	0	2	2	1	0	0	0	0	1	1	0	0	3	2
Total			12	7	5	6	4	2	0	0	0	0	1	2	1	0	10	2

Rank among batters: 2,325 • *Top target (2 home runs)*: Manny Salvo • *Number of pitchers victimized*: 11 • *Total ballparks homered in*: 5 • *First HR*: 05/23/1936 off Bobby Reis

Ron Hassey

RONALD WILLIAM HASSEY
B: 02/27/1953
BL

Year	Tm	Lg	Tot	H	A	0	1	2	3	2	3	4	LO	XN	IP	PH	RHP	LHP
1978	CLE	AL	2	1	1	2	0	0	0	0	0	0	0	0	0	0	1	1
1979	CLE	AL	4	2	2	3	1	0	0	0	0	0	0	0	0	0	4	0
1980	CLE	AL	8	5	3	2	4	2	0	0	0	0	0	0	0	0	8	0
1981	CLE	AL	1	0	1	1	0	0	0	0	0	0	0	0	0	0	1	0
1982	CLE	AL	5	2	3	3	2	0	0	0	0	0	0	1	0	0	4	1
1983	CLE	AL	6	4	2	3	2	1	0	0	0	0	0	0	0	0	4	2
1984	CHI	NL	2	1	1	1	1	0	0	0	0	0	0	0	0	1	2	0
1985	NY	AL	13	3	10	9	1	3	0	2	0	0	0	0	0	0	13	0
1986	NY	AL	6	2	4	2	3	1	0	0	0	0	0	0	0	1	6	0
	CHI	AL	3	3	0	3	0	0	0	0	0	0	0	0	0	0	3	0
	Total		9	5	4	5	3	1	0	0	0	0	0	0	0	1	9	0
1987	CHI	AL	3	1	2	2	1	0	0	0	0	0	0	0	0	0	3	0
1988	OAK	AL	7	3	4	4	2	1	0	0	0	0	0	0	0	0	7	0
1989	OAK	AL	5	3	2	4	1	0	0	0	0	0	0	0	0	0	4	1
1990	OAK	AL	5	2	3	5	0	0	0	0	0	0	0	0	0	0	5	0
1991	MON	NL	1	0	1	1	0	0	0	0	0	0	0	0	0	0	1	0
Total			71	32	39	45	18	8	0	2	0	0	0	1	0	2	66	5

Rank among batters: 731 • Top target (2 home runs): Lamarr Hoyt, Gene Nelson, Mike Witt, Jack Morris, Mike Boddicker, Dennis Lamp, Al Nipper • *Number of pitchers victimized*: 64 • *Total ballparks homered in*: 16 • *First HR*: 05/12/1978 off Nolan Ryan • *LCS HR*—1

Gene Hasson

CHARLES EUGENE HASSON
B: 07/20/1915
BL

Year	Tm	Lg	Tot	H	A	0	1	2	3	2	3	4	LO	XN	IP	PH	RHP	LHP
1937	PHI	AL	3	2	1	0	2	1	0	0	0	0	0	0	0	0	1	2
1938	PHI	AL	1	1	0	0	1	0	0	0	0	0	0	0	0	0	1	0
Total			4	3	1	0	3	1	0	0	0	0	0	0	0	0	2	2

Rank among batters: 3,427 • *Total ballparks homered in*: 2 • *First HR*: 09/09/1937 off Dick Lanahan • *Hit HR in first major league AB*—vs WAS: 09/09/1937 (1)

Charlie Hastings

CHARLES MORTON HASTINGS
B: 11/11/1870 D: 08/03/1934

Year	Tm	Lg	Tot	H	A	0	1	2	3	2	3	4	LO	XN	IP	PH	RHP	LHP
1897	PIT	NL	1	0	1	0	0	1	0	0	0	0	0	0	1	0	0	1

Rank among batters: 4,707 • *Total ballparks homered in*: 1 • *First HR*: 08/11/1897 off Charlie Brown

Bob Hasty

ROBERT KELLER HASTY
B: 05/03/1896 D: 05/28/1972
BR

Year	Tm	Lg	Tot	H	A	0	1	2	3	2	3	4	LO	XN	IP	PH	RHP	LHP
1922	PHI	AL	1	1	0	0	0	1	0	0	0	0	0	0	0	0	1	0

Rank among batters: 4,707 • *Total ballparks homered in*: 1 • *First HR*: 05/15/1922 off Dixie Davis

Billy Hatcher

WILLIAM AUGUSTUS HATCHER
B: 10/04/1960
BR

Year	Tm	Lg	Tot	H	A	0	1	2	3	2	3	4	LO	XN	IP	PH	RHP	LHP
1985	CHI	NL	2	2	0	2	0	0	0	0	0	0	0	0	0	0	2	0

Year	Tm	Lg	Tot	H	A	Men-On				One-Game			LO	XN	IP	PH	RHP	LHP
						0	1	2	3	2	3	4						

Billy Hatcher *continued*

Year	Tm	Lg	Tot	H	A	0	1	2	3	2	3	4	LO	XN	IP	PH	RHP	LHP
1986	HOU	NL	6	2	4	4	1	0	1	0	0	0	0	1	0	0	3	3
1987	HOU	NL	11	3	8	6	3	1	1	0	0	0	0	0	0	0	7	4
1988	HOU	NL	7	3	4	4	3	0	0	0	0	0	0	0	0	0	3	4
1989	HOU	NL	3	0	3	1	1	1	0	0	0	0	0	0	0	0	1	2
	PIT	NL	1	0	1	1	0	0	0	0	0	0	0	0	0	0	1	0
	Total		4	0	4	2	1	1	0	0	0	0	0	0	0	0	2	2
1990	CIN	NL	5	2	3	5	0	0	0	0	0	0	0	0	0	0	4	1
1991	CIN	NL	4	2	2	3	1	0	0	0	0	0	0	0	0	0	3	1
1992	CIN	NL	2	0	2	2	0	0	0	0	0	0	0	0	0	0	0	2
	BOS	AL	1	1	0	1	0	0	0	0	0	0	0	0	0	0	1	0
	Total		3	1	2	3	0	0	0	0	0	0	0	0	0	0	1	2
1993	BOS	AL	9	5	4	3	5	1	0	0	0	0	0	0	0	0	8	1
1994	BOS	AL	1	0	1	1	0	0	0	0	0	0	0	0	0	0	1	0
	PHI	NL	2	0	2	2	0	0	0	0	0	0	0	0	0	0	1	1
	Total		3	0	3	3	0	0	0	0	0	0	0	0	0	0	2	1
Total			54	20	34	35	14	3	2	0	0	0	0	1	0	0	35	19

Rank among batters: 938 • *Top target (2 home runs)*: Dennis Rasmussen, Tom Glavine, Ricky Bones • *Number of pitchers victimized*: 51 • *Total ballparks homered in*: 18 • *First HR*: 06/27/1985 off Ron Darling • *LCS HR*—2

Mickey Hatcher

MICHAEL VAUGHN HATCHER
B: 03/15/1955
BR

Year	Tm	Lg	Tot	H	A	0	1	2	3	2	3	4	LO	XN	IP	PH	RHP	LHP
1979	LA	NL	1	0	1	1	0	0	0	0	0	0	0	0	0	0	1	0
1980	LA	NL	1	1	0	1	0	0	0	0	0	0	0	0	0	0	1	0
1981	MIN	AL	3	3	0	1	1	1	0	0	0	0	0	1	0	0	0	3
1982	MIN	AL	3	2	1	0	2	1	0	0	0	0	0	0	0	0	2	1
1983	MIN	AL	9	6	3	5	3	1	0	0	0	0	0	0	0	1	4	5
1984	MIN	AL	5	4	1	2	2	1	0	0	0	0	0	0	0	0	2	3
1985	MIN	AL	3	1	2	1	1	1	0	0	0	0	0	0	0	0	2	1
1986	MIN	AL	3	1	2	1	2	0	0	0	0	0	0	0	0	0	1	2
1987	LA	NL	7	4	3	4	3	0	0	0	0	0	0	0	0	0	3	4
1988	LA	NL	1	0	1	0	0	1	0	0	0	0	0	0	0	0	0	1
1989	LA	NL	2	0	2	1	1	0	0	0	0	0	0	0	0	0	0	2
Total			38	22	16	17	15	6	0	0	0	0	0	1	0	1	16	22

Rank among batters: 1,225 • Top target (2 home runs): Mike Armstrong, Tom Burgmeier, Ron Guidry, Bob Kipper, Jim Acker • *Number of pitchers victimized*: 33 • *Total ballparks homered in*: 14 • *First HR*: 08/10/1979 off Tom Griffin • *World Series HR*—2

Fred Hatfield

FRED JAMES HATFIELD
B: 03/18/1925
BL

Year	Tm	Lg	Tot	H	A	0	1	2	3	2	3	4	LO	XN	IP	PH	RHP	LHP
1951	BOS	AL	2	1	1	1	1	0	0	0	0	0	0	1	0	0	2	0
1952	BOS	AL	1	1	0	1	0	0	0	0	0	0	0	0	0	0	1	0
	DET	AL	2	2	0	1	1	0	0	0	0	0	0	0	0	0	2	0
	Total		3	3	0	2	1	0	0	0	0	0	0	0	0	0	3	0
1953	DET	AL	3	1	2	3	0	0	0	0	0	0	0	0	0	1	3	0
1954	DET	AL	2	0	2	0	2	0	0	0	0	0	0	1	0	1	2	0
1955	DET	AL	8	4	4	7	1	0	0	0	0	0	0	1	0	0	8	0
1956	CHI	AL	7	3	4	3	3	1	0	1	0	0	0	1	0	1	5	2
Total			25	12	13	16	8	1	0	1	0	0	0	4	0	3	23	2

Rank among batters: 1,608 • *Top target (2 home runs)*: Ray Narleski, Hal Brown • *Number of pitchers victimized*: 23 • *Total ballparks homered in*: 8 • *First HR*: 08/17/1951 off Connie Marrero

Gil Hatfield

GILBERT HATFIELD
B: 01/27/1855 D: 05/27/1921

Year	Tm	Lg	Tot	H	A	0	1	2	3	2	3	4	LO	XN	IP	PH	RHP	LHP
1889	NY	NL	1	1	0	0	1	0	0	0	0	0	0	0	0	0	1	0
1890	NY	PL	2	1	1	2	0	0	0	0	0	0	0	0	1	0	0	2
1891	WAS	AA	1	1	0	0	0	0	1	0	0	0	0	0	0	0	0	1
1893	BRO	NL	2	1	1	2	0	0	0	0	0	0	0	0	0	0	1	0
Total			6	4	2	4	1	0	1	0	0	0	0	0	1	0	2	3

Rank among batters: 2,988 • *Total ballparks homered in*: 6 • *First HR*: 05/24/1889 off Frank Dwyer

Year	Tm	Lg	Tot	H	A	Men-On 0	1	2	3	One-Game 2	3	4	LO	XN	IP	PH	RHP	LHP

Grady Hatton

GRADY EDGEBERT HATTON
B: 10/07/1922
BL

Year	Tm	Lg	Tot	H	A	0	1	2	3	2	3	4	LO	XN	IP	PH	RHP	LHP
1946	CIN	NL	14	9	5	8	5	1	0	0	0	0	0	0	0	0	12	2
1947	CIN	NL	16	11	5	8	7	1	0	0	0	0	0	0	0	0	14	2
1948	CIN	NL	9	6	3	5	2	1	1	0	0	0	0	0	0	0	5	4
1949	CIN	NL	11	9	2	6	3	0	2	0	0	0	2	0	0	0	7	4
1950	CIN	NL	11	9	2	6	5	0	0	0	0	0	0	0	0	0	8	3
1951	CIN	NL	4	2	2	3	1	0	0	0	0	0	0	0	0	0	2	2
1952	CIN	NL	9	5	4	5	2	2	0	0	0	0	1	0	0	0	9	0
1953	CIN	NL	7	3	4	2	4	1	0	0	0	0	1	0	0	3	6	1
1954	BOS	AL	5	0	5	4	0	1	0	0	0	0	0	0	0	0	5	0
1955	BOS	AL	4	2	2	3	0	0	1	0	0	0	0	0	0	0	2	2
1956	BAL	AL	1	0	1	0	1	0	0	0	0	0	0	0	0	0	1	0
Total			91	56	35	50	30	7	4	0	0	0	4	0	0	3	71	20

Rank among batters: 559 • *Top target (4 home runs)*: Red Barrett • *Number of pitchers victimized*: 66 • *Total ballparks homered in*: 12 • *First HR*: 04/18/1946 off Hi Bithorn

Arnold Hauser

ARNOLD GEORGE HAUSER
B: 09/25/1888 D: 05/22/1966
BR

Year	Tm	Lg	Tot	H	A	0	1	2	3	2	3	4	LO	XN	IP	PH	RHP	LHP
1910	STL	NL	2	1	1	1	1	0	0	0	0	0	0	0	1	0	2	0
1911	STL	NL	3	3	0	2	1	0	0	0	0	0	0	0	3	0	2	1
1912	STL	NL	1	0	1	1	0	0	0	0	0	0	0	0	1	0	1	0
Total			6	4	2	4	2	0	0	0	0	0	0	0	5	0	5	1

Rank among batters: 2,988 • *Total ballparks homered in*: 3 • *First HR*: 07/11/1910 off Cliff Curtis

Joe Hauser

JOSEPH JOHN HAUSER
B: 01/12/1899
BL

Year	Tm	Lg	Tot	H	A	0	1	2	3	2	3	4	LO	XN	IP	PH	RHP	LHP
1922	PHI	AL	9	5	4	6	2	1	0	0	0	0	0	0	0	1	9	0
1923	PHI	AL	17	5	12	10	5	2	0	1	0	0	0	0	0	0	13	4
1924	PHI	AL	27	13	14	13	8	6	0	1	1	0	0	1	0	0	21	6
1926	PHI	AL	8	7	1	5	3	0	0	0	0	0	0	0	0	1	6	2
1928	PHI	AL	16	13	3	9	5	2	0	2	0	0	0	0	0	0	12	4
1929	CLE	AL	3	2	1	2	0	1	0	0	0	0	0	0	0	2	3	0
Total			80	45	35	45	23	12	0	4	1	0	0	1	0	4	64	16

Rank among batters: 650 • *Top target (5 home runs)*: Ray Kolp, Walter Johnson • *Number of pitchers victimized*: 51 • *Total ballparks homered in*: 8 • *First HR*: 06/20/1922 off Elam Vangilder

George Hausmann

GEORGE JOHN HAUSMANN
B: 02/11/1916
BR

Year	Tm	Lg	Tot	H	A	0	1	2	3	2	3	4	LO	XN	IP	PH	RHP	LHP
1944	NY	NL	1	1	0	1	0	0	0	0	0	0	0	0	1	0	0	1
1945	NY	NL	2	2	0	2	0	0	0	0	0	0	0	0	0	0	1	1
Total			3	3	0	3	0	0	0	0	0	0	0	0	1	0	1	2

Rank among batters: 3,735 • *Total ballparks homered in*: 1 • *First HR*: 08/01/1944 off Clyde Shoun

Bill Hawes

WILLIAM HILDRETH HAWES
B: 11/17/1853 D: 06/16/1940
BR

Year	Tm	Lg	Tot	H	A	0	1	2	3	2	3	4	LO	XN	IP	PH	RHP	LHP
1884	CIN	UA	4	3	1	2	2	0	0	0	0	0	0	0	1	0	2	0

Rank among batters: 3,427 • *Top target (2 home runs)*: Walter Burke • *Number of pitchers victimized*: 3 • *Total ballparks homered in*: 2 • *First HR*: 05/08/1884 off Bill Sweeney

Bill Hawke

WILLIAM VICTOR HAWKE
B: 04/28/1870 D: 12/11/1902
BR

Year	Tm	Lg	Tot	H	A	0	1	2	3	2	3	4	LO	XN	IP	PH	RHP	LHP
1893	BAL	NL	1	1	0	1	0	0	0	0	0	0	0	0	0	0	1	0

Bill Hawke *continued*

Year	Tm	Lg	Tot	H	A	Men-On 0	1	2	3	One-Game 2	3	4	LO	XN	IP	PH	RHP	LHP
1894	BAL	NL	1	0	1	0	0	1	0	0	0	0	0	0	0	0	1	0
Total			2	1	1	1	0	1	0	0	0	0	0	0	0	0	2	0

Rank among batters: 4,129 • *Top target (2 home runs)*: Harry Staley • *Number of pitchers victimized*: 1 • *Total ballparks homered in*: 2 • *First HR*: 08/12/1893 off Harry Staley

Chicken Hawks

NELSON LOUIS HAWKS
B: 02/03/1896 D: 05/26/1973
BL

Year	Tm	Lg	Tot	H	A	Men-On 0	1	2	3	One-Game 2	3	4	LO	XN	IP	PH	RHP	LHP
1921	NY	AL	2	1	1	1	1	0	0	0	0	0	1	0	2	0	2	0
1925	PHI	NL	5	4	1	1	3	0	1	0	0	0	0	0	0	0	2	3
Total			7	5	2	2	4	0	1	0	0	0	1	0	2	0	4	3

Rank among batters: 2,834 • *Total ballparks homered in*: 4 • *First HR*: 06/13/1921 off Howard Ehmke

Pink Hawley

EMERSON P. HAWLEY
B: 12/05/1872 D: 09/19/1938
BL

Year	Tm	Lg	Tot	H	A	Men-On 0	1	2	3	One-Game 2	3	4	LO	XN	IP	PH	RHP	LHP
1892	STL	NL	1	1	0	1	0	0	0	0	0	0	0	0	0	0	1	0
1894	STL	NL	2	2	0	1	1	0	0	0	0	0	0	0	1	0	0	1
1895	PIT	NL	5	1	4	4	1	0	0	0	0	0	0	0	1	0	3	1
1896	PIT	NL	1	0	1	1	0	0	0	0	0	0	0	0	0	0	0	1
1898	CIN	NL	1	0	1	0	0	1	0	0	0	0	0	0	0	0	0	0
1900	NY	NL	1	1	0	1	0	0	0	0	0	0	0	0	0	0	1	0
Total			11	5	6	8	2	1	0	0	0	0	0	0	2	0	5	3

Rank among batters: 2,419 • *Total ballparks homered in*: 6 • *First HR*: 10/12/1892 off Ben Sanders

Hal Haydel

JOHN HAROLD HAYDEL
B: 07/09/1944
BR

Year	Tm	Lg	Tot	H	A	Men-On 0	1	2	3	One-Game 2	3	4	LO	XN	IP	PH	RHP	LHP
1970	MIN	AL	1	1	0	1	0	0	0	0	0	0	0	0	0	0	0	1

Rank among batters: 4,707 • *Total ballparks homered in*: 1 • *First HR*: 09/07/1970 off Al Downing

Jack Hayden

JOHN FRANCIS HAYDEN
B: 10/21/1880 D: 08/03/1942
BL

Year	Tm	Lg	Tot	H	A	Men-On 0	1	2	3	One-Game 2	3	4	LO	XN	IP	PH	RHP	LHP
1906	BOS	AL	1	0	1	1	0	0	0	0	0	0	1	0	1	0	1	0

Rank among batters: 4,707 • *Total ballparks homered in*: 1 • *First HR*: 09/11/1906 off Walter Clarkson

Charlie Hayes

CHARLES DEWAYNE HAYES
B: 05/29/1965
BR

Year	Tm	Lg	Tot	H	A	Men-On 0	1	2	3	One-Game 2	3	4	LO	XN	IP	PH	RHP	LHP
1989	PHI	NL	8	3	5	5	1	2	0	0	0	0	0	0	0	0	7	1
1990	PHI	NL	10	3	7	5	4	1	0	0	0	0	0	0	0	0	5	5
1991	PHI	NL	12	6	6	7	2	2	1	0	0	0	0	0	0	0	8	4
1992	NY	AL	18	7	11	12	5	1	0	1	0	0	0	0	0	0	12	6
1993	COL	NL	25	17	8	11	7	6	1	1	0	0	0	0	0	0	20	5
1994	COL	NL	10	4	6	7	2	1	0	0	0	0	0	0	0	0	6	4
1995	PHI	NL	11	6	5	7	2	2	0	0	0	0	0	2	0	0	8	3
Total			94	46	48	54	23	15	2	2	0	0	0	2	0	0	66	28

Rank among batters: 535 • Top target (2 home runs): Rick Reed, Ron Darling, Brian Barnes, Jose Guzman, Kevin Gross, Donovan Osborne, Jay Howell, Steve Avery, Dave Burba, Zane Smith, Ramon Martinez, John Smoltz • *Number of pitchers victimized*: 82 • *Total ballparks homered in*: 21 • *First HR*: 07/07/1989 off John Smoltz

Frankie Hayes

FRANK WITMAN HAYES
B: 10/13/1914 D: 06/22/1955
BR

Year	Tm	Lg	Tot	H	A	Men-On 0	1	2	3	One-Game 2	3	4	LO	XN	IP	PH	RHP	LHP
1934	PHI	AL	6	4	2	3	2	1	0	0	0	0	0	1	0	1	6	0

Year	Tm	Lg	Tot	H	A	Men-On 0	1	2	3	One-Game 2	3	4	LO	XN	IP	PH	RHP	LHP

Frankie Hayes *continued*

Year	Tm	Lg	Tot	H	A	Men-On 0	1	2	3	One-Game 2	3	4	LO	XN	IP	PH	RHP	LHP
1936	PHI	AL	10	6	4	4	6	0	0	0	0	0	0	1	0	0	10	0
1937	PHI	AL	10	8	2	6	2	2	0	0	0	0	0	0	0	0	10	0
1938	PHI	AL	11	6	5	3	7	1	0	0	0	0	0	0	0	2	10	1
1939	PHI	AL	20	12	8	8	7	4	1	1	0	0	0	0	0	0	16	4
1940	PHI	AL	16	8	8	11	3	2	0	2	0	0	0	0	0	0	13	3
1941	PHI	AL	12	10	2	10	1	0	1	1	0	0	0	1	0	0	11	1
1942	STL	AL	2	1	1	0	1	1	0	0	0	0	0	0	0	0	2	0
1943	STL	AL	5	3	2	3	2	0	0	0	0	0	0	0	0	1	5	0
1944	PHI	AL	13	6	7	7	4	0	2	1	0	0	0	0	0	0	11	2
1945	PHI	AL	3	1	2	1	1	0	1	0	0	0	0	0	0	0	3	0
	CLE	AL	6	1	5	5	0	1	0	1	0	0	0	0	0	0	5	1
	Total		9	2	7	6	1	1	1	1	0	0	0	0	0	0	8	1
1946	CLE	AL	3	1	2	1	2	0	0	0	0	0	0	0	0	0	3	0
	CHI	AL	2	1	1	1	0	1	0	0	0	0	0	0	0	0	1	1
	Total		5	2	3	2	2	1	0	0	0	0	0	0	0	0	4	1
Total			119	68	51	63	38	13	5	6	0	0	0	3	0	4	106	13

Rank among batters: 392 • *Top target (4 home runs)*: Johnny Marcum, Bob Harris • *Number of pitchers victimized*: 82 • *Total ballparks homered in*: 8 • *First HR*: 04/18/1934 off Red Ruffing

Jackie Hayes

JOHN J. HAYES
B: 06/27/1861

Year	Tm	Lg	Tot	H	A	Men-On 0	1	2	3	One-Game 2	3	4	LO	XN	IP	PH	RHP	LHP
1882	WOR	NL	4	0	4	2	2	0	0	0	0	0	0	0	0	0	4	0
1883	PIT	AA	3	3	0	0	2	1	0	0	0	0	0	0	1	0	2	1
1886	WAS	NL	3	3	0	1	2	0	0	0	0	0	0	0	0	0	3	0
Total			10	6	4	3	6	1	0	0	0	0	0	0	1	0	9	1

Rank among batters: 2,500 • *Top target (2 home runs)*: Fred Goldsmith • *Number of pitchers victimized*: 9 • *Total ballparks homered in*: 5 • *First HR*: 05/03/1882 off Jim Whitney

Jackie Hayes

MINTER CARNEY HAYES
B: 07/19/1906 D: 02/09/1983
BR

Year	Tm	Lg	Tot	H	A	Men-On 0	1	2	3	One-Game 2	3	4	LO	XN	IP	PH	RHP	LHP
1929	WAS	AL	2	1	1	1	0	1	0	0	0	0	0	0	1	0	1	1
1930	WAS	AL	1	0	1	1	0	0	0	0	0	0	0	0	0	0	1	0
1932	CHI	AL	2	0	2	2	0	0	0	0	0	0	0	0	0	0	2	0
1933	CHI	AL	2	2	0	2	0	0	0	0	0	0	1	0	0	0	2	0
1934	CHI	AL	1	1	0	0	1	0	0	0	0	0	0	0	0	0	0	1
1935	CHI	AL	4	4	0	2	1	1	0	0	0	0	0	0	1	0	3	1
1936	CHI	AL	5	2	3	2	2	1	0	0	0	0	0	0	0	0	5	0
1937	CHI	AL	2	1	1	0	2	0	0	0	0	0	0	0	1	0	2	0
1938	CHI	AL	1	0	1	1	0	0	0	0	0	0	0	0	0	0	0	1
Total			20	11	9	11	6	3	0	0	0	0	1	0	3	0	16	4

Rank among batters: 1,810 • *Top target (3 home runs)*: Vic Sorrell • *Number of pitchers victimized*: 18 • *Total ballparks homered in*: 6 • *First HR*: 08/04/1929 off Emil Yde

Von Hayes

VON FRANCIS HAYES
B: 08/31/1958
BL

Year	Tm	Lg	Tot	H	A	Men-On 0	1	2	3	One-Game 2	3	4	LO	XN	IP	PH	RHP	LHP
1981	CLE	AL	1	0	1	1	0	0	0	0	0	0	0	0	0	0	1	0
1982	CLE	AL	14	3	11	4	5	5	0	0	0	0	0	0	0	0	11	3
1983	PHI	NL	6	3	3	4	2	0	0	0	0	0	0	0	0	0	6	0
1984	PHI	NL	16	10	6	12	3	1	0	2	0	0	0	0	0	2	14	2
1985	PHI	NL	13	12	1	8	3	1	1	1	0	0	1	0	1	1	9	4
1986	PHI	NL	19	11	8	11	6	1	1	1	0	0	0	0	0	0	16	3
1987	PHI	NL	21	14	7	13	5	3	0	2	0	0	0	0	0	0	18	3
1988	PHI	NL	6	2	4	4	2	0	0	0	0	0	0	1	0	0	4	2
1989	PHI	NL	26	15	11	13	10	3	0	4	1	0	0	0	1	0	18	8
1990	PHI	NL	17	10	7	10	5	2	0	0	0	0	0	0	0	0	12	5
1992	CAL	AL	4	2	2	1	2	1	0	0	0	0	0	0	0	0	4	0
Total			143	82	61	81	43	17	2	10	1	0	1	1	2	3	113	30

Rank among batters: 307 • *Top target (5 home runs)*: Tom Browning, Rick Sutcliffe • *Number of pitchers victimized*: 108 • *Total ballparks homered in*: 19 • *First HR*: 09/07/1981 off Jim Palmer • *2 HR in 1 inning*—vs NY: 06/11/1985

Joe Haynes

JOSEPH WALTON HAYNES
B: 09/21/1917 D: 01/06/1967
BR

Year	Tm	Lg	Tot	H	A	Men-On 0	1	2	3	One-Game 2	3	4	LO	XN	IP	PH	RHP	LHP
1951	WAS	AL	1	0	1	1	0	0	0	0	0	0	0	0	0	0	0	1

Rank among batters: 4,707 • *Total ballparks homered in*: 1 • *First HR*: 08/24/1951 off Ted Gray

Ray Hayworth

RAYMOND HALL HAYWORTH
B: 01/29/1904
BR

Year	Tm	Lg	Tot	H	A	Men-On 0	1	2	3	One-Game 2	3	4	LO	XN	IP	PH	RHP	LHP
1932	DET	AL	2	0	2	2	0	0	0	0	0	0	0	0	0	0	1	1
1933	DET	AL	1	0	1	0	1	0	0	0	0	0	0	0	0	0	1	0
1936	DET	AL	1	1	0	0	0	1	0	0	0	0	0	0	0	0	0	1
1937	DET	AL	1	0	1	1	0	0	0	0	0	0	0	0	0	0	1	0
Total			5	1	4	3	1	1	0	0	0	0	0	0	0	0	3	2

Rank among batters: 3,191 • *Total ballparks homered in*: 4 • *First HR*: 05/30/1932 off Bob Cooney

Red Hayworth

MYRON CLAUDE HAYWORTH
B: 05/14/1915
BR

Year	Tm	Lg	Tot	H	A	Men-On 0	1	2	3	One-Game 2	3	4	LO	XN	IP	PH	RHP	LHP
1944	STL	AL	1	1	0	0	0	1	0	0	0	0	0	0	0	0	1	0

Rank among batters: 4,707 • *Total ballparks homered in*: 1 • *First HR*: 07/26/1944 off Luke Hamlin

Bob Hazle

ROBERT SIDNEY HAZLE
B: 12/09/1930 D: 04/25/1992
BL

Year	Tm	Lg	Tot	H	A	Men-On 0	1	2	3	One-Game 2	3	4	LO	XN	IP	PH	RHP	LHP
1957	MIL	NL	7	2	5	4	1	2	0	1	0	0	0	1	0	0	6	1
1958	DET	AL	2	2	0	2	0	0	0	0	0	0	0	0	0	2	2	0
Total			9	4	5	6	1	2	0	1	0	0	0	1	0	2	8	1

Rank among batters: 2,587 • *Total ballparks homered in*: 6 • *First HR*: 08/09/1957 off Lindy McDaniel

Egyptian Healy

JOHN J. HEALY
B: 10/27/1866 D: 03/16/1899
BR

Year	Tm	Lg	Tot	H	A	Men-On 0	1	2	3	One-Game 2	3	4	LO	XN	IP	PH	RHP	LHP
1887	IND	NL	3	1	2	2	1	0	0	0	0	0	0	0	0	0	2	1
1888	IND	NL	1	1	0	0	1	0	0	0	0	0	0	0	0	0	0	1
1889	WAS	NL	1	1	0	1	0	0	0	0	0	0	0	0	0	0	1	0
1890	TOL	AA	1	0	1	0	1	0	0	0	0	0	0	0	0	0	1	0
Total			6	3	3	3	3	0	0	0	0	0	0	0	0	0	4	2

Rank among batters: 2,988 • *Total ballparks homered in*: 6 • *First HR*: 05/19/1887 off Tim Keefe

Fran Healy

FRANCIS XAVIER HEALY
B: 09/06/1946
BR

Year	Tm	Lg	Tot	H	A	Men-On 0	1	2	3	One-Game 2	3	4	LO	XN	IP	PH	RHP	LHP
1971	SF	NL	2	2	0	1	1	0	0	0	0	0	0	1	0	1	2	0
1972	SF	NL	1	0	1	0	0	1	0	0	0	0	0	0	0	0	1	0
1973	KC	AL	6	2	4	2	3	1	0	0	0	0	0	0	1	0	3	3
1974	KC	AL	9	5	4	6	3	0	0	0	0	0	0	0	0	0	5	4
1975	KC	AL	2	0	2	1	0	1	0	0	0	0	0	1	0	0	2	0
Total			20	9	11	10	7	3	0	0	0	0	0	2	1	1	13	7

Rank among batters: 1,810 • *Total ballparks homered in*: 9 • *First HR*: 04/15/1971 off Jim Ray

Bunny Hearn

BUNN HEARN
B: 05/21/1891 D: 10/19/1959
BL

Year	Tm	Lg	Tot	H	A	Men-On 0	1	2	3	One-Game 2	3	4	LO	XN	IP	PH	RHP	LHP
1910	STL	NL	1	0	1	1	0	0	0	0	0	0	0	0	0	0	1	0

Rank among batters: 4,707 • *Total ballparks homered in*: 1 • *First HR*: 10/10/1910 off Orlie Weaver

Ed Hearn

EDWARD JOHN HEARN
B: 08/23/1960
BR

Year	Tm	Lg	Tot	H	A	Men-On 0	1	2	3	One-Game 2	3	4	LO	XN	IP	PH	RHP	LHP
1986	NY	NL	4	4	0	3	0	1	0	0	0	0	0	0	0	0	2	2

Rank among batters: 3,427 • *Total ballparks homered in*: 1 • *First HR*: 06/15/1986 off Cecilio Guante

Jim Hearn

JAMES TOLBERT HEARN
B: 04/11/1921
BR

Year	Tm	Lg	Tot	H	A	Men-On 0	1	2	3	One-Game 2	3	4	LO	XN	IP	PH	RHP	LHP
1951	NY	NL	1	1	0	0	1	0	0	0	0	0	0	0	0	0	1	0
1952	NY	NL	3	2	1	1	2	0	0	0	0	0	0	0	0	0	1	2
1954	NY	NL	1	1	0	0	1	0	0	0	0	0	0	0	1	0	1	0
1955	NY	NL	4	4	0	3	1	0	0	1	0	0	0	0	1	0	2	2
Total			9	8	1	4	5	0	0	1	0	0	0	0	2	0	5	4

Rank among batters: 2,587 • *Total ballparks homered in*: 2 • *First HR*: 06/02/1951 off Junior Walsh

Jeff Heath

JOHN GEOFFREY HEATH
B: 04/01/1915 D: 12/09/1975
BL

Year	Tm	Lg	Tot	H	A	Men-On 0	1	2	3	One-Game 2	3	4	LO	XN	IP	PH	RHP	LHP
1936	CLE	AL	1	1	0	1	0	0	0	0	0	0	0	0	0	0	1	0
1938	CLE	AL	21	12	9	8	9	3	1	1	0	0	0	0	0	0	20	1
1939	CLE	AL	14	8	6	7	7	0	0	1	0	0	0	0	2	0	11	3
1940	CLE	AL	14	8	6	9	3	2	0	2	0	0	0	0	0	1	12	2
1941	CLE	AL	24	14	10	12	7	5	0	2	0	0	0	0	0	0	21	3
1942	CLE	AL	10	2	8	6	3	1	0	1	0	0	0	0	0	0	9	1
1943	CLE	AL	18	9	9	9	7	2	0	2	0	0	0	3	1	0	17	1
1944	CLE	AL	5	4	1	3	1	1	0	0	0	0	0	0	0	2	5	0
1945	CLE	AL	15	7	8	3	4	8	0	1	0	0	0	1	1	0	14	1
1946	WAS	AL	4	2	2	2	2	0	0	0	0	0	0	0	0	0	2	2
	STL	AL	12	7	5	6	4	2	0	0	0	0	0	1	0	0	12	0
	Total		16	9	7	8	6	2	0	0	0	0	0	1	0	0	14	2
1947	STL	AL	27	14	13	9	13	3	2	3	0	0	0	2	0	0	24	3
1948	BOS	NL	20	6	14	14	3	2	1	0	0	0	0	0	1	0	20	0
1949	BOS	NL	9	4	5	6	2	1	0	1	0	0	0	1	0	1	9	0
Total			194	98	96	95	65	30	4	14	0	0	0	8	5	4	177	17

Rank among batters: 194 • *Top target (6 home runs)*: Atley Donald • *Number of pitchers victimized*: 119 • *Total ballparks homered in*: 15 • *First HR*: 09/13/1936 off Herman Fink

Mike Heath

MICHAEL THOMAS HEATH
B: 02/05/1955
BR

Year	Tm	Lg	Tot	H	A	Men-On 0	1	2	3	One-Game 2	3	4	LO	XN	IP	PH	RHP	LHP
1979	OAK	AL	3	2	1	2	1	0	0	1	0	0	0	0	0	0	2	1
1980	OAK	AL	1	1	0	0	1	0	0	0	0	0	0	0	0	0	1	0
1981	OAK	AL	8	4	4	4	4	0	0	0	0	0	0	1	0	0	4	4
1982	OAK	AL	3	3	0	2	1	0	0	0	0	0	0	0	0	0	1	2
1983	OAK	AL	6	5	1	5	1	0	0	0	0	0	0	0	0	0	2	4
1984	OAK	AL	13	8	5	9	3	1	0	0	0	0	0	0	0	0	8	5
1985	OAK	AL	13	8	5	8	3	2	0	0	0	0	0	1	1	0	8	5
1986	STL	NL	4	1	3	1	2	1	0	0	0	0	0	0	0	0	0	4
	DET	AL	4	3	1	2	1	1	0	0	0	0	0	0	1	0	2	2
	Total		8	4	4	3	3	2	0	0	0	0	0	0	1	0	2	6
1987	DET	AL	8	8	0	4	3	1	0	0	0	0	0	0	0	0	3	5
1988	DET	AL	5	4	1	5	0	0	0	1	0	0	0	0	0	0	0	5
1989	DET	AL	10	5	5	6	2	2	0	2	0	0	0	0	0	0	5	5
1990	DET	AL	7	3	4	4	2	1	0	0	0	0	0	1	0	0	4	3
1991	ATL	NL	1	1	0	1	0	0	0	0	0	0	0	0	0	0	0	1
Total			86	56	30	53	24	9	0	4	0	0	0	3	2	0	40	46

Rank among batters: 602 • *Top target (3 home runs)*: Frank Tanana, Mark Langston, Curt Young • *Number of pitchers victimized*: 74 • *Total ballparks homered in*: 18 • *First HR*: 06/19/1979 off Dennis Leonard • *LCS HR*—1

Tommy Heath

THOMAS GEORGE HEATH
B: 08/18/1913 D: 02/26/1967
BR

Year	Tm	Lg	Tot	H	A	Men-On 0	1	2	3	One-Game 2	3	4	LO	XN	IP	PH	RHP	LHP
1937	STL	AL	1	1	0	1	0	0	0	0	0	0	0	0	0	0	0	1

Year	Tm	Lg	Tot	H	A	Men-On 0	1	2	3	One-Game 2	3	4	LO	XN	IP	PH	RHP	LHP

Tommy Heath *continued*

Year	Tm	Lg	Tot	H	A	0	1	2	3	2	3	4	LO	XN	IP	PH	RHP	LHP
1938	STL	AL	2	1	1	2	0	0	0	0	0	0	0	0	0	0	1	1
Total			3	2	1	3	0	0	0	0	0	0	0	0	0	0	1	2

Rank among batters: 3,735 • *Total ballparks homered in*: 2 • *First HR*: 07/24/1937 off Ken Chase

Cliff Heathcote

CLIFTON EARL HEATHCOTE
B: 01/24/1898 D: 01/19/1939
BL

Year	Tm	Lg	Tot	H	A	0	1	2	3	2	3	4	LO	XN	IP	PH	RHP	LHP
1918	STL	NL	4	3	1	0	1	3	0	0	0	0	0	0	1	0	4	0
1919	STL	NL	1	0	1	0	0	1	0	0	0	0	0	0	1	0	1	0
1920	STL	NL	3	2	1	2	0	1	0	0	0	0	0	0	0	0	2	1
1922	CHI	NL	1	0	1	0	0	1	0	0	0	0	0	0	0	0	1	0
1923	CHI	NL	1	1	0	1	0	0	0	0	0	0	0	0	0	0	1	0
1925	CHI	NL	5	3	2	2	3	0	0	0	0	0	0	0	1	0	4	1
1926	CHI	NL	10	8	2	5	4	1	0	1	0	0	0	1	2	0	8	2
1927	CHI	NL	2	2	0	1	1	0	0	0	0	0	0	0	0	0	2	0
1928	CHI	NL	3	1	2	3	0	0	0	0	0	0	0	0	0	0	3	0
1929	CHI	NL	2	1	1	2	0	0	0	0	0	0	0	0	0	0	2	0
1930	CHI	NL	9	5	4	8	1	0	0	1	0	0	0	0	0	1	7	2
1932	PHI	NL	1	1	0	0	1	0	0	0	0	0	0	0	0	0	1	0
Total			42	27	15	24	11	7	0	2	0	0	0	1	5	1	36	6

Rank among batters: 1,138 • *Top target (3 home runs)*: Ray Kremer • *Number of pitchers victimized*: 34 • *Total ballparks homered in*: 8 • *First HR*: 06/13/1918 off Erskine Mayer • *Hit for Cycle*—@PHI: 06/13/1918

Richie Hebner

RICHARD JOSEPH HEBNER
B: 11/26/1947
BL

Year	Tm	Lg	Tot	H	A	0	1	2	3	2	3	4	LO	XN	IP	PH	RHP	LHP
1969	PIT	NL	8	3	5	7	1	0	0	0	0	0	0	0	0	0	7	1
1970	PIT	NL	11	5	6	6	4	1	0	1	0	0	0	0	0	0	11	0
1971	PIT	NL	17	9	8	8	7	2	0	1	0	0	0	1	0	1	16	1
1972	PIT	NL	19	9	10	9	5	5	0	1	0	0	0	1	0	0	13	6
1973	PIT	NL	25	11	14	18	6	1	0	0	0	0	0	2	1	0	22	3
1974	PIT	NL	18	4	14	12	4	2	0	2	0	0	0	0	0	0	15	3
1975	PIT	NL	15	11	4	10	3	2	0	0	0	0	0	0	0	0	11	4
1976	PIT	NL	8	2	6	6	2	0	0	0	0	0	0	1	0	0	5	3
1977	PHI	NL	18	13	5	8	8	1	1	2	0	0	0	1	0	0	17	1
1978	PHI	NL	17	14	3	12	4	1	0	1	0	0	0	0	0	0	16	1
1979	NY	NL	10	6	4	4	5	1	0	1	0	0	0	1	0	0	8	2
1980	DET	AL	12	10	2	4	4	3	1	2	0	0	0	0	0	2	10	2
1981	DET	AL	5	4	1	2	2	1	0	1	0	0	0	0	0	0	4	1
1982	DET	AL	8	6	2	4	2	0	0	1	0	0	0	0	0	0	7	1
	PIT	NL	2	2	0	0	0	1	1	0	0	0	0	0	0	0	1	1
	Total		10	8	2	6	2	1	1	1	0	0	0	0	0	0	8	2
1983	PIT	NL	5	3	2	3	0	1	1	0	0	0	0	1	0	2	5	0
1984	CHI	NL	2	1	1	2	0	0	0	0	0	0	0	0	0	1	2	0
1985	CHI	NL	3	2	1	2	0	1	0	0	0	0	0	0	0	1	3	0
Total			203	115	88	119	57	23	4	13	0	0	0	8	1	7	173	30

Rank among batters: 177 • *Top target (5 home runs)*: Bill Stoneman, Ferguson Jenkins, Bob Gibson • *Number of pitchers victimized*: 140 • *Total ballparks homered in*: 22 • *First HR*: 05/04/1969 off Mudcat Grant • *World Series HR*—1; *LCS HR*—3

Guy Hecker

GUY JACKSON HECKER
B: 04/03/1856 D: 12/03/1938
BR

Year	Tm	Lg	Tot	H	A	0	1	2	3	2	3	4	LO	XN	IP	PH	RHP	LHP
1882	LOU	AA	3	0	3	2	1	0	0	0	0	0	0	0	0	0	2	0
1883	LOU	AA	1	1	0	0	0	1	0	0	0	0	0	0	0	0	1	0
1884	LOU	AA	4	0	4	1	1	2	0	0	0	0	0	0	0	0	2	0
1885	LOU	AA	2	2	0	1	1	0	0	0	0	0	0	0	1	0	2	0
1886	LOU	AA	4	3	1	2	1	1	0	0	1	0	0	0	3	0	3	0
1887	LOU	AA	4	2	2	3	1	0	0	0	0	0	0	0	0	0	1	2
1889	LOU	AA	1	1	0	0	0	1	0	0	0	0	0	0	0	0	1	0
Total			19	9	10	9	5	5	0	0	1	0	0	0	4	0	12	1

Rank among batters: 1,861 • *Top target (3 home runs)*: Dick Conway • *Number of pitchers victimized*: 16 • *Total ballparks homered in*: 8 • *First HR*: 05/30/1882 off Harry Arundel

Danny Heep

DANIEL WILLIAM HEEP
B: 07/03/1957
BL

Year	Tm	Lg	Tot	H	A	Men-On 0	Men-On 1	Men-On 2	Men-On 3	One-Game 2	One-Game 3	One-Game 4	LO	XN	IP	PH	RHP	LHP
1982	HOU	NL	4	1	3	2	1	1	0	0	0	0	0	0	0	0	4	0
1983	NY	NL	8	6	2	8	0	0	0	0	0	0	0	0	0	4	8	0
1984	NY	NL	1	1	0	1	0	0	0	0	0	0	0	0	0	0	1	0
1985	NY	NL	7	2	5	3	3	1	0	0	0	0	0	0	0	0	7	0
1986	NY	NL	5	3	2	1	3	1	0	0	0	0	0	0	0	0	5	0
1989	BOS	AL	5	1	4	2	1	2	0	0	0	0	0	1	0	1	5	0
Total			30	14	16	17	8	5	0	0	0	0	0	1	0	5	30	0

Rank among batters: 1,437 • *Top target (3 home runs)*: Charlie Lea • *Number of pitchers victimized*: 27 • *Total ballparks homered in*: 13 • *First HR*: 05/14/1982 off Dick Tidrow

Bob Heffner

ROBERT FREDERIC HEFFNER
B: 09/13/1938
BR

Year	Tm	Lg	Tot	H	A	Men-On 0	Men-On 1	Men-On 2	Men-On 3	One-Game 2	One-Game 3	One-Game 4	LO	XN	IP	PH	RHP	LHP
1964	BOS	AL	1	0	1	1	0	0	0	0	0	0	0	0	0	0	1	0

Rank among batters: 4,707 • *Total ballparks homered in*: 1 • *First HR*: 05/12/1964 off Mudcat Grant

Don Heffner

DONALD HENRY HEFFNER
B: 02/08/1911 D: 08/01/1989
BR

Year	Tm	Lg	Tot	H	A	Men-On 0	Men-On 1	Men-On 2	Men-On 3	One-Game 2	One-Game 3	One-Game 4	LO	XN	IP	PH	RHP	LHP
1938	STL	AL	2	1	1	0	1	1	0	0	0	0	0	0	0	0	2	0
1939	STL	AL	1	1	0	0	1	0	0	0	0	0	0	0	0	0	1	0
1940	STL	AL	3	3	0	3	0	0	0	0	0	0	0	0	0	0	2	1
Total			6	5	1	3	2	1	0	0	0	0	0	0	0	0	5	1

Rank among batters: 2,988 • *Total ballparks homered in*: 2 • *First HR*: 08/20/1938 off Roxie Lawson

Jim Hegan

JAMES EDWARD HEGAN
B: 08/03/1920 D: 06/17/1984
BR

Year	Tm	Lg	Tot	H	A	Men-On 0	Men-On 1	Men-On 2	Men-On 3	One-Game 2	One-Game 3	One-Game 4	LO	XN	IP	PH	RHP	LHP
1941	CLE	AL	1	0	1	1	0	0	0	0	0	0	0	0	0	0	1	0
1947	CLE	AL	4	2	2	1	3	0	0	0	0	0	0	0	0	0	3	1
1948	CLE	AL	14	9	5	7	6	0	1	1	0	0	0	0	0	0	9	5
1949	CLE	AL	8	6	2	5	2	1	0	0	0	0	0	1	0	0	3	5
1950	CLE	AL	14	8	6	11	1	1	1	1	0	0	0	1	0	0	10	4
1951	CLE	AL	6	3	3	3	2	1	0	0	0	0	0	0	0	0	4	2
1952	CLE	AL	4	4	0	1	2	1	0	0	0	0	0	0	0	0	4	0
1953	CLE	AL	9	7	2	6	2	1	0	0	0	0	0	0	0	0	4	5
1954	CLE	AL	11	7	4	8	2	1	0	0	0	0	0	0	0	0	7	4
1955	CLE	AL	9	3	6	6	2	0	1	0	0	0	0	0	0	0	2	7
1956	CLE	AL	6	4	2	3	2	0	1	0	0	0	0	0	0	0	4	2
1957	CLE	AL	4	4	0	2	2	0	0	0	0	0	0	0	0	0	0	4
1958	DET	AL	1	0	1	1	0	0	0	0	0	0	0	0	0	0	1	0
1960	CHI	NL	1	0	1	0	1	0	0	0	0	0	0	0	0	0	1	0
Total			92	57	35	55	27	6	4	2	0	0	0	2	0	0	53	39

Rank among batters: 554 • *Top target (7 home runs)*: Bobby Shantz • *Number of pitchers victimized*: 62 • *Total ballparks homered in*: 10 • *First HR*: 09/09/1941 off Tom Ferrick • *World Series HR*—1

Mike Hegan

JAMES MICHAEL HEGAN
B: 07/21/1942
BL

Year	Tm	Lg	Tot	H	A	Men-On 0	Men-On 1	Men-On 2	Men-On 3	One-Game 2	One-Game 3	One-Game 4	LO	XN	IP	PH	RHP	LHP
1967	NY	AL	1	1	0	1	0	0	0	0	0	0	0	1	0	0	0	1
1969	SEA	AL	8	4	4	5	2	1	0	1	0	0	0	1	0	1	6	2
1970	MIL	AL	11	5	6	5	5	1	0	0	0	0	0	0	0	0	7	4
1971	MIL	AL	4	3	1	3	1	0	0	0	0	0	0	0	0	0	3	1
1972	OAK	AL	1	0	1	1	0	0	0	0	0	0	0	0	0	0	1	0
1973	OAK	AL	1	0	1	1	0	0	0	0	0	0	0	0	0	1	1	0
	NY	AL	6	4	2	4	1	1	0	0	0	0	0	0	0	0	4	2
	Total		7	4	3	5	1	1	0	0	0	0	0	0	0	1	5	2
1974	NY	AL	2	1	1	1	0	1	0	0	0	0	0	0	0	0	1	1
	MIL	AL	7	5	2	2	3	2	0	1	0	0	0	1	0	1	5	2

Mike Hegan *continued*

Year	Tm	Lg	Tot	H	A	Men-On 0	Men-On 1	Men-On 2	Men-On 3	One-Game 2	One-Game 3	One-Game 4	LO	XN	IP	PH	RHP	LHP
1974	Total		9	6	3	3	3	3	0	1	0	0	0	1	0	1	6	3
1975	MIL	AL	5	4	1	5	0	0	0	1	0	0	0	0	0	0	5	0
1976	MIL	AL	5	1	4	3	2	0	0	0	0	0	0	0	0	0	5	0
1977	MIL	AL	2	0	2	2	0	0	0	0	0	0	0	0	0	1	2	0
Total			53	28	25	33	14	6	0	3	0	0	0	3	0	4	40	13

Rank among batters: 953 • *Top target (3 home runs)*: Mike Cuellar, Rick Wise • *Number of pitchers victimized*: 47 • *Total ballparks homered in*: 12 • *First HR*: 09/01/1967 off Dick Lines • *Hit for Cycle—@DET*: 09/03/1976

Jack Heidemann

JACK SEALE HEIDEMANN
B: 07/11/1949
BR

Year	Tm	Lg	Tot	H	A	Men-On 0	Men-On 1	Men-On 2	Men-On 3	One-Game 2	One-Game 3	One-Game 4	LO	XN	IP	PH	RHP	LHP
1970	CLE	AL	6	4	2	6	0	0	0	0	0	0	0	0	0	0	5	1
1975	NY	NL	1	1	0	1	0	0	0	0	0	0	0	0	0	0	0	1
1976	MIL	AL	2	0	2	2	0	0	0	0	0	0	0	0	0	0	0	2
Total			9	5	4	9	0	0	0	0	0	0	0	0	0	0	5	4

Rank among batters: 2,587 • *Total ballparks homered in*: 5 • *First HR*: 05/24/1970 off John Cumberland

John Heidrick

JOHN EMMETT HEIDRICK
B: 07/29/1876 D: 01/20/1916
BL

Year	Tm	Lg	Tot	H	A	Men-On 0	Men-On 1	Men-On 2	Men-On 3	One-Game 2	One-Game 3	One-Game 4	LO	XN	IP	PH	RHP	LHP
1899	STL	NL	2	2	0	2	0	0	0	0	0	0	0	0	0	0	1	1
1900	STL	NL	2	2	0	1	1	0	0	0	0	0	0	0	0	0	2	0
1901	STL	NL	6	3	3	3	2	1	0	0	0	0	0	0	2	0	6	0
1902	STL	AL	3	2	1	2	0	1	0	0	0	0	0	0	1	0	3	0
1903	STL	AL	1	1	0	1	0	0	0	0	0	0	0	0	1	0	0	1
1904	STL	AL	1	0	1	0	1	0	0	0	0	0	0	0	0	0	0	1
1908	STL	AL	1	0	1	1	0	0	0	0	0	0	0	0	0	0	1	0
Total			16	10	6	10	4	2	0	0	0	0	0	0	4	0	13	3

Rank among batters: 2,029 • *Total ballparks homered in*: 8 • *First HR*: 05/27/1899 off Brickyard Kennedy

Harry Heilmann

HARRY EDWIN HEILMANN
B: 08/03/1894 D: 07/09/1951
BR HOF

Year	Tm	Lg	Tot	H	A	Men-On 0	Men-On 1	Men-On 2	Men-On 3	One-Game 2	One-Game 3	One-Game 4	LO	XN	IP	PH	RHP	LHP
1914	DET	AL	2	2	0	0	2	0	0	0	0	0	0	0	0	0	1	1
1916	DET	AL	2	1	1	2	0	0	0	0	0	0	0	0	0	0	1	1
1917	DET	AL	5	1	4	2	2	1	0	0	0	0	0	0	0	0	3	2
1918	DET	AL	5	2	3	3	2	0	0	0	0	0	0	0	2	0	5	0
1919	DET	AL	8	3	5	3	4	0	1	1	0	0	0	1	1	0	6	2
1920	DET	AL	9	5	4	7	1	1	0	0	0	0	0	0	1	0	7	2
1921	DET	AL	19	7	12	7	5	7	0	1	0	0	0	0	1	0	14	5
1922	DET	AL	21	8	13	13	2	6	0	2	0	0	0	0	1	0	18	3
1923	DET	AL	18	11	7	13	5	0	0	0	0	0	0	0	0	0	13	5
1924	DET	AL	10	5	5	6	4	0	0	1	0	0	0	0	0	0	7	3
1925	DET	AL	13	6	7	11	1	1	0	1	0	0	0	0	0	0	3	10
1926	DET	AL	9	4	5	6	3	0	0	0	0	0	0	0	0	0	6	3
1927	DET	AL	14	10	4	7	6	1	0	1	0	0	0	0	0	0	9	5
1928	DET	AL	14	10	4	8	3	2	1	0	0	0	0	0	0	0	11	3
1929	DET	AL	15	9	6	4	10	1	0	2	0	0	0	0	0	0	10	5
1930	CIN	NL	19	4	15	11	5	2	1	1	0	0	0	0	0	0	13	6
Total			183	88	95	103	55	22	3	10	0	0	0	1	6	0	127	56

Rank among batters: 213 • *Top target (6 home runs)*: Eddie Rommel • *Number of pitchers victimized*: 115 • *Total ballparks homered in*: 14 • *First HR*: 07/05/1914 off Earl Hamilton

Fred Heimach

FREDERICK AMOS HEIMACH
B: 01/27/1901 D: 06/01/1973
BL

Year	Tm	Lg	Tot	H	A	Men-On 0	Men-On 1	Men-On 2	Men-On 3	One-Game 2	One-Game 3	One-Game 4	LO	XN	IP	PH	RHP	LHP
1923	PHI	AL	1	0	1	1	0	0	0	0	0	0	0	0	0	0	1	0
1929	NY	AL	1	1	0	1	0	0	0	0	0	0	0	0	1	0	1	0

Fred Heimach *continued*

Year	Tm	Lg	Tot	H	A	Men-On 0	1	2	3	One-Game 2	3	4	LO	XN	IP	PH	RHP	LHP
1932	BRO	NL	1	1	0	0	1	0	0	0	0	0	0	0	0	0	1	0
Total			3	2	1	2	1	0	0	0	0	0	0	0	1	0	3	0

Rank among batters: 3,735 • *Total ballparks homered in*: 2 • *First HR*: 06/28/1923 off Bob Shawkey

Tom Heintzelman

THOMAS KENNETH HEINTZELMAN
B: 11/03/1946
BR

Year	Tm	Lg	Tot	H	A	Men-On 0	1	2	3	One-Game 2	3	4	LO	XN	IP	PH	RHP	LHP
1974	STL	NL	1	1	0	0	1	0	0	0	0	0	0	0	0	0	0	1
1978	SF	NL	2	1	1	2	0	0	0	0	0	0	0	0	0	1	0	2
Total			3	2	1	2	1	0	0	0	0	0	0	0	0	1	0	3

Rank among batters: 3,735 • *Total ballparks homered in*: 3 • *First HR*: 05/15/1974 off Tug McGraw

Bob Heise

ROBERT LOWELL HEISE
B: 05/12/1947
BR

Year	Tm	Lg	Tot	H	A	Men-On 0	1	2	3	One-Game 2	3	4	LO	XN	IP	PH	RHP	LHP
1970	SF	NL	1	1	0	1	0	0	0	0	0	0	0	0	0	0	0	1

Rank among batters: 4,707 • *Total ballparks homered in*: 1 • *First HR*: 06/30/1970 off Danny Coombs

Al Heist

ALFRED MICHAEL HEIST
B: 10/05/1927
BR

Year	Tm	Lg	Tot	H	A	Men-On 0	1	2	3	One-Game 2	3	4	LO	XN	IP	PH	RHP	LHP
1960	CHI	NL	1	0	1	1	0	0	0	0	0	0	0	0	0	0	0	1
1961	CHI	NL	7	5	2	5	0	1	1	0	0	0	2	0	0	0	5	2
Total			8	5	3	6	0	1	1	0	0	0	2	0	0	0	5	3

Rank among batters: 2,703 • *Total ballparks homered in*: 3 • *First HR*: 09/04/1960 off Curt Simmons

Woodie Held

WOODSON GEORGE HELD
B: 03/25/1932
BR

Year	Tm	Lg	Tot	H	A	Men-On 0	1	2	3	One-Game 2	3	4	LO	XN	IP	PH	RHP	LHP
1957	KC	AL	20	10	10	12	6	1	1	2	0	0	0	0	0	0	17	3
1958	KC	AL	4	2	2	2	2	0	0	0	0	0	0	2	0	0	4	0
	CLE	AL	3	0	3	1	2	0	0	0	0	0	0	0	0	0	3	0
	Total		7	2	5	3	4	0	0	0	0	0	0	2	0	0	7	0
1959	CLE	AL	29	19	10	18	8	1	2	2	0	0	0	1	0	0	27	2
1960	CLE	AL	21	9	12	7	8	5	1	3	0	0	0	0	0	0	18	3
1961	CLE	AL	23	7	16	16	7	0	0	2	0	0	0	0	1	0	16	7
1962	CLE	AL	19	12	7	8	9	2	0	0	0	0	0	0	0	0	13	6
1963	CLE	AL	17	6	11	9	6	1	1	0	0	0	2	1	0	0	12	5
1964	CLE	AL	18	9	9	11	6	1	0	0	0	0	1	2	0	0	13	5
1965	WAS	AL	16	5	11	8	4	4	0	1	0	0	0	0	0	0	10	6
1966	BAL	AL	1	0	1	1	0	0	0	0	0	0	0	0	0	0	0	1
1967	BAL	AL	1	0	1	0	0	1	0	0	0	0	0	0	0	1	0	1
	CAL	AL	4	0	4	2	2	0	0	0	0	0	0	0	0	0	2	2
	Total		5	0	5	2	2	1	0	0	0	0	0	0	0	1	2	3
1969	CHI	AL	3	2	1	3	0	0	0	0	0	0	0	0	0	1	3	0
Total			179	81	98	98	60	16	5	10	0	0	3	6	1	2	138	41

Rank among batters: 221 • *Top target (6 home runs)*: Tom Brewer • *Number of pitchers victimized*: 108 • *Total ballparks homered in*: 13 • *First HR*: 06/23/1957 off Tom Brewer

Hank Helf

HENRY HARTZ HELF
B: 08/26/1913 D: 10/27/1984
BR

Year	Tm	Lg	Tot	H	A	Men-On 0	1	2	3	One-Game 2	3	4	LO	XN	IP	PH	RHP	LHP
1946	STL	AL	6	4	2	5	1	0	0	0	0	0	0	0	0	0	3	3

Rank among batters: 2,988 • *Total ballparks homered in*: 2 • *First HR*: 05/19/1946 off Dick Fowler

Tommy Helms

TOMMY VANN HELMS
B: 05/05/1941
BR

Year	Tm	Lg	Tot	H	A	Men-On				One-Game			LO	XN	IP	PH	RHP	LHP
						0	1	2	3	2	3	4						
1966	CIN	NL	9	4	5	5	3	1	0	0	0	0	0	0	0	0	8	1
1967	CIN	NL	2	0	2	1	1	0	0	0	0	0	0	1	1	0	1	1
1968	CIN	NL	2	2	0	1	1	0	0	0	0	0	0	0	0	0	1	1
1969	CIN	NL	1	0	1	1	0	0	0	0	0	0	0	0	0	0	1	0
1970	CIN	NL	1	1	0	0	1	0	0	0	0	0	0	0	0	0	1	0
1971	CIN	NL	3	0	3	3	0	0	0	0	0	0	0	0	0	0	3	0
1972	HOU	NL	5	1	4	1	1	3	0	0	0	0	0	0	0	0	2	3
1973	HOU	NL	4	1	3	0	3	0	1	0	0	0	0	0	0	0	4	0
1974	HOU	NL	5	3	2	1	3	1	0	0	0	0	0	0	0	0	5	0
1976	PIT	NL	1	1	0	0	1	0	0	0	0	0	0	0	0	1	0	1
1977	BOS	AL	1	1	0	0	1	0	0	0	0	0	0	0	0	0	1	0
Total			34	14	20	13	15	5	1	0	0	0	0	1	1	1	27	7

Rank among batters: 1,315 • *Top target (3 home runs)*: Ron Reed • *Number of pitchers victimized*: 30 • *Total ballparks homered in*: 13 • *First HR*: 04/19/1966 off Steve Blass

George Hemming

GEORGE EARL HEMMING
B: 12/15/1868 D: 06/03/1930
BR

Year	Tm	Lg	Tot	H	A	Men-On				One-Game			LO	XN	IP	PH	RHP	LHP
						0	1	2	3	2	3	4						
1894	LOU	NL	2	0	2	1	1	0	0	0	0	0	0	0	0	0	2	0
1895	BAL	NL	1	0	1	0	0	1	0	0	0	0	0	0	0	0	0	1
Total			3	0	3	1	1	1	0	0	0	0	0	0	0	0	2	1

Rank among batters: 3,735 • *Total ballparks homered in*: 3 • *First HR*: 05/27/1894 off Frank Dwyer

Scott Hemond

SCOTT MATHEW HEMOND
B: 11/18/1965
BR

Year	Tm	Lg	Tot	H	A	Men-On				One-Game			LO	XN	IP	PH	RHP	LHP
						0	1	2	3	2	3	4						
1993	OAK	AL	6	3	3	2	3	1	0	0	0	0	0	0	0	0	4	2
1994	OAK	AL	3	2	1	1	1	1	0	0	0	0	0	0	0	0	2	1
1995	STL	NL	3	3	0	3	0	0	0	0	0	0	0	0	0	0	2	1
Total			12	8	4	6	4	2	0	0	0	0	0	0	0	0	8	4

Rank among batters: 2,325 • *Total ballparks homered in*: 6 • *First HR*: 07/21/1993 off Bill Wertz

Charlie Hemphill

CHARLES JUDSON HEMPHILL
B: 04/20/1876 D: 06/22/1953
BL

Year	Tm	Lg	Tot	H	A	Men-On				One-Game			LO	XN	IP	PH	RHP	LHP
						0	1	2	3	2	3	4						
1899	STL	NL	1	1	0	0	1	0	0	0	0	0	0	0	0	0	0	1
	CLE	NL	2	0	2	0	2	0	0	0	0	0	0	0	1	0	2	0
	Total		3	1	2	2	1	0	0	0	0	0	0	0	1	0	2	1
1901	BOS	AL	3	1	2	1	2	0	0	0	0	0	0	0	0	0	3	0
1902	STL	AL	6	4	2	1	4	1	0	0	0	0	0	0	4	0	4	2
1903	STL	AL	3	2	1	1	1	1	0	0	0	0	0	0	2	0	3	0
1904	STL	AL	2	0	2	0	2	0	0	0	0	0	0	1	2	0	1	1
1906	STL	AL	4	3	1	3	1	0	0	0	0	0	0	0	3	0	3	1
1911	NY	AL	1	1	0	1	0	0	0	0	0	0	0	0	0	0	1	0
Total			22	12	10	9	11	2	0	0	0	0	0	1	12	0	17	5

Rank among batters: 1,719 • *Total ballparks homered in*: 10 • *First HR*: 06/27/1899 off Wiley Piatt

Rollie Hemsley

RALSTON BURDETT HEMSLEY
B: 06/24/1907 D: 07/31/1972
BR

Year	Tm	Lg	Tot	H	A	Men-On				One-Game			LO	XN	IP	PH	RHP	LHP
						0	1	2	3	2	3	4						
1930	PIT	NL	2	0	2	1	1	0	0	0	0	0	0	0	0	0	2	0
1931	CHI	NL	3	1	2	2	1	0	0	0	0	0	0	0	0	0	3	0
1932	CHI	NL	4	1	3	1	2	1	0	0	0	0	0	0	0	0	4	0
1933	STL	AL	1	1	0	0	0	1	0	0	0	0	0	0	1	0	0	1
1934	STL	AL	2	2	0	1	1	0	0	0	0	0	0	0	0	0	1	1
1936	STL	AL	2	0	2	2	0	0	0	0	0	0	0	0	0	0	2	0
1937	STL	AL	3	2	1	2	1	0	0	0	0	0	0	0	0	1	2	1
1938	CLE	AL	2	1	1	1	1	0	0	0	0	0	0	0	0	0	2	0

Rollie Hemsley *continued*

Year	Tm	Lg	Tot	H	A	Men-On 0	1	2	3	One-Game 2	3	4	LO	XN	IP	PH	RHP	LHP
1939	CLE	AL	2	1	1	1	1	0	0	0	0	0	0	0	0	0	1	1
1940	CLE	AL	4	1	3	3	1	0	0	0	0	0	0	0	0	0	2	2
1941	CLE	AL	2	0	2	1	1	0	0	0	0	0	0	0	0	0	1	1
1943	NY	AL	2	1	1	2	0	0	0	0	0	0	0	0	0	0	1	1
1944	NY	AL	2	2	0	1	1	0	0	0	0	0	0	0	0	0	2	0
Total			31	13	18	18	11	2	0	0	0	0	0	0	1	1	23	8

Rank among batters: 1,400 • Top target (2 home runs): Johnny Rigney, Eddie Smith, Thornton Lee, Atley Donald • *Number of pitchers victimized*: 27 • *Total ballparks homered in*: 12 • *First HR*: 04/15/1930 off Red Lucas

Solly Hemus

SOLOMON JOSEPH HEMUS
B: 04/17/1923
BL

Year	Tm	Lg	Tot	H	A	Men-On 0	1	2	3	One-Game 2	3	4	LO	XN	IP	PH	RHP	LHP
1951	STL	NL	2	1	1	1	1	0	0	0	0	0	0	0	0	0	2	0
1952	STL	NL	15	7	8	10	4	0	1	3	0	0	2	0	0	0	6	9
1953	STL	NL	14	7	7	7	7	0	0	0	0	0	1	0	0	0	13	1
1954	STL	NL	2	1	1	1	1	0	0	0	0	0	0	0	0	0	2	0
1955	STL	NL	5	4	1	4	1	0	0	0	0	0	0	0	0	0	4	1
1956	PHI	NL	5	2	3	3	1	0	1	0	0	0	0	0	0	0	5	0
1958	PHI	NL	8	2	6	5	3	0	0	0	0	0	0	0	0	0	6	2
Total			51	24	27	31	18	0	2	3	0	0	3	0	0	0	38	13

Rank among batters: 979 • *Top target (3 home runs)*: Bob Friend • *Number of pitchers victimized*: 42 • *Total ballparks homered in*: 10 • *First HR*: 05/06/1951 off Don Newcombe

Dave Henderson

DAVID LEE HENDERSON
B: 07/21/1958
BR

Year	Tm	Lg	Tot	H	A	Men-On 0	1	2	3	One-Game 2	3	4	LO	XN	IP	PH	RHP	LHP
1981	SEA	AL	6	5	1	4	2	0	0	0	0	0	0	0	0	0	2	4
1982	SEA	AL	14	8	6	5	6	2	1	0	0	0	0	1	0	0	6	8
1983	SEA	AL	17	9	8	9	4	4	0	1	0	0	0	0	2	0	11	6
1984	SEA	AL	14	8	6	12	1	1	0	0	0	0	0	1	0	0	9	5
1985	SEA	AL	14	8	6	8	2	4	0	0	0	0	0	0	0	0	11	3
1986	SEA	AL	14	10	4	9	5	0	0	1	0	0	0	1	0	0	8	6
	BOS	AL	1	0	1	1	0	0	0	0	0	0	0	0	0	0	1	0
	Total		15	10	5	10	5	0	0	1	0	0	0	1	0	0	9	6
1987	BOS	AL	8	4	4	4	3	1	0	0	0	0	0	1	0	1	4	4
1988	OAK	AL	24	12	12	16	5	3	0	0	0	0	0	1	0	0	18	6
1989	OAK	AL	15	10	5	10	5	0	0	0	0	0	0	0	0	0	10	5
1990	OAK	AL	20	11	9	11	9	0	0	1	0	0	0	0	0	0	9	11
1991	OAK	AL	25	15	10	15	5	5	0	0	1	0	0	0	0	0	17	8
1993	OAK	AL	20	7	13	15	3	1	1	1	0	0	0	0	0	0	9	11
1994	KC	AL	5	2	3	3	1	1	0	0	0	0	0	0	0	0	2	3
Total			197	109	88	122	51	22	2	4	1	0	0	5	2	1	117	80

Rank among batters: 189 • *Top target (5 home runs)*: Jim Abbott, Jimmy Key • *Number of pitchers victimized*: 135 • *Total ballparks homered in*: 16 • *First HR*: 04/17/1981 off Steve McCatty • *World Series HR*—4; *LCS HR*—3

Hardie Henderson

JAMES HARDING HENDERSON
B: 10/31/1862 D: 02/06/1903
BR

Year	Tm	Lg	Tot	H	A	Men-On 0	1	2	3	One-Game 2	3	4	LO	XN	IP	PH	RHP	LHP
1883	BAL	AA	1	0	1	0	1	0	0	0	0	0	0	0	0	0	1	0
1885	BAL	AA	1	0	1	1	0	0	0	0	0	0	0	0	0	0	1	0
Total			2	0	2	1	1	0	0	0	0	0	0	0	0	0	2	0

Rank among batters: 4,129 • *Total ballparks homered in*: 2 • *First HR*: 08/07/1883 off Fred Corey

Ken Henderson

KENNETH JOSEPH HENDERSON
B: 06/15/1946
BB

Year	Tm	Lg	Tot	H	A	Men-On 0	1	2	3	One-Game 2	3	4	LO	XN	IP	PH	RHP	LHP
1966	SF	NL	1	1	0	1	0	0	0	0	0	0	0	0	0	0	1	0
1967	SF	NL	4	2	2	3	1	0	0	1	0	0	0	0	0	1	1	3
1969	SF	NL	6	3	3	3	2	1	0	0	0	0	0	0	0	0	5	1

Year	Tm	Lg	Tot	H	A	Men-On 0	1	2	3	One-Game 2	3	4	LO	XN	IP	PH	RHP	LHP

Ken Henderson *continued*

Year	Tm	Lg	Tot	H	A	Men-On 0	1	2	3	One-Game 2	3	4	LO	XN	IP	PH	RHP	LHP
1970	SF	NL	17	9	8	6	6	3	2	0	0	0	0	1	0	0	14	3
1971	SF	NL	15	8	7	12	1	2	0	0	0	0	0	0	0	0	12	3
1972	SF	NL	18	11	7	12	3	3	0	2	0	0	0	0	0	0	17	1
1973	CHI	AL	6	2	4	2	0	3	1	0	0	0	0	0	0	0	4	2
1974	CHI	AL	20	13	7	14	4	2	0	2	0	0	0	0	0	0	17	3
1975	CHI	AL	9	3	6	5	2	2	0	1	0	0	0	0	0	0	6	3
1976	ATL	NL	13	6	7	6	5	2	0	0	0	0	0	0	0	1	12	1
1977	TEX	AL	5	2	3	2	2	1	0	0	0	0	0	1	1	0	3	2
1978	NY	NL	1	1	0	0	1	0	0	0	0	0	0	0	0	0	1	0
	CIN	NL	3	1	2	1	0	2	0	0	0	0	0	1	0	1	2	1
	Total		4	2	2	1	1	2	0	0	0	0	0	1	0	1	3	1
1979	CHI	NL	2	0	2	2	0	0	0	0	0	0	0	0	0	1	1	1
1980	CHI	NL	2	0	2	2	0	0	0	0	0	0	0	0	0	1	2	0
Total			122	62	60	71	27	21	3	6	0	0	0	3	1	5	98	24

Rank among batters: 377 • *Top target (5 home runs)*: Clay Kirby, Dave Goltz • *Number of pitchers victimized*: 89 • *Total ballparks homered in*: 26 • *First HR*: 09/21/1966 off Tommie Sisk • *Switch hit HR in 1 game*—1 time

Rickey Henderson

RICKEY HENLEY HENDERSON
B: 12/25/1957
BR

Year	Tm	Lg	Tot	H	A	Men-On 0	1	2	3	One-Game 2	3	4	LO	XN	IP	PH	RHP	LHP
1979	OAK	AL	1	1	0	1	0	0	0	0	0	0	1	0	0	0	1	0
1980	OAK	AL	9	3	6	4	2	3	0	0	0	0	1	0	1	0	3	6
1981	OAK	AL	6	5	1	5	1	0	0	0	0	0	3	0	0	0	2	4
1982	OAK	AL	10	5	5	6	4	0	0	0	0	0	3	0	0	0	7	3
1983	OAK	AL	9	5	4	6	2	1	0	0	0	0	2	0	0	0	5	4
1984	OAK	AL	16	7	9	8	7	1	0	0	0	0	2	0	0	0	9	7
1985	NY	AL	24	8	16	16	7	1	0	2	0	0	7	0	0	0	12	12
1986	NY	AL	28	13	15	20	5	3	0	1	0	0	9	0	0	0	20	8
1987	NY	AL	17	10	7	13	4	0	0	1	0	0	6	0	0	0	10	7
1988	NY	AL	6	2	4	4	2	0	0	0	0	0	1	0	0	0	2	4
1989	NY	AL	3	1	2	1	1	1	0	0	0	0	1	0	0	0	3	0
	OAK	AL	9	6	3	7	1	1	0	0	0	0	4	0	0	0	8	1
	Total		12	7	5	8	2	2	0	0	0	0	5	0	0	0	11	1
1990	OAK	AL	28	8	20	20	6	2	0	3	0	0	5	1	0	0	19	9
1991	OAK	AL	18	8	10	10	3	4	1	1	0	0	5	0	0	0	10	8
1992	OAK	AL	15	10	5	11	2	2	0	0	0	0	5	1	0	0	10	5
1993	OAK	AL	17	8	9	14	2	1	0	1	0	0	7	1	0	0	7	10
	TOR	AL	4	2	2	4	0	0	0	0	0	0	1	0	0	0	2	2
	Total		21	10	11	18	2	1	0	1	0	0	8	1	0	0	9	12
1994	OAK	AL	6	4	2	5	0	1	0	0	0	0	3	0	0	0	3	3
1995	OAK	AL	9	3	6	6	2	1	0	0	0	0	1	1	0	1	7	2
Total			235	109	126	161	51	22	1	9	0	0	67	4	1	1	140	95

Rank among batters: 135 • *Top target (11 home runs)*: Frank Tanana • *Number of pitchers victimized*: 170 • *Total ballparks homered in*: 19 • *First HR*: 09/17/1979 off Steve Comer • *World Series HR—2; LCS HR—2*

Steve Henderson

STEVEN CURTIS HENDERSON
B: 11/18/1952
BR

Year	Tm	Lg	Tot	H	A	Men-On 0	1	2	3	One-Game 2	3	4	LO	XN	IP	PH	RHP	LHP
1977	NY	NL	12	10	2	3	7	1	1	0	0	0	0	2	0	0	10	2
1978	NY	NL	10	7	3	6	2	1	1	0	0	0	1	0	0	3	5	5
1979	NY	NL	5	2	3	3	2	0	0	0	0	0	0	0	0	0	3	2
1980	NY	NL	8	4	4	3	1	4	0	1	0	0	0	0	1	1	8	0
1981	CHI	NL	5	3	2	2	3	0	0	1	0	0	0	0	0	0	5	0
1982	CHI	NL	2	0	2	1	1	0	0	0	0	0	0	0	0	0	0	2
1983	SEA	AL	10	5	5	8	2	0	0	2	0	0	0	0	0	0	5	5
1984	SEA	AL	10	4	6	7	3	0	0	0	0	0	0	0	1	0	4	6
1985	OAK	AL	3	1	2	2	1	0	0	0	0	0	0	0	0	0	1	2
1987	OAK	AL	3	1	2	2	1	0	0	0	0	0	0	0	0	0	0	3
Total			68	37	31	37	23	6	2	4	0	0	1	2	2	4	41	27

Rank among batters: 767 • *Top target (3 home runs)*: Kent Tekulve, Bruce Sutter, Eddie Solomon • *Number of pitchers victimized*: 57 • *Total ballparks homered in*: 15 • *First HR*: 06/21/1977 off Don Collins

Bob Hendley

CHARLES ROBERT HENDLEY
B: 04/30/1939
BR

Year	Tm	Lg	Tot	H	A	Men-On 0	Men-On 1	Men-On 2	Men-On 3	One-Game 2	One-Game 3	One-Game 4	LO	XN	IP	PH	RHP	LHP
1962	MIL	NL	1	1	0	0	1	0	0	0	0	0	0	0	0	0	1	0

Rank among batters: 4,707 • *Total ballparks homered in*: 1 • *First HR*: 08/04/1962 off Dallas Green

George Hendrick

GEORGE ANDREW HENDRICK
B: 10/18/1949
BR

Year	Tm	Lg	Tot	H	A	Men-On 0	Men-On 1	Men-On 2	Men-On 3	One-Game 2	One-Game 3	One-Game 4	LO	XN	IP	PH	RHP	LHP
1972	OAK	AL	4	3	1	1	2	1	0	0	0	0	0	1	0	0	4	0
1973	CLE	AL	21	14	7	14	6	1	0	1	1	0	0	0	0	0	12	9
1974	CLE	AL	19	12	7	11	5	2	1	3	0	0	0	0	0	0	11	8
1975	CLE	AL	24	13	11	14	6	3	1	2	0	0	0	0	0	0	14	10
1976	CLE	AL	25	11	14	17	6	2	0	2	0	0	0	1	0	0	20	5
1977	SD	NL	23	14	9	13	7	3	0	3	0	0	0	0	0	0	18	5
1978	SD	NL	3	2	1	3	0	0	0	0	0	0	0	0	0	0	3	0
	STL	NL	17	7	10	10	3	3	1	1	0	0	0	0	0	0	9	8
	Total		20	9	11	13	3	3	1	1	0	0	0	0	0	0	12	8
1979	STL	NL	16	7	9	8	6	2	0	1	0	0	0	0	0	0	9	7
1980	STL	NL	25	13	12	14	7	4	0	2	0	0	0	2	0	0	15	10
1981	STL	NL	18	6	12	11	5	2	0	1	0	0	0	2	1	0	11	7
1982	STL	NL	19	10	9	11	6	1	1	2	0	0	0	0	0	0	15	4
1983	STL	NL	18	10	8	8	9	1	0	2	0	0	0	1	0	0	11	7
1984	STL	NL	9	2	7	5	4	0	0	0	0	0	0	0	0	0	6	3
1985	PIT	NL	2	0	2	1	1	0	0	0	0	0	0	0	0	0	2	0
	CAL	AL	2	0	2	1	0	1	0	0	0	0	0	0	0	0	1	1
	Total		4	0	4	2	1	1	0	0	0	0	0	0	0	0	3	1
1986	CAL	AL	14	8	6	10	3	0	1	0	0	0	0	0	0	0	5	9
1987	CAL	AL	5	1	4	1	1	3	0	0	0	0	0	0	0	3	1	4
1988	CAL	AL	3	2	1	1	1	1	0	0	0	0	0	0	0	1	1	2
Total			267	135	132	154	78	30	5	20	1	0	0	7	1	4	168	99

Rank among batters: 94 • *Top target (5 home runs)*: Bob Knepper, Pete Falcone • *Number of pitchers victimized*: 169 • *Total ballparks homered in*: 27 • *First HR*: 05/28/1972 off Steve Kealey

Harvey Hendrick

HARVEY HENDRICK
B: 11/09/1897 D: 10/29/1941
BL

Year	Tm	Lg	Tot	H	A	Men-On 0	Men-On 1	Men-On 2	Men-On 3	One-Game 2	One-Game 3	One-Game 4	LO	XN	IP	PH	RHP	LHP
1923	NY	AL	3	3	0	2	0	0	1	0	0	0	0	0	1	0	1	2
1924	NY	AL	1	1	0	0	0	0	1	0	0	0	0	0	1	0	0	1
1927	BRO	NL	4	3	1	3	1	0	0	0	0	0	0	0	1	0	3	1
1928	BRO	NL	11	8	3	4	6	0	1	0	0	0	0	0	1	1	9	2
1929	BRO	NL	14	1	13	5	5	4	0	1	0	0	0	0	1	0	12	2
1930	BRO	NL	5	3	2	2	1	2	0	0	0	0	0	0	0	1	5	0
1931	CIN	NL	1	0	1	0	0	1	0	0	0	0	0	0	0	0	1	0
1932	STL	NL	1	1	0	0	1	0	0	0	0	0	0	0	0	0	1	0
	CIN	NL	4	1	3	3	1	0	0	0	0	0	0	0	0	0	2	2
	Total		5	2	3	3	2	0	0	0	0	0	0	0	0	0	3	2
1933	CHI	NL	4	2	2	0	1	2	1	0	0	0	0	1	0	1	4	0
Total			48	23	25	19	16	9	4	1	0	0	0	1	5	3	38	10

Rank among batters: 1,024 • *Top target (4 home runs)*: Bob Smith, Phil Collins • *Number of pitchers victimized*: 35 • *Total ballparks homered in*: 9 • *First HR*: 09/25/1923 off Earl Whitehill

Ellie Hendricks

ELROD JEROME HENDRICKS
B: 12/22/1940
BL

Year	Tm	Lg	Tot	H	A	Men-On 0	Men-On 1	Men-On 2	Men-On 3	One-Game 2	One-Game 3	One-Game 4	LO	XN	IP	PH	RHP	LHP
1968	BAL	AL	7	3	4	4	3	0	0	0	0	0	0	0	0	1	7	0
1969	BAL	AL	12	6	6	6	4	2	0	0	0	0	0	0	0	1	12	0
1970	BAL	AL	12	4	8	6	4	1	1	0	0	0	0	0	0	1	9	3
1971	BAL	AL	9	4	5	4	4	1	0	0	0	0	0	0	0	0	9	0
1972	CHI	NL	2	2	0	0	1	1	0	1	0	0	0	0	0	0	2	0
1973	BAL	AL	3	1	2	0	3	0	0	0	0	0	0	1	0	0	3	0
1974	BAL	AL	3	0	3	2	1	0	0	0	0	0	0	0	0	0	3	0

Ellie Hendricks *continued*

Year	Tm	Lg	Tot	H	A	Men-On 0	Men-On 1	Men-On 2	Men-On 3	One-Game 2	One-Game 3	One-Game 4	LO	XN	IP	PH	RHP	LHP
1975	BAL	AL	8	3	5	3	2	2	1	0	0	0	0	1	0	0	7	1
1976	BAL	AL	1	0	1	0	1	0	0	0	0	0	0	0	0	0	1	0
	NY	AL	3	1	2	2	1	0	0	0	0	0	0	0	0	0	2	1
	Total		4	1	3	2	2	0	0	0	0	0	0	0	0	0	3	1
1977	NY	AL	1	1	0	0	1	0	0	0	0	0	0	0	0	0	1	0
1978	BAL	AL	1	0	1	1	0	0	0	0	0	0	0	0	0	0	1	0
Total			62	25	37	28	25	7	2	1	0	0	0	2	0	3	57	5

Rank among batters: 835 • *Top target (4 home runs)*: Denny McLain, Mel Stottlemyre, Marty Pattin • *Number of pitchers victimized*: 45 • *Total ballparks homered in*: 14 • *First HR*: 05/15/1968 off Denny McLain • *World Series HR—1; LCS HR—1*

Claude Hendrix

CLAUDE RAYMOND HENDRIX
B: 04/13/1889 D: 03/22/1944
BR

Year	Tm	Lg	Tot	H	A	Men-On 0	Men-On 1	Men-On 2	Men-On 3	One-Game 2	One-Game 3	One-Game 4	LO	XN	IP	PH	RHP	LHP
1911	PIT	NL	1	1	0	1	0	0	0	0	0	0	0	0	1	0	1	0
1912	PIT	NL	1	1	0	0	1	0	0	0	0	0	0	0	0	0	1	0
1913	PIT	NL	1	1	0	1	0	0	0	0	0	0	0	0	0	0	1	0
1914	CHI	FL	2	1	1	1	1	0	0	0	0	0	0	0	0	0	0	2
1915	CHI	FL	4	2	2	1	3	0	0	0	0	0	0	0	0	1	1	3
1916	CHI	NL	1	1	0	0	1	0	0	0	0	0	0	0	0	0	1	0
1918	CHI	NL	3	3	0	1	1	1	0	0	0	0	0	0	0	0	2	1
1919	CHI	NL	1	0	1	1	0	0	0	0	0	0	0	0	0	0	1	0
Total			14	10	4	6	7	1	0	0	0	0	0	0	1	1	8	6

Rank among batters: 2,169 • *Top target (2 home runs)*: Thomas Seaton • *Number of pitchers victimized*: 13 • *Total ballparks homered in*: 5 • *First HR*: 09/02/1911 off Bob Harmon

Tim Hendryx

TIMOTHY GREEN HENDRYX
B: 01/31/1891 D: 08/14/1957
BR

Year	Tm	Lg	Tot	H	A	Men-On 0	Men-On 1	Men-On 2	Men-On 3	One-Game 2	One-Game 3	One-Game 4	LO	XN	IP	PH	RHP	LHP
1912	CLE	AL	1	1	0	0	0	1	0	0	0	0	0	0	1	0	1	0
1917	NY	AL	5	5	0	4	1	0	0	1	0	0	0	0	0	0	3	2
Total			6	6	0	4	1	1	0	1	0	0	0	0	1	0	4	2

Rank among batters: 2,988 • *Top target (2 home runs)*: Dutch Leonard • *Number of pitchers victimized*: 5 • *Total ballparks homered in*: 2 • *First HR*: 09/27/1912 off Charlie Wheatley

Dave Hengel

DAVID LEE HENGEL
B: 12/18/1961
BR

Year	Tm	Lg	Tot	H	A	Men-On 0	Men-On 1	Men-On 2	Men-On 3	One-Game 2	One-Game 3	One-Game 4	LO	XN	IP	PH	RHP	LHP
1986	SEA	AL	1	0	1	1	0	0	0	0	0	0	0	0	0	0	1	0
1987	SEA	AL	1	1	0	0	0	1	0	0	0	0	0	0	0	1	0	1
1988	SEA	AL	2	2	0	0	2	0	0	0	0	0	0	0	0	0	0	2
Total			4	3	1	1	2	1	0	0	0	0	0	0	0	1	1	3

Rank among batters: 3,427 • *Total ballparks homered in*: 2 • *First HR*: 10/03/1986 off Ken Schrom

Gail Henley

GAIL CURTICE HENLEY
B: 10/15/1928
BL

Year	Tm	Lg	Tot	H	A	Men-On 0	Men-On 1	Men-On 2	Men-On 3	One-Game 2	One-Game 3	One-Game 4	LO	XN	IP	PH	RHP	LHP
1954	PIT	NL	1	0	1	0	1	0	0	0	0	0	0	0	0	0	1	0

Rank among batters: 4,707 • *Total ballparks homered in*: 1 • *First HR*: 04/19/1954 off Jim Hearn

Butch Henline

WALTER JOHN HENLINE
B: 12/20/1894 D: 10/09/1957
BR

Year	Tm	Lg	Tot	H	A	Men-On 0	Men-On 1	Men-On 2	Men-On 3	One-Game 2	One-Game 3	One-Game 4	LO	XN	IP	PH	RHP	LHP
1922	PHI	NL	14	11	3	9	4	1	0	0	1	0	0	0	0	0	11	3
1923	PHI	NL	7	6	1	3	3	1	0	0	0	0	0	0	0	0	5	2
1924	PHI	NL	5	4	1	3	2	0	0	0	0	0	0	0	0	0	4	1
1925	PHI	NL	8	6	2	6	1	1	0	0	0	0	0	0	0	0	7	1
1926	PHI	NL	2	1	1	1	0	1	0	0	0	0	0	0	0	0	2	0
1927	BRO	NL	1	1	0	0	1	0	0	0	0	0	0	0	0	0	1	0

						Men-On				One-Game								
Year	Tm	Lg	Tot	H	A	0	1	2	3	2	3	4	LO	XN	IP	PH	RHP	LHP

Butch Henline *continued*

Year	Tm	Lg	Tot	H	A	0	1	2	3	2	3	4	LO	XN	IP	PH	RHP	LHP
1928	BRO	NL	2	0	2	0	2	0	0	0	0	0	0	0	0	0	2	0
1929	BRO	NL	1	1	0	1	0	0	0	0	0	0	0	0	0	0	0	1
Total			40	30	10	23	13	4	0	0	1	0	0	0	0	0	32	8

Rank among batters: 1,181 • Top target (2 home runs): Virgil Cheeves, Bill Sherdel, Hugh McQuillan, Kent Greenfield • *Number of pitchers victimized*: 36 • *Total ballparks homered in*: 6 • *First HR*: 04/29/1922 off Dutch Ruether

Tommy Henrich

THOMAS DAVID HENRICH
B: 02/20/1913
BL

Year	Tm	Lg	Tot	H	A	0	1	2	3	2	3	4	LO	XN	IP	PH	RHP	LHP
1937	NY	AL	8	1	7	4	2	2	0	1	0	0	0	0	0	0	8	0
1938	NY	AL	22	20	2	10	10	2	0	3	0	0	0	0	0	0	21	1
1939	NY	AL	9	5	4	7	0	2	0	0	0	0	0	0	0	0	9	0
1940	NY	AL	10	7	3	4	6	0	0	1	0	0	0	1	0	0	6	4
1941	NY	AL	31	15	16	14	15	2	0	2	0	0	0	1	0	0	25	6
1942	NY	AL	13	11	2	7	5	1	0	0	0	0	0	1	0	0	12	1
1946	NY	AL	19	10	9	13	5	1	0	3	0	0	0	1	0	0	15	4
1947	NY	AL	16	4	12	9	5	2	0	2	0	0	0	0	0	0	13	3
1948	NY	AL	25	15	10	12	8	1	4	0	0	0	0	1	0	0	20	5
1949	NY	AL	24	20	4	14	6	4	0	1	0	0	0	1	0	0	18	6
1950	NY	AL	6	3	3	1	4	1	0	0	0	0	0	1	0	3	4	2
Total			183	111	72	95	66	18	4	13	0	0	0	7	0	3	151	32

Rank among batters: 213 • *Top target (8 home runs)*: Elden Auker, Bob Feller • *Number of pitchers victimized*: 108 • *Total ballparks homered in*: 9 • *First HR*: 05/16/1937 off George Caster • *World Series HR*—4

Olaf Henriksen

OLAF HENRIKSEN
B: 04/26/1888 D: 10/17/1962
BL

Year	Tm	Lg	Tot	H	A	0	1	2	3	2	3	4	LO	XN	IP	PH	RHP	LHP
1914	BOS	AL	1	1	0	1	0	0	0	0	0	0	0	0	1	0	0	1

Rank among batters: 4,707 • *Total ballparks homered in*: 1 • *First HR*: 10/06/1914 off Harry Harper

Butch Henry

FLOYD BLUFORD HENRY
B: 10/07/1968
BL

Year	Tm	Lg	Tot	H	A	0	1	2	3	2	3	4	LO	XN	IP	PH	RHP	LHP
1992	HOU	NL	1	0	1	0	0	1	0	0	0	0	0	0	1	0	1	0

Rank among batters: 4,707 • *Total ballparks homered in*: 1 • *First HR*: 05/08/1992 off Doug Drabek

John Henry

JOHN PARK HENRY
B: 12/26/1889 D: 11/24/1941
BR

Year	Tm	Lg	Tot	H	A	0	1	2	3	2	3	4	LO	XN	IP	PH	RHP	LHP
1913	WAS	AL	1	1	0	1	0	0	0	0	0	0	0	0	1	0	1	0
1915	WAS	AL	1	0	1	1	0	0	0	0	0	0	0	0	0	0	0	1
Total			2	1	1	2	0	0	0	0	0	0	0	0	1	0	1	1

Rank among batters: 4,129 • *Total ballparks homered in*: 2 • *First HR*: 06/05/1913 off Roy Mitchell

Ron Henry

RONALD BAXTER HENRY
B: 08/07/1936
BR

Year	Tm	Lg	Tot	H	A	0	1	2	3	2	3	4	LO	XN	IP	PH	RHP	LHP
1964	MIN	AL	2	1	1	1	1	0	0	0	0	0	0	0	0	1	2	0

Rank among batters: 4,129 • *Total ballparks homered in*: 2 • *First HR*: 07/12/1964 off Don Lee

Ray Herbert

RAYMOND ERNEST HERBERT
B: 12/15/1929
BR

Year	Tm	Lg	Tot	H	A	0	1	2	3	2	3	4	LO	XN	IP	PH	RHP	LHP
1954	DET	AL	1	0	1	0	1	0	0	0	0	0	0	0	0	0	1	0
1959	KC	AL	1	0	1	0	1	0	0	0	0	0	0	0	0	0	1	0
1961	CHI	AL	2	1	1	2	0	0	0	0	0	0	0	0	0	0	2	0
1962	CHI	AL	2	0	2	2	0	0	0	0	0	0	0	0	0	0	2	0

Ray Herbert *continued*

Year	Tm	Lg	Tot	H	A	Men-On 0	Men-On 1	Men-On 2	Men-On 3	One-Game 2	One-Game 3	One-Game 4	LO	XN	IP	PH	RHP	LHP
1963	CHI	AL	1	1	0	1	0	0	0	0	0	0	0	0	0	0	0	1
Total			7	2	5	5	2	0	0	0	0	0	0	0	0	0	6	1

Rank among batters: 2,834 • *Total ballparks homered in*: 5 • *First HR*: 06/11/1954 off Moe Burtschy

Babe Herman

FLOYD CAVES HERMAN
B: 06/26/1903 D: 11/27/1987
BL

Year	Tm	Lg	Tot	H	A	Men-On 0	Men-On 1	Men-On 2	Men-On 3	One-Game 2	One-Game 3	One-Game 4	LO	XN	IP	PH	RHP	LHP
1926	BRO	NL	11	8	3	4	4	3	0	0	0	0	0	0	0	0	6	5
1927	BRO	NL	14	6	8	4	6	4	0	3	0	0	0	0	1	1	12	2
1928	BRO	NL	12	5	7	4	7	1	0	1	0	0	0	0	1	0	9	3
1929	BRO	NL	21	12	9	10	6	3	2	0	0	0	0	0	4	0	15	6
1930	BRO	NL	35	22	13	20	9	6	0	5	0	0	0	0	1	0	23	12
1931	BRO	NL	18	11	7	9	6	3	0	0	0	0	0	0	0	0	11	7
1932	CIN	NL	16	5	11	10	4	2	0	0	0	0	0	0	2	0	8	8
1933	CHI	NL	16	10	6	5	8	2	1	1	1	0	0	0	0	0	15	1
1934	CHI	NL	14	6	8	6	7	1	0	1	0	0	0	0	0	0	12	2
1935	CIN	NL	10	3	7	3	5	2	0	1	0	0	0	0	1	0	8	2
1936	CIN	NL	13	4	9	6	5	2	0	1	0	0	0	0	0	2	13	0
1945	BRO	NL	1	0	1	1	0	0	0	0	0	0	0	0	0	0	1	0
Total			181	92	89	82	67	29	3	13	1	0	0	0	10	3	133	48

Rank among batters: 218 • *Top target (8 home runs)*: Leo Sweetland • *Number of pitchers victimized*: 88 • *Total ballparks homered in*: 8 • *First HR*: 05/08/1926 off Art Reinhart • *Hit for Cycle*—vs CIN: 05/18/1931; @PIT: 07/24/1931; @STL: 09/30/1933

Billy Herman

WILLIAM JENNINGS BRYAN HERMAN
B: 07/07/1909 D: 09/05/1992
BR HOF

Year	Tm	Lg	Tot	H	A	Men-On 0	Men-On 1	Men-On 2	Men-On 3	One-Game 2	One-Game 3	One-Game 4	LO	XN	IP	PH	RHP	LHP
1932	CHI	NL	1	0	1	1	0	0	0	0	0	0	0	0	0	0	1	0
1934	CHI	NL	3	1	2	3	0	0	0	0	0	0	0	0	0	0	3	0
1935	CHI	NL	7	3	4	4	2	1	0	0	0	0	0	0	0	0	3	4
1936	CHI	NL	5	1	4	2	1	2	0	0	0	0	0	0	0	0	5	0
1937	CHI	NL	8	4	4	4	1	2	1	0	0	0	0	0	0	0	8	0
1938	CHI	NL	1	1	0	1	0	0	0	0	0	0	0	0	0	0	0	1
1939	CHI	NL	7	5	2	4	3	0	0	0	0	0	0	0	0	0	6	1
1940	CHI	NL	5	3	2	4	0	1	0	0	0	0	0	1	0	0	3	2
1941	BRO	NL	3	1	2	3	0	0	0	0	0	0	0	0	0	0	2	1
1942	BRO	NL	2	0	2	2	0	0	0	0	0	0	0	0	0	0	2	0
1943	BRO	NL	2	2	0	1	1	0	0	0	0	0	0	0	0	0	2	0
1946	BOS	NL	3	1	2	3	0	0	0	0	0	0	0	0	0	0	2	1
Total			47	22	25	32	8	6	1	0	0	0	0	1	0	0	37	10

Rank among batters: 1,040 • *Top target (3 home runs)*: Carl Hubbell • *Number of pitchers victimized*: 43 • *Total ballparks homered in*: 9 • *First HR*: 05/24/1932 off Syl Johnson • *World Series HR*—1

Gene Hermanski

EUGENE VICTOR HERMANSKI
B: 05/11/1920
BL

Year	Tm	Lg	Tot	H	A	Men-On 0	Men-On 1	Men-On 2	Men-On 3	One-Game 2	One-Game 3	One-Game 4	LO	XN	IP	PH	RHP	LHP
1947	BRO	NL	7	1	6	4	3	0	0	1	0	0	0	0	1	1	7	0
1948	BRO	NL	15	5	10	8	5	2	0	0	1	0	0	0	0	0	13	2
1949	BRO	NL	8	4	4	5	1	0	2	0	0	0	0	0	0	2	8	0
1950	BRO	NL	7	3	4	6	1	0	0	0	0	0	0	1	0	0	7	0
1951	BRO	NL	1	1	0	1	0	0	0	0	0	0	1	0	0	0	1	0
	CHI	NL	3	2	1	1	1	1	0	0	0	0	0	0	0	1	3	0
	Total		4	3	1	2	1	1	0	0	0	0	1	0	0	1	4	0
1952	CHI	NL	4	2	2	2	2	0	0	0	0	0	0	0	0	0	3	1
1953	PIT	NL	1	1	0	0	0	1	0	0	0	0	0	0	0	0	1	0
Total			46	19	27	27	13	4	2	1	1	0	1	1	1	4	43	3

Rank among batters: 1,060 • *Top target (4 home runs)*: Sheldon Jones • *Number of pitchers victimized*: 33 • *Total ballparks homered in*: 8 • *First HR*: 04/26/1947 off Bill Voiselle

Carlos Hernandez

CARLOS ALBERTO (ALMEIDA) HERNANDEZ
B: 05/24/1967
BR

Year	Tm	Lg	Tot	H	A	Men-On 0	Men-On 1	Men-On 2	Men-On 3	One-Game 2	One-Game 3	One-Game 4	LO	XN	IP	PH	RHP	LHP
1992	LA	NL	3	1	2	1	2	0	0	0	0	0	0	0	0	0	0	3

Year	Tm	Lg	Tot	H	A	Men-On 0	Men-On 1	Men-On 2	Men-On 3	One-Game 2	One-Game 3	One-Game 4	LO	XN	IP	PH	RHP	LHP

Carlos Hernandez *continued*

Year	Tm	Lg	Tot	H	A	0	1	2	3	2	3	4	LO	XN	IP	PH	RHP	LHP
1993	LA	NL	2	1	1	2	0	0	0	0	0	0	0	0	0	0	1	1
1994	LA	NL	2	0	2	1	1	0	0	0	0	0	0	0	0	0	1	1
1995	LA	NL	2	1	1	0	0	2	0	0	0	0	0	0	0	1	0	2
Total			9	3	6	4	3	2	0	0	0	0	0	0	0	1	2	7

Rank among batters: 2,587 • *Total ballparks homered in*: 6 • *First HR*: 07/18/1992 off Kyle Abbott

Enzo Hernandez

ENZO OCTAVIO HERNANDEZ
B: 02/12/1949
BR

Year	Tm	Lg	Tot	H	A	0	1	2	3	2	3	4	LO	XN	IP	PH	RHP	LHP
1972	SD	NL	1	0	1	1	0	0	0	0	0	0	0	0	0	0	1	0
1976	SD	NL	1	0	1	1	0	0	0	0	0	0	0	0	0	0	1	0
Total			2	0	2	2	0	0	0	0	0	0	0	0	0	0	2	0

Rank among batters: 4,129 • *Total ballparks homered in*: 2 • *First HR*: 10/03/1972 off Jim Willoughby

Jackie Hernandez

JACINTO (ZULUETA) HERNANDEZ
B: 09/11/1940
BR

Year	Tm	Lg	Tot	H	A	0	1	2	3	2	3	4	LO	XN	IP	PH	RHP	LHP
1968	MIN	AL	2	2	0	2	0	0	0	0	0	0	0	0	0	0	2	0
1969	KC	AL	4	2	2	1	2	1	0	0	0	0	0	0	0	0	2	2
1970	KC	AL	2	1	1	1	1	0	0	0	0	0	0	0	0	0	1	1
1971	PIT	NL	3	0	3	1	1	1	0	1	0	0	0	0	0	0	2	1
1972	PIT	NL	1	0	1	1	0	0	0	0	0	0	0	0	0	0	1	0
Total			12	5	7	6	4	2	0	1	0	0	0	0	0	0	8	4

Rank among batters: 2,325 • *Top target (2 home runs)*: Jim Hardin • *Number of pitchers victimized*: 11 • *Total ballparks homered in*: 7 • *First HR*: 04/17/1968 off Dick Bosman

Jose Hernandez

JOSE ANTONIO (FIGUEROA) HERNANDEZ
B: 07/14/1969
BR

Year	Tm	Lg	Tot	H	A	0	1	2	3	2	3	4	LO	XN	IP	PH	RHP	LHP
1994	CHI	NL	1	0	1	1	0	0	0	0	0	0	0	0	0	0	0	1
1995	CHI	NL	13	6	7	9	3	0	1	1	0	0	0	0	0	0	9	4
Total			14	6	8	10	3	0	1	1	0	0	0	0	0	0	9	5

Rank among batters: 2,169 • *Top target (2 home runs)*: Mike Dyer • *Number of pitchers victimized*: 13 • *Total ballparks homered in*: 7 • *First HR*: 05/12/1994 off Tom Urbani

Keith Hernandez

KEITH HERNANDEZ
B: 10/20/1953
BL

Year	Tm	Lg	Tot	H	A	0	1	2	3	2	3	4	LO	XN	IP	PH	RHP	LHP
1975	STL	NL	3	0	3	0	2	1	0	0	0	0	0	0	0	1	2	1
1976	STL	NL	7	4	3	5	1	1	0	0	0	0	0	0	0	0	4	3
1977	STL	NL	15	5	10	7	3	2	3	0	0	0	0	0	1	0	7	8
1978	STL	NL	11	4	7	7	4	0	0	0	0	0	0	0	0	0	5	6
1979	STL	NL	11	5	6	3	3	4	1	0	0	0	0	0	0	0	5	6
1980	STL	NL	16	8	8	6	6	4	0	1	0	0	0	0	0	0	12	4
1981	STL	NL	8	4	4	5	2	0	1	0	0	0	0	0	0	0	7	1
1982	STL	NL	7	4	3	4	1	2	0	0	0	0	0	0	0	1	5	2
1983	STL	NL	3	2	1	2	1	0	0	0	0	0	0	0	0	0	1	2
	NY	NL	9	8	1	5	4	0	0	0	0	0	0	0	0	0	8	1
	Total		12	10	2	7	5	0	0	0	0	0	0	0	0	0	9	3
1984	NY	NL	15	10	5	4	9	2	0	0	0	0	0	0	0	0	12	3
1985	NY	NL	10	4	6	5	5	0	0	0	0	0	0	0	0	1	8	2
1986	NY	NL	13	6	7	7	5	1	0	0	0	0	0	0	0	0	9	4
1987	NY	NL	18	6	12	11	3	3	1	1	0	0	0	1	0	0	12	6
1988	NY	NL	11	2	9	3	6	1	1	1	0	0	0	0	0	0	5	6
1989	NY	NL	4	2	2	2	1	1	0	0	0	0	0	0	0	0	3	1
1990	CLE	AL	1	0	1	0	1	0	0	0	0	0	0	0	0	0	1	0
Total			162	74	88	76	57	22	7	3	0	0	0	1	1	3	106	56

Rank among batters: 261 • *Top target (6 home runs)*: Mike Scott • *Number of pitchers victimized*: 122 • *Total ballparks homered in*: 14 • *First HR*: 05/24/1975 off Doug Rau • *Hit for Cycle—@ATL*: 07/04/1985 • *World Series HR*—1; *LCS HR*—1

Leo Hernandez

LEONARDO JESUS HERNANDEZ
B: 11/06/1959
BR

Year	Tm	Lg	Tot	H	A	Men-On 0	1	2	3	One-Game 2	3	4	LO	XN	IP	PH	RHP	LHP
1983	BAL	AL	6	5	1	3	1	2	0	0	0	0	0	0	0	0	4	2
1986	NY	AL	1	0	1	1	0	0	0	0	0	0	0	0	0	0	0	1
Total			7	5	2	4	1	2	0	0	0	0	0	0	0	0	4	3

Rank among batters: 2,834 • *Total ballparks homered in*: 3 • *First HR*: 04/09/1983 off Ed Glynn

Larry Herndon

LARRY DARNELL HERNDON
B: 11/03/1953
BR

Year	Tm	Lg	Tot	H	A	Men-On 0	1	2	3	One-Game 2	3	4	LO	XN	IP	PH	RHP	LHP
1976	SF	NL	2	1	1	2	0	0	0	0	0	0	1	0	0	0	1	1
1977	SF	NL	1	0	1	1	0	0	0	0	0	0	0	0	0	0	1	0
1978	SF	NL	1	0	1	0	1	0	0	0	0	0	0	0	0	0	1	0
1979	SF	NL	7	2	5	7	0	0	0	0	0	0	1	0	0	0	4	3
1980	SF	NL	8	3	5	3	3	2	0	0	0	0	0	1	0	1	3	5
1981	SF	NL	5	4	1	2	3	0	0	0	0	0	0	0	1	0	4	1
1982	DET	AL	23	9	14	10	8	5	0	1	1	0	0	1	0	0	17	6
1983	DET	AL	20	7	13	10	8	2	0	0	0	0	0	0	0	0	9	11
1984	DET	AL	7	3	4	6	1	0	0	0	0	0	0	0	0	1	3	4
1985	DET	AL	12	7	5	10	2	0	0	0	0	0	0	0	0	0	5	7
1986	DET	AL	8	4	4	2	4	1	1	0	0	0	0	0	0	3	2	6
1987	DET	AL	9	7	2	3	5	1	0	1	0	0	0	0	0	0	1	8
1988	DET	AL	4	2	2	3	0	1	0	0	0	0	0	0	0	0	0	4
Total			107	49	58	59	35	12	1	2	1	0	2	2	1	5	51	56

Rank among batters: 449 • *Top target (4 home runs)*: Mike Norris, Scott McGregor • *Number of pitchers victimized*: 84 • *Total ballparks homered in*: 22 • *First HR*: 05/24/1976 off Mike Cosgrove • *World Series HR*—1; *LCS HR*—1

Ed Herr

EDWARD JOSEPH HERR
B: 05/18/1862 D: 07/18/1943
BR

Year	Tm	Lg	Tot	H	A	Men-On 0	1	2	3	One-Game 2	3	4	LO	XN	IP	PH	RHP	LHP
1888	STL	AA	3	3	0	0	2	1	0	0	0	0	0	0	0	0	3	0

Rank among batters: 3,735 • *Total ballparks homered in*: 1 • *First HR*: 06/17/1888 off Billy Serad

Tom Herr

THOMAS MITCHELL HERR
B: 04/04/1956
BB

Year	Tm	Lg	Tot	H	A	Men-On 0	1	2	3	One-Game 2	3	4	LO	XN	IP	PH	RHP	LHP
1983	STL	NL	2	1	1	0	1	1	0	0	0	0	0	0	0	0	2	0
1984	STL	NL	4	1	3	3	1	0	0	0	0	0	1	0	0	0	2	2
1985	STL	NL	8	4	4	5	2	1	0	0	0	0	0	0	0	0	5	3
1986	STL	NL	2	1	1	1	1	0	0	0	0	0	0	0	0	0	1	1
1987	STL	NL	2	1	1	0	1	0	1	0	0	0	0	1	0	0	0	2
1988	STL	NL	1	1	0	1	0	0	0	0	0	0	0	0	0	0	0	1
	MIN	AL	1	0	1	1	0	0	0	0	0	0	0	0	0	0	0	1
	Total		2	1	1	2	0	0	0	0	0	0	0	0	0	0	0	2
1989	PHI	NL	2	0	2	1	1	0	0	0	0	0	0	0	0	0	1	1
1990	PHI	NL	4	3	1	2	2	0	0	0	0	0	0	0	0	0	3	1
	NY	NL	1	1	0	1	0	0	0	0	0	0	0	0	0	0	1	0
	Total		5	4	1	3	2	0	0	0	0	0	0	0	0	0	4	1
1991	NY	NL	1	0	1	1	0	0	0	0	0	0	0	0	0	0	1	0
Total			28	13	15	16	9	2	1	0	0	0	1	1	0	0	16	12

Rank among batters: 1,500 • *Top target (2 home runs)*: Tom Gorman • *Number of pitchers victimized*: 27 • *Total ballparks homered in*: 10 • *First HR*: 05/10/1983 off Andy McGaffigan • *World Series HR*—1; *LCS HR*—1

Jose Herrera

JOSE CONCEPCION (ONTIVEROS) HERRERA
B: 04/08/1942
BR

Year	Tm	Lg	Tot	H	A	Men-On 0	1	2	3	One-Game 2	3	4	LO	XN	IP	PH	RHP	LHP
1969	MON	NL	2	0	2	1	0	1	0	0	0	0	0	0	0	2	0	2

Rank among batters: 4,129 • *Top target (2 home runs)*: George Stone • *Number of pitchers victimized*: 1 • *Total ballparks homered in*: 1 • *First HR*: 07/24/1969 off George Stone

Pancho Herrera

JUAN FRANCISCO (WILLAVICENCIO) HERRERA
B: 06/16/1934
BR

Year	Tm	Lg	Tot	H	A	Men-On 0	Men-On 1	Men-On 2	Men-On 3	One-Game 2	One-Game 3	One-Game 4	LO	XN	IP	PH	RHP	LHP
1958	PHI	NL	1	1	0	1	0	0	0	0	0	0	0	0	0	0	0	1
1960	PHI	NL	17	8	9	12	3	2	0	1	0	0	0	0	0	0	7	10
1961	PHI	NL	13	4	9	5	5	3	0	1	0	0	0	0	0	0	4	9
Total			31	13	18	18	8	5	0	2	0	0	0	0	0	0	11	20

Rank among batters: 1,400 • *Top target (4 home runs)*: Wilmer Mizell • *Number of pitchers victimized*: 20 • *Total ballparks homered in*: 8 • *First HR*: 09/16/1958 off Bill Henry

Ed Herrmann

EDWARD MARTIN HERRMANN
B: 08/27/1946
BL

Year	Tm	Lg	Tot	H	A	Men-On 0	Men-On 1	Men-On 2	Men-On 3	One-Game 2	One-Game 3	One-Game 4	LO	XN	IP	PH	RHP	LHP
1969	CHI	AL	8	2	6	4	2	2	0	0	0	0	0	0	0	0	7	1
1970	CHI	AL	19	9	10	12	3	2	2	1	0	0	0	0	0	0	17	2
1971	CHI	AL	11	6	5	7	2	2	0	1	0	0	0	1	0	0	10	1
1972	CHI	AL	10	5	5	6	2	1	1	0	0	0	0	0	0	0	10	0
1973	CHI	AL	10	5	5	6	2	2	0	0	0	0	0	0	0	0	7	3
1974	CHI	AL	10	4	6	5	4	1	0	1	0	0	0	2	0	0	9	1
1975	NY	AL	6	5	1	4	1	1	0	0	0	0	0	0	0	0	6	0
1976	CAL	AL	2	0	2	1	0	1	0	1	0	0	0	0	0	0	2	0
	HOU	NL	3	2	1	2	0	1	0	0	0	0	0	0	0	0	2	1
	Total		5	2	3	3	0	2	0	1	0	0	0	0	0	0	4	1
1977	HOU	NL	1	0	1	0	1	0	0	0	0	0	0	0	0	0	1	0
Total			80	38	42	47	17	13	3	4	0	0	0	3	0	0	71	9

Rank among batters: 650 • *Top target (4 home runs)*: Jim Perry, Joe Coleman, Marty Pattin • *Number of pitchers victimized*: 56 • *Total ballparks homered in*: 17 • *First HR*: 06/04/1969 off Sonny Siebert

John Herrnstein

JOHN ELLETT HERRNSTEIN
B: 03/31/1938
BL

Year	Tm	Lg	Tot	H	A	Men-On 0	Men-On 1	Men-On 2	Men-On 3	One-Game 2	One-Game 3	One-Game 4	LO	XN	IP	PH	RHP	LHP
1963	PHI	NL	1	0	1	1	0	0	0	0	0	0	0	0	0	1	1	0
1964	PHI	NL	6	3	3	5	1	0	0	0	0	0	0	0	0	1	5	1
1965	PHI	NL	1	0	1	1	0	0	0	0	0	0	0	0	0	0	0	1
Total			8	3	5	7	1	0	0	0	0	0	0	0	0	2	6	2

Rank among batters: 2,703 • *Top target (2 home runs)*: Larry Jackson • *Number of pitchers victimized*: 7 • *Total ballparks homered in*: 5 • *First HR*: 09/24/1963 off Don Larsen

Rick Herrscher

RICHARD FRANKLIN HERRSCHER
B: 11/03/1936
BR

Year	Tm	Lg	Tot	H	A	Men-On 0	Men-On 1	Men-On 2	Men-On 3	One-Game 2	One-Game 3	One-Game 4	LO	XN	IP	PH	RHP	LHP
1962	NY	NL	1	1	0	0	0	1	0	0	0	0	0	0	0	0	0	1

Rank among batters: 4,707 • *Total ballparks homered in*: 1 • *First HR*: 08/05/1962 off Jim O'Toole

Mike Hershberger

NORMAN MICHAEL HERSHBERGER
B: 10/09/1939
BR

Year	Tm	Lg	Tot	H	A	Men-On 0	Men-On 1	Men-On 2	Men-On 3	One-Game 2	One-Game 3	One-Game 4	LO	XN	IP	PH	RHP	LHP
1962	CHI	AL	4	2	2	3	1	0	0	0	0	0	0	1	0	0	4	0
1963	CHI	AL	3	2	1	3	0	0	0	0	0	0	0	0	0	0	1	2
1964	CHI	AL	2	1	1	2	0	0	0	0	0	0	0	0	0	0	0	2
1965	KC	AL	5	2	3	4	1	0	0	0	0	0	0	0	0	0	4	1
1966	KC	AL	2	0	2	2	0	0	0	0	0	0	0	0	0	0	0	2
1967	KC	AL	1	0	1	0	0	1	0	0	0	0	0	0	1	0	0	1
1968	OAK	AL	5	4	1	3	1	1	0	0	0	0	0	0	0	1	1	4
1969	OAK	AL	1	0	1	1	0	0	0	0	0	0	0	0	0	0	0	1
1970	MIL	AL	1	1	0	0	0	1	0	0	0	0	0	0	0	0	0	1
1971	CHI	AL	2	0	2	2	0	0	0	0	0	0	0	0	0	0	0	2
Total			26	12	14	20	3	3	0	0	0	0	0	1	1	1	10	16

Rank among batters: 1,576 • *Top target (2 home runs)*: Dave McNally • *Number of pitchers victimized*: 25 • *Total ballparks homered in*: 10 • *First HR*: 04/29/1962 off Don Schwall

Buck Herzog

CHARLES LINCOLN HERZOG
B: 07/09/1885 D: 09/04/1953
BR

Year	Tm	Lg	Tot	H	A	Men-On 0	1	2	3	One-Game 2	3	4	LO	XN	IP	PH	RHP	LHP
1910	BOS	NL	3	2	1	3	0	0	0	0	0	0	0	0	0	0	3	0
1911	BOS	NL	5	4	1	2	2	1	0	0	0	0	0	0	0	0	3	2
	NY	NL	1	1	0	1	0	0	0	0	0	0	0	0	0	0	1	0
	Total		6	5	1	3	2	1	0	0	0	0	0	0	0	0	4	2
1912	NY	NL	2	1	1	2	0	0	0	0	0	0	0	0	0	0	2	0
1913	NY	NL	3	3	0	2	1	0	0	0	0	0	0	0	0	0	3	0
1914	CIN	NL	1	0	1	0	1	0	0	0	0	0	0	0	1	0	1	0
1915	CIN	NL	1	0	1	1	0	0	0	0	0	0	0	0	1	0	1	0
1916	CIN	NL	1	0	1	0	1	0	0	0	0	0	0	0	1	0	0	1
1917	NY	NL	2	1	1	2	0	0	0	0	0	0	0	0	1	0	2	0
1919	BOS	NL	1	0	1	1	0	0	0	0	0	0	0	0	1	0	1	0
Total			20	12	8	14	5	1	0	0	0	0	0	0	5	0	17	3

Rank among batters: 1,810 • Top target (2 home runs): George Bell, Mordecai Brown, Dan Griner, Slim Sallee • *Number of pitchers victimized*: 16 • *Total ballparks homered in*: 6 • *First HR*: 05/09/1910 off Vic Willis

Whitey Herzog

DORREL NORMAN ELVERT HERZOG
B: 11/09/1931
BL

Year	Tm	Lg	Tot	H	A	Men-On 0	1	2	3	One-Game 2	3	4	LO	XN	IP	PH	RHP	LHP
1956	WAS	AL	4	2	2	3	1	0	0	0	0	0	0	0	0	0	3	1
1959	KC	AL	1	0	1	1	0	0	0	0	0	0	0	0	0	0	1	0
1960	KC	AL	8	4	4	4	2	2	0	0	0	0	0	0	0	1	7	1
1961	BAL	AL	5	2	3	4	1	0	0	0	0	0	0	0	0	0	5	0
1962	BAL	AL	7	3	4	4	2	1	0	0	0	0	0	0	0	3	7	0
Total			25	11	14	16	6	3	0	0	0	0	0	0	0	4	23	2

Rank among batters: 1,608 • *Top target (5 home runs)*: Paul Foytack • *Number of pitchers victimized*: 19 • *Total ballparks homered in*: 9 • *First HR*: 06/06/1956 off Gerry Staley

Otto Hess

OTTO C. HESS
B: 10/10/1878 D: 02/25/1926
BL

Year	Tm	Lg	Tot	H	A	Men-On 0	1	2	3	One-Game 2	3	4	LO	XN	IP	PH	RHP	LHP
1905	CLE	AL	2	1	1	2	0	0	0	0	0	0	0	0	0	0	2	0
1913	BOS	NL	2	1	1	0	2	0	0	0	0	0	0	0	0	0	2	0
1914	BOS	NL	1	1	0	1	0	0	0	0	0	0	0	0	0	0	1	0
Total			5	3	2	3	2	0	0	0	0	0	0	0	0	0	5	0

Rank among batters: 3,191 • *Total ballparks homered in*: 4 • *First HR*: 07/20/1905 off Bill Dinneen

Ed Heusser

EDWARD BURLTON HEUSSER
B: 05/07/1909 D: 03/01/1956
BB

Year	Tm	Lg	Tot	H	A	Men-On 0	1	2	3	One-Game 2	3	4	LO	XN	IP	PH	RHP	LHP
1936	STL	NL	1	0	1	1	0	0	0	0	0	0	0	0	0	0	0	1
1940	PHI	AL	1	0	1	0	1	0	0	0	0	0	0	0	0	0	1	0
1945	CIN	NL	1	0	1	1	0	0	0	0	0	0	0	0	0	0	1	0
Total			3	0	3	2	1	0	0	0	0	0	0	0	0	0	2	1

Rank among batters: 3,735 • *Total ballparks homered in*: 3 • *First HR*: 09/14/1936 off Carl Hubbell

Johnny Heving

JOHN ALOYSIUS HEVING
B: 04/29/1896 D: 12/24/1968
BR

Year	Tm	Lg	Tot	H	A	Men-On 0	1	2	3	One-Game 2	3	4	LO	XN	IP	PH	RHP	LHP
1931	PHI	AL	1	1	0	0	0	1	0	0	0	0	0	0	0	0	0	1

Rank among batters: 4,707 • *Total ballparks homered in*: 1 • *First HR*: 06/13/1931 off Lefty Stewart

Mike Heydon

MICHAEL EDWARD HEYDON
B: 07/15/1874 D: 10/13/1913
BL

Year	Tm	Lg	Tot	H	A	Men-On 0	1	2	3	One-Game 2	3	4	LO	XN	IP	PH	RHP	LHP
1901	STL	NL	1	1	0	0	1	0	0	0	0	0	0	0	0	0	1	0

Year	Tm	Lg	Tot	H	A	Men-On 0	Men-On 1	Men-On 2	Men-On 3	One-Game 2	One-Game 3	One-Game 4	LO	XN	IP	PH	RHP	LHP

Mike Heydon *continued*

Year	Tm	Lg	Tot	H	A	0	1	2	3	2	3	4	LO	XN	IP	PH	RHP	LHP
1905	WAS	AL	1	1	0	1	0	0	0	0	0	0	0	0	0	0	1	0
Total			2	2	0	1	1	0	0	0	0	0	0	0	0	0	2	0

Rank among batters: 4,129 • *Total ballparks homered in*: 2 • *First HR*: 07/20/1901 off Kid Nichols

Jack Hiatt

JACK E. HIATT
B: 07/27/1942
BR

Year	Tm	Lg	Tot	H	A	0	1	2	3	2	3	4	LO	XN	IP	PH	RHP	LHP
1965	SF	NL	1	0	1	1	0	0	0	0	0	0	0	0	0	0	0	1
1967	SF	NL	6	2	4	3	0	2	1	0	0	0	0	0	0	2	4	2
1968	SF	NL	4	1	3	2	2	0	0	0	0	0	0	0	0	0	1	3
1969	SF	NL	7	6	1	1	3	2	1	1	0	0	0	1	0	0	5	2
1970	CHI	NL	2	1	1	1	1	0	0	0	0	0	0	0	0	0	1	1
1971	HOU	NL	1	0	1	1	0	0	0	0	0	0	0	0	0	0	1	0
1972	CAL	AL	1	0	1	1	0	0	0	0	0	0	0	0	0	1	0	1
Total			22	10	12	10	6	4	2	1	0	0	0	1	0	3	12	10

Rank among batters: 1,719 • *Top target (2 home runs)*: Denny Lemaster, Milt Pappas • *Number of pitchers victimized*: 20 • *Total ballparks homered in*: 7 • *First HR*: 04/30/1965 off Sandy Koufax

Phil Hiatt

PHILIP FARRELL HIATT
B: 05/01/1969
BR

Year	Tm	Lg	Tot	H	A	0	1	2	3	2	3	4	LO	XN	IP	PH	RHP	LHP
1993	KC	AL	7	4	3	2	4	1	0	0	0	0	0	0	0	0	5	2
1995	KC	AL	4	1	3	2	2	0	0	0	0	0	0	0	0	1	2	2
Total			11	5	6	4	6	1	0	0	0	0	0	0	0	1	7	4

Rank among batters: 2,419 • *Top target (3 home runs)*: Kevin Tapani • *Number of pitchers victimized*: 9 • *Total ballparks homered in*: 4 • *First HR*: 04/11/1993 off Kevin Tapani

Charlie Hickman

CHARLES TAYLOR HICKMAN
B: 05/04/1876 D: 04/19/1934
BR

Year	Tm	Lg	Tot	H	A	0	1	2	3	2	3	4	LO	XN	IP	PH	RHP	LHP
1897	BOS	NL	1	1	0	1	0	0	0	0	0	0	0	0	0	0	1	0
1900	NY	NL	9	4	5	6	3	0	0	0	0	0	0	0	0	0	8	1
1901	NY	NL	4	3	1	2	2	0	0	0	0	0	0	0	0	0	2	2
1902	BOS	AL	3	1	2	2	1	0	0	0	0	0	0	0	0	0	1	2
	CLE	AL	8	5	3	3	4	1	0	0	0	0	0	1	0	0	4	4
	Total		11	6	5	5	5	1	0	0	0	0	0	1	0	0	5	6
1903	CLE	AL	12	6	6	4	6	2	0	0	0	0	0	1	0	0	8	4
1904	CLE	AL	4	2	2	1	3	0	0	0	0	0	0	0	0	0	3	1
	DET	AL	2	0	2	2	0	0	0	0	0	0	0	0	0	0	1	1
	Total		6	2	4	3	3	0	0	0	0	0	0	0	0	0	4	2
1905	DET	AL	2	2	0	1	1	0	0	1	0	0	0	0	0	0	2	0
	WAS	AL	2	2	0	1	1	0	0	0	0	0	0	1	1	0	2	0
	Total		4	4	0	2	2	0	0	1	0	0	0	1	1	0	4	0
1906	WAS	AL	9	3	6	5	3	1	0	0	0	0	0	1	1	0	8	1
1907	WAS	AL	1	0	1	0	1	0	0	0	0	0	0	0	0	0	1	0
1908	CLE	AL	2	1	1	0	1	1	0	0	0	0	0	0	2	0	2	0
Total			59	30	29	28	26	5	0	1	0	0	0	4	4	0	43	16

Rank among batters: 873 • *Top target (5 home runs)*: Jack Powell • *Number of pitchers victimized*: 37 • *Total ballparks homered in*: 13 • *First HR*: 09/21/1897 off Jack Dunn

Jim Hickman

DAVID JAMES HICKMAN
B: 05/19/1894 D: 12/30/1965
BR

Year	Tm	Lg	Tot	H	A	0	1	2	3	2	3	4	LO	XN	IP	PH	RHP	LHP
1915	BAL	FL	1	0	1	0	1	0	0	0	0	0	0	0	0	0	1	0
1917	BRO	NL	6	3	3	2	2	2	0	0	0	0	0	0	4	0	4	2
1918	BRO	NL	1	0	1	1	0	0	0	0	0	0	0	0	0	0	1	0
Total			8	3	5	3	3	2	0	0	0	0	0	0	4	0	6	2

Rank among batters: 2,703 • *Total ballparks homered in*: 6 • *First HR*: 09/26/1915 off Dan Adams

Jim Hickman

JAMES LUCIUS HICKMAN
B: 05/10/1937
BR

Year	Tm	Lg	Tot	H	A	Men-On 0	1	2	3	One-Game 2	3	4	LO	XN	IP	PH	RHP	LHP
1962	NY	NL	13	8	5	7	4	2	0	1	0	0	1	0	0	1	10	3
1963	NY	NL	17	13	4	13	2	0	2	0	0	0	3	1	0	0	13	4
1964	NY	NL	11	6	5	3	6	1	1	0	0	0	0	0	0	0	6	5
1965	NY	NL	15	4	11	10	2	3	0	1	1	0	0	0	0	1	6	9
1966	NY	NL	4	2	2	2	2	0	0	0	0	0	0	0	0	1	2	2
1968	CHI	NL	5	4	1	4	1	0	0	0	0	0	0	0	0	0	2	3
1969	CHI	NL	21	12	9	16	4	0	1	2	0	0	0	1	0	1	14	7
1970	CHI	NL	32	19	13	13	12	7	0	2	0	0	0	0	0	0	24	8
1971	CHI	NL	19	10	9	11	7	1	0	0	0	0	0	1	0	0	9	10
1972	CHI	NL	17	12	5	7	6	3	1	1	0	0	0	1	0	0	13	4
1973	CHI	NL	3	1	2	1	2	0	0	0	0	0	0	0	0	0	2	1
1974	STL	NL	2	1	1	2	0	0	0	0	0	0	0	0	0	2	1	1
Total			159	92	67	89	48	17	5	7	1	0	4	4	0	6	102	57

Rank among batters: 268 • *Top target (5 home runs)*: Chris Short • *Number of pitchers victimized*: 117 • *Total ballparks homered in*: 17 • *First HR*: 04/28/1962 off Ed Keegan • *Hit for Cycle*—vs STL: 08/07/1963

Jim Hicks

JAMES EDWARD HICKS
B: 05/18/1940
BR

Year	Tm	Lg	Tot	H	A	Men-On 0	1	2	3	One-Game 2	3	4	LO	XN	IP	PH	RHP	LHP
1965	CHI	AL	1	1	0	0	1	0	0	0	0	0	0	0	0	0	0	1
1969	STL	NL	1	0	1	1	0	0	0	0	0	0	0	0	0	0	1	0
	CAL	AL	3	2	1	1	1	1	0	0	0	0	0	0	0	0	0	3
	Total		4	2	2	2	1	1	0	0	0	0	0	0	0	0	1	3
Total			5	3	2	2	2	1	0	0	0	0	0	0	0	0	1	4

Rank among batters: 3,191 • *Total ballparks homered in*: 4 • *First HR*: 09/28/1965 off Hank Aguirre

Joe Hicks

WILLIAM JOSEPH HICKS
B: 04/07/1933
BL

Year	Tm	Lg	Tot	H	A	Men-On 0	1	2	3	One-Game 2	3	4	LO	XN	IP	PH	RHP	LHP
1961	WAS	AL	1	1	0	1	0	0	0	0	0	0	0	0	0	0	1	0
1962	WAS	AL	6	4	2	5	0	1	0	0	0	0	0	0	0	0	6	0
1963	NY	NL	5	5	0	2	1	2	0	0	0	0	0	1	0	1	4	1
Total			12	10	2	8	1	3	0	0	0	0	0	1	0	1	11	1

Rank among batters: 2,325 • *Total ballparks homered in*: 5 • *First HR*: 05/02/1961 off Jim Bunning

Kirby Higbe

WALTER KIRBY HIGBE
B: 04/08/1915 D: 05/06/1985
BR

Year	Tm	Lg	Tot	H	A	Men-On 0	1	2	3	One-Game 2	3	4	LO	XN	IP	PH	RHP	LHP
1943	BRO	NL	1	0	1	1	0	0	0	0	0	0	0	0	0	0	1	0
1947	PIT	NL	1	1	0	1	0	0	0	0	0	0	0	1	0	0	1	0
1948	PIT	NL	1	1	0	1	0	0	0	0	0	0	0	0	0	0	1	0
Total			3	2	1	3	0	0	0	0	0	0	0	1	0	0	3	0

Rank among batters: 3,735 • *Total ballparks homered in*: 2 • *First HR*: 06/26/1943 off Charlie Fuchs

Mahlon Higbee

MAHLON JESSE HIGBEE
B: 08/16/1901 D: 04/07/1968
BR

Year	Tm	Lg	Tot	H	A	Men-On 0	1	2	3	One-Game 2	3	4	LO	XN	IP	PH	RHP	LHP
1922	NY	NL	1	1	0	0	1	0	0	0	0	0	0	0	1	0	1	0

Rank among batters: 4,707 • *Total ballparks homered in*: 1 • *First HR*: 10/01/1922 off Al Yeargin

Mike Higgins

MICHAEL FRANKLIN HIGGINS
B: 05/27/1909 D: 03/21/1969
BR

Year	Tm	Lg	Tot	H	A	Men-On 0	1	2	3	One-Game 2	3	4	LO	XN	IP	PH	RHP	LHP
1933	PHI	AL	13	7	6	10	3	0	0	0	0	0	0	1	0	0	8	5
1934	PHI	AL	16	8	8	8	5	2	1	0	0	0	0	0	2	0	14	2
1935	PHI	AL	23	16	7	11	11	1	0	1	1	0	0	1	0	0	18	5

Mike Higgins *continued*

Year	Tm	Lg	Tot	H	A	Men-On 0	Men-On 1	Men-On 2	Men-On 3	One-Game 2	One-Game 3	One-Game 4	LO	XN	IP	PH	RHP	LHP
1936	PHI	AL	12	6	6	6	4	2	0	0	0	0	0	0	1	0	9	3
1937	BOS	AL	9	5	4	6	2	1	0	1	0	0	0	0	0	0	9	0
1938	BOS	AL	5	3	2	2	1	1	1	0	0	0	0	0	0	0	5	0
1939	DET	AL	8	6	2	3	4	1	0	1	0	0	0	0	0	0	8	0
1940	DET	AL	13	11	2	5	5	2	1	0	1	0	0	0	0	0	11	2
1941	DET	AL	11	5	6	5	4	2	0	1	0	0	0	0	0	0	8	3
1942	DET	AL	11	7	4	8	1	1	1	1	0	0	0	0	0	0	9	2
1943	DET	AL	10	7	3	6	3	1	0	0	0	0	0	0	0	0	7	3
1944	DET	AL	7	4	3	5	2	0	0	0	0	0	0	0	0	0	7	0
1946	BOS	AL	2	2	0	2	0	0	0	0	0	0	0	0	0	0	2	0
Total			140	87	53	77	45	14	4	5	2	0	0	2	3	0	115	25

Rank among batters: 310 • *Top target (7 home runs)*: Jack Knott • *Number of pitchers victimized*: 84 • *Total ballparks homered in*: 9 • *First HR*: 04/14/1933 off Lefty Stewart • *Hit for Cycle*—@WAS: 08/06/1933 • *World Series HR*—1

Bobby Higginson

ROBERT LEIGH HIGGINSON
B: 08/18/1970
BL

Year	Tm	Lg	Tot	H	A	Men-On 0	Men-On 1	Men-On 2	Men-On 3	One-Game 2	One-Game 3	One-Game 4	LO	XN	IP	PH	RHP	LHP
1995	DET	AL	14	10	4	10	3	1	0	1	0	0	0	0	0	0	12	2

Rank among batters: 2,169 • *Total ballparks homered in*: 5 • *First HR*: 05/03/1995 off Jason Grimsley

Andy High

ANDREW AIRD HIGH
B: 11/21/1897 D: 02/22/1981
BL

Year	Tm	Lg	Tot	H	A	Men-On 0	Men-On 1	Men-On 2	Men-On 3	One-Game 2	One-Game 3	One-Game 4	LO	XN	IP	PH	RHP	LHP
1922	BRO	NL	6	3	3	3	3	0	0	0	0	0	1	0	1	0	4	2
1923	BRO	NL	3	0	3	0	3	0	0	0	0	0	0	0	1	0	3	0
1924	BRO	NL	6	2	4	2	3	1	0	0	0	0	0	0	1	0	5	1
1925	BOS	NL	4	1	3	1	3	0	0	0	0	0	0	0	1	0	2	2
1926	BOS	NL	2	2	0	1	1	0	0	0	0	0	0	0	2	0	0	2
1927	BOS	NL	4	1	3	2	2	0	0	1	0	0	0	0	0	1	4	0
1928	STL	NL	6	6	0	4	2	0	0	1	0	0	0	0	0	0	5	1
1929	STL	NL	10	4	6	1	7	2	0	1	0	0	0	0	1	0	7	3
1930	STL	NL	2	1	1	1	1	0	0	0	0	0	0	0	0	1	2	0
1933	CIN	NL	1	0	1	0	0	1	0	0	0	0	0	0	0	1	1	0
Total			44	20	24	15	25	4	0	3	0	0	1	0	7	3	33	11

Rank among batters: 1,095 • *Top target (3 home runs)*: Joe Genewich • *Number of pitchers victimized*: 38 • *Total ballparks homered in*: 8 • *First HR*: 04/27/1922 off Rube Marquard

Charlie High

CHARLES EDWIN HIGH
B: 12/01/1898 D: 09/11/1960
BL

Year	Tm	Lg	Tot	H	A	Men-On 0	Men-On 1	Men-On 2	Men-On 3	One-Game 2	One-Game 3	One-Game 4	LO	XN	IP	PH	RHP	LHP
1920	PHI	AL	1	0	1	0	1	0	0	0	0	0	0	0	0	0	1	0

Rank among batters: 4,707 • *Total ballparks homered in*: 1 • *First HR*: 09/16/1920 off Joe DeBerry

Hugh High

HUGH JENKIN HIGH
B: 10/24/1887 D: 11/16/1962
BL

Year	Tm	Lg	Tot	H	A	Men-On 0	Men-On 1	Men-On 2	Men-On 3	One-Game 2	One-Game 3	One-Game 4	LO	XN	IP	PH	RHP	LHP
1915	NY	AL	1	1	0	1	0	0	0	0	0	0	0	0	0	0	1	0
1916	NY	AL	1	1	0	0	1	0	0	0	0	0	0	0	0	0	1	0
1917	NY	AL	1	0	1	1	0	0	0	0	0	0	0	0	0	0	0	1
Total			3	2	1	2	1	0	0	0	0	0	0	0	0	0	2	1

Rank among batters: 3,735 • *Total ballparks homered in*: 2 • *First HR*: 07/31/1915 off Joe Benz

Dick Higham

RICHARD HIGHAM
B: 07/ /1851 D: 03/18/1905
BL

Year	Tm	Lg	Tot	H	A	Men-On 0	Men-On 1	Men-On 2	Men-On 3	One-Game 2	One-Game 3	One-Game 4	LO	XN	IP	PH	RHP	LHP
1878	PRO	NL	1	0	1	0	0	1	0	0	0	0	0	0	0	0	1	0

Rank among batters: 4,707 • *Total ballparks homered in*: 1 • *First HR*: 05/04/1878 off Tommy Bond

Donnie Hill

DONALD EARL HILL
B: 11/12/1960
BB

Year	Tm	Lg	Tot	H	A	Men-On 0	Men-On 1	Men-On 2	Men-On 3	One-Game 2	One-Game 3	One-Game 4	LO	XN	IP	PH	RHP	LHP
1983	OAK	AL	2	1	1	2	0	0	0	0	0	0	0	0	0	0	1	1
1984	OAK	AL	2	0	2	1	1	0	0	0	0	0	0	0	0	0	2	0
1985	OAK	AL	3	0	3	2	0	1	0	0	0	0	0	0	0	0	3	0
1986	OAK	AL	4	0	4	1	1	2	0	0	0	0	0	0	0	0	3	1
1987	CHI	AL	9	1	8	6	2	1	0	0	0	0	0	0	0	0	4	5
1988	CHI	AL	2	1	1	2	0	0	0	0	0	0	0	0	0	0	1	1
1990	CAL	AL	3	0	3	1	1	1	0	0	0	0	0	1	0	0	2	1
1991	CAL	AL	1	1	0	0	0	1	0	0	0	0	0	0	0	0	1	0
Total			26	4	22	15	5	6	0	0	0	0	0	1	0	0	17	9

Rank among batters: 1,576 • *Top target (2 home runs)*: Doyle Alexander • *Number of pitchers victimized*: 25 • *Total ballparks homered in*: 12 • *First HR*: 08/31/1983 off Shane Rawley

Glenallen Hill

GLENALLEN HILL
B: 03/22/1965
BR

Year	Tm	Lg	Tot	H	A	Men-On 0	Men-On 1	Men-On 2	Men-On 3	One-Game 2	One-Game 3	One-Game 4	LO	XN	IP	PH	RHP	LHP
1989	TOR	AL	1	1	0	0	0	0	1	0	0	0	0	0	0	0	1	0
1990	TOR	AL	12	7	5	8	3	0	1	1	0	0	0	0	0	0	7	5
1991	TOR	AL	3	2	1	2	1	0	0	0	0	0	0	0	0	0	1	2
	CLE	AL	5	1	4	3	2	0	0	0	0	0	0	0	0	0	3	2
	Total		8	3	5	5	3	0	0	0	0	0	0	0	0	0	4	4
1992	CLE	AL	18	7	11	13	2	3	0	3	0	0	0	1	0	0	11	7
1993	CLE	AL	5	0	5	4	1	0	0	1	0	0	0	0	0	1	0	5
	CHI	NL	10	5	5	4	5	1	0	0	0	0	0	0	0	2	3	7
	Total		15	5	10	8	6	1	0	1	0	0	0	0	0	3	3	12
1994	CHI	NL	10	3	7	6	3	1	0	1	0	0	0	0	0	0	7	3
1995	SF	NL	24	13	11	12	7	4	1	0	0	0	0	1	0	1	16	8
Total			88	39	49	52	24	9	3	6	0	0	0	2	0	4	49	39

Rank among batters: 590 • *Top target (4 home runs)*: Frank Tanana • *Number of pitchers victimized*: 76 • *Total ballparks homered in*: 26 • *First HR*: 09/01/1989 off Mark Guthrie

Hugh Hill

HUGH ELLIS HILL
B: 07/21/1879 D: 09/06/1958
BL

Year	Tm	Lg	Tot	H	A	Men-On 0	Men-On 1	Men-On 2	Men-On 3	One-Game 2	One-Game 3	One-Game 4	LO	XN	IP	PH	RHP	LHP
1904	STL	NL	3	1	2	3	0	0	0	0	0	0	0	1	0	0	3	0

Rank among batters: 3,735 • *Total ballparks homered in*: 2 • *First HR*: 10/01/1904 off Red Ames

Hunter Hill

HUNTER BENJAMIN HILL
B: 06/21/1879 D: 02/22/1959
BR

Year	Tm	Lg	Tot	H	A	Men-On 0	Men-On 1	Men-On 2	Men-On 3	One-Game 2	One-Game 3	One-Game 4	LO	XN	IP	PH	RHP	LHP
1905	WAS	AL	1	1	0	1	0	0	0	0	0	0	0	0	0	0	1	0

Rank among batters: 4,707 • *Total ballparks homered in*: 1 • *First HR*: 08/09/1905 off Barney Pelty

Jesse Hill

JESSE TERRILL HILL
B: 01/20/1907 D: 08/31/1993
BR

Year	Tm	Lg	Tot	H	A	Men-On 0	Men-On 1	Men-On 2	Men-On 3	One-Game 2	One-Game 3	One-Game 4	LO	XN	IP	PH	RHP	LHP
1935	NY	AL	4	2	2	2	1	1	0	0	0	0	0	0	0	0	3	1
1937	WAS	AL	1	0	1	1	0	0	0	0	0	0	0	0	0	0	0	1
	PHI	AL	1	0	1	1	0	0	0	0	0	0	0	0	0	0	1	0
	Total		2	0	2	2	0	0	0	0	0	0	0	0	0	0	1	1
Total			6	2	4	4	1	1	0	0	0	0	0	0	0	0	4	2

Rank among batters: 2,988 • *Total ballparks homered in*: 4 • *First HR*: 04/25/1935 off Gordon Rhodes

Ken Hill

KENNETH WADE HILL
B: 12/14/1965
BR

Year	Tm	Lg	Tot	H	A	Men-On 0	Men-On 1	Men-On 2	Men-On 3	One-Game 2	One-Game 3	One-Game 4	LO	XN	IP	PH	RHP	LHP
1992	MON	NL	1	1	0	1	0	0	0	0	0	0	0	0	0	0	1	0

Rank among batters: 4,707 • *Total ballparks homered in*: 1 • *First HR*: 06/24/1992 off Mickey Weston

Marc Hill

MARC KEVIN HILL
B: 02/18/1952
BR

Year	Tm	Lg	Tot	H	A	Men-On 0	1	2	3	One-Game 2	3	4	LO	XN	IP	PH	RHP	LHP
1975	SF	NL	5	2	3	2	2	1	0	0	0	0	0	0	0	1	3	2
1976	SF	NL	3	3	0	0	3	0	0	0	0	0	0	0	0	0	1	2
1977	SF	NL	9	8	1	3	4	2	0	0	0	0	0	0	0	1	4	5
1978	SF	NL	3	1	2	2	1	0	0	0	0	0	0	0	0	0	3	0
1979	SF	NL	3	0	3	2	0	1	0	0	0	0	0	0	0	0	2	1
1980	SEA	AL	2	2	0	2	0	0	0	0	0	0	0	0	0	0	1	1
1982	CHI	AL	3	1	2	2	1	0	0	0	0	0	0	0	0	0	1	2
1983	CHI	AL	1	1	0	1	0	0	0	0	0	0	0	0	0	0	0	1
1984	CHI	AL	5	4	1	3	1	1	0	0	0	0	0	0	0	0	3	2
Total			34	22	12	17	12	5	0	0	0	0	0	0	0	2	18	16

Rank among batters: 1,315 • *Top target (2 home runs)*: Jerry Koosman, Craig Swan, Dan Petry • *Number of pitchers victimized*: 31 • *Total ballparks homered in*: 11 • *First HR*: 04/12/1975 off Carl Morton

Chuck Hiller

CHARLES JOSEPH HILLER
B: 10/01/1934
BL

Year	Tm	Lg	Tot	H	A	Men-On 0	1	2	3	One-Game 2	3	4	LO	XN	IP	PH	RHP	LHP
1961	SF	NL	2	2	0	1	1	0	0	0	0	0	0	0	0	0	2	0
1962	SF	NL	3	1	2	3	0	0	0	0	0	0	0	0	0	0	2	1
1963	SF	NL	6	5	1	2	4	0	0	0	0	0	0	0	0	0	6	0
1964	SF	NL	1	0	1	1	0	0	0	0	0	0	1	0	0	0	1	0
1965	SF	NL	1	0	1	1	0	0	0	0	0	0	0	0	0	1	1	0
	NY	NL	5	2	3	5	0	0	0	0	0	0	1	0	0	0	5	0
	Total		6	2	4	6	0	0	0	0	0	0	1	0	0	1	6	0
1966	NY	NL	2	1	1	2	0	0	0	0	0	0	0	0	0	2	2	0
Total			20	11	9	15	5	0	0	0	0	0	2	0	0	3	19	1

Rank among batters: 1,810 • *Top target (3 home runs)*: Bob Gibson • *Number of pitchers victimized*: 17 • *Total ballparks homered in*: 6 • *First HR*: 05/30/1961 off Jim Brosnan • *World Series HR*—1

Mack Hillis

MALCOLM DAVID HILLIS
B: 07/23/1901 D: 06/16/1961
BR

Year	Tm	Lg	Tot	H	A	Men-On 0	1	2	3	One-Game 2	3	4	LO	XN	IP	PH	RHP	LHP
1928	PIT	NL	1	1	0	1	0	0	0	0	0	0	0	0	0	0	1	0

Rank among batters: 4,707 • *Total ballparks homered in*: 1 • *First HR*: 08/15/1928 off Dazzy Vance

Dave Hilton

JOHN DAVID HILTON
B: 09/15/1950
BR

Year	Tm	Lg	Tot	H	A	Men-On 0	1	2	3	One-Game 2	3	4	LO	XN	IP	PH	RHP	LHP
1973	SD	NL	5	3	2	4	0	1	0	0	0	0	0	0	0	0	4	1
1974	SD	NL	1	0	1	1	0	0	0	0	0	0	0	0	0	0	1	0
Total			6	3	3	5	0	1	0	0	0	0	0	0	0	0	5	1

Rank among batters: 2,988 • *Total ballparks homered in*: 4 • *First HR*: 04/29/1973 off Ferguson Jenkins

Bill Hinchman

WILLIAM WHITE HINCHMAN
B: 04/04/1883 D: 02/20/1963
BR

Year	Tm	Lg	Tot	H	A	Men-On 0	1	2	3	One-Game 2	3	4	LO	XN	IP	PH	RHP	LHP
1907	CLE	AL	1	0	1	1	0	0	0	0	0	0	0	0	0	0	1	0
1908	CLE	AL	6	3	3	0	1	5	0	0	0	0	0	0	1	0	5	1
1909	CLE	AL	2	0	2	0	1	1	0	0	0	0	0	0	0	0	2	0
1915	PIT	NL	5	2	3	2	3	0	0	0	0	0	0	0	3	0	3	2
1916	PIT	NL	4	1	3	1	3	0	0	0	0	0	0	0	1	0	3	1
1917	PIT	NL	2	1	1	0	0	2	0	0	0	0	0	0	0	0	1	1
Total			20	7	13	4	8	8	0	0	0	0	0	0	5	0	15	5

Rank among batters: 1,810 • *Top target (2 home runs)*: Gene Packard • *Number of pitchers victimized*: 19 • *Total ballparks homered in*: 11 • *First HR*: 09/08/1907 off Fred Glade

Paul Hines

PAUL A. HINES
B: 03/01/1852 D: 07/10/1935
BR

Year	Tm	Lg	Tot	H	A	Men-On 0	1	2	3	One-Game 2	3	4	LO	XN	IP	PH	RHP	LHP
1876	CHI	NL	2	0	2	1	0	1	0	0	0	0	0	0	0	0	2	0

Paul Hines *continued*

						Men-On				One-Game								
Year	Tm	Lg	Tot	H	A	0	1	2	3	2	3	4	LO	XN	IP	PH	RHP	LHP
1878	PRO	NL	4	3	1	0	3	1	0	0	0	0	0	0	0	0	4	0
1879	PRO	NL	2	1	1	1	1	0	0	0	0	0	0	1	0	0	2	0
1880	PRO	NL	3	2	1	2	0	1	0	0	0	0	0	0	0	0	1	2
1881	PRO	NL	2	1	1	1	1	0	0	0	0	0	0	0	0	0	2	0
1882	PRO	NL	4	1	3	4	0	0	0	0	0	0	1	0	1	0	3	1
1883	PRO	NL	4	2	2	0	3	1	0	0	0	0	0	0	0	0	2	2
1884	PRO	NL	3	1	2	3	0	0	0	0	0	0	1	0	1	0	2	0
1885	PRO	NL	1	0	1	1	0	0	0	0	0	0	1	0	0	0	1	0
1886	WAS	NL	9	5	4	5	3	0	1	1	0	0	0	0	0	0	7	2
1887	WAS	NL	10	6	4	5	3	1	1	0	0	0	2	0	0	0	5	5
1888	IND	NL	4	2	2	2	1	1	0	0	0	0	1	0	0	0	4	0
1889	IND	NL	6	3	3	2	3	1	0	1	0	0	0	0	0	0	6	0
1890	BOS	NL	2	2	0	2	0	0	0	0	0	0	0	0	0	0	2	0
Total			56	29	27	29	18	7	2	2	0	0	6	1	2	0	43	12

Rank among batters: 913 • *Top target (6 home runs)*: John Clarkson • *Number of pitchers victimized*: 37 • *Total ballparks homered in*: 17 • *First HR*: 06/03/1876 off Joe Borden

Chuck Hinton

CHARLES EDWARD HINTON
B: 05/03/1934
BR

Year	Tm	Lg	Tot	H	A	0	1	2	3	2	3	4	LO	XN	IP	PH	RHP	LHP
1961	WAS	AL	6	3	3	3	3	0	0	0	0	0	1	0	0	0	4	2
1962	WAS	AL	17	9	8	8	6	3	0	0	0	0	1	2	1	0	13	4
1963	WAS	AL	15	8	7	8	5	2	0	0	0	0	0	1	1	0	10	5
1964	WAS	AL	11	6	5	5	3	3	0	0	0	0	0	0	0	0	10	1
1965	CLE	AL	18	11	7	13	2	2	1	0	0	0	0	2	0	0	12	6
1966	CLE	AL	12	8	4	5	3	4	0	1	0	0	0	0	0	1	5	7
1967	CLE	AL	10	6	4	8	2	0	0	0	0	0	2	2	0	0	8	2
1968	CAL	AL	7	3	4	6	0	1	0	0	0	0	1	0	0	0	2	5
1969	CLE	AL	3	3	0	0	3	0	0	0	0	0	0	0	0	2	1	2
1970	CLE	AL	9	8	1	7	2	0	0	0	0	0	0	0	0	2	4	5
1971	CLE	AL	5	5	0	2	2	1	0	0	0	0	0	1	0	0	3	2
Total			113	70	43	65	31	16	1	1	0	0	5	8	2	5	72	41

Rank among batters: 421 • *Top target (4 home runs)*: Luis Tiant • *Number of pitchers victimized*: 88 • *Total ballparks homered in*: 14 • *First HR*: 05/21/1961 off Ron Kline

Tommy Hinzo

THOMAS LEE HINZO
B: 06/18/1964
BB

Year	Tm	Lg	Tot	H	A	0	1	2	3	2	3	4	LO	XN	IP	PH	RHP	LHP
1987	CLE	AL	3	3	0	3	0	0	0	0	0	0	0	0	0	0	1	2

Rank among batters: 3,735 • *Total ballparks homered in*: 1 • *First HR*: 08/09/1987 off John Cerutti

Gene Hiser

GENE TAYLOR HISER
B: 12/11/1948
BL

Year	Tm	Lg	Tot	H	A	0	1	2	3	2	3	4	LO	XN	IP	PH	RHP	LHP
1973	CHI	NL	1	1	0	1	0	0	0	0	0	0	0	0	0	0	1	0

Rank among batters: 4,707 • *Total ballparks homered in*: 1 • *First HR*: 06/29/1973 off Buzz Capra

Larry Hisle

LARRY EUGENE HISLE
B: 05/05/1947
BR

Year	Tm	Lg	Tot	H	A	0	1	2	3	2	3	4	LO	XN	IP	PH	RHP	LHP
1969	PHI	NL	20	11	9	12	6	2	0	2	0	0	0	0	0	0	18	2
1970	PHI	NL	10	4	6	3	7	0	0	0	0	0	0	0	0	0	6	4
1973	MIN	AL	15	6	9	8	6	1	0	1	0	0	0	0	0	0	11	4
1974	MIN	AL	19	12	7	9	4	5	1	0	0	0	1	0	0	0	11	8
1975	MIN	AL	11	7	4	2	3	6	0	0	0	0	0	1	0	0	7	4
1976	MIN	AL	14	6	8	1	10	3	0	0	0	0	0	1	0	0	7	7
1977	MIN	AL	28	12	16	13	7	6	2	1	0	0	0	2	0	0	17	11
1978	MIL	AL	34	20	14	13	13	8	0	3	0	0	0	0	0	0	25	9

						Men-On				One-Game								
Year	**Tm**	**Lg**	**Tot**	**H**	**A**	**0**	**1**	**2**	**3**	**2**	**3**	**4**	**LO**	**XN**	**IP**	**PH**	**RHP**	**LHP**

Larry Hisle *continued*

Year	Tm	Lg	Tot	H	A	0	1	2	3	2	3	4	LO	XN	IP	PH	RHP	LHP
1979	MIL	AL	3	2	1	1	2	0	0	0	0	0	0	0	0	0	3	0
1980	MIL	AL	6	2	4	3	2	1	0	1	0	0	0	0	0	0	5	1
1981	MIL	AL	4	0	4	2	1	1	0	0	0	0	0	0	0	0	3	1
1982	MIL	AL	2	2	0	1	1	0	0	0	0	0	0	0	0	1	0	2
Total			166	84	82	68	62	33	3	8	0	0	1	4	0	1	113	53

Rank among batters: 245 • *Top target (6 home runs)*: Paul Splittorff • *Number of pitchers victimized*: 117 • *Total ballparks homered in*: 25 • *First HR*: 04/21/1969 off Gary Gentry • *Hit for Cycle*—@BAL: 06/04/1976

Billy Hitchcock

WILLIAM CLYDE HITCHCOCK
B: 07/31/1916
BR

Year	Tm	Lg	Tot	H	A	0	1	2	3	2	3	4	LO	XN	IP	PH	RHP	LHP
1947	STL	AL	1	0	1	1	0	0	0	0	0	0	0	1	0	0	1	0
1948	BOS	AL	1	0	1	1	0	0	0	0	0	0	0	0	0	0	1	0
1950	PHI	AL	1	1	0	0	1	0	0	0	0	0	0	0	0	1	0	1
1951	PHI	AL	1	0	1	1	0	0	0	0	0	0	0	0	0	0	0	1
1952	PHI	AL	1	0	1	1	0	0	0	0	0	0	0	0	0	0	1	0
Total			5	1	4	4	1	0	0	0	0	0	0	1	0	1	3	2

Rank among batters: 3,191 • *Total ballparks homered in*: 2 • *First HR*: 06/18/1947 off Fritz Dorish

Myril Hoag

MYRIL OLIVER HOAG
B: 03/09/1908 D: 07/28/1971
BR

Year	Tm	Lg	Tot	H	A	0	1	2	3	2	3	4	LO	XN	IP	PH	RHP	LHP
1932	NY	AL	1	0	1	1	0	0	0	0	0	0	0	0	0	0	1	0
1934	NY	AL	3	3	0	2	1	0	0	0	0	0	0	0	0	0	1	2
1935	NY	AL	1	1	0	1	0	0	0	0	0	0	0	0	0	0	0	1
1936	NY	AL	3	1	2	2	1	0	0	0	0	0	0	0	0	0	1	2
1937	NY	AL	3	1	2	1	1	1	0	0	0	0	0	0	0	0	1	2
1939	STL	AL	10	4	6	6	3	1	0	1	0	0	0	0	0	1	8	2
1940	STL	AL	3	2	1	1	1	1	0	0	0	0	0	0	0	0	1	2
1941	CHI	AL	1	1	0	0	1	0	0	0	0	0	0	0	0	0	1	0
1942	CHI	AL	2	0	2	2	0	0	0	0	0	0	0	0	0	0	1	1
1944	CLE	AL	1	1	0	0	1	0	0	0	0	0	0	0	0	0	0	1
Total			28	14	14	16	9	3	0	1	0	0	0	0	0	1	15	13

Rank among batters: 1,500 • *Top target (3 home runs)*: Lynn Nelson • *Number of pitchers victimized*: 23 • *Total ballparks homered in*: 8 • *First HR*: 09/22/1932 off Roy Mahaffey • *World Series HR*—1

Don Hoak

DONALD ALBERT HOAK
B: 02/05/1928 D: 10/09/1969
BR

Year	Tm	Lg	Tot	H	A	0	1	2	3	2	3	4	LO	XN	IP	PH	RHP	LHP
1954	BRO	NL	7	6	1	6	0	0	1	0	0	0	0	1	0	0	6	1
1955	BRO	NL	5	1	4	3	1	1	0	0	0	0	0	0	0	0	4	1
1956	CHI	NL	5	4	1	3	0	2	0	0	0	0	0	0	0	0	4	1
1957	CIN	NL	19	11	8	10	6	2	1	2	0	0	0	0	0	0	12	7
1958	CIN	NL	6	4	2	4	2	0	0	0	0	0	0	0	0	0	4	2
1959	PIT	NL	8	2	6	6	1	1	0	1	0	0	1	0	0	0	4	4
1960	PIT	NL	16	6	10	5	9	2	0	0	0	0	0	1	0	0	11	5
1961	PIT	NL	12	4	8	8	3	1	0	0	0	0	0	0	1	0	5	7
1962	PIT	NL	5	3	2	3	1	1	0	0	0	0	0	0	0	0	2	3
1963	PHI	NL	6	4	2	4	1	1	0	0	0	0	0	0	0	0	5	1
Total			89	45	44	52	24	11	2	3	0	0	1	2	1	0	57	32

Rank among batters: 584 • *Top target (5 home runs)*: Warren Spahn • *Number of pitchers victimized*: 64 • *Total ballparks homered in*: 11 • *First HR*: 05/27/1954 off Curt Simmons

Ed Hobaugh

EDWARD RUSSELL HOBAUGH
B: 06/27/1934
BR

Year	Tm	Lg	Tot	H	A	0	1	2	3	2	3	4	LO	XN	IP	PH	RHP	LHP
1963	WAS	AL	1	0	1	1	0	0	0	0	0	0	0	0	0	0	1	0

Rank among batters: 4,707 • *Total ballparks homered in*: 1 • *First HR*: 09/02/1963 off Jerry Walker

Year	Tm	Lg	Tot	H	A	Men-On 0	1	2	3	One-Game 2	3	4	LO	XN	IP	PH	RHP	LHP

Glen Hobbie

GLEN FREDERICK HOBBIE
B: 04/24/1936
BR

Year	Tm	Lg	Tot	H	A	0	1	2	3	2	3	4	LO	XN	IP	PH	RHP	LHP
1960	CHI	NL	1	1	0	1	0	0	0	0	0	0	0	0	0	0	0	1
1961	CHI	NL	2	2	0	1	1	0	0	1	0	0	0	0	0	0	2	0
1964	STL	NL	1	0	1	1	0	0	0	0	0	0	0	0	0	0	1	0
Total			4	3	1	3	1	0	0	1	0	0	0	0	0	0	3	1

Rank among batters: 3,427 • *Top target (2 home runs)*: Al Cicotte • *Number of pitchers victimized*: 3 • *Total ballparks homered in*: 2 • *First HR*: 08/25/1960 off Wilmer Mizell

Richard Hoblitzell

RICHARD CARLETON HOBLITZELL
B: 10/26/1888 D: 11/14/1962
BR

Year	Tm	Lg	Tot	H	A	0	1	2	3	2	3	4	LO	XN	IP	PH	RHP	LHP
1909	CIN	NL	4	1	3	2	2	0	0	0	0	0	0	0	3	0	4	0
1910	CIN	NL	4	1	3	1	2	0	1	0	0	0	0	0	2	0	4	0
1911	CIN	NL	11	2	9	4	5	1	1	0	0	0	0	0	4	0	10	1
1912	CIN	NL	2	2	0	0	1	1	0	0	0	0	0	0	2	0	1	1
1913	CIN	NL	3	1	2	0	3	0	0	0	0	0	0	0	3	0	2	1
1915	BOS	AL	2	2	0	1	1	0	0	0	0	0	0	0	2	0	2	0
1917	BOS	AL	1	0	1	0	0	1	0	0	0	0	0	0	0	0	1	0
Total			27	9	18	8	14	3	2	0	0	0	0	0	16	0	24	3

Rank among batters: 1,532 • *Top target (2 home runs)*: Howie Camnitz, Nap Rucker • *Number of pitchers victimized*: 25 • *Total ballparks homered in*: 11 • *First HR*: 05/25/1909 off Tully Sparks

Butch Hobson

CLELL LAVERN HOBSON
B: 08/17/1951
BR

Year	Tm	Lg	Tot	H	A	0	1	2	3	2	3	4	LO	XN	IP	PH	RHP	LHP
1976	BOS	AL	8	5	3	2	5	1	0	0	0	0	0	0	1	0	4	4
1977	BOS	AL	30	12	18	15	7	8	0	0	0	0	0	1	0	0	24	6
1978	BOS	AL	17	12	5	10	2	5	0	0	0	0	0	0	0	0	12	5
1979	BOS	AL	28	15	13	16	10	2	0	0	0	0	0	0	0	0	17	11
1980	BOS	AL	11	4	7	6	3	2	0	1	0	0	0	0	0	0	8	3
1981	CAL	AL	4	1	3	1	2	1	0	0	0	0	0	0	0	0	4	0
Total			98	49	49	50	29	19	0	1	0	0	0	1	1	0	69	29

Rank among batters: 506 • *Top target (3 home runs)*: Dave Frost, Jim Palmer • *Number of pitchers victimized*: 84 • *Total ballparks homered in*: 14 • *First HR*: 06/28/1976 off Rudy May

Oris Hockett

ORIS LEON HOCKETT
B: 09/29/1909 D: 03/23/1969
BL

Year	Tm	Lg	Tot	H	A	0	1	2	3	2	3	4	LO	XN	IP	PH	RHP	LHP
1938	BRO	NL	1	1	0	0	1	0	0	0	0	0	0	0	0	0	1	0
1942	CLE	AL	7	5	2	5	2	0	0	0	0	0	0	0	0	0	6	1
1943	CLE	AL	2	0	2	2	0	0	0	0	0	0	1	0	0	0	2	0
1944	CLE	AL	1	1	0	1	0	0	0	0	0	0	0	0	0	0	1	0
1945	CHI	AL	2	0	2	1	0	0	1	0	0	0	0	0	0	0	2	0
Total			13	7	6	9	3	0	1	0	0	0	1	0	0	0	12	1

Rank among batters: 2,248 • *Top target (2 home runs)*: Dick Fowler • *Number of pitchers victimized*: 12 • *Total ballparks homered in*: 6 • *First HR*: 09/14/1938 off Bucky Walters

Johnny Hodapp

URBAN JOHN HODAPP
B: 09/26/1905 D: 06/14/1980
BR

Year	Tm	Lg	Tot	H	A	0	1	2	3	2	3	4	LO	XN	IP	PH	RHP	LHP
1927	CLE	AL	5	0	5	1	3	1	0	0	0	0	0	0	1	0	2	3
1928	CLE	AL	2	0	2	1	1	0	0	1	0	0	0	0	0	0	2	0
1929	CLE	AL	4	0	4	2	2	0	0	0	0	0	0	0	0	0	1	3
1930	CLE	AL	9	0	9	3	5	1	0	0	0	0	0	0	0	0	4	5
1931	CLE	AL	2	0	2	1	1	0	0	0	0	0	0	0	0	0	0	2
1932	CHI	AL	3	2	1	2	1	0	0	0	0	0	0	0	0	0	3	0
1933	BOS	AL	3	0	3	2	1	0	0	0	0	0	0	0	0	1	2	1
Total			28	2	26	12	14	2	0	1	0	0	0	0	1	1	14	14

Johnny Hodapp *continued*

Rank among batters: 1,500 • *Top target (4 home runs)*: Lefty Stewart • *Number of pitchers victimized*: 20 • *Total ballparks homered in*: 7 • *First HR*: 05/27/1927 off Chet Falk

Gomer Hodge

HAROLD MORRIS HODGE
B: 04/03/1944
BB

Year	Tm	Lg	Tot	H	A	Men-On 0	1	2	3	One-Game 2	3	4	LO	XN	IP	PH	RHP	LHP
1971	CLE	AL	1	0	1	1	0	0	0	0	0	0	0	0	0	1	0	1

Rank among batters: 4,707 • *Total ballparks homered in*: 1 • *First HR*: 09/03/1971 off Rogelio Moret

Gil Hodges

GILBERT RAYMOND HODGES
B: 04/04/1924 D: 04/02/1972
BR

Year	Tm	Lg	Tot	H	A	Men-On 0	1	2	3	One-Game 2	3	4	LO	XN	IP	PH	RHP	LHP
1947	BRO	NL	1	0	1	1	0	0	0	0	0	0	0	0	0	0	1	0
1948	BRO	NL	11	9	2	6	3	2	0	1	0	0	0	0	0	0	6	5
1949	BRO	NL	23	15	8	9	9	3	2	2	0	0	0	0	0	0	15	8
1950	BRO	NL	32	19	13	10	9	11	2	2	0	1	0	0	0	0	24	8
1951	BRO	NL	40	16	24	23	11	4	2	6	0	0	0	0	0	0	33	7
1952	BRO	NL	32	18	14	14	10	6	2	1	0	0	0	0	0	0	27	5
1953	BRO	NL	31	18	13	15	10	5	1	3	0	0	0	1	0	0	28	3
1954	BRO	NL	42	25	17	24	11	6	1	4	0	0	0	1	1	0	38	4
1955	BRO	NL	27	18	9	14	8	4	1	2	0	0	0	0	0	0	23	4
1956	BRO	NL	32	18	14	23	6	3	0	3	0	0	0	0	0	0	30	2
1957	BRO	NL	27	16	11	12	9	4	2	0	0	0	0	0	0	0	23	4
1958	LA	NL	22	13	9	13	6	2	1	1	0	0	0	1	0	0	19	3
1959	LA	NL	25	12	13	16	7	2	0	3	0	0	0	1	0	0	15	10
1960	LA	NL	8	3	5	4	4	0	0	0	0	0	0	0	0	0	6	2
1961	LA	NL	8	3	5	4	2	2	0	0	0	0	0	1	0	0	5	3
1962	NY	NL	9	7	2	8	1	0	0	1	0	0	0	0	1	0	3	6
Total			370	210	160	196	106	54	14	29	0	1	0	5	2	0	296	74

Rank among batters: 38 • *Top target (13 home runs)*: Murry Dickson • *Number of pitchers victimized*: 146 • *Total ballparks homered in*: 12 • *First HR*: 06/18/1947 off Hank Borowy • *Hit for Cycle—@PIT*: 06/25/1949 • *World Series HR—*5; *All-Star HR*—1

Ron Hodges

RONALD WRAY HODGES
B: 06/22/1949
BL

Year	Tm	Lg	Tot	H	A	Men-On 0	1	2	3	One-Game 2	3	4	LO	XN	IP	PH	RHP	LHP
1973	NY	NL	1	1	0	1	0	0	0	0	0	0	0	0	0	0	1	0
1974	NY	NL	4	3	1	2	1	1	0	0	0	0	0	0	0	0	4	0
1975	NY	NL	2	2	0	0	2	0	0	0	0	0	0	1	0	0	1	1
1976	NY	NL	4	1	3	2	1	1	0	0	0	0	0	0	0	0	4	0
1977	NY	NL	1	0	1	1	0	0	0	0	0	0	0	0	0	1	1	0
1981	NY	NL	1	1	0	0	1	0	0	0	0	0	0	0	0	0	0	1
1982	NY	NL	5	3	2	2	1	1	1	0	0	0	0	0	0	0	4	1
1984	NY	NL	1	0	1	1	0	0	0	0	0	0	0	0	0	1	1	0
Total			19	11	8	9	6	3	1	0	0	0	0	1	0	2	16	3

Rank among batters: 1,861 • *Total ballparks homered in*: 5 • *First HR*: 06/17/1973 off Bill Greif

Ralph Hodgin

ELMER RALPH HODGIN
B: 02/10/1916
BL

Year	Tm	Lg	Tot	H	A	Men-On 0	1	2	3	One-Game 2	3	4	LO	XN	IP	PH	RHP	LHP
1943	CHI	AL	1	0	1	1	0	0	0	0	0	0	0	0	0	0	1	0
1944	CHI	AL	1	1	0	0	1	0	0	0	0	0	0	0	0	0	0	1
1947	CHI	AL	1	0	1	1	0	0	0	0	0	0	0	0	0	0	1	0
1948	CHI	AL	1	0	1	1	0	0	0	0	0	0	0	0	0	0	1	0
Total			4	1	3	3	1	0	0	0	0	0	0	0	0	0	3	1

Rank among batters: 3,427 • *Total ballparks homered in*: 3 • *First HR*: 09/12/1943 off Denny Galehouse

Paul Hodgson

PAUL JOSEPH DENIS HODGSON
B: 04/14/1960
BR

Year	Tm	Lg	Tot	H	A	Men-On 0	1	2	3	One-Game 2	3	4	LO	XN	IP	PH	RHP	LHP
1980	TOR	AL	1	0	1	1	0	0	0	0	0	0	0	0	0	0	1	0

Rank among batters: 4,707 • *Total ballparks homered in*: 1 • *First HR*: 09/19/1980 off Dennis Martinez

Billy Hoeft

WILLIAM FREDERICK HOEFT
B: 05/17/1932
BL

Year	Tm	Lg	Tot	H	A	Men-On 0	1	2	3	One-Game 2	3	4	LO	XN	IP	PH	RHP	LHP
1957	DET	AL	3	3	0	1	2	0	0	1	0	0	0	0	0	0	3	0

Rank among batters: 3,735 • *Top target (2 home runs)*: Hal Brown • *Number of pitchers victimized*: 2 • *Total ballparks homered in*: 1 • *First HR*: 06/06/1957 off Pedro Ramos

Art Hoelskoetter

ARTHUR H. HOELSKOETTER
B: 09/30/1882 D: 08/03/1954
BR

Year	Tm	Lg	Tot	H	A	Men-On 0	1	2	3	One-Game 2	3	4	LO	XN	IP	PH	RHP	LHP
1907	STL	NL	2	0	2	1	1	0	0	0	0	0	0	0	1	0	1	1

Rank among batters: 4,129 • *Total ballparks homered in*: 2 • *First HR*: 06/29/1907 off Jake Weimer

Joe Hoerner

JOSEPH WALTER HOERNER
B: 11/12/1936
BR

Year	Tm	Lg	Tot	H	A	Men-On 0	1	2	3	One-Game 2	3	4	LO	XN	IP	PH	RHP	LHP
1966	STL	NL	1	0	1	0	0	1	0	0	0	0	0	0	0	0	1	0

Rank among batters: 4,707 • *Total ballparks homered in*: 1 • *First HR*: 07/22/1966 off Ferguson Jenkins

Bill Hoffer

WILLIAM LEOPOLD HOFFER
B: 11/08/1870 D: 07/21/1959
BR

Year	Tm	Lg	Tot	H	A	Men-On 0	1	2	3	One-Game 2	3	4	LO	XN	IP	PH	RHP	LHP
1897	BAL	NL	1	0	1	1	0	0	0	0	0	0	0	0	0	0	1	0

Rank among batters: 4,707 • *Total ballparks homered in*: 1 • *First HR*: 08/11/1897 off Jack Dunn

Stew Hofferth

STEWART EDWARD HOFFERTH
B: 01/27/1913 D: 03/07/1994
BR

Year	Tm	Lg	Tot	H	A	Men-On 0	1	2	3	One-Game 2	3	4	LO	XN	IP	PH	RHP	LHP
1944	BOS	NL	1	0	1	0	1	0	0	0	0	0	0	0	0	0	1	0
1945	BOS	NL	3	2	1	3	0	0	0	0	0	0	0	1	0	1	1	2
Total			4	2	2	3	1	0	0	0	0	0	0	1	0	1	2	2

Rank among batters: 3,427 • *Total ballparks homered in*: 3 • *First HR*: 09/14/1944 off John Wells

Danny Hoffman

DANIEL JOHN HOFFMAN
B: 03/02/1880 D: 03/14/1922
BL

Year	Tm	Lg	Tot	H	A	Men-On 0	1	2	3	One-Game 2	3	4	LO	XN	IP	PH	RHP	LHP
1903	PHI	AL	2	0	2	0	1	1	0	0	0	0	0	0	1	0	2	0
1904	PHI	AL	3	3	0	3	0	0	0	1	0	0	1	0	2	0	1	2
1905	PHI	AL	1	1	0	1	0	0	0	0	0	0	0	0	0	0	1	0
1907	NY	AL	5	4	1	2	2	1	0	0	0	0	0	0	2	0	4	1
1908	STL	AL	1	0	1	1	0	0	0	0	0	0	0	0	1	0	1	0
1909	STL	AL	2	2	0	2	0	0	0	0	0	0	0	0	2	0	2	0
Total			14	10	4	9	3	2	0	1	0	0	1	0	8	0	11	3

Rank among batters: 2,169 • *Top target (2 home runs)*: Doc White • *Number of pitchers victimized*: 13 • *Total ballparks homered in*: 5 • *First HR*: 05/21/1903 off Frank Kitson

Dutch Hoffman

CLARENCE CASPER HOFFMAN
B: 01/28/1904 D: 12/06/1962
BR

Year	Tm	Lg	Tot	H	A	Men-On 0	1	2	3	One-Game 2	3	4	LO	XN	IP	PH	RHP	LHP
1929	CHI	AL	3	1	2	3	0	0	0	0	0	0	0	0	0	0	2	1

Rank among batters: 3,735 • *Total ballparks homered in*: 2 • *First HR*: 05/19/1929 off Augie Prudhomme

Glenn Hoffman

GLENN EDWARD HOFFMAN
B: 07/07/1958
BR

Year	Tm	Lg	Tot	H	A	Men-On 0	1	2	3	One-Game 2	3	4	LO	XN	IP	PH	RHP	LHP
1980	BOS	AL	4	2	2	0	4	0	0	0	0	0	0	0	0	0	3	1
1981	BOS	AL	1	0	1	1	0	0	0	0	0	0	0	0	0	0	1	0

Year	Tm	Lg	Tot	H	A	Men-On 0	Men-On 1	Men-On 2	Men-On 3	One-Game 2	One-Game 3	One-Game 4	LO	XN	IP	PH	RHP	LHP

Glenn Hoffman *continued*

Year	Tm	Lg	Tot	H	A	Men-On 0	Men-On 1	Men-On 2	Men-On 3	One-Game 2	One-Game 3	One-Game 4	LO	XN	IP	PH	RHP	LHP
1982	BOS	AL	7	6	1	1	5	1	0	0	0	0	0	0	0	0	6	1
1983	BOS	AL	4	3	1	3	0	1	0	0	0	0	0	0	0	0	3	1
1985	BOS	AL	6	2	4	5	1	0	0	0	0	0	0	1	0	0	2	4
1989	CAL	AL	1	0	1	1	0	0	0	0	0	0	0	0	0	0	0	1
Total			23	13	10	11	10	2	0	0	0	0	0	1	0	0	15	8

Rank among batters: 1,686 • *Top target (2 home runs)*: Charlie Hough • *Number of pitchers victimized*: 22 • *Total ballparks homered in*: 6 • *First HR*: 06/06/1980 off Ernie Camacho

Jesse Hoffmeister

JESSE H. HOFFMEISTER

Year	Tm	Lg	Tot	H	A	Men-On 0	Men-On 1	Men-On 2	Men-On 3	One-Game 2	One-Game 3	One-Game 4	LO	XN	IP	PH	RHP	LHP
1897	PIT	NL	3	2	1	2	1	0	0	0	0	0	0	0	0	0	3	0

Rank among batters: 3,735 • *Total ballparks homered in*: 2 • *First HR*: 09/13/1897 off Chick Fraser

Bobby Hofman

ROBERT GEORGE HOFMAN
B: 10/05/1925 D: 04/05/1994
BR

Year	Tm	Lg	Tot	H	A	Men-On 0	Men-On 1	Men-On 2	Men-On 3	One-Game 2	One-Game 3	One-Game 4	LO	XN	IP	PH	RHP	LHP
1952	NY	NL	2	2	0	2	0	0	0	0	0	0	0	0	0	0	0	2
1953	NY	NL	12	5	7	6	4	1	1	2	0	0	0	0	0	3	5	7
1954	NY	NL	8	6	2	1	5	1	1	1	0	0	0	0	0	3	2	6
1955	NY	NL	10	7	3	8	2	0	0	0	0	0	0	0	0	3	7	3
Total			32	20	12	17	11	2	2	3	0	0	0	0	0	9	14	18

Rank among batters: 1,360 • *Top target (3 home runs)*: Harvey Haddix • *Number of pitchers victimized*: 25 • *Total ballparks homered in*: 7 • *First HR*: 09/12/1952 off Ken Raffensberger

Solly Hofman

ARTHUR FREDERICK HOFMAN
B: 10/29/1882 D: 03/10/1956
BR

Year	Tm	Lg	Tot	H	A	Men-On 0	Men-On 1	Men-On 2	Men-On 3	One-Game 2	One-Game 3	One-Game 4	LO	XN	IP	PH	RHP	LHP
1904	CHI	NL	1	0	1	1	0	0	0	0	0	0	0	0	0	0	1	0
1905	CHI	NL	1	0	1	1	0	0	0	0	0	0	0	0	1	0	1	0
1906	CHI	NL	2	1	1	2	0	0	0	0	0	0	0	0	0	0	0	0
1907	CHI	NL	1	0	1	1	0	0	0	0	0	0	0	0	1	0	1	0
1908	CHI	NL	2	1	1	2	0	0	0	0	0	0	0	0	0	0	2	0
1909	CHI	NL	2	1	1	2	0	0	0	0	0	0	0	1	2	0	1	1
1910	CHI	NL	3	2	1	2	1	0	0	0	0	0	0	0	1	0	1	2
1911	CHI	NL	2	1	1	1	1	0	0	0	0	0	0	0	0	0	1	1
1914	BRO	FL	5	2	3	5	0	0	0	0	0	0	0	1	0	0	4	1
Total			19	8	11	17	2	0	0	0	0	0	0	2	5	0	12	5

Rank among batters: 1,861 • *Top target (2 home runs)*: John McCloskey, Hooks Wiltse • *Number of pitchers victimized*: 17 • *Total ballparks homered in*: 10 • *First HR*: 09/30/1904 off Dummy Taylor

Fred Hofmann

FRED HOFMANN
B: 06/10/1894 D: 11/19/1964
BR

Year	Tm	Lg	Tot	H	A	Men-On 0	Men-On 1	Men-On 2	Men-On 3	One-Game 2	One-Game 3	One-Game 4	LO	XN	IP	PH	RHP	LHP
1921	NY	AL	1	1	0	1	0	0	0	0	0	0	0	0	0	0	0	1
1922	NY	AL	2	1	1	1	1	0	0	0	0	0	0	0	0	0	1	1
1923	NY	AL	3	3	0	2	1	0	0	0	0	0	0	0	0	0	2	1
1924	NY	AL	1	0	1	1	0	0	0	0	0	0	0	0	0	0	0	1
Total			7	5	2	5	2	0	0	0	0	0	0	0	0	0	3	4

Rank among batters: 2,834 • *Total ballparks homered in*: 3 • *First HR*: 06/15/1921 off Dickie Kerr

Shanty Hogan

JAMES FRANCIS HOGAN
B: 03/21/1906 D: 04/07/1967
BR

Year	Tm	Lg	Tot	H	A	Men-On 0	Men-On 1	Men-On 2	Men-On 3	One-Game 2	One-Game 3	One-Game 4	LO	XN	IP	PH	RHP	LHP
1927	BOS	NL	3	0	3	2	1	0	0	1	0	0	0	1	0	0	2	1
1928	NY	NL	10	9	1	6	1	2	1	0	0	0	0	0	0	0	8	2
1929	NY	NL	5	5	0	3	2	0	0	1	0	0	0	0	0	0	3	2
1930	NY	NL	13	9	4	8	2	3	0	0	0	0	0	0	0	2	10	3
1931	NY	NL	12	11	1	5	3	4	0	1	0	0	0	0	0	0	8	4
1932	NY	NL	8	6	2	4	1	2	1	0	0	0	0	0	0	0	7	1

Shanty Hogan *continued*

Year	Tm	Lg	Tot	H	A	Men-On 0	1	2	3	One-Game 2	3	4	LO	XN	IP	PH	RHP	LHP
1933	BOS	NL	3	1	2	1	1	1	0	0	0	0	0	0	0	0	3	0
1934	BOS	NL	4	1	3	2	2	0	0	0	0	0	0	0	0	0	3	1
1935	BOS	NL	2	1	1	1	1	0	0	0	0	0	0	0	0	0	2	0
1936	WAS	AL	1	0	1	1	0	0	0	0	0	0	0	0	0	0	1	0
Total			61	43	18	33	14	12	2	3	0	0	0	1	0	2	47	14

Rank among batters: 844 • *Top target (5 home runs)*: Socks Seibold • *Number of pitchers victimized*: 42 • *Total ballparks homered in*: 8 • *First HR*: 06/21/1927 off Burleigh Grimes

Willie Hogan

WILLIAM HENRY HOGAN
B: 09/14/1884 D: 09/28/1974
BR

Year	Tm	Lg	Tot	H	A	Men-On 0	1	2	3	One-Game 2	3	4	LO	XN	IP	PH	RHP	LHP
1911	STL	AL	2	0	2	0	2	0	0	0	0	0	0	0	1	0	2	0
1912	STL	AL	1	0	1	0	0	1	0	0	0	0	0	0	0	0	1	0
Total			3	0	3	0	2	1	0	0	0	0	0	0	1	0	3	0

Rank among batters: 3,735 • *Total ballparks homered in*: 3 • *First HR*: 06/02/1911 off Lew Brockett

Bill Hogg

WILLIAM JOHNSTON HOGG
B: 09/11/1881 D: 12/08/1909
BR

Year	Tm	Lg	Tot	H	A	Men-On 0	1	2	3	One-Game 2	3	4	LO	XN	IP	PH	RHP	LHP
1907	NY	AL	1	1	0	1	0	0	0	0	0	0	0	0	1	0	0	1

Rank among batters: 4,707 • *Total ballparks homered in*: 1 • *First HR*: 07/01/1907 off Oscar Graham

George Hogriever

GEORGE C. HOGRIEVER
B: 03/17/1869 D: 01/26/1961
BR

Year	Tm	Lg	Tot	H	A	Men-On 0	1	2	3	One-Game 2	3	4	LO	XN	IP	PH	RHP	LHP
1895	CIN	NL	2	1	1	1	1	0	0	0	0	0	0	0	0	0	1	0

Rank among batters: 4,129 • *Total ballparks homered in*: 2 • *First HR*: 06/04/1895 off Jim Sullivan

Chief Hogsett

ELON CHESTER HOGSETT
B: 11/02/1903
BL

Year	Tm	Lg	Tot	H	A	Men-On 0	1	2	3	One-Game 2	3	4	LO	XN	IP	PH	RHP	LHP
1930	DET	AL	1	0	1	1	0	0	0	0	0	0	0	0	0	0	1	0
1932	DET	AL	2	0	2	1	1	0	0	1	0	0	0	0	0	0	0	2
1935	DET	AL	2	0	2	1	1	0	0	0	0	0	0	0	0	0	0	2
1937	STL	AL	1	1	0	0	1	0	0	0	0	0	0	0	0	0	1	0
Total			6	1	5	3	3	0	0	1	0	0	0	0	0	0	2	4

Rank among batters: 2,988 • *Top target (2 home runs)*: Tony Freitas • *Number of pitchers victimized*: 5 • *Total ballparks homered in*: 3 • *First HR*: 07/28/1930 off Pete Appleton

Chris Hoiles

CHRISTOPHER ALLEN HOILES
B: 03/20/1965
BR

Year	Tm	Lg	Tot	H	A	Men-On 0	1	2	3	One-Game 2	3	4	LO	XN	IP	PH	RHP	LHP
1990	BAL	AL	1	1	0	0	0	1	0	0	0	0	0	1	0	0	1	0
1991	BAL	AL	11	5	6	10	0	0	1	0	0	0	0	0	0	0	5	6
1992	BAL	AL	20	8	12	17	2	0	1	1	0	0	0	0	0	0	16	4
1993	BAL	AL	29	16	13	15	9	4	1	3	0	0	0	0	0	0	21	8
1994	BAL	AL	19	11	8	10	6	3	0	0	0	0	0	0	0	0	11	8
1995	BAL	AL	19	9	10	11	6	2	0	1	0	0	0	0	0	1	7	12
Total			99	50	49	63	23	10	3	5	0	0	0	1	0	1	61	38

Rank among batters: 503 • *Top target (4 home runs)*: Chuck Finley • *Number of pitchers victimized*: 75 • *Total ballparks homered in*: 16 • *First HR*: 06/27/1990 off Sergio Valdez

Ray Holbert

RAY ARTHUR HOLBERT
B: 09/25/1970
BR

Year	Tm	Lg	Tot	H	A	Men-On 0	1	2	3	One-Game 2	3	4	LO	XN	IP	PH	RHP	LHP
1995	SD	NL	2	1	1	1	0	0	1	0	0	0	0	0	0	0	0	2

Rank among batters: 4,129 • *Total ballparks homered in*: 2 • *First HR*: 07/17/1995 off C.J. Nitkowski

Sammy Holbrook

JAMES MARBURY HOLBROOK
B: 07/17/1910 D: 04/10/1991
BR

Year	Tm	Lg	Tot	H	A	Men-On 0	1	2	3	One-Game 2	3	4	LO	XN	IP	PH	RHP	LHP
1935	WAS	AL	2	0	2	0	2	0	0	1	0	0	0	0	0	0	0	2

Rank among batters: 4,129 • *Total ballparks homered in*: 1 • *First HR*: 06/15/1935 off Russ Van Atta

Walter Holke

WALTER HENRY HOLKE
B: 12/25/1892 D: 10/12/1954
BB

Year	Tm	Lg	Tot	H	A	Men-On 0	1	2	3	One-Game 2	3	4	LO	XN	IP	PH	RHP	LHP
1917	NY	NL	2	1	1	1	1	0	0	0	0	0	0	0	0	0	2	0
1918	NY	NL	1	0	1	0	0	1	0	0	0	0	0	0	0	0	1	0
1920	BOS	NL	3	3	0	0	1	2	0	0	0	0	0	0	3	0	2	1
1921	BOS	NL	3	1	2	2	1	0	0	0	0	0	0	0	2	0	3	0
1923	PHI	NL	7	5	2	2	3	2	0	1	0	0	0	0	2	0	7	0
1924	PHI	NL	6	4	2	3	2	1	0	0	0	0	0	0	0	0	6	0
1925	PHI	NL	1	0	1	0	0	1	0	0	0	0	0	0	0	0	1	0
	CIN	NL	1	0	1	0	1	0	0	0	0	0	0	0	1	0	1	0
	Total		2	0	2	0	1	1	0	0	0	0	0	0	1	0	2	0
Total			24	14	10	8	9	7	0	1	0	0	0	0	8	0	23	1

Rank among batters: 1,643 • *Top target (2 home runs)*: Grover Alexander • *Number of pitchers victimized*: 23 • *Total ballparks homered in*: 6 • *First HR*: 04/27/1917 off Jimmy Lavender

Dutch Holland

ROBERT CLYDE HOLLAND
B: 10/12/1903 D: 06/16/1967
BR

Year	Tm	Lg	Tot	H	A	Men-On 0	1	2	3	One-Game 2	3	4	LO	XN	IP	PH	RHP	LHP
1932	BOS	NL	1	1	0	0	0	0	1	0	0	0	0	0	0	0	1	0
1934	CLE	AL	2	0	2	0	2	0	0	0	0	0	0	0	0	0	1	1
Total			3	1	2	0	2	0	1	0	0	0	0	0	0	0	2	1

Rank among batters: 3,735 • *Total ballparks homered in*: 3 • *First HR*: 09/11/1932 off Larry Benton

Todd Hollandsworth

TODD MATHEW HOLLANDSWORTH
B: 04/20/1973
BL

Year	Tm	Lg	Tot	H	A	Men-On 0	1	2	3	One-Game 2	3	4	LO	XN	IP	PH	RHP	LHP
1995	LA	NL	5	3	2	5	0	0	0	1	0	0	0	0	0	0	4	1

Rank among batters: 3,191 • *Top target (2 home runs)*: Shane Reynolds • *Number of pitchers victimized*: 4 • *Total ballparks homered in*: 3 • *First HR*: 07/18/1995 off Shane Reynolds

Bug Holliday

JAMES WEAR HOLLIDAY
B: 02/08/1867 D: 02/15/1910
BR

Year	Tm	Lg	Tot	H	A	Men-On 0	1	2	3	One-Game 2	3	4	LO	XN	IP	PH	RHP	LHP
1889	CIN	AA	19	14	5	6	8	5	0	1	0	0	3	0	3	0	14	4
1890	CIN	NL	4	3	1	2	1	1	0	0	0	0	0	0	1	0	3	1
1891	CIN	NL	9	6	3	3	6	0	0	0	0	0	0	0	2	0	8	0
1892	CIN	NL	13	10	3	8	4	1	0	1	0	0	1	0	3	0	9	3
1893	CIN	NL	5	4	1	2	2	0	1	1	0	0	0	0	2	0	3	0
1894	CIN	NL	13	8	5	2	6	3	2	2	0	0	0	0	1	0	12	1
1897	CIN	NL	2	0	2	2	0	0	0	0	0	0	0	0	0	1	2	0
Total			65	45	20	25	27	10	3	5	0	0	4	0	12	1	51	9

Rank among batters: 799 • *Top target (4 home runs)*: Harry Staley, Bill Hutchison, Kid Nichols • *Number of pitchers victimized*: 45 • *Total ballparks homered in*: 13 • *First HR*: 04/30/1889 off John McCarty

Al Hollingsworth

ALBERT WAYNE HOLLINGSWORTH
B: 02/25/1908
BL

Year	Tm	Lg	Tot	H	A	Men-On 0	1	2	3	One-Game 2	3	4	LO	XN	IP	PH	RHP	LHP
1936	CIN	NL	1	0	1	0	0	0	1	0	0	0	0	0	0	0	1	0
1945	STL	AL	1	0	1	0	0	1	0	0	0	0	0	0	0	0	1	0
Total			2	0	2	0	0	1	1	0	0	0	0	0	0	0	2	0

Rank among batters: 4,129 • *Total ballparks homered in*: 2 • *First HR*: 05/28/1936 off Lon Warneke

Dave Hollins

DAVID MICHAEL HOLLINS
B: 05/25/1966
BB

Year	Tm	Lg	Tot	H	A	Men-On 0	1	2	3	One-Game 2	3	4	LO	XN	IP	PH	RHP	LHP
1990	PHI	NL	5	2	3	2	2	1	0	0	0	0	0	0	0	3	2	3
1991	PHI	NL	6	3	3	3	2	0	1	0	0	0	0	0	0	1	3	3
1992	PHI	NL	27	14	13	11	14	1	1	1	0	0	0	0	0	0	10	17
1993	PHI	NL	18	9	9	8	7	3	0	0	0	0	0	2	0	0	10	8
1994	PHI	NL	4	1	3	1	3	0	0	0	0	0	0	0	0	0	3	1
1995	PHI	NL	7	5	2	4	2	1	0	0	0	0	0	0	0	0	4	3
Total			67	34	33	29	30	6	2	1	0	0	0	2	0	4	32	35

Rank among batters: 777 • *Top target (6 home runs)*: Butch Henry • *Number of pitchers victimized*: 51 • *Total ballparks homered in*: 13 • *First HR*: 05/26/1990 off Pete Smith • *LCS HR*—2

Stan Hollmig

STANLEY ERNEST HOLLMIG
B: 01/02/1926 D: 12/04/1981
BR

Year	Tm	Lg	Tot	H	A	Men-On 0	1	2	3	One-Game 2	3	4	LO	XN	IP	PH	RHP	LHP
1949	PHI	NL	2	2	0	0	1	1	0	0	0	0	0	0	0	0	1	1

Rank among batters: 4,129 • *Total ballparks homered in*: 1 • *First HR*: 06/07/1949 off Vic Lombardi

Charlie Hollocher

CHARLES JACOB HOLLOCHER
B: 06/11/1896 D: 08/14/1940
BL

Year	Tm	Lg	Tot	H	A	Men-On 0	1	2	3	One-Game 2	3	4	LO	XN	IP	PH	RHP	LHP
1918	CHI	NL	2	1	1	2	0	0	0	0	0	0	0	0	0	0	2	0
1919	CHI	NL	3	0	3	1	1	1	0	0	0	0	0	0	1	0	1	2
1921	CHI	NL	3	1	2	2	1	0	0	0	0	0	0	0	0	0	2	1
1922	CHI	NL	3	2	1	2	0	1	0	0	0	0	0	0	0	0	3	0
1923	CHI	NL	1	0	1	0	1	0	0	0	0	0	0	0	0	0	1	0
1924	CHI	NL	2	1	1	2	0	0	0	0	0	0	0	0	0	0	2	0
Total			14	5	9	9	3	2	0	0	0	0	0	0	1	0	11	3

Rank among batters: 2,169 • *Top target (2 home runs)*: Joe Oeschger • *Number of pitchers victimized*: 13 • *Total ballparks homered in*: 6 • *First HR*: 08/03/1918 off Red Causey

Ed Holly

EDWARD WILLIAM HOLLY
B: 07/06/1879 D: 11/27/1973
BR

Year	Tm	Lg	Tot	H	A	Men-On 0	1	2	3	One-Game 2	3	4	LO	XN	IP	PH	RHP	LHP
1907	STL	NL	1	0	1	1	0	0	0	0	0	0	0	0	0	0	0	1

Rank among batters: 4,707 • *Total ballparks homered in*: 1 • *First HR*: 05/18/1907 off Hooks Wiltse

Wattie Holm

ROSCOE ALBERT HOLM
B: 12/28/1901 D: 05/19/1950
BR

Year	Tm	Lg	Tot	H	A	Men-On 0	1	2	3	One-Game 2	3	4	LO	XN	IP	PH	RHP	LHP
1927	STL	NL	3	2	1	2	1	0	0	0	0	0	0	0	0	0	3	0
1928	STL	NL	3	1	2	0	2	0	1	0	0	0	0	0	0	1	2	1
Total			6	3	3	2	3	0	1	0	0	0	0	0	0	1	5	1

Rank among batters: 2,988 • *Total ballparks homered in*: 4 • *First HR*: 06/09/1927 off Larry Benton

Ducky Holmes

JAMES WILLIAM HOLMES
B: 01/28/1869 D: 08/06/1932
BL

Year	Tm	Lg	Tot	H	A	Men-On 0	1	2	3	One-Game 2	3	4	LO	XN	IP	PH	RHP	LHP
1895	LOU	NL	3	3	0	2	0	1	0	1	0	0	0	0	0	0	2	1
1897	NY	NL	1	1	0	0	0	1	0	0	0	0	0	0	0	0	1	0
1898	BAL	NL	1	0	1	1	0	0	0	0	0	0	0	0	1	0	1	0
1899	BAL	NL	4	1	3	2	2	0	0	0	0	0	0	0	0	0	3	1
1901	DET	AL	4	3	1	2	1	0	1	0	0	0	0	0	2	0	3	1
1902	DET	AL	2	0	2	2	0	0	0	0	0	0	0	0	0	0	1	1
1903	WAS	AL	1	1	0	0	0	1	0	0	0	0	0	0	1	0	1	0
1904	CHI	AL	1	0	1	1	0	0	0	0	0	0	0	0	0	0	0	1
Total			17	9	8	10	3	3	1	1	0	0	0	0	4	0	12	5

Rank among batters: 1,969 • *Top target (3 home runs)*: Cy Young • *Number of pitchers victimized*: 14 • *Total ballparks homered in*: 10 • *First HR*: 09/28/1895 off Cy Young

Year	Tm	Lg	Tot	H	A	Men-On				One-Game			LO	XN	IP	PH	RHP	LHP
						0	1	2	3	2	3	4						

Tommy Holmes

THOMAS FRANCIS HOLMES
B: 03/29/1917
BL

Year	Tm	Lg	Tot	H	A	0	1	2	3	2	3	4	LO	XN	IP	PH	RHP	LHP
1942	BOS	NL	4	0	4	3	0	1	0	0	0	0	1	0	1	0	3	1
1943	BOS	NL	5	3	2	4	1	0	0	0	0	0	0	0	0	0	4	1
1944	BOS	NL	13	10	3	7	4	2	0	0	0	0	1	0	0	0	11	2
1945	BOS	NL	28	19	9	15	12	1	0	3	0	0	0	1	0	0	26	2
1946	BOS	NL	6	2	4	4	1	1	0	0	0	0	0	0	1	0	4	2
1947	BOS	NL	9	3	6	3	5	1	0	2	0	0	1	0	0	0	7	2
1948	BOS	NL	6	4	2	5	1	0	0	0	0	0	0	0	0	0	5	1
1949	BOS	NL	8	5	3	2	5	1	0	0	0	0	0	0	0	1	7	1
1950	BOS	NL	9	5	4	4	4	1	0	1	0	0	0	0	0	0	8	1
Total			88	51	37	47	33	8	0	6	0	0	3	1	2	1	75	13

Rank among batters: 590 • *Top target (4 home runs)*: Larry Jansen • *Number of pitchers victimized*: 61 • *Total ballparks homered in*: 8 • *First HR*: 04/28/1942 off Bill Fleming

Jim Holt

JAMES WILLIAM HOLT
B: 05/27/1944
BL

Year	Tm	Lg	Tot	H	A	0	1	2	3	2	3	4	LO	XN	IP	PH	RHP	LHP
1969	MIN	AL	1	1	0	1	0	0	0	0	0	0	0	0	0	1	1	0
1970	MIN	AL	3	3	0	2	1	0	0	0	0	0	0	1	0	0	3	0
1971	MIN	AL	1	1	0	1	0	0	0	0	0	0	0	1	0	0	1	0
1972	MIN	AL	1	1	0	1	0	0	0	0	0	0	0	0	0	0	1	0
1973	MIN	AL	11	4	7	7	3	1	0	1	0	0	0	0	0	0	8	3
1975	OAK	AL	2	1	1	1	1	0	0	0	0	0	0	0	0	0	2	0
Total			19	11	8	13	5	1	0	1	0	0	0	2	0	1	16	3

Rank among batters: 1,861 • *Total ballparks homered in*: 7 • *First HR*: 09/30/1969 off Danny Murphy

Red Holt

JAMES EMMETT MADISON HOLT
B: 07/25/1894 D: 02/02/1961
BL

Year	Tm	Lg	Tot	H	A	0	1	2	3	2	3	4	LO	XN	IP	PH	RHP	LHP
1925	PHI	AL	1	1	0	1	0	0	0	0	0	0	0	0	0	0	0	1

Rank among batters: 4,707 • *Total ballparks homered in*: 1 • *First HR*: 09/23/1925 off Dave Danforth

Ken Holtzman

KENNETH DALE HOLTZMAN
B: 11/03/1945
BR

Year	Tm	Lg	Tot	H	A	0	1	2	3	2	3	4	LO	XN	IP	PH	RHP	LHP
1969	CHI	NL	1	0	1	0	1	0	0	0	0	0	0	0	0	0	1	0
1971	CHI	NL	1	1	0	1	0	0	0	0	0	0	0	0	0	0	1	0
Total			2	1	1	1	1	0	0	0	0	0	0	0	0	0	2	0

Rank among batters: 4,129 • *Total ballparks homered in*: 2 • *First HR*: 08/31/1969 off Phil Niekro • *World Series HR*—1

Abie Hood

ALBIE LARRISON HOOD
B: 01/31/1903 D: 10/14/1988
BL

Year	Tm	Lg	Tot	H	A	0	1	2	3	2	3	4	LO	XN	IP	PH	RHP	LHP
1925	BOS	NL	1	1	0	1	0	0	0	0	0	0	0	0	1	0	1	0

Rank among batters: 4,707 • *Total ballparks homered in*: 1 • *First HR*: 07/17/1925 off Vic Aldridge

Wally Hood

WALLACE JAMES, SR. HOOD
B: 02/09/1895 D: 05/02/1965
BR

Year	Tm	Lg	Tot	H	A	0	1	2	3	2	3	4	LO	XN	IP	PH	RHP	LHP
1921	BRO	NL	1	0	1	1	0	0	0	0	0	0	0	1	1	0	1	0

Rank among batters: 4,707 • *Total ballparks homered in*: 1 • *First HR*: 05/30/1921 off Hugh McQuillan

Bob Hooper

ROBERT NELSON HOOPER
B: 05/30/1922 D: 03/17/1980
BR

Year	Tm	Lg	Tot	H	A	0	1	2	3	2	3	4	LO	XN	IP	PH	RHP	LHP
1950	PHI	AL	1	1	0	0	1	0	0	0	0	0	0	0	0	0	0	1

Year	Tm	Lg	Tot	H	A	Men-On 0	Men-On 1	Men-On 2	Men-On 3	One-Game 2	One-Game 3	One-Game 4	LO	XN	IP	PH	RHP	LHP

Bob Hooper *continued*

Year	Tm	Lg	Tot	H	A	0	1	2	3	2	3	4	LO	XN	IP	PH	RHP	LHP
1951	PHI	AL	1	0	1	0	0	1	0	0	0	0	0	0	0	0	1	0
1952	PHI	AL	2	2	0	2	0	0	0	0	0	0	0	0	0	0	1	1
Total			4	3	1	2	1	1	0	0	0	0	0	0	0	0	2	2

Rank among batters: 3,427 • *Total ballparks homered in*: 2 • *First HR*: 05/30/1950 off Steve Nagy

Harry Hooper

HARRY BARTHOLOMEW HOOPER
B: 08/24/1887 D: 12/18/1974
BL HOF

Year	Tm	Lg	Tot	H	A	0	1	2	3	2	3	4	LO	XN	IP	PH	RHP	LHP
1910	BOS	AL	2	1	1	2	0	0	0	0	0	0	1	0	1	0	2	0
1911	BOS	AL	4	3	1	1	3	0	0	0	0	0	0	0	0	0	4	0
1912	BOS	AL	2	0	2	1	0	1	0	0	0	0	0	0	1	0	2	0
1913	BOS	AL	4	1	3	3	0	1	0	0	0	0	3	0	1	0	3	1
1914	BOS	AL	1	0	1	1	0	0	0	0	0	0	0	0	0	0	1	0
1915	BOS	AL	2	0	2	0	2	0	0	0	0	0	0	0	0	0	2	0
1916	BOS	AL	1	0	1	0	1	0	0	0	0	0	0	0	0	0	1	0
1917	BOS	AL	3	1	2	1	0	2	0	0	0	0	1	0	0	0	3	0
1918	BOS	AL	1	1	0	0	1	0	0	0	0	0	0	0	1	0	1	0
1919	BOS	AL	3	0	3	3	0	0	0	0	0	0	0	0	0	0	2	1
1920	BOS	AL	7	2	5	7	0	0	0	0	0	0	2	1	0	0	7	0
1921	CHI	AL	8	5	3	7	0	1	0	2	0	0	1	0	0	0	5	3
1922	CHI	AL	11	3	8	8	1	2	0	0	0	0	1	1	2	0	10	1
1923	CHI	AL	10	4	6	5	5	0	0	0	0	0	1	0	0	0	10	0
1924	CHI	AL	10	2	8	6	0	2	2	0	0	0	0	0	0	0	10	0
1925	CHI	AL	6	3	3	4	2	0	0	0	0	0	0	0	2	0	5	1
Total			75	26	49	49	15	9	2	2	0	0	10	2	8	0	68	7

Rank among batters: 699 • *Top target (4 home runs)*: Dixie Davis, Bob Shawkey • *Number of pitchers victimized*: 49 • *Total ballparks homered in*: 11 • *First HR*: 08/22/1910 off Joe Lake • *World Series HR*—2

Burt Hooton

BURT CARLTON HOOTON
B: 02/07/1950
BR

Year	Tm	Lg	Tot	H	A	0	1	2	3	2	3	4	LO	XN	IP	PH	RHP	LHP
1972	CHI	NL	1	1	0	0	0	0	1	0	0	0	0	0	0	0	1	0
1975	LA	NL	1	0	1	1	0	0	0	0	0	0	0	0	0	0	1	0
1980	LA	NL	1	1	0	0	0	1	0	0	0	0	0	0	0	0	0	1
1982	LA	NL	1	0	1	1	0	0	0	0	0	0	0	0	0	0	1	0
Total			4	2	2	2	0	1	1	0	0	0	0	0	0	0	3	1

Rank among batters: 3,427 • *Total ballparks homered in*: 3 • *First HR*: 09/16/1972 off Tom Seaver

Buster Hoover

WILLIAM J. HOOVER
B: 1863 BR

Year	Tm	Lg	Tot	H	A	0	1	2	3	2	3	4	LO	XN	IP	PH	RHP	LHP
1884	PHI	NL	1	1	0	0	1	0	0	0	0	0	0	0	1	0	0	1

Rank among batters: 4,707 • *Total ballparks homered in*: 1 • *First HR*: 08/21/1884 off John Henry

Charlie Hoover

CHARLES E. HOOVER
B: 09/09/1865
BL

Year	Tm	Lg	Tot	H	A	0	1	2	3	2	3	4	LO	XN	IP	PH	RHP	LHP
1889	KC	AA	1	1	0	0	1	0	0	0	0	0	0	0	0	0	1	0

Rank among batters: 4,707 • *Total ballparks homered in*: 1 • *First HR*: 08/12/1889 off William Widner

Joe Hoover

ROBERT JOSEPH HOOVER
B: 04/15/1915 D: 09/02/1965
BR

Year	Tm	Lg	Tot	H	A	0	1	2	3	2	3	4	LO	XN	IP	PH	RHP	LHP
1943	DET	AL	4	2	2	2	1	1	0	0	0	0	0	0	0	0	4	0
1945	DET	AL	1	1	0	1	0	0	0	0	0	0	1	0	0	0	1	0
Total			5	3	2	3	1	1	0	0	0	0	1	0	0	0	5	0

Rank among batters: 3,191 • *Top target (2 home runs)*: Lum Harris • *Number of pitchers victimized*: 4 • *Total ballparks homered in*: 3 • *First HR*: 05/16/1943 off Early Wynn

Gail Hopkins

GAIL EASON HOPKINS
B: 02/19/1943
BL

Year	Tm	Lg	Tot	H	A	Men-On 0	1	2	3	One-Game 2	3	4	LO	XN	IP	PH	RHP	LHP
1969	CHI	AL	8	4	4	5	2	1	0	0	0	0	0	0	0	0	8	0
1970	CHI	AL	6	3	3	4	2	0	0	0	0	0	0	0	0	1	5	1
1971	KC	AL	9	4	5	6	1	2	0	0	0	0	0	0	0	1	9	0
1973	KC	AL	2	1	1	1	1	0	0	0	0	0	0	0	0	0	1	1
Total			25	12	13	16	6	3	0	0	0	0	0	0	0	2	23	2

Rank among batters: 1,608 • Top target (2 home runs): Gene Brabender, Luis Tiant, Tom Bradley, Dick Bosman • *Number of pitchers victimized*: 21 • *Total ballparks homered in*: 12 • *First HR*: 04/13/1969 off Gene Brabender

Marty Hopkins

MEREDITH HILLIARD HOPKINS
B: 02/22/1907 D: 11/20/1963
BR

Year	Tm	Lg	Tot	H	A	Men-On 0	1	2	3	One-Game 2	3	4	LO	XN	IP	PH	RHP	LHP
1934	CHI	AL	2	2	0	0	1	0	1	0	0	0	0	0	0	0	2	0
1935	CHI	AL	2	1	1	2	0	0	0	0	0	0	0	0	0	0	1	1
Total			4	3	1	2	1	0	1	0	0	0	0	0	0	0	3	1

Rank among batters: 3,427 • *Total ballparks homered in*: 2 • *First HR*: 07/29/1934 off Firpo Marberry

Johnny Hopp

JOHN LEONARD HOPP
B: 07/18/1916
BL

Year	Tm	Lg	Tot	H	A	Men-On 0	1	2	3	One-Game 2	3	4	LO	XN	IP	PH	RHP	LHP
1940	STL	NL	1	0	1	1	0	0	0	0	0	0	0	0	0	0	1	0
1941	STL	NL	4	4	0	1	2	1	0	0	0	0	0	0	0	0	4	0
1942	STL	NL	3	3	0	2	0	1	0	0	0	0	0	0	0	0	2	1
1943	STL	NL	2	1	1	1	1	0	0	0	0	0	0	0	0	0	2	0
1944	STL	NL	11	5	6	6	3	2	0	0	0	0	1	0	1	0	11	0
1945	STL	NL	3	3	0	2	0	0	1	0	0	0	0	0	0	0	2	1
1946	BOS	NL	3	1	2	3	0	0	0	1	0	0	0	0	0	0	3	0
1947	BOS	NL	2	0	2	2	0	0	0	0	0	0	0	0	0	0	2	0
1948	PIT	NL	1	0	1	1	0	0	0	0	0	0	0	0	0	0	1	0
1949	PIT	NL	5	2	3	3	1	1	0	0	0	0	0	0	0	0	5	0
1950	PIT	NL	8	2	6	5	2	1	0	1	0	0	0	0	0	0	7	1
	NY	AL	1	0	1	0	0	0	1	0	0	0	0	0	0	1	1	0
	Total		9	2	7	5	2	1	1	1	0	0	0	0	0	1	8	1
1951	NY	AL	2	1	1	2	0	0	0	0	0	0	0	0	0	1	2	0
Total			46	22	24	29	9	6	2	2	0	0	1	0	1	2	43	3

Rank among batters: 1,060 • Top target (2 home runs): Manny Salvo, Rip Sewell, Red Barrett, Ted Wilks, Larry Jansen • *Number of pitchers victimized*: 41 • *Total ballparks homered in*: 9 • *First HR*: 09/02/1940 off Junior Thompson

Sam Horn

SAMUEL LEE HORN
B: 11/02/1963
BL

Year	Tm	Lg	Tot	H	A	Men-On 0	1	2	3	One-Game 2	3	4	LO	XN	IP	PH	RHP	LHP
1987	BOS	AL	14	6	8	9	3	1	1	2	0	0	0	0	0	0	11	3
1988	BOS	AL	2	2	0	1	0	1	0	0	0	0	0	0	0	0	2	0
1990	BAL	AL	14	8	6	8	1	4	1	1	0	0	0	0	0	2	14	0
1991	BAL	AL	23	12	11	9	10	3	1	0	0	0	0	0	0	3	22	1
1992	BAL	AL	5	2	3	3	2	0	0	0	0	0	0	0	0	0	5	0
1993	CLE	AL	4	2	2	3	1	0	0	1	0	0	0	0	0	0	4	0
Total			62	32	30	33	17	9	3	4	0	0	0	0	0	5	58	4

Rank among batters: 835 • *Top target (4 home runs)*: Bret Saberhagen • *Number of pitchers victimized*: 52 • *Total ballparks homered in*: 14 • *First HR*: 07/25/1987 off Stan Clarke

Bob Horner

JAMES ROBERT HORNER
B: 08/06/1957
BR

Year	Tm	Lg	Tot	H	A	Men-On 0	1	2	3	One-Game 2	3	4	LO	XN	IP	PH	RHP	LHP
1978	ATL	NL	23	19	4	13	8	2	0	4	0	0	0	0	0	0	20	3
1979	ATL	NL	33	21	12	20	9	4	0	3	0	0	0	0	0	0	22	11
1980	ATL	NL	35	23	12	22	7	6	0	4	0	0	0	1	0	0	29	6
1981	ATL	NL	15	9	6	12	1	2	0	3	0	0	0	0	0	0	12	3
1982	ATL	NL	32	25	7	17	10	5	0	4	0	0	0	0	0	0	25	7
1983	ATL	NL	20	12	8	12	4	4	0	1	0	0	0	0	0	0	14	6

Year	Tm	Lg	Tot	H	A	Men-On 0	1	2	3	One-Game 2	3	4	LO	XN	IP	PH	RHP	LHP

Bob Horner *continued*

Year	Tm	Lg	Tot	H	A	0	1	2	3	2	3	4	LO	XN	IP	PH	RHP	LHP
1984	ATL	NL	3	0	3	1	2	0	0	0	0	0	0	0	0	0	3	0
1985	ATL	NL	27	13	14	11	12	4	0	5	0	0	0	0	0	0	17	10
1986	ATL	NL	27	20	7	17	8	1	1	1	0	1	0	1	0	0	20	7
1988	STL	NL	3	0	3	3	0	0	0	0	0	0	0	0	0	0	1	2
Total			218	142	76	128	61	28	1	25	0	1	0	2	0	0	163	55

Rank among batters: 155 • *Top target (6 home runs)*: Fernando Valenzuela • *Number of pitchers victimized*: 128 • *Total ballparks homered in*: 12 • *First HR*: 06/16/1978 off Bert Blyleven

Rogers Hornsby

ROGERS HORNSBY
B: 04/27/1896 D: 01/05/1963
BR HOF

Year	Tm	Lg	Tot	H	A	0	1	2	3	2	3	4	LO	XN	IP	PH	RHP	LHP
1916	STL	NL	6	3	3	5	1	0	0	0	0	0	0	0	5	0	5	1
1917	STL	NL	8	4	4	5	1	1	1	0	0	0	0	0	5	0	7	1
1918	STL	NL	5	2	3	2	1	1	1	0	0	0	0	0	3	0	2	3
1919	STL	NL	8	5	3	4	1	2	1	0	0	0	0	0	2	0	5	3
1920	STL	NL	9	2	7	4	4	1	0	1	0	0	0	0	2	0	5	4
1921	STL	NL	21	12	9	8	10	2	1	2	0	0	0	1	3	0	18	3
1922	STL	NL	42	24	18	28	5	8	1	5	0	0	0	0	4	0	36	6
1923	STL	NL	17	11	6	9	3	5	0	3	0	0	0	1	0	0	10	7
1924	STL	NL	25	15	10	17	7	1	0	3	0	0	0	0	2	0	21	4
1925	STL	NL	39	24	15	17	16	5	1	4	0	0	0	0	1	0	31	8
1926	STL	NL	11	5	6	4	4	2	1	0	0	0	0	0	1	0	9	2
1927	NY	NL	26	12	14	7	12	6	1	0	0	0	0	0	1	0	20	6
1928	BOS	NL	21	12	9	11	7	3	0	1	0	0	0	0	0	0	16	5
1929	CHI	NL	39	23	16	19	15	3	2	0	0	0	0	0	1	0	27	12
1930	CHI	NL	2	1	1	0	1	1	0	0	0	0	0	0	0	0	1	1
1931	CHI	NL	16	5	11	7	2	5	2	1	1	0	0	1	0	2	14	2
1932	CHI	NL	1	0	1	1	0	0	0	0	0	0	0	0	0	0	1	0
1933	STL	NL	2	0	2	1	1	0	0	0	0	0	0	0	0	1	2	0
	STL	AL	1	1	0	1	0	0	0	0	0	0	0	0	0	1	0	1
	Total		3	1	2	2	1	0	0	0	0	0	0	0	0	2	2	1
1934	STL	AL	1	1	0	0	1	0	0	0	0	0	0	0	0	1	0	1
1937	STL	AL	1	1	0	1	0	0	0	0	0	0	0	0	0	0	1	0
Total			301	163	138	151	92	46	12	20	1	0	0	3	30	5	231	70

Rank among batters: 66 • *Top target (9 home runs)*: Burleigh Grimes • *Number of pitchers victimized*: 137 • *Total ballparks homered in*: 9 • *First HR*: 05/14/1916 off Jeff Pfeffer

Mike Hornung

MICHAEL JOSEPH HORNUNG
B: 06/12/1857 D: 10/30/1931
BR

Year	Tm	Lg	Tot	H	A	0	1	2	3	2	3	4	LO	XN	IP	PH	RHP	LHP
1880	BUF	NL	1	0	1	1	0	0	0	0	0	0	0	0	0	0	1	0
1881	BOS	NL	2	1	1	2	0	0	0	0	0	0	0	0	0	0	2	0
1882	BOS	NL	1	0	1	0	0	1	0	0	0	0	0	0	0	0	1	0
1883	BOS	NL	8	6	2	3	3	2	0	1	0	0	2	0	3	0	5	3
1884	BOS	NL	7	2	5	5	1	1	0	1	0	0	2	0	0	0	3	0
1885	BOS	NL	1	1	0	1	0	0	0	0	0	0	0	0	0	0	1	0
1886	BOS	NL	2	2	0	0	1	1	0	0	0	0	0	0	0	0	1	0
1887	BOS	NL	5	4	1	4	1	0	0	0	0	0	0	0	0	0	5	0
1888	BOS	NL	3	2	1	1	2	0	0	0	0	0	0	0	1	0	3	0
1889	BAL	AA	1	1	0	1	0	0	0	0	0	0	0	0	0	0	1	0
Total			31	19	12	18	8	5	0	2	0	0	4	0	4	0	23	3

Rank among batters: 1,400 • *Top target (3 home runs)*: Hank O'Day, Mickey Welch • *Number of pitchers victimized*: 23 • *Total ballparks homered in*: 12 • *First HR*: 09/25/1880 off Will White

Tony Horton

ANTHONY DARRIN HORTON
B: 12/06/1944
BR

Year	Tm	Lg	Tot	H	A	0	1	2	3	2	3	4	LO	XN	IP	PH	RHP	LHP
1964	BOS	AL	1	0	1	1	0	0	0	0	0	0	0	0	0	0	1	0
1965	BOS	AL	7	3	4	3	2	2	0	0	0	0	0	2	0	0	4	3
1967	CLE	AL	10	8	2	9	0	0	1	0	0	0	0	2	0	0	8	2
1968	CLE	AL	14	7	7	8	6	0	0	1	0	0	0	1	0	0	10	4

Tony Horton *continued*

Year	Tm	Lg	Tot	H	A	Men-On 0	Men-On 1	Men-On 2	Men-On 3	One-Game 2	One-Game 3	One-Game 4	LO	XN	IP	PH	RHP	LHP
1969	CLE	AL	27	16	11	17	7	3	0	5	0	0	0	0	0	0	21	6
1970	CLE	AL	17	14	3	9	4	3	1	1	1	0	0	0	0	1	6	11
Total			76	48	28	47	19	8	2	7	1	0	0	5	0	1	50	26

Rank among batters: 695 • *Top target (3 home runs)*: Pat Dobson, Jim Hardin, Mike Cuellar • *Number of pitchers victimized*: 56 • *Total ballparks homered in*: 9 • *First HR*: 08/08/1964 off Fred Talbot • *Hit for Cycle*—@BAL: 07/02/1970

Willie Horton

WILLIAM WATTERSON HORTON
B: 10/18/1942
BR

Year	Tm	Lg	Tot	H	A	Men-On 0	Men-On 1	Men-On 2	Men-On 3	One-Game 2	One-Game 3	One-Game 4	LO	XN	IP	PH	RHP	LHP
1963	DET	AL	1	1	0	0	1	0	0	0	0	0	0	0	0	1	1	0
1964	DET	AL	1	0	1	0	1	0	0	0	0	0	0	0	0	0	1	0
1965	DET	AL	29	15	14	12	9	8	0	4	0	0	0	0	0	0	19	10
1966	DET	AL	27	12	15	13	5	8	1	1	0	0	0	2	1	0	14	13
1967	DET	AL	19	10	9	11	5	3	0	3	0	0	0	0	0	0	12	7
1968	DET	AL	36	20	16	26	9	1	0	4	0	0	0	1	0	0	20	16
1969	DET	AL	28	13	15	11	8	6	3	3	0	0	0	0	0	0	20	8
1970	DET	AL	17	13	4	10	3	3	1	3	1	0	0	0	0	0	14	3
1971	DET	AL	22	10	12	13	4	4	1	3	0	0	0	1	1	0	12	10
1972	DET	AL	11	7	4	6	4	1	0	0	0	0	0	1	0	0	8	3
1973	DET	AL	17	6	11	11	4	2	0	1	0	0	0	0	0	0	14	3
1974	DET	AL	15	6	9	9	3	3	0	1	0	0	0	0	0	0	6	9
1975	DET	AL	25	6	19	7	14	4	0	2	0	0	0	0	0	0	14	11
1976	DET	AL	14	5	9	6	7	1	0	0	0	0	0	0	0	1	10	4
1977	TEX	AL	15	7	8	8	6	1	0	1	1	0	0	0	0	0	8	7
1978	CLE	AL	5	0	5	3	1	0	1	0	0	0	0	0	0	0	4	1
	OAK	AL	3	1	2	2	1	0	0	0	0	0	0	0	0	0	1	2
	TOR	AL	3	2	1	1	1	1	0	0	0	0	0	0	0	0	3	0
	Total		11	3	8	6	3	1	1	0	0	0	0	0	0	0	8	3
1979	SEA	AL	29	14	15	14	9	4	2	2	0	0	0	0	0	0	21	8
1980	SEA	AL	8	5	3	2	6	0	0	0	0	0	0	0	0	1	5	3
Total			325	153	172	165	101	50	9	28	2	0	0	5	2	3	207	118

Rank among batters: 56 • *Top target (10 home runs)*: Dave McNally • *Number of pitchers victimized*: 194 • *Total ballparks homered in*: 17 • *First HR*: 09/14/1963 off Robin Roberts • *World Series HR*—1

Dwayne Hosey

DWAYNE SAMUEL HOSEY
B: 03/11/1967
BB

Year	Tm	Lg	Tot	H	A	Men-On 0	Men-On 1	Men-On 2	Men-On 3	One-Game 2	One-Game 3	One-Game 4	LO	XN	IP	PH	RHP	LHP
1995	BOS	AL	3	1	2	2	1	0	0	0	0	0	1	0	0	0	2	1

Rank among batters: 3,735 • *Total ballparks homered in*: 3 • *First HR*: 09/13/1995 off Jimmy Haynes

Steve Hosey

STEVEN BERNARD HOSEY
B: 04/02/1969
BR

Year	Tm	Lg	Tot	H	A	Men-On 0	Men-On 1	Men-On 2	Men-On 3	One-Game 2	One-Game 3	One-Game 4	LO	XN	IP	PH	RHP	LHP
1992	SF	NL	1	1	0	1	0	0	0	0	0	0	0	0	0	0	0	1

Rank among batters: 4,707 • *Total ballparks homered in*: 1 • *First HR*: 09/26/1992 off Greg Swindell

Dave Hoskins

DAVID TAYLOR HOSKINS
B: 08/03/1925 D: 04/02/1970
BL

Year	Tm	Lg	Tot	H	A	Men-On 0	Men-On 1	Men-On 2	Men-On 3	One-Game 2	One-Game 3	One-Game 4	LO	XN	IP	PH	RHP	LHP
1953	CLE	AL	1	0	1	0	0	1	0	0	0	0	0	0	0	0	1	0

Rank among batters: 4,707 • *Total ballparks homered in*: 1 • *First HR*: 05/10/1953 off Virgil Trucks

Tim Hosley

TIMOTHY KENNETH HOSLEY
B: 05/10/1947
BR

Year	Tm	Lg	Tot	H	A	Men-On 0	Men-On 1	Men-On 2	Men-On 3	One-Game 2	One-Game 3	One-Game 4	LO	XN	IP	PH	RHP	LHP
1970	DET	AL	1	0	1	1	0	0	0	0	0	0	0	0	0	0	0	1
1971	DET	AL	2	2	0	0	1	1	0	1	0	0	0	0	0	0	0	2

Tim Hosley *continued*

Year	Tm	Lg	Tot	H	A	Men-On 0	1	2	3	One-Game 2	3	4	LO	XN	IP	PH	RHP	LHP
1975	CHI	NL	6	5	1	4	1	0	1	0	0	0	0	0	0	2	4	2
1976	OAK	AL	1	1	0	0	1	0	0	0	0	0	0	0	0	0	1	0
1977	OAK	AL	1	0	1	1	0	0	0	0	0	0	0	0	0	0	0	1
1981	OAK	AL	1	1	0	0	0	1	0	0	0	0	0	0	0	1	0	1
Total			12	9	3	6	3	2	1	1	0	0	0	0	0	3	5	7

Rank among batters: 2,325 • *Top target (2 home runs)*: Mike Kekich • *Number of pitchers victimized*: 11 • *Total ballparks homered in*: 6 • *First HR*: 09/26/1970 off Fritz Peterson

Dave Hostetler

DAVID ALAN HOSTETLER
B: 03/27/1956
BR

Year	Tm	Lg	Tot	H	A	Men-On 0	1	2	3	One-Game 2	3	4	LO	XN	IP	PH	RHP	LHP
1981	MON	NL	1	0	1	1	0	0	0	0	0	0	0	0	0	0	0	1
1982	TEX	AL	22	10	12	11	9	2	0	3	0	0	0	1	0	0	19	3
1983	TEX	AL	11	2	9	6	5	0	0	1	0	0	0	0	0	0	4	7
1984	TEX	AL	3	2	1	2	1	0	0	0	0	0	0	0	0	0	0	3
Total			37	14	23	20	15	2	0	4	0	0	0	1	0	0	23	14

Rank among batters: 1,252 • *Top target (3 home runs)*: Mike Morgan, Scott McGregor • *Number of pitchers victimized*: 30 • *Total ballparks homered in*: 12 • *First HR*: 10/04/1981 off Pete Falcone

Pete Hotaling

PETER JAMES HOTALING
B: 12/16/1856 D: 07/03/1928
BR

Year	Tm	Lg	Tot	H	A	Men-On 0	1	2	3	One-Game 2	3	4	LO	XN	IP	PH	RHP	LHP
1879	CIN	NL	1	1	0	1	0	0	0	0	0	0	1	0	0	0	1	0
1881	WOR	NL	1	1	0	0	1	0	0	0	0	0	0	0	0	0	1	0
1884	CLE	NL	3	0	3	1	1	0	1	0	0	0	0	0	0	0	2	1
1885	BRO	AA	1	1	0	0	1	0	0	0	0	0	0	0	0	0	1	0
1887	CLE	AA	3	0	3	0	3	0	0	0	0	0	0	0	0	0	3	0
Total			9	3	6	2	6	0	1	0	0	0	1	0	0	0	8	1

Rank among batters: 2,587 • *Total ballparks homered in*: 6 • *First HR*: 05/13/1879 off Tommy Bond

Byron Houck

BYRON SIMON HOUCK
B: 08/28/1891 D: 06/17/1969
BR

Year	Tm	Lg	Tot	H	A	Men-On 0	1	2	3	One-Game 2	3	4	LO	XN	IP	PH	RHP	LHP
1914	BRO	FL	1	1	0	1	0	0	0	0	0	0	0	0	0	0	0	1

Rank among batters: 4,707 • *Total ballparks homered in*: 1 • *First HR*: 07/03/1914 off Joe Houser

Sadie Houck

SARGENT PERRY HOUCK
B: 03/ /1856 D: 05/26/1919
BR

Year	Tm	Lg	Tot	H	A	Men-On 0	1	2	3	One-Game 2	3	4	LO	XN	IP	PH	RHP	LHP
1879	BOS	NL	2	1	1	0	2	0	0	0	0	0	0	0	0	0	2	0
1880	PRO	NL	1	0	1	0	1	0	0	0	0	0	0	0	0	0	1	0
1881	DET	NL	1	1	0	1	0	0	0	0	0	0	0	0	0	0	1	0
Total			4	2	2	1	3	0	0	0	0	0	0	0	0	0	4	0

Rank among batters: 3,427 • *Top target (3 home runs)*: Will White • *Number of pitchers victimized*: 2 • *Total ballparks homered in*: 4 • *First HR*: 05/17/1879 off Will White

Charlie Hough

CHARLES OLIVER HOUGH
B: 01/05/1948
BR

Year	Tm	Lg	Tot	H	A	Men-On 0	1	2	3	One-Game 2	3	4	LO	XN	IP	PH	RHP	LHP
1977	LA	NL	1	0	1	1	0	0	0	0	0	0	0	0	0	0	1	0

Rank among batters: 4,707 • *Total ballparks homered in*: 1 • *First HR*: 04/24/1977 off Bob Johnson

Frank House

HENRY FRANKLIN HOUSE
B: 02/18/1930
BL

Year	Tm	Lg	Tot	H	A	Men-On 0	1	2	3	One-Game 2	3	4	LO	XN	IP	PH	RHP	LHP
1951	DET	AL	1	1	0	1	0	0	0	0	0	0	0	0	0	0	1	0

Frank House *continued*

Year	Tm	Lg	Tot	H	A	Men-On 0	1	2	3	One-Game 2	3	4	LO	XN	IP	PH	RHP	LHP
1954	DET	AL	9	6	3	4	4	1	0	0	0	0	0	0	0	0	9	0
1955	DET	AL	15	10	5	8	4	2	1	0	0	0	0	0	0	0	13	2
1956	DET	AL	10	3	7	6	1	3	0	0	0	0	0	0	0	2	10	0
1957	DET	AL	7	4	3	4	2	1	0	0	0	0	0	0	0	0	7	0
1958	KC	AL	4	1	3	1	2	0	1	0	0	0	0	0	0	1	4	0
1959	KC	AL	1	0	1	0	1	0	0	0	0	0	0	0	0	0	1	0
Total			47	25	22	24	14	7	2	0	0	0	0	0	0	3	45	2

Rank among batters: 1,040 • *Top target (3 home runs)*: Bob Porterfield, Dick Donovan • *Number of pitchers victimized*: 38 • *Total ballparks homered in*: 7 • *First HR*: 09/21/1951 off Steve Gromek

Charlie Householder

CHARLES W. HOUSEHOLDER
B: 1856 D: 12/26/1908
BL

Year	Tm	Lg	Tot	H	A	Men-On 0	1	2	3	One-Game 2	3	4	LO	XN	IP	PH	RHP	LHP
1882	BAL	AA	1	1	0	1	0	0	0	0	0	0	0	0	0	0	1	0
1884	BRO	AA	3	1	2	1	2	0	0	0	0	0	0	0	0	0	2	0
Total			4	2	2	2	2	0	0	0	0	0	0	0	0	0	2	0

Rank among batters: 3,427 • *Total ballparks homered in*: 4 • *First HR*: 07/18/1882 off Tony Mullane

Charlie Householder

CHARLES F. HOUSEHOLDER
B: 1856 BR

Year	Tm	Lg	Tot	H	A	Men-On 0	1	2	3	One-Game 2	3	4	LO	XN	IP	PH	RHP	LHP
1884	CHI	UA	1	1	0	1	0	0	0	0	0	0	0	0	0	0	0	0

Rank among batters: 4,707 • *Total ballparks homered in*: 1 • *First HR*: 07/22/1884 off Ernie Hickman

Paul Householder

PAUL WESLEY HOUSEHOLDER
B: 09/04/1958
BB

Year	Tm	Lg	Tot	H	A	Men-On 0	1	2	3	One-Game 2	3	4	LO	XN	IP	PH	RHP	LHP
1981	CIN	NL	2	0	2	0	2	0	0	0	0	0	0	0	0	0	1	1
1982	CIN	NL	9	6	3	6	3	0	0	0	0	0	0	0	0	0	4	5
1983	CIN	NL	6	5	1	2	2	2	0	0	0	0	0	0	1	0	4	2
1985	MIL	AL	11	3	8	5	4	2	0	0	0	0	0	0	0	0	6	5
1986	MIL	AL	1	1	0	0	0	1	0	0	0	0	0	0	0	0	1	0
Total			29	15	14	13	11	5	0	0	0	0	0	0	1	0	16	13

Rank among batters: 1,465 • *Top target (3 home runs)*: Tim Lollar • *Number of pitchers victimized*: 25 • *Total ballparks homered in*: 16 • *First HR*: 09/05/1981 off Steve Carlton

Ben Houser

BENJAMIN FRANKLIN HOUSER
B: 11/30/1883 D: 01/15/1952
BL

Year	Tm	Lg	Tot	H	A	Men-On 0	1	2	3	One-Game 2	3	4	LO	XN	IP	PH	RHP	LHP
1911	BOS	NL	1	0	1	0	0	0	1	0	0	0	0	0	1	0	1	0
1912	BOS	NL	8	7	1	2	3	3	0	0	0	0	0	0	0	0	5	3
Total			9	7	2	2	3	3	1	0	0	0	0	0	1	0	6	3

Rank among batters: 2,587 • *Total ballparks homered in*: 3 • *First HR*: 10/09/1911 off Toots Shultz

Art Houtteman

ARTHUR JOSEPH HOUTTEMAN
B: 08/07/1927
BR

Year	Tm	Lg	Tot	H	A	Men-On 0	1	2	3	One-Game 2	3	4	LO	XN	IP	PH	RHP	LHP
1953	DET	AL	1	0	1	0	1	0	0	0	0	0	0	0	0	0	1	0
1954	CLE	AL	1	0	1	1	0	0	0	0	0	0	0	0	0	0	1	0
Total			2	0	2	1	1	0	0	0	0	0	0	0	0	0	2	0

Rank among batters: 4,129 • *Total ballparks homered in*: 1 • *First HR*: 05/15/1953 off Carl Scheib

Steve Hovley

STEPHEN EUGENE HOVLEY
B: 12/18/1944
BL

Year	Tm	Lg	Tot	H	A	Men-On 0	1	2	3	One-Game 2	3	4	LO	XN	IP	PH	RHP	LHP
1969	SEA	AL	3	1	2	1	2	0	0	0	0	0	0	0	0	0	3	0

Steve Hovley *continued*

Year	Tm	Lg	Tot	H	A	Men-On 0	1	2	3	One-Game 2	3	4	LO	XN	IP	PH	RHP	LHP
1972	KC	AL	3	1	2	2	1	0	0	0	0	0	0	0	0	0	2	1
1973	KC	AL	2	1	1	1	0	1	0	0	0	0	0	0	0	0	2	0
Total			8	3	5	4	3	1	0	0	0	0	0	0	0	0	7	1

Rank among batters: 2,703 • *Total ballparks homered in*: 7 • *First HR*: 07/04/1969 off Dick Drago

Bruce Howard

BRUCE ERNEST HOWARD
B: 03/23/1943
BB

Year	Tm	Lg	Tot	H	A	Men-On 0	1	2	3	One-Game 2	3	4	LO	XN	IP	PH	RHP	LHP
1968	BAL	AL	1	0	1	1	0	0	0	0	0	0	0	0	0	0	1	0

Rank among batters: 4,707 • *Total ballparks homered in*: 1 • *First HR*: 05/19/1968 off Steve Hargan

David Howard

DAVID WAYNE HOWARD
B: 02/26/1967
BB

Year	Tm	Lg	Tot	H	A	Men-On 0	1	2	3	One-Game 2	3	4	LO	XN	IP	PH	RHP	LHP
1991	KC	AL	1	0	1	0	1	0	0	0	0	0	0	0	0	0	0	1
1992	KC	AL	1	1	0	0	0	1	0	0	0	0	0	0	1	0	1	0
1994	KC	AL	1	0	1	0	1	0	0	0	0	0	0	0	0	0	1	0
Total			3	1	2	0	2	1	0	0	0	0	0	0	1	0	2	1

Rank among batters: 3,735 • *Total ballparks homered in*: 2 • *First HR*: 07/26/1991 off Jimmy Key

Del Howard

GEORGE ELMER HOWARD
B: 12/24/1877 D: 12/24/1956
BL

Year	Tm	Lg	Tot	H	A	Men-On 0	1	2	3	One-Game 2	3	4	LO	XN	IP	PH	RHP	LHP
1905	PIT	NL	2	0	2	2	0	0	0	0	0	0	0	0	0	0	2	0
1906	BOS	NL	1	1	0	0	1	0	0	0	0	0	0	0	0	0	1	0
1907	BOS	NL	1	1	0	1	0	0	0	0	0	0	0	0	0	0	1	0
1908	CHI	NL	1	0	1	1	0	0	0	0	0	0	0	0	0	0	1	0
1909	CHI	NL	1	0	1	0	1	0	0	0	0	0	0	0	0	0	0	1
Total			6	2	4	4	2	0	0	0	0	0	0	0	0	0	5	1

Rank among batters: 2,988 • *Total ballparks homered in*: 4 • *First HR*: 05/09/1905 off Jack Sutthoff

Doug Howard

DOUGLAS LYNN HOWARD
B: 02/06/1948
BR

Year	Tm	Lg	Tot	H	A	Men-On 0	1	2	3	One-Game 2	3	4	LO	XN	IP	PH	RHP	LHP
1975	STL	NL	1	0	1	1	0	0	0	0	0	0	0	0	0	1	1	0

Rank among batters: 4,707 • *Total ballparks homered in*: 1 • *First HR*: 07/24/1975 off Burt Hooton

Elston Howard

ELSTON GENE HOWARD
B: 02/23/1929 D: 12/14/1980
BR

Year	Tm	Lg	Tot	H	A	Men-On 0	1	2	3	One-Game 2	3	4	LO	XN	IP	PH	RHP	LHP
1955	NY	AL	10	6	4	5	3	2	0	0	0	0	0	0	0	1	5	5
1956	NY	AL	5	2	3	2	2	1	0	0	0	0	0	0	0	1	4	1
1957	NY	AL	8	3	5	8	0	0	0	0	0	0	0	0	0	0	7	1
1958	NY	AL	11	3	8	3	5	3	0	0	0	0	0	0	0	0	7	4
1959	NY	AL	18	5	13	8	10	0	0	1	0	0	0	1	0	1	11	7
1960	NY	AL	6	5	1	3	2	1	0	0	0	0	0	0	0	1	6	0
1961	NY	AL	21	10	11	13	5	3	0	1	0	0	0	0	0	1	13	8
1962	NY	AL	21	3	18	5	13	3	0	3	0	0	0	1	0	0	14	7
1963	NY	AL	28	10	18	17	9	2	0	2	0	0	0	0	0	0	13	15
1964	NY	AL	15	3	12	8	4	3	0	0	0	0	0	1	0	0	6	9
1965	NY	AL	9	0	9	4	5	0	0	0	0	0	0	0	0	0	3	6
1966	NY	AL	6	1	5	2	2	1	1	0	0	0	0	0	0	0	2	4
1967	NY	AL	3	2	1	3	0	0	0	0	0	0	0	0	0	0	1	2
	BOS	AL	1	1	0	0	0	1	0	0	0	0	0	0	0	0	0	1
	Total		4	3	1	3	0	1	0	0	0	0	0	0	0	0	1	3

Elston Howard *continued*

Year	Tm	Lg	Tot	H	A	Men-On 0	1	2	3	One-Game 2	3	4	LO	XN	IP	PH	RHP	LHP
1968	BOS	AL	5	0	5	3	1	1	0	0	0	0	0	0	0	0	2	3
Total			167	54	113	84	61	21	1	7	0	0	0	3	0	5	94	73

Rank among batters: 242 • *Top target (5 home runs)*: Juan Pizarro • *Number of pitchers victimized*: 120 • *Total ballparks homered in*: 12 • *First HR*: 05/07/1955 off Tom Hurd • *World Series HR*—5

Frank Howard

FRANK OLIVER HOWARD
B: 08/08/1936
BR

Year	Tm	Lg	Tot	H	A	Men-On 0	1	2	3	One-Game 2	3	4	LO	XN	IP	PH	RHP	LHP
1958	LA	NL	1	0	1	0	1	0	0	0	0	0	0	0	0	0	1	0
1959	LA	NL	1	0	1	0	0	1	0	0	0	0	0	0	0	1	1	0
1960	LA	NL	23	14	9	11	7	3	2	2	0	0	0	0	0	0	16	7
1961	LA	NL	15	4	11	8	6	0	1	2	0	0	0	1	0	2	7	8
1962	LA	NL	31	13	18	16	12	3	0	1	0	0	0	1	0	1	20	11
1963	LA	NL	28	13	15	15	11	2	0	1	0	0	0	1	0	1	16	12
1964	LA	NL	24	11	13	12	8	4	0	1	0	0	0	1	0	0	12	12
1965	WAS	AL	21	5	16	14	4	2	1	1	0	0	0	0	0	0	15	6
1966	WAS	AL	18	13	5	6	10	2	0	0	0	0	0	0	0	0	8	10
1967	WAS	AL	36	19	17	22	9	4	1	4	0	0	0	0	0	0	30	6
1968	WAS	AL	44	18	26	25	15	4	0	6	0	0	0	0	0	0	28	16
1969	WAS	AL	48	27	21	28	15	5	0	4	0	0	0	0	0	0	32	16
1970	WAS	AL	44	24	20	18	19	7	0	3	0	0	0	1	0	0	28	16
1971	WAS	AL	26	10	16	14	10	2	0	0	0	0	0	0	0	0	12	14
1972	TEX	AL	9	8	1	6	2	1	0	0	0	0	0	0	0	0	2	7
	DET	AL	1	1	0	0	0	1	0	0	0	0	0	0	0	0	0	1
	Total		10	9	1	6	2	2	0	0	0	0	0	0	0	0	2	8
1973	DET	AL	12	6	6	7	4	1	0	1	0	0	0	0	0	3	0	12
Total			382	186	196	202	133	42	5	26	0	0	0	5	0	8	228	154

Rank among batters: 31 • *Top target (13 home runs)*: Dave McNally • *Number of pitchers victimized*: 199 • *Total ballparks homered in*: 24 • *First HR*: 09/10/1958 off Robin Roberts • *World Series HR*—1; *All-Star HR*—1

Ivon Howard

IVON CHESTER HOWARD
B: 10/12/1882 D: 03/30/1967
BB

Year	Tm	Lg	Tot	H	A	Men-On 0	1	2	3	One-Game 2	3	4	LO	XN	IP	PH	RHP	LHP
1915	STL	AL	2	1	1	2	0	0	0	0	0	0	0	0	0	0	2	0

Rank among batters: 4,129 • *Total ballparks homered in*: 2 • *First HR*: 06/14/1915 off Ray Keating

Larry Howard

LAWRENCE RAYFORD HOWARD
B: 06/06/1945
BR

Year	Tm	Lg	Tot	H	A	Men-On 0	1	2	3	One-Game 2	3	4	LO	XN	IP	PH	RHP	LHP
1970	HOU	NL	2	0	2	1	1	0	0	1	0	0	0	0	0	0	1	1
1971	HOU	NL	2	1	1	0	1	1	0	0	0	0	0	0	0	0	1	1
1972	HOU	NL	2	1	1	1	1	0	0	0	0	0	0	0	0	0	1	1
Total			6	2	4	2	3	1	0	1	0	0	0	0	0	0	3	3

Rank among batters: 2,988 • *Total ballparks homered in*: 4 • *First HR*: 09/07/1970 off Jerry Nyman

Mike Howard

MICHAEL FREDERIC HOWARD
B: 04/02/1958
BB

Year	Tm	Lg	Tot	H	A	Men-On 0	1	2	3	One-Game 2	3	4	LO	XN	IP	PH	RHP	LHP
1982	NY	NL	1	1	0	1	0	0	0	0	0	0	0	0	0	0	1	0

Rank among batters: 4,707 • *Total ballparks homered in*: 1 • *First HR*: 09/24/1982 off Ron Reed

Thomas Howard

THOMAS SYLVESTER HOWARD
B: 12/11/1964
BB

Year	Tm	Lg	Tot	H	A	Men-On 0	1	2	3	One-Game 2	3	4	LO	XN	IP	PH	RHP	LHP
1991	SD	NL	4	4	0	2	1	1	0	0	0	0	0	0	0	1	3	1
1992	CLE	AL	2	1	1	1	1	0	0	0	0	0	0	0	0	0	0	2
1993	CLE	AL	3	3	0	2	1	0	0	0	0	0	0	0	0	0	2	1

Thomas Howard *continued*

Year	Tm	Lg	Tot	H	A	Men-On				One-Game			LO	XN	IP	PH	RHP	LHP
						0	1	2	3	2	3	4						
1993	CIN	NL	4	2	2	2	1	1	0	0	0	0	1	0	0	0	4	0
	Total		7	5	2	4	2	1	0	0	0	0	1	0	0	0	6	1
1994	CIN	NL	5	4	1	2	2	1	0	0	0	0	0	0	0	0	5	0
1995	CIN	NL	3	1	2	2	0	1	0	0	0	0	0	0	0	1	3	0
Total			21	15	6	11	6	4	0	0	0	0	1	0	0	2	17	4

Rank among batters: 1,768 • *Top target (2 home runs)*: Pete Harnisch • *Number of pitchers victimized*: 20 • *Total ballparks homered in*: 9 • *First HR*: 06/15/1991 off Lester Lancaster

Wilbur Howard

WILBUR LEON HOWARD
B: 01/08/1949
BB

Year	Tm	Lg	Tot	H	A	Men-On				One-Game			LO	XN	IP	PH	RHP	LHP
						0	1	2	3	2	3	4						
1974	HOU	NL	2	1	1	2	0	0	0	0	0	0	0	0	0	0	0	2
1976	HOU	NL	1	0	1	0	1	0	0	0	0	0	0	0	0	0	0	1
1977	HOU	NL	2	1	1	1	0	1	0	0	0	0	0	0	1	1	1	1
1978	HOU	NL	1	1	0	1	0	0	0	0	0	0	0	0	0	0	0	1
Total			6	3	3	4	1	1	0	0	0	0	0	0	1	1	1	5

Rank among batters: 2,988 • *Total ballparks homered in*: 3 • *First HR*: 09/08/1974 off Randy Jones

Jim Howarth

JAMES EUGENE HOWARTH
B: 03/07/1947
BL

Year	Tm	Lg	Tot	H	A	Men-On				One-Game			LO	XN	IP	PH	RHP	LHP
						0	1	2	3	2	3	4						
1972	SF	NL	1	1	0	0	1	0	0	0	0	0	0	0	0	0	0	1

Rank among batters: 4,707 • *Total ballparks homered in*: 1 • *First HR*: 06/30/1972 off Claude Osteen

Art Howe

ARTHUR HENRY HOWE
B: 12/15/1946
BR

Year	Tm	Lg	Tot	H	A	Men-On				One-Game			LO	XN	IP	PH	RHP	LHP
						0	1	2	3	2	3	4						
1974	PIT	NL	1	0	1	1	0	0	0	0	0	0	0	0	0	0	0	1
1975	PIT	NL	1	1	0	1	0	0	0	0	0	0	0	0	0	0	1	0
1977	HOU	NL	8	1	7	4	2	1	1	1	0	0	0	0	0	0	6	2
1978	HOU	NL	7	3	4	5	1	1	0	1	0	0	0	0	0	0	5	2
1979	HOU	NL	6	0	6	6	0	0	0	0	0	0	0	0	0	0	4	2
1980	HOU	NL	10	3	7	6	4	0	0	0	0	0	0	0	0	1	3	7
1981	HOU	NL	3	3	0	2	1	0	0	1	0	0	0	0	0	0	1	2
1982	HOU	NL	5	4	1	2	0	3	0	0	0	0	0	0	1	0	3	2
1984	STL	NL	2	1	1	1	1	0	0	0	0	0	0	0	0	0	1	1
Total			43	16	27	28	9	5	1	3	0	0	0	0	1	1	24	19

Rank among batters: 1,116 • *Top target (3 home runs)*: Vida Blue, John Candelaria, Tom Seaver • *Number of pitchers victimized*: 32 • *Total ballparks homered in*: 11 • *First HR*: 09/11/1974 off Steve Carlton • *LCS HR*—1

Dixie Howell

MILLARD HOWELL
B: 01/07/1920 D: 03/18/1960
BL

Year	Tm	Lg	Tot	H	A	Men-On				One-Game			LO	XN	IP	PH	RHP	LHP
						0	1	2	3	2	3	4						
1956	CHI	AL	2	1	1	1	1	0	0	0	0	0	0	0	0	0	2	0
1957	CHI	AL	3	3	0	3	0	0	0	1	0	0	0	0	0	0	3	0
Total			5	4	1	4	1	0	0	1	0	0	0	0	0	0	5	0

Rank among batters: 3,191 • *Total ballparks homered in*: 2 • *First HR*: 06/27/1956 off Ike Delock

Dixie Howell

HOMER ELLIOTT HOWELL
B: 04/24/1920 D: 10/05/1990
BR

Year	Tm	Lg	Tot	H	A	Men-On				One-Game			LO	XN	IP	PH	RHP	LHP
						0	1	2	3	2	3	4						
1947	PIT	NL	4	4	0	1	2	0	1	1	0	0	0	0	0	0	4	0
1949	CIN	NL	2	1	1	1	1	0	0	0	0	0	0	0	0	1	1	1
1950	CIN	NL	2	2	0	1	1	0	0	0	0	0	0	1	0	0	0	2
1951	CIN	NL	2	0	2	1	0	1	0	0	0	0	0	0	0	0	1	1

Year	Tm	Lg	Tot	H	A	Men-On 0	Men-On 1	Men-On 2	Men-On 3	One-Game 2	One-Game 3	One-Game 4	LO	XN	IP	PH	RHP	LHP

Dixie Howell *continued*

Year	Tm	Lg	Tot	H	A	Men-On 0	Men-On 1	Men-On 2	Men-On 3	One-Game 2	One-Game 3	One-Game 4	LO	XN	IP	PH	RHP	LHP
1952	CIN	NL	2	0	2	1	1	0	0	0	0	0	0	0	0	0	1	1
Total			12	7	5	5	5	1	1	1	0	0	0	1	0	1	7	5

Rank among batters: 2,325 • *Top target (2 home runs)*: Buddy Lively, Turk Lown • *Number of pitchers victimized*: 10 • *Total ballparks homered in*: 5 • *First HR*: 08/13/1947 off Paul Erickson

Harry Howell

HENRY HARRY HOWELL
B: 11/14/1876 D: 05/22/1956
BR

Year	Tm	Lg	Tot	H	A	Men-On 0	Men-On 1	Men-On 2	Men-On 3	One-Game 2	One-Game 3	One-Game 4	LO	XN	IP	PH	RHP	LHP
1900	BRO	NL	1	0	1	0	1	0	0	0	0	0	0	0	0	0	0	1
1901	BAL	AL	2	1	1	2	0	0	0	0	0	0	0	0	0	0	2	0
1902	BAL	AL	2	1	1	1	1	0	0	0	0	0	0	0	0	0	2	0
1903	NY	AL	1	1	0	1	0	0	0	0	0	0	0	0	0	0	0	1
1904	STL	AL	1	1	0	0	1	0	0	0	0	0	0	0	0	0	0	1
1905	STL	AL	1	0	1	1	0	0	0	0	0	0	0	0	0	0	0	1
1907	STL	AL	2	1	1	1	0	1	0	0	0	0	0	0	0	0	0	2
1908	STL	AL	1	1	0	1	0	0	0	0	0	0	0	0	0	0	1	0
Total			11	6	5	7	3	1	0	0	0	0	0	0	0	0	5	6

Rank among batters: 2,419 • *Total ballparks homered in*: 7 • *First HR*: 06/23/1900 off Ed Doheny

Jack Howell

JACK ROBERT HOWELL
B: 08/18/1961
BL

Year	Tm	Lg	Tot	H	A	Men-On 0	Men-On 1	Men-On 2	Men-On 3	One-Game 2	One-Game 3	One-Game 4	LO	XN	IP	PH	RHP	LHP
1985	CAL	AL	5	2	3	3	1	0	1	1	0	0	0	0	0	0	4	1
1986	CAL	AL	4	1	3	3	0	1	0	1	0	0	0	1	0	0	4	0
1987	CAL	AL	23	15	8	13	6	4	0	1	0	0	0	1	0	2	22	1
1988	CAL	AL	16	9	7	8	6	2	0	1	0	0	0	0	0	0	12	4
1989	CAL	AL	20	9	11	11	8	1	0	0	0	0	0	1	0	0	18	2
1990	CAL	AL	8	3	5	5	3	0	0	0	0	0	0	1	0	1	8	0
1991	CAL	AL	2	0	2	1	1	0	0	0	0	0	0	0	0	0	2	0
	SD	NL	6	3	3	3	3	0	0	1	0	0	0	0	1	0	6	0
	Total		8	3	5	4	4	0	0	1	0	0	0	0	1	0	8	0
Total			84	42	42	47	28	8	1	5	0	0	0	4	1	3	76	8

Rank among batters: 617 • *Top target (3 home runs)*: Dave Stieb • *Number of pitchers victimized*: 75 • *Total ballparks homered in*: 15 • *First HR*: 05/30/1985 off Joe Cowley

Roy Howell

ROY LEE HOWELL
B: 12/18/1953
BL

Year	Tm	Lg	Tot	H	A	Men-On 0	Men-On 1	Men-On 2	Men-On 3	One-Game 2	One-Game 3	One-Game 4	LO	XN	IP	PH	RHP	LHP
1974	TEX	AL	1	0	1	1	0	0	0	0	0	0	0	0	0	0	1	0
1975	TEX	AL	10	5	5	8	0	1	1	1	0	0	0	0	0	2	9	1
1976	TEX	AL	8	3	5	6	2	0	0	0	0	0	0	0	0	0	8	0
1977	TOR	AL	10	3	7	9	0	1	0	1	0	0	0	0	0	0	8	2
1978	TOR	AL	8	2	6	6	2	0	0	0	0	0	0	0	0	0	5	3
1979	TOR	AL	15	8	7	9	1	3	2	0	0	0	0	0	0	0	12	3
1980	TOR	AL	10	4	6	6	4	0	0	1	0	0	0	1	1	1	7	3
1981	MIL	AL	6	2	4	4	0	1	1	0	0	0	0	0	0	0	6	0
1982	MIL	AL	4	0	4	2	2	0	0	0	0	0	0	0	0	0	3	1
1983	MIL	AL	4	0	4	2	0	1	1	0	0	0	0	0	0	1	3	1
1984	MIL	AL	4	0	4	3	0	1	0	0	0	0	0	0	0	0	4	0
Total			80	27	53	56	11	8	5	3	0	0	0	1	1	4	66	14

Rank among batters: 650 • *Top target (3 home runs)*: Ed Figueroa, Mike Torrez, Wayne Garland • *Number of pitchers victimized*: 63 • *Total ballparks homered in*: 14 • *First HR*: 09/09/1974 off Ed Figueroa

Bill Howerton

WILLIAM RAY HOWERTON
B: 12/12/1921
BL

Year	Tm	Lg	Tot	H	A	Men-On 0	Men-On 1	Men-On 2	Men-On 3	One-Game 2	One-Game 3	One-Game 4	LO	XN	IP	PH	RHP	LHP
1950	STL	NL	10	6	4	8	1	1	0	0	0	0	0	0	0	1	8	2
1951	STL	NL	1	0	1	0	1	0	0	0	0	0	0	0	0	1	1	0

Bill Howerton *continued*

Year	Tm	Lg	Tot	H	A	Men-On 0	1	2	3	One-Game 2	3	4	LO	XN	IP	PH	RHP	LHP
1951	PIT	NL	11	6	5	7	2	2	0	0	0	0	0	0	0	0	10	1
	Total		12	6	6	7	3	2	0	0	0	0	0	0	0	1	11	1
Total			22	12	10	15	4	3	0	0	0	0	0	0	0	2	19	3

Rank among batters: 1,719 • Top target (2 home runs): Sheldon Jones, Johnny Sain, Paul Minner, Howie Fox • *Number of pitchers victimized*: 18 • *Total ballparks homered in*: 6 • *First HR*: 06/10/1950 off Clint Hartung

Dann Howitt

DANN PAUL JOHN HOWITT
B: 02/13/1964
BL

Year	Tm	Lg	Tot	H	A	Men-On 0	1	2	3	One-Game 2	3	4	LO	XN	IP	PH	RHP	LHP
1991	OAK	AL	1	0	1	1	0	0	0	0	0	0	0	0	0	1	1	0
1992	OAK	AL	1	0	1	1	0	0	0	0	0	0	0	0	0	0	1	0
	SEA	AL	1	1	0	0	1	0	0	0	0	0	0	0	0	0	1	0
	Total		2	1	1	1	1	0	0	0	0	0	0	0	0	0	2	0
1993	SEA	AL	2	1	1	0	1	0	1	0	0	0	0	0	0	0	2	0
Total			5	2	3	2	2	0	1	0	0	0	0	0	0	1	5	0

Rank among batters: 3,191 • *Total ballparks homered in*: 4 • *First HR*: 09/03/1991 off Julio Machado

Dick Howser

RICHARD DALTON HOWSER
B: 05/14/1936 D: 06/17/1987
BR

Year	Tm	Lg	Tot	H	A	Men-On 0	1	2	3	One-Game 2	3	4	LO	XN	IP	PH	RHP	LHP
1961	KC	AL	3	0	3	3	0	0	0	0	0	0	0	0	1	0	2	1
1962	KC	AL	6	4	2	3	2	1	0	0	0	0	0	0	2	0	5	1
1963	CLE	AL	1	0	1	1	0	0	0	0	0	0	0	0	0	0	1	0
1964	CLE	AL	3	2	1	2	0	1	0	0	0	0	1	0	0	0	3	0
1965	CLE	AL	1	0	1	1	0	0	0	0	0	0	0	0	0	0	1	0
1966	CLE	AL	2	0	2	2	0	0	0	0	0	0	0	0	0	0	1	1
Total			16	6	10	12	2	2	0	0	0	0	1	0	3	0	13	3

Rank among batters: 2,029 • *Top target (3 home runs)*: Camilo Pascual • *Number of pitchers victimized*: 14 • *Total ballparks homered in*: 7 • *First HR*: 05/28/1961 off Barry Latman

Dummy Hoy

WILLIAM ELLSWORTH HOY
B: 05/23/1862 D: 12/15/1961
BL

Year	Tm	Lg	Tot	H	A	Men-On 0	1	2	3	One-Game 2	3	4	LO	XN	IP	PH	RHP	LHP
1888	WAS	NL	2	0	2	1	1	0	0	0	0	0	0	0	1	0	1	1
1890	BUF	PL	1	0	1	1	0	0	0	0	0	0	0	0	0	0	0	0
1891	STL	AA	5	3	2	2	2	1	0	0	0	0	1	0	0	0	5	0
1892	WAS	NL	3	2	1	1	2	0	0	0	0	0	0	0	1	0	3	0
1894	CIN	NL	5	3	2	0	3	2	0	0	0	0	0	0	1	0	5	0
1895	CIN	NL	3	1	2	2	1	0	0	0	0	0	1	0	1	0	2	1
1896	CIN	NL	4	1	3	1	3	0	0	0	0	0	0	0	0	0	4	0
1897	CIN	NL	2	1	1	1	1	0	0	0	0	0	0	0	0	0	2	0
1898	LOU	NL	6	5	1	2	3	1	0	0	0	0	0	0	3	0	4	2
1899	LOU	NL	5	3	2	4	0	1	0	0	0	0	1	0	1	0	4	1
1901	CHI	AL	2	1	1	1	0	0	1	0	0	0	0	0	0	0	0	2
1902	CIN	NL	2	2	0	0	2	0	0	0	0	0	0	0	1	0	2	0
Total			40	22	18	16	18	5	1	0	0	0	3	0	9	0	32	7

Rank among batters: 1,181 • *Top target (3 home runs)*: Jack Stivetts • *Number of pitchers victimized*: 35 • *Total ballparks homered in*: 18 • *First HR*: 05/09/1888 off Gus Krock

Kent Hrbek

KENT ALLEN HRBEK
B: 05/21/1960
BL

Year	Tm	Lg	Tot	H	A	Men-On 0	1	2	3	One-Game 2	3	4	LO	XN	IP	PH	RHP	LHP
1981	MIN	AL	1	0	1	1	0	0	0	0	0	0	0	1	0	0	1	0
1982	MIN	AL	23	11	12	16	6	0	1	0	0	0	0	0	1	0	19	4
1983	MIN	AL	16	7	9	7	8	1	0	2	0	0	0	1	0	0	10	6
1984	MIN	AL	27	15	12	12	10	4	1	2	0	0	0	0	1	0	17	10
1985	MIN	AL	21	10	11	10	6	2	3	0	0	0	0	0	0	1	15	6
1986	MIN	AL	29	18	11	17	11	1	0	2	0	0	0	0	0	0	25	4
1987	MIN	AL	34	20	14	18	12	4	0	0	0	0	0	1	0	0	28	6

Kent Hrbek *continued*

Year	Tm	Lg	Tot	H	A	Men-On 0	1	2	3	One-Game 2	3	4	LO	XN	IP	PH	RHP	LHP
1988	MIN	AL	25	13	12	14	11	0	0	5	0	0	0	1	0	0	23	2
1989	MIN	AL	25	17	8	14	4	6	1	3	0	0	0	0	0	1	19	6
1990	MIN	AL	22	8	14	12	7	3	0	0	0	0	0	0	0	0	20	2
1991	MIN	AL	20	11	9	5	12	2	1	0	0	0	0	1	0	1	14	6
1992	MIN	AL	15	10	5	11	2	2	0	0	0	0	0	0	0	0	14	1
1993	MIN	AL	25	12	13	10	10	4	1	2	0	0	0	0	0	0	22	3
1994	MIN	AL	10	4	6	4	5	1	0	0	0	0	0	0	0	0	8	2
Total			293	156	137	151	104	30	8	16	0	0	0	5	2	3	235	58

Rank among batters: 71 • *Top target (7 home runs)*: Jack Morris • *Number of pitchers victimized*: 199 • *Total ballparks homered in*: 18 • *First HR*: 08/24/1981 off George Frazier • *World Series HR*—2; *LCS HR*—1

Glenn Hubbard

GLENN DEE HUBBARD
B: 09/25/1957
BR

Year	Tm	Lg	Tot	H	A	Men-On 0	1	2	3	One-Game 2	3	4	LO	XN	IP	PH	RHP	LHP
1978	ATL	NL	2	1	1	2	0	0	0	0	0	0	0	0	0	0	2	0
1979	ATL	NL	3	0	3	0	0	3	0	0	0	0	0	0	0	0	2	1
1980	ATL	NL	9	6	3	4	4	1	0	0	0	0	0	1	0	0	6	3
1981	ATL	NL	6	4	2	4	1	0	1	0	0	0	0	1	0	0	6	0
1982	ATL	NL	9	7	2	4	3	2	0	0	0	0	0	1	0	0	6	3
1983	ATL	NL	12	6	6	4	7	0	1	0	0	0	0	0	0	0	7	5
1984	ATL	NL	9	3	6	4	4	1	0	0	0	0	0	0	0	0	7	2
1985	ATL	NL	5	3	2	4	0	1	0	0	0	0	0	0	0	0	4	1
1986	ATL	NL	4	4	0	2	1	1	0	0	0	0	0	0	0	0	3	1
1987	ATL	NL	5	3	2	3	2	0	0	0	0	0	0	0	0	0	3	2
1988	OAK	AL	3	3	0	0	2	1	0	0	0	0	0	0	0	0	2	1
1989	OAK	AL	3	2	1	2	0	1	0	0	0	0	0	0	0	0	2	1
Total			70	42	28	33	24	11	2	0	0	0	0	3	0	0	50	20

Rank among batters: 742 • *Top target (3 home runs)*: Bob Welch • *Number of pitchers victimized*: 65 • *Total ballparks homered in*: 13 • *First HR*: 09/23/1978 off Manny Sarmiento

Trent Hubbard

TRENIDAD AVIEL HUBBARD
B: 05/11/1964
BR

Year	Tm	Lg	Tot	H	A	Men-On 0	1	2	3	One-Game 2	3	4	LO	XN	IP	PH	RHP	LHP
1994	COL	NL	1	1	0	0	1	0	0	0	0	0	0	0	0	0	1	0
1995	COL	NL	3	2	1	2	1	0	0	0	0	0	1	0	0	0	3	0
Total			4	3	1	2	2	0	0	0	0	0	1	0	0	0	4	0

Rank among batters: 3,427 • *Total ballparks homered in*: 3 • *First HR*: 07/20/1994 off Willie Banks

Bill Hubbell

WILBERT WILLIAM HUBBELL
B: 06/17/1897 D: 08/03/1980
BR

Year	Tm	Lg	Tot	H	A	Men-On 0	1	2	3	One-Game 2	3	4	LO	XN	IP	PH	RHP	LHP
1921	PHI	NL	1	1	0	1	0	0	0	0	0	0	0	0	0	0	0	1

Rank among batters: 4,707 • *Total ballparks homered in*: 1 • *First HR*: 07/20/1921 off Lefty Tyler

Carl Hubbell

CARL OWEN HUBBELL
B: 06/22/1903 D: 11/21/1988
BR HOF

Year	Tm	Lg	Tot	H	A	Men-On 0	1	2	3	One-Game 2	3	4	LO	XN	IP	PH	RHP	LHP
1932	NY	NL	1	0	1	1	0	0	0	0	0	0	0	0	0	0	1	0
1933	NY	NL	1	1	0	1	0	0	0	0	0	0	0	0	0	0	1	0
1935	NY	NL	1	1	0	1	0	0	0	0	0	0	0	0	0	0	1	0
1939	NY	NL	1	1	0	0	1	0	0	0	0	0	0	0	0	0	1	0
Total			4	3	1	3	1	0	0	0	0	0	0	0	0	0	4	0

Rank among batters: 3,427 • *Total ballparks homered in*: 2 • *First HR*: 08/26/1932 off Dizzy Dean

Ken Hubbs

KENNETH DOUGLASS HUBBS
B: 12/23/1941 D: 02/15/1964
BR

Year	Tm	Lg	Tot	H	A	Men-On 0	1	2	3	One-Game 2	3	4	LO	XN	IP	PH	RHP	LHP
1961	CHI	NL	1	1	0	1	0	0	0	0	0	0	0	0	0	0	0	1

Year	Tm	Lg	Tot	H	A	Men-On 0	Men-On 1	Men-On 2	Men-On 3	One-Game 2	One-Game 3	One-Game 4	LO	XN	IP	PH	RHP	LHP

Ken Hubbs *continued*

Year	Tm	Lg	Tot	H	A	0	1	2	3	2	3	4	LO	XN	IP	PH	RHP	LHP
1962	CHI	NL	5	4	1	4	1	0	0	0	0	0	0	0	0	0	4	1
1963	CHI	NL	8	5	3	5	3	0	0	0	0	0	0	0	0	0	6	2
Total			14	10	4	10	4	0	0	0	0	0	0	0	0	0	10	4

Rank among batters: 2,169 • *Top target (2 home runs)*: Jack Fisher • *Number of pitchers victimized*: 13 • *Total ballparks homered in*: 5 • *First HR*: 09/27/1961 off Curt Simmons

Clarence Huber

CLARENCE BILL HUBER
B: 10/27/1896 D: 02/22/1965
BR

Year	Tm	Lg	Tot	H	A	0	1	2	3	2	3	4	LO	XN	IP	PH	RHP	LHP
1925	PHI	NL	5	5	0	4	1	0	0	0	0	0	0	0	0	0	4	1
1926	PHI	NL	1	1	0	0	1	0	0	0	0	0	0	0	0	0	1	0
Total			6	6	0	4	2	0	0	0	0	0	0	0	0	0	5	1

Rank among batters: 2,988 • *Total ballparks homered in*: 1 • *First HR*: 04/23/1925 off Jesse Petty

Rex Hudler

REX ALLEN HUDLER
B: 09/02/1960
BR

Year	Tm	Lg	Tot	H	A	0	1	2	3	2	3	4	LO	XN	IP	PH	RHP	LHP
1988	MON	NL	4	1	3	3	1	0	0	0	0	0	1	1	0	0	2	2
1989	MON	NL	6	3	3	4	1	1	0	0	0	0	0	0	0	2	1	5
1990	STL	NL	7	2	5	5	2	0	0	0	0	0	0	0	0	2	2	5
1991	STL	NL	1	1	0	1	0	0	0	0	0	0	0	0	0	0	0	1
1992	STL	NL	3	2	1	3	0	0	0	0	0	0	0	0	0	2	1	2
1994	CAL	AL	8	4	4	5	2	1	0	0	0	0	0	0	0	0	5	3
1995	CAL	AL	6	4	2	4	0	2	0	0	0	0	0	0	0	0	2	4
Total			35	17	18	25	6	4	0	0	0	0	1	1	0	6	13	22

Rank among batters: 1,291 • Top target (2 home runs): Joe Magrane, Chris Nabholz, Jamie Moyer, Joe Boever • *Number of pitchers victimized*: 31 • *Total ballparks homered in*: 13 • *First HR*: 08/02/1988 off Jim Gott

Willis Hudlin

GEORGE WILLIS HUDLIN
B: 05/23/1906
BR

Year	Tm	Lg	Tot	H	A	0	1	2	3	2	3	4	LO	XN	IP	PH	RHP	LHP
1927	CLE	AL	1	0	1	0	1	0	0	0	0	0	0	0	0	0	0	1
1933	CLE	AL	1	0	1	1	0	0	0	0	0	0	0	0	0	0	0	1
1934	CLE	AL	1	0	1	1	0	0	0	0	0	0	0	0	0	0	0	1
1935	CLE	AL	1	0	1	0	1	0	0	0	0	0	0	0	0	0	0	1
1939	CLE	AL	1	0	1	1	0	0	0	0	0	0	0	0	0	0	1	0
Total			5	0	5	3	2	0	0	0	0	0	0	0	0	0	1	4

Rank among batters: 3,191 • *Top target (2 home runs)*: Rube Walberg • *Number of pitchers victimized*: 4 • *Total ballparks homered in*: 2 • *First HR*: 08/03/1927 off Rube Walberg

Johnny Hudson

JOHN WILSON HUDSON
B: 06/30/1912 D: 11/07/1970
BR

Year	Tm	Lg	Tot	H	A	0	1	2	3	2	3	4	LO	XN	IP	PH	RHP	LHP
1938	BRO	NL	2	2	0	2	0	0	0	0	0	0	0	0	0	0	2	0
1939	BRO	NL	2	0	2	1	0	1	0	0	0	0	0	0	0	0	2	0
Total			4	2	2	3	0	1	0	0	0	0	0	0	0	0	4	0

Rank among batters: 3,427 • *Total ballparks homered in*: 2 • *First HR*: 05/14/1938 off Jim Turner

Nat Hudson

NATHANIEL P. HUDSON
B: 01/12/1869 D: 03/14/1928
BR

Year	Tm	Lg	Tot	H	A	0	1	2	3	2	3	4	LO	XN	IP	PH	RHP	LHP
1888	STL	AA	2	1	1	2	0	0	0	0	0	0	0	0	1	0	1	1
1889	STL	AA	1	1	0	0	0	1	0	0	0	0	0	0	0	0	1	0
Total			3	2	1	2	0	1	0	0	0	0	0	0	1	0	2	1

Rank among batters: 3,735 • *Total ballparks homered in*: 2 • *First HR*: 06/14/1888 off Toad Ramsey

Year	Tm	Lg	Tot	H	A	Men-On 0	Men-On 1	Men-On 2	Men-On 3	One-Game 2	One-Game 3	One-Game 4	LO	XN	IP	PH	RHP	LHP

Frank Huelsman

FRANK ELMER HUELSMAN
B: 06/05/1874 D: 06/09/1959
BR

Year	Tm	Lg	Tot	H	A	0	1	2	3	2	3	4	LO	XN	IP	PH	RHP	LHP
1904	WAS	AL	2	1	1	2	0	0	0	0	0	0	0	0	0	0	2	0
1905	WAS	AL	3	0	3	1	1	1	0	0	0	0	0	0	1	0	3	0
Total			5	1	4	3	1	1	0	0	0	0	0	0	1	0	5	0

Rank among batters: 3,191 • *Total ballparks homered in*: 5 • *First HR*: 08/20/1904 off Frank Kitson

Mike Huff

MICHAEL KALE HUFF
B: 08/11/1963
BR

Year	Tm	Lg	Tot	H	A	0	1	2	3	2	3	4	LO	XN	IP	PH	RHP	LHP
1989	LA	NL	1	0	1	1	0	0	0	0	0	0	0	0	0	0	0	1
1991	CLE	AL	2	1	1	2	0	0	0	0	0	0	1	0	0	0	1	1
	CHI	AL	1	0	1	1	0	0	0	0	0	0	0	0	0	0	0	1
	Total		3	1	2	3	0	0	0	0	0	0	1	0	0	0	1	2
1993	CHI	AL	1	0	1	1	0	0	0	0	0	0	0	0	0	0	0	1
1994	TOR	AL	3	1	2	3	0	0	0	0	0	0	0	0	0	1	2	1
1995	TOR	AL	1	0	1	1	0	0	0	0	0	0	0	0	0	0	1	0
Total			9	2	7	9	0	0	0	0	0	0	1	0	0	1	4	5

Rank among batters: 2,587 • *Total ballparks homered in*: 9 • *First HR*: 08/15/1989 off Dennis Cook

Ben Huffman

BENJAMIN FRANKLIN HUFFMAN
B: 06/26/1914
BL

Year	Tm	Lg	Tot	H	A	0	1	2	3	2	3	4	LO	XN	IP	PH	RHP	LHP
1937	STL	AL	1	0	1	0	1	0	0	0	0	0	0	0	0	1	1	0

Rank among batters: 4,707 • *Total ballparks homered in*: 1 • *First HR*: 08/01/1937 off Spud Chandler

Miller Huggins

MILLER JAMES HUGGINS
B: 03/27/1879 D: 09/25/1929
BB HOF

Year	Tm	Lg	Tot	H	A	0	1	2	3	2	3	4	LO	XN	IP	PH	RHP	LHP
1904	CIN	NL	2	2	0	1	0	0	1	0	0	0	0	0	2	0	2	0
1905	CIN	NL	1	1	0	0	1	0	0	0	0	0	0	0	1	0	1	0
1907	CIN	NL	1	1	0	1	0	0	0	0	0	0	1	0	1	0	1	0
1910	STL	NL	1	0	1	1	0	0	0	0	0	0	0	0	1	0	1	0
1911	STL	NL	1	0	1	0	1	0	0	0	0	0	0	0	0	0	1	0
1914	STL	NL	1	1	0	0	0	1	0	0	0	0	0	0	1	0	0	1
1915	STL	NL	2	1	1	2	0	0	0	0	0	0	0	0	1	0	0	2
Total			9	6	3	5	2	1	1	0	0	0	1	0	7	0	6	3

Rank among batters: 2,587 • *Top target (2 home runs)*: Harry Gaspar • *Number of pitchers victimized*: 8 • *Total ballparks homered in*: 3 • *First HR*: 05/10/1904 off Ed Poole

Jim Hughes

JAMES JAY HUGHES
B: 01/22/1874 D: 06/02/1924
BR

Year	Tm	Lg	Tot	H	A	0	1	2	3	2	3	4	LO	XN	IP	PH	RHP	LHP
1898	BAL	NL	2	1	1	1	1	0	0	0	0	0	0	0	1	0	1	1
1902	BRO	NL	1	1	0	1	0	0	0	0	0	0	0	0	1	0	1	0
Total			3	2	1	2	1	0	0	0	0	0	0	0	2	0	2	1

Rank among batters: 3,735 • *Total ballparks homered in*: 3 • *First HR*: 09/26/1898 off Frank Killen

Keith Hughes

KEITH WILLS HUGHES
B: 09/12/1963
BL

Year	Tm	Lg	Tot	H	A	0	1	2	3	2	3	4	LO	XN	IP	PH	RHP	LHP
1988	BAL	AL	2	1	1	1	1	0	0	0	0	0	0	0	0	0	2	0

Rank among batters: 4,129 • *Total ballparks homered in*: 2 • *First HR*: 05/07/1988 off Melido Perez

Roy Hughes

ROY JOHN HUGHES
B: 01/11/1911 D: 05/05/1995
BR

Year	Tm	Lg	Tot	H	A	0	1	2	3	2	3	4	LO	XN	IP	PH	RHP	LHP
1937	CLE	AL	1	1	0	1	0	0	0	0	0	0	0	0	1	0	0	1

Roy Hughes *continued*

Year	Tm	Lg	Tot	H	A	Men-On 0	1	2	3	One-Game 2	3	4	LO	XN	IP	PH	RHP	LHP
1938	STL	AL	2	1	1	2	0	0	0	0	0	0	0	0	0	1	2	0
1939	PHI	NL	1	0	1	1	0	0	0	0	0	0	0	0	0	0	1	0
1944	CHI	NL	1	1	0	0	0	1	0	0	0	0	0	0	1	0	1	0
Total			5	3	2	4	0	1	0	0	0	0	0	0	2	1	4	1

Rank among batters: 3,191 • *Total ballparks homered in*: 5 • *First HR*: 05/31/1937 off Jake Wade

Terry Hughes

TERRY WAYNE HUGHES
B: 05/13/1949
BR

Year	Tm	Lg	Tot	H	A	Men-On 0	1	2	3	One-Game 2	3	4	LO	XN	IP	PH	RHP	LHP
1974	BOS	AL	1	0	1	0	1	0	0	0	0	0	0	0	0	0	1	0

Rank among batters: 4,707 • *Total ballparks homered in*: 1 • *First HR*: 06/29/1974 off Milt Wilcox

Tom Hughes

THOMAS JAMES HUGHES
B: 11/29/1878 D: 02/08/1956
BR

Year	Tm	Lg	Tot	H	A	Men-On 0	1	2	3	One-Game 2	3	4	LO	XN	IP	PH	RHP	LHP
1903	BOS	AL	1	0	1	0	1	0	0	0	0	0	0	0	0	0	0	1
1904	WAS	AL	1	0	1	1	0	0	0	0	0	0	0	0	0	0	1	0
1905	WAS	AL	1	0	1	0	1	0	0	0	0	0	0	0	0	0	1	0
1906	WAS	AL	1	0	1	1	0	0	0	0	0	0	0	1	0	0	1	0
1907	WAS	AL	1	0	1	1	0	0	0	0	0	0	0	0	0	0	1	0
1911	WAS	AL	1	1	0	1	0	0	0	0	0	0	0	0	0	0	1	0
Total			6	1	5	4	2	0	0	0	0	0	0	1	0	0	5	1

Rank among batters: 2,988 • *Total ballparks homered in*: 5 • *First HR*: 08/28/1903 off Eddie Plank

Tom Hughes

THOMAS L. HUGHES
B: 01/28/1884 D: 11/01/1961
BR

Year	Tm	Lg	Tot	H	A	Men-On 0	1	2	3	One-Game 2	3	4	LO	XN	IP	PH	RHP	LHP
1909	NY	AL	1	0	1	1	0	0	0	0	0	0	0	0	0	0	1	0
1915	BOS	NL	1	0	1	1	0	0	0	0	0	0	0	0	0	0	1	0
1918	BOS	NL	1	0	1	1	0	0	0	0	0	0	0	0	0	0	1	0
Total			3	0	3	3	0	0	0	0	0	0	0	0	0	0	3	0

Rank among batters: 3,735 • *Total ballparks homered in*: 2 • *First HR*: 08/26/1909 off Bill Dinneen

Jim Hughey

JAMES ULYSSES HUGHEY
B: 03/08/1869 D: 03/29/1945

Year	Tm	Lg	Tot	H	A	Men-On 0	1	2	3	One-Game 2	3	4	LO	XN	IP	PH	RHP	LHP
1898	STL	NL	1	1	0	0	0	1	0	0	0	0	0	0	0	0	1	0

Rank among batters: 4,707 • *Total ballparks homered in*: 1 • *First HR*: 04/24/1898 off Jim Gardner

Emil Huhn

EMIL HUGO HUHN
B: 03/10/1892 D: 09/05/1925
BR

Year	Tm	Lg	Tot	H	A	Men-On 0	1	2	3	One-Game 2	3	4	LO	XN	IP	PH	RHP	LHP
1915	NWK	FL	1	1	0	0	0	1	0	0	0	0	0	0	0	0	1	0

Rank among batters: 4,707 • *Total ballparks homered in*: 1 • *First HR*: 06/13/1915 off Russ Ford

Tim Hulett

TIMOTHY CRAIG HULETT
B: 01/20/1960
BR

Year	Tm	Lg	Tot	H	A	Men-On 0	1	2	3	One-Game 2	3	4	LO	XN	IP	PH	RHP	LHP
1985	CHI	AL	5	2	3	4	0	1	0	0	0	0	0	0	0	1	3	2
1986	CHI	AL	17	7	10	11	5	1	0	1	0	0	0	0	0	0	8	9
1987	CHI	AL	7	3	4	6	1	0	0	0	0	0	0	0	0	0	3	4
1989	BAL	AL	3	2	1	3	0	0	0	0	0	0	0	0	0	0	2	1
1990	BAL	AL	3	2	1	2	1	0	0	0	0	0	0	0	0	1	0	3
1991	BAL	AL	7	1	6	5	1	1	0	0	0	0	0	1	0	0	5	2
1992	BAL	AL	2	1	1	1	0	1	0	0	0	0	0	0	0	0	0	2

Tim Hulett *continued*

Year	Tm	Lg	Tot	H	A	Men-On 0	1	2	3	One-Game 2	3	4	LO	XN	IP	PH	RHP	LHP
1993	BAL	AL	2	2	0	1	0	1	0	0	0	0	0	0	0	0	2	0
1994	BAL	AL	2	2	0	0	2	0	0	0	0	0	0	0	0	0	1	1
Total			48	22	26	33	10	5	0	1	0	0	0	1	0	2	24	24

Rank among batters: 1,024 • Top target (2 home runs): Bryan Oelkers, Rafael Lugo, Bud Black, Frank Tanana • *Number of pitchers victimized*: 44 • *Total ballparks homered in*: 13 • *First HR*: 05/15/1985 off Dennis Martinez

David Hulse

DAVID LINDSEY HULSE
B: 02/25/1968
BL

Year	Tm	Lg	Tot	H	A	Men-On 0	1	2	3	One-Game 2	3	4	LO	XN	IP	PH	RHP	LHP
1993	TEX	AL	1	0	1	1	0	0	0	0	0	0	0	0	0	0	1	0
1994	TEX	AL	1	1	0	1	0	0	0	0	0	0	1	0	0	0	1	0
1995	MIL	AL	3	1	2	0	2	1	0	0	0	0	0	0	1	0	3	0
Total			5	2	3	2	2	1	0	0	0	0	1	0	1	0	5	0

Rank among batters: 3,191 • *Total ballparks homered in*: 5 • *First HR*: 09/26/1993 off Alex Fernandez

Rudy Hulswitt

RUDOLPH EDWARD HULSWITT
B: 02/23/1877 D: 01/16/1950
BR

Year	Tm	Lg	Tot	H	A	Men-On 0	1	2	3	One-Game 2	3	4	LO	XN	IP	PH	RHP	LHP
1903	PHI	NL	1	1	0	0	1	0	0	0	0	0	0	0	1	0	1	0
1904	PHI	NL	1	0	1	0	1	0	0	0	0	0	0	0	0	0	0	1
1908	CIN	NL	1	1	0	1	0	0	0	0	0	0	0	0	1	0	1	0
Total			3	2	1	1	2	0	0	0	0	0	0	0	2	0	2	1

Rank among batters: 3,735 • *Total ballparks homered in*: 3 • *First HR*: 08/21/1903 off Bob Rhoads

Tom Hume

THOMAS HUBERT HUME
B: 03/29/1953
BR

Year	Tm	Lg	Tot	H	A	Men-On 0	1	2	3	One-Game 2	3	4	LO	XN	IP	PH	RHP	LHP
1977	CIN	NL	1	1	0	1	0	0	0	0	0	0	0	0	0	0	0	1

Rank among batters: 4,707 • *Total ballparks homered in*: 1 • *First HR*: 06/15/1977 off Randy Lerch

John Hummel

JOHN EDWIN HUMMEL
B: 04/04/1883 D: 05/18/1959
BR

Year	Tm	Lg	Tot	H	A	Men-On 0	1	2	3	One-Game 2	3	4	LO	XN	IP	PH	RHP	LHP
1906	BRO	NL	1	0	1	0	1	0	0	0	0	0	0	0	1	0	0	1
1907	BRO	NL	3	2	1	2	0	1	0	0	0	0	0	0	2	0	2	1
1908	BRO	NL	4	2	2	3	1	0	0	0	0	0	0	0	4	0	3	1
1909	BRO	NL	4	2	2	2	2	0	0	0	0	0	0	0	3	0	1	3
1910	BRO	NL	5	1	4	3	2	0	0	0	0	0	0	0	2	0	3	2
1911	BRO	NL	5	3	2	3	1	1	0	0	0	0	0	0	1	0	4	1
1912	BRO	NL	5	1	4	1	3	1	0	0	0	0	0	0	3	0	4	1
1913	BRO	NL	2	0	2	0	1	1	0	0	0	0	0	0	1	0	0	2
Total			29	11	18	14	11	4	0	0	0	0	0	0	17	0	17	12

Rank among batters: 1,465 • Top target (2 home runs): Jake Weimer, Vic Willis, Lefty Leifield, Otto Hess • *Number of pitchers victimized*: 25 • *Total ballparks homered in*: 9 • *First HR*: 07/10/1906 off Irish McIlveen

Terry Humphrey

TERRYAL GENE HUMPHREY
B: 08/04/1949
BR

Year	Tm	Lg	Tot	H	A	Men-On 0	1	2	3	One-Game 2	3	4	LO	XN	IP	PH	RHP	LHP
1972	MON	NL	1	0	1	1	0	0	0	0	0	0	0	0	0	0	1	0
1973	MON	NL	1	1	0	0	1	0	0	0	0	0	0	0	0	0	0	1
1976	CAL	AL	1	1	0	0	0	1	0	0	0	0	0	0	0	0	1	0
1977	CAL	AL	2	0	2	2	0	0	0	0	0	0	0	0	0	0	1	1
1978	CAL	AL	1	0	1	1	0	0	0	0	0	0	0	0	0	0	0	1
Total			6	2	4	4	1	1	0	0	0	0	0	0	0	0	3	3

Rank among batters: 2,988 • *Total ballparks homered in*: 5 • *First HR*: 07/29/1972 off Danny Frisella

Mike Humphreys

MICHAEL BUTLER HUMPHREYS
B: 04/10/1967
BR

Year	Tm	Lg	Tot	H	A	Men-On 0	1	2	3	One-Game 2	3	4	LO	XN	IP	PH	RHP	LHP
1993	NY	AL	1	1	0	0	1	0	0	0	0	0	0	0	0	0	1	0

Rank among batters: 4,707 • *Total ballparks homered in*: 1 • *First HR*: 06/02/1993 off Tom Kramer

Randy Hundley

CECIL RANDOLPH HUNDLEY
B: 06/01/1942
BR

Year	Tm	Lg	Tot	H	A	Men-On 0	1	2	3	One-Game 2	3	4	LO	XN	IP	PH	RHP	LHP
1966	CHI	NL	19	13	6	12	5	1	1	1	0	0	0	1	0	0	17	2
1967	CHI	NL	14	7	7	7	5	1	1	1	0	0	0	0	0	0	11	3
1968	CHI	NL	7	5	2	2	5	0	0	0	0	0	0	0	0	0	7	0
1969	CHI	NL	18	8	10	9	6	2	1	0	0	0	0	0	0	0	13	5
1970	CHI	NL	7	6	1	3	3	1	0	0	0	0	0	0	0	0	5	2
1972	CHI	NL	5	4	1	3	1	0	1	0	0	0	0	0	0	0	4	1
1973	CHI	NL	10	6	4	7	2	1	0	0	0	0	0	0	0	0	8	2
1975	SD	NL	2	1	1	0	2	0	0	0	0	0	0	0	0	0	2	0
Total			82	50	32	43	29	6	4	2	0	0	0	1	0	0	67	15

Rank among batters: 637 • *Top target (4 home runs)*: Dave Giusti • *Number of pitchers victimized*: 64 • *Total ballparks homered in*: 12 • *First HR*: 04/19/1966 off Ron Herbel • *Hit for Cycle*—vs HOU: 08/11/1966 (1)

Todd Hundley

TODD RANDOLPH HUNDLEY
B: 05/27/1969
BB

Year	Tm	Lg	Tot	H	A	Men-On 0	1	2	3	One-Game 2	3	4	LO	XN	IP	PH	RHP	LHP
1991	NY	NL	1	1	0	1	0	0	0	0	0	0	0	1	0	1	1	0
1992	NY	NL	7	2	5	4	1	2	0	0	0	0	0	0	0	0	3	4
1993	NY	NL	11	5	6	7	2	1	1	0	0	0	0	0	0	0	11	0
1994	NY	NL	16	8	8	11	3	2	0	2	0	0	0	0	0	1	14	2
1995	NY	NL	15	6	9	7	5	1	2	0	0	0	0	1	1	1	12	3
Total			50	22	28	30	11	6	3	2	0	0	0	2	1	3	41	9

Rank among batters: 991 • Top target (2 home runs): Frank Castillo, Mike Morgan, John Burkett, Pedro Astacio, Jeff Brantley, Steve Trachsel • *Number of pitchers victimized*: 44 • *Total ballparks homered in*: 14 • *First HR*: 09/26/1991 off Bill Landrum • *Switch hit HR in 1 game*—1 time

Bernie Hungling

BERNARD HERMAN HUNGLING
B: 03/05/1896 D: 03/30/1968
BR

Year	Tm	Lg	Tot	H	A	Men-On 0	1	2	3	One-Game 2	3	4	LO	XN	IP	PH	RHP	LHP
1922	BRO	NL	1	0	1	1	0	0	0	0	0	0	0	0	0	0	1	0

Rank among batters: 4,707 • *Total ballparks homered in*: 1 • *First HR*: 05/11/1922 off Babe Adams

Bill Hunnefield

WILLIAM FENTON HUNNEFIELD
B: 01/05/1899 D: 08/28/1976
BB

Year	Tm	Lg	Tot	H	A	Men-On 0	1	2	3	One-Game 2	3	4	LO	XN	IP	PH	RHP	LHP
1926	CHI	AL	3	1	2	2	0	1	0	0	0	0	0	0	0	0	1	2
1927	CHI	AL	2	0	2	2	0	0	0	0	0	0	0	0	0	0	1	1
1928	CHI	AL	2	1	1	1	0	1	0	0	0	0	0	0	0	0	0	2
1930	CHI	AL	1	0	1	1	0	0	0	0	0	0	1	0	0	0	0	1
1931	NY	NL	1	1	0	1	0	0	0	0	0	0	0	0	0	0	0	1
Total			9	3	6	7	0	2	0	0	0	0	1	0	0	0	2	7

Rank among batters: 2,587 • *Top target (2 home runs)*: Rube Walberg • *Number of pitchers victimized*: 8 • *Total ballparks homered in*: 6 • *First HR*: 05/08/1926 off Curly Ogden

Ken Hunt

KENNETH LAWRENCE HUNT
B: 07/13/1934
BR

Year	Tm	Lg	Tot	H	A	Men-On 0	1	2	3	One-Game 2	3	4	LO	XN	IP	PH	RHP	LHP
1961	LA	AL	25	17	8	16	3	6	0	1	0	0	0	1	0	1	17	8
1962	LA	AL	1	0	1	1	0	0	0	0	0	0	0	0	0	0	1	0
1963	LA	AL	5	1	4	3	1	1	0	0	0	0	0	0	0	0	2	3
	WAS	AL	1	0	1	0	1	0	0	0	0	0	0	0	0	0	0	1
	Total		6	1	5	3	2	1	0	0	0	0	0	0	0	0	2	4

Year	Tm	Lg	Tot	H	A	Men-On 0	Men-On 1	Men-On 2	Men-On 3	One-Game 2	One-Game 3	One-Game 4	LO	XN	IP	PH	RHP	LHP

Ken Hunt *continued*

Year	Tm	Lg	Tot	H	A	Men-On 0	Men-On 1	Men-On 2	Men-On 3	One-Game 2	One-Game 3	One-Game 4	LO	XN	IP	PH	RHP	LHP
1964	WAS	AL	1	1	0	1	0	0	0	0	0	0	0	0	0	0	0	1
Total			33	19	14	21	5	7	0	1	0	0	0	1	0	1	20	13

Rank among batters: 1,336 • *Top target (2 home runs)*: Pete Burnside, Jim Kaat • *Number of pitchers victimized*: 31 • *Total ballparks homered in*: 12 • *First HR*: 04/20/1961 off Bob Turley

Randy Hunt

JAMES RANDALL HUNT
B: 01/03/1960
BR

Year	Tm	Lg	Tot	H	A	Men-On 0	Men-On 1	Men-On 2	Men-On 3	One-Game 2	One-Game 3	One-Game 4	LO	XN	IP	PH	RHP	LHP
1986	MON	NL	2	0	2	2	0	0	0	0	0	0	0	0	0	0	2	0

Rank among batters: 4,129 • *Total ballparks homered in*: 2 • *First HR*: 09/23/1986 off Ron Davis

Ron Hunt

RONALD KENNETH HUNT
B: 02/23/1941
BR

Year	Tm	Lg	Tot	H	A	Men-On 0	Men-On 1	Men-On 2	Men-On 3	One-Game 2	One-Game 3	One-Game 4	LO	XN	IP	PH	RHP	LHP
1963	NY	NL	10	2	8	7	3	0	0	0	0	0	0	0	0	0	6	4
1964	NY	NL	6	3	3	5	1	0	0	0	0	0	0	0	0	0	4	2
1965	NY	NL	1	1	0	1	0	0	0	0	0	0	0	0	0	0	1	0
1966	NY	NL	3	1	2	1	1	1	0	0	0	0	0	0	1	0	2	1
1967	LA	NL	3	1	2	3	0	0	0	0	0	0	0	0	0	0	2	1
1968	SF	NL	2	1	1	2	0	0	0	0	0	0	0	0	0	0	2	0
1969	SF	NL	3	1	2	3	0	0	0	0	0	0	0	0	0	0	2	1
1970	SF	NL	6	3	3	3	1	1	1	0	0	0	0	0	0	1	3	3
1971	MON	NL	5	4	1	3	2	0	0	0	0	0	1	0	0	0	1	4
Total			39	17	22	28	8	2	1	0	0	0	1	0	1	1	23	16

Rank among batters: 1,204 • Top target (2 home runs): Dick Ellsworth, Bob Purkey, Sandy Koufax, Billy O'Dell, Tony Cloninger, Ross Grimsley • *Number of pitchers victimized*: 33 • *Total ballparks homered in*: 14 • *First HR*: 04/24/1963 off Bob Buhl

Billy Hunter

GORDON WILLIAM HUNTER
B: 06/04/1928
BR

Year	Tm	Lg	Tot	H	A	Men-On 0	Men-On 1	Men-On 2	Men-On 3	One-Game 2	One-Game 3	One-Game 4	LO	XN	IP	PH	RHP	LHP
1953	STL	AL	1	1	0	0	1	0	0	0	0	0	0	0	0	0	1	0
1954	BAL	AL	2	1	1	0	2	0	0	0	0	0	0	0	0	0	2	0
1955	NY	AL	3	0	3	2	1	0	0	0	0	0	0	1	1	0	1	2
1957	KC	AL	8	6	2	6	2	0	0	1	0	0	0	0	0	0	8	0
1958	KC	AL	2	2	0	0	0	2	0	0	0	0	0	0	0	0	2	0
Total			16	10	6	8	6	2	0	1	0	0	0	1	1	0	14	2

Rank among batters: 2,029 • *Top target (2 home runs)*: Early Wynn, George Susce • *Number of pitchers victimized*: 14 • *Total ballparks homered in*: 7 • *First HR*: 09/26/1953 off Connie Johnson

Brian Hunter

BRIAN RAYNOLD HUNTER
B: 03/04/1968
BR

Year	Tm	Lg	Tot	H	A	Men-On 0	Men-On 1	Men-On 2	Men-On 3	One-Game 2	One-Game 3	One-Game 4	LO	XN	IP	PH	RHP	LHP
1991	ATL	NL	12	7	5	7	3	2	0	0	0	0	0	1	0	1	6	6
1992	ATL	NL	14	9	5	10	4	0	0	0	0	0	0	0	0	2	3	11
1994	PIT	NL	11	4	7	4	5	0	2	0	0	0	0	0	0	0	7	4
	CIN	NL	4	0	4	3	1	0	0	0	0	0	0	0	0	0	4	0
	Total		15	4	11	7	6	0	2	0	0	0	0	0	0	0	11	4
1995	CIN	NL	1	0	1	1	0	0	0	0	0	0	0	0	0	0	0	1
Total			42	20	22	25	13	2	2	0	0	0	0	1	0	3	20	22

Rank among batters: 1,138 • *Top target (3 home runs)*: Pete Schourek • *Number of pitchers victimized*: 36 • *Total ballparks homered in*: 8 • *First HR*: 06/05/1991 off Darrel Akerfelds • *World Series HR*—1; *LCS HR*—1

Brian Hunter

BRIAN LEE HUNTER
B: 03/05/1971
BR

Year	Tm	Lg	Tot	H	A	Men-On 0	Men-On 1	Men-On 2	Men-On 3	One-Game 2	One-Game 3	One-Game 4	LO	XN	IP	PH	RHP	LHP
1995	HOU	NL	2	0	2	2	0	0	0	0	0	0	0	1	0	0	2	0

Rank among batters: 4,129 • *Total ballparks homered in*: 2 • *First HR*: 06/16/1995 off Doug Henry

Year	Tm	Lg	Tot	H	A	Men-On				One-Game			LO	XN	IP	PH	RHP	LHP
						0	1	2	3	2	3	4						

Catfish Hunter

JAMES AUGUSTUS HUNTER
B: 04/08/1946
BR HOF

Year	Tm	Lg	Tot	H	A	0	1	2	3	2	3	4	LO	XN	IP	PH	RHP	LHP
1967	KC	AL	2	0	2	1	1	0	0	0	0	0	0	0	0	0	0	2
1968	OAK	AL	1	0	1	1	0	0	0	0	0	0	0	0	0	0	0	1
1969	OAK	AL	1	1	0	1	0	0	0	0	0	0	0	0	0	0	0	1
1970	OAK	AL	1	0	1	1	0	0	0	0	0	0	0	0	0	0	0	1
1971	OAK	AL	1	0	1	0	1	0	0	0	0	0	0	0	0	0	0	1
Total			6	1	5	4	2	0	0	0	0	0	0	0	0	0	0	6

Rank among batters: 2,988 • *Total ballparks homered in*: 5 • *First HR*: 05/30/1967 off Barry Moore

Herb Hunter

HERBERT HARRISON HUNTER
B: 12/25/1896 D: 07/25/1970
BL

Year	Tm	Lg	Tot	H	A	0	1	2	3	2	3	4	LO	XN	IP	PH	RHP	LHP
1916	NY	NL	1	0	1	0	0	1	0	0	0	0	0	1	1	0	1	0

Rank among batters: 4,707 • *Total ballparks homered in*: 1 • *First HR*: 08/25/1916 off Bob Harmon

Newt Hunter

FREDERICK CREIGHTON HUNTER
B: 01/05/1880 D: 10/26/1963
BR

Year	Tm	Lg	Tot	H	A	0	1	2	3	2	3	4	LO	XN	IP	PH	RHP	LHP
1911	PIT	NL	2	1	1	2	0	0	0	0	0	0	0	0	0	0	2	0

Rank among batters: 4,129 • *Total ballparks homered in*: 2 • *First HR*: 05/03/1911 off Bob Harmon

Steve Huntz

STEPHEN MICHAEL HUNTZ
B: 12/03/1945
BB

Year	Tm	Lg	Tot	H	A	0	1	2	3	2	3	4	LO	XN	IP	PH	RHP	LHP
1969	STL	NL	3	1	2	2	1	0	0	1	0	0	0	1	0	0	1	2
1970	SD	NL	11	3	8	6	5	0	0	0	0	0	0	1	0	0	8	3
1971	CHI	AL	2	2	0	1	0	1	0	1	0	0	0	0	0	0	0	2
Total			16	6	10	9	6	1	0	2	0	0	0	2	0	0	9	7

Rank among batters: 2,029 • *Top target (2 home runs)*: Lowell Palmer, Mickey Lolich • *Number of pitchers victimized*: 14 • *Total ballparks homered in*: 8 • *First HR*: 08/28/1969 off Don Wilson

Clint Hurdle

CLINTON MERRICK HURDLE
B: 07/30/1957
BL

Year	Tm	Lg	Tot	H	A	0	1	2	3	2	3	4	LO	XN	IP	PH	RHP	LHP
1977	KC	AL	2	2	0	1	1	0	0	0	0	0	0	0	0	0	2	0
1978	KC	AL	7	3	4	4	2	1	0	0	0	0	0	0	1	0	4	3
1979	KC	AL	3	1	2	3	0	0	0	0	0	0	0	0	0	0	3	0
1980	KC	AL	10	3	7	4	4	2	0	0	0	0	0	0	1	0	10	0
1981	KC	AL	4	0	4	2	2	0	0	0	0	0	0	0	0	0	3	1
1985	NY	NL	3	2	1	2	1	0	0	0	0	0	0	0	0	0	3	0
1986	STL	NL	3	0	3	1	0	2	0	0	0	0	0	0	0	1	3	0
Total			32	11	21	17	10	5	0	0	0	0	0	0	2	1	28	4

Rank among batters: 1,360 • Top target (2 home runs): Ferguson Jenkins, Glenn Abbott, Steve Stone, Rick Reuschel • *Number of pitchers victimized*: 28 • *Total ballparks homered in*: 15 • *First HR*: 09/18/1977 off Glenn Abbott

Don Hurst

FRANK O'DONNELL HURST
B: 08/12/1905 D: 12/06/1952
BL

Year	Tm	Lg	Tot	H	A	0	1	2	3	2	3	4	LO	XN	IP	PH	RHP	LHP
1928	PHI	NL	19	13	6	10	6	3	0	0	0	0	0	0	0	0	12	7
1929	PHI	NL	31	16	15	16	12	2	1	3	0	0	0	0	0	0	13	18
1930	PHI	NL	17	9	8	9	5	3	0	2	0	0	0	0	0	1	15	2
1931	PHI	NL	11	8	3	7	4	0	0	0	0	0	0	0	0	0	8	3
1932	PHI	NL	24	16	8	9	9	5	1	2	0	0	0	0	0	0	16	8
1933	PHI	NL	8	6	2	6	1	1	0	1	0	0	0	0	0	0	5	3
1934	PHI	NL	2	0	2	1	0	1	0	0	0	0	0	0	0	0	1	1
	CHI	NL	3	3	0	2	1	0	0	0	0	0	0	0	0	0	2	1
	Total		5	3	2	3	1	1	0	0	0	0	0	0	0	0	3	2
Total			115	71	44	60	38	15	2	8	0	0	0	0	0	1	72	43

Year	Tm	Lg	Tot	H	A	Men-On 0	1	2	3	One-Game 2	3	4	LO	XN	IP	PH	RHP	LHP

Don Hurst *continued*

Rank among batters: 415 • *Top target (5 home runs)*: Carl Hubbell, Bill Walker • *Number of pitchers victimized*: 67 • *Total ballparks homered in*: 8 • *First HR*: 05/15/1928 off Red Lucas

Butch Huskey

ROBERT LEON HUSKEY
B: 11/10/1971
BR

Year	Tm	Lg	Tot	H	A	Men-On 0	1	2	3	One-Game 2	3	4	LO	XN	IP	PH	RHP	LHP
1995	NY	NL	3	2	1	1	2	0	0	0	0	0	0	0	0	0	3	0

Rank among batters: 3,735 • *Total ballparks homered in*: 2 • *First HR*: 08/20/1995 off Hideo Nomo

Jeff Huson

JEFFREY KENT HUSON
B: 08/15/1964
BL

Year	Tm	Lg	Tot	H	A	Men-On 0	1	2	3	One-Game 2	3	4	LO	XN	IP	PH	RHP	LHP
1991	TEX	AL	2	1	1	0	1	1	0	0	0	0	0	0	0	0	2	0
1992	TEX	AL	4	0	4	3	1	0	0	0	0	0	0	0	0	0	3	1
1995	BAL	AL	1	0	1	1	0	0	0	0	0	0	0	0	0	0	1	0
Total			7	1	6	4	2	1	0	0	0	0	0	0	0	0	6	1

Rank among batters: 2,834 • *Total ballparks homered in*: 6 • *First HR*: 06/14/1991 off Wade Taylor

Bert Husting

BERTHOLD JUNEAU HUSTING
B: 03/06/1878 D: 09/03/1948
BR

Year	Tm	Lg	Tot	H	A	Men-On 0	1	2	3	One-Game 2	3	4	LO	XN	IP	PH	RHP	LHP
1901	MIL	AL	1	1	0	0	0	1	0	0	0	0	0	0	0	0	1	0

Rank among batters: 4,707 • *Total ballparks homered in*: 1 • *First HR*: 08/05/1901 off Jack Cronin

Joe Hutcheson

JOSEPH JOHNSON HUTCHESON
B: 02/05/1905 D: 02/23/1993
BL

Year	Tm	Lg	Tot	H	A	Men-On 0	1	2	3	One-Game 2	3	4	LO	XN	IP	PH	RHP	LHP
1933	BRO	NL	6	1	5	2	3	1	0	0	0	0	0	0	0	0	5	1

Rank among batters: 2,988 • *Top target (2 home runs)*: Jack Salveson • *Number of pitchers victimized*: 5 • *Total ballparks homered in*: 4 • *First HR*: 07/26/1933 off Hal Schumacher

Fred Hutchinson

FREDERICK CHARLES HUTCHINSON
B: 08/12/1919 D: 11/12/1964
BL

Year	Tm	Lg	Tot	H	A	Men-On 0	1	2	3	One-Game 2	3	4	LO	XN	IP	PH	RHP	LHP
1947	DET	AL	2	1	1	2	0	0	0	0	0	0	0	0	0	1	2	0
1948	DET	AL	1	1	0	1	0	0	0	0	0	0	0	0	0	0	1	0
1953	DET	AL	1	1	0	1	0	0	0	0	0	0	0	0	0	0	1	0
Total			4	3	1	4	0	0	0	0	0	0	0	0	0	1	4	0

Rank among batters: 3,427 • *Total ballparks homered in*: 2 • *First HR*: 08/06/1947 off Mel Harder

Bill Hutchison

WILLIAM FORREST HUTCHISON
B: 12/17/1859 D: 03/19/1926
BR

Year	Tm	Lg	Tot	H	A	Men-On 0	1	2	3	One-Game 2	3	4	LO	XN	IP	PH	RHP	LHP
1889	CHI	NL	1	1	0	1	0	0	0	0	0	0	0	0	0	0	1	0
1890	CHI	NL	2	2	0	1	1	0	0	0	0	0	0	0	0	0	1	1
1891	CHI	NL	2	2	0	2	0	0	0	0	0	0	0	0	1	0	2	0
1892	CHI	NL	1	1	0	0	0	1	0	0	0	0	0	0	0	0	1	0
1894	CHI	NL	6	2	4	4	1	1	0	0	0	0	0	0	1	0	6	0
Total			12	8	4	8	2	2	0	0	0	0	0	0	2	0	11	1

Rank among batters: 2,325 • *Total ballparks homered in*: 7 • *First HR*: 06/19/1889 off Kid Gleason

Jim Hutto

JAMES NEAMON HUTTO
B: 10/17/1947
BR

Year	Tm	Lg	Tot	H	A	Men-On 0	1	2	3	One-Game 2	3	4	LO	XN	IP	PH	RHP	LHP
1970	PHI	NL	3	1	2	2	0	0	1	0	0	0	0	0	0	2	2	1

Rank among batters: 3,735 • *Total ballparks homered in*: 3 • *First HR*: 05/03/1970 off Don McMahon

Tom Hutton

THOMAS GEORGE HUTTON
B: 04/20/1946
BL

Year	Tm	Lg	Tot	H	A	Men-On 0	1	2	3	One-Game 2	3	4	LO	XN	IP	PH	RHP	LHP
1972	PHI	NL	4	4	0	1	2	1	0	0	0	0	0	0	0	0	4	0
1973	PHI	NL	5	2	3	3	1	1	0	1	0	0	0	0	0	0	4	1
1974	PHI	NL	4	3	1	1	1	2	0	1	0	0	0	0	0	2	4	0
1975	PHI	NL	3	1	2	1	2	0	0	0	0	0	0	0	0	1	3	0
1976	PHI	NL	1	0	1	0	0	1	0	0	0	0	0	0	0	0	1	0
1977	PHI	NL	2	1	1	1	1	0	0	0	0	0	0	0	0	0	2	0
1978	TOR	AL	2	0	2	1	1	0	0	0	0	0	0	0	0	0	2	0
1979	MON	NL	1	0	1	0	0	1	0	0	0	0	0	0	0	1	1	0
Total			22	11	11	8	8	6	0	2	0	0	0	0	0	4	21	1

Rank among batters: 1,719 • *Top target (3 home runs)*: Tom Seaver • *Number of pitchers victimized*: 19 • *Total ballparks homered in*: 8 • *First HR*: 05/17/1972 off Bill Hands

Ham Hyatt

ROBERT HAMILTON HYATT
B: 11/01/1884 D: 09/11/1963
BL

Year	Tm	Lg	Tot	H	A	Men-On 0	1	2	3	One-Game 2	3	4	LO	XN	IP	PH	RHP	LHP
1910	PIT	NL	1	0	1	1	0	0	0	0	0	0	0	0	0	0	1	0
1913	PIT	NL	4	1	3	1	3	0	0	0	0	0	0	0	0	3	4	0
1914	PIT	NL	1	0	1	0	1	0	0	0	0	0	0	0	0	1	1	0
1915	STL	NL	2	1	1	1	0	1	0	0	0	0	0	0	0	0	1	1
1918	NY	AL	2	1	1	2	0	0	0	0	0	0	0	0	0	0	2	0
Total			10	3	7	5	4	1	0	0	0	0	0	0	0	4	9	1

Rank among batters: 2,500 • *Top target (2 home runs)*: Christy Mathewson, Bert Humphries • *Number of pitchers victimized*: 8 • *Total ballparks homered in*: 7 • *First HR*: 06/15/1910 off Christy Mathewson

Pete Incaviglia

PETER JOSEPH INCAVIGLIA
B: 04/02/1964
BR

Year	Tm	Lg	Tot	H	A	Men-On 0	1	2	3	One-Game 2	3	4	LO	XN	IP	PH	RHP	LHP
1986	TEX	AL	30	17	13	17	9	2	2	2	0	0	0	0	0	0	18	12
1987	TEX	AL	27	11	16	16	8	3	0	2	0	0	0	1	0	0	14	13
1988	TEX	AL	22	12	10	15	6	1	0	0	0	0	0	0	0	0	13	9
1989	TEX	AL	21	13	8	10	6	4	1	1	0	0	0	0	0	1	15	6
1990	TEX	AL	24	15	9	13	7	4	0	2	0	0	0	0	0	1	16	8
1991	DET	AL	11	6	5	5	4	1	1	0	0	0	0	0	0	0	11	0
1992	HOU	NL	11	6	5	4	6	1	0	1	0	0	0	0	0	1	5	6
1993	PHI	NL	24	15	9	12	6	5	1	3	0	0	0	0	0	0	11	13
1994	PHI	NL	13	6	7	8	1	3	1	0	0	0	0	0	0	1	9	4
Total			183	101	82	100	53	24	6	11	0	0	0	1	0	4	112	71

Rank among batters: 213 • *Top target (4 home runs)*: Scott Bailes, Bud Black, Frank Tanana • *Number of pitchers victimized*: 127 • *Total ballparks homered in*: 26 • *First HR*: 04/11/1986 off Tippy Martinez • *LCS HR*—1

Scotty Ingerton

WILLIAM JOHN INGERTON
B: 04/19/1886 D: 06/15/1956
BR

Year	Tm	Lg	Tot	H	A	Men-On 0	1	2	3	One-Game 2	3	4	LO	XN	IP	PH	RHP	LHP
1911	BOS	NL	5	5	0	2	2	1	0	1	0	0	0	1	0	0	4	1

Rank among batters: 3,191 • *Top target (2 home runs)*: Doc Crandall • *Number of pitchers victimized*: 4 • *Total ballparks homered in*: 1 • *First HR*: 05/06/1911 off Doc Crandall

Garey Ingram

GAREY LAMAR INGRAM
B: 07/25/1970
BR

Year	Tm	Lg	Tot	H	A	Men-On 0	1	2	3	One-Game 2	3	4	LO	XN	IP	PH	RHP	LHP
1994	LA	NL	3	1	2	3	0	0	0	0	0	0	0	0	0	1	2	1

Rank among batters: 3,735 • *Total ballparks homered in*: 3 • *First HR*: 05/19/1994 off Mike Munoz • *Hit HR in first major league AB*—@COL: 05/19/1994

Dane Iorg

DANE CHARLES IORG
B: 05/11/1950
BL

Year	Tm	Lg	Tot	H	A	Men-On 0	1	2	3	One-Game 2	3	4	LO	XN	IP	PH	RHP	LHP
1979	STL	NL	1	0	1	1	0	0	0	0	0	0	0	0	0	1	1	0

Year	Tm	Lg	Tot	H	A	Men-On				One-Game			LO	XN	IP	PH	RHP	LHP
						0	1	2	3	2	3	4						

Dane Iorg *continued*

Year	Tm	Lg	Tot	H	A	0	1	2	3	2	3	4	LO	XN	IP	PH	RHP	LHP
1980	STL	NL	3	1	2	2	0	1	0	1	0	0	0	0	0	0	3	0
1981	STL	NL	2	1	1	2	0	0	0	0	0	0	0	0	0	0	2	0
1984	KC	AL	5	3	2	3	2	0	0	0	0	0	0	0	0	1	5	0
1985	KC	AL	1	0	1	1	0	0	0	0	0	0	0	0	0	0	1	0
1986	SD	NL	2	0	2	1	0	1	0	0	0	0	0	0	0	1	2	0
Total			14	5	9	10	2	2	0	1	0	0	0	0	0	3	14	0

Rank among batters: 2,169 • *Top target (2 home runs)*: Jim Bibby • *Number of pitchers victimized*: 13 • *Total ballparks homered in*: 9 • *First HR*: 05/08/1979 off Ken Forsch

Garth Iorg

GARTH RAY IORG
B: 10/12/1954
BR

Year	Tm	Lg	Tot	H	A	0	1	2	3	2	3	4	LO	XN	IP	PH	RHP	LHP
1980	TOR	AL	2	1	1	1	1	0	0	0	0	0	0	0	0	0	0	2
1982	TOR	AL	1	1	0	1	0	0	0	0	0	0	0	0	0	0	0	1
1983	TOR	AL	2	1	1	0	1	1	0	0	0	0	0	0	0	0	0	2
1984	TOR	AL	1	1	0	0	1	0	0	0	0	0	0	0	0	0	0	1
1985	TOR	AL	7	5	2	4	2	1	0	0	0	0	0	1	0	0	2	5
1986	TOR	AL	3	1	2	1	1	1	0	0	0	0	0	0	0	1	0	3
1987	TOR	AL	4	1	3	3	1	0	0	1	0	0	0	0	0	0	3	1
Total			20	11	9	10	7	3	0	1	0	0	0	1	0	1	5	15

Rank among batters: 1,810 • *Top target (2 home runs)*: Frank Viola, Charlie Hough • *Number of pitchers victimized*: 18 • *Total ballparks homered in*: 6 • *First HR*: 06/22/1980 off Sparky Lyle

Hal Irelan

HAROLD IRELAN
B: 08/05/1890 D: 07/16/1944
BB

Year	Tm	Lg	Tot	H	A	0	1	2	3	2	3	4	LO	XN	IP	PH	RHP	LHP
1914	PHI	NL	1	1	0	1	0	0	0	0	0	0	0	0	0	0	1	0

Rank among batters: 4,707 • *Total ballparks homered in*: 1 • *First HR*: 09/02/1914 off Bill James

Monte Irvin

MONTFORD MERRILL IRVIN
B: 02/25/1919
BR HOF

Year	Tm	Lg	Tot	H	A	0	1	2	3	2	3	4	LO	XN	IP	PH	RHP	LHP
1950	NY	NL	15	9	6	10	3	1	1	0	0	0	0	0	0	0	11	4
1951	NY	NL	24	8	16	9	6	8	1	1	0	0	0	1	0	0	18	6
1952	NY	NL	4	3	1	1	2	1	0	0	0	0	0	0	0	0	2	2
1953	NY	NL	21	7	14	12	5	3	1	0	0	0	0	1	1	0	16	5
1954	NY	NL	19	9	10	13	6	0	0	1	0	0	0	0	0	1	16	3
1955	NY	NL	1	0	1	0	1	0	0	0	0	0	0	0	0	0	0	1
1956	CHI	NL	15	7	8	9	3	2	1	1	0	0	0	1	0	0	9	6
Total			99	43	56	54	26	15	4	3	0	0	0	3	1	1	72	27

Rank among batters: 503 • *Top target (5 home runs)*: Ralph Branca • *Number of pitchers victimized*: 62 • *Total ballparks homered in*: 9 • *First HR*: 05/18/1950 off Dutch Leonard

Arthur Irwin

ARTHUR ALBERT IRWIN
B: 02/14/1858 D: 07/16/1921
BL

Year	Tm	Lg	Tot	H	A	0	1	2	3	2	3	4	LO	XN	IP	PH	RHP	LHP
1880	WOR	NL	1	1	0	0	1	0	0	0	0	0	0	0	0	0	1	0
1884	PRO	NL	2	0	2	2	0	0	0	0	0	0	0	1	0	0	1	0
1887	PHI	NL	2	1	1	0	1	1	0	0	0	0	0	0	0	0	2	0
Total			5	2	3	2	2	1	0	0	0	0	0	1	0	0	4	0

Rank among batters: 3,191 • *Total ballparks homered in*: 5 • *First HR*: 10/01/1880 off George Bradley

Charlie Irwin

CHARLES EDWIN IRWIN
B: 02/15/1869 D: 09/21/1925
BL

Year	Tm	Lg	Tot	H	A	0	1	2	3	2	3	4	LO	XN	IP	PH	RHP	LHP
1894	CHI	NL	8	2	6	1	3	3	1	1	0	0	0	0	0	0	6	0
1896	CIN	NL	1	0	1	0	1	0	0	0	0	0	0	0	0	0	0	0

Charlie Irwin *continued*

Year	Tm	Lg	Tot	H	A	Men-On 0	1	2	3	One-Game 2	3	4	LO	XN	IP	PH	RHP	LHP
1898	CIN	NL	3	1	2	1	2	0	0	0	0	0	0	0	2	0	2	1
1899	CIN	NL	1	0	1	1	0	0	0	0	0	0	0	0	1	0	1	0
1900	CIN	NL	1	0	1	0	1	0	0	0	0	0	0	0	1	0	1	0
1902	BRO	NL	2	1	1	2	0	0	0	0	0	0	0	0	0	0	2	0
Total			16	4	12	5	7	3	1	1	0	0	0	0	4	0	12	1

Rank among batters: 2,029 • *Top target (2 home runs)*: Jack Stivetts • *Number of pitchers victimized*: 15 • *Total ballparks homered in*: 9 • *First HR*: 06/07/1894 off Huyler Westervelt

John Irwin

JOHN IRWIN
B: 07/21/1861 D: 02/28/1934
BL

Year	Tm	Lg	Tot	H	A	Men-On 0	1	2	3	One-Game 2	3	4	LO	XN	IP	PH	RHP	LHP
1884	BOS	UA	1	1	0	0	1	0	0	0	0	0	0	0	0	0	0	0
1887	WAS	NL	2	2	0	0	1	1	0	1	0	0	0	0	0	0	0	2
Total			3	3	0	0	2	1	0	1	0	0	0	0	0	0	0	2

Rank among batters: 3,735 • *Top target (2 home runs)*: Kid Madden • *Number of pitchers victimized*: 2 • *Total ballparks homered in*: 2 • *First HR*: 07/02/1884 off Ernie Hickman

Frank Isbell

WILLIAM FRANK ISBELL
B: 08/21/1875 D: 07/15/1941
BL

Year	Tm	Lg	Tot	H	A	Men-On 0	1	2	3	One-Game 2	3	4	LO	XN	IP	PH	RHP	LHP
1901	CHI	AL	3	2	1	1	1	1	0	0	0	0	0	0	0	0	3	0
1902	CHI	AL	4	2	2	1	2	1	0	0	0	0	0	0	1	0	4	0
1903	CHI	AL	2	1	1	1	0	1	0	0	0	0	0	0	2	0	1	1
1904	CHI	AL	1	0	1	1	0	0	0	0	0	0	0	0	1	0	1	0
1905	CHI	AL	2	1	1	2	0	0	0	0	0	0	0	0	1	0	2	0
1908	CHI	AL	1	0	1	0	1	0	0	0	0	0	0	0	0	0	1	0
Total			13	6	7	6	4	3	0	0	0	0	0	0	5	0	12	1

Rank among batters: 2,248 • *Top target (2 home runs)*: Bill Dinneen • *Number of pitchers victimized*: 12 • *Total ballparks homered in*: 5 • *First HR*: 05/18/1901 off Pink Hawley

Mike Ivie

MICHAEL WILSON IVIE
B: 08/08/1952
BR

Year	Tm	Lg	Tot	H	A	Men-On 0	1	2	3	One-Game 2	3	4	LO	XN	IP	PH	RHP	LHP
1974	SD	NL	1	1	0	0	1	0	0	0	0	0	0	0	0	0	1	0
1975	SD	NL	8	2	6	6	1	0	1	0	0	0	0	0	0	0	5	3
1976	SD	NL	7	4	3	2	4	1	0	0	0	0	0	0	0	0	2	5
1977	SD	NL	9	4	5	3	4	1	1	0	0	0	0	0	0	0	4	5
1978	SF	NL	11	5	6	4	4	1	2	0	0	0	0	0	0	4	5	6
1979	SF	NL	27	10	17	17	6	4	0	4	0	0	0	0	0	1	15	12
1980	SF	NL	4	1	3	3	1	0	0	0	0	0	0	1	0	0	3	1
1982	DET	AL	14	10	4	10	3	1	0	1	0	0	0	0	0	0	5	9
Total			81	37	44	45	24	8	4	5	0	0	0	1	0	5	40	41

Rank among batters: 645 • *Top target (4 home runs)*: Phil Niekro • *Number of pitchers victimized*: 62 • *Total ballparks homered in*: 16 • *First HR*: 09/11/1974 off Don Wilson

Ray Jablonski

RAYMOND LEO JABLONSKI
B: 12/17/1926 D: 11/25/1985
BR

Year	Tm	Lg	Tot	H	A	Men-On 0	1	2	3	One-Game 2	3	4	LO	XN	IP	PH	RHP	LHP
1953	STL	NL	21	11	10	12	2	7	0	1	0	0	0	0	0	0	11	10
1954	STL	NL	12	7	5	6	4	2	0	0	0	0	0	0	0	0	6	6
1955	CIN	NL	9	4	5	5	3	1	0	1	0	0	0	0	0	1	5	4
1956	CIN	NL	15	4	11	9	1	3	2	2	0	0	0	1	0	1	8	7
1957	NY	NL	9	3	6	5	3	1	0	0	0	0	0	0	0	1	6	3
1958	SF	NL	12	5	7	6	4	2	0	0	0	0	0	0	0	1	10	2
1959	STL	NL	3	1	2	2	1	0	0	0	0	0	0	0	0	1	1	2
	KC	AL	2	1	1	2	0	0	0	0	0	0	0	0	0	0	1	1
	Total		5	2	3	4	1	0	0	0	0	0	0	0	0	1	2	3
Total			83	36	47	47	18	16	2	4	0	0	0	1	0	5	48	35

Rank among batters: 628 • *Top target (5 home runs)*: Paul Minner • *Number of pitchers victimized*: 52 • *Total ballparks homered in*: 12 • *First HR*: 04/21/1953 off Harry Perkowski

Year	Tm	Lg	Tot	H	A	Men-On 0	Men-On 1	Men-On 2	Men-On 3	One-Game 2	One-Game 3	One-Game 4	LO	XN	IP	PH	RHP	LHP

Fred Jacklitsch

FREDERICK LAWRENCE JACKLITSCH
B: 05/24/1876 D: 07/18/1937
BR

Year	Tm	Lg	Tot	H	A	0	1	2	3	2	3	4	LO	XN	IP	PH	RHP	LHP
1903	BRO	NL	1	0	1	0	0	1	0	0	0	0	0	0	0	0	1	0
1914	BAL	FL	2	2	0	0	0	2	0	0	0	0	0	0	0	0	2	0
1915	BAL	FL	2	2	0	2	0	0	0	0	0	0	0	0	0	0	2	0
Total			5	4	1	2	0	3	0	0	0	0	0	0	0	0	5	0

Rank among batters: 3,191 • *Total ballparks homered in*: 2 • *First HR*: 09/27/1903 off Jack Sutthoff

Al Jackson

ALVIN NEIL JACKSON
B: 12/25/1935
BL

Year	Tm	Lg	Tot	H	A	0	1	2	3	2	3	4	LO	XN	IP	PH	RHP	LHP
1964	NY	NL	1	1	0	1	0	0	0	0	0	0	0	0	0	0	0	1

Rank among batters: 4,707 • *Total ballparks homered in*: 1 • *First HR*: 07/26/1964 off Warren Spahn

Bill Jackson

WILLIAM RILEY JACKSON
B: 04/04/1881 D: 09/24/1958
BL

Year	Tm	Lg	Tot	H	A	0	1	2	3	2	3	4	LO	XN	IP	PH	RHP	LHP
1915	CHI	FL	1	1	0	0	1	0	0	0	0	0	0	0	0	0	1	0

Rank among batters: 4,707 • *Total ballparks homered in*: 1 • *First HR*: 06/06/1915 off Elmer Knetzer

Bo Jackson

VINCENT EDWARD JACKSON
B: 11/30/1962
BR

Year	Tm	Lg	Tot	H	A	0	1	2	3	2	3	4	LO	XN	IP	PH	RHP	LHP
1986	KC	AL	2	1	1	1	1	0	0	0	0	0	0	0	0	0	2	0
1987	KC	AL	22	14	8	16	4	1	1	3	0	0	0	0	0	0	15	7
1988	KC	AL	25	10	15	17	3	5	0	1	0	0	0	0	0	0	17	8
1989	KC	AL	32	11	21	15	11	5	1	1	0	0	0	2	0	0	26	6
1990	KC	AL	28	12	16	12	8	8	0	1	1	0	0	0	1	1	18	10
1991	CHI	AL	3	3	0	1	2	0	0	0	0	0	0	0	0	1	1	2
1993	CHI	AL	16	9	7	7	5	4	0	0	0	0	0	0	0	1	7	9
1994	CAL	AL	13	10	3	6	5	2	0	0	0	0	0	0	0	1	7	6
Total			141	70	71	75	39	25	2	6	1	0	0	2	1	4	93	48

Rank among batters: 309 • *Top target (4 home runs)*: Erik Hanson • *Number of pitchers victimized*: 107 • *Total ballparks homered in*: 17 • *First HR*: 09/14/1986 off Mike Moore • *All-Star HR*—1

Chuck Jackson

CHARLES LEO JACKSON
B: 03/19/1963
BR

Year	Tm	Lg	Tot	H	A	0	1	2	3	2	3	4	LO	XN	IP	PH	RHP	LHP
1987	HOU	NL	1	0	1	1	0	0	0	0	0	0	0	0	0	0	0	1
1988	HOU	NL	1	0	1	1	0	0	0	0	0	0	0	0	0	0	1	0
Total			2	0	2	2	0	0	0	0	0	0	0	0	0	0	1	1

Rank among batters: 4,129 • *Total ballparks homered in*: 2 • *First HR*: 06/25/1987 off Dave Dravecky

Darrin Jackson

DARRIN JAY JACKSON
B: 08/22/1963
BR

Year	Tm	Lg	Tot	H	A	0	1	2	3	2	3	4	LO	XN	IP	PH	RHP	LHP
1988	CHI	NL	6	3	3	5	1	0	0	1	0	0	0	0	0	2	1	5
1989	CHI	NL	1	0	1	1	0	0	0	0	0	0	0	0	0	0	0	1
	SD	NL	3	1	2	2	0	1	0	0	0	0	0	0	0	0	2	1
	Total		4	1	3	3	0	1	0	0	0	0	0	0	0	0	2	2
1990	SD	NL	3	1	2	3	0	0	0	0	0	0	0	0	0	1	2	1
1991	SD	NL	21	12	9	15	4	1	1	2	0	0	2	1	0	1	11	10
1992	SD	NL	17	11	6	10	4	3	0	1	0	0	0	2	0	0	10	7
1993	TOR	AL	5	4	1	4	1	0	0	0	0	0	0	0	0	0	4	1
	NY	NL	1	0	1	1	0	0	0	0	0	0	0	0	0	0	0	1
	Total		6	4	2	5	1	0	0	0	0	0	0	0	0	0	4	2
1994	CHI	AL	10	4	6	5	1	3	1	1	0	0	0	0	0	1	5	5
Total			67	36	31	46	11	8	2	5	0	0	2	3	0	5	35	32

Rank among batters: 777 • Top target (2 home runs): Tom Browning, Bob Patterson, Bobby Ojeda, Mike Remlinger, Rick Mahler, Danny Jackson, Sid Fernandez, Tom Glavine, Frank Viola • *Number of pitchers victimized*: 58 • *Total ballparks homered in*: 15 • *First HR*: 05/21/1988 off Danny Jackson

Year	Tm	Lg	Tot	H	A	Men-On				One-Game			LO	XN	IP	PH	RHP	LHP
						0	1	2	3	2	3	4						

George Jackson

GEORGE CHRISTOPHER JACKSON
B: 10/14/1882 D: 11/25/1972
BR

Year	Tm	Lg	Tot	H	A	0	1	2	3	2	3	4	LO	XN	IP	PH	RHP	LHP
1912	BOS	NL	4	2	2	1	3	0	0	0	0	0	0	0	0	0	3	1

Rank among batters: 3,427 • *Total ballparks homered in*: 3 • *First HR*: 05/30/1912 off Nap Rucker

Grant Jackson

GRANT DWIGHT JACKSON
B: 09/28/1942
BB

Year	Tm	Lg	Tot	H	A	0	1	2	3	2	3	4	LO	XN	IP	PH	RHP	LHP
1969	PHI	NL	1	0	1	0	0	1	0	0	0	0	0	0	0	0	1	0
1971	BAL	AL	1	0	1	1	0	0	0	0	0	0	0	0	0	0	1	0
Total			2	0	2	1	0	1	0	0	0	0	0	0	0	0	2	0

Rank among batters: 4,129 • *Total ballparks homered in*: 2 • *First HR*: 05/23/1969 off Milt Pappas

Jim Jackson

JAMES BENNER JACKSON
B: 11/28/1877 D: 10/09/1955
BR

Year	Tm	Lg	Tot	H	A	0	1	2	3	2	3	4	LO	XN	IP	PH	RHP	LHP
1901	BAL	AL	2	1	1	2	0	0	0	0	0	0	0	0	0	0	2	0
1905	CLE	AL	2	0	2	2	0	0	0	0	0	0	0	0	1	0	2	0
Total			4	1	3	4	0	0	0	0	0	0	0	0	1	0	4	0

Rank among batters: 3,427 • *Top target (2 home runs)*: Dale Gear • *Number of pitchers victimized*: 3 • *Total ballparks homered in*: 4 • *First HR*: 05/02/1901 off Dale Gear

Joe Jackson

JOSEPH JEFFERSON JACKSON
B: 07/16/1889 D: 12/05/1951
BL

Year	Tm	Lg	Tot	H	A	0	1	2	3	2	3	4	LO	XN	IP	PH	RHP	LHP
1910	CLE	AL	1	1	0	0	1	0	0	0	0	0	0	0	1	0	1	0
1911	CLE	AL	7	2	5	2	3	1	1	0	0	0	0	1	2	0	7	0
1912	CLE	AL	3	1	2	2	1	0	0	0	0	0	0	0	0	0	3	0
1913	CLE	AL	7	3	4	4	1	1	1	0	0	0	0	0	2	0	5	2
1914	CLE	AL	3	1	2	1	1	1	0	0	0	0	0	0	0	0	3	0
1915	CLE	AL	3	1	2	1	2	0	0	0	0	0	0	0	0	0	2	1
	CHI	AL	2	0	2	0	0	2	0	0	0	0	0	0	0	0	1	1
	Total		5	1	4	1	2	2	0	0	0	0	0	0	0	0	3	2
1916	CHI	AL	3	1	2	1	1	1	0	0	0	0	0	0	1	0	3	0
1917	CHI	AL	5	2	3	3	1	1	0	0	0	0	0	0	1	0	4	1
1918	CHI	AL	1	0	1	0	1	0	0	0	0	0	0	0	0	0	1	0
1919	CHI	AL	7	1	6	5	2	0	0	0	0	0	0	1	0	0	6	1
1920	CHI	AL	12	5	7	6	3	1	2	0	0	0	0	0	1	0	11	1
Total			54	18	36	25	17	8	4	0	0	0	0	2	8	0	47	7

Rank among batters: 938 • *Top target (3 home runs)*: Tom Hughes, Joe Bush, Jim Bagby • *Number of pitchers victimized*: 42 • *Total ballparks homered in*: 9 • *First HR*: 09/17/1910 off Bob Groom • *World Series HR*—1

Larry Jackson

LAWRENCE CURTIS JACKSON
B: 06/02/1931 D: 08/28/1990
BR

Year	Tm	Lg	Tot	H	A	0	1	2	3	2	3	4	LO	XN	IP	PH	RHP	LHP
1965	CHI	NL	1	1	0	0	1	0	0	0	0	0	0	0	0	0	1	0
1966	PHI	NL	1	0	1	0	1	0	0	0	0	0	0	0	0	0	1	0
Total			2	1	1	0	2	0	0	0	0	0	0	0	0	0	2	0

Rank among batters: 4,129 • *Total ballparks homered in*: 1 • *First HR*: 05/06/1965 off Don Cardwell

Lou Jackson

LOUIS CLARENCE JACKSON
B: 07/26/1935 D: 05/27/1969
BL

Year	Tm	Lg	Tot	H	A	0	1	2	3	2	3	4	LO	XN	IP	PH	RHP	LHP
1958	CHI	NL	1	0	1	0	1	0	0	0	0	0	0	0	0	1	1	0

Rank among batters: 4,707 • *Total ballparks homered in*: 1 • *First HR*: 08/03/1958 off Ray Semproch

Randy Jackson

RANSOM JOSEPH JACKSON
B: 02/10/1926
BR

Year	Tm	Lg	Tot	H	A	0	1	2	3	2	3	4	LO	XN	IP	PH	RHP	LHP
1950	CHI	NL	3	1	2	2	1	0	0	0	0	0	1	1	0	0	2	1

						Men-On				One-Game								
Year	Tm	Lg	Tot	H	A	0	1	2	3	2	3	4	LO	XN	IP	PH	RHP	LHP

Randy Jackson *continued*

Year	Tm	Lg	Tot	H	A	0	1	2	3	2	3	4	LO	XN	IP	PH	RHP	LHP
1951	CHI	NL	16	7	9	7	7	1	1	2	0	0	0	0	0	0	13	3
1952	CHI	NL	9	4	5	8	1	0	0	0	0	0	0	0	0	0	6	3
1953	CHI	NL	19	13	6	13	3	2	1	1	0	0	0	2	0	0	17	2
1954	CHI	NL	19	13	6	12	4	3	0	2	0	0	0	0	0	0	17	2
1955	CHI	NL	21	11	10	13	7	1	0	1	0	0	0	1	0	0	19	2
1956	BRO	NL	8	4	4	4	3	1	0	0	0	0	0	0	1	0	7	1
1957	BRO	NL	2	1	1	1	0	1	0	0	0	0	0	0	0	0	2	0
1958	LA	NL	1	1	0	1	0	0	0	0	0	0	0	0	0	0	1	0
	CLE	AL	4	0	4	3	0	1	0	0	0	0	0	0	0	1	3	1
	Total		5	1	4	4	0	1	0	0	0	0	0	0	0	1	4	1
1959	CHI	NL	1	0	1	0	0	1	0	0	0	0	0	0	0	0	1	0
Total			103	55	48	64	26	11	2	6	0	0	1	4	1	1	88	15

Rank among batters: 477 • *Top target (4 home runs)*: Don Newcombe, Russ Meyer • *Number of pitchers victimized*: 74 • *Total ballparks homered in*: 12 • *First HR*: 05/05/1950 off Bud Podbielan

Reggie Jackson

REGINALD MARTINEZ JACKSON
B: 05/18/1946
BL HOF

Year	Tm	Lg	Tot	H	A	0	1	2	3	2	3	4	LO	XN	IP	PH	RHP	LHP
1967	KC	AL	1	0	1	1	0	0	0	0	0	0	0	0	0	0	0	1
1968	OAK	AL	29	9	20	19	6	4	0	1	0	0	0	0	2	0	18	11
1969	OAK	AL	47	26	21	28	14	5	0	7	1	0	0	1	1	0	31	16
1970	OAK	AL	23	8	15	13	8	1	1	0	0	0	0	0	0	2	13	10
1971	OAK	AL	32	17	15	24	7	1	0	3	0	0	0	3	1	0	26	6
1972	OAK	AL	25	16	9	17	4	4	0	2	0	0	0	0	0	0	14	11
1973	OAK	AL	32	18	14	17	8	7	0	5	0	0	0	0	0	0	20	12
1974	OAK	AL	29	14	15	14	10	5	0	6	0	0	0	1	0	0	18	11
1975	OAK	AL	36	18	18	20	14	2	0	3	0	0	0	1	0	0	33	3
1976	BAL	AL	27	12	15	9	11	4	3	0	0	0	0	1	0	1	18	9
1977	NY	AL	32	11	21	18	10	3	1	4	0	0	0	1	0	0	19	13
1978	NY	AL	27	17	10	15	6	4	2	1	0	0	0	0	0	0	18	9
1979	NY	AL	29	15	14	19	5	5	0	0	0	0	0	0	0	1	19	10
1980	NY	AL	41	16	25	23	12	5	1	1	0	0	0	1	0	0	22	19
1981	NY	AL	15	7	8	6	6	3	0	0	0	0	0	0	0	0	11	4
1982	CAL	AL	39	21	18	22	13	3	1	1	0	0	0	1	0	0	25	14
1983	CAL	AL	14	7	7	8	3	3	0	0	0	0	0	0	0	1	10	4
1984	CAL	AL	25	15	10	9	10	5	1	1	0	0	0	0	0	0	15	10
1985	CAL	AL	27	15	12	12	12	2	1	3	0	0	0	0	0	0	23	4
1986	CAL	AL	18	11	7	9	7	2	0	2	1	0	0	0	0	0	18	0
1987	OAK	AL	15	7	8	5	9	1	0	0	0	0	0	0	0	1	13	2
Total			563	280	283	308	175	69	11	40	2	0	0	10	4	6	384	179

Rank among batters: 6 • *Top target (8 home runs)*: Wilbur Wood • *Number of pitchers victimized*: 306 • *Total ballparks homered in*: 18 • *First HR*: 09/17/1967 off Jim Weaver • *World Series HR—10; LCS HR—8; All-Star HR—1*

Ron Jackson

RONALD HARRIS JACKSON
B: 10/22/1933
BR

Year	Tm	Lg	Tot	H	A	0	1	2	3	2	3	4	LO	XN	IP	PH	RHP	LHP
1954	CHI	AL	4	2	2	3	0	1	0	0	0	0	0	0	0	0	3	1
1955	CHI	AL	2	2	0	1	1	0	0	0	0	0	0	0	0	1	1	1
1956	CHI	AL	1	1	0	1	0	0	0	0	0	0	0	0	0	0	0	1
1957	CHI	AL	2	0	2	1	0	1	0	0	0	0	0	0	0	0	1	1
1958	CHI	AL	7	4	3	6	0	1	0	0	0	0	0	0	0	1	4	3
1959	CHI	AL	1	1	0	1	0	0	0	0	0	0	0	0	0	0	0	1
Total			17	10	7	13	1	3	0	0	0	0	0	0	0	2	9	8

Rank among batters: 1,969 • *Total ballparks homered in*: 7 • *First HR*: 07/05/1954 off Duane Pillette

Ron Jackson

RONNIE DAMIEN JACKSON
B: 05/09/1953
BR

Year	Tm	Lg	Tot	H	A	0	1	2	3	2	3	4	LO	XN	IP	PH	RHP	LHP
1976	CAL	AL	8	1	7	5	1	1	1	0	0	0	0	0	0	1	7	1
1977	CAL	AL	8	6	2	5	3	0	0	0	0	0	0	0	0	0	3	5
1978	CAL	AL	6	2	4	3	2	1	0	0	0	0	0	0	0	0	5	1
1979	MIN	AL	14	8	6	9	4	1	0	0	0	0	0	0	0	0	9	5

						Men-On				One-Game								
Year	Tm	Lg	Tot	H	A	0	1	2	3	2	3	4	LO	XN	IP	PH	RHP	LHP

Randy Jackson *continued*

Year	Tm	Lg	Tot	H	A	0	1	2	3	2	3	4	LO	XN	IP	PH	RHP	LHP
1980	MIN	AL	5	3	2	4	1	0	0	0	0	0	0	0	0	1	2	3
1981	MIN	AL	4	1	3	2	1	1	0	1	0	0	0	0	0	0	2	2
	DET	AL	1	1	0	1	0	0	0	0	0	0	0	0	0	0	0	1
	Total		5	2	3	3	1	1	0	1	0	0	0	0	0	0	2	3
1982	CAL	AL	2	1	1	2	0	0	0	0	0	0	0	0	0	0	1	1
1983	CAL	AL	8	5	3	3	2	2	1	0	0	0	0	0	0	0	2	6
Total			56	28	28	34	14	6	2	1	0	0	0	0	0	2	31	25

Rank among batters: 913 • *Top target (3 home runs)*: Glenn Abbott • *Number of pitchers victimized*: 45 • *Total ballparks homered in*: 13 • *First HR*: 06/04/1976 off Rick Wise

Sonny Jackson

ROLAND THOMAS JACKSON
B: 07/09/1944
BL

Year	Tm	Lg	Tot	H	A	0	1	2	3	2	3	4	LO	XN	IP	PH	RHP	LHP
1966	HOU	NL	3	3	0	2	1	0	0	0	0	0	1	0	3	0	3	0
1968	ATL	NL	1	1	0	1	0	0	0	0	0	0	0	0	0	0	1	0
1969	ATL	NL	1	0	1	0	1	0	0	0	0	0	0	0	1	0	0	1
1971	ATL	NL	2	1	1	2	0	0	0	0	0	0	0	0	0	0	2	0
Total			7	5	2	5	2	0	0	0	0	0	1	0	4	0	6	1

Rank among batters: 2,834 • *Total ballparks homered in*: 3 • *First HR*: 06/21/1966 off Don Sutton

Travis Jackson

TRAVIS CALVIN JACKSON
B: 11/02/1903 D: 07/27/1987
BR HOF

Year	Tm	Lg	Tot	H	A	0	1	2	3	2	3	4	LO	XN	IP	PH	RHP	LHP
1923	NY	NL	4	1	3	2	2	0	0	0	0	0	0	0	2	0	3	1
1924	NY	NL	11	5	6	6	3	0	2	0	0	0	0	0	1	0	7	4
1925	NY	NL	9	3	6	6	1	1	1	1	0	0	0	0	1	0	6	3
1926	NY	NL	8	8	0	4	3	1	0	0	0	0	0	0	0	0	6	2
1927	NY	NL	14	11	3	8	4	1	1	1	0	0	0	0	1	0	8	6
1928	NY	NL	14	10	4	6	5	3	0	0	0	0	0	0	2	0	7	7
1929	NY	NL	21	16	5	10	7	4	0	4	0	0	0	1	2	0	12	9
1930	NY	NL	13	8	5	4	6	3	0	1	0	0	0	0	0	0	10	3
1931	NY	NL	5	4	1	4	1	0	0	0	0	0	0	0	0	0	3	2
1932	NY	NL	4	2	2	0	3	1	0	0	0	0	0	0	0	0	4	0
1934	NY	NL	16	9	7	6	5	5	0	0	0	0	0	1	1	0	11	5
1935	NY	NL	9	7	2	1	4	4	0	0	0	0	0	0	0	0	7	2
1936	NY	NL	7	5	2	4	1	2	0	1	0	0	0	0	0	0	6	1
Total			135	89	46	61	45	25	4	8	0	0	0	2	10	0	90	45

Rank among batters: 326 • Top target (4 home runs): Clarence Mitchell, Leo Sweetland, Dazzy Vance, Ray Benge, Bob Smith, Watty Clark • *Number of pitchers victimized*: 83 • *Total ballparks homered in*: 8 • *First HR*: 07/02/1923 off Clarence Mitchell

William Jacobson

WILLIAM CHESTER JACOBSON
B: 08/16/1890 D: 01/16/1977
BR

Year	Tm	Lg	Tot	H	A	0	1	2	3	2	3	4	LO	XN	IP	PH	RHP	LHP
1915	STL	AL	1	0	1	1	0	0	0	0	0	0	0	0	0	0	1	0
1917	STL	AL	4	2	2	1	3	0	0	0	0	0	0	0	0	0	2	2
1919	STL	AL	4	2	2	2	1	1	0	0	0	0	0	0	0	0	4	0
1920	STL	AL	9	1	8	2	6	1	0	1	0	0	0	0	0	0	4	5
1921	STL	AL	5	5	0	3	2	0	0	0	0	0	0	0	0	0	4	1
1922	STL	AL	9	7	2	4	2	2	1	1	0	0	0	0	0	0	6	3
1923	STL	AL	8	2	6	3	3	2	0	0	0	0	0	0	2	0	7	1
1924	STL	AL	19	13	6	11	7	1	0	1	0	0	0	0	2	0	10	9
1925	STL	AL	15	7	8	9	3	3	0	2	0	0	0	0	0	0	9	6
1926	STL	AL	2	1	1	1	1	0	0	0	0	0	0	0	0	0	2	0
	BOS	AL	6	3	3	4	1	1	0	0	0	0	0	0	0	0	5	1
	Total		8	4	4	5	2	1	0	0	0	0	0	0	0	0	7	1
1927	PHI	AL	1	1	0	1	0	0	0	0	0	0	0	0	0	0	1	0
Total			83	44	39	42	29	11	1	5	0	0	0	0	4	0	55	28

Rank among batters: 628 • *Top target (4 home runs)*: Howard Ehmke • *Number of pitchers victimized*: 61 • *Total ballparks homered in*: 8 • *First HR*: 09/14/1915 off Walter Ancker • *Hit for Cycle*—@CHI: 04/17/1924

Brook Jacoby

BROOK WALLACE JACOBY
B: 11/23/1959
BR

Year	Tm	Lg	Tot	H	A	Men-On 0	1	2	3	One-Game 2	3	4	LO	XN	IP	PH	RHP	LHP
1984	CLE	AL	7	2	5	6	0	1	0	0	0	0	0	0	0	0	4	3
1985	CLE	AL	20	9	11	9	8	2	1	0	0	0	0	0	0	0	11	9
1986	CLE	AL	17	10	7	9	6	2	0	1	0	0	0	0	0	0	12	5
1987	CLE	AL	32	21	11	27	5	0	0	2	1	0	0	0	0	0	27	5
1988	CLE	AL	9	3	6	7	1	0	1	0	0	0	0	0	0	0	6	3
1989	CLE	AL	13	7	6	6	7	0	0	1	0	0	0	0	0	0	7	6
1990	CLE	AL	14	10	4	10	3	1	0	0	0	0	0	0	0	0	11	3
1991	CLE	AL	4	2	2	3	0	1	0	0	0	0	0	1	0	0	3	1
1992	CLE	AL	4	3	1	3	0	1	0	0	0	0	0	1	0	0	2	2
Total			120	67	53	80	30	8	2	4	1	0	0	2	0	0	83	37

Rank among batters: 388 • *Top target (4 home runs)*: Mark Langston, Frank Tanana • *Number of pitchers victimized*: 88 • *Total ballparks homered in*: 14 • *First HR*: 04/08/1984 off Bud Black

Harry Jacoby

HARRY JACOBY

Year	Tm	Lg	Tot	H	A	Men-On 0	1	2	3	One-Game 2	3	4	LO	XN	IP	PH	RHP	LHP
1882	BAL	AA	1	0	1	1	0	0	0	0	0	0	0	0	0	0	0	0

Rank among batters: 4,707 • *Total ballparks homered in*: 1 • *First HR*: 05/04/1882 off Doc Landis

John Jaha

JOHN EMIL JAHA
B: 05/27/1966
BR

Year	Tm	Lg	Tot	H	A	Men-On 0	1	2	3	One-Game 2	3	4	LO	XN	IP	PH	RHP	LHP
1992	MIL	AL	2	1	1	2	0	0	0	0	0	0	0	0	0	0	1	1
1993	MIL	AL	19	5	14	14	4	1	0	1	0	0	0	1	0	0	13	6
1994	MIL	AL	12	5	7	7	3	2	0	2	0	0	0	0	0	0	7	5
1995	MIL	AL	20	8	12	7	5	5	3	0	0	0	0	1	1	0	18	2
Total			53	19	34	30	12	8	3	3	0	0	0	2	1	0	39	14

Rank among batters: 953 • *Top target (3 home runs)*: Jamie Moyer, Mike Trombley • *Number of pitchers victimized*: 47 • *Total ballparks homered in*: 14 • *First HR*: 07/28/1992 off Rod Nichols

Art Jahn

ARTHUR CHARLES JAHN
B: 12/02/1895 D: 01/09/1948
BR

Year	Tm	Lg	Tot	H	A	Men-On 0	1	2	3	One-Game 2	3	4	LO	XN	IP	PH	RHP	LHP
1928	NY	NL	1	1	0	1	0	0	0	0	0	0	0	0	0	0	0	1

Rank among batters: 4,707 • *Total ballparks homered in*: 1 • *First HR*: 05/02/1928 off Jumbo Elliott

Sig Jakucki

SIGMUND JAKUCKI
B: 08/20/1909 D: 05/29/1979
BR

Year	Tm	Lg	Tot	H	A	Men-On 0	1	2	3	One-Game 2	3	4	LO	XN	IP	PH	RHP	LHP
1944	STL	AL	1	1	0	1	0	0	0	0	0	0	0	0	0	0	1	0
1945	STL	AL	2	1	1	1	1	0	0	0	0	0	0	0	0	0	2	0
Total			3	2	1	2	1	0	0	0	0	0	0	0	0	0	3	0

Rank among batters: 3,735 • *Total ballparks homered in*: 2 • *First HR*: 05/31/1944 off Roger Wolff

Bernie James

ROBERT BYRNE JAMES
B: 09/02/1905 D: 08/01/1994
BB

Year	Tm	Lg	Tot	H	A	Men-On 0	1	2	3	One-Game 2	3	4	LO	XN	IP	PH	RHP	LHP
1933	NY	NL	1	1	0	1	0	0	0	0	0	0	0	0	0	0	1	0

Rank among batters: 4,707 • *Total ballparks homered in*: 1 • *First HR*: 05/30/1933 off Van Mungo

Charlie James

CHARLES WESLEY JAMES
B: 12/22/1937
BR

Year	Tm	Lg	Tot	H	A	Men-On 0	1	2	3	One-Game 2	3	4	LO	XN	IP	PH	RHP	LHP
1960	STL	NL	2	2	0	2	0	0	0	0	0	0	0	0	0	0	1	1

						Men-On				One-Game								
Year	Tm	Lg	Tot	H	A	0	1	2	3	2	3	4	LO	XN	IP	PH	RHP	LHP

Charlie James *continued*

Year	Tm	Lg	Tot	H	A	0	1	2	3	2	3	4	LO	XN	IP	PH	RHP	LHP
1961	STL	NL	4	2	2	2	2	0	0	0	0	0	0	0	0	0	0	4
1962	STL	NL	8	6	2	1	2	4	1	0	0	0	0	0	0	1	5	3
1963	STL	NL	10	7	3	7	1	2	0	1	0	0	0	0	0	2	2	8
1964	STL	NL	5	3	2	4	0	1	0	1	0	0	0	0	0	0	2	3
Total			29	20	9	16	5	7	1	2	0	0	0	0	0	3	10	19

Rank among batters: 1,465 • Top target (2 home runs): Jack Curtis, Harvey Haddix, Billy Pierce, Sandy Koufax • *Number of pitchers victimized*: 25 • *Total ballparks homered in*: 6 • *First HR*: 08/20/1960 off Danny McDevitt

Chris James

DONALD CHRIS JAMES
B: 10/04/1962
BR

Year	Tm	Lg	Tot	H	A	0	1	2	3	2	3	4	LO	XN	IP	PH	RHP	LHP
1986	PHI	NL	1	0	1	0	1	0	0	0	0	0	0	0	0	0	0	1
1987	PHI	NL	17	9	8	10	4	3	0	1	0	0	0	0	0	1	8	9
1988	PHI	NL	19	10	9	10	8	0	1	0	0	0	0	0	0	0	12	7
1989	PHI	NL	2	1	1	0	1	0	1	0	0	0	0	0	0	0	0	2
	SD	NL	11	6	5	7	2	1	1	0	0	0	0	1	0	0	6	5
	Total		13	7	6	7	3	1	2	0	0	0	0	1	0	0	6	7
1990	CLE	AL	12	6	6	10	0	2	0	0	0	0	0	0	0	1	8	4
1991	CLE	AL	5	1	4	2	1	2	0	1	0	0	0	0	0	0	3	2
1992	SF	NL	5	3	2	4	1	0	0	0	0	0	0	0	0	2	3	2
1993	HOU	NL	6	6	0	4	1	1	0	0	0	0	0	0	0	2	0	6
	TEX	AL	3	0	3	2	1	0	0	1	0	0	1	0	0	0	1	2
	Total		9	6	3	6	2	1	0	1	0	0	1	0	0	2	1	8
1994	TEX	AL	7	4	3	6	1	0	0	0	0	0	0	0	0	1	2	5
1995	KC	AL	2	0	2	2	0	0	0	0	0	0	0	0	0	0	1	1
Total			90	46	44	57	21	9	3	3	0	0	1	1	0	7	44	46

Rank among batters: 573 • *Top target (3 home runs)*: Sid Fernandez, Randy Johnson • *Number of pitchers victimized*: 74 • *Total ballparks homered in*: 27 • *First HR*: 04/26/1986 off Larry McWilliams

Cleo James

CLEO JOEL JAMES
B: 08/31/1940
BR

Year	Tm	Lg	Tot	H	A	0	1	2	3	2	3	4	LO	XN	IP	PH	RHP	LHP
1970	CHI	NL	3	3	0	2	1	0	0	0	0	0	0	0	0	0	3	0
1971	CHI	NL	2	1	1	1	1	0	0	0	0	0	0	0	0	0	1	1
Total			5	4	1	3	2	0	0	0	0	0	0	0	0	0	4	1

Rank among batters: 3,191 • *Total ballparks homered in*: 2 • *First HR*: 05/28/1970 off Bruce Dal Canton

Dion James

DION JAMES
B: 11/09/1962
BL

Year	Tm	Lg	Tot	H	A	0	1	2	3	2	3	4	LO	XN	IP	PH	RHP	LHP
1984	MIL	AL	1	1	0	0	1	0	0	0	0	0	0	0	0	0	1	0
1987	ATL	NL	10	5	5	6	1	2	1	0	0	0	4	0	0	0	9	1
1988	ATL	NL	3	1	2	3	0	0	0	0	0	0	0	0	0	1	3	0
1989	ATL	NL	1	0	1	1	0	0	0	0	0	0	0	0	0	0	1	0
	CLE	AL	4	1	3	1	3	0	0	0	0	0	0	0	0	0	4	0
	Total		5	1	4	2	3	0	0	0	0	0	0	0	0	0	5	0
1990	CLE	AL	1	0	1	0	1	0	0	0	0	0	0	0	0	0	1	0
1992	NY	AL	3	2	1	1	1	1	0	0	0	0	0	0	0	1	2	1
1993	NY	AL	7	5	2	7	0	0	0	0	0	0	1	0	0	0	7	0
1995	NY	AL	2	1	1	1	1	0	0	0	0	0	0	0	0	0	2	0
Total			32	16	16	20	8	3	1	0	0	0	5	0	0	2	30	2

Rank among batters: 1,360 • *Top target (2 home runs)*: Jaime Navarro, Kevin Tapani, Danny Darwin • *Number of pitchers victimized*: 29 • *Total ballparks homered in*: 15 • *First HR*: 08/22/1984 off Ken Schrom

Charlie Jamieson

CHARLES DEVINE JAMIESON
B: 02/07/1893 D: 10/27/1969
BL

Year	Tm	Lg	Tot	H	A	0	1	2	3	2	3	4	LO	XN	IP	PH	RHP	LHP
1920	CLE	AL	1	0	1	0	0	1	0	0	0	0	0	0	0	0	1	0
1921	CLE	AL	1	0	1	0	0	1	0	0	0	0	0	0	1	0	0	1
1922	CLE	AL	3	1	2	2	1	0	0	0	0	0	0	0	0	0	3	0

Year	Tm	Lg	Tot	H	A	Men-On 0	1	2	3	One-Game 2	3	4	LO	XN	IP	PH	RHP	LHP

Charlie Jamieson *continued*

Year	Tm	Lg	Tot	H	A	0	1	2	3	2	3	4	LO	XN	IP	PH	RHP	LHP
1923	CLE	AL	2	1	1	1	0	1	0	0	0	0	0	1	0	0	2	0
1924	CLE	AL	3	1	2	3	0	0	0	0	0	0	1	0	2	0	1	2
1925	CLE	AL	4	1	3	3	0	1	0	0	0	0	1	1	0	0	4	0
1926	CLE	AL	2	0	2	0	1	1	0	0	0	0	0	0	1	0	1	1
1928	CLE	AL	1	1	0	0	1	0	0	0	0	0	0	0	1	0	0	1
1930	CLE	AL	1	0	1	0	0	1	0	0	0	0	0	0	0	0	1	0
Total			18	5	13	9	3	6	0	0	0	0	2	2	5	0	13	5

Rank among batters: 1,914 • *Top target (2 home runs)*: Joe Bush, Bob Shawkey • *Number of pitchers victimized*: 16 • *Total ballparks homered in*: 7 • *First HR*: 09/27/1920 off Joe DeBerry

Vic Janowicz

VICTOR FELIX JANOWICZ
B: 02/26/1930
BR

Year	Tm	Lg	Tot	H	A	0	1	2	3	2	3	4	LO	XN	IP	PH	RHP	LHP
1953	PIT	NL	2	1	1	1	1	0	0	0	0	0	0	0	0	0	1	1

Rank among batters: 4,129 • *Total ballparks homered in*: 2 • *First HR*: 08/16/1953 off Preacher Roe

Larry Jansen

LAWRENCE JOSEPH JANSEN
B: 07/16/1920
BR

Year	Tm	Lg	Tot	H	A	0	1	2	3	2	3	4	LO	XN	IP	PH	RHP	LHP
1950	NY	NL	1	1	0	1	0	0	0	0	0	0	0	0	0	0	0	1

Rank among batters: 4,707 • *Total ballparks homered in*: 1 • *First HR*: 07/28/1950 off Al Brazle

Heinie Jantzen

WALTER C. JANTZEN
B: 04/09/1890 D: 04/01/1948
BR

Year	Tm	Lg	Tot	H	A	0	1	2	3	2	3	4	LO	XN	IP	PH	RHP	LHP
1912	STL	AL	1	0	1	0	0	1	0	0	0	0	0	0	1	0	0	1

Rank among batters: 4,707 • *Total ballparks homered in*: 1 • *First HR*: 07/10/1912 off Ray Collins

Hal Janvrin

HAROLD CHANDLER JANVRIN
B: 08/27/1892 D: 03/01/1962
BR

Year	Tm	Lg	Tot	H	A	0	1	2	3	2	3	4	LO	XN	IP	PH	RHP	LHP
1913	BOS	AL	3	0	3	1	2	0	0	1	0	0	0	0	2	0	3	0
1914	BOS	AL	1	0	1	1	0	0	0	0	0	0	0	0	1	0	1	0
1919	WAS	AL	1	0	1	0	1	0	0	0	0	0	0	0	1	0	0	1
1920	STL	NL	1	0	1	1	0	0	0	0	0	0	0	0	0	0	0	1
Total			6	0	6	3	3	0	0	1	0	0	0	0	4	0	4	2

Rank among batters: 2,988 • *Total ballparks homered in*: 4 • *First HR*: 05/18/1913 off Roy Mitchell

Roy Jarvis

LEROY GILBERT JARVIS
B: 06/27/1926 D: 01/13/1990
BR

Year	Tm	Lg	Tot	H	A	0	1	2	3	2	3	4	LO	XN	IP	PH	RHP	LHP
1947	PIT	NL	1	1	0	1	0	0	0	0	0	0	0	0	0	0	1	0

Rank among batters: 4,707 • *Total ballparks homered in*: 1 • *First HR*: 04/18/1947 off Clayton Lambert

Hi Jasper

HENRY W. JASPER
B: 11/15/1880 D: 05/22/1937
BR

Year	Tm	Lg	Tot	H	A	0	1	2	3	2	3	4	LO	XN	IP	PH	RHP	LHP
1916	STL	NL	1	1	0	1	0	0	0	0	0	0	0	0	1	0	0	1

Rank among batters: 4,707 • *Total ballparks homered in*: 1 • *First HR*: 05/05/1916 off Clarence Mitchell

Larry Jaster

LARRY EDWARD JASTER
B: 01/13/1944
BL

Year	Tm	Lg	Tot	H	A	0	1	2	3	2	3	4	LO	XN	IP	PH	RHP	LHP
1966	STL	NL	1	0	1	1	0	0	0	0	0	0	0	0	0	0	1	0

Larry Jaster *continued*

Year	Tm	Lg	Tot	H	A	Men-On 0	Men-On 1	Men-On 2	Men-On 3	One-Game 2	One-Game 3	One-Game 4	LO	XN	IP	PH	RHP	LHP
1968	STL	NL	1	0	1	1	0	0	0	0	0	0	0	0	0	0	1	0
Total			2	0	2	2	0	0	0	0	0	0	0	0	0	0	2	0

Rank among batters: 4,129 • *Total ballparks homered in*: 2 • *First HR*: 09/23/1966 off Larry Jackson

Julian Javier

MANUEL JULIAN (LIRANZO) JAVIER
B: 08/09/1936
BR

Year	Tm	Lg	Tot	H	A	Men-On 0	Men-On 1	Men-On 2	Men-On 3	One-Game 2	One-Game 3	One-Game 4	LO	XN	IP	PH	RHP	LHP
1960	STL	NL	4	0	4	4	0	0	0	0	0	0	1	0	0	0	3	1
1961	STL	NL	2	0	2	1	0	0	1	0	0	0	0	0	0	0	1	1
1962	STL	NL	7	1	6	5	2	0	0	0	0	0	1	0	0	0	5	2
1963	STL	NL	9	5	4	5	4	0	0	0	0	0	0	0	0	0	7	2
1964	STL	NL	12	3	9	3	5	3	1	1	0	0	0	0	0	0	4	8
1965	STL	NL	2	2	0	1	1	0	0	0	0	0	0	0	0	0	1	1
1966	STL	NL	7	1	6	5	2	0	0	1	0	0	0	0	0	0	5	2
1967	STL	NL	14	5	9	6	5	3	0	0	0	0	0	1	1	0	9	5
1968	STL	NL	4	1	3	4	0	0	0	0	0	0	0	1	0	0	3	1
1969	STL	NL	10	8	2	7	3	0	0	0	0	0	1	0	0	0	7	3
1970	STL	NL	2	0	2	2	0	0	0	0	0	0	0	0	0	0	1	1
1971	STL	NL	3	1	2	3	0	0	0	0	0	0	0	0	0	0	0	3
1972	CIN	NL	2	0	2	0	1	1	0	0	0	0	0	0	0	0	0	2
Total			78	27	51	46	23	7	2	2	0	0	3	2	1	0	46	32

Rank among batters: 672 • *Top target (4 home runs)*: Denny Lemaster • *Number of pitchers victimized*: 64 • *Total ballparks homered in*: 16 • *First HR*: 05/30/1960 off Clem Labine • *World Series HR*—1

Stan Javier

STANLEY JULIAN ANTONIO (DEJAVIER) JAVIER
B: 01/09/1964
BB

Year	Tm	Lg	Tot	H	A	Men-On 0	Men-On 1	Men-On 2	Men-On 3	One-Game 2	One-Game 3	One-Game 4	LO	XN	IP	PH	RHP	LHP
1987	OAK	AL	2	1	1	1	0	1	0	0	0	0	0	0	0	0	1	1
1988	OAK	AL	2	0	2	2	0	0	0	0	0	0	0	1	0	0	1	1
1989	OAK	AL	1	1	0	0	1	0	0	0	0	0	0	0	0	0	0	1
1990	LA	NL	3	1	2	3	0	0	0	0	0	0	0	0	0	0	2	1
1991	LA	NL	1	0	1	1	0	0	0	0	0	0	0	0	0	0	1	0
1992	LA	NL	1	1	0	0	0	1	0	0	0	0	0	0	0	1	1	0
1993	CAL	AL	3	0	3	2	1	0	0	0	0	0	0	0	0	0	2	1
1994	OAK	AL	10	1	9	4	6	0	0	1	0	0	0	0	0	0	7	3
1995	OAK	AL	8	3	5	6	1	1	0	0	0	0	0	0	0	0	5	3
Total			31	8	23	19	9	3	0	1	0	0	0	1	0	1	20	11

Rank among batters: 1,400 • *Top target (2 home runs)*: Brian Anderson • *Number of pitchers victimized*: 30 • *Total ballparks homered in*: 15 • *First HR*: 04/22/1987 off Mike Witt

Joey Jay

JOSEPH RICHARD JAY
B: 08/15/1935
BB

Year	Tm	Lg	Tot	H	A	Men-On 0	Men-On 1	Men-On 2	Men-On 3	One-Game 2	One-Game 3	One-Game 4	LO	XN	IP	PH	RHP	LHP
1962	CIN	NL	2	1	1	0	1	1	0	0	0	0	0	0	0	0	2	0

Rank among batters: 4,129 • *Total ballparks homered in*: 2 • *First HR*: 05/01/1962 off Sherman Jones

Tex Jeanes

ERNEST LEE JEANES
B: 12/19/1900 D: 04/05/1973
BR

Year	Tm	Lg	Tot	H	A	Men-On 0	Men-On 1	Men-On 2	Men-On 3	One-Game 2	One-Game 3	One-Game 4	LO	XN	IP	PH	RHP	LHP
1925	WAS	AL	1	1	0	0	0	1	0	0	0	0	0	0	1	0	0	1

Rank among batters: 4,707 • *Total ballparks homered in*: 1 • *First HR*: 09/12/1925 off Buster Ross

Hal Jeffcoat

HAROLD BENTLEY JEFFCOAT
B: 09/06/1924
BR

Year	Tm	Lg	Tot	H	A	Men-On 0	Men-On 1	Men-On 2	Men-On 3	One-Game 2	One-Game 3	One-Game 4	LO	XN	IP	PH	RHP	LHP
1948	CHI	NL	4	3	1	2	2	0	0	0	0	0	0	0	0	1	4	0
1949	CHI	NL	2	2	0	2	0	0	0	0	0	0	1	0	0	0	1	1
1950	CHI	NL	2	0	2	2	0	0	0	0	0	0	0	0	0	0	1	1

Year	Tm	Lg	Tot	H	A	Men-On 0	1	2	3	One-Game 2	3	4	LO	XN	IP	PH	RHP	LHP

Hal Jeffcoat *continued*

Year	Tm	Lg	Tot	H	A	0	1	2	3	2	3	4	LO	XN	IP	PH	RHP	LHP
1951	CHI	NL	4	2	2	2	2	0	0	0	0	0	0	0	0	1	4	0
1952	CHI	NL	4	2	2	2	1	1	0	0	0	0	0	0	0	0	3	1
1953	CHI	NL	4	1	3	2	0	2	0	1	0	0	0	0	0	0	4	0
1954	CHI	NL	1	1	0	0	1	0	0	0	0	0	0	0	0	0	1	0
1955	CHI	NL	1	0	1	1	0	0	0	0	0	0	0	0	0	0	1	0
1957	CIN	NL	4	4	0	3	1	0	0	0	0	0	0	0	0	0	3	1
Total			26	15	11	16	7	3	0	1	0	0	1	0	0	2	22	4

Rank among batters: 1,576 • *Top target (2 home runs)*: Billy Loes • *Number of pitchers victimized*: 25 • *Total ballparks homered in*: 7 • *First HR*: 04/24/1948 off Al Papai

Gregg Jefferies

GREGORY SCOTT JEFFERIES
B: 08/01/1967
BB

Year	Tm	Lg	Tot	H	A	0	1	2	3	2	3	4	LO	XN	IP	PH	RHP	LHP
1988	NY	NL	6	3	3	4	2	0	0	0	0	0	0	0	0	0	2	4
1989	NY	NL	12	7	5	9	2	1	0	1	0	0	2	0	0	0	7	5
1990	NY	NL	15	9	6	11	4	0	0	0	0	0	2	0	0	0	10	5
1991	NY	NL	9	5	4	5	4	0	0	0	0	0	0	0	0	1	8	1
1992	KC	AL	10	3	7	7	1	1	1	0	0	0	2	0	0	0	7	3
1993	STL	NL	16	10	6	8	6	2	0	1	0	0	0	1	0	0	8	8
1994	STL	NL	12	7	5	5	5	2	0	2	0	0	0	0	0	0	10	2
1995	PHI	NL	11	4	7	7	4	0	0	0	0	0	0	0	0	0	7	4
Total			91	48	43	56	28	6	1	4	0	0	6	1	0	1	59	32

Rank among batters: 559 • *Top target (3 home runs)*: John Smiley, Tom Browning, Tom Glavine • *Number of pitchers victimized*: 77 • *Total ballparks homered in*: 21 • *First HR*: 08/29/1988 off Eric Show • *Hit for Cycle*—vs LA: 08/25/1995

Reggie Jefferson

REGINALD JIROD JEFFERSON
B: 09/25/1968
BB

Year	Tm	Lg	Tot	H	A	0	1	2	3	2	3	4	LO	XN	IP	PH	RHP	LHP
1991	CIN	NL	1	1	0	1	0	0	0	0	0	0	0	0	0	0	1	0
	CLE	AL	2	1	1	0	1	0	0	1	0	0	0	0	0	0	2	0
	Total		3	2	1	2	0	0	1	0	0	0	0	0	0	0	3	0
1992	CLE	AL	1	1	0	1	0	0	0	0	0	0	0	0	0	0	0	1
1993	CLE	AL	10	4	6	6	3	1	0	0	0	0	0	0	0	1	9	1
1994	SEA	AL	8	4	4	4	3	1	0	1	0	0	0	0	0	0	8	0
1995	BOS	AL	5	1	4	0	4	0	1	0	0	0	0	0	0	0	5	0
Total			27	12	15	13	10	2	2	1	0	0	0	0	0	1	25	2

Rank among batters: 1,532 • *Top target (2 home runs)*: Bill Wegman, Roger Pavlik, Russell Springer • *Number of pitchers victimized*: 24 • *Total ballparks homered in*: 11 • *First HR*: 05/19/1991 off Andy Benes

Stan Jefferson

STANLEY JEFFERSON
B: 12/04/1962
BB

Year	Tm	Lg	Tot	H	A	0	1	2	3	2	3	4	LO	XN	IP	PH	RHP	LHP
1986	NY	NL	1	1	0	0	0	1	0	0	0	0	0	0	0	0	1	0
1987	SD	NL	8	5	3	6	1	1	0	0	0	0	2	0	0	0	7	1
1988	SD	NL	1	1	0	1	0	0	0	0	0	0	0	0	0	0	1	0
1989	BAL	AL	4	3	1	3	0	1	0	0	0	0	0	0	0	0	3	1
1990	CLE	AL	2	1	1	1	1	0	0	0	0	0	0	0	0	0	2	0
Total			16	11	5	11	2	3	0	0	0	0	2	0	0	0	14	2

Rank among batters: 2,029 • *Top target (2 home runs)*: Rick Mahler • *Number of pitchers victimized*: 15 • *Total ballparks homered in*: 8 • *First HR*: 09/20/1986 off Tom Hume

Irv Jeffries

IRVINE FRANKLIN JEFFRIES
B: 09/10/1905 D: 06/08/1982
BR

Year	Tm	Lg	Tot	H	A	0	1	2	3	2	3	4	LO	XN	IP	PH	RHP	LHP
1930	CHI	AL	2	1	1	1	1	0	0	0	0	0	0	0	0	0	2	0
1931	CHI	AL	2	2	0	2	0	0	0	0	0	0	0	0	0	0	2	0
1934	PHI	NL	4	0	4	3	1	0	0	1	0	0	0	0	0	0	2	2
Total			8	3	5	6	2	0	0	1	0	0	0	0	0	0	6	2

Rank among batters: 2,703 • *Total ballparks homered in*: 3 • *First HR*: 06/12/1930 off Myles Thomas

Chris Jelic

CHRISTOPHER JOHN JELIC
B: 12/16/1963
BR

Year	Tm	Lg	Tot	H	A	Men-On 0	Men-On 1	Men-On 2	Men-On 3	One-Game 2	One-Game 3	One-Game 4	LO	XN	IP	PH	RHP	LHP
1990	NY	NL	1	0	1	1	0	0	0	0	0	0	0	0	0	0	1	0

Rank among batters: 4,707 • *Total ballparks homered in*: 1 • *First HR*: 10/03/1990 off Doug Bair

Steve Jeltz

LARRY STEVEN JELTZ
B: 05/28/1959
BB

Year	Tm	Lg	Tot	H	A	Men-On 0	Men-On 1	Men-On 2	Men-On 3	One-Game 2	One-Game 3	One-Game 4	LO	XN	IP	PH	RHP	LHP
1984	PHI	NL	1	0	1	1	0	0	0	0	0	0	0	0	0	0	0	1
1989	PHI	NL	4	3	1	1	2	1	0	1	0	0	0	0	0	0	3	1
Total			5	3	2	2	2	1	0	1	0	0	0	0	0	0	3	2

Rank among batters: 3,191 • *Total ballparks homered in*: 3 • *First HR*: 09/23/1984 off John Tudor • *Switch hit HR in 1 game*—1 time

Ferguson Jenkins

FERGUSON ARTHUR JENKINS
B: 12/13/1943
BR HOF

Year	Tm	Lg	Tot	H	A	Men-On 0	Men-On 1	Men-On 2	Men-On 3	One-Game 2	One-Game 3	One-Game 4	LO	XN	IP	PH	RHP	LHP
1966	CHI	NL	1	1	0	1	0	0	0	0	0	0	0	0	0	0	1	0
1968	CHI	NL	1	0	1	1	0	0	0	0	0	0	0	0	0	0	1	0
1969	CHI	NL	1	0	1	1	0	0	0	0	0	0	0	0	0	0	1	0
1970	CHI	NL	3	1	2	1	2	0	0	0	0	0	0	0	0	0	3	0
1971	CHI	NL	6	6	0	3	3	0	0	1	0	0	0	0	0	0	4	2
1972	CHI	NL	1	1	0	1	0	0	0	0	0	0	0	0	0	0	1	0
Total			13	9	4	8	5	0	0	1	0	0	0	0	0	0	11	2

Rank among batters: 2,248 • *Total ballparks homered in*: 5 • *First HR*: 04/23/1966 off Don Sutton

Tom Jenkins

THOMAS GRIFFITH JENKINS
B: 04/10/1898 D: 05/03/1979
BL

Year	Tm	Lg	Tot	H	A	Men-On 0	Men-On 1	Men-On 2	Men-On 3	One-Game 2	One-Game 3	One-Game 4	LO	XN	IP	PH	RHP	LHP
1931	STL	AL	3	3	0	1	1	1	0	0	0	0	0	0	0	1	3	0

Rank among batters: 3,735 • *Total ballparks homered in*: 1 • *First HR*: 05/05/1931 off Mel Harder

Doug Jennings

JAMES DOUGLAS JENNINGS
B: 09/30/1964
BL

Year	Tm	Lg	Tot	H	A	Men-On 0	Men-On 1	Men-On 2	Men-On 3	One-Game 2	One-Game 3	One-Game 4	LO	XN	IP	PH	RHP	LHP
1988	OAK	AL	1	0	1	0	1	0	0	0	0	0	0	0	0	0	1	0
1990	OAK	AL	2	1	1	2	0	0	0	0	0	0	0	0	0	0	2	0
1993	CHI	NL	2	2	0	1	0	1	0	0	0	0	0	0	0	2	2	0
Total			5	3	2	3	1	1	0	0	0	0	0	0	0	2	5	0

Rank among batters: 3,191 • *Top target (2 home runs)*: Greg Harris • *Number of pitchers victimized*: 4 • *Total ballparks homered in*: 4 • *First HR*: 04/13/1988 off Ed Nunez

Hughie Jennings

HUGH AMBROSE JENNINGS
B: 04/02/1869 D: 02/01/1928
BR HOF

Year	Tm	Lg	Tot	H	A	Men-On 0	Men-On 1	Men-On 2	Men-On 3	One-Game 2	One-Game 3	One-Game 4	LO	XN	IP	PH	RHP	LHP
1891	LOU	AA	1	0	1	0	1	0	0	0	0	0	0	0	0	0	1	0
1892	LOU	NL	2	0	2	1	1	0	0	0	0	0	0	0	0	0	2	0
1893	BAL	NL	1	1	0	0	1	0	0	0	0	0	0	0	0	0	1	0
1894	BAL	NL	4	4	0	2	2	0	0	0	0	0	0	0	1	0	2	2
1895	BAL	NL	4	4	0	0	3	1	0	0	0	0	0	0	1	0	3	1
1897	BAL	NL	2	0	2	1	1	0	0	0	0	0	0	0	0	0	2	0
1898	BAL	NL	1	0	1	0	1	0	0	0	0	0	0	0	0	0	1	0
1900	BRO	NL	1	0	1	1	0	0	0	0	0	0	0	0	0	0	1	0
1901	PHI	NL	1	0	1	1	0	0	0	0	0	0	0	0	0	0	1	0
1902	PHI	NL	1	0	1	0	0	1	0	0	0	0	0	0	0	0	1	0
Total			18	9	9	6	10	2	0	0	0	0	0	0	2	0	15	3

Rank among batters: 1,914 • *Top target (3 home runs)*: Kid Nichols • *Number of pitchers victimized*: 15 • *Total ballparks homered in*: 5 • *First HR*: 07/16/1891 off Darby O'Brien

Jackie Jensen

JACK EUGENE JENSEN
B: 03/09/1927 D: 07/14/1982
BR

Year	Tm	Lg	Tot	H	A	Men-On 0	1	2	3	One-Game 2	3	4	LO	XN	IP	PH	RHP	LHP
1950	NY	AL	1	0	1	1	0	0	0	0	0	0	0	0	0	0	0	1
1951	NY	AL	8	1	7	4	4	0	0	0	0	0	0	0	0	2	2	6
1952	WAS	AL	10	3	7	5	3	1	1	0	0	0	0	0	0	0	3	7
1953	WAS	AL	10	1	9	5	5	0	0	0	0	0	0	0	0	0	6	4
1954	BOS	AL	25	14	11	13	5	6	1	2	0	0	0	1	0	0	20	5
1955	BOS	AL	26	17	9	13	9	2	2	2	0	0	0	1	0	0	18	8
1956	BOS	AL	20	7	13	12	6	2	0	0	0	0	0	0	0	0	15	5
1957	BOS	AL	23	10	13	10	11	1	1	0	0	0	0	1	0	0	18	5
1958	BOS	AL	35	17	18	13	14	6	2	2	0	0	0	1	0	0	28	7
1959	BOS	AL	28	12	16	14	8	5	1	1	0	0	0	2	0	0	20	8
1961	BOS	AL	13	9	4	7	2	4	0	1	0	0	0	2	0	0	6	7
Total			199	91	108	97	67	27	8	8	0	0	0	8	0	2	136	63

Rank among batters: 187 • *Top target (8 home runs)*: Pedro Ramos • *Number of pitchers victimized*: 106 • *Total ballparks homered in*: 11 • *First HR*: 09/11/1950 off Al Sima

Woody Jensen

FORREST DOCENUS JENSEN
B: 08/11/1907
BL

Year	Tm	Lg	Tot	H	A	Men-On 0	1	2	3	One-Game 2	3	4	LO	XN	IP	PH	RHP	LHP
1931	PIT	NL	3	3	0	1	2	0	0	0	0	0	0	0	2	0	2	1
1935	PIT	NL	8	5	3	5	3	0	0	0	0	0	0	0	0	0	6	2
1936	PIT	NL	10	4	6	6	1	3	0	0	0	0	0	0	0	0	9	1
1937	PIT	NL	5	2	3	3	2	0	0	1	0	0	0	0	0	0	3	2
Total			26	14	12	15	8	3	0	1	0	0	0	0	2	0	20	6

Rank among batters: 1,576 • *Top target (3 home runs)*: Dizzy Dean • *Number of pitchers victimized*: 23 • *Total ballparks homered in*: 5 • *First HR*: 09/07/1931 off Ownie Carroll

Garry Jestadt

GARRY ARTHUR JESTADT
B: 03/19/1947
BR

Year	Tm	Lg	Tot	H	A	Men-On 0	1	2	3	One-Game 2	3	4	LO	XN	IP	PH	RHP	LHP
1972	SD	NL	6	3	3	4	2	0	0	0	0	0	0	0	0	1	6	0

Rank among batters: 2,988 • *Total ballparks homered in*: 4 • *First HR*: 05/14/1972 off Mike Torrez

Johnny Jeter

JOHN JETER
B: 10/24/1944
BR

Year	Tm	Lg	Tot	H	A	Men-On 0	1	2	3	One-Game 2	3	4	LO	XN	IP	PH	RHP	LHP
1969	PIT	NL	1	0	1	0	1	0	0	0	0	0	0	0	0	0	1	0
1970	PIT	NL	2	0	2	1	0	1	0	0	0	0	0	0	0	0	2	0
1971	SD	NL	1	0	1	1	0	0	0	0	0	0	0	0	0	0	1	0
1972	SD	NL	7	2	5	2	4	1	0	1	0	0	0	0	0	0	6	1
1973	CHI	AL	7	3	4	7	0	0	0	0	0	0	2	0	0	0	2	5
Total			18	5	13	11	5	2	0	1	0	0	2	0	0	0	12	6

Rank among batters: 1,914 • *Total ballparks homered in*: 14 • *First HR*: 09/15/1969 off Jeff James

Sam Jethroe

SAMUEL JETHROE
B: 01/20/1918
BB

Year	Tm	Lg	Tot	H	A	Men-On 0	1	2	3	One-Game 2	3	4	LO	XN	IP	PH	RHP	LHP
1950	BOS	NL	18	8	10	10	6	2	0	0	0	0	1	0	0	0	11	7
1951	BOS	NL	18	12	6	10	6	2	0	1	0	0	2	0	0	0	13	5
1952	BOS	NL	13	5	8	6	5	1	1	1	0	0	2	0	0	0	7	6
Total			49	25	24	26	17	5	1	2	0	0	5	0	0	0	31	18

Rank among batters: 1,008 • *Top target (3 home runs)*: Frank Hiller, Preacher Roe, Dave Koslo • *Number of pitchers victimized*: 35 • *Total ballparks homered in*: 8 • *First HR*: 04/18/1950 off Kirby Higbe

Manny Jimenez

MANUEL EMILIO (RIVERA) JIMENEZ
B: 11/19/1938
BL

Year	Tm	Lg	Tot	H	A	Men-On 0	1	2	3	One-Game 2	3	4	LO	XN	IP	PH	RHP	LHP
1962	KC	AL	11	3	8	7	3	1	0	1	0	0	0	0	0	0	7	4

Manny Jimenez *continued*

Year	Tm	Lg	Tot	H	A	Men-On 0	Men-On 1	Men-On 2	Men-On 3	One-Game 2	One-Game 3	One-Game 4	LO	XN	IP	PH	RHP	LHP
1964	KC	AL	12	5	7	5	3	3	1	1	1	0	0	0	0	2	11	1
1967	PIT	NL	2	1	1	2	0	0	0	0	0	0	0	0	0	1	2	0
1968	PIT	NL	1	1	0	0	1	0	0	0	0	0	0	0	0	1	1	0
Total			26	10	16	14	7	4	1	2	1	0	0	0	0	4	21	5

Rank among batters: 1,576 • *Top target (3 home runs)*: Robin Roberts • *Number of pitchers victimized*: 21 • *Total ballparks homered in*: 10 • *First HR*: 04/26/1962 off Sam Jones

Tommy John

THOMAS EDWARD JOHN
B: 05/22/1943
BR

Year	Tm	Lg	Tot	H	A	Men-On 0	Men-On 1	Men-On 2	Men-On 3	One-Game 2	One-Game 3	One-Game 4	LO	XN	IP	PH	RHP	LHP
1965	CHI	AL	1	0	1	1	0	0	0	0	0	0	0	0	0	0	1	0
1966	CHI	AL	2	0	2	2	0	0	0	0	0	0	0	0	0	0	2	0
1968	CHI	AL	1	1	0	0	0	1	0	0	0	0	0	0	0	0	1	0
1977	LA	NL	1	1	0	1	0	0	0	0	0	0	0	0	0	0	1	0
Total			5	2	3	4	0	1	0	0	0	0	0	0	0	0	5	0

Rank among batters: 3,191 • *Total ballparks homered in*: 5 • *First HR*: 09/25/1965 off Bill Stafford

Alex Johnson

ALEXANDER JOHNSON
B: 12/07/1942
BR

Year	Tm	Lg	Tot	H	A	Men-On 0	Men-On 1	Men-On 2	Men-On 3	One-Game 2	One-Game 3	One-Game 4	LO	XN	IP	PH	RHP	LHP
1964	PHI	NL	4	3	1	0	4	0	0	0	0	0	0	0	0	1	0	4
1965	PHI	NL	8	3	5	5	2	1	0	0	0	0	0	0	0	1	3	5
1966	STL	NL	2	0	2	1	1	0	0	0	0	0	0	0	0	0	1	1
1967	STL	NL	1	1	0	1	0	0	0	0	0	0	0	0	0	0	0	1
1968	CIN	NL	2	1	1	2	0	0	0	0	0	0	0	0	1	0	2	0
1969	CIN	NL	17	9	8	9	6	2	0	1	0	0	0	0	1	0	13	4
1970	CAL	AL	14	3	11	9	3	2	0	1	0	0	0	0	0	0	11	3
1971	CAL	AL	2	0	2	1	1	0	0	0	0	0	0	0	0	0	1	1
1972	CLE	AL	8	7	1	4	2	2	0	0	0	0	0	0	0	0	6	2
1973	TEX	AL	8	2	6	7	1	0	0	0	0	0	0	1	0	1	3	5
1974	TEX	AL	4	3	1	2	2	0	0	0	0	0	0	0	0	0	2	2
	NY	AL	1	0	1	1	0	0	0	0	0	0	0	1	0	0	1	0
	Total		5	3	2	3	2	0	0	0	0	0	0	1	0	0	3	2
1975	NY	AL	1	0	1	1	0	0	0	0	0	0	0	0	0	0	0	1
1976	DET	AL	6	4	2	4	0	2	0	0	0	0	0	0	0	0	2	4
Total			78	36	42	47	22	9	0	2	0	0	0	2	2	3	45	33

Rank among batters: 672 • Top target (2 home runs): Bobby Bolin, Bill Stoneman, Grant Jackson, Bill Hands, Wally Bunker, Joe Niekro, Mickey Lolich, Vic Albury, Ken Holtzman, Bill Lee • *Number of pitchers victimized*: 68 • *Total ballparks homered in*: 21 • *First HR*: 08/09/1964 off Willard Hunter

Bill Johnson

WILLIAM F. JOHNSON
B: 09/ /1862 D: 07/17/1942
BL

Year	Tm	Lg	Tot	H	A	Men-On 0	Men-On 1	Men-On 2	Men-On 3	One-Game 2	One-Game 3	One-Game 4	LO	XN	IP	PH	RHP	LHP
1891	BAL	AA	2	2	0	1	0	1	0	0	0	0	0	0	1	0	2	0

Rank among batters: 4,129 • *Total ballparks homered in*: 2 • *First HR*: 04/29/1891 off Gil Hatfield

Bill Johnson

WILLIAM LAWRENCE JOHNSON
B: 10/18/1892 D: 11/03/1950
BL

Year	Tm	Lg	Tot	H	A	Men-On 0	Men-On 1	Men-On 2	Men-On 3	One-Game 2	One-Game 3	One-Game 4	LO	XN	IP	PH	RHP	LHP
1917	PHI	AL	1	1	0	0	0	1	0	0	0	0	0	0	1	0	1	0

Rank among batters: 4,707 • *Total ballparks homered in*: 1 • *First HR*: 06/30/1917 off Doc Ayers

Billy Johnson

WILLIAM RUSSELL JOHNSON
B: 08/30/1918
BR

Year	Tm	Lg	Tot	H	A	Men-On 0	Men-On 1	Men-On 2	Men-On 3	One-Game 2	One-Game 3	One-Game 4	LO	XN	IP	PH	RHP	LHP
1943	NY	AL	5	3	2	2	1	2	0	0	0	0	0	0	0	0	4	1
1946	NY	AL	4	1	3	3	1	0	0	0	0	0	0	0	0	0	3	1
1947	NY	AL	10	4	6	4	3	3	0	0	0	0	0	0	0	0	8	2
1948	NY	AL	12	6	6	6	3	2	1	1	0	0	0	0	0	1	6	6
1949	NY	AL	8	3	5	6	1	1	0	0	0	0	0	0	0	1	2	6

Year	Tm	Lg	Tot	H	A	Men-On 0	1	2	3	One-Game 2	3	4	LO	XN	IP	PH	RHP	LHP

Billy Johnson *continued*

Year	Tm	Lg	Tot	H	A	0	1	2	3	2	3	4	LO	XN	IP	PH	RHP	LHP
1950	NY	AL	6	4	2	4	1	0	1	1	0	0	0	0	0	0	2	4
1951	STL	NL	14	6	8	8	4	2	0	1	0	0	0	0	0	0	6	8
1952	STL	NL	2	1	1	0	1	0	1	0	0	0	0	0	0	0	1	1
Total			61	28	33	33	15	10	3	3	0	0	0	0	0	2	32	29

Rank among batters: 844 • *Top target (2 home runs)*: Early Wynn, Don Black, Joe Haynes, Bill Kennedy, Milton Haefner, Hal Newhouser, Al Sima, Alex Kellner, Jocko Thompson, Don Carlsen, Dave Koslo • *Number of pitchers victimized*: 50 • *Total ballparks homered in*: 13 • *First HR*: 05/07/1943 off Don Black

Bob Johnson

ROBERT LEE JOHNSON
B: 11/26/1906 D: 07/06/1982
BR

Year	Tm	Lg	Tot	H	A	0	1	2	3	2	3	4	LO	XN	IP	PH	RHP	LHP
1933	PHI	AL	21	10	11	14	5	2	0	1	0	0	0	0	0	0	19	2
1934	PHI	AL	34	22	12	23	10	1	0	3	0	0	0	0	1	1	30	4
1935	PHI	AL	28	16	12	15	8	3	2	2	0	0	0	0	0	0	25	3
1936	PHI	AL	25	16	9	12	10	2	1	1	0	0	0	0	0	0	21	4
1937	PHI	AL	25	14	11	9	11	4	1	1	0	0	0	0	1	0	21	4
1938	PHI	AL	30	21	9	15	9	3	3	5	0	0	0	0	0	0	26	4
1939	PHI	AL	23	13	10	10	8	5	0	1	0	0	0	0	0	0	19	4
1940	PHI	AL	31	15	16	14	12	5	0	3	0	0	0	0	0	0	23	8
1941	PHI	AL	22	10	12	5	8	8	1	1	0	0	0	1	0	0	19	3
1942	PHI	AL	13	8	5	7	2	4	0	0	0	0	0	0	0	0	12	1
1943	WAS	AL	7	2	5	2	5	0	0	0	0	0	0	0	0	0	6	1
1944	BOS	AL	17	14	3	12	4	1	0	0	0	0	0	0	0	0	16	1
1945	BOS	AL	12	7	5	8	3	1	0	0	0	0	0	0	0	0	10	2
Total			288	168	120	146	95	39	8	18	0	0	0	1	2	1	247	41

Rank among batters: 77 • *Top target (8 home runs)*: Schoolboy Rowe, Elden Auker • *Number of pitchers victimized*: 139 • *Total ballparks homered in*: 9 • *First HR*: 04/16/1933 off Don Brennan • *Hit for Cycle*—vs DET: 07/06/1944

Bobby Johnson

ROBERT WALLACE JOHNSON
B: 03/04/1936
BR

Year	Tm	Lg	Tot	H	A	0	1	2	3	2	3	4	LO	XN	IP	PH	RHP	LHP
1960	KC	AL	1	0	1	1	0	0	0	0	0	0	0	0	0	0	1	0
1961	WAS	AL	6	1	5	2	2	2	0	0	0	0	0	0	0	0	4	2
1962	WAS	AL	12	8	4	7	5	0	0	0	0	0	0	0	0	0	8	4
1963	BAL	AL	8	3	5	4	3	1	0	0	0	0	0	0	0	0	5	3
1964	BAL	AL	3	2	1	3	0	0	0	0	0	0	0	0	0	0	1	2
1965	BAL	AL	5	3	2	2	3	0	0	0	0	0	0	0	0	0	1	4
1966	BAL	AL	1	0	1	0	1	0	0	0	0	0	0	0	0	0	1	0
1967	NY	NL	5	2	3	4	1	0	0	0	0	0	0	1	0	0	4	1
1969	STL	NL	1	0	1	1	0	0	0	0	0	0	0	0	0	1	1	0
	OAK	AL	1	1	0	1	0	0	0	0	0	0	0	0	0	0	0	1
	Total		2	1	1	2	0	0	0	0	0	0	0	0	0	1	1	1
1970	OAK	AL	1	1	0	1	0	0	0	0	0	0	0	0	0	0	0	1
Total			44	21	23	26	15	3	0	0	0	0	0	1	0	1	26	18

Rank among batters: 1,095 • *Top target (3 home runs)*: Ted Bowsfield • *Number of pitchers victimized*: 38 • *Total ballparks homered in*: 16 • *First HR*: 09/25/1960 off Frank Lary

Bobby Johnson

BOBBY EARL JOHNSON
B: 07/31/1959
BR

Year	Tm	Lg	Tot	H	A	0	1	2	3	2	3	4	LO	XN	IP	PH	RHP	LHP
1981	TEX	AL	2	2	0	2	0	0	0	0	0	0	0	0	0	0	0	2
1982	TEX	AL	2	1	1	2	0	0	0	0	0	0	0	0	0	0	2	0
1983	TEX	AL	5	2	3	2	2	1	0	0	0	0	0	1	0	0	1	4
Total			9	5	4	6	2	1	0	0	0	0	0	1	0	0	3	6

Rank among batters: 2,587 • *Top target (2 home runs)*: Geoff Zahn • *Number of pitchers victimized*: 8 • *Total ballparks homered in*: 5 • *First HR*: 10/02/1981 off Geoff Zahn

Brian Johnson

BRIAN DAVID JOHNSON
B: 01/08/1968
BR

Year	Tm	Lg	Tot	H	A	0	1	2	3	2	3	4	LO	XN	IP	PH	RHP	LHP
1994	SD	NL	3	3	0	2	0	0	1	0	0	0	0	0	0	1	2	1

Year	Tm	Lg	Tot	H	A	Men-On 0	Men-On 1	Men-On 2	Men-On 3	One-Game 2	One-Game 3	One-Game 4	LO	XN	IP	PH	RHP	LHP

Brian Johnson *continued*

Year	Tm	Lg	Tot	H	A	Men-On 0	Men-On 1	Men-On 2	Men-On 3	One-Game 2	One-Game 3	One-Game 4	LO	XN	IP	PH	RHP	LHP
1995	SD	NL	3	1	2	0	1	1	1	0	0	0	0	0	0	1	2	1
Total			6	4	2	2	1	1	2	0	0	0	0	0	0	2	4	2

Rank among batters: 2,988 • *Total ballparks homered in*: 3 • *First HR*: 06/18/1994 off Shane Reynolds

Charles Johnson

CHARLES EDWARD JOHNSON
B: 07/20/1971
BR

Year	Tm	Lg	Tot	H	A	Men-On 0	Men-On 1	Men-On 2	Men-On 3	One-Game 2	One-Game 3	One-Game 4	LO	XN	IP	PH	RHP	LHP
1994	FLO	NL	1	1	0	1	0	0	0	0	0	0	0	0	0	0	1	0
1995	FLO	NL	11	3	8	7	4	0	0	0	0	0	0	0	0	0	8	3
Total			12	4	8	8	4	0	0	0	0	0	0	0	0	0	9	3

Rank among batters: 2,325 • *Total ballparks homered in*: 8 • *First HR*: 05/06/1994 off Curt Schilling

Chief Johnson

GEORGE HOWARD JOHNSON
B: 03/30/1886 D: 06/11/1922
BR

Year	Tm	Lg	Tot	H	A	Men-On 0	Men-On 1	Men-On 2	Men-On 3	One-Game 2	One-Game 3	One-Game 4	LO	XN	IP	PH	RHP	LHP
1913	CIN	NL	1	1	0	1	0	0	0	0	0	0	0	0	1	0	1	0
1914	KC	FL	1	1	0	1	0	0	0	0	0	0	0	0	0	0	1	0
1915	KC	FL	1	0	1	1	0	0	0	0	0	0	0	0	0	0	1	0
Total			3	2	1	3	0	0	0	0	0	0	0	0	1	0	3	0

Rank among batters: 3,735 • *Total ballparks homered in*: 3 • *First HR*: 08/04/1913 off Win Noyes

Cliff Johnson

CLIFFORD JOHNSON
B: 07/22/1947
BR

Year	Tm	Lg	Tot	H	A	Men-On 0	Men-On 1	Men-On 2	Men-On 3	One-Game 2	One-Game 3	One-Game 4	LO	XN	IP	PH	RHP	LHP
1973	HOU	NL	2	2	0	1	1	0	0	0	0	0	0	0	0	0	1	1
1974	HOU	NL	10	5	5	4	5	1	0	0	0	0	0	1	0	5	4	6
1975	HOU	NL	20	10	10	8	9	2	1	0	0	0	0	0	0	1	16	4
1976	HOU	NL	10	5	5	6	3	1	0	0	0	0	0	0	0	1	4	6
1977	HOU	NL	10	7	3	6	3	1	0	1	0	0	0	0	0	2	6	4
	NY	AL	12	3	9	6	4	1	1	1	1	0	0	0	0	1	3	9
	Total		22	10	12	12	7	2	1	2	1	0	0	0	0	3	9	13
1978	NY	AL	6	2	4	3	3	0	0	0	0	0	0	0	0	2	0	6
1979	NY	AL	2	1	1	1	1	0	0	0	0	0	0	0	0	0	0	2
	CLE	AL	18	10	8	8	4	5	1	2	0	0	0	0	0	1	10	8
	Total		20	11	9	9	5	5	1	2	0	0	0	0	0	1	10	10
1980	CLE	AL	2	0	2	1	0	1	0	0	0	0	0	0	0	2	1	1
	CHI	NL	1	1	0	0	0	0	1	0	0	0	0	1	0	0	1	0
	CLE	AL	4	4	0	3	1	0	0	0	0	0	0	1	0	0	4	0
	CHI	NL	9	5	4	3	3	2	1	0	0	0	0	0	0	1	6	3
	Total		16	10	6	7	4	3	2	0	0	0	0	2	0	3	12	4
1981	OAK	AL	17	11	6	9	7	1	0	0	0	0	0	1	0	1	7	10
1982	OAK	AL	7	4	3	4	2	1	0	0	0	0	0	0	0	0	1	6
1983	TOR	AL	22	10	12	13	7	2	0	1	0	0	0	1	0	1	8	14
1984	TOR	AL	16	3	13	10	5	1	0	2	0	0	0	0	0	1	10	6
1985	TEX	AL	12	8	4	6	2	4	0	0	0	0	0	0	0	0	11	1
	TOR	AL	1	1	0	1	0	0	0	0	0	0	0	0	0	0	0	1
	Total		13	9	4	7	2	4	0	0	0	0	0	0	0	0	11	2
1986	TOR	AL	15	11	4	7	6	2	0	0	0	0	0	1	0	1	7	8
Total			196	103	93	100	66	25	5	7	1	0	0	6	0	20	100	96

Rank among batters: 191 • *Top target (7 home runs)*: Jerry Garvin • *Number of pitchers victimized*: 148 • *Total ballparks homered in*: 26 • *First HR*: 09/19/1973 off Rich Troedson • *2 HR in 1 inning*—@TOR: 06/30/1977 • *LCS HR*—1

Darrell Johnson

DARRELL DEAN JOHNSON
B: 08/25/1928
BR

Year	Tm	Lg	Tot	H	A	Men-On 0	Men-On 1	Men-On 2	Men-On 3	One-Game 2	One-Game 3	One-Game 4	LO	XN	IP	PH	RHP	LHP
1957	NY	AL	1	0	1	0	0	1	0	0	0	0	0	0	0	0	1	0
1961	CIN	NL	1	0	1	1	0	0	0	0	0	0	0	0	0	0	0	1
Total			2	0	2	1	0	1	0	0	0	0	0	0	0	0	1	1

Rank among batters: 4,129 • *Total ballparks homered in*: 2 • *First HR*: 06/15/1957 off Virgil Trucks

Dave Johnson

DAVID ALLEN JOHNSON
B: 01/30/1943
BR

Year	Tm	Lg	Tot	H	A	Men-On 0	1	2	3	One-Game 2	3	4	LO	XN	IP	PH	RHP	LHP
1966	BAL	AL	7	3	4	4	1	2	0	1	0	0	0	1	0	0	4	3
1967	BAL	AL	10	3	7	9	1	0	0	0	0	0	0	0	0	0	5	5
1968	BAL	AL	9	3	6	5	2	1	1	0	0	0	0	1	0	0	5	4
1969	BAL	AL	7	2	5	3	4	0	0	0	0	0	0	0	0	0	6	1
1970	BAL	AL	10	5	5	4	4	2	0	0	0	0	0	0	0	0	10	0
1971	BAL	AL	18	8	10	10	6	2	0	1	0	0	0	0	1	0	13	5
1972	BAL	AL	5	4	1	3	2	0	0	0	0	0	0	0	0	0	3	2
1973	ATL	NL	43	26	17	24	11	6	2	3	0	0	0	2	0	1	26	17
1974	ATL	NL	15	7	8	9	4	2	0	1	0	0	0	0	0	0	9	6
1977	PHI	NL	8	3	5	5	3	0	0	1	0	0	0	0	0	1	3	5
1978	PHI	NL	2	2	0	0	0	0	2	0	0	0	0	0	0	2	0	2
	CHI	NL	2	2	0	1	1	0	0	0	0	0	0	0	0	1	1	1
	Total		4	4	0	1	1	0	2	0	0	0	0	0	0	3	1	3
Total			136	68	68	77	39	15	5	7	0	0	0	4	1	5	85	51

Rank among batters: 322 • *Top target (6 home runs)*: Denny McLain • *Number of pitchers victimized*: 101 • *Total ballparks homered in*: 23 • *First HR*: 04/26/1966 off Jim McGlothlin • *LCS HR*—2

Deron Johnson

DERON ROGER JOHNSON
B: 07/17/1938 D: 04/23/1992
BR

Year	Tm	Lg	Tot	H	A	Men-On 0	1	2	3	One-Game 2	3	4	LO	XN	IP	PH	RHP	LHP
1961	KC	AL	8	3	5	5	2	1	0	0	0	0	0	0	0	0	5	3
1964	CIN	NL	21	10	11	12	6	3	0	1	0	0	0	0	0	0	7	14
1965	CIN	NL	32	17	15	14	13	5	0	2	0	0	0	0	0	0	18	14
1966	CIN	NL	24	15	9	11	9	4	0	1	0	0	0	0	0	0	14	10
1967	CIN	NL	13	6	7	5	8	0	0	1	0	0	0	0	0	0	10	3
1968	ATL	NL	8	4	4	4	2	2	0	0	0	0	0	0	0	0	4	4
1969	PHI	NL	17	9	8	9	5	3	0	1	0	0	0	0	0	0	12	5
1970	PHI	NL	27	16	11	11	10	6	0	1	0	0	0	0	0	1	18	9
1971	PHI	NL	34	22	12	16	12	5	1	1	1	0	0	1	0	0	20	14
1972	PHI	NL	9	6	3	5	3	1	0	0	0	0	0	0	0	2	3	6
1973	PHI	NL	1	1	0	0	0	1	0	0	0	0	0	0	0	0	0	1
	OAK	AL	19	8	11	10	5	3	1	0	0	0	0	0	0	0	8	11
	Total		20	9	11	10	5	4	1	0	0	0	0	0	0	0	8	12
1974	OAK	AL	7	4	3	5	2	0	0	0	0	0	0	0	0	0	5	2
	MIL	AL	6	1	5	2	2	0	2	0	0	0	0	0	0	0	1	5
	Total		13	5	8	7	4	0	2	0	0	0	0	0	0	0	6	7
1975	CHI	AL	18	8	10	9	4	5	0	1	0	0	0	0	0	1	9	9
	BOS	AL	1	1	0	0	1	0	0	0	0	0	0	0	0	0	0	1
	Total		19	9	10	9	5	5	0	1	0	0	0	0	0	1	9	10
Total			245	131	114	118	84	39	4	9	1	0	0	1	0	4	134	111

Rank among batters: 117 • Top target (5 home runs): Bob Gibson, Bob Veale, Wade Blasingame, Jerry Koosman • *Number of pitchers victimized*: 155 • *Total ballparks homered in*: 29 • *First HR*: 06/30/1961 off Jack Kralick

Don Johnson

DONALD SPORE JOHNSON
B: 12/07/1911
BR

Year	Tm	Lg	Tot	H	A	Men-On 0	1	2	3	One-Game 2	3	4	LO	XN	IP	PH	RHP	LHP
1944	CHI	NL	2	2	0	2	0	0	0	0	0	0	0	0	0	0	2	0
1945	CHI	NL	2	2	0	2	0	0	0	0	0	0	0	0	0	0	1	1
1946	CHI	NL	1	1	0	0	1	0	0	0	0	0	0	0	0	0	0	1
1947	CHI	NL	3	2	1	3	0	0	0	0	0	0	0	0	0	0	2	1
Total			8	7	1	7	1	0	0	0	0	0	0	0	0	0	5	3

Rank among batters: 2,703 • *Total ballparks homered in*: 2 • *First HR*: 05/03/1944 off Tommy de la Cruz

Ernie Johnson

ERNEST RUDOLPH JOHNSON
B: 04/29/1888 D: 05/01/1952
BL

Year	Tm	Lg	Tot	H	A	Men-On 0	1	2	3	One-Game 2	3	4	LO	XN	IP	PH	RHP	LHP
1915	STL	FL	7	5	2	3	3	1	0	0	0	0	0	0	0	0	5	2
1917	STL	AL	2	2	0	1	1	0	0	0	0	0	0	0	0	0	2	0
1921	CHI	AL	1	0	1	1	0	0	0	0	0	0	0	0	0	0	1	0
1923	NY	AL	1	1	0	1	0	0	0	0	0	0	0	0	0	1	1	0

Ernie Johnson *continued*

Year	Tm	Lg	Tot	H	A	Men-On 0	1	2	3	One-Game 2	3	4	LO	XN	IP	PH	RHP	LHP
1924	NY	AL	3	2	1	1	2	0	0	1	0	0	0	0	1	0	3	0
1925	NY	AL	5	4	1	4	1	0	0	0	0	0	0	1	1	1	3	2
Total			19	14	5	11	7	1	0	1	0	0	0	1	2	2	15	4

Rank among batters: 1,861 • *Total ballparks homered in*: 5 • *First HR*: 05/31/1915 off Clint Rogge

Ernie Johnson

ERNEST THORWALD JOHNSON
B: 06/16/1924
BR

Year	Tm	Lg	Tot	H	A	Men-On 0	1	2	3	One-Game 2	3	4	LO	XN	IP	PH	RHP	LHP
1957	MIL	NL	1	0	1	0	0	1	0	0	0	0	0	0	0	0	1	0

Rank among batters: 4,707 • *Total ballparks homered in*: 1 • *First HR*: 06/05/1957 off Steve Ridzik

Frank Johnson

FRANK HERBERT JOHNSON
B: 07/22/1942
BR

Year	Tm	Lg	Tot	H	A	Men-On 0	1	2	3	One-Game 2	3	4	LO	XN	IP	PH	RHP	LHP
1968	SF	NL	1	1	0	1	0	0	0	0	0	0	0	0	0	0	1	0
1970	SF	NL	3	2	1	1	0	2	0	0	0	0	0	0	0	0	3	0
Total			4	3	1	2	0	2	0	0	0	0	0	0	0	0	4	0

Rank among batters: 3,427 • *Total ballparks homered in*: 2 • *First HR*: 05/14/1968 off Dave Giusti

Hank Johnson

HENRY WARD JOHNSON
B: 05/21/1906 D: 08/20/1982
BR

Year	Tm	Lg	Tot	H	A	Men-On 0	1	2	3	One-Game 2	3	4	LO	XN	IP	PH	RHP	LHP
1928	NY	AL	1	1	0	1	0	0	0	0	0	0	0	0	0	0	1	0
1930	NY	AL	1	1	0	0	0	1	0	0	0	0	0	0	0	0	1	0
Total			2	2	0	1	0	1	0	0	0	0	0	0	0	0	2	0

Rank among batters: 4,129 • *Total ballparks homered in*: 1 • *First HR*: 07/12/1928 off Lil Stoner

Howard Johnson

HOWARD MICHAEL JOHNSON
B: 11/29/1960
BB

Year	Tm	Lg	Tot	H	A	Men-On 0	1	2	3	One-Game 2	3	4	LO	XN	IP	PH	RHP	LHP
1982	DET	AL	4	1	3	2	2	0	0	0	0	0	0	0	0	1	4	0
1983	DET	AL	3	2	1	3	0	0	0	0	0	0	0	0	0	0	3	0
1984	DET	AL	12	4	8	5	2	4	1	0	0	0	0	1	0	0	10	2
1985	NY	NL	11	5	6	7	3	0	1	0	0	0	0	2	0	1	8	3
1986	NY	NL	10	5	5	5	3	2	0	1	0	0	0	1	0	0	8	2
1987	NY	NL	36	13	23	21	8	5	2	1	0	0	0	2	1	0	21	15
1988	NY	NL	24	9	15	17	4	3	0	0	0	0	0	1	0	1	18	6
1989	NY	NL	36	19	17	20	12	4	0	1	0	0	0	1	0	0	29	7
1990	NY	NL	23	13	10	14	5	3	1	0	0	0	2	0	0	0	17	6
1991	NY	NL	38	21	17	23	13	1	1	2	0	0	0	2	0	0	24	14
1992	NY	NL	7	2	5	5	1	1	0	0	0	0	0	0	0	0	4	3
1993	NY	NL	7	3	4	5	2	0	0	0	0	0	0	0	0	0	7	0
1994	COL	NL	10	3	7	4	4	1	1	0	0	0	0	0	0	4	9	1
1995	CHI	NL	7	6	1	3	4	0	0	1	0	0	0	0	0	2	7	0
Total			228	106	122	134	63	24	7	6	0	0	2	10	1	9	169	59

Rank among batters: 140 • *Top target (5 home runs)*: Mike LaCoss, Kevin Gross, Greg Maddux • *Number of pitchers victimized*: 149 • *Total ballparks homered in*: 24 • *First HR*: 04/28/1982 off Pete Redfern • *Switch hit HR in 1 game*—1 time

Jing Johnson

RUSSELL CONWELL JOHNSON
B: 10/09/1894 D: 12/06/1950
BR

Year	Tm	Lg	Tot	H	A	Men-On 0	1	2	3	One-Game 2	3	4	LO	XN	IP	PH	RHP	LHP
1916	PHI	AL	1	1	0	0	1	0	0	0	0	0	0	0	0	0	0	1
1919	PHI	AL	1	1	0	1	0	0	0	0	0	0	0	0	0	0	1	0
Total			2	2	0	1	1	0	0	0	0	0	0	0	0	0	1	1

Rank among batters: 4,129 • *Total ballparks homered in*: 1 • *First HR*: 08/29/1916 off Lefty Williams

Ken Johnson

KENNETH TRAVIS JOHNSON
B: 06/16/1933
BR

Year	Tm	Lg	Tot	H	A	Men-On 0	1	2	3	One-Game 2	3	4	LO	XN	IP	PH	RHP	LHP
1964	HOU	NL	1	0	1	1	0	0	0	0	0	0	0	0	0	0	0	1
1966	ATL	NL	1	1	0	1	0	0	0	0	0	0	0	0	0	0	1	0
Total			2	1	1	2	0	0	0	0	0	0	0	0	0	0	1	1

Rank among batters: 4,129 • *Total ballparks homered in*: 2 • *First HR*: 06/21/1964 off Denny Lemaster

Lamar Johnson

LAMAR JOHNSON
B: 09/02/1950
BR

Year	Tm	Lg	Tot	H	A	Men-On 0	1	2	3	One-Game 2	3	4	LO	XN	IP	PH	RHP	LHP
1975	CHI	AL	1	1	0	1	0	0	0	0	0	0	0	0	0	0	0	1
1976	CHI	AL	4	4	0	2	0	2	0	1	0	0	0	0	0	1	1	3
1977	CHI	AL	18	10	8	9	8	1	0	2	0	0	0	0	0	1	8	10
1978	CHI	AL	8	3	5	3	4	1	0	0	0	0	0	0	0	0	4	4
1979	CHI	AL	12	2	10	6	3	3	0	0	0	0	0	0	0	0	6	6
1980	CHI	AL	13	7	6	6	6	1	0	0	0	0	0	0	0	1	8	5
1981	CHI	AL	1	0	1	1	0	0	0	0	0	0	0	0	0	0	1	0
1982	TEX	AL	7	2	5	2	5	0	0	0	0	0	0	0	0	0	3	4
Total			64	29	35	30	26	8	0	3	0	0	0	0	0	3	31	33

Rank among batters: 815 • *Top target (4 home runs)*: Bill Travers • *Number of pitchers victimized*: 51 • *Total ballparks homered in*: 15 • *First HR*: 09/10/1975 off Frank Tanana

Lance Johnson

KENNETH LANCE JOHNSON
B: 07/06/1963
BL

Year	Tm	Lg	Tot	H	A	Men-On 0	1	2	3	One-Game 2	3	4	LO	XN	IP	PH	RHP	LHP
1990	CHI	AL	1	0	1	0	0	1	0	0	0	0	0	0	0	0	1	0
1992	CHI	AL	3	2	1	3	0	0	0	0	0	0	0	0	0	0	3	0
1994	CHI	AL	3	1	2	1	0	1	1	0	0	0	0	0	0	0	2	1
1995	CHI	AL	10	2	8	7	3	0	0	0	0	0	3	0	0	0	9	1
Total			17	5	12	11	3	2	1	0	0	0	3	0	0	0	15	2

Rank among batters: 1,969 • *Total ballparks homered in*: 11 • *First HR*: 07/12/1990 off Andy Hawkins • *LCS HR*—1

Lou Johnson

LOUIS BROWN JOHNSON
B: 09/22/1934
BR

Year	Tm	Lg	Tot	H	A	Men-On 0	1	2	3	One-Game 2	3	4	LO	XN	IP	PH	RHP	LHP
1962	MIL	NL	2	1	1	1	1	0	0	0	0	0	0	0	0	0	1	1
1965	LA	NL	12	6	6	6	5	1	0	1	0	0	0	2	0	0	11	1
1966	LA	NL	17	8	9	8	4	5	0	2	0	0	0	0	0	0	13	4
1967	LA	NL	11	7	4	6	5	0	0	1	0	0	0	0	0	1	3	8
1968	CHI	NL	1	0	1	1	0	0	0	0	0	0	0	0	0	0	0	1
	CLE	AL	5	3	2	4	1	0	0	1	0	0	0	0	0	1	3	2
	Total		6	3	3	5	1	0	0	1	0	0	0	0	0	1	3	3
Total			48	25	23	26	16	6	0	5	0	0	0	2	0	2	31	17

Rank among batters: 1,024 • Top target (2 home runs): Jim O'Toole, Bob Shaw, Jim Bunning, Dick Kelley, Juan Marichal, Denny Lemaster, Dave Boswell • *Number of pitchers victimized*: 41 • *Total ballparks homered in*: 15 • *First HR*: 08/20/1962 off Billy Pierce • *World Series HR*—2

Mark Johnson

MARK PATRICK JOHNSON
B: 10/17/1967
BL

Year	Tm	Lg	Tot	H	A	Men-On 0	1	2	3	One-Game 2	3	4	LO	XN	IP	PH	RHP	LHP
1995	PIT	NL	13	7	6	8	3	2	0	2	0	0	0	0	0	1	12	1

Rank among batters: 2,248 • *Total ballparks homered in*: 6 • *First HR*: 04/29/1995 off Tyler Green

Otis Johnson

OTIS L. JOHNSON
B: 11/05/1883 D: 11/09/1915
BB

Year	Tm	Lg	Tot	H	A	Men-On 0	1	2	3	One-Game 2	3	4	LO	XN	IP	PH	RHP	LHP
1911	NY	AL	3	2	1	1	2	0	0	0	0	0	0	0	1	0	2	1

Rank among batters: 3,735 • *Total ballparks homered in*: 2 • *First HR*: 04/27/1911 off Charlie Smith

Paul Johnson

PAUL OSCAR JOHNSON
B: 09/02/1896 D: 02/14/1973
BR

Year	Tm	Lg	Tot	H	A	Men-On 0	1	2	3	One-Game 2	3	4	LO	XN	IP	PH	RHP	LHP
1921	PHI	AL	1	1	0	1	0	0	0	0	0	0	0	0	0	0	0	1

Rank among batters: 4,707 • *Total ballparks homered in*: 1 • *First HR*: 09/05/1921 off George Mogridge

Randy Johnson

RANDALL STUART JOHNSON
B: 08/15/1958
BL

Year	Tm	Lg	Tot	H	A	Men-On 0	1	2	3	One-Game 2	3	4	LO	XN	IP	PH	RHP	LHP
1982	MIN	AL	10	7	3	6	3	1	0	0	0	0	0	0	0	1	10	0

Rank among batters: 2,500 • *Total ballparks homered in*: 3 • *First HR*: 04/11/1982 off Ken Forsch

Randy Johnson

RANDALL GLENN JOHNSON
B: 06/10/1956
BR

Year	Tm	Lg	Tot	H	A	Men-On 0	1	2	3	One-Game 2	3	4	LO	XN	IP	PH	RHP	LHP
1983	ATL	NL	1	1	0	0	1	0	0	0	0	0	0	0	0	0	1	0
1984	ATL	NL	5	1	4	3	2	0	0	0	0	0	0	1	0	0	3	2
Total			6	2	4	3	3	0	0	0	0	0	0	1	0	0	4	2

Rank among batters: 2,988 • *Total ballparks homered in*: 5 • *First HR*: 08/31/1983 off Joaquin Andujar

Roy Johnson

ROY CLEVELAND JOHNSON
B: 02/23/1903 D: 09/10/1973
BL

Year	Tm	Lg	Tot	H	A	Men-On 0	1	2	3	One-Game 2	3	4	LO	XN	IP	PH	RHP	LHP
1929	DET	AL	10	7	3	7	2	0	1	0	0	0	4	1	2	0	9	1
1930	DET	AL	2	2	0	2	0	0	0	1	0	0	1	0	0	0	2	0
1931	DET	AL	8	5	3	6	1	1	0	0	0	0	1	0	0	0	4	4
1932	DET	AL	3	3	0	2	1	0	0	0	0	0	1	0	0	0	2	1
	BOS	AL	11	1	10	5	5	0	1	1	0	0	0	0	0	0	10	1
	Total		14	4	10	7	6	0	1	1	0	0	1	0	0	0	12	2
1933	BOS	AL	10	5	5	8	1	1	0	0	0	0	0	0	0	0	8	2
1934	BOS	AL	7	2	5	3	3	1	0	0	0	0	0	1	0	0	6	1
1935	BOS	AL	3	0	3	2	1	0	0	0	0	0	0	0	0	0	1	2
1936	NY	AL	1	1	0	1	0	0	0	0	0	0	0	0	0	0	0	1
1937	BOS	NL	3	0	3	2	1	0	0	0	0	0	1	1	0	1	3	0
Total			58	26	32	38	15	3	2	2	0	0	8	3	2	1	45	13

Rank among batters: 886 • Top target (3 home runs): Wes Ferrell, George Earnshaw, Red Ruffing, General Crowder, George Blaeholder • *Number of pitchers victimized*: 40 • *Total ballparks homered in*: 10 • *First HR*: 04/27/1929 off Ed Strelecki

Roy Johnson

ROY EDWARD JOHNSON
B: 06/27/1959
BL

Year	Tm	Lg	Tot	H	A	Men-On 0	1	2	3	One-Game 2	3	4	LO	XN	IP	PH	RHP	LHP
1984	MON	NL	1	0	1	0	1	0	0	0	0	0	0	0	0	0	1	0

Rank among batters: 4,707 • *Total ballparks homered in*: 1 • *First HR*: 09/12/1984 off Rich Bordi

Spud Johnson

JOHN RALPH JOHNSON
B: 1860 BL

Year	Tm	Lg	Tot	H	A	Men-On 0	1	2	3	One-Game 2	3	4	LO	XN	IP	PH	RHP	LHP
1889	COL	AA	2	1	1	0	1	0	1	0	0	0	0	0	0	0	2	0
1890	COL	AA	1	0	1	0	0	1	0	0	0	0	0	0	0	0	0	0
1891	CLE	NL	1	0	1	0	1	0	0	0	0	0	0	0	0	0	0	0
Total			4	1	3	0	2	1	1	0	0	0	0	0	0	0	2	0

Rank among batters: 3,427 • *Total ballparks homered in*: 4 • *First HR*: 05/17/1889 off Scott Stratton

Stan Johnson

STANLEY LUCIUS JOHNSON
B: 02/12/1937
BL

Year	Tm	Lg	Tot	H	A	Men-On 0	1	2	3	One-Game 2	3	4	LO	XN	IP	PH	RHP	LHP
1960	CHI	AL	1	0	1	1	0	0	0	0	0	0	0	0	0	1	1	0

Rank among batters: 4,707 • *Total ballparks homered in*: 1 • *First HR*: 09/23/1960 off Frank Funk

Syl Johnson

SYLVESTER JOHNSON
B: 12/31/1900 D: 02/20/1985
BR

Year	Tm	Lg	Tot	H	A	Men-On 0	1	2	3	One-Game 2	3	4	LO	XN	IP	PH	RHP	LHP
1923	DET	AL	1	0	1	0	1	0	0	0	0	0	0	0	0	0	0	1
1929	STL	NL	1	0	1	0	1	0	0	0	0	0	0	0	0	0	1	0
1934	CIN	NL	1	0	1	0	1	0	0	0	0	0	0	0	0	0	1	0
1935	PHI	NL	1	1	0	1	0	0	0	0	0	0	0	0	0	0	1	0
Total			4	1	3	1	3	0	0	0	0	0	0	0	0	0	3	1

Rank among batters: 3,427 • *Total ballparks homered in*: 4 • *First HR*: 09/19/1923 off Rube Walberg

Tony Johnson

ANTHONY CLAIR JOHNSON
B: 06/23/1956
BR

Year	Tm	Lg	Tot	H	A	Men-On 0	1	2	3	One-Game 2	3	4	LO	XN	IP	PH	RHP	LHP
1982	TOR	AL	3	1	2	1	1	1	0	0	0	0	0	0	0	0	0	3

Rank among batters: 3,735 • *Total ballparks homered in*: 3 • *First HR*: 05/24/1982 off Scott McGregor

Wallace Johnson

WALLACE DARNELL JOHNSON
B: 12/25/1956
BB

Year	Tm	Lg	Tot	H	A	Men-On 0	1	2	3	One-Game 2	3	4	LO	XN	IP	PH	RHP	LHP
1986	MON	NL	1	1	0	1	0	0	0	0	0	0	0	0	0	1	1	0
1987	MON	NL	1	0	1	1	0	0	0	0	0	0	0	0	0	1	1	0
1989	MON	NL	2	0	2	2	0	0	0	0	0	0	0	0	0	0	1	1
1990	MON	NL	1	0	1	0	1	0	0	0	0	0	0	1	0	1	0	1
Total			5	1	4	4	1	0	0	0	0	0	0	1	0	3	3	2

Rank among batters: 3,191 • *Total ballparks homered in*: 4 • *First HR*: 07/30/1986 off Jim Winn

Walter Johnson

WALTER PERRY JOHNSON
B: 11/06/1887 D: 12/10/1946
BR HOF

Year	Tm	Lg	Tot	H	A	Men-On 0	1	2	3	One-Game 2	3	4	LO	XN	IP	PH	RHP	LHP
1909	WAS	AL	1	1	0	1	0	0	0	0	0	0	0	0	0	0	0	1
1910	WAS	AL	2	0	2	1	1	0	0	0	0	0	0	0	0	0	2	0
1911	WAS	AL	1	0	1	1	0	0	0	0	0	0	0	0	0	0	1	0
1912	WAS	AL	2	1	1	1	0	1	0	0	0	0	0	0	1	0	1	1
1913	WAS	AL	2	0	2	1	1	0	0	0	0	0	0	0	0	0	1	1
1914	WAS	AL	3	0	3	2	0	0	1	0	0	0	0	0	0	0	1	2
1915	WAS	AL	2	0	2	1	1	0	0	0	0	0	0	0	0	0	2	0
1916	WAS	AL	1	1	0	1	0	0	0	0	0	0	0	0	1	0	0	1
1918	WAS	AL	1	0	1	0	1	0	0	0	0	0	0	0	0	0	1	0
1919	WAS	AL	1	0	1	1	0	0	0	0	0	0	0	0	0	0	1	0
1920	WAS	AL	1	0	1	1	0	0	0	0	0	0	0	0	0	0	1	0
1922	WAS	AL	1	1	0	0	0	1	0	0	0	0	0	0	1	0	1	0
1924	WAS	AL	1	0	1	0	1	0	0	0	0	0	0	0	0	0	0	1
1925	WAS	AL	2	0	2	0	2	0	0	0	0	0	0	0	0	1	1	1
1926	WAS	AL	1	0	1	0	0	1	0	0	0	0	0	0	0	0	0	1
1927	WAS	AL	2	1	1	2	0	0	0	0	0	0	0	0	0	0	2	0
Total			24	5	19	13	7	3	1	0	0	0	0	0	3	1	15	9

Rank among batters: 1,643 • *Total ballparks homered in*: 10 • *First HR*: 08/16/1909 off Harry Krause

Doc Johnston

WHEELER ROGER JOHNSTON
B: 09/09/1887 D: 02/17/1961
BL

Year	Tm	Lg	Tot	H	A	Men-On 0	1	2	3	One-Game 2	3	4	LO	XN	IP	PH	RHP	LHP
1912	CLE	AL	1	0	1	0	1	0	0	0	0	0	0	0	1	0	1	0
1913	CLE	AL	2	0	2	1	1	0	0	0	0	0	1	0	1	0	2	0
1915	PIT	NL	5	0	5	1	3	1	0	0	0	0	0	0	2	0	4	1
1919	CLE	AL	1	1	0	1	0	0	0	0	0	0	0	0	1	0	1	0
1920	CLE	AL	2	1	1	0	1	1	0	0	0	0	0	0	1	0	2	0
1921	CLE	AL	2	0	2	1	0	1	0	0	0	0	0	0	1	0	2	0
1922	PHI	AL	1	1	0	1	0	0	0	0	0	0	0	0	0	0	1	0
Total			14	3	11	5	6	3	0	0	0	0	1	0	7	0	13	1

Rank among batters: 2,169 • *Total ballparks homered in*: 9 • *First HR*: 09/06/1912 off Joe Benz

Greg Johnston

GREGORY BERNARD JOHNSTON
B: 02/12/1955
BL

Year	Tm	Lg	Tot	H	A	Men-On 0	1	2	3	One-Game 2	3	4	LO	XN	IP	PH	RHP	LHP
1979	SF	NL	1	0	1	1	0	0	0	0	0	0	0	0	0	0	0	1

Rank among batters: 4,707 • *Total ballparks homered in*: 1 • *First HR*: 08/16/1979 off Doug Capilla

Jimmy Johnston

JAMES HARLE JOHNSTON
B: 12/10/1889 D: 02/14/1967
BR

Year	Tm	Lg	Tot	H	A	Men-On 0	1	2	3	One-Game 2	3	4	LO	XN	IP	PH	RHP	LHP
1914	CHI	NL	1	1	0	1	0	0	0	0	0	0	0	0	0	0	0	1
1916	BRO	NL	1	0	1	1	0	0	0	0	0	0	0	0	0	0	1	0
1919	BRO	NL	1	1	0	0	1	0	0	0	0	0	0	0	1	0	1	0
1920	BRO	NL	1	1	0	1	0	0	0	0	0	0	0	0	0	0	0	1
1921	BRO	NL	5	2	3	5	0	0	0	0	0	0	1	0	2	0	4	1
1922	BRO	NL	4	1	3	3	1	0	0	0	0	0	0	0	0	0	4	0
1923	BRO	NL	4	2	2	2	2	0	0	0	0	0	0	0	0	0	3	1
1924	BRO	NL	2	0	2	2	0	0	0	0	0	0	0	0	0	0	2	0
1925	BRO	NL	2	0	2	2	0	0	0	0	0	0	0	0	1	0	0	2
1926	BOS	NL	1	0	1	1	0	0	0	0	0	0	0	0	0	1	1	0
Total			22	8	14	18	4	0	0	0	0	0	1	0	4	1	16	6

Rank among batters: 1,719 • *Top target (2 home runs)*: Red Causey, Jesse Winters • *Number of pitchers victimized*: 20 • *Total ballparks homered in*: 8 • *First HR*: 05/31/1914 off Dick Niehaus • *Hit for Cycle*—@PHI: 05/25/1922 (1)

Johnny Johnston

JOHN THOMAS JOHNSTON
B: 03/28/1890 D: 03/07/1940
BL

Year	Tm	Lg	Tot	H	A	Men-On 0	1	2	3	One-Game 2	3	4	LO	XN	IP	PH	RHP	LHP
1913	STL	AL	2	2	0	2	0	0	0	0	0	0	0	0	0	0	2	0

Rank among batters: 4,129 • *Total ballparks homered in*: 1 • *First HR*: 05/25/1913 off Joe Lake

Richard Johnston

RICHARD FREDERICK JOHNSTON
B: 04/06/1863 D: 04/04/1934
BR

Year	Tm	Lg	Tot	H	A	Men-On 0	1	2	3	One-Game 2	3	4	LO	XN	IP	PH	RHP	LHP
1884	RIC	AA	2	2	0	0	2	0	0	0	0	0	0	0	0	0	2	0
1885	BOS	NL	1	0	1	0	0	1	0	0	0	0	0	0	0	0	1	0
1886	BOS	NL	1	0	1	0	1	0	0	0	0	0	0	0	1	0	1	0
1887	BOS	NL	5	1	4	3	2	0	0	0	0	0	0	0	0	0	3	2
1888	BOS	NL	12	7	5	11	1	0	0	0	0	0	3	0	2	0	10	2
1889	BOS	NL	5	3	2	0	4	1	0	1	0	0	0	1	0	0	4	1
1890	NY	PL	1	1	0	0	1	0	0	0	0	0	0	0	0	0	1	0
1891	CIN	AA	6	4	2	2	4	0	0	0	0	0	0	0	0	0	4	2
Total			33	18	15	16	15	2	0	1	0	0	3	1	3	0	26	7

Rank among batters: 1,336 • *Top target (3 home runs)*: Gus Krock • *Number of pitchers victimized*: 28 • *Total ballparks homered in*: 12 • *First HR*: 08/30/1884 off Bob Emslie

Jay Johnstone

JOHN WILLIAM JOHNSTONE
B: 11/20/1945
BL

Year	Tm	Lg	Tot	H	A	Men-On 0	1	2	3	One-Game 2	3	4	LO	XN	IP	PH	RHP	LHP
1966	CAL	AL	3	1	2	3	0	0	0	0	0	0	1	0	0	0	2	1
1967	CAL	AL	2	0	2	2	0	0	0	0	0	0	0	0	0	1	1	1
1969	CAL	AL	10	5	5	3	5	1	1	0	0	0	0	0	0	0	7	3
1970	CAL	AL	11	4	7	8	1	1	1	0	0	0	0	0	0	1	11	0
1971	CHI	AL	16	9	7	12	3	1	0	2	0	0	0	0	0	2	16	0
1972	CHI	AL	4	2	2	3	0	1	0	0	0	0	0	0	0	1	3	1
1974	PHI	NL	6	5	1	3	2	1	0	1	0	0	0	0	0	0	6	0
1975	PHI	NL	7	5	2	5	1	1	0	0	0	0	0	1	0	1	7	0
1976	PHI	NL	5	2	3	3	2	0	0	0	0	0	0	0	0	0	3	2
1977	PHI	NL	15	9	6	9	6	0	0	2	0	0	0	0	0	0	14	1
1978	NY	AL	1	0	1	1	0	0	0	0	0	0	0	0	0	0	1	0
1979	NY	AL	1	0	1	0	0	0	1	0	0	0	0	0	0	1	1	0
1980	LA	NL	2	2	0	2	0	0	0	0	0	0	0	0	0	0	2	0
1981	LA	NL	3	1	2	3	0	0	0	0	0	0	0	0	0	3	3	0
1982	CHI	NL	10	7	3	4	3	3	0	1	0	0	0	0	0	0	9	1

Year	Tm	Lg	Tot	H	A	Men-On 0	1	2	3	One-Game 2	3	4	LO	XN	IP	PH	RHP	LHP

Jay Johnstone *continued*

Year	Tm	Lg	Tot	H	A	0	1	2	3	2	3	4	LO	XN	IP	PH	RHP	LHP
1983	CHI	NL	6	4	2	4	1	1	0	0	0	0	0	0	0	1	6	0
Total			102	56	46	65	24	10	3	6	0	0	1	1	0	11	92	10

Rank among batters: 483 • *Top target (3 home runs)*: Joe Coleman, Pat Zachry • *Number of pitchers victimized*: 83 • *Total ballparks homered in*: 24 • *First HR*: 08/17/1966 off Camilo Pascual • *World Series HR*—1

Stan Jok

STANLEY EDWARD JOK
B: 05/03/1926 D: 03/06/1972
BR

Year	Tm	Lg	Tot	H	A	0	1	2	3	2	3	4	LO	XN	IP	PH	RHP	LHP
1955	CHI	AL	1	1	0	1	0	0	0	0	0	0	0	0	0	0	1	0

Rank among batters: 4,707 • *Total ballparks homered in*: 1 • *First HR*: 05/01/1955 off Jim McDonald

Smead Jolley

SMEAD POWELL JOLLEY
B: 01/14/1902 D: 11/17/1991
BL

Year	Tm	Lg	Tot	H	A	0	1	2	3	2	3	4	LO	XN	IP	PH	RHP	LHP
1930	CHI	AL	16	8	8	10	2	4	0	1	0	0	0	0	2	0	14	2
1931	CHI	AL	3	0	3	0	1	2	0	0	0	0	0	0	0	1	3	0
1932	BOS	AL	18	9	9	8	5	5	0	2	0	0	0	0	0	0	16	2
1933	BOS	AL	9	4	5	5	4	0	0	0	0	0	0	0	0	2	7	2
Total			46	21	25	23	12	11	0	3	0	0	0	0	2	3	40	6

Rank among batters: 1,060 • Top target (3 home runs): Roy Mahaffey, Sam Gray, George Earnshaw, Tommy Bridges • *Number of pitchers victimized*: 33 • *Total ballparks homered in*: 8 • *First HR*: 05/22/1930 off George Uhle

Dave Jolly

DAVID JOLLY
B: 10/14/1924 D: 05/27/1963
BR

Year	Tm	Lg	Tot	H	A	0	1	2	3	2	3	4	LO	XN	IP	PH	RHP	LHP
1954	MIL	NL	1	0	1	1	0	0	0	0	0	0	0	0	0	0	0	1

Rank among batters: 4,707 • *Total ballparks homered in*: 1 • *First HR*: 06/27/1954 off Curt Simmons

Bob Jones

ROBERT WALTER JONES
B: 12/02/1889 D: 08/30/1964
BL

Year	Tm	Lg	Tot	H	A	0	1	2	3	2	3	4	LO	XN	IP	PH	RHP	LHP
1919	DET	AL	1	0	1	0	0	1	0	0	0	0	0	0	0	0	1	0
1920	DET	AL	1	0	1	1	0	0	0	0	0	0	0	0	1	0	1	0
1921	DET	AL	1	0	1	1	0	0	0	0	0	0	0	0	0	0	1	0
1922	DET	AL	3	1	2	0	2	1	0	0	0	0	0	0	3	0	3	0
1923	DET	AL	1	0	1	0	1	0	0	0	0	0	0	0	0	0	1	0
Total			7	1	6	2	3	2	0	0	0	0	0	0	4	0	7	0

Rank among batters: 2,834 • *Total ballparks homered in*: 4 • *First HR*: 08/29/1919 off Urban Shocker

Bob Jones

ROBERT OLIVER JONES
B: 10/11/1949
BL

Year	Tm	Lg	Tot	H	A	0	1	2	3	2	3	4	LO	XN	IP	PH	RHP	LHP
1976	CAL	AL	6	2	4	3	3	0	0	1	0	0	0	0	0	0	6	0
1977	CAL	AL	1	0	1	1	0	0	0	0	0	0	0	0	0	0	1	0
1981	TEX	AL	3	1	2	2	1	0	0	0	0	0	0	0	0	0	3	0
1983	TEX	AL	1	1	0	0	1	0	0	0	0	0	0	0	0	1	1	0
1984	TEX	AL	4	1	3	1	2	1	0	0	0	0	0	0	0	1	4	0
1985	TEX	AL	5	5	0	3	1	1	0	1	0	0	0	0	0	2	5	0
Total			20	10	10	10	8	2	0	2	0	0	0	0	0	4	20	0

Rank among batters: 1,810 • *Top target (2 home runs)*: Rick Wise, Mike Norris • *Number of pitchers victimized*: 18 • *Total ballparks homered in*: 8 • *First HR*: 06/19/1976 off Rick Wise

Charles Jones

CHARLES WESLEY JONES
B: 04/30/1850
BR

Year	Tm	Lg	Tot	H	A	0	1	2	3	2	3	4	LO	XN	IP	PH	RHP	LHP
1876	CIN	NL	4	2	2	3	0	1	0	0	0	0	0	0	3	0	4	0

Year	Tm	Lg	Tot	H	A	Men-On				One-Game			LO	XN	IP	PH	RHP	LHP
						0	1	2	3	2	3	4						

Charles Jones *continued*

Year	Tm	Lg	Tot	H	A	0	1	2	3	2	3	4	LO	XN	IP	PH	RHP	LHP
1877	CIN	NL	2	2	0	0	1	1	0	0	0	0	0	0	1	0	2	0
1878	CIN	NL	3	2	1	2	1	0	0	0	0	0	0	0	0	0	3	0
1879	BOS	NL	9	4	5	6	3	0	0	1	0	0	2	0	0	0	9	0
1880	BOS	NL	5	3	2	2	3	0	0	1	0	0	0	0	1	0	4	1
1883	CIN	AA	10	8	2	3	5	2	0	0	0	0	0	0	0	0	10	0
1884	CIN	AA	7	7	0	1	4	2	0	0	0	0	0	0	0	0	5	0
1885	CIN	AA	5	3	2	3	1	1	0	0	0	0	0	0	2	0	4	1
1886	CIN	AA	6	6	0	2	1	2	1	0	0	0	0	0	2	0	3	2
1887	CIN	AA	2	1	1	0	2	0	0	0	0	0	0	0	1	0	2	0
	NY	AA	3	3	0	1	1	1	0	0	0	0	0	0	1	0	1	2
	Total		5	4	1	1	3	1	0	0	0	0	0	0	2	0	3	2
Total			56	41	15	23	22	10	1	2	0	0	2	0	11	0	47	6

Rank among batters: 913 • *Top target (5 home runs)*: George Bradley • *Number of pitchers victimized*: 36 • *Total ballparks homered in*: 15 • *First HR*: 05/02/1876 off Al Spalding • *2 HR in 1 inning*—vs BUF: 06/10/1880

Charlie Jones

CHARLES C. JONES
B: 06/02/1876 D: 04/02/1947
BR

Year	Tm	Lg	Tot	H	A	0	1	2	3	2	3	4	LO	XN	IP	PH	RHP	LHP
1905	WAS	AL	2	2	0	0	2	0	0	0	0	0	0	0	2	0	2	0
1906	WAS	AL	3	1	2	0	1	1	1	0	0	0	0	0	0	0	3	0
Total			5	3	2	0	3	1	1	0	0	0	0	0	2	0	5	0

Rank among batters: 3,191 • *Total ballparks homered in*: 3 • *First HR*: 06/06/1905 off George Mullin

Chipper Jones

LARRY WAYNE JONES
B: 04/24/1972
BB

Year	Tm	Lg	Tot	H	A	0	1	2	3	2	3	4	LO	XN	IP	PH	RHP	LHP
1995	ATL	NL	23	15	8	14	6	3	0	0	0	0	0	0	0	0	20	3

Rank among batters: 1,686 • *Total ballparks homered in*: 7 • *First HR*: 05/09/1995 off Josias Manzanillo • *LCS HR*—3

Chris Jones

CHRISTOPHER CARLOS JONES
B: 12/16/1965
BR

Year	Tm	Lg	Tot	H	A	0	1	2	3	2	3	4	LO	XN	IP	PH	RHP	LHP
1991	CIN	NL	2	0	2	2	0	0	0	0	0	0	0	1	0	1	1	1
1992	HOU	NL	1	1	0	0	1	0	0	0	0	0	0	1	0	0	1	0
1993	COL	NL	6	2	4	0	6	0	0	2	0	0	0	0	0	0	4	2
1995	NY	NL	8	4	4	5	1	2	0	0	0	0	0	1	0	3	5	3
Total			17	7	10	7	8	2	0	2	0	0	0	3	0	4	11	6

Rank among batters: 1,969 • *Total ballparks homered in*: 11 • *First HR*: 09/16/1991 off Tim Crews

Clarence Jones

CLARENCE WOODROW JONES
B: 11/07/1941
BL

Year	Tm	Lg	Tot	H	A	0	1	2	3	2	3	4	LO	XN	IP	PH	RHP	LHP
1967	CHI	NL	2	1	1	1	1	0	0	0	0	0	0	0	0	1	2	0

Rank among batters: 4,129 • *Total ballparks homered in*: 2 • *First HR*: 07/30/1967 off Gary Nolan

Cleon Jones

CLEON JOSEPH JONES
B: 08/04/1942
BR

Year	Tm	Lg	Tot	H	A	0	1	2	3	2	3	4	LO	XN	IP	PH	RHP	LHP
1965	NY	NL	1	0	1	1	0	0	0	0	0	0	0	0	0	0	1	0
1966	NY	NL	8	5	3	7	1	0	0	0	0	0	0	1	0	0	1	7
1967	NY	NL	5	2	3	3	2	0	0	0	0	0	0	0	0	0	3	2
1968	NY	NL	14	10	4	10	2	2	0	0	0	0	0	0	0	0	6	8
1969	NY	NL	12	9	3	7	1	3	1	0	0	0	0	0	0	0	5	7
1970	NY	NL	10	6	4	7	2	1	0	0	0	0	0	0	0	0	10	0
1971	NY	NL	14	6	8	9	4	1	0	0	0	0	0	0	0	0	10	4
1972	NY	NL	5	3	2	3	2	0	0	0	0	0	0	0	0	0	4	1
1973	NY	NL	11	6	5	6	4	1	0	2	0	0	0	0	0	0	7	4

Cleon Jones *continued*

Year	Tm	Lg	Tot	H	A	Men-On 0	1	2	3	One-Game 2	3	4	LO	XN	IP	PH	RHP	LHP
1974	NY	NL	13	6	7	5	8	0	0	0	0	0	0	0	0	0	6	7
Total			93	53	40	58	26	8	1	2	0	0	0	1	0	0	53	40

Rank among batters: 545 • *Top target (3 home runs)*: Ken Holtzman, Ray Sadecki, Gary Nolan • *Number of pitchers victimized*: 72 • *Total ballparks homered in*: 14 • *First HR*: 09/22/1965 off Bob Friend • *World Series HR*—1; *LCS HR*—1

Dalton Jones

JAMES DALTON JONES
B: 12/10/1943
BL

Year	Tm	Lg	Tot	H	A	Men-On 0	1	2	3	One-Game 2	3	4	LO	XN	IP	PH	RHP	LHP
1964	BOS	AL	6	1	5	3	3	0	0	0	0	0	0	0	0	1	5	1
1965	BOS	AL	5	2	3	3	2	0	0	0	0	0	0	0	0	0	5	0
1966	BOS	AL	4	1	3	2	2	0	0	0	0	0	0	0	0	1	4	0
1967	BOS	AL	3	1	2	2	1	0	0	0	0	0	0	1	0	0	2	1
1968	BOS	AL	5	2	3	1	4	0	0	0	0	0	0	0	0	0	5	0
1969	BOS	AL	3	3	0	0	2	1	0	0	0	0	0	1	0	0	3	0
1970	DET	AL	6	4	2	6	0	0	0	0	0	0	1	0	0	0	6	0
1971	DET	AL	5	3	2	3	2	0	0	0	0	0	0	0	0	1	5	0
1972	TEX	AL	4	3	1	2	2	0	0	0	0	0	0	0	0	0	4	0
Total			41	20	21	22	18	1	0	0	0	0	1	2	0	3	39	2

Rank among batters: 1,163 • Top target (2 home runs): Joe Sparma, Mudcat Grant, Earl Wilson, Dick Drago, Stan Bahnsen • *Number of pitchers victimized*: 36 • *Total ballparks homered in*: 11 • *First HR*: 04/18/1964 off Don Mossi

Davy Jones

DAVID JEFFERSON JONES
B: 06/30/1880 D: 03/31/1972
BL

Year	Tm	Lg	Tot	H	A	Men-On 0	1	2	3	One-Game 2	3	4	LO	XN	IP	PH	RHP	LHP
1901	MIL	AL	3	0	3	2	1	0	0	0	0	0	0	0	1	0	3	0
1903	CHI	NL	1	0	1	0	1	0	0	0	0	0	0	0	0	0	1	0
1904	CHI	NL	3	0	3	2	0	0	1	0	0	0	0	0	0	0	3	0
1914	PIT	FL	2	2	0	0	1	0	1	0	0	0	0	0	2	0	1	0
Total			9	2	7	4	3	0	2	0	0	0	0	0	3	0	8	0

Rank among batters: 2,587 • *Total ballparks homered in*: 6 • *First HR*: 09/15/1901 off Nixey Callahan

Deacon Jones

GROVER WILLIAM JONES
B: 04/18/1934
BL

Year	Tm	Lg	Tot	H	A	Men-On 0	1	2	3	One-Game 2	3	4	LO	XN	IP	PH	RHP	LHP
1963	CHI	AL	1	1	0	0	1	0	0	0	0	0	0	0	0	0	1	0

Rank among batters: 4,707 • *Total ballparks homered in*: 1 • *First HR*: 09/28/1963 off Jim Hannan

Earl Jones

EARL LESLIE JONES
B: 06/11/1919 D: 01/24/1989
BL

Year	Tm	Lg	Tot	H	A	Men-On 0	1	2	3	One-Game 2	3	4	LO	XN	IP	PH	RHP	LHP
1945	STL	AL	1	1	0	0	0	1	0	0	0	0	0	0	0	0	1	0

Rank among batters: 4,707 • *Total ballparks homered in*: 1 • *First HR*: 08/10/1945 off Steve Gerkin

Fielder Jones

FIELDER ALLISON JONES
B: 08/13/1871 D: 03/13/1934
BL

Year	Tm	Lg	Tot	H	A	Men-On 0	1	2	3	One-Game 2	3	4	LO	XN	IP	PH	RHP	LHP
1896	BRO	NL	3	3	0	2	0	1	0	0	0	0	0	0	0	0	2	1
1897	BRO	NL	1	0	1	0	0	1	0	0	0	0	0	0	0	0	1	0
1898	BRO	NL	1	0	1	0	1	0	0	0	0	0	0	0	0	0	1	0
1899	BRO	NL	2	2	0	1	1	0	0	0	0	0	0	0	1	0	2	0
1900	BRO	NL	4	4	0	2	1	0	1	0	0	0	0	0	2	0	4	0
1901	CHI	AL	2	0	2	1	1	0	0	0	0	0	0	0	1	0	2	0
1904	CHI	AL	3	0	3	2	1	0	0	0	0	0	0	0	0	0	3	0
1905	CHI	AL	2	0	2	0	2	0	0	0	0	0	0	0	1	0	2	0
1906	CHI	AL	2	1	1	1	0	1	0	0	0	0	0	0	0	0	1	1
1908	CHI	AL	1	0	1	0	1	0	0	0	0	0	0	0	0	0	1	0
Total			21	10	11	9	8	3	1	0	0	0	0	0	5	0	19	2

Rank among batters: 1,768 • *Top target (2 home runs)*: Red Donahue, Jack Powell, Cy Young • *Number of pitchers victimized*: 18 • *Total ballparks homered in*: 9 • *First HR*: 06/11/1896 off Cy Young

Hal Jones

HAROLD MARION JONES
B: 04/09/1936
BR

Year	Tm	Lg	Tot	H	A	Men-On 0	Men-On 1	Men-On 2	Men-On 3	One-Game 2	One-Game 3	One-Game 4	LO	XN	IP	PH	RHP	LHP
1961	CLE	AL	2	1	1	2	0	0	0	0	0	0	0	0	0	0	2	0

Rank among batters: 4,129 • *Total ballparks homered in*: 2 • *First HR*: 09/19/1961 off Bill Kunkel

Jack Jones

RYERSON L. JONES

Year	Tm	Lg	Tot	H	A	Men-On 0	Men-On 1	Men-On 2	Men-On 3	One-Game 2	One-Game 3	One-Game 4	LO	XN	IP	PH	RHP	LHP
1884	CIN	UA	2	1	1	1	1	0	0	0	0	0	0	0	0	0	0	0

Rank among batters: 4,129 • *Top target (2 home runs)*: Walter Burke • *Number of pitchers victimized*: 1 • *Total ballparks homered in*: 2 • *First HR*: 05/14/1884 off Walter Burke

Jake Jones

JAMES MURRELL JONES
B: 11/23/1920
BR

Year	Tm	Lg	Tot	H	A	Men-On 0	Men-On 1	Men-On 2	Men-On 3	One-Game 2	One-Game 3	One-Game 4	LO	XN	IP	PH	RHP	LHP
1946	CHI	AL	3	2	1	1	1	1	0	0	0	0	0	0	0	0	3	0
1947	CHI	AL	3	1	2	3	0	0	0	0	0	0	0	0	0	0	2	1
	BOS	AL	16	13	3	5	7	3	1	1	0	0	0	0	0	0	13	3
	Total		19	14	5	8	7	3	1	1	0	0	0	0	0	0	15	4
1948	BOS	AL	1	0	1	0	1	0	0	0	0	0	0	0	0	0	1	0
Total			23	16	7	9	9	4	1	1	0	0	0	0	0	0	19	4

Rank among batters: 1,686 • *Top target (2 home runs)*: Milo Candini • *Number of pitchers victimized*: 22 • *Total ballparks homered in*: 6 • *First HR*: 05/03/1946 off Norm Brown

Jimmy Jones

JAMES CONDIA JONES
B: 04/20/1964
BR

Year	Tm	Lg	Tot	H	A	Men-On 0	Men-On 1	Men-On 2	Men-On 3	One-Game 2	One-Game 3	One-Game 4	LO	XN	IP	PH	RHP	LHP
1987	SD	NL	1	0	1	0	1	0	0	0	0	0	0	0	0	0	0	1
1988	SD	NL	1	1	0	1	0	0	0	0	0	0	0	0	0	0	1	0
Total			2	1	1	1	1	0	0	0	0	0	0	0	0	0	1	1

Rank among batters: 4,129 • *Total ballparks homered in*: 2 • *First HR*: 07/30/1987 off Guy Hoffman

Lynn Jones

LYNN MORRIS JONES
B: 01/01/1953
BR

Year	Tm	Lg	Tot	H	A	Men-On 0	Men-On 1	Men-On 2	Men-On 3	One-Game 2	One-Game 3	One-Game 4	LO	XN	IP	PH	RHP	LHP
1979	DET	AL	4	3	1	3	1	0	0	0	0	0	0	0	0	0	1	3
1981	DET	AL	2	2	0	1	1	0	0	0	0	0	0	0	0	1	1	1
1984	KC	AL	1	1	0	1	0	0	0	0	0	0	0	0	0	0	0	1
Total			7	6	1	5	2	0	0	0	0	0	0	0	0	1	2	5

Rank among batters: 2,834 • *Total ballparks homered in*: 3 • *First HR*: 04/26/1979 off Jerry Augustine

Mack Jones

MACK JONES
B: 11/06/1938
BL

Year	Tm	Lg	Tot	H	A	Men-On 0	Men-On 1	Men-On 2	Men-On 3	One-Game 2	One-Game 3	One-Game 4	LO	XN	IP	PH	RHP	LHP
1962	MIL	NL	10	6	4	6	2	2	0	0	0	0	0	1	0	0	9	1
1963	MIL	NL	3	1	2	3	0	0	0	0	0	0	0	0	0	0	3	0
1965	MIL	NL	31	14	17	17	13	0	1	1	0	0	1	0	0	0	23	8
1966	ATL	NL	23	15	8	12	9	2	0	1	0	0	0	1	0	0	22	1
1967	ATL	NL	17	12	5	10	6	1	0	2	0	0	0	1	0	0	16	1
1968	CIN	NL	10	4	6	6	3	1	0	1	0	0	0	0	0	0	8	2
1969	MON	NL	22	10	12	10	6	4	2	2	0	0	0	0	0	0	21	1
1970	MON	NL	14	8	6	11	3	0	0	3	0	0	1	0	0	0	13	1
1971	MON	NL	3	3	0	1	1	1	0	1	0	0	0	0	0	0	3	0
Total			133	73	60	76	43	11	3	11	0	0	2	3	0	0	118	15

Rank among batters: 337 • *Top target (4 home runs)*: Bill Hands, Ron Herbel, Juan Marichal • *Number of pitchers victimized*: 83 • *Total ballparks homered in*: 15 • *First HR*: 04/28/1962 off Al Cicotte

Nippy Jones

VERNAL LEROY JONES
B: 06/29/1925 D: 10/03/1995
BR

Year	Tm	Lg	Tot	H	A	Men-On 0	Men-On 1	Men-On 2	Men-On 3	One-Game 2	One-Game 3	One-Game 4	LO	XN	IP	PH	RHP	LHP
1947	STL	NL	1	1	0	1	0	0	0	0	0	0	0	0	0	0	1	0

Nippy Jones *continued*

Year	Tm	Lg	Tot	H	A	Men-On 0	1	2	3	One-Game 2	3	4	LO	XN	IP	PH	RHP	LHP
1948	STL	NL	10	9	1	4	5	1	0	0	0	0	0	0	1	0	6	4
1949	STL	NL	8	3	5	2	4	2	0	1	0	0	0	0	0	0	3	5
1951	STL	NL	3	1	2	1	2	0	0	0	0	0	0	0	0	0	1	2
1952	PHI	NL	1	0	1	0	1	0	0	0	0	0	0	0	0	0	0	1
1957	MIL	NL	2	1	1	1	0	1	0	0	0	0	0	1	0	0	1	1
Total			25	15	10	9	12	4	0	1	0	0	0	1	1	0	12	13

Rank among batters: 1,608 • *Top target (2 home runs)*: Ken Heintzelman, Cliff Chambers • *Number of pitchers victimized*: 23 • *Total ballparks homered in*: 6 • *First HR*: 09/11/1947 off Ralph Branca

Ron Jones

RONALD GLEN JONES
B: 06/11/1964
BL

Year	Tm	Lg	Tot	H	A	Men-On 0	1	2	3	One-Game 2	3	4	LO	XN	IP	PH	RHP	LHP
1988	PHI	NL	8	5	3	4	3	1	0	0	0	0	0	0	0	0	5	3
1989	PHI	NL	2	1	1	2	0	0	0	0	0	0	0	0	0	0	1	1
1990	PHI	NL	3	2	1	1	2	0	0	1	0	0	0	0	0	0	3	0
Total			13	8	5	7	5	1	0	1	0	0	0	0	0	0	9	4

Rank among batters: 2,248 • *Total ballparks homered in*: 5 • *First HR*: 08/26/1988 off Tim Belcher

Ruppert Jones

RUPPERT SANDERSON JONES
B: 03/12/1955
BL

Year	Tm	Lg	Tot	H	A	Men-On 0	1	2	3	One-Game 2	3	4	LO	XN	IP	PH	RHP	LHP
1976	KC	AL	1	0	1	1	0	0	0	0	0	0	0	0	0	0	1	0
1977	SEA	AL	24	17	7	16	8	0	0	1	0	0	0	0	1	0	17	7
1978	SEA	AL	6	4	2	5	1	0	0	0	0	0	0	0	0	0	6	0
1979	SEA	AL	21	17	4	15	4	2	0	1	0	0	0	0	2	0	14	7
1980	NY	AL	9	5	4	4	2	2	1	1	0	0	0	2	0	0	6	3
1981	SD	NL	4	2	2	1	2	1	0	0	0	0	0	0	0	0	4	0
1982	SD	NL	12	6	6	7	4	1	0	0	0	0	0	0	0	0	10	2
1983	SD	NL	12	5	7	6	2	4	0	0	0	0	0	2	0	0	11	1
1984	DET	AL	12	6	6	6	3	3	0	0	0	0	0	0	0	1	12	0
1985	CAL	AL	21	10	11	11	8	1	1	2	0	0	0	1	0	0	19	2
1986	CAL	AL	17	10	7	10	6	1	0	1	0	0	5	0	0	2	15	2
1987	CAL	AL	8	3	5	5	3	0	0	0	0	0	1	1	0	2	7	1
Total			147	85	62	87	43	15	2	6	0	0	6	6	3	5	122	25

Rank among batters: 299 • *Top target (4 home runs)*: Dennis Leonard, Mike Smithson, Dave Stieb • *Number of pitchers victimized*: 118 • *Total ballparks homered in*: 24 • *First HR*: 08/29/1976 off Rick Wise

Sam Jones

SAMUEL POND JONES
B: 07/26/1892 D: 07/06/1966
BR

Year	Tm	Lg	Tot	H	A	Men-On 0	1	2	3	One-Game 2	3	4	LO	XN	IP	PH	RHP	LHP
1921	BOS	AL	2	0	2	0	2	0	0	0	0	0	0	0	0	0	2	0
1922	NY	AL	1	0	1	0	0	1	0	0	0	0	0	0	0	0	0	1
1924	NY	AL	1	0	1	1	0	0	0	0	0	0	0	0	0	0	1	0
1928	WAS	AL	2	0	2	2	0	0	0	0	0	0	0	0	0	0	2	0
Total			6	0	6	3	2	1	0	0	0	0	0	0	0	0	5	1

Rank among batters: 2,988 • *Total ballparks homered in*: 3 • *First HR*: 05/13/1921 off Shovel Hodge

Sam Jones

SAMUEL JONES
B: 12/14/1925 D: 11/05/1971
BR

Year	Tm	Lg	Tot	H	A	Men-On 0	1	2	3	One-Game 2	3	4	LO	XN	IP	PH	RHP	LHP
1962	DET	AL	1	1	0	1	0	0	0	0	0	0	0	0	0	0	1	0

Rank among batters: 4,707 • *Total ballparks homered in*: 1 • *First HR*: 04/26/1962 off Dave Wickersham

Tim Jones

WILLIAM TIMOTHY JONES
B: 12/01/1962
BL

Year	Tm	Lg	Tot	H	A	Men-On 0	1	2	3	One-Game 2	3	4	LO	XN	IP	PH	RHP	LHP
1990	STL	NL	1	1	0	1	0	0	0	0	0	0	0	0	0	0	1	0

Rank among batters: 4,707 • *Total ballparks homered in*: 1 • *First HR*: 08/19/1990 off Brian Fisher

Year	Tm	Lg	Tot	H	A	Men-On 0	Men-On 1	Men-On 2	Men-On 3	One-Game 2	One-Game 3	One-Game 4	LO	XN	IP	PH	RHP	LHP

Tom Jones

THOMAS JONES
B: 01/22/1877 D: 06/21/1923
BR

Year	Tm	Lg	Tot	H	A	0	1	2	3	2	3	4	LO	XN	IP	PH	RHP	LHP
1904	STL	AL	2	0	2	0	1	1	0	0	0	0	0	0	0	0	2	0
1908	STL	AL	1	0	1	0	1	0	0	0	0	0	0	0	0	0	1	0
1910	DET	AL	1	0	1	1	0	0	0	0	0	0	0	0	1	0	0	1
Total			4	0	4	1	2	1	0	0	0	0	0	0	1	0	3	1

Rank among batters: 3,427 • *Total ballparks homered in*: 4 • *First HR*: 05/07/1904 off Ed Walsh • *World Series HR*—1

Tracy Jones

TRACY DONALD JONES
B: 03/31/1961
BR

Year	Tm	Lg	Tot	H	A	0	1	2	3	2	3	4	LO	XN	IP	PH	RHP	LHP
1986	CIN	NL	2	1	1	2	0	0	0	0	0	0	2	0	0	0	0	2
1987	CIN	NL	10	4	6	7	2	1	0	0	0	0	1	0	0	1	5	5
1988	CIN	NL	1	0	1	0	1	0	0	0	0	0	0	0	0	1	0	1
	MON	NL	2	0	2	1	0	1	0	0	0	0	0	0	0	0	1	1
	Total		3	0	3	1	1	1	0	0	0	0	0	0	0	1	1	2
1989	DET	AL	3	3	0	2	0	1	0	0	0	0	0	0	0	0	2	1
1990	DET	AL	4	2	2	4	0	0	0	0	0	0	0	0	0	0	0	4
	SEA	AL	2	1	1	2	0	0	0	0	0	0	0	0	0	0	2	0
	Total		6	3	3	6	0	0	0	0	0	0	0	0	0	0	2	4
1991	SEA	AL	3	1	2	2	0	1	0	0	0	0	0	0	0	0	2	1
Total			27	12	15	20	3	4	0	0	0	0	3	0	0	2	12	15

Rank among batters: 1,532 • *Top target (2 home runs)*: Aurelio Lopez • *Number of pitchers victimized*: 26 • *Total ballparks homered in*: 13 • *First HR*: 05/20/1986 off Tim Conroy

Willie Jones

WILLIE EDWARD JONES
B: 08/16/1925 D: 10/18/1983
BR

Year	Tm	Lg	Tot	H	A	0	1	2	3	2	3	4	LO	XN	IP	PH	RHP	LHP
1948	PHI	NL	2	1	1	1	0	1	0	0	0	0	0	0	0	0	1	1
1949	PHI	NL	19	9	10	11	6	2	0	1	0	0	0	0	0	0	14	5
1950	PHI	NL	25	12	13	14	6	3	2	2	0	0	0	0	0	0	20	5
1951	PHI	NL	22	5	17	11	7	2	2	2	0	0	0	0	0	0	13	9
1952	PHI	NL	18	8	10	8	5	5	0	2	0	0	0	0	0	0	12	6
1953	PHI	NL	19	11	8	11	8	0	0	0	0	0	0	0	0	0	11	8
1954	PHI	NL	12	3	9	10	2	0	0	1	0	0	1	0	0	0	9	3
1955	PHI	NL	16	10	6	11	2	2	1	1	0	0	0	0	0	0	13	3
1956	PHI	NL	17	12	5	9	5	2	1	1	0	0	0	0	0	0	12	5
1957	PHI	NL	9	6	3	6	3	0	0	0	0	0	0	0	0	0	5	4
1958	PHI	NL	14	9	5	7	5	2	0	2	0	0	0	0	0	0	11	3
1959	PHI	NL	7	4	3	4	3	0	0	0	0	0	0	0	0	0	4	3
	CIN	NL	7	3	4	4	1	1	1	0	0	0	0	0	0	0	5	2
	Total		14	7	7	8	4	1	1	0	0	0	0	0	0	0	9	5
1960	CIN	NL	3	2	1	3	0	0	0	0	0	0	0	0	0	0	2	1
Total			190	95	95	110	53	20	7	12	0	0	1	0	0	0	132	58

Rank among batters: 201 • *Top target (6 home runs)*: Murry Dickson • *Number of pitchers victimized*: 112 • *Total ballparks homered in*: 10 • *First HR*: 09/20/1948 off Bob Chesnes

Eddie Joost

EDWIN DAVID JOOST
B: 06/05/1916
BR

Year	Tm	Lg	Tot	H	A	0	1	2	3	2	3	4	LO	XN	IP	PH	RHP	LHP
1940	CIN	NL	1	0	1	0	0	1	0	0	0	0	0	0	0	0	1	0
1941	CIN	NL	4	2	2	2	1	0	1	0	0	0	0	0	0	0	4	0
1942	CIN	NL	6	1	5	4	2	0	0	0	0	0	0	0	0	0	6	0
1943	BOS	NL	2	1	1	1	1	0	0	0	0	0	0	0	0	0	1	1
1947	PHI	AL	13	8	5	7	4	2	0	0	0	0	0	0	0	0	11	2
1948	PHI	AL	16	10	6	13	2	1	0	0	0	0	6	1	0	0	16	0
1949	PHI	AL	23	15	8	13	5	5	0	0	0	0	2	0	0	0	14	9
1950	PHI	AL	18	8	10	13	3	2	0	1	0	0	2	0	0	0	15	3
1951	PHI	AL	19	13	6	12	2	5	0	1	0	0	3	1	0	0	14	5
1952	PHI	AL	20	13	7	12	6	1	1	2	0	0	4	0	0	0	13	7
1953	PHI	AL	6	1	5	5	1	0	0	0	0	0	2	0	0	0	4	2
1954	PHI	AL	1	0	1	1	0	0	0	0	0	0	0	0	0	0	0	1

Eddie Joost *continued*

Year	Tm	Lg	Tot	H	A	Men-On 0	1	2	3	One-Game 2	3	4	LO	XN	IP	PH	RHP	LHP
1955	BOS	AL	5	3	2	2	0	3	0	1	0	0	0	0	0	0	5	0
Total			134	75	59	85	27	20	2	5	0	0	19	2	0	0	104	30

Rank among batters: 331 • *Top target (5 home runs)*: Ray Scarborough, Bob Feller • *Number of pitchers victimized*: 74 • *Total ballparks homered in*: 14 • *First HR*: 06/17/1940 off Boom-Boom Beck

Brian Jordan

BRIAN O'NEAL JORDAN
B: 03/29/1967
BR

Year	Tm	Lg	Tot	H	A	Men-On 0	1	2	3	One-Game 2	3	4	LO	XN	IP	PH	RHP	LHP
1992	STL	NL	5	3	2	2	2	1	0	0	0	0	0	0	0	0	1	4
1993	STL	NL	10	4	6	5	4	0	1	2	0	0	0	0	0	0	3	7
1994	STL	NL	5	4	1	2	3	0	0	0	0	0	0	0	0	1	3	2
1995	STL	NL	22	14	8	11	8	3	0	2	0	0	0	0	0	1	17	5
Total			42	25	17	20	17	4	1	4	0	0	0	0	0	2	24	18

Rank among batters: 1,138 • *Top target (2 home runs)*: Steve Cooke, David Mlicki • *Number of pitchers victimized*: 40 • *Total ballparks homered in*: 12 • *First HR*: 04/29/1992 off Trevor Wilson

Buck Jordan

BAXTER BYERLY JORDAN
B: 01/16/1907 D: 03/18/1993
BL

Year	Tm	Lg	Tot	H	A	Men-On 0	1	2	3	One-Game 2	3	4	LO	XN	IP	PH	RHP	LHP
1932	BOS	NL	2	1	1	2	0	0	0	0	0	0	0	0	0	0	2	0
1933	BOS	NL	4	1	3	2	2	0	0	0	0	0	0	0	0	0	4	0
1934	BOS	NL	2	0	2	2	0	0	0	0	0	0	0	0	0	0	2	0
1935	BOS	NL	5	0	5	3	2	0	0	0	0	0	0	0	0	0	4	1
1936	BOS	NL	3	0	3	1	2	0	0	0	0	0	0	0	0	0	3	0
1937	CIN	NL	1	0	1	1	0	0	0	0	0	0	1	0	0	0	1	0
Total			17	2	15	11	6	0	0	0	0	0	1	0	0	0	16	1

Rank among batters: 1,969 • *Top target (3 home runs)*: Guy Bush • *Number of pitchers victimized*: 13 • *Total ballparks homered in*: 7 • *First HR*: 08/17/1932 off Burleigh Grimes

Jimmy Jordan

JAMES WILLIAM JORDAN
B: 01/13/1908 D: 12/04/1957
BR

Year	Tm	Lg	Tot	H	A	Men-On 0	1	2	3	One-Game 2	3	4	LO	XN	IP	PH	RHP	LHP
1936	BRO	NL	2	2	0	2	0	0	0	0	0	0	1	0	0	0	1	1

Rank among batters: 4,129 • *Total ballparks homered in*: 1 • *First HR*: 07/28/1936 off Ralph Birkofer

Kevin Jordan

KEVIN WAYNE JORDAN
B: 10/09/1969
BR

Year	Tm	Lg	Tot	H	A	Men-On 0	1	2	3	One-Game 2	3	4	LO	XN	IP	PH	RHP	LHP
1995	PHI	NL	2	1	1	0	2	0	0	0	0	0	0	0	0	1	0	2

Rank among batters: 4,129 • *Total ballparks homered in*: 2 • *First HR*: 08/20/1995 off Shawn Barton

Ricky Jordan

PAUL SCOTT JORDAN
B: 05/26/1965
BR

Year	Tm	Lg	Tot	H	A	Men-On 0	1	2	3	One-Game 2	3	4	LO	XN	IP	PH	RHP	LHP
1988	PHI	NL	11	6	5	3	5	3	0	0	0	0	0	0	0	0	5	6
1989	PHI	NL	12	7	5	5	6	1	0	1	0	0	0	0	0	0	8	4
1990	PHI	NL	5	2	3	2	2	0	1	0	0	0	0	0	0	0	3	2
1991	PHI	NL	9	5	4	5	2	1	1	1	0	0	0	0	0	0	5	4
1992	PHI	NL	4	2	2	2	1	1	0	0	0	0	0	0	0	0	1	3
1993	PHI	NL	5	3	2	3	1	1	0	0	0	0	0	0	0	0	3	2
1994	PHI	NL	8	5	3	5	3	0	0	0	0	0	0	0	0	0	5	3
Total			54	30	24	25	20	7	2	2	0	0	0	0	0	0	30	24

Rank among batters: 938 • *Top target (4 home runs)*: Andy Benes • *Number of pitchers victimized*: 45 • *Total ballparks homered in*: 11 • *First HR*: 07/17/1988 off Bob Knepper • *Hit HR in first major league AB*—vs HOU: 07/17/1988

Tim Jordan

TIMOTHY JOSEPH JORDAN
B: 02/14/1879 D: 09/13/1949
BL

Year	Tm	Lg	Tot	H	A	Men-On 0	1	2	3	One-Game 2	3	4	LO	XN	IP	PH	RHP	LHP
1906	BRO	NL	12	8	4	4	3	5	0	0	0	0	0	0	1	0	10	2

Tim Jordan *continued*

Year	Tm	Lg	Tot	H	A	Men-On 0	1	2	3	One-Game 2	3	4	LO	XN	IP	PH	RHP	LHP
1907	BRO	NL	4	1	3	2	1	1	0	0	0	0	0	0	1	0	3	1
1908	BRO	NL	12	7	5	7	4	1	0	1	0	0	0	0	1	0	9	3
1909	BRO	NL	3	3	0	2	1	0	0	0	0	0	0	0	0	0	3	0
1910	BRO	NL	1	0	1	0	0	1	0	0	0	0	0	0	0	1	1	0
Total			32	19	13	15	9	8	0	1	0	0	0	0	3	1	26	6

Rank among batters: 1,360 • *Top target (4 home runs)*: Carl Lundgren • *Number of pitchers victimized*: 23 • *Total ballparks homered in*: 6 • *First HR*: 05/07/1906 off Hooks Wiltse

Tom Jordan

THOMAS JEFFERSON JORDAN
B: 09/05/1919
BR

Year	Tm	Lg	Tot	H	A	Men-On 0	1	2	3	One-Game 2	3	4	LO	XN	IP	PH	RHP	LHP
1946	CLE	AL	1	0	1	1	0	0	0	0	0	0	0	0	0	0	1	0

Rank among batters: 4,707 • *Total ballparks homered in*: 1 • *First HR*: 08/25/1946 off Dave Ferriss

Art Jorgens

ARNDT LUDWIG JORGENS
B: 05/18/1905 D: 03/01/1980
BR

Year	Tm	Lg	Tot	H	A	Men-On 0	1	2	3	One-Game 2	3	4	LO	XN	IP	PH	RHP	LHP
1932	NY	AL	2	1	1	0	2	0	0	0	0	0	0	0	0	0	1	1
1933	NY	AL	2	0	2	0	1	0	1	1	0	0	0	0	0	0	2	0
Total			4	1	3	0	3	0	1	1	0	0	0	0	0	0	3	1

Rank among batters: 3,427 • *Top target (2 home runs)*: Sugar Cain • *Number of pitchers victimized*: 3 • *Total ballparks homered in*: 2 • *First HR*: 06/01/1932 off Rube Walberg

Mike Jorgensen

MICHAEL JORGENSEN
B: 08/16/1948
BL

Year	Tm	Lg	Tot	H	A	Men-On 0	1	2	3	One-Game 2	3	4	LO	XN	IP	PH	RHP	LHP
1970	NY	NL	3	1	2	2	1	0	0	0	0	0	0	0	0	0	2	1
1971	NY	NL	5	5	0	3	2	0	0	1	0	0	0	0	0	0	5	0
1972	MON	NL	13	9	4	6	6	1	0	0	0	0	0	0	0	0	12	1
1973	MON	NL	9	6	3	4	2	2	1	0	0	0	0	0	0	0	9	0
1974	MON	NL	11	9	2	4	7	0	0	1	0	0	1	0	0	0	9	2
1975	MON	NL	18	8	10	9	6	2	1	0	0	0	0	0	0	0	17	1
1976	MON	NL	6	2	4	5	1	0	0	0	0	0	0	0	0	0	6	0
1977	OAK	AL	8	2	6	5	1	1	1	1	0	0	0	0	0	0	4	4
1978	TEX	AL	1	0	1	1	0	0	0	0	0	0	0	0	0	0	1	0
1979	TEX	AL	6	4	2	5	0	1	0	0	0	0	0	0	0	0	5	1
1980	NY	NL	7	5	2	5	1	0	1	0	0	0	0	1	0	0	7	0
1981	NY	NL	3	3	0	1	2	0	0	0	0	0	0	0	0	1	3	0
1982	NY	NL	2	2	0	0	1	1	0	0	0	0	0	0	0	1	2	0
1983	NY	NL	1	1	0	0	1	0	0	0	0	0	0	0	0	1	1	0
	ATL	NL	1	0	1	1	0	0	0	0	0	0	0	0	0	1	1	0
	Total		2	1	1	1	1	0	0	0	0	0	0	0	0	2	2	0
1984	STL	NL	1	0	1	0	0	1	0	0	0	0	0	0	0	0	1	0
Total			95	57	38	51	31	9	4	3	0	0	1	1	0	4	85	10

Rank among batters: 529 • *Top target (4 home runs)*: Rick Reuschel • *Number of pitchers victimized*: 72 • *Total ballparks homered in*: 21 • *First HR*: 04/26/1970 off Sandy Vance

Spider Jorgensen

JOHN DONALD JORGENSEN
B: 11/03/1919
BL

Year	Tm	Lg	Tot	H	A	Men-On 0	1	2	3	One-Game 2	3	4	LO	XN	IP	PH	RHP	LHP
1947	BRO	NL	5	3	2	0	3	2	0	0	0	0	0	0	0	0	3	2
1948	BRO	NL	1	1	0	0	1	0	0	0	0	0	0	0	0	0	1	0
1949	BRO	NL	1	0	1	0	1	0	0	0	0	0	0	0	0	0	1	0
1951	NY	NL	2	2	0	2	0	0	0	0	0	0	0	0	0	1	2	0
Total			9	6	3	2	5	2	0	0	0	0	0	0	0	1	7	2

Rank among batters: 2,587 • *Total ballparks homered in*: 5 • *First HR*: 04/17/1947 off Glenn Elliott

Terry Jorgensen

TERRY ALLEN JORGENSEN
B: 09/02/1966
BR

Year	Tm	Lg	Tot	H	A	Men-On 0	1	2	3	One-Game 2	3	4	LO	XN	IP	PH	RHP	LHP
1993	MIN	AL	1	0	1	0	0	1	0	0	0	0	0	0	0	0	0	1

Terry Jorgensen *continued*

Rank among batters: 4,707 • *Total ballparks homered in*: 1 • *First HR*: 08/29/1993 off Scott Radinsky

Felix Jose

DOMINGO FELIX ANDUJAR JOSE
B: 05/02/1965
BB

Year	Tm	Lg	Tot	H	A	Men-On 0	1	2	3	One-Game 2	3	4	LO	XN	IP	PH	RHP	LHP
1990	OAK	AL	8	3	5	2	4	1	1	0	0	0	0	0	1	0	7	1
	STL	NL	3	2	1	0	2	1	0	0	0	0	0	0	0	0	2	1
	Total		11	5	6	4	5	1	1	0	0	0	0	0	1	0	9	2
1991	STL	NL	8	3	5	3	4	1	0	1	0	0	0	0	0	0	7	1
1992	STL	NL	14	12	2	10	3	0	1	0	0	0	0	3	0	0	8	6
1993	KC	AL	6	2	4	2	3	1	0	0	0	0	0	0	0	0	6	0
1994	KC	AL	11	1	10	6	4	1	0	0	0	0	0	1	0	0	8	3
Total			50	23	27	25	19	4	2	1	0	0	0	4	1	0	38	12

Rank among batters: 991 • *Top target (2 home runs)*: Mark Gardner, Chris Bosio, Jason Bere • *Number of pitchers victimized*: 47 • *Total ballparks homered in*: 19 • *First HR*: 04/24/1990 off Dave Johnson

Rick Joseph

RICARDO EMELINDO (HARRIGAN) JOSEPH
B: 08/24/1939 D: 09/08/1979
BR

Year	Tm	Lg	Tot	H	A	Men-On 0	1	2	3	One-Game 2	3	4	LO	XN	IP	PH	RHP	LHP
1967	PHI	NL	1	1	0	0	0	0	1	0	0	0	0	1	0	1	0	1
1968	PHI	NL	3	1	2	3	0	0	0	0	0	0	0	0	0	2	1	2
1969	PHI	NL	6	1	5	4	1	1	0	0	0	0	0	0	0	0	6	0
1970	PHI	NL	3	0	3	1	2	0	0	0	0	0	0	1	0	3	1	2
Total			13	3	10	8	3	1	1	0	0	0	0	2	0	6	8	5

Rank among batters: 2,248 • *Total ballparks homered in*: 6 • *First HR*: 09/16/1967 off Ron Perranoski

Duane Josephson

DUANE CHARLES JOSEPHSON
B: 06/03/1942
BR

Year	Tm	Lg	Tot	H	A	Men-On 0	1	2	3	One-Game 2	3	4	LO	XN	IP	PH	RHP	LHP
1967	CHI	AL	1	1	0	1	0	0	0	0	0	0	0	0	0	0	0	1
1968	CHI	AL	6	3	3	4	2	0	0	0	0	0	0	0	0	0	6	0
1969	CHI	AL	1	1	0	0	1	0	0	0	0	0	0	0	0	0	1	0
1970	CHI	AL	4	3	1	4	0	0	0	0	0	0	0	0	0	0	3	1
1971	BOS	AL	10	2	8	6	3	1	0	1	0	0	0	0	0	0	6	4
1972	BOS	AL	1	0	1	0	1	0	0	0	0	0	0	0	0	0	1	0
Total			23	10	13	15	7	1	0	1	0	0	0	0	0	0	17	6

Rank among batters: 1,686 • *Top target (2 home runs)*: Pat Dobson • *Number of pitchers victimized*: 22 • *Total ballparks homered in*: 9 • *First HR*: 07/30/1967 off Johnny Podres

Von Joshua

VON EVERETT JOSHUA
B: 05/01/1948
BL

Year	Tm	Lg	Tot	H	A	Men-On 0	1	2	3	One-Game 2	3	4	LO	XN	IP	PH	RHP	LHP
1970	LA	NL	1	1	0	1	0	0	0	0	0	0	0	0	0	0	1	0
1973	LA	NL	2	1	1	1	0	1	0	0	0	0	0	0	0	0	2	0
1974	LA	NL	1	1	0	0	0	1	0	0	0	0	0	0	0	0	1	0
1975	SF	NL	7	3	4	4	3	0	0	0	0	0	1	0	0	0	6	1
1976	MIL	AL	5	3	2	5	0	0	0	0	0	0	2	0	0	0	4	1
1977	MIL	AL	9	3	6	6	3	0	0	0	0	0	2	0	0	0	8	1
1979	LA	NL	3	0	3	2	0	1	0	0	0	0	0	0	0	0	2	1
1980	SD	NL	2	1	1	2	0	0	0	0	0	0	0	0	0	1	2	0
Total			30	13	17	21	6	3	0	0	0	0	5	0	0	1	26	4

Rank among batters: 1,437 • *Top target (2 home runs)*: Larry Dierker • *Number of pitchers victimized*: 29 • *Total ballparks homered in*: 14 • *First HR*: 07/22/1970 off Claude Raymond

Addie Joss

ADRIAN JOSS
B: 04/12/1880 D: 04/14/1911
BR HOF

Year	Tm	Lg	Tot	H	A	Men-On 0	1	2	3	One-Game 2	3	4	LO	XN	IP	PH	RHP	LHP
1909	CLE	AL	1	0	1	0	1	0	0	0	0	0	0	0	0	0	1	0

Rank among batters: 4,707 • *Total ballparks homered in*: 1 • *First HR*: 09/07/1909 off Ed Summers

Bill Joyce

WILLIAM MICHAEL JOYCE
B: 09/21/1865 D: 05/08/1941
BL

Year	Tm	Lg	Tot	H	A	Men-On 0	1	2	3	One-Game 2	3	4	LO	XN	IP	PH	RHP	LHP
1890	BRO	PL	1	0	1	0	0	1	0	0	0	0	0	0	0	0	1	0
1891	BOS	AA	3	3	0	1	1	1	0	0	0	0	0	0	0	0	3	0
1892	BRO	NL	6	2	4	3	3	0	0	0	0	0	0	0	1	0	5	1
1894	WAS	NL	17	9	8	5	9	3	0	0	1	0	1	0	1	0	12	4
1895	WAS	NL	17	9	8	10	4	3	0	1	0	0	0	0	0	0	16	1
1896	WAS	NL	8	3	5	5	2	1	0	2	0	0	0	0	0	0	7	1
	NY	NL	5	5	0	0	4	1	0	1	0	0	0	0	1	0	1	4
	Total		13	8	5	5	6	2	0	3	0	0	0	0	1	0	8	5
1897	NY	NL	3	1	2	2	1	0	0	0	0	0	0	0	0	0	2	1
1898	NY	NL	10	7	3	5	3	2	0	1	0	0	0	1	0	0	9	0
Total			70	39	31	31	27	12	0	5	1	0	1	1	3	0	56	12

Rank among batters: 742 • *Top target (4 home runs)*: Phil Knell, Frank Killen, Gus Weyhing • *Number of pitchers victimized*: 47 • *Total ballparks homered in*: 19 • *First HR*: 06/28/1890 off Henry Gruber • *Hit for Cycle*—@PIT: 05/30/1896 (1)

Bob Joyce

ROBERT EMMETT JOYCE
B: 01/14/1915 D: 12/10/1981
BR

Year	Tm	Lg	Tot	H	A	Men-On 0	1	2	3	One-Game 2	3	4	LO	XN	IP	PH	RHP	LHP
1946	NY	NL	1	0	1	1	0	0	0	0	0	0	0	0	0	0	1	0

Rank among batters: 4,707 • *Total ballparks homered in*: 1 • *First HR*: 05/12/1946 off Bill Lee

Wally Joyner

WALLACE KEITH JOYNER
B: 06/16/1962
BL

Year	Tm	Lg	Tot	H	A	Men-On 0	1	2	3	One-Game 2	3	4	LO	XN	IP	PH	RHP	LHP
1986	CAL	AL	22	11	11	13	7	1	1	2	0	0	0	0	0	0	16	6
1987	CAL	AL	34	19	15	21	10	3	0	3	1	0	0	1	0	0	26	8
1988	CAL	AL	13	6	7	4	7	2	0	1	0	0	0	0	0	0	12	1
1989	CAL	AL	16	8	8	11	4	1	0	0	0	0	0	0	0	0	10	6
1990	CAL	AL	8	5	3	6	1	0	1	0	0	0	0	0	0	0	6	2
1991	CAL	AL	21	10	11	12	5	3	1	1	0	0	0	0	0	0	16	5
1992	KC	AL	9	1	8	4	3	2	0	0	0	0	0	1	0	0	7	2
1993	KC	AL	15	4	11	11	3	0	1	1	0	0	0	0	0	0	13	2
1994	KC	AL	8	2	6	4	2	2	0	0	0	0	0	0	0	0	7	1
1995	KC	AL	12	6	6	8	2	1	1	0	0	0	0	0	0	1	12	0
Total			158	72	86	94	44	15	5	8	1	0	0	2	0	1	125	33

Rank among batters: 271 • *Top target (4 home runs)*: Al Nipper, Dave Stieb • *Number of pitchers victimized*: 130 • *Total ballparks homered in*: 18 • *First HR*: 04/09/1986 off Mark Langston • *LCS HR*—1

Oscar Judd

THOMAS WILLIAM OSCAR JUDD
B: 02/14/1908
BL

Year	Tm	Lg	Tot	H	A	Men-On 0	1	2	3	One-Game 2	3	4	LO	XN	IP	PH	RHP	LHP
1942	BOS	AL	2	1	1	2	0	0	0	0	0	0	0	0	0	0	2	0
1946	PHI	NL	1	0	1	1	0	0	0	0	0	0	0	0	1	0	1	0
Total			3	1	2	3	0	0	0	0	0	0	0	0	1	0	3	0

Rank among batters: 3,735 • *Total ballparks homered in*: 3 • *First HR*: 06/23/1942 off Dizzy Trout

Frank Jude

FRANK JUDE
B: 1884 D: 05/04/1961
BR

Year	Tm	Lg	Tot	H	A	Men-On 0	1	2	3	One-Game 2	3	4	LO	XN	IP	PH	RHP	LHP
1906	CIN	NL	1	1	0	1	0	0	0	0	0	0	0	0	1	0	1	0

Rank among batters: 4,707 • *Total ballparks homered in*: 1 • *First HR*: 07/12/1906 off Dummy Taylor

Jeff Juden

JEFFREY DANIEL JUDEN
B: 01/19/1971
BR

Year	Tm	Lg	Tot	H	A	Men-On 0	1	2	3	One-Game 2	3	4	LO	XN	IP	PH	RHP	LHP
1995	PHI	NL	1	1	0	0	0	0	1	0	0	0	0	0	0	0	0	1

Rank among batters: 4,707 • *Total ballparks homered in*: 1 • *First HR*: 08/25/1995 off John Cummings

Year	Tm	Lg	Tot	H	A	Men-On				One-Game			LO	XN	IP	PH	RHP	LHP
						0	1	2	3	2	3	4						

Joe Judge

JOSEPH IGNATIUS JUDGE
B: 05/25/1894 D: 03/11/1963
BL

Year	Tm	Lg	Tot	H	A	0	1	2	3	2	3	4	LO	XN	IP	PH	RHP	LHP
1917	WAS	AL	2	0	2	2	0	0	0	0	0	0	0	0	1	0	2	0
1918	WAS	AL	1	0	1	0	1	0	0	0	0	0	0	0	1	0	0	1
1919	WAS	AL	2	0	2	2	0	0	0	0	0	0	0	0	0	0	1	1
1920	WAS	AL	5	1	4	4	1	0	0	1	0	0	0	0	0	0	5	0
1921	WAS	AL	7	3	4	5	2	0	0	1	0	0	0	0	3	0	7	0
1922	WAS	AL	10	4	6	4	2	4	0	0	0	0	0	0	2	0	8	2
1923	WAS	AL	2	0	2	0	1	1	0	0	0	0	0	0	0	0	2	0
1924	WAS	AL	3	0	3	3	0	0	0	0	0	0	0	0	0	0	2	1
1925	WAS	AL	8	1	7	4	2	0	2	1	0	0	0	0	2	0	6	2
1926	WAS	AL	7	1	6	3	1	2	1	0	0	0	0	0	0	0	6	1
1927	WAS	AL	2	0	2	1	0	1	0	0	0	0	0	0	0	0	2	0
1928	WAS	AL	3	1	2	0	3	0	0	0	0	0	0	0	2	0	2	1
1929	WAS	AL	6	2	4	3	0	3	0	0	0	0	1	0	1	0	3	3
1930	WAS	AL	10	1	9	7	2	1	0	1	0	0	0	0	0	1	5	5
1932	WAS	AL	3	0	3	2	1	0	0	0	0	0	0	0	0	0	3	0
Total			71	14	57	40	16	12	3	4	0	0	1	0	12	1	54	17

Rank among batters: 731 • *Top target (6 home runs)*: Elam Vangilder, Dixie Davis • *Number of pitchers victimized*: 45 • *Total ballparks homered in*: 9 • *First HR*: 06/30/1917 off Joe Bush • *World Series HR*—1

Wally Judnich

WALTER FRANKLIN JUDNICH
B: 01/24/1917 D: 07/12/1971
BL

Year	Tm	Lg	Tot	H	A	0	1	2	3	2	3	4	LO	XN	IP	PH	RHP	LHP
1940	STL	AL	24	14	10	13	8	3	0	2	0	0	0	1	0	0	23	1
1941	STL	AL	14	9	5	8	3	3	0	0	0	0	0	1	0	1	12	2
1942	STL	AL	17	10	7	8	6	3	0	2	0	0	0	2	0	1	16	1
1946	STL	AL	15	10	5	10	3	2	0	1	0	0	0	0	0	0	15	0
1947	STL	AL	18	10	8	10	8	0	0	1	0	0	0	0	0	0	17	1
1948	CLE	AL	2	1	1	2	0	0	0	0	0	0	0	0	0	0	2	0
Total			90	54	36	51	28	11	0	6	0	0	0	4	0	2	85	5

Rank among batters: 573 • *Top target (4 home runs)*: Sid Hudson • *Number of pitchers victimized*: 60 • *Total ballparks homered in*: 8 • *First HR*: 04/16/1940 off Bobo Newsom

George Jumonville

GEORGE BENEDICT JUMONVILLE
B: 05/16/1917
BR

Year	Tm	Lg	Tot	H	A	0	1	2	3	2	3	4	LO	XN	IP	PH	RHP	LHP
1941	PHI	NL	1	0	1	1	0	0	0	0	0	0	0	0	0	1	0	1

Rank among batters: 4,707 • *Total ballparks homered in*: 1 • *First HR*: 05/20/1941 off Clyde Shoun

Ed Jurak

EDWARD JAMES JURAK
B: 10/24/1957
BR

Year	Tm	Lg	Tot	H	A	0	1	2	3	2	3	4	LO	XN	IP	PH	RHP	LHP
1984	BOS	AL	1	0	1	1	0	0	0	0	0	0	0	0	0	0	1	0

Rank among batters: 4,707 • *Total ballparks homered in*: 1 • *First HR*: 06/17/1984 off Jim Clancy

Billy Jurges

WILLIAM FREDERICK JURGES
B: 05/09/1908
BR

Year	Tm	Lg	Tot	H	A	0	1	2	3	2	3	4	LO	XN	IP	PH	RHP	LHP
1932	CHI	NL	2	0	2	1	1	0	0	0	0	0	0	0	0	0	2	0
1933	CHI	NL	5	2	3	1	3	1	0	0	0	0	0	0	1	0	5	0
1934	CHI	NL	8	6	2	5	2	1	0	0	0	0	0	0	0	0	6	2
1935	CHI	NL	1	0	1	1	0	0	0	0	0	0	0	0	0	0	1	0
1936	CHI	NL	1	0	1	1	0	0	0	0	0	0	0	0	0	0	1	0
1937	CHI	NL	1	1	0	1	0	0	0	0	0	0	0	0	0	0	1	0
1938	CHI	NL	1	0	1	1	0	0	0	0	0	0	0	0	0	0	0	1
1939	NY	NL	6	6	0	2	4	0	0	0	0	0	0	0	0	0	5	1
1940	NY	NL	2	2	0	1	1	0	0	0	0	0	0	0	0	0	2	0
1941	NY	NL	5	4	1	2	3	0	0	0	0	0	0	0	0	0	3	2
1942	NY	NL	2	1	1	1	0	1	0	0	0	0	0	0	0	0	2	0

Billy Jurges *continued*

Year	Tm	Lg	Tot	H	A	Men-On 0	1	2	3	One-Game 2	3	4	LO	XN	IP	PH	RHP	LHP
1943	NY	NL	4	2	2	4	0	0	0	0	0	0	0	0	0	0	4	0
1944	NY	NL	1	1	0	0	1	0	0	0	0	0	0	0	0	1	0	1
1945	NY	NL	3	3	0	2	1	0	0	0	0	0	0	0	0	0	3	0
1947	CHI	NL	1	0	1	0	1	0	0	0	0	0	0	1	0	0	0	1
Total			43	28	15	23	17	3	0	0	0	0	0	1	1	1	35	8

Rank among batters: 1,116 • *Top target (3 home runs)*: Paul Derringer • *Number of pitchers victimized*: 39 • *Total ballparks homered in*: 7 • *First HR*: 06/03/1932 off Steve Swetonic

Dave Justice

DAVID CHRISTOPHER JUSTICE
B: 04/14/1966
BL

Year	Tm	Lg	Tot	H	A	Men-On 0	1	2	3	One-Game 2	3	4	LO	XN	IP	PH	RHP	LHP
1989	ATL	NL	1	1	0	1	0	0	0	0	0	0	0	0	0	0	1	0
1990	ATL	NL	28	19	9	17	8	2	1	3	0	0	0	0	0	1	18	10
1991	ATL	NL	21	11	10	10	9	2	0	2	0	0	0	1	0	0	14	7
1992	ATL	NL	21	10	11	8	11	2	0	1	0	0	0	0	0	0	17	4
1993	ATL	NL	40	18	22	20	14	6	0	2	0	0	0	0	0	0	29	11
1994	ATL	NL	19	9	10	13	3	3	0	1	0	0	0	1	0	1	15	4
1995	ATL	NL	24	15	9	14	6	4	0	1	0	0	0	0	0	0	17	7
Total			154	83	71	83	51	19	1	10	0	0	0	2	0	2	111	43

Rank among batters: 278 • *Top target (4 home runs)*: Andy Benes, Doug Drabek • *Number of pitchers victimized*: 113 • *Total ballparks homered in*: 15 • *First HR*: 09/19/1989 off Mike Scott • *World Series HR—4; LCS HR—3*

Skip Jutze

ALFRED HENRY JUTZE
B: 05/28/1946
BR

Year	Tm	Lg	Tot	H	A	Men-On 0	1	2	3	One-Game 2	3	4	LO	XN	IP	PH	RHP	LHP
1977	SEA	AL	3	2	1	1	0	1	1	0	0	0	0	0	0	0	2	1

Rank among batters: 3,735 • *Total ballparks homered in*: 2 • *First HR*: 04/12/1977 off Mike Pazik

Jim Kaat

JAMES LEE KAAT
B: 11/07/1938
BL

Year	Tm	Lg	Tot	H	A	Men-On 0	1	2	3	One-Game 2	3	4	LO	XN	IP	PH	RHP	LHP
1962	MIN	AL	1	0	1	1	0	0	0	0	0	0	0	0	0	0	1	0
1963	MIN	AL	1	0	1	0	0	1	0	0	0	0	0	0	0	0	1	0
1964	MIN	AL	3	1	2	2	1	0	0	0	0	0	0	0	0	0	3	0
1965	MIN	AL	1	0	1	1	0	0	0	0	0	0	0	0	0	0	1	0
1966	MIN	AL	2	2	0	1	1	0	0	0	0	0	0	0	0	0	1	1
1967	MIN	AL	1	0	1	0	1	0	0	0	0	0	0	0	0	0	1	0
1969	MIN	AL	2	1	1	1	1	0	0	0	0	0	0	0	0	0	2	0
1970	MIN	AL	1	1	0	0	1	0	0	0	0	0	0	0	0	0	1	0
1972	MIN	AL	2	1	1	1	1	0	0	0	0	0	0	0	0	0	2	0
1976	PHI	NL	1	1	0	1	0	0	0	0	0	0	0	0	0	0	1	0
1980	STL	NL	1	1	0	1	0	0	0	0	0	0	0	0	0	0	1	0
Total			16	8	8	9	6	1	0	0	0	0	0	0	0	0	15	1

Rank among batters: 2,029 • *Total ballparks homered in*: 9 • *First HR*: 06/19/1962 off Dom Zanni

Mike Kahoe

MICHAEL JOSEPH KAHOE
B: 09/03/1873 D: 05/14/1949
BR

Year	Tm	Lg	Tot	H	A	Men-On 0	1	2	3	One-Game 2	3	4	LO	XN	IP	PH	RHP	LHP
1900	CIN	NL	1	0	1	1	0	0	0	0	0	0	0	0	0	0	1	0
1901	CHI	NL	1	0	1	1	0	0	0	0	0	0	0	0	0	0	1	0
1902	STL	AL	2	1	1	0	1	1	0	0	0	0	0	0	0	0	1	1
Total			4	1	3	2	1	1	0	0	0	0	0	0	0	0	3	1

Rank among batters: 3,427 • *Total ballparks homered in*: 3 • *First HR*: 09/07/1900 off Vic Willis

Al Kaiser

ALFRED EDWARD KAISER
B: 08/03/1886 D: 04/11/1969
BR

Year	Tm	Lg	Tot	H	A	Men-On 0	1	2	3	One-Game 2	3	4	LO	XN	IP	PH	RHP	LHP
1911	BOS	NL	2	1	1	1	1	0	0	0	0	0	0	0	1	0	1	1

Al Kaiser *continued*

Year	Tm	Lg	Tot	H	A	Men-On 0	1	2	3	One-Game 2	3	4	LO	XN	IP	PH	RHP	LHP
1914	IND	FL	1	0	1	0	0	1	0	0	0	0	0	0	0	0	1	0
Total			3	1	2	1	1	1	0	0	0	0	0	0	1	0	2	1

Rank among batters: 3,735 • *Total ballparks homered in*: 3 • *First HR*: 07/05/1911 off Nap Rucker

Al Kaline

ALBERT WILLIAM KALINE
B: 12/19/1934
BR HOF

Year	Tm	Lg	Tot	H	A	Men-On 0	1	2	3	One-Game 2	3	4	LO	XN	IP	PH	RHP	LHP
1953	DET	AL	1	0	1	1	0	0	0	0	0	0	0	0	0	0	1	0
1954	DET	AL	4	1	3	2	0	1	1	0	0	0	0	0	0	0	2	2
1955	DET	AL	27	16	11	13	9	5	0	2	1	0	0	0	0	0	21	6
1956	DET	AL	27	13	14	11	14	2	0	2	0	0	0	0	0	0	23	4
1957	DET	AL	23	10	13	13	5	5	0	2	0	0	0	1	0	0	22	1
1958	DET	AL	16	11	5	8	4	4	0	1	0	0	0	0	0	0	14	2
1959	DET	AL	27	16	11	15	10	2	0	1	0	0	0	0	1	0	18	9
1960	DET	AL	15	7	8	10	2	2	1	0	0	0	0	1	0	0	11	4
1961	DET	AL	19	8	11	14	4	1	0	0	0	0	0	0	0	0	15	4
1962	DET	AL	29	16	13	13	13	3	0	2	0	0	0	0	0	0	23	6
1963	DET	AL	27	22	5	15	9	3	0	3	0	0	0	2	0	0	17	10
1964	DET	AL	17	9	8	10	6	1	0	0	0	0	0	0	1	0	12	5
1965	DET	AL	18	8	10	8	7	3	0	1	0	0	0	1	0	0	11	7
1966	DET	AL	29	18	11	17	10	2	0	3	0	0	0	1	0	0	22	7
1967	DET	AL	25	15	10	16	8	1	0	1	0	0	0	0	0	0	11	14
1968	DET	AL	10	4	6	5	4	1	0	0	0	0	0	0	0	1	8	2
1969	DET	AL	21	13	8	14	7	0	0	3	0	0	0	0	0	0	6	15
1970	DET	AL	16	9	7	7	8	1	0	0	0	0	0	0	0	0	9	7
1971	DET	AL	15	11	4	6	7	2	0	1	0	0	0	0	0	1	9	6
1972	DET	AL	10	6	4	8	2	0	0	0	0	0	0	0	0	0	4	6
1973	DET	AL	10	6	4	7	2	0	1	0	0	0	0	0	0	0	3	7
1974	DET	AL	13	7	6	6	6	1	0	0	0	0	0	1	0	0	9	4
Total			399	226	173	219	137	40	3	22	1	0	0	7	2	2	271	128

Rank among batters: 26 • *Top target (9 home runs)*: Tom Brewer, Jim Kaat • *Number of pitchers victimized*: 219 • *Total ballparks homered in*: 17 • *First HR*: 09/26/1953 off Dave Hoskins • *2 HR in 1 inning*—vs KC: 04/17/1955 • *World Series HR*—2; *LCS HR*—1; *All-Star HR*—2

Willie Kamm

WILLIAM EDWARD KAMM
B: 02/02/1900 D: 12/21/1988
BR

Year	Tm	Lg	Tot	H	A	Men-On 0	1	2	3	One-Game 2	3	4	LO	XN	IP	PH	RHP	LHP
1923	CHI	AL	6	3	3	3	2	1	0	0	0	0	0	0	0	0	3	3
1924	CHI	AL	6	1	5	5	0	1	0	0	0	0	0	0	0	0	5	1
1925	CHI	AL	6	2	4	5	0	0	1	0	0	0	0	0	0	0	2	4
1928	CHI	AL	1	1	0	1	0	0	0	0	0	0	0	0	0	0	0	1
1929	CHI	AL	3	3	0	3	0	0	0	0	0	0	0	0	0	0	1	2
1930	CHI	AL	3	1	2	2	1	0	0	0	0	0	0	0	0	0	2	1
1932	CLE	AL	3	2	1	0	2	0	1	0	0	0	0	0	0	0	2	1
1933	CLE	AL	1	0	1	1	0	0	0	0	0	0	0	0	0	0	0	1
Total			29	13	16	20	5	2	2	0	0	0	0	0	0	0	15	14

Rank among batters: 1,465 • *Top target (3 home runs)*: Ken Holloway • *Number of pitchers victimized*: 22 • *Total ballparks homered in*: 6 • *First HR*: 05/24/1923 off Ken Holloway

Alex Kampouris

ALEXIS WILLIAM KAMPOURIS
B: 11/13/1912 D: 05/29/1993
BR

Year	Tm	Lg	Tot	H	A	Men-On 0	1	2	3	One-Game 2	3	4	LO	XN	IP	PH	RHP	LHP
1935	CIN	NL	7	2	5	5	2	0	0	0	0	0	0	0	0	0	6	1
1936	CIN	NL	5	1	4	2	2	1	0	0	0	0	0	0	0	0	4	1
1937	CIN	NL	17	1	16	7	5	3	2	1	1	0	0	0	0	0	16	1
1938	CIN	NL	2	1	1	2	0	0	0	0	0	0	1	0	0	0	1	1
	NY	NL	5	5	0	3	1	1	0	0	0	0	0	0	0	0	5	0
	Total		7	6	1	5	1	1	0	0	0	0	1	0	0	0	6	1
1939	NY	NL	5	4	1	5	0	0	0	0	0	0	0	0	0	0	5	0
1941	BRO	NL	2	1	1	0	2	0	0	0	0	0	0	0	0	0	1	1
1943	WAS	AL	2	0	2	2	0	0	0	0	0	0	0	0	0	0	1	1
Total			45	15	30	26	12	5	2	1	1	0	1	0	0	0	39	6

Rank among batters: 1,082 • *Top target (4 home runs)*: Johnny Lanning • *Number of pitchers victimized*: 35 • *Total ballparks homered in*: 9 • *First HR*: 05/19/1935 off Hal Schumacher

John Kane

JOHN FRANCIS KANE
B: 09/24/1882 D: 01/28/1934
BR

Year	Tm	Lg	Tot	H	A	Men-On 0	1	2	3	One-Game 2	3	4	LO	XN	IP	PH	RHP	LHP
1907	CIN	NL	3	0	3	3	0	0	0	0	0	0	1	0	2	0	2	1
1908	CIN	NL	3	2	1	2	0	1	0	0	0	0	0	0	3	0	1	2
1910	CHI	NL	1	0	1	1	0	0	0	0	0	0	0	0	0	0	0	1
Total			7	2	5	6	0	1	0	0	0	0	1	0	5	0	3	4

Rank among batters: 2,834 • *Total ballparks homered in*: 4 • *First HR*: 08/20/1907 off Harry McIntire

Rod Kanehl

RODERICK EDWIN KANEHL
B: 04/01/1934
BR

Year	Tm	Lg	Tot	H	A	Men-On 0	1	2	3	One-Game 2	3	4	LO	XN	IP	PH	RHP	LHP
1962	NY	NL	4	4	0	3	0	0	1	0	0	0	0	0	0	0	2	2
1963	NY	NL	1	1	0	0	1	0	0	0	0	0	0	0	0	0	0	1
1964	NY	NL	1	1	0	1	0	0	0	0	0	0	0	0	0	0	1	0
Total			6	6	0	4	1	0	1	0	0	0	0	0	0	0	3	3

Rank among batters: 2,988 • *Total ballparks homered in*: 2 • *First HR*: 06/01/1962 off Billy Pierce

Heinie Kappel

HENRY KAPPEL
B: 09/ /1863 D: 08/27/1905
BR

Year	Tm	Lg	Tot	H	A	Men-On 0	1	2	3	One-Game 2	3	4	LO	XN	IP	PH	RHP	LHP
1888	CIN	AA	1	0	1	1	0	0	0	0	0	0	0	0	1	0	1	0
1889	COL	AA	3	0	3	0	2	1	0	0	0	0	0	0	0	0	3	0
Total			4	0	4	1	2	1	0	0	0	0	0	0	1	0	4	0

Rank among batters: 3,427 • *Top target (2 home runs)*: Gus Weyhing • *Number of pitchers victimized*: 3 • *Total ballparks homered in*: 3 • *First HR*: 06/07/1888 off Gus Weyhing

Joe Kappel

JOSEPH KAPPEL
B: 04/27/1857 D: 07/08/1929
BR

Year	Tm	Lg	Tot	H	A	Men-On 0	1	2	3	One-Game 2	3	4	LO	XN	IP	PH	RHP	LHP
1890	PHI	AA	1	0	1	0	1	0	0	0	0	0	0	0	0	0	1	0

Rank among batters: 4,707 • *Total ballparks homered in*: 1 • *First HR*: 08/16/1890 off Jack Stivetts

Ed Karger

EDWIN KARGER
B: 05/06/1883 D: 09/09/1957
BR

Year	Tm	Lg	Tot	H	A	Men-On 0	1	2	3	One-Game 2	3	4	LO	XN	IP	PH	RHP	LHP
1906	STL	NL	1	0	1	1	0	0	0	0	0	0	0	0	0	0	1	0
1907	STL	NL	2	1	1	1	1	0	0	0	0	0	0	0	1	0	2	0
1910	BOS	AL	2	2	0	1	1	0	0	0	0	0	0	0	1	0	2	0
1911	BOS	AL	1	1	0	1	0	0	0	0	0	0	0	0	0	0	1	0
Total			6	4	2	4	2	0	0	0	0	0	0	0	2	0	6	0

Rank among batters: 2,988 • *Top target (2 home runs)*: Bob Groom • *Number of pitchers victimized*: 5 • *Total ballparks homered in*: 4 • *First HR*: 08/09/1906 off Gus Dorner

Ron Karkovice

RONALD JOSEPH KARKOVICE
B: 08/08/1963
BR

Year	Tm	Lg	Tot	H	A	Men-On 0	1	2	3	One-Game 2	3	4	LO	XN	IP	PH	RHP	LHP
1986	CHI	AL	4	1	3	3	0	1	0	0	0	0	0	0	0	0	2	2
1987	CHI	AL	2	1	1	0	2	0	0	0	0	0	0	0	0	0	1	1
1988	CHI	AL	3	1	2	2	0	1	0	0	0	0	0	0	0	0	2	1
1989	CHI	AL	3	0	3	0	1	1	1	0	0	0	0	0	0	0	2	1
1990	CHI	AL	6	0	6	5	0	0	1	0	0	0	0	1	1	0	4	2
1991	CHI	AL	5	0	5	1	4	0	0	1	0	0	0	0	0	0	2	3
1992	CHI	AL	13	5	8	7	5	1	0	1	0	0	0	0	0	0	9	4
1993	CHI	AL	20	6	14	11	8	0	1	2	0	0	0	1	0	0	13	7
1994	CHI	AL	11	6	5	7	1	2	1	0	0	0	0	0	0	0	5	6
1995	CHI	AL	13	5	8	8	1	3	1	1	0	0	0	0	0	0	11	2
Total			80	25	55	44	22	9	5	5	0	0	0	2	1	0	51	29

Rank among batters: 650 • *Top target (3 home runs)*: John Farrell, Dave Wells • *Number of pitchers victimized*: 70 • *Total ballparks homered in*: 15 • *First HR*: 08/27/1986 off Danny Jackson

Benn Karr

BENJAMIN JOYCE KARR
B: 11/28/1893 D: 12/08/1968
BL

Year	Tm	Lg	Tot	H	A	Men-On 0	1	2	3	One-Game 2	3	4	LO	XN	IP	PH	RHP	LHP
1920	BOS	AL	1	0	1	0	1	0	0	0	0	0	0	0	0	0	1	0
1925	CLE	AL	1	0	1	1	0	0	0	0	0	0	0	0	0	0	1	0
Total			2	0	2	1	1	0	0	0	0	0	0	0	0	0	2	0

Rank among batters: 4,129 • *Total ballparks homered in*: 2 • *First HR*: 08/10/1920 off Adrian Lynch

Eric Karros

ERIC PETER KARROS
B: 11/04/1967
BR

Year	Tm	Lg	Tot	H	A	Men-On 0	1	2	3	One-Game 2	3	4	LO	XN	IP	PH	RHP	LHP
1992	LA	NL	20	6	14	11	6	3	0	0	0	0	0	0	0	1	12	8
1993	LA	NL	23	13	10	14	4	5	0	2	0	0	0	0	0	0	18	5
1994	LA	NL	14	5	9	11	2	1	0	1	0	0	0	0	0	0	10	4
1995	LA	NL	32	19	13	16	13	3	0	2	0	0	0	2	1	0	28	4
Total			89	43	46	52	25	12	0	5	0	0	0	2	1	1	68	21

Rank among batters: 584 • *Top target (3 home runs)*: Greg Harris • *Number of pitchers victimized*: 73 • *Total ballparks homered in*: 14 • *First HR*: 04/09/1992 off Craig Lefferts • *LCS HR*—2

Eddie Kasko

EDWARD MICHAEL KASKO
B: 06/27/1932
BR

Year	Tm	Lg	Tot	H	A	Men-On 0	1	2	3	One-Game 2	3	4	LO	XN	IP	PH	RHP	LHP
1957	STL	NL	1	0	1	0	1	0	0	0	0	0	0	0	0	0	0	1
1958	STL	NL	2	2	0	0	1	0	1	0	0	0	0	0	0	0	0	2
1959	CIN	NL	2	2	0	2	0	0	0	0	0	0	0	0	0	0	1	1
1960	CIN	NL	6	2	4	3	2	0	1	0	0	0	0	0	0	0	6	0
1961	CIN	NL	2	0	2	1	1	0	0	0	0	0	1	0	0	0	2	0
1962	CIN	NL	4	0	4	2	0	1	1	0	0	0	1	1	0	0	3	1
1963	CIN	NL	3	0	3	2	1	0	0	0	0	0	0	0	0	1	0	3
1965	HOU	NL	1	0	1	0	1	0	0	0	0	0	0	0	0	0	1	0
1966	BOS	AL	1	0	1	1	0	0	0	0	0	0	0	0	0	0	0	1
Total			22	6	16	11	7	1	3	0	0	0	2	1	0	1	13	9

Rank among batters: 1,719 • *Top target (2 home runs)*: Jim Owens, Billy Pierce, Al Jackson • *Number of pitchers victimized*: 19 • *Total ballparks homered in*: 9 • *First HR*: 08/20/1957 off Jim Constable

Jack Katoll

JOHN KATOLL
B: 06/24/1872 D: 06/18/1955
BR

Year	Tm	Lg	Tot	H	A	Men-On 0	1	2	3	One-Game 2	3	4	LO	XN	IP	PH	RHP	LHP
1901	CHI	AL	1	0	1	1	0	0	0	0	0	0	0	0	0	0	0	1

Rank among batters: 4,707 • *Total ballparks homered in*: 1 • *First HR*: 05/12/1901 off Ed Siever

Ray Katt

RAYMOND FREDERICK KATT
B: 05/09/1927
BR

Year	Tm	Lg	Tot	H	A	Men-On 0	1	2	3	One-Game 2	3	4	LO	XN	IP	PH	RHP	LHP
1954	NY	NL	9	6	3	6	2	1	0	0	0	0	0	0	0	0	5	4
1955	NY	NL	7	2	5	5	0	2	0	0	0	0	0	1	0	1	4	3
1956	NY	NL	7	3	4	3	4	0	0	0	0	0	0	0	0	0	4	3
	STL	NL	6	5	1	3	3	0	0	0	0	0	0	0	0	0	4	2
	Total		13	8	5	6	7	0	0	0	0	0	0	0	0	0	8	5
1957	NY	NL	2	1	1	2	0	0	0	0	0	0	0	0	0	0	1	1
1958	STL	NL	1	0	1	1	0	0	0	0	0	0	0	0	0	0	1	0
Total			32	17	15	20	9	3	0	0	0	0	0	1	0	1	19	13

Rank among batters: 1,360 • Top target (2 home runs): Billy Loes, Jackie Collum, Joe Nuxhall, Robin Roberts, Wilmer Mizell • *Number of pitchers victimized*: 27 • *Total ballparks homered in*: 8 • *First HR*: 06/11/1954 off Hal Jeffcoat

Benny Kauff

BENJAMIN MICHAEL KAUFF
B: 01/05/1890 D: 11/17/1961
BL

Year	Tm	Lg	Tot	H	A	Men-On 0	1	2	3	One-Game 2	3	4	LO	XN	IP	PH	RHP	LHP
1914	IND	FL	8	3	5	3	3	2	0	0	0	0	0	1	1	0	7	1
1915	BRO	FL	12	5	7	6	5	1	0	0	0	0	0	1	0	0	8	4

Benny Kauff *continued*

Year	Tm	Lg	Tot	H	A	Men-On 0	Men-On 1	Men-On 2	Men-On 3	One-Game 2	One-Game 3	One-Game 4	LO	XN	IP	PH	RHP	LHP
1916	NY	NL	9	7	2	7	1	0	1	0	0	0	0	0	3	0	8	1
1917	NY	NL	5	2	3	1	4	0	0	0	0	0	0	0	0	0	5	0
1918	NY	NL	2	2	0	1	0	1	0	0	0	0	0	0	0	0	2	0
1919	NY	NL	10	7	3	4	5	1	0	0	0	0	0	0	1	0	8	2
1920	NY	NL	3	3	0	2	1	0	0	0	0	0	0	0	0	0	3	0
Total			49	29	20	24	19	5	1	0	0	0	0	2	5	0	41	8

Rank among batters: 1,008 • Top target (2 home runs): Claude Hendrix, Fred Anderson, Phil Douglas, Jack Scott • *Number of pitchers victimized*: 45 • *Total ballparks homered in*: 11 • *First HR*: 05/21/1914 off Fred Anderson • *World Series HR*—2

Tony Kaufmann

ANTHONY CHARLES KAUFMANN
B: 12/16/1900 D: 06/04/1982
BR

Year	Tm	Lg	Tot	H	A	Men-On 0	Men-On 1	Men-On 2	Men-On 3	One-Game 2	One-Game 3	One-Game 4	LO	XN	IP	PH	RHP	LHP
1922	CHI	NL	1	0	1	0	1	0	0	0	0	0	0	0	0	0	1	0
1923	CHI	NL	2	2	0	1	0	1	0	0	0	0	0	0	0	0	1	1
1924	CHI	NL	1	1	0	1	0	0	0	0	0	0	0	0	0	0	1	0
1925	CHI	NL	2	2	0	1	1	0	0	1	0	0	0	0	0	0	0	2
1926	CHI	NL	1	0	1	0	1	0	0	0	0	0	0	0	0	0	1	0
1927	CHI	NL	1	0	1	1	0	0	0	0	0	0	0	0	0	0	0	1
	PHI	NL	1	1	0	0	1	0	0	0	0	0	0	0	0	0	1	0
	Total		2	1	1	1	1	0	0	0	0	0	0	0	0	0	1	1
Total			9	6	3	4	4	1	0	1	0	0	0	0	0	0	5	4

Rank among batters: 2,587 • *Total ballparks homered in*: 3 • *First HR*: 06/19/1922 off Jesse Winters

Marty Kavanagh

MARTIN JOSEPH KAVANAGH
B: 06/13/1891 D: 07/28/1960
BR

Year	Tm	Lg	Tot	H	A	Men-On 0	Men-On 1	Men-On 2	Men-On 3	One-Game 2	One-Game 3	One-Game 4	LO	XN	IP	PH	RHP	LHP
1914	DET	AL	4	2	2	2	2	0	0	0	0	0	0	0	1	0	3	1
1915	DET	AL	4	3	1	1	2	1	0	0	0	0	0	0	1	0	3	1
1916	CLE	AL	1	1	0	0	0	0	1	0	0	0	0	0	0	1	0	1
1918	STL	NL	1	0	1	0	0	0	1	0	0	0	0	1	1	0	1	0
Total			10	6	4	3	4	1	2	0	0	0	0	1	3	1	7	3

Rank among batters: 2,500 • *Total ballparks homered in*: 5 • *First HR*: 04/28/1914 off Reb Russell

Eddie Kazak

EDWARD TERRANCE KAZAK
B: 07/18/1920
BR

Year	Tm	Lg	Tot	H	A	Men-On 0	Men-On 1	Men-On 2	Men-On 3	One-Game 2	One-Game 3	One-Game 4	LO	XN	IP	PH	RHP	LHP
1949	STL	NL	6	3	3	3	2	0	1	0	0	0	0	0	0	1	3	3
1950	STL	NL	5	1	4	3	2	0	0	0	0	0	0	0	0	1	2	3
Total			11	4	7	6	4	0	1	0	0	0	0	0	0	2	5	6

Rank among batters: 2,419 • *Top target (2 home runs)*: Bill Werle • *Number of pitchers victimized*: 10 • *Total ballparks homered in*: 5 • *First HR*: 05/09/1949 off Joe Hatten

Ted Kazanski

THEODORE STANLEY KAZANSKI
B: 01/25/1934
BR

Year	Tm	Lg	Tot	H	A	Men-On 0	Men-On 1	Men-On 2	Men-On 3	One-Game 2	One-Game 3	One-Game 4	LO	XN	IP	PH	RHP	LHP
1953	PHI	NL	2	2	0	1	0	1	0	0	0	0	0	0	1	0	1	1
1954	PHI	NL	1	0	1	1	0	0	0	0	0	0	0	0	0	0	1	0
1955	PHI	NL	1	0	1	1	0	0	0	0	0	0	0	0	1	0	1	0
1956	PHI	NL	4	3	1	2	0	1	1	0	0	0	0	1	1	0	1	3
1957	PHI	NL	3	2	1	3	0	0	0	0	0	0	0	0	0	0	2	1
1958	PHI	NL	3	0	3	0	1	2	0	0	0	0	0	0	0	0	2	1
Total			14	7	7	8	1	4	1	0	0	0	0	1	3	0	8	6

Rank among batters: 2,169 • *Top target (2 home runs)*: Jim Hearn, Johnny Antonelli • *Number of pitchers victimized*: 12 • *Total ballparks homered in*: 6 • *First HR*: 07/19/1953 off Bubba Church

Steve Kealey

STEVEN WILLIAM KEALEY
B: 05/13/1947
BR

Year	Tm	Lg	Tot	H	A	Men-On 0	Men-On 1	Men-On 2	Men-On 3	One-Game 2	One-Game 3	One-Game 4	LO	XN	IP	PH	RHP	LHP
1971	CHI	AL	1	1	0	0	0	1	0	0	0	0	0	0	0	0	1	0

Steve Kealey *continued*

Rank among batters: 4,707 • *Total ballparks homered in*: 1 • *First HR*: 09/06/1971 off Ray Corbin

Bob Kearney

ROBERT HENRY KEARNEY
B: 10/03/1956
BR

Year	Tm	Lg	Tot	H	A	Men-On 0	1	2	3	One-Game 2	3	4	LO	XN	IP	PH	RHP	LHP
1983	OAK	AL	8	4	4	6	0	2	0	0	0	0	0	0	0	0	6	2
1984	SEA	AL	7	6	1	4	3	0	0	0	0	0	0	0	0	0	4	3
1985	SEA	AL	6	2	4	4	1	1	0	0	0	0	0	0	0	0	3	3
1986	SEA	AL	6	4	2	1	3	2	0	1	0	0	0	0	0	0	4	2
Total			27	16	11	15	7	5	0	1	0	0	0	0	0	0	17	10

Rank among batters: 1,532 • *Top target (3 home runs)*: Milt Wilcox • *Number of pitchers victimized*: 24 • *Total ballparks homered in*: 8 • *First HR*: 05/01/1983 off Milt Wilcox

Ray Keating

RAYMOND HERBERT KEATING
B: 07/21/1891 D: 12/28/1963
BR

Year	Tm	Lg	Tot	H	A	Men-On 0	1	2	3	One-Game 2	3	4	LO	XN	IP	PH	RHP	LHP
1919	BOS	NL	1	0	1	0	1	0	0	0	0	0	0	0	0	0	1	0

Rank among batters: 4,707 • *Total ballparks homered in*: 1 • *First HR*: 08/06/1919 off Grover Alexander

Pat Keedy

CHARLES PATRICK KEEDY
B: 01/10/1958
BR

Year	Tm	Lg	Tot	H	A	Men-On 0	1	2	3	One-Game 2	3	4	LO	XN	IP	PH	RHP	LHP
1985	CAL	AL	1	0	1	1	0	0	0	0	0	0	0	0	0	0	1	0
1987	CHI	AL	2	0	2	2	0	0	0	0	0	0	0	0	0	0	1	1
Total			3	0	3	3	0	0	0	0	0	0	0	0	0	0	2	1

Rank among batters: 3,735 • *Total ballparks homered in*: 3 • *First HR*: 10/06/1985 off Jeff Russell

Tim Keefe

TIMOTHY JOHN KEEFE
B: 01/01/1857 D: 04/23/1933
BR HOF

Year	Tm	Lg	Tot	H	A	Men-On 0	1	2	3	One-Game 2	3	4	LO	XN	IP	PH	RHP	LHP
1882	TRO	NL	1	1	0	1	0	0	0	0	0	0	0	0	0	0	0	1
1884	NY	AA	3	3	0	2	1	0	0	0	0	0	0	0	1	0	2	0
1886	NY	NL	1	0	1	0	1	0	0	0	0	0	0	0	0	0	1	0
1887	NY	NL	2	2	0	1	0	1	0	0	0	0	0	0	0	0	1	1
1888	NY	NL	2	0	2	2	0	0	0	0	0	0	0	0	0	0	1	1
1890	NY	PL	2	1	1	0	2	0	0	0	0	0	0	0	0	0	2	0
1892	PHI	NL	1	1	0	1	0	0	0	0	0	0	0	0	0	0	1	0
Total			12	8	4	7	4	1	0	0	0	0	0	0	1	0	8	3

Rank among batters: 2,325 • *Total ballparks homered in*: 9 • *First HR*: 07/20/1882 off J Richmond

Willie Keeler

WILLIAM HENRY KEELER
B: 03/03/1872 D: 01/01/1923
BL HOF

Year	Tm	Lg	Tot	H	A	Men-On 0	1	2	3	One-Game 2	3	4	LO	XN	IP	PH	RHP	LHP
1893	NY	NL	1	1	0	0	1	0	0	0	0	0	0	0	1	0	1	0
	BRO	NL	1	1	0	0	1	0	0	0	0	0	0	0	1	0	1	0
	Total		2	2	0	0	2	0	0	0	0	0	0	0	2	0	2	0
1894	BAL	NL	5	2	3	1	3	1	0	0	0	0	0	0	3	0	4	1
1895	BAL	NL	4	2	2	1	3	0	0	0	0	0	0	0	4	0	4	0
1896	BAL	NL	4	0	4	0	2	2	0	0	0	0	0	0	3	0	3	0
1898	BAL	NL	1	1	0	0	1	0	0	0	0	0	0	0	1	0	1	0
1899	BRO	NL	1	1	0	0	0	0	1	0	0	0	0	0	1	0	0	1
1900	BRO	NL	4	3	1	0	2	2	0	0	0	0	0	0	4	0	3	1
1901	BRO	NL	2	1	1	2	0	0	0	0	0	0	0	0	2	0	1	1
1904	NY	AL	2	2	0	2	0	0	0	1	0	0	0	0	2	0	2	0
1905	NY	AL	4	3	1	3	0	1	0	0	0	0	0	0	4	0	4	0
1906	NY	AL	2	2	0	1	1	0	0	0	0	0	0	0	2	0	2	0
1908	NY	AL	1	1	0	0	1	0	0	0	0	0	0	0	1	0	1	0

Willie Keeler *continued*

Year	Tm	Lg	Tot	H	A	Men-On 0	1	2	3	One-Game 2	3	4	LO	XN	IP	PH	RHP	LHP
1909	NY	AL	1	1	0	0	1	0	0	0	0	0	0	0	1	0	1	0
Total			33	21	12	10	16	6	1	1	0	0	0	0	30	0	28	4

Rank among batters: 1,336 • Top target (2 home runs): Kid Carsey, Win Mercer, Doc Parker, Barney Pelty • *Number of pitchers victimized*: 29 • *Total ballparks homered in*: 12 • *First HR*: 05/09/1893 off Brickyard Kennedy

Jim Keenan

JAMES W. KEENAN
B: 02/10/1858 D: 09/21/1926
BR

Year	Tm	Lg	Tot	H	A	Men-On 0	1	2	3	One-Game 2	3	4	LO	XN	IP	PH	RHP	LHP
1882	PIT	AA	1	0	1	0	1	0	0	0	0	0	0	0	0	0	1	0
1884	IND	AA	3	2	1	0	2	1	0	0	0	0	0	0	0	0	3	0
1885	CIN	AA	1	0	1	1	0	0	0	0	0	0	0	0	0	0	1	0
1886	CIN	AA	3	2	1	0	1	2	0	0	0	0	0	0	0	0	2	0
1888	CIN	AA	1	0	1	0	1	0	0	0	0	0	0	0	0	0	1	0
1889	CIN	AA	6	2	4	4	0	2	0	0	0	0	0	0	1	0	6	0
1890	CIN	NL	3	2	1	0	2	1	0	0	0	0	0	0	0	0	3	0
1891	CIN	NL	4	1	3	2	2	0	0	0	0	0	0	0	0	0	4	0
Total			22	9	13	7	9	6	0	0	0	0	0	0	1	0	21	0

Rank among batters: 1,719 • *Top target (3 home runs)*: Bob Caruthers, Bill Hutchison • *Number of pitchers victimized*: 16 • *Total ballparks homered in*: 10 • *First HR*: 07/04/1882 off John Schappert

Bill Keister

WILLIAM HOFFMAN KEISTER
B: 08/17/1874 D: 08/19/1924
BL

Year	Tm	Lg	Tot	H	A	Men-On 0	1	2	3	One-Game 2	3	4	LO	XN	IP	PH	RHP	LHP
1899	BAL	NL	3	1	2	1	1	0	1	0	0	0	0	0	0	0	2	1
1900	STL	NL	1	0	1	0	0	1	0	0	0	0	0	0	0	0	1	0
1901	BAL	AL	2	1	1	0	0	2	0	0	0	0	0	0	0	0	2	0
1902	WAS	AL	9	7	2	4	2	3	0	1	0	0	0	0	0	0	5	4
1903	PHI	NL	3	2	1	0	2	1	0	0	0	0	0	0	0	0	2	1
Total			18	11	7	5	5	7	1	1	0	0	0	0	0	0	12	6

Rank among batters: 1,914 • *Top target (2 home runs)*: Pep Deininger, Snake Wiltse • *Number of pitchers victimized*: 16 • *Total ballparks homered in*: 10 • *First HR*: 06/08/1899 off Harley Payne

George Kell

GEORGE CLYDE KELL
B: 08/23/1922
BR HOF

Year	Tm	Lg	Tot	H	A	Men-On 0	1	2	3	One-Game 2	3	4	LO	XN	IP	PH	RHP	LHP
1945	PHI	AL	4	2	2	2	2	0	0	1	0	0	0	0	0	0	2	2
1946	DET	AL	4	2	2	4	0	0	0	0	0	0	0	0	0	0	4	0
1947	DET	AL	5	3	2	4	0	0	1	0	0	0	0	0	0	0	3	2
1948	DET	AL	2	1	1	0	0	1	1	0	0	0	0	0	0	0	2	0
1949	DET	AL	3	1	2	3	0	0	0	0	0	0	0	0	0	0	1	2
1950	DET	AL	8	4	4	4	2	2	0	0	0	0	0	0	0	0	4	4
1951	DET	AL	2	1	1	1	1	0	0	0	0	0	0	0	0	0	2	0
1952	DET	AL	1	1	0	0	1	0	0	0	0	0	0	0	0	0	0	1
	BOS	AL	6	4	2	1	4	1	0	0	0	0	0	0	0	0	6	0
	Total		7	5	2	1	5	1	0	0	0	0	0	0	0	0	6	1
1953	BOS	AL	12	9	3	8	3	1	0	0	0	0	0	0	0	0	11	1
1954	CHI	AL	5	4	1	3	1	1	0	0	0	0	0	0	0	0	2	3
1955	CHI	AL	8	2	6	6	1	0	1	0	0	0	0	0	0	0	6	2
1956	CHI	AL	1	0	1	1	0	0	0	0	0	0	0	0	0	0	0	1
	BAL	AL	8	2	6	5	1	2	0	2	0	0	0	0	0	0	5	3
	Total		9	2	7	6	1	2	0	2	0	0	0	0	0	0	5	4
1957	BAL	AL	9	3	6	5	4	0	0	0	0	0	0	0	0	0	5	4
Total			78	39	39	47	20	8	3	3	0	0	0	0	0	0	53	25

Rank among batters: 672 • *Top target (7 home runs)*: Alex Kellner • *Number of pitchers victimized*: 52 • *Total ballparks homered in*: 10 • *First HR*: 05/11/1945 off Eddie Lopat • *Hit for Cycle*—@PHI: 06/02/1950 (2) • *All-Star HR*—1

Frankie Kelleher

FRANCIS EUGENE KELLEHER
B: 08/22/1916 D: 04/13/1979
BR

Year	Tm	Lg	Tot	H	A	Men-On 0	1	2	3	One-Game 2	3	4	LO	XN	IP	PH	RHP	LHP
1942	CIN	NL	3	2	1	1	2	0	0	0	0	0	0	0	0	0	3	0

Frankie Kelleher *continued*

Rank among batters: 3,735 • *Total ballparks homered in*: 2 • *First HR*: 09/06/1942 off Mort Cooper

John Kelleher

JOHN PATRICK KELLEHER
B: 09/13/1893 D: 08/21/1960
BR

Year	Tm	Lg	Tot	H	A	Men-On 0	Men-On 1	Men-On 2	Men-On 3	One-Game 2	One-Game 3	One-Game 4	LO	XN	IP	PH	RHP	LHP
1921	CHI	NL	4	4	0	4	0	0	0	0	0	0	0	0	0	0	4	0
1923	CHI	NL	6	5	1	4	2	0	0	0	0	0	0	0	0	0	5	1
Total			10	9	1	8	2	0	0	0	0	0	0	0	0	0	9	1

Rank among batters: 2,500 • *Top target (2 home runs)*: Jesse Winters • *Number of pitchers victimized*: 9 • *Total ballparks homered in*: 2 • *First HR*: 06/27/1921 off Johnny Morrison

Charlie Keller

CHARLES ERNEST KELLER
B: 09/12/1916 D: 05/23/1990
BL

Year	Tm	Lg	Tot	H	A	Men-On 0	Men-On 1	Men-On 2	Men-On 3	One-Game 2	One-Game 3	One-Game 4	LO	XN	IP	PH	RHP	LHP
1939	NY	AL	11	5	6	2	7	2	0	0	0	0	0	0	1	1	7	4
1940	NY	AL	21	7	14	13	5	2	1	2	1	0	0	0	2	0	18	3
1941	NY	AL	33	17	16	11	14	6	2	2	0	0	0	2	3	0	23	10
1942	NY	AL	26	13	13	16	6	2	2	1	0	0	0	1	0	0	19	7
1943	NY	AL	31	21	10	20	4	7	0	2	0	0	0	1	1	0	25	6
1945	NY	AL	10	8	2	6	3	0	1	1	0	0	0	0	0	0	9	1
1946	NY	AL	30	18	12	17	8	4	1	1	0	0	0	0	0	0	24	6
1947	NY	AL	13	8	5	4	6	3	0	2	0	0	0	0	0	0	11	2
1948	NY	AL	6	3	3	3	1	2	0	0	0	0	0	0	0	2	6	0
1949	NY	AL	3	2	1	1	2	0	0	0	0	0	0	0	0	0	3	0
1950	DET	AL	2	2	0	1	0	1	0	1	0	0	0	0	0	0	2	0
1951	DET	AL	3	3	0	1	1	1	0	0	0	0	0	0	0	1	3	0
Total			189	107	82	95	57	30	7	12	1	0	0	4	7	4	150	39

Rank among batters: 204 • *Top target (7 home runs)*: Tex Hughson • *Number of pitchers victimized*: 94 • *Total ballparks homered in*: 9 • *First HR*: 05/02/1939 off Fred Hutchinson • *World Series HR*—5; *All-Star HR*—1

Hal Keller

HAROLD KEFAUVER KELLER
B: 07/07/1927
BL

Year	Tm	Lg	Tot	H	A	Men-On 0	Men-On 1	Men-On 2	Men-On 3	One-Game 2	One-Game 3	One-Game 4	LO	XN	IP	PH	RHP	LHP
1950	WAS	AL	1	0	1	0	1	0	0	0	0	0	0	0	0	0	1	0

Rank among batters: 4,707 • *Total ballparks homered in*: 1 • *First HR*: 09/29/1950 off James Atkins

Frank Kellert

FRANK WILLIAM KELLERT
B: 07/06/1924 D: 11/19/1976
BR

Year	Tm	Lg	Tot	H	A	Men-On 0	Men-On 1	Men-On 2	Men-On 3	One-Game 2	One-Game 3	One-Game 4	LO	XN	IP	PH	RHP	LHP
1955	BRO	NL	4	4	0	1	3	0	0	1	0	0	0	0	0	0	4	0
1956	CHI	NL	4	1	3	2	2	0	0	0	0	0	0	0	0	0	1	3
Total			8	5	3	3	5	0	0	1	0	0	0	0	0	0	5	3

Rank among batters: 2,703 • *Top target (2 home runs)*: Warren Hacker • *Number of pitchers victimized*: 7 • *Total ballparks homered in*: 3 • *First HR*: 06/04/1955 off Larry Jackson

Joe Kelley

JOSEPH JAMES KELLEY
B: 12/09/1871 D: 08/14/1943
BR HOF

Year	Tm	Lg	Tot	H	A	Men-On 0	Men-On 1	Men-On 2	Men-On 3	One-Game 2	One-Game 3	One-Game 4	LO	XN	IP	PH	RHP	LHP
1893	BAL	NL	9	4	5	8	1	0	0	0	0	0	0	0	4	0	6	3
1894	BAL	NL	6	1	5	4	0	1	1	0	0	0	0	0	0	0	5	0
1895	BAL	NL	10	3	7	5	2	3	0	1	0	0	0	0	2	0	7	3
1896	BAL	NL	8	4	4	5	1	1	1	0	0	0	1	0	0	0	5	3
1897	BAL	NL	5	1	4	2	2	1	0	0	0	0	0	0	0	0	3	2
1898	BAL	NL	2	0	2	1	1	0	0	0	0	0	0	0	0	0	1	1
1899	BRO	NL	6	3	3	3	3	0	0	0	0	0	0	0	1	0	5	0
1900	BRO	NL	6	4	2	2	2	2	0	0	0	0	0	0	2	0	5	1
1901	BRO	NL	4	2	2	2	1	0	1	1	0	0	0	0	2	0	3	1
1902	BAL	AL	1	0	1	0	0	1	0	0	0	0	0	0	0	0	0	1

Joe Kelley *continued*

Year	Tm	Lg	Tot	H	A	Men-On 0	1	2	3	One-Game 2	3	4	LO	XN	IP	PH	RHP	LHP
1902	CIN	NL	1	0	1	1	0	0	0	0	0	0	1	0	0	0	1	0
	Total		2	0	2	1	0	1	0	0	0	0	1	0	0	0	1	1
1903	CIN	NL	3	1	2	2	1	0	0	0	0	0	1	0	2	0	1	2
1905	CIN	NL	1	0	1	1	0	0	0	0	0	0	0	0	0	0	1	0
1906	CIN	NL	1	0	1	0	1	0	0	0	0	0	0	0	1	0	1	0
1908	BOS	NL	2	2	0	2	0	0	0	0	0	0	0	1	0	0	2	0
Total			65	25	40	38	15	9	3	2	0	0	3	1	14	0	46	16

Rank among batters: 799 • *Top target (5 home runs)*: Win Mercer • *Number of pitchers victimized*: 52 • *Total ballparks homered in*: 17 • *First HR*: 05/26/1893 off George Haddock

Mike Kelley

MICHAEL JOSEPH KELLEY
B: 12/02/1875 D: 06/06/1955
BR

Year	Tm	Lg	Tot	H	A	Men-On 0	1	2	3	One-Game 2	3	4	LO	XN	IP	PH	RHP	LHP
1899	LOU	NL	3	1	2	3	0	0	0	0	0	0	0	0	0	0	2	1

Rank among batters: 3,735 • *Total ballparks homered in*: 3 • *First HR*: 08/17/1899 off Harvey Bailey

Alex Kellner

ALEXANDER RAYMOND KELLNER
B: 08/26/1924
BR

Year	Tm	Lg	Tot	H	A	Men-On 0	1	2	3	One-Game 2	3	4	LO	XN	IP	PH	RHP	LHP
1952	PHI	AL	1	1	0	1	0	0	0	0	0	0	0	0	0	0	0	1
1957	KC	AL	3	1	2	3	0	0	0	0	0	0	0	0	0	0	1	2
Total			4	2	2	4	0	0	0	0	0	0	0	0	0	0	1	3

Rank among batters: 3,427 • *Total ballparks homered in*: 4 • *First HR*: 06/08/1952 off Mickey Harris

Billy Kelly

WILLIAM JOSEPH KELLY
B: 05/01/1886 D: 06/03/1940
BR

Year	Tm	Lg	Tot	H	A	Men-On 0	1	2	3	One-Game 2	3	4	LO	XN	IP	PH	RHP	LHP
1912	PIT	NL	1	0	1	1	0	0	0	0	0	0	0	0	0	0	1	0

Rank among batters: 4,707 • *Total ballparks homered in*: 1 • *First HR*: 06/11/1912 off Maury Kent

Roberto Kelly

ROBERTO CONRADO (GRAY) KELLY
B: 10/01/1964
BR

Year	Tm	Lg	Tot	H	A	Men-On 0	1	2	3	One-Game 2	3	4	LO	XN	IP	PH	RHP	LHP
1987	NY	AL	1	0	1	0	0	1	0	0	0	0	0	0	0	0	0	1
1988	NY	AL	1	1	0	1	0	0	0	0	0	0	1	0	0	0	1	0
1989	NY	AL	9	2	7	8	0	1	0	0	0	0	0	0	0	0	6	3
1990	NY	AL	15	5	10	12	3	0	0	0	0	0	4	0	0	0	10	5
1991	NY	AL	20	11	9	13	2	5	0	1	0	0	0	2	0	0	11	9
1992	NY	AL	10	6	4	6	4	0	0	0	0	0	0	0	0	0	6	4
1993	CIN	NL	9	4	5	8	0	0	1	0	0	0	0	0	0	0	6	3
1994	CIN	NL	3	1	2	1	1	1	0	0	0	0	0	0	0	0	3	0
	ATL	NL	6	3	3	3	3	0	0	0	0	0	2	0	0	0	4	2
	Total		9	4	5	4	4	1	0	0	0	0	2	0	0	0	7	2
1995	MON	NL	1	0	1	1	0	0	0	0	0	0	0	0	0	0	1	0
	LA	NL	6	2	4	4	2	0	0	0	0	0	0	0	0	0	4	2
	Total		7	2	5	5	2	0	0	0	0	0	0	0	0	0	5	2
Total			81	35	46	57	15	8	1	1	0	0	7	2	0	0	52	29

Rank among batters: 645 • Top target (2 home runs): Steve Olin, Greg Swindell, Frank Tanana, Greg Harris, Jaime Navarro, Bill Wegman, Bill Gullickson, Dave Otto, Tom Candiotti, Pete Harnisch • *Number of pitchers victimized*: 71 • *Total ballparks homered in*: 26 • *First HR*: 08/06/1987 off Guillermo Hernandez

George Kelly

GEORGE LANGE KELLY
B: 09/10/1895 D: 10/13/1984
BR HOF

Year	Tm	Lg	Tot	H	A	Men-On 0	1	2	3	One-Game 2	3	4	LO	XN	IP	PH	RHP	LHP
1915	NY	NL	1	0	1	0	1	0	0	0	0	0	0	0	1	0	0	1
1919	NY	NL	1	1	0	1	0	0	0	0	0	0	0	1	0	0	1	0
1920	NY	NL	11	6	5	5	2	3	1	0	0	0	0	1	1	0	6	5

George Kelly *continued*

Year	Tm	Lg	Tot	H	A	Men-On 0	Men-On 1	Men-On 2	Men-On 3	One-Game 2	One-Game 3	One-Game 4	LO	XN	IP	PH	RHP	LHP
1921	NY	NL	23	13	10	9	10	1	3	1	0	0	0	1	2	0	16	7
1922	NY	NL	17	9	8	8	8	0	1	3	0	0	0	1	3	0	11	6
1923	NY	NL	16	6	10	9	5	2	0	1	1	0	0	0	1	0	14	2
1924	NY	NL	21	9	12	5	11	3	2	1	1	0	0	2	1	0	19	2
1925	NY	NL	20	12	8	10	5	5	0	2	0	0	0	1	0	0	17	3
1926	NY	NL	13	5	8	6	4	3	0	1	0	0	0	0	0	0	10	3
1927	CIN	NL	5	1	4	3	1	0	1	0	0	0	0	0	0	0	3	2
1928	CIN	NL	3	1	2	1	0	2	0	0	0	0	0	0	0	0	1	2
1929	CIN	NL	5	1	4	2	3	0	0	1	0	0	0	0	0	0	4	1
1930	CIN	NL	5	4	1	2	3	0	0	0	0	0	0	0	0	0	5	0
	CHI	NL	3	2	1	0	3	0	0	0	0	0	0	0	0	0	2	1
	Total		8	6	2	2	6	0	0	0	0	0	0	0	0	0	7	1
1932	BRO	NL	4	0	4	3	0	1	0	0	0	0	0	0	0	0	3	1
Total			148	70	78	64	56	20	8	10	2	0	0	7	9	0	112	36

Rank among batters: 294 • *Top target (9 home runs)*: Vic Aldridge • *Number of pitchers victimized*: 80 • *Total ballparks homered in*: 10 • *First HR*: 09/23/1915 off Slim Sallee • *World Series HR*—1

Jim Kelly

JAMES ROBERT KELLY
B: 02/01/1884 D: 04/10/1961
BL

Year	Tm	Lg	Tot	H	A	Men-On 0	Men-On 1	Men-On 2	Men-On 3	One-Game 2	One-Game 3	One-Game 4	LO	XN	IP	PH	RHP	LHP
1915	PIT	FL	4	1	3	4	0	0	0	0	0	0	1	0	0	0	4	0

Rank among batters: 3,427 • *Total ballparks homered in*: 3 • *First HR*: 05/11/1915 off Fred Anderson

Joe Kelly

JOSEPH HENRY KELLY
B: 09/23/1886 D: 08/16/1977
BR

Year	Tm	Lg	Tot	H	A	Men-On 0	Men-On 1	Men-On 2	Men-On 3	One-Game 2	One-Game 3	One-Game 4	LO	XN	IP	PH	RHP	LHP
1914	PIT	NL	1	0	1	0	1	0	0	0	0	0	0	0	0	0	1	0
1916	CHI	NL	2	2	0	2	0	0	0	0	0	0	0	0	1	0	0	2
1917	BOS	NL	3	2	1	2	0	1	0	0	0	0	1	0	2	0	2	1
Total			6	4	2	4	1	1	0	0	0	0	1	0	3	0	3	3

Rank among batters: 2,988 • *Top target (2 home runs)*: Bob Steele • *Number of pitchers victimized*: 5 • *Total ballparks homered in*: 4 • *First HR*: 06/06/1914 off Rube Marshall

Joe Kelly

JOSEPH JAMES KELLY
B: 04/23/1900 D: 11/24/1967
BL

Year	Tm	Lg	Tot	H	A	Men-On 0	Men-On 1	Men-On 2	Men-On 3	One-Game 2	One-Game 3	One-Game 4	LO	XN	IP	PH	RHP	LHP
1928	CHI	NL	1	1	0	0	0	1	0	0	0	0	0	0	0	0	1	0

Rank among batters: 4,707 • *Total ballparks homered in*: 1 • *First HR*: 04/19/1928 off Pete Appleton

John Kelly

JOHN FRANCIS KELLY
B: 03/03/1859 D: 04/13/1908
BR

Year	Tm	Lg	Tot	H	A	Men-On 0	Men-On 1	Men-On 2	Men-On 3	One-Game 2	One-Game 3	One-Game 4	LO	XN	IP	PH	RHP	LHP
1884	CIN	UA	1	1	0	1	0	0	0	0	0	0	0	0	0	0	0	1

Rank among batters: 4,707 • *Total ballparks homered in*: 1 • *First HR*: 05/11/1884 off Phenomenal Smith

King Kelly

MICHAEL JOSEPH KELLY
B: 12/31/1857 D: 11/08/1894
BR HOF

Year	Tm	Lg	Tot	H	A	Men-On 0	Men-On 1	Men-On 2	Men-On 3	One-Game 2	One-Game 3	One-Game 4	LO	XN	IP	PH	RHP	LHP
1879	CIN	NL	2	2	0	1	0	1	0	0	0	0	0	0	0	0	2	0
1880	CHI	NL	1	0	1	0	1	0	0	0	0	0	0	0	0	0	1	0
1881	CHI	NL	2	0	2	0	2	0	0	0	0	0	0	0	0	0	2	0
1882	CHI	NL	1	0	1	0	1	0	0	0	0	0	0	0	0	0	1	0
1883	CHI	NL	3	2	1	1	2	0	0	0	0	0	0	0	0	0	3	0
1884	CHI	NL	13	12	1	4	2	3	1	0	0	0	0	0	0	0	11	1
1885	CHI	NL	9	9	0	3	3	3	0	2	0	0	0	0	0	0	6	1
1886	CHI	NL	4	3	1	2	1	1	0	0	0	0	0	0	0	0	4	0
1887	BOS	NL	8	7	1	6	2	0	0	0	0	0	0	0	0	0	7	0

King Kelly *continued*

Year	Tm	Lg	Tot	H	A	Men-On 0	1	2	3	One-Game 2	3	4	LO	XN	IP	PH	RHP	LHP
1888	BOS	NL	9	2	7	3	5	1	0	1	0	0	0	0	0	0	6	3
1889	BOS	NL	9	6	3	5	4	0	0	0	0	0	0	0	0	0	8	1
1890	BOS	PL	4	4	0	1	2	1	0	0	0	0	0	0	0	0	3	1
1891	CIN	AA	1	1	0	0	1	0	0	0	0	0	0	0	0	0	1	0
	BOS	AA	1	1	0	0	1	0	0	0	0	0	0	0	0	0	0	0
	Total		2	2	0	0	2	0	0	0	0	0	0	0	0	0	1	0
1892	BOS	NL	2	2	0	1	0	1	0	0	0	0	0	0	0	0	2	0
Total			69	51	18	27	27	11	1	3	0	0	0	0	0	0	57	7

Rank among batters: 756 • *Top target (5 home runs)*: Charley Radbourn • *Number of pitchers victimized*: 46 • *Total ballparks homered in*: 16 • *First HR*: 05/03/1879 off George Bradley • *World Series HR*—1

Mike Kelly

MICHAEL RAYMOND KELLY
B: 06/02/1970
BR

Year	Tm	Lg	Tot	H	A	Men-On 0	1	2	3	One-Game 2	3	4	LO	XN	IP	PH	RHP	LHP
1994	ATL	NL	2	0	2	2	0	0	0	0	0	0	0	0	0	0	0	2
1995	ATL	NL	3	0	3	1	1	1	0	0	0	0	0	0	0	0	1	2
Total			5	0	5	3	1	1	0	0	0	0	0	0	0	0	1	4

Rank among batters: 3,191 • *Total ballparks homered in*: 5 • *First HR*: 07/18/1994 off Steve Cooke

Pat Kelly

HAROLD PATRICK KELLY
B: 07/30/1944
BL

Year	Tm	Lg	Tot	H	A	Men-On 0	1	2	3	One-Game 2	3	4	LO	XN	IP	PH	RHP	LHP
1968	MIN	AL	1	0	1	1	0	0	0	0	0	0	0	0	0	0	0	1
1969	KC	AL	8	3	5	5	2	1	0	0	0	0	0	0	0	0	6	2
1970	KC	AL	6	2	4	2	3	1	0	0	0	0	0	1	1	0	4	2
1971	CHI	AL	3	2	1	2	1	0	0	0	0	0	1	0	0	0	3	0
1972	CHI	AL	5	3	2	3	1	1	0	0	0	0	1	0	0	0	5	0
1973	CHI	AL	1	1	0	0	0	1	0	0	0	0	0	0	0	0	1	0
1974	CHI	AL	4	1	3	2	2	0	0	0	0	0	1	0	1	0	4	0
1975	CHI	AL	9	4	5	5	2	1	1	0	0	0	2	0	0	0	8	1
1976	CHI	AL	5	1	4	3	2	0	0	0	0	0	0	1	0	0	4	1
1977	BAL	AL	10	9	1	6	1	1	2	1	0	0	0	2	0	0	9	1
1978	BAL	AL	11	4	7	5	5	1	0	2	0	0	0	0	0	1	11	0
1979	BAL	AL	9	6	3	6	1	1	1	0	0	0	0	1	0	3	9	0
1980	BAL	AL	3	1	2	0	1	1	1	0	0	0	0	0	0	2	3	0
1981	CLE	AL	1	1	0	1	0	0	0	0	0	0	0	0	0	0	1	0
Total			76	38	38	41	21	9	5	3	0	0	5	5	2	6	68	8

Rank among batters: 695 • *Top target (4 home runs)*: Dave Rozema • *Number of pitchers victimized*: 61 • *Total ballparks homered in*: 15 • *First HR*: 09/23/1968 off Clyde Wright • *LCS HR*—1

Pat Kelly

PATRICK FRANKLIN KELLY
B: 10/14/1967
BR

Year	Tm	Lg	Tot	H	A	Men-On 0	1	2	3	One-Game 2	3	4	LO	XN	IP	PH	RHP	LHP
1991	NY	AL	3	3	0	1	2	0	0	0	0	0	0	0	0	0	2	1
1992	NY	AL	7	3	4	5	1	1	0	0	0	0	0	0	0	0	4	3
1993	NY	AL	7	4	3	5	2	0	0	0	0	0	0	0	0	0	4	3
1994	NY	AL	3	1	2	2	1	0	0	0	0	0	0	0	0	0	2	1
1995	NY	AL	4	1	3	2	2	0	0	0	0	0	0	0	0	0	1	3
Total			24	12	12	15	8	1	0	0	0	0	0	0	0	0	13	11

Rank among batters: 1,643 • *Top target (2 home runs)*: Dennis Cook • *Number of pitchers victimized*: 23 • *Total ballparks homered in*: 10 • *First HR*: 06/07/1991 off Kenny Rogers

Tom Kelly

JAY THOMAS KELLY
B: 08/15/1950
BL

Year	Tm	Lg	Tot	H	A	Men-On 0	1	2	3	One-Game 2	3	4	LO	XN	IP	PH	RHP	LHP
1975	MIN	AL	1	0	1	1	0	0	0	0	0	0	0	0	0	0	1	0

Rank among batters: 4,707 • *Total ballparks homered in*: 1 • *First HR*: 05/26/1975 off Vern Ruhle

Van Kelly

VAN HOWARD KELLY
B: 03/18/1946
BL

Year	Tm	Lg	Tot	H	A	Men-On 0	Men-On 1	Men-On 2	Men-On 3	One-Game 2	One-Game 3	One-Game 4	LO	XN	IP	PH	RHP	LHP
1969	SD	NL	3	1	2	1	2	0	0	0	0	0	0	0	0	0	3	0
1970	SD	NL	1	0	1	0	1	0	0	0	0	0	0	0	0	0	1	0
Total			4	1	3	1	3	0	0	0	0	0	0	0	0	0	4	0

Rank among batters: 3,427 • *Total ballparks homered in*: 4 • *First HR*: 06/17/1969 off Bill Singer

Ken Keltner

KENNETH FREDERICK KELTNER
B: 10/31/1916 D: 12/12/1991
BR

Year	Tm	Lg	Tot	H	A	Men-On 0	Men-On 1	Men-On 2	Men-On 3	One-Game 2	One-Game 3	One-Game 4	LO	XN	IP	PH	RHP	LHP
1938	CLE	AL	26	10	16	13	11	2	0	3	0	0	0	0	0	0	18	8
1939	CLE	AL	13	0	13	12	1	0	0	0	1	0	0	1	0	0	11	2
1940	CLE	AL	15	6	9	7	4	2	2	1	0	0	0	0	0	0	9	6
1941	CLE	AL	23	14	9	15	4	4	0	0	0	0	0	0	1	0	17	6
1942	CLE	AL	6	4	2	4	2	0	0	0	0	0	0	0	0	0	5	1
1943	CLE	AL	4	0	4	4	0	0	0	1	0	0	0	0	0	0	3	1
1944	CLE	AL	13	3	10	6	4	1	2	0	0	0	0	0	2	0	11	2
1946	CLE	AL	13	3	10	9	4	0	0	2	0	0	0	0	0	0	11	2
1947	CLE	AL	11	5	6	4	4	3	0	0	0	0	0	0	0	0	10	1
1948	CLE	AL	31	14	17	18	7	5	1	3	0	0	0	1	0	0	24	7
1949	CLE	AL	8	5	3	3	3	2	0	1	0	0	0	0	0	0	4	4
Total			163	64	99	95	44	19	5	11	1	0	0	2	3	0	123	40

Rank among batters: 257 • *Top target (6 home runs)*: Joe Dobson • *Number of pitchers victimized*: 93 • *Total ballparks homered in*: 9 • *First HR*: 04/28/1938 off Vitautris Tamulis

John Kelty

JOHN JAMES KELTY
B: 06/ /1866

Year	Tm	Lg	Tot	H	A	Men-On 0	Men-On 1	Men-On 2	Men-On 3	One-Game 2	One-Game 3	One-Game 4	LO	XN	IP	PH	RHP	LHP
1890	PIT	NL	1	1	0	0	0	1	0	0	0	0	0	0	0	0	1	0

Rank among batters: 4,707 • *Total ballparks homered in*: 1 • *First HR*: 04/23/1890 off Joe Sommer

Bill Kemmer

WILLIAM EDWARD KEMMER
B: 11/15/1873 D: 06/08/1945
BR

Year	Tm	Lg	Tot	H	A	Men-On 0	Men-On 1	Men-On 2	Men-On 3	One-Game 2	One-Game 3	One-Game 4	LO	XN	IP	PH	RHP	LHP
1895	LOU	NL	1	0	1	1	0	0	0	0	0	0	0	0	0	0	1	0

Rank among batters: 4,707 • *Total ballparks homered in*: 1 • *First HR*: 06/06/1895 off Brickyard Kennedy

Russ Kemmerer

RUSSELL PAUL KEMMERER
B: 11/01/1931
BR

Year	Tm	Lg	Tot	H	A	Men-On 0	Men-On 1	Men-On 2	Men-On 3	One-Game 2	One-Game 3	One-Game 4	LO	XN	IP	PH	RHP	LHP
1957	WAS	AL	2	1	1	0	2	0	0	0	0	0	0	0	0	0	1	1

Rank among batters: 4,129 • *Total ballparks homered in*: 2 • *First HR*: 07/15/1957 off Glenn Cox

Steve Kemp

STEVEN F. KEMP
B: 08/07/1954
BL

Year	Tm	Lg	Tot	H	A	Men-On 0	Men-On 1	Men-On 2	Men-On 3	One-Game 2	One-Game 3	One-Game 4	LO	XN	IP	PH	RHP	LHP
1977	DET	AL	18	7	11	10	6	2	0	1	0	0	0	0	1	0	13	5
1978	DET	AL	15	9	6	6	3	5	1	0	0	0	0	0	0	0	12	3
1979	DET	AL	26	17	9	14	9	2	1	3	0	0	0	1	0	0	18	8
1980	DET	AL	21	15	6	11	6	3	1	3	0	0	0	0	0	0	15	6
1981	DET	AL	9	6	3	7	2	0	0	0	0	0	0	0	0	0	5	4
1982	CHI	AL	19	4	15	7	9	2	1	1	0	0	0	0	0	0	14	5
1983	NY	AL	12	3	9	4	6	2	0	0	0	0	0	1	1	0	11	1
1984	NY	AL	7	2	5	4	3	0	0	0	0	0	0	0	0	0	6	1
1985	PIT	NL	2	1	1	2	0	0	0	0	0	0	0	0	0	0	2	0
1986	PIT	NL	1	0	1	1	0	0	0	0	0	0	0	0	1	0	1	0
Total			130	64	66	66	44	16	4	8	0	0	0	2	3	0	97	33

Rank among batters: 348 • *Top target (4 home runs)*: Ferguson Jenkins, Dennis Leonard • *Number of pitchers victimized*: 101 • *Total ballparks homered in*: 18 • *First HR*: 04/12/1977 off Bill Singer

Fred Kendall

FRED LYN KENDALL
B: 01/31/1949
BR

Year	Tm	Lg	Tot	H	A	Men-On 0	Men-On 1	Men-On 2	Men-On 3	One-Game 2	One-Game 3	One-Game 4	LO	XN	IP	PH	RHP	LHP
1971	SD	NL	1	1	0	1	0	0	0	0	0	0	0	0	0	0	1	0
1972	SD	NL	6	2	4	4	2	0	0	1	0	0	0	0	0	0	5	1
1973	SD	NL	10	4	6	5	4	1	0	0	0	0	0	0	0	0	4	6
1974	SD	NL	8	3	5	4	3	1	0	0	0	0	0	1	0	0	5	3
1976	SD	NL	2	1	1	1	1	0	0	0	0	0	0	0	0	0	1	1
1977	CLE	AL	3	2	1	2	1	0	0	0	0	0	0	0	0	0	2	1
1979	SD	NL	1	0	1	1	0	0	0	0	0	0	0	0	0	0	0	1
Total			31	13	18	18	11	2	0	1	0	0	0	1	0	0	18	13

Rank among batters: 1,400 • *Top target (2 home runs)*: Balor Moore, Steve Carlton, Doug Rau • *Number of pitchers victimized*: 28 • *Total ballparks homered in*: 11 • *First HR*: 07/07/1971 off Bob Gibson

Eddie Kenna

EDWARD ALOYSIUS KENNA
B: 09/30/1897 D: 08/21/1972
BR

Year	Tm	Lg	Tot	H	A	Men-On 0	Men-On 1	Men-On 2	Men-On 3	One-Game 2	One-Game 3	One-Game 4	LO	XN	IP	PH	RHP	LHP
1928	WAS	AL	1	0	1	1	0	0	0	0	0	0	0	0	0	0	1	0

Rank among batters: 4,707 • *Total ballparks homered in*: 1 • *First HR*: 07/25/1928 off General Crowder

Bob Kennedy

ROBERT DANIEL KENNEDY
B: 08/18/1920
BR

Year	Tm	Lg	Tot	H	A	Men-On 0	Men-On 1	Men-On 2	Men-On 3	One-Game 2	One-Game 3	One-Game 4	LO	XN	IP	PH	RHP	LHP
1940	CHI	AL	3	1	2	1	2	0	0	0	0	0	1	0	0	0	2	1
1941	CHI	AL	1	1	0	0	1	0	0	0	0	0	0	0	0	0	1	0
1946	CHI	AL	5	3	2	4	1	0	0	0	0	0	0	0	0	0	4	1
1947	CHI	AL	6	2	4	4	1	1	0	1	0	0	0	0	1	0	6	0
1949	CLE	AL	9	4	5	5	2	2	0	0	0	0	0	0	1	0	3	6
1950	CLE	AL	9	5	4	7	1	1	0	0	0	0	0	0	0	0	2	7
1951	CLE	AL	7	4	3	5	0	2	0	0	0	0	0	1	0	0	0	7
1953	CLE	AL	3	1	2	2	0	1	0	0	0	0	0	0	0	0	1	2
1954	BAL	AL	6	2	4	2	3	0	1	0	0	0	0	0	0	0	4	2
1955	CHI	AL	9	5	4	3	4	1	1	0	0	0	0	0	0	0	8	1
1956	DET	AL	4	2	2	2	0	1	1	0	0	0	0	0	0	0	2	2
1957	BRO	NL	1	1	0	1	0	0	0	0	0	0	0	0	0	0	1	0
Total			63	31	32	36	15	9	3	1	0	0	1	1	2	0	34	29

Rank among batters: 826 • Top target (2 home runs): Fred Hutchinson, Mickey Harris, Milton Haefner, Lou Brissie, Eddie Lopat, Alex Kellner, Sam Zoldak, Allie Reynolds, Erv Palica • *Number of pitchers victimized*: 54 • *Total ballparks homered in*: 10 • *First HR*: 05/01/1940 off Lefty Grove

Brickyard Kennedy

WILLIAM P. KENNEDY
B: 10/07/1867 D: 09/23/1915
BR

Year	Tm	Lg	Tot	H	A	Men-On 0	Men-On 1	Men-On 2	Men-On 3	One-Game 2	One-Game 3	One-Game 4	LO	XN	IP	PH	RHP	LHP
1897	BRO	NL	1	1	0	1	0	0	0	0	0	0	0	0	0	0	1	0

Rank among batters: 4,707 • *Total ballparks homered in*: 1 • *First HR*: 06/12/1897 off Nixey Callahan

Doc Kennedy

MICHAEL JOSEPH KENNEDY
B: 08/11/1853 D: 05/23/1920
BR

Year	Tm	Lg	Tot	H	A	Men-On 0	Men-On 1	Men-On 2	Men-On 3	One-Game 2	One-Game 3	One-Game 4	LO	XN	IP	PH	RHP	LHP
1879	CLE	NL	1	0	1	1	0	0	0	0	0	0	0	0	0	0	1	0

Rank among batters: 4,707 • *Total ballparks homered in*: 1 • *First HR*: 05/30/1879 off Harry McCormick

Ed Kennedy

EDWARD KENNEDY
B: 04/01/1856 D: 05/22/1905

Year	Tm	Lg	Tot	H	A	Men-On 0	Men-On 1	Men-On 2	Men-On 3	One-Game 2	One-Game 3	One-Game 4	LO	XN	IP	PH	RHP	LHP
1883	NY	AA	2	2	0	0	1	1	0	0	0	0	0	0	0	0	2	0
1884	NY	AA	1	0	1	0	1	0	0	0	0	0	0	0	0	0	0	1
1885	NY	AA	2	1	1	1	1	0	0	0	0	0	0	0	0	0	2	0
Total			5	3	2	1	3	1	0	0	0	0	0	0	0	0	4	1

Rank among batters: 3,191 • *Total ballparks homered in*: 4 • *First HR*: 05/12/1883 off Bobby Mathews

John Kennedy

JOHN EDWARD KENNEDY
B: 05/29/1941
BR

Year	Tm	Lg	Tot	H	A	Men-On				One-Game			LO	XN	IP	PH	RHP	LHP
						0	1	2	3	2	3	4						
1962	WAS	AL	1	1	0	1	0	0	0	0	0	0	0	0	0	1	0	1
1964	WAS	AL	7	6	1	5	1	1	0	1	0	0	0	0	0	0	3	4
1965	LA	NL	1	0	1	1	0	0	0	0	0	0	0	0	0	0	0	1
1966	LA	NL	3	2	1	2	1	0	0	0	0	0	0	0	0	0	2	1
1967	NY	AL	1	1	0	1	0	0	0	0	0	0	0	0	0	0	0	1
1969	SEA	AL	4	0	4	2	2	0	0	0	0	0	0	2	0	0	3	1
1970	MIL	AL	2	2	0	1	0	1	0	0	0	0	0	0	0	0	1	1
	BOS	AL	4	2	2	2	2	0	0	0	0	0	0	0	1	1	2	2
	Total		6	4	2	3	2	1	0	0	0	0	0	0	1	1	3	3
1971	BOS	AL	5	3	2	3	2	0	0	0	0	0	1	0	0	0	5	0
1972	BOS	AL	2	0	2	0	1	1	0	0	0	0	0	0	0	0	2	0
1973	BOS	AL	1	1	0	0	1	0	0	0	0	0	0	0	0	0	0	1
1974	BOS	AL	1	1	0	1	0	0	0	0	0	0	0	0	0	0	0	1
Total			32	19	13	19	10	3	0	1	0	0	1	2	1	2	18	14

Rank among batters: 1,360 • Top target (2 home runs): Bill Spanswick, Dean Chance, Jim Perry, Steve Kline, Mickey Lolich • *Number of pitchers victimized*: 27 • *Total ballparks homered in*: 12 • *First HR*: 09/05/1962 off Dick Stigman • *Hit HR in first major league AB*—vs MIN: 09/05/1962 (1)

Junior Kennedy

JUNIOR RAYMOND KENNEDY
B: 08/09/1950
BR

Year	Tm	Lg	Tot	H	A	Men-On				One-Game			LO	XN	IP	PH	RHP	LHP
						0	1	2	3	2	3	4						
1979	CIN	NL	1	0	1	0	1	0	0	0	0	0	0	0	0	0	0	1
1980	CIN	NL	1	1	0	0	0	0	1	0	0	0	0	0	0	0	1	0
1982	CHI	NL	2	1	1	2	0	0	0	0	0	0	0	0	0	0	2	0
Total			4	2	2	2	1	0	1	0	0	0	0	0	0	0	3	1

Rank among batters: 3,427 • *Total ballparks homered in*: 3 • *First HR*: 07/22/1979 off Guillermo Hernandez

Monita Kennedy

MONITA CALVIN KENNEDY
B: 05/11/1922
BR

Year	Tm	Lg	Tot	H	A	Men-On				One-Game			LO	XN	IP	PH	RHP	LHP
						0	1	2	3	2	3	4						
1949	NY	NL	1	1	0	0	0	0	1	0	0	0	0	0	0	0	0	1

Rank among batters: 4,707 • *Total ballparks homered in*: 1 • *First HR*: 07/03/1949 off Morrie Martin

Terry Kennedy

TERRANCE EDWARD KENNEDY
B: 06/04/1956
BL

Year	Tm	Lg	Tot	H	A	Men-On				One-Game			LO	XN	IP	PH	RHP	LHP
						0	1	2	3	2	3	4						
1979	STL	NL	2	2	0	0	1	0	1	0	0	0	0	0	0	0	1	1
1980	STL	NL	4	1	3	1	1	2	0	1	0	0	0	0	0	0	4	0
1981	SD	NL	2	1	1	1	1	0	0	0	0	0	0	0	0	0	2	0
1982	SD	NL	21	10	11	10	8	3	0	2	0	0	0	0	0	1	17	4
1983	SD	NL	17	7	10	9	6	2	0	0	0	0	0	0	0	0	12	5
1984	SD	NL	14	8	6	10	3	1	0	0	0	0	0	0	0	0	10	4
1985	SD	NL	10	7	3	5	3	2	0	0	0	0	0	0	0	0	7	3
1986	SD	NL	12	7	5	7	2	3	0	0	0	0	0	0	0	1	9	3
1987	BAL	AL	18	11	7	12	4	2	0	0	0	0	0	0	0	0	12	6
1988	BAL	AL	3	2	1	3	0	0	0	0	0	0	0	0	0	0	2	1
1989	SF	NL	5	1	4	4	1	0	0	0	0	0	0	0	0	0	5	0
1990	SF	NL	2	2	0	0	1	0	1	0	0	0	0	0	0	0	2	0
1991	SF	NL	3	2	1	1	2	0	0	0	0	0	0	0	0	0	2	1
Total			113	61	52	63	33	15	2	3	0	0	0	0	0	2	85	28

Rank among batters: 421 • *Top target (3 home runs)*: Rick Honeycutt • *Number of pitchers victimized*: 95 • *Total ballparks homered in*: 19 • *First HR*: 07/01/1979 off Tug McGraw • *World Series HR*—1

Vern Kennedy

LLOYD VERNON KENNEDY
B: 03/20/1907 D: 01/28/1993
BL

Year	Tm	Lg	Tot	H	A	Men-On				One-Game			LO	XN	IP	PH	RHP	LHP
						0	1	2	3	2	3	4						
1937	CHI	AL	2	1	1	2	0	0	0	0	0	0	0	0	0	0	2	0

Vern Kennedy *continued*

Year	Tm	Lg	Tot	H	A	Men-On 0	1	2	3	One-Game 2	3	4	LO	XN	IP	PH	RHP	LHP
1940	STL	AL	2	1	1	0	2	0	0	0	0	0	0	0	0	0	2	0
Total			4	2	2	2	2	0	0	0	0	0	0	0	0	0	4	0

Rank among batters: 3,427 • *Total ballparks homered in*: 4 • *First HR*: 07/14/1937 off Buck Ross

Jerry Kenney

GERALD TENNYSON KENNEY
B: 06/30/1945
BL

Year	Tm	Lg	Tot	H	A	Men-On 0	1	2	3	One-Game 2	3	4	LO	XN	IP	PH	RHP	LHP
1967	NY	AL	1	1	0	0	1	0	0	0	0	0	0	0	1	0	1	0
1969	NY	AL	2	1	1	1	1	0	0	0	0	0	0	0	0	0	2	0
1970	NY	AL	4	1	3	4	0	0	0	0	0	0	0	0	0	0	4	0
Total			7	3	4	5	2	0	0	0	0	0	0	0	1	0	7	0

Rank among batters: 2,834 • *Total ballparks homered in*: 5 • *First HR*: 09/13/1967 off Rickey Clark

Jeff Kent

JEFFREY FRANKLIN KENT
B: 03/07/1968
BR

Year	Tm	Lg	Tot	H	A	Men-On 0	1	2	3	One-Game 2	3	4	LO	XN	IP	PH	RHP	LHP
1992	TOR	AL	8	2	6	4	1	3	0	0	0	0	0	0	0	0	6	2
	NY	NL	3	2	1	1	1	1	1	0	0	0	0	0	0	0	2	1
	Total		11	4	7	5	2	4	0	0	0	0	0	1	0	0	8	3
1993	NY	NL	21	9	12	9	7	4	1	2	0	0	0	1	0	0	21	0
1994	NY	NL	14	10	4	7	3	3	1	2	0	0	0	0	0	0	10	4
1995	NY	NL	20	11	9	15	4	1	0	0	0	0	0	0	0	0	17	3
Total			66	34	32	36	16	12	2	4	0	0	0	2	0	0	56	10

Rank among batters: 786 • *Top target (4 home runs)*: Pat Rapp • *Number of pitchers victimized*: 57 • *Total ballparks homered in*: 19 • *First HR*: 04/14/1992 off Lee Guetterman

Dick Kenworthy

RICHARD LEE KENWORTHY
B: 04/01/1941
BR

Year	Tm	Lg	Tot	H	A	Men-On 0	1	2	3	One-Game 2	3	4	LO	XN	IP	PH	RHP	LHP
1967	CHI	AL	4	1	3	3	1	0	0	0	0	0	0	0	0	0	1	3

Rank among batters: 3,427 • *Total ballparks homered in*: 3 • *First HR*: 05/10/1967 off Frank Bertaina

Duke Kenworthy

WILLIAM JENNINGS KENWORTHY
B: 07/04/1886 D: 09/21/1950
BB

Year	Tm	Lg	Tot	H	A	Men-On 0	1	2	3	One-Game 2	3	4	LO	XN	IP	PH	RHP	LHP
1914	KC	FL	15	12	3	6	6	1	2	3	0	0	0	0	0	0	14	1
1915	KC	FL	3	2	1	2	1	0	0	0	0	0	0	0	0	0	3	0
Total			18	14	4	8	7	1	2	3	0	0	0	0	0	0	17	1

Rank among batters: 1,914 • *Top target (2 home runs)*: Earl Moore, Mike Prendergast • *Number of pitchers victimized*: 16 • *Total ballparks homered in*: 5 • *First HR*: 04/26/1914 off Mike Prendergast

Joe Keough

JOSEPH WILLIAM KEOUGH
B: 01/07/1946
BL

Year	Tm	Lg	Tot	H	A	Men-On 0	1	2	3	One-Game 2	3	4	LO	XN	IP	PH	RHP	LHP
1968	OAK	AL	2	0	2	1	1	0	0	0	0	0	0	0	0	1	2	0
1970	KC	AL	4	2	2	2	2	0	0	0	0	0	0	1	0	0	1	3
1971	KC	AL	3	0	3	2	1	0	0	0	0	0	0	0	0	0	3	0
Total			9	2	7	5	4	0	0	0	0	0	0	1	0	1	6	3

Rank among batters: 2,587 • *Top target (2 home runs)*: Mickey Lolich • *Number of pitchers victimized*: 8 • *Total ballparks homered in*: 6 • *First HR*: 08/07/1968 off Lindy McDaniel • *Hit HR in first major league AB*—@NY: 08/07/1968 (2)

Marty Keough

RICHARD MARTIN KEOUGH
B: 04/14/1935
BL

Year	Tm	Lg	Tot	H	A	Men-On 0	1	2	3	One-Game 2	3	4	LO	XN	IP	PH	RHP	LHP
1958	BOS	AL	1	0	1	1	0	0	0	0	0	0	1	0	0	0	1	0
1959	BOS	AL	7	4	3	6	1	0	0	0	0	0	1	0	0	0	7	0

Marty Keough *continued*

Year	Tm	Lg	Tot	H	A	Men-On 0	1	2	3	One-Game 2	3	4	LO	XN	IP	PH	RHP	LHP
1960	BOS	AL	1	1	0	0	1	0	0	0	0	0	0	0	0	0	1	0
	CLE	AL	3	0	3	1	2	0	0	0	0	0	0	0	0	0	3	0
	Total		4	1	3	1	3	0	0	0	0	0	0	0	0	0	4	0
1961	WAS	AL	9	3	6	6	1	2	0	0	0	0	0	1	2	0	8	1
1962	CIN	NL	7	4	3	5	1	1	0	0	0	0	0	1	1	2	7	0
1963	CIN	NL	6	2	4	4	1	1	0	0	0	0	0	0	0	0	6	0
1964	CIN	NL	9	7	2	5	3	1	0	0	0	0	0	1	0	1	9	0
Total			43	21	22	28	10	5	0	0	0	0	2	3	3	3	42	1

Rank among batters: 1,116 • *Top target (3 home runs)*: Turk Farrell • *Number of pitchers victimized*: 34 • *Total ballparks homered in*: 16 • *First HR*: 06/18/1958 off Ray Moore

John Kerins

JOHN NELSON KERINS
B: 07/15/1858 D: 09/08/1919
BR

Year	Tm	Lg	Tot	H	A	Men-On 0	1	2	3	One-Game 2	3	4	LO	XN	IP	PH	RHP	LHP
1884	IND	AA	6	3	3	2	4	0	0	0	0	0	0	0	0	0	6	0
1885	LOU	AA	3	3	0	2	1	0	0	1	0	0	0	0	1	0	3	0
1886	LOU	AA	4	4	0	2	1	1	0	0	0	0	0	0	0	0	1	2
1887	LOU	AA	5	3	2	2	1	2	0	1	0	0	1	0	1	0	5	0
1888	LOU	AA	2	0	2	1	1	0	0	0	0	0	0	0	0	0	2	0
Total			20	13	7	9	8	3	0	2	0	0	1	0	2	0	17	1

Rank among batters: 1,810 • *Top target (2 home runs)*: Jack Lynch, Dave Foutz, Billy Crowell • *Number of pitchers victimized*: 17 • *Total ballparks homered in*: 7 • *First HR*: 05/27/1884 off Sam Kimber

Bill Kern

WILLIAM GEORGE KERN
B: 02/28/1933
BR

Year	Tm	Lg	Tot	H	A	Men-On 0	1	2	3	One-Game 2	3	4	LO	XN	IP	PH	RHP	LHP
1962	KC	AL	1	0	1	1	0	0	0	0	0	0	0	0	0	0	1	0

Rank among batters: 4,707 • *Total ballparks homered in*: 1 • *First HR*: 09/30/1962 off Jim Bunning

Buddy Kerr

JOHN JOSEPH KERR
B: 11/06/1922
BR

Year	Tm	Lg	Tot	H	A	Men-On 0	1	2	3	One-Game 2	3	4	LO	XN	IP	PH	RHP	LHP
1943	NY	NL	2	2	0	1	0	1	0	0	0	0	0	0	0	0	2	0
1944	NY	NL	9	8	1	6	3	0	0	0	0	0	0	0	1	0	6	3
1945	NY	NL	4	3	1	3	1	0	0	0	0	0	0	0	0	0	3	1
1946	NY	NL	6	6	0	3	3	0	0	0	0	0	0	0	0	0	3	3
1947	NY	NL	7	7	0	4	2	1	0	0	0	0	0	0	0	0	5	2
1950	BOS	NL	2	0	2	1	0	1	0	0	0	0	0	1	0	0	1	1
1951	BOS	NL	1	0	1	1	0	0	0	0	0	0	0	0	0	0	0	1
Total			31	26	5	19	9	3	0	0	0	0	0	1	1	0	20	11

Rank among batters: 1,400 • *Top target (2 home runs)*: Ed Heusser, Kirby Higbe, Ken Heintzelman • *Number of pitchers victimized*: 28 • *Total ballparks homered in*: 4 • *First HR*: 09/08/1943 off Bill Lee • *Hit HR in first major league AB*—vs PHI: 09/08/1943

Doc Kerr

JOHN JONAS KERR
B: 01/17/1882 D: 01/09/1937
BB

Year	Tm	Lg	Tot	H	A	Men-On 0	1	2	3	One-Game 2	3	4	LO	XN	IP	PH	RHP	LHP
1914	PIT	FL	1	0	1	1	0	0	0	0	0	0	0	0	0	0	0	1

Rank among batters: 4,707 • *Total ballparks homered in*: 1 • *First HR*: 08/29/1914 off Bill Bailey

John Kerr

JOHN FRANCIS KERR
B: 11/26/1898 D: 10/19/1993
BR

Year	Tm	Lg	Tot	H	A	Men-On 0	1	2	3	One-Game 2	3	4	LO	XN	IP	PH	RHP	LHP
1929	CHI	AL	1	1	0	1	0	0	0	0	0	0	0	0	0	0	0	1
1930	CHI	AL	3	2	1	2	1	0	0	0	0	0	0	1	1	0	1	2
1931	CHI	AL	2	0	2	0	2	0	0	0	0	0	0	0	0	0	1	1
Total			6	3	3	3	3	0	0	0	0	0	0	1	1	0	2	4

Rank among batters: 2,988 • *Total ballparks homered in*: 3 • *First HR*: 08/21/1929 off Ed Wells

Don Kessinger

DONALD EULON KESSINGER
B: 07/17/1942
BB

Year	Tm	Lg	Tot	H	A	Men-On 0	1	2	3	One-Game 2	3	4	LO	XN	IP	PH	RHP	LHP
1966	CHI	NL	1	1	0	1	0	0	0	0	0	0	0	0	0	0	0	1
1968	CHI	NL	1	1	0	0	1	0	0	0	0	0	0	0	0	0	0	1
1969	CHI	NL	4	0	4	4	0	0	0	0	0	0	2	0	1	0	4	0
1970	CHI	NL	1	1	0	1	0	0	0	0	0	0	0	0	1	0	1	0
1971	CHI	NL	2	2	0	2	0	0	0	0	0	0	1	0	1	0	2	0
1972	CHI	NL	1	0	1	1	0	0	0	0	0	0	0	0	0	0	1	0
1974	CHI	NL	1	0	1	1	0	0	0	0	0	0	1	0	0	0	1	0
1976	STL	NL	1	0	1	0	1	0	0	0	0	0	0	0	0	0	1	0
1978	CHI	AL	1	0	1	0	1	0	0	0	0	0	0	0	0	0	0	1
1979	CHI	AL	1	0	1	0	1	0	0	0	0	0	0	0	0	0	0	1
Total			14	5	9	10	4	0	0	0	0	0	4	0	3	0	10	4

Rank among batters: 2,169 • *Total ballparks homered in*: 9 • *First HR*: 05/14/1966 off Jim O'Toole

Keith Kessinger

ROBERT KEITH KESSINGER
B: 02/19/1967
BB

Year	Tm	Lg	Tot	H	A	Men-On 0	1	2	3	One-Game 2	3	4	LO	XN	IP	PH	RHP	LHP
1993	CIN	NL	1	1	0	1	0	0	0	0	0	0	0	0	0	0	1	0

Rank among batters: 4,707 • *Total ballparks homered in*: 1 • *First HR*: 09/19/1993 off Scott Sanderson

Sam Khalifa

SAM KHALIFA
B: 12/05/1963
BR

Year	Tm	Lg	Tot	H	A	Men-On 0	1	2	3	One-Game 2	3	4	LO	XN	IP	PH	RHP	LHP
1985	PIT	NL	2	1	1	1	0	1	0	0	0	0	0	0	0	0	2	0

Rank among batters: 4,129 • *Total ballparks homered in*: 2 • *First HR*: 07/22/1985 off Robert Castillo

Steve Kiefer

STEVEN GEORGE KIEFER
B: 10/18/1960
BR

Year	Tm	Lg	Tot	H	A	Men-On 0	1	2	3	One-Game 2	3	4	LO	XN	IP	PH	RHP	LHP
1985	OAK	AL	1	0	1	0	0	1	0	0	0	0	0	0	0	0	1	0
1987	MIL	AL	5	4	1	1	2	1	1	0	0	0	0	0	0	1	1	4
1988	MIL	AL	1	0	1	1	0	0	0	0	0	0	0	0	0	0	0	1
Total			7	4	3	2	2	2	1	0	0	0	0	0	0	1	2	5

Rank among batters: 2,834 • *Total ballparks homered in*: 4 • *First HR*: 10/02/1985 off Glen Cook

Leo Kiely

LEO PATRICK KIELY
B: 11/30/1929 D: 01/18/1984
BL

Year	Tm	Lg	Tot	H	A	Men-On 0	1	2	3	One-Game 2	3	4	LO	XN	IP	PH	RHP	LHP
1954	BOS	AL	1	0	1	1	0	0	0	0	0	0	0	0	0	0	0	1

Rank among batters: 4,707 • *Total ballparks homered in*: 1 • *First HR*: 07/09/1954 off Alex Kellner

Pete Kilduff

PETER JOHN KILDUFF
B: 04/04/1893 D: 02/14/1930
BR

Year	Tm	Lg	Tot	H	A	Men-On 0	1	2	3	One-Game 2	3	4	LO	XN	IP	PH	RHP	LHP
1917	NY	NL	1	0	1	0	1	0	0	0	0	0	0	0	0	0	1	0
1921	BRO	NL	3	1	2	3	0	0	0	0	0	0	0	1	0	0	3	0
Total			4	1	3	3	1	0	0	0	0	0	0	1	0	0	4	0

Rank among batters: 3,427 • *Total ballparks homered in*: 3 • *First HR*: 04/25/1917 off Grover Alexander

Darryl Kile

DARRYL ANDREW KILE
B: 12/02/1968
BR

Year	Tm	Lg	Tot	H	A	Men-On 0	1	2	3	One-Game 2	3	4	LO	XN	IP	PH	RHP	LHP
1993	HOU	NL	1	1	0	1	0	0	0	0	0	0	0	0	0	0	1	0

Rank among batters: 4,707 • *Total ballparks homered in*: 1 • *First HR*: 07/03/1993 off Omar Olivares

Year	Tm	Lg	Tot	H	A	Men-On 0	1	2	3	One-Game 2	3	4	LO	XN	IP	PH	RHP	LHP

Harmon Killebrew

HARMON CLAYTON KILLEBREW
B: 06/29/1936
BR HOF

Year	Tm	Lg	Tot	H	A	0	1	2	3	2	3	4	LO	XN	IP	PH	RHP	LHP
1955	WAS	AL	4	3	1	3	1	0	0	0	0	0	0	0	0	0	2	2
1956	WAS	AL	5	0	5	3	1	0	1	1	0	0	0	0	0	0	3	2
1957	WAS	AL	2	2	0	1	1	0	0	0	0	0	0	0	0	1	2	0
1959	WAS	AL	42	22	20	20	16	6	0	5	0	0	0	1	0	0	36	6
1960	WAS	AL	31	12	19	13	14	4	0	4	0	0	1	1	0	0	27	4
1961	MIN	AL	46	29	17	20	19	6	1	2	0	0	0	2	1	0	40	6
1962	MIN	AL	48	20	28	18	20	9	1	4	0	0	0	0	0	0	42	6
1963	MIN	AL	45	26	19	29	11	3	2	1	1	0	0	0	0	0	36	9
1964	MIN	AL	49	26	23	25	19	4	1	6	0	0	0	1	0	0	37	12
1965	MIN	AL	25	11	14	10	12	3	0	1	0	0	0	0	0	0	19	6
1966	MIN	AL	39	24	15	19	18	1	1	4	0	0	0	1	0	0	25	14
1967	MIN	AL	44	21	23	26	17	1	0	4	0	0	0	0	0	0	37	7
1968	MIN	AL	17	5	12	13	4	0	0	1	0	0	0	0	0	1	13	4
1969	MIN	AL	49	28	21	19	19	9	2	5	0	0	0	2	0	0	32	17
1970	MIN	AL	41	16	25	20	14	7	0	2	0	0	1	2	0	0	28	13
1971	MIN	AL	28	15	13	8	13	6	1	3	0	0	0	0	0	1	17	11
1972	MIN	AL	26	12	14	14	8	3	1	0	0	0	0	0	0	0	13	13
1973	MIN	AL	5	2	3	4	1	0	0	0	0	0	0	0	0	0	3	2
1974	MIN	AL	13	9	4	4	9	0	0	1	0	0	0	1	0	3	6	7
1975	KC	AL	14	8	6	7	7	0	0	1	0	0	0	0	0	1	4	10
Total			573	291	282	276	224	62	11	45	1	0	2	11	1	7	422	151

Rank among batters: 5 • *Top target (9 home runs)*: Earl Wilson • *Number of pitchers victimized*: 271 • *Total ballparks homered in*: 18 • *First HR*: 06/24/1955 off Billy Hoeft • *World Series HR*—1; *LCS HR*—2; *All-Star HR*—3

Bill Killefer

WILLIAM LAVIER KILLEFER
B: 10/10/1887 D: 07/03/1960
BR

Year	Tm	Lg	Tot	H	A	0	1	2	3	2	3	4	LO	XN	IP	PH	RHP	LHP
1912	PHI	NL	1	0	1	1	0	0	0	0	0	0	0	0	0	0	0	1
1916	PHI	NL	3	2	1	1	1	1	0	0	0	0	0	0	1	0	2	1
Total			4	2	2	2	1	1	0	0	0	0	0	0	1	0	2	2

Rank among batters: 3,427 • *Top target (2 home runs)*: Rube Marquard • *Number of pitchers victimized*: 3 • *Total ballparks homered in*: 3 • *First HR*: 06/25/1912 off Rube Marquard

Red Killefer

WADE HAMPTON KILLEFER
B: 04/13/1885 D: 09/04/1958
BR

Year	Tm	Lg	Tot	H	A	0	1	2	3	2	3	4	LO	XN	IP	PH	RHP	LHP
1909	DET	AL	1	1	0	1	0	0	0	0	0	0	0	0	0	0	1	0
1915	CIN	NL	1	1	0	1	0	0	0	0	0	0	0	0	1	0	1	0
1916	CIN	NL	1	1	0	0	1	0	0	0	0	0	0	0	1	0	1	0
Total			3	3	0	2	1	0	0	0	0	0	0	0	2	0	3	0

Rank among batters: 3,735 • *Total ballparks homered in*: 2 • *First HR*: 07/21/1909 off Tom Hughes

Frank Killen

FRANK BISSELL KILLEN
B: 11/30/1870 D: 12/03/1939
BL

Year	Tm	Lg	Tot	H	A	0	1	2	3	2	3	4	LO	XN	IP	PH	RHP	LHP
1892	WAS	NL	4	3	1	1	1	2	0	0	0	0	0	0	0	0	2	0
1893	PIT	NL	4	2	2	2	1	1	0	0	0	0	0	0	1	0	4	0
1896	PIT	NL	2	0	2	1	0	1	0	0	0	0	0	0	0	0	2	0
1897	PIT	NL	1	1	0	1	0	0	0	0	0	0	0	0	0	0	1	0
Total			11	6	5	5	2	4	0	0	0	0	0	0	1	0	9	0

Rank among batters: 2,419 • *Total ballparks homered in*: 5 • *First HR*: 06/03/1892 off George Rettger

Matt Kilroy

MATTHEW ALOYSIUS KILROY
B: 06/21/1866 D: 03/02/1940
BL

Year	Tm	Lg	Tot	H	A	0	1	2	3	2	3	4	LO	XN	IP	PH	RHP	LHP
1889	BAL	AA	1	1	0	1	0	0	0	0	0	0	0	0	0	0	1	0

Rank among batters: 4,707 • *Total ballparks homered in*: 1 • *First HR*: 08/01/1889 off Parke Swartzel

Bruce Kimm

BRUCE EDWARD KIMM
B: 06/29/1951
BR

Year	Tm	Lg	Tot	H	A	Men-On 0	1	2	3	One-Game 2	3	4	LO	XN	IP	PH	RHP	LHP
1976	DET	AL	1	1	0	1	0	0	0	0	0	0	0	0	0	0	0	1

Rank among batters: 4,707 • *Total ballparks homered in*: 1 • *First HR*: 08/17/1976 off Frank Tanana

Wally Kimmick

WALTER LYONS KIMMICK
B: 05/30/1897 D: 07/24/1989
BR

Year	Tm	Lg	Tot	H	A	Men-On 0	1	2	3	One-Game 2	3	4	LO	XN	IP	PH	RHP	LHP
1925	PHI	NL	1	1	0	0	1	0	0	0	0	0	0	0	0	0	1	0

Rank among batters: 4,707 • *Total ballparks homered in*: 1 • *First HR*: 05/21/1925 off Harry Biemiller

Chad Kimsey

CLYDE ELIAS KIMSEY
B: 08/06/1906 D: 12/03/1942
BL

Year	Tm	Lg	Tot	H	A	Men-On 0	1	2	3	One-Game 2	3	4	LO	XN	IP	PH	RHP	LHP
1929	STL	AL	2	2	0	2	0	0	0	0	0	0	0	0	0	0	2	0
1930	STL	AL	2	1	1	1	1	0	0	0	0	0	0	0	0	0	2	0
1931	STL	AL	2	2	0	1	1	0	0	0	0	0	0	0	0	1	2	0
Total			6	5	1	4	2	0	0	0	0	0	0	0	0	1	6	0

Rank among batters: 2,988 • *Top target (2 home runs)*: Red Faber • *Number of pitchers victimized*: 5 • *Total ballparks homered in*: 2 • *First HR*: 06/25/1929 off Jimmy Zinn

Jerry Kindall

GERALD DONALD KINDALL
B: 05/27/1935
BR

Year	Tm	Lg	Tot	H	A	Men-On 0	1	2	3	One-Game 2	3	4	LO	XN	IP	PH	RHP	LHP
1957	CHI	NL	6	1	5	4	2	0	0	1	0	0	1	0	0	0	5	1
1960	CHI	NL	2	0	2	1	1	0	0	0	0	0	0	0	0	0	1	1
1961	CHI	NL	9	6	3	4	3	2	0	0	0	0	1	0	0	0	6	3
1962	CLE	AL	13	8	5	5	5	3	0	1	0	0	0	0	0	0	11	2
1963	CLE	AL	5	4	1	2	3	0	0	0	0	0	0	1	0	0	3	2
1964	CLE	AL	2	1	1	2	0	0	0	0	0	0	0	0	0	0	1	1
	MIN	AL	1	1	0	1	0	0	0	0	0	0	0	0	0	0	0	1
	Total		3	2	1	3	0	0	0	0	0	0	0	0	0	0	1	2
1965	MIN	AL	6	3	3	6	0	0	0	0	0	0	0	1	0	1	5	1
Total			44	24	20	25	14	5	0	2	0	0	2	2	0	1	32	12

Rank among batters: 1,095 • *Top target (4 home runs)*: Robin Roberts • *Number of pitchers victimized*: 39 • *Total ballparks homered in*: 13 • *First HR*: 07/05/1957 off Bob Buhl

Ellis Kinder

ELLIS RAYMOND KINDER
B: 07/26/1914 D: 10/16/1968
BR

Year	Tm	Lg	Tot	H	A	Men-On 0	1	2	3	One-Game 2	3	4	LO	XN	IP	PH	RHP	LHP
1950	BOS	AL	1	0	1	0	0	0	1	0	0	0	0	0	0	0	0	1

Rank among batters: 4,707 • *Total ballparks homered in*: 1 • *First HR*: 08/06/1950 off Billy Pierce

Ralph Kiner

RALPH MCPHERRAN KINER
B: 10/27/1922
BR HOF

Year	Tm	Lg	Tot	H	A	Men-On 0	1	2	3	One-Game 2	3	4	LO	XN	IP	PH	RHP	LHP
1946	PIT	NL	23	8	15	9	9	4	1	2	0	0	0	0	0	0	18	5
1947	PIT	NL	51	28	23	27	17	7	0	8	2	0	0	0	0	0	45	6
1948	PIT	NL	40	31	9	20	12	7	1	4	1	0	0	0	0	1	38	2
1949	PIT	NL	54	29	25	28	16	6	4	7	0	0	0	1	0	0	47	7
1950	PIT	NL	47	27	20	25	15	5	2	6	0	0	0	2	0	0	39	8
1951	PIT	NL	42	26	16	25	10	4	3	3	1	0	0	2	0	0	36	6
1952	PIT	NL	37	22	15	15	18	4	0	2	0	0	0	1	0	0	33	4
1953	PIT	NL	7	4	3	1	5	1	0	0	0	0	0	0	0	0	7	0
	CHI	NL	28	15	13	12	9	6	1	3	0	0	0	0	0	0	23	5
	Total		35	19	16	13	14	7	1	3	0	0	0	0	0	0	30	5
1954	CHI	NL	22	9	13	17	5	0	0	1	0	0	0	0	0	0	16	6

Ralph Kiner *continued*

Year	Tm	Lg	Tot	H	A	Men-On 0	Men-On 1	Men-On 2	Men-On 3	One-Game 2	One-Game 3	One-Game 4	LO	XN	IP	PH	RHP	LHP
1955	CLE	AL	18	11	7	11	5	1	1	0	0	0	0	0	0	2	8	10
Total			369	210	159	190	121	45	13	36	4	0	0	6	0	3	310	59

Rank among batters: 39 • *Top target (12 home runs)*: Larry Jansen • *Number of pitchers victimized*: 147 • *Total ballparks homered in*: 14 • *First HR*: 04/18/1946 off Howie Pollet • *Hit for Cycle*—@BRO: 06/25/1950 • *All-Star HR*—3

Edward King

EDWARD LEE KING
B: 12/26/1892 D: 09/16/1967
BR

Year	Tm	Lg	Tot	H	A	Men-On 0	Men-On 1	Men-On 2	Men-On 3	One-Game 2	One-Game 3	One-Game 4	LO	XN	IP	PH	RHP	LHP
1917	PIT	NL	1	1	0	0	1	0	0	0	0	0	0	0	0	0	1	0
1918	PIT	NL	1	1	0	1	0	0	0	0	0	0	0	0	0	0	1	0
1920	NY	NL	7	5	2	4	3	0	0	0	0	0	0	0	1	0	3	4
1921	PHI	NL	4	3	1	1	2	1	0	1	0	0	0	0	0	0	0	4
1922	PHI	NL	2	0	2	0	0	2	0	0	0	0	0	0	0	0	1	1
Total			15	10	5	6	6	3	0	1	0	0	0	0	1	0	6	9

Rank among batters: 2,096 • *Top target (2 home runs)*: Eppa Rixey, Wilbur Cooper • *Number of pitchers victimized*: 13 • *Total ballparks homered in*: 7 • *First HR*: 09/20/1917 off Pol Perritt

Hal King

HAROLD KING
B: 02/01/1944
BL

Year	Tm	Lg	Tot	H	A	Men-On 0	Men-On 1	Men-On 2	Men-On 3	One-Game 2	One-Game 3	One-Game 4	LO	XN	IP	PH	RHP	LHP
1970	ATL	NL	11	5	6	6	2	1	2	0	0	0	0	0	0	0	10	1
1971	ATL	NL	5	4	1	3	2	0	0	0	0	0	0	0	0	0	5	0
1972	TEX	AL	4	0	4	4	0	0	0	0	0	0	0	0	0	0	4	0
1973	CIN	NL	4	1	3	2	0	1	1	0	0	0	0	1	0	3	4	0
Total			24	10	14	15	4	2	3	0	0	0	0	1	0	3	23	1

Rank among batters: 1,643 • *Top target (2 home runs)*: Don Sutton • *Number of pitchers victimized*: 23 • *Total ballparks homered in*: 11 • *First HR*: 04/30/1970 off Ferguson Jenkins

Jeff King

JEFFREY WAYNE KING
B: 12/26/1964
BR

Year	Tm	Lg	Tot	H	A	Men-On 0	Men-On 1	Men-On 2	Men-On 3	One-Game 2	One-Game 3	One-Game 4	LO	XN	IP	PH	RHP	LHP
1989	PIT	NL	5	3	2	4	1	0	0	0	0	0	0	1	0	0	5	0
1990	PIT	NL	14	9	5	8	4	1	1	1	0	0	0	0	0	1	5	9
1991	PIT	NL	4	3	1	1	2	1	0	0	0	0	0	0	0	0	3	1
1992	PIT	NL	14	6	8	12	1	0	1	0	0	0	0	0	0	0	9	5
1993	PIT	NL	9	4	5	4	3	2	0	1	0	0	0	0	0	0	5	4
1994	PIT	NL	5	2	3	4	1	0	0	0	0	0	0	0	0	0	3	2
1995	PIT	NL	18	7	11	7	8	2	1	2	0	0	0	1	0	0	11	7
Total			69	34	35	40	20	6	3	4	0	0	0	2	0	1	41	28

Rank among batters: 756 • Top target (2 home runs): Ron Robinson, Danny Darwin, Bobby Ojeda, Steve Wilson, Greg Swindell, Pete Harnisch, Pete Schourek, Terry Mulholland • *Number of pitchers victimized*: 61 • *Total ballparks homered in*: 13 • *First HR*: 07/25/1989 off Rick Aguilera • *2 HR in 1 inning*—@SF: 08/08/1995

Jim King

JAMES HUBERT KING
B: 08/27/1932
BL

Year	Tm	Lg	Tot	H	A	Men-On 0	Men-On 1	Men-On 2	Men-On 3	One-Game 2	One-Game 3	One-Game 4	LO	XN	IP	PH	RHP	LHP
1955	CHI	NL	11	2	9	5	3	3	0	1	0	0	0	0	0	0	9	2
1956	CHI	NL	15	7	8	10	4	1	0	2	0	0	0	0	0	0	15	0
1958	SF	NL	2	1	1	2	0	0	0	0	0	0	0	0	0	1	2	0
1961	WAS	AL	11	4	7	4	5	1	1	0	0	0	0	0	0	0	11	0
1962	WAS	AL	11	2	9	7	4	0	0	1	0	0	0	1	0	0	8	3
1963	WAS	AL	24	10	14	18	4	2	0	2	0	0	0	0	0	0	20	4
1964	WAS	AL	18	8	10	10	5	3	0	0	1	0	0	0	0	0	18	0
1965	WAS	AL	14	6	8	7	5	2	0	0	0	0	0	1	0	2	13	1
1966	WAS	AL	10	5	5	7	2	0	1	0	0	0	0	0	0	0	9	1
1967	WAS	AL	1	1	0	0	1	0	0	0	0	0	0	0	0	0	1	0
Total			117	46	71	70	33	12	2	6	1	0	0	2	0	3	106	11

Rank among batters: 402 • *Top target (3 home runs)*: Gene Conley, Pedro Ramos, Moe Drabowsky • *Number of pitchers victimized*: 93 • *Total ballparks homered in*: 19 • *First HR*: 05/30/1955 off Gordon Jones • *Hit for Cycle*—@BOS: 05/26/1964

						Men-On				One-Game								
Year	Tm	Lg	Tot	H	A	0	1	2	3	2	3	4	LO	XN	IP	PH	RHP	LHP

Silver King

CHARLES FREDERICK KING
B: 01/11/1868 D: 05/21/1938
BR

Year	Tm	Lg	Tot	H	A	0	1	2	3	2	3	4	LO	XN	IP	PH	RHP	LHP
1888	STL	AA	1	1	0	1	0	0	0	0	0	0	0	0	0	0	1	0
1890	CHI	PL	1	1	0	1	0	0	0	0	0	0	0	0	0	0	1	0
1892	NY	NL	2	2	0	1	1	0	0	0	0	0	0	0	1	0	2	0
Total			4	4	0	3	1	0	0	0	0	0	0	0	1	0	4	0

Rank among batters: 3,427 • *Total ballparks homered in*: 3 • *First HR*: 06/26/1888 off Jersey Bakely

Mike Kingery

MICHAEL SCOTT KINGERY
B: 03/29/1961
BL

Year	Tm	Lg	Tot	H	A	0	1	2	3	2	3	4	LO	XN	IP	PH	RHP	LHP
1986	KC	AL	3	1	2	2	1	0	0	0	0	0	0	0	0	0	3	0
1987	SEA	AL	9	5	4	5	2	1	1	0	0	0	0	0	0	1	8	1
1988	SEA	AL	1	1	0	1	0	0	0	0	0	0	0	0	0	0	1	0
1989	SEA	AL	2	2	0	2	0	0	0	0	0	0	0	0	1	0	2	0
1994	COL	NL	4	0	4	2	1	1	0	0	0	0	0	0	0	0	3	1
1995	COL	NL	8	4	4	7	1	0	0	0	0	0	1	0	0	2	8	0
Total			27	13	14	19	5	2	1	0	0	0	1	0	1	3	25	2

Rank among batters: 1,532 • *Top target (2 home runs)*: Jack Morris, Mike Moore • *Number of pitchers victimized*: 25 • *Total ballparks homered in*: 15 • *First HR*: 07/18/1986 off Ken Schrom

Dave Kingman

DAVID ARTHUR KINGMAN
B: 12/21/1948
BR

Year	Tm	Lg	Tot	H	A	0	1	2	3	2	3	4	LO	XN	IP	PH	RHP	LHP
1971	SF	NL	6	3	3	2	3	0	1	1	0	0	0	0	0	0	4	2
1972	SF	NL	29	17	12	14	10	4	1	4	0	0	0	0	0	0	18	11
1973	SF	NL	24	10	14	17	5	1	1	2	0	0	0	0	0	0	14	10
1974	SF	NL	18	12	6	10	5	3	0	1	0	0	0	0	0	1	11	7
1975	NY	NL	36	14	22	20	10	5	1	3	0	0	0	0	0	0	19	17
1976	NY	NL	37	16	21	18	10	9	0	6	1	0	0	1	0	0	26	11
1977	NY	NL	9	5	4	1	5	3	0	1	0	0	0	0	0	0	6	3
	SD	NL	11	5	6	4	4	1	2	1	0	0	0	0	0	0	6	5
	CAL	AL	2	0	2	0	2	0	0	1	0	0	0	0	0	0	2	0
	NY	AL	4	0	4	2	2	0	0	0	0	0	0	0	0	1	1	3
	Total		26	10	16	7	13	4	2	3	0	0	0	0	0	1	15	11
1978	CHI	NL	28	18	10	11	12	4	1	0	1	0	0	1	0	0	16	12
1979	CHI	NL	48	25	23	30	12	5	1	3	2	0	0	0	0	0	32	16
1980	CHI	NL	18	6	12	8	6	3	1	4	0	0	0	0	0	0	17	1
1981	NY	NL	22	11	11	14	2	4	2	2	0	0	0	1	0	0	17	5
1982	NY	NL	37	19	18	16	11	10	0	2	0	0	0	0	1	0	26	11
1983	NY	NL	13	8	5	7	5	1	0	1	0	0	0	1	0	1	10	3
1984	OAK	AL	35	19	16	11	19	2	3	2	1	0	0	0	0	0	26	9
1985	OAK	AL	30	14	16	18	9	2	1	1	0	0	0	0	0	0	17	13
1986	OAK	AL	35	15	20	25	5	4	1	3	0	0	0	1	0	0	21	14
Total			442	217	225	228	137	61	16	38	5	0	0	5	1	3	289	153

Rank among batters: 21 • *Top target (8 home runs)*: Steve Carlton • *Number of pitchers victimized*: 241 • *Total ballparks homered in*: 25 • *First HR*: 07/31/1971 off Dave Giusti • *Hit for Cycle—*@HOU: 04/16/1972

Walt Kinney

WALTER WILLIAM KINNEY
B: 09/09/1893 D: 07/01/1971
BL

Year	Tm	Lg	Tot	H	A	0	1	2	3	2	3	4	LO	XN	IP	PH	RHP	LHP
1919	PHI	AL	1	0	1	0	0	1	0	0	0	0	0	0	0	0	0	1
1923	PHI	AL	1	0	1	1	0	0	0	0	0	0	0	0	0	0	1	0
Total			2	0	2	1	0	1	0	0	0	0	0	0	0	0	1	1

Rank among batters: 4,129 • *Total ballparks homered in*: 1 • *First HR*: 08/16/1919 off Ernie Koob

Tom Kinslow

THOMAS F. KINSLOW
B: 01/12/1866 D: 02/22/1901
BR

Year	Tm	Lg	Tot	H	A	0	1	2	3	2	3	4	LO	XN	IP	PH	RHP	LHP
1890	BRO	PL	4	3	1	1	0	3	0	1	0	0	0	0	0	0	2	2

Tom Kinslow *continued*

Year	Tm	Lg	Tot	H	A	Men-On 0	1	2	3	One-Game 2	3	4	LO	XN	IP	PH	RHP	LHP
1892	BRO	NL	2	1	1	1	1	0	0	0	0	0	0	0	0	0	2	0
1893	BRO	NL	4	2	2	1	1	2	0	0	0	0	0	0	0	0	3	1
1894	BRO	NL	2	2	0	2	0	0	0	0	0	0	0	0	0	0	2	0
Total			12	8	4	5	2	5	0	1	0	0	0	0	0	0	9	2

Rank among batters: 2,325 • *Top target (2 home runs)*: George Keefe • *Number of pitchers victimized*: 11 • *Total ballparks homered in*: 4 • *First HR*: 06/28/1890 off Henry Gruber

Walt Kinzie

WALTER HARRIS KINZIE
B: 03/16/1857 D: 11/05/1909
BR

Year	Tm	Lg	Tot	H	A	Men-On 0	1	2	3	One-Game 2	3	4	LO	XN	IP	PH	RHP	LHP
1884	CHI	NL	2	1	1	1	1	0	0	0	0	0	0	0	0	0	2	0

Rank among batters: 4,129 • *Total ballparks homered in*: 2 • *First HR*: 05/27/1884 off Billy Serad

LaRue Kirby

LARUE KIRBY
B: 12/30/1889 D: 06/10/1961
BB

Year	Tm	Lg	Tot	H	A	Men-On 0	1	2	3	One-Game 2	3	4	LO	XN	IP	PH	RHP	LHP
1914	STL	FL	2	0	2	2	0	0	0	0	0	0	0	0	0	0	1	0

Rank among batters: 4,129 • *Total ballparks homered in*: 2 • *First HR*: 08/01/1914 off William Burke

Wayne Kirby

WAYNE LEONARD KIRBY
B: 01/22/1964
BL

Year	Tm	Lg	Tot	H	A	Men-On 0	1	2	3	One-Game 2	3	4	LO	XN	IP	PH	RHP	LHP
1992	CLE	AL	1	0	1	1	0	0	0	0	0	0	0	0	0	1	1	0
1993	CLE	AL	6	4	2	1	4	1	0	0	0	0	0	0	0	0	6	0
1994	CLE	AL	5	3	2	4	1	0	0	0	0	0	0	0	0	1	5	0
1995	CLE	AL	1	0	1	1	0	0	0	0	0	0	0	0	0	0	1	0
Total			13	7	6	7	5	1	0	0	0	0	0	0	0	2	13	0

Rank among batters: 2,248 • *Top target (2 home runs)*: Jay Howell • *Number of pitchers victimized*: 12 • *Total ballparks homered in*: 6 • *First HR*: 09/15/1992 off Duane Ward

Jay Kirke

JUDSON FABIAN KIRKE
B: 06/16/1888 D: 08/31/1968
BL

Year	Tm	Lg	Tot	H	A	Men-On 0	1	2	3	One-Game 2	3	4	LO	XN	IP	PH	RHP	LHP
1912	BOS	NL	4	3	1	2	1	1	0	0	0	0	0	0	0	0	4	0
1914	CLE	AL	1	0	1	0	1	0	0	0	0	0	0	0	1	0	1	0
1915	CLE	AL	2	0	2	2	0	0	0	0	0	0	0	0	0	0	2	0
Total			7	3	4	4	2	1	0	0	0	0	0	0	1	0	7	0

Rank among batters: 2,834 • *Total ballparks homered in*: 4 • *First HR*: 06/14/1912 off Art Fromme

Willie Kirkland

WILLIE CHARLES KIRKLAND
B: 02/17/1934
BL

Year	Tm	Lg	Tot	H	A	Men-On 0	1	2	3	One-Game 2	3	4	LO	XN	IP	PH	RHP	LHP
1958	SF	NL	14	7	7	10	4	0	0	0	0	0	0	1	1	0	13	1
1959	SF	NL	22	5	17	16	3	3	0	2	0	0	0	0	0	0	19	3
1960	SF	NL	21	9	12	11	7	3	0	1	0	0	0	0	0	0	13	8
1961	CLE	AL	27	14	13	17	8	2	0	1	1	0	0	0	0	0	25	2
1962	CLE	AL	21	12	9	9	7	5	0	0	0	0	0	1	0	0	21	0
1963	CLE	AL	15	7	8	6	6	3	0	1	0	0	0	3	0	0	13	2
1964	BAL	AL	3	1	2	2	1	0	0	0	0	0	0	0	0	0	3	0
	WAS	AL	5	4	1	3	2	0	0	0	0	0	0	0	0	0	4	1
	Total		8	5	3	5	3	0	0	0	0	0	0	0	0	0	7	1
1965	WAS	AL	14	6	8	7	4	3	0	0	0	0	0	0	0	2	14	0
1966	WAS	AL	6	1	5	3	1	2	0	0	0	0	0	0	0	2	6	0
Total			148	66	82	84	43	21	0	5	1	0	0	5	1	4	131	17

Rank among batters: 294 • Top target (4 home runs): Cal McLish, Ken McBride, Jerry Walker, Don Lee • *Number of pitchers victimized*: 99 • *Total ballparks homered in*: 22 • *First HR*: 04/22/1958 off Lindy McDaniel

Ed Kirkpatrick

EDGAR LEON KIRKPATRICK
B: 10/08/1944
BL

						Men-On				One-Game								
Year	Tm	Lg	Tot	H	A	0	1	2	3	2	3	4	LO	XN	IP	PH	RHP	LHP
1963	LA	AL	2	1	1	2	0	0	0	0	0	0	0	0	0	0	2	0
1964	LA	AL	2	0	2	0	2	0	0	0	0	0	0	1	0	0	2	0
1965	CAL	AL	3	0	3	3	0	0	0	0	0	0	0	0	0	0	3	0
1966	CAL	AL	9	6	3	3	4	2	0	1	0	0	0	0	0	0	9	0
1968	CAL	AL	1	1	0	0	1	0	0	0	0	0	0	0	0	1	1	0
1969	KC	AL	14	7	7	7	5	2	0	3	0	0	0	0	1	0	14	0
1970	KC	AL	18	10	8	14	2	1	1	1	0	0	0	0	0	0	12	6
1971	KC	AL	9	7	2	6	2	1	0	1	0	0	0	0	0	1	8	1
1972	KC	AL	9	2	7	6	2	1	0	0	0	0	0	0	0	0	8	1
1973	KC	AL	6	3	3	1	2	3	0	0	0	0	0	0	0	0	6	0
1974	PIT	NL	6	3	3	2	3	1	0	0	0	0	0	0	0	0	6	0
1975	PIT	NL	5	3	2	3	1	1	0	0	0	0	0	1	0	1	4	1
1977	PIT	NL	1	0	1	0	1	0	0	0	0	0	0	0	0	0	1	0
Total			85	43	42	47	25	12	1	6	0	0	0	2	1	3	76	9

Rank among batters: 612 • *Top target (3 home runs)*: Jim Hannan, Jim McGlothlin • *Number of pitchers victimized*: 72 • *Total ballparks homered in*: 20 • *First HR*: 07/15/1963 off Bill Monbouquette

Enos Kirkpatrick

ENOS CLAIRE KIRKPATRICK
B: 12/08/1885 D: 04/14/1964
BR

						Men-On				One-Game								
Year	Tm	Lg	Tot	H	A	0	1	2	3	2	3	4	LO	XN	IP	PH	RHP	LHP
1913	BRO	NL	1	1	0	0	1	0	0	0	0	0	0	0	1	0	1	0
1914	BAL	FL	2	2	0	1	1	0	0	0	0	0	0	0	0	0	1	1
Total			3	3	0	1	2	0	0	0	0	0	0	0	1	0	2	1

Rank among batters: 3,735 • *Total ballparks homered in*: 2 • *First HR*: 05/21/1913 off Babe Adams

Bruce Kison

BRUCE EUGENE KISON
B: 02/18/1950
BR

						Men-On				One-Game								
Year	Tm	Lg	Tot	H	A	0	1	2	3	2	3	4	LO	XN	IP	PH	RHP	LHP
1977	PIT	NL	1	0	1	1	0	0	0	0	0	0	0	0	0	0	1	0
1978	PIT	NL	1	1	0	1	0	0	0	0	0	0	0	0	0	0	0	1
1979	PIT	NL	1	0	1	0	0	0	1	0	0	0	0	0	0	0	0	1
Total			3	1	2	2	0	0	1	0	0	0	0	0	0	0	1	2

Rank among batters: 3,735 • *Total ballparks homered in*: 3 • *First HR*: 04/23/1977 off Nino Espinosa

Frank Kitson

FRANK R. KITSON
B: 09/11/1869 D: 04/14/1930
BL

						Men-On				One-Game								
Year	Tm	Lg	Tot	H	A	0	1	2	3	2	3	4	LO	XN	IP	PH	RHP	LHP
1901	BRO	NL	1	0	1	0	1	0	0	0	0	0	0	0	0	0	1	0
1902	BRO	NL	1	0	1	1	0	0	0	0	0	0	0	0	0	0	1	0
1904	DET	AL	1	0	1	1	0	0	0	0	0	0	0	0	0	0	1	0
1906	WAS	AL	1	0	1	0	1	0	0	0	0	0	0	0	1	0	1	0
Total			4	0	4	2	2	0	0	0	0	0	0	0	1	0	4	0

Rank among batters: 3,427 • *Total ballparks homered in*: 4 • *First HR*: 09/24/1901 off Bill Phillips

Ron Kittle

RONALD DALE KITTLE
B: 01/05/1958
BR

						Men-On				One-Game								
Year	Tm	Lg	Tot	H	A	0	1	2	3	2	3	4	LO	XN	IP	PH	RHP	LHP
1982	CHI	AL	1	0	1	0	1	0	0	0	0	0	0	0	0	0	0	1
1983	CHI	AL	35	18	17	16	12	7	0	0	0	0	0	0	0	0	22	13
1984	CHI	AL	32	17	15	15	11	6	0	3	0	0	0	0	0	2	20	12
1985	CHI	AL	26	12	14	16	8	2	0	5	0	0	0	0	0	0	16	10
1986	CHI	AL	17	5	12	9	7	1	0	4	0	0	0	0	0	0	14	3
	NY	AL	4	1	3	2	1	1	0	0	0	0	0	0	0	0	0	4
	Total		21	6	15	11	8	2	0	4	0	0	0	0	0	0	14	7
1987	NY	AL	12	7	5	8	4	0	0	0	0	0	0	0	1	0	6	6
1988	CLE	AL	18	7	11	12	4	2	0	2	0	0	0	1	0	3	9	9
1989	CHI	AL	11	6	5	5	4	2	0	0	0	0	0	0	0	0	7	4
1990	CHI	AL	16	7	9	11	4	1	0	3	0	0	0	0	0	1	5	11
	BAL	AL	2	1	1	2	0	0	0	0	0	0	0	0	0	0	0	2

Ron Kittle *continued*

Year	Tm	Lg	Tot	H	A	Men-On 0	1	2	3	One-Game 2	3	4	LO	XN	IP	PH	RHP	LHP
1990	Total		18	8	10	13	4	1	0	3	0	0	0	0	0	1	5	13
1991	CHI	AL	2	0	2	0	2	0	0	0	0	0	0	0	0	0	1	1
Total			176	81	95	96	58	22	0	17	0	0	0	1	1	6	100	76

Rank among batters: 227 • *Top target (9 home runs)*: Bert Blyleven • *Number of pitchers victimized*: 117 • *Total ballparks homered in*: 15 • *First HR*: 10/02/1982 off Frank Viola

Malachi Kittridge

MALACHI JEDDIDAH KITTRIDGE
B: 10/12/1869 D: 06/23/1928
BR

Year	Tm	Lg	Tot	H	A	Men-On 0	1	2	3	One-Game 2	3	4	LO	XN	IP	PH	RHP	LHP
1890	CHI	NL	3	3	0	1	1	0	1	0	0	0	0	0	0	0	3	0
1891	CHI	NL	2	0	2	1	1	0	0	0	0	0	0	0	0	0	2	0
1893	CHI	NL	2	2	0	1	0	0	1	0	0	0	0	0	0	0	0	1
1895	CHI	NL	3	1	2	1	2	0	0	0	0	0	0	0	0	0	3	0
1896	CHI	NL	1	1	0	0	0	1	0	0	0	0	0	0	1	0	0	1
1897	CHI	NL	1	0	1	0	1	0	0	0	0	0	0	0	0	0	0	1
1898	LOU	NL	1	0	1	1	0	0	0	0	0	0	0	0	0	0	0	0
1901	BOS	NL	2	1	1	0	1	1	0	0	0	0	0	0	1	0	1	1
1902	BOS	NL	2	2	0	1	0	1	0	0	0	0	0	0	0	0	2	0
Total			17	10	7	6	6	3	2	0	0	0	0	0	2	0	11	3

Rank among batters: 1,969 • *Top target (2 home runs)*: John Clarkson • *Number of pitchers victimized*: 16 • *Total ballparks homered in*: 9 • *First HR*: 07/22/1890 off Mickey Welch

Billy Klaus

WILLIAM JOSEPH KLAUS
B: 12/09/1928
BL

Year	Tm	Lg	Tot	H	A	Men-On 0	1	2	3	One-Game 2	3	4	LO	XN	IP	PH	RHP	LHP
1955	BOS	AL	7	4	3	3	3	1	0	0	0	0	0	0	0	0	6	1
1956	BOS	AL	7	4	3	3	4	0	0	0	0	0	0	0	0	0	6	1
1957	BOS	AL	10	8	2	5	3	2	0	1	0	0	0	0	0	0	8	2
1958	BOS	AL	1	0	1	1	0	0	0	0	0	0	0	0	0	0	1	0
1959	BAL	AL	3	1	2	1	2	0	0	0	0	0	0	0	0	0	3	0
1960	BAL	AL	1	0	1	0	0	0	1	0	0	0	0	0	0	0	1	0
1961	WAS	AL	7	2	5	3	2	1	1	0	0	0	1	0	0	0	7	0
1962	PHI	NL	4	1	3	2	2	0	0	0	0	0	0	0	0	0	3	1
Total			40	20	20	18	16	4	2	1	0	0	1	0	0	0	35	5

Rank among batters: 1,181 • *Top target (3 home runs)*: Ned Garver • *Number of pitchers victimized*: 34 • *Total ballparks homered in*: 14 • *First HR*: 05/11/1955 off Virgil Trucks

Bobby Klaus

ROBERT FRANCIS KLAUS
B: 12/27/1937
BR

Year	Tm	Lg	Tot	H	A	Men-On 0	1	2	3	One-Game 2	3	4	LO	XN	IP	PH	RHP	LHP
1964	CIN	NL	2	0	2	2	0	0	0	0	0	0	0	0	0	0	2	0
	NY	NL	2	1	1	0	1	0	1	0	0	0	0	0	0	0	0	2
	Total		4	1	3	3	0	1	0	0	0	0	0	0	0	0	2	2
1965	NY	NL	2	1	1	2	0	0	0	0	0	0	0	1	0	0	1	1
Total			6	2	4	5	0	1	0	0	0	0	0	1	0	0	3	3

Rank among batters: 2,988 • *Total ballparks homered in*: 5 • *First HR*: 06/13/1964 off Hal Brown

Chuck Klein

CHARLES HERBERT KLEIN
B: 10/07/1904 D: 03/28/1958
BL HOF

Year	Tm	Lg	Tot	H	A	Men-On 0	1	2	3	One-Game 2	3	4	LO	XN	IP	PH	RHP	LHP
1928	PHI	NL	11	9	2	6	4	1	0	0	0	0	0	0	0	0	10	1
1929	PHI	NL	43	25	18	18	14	8	3	4	0	0	0	0	1	0	31	12
1930	PHI	NL	40	26	14	17	16	7	0	4	0	0	0	1	0	0	26	14
1931	PHI	NL	31	22	9	16	9	6	0	6	0	0	0	0	0	0	25	6
1932	PHI	NL	38	29	9	17	13	5	3	3	0	0	0	0	1	0	27	11
1933	PHI	NL	28	20	8	12	10	6	0	3	0	0	0	1	1	0	25	3
1934	CHI	NL	20	12	8	9	7	3	1	1	0	0	0	1	0	0	18	2
1935	CHI	NL	21	8	13	6	12	3	0	2	0	0	0	0	0	0	20	1
1936	CHI	NL	5	3	2	3	2	0	0	1	0	0	0	0	0	0	5	0
	PHI	NL	20	9	11	10	8	2	0	0	0	1	0	1	0	0	19	1

Chuck Klein *continued*

Year	Tm	Lg	Tot	H	A	Men-On				One-Game			LO	XN	IP	PH	RHP	LHP
						0	1	2	3	2	3	4						
1936	Total		25	12	13	13	10	2	0	1	0	1	0	1	0	0	24	1
1937	PHI	NL	15	13	2	10	4	1	0	2	0	0	0	0	0	0	11	4
1938	PHI	NL	8	4	4	4	1	3	0	0	0	0	0	0	0	1	7	1
1939	PHI	NL	1	1	0	1	0	0	0	0	0	0	0	0	0	0	1	0
	PIT	NL	11	5	6	7	3	1	0	1	0	0	0	0	0	1	9	2
	Total		12	6	6	8	3	1	0	1	0	0	0	0	0	1	10	2
1940	PHI	NL	7	3	4	4	3	0	0	0	0	0	0	0	0	0	6	1
1941	PHI	NL	1	1	0	1	0	0	0	0	0	0	0	0	0	1	1	0
Total			300	190	110	141	106	46	7	27	0	1	0	4	3	3	241	59

Rank among batters: 68 • *Top target (11 home runs)*: Red Lucas • *Number of pitchers victimized*: 128 • *Total ballparks homered in*: 9 • *First HR*: 08/04/1928 off Ray Kremer • *Hit for Cycle*—vs CHI: 07/01/1931; @STL: 05/26/1933 • *World Series HR*—1

Lou Klein

LOUIS FRANK KLEIN
B: 10/22/1918 D: 06/20/1976
BR

Year	Tm	Lg	Tot	H	A	Men-On				One-Game			LO	XN	IP	PH	RHP	LHP
						0	1	2	3	2	3	4						
1943	STL	NL	7	3	4	6	1	0	0	1	0	0	3	0	1	0	5	2
1945	STL	NL	1	1	0	1	0	0	0	0	0	0	0	0	0	0	0	1
1946	STL	NL	1	1	0	1	0	0	0	0	0	0	0	0	0	0	1	0
1949	STL	NL	2	2	0	2	0	0	0	1	0	0	0	0	0	0	1	1
1951	PHI	AL	5	3	2	3	2	0	0	0	0	0	0	0	0	0	5	0
Total			16	10	6	13	3	0	0	2	0	0	3	0	1	0	12	4

Rank among batters: 2,029 • *Top target (2 home runs)*: Ken Trinkle • *Number of pitchers victimized*: 15 • *Total ballparks homered in*: 5 • *First HR*: 05/22/1943 off Harry Feldman

Red Kleinow

JOHN PETER KLEINOW
B: 07/20/1879 D: 10/09/1929
BR

Year	Tm	Lg	Tot	H	A	Men-On				One-Game			LO	XN	IP	PH	RHP	LHP
						0	1	2	3	2	3	4						
1905	NY	AL	1	1	0	0	0	1	0	0	0	0	0	0	1	0	1	0
1908	NY	AL	1	1	0	1	0	0	0	0	0	0	0	0	1	0	0	1
1910	BOS	AL	1	0	1	0	1	0	0	0	0	0	0	0	0	0	1	0
Total			3	2	1	1	1	1	0	0	0	0	0	0	2	0	2	1

Rank among batters: 3,735 • *Total ballparks homered in*: 2 • *First HR*: 06/10/1905 off Cy Morgan

Ryan Klesko

RYAN ANTHONY KLESKO
B: 06/12/1971
BL

Year	Tm	Lg	Tot	H	A	Men-On				One-Game			LO	XN	IP	PH	RHP	LHP
						0	1	2	3	2	3	4						
1993	ATL	NL	2	2	0	1	1	0	0	0	0	0	0	0	0	2	2	0
1994	ATL	NL	17	7	10	10	6	1	0	1	0	0	0	0	0	1	17	0
1995	ATL	NL	23	15	8	13	7	2	1	2	0	0	0	0	0	0	20	3
Total			42	24	18	24	14	3	1	3	0	0	0	0	0	3	39	3

Rank among batters: 1,138 • Top target (2 home runs): Andy Benes, Pedro Martinez, Jim Bullinger, John Burkett, Paul Quantrill • *Number of pitchers victimized*: 37 • *Total ballparks homered in*: 11 • *First HR*: 04/27/1993 off Tim Wakefield • *World Series HR*—3

Ed Klieman

EDWARD FREDERICK KLIEMAN
B: 03/21/1918 D: 11/15/1979
BR

Year	Tm	Lg	Tot	H	A	Men-On				One-Game			LO	XN	IP	PH	RHP	LHP
						0	1	2	3	2	3	4						
1945	CLE	AL	1	0	1	0	0	1	0	0	0	0	0	0	0	0	1	0

Rank among batters: 4,707 • *Total ballparks homered in*: 1 • *First HR*: 08/05/1945 off Nels Potter

Lou Klimchock

LOUIS STEPHEN KLIMCHOCK
B: 10/15/1939
BL

Year	Tm	Lg	Tot	H	A	Men-On				One-Game			LO	XN	IP	PH	RHP	LHP
						0	1	2	3	2	3	4						
1958	KC	AL	1	0	1	1	0	0	0	0	0	0	1	0	0	0	1	0
1959	KC	AL	4	1	3	2	1	1	0	0	0	0	0	0	0	0	3	1
1961	KC	AL	1	0	1	1	0	0	0	0	0	0	0	0	0	1	1	0
1969	CLE	AL	6	2	4	5	1	0	0	0	0	0	0	0	0	0	6	0

Lou Klimchock *continued*

Year	Tm	Lg	Tot	H	A	Men-On 0	Men-On 1	Men-On 2	Men-On 3	One-Game 2	One-Game 3	One-Game 4	LO	XN	IP	PH	RHP	LHP
1970	CLE	AL	1	0	1	1	0	0	0	0	0	0	0	0	0	0	1	0
Total			13	3	10	10	2	1	0	0	0	0	1	0	0	1	12	1

Rank among batters: 2,248 • *Top target (2 home runs)*: Stan Bahnsen • *Number of pitchers victimized*: 12 • *Total ballparks homered in*: 7 • *First HR*: 09/28/1958 off Stover McIlwain

Johnny Kling

JOHN KLING
B: 02/25/1875 D: 01/31/1947
BR

Year	Tm	Lg	Tot	H	A	Men-On 0	Men-On 1	Men-On 2	Men-On 3	One-Game 2	One-Game 3	One-Game 4	LO	XN	IP	PH	RHP	LHP
1903	CHI	NL	3	1	2	2	1	0	0	0	0	0	0	0	1	0	2	1
1904	CHI	NL	2	2	0	1	1	0	0	0	0	0	0	0	0	0	2	0
1905	CHI	NL	1	1	0	1	0	0	0	0	0	0	0	0	0	0	1	0
1906	CHI	NL	2	1	1	0	2	0	0	0	0	0	0	0	1	0	0	2
1907	CHI	NL	1	0	1	1	0	0	0	0	0	0	0	1	0	0	1	0
1908	CHI	NL	4	0	4	1	1	0	2	0	0	0	0	1	0	0	2	2
1910	CHI	NL	2	1	1	0	2	0	0	0	0	0	0	0	1	0	2	0
1911	CHI	NL	1	0	1	1	0	0	0	0	0	0	0	0	0	0	1	0
	BOS	NL	2	2	0	0	1	1	0	0	0	0	0	0	0	0	1	1
	Total		3	2	1	1	1	1	0	0	0	0	0	0	0	0	2	1
1912	BOS	NL	2	2	0	1	1	0	0	0	0	0	0	0	0	0	2	0
Total			20	10	10	8	9	1	2	0	0	0	0	2	3	0	14	6

Rank among batters: 1,810 • *Top target (4 home runs)*: Christy Mathewson • *Number of pitchers victimized*: 16 • *Total ballparks homered in*: 8 • *First HR*: 04/29/1903 off Ed Poole

Johnny Klippstein

JOHN CALVIN KLIPPSTEIN
B: 10/17/1927
BR

Year	Tm	Lg	Tot	H	A	Men-On 0	Men-On 1	Men-On 2	Men-On 3	One-Game 2	One-Game 3	One-Game 4	LO	XN	IP	PH	RHP	LHP
1950	CHI	NL	1	1	0	1	0	0	0	0	0	0	0	0	0	0	0	1
1951	CHI	NL	1	0	1	1	0	0	0	0	0	0	0	0	0	0	1	0
1952	CHI	NL	1	0	1	0	0	1	0	0	0	0	0	0	0	0	1	0
1953	CHI	NL	1	0	1	1	0	0	0	0	0	0	0	0	0	0	1	0
1962	CIN	NL	1	0	1	1	0	0	0	0	0	0	0	1	0	0	1	0
Total			5	1	4	4	0	1	0	0	0	0	0	1	0	0	4	1

Rank among batters: 3,191 • *Total ballparks homered in*: 3 • *First HR*: 07/19/1950 off Bob Chipman

Fred Klobedanz

FREDERICK AUGUSTUS KLOBEDANZ
B: 06/13/1871 D: 04/12/1940
BL

Year	Tm	Lg	Tot	H	A	Men-On 0	Men-On 1	Men-On 2	Men-On 3	One-Game 2	One-Game 3	One-Game 4	LO	XN	IP	PH	RHP	LHP
1896	BOS	NL	2	1	1	1	1	0	0	0	0	0	0	0	0	0	1	1
1897	BOS	NL	1	1	0	1	0	0	0	0	0	0	0	0	0	0	1	0
1898	BOS	NL	3	2	1	0	2	1	0	0	0	0	0	0	0	0	1	2
1899	BOS	NL	1	0	1	0	1	0	0	0	0	0	0	0	0	0	1	0
Total			7	4	3	2	4	1	0	0	0	0	0	0	0	0	4	3

Rank among batters: 2,834 • *Total ballparks homered in*: 4 • *First HR*: 08/27/1896 off Buttons Briggs

Billy Klusman

WILLIAM F. KLUSMAN
B: 03/24/1865 D: 06/24/1907
BR

Year	Tm	Lg	Tot	H	A	Men-On 0	Men-On 1	Men-On 2	Men-On 3	One-Game 2	One-Game 3	One-Game 4	LO	XN	IP	PH	RHP	LHP
1888	BOS	NL	2	0	2	2	0	0	0	1	0	0	0	0	2	0	0	2
1890	STL	AA	1	0	1	1	0	0	0	0	0	0	0	0	1	0	0	0
Total			3	0	3	3	0	0	0	1	0	0	0	0	3	0	0	2

Rank among batters: 3,735 • *Top target (2 home runs)*: Ed Beatin • *Number of pitchers victimized*: 2 • *Total ballparks homered in*: 2 • *First HR*: 07/17/1888 off Ed Beatin

Ted Kluszewski

THEODORE BERNARD KLUSZEWSKI
B: 09/10/1924 D: 03/29/1988
BL

Year	Tm	Lg	Tot	H	A	Men-On 0	Men-On 1	Men-On 2	Men-On 3	One-Game 2	One-Game 3	One-Game 4	LO	XN	IP	PH	RHP	LHP
1948	CIN	NL	12	9	3	6	4	2	0	0	0	0	0	0	0	0	12	0
1949	CIN	NL	8	5	3	5	2	0	1	0	0	0	0	0	0	0	7	1

Ted Kluszewski *continued*

Year	Tm	Lg	Tot	H	A	Men-On 0	1	2	3	One-Game 2	3	4	LO	XN	IP	PH	RHP	LHP
1950	CIN	NL	25	14	11	16	4	5	0	2	0	0	0	1	0	0	18	7
1951	CIN	NL	13	8	5	8	5	0	0	0	0	0	0	0	0	0	10	3
1952	CIN	NL	16	4	12	6	8	1	1	0	0	0	0	0	0	0	13	3
1953	CIN	NL	40	23	17	27	11	2	0	3	0	0	0	1	0	0	27	13
1954	CIN	NL	49	34	15	27	17	5	0	6	0	0	0	0	0	0	36	13
1955	CIN	NL	47	22	25	31	14	2	0	5	0	0	0	1	0	0	27	20
1956	CIN	NL	35	23	12	15	15	4	1	2	1	0	0	1	0	0	26	9
1957	CIN	NL	6	3	3	3	3	0	0	1	0	0	0	0	0	2	5	1
1958	PIT	NL	4	2	2	2	1	1	0	1	0	0	0	1	0	0	4	0
1959	PIT	NL	2	2	0	2	0	0	0	0	0	0	0	1	0	0	2	0
	CHI	AL	2	2	0	0	2	0	0	1	0	0	0	0	0	0	2	0
	Total		4	4	0	2	2	0	0	1	0	0	0	1	0	0	4	0
1960	CHI	AL	5	3	2	2	3	0	0	0	0	0	0	0	0	1	4	1
1961	LA	AL	15	9	6	8	5	2	0	1	0	0	0	0	0	1	15	0
Total			279	163	116	158	94	24	3	22	1	0	0	6	0	4	208	71

Rank among batters: 82 • *Top target (9 home runs)*: Warren Spahn • *Number of pitchers victimized*: 139 • *Total ballparks homered in*: 15 • *First HR*: 04/25/1948 off Hal Gregg • *World Series HR*—3; *All-Star HR*—1

Mickey Klutts

GENE ELLIS KLUTTS
B: 09/20/1954
BR

Year	Tm	Lg	Tot	H	A	Men-On 0	1	2	3	One-Game 2	3	4	LO	XN	IP	PH	RHP	LHP
1977	NY	AL	1	1	0	0	1	0	0	0	0	0	0	0	0	0	1	0
1979	OAK	AL	1	0	1	1	0	0	0	0	0	0	0	0	0	0	0	1
1980	OAK	AL	4	3	1	1	2	1	0	0	0	0	0	0	0	1	1	3
1981	OAK	AL	5	3	2	4	0	1	0	1	0	0	0	0	0	0	1	4
1983	TOR	AL	3	1	2	3	0	0	0	1	0	0	0	0	0	1	3	0
Total			14	8	6	9	3	2	0	2	0	0	0	0	0	2	6	8

Rank among batters: 2,169 • *Top target (2 home runs)*: Manny Castillo • *Number of pitchers victimized*: 13 • *Total ballparks homered in*: 6 • *First HR*: 10/02/1977 off Vern Ruhle

Clyde Kluttz

CLYDE FRANKLIN KLUTTZ
B: 12/12/1917 D: 05/12/1979
BR

Year	Tm	Lg	Tot	H	A	Men-On 0	1	2	3	One-Game 2	3	4	LO	XN	IP	PH	RHP	LHP
1942	BOS	NL	1	0	1	0	0	1	0	0	0	0	0	0	0	0	1	0
1944	BOS	NL	2	1	1	0	2	0	0	0	0	0	0	0	0	0	2	0
1945	NY	NL	4	3	1	3	1	0	0	0	0	0	0	1	0	1	2	2
1947	PIT	NL	6	4	2	2	2	1	1	0	0	0	0	0	0	0	5	1
1948	PIT	NL	4	2	2	3	1	0	0	0	0	0	0	0	0	0	4	0
1951	WAS	AL	1	0	1	0	1	0	0	0	0	0	0	0	0	0	1	0
1952	WAS	AL	1	0	1	1	0	0	0	0	0	0	0	0	0	0	0	1
Total			19	10	9	9	7	2	1	0	0	0	0	1	0	1	15	4

Rank among batters: 1,861 • *Top target (2 home runs)*: Ken Burkhart • *Number of pitchers victimized*: 18 • *Total ballparks homered in*: 7 • *First HR*: 07/03/1942 off Bob Carpenter

Joe Kmak

JOSEPH ROBERT KMAK
B: 05/03/1963
BR

Year	Tm	Lg	Tot	H	A	Men-On 0	1	2	3	One-Game 2	3	4	LO	XN	IP	PH	RHP	LHP
1995	CHI	NL	1	1	0	1	0	0	0	0	0	0	0	0	0	0	1	0

Rank among batters: 4,707 • *Total ballparks homered in*: 1 • *First HR*: 07/29/1995 off Tyler Green

Otto Knabe

FRANZ OTTO KNABE
B: 06/12/1884 D: 05/17/1961
BR

Year	Tm	Lg	Tot	H	A	Men-On 0	1	2	3	One-Game 2	3	4	LO	XN	IP	PH	RHP	LHP
1907	PHI	NL	1	0	1	1	0	0	0	0	0	0	0	0	0	0	1	0
1910	PHI	NL	1	0	1	0	1	0	0	0	0	0	0	0	0	0	1	0
1911	PHI	NL	1	1	0	0	1	0	0	0	0	0	0	0	0	0	0	1
1913	PHI	NL	2	1	1	1	1	0	0	0	0	0	0	0	0	0	2	0
1914	BAL	FL	2	2	0	2	0	0	0	0	0	0	0	0	0	0	1	1

Otto Knabe *continued*

Year	Tm	Lg	Tot	H	A	Men-On 0	1	2	3	One-Game 2	3	4	LO	XN	IP	PH	RHP	LHP
1915	BAL	FL	1	1	0	0	1	0	0	0	0	0	0	0	0	0	1	0
Total			8	5	3	4	4	0	0	0	0	0	0	0	0	0	6	2

Rank among batters: 2,703 • *Total ballparks homered in*: 4 • *First HR*: 09/02/1907 off Vive Lindaman

Frank Knauss

FRANK H. KNAUSS
B: 1868 BL

Year	Tm	Lg	Tot	H	A	Men-On 0	1	2	3	One-Game 2	3	4	LO	XN	IP	PH	RHP	LHP
1890	COL	AA	1	1	0	0	1	0	0	0	0	0	0	0	0	0	0	0

Rank among batters: 4,707 • *Total ballparks homered in*: 1 • *First HR*: 07/12/1890 off Will Callahan

Phil Knell

PHILIP H. KNELL
B: 03/02/1865 D: 06/05/1944
BR

Year	Tm	Lg	Tot	H	A	Men-On 0	1	2	3	One-Game 2	3	4	LO	XN	IP	PH	RHP	LHP
1890	PHI	PL	1	1	0	0	0	1	0	0	0	0	0	0	0	0	0	1
1894	LOU	NL	1	0	1	1	0	0	0	0	0	0	0	0	0	0	1	0
Total			2	1	1	1	0	1	0	0	0	0	0	0	0	0	1	1

Rank among batters: 4,129 • *Total ballparks homered in*: 2 • *First HR*: 05/26/1890 off George Keefe

Bob Knepper

ROBERT WESLEY KNEPPER
B: 05/25/1954
BL

Year	Tm	Lg	Tot	H	A	Men-On 0	1	2	3	One-Game 2	3	4	LO	XN	IP	PH	RHP	LHP
1979	SF	NL	1	1	0	1	0	0	0	0	0	0	0	0	0	0	1	0
1981	HOU	NL	1	1	0	1	0	0	0	0	0	0	0	0	0	0	0	1
1983	HOU	NL	1	0	1	1	0	0	0	0	0	0	0	0	0	0	1	0
1984	HOU	NL	1	0	1	1	0	0	0	0	0	0	0	0	0	0	1	0
1985	HOU	NL	1	0	1	0	1	0	0	0	0	0	0	0	0	0	1	0
1989	HOU	NL	1	0	1	1	0	0	0	0	0	0	0	0	0	0	1	0
Total			6	2	4	5	1	0	0	0	0	0	0	0	0	0	5	1

Rank among batters: 2,988 • *Total ballparks homered in*: 3 • *First HR*: 05/25/1979 off Phil Niekro

Alan Knicely

ALAN LEE KNICELY
B: 05/19/1955
BR

Year	Tm	Lg	Tot	H	A	Men-On 0	1	2	3	One-Game 2	3	4	LO	XN	IP	PH	RHP	LHP
1981	HOU	NL	2	0	2	2	0	0	0	0	0	0	0	0	0	0	2	0
1982	HOU	NL	2	2	0	1	0	1	0	0	0	0	0	0	0	0	2	0
1983	CIN	NL	2	2	0	2	0	0	0	0	0	0	0	0	0	0	1	1
1985	CIN	NL	5	3	2	1	1	3	0	0	0	0	0	0	0	0	4	1
1986	STL	NL	1	0	1	1	0	0	0	0	0	0	0	0	0	0	0	1
Total			12	7	5	7	1	4	0	0	0	0	0	0	0	0	9	3

Rank among batters: 2,325 • *Top target (2 home runs)*: Dennis Eckersley • *Number of pitchers victimized*: 11 • *Total ballparks homered in*: 6 • *First HR*: 10/03/1981 off Bob Welch

Bill Knickerbocker

WILLIAM HART KNICKERBOCKER
B: 12/29/1911 D: 09/08/1963
BR

Year	Tm	Lg	Tot	H	A	Men-On 0	1	2	3	One-Game 2	3	4	LO	XN	IP	PH	RHP	LHP
1933	CLE	AL	2	1	1	0	2	0	0	0	0	0	0	0	0	0	1	1
1934	CLE	AL	4	1	3	3	0	0	1	0	0	0	0	0	0	0	4	0
1936	CLE	AL	8	2	6	4	3	0	1	0	0	0	0	0	0	0	5	3
1937	STL	AL	4	1	3	4	0	0	0	0	0	0	1	0	0	0	3	1
1938	NY	AL	1	1	0	1	0	0	0	0	0	0	0	0	0	0	1	0
1940	NY	AL	1	0	1	0	1	0	0	0	0	0	0	0	0	0	0	1
1941	CHI	AL	7	2	5	4	3	0	0	0	0	0	2	0	0	0	7	0
1942	PHI	AL	1	1	0	1	0	0	0	0	0	0	0	1	0	0	1	0
Total			28	9	19	17	9	0	2	0	0	0	3	1	0	0	22	6

Rank among batters: 1,500 • *Top target (2 home runs)*: Bill Beckmann, Jack Knott • *Number of pitchers victimized*: 26 • *Total ballparks homered in*: 7 • *First HR*: 04/13/1933 off George Uhle

Jack Knight

ELMA RUSSELL KNIGHT
B: 01/12/1895 D: 07/30/1976
BL

Year	Tm	Lg	Tot	H	A	Men-On 0	1	2	3	One-Game 2	3	4	LO	XN	IP	PH	RHP	LHP
1926	PHI	NL	2	0	2	0	1	1	0	1	0	0	0	0	0	0	2	0

Rank among batters: 4,129 • *Total ballparks homered in*: 1 • *First HR*: 06/24/1926 off Jimmy Ring

John Knight

JOHN WESLEY KNIGHT
B: 10/06/1885 D: 12/19/1965
BR

Year	Tm	Lg	Tot	H	A	Men-On 0	1	2	3	One-Game 2	3	4	LO	XN	IP	PH	RHP	LHP
1905	PHI	AL	3	2	1	2	1	0	0	0	0	0	0	0	1	0	3	0
1906	PHI	AL	3	0	3	2	1	0	0	0	0	0	0	0	2	0	3	0
1907	BOS	AL	2	2	0	1	1	0	0	0	0	0	0	0	1	0	1	1
1910	NY	AL	3	0	3	3	0	0	0	0	0	0	0	0	0	0	2	1
1911	NY	AL	3	2	1	1	2	0	0	0	0	0	0	0	0	0	2	1
Total			14	6	8	9	5	0	0	0	0	0	0	0	4	0	11	3

Rank among batters: 2,169 • *Top target (2 home runs)*: Jack Powell • *Number of pitchers victimized*: 13 • *Total ballparks homered in*: 6 • *First HR*: 04/20/1905 off Jack Powell

Joseph Knight

JOSEPH WILLIAM KNIGHT
B: 09/28/1859 D: 10/16/1938
BL

Year	Tm	Lg	Tot	H	A	Men-On 0	1	2	3	One-Game 2	3	4	LO	XN	IP	PH	RHP	LHP
1890	CIN	NL	4	2	2	2	2	0	0	0	0	0	0	0	0	0	2	1

Rank among batters: 3,427 • *Total ballparks homered in*: 3 • *First HR*: 06/23/1890 off John Clarkson

Lon Knight

ALONZO P. KNIGHT
B: 06/16/1853 D: 04/23/1932
BR

Year	Tm	Lg	Tot	H	A	Men-On 0	1	2	3	One-Game 2	3	4	LO	XN	IP	PH	RHP	LHP
1881	DET	NL	1	1	0	0	1	0	0	0	0	0	0	0	0	0	1	0
1883	PHI	AA	1	1	0	0	1	0	0	0	0	0	0	0	1	0	1	0
1884	PHI	AA	1	0	1	0	1	0	0	0	0	0	0	0	0	0	1	0
Total			3	2	1	0	3	0	0	0	0	0	0	0	1	0	3	0

Rank among batters: 3,735 • *Total ballparks homered in*: 3 • *First HR*: 07/30/1881 off Jim Galvin • *Hit for Cycle*—vs PIT: 07/30/1883

Ray Knight

CHARLES RAY KNIGHT
B: 12/28/1952
BR

Year	Tm	Lg	Tot	H	A	Men-On 0	1	2	3	One-Game 2	3	4	LO	XN	IP	PH	RHP	LHP
1977	CIN	NL	1	0	1	0	0	1	0	0	0	0	0	0	0	0	0	1
1978	CIN	NL	1	1	0	0	0	1	0	0	0	0	0	0	0	0	1	0
1979	CIN	NL	10	4	6	5	4	0	1	1	0	0	0	0	0	0	5	5
1980	CIN	NL	14	6	8	4	5	2	3	1	0	0	0	0	0	0	10	4
1981	CIN	NL	6	1	5	6	0	0	0	0	0	0	0	0	0	0	6	0
1982	HOU	NL	6	0	6	3	3	0	0	0	0	0	0	0	0	0	4	2
1983	HOU	NL	9	3	6	6	3	0	0	0	0	0	0	0	0	0	6	3
1984	HOU	NL	2	1	1	1	0	1	0	0	0	0	0	0	0	0	1	1
	NY	NL	1	1	0	1	0	0	0	0	0	0	0	0	0	0	0	1
	Total		3	2	1	2	0	1	0	0	0	0	0	0	0	0	1	2
1985	NY	NL	6	4	2	1	2	3	0	0	0	0	0	0	0	0	1	5
1986	NY	NL	11	7	4	7	4	0	0	1	0	0	0	1	0	0	2	9
1987	BAL	AL	14	8	6	6	7	1	0	0	0	0	0	0	0	0	6	8
1988	DET	AL	3	3	0	1	2	0	0	0	0	0	0	0	0	0	0	3
Total			84	39	45	41	30	9	4	3	0	0	0	1	0	0	42	42

Rank among batters: 617 • *Top target (4 home runs)*: Steve Carlton • *Number of pitchers victimized*: 71 • *Total ballparks homered in*: 17 • *First HR*: 07/02/1977 off Bob Owchinko • *2 HR in 1 inning*—vs NY: 05/13/1980 • *World Series HR*—1

Chuck Knoblauch

EDWARD CHARLES KNOBLAUCH
B: 07/07/1968
BR

Year	Tm	Lg	Tot	H	A	Men-On 0	1	2	3	One-Game 2	3	4	LO	XN	IP	PH	RHP	LHP
1991	MIN	AL	1	1	0	1	0	0	0	0	0	0	0	0	0	0	1	0
1992	MIN	AL	2	0	2	2	0	0	0	0	0	0	1	0	0	0	1	1

Chuck Knoblauch *continued*

Year	Tm	Lg	Tot	H	A	Men-On 0	Men-On 1	Men-On 2	Men-On 3	One-Game 2	One-Game 3	One-Game 4	LO	XN	IP	PH	RHP	LHP
1993	MIN	AL	2	2	0	2	0	0	0	0	0	0	0	0	0	0	2	0
1994	MIN	AL	5	1	4	5	0	0	0	1	0	0	3	0	0	0	3	2
1995	MIN	AL	11	4	7	5	6	0	0	0	0	0	2	0	0	0	7	4
Total			21	8	13	15	6	0	0	1	0	0	6	0	0	0	14	7

Rank among batters: 1,768 • *Top target (2 home runs)*: Mike Moore, Jim Abbott • *Number of pitchers victimized*: 19 • *Total ballparks homered in*: 9 • *First HR*: 08/31/1991 off Mike Mussina

Ray Knode

ROBERT TROXELL KNODE
B: 01/28/1901 D: 04/13/1982
BL

Year	Tm	Lg	Tot	H	A	Men-On 0	Men-On 1	Men-On 2	Men-On 3	One-Game 2	One-Game 3	One-Game 4	LO	XN	IP	PH	RHP	LHP
1923	CLE	AL	2	1	1	1	1	0	0	0	0	0	0	0	0	0	2	0

Rank among batters: 4,129 • *Total ballparks homered in*: 2 • *First HR*: 10/04/1923 off Rasty Wright

Bobby Knoop

ROBERT FRANK KNOOP
B: 10/18/1938
BR

Year	Tm	Lg	Tot	H	A	Men-On 0	Men-On 1	Men-On 2	Men-On 3	One-Game 2	One-Game 3	One-Game 4	LO	XN	IP	PH	RHP	LHP
1964	LA	AL	7	1	6	5	1	0	1	0	0	0	0	0	0	0	4	3
1965	CAL	AL	7	2	5	2	5	0	0	0	0	0	0	0	0	0	5	2
1966	CAL	AL	17	9	8	8	7	2	0	0	0	0	0	0	0	0	12	5
1967	CAL	AL	9	5	4	7	1	1	0	0	0	0	0	0	0	0	6	3
1968	CAL	AL	3	1	2	3	0	0	0	0	0	0	0	0	0	0	2	1
1969	CAL	AL	1	1	0	1	0	0	0	0	0	0	0	0	0	0	1	0
	CHI	AL	6	1	5	2	3	1	0	1	0	0	0	0	1	0	5	1
	Total		7	2	5	3	3	1	0	1	0	0	0	0	1	0	6	1
1970	CHI	AL	5	4	1	3	1	1	0	0	0	0	0	0	0	0	4	1
1971	KC	AL	1	0	1	1	0	0	0	0	0	0	0	0	0	0	0	1
Total			56	24	32	32	18	5	1	1	0	0	0	0	1	0	39	17

Rank among batters: 913 • *Top target (3 home runs)*: Bill Monbouquette, Phil Ortega • *Number of pitchers victimized*: 46 • *Total ballparks homered in*: 11 • *First HR*: 04/17/1964 off Dick Egan

Randy Knorr

RANDY DUANE KNORR
B: 11/12/1968
BR

Year	Tm	Lg	Tot	H	A	Men-On 0	Men-On 1	Men-On 2	Men-On 3	One-Game 2	One-Game 3	One-Game 4	LO	XN	IP	PH	RHP	LHP
1992	TOR	AL	1	0	1	1	0	0	0	0	0	0	0	0	0	0	0	1
1993	TOR	AL	4	2	2	1	1	2	0	0	0	0	0	0	0	0	3	1
1994	TOR	AL	7	4	3	5	2	0	0	1	0	0	0	0	0	0	3	4
1995	TOR	AL	3	2	1	2	1	0	0	0	0	0	0	0	0	0	0	3
Total			15	8	7	9	4	2	0	1	0	0	0	0	0	0	6	9

Rank among batters: 2,096 • *Top target (2 home runs)*: Ricky Bones • *Number of pitchers victimized*: 14 • *Total ballparks homered in*: 8 • *First HR*: 08/16/1992 off Dave Otto

Fritz Knothe

WILFRED EDGAR KNOTHE
B: 05/01/1903 D: 03/27/1963
BR

Year	Tm	Lg	Tot	H	A	Men-On 0	Men-On 1	Men-On 2	Men-On 3	One-Game 2	One-Game 3	One-Game 4	LO	XN	IP	PH	RHP	LHP
1932	BOS	NL	1	1	0	0	0	1	0	0	0	0	0	0	0	0	1	0
1933	BOS	NL	1	1	0	0	1	0	0	0	0	0	0	0	0	0	1	0
Total			2	2	0	0	1	1	0	0	0	0	0	0	0	0	2	0

Rank among batters: 4,129 • *Total ballparks homered in*: 1 • *First HR*: 05/31/1932 off Hal Schumacher

Jimmy Knowles

JAMES KNOWLES
B: 09/ /1856 D: 02/11/1912

Year	Tm	Lg	Tot	H	A	Men-On 0	Men-On 1	Men-On 2	Men-On 3	One-Game 2	One-Game 3	One-Game 4	LO	XN	IP	PH	RHP	LHP
1884	BRO	AA	1	0	1	0	1	0	0	0	0	0	0	0	0	0	0	0
1886	WAS	NL	3	1	2	1	2	0	0	0	0	0	0	0	0	0	2	1
1890	ROC	AA	5	2	3	3	1	0	1	0	0	0	0	0	0	0	5	0
Total			9	3	6	4	4	0	1	0	0	0	0	0	0	0	7	1

Rank among batters: 2,587 • *Top target (2 home runs)*: Jack Stivetts • *Number of pitchers victimized*: 8 • *Total ballparks homered in*: 7 • *First HR*: 08/08/1884 off Wes Curry

Pete Koegel

PETER JOHN KOEGEL
B: 07/31/1947
BR

Year	Tm	Lg	Tot	H	A	Men-On 0	1	2	3	One-Game 2	3	4	LO	XN	IP	PH	RHP	LHP
1970	MIL	AL	1	0	1	1	0	0	0	0	0	0	0	0	0	1	0	1

Rank among batters: 4,707 • *Total ballparks homered in*: 1 • *First HR*: 09/25/1970 off Tommy John

Bernard Koehler

BERNARD JAMES KOEHLER
B: 01/26/1877 D: 05/21/1961
BR

Year	Tm	Lg	Tot	H	A	Men-On 0	1	2	3	One-Game 2	3	4	LO	XN	IP	PH	RHP	LHP
1905	STL	AL	2	1	1	0	2	0	0	0	0	0	0	0	1	0	1	1

Rank among batters: 4,129 • *Total ballparks homered in*: 2 • *First HR*: 09/26/1905 off Louis LeRoy

Len Koenecke

LEONARD GEORGE KOENECKE
B: 01/18/1904 D: 09/17/1935
BL

Year	Tm	Lg	Tot	H	A	Men-On 0	1	2	3	One-Game 2	3	4	LO	XN	IP	PH	RHP	LHP
1932	NY	NL	4	2	2	3	1	0	0	0	0	0	0	0	0	0	4	0
1934	BRO	NL	14	8	6	9	4	1	0	3	0	0	2	0	1	0	10	4
1935	BRO	NL	4	1	3	4	0	0	0	0	0	0	0	0	0	0	4	0
Total			22	11	11	16	5	1	0	3	0	0	2	0	1	0	18	4

Rank among batters: 1,719 • *Top target (2 home runs)*: George Darrow, Hal Schumacher, Waite Hoyt • *Number of pitchers victimized*: 19 • *Total ballparks homered in*: 6 • *First HR*: 04/16/1932 off Ben Cantwell

Mark Koenig

MARK ANTHONY KOENIG
B: 07/19/1904 D: 04/22/1993
BB

Year	Tm	Lg	Tot	H	A	Men-On 0	1	2	3	One-Game 2	3	4	LO	XN	IP	PH	RHP	LHP
1926	NY	AL	5	3	2	2	2	1	0	0	0	0	0	0	1	0	3	2
1927	NY	AL	3	0	3	2	1	0	0	0	0	0	0	0	0	0	1	2
1928	NY	AL	4	1	3	0	4	0	0	0	0	0	0	0	1	1	4	0
1929	NY	AL	3	0	3	2	1	0	0	0	0	0	0	0	1	0	3	0
1930	DET	AL	1	1	0	0	0	1	0	0	0	0	0	0	0	0	1	0
1931	DET	AL	1	0	1	0	1	0	0	0	0	0	0	0	0	0	0	1
1932	CHI	NL	3	3	0	1	1	1	0	0	0	0	0	1	0	0	3	0
1933	CHI	NL	3	2	1	2	0	1	0	0	0	0	0	0	0	1	3	0
1934	CIN	NL	1	1	0	0	1	0	0	0	0	0	0	0	0	0	1	0
1935	NY	NL	3	1	2	1	2	0	0	0	0	0	0	0	0	0	3	0
1936	NY	NL	1	1	0	1	0	0	0	0	0	0	0	0	0	1	1	0
Total			28	13	15	11	13	4	0	0	0	0	0	1	3	3	23	5

Rank among batters: 1,500 • *Top target (2 home runs)*: Lil Stoner • *Number of pitchers victimized*: 27 • *Total ballparks homered in*: 11 • *First HR*: 04/23/1926 off Red Ruffing

Dick Kokos

RICHARD JEROME KOKOS
B: 02/28/1928 D: 04/09/1986
BL

Year	Tm	Lg	Tot	H	A	Men-On 0	1	2	3	One-Game 2	3	4	LO	XN	IP	PH	RHP	LHP
1948	STL	AL	4	1	3	3	1	0	0	0	0	0	0	0	0	0	4	0
1949	STL	AL	23	16	7	10	8	5	0	1	0	0	0	0	0	1	15	8
1950	STL	AL	18	11	7	8	5	4	1	0	0	0	0	0	0	0	11	7
1953	STL	AL	13	5	8	8	5	0	0	1	0	0	1	1	0	1	12	1
1954	BAL	AL	1	0	1	1	0	0	0	0	0	0	0	0	0	1	1	0
Total			59	33	26	30	19	9	1	2	0	0	1	1	0	3	43	16

Rank among batters: 873 • Top target (3 home runs): Lou Brissie, Carl Scheib, Bob Lemon, Steve Gromek, Virgil Trucks • *Number of pitchers victimized*: 41 • *Total ballparks homered in*: 7 • *First HR*: 07/11/1948 off Bob Feller

Gary Kolb

GARY ALAN KOLB
B: 03/13/1940
BL

Year	Tm	Lg	Tot	H	A	Men-On 0	1	2	3	One-Game 2	3	4	LO	XN	IP	PH	RHP	LHP
1963	STL	NL	3	2	1	1	2	0	0	0	0	0	0	0	0	0	2	1
1965	NY	NL	1	1	0	0	0	1	0	0	0	0	0	0	0	0	1	0
1968	PIT	NL	2	0	2	2	0	0	0	0	0	0	0	0	0	1	2	0
Total			6	3	3	3	2	1	0	0	0	0	0	0	0	1	5	1

Rank among batters: 2,988 • *Total ballparks homered in*: 4 • *First HR*: 07/12/1963 off Tony Cloninger

Don Kolloway

DONALD MARTIN KOLLOWAY
B: 08/04/1918 D: 06/30/1994
BR

Year	Tm	Lg	Tot	H	A	Men-On				One-Game			LO	XN	IP	PH	RHP	LHP
						0	1	2	3	2	3	4						
1941	CHI	AL	3	0	3	3	0	0	0	1	0	0	0	0	0	0	1	2
1942	CHI	AL	3	1	2	2	1	0	0	0	0	0	0	0	0	0	3	0
1943	CHI	AL	1	1	0	1	0	0	0	0	0	0	0	0	0	0	1	0
1946	CHI	AL	3	2	1	3	0	0	0	0	0	0	0	0	0	0	3	0
1947	CHI	AL	2	0	2	2	0	0	0	0	0	0	0	0	0	0	2	0
1948	CHI	AL	6	2	4	4	1	1	0	0	0	0	0	0	0	0	5	1
1949	DET	AL	2	2	0	2	0	0	0	0	0	0	0	0	0	0	2	0
1950	DET	AL	6	3	3	4	2	0	0	0	0	0	0	0	0	0	4	2
1951	DET	AL	1	1	0	1	0	0	0	0	0	0	0	0	0	0	1	0
1952	DET	AL	2	0	2	0	1	0	1	0	0	0	0	0	0	2	0	2
Total			29	12	17	22	5	1	1	1	0	0	0	0	0	2	22	7

Rank among batters: 1,465 • *Top target (2 home runs)*: Al Smith, Joe Haynes, Ned Garver, Lou Brissie • *Number of pitchers victimized*: 25 • *Total ballparks homered in*: 6 • *First HR*: 06/28/1941 off Al Smith

Ray Kolp

RAYMOND CARL KOLP
B: 10/01/1894 D: 07/29/1967
BR

Year	Tm	Lg	Tot	H	A	Men-On				One-Game			LO	XN	IP	PH	RHP	LHP
						0	1	2	3	2	3	4						
1928	CIN	NL	1	0	1	1	0	0	0	0	0	0	0	0	0	0	1	0
1930	CIN	NL	1	0	1	1	0	0	0	0	0	0	0	0	0	0	1	0
Total			2	0	2	2	0	0	0	0	0	0	0	0	0	0	2	0

Rank among batters: 4,129 • *Total ballparks homered in*: 2 • *First HR*: 06/01/1928 off Hal Goldsmith

Fred Kommers

FREDERICK RAYMOND KOMMERS
B: 03/31/1886 D: 06/14/1943
BL

Year	Tm	Lg	Tot	H	A	Men-On				One-Game			LO	XN	IP	PH	RHP	LHP
						0	1	2	3	2	3	4						
1914	STL	FL	3	3	0	0	2	1	0	0	0	0	0	0	0	0	3	0
	BAL	FL	1	1	0	0	1	0	0	0	0	0	0	0	0	0	1	0
	Total		4	4	0	1	2	1	0	0	0	0	0	0	0	0	4	0
Total			4	4	0	1	2	1	0	0	0	0	0	0	0	0	4	0

Rank among batters: 3,427 • *Total ballparks homered in*: 2 • *First HR*: 04/16/1914 off Cy Falkenberg

Brad Komminsk

BRAD LYNN KOMMINSK
B: 04/04/1961
BR

Year	Tm	Lg	Tot	H	A	Men-On				One-Game			LO	XN	IP	PH	RHP	LHP
						0	1	2	3	2	3	4						
1984	ATL	NL	8	3	5	2	4	1	1	1	0	0	0	0	1	1	5	3
1985	ATL	NL	4	1	3	3	0	1	0	0	0	0	0	0	0	0	1	3
1989	CLE	AL	8	6	2	2	3	3	0	0	0	0	0	1	0	0	7	1
1990	BAL	AL	3	3	0	3	0	0	0	0	0	0	0	0	0	0	1	2
Total			23	13	10	10	7	5	1	1	0	0	0	1	1	1	14	9

Rank among batters: 1,686 • *Total ballparks homered in*: 9 • *First HR*: 06/05/1984 off Scott Garrelts

Ed Konetchy

EDWARD JOSEPH KONETCHY
B: 09/03/1885 D: 05/27/1947
BR

Year	Tm	Lg	Tot	H	A	Men-On				One-Game			LO	XN	IP	PH	RHP	LHP
						0	1	2	3	2	3	4						
1907	STL	NL	2	1	1	1	1	0	0	0	0	0	0	0	2	0	1	1
1908	STL	NL	5	4	1	3	2	0	0	0	0	0	0	0	5	0	4	1
1909	STL	NL	4	3	1	0	4	0	0	0	0	0	0	0	2	0	3	1
1910	STL	NL	3	0	3	3	0	0	0	0	0	0	0	0	1	0	2	1
1911	STL	NL	6	1	5	1	2	3	0	0	0	0	0	0	0	0	3	3
1912	STL	NL	8	3	5	5	2	1	0	1	0	0	0	0	6	0	5	3
1913	STL	NL	8	3	5	5	2	1	0	0	0	0	0	0	5	0	5	3
1914	PIT	NL	4	0	4	3	0	0	1	0	0	0	0	1	1	0	2	2
1915	PIT	FL	10	1	9	4	4	2	0	0	0	0	0	0	1	0	7	3
1916	BOS	NL	3	0	3	2	1	0	0	0	0	0	0	0	0	0	3	0
1917	BOS	NL	2	2	0	1	1	0	0	0	0	0	0	0	2	0	1	1
1918	BOS	NL	2	1	1	2	0	0	0	0	0	0	0	0	1	0	2	0
1919	BRO	NL	1	0	1	1	0	0	0	0	0	0	0	0	0	0	1	0
1920	BRO	NL	5	2	3	3	1	1	0	0	0	0	0	0	2	0	4	1
1921	BRO	NL	3	1	2	3	0	0	0	0	0	0	0	0	0	0	3	0

Ed Konetchy *continued*

Year	Tm	Lg	Tot	H	A	Men-On 0	Men-On 1	Men-On 2	Men-On 3	One-Game 2	One-Game 3	One-Game 4	LO	XN	IP	PH	RHP	LHP
1921	PHI	NL	8	6	2	3	5	0	0	0	0	0	0	0	0	0	5	3
	Total		11	7	4	6	5	0	0	0	0	0	0	0	0	0	8	3
Total			74	28	46	40	25	8	1	1	0	0	0	1	28	0	51	23

Rank among batters: 707 • *Top target (4 home runs)*: Phil Douglas • *Number of pitchers victimized*: 60 • *Total ballparks homered in*: 16 • *First HR*: 08/13/1907 off Irv Young

Jerry Koosman

JEROME MARTIN KOOSMAN
B: 12/23/1942
BR

Year	Tm	Lg	Tot	H	A	Men-On 0	Men-On 1	Men-On 2	Men-On 3	One-Game 2	One-Game 3	One-Game 4	LO	XN	IP	PH	RHP	LHP
1968	NY	NL	1	1	0	1	0	0	0	0	0	0	0	0	0	0	1	0
1977	NY	NL	1	1	0	1	0	0	0	0	0	0	0	0	0	0	1	0
Total			2	2	0	2	0	0	0	0	0	0	0	0	0	0	2	0

Rank among batters: 4,129 • *Total ballparks homered in*: 1 • *First HR*: 09/18/1968 off Bill Hands

Larry Kopf

WILLIAM LORENZ KOPF
B: 11/03/1890 D: 10/15/1986
BB

Year	Tm	Lg	Tot	H	A	Men-On 0	Men-On 1	Men-On 2	Men-On 3	One-Game 2	One-Game 3	One-Game 4	LO	XN	IP	PH	RHP	LHP
1915	PHI	AL	1	1	0	0	0	1	0	0	0	0	0	0	0	0	1	0
1917	CIN	NL	2	1	1	0	2	0	0	0	0	0	0	0	2	0	1	1
1921	CIN	NL	1	0	1	0	1	0	0	0	0	0	0	0	0	1	0	1
1922	BOS	NL	1	1	0	1	0	0	0	0	0	0	0	0	1	0	1	0
Total			5	3	2	1	3	1	0	0	0	0	0	0	3	1	3	2

Rank among batters: 3,191 • *Total ballparks homered in*: 5 • *First HR*: 06/10/1915 off Rip Hagerman

Merlin Kopp

MERLIN HENRY KOPP
B: 01/02/1892 D: 05/06/1960
BB

Year	Tm	Lg	Tot	H	A	Men-On 0	Men-On 1	Men-On 2	Men-On 3	One-Game 2	One-Game 3	One-Game 4	LO	XN	IP	PH	RHP	LHP
1919	PHI	AL	1	0	1	1	0	0	0	0	0	0	0	0	0	0	1	0

Rank among batters: 4,707 • *Total ballparks homered in*: 1 • *First HR*: 07/15/1919 off Dave Davenport

Joe Koppe

JOSEPH KOPPE
B: 10/19/1930
BR

Year	Tm	Lg	Tot	H	A	Men-On 0	Men-On 1	Men-On 2	Men-On 3	One-Game 2	One-Game 3	One-Game 4	LO	XN	IP	PH	RHP	LHP
1959	PHI	NL	7	6	1	5	1	1	0	0	0	0	1	0	0	0	2	5
1960	PHI	NL	1	0	1	0	0	1	0	0	0	0	0	0	0	0	1	0
1961	LA	AL	5	3	2	4	0	0	1	0	0	0	0	1	0	0	4	1
1962	LA	AL	4	1	3	3	1	0	0	0	0	0	0	0	0	0	3	1
1963	LA	AL	1	0	1	0	1	0	0	0	0	0	0	0	0	0	0	1
1965	CAL	AL	1	0	1	1	0	0	0	0	0	0	0	0	0	0	1	0
Total			19	10	9	13	3	2	1	0	0	0	1	1	0	0	11	8

Rank among batters: 1,861 • *Top target (2 home runs)*: Frank Funk • *Number of pitchers victimized*: 18 • *Total ballparks homered in*: 9 • *First HR*: 07/10/1959 off Wilmer Mizell

Art Kores

ARTHUR EMIL KORES
B: 07/22/1886 D: 03/26/1974
BR

Year	Tm	Lg	Tot	H	A	Men-On 0	Men-On 1	Men-On 2	Men-On 3	One-Game 2	One-Game 3	One-Game 4	LO	XN	IP	PH	RHP	LHP
1915	STL	FL	1	1	0	1	0	0	0	0	0	0	0	0	0	0	1	0

Rank among batters: 4,707 • *Total ballparks homered in*: 1 • *First HR*: 09/25/1915 off Gene Krapp

Andy Kosco

ANDREW JOHN KOSCO
B: 10/05/1941
BR

Year	Tm	Lg	Tot	H	A	Men-On 0	Men-On 1	Men-On 2	Men-On 3	One-Game 2	One-Game 3	One-Game 4	LO	XN	IP	PH	RHP	LHP
1965	MIN	AL	1	0	1	1	0	0	0	0	0	0	0	0	0	0	0	1
1966	MIN	AL	2	2	0	0	1	1	0	0	0	0	0	0	0	1	1	1

Andy Kosco *continued*

Year	Tm	Lg	Tot	H	A	Men-On 0	1	2	3	One-Game 2	3	4	LO	XN	IP	PH	RHP	LHP
1968	NY	AL	15	5	10	10	3	2	0	0	0	0	0	0	0	0	10	5
1969	LA	NL	19	10	9	8	8	2	1	1	0	0	0	0	0	0	10	9
1970	LA	NL	8	3	5	6	2	0	0	0	0	0	0	0	0	0	1	7
1971	MIL	AL	10	4	6	6	2	2	0	0	0	0	0	0	0	2	2	8
1972	CAL	AL	6	3	3	5	1	0	0	0	0	0	0	0	0	0	2	4
	BOS	AL	3	3	0	3	0	0	0	0	0	0	0	0	0	2	3	0
	Total		9	6	3	8	1	0	0	0	0	0	0	0	0	2	5	4
1973	CIN	NL	9	4	5	8	0	1	0	0	0	0	0	0	0	1	3	6
Total			73	34	39	47	17	8	1	1	0	0	0	0	0	6	32	41

Rank among batters: 715 • Top target (3 home runs): Jim Merritt, Denny Lemaster, Dave McNally, George Stone • *Number of pitchers victimized*: 59 • *Total ballparks homered in*: 22 • *First HR*: 08/14/1965 off Sam McDowell

Dave Koslo

GEORGE BERNARD KOSLO
B: 03/31/1920 D: 12/01/1975
BL

Year	Tm	Lg	Tot	H	A	Men-On 0	1	2	3	One-Game 2	3	4	LO	XN	IP	PH	RHP	LHP
1949	NY	NL	2	2	0	0	1	1	0	1	0	0	0	0	0	0	2	0
1950	NY	NL	1	0	1	0	1	0	0	0	0	0	0	0	0	0	1	0
Total			3	2	1	0	2	1	0	1	0	0	0	0	0	0	3	0

Rank among batters: 3,735 • *Total ballparks homered in*: 2 • *First HR*: 07/07/1949 off Hank Borowy

Kevin Koslofski

KEVIN CRAIG KOSLOFSKI
B: 09/24/1966
BL

Year	Tm	Lg	Tot	H	A	Men-On 0	1	2	3	One-Game 2	3	4	LO	XN	IP	PH	RHP	LHP
1992	KC	AL	3	1	2	3	0	0	0	0	0	0	0	0	0	0	3	0
1993	KC	AL	1	0	1	1	0	0	0	0	0	0	0	1	0	0	1	0
Total			4	1	3	4	0	0	0	0	0	0	0	1	0	0	4	0

Rank among batters: 3,427 • *Total ballparks homered in*: 4 • *First HR*: 08/27/1992 off Nolan Ryan

Frank Kostro

FRANK JERRY KOSTRO
B: 08/04/1937
BR

Year	Tm	Lg	Tot	H	A	Men-On 0	1	2	3	One-Game 2	3	4	LO	XN	IP	PH	RHP	LHP
1963	LA	AL	2	1	1	1	1	0	0	0	0	0	0	0	0	1	1	1
1964	MIN	AL	3	0	3	1	2	0	0	0	0	0	0	0	0	0	2	1
Total			5	1	4	2	3	0	0	0	0	0	0	0	0	1	3	2

Rank among batters: 3,191 • *Top target (2 home runs)*: Jack Kralick • *Number of pitchers victimized*: 4 • *Total ballparks homered in*: 3 • *First HR*: 07/20/1963 off Jim Bunning

Sandy Koufax

SANFORD KOUFAX
B: 12/30/1935
BR HOF

Year	Tm	Lg	Tot	H	A	Men-On 0	1	2	3	One-Game 2	3	4	LO	XN	IP	PH	RHP	LHP
1962	LA	NL	1	0	1	1	0	0	0	0	0	0	0	0	0	0	0	1
1963	LA	NL	1	0	1	0	0	1	0	0	0	0	0	0	0	0	0	1
Total			2	0	2	1	0	1	0	0	0	0	0	0	0	0	0	2

Rank among batters: 4,129 • *Total ballparks homered in*: 1 • *First HR*: 06/13/1962 off Warren Spahn

Ernie Koy

ERNEST ANYZ KOY
B: 09/17/1909
BR

Year	Tm	Lg	Tot	H	A	Men-On 0	1	2	3	One-Game 2	3	4	LO	XN	IP	PH	RHP	LHP
1938	BRO	NL	11	5	6	5	5	1	0	0	0	0	0	0	0	0	6	5
1939	BRO	NL	8	5	3	6	0	2	0	0	0	0	0	0	0	1	4	4
1940	BRO	NL	1	1	0	1	0	0	0	0	0	0	0	1	0	0	1	0
	STL	NL	8	3	5	3	5	0	0	0	0	0	0	0	0	0	4	4
	Total		9	4	5	4	5	0	0	0	0	0	0	1	0	0	5	4
1941	STL	NL	2	0	2	2	0	0	0	0	0	0	0	0	0	0	2	0
	CIN	NL	2	2	0	1	1	0	0	0	0	0	0	0	0	0	2	0

Ernie Koy *continued*

Year	Tm	Lg	Tot	H	A	Men-On 0	1	2	3	One-Game 2	3	4	LO	XN	IP	PH	RHP	LHP
1941	Total		4	2	2	3	1	0	0	0	0	0	0	0	0	0	4	0
1942	PHI	NL	4	2	2	2	1	1	0	0	0	0	0	0	0	0	3	1
Total			36	18	18	20	12	4	0	0	0	0	0	1	0	1	22	14

Rank among batters: 1,274 • *Top target (4 home runs)*: Cy Blanton • *Number of pitchers victimized*: 26 • *Total ballparks homered in*: 7 • *First HR*: 04/19/1938 off Wayne LaMaster • *Hit HR in first major league AB*—@PHI: 04/19/1938

Al Kozar

ALBERT KENNETH KOZAR
B: 07/05/1921
BR

Year	Tm	Lg	Tot	H	A	Men-On 0	1	2	3	One-Game 2	3	4	LO	XN	IP	PH	RHP	LHP
1948	WAS	AL	1	0	1	1	0	0	0	0	0	0	0	0	0	0	1	0
1949	WAS	AL	4	1	3	3	0	1	0	0	0	0	1	0	1	0	1	3
1950	CHI	AL	1	0	1	1	0	0	0	0	0	0	0	0	0	0	0	1
Total			6	1	5	5	0	1	0	0	0	0	1	0	1	0	2	4

Rank among batters: 2,988 • *Top target (2 home runs)*: Lou Brissie • *Number of pitchers victimized*: 5 • *Total ballparks homered in*: 4 • *First HR*: 07/03/1948 off Allie Reynolds

Jack Kralick

JOHN FRANCIS KRALICK
B: 06/01/1935
BL

Year	Tm	Lg	Tot	H	A	Men-On 0	1	2	3	One-Game 2	3	4	LO	XN	IP	PH	RHP	LHP
1961	MIN	AL	1	0	1	1	0	0	0	0	0	0	0	0	0	0	1	0
1962	MIN	AL	2	2	0	2	0	0	0	0	0	0	0	0	0	0	2	0
1963	CLE	AL	1	0	1	0	1	0	0	0	0	0	0	0	0	0	1	0
Total			4	2	2	3	1	0	0	0	0	0	0	0	0	0	4	0

Rank among batters: 3,427 • *Total ballparks homered in*: 3 • *First HR*: 08/20/1961 off Jim Donohue

Jack Kramer

JOHN HENRY KRAMER
B: 01/05/1918 D: 05/18/1995
BR

Year	Tm	Lg	Tot	H	A	Men-On 0	1	2	3	One-Game 2	3	4	LO	XN	IP	PH	RHP	LHP
1939	STL	AL	1	0	1	1	0	0	0	0	0	0	0	0	0	0	1	0
1944	STL	AL	2	1	1	1	1	0	0	0	0	0	0	0	0	0	1	1
1948	BOS	AL	1	0	1	0	1	0	0	0	0	0	0	0	0	0	1	0
1950	NY	NL	1	0	1	0	1	0	0	0	0	0	0	0	0	0	1	0
Total			5	1	4	2	3	0	0	0	0	0	0	0	0	0	4	1

Rank among batters: 3,191 • *Total ballparks homered in*: 5 • *First HR*: 09/21/1939 off Denny Galehouse

Ed Kranepool

EDWARD EMIL KRANEPOOL
B: 11/08/1944
BL

Year	Tm	Lg	Tot	H	A	Men-On 0	1	2	3	One-Game 2	3	4	LO	XN	IP	PH	RHP	LHP
1963	NY	NL	2	1	1	2	0	0	0	0	0	0	0	0	0	0	2	0
1964	NY	NL	10	7	3	4	4	2	0	1	0	0	0	0	0	0	8	2
1965	NY	NL	10	6	4	5	5	0	0	1	0	0	0	0	0	0	9	1
1966	NY	NL	16	7	9	8	6	2	0	1	0	0	0	0	0	1	15	1
1967	NY	NL	10	6	4	5	3	2	0	0	0	0	0	0	0	0	10	0
1968	NY	NL	3	1	2	3	0	0	0	0	0	0	0	0	0	0	3	0
1969	NY	NL	11	5	6	7	2	2	0	2	0	0	0	0	0	0	11	0
1971	NY	NL	14	8	6	11	3	0	0	0	0	0	0	0	0	0	13	1
1972	NY	NL	8	6	2	5	3	0	0	0	0	0	0	0	0	0	8	0
1973	NY	NL	1	1	0	0	1	0	0	0	0	0	0	0	0	0	1	0
1974	NY	NL	4	2	2	2	0	2	0	0	0	0	0	0	0	1	4	0
1975	NY	NL	4	4	0	2	1	1	0	0	0	0	0	0	0	0	3	1
1976	NY	NL	10	6	4	5	5	0	0	0	0	0	0	0	0	0	10	0
1977	NY	NL	10	4	6	6	4	0	0	1	0	0	0	0	0	1	10	0
1978	NY	NL	3	2	1	0	1	2	0	0	0	0	0	0	0	3	3	0
1979	NY	NL	2	1	1	1	1	0	0	0	0	0	0	0	0	0	2	0
Total			118	67	51	66	39	13	0	6	0	0	0	0	0	6	112	6

Rank among batters: 396 • *Top target (4 home runs)*: Rick Wise, Dave Giusti, Rick Reuschel • *Number of pitchers victimized*: 78 • *Total ballparks homered in*: 17 • *First HR*: 04/19/1963 off Bob Shaw • *World Series HR*—1

Lew Krausse

LEWIS BERNARD, JR. KRAUSSE
B: 04/25/1943
BR

Year	Tm	Lg	Tot	H	A	Men-On 0	Men-On 1	Men-On 2	Men-On 3	One-Game 2	One-Game 3	One-Game 4	LO	XN	IP	PH	RHP	LHP
1967	KC	AL	1	1	0	1	0	0	0	0	0	0	0	0	0	0	0	1
1969	OAK	AL	4	2	2	2	1	1	0	0	0	0	0	0	0	0	1	3
1974	ATL	NL	1	1	0	0	1	0	0	0	0	0	0	0	0	0	1	0
Total			6	4	2	3	2	1	0	0	0	0	0	0	0	0	2	4

Rank among batters: 2,988 • *Total ballparks homered in*: 5 • *First HR*: 07/22/1967 off Jim O'Toole

Danny Kravitz

DANIEL KRAVITZ
B: 12/21/1930
BL

Year	Tm	Lg	Tot	H	A	Men-On 0	Men-On 1	Men-On 2	Men-On 3	One-Game 2	One-Game 3	One-Game 4	LO	XN	IP	PH	RHP	LHP
1956	PIT	NL	2	2	0	1	0	0	1	0	0	0	0	0	0	0	2	0
1958	PIT	NL	1	1	0	1	0	0	0	0	0	0	0	0	0	0	1	0
1959	PIT	NL	3	2	1	1	2	0	0	0	0	0	0	0	0	0	3	0
1960	KC	AL	4	1	3	2	0	2	0	0	0	0	0	0	1	0	4	0
Total			10	6	4	5	2	2	1	0	0	0	0	0	1	0	10	0

Rank among batters: 2,500 • *Total ballparks homered in*: 6 • *First HR*: 05/11/1956 off Jack Meyer

Mike Kreevich

MICHAEL ANDREAS KREEVICH
B: 06/10/1908 D: 04/25/1994
BR

Year	Tm	Lg	Tot	H	A	Men-On 0	Men-On 1	Men-On 2	Men-On 3	One-Game 2	One-Game 3	One-Game 4	LO	XN	IP	PH	RHP	LHP
1936	CHI	AL	5	2	3	2	2	0	1	0	0	0	0	0	0	0	4	1
1937	CHI	AL	12	7	5	6	4	2	0	0	0	0	0	0	1	0	12	0
1938	CHI	AL	6	3	3	2	3	1	0	1	0	0	0	0	0	0	3	3
1939	CHI	AL	5	5	0	2	2	1	0	0	0	0	0	0	0	0	4	1
1940	CHI	AL	8	5	3	4	4	0	0	0	0	0	0	0	0	0	6	2
1942	PHI	AL	1	1	0	1	0	0	0	0	0	0	0	0	0	0	1	0
1944	STL	AL	5	3	2	4	0	1	0	1	0	0	0	0	0	0	1	4
1945	STL	AL	2	2	0	1	0	0	1	0	0	0	0	0	0	0	2	0
	WAS	AL	1	0	1	1	0	0	0	0	0	0	0	0	0	0	0	1
	Total		3	2	1	2	0	0	1	0	0	0	0	0	0	0	2	1
Total			45	28	17	23	15	5	2	2	0	0	0	0	1	0	33	12

Rank among batters: 1,082 • *Top target (3 home runs)*: Wes Ferrell, Bobo Newsom • *Number of pitchers victimized*: 35 • *Total ballparks homered in*: 7 • *First HR*: 04/15/1936 off Jack Knott

Ray Kremer

REMY PETER KREMER
B: 03/23/1893 D: 02/08/1965
BR

Year	Tm	Lg	Tot	H	A	Men-On 0	Men-On 1	Men-On 2	Men-On 3	One-Game 2	One-Game 3	One-Game 4	LO	XN	IP	PH	RHP	LHP
1926	PIT	NL	1	1	0	0	1	0	0	0	0	0	0	0	0	0	1	0
1927	PIT	NL	2	2	0	1	1	0	0	0	0	0	0	0	0	0	1	1
1929	PIT	NL	1	0	1	1	0	0	0	0	0	0	0	0	0	0	1	0
1930	PIT	NL	1	1	0	1	0	0	0	0	0	0	0	0	0	0	1	0
Total			5	4	1	3	2	0	0	0	0	0	0	0	0	0	4	1

Rank among batters: 3,191 • *Top target (2 home runs)*: Claude Willoughby • *Number of pitchers victimized*: 4 • *Total ballparks homered in*: 2 • *First HR*: 08/18/1926 off Bob Smith

Jimmy Kremers

JAMES EDWARD KREMERS
B: 10/08/1965
BL

Year	Tm	Lg	Tot	H	A	Men-On 0	Men-On 1	Men-On 2	Men-On 3	One-Game 2	One-Game 3	One-Game 4	LO	XN	IP	PH	RHP	LHP
1990	ATL	NL	1	1	0	0	1	0	0	0	0	0	0	0	0	0	1	0

Rank among batters: 4,707 • *Total ballparks homered in*: 1 • *First HR*: 07/15/1990 off Tim Burke

Wayne Krenchicki

WAYNE RICHARD KRENCHICKI
B: 09/17/1954
BL

Year	Tm	Lg	Tot	H	A	Men-On 0	Men-On 1	Men-On 2	Men-On 3	One-Game 2	One-Game 3	One-Game 4	LO	XN	IP	PH	RHP	LHP
1982	CIN	NL	2	0	2	1	0	1	0	0	0	0	0	0	0	1	2	0
1983	DET	AL	1	1	0	1	0	0	0	0	0	0	0	0	0	0	1	0
1984	CIN	NL	6	2	4	5	1	0	0	0	0	0	0	0	0	0	6	0
1985	CIN	NL	4	2	2	2	0	1	1	0	0	0	0	0	0	1	4	0

Wayne Krenchicki *continued*

Year	Tm	Lg	Tot	H	A	Men-On 0	Men-On 1	Men-On 2	Men-On 3	One-Game 2	One-Game 3	One-Game 4	LO	XN	IP	PH	RHP	LHP
1986	MON	NL	2	1	1	2	0	0	0	0	0	0	0	0	0	1	2	0
Total			15	6	9	11	1	2	1	0	0	0	0	0	0	3	15	0

Rank among batters: 2,096 • *Top target (2 home runs)*: Eric Show • *Number of pitchers victimized*: 14 • *Total ballparks homered in*: 10 • *First HR*: 07/07/1982 off Kent Tekulve

Chuck Kress

CHARLES STEVEN KRESS
B: 12/09/1921
BL

Year	Tm	Lg	Tot	H	A	Men-On 0	Men-On 1	Men-On 2	Men-On 3	One-Game 2	One-Game 3	One-Game 4	LO	XN	IP	PH	RHP	LHP
1949	CHI	AL	1	0	1	1	0	0	0	0	0	0	0	0	0	0	1	0

Rank among batters: 4,707 • *Total ballparks homered in*: 1 • *First HR*: 07/01/1949 off Fred Hutchinson

Red Kress

RALPH KRESS
B: 01/02/1907 D: 11/29/1962
BR

Year	Tm	Lg	Tot	H	A	Men-On 0	Men-On 1	Men-On 2	Men-On 3	One-Game 2	One-Game 3	One-Game 4	LO	XN	IP	PH	RHP	LHP
1927	STL	AL	1	0	1	0	1	0	0	0	0	0	0	0	0	0	0	1
1928	STL	AL	3	2	1	2	1	0	0	0	0	0	0	0	0	0	2	1
1929	STL	AL	9	1	8	2	7	0	0	1	0	0	0	0	0	0	6	3
1930	STL	AL	16	7	9	10	6	0	0	0	0	0	0	0	0	0	14	2
1931	STL	AL	16	7	9	9	5	2	0	0	0	0	0	0	0	0	9	7
1932	STL	AL	2	1	1	0	1	1	0	0	0	0	0	0	0	0	2	0
	CHI	AL	9	3	6	7	2	0	0	0	0	0	0	0	0	0	8	1
	Total		11	4	7	7	3	1	0	0	0	0	0	0	0	0	10	1
1933	CHI	AL	10	5	5	6	1	2	1	1	0	0	0	0	0	0	9	1
1934	WAS	AL	4	0	4	2	2	0	0	1	0	0	0	0	1	0	4	0
1935	WAS	AL	2	0	2	2	0	0	0	0	0	0	0	0	0	0	1	1
1936	WAS	AL	8	2	6	4	4	0	0	1	0	0	0	0	0	0	4	4
1938	STL	AL	7	4	3	4	2	0	1	0	0	0	0	0	0	0	5	2
1939	DET	AL	1	0	1	0	1	0	0	0	0	0	0	0	0	1	1	0
1940	DET	AL	1	1	0	1	0	0	0	0	0	0	0	0	0	0	1	0
Total			89	33	56	49	33	5	2	4	0	0	0	0	1	1	66	23

Rank among batters: 584 • *Top target (4 home runs)*: Rube Walberg, Earl Whitehill • *Number of pitchers victimized*: 58 • *Total ballparks homered in*: 8 • *First HR*: 10/02/1927 off Charlie Barnabe

Chad Kreuter

CHADDEN MICHAEL KREUTER
B: 08/26/1964
BB

Year	Tm	Lg	Tot	H	A	Men-On 0	Men-On 1	Men-On 2	Men-On 3	One-Game 2	One-Game 3	One-Game 4	LO	XN	IP	PH	RHP	LHP
1988	TEX	AL	1	0	1	0	0	1	0	0	0	0	0	0	0	0	1	0
1989	TEX	AL	5	2	3	5	0	0	0	0	0	0	0	0	0	0	2	3
1992	DET	AL	2	2	0	1	1	0	0	0	0	0	0	0	0	0	1	1
1993	DET	AL	15	9	6	8	6	0	1	1	0	0	0	0	0	1	11	4
1994	DET	AL	1	1	0	1	0	0	0	0	0	0	0	0	0	0	1	0
1995	SEA	AL	1	0	1	1	0	0	0	0	0	0	0	0	0	0	0	1
Total			25	14	11	16	7	1	1	1	0	0	0	0	0	1	16	9

Rank among batters: 1,608 • *Top target (2 home runs)*: Chuck Finley, Danny Darwin • *Number of pitchers victimized*: 23 • *Total ballparks homered in*: 10 • *First HR*: 09/14/1988 off Dave Stewart • *Switch hit HR in 1 game*—1 time

Frank Kreutzer

FRANKLIN JAMES KREUTZER
B: 02/07/1939
BR

Year	Tm	Lg	Tot	H	A	Men-On 0	Men-On 1	Men-On 2	Men-On 3	One-Game 2	One-Game 3	One-Game 4	LO	XN	IP	PH	RHP	LHP
1965	WAS	AL	1	1	0	0	1	0	0	0	0	0	0	0	0	0	0	1

Rank among batters: 4,707 • *Total ballparks homered in*: 1 • *First HR*: 07/02/1965 off Hank Aguirre

Bill Krieg

WILLIAM FREDERICK KRIEG
B: 01/29/1859 D: 03/25/1930
BR

Year	Tm	Lg	Tot	H	A	Men-On 0	Men-On 1	Men-On 2	Men-On 3	One-Game 2	One-Game 3	One-Game 4	LO	XN	IP	PH	RHP	LHP
1885	BRO	AA	1	1	0	0	0	1	0	0	0	0	0	0	0	0	0	1
1886	WAS	NL	1	1	0	0	1	0	0	0	0	0	0	0	0	0	1	0

						Men-On				One-Game								
Year	Tm Lg		Tot	H	A	0	1	2	3	2	3	4	LO	XN	IP	PH	RHP	LHP

Bill Krieg *continued*

1887	WAS	NL	2	1	1	2	0	0	0	0	0	0	0	0	0	0	2	0
Total			4	3	1	2	1	1	0	0	0	0	0	0	0	0	3	1

Rank among batters: 3,427 • *Top target (2 home runs)*: Charley Radbourn • *Number of pitchers victimized*: 3 • *Total ballparks homered in*: 3 • *First HR*: 06/06/1885 off Ed Morris

Gus Krock

AUGUST H. KROCK
B: 05/09/1866 D: 03/22/1905

1888	CHI	NL	1	1	0	0	1	0	0	0	0	0	0	0	0	0	1	0

Rank among batters: 4,707 • *Total ballparks homered in*: 1 • *First HR*: 09/14/1888 off Tim Keefe

John Kroner

JOHN HAROLD KRONER
B: 11/13/1908 D: 04/26/1968
BR

1936	BOS	AL	4	3	1	3	1	0	0	0	0	0	0	0	0	0	4	0
1937	CLE	AL	2	1	1	2	0	0	0	0	0	0	0	0	0	0	0	2
1938	CLE	AL	1	1	0	0	1	0	0	0	0	0	0	0	0	0	0	1
Total			7	5	2	5	2	0	0	0	0	0	0	0	0	0	4	3

Rank among batters: 2,834 • *Top target (2 home runs)*: Thornton Lee • *Number of pitchers victimized*: 6 • *Total ballparks homered in*: 4 • *First HR*: 06/02/1936 off Denny Galehouse

Rocky Krsnich

ROCCO PETER KRSNICH
B: 08/05/1927
BR

1949	CHI	AL	1	0	1	0	0	1	0	0	0	0	0	0	0	0	1	0
1952	CHI	AL	1	1	0	1	0	0	0	0	0	0	0	0	0	0	1	0
1953	CHI	AL	1	1	0	0	1	0	0	0	0	0	0	0	0	0	0	1
Total			3	2	1	1	1	1	0	0	0	0	0	0	0	0	2	1

Rank among batters: 3,735 • *Total ballparks homered in*: 2 • *First HR*: 09/21/1949 off Ralph Buxton

Ernie Krueger

ERNEST GEORGE KRUEGER
B: 12/27/1890 D: 04/22/1976
BR

1917	BRO	NL	1	0	1	1	0	0	0	0	0	0	0	0	0	0	1	0
1919	BRO	NL	5	0	5	2	2	1	0	1	0	0	0	0	0	0	4	1
1920	BRO	NL	1	0	1	0	1	0	0	0	0	0	0	0	0	0	1	0
1921	BRO	NL	3	2	1	1	1	1	0	0	0	0	0	0	0	0	3	0
1925	CIN	NL	1	1	0	1	0	0	0	0	0	0	0	0	0	0	0	1
Total			11	3	8	5	4	2	0	1	0	0	0	0	0	0	9	2

Rank among batters: 2,419 • *Top target (2 home runs)*: Lou North • *Number of pitchers victimized*: 10 • *Total ballparks homered in*: 6 • *First HR*: 08/14/1917 off Ferdie Schupp

Otto Krueger

ARTHUR WILLIAM KRUEGER
B: 09/17/1876 D: 02/20/1961
BR

1900	STL	NL	1	0	1	0	1	0	0	0	0	0	0	0	1	0	1	0
1901	STL	NL	2	1	1	1	1	0	0	0	0	0	0	0	1	0	2	0
1903	PIT	NL	1	1	0	0	1	0	0	0	0	0	0	0	1	0	1	0
1904	PIT	NL	1	0	1	1	0	0	0	0	0	0	0	0	0	0	1	0
Total			5	2	3	2	3	0	0	0	0	0	0	0	3	0	5	0

Rank among batters: 3,191 • *Total ballparks homered in*: 3 • *First HR*: 10/05/1900 off Ed Scott

Chris Krug

EVERETT BEN KRUG
B: 12/25/1939
BR

1965	CHI	NL	5	3	2	1	2	2	0	0	0	0	0	0	0	0	0	5

Rank among batters: 3,191 • *Top target (2 home runs)*: Curt Simmons • *Number of pitchers victimized*: 4 • *Total ballparks homered in*: 3 • *First HR*: 06/13/1965 off Gerry Arrigo

Year	Tm	Lg	Tot	H	A	Men-On 0	1	2	3	One-Game 2	3	4	LO	XN	IP	PH	RHP	LHP

Martin Krug

MARTIN JOHN KRUG
B: 09/10/1888 D: 06/27/1966
BR

Year	Tm	Lg	Tot	H	A	0	1	2	3	2	3	4	LO	XN	IP	PH	RHP	LHP
1922	CHI	NL	4	1	3	3	1	0	0	0	0	0	0	0	1	0	2	2

Rank among batters: 3,427 • *Total ballparks homered in*: 4 • *First HR*: 06/08/1922 off Red Causey

Art Kruger

ARTHUR T. KRUGER
B: 03/16/1881 D: 11/28/1949
BR

Year	Tm	Lg	Tot	H	A	0	1	2	3	2	3	4	LO	XN	IP	PH	RHP	LHP
1914	KC	FL	4	3	1	2	1	1	0	0	0	0	0	0	0	0	3	1
1915	KC	FL	2	2	0	1	0	0	1	0	0	0	0	0	0	1	0	2
Total			6	5	1	3	1	1	1	0	0	0	0	0	0	1	3	3

Rank among batters: 2,988 • *Top target (2 home runs)*: Al Schulz • *Number of pitchers victimized*: 5 • *Total ballparks homered in*: 2 • *First HR*: 04/26/1914 off Tom McGuire

John Kruk

JOHN MARTIN KRUK
B: 02/09/1961
BL

Year	Tm	Lg	Tot	H	A	0	1	2	3	2	3	4	LO	XN	IP	PH	RHP	LHP
1986	SD	NL	4	1	3	2	2	0	0	0	0	0	0	0	0	0	4	0
1987	SD	NL	20	8	12	10	6	4	0	1	0	0	0	1	1	1	16	4
1988	SD	NL	9	8	1	6	2	0	1	0	0	0	1	0	0	1	6	3
1989	SD	NL	3	2	1	1	2	0	0	0	0	0	0	0	0	0	3	0
	PHI	NL	5	4	1	2	2	0	1	0	0	0	0	1	0	0	5	0
	Total		8	6	2	3	4	0	1	0	0	0	0	1	0	0	8	0
1990	PHI	NL	7	2	5	3	2	2	0	0	0	0	0	0	0	1	5	2
1991	PHI	NL	21	8	13	11	6	3	1	1	0	0	0	1	0	0	17	4
1992	PHI	NL	10	7	3	6	2	2	0	1	0	0	0	0	0	0	9	1
1993	PHI	NL	14	8	6	7	6	1	0	2	0	0	0	1	0	0	9	5
1994	PHI	NL	5	3	2	4	1	0	0	0	0	0	0	0	0	1	4	1
1995	CHI	AL	2	2	0	0	0	1	1	0	0	0	0	0	0	0	2	0
Total			100	53	47	52	31	13	4	5	0	0	1	4	1	4	80	20

Rank among batters: 499 • *Top target (3 home runs)*: Jose Rijo, Frank Castillo, Dwight Gooden • *Number of pitchers victimized*: 84 • *Total ballparks homered in*: 14 • *First HR*: 05/10/1986 off Dennis Eckersley • *LCS HR*—1

Mike Krukow

MICHAEL EDWARD KRUKOW
B: 01/21/1952
BR

Year	Tm	Lg	Tot	H	A	0	1	2	3	2	3	4	LO	XN	IP	PH	RHP	LHP
1979	CHI	NL	1	1	0	1	0	0	0	0	0	0	0	0	0	0	1	0
1980	CHI	NL	1	1	0	1	0	0	0	0	0	0	0	0	0	0	0	1
1983	SF	NL	1	0	1	1	0	0	0	0	0	0	0	0	0	0	1	0
1985	SF	NL	1	1	0	1	0	0	0	0	0	0	0	0	0	0	1	0
1988	SF	NL	1	0	1	1	0	0	0	0	0	0	0	0	0	0	1	0
Total			5	3	2	5	0	0	0	0	0	0	0	0	0	0	4	1

Rank among batters: 3,191 • *Top target (2 home runs)*: Eric Show • *Number of pitchers victimized*: 4 • *Total ballparks homered in*: 3 • *First HR*: 06/27/1979 off Rawly Eastwick

Dick Kryhoski

RICHARD DAVID KRYHOSKI
B: 03/24/1925
BL

Year	Tm	Lg	Tot	H	A	0	1	2	3	2	3	4	LO	XN	IP	PH	RHP	LHP
1949	NY	AL	1	1	0	0	1	0	0	0	0	0	0	0	0	0	1	0
1950	DET	AL	4	2	2	2	1	1	0	0	0	0	0	0	0	0	3	1
1951	DET	AL	12	7	5	7	5	0	0	0	0	0	0	0	0	0	11	1
1952	STL	AL	11	8	3	6	4	1	0	1	0	0	0	0	0	0	11	0
1953	STL	AL	16	9	7	13	2	0	1	1	0	0	0	0	0	1	16	0
1954	BAL	AL	1	0	1	1	0	0	0	0	0	0	0	0	0	0	1	0
Total			45	27	18	29	13	2	1	2	0	0	0	0	0	1	43	2

Rank among batters: 1,082 • *Top target (4 home runs)*: Johnny Sain • *Number of pitchers victimized*: 29 • *Total ballparks homered in*: 8 • *First HR*: 04/29/1949 off Denny Galehouse

Tony Kubek

ANTHONY CHRISTOPHER KUBEK
B: 10/12/1936
BL

Year	Tm	Lg	Tot	H	A	0	1	2	3	2	3	4	LO	XN	IP	PH	RHP	LHP
1957	NY	AL	3	1	2	2	1	0	0	0	0	0	0	0	0	0	2	1

Tony Kubek *continued*

Year	Tm	Lg	Tot	H	A	Men-On 0	1	2	3	One-Game 2	3	4	LO	XN	IP	PH	RHP	LHP
1958	NY	AL	2	2	0	2	0	0	0	0	0	0	0	0	1	0	2	0
1959	NY	AL	6	3	3	4	1	1	0	0	0	0	1	0	0	0	6	0
1960	NY	AL	14	9	5	11	3	0	0	2	0	0	1	0	0	0	12	2
1961	NY	AL	8	4	4	5	3	0	0	0	0	0	0	0	0	1	7	1
1962	NY	AL	4	2	2	3	0	1	0	0	0	0	1	0	0	0	4	0
1963	NY	AL	7	5	2	3	4	0	0	0	0	0	1	0	0	0	6	1
1964	NY	AL	8	3	5	5	3	0	0	0	0	0	3	1	0	0	7	1
1965	NY	AL	5	4	1	3	2	0	0	0	0	0	0	0	1	0	4	1
Total			57	33	24	38	17	2	0	2	0	0	7	1	2	1	50	7

Rank among batters: 902 • *Top target (5 home runs)*: Bill Monbouquette • *Number of pitchers victimized*: 44 • *Total ballparks homered in*: 10 • *First HR*: 05/01/1957 off Frank Lary • *World Series HR*—2

Ted Kubiak

THEODORE ROGER KUBIAK
B: 05/12/1942
BB

Year	Tm	Lg	Tot	H	A	Men-On 0	1	2	3	One-Game 2	3	4	LO	XN	IP	PH	RHP	LHP
1969	OAK	AL	2	1	1	1	1	0	0	0	0	0	0	0	0	0	1	1
1970	MIL	AL	4	3	1	3	0	0	1	0	0	0	0	0	0	0	2	2
1971	MIL	AL	3	2	1	2	0	1	0	0	0	0	0	0	0	0	3	0
	STL	NL	1	1	0	0	0	1	0	0	0	0	0	0	0	0	1	0
	Total		4	3	1	2	0	2	0	0	0	0	0	0	0	0	4	0
1973	OAK	AL	3	3	0	1	2	0	0	0	0	0	0	0	0	0	3	0
Total			13	10	3	7	3	2	1	0	0	0	0	0	0	0	10	3

Rank among batters: 2,248 • *Top target (2 home runs)*: Ed Phillips, Gaylord Perry • *Number of pitchers victimized*: 11 • *Total ballparks homered in*: 5 • *First HR*: 06/22/1969 off Jim Kaat

Jack Kubiszyn

JOHN HENRY KUBISZYN
B: 12/19/1936
BR

Year	Tm	Lg	Tot	H	A	Men-On 0	1	2	3	One-Game 2	3	4	LO	XN	IP	PH	RHP	LHP
1962	CLE	AL	1	1	0	1	0	0	0	0	0	0	0	0	0	0	1	0

Rank among batters: 4,707 • *Total ballparks homered in*: 1 • *First HR*: 08/03/1962 off Bill Fischer

Bill Kuehne

WILLIAM J. KUEHNE
B: 10/24/1858 D: 10/27/1921
BR

Year	Tm	Lg	Tot	H	A	Men-On 0	1	2	3	One-Game 2	3	4	LO	XN	IP	PH	RHP	LHP
1883	COL	AA	1	1	0	0	1	0	0	0	0	0	0	0	0	0	1	0
1884	COL	AA	5	4	1	1	1	3	0	0	0	0	0	0	0	0	4	1
1886	PIT	AA	1	0	1	0	1	0	0	0	0	0	0	0	0	0	1	0
1887	PIT	NL	1	0	1	0	1	0	0	0	0	0	0	0	0	0	0	0
1888	PIT	NL	3	0	3	1	1	1	0	0	0	0	0	0	1	0	1	2
1889	PIT	NL	5	0	5	2	1	2	0	0	0	0	0	0	0	0	4	1
1890	PIT	PL	5	4	1	2	1	2	0	0	0	0	0	0	1	0	4	1
1891	COL	AA	2	1	1	0	1	0	1	0	0	0	0	0	1	0	2	0
	LOU	AA	1	1	0	0	0	1	0	0	0	0	0	0	0	0	1	0
	Total		3	2	1	0	1	1	1	0	0	0	0	0	1	0	3	0
1892	CIN	NL	1	0	1	1	0	0	0	0	0	0	1	0	0	0	1	0
Total			25	11	14	7	8	9	1	0	0	0	1	0	3	0	19	4

Rank among batters: 1,608 • *Top target (3 home runs)*: Gus Krock • *Number of pitchers victimized*: 21 • *Total ballparks homered in*: 11 • *First HR*: 05/02/1883 off Sam Weaver

Harvey Kuenn

HARVEY EDWARD KUENN
B: 12/04/1930 D: 02/28/1988
BR

Year	Tm	Lg	Tot	H	A	Men-On 0	1	2	3	One-Game 2	3	4	LO	XN	IP	PH	RHP	LHP
1953	DET	AL	2	0	2	1	1	0	0	0	0	0	0	0	0	0	0	2
1954	DET	AL	5	2	3	3	1	0	1	0	0	0	1	1	0	0	3	2
1955	DET	AL	8	6	2	5	2	1	0	0	0	0	1	0	0	0	5	3
1956	DET	AL	12	5	7	7	3	2	0	1	0	0	1	0	0	0	7	5
1957	DET	AL	9	8	1	7	2	0	0	0	0	0	1	1	0	0	9	0
1958	DET	AL	8	4	4	6	0	2	0	0	0	0	0	0	0	0	6	2
1959	DET	AL	9	4	5	3	5	1	0	0	0	0	0	0	0	0	7	2
1960	CLE	AL	9	5	4	2	5	2	0	0	0	0	0	1	0	0	9	0

Harvey Kuenn *continued*

Year	Tm	Lg	Tot	H	A	Men-On 0	Men-On 1	Men-On 2	Men-On 3	One-Game 2	One-Game 3	One-Game 4	LO	XN	IP	PH	RHP	LHP
1961	SF	NL	5	2	3	5	0	0	0	0	0	0	0	0	0	0	1	4
1962	SF	NL	10	5	5	5	5	0	0	0	0	0	1	0	0	0	6	4
1963	SF	NL	6	2	4	4	2	0	0	0	0	0	1	0	0	0	1	5
1964	SF	NL	4	2	2	2	2	0	0	0	0	0	1	0	0	0	1	3
Total			87	45	42	50	28	8	1	1	0	0	7	3	0	0	55	32

Rank among batters: 594 • *Top target (6 home runs)*: Cal McLish • *Number of pitchers victimized*: 63 • *Total ballparks homered in*: 15 • *First HR*: 05/10/1953 off Gene Bearden

Joe Kuhel

JOSEPH ANTHONY KUHEL
B: 06/25/1906 D: 02/26/1984
BL

Year	Tm	Lg	Tot	H	A	Men-On 0	Men-On 1	Men-On 2	Men-On 3	One-Game 2	One-Game 3	One-Game 4	LO	XN	IP	PH	RHP	LHP
1931	WAS	AL	8	1	7	5	2	1	0	1	0	0	0	0	1	0	4	4
1932	WAS	AL	4	1	3	3	1	0	0	0	0	0	0	0	1	0	3	1
1933	WAS	AL	11	5	6	6	5	0	0	0	0	0	0	0	2	0	10	1
1934	WAS	AL	3	0	3	1	2	0	0	0	0	0	0	0	0	0	2	1
1935	WAS	AL	2	1	1	1	0	0	1	0	0	0	0	0	0	0	2	0
1936	WAS	AL	16	3	13	8	5	3	0	0	0	0	0	0	0	0	12	4
1937	WAS	AL	6	2	4	3	2	1	0	0	0	0	0	0	0	0	6	0
1938	CHI	AL	8	0	8	4	2	2	0	0	0	0	0	0	0	0	6	2
1939	CHI	AL	15	7	8	9	6	0	0	0	0	0	0	0	0	0	14	1
1940	CHI	AL	27	12	15	15	8	4	0	2	0	0	0	1	0	0	25	2
1941	CHI	AL	12	7	5	10	1	1	0	0	0	0	0	0	0	0	11	1
1942	CHI	AL	4	0	4	2	1	1	0	0	0	0	0	0	0	0	4	0
1943	CHI	AL	5	1	4	4	1	0	0	0	0	0	0	0	0	0	4	1
1944	WAS	AL	4	2	2	2	1	1	0	0	0	0	0	0	2	0	4	0
1945	WAS	AL	2	1	1	1	1	0	0	0	0	0	0	0	1	0	2	0
1946	CHI	AL	4	1	3	3	0	1	0	1	0	0	0	0	0	0	3	1
Total			131	44	87	77	38	15	1	4	0	0	0	1	7	0	112	19

Rank among batters: 342 • *Top target (6 home runs)*: Red Ruffing • *Number of pitchers victimized*: 79 • *Total ballparks homered in*: 8 • *First HR*: 05/28/1931 off Danny MacFayden

Duane Kuiper

DUANE EUGENE KUIPER
B: 06/19/1950
BL

Year	Tm	Lg	Tot	H	A	Men-On 0	Men-On 1	Men-On 2	Men-On 3	One-Game 2	One-Game 3	One-Game 4	LO	XN	IP	PH	RHP	LHP
1977	CLE	AL	1	1	0	1	0	0	0	0	0	0	0	0	0	0	1	0

Rank among batters: 4,707 • *Total ballparks homered in*: 1 • *First HR*: 08/29/1977 off Steve Stone

Jeff Kunkel

JEFFREY WILLIAM KUNKEL
B: 03/25/1962
BR

Year	Tm	Lg	Tot	H	A	Men-On 0	Men-On 1	Men-On 2	Men-On 3	One-Game 2	One-Game 3	One-Game 4	LO	XN	IP	PH	RHP	LHP
1984	TEX	AL	3	1	2	3	0	0	0	0	0	0	0	0	0	0	3	0
1986	TEX	AL	1	1	0	1	0	0	0	0	0	0	0	0	0	0	1	0
1987	TEX	AL	1	0	1	1	0	0	0	0	0	0	0	0	0	0	0	1
1988	TEX	AL	2	2	0	2	0	0	0	0	0	0	0	0	0	0	0	2
1989	TEX	AL	8	8	0	7	1	0	0	1	0	0	1	0	0	0	5	3
1990	TEX	AL	3	1	2	2	1	0	0	0	0	0	0	0	0	0	1	2
Total			18	13	5	16	2	0	0	1	0	0	1	0	0	0	10	8

Rank among batters: 1,914 • *Top target (2 home runs)*: Frank Wills, Shane Rawley • *Number of pitchers victimized*: 16 • *Total ballparks homered in*: 6 • *First HR*: 07/31/1984 off Dennis Martinez

Rusty Kuntz

RUSSELL JAY KUNTZ
B: 02/04/1955
BR

Year	Tm	Lg	Tot	H	A	Men-On 0	Men-On 1	Men-On 2	Men-On 3	One-Game 2	One-Game 3	One-Game 4	LO	XN	IP	PH	RHP	LHP
1983	MIN	AL	3	2	1	3	0	0	0	0	0	0	2	0	0	0	1	2
1984	DET	AL	2	1	1	2	0	0	0	0	0	0	0	0	0	0	1	1
Total			5	3	2	5	0	0	0	0	0	0	2	0	0	0	2	3

Rank among batters: 3,191 • *Top target (2 home runs)*: Floyd Bannister • *Number of pitchers victimized*: 4 • *Total ballparks homered in*: 4 • *First HR*: 06/23/1983 off Floyd Bannister

Whitey Kurowski

GEORGE JOHN KUROWSKI
B: 04/19/1918
BR

Year	Tm	Lg	Tot	H	A	Men-On 0	Men-On 1	Men-On 2	Men-On 3	One-Game 2	One-Game 3	One-Game 4	LO	XN	IP	PH	RHP	LHP
1942	STL	NL	9	5	4	4	5	0	0	0	0	0	0	0	0	0	3	6
1943	STL	NL	13	6	7	7	5	1	0	0	0	0	0	0	0	0	11	2
1944	STL	NL	20	5	15	12	4	4	0	3	0	0	0	1	0	0	14	6
1945	STL	NL	21	8	13	17	3	1	0	2	0	0	0	0	0	0	15	6
1946	STL	NL	14	4	10	8	4	2	0	0	0	0	0	0	0	1	7	7
1947	STL	NL	27	11	16	16	9	2	0	2	0	0	0	1	0	0	17	10
1948	STL	NL	2	0	2	0	2	0	0	0	0	0	0	0	0	0	0	2
Total			106	39	67	64	32	10	0	7	0	0	0	2	0	1	67	39

Rank among batters: 451 • *Top target (7 home runs)*: Preacher Roe • *Number of pitchers victimized*: 72 • *Total ballparks homered in*: 8 • *First HR*: 06/17/1942 off Cliff Melton • *World Series HR*—1

Craig Kusick

CRAIG ROBERT KUSICK
B: 09/30/1948
BR

Year	Tm	Lg	Tot	H	A	Men-On 0	Men-On 1	Men-On 2	Men-On 3	One-Game 2	One-Game 3	One-Game 4	LO	XN	IP	PH	RHP	LHP
1974	MIN	AL	8	2	6	6	2	0	0	0	0	0	0	1	0	0	3	5
1975	MIN	AL	6	4	2	3	2	1	0	0	0	0	0	0	0	1	3	3
1976	MIN	AL	11	6	5	8	1	2	0	0	0	0	0	0	0	0	5	6
1977	MIN	AL	12	3	9	8	2	2	0	1	0	0	0	0	0	2	3	9
1978	MIN	AL	4	2	2	4	0	0	0	0	0	0	0	0	0	1	0	4
1979	MIN	AL	3	2	1	3	0	0	0	1	0	0	0	0	0	0	2	1
	TOR	AL	2	1	1	1	1	0	0	0	0	0	0	1	0	0	1	1
	Total		5	3	2	4	1	0	0	1	0	0	0	1	0	0	3	2
Total			46	20	26	33	8	5	0	2	0	0	0	2	0	4	17	29

Rank among batters: 1,060 • *Top target (4 home runs)*: Frank Tanana • *Number of pitchers victimized*: 37 • *Total ballparks homered in*: 13 • *First HR*: 06/30/1974 off Jim Kaat

Art Kusnyer

ARTHUR WILLIAM KUSNYER
B: 12/19/1945
BR

Year	Tm	Lg	Tot	H	A	Men-On 0	Men-On 1	Men-On 2	Men-On 3	One-Game 2	One-Game 3	One-Game 4	LO	XN	IP	PH	RHP	LHP
1972	CAL	AL	2	0	2	1	1	0	0	0	0	0	0	0	0	0	2	0
1978	KC	AL	1	0	1	1	0	0	0	0	0	0	0	0	0	0	0	1
Total			3	0	3	2	1	0	0	0	0	0	0	0	0	0	2	1

Rank among batters: 3,735 • *Total ballparks homered in*: 3 • *First HR*: 05/21/1972 off Vicente Romo

Jul Kustus

JOSEPH JULIUS KUSTUS
B: 09/05/1882 D: 04/27/1916
BR

Year	Tm	Lg	Tot	H	A	Men-On 0	Men-On 1	Men-On 2	Men-On 3	One-Game 2	One-Game 3	One-Game 4	LO	XN	IP	PH	RHP	LHP
1909	BRO	NL	1	1	0	1	0	0	0	0	0	0	0	0	0	0	0	1

Rank among batters: 4,707 • *Total ballparks homered in*: 1 • *First HR*: 05/13/1909 off Johnny Lush

Randy Kutcher

RANDY SCOTT KUTCHER
B: 04/30/1960
BR

Year	Tm	Lg	Tot	H	A	Men-On 0	Men-On 1	Men-On 2	Men-On 3	One-Game 2	One-Game 3	One-Game 4	LO	XN	IP	PH	RHP	LHP
1986	SF	NL	7	5	2	7	0	0	0	0	0	0	2	0	0	0	6	1
1989	BOS	AL	2	1	1	1	0	1	0	0	0	0	0	0	0	0	0	2
1990	BOS	AL	1	0	1	1	0	0	0	0	0	0	0	0	0	0	0	1
Total			10	6	4	9	0	1	0	0	0	0	2	0	0	0	6	4

Rank among batters: 2,500 • *Total ballparks homered in*: 6 • *First HR*: 06/19/1986 off Craig Lefferts

Joe Kutina

JOSEPH PETER KUTINA
B: 01/16/1885 D: 04/13/1945
BR

Year	Tm	Lg	Tot	H	A	Men-On 0	Men-On 1	Men-On 2	Men-On 3	One-Game 2	One-Game 3	One-Game 4	LO	XN	IP	PH	RHP	LHP
1911	STL	AL	3	1	2	3	0	0	0	0	0	0	0	0	1	0	2	1
1912	STL	AL	1	0	1	0	1	0	0	0	0	0	0	0	0	0	1	0
Total			4	1	3	3	1	0	0	0	0	0	0	0	1	0	3	1

Rank among batters: 3,427 • *Total ballparks homered in*: 4 • *First HR*: 09/16/1911 off Charlie Becker

Year	Tm	Lg	Tot	H	A	Men-On 0	Men-On 1	Men-On 2	Men-On 3	One-Game 2	One-Game 3	One-Game 4	LO	XN	IP	PH	RHP	LHP

Bob Kuzava

ROBERT LEROY KUZAVA
B: 05/28/1923
BB

Year	Tm	Lg	Tot	H	A	0	1	2	3	2	3	4	LO	XN	IP	PH	RHP	LHP
1950	WAS	AL	1	1	0	1	0	0	0	0	0	0	0	0	0	0	1	0

Rank among batters: 4,707 • *Total ballparks homered in*: 1 • *First HR*: 07/02/1950 off Bob Hooper

Chet Laabs

CHESTER PETER LAABS
B: 04/30/1912 D: 01/26/1983
BR

Year	Tm	Lg	Tot	H	A	0	1	2	3	2	3	4	LO	XN	IP	PH	RHP	LHP
1937	DET	AL	8	4	4	4	3	1	0	0	0	0	0	0	0	1	8	0
1938	DET	AL	7	4	3	3	2	0	2	0	0	0	0	0	0	1	7	0
1939	STL	AL	10	5	5	3	4	2	1	1	0	0	0	0	0	0	7	3
1940	STL	AL	10	6	4	5	5	0	0	0	0	0	0	0	0	1	3	7
1941	STL	AL	15	9	6	9	1	5	0	2	0	0	0	1	1	1	11	4
1942	STL	AL	27	15	12	10	10	5	2	1	0	0	0	1	0	0	24	3
1943	STL	AL	17	11	6	6	7	4	0	0	0	0	0	2	0	0	14	3
1944	STL	AL	5	5	0	2	3	0	0	1	0	0	0	0	0	0	3	2
1945	STL	AL	1	0	1	1	0	0	0	0	0	0	0	0	0	0	0	1
1946	STL	AL	16	11	5	7	5	4	0	3	0	0	0	0	0	0	7	9
1947	PHI	AL	1	1	0	0	0	1	0	0	0	0	0	0	0	0	0	1
Total			117	71	46	50	40	22	5	8	0	0	0	4	1	4	84	33

Rank among batters: 402 • *Top target (4 home runs)*: Milton Haefner • *Number of pitchers victimized*: 82 • *Total ballparks homered in*: 9 • *First HR*: 06/19/1937 off Lynn Nelson

Clem Labine

CLEMENT WALTER LABINE
B: 08/06/1926
BR

Year	Tm	Lg	Tot	H	A	0	1	2	3	2	3	4	LO	XN	IP	PH	RHP	LHP
1955	BRO	NL	3	1	2	2	0	1	0	0	0	0	0	0	0	0	2	1

Rank among batters: 3,735 • *Total ballparks homered in*: 3 • *First HR*: 05/05/1955 off Larry Jackson

Coco Laboy

JOSE ALBERTO LABOY
B: 07/03/1940
BR

Year	Tm	Lg	Tot	H	A	0	1	2	3	2	3	4	LO	XN	IP	PH	RHP	LHP
1969	MON	NL	18	12	6	13	4	1	0	0	0	0	0	0	0	0	13	5
1970	MON	NL	5	2	3	3	2	0	0	0	0	0	0	0	0	0	4	1
1971	MON	NL	1	1	0	0	1	0	0	0	0	0	0	0	0	0	0	1
1972	MON	NL	3	2	1	2	1	0	0	0	0	0	0	0	0	0	2	1
1973	MON	NL	1	0	1	1	0	0	0	0	0	0	0	0	0	0	1	0
Total			28	17	11	19	8	1	0	0	0	0	0	0	0	0	20	8

Rank among batters: 1,500 • Top target (2 home runs): Ron Taylor, Phil Niekro, Dock Ellis, Milt Pappas • *Number of pitchers victimized*: 24 • *Total ballparks homered in*: 8 • *First HR*: 04/08/1969 off Ron Taylor

Candy LaChance

GEORGE JOSEPH LACHANCE
B: 02/15/1870 D: 08/18/1932
BB

Year	Tm	Lg	Tot	H	A	0	1	2	3	2	3	4	LO	XN	IP	PH	RHP	LHP
1894	BRO	NL	5	2	3	1	1	3	0	0	0	0	0	0	0	0	3	1
1895	BRO	NL	8	6	2	2	4	1	1	0	0	0	0	0	1	0	8	0
1896	BRO	NL	7	2	5	3	2	2	0	0	0	0	0	0	0	0	7	0
1897	BRO	NL	4	1	3	2	2	0	0	0	0	0	0	0	0	0	3	0
1898	BRO	NL	5	3	2	1	2	1	1	0	0	0	0	0	2	0	5	0
1899	BAL	NL	1	0	1	1	0	0	0	0	0	0	0	0	0	0	1	0
1901	CLE	AL	1	0	1	1	0	0	0	0	0	0	0	0	0	0	1	0
1902	BOS	AL	6	4	2	4	2	0	0	0	0	0	0	0	1	0	4	2
1903	BOS	AL	1	0	1	1	0	0	0	0	0	0	0	0	0	0	0	1
1904	BOS	AL	1	1	0	1	0	0	0	0	0	0	0	0	0	0	1	0
Total			39	19	20	17	13	7	2	0	0	0	0	0	4	0	33	4

Rank among batters: 1,204 • *Top target (2 home runs)*: Bill Hoffer, Al Orth, Ted Lewis • *Number of pitchers victimized*: 36 • *Total ballparks homered in*: 14 • *First HR*: 06/20/1894 off Duke Esper

Rene Lachemann

RENE GEORGE LACHEMANN
B: 05/04/1945
BR

Year	Tm	Lg	Tot	H	A	Men-On 0	Men-On 1	Men-On 2	Men-On 3	One-Game 2	One-Game 3	One-Game 4	LO	XN	IP	PH	RHP	LHP
1965	KC	AL	9	2	7	7	0	2	0	0	0	0	0	0	0	1	4	5

Rank among batters: 2,587 • *Total ballparks homered in*: 6 • *First HR*: 05/13/1965 off Gary Peters

Pete LaCock

RALPH PIERRE LACOCK
B: 01/17/1952
BL

Year	Tm	Lg	Tot	H	A	Men-On 0	Men-On 1	Men-On 2	Men-On 3	One-Game 2	One-Game 3	One-Game 4	LO	XN	IP	PH	RHP	LHP
1974	CHI	NL	1	0	1	1	0	0	0	0	0	0	0	0	0	0	1	0
1975	CHI	NL	6	2	4	4	0	1	1	0	0	0	0	0	0	1	6	0
1976	CHI	NL	8	4	4	5	2	1	0	0	0	0	0	0	0	1	8	0
1977	KC	AL	3	2	1	1	1	1	0	0	0	0	0	0	0	0	3	0
1978	KC	AL	5	3	2	3	0	2	0	0	0	0	0	0	0	0	5	0
1979	KC	AL	3	3	0	1	1	1	0	0	0	0	0	0	0	0	3	0
1980	KC	AL	1	0	1	1	0	0	0	0	0	0	0	0	0	0	1	0
Total			27	14	13	16	4	6	1	0	0	0	0	0	0	2	27	0

Rank among batters: 1,532 • *Top target (2 home runs)*: Bob Forsch, Steve Renko • *Number of pitchers victimized*: 25 • *Total ballparks homered in*: 12 • *First HR*: 08/29/1974 off Andy Messersmith

Mike LaCoss

MICHAEL JAMES LACOSS
B: 05/30/1956
BR

Year	Tm	Lg	Tot	H	A	Men-On 0	Men-On 1	Men-On 2	Men-On 3	One-Game 2	One-Game 3	One-Game 4	LO	XN	IP	PH	RHP	LHP
1986	SF	NL	2	1	1	1	0	1	0	0	0	0	0	0	0	0	1	1

Rank among batters: 4,129 • *Total ballparks homered in*: 2 • *First HR*: 06/23/1986 off Dane Iorg

Guy Lacy

OSCEOLA GUY LACY
B: 06/12/1897 D: 11/19/1953
BR

Year	Tm	Lg	Tot	H	A	Men-On 0	Men-On 1	Men-On 2	Men-On 3	One-Game 2	One-Game 3	One-Game 4	LO	XN	IP	PH	RHP	LHP
1926	CLE	AL	1	1	0	1	0	0	0	0	0	0	0	0	1	0	1	0

Rank among batters: 4,707 • *Total ballparks homered in*: 1 • *First HR*: 06/09/1926 off Bill Morrell

Lee Lacy

LEONDAUS LACY
B: 04/10/1948
BR

Year	Tm	Lg	Tot	H	A	Men-On 0	Men-On 1	Men-On 2	Men-On 3	One-Game 2	One-Game 3	One-Game 4	LO	XN	IP	PH	RHP	LHP
1975	LA	NL	7	4	3	5	1	1	0	0	0	0	0	0	0	1	5	2
1976	ATL	NL	3	2	1	2	1	0	0	0	0	0	0	0	0	0	2	1
1977	LA	NL	6	3	3	5	0	1	0	0	0	0	1	0	0	2	4	2
1978	LA	NL	13	10	3	5	7	1	0	0	0	0	0	0	1	5	8	5
1979	PIT	NL	5	3	2	3	2	0	0	0	0	0	0	0	0	0	0	5
1980	PIT	NL	7	4	3	5	2	0	0	1	0	0	0	0	0	0	0	7
1981	PIT	NL	2	1	1	2	0	0	0	0	0	0	0	0	0	0	1	1
1982	PIT	NL	5	2	3	3	2	0	0	0	0	0	0	0	1	0	1	4
1983	PIT	NL	4	1	3	2	2	0	0	0	0	0	1	0	0	0	1	3
1984	PIT	NL	12	6	6	8	4	0	0	0	0	0	0	2	1	0	5	7
1985	BAL	AL	9	3	6	6	3	0	0	2	0	0	1	1	0	0	4	5
1986	BAL	AL	11	5	6	7	3	1	0	0	1	0	0	0	0	0	6	5
1987	BAL	AL	7	2	5	6	1	0	0	0	0	0	1	0	0	0	3	4
Total			91	46	45	59	28	4	0	3	1	0	4	3	3	8	40	51

Rank among batters: 559 • *Top target (3 home runs)*: Randy Lerch • *Number of pitchers victimized*: 76 • *Total ballparks homered in*: 20 • *First HR*: 05/17/1975 off Jim Rooker

Joe Lafata

JOSEPH JOSEPH LAFATA
B: 08/03/1921
BL

Year	Tm	Lg	Tot	H	A	Men-On 0	Men-On 1	Men-On 2	Men-On 3	One-Game 2	One-Game 3	One-Game 4	LO	XN	IP	PH	RHP	LHP
1947	NY	NL	2	2	0	1	1	0	0	0	0	0	0	0	0	0	2	0
1949	NY	NL	3	0	3	0	1	1	1	0	0	0	0	0	0	0	2	1
Total			5	2	3	1	2	1	1	0	0	0	0	0	0	0	4	1

Rank among batters: 3,191 • *Total ballparks homered in*: 3 • *First HR*: 05/30/1947 off Schoolboy Rowe

Ed Lafitte

EDWARD FRANCIS LAFITTE
B: 04/07/1886 D: 04/12/1971
BR

Year	Tm	Lg	Tot	H	A	Men-On 0	1	2	3	One-Game 2	3	4	LO	XN	IP	PH	RHP	LHP
1911	DET	AL	1	1	0	1	0	0	0	0	0	0	0	0	0	0	1	0
1914	BRO	FL	1	1	0	0	0	0	1	0	0	0	0	0	0	0	1	0
Total			2	2	0	1	0	0	1	0	0	0	0	0	0	0	2	0

Rank among batters: 4,129 • *Total ballparks homered in*: 2 • *First HR*: 08/25/1911 off Walter Johnson

Ty LaForest

BYRON JOSEPH LAFOREST
B: 04/18/1917 D: 05/05/1947
BR

Year	Tm	Lg	Tot	H	A	Men-On 0	1	2	3	One-Game 2	3	4	LO	XN	IP	PH	RHP	LHP
1945	BOS	AL	2	2	0	2	0	0	0	0	0	0	0	0	0	0	2	0

Rank among batters: 4,129 • *Total ballparks homered in*: 1 • *First HR*: 08/26/1945 off Russ Christopher

Mike Laga

MICHAEL RUSSELL LAGA
B: 06/14/1960
BL

Year	Tm	Lg	Tot	H	A	Men-On 0	1	2	3	One-Game 2	3	4	LO	XN	IP	PH	RHP	LHP
1982	DET	AL	3	3	0	2	1	0	0	0	0	0	0	0	0	0	3	0
1985	DET	AL	2	0	2	0	2	0	0	0	0	0	0	0	0	0	2	0
1986	DET	AL	3	2	1	2	1	0	0	0	0	0	0	0	0	0	3	0
	STL	NL	3	1	2	2	1	0	0	0	0	0	0	0	0	0	2	1
	Total		6	3	3	4	2	0	0	0	0	0	0	0	0	0	5	1
1987	STL	NL	1	0	1	1	0	0	0	0	0	0	0	0	0	0	1	0
1988	STL	NL	1	1	0	1	0	0	0	0	0	0	0	0	0	0	1	0
1989	SF	NL	1	0	1	0	1	0	0	0	0	0	0	0	0	0	1	0
1990	SF	NL	2	1	1	1	1	0	0	0	0	0	0	0	0	1	1	1
Total			16	8	8	9	7	0	0	0	0	0	0	0	0	1	14	2

Rank among batters: 2,029 • *Total ballparks homered in*: 11 • *First HR*: 09/03/1982 off Rick Langford

Joe Lahoud

JOSEPH MICHAEL LAHOUD
B: 04/14/1947
BL

Year	Tm	Lg	Tot	H	A	Men-On 0	1	2	3	One-Game 2	3	4	LO	XN	IP	PH	RHP	LHP
1968	BOS	AL	1	0	1	0	1	0	0	0	0	0	0	0	0	0	1	0
1969	BOS	AL	9	1	8	5	4	0	0	0	1	0	0	1	0	0	9	0
1970	BOS	AL	2	1	1	2	0	0	0	0	0	0	0	0	0	0	2	0
1971	BOS	AL	14	9	5	8	5	1	0	1	0	0	0	0	0	1	12	2
1972	MIL	AL	12	7	5	6	6	0	0	0	0	0	0	0	0	1	11	1
1973	MIL	AL	5	1	4	2	1	0	2	1	0	0	1	0	0	1	5	0
1974	CAL	AL	13	6	7	7	6	0	0	1	0	0	0	0	0	0	12	1
1975	CAL	AL	6	2	4	2	3	1	0	1	0	0	0	0	0	0	6	0
1976	TEX	AL	1	0	1	1	0	0	0	0	0	0	0	0	0	0	1	0
1977	KC	AL	2	0	2	2	0	0	0	1	0	0	0	0	0	0	2	0
Total			65	27	38	35	26	2	2	5	1	0	1	1	0	3	61	4

Rank among batters: 799 • Top target (3 home runs): Tom Murphy, Lindy McDaniel, Milt Wilcox, Jim Colborn • *Number of pitchers victimized*: 49 • *Total ballparks homered in*: 15 • *First HR*: 04/11/1968 off Denny McLain

Nap Lajoie

NAPOLEON LAJOIE
B: 09/05/1874 D: 02/07/1959
BR HOF

Year	Tm	Lg	Tot	H	A	Men-On 0	1	2	3	One-Game 2	3	4	LO	XN	IP	PH	RHP	LHP
1896	PHI	NL	4	3	1	2	0	2	0	0	0	0	0	1	3	0	2	1
1897	PHI	NL	9	3	6	3	4	2	0	1	0	0	0	0	0	0	7	2
1898	PHI	NL	6	2	4	1	3	2	0	0	0	0	0	0	0	0	4	2
1899	PHI	NL	6	3	3	4	2	0	0	0	0	0	0	0	0	0	3	3
1900	PHI	NL	7	4	3	2	2	3	0	1	0	0	0	0	0	0	7	0
1901	PHI	AL	14	5	9	6	5	1	2	2	0	0	0	0	1	0	12	2
1902	CLE	AL	7	5	2	3	2	1	1	0	0	0	0	0	0	0	5	2
1903	CLE	AL	7	1	6	3	4	0	0	1	0	0	0	0	1	0	4	3
1904	CLE	AL	5	4	1	1	4	0	0	0	0	0	0	0	0	0	3	2
1905	CLE	AL	2	2	0	1	1	0	0	0	0	0	0	0	0	0	1	1
1907	CLE	AL	2	2	0	1	0	0	1	0	0	0	0	0	0	0	2	0
1908	CLE	AL	2	1	1	1	1	0	0	0	0	0	0	0	1	0	2	0
1909	CLE	AL	1	0	1	0	0	1	0	0	0	0	0	0	0	0	1	0

Year	Tm	Lg	Tot	H	A	Men-On 0	Men-On 1	Men-On 2	Men-On 3	One-Game 2	One-Game 3	One-Game 4	LO	XN	IP	PH	RHP	LHP

Nap Lajoie *continued*

Year	Tm	Lg	Tot	H	A	0	1	2	3	2	3	4	LO	XN	IP	PH	RHP	LHP
1910	CLE	AL	4	2	2	0	4	0	0	0	0	0	0	0	1	0	3	1
1911	CLE	AL	2	0	2	0	2	0	0	0	0	0	0	0	0	0	2	0
1913	CLE	AL	1	0	1	0	1	0	0	0	0	0	0	0	0	0	1	0
1915	PHI	AL	1	0	1	1	0	0	0	0	0	0	0	0	0	0	1	0
1916	PHI	AL	2	2	0	1	1	0	0	0	0	0	0	0	0	0	1	1
Total			82	39	43	30	36	12	4	5	0	0	0	1	7	0	61	20

Rank among batters: 637 • *Top target (5 home runs)*: Jack Powell • *Number of pitchers victimized*: 59 • *Total ballparks homered in*: 19 • *First HR*: 08/20/1896 off Art Herman • *Hit for Cycle*—@CLE: 07/30/1901

Eddie Lake

EDWARD ERVING LAKE
B: 03/18/1916 D: 06/07/1995
BR

Year	Tm	Lg	Tot	H	A	0	1	2	3	2	3	4	LO	XN	IP	PH	RHP	LHP
1940	STL	NL	2	2	0	1	1	0	0	1	0	0	0	0	0	0	1	1
1943	BOS	AL	3	1	2	2	1	0	0	0	0	0	0	0	0	0	3	0
1945	BOS	AL	11	6	5	9	0	2	0	0	0	0	3	0	0	0	8	3
1946	DET	AL	8	6	2	7	1	0	0	1	0	0	2	0	0	0	3	5
1947	DET	AL	12	6	6	9	2	1	0	1	0	0	3	0	0	0	10	2
1948	DET	AL	2	1	1	1	1	0	0	0	0	0	0	0	0	0	1	1
1949	DET	AL	1	1	0	1	0	0	0	0	0	0	0	0	0	0	1	0
Total			39	23	16	30	6	3	0	3	0	0	8	0	0	0	27	12

Rank among batters: 1,204 • *Top target (3 home runs)*: Eddie Lopat, Don Black • *Number of pitchers victimized*: 30 • *Total ballparks homered in*: 9 • *First HR*: 05/07/1940 off Hugh Casey

Fred Lake

FREDERICK LOVETT LAKE
B: 10/16/1866 D: 11/24/1931
BR

Year	Tm	Lg	Tot	H	A	0	1	2	3	2	3	4	LO	XN	IP	PH	RHP	LHP
1894	LOU	NL	1	0	1	1	0	0	0	0	0	0	0	0	0	0	1	0

Rank among batters: 4,707 • *Total ballparks homered in*: 1 • *First HR*: 09/05/1894 off Kid Nichols

Joe Lake

JOSEPH HENRY LAKE
B: 01/06/1881 D: 06/30/1950
BR

Year	Tm	Lg	Tot	H	A	0	1	2	3	2	3	4	LO	XN	IP	PH	RHP	LHP
1908	NY	AL	1	1	0	1	0	0	0	0	0	0	0	0	0	0	1	0
1912	DET	AL	1	1	0	1	0	0	0	0	0	0	0	0	0	0	1	0
1913	DET	AL	1	1	0	1	0	0	0	0	0	0	0	0	0	0	1	0
Total			3	3	0	3	0	0	0	0	0	0	0	0	0	0	3	0

Rank among batters: 3,735 • *Total ballparks homered in*: 2 • *First HR*: 10/02/1908 off Burt Keeley

Steve Lake

STEVEN MICHAEL LAKE
B: 03/14/1957
BR

Year	Tm	Lg	Tot	H	A	0	1	2	3	2	3	4	LO	XN	IP	PH	RHP	LHP
1983	CHI	NL	1	1	0	1	0	0	0	0	0	0	0	0	0	0	1	0
1984	CHI	NL	2	1	1	1	0	1	0	0	0	0	0	0	0	0	1	1
1985	CHI	NL	1	1	0	1	0	0	0	0	0	0	0	0	0	0	1	0
1986	STL	NL	2	0	2	1	0	1	0	0	0	0	0	0	0	0	0	2
1987	STL	NL	2	1	1	1	1	0	0	0	0	0	0	0	0	0	0	2
1988	STL	NL	1	1	0	1	0	0	0	0	0	0	0	0	0	0	1	0
1989	PHI	NL	2	1	1	2	0	0	0	0	0	0	0	0	0	0	1	1
1991	PHI	NL	1	0	1	0	1	0	0	0	0	0	0	0	0	0	1	0
1992	PHI	NL	1	1	0	1	0	0	0	0	0	0	0	0	0	0	0	1
1993	CHI	NL	5	1	4	4	1	0	0	0	0	0	0	0	0	0	2	3
Total			18	8	10	13	3	2	0	0	0	0	0	0	0	0	8	10

Rank among batters: 1,914 • *Total ballparks homered in*: 9 • *First HR*: 04/26/1983 off John Montefusco

Al Lakeman

ALBERT WESLEY LAKEMAN
B: 12/31/1918 D: 05/25/1976
BR

Year	Tm	Lg	Tot	H	A	0	1	2	3	2	3	4	LO	XN	IP	PH	RHP	LHP
1945	CIN	NL	8	4	4	5	3	0	0	0	0	0	0	0	0	0	7	1
1947	PHI	NL	6	3	3	2	2	2	0	0	0	0	0	0	0	0	2	4

Al Lakeman *continued*

Year	Tm	Lg	Tot	H	A	Men-On				One-Game			LO	XN	IP	PH	RHP	LHP
						0	1	2	3	2	3	4						
1948	PHI	NL	1	0	1	1	0	0	0	0	0	0	0	0	0	0	1	0
Total			15	7	8	8	5	2	0	0	0	0	0	0	0	0	10	5

Rank among batters: 2,096 • *Total ballparks homered in*: 7 • *First HR*: 07/01/1945 off Whit Wyatt

Tim Laker

TIMOTHY JOHN LAKER
B: 11/27/1969
BR

Year	Tm	Lg	Tot	H	A	Men-On 0	Men-On 1	Men-On 2	Men-On 3	One-Game 2	One-Game 3	One-Game 4	LO	XN	IP	PH	RHP	LHP
1995	MON	NL	3	1	2	3	0	0	0	0	0	0	0	0	0	0	1	2

Rank among batters: 3,735 • *Total ballparks homered in*: 2 • *First HR*: 05/11/1995 off Norm Charlton

Dan Lally

DANIEL J. LALLY
B: 08/12/1867 D: 04/14/1936
BL

Year	Tm	Lg	Tot	H	A	Men-On 0	Men-On 1	Men-On 2	Men-On 3	One-Game 2	One-Game 3	One-Game 4	LO	XN	IP	PH	RHP	LHP
1891	PIT	NL	1	1	0	0	1	0	0	0	0	0	0	0	0	0	1	0
1897	STL	NL	2	0	2	0	2	0	0	0	0	0	0	0	0	0	2	0
Total			3	1	2	0	3	0	0	0	0	0	0	0	0	0	3	0

Rank among batters: 3,735 • *Top target (2 home runs)*: Ted Lewis • *Number of pitchers victimized*: 2 • *Total ballparks homered in*: 2 • *First HR*: 09/21/1891 off Cy Young

Jack Lamabe

JOHN ALEXANDER LAMABE
B: 10/03/1936
BR

Year	Tm	Lg	Tot	H	A	Men-On 0	Men-On 1	Men-On 2	Men-On 3	One-Game 2	One-Game 3	One-Game 4	LO	XN	IP	PH	RHP	LHP
1963	BOS	AL	1	1	0	0	0	1	0	0	0	0	0	0	0	0	1	0

Rank among batters: 4,707 • *Total ballparks homered in*: 1 • *First HR*: 08/14/1963 off Bill Stafford

Ray Lamanno

RAYMOND SIMOND LAMANNO
B: 11/17/1919 D: 02/09/1994
BR

Year	Tm	Lg	Tot	H	A	Men-On 0	Men-On 1	Men-On 2	Men-On 3	One-Game 2	One-Game 3	One-Game 4	LO	XN	IP	PH	RHP	LHP
1942	CIN	NL	12	7	5	10	0	1	1	0	0	0	0	1	0	1	12	0
1946	CIN	NL	1	1	0	0	1	0	0	0	0	0	0	0	0	0	1	0
1947	CIN	NL	5	1	4	4	1	0	0	0	0	0	0	0	0	0	3	2
Total			18	9	9	14	2	1	1	0	0	0	0	1	0	1	16	2

Rank among batters: 1,914 • *Top target (3 home runs)*: Bill Lohrman • *Number of pitchers victimized*: 14 • *Total ballparks homered in*: 4 • *First HR*: 04/30/1942 off Chet Kehn

Bill Lamar

WILLIAM HARMONG LAMAR
B: 03/21/1897 D: 05/24/1970
BL

Year	Tm	Lg	Tot	H	A	Men-On 0	Men-On 1	Men-On 2	Men-On 3	One-Game 2	One-Game 3	One-Game 4	LO	XN	IP	PH	RHP	LHP
1924	PHI	AL	7	4	3	3	2	2	0	0	0	0	0	1	0	0	7	0
1925	PHI	AL	3	1	2	1	2	0	0	0	0	0	0	0	0	0	3	0
1926	PHI	AL	5	3	2	3	2	0	0	0	0	0	0	0	0	0	4	1
1927	PHI	AL	4	1	3	3	1	0	0	0	0	0	0	0	1	0	4	0
Total			19	9	10	10	7	2	0	0	0	0	0	1	1	0	18	1

Rank among batters: 1,861 • Top target (2 home runs): Rip Collins, Howard Ehmke, Waite Hoyt, Lil Stoner • *Number of pitchers victimized*: 15 • *Total ballparks homered in*: 6 • *First HR*: 07/04/1924 off Howard Ehmke

Laymon Lamb

LAYMON RAYMOND LAMB
B: 03/17/1895 D: 10/05/1955
BR

Year	Tm	Lg	Tot	H	A	Men-On 0	Men-On 1	Men-On 2	Men-On 3	One-Game 2	One-Game 3	One-Game 4	LO	XN	IP	PH	RHP	LHP
1921	STL	AL	1	0	1	0	1	0	0	0	0	0	0	0	0	0	1	0

Rank among batters: 4,707 • *Total ballparks homered in*: 1 • *First HR*: 06/11/1921 off Dave Keefe

Gene Lamont

GENE WILLIAM LAMONT
B: 12/25/1946
BL

Year	Tm	Lg	Tot	H	A	Men-On 0	1	2	3	One-Game 2	3	4	LO	XN	IP	PH	RHP	LHP
1970	DET	AL	1	0	1	1	0	0	0	0	0	0	0	0	0	0	1	0
1974	DET	AL	3	1	2	2	1	0	0	0	0	0	0	0	0	0	3	0
Total			4	1	3	3	1	0	0	0	0	0	0	0	0	0	4	0

Rank among batters: 3,427 • *Total ballparks homered in*: 4 • *First HR*: 09/02/1970 off Cal Koonce • *Hit HR in first major league AB*—@BOS: 09/02/1970 (1)

Bobby LaMotte

ROBERT EUGENE LAMOTTE
B: 02/15/1898 D: 11/02/1970
BR

Year	Tm	Lg	Tot	H	A	Men-On 0	1	2	3	One-Game 2	3	4	LO	XN	IP	PH	RHP	LHP
1922	WAS	AL	1	1	0	0	0	0	1	0	0	0	0	0	0	0	1	0
1925	STL	AL	2	1	1	1	0	0	1	0	0	0	0	0	0	0	1	1
Total			3	2	1	1	0	0	2	0	0	0	0	0	0	0	2	1

Rank among batters: 3,735 • *Total ballparks homered in*: 2 • *First HR*: 08/23/1922 off Dixie Leverett

Keith Lampard

CHRISTOPHER KEITH LAMPARD
B: 12/20/1945
BL

Year	Tm	Lg	Tot	H	A	Men-On 0	1	2	3	One-Game 2	3	4	LO	XN	IP	PH	RHP	LHP
1969	HOU	NL	1	1	0	0	1	0	0	0	0	0	0	0	0	1	1	0

Rank among batters: 4,707 • *Total ballparks homered in*: 1 • *First HR*: 09/19/1969 off Wayne Granger

Tom Lampkin

THOMAS MICHAEL LAMPKIN
B: 03/04/1964
BL

Year	Tm	Lg	Tot	H	A	Men-On 0	1	2	3	One-Game 2	3	4	LO	XN	IP	PH	RHP	LHP
1990	SD	NL	1	1	0	1	0	0	0	0	0	0	0	0	0	0	1	0
1993	MIL	AL	4	1	3	0	3	1	0	0	0	0	0	0	0	0	3	1
1995	SF	NL	1	1	0	0	1	0	0	0	0	0	0	0	0	0	1	0
Total			6	3	3	1	4	1	0	0	0	0	0	0	0	0	5	1

Rank among batters: 2,988 • *Total ballparks homered in*: 6 • *First HR*: 07/28/1990 off Mike Scott

Rick Lancellotti

RICHARD ANTHONY LANCELLOTTI
B: 07/05/1956
BL

Year	Tm	Lg	Tot	H	A	Men-On 0	1	2	3	One-Game 2	3	4	LO	XN	IP	PH	RHP	LHP
1986	SF	NL	2	0	2	0	1	1	0	0	0	0	0	0	0	2	2	0

Rank among batters: 4,129 • *Total ballparks homered in*: 2 • *First HR*: 09/21/1986 off Jeff Dedmon

Rafael Landestoy

RAFAEL SILVALDO (SANTANA) LANDESTOY
B: 05/28/1953
BB

Year	Tm	Lg	Tot	H	A	Men-On 0	1	2	3	One-Game 2	3	4	LO	XN	IP	PH	RHP	LHP
1980	HOU	NL	1	0	1	1	0	0	0	0	0	0	0	0	0	1	0	1
1982	CIN	NL	1	0	1	1	0	0	0	0	0	0	0	0	0	1	0	1
1983	LA	NL	1	0	1	1	0	0	0	0	0	0	0	0	0	0	1	0
1984	LA	NL	1	1	0	1	0	0	0	0	0	0	0	0	0	1	0	1
Total			4	1	3	4	0	0	0	0	0	0	0	0	0	3	1	3

Rank among batters: 3,427 • *Total ballparks homered in*: 4 • *First HR*: 05/09/1980 off Larry McWilliams

Jim Landis

JAMES HENRY LANDIS
B: 03/09/1934
BR

Year	Tm	Lg	Tot	H	A	Men-On 0	1	2	3	One-Game 2	3	4	LO	XN	IP	PH	RHP	LHP
1957	CHI	AL	2	1	1	0	1	1	0	0	0	0	0	0	0	0	2	0
1958	CHI	AL	15	6	9	8	6	1	0	0	0	0	0	0	0	0	7	8
1959	CHI	AL	5	1	4	2	2	1	0	0	0	0	0	0	0	0	3	2
1960	CHI	AL	10	8	2	7	2	1	0	0	0	0	0	2	0	0	7	3
1961	CHI	AL	22	12	10	11	9	2	0	1	0	0	0	1	0	0	17	5

Year	Tm	Lg	Tot	H	A	Men-On				One-Game			LO	XN	IP	PH	RHP	LHP
						0	1	2	3	2	3	4						

Jim Landis *continued*

Year	Tm	Lg	Tot	H	A	0	1	2	3	2	3	4	LO	XN	IP	PH	RHP	LHP
1962	CHI	AL	15	4	11	10	2	2	1	2	0	0	0	0	0	0	9	6
1963	CHI	AL	13	7	6	8	3	2	0	0	0	0	1	0	1	0	6	7
1964	CHI	AL	1	0	1	1	0	0	0	0	0	0	0	0	0	1	0	1
1965	KC	AL	3	2	1	2	0	1	0	0	0	0	0	0	0	0	3	0
1966	CLE	AL	3	1	2	3	0	0	0	0	0	0	1	0	0	1	1	2
1967	HOU	NL	1	0	1	1	0	0	0	0	0	0	0	0	0	0	1	0
	DET	AL	2	1	1	1	1	0	0	0	0	0	1	0	0	1	0	2
	BOS	AL	1	1	0	1	0	0	0	0	0	0	0	0	0	0	0	1
	Total		4	2	2	3	1	0	0	0	0	0	1	0	0	1	1	3
Total			93	44	49	55	26	11	1	3	0	0	3	3	1	3	56	37

Rank among batters: 545 • Top target (3 home runs): Rollie Sheldon, Whitey Ford, Jim Bunning, Don Mossi, Mudcat Grant, Dick Stigman • *Number of pitchers victimized*: 73 • *Total ballparks homered in*: 13 • *First HR*: 05/16/1957 off Evelio Hernandez

Ken Landreaux

KENNETH FRANCIS LANDREAUX
B: 12/22/1954
BL

Year	Tm	Lg	Tot	H	A	0	1	2	3	2	3	4	LO	XN	IP	PH	RHP	LHP
1978	CAL	AL	5	4	1	3	2	0	0	0	0	0	0	0	0	0	5	0
1979	MIN	AL	15	8	7	9	4	2	0	0	0	0	0	1	1	0	11	4
1980	MIN	AL	7	4	3	2	5	0	0	0	0	0	0	0	0	0	4	3
1981	LA	NL	7	3	4	6	1	0	0	1	0	0	0	0	0	0	5	2
1982	LA	NL	7	1	6	2	4	1	0	1	0	0	0	0	0	0	6	1
1983	LA	NL	17	10	7	11	5	0	1	0	0	0	0	0	0	0	17	0
1984	LA	NL	11	5	6	9	2	0	0	0	0	0	0	0	0	0	10	1
1985	LA	NL	12	2	10	10	2	0	0	1	0	0	0	0	1	0	10	2
1986	LA	NL	4	1	3	3	1	0	0	0	0	0	0	0	0	1	4	0
1987	LA	NL	6	4	2	2	3	1	0	0	0	0	0	0	0	1	6	0
Total			91	42	49	57	29	4	1	3	0	0	0	1	2	2	78	13

Rank among batters: 559 • *Top target (3 home runs)*: Dennis Martinez, Mike Torrez, Scott Sanderson • *Number of pitchers victimized*: 76 • *Total ballparks homered in*: 22 • *First HR*: 06/04/1978 off Dennis Eckersley

Hobie Landrith

HOBART NEAL LANDRITH
B: 03/16/1930
BL

Year	Tm	Lg	Tot	H	A	0	1	2	3	2	3	4	LO	XN	IP	PH	RHP	LHP
1953	CIN	NL	3	2	1	2	1	0	0	0	0	0	0	0	0	0	3	0
1954	CIN	NL	5	5	0	2	2	1	0	0	0	0	0	1	0	0	4	1
1955	CIN	NL	4	2	2	4	0	0	0	1	0	0	0	0	0	1	2	2
1956	CHI	NL	4	3	1	1	2	1	0	0	0	0	0	0	0	1	3	1
1957	STL	NL	3	2	1	2	1	0	0	0	0	0	0	0	0	0	3	0
1958	STL	NL	3	2	1	3	0	0	0	0	0	0	0	0	0	0	3	0
1959	SF	NL	3	0	3	0	3	0	0	0	0	0	0	0	0	0	3	0
1960	SF	NL	1	0	1	1	0	0	0	0	0	0	0	0	0	0	1	0
1961	SF	NL	2	2	0	2	0	0	0	0	0	0	0	1	0	0	2	0
1962	NY	NL	1	1	0	0	1	0	0	0	0	0	0	0	0	0	0	1
	BAL	AL	4	1	3	2	2	0	0	0	0	0	0	0	0	0	2	2
	Total		5	2	3	2	3	0	0	0	0	0	0	0	0	0	2	3
1963	WAS	AL	1	0	1	1	0	0	0	0	0	0	0	0	0	0	1	0
Total			34	20	14	20	12	2	0	1	0	0	0	2	0	2	27	7

Rank among batters: 1,315 • *Top target (2 home runs)*: Robin Roberts, Jim Brosnan, Warren Spahn • *Number of pitchers victimized*: 31 • *Total ballparks homered in*: 15 • *First HR*: 07/05/1953 off Bubba Church

Don Landrum

DONALD LEROY LANDRUM
B: 02/16/1936
BL

Year	Tm	Lg	Tot	H	A	0	1	2	3	2	3	4	LO	XN	IP	PH	RHP	LHP
1960	STL	NL	2	1	1	2	0	0	0	0	0	0	1	0	0	0	1	1
1961	STL	NL	1	0	1	1	0	0	0	0	0	0	0	0	1	0	1	0
1962	CHI	NL	1	0	1	0	0	1	0	0	0	0	0	0	0	0	1	0
1963	CHI	NL	1	1	0	1	0	0	0	0	0	0	0	0	0	0	1	0
1965	CHI	NL	6	5	1	1	5	0	0	0	0	0	0	0	0	0	5	1
1966	SF	NL	1	0	1	1	0	0	0	0	0	0	0	0	0	0	0	1
Total			12	7	5	6	5	1	0	0	0	0	1	0	1	0	9	3

Rank among batters: 2,325 • *Total ballparks homered in*: 7 • *First HR*: 09/21/1960 off Don Drysdale

Tito Landrum

TERRY LEE LANDRUM
B: 10/25/1954
BR

Year	Tm	Lg	Tot	H	A	Men-On 0	Men-On 1	Men-On 2	Men-On 3	One-Game 2	One-Game 3	One-Game 4	LO	XN	IP	PH	RHP	LHP
1982	STL	NL	2	0	2	1	1	0	0	0	0	0	0	0	0	0	0	2
1983	BAL	AL	1	0	1	1	0	0	0	0	0	0	0	0	0	0	0	1
1984	STL	NL	3	2	1	0	2	1	0	0	0	0	0	1	0	2	0	3
1985	STL	NL	4	2	2	1	2	1	0	0	0	0	0	0	0	1	1	3
1986	STL	NL	2	2	0	2	0	0	0	0	0	0	0	0	0	0	0	2
1987	LA	NL	1	1	0	1	0	0	0	0	0	0	0	0	0	1	1	0
Total			13	7	6	6	5	2	0	0	0	0	0	1	0	4	2	11

Rank among batters: 2,248 • *Total ballparks homered in*: 6 • *First HR*: 05/13/1982 off Ken Dayley • *World Series HR*—1; *LCS HR*—1

Chappy Lane

GEORGE M. LANE
BR

Year	Tm	Lg	Tot	H	A	Men-On 0	Men-On 1	Men-On 2	Men-On 3	One-Game 2	One-Game 3	One-Game 4	LO	XN	IP	PH	RHP	LHP
1882	PIT	AA	3	2	1	0	0	2	1	0	0	0	0	0	0	0	2	0
1884	TOL	AA	1	0	1	1	0	0	0	0	0	0	0	0	0	0	1	0
Total			4	2	2	1	0	2	1	0	0	0	0	0	0	0	3	0

Rank among batters: 3,427 • *Total ballparks homered in*: 3 • *First HR*: 07/10/1882 off Doc Landis

Marvin Lane

MARVIN LANE
B: 01/18/1950
BR

Year	Tm	Lg	Tot	H	A	Men-On 0	Men-On 1	Men-On 2	Men-On 3	One-Game 2	One-Game 3	One-Game 4	LO	XN	IP	PH	RHP	LHP
1973	DET	AL	1	0	1	0	1	0	0	0	0	0	0	0	0	0	0	1
1974	DET	AL	2	1	1	0	2	0	0	0	0	0	0	0	0	0	0	2
Total			3	1	2	0	3	0	0	0	0	0	0	0	0	0	0	3

Rank among batters: 3,735 • *Top target (2 home runs)*: Fritz Peterson • *Number of pitchers victimized*: 2 • *Total ballparks homered in*: 3 • *First HR*: 09/30/1973 off Fritz Peterson

Don Lang

DONALD CHARLES LANG
B: 03/15/1915
BR

Year	Tm	Lg	Tot	H	A	Men-On 0	Men-On 1	Men-On 2	Men-On 3	One-Game 2	One-Game 3	One-Game 4	LO	XN	IP	PH	RHP	LHP
1938	CIN	NL	1	0	1	0	1	0	0	0	0	0	0	0	0	0	0	1
1948	STL	NL	4	1	3	3	1	0	0	0	0	0	0	0	0	0	1	3
Total			5	1	4	3	2	0	0	0	0	0	0	0	0	0	1	4

Rank among batters: 3,191 • *Total ballparks homered in*: 3 • *First HR*: 08/20/1938 off Roy Henshaw

Bill Lange

WILLIAM ALEXANDER LANGE
B: 06/06/1871 D: 07/23/1950
BR

Year	Tm	Lg	Tot	H	A	Men-On 0	Men-On 1	Men-On 2	Men-On 3	One-Game 2	One-Game 3	One-Game 4	LO	XN	IP	PH	RHP	LHP
1893	CHI	NL	8	4	4	3	2	2	1	0	0	0	0	0	3	0	6	2
1894	CHI	NL	6	2	4	2	3	1	0	0	0	0	0	0	1	0	4	1
1895	CHI	NL	10	4	6	4	3	3	0	0	0	0	0	0	0	0	9	1
1896	CHI	NL	4	3	1	1	0	2	1	0	0	0	0	1	0	0	2	1
1897	CHI	NL	5	4	1	0	5	0	0	0	0	0	0	0	0	0	4	1
1898	CHI	NL	5	2	3	2	1	2	0	0	0	0	0	0	2	0	4	1
1899	CHI	NL	1	0	1	1	0	0	0	0	0	0	0	0	0	0	1	0
Total			39	19	20	13	14	10	2	0	0	0	0	1	6	0	30	6

Rank among batters: 1,204 • *Top target (2 home runs)*: Jouett Meekin, Willie Sudhoff • *Number of pitchers victimized*: 37 • *Total ballparks homered in*: 13 • *First HR*: 05/22/1893 off Cy Young

Sam Langford

ELTON LANGFORD
B: 05/21/1899 D: 07/31/1993
BL

Year	Tm	Lg	Tot	H	A	Men-On 0	Men-On 1	Men-On 2	Men-On 3	One-Game 2	One-Game 3	One-Game 4	LO	XN	IP	PH	RHP	LHP
1927	CLE	AL	1	0	1	0	1	0	0	0	0	0	0	0	0	0	1	0
1928	CLE	AL	4	2	2	1	1	2	0	0	0	0	0	0	0	0	4	0
Total			5	2	3	1	2	2	0	0	0	0	0	0	0	0	5	0

Rank among batters: 3,191 • *Total ballparks homered in*: 3 • *First HR*: 09/15/1927 off Myles Thomas

Hal Lanier

HAROLD CLIFTON LANIER
B: 07/04/1942
BR

Year	Tm	Lg	Tot	H	A	Men-On 0	Men-On 1	Men-On 2	Men-On 3	One-Game 2	One-Game 3	One-Game 4	LO	XN	IP	PH	RHP	LHP
1964	SF	NL	2	1	1	1	0	1	0	0	0	0	0	0	0	0	2	0
1966	SF	NL	3	0	3	3	0	0	0	0	0	0	0	1	0	0	2	1
1970	SF	NL	2	2	0	1	0	1	0	0	0	0	0	0	0	0	1	1
1971	SF	NL	1	0	1	1	0	0	0	0	0	0	0	0	0	0	1	0
Total			8	3	5	6	0	2	0	0	0	0	0	1	0	0	6	2

Rank among batters: 2,703 • *Total ballparks homered in*: 5 • *First HR*: 06/21/1964 off Roger Craig

Ray Lankford

RAYMOND LEWIS LANKFORD
B: 06/05/1967
BL

Year	Tm	Lg	Tot	H	A	Men-On 0	Men-On 1	Men-On 2	Men-On 3	One-Game 2	One-Game 3	One-Game 4	LO	XN	IP	PH	RHP	LHP
1990	STL	NL	3	2	1	2	1	0	0	0	0	0	0	0	0	0	3	0
1991	STL	NL	9	4	5	6	3	0	0	1	0	0	1	0	0	0	9	0
1992	STL	NL	20	13	7	9	8	2	1	0	0	0	1	0	0	0	16	4
1993	STL	NL	7	6	1	4	2	1	0	0	0	0	0	0	0	0	7	0
1994	STL	NL	19	8	11	15	2	2	0	1	0	0	5	2	0	0	16	3
1995	STL	NL	25	16	9	12	9	4	0	0	0	0	0	0	0	0	22	3
Total			83	49	34	48	25	9	1	2	0	0	7	2	0	0	73	10

Rank among batters: 628 • *Top target (4 home runs)*: John Burkett • *Number of pitchers victimized*: 71 • *Total ballparks homered in*: 14 • *First HR*: 09/06/1990 off Mark Gardner • *Hit for Cycle*—vs NY: 09/15/1991

Johnny Lanning

JOHN YOUNG LANNING
B: 09/06/1910 D: 11/08/1989
BR

Year	Tm	Lg	Tot	H	A	Men-On 0	Men-On 1	Men-On 2	Men-On 3	One-Game 2	One-Game 3	One-Game 4	LO	XN	IP	PH	RHP	LHP
1936	BOS	NL	1	0	1	1	0	0	0	0	0	0	0	0	0	0	1	0

Rank among batters: 4,707 • *Total ballparks homered in*: 1 • *First HR*: 05/25/1936 off Fred Frankhouse

Carney Lansford

CARNEY RAY LANSFORD
B: 02/07/1957
BR

Year	Tm	Lg	Tot	H	A	Men-On 0	Men-On 1	Men-On 2	Men-On 3	One-Game 2	One-Game 3	One-Game 4	LO	XN	IP	PH	RHP	LHP
1978	CAL	AL	8	4	4	4	2	2	0	0	0	0	0	0	0	0	5	3
1979	CAL	AL	19	5	14	13	5	1	0	1	1	0	1	0	0	0	16	3
1980	CAL	AL	15	8	7	7	4	4	0	0	0	0	0	0	0	0	10	5
1981	BOS	AL	4	1	3	2	1	1	0	0	0	0	0	0	0	0	2	2
1982	BOS	AL	11	4	7	5	2	3	1	0	0	0	0	1	0	0	8	3
1983	OAK	AL	10	4	6	4	4	1	1	1	0	0	0	0	0	0	6	4
1984	OAK	AL	14	7	7	9	4	1	0	0	0	0	0	0	0	0	10	4
1985	OAK	AL	13	7	6	6	6	1	0	2	0	0	0	1	0	0	10	3
1986	OAK	AL	19	10	9	12	5	2	0	2	0	0	0	1	0	0	13	6
1987	OAK	AL	19	9	10	11	3	5	0	0	0	0	0	1	0	0	11	8
1988	OAK	AL	7	1	6	4	3	0	0	0	0	0	0	0	0	0	7	0
1989	OAK	AL	2	1	1	2	0	0	0	0	0	0	0	0	0	0	1	1
1990	OAK	AL	3	1	2	3	0	0	0	0	0	0	0	0	0	0	2	1
1992	OAK	AL	7	4	3	2	3	1	1	0	0	0	0	0	0	0	6	1
Total			151	66	85	84	42	22	3	6	1	0	1	4	0	0	107	44

Rank among batters: 286 • *Top target (5 home runs)*: Milt Wilcox • *Number of pitchers victimized*: 110 • *Total ballparks homered in*: 16 • *First HR*: 04/24/1978 off Mike Parrott • *World Series HR*—1; *LCS HR*—1

Jody Lansford

JOSEPH DALE LANSFORD
B: 01/15/1961
BR

Year	Tm	Lg	Tot	H	A	Men-On 0	Men-On 1	Men-On 2	Men-On 3	One-Game 2	One-Game 3	One-Game 4	LO	XN	IP	PH	RHP	LHP
1983	SD	NL	1	0	1	0	1	0	0	0	0	0	0	0	0	1	0	1

Rank among batters: 4,707 • *Total ballparks homered in*: 1 • *First HR*: 09/21/1983 off Mark Davis

Mike Lansing

MICHAEL THOMAS LANSING
B: 04/03/1968
BR

Year	Tm	Lg	Tot	H	A	Men-On 0	Men-On 1	Men-On 2	Men-On 3	One-Game 2	One-Game 3	One-Game 4	LO	XN	IP	PH	RHP	LHP
1993	MON	NL	3	1	2	1	1	1	0	0	0	0	0	0	0	0	2	1
1994	MON	NL	5	3	2	2	3	0	0	0	0	0	0	0	0	0	2	3

Mike Lansing *continued*

Year	Tm	Lg	Tot	H	A	Men-On 0	Men-On 1	Men-On 2	Men-On 3	One-Game 2	One-Game 3	One-Game 4	LO	XN	IP	PH	RHP	LHP
1995	MON	NL	10	4	6	4	2	3	1	0	0	0	0	0	0	0	6	4
Total			18	8	10	7	6	4	1	0	0	0	0	0	0	0	10	8

Rank among batters: 1,914 • *Total ballparks homered in*: 8 • *First HR*: 04/09/1993 off Steve Reed

Pete Lapan

PETER NELSON LAPAN
B: 06/25/1891 D: 01/05/1953
BR

Year	Tm	Lg	Tot	H	A	Men-On 0	Men-On 1	Men-On 2	Men-On 3	One-Game 2	One-Game 3	One-Game 4	LO	XN	IP	PH	RHP	LHP
1922	WAS	AL	1	0	1	1	0	0	0	0	0	0	0	1	0	0	1	0

Rank among batters: 4,707 • *Total ballparks homered in*: 1 • *First HR*: 09/29/1922 off Eddie Rommel

Ralph LaPointe

RALPH ROBERT LAPOINTE
B: 01/08/1922 D: 09/13/1967
BR

Year	Tm	Lg	Tot	H	A	Men-On 0	Men-On 1	Men-On 2	Men-On 3	One-Game 2	One-Game 3	One-Game 4	LO	XN	IP	PH	RHP	LHP
1947	PHI	NL	1	0	1	1	0	0	0	0	0	0	1	0	0	0	1	0

Rank among batters: 4,707 • *Total ballparks homered in*: 1 • *First HR*: 09/14/1947 off Mel Queen

Frank LaPorte

FRANK BREYFOGLE LAPORTE
B: 02/06/1880 D: 09/25/1939
BR

Year	Tm	Lg	Tot	H	A	Men-On 0	Men-On 1	Men-On 2	Men-On 3	One-Game 2	One-Game 3	One-Game 4	LO	XN	IP	PH	RHP	LHP
1905	NY	AL	1	0	1	0	0	0	1	0	0	0	0	0	0	0	0	1
1906	NY	AL	2	2	0	1	0	0	1	0	0	0	0	1	1	0	1	1
1908	NY	AL	1	0	1	0	1	0	0	0	0	0	0	0	0	0	1	0
1910	NY	AL	2	2	0	1	1	0	0	0	0	0	0	0	0	0	2	0
1911	STL	AL	2	1	1	1	0	0	1	0	0	0	0	0	1	0	1	1
1912	STL	AL	1	0	1	0	0	1	0	0	0	0	0	0	1	0	1	0
1914	IND	FL	4	1	3	2	1	0	1	0	0	0	0	0	1	0	3	1
1915	NWK	FL	3	1	2	2	0	1	0	0	0	0	0	0	1	0	2	1
Total			16	7	9	7	3	2	4	0	0	0	0	1	5	0	11	5

Rank among batters: 2,029 • *Total ballparks homered in*: 10 • *First HR*: 10/07/1905 off Jesse Tannehill

Jack Lapp

JOHN WALKER LAPP
B: 09/10/1884 D: 02/06/1920
BL

Year	Tm	Lg	Tot	H	A	Men-On 0	Men-On 1	Men-On 2	Men-On 3	One-Game 2	One-Game 3	One-Game 4	LO	XN	IP	PH	RHP	LHP
1911	PHI	AL	1	0	1	1	0	0	0	0	0	0	0	0	0	0	1	0
1912	PHI	AL	1	0	1	1	0	0	0	0	0	0	0	0	0	0	1	0
1913	PHI	AL	1	0	1	0	1	0	0	0	0	0	0	0	0	0	1	0
1915	PHI	AL	2	0	2	1	1	0	0	0	0	0	0	0	0	0	2	0
Total			5	0	5	3	2	0	0	0	0	0	0	0	0	0	5	0

Rank among batters: 3,191 • *Total ballparks homered in*: 4 • *First HR*: 07/22/1911 off Frank Lange

Norm Larker

NORMAN HOWARD JOHN LARKER
B: 12/27/1930
BL

Year	Tm	Lg	Tot	H	A	Men-On 0	Men-On 1	Men-On 2	Men-On 3	One-Game 2	One-Game 3	One-Game 4	LO	XN	IP	PH	RHP	LHP
1958	LA	NL	4	2	2	2	1	1	0	1	0	0	0	0	0	0	4	0
1959	LA	NL	8	2	6	4	2	2	0	0	0	0	0	0	0	1	8	0
1960	LA	NL	5	3	2	1	3	1	0	0	0	0	0	0	0	0	4	1
1961	LA	NL	5	1	4	1	2	1	1	0	0	0	0	0	0	0	5	0
1962	HOU	NL	9	1	8	5	2	1	1	0	0	0	0	0	0	0	8	1
1963	MIL	NL	1	1	0	1	0	0	0	0	0	0	0	0	0	0	1	0
Total			32	10	22	14	10	6	2	1	0	0	0	0	0	1	30	2

Rank among batters: 1,360 • *Top target (3 home runs)*: Joey Jay • *Number of pitchers victimized*: 23 • *Total ballparks homered in*: 11 • *First HR*: 07/01/1958 off Jim Brosnan

Barry Larkin

BARRY LOUIS LARKIN
B: 04/28/1964
BR

Year	Tm	Lg	Tot	H	A	Men-On 0	Men-On 1	Men-On 2	Men-On 3	One-Game 2	One-Game 3	One-Game 4	LO	XN	IP	PH	RHP	LHP
1986	CIN	NL	3	3	0	2	1	0	0	0	0	0	0	0	0	0	1	2
1987	CIN	NL	12	6	6	6	3	3	0	0	0	0	1	0	0	1	7	5

Barry Larkin *continued*

Year	Tm	Lg	Tot	H	A	Men-On 0	Men-On 1	Men-On 2	Men-On 3	One-Game 2	One-Game 3	One-Game 4	LO	XN	IP	PH	RHP	LHP
1988	CIN	NL	12	9	3	9	1	2	0	0	0	0	4	0	0	0	7	5
1989	CIN	NL	4	1	3	3	0	1	0	0	0	0	0	0	0	0	2	2
1990	CIN	NL	7	4	3	5	2	0	0	0	0	0	0	0	0	0	3	4
1991	CIN	NL	20	16	4	12	6	2	0	1	1	0	0	0	0	0	12	8
1992	CIN	NL	12	8	4	8	3	1	0	0	0	0	0	0	0	0	6	6
1993	CIN	NL	8	4	4	4	4	0	0	0	0	0	0	0	0	0	4	4
1994	CIN	NL	9	3	6	6	3	0	0	2	0	0	1	0	0	0	6	3
1995	CIN	NL	15	8	7	7	8	0	0	2	0	0	0	0	0	0	7	8
Total			102	62	40	62	31	9	0	5	1	0	6	0	0	1	55	47

Rank among batters: 483 • *Top target (5 home runs)*: Jim Deshaies • *Number of pitchers victimized*: 80 • *Total ballparks homered in*: 14 • *First HR*: 08/17/1986 off Lamarr Hoyt

Gene Larkin

EUGENE THOMAS LARKIN
B: 10/24/1962
BB

Year	Tm	Lg	Tot	H	A	Men-On 0	Men-On 1	Men-On 2	Men-On 3	One-Game 2	One-Game 3	One-Game 4	LO	XN	IP	PH	RHP	LHP
1987	MIN	AL	4	0	4	4	0	0	0	0	0	0	0	0	0	0	3	1
1988	MIN	AL	8	5	3	3	4	1	0	0	0	0	0	0	0	0	6	2
1989	MIN	AL	6	3	3	3	1	2	0	0	0	0	0	0	0	0	5	1
1990	MIN	AL	5	5	0	3	1	1	0	1	0	0	0	0	1	0	5	0
1991	MIN	AL	2	0	2	1	1	0	0	0	0	0	0	0	0	0	1	1
1992	MIN	AL	6	5	1	3	2	1	0	0	0	0	0	0	0	0	6	0
1993	MIN	AL	1	1	0	0	0	1	0	0	0	0	0	0	0	0	1	0
Total			32	19	13	17	9	6	0	1	0	0	0	0	1	0	27	5

Rank among batters: 1,360 • *Top target (2 home runs)*: Mike Boddicker, Melido Perez • *Number of pitchers victimized*: 30 • *Total ballparks homered in*: 12 • *First HR*: 05/29/1987 off Nate Snell

Henry Larkin

HENRY E. LARKIN
B: 01/12/1860 D: 01/31/1942
BR

Year	Tm	Lg	Tot	H	A	Men-On 0	Men-On 1	Men-On 2	Men-On 3	One-Game 2	One-Game 3	One-Game 4	LO	XN	IP	PH	RHP	LHP
1884	PHI	AA	3	1	2	2	1	0	0	0	0	0	0	0	1	0	2	0
1885	PHI	AA	8	3	5	5	2	1	0	2	0	0	0	0	1	0	5	1
1886	PHI	AA	2	1	1	1	1	0	0	0	0	0	0	0	0	0	2	0
1887	PHI	AA	3	0	3	1	2	0	0	0	0	0	0	0	0	0	1	2
1888	PHI	AA	7	2	5	2	3	2	0	0	0	0	0	0	0	0	7	0
1889	PHI	AA	3	1	2	0	2	1	0	0	0	0	0	0	0	0	2	0
1890	CLE	PL	5	0	5	1	3	1	0	0	0	0	0	0	0	0	3	2
1891	PHI	AA	10	3	7	6	2	2	0	0	0	0	0	0	2	0	7	1
1892	WAS	NL	8	5	3	3	4	1	0	1	0	0	0	0	1	0	5	0
1893	WAS	NL	4	2	2	1	2	1	0	0	0	0	0	0	1	0	4	0
Total			53	18	35	22	22	9	0	3	0	0	0	0	6	0	38	5

Rank among batters: 953 • *Top target (3 home runs)*: George Cobb • *Number of pitchers victimized*: 43 • *Total ballparks homered in*: 17 • *First HR*: 08/25/1884 off Adonis Terry • *Hit for Cycle*—vs PIT: 06/16/1885

Terry Larkin

FRANK S. LARKIN
B: 1856 D: 09/16/1894
BR

Year	Tm	Lg	Tot	H	A	Men-On 0	Men-On 1	Men-On 2	Men-On 3	One-Game 2	One-Game 3	One-Game 4	LO	XN	IP	PH	RHP	LHP
1877	HAR	NL	1	0	1	0	0	1	0	0	0	0	0	0	1	0	1	0

Rank among batters: 4,707 • *Total ballparks homered in*: 1 • *First HR*: 07/07/1877 off Jim Devlin

Sam LaRoque

SAMUEL H.J. LAROQUE
B: 02/26/1864

Year	Tm	Lg	Tot	H	A	Men-On 0	Men-On 1	Men-On 2	Men-On 3	One-Game 2	One-Game 3	One-Game 4	LO	XN	IP	PH	RHP	LHP
1890	PIT	NL	1	0	1	1	0	0	0	0	0	0	0	0	0	0	1	0
1891	LOU	AA	1	0	1	1	0	0	0	0	0	0	0	0	0	0	0	0
Total			2	0	2	2	0	0	0	0	0	0	0	0	0	0	1	0

Rank among batters: 4,129 • *Total ballparks homered in*: 2 • *First HR*: 08/19/1890 off Bill Hutchison

Don Larsen

DON JAMES LARSEN
B: 08/07/1929
BR

Year	Tm	Lg	Tot	H	A	Men-On 0	Men-On 1	Men-On 2	Men-On 3	One-Game 2	One-Game 3	One-Game 4	LO	XN	IP	PH	RHP	LHP
1953	STL	AL	3	2	1	3	0	0	0	0	0	0	0	0	0	0	2	1
1954	BAL	AL	1	0	1	1	0	0	0	0	0	0	0	0	0	0	1	0

Don Larsen *continued*

Year	Tm	Lg	Tot	H	A	Men-On 0	1	2	3	One-Game 2	3	4	LO	XN	IP	PH	RHP	LHP
1955	NY	AL	2	0	2	0	1	1	0	0	0	0	0	0	0	0	1	1
1956	NY	AL	2	1	1	1	0	0	1	0	0	0	0	0	0	0	1	1
1958	NY	AL	4	2	2	3	1	0	0	0	0	0	0	0	0	1	3	1
1961	KC	AL	1	1	0	1	0	0	0	0	0	0	0	0	0	1	1	0
	CHI	AL	1	1	0	1	0	0	0	0	0	0	0	0	0	0	1	0
	Total		2	2	0	2	0	0	0	0	0	0	0	0	0	1	2	0
Total			14	7	7	10	2	1	1	0	0	0	0	0	0	2	10	4

Rank among batters: 2,169 • *Total ballparks homered in*: 8 • *First HR*: 07/05/1953 off Dick Weik

Frank Lary

FRANK STRONG LARY
B: 04/10/1930
BR

Year	Tm	Lg	Tot	H	A	Men-On 0	1	2	3	One-Game 2	3	4	LO	XN	IP	PH	RHP	LHP
1956	DET	AL	1	1	0	1	0	0	0	0	0	0	0	0	1	0	0	1
1958	DET	AL	1	0	1	1	0	0	0	0	0	0	0	0	0	0	1	0
1959	DET	AL	1	1	0	0	1	0	0	0	0	0	0	0	0	0	1	0
1960	DET	AL	2	0	2	1	0	1	0	0	0	0	0	0	0	0	2	0
1961	DET	AL	1	0	1	1	0	0	0	0	0	0	0	0	0	0	1	0
Total			6	2	4	4	1	1	0	0	0	0	0	0	1	0	5	1

Rank among batters: 2,988 • *Total ballparks homered in*: 4 • *First HR*: 04/17/1956 off Alex Kellner

Lyn Lary

LYNFORD HOBART LARY
B: 01/28/1906 D: 01/09/1973
BR

Year	Tm	Lg	Tot	H	A	Men-On 0	1	2	3	One-Game 2	3	4	LO	XN	IP	PH	RHP	LHP
1929	NY	AL	5	3	2	5	0	0	0	0	0	0	0	0	0	0	3	2
1930	NY	AL	3	0	3	1	1	1	0	0	0	0	0	0	0	0	2	1
1931	NY	AL	10	6	4	4	4	1	1	0	0	0	0	0	2	0	6	4
1932	NY	AL	3	2	1	2	1	0	0	0	0	0	0	0	0	0	1	2
1934	BOS	AL	2	1	1	0	2	0	0	0	0	0	0	0	0	0	2	0
1935	STL	AL	2	1	1	1	1	0	0	0	0	0	1	0	0	0	2	0
1936	STL	AL	2	0	2	2	0	0	0	0	0	0	0	0	0	0	2	0
1937	CLE	AL	8	4	4	7	0	1	0	0	0	0	4	0	0	0	6	2
1938	CLE	AL	3	0	3	3	0	0	0	0	0	0	1	0	0	0	2	1
Total			38	17	21	25	9	3	1	0	0	0	6	0	2	0	26	12

Rank among batters: 1,225 • *Top target (3 home runs)*: Milt Gaston • *Number of pitchers victimized*: 33 • *Total ballparks homered in*: 10 • *First HR*: 05/18/1929 off Milt Gaston

Arlie Latham

WALTER ARLINGTON LATHAM
B: 03/15/1860 D: 11/29/1952
BR

Year	Tm	Lg	Tot	H	A	Men-On 0	1	2	3	One-Game 2	3	4	LO	XN	IP	PH	RHP	LHP
1884	STL	AA	1	0	1	0	1	0	0	0	0	0	0	0	0	0	1	0
1885	STL	AA	1	0	1	0	1	0	0	0	0	0	0	0	0	0	0	0
1886	STL	AA	1	1	0	1	0	0	0	0	0	0	0	0	0	0	1	0
1887	STL	AA	2	0	2	1	1	0	0	0	0	0	1	0	1	0	2	0
1888	STL	AA	2	1	1	1	0	1	0	0	0	0	0	0	0	0	0	2
1889	STL	AA	4	3	1	2	1	1	0	1	0	0	2	0	0	0	3	1
1890	CHI	PL	1	0	1	0	1	0	0	0	0	0	0	0	0	0	0	1
1891	CIN	NL	7	3	4	5	1	1	0	0	0	0	0	0	0	0	7	0
1893	CIN	NL	2	1	1	1	1	0	0	0	0	0	0	0	1	0	2	0
1894	CIN	NL	4	3	1	2	1	0	1	0	0	0	0	0	0	0	2	1
1895	CIN	NL	2	0	2	1	0	0	1	0	0	0	0	0	0	0	1	1
Total			27	12	15	14	8	3	2	1	0	0	3	0	2	0	19	6

Rank among batters: 1,532 • *Top target (2 home runs)*: Bert Cunningham, Harry Staley • *Number of pitchers victimized*: 25 • *Total ballparks homered in*: 13 • *First HR*: 08/17/1884 off Gus Shallix • *World Series HR*—1

Barry Latman

ARNOLD BARRY LATMAN
B: 05/21/1936
BR

Year	Tm	Lg	Tot	H	A	Men-On 0	1	2	3	One-Game 2	3	4	LO	XN	IP	PH	RHP	LHP
1962	CLE	AL	1	0	1	1	0	0	0	0	0	0	0	0	0	0	0	1
1963	CLE	AL	1	0	1	1	0	0	0	0	0	0	0	0	0	0	0	1
Total			2	0	2	2	0	0	0	0	0	0	0	0	0	0	0	2

Rank among batters: 4,129 • *Total ballparks homered in*: 2 • *First HR*: 06/03/1962 off Don Mossi

Year	Tm	Lg	Tot	H	A	Men-On 0	1	2	3	One-Game 2	3	4	LO	XN	IP	PH	RHP	LHP

Charlie Lau

CHARLES RICHARD LAU
B: 04/12/1933 D: 03/18/1984
BL

Year	Tm	Lg	Tot	H	A	0	1	2	3	2	3	4	LO	XN	IP	PH	RHP	LHP
1961	BAL	AL	1	1	0	0	1	0	0	0	0	0	0	0	0	0	1	0
1962	BAL	AL	6	2	4	3	3	0	0	1	0	0	0	0	0	0	6	0
1963	KC	AL	3	1	2	2	0	1	0	0	0	0	0	0	0	0	3	0
1964	KC	AL	2	1	1	2	0	0	0	0	0	0	0	1	0	1	2	0
	BAL	AL	1	1	0	1	0	0	0	0	0	0	0	0	0	0	1	0
	Total		3	2	1	3	0	0	0	0	0	0	0	1	0	1	3	0
1965	BAL	AL	2	1	1	1	1	0	0	0	0	0	0	0	0	1	2	0
1967	ATL	NL	1	1	0	0	1	0	0	0	0	0	0	0	0	1	1	0
Total			16	8	8	9	6	1	0	1	0	0	0	1	0	3	16	0

Rank among batters: 2,029 • *Total ballparks homered in*: 8 • *First HR*: 09/04/1961 off Paul Foytack

Billy Lauder

WILLIAM LAUDER
B: 02/23/1874 D: 05/20/1933
BR

Year	Tm	Lg	Tot	H	A	0	1	2	3	2	3	4	LO	XN	IP	PH	RHP	LHP
1898	PHI	NL	2	0	2	0	2	0	0	0	0	0	0	0	0	0	1	1
1899	PHI	NL	3	0	3	0	2	1	0	0	0	0	0	0	0	0	3	0
Total			5	0	5	0	4	1	0	0	0	0	0	0	0	0	4	1

Rank among batters: 3,191 • *Total ballparks homered in*: 4 • *First HR*: 08/24/1898 off Bert Cunningham

Tim Laudner

TIMOTHY JON LAUDNER
B: 06/07/1958
BR

Year	Tm	Lg	Tot	H	A	0	1	2	3	2	3	4	LO	XN	IP	PH	RHP	LHP
1981	MIN	AL	2	2	0	0	2	0	0	0	0	0	0	0	0	0	1	1
1982	MIN	AL	7	2	5	1	3	3	0	0	0	0	0	0	0	0	5	2
1983	MIN	AL	6	2	4	6	0	0	0	0	0	0	0	0	0	0	2	4
1984	MIN	AL	10	3	7	4	6	0	0	0	0	0	0	0	0	0	6	4
1985	MIN	AL	7	5	2	6	1	0	0	0	0	0	0	0	0	0	0	7
1986	MIN	AL	10	9	1	9	1	0	0	0	0	0	0	0	0	0	3	7
1987	MIN	AL	16	7	9	7	7	1	1	1	0	0	0	0	0	0	9	7
1988	MIN	AL	13	8	5	8	2	3	0	2	0	0	0	0	0	0	10	3
1989	MIN	AL	6	2	4	4	1	1	0	1	0	0	0	0	0	0	4	2
Total			77	40	37	45	23	8	1	4	0	0	0	0	0	0	40	37

Rank among batters: 682 • *Top target (3 home runs)*: Floyd Bannister • *Number of pitchers victimized*: 63 • *Total ballparks homered in*: 15 • *First HR*: 08/28/1981 off Dave Rozema • *World Series HR*—1

George Lauzerique

GEORGE ALBERT LAUZERIQUE
B: 07/22/1947
BR

Year	Tm	Lg	Tot	H	A	0	1	2	3	2	3	4	LO	XN	IP	PH	RHP	LHP
1970	MIL	AL	1	0	1	0	0	1	0	0	0	0	0	0	0	0	1	0

Rank among batters: 4,707 • *Total ballparks homered in*: 1 • *First HR*: 04/12/1970 off Tommie Sisk

Cookie Lavagetto

HARRY ARTHUR LAVAGETTO
B: 12/01/1912 D: 08/10/1990
BR

Year	Tm	Lg	Tot	H	A	0	1	2	3	2	3	4	LO	XN	IP	PH	RHP	LHP
1934	PIT	NL	3	0	3	2	1	0	0	0	0	0	0	0	0	0	1	2
1936	PIT	NL	2	1	1	2	0	0	0	0	0	0	0	0	0	0	0	2
1937	BRO	NL	8	5	3	4	3	1	0	1	0	0	0	0	0	0	8	0
1938	BRO	NL	6	3	3	2	2	2	0	0	0	0	0	0	0	0	3	3
1939	BRO	NL	10	6	4	4	4	0	2	0	0	0	0	0	0	0	8	2
1940	BRO	NL	4	2	2	3	0	0	1	0	0	0	0	0	0	0	4	0
1941	BRO	NL	1	0	1	0	1	0	0	0	0	0	0	0	0	0	1	0
1946	BRO	NL	3	1	2	2	1	0	0	0	0	0	0	0	0	0	0	3
1947	BRO	NL	3	2	1	3	0	0	0	0	0	0	0	0	0	1	1	2
Total			40	20	20	22	12	3	3	1	0	0	0	0	0	1	26	14

Rank among batters: 1,181 • Top target (2 home runs): Slick Castleman, Joe Bowman, Harry Gumbert, Dave Koslo • *Number of pitchers victimized*: 36 • *Total ballparks homered in*: 9 • *First HR*: 04/18/1934 off Bill Walker

Year	Tm	Lg	Tot	H	A	Men-On 0	1	2	3	One-Game 2	3	4	LO	XN	IP	PH	RHP	LHP

Mike LaValliere

MICHAEL EUGENE LAVALLIERE
B: 08/18/1960
BL

Year	Tm	Lg	Tot	H	A	Men-On 0	1	2	3	One-Game 2	3	4	LO	XN	IP	PH	RHP	LHP
1986	STL	NL	3	1	2	1	2	0	0	0	0	0	0	0	0	0	2	1
1987	PIT	NL	1	1	0	1	0	0	0	0	0	0	0	0	0	0	1	0
1988	PIT	NL	2	0	2	0	1	1	0	0	0	0	0	0	0	0	2	0
1989	PIT	NL	2	2	0	1	0	1	0	0	0	0	0	0	0	0	2	0
1990	PIT	NL	3	2	1	1	0	2	0	0	0	0	0	0	0	0	1	2
1991	PIT	NL	3	1	2	2	0	0	1	0	0	0	0	0	0	0	3	0
1992	PIT	NL	2	1	1	0	2	0	0	0	0	0	0	0	0	0	2	0
1994	CHI	AL	1	0	1	0	1	0	0	0	0	0	0	0	0	0	1	0
1995	CHI	AL	1	0	1	1	0	0	0	0	0	0	0	1	0	0	0	1
Total			18	8	10	7	6	4	1	0	0	0	0	1	0	0	14	4

Rank among batters: 1,914 • *Total ballparks homered in*: 11 • *First HR*: 06/19/1986 off Kevin Gross

Doc Lavan

JOHN LEONARD LAVAN
B: 10/28/1890 D: 05/29/1952
BR

Year	Tm	Lg	Tot	H	A	Men-On 0	1	2	3	One-Game 2	3	4	LO	XN	IP	PH	RHP	LHP
1914	STL	AL	1	1	0	0	1	0	0	0	0	0	0	0	1	0	1	0
1915	STL	AL	1	0	1	1	0	0	0	0	0	0	0	0	0	0	1	0
1919	STL	NL	1	1	0	0	1	0	0	0	0	0	0	0	1	0	1	0
1920	STL	NL	1	0	1	1	0	0	0	0	0	0	0	0	0	0	1	0
1921	STL	NL	2	1	1	0	2	0	0	0	0	0	0	0	0	0	1	1
1923	STL	NL	1	0	1	0	0	1	0	0	0	0	0	0	0	1	1	0
Total			7	3	4	2	4	1	0	0	0	0	0	0	2	1	6	1

Rank among batters: 2,834 • *Total ballparks homered in*: 5 • *First HR*: 08/16/1914 off Jim Scott

Rudy Law

RUDY KARL LAW
B: 10/07/1956
BL

Year	Tm	Lg	Tot	H	A	Men-On 0	1	2	3	One-Game 2	3	4	LO	XN	IP	PH	RHP	LHP
1980	LA	NL	1	1	0	0	1	0	0	0	0	0	0	0	0	0	1	0
1982	CHI	AL	3	0	3	1	1	1	0	0	0	0	1	0	0	0	2	1
1983	CHI	AL	3	1	2	3	0	0	0	0	0	0	0	0	1	0	3	0
1984	CHI	AL	6	4	2	3	3	0	0	0	0	0	1	0	0	1	6	0
1985	CHI	AL	4	4	0	4	0	0	0	0	0	0	1	0	1	0	4	0
1986	KC	AL	1	1	0	0	1	0	0	0	0	0	0	0	0	0	1	0
Total			18	11	7	11	6	1	0	0	0	0	3	0	2	1	17	1

Rank among batters: 1,914 • *Total ballparks homered in*: 7 • *First HR*: 07/04/1980 off Allen Ripley

Vance Law

VANCE AARON LAW
B: 10/01/1956
BR

Year	Tm	Lg	Tot	H	A	Men-On 0	1	2	3	One-Game 2	3	4	LO	XN	IP	PH	RHP	LHP
1982	CHI	AL	5	2	3	3	2	0	0	0	0	0	0	0	0	0	1	4
1983	CHI	AL	4	1	3	3	0	1	0	0	0	0	0	0	0	0	3	1
1984	CHI	AL	17	11	6	11	5	1	0	1	0	0	0	1	0	0	8	9
1985	MON	NL	10	5	5	6	4	0	0	0	0	0	0	0	1	0	6	4
1986	MON	NL	5	3	2	3	2	0	0	0	0	0	0	0	0	0	1	4
1987	MON	NL	12	3	9	9	2	0	1	0	0	0	0	0	0	0	9	3
1988	CHI	NL	11	5	6	3	4	4	0	1	0	0	0	0	0	0	6	5
1989	CHI	NL	7	4	3	7	0	0	0	1	0	0	0	0	0	0	4	3
Total			71	34	37	45	19	6	1	3	0	0	0	1	1	0	38	33

Rank among batters: 731 • Top target (2 home runs): Ed Hodge, Curt Young, Sid Fernandez, Ed Lynch, Brian Fisher, Jose DeLeon • *Number of pitchers victimized*: 65 • *Total ballparks homered in*: 18 • *First HR*: 06/26/1982 off Gaylord Perry

Vern Law

VERNON SANDERS LAW
B: 03/12/1930
BR

Year	Tm	Lg	Tot	H	A	Men-On 0	1	2	3	One-Game 2	3	4	LO	XN	IP	PH	RHP	LHP
1951	PIT	NL	1	0	1	1	0	0	0	0	0	0	0	0	0	0	1	0
1954	PIT	NL	1	0	1	1	0	0	0	0	0	0	0	0	0	0	1	0
1955	PIT	NL	1	0	1	0	1	0	0	0	0	0	0	0	0	0	0	1
1956	PIT	NL	1	0	1	1	0	0	0	0	0	0	0	0	0	0	0	1
1958	PIT	NL	2	0	2	1	0	1	0	0	0	0	0	0	0	0	2	0

Vern Law *continued*

Year	Tm	Lg	Tot	H	A	Men-On 0	Men-On 1	Men-On 2	Men-On 3	One-Game 2	One-Game 3	One-Game 4	LO	XN	IP	PH	RHP	LHP
1959	PIT	NL	1	0	1	0	1	0	0	0	0	0	0	0	0	0	1	0
1960	PIT	NL	1	0	1	1	0	0	0	0	0	0	0	0	0	0	1	0
1964	PIT	NL	1	0	1	1	0	0	0	0	0	0	0	0	0	0	1	0
1965	PIT	NL	1	0	1	0	0	1	0	0	0	0	0	0	0	0	1	0
1966	PIT	NL	1	0	1	1	0	0	0	0	0	0	0	0	0	0	0	1
Total			11	0	11	7	2	2	0	0	0	0	0	0	0	0	8	3

Rank among batters: 2,419 • *Total ballparks homered in*: 8 • *First HR*: 08/11/1951 off Bob Kelly

Tom Lawless

THOMAS JAMES LAWLESS
B: 12/19/1956
BR

Year	Tm	Lg	Tot	H	A	Men-On 0	Men-On 1	Men-On 2	Men-On 3	One-Game 2	One-Game 3	One-Game 4	LO	XN	IP	PH	RHP	LHP
1984	CIN	NL	1	0	1	1	0	0	0	0	0	0	0	0	0	0	0	1
1988	STL	NL	1	0	1	1	0	0	0	0	0	0	0	0	0	0	0	1
Total			2	0	2	2	0	0	0	0	0	0	0	0	0	0	0	2

Rank among batters: 4,129 • *Total ballparks homered in*: 2 • *First HR*: 04/25/1984 off Ken Dayley • *World Series HR*—1

Bob Lawson

ROBERT BAKER LAWSON
B: 08/23/1876 D: 10/28/1952
BR

Year	Tm	Lg	Tot	H	A	Men-On 0	Men-On 1	Men-On 2	Men-On 3	One-Game 2	One-Game 3	One-Game 4	LO	XN	IP	PH	RHP	LHP
1901	BOS	NL	1	1	0	1	0	0	0	0	0	0	0	0	0	0	1	0

Rank among batters: 4,707 • *Total ballparks homered in*: 1 • *First HR*: 06/19/1901 off Mal Eason

Matt Lawton

MATTHEW III LAWTON
B: 11/03/1971
BL

Year	Tm	Lg	Tot	H	A	Men-On 0	Men-On 1	Men-On 2	Men-On 3	One-Game 2	One-Game 3	One-Game 4	LO	XN	IP	PH	RHP	LHP
1995	MIN	AL	1	1	0	0	1	0	0	0	0	0	0	0	0	0	1	0

Rank among batters: 4,707 • *Total ballparks homered in*: 1 • *First HR*: 09/28/1995 off Dennis Martinez

Hillis Layne

IVORIA HILLIS LAYNE
B: 02/23/1918
BL

Year	Tm	Lg	Tot	H	A	Men-On 0	Men-On 1	Men-On 2	Men-On 3	One-Game 2	One-Game 3	One-Game 4	LO	XN	IP	PH	RHP	LHP
1945	WAS	AL	1	0	1	1	0	0	0	0	0	0	0	0	0	0	1	0

Rank among batters: 4,707 • *Total ballparks homered in*: 1 • *First HR*: 08/25/1945 off Tiny Bonham

Les Layton

LESTER LEE LAYTON
B: 11/18/1921
BR

Year	Tm	Lg	Tot	H	A	Men-On 0	Men-On 1	Men-On 2	Men-On 3	One-Game 2	One-Game 3	One-Game 4	LO	XN	IP	PH	RHP	LHP
1948	NY	NL	2	2	0	2	0	0	0	0	0	0	0	0	0	1	1	1

Rank among batters: 4,129 • *Total ballparks homered in*: 1 • *First HR*: 05/21/1948 off Johnny Schmitz • *Hit HR in first major league AB*—vs CHI: 05/21/1948

Johnny Lazor

JOHN PAUL LAZOR
B: 09/09/1912
BL

Year	Tm	Lg	Tot	H	A	Men-On 0	Men-On 1	Men-On 2	Men-On 3	One-Game 2	One-Game 3	One-Game 4	LO	XN	IP	PH	RHP	LHP
1945	BOS	AL	5	2	3	2	1	2	0	1	0	0	0	0	0	0	5	0
1946	BOS	AL	1	0	1	1	0	0	0	0	0	0	0	0	0	0	1	0
Total			6	2	4	3	1	2	0	1	0	0	0	0	0	0	6	0

Rank among batters: 2,988 • *Top target (2 home runs)*: Leslie Mueller • *Number of pitchers victimized*: 5 • *Total ballparks homered in*: 4 • *First HR*: 06/02/1945 off Art Houtteman

Tony Lazzeri

ANTHONY MICHAEL LAZZERI
B: 12/06/1903 D: 08/06/1946
BR HOF

Year	Tm	Lg	Tot	H	A	Men-On 0	Men-On 1	Men-On 2	Men-On 3	One-Game 2	One-Game 3	One-Game 4	LO	XN	IP	PH	RHP	LHP
1926	NY	AL	18	9	9	5	5	7	1	0	0	0	0	0	2	0	13	5

Tony Lazzeri *continued*

Year	Tm	Lg	Tot	H	A	Men-On 0	1	2	3	One-Game 2	3	4	LO	XN	IP	PH	RHP	LHP
1927	NY	AL	18	11	7	8	6	3	1	1	1	0	0	0	2	0	15	3
1928	NY	AL	10	5	5	6	3	1	0	1	0	0	0	0	0	0	6	4
1929	NY	AL	18	5	13	9	6	3	0	1	0	0	0	0	0	0	5	13
1930	NY	AL	9	4	5	3	3	2	1	0	0	0	0	0	0	0	7	2
1931	NY	AL	8	4	4	4	3	1	0	0	0	0	0	0	2	1	3	5
1932	NY	AL	15	11	4	6	7	1	1	1	0	0	0	0	1	0	13	2
1933	NY	AL	18	7	11	12	1	4	1	1	0	0	0	1	0	0	12	6
1934	NY	AL	14	7	7	8	5	1	0	0	0	0	0	1	0	0	11	3
1935	NY	AL	13	6	7	9	2	1	1	1	0	0	0	0	1	0	9	4
1936	NY	AL	14	3	11	5	5	2	2	1	1	0	0	0	0	0	7	7
1937	NY	AL	14	8	6	7	6	1	0	0	0	0	0	0	0	0	12	2
1938	CHI	NL	5	2	3	3	1	1	0	0	0	0	0	0	0	0	5	0
1939	BRO	NL	3	2	1	3	0	0	0	0	0	0	0	0	0	0	2	1
	NY	NL	1	1	0	0	1	0	0	0	0	0	0	0	0	0	1	0
	Total		4	3	1	3	1	0	0	0	0	0	0	0	0	0	3	1
Total			178	85	93	88	54	28	8	7	2	0	0	2	8	1	121	57

Rank among batters: 225 • *Top target (5 home runs)*: George Earnshaw, Lloyd Brown • *Number of pitchers victimized*: 108 • *Total ballparks homered in*: 13 • *First HR*: 04/27/1926 off Eddie Rommel • *Hit for Cycle—@PHI*: 06/03/1932 • *World Series HR*—4

Freddy Leach

FREDERICK LEACH
B: 11/23/1897 D: 12/10/1981
BL

Year	Tm	Lg	Tot	H	A	Men-On 0	1	2	3	One-Game 2	3	4	LO	XN	IP	PH	RHP	LHP
1923	PHI	NL	1	1	0	0	0	1	0	0	0	0	0	0	0	0	1	0
1924	PHI	NL	2	2	0	1	0	1	0	0	0	0	0	0	0	0	2	0
1925	PHI	NL	5	3	2	1	3	1	0	1	0	0	0	0	0	0	4	1
1926	PHI	NL	11	6	5	5	2	3	1	0	0	0	0	0	1	0	10	1
1927	PHI	NL	12	8	4	7	3	1	1	0	0	0	0	0	0	0	11	1
1928	PHI	NL	13	8	5	6	4	3	0	1	0	0	0	0	0	0	11	2
1929	NY	NL	8	1	7	3	5	0	0	1	0	0	0	0	0	0	6	2
1930	NY	NL	13	7	6	7	3	3	0	1	0	0	0	0	0	0	13	0
1931	NY	NL	6	3	3	4	1	1	0	0	0	0	0	0	0	0	6	0
1932	BOS	NL	1	0	1	1	0	0	0	0	0	0	0	0	0	0	1	0
Total			72	39	33	35	21	14	2	4	0	0	0	0	1	0	65	7

Rank among batters: 723 • *Top target (4 home runs)*: Bob Smith, Dazzy Vance, Ray Kremer • *Number of pitchers victimized*: 47 • *Total ballparks homered in*: 7 • *First HR*: 07/05/1923 off Lou North

Rick Leach

RICHARD MAX LEACH
B: 05/04/1957
BL

Year	Tm	Lg	Tot	H	A	Men-On 0	1	2	3	One-Game 2	3	4	LO	XN	IP	PH	RHP	LHP
1981	DET	AL	1	1	0	0	0	1	0	0	0	0	0	0	0	0	1	0
1982	DET	AL	3	2	1	3	0	0	0	0	0	0	0	0	0	0	3	0
1983	DET	AL	3	1	2	1	2	0	0	0	0	0	0	0	0	1	3	0
1986	TOR	AL	5	4	1	2	1	2	0	0	0	0	0	0	0	1	5	0
1987	TOR	AL	3	3	0	1	0	2	0	0	0	0	0	0	0	0	3	0
1989	TEX	AL	1	0	1	1	0	0	0	0	0	0	0	0	0	0	1	0
1990	SF	NL	2	2	0	1	1	0	0	0	0	0	0	0	0	0	2	0
Total			18	13	5	9	4	5	0	0	0	0	0	0	0	2	18	0

Rank among batters: 1,914 • *Top target (2 home runs)*: Storm Davis • *Number of pitchers victimized*: 17 • *Total ballparks homered in*: 6 • *First HR*: 08/18/1981 off Roger Erickson

Tommy Leach

THOMAS WILLIAM LEACH
B: 11/04/1877 D: 09/29/1969
BR

Year	Tm	Lg	Tot	H	A	Men-On 0	1	2	3	One-Game 2	3	4	LO	XN	IP	PH	RHP	LHP
1899	LOU	NL	5	1	4	2	2	1	0	0	0	0	0	0	3	0	3	1
1900	PIT	NL	1	0	1	0	0	1	0	0	0	0	0	0	1	0	1	0
1901	PIT	NL	2	0	2	2	0	0	0	0	0	0	0	0	2	0	2	0
1902	PIT	NL	6	3	3	4	2	0	0	1	0	0	0	0	3	0	6	0
1903	PIT	NL	7	2	5	2	3	1	1	1	0	0	0	0	7	0	7	0
1904	PIT	NL	2	0	2	2	0	0	0	0	0	0	2	0	2	0	2	0
1905	PIT	NL	2	1	1	0	2	0	0	0	0	0	0	0	2	0	1	1
1906	PIT	NL	1	1	0	0	1	0	0	0	0	0	0	0	1	0	1	0
1907	PIT	NL	4	2	2	2	1	0	1	0	0	0	0	0	3	0	2	2

Tommy Leach *continued*

Year	Tm	Lg	Tot	H	A	Men-On 0	1	2	3	One-Game 2	3	4	LO	XN	IP	PH	RHP	LHP
1908	PIT	NL	5	4	1	4	1	0	0	0	0	0	0	0	5	0	3	2
1909	PIT	NL	6	1	5	4	2	0	0	0	0	0	0	0	3	0	4	2
1910	PIT	NL	4	4	0	2	0	1	1	0	0	0	0	0	3	0	4	0
1911	PIT	NL	3	1	2	1	1	0	1	0	0	0	0	0	3	0	1	2
1912	CHI	NL	2	2	0	1	1	0	0	0	0	0	0	0	2	0	1	1
1913	CHI	NL	6	4	2	3	0	3	0	0	0	0	0	0	6	0	3	3
1914	CHI	NL	7	3	4	5	0	2	0	0	0	0	3	1	3	0	5	2
Total			63	29	34	34	16	9	4	2	0	0	5	1	49	0	46	16

Rank among batters: 826 • *Top target (3 home runs)*: Rube Marquard • *Number of pitchers victimized*: 49 • *Total ballparks homered in*: 11 • *First HR*: 06/03/1899 off Cy Seymour

Frederick Lear

FREDERICK FRANCIS LEAR
B: 04/07/1894 D: 10/13/1955
BR

Year	Tm	Lg	Tot	H	A	Men-On 0	1	2	3	One-Game 2	3	4	LO	XN	IP	PH	RHP	LHP
1919	CHI	NL	1	1	0	0	0	1	0	0	0	0	0	0	0	0	1	0
1920	NY	NL	1	1	0	1	0	0	0	0	0	0	0	0	0	0	0	1
Total			2	2	0	1	0	1	0	0	0	0	0	0	0	0	1	1

Rank among batters: 4,129 • *Total ballparks homered in*: 2 • *First HR*: 06/02/1919 off Erskine Mayer

Jack Leary

JOHN J. LEARY
B: 1858

Year	Tm	Lg	Tot	H	A	Men-On 0	1	2	3	One-Game 2	3	4	LO	XN	IP	PH	RHP	LHP
1882	PIT	AA	1	1	0	0	0	1	0	0	0	0	0	0	1	0	0	0
1883	LOU	AA	3	1	2	1	1	1	0	0	0	0	0	0	0	0	2	1
Total			4	2	2	1	1	2	0	0	0	0	0	0	1	0	2	0

Rank among batters: 3,427 • *Top target (2 home runs)*: Frank Mountain • *Number of pitchers victimized*: 3 • *Total ballparks homered in*: 3 • *First HR*: 07/06/1882 off Doc Landis

Tim Leary

TIMOTHY JAMES LEARY
B: 03/21/1958
BR

Year	Tm	Lg	Tot	H	A	Men-On 0	1	2	3	One-Game 2	3	4	LO	XN	IP	PH	RHP	LHP
1984	NY	NL	1	0	1	1	0	0	0	0	0	0	0	0	0	0	0	1

Rank among batters: 4,707 • *Total ballparks homered in*: 1 • *First HR*: 04/20/1984 off Steve Carlton

Hal Leathers

HAROLD LANGFORD LEATHERS
B: 12/02/1898 D: 04/12/1977
BL

Year	Tm	Lg	Tot	H	A	Men-On 0	1	2	3	One-Game 2	3	4	LO	XN	IP	PH	RHP	LHP
1920	CHI	NL	1	0	1	1	0	0	0	0	0	0	0	0	1	0	1	0

Rank among batters: 4,707 • *Total ballparks homered in*: 1 • *First HR*: 09/21/1920 off Joe Oeschger

DeWitt LeBourveau

DEWITT WILEY LEBOURVEAU
B: 08/24/1894 D: 12/09/1947
BL

Year	Tm	Lg	Tot	H	A	Men-On 0	1	2	3	One-Game 2	3	4	LO	XN	IP	PH	RHP	LHP
1920	PHI	NL	3	1	2	2	1	0	0	0	0	0	1	0	1	0	3	0
1921	PHI	NL	6	4	2	2	4	0	0	1	0	0	0	0	0	0	6	0
1922	PHI	NL	2	2	0	0	2	0	0	0	0	0	0	0	0	2	2	0
Total			11	7	4	4	7	0	0	1	0	0	1	0	1	2	11	0

Rank among batters: 2,419 • *Top target (2 home runs)*: Phil Douglas, Bill Doak • *Number of pitchers victimized*: 9 • *Total ballparks homered in*: 4 • *First HR*: 05/02/1920 off Burleigh Grimes

Bill Lee

WILLIAM CRUTCHER LEE
B: 10/21/1909 D: 06/15/1977
BR

Year	Tm	Lg	Tot	H	A	Men-On 0	1	2	3	One-Game 2	3	4	LO	XN	IP	PH	RHP	LHP
1936	CHI	NL	1	1	0	1	0	0	0	0	0	0	0	0	0	0	0	1
1937	CHI	NL	1	1	0	1	0	0	0	0	0	0	0	0	0	0	1	0
1939	CHI	NL	1	0	1	1	0	0	0	0	0	0	0	0	0	0	1	0

Bill Lee *continued*

Year	Tm	Lg	Tot	H	A	Men-On 0	1	2	3	One-Game 2	3	4	LO	XN	IP	PH	RHP	LHP
1941	CHI	NL	2	0	2	1	1	0	0	1	0	0	0	0	0	0	1	1
Total			5	2	3	4	1	0	0	1	0	0	0	0	0	0	3	2

Rank among batters: 3,191 • *Total ballparks homered in*: 3 • *First HR*: 08/21/1936 off Bill Hallahan

Bill Lee

WILLIAM FRANCIS LEE
B: 12/28/1946
BL

Year	Tm	Lg	Tot	H	A	Men-On 0	1	2	3	One-Game 2	3	4	LO	XN	IP	PH	RHP	LHP
1972	BOS	AL	1	0	1	1	0	0	0	0	0	0	0	0	0	0	1	0
1981	MON	NL	1	1	0	1	0	0	0	0	0	0	0	0	0	0	1	0
Total			2	1	1	2	0	0	0	0	0	0	0	0	0	0	2	0

Rank among batters: 4,129 • *Total ballparks homered in*: 2 • *First HR*: 09/11/1972 off Ray Lamb

Bob Lee

ROBERT DEAN LEE
B: 11/26/1937
BR

Year	Tm	Lg	Tot	H	A	Men-On 0	1	2	3	One-Game 2	3	4	LO	XN	IP	PH	RHP	LHP
1965	CAL	AL	1	1	0	1	0	0	0	0	0	0	0	0	0	0	1	0

Rank among batters: 4,707 • *Total ballparks homered in*: 1 • *First HR*: 05/22/1965 off Eddie Fisher

Cliff Lee

CLIFFORD WALKER LEE
B: 08/04/1896 D: 04/25/1980
BR

Year	Tm	Lg	Tot	H	A	Men-On 0	1	2	3	One-Game 2	3	4	LO	XN	IP	PH	RHP	LHP
1921	PHI	NL	4	2	2	1	2	1	0	0	0	0	0	0	0	0	3	1
1922	PHI	NL	17	17	0	6	6	5	0	3	0	0	0	0	2	0	9	8
1923	PHI	NL	11	9	2	6	5	0	0	2	0	0	0	0	1	1	6	5
1924	PHI	NL	1	1	0	1	0	0	0	0	0	0	0	0	0	1	1	0
1925	CLE	AL	4	3	1	1	3	0	0	0	0	0	0	0	0	0	0	4
1926	CLE	AL	1	1	0	1	0	0	0	0	0	0	0	0	1	0	1	0
Total			38	33	5	16	16	6	0	5	0	0	0	0	4	2	20	18

Rank among batters: 1,225 • *Top target (3 home runs)*: Art Nehf, Pete Donohue, Rube Marquard • *Number of pitchers victimized*: 29 • *Total ballparks homered in*: 5 • *First HR*: 06/07/1921 off Buck Freeman

Don Lee

DONALD EDWARD LEE
B: 02/26/1934
BR

Year	Tm	Lg	Tot	H	A	Men-On 0	1	2	3	One-Game 2	3	4	LO	XN	IP	PH	RHP	LHP
1960	WAS	AL	1	0	1	1	0	0	0	0	0	0	0	0	0	0	1	0

Rank among batters: 4,707 • *Total ballparks homered in*: 1 • *First HR*: 08/09/1960 off Johnny Kucks

Hal Lee

HAROLD BURNHAM LEE
B: 02/15/1905 D: 09/04/1989
BR

Year	Tm	Lg	Tot	H	A	Men-On 0	1	2	3	One-Game 2	3	4	LO	XN	IP	PH	RHP	LHP
1930	BRO	NL	1	1	0	0	0	1	0	0	0	0	0	0	0	1	0	1
1931	PHI	NL	2	1	1	1	1	0	0	0	0	0	0	0	0	0	0	2
1932	PHI	NL	18	10	8	13	4	1	0	2	0	0	0	0	0	0	14	4
1933	BOS	NL	1	0	1	0	0	1	0	0	0	0	0	0	0	0	0	1
1934	BOS	NL	8	3	5	3	3	2	0	0	1	0	0	0	0	0	6	2
1936	BOS	NL	3	0	3	0	0	3	0	0	0	0	0	0	0	0	2	1
Total			33	15	18	17	8	8	0	2	1	0	0	0	0	1	22	11

Rank among batters: 1,336 • *Top target (3 home runs)*: Van Mungo • *Number of pitchers victimized*: 27 • *Total ballparks homered in*: 7 • *First HR*: 07/21/1930 off Al Grabowski

Leron Lee

LERON LEE
B: 03/04/1948
BL

Year	Tm	Lg	Tot	H	A	Men-On 0	1	2	3	One-Game 2	3	4	LO	XN	IP	PH	RHP	LHP
1970	STL	NL	6	3	3	4	1	1	0	0	0	0	0	0	0	0	6	0
1971	STL	NL	1	1	0	1	0	0	0	0	0	0	0	0	0	0	1	0
	SD	NL	4	2	2	2	2	0	0	0	0	0	0	0	0	0	4	0

Leron Lee *continued*

Year	Tm	Lg	Tot	H	A	Men-On 0	1	2	3	One-Game 2	3	4	LO	XN	IP	PH	RHP	LHP
1971	Total		5	3	2	3	2	0	0	0	0	0	0	0	0	0	5	0
1972	SD	NL	12	6	6	8	3	1	0	0	0	0	0	0	0	0	10	2
1973	SD	NL	3	0	3	1	2	0	0	0	0	0	0	0	0	0	3	0
1974	CLE	AL	5	5	0	3	1	0	1	1	0	0	0	0	0	0	3	2
Total			31	17	14	19	9	2	1	1	0	0	0	0	0	0	27	4

Rank among batters: 1,400 • Top target (2 home runs): Steve Renko, Bob Moose, Jack Billingham, Bruce Dal Canton • *Number of pitchers victimized*: 27 • *Total ballparks homered in*: 9 • *First HR*: 04/22/1970 off Ferguson Jenkins

Manuel Lee

MANUEL LORA LEE
B: 06/17/1965
BB

Year	Tm	Lg	Tot	H	A	Men-On 0	1	2	3	One-Game 2	3	4	LO	XN	IP	PH	RHP	LHP
1986	TOR	AL	1	1	0	1	0	0	0	0	0	0	0	0	0	0	1	0
1987	TOR	AL	1	0	1	0	0	1	0	0	0	0	0	0	0	0	1	0
1988	TOR	AL	2	2	0	2	0	0	0	0	0	0	0	0	0	0	0	2
1989	TOR	AL	3	1	2	1	1	1	0	0	0	0	0	0	0	0	2	1
1990	TOR	AL	6	2	4	5	1	0	0	0	0	0	0	0	0	0	0	6
1992	TOR	AL	3	1	2	2	1	0	0	0	0	0	0	0	0	0	3	0
1993	TEX	AL	1	0	1	0	1	0	0	0	0	0	0	0	0	0	1	0
1994	TEX	AL	2	1	1	0	0	2	0	0	0	0	0	0	0	0	2	0
Total			19	8	11	11	4	4	0	0	0	0	0	0	0	0	10	9

Rank among batters: 1,861 • *Top target (2 home runs)*: Mike Smithson, Brian Dubois, Curt Young • *Number of pitchers victimized*: 16 • *Total ballparks homered in*: 12 • *First HR*: 08/29/1986 off Mike Smithson

Thornton Lee

THORNTON STARR LEE
B: 09/13/1906
BL

Year	Tm	Lg	Tot	H	A	Men-On 0	1	2	3	One-Game 2	3	4	LO	XN	IP	PH	RHP	LHP
1938	CHI	AL	4	1	3	4	0	0	0	0	0	0	0	0	0	0	4	0

Rank among batters: 3,427 • *Top target (2 home runs)*: Wes Ferrell • *Number of pitchers victimized*: 3 • *Total ballparks homered in*: 3 • *First HR*: 06/07/1938 off Red Ruffing

Watty Lee

WYATT ARNOLD LEE
B: 08/12/1879 D: 03/06/1936
BL

Year	Tm	Lg	Tot	H	A	Men-On 0	1	2	3	One-Game 2	3	4	LO	XN	IP	PH	RHP	LHP
1902	WAS	AL	4	1	3	0	2	2	0	0	0	0	0	0	0	0	3	1

Rank among batters: 3,427 • *Total ballparks homered in*: 3 • *First HR*: 07/04/1902 off Rube Waddell

Gene Leek

EUGENE HAROLD LEEK
B: 07/15/1936
BR

Year	Tm	Lg	Tot	H	A	Men-On 0	1	2	3	One-Game 2	3	4	LO	XN	IP	PH	RHP	LHP
1959	CLE	AL	1	0	1	0	1	0	0	0	0	0	0	0	0	0	1	0
1961	LA	AL	5	4	1	5	0	0	0	0	0	0	0	1	0	0	3	2
Total			6	4	2	5	1	0	0	0	0	0	0	1	0	0	4	2

Rank among batters: 2,988 • *Total ballparks homered in*: 3 • *First HR*: 04/22/1959 off George Susce

Sam Leever

SAMUEL LEEVER
B: 12/23/1871 D: 05/19/1953
BR

Year	Tm	Lg	Tot	H	A	Men-On 0	1	2	3	One-Game 2	3	4	LO	XN	IP	PH	RHP	LHP
1900	PIT	NL	1	0	1	1	0	0	0	0	0	0	0	0	0	0	1	0
1904	PIT	NL	1	0	1	0	1	0	0	0	0	0	0	0	0	0	1	0
Total			2	0	2	1	1	0	0	0	0	0	0	0	0	0	2	0

Rank among batters: 4,129 • *Total ballparks homered in*: 1 • *First HR*: 07/28/1900 off Kid Nichols

Bill LeFebvre

WILFRED HENRY LEFEBVRE
B: 11/11/1915
BL

Year	Tm	Lg	Tot	H	A	Men-On 0	1	2	3	One-Game 2	3	4	LO	XN	IP	PH	RHP	LHP
1938	BOS	AL	1	1	0	1	0	0	0	0	0	0	0	0	0	0	1	0

Rank among batters: 4,707 • *Total ballparks homered in*: 1 • *First HR*: 06/10/1938 off Monty Stratton • *Hit HR on first major league pitch*—vs CHI: 06/10/1938

Jim Lefebvre

JAMES KENNETH LEFEBVRE
B: 01/07/1942
BB

Year	Tm	Lg	Tot	H	A	Men-On 0	1	2	3	One-Game 2	3	4	LO	XN	IP	PH	RHP	LHP
1965	LA	NL	12	3	9	9	3	0	0	0	0	0	0	0	0	0	4	8
1966	LA	NL	24	11	13	17	5	2	0	3	0	0	0	1	1	0	13	11
1967	LA	NL	8	3	5	5	2	1	0	0	0	0	0	0	0	0	1	7
1968	LA	NL	5	1	4	2	1	2	0	0	0	0	0	0	0	0	2	3
1969	LA	NL	4	3	1	2	1	1	0	0	0	0	0	0	0	0	1	3
1970	LA	NL	4	1	3	1	2	1	0	0	0	0	0	0	0	0	2	2
1971	LA	NL	12	5	7	4	5	3	0	0	0	0	0	0	0	0	8	4
1972	LA	NL	5	3	2	2	1	2	0	0	0	0	0	0	0	1	3	2
Total			74	30	44	42	20	12	0	3	0	0	0	1	1	1	34	40

Rank among batters: 707 • *Top target (3 home runs)*: Wade Blasingame, Jim Bunning, Mike McCormick • *Number of pitchers victimized*: 53 • *Total ballparks homered in*: 13 • *First HR*: 04/24/1965 off Bo Belinsky • *Switch hit HR in 1 game*—1 time • *World Series HR*—1

Joe Lefebvre

JOSEPH HENRY LEFEBVRE
B: 02/22/1956
BL

Year	Tm	Lg	Tot	H	A	Men-On 0	1	2	3	One-Game 2	3	4	LO	XN	IP	PH	RHP	LHP
1980	NY	AL	8	4	4	6	1	1	0	1	0	0	0	0	0	1	8	0
1981	SD	NL	8	0	8	5	1	2	0	1	0	0	0	0	0	2	7	1
1982	SD	NL	4	2	2	3	1	0	0	0	0	0	0	1	0	1	4	0
1983	PHI	NL	8	5	3	5	1	1	1	0	0	0	0	0	0	2	8	0
1984	PHI	NL	3	1	2	1	2	0	0	0	0	0	0	0	0	0	3	0
Total			31	12	19	20	6	4	1	2	0	0	0	1	0	6	30	1

Rank among batters: 1,400 • *Top target (2 home runs)*: Dennis Eckersley, Rick Rhoden • *Number of pitchers victimized*: 29 • *Total ballparks homered in*: 15 • *First HR*: 05/22/1980 off Dave Stieb

Craig Lefferts

CRAIG LINDSAY LEFFERTS
B: 09/29/1957
BL

Year	Tm	Lg	Tot	H	A	Men-On 0	1	2	3	One-Game 2	3	4	LO	XN	IP	PH	RHP	LHP
1986	SD	NL	1	1	0	1	0	0	0	0	0	0	0	1	0	0	1	0

Rank among batters: 4,707 • *Total ballparks homered in*: 1 • *First HR*: 04/25/1986 off Greg Minton

Ron LeFlore

RONALD LEFLORE
B: 06/16/1948
BR

Year	Tm	Lg	Tot	H	A	Men-On 0	1	2	3	One-Game 2	3	4	LO	XN	IP	PH	RHP	LHP
1974	DET	AL	2	2	0	1	1	0	0	0	0	0	0	0	0	0	1	1
1975	DET	AL	8	4	4	7	1	0	0	0	0	0	1	1	1	0	5	3
1976	DET	AL	4	1	3	1	2	1	0	0	0	0	0	0	0	0	3	1
1977	DET	AL	16	8	8	12	4	0	0	1	0	0	0	0	1	1	5	11
1978	DET	AL	12	5	7	11	0	1	0	0	0	0	2	0	0	0	4	8
1979	DET	AL	9	7	2	6	3	0	0	0	0	0	1	0	0	0	4	5
1980	MON	NL	4	1	3	4	0	0	0	1	0	0	2	0	0	0	4	0
1982	CHI	AL	4	3	1	1	2	0	1	0	0	0	0	0	0	0	3	1
Total			59	31	28	43	13	2	1	2	0	0	6	1	2	1	29	30

Rank among batters: 873 • *Top target (5 home runs)*: Jerry Garvin • *Number of pitchers victimized*: 41 • *Total ballparks homered in*: 13 • *First HR*: 08/12/1974 off Nelson Briles

Mike Lehane

MICHAEL PATRICK LEHANE
B: 04/15/1865
BR

Year	Tm	Lg	Tot	H	A	Men-On 0	1	2	3	One-Game 2	3	4	LO	XN	IP	PH	RHP	LHP
1891	COL	AA	1	1	0	0	0	1	0	0	0	0	0	0	0	0	0	1

Rank among batters: 4,707 • *Total ballparks homered in*: 1 • *First HR*: 08/06/1891 off Frank Foreman

Paul Lehner

PAUL EUGENE LEHNER
B: 07/01/1920 D: 12/27/1967
BL

Year	Tm	Lg	Tot	H	A	Men-On 0	1	2	3	One-Game 2	3	4	LO	XN	IP	PH	RHP	LHP
1947	STL	AL	7	5	2	3	1	2	1	0	0	0	0	1	2	0	7	0
1948	STL	AL	2	1	1	2	0	0	0	0	0	0	0	0	0	0	2	0
1949	STL	AL	3	2	1	1	0	2	0	0	0	0	0	0	0	1	3	0
1950	PHI	AL	9	3	6	4	4	1	0	0	0	0	0	1	0	1	5	4

Paul Lehner *continued*

Year	Tm	Lg	Tot	H	A	Men-On 0	1	2	3	One-Game 2	3	4	LO	XN	IP	PH	RHP	LHP
1951	STL	AL	1	0	1	1	0	0	0	0	0	0	0	0	0	0	1	0
Total			22	11	11	11	5	5	1	0	0	0	0	2	2	2	18	4

Rank among batters: 1,719 • *Top target (2 home runs)*: Bill Wight • *Number of pitchers victimized*: 21 • *Total ballparks homered in*: 7 • *First HR*: 05/16/1947 off Fritz Dorish

Hank Leiber

HENRY EDWARD LEIBER
B: 01/17/1911 D: 11/08/1993
BR

Year	Tm	Lg	Tot	H	A	Men-On 0	1	2	3	One-Game 2	3	4	LO	XN	IP	PH	RHP	LHP
1934	NY	NL	2	2	0	1	1	0	0	0	0	0	0	0	0	0	0	2
1935	NY	NL	22	12	10	9	10	3	0	2	0	0	0	1	0	0	18	4
1936	NY	NL	9	6	3	3	3	2	1	0	0	0	0	0	0	0	3	6
1937	NY	NL	4	3	1	2	2	0	0	0	0	0	0	0	0	0	2	2
1938	NY	NL	12	6	6	6	2	3	1	1	0	0	0	0	0	0	8	4
1939	CHI	NL	24	16	8	15	4	4	1	1	1	0	0	0	0	0	22	2
1940	CHI	NL	17	10	7	5	7	4	1	1	0	0	0	0	0	0	13	4
1941	CHI	NL	7	5	2	2	2	2	1	1	0	0	0	1	0	0	5	2
1942	NY	NL	4	3	1	2	1	1	0	0	0	0	0	0	0	0	2	2
Total			101	63	38	45	32	19	5	6	1	0	0	2	0	0	73	28

Rank among batters: 491 • *Top target (5 home runs)*: Larry French • *Number of pitchers victimized*: 64 • *Total ballparks homered in*: 9 • *First HR*: 07/12/1934 off Larry French • *2 HR in 1 inning*—vs CHI: 08/24/1935

Nemo Leibold

HARRY LORAN LEIBOLD
B: 02/17/1892 D: 02/04/1977
BL

Year	Tm	Lg	Tot	H	A	Men-On 0	1	2	3	One-Game 2	3	4	LO	XN	IP	PH	RHP	LHP
1920	CHI	AL	1	1	0	1	0	0	0	0	0	0	0	0	0	0	1	0
1922	BOS	AL	1	0	1	1	0	0	0	0	0	0	0	0	0	0	1	0
1923	WAS	AL	1	0	1	0	1	0	0	0	0	0	0	0	0	0	1	0
Total			3	1	2	2	1	0	0	0	0	0	0	0	0	0	3	0

Rank among batters: 3,735 • *Total ballparks homered in*: 3 • *First HR*: 07/01/1920 off Elam Vangilder

Scott Leius

SCOTT THOMAS LEIUS
B: 09/24/1965
BR

Year	Tm	Lg	Tot	H	A	Men-On 0	1	2	3	One-Game 2	3	4	LO	XN	IP	PH	RHP	LHP
1990	MIN	AL	1	0	1	1	0	0	0	0	0	0	0	0	0	0	0	1
1991	MIN	AL	5	2	3	4	1	0	0	0	0	0	0	1	0	0	2	3
1992	MIN	AL	2	2	0	2	0	0	0	0	0	0	0	0	0	0	2	0
1994	MIN	AL	14	7	7	10	3	1	0	0	0	0	0	0	0	0	14	0
1995	MIN	AL	4	2	2	2	0	2	0	0	0	0	0	0	0	0	3	1
Total			26	13	13	19	4	3	0	0	0	0	0	1	0	0	21	5

Rank among batters: 1,576 • *Total ballparks homered in*: 8 • *First HR*: 09/10/1990 off Jim Abbott • *World Series HR*—1

Jack Lelivelt

JOHN FRANK LELIVELT
B: 11/14/1885 D: 01/20/1941
BL

Year	Tm	Lg	Tot	H	A	Men-On 0	1	2	3	One-Game 2	3	4	LO	XN	IP	PH	RHP	LHP
1912	NY	AL	2	2	0	1	1	0	0	1	0	0	0	0	0	0	2	0

Rank among batters: 4,129 • *Top target (2 home runs)*: Tom Hughes • *Number of pitchers victimized*: 1 • *Total ballparks homered in*: 1 • *First HR*: 10/05/1912 off Tom Hughes

Denny Lemaster

DENVER CLAYTON LEMASTER
B: 02/25/1939
BR

Year	Tm	Lg	Tot	H	A	Men-On 0	1	2	3	One-Game 2	3	4	LO	XN	IP	PH	RHP	LHP
1963	MIL	NL	2	2	0	2	0	0	0	0	0	0	0	0	0	0	1	1
1969	HOU	NL	1	0	1	1	0	0	0	0	0	0	0	0	0	0	0	1
1970	HOU	NL	1	0	1	1	0	0	0	0	0	0	0	0	0	0	1	0
Total			4	2	2	4	0	0	0	0	0	0	0	0	0	0	2	2

Rank among batters: 3,427 • *Total ballparks homered in*: 3 • *First HR*: 06/15/1963 off John Boozer

Johnnie LeMaster

JOHNNIE LEE LEMASTER
B: 06/19/1954
BR

Year	Tm	Lg	Tot	H	A	Men-On 0	1	2	3	One-Game 2	3	4	LO	XN	IP	PH	RHP	LHP
1975	SF	NL	2	1	1	1	1	0	0	0	0	0	0	0	1	0	2	0
1978	SF	NL	1	0	1	0	1	0	0	0	0	0	0	0	0	0	1	0
1979	SF	NL	3	2	1	0	2	1	0	0	0	0	0	0	1	0	1	2
1980	SF	NL	3	0	3	2	1	0	0	0	0	0	0	0	0	0	1	2
1982	SF	NL	2	1	1	1	1	0	0	0	0	0	0	0	0	0	0	2
1983	SF	NL	6	4	2	4	1	1	0	1	0	0	1	0	0	0	4	2
1984	SF	NL	4	1	3	2	1	1	0	0	0	0	0	0	0	0	1	3
1985	PIT	NL	1	0	1	0	1	0	0	0	0	0	0	0	0	0	1	0
Total			22	9	13	10	9	3	0	1	0	0	1	0	2	0	11	11

Rank among batters: 1,719 • *Top target (2 home runs)*: Pete Falcone • *Number of pitchers victimized*: 21 • *Total ballparks homered in*: 9 • *First HR*: 09/02/1975 off Don Sutton • *Hit HR in first major league AB*—vs LA: 09/02/1975

Mark Lemke

MARK ALAN LEMKE
B: 08/13/1965
BB

Year	Tm	Lg	Tot	H	A	Men-On 0	1	2	3	One-Game 2	3	4	LO	XN	IP	PH	RHP	LHP
1989	ATL	NL	2	1	1	1	0	1	0	0	0	0	0	0	0	1	0	2
1991	ATL	NL	2	2	0	2	0	0	0	0	0	0	0	0	0	0	2	0
1992	ATL	NL	6	4	2	6	0	0	0	0	0	0	0	0	0	0	1	5
1993	ATL	NL	7	3	4	5	1	1	0	1	0	0	0	0	0	0	2	5
1994	ATL	NL	3	2	1	1	1	1	0	0	0	0	0	0	0	0	0	3
1995	ATL	NL	5	3	2	4	0	1	0	0	0	0	0	0	1	0	3	2
Total			25	15	10	19	2	4	0	1	0	0	0	0	1	1	8	17

Rank among batters: 1,608 • *Top target (2 home runs)*: Denny Neagle, Curt Schilling • *Number of pitchers victimized*: 23 • *Total ballparks homered in*: 8 • *First HR*: 09/14/1989 off Eric Nolte

Bob Lemon

ROBERT GRANVILLE LEMON
B: 09/22/1920
BL HOF

Year	Tm	Lg	Tot	H	A	Men-On 0	1	2	3	One-Game 2	3	4	LO	XN	IP	PH	RHP	LHP
1946	CLE	AL	1	1	0	1	0	0	0	0	0	0	0	0	0	0	1	0
1947	CLE	AL	2	2	0	2	0	0	0	0	0	0	0	0	0	0	2	0
1948	CLE	AL	5	3	2	3	2	0	0	0	0	0	0	0	0	0	5	0
1949	CLE	AL	7	6	1	3	4	0	0	1	0	0	0	0	0	0	5	2
1950	CLE	AL	6	4	2	3	1	2	0	0	0	0	0	0	0	1	3	3
1951	CLE	AL	3	2	1	2	1	0	0	0	0	0	0	0	0	0	2	1
1952	CLE	AL	2	1	1	1	1	0	0	0	0	0	0	0	0	0	2	0
1953	CLE	AL	2	1	1	2	0	0	0	0	0	0	0	0	0	0	2	0
1954	CLE	AL	2	2	0	1	1	0	0	0	0	0	0	0	0	0	2	0
1955	CLE	AL	1	1	0	1	0	0	0	0	0	0	0	0	0	0	0	1
1956	CLE	AL	5	2	3	2	3	0	0	0	0	0	0	0	0	1	4	1
1957	CLE	AL	1	1	0	1	0	0	0	0	0	0	0	0	0	0	1	0
Total			37	26	11	22	13	2	0	1	0	0	0	0	0	2	29	8

Rank among batters: 1,252 • *Top target (2 home runs)*: Fred Hutchinson, Eddie Lopat, Walt Masterson • *Number of pitchers victimized*: 34 • *Total ballparks homered in*: 8 • *First HR*: 07/29/1946 off Early Wynn

Chet Lemon

CHESTER EARL LEMON
B: 02/12/1955
BR

Year	Tm	Lg	Tot	H	A	Men-On 0	1	2	3	One-Game 2	3	4	LO	XN	IP	PH	RHP	LHP
1976	CHI	AL	4	2	2	1	3	0	0	0	0	0	1	0	0	0	2	2
1977	CHI	AL	19	11	8	9	6	4	0	2	0	0	0	1	0	0	13	6
1978	CHI	AL	13	8	5	9	4	0	0	1	0	0	0	0	0	0	6	7
1979	CHI	AL	17	7	10	6	9	2	0	1	0	0	0	0	0	0	8	9
1980	CHI	AL	11	5	6	8	2	1	0	0	0	0	0	0	0	0	9	2
1981	CHI	AL	9	4	5	4	4	1	0	0	0	0	0	0	0	0	8	1
1982	DET	AL	19	12	7	13	4	2	0	2	0	0	0	0	0	0	13	6
1983	DET	AL	24	14	10	15	5	4	0	1	0	0	0	0	0	0	18	6
1984	DET	AL	20	12	8	12	2	5	1	1	0	0	0	0	0	0	11	9
1985	DET	AL	18	9	9	9	5	4	0	2	0	0	0	0	0	0	10	8
1986	DET	AL	12	7	5	6	4	2	0	1	0	0	0	0	0	0	5	7
1987	DET	AL	20	10	10	12	4	4	0	2	0	0	0	0	0	0	12	8
1988	DET	AL	17	12	5	9	5	3	0	2	0	0	0	0	0	0	8	9

Year	Tm	Lg	Tot	H	A	Men-On 0	1	2	3	One-Game 2	3	4	LO	XN	IP	PH	RHP	LHP

Chet Lemon *continued*

Year	Tm	Lg	Tot	H	A	0	1	2	3	2	3	4	LO	XN	IP	PH	RHP	LHP
1989	DET	AL	7	4	3	2	4	1	0	0	0	0	0	0	0	0	2	5
1990	DET	AL	5	2	3	5	0	0	0	1	0	0	0	0	0	0	2	3
Total			215	119	96	120	61	33	1	16	0	0	1	1	0	0	127	88

Rank among batters: 158 • *Top target (6 home runs)*: Frank Tanana • *Number of pitchers victimized*: 162 • *Total ballparks homered in*: 16 • *First HR*: 05/17/1976 off Frank Tanana • *LCS HR*—2

Jim Lemon

JAMES ROBERT LEMON
B: 03/23/1928
BR

Year	Tm	Lg	Tot	H	A	0	1	2	3	2	3	4	LO	XN	IP	PH	RHP	LHP
1950	CLE	AL	1	1	0	1	0	0	0	0	0	0	0	0	0	0	0	1
1953	CLE	AL	1	0	1	0	1	0	0	0	0	0	0	0	0	0	1	0
1954	WAS	AL	2	0	2	1	1	0	0	0	0	0	0	0	0	0	2	0
1955	WAS	AL	1	1	0	0	1	0	0	0	0	0	0	0	0	1	0	1
1956	WAS	AL	27	21	6	15	9	3	0	1	1	0	0	0	0	0	17	10
1957	WAS	AL	17	12	5	12	4	1	0	0	0	0	0	1	0	0	14	3
1958	WAS	AL	26	11	15	20	5	1	0	2	0	0	0	0	0	0	19	7
1959	WAS	AL	33	21	12	17	12	2	2	2	0	0	0	2	0	0	27	6
1960	WAS	AL	38	22	16	17	15	6	0	3	0	0	0	1	0	0	31	7
1961	MIN	AL	14	9	5	11	3	0	0	1	0	0	0	0	0	0	13	1
1962	MIN	AL	1	0	1	0	1	0	0	0	0	0	0	0	0	1	1	0
1963	PHI	NL	2	2	0	1	1	0	0	0	0	0	0	0	0	1	1	1
	CHI	AL	1	0	1	0	0	1	0	0	0	0	0	0	0	0	0	1
	Total		3	2	1	1	1	1	0	0	0	0	0	0	0	1	1	2
Total			164	100	64	95	53	14	2	9	1	0	0	4	0	3	126	38

Rank among batters: 250 • *Top target (7 home runs)*: Whitey Ford • *Number of pitchers victimized*: 83 • *Total ballparks homered in*: 11 • *First HR*: 09/16/1950 off Al Sima • *2 HR in 1 inning*—vs BOS: 09/05/1959

Don Lenhardt

DONALD EUGENE LENHARDT
B: 10/04/1922
BR

Year	Tm	Lg	Tot	H	A	0	1	2	3	2	3	4	LO	XN	IP	PH	RHP	LHP
1950	STL	AL	22	9	13	11	8	2	1	0	0	0	1	0	0	0	16	6
1951	STL	AL	5	1	4	2	2	1	0	1	0	0	0	0	0	0	2	3
	CHI	AL	10	3	7	3	4	3	0	0	0	0	0	0	0	0	5	5
	Total		15	4	11	5	6	4	0	1	0	0	0	0	0	0	7	8
1952	BOS	AL	7	6	1	4	0	1	2	0	0	0	0	1	1	0	6	1
	DET	AL	3	1	2	0	2	0	1	0	0	0	0	0	0	0	1	2
	STL	AL	1	0	1	0	1	0	0	0	0	0	0	0	1	0	1	0
	Total		11	7	4	4	3	1	3	0	0	0	0	1	2	0	8	3
1953	STL	AL	10	3	7	7	1	2	0	0	0	0	0	0	0	0	3	7
1954	BOS	AL	3	2	1	2	1	0	0	0	0	0	0	0	0	1	2	1
Total			61	25	36	29	19	9	4	1	0	0	1	1	2	1	36	25

Rank among batters: 844 • *Top target (4 home runs)*: Bob Hooper • *Number of pitchers victimized*: 44 • *Total ballparks homered in*: 7 • *First HR*: 04/19/1950 off Bill Connelly

Bob Lennon

ROBERT ALBERT LENNON
B: 09/15/1928
BL

Year	Tm	Lg	Tot	H	A	0	1	2	3	2	3	4	LO	XN	IP	PH	RHP	LHP
1957	CHI	NL	1	0	1	0	0	1	0	0	0	0	0	0	0	0	1	0

Rank among batters: 4,707 • *Total ballparks homered in*: 1 • *First HR*: 04/30/1957 off Sal Maglie

Ed Lennox

JAMES EDGAR LENNOX
B: 11/03/1885 D: 10/26/1939
BR

Year	Tm	Lg	Tot	H	A	0	1	2	3	2	3	4	LO	XN	IP	PH	RHP	LHP
1909	BRO	NL	2	1	1	2	0	0	0	0	0	0	0	0	2	0	2	0
1910	BRO	NL	3	0	3	2	1	0	0	0	0	0	0	0	0	0	1	2
1912	CHI	NL	1	1	0	1	0	0	0	0	0	0	0	0	0	0	1	0
1914	PIT	FL	11	1	10	7	3	1	0	2	0	0	0	0	0	0	7	4
1915	PIT	FL	1	0	1	1	0	0	0	0	0	0	0	0	0	1	0	1
Total			18	3	15	13	4	1	0	2	0	0	0	0	2	1	11	7

Rank among batters: 1,914 • *Top target (2 home runs)*: Nick Cullop • *Number of pitchers victimized*: 17 • *Total ballparks homered in*: 11 • *First HR*: 07/07/1909 off Tom McCarthy • *Hit for Cycle*—@KC: 05/06/1914

Jim Lentine

JAMES MATTHEW LENTINE
B: 07/16/1954
BR

Year	Tm	Lg	Tot	H	A	Men-On 0	Men-On 1	Men-On 2	Men-On 3	One-Game 2	One-Game 3	One-Game 4	LO	XN	IP	PH	RHP	LHP
1980	DET	AL	1	0	1	1	0	0	0	0	0	0	1	0	0	0	0	1

Rank among batters: 4,707 • *Total ballparks homered in*: 1 • *First HR*: 06/08/1980 off Bill Travers

Eddie Leon

EDUARDO ANTONIO LEON
B: 08/11/1946
BR

Year	Tm	Lg	Tot	H	A	Men-On 0	Men-On 1	Men-On 2	Men-On 3	One-Game 2	One-Game 3	One-Game 4	LO	XN	IP	PH	RHP	LHP
1969	CLE	AL	3	1	2	2	0	1	0	0	0	0	0	0	0	0	2	1
1970	CLE	AL	10	9	1	9	1	0	0	0	0	0	0	0	0	0	8	2
1971	CLE	AL	4	3	1	2	1	1	0	0	0	0	0	0	0	0	3	1
1972	CLE	AL	4	4	0	2	0	2	0	0	0	0	0	0	0	0	3	1
1973	CHI	AL	3	1	2	2	1	0	0	0	0	0	0	0	0	0	0	3
Total			24	18	6	17	3	4	0	0	0	0	0	0	0	0	16	8

Rank among batters: 1,643 • *Top target (3 home runs)*: Chuck Dobson • *Number of pitchers victimized*: 20 • *Total ballparks homered in*: 6 • *First HR*: 07/29/1969 off Jerry Nyman

Andy Leonard

ANDREW JACKSON LEONARD
B: 06/01/1846 D: 08/21/1903
BR

Year	Tm	Lg	Tot	H	A	Men-On 0	Men-On 1	Men-On 2	Men-On 3	One-Game 2	One-Game 3	One-Game 4	LO	XN	IP	PH	RHP	LHP
1880	CIN	NL	1	1	0	1	0	0	0	0	0	0	0	0	0	0	1	0

Rank among batters: 4,707 • *Total ballparks homered in*: 1 • *First HR*: 05/24/1880 off Jim Galvin

Jeffrey Leonard

JEFFREY LEONARD
B: 09/22/1955
BR

Year	Tm	Lg	Tot	H	A	Men-On 0	Men-On 1	Men-On 2	Men-On 3	One-Game 2	One-Game 3	One-Game 4	LO	XN	IP	PH	RHP	LHP
1980	HOU	NL	3	3	0	2	1	0	0	0	0	0	0	0	0	1	0	3
1981	SF	NL	4	0	4	3	1	0	0	0	0	0	0	0	0	0	2	2
1982	SF	NL	9	4	5	3	3	2	1	0	0	0	0	0	0	0	7	2
1983	SF	NL	21	9	12	14	5	1	1	1	0	0	0	1	0	0	10	11
1984	SF	NL	21	13	8	10	7	3	1	0	0	0	0	0	0	0	8	13
1985	SF	NL	17	8	9	10	6	1	0	2	0	0	0	0	0	0	10	7
1986	SF	NL	6	2	4	2	1	3	0	0	0	0	0	1	0	1	3	3
1987	SF	NL	19	9	10	13	5	1	0	2	0	0	0	1	0	2	14	5
1988	SF	NL	2	0	2	1	1	0	0	0	0	0	0	0	0	0	1	1
	MIL	AL	8	5	3	3	3	1	1	0	0	0	0	0	0	0	5	3
	Total		10	5	5	4	4	1	1	0	0	0	0	0	0	0	6	4
1989	SEA	AL	24	9	15	14	3	5	2	1	0	0	0	1	0	0	16	8
1990	SEA	AL	10	7	3	3	5	2	0	2	0	0	0	0	0	0	4	6
Total			144	69	75	78	41	19	6	8	0	0	0	4	0	4	80	64

Rank among batters: 306 • *Top target (4 home runs)*: Jerry Reuss • *Number of pitchers victimized*: 114 • *Total ballparks homered in*: 24 • *First HR*: 04/25/1980 off Pete Falcone • *Hit for Cycle*—@CIN: 06/27/1985 • *LCS HR*—4

Joe Leonard

JOSEPH HOWARD LEONARD
B: 11/15/1894 D: 05/01/1920
BL

Year	Tm	Lg	Tot	H	A	Men-On 0	Men-On 1	Men-On 2	Men-On 3	One-Game 2	One-Game 3	One-Game 4	LO	XN	IP	PH	RHP	LHP
1919	WAS	AL	2	1	1	1	1	0	0	0	0	0	0	0	1	0	2	0

Rank among batters: 4,129 • *Total ballparks homered in*: 2 • *First HR*: 07/05/1919 off Bob McGraw

Mark Leonard

MARK DAVID LEONARD
B: 08/14/1964
BL

Year	Tm	Lg	Tot	H	A	Men-On 0	Men-On 1	Men-On 2	Men-On 3	One-Game 2	One-Game 3	One-Game 4	LO	XN	IP	PH	RHP	LHP
1990	SF	NL	1	0	1	1	0	0	0	0	0	0	0	0	0	0	1	0
1991	SF	NL	2	0	2	1	1	0	0	0	0	0	0	0	0	0	2	0
1992	SF	NL	4	3	1	1	3	0	0	0	0	0	0	0	0	1	4	0
1995	SF	NL	1	1	0	0	0	1	0	0	0	0	0	0	0	0	1	0
Total			8	4	4	3	4	1	0	0	0	0	0	0	0	1	8	0

Rank among batters: 2,703 • *Top target (2 home runs)*: Frank Castillo • *Number of pitchers victimized*: 7 • *Total ballparks homered in*: 4 • *First HR*: 09/21/1990 off Mike Morgan

Ted Lepcio

THADDEUS STANLEY LEPCIO
B: 07/28/1930
BR

Year	Tm	Lg	Tot	H	A	Men-On 0	1	2	3	One-Game 2	3	4	LO	XN	IP	PH	RHP	LHP
1952	BOS	AL	5	3	2	5	0	0	0	0	0	0	0	1	0	0	4	1
1953	BOS	AL	4	3	1	3	1	0	0	0	0	0	0	0	0	0	3	1
1954	BOS	AL	8	4	4	3	3	1	1	0	0	0	0	0	0	0	7	1
1955	BOS	AL	6	3	3	3	2	1	0	1	0	0	0	0	0	0	6	0
1956	BOS	AL	15	10	5	9	3	3	0	1	0	0	0	1	0	0	12	3
1957	BOS	AL	9	4	5	5	3	1	0	0	0	0	0	0	0	0	5	4
1958	BOS	AL	6	1	5	4	1	1	0	0	0	0	0	1	0	1	5	1
1959	DET	AL	7	4	3	2	3	1	1	0	0	0	0	0	0	0	7	0
1960	PHI	NL	2	2	0	2	0	0	0	0	0	0	0	0	0	0	0	2
1961	MIN	AL	7	2	5	3	2	1	1	0	0	0	0	0	0	0	7	0
Total			69	36	33	39	18	9	3	2	0	0	0	3	0	1	56	13

Rank among batters: 756 • *Top target (3 home runs)*: Early Wynn, Frank Lary • *Number of pitchers victimized*: 53 • *Total ballparks homered in*: 9 • *First HR*: 04/19/1952 off Morrie Martin

Pete LePine

LOUIS JOSEPH LEPINE
B: 09/05/1876 D: 12/03/1949
BL

Year	Tm	Lg	Tot	H	A	Men-On 0	1	2	3	One-Game 2	3	4	LO	XN	IP	PH	RHP	LHP
1902	DET	AL	1	1	0	1	0	0	0	0	0	0	0	0	0	0	0	1

Rank among batters: 4,707 • *Total ballparks homered in*: 1 • *First HR*: 09/10/1902 off Charlie Shields

Don Leppert

DONALD GEORGE LEPPERT
B: 10/19/1931
BL

Year	Tm	Lg	Tot	H	A	Men-On 0	1	2	3	One-Game 2	3	4	LO	XN	IP	PH	RHP	LHP
1961	PIT	NL	3	3	0	2	1	0	0	0	0	0	0	0	0	0	1	2
1962	PIT	NL	3	1	2	2	1	0	0	0	0	0	0	0	0	0	2	1
1963	WAS	AL	6	4	2	4	0	2	0	0	1	0	0	0	0	0	1	5
1964	WAS	AL	3	1	2	2	1	0	0	0	0	0	0	0	0	0	1	2
Total			15	9	6	10	3	2	0	0	1	0	0	0	0	0	5	10

Rank among batters: 2,096 • *Top target (2 home runs)*: Chet Nichols, Hank Aguirre • *Number of pitchers victimized*: 13 • *Total ballparks homered in*: 8 • *First HR*: 06/18/1961 off Curt Simmons • *Hit HR in first major league AB*—vs STL: 06/18/1961 (1)

Randy Lerch

RANDY LOUIS LERCH
B: 10/09/1954
BL

Year	Tm	Lg	Tot	H	A	Men-On 0	1	2	3	One-Game 2	3	4	LO	XN	IP	PH	RHP	LHP
1978	PHI	NL	3	1	2	2	1	0	0	1	0	0	0	0	0	0	2	1
1979	PHI	NL	1	0	1	1	0	0	0	0	0	0	0	0	0	0	1	0
Total			4	1	3	3	1	0	0	1	0	0	0	0	0	0	3	1

Rank among batters: 3,427 • *Top target (2 home runs)*: Don Robinson • *Number of pitchers victimized*: 3 • *Total ballparks homered in*: 3 • *First HR*: 04/24/1978 off Woodie Fryman

George Lerchen

GEORGE EDWARD LERCHEN
B: 12/01/1922
BB

Year	Tm	Lg	Tot	H	A	Men-On 0	1	2	3	One-Game 2	3	4	LO	XN	IP	PH	RHP	LHP
1952	DET	AL	1	0	1	1	0	0	0	0	0	0	0	0	0	0	1	0

Rank among batters: 4,707 • *Total ballparks homered in*: 1 • *First HR*: 05/06/1952 off Connie Marrero

Walt Lerian

WALTER IRVIN LERIAN
B: 02/10/1903 D: 10/22/1929
BR

Year	Tm	Lg	Tot	H	A	Men-On 0	1	2	3	One-Game 2	3	4	LO	XN	IP	PH	RHP	LHP
1928	PHI	NL	2	1	1	1	0	1	0	0	0	0	0	0	0	1	2	0
1929	PHI	NL	6	2	4	4	1	1	0	0	0	0	0	0	0	0	6	0
Total			8	3	5	5	1	2	0	0	0	0	0	0	0	1	8	0

Rank among batters: 2,703 • *Total ballparks homered in*: 5 • *First HR*: 06/27/1928 off Vic Aldridge

Roy Leslie

ROY REID LESLIE
B: 08/23/1894 D: 04/09/1972
BR

Year	Tm	Lg	Tot	H	A	Men-On 0	1	2	3	One-Game 2	3	4	LO	XN	IP	PH	RHP	LHP
1922	PHI	NL	6	6	0	1	4	1	0	0	0	0	0	0	0	1	5	1

Rank among batters: 2,988 • *Total ballparks homered in*: 1 • *First HR*: 05/25/1922 off Burleigh Grimes

Sam Leslie

SAMUEL ANDREW LESLIE
B: 07/26/1905 D: 01/21/1979
BL

Year	Tm	Lg	Tot	H	A	Men-On 0	1	2	3	One-Game 2	3	4	LO	XN	IP	PH	RHP	LHP
1931	NY	NL	3	2	1	3	0	0	0	0	0	0	0	0	0	2	3	0
1932	NY	NL	1	1	0	1	0	0	0	0	0	0	0	0	0	1	1	0
1933	NY	NL	3	2	1	1	0	2	0	0	0	0	0	0	0	0	3	0
	BRO	NL	5	1	4	3	1	1	0	0	0	0	0	0	0	0	4	1
	Total		8	3	5	4	1	3	0	0	0	0	0	0	0	0	7	1
1934	BRO	NL	9	4	5	6	1	1	1	0	0	0	0	0	1	0	7	2
1935	BRO	NL	5	2	3	4	1	0	0	0	0	0	0	0	0	0	5	0
1936	NY	NL	6	5	1	2	4	0	0	0	0	0	0	0	0	0	5	1
1937	NY	NL	3	2	1	1	1	1	0	0	0	0	0	0	0	0	3	0
1938	NY	NL	1	1	0	1	0	0	0	0	0	0	0	0	0	0	0	1
Total			36	20	16	22	8	5	1	0	0	0	0	0	1	3	31	5

Rank among batters: 1,274 • *Top target (3 home runs)*: Phil Collins, Joe Bowman • *Number of pitchers victimized*: 27 • *Total ballparks homered in*: 6 • *First HR*: 04/25/1931 off Clise Dudley • *Hit for Cycle*—vs PHI: 05/24/1936

Charlie Letchas

CHARLIE LETCHAS
B: 10/03/1915 D: 03/14/1995
BR

Year	Tm	Lg	Tot	H	A	Men-On 0	1	2	3	One-Game 2	3	4	LO	XN	IP	PH	RHP	LHP
1939	PHI	NL	1	1	0	1	0	0	0	0	0	0	0	0	0	0	1	0

Rank among batters: 4,707 • *Total ballparks homered in*: 1 • *First HR*: 09/26/1939 off Jim Turner

Jesse Levan

JESSE ROY LEVAN
B: 07/15/1926
BL

Year	Tm	Lg	Tot	H	A	Men-On 0	1	2	3	One-Game 2	3	4	LO	XN	IP	PH	RHP	LHP
1955	WAS	AL	1	1	0	0	0	1	0	0	0	0	0	0	0	1	1	0

Rank among batters: 4,707 • *Total ballparks homered in*: 1 • *First HR*: 05/08/1955 off Don Johnson

Jim Levey

JAMES JULIUS LEVEY
B: 09/13/1906 D: 03/14/1970
BB

Year	Tm	Lg	Tot	H	A	Men-On 0	1	2	3	One-Game 2	3	4	LO	XN	IP	PH	RHP	LHP
1931	STL	AL	5	2	3	2	1	2	0	0	0	0	1	0	1	0	3	2
1932	STL	AL	4	2	2	2	2	0	0	0	0	0	0	2	0	0	1	3
1933	STL	AL	2	1	1	1	1	0	0	0	0	0	0	0	0	0	1	1
Total			11	5	6	5	4	2	0	0	0	0	1	2	1	0	5	6

Rank among batters: 2,419 • *Total ballparks homered in*: 6 • *First HR*: 04/18/1931 off Tommy Bridges

Charlie Levis

CHARLES H. LEVIS
B: 06/21/1860 D: 10/16/1926
BR

Year	Tm	Lg	Tot	H	A	Men-On 0	1	2	3	One-Game 2	3	4	LO	XN	IP	PH	RHP	LHP
1884	BAL	UA	5	4	1	1	3	1	0	1	0	0	0	0	0	0	1	2

Rank among batters: 3,191 • *Top target (2 home runs)*: Bill Gallagher • *Number of pitchers victimized*: 4 • *Total ballparks homered in*: 2 • *First HR*: 05/05/1884 off Milo Lockwood

Jesse Levis

JESSE LEVIS
B: 04/14/1968
BL

Year	Tm	Lg	Tot	H	A	Men-On 0	1	2	3	One-Game 2	3	4	LO	XN	IP	PH	RHP	LHP
1992	CLE	AL	1	0	1	1	0	0	0	0	0	0	0	0	0	0	1	0

Rank among batters: 4,707 • *Total ballparks homered in*: 1 • *First HR*: 09/26/1992 off Kurt Knudsen

Ed Levy

EDWARD CLARENCE LEVY
B: 10/28/1916
BR

Year	Tm	Lg	Tot	H	A	Men-On 0	Men-On 1	Men-On 2	Men-On 3	One-Game 2	One-Game 3	One-Game 4	LO	XN	IP	PH	RHP	LHP
1944	NY	AL	4	2	2	3	1	0	0	0	0	0	0	0	0	0	3	1

Rank among batters: 3,427 • *Total ballparks homered in*: 3 • *First HR*: 04/19/1944 off Emmett O'Neill

Allan Lewis

ALLAN SYDNEY LEWIS
B: 12/12/1941
BB

Year	Tm	Lg	Tot	H	A	Men-On 0	Men-On 1	Men-On 2	Men-On 3	One-Game 2	One-Game 3	One-Game 4	LO	XN	IP	PH	RHP	LHP
1970	OAK	AL	1	0	1	1	0	0	0	0	0	0	0	0	0	0	0	1

Rank among batters: 4,707 • *Total ballparks homered in*: 1 • *First HR*: 09/27/1970 off Greg Garrett

Bill Lewis

WILLIAM HENRY LEWIS
B: 10/15/1904 D: 10/24/1977
BR

Year	Tm	Lg	Tot	H	A	Men-On 0	Men-On 1	Men-On 2	Men-On 3	One-Game 2	One-Game 3	One-Game 4	LO	XN	IP	PH	RHP	LHP
1933	STL	NL	1	1	0	0	1	0	0	0	0	0	0	0	0	0	1	0

Rank among batters: 4,707 • *Total ballparks homered in*: 1 • *First HR*: 09/13/1933 off Ownie Carroll

Buddy Lewis

JOHN KELLY LEWIS
B: 08/10/1916
BL

Year	Tm	Lg	Tot	H	A	Men-On 0	Men-On 1	Men-On 2	Men-On 3	One-Game 2	One-Game 3	One-Game 4	LO	XN	IP	PH	RHP	LHP
1936	WAS	AL	6	0	6	4	0	2	0	1	0	0	0	0	0	0	6	0
1937	WAS	AL	10	2	8	5	5	0	0	0	0	0	0	0	1	0	7	3
1938	WAS	AL	12	4	8	8	2	2	0	0	0	0	0	0	1	0	11	1
1939	WAS	AL	10	4	6	3	6	1	0	0	0	0	0	0	0	0	6	4
1940	WAS	AL	6	1	5	2	4	0	0	0	0	0	0	0	0	0	5	1
1941	WAS	AL	9	3	6	4	4	1	0	1	0	0	0	0	1	0	8	1
1945	WAS	AL	2	0	2	2	0	0	0	0	0	0	0	0	0	0	1	1
1946	WAS	AL	7	2	5	6	0	1	0	0	0	0	0	1	1	0	5	2
1947	WAS	AL	6	1	5	3	2	1	0	0	0	0	0	0	0	0	4	2
1949	WAS	AL	3	0	3	2	1	0	0	0	0	0	0	0	0	0	2	1
Total			71	17	54	39	24	8	0	2	0	0	0	1	4	0	55	16

Rank among batters: 731 • *Top target (3 home runs)*: Red Ruffing, Harry Eisenstat • *Number of pitchers victimized*: 57 • *Total ballparks homered in*: 9 • *First HR*: 05/13/1936 off Red Evans

Darren Lewis

DARREN JOEL LEWIS
B: 08/28/1967
BR

Year	Tm	Lg	Tot	H	A	Men-On 0	Men-On 1	Men-On 2	Men-On 3	One-Game 2	One-Game 3	One-Game 4	LO	XN	IP	PH	RHP	LHP
1991	SF	NL	1	0	1	1	0	0	0	0	0	0	1	0	0	0	0	1
1992	SF	NL	1	1	0	1	0	0	0	0	0	0	1	0	0	0	0	1
1993	SF	NL	2	2	0	0	2	0	0	0	0	0	0	0	0	0	2	0
1994	SF	NL	4	4	0	3	1	0	0	0	0	0	1	0	0	0	3	1
1995	SF	NL	1	1	0	1	0	0	0	0	0	0	1	0	0	0	1	0
Total			9	8	1	6	3	0	0	0	0	0	4	0	0	0	6	3

Rank among batters: 2,587 • *Total ballparks homered in*: 2 • *First HR*: 08/07/1991 off Charlie Leibrandt

Duffy Lewis

GEORGE EDWARD LEWIS
B: 04/18/1888 D: 06/17/1979
BR

Year	Tm	Lg	Tot	H	A	Men-On 0	Men-On 1	Men-On 2	Men-On 3	One-Game 2	One-Game 3	One-Game 4	LO	XN	IP	PH	RHP	LHP
1910	BOS	AL	8	5	3	3	5	0	0	0	0	0	0	0	1	0	6	2
1911	BOS	AL	7	1	6	5	1	1	0	0	0	0	0	0	2	0	6	1
1912	BOS	AL	6	1	5	4	0	1	1	0	0	0	0	0	2	0	6	0
1914	BOS	AL	2	0	2	0	1	1	0	0	0	0	0	0	1	0	2	0
1915	BOS	AL	2	0	2	1	1	0	0	0	0	0	0	0	1	0	1	1
1916	BOS	AL	1	0	1	0	1	0	0	0	0	0	0	0	0	0	1	0
1917	BOS	AL	1	0	1	1	0	0	0	0	0	0	0	0	0	0	1	0
1919	NY	AL	7	4	3	3	3	1	0	0	0	0	0	0	1	0	7	0
1920	NY	AL	4	2	2	1	1	2	0	0	0	0	0	0	0	0	3	1
Total			38	13	25	18	13	6	1	0	0	0	0	0	8	0	33	5

Duffy Lewis *continued*

Rank among batters: 1,225 • *Top target (3 home runs)*: Jack Warhop • *Number of pitchers victimized*: 34 • *Total ballparks homered in*: 13 • *First HR*: 05/28/1910 off Eddie Plank • *World Series HR*—1

Fred Lewis

FREDERICK MILLER LEWIS
B: 10/13/1858 D: 06/05/1945
BB

Year	Tm	Lg	Tot	H	A	Men-On 0	1	2	3	One-Game 2	3	4	LO	XN	IP	PH	RHP	LHP
1883	STL	AA	1	1	0	0	1	0	0	0	0	0	0	0	0	0	1	0
1885	STL	NL	1	1	0	1	0	0	0	0	0	0	0	0	0	0	1	0
1886	CIN	AA	2	2	0	2	0	0	0	0	0	0	0	0	1	0	0	2
Total			4	4	0	3	1	0	0	0	0	0	0	0	1	0	2	2

Rank among batters: 3,427 • *Total ballparks homered in*: 3 • *First HR*: 09/21/1883 off Bobby Mathews

Jack Lewis

JOHN DAVID LEWIS
B: 02/12/1884 D: 02/25/1956
BR

Year	Tm	Lg	Tot	H	A	Men-On 0	1	2	3	One-Game 2	3	4	LO	XN	IP	PH	RHP	LHP
1914	PIT	FL	1	1	0	1	0	0	0	0	0	0	0	0	0	0	0	1

Rank among batters: 4,707 • *Total ballparks homered in*: 1 • *First HR*: 09/19/1914 off Doc Watson

Johnny Lewis

JOHNNY JOE LEWIS
B: 08/10/1939
BL

Year	Tm	Lg	Tot	H	A	Men-On 0	1	2	3	One-Game 2	3	4	LO	XN	IP	PH	RHP	LHP
1964	STL	NL	2	1	1	2	0	0	0	0	0	0	0	0	0	0	2	0
1965	NY	NL	15	5	10	10	4	1	0	1	0	0	0	1	0	0	12	3
1966	NY	NL	5	3	2	4	1	0	0	0	0	0	0	0	0	0	3	2
Total			22	9	13	16	5	1	0	1	0	0	0	1	0	0	17	5

Rank among batters: 1,719 • *Top target (3 home runs)*: Jim Maloney • *Number of pitchers victimized*: 18 • *Total ballparks homered in*: 9 • *First HR*: 04/18/1964 off Bobby Bolin

Mark Lewis

MARK DAVID LEWIS
B: 11/30/1969
BR

Year	Tm	Lg	Tot	H	A	Men-On 0	1	2	3	One-Game 2	3	4	LO	XN	IP	PH	RHP	LHP
1992	CLE	AL	5	2	3	4	1	0	0	0	0	0	0	0	0	0	3	2
1993	CLE	AL	1	1	0	0	1	0	0	0	0	0	0	0	0	0	1	0
1994	CLE	AL	1	1	0	1	0	0	0	0	0	0	0	0	0	0	0	1
1995	CIN	NL	3	1	2	1	1	1	0	0	0	0	0	0	0	0	1	2
Total			10	5	5	6	3	1	0	0	0	0	0	0	0	0	5	5

Rank among batters: 2,500 • *Total ballparks homered in*: 7 • *First HR*: 04/08/1992 off Bob Milacki • *LCS HR*—1

Phil Lewis

PHILIP LEWIS
B: 10/07/1883 D: 08/08/1959
BR

Year	Tm	Lg	Tot	H	A	Men-On 0	1	2	3	One-Game 2	3	4	LO	XN	IP	PH	RHP	LHP
1905	BRO	NL	3	1	2	1	1	1	0	0	0	0	0	0	1	0	1	2
1908	BRO	NL	1	0	1	0	1	0	0	0	0	0	0	0	1	0	0	1
Total			4	1	3	1	2	1	0	0	0	0	0	0	2	0	1	3

Rank among batters: 3,427 • *Total ballparks homered in*: 4 • *First HR*: 08/12/1905 off Francis Pfeffer

Jim Leyritz

JAMES JOSEPH LEYRITZ
B: 12/27/1963
BR

Year	Tm	Lg	Tot	H	A	Men-On 0	1	2	3	One-Game 2	3	4	LO	XN	IP	PH	RHP	LHP
1990	NY	AL	5	1	4	3	1	1	0	1	0	0	0	0	0	0	3	2
1992	NY	AL	7	3	4	4	2	1	0	0	0	0	0	0	0	0	2	5
1993	NY	AL	14	6	8	6	3	4	1	0	0	0	0	0	0	0	8	6
1994	NY	AL	17	4	13	7	8	1	1	2	0	0	0	1	0	0	11	6
1995	NY	AL	7	3	4	5	1	1	0	0	0	0	0	0	0	0	2	5
Total			50	17	33	25	15	8	2	3	0	0	0	1	0	0	26	24

Rank among batters: 991 • Top target (2 home runs): Wilson Alvarez, Chris Haney, Bobby Thigpen, Carlos Reyes, Jeff Montgomery, Jack Morris, John Cummings • *Number of pitchers victimized*: 43 • *Total ballparks homered in*: 15 • *First HR*: 06/30/1990 off Melido Perez • *LCS HR*—1

Carlos Lezcano

CARLOS MANUEL (RUBIO) LEZCANO
B: 09/30/1955
BR

Year	Tm	Lg	Tot	H	A	Men-On 0	1	2	3	One-Game 2	3	4	LO	XN	IP	PH	RHP	LHP
1980	CHI	NL	3	3	0	1	2	0	0	0	0	0	0	0	0	0	3	0

Rank among batters: 3,735 • *Total ballparks homered in*: 1 • *First HR*: 04/17/1980 off Tom Hausman

Sixto Lezcano

SIXTO JOAQUIN (CURRAS) LEZCANO
B: 11/28/1953
BR

Year	Tm	Lg	Tot	H	A	Men-On 0	1	2	3	One-Game 2	3	4	LO	XN	IP	PH	RHP	LHP
1974	MIL	AL	2	2	0	1	0	1	0	0	0	0	0	0	0	0	0	2
1975	MIL	AL	11	4	7	7	2	2	0	0	0	0	0	0	0	0	7	4
1976	MIL	AL	7	4	3	4	3	0	0	0	0	0	0	0	0	0	7	0
1977	MIL	AL	21	6	15	14	6	1	0	1	0	0	0	1	0	0	17	4
1978	MIL	AL	15	10	5	10	1	2	2	1	0	0	0	0	0	0	12	3
1979	MIL	AL	28	14	14	16	8	4	0	1	0	0	0	1	0	0	19	9
1980	MIL	AL	18	8	10	12	4	1	1	2	0	0	0	0	0	0	11	7
1981	STL	NL	5	2	3	3	2	0	0	0	0	0	0	0	0	0	4	1
1982	SD	NL	16	5	11	9	4	3	0	2	0	0	0	1	0	0	10	6
1983	SD	NL	8	6	2	3	3	2	0	0	0	0	0	0	0	0	5	3
1984	PHI	NL	14	9	5	9	1	4	0	2	0	0	0	0	0	1	9	5
1985	PIT	NL	3	2	1	3	0	0	0	0	0	0	0	0	0	0	0	3
Total			148	72	76	91	34	20	3	9	0	0	0	3	0	1	101	47

Rank among batters: 294 • *Top target (4 home runs)*: Ferguson Jenkins • *Number of pitchers victimized*: 119 • *Total ballparks homered in*: 23 • *First HR*: 09/20/1974 off John Hiller • *LCS HR*—1

Al Libke

ALBERT WALTER LIBKE
B: 09/12/1918
BL

Year	Tm	Lg	Tot	H	A	Men-On 0	1	2	3	One-Game 2	3	4	LO	XN	IP	PH	RHP	LHP
1945	CIN	NL	4	4	0	3	1	0	0	0	0	0	0	0	0	0	4	0
1946	CIN	NL	5	4	1	2	3	0	0	0	0	0	0	0	0	0	5	0
Total			9	8	1	5	4	0	0	0	0	0	0	0	0	0	9	0

Rank among batters: 2,587 • *Top target (2 home runs)*: Hank Wyse • *Number of pitchers victimized*: 8 • *Total ballparks homered in*: 2 • *First HR*: 07/12/1945 off Art Herring

Mike Lieberthal

MICHAEL SCOTT LIEBERTHAL
B: 01/18/1972
BR

Year	Tm	Lg	Tot	H	A	Men-On 0	1	2	3	One-Game 2	3	4	LO	XN	IP	PH	RHP	LHP
1994	PHI	NL	1	1	0	1	0	0	0	0	0	0	0	0	0	0	1	0

Rank among batters: 4,707 • *Total ballparks homered in*: 1 • *First HR*: 07/16/1994 off Ramon Martinez

Bill Lillard

WILLIAM BEVERLY LILLARD
B: 01/10/1918
BR

Year	Tm	Lg	Tot	H	A	Men-On 0	1	2	3	One-Game 2	3	4	LO	XN	IP	PH	RHP	LHP
1940	PHI	AL	1	1	0	1	0	0	0	0	0	0	0	0	0	0	1	0

Rank among batters: 4,707 • *Total ballparks homered in*: 1 • *First HR*: 07/07/1940 off Marv Breuer

Jim Lillie

JAMES J. LILLIE
B: 07/27/1861 D: 11/09/1890

Year	Tm	Lg	Tot	H	A	Men-On 0	1	2	3	One-Game 2	3	4	LO	XN	IP	PH	RHP	LHP
1883	BUF	NL	1	0	1	0	0	0	1	0	0	0	0	0	0	0	0	1
1884	BUF	NL	3	3	0	2	0	1	0	0	0	0	0	0	1	0	2	0
1885	BUF	NL	2	2	0	1	1	0	0	0	0	0	0	0	0	0	0	0
Total			6	5	1	3	1	1	1	0	0	0	0	0	1	0	2	1

Rank among batters: 2,988 • *Total ballparks homered in*: 2 • *First HR*: 09/03/1883 off Dupee Shaw

Derek Lilliquist

DEREK JANSEN LILLIQUIST
B: 02/20/1966
BL

Year	Tm	Lg	Tot	H	A	Men-On 0	1	2	3	One-Game 2	3	4	LO	XN	IP	PH	RHP	LHP
1990	ATL	NL	2	2	0	2	0	0	0	1	0	0	0	0	0	0	2	0

Derek Lilliquist *continued*

Rank among batters: 4,129 • *Top target (2 home runs)*: Ron Darling • *Number of pitchers victimized*: 1 • *Total ballparks homered in*: 1 • *First HR*: 05/01/1990 off Ron Darling

Bob Lillis

ROBERT PERRY LILLIS
B: 06/02/1930
BR

Year	Tm	Lg	Tot	H	A	Men-On 0	Men-On 1	Men-On 2	Men-On 3	One-Game 2	One-Game 3	One-Game 4	LO	XN	IP	PH	RHP	LHP
1958	LA	NL	1	1	0	1	0	0	0	0	0	0	1	0	0	0	1	0
1962	HOU	NL	1	0	1	1	0	0	0	0	0	0	0	0	0	0	1	0
1963	HOU	NL	1	1	0	1	0	0	0	0	0	0	0	0	0	0	1	0
Total			3	2	1	3	0	0	0	0	0	0	1	0	0	0	3	0

Rank among batters: 3,735 • *Total ballparks homered in*: 3 • *First HR*: 09/24/1958 off Bob Mabe

Lou Limmer

LOUIS LIMMER
B: 03/10/1925
BL

Year	Tm	Lg	Tot	H	A	Men-On 0	Men-On 1	Men-On 2	Men-On 3	One-Game 2	One-Game 3	One-Game 4	LO	XN	IP	PH	RHP	LHP
1951	PHI	AL	5	0	5	1	2	1	1	0	0	0	0	0	0	2	4	1
1954	PHI	AL	14	7	7	10	3	1	0	0	0	0	0	0	0	0	11	3
Total			19	7	12	11	5	2	1	0	0	0	0	0	0	2	15	4

Rank among batters: 1,861 • *Total ballparks homered in*: 8 • *First HR*: 04/23/1951 off Vic Raschi

Rufino Linares

RUFINO DE LA CRUZ LINARES
B: 02/28/1951
BR

Year	Tm	Lg	Tot	H	A	Men-On 0	Men-On 1	Men-On 2	Men-On 3	One-Game 2	One-Game 3	One-Game 4	LO	XN	IP	PH	RHP	LHP
1981	ATL	NL	5	5	0	3	1	1	0	0	0	0	0	0	0	0	3	2
1982	ATL	NL	2	2	0	2	0	0	0	0	0	0	0	0	0	0	2	0
1984	ATL	NL	1	1	0	1	0	0	0	0	0	0	0	0	0	0	0	1
1985	CAL	AL	3	0	3	0	1	2	0	0	0	0	0	0	0	0	1	2
Total			11	8	3	6	2	3	0	0	0	0	0	0	0	0	6	5

Rank among batters: 2,419 • *Total ballparks homered in*: 4 • *First HR*: 04/17/1981 off Doyle Alexander

Carl Lind

HENRY CARL LIND
B: 09/19/1903 D: 08/02/1946
BR

Year	Tm	Lg	Tot	H	A	Men-On 0	Men-On 1	Men-On 2	Men-On 3	One-Game 2	One-Game 3	One-Game 4	LO	XN	IP	PH	RHP	LHP
1928	CLE	AL	1	0	1	1	0	0	0	0	0	0	0	0	0	0	1	0

Rank among batters: 4,707 • *Total ballparks homered in*: 1 • *First HR*: 06/28/1928 off Ted Blankenship

Jose Lind

JOSE (SALGADO) LIND
B: 05/01/1964
BR

Year	Tm	Lg	Tot	H	A	Men-On 0	Men-On 1	Men-On 2	Men-On 3	One-Game 2	One-Game 3	One-Game 4	LO	XN	IP	PH	RHP	LHP
1988	PIT	NL	2	1	1	2	0	0	0	0	0	0	0	0	0	0	2	0
1989	PIT	NL	2	2	0	2	0	0	0	0	0	0	0	0	0	0	1	1
1990	PIT	NL	1	1	0	0	1	0	0	0	0	0	0	0	0	0	0	1
1991	PIT	NL	3	2	1	2	0	1	0	0	0	0	0	0	0	0	1	2
1994	KC	AL	1	0	1	1	0	0	0	0	0	0	0	0	0	0	0	1
Total			9	6	3	7	1	1	0	0	0	0	0	0	0	0	4	5

Rank among batters: 2,587 • *Total ballparks homered in*: 4 • *First HR*: 06/03/1988 off John Dopson • *LCS HR*—2

Paul Lindblad

PAUL AARON LINDBLAD
B: 08/09/1941
BL

Year	Tm	Lg	Tot	H	A	Men-On 0	Men-On 1	Men-On 2	Men-On 3	One-Game 2	One-Game 3	One-Game 4	LO	XN	IP	PH	RHP	LHP
1967	KC	AL	1	0	1	1	0	0	0	0	0	0	0	0	0	0	1	0

Rank among batters: 4,707 • *Total ballparks homered in*: 1 • *First HR*: 07/31/1967 off Joe Verbanic

Johnny Lindell

JOHN HARLAN LINDELL
B: 08/30/1916 D: 08/27/1985
BR

Year	Tm	Lg	Tot	H	A	Men-On 0	Men-On 1	Men-On 2	Men-On 3	One-Game 2	One-Game 3	One-Game 4	LO	XN	IP	PH	RHP	LHP
1943	NY	AL	4	2	2	1	3	0	0	1	0	0	0	0	0	0	4	0

Johnny Lindell *continued*

Year	Tm	Lg	Tot	H	A	Men-On 0	Men-On 1	Men-On 2	Men-On 3	One-Game 2	One-Game 3	One-Game 4	LO	XN	IP	PH	RHP	LHP
1944	NY	AL	18	5	13	14	2	1	1	0	0	0	0	1	0	0	15	3
1945	NY	AL	1	0	1	1	0	0	0	0	0	0	0	0	0	0	1	0
1946	NY	AL	10	4	6	4	3	3	0	2	0	0	0	0	0	0	2	8
1947	NY	AL	11	7	4	9	2	0	0	0	0	0	0	0	0	0	4	7
1948	NY	AL	13	4	9	7	6	0	0	0	0	0	0	0	0	0	7	6
1949	NY	AL	6	5	1	6	0	0	0	0	0	0	0	0	0	0	1	5
1950	STL	NL	5	0	5	2	2	1	0	0	0	0	0	0	0	0	1	4
1953	PIT	NL	4	1	3	0	3	1	0	0	0	0	0	0	0	2	3	1
Total			72	28	44	44	21	6	1	3	0	0	0	1	0	2	38	34

Rank among batters: 723 • *Top target (4 home runs)*: Sam Zoldak, Mickey Harris, Hal Newhouser • *Number of pitchers victimized*: 52 • *Total ballparks homered in*: 14 • *First HR*: 06/06/1943 off Steve Sundra

Jim Lindeman

JAMES WILLIAM LINDEMAN
B: 01/10/1962
BR

Year	Tm	Lg	Tot	H	A	Men-On 0	Men-On 1	Men-On 2	Men-On 3	One-Game 2	One-Game 3	One-Game 4	LO	XN	IP	PH	RHP	LHP
1986	STL	NL	1	0	1	1	0	0	0	0	0	0	0	0	0	0	0	1
1987	STL	NL	8	2	6	6	1	1	0	1	0	0	0	0	0	0	4	4
1988	STL	NL	2	0	2	2	0	0	0	0	0	0	0	0	0	0	1	1
1990	DET	AL	2	2	0	2	0	0	0	0	0	0	0	0	0	0	0	2
1992	PHI	NL	1	1	0	0	1	0	0	0	0	0	0	0	0	1	0	1
1994	NY	NL	7	3	4	4	3	0	0	0	0	0	0	1	0	0	2	5
Total			21	8	13	15	5	1	0	1	0	0	0	1	0	1	7	14

Rank among batters: 1,768 • *Top target (3 home runs)*: Bob Kipper • *Number of pitchers victimized*: 18 • *Total ballparks homered in*: 10 • *First HR*: 09/05/1986 off Jim Deshaies • *LCS HR*—1

Freddy Lindstrom

FREDERICK CHARLES LINDSTROM
B: 11/21/1905 D: 10/04/1981
BR HOF

Year	Tm	Lg	Tot	H	A	Men-On 0	Men-On 1	Men-On 2	Men-On 3	One-Game 2	One-Game 3	One-Game 4	LO	XN	IP	PH	RHP	LHP
1925	NY	NL	4	0	4	2	2	0	0	0	0	0	0	0	0	0	3	1
1926	NY	NL	9	6	3	4	3	2	0	0	0	0	0	2	3	0	5	4
1927	NY	NL	7	4	3	4	2	1	0	0	0	0	0	0	0	0	4	3
1928	NY	NL	14	11	3	8	2	4	0	1	0	0	0	0	0	0	5	9
1929	NY	NL	15	10	5	8	4	3	0	1	0	0	0	0	1	0	8	7
1930	NY	NL	22	15	7	15	4	3	0	3	0	0	0	1	1	0	15	7
1931	NY	NL	5	3	2	3	1	1	0	0	0	0	0	0	0	0	3	2
1932	NY	NL	15	11	4	8	3	3	1	0	0	0	0	1	0	0	10	5
1933	PIT	NL	5	1	4	4	0	1	0	1	0	0	0	0	0	0	3	2
1934	PIT	NL	4	1	3	1	1	1	1	0	0	0	0	0	0	1	2	2
1935	CHI	NL	3	2	1	3	0	0	0	0	0	0	0	0	0	0	3	0
Total			103	64	39	60	22	19	2	6	0	0	0	4	5	1	61	42

Rank among batters: 477 • *Top target (5 home runs)*: Jumbo Elliott • *Number of pitchers victimized*: 66 • *Total ballparks homered in*: 8 • *First HR*: 06/01/1925 off Bill Hubbell • *Hit for Cycle*—@PIT: 05/08/1930

Ed Linke

EDWARD KARL LINKE
B: 11/09/1911 D: 06/21/1988
BR

Year	Tm	Lg	Tot	H	A	Men-On 0	Men-On 1	Men-On 2	Men-On 3	One-Game 2	One-Game 3	One-Game 4	LO	XN	IP	PH	RHP	LHP
1935	WAS	AL	1	0	1	0	0	1	0	0	0	0	0	1	0	0	1	0
1936	WAS	AL	1	0	1	1	0	0	0	0	0	0	0	0	0	0	0	1
Total			2	0	2	1	0	1	0	0	0	0	0	1	0	0	1	1

Rank among batters: 4,129 • *Total ballparks homered in*: 2 • *First HR*: 06/14/1935 off Whit Wyatt

Phil Linz

PHILIP FRANCIS LINZ
B: 06/04/1939
BR

Year	Tm	Lg	Tot	H	A	Men-On 0	Men-On 1	Men-On 2	Men-On 3	One-Game 2	One-Game 3	One-Game 4	LO	XN	IP	PH	RHP	LHP
1962	NY	AL	1	1	0	0	1	0	0	0	0	0	0	0	0	0	1	0
1963	NY	AL	2	0	2	2	0	0	0	0	0	0	0	0	0	0	0	2
1964	NY	AL	5	2	3	3	2	0	0	1	0	0	0	0	0	0	3	2
1965	NY	AL	2	1	1	1	1	0	0	0	0	0	0	0	0	0	1	1
1967	PHI	NL	1	1	0	1	0	0	0	0	0	0	0	1	0	1	1	0
Total			11	5	6	7	4	0	0	1	0	0	0	1	0	1	6	5

Phil Linz *continued*

Rank among batters: 2,419 • *Total ballparks homered in*: 6 • *First HR*: 05/23/1962 off Dan Pfister • *World Series HR*—2

Frank Linzy

FRANK ALFRED LINZY
B: 09/15/1940
BR

Year	Tm	Lg	Tot	H	A	Men-On 0	Men-On 1	Men-On 2	Men-On 3	One-Game 2	One-Game 3	One-Game 4	LO	XN	IP	PH	RHP	LHP
1965	SF	NL	1	1	0	1	0	0	0	0	0	0	0	0	0	0	1	0

Rank among batters: 4,707 • *Total ballparks homered in*: 1 • *First HR*: 07/28/1965 off Ray Washburn

Johnny Lipon

JOHN JOSEPH LIPON
B: 11/10/1922
BR

Year	Tm	Lg	Tot	H	A	Men-On 0	Men-On 1	Men-On 2	Men-On 3	One-Game 2	One-Game 3	One-Game 4	LO	XN	IP	PH	RHP	LHP
1948	DET	AL	5	3	2	4	1	0	0	0	0	0	0	0	0	0	2	3
1949	DET	AL	3	1	2	1	1	0	1	0	0	0	0	0	0	0	2	1
1950	DET	AL	2	1	1	2	0	0	0	0	0	0	0	0	0	0	2	0
Total			10	5	5	7	2	0	1	0	0	0	0	0	0	0	6	4

Rank among batters: 2,500 • *Top target (2 home runs)*: Bill Wight, Bob Lemon • *Number of pitchers victimized*: 8 • *Total ballparks homered in*: 5 • *First HR*: 04/30/1948 off Bill Wight

Nelson Liriano

NELSON ARTURO (BONILLA) LIRIANO
B: 06/03/1964
BB

Year	Tm	Lg	Tot	H	A	Men-On 0	Men-On 1	Men-On 2	Men-On 3	One-Game 2	One-Game 3	One-Game 4	LO	XN	IP	PH	RHP	LHP
1987	TOR	AL	2	1	1	0	1	1	0	0	0	0	0	0	0	0	0	2
1988	TOR	AL	3	0	3	3	0	0	0	0	0	0	0	0	0	0	2	1
1989	TOR	AL	5	3	2	3	1	1	0	0	0	0	0	0	0	1	5	0
1990	TOR	AL	1	1	0	1	0	0	0	0	0	0	0	0	0	0	1	0
1993	COL	NL	2	0	2	2	0	0	0	0	0	0	1	0	0	0	2	0
1994	COL	NL	3	2	1	2	1	0	0	0	0	0	0	0	0	0	2	1
1995	PIT	NL	5	2	3	3	0	1	1	0	0	0	0	0	0	0	2	3
Total			21	9	12	14	3	3	1	0	0	0	1	0	0	1	14	7

Rank among batters: 1,768 • *Total ballparks homered in*: 12 • *First HR*: 08/30/1987 off Dave Leiper

Joe Lis

JOSEPH ANTHONY LIS
B: 08/15/1946
BR

Year	Tm	Lg	Tot	H	A	Men-On 0	Men-On 1	Men-On 2	Men-On 3	One-Game 2	One-Game 3	One-Game 4	LO	XN	IP	PH	RHP	LHP
1970	PHI	NL	1	1	0	1	0	0	0	0	0	0	0	0	0	0	0	1
1971	PHI	NL	6	3	3	5	1	0	0	0	0	0	0	0	0	1	1	5
1972	PHI	NL	6	3	3	2	2	2	0	0	0	0	0	0	0	0	5	1
1973	MIN	AL	9	7	2	8	1	0	0	0	0	0	0	1	0	0	7	2
1974	CLE	AL	6	2	4	3	3	0	0	0	0	0	0	0	1	0	3	3
1975	CLE	AL	2	0	2	0	1	1	0	0	0	0	0	0	0	0	1	1
1976	CLE	AL	2	0	2	2	0	0	0	0	0	0	0	0	0	0	2	0
Total			32	16	16	21	8	3	0	0	0	0	0	1	1	1	19	13

Rank among batters: 1,360 • *Top target (2 home runs)*: Ken Holtzman, Paul Splittorff • *Number of pitchers victimized*: 30 • *Total ballparks homered in*: 13 • *First HR*: 09/08/1970 off Steve Carlton

Pat Listach

PATRICK ALAN LISTACH
B: 09/12/1967
BR

Year	Tm	Lg	Tot	H	A	Men-On 0	Men-On 1	Men-On 2	Men-On 3	One-Game 2	One-Game 3	One-Game 4	LO	XN	IP	PH	RHP	LHP
1992	MIL	AL	1	0	1	1	0	0	0	0	0	0	0	0	0	0	0	1
1993	MIL	AL	3	0	3	2	1	0	0	0	0	0	1	0	0	0	1	2
Total			4	0	4	3	1	0	0	0	0	0	1	0	0	0	1	3

Rank among batters: 3,427 • *Total ballparks homered in*: 4 • *First HR*: 09/17/1992 off Scott Taylor

Bryan Little

RICHARD BRYAN LITTLE
B: 10/08/1959
BB

Year	Tm	Lg	Tot	H	A	Men-On 0	Men-On 1	Men-On 2	Men-On 3	One-Game 2	One-Game 3	One-Game 4	LO	XN	IP	PH	RHP	LHP
1983	MON	NL	1	0	1	0	0	1	0	0	0	0	0	0	0	0	1	0

Bryan Little *continued*

Year	Tm	Lg	Tot	H	A	Men-On 0	1	2	3	One-Game 2	3	4	LO	XN	IP	PH	RHP	LHP
1985	CHI	AL	2	2	0	1	0	1	0	0	0	0	0	0	0	0	2	0
Total			3	2	1	1	0	2	0	0	0	0	0	0	0	0	3	0

Rank among batters: 3,735 • *Total ballparks homered in*: 2 • *First HR*: 05/31/1983 off Eddie Whitson

Dennis Littlejohn

DENNIS GERALD LITTLEJOHN
B: 10/04/1954
BR

Year	Tm	Lg	Tot	H	A	Men-On 0	1	2	3	One-Game 2	3	4	LO	XN	IP	PH	RHP	LHP
1979	SF	NL	1	0	1	0	1	0	0	0	0	0	0	0	0	0	0	1

Rank among batters: 4,707 • *Total ballparks homered in*: 1 • *First HR*: 08/21/1979 off Grant Jackson

Greg Litton

JON GREGORY LITTON
B: 07/13/1964
BR

Year	Tm	Lg	Tot	H	A	Men-On 0	1	2	3	One-Game 2	3	4	LO	XN	IP	PH	RHP	LHP
1989	SF	NL	4	3	1	3	0	1	0	0	0	0	0	0	0	1	0	4
1990	SF	NL	1	0	1	1	0	0	0	0	0	0	0	0	0	0	0	1
1991	SF	NL	1	0	1	1	0	0	0	0	0	0	0	0	0	0	1	0
1992	SF	NL	4	2	2	2	1	0	1	0	0	0	0	1	0	2	1	3
1993	SEA	AL	3	3	0	2	1	0	0	0	0	0	0	0	0	0	1	2
Total			13	8	5	9	2	1	1	0	0	0	0	1	0	3	3	10

Rank among batters: 2,248 • *Total ballparks homered in*: 6 • *First HR*: 06/11/1989 off Dennis Rasmussen • *World Series HR*—1

Jack Littrell

JACK NAPIER LITTRELL
B: 01/22/1929
BR

Year	Tm	Lg	Tot	H	A	Men-On 0	1	2	3	One-Game 2	3	4	LO	XN	IP	PH	RHP	LHP
1954	PHI	AL	1	0	1	0	0	1	0	0	0	0	0	0	0	0	0	1
1957	CHI	NL	1	1	0	0	0	1	0	0	0	0	0	0	0	0	1	0
Total			2	1	1	0	0	2	0	0	0	0	0	0	0	0	1	1

Rank among batters: 4,129 • *Total ballparks homered in*: 2 • *First HR*: 09/24/1954 off Art Schallock

Danny Litwhiler

DANIEL WEBSTER LITWHILER
B: 08/31/1916
BR

Year	Tm	Lg	Tot	H	A	Men-On 0	1	2	3	One-Game 2	3	4	LO	XN	IP	PH	RHP	LHP
1940	PHI	NL	5	5	0	3	1	0	1	0	0	0	0	0	0	0	5	0
1941	PHI	NL	18	9	9	9	8	0	1	1	0	0	0	0	0	0	14	4
1942	PHI	NL	9	3	6	7	2	0	0	0	0	0	0	0	0	0	8	1
1943	PHI	NL	5	2	3	5	0	0	0	0	0	0	0	0	0	0	4	1
	STL	NL	7	2	5	4	3	0	0	1	0	0	0	0	0	0	6	1
	Total		12	4	8	9	3	0	0	1	0	0	0	0	0	0	10	2
1944	STL	NL	15	5	10	6	4	4	1	0	0	0	0	0	0	1	11	4
1946	BOS	NL	8	4	4	5	2	1	0	0	0	0	0	0	0	0	2	6
1947	BOS	NL	7	3	4	5	2	0	0	0	0	0	0	0	0	2	2	5
1948	CIN	NL	14	6	8	12	2	0	0	0	0	0	1	1	0	0	9	5
1949	CIN	NL	11	5	6	6	3	2	0	0	0	0	0	0	0	1	4	7
1950	CIN	NL	6	3	3	5	0	1	0	0	0	0	0	0	0	1	0	6
1951	CIN	NL	2	2	0	2	0	0	0	0	0	0	0	0	0	1	0	2
Total			107	49	58	69	27	8	3	2	0	0	1	1	0	6	65	42

Rank among batters: 449 • *Top target (5 home runs)*: Preacher Roe • *Number of pitchers victimized*: 75 • *Total ballparks homered in*: 8 • *First HR*: 09/02/1940 off Red Lynn • *World Series HR*—1

Mickey Livingston

THOMPSON ORVILLE LIVINGSTON
B: 11/15/1914 D: 04/03/1983
BR

Year	Tm	Lg	Tot	H	A	Men-On 0	1	2	3	One-Game 2	3	4	LO	XN	IP	PH	RHP	LHP
1942	PHI	NL	2	1	1	0	2	0	0	0	0	0	0	0	0	1	1	1
1943	PHI	NL	3	1	2	1	2	0	0	0	0	0	0	0	0	0	3	0
	CHI	NL	4	4	0	1	3	0	0	0	0	0	0	0	0	0	4	0
	Total		7	5	2	2	5	0	0	0	0	0	0	0	0	0	7	0
1945	CHI	NL	2	1	1	2	0	0	0	0	0	0	0	0	0	0	2	0

Mickey Livingston *continued*

Year	Tm	Lg	Tot	H	A	Men-On				One-Game			LO	XN	IP	PH	RHP	LHP
						0	1	2	3	2	3	4						
1946	CHI	NL	2	1	1	2	0	0	0	0	0	0	0	0	0	0	0	2
1948	NY	NL	2	0	2	2	0	0	0	0	0	0	0	0	0	0	2	0
1949	NY	NL	4	2	2	2	2	0	0	0	0	0	0	0	0	0	2	2
Total			19	10	9	10	9	0	0	0	0	0	0	0	0	1	14	5

Rank among batters: 1,861 • *Top target (2 home runs)*: Bucky Walters, Warren Spahn, Hank Borowy • *Number of pitchers victimized*: 16 • *Total ballparks homered in*: 7 • *First HR*: 08/07/1942 off Carl Hubbell

Scott Livingstone

SCOTT LOUIS LIVINGSTONE
B: 07/15/1965
BL

Year	Tm	Lg	Tot	H	A	Men-On				One-Game			LO	XN	IP	PH	RHP	LHP
						0	1	2	3	2	3	4						
1991	DET	AL	2	1	1	2	0	0	0	0	0	0	0	0	0	0	1	1
1992	DET	AL	4	2	2	2	0	2	0	0	0	0	0	0	0	0	3	1
1993	DET	AL	2	1	1	2	0	0	0	0	0	0	0	0	0	0	2	0
1994	SD	NL	2	1	1	2	0	0	0	0	0	0	0	0	0	0	1	1
1995	SD	NL	5	1	4	4	1	0	0	0	0	0	0	0	1	1	4	1
Total			15	6	9	12	1	2	0	0	0	0	0	0	1	1	11	4

Rank among batters: 2,096 • *Total ballparks homered in*: 10 • *First HR*: 08/01/1991 off Floyd Bannister

Winston Llenas

WINSTON ENRIQUILLO (DAVILLA) LLENAS
B: 09/23/1943
BR

Year	Tm	Lg	Tot	H	A	Men-On				One-Game			LO	XN	IP	PH	RHP	LHP
						0	1	2	3	2	3	4						
1973	CAL	AL	1	0	1	0	0	1	0	0	0	0	0	0	0	1	0	1
1974	CAL	AL	2	1	1	1	1	0	0	0	0	0	0	0	0	1	0	2
Total			3	1	2	1	1	1	0	0	0	0	0	0	0	2	0	3

Rank among batters: 3,735 • *Total ballparks homered in*: 3 • *First HR*: 06/19/1973 off Wilbur Wood

Hans Lobert

JOHN BERNARD LOBERT
B: 10/18/1881 D: 09/14/1968
BR

Year	Tm	Lg	Tot	H	A	Men-On				One-Game			LO	XN	IP	PH	RHP	LHP
						0	1	2	3	2	3	4						
1907	CIN	NL	1	0	1	1	0	0	0	0	0	0	0	0	1	0	1	0
1908	CIN	NL	4	2	2	4	0	0	0	0	0	0	0	0	4	0	4	0
1909	CIN	NL	4	1	3	2	1	1	0	0	0	0	0	0	4	0	3	1
1910	CIN	NL	3	2	1	1	0	2	0	0	0	0	0	0	3	0	3	0
1911	PHI	NL	9	8	1	3	6	0	0	1	0	0	0	1	0	0	3	6
1912	PHI	NL	2	2	0	0	0	2	0	0	0	0	0	0	0	0	2	0
1913	PHI	NL	7	6	1	6	1	0	0	0	0	0	0	1	2	0	6	1
1914	PHI	NL	1	0	1	0	1	0	0	0	0	0	0	0	0	0	1	0
1917	NY	NL	1	1	0	0	1	0	0	0	0	0	0	0	0	0	0	1
Total			32	22	10	17	10	5	0	1	0	0	0	2	14	0	23	9

Rank among batters: 1,360 • Top target (2 home runs): George Bell, Cliff Curtis, Nap Rucker, Slim Sallee, Bert Humphries • *Number of pitchers victimized*: 27 • *Total ballparks homered in*: 8 • *First HR*: 08/14/1907 off George Ferguson

Harry Lochhead

ROBERT HENRY LOCHHEAD
B: 03/29/1876 D: 08/22/1909
BR

Year	Tm	Lg	Tot	H	A	Men-On				One-Game			LO	XN	IP	PH	RHP	LHP
						0	1	2	3	2	3	4						
1899	CLE	NL	1	0	1	0	1	0	0	0	0	0	0	0	0	0	1	0

Rank among batters: 4,707 • *Total ballparks homered in*: 1 • *First HR*: 09/18/1899 off Bill Dinneen

Don Lock

DON WILSON LOCK
B: 07/27/1936
BR

Year	Tm	Lg	Tot	H	A	Men-On				One-Game			LO	XN	IP	PH	RHP	LHP
						0	1	2	3	2	3	4						
1962	WAS	AL	12	5	7	8	3	1	0	0	0	0	0	0	0	0	10	2
1963	WAS	AL	27	12	15	18	5	3	1	2	0	0	0	2	0	0	18	9
1964	WAS	AL	28	14	14	13	7	8	0	5	0	0	0	2	0	1	17	11
1965	WAS	AL	16	11	5	12	3	0	1	1	0	0	0	1	0	1	13	3
1966	WAS	AL	16	9	7	6	6	4	0	0	0	0	0	1	0	3	13	3
1967	PHI	NL	14	7	7	5	5	4	0	0	0	0	0	0	0	0	1	13

Don Lock *continued*

Year	Tm	Lg	Tot	H	A	Men-On 0	1	2	3	One-Game 2	3	4	LO	XN	IP	PH	RHP	LHP
1968	PHI	NL	8	5	3	3	3	1	1	0	0	0	0	0	0	0	1	7
1969	BOS	AL	1	1	0	1	0	0	0	0	0	0	0	0	0	0	0	1
Total			122	64	58	66	32	21	3	8	0	0	0	6	0	5	73	49

Rank among batters: 377 • *Top target (5 home runs)*: Jim Kaat • *Number of pitchers victimized*: 85 • *Total ballparks homered in*: 16 • *First HR*: 07/17/1962 off Juan Pizarro

Bobby Locke

LAWRENCE DONALD LOCKE
B: 03/03/1934
BR

Year	Tm	Lg	Tot	H	A	Men-On 0	1	2	3	One-Game 2	3	4	LO	XN	IP	PH	RHP	LHP
1959	CLE	AL	1	0	1	0	0	1	0	0	0	0	0	0	0	0	1	0

Rank among batters: 4,707 • *Total ballparks homered in*: 1 • *First HR*: 06/18/1959 off Frank Sullivan

Keith Lockhart

KEITH VIRGIL LOCKHART
B: 11/10/1964
BL

Year	Tm	Lg	Tot	H	A	Men-On 0	1	2	3	One-Game 2	3	4	LO	XN	IP	PH	RHP	LHP
1994	SD	NL	2	2	0	2	0	0	0	1	0	0	0	0	0	0	2	0
1995	KC	AL	6	3	3	3	2	1	0	0	0	0	1	0	0	0	6	0
Total			8	5	3	5	2	1	0	1	0	0	1	0	0	0	8	0

Rank among batters: 2,703 • *Total ballparks homered in*: 5 • *First HR*: 04/08/1994 off Dave Weathers

Gene Locklear

GENE LOCKLEAR
B: 07/19/1949
BL

Year	Tm	Lg	Tot	H	A	Men-On 0	1	2	3	One-Game 2	3	4	LO	XN	IP	PH	RHP	LHP
1973	SD	NL	3	0	3	1	0	2	0	0	0	0	0	0	0	0	3	0
1974	SD	NL	1	0	1	1	0	0	0	0	0	0	0	0	0	1	1	0
1975	SD	NL	5	0	5	4	0	1	0	0	0	0	0	0	0	0	4	1
Total			9	0	9	6	0	3	0	0	0	0	0	0	0	1	8	1

Rank among batters: 2,587 • *Total ballparks homered in*: 7 • *First HR*: 08/03/1973 off Ron Schueler

Whitey Lockman

CARROLL WALTER LOCKMAN
B: 07/25/1926
BL

Year	Tm	Lg	Tot	H	A	Men-On 0	1	2	3	One-Game 2	3	4	LO	XN	IP	PH	RHP	LHP
1945	NY	NL	3	3	0	2	1	0	0	0	0	0	0	0	0	0	1	2
1948	NY	NL	18	12	6	12	4	2	0	1	0	0	0	0	1	0	15	3
1949	NY	NL	11	6	5	7	4	0	0	0	0	0	0	0	0	0	8	3
1950	NY	NL	6	5	1	5	1	0	0	0	0	0	0	0	0	0	3	3
1951	NY	NL	12	10	2	8	2	2	0	0	0	0	0	0	0	0	9	3
1952	NY	NL	13	7	6	6	6	1	0	1	0	0	0	1	0	0	11	2
1953	NY	NL	9	9	0	6	3	0	0	0	0	0	2	0	0	0	8	1
1954	NY	NL	16	12	4	9	4	1	2	0	0	0	1	0	0	1	14	2
1955	NY	NL	15	10	5	9	5	1	0	0	0	0	1	1	0	0	9	6
1956	NY	NL	1	1	0	1	0	0	0	0	0	0	0	0	0	0	1	0
1957	NY	NL	7	6	1	5	2	0	0	1	0	0	1	0	0	0	7	0
1958	SF	NL	2	2	0	2	0	0	0	0	0	0	1	1	0	0	1	1
1960	CIN	NL	1	0	1	1	0	0	0	0	0	0	0	0	0	0	1	0
Total			114	83	31	73	32	7	2	3	0	0	6	3	1	1	88	26

Rank among batters: 419 • *Top target (5 home runs)*: Ralph Branca • *Number of pitchers victimized*: 79 • *Total ballparks homered in*: 10 • *First HR*: 07/05/1945 off George Dockins • *Hit HR in first major league AB*—vs STL: 07/05/1945 • *World Series HR*—1

Skip Lockwood

CLAUDE EDWARD LOCKWOOD
B: 08/17/1946
BR

Year	Tm	Lg	Tot	H	A	Men-On 0	1	2	3	One-Game 2	3	4	LO	XN	IP	PH	RHP	LHP
1970	MIL	AL	1	1	0	1	0	0	0	0	0	0	0	0	0	0	1	0
1971	MIL	AL	1	1	0	1	0	0	0	0	0	0	0	0	0	0	1	0
1978	NY	NL	1	0	1	1	0	0	0	0	0	0	0	0	0	0	1	0
Total			3	2	1	3	0	0	0	0	0	0	0	0	0	0	3	0

Rank among batters: 3,735 • *Total ballparks homered in*: 2 • *First HR*: 05/10/1970 off Jim Hannan

Dario Lodigiani

DARIO ANTONIO LODIGIANI
B: 07/16/1916
BR

Year	Tm	Lg	Tot	H	A	Men-On 0	1	2	3	One-Game 2	3	4	LO	XN	IP	PH	RHP	LHP
1938	PHI	AL	6	5	1	2	2	1	1	0	0	0	0	0	0	0	5	1
1939	PHI	AL	6	1	5	2	4	0	0	0	0	0	0	0	0	0	6	0
1941	CHI	AL	4	0	4	3	1	0	0	1	0	0	0	0	0	0	3	1
Total			16	6	10	7	7	1	1	1	0	0	0	0	0	0	14	2

Rank among batters: 2,029 • *Top target (2 home runs)*: Jack Knott • *Number of pitchers victimized*: 15 • *Total ballparks homered in*: 4 • *First HR*: 04/24/1938 off Emerson Dickman

Kenny Lofton

KENNETH LOFTON
B: 05/31/1967
BL

Year	Tm	Lg	Tot	H	A	Men-On 0	1	2	3	One-Game 2	3	4	LO	XN	IP	PH	RHP	LHP
1992	CLE	AL	5	3	2	3	1	1	0	0	0	0	2	0	0	0	5	0
1993	CLE	AL	1	1	0	0	0	0	1	0	0	0	0	0	0	0	1	0
1994	CLE	AL	12	10	2	11	1	0	0	1	0	0	2	2	0	0	9	3
1995	CLE	AL	7	5	2	4	2	1	0	1	0	0	2	0	0	0	7	0
Total			25	19	6	18	4	2	1	2	0	0	6	2	0	0	22	3

Rank among batters: 1,608 • Top target (2 home runs): Cal Eldred, Sean Bergman, Alex Fernandez, Scott Kamieniecki • *Number of pitchers victimized*: 21 • *Total ballparks homered in*: 7 • *First HR*: 05/07/1992 off Mike Campbell

Johnny Logan

JOHN LOGAN
B: 03/23/1927
BR

Year	Tm	Lg	Tot	H	A	Men-On 0	1	2	3	One-Game 2	3	4	LO	XN	IP	PH	RHP	LHP
1952	BOS	NL	4	0	4	3	1	0	0	0	0	0	0	0	0	0	2	2
1953	MIL	NL	11	3	8	7	2	2	0	0	0	0	0	0	0	0	9	2
1954	MIL	NL	8	4	4	5	3	0	0	1	0	0	0	0	0	0	8	0
1955	MIL	NL	13	3	10	10	1	1	1	0	0	0	0	0	0	0	11	2
1956	MIL	NL	15	6	9	11	4	0	0	0	0	0	0	0	0	0	11	4
1957	MIL	NL	10	3	7	6	4	0	0	0	0	0	0	0	0	0	10	0
1958	MIL	NL	11	3	8	7	2	1	1	0	0	0	0	0	0	0	9	2
1959	MIL	NL	13	6	7	9	2	2	0	0	0	0	0	0	0	0	10	3
1960	MIL	NL	7	3	4	6	1	0	0	0	0	0	0	0	0	0	6	1
1962	PIT	NL	1	1	0	0	0	0	1	0	0	0	0	0	0	0	0	1
Total			93	32	61	64	20	6	3	1	0	0	0	0	0	0	76	17

Rank among batters: 545 • *Top target (6 home runs)*: Bob Friend • *Number of pitchers victimized*: 67 • *Total ballparks homered in*: 10 • *First HR*: 08/15/1952 off Max Lanier • *World Series HR—1*

Pete Lohman

GEORGE F. LOHMAN
B: 10/21/1864 D: 11/21/1928

Year	Tm	Lg	Tot	H	A	Men-On 0	1	2	3	One-Game 2	3	4	LO	XN	IP	PH	RHP	LHP
1891	WAS	AA	1	1	0	1	0	0	0	0	0	0	0	0	0	0	1	0

Rank among batters: 4,707 • *Total ballparks homered in*: 1 • *First HR*: 07/11/1891 off John Dolan

Jack Lohrke

JACK WAYNE LOHRKE
B: 02/25/1924
BR

Year	Tm	Lg	Tot	H	A	Men-On 0	1	2	3	One-Game 2	3	4	LO	XN	IP	PH	RHP	LHP
1947	NY	NL	11	8	3	8	3	0	0	0	0	0	0	0	0	0	6	5
1948	NY	NL	5	4	1	3	2	0	0	0	0	0	0	0	0	0	4	1
1949	NY	NL	5	5	0	5	0	0	0	0	0	0	2	0	0	0	2	3
1951	NY	NL	1	0	1	0	1	0	0	0	0	0	0	0	0	0	0	1
Total			22	17	5	16	6	0	0	0	0	0	2	0	0	0	12	10

Rank among batters: 1,719 • *Top target (2 home runs)*: Clyde Shoun, Howie Fox • *Number of pitchers victimized*: 20 • *Total ballparks homered in*: 4 • *First HR*: 06/09/1947 off Kirby Higbe

Bill Lohrman

WILLIAM LEROY LOHRMAN
B: 05/22/1913
BR

Year	Tm	Lg	Tot	H	A	Men-On 0	1	2	3	One-Game 2	3	4	LO	XN	IP	PH	RHP	LHP
1939	NY	NL	2	2	0	2	0	0	0	0	0	0	0	0	0	0	2	0

Rank among batters: 4,129 • *Total ballparks homered in*: 1 • *First HR*: 07/23/1939 off Bill Lee

Ron Lolich

RONALD JOHN LOLICH
B: 09/19/1946
BR

Year	Tm	Lg	Tot	H	A	Men-On 0	1	2	3	One-Game 2	3	4	LO	XN	IP	PH	RHP	LHP
1972	CLE	AL	2	2	0	1	1	0	0	0	0	0	0	0	0	0	0	2
1973	CLE	AL	2	1	1	1	0	0	1	0	0	0	0	0	0	0	2	0
Total			4	3	1	2	1	0	1	0	0	0	0	0	0	0	2	2

Rank among batters: 3,427 • *Total ballparks homered in*: 2 • *First HR*: 07/10/1972 off Dave Lemonds

Sherm Lollar

JOHN SHERMAN LOLLAR
B: 08/23/1924 D: 09/24/1977
BR

Year	Tm	Lg	Tot	H	A	Men-On 0	1	2	3	One-Game 2	3	4	LO	XN	IP	PH	RHP	LHP
1946	CLE	AL	1	0	1	0	1	0	0	0	0	0	0	0	0	0	1	0
1947	NY	AL	1	1	0	1	0	0	0	0	0	0	0	0	0	0	1	0
1949	STL	AL	8	3	5	3	4	1	0	0	0	0	0	0	0	0	4	4
1950	STL	AL	13	7	6	7	4	1	1	0	0	0	0	0	0	0	7	6
1951	STL	AL	8	7	1	4	2	2	0	0	0	0	0	0	0	0	2	6
1952	CHI	AL	13	5	8	6	5	2	0	0	0	0	0	0	0	0	7	6
1953	CHI	AL	8	5	3	3	3	1	1	0	0	0	0	0	0	0	6	2
1954	CHI	AL	7	4	3	6	1	0	0	0	0	0	0	0	0	0	5	2
1955	CHI	AL	16	11	5	11	4	1	0	1	0	0	0	0	0	0	12	4
1956	CHI	AL	11	5	6	6	4	1	0	1	0	0	0	1	0	0	9	2
1957	CHI	AL	11	4	7	8	2	1	0	0	0	0	0	0	0	0	8	3
1958	CHI	AL	20	12	8	10	6	2	2	1	0	0	0	0	0	0	15	5
1959	CHI	AL	22	11	11	11	8	3	0	2	0	0	0	0	0	0	14	8
1960	CHI	AL	7	3	4	4	3	0	0	0	0	0	0	0	0	0	6	1
1961	CHI	AL	7	4	3	4	0	2	1	0	0	0	0	0	0	1	6	1
1962	CHI	AL	2	1	1	1	1	0	0	0	0	0	0	0	0	0	2	0
Total			155	83	72	85	48	17	5	5	0	0	0	1	0	1	105	50

Rank among batters: 274 • *Top target (8 home runs)*: Alex Kellner • *Number of pitchers victimized*: 96 • *Total ballparks homered in*: 11 • *First HR*: 06/03/1946 off Phil Marchildon • *World Series HR*—1

Tim Lollar

WILLIAM TIMOTHY LOLLAR
B: 03/17/1956
BL

Year	Tm	Lg	Tot	H	A	Men-On 0	1	2	3	One-Game 2	3	4	LO	XN	IP	PH	RHP	LHP
1981	SD	NL	1	0	1	1	0	0	0	0	0	0	0	0	0	0	1	0
1982	SD	NL	3	1	2	3	0	0	0	0	0	0	0	0	0	0	3	0
1983	SD	NL	1	0	1	1	0	0	0	0	0	0	0	0	0	0	1	0
1984	SD	NL	3	3	0	0	1	2	0	0	0	0	0	0	0	0	3	0
Total			8	4	4	5	1	2	0	0	0	0	0	0	0	0	8	0

Rank among batters: 2,703 • *Total ballparks homered in*: 4 • *First HR*: 04/28/1981 off Tom Seaver

Doug Loman

DOUGLAS EDWARD LOMAN
B: 05/09/1958
BL

Year	Tm	Lg	Tot	H	A	Men-On 0	1	2	3	One-Game 2	3	4	LO	XN	IP	PH	RHP	LHP
1984	MIL	AL	2	0	2	2	0	0	0	1	0	0	0	0	0	0	1	1

Rank among batters: 4,129 • *Total ballparks homered in*: 1 • *First HR*: 09/23/1984 off Roy Lee Jackson

Ernie Lombardi

ERNESTO NATALI LOMBARDI
B: 04/06/1908 D: 09/26/1977
BR HOF

Year	Tm	Lg	Tot	H	A	Men-On 0	1	2	3	One-Game 2	3	4	LO	XN	IP	PH	RHP	LHP
1931	BRO	NL	4	2	2	2	2	0	0	0	0	0	0	0	0	1	1	3
1932	CIN	NL	11	3	8	7	3	1	0	0	0	0	0	0	0	0	7	4
1933	CIN	NL	4	1	3	2	2	0	0	0	0	0	0	0	0	0	2	2
1934	CIN	NL	9	4	5	5	3	0	1	0	0	0	0	0	0	1	7	2
1935	CIN	NL	12	3	9	7	4	1	0	1	0	0	0	1	0	1	7	5
1936	CIN	NL	12	4	8	10	0	2	0	0	0	0	0	0	0	0	8	4
1937	CIN	NL	9	2	7	5	4	0	0	0	0	0	0	0	0	1	7	2
1938	CIN	NL	19	10	9	11	7	1	0	1	0	0	0	1	0	0	17	2
1939	CIN	NL	20	8	12	11	7	2	0	1	0	0	0	2	0	0	16	4
1940	CIN	NL	14	7	7	9	2	2	1	1	0	0	0	0	0	0	13	1
1941	CIN	NL	10	3	7	5	4	0	1	0	0	0	0	0	0	0	9	1

Ernie Lombardi *continued*

Year	Tm	Lg	Tot	H	A	Men-On 0	Men-On 1	Men-On 2	Men-On 3	One-Game 2	One-Game 3	One-Game 4	LO	XN	IP	PH	RHP	LHP
1942	BOS	NL	11	4	7	8	3	0	0	0	0	0	0	0	0	0	8	3
1943	NY	NL	10	9	1	8	2	0	0	0	0	0	0	1	0	0	9	1
1944	NY	NL	10	5	5	7	1	1	1	1	0	0	0	0	0	0	9	1
1945	NY	NL	19	10	9	10	5	3	1	1	0	0	0	0	0	0	15	4
1946	NY	NL	12	7	5	8	2	1	1	0	0	0	0	1	0	4	6	6
1947	NY	NL	4	2	2	2	0	2	0	1	0	0	0	0	0	0	4	0
Total			190	84	106	117	51	16	6	7	0	0	0	6	0	8	145	45

Rank among batters: 201 • *Top target (9 home runs)*: Hal Schumacher • *Number of pitchers victimized*: 109 • *Total ballparks homered in*: 9 • *First HR*: 05/26/1931 off Jumbo Elliott

Phil Lombardi

PHILLIP ARDEN LOMBARDI
B: 02/20/1963
BR

Year	Tm	Lg	Tot	H	A	Men-On 0	Men-On 1	Men-On 2	Men-On 3	One-Game 2	One-Game 3	One-Game 4	LO	XN	IP	PH	RHP	LHP
1986	NY	AL	2	0	2	0	2	0	0	0	0	0	0	0	0	1	0	2
1989	NY	NL	1	0	1	1	0	0	0	0	0	0	0	0	0	0	0	1
Total			3	0	3	1	2	0	0	0	0	0	0	0	0	1	0	3

Rank among batters: 3,735 • *Total ballparks homered in*: 3 • *First HR*: 09/02/1986 off Curt Young

Steve Lombardozzi

STEPHEN PAUL LOMBARDOZZI
B: 04/26/1960
BR

Year	Tm	Lg	Tot	H	A	Men-On 0	Men-On 1	Men-On 2	Men-On 3	One-Game 2	One-Game 3	One-Game 4	LO	XN	IP	PH	RHP	LHP
1986	MIN	AL	8	6	2	5	0	2	1	0	0	0	0	0	0	0	5	3
1987	MIN	AL	8	3	5	5	0	3	0	1	0	0	1	0	0	0	6	2
1988	MIN	AL	3	3	0	1	2	0	0	0	0	0	0	0	2	0	3	0
1989	HOU	NL	1	1	0	1	0	0	0	0	0	0	0	0	0	0	1	0
Total			20	13	7	12	2	5	1	1	0	0	1	0	2	0	15	5

Rank among batters: 1,810 • *Total ballparks homered in*: 8 • *First HR*: 04/29/1986 off Ron Guidry • *World Series HR*—1

Jim Lonborg

JAMES REYNOLD LONBORG
B: 04/16/1942
BR

Year	Tm	Lg	Tot	H	A	Men-On 0	Men-On 1	Men-On 2	Men-On 3	One-Game 2	One-Game 3	One-Game 4	LO	XN	IP	PH	RHP	LHP
1968	BOS	AL	1	0	1	1	0	0	0	0	0	0	0	0	0	0	1	0
1970	BOS	AL	1	1	0	1	0	0	0	0	0	0	0	0	0	0	1	0
1974	PHI	NL	1	0	1	0	0	0	1	0	0	0	0	0	0	0	1	0
Total			3	1	2	2	0	0	1	0	0	0	0	0	0	0	3	0

Rank among batters: 3,735 • *Total ballparks homered in*: 3 • *First HR*: 07/16/1968 off Dean Chance

Dale Long

RICHARD DALE LONG
B: 02/06/1926 D: 01/27/1991
BL

Year	Tm	Lg	Tot	H	A	Men-On 0	Men-On 1	Men-On 2	Men-On 3	One-Game 2	One-Game 3	One-Game 4	LO	XN	IP	PH	RHP	LHP
1951	PIT	NL	1	0	1	1	0	0	0	0	0	0	0	0	0	0	1	0
	STL	AL	2	1	1	0	1	1	0	0	0	0	0	0	0	0	2	0
	Total		3	1	2	2	1	0	0	0	0	0	0	0	0	0	3	0
1955	PIT	NL	16	4	12	8	6	2	0	2	0	0	0	0	0	1	12	4
1956	PIT	NL	27	12	15	17	8	2	0	1	0	0	0	0	0	0	16	11
1957	CHI	NL	21	12	9	14	5	2	0	1	0	0	0	0	1	0	19	2
1958	CHI	NL	20	9	11	15	5	0	0	0	0	0	0	2	0	2	15	5
1959	CHI	NL	14	10	4	8	6	0	0	0	0	0	0	0	0	2	13	1
1960	SF	NL	3	0	3	1	1	1	0	0	0	0	0	0	0	3	3	0
	NY	AL	3	2	1	1	2	0	0	0	0	0	0	0	0	0	2	1
	Total		6	2	4	2	3	1	0	0	0	0	0	0	0	3	5	1
1961	WAS	AL	17	4	13	12	4	1	0	0	0	0	0	0	0	0	15	2
1962	WAS	AL	4	3	1	0	2	2	0	0	0	0	0	0	0	0	4	0
	NY	AL	4	3	1	1	2	1	0	0	0	0	0	1	0	0	4	0
	Total		8	6	2	1	4	3	0	0	0	0	0	1	0	0	8	0
Total			132	60	72	79	42	11	0	4	0	0	0	3	1	8	106	26

Rank among batters: 339 • *Top target (8 home runs)*: Sam Jones • *Number of pitchers victimized*: 85 • *Total ballparks homered in*: 20 • *First HR*: 05/05/1951 off Jim Hearn

Herman Long

HERMAN C. LONG
B: 04/13/1866 D: 09/17/1909
BL

Year	Tm	Lg	Tot	H	A	Men-On 0	1	2	3	One-Game 2	3	4	LO	XN	IP	PH	RHP	LHP
1889	KC	AA	3	0	3	1	1	1	0	0	0	0	1	0	1	0	2	1
1890	BOS	NL	8	7	1	3	2	3	0	1	0	0	1	0	2	0	7	1
1891	BOS	NL	9	6	3	4	3	2	0	0	0	0	0	0	1	0	8	1
1892	BOS	NL	6	4	2	3	2	0	1	0	0	0	1	0	0	0	4	2
1893	BOS	NL	6	5	1	4	1	1	0	0	0	0	2	0	1	0	5	0
1894	BOS	NL	12	9	3	7	5	0	0	0	0	0	0	0	0	0	8	2
1895	BOS	NL	9	9	0	4	3	2	0	1	0	0	0	0	0	0	9	0
1896	BOS	NL	6	4	2	5	1	0	0	0	0	0	0	0	0	0	5	1
1897	BOS	NL	3	2	1	1	2	0	0	0	0	0	0	0	0	0	3	0
1898	BOS	NL	6	5	1	3	2	0	1	0	0	0	0	0	0	0	5	0
1899	BOS	NL	6	5	1	3	1	2	0	0	0	0	0	0	0	0	5	0
1900	BOS	NL	12	12	0	6	3	3	0	0	0	0	0	0	1	0	12	0
1901	BOS	NL	3	3	0	1	1	1	0	0	0	0	0	0	0	0	3	0
1902	BOS	NL	2	1	1	0	2	0	0	0	0	0	0	0	0	0	2	0
Total			91	72	19	45	29	15	2	2	0	0	5	0	6	0	77	8

Rank among batters: 559 • *Top target (4 home runs)*: Cy Young, Jack Powell • *Number of pitchers victimized*: 60 • *Total ballparks homered in*: 15 • *First HR*: 04/20/1889 off Toad Ramsey • *Hit for Cycle*—@LOU: 05/09/1896 • *World Series HR*—1

Jeoff Long

JEOFFREY KEITH LONG
B: 10/09/1941
BR

Year	Tm	Lg	Tot	H	A	Men-On 0	1	2	3	One-Game 2	3	4	LO	XN	IP	PH	RHP	LHP
1964	STL	NL	1	1	0	0	1	0	0	0	0	0	0	0	0	0	1	0

Rank among batters: 4,707 • *Total ballparks homered in*: 1 • *First HR*: 05/15/1964 off Bobby Tiefenauer

Jim Long

JAMES M. LONG
B: 11/15/1862 D: 12/12/1932

Year	Tm	Lg	Tot	H	A	Men-On 0	1	2	3	One-Game 2	3	4	LO	XN	IP	PH	RHP	LHP
1893	BAL	NL	2	2	0	1	1	0	0	0	0	0	0	0	1	0	2	0

Rank among batters: 4,129 • *Total ballparks homered in*: 1 • *First HR*: 07/19/1893 off Ed Crane

Tom Long

THOMAS AUGUSTUS LONG
B: 06/01/1890 D: 06/15/1972
BR

Year	Tm	Lg	Tot	H	A	Men-On 0	1	2	3	One-Game 2	3	4	LO	XN	IP	PH	RHP	LHP
1915	STL	NL	2	1	1	0	1	1	0	0	0	0	0	0	1	0	0	2
1916	STL	NL	1	0	1	0	1	0	0	0	0	0	0	0	0	0	1	0
1917	STL	NL	3	2	1	2	1	0	0	0	0	0	0	0	2	0	3	0
Total			6	3	3	2	3	1	0	0	0	0	0	0	3	0	4	2

Rank among batters: 2,988 • *Total ballparks homered in*: 4 • *First HR*: 07/20/1915 off Rube Marquard

Tony Longmire

ANTHONY EUGENE LONGMIRE
B: 08/12/1968
BL

Year	Tm	Lg	Tot	H	A	Men-On 0	1	2	3	One-Game 2	3	4	LO	XN	IP	PH	RHP	LHP
1995	PHI	NL	3	2	1	1	0	2	0	0	0	0	0	0	0	3	2	1

Rank among batters: 3,735 • *Total ballparks homered in*: 2 • *First HR*: 04/26/1995 off Vicente Palacios

Joe Lonnett

JOSEPH PAUL LONNETT
B: 02/07/1927
BR

Year	Tm	Lg	Tot	H	A	Men-On 0	1	2	3	One-Game 2	3	4	LO	XN	IP	PH	RHP	LHP
1957	PHI	NL	5	4	1	4	1	0	0	0	0	0	0	0	1	0	5	0
1959	PHI	NL	1	1	0	0	0	1	0	0	0	0	0	0	0	0	0	1
Total			6	5	1	4	1	1	0	0	0	0	0	0	1	0	5	1

Rank among batters: 2,988 • *Top target (2 home runs)*: Don Elston • *Number of pitchers victimized*: 5 • *Total ballparks homered in*: 2 • *First HR*: 07/04/1957 off Al Worthington

Eddie Lopat

EDMUND WALTER LOPAT
B: 06/21/1918 D: 06/15/1992
BL

Year	Tm	Lg	Tot	H	A	Men-On 0	1	2	3	One-Game 2	3	4	LO	XN	IP	PH	RHP	LHP
1945	CHI	AL	1	1	0	1	0	0	0	0	0	0	0	0	0	0	0	1

Eddie Lopat *continued*

Year	Tm	Lg	Tot	H	A	Men-On 0	Men-On 1	Men-On 2	Men-On 3	One-Game 2	One-Game 3	One-Game 4	LO	XN	IP	PH	RHP	LHP
1949	NY	AL	1	0	1	1	0	0	0	0	0	0	0	0	0	0	1	0
1951	NY	AL	3	2	1	1	1	1	0	0	0	0	0	0	0	0	3	0
Total			5	3	2	3	1	1	0	0	0	0	0	0	0	0	4	1

Rank among batters: 3,191 • *Total ballparks homered in*: 4 • *First HR*: 04/20/1945 off Al Hollingsworth

Stan Lopata

STANLEY EDWARD LOPATA
B: 09/12/1925
BR

Year	Tm	Lg	Tot	H	A	Men-On 0	Men-On 1	Men-On 2	Men-On 3	One-Game 2	One-Game 3	One-Game 4	LO	XN	IP	PH	RHP	LHP
1949	PHI	NL	8	4	4	5	2	1	0	0	0	0	0	0	0	0	6	2
1950	PHI	NL	1	1	0	1	0	0	0	0	0	0	0	0	0	0	1	0
1952	PHI	NL	4	2	2	1	3	0	0	0	0	0	0	0	0	0	1	3
1953	PHI	NL	8	4	4	5	2	1	0	0	0	0	0	0	0	0	2	6
1954	PHI	NL	14	10	4	3	8	3	0	1	0	0	0	1	0	1	3	11
1955	PHI	NL	22	13	9	11	8	2	1	0	0	0	0	1	0	0	11	11
1956	PHI	NL	32	15	17	21	8	3	0	4	0	0	0	1	0	1	28	4
1957	PHI	NL	18	10	8	8	8	2	0	1	0	0	0	1	0	1	12	6
1958	PHI	NL	9	3	6	4	4	1	0	0	0	0	0	0	0	0	4	5
Total			116	62	54	59	43	13	1	6	0	0	0	4	0	3	68	48

Rank among batters: 411 • *Top target (6 home runs)*: Harvey Haddix • *Number of pitchers victimized*: 73 • *Total ballparks homered in*: 10 • *First HR*: 04/24/1949 off Joe Hatten

Davey Lopes

DAVID EARL LOPES
B: 05/03/1945
BR

Year	Tm	Lg	Tot	H	A	Men-On 0	Men-On 1	Men-On 2	Men-On 3	One-Game 2	One-Game 3	One-Game 4	LO	XN	IP	PH	RHP	LHP
1973	LA	NL	6	2	4	3	3	0	0	0	0	0	0	1	0	0	3	3
1974	LA	NL	10	4	6	8	1	1	0	0	1	0	3	0	0	0	7	3
1975	LA	NL	8	2	6	5	1	2	0	0	0	0	0	0	0	0	6	2
1976	LA	NL	4	4	0	4	0	0	0	0	0	0	2	0	0	0	3	1
1977	LA	NL	11	5	6	5	4	2	0	0	0	0	4	1	0	0	7	4
1978	LA	NL	17	10	7	8	6	2	1	0	0	0	4	1	1	0	13	4
1979	LA	NL	28	15	13	19	6	2	1	1	0	0	7	2	1	0	15	13
1980	LA	NL	10	5	5	9	1	0	0	0	0	0	6	0	0	0	7	3
1981	LA	NL	5	3	2	3	1	1	0	0	0	0	2	0	0	0	1	4
1982	OAK	AL	11	5	6	5	4	2	0	1	0	0	0	0	0	0	9	2
1983	OAK	AL	17	10	7	12	4	0	1	1	0	0	0	0	0	0	8	9
1984	OAK	AL	9	6	3	5	3	1	0	0	0	0	0	0	1	0	3	6
1985	CHI	NL	11	6	5	2	6	3	0	0	0	0	0	0	0	1	6	5
1986	CHI	NL	6	4	2	5	1	0	0	0	0	0	0	0	0	0	3	3
	HOU	NL	1	0	1	0	1	0	0	0	0	0	0	0	0	0	1	0
	Total		7	4	3	5	2	0	0	0	0	0	0	0	0	0	4	3
1987	HOU	NL	1	0	1	0	1	0	0	0	0	0	0	0	0	0	0	1
Total			155	81	74	93	43	16	3	3	1	0	28	5	3	1	92	63

Rank among batters: 274 • *Top target (4 home runs)*: Fred Norman, Jack Curtis, Dave Roberts • *Number of pitchers victimized*: 113 • *Total ballparks homered in*: 25 • *First HR*: 05/13/1973 off Jim Barr • *World Series HR*—4; *LCS HR*—2

Al Lopez

ALFONSO RAMON LOPEZ
B: 08/20/1908
BR HOF

Year	Tm	Lg	Tot	H	A	Men-On 0	Men-On 1	Men-On 2	Men-On 3	One-Game 2	One-Game 3	One-Game 4	LO	XN	IP	PH	RHP	LHP
1930	BRO	NL	6	3	3	2	1	3	0	0	0	0	0	0	0	0	1	5
1932	BRO	NL	1	1	0	1	0	0	0	0	0	0	0	0	0	0	1	0
1933	BRO	NL	3	2	1	1	1	1	0	0	0	0	0	0	0	0	3	0
1934	BRO	NL	7	5	2	6	1	0	0	0	0	0	0	0	0	0	6	1
1935	BRO	NL	3	2	1	3	0	0	0	0	0	0	0	1	0	0	2	1
1936	BOS	NL	7	2	5	3	4	0	0	0	0	0	0	0	0	0	6	1
1937	BOS	NL	3	0	3	3	0	0	0	0	0	0	0	0	0	0	3	0
1938	BOS	NL	1	1	0	1	0	0	0	0	0	0	0	0	0	0	1	0
1939	BOS	NL	8	3	5	4	1	2	1	0	0	0	0	0	0	0	7	1
1940	BOS	NL	2	2	0	0	1	1	0	0	0	0	0	0	0	0	2	0
	PIT	NL	1	0	1	0	1	0	0	0	0	0	0	0	0	0	0	1
	Total		3	2	1	0	2	1	0	0	0	0	0	0	0	0	2	1
1941	PIT	NL	5	1	4	2	2	1	0	0	0	0	0	0	0	0	4	1
1942	PIT	NL	1	0	1	1	0	0	0	0	0	0	0	0	0	0	0	1

						Men-On				One-Game								
Year	Tm	Lg	Tot	H	A	0	1	2	3	2	3	4	LO	XN	IP	PH	RHP	LHP

Al Lopez *continued*

Year	Tm	Lg	Tot	H	A	0	1	2	3	2	3	4	LO	XN	IP	PH	RHP	LHP
1943	PIT	NL	1	0	1	0	1	0	0	0	0	0	0	0	0	0	1	0
1944	PIT	NL	1	1	0	1	0	0	0	0	0	0	0	0	0	0	1	0
1946	PIT	NL	1	1	0	0	1	0	0	0	0	0	0	0	0	0	0	1
Total			51	24	27	28	14	8	1	0	0	0	0	1	0	0	38	13

Rank among batters: 979 • Top target (2 home runs): Leo Sweetland, Pat Malone, Bob Smith, Larry French, Bill Swift, Benny Frey, Paul Dean • *Number of pitchers victimized*: 44 • *Total ballparks homered in*: 9 • *First HR*: 05/20/1930 off Leo Sweetland

Carlos Lopez

CARLOS ANTONIO (MORALES) LOPEZ
B: 09/27/1950
BR

Year	Tm	Lg	Tot	H	A	0	1	2	3	2	3	4	LO	XN	IP	PH	RHP	LHP
1977	SEA	AL	8	4	4	5	3	0	0	1	0	0	0	1	0	0	5	3
1978	BAL	AL	4	3	1	2	2	0	0	0	0	0	1	0	0	0	0	4
Total			12	7	5	7	5	0	0	1	0	0	1	1	0	0	5	7

Rank among batters: 2,325 • *Top target (2 home runs)*: Rudy May • *Number of pitchers victimized*: 11 • *Total ballparks homered in*: 5 • *First HR*: 05/03/1977 off Tom Murphy

Hector Lopez

HECTOR HEADLEY (SWAINSON) LOPEZ
B: 07/08/1929
BR

Year	Tm	Lg	Tot	H	A	0	1	2	3	2	3	4	LO	XN	IP	PH	RHP	LHP
1955	KC	AL	15	10	5	10	3	2	0	0	0	0	0	0	0	0	10	5
1956	KC	AL	18	8	10	10	6	2	0	0	0	0	0	0	0	0	12	6
1957	KC	AL	11	7	4	9	2	0	0	1	0	0	0	0	0	0	8	3
1958	KC	AL	17	14	3	8	9	0	0	1	1	0	0	1	0	0	15	2
1959	KC	AL	6	5	1	4	1	1	0	0	0	0	0	0	0	0	4	2
	NY	AL	16	1	15	8	8	0	0	1	0	0	0	0	0	0	11	5
	Total		22	6	16	12	9	1	0	1	0	0	0	0	0	0	15	7
1960	NY	AL	9	4	5	7	2	0	0	1	0	0	0	1	0	0	6	3
1961	NY	AL	3	1	2	1	2	0	0	0	0	0	0	0	0	0	2	1
1962	NY	AL	6	3	3	2	3	1	0	0	0	0	0	0	0	0	3	3
1963	NY	AL	14	5	9	6	6	2	0	0	0	0	0	0	0	0	10	4
1964	NY	AL	10	1	9	7	3	0	0	1	0	0	0	0	0	0	6	4
1965	NY	AL	7	1	6	6	1	0	0	0	0	0	0	0	0	0	3	4
1966	NY	AL	4	1	3	3	0	1	0	0	0	0	0	0	0	0	2	2
Total			136	61	75	81	46	9	0	5	1	0	0	2	0	0	92	44

Rank among batters: 322 • *Top target (6 home runs)*: Pedro Ramos • *Number of pitchers victimized*: 88 • *Total ballparks homered in*: 11 • *First HR*: 06/26/1955 off Don Johnson • *World Series HR*—1

Javier Lopez

JAVIER (TORRES) LOPEZ
B: 11/05/1970
BR

Year	Tm	Lg	Tot	H	A	0	1	2	3	2	3	4	LO	XN	IP	PH	RHP	LHP
1993	ATL	NL	1	0	1	0	1	0	0	0	0	0	0	0	0	0	1	0
1994	ATL	NL	13	4	9	7	4	2	0	2	0	0	0	0	0	0	8	5
1995	ATL	NL	14	8	6	9	3	2	0	0	0	0	0	0	0	0	12	2
Total			28	12	16	16	8	4	0	2	0	0	0	0	0	0	21	7

Rank among batters: 1,500 • *Top target (2 home runs)*: Dave Weathers, Bret Saberhagen • *Number of pitchers victimized*: 26 • *Total ballparks homered in*: 11 • *First HR*: 08/21/1993 off Shawn Boskie • *World Series HR*—1; *LCS HR*—1

Luis Lopez

LUIS MANUEL (SANTOS) LOPEZ
B: 09/04/1970
BB

Year	Tm	Lg	Tot	H	A	0	1	2	3	2	3	4	LO	XN	IP	PH	RHP	LHP
1994	SD	NL	2	2	0	1	0	0	1	0	0	0	0	0	0	0	2	0

Rank among batters: 4,129 • *Total ballparks homered in*: 1 • *First HR*: 05/23/1994 off Mark Portugal

Marcelino Lopez

MARCELINO PONS LOPEZ
B: 09/23/1943
BR

Year	Tm	Lg	Tot	H	A	0	1	2	3	2	3	4	LO	XN	IP	PH	RHP	LHP
1965	CAL	AL	1	0	1	1	0	0	0	0	0	0	0	0	0	0	1	0

Rank among batters: 4,707 • *Total ballparks homered in*: 1 • *First HR*: 07/25/1965 off Earl Wilson

Year	Tm	Lg	Tot	H	A	Men-On 0	1	2	3	One-Game 2	3	4	LO	XN	IP	PH	RHP	LHP

Bris Lord

BRISTOL ROBOTHAM LORD
B: 09/21/1883 D: 11/13/1964
BR

Year	Tm	Lg	Tot	H	A	0	1	2	3	2	3	4	LO	XN	IP	PH	RHP	LHP
1906	PHI	AL	1	1	0	1	0	0	0	0	0	0	0	0	1	0	1	0
1907	PHI	AL	1	1	0	0	1	0	0	0	0	0	0	0	0	0	1	0
1909	CLE	AL	1	1	0	0	1	0	0	0	0	0	0	0	0	0	1	0
1910	PHI	AL	1	1	0	1	0	0	0	0	0	0	0	0	0	0	1	0
1911	PHI	AL	3	0	3	2	0	1	0	0	0	0	0	0	0	0	2	1
1913	BOS	NL	6	2	4	3	1	2	0	0	0	0	0	0	0	0	4	2
Total			13	6	7	7	3	3	0	0	0	0	0	0	1	0	10	3

Rank among batters: 2,248 • *Total ballparks homered in*: 11 • *First HR*: 08/23/1906 off George Mullin

Harry Lord

HARRY DONALD LORD
B: 03/08/1882 D: 08/09/1948
BL

Year	Tm	Lg	Tot	H	A	0	1	2	3	2	3	4	LO	XN	IP	PH	RHP	LHP
1908	BOS	AL	2	2	0	0	2	0	0	0	0	0	0	0	1	0	2	0
1910	BOS	AL	1	1	0	0	0	1	0	0	0	0	0	0	0	0	1	0
1911	CHI	AL	3	1	2	2	0	1	0	0	0	0	0	0	1	0	2	1
1912	CHI	AL	5	2	3	1	4	0	0	0	0	0	0	0	1	0	5	0
1913	CHI	AL	1	1	0	1	0	0	0	0	0	0	0	0	1	0	1	0
1914	CHI	AL	1	1	0	0	0	1	0	0	0	0	0	0	1	0	1	0
1915	BUF	FL	1	1	0	1	0	0	0	0	0	0	0	0	0	0	1	0
Total			14	9	5	5	6	3	0	0	0	0	0	0	5	0	13	1

Rank among batters: 2,169 • *Top target (2 home runs)*: Ray Fisher, Walter Johnson • *Number of pitchers victimized*: 12 • *Total ballparks homered in*: 6 • *First HR*: 08/28/1908 off Jack Powell

Mark Loretta

MARK DAVID LORETTA
B: 08/14/1971
BR

Year	Tm	Lg	Tot	H	A	0	1	2	3	2	3	4	LO	XN	IP	PH	RHP	LHP
1995	MIL	AL	1	0	1	1	0	0	0	0	0	0	0	0	0	0	1	0

Rank among batters: 4,707 • *Total ballparks homered in*: 1 • *First HR*: 09/12/1995 off Jose Lima

Baldy Louden

WILLIAM P. LOUDEN
B: 08/27/1885 D: 12/08/1935
BR

Year	Tm	Lg	Tot	H	A	0	1	2	3	2	3	4	LO	XN	IP	PH	RHP	LHP
1912	DET	AL	1	0	1	0	1	0	0	0	0	0	0	0	1	0	1	0
1914	BUF	FL	6	3	3	4	2	0	0	0	0	0	0	0	2	0	6	0
1915	BUF	FL	4	3	1	3	0	1	0	0	0	0	0	0	0	0	4	0
1916	CIN	NL	1	0	1	1	0	0	0	0	0	0	0	0	1	0	1	0
Total			12	6	6	8	3	1	0	0	0	0	0	0	4	0	12	0

Rank among batters: 2,325 • *Top target (2 home runs)*: Earl Moseley • *Number of pitchers victimized*: 11 • *Total ballparks homered in*: 6 • *First HR*: 07/15/1912 off Charles Hall

Tom Lovett

THOMAS JOSEPH LOVETT
B: 12/07/1863 D: 03/19/1928
BR

Year	Tm	Lg	Tot	H	A	0	1	2	3	2	3	4	LO	XN	IP	PH	RHP	LHP
1889	BRO	AA	2	1	1	0	1	0	1	0	0	0	0	0	0	0	1	1
1890	BRO	NL	1	1	0	1	0	0	0	0	0	0	0	0	0	0	1	0
1894	BOS	NL	1	1	0	1	0	0	0	0	0	0	0	0	0	0	1	0
Total			4	3	1	2	1	0	1	0	0	0	0	0	0	0	3	1

Rank among batters: 3,427 • *Total ballparks homered in*: 3 • *First HR*: 05/27/1889 off Mark Baldwin

Joe Lovitto

JOSEPH LOVITTO
B: 01/06/1951
BB

Year	Tm	Lg	Tot	H	A	0	1	2	3	2	3	4	LO	XN	IP	PH	RHP	LHP
1972	TEX	AL	1	1	0	0	1	0	0	0	0	0	0	0	0	0	0	1
1974	TEX	AL	2	2	0	2	0	0	0	0	0	0	0	0	0	0	2	0
1975	TEX	AL	1	0	1	1	0	0	0	0	0	0	0	0	0	0	0	1
Total			4	3	1	3	1	0	0	0	0	0	0	0	0	0	2	2

Rank among batters: 3,427 • *Total ballparks homered in*: 2 • *First HR*: 06/10/1972 off Dave McNally

Torri Lovullo

SALVATORE ANTHONY LOVULLO
B: 07/25/1965
BB

Year	Tm	Lg	Tot	H	A	Men-On 0	Men-On 1	Men-On 2	Men-On 3	One-Game 2	One-Game 3	One-Game 4	LO	XN	IP	PH	RHP	LHP
1988	DET	AL	1	0	1	1	0	0	0	0	0	0	0	0	0	0	1	0
1989	DET	AL	1	0	1	0	1	0	0	0	0	0	0	0	0	0	0	1
1993	CAL	AL	6	4	2	3	3	0	0	0	0	0	0	0	0	1	5	1
1994	SEA	AL	2	2	0	1	0	1	0	0	0	0	0	0	0	1	2	0
Total			10	6	4	5	4	1	0	0	0	0	0	0	0	2	8	2

Rank among batters: 2,500 • *Total ballparks homered in*: 5 • *First HR*: 09/25/1988 off Jose Bautista

Bobby Lowe

ROBERT LINCOLN LOWE
B: 07/10/1868 D: 12/08/1951
BR

Year	Tm	Lg	Tot	H	A	Men-On 0	Men-On 1	Men-On 2	Men-On 3	One-Game 2	One-Game 3	One-Game 4	LO	XN	IP	PH	RHP	LHP
1890	BOS	NL	2	2	0	2	0	0	0	0	0	0	1	0	0	0	1	0
1891	BOS	NL	6	5	1	4	2	0	0	0	0	0	0	0	0	0	5	1
1892	BOS	NL	3	2	1	0	1	2	0	0	0	0	0	0	0	0	1	0
1893	BOS	NL	14	9	5	7	4	2	1	0	0	0	1	0	1	0	11	2
1894	BOS	NL	17	16	1	9	4	3	1	0	0	1	1	0	0	0	13	2
1895	BOS	NL	7	6	1	4	2	0	1	0	0	0	0	0	0	0	7	0
1896	BOS	NL	2	0	2	1	1	0	0	1	0	0	0	0	1	0	2	0
1897	BOS	NL	5	5	0	0	4	1	0	0	0	0	0	0	0	0	4	1
1898	BOS	NL	4	4	0	3	1	0	0	0	0	0	0	0	0	0	3	1
1899	BOS	NL	4	3	1	3	0	1	0	0	0	0	0	0	0	0	3	1
1900	BOS	NL	3	3	0	2	0	1	0	0	0	0	0	0	0	0	2	1
1901	BOS	NL	3	1	2	1	2	0	0	0	0	0	0	0	1	0	3	0
1906	DET	AL	1	1	0	0	1	0	0	0	0	0	0	0	0	0	1	0
Total			71	57	14	36	22	10	3	1	0	1	3	0	3	0	56	9

Rank among batters: 731 • *Top target (4 home runs)*: Elton Chamberlin, Ad Gumbert • *Number of pitchers victimized*: 51 • *Total ballparks homered in*: 13 • *First HR*: 08/26/1890 off Charlie Heard • *2 HR in 1 inning*—vs CIN: 05/30/1894 (2)

John Lowenstein

JOHN LEE LOWENSTEIN
B: 01/27/1947
BL

Year	Tm	Lg	Tot	H	A	Men-On 0	Men-On 1	Men-On 2	Men-On 3	One-Game 2	One-Game 3	One-Game 4	LO	XN	IP	PH	RHP	LHP
1970	CLE	AL	1	1	0	0	1	0	0	0	0	0	0	0	0	0	1	0
1971	CLE	AL	4	1	3	3	1	0	0	0	0	0	0	0	0	0	4	0
1972	CLE	AL	6	2	4	2	3	1	0	0	0	0	0	0	0	0	6	0
1973	CLE	AL	6	3	3	2	3	1	0	0	0	0	0	0	0	0	6	0
1974	CLE	AL	8	2	6	2	4	1	1	0	0	0	0	0	0	0	4	4
1975	CLE	AL	12	8	4	7	3	2	0	0	0	0	1	0	0	1	12	0
1976	CLE	AL	2	2	0	2	0	0	0	0	0	0	0	0	0	0	2	0
1977	CLE	AL	4	2	2	4	0	0	0	0	0	0	0	1	0	1	4	0
1978	TEX	AL	5	3	2	4	1	0	0	0	0	0	0	1	1	0	5	0
1979	BAL	AL	11	4	7	6	2	2	1	0	0	0	0	0	0	0	11	0
1980	BAL	AL	4	2	2	3	0	1	0	0	0	0	0	0	0	0	4	0
1981	BAL	AL	6	4	2	5	1	0	0	1	0	0	0	0	0	0	6	0
1982	BAL	AL	24	10	14	15	5	4	0	1	0	0	0	2	0	1	24	0
1983	BAL	AL	15	7	8	7	5	1	2	0	0	0	0	0	0	1	15	0
1984	BAL	AL	8	2	6	4	4	0	0	0	0	0	0	0	0	0	8	0
Total			116	53	63	66	33	13	4	2	0	0	1	4	1	4	112	4

Rank among batters: 411 • *Top target (4 home runs)*: Jim Colborn, Doc Medich, Jack Morris • *Number of pitchers victimized*: 83 • *Total ballparks homered in*: 16 • *First HR*: 09/10/1970 off Jim Hannan • *World Series HR*—1; *LCS HR*—1

Turk Lown

OMAR JOSEPH LOWN
B: 05/30/1924
BR

Year	Tm	Lg	Tot	H	A	Men-On 0	Men-On 1	Men-On 2	Men-On 3	One-Game 2	One-Game 3	One-Game 4	LO	XN	IP	PH	RHP	LHP
1956	CHI	NL	1	1	0	0	1	0	0	0	0	0	0	0	0	0	1	0

Rank among batters: 4,707 • *Total ballparks homered in*: 1 • *First HR*: 05/30/1956 off Bob Buhl

Peanuts Lowrey

HARRY LEE LOWREY
B: 08/27/1918 D: 07/02/1986
BR

Year	Tm	Lg	Tot	H	A	Men-On 0	Men-On 1	Men-On 2	Men-On 3	One-Game 2	One-Game 3	One-Game 4	LO	XN	IP	PH	RHP	LHP
1942	CHI	NL	1	1	0	1	0	0	0	0	0	0	1	0	0	0	0	1
1943	CHI	NL	1	0	1	1	0	0	0	0	0	0	0	0	0	0	1	0

Peanuts Lowrey *continued*

Year	Tm	Lg	Tot	H	A	Men-On				One-Game			LO	XN	IP	PH	RHP	LHP
						0	1	2	3	2	3	4						
1945	CHI	NL	7	2	5	3	2	2	0	0	0	0	0	0	0	0	6	1
1946	CHI	NL	4	4	0	3	0	1	0	0	0	0	0	0	0	0	2	2
1947	CHI	NL	5	3	2	2	1	2	0	0	0	0	0	0	0	0	3	2
1948	CHI	NL	2	1	1	2	0	0	0	0	0	0	0	0	0	0	2	0
1949	CHI	NL	2	1	1	2	0	0	0	0	0	0	0	0	0	0	0	2
	CIN	NL	2	1	1	1	1	0	0	0	0	0	0	0	0	0	0	2
	Total		4	2	2	3	1	0	0	0	0	0	0	0	0	0	0	4
1950	CIN	NL	1	1	0	1	0	0	0	0	0	0	0	0	0	0	0	1
	STL	NL	1	0	1	1	0	0	0	0	0	0	1	0	0	0	1	0
	Total		2	1	1	2	0	0	0	0	0	0	1	0	0	0	1	1
1951	STL	NL	5	3	2	4	1	0	0	0	0	0	1	0	0	0	1	4
1952	STL	NL	1	0	1	0	0	1	0	0	0	0	0	0	0	0	0	1
1953	STL	NL	5	1	4	3	1	1	0	0	0	0	0	0	0	2	2	3
Total			37	18	19	24	6	7	0	0	0	0	3	0	0	2	18	19

Rank among batters: 1,252 • *Top target (4 home runs)*: Preacher Roe • *Number of pitchers victimized*: 32 • *Total ballparks homered in*: 8 • *First HR*: 05/01/1942 off Dave Koslo

Dwight Lowry

DWIGHT LOWRY
B: 10/23/1957
BL

Year	Tm	Lg	Tot	H	A	Men-On 0	Men-On 1	Men-On 2	Men-On 3	One-Game 2	One-Game 3	One-Game 4	LO	XN	IP	PH	RHP	LHP
1984	DET	AL	2	1	1	1	1	0	0	0	0	0	0	0	0	0	2	0
1986	DET	AL	3	1	2	2	0	1	0	0	0	0	0	0	0	0	2	1
Total			5	2	3	3	1	1	0	0	0	0	0	0	0	0	4	1

Rank among batters: 3,191 • *Total ballparks homered in*: 4 • *First HR*: 05/20/1984 off Lary Sorensen

Willie Lozado

WILLIAM LOZADO
B: 05/12/1959
BR

Year	Tm	Lg	Tot	H	A	Men-On 0	Men-On 1	Men-On 2	Men-On 3	One-Game 2	One-Game 3	One-Game 4	LO	XN	IP	PH	RHP	LHP
1984	MIL	AL	1	0	1	0	0	1	0	0	0	0	0	0	0	0	1	0

Rank among batters: 4,707 • *Total ballparks homered in*: 1 • *First HR*: 09/11/1984 off Steve Crawford

Hal Luby

HUGH MAX LUBY
B: 06/13/1913 D: 05/04/1986
BR

Year	Tm	Lg	Tot	H	A	Men-On 0	Men-On 1	Men-On 2	Men-On 3	One-Game 2	One-Game 3	One-Game 4	LO	XN	IP	PH	RHP	LHP
1944	NY	NL	2	2	0	1	1	0	0	0	0	0	0	1	0	0	0	2

Rank among batters: 4,129 • *Total ballparks homered in*: 1 • *First HR*: 07/29/1944 off Clyde Shoun

Pat Luby

JOHN PERKINS LUBY
B: 01/ /1869 D: 04/24/1899

Year	Tm	Lg	Tot	H	A	Men-On 0	Men-On 1	Men-On 2	Men-On 3	One-Game 2	One-Game 3	One-Game 4	LO	XN	IP	PH	RHP	LHP
1890	CHI	NL	3	2	1	2	0	1	0	0	0	0	0	0	0	0	2	0
1891	CHI	NL	2	2	0	0	1	1	0	0	0	0	0	0	0	0	2	0
1892	CHI	NL	2	0	2	1	0	1	0	0	0	0	0	0	0	0	2	0
Total			7	4	3	3	1	3	0	0	0	0	0	0	0	0	6	0

Rank among batters: 2,834 • *Total ballparks homered in*: 3 • *First HR*: 06/26/1890 off Tom Lovett

Johnny Lucadello

JOHN LUCADELLO
B: 02/22/1919
BR

Year	Tm	Lg	Tot	H	A	Men-On 0	Men-On 1	Men-On 2	Men-On 3	One-Game 2	One-Game 3	One-Game 4	LO	XN	IP	PH	RHP	LHP
1940	STL	AL	2	2	0	1	1	0	0	1	0	0	0	0	0	0	1	1
1941	STL	AL	2	1	1	2	0	0	0	0	0	0	1	0	0	0	1	1
1946	STL	AL	1	0	1	1	0	0	0	0	0	0	0	0	0	0	1	0
Total			5	3	2	4	1	0	0	1	0	0	1	0	0	0	3	2

Rank among batters: 3,191 • *Total ballparks homered in*: 3 • *First HR*: 09/16/1940 off Marius Russo • *Switch hit HR in 1 game*—1 time

Red Lucas

CHARLES FREDERICK LUCAS
B: 04/28/1902 D: 07/09/1986
BL

Year	Tm	Lg	Tot	H	A	Men-On 0	Men-On 1	Men-On 2	Men-On 3	One-Game 2	One-Game 3	One-Game 4	LO	XN	IP	PH	RHP	LHP
1930	CIN	NL	2	0	2	1	0	1	0	0	0	0	0	0	0	1	2	0

Red Lucas *continued*

Year	Tm	Lg	Tot	H	A	Men-On 0	1	2	3	One-Game 2	3	4	LO	XN	IP	PH	RHP	LHP
1933	CIN	NL	1	1	0	0	0	1	0	0	0	0	0	0	0	1	1	0
Total			3	1	2	1	0	2	0	0	0	0	0	0	0	2	3	0

Rank among batters: 3,735 • *Total ballparks homered in*: 3 • *First HR*: 07/11/1930 off Hap Collard

Fred Luderus

FREDERICK WILLIAM LUDERUS
B: 09/12/1885 D: 01/05/1961
BL

Year	Tm	Lg	Tot	H	A	Men-On 0	1	2	3	One-Game 2	3	4	LO	XN	IP	PH	RHP	LHP
1909	CHI	NL	1	1	0	0	1	0	0	0	0	0	0	0	1	0	1	0
1911	PHI	NL	16	15	1	10	3	2	1	3	0	0	0	1	0	0	16	0
1912	PHI	NL	10	8	2	5	2	2	1	0	0	0	0	0	2	0	10	0
1913	PHI	NL	18	12	6	8	7	3	0	2	0	0	0	0	1	0	17	1
1914	PHI	NL	12	8	4	10	2	0	0	1	0	0	0	0	0	0	11	1
1915	PHI	NL	7	5	2	4	2	1	0	0	0	0	0	0	0	0	7	0
1916	PHI	NL	5	2	3	2	3	0	0	0	0	0	0	0	0	0	4	1
1917	PHI	NL	5	2	3	3	2	0	0	0	0	0	0	0	1	0	5	0
1918	PHI	NL	5	5	0	1	2	1	1	0	0	0	0	0	0	0	4	1
1919	PHI	NL	5	5	0	4	0	1	0	0	0	0	0	0	0	0	5	0
Total			84	63	21	47	24	10	3	6	0	0	0	1	5	0	80	4

Rank among batters: 617 • *Top target (5 home runs)*: Hub Perdue • *Number of pitchers victimized*: 57 • *Total ballparks homered in*: 10 • *First HR*: 09/29/1909 off Lew Moren • *World Series HR*—1

Eddie Lukon

EDWARD PAUL LUKON
B: 08/05/1920
BL

Year	Tm	Lg	Tot	H	A	Men-On 0	1	2	3	One-Game 2	3	4	LO	XN	IP	PH	RHP	LHP
1946	CIN	NL	12	6	6	7	5	0	0	2	0	0	0	0	0	1	12	0
1947	CIN	NL	11	7	4	7	3	1	0	1	0	0	0	0	0	0	10	1
Total			23	13	10	14	8	1	0	3	0	0	0	0	0	1	22	1

Rank among batters: 1,686 • Top target (2 home runs): Mort Cooper, Sheldon Jones, Hank Wyse, Si Johnson • *Number of pitchers victimized*: 19 • *Total ballparks homered in*: 7 • *First HR*: 05/26/1946 off Red Barrett

Mike Lum

MICHAEL KEN-WAI LUM
B: 10/27/1945
BL

Year	Tm	Lg	Tot	H	A	Men-On 0	1	2	3	One-Game 2	3	4	LO	XN	IP	PH	RHP	LHP
1968	ATL	NL	3	2	1	1	2	0	0	0	0	0	0	0	0	1	2	1
1969	ATL	NL	1	1	0	1	0	0	0	0	0	0	0	0	0	0	1	0
1970	ATL	NL	7	5	2	5	2	0	0	0	1	0	1	0	0	0	7	0
1971	ATL	NL	13	7	6	7	3	3	0	2	0	0	0	2	0	0	10	3
1972	ATL	NL	9	5	4	6	1	2	0	1	0	0	0	0	0	1	8	1
1973	ATL	NL	16	12	4	12	3	1	0	0	0	0	0	0	0	0	12	4
1974	ATL	NL	11	6	5	7	2	0	2	0	0	0	0	0	0	0	9	2
1975	ATL	NL	8	6	2	5	3	0	0	0	0	0	0	0	0	1	8	0
1976	CIN	NL	3	0	3	3	0	0	0	0	0	0	0	1	0	1	3	0
1977	CIN	NL	5	2	3	3	1	1	0	0	0	0	0	1	0	0	5	0
1978	CIN	NL	6	3	3	3	2	1	0	0	0	0	0	0	0	2	6	0
1979	ATL	NL	6	4	2	3	2	1	0	0	0	0	0	0	0	3	6	0
1981	CHI	NL	2	2	0	1	1	0	0	0	0	0	0	0	0	1	2	0
Total			90	55	35	57	22	9	2	3	1	0	1	4	0	10	79	11

Rank among batters: 573 • *Top target (3 home runs)*: Tom Phoebus, Steve Rogers, Jim Barr • *Number of pitchers victimized*: 77 • *Total ballparks homered in*: 13 • *First HR*: 06/26/1968 off Rick Wise

Harry Lumley

HARRY G. LUMLEY
B: 09/29/1880 D: 05/22/1938
BL

Year	Tm	Lg	Tot	H	A	Men-On 0	1	2	3	One-Game 2	3	4	LO	XN	IP	PH	RHP	LHP
1904	BRO	NL	9	2	7	4	4	1	0	0	0	0	0	0	3	0	8	1
1905	BRO	NL	7	4	3	3	3	1	0	0	0	0	0	0	0	0	7	0
1906	BRO	NL	9	2	7	7	1	1	0	0	0	0	2	0	3	0	4	5
1907	BRO	NL	9	4	5	3	1	5	0	0	0	0	0	1	1	0	7	2
1908	BRO	NL	4	3	1	4	0	0	0	0	0	0	0	0	0	0	4	0
Total			38	15	23	21	9	8	0	0	0	0	2	1	7	0	30	8

Year	Tm	Lg	Tot	H	A	Men-On 0	1	2	3	One-Game 2	3	4	LO	XN	IP	PH	RHP	LHP

Harry Lumley *continued*

Rank among batters: 1,225 • *Top target (3 home runs)*: Tully Sparks, Bob Ewing • *Number of pitchers victimized*: 29 • *Total ballparks homered in*: 8 • *First HR*: 05/23/1904 off Jack Dunleavy

Jerry Lumpe

JERRY DEAN LUMPE
B: 06/02/1933
BL

Year	Tm	Lg	Tot	H	A	0	1	2	3	2	3	4	LO	XN	IP	PH	RHP	LHP
1958	NY	AL	3	2	1	0	0	3	0	0	0	0	0	0	0	0	3	0
1959	KC	AL	3	2	1	1	2	0	0	0	0	0	0	0	0	0	1	2
1960	KC	AL	8	7	1	5	1	1	1	1	0	0	0	0	0	0	8	0
1961	KC	AL	3	2	1	1	1	1	0	0	0	0	0	1	0	0	2	1
1962	KC	AL	10	6	4	5	5	0	0	0	0	0	0	1	0	0	9	1
1963	KC	AL	5	3	2	2	2	1	0	0	0	0	0	1	0	0	2	3
1964	DET	AL	6	3	3	4	2	0	0	0	0	0	0	0	1	0	6	0
1965	DET	AL	4	3	1	1	3	0	0	0	0	0	0	0	0	0	4	0
1966	DET	AL	1	1	0	0	0	1	0	0	0	0	0	0	0	0	1	0
1967	DET	AL	4	2	2	2	2	0	0	0	0	0	0	0	0	0	4	0
Total			47	31	16	21	18	7	1	1	0	0	0	3	1	0	40	7

Rank among batters: 1,040 • *Top target (4 home runs)*: Ralph Terry • *Number of pitchers victimized*: 39 • *Total ballparks homered in*: 10 • *First HR*: 06/24/1958 off Early Wynn

Don Lund

DONALD ANDREW LUND
B: 05/18/1923
BR

Year	Tm	Lg	Tot	H	A	0	1	2	3	2	3	4	LO	XN	IP	PH	RHP	LHP
1947	BRO	NL	2	0	2	1	1	0	0	0	0	0	0	0	0	1	0	2
1948	BRO	NL	1	0	1	0	0	1	0	0	0	0	0	0	0	0	0	1
	STL	AL	3	1	2	2	0	1	0	0	0	0	0	0	0	0	1	2
	Total		4	1	3	2	0	2	0	0	0	0	0	0	0	0	1	3
1953	DET	AL	9	3	6	4	3	2	0	0	0	0	0	0	1	0	5	4
Total			15	4	11	7	4	4	0	0	0	0	0	0	1	1	6	9

Rank among batters: 2,096 • *Top target (2 home runs)*: Bob Cain, Don Larsen • *Number of pitchers victimized*: 13 • *Total ballparks homered in*: 7 • *First HR*: 09/12/1947 off Howie Pollet

Tony Lupien

ULYSSES JOHN LUPIEN
B: 04/23/1917
BL

Year	Tm	Lg	Tot	H	A	0	1	2	3	2	3	4	LO	XN	IP	PH	RHP	LHP
1942	BOS	AL	3	2	1	3	0	0	0	0	0	0	0	0	0	0	3	0
1943	BOS	AL	4	2	2	2	2	0	0	0	0	0	0	0	0	0	3	1
1944	PHI	NL	5	2	3	4	1	0	0	0	0	0	0	0	0	0	5	0
1948	CHI	AL	6	2	4	4	0	2	0	0	0	0	0	0	0	0	5	1
Total			18	8	10	13	3	2	0	0	0	0	0	0	0	0	16	2

Rank among batters: 1,914 • *Total ballparks homered in*: 10 • *First HR*: 06/30/1942 off Sid Hudson

Al Luplow

ALVIN DAVID LUPLOW
B: 03/13/1939
BL

Year	Tm	Lg	Tot	H	A	0	1	2	3	2	3	4	LO	XN	IP	PH	RHP	LHP
1962	CLE	AL	14	9	5	7	7	0	0	0	0	0	0	1	0	2	13	1
1963	CLE	AL	7	5	2	5	2	0	0	0	0	0	0	0	0	0	7	0
1965	CLE	AL	1	1	0	0	1	0	0	0	0	0	0	0	0	1	1	0
1966	NY	NL	7	1	6	5	1	1	0	1	0	0	0	0	0	0	7	0
1967	NY	NL	3	3	0	3	0	0	0	0	0	0	0	0	0	0	3	0
	PIT	NL	1	0	1	0	0	1	0	0	0	0	0	0	0	0	1	0
	Total		4	3	1	3	0	1	0	0	0	0	0	0	0	0	4	0
Total			33	19	14	20	11	2	0	1	0	0	0	1	0	3	32	1

Rank among batters: 1,336 • *Top target (3 home runs)*: Juan Marichal • *Number of pitchers victimized*: 27 • *Total ballparks homered in*: 10 • *First HR*: 04/17/1962 off Bill Monbouquette

Dolf Luque

ADOLFO DOMINGO DE GUZMAN LUQUE
B: 08/04/1890 D: 07/03/1957
BR

Year	Tm	Lg	Tot	H	A	0	1	2	3	2	3	4	LO	XN	IP	PH	RHP	LHP
1923	CIN	NL	1	0	1	0	1	0	0	0	0	0	0	0	0	0	1	0

Dolf Luque *continued*

Year	Tm	Lg	Tot	H	A	Men-On 0	1	2	3	One-Game 2	3	4	LO	XN	IP	PH	RHP	LHP
1924	CIN	NL	1	1	0	1	0	0	0	0	0	0	0	0	1	0	1	0
1925	CIN	NL	2	0	2	2	0	0	0	0	0	0	0	0	0	0	2	0
1929	CIN	NL	1	0	1	1	0	0	0	0	0	0	0	0	0	0	1	0
Total			5	1	4	4	1	0	0	0	0	0	0	0	1	0	5	0

Rank among batters: 3,191 • *Top target (2 home runs)*: Hugh McQuillan • *Number of pitchers victimized*: 4 • *Total ballparks homered in*: 3 • *First HR*: 08/15/1923 off Hugh McQuillan

Scott Lusader

SCOTT EDWARD LUSADER
B: 09/30/1964
BL

Year	Tm	Lg	Tot	H	A	Men-On 0	1	2	3	One-Game 2	3	4	LO	XN	IP	PH	RHP	LHP
1987	DET	AL	1	1	0	0	1	0	0	0	0	0	0	0	0	0	1	0
1988	DET	AL	1	0	1	0	1	0	0	0	0	0	0	0	0	0	1	0
1989	DET	AL	1	1	0	0	1	0	0	0	0	0	0	0	0	0	1	0
1990	DET	AL	2	1	1	0	1	1	0	0	0	0	0	0	0	0	2	0
Total			5	3	2	0	4	1	0	0	0	0	0	0	0	0	5	0

Rank among batters: 3,191 • *Top target (2 home runs)*: Jack McDowell • *Number of pitchers victimized*: 4 • *Total ballparks homered in*: 3 • *First HR*: 10/02/1987 off Jim Clancy

Billy Lush

WILLIAM LUCAS LUSH
B: 11/10/1873 D: 08/28/1951
BB

Year	Tm	Lg	Tot	H	A	Men-On 0	1	2	3	One-Game 2	3	4	LO	XN	IP	PH	RHP	LHP
1896	WAS	NL	4	3	1	3	1	0	0	0	0	0	0	0	1	0	1	3
1902	BOS	NL	2	2	0	1	1	0	0	0	0	0	0	0	0	0	1	0
1903	DET	AL	1	0	1	1	0	0	0	0	0	0	0	0	0	0	0	1
1904	CLE	AL	1	0	1	0	1	0	0	0	0	0	0	0	0	0	1	0
Total			8	5	3	5	3	0	0	0	0	0	0	0	1	0	3	4

Rank among batters: 2,703 • *Total ballparks homered in*: 5 • *First HR*: 06/10/1896 off Danny Friend

Johnny Lush

JOHN CHARLES LUSH
B: 10/08/1885 D: 11/18/1946
BL

Year	Tm	Lg	Tot	H	A	Men-On 0	1	2	3	One-Game 2	3	4	LO	XN	IP	PH	RHP	LHP
1904	PHI	NL	2	0	2	0	2	0	0	0	0	0	0	0	2	0	2	0

Rank among batters: 4,129 • *Total ballparks homered in*: 2 • *First HR*: 09/08/1904 off Claude Elliott

Lyle Luttrell

LYLE KENNETH LUTTRELL
B: 02/22/1930 D: 07/11/1984
BR

Year	Tm	Lg	Tot	H	A	Men-On 0	1	2	3	One-Game 2	3	4	LO	XN	IP	PH	RHP	LHP
1956	WAS	AL	2	1	1	2	0	0	0	0	0	0	0	0	0	0	1	1

Rank among batters: 4,129 • *Total ballparks homered in*: 2 • *First HR*: 05/31/1956 off Don Larsen

Rube Lutzke

WALTER JOHN LUTZKE
B: 11/17/1897 D: 03/06/1938
BR

Year	Tm	Lg	Tot	H	A	Men-On 0	1	2	3	One-Game 2	3	4	LO	XN	IP	PH	RHP	LHP
1923	CLE	AL	3	0	3	2	1	0	0	0	0	0	0	0	3	0	0	3
1925	CLE	AL	1	1	0	1	0	0	0	0	0	0	0	0	0	0	1	0
Total			4	1	3	3	1	0	0	0	0	0	0	0	3	0	1	3

Rank among batters: 3,427 • *Top target (2 home runs)*: Herb Pennock • *Number of pitchers victimized*: 3 • *Total ballparks homered in*: 3 • *First HR*: 06/11/1923 off Herb Pennock

Greg Luzinski

GREGORY MICHAEL LUZINSKI
B: 11/22/1950
BR

Year	Tm	Lg	Tot	H	A	Men-On 0	1	2	3	One-Game 2	3	4	LO	XN	IP	PH	RHP	LHP
1971	PHI	NL	3	2	1	2	1	0	0	0	0	0	0	0	0	0	3	0
1972	PHI	NL	18	8	10	14	4	0	0	1	0	0	0	0	0	1	13	5
1973	PHI	NL	29	15	14	17	10	2	0	4	0	0	0	1	0	0	21	8
1974	PHI	NL	7	5	2	1	4	2	0	0	0	0	0	0	0	0	5	2

Greg Luzinski *continued*

Year	Tm	Lg	Tot	H	A	Men-On 0	1	2	3	One-Game 2	3	4	LO	XN	IP	PH	RHP	LHP
1975	PHI	NL	34	21	13	23	9	2	0	2	0	0	0	1	0	0	26	8
1976	PHI	NL	21	15	6	7	11	1	2	0	0	0	0	0	0	0	12	9
1977	PHI	NL	39	22	17	19	12	6	2	5	0	0	0	0	0	0	34	5
1978	PHI	NL	35	20	15	18	13	4	0	4	0	0	0	0	0	0	30	5
1979	PHI	NL	18	7	11	8	8	1	1	0	0	0	0	0	0	0	13	5
1980	PHI	NL	19	15	4	12	4	3	0	1	0	0	0	0	0	0	14	5
1981	CHI	AL	21	9	12	12	6	3	0	2	0	0	0	1	0	0	16	5
1982	CHI	AL	18	13	5	10	4	4	0	1	0	0	0	1	0	0	12	6
1983	CHI	AL	32	18	14	17	12	3	0	3	0	0	0	0	0	0	19	13
1984	CHI	AL	13	9	4	7	2	2	2	0	0	0	0	0	0	1	8	5
Total			307	179	128	167	100	33	7	23	0	0	0	4	0	2	226	81

Rank among batters: 63 • *Top target (8 home runs)*: Steve Renko • *Number of pitchers victimized*: 199 • *Total ballparks homered in*: 25 • *First HR*: 09/07/1971 off Reggie Cleveland • *LCS HR*—5; *All-Star HR*—1

Mitch Lyden

MITCHELL SCOTT LYDEN
B: 12/14/1964
BR

Year	Tm	Lg	Tot	H	A	Men-On 0	1	2	3	One-Game 2	3	4	LO	XN	IP	PH	RHP	LHP
1993	FLO	NL	1	0	1	1	0	0	0	0	0	0	0	0	0	0	1	0

Rank among batters: 4,707 • *Total ballparks homered in*: 1 • *First HR*: 06/16/1993 off Jose Bautista • *Hit HR in first major league AB*—@CHI: 06/16/1993

Scott Lydy

DONALD SCOTT LYDY
B: 10/26/1968
BR

Year	Tm	Lg	Tot	H	A	Men-On 0	1	2	3	One-Game 2	3	4	LO	XN	IP	PH	RHP	LHP
1993	OAK	AL	2	1	1	1	1	0	0	0	0	0	0	0	0	0	2	0

Rank among batters: 4,129 • *Total ballparks homered in*: 2 • *First HR*: 08/04/1993 off Tim Leary

Jerry Lynch

GERALD THOMAS LYNCH
B: 07/17/1930
BL

Year	Tm	Lg	Tot	H	A	Men-On 0	1	2	3	One-Game 2	3	4	LO	XN	IP	PH	RHP	LHP
1954	PIT	NL	8	2	6	6	2	0	0	1	0	0	0	0	0	0	7	1
1955	PIT	NL	5	2	3	4	1	0	0	0	0	0	0	0	0	0	5	0
1957	CIN	NL	4	3	1	3	1	0	0	0	0	0	0	1	0	3	4	0
1958	CIN	NL	16	10	6	9	5	2	0	0	0	0	0	0	0	1	14	2
1959	CIN	NL	17	12	5	8	7	2	0	1	0	0	0	0	0	1	17	0
1960	CIN	NL	6	3	3	3	1	1	1	0	0	0	0	0	0	0	6	0
1961	CIN	NL	13	6	7	7	4	2	0	1	0	0	0	0	0	5	12	1
1962	CIN	NL	12	6	6	8	4	0	0	0	0	0	0	0	0	1	12	0
1963	CIN	NL	2	1	1	0	2	0	0	0	0	0	0	0	0	2	2	0
	PIT	NL	10	5	5	5	3	2	0	0	0	0	0	0	0	2	10	0
	Total		12	6	6	5	5	2	0	0	0	0	0	0	0	4	12	0
1964	PIT	NL	16	6	10	6	6	3	1	1	0	0	0	0	0	1	15	1
1965	PIT	NL	5	1	4	4	1	0	0	1	0	0	0	0	0	1	5	0
1966	PIT	NL	1	0	1	1	0	0	0	0	0	0	0	0	0	1	1	0
Total			115	57	58	64	37	12	2	5	0	0	0	1	0	18	110	5

Rank among batters: 415 • *Top target (6 home runs)*: Vern Law • *Number of pitchers victimized*: 77 • *Total ballparks homered in*: 14 • *First HR*: 04/27/1954 off Corky Valentine

Matthew Lynch

MATTHEW DANIEL LYNCH
B: 02/07/1926 D: 06/30/1978
BR

Year	Tm	Lg	Tot	H	A	Men-On 0	1	2	3	One-Game 2	3	4	LO	XN	IP	PH	RHP	LHP
1948	CHI	NL	1	0	1	1	0	0	0	0	0	0	0	0	0	0	1	0

Rank among batters: 4,707 • *Total ballparks homered in*: 1 • *First HR*: 09/14/1948 off Johnny Sain

Fred Lynn

FREDERIC MICHAEL LYNN
B: 02/03/1952
BL

Year	Tm	Lg	Tot	H	A	Men-On 0	1	2	3	One-Game 2	3	4	LO	XN	IP	PH	RHP	LHP
1974	BOS	AL	2	1	1	2	0	0	0	0	0	0	0	0	0	0	2	0

Fred Lynn *continued*

Year	Tm	Lg	Tot	H	A	Men-On 0	1	2	3	One-Game 2	3	4	LO	XN	IP	PH	RHP	LHP
1975	BOS	AL	21	9	12	8	7	6	0	1	1	0	0	0	0	0	17	4
1976	BOS	AL	10	4	6	8	2	0	0	0	0	0	0	0	0	0	8	2
1977	BOS	AL	18	10	8	10	6	2	0	4	0	0	0	0	0	0	16	2
1978	BOS	AL	22	11	11	13	6	3	0	1	0	0	0	1	0	0	18	4
1979	BOS	AL	39	28	11	14	18	7	0	4	0	0	0	0	0	0	34	5
1980	BOS	AL	12	6	6	3	7	2	0	1	0	0	0	1	0	0	11	1
1981	CAL	AL	5	3	2	2	2	1	0	1	0	0	0	0	0	0	2	3
1982	CAL	AL	21	13	8	9	9	2	1	0	0	0	0	0	0	0	14	7
1983	CAL	AL	22	14	8	12	6	3	1	0	0	0	0	0	0	0	16	6
1984	CAL	AL	23	16	7	12	6	5	0	3	0	0	0	0	0	0	17	6
1985	BAL	AL	23	14	9	11	6	5	1	0	0	0	0	0	0	0	19	4
1986	BAL	AL	23	13	10	11	6	5	1	1	0	0	0	0	0	1	16	7
1987	BAL	AL	23	11	12	13	3	5	2	2	0	0	0	0	0	1	18	5
1988	BAL	AL	18	11	7	13	5	0	0	2	0	0	1	0	0	0	17	1
	DET	AL	7	2	5	5	1	0	1	0	0	0	0	0	0	1	4	3
	Total		25	13	12	18	6	0	1	2	0	0	1	0	0	1	21	4
1989	DET	AL	11	9	2	8	1	2	0	1	0	0	0	0	0	0	11	0
1990	SD	NL	6	2	4	5	1	0	0	0	0	0	0	0	0	1	6	0
Total			306	177	129	159	92	48	7	21	1	0	1	2	0	4	246	60

Rank among batters: 65 • *Top target (7 home runs)*: Dan Petry • *Number of pitchers victimized*: 206 • *Total ballparks homered in*: 19 • *First HR*: 09/15/1974 off Jim Slaton • *Hit for Cycle*—vs MIN: 05/13/1980 • *World Series HR*—1; *LCS HR*—1; *All-Star HR*—4

Al Lyons

ALBERT HAROLD LYONS
B: 07/18/1918 D: 12/20/1965
BR

Year	Tm	Lg	Tot	H	A	Men-On 0	1	2	3	One-Game 2	3	4	LO	XN	IP	PH	RHP	LHP
1947	PIT	NL	1	1	0	1	0	0	0	0	0	0	0	0	0	0	1	0

Rank among batters: 4,707 • *Total ballparks homered in*: 1 • *First HR*: 09/23/1947 off Jim Hearn

Barry Lyons

BARRY STEPHEN LYONS
B: 06/03/1960
BR

Year	Tm	Lg	Tot	H	A	Men-On 0	1	2	3	One-Game 2	3	4	LO	XN	IP	PH	RHP	LHP
1987	NY	NL	4	4	0	2	0	1	1	0	0	0	0	0	0	1	3	1
1989	NY	NL	3	1	2	3	0	0	0	0	0	0	0	0	0	0	0	3
1990	NY	NL	2	1	1	0	2	0	0	0	0	0	0	1	0	0	2	0
	LA	NL	1	0	1	0	1	0	0	0	0	0	0	0	0	1	0	1
	Total		3	1	2	0	3	0	0	0	0	0	0	1	0	1	2	1
1995	CHI	AL	5	3	2	2	1	2	0	0	0	0	0	0	0	0	3	2
Total			15	9	6	7	4	3	1	0	0	0	0	1	0	2	8	7

Rank among batters: 2,096 • *Total ballparks homered in*: 8 • *First HR*: 04/26/1987 off Pat Perry

Denny Lyons

DENNIS PATRICK ALOYSIUS LYONS
B: 03/12/1866 D: 01/03/1929
BR

Year	Tm	Lg	Tot	H	A	Men-On 0	1	2	3	One-Game 2	3	4	LO	XN	IP	PH	RHP	LHP
1887	PHI	AA	6	4	2	2	4	0	0	0	0	0	0	0	2	0	3	1
1888	PHI	AA	6	5	1	4	2	0	0	1	0	0	0	0	0	0	4	2
1889	PHI	AA	9	7	2	7	2	0	0	1	0	0	0	0	1	0	8	0
1890	PHI	AA	7	6	1	5	2	0	0	1	0	0	0	0	0	0	4	2
1891	STL	AA	11	8	3	6	3	2	0	0	0	0	0	0	1	0	9	1
1892	NY	NL	8	7	1	6	1	0	1	0	0	0	0	0	1	0	7	1
1893	PIT	NL	3	1	2	1	2	0	0	0	0	0	0	0	0	0	2	1
1894	PIT	NL	4	2	2	1	2	1	0	0	0	0	0	0	1	0	2	2
1895	STL	NL	2	2	0	2	0	0	0	0	0	0	0	0	1	0	1	1
1896	PIT	NL	4	1	3	2	1	1	0	0	0	0	0	0	0	0	4	0
1897	PIT	NL	2	1	1	1	0	1	0	0	0	0	0	0	0	0	2	0
Total			62	44	18	37	19	5	1	3	0	0	0	0	7	0	46	10

Rank among batters: 835 • Top target (2 home runs): Henry Porter, Parke Swartzel, Scott Stratton, Fred Smith, Jersey Bakely, Will Callahan, Jack Stivetts, Red Ehret, Gus Weyhing, Kid Nichols • *Number of pitchers victimized*: 52 • *Total ballparks homered in*: 16 • *First HR*: 05/28/1887 off Jumbo McGinnis

Harry Lyons

HARRY P. LYONS
B: 03/25/1866 D: 06/30/1912
BR

Year	Tm	Lg	Tot	H	A	Men-On 0	1	2	3	One-Game 2	3	4	LO	XN	IP	PH	RHP	LHP
1888	STL	AA	4	1	3	1	1	2	0	0	0	0	0	0	0	0	1	3

Harry Lyons *continued*

Year	Tm	Lg	Tot	H	A	Men-On 0	Men-On 1	Men-On 2	Men-On 3	One-Game 2	One-Game 3	One-Game 4	LO	XN	IP	PH	RHP	LHP
1890	ROC	AA	3	1	2	2	0	1	0	0	0	0	0	0	0	0	3	0
Total			7	2	5	3	1	3	0	0	0	0	0	0	0	0	4	1

Rank among batters: 2,834 • *Top target (2 home runs)*: Tony Mullane • *Number of pitchers victimized*: 6 • *Total ballparks homered in*: 6 • *First HR*: 05/21/1888 off Phenomenal Smith

Steve Lyons

STEPHEN JOHN LYONS
B: 06/03/1960
BL

Year	Tm	Lg	Tot	H	A	Men-On 0	Men-On 1	Men-On 2	Men-On 3	One-Game 2	One-Game 3	One-Game 4	LO	XN	IP	PH	RHP	LHP
1985	BOS	AL	5	4	1	2	2	1	0	1	0	0	0	0	0	0	4	1
1986	BOS	AL	1	1	0	1	0	0	0	0	0	0	0	0	0	1	1	0
1987	CHI	AL	1	0	1	0	1	0	0	0	0	0	0	0	0	0	1	0
1988	CHI	AL	5	1	4	3	2	0	0	0	0	0	0	0	0	0	2	3
1989	CHI	AL	2	0	2	0	1	0	1	0	0	0	0	0	0	0	2	0
1990	CHI	AL	1	0	1	1	0	0	0	0	0	0	0	0	0	0	1	0
1991	BOS	AL	4	2	2	3	1	0	0	0	0	0	0	0	0	0	3	1
Total			19	8	11	10	7	1	1	1	0	0	0	0	0	1	14	5

Rank among batters: 1,861 • *Top target (2 home runs)*: Jose Guzman • *Number of pitchers victimized*: 18 • *Total ballparks homered in*: 9 • *First HR*: 05/27/1985 off Ken Schrom

Ted Lyons

THEODORE AMAR LYONS
B: 12/28/1900 D: 07/25/1986
BB HOF

Year	Tm	Lg	Tot	H	A	Men-On 0	Men-On 1	Men-On 2	Men-On 3	One-Game 2	One-Game 3	One-Game 4	LO	XN	IP	PH	RHP	LHP
1927	CHI	AL	1	0	1	1	0	0	0	0	0	0	0	0	0	0	1	0
1930	CHI	AL	1	0	1	1	0	0	0	0	0	0	0	0	0	0	1	0
1932	CHI	AL	1	0	1	1	0	0	0	0	0	0	0	0	0	0	1	0
1933	CHI	AL	1	1	0	0	1	0	0	0	0	0	0	0	0	0	1	0
1934	CHI	AL	1	1	0	0	1	0	0	0	0	0	0	0	0	0	1	0
Total			5	2	3	3	2	0	0	0	0	0	0	0	0	0	5	0

Rank among batters: 3,191 • *Total ballparks homered in*: 3 • *First HR*: 05/02/1927 off Ken Holloway

Jim Lyttle

JAMES LAWRENCE LYTTLE
B: 05/20/1946
BL

Year	Tm	Lg	Tot	H	A	Men-On 0	Men-On 1	Men-On 2	Men-On 3	One-Game 2	One-Game 3	One-Game 4	LO	XN	IP	PH	RHP	LHP
1970	NY	AL	3	3	0	3	0	0	0	0	0	0	0	0	0	0	3	0
1971	NY	AL	1	0	1	1	0	0	0	0	0	0	0	0	0	0	1	0
1973	MON	NL	4	2	2	2	2	0	0	0	0	0	0	0	0	1	4	0
1976	MON	NL	1	0	1	0	0	1	0	0	0	0	0	0	0	1	1	0
Total			9	5	4	6	2	1	0	0	0	0	0	0	0	2	9	0

Rank among batters: 2,587 • *Total ballparks homered in*: 6 • *First HR*: 08/11/1970 off Gerald Janeski

Duke Maas

DUANE FREDERICK MAAS
B: 01/31/1929 D: 12/07/1976
BR

Year	Tm	Lg	Tot	H	A	Men-On 0	Men-On 1	Men-On 2	Men-On 3	One-Game 2	One-Game 3	One-Game 4	LO	XN	IP	PH	RHP	LHP
1957	DET	AL	1	1	0	0	1	0	0	0	0	0	0	0	0	0	1	0

Rank among batters: 4,707 • *Total ballparks homered in*: 1 • *First HR*: 06/14/1957 off Frank Sullivan

Kevin Maas

KEVIN CHRISTIAN MAAS
B: 01/20/1965
BL

Year	Tm	Lg	Tot	H	A	Men-On 0	Men-On 1	Men-On 2	Men-On 3	One-Game 2	One-Game 3	One-Game 4	LO	XN	IP	PH	RHP	LHP
1990	NY	AL	21	12	9	15	5	1	0	2	0	0	0	0	0	0	18	3
1991	NY	AL	23	8	15	16	3	4	0	1	0	0	0	1	0	0	14	9
1992	NY	AL	11	7	4	8	1	2	0	0	0	0	0	0	0	1	10	1
1993	NY	AL	9	7	2	4	2	3	0	1	0	0	0	0	0	1	9	0
1995	MIN	AL	1	1	0	1	0	0	0	0	0	0	0	0	0	0	1	0
Total			65	35	30	44	11	10	0	4	0	0	0	1	0	2	52	13

Rank among batters: 799 • Top target (2 home runs): Adam Peterson, Walt Terrell, Nolan Ryan, Greg Swindell, Paul Gibson, Greg Hibbard, Tom Candiotti, Bill Wegman, Kevin Tapani, Rick Sutcliffe, Jeff Montgomery • *Number of pitchers victimized*: 54 • *Total ballparks homered in*: 12 • *First HR*: 07/04/1990 off Bret Saberhagen

Year	Tm	Lg	Tot	H	A	Men-On 0	1	2	3	One-Game 2	3	4	LO	XN	IP	PH	RHP	LHP

John Mabry

JOHN STEVEN MABRY
B: 10/17/1970
BL

Year	Tm	Lg	Tot	H	A	0	1	2	3	2	3	4	LO	XN	IP	PH	RHP	LHP
1995	STL	NL	5	2	3	3	2	0	0	0	0	0	1	0	0	0	3	2

Rank among batters: 3,191 • *Total ballparks homered in*: 3 • *First HR*: 07/03/1995 off Gabe White

Mike Macfarlane

MICHAEL ANDREW MACFARLANE
B: 04/12/1964
BR

Year	Tm	Lg	Tot	H	A	0	1	2	3	2	3	4	LO	XN	IP	PH	RHP	LHP
1988	KC	AL	4	2	2	1	2	1	0	0	0	0	0	0	0	0	3	1
1989	KC	AL	2	0	2	1	0	1	0	0	0	0	0	0	0	0	2	0
1990	KC	AL	6	1	5	4	1	0	1	0	0	0	0	0	0	0	4	2
1991	KC	AL	13	6	7	10	2	0	1	1	0	0	0	0	0	0	8	5
1992	KC	AL	17	7	10	11	5	1	0	0	0	0	0	0	0	0	10	7
1993	KC	AL	20	7	13	11	7	2	0	0	0	0	0	0	0	0	16	4
1994	KC	AL	14	9	5	5	5	3	1	1	0	0	0	1	0	0	11	3
1995	BOS	AL	15	7	8	10	2	2	1	0	0	0	0	0	0	0	7	8
Total			91	39	52	53	24	10	4	2	0	0	0	1	0	0	61	30

Rank among batters: 559 • Top target (3 home runs): Bill Gullickson, Jason Bere, Mike Mussina, Pat Hentgen • *Number of pitchers victimized*: 71 • *Total ballparks homered in*: 17 • *First HR*: 05/21/1988 off Scott Bailes

Danny MacFayden

DANIEL KNOWLES MACFAYDEN
B: 06/10/1905 D: 08/26/1972
BR

Year	Tm	Lg	Tot	H	A	0	1	2	3	2	3	4	LO	XN	IP	PH	RHP	LHP
1927	BOS	AL	1	0	1	1	0	0	0	0	0	0	0	0	0	0	1	0

Rank among batters: 4,707 • *Total ballparks homered in*: 1 • *First HR*: 05/22/1927 off Sam Jones

Ken Macha

KENNETH EDWARD MACHA
B: 09/29/1950
BR

Year	Tm	Lg	Tot	H	A	0	1	2	3	2	3	4	LO	XN	IP	PH	RHP	LHP
1980	MON	NL	1	1	0	1	0	0	0	0	0	0	0	0	0	0	1	0

Rank among batters: 4,707 • *Total ballparks homered in*: 1 • *First HR*: 05/04/1980 off Ed Halicki

Dave Machemer

DAVID RITCHIE MACHEMER
B: 05/24/1951
BR

Year	Tm	Lg	Tot	H	A	0	1	2	3	2	3	4	LO	XN	IP	PH	RHP	LHP
1978	CAL	AL	1	0	1	1	0	0	0	0	0	0	1	0	0	0	0	1

Rank among batters: 4,707 • *Total ballparks homered in*: 1 • *First HR*: 06/21/1978 off Geoff Zahn • *Hit HR in first major league AB*—@MIN: 06/21/1978

Connie Mack

CORNELIUS ALEXANDER MACK
B: 12/22/1862 D: 02/08/1956
BR HOF

Year	Tm	Lg	Tot	H	A	0	1	2	3	2	3	4	LO	XN	IP	PH	RHP	LHP
1888	WAS	NL	3	2	1	1	1	1	0	0	0	0	0	0	0	0	2	1
1892	PIT	NL	1	1	0	0	0	1	0	0	0	0	0	0	0	0	1	0
1894	PIT	NL	1	0	1	0	0	1	0	0	0	0	0	0	0	0	0	1
Total			5	3	2	1	1	3	0	0	0	0	0	0	0	0	3	2

Rank among batters: 3,191 • *Total ballparks homered in*: 4 • *First HR*: 09/21/1888 off John Tener

Denny Mack

DENNIS JOSEPH MACK
B: 1851 D: 04/10/1888
BR

Year	Tm	Lg	Tot	H	A	0	1	2	3	2	3	4	LO	XN	IP	PH	RHP	LHP
1876	STL	NL	1	0	1	1	0	0	0	0	0	0	0	0	0	0	1	0

Rank among batters: 4,707 • *Total ballparks homered in*: 1 • *First HR*: 09/13/1876 off Jack Manning

Joseph Mack

JOSEPH JOHN MACK
B: 01/04/1912
BB

Year	Tm	Lg	Tot	H	A	Men-On 0	1	2	3	One-Game 2	3	4	LO	XN	IP	PH	RHP	LHP
1945	BOS	NL	3	2	1	3	0	0	0	0	0	0	0	0	0	0	3	0

Rank among batters: 3,735 • *Total ballparks homered in*: 2 • *First HR*: 04/17/1945 off Bill Voiselle

Ray Mack

RAYMOND JAMES MACK
B: 08/31/1916 D: 05/07/1969
BR

Year	Tm	Lg	Tot	H	A	Men-On 0	1	2	3	One-Game 2	3	4	LO	XN	IP	PH	RHP	LHP
1939	CLE	AL	1	1	0	1	0	0	0	0	0	0	0	0	0	0	0	1
1940	CLE	AL	12	4	8	6	5	0	1	0	0	0	0	0	2	0	6	6
1941	CLE	AL	9	3	6	7	1	1	0	0	0	0	0	0	0	0	6	3
1942	CLE	AL	2	0	2	1	1	0	0	0	0	0	0	0	0	0	2	0
1943	CLE	AL	7	1	6	4	1	2	0	0	0	0	0	1	0	0	7	0
1946	CLE	AL	1	0	1	1	0	0	0	0	0	0	0	0	0	0	0	1
1947	CHI	NL	2	2	0	2	0	0	0	0	0	0	0	0	0	0	0	2
Total			34	11	23	22	8	3	1	0	0	0	0	1	2	0	21	13

Rank among batters: 1,315 • Top target (2 home runs): Lefty Grove, Fritz Ostermueller, Chubby Dean, Spud Chandler • *Number of pitchers victimized*: 30 • *Total ballparks homered in*: 10 • *First HR*: 08/27/1939 off Fritz Ostermueller

Reddy Mack

JOSEPH MACK
B: 05/02/1866 D: 12/30/1916

Year	Tm	Lg	Tot	H	A	Men-On 0	1	2	3	One-Game 2	3	4	LO	XN	IP	PH	RHP	LHP
1886	LOU	AA	1	1	0	1	0	0	0	0	0	0	0	0	1	0	0	1
1887	LOU	AA	1	1	0	0	0	1	0	0	0	0	0	0	0	0	0	0
1888	LOU	AA	3	1	2	2	1	0	0	0	0	0	1	0	0	0	2	1
1889	BAL	AA	1	0	1	1	0	0	0	0	0	0	0	0	0	0	1	0
Total			6	3	3	4	1	1	0	0	0	0	1	0	1	0	3	2

Rank among batters: 2,988 • *Total ballparks homered in*: 4 • *First HR*: 08/15/1886 off Matt Kilroy

Shane Mack

SHANE LEE MACK
B: 12/07/1963
BR

Year	Tm	Lg	Tot	H	A	Men-On 0	1	2	3	One-Game 2	3	4	LO	XN	IP	PH	RHP	LHP
1987	SD	NL	4	2	2	3	1	0	0	0	0	0	1	0	0	0	0	4
1990	MIN	AL	8	5	3	6	2	0	0	0	0	0	0	0	0	0	3	5
1991	MIN	AL	18	4	14	8	5	3	2	1	0	0	0	0	0	1	9	9
1992	MIN	AL	16	10	6	10	4	1	1	0	0	0	4	0	0	0	12	4
1993	MIN	AL	10	3	7	3	4	3	0	1	0	0	1	0	0	0	8	2
1994	MIN	AL	15	8	7	9	3	2	1	0	0	0	0	0	1	0	10	5
Total			71	32	39	39	19	9	4	2	0	0	6	0	1	1	42	29

Rank among batters: 731 • *Top target (3 home runs)*: Scott Sanderson, Ben McDonald • *Number of pitchers victimized*: 59 • *Total ballparks homered in*: 18 • *First HR*: 06/13/1987 off Atlee Hammaker

Pete Mackanin

PETER MACKANIN
B: 08/01/1951
BR

Year	Tm	Lg	Tot	H	A	Men-On 0	1	2	3	One-Game 2	3	4	LO	XN	IP	PH	RHP	LHP
1975	MON	NL	12	7	5	12	0	0	0	0	0	0	0	0	0	0	6	6
1976	MON	NL	8	4	4	6	1	1	0	0	0	0	0	0	0	0	4	4
1977	MON	NL	1	0	1	0	1	0	0	0	0	0	0	0	0	0	1	0
1979	PHI	NL	1	1	0	1	0	0	0	0	0	0	0	0	0	0	0	1
1980	MIN	AL	4	4	0	2	1	1	0	0	0	0	0	0	0	0	2	2
1981	MIN	AL	4	3	1	2	2	0	0	0	0	0	0	0	0	1	2	2
Total			30	19	11	23	5	2	0	0	0	0	0	0	0	1	15	15

Rank among batters: 1,437 • *Top target (2 home runs)*: Bill Bonham, Jack Billingham, Tom Underwood • *Number of pitchers victimized*: 27 • *Total ballparks homered in*: 11 • *First HR*: 05/17/1975 off Fred Norman

Felix Mackiewicz

FELIX THADDEUS MACKIEWICZ
B: 11/20/1917 D: 12/20/1993
BR

Year	Tm	Lg	Tot	H	A	Men-On 0	1	2	3	One-Game 2	3	4	LO	XN	IP	PH	RHP	LHP
1945	CLE	AL	2	0	2	0	1	1	0	0	0	0	0	0	0	0	2	0

Rank among batters: 4,129 • *Total ballparks homered in*: 2 • *First HR*: 05/08/1945 off Orval Grove

Max Macon

MAX CULLEN MACON
B: 10/14/1915 D: 08/05/1989
BL

Year	Tm	Lg	Tot	H	A	Men-On				One-Game			LO	XN	IP	PH	RHP	LHP
						0	1	2	3	2	3	4						
1944	BOS	NL	3	3	0	2	1	0	0	0	0	0	0	0	0	0	2	1

Rank among batters: 3,735 • *Total ballparks homered in*: 1 • *First HR*: 05/31/1944 off Max Lanier

Jimmy Macullar

JAMES F. MACULLAR
B: 01/16/1855 D: 04/08/1924
BR

Year	Tm	Lg	Tot	H	A	Men-On				One-Game			LO	XN	IP	PH	RHP	LHP
						0	1	2	3	2	3	4						
1884	BAL	AA	4	2	2	3	1	0	0	1	0	0	0	0	0	0	3	0
1885	BAL	AA	3	3	0	1	2	0	0	0	0	0	0	0	0	0	2	0
Total			7	5	2	4	3	0	0	1	0	0	0	0	0	0	5	0

Rank among batters: 2,834 • *Total ballparks homered in*: 2 • *First HR*: 05/29/1884 off Will White

Kid Madden

MICHAEL JOSEPH MADDEN
B: 10/02/1867 D: 03/16/1896

Year	Tm	Lg	Tot	H	A	Men-On				One-Game			LO	XN	IP	PH	RHP	LHP
						0	1	2	3	2	3	4						
1887	BOS	NL	1	1	0	1	0	0	0	0	0	0	0	0	0	0	1	0
1891	BAL	AA	1	1	0	1	0	0	0	0	0	0	1	0	0	0	1	0
Total			2	2	0	2	0	0	0	0	0	0	1	0	0	0	2	0

Rank among batters: 4,129 • *Total ballparks homered in*: 2 • *First HR*: 08/27/1887 off Jim Galvin

Clarence Maddern

CLARENCE JAMES MADDERN
B: 09/26/1921 D: 08/09/1986
BR

Year	Tm	Lg	Tot	H	A	Men-On				One-Game			LO	XN	IP	PH	RHP	LHP
						0	1	2	3	2	3	4						
1948	CHI	NL	4	1	3	2	1	1	0	1	0	0	0	0	0	1	4	0
1949	CHI	NL	1	1	0	1	0	0	0	0	0	0	0	0	0	0	0	1
Total			5	2	3	3	1	1	0	1	0	0	0	0	0	1	4	1

Rank among batters: 3,191 • *Top target (2 home runs)*: Clint Hartung • *Number of pitchers victimized*: 4 • *Total ballparks homered in*: 2 • *First HR*: 05/21/1948 off Sheldon Jones

Elliott Maddox

ELLIOTT MADDOX
B: 12/21/1947
BR

Year	Tm	Lg	Tot	H	A	Men-On				One-Game			LO	XN	IP	PH	RHP	LHP
						0	1	2	3	2	3	4						
1970	DET	AL	3	2	1	2	1	0	0	0	0	0	0	1	0	0	2	1
1971	WAS	AL	1	1	0	0	0	1	0	0	0	0	0	0	0	0	0	1
1973	TEX	AL	1	1	0	0	0	1	0	0	0	0	0	0	0	0	1	0
1974	NY	AL	3	2	1	2	1	0	0	0	0	0	0	0	0	0	0	3
1975	NY	AL	1	1	0	0	0	1	0	0	0	0	0	0	0	0	1	0
1977	BAL	AL	2	1	1	1	1	0	0	0	0	0	0	0	0	0	1	1
1978	NY	NL	2	0	2	1	1	0	0	0	0	0	0	0	0	0	1	1
1979	NY	NL	1	0	1	1	0	0	0	0	0	0	0	0	0	0	1	0
1980	NY	NL	4	2	2	4	0	0	0	0	0	0	0	0	0	0	3	1
Total			18	10	8	11	4	3	0	0	0	0	0	1	0	0	10	8

Rank among batters: 1,914 • *Top target (2 home runs)*: Dennis Lamp • *Number of pitchers victimized*: 17 • *Total ballparks homered in*: 10 • *First HR*: 04/29/1970 off Mike Hedlund

Garry Maddox

GARRY LEE MADDOX
B: 09/01/1949
BR

Year	Tm	Lg	Tot	H	A	Men-On				One-Game			LO	XN	IP	PH	RHP	LHP
						0	1	2	3	2	3	4						
1972	SF	NL	12	7	5	4	4	3	1	1	0	0	0	0	0	0	9	3
1973	SF	NL	11	5	6	4	5	2	0	1	0	0	0	0	1	0	7	4
1974	SF	NL	8	5	3	5	1	2	0	1	0	0	0	0	1	0	5	3
1975	SF	NL	1	0	1	0	1	0	0	0	0	0	0	0	0	0	0	1
	PHI	NL	4	2	2	3	0	1	0	0	0	0	0	0	0	0	3	1
	Total		5	2	3	3	1	1	0	0	0	0	0	0	0	0	3	2
1976	PHI	NL	6	3	3	3	1	1	1	0	0	0	0	0	0	0	5	1
1977	PHI	NL	14	8	6	8	5	1	0	0	0	0	2	0	0	0	11	3
1978	PHI	NL	11	7	4	5	4	2	0	0	0	0	0	0	0	0	8	3

Year	Tm	Lg	Tot	H	A	Men-On 0	1	2	3	One-Game 2	3	4	LO	XN	IP	PH	RHP	LHP

Garry Maddox *continued*

Year	Tm	Lg	Tot	H	A	0	1	2	3	2	3	4	LO	XN	IP	PH	RHP	LHP
1979	PHI	NL	13	6	7	10	0	2	1	0	0	0	0	0	0	0	9	4
1980	PHI	NL	11	6	5	6	4	1	0	0	0	0	0	0	0	0	8	3
1981	PHI	NL	5	5	0	3	0	2	0	0	0	0	0	0	0	0	2	3
1982	PHI	NL	8	3	5	3	3	1	1	0	0	0	0	0	0	0	7	1
1983	PHI	NL	4	2	2	4	0	0	0	0	0	0	0	0	0	0	3	1
1984	PHI	NL	5	3	2	2	3	0	0	0	0	0	0	0	0	0	2	3
1985	PHI	NL	4	2	2	4	0	0	0	0	0	0	1	0	0	0	2	2
Total			117	64	53	64	31	18	4	3	0	0	3	0	2	0	81	36

Rank among batters: 402 • *Top target (4 home runs)*: Ray Burris • *Number of pitchers victimized*: 94 • *Total ballparks homered in*: 12 • *First HR*: 05/26/1972 off Ron Reed • *World Series HR*—1

Greg Maddux

GREGORY ALAN MADDUX
B: 04/14/1966
BR

Year	Tm	Lg	Tot	H	A	0	1	2	3	2	3	4	LO	XN	IP	PH	RHP	LHP
1991	CHI	NL	1	0	1	1	0	0	0	0	0	0	0	0	0	0	1	0
1992	CHI	NL	1	1	0	1	0	0	0	0	0	0	0	0	0	0	0	1
Total			2	1	1	2	0	0	0	0	0	0	0	0	0	0	1	1

Rank among batters: 4,129 • *Total ballparks homered in*: 2 • *First HR*: 06/16/1991 off Jose Melendez

Scotti Madison

CHARLES SCOTT MADISON
B: 09/12/1959
BB

Year	Tm	Lg	Tot	H	A	0	1	2	3	2	3	4	LO	XN	IP	PH	RHP	LHP
1989	CIN	NL	1	0	1	0	1	0	0	0	0	0	0	0	0	0	0	1

Rank among batters: 4,707 • *Total ballparks homered in*: 1 • *First HR*: 08/08/1989 off Craig Lefferts

Ed Madjeski

EDWARD WILLIAM MADJESKI
B: 07/20/1908 D: 11/11/1994
BR

Year	Tm	Lg	Tot	H	A	0	1	2	3	2	3	4	LO	XN	IP	PH	RHP	LHP
1934	CHI	AL	5	3	2	1	4	0	0	0	0	0	0	0	0	0	4	1

Rank among batters: 3,191 • *Total ballparks homered in*: 2 • *First HR*: 06/08/1934 off Firpo Marberry

Bill Madlock

BILL MADLOCK
B: 01/02/1951
BR

Year	Tm	Lg	Tot	H	A	0	1	2	3	2	3	4	LO	XN	IP	PH	RHP	LHP
1973	TEX	AL	1	1	0	0	1	0	0	0	0	0	0	0	0	0	0	1
1974	CHI	NL	9	7	2	6	2	0	1	1	0	0	0	0	0	1	8	1
1975	CHI	NL	7	6	1	5	2	0	0	1	0	0	0	0	0	0	3	4
1976	CHI	NL	15	11	4	11	3	0	1	0	0	0	0	0	0	0	9	6
1977	SF	NL	12	6	6	8	3	1	0	2	0	0	0	0	0	0	8	4
1978	SF	NL	15	5	10	12	2	1	0	1	0	0	4	0	0	0	10	5
1979	SF	NL	7	1	6	6	1	0	0	0	0	0	0	0	0	0	5	2
	PIT	NL	7	2	5	2	5	0	0	0	0	0	0	0	0	0	5	2
	Total		14	3	11	8	6	0	0	0	0	0	0	0	0	0	10	4
1980	PIT	NL	10	7	3	4	6	0	0	1	0	0	0	0	0	0	7	3
1981	PIT	NL	6	2	4	3	3	0	0	0	0	0	0	0	0	0	4	2
1982	PIT	NL	19	13	6	11	7	0	1	0	0	0	0	1	0	0	13	6
1983	PIT	NL	12	8	4	8	4	0	0	0	0	0	0	0	0	0	6	6
1984	PIT	NL	4	1	3	4	0	0	0	1	0	0	0	0	0	0	2	2
1985	PIT	NL	10	6	4	6	4	0	0	1	0	0	0	0	0	0	7	3
	LA	NL	2	0	2	1	1	0	0	0	0	0	0	0	0	0	1	1
	Total		12	6	6	7	5	0	0	1	0	0	0	0	0	0	8	4
1986	LA	NL	10	4	6	3	5	2	0	0	0	0	0	0	0	0	4	6
1987	LA	NL	3	1	2	2	1	0	0	0	0	0	0	0	0	0	2	1
	DET	AL	14	7	7	8	6	0	0	0	1	0	0	0	0	0	7	7
Total			163	88	75	100	56	4	3	8	1	0	4	1	0	1	101	62

Rank among batters: 257 • *Top target (4 home runs)*: Burt Hooton, Bob Welch, Jerry Reuss • *Number of pitchers victimized*: 115 • *Total ballparks homered in*: 21 • *First HR*: 09/17/1973 off Jim Kaat • *LCS HR*—4

Dave Magadan

DAVID JOSEPH MAGADAN
B: 09/30/1962
BL

Year	Tm	Lg	Tot	H	A	Men-On 0	1	2	3	One-Game 2	3	4	LO	XN	IP	PH	RHP	LHP
1987	NY	NL	3	2	1	3	0	0	0	0	0	0	0	0	0	2	1	2
1988	NY	NL	1	1	0	0	1	0	0	0	0	0	0	0	0	0	1	0
1989	NY	NL	4	3	1	3	1	0	0	0	0	0	0	1	0	0	4	0
1990	NY	NL	6	2	4	3	3	0	0	0	0	0	0	0	0	0	4	2
1991	NY	NL	4	2	2	2	1	1	0	0	0	0	0	0	0	0	4	0
1992	NY	NL	3	2	1	1	0	2	0	0	0	0	0	0	0	0	3	0
1993	FLO	NL	4	3	1	2	2	0	0	0	0	0	0	0	0	0	4	0
	SEA	AL	1	0	1	0	1	0	0	0	0	0	0	0	0	0	1	0
	Total		5	3	2	2	3	0	0	0	0	0	0	0	0	0	5	0
1994	FLO	NL	1	1	0	0	1	0	0	0	0	0	0	0	0	0	1	0
1995	HOU	NL	2	0	2	2	0	0	0	0	0	0	0	0	0	0	2	0
Total			29	16	13	16	10	3	0	0	0	0	0	1	0	2	25	4

Rank among batters: 1,465 • *Total ballparks homered in*: 9 • *First HR*: 04/20/1987 off John Smiley

Lee Magee

LEO CHRISTOPHER MAGEE
B: 06/04/1889 D: 03/14/1966
BB

Year	Tm	Lg	Tot	H	A	Men-On 0	1	2	3	One-Game 2	3	4	LO	XN	IP	PH	RHP	LHP
1913	STL	NL	2	2	0	0	1	0	1	0	0	0	0	0	0	0	2	0
1914	STL	NL	2	2	0	1	1	0	0	0	0	0	0	0	1	0	2	0
1915	BRO	FL	4	3	1	0	4	0	0	0	0	0	0	0	0	0	3	1
1916	NY	AL	3	2	1	1	1	1	0	0	0	0	0	0	0	0	1	2
1919	CHI	NL	1	1	0	1	0	0	0	0	0	0	0	0	0	0	0	1
Total			12	10	2	3	7	1	1	0	0	0	0	0	1	0	8	4

Rank among batters: 2,325 • *Top target (2 home runs)*: Doc Crandall • *Number of pitchers victimized*: 11 • *Total ballparks homered in*: 6 • *First HR*: 04/18/1913 off Jimmy Lavender

Sherry Magee

SHERWOOD ROBERT MAGEE
B: 08/06/1884 D: 03/13/1929
BR

Year	Tm	Lg	Tot	H	A	Men-On 0	1	2	3	One-Game 2	3	4	LO	XN	IP	PH	RHP	LHP
1904	PHI	NL	3	2	1	1	1	1	0	0	0	0	0	1	2	0	3	0
1905	PHI	NL	5	1	4	3	2	0	0	0	0	0	0	0	1	0	4	1
1906	PHI	NL	6	1	5	4	2	0	0	0	0	0	0	0	3	0	5	1
1907	PHI	NL	4	1	3	0	4	0	0	0	0	0	0	0	4	0	2	2
1908	PHI	NL	2	0	2	1	1	0	0	0	0	0	0	0	2	0	1	1
1909	PHI	NL	2	1	1	1	1	0	0	0	0	0	0	0	0	0	2	0
1910	PHI	NL	6	3	3	4	0	1	1	0	0	0	0	0	0	0	3	3
1911	PHI	NL	15	10	5	8	6	1	0	0	0	0	0	0	2	0	12	3
1912	PHI	NL	6	3	3	2	3	1	0	1	0	0	0	0	1	0	5	1
1913	PHI	NL	11	8	3	4	3	4	0	1	0	0	0	0	1	0	7	4
1914	PHI	NL	15	12	3	7	6	2	0	1	0	0	0	0	2	0	12	3
1915	BOS	NL	2	0	2	0	2	0	0	0	0	0	0	0	0	0	2	0
1916	BOS	NL	3	2	1	2	0	0	1	0	0	0	0	0	2	0	2	1
1917	BOS	NL	1	0	1	0	1	0	0	0	0	0	0	0	0	0	1	0
1918	CIN	NL	2	1	1	0	1	1	0	0	0	0	0	0	1	0	1	1
Total			83	45	38	37	33	11	2	3	0	0	0	1	21	0	62	21

Rank among batters: 628 • *Top target (5 home runs)*: Rube Marquard • *Number of pitchers victimized*: 57 • *Total ballparks homered in*: 12 • *First HR*: 09/08/1904 off Dummy Taylor

Harl Maggert

HARL VESTIN MAGGERT
B: 02/13/1883 D: 01/07/1963
BL

Year	Tm	Lg	Tot	H	A	Men-On 0	1	2	3	One-Game 2	3	4	LO	XN	IP	PH	RHP	LHP
1912	PHI	AL	1	1	0	1	0	0	0	0	0	0	0	0	0	0	1	0

Rank among batters: 4,707 • *Total ballparks homered in*: 1 • *First HR*: 07/22/1912 off Mack Allison

Harl Maggert

HARL WARREN MAGGERT
B: 05/14/1914 D: 07/10/1986
BR

Year	Tm	Lg	Tot	H	A	Men-On 0	1	2	3	One-Game 2	3	4	LO	XN	IP	PH	RHP	LHP
1938	BOS	NL	3	2	1	2	0	0	1	0	0	0	0	0	0	2	1	2

Rank among batters: 3,735 • *Total ballparks homered in*: 2 • *First HR*: 04/30/1938 off Al Smith

Sal Maglie

SALVATORE ANTHONY MAGLIE
B: 04/26/1917 D: 12/28/1992
BR

						Men-On				One-Game								
Year	Tm	Lg	Tot	H	A	0	1	2	3	2	3	4	LO	XN	IP	PH	RHP	LHP
1951	NY	NL	1	0	1	1	0	0	0	0	0	0	0	0	0	0	0	1
1958	NY	AL	1	0	1	0	0	1	0	0	0	0	0	0	0	0	1	0
Total			2	0	2	1	0	1	0	0	0	0	0	0	0	0	1	1

Rank among batters: 4,129 • *Total ballparks homered in*: 2 • *First HR*: 06/16/1951 off Paul LaPalme

George Magoon

GEORGE HENRY MAGOON
B: 03/27/1875 D: 12/06/1943
BR

						Men-On				One-Game								
Year	Tm	Lg	Tot	H	A	0	1	2	3	2	3	4	LO	XN	IP	PH	RHP	LHP
1898	BRO	NL	1	1	0	0	1	0	0	0	0	0	0	0	0	0	1	0
1901	CIN	NL	1	0	1	0	1	0	0	0	0	0	0	0	1	0	1	0
Total			2	1	1	0	2	0	0	0	0	0	0	0	1	0	2	0

Rank among batters: 4,129 • *Total ballparks homered in*: 2 • *First HR*: 08/16/1898 off Zeke Wilson

Joe Magrane

JOSEPH DAVID MAGRANE
B: 07/02/1964
BR

						Men-On				One-Game								
Year	Tm	Lg	Tot	H	A	0	1	2	3	2	3	4	LO	XN	IP	PH	RHP	LHP
1987	STL	NL	1	1	0	1	0	0	0	0	0	0	0	0	0	0	1	0
1988	STL	NL	1	0	1	0	0	1	0	0	0	0	0	0	0	0	1	0
1989	STL	NL	1	0	1	1	0	0	0	0	0	0	0	0	0	0	1	0
1992	STL	NL	1	0	1	1	0	0	0	0	0	0	0	0	0	0	0	1
Total			4	1	3	3	0	1	0	0	0	0	0	0	0	0	3	1

Rank among batters: 3,427 • *Total ballparks homered in*: 4 • *First HR*: 09/19/1987 off Scott Sanderson

Freddie Maguire

FREDERICK EDWARD MAGUIRE
B: 05/10/1899 D: 11/03/1961
BR

						Men-On				One-Game								
Year	Tm	Lg	Tot	H	A	0	1	2	3	2	3	4	LO	XN	IP	PH	RHP	LHP
1928	CHI	NL	1	0	1	1	0	0	0	0	0	0	0	0	0	0	1	0

Rank among batters: 4,707 • *Total ballparks homered in*: 1 • *First HR*: 04/11/1928 off Dolf Luque

Jack Maguire

JACK MAGUIRE
B: 02/05/1925
BR

						Men-On				One-Game								
Year	Tm	Lg	Tot	H	A	0	1	2	3	2	3	4	LO	XN	IP	PH	RHP	LHP
1951	NY	NL	1	1	0	1	0	0	0	0	0	0	0	0	0	0	0	1
	STL	AL	1	0	1	0	1	0	0	0	0	0	0	0	0	0	0	1
	Total		2	1	1	2	0	0	0	0	0	0	0	0	0	0	0	2
Total			2	1	1	2	0	0	0	0	0	0	0	0	0	0	0	2

Rank among batters: 4,129 • *Total ballparks homered in*: 2 • *First HR*: 04/27/1951 off Warren Spahn

Art Mahaffey

ARTHUR MAHAFFEY
B: 06/04/1938
BR

						Men-On				One-Game								
Year	Tm	Lg	Tot	H	A	0	1	2	3	2	3	4	LO	XN	IP	PH	RHP	LHP
1962	PHI	NL	2	1	1	0	1	0	1	0	0	0	0	0	0	0	2	0
1964	PHI	NL	1	0	1	0	0	1	0	0	0	0	0	0	0	0	0	1
Total			3	1	2	0	1	1	1	0	0	0	0	0	0	0	2	1

Rank among batters: 3,735 • *Total ballparks homered in*: 3 • *First HR*: 05/19/1962 off Glen Hobbie

Roy Mahaffey

LEE ROY MAHAFFEY
B: 02/09/1903 D: 07/23/1969
BR

						Men-On				One-Game								
Year	Tm	Lg	Tot	H	A	0	1	2	3	2	3	4	LO	XN	IP	PH	RHP	LHP
1930	PHI	AL	1	0	1	1	0	0	0	0	0	0	0	0	0	0	1	0
1931	PHI	AL	2	1	1	1	1	0	0	0	0	0	0	0	0	0	2	0
1932	PHI	AL	1	1	0	1	0	0	0	0	0	0	0	0	0	0	0	1
Total			4	2	2	3	1	0	0	0	0	0	0	0	0	0	3	1

Rank among batters: 3,427 • *Total ballparks homered in*: 3 • *First HR*: 06/06/1930 off Rip Collins

Year	Tm	Lg	Tot	H	A	Men-On 0	Men-On 1	Men-On 2	Men-On 3	One-Game 2	One-Game 3	One-Game 4	LO	XN	IP	PH	RHP	LHP

Art Mahan

ARTHUR LEO MAHAN
B: 06/08/1913
BL

Year	Tm	Lg	Tot	H	A	0	1	2	3	2	3	4	LO	XN	IP	PH	RHP	LHP
1940	PHI	NL	2	1	1	0	1	1	0	0	0	0	0	0	0	0	1	1

Rank among batters: 4,129 • *Total ballparks homered in*: 2 • *First HR*: 06/26/1940 off Rip Sewell

Ron Mahay

RONALD MATTHEW MAHAY
B: 06/28/1971
BL

Year	Tm	Lg	Tot	H	A	0	1	2	3	2	3	4	LO	XN	IP	PH	RHP	LHP
1995	BOS	AL	1	0	1	1	0	0	0	0	0	0	0	0	0	0	1	0

Rank among batters: 4,707 • *Total ballparks homered in*: 1 • *First HR*: 05/26/1995 off Mike Butcher

Greg Mahlberg

GREGORY JOHN MAHLBERG
B: 08/08/1952
BR

Year	Tm	Lg	Tot	H	A	0	1	2	3	2	3	4	LO	XN	IP	PH	RHP	LHP
1979	TEX	AL	1	0	1	1	0	0	0	0	0	0	0	0	0	0	0	1

Rank among batters: 4,707 • *Total ballparks homered in*: 1 • *First HR*: 09/03/1979 off Floyd Bannister

Rick Mahler

RICHARD KEITH MAHLER
B: 08/05/1953
BR

Year	Tm	Lg	Tot	H	A	0	1	2	3	2	3	4	LO	XN	IP	PH	RHP	LHP
1982	ATL	NL	1	1	0	0	1	0	0	0	0	0	0	0	0	0	1	0

Rank among batters: 4,707 • *Total ballparks homered in*: 1 • *First HR*: 06/23/1982 off Alejandro Pena

Jim Mahoney

JAMES THOMAS MAHONEY
B: 05/26/1934
BR

Year	Tm	Lg	Tot	H	A	0	1	2	3	2	3	4	LO	XN	IP	PH	RHP	LHP
1959	BOS	AL	1	1	0	0	0	1	0	0	0	0	0	0	0	0	1	0
1962	CLE	AL	3	3	0	3	0	0	0	0	0	0	0	0	0	0	3	0
Total			4	4	0	3	0	1	0	0	0	0	0	0	0	0	4	0

Rank among batters: 3,427 • *Total ballparks homered in*: 2 • *First HR*: 09/14/1959 off Turk Lown

Bob Maier

ROBERT PHILLIP MAIER
B: 09/05/1915 D: 08/04/1993
BR

Year	Tm	Lg	Tot	H	A	0	1	2	3	2	3	4	LO	XN	IP	PH	RHP	LHP
1945	DET	AL	1	0	1	0	1	0	0	0	0	0	0	0	0	0	0	1

Rank among batters: 4,707 • *Total ballparks homered in*: 1 • *First HR*: 08/28/1945 off Sam Zoldak

Willard Mains

WILLARD EBEN MAINS
B: 07/07/1868 D: 05/23/1923

Year	Tm	Lg	Tot	H	A	0	1	2	3	2	3	4	LO	XN	IP	PH	RHP	LHP
1891	CIN	AA	1	1	0	1	0	0	0	0	0	0	0	0	0	0	1	0

Rank among batters: 4,707 • *Total ballparks homered in*: 1 • *First HR*: 05/02/1891 off Clark Griffith

Fritz Maisel

FREDERICK CHARLES MAISEL
B: 12/23/1889 D: 04/22/1967
BR

Year	Tm	Lg	Tot	H	A	0	1	2	3	2	3	4	LO	XN	IP	PH	RHP	LHP
1914	NY	AL	2	1	1	2	0	0	0	0	0	0	1	0	1	0	1	1
1915	NY	AL	4	2	2	4	0	0	0	0	0	0	2	0	1	0	3	1
Total			6	3	3	6	0	0	0	0	0	0	3	0	2	0	4	2

Rank among batters: 2,988 • *Total ballparks homered in*: 4 • *First HR*: 09/03/1914 off Doc Ayers

Hank Majeski

HENRY MAJESKI
B: 12/13/1916 D: 08/09/1991
BR

Year	Tm	Lg	Tot	H	A	0	1	2	3	2	3	4	LO	XN	IP	PH	RHP	LHP
1939	BOS	NL	7	3	4	5	1	0	1	0	0	0	0	0	0	0	4	3

Hank Majeski *continued*

Year	Tm	Lg	Tot	H	A	Men-On 0	1	2	3	One-Game 2	3	4	LO	XN	IP	PH	RHP	LHP
1946	PHI	AL	1	1	0	1	0	0	0	0	0	0	0	0	0	0	1	0
1947	PHI	AL	8	2	6	5	3	0	0	0	0	0	0	0	0	0	8	0
1948	PHI	AL	12	7	5	4	7	1	0	0	0	0	0	0	0	0	9	3
1949	PHI	AL	9	3	6	6	3	0	0	0	0	0	0	0	0	0	7	2
1950	CHI	AL	6	5	1	3	2	1	0	1	0	0	0	0	0	0	3	3
1951	PHI	AL	5	3	2	5	0	0	0	0	0	0	0	0	0	0	4	1
1952	PHI	AL	2	2	0	1	1	0	0	0	0	0	0	0	0	0	2	0
1953	CLE	AL	2	2	0	2	0	0	0	0	0	0	0	0	0	1	2	0
1954	CLE	AL	3	0	3	1	0	2	0	0	0	0	0	0	0	0	2	1
1955	CLE	AL	2	1	1	2	0	0	0	0	0	0	0	0	0	0	1	1
Total			57	29	28	35	17	4	1	1	0	0	0	0	0	1	43	14

Rank among batters: 902 • *Top target (3 home runs)*: Early Wynn, Virgil Trucks, Ellis Kinder • *Number of pitchers victimized*: 43 • *Total ballparks homered in*: 11 • *First HR*: 06/16/1939 off Bob Klinger • *World Series HR*—1

John Malarkey

JOHN S. MALARKEY
B: 05/04/1872 D: 10/29/1949

Year	Tm	Lg	Tot	H	A	Men-On 0	1	2	3	One-Game 2	3	4	LO	XN	IP	PH	RHP	LHP
1902	BOS	NL	1	1	0	1	0	0	0	0	0	0	0	1	0	0	1	0

Rank among batters: 4,707 • *Total ballparks homered in*: 1 • *First HR*: 09/11/1902 off Mike O'Neill

Charlie Malay

CHARLES FRANCIS MALAY
B: 06/13/1879 D: 09/18/1949
BB

Year	Tm	Lg	Tot	H	A	Men-On 0	1	2	3	One-Game 2	3	4	LO	XN	IP	PH	RHP	LHP
1905	BRO	NL	1	1	0	0	0	1	0	0	0	0	0	0	1	0	0	1

Rank among batters: 4,707 • *Total ballparks homered in*: 1 • *First HR*: 07/12/1905 off Patsy Flaherty

Candy Maldonado

CANDIDO (GUADARRAMA) MALDONADO
B: 09/05/1960
BR

Year	Tm	Lg	Tot	H	A	Men-On 0	1	2	3	One-Game 2	3	4	LO	XN	IP	PH	RHP	LHP
1983	LA	NL	1	1	0	0	1	0	0	0	0	0	0	0	0	1	1	0
1984	LA	NL	5	1	4	5	0	0	0	0	0	0	0	1	0	2	1	4
1985	LA	NL	5	2	3	5	0	0	0	0	0	0	0	0	0	1	0	5
1986	SF	NL	18	6	12	7	6	3	2	2	0	0	0	1	0	4	12	6
1987	SF	NL	20	14	6	14	5	0	1	2	0	0	0	0	0	1	14	6
1988	SF	NL	12	5	7	7	4	1	0	0	0	0	0	0	0	0	11	1
1989	SF	NL	9	1	8	7	2	0	0	1	0	0	0	0	0	0	7	2
1990	CLE	AL	22	12	10	13	5	4	0	1	0	0	0	0	0	0	12	10
1991	MIL	AL	5	3	2	0	4	1	0	0	0	0	0	0	0	0	5	0
	TOR	AL	7	4	3	4	3	0	0	0	0	0	0	0	0	0	4	3
	Total		12	7	5	4	7	1	0	0	0	0	0	0	0	0	9	3
1992	TOR	AL	20	8	12	10	10	0	0	0	0	0	0	0	0	0	16	4
1993	CHI	NL	3	1	2	1	1	1	0	0	0	0	0	0	0	1	1	2
	CLE	AL	5	4	1	1	3	1	0	0	0	0	0	0	0	0	2	3
	Total		8	5	3	2	4	2	0	0	0	0	0	0	0	1	3	5
1994	CLE	AL	5	4	1	3	2	0	0	0	0	0	0	0	0	1	1	4
1995	TOR	AL	7	5	2	3	3	1	0	0	0	0	0	0	0	0	3	4
	TEX	AL	2	2	0	1	0	1	0	0	0	0	0	0	0	0	1	1
	Total		9	7	2	4	3	2	0	0	0	0	0	0	0	0	4	5
Total			146	73	73	81	49	13	3	6	0	0	0	2	0	11	91	55

Rank among batters: 302 • Top target (3 home runs): Dennis Martinez, Scott Sanderson, Bob Welch, Mike Mussina • *Number of pitchers victimized*: 119 • *Total ballparks homered in*: 29 • *First HR*: 08/15/1983 off Fred Breining • *Hit for Cycle*—@STL: 05/04/1987 • *World Series HR*—1; *LCS HR*—2

Jim Maler

JAMES MICHAEL MALER
B: 08/16/1958
BR

Year	Tm	Lg	Tot	H	A	Men-On 0	1	2	3	One-Game 2	3	4	LO	XN	IP	PH	RHP	LHP
1982	SEA	AL	4	1	3	2	1	0	1	0	0	0	0	0	0	0	3	1
1983	SEA	AL	1	1	0	0	1	0	0	0	0	0	0	0	0	1	0	1
Total			5	2	3	2	2	0	1	0	0	0	0	0	0	1	3	2

Rank among batters: 3,191 • *Total ballparks homered in*: 3 • *First HR*: 04/06/1982 off Pete Redfern

Year	Tm	Lg	Tot	H	A	Men-On 0	1	2	3	One-Game 2	3	4	LO	XN	IP	PH	RHP	LHP

Bobby Malkmus

ROBERT EDWARD MALKMUS
B: 07/04/1931
BR

Year	Tm	Lg	Tot	H	A	0	1	2	3	2	3	4	LO	XN	IP	PH	RHP	LHP
1960	PHI	NL	1	1	0	0	0	0	1	0	0	0	0	0	0	0	1	0
1961	PHI	NL	7	4	3	6	1	0	0	0	0	0	2	0	0	0	3	4
Total			8	5	3	6	1	0	1	0	0	0	2	0	0	0	4	4

Rank among batters: 2,703 • *Total ballparks homered in*: 4 • *First HR*: 09/15/1960 off Sam Jones

Les Mallon

LESLIE CLYDE MALLON
B: 11/21/1905 D: 04/17/1991
BR

Year	Tm	Lg	Tot	H	A	0	1	2	3	2	3	4	LO	XN	IP	PH	RHP	LHP
1931	PHI	NL	1	1	0	1	0	0	0	0	0	0	0	0	0	0	1	0
1932	PHI	NL	5	3	2	4	1	0	0	0	0	0	1	0	0	0	1	4
1935	BOS	NL	2	1	1	2	0	0	0	0	0	0	0	0	0	0	2	0
Total			8	5	3	7	1	0	0	0	0	0	1	0	0	0	4	4

Rank among batters: 2,703 • *Top target (2 home runs)*: Jim Mooney • *Number of pitchers victimized*: 7 • *Total ballparks homered in*: 3 • *First HR*: 06/19/1931 off Ed Strelecki

Eddie Malone

EDWARD RUSSELL MALONE
B: 06/16/1920
BR

Year	Tm	Lg	Tot	H	A	0	1	2	3	2	3	4	LO	XN	IP	PH	RHP	LHP
1949	CHI	AL	1	0	1	1	0	0	0	0	0	0	0	0	0	0	0	1

Rank among batters: 4,707 • *Total ballparks homered in*: 1 • *First HR*: 09/14/1949 off Lloyd Hittle

Lew Malone

LEWIS ALOYSIUS MALONE
B: 03/13/1897 D: 02/17/1972
BR

Year	Tm	Lg	Tot	H	A	0	1	2	3	2	3	4	LO	XN	IP	PH	RHP	LHP
1915	PHI	AL	1	1	0	0	1	0	0	0	0	0	0	0	0	0	0	1

Rank among batters: 4,707 • *Total ballparks homered in*: 1 • *First HR*: 09/03/1915 off Vean Gregg

Pat Malone

PERCE LEIGH MALONE
B: 09/25/1902 D: 05/13/1943
BL

Year	Tm	Lg	Tot	H	A	0	1	2	3	2	3	4	LO	XN	IP	PH	RHP	LHP
1928	CHI	NL	1	1	0	0	1	0	0	0	0	0	0	0	0	0	1	0
1929	CHI	NL	2	1	1	1	0	1	0	0	0	0	0	0	0	0	2	0
1930	CHI	NL	4	3	1	1	3	0	0	0	0	0	0	0	0	0	3	1
1931	CHI	NL	1	1	0	1	0	0	0	0	0	0	0	0	0	0	0	1
1932	CHI	NL	1	1	0	1	0	0	0	0	0	0	0	0	0	0	1	0
Total			9	7	2	4	4	1	0	0	0	0	0	0	0	0	7	2

Rank among batters: 2,587 • *Total ballparks homered in*: 3 • *First HR*: 07/14/1928 off Augie Walsh

Billy Maloney

WILLIAM ALPHONSE MALONEY
B: 06/05/1878 D: 09/02/1960
BL

Year	Tm	Lg	Tot	H	A	0	1	2	3	2	3	4	LO	XN	IP	PH	RHP	LHP
1902	CIN	NL	1	1	0	0	0	1	0	0	0	0	0	0	1	0	1	0
1905	CHI	NL	2	1	1	0	0	1	1	0	0	0	0	0	0	0	2	0
1908	BRO	NL	3	2	1	3	0	0	0	0	0	0	0	0	0	1	1	2
Total			6	4	2	3	0	2	1	0	0	0	0	0	1	1	4	2

Rank among batters: 2,988 • *Total ballparks homered in*: 4 • *First HR*: 08/23/1902 off Chick Fraser

Jim Maloney

JAMES WILLIAM MALONEY
B: 06/02/1940
BL

Year	Tm	Lg	Tot	H	A	0	1	2	3	2	3	4	LO	XN	IP	PH	RHP	LHP
1961	CIN	NL	1	0	1	0	1	0	0	0	0	0	0	0	0	0	1	0
1964	CIN	NL	1	1	0	0	0	1	0	0	0	0	0	0	0	0	0	1
1968	CIN	NL	2	0	2	1	1	0	0	0	0	0	0	0	0	0	2	0
1969	CIN	NL	3	2	1	3	0	0	0	0	0	0	0	0	0	0	3	0
Total			7	3	4	4	2	1	0	0	0	0	0	0	0	0	6	1

Jim Maloney *continued*

Rank among batters: 2,834 • *Total ballparks homered in*: 5 • *First HR*: 05/30/1961 off Sam Jones

Frank Malzone

FRANK JAMES MALZONE
B: 02/28/1930
BR

Year	Tm	Lg	Tot	H	A	Men-On 0	Men-On 1	Men-On 2	Men-On 3	One-Game 2	One-Game 3	One-Game 4	LO	XN	IP	PH	RHP	LHP
1956	BOS	AL	2	1	1	0	2	0	0	0	0	0	0	0	0	0	2	0
1957	BOS	AL	15	8	7	6	7	1	1	2	0	0	0	1	0	0	12	3
1958	BOS	AL	15	10	5	8	4	2	1	1	0	0	0	0	0	0	14	1
1959	BOS	AL	19	5	14	12	5	2	0	2	0	0	0	1	0	0	18	1
1960	BOS	AL	14	7	7	6	8	0	0	0	0	0	0	0	0	0	10	4
1961	BOS	AL	14	6	8	9	0	5	0	2	0	0	0	0	0	0	11	3
1962	BOS	AL	21	10	11	11	5	5	0	2	0	0	0	0	0	0	17	4
1963	BOS	AL	15	11	4	8	4	3	0	1	0	0	0	1	0	0	10	5
1964	BOS	AL	13	9	4	8	4	1	0	2	0	0	0	0	0	0	12	1
1965	BOS	AL	3	1	2	0	3	0	0	0	0	0	0	0	0	0	0	3
1966	CAL	AL	2	0	2	1	0	1	0	0	0	0	0	0	0	0	2	0
Total			133	68	65	69	42	20	2	12	0	0	0	3	0	0	108	25

Rank among batters: 337 • *Top target (6 home runs)*: Ralph Terry, Pedro Ramos • *Number of pitchers victimized*: 81 • *Total ballparks homered in*: 12 • *First HR*: 05/03/1956 off Duke Maas • *All-Star HR*—1

Al Mamaux

ALBERT LEON MAMAUX
B: 05/30/1894 D: 01/02/1963
BR

Year	Tm	Lg	Tot	H	A	Men-On 0	Men-On 1	Men-On 2	Men-On 3	One-Game 2	One-Game 3	One-Game 4	LO	XN	IP	PH	RHP	LHP
1922	BRO	NL	1	0	1	1	0	0	0	0	0	0	0	0	0	0	1	0

Rank among batters: 4,707 • *Total ballparks homered in*: 1 • *First HR*: 05/27/1922 off Lee Meadows

Frank Mancuso

FRANK OCTAVIUS MANCUSO
B: 05/23/1918
BR

Year	Tm	Lg	Tot	H	A	Men-On 0	Men-On 1	Men-On 2	Men-On 3	One-Game 2	One-Game 3	One-Game 4	LO	XN	IP	PH	RHP	LHP
1944	STL	AL	1	1	0	0	1	0	0	0	0	0	0	0	0	0	1	0
1945	STL	AL	1	0	1	1	0	0	0	0	0	0	0	0	0	0	1	0
1946	STL	AL	3	0	3	2	1	0	0	0	0	0	0	0	0	0	3	0
Total			5	1	4	3	2	0	0	0	0	0	0	0	0	0	5	0

Rank among batters: 3,191 • *Total ballparks homered in*: 5 • *First HR*: 06/03/1944 off Luke Hamlin

Gus Mancuso

AUGUST RODNEY MANCUSO
B: 12/05/1905 D: 10/26/1984
BR

Year	Tm	Lg	Tot	H	A	Men-On 0	Men-On 1	Men-On 2	Men-On 3	One-Game 2	One-Game 3	One-Game 4	LO	XN	IP	PH	RHP	LHP
1930	STL	NL	7	2	5	3	3	1	0	1	0	0	0	0	0	0	5	2
1931	STL	NL	1	1	0	1	0	0	0	0	0	0	0	0	0	0	0	1
1932	STL	NL	5	1	4	3	1	1	0	0	0	0	0	0	0	0	2	3
1933	NY	NL	6	3	3	4	1	1	0	0	0	0	0	1	0	1	4	2
1934	NY	NL	7	5	2	6	1	0	0	1	0	0	0	0	0	0	7	0
1935	NY	NL	5	5	0	5	0	0	0	1	0	0	0	0	0	0	5	0
1936	NY	NL	9	8	1	5	2	2	0	0	0	0	0	0	0	0	9	0
1937	NY	NL	4	4	0	2	1	1	0	0	0	0	0	0	0	0	2	2
1938	NY	NL	2	2	0	1	0	0	1	0	0	0	0	0	0	0	2	0
1939	CHI	NL	2	0	2	2	0	0	0	0	0	0	0	0	0	0	2	0
1941	STL	NL	2	0	2	2	0	0	0	0	0	0	0	0	0	0	0	2
1943	NY	NL	2	2	0	1	1	0	0	0	0	0	0	0	0	1	2	0
1944	NY	NL	1	1	0	1	0	0	0	0	0	0	0	0	0	0	1	0
Total			53	34	19	36	10	6	1	3	0	0	0	1	0	2	41	12

Rank among batters: 953 • *Top target (5 home runs)*: Waite Hoyt • *Number of pitchers victimized*: 42 • *Total ballparks homered in*: 8 • *First HR*: 06/13/1930 off Ed Brandt

Angel Mangual

ANGEL LUIS (GUILBE) MANGUAL
B: 03/19/1947
BR

Year	Tm	Lg	Tot	H	A	Men-On 0	Men-On 1	Men-On 2	Men-On 3	One-Game 2	One-Game 3	One-Game 4	LO	XN	IP	PH	RHP	LHP
1971	OAK	AL	4	3	1	2	1	1	0	0	0	0	0	0	0	1	2	2

Angel Mangual *continued*

Year	Tm	Lg	Tot	H	A	Men-On				One-Game			LO	XN	IP	PH	RHP	LHP
						0	1	2	3	2	3	4						
1972	OAK	AL	5	2	3	3	0	2	0	0	0	0	0	0	0	1	2	3
1973	OAK	AL	3	1	2	2	0	1	0	0	0	0	0	1	0	0	3	0
1974	OAK	AL	9	4	5	5	1	2	1	0	0	0	0	0	0	0	8	1
1975	OAK	AL	1	0	1	1	0	0	0	0	0	0	0	0	0	0	0	1
Total			22	10	12	13	2	6	1	0	0	0	0	1	0	2	15	7

Rank among batters: 1,719 • *Top target (2 home runs)*: Dick Drago, Joe Decker, Stan Bahnsen • *Number of pitchers victimized*: 19 • *Total ballparks homered in*: 8 • *First HR*: 04/27/1971 off Dave McNally

Pepe Mangual

JOSE MANUEL (GUILBE) MANGUAL
B: 05/23/1952
BR

Year	Tm	Lg	Tot	H	A	Men-On				One-Game			LO	XN	IP	PH	RHP	LHP
						0	1	2	3	2	3	4						
1973	MON	NL	3	1	2	2	1	0	0	0	0	0	0	0	0	0	2	1
1975	MON	NL	9	4	5	6	2	1	0	0	0	0	2	0	0	0	6	3
1976	MON	NL	3	1	2	3	0	0	0	0	0	0	1	0	0	0	3	0
	NY	NL	1	0	1	1	0	0	0	0	0	0	0	0	0	0	0	1
	Total		4	1	3	4	0	0	0	0	0	0	1	0	0	0	3	1
Total			16	6	10	12	3	1	0	0	0	0	3	0	0	0	11	5

Rank among batters: 2,029 • *Top target (2 home runs)*: Tom Griffin • *Number of pitchers victimized*: 15 • *Total ballparks homered in*: 8 • *First HR*: 04/08/1973 off Burt Hooton

Clyde Manion

CLYDE JENNINGS MANION
B: 10/30/1896 D: 09/04/1967
BR

Year	Tm	Lg	Tot	H	A	Men-On				One-Game			LO	XN	IP	PH	RHP	LHP
						0	1	2	3	2	3	4						
1928	STL	AL	2	1	1	2	0	0	0	0	0	0	0	0	0	1	2	0
1930	STL	AL	1	0	1	1	0	0	0	0	0	0	0	0	0	0	1	0
Total			3	1	2	3	0	0	0	0	0	0	0	0	0	1	3	0

Rank among batters: 3,735 • *Total ballparks homered in*: 3 • *First HR*: 04/13/1928 off Sam Gibson

Phil Mankowski

PHILIP ANTHONY MANKOWSKI
B: 01/09/1953
BL

Year	Tm	Lg	Tot	H	A	Men-On				One-Game			LO	XN	IP	PH	RHP	LHP
						0	1	2	3	2	3	4						
1976	DET	AL	1	0	1	1	0	0	0	0	0	0	0	0	0	0	1	0
1977	DET	AL	3	3	0	2	1	0	0	0	0	0	0	0	0	1	2	1
1978	DET	AL	4	3	1	1	2	1	0	0	0	0	0	0	0	0	4	0
Total			8	6	2	4	3	1	0	0	0	0	0	0	0	1	7	1

Rank among batters: 2,703 • *Top target (2 home runs)*: Dennis Eckersley, Dick Tidrow • *Number of pitchers victimized*: 6 • *Total ballparks homered in*: 3 • *First HR*: 09/28/1976 off Dennis Eckersley

Fred Mann

FRED J. MANN
B: 04/01/1858 D: 04/16/1916
BL

Year	Tm	Lg	Tot	H	A	Men-On				One-Game			LO	XN	IP	PH	RHP	LHP
						0	1	2	3	2	3	4						
1883	COL	AA	1	0	1	1	0	0	0	0	0	0	0	0	0	0	1	0
1884	COL	AA	7	5	2	1	4	2	0	0	0	0	0	0	0	0	6	0
1886	PIT	AA	2	0	2	1	0	0	1	0	0	0	0	0	0	0	0	0
1887	CLE	AA	2	1	1	0	1	0	1	0	0	0	0	0	1	0	1	1
Total			12	6	6	3	5	2	2	0	0	0	0	0	1	0	8	1

Rank among batters: 2,325 • *Total ballparks homered in*: 8 • *First HR*: 07/30/1883 off Will White

Kelly Mann

KELLY JOHN MANN
B: 08/17/1967
BR

Year	Tm	Lg	Tot	H	A	Men-On				One-Game			LO	XN	IP	PH	RHP	LHP
						0	1	2	3	2	3	4						
1990	ATL	NL	1	0	1	1	0	0	0	0	0	0	0	0	0	0	0	1

Rank among batters: 4,707 • *Total ballparks homered in*: 1 • *First HR*: 09/25/1990 off Norm Charlton

Les Mann

LESLIE MANN
B: 11/18/1893 D: 01/14/1962
BR

Year	Tm	Lg	Tot	H	A	Men-On				One-Game			LO	XN	IP	PH	RHP	LHP
						0	1	2	3	2	3	4						
1913	BOS	NL	3	0	3	0	1	2	0	0	0	0	0	0	0	0	2	1

Les Mann *continued*

Year	Tm	Lg	Tot	H	A	Men-On				One-Game			LO	XN	IP	PH	RHP	LHP
						0	1	2	3	2	3	4						
1914	BOS	NL	4	2	2	2	2	0	0	0	0	0	0	0	2	0	2	2
1915	CHI	FL	4	1	3	2	2	0	0	0	0	0	0	0	0	0	3	1
1916	CHI	NL	2	2	0	2	0	0	0	0	0	0	0	0	0	0	0	2
1917	CHI	NL	1	1	0	0	1	0	0	0	0	0	0	0	0	0	1	0
1918	CHI	NL	2	0	2	1	1	0	0	0	0	0	0	0	1	0	1	1
1919	CHI	NL	1	0	1	1	0	0	0	0	0	0	0	0	0	0	1	0
	BOS	NL	3	1	2	1	2	0	0	0	0	0	0	0	1	0	2	1
	Total		4	1	3	2	2	0	0	0	0	0	0	0	1	0	3	1
1920	BOS	NL	3	1	2	1	1	1	0	0	0	0	0	0	1	0	0	3
1921	STL	NL	7	6	1	5	1	1	0	1	0	0	4	0	0	0	1	6
1922	STL	NL	2	2	0	1	0	0	1	0	0	0	1	0	0	0	0	2
1923	STL	NL	5	1	4	4	0	1	0	1	0	0	0	0	1	1	0	5
1925	BOS	NL	2	1	1	1	1	0	0	0	0	0	0	0	1	0	0	2
1926	BOS	NL	1	0	1	0	1	0	0	0	0	0	0	0	1	0	1	0
1927	NY	NL	2	2	0	1	1	0	0	0	0	0	1	0	0	0	0	2
1928	NY	NL	2	1	1	0	2	0	0	0	0	0	0	0	0	0	0	2
Total			44	21	23	22	16	5	1	2	0	0	6	0	8	1	14	30

Rank among batters: 1,095 • *Top target (4 home runs)*: Art Nehf • *Number of pitchers victimized*: 29 • *Total ballparks homered in*: 13 • *First HR*: 05/02/1913 off Frank Allen

Jack Manning

JOHN E. MANNING
B: 12/20/1853 D: 08/15/1929
BR

Year	Tm	Lg	Tot	H	A	0	1	2	3	2	3	4	LO	XN	IP	PH	RHP	LHP
1876	BOS	NL	2	2	0	2	0	0	0	0	0	0	0	0	0	0	2	0
1880	CIN	NL	2	2	0	2	0	0	0	0	0	0	0	0	0	0	2	0
1884	PHI	NL	5	0	5	1	3	1	0	0	1	0	0	0	0	0	5	0
1885	PHI	NL	3	0	3	1	2	0	0	0	0	0	1	1	0	0	3	0
1886	BAL	AA	1	1	0	0	1	0	0	0	0	0	0	0	1	0	1	0
Total			13	5	8	6	6	1	0	0	1	0	1	1	1	0	13	0

Rank among batters: 2,248 • *Top target (3 home runs)*: John Clarkson • *Number of pitchers victimized*: 10 • *Total ballparks homered in*: 7 • *First HR*: 08/03/1876 off George Zettlein

Jim Manning

JAMES H. MANNING
B: 01/31/1862 D: 10/22/1929
BB

Year	Tm	Lg	Tot	H	A	0	1	2	3	2	3	4	LO	XN	IP	PH	RHP	LHP
1884	BOS	NL	2	1	1	2	0	0	0	0	0	0	0	0	1	0	2	0
1885	BOS	NL	2	0	2	1	0	1	0	0	0	0	0	0	0	0	2	0
	DET	NL	1	1	0	0	1	0	0	0	0	0	0	0	0	0	0	1
	Total		3	1	2	1	1	1	0	0	0	0	0	0	0	0	2	1
1889	KC	AA	3	1	2	2	0	1	0	0	0	0	0	0	0	0	3	0
Total			8	3	5	5	1	2	0	0	0	0	0	0	1	0	7	1

Rank among batters: 2,703 • *Top target (2 home runs)*: Jim Galvin, John Coleman • *Number of pitchers victimized*: 6 • *Total ballparks homered in*: 7 • *First HR*: 05/29/1884 off John Coleman

Rick Manning

RICHARD EUGENE MANNING
B: 09/02/1954
BL

Year	Tm	Lg	Tot	H	A	0	1	2	3	2	3	4	LO	XN	IP	PH	RHP	LHP
1975	CLE	AL	3	2	1	1	1	0	1	0	0	0	0	0	1	0	1	2
1976	CLE	AL	6	2	4	5	0	0	1	0	0	0	0	1	0	0	4	2
1977	CLE	AL	5	0	5	3	1	1	0	0	0	0	1	0	0	0	3	2
1978	CLE	AL	3	1	2	3	0	0	0	0	0	0	1	0	0	0	2	1
1979	CLE	AL	3	1	2	1	1	0	1	0	0	0	0	0	0	0	1	2
1980	CLE	AL	3	3	0	1	1	1	0	0	0	0	0	0	0	0	3	0
1981	CLE	AL	4	2	2	2	2	0	0	0	0	0	0	0	0	0	3	1
1982	CLE	AL	8	1	7	5	3	0	0	0	0	0	0	0	0	0	6	2
1983	CLE	AL	1	0	1	1	0	0	0	0	0	0	0	0	0	0	1	0
	MIL	AL	3	2	1	3	0	0	0	0	0	0	0	1	0	0	2	1
	Total		4	2	2	4	0	0	0	0	0	0	0	1	0	0	3	1
1984	MIL	AL	7	1	6	5	1	1	0	0	0	0	0	0	0	0	5	2
1985	MIL	AL	2	1	1	0	1	1	0	0	0	0	0	0	0	0	1	1
1986	MIL	AL	8	4	4	4	2	2	0	0	0	0	0	0	0	0	7	1
Total			56	20	36	34	13	6	3	0	0	0	2	2	1	0	39	17

Rank among batters: 913 • Top target (2 home runs): Ken Holtzman, Doug Bird, Scott McGregor, Jerry Augustine, Luis Leal, Mike Moore • *Number of pitchers victimized*: 50 • *Total ballparks homered in*: 14 • *First HR*: 07/11/1975 off Mickey Scott

Tim Manning

TIMOTHY EDWARD MANNING
B: 12/03/1853 D: 06/11/1934
BR

Year	Tm	Lg	Tot	H	A	Men-On 0	1	2	3	One-Game 2	3	4	LO	XN	IP	PH	RHP	LHP
1884	BAL	AA	2	2	0	2	0	0	0	0	0	0	0	0	0	0	2	0

Rank among batters: 4,129 • *Total ballparks homered in*: 1 • *First HR*: 05/03/1884 off Tim Keefe

Don Manno

DONALD D. MANNO
B: 05/15/1915
BR

Year	Tm	Lg	Tot	H	A	Men-On 0	1	2	3	One-Game 2	3	4	LO	XN	IP	PH	RHP	LHP
1940	BOS	NL	1	0	1	0	0	0	1	0	0	0	0	0	0	0	0	1

Rank among batters: 4,707 • *Total ballparks homered in*: 1 • *First HR*: 09/26/1940 off Wes Flowers

Fred Manrique

FRED ELOY (REYES) MANRIQUE
B: 11/05/1961
BR

Year	Tm	Lg	Tot	H	A	Men-On 0	1	2	3	One-Game 2	3	4	LO	XN	IP	PH	RHP	LHP
1985	MON	NL	1	1	0	1	0	0	0	0	0	0	1	0	0	0	0	1
1986	STL	NL	1	0	1	1	0	0	0	0	0	0	0	0	0	1	0	1
1987	CHI	AL	4	2	2	2	0	2	0	0	0	0	0	0	0	0	2	2
1988	CHI	AL	5	3	2	3	1	1	0	0	0	0	0	0	0	0	3	2
1989	CHI	AL	2	1	1	0	2	0	0	0	0	0	0	0	0	0	1	1
	TEX	AL	2	0	2	1	1	0	0	0	0	0	0	0	0	0	2	0
	Total		4	1	3	1	3	0	0	0	0	0	0	0	0	0	3	1
1990	MIN	AL	5	3	2	1	2	2	0	0	0	0	0	0	0	0	4	1
Total			20	10	10	9	6	5	0	0	0	0	1	0	0	1	12	8

Rank among batters: 1,810 • *Top target (2 home runs)*: Jeff Robinson, Brian Holton • *Number of pitchers victimized*: 18 • *Total ballparks homered in*: 11 • *First HR*: 10/03/1985 off Shane Rawley

Mike Mansell

MICHAEL R. MANSELL
B: 01/15/1858 D: 12/04/1902
BL

Year	Tm	Lg	Tot	H	A	Men-On 0	1	2	3	One-Game 2	3	4	LO	XN	IP	PH	RHP	LHP
1879	SYR	NL	1	0	1	0	1	0	0	0	0	0	0	0	0	0	1	0
1880	CIN	NL	2	1	1	2	0	0	0	0	0	0	0	0	0	0	2	0
1882	PIT	AA	2	1	1	1	1	0	0	0	0	0	0	0	0	0	1	0
1883	PIT	AA	3	2	1	2	1	0	0	0	0	0	0	0	0	0	2	0
1884	PIT	AA	1	1	0	0	0	1	0	0	0	0	0	0	0	0	0	0
Total			9	5	4	5	3	1	0	0	0	0	0	0	0	0	6	0

Rank among batters: 2,587 • *Top target (2 home runs)*: Will White • *Number of pitchers victimized*: 8 • *Total ballparks homered in*: 5 • *First HR*: 08/27/1879 off Tommy Bond

Felix Mantilla

FELIX (LAMELA) MANTILLA
B: 07/29/1934
BR

Year	Tm	Lg	Tot	H	A	Men-On 0	1	2	3	One-Game 2	3	4	LO	XN	IP	PH	RHP	LHP
1957	MIL	NL	4	2	2	0	3	1	0	0	0	0	0	0	0	0	2	2
1958	MIL	NL	7	3	4	6	1	0	0	0	0	0	1	0	0	0	1	6
1959	MIL	NL	3	2	1	1	1	1	0	0	0	0	0	0	0	0	1	2
1960	MIL	NL	3	1	2	3	0	0	0	0	0	0	0	0	0	0	3	0
1961	MIL	NL	1	1	0	0	1	0	0	0	0	0	0	0	0	0	0	1
1962	NY	NL	11	5	6	6	3	2	0	0	0	0	1	1	0	1	10	1
1963	BOS	AL	6	2	4	4	2	0	0	0	0	0	1	0	0	0	3	3
1964	BOS	AL	30	19	11	16	12	2	0	3	0	0	2	0	0	1	20	10
1965	BOS	AL	18	11	7	7	6	4	1	0	0	0	0	0	0	0	15	3
1966	HOU	NL	6	2	4	1	3	2	0	0	0	0	0	0	0	2	4	2
Total			89	48	41	44	32	12	1	3	0	0	5	1	0	4	59	30

Rank among batters: 584 • *Top target (3 home runs)*: John Wyatt, Jim Kaat, Luis Tiant, Mudcat Grant • *Number of pitchers victimized*: 68 • *Total ballparks homered in*: 20 • *First HR*: 06/29/1957 off Red Swanson

Mickey Mantle

MICKEY CHARLES MANTLE
B: 10/20/1931 D: 08/13/1995
BB HOF

Year	Tm	Lg	Tot	H	A	Men-On 0	1	2	3	One-Game 2	3	4	LO	XN	IP	PH	RHP	LHP
1951	NY	AL	13	7	6	4	5	4	0	0	0	0	1	0	0	0	11	2

Mickey Mantle *continued*

Year	Tm	Lg	Tot	H	A	Men-On 0	1	2	3	One-Game 2	3	4	LO	XN	IP	PH	RHP	LHP
1952	NY	AL	23	11	12	14	4	3	2	1	0	0	0	0	0	0	11	12
1953	NY	AL	21	8	13	5	10	5	1	0	0	0	0	0	1	1	8	13
1954	NY	AL	27	14	13	19	6	2	0	1	0	0	0	1	0	0	20	7
1955	NY	AL	37	19	18	21	9	6	1	3	1	0	0	1	0	0	27	10
1956	NY	AL	52	27	25	29	16	6	1	7	0	0	0	1	0	0	39	13
1957	NY	AL	34	14	20	20	12	2	0	1	0	0	0	2	0	0	26	8
1958	NY	AL	42	21	21	27	10	5	0	3	0	0	0	0	3	0	34	8
1959	NY	AL	31	18	13	15	13	3	0	2	0	0	0	3	1	0	25	6
1960	NY	AL	40	23	17	22	12	6	0	4	0	0	0	2	0	0	24	16
1961	NY	AL	54	24	30	27	17	9	1	8	0	0	0	2	1	0	43	11
1962	NY	AL	30	16	14	17	9	3	1	5	0	0	0	0	0	1	26	4
1963	NY	AL	15	8	7	8	5	2	0	1	0	0	0	1	0	2	8	7
1964	NY	AL	35	16	19	17	13	5	0	2	0	0	0	0	0	0	20	15
1965	NY	AL	19	9	10	14	3	1	1	0	0	0	0	0	0	0	9	10
1966	NY	AL	23	11	12	15	4	3	1	4	0	0	0	0	0	1	14	9
1967	NY	AL	22	10	12	15	6	1	0	1	0	0	0	1	0	1	17	5
1968	NY	AL	18	10	8	8	9	1	0	2	0	0	0	0	0	1	11	7
Total			536	266	270	297	163	67	9	45	1	0	1	14	6	7	373	163

Rank among batters: 8 • *Top target (13 home runs)*: Early Wynn • *Number of pitchers victimized*: 224 • *Total ballparks homered in*: 16 • *First HR*: 05/01/1951 off Randy Gumpert • *Switch hit HR in 1 game*—10 times • *Hit for Cycle*—vs CHI: 07/23/1957 • *World Series HR*—18; *All-Star HR*—2

Jeff Manto

JEFFREY PAUL MANTO
B: 08/23/1964
BR

Year	Tm	Lg	Tot	H	A	Men-On 0	1	2	3	One-Game 2	3	4	LO	XN	IP	PH	RHP	LHP
1990	CLE	AL	2	1	1	1	0	1	0	0	0	0	0	0	0	0	2	0
1991	CLE	AL	2	0	2	2	0	0	0	0	0	0	0	1	0	0	2	0
1995	BAL	AL	17	12	5	9	7	1	0	2	0	0	0	0	0	1	10	7
Total			21	13	8	12	7	2	0	2	0	0	0	1	0	1	14	7

Rank among batters: 1,768 • *Top target (2 home runs)*: Russell Springer • *Number of pitchers victimized*: 20 • *Total ballparks homered in*: 9 • *First HR*: 08/04/1990 off Jimmy Jones

Chuck Manuel

CHARLES FUQUA MANUEL
B: 01/04/1944
BL

Year	Tm	Lg	Tot	H	A	Men-On 0	1	2	3	One-Game 2	3	4	LO	XN	IP	PH	RHP	LHP
1969	MIN	AL	2	0	2	1	0	1	0	0	0	0	0	0	0	0	1	1
1970	MIN	AL	1	0	1	1	0	0	0	0	0	0	0	0	0	1	1	0
1972	MIN	AL	1	0	1	1	0	0	0	0	0	0	0	0	0	1	1	0
Total			4	0	4	3	0	1	0	0	0	0	0	0	0	2	3	1

Rank among batters: 3,427 • *Total ballparks homered in*: 4 • *First HR*: 04/26/1969 off Don Secrist

Jerry Manuel

JERRY MANUEL
B: 12/23/1953
BB

Year	Tm	Lg	Tot	H	A	Men-On 0	1	2	3	One-Game 2	3	4	LO	XN	IP	PH	RHP	LHP
1981	MON	NL	3	2	1	1	1	1	0	0	0	0	0	0	0	0	3	0

Rank among batters: 3,735 • *Total ballparks homered in*: 2 • *First HR*: 04/26/1981 off Jeff Reardon

Heinie Manush

HENRY EMMETT MANUSH
B: 07/20/1901 D: 05/12/1971
BL HOF

Year	Tm	Lg	Tot	H	A	Men-On 0	1	2	3	One-Game 2	3	4	LO	XN	IP	PH	RHP	LHP
1923	DET	AL	4	2	2	2	2	0	0	0	0	0	0	0	0	1	4	0
1924	DET	AL	9	3	6	5	2	0	2	0	0	0	0	0	1	0	9	0
1925	DET	AL	5	1	4	4	1	0	0	0	0	0	0	0	0	1	4	1
1926	DET	AL	14	8	6	7	5	2	0	0	0	0	0	0	2	0	10	4
1927	DET	AL	6	1	5	2	2	2	0	0	0	0	0	0	0	1	5	1
1928	STL	AL	13	13	0	8	2	3	0	1	0	0	0	0	0	0	9	4
1929	STL	AL	6	3	3	2	2	1	1	0	0	0	0	0	0	0	5	1
1930	STL	AL	2	1	1	1	1	0	0	0	0	0	0	0	0	0	2	0
	WAS	AL	7	2	5	3	4	0	0	1	0	0	0	0	0	0	7	0
	Total		9	3	6	4	5	0	0	1	0	0	0	0	0	0	9	0

Heinie Manush *continued*

Year	Tm	Lg	Tot	H	A	Men-On 0	1	2	3	One-Game 2	3	4	LO	XN	IP	PH	RHP	LHP
1931	WAS	AL	6	1	5	5	1	0	0	0	0	0	0	0	0	0	6	0
1932	WAS	AL	14	6	8	4	5	5	0	0	0	0	0	1	1	1	11	3
1933	WAS	AL	5	0	5	3	1	0	1	0	0	0	0	0	0	0	5	0
1934	WAS	AL	11	4	7	4	4	2	1	2	0	0	0	0	2	0	8	3
1935	WAS	AL	4	0	4	2	0	1	1	1	0	0	0	0	0	0	4	0
1937	BRO	NL	4	2	2	1	1	2	0	0	0	0	0	0	0	0	3	1
Total			110	47	63	53	33	18	6	5	0	0	0	1	6	4	92	18

Rank among batters: 436 • *Top target (4 home runs)*: Ted Lyons, Willis Hudlin • *Number of pitchers victimized*: 76 • *Total ballparks homered in*: 11 • *First HR*: 06/20/1923 off Joe Bush

Kirt Manwaring

KIRT DEAN MANWARING
B: 07/15/1965
BR

Year	Tm	Lg	Tot	H	A	Men-On 0	1	2	3	One-Game 2	3	4	LO	XN	IP	PH	RHP	LHP
1988	SF	NL	1	0	1	1	0	0	0	0	0	0	0	0	0	0	1	0
1992	SF	NL	4	1	3	4	0	0	0	0	0	0	0	0	0	0	4	0
1993	SF	NL	5	3	2	4	1	0	0	0	0	0	0	0	0	0	3	2
1994	SF	NL	1	0	1	1	0	0	0	0	0	0	0	0	0	0	0	1
1995	SF	NL	4	4	0	3	1	0	0	1	0	0	0	0	0	0	1	3
Total			15	8	7	13	2	0	0	1	0	0	0	0	0	0	9	6

Rank among batters: 2,096 • *Top target (2 home runs)*: Greg Swindell • *Number of pitchers victimized*: 14 • *Total ballparks homered in*: 6 • *First HR*: 09/19/1988 off Rick Mahler

Cliff Mapes

CLIFFORD FRANKLIN MAPES
B: 03/13/1922
BL

Year	Tm	Lg	Tot	H	A	Men-On 0	1	2	3	One-Game 2	3	4	LO	XN	IP	PH	RHP	LHP
1948	NY	AL	1	1	0	1	0	0	0	0	0	0	0	0	0	0	0	1
1949	NY	AL	7	5	2	4	3	0	0	0	0	0	0	0	0	0	6	1
1950	NY	AL	12	9	3	6	3	3	0	0	0	0	0	0	0	0	9	3
1951	NY	AL	2	1	1	2	0	0	0	0	0	0	0	0	0	0	2	0
	STL	AL	7	3	4	4	2	1	0	0	0	0	0	0	1	1	6	1
	Total		9	4	5	6	2	1	0	0	0	0	0	0	1	1	8	1
1952	DET	AL	9	6	3	7	2	0	0	0	0	0	0	1	0	1	9	0
Total			38	25	13	24	10	4	0	0	0	0	0	1	1	2	32	6

Rank among batters: 1,225 • *Top target (5 home runs)*: Bob Lemon • *Number of pitchers victimized*: 28 • *Total ballparks homered in*: 7 • *First HR*: 07/21/1948 off Sam Zoldak

Rabbit Maranville

WALTER JAMES VINCENT MARANVILLE
B: 11/11/1891 D: 01/05/1954
BR HOF

Year	Tm	Lg	Tot	H	A	Men-On 0	1	2	3	One-Game 2	3	4	LO	XN	IP	PH	RHP	LHP
1913	BOS	NL	2	0	2	0	1	1	0	0	0	0	0	0	2	0	1	1
1914	BOS	NL	4	2	2	2	0	0	2	0	0	0	0	1	3	0	2	2
1915	BOS	NL	2	1	1	0	1	1	0	0	0	0	0	0	2	0	2	0
1916	BOS	NL	4	3	1	3	0	1	0	0	0	0	3	0	4	0	4	0
1917	BOS	NL	3	2	1	1	1	1	0	0	0	0	0	0	3	0	3	0
1919	BOS	NL	5	2	3	1	3	1	0	1	0	0	0	0	4	0	2	3
1920	BOS	NL	1	1	0	1	0	0	0	0	0	0	0	0	1	0	1	0
1921	PIT	NL	1	0	1	1	0	0	0	0	0	0	0	0	0	0	0	1
1923	PIT	NL	1	0	1	0	1	0	0	0	0	0	0	0	1	0	0	1
1924	PIT	NL	2	2	0	1	1	0	0	0	0	0	1	0	1	0	2	0
1928	STL	NL	1	0	1	0	0	1	0	0	0	0	0	0	0	0	1	0
1930	BOS	NL	2	2	0	1	1	0	0	0	0	0	0	0	1	0	2	0
Total			28	15	13	11	9	6	2	1	0	0	4	1	22	0	20	8

Rank among batters: 1,500 • *Top target (2 home runs)*: Slim Sallee, Eppa Rixey, Freddie Fitzsimmons • *Number of pitchers victimized*: 25 • *Total ballparks homered in*: 8 • *First HR*: 06/09/1913 off Slim Sallee

Firpo Marberry

FREDERICK MARBERRY
B: 11/30/1898 D: 06/30/1976
BR

Year	Tm	Lg	Tot	H	A	Men-On 0	1	2	3	One-Game 2	3	4	LO	XN	IP	PH	RHP	LHP
1931	WAS	AL	1	0	1	1	0	0	0	0	0	0	0	0	0	0	1	0

Rank among batters: 4,707 • *Total ballparks homered in*: 1 • *First HR*: 08/16/1931 off Sam Gray

Phil Marchildon

PHILIP JOSEPH MARCHILDON
B: 10/25/1913
BR

Year	Tm	Lg	Tot	H	A	Men-On 0	Men-On 1	Men-On 2	Men-On 3	One-Game 2	One-Game 3	One-Game 4	LO	XN	IP	PH	RHP	LHP
1947	PHI	AL	1	1	0	1	0	0	0	0	0	0	0	0	0	0	1	0

Rank among batters: 4,707 • *Total ballparks homered in*: 1 • *First HR*: 08/09/1947 off Sid Hudson

Johnny Marcum

JOHN ALFRED MARCUM
B: 09/09/1909 D: 09/10/1984
BL

Year	Tm	Lg	Tot	H	A	Men-On 0	Men-On 1	Men-On 2	Men-On 3	One-Game 2	One-Game 3	One-Game 4	LO	XN	IP	PH	RHP	LHP
1934	PHI	AL	1	0	1	1	0	0	0	0	0	0	0	0	0	1	1	0
1935	PHI	AL	2	2	0	2	0	0	0	0	0	0	0	0	0	0	2	0
1936	BOS	AL	2	1	1	2	0	0	0	0	0	0	0	0	0	0	2	0
Total			5	3	2	5	0	0	0	0	0	0	0	0	0	1	5	0

Rank among batters: 3,191 • *Total ballparks homered in*: 3 • *First HR*: 09/12/1934 off Monte Pearson

Joe Margoneri

JOSEPH EMANUEL MARGONERI
B: 01/13/1930
BL

Year	Tm	Lg	Tot	H	A	Men-On 0	Men-On 1	Men-On 2	Men-On 3	One-Game 2	One-Game 3	One-Game 4	LO	XN	IP	PH	RHP	LHP
1956	NY	NL	1	1	0	1	0	0	0	0	0	0	0	0	0	0	1	0

Rank among batters: 4,707 • *Total ballparks homered in*: 1 • *First HR*: 08/04/1956 off Warren Hacker

Juan Marichal

JUAN ANTONIO (SANCHEZ) MARICHAL
B: 10/20/1937
BR HOF

Year	Tm	Lg	Tot	H	A	Men-On 0	Men-On 1	Men-On 2	Men-On 3	One-Game 2	One-Game 3	One-Game 4	LO	XN	IP	PH	RHP	LHP
1963	SF	NL	1	0	1	1	0	0	0	0	0	0	0	0	0	0	1	0
1966	SF	NL	1	1	0	1	0	0	0	0	0	0	0	0	0	0	1	0
1971	SF	NL	2	1	1	0	1	1	0	0	0	0	0	0	0	0	2	0
Total			4	2	2	2	1	1	0	0	0	0	0	0	0	0	4	0

Rank among batters: 3,427 • *Total ballparks homered in*: 3 • *First HR*: 09/12/1963 off Tracy Stallard

Marty Marion

MARTIN WHITEFORD MARION
B: 12/01/1917
BR

Year	Tm	Lg	Tot	H	A	Men-On 0	Men-On 1	Men-On 2	Men-On 3	One-Game 2	One-Game 3	One-Game 4	LO	XN	IP	PH	RHP	LHP
1940	STL	NL	3	1	2	2	1	0	0	0	0	0	0	0	0	0	2	1
1941	STL	NL	3	0	3	0	3	0	0	0	0	0	0	0	0	0	3	0
1943	STL	NL	1	0	1	1	0	0	0	0	0	0	0	0	0	0	0	1
1944	STL	NL	6	2	4	3	2	1	0	1	0	0	0	0	2	0	5	1
1945	STL	NL	1	1	0	0	1	0	0	0	0	0	0	0	0	0	1	0
1946	STL	NL	3	0	3	2	1	0	0	0	0	0	0	0	0	0	1	2
1947	STL	NL	4	1	3	2	1	1	0	0	0	0	0	0	0	0	4	0
1948	STL	NL	4	0	4	2	1	1	0	0	0	0	0	0	0	0	4	0
1949	STL	NL	5	1	4	2	3	0	0	0	0	0	0	0	0	0	3	2
1950	STL	NL	4	3	1	2	0	1	1	0	0	0	0	0	0	0	1	3
1952	STL	AL	2	0	2	1	0	1	0	0	0	0	0	0	0	0	2	0
Total			36	9	27	17	13	5	1	1	0	0	0	0	2	0	26	10

Rank among batters: 1,274 • *Top target (3 home runs)*: Jim Tobin • *Number of pitchers victimized*: 31 • *Total ballparks homered in*: 9 • *First HR*: 08/27/1940 off Jim Tobin • *World Series HR*—1

Red Marion

JOHN WYETH MARION
B: 03/14/1914 D: 03/13/1975
BR

Year	Tm	Lg	Tot	H	A	Men-On 0	Men-On 1	Men-On 2	Men-On 3	One-Game 2	One-Game 3	One-Game 4	LO	XN	IP	PH	RHP	LHP
1935	WAS	AL	1	0	1	1	0	0	0	0	0	0	0	0	0	0	0	1

Rank among batters: 4,707 • *Total ballparks homered in*: 1 • *First HR*: 09/28/1935 off Woody Upchurch

Roger Maris

ROGER EUGENE MARIS
B: 09/10/1934 D: 12/14/1985
BL

Year	Tm	Lg	Tot	H	A	Men-On 0	Men-On 1	Men-On 2	Men-On 3	One-Game 2	One-Game 3	One-Game 4	LO	XN	IP	PH	RHP	LHP
1957	CLE	AL	14	8	6	7	6	0	1	1	0	0	0	1	0	0	12	2

Year	Tm	Lg	Tot	H	A	Men-On				One-Game			LO	XN	IP	PH	RHP	LHP
						0	1	2	3	2	3	4						

Roger Maris *continued*

Year	Tm	Lg	Tot	H	A	Men-On 0	Men-On 1	Men-On 2	Men-On 3	One-Game 2	One-Game 3	One-Game 4	LO	XN	IP	PH	RHP	LHP
1958	CLE	AL	9	0	9	5	4	0	0	1	0	0	2	0	0	0	5	4
	KC	AL	19	10	9	11	5	1	2	2	0	0	0	1	1	0	17	2
	Total		28	10	18	16	9	1	2	3	0	0	2	1	1	0	22	6
1959	KC	AL	16	6	10	9	3	3	1	1	0	0	0	0	0	0	12	4
1960	NY	AL	39	13	26	18	17	4	0	6	0	0	0	0	1	0	34	5
1961	NY	AL	61	30	31	33	19	9	0	7	0	0	0	1	0	0	49	12
1962	NY	AL	33	19	14	17	7	8	1	3	0	0	0	1	0	0	22	11
1963	NY	AL	23	11	12	15	6	2	0	1	0	0	0	0	0	0	16	7
1964	NY	AL	26	10	16	14	10	2	0	2	0	0	0	0	1	1	21	5
1965	NY	AL	8	4	4	5	3	0	0	0	0	0	0	0	0	0	5	3
1966	NY	AL	13	7	6	7	5	1	0	0	0	0	0	0	0	2	12	1
1967	STL	NL	9	4	5	6	2	1	0	0	0	0	0	1	0	0	7	2
1968	STL	NL	5	0	5	1	3	1	0	1	0	0	0	0	0	0	5	0
Total			275	122	153	148	90	32	5	25	0	0	2	5	3	3	217	58

Rank among batters: 85 • *Top target (9 home runs)*: Jim Perry • *Number of pitchers victimized*: 154 • *Total ballparks homered in*: 19 • *First HR*: 04/18/1957 off Jack Crimian • *World Series HR*—6

Rube Marquard

RICHARD WILLIAM MARQUARD
B: 10/09/1889 D: 06/01/1980
BB HOF

Year	Tm	Lg	Tot	H	A	Men-On 0	Men-On 1	Men-On 2	Men-On 3	One-Game 2	One-Game 3	One-Game 4	LO	XN	IP	PH	RHP	LHP
1911	NY	NL	1	1	0	1	0	0	0	0	0	0	0	0	0	0	1	0

Rank among batters: 4,707 • *Total ballparks homered in*: 1 • *First HR*: 07/08/1911 off Harry McIntire

Gonzalo Marquez

GONZALO ENRIQUE (MOYA) MARQUEZ
B: 03/31/1946 D: 12/20/1984
BL

Year	Tm	Lg	Tot	H	A	Men-On 0	Men-On 1	Men-On 2	Men-On 3	One-Game 2	One-Game 3	One-Game 4	LO	XN	IP	PH	RHP	LHP
1973	CHI	NL	1	1	0	1	0	0	0	0	0	0	0	0	0	0	1	0

Rank among batters: 4,707 • *Total ballparks homered in*: 1 • *First HR*: 09/21/1973 off Steve Rogers

Bob Marquis

ROBERT RUDOLPH MARQUIS
B: 12/23/1924
BL

Year	Tm	Lg	Tot	H	A	Men-On 0	Men-On 1	Men-On 2	Men-On 3	One-Game 2	One-Game 3	One-Game 4	LO	XN	IP	PH	RHP	LHP
1953	CIN	NL	2	2	0	2	0	0	0	0	0	0	0	0	0	0	2	0

Rank among batters: 4,129 • *Total ballparks homered in*: 1 • *First HR*: 05/08/1953 off Stu Miller

Lefty Marr

CHARLES W. MARR
B: 09/19/1862 D: 01/11/1912
BL

Year	Tm	Lg	Tot	H	A	Men-On 0	Men-On 1	Men-On 2	Men-On 3	One-Game 2	One-Game 3	One-Game 4	LO	XN	IP	PH	RHP	LHP
1889	COL	AA	1	0	1	0	0	1	0	0	0	0	0	0	0	0	0	1
1890	CIN	NL	1	1	0	1	0	0	0	0	0	0	0	0	1	0	1	0
Total			2	1	1	1	0	1	0	0	0	0	0	0	1	0	1	1

Rank among batters: 4,129 • *Total ballparks homered in*: 1 • *First HR*: 07/11/1889 off Mike Smith

Oreste Marrero

ORESTE VILATO (VAZQUEZ) MARRERO
B: 10/31/1969
BL

Year	Tm	Lg	Tot	H	A	Men-On 0	Men-On 1	Men-On 2	Men-On 3	One-Game 2	One-Game 3	One-Game 4	LO	XN	IP	PH	RHP	LHP
1993	MON	NL	1	1	0	0	1	0	0	0	0	0	0	0	0	0	1	0

Rank among batters: 4,707 • *Total ballparks homered in*: 1 • *First HR*: 09/08/1993 off Mo Sanford

William Marriott

WILLIAM EARL MARRIOTT
B: 08/18/1893 D: 08/11/1969
BL

Year	Tm	Lg	Tot	H	A	Men-On 0	Men-On 1	Men-On 2	Men-On 3	One-Game 2	One-Game 3	One-Game 4	LO	XN	IP	PH	RHP	LHP
1925	BOS	NL	1	1	0	1	0	0	0	0	0	0	0	0	1	0	1	0

William Marriott *continued*

Year	Tm	Lg	Tot	H	A	Men-On 0	Men-On 1	Men-On 2	Men-On 3	One-Game 2	One-Game 3	One-Game 4	LO	XN	IP	PH	RHP	LHP
1926	BRO	NL	3	2	1	2	1	0	0	1	0	0	0	0	1	0	3	0
Total			4	3	1	3	1	0	0	1	0	0	0	0	2	0	4	0

Rank among batters: 3,427 • *Top target (2 home runs)*: Claude Willoughby • *Number of pitchers victimized*: 3 • *Total ballparks homered in*: 3 • *First HR*: 05/12/1925 off Sheriff Blake

Armando Marsans

ARMANDO MARSANS
B: 10/03/1887 D: 09/03/1960
BR

Year	Tm	Lg	Tot	H	A	Men-On 0	Men-On 1	Men-On 2	Men-On 3	One-Game 2	One-Game 3	One-Game 4	LO	XN	IP	PH	RHP	LHP
1912	CIN	NL	1	0	1	0	1	0	0	0	0	0	0	0	0	0	0	1
1916	STL	AL	1	0	1	1	0	0	0	0	0	0	0	0	0	0	1	0
Total			2	0	2	1	1	0	0	0	0	0	0	0	0	0	1	1

Rank among batters: 4,129 • *Total ballparks homered in*: 1 • *First HR*: 08/01/1912 off Hooks Wiltse

Fred Marsh

FRED FRANCIS MARSH
B: 01/05/1924
BR

Year	Tm	Lg	Tot	H	A	Men-On 0	Men-On 1	Men-On 2	Men-On 3	One-Game 2	One-Game 3	One-Game 4	LO	XN	IP	PH	RHP	LHP
1951	STL	AL	4	1	3	3	1	0	0	0	0	0	0	0	0	0	3	1
1952	STL	AL	2	2	0	1	0	1	0	0	0	0	1	0	0	0	2	0
1953	CHI	AL	2	0	2	2	0	0	0	0	0	0	0	0	0	0	2	0
1955	BAL	AL	2	1	1	1	0	1	0	0	0	0	1	0	0	0	1	1
Total			10	4	6	7	1	2	0	0	0	0	2	0	0	0	8	2

Rank among batters: 2,500 • *Top target (2 home runs)*: Bob Lemon • *Number of pitchers victimized*: 9 • *Total ballparks homered in*: 6 • *First HR*: 05/27/1951 off Gene Bearden

Tom Marsh

THOMAS OWEN MARSH
B: 12/27/1965
BR

Year	Tm	Lg	Tot	H	A	Men-On 0	Men-On 1	Men-On 2	Men-On 3	One-Game 2	One-Game 3	One-Game 4	LO	XN	IP	PH	RHP	LHP
1992	PHI	NL	2	1	1	1	0	0	1	0	0	0	0	0	0	0	1	1
1995	PHI	NL	3	1	2	1	2	0	0	1	0	0	0	0	0	0	2	1
Total			5	2	3	2	2	0	1	1	0	0	0	0	0	0	3	2

Rank among batters: 3,191 • *Total ballparks homered in*: 3 • *First HR*: 06/14/1992 off Rheal Cormier

Dave Marshall

DAVID LEWIS MARSHALL
B: 01/14/1943
BL

Year	Tm	Lg	Tot	H	A	Men-On 0	Men-On 1	Men-On 2	Men-On 3	One-Game 2	One-Game 3	One-Game 4	LO	XN	IP	PH	RHP	LHP
1968	SF	NL	1	1	0	0	1	0	0	0	0	0	0	0	0	0	1	0
1969	SF	NL	2	1	1	1	0	1	0	0	0	0	0	0	0	0	2	0
1970	NY	NL	6	1	5	4	0	1	1	0	0	0	0	0	0	2	6	0
1971	NY	NL	3	2	1	0	2	0	1	0	0	0	0	0	0	1	3	0
1972	NY	NL	4	0	4	4	0	0	0	0	0	0	0	0	0	0	3	1
Total			16	5	11	9	3	2	2	0	0	0	0	0	0	3	15	1

Rank among batters: 2,029 • *Top target (2 home runs)*: Carl Morton • *Number of pitchers victimized*: 15 • *Total ballparks homered in*: 8 • *First HR*: 05/05/1968 off Ray Washburn

Doc Marshall

WILLIAM RIDDLE MARSHALL
B: 09/22/1875 D: 12/11/1959
BR

Year	Tm	Lg	Tot	H	A	Men-On 0	Men-On 1	Men-On 2	Men-On 3	One-Game 2	One-Game 3	One-Game 4	LO	XN	IP	PH	RHP	LHP
1907	STL	NL	2	1	1	2	0	0	0	0	0	0	0	0	0	0	1	1

Rank among batters: 4,129 • *Total ballparks homered in*: 2 • *First HR*: 04/28/1907 off Jack Taylor

Jim Marshall

RUFUS JAMES MARSHALL
B: 05/25/1931
BL

Year	Tm	Lg	Tot	H	A	Men-On 0	Men-On 1	Men-On 2	Men-On 3	One-Game 2	One-Game 3	One-Game 4	LO	XN	IP	PH	RHP	LHP
1958	BAL	AL	5	5	0	4	1	0	0	0	0	0	0	0	0	1	5	0
	CHI	NL	5	4	1	0	3	2	0	0	1	0	0	0	0	0	5	0
	Total		10	9	1	7	3	0	0	1	0	0	0	0	0	1	10	0

Jim Marshall *continued*

Year	Tm	Lg	Tot	H	A	Men-On 0	1	2	3	One-Game 2	3	4	LO	XN	IP	PH	RHP	LHP
1959	CHI	NL	11	4	7	8	1	2	0	1	0	0	0	0	0	1	11	0
1960	SF	NL	2	1	1	2	0	0	0	0	0	0	0	0	0	0	2	0
1961	SF	NL	1	1	0	1	0	0	0	0	0	0	0	0	0	1	0	1
1962	NY	NL	3	3	0	3	0	0	0	0	0	0	0	0	0	0	3	0
	PIT	NL	2	0	2	1	0	1	0	0	0	0	0	0	0	0	2	0
	Total		5	3	2	4	0	1	0	0	0	0	0	0	0	0	5	0
Total			29	18	11	22	4	3	0	2	0	0	0	0	0	3	28	1

Rank among batters: 1,465 • *Top target (2 home runs)*: Lindy McDaniel, Ron Kline • *Number of pitchers victimized*: 27 • *Total ballparks homered in*: 9 • *First HR*: 05/01/1958 off Jim Wilson

Max Marshall

MILO MAX MARSHALL
B: 09/18/1913
BL

Year	Tm	Lg	Tot	H	A	Men-On 0	1	2	3	One-Game 2	3	4	LO	XN	IP	PH	RHP	LHP
1942	CIN	NL	7	4	3	5	1	1	0	0	0	0	0	0	0	0	7	0
1943	CIN	NL	4	1	3	3	1	0	0	0	0	0	0	0	1	1	4	0
1944	CIN	NL	4	0	4	2	2	0	0	0	0	0	0	0	0	0	4	0
Total			15	5	10	10	4	1	0	0	0	0	0	0	1	1	15	0

Rank among batters: 2,096 • *Top target (3 home runs)*: Bill Lohrman • *Number of pitchers victimized*: 11 • *Total ballparks homered in*: 5 • *First HR*: 05/16/1942 off Bill Lohrman

Mike Marshall

MICHAEL GRANT MARSHALL
B: 01/15/1943
BR

Year	Tm	Lg	Tot	H	A	Men-On 0	1	2	3	One-Game 2	3	4	LO	XN	IP	PH	RHP	LHP
1969	SEA	AL	1	0	1	1	0	0	0	0	0	0	0	0	0	0	1	0

Rank among batters: 4,707 • *Total ballparks homered in*: 1 • *First HR*: 05/18/1969 off Fred Wenz

Mike Marshall

MICHAEL ALLEN MARSHALL
B: 01/12/1960
BR

Year	Tm	Lg	Tot	H	A	Men-On 0	1	2	3	One-Game 2	3	4	LO	XN	IP	PH	RHP	LHP
1982	LA	NL	5	2	3	4	1	0	0	0	0	0	0	0	0	1	3	2
1983	LA	NL	17	9	8	9	6	1	1	1	0	0	0	1	0	0	15	2
1984	LA	NL	21	11	10	10	7	3	1	1	0	0	0	1	0	0	13	8
1985	LA	NL	28	15	13	17	9	0	2	1	0	0	0	0	0	0	20	8
1986	LA	NL	19	13	6	12	5	2	0	3	0	0	0	2	0	0	10	9
1987	LA	NL	16	5	11	6	7	2	1	2	0	0	0	1	0	0	11	5
1988	LA	NL	20	9	11	9	9	1	1	1	0	0	0	0	0	0	16	4
1989	LA	NL	11	6	5	4	6	1	0	0	0	0	0	0	0	0	4	7
1990	NY	NL	6	4	2	3	2	0	1	0	0	0	0	1	0	0	3	3
	BOS	AL	4	3	1	3	1	0	0	0	0	0	0	0	0	0	3	1
	Total		10	7	3	6	3	0	1	0	0	0	0	1	0	0	6	4
1991	BOS	AL	1	1	0	1	0	0	0	0	0	0	0	0	0	0	1	0
Total			148	78	70	78	53	10	7	9	0	0	0	6	0	1	99	49

Rank among batters: 294 • *Top target (7 home runs)*: Bob Knepper • *Number of pitchers victimized*: 101 • *Total ballparks homered in*: 14 • *First HR*: 06/29/1982 off Floyd Chiffer • *World Series HR*—1; *LCS HR*—2

Willard Marshall

WILLARD WARREN MARSHALL
B: 02/08/1921
BL

Year	Tm	Lg	Tot	H	A	Men-On 0	1	2	3	One-Game 2	3	4	LO	XN	IP	PH	RHP	LHP
1942	NY	NL	11	8	3	5	2	3	1	1	0	0	0	1	0	0	9	2
1946	NY	NL	13	11	2	9	4	0	0	0	0	0	0	0	0	0	6	7
1947	NY	NL	36	25	11	19	13	4	0	1	1	0	0	1	0	0	30	6
1948	NY	NL	14	9	5	11	1	2	0	0	0	0	0	0	0	0	10	4
1949	NY	NL	12	10	2	8	1	3	0	0	0	0	0	0	0	0	9	3
1950	BOS	NL	5	3	2	1	2	2	0	0	0	0	0	0	0	0	4	1
1951	BOS	NL	11	4	7	4	6	1	0	0	0	0	0	0	0	0	8	3
1952	BOS	NL	2	1	1	2	0	0	0	0	0	0	0	0	0	0	2	0
	CIN	NL	8	6	2	4	3	1	0	0	0	0	0	0	0	0	8	0
	Total		10	7	3	6	3	1	0	0	0	0	0	0	0	0	10	0
1953	CIN	NL	17	9	8	5	9	3	0	1	0	0	0	0	0	0	14	3

Willard Marshall *continued*

Year	Tm	Lg	Tot	H	A	Men-On 0	1	2	3	One-Game 2	3	4	LO	XN	IP	PH	RHP	LHP
1954	CHI	AL	1	1	0	1	0	0	0	0	0	0	0	0	0	1	1	0
Total			130	87	43	69	41	19	1	3	1	0	0	2	0	1	101	29

Rank among batters: 348 • *Top target (6 home runs)*: Ralph Branca • *Number of pitchers victimized*: 91 • *Total ballparks homered in*: 9 • *First HR*: 04/15/1942 off Kirby Higbe

Al Martin

ALBERT LEE MARTIN
B: 11/24/1967
BL

Year	Tm	Lg	Tot	H	A	Men-On 0	1	2	3	One-Game 2	3	4	LO	XN	IP	PH	RHP	LHP
1993	PIT	NL	18	15	3	11	5	2	0	0	0	0	0	0	0	1	17	1
1994	PIT	NL	9	6	3	4	5	0	0	0	0	0	0	0	0	0	8	1
1995	PIT	NL	13	8	5	8	4	1	0	0	0	0	4	0	0	1	12	1
Total			40	29	11	23	14	3	0	0	0	0	4	0	0	2	37	3

Rank among batters: 1,181 • Top target (2 home runs): Charlie Hough, Jeff Shaw, Scott Sanders, Tom Candiotti, Jose Bautista • *Number of pitchers victimized*: 35 • *Total ballparks homered in*: 10 • *First HR*: 04/10/1993 off Jeff Brantley

Babe Martin

BORIS MICHAEL MARTIN
B: 03/28/1920
BR

Year	Tm	Lg	Tot	H	A	Men-On 0	1	2	3	One-Game 2	3	4	LO	XN	IP	PH	RHP	LHP
1945	STL	AL	2	0	2	0	2	0	0	0	0	0	0	0	0	0	2	0

Rank among batters: 4,129 • *Total ballparks homered in*: 1 • *First HR*: 05/27/1945 off Hank Borowy

Billy Martin

ALFRED MANUEL MARTIN
B: 05/16/1928 D: 12/25/1989
BR

Year	Tm	Lg	Tot	H	A	Men-On 0	1	2	3	One-Game 2	3	4	LO	XN	IP	PH	RHP	LHP
1950	NY	AL	1	0	1	0	0	1	0	0	0	0	0	0	0	0	0	1
1952	NY	AL	3	1	2	1	2	0	0	0	0	0	0	0	0	0	2	1
1953	NY	AL	15	7	8	9	5	1	0	0	0	0	0	1	0	0	7	8
1955	NY	AL	1	0	1	0	0	1	0	0	0	0	0	0	1	0	1	0
1956	NY	AL	9	2	7	5	4	0	0	0	0	0	2	0	0	0	6	3
1957	NY	AL	1	0	1	0	1	0	0	0	0	0	0	0	0	0	1	0
	KC	AL	9	5	4	8	1	0	0	0	0	0	0	0	0	0	6	3
	Total		10	5	5	8	2	0	0	0	0	0	0	0	0	0	7	3
1958	DET	AL	7	3	4	3	2	2	0	1	0	0	0	0	0	0	7	0
1959	CLE	AL	9	5	4	6	2	1	0	0	0	0	1	0	1	0	9	0
1960	CIN	NL	3	0	3	2	0	1	0	0	0	0	1	0	0	0	2	1
1961	MIN	AL	6	4	2	3	1	2	0	0	0	0	0	0	0	0	5	1
Total			64	27	37	37	18	9	0	1	0	0	4	1	2	0	46	18

Rank among batters: 815 • *Top target (3 home runs)*: Frank Sullivan • *Number of pitchers victimized*: 54 • *Total ballparks homered in*: 13 • *First HR*: 08/06/1950 off Sam Zoldak • *World Series HR—5*

Gene Martin

THOMAS EUGENE MARTIN
B: 01/12/1947
BL

Year	Tm	Lg	Tot	H	A	Men-On 0	1	2	3	One-Game 2	3	4	LO	XN	IP	PH	RHP	LHP
1968	WAS	AL	1	0	1	1	0	0	0	0	0	0	0	0	0	1	1	0

Rank among batters: 4,707 • *Total ballparks homered in*: 1 • *First HR*: 09/08/1968 off Stan Bahnsen

Hersh Martin

HERSHEL RAY MARTIN
B: 09/19/1909 D: 11/17/1980
BB

Year	Tm	Lg	Tot	H	A	Men-On 0	1	2	3	One-Game 2	3	4	LO	XN	IP	PH	RHP	LHP
1937	PHI	NL	8	3	5	7	1	0	0	0	0	0	0	0	0	0	5	3
1938	PHI	NL	3	3	0	3	0	0	0	0	0	0	0	0	0	0	2	1
1939	PHI	NL	1	0	1	0	1	0	0	0	0	0	0	0	0	0	1	0
1944	NY	AL	9	7	2	3	4	2	0	3	0	0	0	0	0	1	9	0
1945	NY	AL	7	5	2	3	4	0	0	0	0	0	0	0	0	0	7	0
Total			28	18	10	16	10	2	0	3	0	0	0	0	0	1	24	4

Rank among batters: 1,500 • *Top target (3 home runs)*: Joe Haynes • *Number of pitchers victimized*: 22 • *Total ballparks homered in*: 8 • *First HR*: 05/07/1937 off Joe Bowman

J.C. Martin

JOSEPH CLIFTON MARTIN
B: 12/13/1936
BL

Year	Tm	Lg	Tot	H	A	Men-On 0	1	2	3	One-Game 2	3	4	LO	XN	IP	PH	RHP	LHP
1961	CHI	AL	5	4	1	1	3	1	0	0	0	0	0	0	0	0	4	1
1963	CHI	AL	5	4	1	3	1	1	0	0	0	0	0	0	0	0	5	0
1964	CHI	AL	4	0	4	3	1	0	0	0	0	0	0	0	0	0	3	1
1965	CHI	AL	2	0	2	2	0	0	0	0	0	0	0	0	0	0	2	0
1966	CHI	AL	2	0	2	0	2	0	0	0	0	0	0	0	0	0	2	0
1967	CHI	AL	4	4	0	2	2	0	0	0	0	0	0	0	0	0	3	1
1968	NY	NL	3	3	0	1	2	0	0	0	0	0	0	0	0	0	3	0
1969	NY	NL	4	1	3	2	2	0	0	0	0	0	0	0	0	0	3	1
1970	CHI	NL	1	1	0	1	0	0	0	0	0	0	0	0	0	0	0	1
1971	CHI	NL	2	1	1	0	2	0	0	0	0	0	0	0	0	0	2	0
Total			32	18	14	15	15	2	0	0	0	0	0	0	0	0	27	5

Rank among batters: 1,360 • *Top target (2 home runs)*: Camilo Pascual • *Number of pitchers victimized*: 31 • *Total ballparks homered in*: 13 • *First HR*: 04/22/1961 off Mike Fornieles

Jerry Martin

JERRY LINDSEY MARTIN
B: 05/11/1949
BR

Year	Tm	Lg	Tot	H	A	Men-On 0	1	2	3	One-Game 2	3	4	LO	XN	IP	PH	RHP	LHP
1975	PHI	NL	2	1	1	0	1	0	1	0	0	0	0	0	0	0	1	1
1976	PHI	NL	2	1	1	1	1	0	0	0	0	0	0	0	0	0	0	2
1977	PHI	NL	6	3	3	6	0	0	0	0	0	0	0	0	0	0	2	4
1978	PHI	NL	9	3	6	5	2	2	0	0	0	0	2	0	0	3	1	8
1979	CHI	NL	19	13	6	8	9	2	0	1	0	0	0	2	0	1	9	10
1980	CHI	NL	23	13	10	13	5	4	1	2	0	0	0	0	0	0	17	6
1981	SF	NL	4	3	1	2	1	0	1	0	0	0	0	0	0	0	4	0
1982	KC	AL	15	6	9	10	4	1	0	0	0	0	0	0	0	0	8	7
1983	KC	AL	2	1	1	2	0	0	0	0	0	0	0	0	1	0	1	1
1984	NY	NL	3	0	3	2	1	0	0	0	0	0	0	0	0	0	0	3
Total			85	44	41	49	24	9	3	3	0	0	2	2	1	4	43	42

Rank among batters: 612 • *Top target (5 home runs)*: John Candelaria • *Number of pitchers victimized*: 64 • *Total ballparks homered in*: 19 • *First HR*: 05/28/1975 off Pete Falcone • *LCS HR*—1

Norberto Martin

NORBERTO ENRIQUE (MCDONALD) MARTIN
B: 12/10/1966
BR

Year	Tm	Lg	Tot	H	A	Men-On 0	1	2	3	One-Game 2	3	4	LO	XN	IP	PH	RHP	LHP
1994	CHI	AL	1	0	1	0	0	0	1	0	0	0	0	0	0	0	0	1
1995	CHI	AL	2	1	1	2	0	0	0	0	0	0	0	0	0	0	1	1
Total			3	1	2	2	0	0	1	0	0	0	0	0	0	0	1	2

Rank among batters: 3,735 • *Total ballparks homered in*: 3 • *First HR*: 06/04/1994 off Jim Poole

Pepper Martin

JOHN LEONARD ROOSEVELT MARTIN
B: 02/29/1904 D: 03/05/1965
BR

Year	Tm	Lg	Tot	H	A	Men-On 0	1	2	3	One-Game 2	3	4	LO	XN	IP	PH	RHP	LHP
1931	STL	NL	7	3	4	3	3	1	0	1	0	0	0	0	0	0	5	2
1932	STL	NL	4	4	0	2	2	0	0	0	0	0	0	0	0	0	3	1
1933	STL	NL	8	5	3	3	2	3	0	0	0	0	0	2	1	0	5	3
1934	STL	NL	5	1	4	3	2	0	0	0	0	0	0	1	0	0	4	1
1935	STL	NL	9	1	8	7	1	0	1	1	0	0	1	0	2	0	8	1
1936	STL	NL	11	5	6	4	4	2	1	1	0	0	0	0	0	0	7	4
1937	STL	NL	5	2	3	5	0	0	0	0	0	0	0	0	0	0	5	0
1938	STL	NL	2	0	2	1	0	1	0	0	0	0	0	0	0	0	2	0
1939	STL	NL	3	1	2	1	1	1	0	0	0	0	0	0	0	0	3	0
1940	STL	NL	3	0	3	2	0	0	1	0	0	0	0	0	0	0	0	3
1944	STL	NL	2	0	2	2	0	0	0	0	0	0	1	0	0	0	0	2
Total			59	22	37	33	15	8	3	3	0	0	2	3	3	0	42	17

Rank among batters: 873 • *Top target (4 home runs)*: Carl Hubbell • *Number of pitchers victimized*: 43 • *Total ballparks homered in*: 8 • *First HR*: 05/07/1931 off Claude Willoughby • *Hit for Cycle*—@PHI: 05/05/1933 • *World Series HR*—1

Speed Martin

ELWOOD GOOD MARTIN
B: 09/15/1893 D: 06/14/1983
BR

Year	Tm	Lg	Tot	H	A	Men-On 0	1	2	3	One-Game 2	3	4	LO	XN	IP	PH	RHP	LHP
1920	CHI	NL	1	0	1	0	0	1	0	0	0	0	0	0	0	0	1	0

						Men-On				One-Game								
Year	Tm	Lg	Tot	H	A	0	1	2	3	2	3	4	LO	XN	IP	PH	RHP	LHP

Speed Martin *continued*

Rank among batters: 4,707 • *Total ballparks homered in*: 1 • *First HR*: 09/18/1920 off George Smith

Stu Martin

STUART MCGUIRE MARTIN
B: 11/17/1913
BL

Year	Tm	Lg	Tot	H	A	0	1	2	3	2	3	4	LO	XN	IP	PH	RHP	LHP
1936	STL	NL	6	2	4	2	1	3	0	0	0	0	0	0	0	0	6	0
1937	STL	NL	1	1	0	1	0	0	0	0	0	0	0	0	0	0	1	0
1938	STL	NL	1	0	1	1	0	0	0	0	0	0	0	0	0	0	0	1
1939	STL	NL	3	1	2	2	0	1	0	0	0	0	0	0	0	1	3	0
1940	STL	NL	4	4	0	2	2	0	0	1	0	0	0	0	1	0	3	1
1942	PIT	NL	1	1	0	0	1	0	0	0	0	0	0	0	0	0	1	0
Total			16	9	7	8	4	4	0	1	0	0	0	0	1	1	14	2

Rank among batters: 2,029 • *Top target (2 home runs)*: Bill Lee, Hugh Casey • *Number of pitchers victimized*: 14 • *Total ballparks homered in*: 6 • *First HR*: 05/14/1936 off Fred Frankhouse

Buck Martinez

JOHN ALBERT MARTINEZ
B: 11/07/1948
BR

Year	Tm	Lg	Tot	H	A	0	1	2	3	2	3	4	LO	XN	IP	PH	RHP	LHP
1969	KC	AL	4	2	2	3	0	1	0	0	0	0	0	0	0	0	3	1
1973	KC	AL	1	1	0	1	0	0	0	0	0	0	0	0	0	0	1	0
1974	KC	AL	1	0	1	0	0	1	0	0	0	0	0	0	0	0	1	0
1975	KC	AL	3	1	2	2	1	0	0	0	0	0	0	0	0	0	1	2
1976	KC	AL	5	2	3	3	2	0	0	0	0	0	0	0	0	0	2	3
1977	KC	AL	1	1	0	1	0	0	0	0	0	0	0	0	0	0	1	0
1978	MIL	AL	1	0	1	1	0	0	0	0	0	0	0	0	0	0	1	0
1979	MIL	AL	4	0	4	4	0	0	0	0	0	0	0	0	0	0	1	3
1980	MIL	AL	3	1	2	3	0	0	0	0	0	0	0	0	0	0	2	1
1981	TOR	AL	4	3	1	2	1	1	0	0	0	0	0	0	0	0	1	3
1982	TOR	AL	10	6	4	8	1	1	0	0	0	0	0	0	0	0	3	7
1983	TOR	AL	10	5	5	5	4	0	1	0	0	0	0	0	0	1	1	9
1984	TOR	AL	5	2	3	2	3	0	0	1	0	0	0	0	0	0	2	3
1985	TOR	AL	4	2	2	2	2	0	0	0	0	0	0	1	0	0	1	3
1986	TOR	AL	2	1	1	2	0	0	0	0	0	0	0	0	0	1	0	2
Total			58	27	31	39	14	4	1	1	0	0	0	1	0	2	21	37

Rank among batters: 886 • *Top target (3 home runs)*: Larry Gura, Floyd Bannister • *Number of pitchers victimized*: 51 • *Total ballparks homered in*: 16 • *First HR*: 06/28/1969 off Dave Boswell

Carlos Martinez

CARLOS ALBERTO ESCOBAR MARTINEZ
B: 08/11/1964
BR

Year	Tm	Lg	Tot	H	A	0	1	2	3	2	3	4	LO	XN	IP	PH	RHP	LHP
1989	CHI	AL	5	2	3	5	0	0	0	0	0	0	0	0	0	0	3	2
1990	CHI	AL	4	2	2	3	0	1	0	0	0	0	0	0	0	0	3	1
1991	CLE	AL	5	3	2	4	1	0	0	0	0	0	0	0	0	0	1	4
1992	CLE	AL	5	2	3	3	1	0	1	1	0	0	0	1	0	0	4	1
1993	CLE	AL	5	2	3	2	1	2	0	0	0	0	0	0	0	1	3	2
1995	CAL	AL	1	0	1	1	0	0	0	0	0	0	0	0	0	0	0	1
Total			25	11	14	18	3	3	1	1	0	0	0	1	0	1	14	11

Rank among batters: 1,608 • *Top target (2 home runs)*: Tom Candiotti, Ron Darling • *Number of pitchers victimized*: 23 • *Total ballparks homered in*: 9 • *First HR*: 05/27/1989 off John Cerutti

Carmelo Martinez

CARMELO (SALGADO) MARTINEZ
B: 07/28/1960
BR

Year	Tm	Lg	Tot	H	A	0	1	2	3	2	3	4	LO	XN	IP	PH	RHP	LHP
1983	CHI	NL	6	2	4	4	0	2	0	0	0	0	0	0	0	0	5	1
1984	SD	NL	13	6	7	7	4	2	0	0	0	0	0	0	1	0	11	2
1985	SD	NL	21	15	6	12	5	3	1	2	0	0	0	0	0	0	13	8
1986	SD	NL	9	6	3	5	4	0	0	0	0	0	0	0	0	2	2	7
1987	SD	NL	15	10	5	11	1	3	0	1	0	0	0	0	0	0	7	8
1988	SD	NL	18	11	7	10	7	1	0	2	0	0	0	0	0	0	11	7
1989	SD	NL	6	2	4	2	1	2	1	0	0	0	0	0	0	1	4	2
1990	PHI	NL	8	4	4	5	1	1	1	0	0	0	0	0	0	0	5	3
	PIT	NL	2	2	0	0	2	0	0	0	0	0	0	0	0	0	0	2

Carmelo Martinez *continued*

Year	Tm	Lg	Tot	H	A	Men-On 0	1	2	3	One-Game 2	3	4	LO	XN	IP	PH	RHP	LHP
1990	Total		10	6	4	5	3	1	1	0	0	0	0	0	0	0	5	5
1991	KC	AL	4	3	1	3	0	1	0	0	0	0	0	0	0	2	2	2
	CIN	NL	6	2	4	5	1	0	0	0	0	0	0	0	0	1	6	0
	Total		10	5	5	8	1	1	0	0	0	0	0	0	0	3	8	2
Total			108	63	45	64	26	15	3	5	0	0	0	0	1	6	66	42

Rank among batters: 443 • *Top target (4 home runs)*: Atlee Hammaker • *Number of pitchers victimized*: 91 • *Total ballparks homered in*: 14 • *First HR*: 08/22/1983 off Frank Pastore • *Hit HR in first major league AB*—vs CIN: 08/22/1983

Chito Martinez

REYENALDO IGNACIO MARTINEZ
B: 12/19/1965
BL

Year	Tm	Lg	Tot	H	A	Men-On 0	1	2	3	One-Game 2	3	4	LO	XN	IP	PH	RHP	LHP
1991	BAL	AL	13	8	5	7	5	1	0	1	0	0	0	0	0	1	12	1
1992	BAL	AL	5	2	3	2	2	1	0	0	0	0	0	0	0	0	3	2
Total			18	10	8	9	7	2	0	1	0	0	0	0	0	1	15	3

Rank among batters: 1,914 • *Top target (2 home runs)*: Mark Leiter • *Number of pitchers victimized*: 17 • *Total ballparks homered in*: 8 • *First HR*: 07/11/1991 off Gene Nelson

Dave Martinez

DAVID MARTINEZ
B: 09/26/1964
BL

Year	Tm	Lg	Tot	H	A	Men-On 0	1	2	3	One-Game 2	3	4	LO	XN	IP	PH	RHP	LHP
1986	CHI	NL	1	1	0	1	0	0	0	0	0	0	0	0	0	0	1	0
1987	CHI	NL	8	5	3	7	1	0	0	0	0	0	2	0	0	0	7	1
1988	CHI	NL	4	2	2	1	2	0	1	0	0	0	0	0	0	0	2	2
	MON	NL	2	0	2	2	0	0	0	1	0	0	0	0	0	0	2	0
	Total		6	2	4	3	2	0	1	1	0	0	0	0	0	0	4	2
1989	MON	NL	3	1	2	3	0	0	0	1	0	0	1	0	0	0	3	0
1990	MON	NL	11	5	6	7	4	0	0	1	0	0	0	0	0	0	10	1
1991	MON	NL	7	3	4	7	0	0	0	1	0	0	0	0	0	0	7	0
1992	CIN	NL	3	3	0	2	1	0	0	0	0	0	0	0	0	0	3	0
1993	SF	NL	5	1	4	4	0	1	0	1	0	0	1	0	0	0	5	0
1994	SF	NL	4	1	3	4	0	0	0	0	0	0	0	0	0	0	4	0
1995	CHI	AL	5	2	3	2	1	1	1	0	0	0	0	0	0	0	5	0
Total			53	24	29	40	9	2	2	5	0	0	4	0	0	0	49	4

Rank among batters: 953 • *Top target (3 home runs)*: Mike Bielecki, Jose Rijo • *Number of pitchers victimized*: 42 • *Total ballparks homered in*: 17 • *First HR*: 07/19/1986 off Mike Krukow

Domingo Martinez

DOMINGO EMILIO (LAFONTAINE) MARTINEZ
B: 08/04/1967
BR

Year	Tm	Lg	Tot	H	A	Men-On 0	1	2	3	One-Game 2	3	4	LO	XN	IP	PH	RHP	LHP
1992	TOR	AL	1	1	0	0	1	0	0	0	0	0	0	0	0	0	0	1
1993	TOR	AL	1	0	1	1	0	0	0	0	0	0	0	0	0	0	0	1
Total			2	1	1	1	1	0	0	0	0	0	0	0	0	0	0	2

Rank among batters: 4,129 • *Total ballparks homered in*: 2 • *First HR*: 09/18/1992 off Mike Jeffcoat

Edgar Martinez

EDGAR MARTINEZ
B: 01/02/1963
BR

Year	Tm	Lg	Tot	H	A	Men-On 0	1	2	3	One-Game 2	3	4	LO	XN	IP	PH	RHP	LHP
1989	SEA	AL	2	0	2	1	1	0	0	0	0	0	0	0	0	0	1	1
1990	SEA	AL	11	3	8	5	5	1	0	1	0	0	0	1	0	0	5	6
1991	SEA	AL	14	8	6	9	4	1	0	1	0	0	0	0	0	0	12	2
1992	SEA	AL	18	11	7	9	4	4	1	1	0	0	0	0	0	0	14	4
1993	SEA	AL	4	1	3	3	1	0	0	0	0	0	0	0	0	1	4	0
1994	SEA	AL	13	4	9	7	4	2	0	1	0	0	0	0	0	0	9	4
1995	SEA	AL	29	16	13	15	8	5	1	2	0	0	0	0	0	0	21	8
Total			91	43	48	49	27	13	2	6	0	0	0	1	0	1	66	25

Rank among batters: 559 • *Top target (3 home runs)*: Ricky Bones • *Number of pitchers victimized*: 75 • *Total ballparks homered in*: 16 • *First HR*: 05/06/1989 off Jeff Ballard • *LCS HR*—2

Hector Martinez

RODOLFO HECTOR MARTINEZ
B: 05/11/1939
BR

Year	Tm	Lg	Tot	H	A	Men-On 0	1	2	3	One-Game 2	3	4	LO	XN	IP	PH	RHP	LHP
1963	KC	AL	1	0	1	1	0	0	0	0	0	0	0	0	0	0	1	0

Rank among batters: 4,707 • *Total ballparks homered in*: 1 • *First HR*: 05/24/1963 off Ken McBride

Jose Martinez

JOSE (AZCUIZ) MARTINEZ
B: 07/26/1941
BR

Year	Tm	Lg	Tot	H	A	Men-On 0	1	2	3	One-Game 2	3	4	LO	XN	IP	PH	RHP	LHP
1969	PIT	NL	1	0	1	0	0	0	1	0	0	0	0	0	0	0	1	0

Rank among batters: 4,707 • *Total ballparks homered in*: 1 • *First HR*: 09/08/1969 off Claude Raymond

Ramon Martinez

RAMON JAIME MARTINEZ
B: 03/22/1968
BR

Year	Tm	Lg	Tot	H	A	Men-On 0	1	2	3	One-Game 2	3	4	LO	XN	IP	PH	RHP	LHP
1991	LA	NL	1	1	0	1	0	0	0	0	0	0	0	0	0	0	0	1

Rank among batters: 4,707 • *Total ballparks homered in*: 1 • *First HR*: 09/22/1991 off Tom Glavine

Sandy Martinez

ANGEL SANDY (MARTINEZ) MARTINEZ
B: 10/03/1972
BL

Year	Tm	Lg	Tot	H	A	Men-On 0	1	2	3	One-Game 2	3	4	LO	XN	IP	PH	RHP	LHP
1995	TOR	AL	2	1	1	0	1	1	0	0	0	0	0	0	0	0	2	0

Rank among batters: 4,129 • *Total ballparks homered in*: 2 • *First HR*: 06/27/1995 off Roger Clemens

Ted Martinez

TEODORO NOEL (ENCARNACION) MARTINEZ
B: 12/10/1947
BR

Year	Tm	Lg	Tot	H	A	Men-On 0	1	2	3	One-Game 2	3	4	LO	XN	IP	PH	RHP	LHP
1971	NY	NL	1	0	1	1	0	0	0	0	0	0	1	0	0	0	1	0
1972	NY	NL	1	0	1	0	0	1	0	0	0	0	0	0	0	0	1	0
1973	NY	NL	1	1	0	1	0	0	0	0	0	0	0	0	0	0	0	1
1974	NY	NL	2	1	1	1	1	0	0	0	0	0	0	0	0	0	2	0
1977	LA	NL	1	0	1	0	1	0	0	0	0	0	0	0	0	0	1	0
1978	LA	NL	1	0	1	0	0	1	0	0	0	0	0	0	0	0	1	0
Total			7	2	5	3	2	2	0	0	0	0	1	0	0	0	6	1

Rank among batters: 2,834 • *Total ballparks homered in*: 5 • *First HR*: 09/17/1971 off Nelson Briles

Tino Martinez

CONSTANTINO MARTINEZ
B: 12/07/1967
BL

Year	Tm	Lg	Tot	H	A	Men-On 0	1	2	3	One-Game 2	3	4	LO	XN	IP	PH	RHP	LHP
1991	SEA	AL	4	3	1	4	0	0	0	0	0	0	0	0	0	0	3	1
1992	SEA	AL	16	10	6	13	1	1	1	0	0	0	0	0	0	0	13	3
1993	SEA	AL	17	9	8	9	3	5	0	0	0	0	0	0	0	0	12	5
1994	SEA	AL	20	8	12	13	4	3	0	0	0	0	0	0	0	0	16	4
1995	SEA	AL	31	14	17	18	4	7	2	3	0	0	0	1	0	0	21	10
Total			88	44	44	57	12	16	3	3	0	0	0	1	0	0	65	23

Rank among batters: 590 • Top target (3 home runs): Melido Perez, Alex Fernandez, Brian Anderson, Dennis Eckersley • *Number of pitchers victimized*: 69 • *Total ballparks homered in*: 14 • *First HR*: 08/26/1991 off Julio Machado • *LCS HR*—1

Joe Marty

JOSEPH ANTON MARTY
B: 09/01/1913 D: 10/04/1984
BR

Year	Tm	Lg	Tot	H	A	Men-On 0	1	2	3	One-Game 2	3	4	LO	XN	IP	PH	RHP	LHP
1937	CHI	NL	5	2	3	5	0	0	0	0	0	0	0	0	0	0	4	1
1938	CHI	NL	7	4	3	4	2	1	0	0	0	0	0	0	0	0	5	2
1939	CHI	NL	2	0	2	1	1	0	0	0	0	0	0	0	0	0	1	1
	PHI	NL	9	4	5	5	4	0	0	0	0	0	1	0	0	1	7	2
	Total		11	4	7	6	5	0	0	0	0	0	1	0	0	1	8	3
1940	PHI	NL	13	7	6	8	5	0	0	2	0	0	0	0	0	0	9	4

Joe Marty *continued*

Year	Tm	Lg	Tot	H	A	Men-On 0	Men-On 1	Men-On 2	Men-On 3	One-Game 2	One-Game 3	One-Game 4	LO	XN	IP	PH	RHP	LHP
1941	PHI	NL	8	5	3	8	0	0	0	0	0	0	1	0	0	0	8	0
Total			44	22	22	31	12	1	0	2	0	0	2	0	0	1	34	10

Rank among batters: 1,095 • *Top target (3 home runs)*: Claude Passeau, Roy Joiner, Charlie Root • *Number of pitchers victimized*: 34 • *Total ballparks homered in*: 9 • *First HR*: 05/04/1937 off Pete Sivess • *World Series HR*—1

Bob Martyn

ROBERT GORDON MARTYN
B: 08/15/1930
BL

Year	Tm	Lg	Tot	H	A	Men-On 0	Men-On 1	Men-On 2	Men-On 3	One-Game 2	One-Game 3	One-Game 4	LO	XN	IP	PH	RHP	LHP
1957	KC	AL	1	0	1	0	1	0	0	0	0	0	0	0	0	0	1	0
1958	KC	AL	2	2	0	1	1	0	0	0	0	0	0	0	0	0	2	0
Total			3	2	1	1	2	0	0	0	0	0	0	0	0	0	3	0

Rank among batters: 3,735 • *Total ballparks homered in*: 2 • *First HR*: 09/15/1957 off Bob Turley

John Marzano

JOHN ROBERT MARZANO
B: 02/14/1963
BR

Year	Tm	Lg	Tot	H	A	Men-On 0	Men-On 1	Men-On 2	Men-On 3	One-Game 2	One-Game 3	One-Game 4	LO	XN	IP	PH	RHP	LHP
1987	BOS	AL	5	4	1	2	2	1	0	1	0	0	0	0	0	0	5	0
1989	BOS	AL	1	1	0	1	0	0	0	0	0	0	0	0	0	0	1	0
Total			6	5	1	3	2	1	0	1	0	0	0	0	0	0	6	0

Rank among batters: 2,988 • *Top target (2 home runs)*: Jose Guzman, Greg Harris • *Number of pitchers victimized*: 4 • *Total ballparks homered in*: 2 • *First HR*: 08/03/1987 off Jose Guzman

Clyde Mashore

CLYDE WAYNE MASHORE
B: 05/29/1945
BR

Year	Tm	Lg	Tot	H	A	Men-On 0	Men-On 1	Men-On 2	Men-On 3	One-Game 2	One-Game 3	One-Game 4	LO	XN	IP	PH	RHP	LHP
1970	MON	NL	1	1	0	0	1	0	0	0	0	0	0	0	0	0	0	1
1971	MON	NL	1	0	1	1	0	0	0	0	0	0	0	0	0	1	0	1
1972	MON	NL	3	2	1	2	0	1	0	0	0	0	0	0	0	0	0	3
1973	MON	NL	3	0	3	0	2	1	0	0	0	0	0	0	0	2	1	2
Total			8	3	5	3	3	2	0	0	0	0	0	0	0	3	1	7

Rank among batters: 2,703 • *Total ballparks homered in*: 6 • *First HR*: 09/14/1970 off Ray Sadecki

Phil Masi

PHILIP SAMUEL MASI
B: 01/06/1916 D: 03/29/1990
BR

Year	Tm	Lg	Tot	H	A	Men-On 0	Men-On 1	Men-On 2	Men-On 3	One-Game 2	One-Game 3	One-Game 4	LO	XN	IP	PH	RHP	LHP
1939	BOS	NL	1	0	1	0	1	0	0	0	0	0	0	0	0	0	1	0
1940	BOS	NL	1	1	0	1	0	0	0	0	0	0	0	0	0	0	1	0
1941	BOS	NL	3	0	3	2	1	0	0	1	0	0	0	0	0	0	1	2
1943	BOS	NL	2	2	0	0	1	0	1	0	0	0	0	0	0	0	0	2
1944	BOS	NL	3	3	0	2	0	1	0	0	0	0	0	0	0	0	2	1
1945	BOS	NL	7	4	3	4	3	0	0	0	0	0	0	0	0	0	5	2
1946	BOS	NL	3	1	2	2	0	1	0	0	0	0	0	0	1	0	2	1
1947	BOS	NL	9	1	8	6	0	3	0	0	0	0	0	0	0	1	5	4
1948	BOS	NL	5	2	3	2	3	0	0	0	0	0	0	0	0	0	1	4
1949	PIT	NL	2	2	0	1	1	0	0	0	0	0	0	1	0	0	2	0
1950	CHI	AL	7	4	3	5	2	0	0	0	0	0	0	0	0	0	3	4
1951	CHI	AL	4	0	4	3	1	0	0	1	0	0	0	0	0	0	2	2
Total			47	20	27	28	13	5	1	2	0	0	0	1	1	1	25	22

Rank among batters: 1,040 • *Top target (3 home runs)*: Clyde Shoun • *Number of pitchers victimized*: 40 • *Total ballparks homered in*: 13 • *First HR*: 08/13/1939 off Hugh Casey

Leech Maskrey

SAMUEL LEECH MASKREY
B: 02/11/1854 D: 04/01/1922
BR

Year	Tm	Lg	Tot	H	A	Men-On 0	Men-On 1	Men-On 2	Men-On 3	One-Game 2	One-Game 3	One-Game 4	LO	XN	IP	PH	RHP	LHP
1883	LOU	AA	1	0	1	0	1	0	0	0	0	0	0	0	0	0	1	0
1885	LOU	AA	1	1	0	1	0	0	0	0	0	0	0	0	0	0	1	0
Total			2	1	1	1	1	0	0	0	0	0	0	0	0	0	2	0

Rank among batters: 4,129 • *Total ballparks homered in*: 2 • *First HR*: 08/13/1883 off Will White

Year	Tm	Lg	Tot	H	A	Men-On 0	1	2	3	One-Game 2	3	4	LO	XN	IP	PH	RHP	LHP

Don Mason

DONALD STETSON MASON
B: 12/20/1944
BL

Year	Tm	Lg	Tot	H	A	0	1	2	3	2	3	4	LO	XN	IP	PH	RHP	LHP
1966	SF	NL	1	0	1	1	0	0	0	0	0	0	0	0	0	0	1	0
1971	SD	NL	2	0	2	2	0	0	0	0	0	0	0	0	0	0	2	0
Total			3	0	3	3	0	0	0	0	0	0	0	0	0	0	3	0

Rank among batters: 3,735 • *Total ballparks homered in*: 3 • *First HR*: 06/24/1966 off Sammy Ellis

Jim Mason

JAMES PERCY MASON
B: 08/14/1950
BL

Year	Tm	Lg	Tot	H	A	0	1	2	3	2	3	4	LO	XN	IP	PH	RHP	LHP
1973	TEX	AL	3	1	2	2	1	0	0	0	0	0	0	1	0	0	3	0
1974	NY	AL	5	3	2	3	2	0	0	0	0	0	0	0	0	0	4	1
1975	NY	AL	2	2	0	1	1	0	0	0	0	0	0	0	0	0	2	0
1976	NY	AL	1	0	1	1	0	0	0	0	0	0	0	0	0	0	1	0
1977	TEX	AL	1	0	1	1	0	0	0	0	0	0	0	0	0	0	1	0
Total			12	6	6	8	4	0	0	0	0	0	0	1	0	0	11	1

Rank among batters: 2,325 • *Top target (2 home runs)*: Bill Hands • *Number of pitchers victimized*: 11 • *Total ballparks homered in*: 7 • *First HR*: 06/18/1973 off Bill Hands • *World Series HR*—1

Dan Masteller

DAN PATRICK MASTELLER
B: 03/17/1968
BL

Year	Tm	Lg	Tot	H	A	0	1	2	3	2	3	4	LO	XN	IP	PH	RHP	LHP
1995	MIN	AL	3	1	2	2	1	0	0	0	0	0	0	0	0	1	3	0

Rank among batters: 3,735 • *Total ballparks homered in*: 3 • *First HR*: 07/28/1995 off Jack McDowell

Victor Mata

VICTOR JOSE (ABREU) MATA
B: 06/17/1961
BR

Year	Tm	Lg	Tot	H	A	0	1	2	3	2	3	4	LO	XN	IP	PH	RHP	LHP
1984	NY	AL	1	1	0	1	0	0	0	0	0	0	0	0	0	0	0	1

Rank among batters: 4,707 • *Total ballparks homered in*: 1 • *First HR*: 08/05/1984 off Neal Heaton

Tommy Matchick

JOHN THOMAS MATCHICK
B: 09/07/1943
BL

Year	Tm	Lg	Tot	H	A	0	1	2	3	2	3	4	LO	XN	IP	PH	RHP	LHP
1968	DET	AL	3	3	0	1	2	0	0	0	0	0	0	0	0	0	3	0
1971	MIL	AL	1	1	0	1	0	0	0	0	0	0	0	0	0	0	1	0
Total			4	4	0	2	2	0	0	0	0	0	0	0	0	0	4	0

Rank among batters: 3,427 • *Total ballparks homered in*: 2 • *First HR*: 07/02/1968 off Larry Sherry

Mike Matheny

MICHAEL SCOTT MATHENY
B: 09/22/1970
BR

Year	Tm	Lg	Tot	H	A	0	1	2	3	2	3	4	LO	XN	IP	PH	RHP	LHP
1994	MIL	AL	1	1	0	1	0	0	0	0	0	0	0	0	0	0	0	1

Rank among batters: 4,707 • *Total ballparks homered in*: 1 • *First HR*: 07/21/1994 off Jim Deshaies

Bobby Mathews

ROBERT T. MATHEWS
B: 11/21/1851 D: 04/17/1898
BR

Year	Tm	Lg	Tot	H	A	0	1	2	3	2	3	4	LO	XN	IP	PH	RHP	LHP
1879	PRO	NL	1	1	0	0	1	0	0	0	0	0	0	0	0	0	1	0

Rank among batters: 4,707 • *Total ballparks homered in*: 1 • *First HR*: 06/27/1879 off Tommy Bond

Eddie Mathews

EDWIN LEE MATHEWS
B: 10/13/1931
BL HOF

Year	Tm	Lg	Tot	H	A	0	1	2	3	2	3	4	LO	XN	IP	PH	RHP	LHP
1952	BOS	NL	25	11	14	19	4	2	0	0	1	0	0	1	0	0	18	7

Year	Tm	Lg	Tot	H	A	Men-On 0	1	2	3	One-Game 2	3	4	LO	XN	IP	PH	RHP	LHP

Eddie Mathews *continued*

Year	Tm	Lg	Tot	H	A	Men-On 0	1	2	3	One-Game 2	3	4	LO	XN	IP	PH	RHP	LHP
1953	MIL	NL	47	17	30	20	21	4	2	6	0	0	0	1	0	0	35	12
1954	MIL	NL	40	16	24	22	14	2	2	6	0	0	0	0	0	0	31	9
1955	MIL	NL	41	20	21	19	19	3	0	4	0	0	0	0	0	1	37	4
1956	MIL	NL	37	15	22	19	15	3	0	2	0	0	0	0	0	0	34	3
1957	MIL	NL	32	13	19	18	10	4	0	2	0	0	0	1	0	0	31	1
1958	MIL	NL	31	17	14	20	8	3	0	4	0	0	0	0	0	0	24	7
1959	MIL	NL	46	20	26	22	18	5	1	6	0	0	0	0	0	0	37	9
1960	MIL	NL	39	23	16	18	15	6	0	5	0	0	0	1	0	0	34	5
1961	MIL	NL	32	14	18	18	14	0	0	3	0	0	0	1	0	0	17	15
1962	MIL	NL	29	18	11	16	10	2	1	3	0	0	0	1	0	0	20	9
1963	MIL	NL	23	11	12	13	5	5	0	1	0	0	0	0	0	0	19	4
1964	MIL	NL	23	10	13	10	10	3	0	0	0	0	0	0	0	0	22	1
1965	MIL	NL	32	17	15	13	12	6	1	2	0	0	0	0	0	0	28	4
1966	ATL	NL	16	9	7	12	3	0	1	2	0	0	0	0	1	0	15	1
1967	HOU	NL	10	3	7	5	3	2	0	0	0	0	0	0	0	1	8	2
	DET	AL	6	3	3	5	1	0	0	1	0	0	0	0	0	0	5	1
	Total		16	6	10	10	4	2	0	1	0	0	0	0	0	1	13	3
1968	DET	AL	3	1	2	1	1	1	0	1	0	0	0	0	0	0	3	0
Total			512	238	274	270	183	51	8	48	1	0	0	6	1	2	418	94

Rank among batters: 12 • *Top target (14 home runs)*: Bob Friend • *Number of pitchers victimized*: 199 • *Total ballparks homered in*: 24 • *First HR*: 04/19/1952 off Ken Heintzelman • *World Series HR—*1; *All-Star HR—*2

Nelson Mathews

NELSON ELMER MATHEWS
B: 07/21/1941
BR

Year	Tm	Lg	Tot	H	A	Men-On 0	1	2	3	One-Game 2	3	4	LO	XN	IP	PH	RHP	LHP
1962	CHI	NL	2	2	0	0	0	1	1	0	0	0	0	0	0	0	2	0
1963	CHI	NL	4	1	3	2	1	1	0	0	0	0	0	0	0	0	2	2
1964	KC	AL	14	11	3	8	3	1	2	1	0	0	0	1	1	0	10	4
1965	KC	AL	2	1	1	1	1	0	0	0	0	0	0	0	0	0	0	2
Total			22	15	7	11	5	3	3	1	0	0	0	1	1	0	14	8

Rank among batters: 1,719 • *Top target (2 home runs)*: Wally Bunker • *Number of pitchers victimized*: 21 • *Total ballparks homered in*: 8 • *First HR*: 09/16/1962 off Stan Williams

Christy Mathewson

CHRISTOPHER MATHEWSON
B: 08/12/1878 D: 10/07/1925
BR HOF

Year	Tm	Lg	Tot	H	A	Men-On 0	1	2	3	One-Game 2	3	4	LO	XN	IP	PH	RHP	LHP
1902	NY	NL	2	2	0	1	1	0	0	0	0	0	0	0	0	0	1	0
1903	NY	NL	1	0	1	0	0	1	0	0	0	0	0	0	0	0	1	0
1905	NY	NL	2	2	0	0	1	1	0	0	0	0	0	0	0	0	2	0
1909	NY	NL	1	1	0	1	0	0	0	0	0	0	0	0	0	0	1	0
1910	NY	NL	1	0	1	1	0	0	0	0	0	0	0	0	0	0	1	0
Total			7	5	2	3	2	2	0	0	0	0	0	0	0	0	6	0

Rank among batters: 2,834 • *Total ballparks homered in*: 3 • *First HR*: 05/01/1902 off Cy Vorhees

John Matias

JOHN ROY MATIAS
B: 08/15/1944
BL

Year	Tm	Lg	Tot	H	A	Men-On 0	1	2	3	One-Game 2	3	4	LO	XN	IP	PH	RHP	LHP
1970	CHI	AL	2	1	1	1	1	0	0	0	0	0	0	0	0	0	2	0

Rank among batters: 4,129 • *Total ballparks homered in*: 2 • *First HR*: 04/15/1970 off Chuck Dobson

Gary Matthews

GARY NATHANIEL MATTHEWS
B: 07/05/1950
BR

Year	Tm	Lg	Tot	H	A	Men-On 0	1	2	3	One-Game 2	3	4	LO	XN	IP	PH	RHP	LHP
1972	SF	NL	4	2	2	2	2	0	0	1	0	0	0	0	0	0	1	3
1973	SF	NL	12	5	7	9	3	0	0	0	0	0	0	0	0	0	6	6
1974	SF	NL	16	7	9	6	6	3	1	0	0	0	0	1	0	0	13	3
1975	SF	NL	12	4	8	7	3	2	0	1	0	0	0	1	0	0	7	5
1976	SF	NL	20	11	9	10	8	2	0	2	1	0	0	1	0	0	13	7
1977	ATL	NL	17	14	3	10	6	0	1	1	0	0	0	0	0	0	12	5

Gary Matthews *continued*

Year	Tm	Lg	Tot	H	A	Men-On 0	Men-On 1	Men-On 2	Men-On 3	One-Game 2	One-Game 3	One-Game 4	LO	XN	IP	PH	RHP	LHP
1978	ATL	NL	18	10	8	13	2	3	0	1	0	0	0	1	0	0	12	6
1979	ATL	NL	27	18	9	17	7	2	1	3	0	0	0	0	1	0	22	5
1980	ATL	NL	19	9	10	9	8	2	0	3	0	0	0	1	0	1	17	2
1981	PHI	NL	9	5	4	3	2	4	0	0	0	0	0	1	0	0	6	3
1982	PHI	NL	19	10	9	11	6	2	0	1	0	0	0	1	0	0	14	5
1983	PHI	NL	10	3	7	7	1	2	0	0	0	0	0	0	0	0	8	2
1984	CHI	NL	14	8	6	8	4	2	0	0	0	0	0	0	0	0	9	5
1985	CHI	NL	13	8	5	6	4	3	0	0	0	0	0	0	0	1	9	4
1986	CHI	NL	21	11	10	15	4	2	0	2	0	0	0	0	0	0	15	6
1987	SEA	AL	3	2	1	2	1	0	0	0	0	0	0	0	0	0	2	1
Total			234	127	107	135	67	29	3	15	1	0	0	7	1	2	166	68

Rank among batters: 139 • *Top target (7 home runs)*: Don Sutton • *Number of pitchers victimized*: 156 • *Total ballparks homered in*: 15 • *First HR*: 09/16/1972 off Ron Reed • *World Series HR—1; LCS HR—6*

Wid Matthews

WID CURRY MATTHEWS
B: 10/20/1896 D: 10/05/1965
BL

Year	Tm	Lg	Tot	H	A	Men-On 0	Men-On 1	Men-On 2	Men-On 3	One-Game 2	One-Game 3	One-Game 4	LO	XN	IP	PH	RHP	LHP
1923	PHI	AL	1	1	0	1	0	0	0	0	0	0	0	0	0	0	1	0

Rank among batters: 4,707 • *Total ballparks homered in*: 1 • *First HR*: 05/25/1923 off Bob Shawkey

Wally Mattick

WALTER JOSEPH MATTICK
B: 03/12/1887 D: 11/05/1968
BR

Year	Tm	Lg	Tot	H	A	Men-On 0	Men-On 1	Men-On 2	Men-On 3	One-Game 2	One-Game 3	One-Game 4	LO	XN	IP	PH	RHP	LHP
1912	CHI	AL	1	1	0	0	0	1	0	0	0	0	0	0	0	0	1	0

Rank among batters: 4,707 • *Total ballparks homered in*: 1 • *First HR*: 07/06/1912 off Joe Lake

Mike Mattimore

MICHAEL JOSEPH MATTIMORE
B: 1859 D: 04/28/1931
BL

Year	Tm	Lg	Tot	H	A	Men-On 0	Men-On 1	Men-On 2	Men-On 3	One-Game 2	One-Game 3	One-Game 4	LO	XN	IP	PH	RHP	LHP
1889	PHI	AA	1	0	1	0	1	0	0	0	0	0	0	0	0	0	1	0

Rank among batters: 4,707 • *Total ballparks homered in*: 1 • *First HR*: 05/16/1889 off John McCarty

Don Mattingly

DONALD ARTHUR MATTINGLY
B: 04/20/1961
BL

Year	Tm	Lg	Tot	H	A	Men-On 0	Men-On 1	Men-On 2	Men-On 3	One-Game 2	One-Game 3	One-Game 4	LO	XN	IP	PH	RHP	LHP
1983	NY	AL	4	0	4	4	0	0	0	0	0	0	1	0	0	0	2	2
1984	NY	AL	23	12	11	12	6	5	0	0	0	0	0	0	1	0	18	5
1985	NY	AL	35	22	13	19	13	3	0	5	0	0	0	0	0	0	17	18
1986	NY	AL	31	17	14	19	8	4	0	2	0	0	1	0	0	0	26	5
1987	NY	AL	30	17	13	13	8	3	6	2	0	0	0	0	0	0	19	11
1988	NY	AL	18	11	7	8	8	2	0	2	0	0	0	0	0	0	15	3
1989	NY	AL	23	19	4	12	10	1	0	2	0	0	0	1	0	0	15	8
1990	NY	AL	5	4	1	2	2	1	0	0	0	0	0	0	0	0	5	0
1991	NY	AL	9	7	2	5	4	0	0	0	0	0	0	0	0	0	5	4
1992	NY	AL	14	6	8	6	7	1	0	0	0	0	0	0	0	0	12	2
1993	NY	AL	17	8	9	10	5	2	0	0	0	0	0	1	0	0	12	5
1994	NY	AL	6	3	3	1	3	2	0	0	0	0	0	0	0	1	5	1
1995	NY	AL	7	5	2	5	2	0	0	0	0	0	0	0	0	0	5	2
Total			222	131	91	116	76	24	6	13	0	0	2	2	1	1	156	66

Rank among batters: 148 • Top target (4 home runs): Tom Candiotti, Charlie Hough, Jack Morris, Mark Gubicza • *Number of pitchers victimized*: 154 • *Total ballparks homered in*: 17 • *First HR*: 06/24/1983 off John Tudor • *LCS HR—1*

Len Matuszek

LEONARD JAMES MATUSZEK
B: 09/27/1954
BL

Year	Tm	Lg	Tot	H	A	Men-On 0	Men-On 1	Men-On 2	Men-On 3	One-Game 2	One-Game 3	One-Game 4	LO	XN	IP	PH	RHP	LHP
1983	PHI	NL	4	2	2	2	1	1	0	0	0	0	0	0	0	0	4	0
1984	PHI	NL	12	5	7	7	4	1	0	0	0	0	0	0	0	3	12	0

Len Matuszek *continued*

Year	Tm	Lg	Tot	H	A	Men-On 0	Men-On 1	Men-On 2	Men-On 3	One-Game 2	One-Game 3	One-Game 4	LO	XN	IP	PH	RHP	LHP
1985	TOR	AL	2	1	1	2	0	0	0	0	0	0	0	0	0	0	2	0
	LA	NL	3	0	3	2	1	0	0	0	0	0	0	0	0	0	3	0
	Total		5	1	4	4	1	0	0	0	0	0	0	0	0	0	5	0
1986	LA	NL	9	7	2	3	3	3	0	1	0	0	0	0	0	1	9	0
Total			30	15	15	16	9	5	0	1	0	0	0	0	0	4	30	0

Rank among batters: 1,437 • *Top target (2 home runs)*: Eric Show, Andy Hawkins • *Number of pitchers victimized*: 28 • *Total ballparks homered in*: 10 • *First HR*: 09/14/1983 off Ray Burris

Gene Mauch

GENE WILLIAM MAUCH
B: 11/18/1925
BR

Year	Tm	Lg	Tot	H	A	Men-On 0	Men-On 1	Men-On 2	Men-On 3	One-Game 2	One-Game 3	One-Game 4	LO	XN	IP	PH	RHP	LHP
1948	CHI	NL	1	1	0	1	0	0	0	0	0	0	0	0	0	0	1	0
1949	CHI	NL	1	1	0	0	0	1	0	0	0	0	0	0	0	0	0	1
1950	BOS	NL	1	0	1	0	0	1	0	0	0	0	0	0	0	0	1	0
1957	BOS	AL	2	1	1	2	0	0	0	0	0	0	0	0	0	0	2	0
Total			5	3	2	3	0	2	0	0	0	0	0	0	0	0	4	1

Rank among batters: 3,191 • *Total ballparks homered in*: 4 • *First HR*: 06/30/1948 off Jim Hearn

Al Maul

ALBERT JOSEPH MAUL
B: 10/09/1865 D: 05/03/1958
BR

Year	Tm	Lg	Tot	H	A	Men-On 0	Men-On 1	Men-On 2	Men-On 3	One-Game 2	One-Game 3	One-Game 4	LO	XN	IP	PH	RHP	LHP
1887	PHI	NL	1	1	0	1	0	0	0	0	0	0	0	0	0	0	0	1
1889	PIT	NL	4	1	3	2	2	0	0	1	0	0	0	0	0	0	4	0
1894	WAS	NL	2	1	1	1	1	0	0	0	0	0	0	0	1	0	2	0
Total			7	3	4	4	3	0	0	1	0	0	0	0	1	0	6	1

Rank among batters: 2,834 • *Total ballparks homered in*: 6 • *First HR*: 06/17/1887 off Dupee Shaw

Mark Mauldin

MARSHALL REESE MAULDIN
B: 11/05/1914 D: 09/02/1990
BR

Year	Tm	Lg	Tot	H	A	Men-On 0	Men-On 1	Men-On 2	Men-On 3	One-Game 2	One-Game 3	One-Game 4	LO	XN	IP	PH	RHP	LHP
1934	CHI	AL	1	1	0	1	0	0	0	0	0	0	0	0	0	0	1	0

Rank among batters: 4,707 • *Total ballparks homered in*: 1 • *First HR*: 09/22/1934 off Oral Hildebrand

Carmen Mauro

CARMEN LOUIS MAURO
B: 11/10/1926
BL

Year	Tm	Lg	Tot	H	A	Men-On 0	Men-On 1	Men-On 2	Men-On 3	One-Game 2	One-Game 3	One-Game 4	LO	XN	IP	PH	RHP	LHP
1948	CHI	NL	1	0	1	1	0	0	0	0	0	0	0	0	1	0	1	0
1950	CHI	NL	1	0	1	1	0	0	0	0	0	0	0	1	0	0	1	0
Total			2	0	2	2	0	0	0	0	0	0	0	1	1	0	2	0

Rank among batters: 4,129 • *Total ballparks homered in*: 2 • *First HR*: 10/03/1948 off Murry Dickson

Dal Maxvill

CHARLES DALLAN MAXVILL
B: 02/18/1939
BR

Year	Tm	Lg	Tot	H	A	Men-On 0	Men-On 1	Men-On 2	Men-On 3	One-Game 2	One-Game 3	One-Game 4	LO	XN	IP	PH	RHP	LHP
1962	STL	NL	1	0	1	0	0	1	0	0	0	0	0	0	0	0	0	1
1967	STL	NL	1	1	0	1	0	0	0	0	0	0	0	0	1	0	0	1
1968	STL	NL	1	1	0	1	0	0	0	0	0	0	0	0	0	0	0	1
1969	STL	NL	2	1	1	1	0	0	1	0	0	0	0	0	0	0	1	1
1972	STL	NL	1	1	0	1	0	0	0	0	0	0	0	0	1	0	1	0
Total			6	4	2	4	0	1	1	0	0	0	0	0	2	0	2	4

Rank among batters: 2,988 • *Total ballparks homered in*: 3 • *First HR*: 08/19/1962 off Al Jackson

Charlie Maxwell

CHARLES RICHARD MAXWELL
B: 04/08/1927
BL

Year	Tm	Lg	Tot	H	A	Men-On 0	Men-On 1	Men-On 2	Men-On 3	One-Game 2	One-Game 3	One-Game 4	LO	XN	IP	PH	RHP	LHP
1951	BOS	AL	3	2	1	0	1	1	1	0	0	0	0	0	0	3	3	0

						Men-On				One-Game								
Year	Tm	Lg	Tot	H	A	0	1	2	3	2	3	4	LO	XN	IP	PH	RHP	LHP

Charlie Maxwell *continued*

Year	Tm	Lg	Tot	H	A	0	1	2	3	2	3	4	LO	XN	IP	PH	RHP	LHP
1955	DET	AL	7	4	3	3	4	0	0	0	0	0	0	0	0	1	7	0
1956	DET	AL	28	14	14	19	7	1	1	2	0	0	0	0	0	0	25	3
1957	DET	AL	24	15	9	13	8	3	0	2	0	0	0	0	0	0	22	2
1958	DET	AL	13	9	4	6	4	2	1	0	0	0	0	0	0	0	13	0
1959	DET	AL	31	21	10	14	9	7	1	2	1	0	0	0	0	1	26	5
1960	DET	AL	24	16	8	12	10	2	0	3	0	0	0	5	0	0	21	3
1961	DET	AL	5	3	2	3	1	1	0	0	0	0	0	0	0	3	5	0
1962	DET	AL	1	1	0	1	0	0	0	0	0	0	0	0	0	0	1	0
	CHI	AL	9	3	6	5	1	2	1	1	0	0	0	0	0	0	9	0
	Total		10	4	6	6	1	2	1	1	0	0	0	0	0	0	10	0
1963	CHI	AL	3	1	2	2	1	0	0	0	0	0	0	0	0	0	3	0
Total			148	89	59	78	46	19	5	10	1	0	0	5	0	8	135	13

Rank among batters: 294 • *Top target (6 home runs)*: Pedro Ramos, Dick Donovan • *Number of pitchers victimized*: 82 • *Total ballparks homered in*: 10 • *First HR*: 07/17/1951 off Bob Feller

Carlos May

CARLOS MAY
B: 05/17/1948
BL

Year	Tm	Lg	Tot	H	A	0	1	2	3	2	3	4	LO	XN	IP	PH	RHP	LHP
1969	CHI	AL	18	8	10	13	4	0	1	2	0	0	2	0	0	1	14	4
1970	CHI	AL	12	9	3	5	4	3	0	0	0	0	0	0	0	0	11	1
1971	CHI	AL	7	2	5	3	2	1	1	0	0	0	0	0	1	0	6	1
1972	CHI	AL	12	9	3	7	2	2	1	2	0	0	0	0	0	0	10	2
1973	CHI	AL	20	13	7	10	5	5	0	1	0	0	0	0	0	0	16	4
1974	CHI	AL	8	4	4	3	4	1	0	1	0	0	0	0	0	0	7	1
1975	CHI	AL	8	2	6	7	1	0	0	0	0	0	0	1	0	0	6	2
1976	NY	AL	3	1	2	1	0	2	0	0	0	0	0	0	0	0	3	0
1977	NY	AL	2	1	1	1	1	0	0	0	0	0	0	0	0	0	2	0
Total			90	49	41	50	23	14	3	6	0	0	2	1	1	1	75	15

Rank among batters: 573 • *Top target (3 home runs)*: Marty Pattin, Catfish Hunter, Luis Tiant • *Number of pitchers victimized*: 70 • *Total ballparks homered in*: 15 • *First HR*: 04/09/1969 off Jim Nash

Dave May

DAVID LAFRANCE MAY
B: 12/23/1943
BL

Year	Tm	Lg	Tot	H	A	0	1	2	3	2	3	4	LO	XN	IP	PH	RHP	LHP
1967	BAL	AL	1	0	1	0	1	0	0	0	0	0	0	0	0	0	1	0
1969	BAL	AL	3	1	2	2	1	0	0	0	0	0	0	0	0	1	3	0
1970	BAL	AL	1	1	0	0	1	0	0	0	0	0	0	1	0	0	1	0
	MIL	AL	7	5	2	4	3	0	0	0	0	0	0	0	0	0	6	1
	Total		8	6	2	4	4	0	0	0	0	0	0	1	0	0	7	1
1971	MIL	AL	16	5	11	11	2	3	0	0	0	0	0	0	0	0	15	1
1972	MIL	AL	9	3	6	6	3	0	0	0	0	0	0	0	0	0	7	2
1973	MIL	AL	25	13	12	12	11	0	2	3	0	0	0	3	1	0	16	9
1974	MIL	AL	10	2	8	8	1	1	0	1	0	0	2	0	0	0	8	2
1975	ATL	NL	12	7	5	7	3	1	1	0	0	0	0	0	0	2	10	2
1976	ATL	NL	3	1	2	1	2	0	0	0	0	0	0	0	0	0	3	0
1977	TEX	AL	7	2	5	3	2	2	0	0	0	0	0	0	0	0	7	0
1978	MIL	AL	2	0	2	2	0	0	0	0	0	0	0	0	0	0	2	0
Total			96	40	56	56	30	7	3	4	0	0	2	4	1	3	79	17

Rank among batters: 520 • *Top target (5 home runs)*: Mel Stottlemyre • *Number of pitchers victimized*: 76 • *Total ballparks homered in*: 23 • *First HR*: 07/30/1967 off Stan Williams

Derrick May

DERRICK BRANT MAY
B: 07/14/1968
BL

Year	Tm	Lg	Tot	H	A	0	1	2	3	2	3	4	LO	XN	IP	PH	RHP	LHP
1990	CHI	NL	1	1	0	0	0	1	0	0	0	0	0	0	0	0	1	0
1991	CHI	NL	1	1	0	1	0	0	0	0	0	0	0	0	0	1	1	0
1992	CHI	NL	8	3	5	2	2	4	0	1	0	0	0	1	0	1	7	1
1993	CHI	NL	10	3	7	3	3	3	1	1	0	0	0	0	0	0	6	4
1994	CHI	NL	8	5	3	6	1	1	0	0	0	0	0	1	0	0	6	2
1995	MIL	AL	1	1	0	0	0	1	0	0	0	0	0	0	0	0	1	0
	HOU	NL	8	3	5	2	4	1	1	0	0	0	0	0	0	2	8	0

Year	Tm	Lg	Tot	H	A	Men-On 0	Men-On 1	Men-On 2	Men-On 3	One-Game 2	One-Game 3	One-Game 4	LO	XN	IP	PH	RHP	LHP

Derrick May *continued*

Year	Tm	Lg	Tot	H	A	0	1	2	3	2	3	4	LO	XN	IP	PH	RHP	LHP
1995	Total		9	4	5	2	4	2	1	0	0	0	0	0	0	2	9	0
Total			37	17	20	14	10	11	2	2	0	0	0	2	0	4	30	7

Rank among batters: 1,252 • Top target (2 home runs): Brad Brink, Dennis Martinez, Greg Harris, Ramon Martinez • *Number of pitchers victimized*: 33 • *Total ballparks homered in*: 13 • *First HR*: 09/19/1990 off Ted Power

Jakie May

FRANK SPRUIELL MAY
B: 11/25/1895 D: 06/03/1970
BR

Year	Tm	Lg	Tot	H	A	0	1	2	3	2	3	4	LO	XN	IP	PH	RHP	LHP
1918	STL	NL	1	1	0	0	0	1	0	0	0	0	0	0	0	0	1	0
1924	CIN	NL	1	0	1	1	0	0	0	0	0	0	0	0	0	0	0	1
Total			2	1	1	1	0	1	0	0	0	0	0	0	0	0	1	1

Rank among batters: 4,129 • *Total ballparks homered in*: 2 • *First HR*: 07/05/1918 off Roy Walker

Jerry May

JERRY LEE MAY
B: 12/14/1943
BR

Year	Tm	Lg	Tot	H	A	0	1	2	3	2	3	4	LO	XN	IP	PH	RHP	LHP
1966	PIT	NL	1	0	1	1	0	0	0	0	0	0	0	0	0	0	0	1
1967	PIT	NL	3	2	1	2	1	0	0	0	0	0	0	0	0	0	2	1
1968	PIT	NL	1	1	0	1	0	0	0	0	0	0	0	0	0	0	1	0
1969	PIT	NL	7	3	4	5	0	1	1	0	0	0	0	0	0	1	5	2
1970	PIT	NL	1	0	1	0	0	1	0	0	0	0	0	0	0	0	1	0
1971	KC	AL	1	1	0	0	1	0	0	0	0	0	0	0	0	0	1	0
1972	KC	AL	1	0	1	0	1	0	0	0	0	0	0	0	0	0	0	1
Total			15	7	8	9	3	2	1	0	0	0	0	0	0	1	10	5

Rank among batters: 2,096 • *Total ballparks homered in*: 8 • *First HR*: 08/18/1966 off Rob Gardner

Lee May

LEE ANDREW MAY
B: 05/23/1943
BR

Year	Tm	Lg	Tot	H	A	0	1	2	3	2	3	4	LO	XN	IP	PH	RHP	LHP
1966	CIN	NL	2	2	0	1	0	1	0	0	0	0	0	0	0	0	1	1
1967	CIN	NL	12	8	4	6	4	2	0	0	0	0	0	0	0	0	7	5
1968	CIN	NL	22	11	11	13	8	1	0	2	0	0	0	0	0	0	15	7
1969	CIN	NL	38	23	15	18	14	5	1	6	0	0	0	2	0	0	29	9
1970	CIN	NL	34	21	13	23	8	0	3	2	0	0	0	3	0	0	22	12
1971	CIN	NL	39	19	20	23	12	4	0	6	0	0	0	0	0	0	28	11
1972	HOU	NL	29	13	16	16	8	5	0	2	0	0	0	0	0	0	25	4
1973	HOU	NL	28	10	18	13	10	3	2	2	1	0	0	1	0	0	22	6
1974	HOU	NL	24	18	6	16	7	1	0	3	0	0	0	0	0	0	16	8
1975	BAL	AL	20	8	12	12	3	5	0	2	0	0	0	0	0	0	16	4
1976	BAL	AL	25	12	13	10	8	6	1	2	0	0	0	1	0	0	16	9
1977	BAL	AL	27	11	16	9	11	5	2	2	0	0	0	0	0	0	24	3
1978	BAL	AL	25	11	14	15	9	1	0	4	0	0	0	0	0	0	13	12
1979	BAL	AL	19	8	11	11	5	1	2	1	0	0	0	0	0	0	13	6
1980	BAL	AL	7	3	4	7	0	0	0	0	0	0	0	0	0	0	4	3
1982	KC	AL	3	1	2	1	2	0	0	0	0	0	0	0	0	0	1	2
Total			354	179	175	194	109	40	11	34	1	0	0	7	0	0	252	102

Rank among batters: 43 • *Top target (6 home runs)*: Jerry Koosman, Reggie Cleveland • *Number of pitchers victimized*: 213 • *Total ballparks homered in*: 29 • *First HR*: 09/24/1966 off Bob Shaw • *2 HR in 1 inning*—vs CHI: 04/29/1974 • *World Series HR*—2

Milt May

MILTON SCOTT MAY
B: 08/01/1950
BL

Year	Tm	Lg	Tot	H	A	0	1	2	3	2	3	4	LO	XN	IP	PH	RHP	LHP
1971	PIT	NL	6	5	1	3	3	0	0	0	0	0	0	0	0	0	5	1
1973	PIT	NL	7	5	2	4	2	1	0	0	0	0	0	0	1	0	6	1
1974	HOU	NL	7	3	4	2	4	0	1	0	0	0	0	0	0	1	5	2
1975	HOU	NL	4	1	3	1	2	1	0	0	0	0	0	0	0	0	4	0
1977	DET	AL	12	7	5	10	1	0	1	1	0	0	0	2	0	1	8	4
1978	DET	AL	10	7	3	5	3	2	0	0	0	0	0	0	0	0	9	1
1979	CHI	AL	7	3	4	5	2	0	0	0	0	0	0	0	0	0	7	0
1980	SF	NL	6	1	5	3	1	1	1	0	0	0	0	0	0	0	5	1
1981	SF	NL	2	1	1	1	0	1	0	0	0	0	0	1	0	1	2	0

Year	Tm	Lg	Tot	H	A	Men-On 0	1	2	3	One-Game 2	3	4	LO	XN	IP	PH	RHP	LHP

Milt May *continued*

Year	Tm	Lg	Tot	H	A	0	1	2	3	2	3	4	LO	XN	IP	PH	RHP	LHP
1982	SF	NL	9	4	5	7	2	0	0	1	0	0	0	1	0	1	7	2
1983	SF	NL	6	4	2	4	1	1	0	0	0	0	0	0	0	0	6	0
1984	PIT	NL	1	1	0	1	0	0	0	0	0	0	0	0	0	0	1	0
Total			77	42	35	46	21	7	3	2	0	0	0	4	1	4	65	12

Rank among batters: 682 • Top target (2 home runs): Bill Hands, Don Wilson, Dave Lemanczyk, Ferguson Jenkins, Paul Mitchell, Doyle Alexander, Ray Burris, Mario Soto, Don Robinson, Bob Welch • *Number of pitchers victimized*: 67 • *Total ballparks homered in*: 22 • *First HR*: 05/29/1971 off Bill Hands

Pinky May

MERRILL GLEND MAY
B: 01/18/1911
BR

Year	Tm	Lg	Tot	H	A	0	1	2	3	2	3	4	LO	XN	IP	PH	RHP	LHP
1939	PHI	NL	2	0	2	0	2	0	0	0	0	0	0	0	0	0	2	0
1940	PHI	NL	1	0	1	1	0	0	0	0	0	0	0	0	0	0	0	1
1943	PHI	NL	1	0	1	1	0	0	0	0	0	0	0	0	0	0	0	1
Total			4	0	4	2	2	0	0	0	0	0	0	0	0	0	2	2

Rank among batters: 3,427 • *Top target (2 home runs)*: Cliff Melton • *Number of pitchers victimized*: 3 • *Total ballparks homered in*: 1 • *First HR*: 08/12/1939 off Manny Salvo

John Mayberry

JOHN CLAIBORN MAYBERRY
B: 02/18/1949
BL

Year	Tm	Lg	Tot	H	A	0	1	2	3	2	3	4	LO	XN	IP	PH	RHP	LHP
1970	HOU	NL	5	2	3	3	1	1	0	1	0	0	0	0	0	1	4	1
1971	HOU	NL	7	1	6	5	1	1	0	1	0	0	0	0	0	0	5	2
1972	KC	AL	25	13	12	10	8	6	1	1	0	0	0	0	0	0	14	11
1973	KC	AL	26	14	12	13	9	4	0	1	0	0	0	0	0	0	21	5
1974	KC	AL	22	9	13	12	9	1	0	0	0	0	0	0	0	0	11	11
1975	KC	AL	34	11	23	23	8	3	0	2	1	0	0	1	0	0	27	7
1976	KC	AL	13	10	3	7	3	3	0	2	0	0	0	1	0	0	10	3
1977	KC	AL	23	7	16	9	10	4	0	1	1	0	0	0	0	1	14	9
1978	TOR	AL	22	12	10	14	6	2	0	3	0	0	0	0	0	1	17	5
1979	TOR	AL	21	13	8	14	3	4	0	1	0	0	0	0	0	0	20	1
1980	TOR	AL	30	10	20	19	8	3	0	4	0	0	0	0	0	0	22	8
1981	TOR	AL	17	10	7	8	7	2	0	1	0	0	0	0	0	0	11	6
1982	TOR	AL	2	2	0	2	0	0	0	1	0	0	0	1	0	0	1	1
	NY	AL	8	2	6	6	1	1	0	0	0	0	0	0	0	1	7	1
	Total		10	4	6	8	1	1	0	1	0	0	0	1	0	1	8	2
Total			255	116	139	145	74	35	1	19	2	0	0	3	0	4	184	71

Rank among batters: 101 • *Top target (8 home runs)*: Gaylord Perry • *Number of pitchers victimized*: 157 • *Total ballparks homered in*: 22 • *First HR*: 04/15/1970 off Gaylord Perry • *Hit for Cycle*—vs CHI: 08/05/1977 • *LCS HR*—2

Lee Maye

ARTHUR LEE MAYE
B: 12/11/1934
BL

Year	Tm	Lg	Tot	H	A	0	1	2	3	2	3	4	LO	XN	IP	PH	RHP	LHP
1959	MIL	NL	4	3	1	1	2	1	0	0	0	0	0	0	1	0	4	0
1961	MIL	NL	14	5	9	9	3	1	1	0	0	0	0	0	0	0	13	1
1962	MIL	NL	10	7	3	4	5	1	0	1	0	0	0	0	0	0	8	2
1963	MIL	NL	11	7	4	8	2	1	0	0	0	0	1	0	0	0	11	0
1964	MIL	NL	10	7	3	7	3	0	0	0	0	0	0	0	0	0	8	2
1965	MIL	NL	2	2	0	1	1	0	0	0	0	0	0	0	0	0	1	1
	HOU	NL	3	1	2	2	0	1	0	0	0	0	0	0	0	0	1	2
	Total		5	3	2	3	1	1	0	0	0	0	0	0	0	0	2	3
1966	HOU	NL	9	3	6	7	1	1	0	0	0	0	0	0	0	0	8	1
1967	CLE	AL	9	5	4	7	2	0	0	0	0	0	1	0	1	2	8	1
1968	CLE	AL	4	3	1	3	1	0	0	0	0	0	1	0	0	0	4	0
1969	CLE	AL	1	1	0	0	1	0	0	0	0	0	0	0	0	0	1	0
	WAS	AL	9	4	5	6	2	0	1	0	0	0	0	0	0	0	9	0
	Total		10	5	5	6	3	0	1	0	0	0	0	0	0	0	10	0
1970	WAS	AL	7	7	0	4	1	2	0	0	0	0	1	0	0	1	7	0
1971	CHI	AL	1	0	1	0	1	0	0	0	0	0	0	0	0	0	1	0
Total			94	55	39	59	25	8	2	1	0	0	4	0	2	3	84	10

Rank among batters: 535 • *Top target (4 home runs)*: Glen Hobbie • *Number of pitchers victimized*: 71 • *Total ballparks homered in*: 21 • *First HR*: 09/07/1959 off Bob Friend

Ed Mayer

EDWARD H. MAYER
B: 08/16/1866 D: 05/18/1913

Year	Tm	Lg	Tot	H	A	Men-On 0	1	2	3	One-Game 2	3	4	LO	XN	IP	PH	RHP	LHP
1890	PHI	NL	1	1	0	0	0	1	0	0	0	0	0	0	0	0	1	0

Rank among batters: 4,707 • *Total ballparks homered in*: 1 • *First HR*: 06/20/1890 off Kirtley Baker

Erskine Mayer

ERSKINE JOHN MAYER
B: 01/16/1889 D: 03/10/1957
BR

Year	Tm	Lg	Tot	H	A	Men-On 0	1	2	3	One-Game 2	3	4	LO	XN	IP	PH	RHP	LHP
1914	PHI	NL	1	0	1	1	0	0	0	0	0	0	0	0	0	0	1	0
1915	PHI	NL	1	1	0	1	0	0	0	0	0	0	0	0	0	0	0	1
Total			2	1	1	2	0	0	0	0	0	0	0	0	0	0	1	1

Rank among batters: 4,129 • *Total ballparks homered in*: 2 • *First HR*: 07/01/1914 off Iron Davis

Sam Mayer

SAMUEL FRANKEL MAYER
B: 02/28/1893 D: 07/01/1962
BR

Year	Tm	Lg	Tot	H	A	Men-On 0	1	2	3	One-Game 2	3	4	LO	XN	IP	PH	RHP	LHP
1915	WAS	AL	1	0	1	1	0	0	0	0	0	0	0	0	0	0	1	0

Rank among batters: 4,707 • *Total ballparks homered in*: 1 • *First HR*: 09/06/1915 off Jack Nabors

Buster Maynard

JAMES WALTER MAYNARD
B: 03/25/1913 D: 09/07/1977
BR

Year	Tm	Lg	Tot	H	A	Men-On 0	1	2	3	One-Game 2	3	4	LO	XN	IP	PH	RHP	LHP
1940	NY	NL	1	1	0	1	0	0	0	0	0	0	1	0	0	0	0	1
1942	NY	NL	4	2	2	1	2	1	0	0	0	0	0	0	0	1	2	2
1943	NY	NL	9	5	4	7	1	1	0	1	0	0	2	0	0	0	5	4
Total			14	8	6	9	3	2	0	1	0	0	3	0	0	1	7	7

Rank among batters: 2,169 • *Top target (2 home runs)*: Al Gerheauser, Paul Derringer • *Number of pitchers victimized*: 12 • *Total ballparks homered in*: 4 • *First HR*: 09/18/1940 off Larry French

Brent Mayne

BRENT DANEM MAYNE
B: 04/19/1968
BL

Year	Tm	Lg	Tot	H	A	Men-On 0	1	2	3	One-Game 2	3	4	LO	XN	IP	PH	RHP	LHP
1991	KC	AL	3	2	1	0	3	0	0	0	0	0	0	0	2	1	3	0
1993	KC	AL	2	0	2	2	0	0	0	0	0	0	0	0	0	0	2	0
1994	KC	AL	2	1	1	0	1	0	1	0	0	0	0	0	0	0	2	0
1995	KC	AL	1	1	0	1	0	0	0	0	0	0	0	0	0	0	1	0
Total			8	4	4	3	4	0	1	0	0	0	0	0	2	1	8	0

Rank among batters: 2,703 • *Total ballparks homered in*: 5 • *First HR*: 08/01/1991 off Julio Machado

Eddie Mayo

EDWARD JOSEPH MAYO
B: 04/15/1910
BL

Year	Tm	Lg	Tot	H	A	Men-On 0	1	2	3	One-Game 2	3	4	LO	XN	IP	PH	RHP	LHP
1936	NY	NL	1	0	1	1	0	0	0	0	0	0	0	0	0	0	1	0
1937	BOS	NL	1	0	1	0	1	0	0	0	0	0	0	1	0	0	1	0
1938	BOS	NL	1	0	1	1	0	0	0	0	0	0	0	0	0	0	1	0
1944	DET	AL	5	2	3	3	1	1	0	0	0	0	0	0	0	0	5	0
1945	DET	AL	10	8	2	5	3	2	0	1	0	0	0	0	0	0	10	0
1947	DET	AL	6	4	2	4	1	1	0	1	0	0	0	0	0	0	5	1
1948	DET	AL	2	1	1	1	0	1	0	0	0	0	0	0	0	0	1	1
Total			26	15	11	15	6	5	0	2	0	0	0	1	0	0	24	2

Rank among batters: 1,576 • *Top target (2 home runs)*: Atley Donald, Jack Kramer, Spec Shea • *Number of pitchers victimized*: 23 • *Total ballparks homered in*: 6 • *First HR*: 06/06/1936 off Ed Heusser

Jackie Mayo

JOHN LEWIS MAYO
B: 07/26/1925
BL

Year	Tm	Lg	Tot	H	A	Men-On 0	1	2	3	One-Game 2	3	4	LO	XN	IP	PH	RHP	LHP
1952	PHI	NL	1	1	0	1	0	0	0	0	0	0	0	0	0	0	1	0

Rank among batters: 4,707 • *Total ballparks homered in*: 1 • *First HR*: 05/15/1952 off Ewell Blackwell

Al Mays

ALBERT C. MAYS
B: 05/17/1865 D: 05/17/1905
BR

Year	Tm	Lg	Tot	H	A	Men-On 0	1	2	3	One-Game 2	3	4	LO	XN	IP	PH	RHP	LHP
1886	NY	AA	1	0	1	0	1	0	0	0	0	0	0	0	0	0	1	0
1887	NY	AA	2	1	1	0	0	2	0	0	0	0	0	0	0	0	2	0
Total			3	1	2	0	1	2	0	0	0	0	0	0	0	0	3	0

Rank among batters: 3,735 • *Total ballparks homered in*: 3 • *First HR*: 06/30/1886 off Nat Hudson

Carl Mays

CARL WILLIAM MAYS
B: 11/12/1891 D: 04/04/1971
BL

Year	Tm	Lg	Tot	H	A	Men-On 0	1	2	3	One-Game 2	3	4	LO	XN	IP	PH	RHP	LHP
1921	NY	AL	2	1	1	1	0	1	0	0	0	0	0	0	0	0	2	0
1923	NY	AL	1	1	0	1	0	0	0	0	0	0	0	0	0	0	0	1
1924	CIN	NL	1	0	1	0	1	0	0	0	0	0	0	0	0	0	1	0
1927	CIN	NL	1	0	1	1	0	0	0	0	0	0	0	0	0	0	1	0
Total			5	2	3	3	1	1	0	0	0	0	0	0	0	0	4	1

Rank among batters: 3,191 • *Total ballparks homered in*: 5 • *First HR*: 06/10/1921 off Jim Bagby

Willie Mays

WILLIE HOWARD MAYS
B: 05/06/1931
BR HOF

Year	Tm	Lg	Tot	H	A	Men-On 0	1	2	3	One-Game 2	3	4	LO	XN	IP	PH	RHP	LHP
1951	NY	NL	20	13	7	11	6	3	0	2	0	0	0	3	0	0	12	8
1952	NY	NL	4	2	2	3	1	0	0	0	0	0	0	0	0	0	3	1
1954	NY	NL	41	20	21	24	14	3	0	4	0	0	0	1	2	0	27	14
1955	NY	NL	51	22	29	28	20	2	1	9	0	0	0	4	1	0	34	17
1956	NY	NL	36	20	16	24	9	3	0	4	0	0	0	0	0	0	29	7
1957	NY	NL	35	17	18	19	12	4	0	2	0	0	0	2	1	0	24	11
1958	SF	NL	29	16	13	15	9	4	1	3	0	0	0	1	0	0	21	8
1959	SF	NL	34	16	18	19	11	4	0	2	0	0	0	2	0	1	25	9
1960	SF	NL	29	12	17	15	9	4	1	3	0	0	0	0	2	0	16	13
1961	SF	NL	40	21	19	17	18	3	2	3	1	1	0	1	0	1	30	10
1962	SF	NL	49	28	21	24	17	7	1	6	0	0	0	1	0	0	32	17
1963	SF	NL	38	20	18	24	9	5	0	1	1	0	0	3	1	0	26	12
1964	SF	NL	47	25	22	28	14	5	0	8	0	0	0	0	0	1	30	17
1965	SF	NL	52	24	28	27	19	6	0	4	0	0	0	0	0	0	40	12
1966	SF	NL	37	16	21	14	19	4	0	0	0	0	0	0	1	0	25	12
1967	SF	NL	22	13	9	14	5	2	1	2	0	0	0	1	0	0	13	9
1968	SF	NL	23	12	11	15	6	2	0	2	0	0	0	1	0	0	13	10
1969	SF	NL	13	7	6	7	4	2	0	0	0	0	0	1	0	2	11	2
1970	SF	NL	28	15	13	15	11	2	0	5	0	0	0	0	0	0	24	4
1971	SF	NL	18	9	9	11	5	1	1	0	0	0	0	1	0	0	9	9
1972	NY	NL	8	3	5	6	2	0	0	0	0	0	0	0	0	0	6	2
1973	NY	NL	6	4	2	5	0	1	0	0	0	0	0	0	0	0	1	5
Total			660	335	325	365	220	67	8	60	2	1	0	22	8	5	451	209

Rank among batters: 3 • *Top target (18 home runs)*: Warren Spahn • *Number of pitchers victimized*: 267 • *Total ballparks homered in*: 22 • *First HR*: 05/28/1951 off Warren Spahn • *LCS HR*—1; *All-Star HR*—3

Bill Mazeroski

WILLIAM STANLEY MAZEROSKI
B: 09/05/1936
BR

Year	Tm	Lg	Tot	H	A	Men-On 0	1	2	3	One-Game 2	3	4	LO	XN	IP	PH	RHP	LHP
1956	PIT	NL	3	1	2	0	3	0	0	0	0	0	0	0	0	0	3	0
1957	PIT	NL	8	0	8	5	3	0	0	0	0	0	0	0	0	1	5	3
1958	PIT	NL	19	8	11	9	8	2	0	2	0	0	0	0	0	0	13	6
1959	PIT	NL	7	2	5	6	1	0	0	1	0	0	0	0	0	0	5	2
1960	PIT	NL	11	5	6	5	4	2	0	0	0	0	0	0	0	0	7	4
1961	PIT	NL	13	4	9	8	4	1	0	2	0	0	0	0	0	0	12	1
1962	PIT	NL	14	4	10	6	6	1	1	1	0	0	0	0	0	0	11	3
1963	PIT	NL	8	2	6	5	1	2	0	0	0	0	0	0	0	0	5	3
1964	PIT	NL	10	5	5	4	5	1	0	0	0	0	0	0	1	0	8	2
1965	PIT	NL	6	1	5	4	2	0	0	0	0	0	0	0	0	0	3	3
1966	PIT	NL	16	6	10	9	3	2	2	2	0	0	0	1	0	0	13	3
1967	PIT	NL	9	3	6	5	3	1	0	0	0	0	0	0	0	0	5	4
1968	PIT	NL	3	2	1	2	1	0	0	0	0	0	0	0	0	0	3	0
1969	PIT	NL	3	1	2	2	1	0	0	0	0	0	0	0	0	0	1	2

						Men-On				One-Game								
Year	Tm	Lg	Tot	H	A	0	1	2	3	2	3	4	LO	XN	IP	PH	RHP	LHP

Bill Mazeroski *continued*

Year	Tm	Lg	Tot	H	A	0	1	2	3	2	3	4	LO	XN	IP	PH	RHP	LHP
1970	PIT	NL	7	1	6	5	1	1	0	0	0	0	0	1	0	0	7	0
1971	PIT	NL	1	0	1	0	1	0	0	0	0	0	0	0	0	0	0	1
Total			138	45	93	75	47	13	3	8	0	0	0	2	1	1	101	37

Rank among batters: 314 • *Top target (5 home runs)*: Don Newcombe, Stan Williams • *Number of pitchers victimized*: 99 • *Total ballparks homered in*: 20 • *First HR*: 08/16/1956 off Robin Roberts • *World Series HR*—2

Mel Mazzera

MELVIN LEONARD MAZZERA
B: 01/31/1914
BL

Year	Tm	Lg	Tot	H	A	0	1	2	3	2	3	4	LO	XN	IP	PH	RHP	LHP
1935	STL	AL	1	0	1	1	0	0	0	0	0	0	0	0	0	0	1	0
1938	STL	AL	6	6	0	4	1	1	0	0	0	0	0	0	0	0	6	0
1939	STL	AL	3	2	1	1	2	0	0	1	0	0	0	0	0	0	3	0
Total			10	8	2	6	3	1	0	1	0	0	0	0	0	0	10	0

Rank among batters: 2,500 • *Top target (2 home runs)*: Ted Lyons • *Number of pitchers victimized*: 9 • *Total ballparks homered in*: 3 • *First HR*: 09/25/1935 off Ray Phelps

Lee Mazzilli

LEE LOUIS MAZZILLI
B: 03/25/1955
BB

Year	Tm	Lg	Tot	H	A	0	1	2	3	2	3	4	LO	XN	IP	PH	RHP	LHP
1976	NY	NL	2	1	1	0	1	1	0	0	0	0	0	0	0	1	1	1
1977	NY	NL	6	3	3	3	3	0	0	0	0	0	0	0	0	0	5	1
1978	NY	NL	16	8	8	10	5	0	1	1	0	0	1	0	0	0	11	5
1979	NY	NL	15	6	9	6	6	3	0	1	0	0	0	1	0	0	10	5
1980	NY	NL	16	10	6	8	5	3	0	1	0	0	1	0	1	0	6	10
1981	NY	NL	6	1	5	4	2	0	0	0	0	0	0	0	0	0	5	1
1982	TEX	AL	4	2	2	1	3	0	0	0	0	0	0	0	0	0	2	2
	NY	AL	6	3	3	2	2	2	0	0	0	0	0	0	0	0	1	5
	Total		10	5	5	3	5	2	0	0	0	0	0	0	0	0	3	7
1983	PIT	NL	5	1	4	3	2	0	0	0	0	0	0	0	0	0	5	0
1984	PIT	NL	4	3	1	4	0	0	0	0	0	0	0	0	0	1	4	0
1985	PIT	NL	1	0	1	1	0	0	0	0	0	0	0	0	0	0	1	0
1986	PIT	NL	1	0	1	0	1	0	0	0	0	0	0	0	0	0	1	0
	NY	NL	2	1	1	1	1	0	0	0	0	0	0	0	0	0	1	1
	Total		3	1	2	1	2	0	0	0	0	0	0	0	0	0	2	1
1987	NY	NL	3	3	0	2	0	1	0	0	0	0	0	0	0	2	1	2
1989	NY	NL	2	1	1	1	0	1	0	0	0	0	0	0	0	1	2	0
	TOR	AL	4	2	2	3	1	0	0	0	0	0	0	0	0	1	4	0
	Total		6	3	3	4	1	1	0	0	0	0	0	0	0	2	6	0
Total			93	45	48	49	32	11	1	3	0	0	2	1	1	6	60	33

Rank among batters: 545 • *Top target (3 home runs)*: Steve Carlton, Bob Sykes, Rick Reuschel • *Number of pitchers victimized*: 77 • *Total ballparks homered in*: 20 • *First HR*: 09/08/1976 off Darold Knowles • *Switch hit HR in 1 game*—1 time • *All-Star HR*—1

Bill McAfee

WILLIAM FORT MCAFEE
B: 09/07/1907 D: 07/08/1958
BR

Year	Tm	Lg	Tot	H	A	0	1	2	3	2	3	4	LO	XN	IP	PH	RHP	LHP
1933	WAS	AL	1	0	1	1	0	0	0	0	0	0	0	0	0	0	1	0

Rank among batters: 4,707 • *Total ballparks homered in*: 1 • *First HR*: 07/24/1933 off George Earnshaw

Jimmy McAleer

JAMES ROBERT MCALEER
B: 07/10/1864 D: 04/29/1931
BR

Year	Tm	Lg	Tot	H	A	0	1	2	3	2	3	4	LO	XN	IP	PH	RHP	LHP
1890	CLE	PL	1	1	0	0	0	1	0	0	0	0	0	0	0	0	1	0
1891	CLE	NL	1	0	1	1	0	0	0	0	0	0	0	0	0	0	1	0
1892	CLE	NL	4	0	4	3	0	0	1	0	0	0	0	0	1	0	3	1
1893	CLE	NL	2	0	2	1	1	0	0	0	0	0	0	0	0	0	2	0
1894	CLE	NL	2	0	2	1	1	0	0	0	0	0	0	0	0	0	1	0
1896	CLE	NL	1	0	1	1	0	0	0	0	0	0	0	0	0	0	1	0
Total			11	1	10	7	2	1	1	0	0	0	0	0	1	0	9	1

Rank among batters: 2,419 • *Top target (2 home runs)*: Brickyard Kennedy • *Number of pitchers victimized*: 10 • *Total ballparks homered in*: 7 • *First HR*: 08/13/1890 off Bert Cunningham

Year	Tm	Lg	Tot	H	A	Men-On 0	1	2	3	One-Game 2	3	4	LO	XN	IP	PH	RHP	LHP

Sport McAllister

LEWIS WILLIAM MCALLISTER
B: 07/23/1874 D: 07/17/1962
BB

Year	Tm	Lg	Tot	H	A	0	1	2	3	2	3	4	LO	XN	IP	PH	RHP	LHP
1899	CLE	NL	1	0	1	1	0	0	0	0	0	0	0	0	0	0	1	0
1901	DET	AL	3	3	0	0	1	2	0	0	0	0	0	0	0	0	3	0
1902	DET	AL	1	1	0	0	0	1	0	0	0	0	0	0	0	0	1	0
Total			5	4	1	1	1	3	0	0	0	0	0	0	0	0	5	0

Rank among batters: 3,191 • *Total ballparks homered in*: 3 • *First HR*: 08/19/1899 off Sam Leever

Ernie McAnally

ERNEST LEE MCANALLY
B: 08/15/1946
BR

Year	Tm	Lg	Tot	H	A	0	1	2	3	2	3	4	LO	XN	IP	PH	RHP	LHP
1971	MON	NL	1	0	1	0	0	1	0	0	0	0	0	0	0	0	0	1

Rank among batters: 4,707 • *Total ballparks homered in*: 1 • *First HR*: 09/02/1971 off Juan Pizarro

Dick McAuliffe

RICHARD JOHN MCAULIFFE
B: 11/29/1939
BL

Year	Tm	Lg	Tot	H	A	0	1	2	3	2	3	4	LO	XN	IP	PH	RHP	LHP
1961	DET	AL	6	1	5	4	2	0	0	0	0	0	1	0	0	0	5	1
1962	DET	AL	12	5	7	7	2	3	0	0	0	0	0	0	0	0	8	4
1963	DET	AL	13	8	5	7	3	2	1	0	0	0	0	0	0	0	11	2
1964	DET	AL	24	13	11	14	8	1	1	1	0	0	0	2	0	0	20	4
1965	DET	AL	15	12	3	7	5	2	1	1	0	0	2	1	1	0	13	2
1966	DET	AL	23	9	14	16	4	2	1	1	0	0	5	0	0	1	19	4
1967	DET	AL	22	13	9	19	2	0	1	1	0	0	3	1	1	0	16	6
1968	DET	AL	16	10	6	14	2	0	0	0	0	0	2	0	0	0	13	3
1969	DET	AL	11	7	4	8	2	1	0	0	0	0	2	1	0	1	9	2
1970	DET	AL	12	7	5	7	4	0	1	1	0	0	2	0	0	0	11	1
1971	DET	AL	18	10	8	13	2	3	0	0	0	0	2	0	0	1	17	1
1972	DET	AL	8	3	5	4	2	2	0	1	0	0	0	0	0	0	8	0
1973	DET	AL	12	8	4	3	3	4	2	1	0	0	0	0	0	0	10	2
1974	BOS	AL	5	3	2	3	1	1	0	0	0	0	0	0	0	1	4	1
Total			197	109	88	126	42	21	8	7	0	0	19	5	2	4	164	33

Rank among batters: 189 • *Top target (6 home runs)*: Dean Chance • *Number of pitchers victimized*: 131 • *Total ballparks homered in*: 15 • *First HR*: 06/23/1961 off Dick Stigman • *World Series HR*—1; *LCS HR*—1; *All-Star HR*—1

Wickey McAvoy

JAMES EUGENE MCAVOY
B: 10/22/1894 D: 07/06/1973
BR

Year	Tm	Lg	Tot	H	A	0	1	2	3	2	3	4	LO	XN	IP	PH	RHP	LHP
1917	PHI	AL	1	1	0	1	0	0	0	0	0	0	0	0	0	0	1	0

Rank among batters: 4,707 • *Total ballparks homered in*: 1 • *First HR*: 09/28/1917 off Hooks Dauss

Al McBean

ALVIN O'NEAL MCBEAN
B: 05/15/1938
BR

Year	Tm	Lg	Tot	H	A	0	1	2	3	2	3	4	LO	XN	IP	PH	RHP	LHP
1961	PIT	NL	1	0	1	0	1	0	0	0	0	0	0	0	0	0	1	0
1963	PIT	NL	1	0	1	1	0	0	0	0	0	0	0	1	0	0	1	0
1968	PIT	NL	1	1	0	0	0	0	1	0	0	0	0	0	0	0	0	1
Total			3	1	2	1	1	0	1	0	0	0	0	1	0	0	2	1

Rank among batters: 3,735 • *Total ballparks homered in*: 3 • *First HR*: 08/05/1961 off Jay Hook

Algie McBride

ALGERNON GRIGGS MCBRIDE
B: 05/23/1869 D: 01/10/1956
BL

Year	Tm	Lg	Tot	H	A	0	1	2	3	2	3	4	LO	XN	IP	PH	RHP	LHP
1896	CHI	NL	1	0	1	1	0	0	0	0	0	0	0	0	1	0	0	1
1898	CIN	NL	2	1	1	2	0	0	0	0	0	0	0	0	2	0	2	0
1899	CIN	NL	1	0	1	1	0	0	0	0	0	0	1	0	0	0	1	0
1900	CIN	NL	4	2	2	1	3	0	0	0	0	0	0	0	2	0	3	1
1901	CIN	NL	2	1	1	1	1	0	0	0	0	0	0	0	2	0	2	0
	NY	NL	2	2	0	2	0	0	0	0	0	0	0	0	0	0	2	0
	Total		4	3	1	3	1	0	0	0	0	0	0	0	2	0	4	0

Year	Tm	Lg	Tot	H	A	Men-On				One-Game			LO	XN	IP	PH	RHP	LHP
						0	1	2	3	2	3	4						

Algie McBride *continued*

Year	Tm	Lg	Tot	H	A	0	1	2	3	2	3	4	LO	XN	IP	PH	RHP	LHP
Total			12	6	6	8	4	0	0	0	0	0	1	0	7	0	10	2

Rank among batters: 2,325 • *Top target (3 home runs)*: Jack Powell • *Number of pitchers victimized*: 9 • *Total ballparks homered in*: 6 • *First HR*: 05/29/1896 off Harley Payne

Bake McBride

ARNOLD RAY MCBRIDE
B: 02/03/1949
BL

Year	Tm	Lg	Tot	H	A	0	1	2	3	2	3	4	LO	XN	IP	PH	RHP	LHP
1974	STL	NL	6	4	2	2	3	1	0	0	0	0	0	1	1	0	4	2
1975	STL	NL	5	4	1	3	1	1	0	1	0	0	2	0	2	0	3	2
1976	STL	NL	3	1	2	1	2	0	0	0	0	0	0	0	0	1	3	0
1977	STL	NL	4	1	3	2	2	0	0	0	0	0	0	0	0	0	3	1
	PHI	NL	11	5	6	5	4	2	0	0	0	0	0	1	0	0	10	1
	Total		15	6	9	7	6	2	0	0	0	0	0	1	0	0	13	2
1978	PHI	NL	10	6	4	6	2	1	1	0	0	0	3	0	0	1	9	1
1979	PHI	NL	12	6	6	4	4	4	0	1	0	0	3	0	1	1	10	2
1980	PHI	NL	9	4	5	6	1	2	0	0	0	0	0	0	0	0	7	2
1981	PHI	NL	2	1	1	1	0	1	0	0	0	0	0	0	0	0	2	0
1983	CLE	AL	1	0	1	1	0	0	0	0	0	0	0	0	0	0	0	1
Total			63	32	31	31	19	12	1	2	0	0	8	2	4	3	51	12

Rank among batters: 826 • *Top target (5 home runs)*: Rick Reuschel • *Number of pitchers victimized*: 49 • *Total ballparks homered in*: 11 • *First HR*: 04/14/1974 off Bob Moose • *World Series HR*—1; *LCS HR*—2

George McBride

GEORGE FLORIAN MCBRIDE
B: 11/20/1880 D: 07/02/1973
BR

Year	Tm	Lg	Tot	H	A	0	1	2	3	2	3	4	LO	XN	IP	PH	RHP	LHP
1905	STL	NL	2	1	1	0	2	0	0	0	0	0	0	0	1	0	2	0
1910	WAS	AL	1	0	1	0	1	0	0	0	0	0	0	0	0	0	1	0
1912	WAS	AL	1	0	1	0	1	0	0	0	0	0	0	0	0	0	1	0
1913	WAS	AL	1	1	0	0	1	0	0	0	0	0	0	0	1	0	0	1
1915	WAS	AL	1	0	1	1	0	0	0	0	0	0	0	1	0	0	0	1
1916	WAS	AL	1	1	0	0	0	1	0	0	0	0	0	0	1	0	1	0
Total			7	3	4	1	5	1	0	0	0	0	0	1	3	0	5	2

Rank among batters: 2,834 • *Total ballparks homered in*: 6 • *First HR*: 08/29/1905 off Red Ames

Ken McBride

KENNETH FAYE MCBRIDE
B: 08/12/1935
BR

Year	Tm	Lg	Tot	H	A	0	1	2	3	2	3	4	LO	XN	IP	PH	RHP	LHP
1962	LA	AL	1	0	1	1	0	0	0	0	0	0	0	0	0	0	1	0

Rank among batters: 4,707 • *Total ballparks homered in*: 1 • *First HR*: 06/19/1962 off John Wyatt

Pete McBride

PETER WILLIAM MCBRIDE
B: 07/09/1875 D: 07/03/1944
BR

Year	Tm	Lg	Tot	H	A	0	1	2	3	2	3	4	LO	XN	IP	PH	RHP	LHP
1899	STL	NL	1	0	1	1	0	0	0	0	0	0	0	0	0	0	1	0

Rank among batters: 4,707 • *Total ballparks homered in*: 1 • *First HR*: 07/12/1899 off Jack Dunn

Tom McBride

THOMAS RAYMOND MCBRIDE
B: 11/02/1914
BR

Year	Tm	Lg	Tot	H	A	0	1	2	3	2	3	4	LO	XN	IP	PH	RHP	LHP
1945	BOS	AL	1	0	1	0	0	1	0	0	0	0	0	0	0	0	1	0
1948	WAS	AL	1	1	0	0	0	0	1	0	0	0	0	0	1	0	0	1
Total			2	1	1	0	0	1	1	0	0	0	0	0	1	0	1	1

Rank among batters: 4,129 • *Total ballparks homered in*: 2 • *First HR*: 06/27/1945 off Buck Ross

Joe McCabe

JOSEPH ROBERT MCCABE
B: 08/27/1938
BR

Year	Tm	Lg	Tot	H	A	0	1	2	3	2	3	4	LO	XN	IP	PH	RHP	LHP
1965	WAS	AL	1	0	1	1	0	0	0	0	0	0	0	0	0	0	0	1

Joe McCabe *continued*

Rank among batters: 4,707 • *Total ballparks homered in*: 1 • *First HR*: 05/02/1965 off Jack Kralick

Brian McCall

BRIAN ALLEN MCCALL
B: 01/25/1943
BL

Year	Tm	Lg	Tot	H	A	Men-On 0	1	2	3	One-Game 2	3	4	LO	XN	IP	PH	RHP	LHP
1962	CHI	AL	2	0	2	1	1	0	0	1	0	0	0	0	0	0	2	0

Rank among batters: 4,129 • *Total ballparks homered in*: 1 • *First HR*: 09/30/1962 off Bill Stafford

Jack McCandless

SCOTT COOK MCCANDLESS
B: 05/05/1891 D: 08/17/1961
BL

Year	Tm	Lg	Tot	H	A	Men-On 0	1	2	3	One-Game 2	3	4	LO	XN	IP	PH	RHP	LHP
1915	BAL	FL	5	3	2	4	1	0	0	0	0	0	1	0	0	0	3	2

Rank among batters: 3,191 • *Total ballparks homered in*: 3 • *First HR*: 07/01/1915 off Frank Allen

Bill McCarren

WILLIAM JOSEPH MCCARREN
B: 11/04/1895 D: 09/11/1983
BR

Year	Tm	Lg	Tot	H	A	Men-On 0	1	2	3	One-Game 2	3	4	LO	XN	IP	PH	RHP	LHP
1923	BRO	NL	3	1	2	2	1	0	0	0	0	0	0	0	1	0	3	0

Rank among batters: 3,735 • *Total ballparks homered in*: 3 • *First HR*: 06/13/1923 off Tiny Osborne

Alex McCarthy

ALEXANDER GEORGE MCCARTHY
B: 05/12/1888 D: 03/12/1978
BR

Year	Tm	Lg	Tot	H	A	Men-On 0	1	2	3	One-Game 2	3	4	LO	XN	IP	PH	RHP	LHP
1911	PIT	NL	2	2	0	0	1	1	0	0	0	0	0	0	1	0	2	0
1912	PIT	NL	1	1	0	0	1	0	0	0	0	0	0	0	0	0	0	1
1914	PIT	NL	1	0	1	1	0	0	0	0	0	0	0	0	0	0	1	0
1915	CHI	NL	1	1	0	0	1	0	0	0	0	0	0	0	1	0	1	0
Total			5	4	1	1	3	1	0	0	0	0	0	0	2	0	4	1

Rank among batters: 3,191 • *Total ballparks homered in*: 3 • *First HR*: 07/05/1911 off Rube Geyer

Jack McCarthy

JOHN ARTHUR MCCARTHY
B: 03/26/1869 D: 09/11/1931
BL

Year	Tm	Lg	Tot	H	A	Men-On 0	1	2	3	One-Game 2	3	4	LO	XN	IP	PH	RHP	LHP
1898	PIT	NL	4	2	2	3	0	1	0	0	0	0	0	0	0	0	3	1
1899	PIT	NL	3	1	2	2	1	0	0	0	0	0	0	0	0	0	3	0
Total			7	3	4	5	1	1	0	0	0	0	0	0	0	0	6	1

Rank among batters: 2,834 • *Total ballparks homered in*: 4 • *First HR*: 04/18/1898 off Dad Clarke

Johnny McCarthy

JOHN JOSEPH MCCARTHY
B: 01/07/1910 D: 09/13/1973
BL

Year	Tm	Lg	Tot	H	A	Men-On 0	1	2	3	One-Game 2	3	4	LO	XN	IP	PH	RHP	LHP
1934	BRO	NL	1	1	0	0	0	1	0	0	0	0	0	0	0	0	1	0
1936	NY	NL	1	0	1	0	1	0	0	0	0	0	0	0	0	0	1	0
1937	NY	NL	10	7	3	4	5	1	0	1	0	0	0	0	1	0	8	2
1938	NY	NL	8	6	2	3	0	5	0	0	0	0	0	0	1	0	6	2
1939	NY	NL	1	1	0	1	0	0	0	0	0	0	0	0	0	1	1	0
1943	BOS	NL	2	2	0	1	1	0	0	0	0	0	0	0	0	0	2	0
1948	NY	NL	2	1	1	1	1	0	0	0	0	0	0	0	0	1	1	1
Total			25	18	7	10	8	7	0	1	0	0	0	0	2	2	20	5

Rank among batters: 1,608 • *Top target (2 home runs)*: Si Johnson, Luke Hamlin, Rip Sewell • *Number of pitchers victimized*: 22 • *Total ballparks homered in*: 5 • *First HR*: 09/23/1934 off Syl Johnson

Tommy McCarthy

THOMAS FRANCIS MICHAEL MCCARTHY
B: 07/24/1863 D: 08/05/1922
BR HOF

Year	Tm	Lg	Tot	H	A	Men-On 0	1	2	3	One-Game 2	3	4	LO	XN	IP	PH	RHP	LHP
1888	STL	AA	1	1	0	1	0	0	0	0	0	0	0	0	0	0	0	1

Tommy McCarthy *continued*

Year	Tm	Lg	Tot	H	A	Men-On				One-Game			LO	XN	IP	PH	RHP	LHP
						0	1	2	3	2	3	4						
1889	STL	AA	2	2	0	1	0	1	0	0	0	0	1	0	0	0	2	0
1890	STL	AA	6	6	0	2	4	0	0	0	0	0	0	0	0	0	4	1
1891	STL	AA	8	5	3	2	4	1	1	0	0	0	0	0	0	0	7	0
1892	BOS	NL	4	3	1	1	3	0	0	1	0	0	1	0	0	0	4	0
1893	BOS	NL	5	3	2	0	4	1	0	0	0	0	0	0	0	0	4	1
1894	BOS	NL	13	10	3	7	5	1	0	3	0	0	0	0	0	0	12	1
1895	BOS	NL	2	2	0	1	0	0	1	0	0	0	0	0	0	0	2	0
1896	BRO	NL	3	3	0	2	0	1	0	0	0	0	0	0	1	0	2	1
Total			44	35	9	17	20	5	2	4	0	0	2	0	1	0	37	4

Rank among batters: 1,095 • *Top target (4 home runs)*: Adonis Terry • *Number of pitchers victimized*: 35 • *Total ballparks homered in*: 10 • *First HR*: 06/14/1888 off Toad Ramsey • *World Series HR*—1

David McCarty

DAVID ANDREW MCCARTY
B: 11/23/1969
BR

Year	Tm	Lg	Tot	H	A	Men-On				One-Game			LO	XN	IP	PH	RHP	LHP
						0	1	2	3	2	3	4						
1993	MIN	AL	2	2	0	2	0	0	0	0	0	0	0	0	0	0	2	0
1994	MIN	AL	1	1	0	0	1	0	0	0	0	0	0	0	0	0	0	1
Total			3	3	0	2	1	0	0	0	0	0	0	0	0	0	2	1

Rank among batters: 3,735 • *Total ballparks homered in*: 1 • *First HR*: 06/02/1993 off Roger Pavlik

Lew McCarty

GEORGE LEWIS MCCARTY
B: 11/17/1888 D: 06/09/1930
BR

Year	Tm	Lg	Tot	H	A	Men-On				One-Game			LO	XN	IP	PH	RHP	LHP
						0	1	2	3	2	3	4						
1914	BRO	NL	1	1	0	0	1	0	0	0	0	0	0	0	0	0	0	1
1917	NY	NL	2	2	0	0	2	0	0	0	0	0	0	0	0	0	2	0
1919	NY	NL	2	2	0	0	1	1	0	0	0	0	0	0	0	0	1	1
Total			5	5	0	0	4	1	0	0	0	0	0	0	0	0	3	2

Rank among batters: 3,191 • *Total ballparks homered in*: 2 • *First HR*: 09/22/1914 off Eral Yingling

Tim McCarver

JAMES TIMOTHY MCCARVER
B: 10/16/1941
BL

Year	Tm	Lg	Tot	H	A	Men-On				One-Game			LO	XN	IP	PH	RHP	LHP
						0	1	2	3	2	3	4						
1961	STL	NL	1	1	0	1	0	0	0	0	0	0	0	0	0	0	1	0
1963	STL	NL	4	2	2	1	0	2	1	0	0	0	0	0	1	0	2	2
1964	STL	NL	9	7	2	5	4	0	0	0	0	0	0	0	1	0	9	0
1965	STL	NL	11	9	2	6	4	0	1	0	0	0	0	0	0	0	9	2
1966	STL	NL	12	8	4	4	6	2	0	1	0	0	0	0	0	0	8	4
1967	STL	NL	14	7	7	8	3	2	1	0	0	0	0	0	0	1	12	2
1968	STL	NL	5	3	2	4	1	0	0	0	0	0	0	0	0	0	3	2
1969	STL	NL	7	2	5	4	1	1	1	0	0	0	0	0	0	0	6	1
1970	PHI	NL	4	1	3	2	2	0	0	0	0	0	0	0	0	0	3	1
1971	PHI	NL	8	6	2	2	4	2	0	0	0	0	0	0	0	1	8	0
1972	PHI	NL	2	1	1	2	0	0	0	0	0	0	0	0	0	0	2	0
	MON	NL	5	3	2	4	1	0	0	0	0	0	0	0	0	0	4	1
	Total		7	4	3	6	1	0	0	0	0	0	0	0	0	0	6	1
1973	STL	NL	3	2	1	0	2	0	1	0	0	0	0	0	0	1	3	0
1975	PHI	NL	1	1	0	1	0	0	0	0	0	0	0	0	0	0	1	0
1976	PHI	NL	3	2	1	1	1	1	0	0	0	0	0	0	0	0	3	0
1977	PHI	NL	6	3	3	3	1	1	1	1	0	0	0	0	0	1	6	0
1978	PHI	NL	1	0	1	0	0	1	0	0	0	0	0	0	0	0	1	0
1979	PHI	NL	1	1	0	0	0	1	0	0	0	0	0	0	0	0	1	0
Total			97	59	38	48	30	13	6	2	0	0	0	0	2	4	82	15

Rank among batters: 515 • *Top target (5 home runs)*: Jim Bunning • *Number of pitchers victimized*: 80 • *Total ballparks homered in*: 17 • *First HR*: 07/13/1961 off Tony Cloninger • *World Series HR*—2

Al McCauley

ALLEN A. MCCAULEY
B: 03/04/1863 D: 08/24/1917
BL

Year	Tm	Lg	Tot	H	A	Men-On				One-Game			LO	XN	IP	PH	RHP	LHP
						0	1	2	3	2	3	4						
1890	PHI	NL	1	0	1	0	1	0	0	0	0	0	0	0	0	0	1	0

Al McCauley *continued*

Year	Tm	Lg	Tot	H	A	Men-On 0	1	2	3	One-Game 2	3	4	LO	XN	IP	PH	RHP	LHP
1891	WAS	AA	1	0	1	0	1	0	0	0	0	0	0	0	0	0	1	0
Total			2	0	2	0	2	0	0	0	0	0	0	0	0	0	2	0

Rank among batters: 4,129 • *Total ballparks homered in*: 2 • *First HR*: 06/14/1890 off Kid Nichols

Pat McCauley

PATRICK M. MCCAULEY
B: 06/10/1870 D: 01/23/1917

Year	Tm	Lg	Tot	H	A	Men-On 0	1	2	3	One-Game 2	3	4	LO	XN	IP	PH	RHP	LHP
1896	WAS	NL	3	1	2	1	1	1	0	0	0	0	0	0	1	0	1	2

Rank among batters: 3,735 • *Total ballparks homered in*: 3 • *First HR*: 04/17/1896 off Ed Doheny

Bill McClellan

WILLIAM HENRY MCCLELLAN
B: 03/22/1856 D: 07/03/1929
BL

Year	Tm	Lg	Tot	H	A	Men-On 0	1	2	3	One-Game 2	3	4	LO	XN	IP	PH	RHP	LHP
1883	PHI	NL	1	0	1	1	0	0	0	0	0	0	0	0	0	0	1	0
1884	PHI	NL	3	0	3	3	0	0	0	0	0	0	0	0	0	0	3	0
1886	BRO	AA	1	1	0	0	0	1	0	0	0	0	0	0	0	0	1	0
1887	BRO	AA	1	1	0	1	0	0	0	0	0	0	0	0	0	0	1	0
Total			6	2	4	5	0	1	0	0	0	0	0	0	0	0	6	0

Rank among batters: 2,988 • *Total ballparks homered in*: 4 • *First HR*: 06/20/1883 off Jim Whitney

Harvey McClellan

HARVEY MCDOWELL MCCLELLAN
B: 12/22/1894 D: 11/06/1925
BR

Year	Tm	Lg	Tot	H	A	Men-On 0	1	2	3	One-Game 2	3	4	LO	XN	IP	PH	RHP	LHP
1921	CHI	AL	1	0	1	0	0	1	0	0	0	0	0	0	0	0	1	0
1922	CHI	AL	2	0	2	1	0	1	0	0	0	0	0	0	0	0	2	0
1923	CHI	AL	1	0	1	1	0	0	0	0	0	0	0	1	0	0	1	0
Total			4	0	4	2	0	2	0	0	0	0	0	1	0	0	4	0

Rank among batters: 3,427 • *Total ballparks homered in*: 3 • *First HR*: 07/30/1921 off Bob Hasty

Lloyd McClendon

LLOYD GLENN MCCLENDON
B: 01/11/1959
BR

Year	Tm	Lg	Tot	H	A	Men-On 0	1	2	3	One-Game 2	3	4	LO	XN	IP	PH	RHP	LHP
1987	CIN	NL	2	0	2	1	1	0	0	0	0	0	0	0	0	1	1	1
1988	CIN	NL	3	0	3	0	3	0	0	0	0	0	0	0	0	1	2	1
1989	CHI	NL	12	9	3	9	2	1	0	0	0	0	0	0	0	1	6	6
1990	CHI	NL	1	0	1	0	0	0	1	0	0	0	0	0	0	0	0	1
	PIT	NL	1	0	1	0	1	0	0	0	0	0	0	0	0	1	0	1
	Total		2	0	2	0	1	0	1	0	0	0	0	0	0	1	0	2
1991	PIT	NL	7	2	5	4	2	1	0	1	0	0	0	0	0	2	1	6
1992	PIT	NL	3	3	0	2	0	0	1	0	0	0	0	0	0	0	1	2
1993	PIT	NL	2	1	1	2	0	0	0	0	0	0	0	0	0	0	2	0
1994	PIT	NL	4	2	2	3	1	0	0	0	0	0	0	0	0	2	1	3
Total			35	17	18	21	10	2	2	1	0	0	0	0	0	8	14	21

Rank among batters: 1,291 • *Top target (2 home runs)*: Dennis Rasmussen, Tom Glavine, Sid Fernandez • *Number of pitchers victimized*: 32 • *Total ballparks homered in*: 8 • *First HR*: 05/17/1987 off Lee Tunnell • *LCS HR*—1

Amby McConnell

AMBROSE MOSES MCCONNELL
B: 04/29/1883 D: 05/20/1942
BL

Year	Tm	Lg	Tot	H	A	Men-On 0	1	2	3	One-Game 2	3	4	LO	XN	IP	PH	RHP	LHP
1908	BOS	AL	2	1	1	1	0	1	0	0	0	0	0	0	1	0	2	0
1911	CHI	AL	1	0	1	0	1	0	0	0	0	0	0	0	0	0	1	0
Total			3	1	2	1	1	1	0	0	0	0	0	0	1	0	3	0

Rank among batters: 3,735 • *Total ballparks homered in*: 3 • *First HR*: 06/07/1908 off Ed Summers

George McConnell

GEORGE NEELY MCCONNELL
B: 09/16/1877 D: 05/10/1964
BR

Year	Tm	Lg	Tot	H	A	Men-On 0	1	2	3	One-Game 2	3	4	LO	XN	IP	PH	RHP	LHP
1915	CHI	FL	1	0	1	0	1	0	0	0	0	0	0	0	0	0	1	0

Rank among batters: 4,707 • *Total ballparks homered in*: 1 • *First HR*: 08/16/1915 off George Suggs

Year	Tm	Lg	Tot	H	A	Men-On				One-Game			LO	XN	IP	PH	RHP	LHP
						0	1	2	3	2	3	4						

Barry McCormick

WILLIAM J. MCCORMICK
B: 12/25/1874 D: 01/28/1956

Year	Tm	Lg	Tot	H	A	0	1	2	3	2	3	4	LO	XN	IP	PH	RHP	LHP
1896	CHI	NL	1	1	0	0	1	0	0	0	0	0	0	0	0	0	1	0
1897	CHI	NL	2	1	1	0	1	1	0	0	0	0	0	0	0	0	2	0
1898	CHI	NL	2	1	1	1	0	1	0	0	0	0	0	0	0	0	2	0
1899	CHI	NL	2	2	0	0	1	1	0	0	0	0	0	0	0	0	2	0
1900	CHI	NL	3	1	2	1	1	1	0	0	0	0	0	0	0	0	2	1
1901	CHI	NL	1	0	1	1	0	0	0	0	0	0	0	0	1	0	0	1
1902	STL	AL	3	2	1	3	0	0	0	0	0	0	0	0	0	0	2	1
1903	STL	AL	1	0	1	1	0	0	0	0	0	0	0	0	0	0	1	0
Total			15	8	7	7	4	4	0	0	0	0	0	0	1	0	12	3

Rank among batters: 2,096 • *Top target (2 home runs)*: Cowboy Jones • *Number of pitchers victimized*: 14 • *Total ballparks homered in*: 9 • *First HR*: 07/01/1896 off Zeke Wilson

Frank McCormick

FRANK ANDREW MCCORMICK
B: 06/09/1911 D: 11/21/1982
BR

Year	Tm	Lg	Tot	H	A	0	1	2	3	2	3	4	LO	XN	IP	PH	RHP	LHP
1938	CIN	NL	5	3	2	2	2	1	0	0	0	0	0	0	0	0	4	1
1939	CIN	NL	18	11	7	8	8	1	1	0	0	0	0	0	0	0	18	0
1940	CIN	NL	19	10	9	10	4	4	1	0	0	0	0	0	0	0	18	1
1941	CIN	NL	17	11	6	13	1	3	0	1	0	0	0	0	0	0	17	0
1942	CIN	NL	13	8	5	5	7	1	0	0	0	0	0	0	0	0	13	0
1943	CIN	NL	8	3	5	5	2	0	1	0	0	0	0	1	0	0	7	1
1944	CIN	NL	20	7	13	6	7	7	0	1	0	0	0	2	0	0	19	1
1945	CIN	NL	10	3	7	4	3	3	0	0	0	0	0	1	0	0	10	0
1946	PHI	NL	11	5	6	5	3	2	1	0	0	0	0	0	0	0	10	1
1947	PHI	NL	1	1	0	1	0	0	0	0	0	0	0	0	0	0	1	0
	BOS	NL	2	0	2	1	0	1	0	0	0	0	0	0	0	0	1	1
	Total		3	1	2	2	0	1	0	0	0	0	0	0	0	0	2	1
1948	BOS	NL	4	0	4	2	2	0	0	0	0	0	0	0	0	0	1	3
Total			128	62	66	62	39	23	4	2	0	0	0	4	0	0	119	9

Rank among batters: 356 • *Top target (6 home runs)*: Harry Feldman • *Number of pitchers victimized*: 84 • *Total ballparks homered in*: 8 • *First HR*: 04/28/1938 off Bill Lee

Harry McCormick

PATRICK HENRY MCCORMICK
B: 10/25/1855 D: 08/08/1889
BR

Year	Tm	Lg	Tot	H	A	0	1	2	3	2	3	4	LO	XN	IP	PH	RHP	LHP
1879	SYR	NL	1	1	0	1	0	0	0	0	0	0	0	0	0	0	1	0

Rank among batters: 4,707 • *Total ballparks homered in*: 1 • *First HR*: 07/26/1879 off Tommy Bond

Jim McCormick

JAMES MCCORMICK
B: 11/03/1856 D: 03/10/1918
BR

Year	Tm	Lg	Tot	H	A	0	1	2	3	2	3	4	LO	XN	IP	PH	RHP	LHP
1882	CLE	NL	2	1	1	1	0	0	0	0	0	0	0	0	0	0	2	0
1886	CHI	NL	2	1	1	1	1	0	0	0	0	0	0	0	0	0	2	0
Total			4	2	2	2	1	0	0	0	0	0	0	0	0	0	4	0

Rank among batters: 3,427 • *Total ballparks homered in*: 4 • *First HR*: 08/19/1882 off Frank Mountain

Mike McCormick

MYRON WINTHROP MCCORMICK
B: 05/06/1917 D: 04/14/1976
BR

Year	Tm	Lg	Tot	H	A	0	1	2	3	2	3	4	LO	XN	IP	PH	RHP	LHP
1940	CIN	NL	1	0	1	1	0	0	0	0	0	0	0	1	0	0	1	0
1941	CIN	NL	4	2	2	1	1	2	0	0	0	0	0	0	0	0	4	0
1942	CIN	NL	1	0	1	1	0	0	0	0	0	0	0	0	1	0	1	0
1946	BOS	NL	1	0	1	1	0	0	0	0	0	0	0	0	0	0	0	1
1947	BOS	NL	3	0	3	3	0	0	0	0	0	0	0	0	0	1	2	1
1948	BOS	NL	1	0	1	1	0	0	0	0	0	0	0	0	0	0	0	1
1949	BRO	NL	2	1	1	1	0	1	0	0	0	0	0	0	0	1	0	2
1951	WAS	AL	1	0	1	0	0	0	1	0	0	0	0	0	0	0	0	1
Total			14	3	11	9	1	3	1	0	0	0	0	1	1	2	8	6

Rank among batters: 2,169 • *Total ballparks homered in*: 7 • *First HR*: 05/14/1940 off Newt Kimball

Mike McCormick

MICHAEL FRANCIS MCCORMICK
B: 09/29/1938
BL

Year	Tm	Lg	Tot	H	A	Men-On 0	1	2	3	One-Game 2	3	4	LO	XN	IP	PH	RHP	LHP
1962	SF	NL	1	0	1	1	0	0	0	0	0	0	0	0	0	0	0	1
1963	BAL	AL	1	0	1	1	0	0	0	0	0	0	0	0	0	0	0	1
1966	WAS	AL	2	0	2	2	0	0	0	0	0	0	0	0	0	0	2	0
1967	SF	NL	1	0	1	0	1	0	0	0	0	0	0	0	0	0	1	0
1968	SF	NL	1	1	0	0	1	0	0	0	0	0	0	0	0	0	1	0
1969	SF	NL	1	0	1	1	0	0	0	0	0	0	0	1	0	0	1	0
Total			7	1	6	5	2	0	0	0	0	0	0	1	0	0	5	2

Rank among batters: 2,834 • *Total ballparks homered in*: 7 • *First HR*: 05/09/1962 off Curt Simmons

Moose McCormick

HARRY ELWOOD MCCORMICK
B: 02/28/1881 D: 07/09/1962
BL

Year	Tm	Lg	Tot	H	A	Men-On 0	1	2	3	One-Game 2	3	4	LO	XN	IP	PH	RHP	LHP
1904	NY	NL	1	1	0	0	0	1	0	0	0	0	0	0	0	0	1	0
	PIT	NL	2	0	2	0	1	1	0	0	0	0	0	0	1	0	2	0
	Total		3	1	2	1	1	1	0	0	0	0	0	0	1	0	3	0
1909	NY	NL	3	3	0	3	0	0	0	0	0	0	0	0	1	0	1	2
Total			6	4	2	4	1	1	0	0	0	0	0	0	2	0	4	2

Rank among batters: 2,988 • *Total ballparks homered in*: 2 • *First HR*: 04/25/1904 off Ed Poole

Barney McCosky

WILLIAM BARNEY MCCOSKY
B: 04/11/1917
BL

Year	Tm	Lg	Tot	H	A	Men-On 0	1	2	3	One-Game 2	3	4	LO	XN	IP	PH	RHP	LHP
1939	DET	AL	4	1	3	3	0	1	0	0	0	0	1	0	0	0	4	0
1940	DET	AL	4	2	2	3	0	1	0	1	0	0	1	0	1	0	2	2
1941	DET	AL	3	2	1	1	0	2	0	0	0	0	0	0	0	0	3	0
1942	DET	AL	7	5	2	4	3	0	0	0	0	0	0	0	1	0	7	0
1946	DET	AL	1	1	0	0	1	0	0	0	0	0	0	0	0	0	1	0
	PHI	AL	1	1	0	1	0	0	0	0	0	0	0	0	1	0	1	0
	Total		2	2	0	1	1	0	0	0	0	0	0	0	1	0	2	0
1947	PHI	AL	1	0	1	1	0	0	0	0	0	0	0	0	0	0	1	0
1951	PHI	AL	1	0	1	1	0	0	0	0	0	0	0	0	0	0	1	0
	CIN	NL	1	1	0	0	1	0	0	0	0	0	0	0	0	0	1	0
	Total		2	1	1	1	1	0	0	0	0	0	0	0	0	0	2	0
1952	CLE	AL	1	0	1	1	0	0	0	0	0	0	0	0	0	1	1	0
Total			24	13	11	15	5	4	0	1	0	0	2	0	3	1	22	2

Rank among batters: 1,643 • Top target (2 home runs): Al Milnar, Johnny Niggeling, Joe Haynes, Vic Raschi • *Number of pitchers victimized*: 20 • *Total ballparks homered in*: 7 • *First HR*: 04/21/1939 off Bob Feller

Willie McCovey

WILLIE LEE MCCOVEY
B: 01/10/1938
BL HOF

Year	Tm	Lg	Tot	H	A	Men-On 0	1	2	3	One-Game 2	3	4	LO	XN	IP	PH	RHP	LHP
1959	SF	NL	13	8	5	9	4	0	0	1	0	0	0	0	0	0	8	5
1960	SF	NL	13	4	9	6	4	2	1	1	0	0	0	0	0	1	13	0
1961	SF	NL	18	9	9	12	4	2	0	2	0	0	0	0	0	2	18	0
1962	SF	NL	20	12	8	11	5	4	0	3	0	0	0	0	0	2	19	1
1963	SF	NL	44	26	18	25	16	3	0	4	1	0	0	1	0	0	37	7
1964	SF	NL	18	8	10	11	6	0	1	0	1	0	0	0	0	1	14	4
1965	SF	NL	39	22	17	21	11	6	1	2	0	0	0	1	0	1	29	10
1966	SF	NL	36	22	14	17	15	3	1	2	1	0	0	2	0	2	28	8
1967	SF	NL	31	13	18	15	7	6	3	1	0	0	0	0	1	0	23	8
1968	SF	NL	36	20	16	21	6	8	1	3	0	0	0	1	0	0	27	9
1969	SF	NL	45	22	23	22	18	3	2	5	0	0	0	0	0	0	38	7
1970	SF	NL	39	16	23	18	13	6	2	5	0	0	0	1	0	0	32	7
1971	SF	NL	18	9	9	7	6	4	1	1	0	0	0	1	0	1	14	4
1972	SF	NL	14	8	6	8	5	0	1	1	0	0	0	0	0	0	11	3
1973	SF	NL	29	21	8	19	6	4	0	4	0	0	0	1	0	0	23	6
1974	SD	NL	22	10	12	14	4	3	1	1	0	0	0	0	0	0	20	2
1975	SD	NL	23	11	12	13	6	3	1	1	0	0	0	0	0	2	20	3
1976	SD	NL	7	4	3	4	1	2	0	0	0	0	0	0	0	1	7	0
1977	SF	NL	28	6	22	12	12	2	2	3	0	0	0	0	0	0	21	7

Willie McCovey *continued*

Year	Tm	Lg	Tot	H	A	Men-On 0	1	2	3	One-Game 2	3	4	LO	XN	IP	PH	RHP	LHP
1978	SF	NL	12	4	8	7	3	2	0	0	0	0	0	0	0	1	5	7
1979	SF	NL	15	9	6	8	3	4	0	1	0	0	0	2	0	2	13	2
1980	SF	NL	1	0	1	1	0	0	0	0	0	0	0	0	0	0	1	0
Total			521	264	257	281	155	67	18	41	3	0	0	10	1	16	421	100

Rank among batters: 10 • *Top target (12 home runs)*: Don Drysdale • *Number of pitchers victimized*: 245 • *Total ballparks homered in*: 22 • *First HR*: 08/02/1959 off Ron Kline • *2 HR in 1 inning*—vs HOU: 04/12/1973; @CIN: 06/27/1977 • *World Series HR*—1; *LCS HR*—2; *All-Star HR*—2

Benny McCoy

BENJAMIN JENISON MCCOY
B: 11/09/1915
BL

Year	Tm	Lg	Tot	H	A	Men-On 0	1	2	3	One-Game 2	3	4	LO	XN	IP	PH	RHP	LHP
1939	DET	AL	1	1	0	0	1	0	0	0	0	0	0	0	0	0	1	0
1940	PHI	AL	7	2	5	2	3	2	0	0	0	0	0	0	0	0	6	1
1941	PHI	AL	8	4	4	4	2	1	1	0	0	0	0	0	0	0	8	0
Total			16	7	9	6	6	3	1	0	0	0	0	0	0	0	15	1

Rank among batters: 2,029 • *Total ballparks homered in*: 6 • *First HR*: 08/14/1939 off Willis Hudlin

Tommy McCraw

TOMMY LEE MCCRAW
B: 11/21/1940
BL

Year	Tm	Lg	Tot	H	A	Men-On 0	1	2	3	One-Game 2	3	4	LO	XN	IP	PH	RHP	LHP
1963	CHI	AL	6	2	4	1	2	3	0	1	0	0	0	0	0	0	5	1
1964	CHI	AL	6	2	4	5	1	0	0	0	0	0	1	0	0	0	4	2
1965	CHI	AL	5	3	2	2	2	0	1	0	0	0	0	0	0	0	4	1
1966	CHI	AL	5	3	2	2	2	0	1	1	0	0	0	0	0	0	4	1
1967	CHI	AL	11	3	8	4	4	3	0	1	1	0	0	0	0	0	6	5
1968	CHI	AL	9	3	6	4	2	2	1	0	0	0	0	0	0	0	7	2
1969	CHI	AL	2	2	0	1	1	0	0	0	0	0	0	0	0	0	2	0
1970	CHI	AL	6	0	6	4	2	0	0	0	0	0	0	0	0	0	4	2
1971	WAS	AL	7	3	4	6	1	0	0	0	0	0	0	1	1	3	7	0
1972	CLE	AL	7	3	4	4	2	1	0	0	0	0	0	0	1	1	4	3
1973	CAL	AL	3	0	3	2	1	0	0	0	0	0	0	0	0	0	3	0
1974	CAL	AL	3	1	2	2	1	0	0	1	0	0	0	0	0	0	2	1
	CLE	AL	3	2	1	2	1	0	0	0	0	0	0	0	0	0	2	1
	Total		6	3	3	4	2	0	0	1	0	0	0	0	0	0	4	2
1975	CLE	AL	2	1	1	1	1	0	0	0	0	0	0	0	0	0	1	1
Total			75	28	47	40	23	9	3	4	1	0	1	1	2	4	55	20

Rank among batters: 699 • *Top target (3 home runs)*: Mel Stottlemyre, Catfish Hunter, Luis Tiant • *Number of pitchers victimized*: 62 • *Total ballparks homered in*: 14 • *First HR*: 06/19/1963 off Dick Stigman

Tom McCreery

THOMAS LIVINGSTON MCCREERY
B: 10/19/1874 D: 07/03/1941
BB

Year	Tm	Lg	Tot	H	A	Men-On 0	1	2	3	One-Game 2	3	4	LO	XN	IP	PH	RHP	LHP
1896	LOU	NL	7	6	1	4	3	0	0	0	0	0	0	0	1	0	6	1
1897	LOU	NL	4	3	1	2	1	1	0	0	1	0	0	0	3	0	4	0
	NY	NL	1	1	0	1	0	0	0	0	0	0	0	0	0	0	1	0
	Total		5	4	1	3	1	1	0	0	1	0	0	0	3	0	5	0
1898	NY	NL	1	1	0	0	0	1	0	0	0	0	0	0	0	0	1	0
	PIT	NL	2	2	0	1	0	1	0	0	0	0	0	0	1	0	1	1
	Total		3	3	0	1	0	2	0	0	0	0	0	0	1	0	2	1
1899	PIT	NL	2	1	1	2	0	0	0	0	0	0	0	0	1	0	1	0
1900	PIT	NL	1	1	0	1	0	0	0	0	0	0	0	0	0	0	0	1
1901	BRO	NL	3	3	0	2	0	1	0	0	0	0	0	0	1	0	2	1
1902	BRO	NL	4	3	1	3	0	1	0	0	0	0	0	0	1	0	4	0
1903	BOS	NL	1	0	1	0	1	0	0	0	0	0	0	0	1	0	1	0
Total			26	21	5	16	5	5	0	0	1	0	0	0	9	0	21	4

Rank among batters: 1,576 • *Top target (3 home runs)*: Jack Taylor • *Number of pitchers victimized*: 21 • *Total ballparks homered in*: 6 • *First HR*: 05/14/1896 off Bert Inks

Clyde McCullough

CLYDE EDWARD MCCULLOUGH
B: 03/04/1917 D: 09/18/1982
BR

Year	Tm	Lg	Tot	H	A	Men-On 0	1	2	3	One-Game 2	3	4	LO	XN	IP	PH	RHP	LHP
1941	CHI	NL	9	1	8	3	2	4	0	0	0	0	0	0	0	0	7	2

Clyde McCullough *continued*

Year	Tm	Lg	Tot	H	A	Men-On 0	1	2	3	One-Game 2	3	4	LO	XN	IP	PH	RHP	LHP
1942	CHI	NL	5	1	4	4	1	0	0	0	1	0	0	0	0	0	5	0
1943	CHI	NL	2	0	2	1	1	0	0	0	0	0	0	0	0	0	1	1
1946	CHI	NL	4	1	3	1	2	1	0	0	0	0	0	1	0	0	2	2
1947	CHI	NL	3	2	1	2	1	0	0	0	0	0	0	0	0	0	2	1
1948	CHI	NL	1	0	1	1	0	0	0	0	0	0	0	0	0	0	1	0
1949	PIT	NL	4	2	2	3	1	0	0	0	0	0	0	0	0	0	3	1
1950	PIT	NL	6	5	1	5	1	0	0	0	0	0	0	0	0	0	5	1
1951	PIT	NL	8	5	3	5	3	0	0	0	0	0	0	0	0	0	7	1
1952	PIT	NL	1	0	1	1	0	0	0	0	0	0	0	0	0	0	1	0
1953	CHI	NL	6	2	4	4	2	0	0	0	0	0	0	0	0	0	5	1
1954	CHI	NL	3	1	2	2	0	0	1	0	0	0	0	0	0	0	2	1
Total			52	20	32	32	14	5	1	0	1	0	0	1	0	0	41	11

Rank among batters: 965 • *Top target (3 home runs)*: Tommy Hughes • *Number of pitchers victimized*: 45 • *Total ballparks homered in*: 9 • *First HR*: 04/20/1941 off Max Lanier

Harry McCurdy

HARRY HENRY MCCURDY
B: 09/15/1899 D: 07/21/1972
BL

Year	Tm	Lg	Tot	H	A	Men-On 0	1	2	3	One-Game 2	3	4	LO	XN	IP	PH	RHP	LHP
1926	CHI	AL	1	1	0	1	0	0	0	0	0	0	0	0	0	0	1	0
1927	CHI	AL	1	0	1	0	0	1	0	0	0	0	0	0	0	0	1	0
1928	CHI	AL	2	0	2	0	1	0	1	0	0	0	0	0	0	0	2	0
1930	PHI	NL	1	0	1	1	0	0	0	0	0	0	0	0	0	0	1	0
1931	PHI	NL	1	1	0	1	0	0	0	0	0	0	0	0	0	0	1	0
1932	PHI	NL	1	1	0	0	1	0	0	0	0	0	0	0	0	0	1	0
1933	PHI	NL	2	2	0	0	1	1	0	0	0	0	0	0	0	2	2	0
Total			9	5	4	3	3	2	1	0	0	0	0	0	0	2	9	0

Rank among batters: 2,587 • *Total ballparks homered in*: 6 • *First HR*: 09/06/1926 off Rip Collins

Lindy McDaniel

LYNDALL DALE MCDANIEL
B: 12/13/1935
BR

Year	Tm	Lg	Tot	H	A	Men-On 0	1	2	3	One-Game 2	3	4	LO	XN	IP	PH	RHP	LHP
1957	STL	NL	1	0	1	1	0	0	0	0	0	0	0	0	0	0	1	0
1963	CHI	NL	1	1	0	1	0	0	0	0	0	0	0	1	0	0	0	1
1972	NY	AL	1	0	1	1	0	0	0	0	0	0	0	0	0	0	0	1
Total			3	1	2	3	0	0	0	0	0	0	0	1	0	0	1	2

Rank among batters: 3,735 • *Total ballparks homered in*: 3 • *First HR*: 05/04/1957 off Roger Craig

Mickey McDermott

MAURICE JOSEPH MCDERMOTT
B: 04/29/1928
BL

Year	Tm	Lg	Tot	H	A	Men-On 0	1	2	3	One-Game 2	3	4	LO	XN	IP	PH	RHP	LHP
1951	BOS	AL	1	1	0	0	0	1	0	0	0	0	0	0	0	0	1	0
1952	BOS	AL	1	0	1	0	0	1	0	0	0	0	0	0	0	0	1	0
1953	BOS	AL	1	0	1	1	0	0	0	0	0	0	0	0	0	0	1	0
1955	WAS	AL	1	0	1	1	0	0	0	0	0	0	0	0	0	0	0	1
1956	NY	AL	1	1	0	1	0	0	0	0	0	0	0	0	1	0	1	0
1957	KC	AL	4	1	3	3	1	0	0	0	0	0	0	0	0	2	4	0
Total			9	3	6	6	1	2	0	0	0	0	0	0	1	2	8	1

Rank among batters: 2,587 • *Total ballparks homered in*: 6 • *First HR*: 08/03/1951 off Dizzy Trout

Dave McDonald

DAVID BRUCE MCDONALD
B: 05/20/1943
BL

Year	Tm	Lg	Tot	H	A	Men-On 0	1	2	3	One-Game 2	3	4	LO	XN	IP	PH	RHP	LHP
1971	MON	NL	1	1	0	1	0	0	0	0	0	0	0	0	0	0	1	0

Rank among batters: 4,707 • *Total ballparks homered in*: 1 • *First HR*: 07/02/1971 off Rick Wise

Ed McDonald

EDWARD C. MCDONALD
B: 10/28/1886 D: 03/11/1946
BR

Year	Tm	Lg	Tot	H	A	Men-On 0	1	2	3	One-Game 2	3	4	LO	XN	IP	PH	RHP	LHP
1911	BOS	NL	1	0	1	0	1	0	0	0	0	0	0	0	0	0	1	0

Ed McDonald *continued*

Year	Tm	Lg	Tot	H	A	Men-On 0	1	2	3	One-Game 2	3	4	LO	XN	IP	PH	RHP	LHP
1912	BOS	NL	2	0	2	2	0	0	0	0	0	0	1	0	0	0	2	0
Total			3	0	3	2	1	0	0	0	0	0	1	0	0	0	3	0

Rank among batters: 3,735 • *Total ballparks homered in*: 2 • *First HR*: 09/29/1911 off Harry Gaspar

Tex McDonald

CHARLES C. MCDONALD
B: 01/31/1891 D: 03/31/1943
BL

Year	Tm	Lg	Tot	H	A	Men-On 0	1	2	3	One-Game 2	3	4	LO	XN	IP	PH	RHP	LHP
1912	CIN	NL	1	0	1	1	0	0	0	0	0	0	0	0	0	0	1	0
1914	PIT	FL	3	0	3	1	1	1	0	0	0	0	0	0	0	0	3	0
	BUF	FL	3	1	2	1	2	0	0	0	0	0	0	0	0	0	3	0
	Total		6	1	5	2	3	1	0	0	0	0	0	0	0	0	6	0
1915	BUF	FL	6	3	3	5	1	0	0	0	0	0	0	0	0	0	6	0
Total			13	4	9	8	4	1	0	0	0	0	0	0	0	0	13	0

Rank among batters: 2,248 • *Top target (2 home runs)*: Cy Falkenberg • *Number of pitchers victimized*: 12 • *Total ballparks homered in*: 7 • *First HR*: 06/12/1912 off George Chalmers

Gil McDougald

GILBERT JAMES MCDOUGALD
B: 05/19/1928
BR

Year	Tm	Lg	Tot	H	A	Men-On 0	1	2	3	One-Game 2	3	4	LO	XN	IP	PH	RHP	LHP
1951	NY	AL	14	7	7	7	6	0	1	0	0	0	0	0	1	0	11	3
1952	NY	AL	11	1	10	5	3	3	0	1	0	0	0	0	0	0	5	6
1953	NY	AL	10	3	7	5	2	3	0	0	0	0	1	1	0	0	4	6
1954	NY	AL	12	2	10	7	1	3	1	0	0	0	3	0	0	0	7	5
1955	NY	AL	13	4	9	11	2	0	0	0	0	0	1	0	0	0	10	3
1956	NY	AL	13	2	11	7	2	4	0	0	0	0	1	0	0	0	8	5
1957	NY	AL	13	6	7	8	5	0	0	1	0	0	0	0	0	0	12	1
1958	NY	AL	14	4	10	5	5	4	0	1	0	0	0	0	0	0	11	3
1959	NY	AL	4	0	4	3	1	0	0	0	0	0	0	0	0	0	3	1
1960	NY	AL	8	0	8	6	1	1	0	1	0	0	1	0	0	0	7	1
Total			112	29	83	64	28	18	2	4	0	0	7	1	1	0	78	34

Rank among batters: 429 • *Top target (6 home runs)*: Bob Lemon, Early Wynn • *Number of pitchers victimized*: 74 • *Total ballparks homered in*: 10 • *First HR*: 05/03/1951 off Bobby Herrera • *World Series HR*—7

Oddibe McDowell

ODDIBE MCDOWELL
B: 08/25/1962
BL

Year	Tm	Lg	Tot	H	A	Men-On 0	1	2	3	One-Game 2	3	4	LO	XN	IP	PH	RHP	LHP
1985	TEX	AL	18	10	8	14	4	0	0	0	0	0	2	0	0	1	15	3
1986	TEX	AL	18	8	10	15	2	1	0	1	0	0	4	1	0	1	15	3
1987	TEX	AL	14	5	9	10	2	1	1	1	0	0	1	1	0	0	12	2
1988	TEX	AL	6	4	2	6	0	0	0	0	0	0	1	0	0	0	4	2
1989	CLE	AL	3	1	2	0	2	1	0	0	0	0	0	0	0	1	3	0
	ATL	NL	7	2	5	5	2	0	0	1	0	0	2	0	0	1	7	0
	Total		10	3	7	5	4	1	0	1	0	0	2	0	0	2	10	0
1990	ATL	NL	7	4	3	4	1	2	0	0	0	0	2	1	0	0	7	0
1994	TEX	AL	1	1	0	1	0	0	0	0	0	0	0	0	0	0	1	0
Total			74	35	39	55	13	5	1	3	0	0	12	3	0	4	64	10

Rank among batters: 707 • *Top target (5 home runs)*: Bert Blyleven • *Number of pitchers victimized*: 59 • *Total ballparks homered in*: 21 • *First HR*: 06/08/1985 off Keith Atherton • *Hit for Cycle*—vs CLE: 07/23/1985

Sam McDowell

SAMUEL EDWARD MCDOWELL
B: 09/21/1942
BL

Year	Tm	Lg	Tot	H	A	Men-On 0	1	2	3	One-Game 2	3	4	LO	XN	IP	PH	RHP	LHP
1967	CLE	AL	1	0	1	0	1	0	0	0	0	0	0	0	0	0	1	0
1970	CLE	AL	1	1	0	1	0	0	0	0	0	0	0	0	0	0	1	0
Total			2	1	1	1	1	0	0	0	0	0	0	0	0	0	2	0

Rank among batters: 4,129 • *Total ballparks homered in*: 2 • *First HR*: 05/21/1967 off Bucky Brandon

Pryor McElveen

PRYOR MYNATT MCELVEEN
B: 11/05/1881 D: 10/27/1951
BR

Year	Tm	Lg	Tot	H	A	Men-On 0	Men-On 1	Men-On 2	Men-On 3	One-Game 2	One-Game 3	One-Game 4	LO	XN	IP	PH	RHP	LHP
1909	BRO	NL	3	2	1	1	0	2	0	0	0	0	0	0	1	0	2	1
1910	BRO	NL	1	1	0	1	0	0	0	0	0	0	0	0	1	0	1	0
Total			4	3	1	2	0	2	0	0	0	0	0	0	2	0	3	1

Rank among batters: 3,427 • *Total ballparks homered in*: 2 • *First HR*: 07/20/1909 off Jack Pfiester

Ed McFarland

EDWARD WILLIAM MCFARLAND
B: 08/03/1874 D: 11/28/1959
BR

Year	Tm	Lg	Tot	H	A	Men-On 0	Men-On 1	Men-On 2	Men-On 3	One-Game 2	One-Game 3	One-Game 4	LO	XN	IP	PH	RHP	LHP
1896	STL	NL	3	3	0	2	1	0	0	0	0	0	0	0	1	0	2	1
1897	STL	NL	1	1	0	0	1	0	0	0	0	0	0	0	0	0	1	0
	PHI	NL	1	0	1	0	1	0	0	0	0	0	0	0	0	0	0	1
	Total		2	1	1	0	2	0	0	0	0	0	0	0	0	0	1	1
1898	PHI	NL	3	2	1	1	2	0	0	0	0	0	0	0	0	0	2	1
1899	PHI	NL	2	0	2	2	0	0	0	0	0	0	0	0	0	0	1	1
1901	PHI	NL	1	1	0	1	0	0	0	0	0	0	0	0	0	0	1	0
1902	CHI	AL	1	0	1	1	0	0	0	0	0	0	0	0	0	0	1	0
1903	CHI	AL	1	0	1	1	0	0	0	0	0	0	0	0	0	0	1	0
Total			13	7	6	8	5	0	0	0	0	0	0	0	1	0	9	4

Rank among batters: 2,248 • *Total ballparks homered in*: 6 • *First HR*: 04/22/1896 off Danny Friend

Herm McFarland

HERMAS WALTER MCFARLAND
B: 03/11/1870 D: 09/21/1935
BL

Year	Tm	Lg	Tot	H	A	Men-On 0	Men-On 1	Men-On 2	Men-On 3	One-Game 2	One-Game 3	One-Game 4	LO	XN	IP	PH	RHP	LHP
1896	LOU	NL	1	1	0	0	0	0	1	0	0	0	0	0	0	0	1	0
1901	CHI	AL	4	3	1	3	0	0	1	0	0	0	0	0	0	0	3	1
1902	BAL	AL	3	1	2	1	1	0	1	0	0	0	0	0	1	0	3	0
1903	NY	AL	5	4	1	3	2	0	0	0	0	0	0	0	0	0	5	0
Total			13	9	4	7	3	0	3	0	0	0	0	0	1	0	12	1

Rank among batters: 2,248 • *Top target (2 home runs)*: Cy Young • *Number of pitchers victimized*: 12 • *Total ballparks homered in*: 8 • *First HR*: 05/05/1896 off Dad Clarke

Orlando McFarlane

ORLANDO DEJESUS (QUESADA) MCFARLANE
B: 06/28/1938
BR

Year	Tm	Lg	Tot	H	A	Men-On 0	Men-On 1	Men-On 2	Men-On 3	One-Game 2	One-Game 3	One-Game 4	LO	XN	IP	PH	RHP	LHP
1966	DET	AL	5	2	3	3	2	0	0	0	0	0	0	0	0	0	5	0

Rank among batters: 3,191 • *Total ballparks homered in*: 4 • *First HR*: 04/14/1966 off Bob Friend

Patsy McGaffigan

MARK ANDREW MCGAFFIGAN
B: 09/12/1888 D: 12/22/1940
BR

Year	Tm	Lg	Tot	H	A	Men-On 0	Men-On 1	Men-On 2	Men-On 3	One-Game 2	One-Game 3	One-Game 4	LO	XN	IP	PH	RHP	LHP
1918	PHI	NL	1	1	0	1	0	0	0	0	0	0	0	0	0	0	0	1

Rank among batters: 4,707 • *Total ballparks homered in*: 1 • *First HR*: 06/05/1918 off Rube Bressler

Dan McGann

DENNIS LAWRENCE MCGANN
B: 07/15/1871 D: 12/13/1910
BB

Year	Tm	Lg	Tot	H	A	Men-On 0	Men-On 1	Men-On 2	Men-On 3	One-Game 2	One-Game 3	One-Game 4	LO	XN	IP	PH	RHP	LHP
1896	BOS	NL	2	1	1	2	0	0	0	0	0	0	0	0	0	0	2	0
1898	BAL	NL	5	2	3	0	3	1	1	0	0	0	0	0	0	0	5	0
1899	BRO	NL	2	1	1	0	1	1	0	0	0	0	0	0	0	0	2	0
	WAS	NL	5	2	3	4	1	0	0	0	0	0	0	0	0	0	4	1
	Total		7	3	4	4	2	1	0	0	0	0	0	0	0	0	6	1
1900	STL	NL	4	3	1	1	2	1	0	0	0	0	0	0	1	0	4	0
1901	STL	NL	6	3	3	3	2	1	0	0	0	0	0	0	2	0	3	3
1903	NY	NL	3	2	1	0	2	0	1	0	0	0	0	0	0	0	3	0
1904	NY	NL	6	4	2	5	1	0	0	1	0	0	0	0	0	0	5	1
1905	NY	NL	5	4	1	3	1	1	0	1	0	0	0	0	0	0	5	0

Dan McGann *continued*

Year	Tm	Lg	Tot	H	A	Men-On 0	1	2	3	One-Game 2	3	4	LO	XN	IP	PH	RHP	LHP
1907	NY	NL	2	1	1	2	0	0	0	0	0	0	0	0	0	0	1	1
1908	BOS	NL	2	2	0	2	0	0	0	0	0	0	0	0	0	0	2	0
Total			42	25	17	22	13	5	2	2	0	0	0	0	3	0	36	6

Rank among batters: 1,138 • *Top target (3 home runs)*: Sam Leever • *Number of pitchers victimized*: 35 • *Total ballparks homered in*: 12 • *First HR*: 09/05/1896 off Nig Cuppy

Chippy McGarr

JAMES B. MCGARR
B: 05/10/1863 D: 06/06/1904
BR

Year	Tm	Lg	Tot	H	A	Men-On 0	1	2	3	One-Game 2	3	4	LO	XN	IP	PH	RHP	LHP
1886	PHI	AA	2	1	1	1	0	1	0	0	0	0	0	0	0	0	1	1
1887	PHI	AA	1	0	1	0	1	0	0	0	0	0	0	0	0	0	0	1
1890	BOS	NL	1	0	1	1	0	0	0	0	0	0	0	0	1	0	1	0
1894	CLE	NL	2	1	1	1	1	0	0	0	0	0	0	0	0	0	2	0
1895	CLE	NL	2	0	2	2	0	0	0	0	0	0	0	0	0	0	2	0
1896	CLE	NL	1	1	0	1	0	0	0	0	0	0	0	0	0	0	1	0
Total			9	3	6	6	2	1	0	0	0	0	0	0	1	0	7	0

Rank among batters: 2,587 • *Top target (2 home runs)*: Tony Mullane, Jack Stivetts • *Number of pitchers victimized*: 7 • *Total ballparks homered in*: 6 • *First HR*: 09/23/1886 off Nat Hudson • *Hit for Cycle*—vs STL: 09/23/1886

Jack McGeachey

JOHN CHARLES MCGEACHEY
B: 05/13/1864 D: 04/05/1930
BR

Year	Tm	Lg	Tot	H	A	Men-On 0	1	2	3	One-Game 2	3	4	LO	XN	IP	PH	RHP	LHP
1886	STL	NL	2	1	1	0	2	0	0	0	0	0	0	0	0	0	2	0
1887	IND	NL	1	1	0	0	0	0	1	0	0	0	0	0	0	0	0	0
1889	IND	NL	2	2	0	1	1	0	0	0	0	0	0	0	1	0	2	0
1890	BRO	PL	1	0	1	0	1	0	0	0	0	0	0	0	1	0	1	0
1891	PHI	AA	2	2	0	1	1	0	0	1	0	0	0	0	1	0	1	1
	BOS	AA	1	1	0	1	0	0	0	0	0	0	0	0	0	0	1	0
	Total		3	3	0	2	1	0	0	1	0	0	0	0	1	0	2	1
Total			9	7	2	3	5	0	1	1	0	0	0	0	3	0	7	1

Rank among batters: 2,587 • *Total ballparks homered in*: 7 • *First HR*: 08/07/1886 off Tony Madigan

Willie McGee

WILLIE DEAN MCGEE
B: 11/02/1958
BB

Year	Tm	Lg	Tot	H	A	Men-On 0	1	2	3	One-Game 2	3	4	LO	XN	IP	PH	RHP	LHP
1982	STL	NL	4	2	2	1	1	1	1	0	0	0	0	0	1	0	2	2
1983	STL	NL	5	4	1	2	2	1	0	0	0	0	0	0	1	0	3	2
1984	STL	NL	6	2	4	3	3	0	0	0	0	0	0	1	0	0	1	5
1985	STL	NL	10	3	7	5	2	3	0	0	0	0	0	0	0	0	3	7
1986	STL	NL	7	7	0	5	2	0	0	1	0	0	0	0	0	0	2	5
1987	STL	NL	11	6	5	2	6	3	0	0	0	0	0	0	0	0	5	6
1988	STL	NL	3	1	2	2	1	0	0	0	0	0	0	0	0	0	3	0
1989	STL	NL	3	1	2	2	1	0	0	0	0	0	0	0	0	0	1	2
1990	STL	NL	3	1	2	3	0	0	0	0	0	0	0	0	0	0	1	2
1991	SF	NL	4	2	2	3	1	0	0	0	0	0	0	0	0	0	2	2
1992	SF	NL	1	0	1	1	0	0	0	0	0	0	0	0	0	0	0	1
1993	SF	NL	4	0	4	3	1	0	0	0	0	0	0	0	0	0	3	1
1994	SF	NL	5	2	3	4	1	0	0	0	0	0	0	0	1	0	3	2
1995	BOS	AL	2	1	1	2	0	0	0	0	0	0	0	0	0	0	0	2
Total			68	32	36	38	21	8	1	1	0	0	0	1	3	0	29	39

Rank among batters: 767 • *Top target (3 home runs)*: Bobby Ojeda • *Number of pitchers victimized*: 58 • *Total ballparks homered in*: 14 • *First HR*: 07/20/1982 off Ken Dayley • *Hit for Cycle*—@CHI: 06/23/1984 • *World Series HR*—3; *LCS HR*—1

Bill McGhee

WILLIAM MAC MCGHEE
B: 09/05/1905 D: 03/10/1984
BL

Year	Tm	Lg	Tot	H	A	Men-On 0	1	2	3	One-Game 2	3	4	LO	XN	IP	PH	RHP	LHP
1944	PHI	AL	1	0	1	1	0	0	0	0	0	0	0	0	0	0	0	1

Rank among batters: 4,707 • *Total ballparks homered in*: 1 • *First HR*: 09/03/1944 off Clem Dreisewerd

Ed McGhee

WARREN EDWARD MCGHEE
B: 09/29/1924 D: 02/13/1986
BR

Year	Tm	Lg	Tot	H	A	Men-On 0	1	2	3	One-Game 2	3	4	LO	XN	IP	PH	RHP	LHP
1953	PHI	AL	1	1	0	0	1	0	0	0	0	0	0	0	0	0	1	0
1954	PHI	AL	2	1	1	1	1	0	0	0	0	0	0	0	0	0	2	0
Total			3	2	1	1	2	0	0	0	0	0	0	0	0	0	3	0

Rank among batters: 3,735 • *Total ballparks homered in*: 2 • *First HR*: 08/05/1953 off Fritz Dorish

Dan McGinn

DANIEL MICHAEL MCGINN
B: 11/29/1943
BL

Year	Tm	Lg	Tot	H	A	Men-On 0	1	2	3	One-Game 2	3	4	LO	XN	IP	PH	RHP	LHP
1969	MON	NL	1	0	1	1	0	0	0	0	0	0	0	0	0	0	1	0

Rank among batters: 4,707 • *Total ballparks homered in*: 1 • *First HR*: 04/08/1969 off Tom Seaver

Jumbo McGinnis

GEORGE WASHINGTON MCGINNIS
B: 02/22/1864 D: 05/18/1934

Year	Tm	Lg	Tot	H	A	Men-On 0	1	2	3	One-Game 2	3	4	LO	XN	IP	PH	RHP	LHP
1885	STL	AA	1	1	0	0	0	1	0	0	0	0	0	0	0	0	0	0
1886	BAL	AA	1	0	1	1	0	0	0	0	0	0	0	0	0	0	1	0
Total			2	1	1	1	0	1	0	0	0	0	0	0	0	0	1	0

Rank among batters: 4,129 • *Total ballparks homered in*: 1 • *First HR*: 07/07/1885 off Franklin Gardner

John McGlone

JOHN T. MCGLONE
B: 1864 D: 11/24/1927

Year	Tm	Lg	Tot	H	A	Men-On 0	1	2	3	One-Game 2	3	4	LO	XN	IP	PH	RHP	LHP
1888	CLE	AA	1	1	0	0	1	0	0	0	0	0	0	0	1	0	1	0

Rank among batters: 4,707 • *Total ballparks homered in*: 1 • *First HR*: 06/06/1888 off Guy Hecker

Jim McGlothlin

JAMES MILTON MCGLOTHLIN
B: 10/06/1943 D: 12/23/1975
BR

Year	Tm	Lg	Tot	H	A	Men-On 0	1	2	3	One-Game 2	3	4	LO	XN	IP	PH	RHP	LHP
1970	CIN	NL	1	0	1	1	0	0	0	0	0	0	0	0	0	0	0	1
1971	CIN	NL	1	0	1	1	0	0	0	0	0	0	0	0	0	0	1	0
1972	CIN	NL	1	1	0	1	0	0	0	0	0	0	0	0	0	0	0	1
Total			3	1	2	3	0	0	0	0	0	0	0	0	0	0	1	2

Rank among batters: 3,735 • *Total ballparks homered in*: 2 • *First HR*: 09/19/1970 off Steve Barber

Beauty McGowan

FRANK BERNARD MCGOWAN
B: 11/08/1901 D: 05/06/1982
BL

Year	Tm	Lg	Tot	H	A	Men-On 0	1	2	3	One-Game 2	3	4	LO	XN	IP	PH	RHP	LHP
1922	PHI	AL	1	0	1	1	0	0	0	0	0	0	0	0	0	0	1	0
1923	PHI	AL	1	0	1	1	0	0	0	0	0	0	0	0	0	0	1	0
1928	STL	AL	2	2	0	1	1	0	0	0	0	0	0	0	1	0	1	1
1929	STL	AL	2	1	1	1	1	0	0	0	0	0	0	0	0	0	1	1
Total			6	3	3	4	2	0	0	0	0	0	0	0	1	0	4	2

Rank among batters: 2,988 • *Total ballparks homered in*: 3 • *First HR*: 08/02/1922 off Urban Shocker

Bob McGraw

ROBERT EMMETT MCGRAW
B: 04/10/1895 D: 06/02/1978
BR

Year	Tm	Lg	Tot	H	A	Men-On 0	1	2	3	One-Game 2	3	4	LO	XN	IP	PH	RHP	LHP
1927	STL	NL	1	1	0	1	0	0	0	0	0	0	0	0	0	0	1	0

Rank among batters: 4,707 • *Total ballparks homered in*: 1 • *First HR*: 07/30/1927 off Freddie Fitzsimmons

John McGraw

JOHN JOSEPH MCGRAW
B: 04/07/1873 D: 02/25/1934
BL HOF

Year	Tm	Lg	Tot	H	A	Men-On 0	1	2	3	One-Game 2	3	4	LO	XN	IP	PH	RHP	LHP
1892	BAL	NL	1	0	1	0	0	1	0	0	0	0	0	0	0	0	1	0

John McGraw *continued*

Year	Tm	Lg	Tot	H	A	Men-On 0	Men-On 1	Men-On 2	Men-On 3	One-Game 2	One-Game 3	One-Game 4	LO	XN	IP	PH	RHP	LHP
1893	BAL	NL	5	3	2	2	2	0	1	0	0	0	1	0	3	0	3	0
1894	BAL	NL	1	0	1	0	1	0	0	0	0	0	0	0	0	0	1	0
1895	BAL	NL	2	0	2	0	2	0	0	0	0	0	0	0	0	0	2	0
1899	BAL	NL	1	1	0	0	1	0	0	0	0	0	0	0	0	0	1	0
1900	STL	NL	2	1	1	2	0	0	0	0	0	0	0	0	0	0	2	0
1902	BAL	AL	1	1	0	0	1	0	0	0	0	0	0	0	0	0	0	1
Total			13	6	7	4	7	1	1	0	0	0	1	0	3	0	10	1

Rank among batters: 2,248 • *Top target (2 home runs)*: Kid Nichols • *Number of pitchers victimized*: 12 • *Total ballparks homered in*: 8 • *First HR*: 10/01/1892 off George Haddock

Tug McGraw

FRANK EDWIN MCGRAW
B: 08/30/1944
BR

Year	Tm	Lg	Tot	H	A	Men-On 0	Men-On 1	Men-On 2	Men-On 3	One-Game 2	One-Game 3	One-Game 4	LO	XN	IP	PH	RHP	LHP
1971	NY	NL	1	0	1	1	0	0	0	0	0	0	0	0	0	0	1	0

Rank among batters: 4,707 • *Total ballparks homered in*: 1 • *First HR*: 09/08/1971 off Carl Morton

Fred McGriff

FREDERICK STANLEY MCGRIFF
B: 10/31/1963
BL

Year	Tm	Lg	Tot	H	A	Men-On 0	Men-On 1	Men-On 2	Men-On 3	One-Game 2	One-Game 3	One-Game 4	LO	XN	IP	PH	RHP	LHP
1987	TOR	AL	20	7	13	14	4	2	0	1	0	0	0	0	0	1	19	1
1988	TOR	AL	34	18	16	19	12	3	0	4	0	0	0	0	0	1	29	5
1989	TOR	AL	36	18	18	21	11	3	1	4	0	0	0	1	0	0	31	5
1990	TOR	AL	35	14	21	24	9	2	0	3	0	0	0	2	0	0	27	8
1991	SD	NL	31	18	13	17	8	4	2	3	0	0	0	1	0	0	17	14
1992	SD	NL	35	21	14	19	14	1	1	2	0	0	0	0	0	0	22	13
1993	SD	NL	18	7	11	11	7	0	0	0	0	0	0	2	0	0	14	4
	ATL	NL	19	8	11	10	5	3	1	3	0	0	0	0	1	0	15	4
	Total		37	15	22	21	12	3	1	3	0	0	0	2	1	0	29	8
1994	ATL	NL	34	13	21	16	11	7	0	2	0	0	0	1	0	0	24	10
1995	ATL	NL	27	15	12	14	9	4	0	2	0	0	0	0	0	0	21	6
Total			289	139	150	165	90	29	5	24	0	0	0	7	1	2	219	70

Rank among batters: 76 • *Top target (5 home runs)*: Jose Rijo • *Number of pitchers victimized*: 212 • *Total ballparks homered in*: 30 • *First HR*: 04/17/1987 off Bob Stanley • *World Series HR*—2; *LCS HR*—3; *All-Star HR*—1

Terry McGriff

TERENCE ROY MCGRIFF
B: 09/23/1963
BR

Year	Tm	Lg	Tot	H	A	Men-On 0	Men-On 1	Men-On 2	Men-On 3	One-Game 2	One-Game 3	One-Game 4	LO	XN	IP	PH	RHP	LHP
1987	CIN	NL	2	1	1	0	1	0	1	0	0	0	0	0	0	0	2	0
1988	CIN	NL	1	1	0	1	0	0	0	0	0	0	0	0	0	0	0	1
Total			3	2	1	1	1	0	1	0	0	0	0	0	0	0	2	1

Rank among batters: 3,735 • *Total ballparks homered in*: 2 • *First HR*: 07/30/1987 off Lance McCullers

Bill McGuire

WILLIAM PATRICK MCGUIRE
B: 02/14/1964
BR

Year	Tm	Lg	Tot	H	A	Men-On 0	Men-On 1	Men-On 2	Men-On 3	One-Game 2	One-Game 3	One-Game 4	LO	XN	IP	PH	RHP	LHP
1989	SEA	AL	1	0	1	0	0	1	0	0	0	0	0	0	0	0	0	1

Rank among batters: 4,707 • *Total ballparks homered in*: 1 • *First HR*: 06/11/1989 off Bud Black

Deacon McGuire

JAMES THOMAS MCGUIRE
B: 11/18/1863 D: 10/31/1936
BR

Year	Tm	Lg	Tot	H	A	Men-On 0	Men-On 1	Men-On 2	Men-On 3	One-Game 2	One-Game 3	One-Game 4	LO	XN	IP	PH	RHP	LHP
1884	TOL	AA	1	1	0	1	0	0	0	0	0	0	0	0	0	0	0	0
1886	PHI	NL	2	2	0	1	0	1	0	0	0	0	0	0	0	0	1	1
1887	PHI	NL	2	1	1	1	0	1	0	0	0	0	0	0	0	0	1	1
1888	CLE	AA	1	0	1	0	1	0	0	0	0	0	0	0	0	0	1	0
1890	ROC	AA	4	2	2	0	3	0	1	0	0	0	0	0	0	0	3	1
1891	WAS	AA	3	2	1	1	1	1	0	0	0	0	0	0	0	0	3	0
1892	WAS	NL	4	3	1	4	0	0	0	0	0	0	0	0	1	0	4	0

						Men-On				One-Game								
Year	Tm	Lg	Tot	H	A	0	1	2	3	2	3	4	LO	XN	IP	PH	RHP	LHP

Deacon McGuire *continued*

Year	Tm	Lg	Tot	H	A	0	1	2	3	2	3	4	LO	XN	IP	PH	RHP	LHP
1893	WAS	NL	1	0	1	1	0	0	0	0	0	0	0	0	1	0	0	0
1894	WAS	NL	6	3	3	2	3	1	0	0	0	0	0	0	0	0	4	1
1895	WAS	NL	10	7	3	5	2	3	0	0	0	0	0	0	0	0	10	0
1896	WAS	NL	2	0	2	1	0	1	0	0	0	0	0	0	0	0	1	1
1897	WAS	NL	4	3	1	1	2	1	0	0	0	0	0	0	0	0	3	1
1898	WAS	NL	1	0	1	1	0	0	0	0	0	0	0	0	0	0	1	0
1899	WAS	NL	1	1	0	1	0	0	0	0	0	0	0	0	0	0	1	0
1902	DET	AL	2	1	1	0	0	1	1	0	0	0	0	0	0	0	1	1
1907	BOS	AL	1	1	0	1	0	0	0	0	0	0	0	1	0	1	0	1
Total			45	27	18	21	12	10	2	0	0	0	0	1	2	1	34	8

Rank among batters: 1,082 • *Top target (3 home runs)*: Sadie McMahon, Kid Nichols, Brickyard Kennedy • *Number of pitchers victimized*: 36 • *Total ballparks homered in*: 20 • *First HR*: 08/13/1884 off Larry McKeon

Tom McGuire

THOMAS PATRICK MCGUIRE
B: 02/01/1892 D: 12/07/1959
BR

Year	Tm	Lg	Tot	H	A	0	1	2	3	2	3	4	LO	XN	IP	PH	RHP	LHP
1914	CHI	FL	1	0	1	1	0	0	0	0	0	0	0	0	0	0	1	0

Rank among batters: 4,707 • *Total ballparks homered in*: 1 • *First HR*: 08/06/1914 off George Suggs

Mark McGwire

MARK DAVID MCGWIRE
B: 10/01/1963
BR

Year	Tm	Lg	Tot	H	A	0	1	2	3	2	3	4	LO	XN	IP	PH	RHP	LHP
1986	OAK	AL	3	1	2	2	1	0	0	0	0	0	0	0	0	1	1	2
1987	OAK	AL	49	21	28	32	13	4	0	6	1	0	0	3	0	0	33	16
1988	OAK	AL	32	12	20	15	9	7	1	0	0	0	0	2	0	1	21	11
1989	OAK	AL	33	12	21	17	10	4	2	3	0	0	0	0	0	0	27	6
1990	OAK	AL	39	14	25	20	15	3	1	5	0	0	0	1	0	0	28	11
1991	OAK	AL	22	15	7	8	8	6	0	3	0	0	0	1	0	1	17	5
1992	OAK	AL	42	24	18	27	11	3	1	5	0	0	0	0	0	0	28	14
1993	OAK	AL	9	5	4	6	2	1	0	3	0	0	0	0	0	0	6	3
1994	OAK	AL	9	6	3	4	4	1	0	0	0	0	0	0	0	0	5	4
1995	OAK	AL	39	15	24	16	17	5	1	4	1	0	0	0	1	0	25	14
Total			277	125	152	147	90	34	6	29	2	0	0	7	1	3	191	86

Rank among batters: 83 • *Top target (7 home runs)*: Frank Tanana • *Number of pitchers victimized*: 176 • *Total ballparks homered in*: 18 • *First HR*: 08/25/1986 off Walt Terrell • *World Series HR*—1; *LCS HR*—3

John McHale

JOHN JOSEPH MCHALE
B: 09/21/1921
BL

Year	Tm	Lg	Tot	H	A	0	1	2	3	2	3	4	LO	XN	IP	PH	RHP	LHP
1947	DET	AL	3	3	0	1	2	0	0	1	0	0	0	0	0	0	3	0

Rank among batters: 3,735 • *Top target (2 home runs)*: Nels Potter • *Number of pitchers victimized*: 2 • *Total ballparks homered in*: 1 • *First HR*: 05/30/1947 off Nels Potter

Austin McHenry

AUSTIN BUSH MCHENRY
B: 09/22/1895 D: 11/27/1922
BR

Year	Tm	Lg	Tot	H	A	0	1	2	3	2	3	4	LO	XN	IP	PH	RHP	LHP
1918	STL	NL	1	1	0	0	1	0	0	0	0	0	0	0	0	0	1	0
1919	STL	NL	1	1	0	0	1	0	0	0	0	0	0	0	1	0	1	0
1920	STL	NL	10	3	7	3	5	2	0	0	0	0	0	0	0	1	5	5
1921	STL	NL	17	6	11	12	0	5	0	1	0	0	0	0	1	0	14	3
1922	STL	NL	5	2	3	3	2	0	0	1	0	0	0	0	0	0	2	3
Total			34	13	21	18	9	7	0	2	0	0	0	0	2	1	23	11

Rank among batters: 1,315 • Top target (2 home runs): Art Nehf, Fred Toney, Bill Hubbell, Dana Fillingim, Virgil Cheeves, Philip Weinert, Percy Jones • *Number of pitchers victimized*: 27 • *Total ballparks homered in*: 8 • *First HR*: 07/12/1918 off Elmer Jacobs

Stuffy McInnis

JOHN PHALEN MCINNIS
B: 09/19/1890 D: 02/16/1960
BR

Year	Tm	Lg	Tot	H	A	0	1	2	3	2	3	4	LO	XN	IP	PH	RHP	LHP
1909	PHI	AL	1	1	0	0	1	0	0	0	0	0	0	0	1	0	1	0

Stuffy McInnis *continued*

Year	Tm	Lg	Tot	H	A	Men-On 0	1	2	3	One-Game 2	3	4	LO	XN	IP	PH	RHP	LHP
1911	PHI	AL	3	0	3	1	1	0	1	0	0	0	0	0	1	0	2	1
1912	PHI	AL	3	3	0	1	1	1	0	1	0	0	0	0	2	0	1	2
1913	PHI	AL	4	2	2	3	0	1	0	0	0	0	0	0	3	0	4	0
1914	PHI	AL	1	0	1	0	1	0	0	0	0	0	0	0	1	0	0	1
1916	PHI	AL	1	1	0	0	0	1	0	0	0	0	0	0	0	0	0	1
1919	BOS	AL	1	1	0	1	0	0	0	0	0	0	0	0	1	0	0	1
1920	BOS	AL	2	0	2	1	0	0	1	0	0	0	0	0	1	0	2	0
1922	CLE	AL	1	1	0	1	0	0	0	0	0	0	0	0	1	0	1	0
1923	BOS	NL	2	0	2	0	1	0	1	0	0	0	0	0	0	0	1	1
1924	BOS	NL	1	0	1	1	0	0	0	0	0	0	0	0	0	0	1	0
Total			20	9	11	9	5	3	3	1	0	0	0	0	11	0	13	7

Rank among batters: 1,810 • *Top target (2 home runs)*: Vean Gregg • *Number of pitchers victimized*: 19 • *Total ballparks homered in*: 9 • *First HR*: 09/22/1909 off Jack Gilligan

Harry McIntire

JOHN REID MCINTIRE
B: 01/11/1879 D: 01/09/1949
BR

Year	Tm	Lg	Tot	H	A	Men-On 0	1	2	3	One-Game 2	3	4	LO	XN	IP	PH	RHP	LHP
1905	BRO	NL	1	1	0	1	0	0	0	0	0	0	0	0	1	0	1	0
1910	CHI	NL	1	1	0	0	1	0	0	0	0	0	0	0	0	0	1	0
Total			2	2	0	1	1	0	0	0	0	0	0	0	1	0	2	0

Rank among batters: 4,129 • *Total ballparks homered in*: 2 • *First HR*: 07/04/1905 off Chick Fraser

Tim McIntosh

TIMOTHY ALLEN MCINTOSH
B: 03/21/1965
BR

Year	Tm	Lg	Tot	H	A	Men-On 0	1	2	3	One-Game 2	3	4	LO	XN	IP	PH	RHP	LHP
1990	MIL	AL	1	1	0	1	0	0	0	0	0	0	0	0	0	0	0	1
1991	MIL	AL	1	1	0	1	0	0	0	0	0	0	0	0	0	0	0	1
Total			2	2	0	2	0	0	0	0	0	0	0	0	0	0	0	2

Rank among batters: 4,129 • *Total ballparks homered in*: 1 • *First HR*: 09/28/1990 off Steve Adkins

Matty McIntyre

MATTHEW W. MCINTYRE
B: 06/12/1880 D: 04/02/1920
BL

Year	Tm	Lg	Tot	H	A	Men-On 0	1	2	3	One-Game 2	3	4	LO	XN	IP	PH	RHP	LHP
1904	DET	AL	2	0	2	0	1	1	0	0	0	0	0	0	0	0	2	0
1909	DET	AL	1	1	0	0	1	0	0	0	0	0	0	0	0	0	1	0
1911	CHI	AL	1	1	0	0	1	0	0	0	0	0	0	0	0	0	1	0
Total			4	2	2	0	3	1	0	0	0	0	0	0	0	0	4	0

Rank among batters: 3,427 • *Total ballparks homered in*: 3 • *First HR*: 09/14/1904 off Willie Sudhoff

Otto McIvor

EDWARD OTTO MCIVOR
B: 07/26/1884 D: 05/04/1954
BB

Year	Tm	Lg	Tot	H	A	Men-On 0	1	2	3	One-Game 2	3	4	LO	XN	IP	PH	RHP	LHP
1911	STL	NL	1	0	1	0	1	0	0	0	0	0	0	0	0	0	1	0

Rank among batters: 4,707 • *Total ballparks homered in*: 1 • *First HR*: 07/19/1911 off Bill Schardt

Archie McKain

ARCHIE RICHARD MCKAIN
B: 05/12/1911 D: 05/21/1985
BB

Year	Tm	Lg	Tot	H	A	Men-On 0	1	2	3	One-Game 2	3	4	LO	XN	IP	PH	RHP	LHP
1939	DET	AL	2	0	2	2	0	0	0	0	0	0	0	0	0	0	2	0

Rank among batters: 4,129 • *Total ballparks homered in*: 2 • *First HR*: 05/14/1939 off Roxie Lawson

Dave McKay

DAVID LAWRENCE MCKAY
B: 03/14/1950
BB

Year	Tm	Lg	Tot	H	A	Men-On 0	1	2	3	One-Game 2	3	4	LO	XN	IP	PH	RHP	LHP
1975	MIN	AL	2	1	1	1	1	0	0	0	0	0	0	0	0	0	2	0
1977	TOR	AL	3	2	1	2	1	0	0	0	0	0	0	0	0	0	1	2

Dave McKay *continued*

Year	Tm	Lg	Tot	H	A	Men-On				One-Game			LO	XN	IP	PH	RHP	LHP
						0	1	2	3	2	3	4						
1978	TOR	AL	7	4	3	6	1	0	0	0	0	0	0	1	0	0	1	6
1980	OAK	AL	1	0	1	1	0	0	0	0	0	0	0	0	0	0	1	0
1981	OAK	AL	4	1	3	4	0	0	0	0	0	0	0	0	0	0	1	3
1982	OAK	AL	4	1	3	1	3	0	0	0	0	0	0	0	0	0	2	2
Total			21	9	12	15	6	0	0	0	0	0	0	1	0	0	8	13

Rank among batters: 1,768 • *Top target (2 home runs)*: Larry Gura • *Number of pitchers victimized*: 20 • *Total ballparks homered in*: 11 • *First HR*: 08/22/1975 off Vern Ruhle • *Hit HR in first major league AB*—vs DET: 08/22/1975 • *LCS HR*—1

Ed McKean

EDWIN JOHN MCKEAN
B: 06/06/1864 D: 08/16/1919
BR

Year	Tm	Lg	Tot	H	A	Men-On 0	1	2	3	One-Game 2	3	4	LO	XN	IP	PH	RHP	LHP
1887	CLE	AA	2	0	2	0	1	1	0	0	0	0	0	0	0	0	2	0
1888	CLE	AA	6	4	2	5	1	0	0	0	0	0	0	0	3	0	4	2
1889	CLE	NL	5	1	4	2	2	1	0	0	0	0	0	1	0	0	5	0
1890	CLE	NL	7	7	0	2	4	1	0	1	0	0	1	0	0	0	4	3
1891	CLE	NL	6	1	5	4	2	0	0	1	0	0	0	0	1	0	6	0
1893	CLE	NL	4	1	3	2	1	1	0	0	0	0	0	0	1	0	4	0
1894	CLE	NL	8	2	6	3	5	0	0	0	0	0	0	0	2	0	7	1
1895	CLE	NL	8	2	6	1	5	1	1	0	0	0	0	0	1	0	7	1
1896	CLE	NL	7	1	6	3	4	0	0	0	0	0	0	0	0	0	6	1
1897	CLE	NL	2	0	2	2	0	0	0	0	0	0	0	0	0	0	1	1
1898	CLE	NL	9	3	6	3	4	2	0	0	0	0	0	0	0	0	6	3
1899	STL	NL	3	2	1	2	1	0	0	0	0	0	0	1	0	0	2	1
Total			67	24	43	29	30	7	1	2	0	0	1	2	8	0	54	12

Rank among batters: 777 • *Top target (4 home runs)*: Bill Hutchison, Kid Carsey • *Number of pitchers victimized*: 48 • *Total ballparks homered in*: 19 • *First HR*: 04/30/1887 off Dave Foutz

Bill McKechnie

WILLIAM BOYD MCKECHNIE
B: 08/07/1886 D: 10/29/1965
BB HOF

Year	Tm	Lg	Tot	H	A	Men-On 0	1	2	3	One-Game 2	3	4	LO	XN	IP	PH	RHP	LHP
1911	PIT	NL	2	2	0	1	1	0	0	1	0	0	0	0	2	0	2	0
1914	IND	FL	2	1	1	1	1	0	0	0	0	0	0	0	1	0	1	1
1915	NWK	FL	1	0	1	0	1	0	0	0	0	0	0	0	0	0	1	0
1918	PIT	NL	2	1	1	2	0	0	0	0	0	0	0	0	2	0	1	1
1920	PIT	NL	1	1	0	1	0	0	0	0	0	0	0	0	1	0	1	0
Total			8	5	3	5	3	0	0	1	0	0	0	0	6	0	6	2

Rank among batters: 2,703 • *Total ballparks homered in*: 5 • *First HR*: 09/02/1911 off Rube Geyer

Red McKee

RAYMOND ELLIS MCKEE
B: 07/20/1890 D: 08/05/1972
BL

Year	Tm	Lg	Tot	H	A	Men-On 0	1	2	3	One-Game 2	3	4	LO	XN	IP	PH	RHP	LHP
1913	DET	AL	1	0	1	0	0	1	0	0	0	0	0	0	0	0	1	0
1915	DET	AL	1	0	1	1	0	0	0	0	0	0	0	0	0	0	1	0
Total			2	0	2	1	0	1	0	0	0	0	0	0	0	0	2	0

Rank among batters: 4,129 • *Total ballparks homered in*: 2 • *First HR*: 06/21/1913 off Cy Falkenberg

Russ McKelvy

RUSSELL ERRETT MCKELVY
B: 09/08/1856 D: 10/19/1915
BR

Year	Tm	Lg	Tot	H	A	Men-On 0	1	2	3	One-Game 2	3	4	LO	XN	IP	PH	RHP	LHP
1878	IND	NL	2	0	2	1	0	1	0	0	0	0	0	0	1	0	1	1

Rank among batters: 4,129 • *Total ballparks homered in*: 2 • *First HR*: 06/01/1878 off Robert Mitchell

Rich McKinney

CHARLES RICHARD MCKINNEY
B: 11/22/1946
BR

Year	Tm	Lg	Tot	H	A	Men-On 0	1	2	3	One-Game 2	3	4	LO	XN	IP	PH	RHP	LHP
1970	CHI	AL	4	4	0	2	2	0	0	0	0	0	0	0	0	0	3	1
1971	CHI	AL	8	1	7	6	1	1	0	0	0	0	0	0	0	0	4	4
1972	NY	AL	1	0	1	1	0	0	0	0	0	0	0	0	0	0	1	0
1973	OAK	AL	1	1	0	1	0	0	0	0	0	0	0	0	0	0	0	1

Rich McKinney *continued*

Year	Tm	Lg	Tot	H	A	Men-On 0	1	2	3	One-Game 2	3	4	LO	XN	IP	PH	RHP	LHP
1977	OAK	AL	6	4	2	5	1	0	0	0	0	0	0	0	0	3	2	4
Total			20	10	10	15	4	1	0	0	0	0	0	0	0	3	10	10

Rank among batters: 1,810 • *Top target (2 home runs)*: Jim Kaat, Sonny Siebert, Paul Splittorff • *Number of pitchers victimized*: 17 • *Total ballparks homered in*: 8 • *First HR*: 09/21/1970 off Jim York

Alex McKinnon

ALEXANDER J. MCKINNON
B: 08/14/1856 D: 07/24/1887
BR

Year	Tm	Lg	Tot	H	A	Men-On 0	1	2	3	One-Game 2	3	4	LO	XN	IP	PH	RHP	LHP
1884	NY	NL	3	2	1	1	1	0	1	0	0	0	0	0	0	0	2	0
1885	STL	NL	1	1	0	1	0	0	0	0	0	0	0	0	0	0	1	0
1886	STL	NL	8	5	3	3	5	0	0	0	0	0	0	0	0	0	5	2
1887	PIT	NL	1	0	1	0	1	0	0	0	0	0	0	0	0	0	0	1
Total			13	8	5	5	7	0	1	0	0	0	0	0	0	0	8	3

Rank among batters: 2,248 • *Top target (2 home runs)*: Dan Casey, John Clarkson • *Number of pitchers victimized*: 11 • *Total ballparks homered in*: 6 • *First HR*: 05/01/1884 off Larry Corcoran

Jeff McKnight

JEFFERSON ALAN MCKNIGHT
B: 02/18/1963
BB

Year	Tm	Lg	Tot	H	A	Men-On 0	1	2	3	One-Game 2	3	4	LO	XN	IP	PH	RHP	LHP
1990	BAL	AL	1	1	0	1	0	0	0	0	0	0	0	0	0	0	1	0
1992	NY	NL	2	1	1	0	2	0	0	0	0	0	0	0	0	0	2	0
1993	NY	NL	2	2	0	0	1	1	0	0	0	0	0	0	0	1	2	0
Total			5	4	1	1	3	1	0	0	0	0	0	0	0	1	5	0

Rank among batters: 3,191 • *Total ballparks homered in*: 3 • *First HR*: 09/12/1990 off Jack Morris

Denny McLain

DENNIS DALE MCLAIN
B: 03/29/1944
BR

Year	Tm	Lg	Tot	H	A	Men-On 0	1	2	3	One-Game 2	3	4	LO	XN	IP	PH	RHP	LHP
1963	DET	AL	1	1	0	1	0	0	0	0	0	0	0	0	0	0	1	0

Rank among batters: 4,707 • *Total ballparks homered in*: 1 • *First HR*: 09/21/1963 off Fritz Ackley

Polly McLarry

HOWARD ZELL MCLARRY
B: 03/25/1891 D: 11/04/1971
BL

Year	Tm	Lg	Tot	H	A	Men-On 0	1	2	3	One-Game 2	3	4	LO	XN	IP	PH	RHP	LHP
1915	CHI	NL	1	1	0	1	0	0	0	0	0	0	0	0	0	0	1	0

Rank among batters: 4,707 • *Total ballparks homered in*: 1 • *First HR*: 07/31/1915 off Hank Ritter

Bernard McLaughlin

BERNARD MCLAUGHLIN
B: 1857 D: 02/13/1921
BR

Year	Tm	Lg	Tot	H	A	Men-On 0	1	2	3	One-Game 2	3	4	LO	XN	IP	PH	RHP	LHP
1887	PHI	NL	1	0	1	1	0	0	0	0	0	0	0	0	0	0	1	0
1890	SYR	AA	2	0	2	2	0	0	0	0	0	0	0	0	1	0	2	0
Total			3	0	3	3	0	0	0	0	0	0	0	0	1	0	3	0

Rank among batters: 3,735 • *Total ballparks homered in*: 3 • *First HR*: 06/25/1887 off John Cahill

Francis McLaughlin

FRANCIS EDWARD MCLAUGHLIN
B: 06/19/1856 D: 04/05/1917
BR

Year	Tm	Lg	Tot	H	A	Men-On 0	1	2	3	One-Game 2	3	4	LO	XN	IP	PH	RHP	LHP
1882	WOR	NL	1	1	0	1	0	0	0	0	0	0	0	0	0	0	1	0
1883	PIT	AA	1	1	0	1	0	0	0	0	0	0	0	0	0	0	0	0
1884	CIN	UA	2	1	1	1	1	0	0	0	0	0	0	0	0	0	2	0
	KC	UA	1	0	1	1	0	0	0	0	0	0	0	0	0	0	1	0

Francis McLaughlin *continued*

Year	Tm	Lg	Tot	H	A	Men-On 0	1	2	3	One-Game 2	3	4	LO	XN	IP	PH	RHP	LHP
1884	Total		3	1	2	2	1	0	0	0	0	0	0	0	0	0	3	0
Total			5	3	2	4	1	0	0	0	0	0	0	0	0	0	4	0

Rank among batters: 3,191 • *Top target (2 home runs)*: Hugh Daily • *Number of pitchers victimized*: 4 • *Total ballparks homered in*: 5 • *First HR*: 08/24/1882 off Fred Goldsmith

Tom McLaughlin

THOMAS MCLAUGHLIN
B: 03/28/1860 D: 07/21/1921

Year	Tm	Lg	Tot	H	A	Men-On 0	1	2	3	One-Game 2	3	4	LO	XN	IP	PH	RHP	LHP
1885	LOU	AA	2	2	0	0	1	1	0	0	0	0	0	0	1	0	2	0

Rank among batters: 4,129 • *Total ballparks homered in*: 1 • *First HR*: 07/05/1885 off Jack Lynch

Larry McLean

JOHN BANNERMAN MCLEAN
B: 07/18/1881 D: 03/24/1921
BR

Year	Tm	Lg	Tot	H	A	Men-On 0	1	2	3	One-Game 2	3	4	LO	XN	IP	PH	RHP	LHP
1908	CIN	NL	1	0	1	0	1	0	0	0	0	0	0	0	0	1	1	0
1909	CIN	NL	2	0	2	2	0	0	0	0	0	0	0	0	1	0	1	1
1910	CIN	NL	2	0	2	0	1	1	0	0	0	0	0	0	0	1	1	1
1912	CIN	NL	1	0	1	0	0	1	0	0	0	0	0	0	0	0	1	0
Total			6	0	6	2	2	2	0	0	0	0	0	0	1	2	4	2

Rank among batters: 2,988 • *Total ballparks homered in*: 4 • *First HR*: 06/26/1908 off Chick Fraser

Mark McLemore

MARK TREMELL MCLEMORE
B: 10/04/1964
BB

Year	Tm	Lg	Tot	H	A	Men-On 0	1	2	3	One-Game 2	3	4	LO	XN	IP	PH	RHP	LHP
1987	CAL	AL	3	3	0	2	1	0	0	0	0	0	0	1	0	0	2	1
1988	CAL	AL	2	1	1	1	1	0	0	0	0	0	0	0	0	0	2	0
1993	BAL	AL	4	2	2	3	1	0	0	0	0	0	0	0	0	0	4	0
1994	BAL	AL	3	2	1	1	2	0	0	0	0	0	0	0	0	0	3	0
1995	TEX	AL	5	3	2	1	3	1	0	0	0	0	0	0	0	0	4	1
Total			17	11	6	8	8	1	0	0	0	0	0	1	0	0	15	2

Rank among batters: 1,969 • *Top target (2 home runs)*: Ricky Bones • *Number of pitchers victimized*: 16 • *Total ballparks homered in*: 8 • *First HR*: 07/02/1987 off Mark Clear

Cal McLish

CALVIN COOLIDGE JULIUS CAESAR TUSKAHOMA MCLISH
B: 12/01/1925
BB

Year	Tm	Lg	Tot	H	A	Men-On 0	1	2	3	One-Game 2	3	4	LO	XN	IP	PH	RHP	LHP
1949	CHI	NL	1	1	0	1	0	0	0	0	0	0	0	0	0	0	1	0
1957	CLE	AL	2	1	1	1	0	1	0	0	0	0	0	0	0	0	1	1
Total			3	2	1	2	0	1	0	0	0	0	0	0	0	0	2	1

Rank among batters: 3,735 • *Total ballparks homered in*: 3 • *First HR*: 05/22/1949 off Johnny Sain

Jack McMahon

JOHN HENRY MCMAHON
B: 10/15/1869 D: 12/30/1894
BR

Year	Tm	Lg	Tot	H	A	Men-On 0	1	2	3	One-Game 2	3	4	LO	XN	IP	PH	RHP	LHP
1892	NY	NL	1	1	0	0	0	1	0	0	0	0	0	0	0	0	1	0

Rank among batters: 4,707 • *Total ballparks homered in*: 1 • *First HR*: 09/06/1892 off Ad Gumbert

Sadie McMahon

JOHN JOSEPH MCMAHON
B: 09/19/1867 D: 02/20/1954
BR

Year	Tm	Lg	Tot	H	A	Men-On 0	1	2	3	One-Game 2	3	4	LO	XN	IP	PH	RHP	LHP
1890	PHI	AA	2	1	1	1	1	0	0	0	0	0	0	0	1	0	0	1
1891	BAL	AA	1	0	1	0	0	1	0	0	0	0	0	0	0	0	0	0
Total			3	1	2	1	1	1	0	0	0	0	0	0	1	0	0	1

Rank among batters: 3,735 • *Total ballparks homered in*: 2 • *First HR*: 05/22/1890 off Ed Cushman

Year	Tm	Lg	Tot	H	A	Men-On 0	1	2	3	One-Game 2	3	4	LO	XN	IP	PH	RHP	LHP

Jim McManus

JAMES MICHAEL MCMANUS
B: 07/20/1936
BL

Year	Tm	Lg	Tot	H	A	Men-On 0	1	2	3	One-Game 2	3	4	LO	XN	IP	PH	RHP	LHP
1960	KC	AL	1	1	0	1	0	0	0	0	0	0	0	0	0	0	1	0

Rank among batters: 4,707 • *Total ballparks homered in*: 1 • *First HR*: 09/30/1960 off Frank Lary

Marty McManus

MARTIN JOSEPH MCMANUS
B: 03/14/1900 D: 02/18/1966
BR

Year	Tm	Lg	Tot	H	A	Men-On 0	1	2	3	One-Game 2	3	4	LO	XN	IP	PH	RHP	LHP
1921	STL	AL	3	2	1	1	0	2	0	0	0	0	0	0	0	0	1	2
1922	STL	AL	11	6	5	4	5	2	0	0	0	0	0	0	1	0	8	3
1923	STL	AL	15	10	5	7	4	4	0	1	0	0	0	0	0	0	10	5
1924	STL	AL	5	2	3	3	2	0	0	1	0	0	0	0	0	0	3	2
1925	STL	AL	13	8	5	6	5	2	0	0	0	0	0	0	0	0	7	5
1926	STL	AL	9	7	2	5	4	0	0	0	0	0	0	0	0	0	4	5
1927	DET	AL	9	5	4	4	3	1	1	0	0	0	0	1	0	0	7	2
1928	DET	AL	8	5	3	5	3	0	0	0	0	0	0	0	0	0	7	1
1929	DET	AL	18	12	6	7	8	1	2	1	0	0	0	0	0	0	13	5
1930	DET	AL	9	5	4	6	1	2	0	0	0	0	0	0	0	0	9	0
1931	DET	AL	3	3	0	2	1	0	0	0	0	0	0	0	0	0	1	2
	BOS	AL	1	0	1	0	1	0	0	0	0	0	0	0	0	0	1	0
	Total		4	3	1	2	2	0	0	0	0	0	0	0	0	0	2	2
1932	BOS	AL	5	2	3	4	1	0	0	0	0	0	0	1	0	0	3	2
1933	BOS	AL	3	3	0	2	1	0	0	0	0	0	0	0	0	0	3	0
1934	BOS	NL	8	4	4	5	2	0	1	0	0	0	0	0	0	0	8	0
Total			120	74	46	61	41	14	4	3	0	0	0	2	1	0	85	34

Rank among batters: 388 • *Top target (6 home runs)*: Tommy Thomas • *Number of pitchers victimized*: 80 • *Total ballparks homered in*: 12 • *First HR*: 06/30/1921 off Dickie Kerr

Norm McMillan

NORMAN ALEXIS MCMILLAN
B: 10/05/1895 D: 09/28/1969
BR

Year	Tm	Lg	Tot	H	A	Men-On 0	1	2	3	One-Game 2	3	4	LO	XN	IP	PH	RHP	LHP
1928	CHI	NL	1	1	0	1	0	0	0	0	0	0	0	0	0	0	1	0
1929	CHI	NL	5	2	3	2	1	1	1	0	0	0	0	0	1	0	4	1
Total			6	3	3	3	1	1	1	0	0	0	0	0	1	0	5	1

Rank among batters: 2,988 • *Total ballparks homered in*: 4 • *First HR*: 08/15/1928 off Joe Genewich

Roy McMillan

ROY DAVID MCMILLAN
B: 07/17/1930
BR

Year	Tm	Lg	Tot	H	A	Men-On 0	1	2	3	One-Game 2	3	4	LO	XN	IP	PH	RHP	LHP
1951	CIN	NL	1	1	0	1	0	0	0	0	0	0	0	0	0	1	0	1
1952	CIN	NL	7	3	4	6	0	1	0	0	0	0	0	0	0	0	5	2
1953	CIN	NL	5	1	4	4	1	0	0	0	0	0	0	0	0	0	4	1
1954	CIN	NL	4	2	2	2	2	0	0	0	0	0	0	0	0	0	1	3
1955	CIN	NL	1	0	1	0	1	0	0	0	0	0	0	0	0	0	0	1
1956	CIN	NL	3	1	2	1	2	0	0	0	0	0	0	0	0	0	1	2
1957	CIN	NL	1	1	0	0	1	0	0	0	0	0	0	1	0	0	1	0
1958	CIN	NL	1	0	1	1	0	0	0	0	0	0	0	0	0	0	1	0
1959	CIN	NL	9	5	4	7	1	1	0	0	0	0	0	0	0	0	6	3
1960	CIN	NL	10	3	7	7	1	2	0	1	0	0	1	0	0	0	6	4
1961	MIL	NL	7	2	5	6	0	1	0	0	0	0	0	0	0	0	4	3
1962	MIL	NL	12	4	8	7	3	2	0	0	0	0	1	0	0	0	8	4
1963	MIL	NL	4	1	3	3	1	0	0	0	0	0	0	0	0	0	1	3
1964	NY	NL	1	1	0	0	1	0	0	0	0	0	0	0	0	0	1	0
1965	NY	NL	1	1	0	1	0	0	0	0	0	0	0	0	0	0	0	1
1966	NY	NL	1	0	1	1	0	0	0	0	0	0	0	0	0	0	1	0
Total			68	26	42	47	14	7	0	1	0	0	2	1	0	1	40	28

Rank among batters: 767 • *Top target (3 home runs)*: Warren Spahn • *Number of pitchers victimized*: 54 • *Total ballparks homered in*: 12 • *First HR*: 06/21/1951 off Preacher Roe

Ken McMullen

KENNETH LEE MCMULLEN
B: 06/01/1942
BR

Year	Tm	Lg	Tot	H	A	Men-On 0	1	2	3	One-Game 2	3	4	LO	XN	IP	PH	RHP	LHP
1963	LA	NL	5	4	1	3	1	0	1	0	0	0	0	0	0	0	3	2
1964	LA	NL	1	0	1	0	1	0	0	0	0	0	0	0	0	0	0	1

Year	Tm	Lg	Tot	H	A	Men-On				One-Game			LO	XN	IP	PH	RHP	LHP
						0	1	2	3	2	3	4						

Ken McMullen *continued*

Year	Tm	Lg	Tot	H	A	0	1	2	3	2	3	4	LO	XN	IP	PH	RHP	LHP
1965	WAS	AL	18	10	8	13	4	1	0	0	0	0	0	1	0	0	11	7
1966	WAS	AL	13	6	7	7	4	2	0	0	0	0	0	0	0	1	7	6
1967	WAS	AL	16	7	9	9	3	3	1	2	0	0	0	1	0	0	7	9
1968	WAS	AL	20	10	10	13	2	5	0	3	0	0	0	2	0	0	12	8
1969	WAS	AL	19	13	6	11	5	3	0	1	0	0	0	1	1	0	12	7
1970	CAL	AL	14	6	8	4	8	2	0	0	0	0	0	1	0	0	11	3
1971	CAL	AL	21	8	13	12	8	1	0	0	0	0	0	0	1	0	16	5
1972	CAL	AL	9	4	5	5	2	2	0	0	0	0	0	0	0	0	6	3
1973	LA	NL	5	4	1	3	1	1	0	0	0	0	0	1	0	2	1	4
1974	LA	NL	3	1	2	1	2	0	0	0	0	0	0	0	0	2	2	1
1975	LA	NL	2	1	1	0	0	1	1	0	0	0	0	0	0	2	0	2
1976	OAK	AL	5	4	1	2	2	1	0	0	0	0	0	0	0	1	3	2
1977	MIL	AL	5	2	3	1	4	0	0	0	0	0	0	0	0	2	2	3
Total			156	80	76	84	47	22	3	6	0	0	0	7	2	10	93	63

Rank among batters: 272 • *Top target (4 home runs)*: Sam McDowell • *Number of pitchers victimized*: 114 • *Total ballparks homered in*: 18 • *First HR*: 04/22/1963 off Bob Hendley

Fred McMullin

FREDERICK WILLIAM MCMULLIN
B: 10/13/1891 D: 11/21/1952
BR

Year	Tm	Lg	Tot	H	A	0	1	2	3	2	3	4	LO	XN	IP	PH	RHP	LHP
1918	CHI	AL	1	1	0	0	1	0	0	0	0	0	0	0	0	0	1	0

Rank among batters: 4,707 • *Total ballparks homered in*: 1 • *First HR*: 08/01/1918 off Eddie Matteson

Eric McNair

DONALD ERIC MCNAIR
B: 04/12/1909 D: 03/11/1949
BR

Year	Tm	Lg	Tot	H	A	0	1	2	3	2	3	4	LO	XN	IP	PH	RHP	LHP
1931	PHI	AL	5	2	3	3	2	0	0	0	0	0	0	1	0	0	5	0
1932	PHI	AL	18	14	4	9	7	1	1	1	0	0	0	0	0	0	14	4
1933	PHI	AL	7	4	3	4	1	2	0	0	0	0	1	0	0	0	5	2
1934	PHI	AL	17	8	9	9	4	4	0	1	0	0	1	1	0	0	14	3
1935	PHI	AL	4	1	3	2	1	1	0	0	0	0	0	0	0	0	4	0
1936	BOS	AL	4	3	1	2	2	0	0	0	0	0	0	0	0	0	4	0
1937	BOS	AL	12	7	5	6	4	2	0	0	0	0	0	0	0	1	9	3
1939	CHI	AL	7	6	1	1	5	1	0	0	0	0	0	0	0	0	5	2
1940	CHI	AL	7	2	5	5	2	0	0	0	0	0	0	0	0	0	6	1
1942	DET	AL	1	0	1	1	0	0	0	0	0	0	0	0	0	0	0	1
Total			82	47	35	42	28	11	1	2	0	0	2	2	0	1	66	16

Rank among batters: 637 • *Top target (4 home runs)*: Vic Sorrell • *Number of pitchers victimized*: 55 • *Total ballparks homered in*: 9 • *First HR*: 05/21/1931 off Tommy Bridges

Dave McNally

DAVID ARTHUR MCNALLY
B: 10/31/1942
BR

Year	Tm	Lg	Tot	H	A	0	1	2	3	2	3	4	LO	XN	IP	PH	RHP	LHP
1968	BAL	AL	3	2	1	1	1	0	1	0	0	0	0	0	0	0	3	0
1969	BAL	AL	1	1	0	0	1	0	0	0	0	0	0	0	0	0	1	0
1970	BAL	AL	1	1	0	0	1	0	0	0	0	0	0	0	0	0	1	0
1971	BAL	AL	2	2	0	0	2	0	0	0	0	0	0	0	0	0	1	1
1972	BAL	AL	2	0	2	1	1	0	0	0	0	0	0	0	0	0	1	1
Total			9	6	3	2	6	0	1	0	0	0	0	0	0	0	7	2

Rank among batters: 2,587 • *Total ballparks homered in*: 4 • *First HR*: 07/20/1968 off Denny McLain • *World Series HR*—2

Mike McNally

MICHAEL JOSEPH MCNALLY
B: 09/09/1892 D: 05/29/1965
BR

Year	Tm	Lg	Tot	H	A	0	1	2	3	2	3	4	LO	XN	IP	PH	RHP	LHP
1921	NY	AL	1	1	0	1	0	0	0	0	0	0	0	0	0	0	0	1

Rank among batters: 4,707 • *Total ballparks homered in*: 1 • *First HR*: 09/18/1921 off Dutch Leonard

Jim McNamara

JAMES PATRICK MCNAMARA
B: 06/10/1965
BL

Year	Tm	Lg	Tot	H	A	0	1	2	3	2	3	4	LO	XN	IP	PH	RHP	LHP
1992	SF	NL	1	1	0	0	1	0	0	0	0	0	0	0	0	0	1	0

Jim McNamara *continued*

Rank among batters: 4,707 • *Total ballparks homered in*: 1 • *First HR*: 04/17/1992 off Dwayne Henry

Earl McNeely

GEORGE EARL MCNEELY
B: 05/12/1898 D: 07/16/1971
BR

						Men-On				One-Game								
Year	Tm	Lg	Tot	H	A	0	1	2	3	2	3	4	LO	XN	IP	PH	RHP	LHP
1925	WAS	AL	3	0	3	3	0	0	0	1	0	0	0	0	0	0	1	2
1929	STL	AL	1	1	0	0	1	0	0	0	0	0	0	0	0	0	0	1
Total			4	1	3	3	1	0	0	1	0	0	0	0	0	0	1	3

Rank among batters: 3,427 • *Total ballparks homered in*: 3 • *First HR*: 06/26/1925 off Lefty Grove

Jerry McNertney

GERALD EDWARD MCNERTNEY
B: 08/07/1936
BR

						Men-On				One-Game								
Year	Tm	Lg	Tot	H	A	0	1	2	3	2	3	4	LO	XN	IP	PH	RHP	LHP
1964	CHI	AL	3	0	3	2	0	0	1	0	0	0	0	0	0	0	2	1
1967	CHI	AL	3	2	1	2	0	1	0	0	0	0	0	0	0	0	1	2
1968	CHI	AL	3	0	3	3	0	0	0	0	0	0	0	0	0	0	2	1
1969	SEA	AL	8	5	3	3	2	3	0	0	0	0	0	0	0	0	3	5
1970	MIL	AL	6	2	4	4	2	0	0	0	0	0	0	0	0	1	4	2
1971	STL	NL	4	2	2	2	2	0	0	0	0	0	0	0	0	0	3	1
Total			27	11	16	16	6	4	1	0	0	0	0	0	0	1	15	12

Rank among batters: 1,532 • *Top target (2 home runs)*: Phil Regan • *Number of pitchers victimized*: 26 • *Total ballparks homered in*: 13 • *First HR*: 05/30/1964 off Phil Regan

Pat McNulty

PATRICK HOWARD MCNULTY
B: 02/27/1899 D: 05/04/1963
BL

						Men-On				One-Game								
Year	Tm	Lg	Tot	H	A	0	1	2	3	2	3	4	LO	XN	IP	PH	RHP	LHP
1925	CLE	AL	6	3	3	3	1	2	0	0	0	0	0	0	3	0	6	0

Rank among batters: 2,988 • *Total ballparks homered in*: 3 • *First HR*: 04/14/1925 off Dixie Davis

Bid McPhee

JOHN ALEXANDER MCPHEE
B: 11/01/1859 D: 01/03/1943
BR

						Men-On				One-Game								
Year	Tm	Lg	Tot	H	A	0	1	2	3	2	3	4	LO	XN	IP	PH	RHP	LHP
1882	CIN	AA	1	0	1	1	0	0	0	0	0	0	0	0	0	0	1	0
1883	CIN	AA	2	2	0	0	1	1	0	0	0	0	0	0	0	0	1	0
1884	CIN	AA	5	3	2	3	1	1	0	1	0	0	0	0	0	0	5	0
1886	CIN	AA	8	6	2	3	3	2	0	0	0	0	0	0	0	0	4	1
1887	CIN	AA	2	2	0	2	0	0	0	0	0	0	0	0	1	0	0	2
1888	CIN	AA	4	4	0	3	1	0	0	0	0	0	0	0	2	0	4	0
1889	CIN	AA	5	5	0	1	3	0	1	1	0	0	0	0	0	0	4	1
1890	CIN	NL	3	2	1	3	0	0	0	0	0	0	1	0	0	0	3	0
1891	CIN	NL	6	5	1	4	1	1	0	0	0	0	0	0	0	0	4	2
1892	CIN	NL	4	3	1	1	2	0	1	0	0	0	0	0	0	0	4	0
1893	CIN	NL	3	2	1	2	0	1	0	0	0	0	0	0	0	0	2	1
1894	CIN	NL	5	3	2	1	2	1	1	0	0	0	0	0	1	0	5	0
1895	CIN	NL	1	0	1	1	0	0	0	0	0	0	0	0	0	0	1	0
1896	CIN	NL	1	1	0	1	0	0	0	0	0	0	0	0	1	0	1	0
1897	CIN	NL	1	0	1	0	0	1	0	0	0	0	0	0	0	0	1	0
1898	CIN	NL	1	0	1	1	0	0	0	0	0	0	0	0	0	0	1	0
1899	CIN	NL	1	0	1	0	1	0	0	0	0	0	0	0	0	0	1	0
Total			53	38	15	27	15	8	3	2	0	0	1	0	5	0	42	7

Rank among batters: 953 • *Top target (4 home runs)*: Jack Lynch • *Number of pitchers victimized*: 40 • *Total ballparks homered in*: 14 • *First HR*: 05/19/1882 off Harry Arundel • *Hit for Cycle*—vs BAL: 08/26/1887

Mox McQuery

WILLIAM THOMAS MCQUERY
B: 06/28/1861 D: 06/12/1900

						Men-On				One-Game								
Year	Tm	Lg	Tot	H	A	0	1	2	3	2	3	4	LO	XN	IP	PH	RHP	LHP
1884	CIN	UA	2	1	1	2	0	0	0	0	0	0	0	0	0	0	2	0
1885	DET	NL	3	3	0	1	2	0	0	0	0	0	0	0	0	0	2	1
1886	KC	NL	4	1	3	1	2	1	0	0	0	0	0	0	0	0	3	1

Mox McQuery *continued*

Year	Tm	Lg	Tot	H	A	Men-On 0	1	2	3	One-Game 2	3	4	LO	XN	IP	PH	RHP	LHP
1890	SYR	AA	2	0	2	1	1	0	0	0	0	0	0	0	0	0	0	2
1891	WAS	AA	2	1	1	2	0	0	0	0	0	0	0	0	0	0	2	0
Total			13	6	7	7	5	1	0	0	0	0	0	0	0	0	9	4

Rank among batters: 2,248 • *Top target (2 home runs)*: Charlie Buffinton • *Number of pitchers victimized*: 12 • *Total ballparks homered in*: 11 • *First HR*: 08/20/1884 off Al Atkinson • *Hit for Cycle*—vs PRO: 09/28/1885

Hugh McQuillan

HUGH A. MCQUILLAN
B: 09/15/1897 D: 08/26/1947
BR

Year	Tm	Lg	Tot	H	A	Men-On 0	1	2	3	One-Game 2	3	4	LO	XN	IP	PH	RHP	LHP
1920	BOS	NL	1	0	1	1	0	0	0	0	0	0	0	0	0	0	1	0
1921	BOS	NL	1	0	1	0	1	0	0	0	0	0	0	0	0	0	1	0
Total			2	0	2	1	1	0	0	0	0	0	0	0	0	0	2	0

Rank among batters: 4,129 • *Total ballparks homered in*: 1 • *First HR*: 09/23/1920 off Bill Hubbell

Glenn McQuillen

GLENN RICHARD MCQUILLEN
B: 04/19/1915 D: 06/08/1989
BR

Year	Tm	Lg	Tot	H	A	Men-On 0	1	2	3	One-Game 2	3	4	LO	XN	IP	PH	RHP	LHP
1942	STL	AL	3	1	2	3	0	0	0	0	0	0	0	0	0	0	2	1
1946	STL	AL	1	0	1	1	0	0	0	0	0	0	0	0	0	0	0	1
Total			4	1	3	4	0	0	0	0	0	0	0	0	0	0	2	2

Rank among batters: 3,427 • *Total ballparks homered in*: 4 • *First HR*: 04/29/1942 off Spud Chandler

George McQuinn

GEORGE HARTLEY MCQUINN
B: 05/29/1910 D: 12/24/1978
BL

Year	Tm	Lg	Tot	H	A	Men-On 0	1	2	3	One-Game 2	3	4	LO	XN	IP	PH	RHP	LHP
1938	STL	AL	12	7	5	5	5	2	0	0	0	0	0	0	0	0	11	1
1939	STL	AL	20	12	8	10	8	2	0	2	0	0	0	0	0	0	19	1
1940	STL	AL	16	8	8	9	5	2	0	2	0	0	0	2	0	0	15	1
1941	STL	AL	18	11	7	9	6	3	0	2	0	0	0	1	0	0	15	3
1942	STL	AL	12	8	4	6	5	1	0	1	0	0	0	0	0	0	11	1
1943	STL	AL	12	7	5	4	6	2	0	0	0	0	0	0	0	0	11	1
1944	STL	AL	11	7	4	3	7	1	0	1	0	0	0	0	0	0	11	0
1945	STL	AL	7	4	3	4	3	0	0	0	0	0	0	0	0	1	7	0
1946	PHI	AL	3	0	3	2	1	0	0	0	0	0	0	0	0	0	2	1
1947	NY	AL	13	7	6	7	4	2	0	1	0	0	0	0	0	0	11	2
1948	NY	AL	11	7	4	6	3	2	0	0	0	0	0	0	0	0	11	0
Total			135	78	57	65	53	17	0	9	0	0	0	3	0	1	124	11

Rank among batters: 326 • *Top target (5 home runs)*: Tex Hughson • *Number of pitchers victimized*: 88 • *Total ballparks homered in*: 9 • *First HR*: 04/27/1938 off Tommy Bridges • *Hit for Cycle*—vs BOS: 07/19/1941 (1) • *World Series HR*—1

Brian McRae

BRIAN WESLEY MCRAE
B: 08/27/1967
BB

Year	Tm	Lg	Tot	H	A	Men-On 0	1	2	3	One-Game 2	3	4	LO	XN	IP	PH	RHP	LHP
1990	KC	AL	2	1	1	1	0	1	0	0	0	0	0	0	0	0	1	1
1991	KC	AL	8	3	5	3	3	1	1	1	0	0	0	0	2	0	6	2
1992	KC	AL	4	2	2	1	2	1	0	0	0	0	0	0	2	0	1	3
1993	KC	AL	12	5	7	6	5	1	0	0	0	0	0	0	1	0	7	5
1994	KC	AL	4	2	2	3	1	0	0	0	0	0	0	0	0	0	3	1
1995	CHI	NL	12	6	6	11	0	0	1	0	0	0	3	1	0	0	10	2
Total			42	19	23	25	11	4	2	1	0	0	3	1	5	0	28	14

Rank among batters: 1,138 • *Top target (2 home runs)*: Chuck Finley • *Number of pitchers victimized*: 41 • *Total ballparks homered in*: 14 • *First HR*: 08/26/1990 off Keith Comstock

Hal McRae

HAROLD ABRAHAM MCRAE
B: 07/10/1945
BR

Year	Tm	Lg	Tot	H	A	Men-On 0	1	2	3	One-Game 2	3	4	LO	XN	IP	PH	RHP	LHP
1970	CIN	NL	8	5	3	7	1	0	0	1	0	0	0	0	0	1	1	7

Hal McRae *continued*

Year	Tm	Lg	Tot	H	A	Men-On 0	Men-On 1	Men-On 2	Men-On 3	One-Game 2	One-Game 3	One-Game 4	LO	XN	IP	PH	RHP	LHP
1971	CIN	NL	9	6	3	8	0	1	0	1	0	0	0	0	0	0	3	6
1972	CIN	NL	5	2	3	2	2	0	1	0	0	0	0	0	0	3	0	5
1973	KC	AL	9	2	7	6	2	1	0	1	0	0	0	0	0	0	2	7
1974	KC	AL	15	9	6	8	5	1	1	0	0	0	0	0	0	0	9	6
1975	KC	AL	5	2	3	3	1	1	0	0	0	0	0	0	0	0	2	3
1976	KC	AL	8	4	4	4	3	1	0	0	0	0	0	0	0	0	3	5
1977	KC	AL	21	8	13	15	5	1	0	1	0	0	0	0	0	0	12	9
1978	KC	AL	16	8	8	12	3	1	0	0	0	0	0	0	0	0	8	8
1979	KC	AL	10	5	5	6	2	2	0	0	0	0	0	1	0	0	5	5
1980	KC	AL	14	6	8	7	4	3	0	1	0	0	0	0	1	0	9	5
1981	KC	AL	7	2	5	6	1	0	0	0	0	0	0	0	0	0	6	1
1982	KC	AL	27	12	15	12	10	4	1	1	0	0	0	1	1	0	13	14
1983	KC	AL	12	5	7	9	2	1	0	0	0	0	0	0	0	0	7	5
1984	KC	AL	3	2	1	1	2	0	0	0	0	0	0	0	0	0	0	3
1985	KC	AL	14	7	7	5	8	1	0	1	0	0	0	0	0	1	6	8
1986	KC	AL	7	1	6	3	4	0	0	0	0	0	0	1	0	1	2	5
1987	KC	AL	1	1	0	1	0	0	0	0	0	0	0	0	0	0	0	1
Total			191	87	104	115	55	18	3	7	0	0	0	3	2	6	88	103

Rank among batters: 200 • *Top target (6 home runs)*: Ken Holtzman, Frank Tanana • *Number of pitchers victimized*: 133 • *Total ballparks homered in*: 24 • *First HR*: 04/17/1970 off Don McMahon • *LCS HR*—1

Kevin McReynolds

WALTER KEVIN MCREYNOLDS
B: 10/16/1959
BR

Year	Tm	Lg	Tot	H	A	Men-On 0	Men-On 1	Men-On 2	Men-On 3	One-Game 2	One-Game 3	One-Game 4	LO	XN	IP	PH	RHP	LHP
1983	SD	NL	4	3	1	3	1	0	0	0	0	0	0	0	0	0	3	1
1984	SD	NL	20	10	10	16	2	2	0	0	0	0	0	2	0	1	11	9
1985	SD	NL	15	6	9	8	4	3	0	0	0	0	0	0	0	0	12	3
1986	SD	NL	26	14	12	12	10	3	1	2	0	0	0	0	0	0	16	10
1987	NY	NL	29	18	11	18	7	4	0	3	0	0	0	0	0	0	17	12
1988	NY	NL	27	13	14	16	5	4	2	2	0	0	0	1	0	0	15	12
1989	NY	NL	22	12	10	15	3	3	1	0	0	0	0	1	0	0	13	9
1990	NY	NL	24	11	13	14	4	5	1	4	0	0	0	1	0	0	20	4
1991	NY	NL	16	7	9	7	3	5	1	0	0	0	0	2	0	1	11	5
1992	KC	AL	13	4	9	7	6	0	0	0	0	0	0	0	0	0	8	5
1993	KC	AL	11	8	3	9	2	0	0	0	0	0	0	0	0	0	9	2
1994	NY	NL	4	3	1	3	0	1	0	1	0	0	0	0	0	0	3	1
Total			211	109	102	128	47	30	6	12	0	0	0	7	0	2	138	73

Rank among batters: 162 • *Top target (6 home runs)*: Bryn Smith • *Number of pitchers victimized*: 132 • *Total ballparks homered in*: 20 • *First HR*: 06/02/1983 off Ron Reed • *Hit for Cycle*—@STL: 08/01/1989 • *LCS HR*—3

Jim McTamany

JAMES EDWARD MCTAMANY
B: 07/01/1863 D: 04/16/1916
BR

Year	Tm	Lg	Tot	H	A	Men-On 0	Men-On 1	Men-On 2	Men-On 3	One-Game 2	One-Game 3	One-Game 4	LO	XN	IP	PH	RHP	LHP
1885	BRO	AA	1	1	0	1	0	0	0	0	0	0	0	0	0	0	1	0
1886	BRO	AA	2	2	0	0	1	1	0	1	0	0	0	0	0	0	2	0
1887	BRO	AA	1	1	0	1	0	0	0	0	0	0	0	0	0	0	0	1
1888	KC	AA	4	4	0	1	1	2	0	1	0	0	1	0	0	0	2	2
1889	COL	AA	4	2	2	3	1	0	0	0	0	0	1	0	0	0	3	1
1890	COL	AA	1	1	0	1	0	0	0	0	0	0	1	0	0	0	1	0
1891	COL	AA	3	1	2	2	0	1	0	0	0	0	0	0	2	0	3	0
	PHI	AA	3	1	2	2	1	0	0	0	0	0	1	0	1	0	2	1
	Total		6	2	4	4	1	1	0	0	0	0	1	0	3	0	5	1
Total			19	13	6	11	4	4	0	2	0	0	4	0	3	0	14	5

Rank among batters: 1,861 • *Top target (2 home runs)*: Al Atkinson, Mike Mattimore, Elton Chamberlin • *Number of pitchers victimized*: 16 • *Total ballparks homered in*: 10 • *First HR*: 09/03/1885 off Douglass Crothers

Cal McVey

CALVIN ALEXANDER MCVEY
B: 08/30/1850 D: 08/20/1926
BR

Year	Tm	Lg	Tot	H	A	Men-On 0	Men-On 1	Men-On 2	Men-On 3	One-Game 2	One-Game 3	One-Game 4	LO	XN	IP	PH	RHP	LHP
1876	CHI	NL	1	0	1	0	1	0	0	0	0	0	0	0	0	0	1	0
1878	CIN	NL	2	2	0	0	2	0	0	0	0	0	0	0	0	0	2	0
Total			3	2	1	0	3	0	0	0	0	0	0	0	0	0	3	0

Year	Tm	Lg	Tot	H	A	Men-On 0	1	2	3	One-Game 2	3	4	LO	XN	IP	PH	RHP	LHP

Cal McVey *continued*

Rank among batters: 3,735 • *Total ballparks homered in*: 2 • *First HR*: 09/09/1876 off Bobby Mathews

Bob Meacham

ROBERT ANDREW MEACHAM
B: 08/25/1960
BB

Year	Tm	Lg	Tot	H	A	0	1	2	3	2	3	4	LO	XN	IP	PH	RHP	LHP
1984	NY	AL	2	1	1	1	1	0	0	0	0	0	0	0	0	0	2	0
1985	NY	AL	1	1	0	1	0	0	0	0	0	0	0	0	0	0	1	0
1987	NY	AL	5	2	3	3	2	0	0	0	0	0	1	0	0	0	2	3
Total			8	4	4	5	3	0	0	0	0	0	1	0	0	0	5	3

Rank among batters: 2,703 • *Top target (2 home runs)*: Ron Romanick • *Number of pitchers victimized*: 7 • *Total ballparks homered in*: 4 • *First HR*: 08/21/1984 off Ron Romanick

Charlie Mead

CHARLES RICHARD MEAD
B: 04/09/1921
BL

Year	Tm	Lg	Tot	H	A	0	1	2	3	2	3	4	LO	XN	IP	PH	RHP	LHP
1943	NY	NL	1	0	1	1	0	0	0	0	0	0	0	0	0	0	1	0
1944	NY	NL	1	1	0	0	1	0	0	0	0	0	0	0	0	0	1	0
1945	NY	NL	1	1	0	0	0	1	0	0	0	0	0	0	0	0	0	1
Total			3	2	1	1	1	1	0	0	0	0	0	0	0	0	2	1

Rank among batters: 3,735 • *Total ballparks homered in*: 2 • *First HR*: 09/24/1943 off Ray Starr

Lee Meadows

HENRY LEE MEADOWS
B: 07/12/1894 D: 01/29/1963
BL

Year	Tm	Lg	Tot	H	A	0	1	2	3	2	3	4	LO	XN	IP	PH	RHP	LHP
1921	PHI	NL	3	3	0	1	1	0	1	0	0	0	0	0	0	0	2	1
1923	PHI	NL	1	1	0	0	0	1	0	0	0	0	0	0	0	0	0	1
1925	PIT	NL	1	1	0	0	1	0	0	0	0	0	0	0	0	0	0	1
Total			5	5	0	1	2	1	1	0	0	0	0	0	0	0	2	3

Rank among batters: 3,191 • *Total ballparks homered in*: 2 • *First HR*: 04/16/1921 off Slim Sallee

Louie Meadows

MICHAEL RAY MEADOWS
B: 04/29/1961
BL

Year	Tm	Lg	Tot	H	A	0	1	2	3	2	3	4	LO	XN	IP	PH	RHP	LHP
1988	HOU	NL	2	1	1	2	0	0	0	0	0	0	0	0	0	1	2	0
1989	HOU	NL	3	3	0	2	0	0	1	0	0	0	0	0	0	0	3	0
Total			5	4	1	4	0	0	1	0	0	0	0	0	0	1	5	0

Rank among batters: 3,191 • *Total ballparks homered in*: 2 • *First HR*: 07/01/1988 off Terry Leach

Pat Meares

PATRICK JAMES MEARES
B: 09/06/1968
BR

Year	Tm	Lg	Tot	H	A	0	1	2	3	2	3	4	LO	XN	IP	PH	RHP	LHP
1994	MIN	AL	2	0	2	1	1	0	0	1	0	0	0	0	0	0	2	0
1995	MIN	AL	12	3	9	9	2	1	0	0	0	0	1	0	0	0	7	5
Total			14	3	11	10	3	1	0	1	0	0	1	0	0	0	9	5

Rank among batters: 2,169 • *Top target (2 home runs)*: Randy Johnson • *Number of pitchers victimized*: 13 • *Total ballparks homered in*: 8 • *First HR*: 06/19/1994 off Mike Oquist

Luis Medina

LUIS MAIN MEDINA
B: 03/26/1963
BR

Year	Tm	Lg	Tot	H	A	0	1	2	3	2	3	4	LO	XN	IP	PH	RHP	LHP
1988	CLE	AL	6	4	2	4	2	0	0	1	0	0	0	0	0	0	2	4
1989	CLE	AL	4	1	3	3	1	0	0	0	0	0	0	0	0	0	0	4
Total			10	5	5	7	3	0	0	1	0	0	0	0	0	0	2	8

Rank among batters: 2,500 • *Top target (2 home runs)*: Tommy John, Jimmy Key • *Number of pitchers victimized*: 8 • *Total ballparks homered in*: 5 • *First HR*: 09/07/1988 off Tommy John

Joe Medwick

JOSEPH MICHAEL MEDWICK
B: 11/24/1911 D: 03/21/1975
BR HOF

Year	Tm	Lg	Tot	H	A	Men-On 0	1	2	3	One-Game 2	3	4	LO	XN	IP	PH	RHP	LHP
1932	STL	NL	2	0	2	1	1	0	0	0	0	0	0	0	0	0	2	0
1933	STL	NL	18	7	11	11	4	3	0	1	0	0	0	0	0	0	14	4
1934	STL	NL	18	8	10	10	6	1	1	1	0	0	0	1	0	0	14	4
1935	STL	NL	23	13	10	12	10	1	0	3	0	0	0	1	1	0	16	7
1936	STL	NL	18	6	12	10	5	3	0	1	0	0	0	0	0	0	13	5
1937	STL	NL	31	18	13	14	11	5	1	4	0	0	0	0	0	0	23	8
1938	STL	NL	21	13	8	10	8	3	0	0	0	0	0	0	0	0	15	6
1939	STL	NL	14	10	4	7	7	0	0	0	0	0	0	0	0	0	11	3
1940	STL	NL	3	2	1	2	1	0	0	0	0	0	0	0	0	0	3	0
	BRO	NL	14	3	11	8	3	2	1	0	0	0	0	0	0	0	11	3
	Total		17	5	12	10	4	2	1	0	0	0	0	0	0	0	14	3
1941	BRO	NL	18	12	6	8	7	3	0	0	0	0	0	0	0	0	11	7
1942	BRO	NL	4	2	2	2	1	1	0	0	0	0	0	0	0	0	1	3
1943	NY	NL	5	3	2	2	0	3	0	0	0	0	0	0	0	0	3	2
1944	NY	NL	7	5	2	4	2	1	0	0	0	0	0	0	0	0	6	1
1945	NY	NL	3	2	1	1	2	0	0	0	0	0	0	0	0	0	2	1
1946	BRO	NL	2	1	1	0	1	1	0	0	0	0	0	0	0	0	0	2
1947	STL	NL	4	2	2	1	1	2	0	0	0	0	0	0	0	0	0	4
Total			205	107	98	103	70	29	3	10	0	0	0	2	1	0	145	60

Rank among batters: 173 • *Top target (7 home runs)*: Jim Turner • *Number of pitchers victimized*: 109 • *Total ballparks homered in*: 9 • *First HR*: 09/10/1932 off Freddie Fitzsimmons • *Hit for Cycle—*@CIN: 06/29/1935 • *World Series HR*—1; *All-Star HR*—1

Jouett Meekin

GEORGE JOUETT MEEKIN
B: 02/21/1867 D: 12/14/1944
BR

Year	Tm	Lg	Tot	H	A	Men-On 0	1	2	3	One-Game 2	3	4	LO	XN	IP	PH	RHP	LHP
1891	LOU	AA	1	0	1	1	0	0	0	0	0	0	0	0	0	0	0	0
1892	WAS	NL	2	1	1	2	0	0	0	0	0	0	0	0	0	0	2	0
1893	WAS	NL	3	2	1	3	0	0	0	0	0	0	0	0	2	0	3	0
1894	NY	NL	5	4	1	1	4	0	0	0	0	0	0	1	1	0	5	0
1895	NY	NL	1	0	1	0	0	1	0	0	0	0	0	0	0	0	1	0
1896	NY	NL	2	2	0	0	1	1	0	0	0	0	0	0	0	0	2	0
1899	NY	NL	1	0	1	0	1	0	0	0	0	0	0	0	0	0	0	1
Total			15	9	6	7	6	2	0	0	0	0	0	1	3	0	13	1

Rank among batters: 2,096 • *Top target (2 home runs)*: Ad Gumbert, Kid Nichols • *Number of pitchers victimized*: 13 • *Total ballparks homered in*: 8 • *First HR*: 09/30/1891 off George Davies

Sammy Meeks

SAMUEL MACK MEEKS
B: 04/23/1923
BR

Year	Tm	Lg	Tot	H	A	Men-On 0	1	2	3	One-Game 2	3	4	LO	XN	IP	PH	RHP	LHP
1949	CIN	NL	2	2	0	1	1	0	0	0	0	0	0	0	0	0	1	1
1950	CIN	NL	1	1	0	1	0	0	0	0	0	0	0	0	0	0	0	1
Total			3	3	0	2	1	0	0	0	0	0	0	0	0	0	1	2

Rank among batters: 3,735 • *Total ballparks homered in*: 1 • *First HR*: 09/22/1949 off Monita Kennedy

Dave Meier

DAVID KEITH MEIER
B: 08/08/1959
BR

Year	Tm	Lg	Tot	H	A	Men-On 0	1	2	3	One-Game 2	3	4	LO	XN	IP	PH	RHP	LHP
1985	MIN	AL	1	1	0	0	0	1	0	0	0	0	0	0	0	0	0	1

Rank among batters: 4,707 • *Total ballparks homered in*: 1 • *First HR*: 10/01/1985 off Floyd Bannister

Frank Meinke

FRANK LOUIS MEINKE
B: 10/18/1863 D: 11/08/1931
BR

Year	Tm	Lg	Tot	H	A	Men-On 0	1	2	3	One-Game 2	3	4	LO	XN	IP	PH	RHP	LHP
1884	DET	NL	6	1	5	0	4	2	0	1	0	0	0	0	0	0	4	0

Rank among batters: 2,988 • *Top target (2 home runs)*: George Crosby • *Number of pitchers victimized*: 5 • *Total ballparks homered in*: 4 • *First HR*: 05/29/1884 off Larry Corcoran

Year	Tm	Lg	Tot	H	A	Men-On 0	Men-On 1	Men-On 2	Men-On 3	One-Game 2	One-Game 3	One-Game 4	LO	XN	IP	PH	RHP	LHP

John Meister

JOHN F. MEISTER
B: 05/10/1863 D: 01/28/1923

Year	Tm	Lg	Tot	H	A	0	1	2	3	2	3	4	LO	XN	IP	PH	RHP	LHP
1886	NY	AA	2	1	1	1	1	0	0	0	0	0	0	0	0	0	1	1
1887	NY	AA	1	0	1	0	1	0	0	0	0	0	0	0	0	0	1	0
Total			3	1	2	1	2	0	0	0	0	0	0	0	0	0	2	1

Rank among batters: 3,735 • *Total ballparks homered in*: 3 • *First HR*: 08/28/1886 off Cyclone Miller

Roberto Mejia

ROBERTO ANTONIO (DIAZ) MEJIA
B: 04/14/1972
BR

Year	Tm	Lg	Tot	H	A	0	1	2	3	2	3	4	LO	XN	IP	PH	RHP	LHP
1993	COL	NL	5	3	2	4	1	0	0	0	0	0	0	0	0	0	3	2
1994	COL	NL	4	1	3	2	2	0	0	0	0	0	0	0	0	0	3	1
1995	COL	NL	1	1	0	1	0	0	0	0	0	0	0	0	0	0	1	0
Total			10	5	5	7	3	0	0	0	0	0	0	0	0	0	7	3

Rank among batters: 2,500 • *Total ballparks homered in*: 7 • *First HR*: 07/23/1993 off Allen Watson

Ramon Mejias

RAMON (GOMEZ) MEJIAS
B: 08/09/1930
BR

Year	Tm	Lg	Tot	H	A	0	1	2	3	2	3	4	LO	XN	IP	PH	RHP	LHP
1955	PIT	NL	3	2	1	1	2	0	0	0	0	0	0	0	0	0	1	2
1957	PIT	NL	2	0	2	1	1	0	0	0	0	0	1	0	0	0	0	2
1958	PIT	NL	5	0	5	4	1	0	0	0	1	0	1	0	0	0	2	3
1959	PIT	NL	7	1	6	4	3	0	0	0	0	0	0	1	0	0	4	3
1962	HOU	NL	24	12	12	12	7	5	0	2	0	0	0	0	1	0	20	4
1963	BOS	AL	11	8	3	5	5	1	0	2	0	0	0	0	0	0	10	1
1964	BOS	AL	2	2	0	2	0	0	0	0	0	0	0	0	0	0	1	1
Total			54	25	29	29	19	6	0	4	1	0	2	1	1	0	38	16

Rank among batters: 938 • *Top target (4 home runs)*: Warren Spahn • *Number of pitchers victimized*: 45 • *Total ballparks homered in*: 16 • *First HR*: 04/14/1955 off Herm Wehmeier

Sam Mejias

SAMUEL ELIAS MEJIAS
B: 05/09/1952
BR

Year	Tm	Lg	Tot	H	A	0	1	2	3	2	3	4	LO	XN	IP	PH	RHP	LHP
1977	MON	NL	3	1	2	2	1	0	0	0	0	0	0	0	0	1	3	0
1980	CIN	NL	1	1	0	1	0	0	0	0	0	0	0	0	0	0	1	0
Total			4	2	2	3	1	0	0	0	0	0	0	0	0	1	4	0

Rank among batters: 3,427 • *Total ballparks homered in*: 4 • *First HR*: 06/05/1977 off Clay Carroll

Sam Mele

SABATH ANTHONY MELE
B: 01/23/1923
BR

Year	Tm	Lg	Tot	H	A	0	1	2	3	2	3	4	LO	XN	IP	PH	RHP	LHP
1947	BOS	AL	12	8	4	7	3	2	0	0	0	0	1	0	0	1	10	2
1948	BOS	AL	2	1	1	0	2	0	0	0	0	0	0	0	0	0	1	1
1949	WAS	AL	3	3	0	2	1	0	0	0	0	0	0	0	0	0	0	3
1950	WAS	AL	12	0	12	4	3	5	0	0	0	0	0	0	0	0	6	6
1951	WAS	AL	5	1	4	2	2	0	1	0	0	0	0	0	0	0	3	2
1952	WAS	AL	2	0	2	1	1	0	0	0	0	0	0	0	0	0	1	1
	CHI	AL	14	8	6	8	3	3	0	1	0	0	0	1	0	1	10	4
	Total		16	8	8	9	4	3	0	1	0	0	0	1	0	1	11	5
1953	CHI	AL	12	6	6	6	5	0	1	0	0	0	0	1	0	1	6	6
1954	BAL	AL	5	1	4	1	4	0	0	0	0	0	0	0	0	0	3	2
	BOS	AL	7	4	3	3	2	2	0	0	0	0	1	0	0	1	4	3
	Total		12	5	7	4	6	2	0	0	0	0	1	0	0	1	7	5
1955	CIN	NL	2	1	1	1	1	0	0	0	0	0	0	0	0	1	1	1
1956	CLE	AL	4	1	3	4	0	0	0	0	0	0	0	0	0	1	1	3
Total			80	34	46	39	27	12	2	1	0	0	2	2	0	6	46	34

Rank among batters: 650 • *Top target (4 home runs)*: Ray Scarborough • *Number of pitchers victimized*: 64 • *Total ballparks homered in*: 10 • *First HR*: 04/22/1947 off Bill Bevens

Francisco Melendez

FRANCISCO JAVIER (VILLEGAS) MELENDEZ
B: 01/25/1964
BL

Year	Tm	Lg	Tot	H	A	Men-On 0	Men-On 1	Men-On 2	Men-On 3	One-Game 2	One-Game 3	One-Game 4	LO	XN	IP	PH	RHP	LHP
1987	SF	NL	1	1	0	1	0	0	0	0	0	0	0	0	0	1	1	0

Rank among batters: 4,707 • *Total ballparks homered in*: 1 • *First HR*: 10/02/1987 off Kevin Coffman

Luis Melendez

LUIS ANTONIO (SANTANA) MELENDEZ
B: 08/11/1949
BR

Year	Tm	Lg	Tot	H	A	Men-On 0	Men-On 1	Men-On 2	Men-On 3	One-Game 2	One-Game 3	One-Game 4	LO	XN	IP	PH	RHP	LHP
1972	STL	NL	5	3	2	2	2	0	1	0	0	0	0	0	0	1	3	2
1973	STL	NL	2	0	2	0	0	1	1	0	0	0	0	0	0	0	1	1
1975	STL	NL	2	0	2	2	0	0	0	0	0	0	0	0	0	0	0	2
Total			9	3	6	4	2	1	2	0	0	0	0	0	0	1	4	5

Rank among batters: 2,587 • *Total ballparks homered in*: 7 • *First HR*: 05/02/1972 off Don Gullett

Ski Melillo

OSCAR DONALD MELILLO
B: 08/04/1899 D: 11/14/1963
BR

Year	Tm	Lg	Tot	H	A	Men-On 0	Men-On 1	Men-On 2	Men-On 3	One-Game 2	One-Game 3	One-Game 4	LO	XN	IP	PH	RHP	LHP
1926	STL	AL	1	1	0	1	0	0	0	0	0	0	0	0	0	0	0	1
1929	STL	AL	5	1	4	3	2	0	0	0	0	0	0	0	0	0	4	1
1930	STL	AL	5	3	2	4	1	0	0	0	0	0	0	0	1	0	3	2
1931	STL	AL	2	1	1	0	2	0	0	0	0	0	0	0	0	0	2	0
1932	STL	AL	3	2	1	2	1	0	0	0	0	0	0	0	0	0	1	2
1933	STL	AL	3	2	1	0	1	2	0	0	0	0	0	0	1	0	0	3
1934	STL	AL	2	2	0	0	0	2	0	0	0	0	0	0	0	0	1	1
1935	BOS	AL	1	0	1	1	0	0	0	0	0	0	1	0	0	0	1	0
Total			22	12	10	11	7	4	0	0	0	0	1	0	2	0	12	10

Rank among batters: 1,719 • *Top target (3 home runs)*: Lefty Gomez • *Number of pitchers victimized*: 20 • *Total ballparks homered in*: 7 • *First HR*: 06/18/1926 off Dutch Ruether • *Hit for Cycle—@CLE*: 05/23/1929 (2)

Paul Meloan

PAUL B. MELOAN
B: 08/23/1888 D: 02/11/1950
BL

Year	Tm	Lg	Tot	H	A	Men-On 0	Men-On 1	Men-On 2	Men-On 3	One-Game 2	One-Game 3	One-Game 4	LO	XN	IP	PH	RHP	LHP
1911	STL	AL	3	1	2	3	0	0	0	0	0	0	0	1	0	0	3	0

Rank among batters: 3,735 • *Top target (2 home runs)*: Ray Caldwell • *Number of pitchers victimized*: 2 • *Total ballparks homered in*: 3 • *First HR*: 05/21/1911 off Ray Caldwell

Bill Melton

WILLIAM EDWIN MELTON
B: 07/07/1945
BR

Year	Tm	Lg	Tot	H	A	Men-On 0	Men-On 1	Men-On 2	Men-On 3	One-Game 2	One-Game 3	One-Game 4	LO	XN	IP	PH	RHP	LHP
1968	CHI	AL	2	1	1	1	1	0	0	0	0	0	0	0	0	0	1	1
1969	CHI	AL	23	13	10	14	6	2	1	0	1	0	0	2	0	0	17	6
1970	CHI	AL	33	23	10	23	7	3	0	2	0	0	0	1	0	0	21	12
1971	CHI	AL	33	16	17	18	10	3	2	1	0	0	1	1	0	0	23	10
1972	CHI	AL	7	5	2	2	1	4	0	0	0	0	0	0	0	0	5	2
1973	CHI	AL	20	13	7	10	9	1	0	0	0	0	0	0	0	0	13	7
1974	CHI	AL	21	11	10	11	8	2	0	0	0	0	0	0	0	0	12	9
1975	CHI	AL	15	8	7	7	4	3	1	0	0	0	0	0	0	0	11	4
1976	CAL	AL	6	3	3	5	1	0	0	0	0	0	0	0	0	0	4	2
Total			160	93	67	91	47	18	4	3	1	0	1	4	0	0	107	53

Rank among batters: 263 • *Top target (5 home runs)*: Sonny Siebert • *Number of pitchers victimized*: 100 • *Total ballparks homered in*: 15 • *First HR*: 09/11/1968 off Fritz Peterson

Rube Melton

REUBEN FRANKLIN MELTON
B: 02/27/1917 D: 09/11/1971
BR

Year	Tm	Lg	Tot	H	A	Men-On 0	Men-On 1	Men-On 2	Men-On 3	One-Game 2	One-Game 3	One-Game 4	LO	XN	IP	PH	RHP	LHP
1942	PHI	NL	1	0	1	0	1	0	0	0	0	0	0	0	1	0	1	0

Rank among batters: 4,707 • *Total ballparks homered in*: 1 • *First HR*: 07/14/1942 off Ray Starr

Bob Melvin

ROBERT PAUL MELVIN
B: 10/28/1961
BR

Year	Tm	Lg	Tot	H	A	Men-On 0	1	2	3	One-Game 2	3	4	LO	XN	IP	PH	RHP	LHP
1986	SF	NL	5	2	3	3	2	0	0	0	0	0	0	0	0	0	2	3
1987	SF	NL	11	6	5	9	1	1	0	2	0	0	0	0	0	0	6	5
1988	SF	NL	8	4	4	4	3	1	0	0	0	0	0	0	0	0	5	3
1989	BAL	AL	1	0	1	0	0	1	0	0	0	0	0	0	0	0	0	1
1990	BAL	AL	5	3	2	2	3	0	0	0	0	0	0	0	0	0	2	3
1991	BAL	AL	1	0	1	1	0	0	0	0	0	0	0	0	0	0	1	0
1993	BOS	AL	3	1	2	1	2	0	0	0	0	0	0	0	0	0	2	1
1994	NY	AL	1	1	0	0	0	1	0	0	0	0	0	0	0	0	0	1
Total			35	17	18	20	11	4	0	2	0	0	0	0	0	0	18	17

Rank among batters: 1,291 • *Top target (3 home runs)*: Fernando Valenzuela • *Number of pitchers victimized*: 32 • *Total ballparks homered in*: 14 • *First HR*: 06/18/1986 off Mark Thurmond

Mario Mendoza

MARIO (AIZPURU) MENDOZA
B: 12/26/1950
BR

Year	Tm	Lg	Tot	H	A	Men-On 0	1	2	3	One-Game 2	3	4	LO	XN	IP	PH	RHP	LHP
1978	PIT	NL	1	1	0	1	0	0	0	0	0	0	0	0	0	0	1	0
1979	SEA	AL	1	1	0	1	0	0	0	0	0	0	0	0	1	0	1	0
1980	SEA	AL	2	2	0	2	0	0	0	0	0	0	0	0	0	0	1	1
Total			4	4	0	4	0	0	0	0	0	0	0	0	1	0	3	1

Rank among batters: 3,427 • *Total ballparks homered in*: 2 • *First HR*: 04/29/1978 off Jim Barr

Denis Menke

DENIS JOHN MENKE
B: 07/21/1940
BR

Year	Tm	Lg	Tot	H	A	Men-On 0	1	2	3	One-Game 2	3	4	LO	XN	IP	PH	RHP	LHP
1962	MIL	NL	2	1	1	0	1	0	1	0	0	0	0	0	0	0	1	1
1963	MIL	NL	11	7	4	6	1	4	0	0	0	0	1	0	0	0	7	4
1964	MIL	NL	20	12	8	13	5	2	0	1	0	0	2	1	1	0	16	4
1965	MIL	NL	4	2	2	3	0	1	0	0	0	0	0	0	0	0	3	1
1966	ATL	NL	15	10	5	8	3	4	0	1	0	0	0	0	0	0	11	4
1967	ATL	NL	7	4	3	4	2	1	0	0	0	0	0	0	0	0	4	3
1968	HOU	NL	6	1	5	3	1	2	0	0	0	0	0	0	0	0	5	1
1969	HOU	NL	10	5	5	5	3	1	1	0	0	0	0	0	0	0	6	4
1970	HOU	NL	13	7	6	6	4	2	1	1	0	0	0	0	0	0	10	3
1971	HOU	NL	1	1	0	1	0	0	0	0	0	0	0	0	0	0	1	0
1972	CIN	NL	9	7	2	6	2	1	0	0	0	0	0	0	0	0	6	3
1973	CIN	NL	3	2	1	2	1	0	0	0	0	0	0	0	0	0	1	2
Total			101	59	42	57	23	18	3	3	0	0	3	1	1	0	71	30

Rank among batters: 491 • *Top target (4 home runs)*: Ferguson Jenkins • *Number of pitchers victimized*: 71 • *Total ballparks homered in*: 15 • *First HR*: 05/15/1962 off Earl Francis • *World Series HR*—1; *LCS HR*—1

Mike Menosky

MICHAEL WILLIAM MENOSKY
B: 10/16/1894 D: 04/11/1983
BL

Year	Tm	Lg	Tot	H	A	Men-On 0	1	2	3	One-Game 2	3	4	LO	XN	IP	PH	RHP	LHP
1914	PIT	FL	2	0	2	2	0	0	0	0	0	0	0	0	0	1	2	0
1917	WAS	AL	1	1	0	0	0	0	1	0	0	0	0	0	0	0	1	0
1919	WAS	AL	6	1	5	3	2	1	0	1	0	0	0	0	0	1	6	0
1920	BOS	AL	3	0	3	2	0	1	0	0	0	0	0	0	0	0	3	0
1921	BOS	AL	3	1	2	2	0	1	0	0	0	0	0	0	0	0	3	0
1922	BOS	AL	3	0	3	3	0	0	0	0	0	0	1	0	0	1	3	0
Total			18	3	15	12	2	3	1	1	0	0	1	0	0	3	18	0

Rank among batters: 1,914 • *Top target (2 home runs)*: Allen Russell, Bernie Boland, Howard Ehmke • *Number of pitchers victimized*: 15 • *Total ballparks homered in*: 8 • *First HR*: 05/08/1914 off Doc Crandall

Ed Mensor

EDWARD MENSOR
B: 11/07/1886 D: 04/20/1970
BB

Year	Tm	Lg	Tot	H	A	Men-On 0	1	2	3	One-Game 2	3	4	LO	XN	IP	PH	RHP	LHP
1914	PIT	NL	1	1	0	1	0	0	0	0	0	0	1	0	1	0	1	0

Rank among batters: 4,707 • *Total ballparks homered in*: 1 • *First HR*: 07/15/1914 off Ed Reulbach

Rudy Meoli

RUDOLPH BARTHOLOMEW MEOLI
B: 05/01/1951
BL

Year	Tm	Lg	Tot	H	A	Men-On 0	1	2	3	One-Game 2	3	4	LO	XN	IP	PH	RHP	LHP
1973	CAL	AL	2	0	2	1	1	0	0	0	0	0	0	0	1	0	2	0

Rank among batters: 4,129 • *Total ballparks homered in*: 2 • *First HR*: 07/14/1973 off Joe Coleman

Orlando Mercado

ORLANDO (RODRIGUEZ) MERCADO
B: 11/07/1961
BR

Year	Tm	Lg	Tot	H	A	Men-On 0	1	2	3	One-Game 2	3	4	LO	XN	IP	PH	RHP	LHP
1982	SEA	AL	1	1	0	0	0	0	1	0	0	0	0	0	0	0	1	0
1983	SEA	AL	1	1	0	0	1	0	0	0	0	0	0	0	0	0	0	1
1986	TEX	AL	1	1	0	1	0	0	0	0	0	0	0	0	0	0	0	1
1988	OAK	AL	1	1	0	1	0	0	0	0	0	0	0	0	0	0	0	1
1990	NY	NL	3	2	1	2	1	0	0	0	0	0	0	0	0	0	1	2
Total			7	6	1	4	2	0	1	0	0	0	0	0	0	0	2	5

Rank among batters: 2,834 • *Top target (2 home runs)*: Charlie Leibrandt • *Number of pitchers victimized*: 6 • *Total ballparks homered in*: 5 • *First HR*: 09/19/1982 off Steve Comer

Orlando Merced

ORLANDO LUIS (VILLANUEVA) MERCED
B: 11/02/1966
BB

Year	Tm	Lg	Tot	H	A	Men-On 0	1	2	3	One-Game 2	3	4	LO	XN	IP	PH	RHP	LHP
1991	PIT	NL	10	5	5	4	2	3	1	0	0	0	0	1	0	1	10	0
1992	PIT	NL	6	4	2	2	2	2	0	0	0	0	0	0	0	0	6	0
1993	PIT	NL	8	3	5	2	3	3	0	0	0	0	0	0	0	1	8	0
1994	PIT	NL	9	4	5	4	2	3	0	0	0	0	0	0	0	0	6	3
1995	PIT	NL	15	8	7	8	4	3	0	1	0	0	0	0	0	1	10	5
Total			48	24	24	20	13	14	1	1	0	0	0	1	0	3	40	8

Rank among batters: 1,024 • Top target (2 home runs): Dave Smith, Jimmy Jones, Shawn Boskie, Pete Harnisch • *Number of pitchers victimized*: 44 • *Total ballparks homered in*: 13 • *First HR*: 05/03/1991 off Pete Harnisch • *LCS HR*—1

Win Mercer

GEORGE BARCLAY MERCER
B: 06/20/1874 D: 01/12/1903
BR

Year	Tm	Lg	Tot	H	A	Men-On 0	1	2	3	One-Game 2	3	4	LO	XN	IP	PH	RHP	LHP
1894	WAS	NL	2	2	0	1	1	0	0	0	0	0	0	0	0	0	2	0
1895	WAS	NL	1	1	0	1	0	0	0	0	0	0	0	0	0	0	1	0
1896	WAS	NL	1	1	0	1	0	0	0	0	0	0	0	0	0	0	1	0
1898	WAS	NL	2	1	1	1	0	1	0	0	0	0	0	0	1	0	1	1
1899	WAS	NL	1	1	0	1	0	0	0	0	0	0	0	0	0	0	1	0
Total			7	6	1	5	1	1	0	0	0	0	0	0	1	0	6	1

Rank among batters: 2,834 • *Top target (2 home runs)*: Kid Carsey • *Number of pitchers victimized*: 6 • *Total ballparks homered in*: 2 • *First HR*: 06/01/1894 off Ad Gumbert

Fred Merkle

FREDERICK CHARLES MERKLE
B: 12/20/1888 D: 03/02/1956
BR

Year	Tm	Lg	Tot	H	A	Men-On 0	1	2	3	One-Game 2	3	4	LO	XN	IP	PH	RHP	LHP
1908	NY	NL	1	1	0	0	0	1	0	0	0	0	0	0	0	1	0	1
1910	NY	NL	4	2	2	4	0	0	0	0	0	0	0	0	0	0	3	1
1911	NY	NL	12	7	5	5	4	3	0	1	0	0	0	0	0	0	12	0
1912	NY	NL	11	6	5	7	3	1	0	1	0	0	0	0	0	0	9	2
1913	NY	NL	2	2	0	1	0	1	0	0	0	0	0	0	1	0	1	1
1914	NY	NL	7	5	2	4	1	2	0	0	0	0	0	0	1	0	6	1
1915	NY	NL	4	2	2	1	3	0	0	0	0	0	0	0	0	0	4	0
1916	NY	NL	7	3	4	6	1	0	0	0	0	0	0	0	1	0	4	3
1917	CHI	NL	3	2	1	1	2	0	0	0	0	0	0	0	1	0	2	1
1918	CHI	NL	3	2	1	2	0	1	0	0	0	0	0	0	1	0	2	1
1919	CHI	NL	3	2	1	2	1	0	0	0	0	0	0	0	0	0	3	0
1920	CHI	NL	3	2	1	1	1	1	0	0	0	0	0	0	0	0	3	0
Total			60	36	24	34	16	10	0	2	0	0	0	0	5	1	49	11

Rank among batters: 863 • *Top target (5 home runs)*: Grover Alexander • *Number of pitchers victimized*: 45 • *Total ballparks homered in*: 11 • *First HR*: 06/23/1908 off Patsy Flaherty • *World Series HR*—1

Lloyd Merriman

LLOYD ARCHER MERRIMAN
B: 08/02/1924
BL

Year	Tm	Lg	Tot	H	A	Men-On 0	1	2	3	One-Game 2	3	4	LO	XN	IP	PH	RHP	LHP
1949	CIN	NL	4	2	2	2	1	1	0	0	0	0	0	0	0	0	4	0
1950	CIN	NL	2	2	0	0	1	1	0	0	0	0	0	0	0	0	2	0
1951	CIN	NL	5	4	1	1	3	1	0	0	0	0	0	0	0	0	4	1
1955	CHI	NL	1	1	0	1	0	0	0	0	0	0	1	0	0	0	1	0
Total			12	9	3	4	5	3	0	0	0	0	1	0	0	0	11	1

Rank among batters: 2,325 • *Top target (3 home runs)*: Gerry Staley • *Number of pitchers victimized*: 10 • *Total ballparks homered in*: 4 • *First HR*: 04/24/1949 off Hugh Casey

Bill Merritt

WILLIAM HENRY MERRITT
B: 07/30/1870 D: 11/17/1937
BR

Year	Tm	Lg	Tot	H	A	Men-On 0	1	2	3	One-Game 2	3	4	LO	XN	IP	PH	RHP	LHP
1892	LOU	NL	1	0	1	0	0	1	0	0	0	0	0	0	0	0	0	1
1893	BOS	NL	3	3	0	1	2	0	0	1	0	0	0	0	0	0	3	0
1894	PIT	NL	1	0	1	1	0	0	0	0	0	0	0	0	0	0	1	0
	CIN	NL	1	1	0	0	1	0	0	0	0	0	0	0	0	0	1	0
	Total		2	1	1	1	1	0	0	0	0	0	0	0	0	0	2	0
1896	PIT	NL	1	1	0	1	0	0	0	0	0	0	0	0	0	0	1	0
1897	PIT	NL	1	0	1	0	1	0	0	0	0	0	0	0	0	0	0	1
Total			8	5	3	3	4	1	0	1	0	0	0	0	0	0	6	2

Rank among batters: 2,703 • *Top target (3 home runs)*: Jack Taylor • *Number of pitchers victimized*: 6 • *Total ballparks homered in*: 5 • *First HR*: 10/11/1892 off Ted Breitenstein

Jim Merritt

JAMES JOSEPH MERRITT
B: 12/09/1943
BL

Year	Tm	Lg	Tot	H	A	Men-On 0	1	2	3	One-Game 2	3	4	LO	XN	IP	PH	RHP	LHP
1969	CIN	NL	1	0	1	1	0	0	0	0	0	0	0	0	0	0	1	0
1970	CIN	NL	3	1	2	2	0	1	0	0	0	0	0	0	0	0	3	0
Total			4	1	3	3	0	1	0	0	0	0	0	0	0	0	4	0

Rank among batters: 3,427 • *Total ballparks homered in*: 4 • *First HR*: 07/24/1969 off Gary Gentry

Jack Merson

JOHN WARREN MERSON
B: 01/17/1922
BR

Year	Tm	Lg	Tot	H	A	Men-On 0	1	2	3	One-Game 2	3	4	LO	XN	IP	PH	RHP	LHP
1951	PIT	NL	1	1	0	0	1	0	0	0	0	0	0	0	0	0	1	0
1952	PIT	NL	5	4	1	5	0	0	0	0	0	0	0	0	0	0	3	2
Total			6	5	1	5	1	0	0	0	0	0	0	0	0	0	4	2

Rank among batters: 2,988 • *Top target (2 home runs)*: Herm Wehmeier • *Number of pitchers victimized*: 5 • *Total ballparks homered in*: 2 • *First HR*: 09/28/1951 off Herm Wehmeier

Sam Mertes

SAMUEL BLAIR MERTES
B: 08/06/1872 D: 03/11/1945
BR

Year	Tm	Lg	Tot	H	A	Men-On 0	1	2	3	One-Game 2	3	4	LO	XN	IP	PH	RHP	LHP
1898	CHI	NL	1	1	0	0	0	1	0	0	0	0	0	0	1	0	1	0
1899	CHI	NL	9	5	4	2	6	1	0	1	0	0	0	0	2	0	7	2
1900	CHI	NL	7	2	5	5	1	1	0	1	0	0	2	0	0	0	4	3
1901	CHI	AL	5	2	3	2	1	2	0	0	0	0	0	0	1	0	2	3
1902	CHI	AL	1	0	1	0	0	1	0	0	0	0	0	1	0	0	1	0
1903	NY	NL	7	2	5	3	1	3	0	0	0	0	0	0	1	0	4	3
1904	NY	NL	4	2	2	4	0	0	0	0	0	0	0	0	0	0	4	0
1905	NY	NL	5	5	0	2	1	1	1	0	0	0	0	0	1	0	4	1
1906	NY	NL	1	0	1	1	0	0	0	0	0	0	0	0	0	0	1	0
Total			40	19	21	19	10	10	1	2	0	0	2	1	6	0	28	12

Rank among batters: 1,181 • *Top target (3 home runs)*: Bill Dinneen, Jack Cronin • *Number of pitchers victimized*: 35 • *Total ballparks homered in*: 14 • *First HR*: 06/29/1898 off Jouett Meekin • *Hit for Cycle*—vs STL: 10/04/1904 (1)

Lennie Merullo

LEONARD RICHARD MERULLO
B: 05/05/1917
BR

Year	Tm	Lg	Tot	H	A	Men-On 0	1	2	3	One-Game 2	3	4	LO	XN	IP	PH	RHP	LHP
1942	CHI	NL	2	1	1	0	1	1	0	0	0	0	0	0	0	0	1	1

Lennie Merullo *continued*

Year	Tm	Lg	Tot	H	A	Men-On 0	1	2	3	One-Game 2	3	4	LO	XN	IP	PH	RHP	LHP
1943	CHI	NL	1	0	1	1	0	0	0	0	0	0	0	0	0	0	1	0
1944	CHI	NL	1	1	0	0	0	0	1	0	0	0	0	0	0	0	1	0
1945	CHI	NL	2	1	1	0	2	0	0	0	0	0	0	0	0	0	2	0
Total			6	3	3	1	3	1	1	0	0	0	0	0	0	0	5	1

Rank among batters: 2,988 • *Total ballparks homered in*: 4 • *First HR*: 05/29/1942 off Paul Derringer

Matt Merullo

MATTHEW BATES MERULLO
B: 08/04/1965
BL

Year	Tm	Lg	Tot	H	A	Men-On 0	1	2	3	One-Game 2	3	4	LO	XN	IP	PH	RHP	LHP
1989	CHI	AL	1	1	0	1	0	0	0	0	0	0	0	0	0	0	0	1
1991	CHI	AL	5	1	4	4	1	0	0	0	0	0	0	0	0	2	5	0
1995	MIN	AL	1	1	0	0	0	0	1	0	0	0	0	0	0	0	0	1
Total			7	3	4	5	1	0	1	0	0	0	0	0	0	2	5	2

Rank among batters: 2,834 • *Total ballparks homered in*: 7 • *First HR*: 04/14/1989 off Rick Honeycutt

Stephen Mesner

STEPHEN MATHIAS MESNER
B: 01/13/1918 D: 04/06/1981
BR

Year	Tm	Lg	Tot	H	A	Men-On 0	1	2	3	One-Game 2	3	4	LO	XN	IP	PH	RHP	LHP
1944	CIN	NL	1	0	1	0	0	0	1	0	0	0	0	0	0	0	1	0
1945	CIN	NL	1	0	1	1	0	0	0	0	0	0	0	0	0	0	1	0
Total			2	0	2	1	0	0	1	0	0	0	0	0	0	0	2	0

Rank among batters: 4,129 • *Total ballparks homered in*: 2 • *First HR*: 09/27/1944 off Bill Voiselle

Andy Messersmith

JOHN ALEXANDER MESSERSMITH
B: 08/06/1945
BR

Year	Tm	Lg	Tot	H	A	Men-On 0	1	2	3	One-Game 2	3	4	LO	XN	IP	PH	RHP	LHP
1970	CAL	AL	1	1	0	1	0	0	0	0	0	0	0	0	0	0	0	1
1971	CAL	AL	2	1	1	1	1	0	0	0	0	0	0	0	0	0	2	0
1974	LA	NL	1	0	1	1	0	0	0	0	0	0	0	0	0	0	1	0
1977	ATL	NL	1	1	0	1	0	0	0	0	0	0	0	0	0	0	1	0
Total			5	3	2	4	1	0	0	0	0	0	0	0	0	0	4	1

Rank among batters: 3,191 • *Total ballparks homered in*: 4 • *First HR*: 05/09/1970 off Mike Kekich

Bud Metheny

ARTHUR BEAUREGARD METHENY
B: 06/01/1915
BL

Year	Tm	Lg	Tot	H	A	Men-On 0	1	2	3	One-Game 2	3	4	LO	XN	IP	PH	RHP	LHP
1943	NY	AL	9	5	4	6	3	0	0	0	0	0	0	0	0	0	9	0
1944	NY	AL	14	12	2	8	5	1	0	0	0	0	0	0	0	0	12	2
1945	NY	AL	8	5	3	2	5	1	0	1	0	0	0	0	0	0	8	0
Total			31	22	9	16	13	2	0	1	0	0	0	0	0	0	29	2

Rank among batters: 1,400 • Top target (2 home runs): Bob Muncrief, Gordon Maltzberger, Dutch Leonard, Bobo Newsom, Bill Dietrich, Earl Caldwell • *Number of pitchers victimized*: 25 • *Total ballparks homered in*: 6 • *First HR*: 07/11/1943 off Gordon Maltzberger

George Metkovich

GEORGE MICHAEL METKOVICH
B: 10/08/1920 D: 05/17/1995
BL

Year	Tm	Lg	Tot	H	A	Men-On 0	1	2	3	One-Game 2	3	4	LO	XN	IP	PH	RHP	LHP
1943	BOS	AL	5	2	3	4	0	1	0	0	0	0	0	0	0	0	5	0
1944	BOS	AL	9	4	5	7	1	1	0	0	0	0	0	0	1	0	9	0
1945	BOS	AL	5	1	4	1	4	0	0	0	0	0	0	0	0	0	4	1
1946	BOS	AL	4	2	2	1	2	1	0	0	0	0	0	0	0	0	4	0
1947	CLE	AL	5	1	4	4	1	0	0	0	0	0	0	0	0	0	5	0
1949	CHI	AL	5	0	5	3	2	0	0	1	0	0	0	0	0	0	4	1
1951	PIT	NL	3	1	2	2	1	0	0	0	0	0	0	0	0	0	3	0
1952	PIT	NL	7	3	4	1	5	1	0	1	0	0	0	0	0	0	7	0
1953	PIT	NL	1	0	1	0	1	0	0	0	0	0	0	0	0	1	1	0
	CHI	NL	2	2	0	2	0	0	0	0	0	0	0	0	0	0	2	0
	Total		3	2	1	2	1	0	0	0	0	0	0	0	0	1	3	0

George Metkovich *continued*

Year	Tm	Lg	Tot	H	A	Men-On				One-Game			LO	XN	IP	PH	RHP	LHP
						0	1	2	3	2	3	4						
1954	MIL	NL	1	0	1	1	0	0	0	0	0	0	0	0	0	0	0	1
Total			47	16	31	26	17	4	0	2	0	0	0	0	1	1	44	3

Rank among batters: 1,040 • Top target (2 home runs): Ray Poat, Orval Grove, Virgil Trucks, Bobo Newsom, Joe Coleman, Bob Lemon, Max Surkont • *Number of pitchers victimized*: 40 • *Total ballparks homered in*: 14 • *First HR*: 07/24/1943 off Bobo Newsom

Charlie Metro

CHARLES METRO
B: 04/28/1919
BR

Year	Tm	Lg	Tot	H	A	Men-On				One-Game			LO	XN	IP	PH	RHP	LHP
						0	1	2	3	2	3	4						
1945	PHI	AL	3	1	2	3	0	0	0	0	0	0	0	0	0	0	3	0

Rank among batters: 3,735 • *Total ballparks homered in*: 2 • *First HR*: 06/12/1945 off Jim Wilson

Roger Metzger

ROGER HENRY METZGER
B: 10/10/1947
BB

Year	Tm	Lg	Tot	H	A	Men-On				One-Game			LO	XN	IP	PH	RHP	LHP
						0	1	2	3	2	3	4						
1972	HOU	NL	2	0	2	1	0	1	0	0	0	0	0	1	0	0	2	0
1973	HOU	NL	1	0	1	1	0	0	0	0	0	0	1	0	0	0	1	0
1975	HOU	NL	2	0	2	1	1	0	0	0	0	0	0	0	0	0	1	1
Total			5	0	5	3	1	1	0	0	0	0	1	1	0	0	4	1

Rank among batters: 3,191 • *Total ballparks homered in*: 5 • *First HR*: 05/10/1972 off Bob Gibson

Alex Metzler

ALEXANDER METZLER
B: 01/04/1903 D: 11/30/1973
BL

Year	Tm	Lg	Tot	H	A	Men-On				One-Game			LO	XN	IP	PH	RHP	LHP
						0	1	2	3	2	3	4						
1927	CHI	AL	3	1	2	2	1	0	0	0	0	0	1	0	1	0	3	0
1928	CHI	AL	3	1	2	1	2	0	0	0	0	0	0	0	0	1	3	0
1929	CHI	AL	2	0	2	0	1	1	0	0	0	0	0	0	0	0	2	0
1930	STL	AL	1	1	0	0	0	1	0	0	0	0	0	0	0	0	1	0
Total			9	3	6	3	4	2	0	0	0	0	1	0	1	1	9	0

Rank among batters: 2,587 • *Total ballparks homered in*: 6 • *First HR*: 05/10/1927 off Sloppy Thurston

Hensley Meulens

HENSLEY FILEMON ACASIO MEULENS
B: 06/23/1967
BR

Year	Tm	Lg	Tot	H	A	Men-On				One-Game			LO	XN	IP	PH	RHP	LHP
						0	1	2	3	2	3	4						
1990	NY	AL	3	2	1	2	0	1	0	0	0	0	0	0	0	0	2	1
1991	NY	AL	6	4	2	3	3	0	0	0	0	0	0	0	0	1	1	5
1992	NY	AL	1	1	0	1	0	0	0	0	0	0	0	0	0	0	1	0
1993	NY	AL	2	1	1	2	0	0	0	0	0	0	0	0	0	0	1	1
Total			12	8	4	8	3	1	0	0	0	0	0	0	0	1	5	7

Rank among batters: 2,325 • *Total ballparks homered in*: 4 • *First HR*: 09/12/1990 off Charlie Hough

Bob Meusel

ROBERT WILLIAM MEUSEL
B: 07/19/1896 D: 11/28/1977
BR

Year	Tm	Lg	Tot	H	A	Men-On				One-Game			LO	XN	IP	PH	RHP	LHP
						0	1	2	3	2	3	4						
1920	NY	AL	11	6	5	6	3	2	0	0	0	0	0	0	1	0	8	3
1921	NY	AL	24	14	10	8	4	11	1	2	0	0	0	0	1	0	15	9
1922	NY	AL	16	9	7	10	1	5	0	1	0	0	0	0	0	0	11	5
1923	NY	AL	9	5	4	6	0	3	0	0	0	0	0	0	5	0	0	9
1924	NY	AL	12	7	5	8	2	2	0	0	0	0	0	0	1	0	8	4
1925	NY	AL	33	16	17	15	13	5	0	5	0	0	0	1	3	0	16	17
1926	NY	AL	12	5	7	8	2	2	0	0	0	0	0	0	0	0	6	6
1927	NY	AL	8	3	5	5	2	1	0	0	0	0	0	0	1	0	7	1
1928	NY	AL	11	6	5	6	1	3	1	0	0	0	0	0	0	0	8	3
1929	NY	AL	10	2	8	4	3	2	1	0	0	0	0	1	2	0	4	6
1930	CIN	NL	10	3	7	6	3	1	0	0	0	0	0	0	0	0	8	2
Total			156	76	80	82	34	37	3	8	0	0	0	2	14	0	91	65

Rank among batters: 272 • *Top target (6 home runs)*: Ted Blankenship • *Number of pitchers victimized*: 95 • *Total ballparks homered in*: 14 • *First HR*: 06/02/1920 off Jim Shaw • *Hit for Cycle*—@WAS: 05/07/1921; @PHI: 07/03/1922; @DET: 07/26/1928 (1) • *World Series HR*—1

Irish Meusel

EMIL FREDERICK MEUSEL
B: 06/09/1893 D: 03/01/1963
BR

Year	Tm	Lg	Tot	H	A	Men-On 0	Men-On 1	Men-On 2	Men-On 3	One-Game 2	One-Game 3	One-Game 4	LO	XN	IP	PH	RHP	LHP
1918	PHI	NL	4	2	2	1	1	1	1	0	0	0	0	0	2	0	3	1
1919	PHI	NL	5	4	1	2	2	1	0	0	0	0	0	0	1	0	4	1
1920	PHI	NL	14	12	2	7	5	2	0	1	0	0	0	0	0	0	9	5
1921	PHI	NL	12	8	4	8	3	1	0	0	0	0	0	0	0	0	8	4
	NY	NL	2	1	1	1	1	0	0	0	0	0	0	0	0	0	1	1
	Total		14	9	5	9	4	1	0	0	0	0	0	0	0	0	9	5
1922	NY	NL	16	8	8	7	6	2	1	1	0	0	0	0	0	0	11	5
1923	NY	NL	19	8	11	10	4	5	0	2	0	0	0	0	2	0	13	6
1924	NY	NL	6	2	4	3	2	1	0	0	0	0	0	0	0	0	5	1
1925	NY	NL	21	9	12	10	9	2	0	3	0	0	0	0	0	0	13	8
1926	NY	NL	6	2	4	4	2	0	0	0	0	0	0	0	0	0	3	3
1927	BRO	NL	1	0	1	0	0	1	0	0	0	0	0	0	0	0	1	0
Total			106	56	50	53	35	16	2	7	0	0	0	0	5	0	71	35

Rank among batters: 451 • *Top target (5 home runs)*: Burleigh Grimes, Wilbur Cooper • *Number of pitchers victimized*: 65 • *Total ballparks homered in*: 8 • *First HR*: 08/08/1918 off Cy Slapnicka • *World Series HR*—3

Benny Meyer

BERNHARD MEYER
B: 01/01/1888 D: 02/06/1974
BR

Year	Tm	Lg	Tot	H	A	Men-On 0	Men-On 1	Men-On 2	Men-On 3	One-Game 2	One-Game 3	One-Game 4	LO	XN	IP	PH	RHP	LHP
1913	BRO	NL	1	0	1	0	1	0	0	0	0	0	0	0	1	0	1	0
1914	BAL	FL	5	5	0	3	1	1	0	0	0	0	1	0	0	0	5	0
1915	BUF	FL	1	1	0	1	0	0	0	0	0	0	0	0	0	0	1	0
Total			7	6	1	4	2	1	0	0	0	0	1	0	1	0	7	0

Rank among batters: 2,834 • *Total ballparks homered in*: 3 • *First HR*: 06/09/1913 off Babe Adams

Billy Meyer

WILLIAM ADAM MEYER
B: 01/14/1892 D: 03/31/1957
BR

Year	Tm	Lg	Tot	H	A	Men-On 0	Men-On 1	Men-On 2	Men-On 3	One-Game 2	One-Game 3	One-Game 4	LO	XN	IP	PH	RHP	LHP
1916	PHI	AL	1	0	1	0	1	0	0	0	0	0	0	0	1	0	0	1

Rank among batters: 4,707 • *Total ballparks homered in*: 1 • *First HR*: 05/31/1916 off Nick Cullop

Dan Meyer

DANIEL THOMAS MEYER
B: 08/03/1952
BL

Year	Tm	Lg	Tot	H	A	Men-On 0	Men-On 1	Men-On 2	Men-On 3	One-Game 2	One-Game 3	One-Game 4	LO	XN	IP	PH	RHP	LHP
1974	DET	AL	3	1	2	2	1	0	0	1	0	0	0	0	0	0	2	1
1975	DET	AL	8	8	0	5	2	1	0	0	0	0	0	0	0	1	8	0
1976	DET	AL	2	2	0	0	2	0	0	0	0	0	0	0	0	1	2	0
1977	SEA	AL	22	13	9	12	4	6	0	1	0	0	0	0	0	0	17	5
1978	SEA	AL	8	4	4	4	3	1	0	0	0	0	0	0	0	0	6	2
1979	SEA	AL	20	11	9	14	3	1	2	0	0	0	0	0	0	1	14	6
1980	SEA	AL	11	7	4	6	5	0	0	1	0	0	0	1	1	0	11	0
1981	SEA	AL	3	2	1	1	2	0	0	0	0	0	0	0	0	0	1	2
1982	OAK	AL	8	3	5	3	3	2	0	1	0	0	0	0	0	0	8	0
1983	OAK	AL	1	1	0	1	0	0	0	0	0	0	0	0	0	0	1	0
Total			86	52	34	48	25	11	2	4	0	0	0	1	1	3	70	16

Rank among batters: 602 • *Top target (4 home runs)*: Mike Torrez • *Number of pitchers victimized*: 65 • *Total ballparks homered in*: 15 • *First HR*: 09/20/1974 off Bill Champion

Dutch Meyer

LAMBERT DALTON MEYER
B: 10/06/1915
BR

Year	Tm	Lg	Tot	H	A	Men-On 0	Men-On 1	Men-On 2	Men-On 3	One-Game 2	One-Game 3	One-Game 4	LO	XN	IP	PH	RHP	LHP
1941	DET	AL	1	1	0	1	0	0	0	0	0	0	0	0	0	1	1	0
1942	DET	AL	2	2	0	0	2	0	0	0	0	0	0	0	0	0	2	0
1945	CLE	AL	7	4	3	5	2	0	0	0	0	0	0	0	0	0	5	2
Total			10	7	3	6	4	0	0	0	0	0	0	0	0	1	8	2

Rank among batters: 2,500 • *Total ballparks homered in*: 5 • *First HR*: 08/26/1941 off Phil Marchildon

Jack Meyer

JOHN ROBERT MEYER
B: 03/23/1932 D: 03/06/1967
BR

Year	Tm	Lg	Tot	H	A	Men-On 0	Men-On 1	Men-On 2	Men-On 3	One-Game 2	One-Game 3	One-Game 4	LO	XN	IP	PH	RHP	LHP
1956	PHI	NL	1	0	1	1	0	0	0	0	0	0	0	1	0	0	1	0

Rank among batters: 4,707 • *Total ballparks homered in*: 1 • *First HR*: 04/29/1956 off Hoyt Wilhelm

Joey Meyer

TANNER JOE MEYER
B: 05/10/1962
BR

Year	Tm	Lg	Tot	H	A	Men-On 0	Men-On 1	Men-On 2	Men-On 3	One-Game 2	One-Game 3	One-Game 4	LO	XN	IP	PH	RHP	LHP
1988	MIL	AL	11	5	6	6	4	1	0	0	0	0	0	0	0	0	4	7
1989	MIL	AL	7	5	2	4	3	0	0	0	0	0	0	0	0	1	5	2
Total			18	10	8	10	7	1	0	0	0	0	0	0	0	1	9	9

Rank among batters: 1,914 • *Top target (2 home runs)*: John Candelaria • *Number of pitchers victimized*: 17 • *Total ballparks homered in*: 7 • *First HR*: 04/17/1988 off John Candelaria

Russ Meyer

RUSSELL CHARLES MEYER
B: 10/25/1923
BB

Year	Tm	Lg	Tot	H	A	Men-On 0	Men-On 1	Men-On 2	Men-On 3	One-Game 2	One-Game 3	One-Game 4	LO	XN	IP	PH	RHP	LHP
1952	PHI	NL	1	0	1	0	1	0	0	0	0	0	0	0	0	0	1	0

Rank among batters: 4,707 • *Total ballparks homered in*: 1 • *First HR*: 08/07/1952 off Sheldon Jones

Chief Meyers

JOHN TORTES MEYERS
B: 07/29/1880 D: 07/25/1971
BR

Year	Tm	Lg	Tot	H	A	Men-On 0	Men-On 1	Men-On 2	Men-On 3	One-Game 2	One-Game 3	One-Game 4	LO	XN	IP	PH	RHP	LHP
1909	NY	NL	1	1	0	0	0	0	1	0	0	0	0	0	1	0	1	0
1910	NY	NL	1	1	0	0	0	1	0	0	0	0	0	0	0	0	1	0
1911	NY	NL	1	1	0	0	1	0	0	0	0	0	0	0	1	0	0	1
1912	NY	NL	6	4	2	5	0	0	1	0	0	0	0	0	0	0	3	3
1913	NY	NL	3	3	0	2	1	0	0	0	0	0	0	0	0	0	2	1
1914	NY	NL	1	0	1	0	1	0	0	0	0	0	0	0	0	0	0	1
1915	NY	NL	1	1	0	1	0	0	0	0	0	0	0	0	0	0	1	0
Total			14	11	3	8	3	1	2	0	0	0	0	0	2	0	8	6

Rank among batters: 2,169 • *Total ballparks homered in*: 4 • *First HR*: 09/11/1909 off Elmer Knetzer • *Hit for Cycle*—vs CHI: 06/10/1912

Gene Michael

EUGENE RICHARD MICHAEL
B: 06/02/1938
BB

Year	Tm	Lg	Tot	H	A	Men-On 0	Men-On 1	Men-On 2	Men-On 3	One-Game 2	One-Game 3	One-Game 4	LO	XN	IP	PH	RHP	LHP
1968	NY	AL	1	0	1	1	0	0	0	0	0	0	0	0	0	0	1	0
1969	NY	AL	2	2	0	1	1	0	0	0	0	0	0	0	0	0	1	1
1970	NY	AL	2	1	1	2	0	0	0	0	0	0	0	0	0	0	2	0
1971	NY	AL	3	1	2	2	1	0	0	0	0	0	1	1	0	0	0	3
1972	NY	AL	1	1	0	0	0	1	0	0	0	0	0	0	0	0	1	0
1973	NY	AL	3	2	1	1	1	1	0	0	0	0	0	0	0	0	3	0
1975	DET	AL	3	0	3	2	0	1	0	0	0	0	0	0	0	0	2	1
Total			15	7	8	9	3	3	0	0	0	0	1	1	0	0	10	5

Rank among batters: 2,096 • *Total ballparks homered in*: 6 • *First HR*: 04/20/1968 off Jim Perry

Cass Michaels

CASIMIR EUGENE MICHAELS
B: 03/04/1926 D: 11/12/1982
BR

Year	Tm	Lg	Tot	H	A	Men-On 0	Men-On 1	Men-On 2	Men-On 3	One-Game 2	One-Game 3	One-Game 4	LO	XN	IP	PH	RHP	LHP
1945	CHI	AL	2	1	1	1	1	0	0	0	0	0	0	0	0	0	2	0
1946	CHI	AL	1	0	1	1	0	0	0	0	0	0	0	0	0	0	0	1
1947	CHI	AL	3	1	2	3	0	0	0	0	0	0	0	0	1	0	2	1
1948	CHI	AL	5	3	2	3	2	0	0	0	0	0	0	0	0	0	3	2
1949	CHI	AL	6	2	4	4	0	2	0	0	0	0	0	0	0	0	3	3
1950	CHI	AL	4	2	2	3	1	0	0	0	0	0	0	0	0	0	4	0
	WAS	AL	4	1	3	2	2	0	0	0	0	0	0	0	0	0	3	1
	Total		8	3	5	5	3	0	0	0	0	0	0	0	0	0	7	1
1951	WAS	AL	4	2	2	1	2	0	1	0	0	0	0	0	0	0	2	2

Cass Michaels *continued*

Year	Tm	Lg	Tot	H	A	Men-On 0	1	2	3	One-Game 2	3	4	LO	XN	IP	PH	RHP	LHP
1952	WAS	AL	1	0	1	0	1	0	0	0	0	0	0	0	0	0	0	1
	STL	AL	3	2	1	0	3	0	0	0	0	0	0	0	0	0	3	0
	PHI	AL	1	1	0	1	0	0	0	0	0	0	0	0	0	0	1	0
	Total		5	3	2	1	4	0	0	0	0	0	0	0	0	0	4	1
1953	PHI	AL	12	3	9	6	4	2	0	0	0	0	0	2	0	0	7	5
1954	CHI	AL	7	2	5	2	4	0	1	0	0	0	0	0	0	0	3	4
Total			53	20	33	27	20	4	2	0	0	0	0	2	1	0	33	20

Rank among batters: 953 • *Top target (3 home runs)*: Billy Pierce • *Number of pitchers victimized*: 40 • *Total ballparks homered in*: 9 • *First HR*: 06/13/1945 off Ed Klieman

Ed Mierkowicz

EDWARD FRANK MIERKOWICZ
B: 03/06/1924
BR

Year	Tm	Lg	Tot	H	A	Men-On 0	1	2	3	One-Game 2	3	4	LO	XN	IP	PH	RHP	LHP
1947	DET	AL	1	1	0	1	0	0	0	0	0	0	0	0	0	0	0	1

Rank among batters: 4,707 • *Total ballparks homered in*: 1 • *First HR*: 08/10/1947 off Eddie Lopat

Matt Mieske

MATTHEW TODD MIESKE
B: 02/13/1968
BR

Year	Tm	Lg	Tot	H	A	Men-On 0	1	2	3	One-Game 2	3	4	LO	XN	IP	PH	RHP	LHP
1993	MIL	AL	3	1	2	2	1	0	0	0	0	0	0	0	0	0	1	2
1994	MIL	AL	10	7	3	7	1	2	0	1	0	0	0	0	0	0	3	7
1995	MIL	AL	12	3	9	3	4	3	2	0	0	0	0	1	0	2	3	9
Total			25	11	14	12	6	5	2	1	0	0	0	1	0	2	7	18

Rank among batters: 1,608 • *Total ballparks homered in*: 11 • *First HR*: 05/09/1993 off Joe Hesketh

Larry Miggins

LAWRENCE EDWARD MIGGINS
B: 08/20/1925
BR

Year	Tm	Lg	Tot	H	A	Men-On 0	1	2	3	One-Game 2	3	4	LO	XN	IP	PH	RHP	LHP
1952	STL	NL	2	0	2	0	2	0	0	0	0	0	0	0	0	0	0	2

Rank among batters: 4,129 • *Total ballparks homered in*: 2 • *First HR*: 05/13/1952 off Preacher Roe

Eddie Miksis

EDWARD THOMAS MIKSIS
B: 09/11/1926
BR

Year	Tm	Lg	Tot	H	A	Men-On 0	1	2	3	One-Game 2	3	4	LO	XN	IP	PH	RHP	LHP
1947	BRO	NL	4	3	1	4	0	0	0	0	0	0	0	0	0	0	3	1
1948	BRO	NL	2	1	1	1	0	1	0	0	0	0	0	0	0	0	0	2
1949	BRO	NL	1	1	0	0	1	0	0	0	0	0	0	0	0	0	1	0
1950	BRO	NL	2	2	0	1	1	0	0	0	0	0	1	0	0	0	1	1
1951	CHI	NL	4	2	2	4	0	0	0	0	0	0	2	0	0	0	2	2
1952	CHI	NL	2	1	1	1	1	0	0	0	0	0	0	0	0	0	0	2
1953	CHI	NL	8	5	3	8	0	0	0	0	0	0	0	1	0	0	7	1
1954	CHI	NL	2	1	1	2	0	0	0	0	0	0	0	1	0	0	2	0
1955	CHI	NL	9	6	3	4	5	0	0	0	0	0	1	0	0	0	6	3
1956	CHI	NL	9	4	5	7	1	1	0	0	0	0	2	0	0	0	7	2
1957	STL	NL	1	0	1	1	0	0	0	0	0	0	0	0	0	0	0	1
Total			44	26	18	33	9	2	0	0	0	0	6	2	0	0	29	15

Rank among batters: 1,095 • *Top target (3 home runs)*: Jim Hearn • *Number of pitchers victimized*: 39 • *Total ballparks homered in*: 8 • *First HR*: 05/28/1947 off Hub Andrews

Clyde Milan

JESSE CLYDE MILAN
B: 03/25/1887 D: 03/03/1953
BL

Year	Tm	Lg	Tot	H	A	Men-On 0	1	2	3	One-Game 2	3	4	LO	XN	IP	PH	RHP	LHP
1908	WAS	AL	1	0	1	0	0	1	0	0	0	0	0	0	1	0	1	0
1909	WAS	AL	1	1	0	1	0	0	0	0	0	0	0	0	1	0	0	1
1911	WAS	AL	3	2	1	3	0	0	0	0	0	0	1	0	2	0	2	1
1912	WAS	AL	1	1	0	0	0	1	0	0	0	0	0	0	1	0	1	0
1913	WAS	AL	3	2	1	2	1	0	0	0	0	0	0	0	2	0	3	0

Year	Tm	Lg	Tot	H	A	Men-On 0	Men-On 1	Men-On 2	Men-On 3	One-Game 2	One-Game 3	One-Game 4	LO	XN	IP	PH	RHP	LHP

Clyde Milan *continued*

Year	Tm	Lg	Tot	H	A	0	1	2	3	2	3	4	LO	XN	IP	PH	RHP	LHP
1914	WAS	AL	1	1	0	1	0	0	0	0	0	0	0	0	1	0	1	0
1915	WAS	AL	2	2	0	2	0	0	0	0	0	0	0	0	2	0	2	0
1916	WAS	AL	1	0	1	1	0	0	0	0	0	0	0	0	0	0	1	0
1920	WAS	AL	3	0	3	1	2	0	0	0	0	0	0	0	2	0	3	0
1921	WAS	AL	1	1	0	1	0	0	0	0	0	0	0	0	1	0	0	1
Total			17	10	7	12	3	2	0	0	0	0	1	0	13	0	14	3

Rank among batters: 1,969 • *Top target (2 home runs)*: Doc White • *Number of pitchers victimized*: 16 • *Total ballparks homered in*: 6 • *First HR*: 10/02/1908 off Joe Lake

Larry Milbourne

LAWRENCE WILLIAM MILBOURNE
B: 02/14/1951
BB

Year	Tm	Lg	Tot	H	A	0	1	2	3	2	3	4	LO	XN	IP	PH	RHP	LHP
1975	HOU	NL	1	1	0	0	1	0	0	0	0	0	0	0	0	0	0	1
1977	SEA	AL	2	2	0	1	1	0	0	0	0	0	0	0	0	0	2	0
1978	SEA	AL	2	2	0	1	0	0	1	1	0	0	0	0	0	0	1	1
1979	SEA	AL	2	1	1	1	1	0	0	0	0	0	0	0	0	0	1	1
1981	NY	AL	1	1	0	1	0	0	0	0	0	0	0	0	1	0	1	0
1982	CLE	AL	2	1	1	0	2	0	0	0	0	0	0	0	0	0	0	2
1984	SEA	AL	1	1	0	1	0	0	0	0	0	0	0	0	0	0	0	1
Total			11	9	2	5	5	0	1	1	0	0	0	0	1	0	5	6

Rank among batters: 2,419 • *Total ballparks homered in*: 5 • *First HR*: 09/23/1975 off Fred Norman • *Switch hit HR in 1 game—*

Dee Miles

WILSON DANIEL MILES
B: 02/15/1909 D: 11/02/1976
BL

Year	Tm	Lg	Tot	H	A	0	1	2	3	2	3	4	LO	XN	IP	PH	RHP	LHP
1939	PHI	AL	1	1	0	0	1	0	0	0	0	0	0	1	0	1	1	0
1940	PHI	AL	1	0	1	1	0	0	0	0	0	0	0	0	0	0	1	0
Total			2	1	1	1	1	0	0	0	0	0	0	1	0	1	2	0

Rank among batters: 4,129 • *Total ballparks homered in*: 2 • *First HR*: 09/14/1939 off Clint Brown

Mike Miley

MICHAEL WILFRED MILEY
B: 03/30/1953 D: 01/06/1977
BB

Year	Tm	Lg	Tot	H	A	0	1	2	3	2	3	4	LO	XN	IP	PH	RHP	LHP
1975	CAL	AL	4	2	2	2	1	1	0	0	0	0	0	1	0	0	1	3

Rank among batters: 3,427 • *Total ballparks homered in*: 3 • *First HR*: 07/13/1975 off Dave LaRoche

Felix Millan

FELIX BERNARDO (MARTINEZ) MILLAN
B: 08/21/1943
BR

Year	Tm	Lg	Tot	H	A	0	1	2	3	2	3	4	LO	XN	IP	PH	RHP	LHP
1967	ATL	NL	2	1	1	2	0	0	0	0	0	0	0	0	0	0	2	0
1968	ATL	NL	1	0	1	1	0	0	0	0	0	0	0	0	0	0	0	1
1969	ATL	NL	6	5	1	5	0	0	1	0	0	0	0	0	0	0	5	1
1970	ATL	NL	2	2	0	2	0	0	0	0	0	0	0	0	0	0	1	1
1971	ATL	NL	2	1	1	1	1	0	0	0	0	0	0	0	0	0	2	0
1972	ATL	NL	1	1	0	1	0	0	0	0	0	0	0	0	0	0	1	0
1973	NY	NL	3	1	2	1	2	0	0	0	0	0	0	0	0	0	2	1
1974	NY	NL	1	0	1	0	1	0	0	0	0	0	0	0	0	0	1	0
1975	NY	NL	1	1	0	1	0	0	0	0	0	0	0	0	0	0	0	1
1976	NY	NL	1	0	1	0	1	0	0	0	0	0	0	0	0	0	1	0
1977	NY	NL	2	1	1	2	0	0	0	0	0	0	0	0	0	0	0	2
Total			22	13	9	16	5	0	1	0	0	0	0	0	0	0	15	7

Rank among batters: 1,719 • *Top target (2 home runs)*: Larry Jaster • *Number of pitchers victimized*: 21 • *Total ballparks homered in*: 9 • *First HR*: 09/28/1967 off Sammy Ellis

Bing Miller

EDMUND JOHN MILLER
B: 08/30/1894 D: 05/07/1966
BR

Year	Tm	Lg	Tot	H	A	0	1	2	3	2	3	4	LO	XN	IP	PH	RHP	LHP
1921	WAS	AL	9	1	8	6	3	0	0	0	0	0	0	0	1	0	7	2

Bing Miller *continued*

Year	Tm	Lg	Tot	H	A	Men-On 0	Men-On 1	Men-On 2	Men-On 3	One-Game 2	One-Game 3	One-Game 4	LO	XN	IP	PH	RHP	LHP
1922	PHI	AL	21	14	7	13	5	3	0	2	0	0	0	0	0	0	19	2
1923	PHI	AL	12	6	6	8	4	0	0	0	0	0	0	0	0	0	11	1
1924	PHI	AL	6	2	4	3	2	1	0	0	0	0	0	0	0	0	5	1
1925	PHI	AL	10	4	6	6	3	1	0	0	0	0	0	0	0	0	8	2
1926	PHI	AL	2	0	2	1	1	0	0	0	0	0	0	0	0	1	1	1
	STL	AL	4	1	3	3	1	0	0	0	0	0	0	0	0	0	3	1
	Total		6	1	5	4	2	0	0	0	0	0	0	0	0	1	4	2
1927	STL	AL	5	4	1	4	0	1	0	0	0	0	0	0	1	0	2	3
1928	PHI	AL	8	5	3	4	1	3	0	0	0	0	0	0	0	0	6	2
1929	PHI	AL	8	5	3	6	2	0	0	0	0	0	0	0	0	0	8	0
1930	PHI	AL	9	3	6	7	0	2	0	0	0	0	0	1	2	0	7	2
1931	PHI	AL	8	3	5	6	1	1	0	0	0	0	0	0	0	0	7	1
1932	PHI	AL	7	5	2	3	3	1	0	1	0	0	0	0	0	0	6	1
1933	PHI	AL	2	2	0	1	0	1	0	0	0	0	0	0	0	0	2	0
1934	PHI	AL	1	0	1	1	0	0	0	0	0	0	0	0	0	0	1	0
1935	BOS	AL	3	1	2	1	2	0	0	0	0	0	0	0	0	0	2	1
1936	BOS	AL	1	0	1	0	1	0	0	0	0	0	0	0	0	0	1	0
Total			116	56	60	73	29	14	0	3	0	0	0	1	4	1	96	20

Rank among batters: 411 • *Top target (5 home runs)*: Urban Shocker, Sloppy Thurston • *Number of pitchers victimized*: 80 • *Total ballparks homered in*: 10 • *First HR*: 06/12/1921 off George Uhle

Bob Miller

ROBERT JOHN MILLER
B: 06/16/1926
BR

Year	Tm	Lg	Tot	H	A	Men-On 0	Men-On 1	Men-On 2	Men-On 3	One-Game 2	One-Game 3	One-Game 4	LO	XN	IP	PH	RHP	LHP
1954	PHI	NL	1	1	0	1	0	0	0	0	0	0	0	0	0	0	1	0
1957	PHI	NL	1	0	1	0	1	0	0	0	0	0	0	0	0	0	1	0
Total			2	1	1	1	1	0	0	0	0	0	0	0	0	0	2	0

Rank among batters: 4,129 • *Total ballparks homered in*: 2 • *First HR*: 04/19/1954 off Don Newcombe

Bruce Miller

CHARLES BRUCE MILLER
B: 03/04/1947
BR

Year	Tm	Lg	Tot	H	A	Men-On 0	Men-On 1	Men-On 2	Men-On 3	One-Game 2	One-Game 3	One-Game 4	LO	XN	IP	PH	RHP	LHP
1975	SF	NL	1	0	1	1	0	0	0	0	0	0	0	0	0	0	1	0

Rank among batters: 4,707 • *Total ballparks homered in*: 1 • *First HR*: 07/31/1975 off Clay Kirby

Darrell Miller

DARRELL KEITH MILLER
B: 02/26/1958
BR

Year	Tm	Lg	Tot	H	A	Men-On 0	Men-On 1	Men-On 2	Men-On 3	One-Game 2	One-Game 3	One-Game 4	LO	XN	IP	PH	RHP	LHP
1985	CAL	AL	2	0	2	1	1	0	0	0	0	0	0	0	0	0	2	0
1987	CAL	AL	4	3	1	4	0	0	0	0	0	0	0	0	0	0	2	2
1988	CAL	AL	2	0	2	1	1	0	0	0	0	0	0	0	0	0	1	1
Total			8	3	5	6	2	0	0	0	0	0	0	0	0	0	5	3

Rank among batters: 2,703 • *Total ballparks homered in*: 6 • *First HR*: 09/29/1985 off Vern Ruhle

Doc Miller

ROY OSCAR MILLER
B: 02/04/1883 D: 07/31/1938
BL

Year	Tm	Lg	Tot	H	A	Men-On 0	Men-On 1	Men-On 2	Men-On 3	One-Game 2	One-Game 3	One-Game 4	LO	XN	IP	PH	RHP	LHP
1910	BOS	NL	3	3	0	2	1	0	0	0	0	0	0	0	0	0	3	0
1911	BOS	NL	7	5	2	4	2	1	0	1	0	0	0	0	0	0	7	0
1912	BOS	NL	2	1	1	2	0	0	0	0	0	0	0	0	0	0	1	1
Total			12	9	3	8	3	1	0	1	0	0	0	0	0	0	11	1

Rank among batters: 2,325 • *Top target (2 home runs)*: Elmer Steele, Art Fromme • *Number of pitchers victimized*: 10 • *Total ballparks homered in*: 4 • *First HR*: 07/07/1910 off Bugs Raymond

Doggie Miller

GEORGE FREDERICK MILLER
B: 08/15/1864 D: 04/06/1909
BR

Year	Tm	Lg	Tot	H	A	Men-On 0	Men-On 1	Men-On 2	Men-On 3	One-Game 2	One-Game 3	One-Game 4	LO	XN	IP	PH	RHP	LHP
1886	PIT	AA	2	0	2	2	0	0	0	1	0	0	0	0	1	0	0	0

Doggie Miller *continued*

Year	Tm	Lg	Tot	H	A	Men-On 0	Men-On 1	Men-On 2	Men-On 3	One-Game 2	One-Game 3	One-Game 4	LO	XN	IP	PH	RHP	LHP
1887	PIT	NL	1	0	1	0	0	1	0	0	0	0	0	0	0	0	1	0
1889	PIT	NL	6	4	2	2	2	2	0	0	0	0	0	0	0	0	5	1
1890	PIT	NL	4	0	4	1	1	2	0	0	0	0	0	0	0	0	3	0
1891	PIT	NL	4	1	3	1	2	1	0	0	0	0	0	0	0	0	3	1
1892	PIT	NL	2	2	0	0	1	1	0	0	0	0	0	0	1	0	1	1
1894	STL	NL	8	3	5	5	2	1	0	0	0	0	0	0	1	0	7	0
1895	STL	NL	5	5	0	1	3	0	1	0	0	0	0	0	0	0	4	0
1896	LOU	NL	1	0	1	1	0	0	0	0	0	0	0	0	0	0	0	1
Total			33	15	18	13	11	8	1	1	0	0	0	0	3	0	24	2

Rank among batters: 1,336 • Top target (2 home runs): Larry McKeon, Henry Boyle, John Clarkson, Tony Mullane, Kid Gleason • *Number of pitchers victimized*: 28 • *Total ballparks homered in*: 14 • *First HR*: 04/21/1886 off Larry McKeon

Dots Miller

JOHN BARNEY MILLER
B: 09/09/1886 D: 09/05/1923
BR

Year	Tm	Lg	Tot	H	A	Men-On 0	Men-On 1	Men-On 2	Men-On 3	One-Game 2	One-Game 3	One-Game 4	LO	XN	IP	PH	RHP	LHP
1909	PIT	NL	3	1	2	2	0	1	0	0	0	0	0	0	2	0	2	1
1910	PIT	NL	1	0	1	0	1	0	0	0	0	0	0	0	1	0	0	1
1911	PIT	NL	6	2	4	4	1	1	0	0	0	0	0	0	0	0	4	2
1912	PIT	NL	4	2	2	2	2	0	0	0	0	0	0	0	1	0	2	2
1913	PIT	NL	7	2	5	2	4	1	0	0	0	0	0	1	0	0	5	2
1914	STL	NL	4	1	3	3	1	0	0	0	0	0	0	0	2	0	1	3
1915	STL	NL	2	1	1	0	1	0	1	0	0	0	0	0	1	0	0	2
1916	STL	NL	1	0	1	0	1	0	0	0	0	0	0	0	0	0	0	1
1917	STL	NL	2	1	1	1	1	0	0	0	0	0	0	0	1	0	1	1
1919	STL	NL	1	0	1	1	0	0	0	0	0	0	0	0	1	0	0	1
1920	PHI	NL	1	0	1	1	0	0	0	0	0	0	0	0	0	0	0	1
Total			32	10	22	16	12	3	1	0	0	0	0	1	9	0	15	17

Rank among batters: 1,360 • Top target (2 home runs): Cliff Curtis, Thomas Seaton, Eral Yingling, Wilbur Cooper, Clarence Mitchell • *Number of pitchers victimized*: 27 • *Total ballparks homered in*: 11 • *First HR*: 07/14/1909 off Nap Rucker

Dusty Miller

CHARLES BRADLEY MILLER
B: 09/10/1868 D: 09/03/1945
BL

Year	Tm	Lg	Tot	H	A	Men-On 0	Men-On 1	Men-On 2	Men-On 3	One-Game 2	One-Game 3	One-Game 4	LO	XN	IP	PH	RHP	LHP
1890	STL	AA	1	1	0	0	1	0	0	0	0	0	0	0	0	0	1	0
1895	CIN	NL	10	2	8	3	4	3	0	0	0	0	0	1	3	0	7	2
1896	CIN	NL	4	2	2	4	0	0	0	0	0	0	0	0	1	0	2	2
1897	CIN	NL	4	1	3	3	1	0	0	0	0	0	0	0	1	0	3	1
1898	CIN	NL	3	0	3	0	3	0	0	0	0	0	0	0	0	0	2	0
Total			22	6	16	10	9	3	0	0	0	0	0	1	5	0	15	5

Rank among batters: 1,719 • *Top target (2 home runs)*: Dan Daub • *Number of pitchers victimized*: 21 • *Total ballparks homered in*: 10 • *First HR*: 08/25/1890 off George Meakim

Eddie Miller

EDWARD ROBERT MILLER
B: 11/26/1916
BR

Year	Tm	Lg	Tot	H	A	Men-On 0	Men-On 1	Men-On 2	Men-On 3	One-Game 2	One-Game 3	One-Game 4	LO	XN	IP	PH	RHP	LHP
1939	BOS	NL	4	2	2	3	0	1	0	0	0	0	0	0	0	0	4	0
1940	BOS	NL	14	4	10	4	7	2	1	0	0	0	0	1	0	0	11	3
1941	BOS	NL	6	0	6	2	2	2	0	0	0	0	0	0	0	0	6	0
1942	BOS	NL	6	2	4	3	1	1	1	0	0	0	0	0	1	0	5	1
1943	CIN	NL	2	0	2	1	1	0	0	0	0	0	0	0	0	0	2	0
1944	CIN	NL	4	0	4	1	1	2	0	0	0	0	0	0	0	0	3	1
1945	CIN	NL	13	5	8	7	4	2	0	1	0	0	0	0	0	0	13	0
1946	CIN	NL	6	2	4	4	1	1	0	0	0	0	0	1	0	0	5	1
1947	CIN	NL	19	5	14	10	7	1	1	2	0	0	0	0	0	0	16	3
1948	PHI	NL	14	7	7	12	2	0	0	0	0	0	0	0	0	0	12	2
1949	PHI	NL	6	2	4	3	1	1	1	1	0	0	0	0	0	0	4	2
1950	STL	NL	3	3	0	1	1	1	0	0	0	0	0	0	0	0	3	0
Total			97	32	65	51	28	14	4	4	0	0	0	2	1	0	84	13

Rank among batters: 515 • *Top target (4 home runs)*: Clint Hartung • *Number of pitchers victimized*: 69 • *Total ballparks homered in*: 8 • *First HR*: 04/22/1939 off Bill Lohrman

Eddie Miller

EDWARD LEE MILLER
B: 06/29/1957
BB

Year	Tm	Lg	Tot	H	A	Men-On 0	Men-On 1	Men-On 2	Men-On 3	One-Game 2	One-Game 3	One-Game 4	LO	XN	IP	PH	RHP	LHP
1984	SD	NL	1	0	1	1	0	0	0	0	0	0	0	0	0	0	1	0

Rank among batters: 4,707 • *Total ballparks homered in*: 1 • *First HR*: 09/30/1984 off Pascual Perez

Elmer Miller

ELMER MILLER
B: 07/28/1890 D: 11/28/1944
BR

Year	Tm	Lg	Tot	H	A	Men-On 0	Men-On 1	Men-On 2	Men-On 3	One-Game 2	One-Game 3	One-Game 4	LO	XN	IP	PH	RHP	LHP
1916	NY	AL	1	0	1	1	0	0	0	0	0	0	0	0	0	0	1	0
1917	NY	AL	3	2	1	1	0	2	0	0	0	0	0	0	1	0	1	2
1918	NY	AL	1	0	1	1	0	0	0	0	0	0	0	0	0	0	1	0
1921	NY	AL	4	2	2	3	0	1	0	0	0	0	0	0	1	0	2	2
1922	NY	AL	3	2	1	2	0	1	0	0	0	0	0	0	0	0	1	2
	BOS	AL	4	0	4	3	0	1	0	1	0	0	0	0	0	0	3	1
	Total		7	2	5	5	0	2	0	1	0	0	0	0	0	0	4	3
Total			16	6	10	11	0	5	0	1	0	0	0	0	2	0	9	7

Rank among batters: 2,029 • *Top target (3 home runs)*: Red Oldham • *Number of pitchers victimized*: 12 • *Total ballparks homered in*: 6 • *First HR*: 07/29/1916 off Dave Davenport

Elmer Miller

ELMER JOSEPH MILLER
B: 04/17/1903 D: 01/08/1987
BL

Year	Tm	Lg	Tot	H	A	Men-On 0	Men-On 1	Men-On 2	Men-On 3	One-Game 2	One-Game 3	One-Game 4	LO	XN	IP	PH	RHP	LHP
1929	PHI	NL	1	0	1	1	0	0	0	0	0	0	0	0	0	0	1	0

Rank among batters: 4,707 • *Total ballparks homered in*: 1 • *First HR*: 07/24/1929 off Syl Johnson

Hack Miller

LAWRENCE H. MILLER
B: 01/01/1894 D: 09/17/1971
BR

Year	Tm	Lg	Tot	H	A	Men-On 0	Men-On 1	Men-On 2	Men-On 3	One-Game 2	One-Game 3	One-Game 4	LO	XN	IP	PH	RHP	LHP
1922	CHI	NL	12	8	4	4	5	2	1	2	0	0	0	0	0	0	4	8
1923	CHI	NL	20	14	6	10	7	2	1	1	0	0	0	0	1	1	12	8
1924	CHI	NL	4	0	4	3	1	0	0	0	0	0	0	0	0	1	1	3
1925	CHI	NL	2	1	1	2	0	0	0	0	0	0	0	0	0	0	2	0
Total			38	23	15	19	13	4	2	3	0	0	0	0	1	2	19	19

Rank among batters: 1,225 • *Top target (4 home runs)*: Art Nehf • *Number of pitchers victimized*: 25 • *Total ballparks homered in*: 7 • *First HR*: 04/21/1922 off Eppa Rixey

Hack Miller

JAMES ELDRIDGE MILLER
B: 02/13/1913 D: 11/21/1966
BR

Year	Tm	Lg	Tot	H	A	Men-On 0	Men-On 1	Men-On 2	Men-On 3	One-Game 2	One-Game 3	One-Game 4	LO	XN	IP	PH	RHP	LHP
1944	DET	AL	1	0	1	0	0	1	0	0	0	0	0	0	0	0	0	1

Rank among batters: 4,707 • *Total ballparks homered in*: 1 • *First HR*: 04/23/1944 off Al Smith • *Hit HR in first major league AB*—@CLE: 04/23/1944 (2)

Joe Miller

JOSEPH A. MILLER
B: 02/17/1861 D: 04/23/1928
BR

Year	Tm	Lg	Tot	H	A	Men-On 0	Men-On 1	Men-On 2	Men-On 3	One-Game 2	One-Game 3	One-Game 4	LO	XN	IP	PH	RHP	LHP
1884	TOL	AA	1	0	1	0	1	0	0	0	0	0	0	0	0	0	1	0

Rank among batters: 4,707 • *Total ballparks homered in*: 1 • *First HR*: 07/19/1884 off Tommy Bond

John Miller

JOHN ALLEN MILLER
B: 03/14/1944
BR

Year	Tm	Lg	Tot	H	A	Men-On 0	Men-On 1	Men-On 2	Men-On 3	One-Game 2	One-Game 3	One-Game 4	LO	XN	IP	PH	RHP	LHP
1966	NY	AL	1	0	1	0	1	0	0	0	0	0	0	0	0	0	1	0
1969	LA	NL	1	0	1	1	0	0	0	0	0	0	0	0	0	1	0	1
Total			2	0	2	1	1	0	0	0	0	0	0	0	0	1	1	1

Rank among batters: 4,129 • *Total ballparks homered in*: 2 • *First HR*: 09/11/1966 off Lee Stange • *Hit HR in first major league AB*—@BOS: 09/11/1966

Keith Miller

KEITH ALAN MILLER
B: 06/12/1963
BR

Year	Tm	Lg	Tot	H	A	Men-On 0	1	2	3	One-Game 2	3	4	LO	XN	IP	PH	RHP	LHP
1988	NY	NL	1	1	0	1	0	0	0	0	0	0	0	0	0	0	0	1
1989	NY	NL	1	0	1	1	0	0	0	0	0	0	0	0	0	0	0	1
1990	NY	NL	1	1	0	0	1	0	0	0	0	0	0	0	0	0	1	0
1991	NY	NL	4	2	2	4	0	0	0	0	0	0	0	1	0	0	3	1
1992	KC	AL	4	1	3	3	1	0	0	0	0	0	1	0	0	0	4	0
1995	KC	AL	1	0	1	0	1	0	0	0	0	0	0	0	0	0	0	1
Total			12	5	7	9	3	0	0	0	0	0	1	1	0	0	8	4

Rank among batters: 2,325 • *Total ballparks homered in*: 9 • *First HR*: 07/01/1988 off Jim Deshaies

Norm Miller

NORMAN CALVIN MILLER
B: 02/05/1946
BL

Year	Tm	Lg	Tot	H	A	Men-On 0	1	2	3	One-Game 2	3	4	LO	XN	IP	PH	RHP	LHP
1966	HOU	NL	1	1	0	0	0	1	0	0	0	0	0	0	0	0	0	1
1967	HOU	NL	1	0	1	0	0	1	0	0	0	0	0	0	0	0	1	0
1968	HOU	NL	6	3	3	5	0	0	1	0	0	0	1	0	0	0	5	1
1969	HOU	NL	4	2	2	3	0	1	0	0	0	0	0	0	0	0	3	1
1970	HOU	NL	4	2	2	1	1	2	0	0	0	0	0	0	0	2	4	0
1971	HOU	NL	2	0	2	1	0	1	0	0	0	0	0	0	0	1	1	1
1972	HOU	NL	4	2	2	2	2	0	0	0	0	0	0	0	0	0	3	1
1973	ATL	NL	1	1	0	0	0	1	0	0	0	0	0	0	0	0	1	0
1974	ATL	NL	1	0	1	1	0	0	0	0	0	0	0	0	0	1	1	0
Total			24	11	13	13	3	7	1	0	0	0	1	0	0	4	19	5

Rank among batters: 1,643 • *Total ballparks homered in*: 9 • *First HR*: 09/17/1966 off John Morris

Orlando Miller

ORLANDO (SALMON) MILLER
B: 01/13/1969
BR

Year	Tm	Lg	Tot	H	A	Men-On 0	1	2	3	One-Game 2	3	4	LO	XN	IP	PH	RHP	LHP
1994	HOU	NL	2	0	2	1	1	0	0	1	0	0	0	0	0	0	2	0
1995	HOU	NL	5	1	4	2	2	1	0	1	0	0	0	0	0	0	5	0
Total			7	1	6	3	3	1	0	2	0	0	0	0	0	0	7	0

Rank among batters: 2,834 • *Top target (3 home runs)*: Esteban Loaiza • *Number of pitchers victimized*: 5 • *Total ballparks homered in*: 4 • *First HR*: 07/10/1994 off Kevin Foster

Otto Miller

LOWELL OTTO MILLER
B: 06/01/1889 D: 03/29/1962
BR

Year	Tm	Lg	Tot	H	A	Men-On 0	1	2	3	One-Game 2	3	4	LO	XN	IP	PH	RHP	LHP
1912	BRO	NL	1	1	0	0	1	0	0	0	0	0	0	0	0	0	0	1
1916	BRO	NL	1	1	0	1	0	0	0	0	0	0	0	0	0	0	0	1
1917	BRO	NL	1	1	0	0	1	0	0	0	0	0	0	0	1	0	1	0
1921	BRO	NL	1	1	0	1	0	0	0	0	0	0	0	0	0	0	1	0
1922	BRO	NL	1	0	1	0	1	0	0	0	0	0	0	0	0	0	1	0
Total			5	4	1	2	3	0	0	0	0	0	0	0	1	0	3	2

Rank among batters: 3,191 • *Total ballparks homered in*: 3 • *First HR*: 07/27/1912 off Rube Benton

Ox Miller

JOHN ANTHONY MILLER
B: 05/04/1915
BR

Year	Tm	Lg	Tot	H	A	Men-On 0	1	2	3	One-Game 2	3	4	LO	XN	IP	PH	RHP	LHP
1947	CHI	NL	1	0	1	0	0	0	1	0	0	0	0	0	0	0	1	0

Rank among batters: 4,707 • *Total ballparks homered in*: 1 • *First HR*: 09/07/1947 off Kirby Higbe

Ralph Miller

RALPH JOSEPH MILLER
B: 02/29/1896 D: 03/18/1939
BR

Year	Tm	Lg	Tot	H	A	Men-On 0	1	2	3	One-Game 2	3	4	LO	XN	IP	PH	RHP	LHP
1921	PHI	NL	3	3	0	2	0	0	1	0	0	0	0	0	0	0	3	0

Rank among batters: 3,735 • *Total ballparks homered in*: 1 • *First HR*: 04/28/1921 off Jack Scott

						Men-On				One-Game								
Year	Tm	Lg	Tot	H	A	0	1	2	3	2	3	4	LO	XN	IP	PH	RHP	LHP

Rick Miller

RICHARD ALAN MILLER
B: 04/19/1948
BL

Year	Tm	Lg	Tot	H	A	0	1	2	3	2	3	4	LO	XN	IP	PH	RHP	LHP
1971	BOS	AL	1	0	1	0	0	1	0	0	0	0	0	0	0	0	1	0
1972	BOS	AL	3	0	3	1	1	1	0	0	0	0	0	1	0	0	3	0
1973	BOS	AL	6	1	5	5	0	1	0	0	0	0	1	0	0	0	6	0
1974	BOS	AL	5	3	2	2	2	0	1	0	0	0	0	0	0	0	5	0
1978	CAL	AL	1	1	0	0	0	0	1	0	0	0	0	0	0	0	1	0
1979	CAL	AL	2	1	1	1	0	1	0	0	0	0	0	0	0	0	2	0
1980	CAL	AL	2	0	2	1	1	0	0	0	0	0	1	0	0	0	2	0
1981	BOS	AL	2	2	0	0	0	2	0	0	0	0	0	0	0	0	1	1
1982	BOS	AL	4	1	3	1	2	0	1	0	0	0	0	0	0	0	4	0
1983	BOS	AL	2	0	2	1	0	1	0	0	0	0	0	0	0	0	2	0
Total			28	9	19	12	6	7	3	0	0	0	2	1	0	0	27	1

Rank among batters: 1,500 • *Top target (2 home runs)*: Catfish Hunter • *Number of pitchers victimized*: 27 • *Total ballparks homered in*: 9 • *First HR*: 09/16/1971 off Rich Hand

Ward Miller

WARD TAYLOR MILLER
B: 07/05/1884 D: 09/04/1958
BL

Year	Tm	Lg	Tot	H	A	0	1	2	3	2	3	4	LO	XN	IP	PH	RHP	LHP
1913	CHI	NL	1	0	1	0	1	0	0	0	0	0	0	0	0	0	1	0
1914	STL	FL	4	2	2	1	3	0	0	0	0	0	0	0	0	0	3	1
1915	STL	FL	1	0	1	1	0	0	0	0	0	0	0	0	0	0	1	0
1916	STL	AL	1	1	0	1	0	0	0	0	0	0	0	0	0	0	1	0
1917	STL	AL	1	1	0	1	0	0	0	0	0	0	0	0	0	1	1	0
Total			8	4	4	4	4	0	0	0	0	0	0	0	0	1	7	1

Rank among batters: 2,703 • *Total ballparks homered in*: 4 • *First HR*: 07/22/1913 off Grover Alexander

Billy Milligan

WILLIAM JOSEPH MILLIGAN
B: 08/19/1878 D: 10/14/1928
BR

Year	Tm	Lg	Tot	H	A	0	1	2	3	2	3	4	LO	XN	IP	PH	RHP	LHP
1901	PHI	AL	1	0	1	1	0	0	0	0	0	0	0	0	0	0	0	1

Rank among batters: 4,707 • *Total ballparks homered in*: 1 • *First HR*: 06/26/1901 off Case Patten

Jocko Milligan

JOHN MILLIGAN
B: 08/08/1861 D: 08/29/1923
BR

Year	Tm	Lg	Tot	H	A	0	1	2	3	2	3	4	LO	XN	IP	PH	RHP	LHP
1884	PHI	AA	3	2	1	1	1	1	0	0	0	0	0	0	0	0	1	1
1885	PHI	AA	2	2	0	1	1	0	0	0	0	0	0	0	0	0	1	1
1886	PHI	AA	5	4	1	2	2	1	0	0	0	0	0	0	0	0	3	1
1887	PHI	AA	2	2	0	0	2	0	0	0	0	0	0	0	0	0	2	0
1888	STL	AA	5	4	1	2	1	1	1	0	0	0	0	0	0	0	3	1
1889	STL	AA	12	10	2	6	2	4	0	3	0	0	0	0	0	0	8	4
1890	PHI	PL	3	0	3	2	0	1	0	0	0	0	0	0	0	0	3	0
1891	PHI	AA	11	4	7	6	3	2	0	0	0	0	0	0	1	0	9	1
1892	WAS	NL	4	1	3	3	1	0	0	0	0	0	0	0	0	0	3	0
1893	BAL	NL	1	0	1	0	0	1	0	0	0	0	0	0	0	0	0	1
	NY	NL	1	0	1	0	1	0	0	0	0	0	0	0	0	0	1	0
	Total		2	0	2	0	1	1	0	0	0	0	0	0	0	0	1	1
Total			49	29	20	23	14	11	1	3	0	0	0	0	1	0	34	7

Rank among batters: 1,008 • *Top target (4 home runs)*: Bert Cunningham • *Number of pitchers victimized*: 34 • *Total ballparks homered in*: 16 • *First HR*: 06/13/1884 off Larry McKeon

Randy Milligan

RANDY ANDRE MILLIGAN
B: 11/27/1961
BR

Year	Tm	Lg	Tot	H	A	0	1	2	3	2	3	4	LO	XN	IP	PH	RHP	LHP
1988	PIT	NL	3	1	2	2	1	0	0	0	0	0	0	0	0	1	1	2
1989	BAL	AL	12	6	6	6	2	4	0	0	0	0	0	1	0	0	6	6
1990	BAL	AL	20	11	9	17	1	2	0	2	1	0	0	1	0	0	12	8
1991	BAL	AL	16	8	8	11	2	2	1	2	0	0	0	0	0	0	11	5

Randy Milligan *continued*

Year	Tm	Lg	Tot	H	A	Men-On 0	1	2	3	One-Game 2	3	4	LO	XN	IP	PH	RHP	LHP
1992	BAL	AL	11	7	4	6	4	0	1	2	0	0	0	0	0	0	8	3
1993	CIN	NL	6	5	1	5	0	1	0	1	0	0	0	0	0	0	2	4
1994	MON	NL	2	1	1	0	2	0	0	0	0	0	0	0	0	1	1	1
Total			70	39	31	47	12	9	2	7	1	0	0	2	0	2	41	29

Rank among batters: 742 • *Top target (6 home runs)*: Greg Swindell • *Number of pitchers victimized*: 57 • *Total ballparks homered in*: 20 • *First HR*: 04/30/1988 off Candy Sierra

Brad Mills

JAMES BRADLEY MILLS
B: 01/19/1957
BL

Year	Tm	Lg	Tot	H	A	Men-On 0	1	2	3	One-Game 2	3	4	LO	XN	IP	PH	RHP	LHP
1982	MON	NL	1	1	0	1	0	0	0	0	0	0	0	0	0	1	1	0

Rank among batters: 4,707 • *Total ballparks homered in*: 1 • *First HR*: 08/10/1982 off Randy Martz

Buster Mills

COLONEL BUSTER MILLS
B: 09/16/1908 D: 12/01/1991
BR

Year	Tm	Lg	Tot	H	A	Men-On 0	1	2	3	One-Game 2	3	4	LO	XN	IP	PH	RHP	LHP
1934	STL	NL	1	0	1	0	1	0	0	0	0	0	0	0	0	0	1	0
1935	BRO	NL	1	0	1	0	0	1	0	0	0	0	0	0	0	0	1	0
1937	BOS	AL	7	2	5	5	2	0	0	0	0	0	1	0	1	0	6	1
1938	STL	AL	3	1	2	2	0	1	0	0	0	0	0	0	0	0	1	2
1940	NY	AL	1	1	0	0	1	0	0	0	0	0	0	0	0	0	0	1
1942	CLE	AL	1	0	1	1	0	0	0	0	0	0	0	0	0	0	0	1
Total			14	4	10	8	4	2	0	0	0	0	1	0	1	0	9	5

Rank among batters: 2,169 • *Top target (2 home runs)*: George Caster • *Number of pitchers victimized*: 13 • *Total ballparks homered in*: 7 • *First HR*: 04/29/1934 off Pat Malone

Lefty Mills

HOWARD ROBINSON MILLS
B: 05/12/1910 D: 09/23/1982
BL

Year	Tm	Lg	Tot	H	A	Men-On 0	1	2	3	One-Game 2	3	4	LO	XN	IP	PH	RHP	LHP
1939	STL	AL	1	1	0	1	0	0	0	0	0	0	0	0	0	0	1	0

Rank among batters: 4,707 • *Total ballparks homered in*: 1 • *First HR*: 07/06/1939 off Al Benton

Al Milnar

ALBERT JOSEPH MILNAR
B: 12/26/1913
BL

Year	Tm	Lg	Tot	H	A	Men-On 0	1	2	3	One-Game 2	3	4	LO	XN	IP	PH	RHP	LHP
1938	CLE	AL	1	1	0	0	1	0	0	0	0	0	0	0	0	0	1	0
1941	CLE	AL	2	0	2	0	2	0	0	0	0	0	0	0	0	0	2	0
1942	CLE	AL	1	1	0	1	0	0	0	0	0	0	0	0	0	0	1	0
Total			4	2	2	1	3	0	0	0	0	0	0	0	0	0	4	0

Rank among batters: 3,427 • *Total ballparks homered in*: 3 • *First HR*: 09/10/1938 off Bobo Newsom

Pete Milne

WILLIAM JAMES MILNE
B: 04/10/1925
BL

Year	Tm	Lg	Tot	H	A	Men-On 0	1	2	3	One-Game 2	3	4	LO	XN	IP	PH	RHP	LHP
1949	NY	NL	1	1	0	0	0	0	1	0	0	0	0	0	1	1	1	0

Rank among batters: 4,707 • *Total ballparks homered in*: 1 • *First HR*: 04/27/1949 off Pat McGlothin

Eddie Milner

EDWARD JAMES MILNER
B: 05/21/1955
BL

Year	Tm	Lg	Tot	H	A	Men-On 0	1	2	3	One-Game 2	3	4	LO	XN	IP	PH	RHP	LHP
1982	CIN	NL	4	1	3	2	1	1	0	0	0	0	0	0	0	0	4	0
1983	CIN	NL	9	3	6	8	1	0	0	0	0	0	2	0	0	0	8	1
1984	CIN	NL	7	5	2	4	1	2	0	0	0	0	2	0	0	0	6	1
1985	CIN	NL	3	1	2	2	1	0	0	0	0	0	1	0	0	0	3	0
1986	CIN	NL	15	8	7	12	2	1	0	1	0	0	0	0	0	0	15	0

Eddie Milner *continued*

Year	Tm	Lg	Tot	H	A	Men-On 0	1	2	3	One-Game 2	3	4	LO	XN	IP	PH	RHP	LHP
1987	SF	NL	4	4	0	4	0	0	0	0	0	0	2	0	0	0	4	0
Total			42	22	20	32	6	4	0	1	0	0	7	0	0	0	40	2

Rank among batters: 1,138 • Top target (2 home runs): Dennis Eckersley, Pascual Perez, Ron Darling, Eddie Whitson, Mike Scott • *Number of pitchers victimized*: 37 • *Total ballparks homered in*: 9 • *First HR*: 05/29/1982 off Steve Rogers

John Milner

JOHN DAVID MILNER
B: 12/28/1949
BL

Year	Tm	Lg	Tot	H	A	Men-On 0	1	2	3	One-Game 2	3	4	LO	XN	IP	PH	RHP	LHP
1972	NY	NL	17	9	8	13	2	2	0	0	0	0	0	0	0	0	13	4
1973	NY	NL	23	11	12	12	5	4	2	1	0	0	0	0	0	0	18	5
1974	NY	NL	20	9	11	15	5	0	0	1	0	0	0	1	0	0	16	4
1975	NY	NL	7	3	4	4	1	2	0	0	0	0	0	0	0	0	7	0
1976	NY	NL	15	7	8	6	5	1	3	1	0	0	0	0	0	0	12	3
1977	NY	NL	12	6	6	7	5	0	0	1	0	0	0	0	0	0	11	1
1978	PIT	NL	6	1	5	1	2	1	2	0	0	0	0	1	0	1	4	2
1979	PIT	NL	16	7	9	6	6	2	2	1	0	0	0	0	0	1	12	4
1980	PIT	NL	8	2	6	6	2	0	0	0	0	0	0	0	0	0	8	0
1981	PIT	NL	2	1	1	0	1	1	0	0	0	0	0	0	0	2	2	0
	MON	NL	3	1	2	1	1	1	0	0	0	0	0	0	0	0	3	0
	Total		5	2	3	1	2	2	0	0	0	0	0	0	0	2	5	0
1982	PIT	NL	2	1	1	1	0	0	1	0	0	0	0	0	0	2	2	0
Total			131	58	73	72	35	14	10	5	0	0	0	2	0	6	108	23

Rank among batters: 342 • *Top target (6 home runs)*: Lynn McGlothen • *Number of pitchers victimized*: 97 • *Total ballparks homered in*: 12 • *First HR*: 05/17/1972 off Denny Lemaster

Don Mincher

DONALD RAY MINCHER
B: 06/24/1938
BL

Year	Tm	Lg	Tot	H	A	Men-On 0	1	2	3	One-Game 2	3	4	LO	XN	IP	PH	RHP	LHP
1960	WAS	AL	2	1	1	2	0	0	0	0	0	0	0	0	0	0	1	1
1961	MIN	AL	5	4	1	3	2	0	0	0	0	0	0	0	0	0	4	1
1962	MIN	AL	9	4	5	4	1	2	2	1	0	0	0	0	0	2	8	1
1963	MIN	AL	17	10	7	11	2	3	1	3	0	0	0	0	0	0	14	3
1964	MIN	AL	23	10	13	13	3	6	1	1	0	0	0	1	0	4	22	1
1965	MIN	AL	22	13	9	14	4	4	0	3	0	0	0	1	0	1	21	1
1966	MIN	AL	14	10	4	6	5	2	1	1	0	0	0	0	0	0	8	6
1967	CAL	AL	25	14	11	10	10	5	0	1	0	0	0	0	0	0	18	7
1968	CAL	AL	13	5	8	7	5	1	0	2	0	0	0	0	0	0	13	0
1969	SEA	AL	25	13	12	11	11	2	1	1	0	0	0	0	0	1	23	2
1970	OAK	AL	27	14	13	16	9	2	0	3	0	0	0	0	0	0	20	7
1971	OAK	AL	2	1	1	2	0	0	0	0	0	0	0	0	0	0	0	2
	WAS	AL	10	5	5	3	6	0	1	0	0	0	0	1	0	2	9	1
	Total		12	6	6	5	6	0	1	0	0	0	0	1	0	2	9	3
1972	TEX	AL	6	3	3	2	2	2	0	0	0	0	0	0	0	0	6	0
Total			200	107	93	104	60	29	7	16	0	0	0	3	0	10	167	33

Rank among batters: 183 • *Top target (5 home runs)*: Steve Ridzik, Milt Pappas, Joe Horlen • *Number of pitchers victimized*: 126 • *Total ballparks homered in*: 16 • *First HR*: 04/25/1960 off Milt Pappas • *World Series HR*—1

Paul Minner

PAUL EDISON MINNER
B: 07/30/1923
BL

Year	Tm	Lg	Tot	H	A	Men-On 0	1	2	3	One-Game 2	3	4	LO	XN	IP	PH	RHP	LHP
1950	CHI	NL	1	1	0	1	0	0	0	0	0	0	0	0	0	0	1	0
1951	CHI	NL	1	0	1	1	0	0	0	0	0	0	0	0	0	0	1	0
1952	CHI	NL	1	1	0	1	0	0	0	0	0	0	0	0	0	0	1	0
1953	CHI	NL	1	0	1	0	1	0	0	0	0	0	0	0	0	0	1	0
1954	CHI	NL	2	1	1	0	2	0	0	0	0	0	0	0	0	0	2	0
Total			6	3	3	3	3	0	0	0	0	0	0	0	0	0	6	0

Rank among batters: 2,988 • *Total ballparks homered in*: 4 • *First HR*: 08/24/1950 off Max Surkont

Minnie Minoso

SATURNINO ORESTES ARMAS (ARRIETA) MINOSO
B: 11/29/1922
BR

Year	Tm	Lg	Tot	H	A	Men-On 0	1	2	3	One-Game 2	3	4	LO	XN	IP	PH	RHP	LHP
1949	CLE	AL	1	1	0	1	0	0	0	0	0	0	0	0	0	0	1	0

Year	Tm	Lg	Tot	H	A	Men-On 0	Men-On 1	Men-On 2	Men-On 3	One-Game 2	One-Game 3	One-Game 4	LO	XN	IP	PH	RHP	LHP

Minnie Minoso *continued*

Year	Tm	Lg	Tot	H	A	Men-On 0	Men-On 1	Men-On 2	Men-On 3	One-Game 2	One-Game 3	One-Game 4	LO	XN	IP	PH	RHP	LHP
1951	CHI	AL	10	7	3	7	3	0	0	0	0	0	0	1	0	0	7	3
1952	CHI	AL	13	4	9	9	2	2	0	1	0	0	0	1	0	0	9	4
1953	CHI	AL	15	5	10	4	6	5	0	1	0	0	0	0	0	0	11	4
1954	CHI	AL	19	7	12	7	6	5	1	0	0	0	0	0	0	0	15	4
1955	CHI	AL	10	5	5	3	6	1	0	1	0	0	1	0	0	0	5	5
1956	CHI	AL	21	11	10	10	7	4	0	2	0	0	0	0	0	0	11	10
1957	CHI	AL	12	3	9	7	3	1	1	1	0	0	0	1	0	0	11	1
1958	CLE	AL	24	11	13	13	6	5	0	0	0	0	1	2	0	0	19	5
1959	CLE	AL	21	7	14	9	4	6	2	1	0	0	0	0	0	0	20	1
1960	CHI	AL	20	9	11	12	5	2	1	1	0	0	0	0	0	0	19	1
1961	CHI	AL	14	11	3	9	4	1	0	1	0	0	0	1	0	0	13	1
1962	STL	NL	1	0	1	1	0	0	0	0	0	0	0	0	0	0	1	0
1963	WAS	AL	4	3	1	1	1	1	1	0	0	0	0	0	0	1	0	4
1964	CHI	AL	1	1	0	0	0	1	0	0	0	0	0	0	0	1	0	1
Total			186	85	101	93	53	34	6	9	0	0	2	6	0	2	142	44

Rank among batters: 208 • *Top target (6 home runs)*: Early Wynn, Jim Bunning • *Number of pitchers victimized*: 112 • *Total ballparks homered in*: 12 • *First HR*: 05/05/1949 off Jack Kramer

Greg Minton

GREGORY BRIAN MINTON
B: 07/29/1951
BB

Year	Tm	Lg	Tot	H	A	Men-On 0	Men-On 1	Men-On 2	Men-On 3	One-Game 2	One-Game 3	One-Game 4	LO	XN	IP	PH	RHP	LHP
1983	SF	NL	1	0	1	0	1	0	0	0	0	0	0	0	0	0	1	0

Rank among batters: 4,707 • *Total ballparks homered in*: 1 • *First HR*: 09/27/1983 off Gene Garber

Willie Miranda

GUILLERMO (PEREZ) MIRANDA
B: 05/24/1926
BB

Year	Tm	Lg	Tot	H	A	Men-On 0	Men-On 1	Men-On 2	Men-On 3	One-Game 2	One-Game 3	One-Game 4	LO	XN	IP	PH	RHP	LHP
1953	NY	AL	1	1	0	1	0	0	0	0	0	0	0	0	0	0	1	0
1954	NY	AL	1	1	0	0	1	0	0	0	0	0	0	0	0	0	0	1
1955	BAL	AL	1	0	1	1	0	0	0	0	0	0	0	0	1	0	1	0
1956	BAL	AL	2	0	2	2	0	0	0	0	0	0	0	0	0	0	1	1
1958	BAL	AL	1	0	1	1	0	0	0	0	0	0	0	0	0	0	1	0
Total			6	2	4	5	1	0	0	0	0	0	0	0	1	0	4	2

Rank among batters: 2,988 • *Total ballparks homered in*: 4 • *First HR*: 06/24/1953 off Saul Rogovin

Bobby Mitchell

ROBERT VANCE MITCHELL
B: 10/22/1943
BR

Year	Tm	Lg	Tot	H	A	Men-On 0	Men-On 1	Men-On 2	Men-On 3	One-Game 2	One-Game 3	One-Game 4	LO	XN	IP	PH	RHP	LHP
1971	MIL	AL	2	2	0	0	1	1	0	0	0	0	0	0	0	0	1	1
1973	MIL	AL	5	3	2	1	3	1	0	0	0	0	0	0	0	0	1	4
1974	MIL	AL	5	1	4	5	0	0	0	0	0	0	0	1	0	0	2	3
1975	MIL	AL	9	5	4	3	2	4	0	1	0	0	0	0	0	0	2	7
Total			21	11	10	9	6	6	0	1	0	0	0	1	0	0	6	15

Rank among batters: 1,768 • *Top target (2 home runs)*: Wilbur Wood, Larry Gura • *Number of pitchers victimized*: 19 • *Total ballparks homered in*: 8 • *First HR*: 08/01/1971 off Jim Shellenback

Bobby Mitchell

ROBERT VAN MITCHELL
B: 04/07/1955
BL

Year	Tm	Lg	Tot	H	A	Men-On 0	Men-On 1	Men-On 2	Men-On 3	One-Game 2	One-Game 3	One-Game 4	LO	XN	IP	PH	RHP	LHP
1982	MIN	AL	2	1	1	2	0	0	0	0	0	0	0	0	0	0	2	0
1983	MIN	AL	1	1	0	1	0	0	0	0	0	0	0	0	0	0	1	0
Total			3	2	1	3	0	0	0	0	0	0	0	0	0	0	3	0

Rank among batters: 3,735 • *Total ballparks homered in*: 2 • *First HR*: 04/23/1982 off Larry Andersen

Clarence Mitchell

CLARENCE ELMER MITCHELL
B: 02/22/1891 D: 11/06/1963
BL

Year	Tm	Lg	Tot	H	A	Men-On 0	Men-On 1	Men-On 2	Men-On 3	One-Game 2	One-Game 3	One-Game 4	LO	XN	IP	PH	RHP	LHP
1919	BRO	NL	1	1	0	1	0	0	0	0	0	0	0	0	0	1	1	0
1922	BRO	NL	3	1	2	0	2	1	0	0	0	0	0	1	0	1	3	0

Clarence Mitchell *continued*

Year	Tm	Lg	Tot	H	A	Men-On 0	Men-On 1	Men-On 2	Men-On 3	One-Game 2	One-Game 3	One-Game 4	LO	XN	IP	PH	RHP	LHP
1923	PHI	NL	1	0	1	1	0	0	0	0	0	0	0	0	0	0	1	0
1927	PHI	NL	1	0	1	0	1	0	0	0	0	0	0	0	0	0	1	0
1931	NY	NL	1	1	0	1	0	0	0	0	0	0	0	0	0	0	1	0
Total			7	3	4	3	3	1	0	0	0	0	0	1	0	2	7	0

Rank among batters: 2,834 • *Total ballparks homered in*: 5 • *First HR*: 06/24/1919 off Fred Toney

Dale Mitchell

LOREN DALE MITCHELL
B: 08/23/1921 D: 01/05/1987
BL

Year	Tm	Lg	Tot	H	A	Men-On 0	Men-On 1	Men-On 2	Men-On 3	One-Game 2	One-Game 3	One-Game 4	LO	XN	IP	PH	RHP	LHP
1947	CLE	AL	1	1	0	0	1	0	0	0	0	0	0	0	0	0	1	0
1948	CLE	AL	4	3	1	3	1	0	0	0	0	0	2	0	0	0	3	1
1949	CLE	AL	3	2	1	2	0	1	0	0	0	0	0	0	0	0	3	0
1950	CLE	AL	3	1	2	2	0	1	0	0	0	0	0	0	0	0	3	0
1951	CLE	AL	11	4	7	4	4	2	1	1	0	0	2	0	0	0	5	6
1952	CLE	AL	5	4	1	5	0	0	0	0	0	0	0	0	0	0	3	2
1953	CLE	AL	13	7	6	8	4	1	0	0	0	0	1	0	1	0	10	3
1954	CLE	AL	1	0	1	0	1	0	0	0	0	0	0	0	0	1	1	0
Total			41	22	19	24	11	5	1	1	0	0	5	0	1	1	29	12

Rank among batters: 1,163 • Top target (2 home runs): Dick Fowler, Bob Cain, Julio Moreno, Marlin Stuart, Whitey Ford • *Number of pitchers victimized*: 36 • *Total ballparks homered in*: 6 • *First HR*: 06/06/1947 off Carl Scheib • *World Series HR*—1

Johnny Mitchell

JOHN FRANKLIN MITCHELL
B: 08/09/1894 D: 11/04/1965
BB

Year	Tm	Lg	Tot	H	A	Men-On 0	Men-On 1	Men-On 2	Men-On 3	One-Game 2	One-Game 3	One-Game 4	LO	XN	IP	PH	RHP	LHP
1922	BOS	AL	1	0	1	1	0	0	0	0	0	0	0	0	0	0	1	0
1924	BRO	NL	1	1	0	1	0	0	0	0	0	0	0	0	0	0	1	0
Total			2	1	1	2	0	0	0	0	0	0	0	0	0	0	2	0

Rank among batters: 4,129 • *Total ballparks homered in*: 2 • *First HR*: 09/05/1922 off Waite Hoyt

Keith Mitchell

KEITH ALEXANDER MITCHELL
B: 08/06/1969
BR

Year	Tm	Lg	Tot	H	A	Men-On 0	Men-On 1	Men-On 2	Men-On 3	One-Game 2	One-Game 3	One-Game 4	LO	XN	IP	PH	RHP	LHP
1991	ATL	NL	2	1	1	2	0	0	0	0	0	0	1	0	0	0	2	0
1994	SEA	AL	5	2	3	2	2	1	0	1	0	0	0	0	0	0	3	2
Total			7	3	4	4	2	1	0	1	0	0	1	0	0	0	5	2

Rank among batters: 2,834 • *Total ballparks homered in*: 5 • *First HR*: 08/11/1991 off Darryl Kile

Kevin Mitchell

KEVIN DARNELL MITCHELL
B: 01/13/1962
BR

Year	Tm	Lg	Tot	H	A	Men-On 0	Men-On 1	Men-On 2	Men-On 3	One-Game 2	One-Game 3	One-Game 4	LO	XN	IP	PH	RHP	LHP
1986	NY	NL	12	4	8	7	5	0	0	0	0	0	0	0	0	0	5	7
1987	SD	NL	7	2	5	4	3	0	0	1	0	0	0	0	0	0	3	4
	SF	NL	15	7	8	7	5	3	0	1	0	0	0	0	0	0	9	6
	Total		22	9	13	11	8	3	0	2	0	0	0	0	0	0	12	10
1988	SF	NL	19	10	9	12	5	2	0	0	0	0	0	1	0	0	14	5
1989	SF	NL	47	22	25	25	16	6	0	6	0	0	0	1	0	0	28	19
1990	SF	NL	35	15	20	24	10	1	0	1	1	0	0	2	0	0	26	9
1991	SF	NL	27	9	18	15	8	4	0	2	0	0	0	1	0	0	20	7
1992	SEA	AL	9	5	4	4	2	2	1	2	0	0	0	0	0	0	4	5
1993	CIN	NL	19	10	9	13	4	2	0	2	0	0	0	0	0	0	11	8
1994	CIN	NL	30	18	12	19	9	2	0	4	0	0	0	2	0	1	21	9
Total			220	102	118	130	67	22	1	19	1	0	0	7	0	1	141	79

Rank among batters: 149 • *Top target (5 home runs)*: Dennis Martinez, Bruce Hurst, Andy Benes • *Number of pitchers victimized*: 142 • *Total ballparks homered in*: 18 • *First HR*: 04/27/1986 off John Tudor • *World Series HR*—1; *LCS HR*—3

Mike Mitchell

MICHAEL FRANCIS MITCHELL
B: 12/12/1879 D: 07/16/1961
BR

Year	Tm	Lg	Tot	H	A	Men-On 0	Men-On 1	Men-On 2	Men-On 3	One-Game 2	One-Game 3	One-Game 4	LO	XN	IP	PH	RHP	LHP
1907	CIN	NL	3	0	3	3	0	0	0	0	0	0	0	0	2	0	3	0

Mike Mitchell *continued*

Year	Tm	Lg	Tot	H	A	Men-On 0	1	2	3	One-Game 2	3	4	LO	XN	IP	PH	RHP	LHP
1908	CIN	NL	1	1	0	1	0	0	0	0	0	0	0	1	1	0	1	0
1909	CIN	NL	4	1	3	3	0	1	0	0	0	0	0	0	3	0	4	0
1910	CIN	NL	5	1	4	2	3	0	0	0	0	0	0	0	3	0	5	0
1911	CIN	NL	2	0	2	1	1	0	0	0	0	0	0	0	0	0	2	0
1912	CIN	NL	4	2	2	3	1	0	0	0	0	0	0	0	2	0	3	1
1913	CHI	NL	4	3	1	2	1	1	0	0	0	0	0	0	0	0	2	2
	PIT	NL	1	0	1	0	1	0	0	0	0	0	0	0	0	0	1	0
	Total		5	3	2	2	2	1	0	0	0	0	0	0	0	0	3	2
1914	PIT	NL	2	0	2	1	0	1	0	0	0	0	0	0	1	0	2	0
	WAS	AL	1	0	1	1	0	0	0	0	0	0	0	0	0	0	1	0
	Total		3	0	3	2	0	1	0	0	0	0	0	0	1	0	3	0
Total			27	8	19	17	7	3	0	0	0	0	0	1	12	0	24	3

Rank among batters: 1,532 • *Top target (2 home runs)*: Harry McIntire, Buster Brown • *Number of pitchers victimized*: 25 • *Total ballparks homered in*: 10 • *First HR*: 05/10/1907 off Vive Lindaman • *Hit for Cycle*—@NY: 08/19/1911 (2)

George Mitterwald

GEORGE EUGENE MITTERWALD
B: 06/07/1945
BR

Year	Tm	Lg	Tot	H	A	Men-On 0	1	2	3	One-Game 2	3	4	LO	XN	IP	PH	RHP	LHP
1969	MIN	AL	5	1	4	4	1	0	0	0	0	0	0	0	0	0	1	4
1970	MIN	AL	15	9	6	6	7	2	0	0	0	0	0	1	0	0	8	7
1971	MIN	AL	13	6	7	8	2	3	0	1	0	0	0	0	0	0	5	8
1972	MIN	AL	1	1	0	1	0	0	0	0	0	0	0	0	0	0	1	0
1973	MIN	AL	16	12	4	8	4	4	0	1	0	0	0	1	0	0	11	5
1974	CHI	NL	7	4	3	4	2	0	1	0	1	0	0	0	0	0	5	2
1975	CHI	NL	5	2	3	4	1	0	0	0	0	0	0	0	0	1	0	5
1976	CHI	NL	5	4	1	3	2	0	0	0	0	0	0	0	0	0	3	2
1977	CHI	NL	9	6	3	6	2	1	0	1	0	0	0	1	0	0	5	4
Total			76	45	31	44	21	10	1	3	1	0	0	3	0	1	39	37

Rank among batters: 695 • *Top target (3 home runs)*: Rudy May • *Number of pitchers victimized*: 64 • *Total ballparks homered in*: 23 • *First HR*: 04/11/1969 off George Brunet

Johnny Mize

JOHN ROBERT MIZE
B: 01/07/1913 D: 06/02/1993
BL HOF

Year	Tm	Lg	Tot	H	A	Men-On 0	1	2	3	One-Game 2	3	4	LO	XN	IP	PH	RHP	LHP
1936	STL	NL	19	8	11	8	6	4	1	1	0	0	0	1	0	2	16	3
1937	STL	NL	25	15	10	12	9	4	0	2	0	0	0	0	0	0	20	5
1938	STL	NL	27	22	5	13	9	5	0	1	2	0	0	0	0	0	25	2
1939	STL	NL	28	15	13	14	11	3	0	3	0	0	0	0	0	0	26	2
1940	STL	NL	43	25	18	24	13	6	0	4	2	0	0	1	0	0	29	14
1941	STL	NL	16	7	9	7	5	3	1	0	0	0	0	0	0	0	15	1
1942	NY	NL	26	16	10	14	9	3	0	0	0	0	0	1	1	0	17	9
1946	NY	NL	22	12	10	11	6	4	1	2	0	0	0	1	0	0	15	7
1947	NY	NL	51	29	22	26	15	8	2	3	1	0	0	0	0	0	36	15
1948	NY	NL	40	25	15	21	13	6	0	4	0	0	0	1	0	0	30	10
1949	NY	NL	18	13	5	5	10	3	0	1	0	0	0	1	0	0	12	6
	NY	AL	1	0	1	0	1	0	0	0	0	0	0	0	0	0	1	0
	Total		19	13	6	5	11	3	0	1	0	0	0	1	0	0	13	6
1950	NY	AL	25	14	11	10	11	4	0	2	1	0	0	0	0	0	19	6
1951	NY	AL	10	7	3	7	3	0	0	1	0	0	0	0	0	0	6	4
1952	NY	AL	4	2	2	2	1	0	1	0	0	0	0	0	0	2	3	1
1953	NY	AL	4	2	2	1	1	2	0	0	0	0	0	0	0	3	4	0
Total			359	212	147	175	123	55	6	24	6	0	0	6	1	7	274	85

Rank among batters: 41 • *Top target (6 home runs)*: Bill Lee, Murry Dickson • *Number of pitchers victimized*: 168 • *Total ballparks homered in*: 15 • *First HR*: 04/30/1936 off Harry Gumbert • *Hit for Cycle*—vs NY: 07/13/1940 (1) • *World Series HR*—3; *All-Star HR*—1

Wilmer Mizell

WILMER DAVID MIZELL
B: 08/13/1930
BR

Year	Tm	Lg	Tot	H	A	Men-On 0	1	2	3	One-Game 2	3	4	LO	XN	IP	PH	RHP	LHP
1953	STL	NL	1	0	1	1	0	0	0	0	0	0	0	0	0	0	1	0

Rank among batters: 4,707 • *Total ballparks homered in*: 1 • *First HR*: 05/26/1953 off Turk Lown

John Mizerock

JOHN JOSEPH MIZEROCK
B: 12/08/1960
BL

Year	Tm	Lg	Tot	H	A	Men-On 0	1	2	3	One-Game 2	3	4	LO	XN	IP	PH	RHP	LHP
1983	HOU	NL	1	0	1	1	0	0	0	0	0	0	0	0	0	0	1	0
1986	HOU	NL	1	0	1	1	0	0	0	0	0	0	0	0	0	0	1	0
Total			2	0	2	2	0	0	0	0	0	0	0	0	0	0	2	0

Rank among batters: 4,129 • *Total ballparks homered in*: 2 • *First HR*: 08/16/1983 off Charlie Puleo

Dave Moates

DAVID ALLEN MOATES
B: 01/30/1948
BL

Year	Tm	Lg	Tot	H	A	Men-On 0	1	2	3	One-Game 2	3	4	LO	XN	IP	PH	RHP	LHP
1975	TEX	AL	3	2	1	3	0	0	0	0	0	0	1	0	0	0	3	0

Rank among batters: 3,735 • *Total ballparks homered in*: 2 • *First HR*: 07/21/1975 off Luis Tiant

Danny Moeller

DANIEL EDWARD MOELLER
B: 03/23/1885 D: 04/14/1951
BB

Year	Tm	Lg	Tot	H	A	Men-On 0	1	2	3	One-Game 2	3	4	LO	XN	IP	PH	RHP	LHP
1912	WAS	AL	6	4	2	4	1	1	0	0	0	0	1	0	3	0	6	0
1913	WAS	AL	5	3	2	3	0	2	0	0	0	0	2	0	2	0	3	2
1914	WAS	AL	1	1	0	1	0	0	0	0	0	0	1	0	0	0	1	0
1915	WAS	AL	2	0	2	2	0	0	0	0	0	0	0	0	0	0	1	1
1916	WAS	AL	1	0	1	1	0	0	0	0	0	0	1	0	0	0	1	0
Total			15	8	7	11	1	3	0	0	0	0	5	0	5	0	12	3

Rank among batters: 2,096 • *Top target (2 home runs)*: George Baumgardner, Jean Dubuc • *Number of pitchers victimized*: 13 • *Total ballparks homered in*: 7 • *First HR*: 07/04/1912 off Jack Quinn

George Mogridge

GEORGE ANTHONY MOGRIDGE
B: 02/18/1889 D: 03/04/1962
BL

Year	Tm	Lg	Tot	H	A	Men-On 0	1	2	3	One-Game 2	3	4	LO	XN	IP	PH	RHP	LHP
1922	WAS	AL	1	0	1	1	0	0	0	0	0	0	0	0	0	0	1	0

Rank among batters: 4,707 • *Total ballparks homered in*: 1 • *First HR*: 08/03/1922 off Ted Blankenship

Johnny Mokan

JOHN LEO MOKAN
B: 09/23/1895 D: 02/10/1985
BR

Year	Tm	Lg	Tot	H	A	Men-On 0	1	2	3	One-Game 2	3	4	LO	XN	IP	PH	RHP	LHP
1922	PHI	NL	3	3	0	1	0	1	1	0	0	0	0	0	0	0	0	3
1923	PHI	NL	10	9	1	5	2	3	0	2	0	0	0	0	0	0	6	4
1924	PHI	NL	7	2	5	5	1	1	0	0	0	0	0	0	0	0	5	2
1925	PHI	NL	6	4	2	3	3	0	0	0	0	0	0	0	0	0	2	4
1926	PHI	NL	6	4	2	0	2	4	0	0	0	0	0	0	0	0	2	4
Total			32	22	10	14	8	9	1	2	0	0	0	0	0	0	15	17

Rank among batters: 1,360 • *Top target (3 home runs)*: Jack Bentley, Wilbur Cooper • *Number of pitchers victimized*: 26 • *Total ballparks homered in*: 5 • *First HR*: 08/02/1922 off Percy Jones

Bob Molinaro

ROBERT JOSEPH MOLINARO
B: 05/21/1950
BL

Year	Tm	Lg	Tot	H	A	Men-On 0	1	2	3	One-Game 2	3	4	LO	XN	IP	PH	RHP	LHP
1978	CHI	AL	6	2	4	6	0	0	0	0	0	0	0	0	0	0	6	0
1980	CHI	AL	5	0	5	4	1	0	0	0	0	0	0	0	0	1	5	0
1981	CHI	AL	1	0	1	0	1	0	0	0	0	0	0	0	0	1	1	0
1982	CHI	NL	1	0	1	1	0	0	0	0	0	0	0	0	0	1	1	0
1983	PHI	NL	1	0	1	1	0	0	0	0	0	0	0	0	0	1	1	0
Total			14	2	12	12	2	0	0	0	0	0	0	0	0	4	14	0

Rank among batters: 2,169 • *Top target (2 home runs)*: Glenn Abbott, Ferguson Jenkins • *Number of pitchers victimized*: 12 • *Total ballparks homered in*: 9 • *First HR*: 06/25/1978 off Roger Erickson

Paul Molitor

PAUL LEO MOLITOR
B: 08/22/1956
BR

Year	Tm	Lg	Tot	H	A	Men-On 0	1	2	3	One-Game 2	3	4	LO	XN	IP	PH	RHP	LHP
1978	MIL	AL	6	4	2	4	1	1	0	0	0	0	1	1	0	0	5	1
1979	MIL	AL	9	3	6	7	1	1	0	0	0	0	2	0	0	0	5	4

Paul Molitor *continued*

Year	Tm	Lg	Tot	H	A	Men-On 0	1	2	3	One-Game 2	3	4	LO	XN	IP	PH	RHP	LHP
1980	MIL	AL	9	2	7	8	0	1	0	0	0	0	2	0	0	0	4	5
1981	MIL	AL	2	1	1	1	0	0	1	0	0	0	0	0	0	0	2	0
1982	MIL	AL	19	9	10	11	5	3	0	0	1	0	3	0	0	0	15	4
1983	MIL	AL	15	9	6	14	1	0	0	0	0	0	3	0	0	0	6	9
1985	MIL	AL	10	6	4	9	1	0	0	0	0	0	1	0	0	0	5	5
1986	MIL	AL	9	5	4	6	1	2	0	1	0	0	3	0	0	0	8	1
1987	MIL	AL	16	7	9	8	4	4	0	0	0	0	3	0	0	0	13	3
1988	MIL	AL	13	9	4	8	3	2	0	1	0	0	5	0	0	0	9	4
1989	MIL	AL	11	6	5	9	2	0	0	1	0	0	2	0	0	0	7	4
1990	MIL	AL	12	6	6	7	4	1	0	0	0	0	2	0	0	0	7	5
1991	MIL	AL	17	7	10	13	2	2	0	0	0	0	6	0	0	0	12	5
1992	MIL	AL	12	4	8	6	4	2	0	1	0	0	0	0	0	0	6	6
1993	TOR	AL	22	13	9	14	6	2	0	1	0	0	0	0	0	0	15	7
1994	TOR	AL	14	8	6	5	7	1	1	3	0	0	0	0	1	0	9	5
1995	TOR	AL	15	6	9	9	5	1	0	0	0	0	0	0	1	0	11	4
Total			211	105	106	139	47	23	2	8	1	0	33	1	2	0	139	72

Rank among batters: 162 • *Top target (4 home runs)*: Mike Smithson, Dennis Eckersley • *Number of pitchers victimized*: 167 • *Total ballparks homered in*: 19 • *First HR*: 04/08/1978 off Joe Kerrigan • *Hit for Cycle*—@MIN: 05/15/1991 • *World Series HR*—2; *LCS HR*—4

Fritz Mollwitz

FREDERICK AUGUST MOLLWITZ
B: 06/16/1890 D: 10/03/1967
BR

Year	Tm	Lg	Tot	H	A	Men-On 0	1	2	3	One-Game 2	3	4	LO	XN	IP	PH	RHP	LHP
1915	CIN	NL	1	1	0	1	0	0	0	0	0	0	0	0	1	0	1	0

Rank among batters: 4,707 • *Total ballparks homered in*: 1 • *First HR*: 09/19/1915 off Dick Rudolph

Rick Monday

ROBERT JAMES MONDAY
B: 11/20/1945
BL

Year	Tm	Lg	Tot	H	A	Men-On 0	1	2	3	One-Game 2	3	4	LO	XN	IP	PH	RHP	LHP
1967	KC	AL	14	4	10	9	3	2	0	0	0	0	0	1	2	0	8	6
1968	OAK	AL	8	5	3	4	3	1	0	1	0	0	0	0	0	1	4	4
1969	OAK	AL	12	2	10	4	5	1	2	0	0	0	0	0	0	0	8	4
1970	OAK	AL	10	5	5	8	1	1	0	0	0	0	0	0	0	0	8	2
1971	OAK	AL	18	8	10	11	6	1	0	1	0	0	0	0	0	0	17	1
1972	CHI	NL	11	5	6	9	1	1	0	1	1	0	0	0	0	0	11	0
1973	CHI	NL	26	17	9	14	10	1	1	4	0	0	6	0	0	0	22	4
1974	CHI	NL	20	12	8	13	5	2	0	1	0	0	3	0	1	0	15	5
1975	CHI	NL	17	12	5	9	4	4	0	0	0	0	0	0	0	1	13	4
1976	CHI	NL	32	20	12	19	7	6	0	3	0	0	8	2	0	1	25	7
1977	LA	NL	15	6	9	7	8	0	0	1	0	0	0	0	0	0	12	3
1978	LA	NL	19	11	8	13	1	5	0	3	0	0	0	0	0	0	19	0
1980	LA	NL	10	3	7	6	3	1	0	0	0	0	0	0	0	1	9	1
1981	LA	NL	11	4	7	7	4	0	0	1	0	0	0	1	0	1	9	2
1982	LA	NL	11	7	4	6	2	2	1	1	0	0	0	0	0	1	11	0
1983	LA	NL	6	4	2	5	1	0	0	1	0	0	0	0	0	0	6	0
1984	LA	NL	1	0	1	0	0	1	0	0	0	0	0	0	0	1	1	0
Total			241	125	116	144	64	29	4	18	1	0	17	4	3	7	198	43

Rank among batters: 125 • *Top target (11 home runs)*: Tom Seaver • *Number of pitchers victimized*: 163 • *Total ballparks homered in*: 26 • *First HR*: 04/29/1967 off Don McMahon • *LCS HR*—1

Raul Mondesi

RAUL RAMON (AVELINO) MONDESI
B: 03/12/1971
BR

Year	Tm	Lg	Tot	H	A	Men-On 0	1	2	3	One-Game 2	3	4	LO	XN	IP	PH	RHP	LHP
1993	LA	NL	4	2	2	1	3	0	0	0	0	0	0	1	0	0	2	2
1994	LA	NL	16	10	6	12	1	3	0	0	0	0	0	1	0	0	12	4
1995	LA	NL	26	13	13	8	16	1	1	3	0	0	0	0	1	0	21	5
Total			46	25	21	21	20	4	1	3	0	0	0	2	1	0	35	11

Rank among batters: 1,060 • *Top target (2 home runs)*: John Smoltz, Mark Thompson • *Number of pitchers victimized*: 44 • *Total ballparks homered in*: 13 • *First HR*: 07/31/1993 off Bob Scanlan

Don Money

DONALD WAYNE MONEY
B: 06/07/1947
BR

Year	Tm	Lg	Tot	H	A	Men-On 0	1	2	3	One-Game 2	3	4	LO	XN	IP	PH	RHP	LHP
1969	PHI	NL	6	3	3	4	1	1	0	1	0	0	0	0	0	0	5	1

Don Money *continued*

Year	Tm	Lg	Tot	H	A	Men-On 0	Men-On 1	Men-On 2	Men-On 3	One-Game 2	One-Game 3	One-Game 4	LO	XN	IP	PH	RHP	LHP
1970	PHI	NL	14	8	6	6	5	3	0	2	0	0	0	0	0	0	10	4
1971	PHI	NL	7	6	1	5	1	1	0	0	0	0	0	0	0	0	6	1
1972	PHI	NL	15	9	6	8	4	3	0	3	0	0	0	0	0	0	9	6
1973	MIL	AL	11	6	5	7	2	2	0	1	0	0	0	0	0	0	8	3
1974	MIL	AL	15	8	7	10	3	1	1	0	0	0	4	0	0	0	10	5
1975	MIL	AL	15	8	7	12	2	1	0	3	0	0	4	0	0	0	11	4
1976	MIL	AL	12	5	7	7	4	1	0	0	0	0	2	0	0	0	9	3
1977	MIL	AL	25	10	15	16	7	1	1	2	0	0	0	2	0	1	21	4
1978	MIL	AL	14	8	6	11	2	1	0	1	0	0	0	0	0	0	10	4
1979	MIL	AL	6	5	1	5	1	0	0	0	0	0	0	0	0	0	5	1
1980	MIL	AL	17	10	7	8	5	3	1	1	0	0	0	0	0	0	10	7
1981	MIL	AL	2	1	1	2	0	0	0	0	0	0	0	0	0	0	0	2
1982	MIL	AL	16	6	10	9	7	0	0	1	0	0	0	0	0	0	7	9
1983	MIL	AL	1	1	0	1	0	0	0	0	0	0	0	0	0	0	1	0
Total			176	94	82	111	44	18	3	15	0	0	10	2	0	1	122	54

Rank among batters: 227 • *Top target (6 home runs)*: Ferguson Jenkins • *Number of pitchers victimized*: 124 • *Total ballparks homered in*: 23 • *First HR*: 04/08/1969 off Ferguson Jenkins

John Monroe

JOHN ALLEN MONROE
B: 08/24/1898 D: 06/19/1956
BL

Year	Tm	Lg	Tot	H	A	Men-On 0	Men-On 1	Men-On 2	Men-On 3	One-Game 2	One-Game 3	One-Game 4	LO	XN	IP	PH	RHP	LHP
1921	NY	NL	1	0	1	0	1	0	0	0	0	0	0	0	0	0	1	0
	PHI	NL	1	0	1	0	0	1	0	0	0	0	0	0	1	0	1	0
	Total		2	0	2	0	2	0	0	0	0	0	0	0	1	0	2	0
Total			2	0	2	0	2	0	0	0	0	0	0	0	1	0	2	0

Rank among batters: 4,129 • *Total ballparks homered in*: 2 • *First HR*: 06/12/1921 off Bill Pertica

Ed Montague

EDWARD FRANCIS MONTAGUE
B: 07/24/1905 D: 06/17/1988
BR

Year	Tm	Lg	Tot	H	A	Men-On 0	Men-On 1	Men-On 2	Men-On 3	One-Game 2	One-Game 3	One-Game 4	LO	XN	IP	PH	RHP	LHP
1930	CLE	AL	1	1	0	1	0	0	0	0	0	0	0	0	0	0	1	0
1931	CLE	AL	1	0	1	1	0	0	0	0	0	0	0	0	0	0	1	0
Total			2	1	1	2	0	0	0	0	0	0	0	0	0	0	2	0

Rank among batters: 4,129 • *Total ballparks homered in*: 2 • *First HR*: 07/19/1930 off Firpo Marberry

Willie Montanez

GUILLERMO (NARANJO) MONTANEZ
B: 04/01/1948
BL

Year	Tm	Lg	Tot	H	A	Men-On 0	Men-On 1	Men-On 2	Men-On 3	One-Game 2	One-Game 3	One-Game 4	LO	XN	IP	PH	RHP	LHP
1971	PHI	NL	30	14	16	16	13	1	0	3	0	0	0	2	0	0	25	5
1972	PHI	NL	13	8	5	5	7	1	0	0	0	0	0	0	0	0	10	3
1973	PHI	NL	11	9	2	2	6	3	0	0	0	0	0	0	0	0	10	1
1974	PHI	NL	7	4	3	3	3	0	1	0	0	0	0	0	0	0	5	2
1975	PHI	NL	2	0	2	1	1	0	0	0	0	0	0	0	0	0	2	0
	SF	NL	8	5	3	5	1	2	0	0	0	0	0	0	0	0	6	2
	Total		10	5	5	6	2	2	0	0	0	0	0	0	0	0	8	2
1976	SF	NL	2	2	0	1	1	0	0	0	0	0	0	0	0	0	2	0
	ATL	NL	9	5	4	3	4	2	0	1	0	0	0	0	0	0	8	1
	Total		11	7	4	4	5	2	0	1	0	0	0	0	0	0	10	1
1977	ATL	NL	20	14	6	12	8	0	0	0	0	0	0	0	0	0	13	7
1978	NY	NL	17	7	10	6	7	4	0	1	0	0	0	1	0	0	13	4
1979	NY	NL	5	1	4	1	3	1	0	0	0	0	0	0	0	0	3	2
	TEX	AL	8	4	4	6	0	1	1	0	0	0	0	1	0	0	5	3
	Total		13	5	8	7	3	2	1	0	0	0	0	1	0	0	8	5
1980	SD	NL	6	3	3	1	5	0	0	1	0	0	0	0	0	0	5	1
1981	PIT	NL	1	1	0	1	0	0	0	0	0	0	0	0	0	1	1	0
Total			139	77	62	63	59	15	2	6	0	0	0	4	0	1	108	31

Rank among batters: 311 • *Top target (5 home runs)*: Ron Reed, Ray Burris • *Number of pitchers victimized*: 108 • *Total ballparks homered in*: 17 • *First HR*: 04/14/1971 off Bob Moose

John Montefusco

JOHN JOSEPH MONTEFUSCO
B: 05/25/1950
BR

Year	Tm	Lg	Tot	H	A	Men-On 0	Men-On 1	Men-On 2	Men-On 3	One-Game 2	One-Game 3	One-Game 4	LO	XN	IP	PH	RHP	LHP
1974	SF	NL	2	1	1	1	1	0	0	0	0	0	0	0	0	0	2	0

Year	Tm	Lg	Tot	H	A	Men-On 0	1	2	3	One-Game 2	3	4	LO	XN	IP	PH	RHP	LHP

John Montefusco *continued*

Year	Tm	Lg	Tot	H	A	0	1	2	3	2	3	4	LO	XN	IP	PH	RHP	LHP
1975	SF	NL	1	1	0	1	0	0	0	0	0	0	0	0	0	0	1	0
1977	SF	NL	1	0	1	1	0	0	0	0	0	0	0	0	0	0	1	0
Total			4	2	2	3	1	0	0	0	0	0	0	0	0	0	4	0

Rank among batters: 3,427 • *Total ballparks homered in*: 3 • *First HR*: 09/03/1974 off Charlie Hough • *Hit HR in first major league AB*—@LA: 09/03/1974

Felipe Montemayor

FELIPE ANGEL MONTEMAYOR
B: 02/07/1930
BL

Year	Tm	Lg	Tot	H	A	0	1	2	3	2	3	4	LO	XN	IP	PH	RHP	LHP
1955	PIT	NL	2	2	0	0	2	0	0	0	0	0	0	0	0	0	2	0

Rank among batters: 4,129 • *Total ballparks homered in*: 1 • *First HR*: 05/01/1955 off Floyd Wooldridge

Bob Montgomery

ROBERT EDWARD MONTGOMERY
B: 04/16/1944
BR

Year	Tm	Lg	Tot	H	A	0	1	2	3	2	3	4	LO	XN	IP	PH	RHP	LHP
1970	BOS	AL	1	0	1	1	0	0	0	0	0	0	0	0	0	0	1	0
1971	BOS	AL	2	1	1	0	1	0	1	0	0	0	0	0	0	0	1	1
1972	BOS	AL	2	0	2	1	0	1	0	0	0	0	0	0	0	0	1	1
1973	BOS	AL	7	5	2	4	2	0	1	1	0	0	0	2	0	0	6	1
1974	BOS	AL	4	1	3	1	3	0	0	0	0	0	0	0	0	0	3	1
1975	BOS	AL	2	2	0	1	1	0	0	0	0	0	0	0	0	0	2	0
1976	BOS	AL	3	2	1	1	1	1	0	0	0	0	0	0	0	0	1	2
1977	BOS	AL	2	2	0	1	1	0	0	0	0	0	0	0	0	0	2	0
Total			23	13	10	10	9	2	2	1	0	0	0	2	0	0	17	6

Rank among batters: 1,686 • *Top target (2 home runs)*: Doug Bird, Jim Palmer, Jim Colborn • *Number of pitchers victimized*: 20 • *Total ballparks homered in*: 7 • *First HR*: 09/11/1970 off Jim Palmer

Wally Moon

WALLACE WADE MOON
B: 04/03/1930
BL

Year	Tm	Lg	Tot	H	A	0	1	2	3	2	3	4	LO	XN	IP	PH	RHP	LHP
1954	STL	NL	12	8	4	8	3	0	1	0	0	0	2	1	0	0	8	4
1955	STL	NL	19	15	4	8	8	1	2	1	0	0	0	1	0	0	16	3
1956	STL	NL	16	8	8	12	1	2	1	1	0	0	0	0	0	0	14	2
1957	STL	NL	24	13	11	15	6	3	0	1	0	0	0	0	1	0	15	9
1958	STL	NL	7	6	1	5	1	1	0	0	0	0	0	0	0	0	7	0
1959	LA	NL	19	14	5	14	2	3	0	1	0	0	0	0	0	0	16	3
1960	LA	NL	13	9	4	4	5	3	1	0	0	0	0	1	2	0	11	2
1961	LA	NL	17	14	3	13	2	2	0	2	0	0	0	0	1	0	15	2
1962	LA	NL	4	2	2	3	1	0	0	0	0	0	0	0	0	0	3	1
1963	LA	NL	8	1	7	7	1	0	0	0	0	0	0	0	0	0	8	0
1964	LA	NL	2	1	1	1	1	0	0	0	0	0	0	0	0	0	2	0
1965	LA	NL	1	0	1	1	0	0	0	0	0	0	0	0	0	0	1	0
Total			142	91	51	91	31	15	5	6	0	0	2	3	4	0	116	26

Rank among batters: 308 • *Top target (9 home runs)*: Robin Roberts • *Number of pitchers victimized*: 82 • *Total ballparks homered in*: 13 • *First HR*: 04/13/1954 off Paul Minner • *Hit HR in first major league AB*—vs CHI: 04/13/1954 • *World Series HR*—1

Anse Moore

ANSEL WINN MOORE
B: 09/22/1917 D: 10/29/1993
BL

Year	Tm	Lg	Tot	H	A	0	1	2	3	2	3	4	LO	XN	IP	PH	RHP	LHP
1946	DET	AL	1	1	0	1	0	0	0	0	0	0	0	0	0	0	1	0

Rank among batters: 4,707 • *Total ballparks homered in*: 1 • *First HR*: 05/14/1946 off Roger Wolff

Archie Moore

ARCHIE FRANCIS MOORE
B: 08/30/1941
BL

Year	Tm	Lg	Tot	H	A	0	1	2	3	2	3	4	LO	XN	IP	PH	RHP	LHP
1965	NY	AL	1	1	0	0	1	0	0	0	0	0	0	0	0	0	1	0

Rank among batters: 4,707 • *Total ballparks homered in*: 1 • *First HR*: 09/08/1965 off Jim Duckworth

Charlie Moore

CHARLES WILLIAM MOORE
B: 06/21/1953
BR

Year	Tm	Lg	Tot	H	A	Men-On 0	1	2	3	One-Game 2	3	4	LO	XN	IP	PH	RHP	LHP
1975	MIL	AL	1	0	1	1	0	0	0	0	0	0	0	0	0	0	0	1
1976	MIL	AL	3	1	2	3	0	0	0	0	0	0	0	0	0	0	3	0
1977	MIL	AL	5	2	3	3	2	0	0	0	0	0	0	0	0	0	5	0
1978	MIL	AL	5	4	1	2	3	0	0	0	0	0	0	0	0	0	3	2
1979	MIL	AL	5	2	3	2	2	1	0	0	0	0	0	0	0	0	4	1
1980	MIL	AL	2	1	1	1	0	1	0	0	0	0	0	0	0	0	2	0
1981	MIL	AL	1	1	0	1	0	0	0	0	0	0	0	0	0	0	0	1
1982	MIL	AL	6	3	3	3	3	0	0	0	0	0	0	0	0	0	2	4
1983	MIL	AL	2	1	1	2	0	0	0	0	0	0	0	0	0	0	0	2
1984	MIL	AL	2	1	1	1	1	0	0	0	0	0	0	0	0	0	0	2
1986	MIL	AL	3	2	1	3	0	0	0	0	0	0	0	0	0	0	2	1
1987	TOR	AL	1	1	0	0	1	0	0	0	0	0	0	0	0	0	1	0
Total			36	19	17	22	12	2	0	0	0	0	0	0	0	0	22	14

Rank among batters: 1,274 • *Top target (2 home runs)*: Ferguson Jenkins, Tom Underwood • *Number of pitchers victimized*: 34 • *Total ballparks homered in*: 12 • *First HR*: 08/16/1975 off Ken Holtzman • *Hit for Cycle—*@CAL: 10/01/1980

Dee Moore

D C MOORE
B: 04/06/1914
BR

Year	Tm	Lg	Tot	H	A	Men-On 0	1	2	3	One-Game 2	3	4	LO	XN	IP	PH	RHP	LHP
1943	PHI	NL	1	0	1	1	0	0	0	0	0	0	0	0	0	0	0	1

Rank among batters: 4,707 • *Total ballparks homered in*: 1 • *First HR*: 07/28/1943 off Harry Brecheen

Eddie Moore

GRAHAM EDWARD MOORE
B: 01/18/1899 D: 02/10/1976
BR

Year	Tm	Lg	Tot	H	A	Men-On 0	1	2	3	One-Game 2	3	4	LO	XN	IP	PH	RHP	LHP
1924	PIT	NL	2	2	0	2	0	0	0	0	0	0	1	0	2	0	2	0
1925	PIT	NL	6	1	5	4	2	0	0	0	0	0	0	0	1	0	4	2
1927	BOS	NL	1	1	0	0	1	0	0	0	0	0	0	0	1	0	1	0
1928	BOS	NL	2	1	1	2	0	0	0	0	0	0	0	0	0	0	2	0
1930	BRO	NL	1	1	0	1	0	0	0	0	0	0	0	0	0	0	0	1
1932	NY	NL	1	1	0	1	0	0	0	0	0	0	0	0	0	0	0	1
Total			13	7	6	10	3	0	0	0	0	0	1	0	4	0	9	4

Rank among batters: 2,248 • *Total ballparks homered in*: 7 • *First HR*: 08/27/1924 off Hal Carlson • *World Series HR*—1

Gene Moore

EUGENE, JR. MOORE
B: 08/26/1909 D: 03/12/1978
BL

Year	Tm	Lg	Tot	H	A	Men-On 0	1	2	3	One-Game 2	3	4	LO	XN	IP	PH	RHP	LHP
1936	BOS	NL	13	4	9	11	2	0	0	1	0	0	1	0	0	0	13	0
1937	BOS	NL	16	7	9	10	6	0	0	0	0	0	0	0	0	0	16	0
1938	BOS	NL	3	0	3	1	0	0	2	0	0	0	0	0	0	0	2	1
1939	BRO	NL	3	1	2	1	1	1	0	0	0	0	0	0	0	0	3	0
1940	BOS	NL	5	1	4	3	2	0	0	0	0	0	0	0	0	0	5	0
1941	BOS	NL	5	4	1	4	1	0	0	1	0	0	0	0	0	0	5	0
1943	WAS	AL	2	1	1	2	0	0	0	0	0	0	0	0	0	0	2	0
1944	STL	AL	6	6	0	3	0	2	1	0	0	0	0	0	0	1	6	0
1945	STL	AL	5	3	2	3	2	0	0	0	0	0	0	1	1	0	4	1
Total			58	27	31	38	14	3	3	2	0	0	1	1	1	1	56	2

Rank among batters: 886 • *Top target (7 home runs)*: Charlie Root • *Number of pitchers victimized*: 43 • *Total ballparks homered in*: 12 • *First HR*: 04/20/1936 off George Earnshaw

Harry Moore

HENRY S. MOORE

Year	Tm	Lg	Tot	H	A	Men-On 0	1	2	3	One-Game 2	3	4	LO	XN	IP	PH	RHP	LHP
1884	WAS	UA	1	1	0	1	0	0	0	0	0	0	0	0	0	0	1	0

Rank among batters: 4,707 • *Total ballparks homered in*: 1 • *First HR*: 07/14/1884 off Hugh Daily

Jerrie Moore

JEREMIAH S. MOORE
D: 09/26/1890
BL

Year	Tm	Lg	Tot	H	A	Men-On 0	1	2	3	One-Game 2	3	4	LO	XN	IP	PH	RHP	LHP
1884	ALT	UA	1	0	1	1	0	0	0	0	0	0	0	0	0	0	1	0

Jerrie Moore *continued*

Rank among batters: 4,707 • *Total ballparks homered in*: 1 • *First HR*: 04/17/1884 off George Bradley

Jimmy Moore

JAMES WILLIAM MOORE
B: 04/24/1903 D: 03/07/1986
BR

Year	Tm	Lg	Tot	H	A	Men-On 0	1	2	3	One-Game 2	3	4	LO	XN	IP	PH	RHP	LHP
1930	PHI	AL	2	1	1	1	1	0	0	0	0	0	0	0	0	0	1	1
1931	PHI	AL	2	1	1	2	0	0	0	0	0	0	0	0	0	0	2	0
Total			4	2	2	3	1	0	0	0	0	0	0	0	0	0	3	1

Rank among batters: 3,427 • *Total ballparks homered in*: 3 • *First HR*: 09/03/1930 off Milt Gaston

Jo Jo Moore

JOSEPH GREGG MOORE
B: 12/25/1908
BL

Year	Tm	Lg	Tot	H	A	Men-On 0	1	2	3	One-Game 2	3	4	LO	XN	IP	PH	RHP	LHP
1932	NY	NL	2	2	0	2	0	0	0	0	0	0	0	0	0	0	2	0
1934	NY	NL	15	8	7	8	5	1	1	1	0	0	1	0	0	1	13	2
1935	NY	NL	15	13	2	7	6	2	0	1	0	0	1	0	1	0	13	2
1936	NY	NL	7	3	4	6	1	0	0	0	0	0	0	0	1	0	7	0
1937	NY	NL	6	6	0	4	2	0	0	0	0	0	0	0	0	0	4	2
1938	NY	NL	11	10	1	5	1	5	0	0	0	0	0	0	2	0	7	4
1939	NY	NL	10	8	2	8	1	1	0	1	0	0	1	0	0	1	8	2
1940	NY	NL	6	4	2	4	2	0	0	0	0	0	1	0	0	0	5	1
1941	NY	NL	7	5	2	3	3	1	0	0	0	0	0	0	0	0	7	0
Total			79	59	20	47	21	10	1	3	0	0	4	0	4	2	66	13

Rank among batters: 661 • *Top target (4 home runs)*: Larry French, Lon Warneke, Paul Derringer • *Number of pitchers victimized*: 52 • *Total ballparks homered in*: 7 • *First HR*: 07/27/1932 off Glenn Spencer • *World Series HR*—1

Johnny Moore

JOHN FRANCIS MOORE
B: 03/23/1902 D: 04/04/1991
BL

Year	Tm	Lg	Tot	H	A	Men-On 0	1	2	3	One-Game 2	3	4	LO	XN	IP	PH	RHP	LHP
1929	CHI	NL	2	2	0	1	1	0	0	0	0	0	0	0	0	0	2	0
1931	CHI	NL	2	1	1	1	0	1	0	0	0	0	0	0	0	0	2	0
1932	CHI	NL	13	7	6	4	8	1	0	0	0	0	0	0	0	0	12	1
1933	CIN	NL	1	0	1	1	0	0	0	0	0	0	0	0	0	0	1	0
1934	PHI	NL	11	8	3	5	6	0	0	0	0	0	0	0	0	0	7	4
1935	PHI	NL	19	11	8	10	9	0	0	2	0	0	0	1	0	0	14	5
1936	PHI	NL	16	15	1	9	6	1	0	1	1	0	0	1	0	0	10	6
1937	PHI	NL	9	4	5	1	6	2	0	1	0	0	0	0	0	0	8	1
Total			73	48	25	32	36	5	0	4	1	0	0	2	0	0	56	17

Rank among batters: 715 • *Top target (4 home runs)*: Watty Clark, Hal Schumacher • *Number of pitchers victimized*: 49 • *Total ballparks homered in*: 6 • *First HR*: 06/07/1929 off Johnny Morrison

Junior Moore

ALVIN EARL MOORE
B: 01/25/1953
BR

Year	Tm	Lg	Tot	H	A	Men-On 0	1	2	3	One-Game 2	3	4	LO	XN	IP	PH	RHP	LHP
1977	ATL	NL	5	3	2	4	0	0	1	0	0	0	0	1	0	0	3	2
1979	CHI	AL	1	1	0	1	0	0	0	0	0	0	0	0	0	0	0	1
1980	CHI	AL	1	0	1	1	0	0	0	0	0	0	0	0	0	0	1	0
Total			7	4	3	6	0	0	1	0	0	0	0	1	0	0	4	3

Rank among batters: 2,834 • *Total ballparks homered in*: 5 • *First HR*: 05/25/1977 off Tom Griffin

Kelvin Moore

KELVIN ORLANDO MOORE
B: 09/26/1957
BR

Year	Tm	Lg	Tot	H	A	Men-On 0	1	2	3	One-Game 2	3	4	LO	XN	IP	PH	RHP	LHP
1981	OAK	AL	1	0	1	1	0	0	0	0	0	0	0	0	0	0	0	1
1982	OAK	AL	2	2	0	2	0	0	0	0	0	0	0	0	0	0	1	1
1983	OAK	AL	5	1	4	3	2	0	0	1	0	0	0	0	0	0	5	0
Total			8	3	5	6	2	0	0	1	0	0	0	0	0	0	6	2

Rank among batters: 2,703 • *Total ballparks homered in*: 4 • *First HR*: 10/03/1981 off Mike Jones

Randy Moore

RANDOLPH EDWARD MOORE
B: 06/21/1906 D: 06/12/1992
BL

Year	Tm	Lg	Tot	H	A	Men-On 0	Men-On 1	Men-On 2	Men-On 3	One-Game 2	One-Game 3	One-Game 4	LO	XN	IP	PH	RHP	LHP
1930	BOS	NL	2	1	1	1	1	0	0	0	0	0	0	0	0	0	1	1
1931	BOS	NL	3	1	2	1	1	1	0	1	0	0	0	0	0	0	3	0
1932	BOS	NL	3	1	2	1	1	1	0	0	0	0	0	0	0	0	3	0
1933	BOS	NL	8	1	7	5	1	2	0	0	0	0	0	1	0	0	7	1
1934	BOS	NL	7	1	6	4	3	0	0	0	0	0	0	0	0	0	6	1
1935	BOS	NL	4	0	4	3	1	0	0	0	0	0	0	0	0	0	4	0
Total			27	5	22	15	8	4	0	1	0	0	0	1	0	0	24	3

Rank among batters: 1,532 • *Top target (2 home runs)*: Sloppy Thurston, Cy Moore, Reggie Grabowski, Pat Malone, Charlie Root, Tex Carleton • *Number of pitchers victimized*: 21 • *Total ballparks homered in*: 7 • *First HR*: 05/13/1930 off Pat Malone

Ray Moore

RAYMOND LEROY MOORE
B: 06/01/1926 D: 03/02/1995
BR

Year	Tm	Lg	Tot	H	A	Men-On 0	Men-On 1	Men-On 2	Men-On 3	One-Game 2	One-Game 3	One-Game 4	LO	XN	IP	PH	RHP	LHP
1956	BAL	AL	2	1	1	0	1	1	0	0	0	0	0	0	0	0	1	1
1957	BAL	AL	3	3	0	3	0	0	0	0	0	0	0	0	0	0	3	0
1958	CHI	AL	1	0	1	1	0	0	0	0	0	0	0	0	0	0	1	0
Total			6	4	2	4	1	1	0	0	0	0	0	0	0	0	5	1

Rank among batters: 2,988 • *Total ballparks homered in*: 3 • *First HR*: 06/29/1956 off Mel Parnell

Roy Moore

ROY DANIEL MOORE
B: 10/26/1898 D: 04/05/1951
BB

Year	Tm	Lg	Tot	H	A	Men-On 0	Men-On 1	Men-On 2	Men-On 3	One-Game 2	One-Game 3	One-Game 4	LO	XN	IP	PH	RHP	LHP
1920	PHI	AL	1	1	0	0	1	0	0	0	0	0	0	0	0	0	1	0
1921	PHI	AL	3	2	1	3	0	0	0	0	0	0	0	0	0	0	3	0
Total			4	3	1	3	1	0	0	0	0	0	0	0	0	0	4	0

Rank among batters: 3,427 • *Total ballparks homered in*: 2 • *First HR*: 05/25/1920 off Roy Wilkinson

Terry Moore

TERRY BLUFORD MOORE
B: 05/27/1912 D: 03/29/1995
BR

Year	Tm	Lg	Tot	H	A	Men-On 0	Men-On 1	Men-On 2	Men-On 3	One-Game 2	One-Game 3	One-Game 4	LO	XN	IP	PH	RHP	LHP
1935	STL	NL	6	3	3	4	2	0	0	0	0	0	0	0	0	0	2	4
1936	STL	NL	5	2	3	3	2	0	0	0	0	0	1	0	1	0	5	0
1937	STL	NL	5	3	2	1	1	3	0	0	0	0	1	1	0	0	4	1
1938	STL	NL	4	3	1	3	0	0	1	0	0	0	2	0	0	0	2	2
1939	STL	NL	17	9	8	9	6	2	0	1	0	0	0	0	2	0	15	2
1940	STL	NL	17	10	7	12	3	2	0	2	0	0	0	0	0	0	11	6
1941	STL	NL	6	5	1	5	1	0	0	0	0	0	0	0	0	0	4	2
1942	STL	NL	6	2	4	5	1	0	0	0	0	0	0	0	0	0	4	2
1946	STL	NL	3	2	1	1	0	2	0	0	0	0	0	0	0	0	0	3
1947	STL	NL	7	1	6	6	1	0	0	0	0	0	0	0	0	0	3	4
1948	STL	NL	4	2	2	3	0	1	0	0	0	0	0	1	0	0	2	2
Total			80	42	38	52	17	10	1	3	0	0	4	2	3	0	52	28

Rank among batters: 650 • *Top target (3 home runs)*: Carl Hubbell, Vito Tamulis, Bucky Walters, Paul Derringer, Hal Schumacher, Ken Heintzelman • *Number of pitchers victimized*: 55 • *Total ballparks homered in*: 9 • *First HR*: 05/05/1935 off Ed Brandt

Wilcy Moore

WILLIAM WILCY MOORE
B: 05/20/1897 D: 03/29/1963
BR

Year	Tm	Lg	Tot	H	A	Men-On 0	Men-On 1	Men-On 2	Men-On 3	One-Game 2	One-Game 3	One-Game 4	LO	XN	IP	PH	RHP	LHP
1927	NY	AL	1	1	0	1	0	0	0	0	0	0	0	0	0	0	1	0

Rank among batters: 4,707 • *Total ballparks homered in*: 1 • *First HR*: 09/16/1927 off Ted Blankenship

Bob Moose

ROBERT RALPH MOOSE
B: 10/09/1947 D: 10/09/1976
BR

Year	Tm	Lg	Tot	H	A	Men-On 0	Men-On 1	Men-On 2	Men-On 3	One-Game 2	One-Game 3	One-Game 4	LO	XN	IP	PH	RHP	LHP
1976	PIT	NL	1	0	1	1	0	0	0	0	0	0	0	0	0	0	1	0

Rank among batters: 4,707 • *Total ballparks homered in*: 1 • *First HR*: 06/11/1976 off Bruce Dal Canton

Year	Tm	Lg	Tot	H	A	Men-On				One-Game			LO	XN	IP	PH	RHP	LHP
						0	1	2	3	2	3	4						

Andres Mora

ANDRES (IBARA) MORA
B: 05/25/1955
BR

Year	Tm	Lg	Tot	H	A	0	1	2	3	2	3	4	LO	XN	IP	PH	RHP	LHP
1976	BAL	AL	6	2	4	3	2	1	0	0	0	0	0	0	0	1	3	3
1977	BAL	AL	13	8	5	5	6	2	0	1	0	0	0	0	0	2	6	7
1978	BAL	AL	8	5	3	7	1	0	0	1	0	0	0	0	0	0	2	6
Total			27	15	12	15	9	3	0	2	0	0	0	0	0	3	11	16

Rank among batters: 1,532 • *Top target (2 home runs)*: Dave Goltz, Ken Kravec • *Number of pitchers victimized*: 25 • *Total ballparks homered in*: 9 • *First HR*: 04/17/1976 off Paul Lindblad

Jerry Morales

JULIO RUBEN (TORRES) MORALES
B: 02/18/1949
BR

Year	Tm	Lg	Tot	H	A	0	1	2	3	2	3	4	LO	XN	IP	PH	RHP	LHP
1969	SD	NL	1	0	1	1	0	0	0	0	0	0	0	0	0	0	1	0
1970	SD	NL	1	0	1	1	0	0	0	0	0	0	0	0	0	0	0	1
1972	SD	NL	4	2	2	2	2	0	0	0	0	0	0	0	0	1	4	0
1973	SD	NL	9	6	3	8	1	0	0	0	0	0	2	0	0	2	6	3
1974	CHI	NL	15	7	8	10	3	1	1	1	0	0	0	0	0	0	11	4
1975	CHI	NL	12	7	5	5	5	2	0	0	0	0	0	0	0	0	10	2
1976	CHI	NL	16	12	4	9	7	0	0	1	0	0	0	1	0	1	13	3
1977	CHI	NL	11	5	6	8	2	1	0	0	0	0	0	0	0	0	7	4
1978	STL	NL	4	0	4	2	2	0	0	0	0	0	0	0	0	0	2	2
1979	DET	AL	14	7	7	9	5	0	0	2	0	0	0	0	0	0	1	13
1980	NY	NL	3	1	2	3	0	0	0	0	0	0	0	0	0	0	1	2
1981	CHI	NL	1	1	0	0	1	0	0	0	0	0	0	0	0	1	0	1
1982	CHI	NL	4	3	1	2	0	2	0	0	0	0	0	0	0	2	2	2
Total			95	51	44	60	28	6	1	4	0	0	2	1	0	7	58	37

Rank among batters: 529 • *Top target (4 home runs)*: Steve Rogers • *Number of pitchers victimized*: 73 • *Total ballparks homered in*: 21 • *First HR*: 09/10/1969 off Tony Cloninger

Jose Morales

JOSE MANUEL MORALES
B: 12/30/1944
BR

Year	Tm	Lg	Tot	H	A	0	1	2	3	2	3	4	LO	XN	IP	PH	RHP	LHP
1974	MON	NL	1	1	0	0	0	1	0	0	0	0	0	0	0	1	0	1
1975	MON	NL	2	2	0	2	0	0	0	0	0	0	0	0	0	1	1	1
1976	MON	NL	4	2	2	0	2	2	0	0	0	0	0	0	0	3	3	1
1977	MON	NL	1	0	1	1	0	0	0	0	0	0	0	0	0	0	1	0
1978	MIN	AL	2	1	1	2	0	0	0	0	0	0	0	0	0	0	0	2
1979	MIN	AL	2	1	1	1	0	1	0	0	0	0	0	0	0	0	2	0
1980	MIN	AL	8	3	5	2	2	3	1	1	0	0	0	0	0	2	2	6
1981	BAL	AL	2	0	2	1	0	1	0	0	0	0	0	1	0	1	2	0
1982	LA	NL	1	1	0	1	0	0	0	0	0	0	0	0	0	1	0	1
1983	LA	NL	3	0	3	2	1	0	0	0	0	0	0	0	0	3	2	1
Total			26	11	15	12	5	8	1	1	0	0	0	1	0	12	13	13

Rank among batters: 1,576 • *Total ballparks homered in*: 15 • *First HR*: 09/15/1974 off Ken Brett

Rich Morales

RICHARD ANGELO MORALES
B: 09/20/1943
BR

Year	Tm	Lg	Tot	H	A	0	1	2	3	2	3	4	LO	XN	IP	PH	RHP	LHP
1970	CHI	AL	1	0	1	1	0	0	0	0	0	0	0	0	0	0	0	1
1971	CHI	AL	2	0	2	2	0	0	0	0	0	0	0	0	0	0	2	0
1972	CHI	AL	2	1	1	2	0	0	0	0	0	0	0	0	0	0	1	1
1974	SD	NL	1	0	1	0	1	0	0	0	0	0	0	0	0	0	0	1
Total			6	1	5	5	1	0	0	0	0	0	0	0	0	0	3	3

Rank among batters: 2,988 • *Total ballparks homered in*: 5 • *First HR*: 09/13/1970 off Jim Kaat

Al Moran

RICHARD ALAN MORAN
B: 12/05/1938
BR

Year	Tm	Lg	Tot	H	A	0	1	2	3	2	3	4	LO	XN	IP	PH	RHP	LHP
1963	NY	NL	1	1	0	0	1	0	0	0	0	0	0	0	0	0	0	1

Rank among batters: 4,707 • *Total ballparks homered in*: 1 • *First HR*: 08/31/1963 off Warren Spahn

Bill Moran

WILLIAM L. MORAN
B: 10/10/1869 D: 04/08/1916

Year	Tm	Lg	Tot	H	A	Men-On 0	Men-On 1	Men-On 2	Men-On 3	One-Game 2	One-Game 3	One-Game 4	LO	XN	IP	PH	RHP	LHP
1895	CHI	NL	1	1	0	0	1	0	0	0	0	0	0	0	0	0	0	0

Rank among batters: 4,707 • *Total ballparks homered in*: 1 • *First HR*: 05/22/1895 off George Hodson

Billy Moran

WILLIAM NELSON MORAN
B: 11/27/1933
BR

Year	Tm	Lg	Tot	H	A	Men-On 0	Men-On 1	Men-On 2	Men-On 3	One-Game 2	One-Game 3	One-Game 4	LO	XN	IP	PH	RHP	LHP
1958	CLE	AL	1	0	1	0	0	1	0	0	0	0	0	0	0	0	0	1
1961	LA	AL	2	2	0	0	2	0	0	0	0	0	0	0	0	0	2	0
1962	LA	AL	17	9	8	9	6	2	0	1	0	0	0	1	0	0	13	4
1963	LA	AL	7	4	3	6	1	0	0	0	0	0	0	0	0	0	7	0
1964	CLE	AL	1	1	0	1	0	0	0	0	0	0	0	0	0	0	1	0
Total			28	16	12	16	9	3	0	1	0	0	0	1	0	0	23	5

Rank among batters: 1,500 • Top target (2 home runs): Georges Maranda, Pete Burnside, Ralph Terry, Eddie Fisher, Jim Bunning, Dave Wickersham • *Number of pitchers victimized*: 22 • *Total ballparks homered in*: 9 • *First HR*: 06/13/1958 off Chuck Stobbs

Charles Moran

CHARLES VINCENT MORAN
B: 03/26/1879 D: 04/11/1934

Year	Tm	Lg	Tot	H	A	Men-On 0	Men-On 1	Men-On 2	Men-On 3	One-Game 2	One-Game 3	One-Game 4	LO	XN	IP	PH	RHP	LHP
1903	WAS	AL	1	1	0	1	0	0	0	0	0	0	0	0	0	0	0	1

Rank among batters: 4,707 • *Total ballparks homered in*: 1 • *First HR*: 07/18/1903 off Patsy Flaherty

Herbie Moran

JOHN HERBERT MORAN
B: 02/16/1884 D: 09/21/1954
BL

Year	Tm	Lg	Tot	H	A	Men-On 0	Men-On 1	Men-On 2	Men-On 3	One-Game 2	One-Game 3	One-Game 4	LO	XN	IP	PH	RHP	LHP
1912	BRO	NL	1	1	0	1	0	0	0	0	0	0	1	0	1	0	0	1
1914	CIN	NL	1	0	1	1	0	0	0	0	0	0	0	0	1	0	1	0
Total			2	1	1	2	0	0	0	0	0	0	1	0	2	0	1	1

Rank among batters: 4,129 • *Total ballparks homered in*: 2 • *First HR*: 06/14/1912 off Joe Willis

Pat Moran

PATRICK JOSEPH MORAN
B: 02/07/1876 D: 03/07/1924
BR

Year	Tm	Lg	Tot	H	A	Men-On 0	Men-On 1	Men-On 2	Men-On 3	One-Game 2	One-Game 3	One-Game 4	LO	XN	IP	PH	RHP	LHP
1901	BOS	NL	2	1	1	2	0	0	0	0	0	0	0	0	0	0	2	0
1902	BOS	NL	1	1	0	1	0	0	0	0	0	0	0	0	0	0	1	0
1903	BOS	NL	7	5	2	4	2	0	1	0	0	0	0	0	0	1	6	1
1904	BOS	NL	4	3	1	3	0	1	0	0	0	0	0	0	0	0	3	1
1905	BOS	NL	2	2	0	2	0	0	0	0	0	0	0	0	0	0	2	0
1907	CHI	NL	1	1	0	1	0	0	0	0	0	0	0	1	1	0	1	0
1909	CHI	NL	1	0	1	0	1	0	0	0	0	0	0	0	0	0	1	0
Total			18	13	5	13	3	1	1	0	0	0	0	1	1	1	16	2

Rank among batters: 1,914 • *Top target (2 home runs)*: Mordecai Brown, Bob Wicker, Joe McGinnity • *Number of pitchers victimized*: 15 • *Total ballparks homered in*: 4 • *First HR*: 07/20/1901 off Willie Sudhoff

Sam Moran

SAMUEL MORAN
B: 09/16/1870 D: 08/29/1897

Year	Tm	Lg	Tot	H	A	Men-On 0	Men-On 1	Men-On 2	Men-On 3	One-Game 2	One-Game 3	One-Game 4	LO	XN	IP	PH	RHP	LHP
1895	PIT	NL	1	0	1	1	0	0	0	0	0	0	0	0	0	0	1	0

Rank among batters: 4,707 • *Total ballparks homered in*: 1 • *First HR*: 09/28/1895 off Dewey McDougal

Mickey Morandini

MICHAEL ROBERT MORANDINI
B: 04/22/1966
BL

Year	Tm	Lg	Tot	H	A	Men-On 0	Men-On 1	Men-On 2	Men-On 3	One-Game 2	One-Game 3	One-Game 4	LO	XN	IP	PH	RHP	LHP
1990	PHI	NL	1	1	0	1	0	0	0	0	0	0	0	0	0	0	1	0
1991	PHI	NL	1	1	0	0	0	1	0	0	0	0	0	0	0	0	1	0
1992	PHI	NL	3	2	1	1	2	0	0	0	0	0	0	0	1	0	2	1
1993	PHI	NL	3	2	1	1	1	0	1	0	0	0	0	0	0	1	2	1
1994	PHI	NL	2	1	1	2	0	0	0	0	0	0	0	0	0	0	2	0

Mickey Morandini *continued*

Year	Tm	Lg	Tot	H	A	Men-On 0	Men-On 1	Men-On 2	Men-On 3	One-Game 2	One-Game 3	One-Game 4	LO	XN	IP	PH	RHP	LHP
1995	PHI	NL	6	3	3	3	2	1	0	0	0	0	0	1	0	1	5	1
Total			16	10	6	8	5	2	1	0	0	0	0	1	1	2	13	3

Rank among batters: 2,029 • *Top target (2 home runs)*: Mark Portugal, Sergio Valdez • *Number of pitchers victimized*: 14 • *Total ballparks homered in*: 6 • *First HR*: 09/22/1990 off Scott Anderson

Mike Mordecai

MICHAEL HOWARD MORDECAI
B: 12/13/1967
BB

Year	Tm	Lg	Tot	H	A	Men-On 0	Men-On 1	Men-On 2	Men-On 3	One-Game 2	One-Game 3	One-Game 4	LO	XN	IP	PH	RHP	LHP
1994	ATL	NL	1	1	0	0	0	1	0	0	0	0	0	0	0	0	1	0
1995	ATL	NL	3	1	2	2	0	1	0	0	0	0	0	0	0	1	1	2
Total			4	2	2	2	0	2	0	0	0	0	0	0	0	1	2	2

Rank among batters: 3,427 • *Total ballparks homered in*: 3 • *First HR*: 05/10/1994 off Doug Jones

Ray Morehart

RAYMOND ANDERSON MOREHART
B: 12/02/1899 D: 01/13/1989
BL

Year	Tm	Lg	Tot	H	A	Men-On 0	Men-On 1	Men-On 2	Men-On 3	One-Game 2	One-Game 3	One-Game 4	LO	XN	IP	PH	RHP	LHP
1927	NY	AL	1	1	0	0	0	1	0	0	0	0	0	0	1	0	0	1

Rank among batters: 4,707 • *Total ballparks homered in*: 1 • *First HR*: 06/09/1927 off Bert Cole

Keith Moreland

BOBBY KEITH MORELAND
B: 05/02/1954
BR

Year	Tm	Lg	Tot	H	A	Men-On 0	Men-On 1	Men-On 2	Men-On 3	One-Game 2	One-Game 3	One-Game 4	LO	XN	IP	PH	RHP	LHP
1980	PHI	NL	4	1	3	2	1	0	1	0	0	0	0	0	0	0	4	0
1981	PHI	NL	6	4	2	5	0	1	0	2	0	0	0	0	0	0	6	0
1982	CHI	NL	15	8	7	7	4	4	0	1	0	0	0	0	0	1	10	5
1983	CHI	NL	16	8	8	5	10	1	0	0	0	0	0	0	0	0	9	7
1984	CHI	NL	16	13	3	10	2	3	1	2	0	0	0	0	0	0	9	7
1985	CHI	NL	14	11	3	6	5	3	0	1	0	0	0	1	0	0	11	3
1986	CHI	NL	12	8	4	7	3	2	0	1	0	0	0	1	0	0	7	5
1987	CHI	NL	27	19	8	15	10	1	1	1	0	0	0	0	0	0	24	3
1988	SD	NL	5	3	2	4	1	0	0	0	0	0	0	0	0	0	3	2
1989	DET	AL	5	2	3	2	1	2	0	0	0	0	0	0	0	0	3	2
	BAL	AL	1	0	1	0	1	0	0	0	0	0	0	0	0	0	1	0
	Total		6	2	4	2	2	2	0	0	0	0	0	0	0	0	4	2
Total			121	77	44	63	38	17	3	8	0	0	0	2	0	1	87	34

Rank among batters: 382 • *Top target (5 home runs)*: Bill Gullickson, Kevin Gross • *Number of pitchers victimized*: 92 • *Total ballparks homered in*: 16 • *First HR*: 05/21/1980 off Tom Seaver • *LCS HR*—1

Jose Moreno

JOSE DE LOS SANTOS MAURICIO MORENO
B: 11/01/1957
BB

Year	Tm	Lg	Tot	H	A	Men-On 0	Men-On 1	Men-On 2	Men-On 3	One-Game 2	One-Game 3	One-Game 4	LO	XN	IP	PH	RHP	LHP
1980	NY	NL	2	1	1	1	1	0	0	0	0	0	0	0	0	1	2	0

Rank among batters: 4,129 • *Total ballparks homered in*: 2 • *First HR*: 06/18/1980 off John Montefusco

Omar Moreno

OMAR RENAN (QUINTERO) MORENO
B: 10/24/1952
BL

Year	Tm	Lg	Tot	H	A	Men-On 0	Men-On 1	Men-On 2	Men-On 3	One-Game 2	One-Game 3	One-Game 4	LO	XN	IP	PH	RHP	LHP
1976	PIT	NL	2	0	2	1	1	0	0	0	0	0	0	0	0	0	2	0
1977	PIT	NL	7	3	4	5	1	1	0	0	0	0	0	0	0	0	5	2
1978	PIT	NL	2	1	1	2	0	0	0	0	0	0	0	0	1	0	1	1
1979	PIT	NL	8	1	7	6	1	1	0	0	0	0	2	0	0	0	6	2
1980	PIT	NL	2	1	1	2	0	0	0	0	0	0	1	0	1	0	2	0
1981	PIT	NL	1	0	1	1	0	0	0	0	0	0	1	0	0	0	1	0
1982	PIT	NL	3	1	2	2	1	0	0	0	0	0	1	0	0	0	2	1
1983	NY	AL	1	1	0	0	0	1	0	0	0	0	0	0	0	0	0	1
1984	NY	AL	4	2	2	2	2	0	0	0	0	0	0	0	0	0	4	0
1985	NY	AL	1	1	0	1	0	0	0	0	0	0	0	0	0	0	1	0

Omar Moreno *continued*

Year	Tm	Lg	Tot	H	A	Men-On 0	1	2	3	One-Game 2	3	4	LO	XN	IP	PH	RHP	LHP
1985	KC	AL	2	2	0	1	0	1	0	0	0	0	1	0	1	0	2	0
	Total		3	3	0	2	0	1	0	0	0	0	1	0	1	0	3	0
1986	ATL	NL	4	3	1	1	1	2	0	0	0	0	0	0	0	1	4	0
Total			37	16	21	24	7	6	0	0	0	0	6	0	3	1	30	7

Rank among batters: 1,252 • *Top target (3 home runs)*: Don Sutton • *Number of pitchers victimized*: 32 • *Total ballparks homered in*: 14 • *First HR*: 08/13/1976 off Joe Niekro

Bobby Morgan

ROBERT MORRIS MORGAN
B: 06/29/1926
BR

Year	Tm	Lg	Tot	H	A	Men-On 0	1	2	3	One-Game 2	3	4	LO	XN	IP	PH	RHP	LHP
1950	BRO	NL	7	0	7	4	2	1	0	1	0	0	1	0	0	0	5	2
1952	BRO	NL	7	5	2	5	2	0	0	1	0	0	2	0	0	0	6	1
1953	BRO	NL	7	7	0	4	3	0	0	0	0	0	0	0	0	0	6	1
1954	PHI	NL	14	8	6	11	2	0	1	1	0	0	0	0	0	0	7	7
1955	PHI	NL	10	6	4	5	2	3	0	0	0	0	1	0	0	1	7	3
1956	STL	NL	3	1	2	1	2	0	0	0	0	0	0	0	0	0	2	1
1957	CHI	NL	5	3	2	3	2	0	0	0	0	0	0	0	0	0	3	2
Total			53	30	23	33	15	4	1	3	0	0	4	0	0	1	36	17

Rank among batters: 953 • *Top target (3 home runs)*: Frank Smith, Howie Pollet • *Number of pitchers victimized*: 45 • *Total ballparks homered in*: 7 • *First HR*: 06/05/1950 off Paul Minner

Ed Morgan

EDWARD CARRE MORGAN
B: 05/22/1904 D: 04/09/1980
BR

Year	Tm	Lg	Tot	H	A	Men-On 0	1	2	3	One-Game 2	3	4	LO	XN	IP	PH	RHP	LHP
1928	CLE	AL	4	2	2	1	0	3	0	0	0	0	0	1	0	0	4	0
1929	CLE	AL	2	0	2	2	0	0	0	0	0	0	0	0	1	0	0	2
1930	CLE	AL	26	14	12	9	14	3	0	1	0	0	1	0	0	0	19	7
1931	CLE	AL	11	7	4	5	2	4	0	0	0	0	0	0	0	0	9	2
1932	CLE	AL	4	2	2	4	0	0	0	0	0	0	0	0	0	0	3	1
1933	CLE	AL	1	1	0	1	0	0	0	0	0	0	0	0	0	0	0	1
1934	BOS	AL	3	1	2	0	0	2	1	0	0	0	0	0	0	0	3	0
Total			51	27	24	22	16	12	1	1	0	0	1	1	1	0	38	13

Rank among batters: 979 • *Top target (4 home runs)*: Roy Mahaffey • *Number of pitchers victimized*: 33 • *Total ballparks homered in*: 8 • *First HR*: 06/25/1928 off Dick Coffman

Eddie Morgan

EDWIN WILLIS MORGAN
B: 11/19/1914 D: 06/27/1982
BL

Year	Tm	Lg	Tot	H	A	Men-On 0	1	2	3	One-Game 2	3	4	LO	XN	IP	PH	RHP	LHP
1936	STL	NL	1	1	0	0	1	0	0	0	0	0	0	0	0	1	1	0

Rank among batters: 4,707 • *Total ballparks homered in*: 1 • *First HR*: 04/14/1936 off Lon Warneke • *Hit HR on first major league pitch*—vs CHI: 04/14/1936

Joe Morgan

JOSEPH MICHAEL MORGAN
B: 11/19/1930
BL

Year	Tm	Lg	Tot	H	A	Men-On 0	1	2	3	One-Game 2	3	4	LO	XN	IP	PH	RHP	LHP
1960	CLE	AL	2	1	1	2	0	0	0	0	0	0	0	0	0	0	2	0

Rank among batters: 4,129 • *Total ballparks homered in*: 2 • *First HR*: 08/30/1960 off Chuck Estrada

Joe Morgan

JOE LEONARD MORGAN
B: 09/19/1943
BL HOF

Year	Tm	Lg	Tot	H	A	Men-On 0	1	2	3	One-Game 2	3	4	LO	XN	IP	PH	RHP	LHP
1965	HOU	NL	14	4	10	13	1	0	0	2	0	0	4	0	0	0	11	3
1966	HOU	NL	5	3	2	4	0	1	0	0	0	0	2	0	0	0	3	2
1967	HOU	NL	6	2	4	3	2	1	0	0	0	0	0	0	0	0	4	2
1969	HOU	NL	15	7	8	12	2	1	0	0	0	0	2	1	0	0	14	1
1970	HOU	NL	8	4	4	5	3	0	0	0	0	0	0	1	1	0	7	1
1971	HOU	NL	13	4	9	8	4	1	0	0	0	0	0	1	0	0	11	2
1972	CIN	NL	16	9	7	7	8	1	0	1	0	0	0	0	0	0	15	1

Joe Morgan *continued*

Year	Tm	Lg	Tot	H	A	Men-On 0	1	2	3	One-Game 2	3	4	LO	XN	IP	PH	RHP	LHP
1973	CIN	NL	26	9	17	12	13	1	0	2	0	0	0	0	1	1	22	4
1974	CIN	NL	22	13	9	10	9	2	1	1	0	0	0	0	0	0	18	4
1975	CIN	NL	17	10	7	9	5	3	0	0	0	0	0	0	0	0	13	4
1976	CIN	NL	27	13	14	12	6	7	2	3	0	0	0	0	0	0	24	3
1977	CIN	NL	22	11	11	8	8	5	1	1	0	0	0	0	0	0	14	8
1978	CIN	NL	13	6	7	5	6	2	0	0	0	0	0	0	0	0	9	4
1979	CIN	NL	9	4	5	9	0	0	0	0	0	0	0	0	0	0	5	4
1980	HOU	NL	11	2	9	7	4	0	0	0	0	0	2	0	0	0	8	3
1981	SF	NL	8	4	4	6	2	0	0	0	0	0	0	0	0	0	7	1
1982	SF	NL	14	6	8	10	2	2	0	0	0	0	1	0	0	0	8	6
1983	PHI	NL	16	9	7	8	5	3	0	3	0	0	2	0	0	0	15	1
1984	OAK	AL	6	2	4	5	0	1	0	0	0	0	0	0	0	0	4	2
Total			268	122	146	153	80	31	4	13	0	0	13	3	2	1	212	56

Rank among batters: 91 • *Top target (7 home runs)*: Don Sutton • *Number of pitchers victimized*: 170 • *Total ballparks homered in*: 21 • *First HR*: 05/08/1965 off Lindy McDaniel • *World Series HR*—3; *LCS HR*—2; *All-Star HR*—1

Ray Morgan

RAYMOND CARYLL MORGAN
B: 06/14/1889 D: 02/15/1940
BR

Year	Tm	Lg	Tot	H	A	Men-On 0	1	2	3	One-Game 2	3	4	LO	XN	IP	PH	RHP	LHP
1912	WAS	AL	1	0	1	1	0	0	0	0	0	0	0	0	1	0	1	0
1914	WAS	AL	1	1	0	1	0	0	0	0	0	0	0	0	0	0	1	0
1916	WAS	AL	1	0	1	1	0	0	0	0	0	0	0	0	0	0	1	0
1917	WAS	AL	1	0	1	1	0	0	0	0	0	0	0	0	0	0	1	0
Total			4	1	3	4	0	0	0	0	0	0	0	0	1	0	4	0

Rank among batters: 3,427 • *Total ballparks homered in*: 3 • *First HR*: 06/05/1912 off Joe Benz

Red Morgan

JAMES EDWARD MORGAN
B: 10/06/1883 D: 03/25/1981

Year	Tm	Lg	Tot	H	A	Men-On 0	1	2	3	One-Game 2	3	4	LO	XN	IP	PH	RHP	LHP
1906	BOS	AL	1	1	0	0	1	0	0	0	0	0	0	0	1	0	1	0

Rank among batters: 4,707 • *Total ballparks homered in*: 1 • *First HR*: 07/24/1906 off Bob Rhoads

Tom Morgan

TOM STEPHEN MORGAN
B: 05/20/1930 D: 01/13/1987
BR

Year	Tm	Lg	Tot	H	A	Men-On 0	1	2	3	One-Game 2	3	4	LO	XN	IP	PH	RHP	LHP
1951	NY	AL	1	1	0	1	0	0	0	0	0	0	0	0	0	0	1	0
1952	NY	AL	1	1	0	0	1	0	0	0	0	0	0	0	0	0	0	1
1954	NY	AL	1	0	1	0	1	0	0	0	0	0	0	0	0	0	1	0
1959	DET	AL	2	1	1	2	0	0	0	0	0	0	0	0	0	0	1	1
Total			5	3	2	3	2	0	0	0	0	0	0	0	0	0	3	2

Rank among batters: 3,191 • *Total ballparks homered in*: 3 • *First HR*: 08/01/1951 off Virgil Trucks

Gene Moriarity

EUGENE JOHN MORIARITY
B: 01/05/1865
BL

Year	Tm	Lg	Tot	H	A	Men-On 0	1	2	3	One-Game 2	3	4	LO	XN	IP	PH	RHP	LHP
1892	STL	NL	3	1	2	1	2	0	0	0	0	0	0	0	0	0	3	0

Rank among batters: 3,735 • *Total ballparks homered in*: 3 • *First HR*: 09/08/1892 off Jack Stivetts

Ed Moriarty

EDWARD JEROME MORIARTY
B: 10/12/1912 D: 09/29/1991
BR

Year	Tm	Lg	Tot	H	A	Men-On 0	1	2	3	One-Game 2	3	4	LO	XN	IP	PH	RHP	LHP
1935	BOS	NL	1	1	0	1	0	0	0	0	0	0	0	0	0	0	1	0

Rank among batters: 4,707 • *Total ballparks homered in*: 1 • *First HR*: 06/22/1935 off Charlie Root

George Moriarty

GEORGE JOSEPH MORIARTY
B: 06/07/1884 D: 04/08/1964
BR

Year	Tm	Lg	Tot	H	A	Men-On 0	1	2	3	One-Game 2	3	4	LO	XN	IP	PH	RHP	LHP
1909	DET	AL	1	1	0	0	1	0	0	0	0	0	0	0	0	0	0	1

George Moriarty *continued*

Year	Tm	Lg	Tot	H	A	Men-On 0	1	2	3	One-Game 2	3	4	LO	XN	IP	PH	RHP	LHP
1910	DET	AL	2	2	0	0	1	1	0	0	0	0	0	0	0	0	2	0
1911	DET	AL	1	1	0	1	0	0	0	0	0	0	0	0	1	0	1	0
1914	DET	AL	1	0	1	1	0	0	0	0	0	0	0	0	0	0	1	0
Total			5	4	1	2	2	1	0	0	0	0	0	0	1	0	4	1

Rank among batters: 3,191 • *Total ballparks homered in*: 2 • *First HR*: 09/02/1909 off Ray Collins

Russ Morman

RUSSELL LEE MORMAN
B: 04/28/1962
BR

Year	Tm	Lg	Tot	H	A	Men-On 0	1	2	3	One-Game 2	3	4	LO	XN	IP	PH	RHP	LHP
1986	CHI	AL	4	1	3	3	1	0	0	0	0	0	0	0	0	0	2	2
1990	KC	AL	1	0	1	1	0	0	0	0	0	0	0	0	0	0	0	1
1994	FLO	NL	1	0	1	1	0	0	0	0	0	0	0	0	0	0	0	1
1995	FLO	NL	3	1	2	3	0	0	0	0	0	0	0	0	0	0	2	1
Total			9	2	7	8	1	0	0	0	0	0	0	0	0	0	4	5

Rank among batters: 2,587 • *Total ballparks homered in*: 9 • *First HR*: 08/03/1986 off Randy O'Neal

John Morrill

JOHN FRANCIS MORRILL
B: 02/19/1855 D: 04/02/1932
BR

Year	Tm	Lg	Tot	H	A	Men-On 0	1	2	3	One-Game 2	3	4	LO	XN	IP	PH	RHP	LHP
1880	BOS	NL	2	2	0	0	2	0	0	0	0	0	0	0	0	0	2	0
1881	BOS	NL	1	1	0	1	0	0	0	0	0	0	0	0	0	0	1	0
1882	BOS	NL	2	1	1	1	1	0	0	0	0	0	0	0	0	0	1	1
1883	BOS	NL	6	2	4	2	2	2	0	1	0	0	0	0	0	0	4	2
1884	BOS	NL	3	1	2	1	2	0	0	0	0	0	0	0	0	0	3	0
1885	BOS	NL	4	0	4	2	2	0	0	0	0	0	0	0	0	0	2	1
1886	BOS	NL	7	6	1	2	4	1	0	0	0	0	0	0	0	0	6	1
1887	BOS	NL	12	7	5	4	7	0	1	0	0	0	0	0	0	0	10	2
1888	BOS	NL	4	1	3	1	3	0	0	0	0	0	0	0	0	0	3	1
1889	WAS	NL	2	2	0	2	0	0	0	1	0	0	0	0	0	0	2	0
Total			43	23	20	16	23	3	1	2	0	0	0	0	0	0	34	8

Rank among batters: 1,116 • *Top target (3 home runs)*: Monte Ward, Stump Wiedman, Jim Galvin • *Number of pitchers victimized*: 31 • *Total ballparks homered in*: 12 • *First HR*: 05/19/1880 off Monte Ward

Ed Morris

EDWARD MORRIS
B: 09/29/1862 D: 04/12/1937
BR

Year	Tm	Lg	Tot	H	A	Men-On 0	1	2	3	One-Game 2	3	4	LO	XN	IP	PH	RHP	LHP
1886	PIT	AA	1	0	1	0	0	1	0	0	0	0	0	0	0	0	0	1

Rank among batters: 4,707 • *Total ballparks homered in*: 1 • *First HR*: 06/12/1886 off Tony Mullane

Ed Morris

WALTER EDWARD MORRIS
B: 12/07/1899 D: 03/03/1932
BR

Year	Tm	Lg	Tot	H	A	Men-On 0	1	2	3	One-Game 2	3	4	LO	XN	IP	PH	RHP	LHP
1929	BOS	AL	1	1	0	1	0	0	0	0	0	0	0	0	0	0	1	0

Rank among batters: 4,707 • *Total ballparks homered in*: 1 • *First HR*: 05/26/1929 off Waite Hoyt

Hal Morris

WILLIAM HAROLD MORRIS
B: 04/09/1965
BL

Year	Tm	Lg	Tot	H	A	Men-On 0	1	2	3	One-Game 2	3	4	LO	XN	IP	PH	RHP	LHP
1990	CIN	NL	7	3	4	5	1	1	0	0	0	0	0	0	0	0	7	0
1991	CIN	NL	14	9	5	12	1	1	0	0	0	0	0	0	0	1	13	1
1992	CIN	NL	6	3	3	3	2	1	0	0	0	0	0	1	0	0	5	1
1993	CIN	NL	7	2	5	5	1	1	0	1	0	0	0	0	0	0	7	0
1994	CIN	NL	10	5	5	5	4	0	1	0	0	0	0	1	0	0	10	0
1995	CIN	NL	11	6	5	7	3	1	0	0	0	0	0	0	0	0	11	0
Total			55	28	27	37	12	5	1	1	0	0	0	2	0	1	53	2

Rank among batters: 926 • *Top target (2 home runs)*: John Burkett • *Number of pitchers victimized*: 54 • *Total ballparks homered in*: 14 • *First HR*: 07/05/1990 off Ken Howell

John Morris

JOHN DANIEL MORRIS
B: 02/23/1961
BL

Year	Tm	Lg	Tot	H	A	Men-On 0	Men-On 1	Men-On 2	Men-On 3	One-Game 2	One-Game 3	One-Game 4	LO	XN	IP	PH	RHP	LHP
1986	STL	NL	1	1	0	1	0	0	0	0	0	0	0	0	0	0	1	0
1987	STL	NL	3	1	2	2	1	0	0	0	0	0	0	0	0	0	3	0
1989	STL	NL	2	2	0	1	1	0	0	0	0	0	0	0	0	0	2	0
1991	PHI	NL	1	1	0	1	0	0	0	0	0	0	0	1	0	0	1	0
1992	CAL	AL	1	0	1	1	0	0	0	0	0	0	0	0	0	0	1	0
Total			8	5	3	6	2	0	0	0	0	0	0	1	0	0	8	0

Rank among batters: 2,703 • *Total ballparks homered in*: 4 • *First HR*: 09/24/1986 off Kevin Gross

Guy Morrison

WALTER GUY MORRISON
B: 08/29/1895 D: 08/14/1934
BR

Year	Tm	Lg	Tot	H	A	Men-On 0	Men-On 1	Men-On 2	Men-On 3	One-Game 2	One-Game 3	One-Game 4	LO	XN	IP	PH	RHP	LHP
1927	BOS	NL	1	0	1	1	0	0	0	0	0	0	0	0	0	0	0	1

Rank among batters: 4,707 • *Total ballparks homered in*: 1 • *First HR*: 09/20/1927 off Percy Jones

Jim Morrison

JAMES FORREST MORRISON
B: 09/23/1952
BR

Year	Tm	Lg	Tot	H	A	Men-On 0	Men-On 1	Men-On 2	Men-On 3	One-Game 2	One-Game 3	One-Game 4	LO	XN	IP	PH	RHP	LHP
1978	PHI	NL	3	3	0	1	2	0	0	0	0	0	0	0	0	0	2	1
1979	CHI	AL	14	9	5	13	1	0	0	1	0	0	4	1	0	0	6	8
1980	CHI	AL	15	5	10	9	3	3	0	0	0	0	0	0	0	0	9	6
1981	CHI	AL	10	3	7	7	3	0	0	0	0	0	0	0	0	0	8	2
1982	CHI	AL	7	3	4	6	1	0	0	1	0	0	0	0	0	0	5	2
	PIT	NL	4	2	2	4	0	0	0	0	0	0	0	0	0	0	2	2
	Total		11	5	6	10	1	0	0	1	0	0	0	0	0	0	7	4
1983	PIT	NL	6	2	4	5	0	1	0	0	0	0	0	0	0	0	1	5
1984	PIT	NL	11	6	5	8	2	1	0	0	0	0	0	0	0	0	7	4
1985	PIT	NL	4	2	2	3	1	0	0	0	0	0	0	0	0	1	3	1
1986	PIT	NL	23	11	12	12	9	1	1	1	0	0	0	0	0	0	17	6
1987	PIT	NL	9	6	3	5	3	1	0	2	0	0	0	2	0	0	4	5
	DET	AL	4	1	3	3	0	1	0	0	0	0	0	0	0	0	3	1
	Total		13	7	6	8	3	2	0	2	0	0	0	2	0	0	7	6
1988	ATL	NL	2	2	0	1	0	1	0	0	0	0	0	0	0	1	0	2
Total			112	55	57	77	25	9	1	5	0	0	4	3	0	2	67	45

Rank among batters: 429 • *Top target (3 home runs)*: Rick Honeycutt, Ron Robinson, Greg Mathews • *Number of pitchers victimized*: 97 • *Total ballparks homered in*: 26 • *First HR*: 05/10/1978 off Mark Lemongello

Jon Morrison

JONATHAN W. MORRISON
B: 1859 BL

Year	Tm	Lg	Tot	H	A	Men-On 0	Men-On 1	Men-On 2	Men-On 3	One-Game 2	One-Game 3	One-Game 4	LO	XN	IP	PH	RHP	LHP
1884	IND	AA	1	0	1	1	0	0	0	0	0	0	0	0	0	0	1	0

Rank among batters: 4,707 • *Total ballparks homered in*: 1 • *First HR*: 08/27/1884 off Gus Shallix

Mike Morrison

MICHAEL MORRISON
B: 02/06/1867 D: 06/16/1955
BR

Year	Tm	Lg	Tot	H	A	Men-On 0	Men-On 1	Men-On 2	Men-On 3	One-Game 2	One-Game 3	One-Game 4	LO	XN	IP	PH	RHP	LHP
1890	SYR	AA	1	1	0	0	1	0	0	0	0	0	0	0	0	0	0	1

Rank among batters: 4,707 • *Total ballparks homered in*: 1 • *First HR*: 06/24/1890 off Mike Mattimore

Bubba Morton

WYCLIFFE NATHANIEL MORTON
B: 12/13/1931
BR

Year	Tm	Lg	Tot	H	A	Men-On 0	Men-On 1	Men-On 2	Men-On 3	One-Game 2	One-Game 3	One-Game 4	LO	XN	IP	PH	RHP	LHP
1961	DET	AL	2	1	1	0	1	1	0	0	0	0	0	0	0	0	1	1
1962	DET	AL	4	4	0	4	0	0	0	0	0	0	0	0	0	0	0	4
1968	CAL	AL	1	1	0	1	0	0	0	0	0	0	0	0	0	0	0	1
1969	CAL	AL	7	3	4	6	1	0	0	0	0	0	0	0	0	0	0	7
Total			14	9	5	11	2	1	0	0	0	0	0	0	0	0	1	13

Rank among batters: 2,169 • *Top target (3 home runs)*: Tommy John • *Number of pitchers victimized*: 11 • *Total ballparks homered in*: 5 • *First HR*: 06/04/1961 off Jim Kaat

Carl Morton

CARL WENDLE MORTON
B: 01/18/1944 D: 04/12/1983
BR

						Men-On				One-Game								
Year	**Tm**	**Lg**	**Tot**	**H**	**A**	**0**	**1**	**2**	**3**	**2**	**3**	**4**	**LO**	**XN**	**IP**	**PH**	**RHP**	**LHP**
1970	MON	NL	2	1	1	0	2	0	0	0	0	0	0	0	0	0	1	1
1971	MON	NL	2	0	2	1	1	0	0	0	0	0	0	0	0	0	2	0
1973	ATL	NL	3	3	0	2	1	0	0	0	0	0	0	0	0	0	1	2
Total			7	4	3	3	4	0	0	0	0	0	0	0	0	0	4	3

Rank among batters: 2,834 • *Total ballparks homered in*: 5 • *First HR*: 07/21/1970 off Don Sutton

Walt Moryn

WALTER JOSEPH MORYN
B: 04/12/1926
BL

						Men-On				One-Game								
Year	**Tm**	**Lg**	**Tot**	**H**	**A**	**0**	**1**	**2**	**3**	**2**	**3**	**4**	**LO**	**XN**	**IP**	**PH**	**RHP**	**LHP**
1954	BRO	NL	2	0	2	0	2	0	0	0	0	0	0	0	0	1	2	0
1955	BRO	NL	1	0	1	1	0	0	0	0	0	0	0	0	0	0	1	0
1956	CHI	NL	23	7	16	15	7	1	0	3	0	0	0	0	1	0	20	3
1957	CHI	NL	19	12	7	10	6	2	1	1	0	0	0	1	0	0	14	5
1958	CHI	NL	26	15	11	11	13	2	0	3	1	0	0	0	0	1	19	7
1959	CHI	NL	14	7	7	7	4	3	0	0	0	0	0	0	1	0	11	3
1960	CHI	NL	2	0	2	1	1	0	0	0	0	0	0	0	0	1	2	0
	STL	NL	11	6	5	5	5	1	0	0	0	0	0	1	0	0	10	1
	Total		13	6	7	6	6	1	0	0	0	0	0	1	0	1	12	1
1961	PIT	NL	3	1	2	1	1	1	0	1	0	0	0	0	0	0	3	0
Total			101	48	53	51	39	10	1	8	1	0	0	2	2	3	82	19

Rank among batters: 491 • *Top target (6 home runs)*: Robin Roberts • *Number of pitchers victimized*: 64 • *Total ballparks homered in*: 10 • *First HR*: 07/05/1954 off Johnny Hetki

Ross Moschitto

ROSAIRE ALLEN MOSCHITTO
B: 02/15/1945
BR

						Men-On				One-Game								
Year	**Tm**	**Lg**	**Tot**	**H**	**A**	**0**	**1**	**2**	**3**	**2**	**3**	**4**	**LO**	**XN**	**IP**	**PH**	**RHP**	**LHP**
1965	NY	AL	1	1	0	0	1	0	0	0	0	0	0	0	0	0	1	0

Rank among batters: 4,707 • *Total ballparks homered in*: 1 • *First HR*: 06/18/1965 off Jim Perry

Lloyd Moseby

LLOYD ANTHONY MOSEBY
B: 11/05/1959
BL

						Men-On				One-Game								
Year	**Tm**	**Lg**	**Tot**	**H**	**A**	**0**	**1**	**2**	**3**	**2**	**3**	**4**	**LO**	**XN**	**IP**	**PH**	**RHP**	**LHP**
1980	TOR	AL	9	4	5	4	4	1	0	0	0	0	0	0	0	0	7	2
1981	TOR	AL	9	3	6	6	2	1	0	0	0	0	1	0	1	0	6	3
1982	TOR	AL	9	4	5	6	3	0	0	0	0	0	0	0	0	0	3	6
1983	TOR	AL	18	13	5	8	10	0	0	3	0	0	0	0	1	0	14	4
1984	TOR	AL	18	10	8	9	7	1	1	0	0	0	0	0	0	0	16	2
1985	TOR	AL	18	11	7	9	9	0	0	1	0	0	0	0	0	0	11	7
1986	TOR	AL	21	11	10	12	7	1	1	2	0	0	1	1	0	0	15	6
1987	TOR	AL	26	15	11	11	10	5	0	2	0	0	0	0	0	0	21	5
1988	TOR	AL	10	2	8	6	3	1	0	0	0	0	0	0	0	0	8	2
1989	TOR	AL	11	4	7	6	4	0	1	0	0	0	3	0	0	0	9	2
1990	DET	AL	14	8	6	10	2	1	1	0	0	0	0	0	0	0	12	2
1991	DET	AL	6	4	2	3	2	1	0	0	0	0	0	0	0	0	5	1
Total			169	89	80	90	63	12	4	8	0	0	5	1	2	0	127	42

Rank among batters: 238 • *Top target (6 home runs)*: Mike Smithson • *Number of pitchers victimized*: 126 • *Total ballparks homered in*: 16 • *First HR*: 05/25/1980 off Tommy John • *LCS HR*—1

Jerry Moses

GERALD BRAHEEN MOSES
B: 08/09/1946
BR

						Men-On				One-Game								
Year	**Tm**	**Lg**	**Tot**	**H**	**A**	**0**	**1**	**2**	**3**	**2**	**3**	**4**	**LO**	**XN**	**IP**	**PH**	**RHP**	**LHP**
1965	BOS	AL	1	1	0	1	0	0	0	0	0	0	0	0	0	1	1	0
1968	BOS	AL	2	1	1	0	2	0	0	0	0	0	0	0	0	0	0	2
1969	BOS	AL	4	4	0	2	1	0	1	0	0	0	0	0	0	0	3	1
1970	BOS	AL	6	3	3	3	1	2	0	0	0	0	0	0	0	1	5	1
1971	CAL	AL	4	1	3	1	3	0	0	1	0	0	0	0	0	0	2	2
1972	CLE	AL	4	3	1	3	1	0	0	0	0	0	0	0	0	0	1	3

Year	Tm	Lg	Tot	H	A	Men-On 0	Men-On 1	Men-On 2	Men-On 3	One-Game 2	One-Game 3	One-Game 4	LO	XN	IP	PH	RHP	LHP

Jerry Moses *continued*

Year	Tm	Lg	Tot	H	A	0	1	2	3	2	3	4	LO	XN	IP	PH	RHP	LHP
1974	DET	AL	4	2	2	3	1	0	0	0	0	0	0	0	0	0	1	3
Total			25	15	10	13	9	2	1	1	0	0	0	0	0	2	13	12

Rank among batters: 1,608 • *Top target (2 home runs)*: Al Downing, Bert Blyleven • *Number of pitchers victimized*: 23 • *Total ballparks homered in*: 9 • *First HR*: 05/25/1965 off Mudcat Grant

John Moses

JOHN WILLIAM MOSES
B: 08/09/1957
BB

Year	Tm	Lg	Tot	H	A	0	1	2	3	2	3	4	LO	XN	IP	PH	RHP	LHP
1982	SEA	AL	1	1	0	1	0	0	0	0	0	0	0	0	0	0	1	0
1986	SEA	AL	3	2	1	3	0	0	0	0	0	0	0	0	0	0	1	2
1987	SEA	AL	3	2	1	1	2	0	0	0	0	0	1	0	0	0	2	1
1988	MIN	AL	2	0	2	1	1	0	0	0	0	0	0	0	0	0	2	0
1989	MIN	AL	1	0	1	0	1	0	0	0	0	0	0	0	0	0	1	0
1990	MIN	AL	1	0	1	0	1	0	0	0	0	0	0	0	0	0	1	0
Total			11	5	6	6	5	0	0	0	0	0	1	0	0	0	8	3

Rank among batters: 2,419 • *Total ballparks homered in*: 5 • *First HR*: 09/23/1982 off Chico Escarrega

Wally Moses

WALLACE MOSES
B: 10/08/1910 D: 10/10/1990
BL

Year	Tm	Lg	Tot	H	A	0	1	2	3	2	3	4	LO	XN	IP	PH	RHP	LHP
1935	PHI	AL	5	1	4	4	1	0	0	0	0	0	1	0	1	0	5	0
1936	PHI	AL	7	3	4	3	2	2	0	0	0	0	0	1	0	0	7	0
1937	PHI	AL	25	10	15	14	10	1	0	2	0	0	4	1	0	0	24	1
1938	PHI	AL	8	1	7	6	1	1	0	0	0	0	2	0	0	0	7	1
1939	PHI	AL	3	0	3	2	0	1	0	0	0	0	0	0	0	0	3	0
1940	PHI	AL	9	2	7	3	4	2	0	0	0	0	0	0	0	0	8	1
1941	PHI	AL	4	2	2	1	3	0	0	0	0	0	0	0	0	1	3	1
1942	CHI	AL	7	1	6	2	4	1	0	0	0	0	0	0	0	0	6	1
1943	CHI	AL	3	2	1	2	1	0	0	0	0	0	1	0	0	0	3	0
1944	CHI	AL	3	0	3	3	0	0	0	0	0	0	1	1	0	0	3	0
1945	CHI	AL	2	1	1	0	2	0	0	0	0	0	0	0	0	0	2	0
1946	CHI	AL	4	1	3	4	0	0	0	0	0	0	0	0	0	0	4	0
	BOS	AL	2	1	1	2	0	0	0	0	0	0	0	0	0	0	2	0
	Total		6	2	4	6	0	0	0	0	0	0	0	0	0	0	6	0
1947	BOS	AL	2	0	2	1	1	0	0	0	0	0	1	0	0	0	2	0
1948	BOS	AL	2	0	2	2	0	0	0	0	0	0	0	0	0	0	2	0
1949	PHI	AL	1	0	1	0	1	0	0	0	0	0	0	1	0	1	1	0
1950	PHI	AL	2	0	2	0	1	0	1	0	0	0	0	0	0	0	2	0
Total			89	25	64	49	31	8	1	2	0	0	10	4	1	2	84	5

Rank among batters: 584 • *Top target (5 home runs)*: Oral Hildebrand • *Number of pitchers victimized*: 64 • *Total ballparks homered in*: 9 • *First HR*: 04/19/1935 off Pat Malone

Paul Moskau

PAUL RICHARD MOSKAU
B: 12/20/1953
BR

Year	Tm	Lg	Tot	H	A	0	1	2	3	2	3	4	LO	XN	IP	PH	RHP	LHP
1977	CIN	NL	1	0	1	1	0	0	0	0	0	0	0	0	0	0	0	1
1978	CIN	NL	1	1	0	0	0	1	0	0	0	0	0	0	0	0	1	0
Total			2	1	1	1	0	1	0	0	0	0	0	0	0	0	1	1

Rank among batters: 4,129 • *Total ballparks homered in*: 2 • *First HR*: 06/21/1977 off Randy Lerch

Jim Mosolf

JAMES FREDERICK MOSOLF
B: 08/21/1905 D: 12/28/1979
BL

Year	Tm	Lg	Tot	H	A	0	1	2	3	2	3	4	LO	XN	IP	PH	RHP	LHP
1931	PIT	NL	1	1	0	0	1	0	0	0	0	0	0	0	0	0	1	0
1933	CHI	NL	1	0	1	0	1	0	0	0	0	0	0	0	0	0	1	0
Total			2	1	1	0	2	0	0	0	0	0	0	0	0	0	2	0

Rank among batters: 4,129 • *Total ballparks homered in*: 2 • *First HR*: 06/03/1931 off Bruce Cunningham

Les Moss

JOHN LESTER MOSS
B: 05/14/1925
BR

Year	Tm	Lg	Tot	H	A	Men-On 0	Men-On 1	Men-On 2	Men-On 3	One-Game 2	One-Game 3	One-Game 4	LO	XN	IP	PH	RHP	LHP
1947	STL	AL	6	3	3	1	4	1	0	0	0	0	0	0	0	0	5	1
1948	STL	AL	14	5	9	7	5	2	0	0	0	0	0	0	0	0	11	3
1949	STL	AL	10	3	7	3	5	2	0	0	0	0	0	0	0	0	8	2
1950	STL	AL	8	2	6	6	1	1	0	0	0	0	0	0	0	2	4	4
1951	STL	AL	1	1	0	1	0	0	0	0	0	0	0	0	0	0	0	1
	BOS	AL	3	2	1	2	0	0	1	0	0	0	0	0	0	0	1	2
	Total		4	3	1	3	0	0	1	0	0	0	0	0	0	0	1	3
1952	STL	AL	3	0	3	3	0	0	0	0	0	0	0	0	0	0	1	2
1953	STL	AL	2	1	1	2	0	0	0	0	0	0	0	0	0	0	0	2
1955	BAL	AL	2	0	2	2	0	0	0	0	0	0	0	0	0	0	2	0
	CHI	AL	2	1	1	0	1	1	0	0	0	0	0	0	0	0	2	0
	Total		4	1	3	2	1	1	0	0	0	0	0	0	0	0	4	0
1956	CHI	AL	10	4	6	5	4	1	0	2	0	0	0	0	0	0	4	6
1957	CHI	AL	2	1	1	2	0	0	0	0	0	0	0	0	0	0	2	0
Total			63	23	40	34	20	8	1	2	0	0	0	0	0	2	40	23

Rank among batters: 826 • *Top target (3 home runs)*: Joe Dobson, Bob Feller, Chuck Stobbs • *Number of pitchers victimized*: 48 • *Total ballparks homered in*: 9 • *First HR*: 06/08/1947 off Karl Drews

Don Mossi

DONALD LOUIS MOSSI
B: 01/11/1929
BL

Year	Tm	Lg	Tot	H	A	Men-On 0	Men-On 1	Men-On 2	Men-On 3	One-Game 2	One-Game 3	One-Game 4	LO	XN	IP	PH	RHP	LHP
1959	DET	AL	1	0	1	1	0	0	0	0	0	0	0	0	0	0	1	0
1961	DET	AL	1	1	0	1	0	0	0	0	0	0	0	0	0	0	0	1
Total			2	1	1	2	0	0	0	0	0	0	0	0	0	0	1	1

Rank among batters: 4,129 • *Total ballparks homered in*: 2 • *First HR*: 08/30/1959 off Tom Sturdivant

John Mostil

JOHN ANTHONY MOSTIL
B: 06/01/1896 D: 12/10/1970
BR

Year	Tm	Lg	Tot	H	A	Men-On 0	Men-On 1	Men-On 2	Men-On 3	One-Game 2	One-Game 3	One-Game 4	LO	XN	IP	PH	RHP	LHP
1921	CHI	AL	3	0	3	1	2	0	0	0	0	0	0	0	1	0	2	1
1922	CHI	AL	7	2	5	4	3	0	0	0	0	0	0	0	1	0	5	2
1923	CHI	AL	3	0	3	2	1	0	0	0	0	0	0	0	2	0	2	1
1924	CHI	AL	4	0	4	1	2	1	0	1	0	0	1	0	0	0	2	2
1925	CHI	AL	2	2	0	1	1	0	0	0	0	0	0	1	0	0	0	2
1926	CHI	AL	4	1	3	3	0	1	0	0	0	0	1	0	0	0	3	1
Total			23	5	18	12	9	2	0	1	0	0	2	1	4	0	14	9

Rank among batters: 1,686 • *Top target (2 home runs)*: Sam Jones, Tom Zachary, Milt Gaston • *Number of pitchers victimized*: 20 • *Total ballparks homered in*: 8 • *First HR*: 04/18/1921 off Urban Shocker

Andy Mota

ANDRES ALBERTO (MATOS) MOTA
B: 03/04/1966
BR

Year	Tm	Lg	Tot	H	A	Men-On 0	Men-On 1	Men-On 2	Men-On 3	One-Game 2	One-Game 3	One-Game 4	LO	XN	IP	PH	RHP	LHP
1991	HOU	NL	1	0	1	0	1	0	0	0	0	0	0	0	0	0	1	0

Rank among batters: 4,707 • *Total ballparks homered in*: 1 • *First HR*: 09/04/1991 off Terry Bross

Manny Mota

MANUEL RAFAEL (GERONIMO) MOTA
B: 02/18/1938
BR

Year	Tm	Lg	Tot	H	A	Men-On 0	Men-On 1	Men-On 2	Men-On 3	One-Game 2	One-Game 3	One-Game 4	LO	XN	IP	PH	RHP	LHP
1964	PIT	NL	5	4	1	2	2	1	0	0	0	0	0	0	0	1	2	3
1965	PIT	NL	4	2	2	4	0	0	0	0	0	0	0	1	0	1	4	0
1966	PIT	NL	5	0	5	3	2	0	0	0	0	0	0	0	0	0	4	1
1967	PIT	NL	4	4	0	3	1	0	0	0	0	0	0	0	1	0	1	3
1968	PIT	NL	1	0	1	1	0	0	0	0	0	0	0	0	0	1	0	1
1969	LA	NL	3	2	1	1	1	1	0	0	0	0	0	0	1	0	0	3
1970	LA	NL	3	2	1	3	0	0	0	0	0	0	0	0	0	0	1	2
1972	LA	NL	5	3	2	3	2	0	0	0	0	0	0	0	1	0	1	4
1977	LA	NL	1	1	0	1	0	0	0	0	0	0	0	0	0	1	1	0
Total			31	18	13	21	8	2	0	0	0	0	0	1	3	4	14	17

Year	Tm	Lg	Tot	H	A	Men-On 0	Men-On 1	Men-On 2	Men-On 3	One-Game 2	One-Game 3	One-Game 4	LO	XN	IP	PH	RHP	LHP

Manny Mota *continued*

Rank among batters: 1,400 • *Top target (2 home runs)*: Jim Bunning, Steve Carlton, George Stone • *Number of pitchers victimized*: 28 • *Total ballparks homered in*: 11 • *First HR*: 05/26/1964 off Chris Short

Darryl Motley

DARRYL DEWAYNE MOTLEY
B: 01/21/1960
BR

Year	Tm	Lg	Tot	H	A	Men-On 0	Men-On 1	Men-On 2	Men-On 3	One-Game 2	One-Game 3	One-Game 4	LO	XN	IP	PH	RHP	LHP
1981	KC	AL	2	0	2	2	0	0	0	0	0	0	0	0	0	0	1	1
1983	KC	AL	3	2	1	2	1	0	0	0	0	0	0	0	0	0	1	2
1984	KC	AL	15	5	10	8	6	0	1	2	0	0	1	0	0	0	9	6
1985	KC	AL	17	6	11	10	3	4	0	0	0	0	0	0	0	0	9	8
1986	KC	AL	7	3	4	5	1	0	1	1	0	0	0	0	0	0	4	3
Total			44	16	28	27	11	4	2	3	0	0	1	0	0	0	24	20

Rank among batters: 1,095 • *Top target (3 home runs)*: Don Sutton, Frank Viola • *Number of pitchers victimized*: 37 • *Total ballparks homered in*: 12 • *First HR*: 08/25/1981 off Jack Morris • *World Series HR*—1

Curt Motton

CURTELL HOWARD MOTTON
B: 09/24/1940
BR

Year	Tm	Lg	Tot	H	A	Men-On 0	Men-On 1	Men-On 2	Men-On 3	One-Game 2	One-Game 3	One-Game 4	LO	XN	IP	PH	RHP	LHP
1967	BAL	AL	2	1	1	1	1	0	0	0	0	0	0	0	0	0	2	0
1968	BAL	AL	8	3	5	4	2	2	0	0	0	0	0	0	0	2	1	7
1969	BAL	AL	6	2	4	2	4	0	0	1	0	0	0	1	0	2	1	5
1970	BAL	AL	3	2	1	0	1	2	0	0	0	0	0	0	0	0	1	2
1971	BAL	AL	4	3	1	2	1	0	1	0	0	0	0	0	0	1	0	4
1972	MIL	AL	1	0	1	1	0	0	0	0	0	0	0	0	0	0	0	1
1973	BAL	AL	1	1	0	0	0	1	0	0	0	0	0	0	0	0	0	1
Total			25	12	13	10	9	5	1	1	0	0	0	1	0	5	5	20

Rank among batters: 1,608 • *Top target (3 home runs)*: Rudy May • *Number of pitchers victimized*: 22 • *Total ballparks homered in*: 9 • *First HR*: 07/13/1967 off Galen Cisco

Frank Motz

FRANK H. MOTZ
B: 10/01/1869 D: 03/18/1944

Year	Tm	Lg	Tot	H	A	Men-On 0	Men-On 1	Men-On 2	Men-On 3	One-Game 2	One-Game 3	One-Game 4	LO	XN	IP	PH	RHP	LHP
1893	CIN	NL	2	2	0	1	0	1	0	0	0	0	0	0	0	0	1	1

Rank among batters: 4,129 • *Total ballparks homered in*: 1 • *First HR*: 09/18/1893 off Bill Hawke

Frank Mountain

FRANK HENRY MOUNTAIN
B: 05/17/1860 D: 11/19/1939
BR

Year	Tm	Lg	Tot	H	A	Men-On 0	Men-On 1	Men-On 2	Men-On 3	One-Game 2	One-Game 3	One-Game 4	LO	XN	IP	PH	RHP	LHP
1882	WOR	NL	2	2	0	2	0	0	0	0	0	0	0	0	1	0	2	0
1883	COL	AA	3	0	3	3	0	0	0	0	0	0	0	0	0	0	3	0
1884	COL	AA	4	1	3	3	1	0	0	0	0	0	0	0	0	0	4	0
Total			9	3	6	8	1	0	0	0	0	0	0	0	1	0	9	0

Rank among batters: 2,587 • *Top target (2 home runs)*: Fred Corey, Bob Barr • *Number of pitchers victimized*: 7 • *Total ballparks homered in*: 7 • *First HR*: 07/25/1882 off Charley Radbourn

James Mouton

JAMES RALEIGH MOUTON
B: 12/29/1968
BR

Year	Tm	Lg	Tot	H	A	Men-On 0	Men-On 1	Men-On 2	Men-On 3	One-Game 2	One-Game 3	One-Game 4	LO	XN	IP	PH	RHP	LHP
1994	HOU	NL	2	1	1	0	1	0	1	0	0	0	0	0	0	0	1	1
1995	HOU	NL	4	2	2	3	1	0	0	0	0	0	0	1	0	1	1	3
Total			6	3	3	3	2	0	1	0	0	0	0	1	0	1	2	4

Rank among batters: 2,988 • *Total ballparks homered in*: 4 • *First HR*: 04/23/1994 off Vicente Palacios

Lyle Mouton

LYLE JOSEPH MOUTON
B: 05/13/1969
BR

Year	Tm	Lg	Tot	H	A	Men-On 0	Men-On 1	Men-On 2	Men-On 3	One-Game 2	One-Game 3	One-Game 4	LO	XN	IP	PH	RHP	LHP
1995	CHI	AL	5	4	1	3	1	1	0	0	0	0	0	0	0	1	3	2

Rank among batters: 3,191 • *Total ballparks homered in*: 2 • *First HR*: 06/14/1995 off Rick Honeycutt

Year	Tm	Lg	Tot	H	A	Men-On				One-Game			LO	XN	IP	PH	RHP	LHP
						0	1	2	3	2	3	4						

Mike Mowrey

HARRY HARLAN MOWREY
B: 04/20/1884 D: 03/20/1947
BR

Year	Tm	Lg	Tot	H	A	0	1	2	3	2	3	4	LO	XN	IP	PH	RHP	LHP
1907	CIN	NL	1	0	1	0	1	0	0	0	0	0	0	0	1	0	1	0
1910	STL	NL	2	0	2	1	1	0	0	0	0	0	0	0	1	0	2	0
1912	STL	NL	2	0	2	1	1	0	0	0	0	0	0	0	0	0	0	2
1914	PIT	NL	1	0	1	0	1	0	0	0	0	0	0	0	1	0	1	0
1915	PIT	FL	1	0	1	1	0	0	0	0	0	0	0	0	0	0	1	0
Total			7	0	7	3	4	0	0	0	0	0	0	0	3	0	5	2

Rank among batters: 2,834 • *Total ballparks homered in*: 6 • *First HR*: 08/14/1907 off Joe McGinnity

Joe Mowry

JOSEPH ALOYSIUS MOWRY
B: 04/06/1908 D: 02/09/1994
BB

Year	Tm	Lg	Tot	H	A	0	1	2	3	2	3	4	LO	XN	IP	PH	RHP	LHP
1934	BOS	NL	1	0	1	1	0	0	0	0	0	0	0	0	0	0	1	0
1935	BOS	NL	1	0	1	1	0	0	0	0	0	0	0	0	0	0	1	0
Total			2	0	2	2	0	0	0	0	0	0	0	0	0	0	2	0

Rank among batters: 4,129 • *Total ballparks homered in*: 1 • *First HR*: 05/06/1934 off Burleigh Grimes

Mike Moynahan

MICHAEL MOYNAHAN
B: 1856 D: 04/09/1899
BL

Year	Tm	Lg	Tot	H	A	0	1	2	3	2	3	4	LO	XN	IP	PH	RHP	LHP
1883	PHI	AA	1	1	0	0	1	0	0	0	0	0	0	0	1	0	1	0

Rank among batters: 4,707 • *Total ballparks homered in*: 1 • *First HR*: 07/28/1883 off Jack Neagle

Don Mueller

DONALD FREDERICK MUELLER
B: 04/14/1927
BL

Year	Tm	Lg	Tot	H	A	0	1	2	3	2	3	4	LO	XN	IP	PH	RHP	LHP
1948	NY	NL	1	0	1	0	0	1	0	0	0	0	0	0	0	1	1	0
1950	NY	NL	7	4	3	3	2	1	1	0	0	0	0	0	0	0	7	0
1951	NY	NL	16	12	4	10	5	1	0	1	1	0	0	0	1	0	16	0
1952	NY	NL	12	8	4	10	2	0	0	0	0	0	1	1	0	0	12	0
1953	NY	NL	6	5	1	3	3	0	0	0	0	0	0	0	0	0	5	1
1954	NY	NL	4	4	0	3	0	0	1	0	0	0	0	0	1	0	1	3
1955	NY	NL	8	7	1	6	1	1	0	0	0	0	0	0	1	0	4	4
1956	NY	NL	5	4	1	4	1	0	0	0	0	0	1	0	0	1	3	2
1957	NY	NL	6	6	0	4	0	2	0	1	0	0	0	0	0	1	6	0
Total			65	50	15	43	14	6	2	2	1	0	2	1	3	3	55	10

Rank among batters: 799 • *Top target (4 home runs)*: Murry Dickson • *Number of pitchers victimized*: 51 • *Total ballparks homered in*: 9 • *First HR*: 08/25/1948 off Jess Dobernic • *Hit for Cycle*—vs PIT: 07/11/1954 (1)

Heinie Mueller

CLARENCE FRANCIS MUELLER
B: 09/16/1899 D: 01/23/1975
BL

Year	Tm	Lg	Tot	H	A	0	1	2	3	2	3	4	LO	XN	IP	PH	RHP	LHP
1921	STL	NL	1	1	0	1	0	0	0	0	0	0	0	0	0	0	1	0
1922	STL	NL	3	3	0	1	1	1	0	0	0	0	0	0	0	1	3	0
1923	STL	NL	5	0	5	5	0	0	0	1	0	0	0	1	0	0	5	0
1924	STL	NL	2	1	1	1	1	0	0	0	0	0	0	0	0	0	2	0
1925	STL	NL	1	0	1	0	1	0	0	0	0	0	0	0	1	0	1	0
1926	STL	NL	3	3	0	1	1	1	0	0	0	0	0	0	0	0	3	0
	NY	NL	4	2	2	2	1	1	0	1	0	0	0	0	0	0	4	0
	Total		7	5	2	3	2	2	0	1	0	0	0	0	0	0	7	0
1927	NY	NL	3	3	0	3	0	0	0	0	0	0	1	0	0	1	3	0
Total			22	13	9	14	5	3	0	2	0	0	1	1	1	2	22	0

Rank among batters: 1,719 • *Top target (3 home runs)*: Mule Watson • *Number of pitchers victimized*: 17 • *Total ballparks homered in*: 5 • *First HR*: 09/30/1921 off Hal Carlson

Heinie Mueller

EMMETT JEROME MUELLER
B: 07/20/1912 D: 10/03/1986
BB

Year	Tm	Lg	Tot	H	A	0	1	2	3	2	3	4	LO	XN	IP	PH	RHP	LHP
1938	PHI	NL	4	2	2	2	1	1	0	0	0	0	1	0	0	0	4	0
1939	PHI	NL	9	1	8	7	0	2	0	0	0	0	1	0	0	0	7	2

Year	Tm	Lg	Tot	H	A	Men-On 0	Men-On 1	Men-On 2	Men-On 3	One-Game 2	One-Game 3	One-Game 4	LO	XN	IP	PH	RHP	LHP

Heinie Mueller *continued*

Year	Tm	Lg	Tot	H	A	0	1	2	3	2	3	4	LO	XN	IP	PH	RHP	LHP
1940	PHI	NL	3	1	2	2	0	0	1	0	0	0	0	0	0	0	3	0
1941	PHI	NL	1	1	0	1	0	0	0	0	0	0	0	0	0	0	1	0
Total			17	5	12	12	1	3	1	0	0	0	2	0	0	0	15	2

Rank among batters: 1,969 • *Total ballparks homered in*: 7 • *First HR*: 04/19/1938 off Van Mungo • *Hit HR in first major league AB*—vs BRO: 04/19/1938

Leslie Mueller

LESLIE CLYDE MUELLER
B: 03/04/1919
BR

Year	Tm	Lg	Tot	H	A	0	1	2	3	2	3	4	LO	XN	IP	PH	RHP	LHP
1945	DET	AL	1	1	0	0	1	0	0	0	0	0	0	0	0	0	1	0

Rank among batters: 4,707 • *Total ballparks homered in*: 1 • *First HR*: 06/09/1945 off Joe Haynes

Ray Mueller

RAY COLEMAN MUELLER
B: 03/08/1912 D: 06/29/1994
BR

Year	Tm	Lg	Tot	H	A	0	1	2	3	2	3	4	LO	XN	IP	PH	RHP	LHP
1935	BOS	NL	3	2	1	2	1	0	0	0	0	0	0	0	0	0	2	1
1937	BOS	NL	2	2	0	1	0	0	1	0	0	0	0	1	0	0	2	0
1938	BOS	NL	4	3	1	3	1	0	0	0	0	0	0	0	0	0	3	1
1939	PIT	NL	2	1	1	1	1	0	0	0	0	0	0	0	0	0	2	0
1943	CIN	NL	8	4	4	5	0	3	0	2	0	0	0	0	0	0	6	2
1944	CIN	NL	10	2	8	6	4	0	0	0	0	0	0	0	0	0	9	1
1946	CIN	NL	8	3	5	7	1	0	0	1	0	0	0	0	0	0	7	1
1947	CIN	NL	6	3	3	4	0	2	0	0	0	0	0	0	0	0	5	1
1949	CIN	NL	1	1	0	0	0	1	0	0	0	0	0	0	0	0	1	0
	NY	NL	5	4	1	4	0	1	0	1	0	0	0	0	0	0	2	3
	Total		6	5	1	4	0	2	0	1	0	0	0	0	0	0	3	3
1950	PIT	NL	6	2	4	2	3	1	0	0	0	0	0	0	0	0	6	0
1951	BOS	NL	1	1	0	0	0	1	0	0	0	0	0	0	0	0	0	1
Total			56	28	28	35	11	9	1	4	0	0	0	1	0	0	45	11

Rank among batters: 913 • *Top target (3 home runs)*: Vern Bickford • *Number of pitchers victimized*: 46 • *Total ballparks homered in*: 8 • *First HR*: 05/31/1935 off Carl Hubbell

Walter Mueller

WALTER JOHN MUELLER
B: 12/06/1894 D: 08/16/1971
BR

Year	Tm	Lg	Tot	H	A	0	1	2	3	2	3	4	LO	XN	IP	PH	RHP	LHP
1922	PIT	NL	2	1	1	1	0	1	0	0	0	0	0	0	1	0	2	0

Rank among batters: 4,129 • *Total ballparks homered in*: 2 • *First HR*: 05/07/1922 off Grover Alexander • *Hit HR on first major league pitch*—@CHI: 05/07/1922

Billy Muffett

BILLY ARNOLD MUFFETT
B: 09/21/1930
BR

Year	Tm	Lg	Tot	H	A	0	1	2	3	2	3	4	LO	XN	IP	PH	RHP	LHP
1961	BOS	AL	1	1	0	1	0	0	0	0	0	0	0	0	0	0	1	0

Rank among batters: 4,707 • *Total ballparks homered in*: 1 • *First HR*: 09/16/1961 off Jack Fisher

Mike Muldoon

MICHAEL D. MULDOON
B: 1858

Year	Tm	Lg	Tot	H	A	0	1	2	3	2	3	4	LO	XN	IP	PH	RHP	LHP
1882	CLE	NL	6	0	6	2	1	0	0	2	0	0	0	0	0	0	3	3
1884	CLE	NL	2	1	1	1	1	0	0	0	0	0	0	0	0	0	1	1
1885	BAL	AA	2	2	0	1	0	1	0	0	0	0	0	0	1	0	1	0
Total			10	3	7	4	2	1	0	2	0	0	0	0	1	0	5	4

Rank among batters: 2,500 • *Top target (3 home runs)*: Lee Richmond • *Number of pitchers victimized*: 7 • *Total ballparks homered in*: 5 • *First HR*: 06/15/1882 off Monte Ward

Terry Mulholland

TERENCE JOHN MULHOLLAND
B: 03/09/1963
BR

Year	Tm	Lg	Tot	H	A	0	1	2	3	2	3	4	LO	XN	IP	PH	RHP	LHP
1995	SF	NL	1	0	1	1	0	0	0	0	0	0	0	0	0	0	1	0

Year	Tm	Lg	Tot	H	A	Men-On 0	1	2	3	One-Game 2	3	4	LO	XN	IP	PH	RHP	LHP

Terry Mulholland *continued*

Rank among batters: 4,707 • *Total ballparks homered in*: 1 • *First HR*: 08/18/1995 off Tyler Green

Tony Mullane

ANTHONY JOHN MULLANE
B: 01/30/1859 D: 04/25/1944
BB

Year	Tm	Lg	Tot	H	A	0	1	2	3	2	3	4	LO	XN	IP	PH	RHP	LHP
1884	TOL	AA	3	2	1	2	1	0	0	0	0	0	0	0	0	0	2	0
1887	CIN	AA	3	2	1	1	2	0	0	0	0	0	0	0	0	0	2	1
1888	CIN	AA	1	1	0	0	0	1	0	0	0	0	0	0	0	0	1	0
1893	CIN	NL	1	0	1	0	1	0	0	0	0	0	0	0	0	0	1	0
Total			8	5	3	3	4	1	0	0	0	0	0	0	0	0	6	1

Rank among batters: 2,703 • *Total ballparks homered in*: 5 • *First HR*: 06/12/1884 off Tim Keefe

Joe Mulligan

EDWARD JOSEPH MULLIGAN
B: 08/27/1894 D: 03/15/1982
BR

Year	Tm	Lg	Tot	H	A	0	1	2	3	2	3	4	LO	XN	IP	PH	RHP	LHP
1921	CHI	AL	1	0	1	0	1	0	0	0	0	0	0	0	1	0	0	1

Rank among batters: 4,707 • *Total ballparks homered in*: 1 • *First HR*: 06/03/1921 off George Mogridge

George Mullin

GEORGE JOSEPH MULLIN
B: 07/04/1880 D: 01/07/1944
BR

Year	Tm	Lg	Tot	H	A	0	1	2	3	2	3	4	LO	XN	IP	PH	RHP	LHP
1903	DET	AL	1	0	1	0	1	0	0	0	0	0	0	0	0	0	1	0
1908	DET	AL	1	1	0	1	0	0	0	0	0	0	0	0	1	0	1	0
1910	DET	AL	1	1	0	1	0	0	0	0	0	0	0	0	1	0	0	1
Total			3	2	1	2	1	0	0	0	0	0	0	0	2	0	2	1

Rank among batters: 3,735 • *Total ballparks homered in*: 2 • *First HR*: 09/19/1903 off Weldon Henley

Jim Mullin

JAMES HENRY MULLIN
B: 10/16/1883 D: 01/24/1925
BR

Year	Tm	Lg	Tot	H	A	0	1	2	3	2	3	4	LO	XN	IP	PH	RHP	LHP
1904	PHI	AL	1	1	0	1	0	0	0	0	0	0	0	0	0	0	0	1

Rank among batters: 4,707 • *Total ballparks homered in*: 1 • *First HR*: 07/11/1904 off Beany Jacobson

Pat Mullin

PATRICK JOSEPH MULLIN
B: 11/01/1917
BL

Year	Tm	Lg	Tot	H	A	0	1	2	3	2	3	4	LO	XN	IP	PH	RHP	LHP
1941	DET	AL	5	2	3	1	4	0	0	0	0	0	0	0	1	0	5	0
1946	DET	AL	3	2	1	0	2	0	1	0	0	0	0	0	0	0	3	0
1947	DET	AL	15	10	5	9	5	1	0	2	0	0	0	0	0	1	12	3
1948	DET	AL	23	11	12	12	8	3	0	0	0	0	0	0	0	0	20	3
1949	DET	AL	12	6	6	5	5	2	0	0	1	0	0	0	0	1	10	2
1950	DET	AL	6	4	2	1	4	1	0	0	0	0	0	0	1	0	6	0
1951	DET	AL	12	8	4	7	3	2	0	1	0	0	0	1	0	1	11	1
1952	DET	AL	7	7	0	2	4	0	1	0	0	0	0	0	0	0	7	0
1953	DET	AL	4	2	2	3	1	0	0	0	0	0	0	0	0	1	4	0
Total			87	52	35	40	36	9	2	3	1	0	0	1	2	4	78	9

Rank among batters: 594 • *Top target (5 home runs)*: Bob Feller • *Number of pitchers victimized*: 56 • *Total ballparks homered in*: 8 • *First HR*: 05/16/1941 off Bill Beckmann

Rance Mulliniks

STEVEN RANCE MULLINIKS
B: 01/15/1956
BL

Year	Tm	Lg	Tot	H	A	0	1	2	3	2	3	4	LO	XN	IP	PH	RHP	LHP
1977	CAL	AL	3	2	1	0	3	0	0	0	0	0	0	0	0	0	3	0
1978	CAL	AL	1	1	0	1	0	0	0	0	0	0	0	0	0	0	1	0
1979	CAL	AL	1	0	1	1	0	0	0	0	0	0	0	0	0	0	0	1
1982	TOR	AL	4	2	2	2	2	0	0	0	0	0	0	0	0	0	4	0

Rance Mulliniks *continued*

Year	Tm	Lg	Tot	H	A	Men-On 0	Men-On 1	Men-On 2	Men-On 3	One-Game 2	One-Game 3	One-Game 4	LO	XN	IP	PH	RHP	LHP
1983	TOR	AL	10	4	6	6	2	2	0	0	0	0	0	0	0	1	9	1
1984	TOR	AL	3	1	2	2	1	0	0	0	0	0	0	0	0	0	3	0
1985	TOR	AL	10	4	6	7	3	0	0	0	0	0	0	1	0	1	10	0
1986	TOR	AL	11	5	6	6	3	2	0	1	0	0	0	0	0	0	11	0
1987	TOR	AL	11	6	5	6	4	1	0	2	0	0	0	0	0	0	10	1
1988	TOR	AL	12	7	5	7	3	2	0	0	0	0	0	0	0	0	11	1
1989	TOR	AL	3	1	2	1	1	0	1	0	0	0	0	0	0	0	3	0
1990	TOR	AL	2	1	1	2	0	0	0	0	0	0	0	0	0	0	2	0
1991	TOR	AL	2	1	1	2	0	0	0	0	0	0	0	0	1	0	2	0
Total			73	35	38	43	22	7	1	3	0	0	0	1	1	2	69	4

Rank among batters: 715 • Top target (2 home runs): Dennis Eckersley, Ken Schrom, Joel Davis, Mike Brown, Don Sutton, Jack Morris, Ken Dixon, Jeff Russell • *Number of pitchers victimized*: 65 • *Total ballparks homered in*: 14 • *First HR*: 07/04/1977 off Rick Langford • *LCS HR*—1

Fran Mullins

FRANCIS JOSEPH MULLINS
B: 05/14/1957
BR

Year	Tm	Lg	Tot	H	A	Men-On 0	Men-On 1	Men-On 2	Men-On 3	One-Game 2	One-Game 3	One-Game 4	LO	XN	IP	PH	RHP	LHP
1984	SF	NL	2	2	0	1	1	0	0	0	0	0	0	0	0	0	1	1

Rank among batters: 4,129 • *Total ballparks homered in*: 1 • *First HR*: 05/11/1984 off Charlie Lea

Joe Mulvey

JOSEPH H. MULVEY
B: 10/27/1858 D: 08/21/1928
BR

Year	Tm	Lg	Tot	H	A	Men-On 0	Men-On 1	Men-On 2	Men-On 3	One-Game 2	One-Game 3	One-Game 4	LO	XN	IP	PH	RHP	LHP
1884	PHI	NL	2	0	2	1	0	1	0	0	0	0	0	0	2	0	1	0
1885	PHI	NL	6	2	4	3	3	0	0	0	0	0	0	0	0	0	4	2
1886	PHI	NL	2	1	1	1	1	0	0	0	0	0	0	0	0	0	2	0
1887	PHI	NL	2	0	2	1	1	0	0	0	0	0	0	0	0	0	2	0
1889	PHI	NL	6	3	3	2	2	1	1	1	0	0	0	0	3	0	5	1
1890	PHI	PL	5	1	4	2	3	0	0	0	0	0	0	0	1	0	4	1
1891	PHI	AA	5	2	3	3	0	2	0	0	0	0	0	0	2	0	4	1
Total			28	9	19	13	10	4	1	1	0	0	0	0	8	0	22	5

Rank among batters: 1,500 • *Top target (2 home runs)*: John Clarkson, John Tener • *Number of pitchers victimized*: 26 • *Total ballparks homered in*: 14 • *First HR*: 07/07/1884 off Frank Meinke

Jerry Mumphrey

JERRY WAYNE MUMPHREY
B: 09/09/1952
BB

Year	Tm	Lg	Tot	H	A	Men-On 0	Men-On 1	Men-On 2	Men-On 3	One-Game 2	One-Game 3	One-Game 4	LO	XN	IP	PH	RHP	LHP
1976	STL	NL	1	0	1	1	0	0	0	0	0	0	0	0	0	0	0	1
1977	STL	NL	2	0	2	2	0	0	0	0	0	0	0	0	0	0	2	0
1978	STL	NL	2	1	1	0	1	1	0	0	0	0	0	0	0	0	2	0
1979	STL	NL	3	2	1	1	1	1	0	0	0	0	0	0	1	0	3	0
1980	SD	NL	4	1	3	2	1	1	0	0	0	0	0	0	0	1	4	0
1981	NY	AL	6	3	3	4	2	0	0	0	0	0	0	1	0	0	5	1
1982	NY	AL	9	6	3	6	1	2	0	0	0	0	0	1	0	0	8	1
1983	NY	AL	7	1	6	6	1	0	0	0	0	0	1	0	1	0	5	2
	HOU	NL	1	1	0	0	0	1	0	0	0	0	0	0	0	0	1	0
	Total		8	2	6	6	1	1	0	0	0	0	1	0	1	0	6	2
1984	HOU	NL	9	1	8	2	7	0	0	1	0	0	0	0	0	0	9	0
1985	HOU	NL	8	4	4	4	3	1	0	0	0	0	0	0	0	0	8	0
1986	CHI	NL	5	4	1	2	2	1	0	0	0	0	0	0	0	1	5	0
1987	CHI	NL	13	7	6	10	2	1	0	0	0	0	0	0	0	2	13	0
Total			70	31	39	40	21	9	0	1	0	0	1	2	2	4	65	5

Rank among batters: 742 • *Top target (4 home runs)*: Kevin Gross • *Number of pitchers victimized*: 61 • *Total ballparks homered in*: 22 • *First HR*: 09/17/1976 off Gerry Hannahs

Red Munger

GEORGE DAVID MUNGER
B: 10/04/1918
BR

Year	Tm	Lg	Tot	H	A	Men-On 0	Men-On 1	Men-On 2	Men-On 3	One-Game 2	One-Game 3	One-Game 4	LO	XN	IP	PH	RHP	LHP
1949	STL	NL	1	1	0	1	0	0	0	0	0	0	0	0	0	0	0	1

Rank among batters: 4,707 • *Total ballparks homered in*: 1 • *First HR*: 06/26/1949 off Glenn Elliott

Year	Tm	Lg	Tot	H	A	Men-On 0	Men-On 1	Men-On 2	Men-On 3	One-Game 2	One-Game 3	One-Game 4	LO	XN	IP	PH	RHP	LHP

Bobby Munoz

ROBERTO (SBERT) MUNOZ
B: 03/03/1968
BR

Year	Tm	Lg	Tot	H	A	0	1	2	3	2	3	4	LO	XN	IP	PH	RHP	LHP
1994	PHI	NL	1	1	0	0	0	1	0	0	0	0	0	0	0	0	0	1

Rank among batters: 4,707 • *Total ballparks homered in*: 1 • *First HR*: 06/25/1994 off Kent Mercker

Pedro Munoz

PEDRO JAVIER (GONZALEZ) MUNOZ
B: 09/19/1968
BR

Year	Tm	Lg	Tot	H	A	0	1	2	3	2	3	4	LO	XN	IP	PH	RHP	LHP
1991	MIN	AL	7	4	3	3	1	2	1	0	0	0	0	0	0	0	4	3
1992	MIN	AL	12	8	4	4	3	5	0	0	0	0	0	0	0	0	9	3
1993	MIN	AL	13	2	11	9	2	2	0	3	0	0	0	2	0	0	7	6
1994	MIN	AL	11	5	6	8	2	1	0	1	0	0	0	0	0	0	6	5
1995	MIN	AL	18	10	8	10	8	0	0	1	0	0	0	0	0	1	12	6
Total			61	29	32	34	16	10	1	5	0	0	0	2	0	1	38	23

Rank among batters: 844 • *Top target (3 home runs)*: Storm Davis, Jim Abbott • *Number of pitchers victimized*: 50 • *Total ballparks homered in*: 13 • *First HR*: 05/16/1991 off Darren Holmes

Joe Munson

JOSEPH MARTIN NAPOLEON MUNSON
B: 11/06/1899 D: 02/24/1991
BL

Year	Tm	Lg	Tot	H	A	0	1	2	3	2	3	4	LO	XN	IP	PH	RHP	LHP
1926	CHI	NL	3	3	0	1	1	1	0	1	0	0	0	0	0	0	3	0

Rank among batters: 3,735 • *Total ballparks homered in*: 1 • *First HR*: 04/29/1926 off Syl Johnson

Thurman Munson

THURMAN LEE MUNSON
B: 06/07/1947 D: 08/02/1979
BR

Year	Tm	Lg	Tot	H	A	0	1	2	3	2	3	4	LO	XN	IP	PH	RHP	LHP
1969	NY	AL	1	1	0	1	0	0	0	0	0	0	0	0	0	0	1	0
1970	NY	AL	6	1	5	3	2	1	0	0	0	0	0	0	0	0	2	4
1971	NY	AL	10	4	6	6	3	1	0	0	0	0	0	0	0	0	4	6
1972	NY	AL	7	3	4	3	3	1	0	0	0	0	0	1	0	0	4	3
1973	NY	AL	20	7	13	11	8	1	0	1	0	0	0	0	0	0	8	12
1974	NY	AL	13	7	6	5	7	1	0	0	0	0	0	1	0	0	7	6
1975	NY	AL	12	4	8	4	7	1	0	0	0	0	0	0	0	0	8	4
1976	NY	AL	17	5	12	9	6	2	0	0	0	0	0	1	0	0	6	11
1977	NY	AL	18	8	10	11	6	1	0	0	0	0	0	0	0	0	11	7
1978	NY	AL	6	2	4	4	2	0	0	0	0	0	0	0	0	0	2	4
1979	NY	AL	3	0	3	0	3	0	0	0	0	0	0	0	0	0	3	0
Total			113	42	71	57	47	9	0	1	0	0	0	3	0	0	56	57

Rank among batters: 421 • *Top target (4 home runs)*: Mickey Lolich, Ross Grimsley • *Number of pitchers victimized*: 84 • *Total ballparks homered in*: 14 • *First HR*: 08/10/1969 off Lew Krausse • *World Series HR*—1; *LCS HR*—2

John Munyan

JOHN B. MUNYAN
B: 11/14/1860 D: 02/18/1945

Year	Tm	Lg	Tot	H	A	0	1	2	3	2	3	4	LO	XN	IP	PH	RHP	LHP
1890	STL	AA	4	3	1	1	1	2	0	0	0	0	0	0	0	0	2	1

Rank among batters: 3,427 • *Total ballparks homered in*: 2 • *First HR*: 06/08/1890 off Ed Cushman

Bobby Murcer

BOBBY RAY MURCER
B: 05/20/1946
BL

Year	Tm	Lg	Tot	H	A	0	1	2	3	2	3	4	LO	XN	IP	PH	RHP	LHP
1965	NY	AL	1	0	1	0	1	0	0	0	0	0	0	0	0	0	1	0
1969	NY	AL	26	14	12	17	7	2	0	3	0	0	0	0	0	0	16	10
1970	NY	AL	23	16	7	15	7	1	0	1	1	0	0	0	0	0	12	11
1971	NY	AL	25	11	14	11	11	2	1	2	0	0	0	0	0	1	14	11
1972	NY	AL	33	18	15	19	8	5	1	1	0	0	0	1	0	1	24	9
1973	NY	AL	22	19	3	10	6	6	0	1	1	0	0	0	0	0	17	5
1974	NY	AL	10	2	8	4	6	0	0	1	0	0	0	0	0	0	6	4
1975	SF	NL	11	5	6	4	6	1	0	1	0	0	0	0	0	0	8	3
1976	SF	NL	23	12	11	9	9	4	1	3	0	0	0	0	0	0	13	10

Bobby Murcer *continued*

Year	Tm	Lg	Tot	H	A	Men-On 0	1	2	3	One-Game 2	3	4	LO	XN	IP	PH	RHP	LHP
1977	CHI	NL	27	17	10	18	6	3	0	2	0	0	0	0	0	1	14	13
1978	CHI	NL	9	3	6	4	2	2	1	0	0	0	0	0	0	1	8	1
1979	CHI	NL	7	3	4	2	4	1	0	1	0	0	0	0	0	0	6	1
	NY	AL	8	7	1	4	2	2	0	2	0	0	1	0	0	0	7	1
	Total		15	10	5	6	6	3	0	3	0	0	1	0	0	0	13	2
1980	NY	AL	13	7	6	7	4	1	1	1	0	0	0	0	0	0	12	1
1981	NY	AL	6	4	2	2	1	2	1	0	0	0	0	0	0	3	6	0
1982	NY	AL	7	3	4	2	2	2	1	0	0	0	0	2	0	2	6	1
1983	NY	AL	1	1	0	1	0	0	0	0	0	0	0	0	0	0	1	0
Total			252	142	110	129	82	34	7	19	2	0	1	3	0	9	171	81

Rank among batters: 106 • *Top target (6 home runs)*: Gene Garber • *Number of pitchers victimized*: 180 • *Total ballparks homered in*: 28 • *First HR*: 09/14/1965 off Jim Duckworth • *Hit for Cycle*—vs TEX: 08/29/1972 (1)

Tim Murnane

TIMOTHY HAYES MURNANE
B: 06/04/1852 D: 02/07/1917
BL

Year	Tm	Lg	Tot	H	A	Men-On 0	1	2	3	One-Game 2	3	4	LO	XN	IP	PH	RHP	LHP
1876	BOS	NL	2	1	1	2	0	0	0	0	0	0	0	0	0	0	2	0
1877	BOS	NL	1	0	1	1	0	0	0	0	0	0	0	0	1	0	1	0
Total			3	1	2	3	0	0	0	0	0	0	0	0	1	0	3	0

Rank among batters: 3,735 • *Total ballparks homered in*: 3 • *First HR*: 06/24/1876 off Dory Dean

Billy Murphy

WILLIAM EUGENE MURPHY
B: 05/07/1944
BR

Year	Tm	Lg	Tot	H	A	Men-On 0	1	2	3	One-Game 2	3	4	LO	XN	IP	PH	RHP	LHP
1966	NY	NL	3	2	1	2	0	1	0	0	0	0	0	0	0	1	1	2

Rank among batters: 3,735 • *Total ballparks homered in*: 2 • *First HR*: 05/13/1966 off Ray Sadecki

Buzz Murphy

ROBERT R. MURPHY
B: 04/26/1895 D: 05/11/1938
BL

Year	Tm	Lg	Tot	H	A	Men-On 0	1	2	3	One-Game 2	3	4	LO	XN	IP	PH	RHP	LHP
1918	BOS	NL	1	0	1	0	1	0	0	0	0	0	0	0	0	0	1	0

Rank among batters: 4,707 • *Total ballparks homered in*: 1 • *First HR*: 07/21/1918 off Jimmy Ring

Con Murphy

CORNELIUS B. MURPHY
B: 10/15/1863 D: 08/01/1914

Year	Tm	Lg	Tot	H	A	Men-On 0	1	2	3	One-Game 2	3	4	LO	XN	IP	PH	RHP	LHP
1890	BRO	AA	1	0	1	0	1	0	0	0	0	0	0	0	0	0	0	1

Rank among batters: 4,707 • *Total ballparks homered in*: 1 • *First HR*: 08/17/1890 off Ed Cushman

Dale Murphy

DALE BRYAN MURPHY
B: 03/12/1956
BR

Year	Tm	Lg	Tot	H	A	Men-On 0	1	2	3	One-Game 2	3	4	LO	XN	IP	PH	RHP	LHP
1977	ATL	NL	2	0	2	2	0	0	0	1	0	0	0	1	0	0	1	1
1978	ATL	NL	23	17	6	12	7	2	2	1	0	0	0	0	0	0	17	6
1979	ATL	NL	21	12	9	12	5	4	0	2	1	0	0	0	0	0	16	5
1980	ATL	NL	33	17	16	18	10	4	1	1	0	0	0	0	0	0	25	8
1981	ATL	NL	13	8	5	5	5	3	0	1	0	0	0	0	0	0	9	4
1982	ATL	NL	36	24	12	17	16	3	0	2	0	0	0	0	0	0	25	11
1983	ATL	NL	36	17	19	14	17	5	0	6	0	0	0	1	0	0	31	5
1984	ATL	NL	36	18	18	18	15	3	0	2	0	0	0	1	1	0	21	15
1985	ATL	NL	37	19	18	18	14	5	0	2	0	0	0	1	0	0	27	10
1986	ATL	NL	29	17	12	13	11	5	0	3	0	0	0	0	0	1	20	9
1987	ATL	NL	44	25	19	25	12	6	1	5	0	0	0	0	0	0	30	14
1988	ATL	NL	24	14	10	17	3	4	0	2	0	0	0	1	0	0	15	9
1989	ATL	NL	20	9	11	6	6	8	0	2	0	0	0	0	0	0	15	5
1990	ATL	NL	17	8	9	5	7	5	0	1	0	0	0	0	0	0	9	8
	PHI	NL	7	1	6	4	3	0	0	0	0	0	0	0	0	0	3	4
	Total		24	9	15	9	10	5	0	1	0	0	0	0	0	0	12	12

Dale Murphy *continued*

Year	Tm	Lg	Tot	H	A	Men-On 0	1	2	3	One-Game 2	3	4	LO	XN	IP	PH	RHP	LHP
1991	PHI	NL	18	9	9	12	4	1	1	0	0	0	0	1	0	0	13	5
1992	PHI	NL	2	2	0	1	1	0	0	0	0	0	0	0	0	0	1	1
Total			398	217	181	199	136	58	5	31	1	0	0	6	1	1	278	120

Rank among batters: 27 • *Top target (8 home runs)*: Bob Knepper, Fernando Valenzuela • *Number of pitchers victimized*: 210 • *Total ballparks homered in*: 12 • *First HR*: 09/15/1977 off Randy Jones • *2 HR in 1 inning*—vs SF: 07/27/1989 • *All-Star HR*—1

Danny Murphy

DANIEL FRANCIS MURPHY
B: 08/11/1876 D: 11/22/1955
BR

Year	Tm	Lg	Tot	H	A	Men-On 0	1	2	3	One-Game 2	3	4	LO	XN	IP	PH	RHP	LHP
1902	PHI	AL	1	0	1	0	0	1	0	0	0	0	0	0	1	0	1	0
1903	PHI	AL	1	1	0	0	0	1	0	0	0	0	0	0	0	0	1	0
1904	PHI	AL	7	3	4	3	1	2	1	0	0	0	0	0	4	0	4	3
1905	PHI	AL	6	4	2	3	2	1	0	0	0	0	0	0	3	0	5	1
1906	PHI	AL	2	0	2	1	1	0	0	0	0	0	0	0	1	0	0	2
1907	PHI	AL	2	0	2	2	0	0	0	0	0	0	0	0	1	0	1	1
1908	PHI	AL	4	4	0	1	1	0	2	0	0	0	0	0	1	0	3	1
1909	PHI	AL	5	2	3	4	0	1	0	0	0	0	0	0	3	0	4	1
1910	PHI	AL	4	3	1	3	1	0	0	0	0	0	0	0	4	0	3	1
1911	PHI	AL	6	2	4	4	1	1	0	0	0	0	0	0	4	0	6	0
1912	PHI	AL	2	1	1	0	2	0	0	0	0	0	0	0	0	0	1	1
1914	BRO	FL	4	1	3	1	1	2	0	0	0	0	0	0	0	0	3	1
Total			44	21	23	22	10	9	3	0	0	0	0	0	22	0	32	12

Rank among batters: 1,095 • *Top target (3 home runs)*: Jesse Tannehill, Doc White, George Mullin • *Number of pitchers victimized*: 36 • *Total ballparks homered in*: 15 • *First HR*: 07/08/1902 off Cy Young • *Hit for Cycle*—vs STL: 08/25/1910 • *World Series HR*—1

Danny Murphy

DANIEL FRANCIS MURPHY
B: 08/23/1942
BL

Year	Tm	Lg	Tot	H	A	Men-On 0	1	2	3	One-Game 2	3	4	LO	XN	IP	PH	RHP	LHP
1960	CHI	NL	1	0	1	0	0	1	0	0	0	0	0	0	0	0	1	0
1961	CHI	NL	2	2	0	2	0	0	0	1	0	0	0	0	0	0	2	0
1970	CHI	AL	1	1	0	1	0	0	0	0	0	0	0	0	0	0	1	0
Total			4	3	1	3	0	1	0	1	0	0	0	0	0	0	4	0

Rank among batters: 3,427 • *Top target (2 home runs)*: Larry Jackson • *Number of pitchers victimized*: 3 • *Total ballparks homered in*: 3 • *First HR*: 09/13/1960 off Bob Purkey

Dwayne Murphy

DWAYNE KEITH MURPHY
B: 03/18/1955
BL

Year	Tm	Lg	Tot	H	A	Men-On 0	1	2	3	One-Game 2	3	4	LO	XN	IP	PH	RHP	LHP
1979	OAK	AL	11	4	7	7	3	1	0	0	0	0	1	0	0	0	10	1
1980	OAK	AL	13	5	8	6	7	0	0	0	0	0	0	0	0	0	9	4
1981	OAK	AL	15	7	8	7	4	3	1	0	0	0	0	2	0	0	11	4
1982	OAK	AL	27	15	12	15	11	1	0	0	0	0	0	0	0	0	18	9
1983	OAK	AL	17	12	5	8	6	1	2	0	0	0	0	1	0	0	14	3
1984	OAK	AL	33	12	21	23	6	4	0	3	0	0	0	1	0	0	25	8
1985	OAK	AL	20	5	15	13	6	1	0	1	0	0	0	1	0	0	13	7
1986	OAK	AL	9	5	4	6	3	0	0	0	0	0	0	0	1	0	8	1
1987	OAK	AL	8	2	6	5	3	0	0	0	0	0	0	0	0	0	6	2
1988	DET	AL	4	2	2	1	2	1	0	0	0	0	0	0	0	0	3	1
1989	PHI	NL	9	4	5	5	4	0	0	0	0	0	0	0	0	2	8	1
Total			166	73	93	96	55	12	3	4	0	0	1	5	1	2	125	41

Rank among batters: 245 • *Top target (6 home runs)*: Scott McGregor • *Number of pitchers victimized*: 123 • *Total ballparks homered in*: 20 • *First HR*: 05/06/1979 off Catfish Hunter • *LCS HR*—1

Ed Murphy

EDWARD J. MURPHY
B: 01/22/1877 D: 01/29/1935

Year	Tm	Lg	Tot	H	A	Men-On 0	1	2	3	One-Game 2	3	4	LO	XN	IP	PH	RHP	LHP
1901	STL	NL	1	1	0	0	1	0	0	0	0	0	0	0	0	0	1	0

Rank among batters: 4,707 • *Total ballparks homered in*: 1 • *First HR*: 07/13/1901 off Willie Mills

Eddie Murphy

JOHN EDWARD MURPHY
B: 10/02/1891 D: 02/21/1969
BL

Year	Tm	Lg	Tot	H	A	Men-On 0	Men-On 1	Men-On 2	Men-On 3	One-Game 2	One-Game 3	One-Game 4	LO	XN	IP	PH	RHP	LHP
1913	PHI	AL	1	1	0	1	0	0	0	0	0	0	0	0	0	0	1	0
1914	PHI	AL	3	0	3	3	0	0	0	0	0	0	1	0	0	0	2	1
Total			4	1	3	4	0	0	0	0	0	0	1	0	0	0	3	1

Rank among batters: 3,427 • *Total ballparks homered in*: 4 • *First HR*: 10/03/1913 off Ray Caldwell

Frank Murphy

FRANCIS PATRICK MURPHY
B: 04/16/1875 D: 11/04/1912

Year	Tm	Lg	Tot	H	A	Men-On 0	Men-On 1	Men-On 2	Men-On 3	One-Game 2	One-Game 3	One-Game 4	LO	XN	IP	PH	RHP	LHP
1901	BOS	NL	1	1	0	1	0	0	0	0	0	0	0	0	0	0	1	0

Rank among batters: 4,707 • *Total ballparks homered in*: 1 • *First HR*: 08/08/1901 off Bill Duggleby

Larry Murphy

LAWRENCE PATRICK MURPHY
BL

Year	Tm	Lg	Tot	H	A	Men-On 0	Men-On 1	Men-On 2	Men-On 3	One-Game 2	One-Game 3	One-Game 4	LO	XN	IP	PH	RHP	LHP
1891	WAS	AA	1	0	1	0	0	1	0	0	0	0	0	0	0	0	1	0

Rank among batters: 4,707 • *Total ballparks homered in*: 1 • *First HR*: 09/22/1891 off George Rettger

Morgan Murphy

MORGAN EDWARD MURPHY
B: 02/14/1867 D: 10/03/1938
BR

Year	Tm	Lg	Tot	H	A	Men-On 0	Men-On 1	Men-On 2	Men-On 3	One-Game 2	One-Game 3	One-Game 4	LO	XN	IP	PH	RHP	LHP
1890	BOS	PL	2	2	0	2	0	0	0	0	0	0	0	0	0	0	2	0
1891	BOS	AA	4	2	2	4	0	0	0	0	0	0	0	0	0	0	1	1
1892	CIN	NL	2	1	1	0	2	0	0	0	0	0	0	0	0	0	2	0
1893	CIN	NL	1	0	1	1	0	0	0	0	0	0	0	0	0	0	1	0
1894	CIN	NL	1	1	0	0	0	1	0	0	0	0	0	0	0	0	1	0
Total			10	6	4	7	2	1	0	0	0	0	0	0	0	0	7	1

Rank among batters: 2,500 • *Total ballparks homered in*: 7 • *First HR*: 05/30/1890 off Alex Ferson

Pat Murphy

PATRICK J. MURPHY
B: 01/02/1857 D: 05/16/1927

Year	Tm	Lg	Tot	H	A	Men-On 0	Men-On 1	Men-On 2	Men-On 3	One-Game 2	One-Game 3	One-Game 4	LO	XN	IP	PH	RHP	LHP
1889	NY	NL	1	0	1	0	1	0	0	0	0	0	0	0	0	0	1	0

Rank among batters: 4,707 • *Total ballparks homered in*: 1 • *First HR*: 09/27/1889 off John Tener

Tom Murphy

THOMAS ANDREW MURPHY
B: 12/30/1945
BR

Year	Tm	Lg	Tot	H	A	Men-On 0	Men-On 1	Men-On 2	Men-On 3	One-Game 2	One-Game 3	One-Game 4	LO	XN	IP	PH	RHP	LHP
1970	CAL	AL	1	0	1	1	0	0	0	0	0	0	0	0	0	0	1	0

Rank among batters: 4,707 • *Total ballparks homered in*: 1 • *First HR*: 09/21/1970 off Lew Krausse

Willie Murphy

WILLIAM N. MURPHY
B: 1865 BL

Year	Tm	Lg	Tot	H	A	Men-On 0	Men-On 1	Men-On 2	Men-On 3	One-Game 2	One-Game 3	One-Game 4	LO	XN	IP	PH	RHP	LHP
1884	CLE	NL	1	0	1	1	0	0	0	0	0	0	0	0	0	0	1	0

Rank among batters: 4,707 • *Total ballparks homered in*: 1 • *First HR*: 06/07/1884 off Fred Goldsmith

Eddie Murray

EDDIE CLARENCE MURRAY
B: 02/24/1956
BB

Year	Tm	Lg	Tot	H	A	Men-On 0	Men-On 1	Men-On 2	Men-On 3	One-Game 2	One-Game 3	One-Game 4	LO	XN	IP	PH	RHP	LHP
1977	BAL	AL	27	14	13	18	7	2	0	2	0	0	0	1	0	0	20	7
1978	BAL	AL	27	10	17	17	6	3	1	1	0	0	0	3	0	0	21	6
1979	BAL	AL	25	10	15	14	7	3	1	0	1	0	0	0	0	0	16	9
1980	BAL	AL	32	10	22	16	11	5	0	1	1	0	0	1	0	0	23	9
1981	BAL	AL	22	12	10	8	10	2	2	1	0	0	0	0	0	0	16	6
1982	BAL	AL	32	18	14	14	9	7	2	2	0	0	0	2	0	0	21	11

Eddie Murray *continued*

Year	Tm	Lg	Tot	H	A	Men-On 0	Men-On 1	Men-On 2	Men-On 3	One-Game 2	One-Game 3	One-Game 4	LO	XN	IP	PH	RHP	LHP
1983	BAL	AL	33	16	17	16	15	1	1	2	0	0	0	0	0	0	21	12
1984	BAL	AL	29	18	11	13	9	5	2	0	0	0	0	1	0	0	24	5
1985	BAL	AL	31	15	16	15	9	4	3	0	1	0	0	0	0	0	21	10
1986	BAL	AL	17	9	8	6	6	3	2	2	0	0	0	0	0	0	11	6
1987	BAL	AL	30	14	16	15	11	4	0	3	0	0	0	1	0	0	19	11
1988	BAL	AL	28	14	14	13	10	5	0	2	0	0	0	0	0	0	21	7
1989	LA	NL	20	4	16	5	8	6	1	2	0	0	0	0	0	1	16	4
1990	LA	NL	26	12	14	12	11	3	0	3	0	0	0	1	0	0	18	8
1991	LA	NL	19	11	8	10	6	3	0	0	0	0	0	0	0	1	13	6
1992	NY	NL	16	7	9	8	4	2	2	0	0	0	0	0	0	0	13	3
1993	NY	NL	27	15	12	11	13	3	0	1	0	0	0	0	0	0	19	8
1994	CLE	AL	17	7	10	8	7	2	0	3	0	0	0	0	0	0	12	5
1995	CLE	AL	21	11	10	12	7	2	0	2	0	0	0	0	0	0	18	3
Total			479	227	252	231	166	65	17	27	3	0	0	10	0	2	343	136

Rank among batters: 16 • *Top target (6 home runs)*: Milt Wilcox, Bert Blyleven, Frank Tanana • *Number of pitchers victimized*: 307 • *Total ballparks homered in*: 31 • *First HR*: 04/18/1977 off Pat Dobson • *Switch hit HR in 1 game*—11 time • *World Series HR*—4; *LCS HR*—4

George Murray

GEORGE KING MURRAY
B: 09/23/1898 D: 10/18/1955
BR

Year	Tm	Lg	Tot	H	A	Men-On 0	Men-On 1	Men-On 2	Men-On 3	One-Game 2	One-Game 3	One-Game 4	LO	XN	IP	PH	RHP	LHP
1922	NY	AL	1	1	0	0	0	1	0	0	0	0	0	0	0	0	1	0

Rank among batters: 4,707 • *Total ballparks homered in*: 1 • *First HR*: 05/17/1922 off George Uhle

Jim Murray

JAMES OSCAR MURRAY
B: 01/16/1878 D: 04/25/1945
BR

Year	Tm	Lg	Tot	H	A	Men-On 0	Men-On 1	Men-On 2	Men-On 3	One-Game 2	One-Game 3	One-Game 4	LO	XN	IP	PH	RHP	LHP
1911	STL	AL	3	2	1	3	0	0	0	0	0	0	0	0	0	0	3	0

Rank among batters: 3,735 • *Total ballparks homered in*: 2 • *First HR*: 04/19/1911 off Jim Scott

Larry Murray

LARRY MURRAY
B: 04/01/1953
BB

Year	Tm	Lg	Tot	H	A	Men-On 0	Men-On 1	Men-On 2	Men-On 3	One-Game 2	One-Game 3	One-Game 4	LO	XN	IP	PH	RHP	LHP
1977	OAK	AL	1	1	0	1	0	0	0	0	0	0	0	0	0	0	0	1
1979	OAK	AL	2	2	0	0	2	0	0	0	0	0	0	0	1	0	1	1
Total			3	3	0	1	2	0	0	0	0	0	0	0	1	0	1	2

Rank among batters: 3,735 • *Total ballparks homered in*: 1 • *First HR*: 07/27/1977 off Ken Brett

Ray Murray

RAYMOND LEE MURRAY
B: 10/12/1917
BR

Year	Tm	Lg	Tot	H	A	Men-On 0	Men-On 1	Men-On 2	Men-On 3	One-Game 2	One-Game 3	One-Game 4	LO	XN	IP	PH	RHP	LHP
1950	CLE	AL	1	1	0	1	0	0	0	0	0	0	0	0	0	0	0	1
1952	PHI	AL	1	1	0	0	1	0	0	0	0	0	0	0	0	0	0	1
1953	PHI	AL	6	5	1	3	2	1	0	0	0	0	0	0	0	0	5	1
Total			8	7	1	4	3	1	0	0	0	0	0	0	0	0	5	3

Rank among batters: 2,703 • *Total ballparks homered in*: 3 • *First HR*: 05/21/1950 off Eddie Lopat

Red Murray

JOHN JOSEPH MURRAY
B: 03/04/1884 D: 12/04/1958
BR

Year	Tm	Lg	Tot	H	A	Men-On 0	Men-On 1	Men-On 2	Men-On 3	One-Game 2	One-Game 3	One-Game 4	LO	XN	IP	PH	RHP	LHP
1906	STL	NL	1	0	1	0	1	0	0	0	0	0	0	0	0	0	0	1
1907	STL	NL	7	4	3	3	3	1	0	0	0	0	0	0	3	0	5	2
1908	STL	NL	7	2	5	4	2	1	0	0	0	0	0	0	1	0	6	1
1909	NY	NL	7	3	4	3	3	1	0	0	0	0	0	0	1	0	5	2
1910	NY	NL	4	4	0	1	2	0	1	0	0	0	0	0	2	0	1	3
1911	NY	NL	3	3	0	1	2	0	0	0	0	0	0	0	0	0	1	2
1912	NY	NL	3	3	0	2	1	0	0	0	0	0	0	0	0	0	3	0
1913	NY	NL	2	0	2	0	2	0	0	0	0	0	0	0	0	0	2	0

Red Murray *continued*

Year	Tm	Lg	Tot	H	A	Men-On 0	1	2	3	One-Game 2	3	4	LO	XN	IP	PH	RHP	LHP
1915	NY	NL	3	3	0	0	2	1	0	0	0	0	0	0	1	0	2	1
Total			37	22	15	14	18	4	1	0	0	0	0	0	8	0	25	12

Rank among batters: 1,252 • *Top target (5 home runs)*: Vive Lindaman • *Number of pitchers victimized*: 27 • *Total ballparks homered in*: 9 • *First HR*: 09/26/1906 off Patrick Dolan

Rich Murray

RICHARD DALE MURRAY
B: 07/06/1957
BR

Year	Tm	Lg	Tot	H	A	Men-On 0	1	2	3	One-Game 2	3	4	LO	XN	IP	PH	RHP	LHP
1980	SF	NL	4	1	3	1	3	0	0	0	0	0	0	0	0	0	1	3

Rank among batters: 3,427 • *Total ballparks homered in*: 4 • *First HR*: 06/11/1980 off Randy Lerch

Ivan Murrell

IVAN AUGUSTUS (PETERS) MURRELL
B: 04/24/1945
BR

Year	Tm	Lg	Tot	H	A	Men-On 0	1	2	3	One-Game 2	3	4	LO	XN	IP	PH	RHP	LHP
1969	SD	NL	3	2	1	1	2	0	0	0	0	0	0	0	0	0	3	0
1970	SD	NL	12	8	4	9	2	1	0	1	0	0	0	1	0	1	10	2
1971	SD	NL	7	4	3	4	2	1	0	0	0	0	0	1	0	1	4	3
1973	SD	NL	9	3	6	7	2	0	0	0	0	0	0	0	0	0	6	3
1974	ATL	NL	2	1	1	2	0	0	0	0	0	0	0	0	0	1	1	1
Total			33	18	15	23	8	2	0	1	0	0	0	2	0	3	24	9

Rank among batters: 1,336 • *Top target (2 home runs)*: Scipio Spinks, Dock Ellis, Steve Carlton • *Number of pitchers victimized*: 30 • *Total ballparks homered in*: 11 • *First HR*: 07/12/1969 off Gary Neibauer

Danny Murtaugh

DANIEL EDWARD MURTAUGH
B: 10/08/1917 D: 12/02/1976
BR

Year	Tm	Lg	Tot	H	A	Men-On 0	1	2	3	One-Game 2	3	4	LO	XN	IP	PH	RHP	LHP
1943	PHI	NL	1	0	1	1	0	0	0	0	0	0	0	0	0	0	1	0
1946	PHI	NL	1	0	1	0	1	0	0	0	0	0	0	0	0	0	1	0
1948	PIT	NL	1	1	0	0	0	0	1	0	0	0	0	0	0	0	1	0
1949	PIT	NL	2	1	1	2	0	0	0	0	0	0	0	0	0	0	1	1
1950	PIT	NL	2	1	1	1	1	0	0	0	0	0	0	0	0	0	1	1
1951	PIT	NL	1	0	1	1	0	0	0	0	0	0	0	0	0	0	1	0
Total			8	3	5	5	2	0	1	0	0	0	0	0	0	0	6	2

Rank among batters: 2,703 • *Total ballparks homered in*: 3 • *First HR*: 05/31/1943 off Dick Barrett

Tony Muser

ANTHONY JOSEPH MUSER
B: 08/01/1947
BL

Year	Tm	Lg	Tot	H	A	Men-On 0	1	2	3	One-Game 2	3	4	LO	XN	IP	PH	RHP	LHP
1972	CHI	AL	1	1	0	0	1	0	0	0	0	0	0	0	0	0	1	0
1973	CHI	AL	4	2	2	4	0	0	0	0	0	0	0	0	0	0	3	1
1974	CHI	AL	1	0	1	0	1	0	0	0	0	0	0	0	0	0	1	0
1976	BAL	AL	1	0	1	0	1	0	0	0	0	0	0	1	0	0	1	0
Total			7	3	4	4	3	0	0	0	0	0	0	1	0	0	6	1

Rank among batters: 2,834 • *Total ballparks homered in*: 5 • *First HR*: 09/22/1972 off Jim Panther

Stan Musial

STANLEY FRANK MUSIAL
B: 11/21/1920
BL HOF

Year	Tm	Lg	Tot	H	A	Men-On 0	1	2	3	One-Game 2	3	4	LO	XN	IP	PH	RHP	LHP
1941	STL	NL	1	0	1	0	1	0	0	0	0	0	0	0	0	0	1	0
1942	STL	NL	10	8	2	3	5	1	1	1	0	0	0	1	0	0	10	0
1943	STL	NL	13	7	6	7	5	1	0	2	0	0	0	0	1	0	12	1
1944	STL	NL	12	5	7	1	8	3	0	0	0	0	0	0	2	0	10	2
1946	STL	NL	16	10	6	11	5	0	0	0	0	0	0	2	0	0	13	3
1947	STL	NL	19	5	14	9	7	2	1	1	0	0	0	0	2	0	12	7
1948	STL	NL	39	16	23	21	16	1	1	1	0	0	0	1	0	0	21	18
1949	STL	NL	36	13	23	21	9	6	0	6	0	0	0	0	1	0	15	21
1950	STL	NL	28	15	13	12	12	4	0	2	0	0	0	1	1	0	14	14

Stan Musial *continued*

Year	Tm	Lg	Tot	H	A	Men-On 0	1	2	3	One-Game 2	3	4	LO	XN	IP	PH	RHP	LHP
1951	STL	NL	32	19	13	19	8	5	0	4	0	0	0	1	2	1	24	8
1952	STL	NL	21	10	11	10	9	2	0	1	0	0	0	0	0	0	15	6
1953	STL	NL	30	15	15	15	12	3	0	2	0	0	0	0	0	0	21	9
1954	STL	NL	35	19	16	16	11	7	1	5	1	0	0	1	0	0	20	15
1955	STL	NL	33	22	11	17	13	2	1	2	0	0	0	0	0	0	18	15
1956	STL	NL	27	14	13	12	10	3	2	1	0	0	0	0	0	0	17	10
1957	STL	NL	29	12	17	12	14	2	1	2	0	0	0	2	0	0	20	9
1958	STL	NL	17	13	4	8	8	1	0	2	0	0	0	0	0	0	11	6
1959	STL	NL	14	10	4	8	5	1	0	1	0	0	0	0	0	0	11	3
1960	STL	NL	17	10	7	11	5	1	0	0	0	0	0	1	0	0	15	2
1961	STL	NL	15	11	4	4	7	3	1	2	0	0	0	0	0	0	13	2
1962	STL	NL	19	10	9	9	5	5	0	0	1	0	0	1	0	1	17	2
1963	STL	NL	12	8	4	6	5	1	0	0	0	0	0	0	0	0	10	2
Total			475	252	223	232	180	54	9	35	2	0	0	11	9	2	320	155

Rank among batters: 17 • *Top target (17 home runs)*: Warren Spahn • *Number of pitchers victimized*: 215 • *Total ballparks homered in*: 12 • *First HR*: 09/23/1941 off Rip Sewell • *Hit for Cycle*—@BRO: 07/24/1949 • *World Series HR*—1; *All-Star HR*—6

George Myatt

GEORGE EDWARD MYATT
B: 06/14/1914
BL

Year	Tm	Lg	Tot	H	A	Men-On 0	1	2	3	One-Game 2	3	4	LO	XN	IP	PH	RHP	LHP
1938	NY	NL	3	2	1	3	0	0	0	0	0	0	0	0	0	0	3	0
1945	WAS	AL	1	0	1	1	0	0	0	0	0	0	0	0	0	0	1	0
Total			4	2	2	4	0	0	0	0	0	0	0	0	0	0	4	0

Rank among batters: 3,427 • *Total ballparks homered in*: 3 • *First HR*: 08/17/1938 off Bill Posedel

Glenn Myatt

GLENN CALVIN MYATT
B: 07/09/1897 D: 08/09/1969
BL

Year	Tm	Lg	Tot	H	A	Men-On 0	1	2	3	One-Game 2	3	4	LO	XN	IP	PH	RHP	LHP
1923	CLE	AL	3	1	2	2	0	1	0	0	0	0	0	1	0	1	3	0
1924	CLE	AL	8	2	6	1	4	3	0	1	0	0	0	0	0	1	8	0
1925	CLE	AL	11	6	5	7	4	0	0	0	0	0	0	0	0	0	9	2
1927	CLE	AL	2	2	0	2	0	0	0	0	0	0	0	0	0	0	2	0
1928	CLE	AL	1	0	1	1	0	0	0	0	0	0	0	0	0	0	1	0
1929	CLE	AL	1	1	0	0	0	1	0	0	0	0	0	0	0	0	1	0
1930	CLE	AL	2	2	0	1	1	0	0	0	0	0	0	0	0	0	2	0
1931	CLE	AL	1	1	0	0	1	0	0	0	0	0	0	0	0	0	1	0
1932	CLE	AL	8	2	6	3	4	1	0	0	0	0	0	0	0	0	8	0
1935	NY	NL	1	1	0	0	1	0	0	0	0	0	0	0	0	1	1	0
Total			38	18	20	17	15	6	0	1	0	0	0	1	0	3	36	2

Rank among batters: 1,225 • *Top target (5 home runs)*: Bob Shawkey • *Number of pitchers victimized*: 25 • *Total ballparks homered in*: 7 • *First HR*: 06/10/1923 off Waite Hoyt

Buddy Myer

CHARLES SOLOMON MYER
B: 03/16/1904 D: 10/31/1974
BL

Year	Tm	Lg	Tot	H	A	Men-On 0	1	2	3	One-Game 2	3	4	LO	XN	IP	PH	RHP	LHP
1926	WAS	AL	1	0	1	0	1	0	0	0	0	0	0	0	0	0	1	0
1927	BOS	AL	2	0	2	2	0	0	0	0	0	0	0	0	2	0	2	0
1928	BOS	AL	1	0	1	1	0	0	0	0	0	0	0	0	1	0	1	0
1929	WAS	AL	3	3	0	1	0	2	0	0	0	0	1	0	3	0	2	1
1930	WAS	AL	2	2	0	0	1	1	0	0	0	0	0	0	2	0	1	1
1931	WAS	AL	4	2	2	3	1	0	0	0	0	0	1	0	3	0	3	1
1932	WAS	AL	5	3	2	3	1	0	1	0	0	0	1	0	1	0	5	0
1933	WAS	AL	4	0	4	3	1	0	0	0	0	0	1	0	0	0	4	0
1934	WAS	AL	3	0	3	1	2	0	0	0	0	0	0	0	0	0	3	0
1935	WAS	AL	5	1	4	1	4	0	0	0	0	0	0	0	1	0	4	1
1937	WAS	AL	1	1	0	0	1	0	0	0	0	0	0	0	0	0	1	0
1938	WAS	AL	6	3	3	1	2	2	1	0	0	0	0	0	2	0	4	2
1939	WAS	AL	1	0	1	1	0	0	0	0	0	0	0	0	0	0	1	0
Total			38	15	23	17	14	5	2	0	0	0	4	0	15	0	32	6

Rank among batters: 1,225 • Top target (2 home runs): George Blaeholder, Dick Coffman, Earl Whitehill, Bump Hadley • *Number of pitchers victimized*: 34 • *Total ballparks homered in*: 6 • *First HR*: 06/02/1926 off Urban Shocker

Year	Tm	Lg	Tot	H	A	Men-On 0	1	2	3	One-Game 2	3	4	LO	XN	IP	PH	RHP	LHP

Al Myers

JAMES ALBERT MYERS
B: 10/22/1863 D: 12/24/1927
BR

Year	Tm	Lg	Tot	H	A	0	1	2	3	2	3	4	LO	XN	IP	PH	RHP	LHP
1885	PHI	NL	1	0	1	0	1	0	0	0	0	0	0	0	0	0	1	0
1886	KC	NL	4	0	4	2	1	0	1	0	0	0	0	0	0	0	4	0
1887	WAS	NL	2	1	1	2	0	0	0	0	0	0	0	0	0	0	1	1
1888	WAS	NL	2	1	1	1	0	1	0	0	0	0	0	0	0	0	2	0
1890	PHI	NL	2	2	0	0	1	0	1	0	0	0	0	0	2	0	2	0
1891	PHI	NL	2	0	2	1	1	0	0	0	0	0	0	0	0	0	1	0
Total			13	4	9	6	4	1	2	0	0	0	0	0	2	0	11	1

Rank among batters: 2,248 • *Total ballparks homered in*: 9 • *First HR*: 10/09/1885 off Jim McCormick

Billy Myers

WILLIAM HARRISON MYERS
B: 08/14/1910
BR

Year	Tm	Lg	Tot	H	A	0	1	2	3	2	3	4	LO	XN	IP	PH	RHP	LHP
1935	CIN	NL	5	2	3	1	4	0	0	0	0	0	0	0	0	0	3	2
1936	CIN	NL	6	0	6	4	1	1	0	0	0	0	0	1	0	0	5	1
1937	CIN	NL	7	1	6	4	3	0	0	0	0	0	0	0	0	0	6	1
1938	CIN	NL	12	5	7	9	2	1	0	0	0	0	0	1	0	0	8	4
1939	CIN	NL	9	7	2	2	5	1	1	1	0	0	0	0	0	0	9	0
1940	CIN	NL	5	4	1	2	3	0	0	0	0	0	0	0	0	0	3	2
1941	CHI	NL	1	0	1	1	0	0	0	0	0	0	0	0	0	0	0	1
Total			45	19	26	23	18	3	1	1	0	0	0	2	0	0	34	11

Rank among batters: 1,082 • *Top target (3 home runs)*: Hal Schumacher • *Number of pitchers victimized*: 36 • *Total ballparks homered in*: 8 • *First HR*: 05/09/1935 off Ray Benge

George Myers

GEORGE D. MYERS
B: 11/13/1860 D: 12/14/1926
BR

Year	Tm	Lg	Tot	H	A	0	1	2	3	2	3	4	LO	XN	IP	PH	RHP	LHP
1884	BUF	NL	2	1	1	1	0	1	0	0	0	0	0	0	0	0	1	1
1887	IND	NL	1	1	0	0	0	1	0	0	0	0	0	0	0	0	0	1
1888	IND	NL	2	2	0	2	0	0	0	0	0	0	0	0	0	0	0	2
Total			5	4	1	3	0	2	0	0	0	0	0	0	0	0	1	4

Rank among batters: 3,191 • *Total ballparks homered in*: 4 • *First HR*: 06/05/1884 off Fred Goldsmith

Greg Myers

GREGORY RICHARD MYERS
B: 04/14/1966
BL

Year	Tm	Lg	Tot	H	A	0	1	2	3	2	3	4	LO	XN	IP	PH	RHP	LHP
1990	TOR	AL	5	3	2	3	0	2	0	0	0	0	0	0	0	0	5	0
1991	TOR	AL	8	5	3	5	3	0	0	0	0	0	0	0	0	0	7	1
1992	TOR	AL	1	0	1	0	0	1	0	0	0	0	0	0	0	0	1	0
1993	CAL	AL	7	4	3	6	1	0	0	0	0	0	0	0	0	2	7	0
1994	CAL	AL	2	1	1	1	1	0	0	0	0	0	0	0	0	0	2	0
1995	CAL	AL	9	6	3	6	3	0	0	0	0	0	0	1	0	0	9	0
Total			32	19	13	21	8	3	0	0	0	0	0	1	0	2	31	1

Rank among batters: 1,360 • *Top target (2 home runs)*: Hipolito Pichardo • *Number of pitchers victimized*: 31 • *Total ballparks homered in*: 11 • *First HR*: 04/20/1990 off Luis Aquino

Hap Myers

RALPH EDWARD MYERS
B: 04/08/1888 D: 06/30/1967
BR

Year	Tm	Lg	Tot	H	A	0	1	2	3	2	3	4	LO	XN	IP	PH	RHP	LHP
1913	BOS	NL	2	1	1	1	1	0	0	0	0	0	0	0	1	0	1	1
1914	BRO	FL	1	1	0	0	0	1	0	0	0	0	0	0	0	0	1	0
1915	BRO	FL	1	0	1	0	1	0	0	0	0	0	0	0	0	0	0	1
Total			4	2	2	1	2	1	0	0	0	0	0	0	1	0	2	2

Rank among batters: 3,427 • *Total ballparks homered in*: 4 • *First HR*: 06/13/1913 off Red Ames

Hi Myers

HENRY HARRISON MYERS
B: 04/27/1889 D: 05/01/1965
BR

Year	Tm	Lg	Tot	H	A	0	1	2	3	2	3	4	LO	XN	IP	PH	RHP	LHP
1915	BRO	NL	2	2	0	2	0	0	0	0	0	0	1	0	1	0	1	1

Hi Myers *continued*

Year	Tm	Lg	Tot	H	A	Men-On 0	Men-On 1	Men-On 2	Men-On 3	One-Game 2	One-Game 3	One-Game 4	LO	XN	IP	PH	RHP	LHP
1916	BRO	NL	3	3	0	2	1	0	0	0	0	0	0	0	3	0	1	2
1917	BRO	NL	1	1	0	0	0	1	0	0	0	0	0	0	1	0	1	0
1918	BRO	NL	4	1	3	1	2	1	0	0	0	0	0	0	1	0	3	1
1919	BRO	NL	5	1	4	1	2	2	0	0	0	0	0	1	2	0	2	3
1920	BRO	NL	4	3	1	4	0	0	0	0	0	0	0	0	0	0	2	2
1921	BRO	NL	4	1	3	3	0	1	0	0	0	0	0	0	0	0	4	0
1922	BRO	NL	6	3	3	4	2	0	0	0	0	0	0	1	1	0	6	0
1923	STL	NL	2	0	2	0	1	1	0	0	0	0	0	0	2	0	2	0
1924	STL	NL	1	0	1	0	0	1	0	0	0	0	0	0	0	0	0	1
Total			32	15	17	17	8	7	0	0	0	0	1	2	11	0	22	10

Rank among batters: 1,360 • *Top target (3 home runs)*: Gene Packard • *Number of pitchers victimized*: 26 • *Total ballparks homered in*: 6 • *First HR*: 07/15/1915 off Red Ames • *World Series HR*—1

Lynn Myers

LYNNWOOD LINCOLN MYERS
B: 02/23/1914
BR

Year	Tm	Lg	Tot	H	A	Men-On 0	Men-On 1	Men-On 2	Men-On 3	One-Game 2	One-Game 3	One-Game 4	LO	XN	IP	PH	RHP	LHP
1938	STL	NL	1	0	1	1	0	0	0	0	0	0	0	0	0	0	1	0

Rank among batters: 4,707 • *Total ballparks homered in*: 1 • *First HR*: 08/15/1938 off Clay Bryant

Tim Naehring

TIMOTHY JAMES NAEHRING
B: 02/01/1967
BR

Year	Tm	Lg	Tot	H	A	Men-On 0	Men-On 1	Men-On 2	Men-On 3	One-Game 2	One-Game 3	One-Game 4	LO	XN	IP	PH	RHP	LHP
1990	BOS	AL	2	2	0	1	1	0	0	0	0	0	0	0	0	0	1	1
1992	BOS	AL	3	0	3	2	1	0	0	0	0	0	0	1	0	0	1	2
1993	BOS	AL	1	0	1	1	0	0	0	0	0	0	0	0	0	0	1	0
1994	BOS	AL	7	4	3	5	1	1	0	1	0	0	0	0	0	0	5	2
1995	BOS	AL	10	5	5	6	2	2	0	0	0	0	0	0	0	0	7	3
Total			23	11	12	15	5	3	0	1	0	0	0	1	0	0	15	8

Rank among batters: 1,686 • *Total ballparks homered in*: 9 • *First HR*: 07/18/1990 off David West • *LCS HR*—1

Bill Nagel

WILLIAM TAYLOR NAGEL
B: 08/19/1915 D: 10/08/1981
BR

Year	Tm	Lg	Tot	H	A	Men-On 0	Men-On 1	Men-On 2	Men-On 3	One-Game 2	One-Game 3	One-Game 4	LO	XN	IP	PH	RHP	LHP
1939	PHI	AL	12	6	6	10	2	0	0	1	0	0	0	0	0	0	8	4
1945	CHI	AL	3	0	3	2	1	0	0	0	0	0	0	0	0	0	2	1
Total			15	6	9	12	3	0	0	1	0	0	0	0	0	0	10	5

Rank among batters: 2,096 • *Top target (2 home runs)*: Dutch Leonard, Bob Harris, Atley Donald • *Number of pitchers victimized*: 12 • *Total ballparks homered in*: 7 • *First HR*: 05/08/1939 off Bob Harris

Russ Nagelson

RUSSELL CHARLES NAGELSON
B: 09/19/1944
BL

Year	Tm	Lg	Tot	H	A	Men-On 0	Men-On 1	Men-On 2	Men-On 3	One-Game 2	One-Game 3	One-Game 4	LO	XN	IP	PH	RHP	LHP
1970	CLE	AL	1	0	1	1	0	0	0	0	0	0	0	0	0	0	1	0

Rank among batters: 4,707 • *Total ballparks homered in*: 1 • *First HR*: 04/12/1970 off Mel Stottlemyre

Tom Nagle

THOMAS EDWARD NAGLE
B: 10/30/1865 D: 03/09/1946
BR

Year	Tm	Lg	Tot	H	A	Men-On 0	Men-On 1	Men-On 2	Men-On 3	One-Game 2	One-Game 3	One-Game 4	LO	XN	IP	PH	RHP	LHP
1890	CHI	NL	1	1	0	1	0	0	0	0	0	0	0	0	0	0	1	0

Rank among batters: 4,707 • *Total ballparks homered in*: 1 • *First HR*: 09/12/1890 off Cy Young

Steve Nagy

STEPHEN NAGY
B: 05/28/1919
BL

Year	Tm	Lg	Tot	H	A	Men-On 0	Men-On 1	Men-On 2	Men-On 3	One-Game 2	One-Game 3	One-Game 4	LO	XN	IP	PH	RHP	LHP
1950	WAS	AL	1	1	0	1	0	0	0	0	0	0	0	0	1	0	0	1

Rank among batters: 4,707 • *Total ballparks homered in*: 1 • *First HR*: 04/28/1950 off Joe Page

Bill Nahorodny

WILLIAM GERARD NAHORODNY
B: 08/31/1953
BR

Year	Tm	Lg	Tot	H	A	Men-On 0	Men-On 1	Men-On 2	Men-On 3	One-Game 2	One-Game 3	One-Game 4	LO	XN	IP	PH	RHP	LHP
1977	CHI	AL	1	1	0	1	0	0	0	0	0	0	0	0	0	0	0	1
1978	CHI	AL	8	4	4	5	3	0	0	0	0	0	0	0	0	0	5	3
1979	CHI	AL	6	3	3	3	3	0	0	1	0	0	0	0	0	1	2	4
1980	ATL	NL	5	2	3	3	2	0	0	0	0	0	0	0	0	0	3	2
1982	CLE	AL	4	1	3	1	3	0	0	0	0	0	0	0	0	1	0	4
1984	SEA	AL	1	0	1	0	1	0	0	0	0	0	0	0	0	0	1	0
Total			25	11	14	13	12	0	0	1	0	0	0	0	0	2	11	14

Rank among batters: 1,608 • *Top target (3 home runs)*: Larry Gura • *Number of pitchers victimized*: 21 • *Total ballparks homered in*: 13 • *First HR*: 09/18/1977 off Balor Moore

Doc Nance

WILLIAM G. NANCE
B: 08/02/1876 D: 05/28/1958
BR

Year	Tm	Lg	Tot	H	A	Men-On 0	Men-On 1	Men-On 2	Men-On 3	One-Game 2	One-Game 3	One-Game 4	LO	XN	IP	PH	RHP	LHP
1897	LOU	NL	3	1	2	1	1	1	0	0	0	0	0	0	0	0	0	2
1898	LOU	NL	1	0	1	0	0	1	0	0	0	0	0	0	0	0	0	1
1901	DET	AL	3	2	1	1	1	1	0	0	0	0	0	0	0	0	2	1
Total			7	3	4	2	2	3	0	0	0	0	0	0	0	0	2	4

Rank among batters: 2,834 • *Total ballparks homered in*: 6 • *First HR*: 08/20/1897 off Mike Sullivan

Hal Naragon

HAROLD RICHARD NARAGON
B: 10/01/1928
BL

Year	Tm	Lg	Tot	H	A	Men-On 0	Men-On 1	Men-On 2	Men-On 3	One-Game 2	One-Game 3	One-Game 4	LO	XN	IP	PH	RHP	LHP
1955	CLE	AL	1	1	0	1	0	0	0	0	0	0	0	0	0	0	1	0
1956	CLE	AL	3	1	2	2	1	0	0	0	0	0	0	0	0	0	3	0
1961	MIN	AL	2	2	0	2	0	0	0	0	0	0	0	0	0	0	2	0
Total			6	4	2	5	1	0	0	0	0	0	0	0	0	0	6	0

Rank among batters: 2,988 • *Total ballparks homered in*: 3 • *First HR*: 08/10/1955 off Jim Bunning

Ray Narleski

RAYMOND EDMOND NARLESKI
B: 11/25/1928
BR

Year	Tm	Lg	Tot	H	A	Men-On 0	Men-On 1	Men-On 2	Men-On 3	One-Game 2	One-Game 3	One-Game 4	LO	XN	IP	PH	RHP	LHP
1957	CLE	AL	1	0	1	0	0	1	0	0	0	0	0	0	0	0	1	0

Rank among batters: 4,707 • *Total ballparks homered in*: 1 • *First HR*: 06/23/1957 off Russ Kemmerer

Jerry Narron

JERRY AUSTIN NARRON
B: 01/15/1956
BL

Year	Tm	Lg	Tot	H	A	Men-On 0	Men-On 1	Men-On 2	Men-On 3	One-Game 2	One-Game 3	One-Game 4	LO	XN	IP	PH	RHP	LHP
1979	NY	AL	4	1	3	2	1	1	0	0	0	0	0	0	0	0	3	1
1980	SEA	AL	4	3	1	1	1	2	0	0	0	0	0	0	0	1	4	0
1981	SEA	AL	3	1	2	2	0	1	0	0	0	0	0	1	0	0	3	0
1983	CAL	AL	1	0	1	1	0	0	0	0	0	0	0	0	0	0	1	0
1984	CAL	AL	3	0	3	2	1	0	0	0	0	0	0	0	0	2	3	0
1985	CAL	AL	5	3	2	3	0	1	1	0	0	0	0	0	0	1	5	0
1986	CAL	AL	1	0	1	1	0	0	0	0	0	0	0	0	0	0	1	0
Total			21	8	13	12	3	5	1	0	0	0	0	1	0	4	20	1

Rank among batters: 1,768 • *Top target (2 home runs)*: Bill Caudill • *Number of pitchers victimized*: 20 • *Total ballparks homered in*: 12 • *First HR*: 07/01/1979 off Dennis Eckersley

Buster Narum

LESLIE FERDINAND NARUM
B: 11/16/1940
BR

Year	Tm	Lg	Tot	H	A	Men-On 0	Men-On 1	Men-On 2	Men-On 3	One-Game 2	One-Game 3	One-Game 4	LO	XN	IP	PH	RHP	LHP
1963	BAL	AL	1	0	1	0	1	0	0	0	0	0	0	0	0	0	0	1
1964	WAS	AL	1	1	0	1	0	0	0	0	0	0	0	0	0	0	1	0
1965	WAS	AL	1	1	0	1	0	0	0	0	0	0	0	0	0	0	1	0
Total			3	2	1	2	1	0	0	0	0	0	0	0	0	0	2	1

Rank among batters: 3,735 • *Total ballparks homered in*: 2 • *First HR*: 05/03/1963 off Don Mossi • *Hit HR in first major league AB—@DET*: 05/03/1963

Year	Tm	Lg	Tot	H	A	Men-On 0	Men-On 1	Men-On 2	Men-On 3	One-Game 2	One-Game 3	One-Game 4	LO	XN	IP	PH	RHP	LHP

Billy Nash

WILLIAM MITCHELL NASH
B: 06/24/1865 D: 11/15/1929
BR

Year	Tm	Lg	Tot	H	A	Men-On 0	Men-On 1	Men-On 2	Men-On 3	One-Game 2	One-Game 3	One-Game 4	LO	XN	IP	PH	RHP	LHP
1884	RIC	AA	1	0	1	0	1	0	0	0	0	0	0	0	0	0	1	0
1886	BOS	NL	1	0	1	1	0	0	0	0	0	0	0	0	0	0	1	0
1887	BOS	NL	6	2	4	4	0	2	0	0	0	0	0	0	1	0	6	0
1888	BOS	NL	4	2	2	2	1	1	0	0	0	0	0	0	1	0	4	0
1889	BOS	NL	3	1	2	2	0	1	0	0	0	0	0	0	0	0	3	0
1890	BOS	PL	5	5	0	3	1	1	0	0	0	0	0	0	0	0	3	1
1891	BOS	NL	5	2	3	3	2	0	0	0	0	0	0	0	1	0	3	0
1892	BOS	NL	4	2	2	2	2	0	0	0	0	0	0	0	0	0	3	1
1893	BOS	NL	10	6	4	4	3	3	0	0	0	0	0	1	1	0	7	2
1894	BOS	NL	8	7	1	5	1	1	1	0	0	0	0	0	0	0	7	1
1895	BOS	NL	10	9	1	2	5	2	1	0	0	0	0	0	0	0	9	1
1896	PHI	NL	3	1	2	1	1	1	0	0	0	0	0	0	0	0	2	1
Total			60	37	23	29	17	12	2	0	0	0	0	1	4	0	49	6

Rank among batters: 863 • Top target (2 home runs): Pete Conway, Hank O'Day, Pretzels Getzien, Ed Crane, Ed Stein, Al Maul, Dad Clarkson, Kid Carsey, Ted Breitenstein • *Number of pitchers victimized*: 51 • *Total ballparks homered in*: 19 • *First HR*: 09/15/1884 off Dave Foutz

Jim Nash

JAMES EDWIN NASH
B: 02/09/1945
BR

Year	Tm	Lg	Tot	H	A	Men-On 0	Men-On 1	Men-On 2	Men-On 3	One-Game 2	One-Game 3	One-Game 4	LO	XN	IP	PH	RHP	LHP
1968	OAK	AL	2	2	0	2	0	0	0	0	0	0	0	0	0	0	1	1
1970	ATL	NL	2	1	1	1	1	0	0	0	0	0	0	0	0	0	1	1
Total			4	3	1	3	1	0	0	0	0	0	0	0	0	0	2	2

Rank among batters: 3,427 • *Total ballparks homered in*: 3 • *First HR*: 05/22/1968 off Stan Williams

Bobby Natal

ROBERT MARCEL NATAL
B: 11/13/1965
BR

Year	Tm	Lg	Tot	H	A	Men-On 0	Men-On 1	Men-On 2	Men-On 3	One-Game 2	One-Game 3	One-Game 4	LO	XN	IP	PH	RHP	LHP
1993	FLO	NL	1	0	1	1	0	0	0	0	0	0	0	0	0	0	1	0
1995	FLO	NL	2	2	0	2	0	0	0	0	0	0	0	0	0	0	1	1
Total			3	2	1	3	0	0	0	0	0	0	0	0	0	0	2	1

Rank among batters: 3,735 • *Total ballparks homered in*: 2 • *First HR*: 07/04/1993 off John Smoltz

Earl Naylor

EARL EUGENE NAYLOR
B: 05/19/1919 D: 01/16/1990
BR

Year	Tm	Lg	Tot	H	A	Men-On 0	Men-On 1	Men-On 2	Men-On 3	One-Game 2	One-Game 3	One-Game 4	LO	XN	IP	PH	RHP	LHP
1943	PHI	NL	3	2	1	2	0	1	0	0	0	0	0	0	0	0	3	0

Rank among batters: 3,735 • *Total ballparks homered in*: 2 • *First HR*: 04/29/1943 off Kirby Higbe

Rollie Naylor

ROLEINE CECIL NAYLOR
B: 02/04/1892 D: 06/18/1966
BR

Year	Tm	Lg	Tot	H	A	Men-On 0	Men-On 1	Men-On 2	Men-On 3	One-Game 2	One-Game 3	One-Game 4	LO	XN	IP	PH	RHP	LHP
1922	PHI	AL	1	1	0	1	0	0	0	0	0	0	0	0	0	0	1	0

Rank among batters: 4,707 • *Total ballparks homered in*: 1 • *First HR*: 07/08/1922 off Charlie Robertson

Denny Neagle

DENNIS EDWARD NEAGLE
B: 09/13/1968
BL

Year	Tm	Lg	Tot	H	A	Men-On 0	Men-On 1	Men-On 2	Men-On 3	One-Game 2	One-Game 3	One-Game 4	LO	XN	IP	PH	RHP	LHP
1994	PIT	NL	1	1	0	0	1	0	0	0	0	0	0	0	0	0	1	0
1995	PIT	NL	1	0	1	0	0	0	1	0	0	0	0	0	0	0	1	0
Total			2	1	1	0	1	0	1	0	0	0	0	0	0	0	2	0

Rank among batters: 4,129 • *Total ballparks homered in*: 2 • *First HR*: 07/25/1994 off Willie Banks

Charlie Neal

CHARLES LENARD NEAL
B: 01/30/1931
BR

Year	Tm	Lg	Tot	H	A	Men-On 0	Men-On 1	Men-On 2	Men-On 3	One-Game 2	One-Game 3	One-Game 4	LO	XN	IP	PH	RHP	LHP
1956	BRO	NL	2	0	2	1	1	0	0	0	0	0	0	0	0	0	1	1

Year	Tm	Lg	Tot	H	A	Men-On 0	1	2	3	One-Game 2	3	4	LO	XN	IP	PH	RHP	LHP

Charlie Neal *continued*

Year	Tm	Lg	Tot	H	A	Men-On 0	1	2	3	One-Game 2	3	4	LO	XN	IP	PH	RHP	LHP
1957	BRO	NL	12	6	6	6	4	2	0	1	0	0	2	0	0	0	12	0
1958	LA	NL	22	14	8	11	8	3	0	2	0	0	0	0	0	0	20	2
1959	LA	NL	19	13	6	12	6	1	0	2	0	0	0	0	0	0	18	1
1960	LA	NL	8	5	3	6	1	1	0	0	0	0	0	1	0	0	7	1
1961	LA	NL	10	6	4	4	6	0	0	0	0	0	0	0	0	0	7	3
1962	NY	NL	11	7	4	9	1	1	0	1	0	0	0	0	0	0	9	2
1963	NY	NL	3	2	1	3	0	0	0	0	0	0	1	0	1	0	2	1
Total			87	53	34	52	27	8	0	6	0	0	3	1	1	0	76	11

Rank among batters: 594 • *Top target (5 home runs)*: Lew Burdette • *Number of pitchers victimized*: 54 • *Total ballparks homered in*: 10 • *First HR*: 04/21/1956 off Bob Friend • *World Series HR*—2

Greasy Neale

ALFRED EARLE NEALE
B: 11/05/1891 D: 11/02/1973
BL

Year	Tm	Lg	Tot	H	A	Men-On 0	1	2	3	One-Game 2	3	4	LO	XN	IP	PH	RHP	LHP
1917	CIN	NL	3	2	1	0	3	0	0	0	0	0	0	0	3	0	3	0
1918	CIN	NL	1	0	1	0	1	0	0	0	0	0	0	0	1	0	1	0
1919	CIN	NL	1	1	0	1	0	0	0	0	0	0	0	0	1	0	0	1
1920	CIN	NL	3	0	3	1	2	0	0	0	0	0	0	0	3	0	3	0
Total			8	3	5	2	6	0	0	0	0	0	0	0	8	0	7	1

Rank among batters: 2,703 • *Total ballparks homered in*: 5 • *First HR*: 06/11/1917 off Laurence Cheney

Joe Neale

JOSEPH HUNT NEALE
B: 05/07/1866 D: 12/30/1913
BR

Year	Tm	Lg	Tot	H	A	Men-On 0	1	2	3	One-Game 2	3	4	LO	XN	IP	PH	RHP	LHP
1891	STL	AA	1	1	0	1	0	0	0	0	0	0	0	0	0	0	1	0

Rank among batters: 4,707 • *Total ballparks homered in*: 1 • *First HR*: 04/10/1891 off Frank Dwyer

Jim Nealon

JAMES JOSEPH NEALON
B: 12/15/1884 D: 04/02/1910
BR

Year	Tm	Lg	Tot	H	A	Men-On 0	1	2	3	One-Game 2	3	4	LO	XN	IP	PH	RHP	LHP
1906	PIT	NL	3	2	1	1	1	1	0	0	0	0	0	0	2	0	2	1

Rank among batters: 3,735 • *Total ballparks homered in*: 2 • *First HR*: 05/05/1906 off Fred Beebe

Tom Needham

THOMAS J. NEEDHAM
B: 04/07/1879 D: 12/13/1926
BR

Year	Tm	Lg	Tot	H	A	Men-On 0	1	2	3	One-Game 2	3	4	LO	XN	IP	PH	RHP	LHP
1904	BOS	NL	4	2	2	3	1	0	0	0	0	0	0	0	1	0	3	1
1905	BOS	NL	2	2	0	2	0	0	0	0	0	0	0	0	0	0	2	0
1906	BOS	NL	1	0	1	1	0	0	0	0	0	0	0	0	0	0	1	0
1907	BOS	NL	1	0	1	0	1	0	0	0	0	0	0	0	0	0	0	1
Total			8	4	4	6	2	0	0	0	0	0	0	0	1	0	6	2

Rank among batters: 2,703 • *Total ballparks homered in*: 5 • *First HR*: 06/28/1904 off Oscar Jones

Troy Neel

TROY LEE NEEL
B: 09/14/1965
BL

Year	Tm	Lg	Tot	H	A	Men-On 0	1	2	3	One-Game 2	3	4	LO	XN	IP	PH	RHP	LHP
1992	OAK	AL	3	2	1	0	3	0	0	0	0	0	0	0	0	0	2	1
1993	OAK	AL	19	11	8	14	2	3	0	2	0	0	0	0	0	0	15	4
1994	OAK	AL	15	6	9	9	5	1	0	1	0	0	0	0	0	1	8	7
Total			37	19	18	23	10	4	0	3	0	0	0	0	0	1	25	12

Rank among batters: 1,252 • Top target (2 home runs): John Dopson, Paul Quantrill, Willie Banks, Pat Hentgen, Dave Wells, Kenny Rogers • *Number of pitchers victimized*: 31 • *Total ballparks homered in*: 11 • *First HR*: 07/06/1992 off Jeff Mutis

Cal Neeman

CALVIN AMANDUS NEEMAN
B: 02/18/1929
BR

Year	Tm	Lg	Tot	H	A	Men-On 0	1	2	3	One-Game 2	3	4	LO	XN	IP	PH	RHP	LHP
1957	CHI	NL	10	5	5	6	3	1	0	0	0	0	0	1	0	0	6	4

Cal Neeman *continued*

Year	Tm	Lg	Tot	H	A	Men-On 0	Men-On 1	Men-On 2	Men-On 3	One-Game 2	One-Game 3	One-Game 4	LO	XN	IP	PH	RHP	LHP
1958	CHI	NL	12	6	6	8	2	2	0	0	0	0	0	1	0	0	2	10
1959	CHI	NL	3	2	1	1	1	1	0	0	0	0	0	1	1	0	2	1
1960	PHI	NL	4	3	1	1	2	1	0	0	0	0	0	0	0	0	3	1
1962	PIT	NL	1	1	0	0	1	0	0	0	0	0	0	0	0	0	1	0
Total			30	17	13	16	9	5	0	0	0	0	0	3	1	0	14	16

Rank among batters: 1,437 • *Top target (5 home runs)*: Harvey Haddix • *Number of pitchers victimized*: 24 • *Total ballparks homered in*: 8 • *First HR*: 04/23/1957 off Lew Burdette

Art Nehf

ARTHUR NEUKOM NEHF
B: 07/31/1892 D: 12/18/1960
BL

Year	Tm	Lg	Tot	H	A	Men-On 0	Men-On 1	Men-On 2	Men-On 3	One-Game 2	One-Game 3	One-Game 4	LO	XN	IP	PH	RHP	LHP
1919	NY	NL	1	1	0	1	0	0	0	0	0	0	0	0	0	0	1	0
1922	NY	NL	1	1	0	1	0	0	0	0	0	0	0	0	0	0	0	1
1924	NY	NL	5	4	1	3	2	0	0	1	0	0	0	0	0	0	4	1
1928	CHI	NL	1	1	0	0	1	0	0	0	0	0	0	0	0	0	1	0
Total			8	7	1	5	3	0	0	1	0	0	0	0	0	0	6	2

Rank among batters: 2,703 • *Top target (4 home runs)*: Johnny Stuart • *Number of pitchers victimized*: 5 • *Total ballparks homered in*: 3 • *First HR*: 09/27/1919 off Brad Hogg

Gary Neibauer

GARY WAYNE NEIBAUER
B: 10/29/1944
BR

Year	Tm	Lg	Tot	H	A	Men-On 0	Men-On 1	Men-On 2	Men-On 3	One-Game 2	One-Game 3	One-Game 4	LO	XN	IP	PH	RHP	LHP
1973	ATL	NL	1	1	0	1	0	0	0	0	0	0	0	0	0	0	0	1

Rank among batters: 4,707 • *Total ballparks homered in*: 1 • *First HR*: 08/04/1973 off Randy Jones

Bob Neighbors

ROBERT OTIS NEIGHBORS
B: 11/09/1917 D: 08/08/1952
BR

Year	Tm	Lg	Tot	H	A	Men-On 0	Men-On 1	Men-On 2	Men-On 3	One-Game 2	One-Game 3	One-Game 4	LO	XN	IP	PH	RHP	LHP
1939	STL	AL	1	0	1	1	0	0	0	0	0	0	0	0	0	0	1	0

Rank among batters: 4,707 • *Total ballparks homered in*: 1 • *First HR*: 09/21/1939 off Denny Galehouse

Bernie Neis

BERNARD EDMUND NEIS
B: 09/26/1895 D: 11/29/1972
BB

Year	Tm	Lg	Tot	H	A	Men-On 0	Men-On 1	Men-On 2	Men-On 3	One-Game 2	One-Game 3	One-Game 4	LO	XN	IP	PH	RHP	LHP
1920	BRO	NL	2	2	0	2	0	0	0	0	0	0	0	0	0	0	1	1
1921	BRO	NL	4	2	2	2	1	1	0	0	0	0	0	0	0	0	2	2
1922	BRO	NL	1	0	1	0	1	0	0	0	0	0	0	0	0	0	0	1
1923	BRO	NL	5	3	2	2	1	2	0	0	0	0	0	0	0	0	2	3
1924	BRO	NL	4	2	2	3	1	0	0	0	0	0	2	0	0	0	2	2
1925	BOS	NL	5	2	3	5	0	0	0	1	0	0	0	0	1	0	2	3
1927	CLE	AL	4	1	3	3	0	1	0	0	0	0	0	0	0	0	2	2
Total			25	12	13	17	4	4	0	1	0	0	2	0	1	0	11	14

Rank among batters: 1,608 • *Top target (3 home runs)*: Clarence Mitchell • *Number of pitchers victimized*: 21 • *Total ballparks homered in*: 8 • *First HR*: 04/18/1920 off Dick Rudolph

Candy Nelson

JOHN W. NELSON
B: 03/12/1854 D: 09/04/1910
BL

Year	Tm	Lg	Tot	H	A	Men-On 0	Men-On 1	Men-On 2	Men-On 3	One-Game 2	One-Game 3	One-Game 4	LO	XN	IP	PH	RHP	LHP
1881	WOR	NL	1	1	0	0	0	1	0	0	0	0	0	0	0	0	1	0
1884	NY	AA	1	0	1	1	0	0	0	0	0	0	0	0	0	0	1	0
1885	NY	AA	1	0	1	1	0	0	0	0	0	0	0	0	1	0	1	0
Total			3	1	2	2	0	1	0	0	0	0	0	0	1	0	3	0

Rank among batters: 3,735 • *Total ballparks homered in*: 3 • *First HR*: 09/27/1881 off Stump Wiedman

Dave Nelson

DAVID EARL NELSON
B: 06/20/1944
BR

Year	Tm	Lg	Tot	H	A	Men-On 0	Men-On 1	Men-On 2	Men-On 3	One-Game 2	One-Game 3	One-Game 4	LO	XN	IP	PH	RHP	LHP
1971	WAS	AL	5	3	2	4	0	1	0	0	0	0	2	0	0	0	2	3

Dave Nelson *continued*

Year	Tm	Lg	Tot	H	A	Men-On 0	Men-On 1	Men-On 2	Men-On 3	One-Game 2	One-Game 3	One-Game 4	LO	XN	IP	PH	RHP	LHP
1972	TEX	AL	2	1	1	2	0	0	0	0	0	0	1	0	0	0	2	0
1973	TEX	AL	7	2	5	3	3	1	0	1	0	0	2	0	0	0	5	2
1974	TEX	AL	3	1	2	0	1	2	0	0	0	0	0	0	0	0	3	0
1975	TEX	AL	2	1	1	2	0	0	0	0	0	0	0	0	0	0	0	2
1976	KC	AL	1	0	1	0	1	0	0	0	0	0	0	0	0	0	1	0
Total			20	8	12	11	5	4	0	1	0	0	5	0	0	0	13	7

Rank among batters: 1,810 • *Top target (3 home runs)*: Eddie Fisher • *Number of pitchers victimized*: 17 • *Total ballparks homered in*: 9 • *First HR*: 06/18/1971 off Sonny Siebert

Jamie Nelson

JAMES VICTOR NELSON
B: 09/05/1959
BR

Year	Tm	Lg	Tot	H	A	Men-On 0	Men-On 1	Men-On 2	Men-On 3	One-Game 2	One-Game 3	One-Game 4	LO	XN	IP	PH	RHP	LHP
1983	SEA	AL	1	1	0	0	1	0	0	0	0	0	0	0	0	0	0	1

Rank among batters: 4,707 • *Total ballparks homered in*: 1 • *First HR*: 07/21/1983 off Bobby Ojeda

Lynn Nelson

LYNN BERNARD NELSON
B: 02/24/1905 D: 02/15/1955
BL

Year	Tm	Lg	Tot	H	A	Men-On 0	Men-On 1	Men-On 2	Men-On 3	One-Game 2	One-Game 3	One-Game 4	LO	XN	IP	PH	RHP	LHP
1937	PHI	AL	4	2	2	2	1	0	1	0	0	0	0	0	0	2	4	0
1940	DET	AL	1	1	0	0	1	0	0	0	0	0	0	0	0	1	1	0
Total			5	3	2	2	2	0	1	0	0	0	0	0	0	3	5	0

Rank among batters: 3,191 • *Top target (2 home runs)*: Ivy Andrews • *Number of pitchers victimized*: 4 • *Total ballparks homered in*: 4 • *First HR*: 07/10/1937 off Johnny Marcum

Red Nelson

ALBERT FRANCIS NELSON
B: 05/19/1886 D: 10/26/1956
BR

Year	Tm	Lg	Tot	H	A	Men-On 0	Men-On 1	Men-On 2	Men-On 3	One-Game 2	One-Game 3	One-Game 4	LO	XN	IP	PH	RHP	LHP
1910	STL	AL	1	1	0	1	0	0	0	0	0	0	0	0	0	0	1	0

Rank among batters: 4,707 • *Total ballparks homered in*: 1 • *First HR*: 10/02/1910 off Ralph Works

Ricky Nelson

RICKY LEE NELSON
B: 05/08/1959
BL

Year	Tm	Lg	Tot	H	A	Men-On 0	Men-On 1	Men-On 2	Men-On 3	One-Game 2	One-Game 3	One-Game 4	LO	XN	IP	PH	RHP	LHP
1983	SEA	AL	5	1	4	4	0	1	0	0	0	0	0	0	0	0	5	0
1984	SEA	AL	1	0	1	1	0	0	0	0	0	0	0	0	0	0	1	0
Total			6	1	5	5	0	1	0	0	0	0	0	0	0	0	6	0

Rank among batters: 2,988 • *Total ballparks homered in*: 6 • *First HR*: 05/20/1983 off Tom Tellmann

Rob Nelson

ROBERT AUGUSTUS NELSON
B: 05/17/1964
BL

Year	Tm	Lg	Tot	H	A	Men-On 0	Men-On 1	Men-On 2	Men-On 3	One-Game 2	One-Game 3	One-Game 4	LO	XN	IP	PH	RHP	LHP
1988	SD	NL	1	1	0	1	0	0	0	0	0	0	0	0	0	0	1	0
1989	SD	NL	3	1	2	1	1	1	0	0	0	0	0	0	0	0	3	0
Total			4	2	2	2	1	1	0	0	0	0	0	0	0	0	4	0

Rank among batters: 3,427 • *Total ballparks homered in*: 3 • *First HR*: 09/27/1988 off Tim Leary

Rocky Nelson

GLENN RICHARD NELSON
B: 11/18/1924
BL

Year	Tm	Lg	Tot	H	A	Men-On 0	Men-On 1	Men-On 2	Men-On 3	One-Game 2	One-Game 3	One-Game 4	LO	XN	IP	PH	RHP	LHP
1949	STL	NL	4	2	2	1	1	2	0	0	0	0	0	0	1	0	4	0
1950	STL	NL	1	1	0	0	1	0	0	0	0	0	0	0	0	0	0	1
1951	PIT	NL	1	0	1	1	0	0	0	0	0	0	0	0	0	1	1	0
1956	BRO	NL	4	2	2	3	1	0	0	0	0	0	0	0	0	0	4	0
	STL	NL	3	1	2	0	3	0	0	0	0	0	0	0	0	2	3	0
	Total		7	3	4	3	4	0	0	0	0	0	0	0	0	2	7	0
1959	PIT	NL	6	6	0	2	4	0	0	1	0	0	0	0	0	1	5	1
1960	PIT	NL	7	5	2	4	1	2	0	1	0	0	0	1	0	0	7	0

Rocky Nelson *continued*

						Men-On				One-Game								
Year	Tm	Lg	Tot	H	A	0	1	2	3	2	3	4	LO	XN	IP	PH	RHP	LHP
1961	PIT	NL	5	1	4	4	0	1	0	0	0	0	0	0	0	1	5	0
Total			31	18	13	15	11	5	0	2	0	0	0	1	1	5	29	2

Rank among batters: 1,400 • Top target (2 home runs): Clint Hartung, Bob Buhl, Sam Jones, Don Drysdale, Bob Purkey • *Number of pitchers victimized*: 26 • *Total ballparks homered in*: 9 • *First HR*: 04/30/1949 off Bob Rush • *World Series HR*—1

Dick Nen

RICHARD LEROY NEN
B: 09/24/1939
BL

						Men-On				One-Game								
Year	Tm	Lg	Tot	H	A	0	1	2	3	2	3	4	LO	XN	IP	PH	RHP	LHP
1963	LA	NL	1	0	1	1	0	0	0	0	0	0	0	0	0	0	1	0
1965	WAS	AL	6	3	3	4	1	0	1	0	0	0	0	0	0	0	6	0
1966	WAS	AL	6	0	6	2	3	1	0	0	0	0	0	0	0	0	5	1
1967	WAS	AL	6	4	2	4	1	1	0	0	0	0	0	0	0	1	6	0
1968	CHI	NL	2	1	1	0	2	0	0	0	0	0	0	0	0	1	2	0
Total			21	8	13	11	7	2	1	0	0	0	0	0	0	2	20	1

Rank among batters: 1,768 • *Top target (3 home runs)*: Luis Tiant, Catfish Hunter • *Number of pitchers victimized*: 17 • *Total ballparks homered in*: 10 • *First HR*: 09/18/1963 off Ron Taylor

Jack Ness

JOHN CHARLES NESS
B: 11/11/1885 D: 12/03/1957
BR

						Men-On				One-Game								
Year	Tm	Lg	Tot	H	A	0	1	2	3	2	3	4	LO	XN	IP	PH	RHP	LHP
1916	CHI	AL	1	1	0	1	0	0	0	0	0	0	0	0	0	0	0	1

Rank among batters: 4,707 • *Total ballparks homered in*: 1 • *First HR*: 08/07/1916 off Dutch Leonard

Graig Nettles

GRAIG NETTLES
B: 08/20/1944
BL

						Men-On				One-Game								
Year	Tm	Lg	Tot	H	A	0	1	2	3	2	3	4	LO	XN	IP	PH	RHP	LHP
1968	MIN	AL	5	1	4	4	0	1	0	1	0	0	0	0	0	0	5	0
1969	MIN	AL	7	2	5	5	0	2	0	0	0	0	0	0	0	2	7	0
1970	CLE	AL	26	13	13	14	9	3	0	1	0	0	1	0	0	2	22	4
1971	CLE	AL	28	15	13	17	10	1	0	1	0	0	1	0	0	0	20	8
1972	CLE	AL	17	11	6	10	6	1	0	0	0	0	0	1	0	0	7	10
1973	NY	AL	22	12	10	12	8	2	0	1	0	0	0	1	0	0	12	10
1974	NY	AL	22	9	13	13	7	1	1	3	0	0	0	1	0	0	13	9
1975	NY	AL	21	14	7	11	7	3	0	2	0	0	0	0	0	0	15	6
1976	NY	AL	32	18	14	15	11	5	1	4	0	0	0	1	0	0	22	10
1977	NY	AL	37	18	19	22	7	8	0	3	0	0	0	0	0	0	25	12
1978	NY	AL	27	16	11	18	6	3	0	2	0	0	0	1	0	0	18	9
1979	NY	AL	20	11	9	10	9	1	0	1	0	0	0	1	0	0	12	8
1980	NY	AL	16	11	5	10	5	1	0	0	0	0	0	2	0	1	12	4
1981	NY	AL	15	11	4	9	5	1	0	1	0	0	0	1	0	0	10	5
1982	NY	AL	18	10	8	10	6	1	1	1	0	0	0	0	0	0	15	3
1983	NY	AL	20	11	9	12	5	3	0	1	0	0	0	0	0	1	16	4
1984	SD	NL	20	11	9	10	10	0	0	2	0	0	0	1	0	1	19	1
1985	SD	NL	15	6	9	12	3	0	0	1	0	0	0	0	0	0	11	4
1986	SD	NL	16	13	3	6	7	3	0	2	0	0	0	1	0	1	13	3
1987	ATL	NL	5	2	3	1	2	1	1	0	0	0	0	0	0	3	5	0
1988	MON	NL	1	1	0	1	0	0	0	0	0	0	0	0	0	1	1	0
Total			390	216	174	222	123	41	4	27	0	0	2	11	0	12	280	110

Rank among batters: 28 • *Top target (9 home runs)*: Jim Palmer, Luis Tiant • *Number of pitchers victimized*: 236 • *Total ballparks homered in*: 28 • *First HR*: 09/06/1968 off Denny McLain • *LCS HR*—5

Jim Nettles

JAMES WILLIAM NETTLES
B: 03/02/1947
BL

						Men-On				One-Game								
Year	Tm	Lg	Tot	H	A	0	1	2	3	2	3	4	LO	XN	IP	PH	RHP	LHP
1971	MIN	AL	6	3	3	3	2	0	1	0	0	0	0	1	1	0	4	2
1972	MIN	AL	4	1	3	3	0	1	0	0	0	0	0	0	0	1	3	1
1974	DET	AL	6	5	1	1	4	1	0	1	0	0	0	0	0	0	6	0
Total			16	9	7	7	6	2	1	1	0	0	0	1	1	1	13	3

Year	Tm	Lg	Tot	H	A	Men-On 0	1	2	3	One-Game 2	3	4	LO	XN	IP	PH	RHP	LHP

Jim Nettles *continued*

Rank among batters: 2,029 • *Top target (2 home runs)*: Joe Decker • *Number of pitchers victimized*: 15 • *Total ballparks homered in*: 6 • *First HR*: 07/11/1971 off Tom Burgmeier

Johnny Neun

JOHN HENRY NEUN
B: 10/28/1900 D: 03/28/1990
BB

Year	Tm	Lg	Tot	H	A	Men-On 0	1	2	3	One-Game 2	3	4	LO	XN	IP	PH	RHP	LHP
1930	BOS	NL	2	0	2	2	0	0	0	0	0	0	0	0	1	0	1	1

Rank among batters: 4,129 • *Total ballparks homered in*: 2 • *First HR*: 05/01/1930 off Larry French

Phil Nevin

PHILLIP JOSEPH NEVIN
B: 01/19/1971
BR

Year	Tm	Lg	Tot	H	A	Men-On 0	1	2	3	One-Game 2	3	4	LO	XN	IP	PH	RHP	LHP
1995	DET	AL	2	2	0	2	0	0	0	0	0	0	0	0	0	0	2	0

Rank among batters: 4,129 • *Total ballparks homered in*: 1 • *First HR*: 09/03/1995 off Albie Lopez

Don Newcombe

DONALD NEWCOMBE
B: 06/14/1926
BL

Year	Tm	Lg	Tot	H	A	Men-On 0	1	2	3	One-Game 2	3	4	LO	XN	IP	PH	RHP	LHP
1950	BRO	NL	1	0	1	1	0	0	0	0	0	0	0	0	0	0	0	1
1955	BRO	NL	7	4	3	3	3	1	0	2	0	0	0	0	0	0	7	0
1956	BRO	NL	2	2	0	1	1	0	0	1	0	0	0	0	0	0	2	0
1957	BRO	NL	1	0	1	1	0	0	0	0	0	0	0	0	0	0	1	0
1958	CIN	NL	1	1	0	0	1	0	0	0	0	0	0	0	0	0	1	0
1959	CIN	NL	3	1	2	2	1	0	0	0	0	0	0	0	0	0	3	0
Total			15	8	7	8	6	1	0	3	0	0	0	0	0	0	14	1

Rank among batters: 2,096 • *Top target (2 home runs)*: Ron Kline, Tom Poholsky • *Number of pitchers victimized*: 13 • *Total ballparks homered in*: 6 • *First HR*: 07/04/1950 off Monita Kennedy

Marc Newfield

MARC ALEXANDER NEWFIELD
B: 10/19/1972
BR

Year	Tm	Lg	Tot	H	A	Men-On 0	1	2	3	One-Game 2	3	4	LO	XN	IP	PH	RHP	LHP
1993	SEA	AL	1	1	0	1	0	0	0	0	0	0	0	0	0	0	0	1
1994	SEA	AL	1	0	1	0	1	0	0	0	0	0	0	0	0	0	0	1
1995	SEA	AL	3	0	3	1	1	1	0	0	0	0	0	0	1	0	2	1
	SD	NL	1	1	0	1	0	0	0	0	0	0	0	0	0	0	0	1
	Total		4	1	3	2	1	1	0	0	0	0	0	0	1	0	2	2
Total			6	2	4	3	2	1	0	0	0	0	0	0	1	0	2	4

Rank among batters: 2,988 • *Total ballparks homered in*: 5 • *First HR*: 07/11/1993 off Jeff Mutis

Hal Newhouser

HAROLD NEWHOUSER
B: 05/20/1921
BL

Year	Tm	Lg	Tot	H	A	Men-On 0	1	2	3	One-Game 2	3	4	LO	XN	IP	PH	RHP	LHP
1946	DET	AL	2	1	1	1	0	1	0	0	0	0	0	0	0	0	1	1

Rank among batters: 4,129 • *Total ballparks homered in*: 2 • *First HR*: 06/26/1946 off Bill Butland

Al Newman

ALBERT DWAYNE NEWMAN
B: 06/30/1960
BB

Year	Tm	Lg	Tot	H	A	Men-On 0	1	2	3	One-Game 2	3	4	LO	XN	IP	PH	RHP	LHP
1986	MON	NL	1	0	1	0	1	0	0	0	0	0	0	0	0	0	0	1

Rank among batters: 4,707 • *Total ballparks homered in*: 1 • *First HR*: 07/06/1986 off Zane Smith

Fred Newman

FREDERICK WILLIAM NEWMAN
B: 02/21/1942 D: 06/24/1987
BR

Year	Tm	Lg	Tot	H	A	Men-On 0	1	2	3	One-Game 2	3	4	LO	XN	IP	PH	RHP	LHP
1964	LA	AL	1	0	1	1	0	0	0	0	0	0	0	0	0	0	1	0

Year	Tm	Lg	Tot	H	A	Men-On				One-Game			LO	XN	IP	PH	RHP	LHP
						0	1	2	3	2	3	4						

Fred Newman *continued*

Year	Tm	Lg	Tot	H	A	0	1	2	3	2	3	4	LO	XN	IP	PH	RHP	LHP
1965	CAL	AL	1	0	1	1	0	0	0	0	0	0	0	0	0	0	0	1
Total			2	0	2	2	0	0	0	0	0	0	0	0	0	0	1	1

Rank among batters: 4,129 • *Total ballparks homered in*: 2 • *First HR*: 09/12/1964 off Pete Charton

Jeff Newman

JEFFREY LYNN NEWMAN
B: 09/11/1948
BR

Year	Tm	Lg	Tot	H	A	0	1	2	3	2	3	4	LO	XN	IP	PH	RHP	LHP
1977	OAK	AL	4	2	2	3	1	0	0	0	0	0	0	0	0	0	4	0
1978	OAK	AL	9	4	5	6	2	1	0	0	0	0	0	0	0	2	4	5
1979	OAK	AL	22	9	13	15	4	3	0	1	0	0	0	0	0	0	17	5
1980	OAK	AL	15	7	8	8	7	0	0	0	0	0	0	0	0	0	8	7
1981	OAK	AL	3	2	1	3	0	0	0	0	0	0	0	0	0	0	2	1
1982	OAK	AL	6	3	3	2	4	0	0	0	0	0	0	0	0	0	3	3
1983	BOS	AL	3	0	3	3	0	0	0	0	0	0	0	0	0	0	2	1
1984	BOS	AL	1	0	1	1	0	0	0	0	0	0	0	0	0	0	1	0
Total			63	27	36	41	18	4	0	1	0	0	0	0	0	2	41	22

Rank among batters: 826 • *Top target (4 home runs)*: Mike Caldwell • *Number of pitchers victimized*: 52 • *Total ballparks homered in*: 12 • *First HR*: 07/10/1977 off Doug Bird

Patrick Newnam

PATRICK HENRY NEWNAM
B: 12/10/1880 D: 06/20/1938
BL

Year	Tm	Lg	Tot	H	A	0	1	2	3	2	3	4	LO	XN	IP	PH	RHP	LHP
1910	STL	AL	2	0	2	1	1	0	0	0	0	0	0	0	0	0	1	1

Rank among batters: 4,129 • *Total ballparks homered in*: 1 • *First HR*: 08/22/1910 off Eddie Cicotte

Bobo Newsom

LOUIS NORMAN NEWSOM
B: 08/11/1907 D: 12/07/1962
BR

Year	Tm	Lg	Tot	H	A	0	1	2	3	2	3	4	LO	XN	IP	PH	RHP	LHP
1937	WAS	AL	1	0	1	1	0	0	0	0	0	0	0	0	0	0	1	0

Rank among batters: 4,707 • *Total ballparks homered in*: 1 • *First HR*: 05/08/1937 off Schoolboy Rowe

Skeeter Newsome

LAMAR ASHBY NEWSOME
B: 10/18/1910 D: 08/31/1989
BR

Year	Tm	Lg	Tot	H	A	0	1	2	3	2	3	4	LO	XN	IP	PH	RHP	LHP
1935	PHI	AL	1	1	0	1	0	0	0	0	0	0	0	0	0	0	1	0
1937	PHI	AL	1	0	1	1	0	0	0	0	0	0	0	0	0	0	1	0
1941	BOS	AL	2	1	1	2	0	0	0	0	0	0	1	0	0	0	2	0
1943	BOS	AL	1	1	0	0	1	0	0	0	0	0	0	0	0	0	1	0
1945	BOS	AL	1	0	1	0	1	0	0	0	0	0	0	0	0	0	1	0
1946	PHI	NL	1	1	0	0	1	0	0	0	0	0	0	0	0	0	1	0
1947	PHI	NL	2	0	2	1	0	0	1	0	0	0	0	0	0	0	2	0
Total			9	4	5	5	3	0	1	0	0	0	1	0	0	0	9	0

Rank among batters: 2,587 • *Top target (2 home runs)*: Bobo Newsom • *Number of pitchers victimized*: 8 • *Total ballparks homered in*: 5 • *First HR*: 09/28/1935 off Bobo Newsom

Warren Newson

WARREN DALE NEWSON
B: 07/03/1964
BL

Year	Tm	Lg	Tot	H	A	0	1	2	3	2	3	4	LO	XN	IP	PH	RHP	LHP
1991	CHI	AL	4	1	3	3	0	1	0	0	0	0	0	0	0	0	4	0
1992	CHI	AL	1	1	0	1	0	0	0	0	0	0	0	0	0	0	1	0
1993	CHI	AL	2	2	0	2	0	0	0	0	0	0	0	0	0	0	2	0
1994	CHI	AL	2	2	0	2	0	0	0	0	0	0	0	0	0	0	2	0
1995	CHI	AL	3	3	0	3	0	0	0	0	0	0	0	0	0	0	3	0
	SEA	AL	2	1	1	2	0	0	0	0	0	0	0	0	0	0	2	0
	Total		5	4	1	5	0	0	0	0	0	0	0	0	0	0	5	0
Total			14	10	4	13	0	1	0	0	0	0	0	0	0	0	14	0

Rank among batters: 2,169 • *Top target (2 home runs)*: Pat Mahomes • *Number of pitchers victimized*: 13 • *Total ballparks homered in*: 6 • *First HR*: 07/14/1991 off Mark Knudson • *LCS HR*—1

Gus Niarhos

CONSTANTINE GREGORY NIARHOS
B: 12/06/1920
BR

Year	Tm	Lg	Tot	H	A	Men-On 0	1	2	3	One-Game 2	3	4	LO	XN	IP	PH	RHP	LHP
1951	CHI	AL	1	0	1	1	0	0	0	0	0	0	0	0	0	0	0	1

Rank among batters: 4,707 • *Total ballparks homered in*: 1 • *First HR*: 09/19/1951 off Bob Kuzava

Simon Nicholls

SIMON BURDETTE NICHOLLS
B: 07/18/1882 D: 03/12/1911
BL

Year	Tm	Lg	Tot	H	A	Men-On 0	1	2	3	One-Game 2	3	4	LO	XN	IP	PH	RHP	LHP
1908	PHI	AL	4	0	4	3	1	0	0	0	0	0	0	0	1	0	4	0

Rank among batters: 3,427 • *Total ballparks homered in*: 3 • *First HR*: 04/17/1908 off Al Orth

Art Nichols

ARTHUR FRANCIS NICHOLS
B: 07/14/1871 D: 08/09/1945
BR

Year	Tm	Lg	Tot	H	A	Men-On 0	1	2	3	One-Game 2	3	4	LO	XN	IP	PH	RHP	LHP
1899	CHI	NL	1	0	1	1	0	0	0	0	0	0	0	0	0	0	1	0
1901	STL	NL	1	0	1	1	0	0	0	0	0	0	0	0	1	0	1	0
1902	STL	NL	1	1	0	0	0	1	0	0	0	0	0	0	1	0	1	0
Total			3	1	2	2	0	1	0	0	0	0	0	0	2	0	3	0

Rank among batters: 3,735 • *Total ballparks homered in*: 3 • *First HR*: 06/08/1899 off Win Mercer

Kid Nichols

CHARLES AUGUSTUS NICHOLS
B: 09/14/1869 D: 04/11/1953
BB HOF

Year	Tm	Lg	Tot	H	A	Men-On 0	1	2	3	One-Game 2	3	4	LO	XN	IP	PH	RHP	LHP
1892	BOS	NL	2	1	1	1	0	0	1	0	0	0	0	0	0	0	2	0
1893	BOS	NL	2	0	2	0	2	0	0	0	0	0	0	0	0	0	2	0
1896	BOS	NL	1	0	1	0	0	1	0	0	0	0	0	0	0	0	1	0
1897	BOS	NL	3	1	2	0	2	1	0	0	0	0	0	0	0	0	3	0
1898	BOS	NL	2	2	0	1	1	0	0	0	0	0	0	0	0	0	1	1
1899	BOS	NL	1	1	0	1	0	0	0	0	0	0	0	0	0	0	1	0
1900	BOS	NL	1	1	0	0	1	0	0	0	0	0	0	0	0	0	1	0
1901	BOS	NL	4	3	1	3	1	0	0	0	0	0	0	0	1	0	3	1
Total			16	9	7	6	7	2	1	0	0	0	0	0	1	0	14	2

Rank among batters: 2,029 • *Total ballparks homered in*: 9 • *First HR*: 07/29/1892 off Gus Weyhing

Reid Nichols

THOMAS REID NICHOLS
B: 08/05/1958
BR

Year	Tm	Lg	Tot	H	A	Men-On 0	1	2	3	One-Game 2	3	4	LO	XN	IP	PH	RHP	LHP
1982	BOS	AL	7	1	6	3	3	1	0	1	0	0	0	1	0	0	5	2
1983	BOS	AL	6	3	3	4	2	0	0	0	0	0	0	0	0	0	2	4
1984	BOS	AL	1	1	0	0	0	1	0	0	0	0	0	0	0	1	0	1
1985	BOS	AL	1	0	1	1	0	0	0	0	0	0	0	0	0	0	0	1
	CHI	AL	1	0	1	0	1	0	0	0	0	0	0	0	0	0	0	1
	Total		2	0	2	1	1	0	0	0	0	0	0	0	0	0	0	2
1986	CHI	AL	2	2	0	2	0	0	0	0	0	0	0	0	0	0	2	0
1987	MON	NL	4	3	1	1	2	1	0	0	0	0	0	0	0	0	0	4
Total			22	10	12	11	8	3	0	1	0	0	0	1	0	1	9	13

Rank among batters: 1,719 • *Top target (2 home runs)*: Bill Caudill, Bill Krueger • *Number of pitchers victimized*: 20 • *Total ballparks homered in*: 10 • *First HR*: 05/28/1982 off Floyd Bannister

Bill Nicholson

WILLIAM BECK NICHOLSON
B: 12/11/1914
BL

Year	Tm	Lg	Tot	H	A	Men-On 0	1	2	3	One-Game 2	3	4	LO	XN	IP	PH	RHP	LHP
1939	CHI	NL	5	2	3	5	0	0	0	0	0	0	0	0	0	0	5	0
1940	CHI	NL	25	14	11	8	9	6	2	1	0	0	0	1	0	2	25	0
1941	CHI	NL	26	10	16	14	6	4	2	0	0	0	0	1	0	0	19	7
1942	CHI	NL	21	12	9	12	8	1	0	1	0	0	0	1	0	0	17	4
1943	CHI	NL	29	14	15	9	17	3	0	3	0	0	0	1	0	0	25	4
1944	CHI	NL	33	14	19	17	14	0	2	2	1	0	0	0	0	0	28	5
1945	CHI	NL	13	6	7	5	6	2	0	1	0	0	0	0	0	0	12	1

Bill Nicholson *continued*

						Men-On				One-Game								
Year	Tm	Lg	Tot	H	A	0	1	2	3	2	3	4	LO	XN	IP	PH	RHP	LHP
1946	CHI	NL	8	2	6	4	2	1	1	0	0	0	0	0	0	1	5	3
1947	CHI	NL	26	8	18	17	7	1	1	4	0	0	0	1	0	0	15	11
1948	CHI	NL	19	7	12	15	4	0	0	0	0	0	0	0	0	0	14	5
1949	PHI	NL	11	4	7	8	1	2	0	0	0	0	0	0	0	0	10	1
1950	PHI	NL	3	2	1	0	2	1	0	0	0	0	0	0	0	2	2	1
1951	PHI	NL	8	2	6	4	4	0	0	0	0	0	0	0	0	0	8	0
1952	PHI	NL	6	2	4	2	2	2	0	0	0	0	0	0	0	3	5	1
1953	PHI	NL	2	0	2	0	2	0	0	0	0	0	0	0	0	0	2	0
Total			235	99	136	120	84	23	8	12	1	0	0	5	0	8	192	43

Rank among batters: 135 • *Top target (7 home runs)*: Curt Davis, Bill Voiselle • *Number of pitchers victimized*: 135 • *Total ballparks homered in*: 8 • *First HR*: 08/01/1939 off Bill Kerksieck

Dave Nicholson

DAVID LAWRENCE NICHOLSON
B: 08/29/1939
BR

						Men-On				One-Game								
Year	Tm	Lg	Tot	H	A	0	1	2	3	2	3	4	LO	XN	IP	PH	RHP	LHP
1960	BAL	AL	5	1	4	4	0	1	0	0	0	0	0	0	0	0	1	4
1962	BAL	AL	9	2	7	7	2	0	0	1	0	0	0	0	0	0	5	4
1963	CHI	AL	22	15	7	11	8	1	2	1	0	0	0	1	0	0	9	13
1964	CHI	AL	13	7	6	6	3	4	0	1	0	0	0	0	0	1	8	5
1965	CHI	AL	2	1	1	1	1	0	0	0	0	0	0	0	0	0	1	1
1966	HOU	NL	10	7	3	7	2	1	0	1	0	0	0	0	0	0	2	8
Total			61	33	28	36	16	7	2	4	0	0	0	1	0	1	26	35

Rank among batters: 844 • *Top target (3 home runs)*: Don Mossi, Jim Kaat • *Number of pitchers victimized*: 48 • *Total ballparks homered in*: 13 • *First HR*: 06/25/1960 off Ken Johnson

Fred Nicholson

FRED NICHOLSON
B: 09/01/1894 D: 01/23/1972
BR

						Men-On				One-Game								
Year	Tm	Lg	Tot	H	A	0	1	2	3	2	3	4	LO	XN	IP	PH	RHP	LHP
1919	PIT	NL	1	0	1	1	0	0	0	0	0	0	1	0	0	0	1	0
1920	PIT	NL	4	1	3	1	3	0	0	0	0	0	0	0	0	2	4	0
1921	BOS	NL	5	1	4	3	2	0	0	0	0	0	0	1	1	1	1	4
1922	BOS	NL	2	0	2	2	0	0	0	1	0	0	0	0	1	0	0	2
Total			12	2	10	7	5	0	0	1	0	0	1	1	2	3	6	6

Rank among batters: 2,325 • Top target (2 home runs): Ferdie Schupp, Art Nehf, Bill Sherdel, Eppa Rixey • *Number of pitchers victimized*: 8 • *Total ballparks homered in*: 7 • *First HR*: 09/26/1919 off Ferdie Schupp

Parson Nicholson

THOMAS C. NICHOLSON
B: 04/14/1863 D: 02/28/1917

						Men-On				One-Game								
Year	Tm	Lg	Tot	H	A	0	1	2	3	2	3	4	LO	XN	IP	PH	RHP	LHP
1888	DET	NL	1	0	1	0	1	0	0	0	0	0	0	0	0	0	1	0
1890	TOL	AA	4	3	1	1	3	0	0	0	0	0	0	0	0	0	1	1
Total			5	3	2	1	4	0	0	0	0	0	0	0	0	0	2	1

Rank among batters: 3,191 • *Top target (2 home runs)*: Charlie McCullough • *Number of pitchers victimized*: 4 • *Total ballparks homered in*: 3 • *First HR*: 10/13/1888 off Hank O'Day

Hugh Nicol

HUGH N. NICOL
B: 01/01/1858 D: 06/27/1921
BR

						Men-On				One-Game								
Year	Tm	Lg	Tot	H	A	0	1	2	3	2	3	4	LO	XN	IP	PH	RHP	LHP
1882	CHI	NL	1	0	1	1	0	0	0	0	0	0	0	0	0	0	1	0
1887	CIN	AA	1	1	0	1	0	0	0	0	0	0	0	0	0	0	1	0
1888	CIN	AA	1	1	0	0	1	0	0	0	0	0	0	0	0	0	1	0
1889	CIN	AA	2	2	0	1	1	0	0	0	0	0	0	0	0	0	2	0
Total			5	4	1	3	2	0	0	0	0	0	0	0	0	0	5	0

Rank among batters: 3,191 • *Total ballparks homered in*: 2 • *First HR*: 06/09/1882 off Monte Ward

Steve Nicosia

STEVEN RICHARD NICOSIA
B: 08/06/1955
BR

						Men-On				One-Game								
Year	Tm	Lg	Tot	H	A	0	1	2	3	2	3	4	LO	XN	IP	PH	RHP	LHP
1979	PIT	NL	4	2	2	4	0	0	0	0	0	0	0	0	0	0	0	4

Steve Nicosia *continued*

Year	Tm	Lg	Tot	H	A	Men-On				One-Game			LO	XN	IP	PH	RHP	LHP
						0	1	2	3	2	3	4						
1980	PIT	NL	1	1	0	0	1	0	0	0	0	0	0	0	0	0	0	1
1981	PIT	NL	2	2	0	2	0	0	0	0	0	0	0	0	0	0	2	0
1982	PIT	NL	1	1	0	1	0	0	0	0	0	0	0	0	0	0	0	1
1983	PIT	NL	1	0	1	1	0	0	0	0	0	0	0	0	0	0	0	1
1984	SF	NL	2	2	0	1	1	0	0	0	0	0	0	0	0	0	0	2
Total			11	8	3	9	2	0	0	0	0	0	0	0	0	0	2	9

Rank among batters: 2,419 • *Total ballparks homered in*: 5 • *First HR*: 04/07/1979 off Ross Grimsley

Bert Niehoff

JOHN ALBERT NIEHOFF
B: 05/13/1884 D: 12/08/1974
BR

Year	Tm	Lg	Tot	H	A	Men-On				One-Game			LO	XN	IP	PH	RHP	LHP
						0	1	2	3	2	3	4						
1914	CIN	NL	4	1	3	2	2	0	0	0	0	0	0	0	1	0	2	2
1915	PHI	NL	2	2	0	2	0	0	0	0	0	0	0	0	0	0	2	0
1916	PHI	NL	4	3	1	2	1	1	0	0	0	0	0	1	0	0	2	2
1917	PHI	NL	2	2	0	2	0	0	0	0	0	0	0	0	0	0	2	0
Total			12	8	4	8	3	1	0	0	0	0	0	1	1	0	8	4

Rank among batters: 2,325 • *Total ballparks homered in*: 5 • *First HR*: 04/22/1914 off George Pearce

Joe Niekro

JOSEPH FRANKLIN NIEKRO
B: 11/07/1944
BR

Year	Tm	Lg	Tot	H	A	Men-On				One-Game			LO	XN	IP	PH	RHP	LHP
						0	1	2	3	2	3	4						
1976	HOU	NL	1	0	1	1	0	0	0	0	0	0	0	0	0	0	1	0

Rank among batters: 4,707 • *Total ballparks homered in*: 1 • *First HR*: 05/29/1976 off Phil Niekro

Phil Niekro

PHILIP HENRY NIEKRO
B: 04/01/1939
BR

Year	Tm	Lg	Tot	H	A	Men-On				One-Game			LO	XN	IP	PH	RHP	LHP
						0	1	2	3	2	3	4						
1968	ATL	NL	2	1	1	1	0	1	0	0	0	0	0	0	0	0	2	0
1970	ATL	NL	1	1	0	1	0	0	0	0	0	0	0	0	0	0	1	0
1972	ATL	NL	1	0	1	1	0	0	0	0	0	0	0	0	0	0	0	1
1973	ATL	NL	1	0	1	1	0	0	0	0	0	0	0	0	0	0	1	0
1976	ATL	NL	1	1	0	0	0	1	0	0	0	0	0	0	0	0	1	0
1982	ATL	NL	1	0	1	0	1	0	0	0	0	0	0	0	0	0	1	0
Total			7	3	4	4	1	2	0	0	0	0	0	0	0	0	6	1

Rank among batters: 2,834 • *Total ballparks homered in*: 5 • *First HR*: 04/12/1968 off John Tsitouris

Bob Nieman

ROBERT CHARLES NIEMAN
B: 01/26/1927 D: 03/10/1985
BR

Year	Tm	Lg	Tot	H	A	Men-On				One-Game			LO	XN	IP	PH	RHP	LHP
						0	1	2	3	2	3	4						
1951	STL	AL	2	0	2	1	1	0	0	1	0	0	0	0	0	0	0	2
1952	STL	AL	18	12	6	12	4	2	0	1	0	0	0	0	0	0	9	9
1953	DET	AL	15	12	3	11	4	0	0	0	0	0	0	1	0	0	12	3
1954	DET	AL	8	5	3	4	2	1	1	0	0	0	0	0	0	1	7	1
1955	CHI	AL	11	6	5	4	4	2	1	1	0	0	0	0	0	0	6	5
1956	CHI	AL	2	1	1	2	0	0	0	0	0	0	0	0	0	0	0	2
	BAL	AL	12	6	6	5	4	3	0	0	0	0	0	1	1	0	9	3
	Total		14	7	7	7	4	3	0	0	0	0	0	1	1	0	9	5
1957	BAL	AL	13	3	10	10	2	1	0	0	0	0	0	1	0	0	10	3
1958	BAL	AL	16	2	14	8	7	1	0	2	0	0	0	0	0	0	11	5
1959	BAL	AL	21	10	11	14	6	1	0	2	0	0	0	0	0	0	10	11
1960	STL	NL	4	4	0	4	0	0	0	0	0	0	0	0	0	1	1	3
1961	CLE	AL	2	0	2	2	0	0	0	0	0	0	0	0	0	1	0	2
1962	SF	NL	1	1	0	1	0	0	0	0	0	0	0	0	0	1	0	1
Total			125	62	63	78	34	11	2	7	0	0	0	3	1	4	75	50

Rank among batters: 366 • Top target (4 home runs): Bobby Shantz, Mickey McDermott, Tom Gorman, Ray Narleski • *Number of pitchers victimized*: 82 • *Total ballparks homered in*: 12 • *First HR*: 09/13/1951 off Mickey McDermott • *Hit HR in first major league AB*—@BOS: 09/13/1951

Butch Nieman

ELMER LEROY NIEMAN
B: 02/08/1918 D: 11/02/1993
BL

Year	Tm	Lg	Tot	H	A	Men-On 0	1	2	3	One-Game 2	3	4	LO	XN	IP	PH	RHP	LHP
1943	BOS	NL	7	5	2	1	5	1	0	0	0	0	0	2	0	0	6	1
1944	BOS	NL	16	12	4	10	4	2	0	4	0	0	0	1	0	0	16	0
1945	BOS	NL	14	9	5	3	4	6	1	0	0	0	0	1	0	5	13	1
Total			37	26	11	14	13	9	1	4	0	0	0	4	0	5	35	2

Rank among batters: 1,252 • *Top target (4 home runs)*: Ray Starr • *Number of pitchers victimized*: 29 • *Total ballparks homered in*: 5 • *First HR*: 07/30/1943 off Ray Starr

Al Niemiec

ALFRED JOSEPH NIEMIEC
B: 05/18/1911
BR

Year	Tm	Lg	Tot	H	A	Men-On 0	1	2	3	One-Game 2	3	4	LO	XN	IP	PH	RHP	LHP
1936	PHI	AL	1	1	0	1	0	0	0	0	0	0	0	0	0	0	1	0

Rank among batters: 4,707 • *Total ballparks homered in*: 1 • *First HR*: 08/14/1936 off Red Ruffing

Tom Nieto

THOMAS ANDREW NIETO
B: 10/27/1960
BR

Year	Tm	Lg	Tot	H	A	Men-On 0	1	2	3	One-Game 2	3	4	LO	XN	IP	PH	RHP	LHP
1984	STL	NL	3	2	1	0	2	1	0	0	0	0	0	0	1	0	1	2
1986	MON	NL	1	1	0	1	0	0	0	0	0	0	0	1	0	0	1	0
1987	MIN	AL	1	0	1	0	0	1	0	0	0	0	0	0	0	0	0	1
Total			5	3	2	1	2	2	0	0	0	0	0	1	1	0	2	3

Rank among batters: 3,191 • *Total ballparks homered in*: 4 • *First HR*: 05/11/1984 off Jeff Russell

Melvin Nieves

MELVIN (RAMOS) NIEVES
B: 12/28/1971
BB

Year	Tm	Lg	Tot	H	A	Men-On 0	1	2	3	One-Game 2	3	4	LO	XN	IP	PH	RHP	LHP
1993	SD	NL	2	2	0	2	0	0	0	0	0	0	0	0	0	0	1	1
1994	SD	NL	1	0	1	1	0	0	0	0	0	0	0	0	0	0	0	1
1995	SD	NL	14	5	9	9	3	0	2	0	0	0	0	2	0	1	9	5
Total			17	7	10	12	3	0	2	0	0	0	0	2	0	1	10	7

Rank among batters: 1,969 • *Top target (2 home runs)*: Mike Munoz • *Number of pitchers victimized*: 16 • *Total ballparks homered in*: 9 • *First HR*: 09/08/1993 off Chris Hammond

Harry Niles

HERBERT CLYDE NILES
B: 09/10/1880 D: 04/18/1953
BR

Year	Tm	Lg	Tot	H	A	Men-On 0	1	2	3	One-Game 2	3	4	LO	XN	IP	PH	RHP	LHP
1906	STL	AL	2	2	0	0	2	0	0	0	0	0	0	0	2	0	2	0
1907	STL	AL	2	1	1	1	0	1	0	0	0	0	0	0	2	0	1	1
1908	NY	AL	4	4	0	3	1	0	0	0	0	0	0	0	4	0	3	1
	BOS	AL	1	1	0	0	1	0	0	0	0	0	0	0	1	0	1	0
	Total		5	5	0	3	2	0	0	0	0	0	0	0	5	0	4	1
1909	BOS	AL	1	1	0	0	1	0	0	0	0	0	0	0	1	0	1	0
1910	BOS	AL	1	1	0	1	0	0	0	0	0	0	0	0	1	0	1	0
	CLE	AL	1	0	1	0	1	0	0	0	0	0	0	0	1	0	1	0
	Total		2	1	1	1	1	0	0	0	0	0	0	0	2	0	2	0
Total			12	10	2	5	6	1	0	0	0	0	0	0	12	0	10	2

Rank among batters: 2,325 • *Top target (2 home runs)*: George Winter, George Mullin • *Number of pitchers victimized*: 10 • *Total ballparks homered in*: 3 • *First HR*: 06/17/1906 off Tom Hughes

Rabbit Nill

GEORGE CHARLES NILL
B: 07/14/1881 D: 05/24/1962
BR

Year	Tm	Lg	Tot	H	A	Men-On 0	1	2	3	One-Game 2	3	4	LO	XN	IP	PH	RHP	LHP
1905	WAS	AL	3	1	2	2	1	0	0	0	0	0	0	0	1	0	3	0

Rank among batters: 3,735 • *Total ballparks homered in*: 3 • *First HR*: 08/23/1905 off Bill Donovan

Dave Nilsson

DAVID WAYNE NILSSON
B: 12/14/1969
BL

Year	Tm	Lg	Tot	H	A	Men-On 0	1	2	3	One-Game 2	3	4	LO	XN	IP	PH	RHP	LHP
1992	MIL	AL	4	1	3	2	2	0	0	0	0	0	0	0	0	0	4	0

Dave Nilsson *continued*

Year	Tm	Lg	Tot	H	A	Men-On 0	1	2	3	One-Game 2	3	4	LO	XN	IP	PH	RHP	LHP
1993	MIL	AL	7	5	2	4	3	0	0	0	0	0	0	1	0	0	5	2
1994	MIL	AL	12	4	8	6	2	3	1	0	0	0	0	0	0	0	10	2
1995	MIL	AL	12	7	5	4	5	2	1	0	0	0	0	0	0	0	10	2
Total			35	17	18	16	12	5	2	0	0	0	0	1	0	0	29	6

Rank among batters: 1,291 • *Top target (2 home runs)*: Alex Fernandez, Dave Stewart • *Number of pitchers victimized*: 33 • *Total ballparks homered in*: 13 • *First HR*: 05/22/1992 off Melido Perez

Al Nixon

ALBERT RICHARD NIXON
B: 04/11/1886 D: 11/09/1960
BR

Year	Tm	Lg	Tot	H	A	Men-On 0	1	2	3	One-Game 2	3	4	LO	XN	IP	PH	RHP	LHP
1921	BOS	NL	1	0	1	0	1	0	0	0	0	0	0	0	0	0	0	1
1922	BOS	NL	2	0	2	0	1	1	0	0	0	0	0	0	1	0	1	1
1926	PHI	NL	4	2	2	2	2	0	0	1	0	0	0	1	0	0	1	3
Total			7	2	5	2	4	1	0	1	0	0	0	1	1	0	2	5

Rank among batters: 2,834 • *Top target (2 home runs)*: Eppa Rixey • *Number of pitchers victimized*: 6 • *Total ballparks homered in*: 5 • *First HR*: 09/20/1921 off Bill Sherdel

Donell Nixon

ROBERT DONELL NIXON
B: 12/31/1961
BR

Year	Tm	Lg	Tot	H	A	Men-On 0	1	2	3	One-Game 2	3	4	LO	XN	IP	PH	RHP	LHP
1987	SEA	AL	3	2	1	2	0	1	0	0	0	0	1	0	0	0	2	1
1989	SF	NL	1	0	1	1	0	0	0	0	0	0	0	0	0	0	1	0
Total			4	2	2	3	0	1	0	0	0	0	1	0	0	0	3	1

Rank among batters: 3,427 • *Total ballparks homered in*: 3 • *First HR*: 07/24/1987 off Bruce Hurst

Otis Nixon

OTIS JUNIOR NIXON
B: 01/09/1959
BB

Year	Tm	Lg	Tot	H	A	Men-On 0	1	2	3	One-Game 2	3	4	LO	XN	IP	PH	RHP	LHP
1985	CLE	AL	3	1	2	2	1	0	0	0	0	0	2	0	0	0	2	1
1990	MON	NL	1	0	1	1	0	0	0	0	0	0	0	0	0	0	0	1
1992	ATL	NL	2	1	1	0	2	0	0	0	0	0	0	0	0	0	0	2
1993	ATL	NL	1	1	0	1	0	0	0	0	0	0	1	0	0	0	0	1
Total			7	3	4	4	3	0	0	0	0	0	3	0	0	0	2	5

Rank among batters: 2,834 • *Top target (2 home runs)*: Trevor Wilson • *Number of pitchers victimized*: 6 • *Total ballparks homered in*: 6 • *First HR*: 07/20/1985 off Floyd Bannister

Russ Nixon

RUSSELL EUGENE NIXON
B: 02/19/1935
BL

Year	Tm	Lg	Tot	H	A	Men-On 0	1	2	3	One-Game 2	3	4	LO	XN	IP	PH	RHP	LHP
1957	CLE	AL	2	0	2	0	1	1	0	0	0	0	0	0	0	0	2	0
1958	CLE	AL	9	7	2	7	2	0	0	1	0	0	0	0	0	0	9	0
1959	CLE	AL	1	0	1	0	0	1	0	0	0	0	0	0	0	0	1	0
1960	CLE	AL	1	0	1	1	0	0	0	0	0	0	0	1	0	0	1	0
	BOS	AL	5	1	4	2	3	0	0	0	0	0	0	0	0	0	5	0
	Total		6	1	5	3	3	0	0	0	0	0	0	1	0	0	6	0
1961	BOS	AL	1	0	1	0	1	0	0	0	0	0	0	0	0	0	1	0
1962	BOS	AL	1	0	1	1	0	0	0	0	0	0	0	0	0	0	1	0
1963	BOS	AL	5	3	2	3	1	1	0	1	0	0	0	0	0	0	5	0
1964	BOS	AL	1	1	0	0	1	0	0	0	0	0	0	0	0	1	0	1
1967	MIN	AL	1	0	1	1	0	0	0	0	0	0	0	0	0	0	0	1
Total			27	12	15	15	9	3	0	2	0	0	0	1	0	1	25	2

Rank among batters: 1,532 • *Top target (5 home runs)*: Jim Bunning • *Number of pitchers victimized*: 20 • *Total ballparks homered in*: 8 • *First HR*: 06/25/1957 off Tom Sturdivant

Willard Nixon

WILLARD LEE NIXON
B: 06/17/1928
BL

Year	Tm	Lg	Tot	H	A	Men-On 0	1	2	3	One-Game 2	3	4	LO	XN	IP	PH	RHP	LHP
1951	BOS	AL	1	0	1	1	0	0	0	0	0	0	0	0	0	0	1	0

Willard Nixon *continued*

Year	Tm	Lg	Tot	H	A	Men-On				One-Game			LO	XN	IP	PH	RHP	LHP
						0	1	2	3	2	3	4						
1954	BOS	AL	1	0	1	1	0	0	0	0	0	0	0	0	0	0	1	0
Total			2	0	2	2	0	0	0	0	0	0	0	0	0	0	2	0

Rank among batters: 4,129 • *Total ballparks homered in*: 2 • *First HR*: 05/07/1951 off Ned Garver

Ray Noble

RAFAEL MIGUEL (MAGEE) NOBLE
B: 03/15/1919
BR

Year	Tm	Lg	Tot	H	A	Men-On				One-Game			LO	XN	IP	PH	RHP	LHP
						0	1	2	3	2	3	4						
1951	NY	NL	5	5	0	3	2	0	0	1	0	0	0	0	0	1	1	4
1953	NY	NL	4	3	1	2	0	2	0	0	0	0	0	0	0	0	3	1
Total			9	8	1	5	2	2	0	1	0	0	0	0	0	1	4	5

Rank among batters: 2,587 • *Total ballparks homered in*: 2 • *First HR*: 04/27/1951 off Warren Spahn

Junior Noboa

MILCIADES ARTURO (DIAZ) NOBOA
B: 11/10/1964
BR

Year	Tm	Lg	Tot	H	A	Men-On				One-Game			LO	XN	IP	PH	RHP	LHP
						0	1	2	3	2	3	4						
1991	MON	NL	1	0	1	1	0	0	0	0	0	0	0	0	0	1	0	1

Rank among batters: 4,707 • *Total ballparks homered in*: 1 • *First HR*: 05/24/1991 off Paul Assenmacher

Paul Noce

PAUL DAVID NOCE
B: 12/16/1959
BR

Year	Tm	Lg	Tot	H	A	Men-On				One-Game			LO	XN	IP	PH	RHP	LHP
						0	1	2	3	2	3	4						
1987	CHI	NL	3	3	0	2	0	1	0	0	0	0	0	0	0	0	3	0

Rank among batters: 3,735 • *Total ballparks homered in*: 1 • *First HR*: 07/03/1987 off Kelly Downs

Matt Nokes

MATTHEW DODGE NOKES
B: 10/31/1963
BL

Year	Tm	Lg	Tot	H	A	Men-On				One-Game			LO	XN	IP	PH	RHP	LHP
						0	1	2	3	2	3	4						
1985	SF	NL	2	1	1	0	2	0	0	0	0	0	0	0	0	0	2	0
1986	DET	AL	1	0	1	1	0	0	0	0	0	0	0	0	0	0	1	0
1987	DET	AL	32	14	18	20	8	2	2	3	0	0	0	0	0	0	28	4
1988	DET	AL	16	9	7	10	4	2	0	2	0	0	0	0	0	0	14	2
1989	DET	AL	9	7	2	2	5	1	1	0	0	0	0	0	0	0	7	2
1990	DET	AL	3	1	2	3	0	0	0	0	0	0	0	0	0	0	3	0
	NY	AL	8	3	5	5	1	2	0	0	0	0	0	0	0	2	8	0
	Total		11	4	7	8	1	2	0	0	0	0	0	0	0	2	11	0
1991	NY	AL	24	13	11	11	9	3	1	5	0	0	0	0	0	0	18	6
1992	NY	AL	22	18	4	10	7	4	1	1	0	0	0	0	0	1	17	5
1993	NY	AL	10	4	6	5	3	2	0	2	0	0	0	1	0	2	8	2
1994	NY	AL	7	6	1	3	3	0	1	2	0	0	0	0	0	0	6	1
1995	BAL	AL	2	1	1	0	1	1	0	0	0	0	0	0	0	0	2	0
Total			136	77	59	70	43	17	6	15	0	0	0	1	0	5	114	22

Rank among batters: 322 • *Top target (7 home runs)*: Todd Stottlemyre • *Number of pitchers victimized*: 102 • *Total ballparks homered in*: 19 • *First HR*: 09/09/1985 off Mike Scott • *LCS HR*—1

Gary Nolan

GARY LYNN NOLAN
B: 05/27/1948
BR

Year	Tm	Lg	Tot	H	A	Men-On				One-Game			LO	XN	IP	PH	RHP	LHP
						0	1	2	3	2	3	4						
1968	CIN	NL	1	0	1	0	0	1	0	0	0	0	0	0	0	0	0	1

Rank among batters: 4,707 • *Total ballparks homered in*: 1 • *First HR*: 06/29/1968 off Ray Sadecki

Joe Nolan

JOSEPH WILLIAM NOLAN
B: 05/12/1951
BL

Year	Tm	Lg	Tot	H	A	Men-On				One-Game			LO	XN	IP	PH	RHP	LHP
						0	1	2	3	2	3	4						
1977	ATL	NL	3	1	2	3	0	0	0	0	0	0	0	0	0	2	3	0

Year	Tm	Lg	Tot	H	A	Men-On 0	1	2	3	One-Game 2	3	4	LO	XN	IP	PH	RHP	LHP

Joe Nolan *continued*

Year	Tm	Lg	Tot	H	A	0	1	2	3	2	3	4	LO	XN	IP	PH	RHP	LHP
1978	ATL	NL	4	3	1	3	1	0	0	1	0	0	0	0	0	0	4	0
1979	ATL	NL	4	2	2	2	2	0	0	0	0	0	0	0	0	0	4	0
1980	CIN	NL	3	3	0	3	0	0	0	0	0	0	0	0	0	0	3	0
1981	CIN	NL	1	1	0	1	0	0	0	0	0	0	0	0	0	0	1	0
1982	BAL	AL	6	3	3	3	1	1	1	0	0	0	0	2	0	1	6	0
1983	BAL	AL	5	2	3	3	1	0	1	0	0	0	0	0	0	0	4	1
1984	BAL	AL	1	0	1	1	0	0	0	0	0	0	0	0	0	1	1	0
Total			27	15	12	19	5	1	2	1	0	0	0	2	0	4	26	1

Rank among batters: 1,532 • *Top target (3 home runs)*: Steve Rogers • *Number of pitchers victimized*: 23 • *Total ballparks homered in*: 12 • *First HR*: 07/24/1977 off Bruce Kison

Pete Noonan

PETER JOHN NOONAN
B: 11/24/1881 D: 02/11/1965
BR

Year	Tm	Lg	Tot	H	A	0	1	2	3	2	3	4	LO	XN	IP	PH	RHP	LHP
1904	PHI	AL	2	1	1	1	1	0	0	0	0	0	0	0	0	0	2	0
1906	STL	NL	1	1	0	1	0	0	0	0	0	0	0	0	0	0	1	0
1907	STL	NL	1	0	1	0	1	0	0	0	0	0	0	0	0	0	1	0
Total			4	2	2	2	2	0	0	0	0	0	0	0	0	0	4	0

Rank among batters: 3,427 • *Total ballparks homered in*: 4 • *First HR*: 09/15/1904 off Tom Hughes

Wayne Nordhagen

WAYNE OREN NORDHAGEN
B: 07/04/1948
BR

Year	Tm	Lg	Tot	H	A	0	1	2	3	2	3	4	LO	XN	IP	PH	RHP	LHP
1977	CHI	AL	4	1	3	1	2	1	0	1	0	0	0	0	0	0	1	3
1978	CHI	AL	5	3	2	2	2	1	0	0	0	0	0	0	0	2	2	3
1979	CHI	AL	7	4	3	6	0	0	1	1	0	0	0	0	0	0	1	6
1980	CHI	AL	15	10	5	11	2	2	0	1	0	0	0	0	0	0	6	9
1981	CHI	AL	6	3	3	4	2	0	0	0	0	0	0	0	1	0	5	1
1982	TOR	AL	1	1	0	0	1	0	0	0	0	0	0	0	0	0	0	1
1983	CHI	NL	1	0	1	1	0	0	0	0	0	0	0	0	0	0	0	1
Total			39	22	17	25	9	4	1	3	0	0	0	0	1	2	15	24

Rank among batters: 1,204 • *Top target (3 home runs)*: Rick Honeycutt, Paul Splittorff • *Number of pitchers victimized*: 31 • *Total ballparks homered in*: 12 • *First HR*: 08/25/1977 off Rudy May

Irv Noren

IRVING ARNOLD NOREN
B: 11/29/1924
BL

Year	Tm	Lg	Tot	H	A	0	1	2	3	2	3	4	LO	XN	IP	PH	RHP	LHP
1950	WAS	AL	14	6	8	4	7	3	0	1	0	0	0	0	0	0	10	4
1951	WAS	AL	8	4	4	4	4	0	0	1	0	0	0	0	1	0	7	1
1952	NY	AL	5	2	3	3	2	0	0	0	0	0	0	0	0	0	3	2
1953	NY	AL	6	2	4	2	2	2	0	0	0	0	0	0	0	1	5	1
1954	NY	AL	12	8	4	9	3	0	0	1	0	0	0	0	0	1	12	0
1955	NY	AL	8	5	3	4	3	0	1	1	0	0	0	2	1	0	8	0
1957	KC	AL	2	2	0	1	1	0	0	1	0	0	0	0	0	0	2	0
	STL	NL	1	0	1	1	0	0	0	0	0	0	0	0	0	0	1	0
	Total		3	2	1	2	1	0	0	1	0	0	0	0	0	0	3	0
1958	STL	NL	4	0	4	4	0	0	0	0	0	0	0	0	0	1	4	0
1959	CHI	NL	4	3	1	4	0	0	0	0	0	0	0	0	0	0	4	0
1960	LA	NL	1	1	0	1	0	0	0	0	0	0	0	0	0	1	1	0
Total			65	33	32	37	22	5	1	5	0	0	0	2	2	4	57	8

Rank among batters: 799 • *Top target (4 home runs)*: Joe Coleman • *Number of pitchers victimized*: 46 • *Total ballparks homered in*: 13 • *First HR*: 04/28/1950 off Joe Page

Dan Norman

DANIEL EDMUND NORMAN
B: 01/11/1955
BR

Year	Tm	Lg	Tot	H	A	0	1	2	3	2	3	4	LO	XN	IP	PH	RHP	LHP
1978	NY	NL	4	1	3	3	1	0	0	1	0	0	0	0	0	0	1	3
1979	NY	NL	3	0	3	1	1	1	0	0	0	0	0	0	0	1	1	2
1980	NY	NL	2	1	1	2	0	0	0	0	0	0	0	0	0	2	1	1

Year	Tm	Lg	Tot	H	A	Men-On 0	Men-On 1	Men-On 2	Men-On 3	One-Game 2	One-Game 3	One-Game 4	LO	XN	IP	PH	RHP	LHP

Dan Norman *continued*

Year	Tm	Lg	Tot	H	A	0	1	2	3	2	3	4	LO	XN	IP	PH	RHP	LHP
1982	MON	NL	2	2	0	2	0	0	0	0	0	0	0	0	0	0	0	2
Total			11	4	7	8	2	1	0	1	0	0	0	0	0	3	3	8

Rank among batters: 2,419 • *Top target (3 home runs)*: John Candelaria • *Number of pitchers victimized*: 9 • *Total ballparks homered in*: 6 • *First HR*: 09/06/1978 off Ross Grimsley

Jim Norris

JAMES FRANCIS NORRIS
B: 12/20/1948
BL

Year	Tm	Lg	Tot	H	A	0	1	2	3	2	3	4	LO	XN	IP	PH	RHP	LHP
1977	CLE	AL	2	0	2	0	2	0	0	0	0	0	0	0	0	0	2	0
1978	CLE	AL	2	0	2	2	0	0	0	0	0	0	0	0	0	0	2	0
1979	CLE	AL	3	2	1	1	1	1	0	1	0	0	1	0	0	0	3	0
Total			7	2	5	3	3	1	0	1	0	0	1	0	0	0	7	0

Rank among batters: 2,834 • *Top target (2 home runs)*: Dennis Eckersley, Jack Morris • *Number of pitchers victimized*: 5 • *Total ballparks homered in*: 4 • *First HR*: 04/10/1977 off Reggie Cleveland

Leo Norris

LEO JOHN NORRIS
B: 05/17/1908 D: 02/13/1987
BR

Year	Tm	Lg	Tot	H	A	0	1	2	3	2	3	4	LO	XN	IP	PH	RHP	LHP
1936	PHI	NL	11	6	5	4	2	5	0	0	0	0	0	0	0	0	9	2
1937	PHI	NL	9	7	2	8	1	0	0	0	0	0	2	0	0	0	7	2
Total			20	13	7	12	3	5	0	0	0	0	2	0	0	0	16	4

Rank among batters: 1,810 • *Top target (3 home runs)*: Dizzy Dean • *Number of pitchers victimized*: 16 • *Total ballparks homered in*: 6 • *First HR*: 04/23/1936 off Bob Brown

Bill North

WILLIAM ALEX NORTH
B: 05/15/1948
BB

Year	Tm	Lg	Tot	H	A	0	1	2	3	2	3	4	LO	XN	IP	PH	RHP	LHP
1973	OAK	AL	5	0	5	5	0	0	0	0	0	0	0	0	0	0	1	4
1974	OAK	AL	4	1	3	3	1	0	0	0	0	0	0	0	0	0	0	4
1975	OAK	AL	1	1	0	1	0	0	0	0	0	0	0	0	0	0	0	1
1976	OAK	AL	2	2	0	2	0	0	0	0	0	0	1	0	0	0	0	2
1977	OAK	AL	1	0	1	1	0	0	0	0	0	0	0	0	0	0	0	1
1979	SF	NL	5	5	0	5	0	0	0	0	0	0	4	0	0	0	0	5
1980	SF	NL	1	0	1	1	0	0	0	0	0	0	0	0	0	0	1	0
1981	SF	NL	1	0	1	0	0	0	1	0	0	0	0	0	0	0	1	0
Total			20	9	11	18	1	0	1	0	0	0	5	0	0	0	3	17

Rank among batters: 1,810 • *Top target (2 home runs)*: Frank Tanana, Ross Grimsley • *Number of pitchers victimized*: 18 • *Total ballparks homered in*: 11 • *First HR*: 05/17/1973 off Rudy May

Lou North

LOUIS ALEXANDER NORTH
B: 06/15/1891 D: 05/16/1974
BR

Year	Tm	Lg	Tot	H	A	0	1	2	3	2	3	4	LO	XN	IP	PH	RHP	LHP
1922	STL	NL	1	0	1	1	0	0	0	0	0	0	0	0	0	0	1	0

Rank among batters: 4,707 • *Total ballparks homered in*: 1 • *First HR*: 09/13/1922 off Bill Hubbell

Hub Northen

HUBBARD ELWIN NORTHEN
B: 08/16/1885 D: 10/01/1947
BL

Year	Tm	Lg	Tot	H	A	0	1	2	3	2	3	4	LO	XN	IP	PH	RHP	LHP
1912	BRO	NL	3	0	3	0	3	0	0	0	0	0	0	0	0	0	3	0

Rank among batters: 3,735 • *Total ballparks homered in*: 3 • *First HR*: 06/25/1912 off Hub Perdue

Ron Northey

RONALD JAMES NORTHEY
B: 04/26/1920 D: 04/16/1971
BL

Year	Tm	Lg	Tot	H	A	0	1	2	3	2	3	4	LO	XN	IP	PH	RHP	LHP
1942	PHI	NL	5	2	3	5	0	0	0	0	0	0	0	0	2	0	4	1

Ron Northey *continued*

Year	Tm	Lg	Tot	H	A	Men-On 0	1	2	3	One-Game 2	3	4	LO	XN	IP	PH	RHP	LHP
1943	PHI	NL	16	8	8	13	3	0	0	1	0	0	0	1	0	0	16	0
1944	PHI	NL	22	7	15	13	8	0	1	1	0	0	0	1	0	0	19	3
1946	PHI	NL	16	5	11	8	5	2	1	1	0	0	0	0	0	0	16	0
1947	STL	NL	15	7	8	8	5	1	1	1	0	0	0	0	0	2	13	2
1948	STL	NL	13	6	7	7	3	1	2	0	0	0	0	0	0	1	13	0
1949	STL	NL	7	4	3	4	0	1	2	0	0	0	0	0	0	0	7	0
1950	CIN	NL	5	4	1	4	1	0	0	0	0	0	0	0	0	0	3	2
	CHI	NL	4	2	2	1	1	1	1	0	0	0	0	0	0	1	2	2
	Total		9	6	3	5	2	1	1	0	0	0	0	0	0	1	5	4
1955	CHI	AL	1	0	1	0	1	0	0	0	0	0	0	0	0	1	1	0
1956	CHI	AL	3	1	2	0	2	1	0	0	0	0	0	0	0	3	3	0
1957	PHI	NL	1	0	1	0	1	0	0	0	0	0	0	0	0	1	1	0
Total			108	46	62	63	30	7	8	4	0	0	0	2	2	9	98	10

Rank among batters: 443 • *Top target (6 home runs)*: Bill Voiselle • *Number of pitchers victimized*: 72 • *Total ballparks homered in*: 12 • *First HR*: 04/18/1942 off Hugh Casey

Scott Northey

SCOTT RICHARD NORTHEY
B: 10/15/1946
BR

Year	Tm	Lg	Tot	H	A	Men-On 0	1	2	3	One-Game 2	3	4	LO	XN	IP	PH	RHP	LHP
1969	KC	AL	1	0	1	0	0	1	0	0	0	0	0	0	0	0	0	1

Rank among batters: 4,707 • *Total ballparks homered in*: 1 • *First HR*: 09/28/1969 off Gary Peters

Jim Northrup

JAMES THOMAS NORTHRUP
B: 11/24/1939
BL

Year	Tm	Lg	Tot	H	A	Men-On 0	1	2	3	One-Game 2	3	4	LO	XN	IP	PH	RHP	LHP
1965	DET	AL	2	2	0	1	1	0	0	0	0	0	0	1	0	1	2	0
1966	DET	AL	16	10	6	7	6	2	1	0	0	0	0	0	0	1	12	4
1967	DET	AL	10	7	3	3	4	1	2	0	0	0	0	0	0	0	8	2
1968	DET	AL	21	10	11	8	8	1	4	5	0	0	0	0	0	0	17	4
1969	DET	AL	25	13	12	15	9	1	0	1	0	0	0	1	0	0	16	9
1970	DET	AL	24	13	11	11	9	3	1	2	0	0	0	0	0	0	17	7
1971	DET	AL	16	9	7	12	0	4	0	2	0	0	0	2	0	0	15	1
1972	DET	AL	8	5	3	5	3	0	0	0	0	0	0	0	0	0	8	0
1973	DET	AL	12	9	3	9	1	2	0	2	0	0	2	0	0	0	10	2
1974	DET	AL	11	9	2	7	2	2	0	1	0	0	0	0	0	0	10	1
	MON	NL	2	0	2	1	1	0	0	0	0	0	0	0	0	0	2	0
	BAL	AL	1	0	1	0	1	0	0	0	0	0	0	0	0	1	1	0
	Total		14	9	5	8	4	2	0	1	0	0	0	0	0	1	13	1
1975	BAL	AL	5	0	5	1	4	0	0	0	0	0	0	0	0	1	5	0
Total			153	87	66	80	49	16	8	13	0	0	2	4	0	4	123	30

Rank among batters: 280 • *Top target (5 home runs)*: Pat Dobson • *Number of pitchers victimized*: 108 • *Total ballparks homered in*: 15 • *First HR*: 05/22/1965 off Robin Roberts • *World Series HR—2*

Willie Norwood

WILLIE NORWOOD
B: 11/07/1950
BR

Year	Tm	Lg	Tot	H	A	Men-On 0	1	2	3	One-Game 2	3	4	LO	XN	IP	PH	RHP	LHP
1977	MIN	AL	3	1	2	2	1	0	0	1	0	0	0	0	0	0	1	2
1978	MIN	AL	8	4	4	6	1	1	0	0	0	0	1	2	0	0	4	4
1979	MIN	AL	6	2	4	4	2	0	0	0	0	0	0	0	0	0	4	2
1980	MIN	AL	1	0	1	0	1	0	0	0	0	0	0	0	0	0	0	1
Total			18	7	11	12	5	1	0	1	0	0	1	2	0	0	9	9

Rank among batters: 1,914 • *Top target (2 home runs)*: Jim Umbarger • *Number of pitchers victimized*: 17 • *Total ballparks homered in*: 9 • *First HR*: 09/18/1977 off Jim Umbarger

Joe Nossek

JOSEPH RUDOLPH NOSSEK
B: 11/08/1940
BR

Year	Tm	Lg	Tot	H	A	Men-On 0	1	2	3	One-Game 2	3	4	LO	XN	IP	PH	RHP	LHP
1965	MIN	AL	2	1	1	1	0	1	0	0	0	0	0	0	0	0	1	1

Joe Nossek *continued*

Year	Tm	Lg	Tot	H	A	Men-On 0	1	2	3	One-Game 2	3	4	LO	XN	IP	PH	RHP	LHP
1966	KC	AL	1	1	0	0	1	0	0	0	0	0	0	0	1	0	0	1
Total			3	2	1	1	1	1	0	0	0	0	0	0	1	0	1	2

Rank among batters: 3,735 • *Total ballparks homered in*: 3 • *First HR*: 06/13/1965 off Hank Aguirre

Lou Novikoff

LOUIS ALEXANDER NOVIKOFF
B: 10/12/1915 D: 09/30/1970
BR

Year	Tm	Lg	Tot	H	A	Men-On 0	1	2	3	One-Game 2	3	4	LO	XN	IP	PH	RHP	LHP
1941	CHI	NL	5	3	2	4	0	1	0	0	0	0	0	0	0	0	4	1
1942	CHI	NL	7	3	4	4	2	1	0	0	0	0	0	0	0	0	4	3
1944	CHI	NL	3	1	2	3	0	0	0	0	0	0	0	0	0	2	1	2
Total			15	7	8	11	2	2	0	0	0	0	0	0	0	2	9	6

Rank among batters: 2,096 • *Total ballparks homered in*: 5 • *First HR*: 04/17/1941 off Rip Sewell

Les Nunamaker

LESLIE GRANT NUNAMAKER
B: 01/25/1889 D: 11/14/1938
BR

Year	Tm	Lg	Tot	H	A	Men-On 0	1	2	3	One-Game 2	3	4	LO	XN	IP	PH	RHP	LHP
1914	NY	AL	2	2	0	1	1	0	0	0	0	0	0	0	0	0	1	1

Rank among batters: 4,129 • *Total ballparks homered in*: 1 • *First HR*: 05/20/1914 off Harry Hoch

Jon Nunnally

JONATHAN KEITH NUNNALLY
B: 11/09/1971
BL

Year	Tm	Lg	Tot	H	A	Men-On 0	1	2	3	One-Game 2	3	4	LO	XN	IP	PH	RHP	LHP
1995	KC	AL	14	6	8	10	3	1	0	1	0	0	1	2	0	1	13	1

Rank among batters: 2,169 • *Total ballparks homered in*: 8 • *First HR*: 04/29/1995 off Melido Perez • *Hit HR in first major league AB*—vs NY: 04/29/1995

Joe Nuxhall

JOSEPH HENRY NUXHALL
B: 07/30/1928
BL

Year	Tm	Lg	Tot	H	A	Men-On 0	1	2	3	One-Game 2	3	4	LO	XN	IP	PH	RHP	LHP
1953	CIN	NL	3	0	3	2	0	1	0	0	0	0	0	0	0	0	3	0
1954	CIN	NL	3	2	1	3	0	0	0	0	0	0	0	0	0	0	2	1
1955	CIN	NL	3	0	3	2	0	1	0	0	0	0	0	0	0	0	3	0
1956	CIN	NL	2	2	0	2	0	0	0	0	0	0	0	0	0	0	1	1
1961	KC	AL	2	1	1	1	0	1	0	0	0	0	0	0	0	0	1	1
1962	CIN	NL	1	0	1	1	0	0	0	0	0	0	0	0	0	0	1	0
1964	CIN	NL	1	0	1	1	0	0	0	0	0	0	0	0	0	0	1	0
Total			15	5	10	12	0	3	0	0	0	0	0	0	0	0	12	3

Rank among batters: 2,096 • *Top target (2 home runs)*: Max Surkont, Murry Dickson, Vern Law • *Number of pitchers victimized*: 12 • *Total ballparks homered in*: 7 • *First HR*: 06/07/1953 off Roy Face

Charlie Nyce

CHARLES REIFF NYCE
B: 07/01/1870 D: 05/09/1908

Year	Tm	Lg	Tot	H	A	Men-On 0	1	2	3	One-Game 2	3	4	LO	XN	IP	PH	RHP	LHP
1895	BOS	NL	2	2	0	0	2	0	0	0	0	0	0	0	0	0	2	0

Rank among batters: 4,129 • *Total ballparks homered in*: 1 • *First HR*: 05/30/1895 off Dad Clarkson

Chris Nyman

CHRISTOPHER CURTIS NYMAN
B: 06/06/1955
BR

Year	Tm	Lg	Tot	H	A	Men-On 0	1	2	3	One-Game 2	3	4	LO	XN	IP	PH	RHP	LHP
1983	CHI	AL	2	1	1	1	1	0	0	0	0	0	0	0	0	0	0	2

Rank among batters: 4,129 • *Total ballparks homered in*: 2 • *First HR*: 06/02/1983 off Larry Gura

Nyls Nyman

NYLS WALLACE REX NYMAN
B: 03/07/1954
BL

Year	Tm	Lg	Tot	H	A	Men-On 0	1	2	3	One-Game 2	3	4	LO	XN	IP	PH	RHP	LHP
1975	CHI	AL	2	0	2	2	0	0	0	0	0	0	0	0	0	0	2	0

Year	Tm	Lg	Tot	H	A	Men-On 0	1	2	3	One-Game 2	3	4	LO	XN	IP	PH	RHP	LHP

Nyls Nyman *continued*

Rank among batters: 4,129 • *Total ballparks homered in*: 2 • *First HR*: 08/23/1975 off Jim Willoughby

Mike O'Berry

PRESTON MICHAEL O'BERRY
B: 04/20/1954
BR

Year	Tm	Lg	Tot	H	A	0	1	2	3	2	3	4	LO	XN	IP	PH	RHP	LHP
1979	BOS	AL	1	0	1	1	0	0	0	0	0	0	0	0	0	0	0	1
1981	CIN	NL	1	0	1	1	0	0	0	0	0	0	0	0	0	0	1	0
1983	CAL	AL	1	1	0	0	1	0	0	0	0	0	0	0	0	0	0	1
Total			3	1	2	2	1	0	0	0	0	0	0	0	0	0	1	2

Rank among batters: 3,735 • *Total ballparks homered in*: 3 • *First HR*: 06/17/1979 off Ken Kravec

Billy O'Brien

WILLIAM SMITH O'BRIEN
B: 03/14/1860 D: 05/26/1911
BR

Year	Tm	Lg	Tot	H	A	0	1	2	3	2	3	4	LO	XN	IP	PH	RHP	LHP
1887	WAS	NL	19	11	8	8	10	1	0	2	0	0	0	0	0	0	13	6
1888	WAS	NL	9	8	1	5	3	1	0	0	0	0	0	0	0	0	7	2
1890	BRO	AA	4	1	3	1	3	0	0	0	0	0	0	0	0	0	1	2
Total			32	20	12	14	16	2	0	2	0	0	0	0	0	0	21	10

Rank among batters: 1,360 • Top target (2 home runs): Jack McGeachey, Charlie Buffinton, Cannonball Titcomb, Ed Morris, Pretzels Getzien, George Van Haltren, Mickey Welch, Bill Burdick • *Number of pitchers victimized*: 24 • *Total ballparks homered in*: 8 • *First HR*: 05/03/1887 off Mike Mattimore

Charlie O'Brien

CHARLES HUGH O'BRIEN
B: 05/01/1960
BR

Year	Tm	Lg	Tot	H	A	0	1	2	3	2	3	4	LO	XN	IP	PH	RHP	LHP
1988	MIL	AL	2	2	0	1	1	0	0	0	0	0	0	0	0	0	1	1
1989	MIL	AL	6	4	2	3	1	2	0	0	0	0	0	0	0	0	3	3
1991	NY	NL	2	1	1	1	1	0	0	0	0	0	0	0	0	0	1	1
1992	NY	NL	2	1	1	1	1	0	0	0	0	0	0	0	0	0	1	1
1993	NY	NL	4	1	3	3	1	0	0	0	0	0	0	2	0	0	3	1
1994	ATL	NL	8	6	2	4	3	1	0	0	0	0	0	0	0	0	6	2
1995	ATL	NL	9	4	5	5	3	1	0	0	0	0	0	0	0	0	8	1
Total			33	19	14	18	11	4	0	0	0	0	0	2	0	0	23	10

Rank among batters: 1,336 • *Top target (2 home runs)*: Bob Tewksbury • *Number of pitchers victimized*: 32 • *Total ballparks homered in*: 12 • *First HR*: 07/18/1988 off Floyd Bannister • *LCS HR*—1

Darby O'Brien

WILLIAM D. O'BRIEN
B: 09/01/1863 D: 06/15/1893
BR

Year	Tm	Lg	Tot	H	A	0	1	2	3	2	3	4	LO	XN	IP	PH	RHP	LHP
1887	NY	AA	5	1	4	0	1	4	0	1	0	0	0	0	0	0	5	0
1888	BRO	AA	2	1	1	1	1	0	0	0	0	0	0	0	0	0	1	1
1889	BRO	AA	5	4	1	1	3	1	0	0	0	0	0	0	0	0	5	0
1890	BRO	NL	2	2	0	0	1	1	0	0	0	0	0	0	0	0	1	1
1891	BRO	NL	5	1	4	1	0	4	0	0	0	0	0	0	1	0	4	1
1892	BRO	NL	1	0	1	1	0	0	0	0	0	0	0	0	0	0	1	0
Total			20	9	11	4	6	10	0	1	0	0	0	0	1	0	17	2

Rank among batters: 1,810 • *Top target (2 home runs)*: Joe Neale, Gus Weyhing • *Number of pitchers victimized*: 18 • *Total ballparks homered in*: 12 • *First HR*: 07/10/1887 off Billy Serad

Jack O'Brien

JOHN K. O'BRIEN
B: 06/12/1860 D: 11/20/1910
BR

Year	Tm	Lg	Tot	H	A	0	1	2	3	2	3	4	LO	XN	IP	PH	RHP	LHP
1882	PHI	AA	3	2	1	1	1	1	0	0	0	0	0	0	0	0	0	0
1884	PHI	AA	1	1	0	0	1	0	0	0	0	0	0	0	0	0	1	0
1885	PHI	AA	2	1	1	0	0	2	0	0	0	0	0	0	0	0	2	0
1887	BRO	AA	1	0	1	0	1	0	0	0	0	0	0	0	0	0	1	0
1890	PHI	AA	4	1	3	1	3	0	0	1	0	0	0	1	0	0	3	0
Total			11	5	6	2	6	3	0	1	0	0	0	1	0	0	7	0

Year	Tm	Lg	Tot	H	A	Men-On 0	1	2	3	One-Game 2	3	4	LO	XN	IP	PH	RHP	LHP

Jack O'Brien *continued*

Rank among batters: 2,419 • *Top target (2 home runs)*: Jack Stivetts • *Number of pitchers victimized*: 10 • *Total ballparks homered in*: 5 • *First HR*: 05/17/1882 off John Reccius

Jack O'Brien

JOHN JOSEPH O'BRIEN
B: 02/05/1873 D: 06/10/1933
BL

Year	Tm	Lg	Tot	H	A	0	1	2	3	2	3	4	LO	XN	IP	PH	RHP	LHP
1899	WAS	NL	6	3	3	4	1	1	0	0	0	0	0	0	0	0	6	0
1903	BOS	AL	3	3	0	1	1	1	0	0	0	0	0	0	0	0	3	0
Total			9	6	3	5	2	2	0	0	0	0	0	0	0	0	9	0

Rank among batters: 2,587 • *Top target (2 home runs)*: Jack Powell, Jack Chesbro • *Number of pitchers victimized*: 7 • *Total ballparks homered in*: 4 • *First HR*: 06/20/1899 off Jack Powell

John O'Brien

JOHN J. O'BRIEN
B: 07/14/1870 D: 05/13/1913
BL

Year	Tm	Lg	Tot	H	A	0	1	2	3	2	3	4	LO	XN	IP	PH	RHP	LHP
1895	LOU	NL	1	0	1	0	0	1	0	0	0	0	0	0	0	0	1	0
1896	LOU	NL	2	1	1	1	0	1	0	0	0	0	0	0	0	0	0	2
	WAS	NL	4	2	2	0	3	1	0	0	0	0	0	0	0	0	4	0
	Total		6	3	3	1	3	2	0	0	0	0	0	0	0	0	4	2
1897	WAS	NL	3	3	0	2	0	1	0	0	0	0	0	0	1	0	3	0
1899	BAL	NL	1	0	1	0	1	0	0	0	0	0	0	0	0	0	1	0
	PIT	NL	1	0	1	1	0	0	0	0	0	0	0	0	0	0	1	0
Total			12	6	6	4	4	4	0	0	0	0	0	0	1	0	9	2

Rank among batters: 2,325 • *Top target (2 home runs)*: Jack Taylor • *Number of pitchers victimized*: 11 • *Total ballparks homered in*: 6 • *First HR*: 09/15/1895 off Doc Parker

Johnny O'Brien

JOHN THOMAS O'BRIEN
B: 12/11/1930
BR

Year	Tm	Lg	Tot	H	A	0	1	2	3	2	3	4	LO	XN	IP	PH	RHP	LHP
1953	PIT	NL	2	2	0	0	1	1	0	0	0	0	0	0	0	0	1	1
1955	PIT	NL	1	0	1	1	0	0	0	0	0	0	0	0	0	0	0	1
1959	MIL	NL	1	1	0	1	0	0	0	0	0	0	0	0	0	0	1	0
Total			4	3	1	2	1	1	0	0	0	0	0	0	0	0	2	2

Rank among batters: 3,427 • *Total ballparks homered in*: 3 • *First HR*: 08/25/1953 off Harry Perkowski

Pete O'Brien

PETER JAMES O'BRIEN
B: 06/16/1867 D: 06/30/1937
BR

Year	Tm	Lg	Tot	H	A	0	1	2	3	2	3	4	LO	XN	IP	PH	RHP	LHP
1890	CHI	NL	3	3	0	0	2	1	0	0	0	0	0	0	0	0	2	0

Rank among batters: 3,735 • *Total ballparks homered in*: 1 • *First HR*: 05/02/1890 off Henry Jones

Pete O'Brien

PETER J. O'BRIEN
B: 06/17/1877 D: 01/31/1917
BL

Year	Tm	Lg	Tot	H	A	0	1	2	3	2	3	4	LO	XN	IP	PH	RHP	LHP
1901	CIN	NL	1	1	0	0	0	1	0	0	0	0	0	0	1	0	1	0
1906	STL	AL	2	2	0	1	0	1	0	0	0	0	0	0	0	0	2	0
Total			3	3	0	1	0	2	0	0	0	0	0	0	1	0	3	0

Rank among batters: 3,735 • *Total ballparks homered in*: 2 • *First HR*: 09/22/1901 off Bill Magee

Pete O'Brien

PETER MICHAEL O'BRIEN
B: 02/09/1958
BL

Year	Tm	Lg	Tot	H	A	0	1	2	3	2	3	4	LO	XN	IP	PH	RHP	LHP
1982	TEX	AL	4	2	2	3	1	0	0	0	0	0	0	0	0	0	3	1
1983	TEX	AL	8	4	4	4	2	2	0	0	0	0	0	0	0	0	8	0
1984	TEX	AL	18	7	11	12	3	3	0	1	0	0	0	0	0	0	16	2
1985	TEX	AL	22	12	10	15	7	0	0	0	0	0	0	0	0	0	20	2

Pete O'Brien *continued*

Year	Tm	Lg	Tot	H	A	Men-On 0	Men-On 1	Men-On 2	Men-On 3	One-Game 2	One-Game 3	One-Game 4	LO	XN	IP	PH	RHP	LHP
1986	TEX	AL	23	11	12	11	8	4	0	1	0	0	0	1	0	0	19	4
1987	TEX	AL	23	9	14	15	6	1	1	2	0	0	0	2	0	0	20	3
1988	TEX	AL	16	6	10	11	4	0	1	2	0	0	0	1	0	1	13	3
1989	CLE	AL	12	5	7	8	4	0	0	0	0	0	0	0	0	0	8	4
1990	SEA	AL	5	3	2	5	0	0	0	0	0	0	0	0	0	0	4	1
1991	SEA	AL	17	12	5	8	8	1	0	1	0	0	0	1	0	0	13	4
1992	SEA	AL	14	6	8	9	3	2	0	0	0	0	0	0	0	0	13	1
1993	SEA	AL	7	1	6	4	1	1	1	0	0	0	0	0	0	0	7	0
Total			169	78	91	105	47	14	3	7	0	0	0	5	0	1	144	25

Rank among batters: 238 • *Top target (5 home runs)*: Mike Witt • *Number of pitchers victimized*: 125 • *Total ballparks homered in*: 16 • *First HR*: 09/10/1982 off Gaylord Perry

Syd O'Brien

SYDNEY LLOYD O'BRIEN
B: 12/18/1944
BR

Year	Tm	Lg	Tot	H	A	Men-On 0	Men-On 1	Men-On 2	Men-On 3	One-Game 2	One-Game 3	One-Game 4	LO	XN	IP	PH	RHP	LHP
1969	BOS	AL	9	6	3	6	3	0	0	0	0	0	2	0	0	0	7	2
1970	CHI	AL	8	6	2	3	4	1	0	0	0	0	1	0	0	0	6	2
1971	CAL	AL	5	3	2	2	3	0	0	0	0	0	0	1	0	1	4	1
1972	CAL	AL	1	0	1	1	0	0	0	0	0	0	0	0	0	1	0	1
	MIL	AL	1	1	0	0	1	0	0	0	0	0	0	0	0	0	1	0
	Total		2	1	1	1	1	0	0	0	0	0	0	0	0	1	1	1
Total			24	16	8	12	11	1	0	0	0	0	3	1	0	2	18	6

Rank among batters: 1,643 • *Top target (2 home runs)*: Jim Hannan • *Number of pitchers victimized*: 23 • *Total ballparks homered in*: 9 • *First HR*: 05/06/1969 off Bucky Brandon

Tom O'Brien

THOMAS H. O'BRIEN
B: 06/22/1860 D: 04/21/1921
BR

Year	Tm	Lg	Tot	H	A	Men-On 0	Men-On 1	Men-On 2	Men-On 3	One-Game 2	One-Game 3	One-Game 4	LO	XN	IP	PH	RHP	LHP
1884	BOS	UA	4	1	3	0	3	1	0	0	0	0	0	0	0	0	2	0

Rank among batters: 3,427 • *Total ballparks homered in*: 4 • *First HR*: 06/04/1884 off Bill Sweeney

Tom O'Brien

THOMAS J. O'BRIEN
B: 02/20/1873 D: 02/04/1901

Year	Tm	Lg	Tot	H	A	Men-On 0	Men-On 1	Men-On 2	Men-On 3	One-Game 2	One-Game 3	One-Game 4	LO	XN	IP	PH	RHP	LHP
1898	PIT	NL	1	0	1	1	0	0	0	0	0	0	0	0	0	0	1	0
1899	NY	NL	6	2	4	1	4	1	0	0	0	0	0	0	1	0	4	1
1900	PIT	NL	3	3	0	2	0	1	0	0	0	0	0	0	0	0	1	2
Total			10	5	5	4	4	2	0	0	0	0	0	0	1	0	6	3

Rank among batters: 2,500 • *Top target (2 home runs)*: Brickyard Kennedy • *Number of pitchers victimized*: 9 • *Total ballparks homered in*: 6 • *First HR*: 09/20/1898 off Brickyard Kennedy

Tommy O'Brien

THOMAS EDWARD O'BRIEN
B: 12/19/1918 D: 11/05/1978
BR

Year	Tm	Lg	Tot	H	A	Men-On 0	Men-On 1	Men-On 2	Men-On 3	One-Game 2	One-Game 3	One-Game 4	LO	XN	IP	PH	RHP	LHP
1943	PIT	NL	2	1	1	1	0	1	0	0	0	0	0	0	0	0	1	1
1944	PIT	NL	3	1	2	2	1	0	0	1	0	0	0	0	0	0	0	3
1949	BOS	AL	3	1	2	2	1	0	0	0	0	0	0	0	0	0	2	1
Total			8	3	5	5	2	1	0	1	0	0	0	0	0	0	3	5

Rank among batters: 2,703 • *Top target (2 home runs)*: Bob Chipman • *Number of pitchers victimized*: 7 • *Total ballparks homered in*: 6 • *First HR*: 07/27/1943 off Ken Chase

Danny O'Connell

DANIEL FRANCIS O'CONNELL
B: 01/21/1927 D: 10/02/1969
BR

Year	Tm	Lg	Tot	H	A	Men-On 0	Men-On 1	Men-On 2	Men-On 3	One-Game 2	One-Game 3	One-Game 4	LO	XN	IP	PH	RHP	LHP
1950	PIT	NL	8	6	2	5	2	1	0	0	0	0	0	0	0	0	6	2
1953	PIT	NL	7	4	3	4	2	1	0	1	0	0	0	0	0	0	4	3
1954	MIL	NL	2	0	2	1	0	1	0	0	0	0	0	0	0	0	1	1
1955	MIL	NL	6	0	6	4	1	1	0	1	0	0	0	1	0	0	3	3

Danny O'Connell *continued*

Year	Tm	Lg	Tot	H	A	Men-On 0	1	2	3	One-Game 2	3	4	LO	XN	IP	PH	RHP	LHP
1956	MIL	NL	2	0	2	1	0	1	0	0	0	0	0	0	0	0	1	1
1957	MIL	NL	1	0	1	1	0	0	0	0	0	0	0	0	0	0	1	0
	NY	NL	7	5	2	3	2	2	0	0	0	0	0	1	0	0	6	1
	Total		8	5	3	4	2	2	0	0	0	0	0	1	0	0	7	1
1958	SF	NL	3	0	3	2	1	0	0	1	0	0	0	0	0	0	3	0
1961	WAS	AL	1	0	1	0	1	0	0	0	0	0	0	0	0	0	1	0
1962	WAS	AL	2	1	1	2	0	0	0	0	0	0	0	0	0	0	2	0
Total			39	16	23	23	9	7	0	3	0	0	0	2	0	0	28	11

Rank among batters: 1,204 • Top target (2 home runs): Warren Spahn, Johnny Antonelli, Jim Hearn, Harvey Haddix, Don Drysdale • *Number of pitchers victimized*: 34 • *Total ballparks homered in*: 11 • *First HR*: 07/16/1950 off Vern Bickford

Jimmy O'Connell

JAMES JOSEPH O'CONNELL
B: 02/11/1901 D: 11/11/1976
BL

Year	Tm	Lg	Tot	H	A	Men-On 0	1	2	3	One-Game 2	3	4	LO	XN	IP	PH	RHP	LHP
1923	NY	NL	6	4	2	3	2	1	0	0	0	0	0	0	0	0	6	0
1924	NY	NL	2	2	0	0	2	0	0	0	0	0	0	0	0	0	2	0
Total			8	6	2	3	4	1	0	0	0	0	0	0	0	0	8	0

Rank among batters: 2,703 • *Top target (2 home runs)*: Petie Behan, Bill Hubbell • *Number of pitchers victimized*: 6 • *Total ballparks homered in*: 2 • *First HR*: 05/27/1923 off Petie Behan

Frank O'Connor

FRANK HENRY O'CONNOR
B: 09/15/1870 D: 12/26/1913
BL

Year	Tm	Lg	Tot	H	A	Men-On 0	1	2	3	One-Game 2	3	4	LO	XN	IP	PH	RHP	LHP
1893	PHI	NL	1	0	1	0	0	1	0	0	0	0	0	0	0	0	1	0

Rank among batters: 4,707 • *Total ballparks homered in*: 1 • *First HR*: 08/07/1893 off Bill Hawke

Jack O'Connor

JOHN JOSEPH O'CONNOR
B: 06/02/1869 D: 11/14/1937
BR

Year	Tm	Lg	Tot	H	A	Men-On 0	1	2	3	One-Game 2	3	4	LO	XN	IP	PH	RHP	LHP
1888	CIN	AA	1	1	0	1	0	0	0	0	0	0	0	0	0	0	1	0
1889	COL	AA	4	0	4	2	1	1	0	0	0	0	0	0	0	0	4	0
1890	COL	AA	2	0	2	1	1	0	0	0	0	0	0	0	0	0	0	1
1892	CLE	NL	1	0	1	0	1	0	0	0	0	0	0	0	0	0	1	0
1893	CLE	NL	4	2	2	1	1	1	1	0	0	0	0	0	1	0	2	2
1894	CLE	NL	2	0	2	1	0	0	1	0	0	0	0	0	0	0	2	0
1896	CLE	NL	1	0	1	0	0	1	0	0	0	0	0	0	0	0	1	0
1897	CLE	NL	2	1	1	1	0	1	0	0	0	0	0	0	0	0	0	2
1898	CLE	NL	1	0	1	0	0	1	0	0	0	0	0	0	0	0	1	0
1902	PIT	NL	1	1	0	0	0	1	0	0	0	0	0	0	1	0	0	1
Total			19	5	14	7	4	6	2	0	0	0	0	0	2	0	12	6

Rank among batters: 1,861 • *Top target (2 home runs)*: Jack Stivetts • *Number of pitchers victimized*: 18 • *Total ballparks homered in*: 14 • *First HR*: 05/05/1888 off Frank Hafner

Hank O'Day

HENRY FRANCIS O'DAY
B: 07/08/1862 D: 07/02/1935

Year	Tm	Lg	Tot	H	A	Men-On 0	1	2	3	One-Game 2	3	4	LO	XN	IP	PH	RHP	LHP
1890	NY	PL	1	0	1	0	1	0	0	0	0	0	0	0	0	0	1	0

Rank among batters: 4,707 • *Total ballparks homered in*: 1 • *First HR*: 08/08/1890 off Ad Gumbert

Ken O'Dea

JAMES KENNETH O'DEA
B: 03/16/1913 D: 12/17/1985
BL

Year	Tm	Lg	Tot	H	A	Men-On 0	1	2	3	One-Game 2	3	4	LO	XN	IP	PH	RHP	LHP
1935	CHI	NL	6	4	2	3	2	1	0	0	0	0	0	1	0	0	5	1
1936	CHI	NL	2	2	0	1	1	0	0	0	0	0	0	0	0	0	2	0
1937	CHI	NL	4	2	2	1	2	1	0	0	0	0	0	0	0	0	2	2
1938	CHI	NL	3	2	1	2	1	0	0	0	0	0	0	0	0	0	3	0
1939	NY	NL	3	2	1	3	0	0	0	0	0	0	0	1	0	1	3	0
1941	NY	NL	3	1	2	1	1	0	1	0	0	0	0	0	0	1	3	0
1942	STL	NL	5	3	2	2	2	0	1	0	0	0	0	1	0	0	4	1
1943	STL	NL	3	3	0	0	3	0	0	0	0	0	0	0	0	1	3	0

Ken O'Dea *continued*

Year	Tm	Lg	Tot	H	A	Men-On 0	Men-On 1	Men-On 2	Men-On 3	One-Game 2	One-Game 3	One-Game 4	LO	XN	IP	PH	RHP	LHP
1944	STL	NL	6	4	2	1	3	2	0	0	0	0	0	0	0	2	6	0
1945	STL	NL	4	1	3	2	0	2	0	0	0	0	0	0	0	0	4	0
1946	STL	NL	1	1	0	1	0	0	0	0	0	0	0	0	0	0	1	0
Total			40	25	15	17	15	6	2	0	0	0	0	3	0	5	36	4

Rank among batters: 1,181 • *Top target (3 home runs)*: Claude Passeau, Rip Sewell • *Number of pitchers victimized*: 33 • *Total ballparks homered in*: 8 • *First HR*: 06/05/1935 off Gene Schott • *World Series HR*—1

Paul O'Dea

PAUL O'DEA
B: 07/03/1920 D: 12/11/1978
BL

Year	Tm	Lg	Tot	H	A	Men-On 0	Men-On 1	Men-On 2	Men-On 3	One-Game 2	One-Game 3	One-Game 4	LO	XN	IP	PH	RHP	LHP
1945	CLE	AL	1	1	0	1	0	0	0	0	0	0	0	0	0	0	1	0

Rank among batters: 4,707 • *Total ballparks homered in*: 1 • *First HR*: 05/19/1945 off Don Black

Billy O'Dell

WILLIAM OLIVER O'DELL
B: 02/10/1933
BB

Year	Tm	Lg	Tot	H	A	Men-On 0	Men-On 1	Men-On 2	Men-On 3	One-Game 2	One-Game 3	One-Game 4	LO	XN	IP	PH	RHP	LHP
1958	BAL	AL	1	0	1	1	0	0	0	0	0	0	0	0	0	0	1	0
1959	BAL	AL	1	1	0	0	1	0	0	0	0	0	0	0	1	0	0	1
Total			2	1	1	1	1	0	0	0	0	0	0	0	1	0	1	1

Rank among batters: 4,129 • *Total ballparks homered in*: 2 • *First HR*: 05/24/1958 off Bob Keegan

George O'Donnell

GEORGE DANA O'DONNELL
B: 05/27/1929
BR

Year	Tm	Lg	Tot	H	A	Men-On 0	Men-On 1	Men-On 2	Men-On 3	One-Game 2	One-Game 3	One-Game 4	LO	XN	IP	PH	RHP	LHP
1954	PIT	NL	1	0	1	0	1	0	0	0	0	0	0	0	0	0	0	1

Rank among batters: 4,707 • *Total ballparks homered in*: 1 • *First HR*: 07/10/1954 off Windy McCall

John O'Donoghue

JOHN EUGENE O'DONOGHUE
B: 10/07/1939
BR

Year	Tm	Lg	Tot	H	A	Men-On 0	Men-On 1	Men-On 2	Men-On 3	One-Game 2	One-Game 3	One-Game 4	LO	XN	IP	PH	RHP	LHP
1964	KC	AL	1	0	1	0	1	0	0	0	0	0	0	0	0	0	1	0
1965	KC	AL	1	0	1	1	0	0	0	0	0	0	0	0	0	0	1	0
1967	CLE	AL	1	0	1	0	0	0	1	0	0	0	0	0	0	0	1	0
Total			3	0	3	1	1	0	1	0	0	0	0	0	0	0	3	0

Rank among batters: 3,735 • *Top target (2 home runs)*: Buster Narum • *Number of pitchers victimized*: 2 • *Total ballparks homered in*: 2 • *First HR*: 06/09/1964 off Buster Narum

Lefty O'Doul

FRANCIS JOSEPH O'DOUL
B: 03/04/1897 D: 12/07/1969
BL

Year	Tm	Lg	Tot	H	A	Men-On 0	Men-On 1	Men-On 2	Men-On 3	One-Game 2	One-Game 3	One-Game 4	LO	XN	IP	PH	RHP	LHP
1928	NY	NL	8	7	1	5	3	0	0	2	0	0	0	0	0	0	8	0
1929	PHI	NL	32	19	13	18	9	5	0	2	0	0	0	1	0	0	23	9
1930	PHI	NL	22	13	9	14	4	4	0	1	0	0	0	0	0	2	16	6
1931	BRO	NL	7	7	0	4	3	0	0	0	0	0	0	0	0	0	5	2
1932	BRO	NL	21	13	8	14	6	1	0	3	0	0	0	1	0	0	19	2
1933	BRO	NL	5	3	2	3	2	0	0	1	0	0	0	0	0	0	5	0
	NY	NL	9	6	3	5	4	0	0	1	0	0	0	0	0	0	9	0
	Total		14	9	5	8	6	0	0	2	0	0	0	0	0	0	14	0
1934	NY	NL	9	7	2	1	5	2	1	0	0	0	0	0	0	3	9	0
Total			113	75	38	64	36	12	1	10	0	0	0	2	0	5	94	19

Rank among batters: 421 • *Top target (5 home runs)*: Carl Hubbell, Fred Frankhouse, Red Lucas • *Number of pitchers victimized*: 66 • *Total ballparks homered in*: 7 • *First HR*: 04/15/1928 off Jimmy Ring

Bob O'Farrell

ROBERT ARTHUR O'FARRELL
B: 10/19/1896 D: 02/20/1988
BR

Year	Tm	Lg	Tot	H	A	Men-On 0	Men-On 1	Men-On 2	Men-On 3	One-Game 2	One-Game 3	One-Game 4	LO	XN	IP	PH	RHP	LHP
1918	CHI	NL	1	0	1	1	0	0	0	0	0	0	0	0	0	0	1	0

Bob O'Farrell *continued*

						Men-On				One-Game								
Year	**Tm**	**Lg**	**Tot**	**H**	**A**	**0**	**1**	**2**	**3**	**2**	**3**	**4**	**LO**	**XN**	**IP**	**PH**	**RHP**	**LHP**
1920	CHI	NL	3	0	3	1	2	0	0	0	0	0	0	1	1	0	2	1
1921	CHI	NL	4	4	0	2	1	0	1	0	0	0	0	0	0	0	4	0
1922	CHI	NL	4	1	3	1	2	1	0	0	0	0	0	0	0	0	3	1
1923	CHI	NL	12	10	2	6	4	1	1	1	0	0	0	0	0	0	7	5
1924	CHI	NL	3	2	1	2	1	0	0	0	0	0	0	0	0	0	2	1
1925	STL	NL	3	2	1	1	1	1	0	0	0	0	0	0	0	0	2	1
1926	STL	NL	7	4	3	3	2	2	0	0	0	0	0	0	0	0	5	2
1928	NY	NL	2	1	1	1	0	0	1	0	0	0	0	0	0	0	1	1
1929	NY	NL	4	2	2	1	3	0	0	0	0	0	0	0	0	0	2	2
1930	NY	NL	4	3	1	1	2	1	0	0	0	0	0	0	1	0	4	0
1931	NY	NL	1	0	1	0	1	0	0	0	0	0	0	0	0	0	0	1
1933	STL	NL	2	0	2	1	1	0	0	1	0	0	0	0	0	0	2	0
1934	CIN	NL	1	0	1	1	0	0	0	0	0	0	0	0	0	0	1	0
Total			51	29	22	22	20	6	3	2	0	0	0	1	2	0	36	15

Rank among batters: 979 • Top target (2 home runs): Jack Bentley, Jeff Pfeffer, Jimmy Ring, Win Ballou, Erv Brame, Red Lucas, Bill Sherdel, Hal Schumacher • *Number of pitchers victimized*: 43 • *Total ballparks homered in*: 9 • *First HR*: 07/25/1918 off Joe Oeschger

Bill O'Hara

WILLIAM ALEXANDER O'HARA
B: 08/14/1883 D: 06/15/1931
BL

						Men-On				One-Game								
Year	**Tm**	**Lg**	**Tot**	**H**	**A**	**0**	**1**	**2**	**3**	**2**	**3**	**4**	**LO**	**XN**	**IP**	**PH**	**RHP**	**LHP**
1909	NY	NL	1	1	0	0	1	0	0	0	0	0	0	0	1	0	0	1

Rank among batters: 4,707 • *Total ballparks homered in*: 1 • *First HR*: 05/13/1909 off Rube Kroh

Charley O'Leary

CHARLES TIMOTHY O'LEARY
B: 10/15/1882 D: 01/06/1941
BR

						Men-On				One-Game								
Year	**Tm**	**Lg**	**Tot**	**H**	**A**	**0**	**1**	**2**	**3**	**2**	**3**	**4**	**LO**	**XN**	**IP**	**PH**	**RHP**	**LHP**
1904	DET	AL	1	1	0	1	0	0	0	0	0	0	0	0	0	0	1	0
1906	DET	AL	2	1	1	1	0	1	0	0	0	0	0	0	0	0	1	1
Total			3	2	1	2	0	1	0	0	0	0	0	0	0	0	2	1

Rank among batters: 3,735 • *Total ballparks homered in*: 2 • *First HR*: 06/08/1904 off Bill Dinneen

Dan O'Leary

DANIEL O'LEARY
B: 10/22/1856 D: 06/24/1922
BL

						Men-On				One-Game								
Year	**Tm**	**Lg**	**Tot**	**H**	**A**	**0**	**1**	**2**	**3**	**2**	**3**	**4**	**LO**	**XN**	**IP**	**PH**	**RHP**	**LHP**
1884	CIN	UA	1	1	0	0	1	0	0	0	0	0	0	0	0	0	0	0

Rank among batters: 4,707 • *Total ballparks homered in*: 1 • *First HR*: 05/17/1884 off Walter Burke

Troy O'Leary

TROY FRANKLIN O'LEARY
B: 08/04/1969
BL

						Men-On				One-Game								
Year	**Tm**	**Lg**	**Tot**	**H**	**A**	**0**	**1**	**2**	**3**	**2**	**3**	**4**	**LO**	**XN**	**IP**	**PH**	**RHP**	**LHP**
1994	MIL	AL	2	0	2	2	0	0	0	0	0	0	0	0	0	0	2	0
1995	BOS	AL	10	5	5	5	3	2	0	1	0	0	1	1	0	1	10	0
Total			12	5	7	7	3	2	0	1	0	0	1	1	0	1	12	0

Rank among batters: 2,325 • *Top target (2 home runs)*: Brad Radke • *Number of pitchers victimized*: 11 • *Total ballparks homered in*: 4 • *First HR*: 05/17/1994 off Dennis Martinez

Tom O'Malley

THOMAS PATRICK O'MALLEY
B: 12/25/1960
BL

						Men-On				One-Game								
Year	**Tm**	**Lg**	**Tot**	**H**	**A**	**0**	**1**	**2**	**3**	**2**	**3**	**4**	**LO**	**XN**	**IP**	**PH**	**RHP**	**LHP**
1982	SF	NL	2	0	2	1	1	0	0	0	0	0	0	0	0	0	2	0
1983	SF	NL	5	3	2	5	0	0	0	0	0	0	0	0	0	0	4	1
1985	BAL	AL	1	0	1	0	1	0	0	0	0	0	0	0	0	0	1	0
1986	BAL	AL	1	1	0	1	0	0	0	0	0	0	0	0	0	0	1	0
1987	TEX	AL	1	0	1	0	0	1	0	0	0	0	0	0	0	0	1	0
1990	NY	NL	3	1	2	2	1	0	0	0	0	0	0	1	0	1	3	0
Total			13	5	8	9	3	1	0	0	0	0	0	1	0	1	12	1

Rank among batters: 2,248 • *Total ballparks homered in*: 7 • *First HR*: 05/09/1982 off Pat Zachry

Ollie O'Mara

OLIVER EDWARD O'MARA
B: 03/08/1891 D: 10/24/1989
BR

Year	Tm	Lg	Tot	H	A	Men-On 0	1	2	3	One-Game 2	3	4	LO	XN	IP	PH	RHP	LHP
1914	BRO	NL	1	0	1	1	0	0	0	0	0	0	0	0	0	0	0	1
1918	BRO	NL	1	0	1	1	0	0	0	0	0	0	0	0	0	0	1	0
Total			2	0	2	2	0	0	0	0	0	0	0	0	0	0	1	1

Rank among batters: 4,129 • *Total ballparks homered in*: 2 • *First HR*: 07/20/1914 off Slim Sallee

Mickey O'Neil

GEORGE MICHAEL O'NEIL
B: 04/12/1900 D: 04/08/1964
BR

Year	Tm	Lg	Tot	H	A	Men-On 0	1	2	3	One-Game 2	3	4	LO	XN	IP	PH	RHP	LHP
1921	BOS	NL	2	2	0	0	0	2	0	0	0	0	0	0	2	0	2	0
1925	BOS	NL	2	0	2	2	0	0	0	0	0	0	0	0	1	0	1	1
Total			4	2	2	2	0	2	0	0	0	0	0	0	3	0	3	1

Rank among batters: 3,427 • *Total ballparks homered in*: 2 • *First HR*: 04/13/1921 off Leon Cadore

Bill O'Neill

WILLIAM JOHN O'NEILL
B: 01/22/1880 D: 07/20/1920
BB

Year	Tm	Lg	Tot	H	A	Men-On 0	1	2	3	One-Game 2	3	4	LO	XN	IP	PH	RHP	LHP
1904	WAS	AL	1	0	1	1	0	0	0	0	0	0	1	0	0	0	1	0
1906	CHI	AL	1	0	1	0	1	0	0	0	0	0	0	0	0	0	1	0
Total			2	0	2	1	1	0	0	0	0	0	1	0	0	0	2	0

Rank among batters: 4,129 • *Total ballparks homered in*: 2 • *First HR*: 09/05/1904 off George Winter

Emmett O'Neill

ROBERT EMMETT O'NEILL
B: 01/13/1918 D: 10/11/1993
BR

Year	Tm	Lg	Tot	H	A	Men-On 0	1	2	3	One-Game 2	3	4	LO	XN	IP	PH	RHP	LHP
1945	BOS	AL	1	1	0	0	0	1	0	0	0	0	0	0	0	0	1	0

Rank among batters: 4,707 • *Total ballparks homered in*: 1 • *First HR*: 06/01/1945 off Walter Wilson

Jack O'Neill

JOHN JOSEPH O'NEILL
B: 01/10/1873 D: 06/25/1935
BR

Year	Tm	Lg	Tot	H	A	Men-On 0	1	2	3	One-Game 2	3	4	LO	XN	IP	PH	RHP	LHP
1904	CHI	NL	1	0	1	0	0	0	1	0	0	0	0	0	0	0	1	0

Rank among batters: 4,707 • *Total ballparks homered in*: 1 • *First HR*: 08/17/1904 off Tom Fisher

Jim O'Neill

JAMES LEO O'NEILL
B: 02/23/1893 D: 09/05/1976
BR

Year	Tm	Lg	Tot	H	A	Men-On 0	1	2	3	One-Game 2	3	4	LO	XN	IP	PH	RHP	LHP
1920	WAS	AL	1	0	1	0	1	0	0	0	0	0	0	0	0	0	0	1

Rank among batters: 4,707 • *Total ballparks homered in*: 1 • *First HR*: 04/20/1920 off Pat Martin

Mike O'Neill

MICHAEL JOYCE O'NEILL
B: 09/07/1877 D: 08/12/1959
BR

Year	Tm	Lg	Tot	H	A	Men-On 0	1	2	3	One-Game 2	3	4	LO	XN	IP	PH	RHP	LHP
1902	STL	NL	2	0	2	1	0	0	1	0	0	0	0	0	1	1	2	0

Rank among batters: 4,129 • *Total ballparks homered in*: 2 • *First HR*: 06/03/1902 off Togie Pittinger

Paul O'Neill

PAUL ANDREW O'NEILL
B: 02/25/1963
BL

Year	Tm	Lg	Tot	H	A	Men-On 0	1	2	3	One-Game 2	3	4	LO	XN	IP	PH	RHP	LHP
1987	CIN	NL	7	4	3	4	3	0	0	0	0	0	0	0	0	2	7	0
1988	CIN	NL	16	12	4	8	7	1	0	1	0	0	0	0	0	0	15	1
1989	CIN	NL	15	11	4	6	5	3	1	1	0	0	0	0	0	0	11	4
1990	CIN	NL	16	10	6	7	6	3	0	2	0	0	0	0	0	0	13	3

Paul O'Neill *continued*

Year	Tm	Lg	Tot	H	A	Men-On 0	1	2	3	One-Game 2	3	4	LO	XN	IP	PH	RHP	LHP
1991	CIN	NL	28	20	8	12	11	5	0	2	0	0	0	1	0	0	25	3
1992	CIN	NL	14	6	8	12	2	0	0	0	0	0	0	0	0	0	12	2
1993	NY	AL	20	8	12	17	3	0	0	0	0	0	0	0	0	0	18	2
1994	NY	AL	21	10	11	10	8	2	1	2	0	0	0	1	0	0	14	7
1995	NY	AL	22	12	10	11	6	5	0	1	1	0	0	0	0	0	13	9
Total			159	93	66	87	51	19	2	9	1	0	0	2	0	2	128	31

Rank among batters: 268 • *Top target (5 home runs)*: Don Robinson, Tim Belcher, Kevin Gross • *Number of pitchers victimized*: 113 • *Total ballparks homered in*: 27 • *First HR*: 05/09/1987 off Kevin Gross • *LCS HR*—4

Steve O'Neill

STEPHEN FRANCIS O'NEILL
B: 07/06/1891 D: 01/26/1962
BR

Year	Tm	Lg	Tot	H	A	Men-On 0	1	2	3	One-Game 2	3	4	LO	XN	IP	PH	RHP	LHP
1915	CLE	AL	2	2	0	1	1	0	0	0	0	0	0	0	0	0	1	1
1918	CLE	AL	1	0	1	1	0	0	0	0	0	0	0	0	0	0	1	0
1919	CLE	AL	2	1	1	1	0	1	0	0	0	0	0	0	0	0	2	0
1920	CLE	AL	3	0	3	3	0	0	0	0	0	0	0	0	1	0	2	1
1921	CLE	AL	1	0	1	1	0	0	0	0	0	0	0	0	0	0	1	0
1922	CLE	AL	2	0	2	2	0	0	0	0	0	0	0	0	0	0	2	0
1925	NY	AL	1	1	0	1	0	0	0	0	0	0	0	0	0	0	1	0
1927	STL	AL	1	1	0	0	1	0	0	0	0	0	0	0	0	0	1	0
Total			13	5	8	10	2	1	0	0	0	0	0	0	1	0	11	2

Rank among batters: 2,248 • *Top target (2 home runs)*: Eddie Rommel • *Number of pitchers victimized*: 12 • *Total ballparks homered in*: 6 • *First HR*: 07/09/1915 off Ray Fisher

Tip O'Neill

JAMES EDWARD O'NEILL
B: 05/25/1858 D: 12/31/1915
BR

Year	Tm	Lg	Tot	H	A	Men-On 0	1	2	3	One-Game 2	3	4	LO	XN	IP	PH	RHP	LHP
1884	STL	AA	3	1	2	2	1	0	0	0	0	0	0	0	0	0	3	0
1885	STL	AA	3	2	1	2	0	1	0	1	0	0	0	0	1	0	2	0
1886	STL	AA	3	1	2	2	0	1	0	0	0	0	0	0	0	0	1	0
1887	STL	AA	14	10	4	7	4	3	0	1	0	0	0	0	1	0	8	5
1888	STL	AA	5	3	2	4	1	0	0	0	0	0	0	0	2	0	3	1
1889	STL	AA	9	8	1	5	3	1	0	0	0	0	0	0	0	0	7	2
1890	CHI	PL	3	1	2	2	1	0	0	0	0	0	0	0	0	0	3	0
1891	STL	AA	10	8	2	3	4	3	0	0	0	0	0	0	2	0	8	1
1892	CIN	NL	2	2	0	0	2	0	0	0	0	0	0	0	1	0	2	0
Total			52	36	16	27	16	9	0	2	0	0	0	0	7	0	37	6

Rank among batters: 965 • *Top target (3 home runs)*: Tony Mullane, Gus Weyhing • *Number of pitchers victimized*: 38 • *Total ballparks homered in*: 14 • *First HR*: 06/19/1884 off Bob Barr • *Hit for Cycle*—vs CLE: 04/30/1887; vs LOU: 05/07/1887 • *World Series HR*—5

Frank O'Rourke

JAMES FRANCIS O'ROURKE
B: 11/28/1894 D: 05/14/1986
BR

Year	Tm	Lg	Tot	H	A	Men-On 0	1	2	3	One-Game 2	3	4	LO	XN	IP	PH	RHP	LHP
1921	WAS	AL	3	2	1	0	2	1	0	0	0	0	0	0	1	0	1	2
1922	BOS	AL	1	0	1	1	0	0	0	0	0	0	0	0	0	0	1	0
1925	DET	AL	5	5	0	2	3	0	0	0	0	0	0	0	1	0	5	0
1926	DET	AL	1	0	1	1	0	0	0	0	0	0	0	0	0	0	1	0
1927	STL	AL	1	1	0	1	0	0	0	0	0	0	0	1	0	0	0	1
1928	STL	AL	1	1	0	0	1	0	0	0	0	0	0	0	0	0	1	0
1929	STL	AL	2	1	1	2	0	0	0	0	0	0	0	0	1	0	1	1
1930	STL	AL	1	0	1	0	1	0	0	0	0	0	0	0	0	0	1	0
Total			15	10	5	7	7	1	0	0	0	0	0	1	3	0	11	4

Rank among batters: 2,096 • *Total ballparks homered in*: 6 • *First HR*: 06/24/1921 off Carl Mays

Jim O'Rourke

JAMES HENRY O'ROURKE
B: 09/01/1850 D: 01/08/1919
BR HOF

Year	Tm	Lg	Tot	H	A	Men-On 0	1	2	3	One-Game 2	3	4	LO	XN	IP	PH	RHP	LHP
1876	BOS	NL	2	1	1	1	1	0	0	0	0	0	0	0	0	0	2	0
1878	BOS	NL	1	1	0	1	0	0	0	0	0	0	0	0	0	0	1	0
1879	PRO	NL	1	1	0	0	0	1	0	0	0	0	0	0	0	0	1	0

						Men-On				One-Game								
Year	Tm	Lg	Tot	H	A	0	1	2	3	2	3	4	LO	XN	IP	PH	RHP	LHP

Jim O'Rourke *continued*

Year	Tm	Lg	Tot	H	A	0	1	2	3	2	3	4	LO	XN	IP	PH	RHP	LHP
1880	BOS	NL	6	3	3	5	1	0	0	1	0	0	0	0	1	0	4	1
1882	BUF	NL	2	1	1	1	0	1	0	0	0	0	0	0	0	0	2	0
1883	BUF	NL	1	1	0	1	0	0	0	0	0	0	0	0	0	0	1	0
1884	BUF	NL	5	2	3	2	2	0	0	0	0	0	0	0	1	0	5	0
1885	NY	NL	5	3	2	3	2	0	0	0	0	0	1	0	0	0	5	0
1886	NY	NL	1	0	1	1	0	0	0	0	0	0	0	0	1	0	0	1
1887	NY	NL	3	1	2	1	2	0	0	0	0	0	0	0	0	0	2	1
1888	NY	NL	4	3	1	2	1	1	0	0	0	0	0	0	1	0	1	3
1889	NY	NL	3	1	2	1	2	0	0	0	0	0	0	0	0	0	2	1
1890	NY	PL	9	4	5	2	4	2	1	0	0	0	0	0	3	0	6	2
1891	NY	NL	5	4	1	2	1	2	0	0	0	0	0	0	2	0	4	1
1893	WAS	NL	2	1	1	1	1	0	0	0	0	0	0	0	1	0	2	0
Total			50	27	23	24	17	7	1	1	0	0	1	0	10	0	38	10

Rank among batters: 991 • *Top target (5 home runs)*: Larry Corcoran • *Number of pitchers victimized*: 37 • *Total ballparks homered in*: 22 • *First HR*: 06/15/1876 off George Bradley • *Hit for Cycle*—vs CHI: 06/16/1884 • *World Series HR*—2

John O'Rourke

JOHN O'ROURKE
B: 08/23/1849 D: 06/23/1911
BL

Year	Tm	Lg	Tot	H	A	0	1	2	3	2	3	4	LO	XN	IP	PH	RHP	LHP
1879	BOS	NL	6	3	3	2	2	2	0	1	0	0	0	0	1	0	6	0
1880	BOS	NL	3	2	1	2	1	0	0	0	0	0	0	0	0	0	3	0
1883	NY	AA	2	1	1	2	0	0	0	0	0	0	0	0	0	0	2	0
Total			11	6	5	6	3	2	0	1	0	0	0	0	1	0	11	0

Rank among batters: 2,419 • *Top target (4 home runs)*: Will White • *Number of pitchers victimized*: 6 • *Total ballparks homered in*: 6 • *First HR*: 06/28/1879 off Monte Ward

Tom O'Rourke

THOMAS JOSEPH O'ROURKE
B: 10/ /1865 D: 07/19/1929

Year	Tm	Lg	Tot	H	A	0	1	2	3	2	3	4	LO	XN	IP	PH	RHP	LHP
1890	SYR	AA	1	0	1	1	0	0	0	0	0	0	0	0	0	0	1	0

Rank among batters: 4,707 • *Total ballparks homered in*: 1 • *First HR*: 10/02/1890 off Jack Stivetts

Rebel Oakes

ENNIS TELFAIR OAKES
B: 12/17/1886 D: 02/29/1948
BL

Year	Tm	Lg	Tot	H	A	0	1	2	3	2	3	4	LO	XN	IP	PH	RHP	LHP
1909	CIN	NL	3	1	2	3	0	0	0	0	0	0	0	0	2	0	3	0
1911	STL	NL	2	2	0	0	1	1	0	0	0	0	0	0	2	0	2	0
1912	STL	NL	3	1	2	1	2	0	0	0	0	0	0	0	0	0	2	1
1914	PIT	FL	7	3	4	2	4	1	0	0	0	0	0	0	0	0	7	0
Total			15	7	8	6	7	2	0	0	0	0	0	0	4	0	14	1

Rank among batters: 2,096 • *Total ballparks homered in*: 6 • *First HR*: 07/27/1909 off Vic Willis

Prince Oana

HENRY KUAHANE OANA
B: 01/22/1908 D: 06/19/1976
BR

Year	Tm	Lg	Tot	H	A	0	1	2	3	2	3	4	LO	XN	IP	PH	RHP	LHP
1943	DET	AL	1	1	0	0	0	1	0	0	0	0	0	0	0	0	1	0

Rank among batters: 4,707 • *Total ballparks homered in*: 1 • *First HR*: 07/03/1943 off Atley Donald

Johnny Oates

JOHNNY LANE OATES
B: 01/21/1946
BL

Year	Tm	Lg	Tot	H	A	0	1	2	3	2	3	4	LO	XN	IP	PH	RHP	LHP
1972	BAL	AL	4	2	2	3	0	1	0	0	0	0	0	0	0	0	4	0
1973	ATL	NL	4	2	2	2	2	0	0	0	0	0	0	0	0	0	1	3
1974	ATL	NL	1	1	0	1	0	0	0	0	0	0	0	0	0	0	1	0
1975	PHI	NL	1	1	0	1	0	0	0	0	0	0	0	0	0	0	1	0
1977	LA	NL	3	2	1	2	1	0	0	0	0	0	0	0	0	0	3	0
1980	NY	AL	1	1	0	1	0	0	0	0	0	0	0	0	0	0	0	1
Total			14	9	5	10	3	1	0	0	0	0	0	0	0	0	10	4

Rank among batters: 2,169 • *Total ballparks homered in*: 9 • *First HR*: 05/06/1972 off Dick Drago

Sherman Obando

SHERMAN OMAR (GAINOR) OBANDO
B: 01/23/1970
BR

Year	Tm	Lg	Tot	H	A	Men-On 0	1	2	3	One-Game 2	3	4	LO	XN	IP	PH	RHP	LHP
1993	BAL	AL	3	2	1	2	0	1	0	0	0	0	0	0	0	0	1	2

Rank among batters: 3,735 • *Total ballparks homered in*: 2 • *First HR*: 05/19/1993 off Mark Clark

Ken Oberkfell

KENNETH RAY OBERKFELL
B: 05/04/1956
BL

Year	Tm	Lg	Tot	H	A	Men-On 0	1	2	3	One-Game 2	3	4	LO	XN	IP	PH	RHP	LHP
1979	STL	NL	1	1	0	0	1	0	0	0	0	0	0	0	0	0	1	0
1980	STL	NL	3	0	3	1	2	0	0	0	0	0	0	0	1	0	3	0
1981	STL	NL	2	0	2	1	1	0	0	0	0	0	0	0	0	0	1	1
1982	STL	NL	2	1	1	2	0	0	0	0	0	0	0	0	0	0	2	0
1983	STL	NL	3	0	3	2	1	0	0	0	0	0	0	0	0	0	3	0
1984	ATL	NL	1	1	0	0	1	0	0	0	0	0	0	0	0	0	1	0
1985	ATL	NL	3	2	1	1	2	0	0	0	0	0	0	0	0	0	3	0
1986	ATL	NL	5	2	3	3	0	2	0	0	0	0	0	1	0	0	3	2
1987	ATL	NL	3	2	1	2	1	0	0	0	0	0	0	0	0	0	3	0
1988	ATL	NL	3	1	2	2	1	0	0	0	0	0	0	0	0	0	3	0
1989	SF	NL	2	1	1	1	0	1	0	0	0	0	0	0	0	1	2	0
1990	HOU	NL	1	0	1	0	0	1	0	0	0	0	0	0	0	0	1	0
Total			29	11	18	15	10	4	0	0	0	0	0	1	1	1	26	3

Rank among batters: 1,465 • Top target (2 home runs): Lamarr Hoyt, Chris Welsh, Eric Show, Ron Darling • *Number of pitchers victimized*: 25 • *Total ballparks homered in*: 10 • *First HR*: 05/13/1979 off Phil Niekro

Blue Moon Odom

JOHNNY LEE ODOM
B: 05/29/1945
BR

Year	Tm	Lg	Tot	H	A	Men-On 0	1	2	3	One-Game 2	3	4	LO	XN	IP	PH	RHP	LHP
1968	OAK	AL	1	0	1	1	0	0	0	0	0	0	0	0	0	0	0	1
1969	OAK	AL	5	4	1	3	0	2	0	0	0	0	0	0	0	0	4	1
1970	OAK	AL	3	1	2	2	1	0	0	0	0	0	0	0	0	0	3	0
1971	OAK	AL	1	1	0	1	0	0	0	0	0	0	0	0	0	0	0	1
1972	OAK	AL	2	1	1	2	0	0	0	0	0	0	0	0	0	0	1	1
Total			12	7	5	9	1	2	0	0	0	0	0	0	0	0	8	4

Rank among batters: 2,325 • *Total ballparks homered in*: 5 • *First HR*: 06/12/1968 off Billy Rohr

Fred Odwell

FREDERICK WILLIAM ODWELL
B: 09/25/1872 D: 08/19/1948
BL

Year	Tm	Lg	Tot	H	A	Men-On 0	1	2	3	One-Game 2	3	4	LO	XN	IP	PH	RHP	LHP
1904	CIN	NL	1	0	1	1	0	0	0	0	0	0	0	0	0	0	1	0
1905	CIN	NL	9	2	7	3	5	1	0	0	0	0	0	0	4	0	8	1
Total			10	2	8	4	5	1	0	0	0	0	0	0	4	0	9	1

Rank among batters: 2,500 • *Top target (2 home runs)*: Kaiser Wilhelm • *Number of pitchers victimized*: 9 • *Total ballparks homered in*: 6 • *First HR*: 08/03/1904 off Tully Sparks

Chuck Oertel

CHARLES FRANK OERTEL
B: 03/12/1931
BL

Year	Tm	Lg	Tot	H	A	Men-On 0	1	2	3	One-Game 2	3	4	LO	XN	IP	PH	RHP	LHP
1958	BAL	AL	1	0	1	1	0	0	0	0	0	0	0	0	0	0	1	0

Rank among batters: 4,707 • *Total ballparks homered in*: 1 • *First HR*: 09/13/1958 off Jim Bunning

Ron Oester

RONALD JOHN OESTER
B: 05/05/1956
BB

Year	Tm	Lg	Tot	H	A	Men-On 0	1	2	3	One-Game 2	3	4	LO	XN	IP	PH	RHP	LHP
1980	CIN	NL	2	0	2	1	0	1	0	0	0	0	0	0	0	0	0	2
1981	CIN	NL	5	3	2	4	0	0	1	0	0	0	0	1	0	0	5	0
1982	CIN	NL	9	4	5	6	3	0	0	1	0	0	0	1	0	0	9	0
1983	CIN	NL	11	6	5	6	3	2	0	0	0	0	0	1	0	0	10	1
1984	CIN	NL	3	2	1	3	0	0	0	0	0	0	0	0	0	0	2	1
1985	CIN	NL	1	0	1	0	1	0	0	0	0	0	0	0	0	0	1	0

Year	Tm	Lg	Tot	H	A	Men-On 0	1	2	3	One-Game 2	3	4	LO	XN	IP	PH	RHP	LHP

Ron Oester *continued*

Year	Tm	Lg	Tot	H	A	Men-On 0	1	2	3	One-Game 2	3	4	LO	XN	IP	PH	RHP	LHP
1986	CIN	NL	8	6	2	5	2	1	0	1	0	0	0	0	0	0	7	1
1987	CIN	NL	2	0	2	1	1	0	0	0	0	0	0	1	0	0	2	0
1989	CIN	NL	1	1	0	1	0	0	0	0	0	0	0	0	0	0	1	0
Total			42	22	20	27	10	4	1	2	0	0	0	4	0	0	37	5

Rank among batters: 1,138 • *Top target (3 home runs)*: Phil Niekro • *Number of pitchers victimized*: 38 • *Total ballparks homered in*: 10 • *First HR*: 07/28/1980 off Fred Norman

Jose Offerman

JOSE ANTONIO (DONO) OFFERMAN
B: 11/08/1968
BB

Year	Tm	Lg	Tot	H	A	Men-On 0	1	2	3	One-Game 2	3	4	LO	XN	IP	PH	RHP	LHP
1990	LA	NL	1	1	0	1	0	0	0	0	0	0	1	0	0	0	1	0
1992	LA	NL	1	1	0	1	0	0	0	0	0	0	0	0	0	0	0	1
1993	LA	NL	1	1	0	1	0	0	0	0	0	0	0	0	0	0	0	1
1994	LA	NL	1	0	1	1	0	0	0	0	0	0	0	0	0	0	1	0
1995	LA	NL	4	2	2	3	1	0	0	0	0	0	0	0	0	0	3	1
Total			8	5	3	7	1	0	0	0	0	0	1	0	0	0	5	3

Rank among batters: 2,703 • *Total ballparks homered in*: 3 • *First HR*: 08/19/1990 off Dennis Martinez • *Hit HR in first major league AB*—vs MON: 08/19/1990

Rowland Office

ROWLAND JOHNIE OFFICE
B: 10/25/1952
BL

Year	Tm	Lg	Tot	H	A	Men-On 0	1	2	3	One-Game 2	3	4	LO	XN	IP	PH	RHP	LHP
1974	ATL	NL	3	1	2	2	1	0	0	0	0	0	0	0	0	0	3	0
1975	ATL	NL	3	2	1	1	0	2	0	0	0	0	0	0	0	0	3	0
1976	ATL	NL	4	0	4	1	1	2	0	0	0	0	1	0	0	0	3	1
1977	ATL	NL	5	5	0	3	2	0	0	0	0	0	0	0	0	0	5	0
1978	ATL	NL	9	5	4	6	0	3	0	0	0	0	0	0	0	1	9	0
1979	ATL	NL	2	0	2	0	1	1	0	0	0	0	0	0	0	1	2	0
1980	MON	NL	6	5	1	5	1	0	0	0	0	0	0	0	0	1	6	0
Total			32	18	14	18	6	8	0	0	0	0	1	0	0	3	31	1

Rank among batters: 1,360 • *Top target (2 home runs)*: Don Sutton, Dennis Lamp • *Number of pitchers victimized*: 30 • *Total ballparks homered in*: 10 • *First HR*: 05/12/1974 off Jim Barr

Ben Oglivie

BENJAMIN AMBROSIO OGLIVIE
B: 02/11/1949
BL

Year	Tm	Lg	Tot	H	A	Men-On 0	1	2	3	One-Game 2	3	4	LO	XN	IP	PH	RHP	LHP
1972	BOS	AL	8	4	4	4	4	0	0	1	0	0	0	1	0	1	6	2
1973	BOS	AL	2	1	1	2	0	0	0	0	0	0	0	1	0	0	2	0
1974	DET	AL	4	2	2	3	0	1	0	0	0	0	0	0	0	0	4	0
1975	DET	AL	9	6	3	5	4	0	0	0	0	0	0	0	1	0	7	2
1976	DET	AL	15	8	7	6	9	0	0	1	0	0	0	1	1	3	13	2
1977	DET	AL	21	9	12	12	8	1	0	1	0	0	0	0	0	0	18	3
1978	MIL	AL	18	6	12	8	8	2	0	0	0	0	0	0	0	0	17	1
1979	MIL	AL	29	16	13	18	9	1	1	2	1	0	0	1	0	1	23	6
1980	MIL	AL	41	15	26	24	12	4	1	4	0	0	0	0	2	0	29	12
1981	MIL	AL	14	3	11	4	6	4	0	0	0	0	0	1	0	0	11	3
1982	MIL	AL	34	16	18	19	11	3	1	0	1	0	0	0	0	0	25	9
1983	MIL	AL	13	8	5	6	4	2	1	0	1	0	0	0	0	0	7	6
1984	MIL	AL	12	7	5	7	4	1	0	0	0	0	0	1	0	0	10	2
1985	MIL	AL	10	4	6	3	5	2	0	0	0	0	0	0	0	0	8	2
1986	MIL	AL	5	2	3	2	3	0	0	1	0	0	0	0	0	0	5	0
Total			235	107	128	123	87	21	4	10	3	0	1	6	4	5	185	50

Rank among batters: 135 • *Top target (6 home runs)*: Dennis Eckersley • *Number of pitchers victimized*: 154 • *Total ballparks homered in*: 15 • *First HR*: 05/14/1972 off Catfish Hunter • *World Series HR*—1; *LCS HR*—1

Bruce Ogrodowski

AMBROSE FRANCIS OGRODOWSKI
B: 02/17/1912 D: 03/05/1956
BR

Year	Tm	Lg	Tot	H	A	Men-On 0	1	2	3	One-Game 2	3	4	LO	XN	IP	PH	RHP	LHP
1936	STL	NL	1	1	0	0	1	0	0	0	0	0	0	0	0	0	1	0

Bruce Ogrodowski *continued*

						Men-On				One-Game								
Year	Tm	Lg	Tot	H	A	0	1	2	3	2	3	4	LO	XN	IP	PH	RHP	LHP
1937	STL	NL	3	1	2	3	0	0	0	0	0	0	0	0	0	0	3	0
Total			4	2	2	3	1	0	0	0	0	0	0	0	0	0	4	0

Rank among batters: 3,427 • *Total ballparks homered in*: 3 • *First HR*: 05/01/1936 off George Earnshaw

Bobby Ojeda

ROBERT MICHAEL OJEDA
B: 12/17/1957
BL

Year	Tm	Lg	Tot	H	A	0	1	2	3	2	3	4	LO	XN	IP	PH	RHP	LHP
1991	LA	NL	1	0	1	0	1	0	0	0	0	0	0	0	0	0	1	0

Rank among batters: 4,707 • *Total ballparks homered in*: 1 • *First HR*: 07/11/1991 off Mark Gardner

Red Oldham

JOHN CYRUS OLDHAM
B: 07/15/1893 D: 01/28/1961
BB

Year	Tm	Lg	Tot	H	A	0	1	2	3	2	3	4	LO	XN	IP	PH	RHP	LHP
1921	DET	AL	2	0	2	1	1	0	0	0	0	0	0	0	0	0	2	0

Rank among batters: 4,129 • *Total ballparks homered in*: 2 • *First HR*: 07/07/1921 off Roy Wilkinson

Bob Oldis

ROBERT CARL OLDIS
B: 01/05/1928
BR

Year	Tm	Lg	Tot	H	A	0	1	2	3	2	3	4	LO	XN	IP	PH	RHP	LHP
1962	PHI	NL	1	0	1	1	0	0	0	0	0	0	0	0	0	0	0	1

Rank among batters: 4,707 • *Total ballparks homered in*: 1 • *First HR*: 08/09/1962 off Pete Richert

Rube Oldring

REUBEN HENRY OLDRING
B: 05/30/1884 D: 09/09/1961
BR

Year	Tm	Lg	Tot	H	A	0	1	2	3	2	3	4	LO	XN	IP	PH	RHP	LHP
1905	NY	AL	1	0	1	1	0	0	0	0	0	0	0	0	0	0	1	0
1907	PHI	AL	1	0	1	0	1	0	0	0	0	0	0	0	0	0	1	0
1908	PHI	AL	1	0	1	0	0	1	0	0	0	0	0	0	0	0	1	0
1909	PHI	AL	1	0	1	0	1	0	0	0	0	0	0	0	1	0	1	0
1910	PHI	AL	4	1	3	4	0	0	0	0	0	0	0	0	2	0	4	0
1911	PHI	AL	3	0	3	1	1	1	0	0	0	0	0	0	1	0	2	1
1912	PHI	AL	1	0	1	1	0	0	0	0	0	0	0	0	0	0	1	0
1913	PHI	AL	5	3	2	3	2	0	0	0	0	0	0	0	0	0	5	0
1914	PHI	AL	3	3	0	1	1	1	0	0	0	0	0	0	0	0	3	0
1915	PHI	AL	6	5	1	2	3	1	0	0	0	0	0	0	0	0	4	2
1916	NY	AL	1	0	1	0	0	0	1	0	0	0	0	0	0	0	1	0
Total			27	12	15	13	9	4	1	0	0	0	0	0	4	0	24	3

Rank among batters: 1,532 • *Top target (2 home runs)*: Ed Summers, Rube Foster, Ray Keating • *Number of pitchers victimized*: 24 • *Total ballparks homered in*: 10 • *First HR*: 10/07/1905 off George Winter • *World Series HR*—1

John Olerud

JOHN GARRETT OLERUD
B: 08/05/1968
BL

Year	Tm	Lg	Tot	H	A	0	1	2	3	2	3	4	LO	XN	IP	PH	RHP	LHP
1990	TOR	AL	14	11	3	8	5	1	0	1	0	0	0	0	0	0	11	3
1991	TOR	AL	17	7	10	12	4	1	0	1	0	0	0	1	0	0	14	3
1992	TOR	AL	16	4	12	9	5	2	0	1	0	0	0	1	0	0	13	3
1993	TOR	AL	24	9	15	15	7	2	0	1	0	0	0	0	0	0	20	4
1994	TOR	AL	12	6	6	6	5	1	0	1	0	0	0	0	0	0	9	3
1995	TOR	AL	8	1	7	6	1	0	1	1	0	0	0	0	0	0	7	1
Total			91	38	53	56	27	7	1	6	0	0	0	2	0	0	74	17

Rank among batters: 559 • *Top target (3 home runs)*: John Farrell, David Cone, Ben McDonald • *Number of pitchers victimized*: 75 • *Total ballparks homered in*: 16 • *First HR*: 04/18/1990 off Pete Harnisch • *World Series HR*—1; *LCS HR*—1

Frank Olin

FRANKLIN WALTER OLIN
B: 01/09/1860 D: 05/20/1951
BL

Year	Tm	Lg	Tot	H	A	0	1	2	3	2	3	4	LO	XN	IP	PH	RHP	LHP
1884	TOL	AA	1	0	1	1	0	0	0	0	0	0	0	0	0	0	1	0

Frank Olin *continued*

Rank among batters: 4,707 • *Total ballparks homered in*: 1 • *First HR*: 09/29/1884 off Hardie Henderson

Jose Oliva

JOSE (GALVEZ) OLIVA
B: 03/03/1971
BR

Year	Tm	Lg	Tot	H	A	Men-On 0	1	2	3	One-Game 2	3	4	LO	XN	IP	PH	RHP	LHP
1994	ATL	NL	6	4	2	5	0	1	0	1	0	0	0	0	0	0	4	2
1995	ATL	NL	5	1	4	2	3	0	0	0	0	0	0	0	0	0	3	2
	STL	NL	2	1	1	1	1	0	0	0	0	0	0	0	0	0	2	0
Total			13	6	7	8	4	1	0	1	0	0	0	0	0	0	9	4

Rank among batters: 2,248 • *Total ballparks homered in*: 8 • *First HR*: 07/10/1994 off Allen Watson

Tony Oliva

PEDRO (LOPEZ) OLIVA
B: 07/20/1940
BL

Year	Tm	Lg	Tot	H	A	Men-On 0	1	2	3	One-Game 2	3	4	LO	XN	IP	PH	RHP	LHP
1964	MIN	AL	32	17	15	17	10	4	1	4	0	0	0	2	2	0	28	4
1965	MIN	AL	16	5	11	7	7	2	0	2	0	0	0	0	0	0	15	1
1966	MIN	AL	25	18	7	18	4	3	0	2	0	0	0	1	1	0	20	5
1967	MIN	AL	17	9	8	12	3	2	0	1	0	0	0	0	0	0	17	0
1968	MIN	AL	18	7	11	7	10	1	0	2	0	0	0	0	0	0	18	0
1969	MIN	AL	24	11	13	14	6	4	0	3	0	0	0	1	0	0	18	6
1970	MIN	AL	23	6	17	8	11	4	0	0	0	0	0	0	0	0	18	5
1971	MIN	AL	22	9	13	13	6	3	0	1	0	0	0	0	0	0	13	9
1973	MIN	AL	16	5	11	10	4	1	1	1	1	0	0	0	0	0	14	2
1974	MIN	AL	13	4	9	8	2	3	0	1	0	0	0	0	0	0	9	4
1975	MIN	AL	13	4	9	10	1	1	1	0	0	0	0	0	0	1	11	2
1976	MIN	AL	1	0	1	0	1	0	0	0	0	0	0	0	0	1	1	0
Total			220	95	125	124	65	28	3	17	1	0	0	4	3	2	182	38

Rank among batters: 149 • *Top target (8 home runs)*: Catfish Hunter • *Number of pitchers victimized*: 121 • *Total ballparks homered in*: 15 • *First HR*: 04/18/1964 off Steve Ridzik • *World Series HR*—1; *LCS HR*—2

Omar Olivares

OMAR (PALQU) OLIVARES
B: 07/06/1967
BR

Year	Tm	Lg	Tot	H	A	Men-On 0	1	2	3	One-Game 2	3	4	LO	XN	IP	PH	RHP	LHP
1990	STL	NL	1	0	1	1	0	0	0	0	0	0	0	0	0	0	1	0
1992	STL	NL	1	0	1	0	1	0	0	0	0	0	0	0	0	0	1	0
1994	STL	NL	1	0	1	1	0	0	0	0	0	0	0	0	0	0	1	0
1995	PHI	NL	1	1	0	0	1	0	0	0	0	0	0	0	0	1	1	0
Total			4	1	3	2	2	0	0	0	0	0	0	0	0	1	4	0

Rank among batters: 3,427 • *Total ballparks homered in*: 4 • *First HR*: 09/08/1990 off Rick Sutcliffe

Al Oliver

ALBERT OLIVER
B: 10/14/1946
BL

Year	Tm	Lg	Tot	H	A	Men-On 0	1	2	3	One-Game 2	3	4	LO	XN	IP	PH	RHP	LHP
1969	PIT	NL	17	7	10	8	6	2	1	1	0	0	0	0	1	0	14	3
1970	PIT	NL	12	2	10	8	3	0	1	0	0	0	0	1	0	0	10	2
1971	PIT	NL	14	3	11	8	5	1	0	1	0	0	0	0	0	0	10	4
1972	PIT	NL	12	5	7	5	3	4	0	1	0	0	0	0	0	0	12	0
1973	PIT	NL	20	7	13	9	9	1	1	1	0	0	0	0	0	0	15	5
1974	PIT	NL	11	4	7	4	6	1	0	1	0	0	0	0	0	0	8	3
1975	PIT	NL	18	9	9	7	9	1	1	0	0	0	0	0	0	0	11	7
1976	PIT	NL	12	9	3	6	4	2	0	0	0	0	0	0	0	0	6	6
1977	PIT	NL	19	12	7	13	4	2	0	0	0	0	0	0	0	1	15	4
1978	TEX	AL	14	6	8	10	3	1	0	0	0	0	0	0	0	0	10	4
1979	TEX	AL	12	8	4	8	4	0	0	1	1	0	0	0	0	0	11	1
1980	TEX	AL	19	8	11	13	4	1	1	0	1	0	0	0	0	0	15	4
1981	TEX	AL	4	3	1	2	2	0	0	0	0	0	0	0	0	0	2	2
1982	MON	NL	22	12	10	11	8	3	0	1	0	0	0	0	0	1	15	7
1983	MON	NL	8	5	3	4	2	0	2	1	0	0	0	0	0	0	7	1
1985	TOR	AL	5	1	4	2	2	1	0	0	0	0	0	1	0	0	4	1
Total			219	101	118	118	74	20	7	8	2	0	0	2	1	2	165	54

Rank among batters: 152 • *Top target (4 home runs)*: Bob Gibson, Don Sutton • *Number of pitchers victimized*: 158 • *Total ballparks homered in*: 30 • *First HR*: 04/17/1969 off Cal Koonce • *LCS HR*—3

Bob Oliver

ROBERT LEE OLIVER
B: 02/08/1943
BR

Year	Tm	Lg	Tot	H	A	Men-On 0	1	2	3	One-Game 2	3	4	LO	XN	IP	PH	RHP	LHP
1969	KC	AL	13	5	8	4	7	1	1	0	0	0	0	0	0	1	11	2
1970	KC	AL	27	11	16	12	9	6	0	3	0	0	0	1	0	0	21	6
1971	KC	AL	8	1	7	3	2	2	1	1	0	0	0	0	0	1	5	3
1972	KC	AL	1	1	0	1	0	0	0	0	0	0	0	0	0	0	0	1
	CAL	AL	19	10	9	8	9	2	0	0	0	0	0	1	0	0	13	6
	Total		20	11	9	9	9	2	0	0	0	0	0	1	0	0	13	7
1973	CAL	AL	18	6	12	8	6	4	0	0	0	0	0	0	0	0	10	8
1974	CAL	AL	8	7	1	5	2	1	0	1	0	0	0	0	0	0	4	4
Total			94	41	53	41	35	16	2	5	0	0	0	2	0	2	64	30

Rank among batters: 535 • *Top target (4 home runs)*: Lew Krausse • *Number of pitchers victimized*: 68 • *Total ballparks homered in*: 15 • *First HR*: 04/29/1969 off Dick Woodson

Gene Oliver

EUGENE GEORGE OLIVER
B: 03/22/1935
BR

Year	Tm	Lg	Tot	H	A	Men-On 0	1	2	3	One-Game 2	3	4	LO	XN	IP	PH	RHP	LHP
1959	STL	NL	6	2	4	2	3	1	0	0	0	0	0	0	0	0	3	3
1961	STL	NL	4	1	3	2	2	0	0	0	0	0	0	0	0	0	2	2
1962	STL	NL	14	4	10	10	2	2	0	0	0	0	0	0	0	0	6	8
1963	STL	NL	6	2	4	2	4	0	0	0	0	0	0	1	1	0	3	3
	MIL	NL	11	5	6	4	5	1	1	1	0	0	0	0	0	0	6	5
	Total		17	7	10	6	9	1	1	1	0	0	0	1	1	0	9	8
1964	MIL	NL	13	8	5	7	3	2	1	1	0	0	0	0	0	1	5	8
1965	MIL	NL	21	9	12	15	6	0	0	4	0	0	0	1	1	0	17	4
1966	ATL	NL	8	8	0	3	4	1	0	1	1	0	0	0	0	0	5	3
1967	ATL	NL	3	3	0	2	1	0	0	0	0	0	0	0	0	0	2	1
	PHI	NL	7	5	2	5	2	0	0	0	0	0	0	0	0	0	4	3
	Total		10	8	2	7	3	0	0	0	0	0	0	0	0	0	6	4
Total			93	47	46	52	32	7	2	7	1	0	0	2	2	1	53	40

Rank among batters: 545 • *Top target (4 home runs)*: Joe Nuxhall, Sandy Koufax • *Number of pitchers victimized*: 63 • *Total ballparks homered in*: 11 • *First HR*: 06/07/1959 off Ruben Gomez

Joe Oliver

JOSEPH MELTON OLIVER
B: 07/24/1965
BR

Year	Tm	Lg	Tot	H	A	Men-On 0	1	2	3	One-Game 2	3	4	LO	XN	IP	PH	RHP	LHP
1989	CIN	NL	3	1	2	2	1	0	0	0	0	0	0	0	0	0	2	1
1990	CIN	NL	8	3	5	4	2	2	0	1	0	0	0	0	0	0	3	5
1991	CIN	NL	11	7	4	3	5	2	1	0	0	0	0	0	0	0	3	8
1992	CIN	NL	10	7	3	4	3	3	0	0	0	0	0	0	0	0	6	4
1993	CIN	NL	14	7	7	5	4	4	1	1	0	0	0	0	0	0	8	6
1994	CIN	NL	1	1	0	0	1	0	0	0	0	0	0	0	0	0	0	1
1995	MIL	AL	12	4	8	6	3	2	1	0	0	0	0	0	0	0	11	1
Total			59	30	29	24	19	13	3	2	0	0	0	0	0	0	33	26

Rank among batters: 873 • *Top target (3 home runs)*: Zane Smith, Bud Black • *Number of pitchers victimized*: 49 • *Total ballparks homered in*: 19 • *First HR*: 08/18/1989 off Ricky Horton

Nate Oliver

NATHANIEL OLIVER
B: 12/13/1940
BR

Year	Tm	Lg	Tot	H	A	Men-On 0	1	2	3	One-Game 2	3	4	LO	XN	IP	PH	RHP	LHP
1963	LA	NL	1	0	1	1	0	0	0	0	0	0	0	0	0	0	1	0
1969	CHI	NL	1	1	0	0	1	0	0	0	0	0	0	0	0	0	1	0
Total			2	1	1	1	1	0	0	0	0	0	0	0	0	0	2	0

Rank among batters: 4,129 • *Total ballparks homered in*: 2 • *First HR*: 07/13/1963 off Larry Bearnarth

Luis Olmo

LUIS FRANCISCO OLMO
B: 08/11/1919
BR

Year	Tm	Lg	Tot	H	A	Men-On 0	1	2	3	One-Game 2	3	4	LO	XN	IP	PH	RHP	LHP
1943	BRO	NL	4	1	3	3	1	0	0	0	0	0	0	0	1	0	4	0
1944	BRO	NL	9	4	5	3	3	3	0	0	0	0	0	0	1	0	7	2
1945	BRO	NL	10	2	8	3	5	0	2	0	0	0	0	0	0	0	6	4
1949	BRO	NL	1	1	0	1	0	0	0	0	0	0	0	0	0	0	0	1

Luis Olmo *continued*

Year	Tm	Lg	Tot	H	A	Men-On 0	1	2	3	One-Game 2	3	4	LO	XN	IP	PH	RHP	LHP
1950	BOS	NL	5	2	3	3	2	0	0	0	0	0	0	0	0	0	1	4
Total			29	10	19	13	11	3	2	0	0	0	0	0	2	0	18	11

Rank among batters: 1,465 • *Top target (3 home runs)*: Ken Raffensberger • *Number of pitchers victimized*: 24 • *Total ballparks homered in*: 8 • *First HR*: 07/26/1943 off Max Butcher • *World Series HR*—1

Barney Olsen

BERNARD CHARLES OLSEN
B: 09/11/1919 D: 03/30/1977
BR

Year	Tm	Lg	Tot	H	A	Men-On 0	1	2	3	One-Game 2	3	4	LO	XN	IP	PH	RHP	LHP
1941	CHI	NL	1	0	1	1	0	0	0	0	0	0	0	0	0	0	0	1

Rank among batters: 4,707 • *Total ballparks homered in*: 1 • *First HR*: 08/26/1941 off Lefty Hoerst

Vern Olsen

VERN JARL OLSEN
B: 03/16/1918 D: 07/13/1989
BR

Year	Tm	Lg	Tot	H	A	Men-On 0	1	2	3	One-Game 2	3	4	LO	XN	IP	PH	RHP	LHP
1941	CHI	NL	1	0	1	0	0	1	0	0	0	0	0	0	0	0	1	0

Rank among batters: 4,707 • *Total ballparks homered in*: 1 • *First HR*: 05/08/1941 off Isaac Pearson

Greg Olson

GREGORY WILLIAM OLSON
B: 09/06/1960
BR

Year	Tm	Lg	Tot	H	A	Men-On 0	1	2	3	One-Game 2	3	4	LO	XN	IP	PH	RHP	LHP
1990	ATL	NL	7	4	3	3	1	2	1	1	0	0	0	0	0	0	2	5
1991	ATL	NL	6	6	0	4	2	0	0	0	0	0	0	0	0	0	4	2
1992	ATL	NL	3	0	3	3	0	0	0	0	0	0	0	0	0	0	2	1
1993	ATL	NL	4	3	1	0	2	2	0	0	0	0	0	0	0	0	1	3
Total			20	13	7	10	5	4	1	1	0	0	0	0	0	0	9	11

Rank among batters: 1,810 • *Total ballparks homered in*: 6 • *First HR*: 05/08/1990 off Steve Wilson • *LCS HR*—1

Ivy Olson

IVAN MASSIE OLSON
B: 10/14/1885 D: 09/01/1965
BR

Year	Tm	Lg	Tot	H	A	Men-On 0	1	2	3	One-Game 2	3	4	LO	XN	IP	PH	RHP	LHP
1911	CLE	AL	1	1	0	0	0	0	1	0	0	0	0	0	1	0	1	0
1914	CLE	AL	1	1	0	0	0	1	0	0	0	0	0	0	1	0	0	1
1916	BRO	NL	1	0	1	1	0	0	0	0	0	0	0	0	0	0	1	0
1917	BRO	NL	2	1	1	2	0	0	0	0	0	0	0	0	0	0	0	2
1918	BRO	NL	1	1	0	1	0	0	0	0	0	0	0	0	0	0	0	1
1919	BRO	NL	1	1	0	1	0	0	0	0	0	0	0	0	1	0	1	0
1920	BRO	NL	1	0	1	0	1	0	0	0	0	0	0	0	0	0	0	1
1921	BRO	NL	3	0	3	2	1	0	0	0	0	0	1	0	1	0	2	1
1922	BRO	NL	1	0	1	1	0	0	0	0	0	0	0	0	0	0	1	0
1923	BRO	NL	1	0	1	0	0	1	0	0	0	0	0	0	0	0	1	0
Total			13	5	8	8	2	2	1	0	0	0	1	0	4	0	7	6

Rank among batters: 2,248 • *Total ballparks homered in*: 8 • *First HR*: 05/18/1911 off Tom Hughes

Karl Olson

KARL ARTHUR OLSON
B: 07/06/1930
BR

Year	Tm	Lg	Tot	H	A	Men-On 0	1	2	3	One-Game 2	3	4	LO	XN	IP	PH	RHP	LHP
1953	BOS	AL	1	0	1	0	1	0	0	0	0	0	0	0	0	0	1	0
1954	BOS	AL	1	0	1	0	0	1	0	0	0	0	0	0	0	0	1	0
1956	WAS	AL	4	3	1	3	1	0	0	1	0	0	0	0	0	0	4	0
Total			6	3	3	3	2	1	0	1	0	0	0	0	0	0	6	0

Rank among batters: 2,988 • *Top target (2 home runs)*: Don Larsen • *Number of pitchers victimized*: 5 • *Total ballparks homered in*: 3 • *First HR*: 09/03/1953 off Steve Gromek

Eddie Onslow

EDWARD JOSEPH ONSLOW
B: 02/17/1893 D: 05/08/1981
BL

Year	Tm	Lg	Tot	H	A	Men-On 0	1	2	3	One-Game 2	3	4	LO	XN	IP	PH	RHP	LHP
1912	DET	AL	1	0	1	0	0	0	1	0	0	0	0	0	1	0	1	0

Rank among batters: 4,707 • *Total ballparks homered in*: 1 • *First HR*: 08/22/1912 off Tom Hughes

Steve Ontiveros

STEVEN ROBERT ONTIVEROS
B: 10/26/1951
BB

Year	Tm	Lg	Tot	H	A	Men-On 0	Men-On 1	Men-On 2	Men-On 3	One-Game 2	One-Game 3	One-Game 4	LO	XN	IP	PH	RHP	LHP
1973	SF	NL	1	0	1	0	1	0	0	0	0	0	0	0	0	1	1	0
1974	SF	NL	4	3	1	3	1	0	0	0	0	0	0	0	0	0	4	0
1975	SF	NL	3	1	2	3	0	0	0	0	0	0	0	0	0	0	3	0
1977	CHI	NL	10	5	5	7	1	2	0	0	0	0	0	0	0	0	8	2
1978	CHI	NL	1	0	1	0	1	0	0	0	0	0	0	0	0	0	1	0
1979	CHI	NL	4	1	3	1	2	1	0	0	0	0	0	0	0	0	3	1
1980	CHI	NL	1	1	0	1	0	0	0	0	0	0	0	0	0	0	1	0
Total			24	11	13	15	6	3	0	0	0	0	0	0	0	1	21	3

Rank among batters: 1,643 • *Top target (2 home runs)*: Tom Seaver, Tom Griffin • *Number of pitchers victimized*: 22 • *Total ballparks homered in*: 6 • *First HR*: 09/13/1973 off Gary Ross

Jose Oquendo

JOSE MANUEL (CONTRERAS) OQUENDO
B: 07/04/1963
BB

Year	Tm	Lg	Tot	H	A	Men-On 0	Men-On 1	Men-On 2	Men-On 3	One-Game 2	One-Game 3	One-Game 4	LO	XN	IP	PH	RHP	LHP
1983	NY	NL	1	0	1	1	0	0	0	0	0	0	0	0	0	0	0	1
1987	STL	NL	1	0	1	0	1	0	0	0	0	0	0	0	0	1	0	1
1988	STL	NL	7	4	3	3	2	2	0	0	0	0	0	1	0	0	0	7
1989	STL	NL	1	0	1	1	0	0	0	0	0	0	0	0	0	0	1	0
1990	STL	NL	1	1	0	1	0	0	0	0	0	0	0	0	0	0	0	1
1991	STL	NL	1	0	1	1	0	0	0	0	0	0	0	0	0	0	0	1
1995	STL	NL	2	0	2	1	1	0	0	0	0	0	0	0	0	1	0	2
Total			14	5	9	8	4	2	0	0	0	0	0	1	0	2	1	13

Rank among batters: 2,169 • *Top target (2 home runs)*: Craig Lefferts, Tom Browning • *Number of pitchers victimized*: 12 • *Total ballparks homered in*: 8 • *First HR*: 08/21/1983 off Gary Lavelle • *LCS HR*—1

Joe Orengo

JOSEPH CHARLES ORENGO
B: 11/29/1914 D: 07/24/1988
BR

Year	Tm	Lg	Tot	H	A	Men-On 0	Men-On 1	Men-On 2	Men-On 3	One-Game 2	One-Game 3	One-Game 4	LO	XN	IP	PH	RHP	LHP
1940	STL	NL	7	3	4	6	1	0	0	0	0	0	0	0	0	0	4	3
1941	NY	NL	4	4	0	1	3	0	0	0	0	0	0	0	0	1	3	1
1943	NY	NL	6	5	1	4	2	0	0	0	0	0	0	0	1	0	5	1
Total			17	12	5	11	6	0	0	0	0	0	0	0	1	1	12	5

Rank among batters: 1,969 • *Total ballparks homered in*: 5 • *First HR*: 05/13/1940 off Johnny Vander Meer

Dave Orr

DAVID L. ORR
B: 09/29/1859 D: 06/03/1915
BR

Year	Tm	Lg	Tot	H	A	Men-On 0	Men-On 1	Men-On 2	Men-On 3	One-Game 2	One-Game 3	One-Game 4	LO	XN	IP	PH	RHP	LHP
1883	NY	AA	2	0	2	1	0	1	0	1	0	0	0	0	0	0	2	0
1884	NY	AA	9	4	5	2	4	3	0	1	0	0	0	0	0	0	6	0
1885	NY	AA	6	3	3	4	1	0	1	0	0	0	0	0	3	0	5	0
1886	NY	AA	7	4	3	4	3	0	0	0	0	0	0	0	2	0	4	2
1887	NY	AA	2	1	1	0	1	1	0	0	0	0	0	0	0	0	1	1
1888	BRO	AA	1	1	0	0	1	0	0	0	0	0	0	0	1	0	1	0
1889	COL	AA	4	3	1	2	0	1	1	0	0	0	0	1	0	0	4	0
1890	BRO	PL	6	3	3	1	2	3	0	0	0	0	0	0	0	0	2	3
Total			37	19	18	14	12	9	2	2	0	0	0	1	6	0	25	4

Rank among batters: 1,252 • *Top target (3 home runs)*: Jumbo McGinnis • *Number of pitchers victimized*: 29 • *Total ballparks homered in*: 16 • *First HR*: 09/22/1883 off Ed Dundon • *Hit for Cycle*—vs STL: 06/12/1885; @BAL: 08/10/1887

Ernie Orsatti

ERNEST RALPH ORSATTI
B: 09/08/1902 D: 09/04/1968
BL

Year	Tm	Lg	Tot	H	A	Men-On 0	Men-On 1	Men-On 2	Men-On 3	One-Game 2	One-Game 3	One-Game 4	LO	XN	IP	PH	RHP	LHP
1928	STL	NL	3	3	0	2	1	0	0	0	0	0	0	0	0	0	2	1
1929	STL	NL	3	3	0	3	0	0	0	0	0	0	0	0	1	0	3	0
1930	STL	NL	1	1	0	0	1	0	0	0	0	0	0	0	0	0	1	0
1932	STL	NL	2	1	1	1	1	0	0	0	0	0	0	0	0	0	1	1
1935	STL	NL	1	1	0	1	0	0	0	0	0	0	0	0	0	0	1	0
Total			10	9	1	7	3	0	0	0	0	0	0	0	1	0	8	2

Rank among batters: 2,500 • *Top target (2 home runs)*: Carl Hubbell • *Number of pitchers victimized*: 9 • *Total ballparks homered in*: 2 • *First HR*: 08/18/1928 off Carl Hubbell

John Orsino

JOHN JOSEPH ORSINO
B: 04/22/1938
BR

Year	Tm	Lg	Tot	H	A	Men-On 0	Men-On 1	Men-On 2	Men-On 3	One-Game 2	One-Game 3	One-Game 4	LO	XN	IP	PH	RHP	LHP
1961	SF	NL	4	0	4	2	1	1	0	1	0	0	0	0	0	0	1	3
1963	BAL	AL	19	11	8	9	9	1	0	1	0	0	0	0	0	0	17	2
1964	BAL	AL	8	5	3	7	1	0	0	0	0	0	0	0	0	1	7	1
1965	BAL	AL	9	5	4	7	1	1	0	0	0	0	0	1	0	1	4	5
Total			40	21	19	25	12	3	0	2	0	0	0	1	0	2	29	11

Rank among batters: 1,181 • *Top target (4 home runs)*: Earl Wilson • *Number of pitchers victimized*: 32 • *Total ballparks homered in*: 9 • *First HR*: 07/23/1961 off Jim O'Toole

Joe Orsulak

JOSEPH MICHAEL ORSULAK
B: 05/31/1962
BL

Year	Tm	Lg	Tot	H	A	Men-On 0	Men-On 1	Men-On 2	Men-On 3	One-Game 2	One-Game 3	One-Game 4	LO	XN	IP	PH	RHP	LHP
1986	PIT	NL	2	0	2	2	0	0	0	0	0	0	0	0	0	0	2	0
1988	BAL	AL	8	3	5	6	1	1	0	0	0	0	2	0	0	0	8	0
1989	BAL	AL	7	0	7	5	2	0	0	1	0	0	0	0	0	1	7	0
1990	BAL	AL	11	9	2	5	3	3	0	1	0	0	0	0	0	0	11	0
1991	BAL	AL	5	3	2	2	2	0	1	0	0	0	0	0	0	1	5	0
1992	BAL	AL	4	2	2	2	1	1	0	0	0	0	0	0	0	0	4	0
1993	NY	NL	8	5	3	8	0	0	0	0	0	0	0	0	0	0	8	0
1994	NY	NL	8	4	4	3	2	2	1	0	0	0	0	1	0	1	8	0
1995	NY	NL	1	1	0	0	0	1	0	0	0	0	0	0	0	1	1	0
Total			54	27	27	33	11	8	2	2	0	0	2	1	0	4	54	0

Rank among batters: 938 • *Top target (3 home runs)*: Scott Sanderson • *Number of pitchers victimized*: 45 • *Total ballparks homered in*: 21 • *First HR*: 04/19/1986 off Scott Sanderson

Jorge Orta

JORGE (NUNEZ) ORTA
B: 11/26/1950
BL

Year	Tm	Lg	Tot	H	A	Men-On 0	Men-On 1	Men-On 2	Men-On 3	One-Game 2	One-Game 3	One-Game 4	LO	XN	IP	PH	RHP	LHP
1972	CHI	AL	3	0	3	3	0	0	0	0	0	0	0	1	0	0	2	1
1973	CHI	AL	6	2	4	3	3	0	0	0	0	0	0	0	0	1	4	2
1974	CHI	AL	10	1	9	5	4	1	0	2	0	0	0	1	0	0	9	1
1975	CHI	AL	11	6	5	5	6	0	0	0	0	0	0	0	0	0	11	0
1976	CHI	AL	14	8	6	11	3	0	0	0	0	0	0	0	0	0	13	1
1977	CHI	AL	11	7	4	6	4	1	0	0	0	0	0	0	0	1	10	1
1978	CHI	AL	13	9	4	6	5	2	0	1	0	0	0	0	0	0	13	0
1979	CHI	AL	11	5	6	5	5	1	0	0	0	0	0	0	0	0	11	0
1980	CLE	AL	10	6	4	5	4	0	1	0	0	0	0	0	0	0	10	0
1981	CLE	AL	5	2	3	5	0	0	0	0	0	0	0	1	0	0	4	1
1982	LA	NL	2	1	1	1	1	0	0	0	0	0	0	0	0	1	2	0
1983	TOR	AL	10	7	3	6	2	2	0	0	0	0	0	0	1	0	10	0
1984	KC	AL	9	3	6	5	3	1	0	0	0	0	0	0	0	0	9	0
1985	KC	AL	4	1	3	1	2	1	0	0	0	0	0	0	0	0	4	0
1986	KC	AL	9	5	4	4	5	0	0	1	0	0	0	0	2	0	9	0
1987	KC	AL	2	0	2	2	0	0	0	0	0	0	0	0	0	0	2	0
Total			130	63	67	73	47	9	1	4	0	0	0	3	3	3	123	7

Rank among batters: 348 • *Top target (5 home runs)*: Doug Bird • *Number of pitchers victimized*: 92 • *Total ballparks homered in*: 17 • *First HR*: 04/30/1972 off Mike Kilkenny

Frank Ortenzio

FRANK JOSEPH ORTENZIO
B: 02/24/1951
BR

Year	Tm	Lg	Tot	H	A	Men-On 0	Men-On 1	Men-On 2	Men-On 3	One-Game 2	One-Game 3	One-Game 4	LO	XN	IP	PH	RHP	LHP
1973	KC	AL	1	0	1	0	1	0	0	0	0	0	0	0	0	0	1	0

Rank among batters: 4,707 • *Total ballparks homered in*: 1 • *First HR*: 09/29/1973 off Don Durham

Al Orth

ALBERT LEWIS ORTH
B: 09/05/1872 D: 10/08/1948
BL

Year	Tm	Lg	Tot	H	A	Men-On 0	Men-On 1	Men-On 2	Men-On 3	One-Game 2	One-Game 3	One-Game 4	LO	XN	IP	PH	RHP	LHP
1895	PHI	NL	1	1	0	0	1	0	0	0	0	0	0	0	0	0	1	0
1896	PHI	NL	1	1	0	0	1	0	0	0	0	0	0	0	0	0	1	0
1897	PHI	NL	1	0	1	1	0	0	0	0	0	0	0	0	1	0	1	0
1898	PHI	NL	1	1	0	0	1	0	0	0	0	0	0	0	0	0	1	0

Al Orth *continued*

Year	Tm	Lg	Tot	H	A	Men-On 0	1	2	3	One-Game 2	3	4	LO	XN	IP	PH	RHP	LHP
1899	PHI	NL	1	1	0	0	0	1	0	0	0	0	0	0	0	0	1	0
1900	PHI	NL	1	1	0	0	0	1	0	0	0	0	0	0	0	0	1	0
1901	PHI	NL	1	1	0	1	0	0	0	0	0	0	0	0	0	0	1	0
1902	WAS	AL	2	0	2	2	0	0	0	0	0	0	0	0	0	0	2	0
1905	NY	AL	1	0	1	1	0	0	0	0	0	0	0	0	1	0	1	0
1906	NY	AL	1	1	0	0	1	0	0	0	0	0	0	0	0	0	0	1
1907	NY	AL	1	0	1	1	0	0	0	0	0	0	0	0	1	0	1	0
Total			12	7	5	6	4	2	0	0	0	0	0	0	3	0	11	1

Rank among batters: 2,325 • *Top target (2 home runs)*: Red Donahue • *Number of pitchers victimized*: 11 • *Total ballparks homered in*: 5 • *First HR*: 09/02/1895 off Pink Hawley

Javier Ortiz

JAVIER VICTOR ORTIZ
B: 01/22/1963
BR

Year	Tm	Lg	Tot	H	A	Men-On 0	1	2	3	One-Game 2	3	4	LO	XN	IP	PH	RHP	LHP
1990	HOU	NL	1	1	0	1	0	0	0	0	0	0	0	0	0	0	0	1
1991	HOU	NL	1	0	1	1	0	0	0	0	0	0	0	0	0	0	1	0
Total			2	1	1	2	0	0	0	0	0	0	0	0	0	0	1	1

Rank among batters: 4,129 • *Total ballparks homered in*: 2 • *First HR*: 07/12/1990 off Bruce Ruffin

Junior Ortiz

ADALBERTO (COLON) ORTIZ
B: 10/24/1959
BR

Year	Tm	Lg	Tot	H	A	Men-On 0	1	2	3	One-Game 2	3	4	LO	XN	IP	PH	RHP	LHP
1985	PIT	NL	1	0	1	1	0	0	0	0	0	0	0	0	0	0	1	0
1987	PIT	NL	1	0	1	1	0	0	0	0	0	0	0	0	0	0	1	0
1988	PIT	NL	2	1	1	2	0	0	0	0	0	0	0	0	0	0	1	1
1989	PIT	NL	1	0	1	0	1	0	0	0	0	0	0	0	0	0	0	1
Total			5	1	4	4	1	0	0	0	0	0	0	0	0	0	3	2

Rank among batters: 3,191 • *Total ballparks homered in*: 4 • *First HR*: 10/02/1985 off Jay Baller

Luis Ortiz

LUIS ALBERTO (GALARZA) ORTIZ
B: 05/25/1970
BR

Year	Tm	Lg	Tot	H	A	Men-On 0	1	2	3	One-Game 2	3	4	LO	XN	IP	PH	RHP	LHP
1995	TEX	AL	1	1	0	1	0	0	0	0	0	0	0	0	0	0	0	1

Rank among batters: 4,707 • *Total ballparks homered in*: 1 • *First HR*: 06/04/1995 off Eddie Guardado

Roberto Ortiz

ROBERTO GONZALO (NUNEZ) ORTIZ
B: 06/30/1915 D: 09/15/1971
BR

Year	Tm	Lg	Tot	H	A	Men-On 0	1	2	3	One-Game 2	3	4	LO	XN	IP	PH	RHP	LHP
1941	WAS	AL	1	0	1	0	1	0	0	0	0	0	0	0	0	0	1	0
1942	WAS	AL	1	1	0	0	1	0	0	0	0	0	0	0	0	0	1	0
1944	WAS	AL	5	3	2	4	1	0	0	0	0	0	0	0	1	0	5	0
1949	WAS	AL	1	0	1	0	0	1	0	0	0	0	0	0	0	0	0	1
Total			8	4	4	4	3	1	0	0	0	0	0	0	1	0	7	1

Rank among batters: 2,703 • *Total ballparks homered in*: 3 • *First HR*: 09/06/1941 off Bill Beckmann

John Orton

JOHN ANDREW ORTON
B: 12/08/1965
BR

Year	Tm	Lg	Tot	H	A	Men-On 0	1	2	3	One-Game 2	3	4	LO	XN	IP	PH	RHP	LHP
1990	CAL	AL	1	0	1	1	0	0	0	0	0	0	0	0	0	0	1	0
1992	CAL	AL	2	1	1	1	0	1	0	0	0	0	0	0	0	0	1	1
1993	CAL	AL	1	0	1	1	0	0	0	0	0	0	0	0	0	0	1	0
Total			4	1	3	3	0	1	0	0	0	0	0	0	0	0	3	1

Rank among batters: 3,427 • *Total ballparks homered in*: 4 • *First HR*: 04/27/1990 off Tim Leary

Fred Osborn

WILFRED PEARL OSBORN
B: 11/28/1883 D: 09/02/1954
BL

Year	Tm	Lg	Tot	H	A	Men-On 0	1	2	3	One-Game 2	3	4	LO	XN	IP	PH	RHP	LHP
1908	PHI	NL	2	0	2	1	1	0	0	0	0	0	0	0	1	0	2	0

Fred Osborn *continued*

Rank among batters: 4,129 • *Total ballparks homered in*: 2 • *First HR*: 06/29/1908 off Jake Boultes

Bobo Osborne

LAWRENCE SIDNEY OSBORNE
B: 10/12/1935
BL

Year	Tm	Lg	Tot	H	A	Men-On 0	Men-On 1	Men-On 2	Men-On 3	One-Game 2	One-Game 3	One-Game 4	LO	XN	IP	PH	RHP	LHP
1959	DET	AL	3	2	1	2	1	0	0	0	0	0	0	0	0	0	2	1
1961	DET	AL	2	1	1	1	1	0	0	0	0	0	0	0	0	0	2	0
1963	WAS	AL	12	5	7	7	5	0	0	1	0	0	0	0	0	0	10	2
Total			17	8	9	10	7	0	0	1	0	0	0	0	0	0	14	3

Rank among batters: 1,969 • *Top target (2 home runs)*: Whitey Ford • *Number of pitchers victimized*: 16 • *Total ballparks homered in*: 6 • *First HR*: 04/29/1959 off Arnie Portocarrero

Fred Osborne

FREDERICK W. OSBORNE
B: 05/ /1865

Year	Tm	Lg	Tot	H	A	Men-On 0	Men-On 1	Men-On 2	Men-On 3	One-Game 2	One-Game 3	One-Game 4	LO	XN	IP	PH	RHP	LHP
1890	PIT	NL	1	0	1	1	0	0	0	0	0	0	0	0	0	0	0	1

Rank among batters: 4,707 • *Total ballparks homered in*: 1 • *First HR*: 08/07/1890 off Frank Foreman

Champ Osteen

JAMES CHAMPLIN OSTEEN
B: 02/24/1877 D: 12/14/1962
BL

Year	Tm	Lg	Tot	H	A	Men-On 0	Men-On 1	Men-On 2	Men-On 3	One-Game 2	One-Game 3	One-Game 4	LO	XN	IP	PH	RHP	LHP
1904	NY	AL	2	1	1	2	0	0	0	0	0	0	0	0	1	0	2	0

Rank among batters: 4,129 • *Total ballparks homered in*: 2 • *First HR*: 06/16/1904 off Willie Sudhoff

Claude Osteen

CLAUDE WILSON OSTEEN
B: 08/09/1939
BL

Year	Tm	Lg	Tot	H	A	Men-On 0	Men-On 1	Men-On 2	Men-On 3	One-Game 2	One-Game 3	One-Game 4	LO	XN	IP	PH	RHP	LHP
1963	WAS	AL	1	0	1	0	1	0	0	0	0	0	0	0	0	0	1	0
1964	WAS	AL	1	1	0	1	0	0	0	0	0	0	0	0	0	0	1	0
1966	LA	NL	1	0	1	1	0	0	0	0	0	0	0	0	0	0	1	0
1967	LA	NL	2	0	2	2	0	0	0	0	0	0	0	0	0	0	2	0
1969	LA	NL	1	1	0	1	0	0	0	0	0	0	0	0	0	0	1	0
1970	LA	NL	1	0	1	0	1	0	0	0	0	0	0	0	0	0	1	0
1972	LA	NL	1	0	1	1	0	0	0	0	0	0	0	0	0	0	1	0
Total			8	2	6	6	2	0	0	0	0	0	0	0	0	0	8	0

Rank among batters: 2,703 • *Total ballparks homered in*: 7 • *First HR*: 09/04/1963 off Jim Bouton

Johnny Ostrowski

JOHN THADDEUS OSTROWSKI
B: 10/17/1917 D: 11/13/1992
BR

Year	Tm	Lg	Tot	H	A	Men-On 0	Men-On 1	Men-On 2	Men-On 3	One-Game 2	One-Game 3	One-Game 4	LO	XN	IP	PH	RHP	LHP
1946	CHI	NL	3	0	3	2	1	0	0	0	0	0	0	0	0	0	2	1
1949	CHI	AL	5	1	4	4	1	0	0	0	0	0	0	0	0	1	4	1
1950	CHI	AL	2	0	2	2	0	0	0	0	0	0	0	0	0	0	1	1
	WAS	AL	4	3	1	2	1	1	0	0	0	0	0	0	0	0	2	2
	Total		6	3	3	4	1	1	0	0	0	0	0	0	0	0	3	3
Total			14	4	10	10	3	1	0	0	0	0	0	0	0	1	9	5

Rank among batters: 2,169 • *Top target (2 home runs)*: Ellis Kinder, Early Wynn • *Number of pitchers victimized*: 12 • *Total ballparks homered in*: 9 • *First HR*: 08/11/1946 off Johnny Lanning

Amos Otis

AMOS JOSEPH OTIS
B: 04/26/1947
BR

Year	Tm	Lg	Tot	H	A	Men-On 0	Men-On 1	Men-On 2	Men-On 3	One-Game 2	One-Game 3	One-Game 4	LO	XN	IP	PH	RHP	LHP
1970	KC	AL	11	6	5	9	2	0	0	1	0	0	0	0	0	0	4	7
1971	KC	AL	15	3	12	10	3	2	0	0	0	0	0	0	0	0	12	3
1972	KC	AL	11	2	9	5	3	3	0	0	0	0	0	0	0	0	6	5
1973	KC	AL	26	11	15	15	7	4	0	1	0	0	0	0	0	0	16	10
1974	KC	AL	12	3	9	6	5	1	0	0	0	0	0	0	0	0	6	6
1975	KC	AL	9	6	3	6	3	0	0	0	0	0	1	0	2	0	5	4

Year	Tm	Lg	Tot	H	A	Men-On 0	1	2	3	One-Game 2	3	4	LO	XN	IP	PH	RHP	LHP

Amos Otis *continued*

Year	Tm	Lg	Tot	H	A	0	1	2	3	2	3	4	LO	XN	IP	PH	RHP	LHP
1976	KC	AL	18	10	8	8	7	3	0	1	0	0	0	0	0	0	12	6
1977	KC	AL	17	7	10	8	8	1	0	0	0	0	0	0	1	1	12	5
1978	KC	AL	22	11	11	8	11	2	1	1	0	0	0	0	1	0	15	7
1979	KC	AL	18	10	8	8	8	2	0	0	0	0	0	0	1	1	10	8
1980	KC	AL	10	4	6	8	2	0	0	1	0	0	0	0	0	0	7	3
1981	KC	AL	9	4	5	4	5	0	0	0	0	0	0	1	0	0	4	5
1982	KC	AL	11	5	6	3	5	2	1	1	0	0	0	0	1	0	8	3
1983	KC	AL	4	3	1	1	3	0	0	0	0	0	0	0	0	0	2	2
Total			193	85	108	99	72	20	2	6	0	0	1	1	6	2	119	74

Rank among batters: 197 • *Top target (4 home runs)*: Mickey Lolich, Bill Lee, Jim Slaton • *Number of pitchers victimized*: 137 • *Total ballparks homered in*: 16 • *First HR*: 04/24/1970 off Mike Cuellar • *World Series HR*—3

Billy Ott

WILLIAM JOSEPH OTT
B: 11/23/1940
BB

Year	Tm	Lg	Tot	H	A	0	1	2	3	2	3	4	LO	XN	IP	PH	RHP	LHP
1962	CHI	NL	1	1	0	1	0	0	0	0	0	0	0	0	0	0	1	0

Rank among batters: 4,707 • *Total ballparks homered in*: 1 • *First HR*: 09/17/1962 off Ray Washburn

Ed Ott

NATHAN EDWARD OTT
B: 07/11/1951
BL

Year	Tm	Lg	Tot	H	A	0	1	2	3	2	3	4	LO	XN	IP	PH	RHP	LHP
1977	PIT	NL	7	2	5	4	3	0	0	0	0	0	0	0	0	0	6	1
1978	PIT	NL	9	5	4	7	2	0	0	1	0	0	0	1	0	0	7	2
1979	PIT	NL	7	4	3	4	2	0	1	0	0	0	0	0	0	0	4	3
1980	PIT	NL	8	6	2	7	1	0	0	1	0	0	0	0	0	0	8	0
1981	CAL	AL	2	0	2	1	1	0	0	0	0	0	0	0	0	0	2	0
Total			33	17	16	23	9	0	1	2	0	0	0	1	0	0	27	6

Rank among batters: 1,336 • *Top target (3 home runs)*: Bob Welch • *Number of pitchers victimized*: 28 • *Total ballparks homered in*: 12 • *First HR*: 05/02/1977 off Buzz Capra

Mel Ott

MELVIN THOMAS OTT
B: 03/02/1909 D: 11/21/1958
BL HOF

Year	Tm	Lg	Tot	H	A	0	1	2	3	2	3	4	LO	XN	IP	PH	RHP	LHP
1927	NY	NL	1	1	0	1	0	0	0	0	0	0	0	0	1	0	1	0
1928	NY	NL	18	9	9	8	9	1	0	2	0	0	0	0	0	0	17	1
1929	NY	NL	42	20	22	13	23	6	0	3	0	0	0	1	1	0	27	15
1930	NY	NL	25	21	4	11	6	8	0	2	1	0	0	0	0	0	17	8
1931	NY	NL	29	20	9	12	13	4	0	2	0	0	0	0	0	0	26	3
1932	NY	NL	38	24	14	18	11	9	0	5	0	0	0	0	0	0	28	10
1933	NY	NL	23	13	10	9	9	3	2	2	0	0	0	0	0	0	16	7
1934	NY	NL	35	16	19	14	12	9	0	7	0	0	0	0	0	0	28	7
1935	NY	NL	31	19	12	15	8	7	1	1	0	0	0	0	0	0	28	3
1936	NY	NL	33	18	15	13	12	8	0	5	0	0	0	1	0	0	32	1
1937	NY	NL	31	15	16	18	8	5	0	3	0	0	0	1	0	0	19	12
1938	NY	NL	36	20	16	17	12	6	1	2	0	0	0	2	0	0	20	16
1939	NY	NL	27	15	12	12	10	5	0	1	0	0	0	1	0	0	25	2
1940	NY	NL	19	12	7	12	4	3	0	1	0	0	0	0	0	0	16	3
1941	NY	NL	27	19	8	12	11	3	1	4	0	0	0	0	0	0	24	3
1942	NY	NL	30	23	7	17	10	1	2	2	0	0	0	0	0	0	22	8
1943	NY	NL	18	18	0	10	8	0	0	0	0	0	0	1	0	1	15	3
1944	NY	NL	26	21	5	11	12	3	0	5	0	0	0	0	0	0	23	3
1945	NY	NL	21	18	3	12	6	3	0	1	0	0	0	0	0	2	16	5
1946	NY	NL	1	1	0	0	1	0	0	0	0	0	0	0	0	0	0	1
Total			511	323	188	235	185	84	7	48	1	0	0	7	2	3	400	111

Rank among batters: 14 • *Top target (13 home runs)*: Lon Warneke • *Number of pitchers victimized*: 199 • *Total ballparks homered in*: 8 • *First HR*: 07/18/1927 off Hal Carlson • *Hit for Cycle*—@BOS: 05/16/1929 (2) • *World Series HR*—4

Billy Otterson

WILLIAM JOHN OTTERSON
B: 05/04/1862 D: 09/21/1940
BR

Year	Tm	Lg	Tot	H	A	0	1	2	3	2	3	4	LO	XN	IP	PH	RHP	LHP
1887	BRO	AA	2	2	0	1	0	0	1	0	0	0	0	0	0	0	1	0

Billy Otterson *continued*

Rank among batters: 4,129 • *Total ballparks homered in*: 2 • *First HR*: 09/09/1887 off Mike Morrison

Chink Outen

WILLIAM AUSTIN OUTEN
B: 06/17/1905 D: 09/11/1961
BL

Year	Tm	Lg	Tot	H	A	Men-On 0	1	2	3	One-Game 2	3	4	LO	XN	IP	PH	RHP	LHP
1933	BRO	NL	4	3	1	3	1	0	0	0	0	0	0	1	0	1	3	1

Rank among batters: 3,427 • *Total ballparks homered in*: 2 • *First HR*: 06/28/1933 off Paul Derringer

Jimmy Outlaw

JAMES PAULUS OUTLAW
B: 01/20/1913
BR

Year	Tm	Lg	Tot	H	A	Men-On 0	1	2	3	One-Game 2	3	4	LO	XN	IP	PH	RHP	LHP
1943	DET	AL	1	1	0	1	0	0	0	0	0	0	0	0	0	0	0	1
1944	DET	AL	3	1	2	0	1	1	1	0	0	0	0	0	1	0	3	0
1946	DET	AL	2	1	1	2	0	0	0	0	0	0	0	0	0	0	2	0
Total			6	3	3	3	1	1	1	0	0	0	0	0	1	0	5	1

Rank among batters: 2,988 • *Top target (2 home runs)*: Tex Hughson • *Number of pitchers victimized*: 5 • *Total ballparks homered in*: 4 • *First HR*: 09/09/1943 off Al Smith

Orval Overall

ORVAL OVERALL
B: 02/02/1881 D: 07/14/1947
BB

Year	Tm	Lg	Tot	H	A	Men-On 0	1	2	3	One-Game 2	3	4	LO	XN	IP	PH	RHP	LHP
1909	CHI	NL	2	1	1	1	1	0	0	0	0	0	0	0	0	0	2	0

Rank among batters: 4,129 • *Total ballparks homered in*: 2 • *First HR*: 07/08/1909 off Lew Moren

Dave Owen

DAVE OWEN
B: 04/25/1958
BB

Year	Tm	Lg	Tot	H	A	Men-On 0	1	2	3	One-Game 2	3	4	LO	XN	IP	PH	RHP	LHP
1984	CHI	NL	1	0	1	1	0	0	0	0	0	0	0	0	0	0	1	0

Rank among batters: 4,707 • *Total ballparks homered in*: 1 • *First HR*: 07/05/1984 off Bill Laskey

Frank Owen

FRANK MALCOLM OWEN
B: 12/23/1879 D: 11/24/1942
BB

Year	Tm	Lg	Tot	H	A	Men-On 0	1	2	3	One-Game 2	3	4	LO	XN	IP	PH	RHP	LHP
1904	CHI	AL	2	0	2	1	1	0	0	0	0	0	0	1	0	0	2	0

Rank among batters: 4,129 • *Total ballparks homered in*: 2 • *First HR*: 05/21/1904 off Jack Powell

Larry Owen

LAWRENCE THOMAS OWEN
B: 05/31/1955
BR

Year	Tm	Lg	Tot	H	A	Men-On 0	1	2	3	One-Game 2	3	4	LO	XN	IP	PH	RHP	LHP
1985	ATL	NL	2	2	0	1	1	0	0	1	0	0	0	0	0	0	0	2
1987	KC	AL	5	2	3	3	2	0	0	0	0	0	0	0	0	0	0	5
1988	KC	AL	1	0	1	1	0	0	0	0	0	0	0	0	0	0	1	0
Total			8	4	4	5	3	0	0	1	0	0	0	0	0	0	1	7

Rank among batters: 2,703 • *Total ballparks homered in*: 5 • *First HR*: 09/19/1985 off Tom Browning

Marv Owen

MARVIN JAMES OWEN
B: 03/22/1906 D: 06/22/1991
BR

Year	Tm	Lg	Tot	H	A	Men-On 0	1	2	3	One-Game 2	3	4	LO	XN	IP	PH	RHP	LHP
1931	DET	AL	3	1	2	2	1	0	0	0	0	0	0	0	0	0	3	0
1933	DET	AL	2	1	1	1	0	1	0	0	0	0	0	0	0	0	2	0
1934	DET	AL	8	3	5	5	2	1	0	0	0	0	0	0	0	0	6	2
1935	DET	AL	2	0	2	1	0	1	0	0	0	0	0	0	0	0	1	1
1936	DET	AL	9	6	3	5	3	1	0	1	0	0	0	1	0	0	8	1
1937	DET	AL	1	0	1	1	0	0	0	0	0	0	0	0	0	0	1	0

Marv Owen *continued*

Year	Tm	Lg	Tot	H	A	Men-On 0	1	2	3	One-Game 2	3	4	LO	XN	IP	PH	RHP	LHP
1938	CHI	AL	6	1	5	5	1	0	0	0	0	0	0	0	0	0	5	1
Total			31	12	19	20	7	4	0	1	0	0	0	1	0	0	26	5

Rank among batters: 1,400 • *Top target (3 home runs)*: George Blaeholder, Oral Hildebrand • *Number of pitchers victimized*: 23 • *Total ballparks homered in*: 7 • *First HR*: 05/07/1931 off Red Faber

Mickey Owen

ARNOLD MALCOLM OWEN
B: 04/04/1916
BR

Year	Tm	Lg	Tot	H	A	Men-On 0	1	2	3	One-Game 2	3	4	LO	XN	IP	PH	RHP	LHP
1938	STL	NL	4	1	3	3	1	0	0	0	0	0	0	0	0	0	2	2
1939	STL	NL	3	2	1	3	0	0	0	0	0	0	0	0	0	0	2	1
1941	BRO	NL	1	0	1	1	0	0	0	0	0	0	0	0	0	0	1	0
1944	BRO	NL	1	0	1	0	1	0	0	0	0	0	0	0	0	0	1	0
1949	CHI	NL	2	0	2	0	2	0	0	0	0	0	0	0	0	0	0	2
1950	CHI	NL	2	1	1	2	0	0	0	0	0	0	0	0	0	0	1	1
1954	BOS	AL	1	1	0	0	0	0	1	0	0	0	0	0	0	0	1	0
Total			14	5	9	9	4	0	1	0	0	0	0	0	0	0	8	6

Rank among batters: 2,169 • *Total ballparks homered in*: 8 • *First HR*: 05/18/1938 off Buck Marrow • *All-Star HR*—1

Spike Owen

SPIKE DEE OWEN
B: 04/19/1961
BB

Year	Tm	Lg	Tot	H	A	Men-On 0	1	2	3	One-Game 2	3	4	LO	XN	IP	PH	RHP	LHP
1983	SEA	AL	2	1	1	2	0	0	0	0	0	0	1	0	0	0	1	1
1984	SEA	AL	3	2	1	1	1	1	0	0	0	0	0	0	0	0	2	1
1985	SEA	AL	6	3	3	4	2	0	0	0	0	0	0	0	0	0	5	1
1986	BOS	AL	1	0	1	1	0	0	0	0	0	0	0	0	0	0	0	1
1987	BOS	AL	2	2	0	1	1	0	0	0	0	0	0	1	0	0	0	2
1988	BOS	AL	5	2	3	4	1	0	0	0	0	0	1	0	0	0	1	4
1989	MON	NL	6	5	1	1	4	1	0	0	0	0	0	1	0	0	4	2
1990	MON	NL	5	2	3	5	0	0	0	0	0	0	0	0	0	0	2	3
1991	MON	NL	3	1	2	2	1	0	0	0	0	0	0	0	0	0	2	1
1992	MON	NL	7	3	4	6	1	0	0	0	0	0	0	0	0	0	3	4
1993	NY	AL	2	1	1	1	0	1	0	0	0	0	0	0	0	0	1	1
1994	CAL	AL	3	2	1	2	1	0	0	0	0	0	1	0	0	0	0	3
1995	CAL	AL	1	0	1	1	0	0	0	0	0	0	0	0	0	0	1	0
Total			46	24	22	31	12	3	0	0	0	0	3	2	0	0	22	24

Rank among batters: 1,060 • *Top target (2 home runs)*: Eddie Whitson, Jim Deshaies, Terry Mulholland • *Number of pitchers victimized*: 43 • *Total ballparks homered in*: 19 • *First HR*: 07/13/1983 off Doug Bird

Frank Owens

FRANK WALTER OWENS
B: 01/26/1886 D: 07/02/1958
BR

Year	Tm	Lg	Tot	H	A	Men-On 0	1	2	3	One-Game 2	3	4	LO	XN	IP	PH	RHP	LHP
1914	BRO	FL	2	0	2	2	0	0	0	0	0	0	0	0	0	0	1	1
1915	BAL	FL	3	3	0	3	0	0	0	0	0	0	0	1	0	0	3	0
Total			5	3	2	5	0	0	0	0	0	0	0	1	0	0	4	1

Rank among batters: 3,191 • *Total ballparks homered in*: 2 • *First HR*: 04/22/1914 off George Suggs

Jayhawk Owens

CLAUDE JAYHAWK OWENS
B: 02/10/1969
BR

Year	Tm	Lg	Tot	H	A	Men-On 0	1	2	3	One-Game 2	3	4	LO	XN	IP	PH	RHP	LHP
1993	COL	NL	3	2	1	3	0	0	0	1	0	0	0	0	0	0	2	1
1995	COL	NL	4	3	1	2	2	0	0	1	0	0	0	0	0	0	2	2
Total			7	5	2	5	2	0	0	2	0	0	0	0	0	0	4	3

Rank among batters: 2,834 • *Top target (2 home runs)*: Rene Arocha • *Number of pitchers victimized*: 6 • *Total ballparks homered in*: 4 • *First HR*: 06/25/1993 off Bryan Hickerson

Red Owens

THOMAS LLEWELLYN OWENS
B: 11/01/1874 D: 08/20/1952
BR

Year	Tm	Lg	Tot	H	A	Men-On 0	1	2	3	One-Game 2	3	4	LO	XN	IP	PH	RHP	LHP
1905	BRO	NL	1	1	0	0	1	0	0	0	0	0	0	0	0	0	1	0

Red Owens *continued*

Rank among batters: 4,707 • *Total ballparks homered in*: 1 • *First HR*: 05/23/1905 off Jake Thielman

Andy Oyler

ANDREW PAUL OYLER
B: 05/05/1880 D: 10/24/1970
BR

Year	Tm	Lg	Tot	H	A	Men-On 0	1	2	3	One-Game 2	3	4	LO	XN	IP	PH	RHP	LHP
1902	BAL	AL	1	1	0	0	0	1	0	0	0	0	0	0	1	0	1	0

Rank among batters: 4,707 • *Total ballparks homered in*: 1 • *First HR*: 05/27/1902 off Roy Patterson

Ray Oyler

RAYMOND FRANCIS OYLER
B: 08/04/1938 D: 01/26/1981
BR

Year	Tm	Lg	Tot	H	A	Men-On 0	1	2	3	One-Game 2	3	4	LO	XN	IP	PH	RHP	LHP
1965	DET	AL	5	3	2	4	1	0	0	0	0	0	0	0	0	0	2	3
1966	DET	AL	1	0	1	1	0	0	0	0	0	0	0	0	0	0	1	0
1967	DET	AL	1	1	0	0	0	1	0	0	0	0	0	0	0	0	1	0
1968	DET	AL	1	1	0	1	0	0	0	0	0	0	0	0	0	0	0	1
1969	SEA	AL	7	5	2	5	2	0	0	0	0	0	0	0	0	0	4	3
Total			15	10	5	11	3	1	0	0	0	0	0	0	0	0	8	7

Rank among batters: 2,096 • *Top target (2 home runs)*: Dave McNally, George Brunet • *Number of pitchers victimized*: 13 • *Total ballparks homered in*: 7 • *First HR*: 07/21/1965 off Jack Kralick

Jim Paciorek

JAMES JOSEPH PACIOREK
B: 06/07/1960
BR

Year	Tm	Lg	Tot	H	A	Men-On 0	1	2	3	One-Game 2	3	4	LO	XN	IP	PH	RHP	LHP
1987	MIL	AL	2	1	1	2	0	0	0	0	0	0	0	0	0	0	0	2

Rank among batters: 4,129 • *Total ballparks homered in*: 2 • *First HR*: 05/13/1987 off Curt Young

Tom Paciorek

THOMAS MARIAN PACIOREK
B: 11/02/1946
BR

Year	Tm	Lg	Tot	H	A	Men-On 0	1	2	3	One-Game 2	3	4	LO	XN	IP	PH	RHP	LHP
1972	LA	NL	1	0	1	1	0	0	0	0	0	0	0	0	0	0	0	1
1973	LA	NL	5	2	3	3	2	0	0	0	0	0	0	0	0	0	3	2
1974	LA	NL	1	1	0	0	0	1	0	0	0	0	0	0	0	1	0	1
1975	LA	NL	1	0	1	0	0	1	0	0	0	0	0	0	0	0	0	1
1976	ATL	NL	4	2	2	2	1	0	1	0	0	0	0	0	1	0	3	1
1977	ATL	NL	3	0	3	1	2	0	0	0	0	0	0	0	0	0	2	1
1978	SEA	AL	4	3	1	1	2	1	0	0	0	0	0	0	0	0	3	1
1979	SEA	AL	6	6	0	2	0	4	0	0	0	0	0	0	0	1	2	4
1980	SEA	AL	15	11	4	5	9	1	0	0	0	0	0	0	0	0	8	7
1981	SEA	AL	14	7	7	8	3	3	0	1	0	0	0	0	0	0	10	4
1982	CHI	AL	11	0	11	4	4	3	0	1	0	0	0	0	0	0	8	3
1983	CHI	AL	9	4	5	4	3	2	0	0	0	0	0	0	0	0	4	5
1984	CHI	AL	4	2	2	3	1	0	0	0	0	0	0	0	0	1	1	3
1985	NY	NL	1	1	0	0	1	0	0	0	0	0	0	0	0	0	0	1
1986	TEX	AL	4	0	4	4	0	0	0	0	0	0	0	0	0	0	2	2
1987	TEX	AL	3	2	1	1	2	0	0	0	0	0	0	0	0	0	0	3
Total			86	41	45	39	30	16	1	2	0	0	0	0	1	3	46	40

Rank among batters: 602 • *Top target (3 home runs)*: Mike Flanagan • *Number of pitchers victimized*: 77 • *Total ballparks homered in*: 25 • *First HR*: 10/04/1972 off Larry Jaster

Gene Packard

EUGENE MILO PACKARD
B: 07/13/1887 D: 05/19/1959
BL

Year	Tm	Lg	Tot	H	A	Men-On 0	1	2	3	One-Game 2	3	4	LO	XN	IP	PH	RHP	LHP
1914	KC	FL	1	1	0	1	0	0	0	0	0	0	0	0	0	0	1	0
1915	KC	FL	1	0	1	1	0	0	0	0	0	0	0	0	0	0	1	0
Total			2	1	1	2	0	0	0	0	0	0	0	0	0	0	2	0

Rank among batters: 4,129 • *Total ballparks homered in*: 2 • *First HR*: 08/22/1914 off Howie Camnitz

Dick Padden

RICHARD JOSEPH PADDEN
B: 09/17/1870 D: 10/31/1922
BR

Year	Tm	Lg	Tot	H	A	Men-On 0	Men-On 1	Men-On 2	Men-On 3	One-Game 2	One-Game 3	One-Game 4	LO	XN	IP	PH	RHP	LHP
1896	PIT	NL	2	0	2	1	1	0	0	0	0	0	0	0	0	0	2	0
1897	PIT	NL	2	1	1	1	1	0	0	0	0	0	0	0	0	0	2	0
1898	PIT	NL	2	2	0	1	1	0	0	0	0	0	0	0	0	0	2	0
1899	WAS	NL	2	0	2	2	0	0	0	0	0	0	0	0	0	0	1	1
1901	STL	NL	2	1	1	1	1	0	0	0	0	0	0	0	1	0	1	1
1902	STL	AL	1	0	1	1	0	0	0	0	0	0	0	0	0	0	1	0
Total			11	4	7	7	4	0	0	0	0	0	0	0	1	0	9	2

Rank among batters: 2,419 • *Total ballparks homered in*: 7 • *First HR*: 08/20/1896 off Brickyard Kennedy

Tom Padden

THOMAS FRANCIS PADDEN
B: 10/06/1908 D: 06/11/1973
BR

Year	Tm	Lg	Tot	H	A	Men-On 0	Men-On 1	Men-On 2	Men-On 3	One-Game 2	One-Game 3	One-Game 4	LO	XN	IP	PH	RHP	LHP
1935	PIT	NL	1	0	1	1	0	0	0	0	0	0	0	0	0	0	0	1
1936	PIT	NL	1	0	1	0	1	0	0	0	0	0	0	0	0	0	0	1
Total			2	0	2	1	1	0	0	0	0	0	0	0	0	0	0	2

Rank among batters: 4,129 • *Total ballparks homered in*: 2 • *First HR*: 08/26/1935 off Al Smith

Delmer Paddock

DELMER HAROLD PADDOCK
B: 06/08/1887 D: 02/06/1952
BL

Year	Tm	Lg	Tot	H	A	Men-On 0	Men-On 1	Men-On 2	Men-On 3	One-Game 2	One-Game 3	One-Game 4	LO	XN	IP	PH	RHP	LHP
1912	NY	AL	1	1	0	0	1	0	0	0	0	0	0	0	0	0	0	1

Rank among batters: 4,707 • *Total ballparks homered in*: 1 • *First HR*: 08/28/1912 off Vean Gregg

Don Padgett

DON WILSON PADGETT
B: 12/05/1911 D: 12/09/1980
BL

Year	Tm	Lg	Tot	H	A	Men-On 0	Men-On 1	Men-On 2	Men-On 3	One-Game 2	One-Game 3	One-Game 4	LO	XN	IP	PH	RHP	LHP
1937	STL	NL	10	6	4	2	6	2	0	0	0	0	0	0	0	0	8	2
1938	STL	NL	8	7	1	3	3	1	1	0	0	0	0	0	0	0	8	0
1939	STL	NL	5	5	0	1	2	1	1	0	0	0	0	0	0	2	5	0
1940	STL	NL	6	4	2	2	3	1	0	0	0	0	0	0	1	1	6	0
1941	STL	NL	5	4	1	2	1	2	0	0	0	0	0	1	0	0	5	0
1946	BRO	NL	1	0	1	0	0	1	0	0	0	0	0	1	0	1	1	0
	BOS	NL	2	1	1	0	1	1	0	0	0	0	0	0	0	0	2	0
	Total		3	1	2	0	1	2	0	0	0	0	0	1	0	1	3	0
Total			37	27	10	10	16	9	2	0	0	0	0	2	1	4	35	2

Rank among batters: 1,252 • *Top target (3 home runs)*: Max Butcher • *Number of pitchers victimized*: 30 • *Total ballparks homered in*: 8 • *First HR*: 05/27/1937 off Jim Turner

Ernie Padgett

ERNEST KITCHEN PADGETT
B: 03/01/1899 D: 04/15/1957
BR

Year	Tm	Lg	Tot	H	A	Men-On 0	Men-On 1	Men-On 2	Men-On 3	One-Game 2	One-Game 3	One-Game 4	LO	XN	IP	PH	RHP	LHP
1924	BOS	NL	1	1	0	0	1	0	0	0	0	0	0	0	1	0	1	0

Rank among batters: 4,707 • *Total ballparks homered in*: 1 • *First HR*: 06/30/1924 off Johnny Couch

Dennis Paepke

DENNIS RAY PAEPKE
B: 04/17/1945
BR

Year	Tm	Lg	Tot	H	A	Men-On 0	Men-On 1	Men-On 2	Men-On 3	One-Game 2	One-Game 3	One-Game 4	LO	XN	IP	PH	RHP	LHP
1971	KC	AL	2	0	2	1	1	0	0	0	0	0	0	0	0	0	0	2

Rank among batters: 4,129 • *Total ballparks homered in*: 2 • *First HR*: 05/26/1971 off Wilbur Wood

Andy Pafko

ANDREW PAFKO
B: 02/25/1921
BR

Year	Tm	Lg	Tot	H	A	Men-On 0	Men-On 1	Men-On 2	Men-On 3	One-Game 2	One-Game 3	One-Game 4	LO	XN	IP	PH	RHP	LHP
1944	CHI	NL	6	3	3	2	4	0	0	0	0	0	0	0	0	0	4	2
1945	CHI	NL	12	6	6	5	3	2	2	0	0	0	0	0	1	0	11	1
1946	CHI	NL	3	1	2	1	2	0	0	0	0	0	0	0	0	0	0	3

Andy Pafko *continued*

Year	Tm	Lg	Tot	H	A	Men-On 0	1	2	3	One-Game 2	3	4	LO	XN	IP	PH	RHP	LHP
1947	CHI	NL	13	3	10	7	6	0	0	0	0	0	0	0	0	0	7	6
1948	CHI	NL	26	17	9	14	8	4	0	1	0	0	0	0	0	0	19	7
1949	CHI	NL	18	11	7	6	8	2	2	2	0	0	0	1	0	0	10	8
1950	CHI	NL	36	16	20	22	7	7	0	2	1	0	0	1	0	0	28	8
1951	CHI	NL	12	3	9	9	1	1	1	2	0	0	0	0	0	0	10	2
	BRO	NL	18	8	10	10	5	3	0	0	0	0	0	0	0	0	14	4
	Total		30	11	19	19	6	4	1	2	0	0	0	0	0	0	24	6
1952	BRO	NL	19	12	7	14	2	2	1	3	0	0	0	3	0	0	13	6
1953	MIL	NL	17	7	10	10	5	2	0	2	0	0	0	1	0	0	15	2
1954	MIL	NL	14	3	11	10	3	1	0	1	0	0	0	0	0	0	10	4
1955	MIL	NL	5	2	3	2	2	1	0	0	0	0	0	0	0	1	4	1
1956	MIL	NL	2	0	2	0	2	0	0	0	0	0	0	0	0	1	0	2
1957	MIL	NL	8	5	3	6	2	0	0	1	0	0	0	0	0	2	3	5
1958	MIL	NL	3	0	3	2	0	1	0	0	0	0	0	0	0	0	2	1
1959	MIL	NL	1	1	0	1	0	0	0	0	0	0	0	0	0	0	0	1
Total			213	98	115	121	60	26	6	14	1	0	0	6	1	4	150	63

Rank among batters: 161 • *Top target (9 home runs)*: Murry Dickson • *Number of pitchers victimized*: 120 • *Total ballparks homered in*: 9 • *First HR*: 05/30/1944 off Ewald Pyle

Jose Pagan

JOSE ANTONIO (RODRIGUEZ) PAGAN
B: 05/05/1935
BR

Year	Tm	Lg	Tot	H	A	Men-On 0	1	2	3	One-Game 2	3	4	LO	XN	IP	PH	RHP	LHP
1961	SF	NL	5	1	4	4	1	0	0	1	0	0	0	1	0	0	5	0
1962	SF	NL	7	3	4	4	3	0	0	0	0	0	0	0	0	0	5	2
1963	SF	NL	6	2	4	4	1	1	0	0	0	0	0	0	0	0	5	1
1964	SF	NL	1	0	1	0	1	0	0	0	0	0	0	0	0	0	1	0
1966	PIT	NL	4	0	4	2	2	0	0	0	0	0	0	0	0	0	2	2
1967	PIT	NL	1	0	1	1	0	0	0	0	0	0	0	0	0	0	0	1
1968	PIT	NL	4	2	2	3	1	0	0	0	0	0	0	0	0	0	4	0
1969	PIT	NL	9	0	9	4	4	1	0	1	0	0	0	0	0	3	4	5
1970	PIT	NL	7	2	5	4	2	1	0	1	0	0	0	0	0	0	4	3
1971	PIT	NL	5	0	5	3	1	1	0	1	0	0	0	0	0	0	3	2
1972	PIT	NL	3	2	1	3	0	0	0	0	0	0	0	0	0	1	1	2
Total			52	12	40	32	16	4	0	4	0	0	0	1	0	4	34	18

Rank among batters: 965 • *Top target (3 home runs)*: Lew Burdette • *Number of pitchers victimized*: 45 • *Total ballparks homered in*: 16 • *First HR*: 04/30/1961 off Lew Burdette • *World Series HR*—1

Joe Page

JOSEPH FRANCIS PAGE
B: 10/28/1917 D: 04/21/1980
BL

Year	Tm	Lg	Tot	H	A	Men-On 0	1	2	3	One-Game 2	3	4	LO	XN	IP	PH	RHP	LHP
1946	NY	AL	1	1	0	1	0	0	0	0	0	0	0	0	0	0	1	0
1947	NY	AL	1	0	1	1	0	0	0	0	0	0	0	0	0	0	1	0
Total			2	1	1	2	0	0	0	0	0	0	0	0	0	0	2	0

Rank among batters: 4,129 • *Total ballparks homered in*: 2 • *First HR*: 05/04/1946 off George Caster

Mitchell Page

MITCHELL OTIS PAGE
B: 10/15/1951
BL

Year	Tm	Lg	Tot	H	A	Men-On 0	1	2	3	One-Game 2	3	4	LO	XN	IP	PH	RHP	LHP
1977	OAK	AL	21	10	11	12	5	4	0	3	0	0	0	0	0	0	17	4
1978	OAK	AL	17	10	7	11	4	1	1	0	0	0	0	0	0	0	11	6
1979	OAK	AL	9	4	5	5	4	0	0	0	0	0	0	0	0	0	8	1
1980	OAK	AL	17	8	9	15	2	0	0	3	0	0	0	0	0	0	13	4
1981	OAK	AL	4	2	2	2	2	0	0	0	0	0	0	0	0	1	4	0
1982	OAK	AL	4	2	2	3	1	0	0	0	0	0	0	0	0	0	4	0
Total			72	36	36	48	18	5	1	6	0	0	0	0	0	1	57	15

Rank among batters: 723 • *Top target (4 home runs)*: Ferguson Jenkins • *Number of pitchers victimized*: 59 • *Total ballparks homered in*: 13 • *First HR*: 04/13/1977 off Wayne Simpson

Karl Pagel

KARL DOUGLAS PAGEL
B: 03/29/1955
BL

Year	Tm	Lg	Tot	H	A	Men-On 0	1	2	3	One-Game 2	3	4	LO	XN	IP	PH	RHP	LHP
1981	CLE	AL	1	1	0	0	1	0	0	0	0	0	0	0	0	1	1	0

Year	Tm	Lg	Tot	H	A	Men-On 0	Men-On 1	Men-On 2	Men-On 3	One-Game 2	One-Game 3	One-Game 4	LO	XN	IP	PH	RHP	LHP

Karl Pagel *continued*

Rank among batters: 4,707 • *Total ballparks homered in*: 1 • *First HR*: 09/15/1981 off Dennis Martinez

Jim Pagliaroni

JAMES VINCENT PAGLIARONI
B: 12/08/1937
BR

Year	Tm	Lg	Tot	H	A	Men-On 0	Men-On 1	Men-On 2	Men-On 3	One-Game 2	One-Game 3	One-Game 4	LO	XN	IP	PH	RHP	LHP
1960	BOS	AL	2	1	1	1	1	0	0	0	0	0	0	0	0	0	0	2
1961	BOS	AL	16	11	5	10	4	1	1	0	0	0	0	1	0	1	11	5
1962	BOS	AL	11	5	6	8	1	2	0	0	0	0	0	0	0	0	9	2
1963	PIT	NL	11	6	5	9	0	2	0	0	0	0	0	0	0	0	8	3
1964	PIT	NL	10	7	3	4	4	1	1	0	0	0	0	0	0	0	7	3
1965	PIT	NL	17	5	12	9	4	4	0	1	0	0	0	0	0	0	13	4
1966	PIT	NL	11	4	7	6	3	2	0	0	0	0	0	0	0	0	8	3
1968	OAK	AL	6	5	1	4	2	0	0	0	0	0	0	0	0	0	3	3
1969	OAK	AL	1	1	0	1	0	0	0	0	0	0	0	0	0	0	0	1
	SEA	AL	5	5	0	3	2	0	0	0	0	0	0	1	0	1	1	4
	Total		6	6	0	4	2	0	0	0	0	0	0	1	0	1	1	5
Total			90	50	40	55	21	12	2	1	0	0	0	2	0	2	60	30

Rank among batters: 573 • *Top target (3 home runs)*: Bud Daley, Bob Buhl • *Number of pitchers victimized*: 78 • *Total ballparks homered in*: 22 • *First HR*: 08/06/1960 off Pete Burnside

Mike Pagliarulo

MICHAEL TIMOTHY PAGLIARULO
B: 03/15/1960
BL

Year	Tm	Lg	Tot	H	A	Men-On 0	Men-On 1	Men-On 2	Men-On 3	One-Game 2	One-Game 3	One-Game 4	LO	XN	IP	PH	RHP	LHP
1984	NY	AL	7	4	3	2	4	0	1	0	0	0	0	0	0	0	7	0
1985	NY	AL	19	8	11	8	10	1	0	1	0	0	0	0	0	1	17	2
1986	NY	AL	28	14	14	18	5	5	0	2	0	0	0	0	0	0	26	2
1987	NY	AL	32	17	15	18	12	0	2	4	0	0	0	2	0	0	28	4
1988	NY	AL	15	8	7	4	8	2	1	1	0	0	0	0	0	0	10	5
1989	NY	AL	4	3	1	4	0	0	0	0	0	0	0	0	0	0	4	0
	SD	NL	3	2	1	1	1	1	0	0	0	0	0	0	0	0	3	0
	Total		7	5	2	5	1	1	0	0	0	0	0	0	0	0	7	0
1990	SD	NL	7	1	6	6	1	0	0	0	0	0	0	0	0	1	3	4
1991	MIN	AL	6	4	2	4	1	1	0	1	0	0	0	0	1	0	6	0
1993	MIN	AL	3	2	1	0	1	2	0	0	0	0	0	0	0	1	3	0
	BAL	AL	6	3	3	2	2	1	1	0	0	0	0	0	0	0	6	0
	Total		9	5	4	2	3	3	1	0	0	0	0	0	0	1	9	0
1995	TEX	AL	4	1	3	3	1	0	0	0	0	0	0	0	1	0	4	0
Total			134	67	67	70	46	13	5	9	0	0	0	2	2	3	117	17

Rank among batters: 331 • *Top target (5 home runs)*: Don Sutton • *Number of pitchers victimized*: 98 • *Total ballparks homered in*: 21 • *First HR*: 07/13/1984 off Bret Saberhagen • *World Series HR*—1; *LCS HR*—1

Tom Pagnozzi

THOMAS ALAN PAGNOZZI
B: 07/30/1962
BR

Year	Tm	Lg	Tot	H	A	Men-On 0	Men-On 1	Men-On 2	Men-On 3	One-Game 2	One-Game 3	One-Game 4	LO	XN	IP	PH	RHP	LHP
1987	STL	NL	2	2	0	1	0	0	1	0	0	0	0	0	0	0	0	2
1990	STL	NL	2	2	0	2	0	0	0	0	0	0	0	0	0	0	1	1
1991	STL	NL	2	2	0	1	0	1	0	0	0	0	0	0	0	0	0	2
1992	STL	NL	7	3	4	4	3	0	0	0	0	0	0	0	0	0	3	4
1993	STL	NL	7	1	6	6	1	0	0	0	0	0	0	0	0	0	5	2
1994	STL	NL	7	2	5	2	4	0	1	0	0	0	0	0	0	0	6	1
1995	STL	NL	2	1	1	1	1	0	0	0	0	0	0	0	0	0	2	0
Total			29	13	16	17	9	1	2	0	0	0	0	0	0	0	17	12

Rank among batters: 1,465 • *Total ballparks homered in*: 10 • *First HR*: 04/19/1987 off Sid Fernandez

Rey Palacios

ROBERT REY PALACIOS
B: 11/08/1962
BR

Year	Tm	Lg	Tot	H	A	Men-On 0	Men-On 1	Men-On 2	Men-On 3	One-Game 2	One-Game 3	One-Game 4	LO	XN	IP	PH	RHP	LHP
1989	KC	AL	1	0	1	0	1	0	0	0	0	0	0	0	0	0	0	1
1990	KC	AL	2	1	1	1	0	0	1	0	0	0	0	1	0	0	1	1
Total			3	1	2	1	1	0	1	0	0	0	0	1	0	0	1	2

Rank among batters: 3,735 • *Total ballparks homered in*: 3 • *First HR*: 06/17/1989 off Scott Bailes

Erv Palica

ERVIN MARTIN PALICA
B: 02/09/1928 D: 05/29/1982
BR

Year	Tm	Lg	Tot	H	A	Men-On 0	1	2	3	One-Game 2	3	4	LO	XN	IP	PH	RHP	LHP
1950	BRO	NL	1	0	1	0	0	0	1	0	0	0	0	0	0	0	1	0

Rank among batters: 4,707 • *Total ballparks homered in*: 1 • *First HR*: 09/24/1950 off Bubba Church

Rafael Palmeiro

RAFAEL (CORRALES) PALMEIRO
B: 09/24/1964
BL

Year	Tm	Lg	Tot	H	A	Men-On 0	1	2	3	One-Game 2	3	4	LO	XN	IP	PH	RHP	LHP
1986	CHI	NL	3	1	2	1	1	1	0	0	0	0	0	0	0	0	3	0
1987	CHI	NL	14	5	9	9	4	1	0	0	0	0	0	0	0	2	13	1
1988	CHI	NL	8	8	0	6	1	0	1	1	0	0	0	0	0	0	6	2
1989	TEX	AL	8	4	4	4	4	0	0	0	0	0	0	0	0	0	6	2
1990	TEX	AL	14	9	5	8	6	0	0	0	0	0	0	1	0	0	9	5
1991	TEX	AL	26	12	14	14	10	2	0	2	0	0	0	1	0	0	17	9
1992	TEX	AL	22	8	14	13	6	2	1	1	0	0	0	1	0	0	17	5
1993	TEX	AL	37	22	15	21	14	2	0	5	0	0	0	2	0	0	35	2
1994	BAL	AL	23	11	12	15	6	2	0	0	0	0	0	1	0	0	13	10
1995	BAL	AL	39	21	18	21	13	5	0	4	0	0	0	1	0	0	28	11
Total			194	101	93	112	65	15	2	13	0	0	0	7	0	2	147	47

Rank among batters: 194 • *Top target (4 home runs)*: Bill Gullickson, Mark Langston • *Number of pitchers victimized*: 140 • *Total ballparks homered in*: 25 • *First HR*: 09/09/1986 off Kevin Gross

David Palmer

DAVID WILLIAM PALMER
B: 08/19/1957
BR

Year	Tm	Lg	Tot	H	A	Men-On 0	1	2	3	One-Game 2	3	4	LO	XN	IP	PH	RHP	LHP
1984	MON	NL	1	0	1	0	1	0	0	0	0	0	0	0	0	0	0	1
1986	ATL	NL	1	0	1	1	0	0	0	0	0	0	0	0	0	0	1	0
1987	ATL	NL	1	0	1	0	0	1	0	0	0	0	0	0	0	0	1	0
1988	PHI	NL	2	1	1	2	0	0	0	0	0	0	0	0	0	0	2	0
Total			5	1	4	3	1	1	0	0	0	0	0	0	0	0	4	1

Rank among batters: 3,191 • *Total ballparks homered in*: 5 • *First HR*: 04/07/1984 off Pete Falcone

Dean Palmer

DEAN WILLIAM PALMER
B: 12/27/1968
BR

Year	Tm	Lg	Tot	H	A	Men-On 0	1	2	3	One-Game 2	3	4	LO	XN	IP	PH	RHP	LHP
1991	TEX	AL	15	6	9	6	5	4	0	1	0	0	0	1	0	1	6	9
1992	TEX	AL	26	11	15	13	10	1	2	1	0	0	0	0	0	1	18	8
1993	TEX	AL	33	12	21	14	14	4	1	2	0	0	0	0	0	0	27	6
1994	TEX	AL	19	11	8	10	5	3	1	3	0	0	0	0	0	0	15	4
1995	TEX	AL	9	5	4	6	3	0	0	2	0	0	0	1	0	0	6	3
Total			102	45	57	49	37	12	4	9	0	0	0	2	0	2	72	30

Rank among batters: 483 • Top target (3 home runs): Bill Wegman, Bobby Witt, Bill Gullickson, Charles Nagy, Mark Langston, Danny Darwin • *Number of pitchers victimized*: 77 • *Total ballparks homered in*: 15 • *First HR*: 06/27/1991 off Rick Honeycutt

Jim Palmer

JAMES ALVIN PALMER
B: 10/15/1945
BR HOF

Year	Tm	Lg	Tot	H	A	Men-On 0	1	2	3	One-Game 2	3	4	LO	XN	IP	PH	RHP	LHP
1965	BAL	AL	1	1	0	0	1	0	0	0	0	0	0	0	0	0	1	0
1966	BAL	AL	1	0	1	0	1	0	0	0	0	0	0	0	0	0	1	0
1970	BAL	AL	1	1	0	1	0	0	0	0	0	0	0	0	0	0	1	0
Total			3	2	1	1	2	0	0	0	0	0	0	0	0	0	3	0

Rank among batters: 3,735 • *Total ballparks homered in*: 2 • *First HR*: 05/16/1965 off Jim Bouton

Lowell Palmer

LOWELL RAYMOND PALMER
B: 08/18/1947
BR

Year	Tm	Lg	Tot	H	A	Men-On 0	1	2	3	One-Game 2	3	4	LO	XN	IP	PH	RHP	LHP
1969	PHI	NL	1	1	0	1	0	0	0	0	0	0	0	0	0	0	1	0

Rank among batters: 4,707 • *Total ballparks homered in*: 1 • *First HR*: 07/19/1969 off Bill Hands

Stan Palys

STANLEY FRANCIS PALYS
B: 05/01/1930
BR

Year	Tm	Lg	Tot	H	A	Men-On 0	Men-On 1	Men-On 2	Men-On 3	One-Game 2	One-Game 3	One-Game 4	LO	XN	IP	PH	RHP	LHP
1955	PHI	NL	1	1	0	1	0	0	0	0	0	0	0	0	0	0	1	0
	CIN	NL	7	3	4	0	3	4	0	0	1	0	0	0	0	0	2	5
	Total		8	4	4	4	4	0	0	1	0	0	0	0	0	0	3	5
1956	CIN	NL	2	0	2	2	0	0	0	0	0	0	0	0	0	1	1	1
Total			10	4	6	6	4	0	0	1	0	0	0	0	0	1	4	6

Rank among batters: 2,500 • *Total ballparks homered in*: 5 • *First HR*: 04/23/1955 off Bob Friend

Jim Pankovits

JAMES FRANKLIN PANKOVITS
B: 08/06/1955
BR

Year	Tm	Lg	Tot	H	A	Men-On 0	Men-On 1	Men-On 2	Men-On 3	One-Game 2	One-Game 3	One-Game 4	LO	XN	IP	PH	RHP	LHP
1984	HOU	NL	1	0	1	0	0	1	0	0	0	0	0	0	0	1	0	1
1985	HOU	NL	4	2	2	3	0	0	1	0	0	0	0	0	0	0	1	3
1986	HOU	NL	1	0	1	1	0	0	0	0	0	0	0	0	0	1	1	0
1987	HOU	NL	1	0	1	1	0	0	0	0	0	0	0	0	0	0	0	1
1988	HOU	NL	2	0	2	2	0	0	0	0	0	0	0	0	0	0	0	2
Total			9	2	7	7	0	1	1	0	0	0	0	0	0	2	2	7

Rank among batters: 2,587 • *Total ballparks homered in*: 4 • *First HR*: 08/11/1984 off Johnny Franco

Ken Pape

KENNETH WAYNE PAPE
B: 10/01/1951
BR

Year	Tm	Lg	Tot	H	A	Men-On 0	Men-On 1	Men-On 2	Men-On 3	One-Game 2	One-Game 3	One-Game 4	LO	XN	IP	PH	RHP	LHP
1976	TEX	AL	1	0	1	0	1	0	0	0	0	0	0	0	0	0	1	0

Rank among batters: 4,707 • *Total ballparks homered in*: 1 • *First HR*: 09/19/1976 off Dick Bosman

Stan Papi

STANLEY GERARD PAPI
B: 02/04/1951
BR

Year	Tm	Lg	Tot	H	A	Men-On 0	Men-On 1	Men-On 2	Men-On 3	One-Game 2	One-Game 3	One-Game 4	LO	XN	IP	PH	RHP	LHP
1979	BOS	AL	1	0	1	0	1	0	0	0	0	0	0	0	0	0	0	1
1980	DET	AL	3	3	0	0	2	1	0	0	0	0	0	0	0	0	0	3
1981	DET	AL	3	1	2	1	2	0	0	0	0	0	0	0	0	0	1	2
Total			7	4	3	1	5	1	0	0	0	0	0	0	0	0	1	6

Rank among batters: 2,834 • *Total ballparks homered in*: 4 • *First HR*: 08/26/1979 off Paul Splittorff

Erik Pappas

ERIK DANIEL PAPPAS
B: 04/25/1966
BR

Year	Tm	Lg	Tot	H	A	Men-On 0	Men-On 1	Men-On 2	Men-On 3	One-Game 2	One-Game 3	One-Game 4	LO	XN	IP	PH	RHP	LHP
1993	STL	NL	1	1	0	0	1	0	0	0	0	0	0	0	0	0	0	1

Rank among batters: 4,707 • *Total ballparks homered in*: 1 • *First HR*: 06/14/1993 off Denny Neagle

Milt Pappas

MILTON STEPHEN PAPPAS
B: 05/11/1939
BR

Year	Tm	Lg	Tot	H	A	Men-On 0	Men-On 1	Men-On 2	Men-On 3	One-Game 2	One-Game 3	One-Game 4	LO	XN	IP	PH	RHP	LHP
1958	BAL	AL	1	0	1	1	0	0	0	0	0	0	0	0	0	0	1	0
1960	BAL	AL	1	1	0	0	1	0	0	0	0	0	0	0	0	0	0	1
1961	BAL	AL	3	0	3	3	0	0	0	1	0	0	0	0	0	0	3	0
1962	BAL	AL	4	1	3	3	1	0	0	0	0	0	0	0	0	0	4	0
1963	BAL	AL	2	1	1	0	1	1	0	0	0	0	0	0	0	0	2	0
1966	CIN	NL	1	1	0	1	0	0	0	0	0	0	0	0	0	0	1	0
1967	CIN	NL	1	1	0	1	0	0	0	0	0	0	0	0	0	0	1	0
1968	ATL	NL	1	1	0	0	0	1	0	0	0	0	0	0	0	0	1	0
1969	ATL	NL	2	1	1	1	1	0	0	0	0	0	0	0	0	0	0	2
1970	CHI	NL	2	2	0	1	1	0	0	0	0	0	0	0	0	0	2	0
1972	CHI	NL	1	1	0	0	1	0	0	0	0	0	0	0	0	0	0	1
1973	CHI	NL	1	1	0	1	0	0	0	0	0	0	0	0	0	0	1	0
Total			20	11	9	12	6	2	0	1	0	0	0	0	0	0	16	4

Rank among batters: 1,810 • *Top target (2 home runs)*: Pedro Ramos, Ron Reed • *Number of pitchers victimized*: 18 • *Total ballparks homered in*: 11 • *First HR*: 07/24/1958 off Gerry Staley

Craig Paquette

CRAIG HAROLD PAQUETTE
B: 03/28/1969
BR

Year	Tm	Lg	Tot	H	A	Men-On 0	Men-On 1	Men-On 2	Men-On 3	One-Game 2	One-Game 3	One-Game 4	LO	XN	IP	PH	RHP	LHP
1993	OAK	AL	12	8	4	6	3	3	0	0	0	0	0	0	0	0	7	5
1995	OAK	AL	13	8	5	7	4	1	1	2	0	0	0	0	0	0	7	6
Total			25	16	9	13	7	4	1	2	0	0	0	0	0	0	14	11

Rank among batters: 1,608 • *Top target (3 home runs)*: Brad Radke • *Number of pitchers victimized*: 23 • *Total ballparks homered in*: 5 • *First HR*: 06/12/1993 off Jim Deshaies

Al Pardo

ALBERTO JUDAS PARDO
B: 09/08/1962
BB

Year	Tm	Lg	Tot	H	A	Men-On 0	Men-On 1	Men-On 2	Men-On 3	One-Game 2	One-Game 3	One-Game 4	LO	XN	IP	PH	RHP	LHP
1986	BAL	AL	1	0	1	1	0	0	0	0	0	0	0	0	0	0	1	0

Rank among batters: 4,707 • *Total ballparks homered in*: 1 • *First HR*: 07/10/1986 off Joe Cowley

Johnny Paredes

JOHNNY ALFONSO (ISAMBERT) PAREDES
B: 09/02/1962
BR

Year	Tm	Lg	Tot	H	A	Men-On 0	Men-On 1	Men-On 2	Men-On 3	One-Game 2	One-Game 3	One-Game 4	LO	XN	IP	PH	RHP	LHP
1988	MON	NL	1	0	1	0	0	1	0	0	0	0	0	1	0	0	1	0

Rank among batters: 4,707 • *Total ballparks homered in*: 1 • *First HR*: 05/01/1988 off Jeff Heathcock

Freddy Parent

FREDERICK ALFRED PARENT
B: 11/25/1875 D: 11/02/1972
BR

Year	Tm	Lg	Tot	H	A	Men-On 0	Men-On 1	Men-On 2	Men-On 3	One-Game 2	One-Game 3	One-Game 4	LO	XN	IP	PH	RHP	LHP
1901	BOS	AL	4	2	2	1	2	1	0	0	0	0	0	0	0	0	3	1
1902	BOS	AL	3	1	2	1	2	0	0	0	0	0	0	0	0	0	2	1
1903	BOS	AL	4	4	0	1	3	0	0	0	0	0	0	0	0	0	0	4
1904	BOS	AL	6	3	3	3	2	0	1	0	0	0	0	0	2	0	3	3
1906	BOS	AL	1	0	1	1	0	0	0	0	0	0	0	0	1	0	1	0
1907	BOS	AL	1	1	0	0	1	0	0	0	0	0	0	0	0	0	1	0
1910	CHI	AL	1	0	1	0	1	0	0	0	0	0	0	0	0	0	0	1
Total			20	11	9	7	11	1	1	0	0	0	0	0	3	0	10	10

Rank among batters: 1,810 • *Top target (2 home runs)*: Bill Carrick, Rube Waddell • *Number of pitchers victimized*: 18 • *Total ballparks homered in*: 6 • *First HR*: 06/02/1901 off Bill Reidy

Mark Parent

MARK ALAN PARENT
B: 09/16/1961
BR

Year	Tm	Lg	Tot	H	A	Men-On 0	Men-On 1	Men-On 2	Men-On 3	One-Game 2	One-Game 3	One-Game 4	LO	XN	IP	PH	RHP	LHP
1988	SD	NL	6	4	2	2	3	1	0	2	0	0	0	1	0	1	3	3
1989	SD	NL	7	6	1	5	1	1	0	0	0	0	0	0	0	1	5	2
1990	SD	NL	3	1	2	3	0	0	0	0	0	0	0	0	0	0	1	2
1992	BAL	AL	2	0	2	2	0	0	0	0	0	0	0	0	0	0	1	1
1993	BAL	AL	4	1	3	2	1	1	0	0	0	0	0	0	0	0	2	2
1994	CHI	NL	3	0	3	1	2	0	0	0	0	0	0	0	0	0	1	2
1995	PIT	NL	15	5	10	10	4	1	0	0	0	0	0	0	0	0	7	8
	CHI	NL	3	2	1	2	1	0	0	0	0	0	0	0	0	0	2	1
	Total		18	7	11	12	5	1	0	0	0	0	0	0	0	0	9	9
Total			43	19	24	27	12	4	0	2	0	0	0	1	0	2	22	21

Rank among batters: 1,116 • Top target (2 home runs): Greg Swindell, Bryan Hickerson, Bill VanLandingham, Fernando Valenzuela • *Number of pitchers victimized*: 39 • *Total ballparks homered in*: 17 • *First HR*: 08/14/1988 off Joaquin Andujar

Kelly Paris

KELLY JAY PARIS
B: 10/17/1957
BR

Year	Tm	Lg	Tot	H	A	Men-On 0	Men-On 1	Men-On 2	Men-On 3	One-Game 2	One-Game 3	One-Game 4	LO	XN	IP	PH	RHP	LHP
1988	CHI	AL	3	0	3	1	1	1	0	1	0	0	0	0	0	0	0	3

Rank among batters: 3,735 • *Top target (2 home runs)*: Mark Langston • *Number of pitchers victimized*: 2 • *Total ballparks homered in*: 2 • *First HR*: 08/07/1988 off Chuck Finley

Year	Tm	Lg	Tot	H	A	Men-On 0	Men-On 1	Men-On 2	Men-On 3	One-Game 2	One-Game 3	One-Game 4	LO	XN	IP	PH	RHP	LHP

Ace Parker

CLARENCE MCKAY PARKER
B: 05/17/1912
BR

Year	Tm	Lg	Tot	H	A	0	1	2	3	2	3	4	LO	XN	IP	PH	RHP	LHP
1937	PHI	AL	2	1	1	0	1	1	0	0	0	0	0	0	0	1	2	0

Rank among batters: 4,129 • *Total ballparks homered in*: 2 • *First HR*: 04/30/1937 off Wes Ferrell • *Hit HR in first major league AB*—@BOS: 04/30/1937

Billy Parker

WILLIAM DAVID PARKER
B: 01/14/1947
BR

Year	Tm	Lg	Tot	H	A	0	1	2	3	2	3	4	LO	XN	IP	PH	RHP	LHP
1971	CAL	AL	1	1	0	1	0	0	0	0	0	0	0	1	0	0	1	0
1972	CAL	AL	2	0	2	2	0	0	0	0	0	0	0	0	0	0	0	2
Total			3	1	2	3	0	0	0	0	0	0	0	1	0	0	1	2

Rank among batters: 3,735 • *Total ballparks homered in*: 3 • *First HR*: 09/09/1971 off Floyd Weaver

Dave Parker

DAVID GENE PARKER
B: 06/09/1951
BL

Year	Tm	Lg	Tot	H	A	0	1	2	3	2	3	4	LO	XN	IP	PH	RHP	LHP
1973	PIT	NL	4	2	2	2	1	1	0	0	0	0	0	0	0	0	4	0
1974	PIT	NL	4	3	1	1	0	2	1	0	0	0	0	1	0	1	4	0
1975	PIT	NL	25	10	15	10	9	6	0	1	0	0	0	0	0	1	18	7
1976	PIT	NL	13	5	8	8	4	1	0	1	0	0	0	0	0	0	11	2
1977	PIT	NL	21	10	11	10	9	1	1	3	0	0	0	0	0	0	14	7
1978	PIT	NL	30	14	16	11	14	5	0	3	0	0	0	1	0	0	20	10
1979	PIT	NL	25	14	11	15	7	3	0	0	0	0	0	0	2	0	12	13
1980	PIT	NL	17	10	7	6	9	2	0	2	0	0	0	0	0	0	11	6
1981	PIT	NL	9	4	5	3	2	4	0	0	0	0	0	0	0	0	7	2
1982	PIT	NL	6	4	2	5	0	1	0	1	0	0	0	0	0	0	6	0
1983	PIT	NL	12	6	6	5	7	0	0	0	0	0	0	0	0	0	5	7
1984	CIN	NL	16	10	6	8	4	3	1	0	0	0	0	0	0	0	11	5
1985	CIN	NL	34	16	18	16	13	3	2	2	0	0	0	0	0	0	27	7
1986	CIN	NL	31	17	14	9	12	8	2	1	0	0	0	0	0	1	21	10
1987	CIN	NL	26	14	12	11	11	4	0	2	0	0	0	0	0	0	18	8
1988	OAK	AL	12	6	6	3	7	2	0	0	0	0	0	0	0	1	10	2
1989	OAK	AL	22	10	12	12	6	3	1	1	0	0	0	1	0	0	16	6
1990	MIL	AL	21	9	12	13	6	2	0	1	0	0	0	0	0	0	15	6
1991	CAL	AL	11	6	5	6	3	2	0	0	0	0	0	0	0	0	7	4
Total			339	170	169	154	124	53	8	18	0	0	0	3	2	4	237	102

Rank among batters: 48 • *Top target (6 home runs)*: Steve Carlton, Andy Hawkins • *Number of pitchers victimized*: 220 • *Total ballparks homered in*: 25 • *First HR*: 07/22/1973 off Steve Arlin • *World Series HR*—1; *LCS HR*—2; *All-Star HR*—1

Rick Parker

RICHARD ALAN PARKER
B: 03/20/1963
BR

Year	Tm	Lg	Tot	H	A	0	1	2	3	2	3	4	LO	XN	IP	PH	RHP	LHP
1990	SF	NL	2	0	2	1	0	1	0	0	0	0	0	0	0	0	0	2

Rank among batters: 4,129 • *Total ballparks homered in*: 2 • *First HR*: 06/08/1990 off Derek Lilliquist

Wes Parker

MAURICE WESLEY PARKER
B: 11/13/1939
BB

Year	Tm	Lg	Tot	H	A	0	1	2	3	2	3	4	LO	XN	IP	PH	RHP	LHP
1964	LA	NL	3	0	3	3	0	0	0	0	0	0	0	0	0	0	1	2
1965	LA	NL	8	3	5	4	4	0	0	0	0	0	0	1	0	0	6	2
1966	LA	NL	12	4	8	7	3	2	0	1	0	0	0	0	0	0	8	4
1967	LA	NL	5	1	4	3	1	1	0	0	0	0	1	0	1	0	3	2
1968	LA	NL	3	2	1	3	0	0	0	0	0	0	0	0	0	0	2	1
1969	LA	NL	13	5	8	7	6	0	0	0	0	0	0	0	0	0	5	8
1970	LA	NL	10	3	7	6	4	0	0	0	0	0	0	0	0	0	3	7
1971	LA	NL	6	2	4	3	3	0	0	0	0	0	0	0	0	0	5	1
1972	LA	NL	4	2	2	2	2	0	0	0	0	0	0	0	0	0	2	2
Total			64	22	42	38	23	3	0	1	0	0	1	1	1	0	35	29

Rank among batters: 815 • *Top target (3 home runs)*: Jack Fisher, Ray Sadecki • *Number of pitchers victimized*: 55 • *Total ballparks homered in*: 12 • *First HR*: 08/31/1964 off Ron Taylor • *Switch hit HR in 1 game*—1 time • *Hit for Cycle*—@NY: 05/07/1970 • *World Series HR*—1

Year	Tm	Lg	Tot	H	A	Men-On 0	Men-On 1	Men-On 2	Men-On 3	One-Game 2	One-Game 3	One-Game 4	LO	XN	IP	PH	RHP	LHP

Frank Parkinson

FRANK JOSEPH PARKINSON
B: 03/23/1895 D: 07/04/1960
BR

Year	Tm	Lg	Tot	H	A	0	1	2	3	2	3	4	LO	XN	IP	PH	RHP	LHP
1921	PHI	NL	5	5	0	3	2	0	0	0	0	0	0	0	0	0	5	0
1922	PHI	NL	15	14	1	7	4	4	0	1	0	0	0	0	0	0	12	3
1923	PHI	NL	3	2	1	1	1	1	0	0	0	0	0	0	0	0	0	3
1924	PHI	NL	1	1	0	1	0	0	0	0	0	0	0	0	0	0	1	0
Total			24	22	2	12	7	5	0	1	0	0	0	0	0	0	18	6

Rank among batters: 1,643 • *Top target (2 home runs)*: Vic Aldridge, Pete Donohue, Tony Kaufmann • *Number of pitchers victimized*: 21 • *Total ballparks homered in*: 3 • *First HR*: 06/27/1921 off Phil Douglas

Art Parks

ARTIE WILLIAM PARKS
B: 11/01/1911 D: 12/06/1989
BL

Year	Tm	Lg	Tot	H	A	0	1	2	3	2	3	4	LO	XN	IP	PH	RHP	LHP
1939	BRO	NL	1	0	1	1	0	0	0	0	0	0	0	0	0	0	1	0

Rank among batters: 4,707 • *Total ballparks homered in*: 1 • *First HR*: 08/10/1939 off Boom-Boom Beck

Derek Parks

DEREK GAVIN PARKS
B: 09/29/1968
BR

Year	Tm	Lg	Tot	H	A	0	1	2	3	2	3	4	LO	XN	IP	PH	RHP	LHP
1994	MIN	AL	1	0	1	1	0	0	0	0	0	0	0	0	0	0	0	1

Rank among batters: 4,707 • *Total ballparks homered in*: 1 • *First HR*: 06/18/1994 off Sid Fernandez

Leroy Parmelee

LEROY EARL PARMELEE
B: 04/25/1907 D: 08/31/1981
BR

Year	Tm	Lg	Tot	H	A	0	1	2	3	2	3	4	LO	XN	IP	PH	RHP	LHP
1933	NY	NL	1	0	1	0	0	1	0	0	0	0	0	0	0	0	1	0
1934	NY	NL	2	1	1	1	0	0	1	0	0	0	0	0	0	0	2	0
1937	CHI	NL	2	1	1	1	0	1	0	0	0	0	0	0	0	0	2	0
Total			5	2	3	2	0	2	1	0	0	0	0	0	0	0	5	0

Rank among batters: 3,191 • *Total ballparks homered in*: 4 • *First HR*: 05/23/1933 off Red Lucas

Mel Parnell

MELVIN LLOYD PARNELL
B: 06/13/1922
BL

Year	Tm	Lg	Tot	H	A	0	1	2	3	2	3	4	LO	XN	IP	PH	RHP	LHP
1952	BOS	AL	1	0	1	1	0	0	0	0	0	0	0	0	0	0	1	0

Rank among batters: 4,707 • *Total ballparks homered in*: 1 • *First HR*: 09/15/1952 off Lou Kretlow

Lance Parrish

LANCE MICHAEL PARRISH
B: 06/15/1956
BR

Year	Tm	Lg	Tot	H	A	0	1	2	3	2	3	4	LO	XN	IP	PH	RHP	LHP
1977	DET	AL	3	2	1	3	0	0	0	0	0	0	0	0	0	0	0	3
1978	DET	AL	14	7	7	7	6	0	1	1	0	0	0	2	0	0	1	13
1979	DET	AL	19	8	11	17	2	0	0	2	0	0	0	0	0	0	8	11
1980	DET	AL	24	7	17	13	6	5	0	2	0	0	0	0	0	1	8	16
1981	DET	AL	10	8	2	5	4	1	0	1	0	0	0	1	0	0	4	6
1982	DET	AL	32	22	10	17	13	2	0	4	0	0	0	2	0	0	20	12
1983	DET	AL	27	12	15	15	9	1	2	0	0	0	0	2	0	0	18	9
1984	DET	AL	33	13	20	17	11	4	1	1	0	0	0	2	0	0	19	14
1985	DET	AL	28	11	17	15	10	2	1	3	0	0	0	0	0	0	19	9
1986	DET	AL	22	8	14	14	5	3	0	4	0	0	0	0	0	0	17	5
1987	PHI	NL	17	5	12	6	6	4	1	0	0	0	0	1	0	0	11	6
1988	PHI	NL	15	11	4	6	7	2	0	0	0	0	0	0	0	0	11	4
1989	CAL	AL	17	8	9	11	5	1	0	0	0	0	0	0	0	0	10	7
1990	CAL	AL	24	14	10	11	10	2	1	1	0	0	0	1	0	0	17	7
1991	CAL	AL	19	9	10	12	7	0	0	1	0	0	0	0	0	0	17	2
1992	CAL	AL	4	1	3	2	1	1	0	0	0	0	0	0	0	0	4	0
	SEA	AL	8	6	2	6	0	2	0	1	0	0	0	0	0	0	4	4
	Total		12	7	5	8	1	3	0	1	0	0	0	0	0	0	8	4
1993	CLE	AL	1	1	0	0	1	0	0	0	0	0	0	0	0	0	1	0

Lance Parrish *continued*

Year	Tm	Lg	Tot	H	A	Men-On 0	1	2	3	One-Game 2	3	4	LO	XN	IP	PH	RHP	LHP
1994	PIT	NL	3	3	0	3	0	0	0	0	0	0	0	0	0	0	2	1
1995	TOR	AL	4	4	0	2	1	1	0	1	0	0	0	0	0	0	4	0
Total			324	160	164	182	104	31	7	22	0	0	0	11	0	1	195	129

Rank among batters: 57 • *Top target (6 home runs)*: Ron Guidry, Bruce Hurst, Mike Flanagan • *Number of pitchers victimized*: 221 • *Total ballparks homered in*: 26 • *First HR*: 09/07/1977 off Earl Stephenson • *World Series HR*—1; *LCS HR*—1

Larry Parrish

LARRY ALTON PARRISH
B: 11/10/1953
BR

Year	Tm	Lg	Tot	H	A	Men-On 0	1	2	3	One-Game 2	3	4	LO	XN	IP	PH	RHP	LHP
1975	MON	NL	10	5	5	8	1	1	0	0	0	0	0	1	0	0	6	4
1976	MON	NL	11	4	7	6	4	1	0	1	0	0	0	0	0	0	10	1
1977	MON	NL	11	4	7	6	3	2	0	1	1	0	0	0	0	1	6	5
1978	MON	NL	15	4	11	8	3	3	1	0	1	0	0	0	0	0	8	7
1979	MON	NL	30	14	16	16	12	2	0	2	0	0	0	0	0	0	28	2
1980	MON	NL	15	6	9	8	5	2	0	0	1	0	0	1	0	0	13	2
1981	MON	NL	8	3	5	5	2	1	0	0	0	0	0	0	0	0	5	3
1982	TEX	AL	17	6	11	7	3	4	3	1	0	0	0	1	0	0	12	5
1983	TEX	AL	26	10	16	13	9	4	0	2	0	0	0	0	0	0	19	7
1984	TEX	AL	22	11	11	11	6	4	1	2	0	0	0	1	0	0	14	8
1985	TEX	AL	17	8	9	10	5	2	0	1	1	0	0	0	0	0	9	8
1986	TEX	AL	28	14	14	18	7	3	0	2	0	0	0	0	1	0	17	11
1987	TEX	AL	32	16	16	13	12	7	0	1	0	0	0	0	0	0	18	14
1988	TEX	AL	7	4	3	6	1	0	0	0	0	0	0	0	0	0	5	2
	BOS	AL	7	3	4	4	3	0	0	0	0	0	0	1	0	0	6	1
	Total		14	7	7	10	4	0	0	0	0	0	0	1	0	0	11	3
Total			256	112	144	139	76	36	5	13	4	0	0	5	1	1	176	80

Rank among batters: 98 • *Top target (6 home runs)*: Ron Guidry • *Number of pitchers victimized*: 179 • *Total ballparks homered in*: 26 • *First HR*: 04/16/1975 off Dock Ellis

Jiggs Parrott

WALTER EDWARD PARROTT
B: 07/14/1871 D: 04/16/1898

Year	Tm	Lg	Tot	H	A	Men-On 0	1	2	3	One-Game 2	3	4	LO	XN	IP	PH	RHP	LHP
1892	CHI	NL	2	0	2	1	1	0	0	0	0	0	0	0	1	0	2	0
1893	CHI	NL	1	1	0	0	0	0	1	0	0	0	0	0	0	0	1	0
1894	CHI	NL	3	0	3	2	1	0	0	0	0	0	0	0	0	0	2	0
Total			6	1	5	3	2	0	1	0	0	0	0	0	1	0	5	0

Rank among batters: 2,988 • *Total ballparks homered in*: 5 • *First HR*: 07/23/1892 off Kid Nichols

Tom Parrott

THOMAS WILLIAM PARROTT
B: 04/10/1868 D: 01/01/1932
BR

Year	Tm	Lg	Tot	H	A	Men-On 0	1	2	3	One-Game 2	3	4	LO	XN	IP	PH	RHP	LHP
1893	CIN	NL	1	1	0	1	0	0	0	0	0	0	0	0	0	0	1	0
1894	CIN	NL	4	4	0	3	1	0	0	0	0	0	0	0	1	0	3	1
1895	CIN	NL	3	0	3	2	1	0	0	0	0	0	0	0	0	0	2	1
1896	STL	NL	7	4	3	5	2	0	0	0	0	0	0	0	0	0	6	1
Total			15	9	6	11	4	0	0	0	0	0	0	0	1	0	12	3

Rank among batters: 2,096 • *Total ballparks homered in*: 7 • *First HR*: 09/18/1893 off Bill Hawke • *Hit for Cycle*—vs NY: 09/28/1894

Bill Parsons

WILLIAM RAYMOND PARSONS
B: 08/17/1948
BR

Year	Tm	Lg	Tot	H	A	Men-On 0	1	2	3	One-Game 2	3	4	LO	XN	IP	PH	RHP	LHP
1971	MIL	AL	1	0	1	1	0	0	0	0	0	0	0	0	0	0	1	0

Rank among batters: 4,707 • *Total ballparks homered in*: 1 • *First HR*: 06/15/1971 off Jim Palmer

Casey Parsons

CASEY ROBERT PARSONS
B: 04/14/1954
BL

Year	Tm	Lg	Tot	H	A	Men-On 0	1	2	3	One-Game 2	3	4	LO	XN	IP	PH	RHP	LHP
1981	SEA	AL	1	0	1	0	1	0	0	0	0	0	0	0	0	0	1	0

Year	Tm	Lg	Tot	H	A	Men-On 0	Men-On 1	Men-On 2	Men-On 3	One-Game 2	One-Game 3	One-Game 4	LO	XN	IP	PH	RHP	LHP

Casey Parsons *continued*

Year	Tm	Lg	Tot	H	A	0	1	2	3	2	3	4	LO	XN	IP	PH	RHP	LHP
1987	CLE	AL	1	1	0	0	0	0	1	0	0	0	0	0	0	1	1	0
Total			2	1	1	0	1	0	1	0	0	0	0	0	0	1	2	0

Rank among batters: 4,129 • *Total ballparks homered in*: 2 • *First HR*: 09/07/1981 off Richard Dotson

Dixie Parsons

EDWARD DIXON PARSONS
B: 05/12/1916 D: 10/31/1991
BR

Year	Tm	Lg	Tot	H	A	0	1	2	3	2	3	4	LO	XN	IP	PH	RHP	LHP
1942	DET	AL	2	1	1	2	0	0	0	0	0	0	0	0	0	0	2	0

Rank among batters: 4,129 • *Total ballparks homered in*: 2 • *First HR*: 05/22/1942 off Johnny Humphries

Roy Partee

ROY ROBERT PARTEE
B: 09/07/1917
BR

Year	Tm	Lg	Tot	H	A	0	1	2	3	2	3	4	LO	XN	IP	PH	RHP	LHP
1944	BOS	AL	2	2	0	2	0	0	0	0	0	0	0	0	0	0	2	0

Rank among batters: 4,129 • *Total ballparks homered in*: 1 • *First HR*: 06/08/1944 off Atley Donald

Jay Partridge

JAMES BUGG PARTRIDGE
B: 11/15/1902 D: 01/14/1974
BL

Year	Tm	Lg	Tot	H	A	0	1	2	3	2	3	4	LO	XN	IP	PH	RHP	LHP
1927	BRO	NL	7	3	4	6	1	0	0	0	0	0	1	0	0	0	5	2

Rank among batters: 2,834 • *Total ballparks homered in*: 4 • *First HR*: 04/14/1927 off Foster Edwards

Ben Paschal

BENJAMIN EDWIN PASCHAL
B: 10/13/1895 D: 11/10/1974
BR

Year	Tm	Lg	Tot	H	A	0	1	2	3	2	3	4	LO	XN	IP	PH	RHP	LHP
1925	NY	AL	12	4	8	6	4	2	0	2	0	0	0	0	2	0	3	9
1926	NY	AL	7	4	3	4	3	0	0	0	0	0	0	0	1	0	2	5
1927	NY	AL	2	2	0	1	1	0	0	1	0	0	0	0	0	0	1	1
1928	NY	AL	1	1	0	1	0	0	0	0	0	0	0	0	0	0	1	0
1929	NY	AL	2	2	0	1	1	0	0	0	0	0	0	0	1	1	0	2
Total			24	13	11	13	9	2	0	3	0	0	0	0	4	1	7	17

Rank among batters: 1,643 • *Top target (2 home runs)*: Buster Ross, Sherry Smith • *Number of pitchers victimized*: 22 • *Total ballparks homered in*: 7 • *First HR*: 04/14/1925 off George Mogridge

Camilo Pascual

CAMILO ALBERTO (LUS) PASCUAL
B: 01/20/1934
BR

Year	Tm	Lg	Tot	H	A	0	1	2	3	2	3	4	LO	XN	IP	PH	RHP	LHP
1960	WAS	AL	1	0	1	0	0	0	1	0	0	0	0	0	0	0	1	0
1962	MIN	AL	2	2	0	1	1	0	0	0	0	0	0	0	0	0	2	0
1965	MIN	AL	2	1	1	1	0	0	1	0	0	0	0	0	0	0	2	0
Total			5	3	2	2	1	0	2	0	0	0	0	0	0	0	5	0

Rank among batters: 3,191 • *Total ballparks homered in*: 3 • *First HR*: 08/14/1960 off Bob Turley

Dode Paskert

GEORGE HENRY PASKERT
B: 08/28/1881 D: 02/12/1959
BR

Year	Tm	Lg	Tot	H	A	0	1	2	3	2	3	4	LO	XN	IP	PH	RHP	LHP
1907	CIN	NL	1	1	0	0	1	0	0	0	0	0	0	0	1	0	1	0
1908	CIN	NL	1	1	0	1	0	0	0	0	0	0	0	0	0	0	0	1
1910	CIN	NL	2	0	2	2	0	0	0	0	0	0	0	0	2	0	2	0
1911	PHI	NL	4	4	0	2	2	0	0	0	0	0	0	0	0	0	4	0
1912	PHI	NL	2	0	2	1	0	1	0	0	0	0	0	0	0	0	1	1
1913	PHI	NL	4	4	0	3	1	0	0	0	0	0	1	0	0	1	3	1
1914	PHI	NL	3	2	1	2	1	0	0	0	0	0	1	0	1	0	3	0
1915	PHI	NL	3	2	1	1	2	0	0	0	0	0	0	0	0	0	3	0
1916	PHI	NL	8	8	0	8	0	0	0	0	0	0	2	0	0	0	8	0

Dode Paskert *continued*

Year	Tm	Lg	Tot	H	A	Men-On 0	1	2	3	One-Game 2	3	4	LO	XN	IP	PH	RHP	LHP
1917	PHI	NL	4	4	0	3	1	0	0	0	0	0	1	0	0	0	4	0
1918	CHI	NL	3	1	2	1	2	0	0	0	0	0	0	0	1	0	3	0
1919	CHI	NL	2	2	0	0	1	1	0	0	0	0	0	0	0	0	2	0
1920	CHI	NL	5	4	1	3	2	0	0	0	0	0	0	0	1	0	3	2
Total			42	33	9	27	13	2	0	0	0	0	5	0	6	1	37	5

Rank among batters: 1,138 • Top target (2 home runs): Doc Crandall, Jimmy Lavender, Laurence Cheney, Bob Harmon, Pat Ragan, Mike Prendergast, Bill Doak • *Number of pitchers victimized*: 35 • *Total ballparks homered in*: 8 • *First HR*: 10/06/1907 off Babe Adams

Kevin Pasley

KEVIN PATRICK PASLEY
B: 07/22/1953
BR

Year	Tm	Lg	Tot	H	A	Men-On 0	1	2	3	One-Game 2	3	4	LO	XN	IP	PH	RHP	LHP
1978	SEA	AL	1	1	0	0	1	0	0	0	0	0	0	0	0	0	1	0

Rank among batters: 4,707 • *Total ballparks homered in*: 1 • *First HR*: 10/01/1978 off Ferguson Jenkins

Dan Pasqua

DANIEL ANTHONY PASQUA
B: 10/17/1961
BL

Year	Tm	Lg	Tot	H	A	Men-On 0	1	2	3	One-Game 2	3	4	LO	XN	IP	PH	RHP	LHP
1985	NY	AL	9	7	2	4	3	2	0	1	0	0	0	0	0	0	9	0
1986	NY	AL	16	9	7	12	3	1	0	1	0	0	0	0	1	1	13	3
1987	NY	AL	17	6	11	9	6	2	0	0	0	0	0	0	0	3	17	0
1988	CHI	AL	20	11	9	14	5	1	0	4	0	0	0	1	0	0	20	0
1989	CHI	AL	11	5	6	7	3	1	0	1	0	0	0	0	0	0	8	3
1990	CHI	AL	13	4	9	6	5	2	0	1	0	0	0	1	0	0	13	0
1991	CHI	AL	18	10	8	10	6	2	0	1	0	0	0	0	0	0	16	2
1992	CHI	AL	6	2	4	3	2	0	1	0	0	0	0	0	0	0	6	0
1993	CHI	AL	5	2	3	0	3	2	0	0	0	0	0	0	0	0	3	2
1994	CHI	AL	2	1	1	1	0	1	0	0	0	0	0	0	0	0	2	0
Total			117	57	60	66	36	14	1	9	0	0	0	2	1	4	107	10

Rank among batters: 402 • *Top target (4 home runs)*: Bill Wegman • *Number of pitchers victimized*: 86 • *Total ballparks homered in*: 16 • *First HR*: 05/30/1985 off Ron Romanick

Claude Passeau

CLAUDE WILLIAM PASSEAU
B: 04/09/1909
BR

Year	Tm	Lg	Tot	H	A	Men-On 0	1	2	3	One-Game 2	3	4	LO	XN	IP	PH	RHP	LHP
1936	PHI	NL	2	1	1	1	1	0	0	0	0	0	0	0	0	0	2	0
1937	PHI	NL	1	1	0	0	0	1	0	0	0	0	0	0	0	0	1	0
1939	CHI	NL	1	1	0	1	0	0	0	0	0	0	0	0	0	0	1	0
1940	CHI	NL	1	1	0	1	0	0	0	0	0	0	0	0	0	0	0	1
1941	CHI	NL	3	1	2	2	0	0	1	0	0	0	0	0	0	0	1	2
1942	CHI	NL	2	0	2	1	1	0	0	0	0	0	0	0	0	0	2	0
1945	CHI	NL	2	1	1	1	0	1	0	0	0	0	0	0	0	0	2	0
1946	CHI	NL	3	2	1	1	2	0	0	0	0	0	0	0	0	0	2	1
Total			15	8	7	8	4	2	1	0	0	0	0	0	0	0	11	4

Rank among batters: 2,096 • *Total ballparks homered in*: 7 • *First HR*: 08/18/1936 off Bobby Reis

Frank Pastore

FRANK ENRICO PASTORE
B: 08/21/1957
BR

Year	Tm	Lg	Tot	H	A	Men-On 0	1	2	3	One-Game 2	3	4	LO	XN	IP	PH	RHP	LHP
1982	CIN	NL	1	1	0	1	0	0	0	0	0	0	0	0	0	0	1	0
1983	CIN	NL	1	0	1	0	1	0	0	0	0	0	0	0	0	0	1	0
Total			2	1	1	1	1	0	0	0	0	0	0	0	0	0	2	0

Rank among batters: 4,129 • *Total ballparks homered in*: 2 • *First HR*: 08/23/1982 off Bill Gullickson

Cliff Pastornicky

CLIFFORD SCOT PASTORNICKY
B: 11/18/1958
BR

Year	Tm	Lg	Tot	H	A	Men-On 0	1	2	3	One-Game 2	3	4	LO	XN	IP	PH	RHP	LHP
1983	KC	AL	2	2	0	0	1	1	0	0	0	0	0	0	0	0	1	1

Rank among batters: 4,129 • *Total ballparks homered in*: 1 • *First HR*: 06/19/1983 off Matt Young

Year	Tm	Lg	Tot	H	A	Men-On 0	Men-On 1	Men-On 2	Men-On 3	One-Game 2	One-Game 3	One-Game 4	LO	XN	IP	PH	RHP	LHP

Freddie Patek

FREDERICK JOSEPH PATEK
B: 10/09/1944
BR

Year	Tm	Lg	Tot	H	A	0	1	2	3	2	3	4	LO	XN	IP	PH	RHP	LHP
1968	PIT	NL	2	1	1	1	0	1	0	0	0	0	0	0	0	0	1	1
1969	PIT	NL	5	3	2	4	1	0	0	0	0	0	0	0	0	0	4	1
1970	PIT	NL	1	1	0	0	0	1	0	0	0	0	0	0	0	0	1	0
1971	KC	AL	6	1	5	4	2	0	0	0	0	0	3	0	1	0	4	2
1973	KC	AL	5	3	2	5	0	0	0	0	0	0	2	0	0	0	4	1
1974	KC	AL	3	2	1	3	0	0	0	0	0	0	0	0	0	0	1	2
1975	KC	AL	5	1	4	4	1	0	0	0	0	0	1	0	1	0	3	2
1976	KC	AL	1	0	1	1	0	0	0	0	0	0	0	0	0	0	1	0
1977	KC	AL	5	1	4	3	2	0	0	0	0	0	0	0	0	0	3	2
1978	KC	AL	2	0	2	0	2	0	0	0	0	0	0	0	0	0	2	0
1979	KC	AL	1	0	1	0	0	1	0	0	0	0	0	0	0	0	0	1
1980	CAL	AL	5	2	3	2	2	1	0	0	1	0	0	0	0	0	3	2
Total			41	15	26	27	10	4	0	0	1	0	6	0	2	0	27	14

Rank among batters: 1,163 • Top target (2 home runs): Stan Bahnsen, Gaylord Perry, Dick Drago, Jerry Koosman • *Number of pitchers victimized*: 37 • *Total ballparks homered in*: 16 • *First HR*: 06/15/1968 off Don Wilson • *Hit for Cycle*—@MIN: 07/09/1971 • *LCS HR*—1

Bob Patrick

ROBERT LEE PATRICK
B: 10/27/1917
BR

Year	Tm	Lg	Tot	H	A	0	1	2	3	2	3	4	LO	XN	IP	PH	RHP	LHP
1942	DET	AL	1	1	0	1	0	0	0	0	0	0	0	0	0	0	0	1

Rank among batters: 4,707 • *Total ballparks homered in*: 1 • *First HR*: 04/24/1942 off Eddie Smith

Case Patten

CASE LYMAN PATTEN
B: 05/07/1876 D: 05/31/1935
BB

Year	Tm	Lg	Tot	H	A	0	1	2	3	2	3	4	LO	XN	IP	PH	RHP	LHP
1901	WAS	AL	1	1	0	1	0	0	0	0	0	0	0	0	0	0	1	0
1906	WAS	AL	1	0	1	1	0	0	0	0	0	0	0	0	0	0	1	0
Total			2	1	1	2	0	0	0	0	0	0	0	0	0	0	2	0

Rank among batters: 4,129 • *Total ballparks homered in*: 2 • *First HR*: 08/20/1901 off Clark Griffith

John Patterson

JOHN ALLEN PATTERSON
B: 02/11/1967
BB

Year	Tm	Lg	Tot	H	A	0	1	2	3	2	3	4	LO	XN	IP	PH	RHP	LHP
1993	SF	NL	1	0	1	1	0	0	0	0	0	0	0	0	0	1	1	0
1994	SF	NL	3	2	1	0	2	0	1	0	0	0	0	0	0	0	3	0
1995	SF	NL	1	1	0	1	0	0	0	0	0	0	0	0	0	0	1	0
Total			5	3	2	2	2	0	1	0	0	0	0	0	0	1	5	0

Rank among batters: 3,191 • *Total ballparks homered in*: 3 • *First HR*: 09/01/1993 off Mark Wohlers

Mike Patterson

MICHAEL LEE PATTERSON
B: 01/26/1958
BL

Year	Tm	Lg	Tot	H	A	0	1	2	3	2	3	4	LO	XN	IP	PH	RHP	LHP
1982	NY	AL	1	1	0	1	0	0	0	0	0	0	0	0	0	0	1	0

Rank among batters: 4,707 • *Total ballparks homered in*: 1 • *First HR*: 05/21/1982 off John Pacella

Pat Patterson

WILLIAM JENNINGS BRYAN PATTERSON
B: 01/29/1901 D: 10/01/1977
BR

Year	Tm	Lg	Tot	H	A	0	1	2	3	2	3	4	LO	XN	IP	PH	RHP	LHP
1921	NY	NL	1	0	1	0	1	0	0	0	0	0	0	0	0	0	1	0

Rank among batters: 4,707 • *Total ballparks homered in*: 1 • *First HR*: 06/25/1921 off Lee Meadows

Roy Patterson

ROY LEWIS PATTERSON
B: 12/17/1876 D: 04/14/1953
BR

Year	Tm	Lg	Tot	H	A	0	1	2	3	2	3	4	LO	XN	IP	PH	RHP	LHP
1901	CHI	AL	1	0	1	0	0	1	0	0	0	0	0	0	1	0	1	0

Rank among batters: 4,707 • *Total ballparks homered in*: 1 • *First HR*: 06/13/1901 off Joe McGinnity

Marty Pattin

MARTIN WILLIAM PATTIN
B: 04/06/1943
BR

						Men-On				One-Game								
Year	Tm	Lg	Tot	H	A	0	1	2	3	2	3	4	LO	XN	IP	PH	RHP	LHP
1972	BOS	AL	2	2	0	0	2	0	0	0	0	0	0	0	0	0	2	0

Rank among batters: 4,129 • *Top target (2 home runs)*: Bill Parsons • *Number of pitchers victimized*: 1 • *Total ballparks homered in*: 1 • *First HR*: 07/01/1972 off Bill Parsons

Carlos Paula

CARLOS (CONILL) PAULA
B: 11/28/1927 D: 04/25/1983
BR

						Men-On				One-Game								
Year	Tm	Lg	Tot	H	A	0	1	2	3	2	3	4	LO	XN	IP	PH	RHP	LHP
1955	WAS	AL	6	1	5	4	2	0	0	0	0	0	0	0	0	2	4	2
1956	WAS	AL	3	2	1	2	0	1	0	0	0	0	0	0	0	1	2	1
Total			9	3	6	6	2	1	0	0	0	0	0	0	0	3	6	3

Rank among batters: 2,587 • *Total ballparks homered in*: 6 • *First HR*: 04/27/1955 off Early Wynn

Gene Paulette

EUGENE EDWARD PAULETTE
B: 05/26/1891 D: 02/08/1966
BR

						Men-On				One-Game								
Year	Tm	Lg	Tot	H	A	0	1	2	3	2	3	4	LO	XN	IP	PH	RHP	LHP
1919	PHI	NL	1	0	1	0	0	0	1	0	0	0	0	0	0	0	1	0
1920	PHI	NL	1	1	0	0	0	1	0	0	0	0	0	0	0	0	1	0
Total			2	1	1	0	0	1	1	0	0	0	0	0	0	0	2	0

Rank among batters: 4,129 • *Total ballparks homered in*: 2 • *First HR*: 08/11/1919 off Hod Eller

Don Pavletich

DONALD STEPHEN PAVLETICH
B: 07/13/1938
BR

						Men-On				One-Game								
Year	Tm	Lg	Tot	H	A	0	1	2	3	2	3	4	LO	XN	IP	PH	RHP	LHP
1962	CIN	NL	1	1	0	0	1	0	0	0	0	0	0	0	0	1	0	1
1963	CIN	NL	5	2	3	3	2	0	0	0	0	0	0	0	0	0	0	5
1964	CIN	NL	5	5	0	2	3	0	0	0	0	0	0	0	0	0	4	1
1965	CIN	NL	8	3	5	4	4	0	0	0	0	0	0	1	0	0	2	6
1966	CIN	NL	12	5	7	11	0	1	0	0	0	0	0	1	0	1	8	4
1967	CIN	NL	6	4	2	4	1	0	1	1	0	0	0	0	0	1	2	4
1968	CIN	NL	2	2	0	1	1	0	0	0	0	0	0	0	0	0	1	1
1969	CHI	AL	6	3	3	4	2	0	0	0	0	0	0	0	0	0	1	5
1971	BOS	AL	1	0	1	1	0	0	0	0	0	0	0	0	0	0	1	0
Total			46	25	21	30	14	1	1	1	0	0	0	2	0	3	19	27

Rank among batters: 1,060 • *Top target (3 home runs)*: Denny Lemaster, Ferguson Jenkins • *Number of pitchers victimized*: 37 • *Total ballparks homered in*: 15 • *First HR*: 07/27/1962 off Jack Curtis

Fred Payne

FREDERICK THOMAS PAYNE
B: 09/02/1880 D: 01/16/1954
BR

						Men-On				One-Game								
Year	Tm	Lg	Tot	H	A	0	1	2	3	2	3	4	LO	XN	IP	PH	RHP	LHP
1911	CHI	AL	1	0	1	1	0	0	0	0	0	0	0	0	1	0	1	0

Rank among batters: 4,707 • *Total ballparks homered in*: 1 • *First HR*: 05/05/1911 off Hi West

Johnny Peacock

JOHN GASTON PEACOCK
B: 01/10/1910 D: 10/17/1981
BL

						Men-On				One-Game								
Year	Tm	Lg	Tot	H	A	0	1	2	3	2	3	4	LO	XN	IP	PH	RHP	LHP
1938	BOS	AL	1	0	1	1	0	0	0	0	0	0	0	0	0	0	1	0

Rank among batters: 4,707 • *Total ballparks homered in*: 1 • *First HR*: 09/27/1938 off Buck Ross

Albie Pearson

ALBERT GREGORY PEARSON
B: 09/12/1934
BL

						Men-On				One-Game								
Year	Tm	Lg	Tot	H	A	0	1	2	3	2	3	4	LO	XN	IP	PH	RHP	LHP
1958	WAS	AL	3	1	2	0	2	1	0	0	0	0	0	0	1	0	3	0
1960	BAL	AL	1	0	1	0	0	0	1	0	0	0	0	0	0	0	1	0
1961	LA	AL	7	5	2	5	1	1	0	0	0	0	2	0	0	1	6	1

Albie Pearson *continued*

Year	Tm	Lg	Tot	H	A	Men-On 0	Men-On 1	Men-On 2	Men-On 3	One-Game 2	One-Game 3	One-Game 4	LO	XN	IP	PH	RHP	LHP
1962	LA	AL	5	1	4	3	2	0	0	0	0	0	2	0	0	0	3	2
1963	LA	AL	6	2	4	4	1	1	0	0	0	0	1	0	0	0	5	1
1964	LA	AL	2	1	1	0	2	0	0	0	0	0	0	0	0	0	2	0
1965	CAL	AL	4	3	1	4	0	0	0	0	0	0	0	0	0	0	4	0
Total			28	13	15	16	8	3	1	0	0	0	5	0	1	1	24	4

Rank among batters: 1,500 • *Top target (3 home runs)*: Bob Turley, Whitey Ford • *Number of pitchers victimized*: 22 • *Total ballparks homered in*: 10 • *First HR*: 07/28/1958 off Early Wynn

Isaac Pearson

ISAAC OVERTON PEARSON
B: 03/01/1917 D: 03/17/1985
BR

Year	Tm	Lg	Tot	H	A	Men-On 0	Men-On 1	Men-On 2	Men-On 3	One-Game 2	One-Game 3	One-Game 4	LO	XN	IP	PH	RHP	LHP
1946	PHI	NL	1	1	0	1	0	0	0	0	0	0	0	0	0	0	1	0

Rank among batters: 4,707 • *Total ballparks homered in*: 1 • *First HR*: 05/23/1946 off Ed Bahr

Monte Pearson

MONTGOMERY MARCELLUS PEARSON
B: 09/02/1909 D: 01/27/1978
BR

Year	Tm	Lg	Tot	H	A	Men-On 0	Men-On 1	Men-On 2	Men-On 3	One-Game 2	One-Game 3	One-Game 4	LO	XN	IP	PH	RHP	LHP
1934	CLE	AL	1	0	1	0	1	0	0	0	0	0	0	0	0	0	1	0
1936	NY	AL	1	1	0	0	1	0	0	0	0	0	0	0	0	0	1	0
Total			2	1	1	0	2	0	0	0	0	0	0	0	0	0	2	0

Rank among batters: 4,129 • *Total ballparks homered in*: 2 • *First HR*: 09/03/1934 off George Blaeholder

George Pechiney

GEORGE ADOLPHE PECHINEY
B: 09/20/1861 D: 07/14/1943
BR

Year	Tm	Lg	Tot	H	A	Men-On 0	Men-On 1	Men-On 2	Men-On 3	One-Game 2	One-Game 3	One-Game 4	LO	XN	IP	PH	RHP	LHP
1886	CIN	AA	1	0	1	1	0	0	0	0	0	0	0	0	0	0	0	1

Rank among batters: 4,707 • *Total ballparks homered in*: 1 • *First HR*: 09/20/1886 off Cyclone Miller

Hal Peck

HAROLD ARTHUR PECK
B: 04/20/1917 D: 04/13/1995
BL

Year	Tm	Lg	Tot	H	A	Men-On 0	Men-On 1	Men-On 2	Men-On 3	One-Game 2	One-Game 3	One-Game 4	LO	XN	IP	PH	RHP	LHP
1945	PHI	AL	5	1	4	4	1	0	0	0	0	0	0	1	0	0	5	0
1946	PHI	AL	2	0	2	2	0	0	0	0	0	0	0	0	0	0	1	1
1947	CLE	AL	8	4	4	5	2	1	0	1	0	0	1	0	0	0	6	2
Total			15	5	10	11	3	1	0	1	0	0	1	1	0	0	12	3

Rank among batters: 2,096 • *Top target (2 home runs)*: Eddie Lopat • *Number of pitchers victimized*: 14 • *Total ballparks homered in*: 8 • *First HR*: 05/12/1945 off Sig Jakucki

Roger Peckinpaugh

ROGER THORPE PECKINPAUGH
B: 02/05/1891 D: 11/17/1977
BR

Year	Tm	Lg	Tot	H	A	Men-On 0	Men-On 1	Men-On 2	Men-On 3	One-Game 2	One-Game 3	One-Game 4	LO	XN	IP	PH	RHP	LHP
1912	CLE	AL	1	0	1	1	0	0	0	0	0	0	0	0	0	0	1	0
1913	NY	AL	1	0	1	0	0	0	1	0	0	0	0	0	0	0	1	0
1914	NY	AL	3	2	1	0	3	0	0	0	0	0	0	0	0	0	1	2
1915	NY	AL	5	5	0	5	0	0	0	0	0	0	0	0	0	0	4	1
1916	NY	AL	4	2	2	1	3	0	0	0	0	0	0	0	0	0	4	0
1919	NY	AL	7	6	1	4	1	2	0	1	0	0	0	0	1	0	3	4
1920	NY	AL	8	8	0	6	1	1	0	1	0	0	2	0	1	0	5	3
1921	NY	AL	8	6	2	3	5	0	0	0	0	0	0	1	0	0	6	2
1922	WAS	AL	2	1	1	1	1	0	0	0	0	0	0	0	1	0	2	0
1923	WAS	AL	2	1	1	1	1	0	0	0	0	0	0	0	1	0	1	1
1924	WAS	AL	2	0	2	2	0	0	0	0	0	0	0	0	1	0	0	2
1925	WAS	AL	4	0	4	2	1	1	0	1	0	0	0	0	0	0	0	4
1926	WAS	AL	1	0	1	1	0	0	0	0	0	0	0	0	1	0	1	0
Total			48	31	17	27	16	4	1	3	0	0	2	1	6	0	29	19

Rank among batters: 1,024 • *Top target (4 home runs)*: Eric Erickson, Herb Pennock, Rube Walberg • *Number of pitchers victimized*: 31 • *Total ballparks homered in*: 7 • *First HR*: 07/19/1912 off Russ Ford • *World Series HR*—1

Year	Tm	Lg	Tot	H	A	Men-On 0	1	2	3	One-Game 2	3	4	LO	XN	IP	PH	RHP	LHP

Bill Pecota

WILLIAM JOSEPH PECOTA
B: 02/16/1960
BR

Year	Tm	Lg	Tot	H	A	0	1	2	3	2	3	4	LO	XN	IP	PH	RHP	LHP
1987	KC	AL	3	0	3	2	1	0	0	0	0	0	0	0	0	0	1	2
1988	KC	AL	1	0	1	1	0	0	0	0	0	0	0	0	0	0	1	0
1989	KC	AL	3	0	3	2	1	0	0	1	0	0	0	0	0	0	3	0
1990	KC	AL	5	3	2	4	1	0	0	0	0	0	0	0	1	0	3	2
1991	KC	AL	6	4	2	3	1	2	0	0	0	0	0	0	1	0	4	2
1992	NY	NL	2	1	1	1	1	0	0	0	0	0	0	1	0	1	0	2
1994	ATL	NL	2	1	1	2	0	0	0	0	0	0	0	0	0	0	2	0
Total			22	9	13	15	5	2	0	1	0	0	0	1	2	1	14	8

Rank among batters: 1,719 • *Top target (2 home runs)*: Randy Johnson • *Number of pitchers victimized*: 21 • *Total ballparks homered in*: 12 • *First HR*: 05/08/1987 off Rich Yett

Les Peden

LESLIE EARL PEDEN
B: 09/17/1923
BR

Year	Tm	Lg	Tot	H	A	0	1	2	3	2	3	4	LO	XN	IP	PH	RHP	LHP
1953	WAS	AL	1	0	1	1	0	0	0	0	0	0	0	0	0	0	1	0

Rank among batters: 4,707 • *Total ballparks homered in*: 1 • *First HR*: 04/29/1953 off Saul Rogovin

Al Pedrique

ALFREDO JOSE (GARCIA) PEDRIQUE
B: 08/11/1960
BR

Year	Tm	Lg	Tot	H	A	0	1	2	3	2	3	4	LO	XN	IP	PH	RHP	LHP
1987	PIT	NL	1	0	1	0	0	1	0	0	0	0	0	0	0	0	1	0

Rank among batters: 4,707 • *Total ballparks homered in*: 1 • *First HR*: 07/20/1987 off Mike LaCoss

Homer Peel

HOMER HEFNER PEEL
B: 10/10/1902
BR

Year	Tm	Lg	Tot	H	A	0	1	2	3	2	3	4	LO	XN	IP	PH	RHP	LHP
1933	NY	NL	1	1	0	0	0	0	1	0	0	0	0	0	0	0	0	1
1934	NY	NL	1	1	0	0	1	0	0	0	0	0	0	0	0	1	0	1
Total			2	2	0	0	1	0	1	0	0	0	0	0	0	1	0	2

Rank among batters: 4,129 • *Total ballparks homered in*: 1 • *First HR*: 06/08/1933 off Snipe Hansen

Steve Pegues

STEVEN ANTONE PEGUES
B: 05/21/1968
BR

Year	Tm	Lg	Tot	H	A	0	1	2	3	2	3	4	LO	XN	IP	PH	RHP	LHP
1995	PIT	NL	6	5	1	4	2	0	0	1	0	0	0	0	0	0	3	3

Rank among batters: 2,988 • *Top target (2 home runs)*: Steve Mintz • *Number of pitchers victimized*: 5 • *Total ballparks homered in*: 2 • *First HR*: 06/19/1995 off Steve Mintz

Heinie Peitz

HENRY CLEMENT PEITZ
B: 11/28/1870 D: 10/23/1943
BR

Year	Tm	Lg	Tot	H	A	0	1	2	3	2	3	4	LO	XN	IP	PH	RHP	LHP
1893	STL	NL	1	0	1	0	1	0	0	0	0	0	0	0	0	0	1	0
1894	STL	NL	3	1	2	2	1	0	0	1	0	0	0	0	0	0	2	1
1895	STL	NL	2	1	1	1	1	0	0	0	0	0	0	0	1	0	2	0
1896	CIN	NL	2	1	1	1	1	0	0	0	0	0	0	0	0	0	1	1
1897	CIN	NL	1	1	0	1	0	0	0	0	0	0	0	0	0	0	1	0
1898	CIN	NL	1	0	1	0	0	1	0	0	0	0	0	0	0	0	1	0
1899	CIN	NL	1	0	1	1	0	0	0	0	0	0	0	0	1	0	1	0
1900	CIN	NL	2	2	0	1	1	0	0	0	0	0	0	0	1	0	2	0
1901	CIN	NL	1	1	0	1	0	0	0	0	0	0	0	0	0	0	1	0
1902	CIN	NL	1	1	0	0	0	1	0	0	0	0	0	0	1	0	1	0
1904	CIN	NL	1	0	1	0	0	1	0	0	0	0	0	0	0	0	1	0
Total			16	8	8	8	5	3	0	1	0	0	0	0	4	0	14	2

Rank among batters: 2,029 • *Top target (2 home runs)*: Tom Parrott • *Number of pitchers victimized*: 15 • *Total ballparks homered in*: 8 • *First HR*: 06/14/1893 off Harry Staley

Year	Tm	Lg	Tot	H	A	Men-On				One-Game			LO	XN	IP	PH	RHP	LHP
						0	1	2	3	2	3	4						

Eddie Pellagrini

EDWARD CHARLES PELLAGRINI
B: 03/13/1918
BR

Year	Tm	Lg	Tot	H	A	0	1	2	3	2	3	4	LO	XN	IP	PH	RHP	LHP
1946	BOS	AL	2	2	0	2	0	0	0	0	0	0	0	0	0	0	2	0
1947	BOS	AL	4	2	2	4	0	0	0	0	0	0	1	0	0	0	4	0
1948	STL	AL	2	2	0	1	0	1	0	0	0	0	0	0	0	0	2	0
1949	STL	AL	2	2	0	2	0	0	0	0	0	0	0	0	0	0	1	1
1951	PHI	NL	5	1	4	3	2	0	0	0	0	0	0	1	0	0	5	0
1952	CIN	NL	1	0	1	1	0	0	0	0	0	0	0	1	0	0	1	0
1953	PIT	NL	4	1	3	1	2	1	0	0	0	0	0	0	0	2	2	2
Total			20	10	10	14	4	2	0	0	0	0	1	2	0	2	17	3

Rank among batters: 1,810 • *Top target (2 home runs)*: Early Wynn, Sid Hudson • *Number of pitchers victimized*: 18 • *Total ballparks homered in*: 9 • *First HR*: 04/22/1946 off Sid Hudson • *Hit HR in first major league AB*—vs WAS: 04/22/1946

Dan Peltier

DANIEL EDWARD PELTIER
B: 06/30/1968
BL

Year	Tm	Lg	Tot	H	A	0	1	2	3	2	3	4	LO	XN	IP	PH	RHP	LHP
1993	TEX	AL	1	1	0	0	1	0	0	0	0	0	0	0	0	0	1	0

Rank among batters: 4,707 • *Total ballparks homered in*: 1 • *First HR*: 06/05/1993 off Bob Wickman

John Peltz

JOHN PELTZ
B: 04/23/1861 D: 02/27/1906
BR

Year	Tm	Lg	Tot	H	A	0	1	2	3	2	3	4	LO	XN	IP	PH	RHP	LHP
1884	IND	AA	3	2	1	1	1	1	0	0	0	0	0	0	1	0	3	0
1890	BRO	AA	1	1	0	0	0	1	0	0	0	0	0	0	0	0	1	0
Total			4	3	1	1	1	2	0	0	0	0	0	0	1	0	4	0

Rank among batters: 3,427 • *Total ballparks homered in*: 3 • *First HR*: 05/16/1884 off Tip O'Neill

Alejandro Pena

ALEJANDRO (VASQUEZ) PENA
B: 06/25/1959
BR

Year	Tm	Lg	Tot	H	A	0	1	2	3	2	3	4	LO	XN	IP	PH	RHP	LHP
1983	LA	NL	1	0	1	1	0	0	0	0	0	0	0	0	0	0	1	0

Rank among batters: 4,707 • *Total ballparks homered in*: 1 • *First HR*: 07/23/1983 off John Stuper

Bert Pena

ADALBERTO (RIVERA) PENA
B: 07/11/1959
BR

Year	Tm	Lg	Tot	H	A	0	1	2	3	2	3	4	LO	XN	IP	PH	RHP	LHP
1984	HOU	NL	1	0	1	1	0	0	0	0	0	0	0	0	0	0	0	1

Rank among batters: 4,707 • *Total ballparks homered in*: 1 • *First HR*: 09/02/1984 off Ricky Horton

Geronimo Pena

GERONIMO (MARTINEZ) PENA
B: 03/29/1967
BB

Year	Tm	Lg	Tot	H	A	0	1	2	3	2	3	4	LO	XN	IP	PH	RHP	LHP
1991	STL	NL	5	1	4	5	0	0	0	0	0	0	0	1	0	0	2	3
1992	STL	NL	7	4	3	4	3	0	0	0	0	0	2	0	0	0	4	3
1993	STL	NL	5	2	3	3	1	1	0	0	0	0	0	0	0	0	2	3
1994	STL	NL	11	7	4	7	2	2	0	1	0	0	0	0	0	1	7	4
1995	STL	NL	1	1	0	1	0	0	0	0	0	0	0	0	0	0	1	0
Total			29	15	14	20	6	3	0	1	0	0	2	1	0	1	16	13

Rank among batters: 1,465 • *Top target (3 home runs)*: Gregory Harris • *Number of pitchers victimized*: 26 • *Total ballparks homered in*: 11 • *First HR*: 04/28/1991 off Steven Frey • *Switch hit HR in 1 game*—1 time

Orlando Pena

ORLANDO GREGORIO (QUEVARA) PENA
B: 11/17/1933
BR

Year	Tm	Lg	Tot	H	A	0	1	2	3	2	3	4	LO	XN	IP	PH	RHP	LHP
1963	KC	AL	1	1	0	0	0	0	1	0	0	0	0	0	0	0	0	1
1964	KC	AL	1	1	0	1	0	0	0	0	0	0	0	0	0	0	1	0
Total			2	2	0	1	0	0	1	0	0	0	0	0	0	0	1	1

Rank among batters: 4,129 • *Total ballparks homered in*: 1 • *First HR*: 05/31/1963 off Claude Osteen

Year	Tm	Lg	Tot	H	A	Men-On 0	Men-On 1	Men-On 2	Men-On 3	One-Game 2	One-Game 3	One-Game 4	LO	XN	IP	PH	RHP	LHP

Roberto Pena

ROBERTO CESAR PENA
B: 04/17/1937 D: 07/23/1982
BR

Year	Tm	Lg	Tot	H	A	0	1	2	3	2	3	4	LO	XN	IP	PH	RHP	LHP
1965	CHI	NL	2	2	0	2	0	0	0	0	0	0	0	0	0	0	1	1
1968	PHI	NL	1	0	1	1	0	0	0	0	0	0	0	0	0	0	0	1
1969	SD	NL	4	2	2	1	2	0	1	0	0	0	0	0	0	0	2	2
1970	MIL	AL	3	2	1	1	1	0	1	0	0	0	0	0	1	0	1	2
1971	MIL	AL	3	0	3	2	1	0	0	0	0	0	0	0	0	0	2	1
Total			13	6	7	7	4	0	2	0	0	0	0	0	1	0	6	7

Rank among batters: 2,248 • *Top target (2 home runs)*: Steve Carlton • *Number of pitchers victimized*: 12 • *Total ballparks homered in*: 9 • *First HR*: 04/12/1965 off Bob Gibson

Tony Pena

ANTONIO FRANCESCO (PADILLA) PENA
B: 06/04/1957
BR

Year	Tm	Lg	Tot	H	A	0	1	2	3	2	3	4	LO	XN	IP	PH	RHP	LHP
1981	PIT	NL	2	1	1	2	0	0	0	0	0	0	0	0	0	0	0	2
1982	PIT	NL	11	5	6	6	1	3	1	1	0	0	0	0	0	0	8	3
1983	PIT	NL	15	8	7	11	2	2	0	1	0	0	0	0	0	0	12	3
1984	PIT	NL	15	7	8	8	3	2	2	1	0	0	0	0	0	0	8	7
1985	PIT	NL	10	2	8	5	2	3	0	1	0	0	0	3	0	0	8	2
1986	PIT	NL	10	5	5	9	1	0	0	0	0	0	0	0	0	0	6	4
1987	STL	NL	5	1	4	1	2	2	0	0	0	0	0	0	0	0	2	3
1988	STL	NL	10	4	6	6	2	2	0	1	0	0	0	1	0	0	5	5
1989	STL	NL	4	3	1	4	0	0	0	0	0	0	0	0	0	0	2	2
1990	BOS	AL	7	3	4	5	1	1	0	0	0	0	0	0	0	0	2	5
1991	BOS	AL	5	2	3	3	2	0	0	0	0	0	0	0	0	0	1	4
1992	BOS	AL	1	1	0	1	0	0	0	0	0	0	0	0	0	0	0	1
1993	BOS	AL	4	2	2	3	1	0	0	0	0	0	0	0	0	0	3	1
1994	CLE	AL	2	1	1	2	0	0	0	0	0	0	0	0	0	0	0	2
1995	CLE	AL	5	1	4	3	1	1	0	0	0	0	0	0	0	0	4	1
Total			106	46	60	69	18	16	3	5	0	0	0	4	0	0	61	45

Rank among batters: 451 • *Top target (4 home runs)*: Scott Sanderson • *Number of pitchers victimized*: 85 • *Total ballparks homered in*: 24 • *First HR*: 05/08/1981 off Bob Shirley • *LCS HR*—1

Jim Pendleton

JAMES EDWARD PENDLETON
B: 01/07/1924
BR

Year	Tm	Lg	Tot	H	A	0	1	2	3	2	3	4	LO	XN	IP	PH	RHP	LHP
1953	MIL	NL	7	1	6	3	2	2	0	0	1	0	0	0	1	0	6	1
1954	MIL	NL	1	0	1	0	0	1	0	0	0	0	0	0	0	1	1	0
1959	CIN	NL	3	2	1	2	1	0	0	0	0	0	0	0	0	1	2	1
1962	HOU	NL	8	4	4	6	1	1	0	0	0	0	0	0	0	0	5	3
Total			19	7	12	11	4	4	0	0	1	0	0	0	1	2	14	5

Rank among batters: 1,861 • *Top target (2 home runs)*: Jim Waugh • *Number of pitchers victimized*: 18 • *Total ballparks homered in*: 9 • *First HR*: 06/03/1953 off Ben Wade

Terry Pendleton

TERRY LEE PENDLETON
B: 07/16/1960
BB

Year	Tm	Lg	Tot	H	A	0	1	2	3	2	3	4	LO	XN	IP	PH	RHP	LHP
1984	STL	NL	1	0	1	0	1	0	0	0	0	0	0	0	0	0	1	0
1985	STL	NL	5	3	2	3	0	0	2	0	0	0	0	0	1	0	3	2
1986	STL	NL	1	0	1	1	0	0	0	0	0	0	0	0	0	0	1	0
1987	STL	NL	12	5	7	5	7	0	0	0	0	0	0	0	0	0	8	4
1988	STL	NL	6	3	3	5	1	0	0	0	0	0	0	0	0	0	5	1
1989	STL	NL	13	8	5	8	5	0	0	0	0	0	0	0	0	0	11	2
1990	STL	NL	6	6	0	3	3	0	0	0	0	0	0	0	0	0	2	4
1991	ATL	NL	22	13	9	13	7	2	0	2	0	0	0	0	0	0	18	4
1992	ATL	NL	21	13	8	11	7	2	1	0	0	0	0	0	0	0	13	8
1993	ATL	NL	17	9	8	9	6	2	0	1	0	0	0	0	0	0	13	4
1994	ATL	NL	7	3	4	6	1	0	0	0	0	0	0	0	0	0	6	1
1995	FLO	NL	14	8	6	6	6	2	0	0	0	0	0	0	0	0	11	3
Total			125	71	54	70	44	8	3	3	0	0	0	0	1	0	92	33

Rank among batters: 366 • *Top target (4 home runs)*: Roger McDowell • *Number of pitchers victimized*: 100 • *Total ballparks homered in*: 15 • *First HR*: 08/22/1984 off Mario Soto • *World Series HR*—2; *LCS HR*—1

Herb Pennock

HERBERT JEFFERIS PENNOCK
B: 02/10/1894 D: 01/30/1948
BB HOF

Year	Tm	Lg	Tot	H	A	Men-On 0	Men-On 1	Men-On 2	Men-On 3	One-Game 2	One-Game 3	One-Game 4	LO	XN	IP	PH	RHP	LHP
1921	BOS	AL	1	1	0	0	1	0	0	0	0	0	0	0	1	0	1	0
1924	NY	AL	2	2	0	1	0	1	0	0	0	0	0	0	0	0	2	0
1931	NY	AL	1	1	0	1	0	0	0	0	0	0	0	0	0	0	1	0
Total			4	4	0	2	1	1	0	0	0	0	0	0	1	0	4	0

Rank among batters: 3,427 • *Total ballparks homered in*: 2 • *First HR*: 06/22/1921 off Bob Shawkey

Jimmy Peoples

JAMES ELSWORTH PEOPLES
B: 10/08/1863 D: 08/29/1920

Year	Tm	Lg	Tot	H	A	Men-On 0	Men-On 1	Men-On 2	Men-On 3	One-Game 2	One-Game 3	One-Game 4	LO	XN	IP	PH	RHP	LHP
1884	CIN	AA	1	1	0	1	0	0	0	0	0	0	0	0	0	0	1	0
1885	BRO	AA	1	0	1	1	0	0	0	0	0	0	0	0	0	0	0	0
1886	BRO	AA	3	1	2	1	1	1	0	0	0	0	0	0	0	0	2	0
1887	BRO	AA	1	1	0	1	0	0	0	0	0	0	0	0	0	0	1	0
1889	COL	AA	1	1	0	0	0	1	0	0	0	0	0	0	0	0	0	1
Total			7	4	3	4	1	2	0	0	0	0	0	0	0	0	4	1

Rank among batters: 2,834 • *Total ballparks homered in*: 6 • *First HR*: 07/08/1884 off Sam Kimber

Joe Pepitone

JOSEPH ANTHONY PEPITONE
B: 10/09/1940
BL

Year	Tm	Lg	Tot	H	A	Men-On 0	Men-On 1	Men-On 2	Men-On 3	One-Game 2	One-Game 3	One-Game 4	LO	XN	IP	PH	RHP	LHP
1962	NY	AL	7	5	2	3	3	1	0	1	0	0	0	0	0	2	6	1
1963	NY	AL	27	17	10	16	7	3	1	2	0	0	0	0	1	0	21	6
1964	NY	AL	28	14	14	16	6	5	1	2	0	0	0	0	0	0	21	7
1965	NY	AL	18	14	4	5	8	4	1	2	0	0	0	0	0	0	16	2
1966	NY	AL	31	16	15	19	11	1	0	0	0	0	0	0	0	0	19	12
1967	NY	AL	13	9	4	4	8	1	0	1	0	0	0	0	0	1	10	3
1968	NY	AL	15	6	9	8	5	1	1	1	0	0	0	0	0	0	14	1
1969	NY	AL	27	15	12	17	6	3	1	0	0	0	0	2	0	1	19	8
1970	HOU	NL	14	6	8	9	3	1	1	0	0	0	0	0	0	0	12	2
	CHI	NL	12	4	8	6	3	2	1	0	0	0	0	0	1	0	9	3
	Total		26	10	16	15	6	3	2	0	0	0	0	0	1	0	21	5
1971	CHI	NL	16	7	9	10	4	2	0	0	0	0	0	1	0	0	13	3
1972	CHI	NL	8	3	5	6	1	1	0	0	0	0	0	0	0	0	7	1
1973	CHI	NL	3	0	3	1	1	1	0	0	0	0	0	0	0	0	3	0
Total			219	116	103	120	66	26	7	9	0	0	0	3	2	4	170	49

Rank among batters: 152 • *Top target (6 home runs)*: Mickey Lolich • *Number of pitchers victimized*: 142 • *Total ballparks homered in*: 25 • *First HR*: 05/05/1962 off Marty Kutyna • *2 HR in 1 inning*—vs KC: 05/23/1962 • *World Series HR*—1

Roy Pepper

RAYMOND WATSON PEPPER
B: 08/05/1905
BR

Year	Tm	Lg	Tot	H	A	Men-On 0	Men-On 1	Men-On 2	Men-On 3	One-Game 2	One-Game 3	One-Game 4	LO	XN	IP	PH	RHP	LHP
1933	STL	NL	1	0	1	0	1	0	0	0	0	0	0	0	0	0	1	0
1934	STL	AL	7	5	2	0	4	3	0	1	0	0	0	0	0	0	2	5
1935	STL	AL	4	1	3	1	3	0	0	0	0	0	0	0	1	0	1	3
1936	STL	AL	2	1	1	2	0	0	0	0	0	0	0	0	0	1	1	1
Total			14	7	7	3	8	3	0	1	0	0	0	0	1	1	5	9

Rank among batters: 2,169 • *Top target (3 home runs)*: Carl Fischer • *Number of pitchers victimized*: 10 • *Total ballparks homered in*: 7 • *First HR*: 04/30/1933 off Guy Bush

Jack Perconte

JOHN PATRICK PERCONTE
B: 08/31/1954
BL

Year	Tm	Lg	Tot	H	A	Men-On 0	Men-On 1	Men-On 2	Men-On 3	One-Game 2	One-Game 3	One-Game 4	LO	XN	IP	PH	RHP	LHP
1985	SEA	AL	2	2	0	2	0	0	0	0	0	0	2	0	0	0	2	0

Rank among batters: 4,129 • *Total ballparks homered in*: 1 • *First HR*: 05/17/1985 off Ken Dixon

Carlos Perez

CARLOS (GROSS) PEREZ
B: 04/14/1971
BL

Year	Tm	Lg	Tot	H	A	Men-On 0	Men-On 1	Men-On 2	Men-On 3	One-Game 2	One-Game 3	One-Game 4	LO	XN	IP	PH	RHP	LHP
1995	MON	NL	1	0	1	1	0	0	0	0	0	0	0	0	0	0	1	0

Year	Tm	Lg	Tot	H	A	Men-On 0	Men-On 1	Men-On 2	Men-On 3	One-Game 2	One-Game 3	One-Game 4	LO	XN	IP	PH	RHP	LHP

Carlos Perez *continued*

Rank among batters: 4,707 • *Total ballparks homered in*: 1 • *First HR*: 05/11/1995 off Mike Williams

Eddie Perez

EDUARDO PEREZ
B: 05/04/1968
BR

Year	Tm	Lg	Tot	H	A	Men-On 0	Men-On 1	Men-On 2	Men-On 3	One-Game 2	One-Game 3	One-Game 4	LO	XN	IP	PH	RHP	LHP
1995	ATL	NL	1	0	1	0	1	0	0	0	0	0	0	0	0	0	1	0

Rank among batters: 4,707 • *Total ballparks homered in*: 1 • *First HR*: 09/15/1995 off Michael Jackson

Eduardo Perez

EDUARDO ATANACIO PEREZ
B: 09/11/1969
BR

Year	Tm	Lg	Tot	H	A	Men-On 0	Men-On 1	Men-On 2	Men-On 3	One-Game 2	One-Game 3	One-Game 4	LO	XN	IP	PH	RHP	LHP
1993	CAL	AL	4	2	2	1	2	1	0	0	0	0	0	0	0	0	4	0
1994	CAL	AL	5	3	2	3	1	1	0	2	0	0	0	0	0	0	3	2
1995	CAL	AL	1	0	1	0	1	0	0	0	0	0	0	0	0	1	0	1
Total			10	5	5	4	4	2	0	2	0	0	0	0	0	1	7	3

Rank among batters: 2,500 • *Top target (2 home runs)*: Dave Stewart • *Number of pitchers victimized*: 9 • *Total ballparks homered in*: 4 • *First HR*: 07/27/1993 off Kevin Campbell

Marty Perez

MARTIN ROMAN PEREZ
B: 02/28/1947
BR

Year	Tm	Lg	Tot	H	A	Men-On 0	Men-On 1	Men-On 2	Men-On 3	One-Game 2	One-Game 3	One-Game 4	LO	XN	IP	PH	RHP	LHP
1971	ATL	NL	4	3	1	2	1	1	0	0	0	0	0	0	0	0	1	3
1972	ATL	NL	1	1	0	0	0	1	0	0	0	0	0	0	0	0	1	0
1973	ATL	NL	8	7	1	4	3	1	0	0	0	0	0	0	1	0	2	6
1974	ATL	NL	2	1	1	1	0	1	0	0	0	0	0	0	0	0	1	1
1975	ATL	NL	2	1	1	2	0	0	0	0	0	0	0	0	0	0	2	0
1976	ATL	NL	1	1	0	0	1	0	0	0	0	0	0	0	0	0	0	1
	SF	NL	2	0	2	1	1	0	0	0	0	0	0	0	0	0	1	1
	Total		3	1	2	1	2	0	0	0	0	0	0	0	0	0	1	2
1977	OAK	AL	2	1	1	2	0	0	0	0	0	0	0	0	0	0	0	2
Total			22	15	7	12	6	4	0	0	0	0	0	0	1	0	8	14

Rank among batters: 1,719 • *Top target (2 home runs)*: Jim Barr • *Number of pitchers victimized*: 21 • *Total ballparks homered in*: 7 • *First HR*: 06/19/1971 off Jim Merritt

Robert Perez

ROBERT ALEXANDER (JIMENEZ) PEREZ
B: 06/04/1969
BR

Year	Tm	Lg	Tot	H	A	Men-On 0	Men-On 1	Men-On 2	Men-On 3	One-Game 2	One-Game 3	One-Game 4	LO	XN	IP	PH	RHP	LHP
1995	TOR	AL	1	1	0	1	0	0	0	0	0	0	0	0	0	0	0	1

Rank among batters: 4,707 • *Total ballparks homered in*: 1 • *First HR*: 09/17/1995 off Brian Givens

Tomas Perez

TOMAS ORLANDO PEREZ
B: 12/29/1973
BR

Year	Tm	Lg	Tot	H	A	Men-On 0	Men-On 1	Men-On 2	Men-On 3	One-Game 2	One-Game 3	One-Game 4	LO	XN	IP	PH	RHP	LHP
1995	TOR	AL	1	1	0	0	1	0	0	0	0	0	0	0	0	0	0	1

Rank among batters: 4,707 • *Total ballparks homered in*: 1 • *First HR*: 07/29/1995 off Steve Wojciechowski

Tony Perez

ATANASIO (RIGAL) PEREZ
B: 05/14/1942
BR

Year	Tm	Lg	Tot	H	A	Men-On 0	Men-On 1	Men-On 2	Men-On 3	One-Game 2	One-Game 3	One-Game 4	LO	XN	IP	PH	RHP	LHP
1965	CIN	NL	12	7	5	3	5	3	1	0	0	0	0	0	0	3	3	9
1966	CIN	NL	4	4	0	0	4	0	0	0	0	0	0	0	0	0	2	2
1967	CIN	NL	26	11	15	11	14	1	0	1	0	0	0	0	0	0	18	8
1968	CIN	NL	18	5	13	11	6	1	0	0	0	0	0	0	0	0	15	3
1969	CIN	NL	37	15	22	19	13	5	0	2	0	0	0	1	0	0	32	5
1970	CIN	NL	40	19	21	18	14	7	1	3	0	0	0	0	0	0	32	8
1971	CIN	NL	25	11	14	12	8	5	0	1	0	0	0	1	0	0	19	6
1972	CIN	NL	21	11	10	14	4	3	0	0	0	0	0	0	0	0	13	8
1973	CIN	NL	27	9	18	14	10	2	1	2	0	0	0	3	0	0	17	10
1974	CIN	NL	28	17	11	17	9	2	0	0	0	0	0	2	0	0	18	10

Tony Perez *continued*

Year	Tm	Lg	Tot	H	A	Men-On				One-Game			LO	XN	IP	PH	RHP	LHP
						0	1	2	3	2	3	4						
1975	CIN	NL	20	12	8	7	12	0	1	0	0	0	0	1	0	0	16	4
1976	CIN	NL	19	9	10	11	6	2	0	1	0	0	0	0	0	2	10	9
1977	MON	NL	19	8	11	9	9	1	0	1	0	0	0	0	0	0	11	8
1978	MON	NL	14	5	9	9	5	0	0	1	0	0	0	0	0	0	7	7
1979	MON	NL	13	7	6	8	4	1	0	1	0	0	0	1	0	0	10	3
1980	BOS	AL	25	9	16	12	8	4	1	3	0	0	0	0	0	0	15	10
1981	BOS	AL	9	7	2	2	4	3	0	1	0	0	0	0	0	0	5	4
1982	BOS	AL	6	5	1	4	2	0	0	0	0	0	0	0	0	2	1	5
1983	PHI	NL	6	3	3	2	2	2	0	0	0	0	0	0	0	0	4	2
1984	CIN	NL	2	2	0	0	2	0	0	0	0	0	0	1	0	1	1	1
1985	CIN	NL	6	4	2	4	0	1	1	0	0	0	0	0	0	1	0	6
1986	CIN	NL	2	2	0	1	1	0	0	0	0	0	0	0	0	0	1	1
Total			379	182	197	188	142	43	6	17	0	0	0	10	0	9	250	129

Rank among batters: 33 • *Top target (9 home runs)*: Phil Niekro • *Number of pitchers victimized*: 230 • *Total ballparks homered in*: 28 • *First HR*: 04/13/1965 off Denny Lemaster • *World Series HR*—3; *LCS HR*—3; *All-Star HR*—1

Broderick Perkins

BRODERICK PHILLIP PERKINS
B: 11/23/1954
BL

Year	Tm	Lg	Tot	H	A	Men-On				One-Game			LO	XN	IP	PH	RHP	LHP
						0	1	2	3	2	3	4						
1978	SD	NL	2	0	2	1	1	0	0	0	0	0	0	0	0	0	2	0
1980	SD	NL	2	1	1	2	0	0	0	0	0	0	0	0	0	0	2	0
1981	SD	NL	2	1	1	1	0	1	0	0	0	0	0	0	0	0	2	0
1982	SD	NL	2	0	2	2	0	0	0	0	0	0	0	0	0	0	2	0
Total			8	2	6	6	1	1	0	0	0	0	0	0	0	0	8	0

Rank among batters: 2,703 • *Total ballparks homered in*: 5 • *First HR*: 07/13/1978 off Rick Reuschel

Cy Perkins

RALPH FOSTER PERKINS
B: 02/27/1896 D: 10/02/1963
BR

Year	Tm	Lg	Tot	H	A	Men-On				One-Game			LO	XN	IP	PH	RHP	LHP
						0	1	2	3	2	3	4						
1918	PHI	AL	1	1	0	0	0	1	0	0	0	0	0	0	0	0	1	0
1919	PHI	AL	2	2	0	1	0	1	0	0	0	0	0	0	0	0	2	0
1920	PHI	AL	5	5	0	4	1	0	0	0	0	0	0	0	0	0	4	1
1921	PHI	AL	12	10	2	8	4	0	0	1	0	0	0	0	0	0	6	6
1922	PHI	AL	6	5	1	3	2	1	0	0	0	0	0	0	0	0	4	2
1923	PHI	AL	2	2	0	2	0	0	0	0	0	0	0	0	0	0	1	1
1925	PHI	AL	1	0	1	1	0	0	0	0	0	0	0	0	0	0	0	1
1927	PHI	AL	1	1	0	0	1	0	0	0	0	0	0	0	0	1	0	1
Total			30	26	4	19	8	3	0	1	0	0	0	0	0	1	18	12

Rank among batters: 1,437 • Top target (2 home runs): Tom Zachary, George Mogridge, Elam Vangilder, Red Faber, Ray Kolp • *Number of pitchers victimized*: 25 • *Total ballparks homered in*: 4 • *First HR*: 05/08/1918 off Ray Caldwell

Harry Perkowski

HARRY WALTER PERKOWSKI
B: 09/06/1922
BL

Year	Tm	Lg	Tot	H	A	Men-On				One-Game			LO	XN	IP	PH	RHP	LHP
						0	1	2	3	2	3	4						
1954	CIN	NL	1	1	0	0	1	0	0	0	0	0	0	0	0	0	1	0

Rank among batters: 4,707 • *Total ballparks homered in*: 1 • *First HR*: 06/11/1954 off Bob Milliken

George Perring

GEORGE WILSON PERRING
B: 08/13/1884 D: 08/20/1960
BR

Year	Tm	Lg	Tot	H	A	Men-On				One-Game			LO	XN	IP	PH	RHP	LHP
						0	1	2	3	2	3	4						
1914	KC	FL	2	2	0	1	1	0	0	0	0	0	0	0	0	0	2	0
1915	KC	FL	7	6	1	4	2	1	0	1	0	0	0	0	0	0	6	1
Total			9	8	1	5	3	1	0	1	0	0	0	0	0	0	8	1

Rank among batters: 2,587 • *Top target (2 home runs)*: Dave Black • *Number of pitchers victimized*: 8 • *Total ballparks homered in*: 2 • *First HR*: 04/18/1914 off Tom McGuire

Bob Perry

MELVIN GRAY PERRY
B: 09/14/1934
BR

Year	Tm	Lg	Tot	H	A	Men-On				One-Game			LO	XN	IP	PH	RHP	LHP
						0	1	2	3	2	3	4						
1963	LA	AL	3	0	3	0	2	1	0	0	0	0	0	0	0	0	1	2

Year	Tm	Lg	Tot	H	A	Men-On 0	Men-On 1	Men-On 2	Men-On 3	One-Game 2	One-Game 3	One-Game 4	LO	XN	IP	PH	RHP	LHP

Bob Perry *continued*

Year	Tm	Lg	Tot	H	A	0	1	2	3	2	3	4	LO	XN	IP	PH	RHP	LHP
1964	LA	AL	3	1	2	2	0	1	0	0	0	0	0	0	0	0	3	0
Total			6	1	5	2	2	2	0	0	0	0	0	0	0	0	4	2

Rank among batters: 2,988 • *Total ballparks homered in*: 5 • *First HR*: 05/19/1963 off Whitey Ford

Gaylord Perry

GAYLORD JACKSON PERRY
B: 09/15/1938
BR HOF

Year	Tm	Lg	Tot	H	A	0	1	2	3	2	3	4	LO	XN	IP	PH	RHP	LHP
1969	SF	NL	1	1	0	1	0	0	0	0	0	0	0	0	0	0	0	1
1970	SF	NL	1	1	0	0	1	0	0	0	0	0	0	0	0	0	1	0
1971	SF	NL	1	0	1	1	0	0	0	0	0	0	0	0	0	0	1	0
1972	CLE	AL	1	1	0	0	1	0	0	0	0	0	0	0	0	0	1	0
1979	SD	NL	1	1	0	1	0	0	0	0	0	0	0	0	0	0	1	0
1981	ATL	NL	1	0	1	1	0	0	0	0	0	0	0	0	0	0	1	0
Total			6	4	2	4	2	0	0	0	0	0	0	0	0	0	5	1

Rank among batters: 2,988 • *Total ballparks homered in*: 5 • *First HR*: 07/20/1969 off Claude Osteen

Gerald Perry

GERALD JUNE PERRY
B: 10/30/1960
BL

Year	Tm	Lg	Tot	H	A	0	1	2	3	2	3	4	LO	XN	IP	PH	RHP	LHP
1983	ATL	NL	1	0	1	1	0	0	0	0	0	0	0	0	0	0	1	0
1984	ATL	NL	7	3	4	5	1	1	0	0	0	0	0	0	0	0	6	1
1985	ATL	NL	3	3	0	1	2	0	0	0	0	0	0	0	0	1	2	1
1986	ATL	NL	2	2	0	1	1	0	0	0	0	0	0	0	0	0	1	1
1987	ATL	NL	12	2	10	5	3	4	0	0	0	0	0	0	0	0	7	5
1988	ATL	NL	8	4	4	3	4	1	0	0	0	0	0	0	0	0	5	3
1989	ATL	NL	4	2	2	2	1	1	0	0	0	0	0	0	0	0	1	3
1990	KC	AL	8	3	5	7	0	0	1	0	0	0	0	0	0	0	7	1
1991	STL	NL	6	1	5	4	2	0	0	0	0	0	0	0	0	1	4	2
1992	STL	NL	1	1	0	0	1	0	0	0	0	0	0	0	0	1	1	0
1993	STL	NL	4	3	1	3	0	1	0	0	0	0	0	0	0	3	4	0
1994	STL	NL	3	1	2	3	0	0	0	0	0	0	0	0	0	1	3	0
Total			59	25	34	35	15	8	1	0	0	0	0	0	0	7	42	17

Rank among batters: 873 • *Top target (3 home runs)*: Scott Garrelts • *Number of pitchers victimized*: 52 • *Total ballparks homered in*: 17 • *First HR*: 08/19/1983 off Chuck Rainey

Herbert Perry

HERBERT EDWARD PERRY
B: 09/15/1969
BR

Year	Tm	Lg	Tot	H	A	0	1	2	3	2	3	4	LO	XN	IP	PH	RHP	LHP
1995	CLE	AL	3	3	0	2	1	0	0	1	0	0	0	0	0	0	0	3

Rank among batters: 3,735 • *Top target (2 home runs)*: Andy Pettitte • *Number of pitchers victimized*: 2 • *Total ballparks homered in*: 1 • *First HR*: 06/17/1995 off Andy Pettitte

Jim Perry

JAMES EVAN PERRY
B: 10/30/1935
BB

Year	Tm	Lg	Tot	H	A	0	1	2	3	2	3	4	LO	XN	IP	PH	RHP	LHP
1966	MIN	AL	1	0	1	1	0	0	0	0	0	0	0	0	0	0	0	1
1967	MIN	AL	1	1	0	0	1	0	0	0	0	0	0	0	0	0	1	0
1968	MIN	AL	2	1	1	1	0	1	0	0	0	0	0	0	0	0	1	1
1970	MIN	AL	1	1	0	1	0	0	0	0	0	0	0	0	0	0	0	1
Total			5	3	2	3	1	1	0	0	0	0	0	0	0	0	2	3

Rank among batters: 3,191 • *Top target (2 home runs)*: Dave McNally • *Number of pitchers victimized*: 4 • *Total ballparks homered in*: 3 • *First HR*: 07/03/1966 off Dave McNally

Pat Perry

WILLIAM PATRICK PERRY
B: 02/04/1959
BL

Year	Tm	Lg	Tot	H	A	0	1	2	3	2	3	4	LO	XN	IP	PH	RHP	LHP
1988	CHI	NL	1	1	0	0	1	0	0	0	0	0	0	0	0	0	1	0

Rank among batters: 4,707 • *Total ballparks homered in*: 1 • *First HR*: 08/06/1988 off Mike Maddux

Scott Perry

HERBERT SCOTT PERRY
B: 04/17/1891 D: 10/27/1959
BL

Year	Tm	Lg	Tot	H	A	Men-On 0	1	2	3	One-Game 2	3	4	LO	XN	IP	PH	RHP	LHP
1920	PHI	AL	1	1	0	1	0	0	0	0	0	0	0	0	0	0	0	1

Rank among batters: 4,707 • *Total ballparks homered in*: 1 • *First HR*: 05/26/1920 off Lefty Williams

Johnny Pesky

JOHN MICHAEL PESKY
B: 09/27/1919
BL

Year	Tm	Lg	Tot	H	A	Men-On 0	1	2	3	One-Game 2	3	4	LO	XN	IP	PH	RHP	LHP
1942	BOS	AL	2	1	1	0	1	1	0	0	0	0	0	0	0	0	2	0
1946	BOS	AL	2	2	0	1	1	0	0	0	0	0	0	0	0	0	2	0
1948	BOS	AL	3	0	3	0	2	1	0	0	0	0	0	0	0	0	3	0
1949	BOS	AL	2	0	2	0	2	0	0	0	0	0	0	0	0	0	1	1
1950	BOS	AL	1	1	0	0	1	0	0	0	0	0	0	0	0	0	1	0
1951	BOS	AL	3	2	1	1	2	0	0	0	0	0	0	0	0	0	2	1
1952	DET	AL	1	1	0	0	1	0	0	0	0	0	0	0	0	0	1	0
1953	DET	AL	2	2	0	1	0	1	0	0	0	0	0	0	0	0	2	0
1954	DET	AL	1	1	0	1	0	0	0	0	0	0	0	1	0	1	1	0
Total			17	10	7	4	10	3	0	0	0	0	0	1	0	1	15	2

Rank among batters: 1,969 • *Top target (2 home runs)*: Dick Fowler, Eddie Lopat • *Number of pitchers victimized*: 15 • *Total ballparks homered in*: 5 • *First HR*: 07/24/1942 off Bob Muncrief

Roberto Petagine

ROBERTO ANTONIO (GUERRA) PETAGINE
B: 06/07/1971
BL

Year	Tm	Lg	Tot	H	A	Men-On 0	1	2	3	One-Game 2	3	4	LO	XN	IP	PH	RHP	LHP
1995	SD	NL	3	2	1	2	0	1	0	0	0	0	0	0	0	1	3	0

Rank among batters: 3,735 • *Total ballparks homered in*: 2 • *First HR*: 04/28/1995 off Jeff Brantley

Gary Peters

GARY CHARLES PETERS
B: 04/21/1937
BL

Year	Tm	Lg	Tot	H	A	Men-On 0	1	2	3	One-Game 2	3	4	LO	XN	IP	PH	RHP	LHP
1963	CHI	AL	3	1	2	2	1	0	0	0	0	0	0	0	0	0	2	1
1964	CHI	AL	4	3	1	1	1	2	0	0	0	0	0	1	0	1	3	1
1965	CHI	AL	1	0	1	0	0	1	0	0	0	0	0	0	0	0	1	0
1966	CHI	AL	1	0	1	1	0	0	0	0	0	0	0	0	0	0	1	0
1967	CHI	AL	2	0	2	1	1	0	0	0	0	0	0	0	0	0	1	1
1968	CHI	AL	2	2	0	1	0	0	1	0	0	0	0	0	0	1	1	1
1969	CHI	AL	2	0	2	2	0	0	0	0	0	0	0	0	0	0	2	0
1970	BOS	AL	1	0	1	0	0	1	0	0	0	0	0	0	0	0	1	0
1971	BOS	AL	3	1	2	0	1	2	0	0	0	0	0	0	0	2	3	0
Total			19	7	12	8	4	6	1	0	0	0	0	1	0	4	15	4

Rank among batters: 1,861 • *Top target (2 home runs)*: Gary Bell • *Number of pitchers victimized*: 18 • *Total ballparks homered in*: 9 • *First HR*: 05/06/1963 off Ted Bowsfield

John Peters

JOHN PAUL PETERS
B: 04/08/1850 D: 01/04/1924
BR

Year	Tm	Lg	Tot	H	A	Men-On 0	1	2	3	One-Game 2	3	4	LO	XN	IP	PH	RHP	LHP
1876	CHI	NL	1	1	0	1	0	0	0	0	0	0	0	0	1	0	1	0
1879	CHI	NL	1	1	0	1	0	0	0	0	0	0	0	0	1	0	0	1
Total			2	2	0	2	0	0	0	0	0	0	0	0	2	0	1	1

Rank among batters: 4,129 • *Total ballparks homered in*: 2 • *First HR*: 07/13/1876 off Dick McBride

John Peters

JOHN WILLIAM PETERS
B: 07/14/1893 D: 02/21/1932
BR

Year	Tm	Lg	Tot	H	A	Men-On 0	1	2	3	One-Game 2	3	4	LO	XN	IP	PH	RHP	LHP
1921	PHI	NL	3	3	0	3	0	0	0	0	0	0	0	0	0	0	3	0
1922	PHI	NL	4	4	0	1	2	1	0	1	0	0	0	0	0	1	2	2
Total			7	7	0	4	2	1	0	1	0	0	0	0	0	1	5	2

Rank among batters: 2,834 • *Top target (2 home runs)*: Dutch Ruether • *Number of pitchers victimized*: 6 • *Total ballparks homered in*: 1 • *First HR*: 07/16/1921 off Dolf Luque

Year	Tm	Lg	Tot	H	A	Men-On 0	1	2	3	One-Game 2	3	4	LO	XN	IP	PH	RHP	LHP

Rick Peters

RICHARD DEVIN PETERS
B: 11/21/1955
BB

Year	Tm	Lg	Tot	H	A	0	1	2	3	2	3	4	LO	XN	IP	PH	RHP	LHP
1980	DET	AL	2	0	2	1	0	0	1	0	0	0	0	0	0	0	2	0

Rank among batters: 4,129 • *Total ballparks homered in*: 2 • *First HR*: 05/27/1980 off Mike Griffin

Rusty Peters

RUSSELL DIXON PETERS
B: 12/14/1914
BR

Year	Tm	Lg	Tot	H	A	0	1	2	3	2	3	4	LO	XN	IP	PH	RHP	LHP
1936	PHI	AL	3	2	1	2	1	0	0	0	0	0	0	0	0	0	3	0
1937	PHI	AL	3	0	3	1	1	1	0	0	0	0	0	0	0	0	3	0
1943	CLE	AL	1	0	1	1	0	0	0	0	0	0	0	0	0	0	1	0
1944	CLE	AL	1	0	1	0	1	0	0	0	0	0	0	0	0	0	1	0
Total			8	2	6	4	3	1	0	0	0	0	0	0	0	0	8	0

Rank among batters: 2,703 • *Top target (2 home runs)*: Jack Knott • *Number of pitchers victimized*: 7 • *Total ballparks homered in*: 4 • *First HR*: 04/28/1936 off Ivy Andrews

Bob Peterson

ROBERT A. PETERSON
B: 07/16/1884 D: 11/27/1962
BR

Year	Tm	Lg	Tot	H	A	0	1	2	3	2	3	4	LO	XN	IP	PH	RHP	LHP
1906	BOS	AL	1	1	0	1	0	0	0	0	0	0	0	0	0	0	1	0

Rank among batters: 4,707 • *Total ballparks homered in*: 1 • *First HR*: 10/06/1906 off Tom Hughes

Cap Peterson

CHARLES ANDREW PETERSON
B: 08/15/1942 D: 05/16/1980
BR

Year	Tm	Lg	Tot	H	A	0	1	2	3	2	3	4	LO	XN	IP	PH	RHP	LHP
1963	SF	NL	1	0	1	1	0	0	0	0	0	0	0	0	0	0	0	1
1964	SF	NL	1	1	0	0	1	0	0	0	0	0	0	0	0	1	1	0
1965	SF	NL	3	3	0	2	0	1	0	0	0	0	0	0	0	0	0	3
1966	SF	NL	2	2	0	0	1	1	0	0	0	0	0	0	0	0	1	1
1967	WAS	AL	8	5	3	4	2	2	0	1	0	0	0	1	0	1	5	3
1968	WAS	AL	3	2	1	3	0	0	0	0	0	0	0	0	0	1	2	1
1969	CLE	AL	1	0	1	0	0	1	0	0	0	0	0	0	0	0	1	0
Total			19	13	6	10	4	5	0	1	0	0	0	1	0	3	10	9

Rank among batters: 1,861 • *Top target (2 home runs)*: Sandy Koufax, Joe Horlen, Sammy Ellis • *Number of pitchers victimized*: 16 • *Total ballparks homered in*: 7 • *First HR*: 05/30/1963 off Joe Nuxhall

Fritz Peterson

FRED INGLES PETERSON
B: 02/08/1942
BB

Year	Tm	Lg	Tot	H	A	0	1	2	3	2	3	4	LO	XN	IP	PH	RHP	LHP
1970	NY	AL	2	2	0	1	1	0	0	0	0	0	0	0	0	0	0	2

Rank among batters: 4,129 • *Total ballparks homered in*: 1 • *First HR*: 04/28/1970 off Clyde Wright

Hardy Peterson

HARDING WILLIAM PETERSON
B: 10/17/1929
BR

Year	Tm	Lg	Tot	H	A	0	1	2	3	2	3	4	LO	XN	IP	PH	RHP	LHP
1955	PIT	NL	1	0	1	0	1	0	0	0	0	0	0	0	0	0	0	1
1957	PIT	NL	2	0	2	2	0	0	0	0	0	0	0	0	0	0	1	1
Total			3	0	3	2	1	0	0	0	0	0	0	0	0	0	1	2

Rank among batters: 3,735 • *Total ballparks homered in*: 3 • *First HR*: 08/14/1955 off Johnny Antonelli

Geno Petralli

EUGENE JAMES PETRALLI
B: 09/25/1959
BB

Year	Tm	Lg	Tot	H	A	0	1	2	3	2	3	4	LO	XN	IP	PH	RHP	LHP
1986	TEX	AL	2	1	1	1	1	0	0	0	0	0	0	0	0	1	2	0
1987	TEX	AL	7	4	3	6	0	1	0	1	0	0	0	0	0	2	7	0
1988	TEX	AL	7	1	6	6	1	0	0	0	0	0	0	0	0	1	7	0

Geno Petralli *continued*

Year	Tm	Lg	Tot	H	A	Men-On				One-Game			LO	XN	IP	PH	RHP	LHP
						0	1	2	3	2	3	4						
1989	TEX	AL	4	1	3	2	1	1	0	0	0	0	0	0	0	1	4	0
1991	TEX	AL	2	0	2	1	0	1	0	0	0	0	0	0	0	0	2	0
1992	TEX	AL	1	0	1	0	0	1	0	0	0	0	0	0	0	1	1	0
1993	TEX	AL	1	1	0	1	0	0	0	0	0	0	0	0	0	0	1	0
Total			24	8	16	17	3	4	0	1	0	0	0	0	0	6	24	0

Rank among batters: 1,643 • *Top target (2 home runs)*: Roger Clemens, Mike Boddicker, Melido Perez • *Number of pitchers victimized*: 21 • *Total ballparks homered in*: 9 • *First HR*: 07/13/1986 off Phil Niekro

Rico Petrocelli

AMERICO PETER PETROCELLI
B: 06/27/1943
BR

Year	Tm	Lg	Tot	H	A	Men-On 0	1	2	3	One-Game 2	3	4	LO	XN	IP	PH	RHP	LHP
1965	BOS	AL	13	10	3	10	1	2	0	1	0	0	0	0	0	0	7	6
1966	BOS	AL	18	10	8	12	4	0	2	1	0	0	1	0	0	0	16	2
1967	BOS	AL	17	10	7	10	6	1	0	1	0	0	0	0	0	0	9	8
1968	BOS	AL	12	4	8	8	4	0	0	0	0	0	0	0	0	0	9	3
1969	BOS	AL	40	22	18	23	13	3	1	2	0	0	0	2	0	0	31	9
1970	BOS	AL	29	20	9	14	8	5	2	1	0	0	0	0	0	0	21	8
1971	BOS	AL	28	18	10	17	8	3	0	1	0	0	0	1	0	0	21	7
1972	BOS	AL	15	13	2	7	3	2	3	0	0	0	0	0	0	0	11	4
1973	BOS	AL	13	9	4	8	3	2	0	0	0	0	0	0	0	0	8	5
1974	BOS	AL	15	10	5	6	7	1	1	2	0	0	0	0	0	0	10	5
1975	BOS	AL	7	5	2	3	2	2	0	0	0	0	0	0	0	0	2	5
1976	BOS	AL	3	3	0	1	1	1	0	0	0	0	0	0	0	0	3	0
Total			210	134	76	119	60	22	9	9	0	0	1	3	0	0	148	62

Rank among batters: 166 • *Top target (6 home runs)*: Mickey Lolich • *Number of pitchers victimized*: 125 • *Total ballparks homered in*: 13 • *First HR*: 06/20/1965 off Gary Peters • *World Series HR*—2; *LCS HR*—1

Joe Pettini

JOSEPH PAUL PETTINI
B: 01/26/1955
BR

Year	Tm	Lg	Tot	H	A	Men-On 0	1	2	3	One-Game 2	3	4	LO	XN	IP	PH	RHP	LHP
1980	SF	NL	1	0	1	1	0	0	0	0	0	0	0	0	0	0	0	1

Rank among batters: 4,707 • *Total ballparks homered in*: 1 • *First HR*: 07/23/1980 off Guillermo Hernandez

Gary Pettis

GARY GEORGE PETTIS
B: 04/03/1958
BB

Year	Tm	Lg	Tot	H	A	Men-On 0	1	2	3	One-Game 2	3	4	LO	XN	IP	PH	RHP	LHP
1982	CAL	AL	1	1	0	1	0	0	0	0	0	0	0	0	0	0	1	0
1983	CAL	AL	3	3	0	2	1	0	0	0	0	0	0	0	1	0	3	0
1984	CAL	AL	2	1	1	1	0	0	1	0	0	0	1	0	0	0	2	0
1985	CAL	AL	1	0	1	0	0	1	0	0	0	0	0	0	0	0	1	0
1986	CAL	AL	5	1	4	2	1	2	0	0	0	0	1	0	0	0	3	2
1987	CAL	AL	1	1	0	1	0	0	0	0	0	0	0	0	1	0	0	1
1988	DET	AL	3	0	3	1	1	1	0	0	0	0	0	0	0	0	3	0
1989	DET	AL	1	1	0	1	0	0	0	0	0	0	1	0	0	0	1	0
1990	TEX	AL	3	3	0	3	0	0	0	0	0	0	0	0	0	0	3	0
1992	DET	AL	1	1	0	1	0	0	0	0	0	0	0	0	0	0	1	0
Total			21	12	9	13	3	4	1	0	0	0	3	0	2	0	18	3

Rank among batters: 1,768 • *Top target (2 home runs)*: Dan Petry, Mike Mason • *Number of pitchers victimized*: 19 • *Total ballparks homered in*: 8 • *First HR*: 10/03/1982 off Danny Darwin • *LCS HR*—1

Bob Pettit

ROBERT HENRY PETTIT
B: 07/19/1861 D: 11/01/1910
BL

Year	Tm	Lg	Tot	H	A	Men-On 0	1	2	3	One-Game 2	3	4	LO	XN	IP	PH	RHP	LHP
1887	CHI	NL	2	2	0	1	1	0	0	0	0	0	0	0	0	0	1	1
1888	CHI	NL	4	2	2	2	2	0	0	0	0	0	0	0	1	0	3	1
1891	MIL	AA	1	1	0	0	1	0	0	0	0	0	0	0	0	0	0	1
Total			7	5	2	3	4	0	0	0	0	0	0	0	1	0	4	3

Rank among batters: 2,834 • *Top target (2 home runs)*: Lev Shreve, Dan Casey • *Number of pitchers victimized*: 5 • *Total ballparks homered in*: 3 • *First HR*: 09/10/1887 off Lev Shreve

Year	Tm	Lg	Tot	H	A	Men-On 0	1	2	3	One-Game 2	3	4	LO	XN	IP	PH	RHP	LHP

Charlie Petty

CHARLES E. PETTY
B: 01/28/1866

Year	Tm	Lg	Tot	H	A	Men-On 0	1	2	3	One-Game 2	3	4	LO	XN	IP	PH	RHP	LHP
1893	NY	NL	1	1	0	1	0	0	0	0	0	0	0	0	0	0	1	0

Rank among batters: 4,707 • *Total ballparks homered in*: 1 • *First HR*: 09/02/1893 off Bill Whitrock

Francis Pfeffer

FRANCIS XAVIER PFEFFER
B: 03/31/1882 D: 12/19/1954
BR

Year	Tm	Lg	Tot	H	A	Men-On 0	1	2	3	One-Game 2	3	4	LO	XN	IP	PH	RHP	LHP
1906	BOS	NL	1	0	1	1	0	0	0	0	0	0	0	0	0	0	1	0
1911	BOS	NL	1	0	1	0	1	0	0	0	0	0	0	0	0	0	1	0
Total			2	0	2	1	1	0	0	0	0	0	0	0	0	0	2	0

Rank among batters: 4,129 • *Total ballparks homered in*: 2 • *First HR*: 05/12/1906 off Jack Taylor

Fred Pfeffer

NATHANIEL FREDERICK PFEFFER
B: 03/17/1860 D: 04/10/1932
BR

Year	Tm	Lg	Tot	H	A	Men-On 0	1	2	3	One-Game 2	3	4	LO	XN	IP	PH	RHP	LHP
1882	TRO	NL	1	1	0	0	1	0	0	0	0	0	0	0	0	0	1	0
1883	CHI	NL	1	1	0	0	0	1	0	0	0	0	0	0	0	0	1	0
1884	CHI	NL	25	25	0	7	5	8	1	2	0	0	0	0	0	0	20	3
1885	CHI	NL	5	5	0	3	1	1	0	0	0	0	0	0	0	0	5	0
1886	CHI	NL	7	7	0	3	1	3	0	0	0	0	0	0	1	0	5	2
1887	CHI	NL	16	14	2	7	7	2	0	0	0	0	0	0	0	0	13	3
1888	CHI	NL	8	7	1	4	3	1	0	0	0	0	0	0	2	0	7	1
1889	CHI	NL	7	6	1	4	1	2	0	0	0	0	0	1	0	0	6	1
1890	CHI	PL	5	4	1	2	1	2	0	0	0	0	0	0	0	0	4	1
1891	CHI	NL	7	6	1	3	3	1	0	0	0	0	0	0	0	0	5	1
1892	LOU	NL	2	1	1	1	1	0	0	0	0	0	0	0	1	0	1	0
1893	LOU	NL	3	1	2	2	1	0	0	0	0	0	0	0	0	0	2	1
1894	LOU	NL	5	2	3	1	3	1	0	0	0	0	0	0	0	0	4	0
1896	CHI	NL	2	1	1	2	0	0	0	0	0	0	0	0	0	0	2	0
Total			94	81	13	39	28	22	1	2	0	0	0	1	4	0	76	12

Rank among batters: 535 • *Top target (8 home runs)*: Charley Radbourn • *Number of pitchers victimized*: 57 • *Total ballparks homered in*: 16 • *First HR*: 06/16/1882 off Stump Wiedman • *World Series HR*—2

Bobby Pfeil

ROBERT RAYMOND PFEIL
B: 11/13/1943
BR

Year	Tm	Lg	Tot	H	A	Men-On 0	1	2	3	One-Game 2	3	4	LO	XN	IP	PH	RHP	LHP
1971	PHI	NL	2	2	0	1	1	0	0	1	0	0	0	0	0	0	2	0

Rank among batters: 4,129 • *Top target (2 home runs)*: Larry Dierker • *Number of pitchers victimized*: 1 • *Total ballparks homered in*: 1 • *First HR*: 07/27/1971 off Larry Dierker

Art Phelan

ARTHUR THOMAS PHELAN
B: 08/14/1887 D: 12/27/1964
BR

Year	Tm	Lg	Tot	H	A	Men-On 0	1	2	3	One-Game 2	3	4	LO	XN	IP	PH	RHP	LHP
1912	CIN	NL	3	0	3	1	2	0	0	0	0	0	0	0	1	0	3	0
1913	CHI	NL	2	1	1	1	0	1	0	0	0	0	0	0	1	1	0	2
1915	CHI	NL	3	2	1	1	2	0	0	0	0	0	0	0	1	0	2	1
Total			8	3	5	3	4	1	0	0	0	0	0	0	3	1	5	3

Rank among batters: 2,703 • *Top target (2 home runs)*: Cliff Curtis • *Number of pitchers victimized*: 7 • *Total ballparks homered in*: 4 • *First HR*: 05/27/1912 off Ed Reulbach

Dick Phelan

JAMES DICKSON PHELAN
B: 12/10/1854 D: 02/13/1931
BR

Year	Tm	Lg	Tot	H	A	Men-On 0	1	2	3	One-Game 2	3	4	LO	XN	IP	PH	RHP	LHP
1884	BAL	UA	3	2	1	1	1	1	0	0	0	0	0	0	0	0	1	1
1885	BUF	NL	1	0	1	0	1	0	0	0	0	0	0	0	0	0	0	0
Total			4	2	2	1	2	1	0	0	0	0	0	0	0	0	1	1

Rank among batters: 3,427 • *Total ballparks homered in*: 3 • *First HR*: 06/05/1884 off Tommy Bond

Babe Phelps

ERNEST GORDON PHELPS
B: 04/16/1908 D: 12/10/1992
BL

Year	Tm	Lg	Tot	H	A	Men-On 0	1	2	3	One-Game 2	3	4	LO	XN	IP	PH	RHP	LHP
1934	CHI	NL	2	1	1	1	1	0	0	0	0	0	0	0	0	1	2	0
1935	BRO	NL	5	3	2	1	3	1	0	0	0	0	0	0	0	1	4	1
1936	BRO	NL	5	3	2	3	1	1	0	0	0	0	0	0	0	0	4	1
1937	BRO	NL	7	5	2	3	2	2	0	0	0	0	0	0	0	0	4	3
1938	BRO	NL	5	4	1	3	2	0	0	0	0	0	0	0	0	0	5	0
1939	BRO	NL	6	4	2	5	1	0	0	0	0	0	0	0	0	0	5	1
1940	BRO	NL	13	9	4	4	7	1	1	1	0	0	0	0	0	1	13	0
1941	BRO	NL	2	1	1	1	0	1	0	0	0	0	0	0	0	0	2	0
1942	PIT	NL	9	3	6	8	1	0	0	1	0	0	0	0	0	0	9	0
Total			54	33	21	29	18	6	1	2	0	0	0	0	0	3	48	6

Rank among batters: 938 • *Top target (3 home runs)*: Tex Carleton, Claude Passeau, Thomas Earley • *Number of pitchers victimized*: 42 • *Total ballparks homered in*: 8 • *First HR*: 05/08/1934 off Phil Collins

Ed Phelps

EDWARD JAYKILL PHELPS
B: 03/03/1879 D: 01/31/1942
BR

Year	Tm	Lg	Tot	H	A	Men-On 0	1	2	3	One-Game 2	3	4	LO	XN	IP	PH	RHP	LHP
1903	PIT	NL	2	1	1	0	2	0	0	0	0	0	0	0	0	0	2	0
1906	CIN	NL	1	1	0	1	0	0	0	0	0	0	0	0	0	0	1	0
Total			3	2	1	1	2	0	0	0	0	0	0	0	0	0	3	0

Rank among batters: 3,735 • *Total ballparks homered in*: 3 • *First HR*: 05/26/1903 off Togie Pittinger

Ken Phelps

KENNETH ALLEN PHELPS
B: 08/06/1954
BL

Year	Tm	Lg	Tot	H	A	Men-On 0	1	2	3	One-Game 2	3	4	LO	XN	IP	PH	RHP	LHP
1983	SEA	AL	7	6	1	5	2	0	0	0	0	0	0	0	0	0	6	1
1984	SEA	AL	24	13	11	15	6	3	0	3	0	0	0	0	0	1	23	1
1985	SEA	AL	9	5	4	3	4	1	1	0	0	0	0	0	0	1	9	0
1986	SEA	AL	24	15	9	13	8	3	0	1	0	0	0	0	0	2	23	1
1987	SEA	AL	27	15	12	16	9	2	0	5	0	0	0	0	0	0	24	3
1988	SEA	AL	14	6	8	7	5	2	0	0	0	0	0	0	0	0	14	0
	NY	AL	10	6	4	5	2	3	0	0	0	0	0	1	0	0	9	1
	Total		24	12	12	12	7	5	0	0	0	0	0	1	0	0	23	1
1989	NY	AL	7	4	3	2	4	1	0	0	0	0	0	0	0	3	7	0
1990	OAK	AL	1	1	0	1	0	0	0	0	0	0	0	0	0	1	1	0
Total			123	71	52	67	40	15	1	9	0	0	0	1	0	8	116	7

Rank among batters: 372 • *Top target (4 home runs)*: Jim Clancy, Doyle Alexander • *Number of pitchers victimized*: 81 • *Total ballparks homered in*: 15 • *First HR*: 04/12/1983 off Mike Witt

Ray Phelps

RAYMOND CLIFFORD PHELPS
B: 12/11/1903 D: 07/07/1971
BR

Year	Tm	Lg	Tot	H	A	Men-On 0	1	2	3	One-Game 2	3	4	LO	XN	IP	PH	RHP	LHP
1930	BRO	NL	1	1	0	1	0	0	0	0	0	0	0	0	0	0	0	1

Rank among batters: 4,707 • *Total ballparks homered in*: 1 • *First HR*: 07/17/1930 off Bud Teachout

Dave Philley

DAVID EARL PHILLEY
B: 05/16/1920
BB

Year	Tm	Lg	Tot	H	A	Men-On 0	1	2	3	One-Game 2	3	4	LO	XN	IP	PH	RHP	LHP
1947	CHI	AL	2	0	2	0	1	1	0	0	0	0	0	0	0	0	2	0
1948	CHI	AL	5	1	4	3	2	0	0	0	0	0	0	0	0	0	5	0
1950	CHI	AL	14	6	8	6	4	4	0	1	0	0	0	0	1	0	5	9
1951	PHI	AL	7	3	4	5	1	0	1	0	0	0	0	0	0	0	2	5
1952	PHI	AL	7	3	4	4	3	0	0	0	0	0	0	0	0	0	2	5
1953	PHI	AL	9	2	7	7	1	1	0	0	0	0	0	0	0	0	5	4
1954	CLE	AL	12	4	8	7	1	3	1	0	0	0	0	1	0	0	5	7
1955	CLE	AL	2	1	1	2	0	0	0	0	0	0	0	0	0	0	2	0
	BAL	AL	6	1	5	3	2	0	1	0	0	0	0	0	0	0	2	4
	Total		8	2	6	5	2	0	1	0	0	0	0	0	0	0	4	4
1956	BAL	AL	1	0	1	0	0	1	0	0	0	0	0	0	0	0	1	0

Dave Philley *continued*

Year	Tm	Lg	Tot	H	A	Men-On 0	Men-On 1	Men-On 2	Men-On 3	One-Game 2	One-Game 3	One-Game 4	LO	XN	IP	PH	RHP	LHP
1956	CHI	AL	4	2	2	3	1	0	0	0	0	0	0	0	0	0	2	2
	Total		5	2	3	3	1	1	0	0	0	0	0	0	0	0	3	2
1957	DET	AL	2	0	2	1	0	1	0	0	0	0	0	0	0	0	1	1
1958	PHI	NL	3	0	3	1	1	1	0	0	0	0	0	0	0	1	3	0
1959	PHI	NL	7	1	6	3	3	1	0	0	0	0	0	0	0	0	6	1
1960	SF	NL	1	1	0	0	0	1	0	0	0	0	0	0	0	1	1	0
	BAL	AL	1	0	1	0	1	0	0	0	0	0	0	0	0	0	1	0
	Total		2	1	1	0	1	1	0	0	0	0	0	0	0	1	2	0
1961	BAL	AL	1	1	0	1	0	0	0	0	0	0	0	0	0	0	0	1
Total			84	26	58	46	21	14	3	1	0	0	0	1	1	2	45	39

Rank among batters: 617 • *Top target (4 home runs)*: Alex Kellner, Billy Pierce • *Number of pitchers victimized*: 66 • *Total ballparks homered in*: 15 • *First HR*: 06/15/1947 off Joe Dobson

Deacon Phillippe

CHARLES LOUIS PHILLIPPE
B: 05/23/1872 D: 03/30/1952
BR

Year	Tm	Lg	Tot	H	A	Men-On 0	Men-On 1	Men-On 2	Men-On 3	One-Game 2	One-Game 3	One-Game 4	LO	XN	IP	PH	RHP	LHP
1901	PIT	NL	1	0	1	0	0	1	0	0	0	0	0	0	0	0	1	0
1902	PIT	NL	1	0	1	1	0	0	0	0	0	0	0	0	0	0	1	0
1910	PIT	NL	1	1	0	0	0	0	1	0	0	0	0	0	1	0	0	1
Total			3	1	2	1	0	1	1	0	0	0	0	0	1	0	2	1

Rank among batters: 3,735 • *Total ballparks homered in*: 2 • *First HR*: 09/05/1901 off Al Maul

Adolfo Phillips

ADOLFO EMILIO (LOPEZ) PHILLIPS
B: 12/16/1941
BR

Year	Tm	Lg	Tot	H	A	Men-On 0	Men-On 1	Men-On 2	Men-On 3	One-Game 2	One-Game 3	One-Game 4	LO	XN	IP	PH	RHP	LHP
1965	PHI	NL	3	2	1	2	1	0	0	1	0	0	1	0	0	0	1	2
1966	CHI	NL	16	12	4	10	4	2	0	0	0	0	2	0	1	1	15	1
1967	CHI	NL	17	9	8	8	3	5	1	0	1	0	0	0	0	0	13	4
1968	CHI	NL	13	7	6	9	3	1	0	1	0	0	0	0	0	0	12	1
1969	MON	NL	4	4	0	3	1	0	0	0	0	0	0	0	0	0	2	2
1970	MON	NL	6	4	2	4	2	0	0	0	0	0	0	0	1	0	2	4
Total			59	38	21	36	14	8	1	2	1	0	3	0	2	1	45	14

Rank among batters: 873 • *Top target (3 home runs)*: Ken Johnson • *Number of pitchers victimized*: 48 • *Total ballparks homered in*: 11 • *First HR*: 09/06/1965 off Barney Schultz

Bill Phillips

WILLIAM B. PHILLIPS
B: 1857 D: 10/07/1900
BR

Year	Tm	Lg	Tot	H	A	Men-On 0	Men-On 1	Men-On 2	Men-On 3	One-Game 2	One-Game 3	One-Game 4	LO	XN	IP	PH	RHP	LHP
1880	CLE	NL	1	0	1	0	0	1	0	0	0	0	0	0	0	0	0	1
1881	CLE	NL	1	0	1	1	0	0	0	0	0	0	0	0	0	0	1	0
1882	CLE	NL	4	3	1	4	0	0	0	0	0	0	0	0	0	0	4	0
1883	CLE	NL	2	0	2	2	0	0	0	0	0	0	0	0	0	0	1	1
1884	CLE	NL	3	2	1	2	1	0	0	0	0	0	0	0	0	0	2	0
1885	BRO	AA	3	1	2	1	1	1	0	0	0	0	0	0	0	0	3	0
1887	BRO	AA	2	1	1	0	2	0	0	0	0	0	0	0	0	0	1	1
1888	KC	AA	1	1	0	0	0	1	0	0	0	0	0	0	0	0	0	1
Total			17	8	9	10	4	3	0	0	0	0	0	0	0	0	12	4

Rank among batters: 1,969 • *Top target (2 home runs)*: Hugh Daily • *Number of pitchers victimized*: 16 • *Total ballparks homered in*: 11 • *First HR*: 06/14/1880 off J Richmond

Bubba Phillips

JOHN MELVIN PHILLIPS
B: 02/24/1928 D: 06/22/1993
BR

Year	Tm	Lg	Tot	H	A	Men-On 0	Men-On 1	Men-On 2	Men-On 3	One-Game 2	One-Game 3	One-Game 4	LO	XN	IP	PH	RHP	LHP
1955	DET	AL	3	2	1	2	1	0	0	0	0	0	0	0	0	0	2	1
1956	CHI	AL	2	2	0	2	0	0	0	0	0	0	0	0	0	0	1	1
1957	CHI	AL	7	1	6	6	1	0	0	1	0	0	0	0	0	0	4	3
1958	CHI	AL	5	2	3	3	2	0	0	0	0	0	0	0	1	0	5	0
1959	CHI	AL	5	3	2	4	1	0	0	0	0	0	0	0	0	0	2	3
1960	CLE	AL	4	2	2	1	2	1	0	1	0	0	0	0	0	0	3	1

Bubba Phillips *continued*

Year	Tm	Lg	Tot	H	A	Men-On 0	1	2	3	One-Game 2	3	4	LO	XN	IP	PH	RHP	LHP
1961	CLE	AL	18	7	11	10	4	2	2	1	0	0	0	1	0	0	12	6
1962	CLE	AL	10	7	3	6	3	1	0	0	0	0	0	0	0	0	8	2
1963	DET	AL	5	2	3	3	1	1	0	0	0	0	0	0	0	1	2	3
1964	DET	AL	3	2	1	2	1	0	0	0	0	0	0	0	0	0	1	2
Total			62	30	32	39	16	5	2	3	0	0	0	1	1	1	40	22

Rank among batters: 835 • Top target (3 home runs): Ned Garver, Frank Baumann, Jim Coates, Gene Conley • *Number of pitchers victimized*: 46 • *Total ballparks homered in*: 11 • *First HR*: 05/29/1955 off Mike Fornieles

Buz Phillips

ALBERT ABERNATHY PHILLIPS
B: 05/25/1904 D: 11/06/1964
BR

Year	Tm	Lg	Tot	H	A	Men-On 0	1	2	3	One-Game 2	3	4	LO	XN	IP	PH	RHP	LHP
1930	PHI	NL	1	1	0	0	1	0	0	0	0	0	0	0	0	0	0	1

Rank among batters: 4,707 • *Total ballparks homered in*: 1 • *First HR*: 09/12/1930 off Bud Teachout

Damon Phillips

DAMON ROSWELL PHILLIPS
B: 06/08/1919
BR

Year	Tm	Lg	Tot	H	A	Men-On 0	1	2	3	One-Game 2	3	4	LO	XN	IP	PH	RHP	LHP
1944	BOS	NL	1	0	1	0	1	0	0	0	0	0	0	0	1	0	0	1

Rank among batters: 4,707 • *Total ballparks homered in*: 1 • *First HR*: 05/12/1944 off Cookie Cuccurullo

Dick Phillips

RICHARD EUGENE PHILLIPS
B: 11/24/1931
BL

Year	Tm	Lg	Tot	H	A	Men-On 0	1	2	3	One-Game 2	3	4	LO	XN	IP	PH	RHP	LHP
1963	WAS	AL	10	6	4	7	3	0	0	0	0	0	0	1	0	0	8	2
1964	WAS	AL	2	1	1	2	0	0	0	0	0	0	0	0	0	0	1	1
Total			12	7	5	9	3	0	0	0	0	0	0	1	0	0	9	3

Rank among batters: 2,325 • *Total ballparks homered in*: 5 • *First HR*: 07/06/1963 off Ken McBride

Eddie Phillips

EDWARD DAVID PHILLIPS
B: 02/17/1901 D: 01/26/1968
BR

Year	Tm	Lg	Tot	H	A	Men-On 0	1	2	3	One-Game 2	3	4	LO	XN	IP	PH	RHP	LHP
1929	DET	AL	2	1	1	1	1	0	0	0	0	0	0	0	0	0	1	1
1931	PIT	NL	7	3	4	6	0	0	1	0	0	0	0	0	0	0	2	5
1932	NY	AL	2	1	1	2	0	0	0	0	0	0	0	0	0	0	2	0
1934	WAS	AL	2	1	1	2	0	0	0	0	0	0	0	0	0	0	2	0
1935	CLE	AL	1	1	0	0	1	0	0	0	0	0	0	0	0	0	1	0
Total			14	7	7	11	2	0	1	0	0	0	0	0	0	0	8	6

Rank among batters: 2,169 • *Total ballparks homered in*: 8 • *First HR*: 05/15/1929 off Rube Walberg

J.R. Phillips

CHARLES GENE PHILLIPS
B: 04/29/1970
BL

Year	Tm	Lg	Tot	H	A	Men-On 0	1	2	3	One-Game 2	3	4	LO	XN	IP	PH	RHP	LHP
1993	SF	NL	1	0	1	0	1	0	0	0	0	0	0	0	0	0	1	0
1994	SF	NL	1	0	1	1	0	0	0	0	0	0	0	0	0	0	1	0
1995	SF	NL	9	5	4	5	3	1	0	1	0	0	0	1	0	0	8	1
Total			11	5	6	6	4	1	0	1	0	0	0	1	0	0	10	1

Rank among batters: 2,419 • *Top target (2 home runs)*: Steve Parris • *Number of pitchers victimized*: 10 • *Total ballparks homered in*: 6 • *First HR*: 09/04/1993 off Rene Arocha

Jack Phillips

JACK DORN PHILLIPS
B: 09/06/1921
BR

Year	Tm	Lg	Tot	H	A	Men-On 0	1	2	3	One-Game 2	3	4	LO	XN	IP	PH	RHP	LHP
1947	NY	AL	1	0	1	1	0	0	0	0	0	0	0	0	0	0	1	0
1949	NY	AL	1	1	0	0	0	1	0	0	0	0	0	0	0	0	0	1
1950	PIT	NL	5	3	2	4	0	0	1	0	0	0	0	0	0	1	3	2

Jack Phillips *continued*

Year	Tm	Lg	Tot	H	A	Men-On				One-Game			LO	XN	IP	PH	RHP	LHP
						0	1	2	3	2	3	4						
1955	DET	AL	1	1	0	0	1	0	0	0	0	0	0	0	0	0	0	1
1956	DET	AL	1	1	0	1	0	0	0	0	0	0	0	0	0	0	0	1
Total			9	6	3	6	1	1	1	0	0	0	0	0	0	1	4	5

Rank among batters: 2,587 • *Total ballparks homered in*: 6 • *First HR*: 09/21/1947 off Joe Coleman

Mike Phillips

MICHAEL DWAINE PHILLIPS
B: 08/19/1950
BL

Year	Tm	Lg	Tot	H	A	Men-On				One-Game			LO	XN	IP	PH	RHP	LHP
						0	1	2	3	2	3	4						
1973	SF	NL	1	1	0	1	0	0	0	0	0	0	0	0	0	0	1	0
1974	SF	NL	2	2	0	1	0	1	0	0	0	0	0	0	0	0	2	0
1975	NY	NL	1	0	1	0	1	0	0	0	0	0	0	0	0	0	1	0
1976	NY	NL	4	0	4	3	1	0	0	0	0	0	1	0	0	0	4	0
1977	NY	NL	1	1	0	1	0	0	0	0	0	0	0	0	0	0	0	1
1978	STL	NL	1	0	1	0	0	1	0	0	0	0	0	1	0	0	1	0
1979	STL	NL	1	0	1	0	1	0	0	0	0	0	0	0	0	0	1	0
Total			11	4	7	6	3	2	0	0	0	0	1	1	0	0	10	1

Rank among batters: 2,419 • *Top target (2 home runs)*: Steve Arlin, Ray Burris • *Number of pitchers victimized*: 9 • *Total ballparks homered in*: 5 • *First HR*: 09/22/1973 off Steve Arlin • *Hit for Cycle—*@CHI: 06/25/1976

Tony Phillips

KEITH ANTHONY PHILLIPS
B: 04/25/1959
BB

Year	Tm	Lg	Tot	H	A	Men-On				One-Game			LO	XN	IP	PH	RHP	LHP
						0	1	2	3	2	3	4						
1983	OAK	AL	4	1	3	2	2	0	0	0	0	0	0	1	0	0	3	1
1984	OAK	AL	4	2	2	2	0	2	0	0	0	0	0	0	0	0	3	1
1985	OAK	AL	4	2	2	3	1	0	0	0	0	0	0	0	0	0	2	2
1986	OAK	AL	5	3	2	5	0	0	0	0	0	0	2	0	0	0	2	3
1987	OAK	AL	10	5	5	4	4	1	1	0	0	0	0	0	0	0	7	3
1988	OAK	AL	2	2	0	1	1	0	0	0	0	0	0	0	0	0	2	0
1989	OAK	AL	4	2	2	1	3	0	0	0	0	0	0	0	0	0	4	0
1990	DET	AL	8	4	4	3	4	1	0	0	0	0	0	0	0	0	6	2
1991	DET	AL	17	9	8	14	2	1	0	0	0	0	2	0	0	1	6	11
1992	DET	AL	10	3	7	7	0	3	0	0	0	0	4	0	0	0	5	5
1993	DET	AL	7	3	4	5	0	2	0	0	0	0	2	0	0	0	7	0
1994	DET	AL	19	12	7	14	3	2	0	2	0	0	5	0	0	0	15	4
1995	CAL	AL	27	13	14	20	3	4	0	1	0	0	6	0	0	0	20	7
Total			121	61	60	81	23	16	1	3	0	0	21	1	0	1	82	39

Rank among batters: 382 • *Top target (4 home runs)*: Scott Erickson, Pat Hentgen • *Number of pitchers victimized*: 102 • *Total ballparks homered in*: 19 • *First HR*: 04/16/1983 off Matt Young • *Hit for Cycle—*@BAL: 05/16/1986 • *World Series HR—*1

Tom Phoebus

THOMAS HAROLD PHOEBUS
B: 04/07/1942
BR

Year	Tm	Lg	Tot	H	A	Men-On				One-Game			LO	XN	IP	PH	RHP	LHP
						0	1	2	3	2	3	4						
1967	BAL	AL	1	0	1	1	0	0	0	0	0	0	0	0	0	0	1	0
1968	BAL	AL	1	1	0	1	0	0	0	0	0	0	0	0	0	0	0	1
Total			2	1	1	2	0	0	0	0	0	0	0	0	0	0	1	1

Rank among batters: 4,129 • *Total ballparks homered in*: 2 • *First HR*: 06/06/1967 off Jim Coates

Mike Piazza

MICHAEL JOSEPH PIAZZA
B: 09/04/1968
BR

Year	Tm	Lg	Tot	H	A	Men-On				One-Game			LO	XN	IP	PH	RHP	LHP
						0	1	2	3	2	3	4						
1992	LA	NL	1	1	0	0	0	1	0	0	0	0	0	0	0	0	1	0
1993	LA	NL	35	21	14	23	8	4	0	5	0	0	0	0	0	0	22	13
1994	LA	NL	24	13	11	8	9	5	2	0	0	0	0	0	0	0	17	7
1995	LA	NL	32	9	23	14	13	3	2	6	0	0	0	0	1	1	24	8
Total			92	44	48	45	30	13	4	11	0	0	0	0	1	1	64	28

Rank among batters: 554 • Top target (3 home runs): Mark Portugal, Steve Reed, Greg Swindell, Paul Wagner • *Number of pitchers victimized*: 72 • *Total ballparks homered in*: 15 • *First HR*: 09/12/1992 off Steve Reed • *LCS HR—*1; *All-Star HR—*1

Rob Picciolo

ROBERT MICHAEL PICCIOLO
B: 02/04/1953
BR

Year	Tm	Lg	Tot	H	A	Men-On 0	1	2	3	One-Game 2	3	4	LO	XN	IP	PH	RHP	LHP
1977	OAK	AL	2	0	2	2	0	0	0	0	0	0	0	0	0	0	2	0
1978	OAK	AL	2	0	2	1	1	0	0	0	0	0	0	0	0	0	1	1
1979	OAK	AL	2	1	1	2	0	0	0	0	0	0	0	0	0	0	2	0
1980	OAK	AL	5	2	3	2	2	1	0	0	0	0	0	0	0	0	1	4
1981	OAK	AL	4	4	0	4	0	0	0	0	0	0	0	0	0	0	1	3
1984	CAL	AL	1	0	1	1	0	0	0	0	0	0	0	0	1	0	1	0
1985	OAK	AL	1	0	1	0	1	0	0	0	0	0	0	0	0	0	0	1
Total			17	7	10	12	4	1	0	0	0	0	0	0	1	0	8	9

Rank among batters: 1,969 • *Top target (2 home runs)*: Moose Haas, Jerry Koosman • *Number of pitchers victimized*: 15 • *Total ballparks homered in*: 8 • *First HR*: 04/15/1977 off Paul Thormodsgard

Val Picinich

VALENTINE JOHN PICINICH
B: 09/08/1896 D: 12/05/1942
BR

Year	Tm	Lg	Tot	H	A	Men-On 0	1	2	3	One-Game 2	3	4	LO	XN	IP	PH	RHP	LHP
1919	WAS	AL	3	0	3	2	1	0	0	0	0	0	0	0	0	0	3	0
1920	WAS	AL	3	0	3	1	0	2	0	0	0	0	0	0	0	0	1	2
1923	BOS	AL	2	0	2	0	1	1	0	0	0	0	0	0	1	0	2	0
1924	BOS	AL	1	1	0	0	1	0	0	0	0	0	0	0	1	0	0	1
1925	BOS	AL	1	0	1	1	0	0	0	0	0	0	0	0	0	0	1	0
1926	CIN	NL	2	2	0	0	1	1	0	0	0	0	0	0	1	0	0	2
1928	CIN	NL	7	0	7	4	1	2	0	1	0	0	0	0	1	0	5	2
1929	BRO	NL	4	2	2	2	2	0	0	0	0	0	0	0	1	0	3	1
1931	BRO	NL	1	0	1	1	0	0	0	0	0	0	0	0	0	0	0	1
1932	BRO	NL	1	0	1	1	0	0	0	0	0	0	0	0	0	1	0	1
1933	PIT	NL	1	0	1	1	0	0	0	0	0	0	0	0	0	0	1	0
Total			26	5	21	13	7	6	0	1	0	0	0	0	5	1	16	10

Rank among batters: 1,576 • *Top target (2 home runs)*: Bill Walker • *Number of pitchers victimized*: 25 • *Total ballparks homered in*: 12 • *First HR*: 06/28/1919 off Scott Perry

Charlie Pick

CHARLES THOMAS PICK
B: 04/10/1888 D: 06/26/1954
BL

Year	Tm	Lg	Tot	H	A	Men-On 0	1	2	3	One-Game 2	3	4	LO	XN	IP	PH	RHP	LHP
1919	BOS	NL	1	1	0	1	0	0	0	0	0	0	1	0	1	0	0	1
1920	BOS	NL	2	0	2	1	1	0	0	0	0	0	0	0	0	0	1	1
Total			3	1	2	2	1	0	0	0	0	0	1	0	1	0	1	2

Rank among batters: 3,735 • *Total ballparks homered in*: 3 • *First HR*: 08/21/1919 off Slim Sallee

Eddie Pick

EDGAR EVERETT PICK
B: 05/07/1899 D: 05/13/1967
BB

Year	Tm	Lg	Tot	H	A	Men-On 0	1	2	3	One-Game 2	3	4	LO	XN	IP	PH	RHP	LHP
1927	CHI	NL	2	0	2	2	0	0	0	0	0	0	0	0	0	0	2	0

Rank among batters: 4,129 • *Total ballparks homered in*: 2 • *First HR*: 06/25/1927 off Vic Aldridge

Ollie Pickering

OLIVER DANIEL PICKERING
B: 04/09/1870 D: 01/20/1952
BL

Year	Tm	Lg	Tot	H	A	Men-On 0	1	2	3	One-Game 2	3	4	LO	XN	IP	PH	RHP	LHP
1896	LOU	NL	1	1	0	0	1	0	0	0	0	0	0	0	1	0	1	0
1897	LOU	NL	1	1	0	1	0	0	0	0	0	0	0	0	1	0	1	0
	CLE	NL	1	0	1	1	0	0	0	0	0	0	0	0	0	0	1	0
	Total		2	1	1	2	0	0	0	0	0	0	0	0	1	0	2	0
1902	CLE	AL	3	1	2	2	0	1	0	0	0	0	1	0	0	0	3	0
1903	PHI	AL	1	1	0	1	0	0	0	0	0	0	0	1	0	0	1	0
1908	WAS	AL	2	1	1	1	0	1	0	0	0	0	0	0	0	0	2	0
Total			9	5	4	6	1	2	0	0	0	0	1	1	2	0	9	0

Rank among batters: 2,587 • *Total ballparks homered in*: 8 • *First HR*: 09/12/1896 off Billy Rhines

Urbane Pickering

URBANE HENRY PICKERING
B: 06/03/1899 D: 05/13/1970
BR

						Men-On				One-Game								
Year	Tm	Lg	Tot	H	A	0	1	2	3	2	3	4	LO	XN	IP	PH	RHP	LHP
1931	BOS	AL	9	1	8	6	1	2	0	1	0	0	0	0	0	0	6	3
1932	BOS	AL	2	0	2	2	0	0	0	0	0	0	0	0	0	0	2	0
Total			11	1	10	8	1	2	0	1	0	0	0	0	0	0	8	3

Rank among batters: 2,419 • *Top target (2 home runs)*: Lefty Stewart, George Earnshaw • *Number of pitchers victimized*: 9 • *Total ballparks homered in*: 6 • *First HR*: 05/04/1931 off Bill Shores

John Pickett

JOHN THOMAS PICKETT
B: 02/20/1866 D: 07/04/1922
BR

						Men-On				One-Game								
Year	Tm	Lg	Tot	H	A	0	1	2	3	2	3	4	LO	XN	IP	PH	RHP	LHP
1890	PHI	PL	4	2	2	2	1	1	0	0	0	0	0	0	0	0	3	1
1892	BAL	NL	1	1	0	0	1	0	0	0	0	0	0	0	0	0	1	0
Total			5	3	2	2	2	1	0	0	0	0	0	0	0	0	4	1

Rank among batters: 3,191 • *Total ballparks homered in*: 4 • *First HR*: 06/26/1890 off Lady Baldwin

Jack Pierce

LAVERN JACK PIERCE
B: 06/02/1948
BL

						Men-On				One-Game								
Year	Tm	Lg	Tot	H	A	0	1	2	3	2	3	4	LO	XN	IP	PH	RHP	LHP
1975	DET	AL	8	5	3	4	4	0	0	0	0	0	0	0	0	0	7	1

Rank among batters: 2,703 • *Total ballparks homered in*: 4 • *First HR*: 06/05/1975 off Bill Singer

Jim Piersall

JAMES ANTHONY PIERSALL
B: 11/14/1929
BR

						Men-On				One-Game								
Year	Tm	Lg	Tot	H	A	0	1	2	3	2	3	4	LO	XN	IP	PH	RHP	LHP
1952	BOS	AL	1	1	0	1	0	0	0	0	0	0	0	0	0	0	1	0
1953	BOS	AL	3	1	2	2	1	0	0	0	0	0	0	0	1	0	2	1
1954	BOS	AL	8	5	3	6	1	1	0	0	0	0	0	0	0	0	5	3
1955	BOS	AL	13	10	3	5	6	2	0	0	0	0	0	0	0	0	6	7
1956	BOS	AL	14	7	7	8	6	0	0	1	0	0	0	0	1	0	10	4
1957	BOS	AL	19	9	10	12	4	3	0	0	0	0	1	0	0	0	12	7
1958	BOS	AL	8	6	2	5	2	1	0	0	0	0	2	0	0	0	7	1
1959	CLE	AL	4	1	3	2	1	1	0	0	0	0	0	0	0	0	2	2
1960	CLE	AL	18	7	11	8	8	2	0	1	0	0	2	1	0	0	11	7
1961	CLE	AL	6	4	2	2	3	1	0	0	0	0	0	0	0	0	6	0
1962	WAS	AL	4	2	2	2	2	0	0	0	0	0	0	1	0	0	2	2
1963	WAS	AL	1	1	0	1	0	0	0	0	0	0	0	0	0	0	1	0
	NY	NL	1	1	0	1	0	0	0	0	0	0	0	0	0	0	1	0
	Total		2	2	0	2	0	0	0	0	0	0	0	0	0	0	2	0
1964	LA	AL	2	0	2	1	1	0	0	0	0	0	1	0	0	0	1	1
1965	CAL	AL	2	1	1	1	1	0	0	0	0	0	0	0	0	0	1	1
Total			104	56	48	57	36	11	0	2	0	0	6	2	2	0	68	36

Rank among batters: 469 • *Top target (5 home runs)*: Billy Pierce • *Number of pitchers victimized*: 76 • *Total ballparks homered in*: 14 • *First HR*: 06/09/1952 off Art Houtteman

Tony Piet

ANTHONY FRANCIS PIET
B: 12/07/1906 D: 12/01/1981
BR

						Men-On				One-Game								
Year	Tm	Lg	Tot	H	A	0	1	2	3	2	3	4	LO	XN	IP	PH	RHP	LHP
1932	PIT	NL	7	2	5	4	1	1	1	1	0	0	0	2	1	0	3	4
1933	PIT	NL	1	0	1	0	1	0	0	0	0	0	0	0	0	0	1	0
1934	CIN	NL	1	0	1	0	0	1	0	0	0	0	0	0	0	0	1	0
1935	CHI	AL	3	2	1	0	3	0	0	0	0	0	0	0	1	0	2	1
1936	CHI	AL	7	3	4	5	2	0	0	0	0	0	0	0	0	0	7	0
1937	CHI	AL	4	4	0	2	1	1	0	0	0	0	0	0	0	0	4	0
Total			23	11	12	11	8	3	1	1	0	0	0	2	2	0	18	5

Rank among batters: 1,686 • *Top target (2 home runs)*: Hi Bell, Bill Walker • *Number of pitchers victimized*: 21 • *Total ballparks homered in*: 10 • *First HR*: 06/03/1932 off Jakie May

Joe Pignatano

JOSEPH BENJAMIN PIGNATANO
B: 08/04/1929
BR

						Men-On				One-Game								
Year	Tm	Lg	Tot	H	A	0	1	2	3	2	3	4	LO	XN	IP	PH	RHP	LHP
1958	LA	NL	9	5	4	6	2	1	0	0	0	0	0	1	0	0	5	4

Year	Tm	Lg	Tot	H	A	Men-On 0	Men-On 1	Men-On 2	Men-On 3	One-Game 2	One-Game 3	One-Game 4	LO	XN	IP	PH	RHP	LHP

Joe Pignatano *continued*

Year	Tm	Lg	Tot	H	A	0	1	2	3	2	3	4	LO	XN	IP	PH	RHP	LHP
1959	LA	NL	1	1	0	0	0	1	0	0	0	0	0	0	0	0	1	0
1960	LA	NL	2	2	0	2	0	0	0	0	0	0	0	0	0	0	1	1
1961	KC	AL	4	0	4	1	3	0	0	0	0	0	0	0	0	0	2	2
Total			16	8	8	9	5	2	0	0	0	0	0	1	0	0	9	7

Rank among batters: 2,029 • *Top target (2 home runs)*: Joe Nuxhall • *Number of pitchers victimized*: 15 • *Total ballparks homered in*: 7 • *First HR*: 06/18/1958 off Robin Roberts

Jess Pike

JESS WILLARD PIKE
B: 07/31/1915 D: 03/28/1984
BL

Year	Tm	Lg	Tot	H	A	0	1	2	3	2	3	4	LO	XN	IP	PH	RHP	LHP
1946	NY	NL	1	1	0	0	0	1	0	0	0	0	0	0	0	0	0	1

Rank among batters: 4,707 • *Total ballparks homered in*: 1 • *First HR*: 04/28/1946 off Joe Hatten

Lip Pike

LIPMAN EMANUEL PIKE
B: 05/25/1845 D: 10/10/1893
BL

Year	Tm	Lg	Tot	H	A	0	1	2	3	2	3	4	LO	XN	IP	PH	RHP	LHP
1876	STL	NL	1	1	0	1	0	0	0	0	0	0	0	0	0	0	1	0
1877	CIN	NL	4	2	2	4	0	0	0	0	0	0	1	0	0	0	4	0
Total			5	3	2	5	0	0	0	0	0	0	1	0	0	0	5	0

Rank among batters: 3,191 • *Top target (2 home runs)*: Tommy Bond • *Number of pitchers victimized*: 4 • *Total ballparks homered in*: 4 • *First HR*: 07/13/1876 off Tommy Bond

Al Pilarcik

ALFRED JAMES PILARCIK
B: 07/03/1930
BL

Year	Tm	Lg	Tot	H	A	0	1	2	3	2	3	4	LO	XN	IP	PH	RHP	LHP
1956	KC	AL	4	3	1	3	1	0	0	0	0	0	0	0	0	0	4	0
1957	BAL	AL	9	2	7	6	2	1	0	0	0	0	0	0	0	0	8	1
1958	BAL	AL	1	1	0	1	0	0	0	0	0	0	0	0	0	0	1	0
1959	BAL	AL	3	1	2	2	0	1	0	0	0	0	0	1	0	0	2	1
1960	BAL	AL	4	2	2	2	1	1	0	0	0	0	0	0	0	0	4	0
1961	CHI	AL	1	0	1	0	0	1	0	0	0	0	0	0	0	0	1	0
Total			22	9	13	14	4	4	0	0	0	0	0	1	0	0	20	2

Rank among batters: 1,719 • *Top target (2 home runs)*: Bob Keegan • *Number of pitchers victimized*: 21 • *Total ballparks homered in*: 9 • *First HR*: 07/26/1956 off Frank Sullivan

Duane Pillette

DUANE XAVIER PILLETTE
B: 07/24/1922
BR

Year	Tm	Lg	Tot	H	A	0	1	2	3	2	3	4	LO	XN	IP	PH	RHP	LHP
1953	STL	AL	1	0	1	1	0	0	0	0	0	0	0	0	0	0	1	0

Rank among batters: 4,707 • *Total ballparks homered in*: 1 • *First HR*: 06/27/1953 off Marion Fricano

George Pinckney

GEORGE BURTON PINCKNEY
B: 01/11/1862 D: 11/10/1926
BR

Year	Tm	Lg	Tot	H	A	0	1	2	3	2	3	4	LO	XN	IP	PH	RHP	LHP
1887	BRO	AA	3	3	0	1	0	1	0	0	0	0	0	0	0	0	2	0
1888	BRO	AA	4	4	0	2	1	1	0	0	0	0	0	0	0	0	3	1
1889	BRO	AA	4	2	2	1	3	0	0	0	0	0	0	0	2	0	2	2
1890	BRO	NL	7	6	1	3	4	0	0	0	0	0	0	0	2	0	6	1
1891	BRO	NL	2	1	1	2	0	0	0	0	0	0	0	0	0	0	2	0
1893	LOU	NL	1	0	1	0	1	0	0	0	0	0	0	0	0	0	1	0
Total			21	16	5	9	9	2	0	0	0	0	0	0	4	0	16	4

Rank among batters: 1,768 • *Top target (2 home runs)*: Guy Hecker • *Number of pitchers victimized*: 20 • *Total ballparks homered in*: 8 • *First HR*: 06/08/1887 off George Pechiney

Babe Pinelli

RALPH ARTHUR PINELLI
B: 10/18/1895 D: 10/22/1984
BR

Year	Tm	Lg	Tot	H	A	0	1	2	3	2	3	4	LO	XN	IP	PH	RHP	LHP
1918	CHI	AL	1	0	1	1	0	0	0	0	0	0	0	0	1	0	1	0

Babe Pinelli *continued*

Year	Tm	Lg	Tot	H	A	Men-On 0	1	2	3	One-Game 2	3	4	LO	XN	IP	PH	RHP	LHP
1922	CIN	NL	1	1	0	0	0	1	0	0	0	0	0	0	1	0	0	1
1925	CIN	NL	2	1	1	2	0	0	0	0	0	0	0	0	1	0	0	2
1927	CIN	NL	1	0	1	1	0	0	0	0	0	0	0	0	1	0	1	0
Total			5	2	3	4	0	1	0	0	0	0	0	0	4	0	2	3

Rank among batters: 3,191 • *Total ballparks homered in*: 4 • *First HR*: 08/11/1918 off Johnny Enzmann

Lou Piniella

LOUIS VICTOR PINIELLA
B: 08/28/1943
BR

Year	Tm	Lg	Tot	H	A	Men-On 0	1	2	3	One-Game 2	3	4	LO	XN	IP	PH	RHP	LHP
1969	KC	AL	11	5	6	5	5	1	0	0	0	0	0	0	1	0	5	6
1970	KC	AL	11	7	4	3	4	4	0	0	0	0	0	0	0	1	8	3
1971	KC	AL	3	2	1	2	0	1	0	0	0	0	0	0	0	0	1	2
1972	KC	AL	11	3	8	7	3	1	0	0	0	0	0	0	0	0	8	3
1973	KC	AL	9	3	6	5	3	0	1	0	0	0	0	0	0	0	4	5
1974	NY	AL	9	1	8	6	2	1	0	0	0	0	0	0	0	0	2	7
1976	NY	AL	3	2	1	2	1	0	0	0	0	0	0	0	0	0	1	2
1977	NY	AL	12	4	8	9	3	0	0	0	0	0	0	0	0	0	7	5
1978	NY	AL	6	4	2	3	2	1	0	0	0	0	0	0	0	0	0	6
1979	NY	AL	11	3	8	6	3	2	0	0	0	0	0	0	0	1	1	10
1980	NY	AL	2	1	1	0	1	1	0	0	0	0	0	0	0	0	1	1
1981	NY	AL	5	0	5	5	0	0	0	0	0	0	0	0	0	0	0	5
1982	NY	AL	6	1	5	4	2	0	0	0	0	0	0	0	0	0	1	5
1983	NY	AL	2	1	1	1	1	0	0	0	0	0	0	0	0	0	0	2
1984	NY	AL	1	1	0	1	0	0	0	0	0	0	0	0	0	0	0	1
Total			102	38	64	59	30	12	1	0	0	0	0	0	1	2	39	63

Rank among batters: 483 • *Top target (3 home runs)*: Francisco Barrios, Frank Tanana • *Number of pitchers victimized*: 83 • *Total ballparks homered in*: 16 • *First HR*: 04/20/1969 off Jim Nash • *LCS HR*—3

Vada Pinson

VADA EDWARD PINSON
B: 08/11/1938 D: 10/21/1995
BL

Year	Tm	Lg	Tot	H	A	Men-On 0	1	2	3	One-Game 2	3	4	LO	XN	IP	PH	RHP	LHP
1958	CIN	NL	1	0	1	0	0	0	1	0	0	0	0	0	0	0	1	0
1959	CIN	NL	20	13	7	10	9	1	0	1	0	0	0	0	0	0	19	1
1960	CIN	NL	20	11	9	13	4	1	2	1	0	0	0	0	0	0	15	5
1961	CIN	NL	16	9	7	8	4	3	1	1	0	0	0	1	0	0	10	6
1962	CIN	NL	23	14	9	10	9	4	0	1	0	0	0	1	2	0	20	3
1963	CIN	NL	22	14	8	13	5	4	0	1	0	0	0	0	1	0	16	6
1964	CIN	NL	23	11	12	17	4	2	0	3	0	0	0	0	0	0	19	4
1965	CIN	NL	22	16	6	11	6	4	1	0	0	0	0	0	0	0	18	4
1966	CIN	NL	16	9	7	7	5	3	1	1	0	0	0	0	0	0	13	3
1967	CIN	NL	18	9	9	11	6	1	0	0	0	0	0	1	0	0	15	3
1968	CIN	NL	5	4	1	4	0	1	0	0	0	0	0	0	0	0	4	1
1969	STL	NL	10	4	6	5	4	1	0	0	0	0	0	0	0	0	7	3
1970	CLE	AL	24	19	5	14	8	1	1	1	0	0	1	0	0	0	19	5
1971	CLE	AL	11	8	3	8	2	1	0	0	0	0	2	0	0	0	10	1
1972	CAL	AL	7	1	6	5	0	2	0	0	0	0	0	0	0	0	7	0
1973	CAL	AL	8	5	3	5	2	1	0	0	0	0	0	0	0	0	8	0
1974	KC	AL	6	3	3	3	2	0	1	0	0	0	0	0	0	0	6	0
1975	KC	AL	4	1	3	4	0	0	0	0	0	0	1	0	0	0	4	0
Total			256	151	105	148	70	30	8	10	0	0	4	3	3	0	211	45

Rank among batters: 98 • *Top target (7 home runs)*: Mike McCormick • *Number of pitchers victimized*: 162 • *Total ballparks homered in*: 27 • *First HR*: 04/18/1958 off Ron Kline

George Pipgras

GEORGE WILLIAM PIPGRAS
B: 12/20/1899 D: 10/19/1986
BR

Year	Tm	Lg	Tot	H	A	Men-On 0	1	2	3	One-Game 2	3	4	LO	XN	IP	PH	RHP	LHP
1927	NY	AL	1	1	0	1	0	0	0	0	0	0	0	0	0	0	1	0
1930	NY	AL	1	0	1	1	0	0	0	0	0	0	0	0	0	0	1	0
Total			2	1	1	2	0	0	0	0	0	0	0	0	0	0	2	0

Rank among batters: 4,129 • *Total ballparks homered in*: 2 • *First HR*: 06/12/1927 off George Uhle

Year	Tm	Lg	Tot	H	A	Men-On 0	Men-On 1	Men-On 2	Men-On 3	One-Game 2	One-Game 3	One-Game 4	LO	XN	IP	PH	RHP	LHP

Wally Pipp

WALTER CLEMENT PIPP
B: 02/17/1893 D: 01/11/1965
BL

Year	Tm	Lg	Tot	H	A	0	1	2	3	2	3	4	LO	XN	IP	PH	RHP	LHP
1915	NY	AL	4	4	0	3	0	1	0	0	0	0	0	0	1	0	3	1
1916	NY	AL	12	8	4	6	3	3	0	0	0	0	0	0	2	0	10	2
1917	NY	AL	9	6	3	5	1	3	0	0	0	0	0	0	1	0	7	2
1918	NY	AL	2	0	2	0	1	1	0	0	0	0	0	0	0	0	2	0
1919	NY	AL	7	4	3	3	2	2	0	0	0	0	0	0	1	0	5	2
1920	NY	AL	11	6	5	4	5	2	0	0	0	0	0	1	1	0	11	0
1921	NY	AL	8	4	4	7	0	1	0	0	0	0	0	0	1	0	8	0
1922	NY	AL	9	6	3	4	4	1	0	0	0	0	0	1	1	0	7	2
1923	NY	AL	6	4	2	3	2	0	1	0	0	0	0	1	2	0	6	0
1924	NY	AL	9	8	1	5	4	0	0	0	0	0	0	1	3	0	9	0
1925	NY	AL	3	1	2	3	0	0	0	0	0	0	0	0	0	0	0	3
1926	CIN	NL	6	2	4	2	2	1	1	0	0	0	0	0	1	0	5	1
1927	CIN	NL	2	0	2	0	1	1	0	0	0	0	0	0	0	0	1	1
1928	CIN	NL	2	0	2	1	1	0	0	1	0	0	0	0	0	0	2	0
Total			90	53	37	46	26	16	2	1	0	0	0	4	14	0	76	14

Rank among batters: 573 • *Top target (5 home runs)*: Hooks Dauss • *Number of pitchers victimized*: 66 • *Total ballparks homered in*: 10 • *First HR*: 06/14/1915 off Harry Hoch

Greg Pirkl

GREGORY DANIEL PIRKL
B: 08/07/1970
BR

Year	Tm	Lg	Tot	H	A	0	1	2	3	2	3	4	LO	XN	IP	PH	RHP	LHP
1993	SEA	AL	1	1	0	0	0	1	0	0	0	0	0	0	0	0	0	1
1994	SEA	AL	6	2	4	3	3	0	0	0	0	0	0	0	0	1	2	4
Total			7	3	4	3	3	1	0	0	0	0	0	0	0	1	2	5

Rank among batters: 2,834 • *Total ballparks homered in*: 4 • *First HR*: 08/14/1993 off Mark Langston

Jim Pisoni

JAMES PETE PISONI
B: 08/14/1929
BR

Year	Tm	Lg	Tot	H	A	0	1	2	3	2	3	4	LO	XN	IP	PH	RHP	LHP
1953	STL	AL	1	1	0	1	0	0	0	0	0	0	0	0	0	0	1	0
1956	KC	AL	2	2	0	1	1	0	0	0	0	0	0	0	0	0	2	0
1957	KC	AL	3	3	0	2	0	0	1	0	0	0	0	0	0	0	2	1
Total			6	6	0	4	1	0	1	0	0	0	0	0	0	0	5	1

Rank among batters: 2,988 • *Total ballparks homered in*: 2 • *First HR*: 09/26/1953 off Connie Johnson

Skip Pitlock

LEE PATRICK THOMAS PITLOCK
B: 11/06/1947
BL

Year	Tm	Lg	Tot	H	A	0	1	2	3	2	3	4	LO	XN	IP	PH	RHP	LHP
1970	SF	NL	1	1	0	1	0	0	0	0	0	0	0	0	1	0	0	1

Rank among batters: 4,707 • *Total ballparks homered in*: 1 • *First HR*: 08/08/1970 off Wade Blasingame

Clarke Pittenger

CLARKE ALONZO PITTENGER
B: 02/24/1899 D: 11/04/1977
BR

Year	Tm	Lg	Tot	H	A	0	1	2	3	2	3	4	LO	XN	IP	PH	RHP	LHP
1927	CIN	NL	1	1	0	0	0	1	0	0	0	0	0	0	1	0	1	0

Rank among batters: 4,707 • *Total ballparks homered in*: 1 • *First HR*: 09/11/1927 off Hugh McQuillan

Togie Pittinger

CHARLES RENO PITTINGER
B: 01/12/1872 D: 01/14/1909
BL

Year	Tm	Lg	Tot	H	A	0	1	2	3	2	3	4	LO	XN	IP	PH	RHP	LHP
1903	BOS	NL	1	0	1	1	0	0	0	0	0	0	0	0	0	0	1	0

Rank among batters: 4,707 • *Total ballparks homered in*: 1 • *First HR*: 07/27/1903 off Dummy Taylor

Juan Pizarro

JUAN ROMAN (CORDOVA) PIZARRO
B: 02/07/1937
BL

Year	Tm	Lg	Tot	H	A	0	1	2	3	2	3	4	LO	XN	IP	PH	RHP	LHP
1957	MIL	NL	1	0	1	1	0	0	0	0	0	0	0	0	0	0	1	0

Year	Tm	Lg	Tot	H	A	Men-On 0	1	2	3	One-Game 2	3	4	LO	XN	IP	PH	RHP	LHP

Juan Pizarro *continued*

Year	Tm	Lg	Tot	H	A	Men-On 0	1	2	3	One-Game 2	3	4	LO	XN	IP	PH	RHP	LHP
1963	CHI	AL	2	1	1	1	1	0	0	0	0	0	0	0	0	0	2	0
1964	CHI	AL	3	1	2	2	0	1	0	0	0	0	0	0	0	0	3	0
1965	CHI	AL	1	0	1	0	1	0	0	0	0	0	0	0	0	0	1	0
1971	CHI	NL	1	0	1	1	0	0	0	0	0	0	0	0	0	0	1	0
Total			8	2	6	5	2	1	0	0	0	0	0	0	0	0	8	0

Rank among batters: 2,703 • *Top target (2 home runs)*: Ken McBride • *Number of pitchers victimized*: 7 • *Total ballparks homered in*: 7 • *First HR*: 05/10/1957 off Sam Jones

Eddie Plank

EDWARD STEWART PLANK
B: 08/31/1875 D: 02/24/1926
BL HOF

Year	Tm	Lg	Tot	H	A	Men-On 0	1	2	3	One-Game 2	3	4	LO	XN	IP	PH	RHP	LHP
1903	PHI	AL	1	0	1	1	0	0	0	0	0	0	0	0	1	0	1	0
1907	PHI	AL	1	0	1	1	0	0	0	0	0	0	0	0	1	0	1	0
1909	PHI	AL	1	1	0	1	0	0	0	0	0	0	0	0	0	0	1	0
Total			3	1	2	3	0	0	0	0	0	0	0	0	2	0	3	0

Rank among batters: 3,735 • *Total ballparks homered in*: 3 • *First HR*: 05/02/1903 off Cy Young

Phil Plantier

PHILLIP ALAN PLANTIER
B: 01/27/1969
BL

Year	Tm	Lg	Tot	H	A	Men-On 0	1	2	3	One-Game 2	3	4	LO	XN	IP	PH	RHP	LHP
1991	BOS	AL	11	6	5	7	2	2	0	1	0	0	0	0	0	1	8	3
1992	BOS	AL	7	5	2	4	3	0	0	0	0	0	0	0	0	1	7	0
1993	SD	NL	34	16	18	15	11	7	1	3	0	0	0	1	0	0	27	7
1994	SD	NL	18	7	11	12	6	0	0	1	0	0	0	1	0	0	12	6
1995	HOU	NL	4	0	4	1	1	2	0	0	0	0	0	0	0	0	3	1
	SD	NL	5	1	4	4	1	0	0	1	0	0	0	0	0	1	3	2
	Total		9	1	8	5	2	2	0	1	0	0	0	0	0	1	6	3
Total			79	35	44	43	24	11	1	6	0	0	0	2	0	3	60	19

Rank among batters: 661 • *Top target (3 home runs)*: Scott Sanderson, Mike Morgan • *Number of pitchers victimized*: 66 • *Total ballparks homered in*: 20 • *First HR*: 08/16/1991 off Storm Davis

Elmo Plaskett

ELMO ALEXANDER PLASKETT
B: 06/27/1938
BR

Year	Tm	Lg	Tot	H	A	Men-On 0	1	2	3	One-Game 2	3	4	LO	XN	IP	PH	RHP	LHP
1962	PIT	NL	1	1	0	0	0	1	0	0	0	0	0	0	0	0	0	1

Rank among batters: 4,707 • *Total ballparks homered in*: 1 • *First HR*: 09/17/1962 off Mike McCormick

Whitey Platt

MIZELL GEORGE PLATT
B: 08/21/1920 D: 07/27/1970
BR

Year	Tm	Lg	Tot	H	A	Men-On 0	1	2	3	One-Game 2	3	4	LO	XN	IP	PH	RHP	LHP
1946	CHI	AL	3	2	1	2	0	1	0	0	0	0	0	0	0	0	1	2
1948	STL	AL	7	3	4	4	3	0	0	0	0	0	0	0	0	0	5	2
1949	STL	AL	3	1	2	3	0	0	0	0	0	0	0	0	0	0	2	1
Total			13	6	7	9	3	1	0	0	0	0	0	0	0	0	8	5

Rank among batters: 2,248 • *Total ballparks homered in*: 5 • *First HR*: 05/20/1946 off Dutch Leonard

Herb Plews

HERBERT EUGENE PLEWS
B: 06/14/1928
BL

Year	Tm	Lg	Tot	H	A	Men-On 0	1	2	3	One-Game 2	3	4	LO	XN	IP	PH	RHP	LHP
1956	WAS	AL	1	1	0	1	0	0	0	0	0	0	0	0	0	0	1	0
1957	WAS	AL	1	0	1	1	0	0	0	0	0	0	0	0	0	0	1	0
1958	WAS	AL	2	0	2	2	0	0	0	0	0	0	0	0	0	0	2	0
Total			4	1	3	4	0	0	0	0	0	0	0	0	0	0	4	0

Rank among batters: 3,427 • *Top target (2 home runs)*: Bob Keegan, Jim Bunning • *Number of pitchers victimized*: 2 • *Total ballparks homered in*: 3 • *First HR*: 08/28/1956 off Bob Keegan

Bill Plummer

WILLIAM FRANCIS PLUMMER
B: 03/21/1947
BR

Year	Tm	Lg	Tot	H	A	Men-On 0	1	2	3	One-Game 2	3	4	LO	XN	IP	PH	RHP	LHP
1972	CIN	NL	2	0	2	2	0	0	0	0	0	0	0	0	0	0	1	1
1973	CIN	NL	2	0	2	0	1	1	0	0	0	0	0	0	0	0	1	1
1974	CIN	NL	2	0	2	1	1	0	0	1	0	0	0	0	0	0	0	2
1975	CIN	NL	1	0	1	0	1	0	0	0	0	0	0	0	0	0	0	1
1976	CIN	NL	4	3	1	3	0	0	1	0	0	0	0	0	0	0	2	2
1977	CIN	NL	1	1	0	0	0	1	0	0	0	0	0	0	0	0	1	0
1978	SEA	AL	2	1	1	1	1	0	0	0	0	0	0	0	0	0	1	1
Total			14	5	9	7	4	2	1	1	0	0	0	0	0	0	6	8

Rank among batters: 2,169 • *Top target (2 home runs)*: Steve Carlton • *Number of pitchers victimized*: 13 • *Total ballparks homered in*: 8 • *First HR*: 08/22/1972 off Mike Marshall

Ray Poat

RAYMOND WILLIS POAT
B: 12/19/1917 D: 04/29/1990
BR

Year	Tm	Lg	Tot	H	A	Men-On 0	1	2	3	One-Game 2	3	4	LO	XN	IP	PH	RHP	LHP
1947	NY	NL	1	1	0	1	0	0	0	0	0	0	0	0	0	0	0	1

Rank among batters: 4,707 • *Total ballparks homered in*: 1 • *First HR*: 08/27/1947 off Harry Brecheen

Biff Pocoroba

BIFF BENEDICT POCOROBA
B: 07/25/1953
BB

Year	Tm	Lg	Tot	H	A	Men-On 0	1	2	3	One-Game 2	3	4	LO	XN	IP	PH	RHP	LHP
1975	ATL	NL	1	0	1	1	0	0	0	0	0	0	0	0	0	0	1	0
1977	ATL	NL	8	4	4	4	2	1	1	0	0	0	0	0	0	1	8	0
1978	ATL	NL	6	2	4	1	2	2	1	0	0	0	0	0	0	0	5	1
1980	ATL	NL	2	1	1	2	0	0	0	0	0	0	0	0	0	2	2	0
1982	ATL	NL	2	2	0	2	0	0	0	0	0	0	0	0	0	0	2	0
1983	ATL	NL	2	2	0	1	1	0	0	0	0	0	0	0	0	0	2	0
Total			21	11	10	11	5	3	2	0	0	0	0	0	0	3	20	1

Rank among batters: 1,768 • *Top target (2 home runs)*: Bill Atkinson, Larry Christenson • *Number of pitchers victimized*: 19 • *Total ballparks homered in*: 7 • *First HR*: 06/28/1975 off Wayne Granger

Johnny Podres

JOHN JOSEPH PODRES
B: 09/30/1932
BL

Year	Tm	Lg	Tot	H	A	Men-On 0	1	2	3	One-Game 2	3	4	LO	XN	IP	PH	RHP	LHP
1962	LA	NL	1	0	1	1	0	0	0	0	0	0	0	0	0	0	1	0
1963	LA	NL	1	0	1	0	1	0	0	0	0	0	0	0	0	0	1	0
Total			2	0	2	1	1	0	0	0	0	0	0	0	0	0	2	0

Rank among batters: 4,129 • *Total ballparks homered in*: 2 • *First HR*: 08/14/1962 off Al McBean

Jimmy Pofahl

JAMES WILLARD POFAHL
B: 06/18/1917 D: 09/14/1984
BR

Year	Tm	Lg	Tot	H	A	Men-On 0	1	2	3	One-Game 2	3	4	LO	XN	IP	PH	RHP	LHP
1940	WAS	AL	2	2	0	2	0	0	0	0	0	0	0	0	2	0	1	1

Rank among batters: 4,129 • *Total ballparks homered in*: 1 • *First HR*: 05/09/1940 off Thornton Lee

John Poff

JOHN WILLIAM POFF
B: 10/23/1952
BL

Year	Tm	Lg	Tot	H	A	Men-On 0	1	2	3	One-Game 2	3	4	LO	XN	IP	PH	RHP	LHP
1980	MIL	AL	1	0	1	1	0	0	0	0	0	0	0	0	0	0	1	0

Rank among batters: 4,707 • *Total ballparks homered in*: 1 • *First HR*: 09/27/1980 off Rick Langford

Aaron Pointer

AARON ELTON POINTER
B: 04/19/1942
BR

Year	Tm	Lg	Tot	H	A	Men-On 0	1	2	3	One-Game 2	3	4	LO	XN	IP	PH	RHP	LHP
1966	HOU	NL	1	0	1	1	0	0	0	0	0	0	0	0	0	0	0	1

Year	Tm	Lg	Tot	H	A	Men-On 0	1	2	3	One-Game 2	3	4	LO	XN	IP	PH	RHP	LHP

Aaron Pointer *continued*

1967	HOU	NL	1	0	1	0	0	1	0	0	0	0	0	0	0	0	1	0
Total			2	0	2	1	0	1	0	0	0	0	0	0	0	0	1	1

Rank among batters: 4,129 • *Total ballparks homered in*: 1 • *First HR*: 09/29/1966 off Joe Nuxhall

Gus Polidor

GUSTAVO ADOLFO (GONZALEZ) POLIDOR
B: 10/26/1961 D: 04/28/1995
BR

1987	CAL	AL	2	0	2	2	0	0	0	0	0	0	0	0	0	0	1	1

Rank among batters: 4,129 • *Total ballparks homered in*: 2 • *First HR*: 07/27/1987 off Dave Stewart

Luis Polonia

LUIS ANDREW (ALMONTE) POLONIA
B: 12/10/1964
BL

1987	OAK	AL	4	1	3	2	2	0	0	0	0	0	1	0	0	0	4	0
1988	OAK	AL	2	1	1	1	1	0	0	0	0	0	0	0	0	0	2	0
1989	OAK	AL	1	0	1	0	1	0	0	0	0	0	0	0	0	0	1	0
	NY	AL	2	1	1	0	2	0	0	0	0	0	0	0	0	0	2	0
	Total		3	1	2	0	3	0	0	0	0	0	0	0	0	0	3	0
1990	CAL	AL	2	2	0	1	0	0	1	0	0	0	0	0	1	0	2	0
1991	CAL	AL	2	1	1	2	0	0	0	0	0	0	1	0	1	0	2	0
1993	CAL	AL	1	0	1	1	0	0	0	0	0	0	0	0	0	0	1	0
1994	NY	AL	1	0	1	0	1	0	0	0	0	0	0	0	0	0	1	0
1995	NY	AL	2	2	0	2	0	0	0	0	0	0	1	0	0	0	1	1
Total			17	8	9	9	7	0	1	0	0	0	3	0	2	0	16	1

Rank among batters: 1,969 • *Top target (2 home runs)*: Tim Leary • *Number of pitchers victimized*: 16 • *Total ballparks homered in*: 8 • *First HR*: 04/28/1987 off Calvin Schiraldi • *World Series HR—1*

Carlos Ponce

CARLOS ANTONIO (DIAZ) PONCE
B: 02/07/1959
BR

1985	MIL	AL	1	1	0	1	0	0	0	0	0	0	0	0	0	0	0	1

Rank among batters: 4,707 • *Total ballparks homered in*: 1 • *First HR*: 08/18/1985 off Britt Burns

Harlon Pool

HARLIN WELTY POOL
B: 03/12/1908 D: 02/15/1963
BL

1934	CIN	NL	2	0	2	0	1	0	1	0	0	0	0	0	0	0	2	0

Rank among batters: 4,129 • *Total ballparks homered in*: 2 • *First HR*: 07/08/1934 off Paul Dean

Ed Poole

EDWARD T. POOLE
B: 09/07/1874 D: 03/11/1919
BR

1900	PIT	NL	1	1	0	0	1	0	0	0	0	0	0	0	0	0	1	0
1901	PIT	NL	1	1	0	0	0	1	0	0	0	0	0	0	0	0	1	0
Total			2	2	0	0	1	1	0	0	0	0	0	0	0	0	2	0

Rank among batters: 4,129 • *Total ballparks homered in*: 1 • *First HR*: 10/12/1900 off Nixey Callahan

Jim Poole

JAMES ROBERT POOLE
B: 05/12/1895 D: 01/02/1975
BL

1925	PHI	AL	5	2	3	3	2	0	0	0	0	0	0	0	1	0	5	0
1926	PHI	AL	8	4	4	3	4	1	0	0	0	0	0	1	0	0	7	1
Total			13	6	7	6	6	1	0	0	0	0	0	1	1	0	12	1

Rank among batters: 2,248 • *Top target (2 home runs)*: Alex Ferguson • *Number of pitchers victimized*: 12 • *Total ballparks homered in*: 5 • *First HR*: 04/14/1925 off Alex Ferguson

Tom Poorman

THOMAS IVERSON POORMAN
B: 10/14/1857 D: 02/18/1905
BL

Year	Tm	Lg	Tot	H	A	Men-On 0	1	2	3	One-Game 2	3	4	LO	XN	IP	PH	RHP	LHP
1885	BOS	NL	3	0	3	0	3	0	0	0	0	0	0	0	0	0	3	0
1886	BOS	NL	3	3	0	1	2	0	0	0	0	0	0	0	0	0	3	0
1887	PHI	AA	4	3	1	2	2	0	0	0	0	0	1	0	1	0	4	0
1888	PHI	AA	2	1	1	0	1	1	0	0	0	0	0	0	0	0	2	0
Total			12	7	5	3	8	1	0	0	0	0	1	0	1	0	12	0

Rank among batters: 2,325 • *Top target (2 home runs)*: Mike Morrison • *Number of pitchers victimized*: 11 • *Total ballparks homered in*: 6 • *First HR*: 07/22/1885 off Pete Wood

Dave Pope

DAVID POPE
B: 06/17/1925
BL

Year	Tm	Lg	Tot	H	A	Men-On 0	1	2	3	One-Game 2	3	4	LO	XN	IP	PH	RHP	LHP
1952	CLE	AL	1	0	1	0	0	1	0	0	0	0	0	0	0	0	0	1
1954	CLE	AL	4	4	0	3	1	0	0	0	0	0	0	0	0	1	4	0
1955	CLE	AL	6	5	1	1	3	1	1	0	0	0	0	0	0	0	4	2
	BAL	AL	1	1	0	0	1	0	0	0	0	0	0	0	0	0	1	0
	Total		7	6	1	1	4	1	1	0	0	0	0	0	0	0	5	2
Total			12	10	2	4	5	2	1	0	0	0	0	0	0	1	9	3

Rank among batters: 2,325 • *Top target (2 home runs)*: Ned Garver • *Number of pitchers victimized*: 11 • *Total ballparks homered in*: 4 • *First HR*: 09/28/1952 off Ted Gray

Paul Popovich

PAUL EDWARD POPOVICH
B: 08/18/1940
BB

Year	Tm	Lg	Tot	H	A	Men-On 0	1	2	3	One-Game 2	3	4	LO	XN	IP	PH	RHP	LHP
1968	LA	NL	2	1	1	2	0	0	0	0	0	0	0	0	0	0	0	2
1969	CHI	NL	1	0	1	0	1	0	0	0	0	0	0	0	0	0	0	1
1970	CHI	NL	4	1	3	2	2	0	0	0	0	0	1	0	0	0	3	1
1971	CHI	NL	4	2	2	0	2	1	1	0	0	0	0	0	0	0	1	3
1972	CHI	NL	1	1	0	1	0	0	0	0	0	0	0	0	0	0	0	1
1973	CHI	NL	2	1	1	1	0	1	0	0	0	0	0	0	0	0	0	2
Total			14	6	8	6	5	2	1	0	0	0	1	0	0	0	4	10

Rank among batters: 2,169 • *Top target (2 home runs)*: Jerry Koosman • *Number of pitchers victimized*: 13 • *Total ballparks homered in*: 8 • *First HR*: 06/09/1968 off Woodie Fryman

Tom Poquette

THOMAS ARTHUR POQUETTE
B: 10/30/1951
BL

Year	Tm	Lg	Tot	H	A	Men-On 0	1	2	3	One-Game 2	3	4	LO	XN	IP	PH	RHP	LHP
1976	KC	AL	2	1	1	1	1	0	0	0	0	0	0	0	1	0	2	0
1977	KC	AL	2	1	1	1	1	0	0	0	0	0	1	0	0	0	2	0
1978	KC	AL	4	1	3	2	1	1	0	0	0	0	0	0	0	1	4	0
1979	BOS	AL	2	2	0	1	0	1	0	0	0	0	0	0	0	0	2	0
Total			10	5	5	5	3	2	0	0	0	0	1	0	1	1	10	0

Rank among batters: 2,500 • *Total ballparks homered in*: 7 • *First HR*: 06/15/1976 off Steve Grilli

Darrell Porter

DARRELL RAY PORTER
B: 01/17/1952
BL

Year	Tm	Lg	Tot	H	A	Men-On 0	1	2	3	One-Game 2	3	4	LO	XN	IP	PH	RHP	LHP
1971	MIL	AL	2	2	0	1	0	1	0	0	0	0	0	0	0	0	1	1
1972	MIL	AL	1	1	0	1	0	0	0	0	0	0	0	0	0	0	1	0
1973	MIL	AL	16	7	9	7	4	4	1	0	0	0	0	0	0	0	15	1
1974	MIL	AL	12	7	5	7	3	0	2	0	0	0	0	0	0	1	10	2
1975	MIL	AL	18	9	9	9	8	1	0	1	0	0	0	0	0	0	14	4
1976	MIL	AL	5	3	2	3	2	0	0	0	0	0	0	0	0	0	4	1
1977	KC	AL	16	4	12	11	5	0	0	2	0	0	0	0	0	0	13	3
1978	KC	AL	18	7	11	13	4	1	0	2	0	0	0	0	1	0	13	5
1979	KC	AL	20	8	12	11	4	5	0	0	0	0	0	0	0	0	14	6
1980	KC	AL	7	1	6	3	4	0	0	0	0	0	0	0	0	0	2	5
1981	STL	NL	6	2	4	4	1	0	1	0	0	0	0	0	0	0	5	1
1982	STL	NL	12	3	9	6	5	1	0	1	0	0	0	0	0	0	11	1

Darrell Porter *continued*

Year	Tm	Lg	Tot	H	A	Men-On 0	1	2	3	One-Game 2	3	4	LO	XN	IP	PH	RHP	LHP
1983	STL	NL	15	5	10	6	6	2	1	1	0	0	0	0	0	0	14	1
1984	STL	NL	11	4	7	3	6	1	1	0	0	0	0	1	0	0	6	5
1985	STL	NL	10	4	6	7	0	3	0	0	0	0	0	0	0	1	9	1
1986	TEX	AL	12	6	6	7	3	1	1	1	0	0	0	0	0	1	12	0
1987	TEX	AL	7	4	3	5	1	1	0	0	0	0	0	0	0	3	7	0
Total			188	77	111	104	56	21	7	8	0	0	0	1	1	6	151	37

Rank among batters: 207 • *Top target (5 home runs)*: Mike Krukow • *Number of pitchers victimized*: 147 • *Total ballparks homered in*: 26 • *First HR*: 09/14/1971 off Tom Bradley • *World Series HR*—1

Dick Porter

RICHARD TWILLEY PORTER
B: 12/30/1901 D: 09/24/1974
BL

Year	Tm	Lg	Tot	H	A	Men-On 0	1	2	3	One-Game 2	3	4	LO	XN	IP	PH	RHP	LHP
1929	CLE	AL	1	1	0	1	0	0	0	0	0	0	0	0	0	0	1	0
1930	CLE	AL	4	2	2	1	1	1	1	0	0	0	0	1	1	0	4	0
1931	CLE	AL	1	0	1	1	0	0	0	0	0	0	0	0	0	0	1	0
1932	CLE	AL	4	4	0	2	2	0	0	0	0	0	0	0	0	0	2	2
1934	CLE	AL	1	0	1	1	0	0	0	0	0	0	1	0	0	0	1	0
Total			11	7	4	6	3	1	1	0	0	0	1	1	1	0	9	2

Rank among batters: 2,419 • *Top target (2 home runs)*: Hank Johnson • *Number of pitchers victimized*: 10 • *Total ballparks homered in*: 5 • *First HR*: 07/13/1929 off Sam Jones

Henry Porter

HENRY PORTER
B: 06/ /1858 D: 12/30/1906
BR

Year	Tm	Lg	Tot	H	A	Men-On 0	1	2	3	One-Game 2	3	4	LO	XN	IP	PH	RHP	LHP
1887	BRO	AA	1	0	1	0	1	0	0	0	0	0	0	0	0	0	1	0

Rank among batters: 4,707 • *Total ballparks homered in*: 1 • *First HR*: 08/28/1887 off Guy Hecker

Jay Porter

J W PORTER
B: 01/17/1933
BR

Year	Tm	Lg	Tot	H	A	Men-On 0	1	2	3	One-Game 2	3	4	LO	XN	IP	PH	RHP	LHP
1957	DET	AL	2	2	0	1	1	0	0	0	0	0	0	0	0	0	1	1
1958	CLE	AL	4	3	1	1	2	1	0	0	0	0	0	0	0	2	2	2
1959	WAS	AL	1	1	0	1	0	0	0	0	0	0	0	0	0	0	1	0
	STL	NL	1	1	0	1	0	0	0	0	0	0	0	0	0	0	0	1
	Total		2	2	0	2	0	0	0	0	0	0	0	0	0	0	1	1
Total			8	7	1	4	3	1	0	0	0	0	0	0	0	2	4	4

Rank among batters: 2,703 • *Total ballparks homered in*: 4 • *First HR*: 06/07/1957 off Don Larsen

Bob Porterfield

ERWIN COOLEDGE PORTERFIELD
B: 08/10/1923 D: 04/28/1980
BR

Year	Tm	Lg	Tot	H	A	Men-On 0	1	2	3	One-Game 2	3	4	LO	XN	IP	PH	RHP	LHP
1953	WAS	AL	3	0	3	0	1	1	1	0	0	0	0	0	0	0	1	2
1954	WAS	AL	1	0	1	1	0	0	0	0	0	0	0	0	0	0	0	1
1956	BOS	AL	1	0	1	1	0	0	0	0	0	0	0	0	0	0	1	0
1958	PIT	NL	1	0	1	0	1	0	0	0	0	0	0	0	0	0	1	0
Total			6	0	6	2	2	1	1	0	0	0	0	0	0	0	3	3

Rank among batters: 2,988 • *Total ballparks homered in*: 4 • *First HR*: 05/05/1953 off Bill Wight

Arnie Portocarrero

ARNOLD MARIO PORTOCARRERO
B: 07/05/1931 D: 06/21/1986
BR

Year	Tm	Lg	Tot	H	A	Men-On 0	1	2	3	One-Game 2	3	4	LO	XN	IP	PH	RHP	LHP
1954	PHI	AL	1	1	0	1	0	0	0	0	0	0	0	0	0	0	1	0
1955	KC	AL	1	1	0	0	1	0	0	0	0	0	0	0	0	0	0	1
1958	BAL	AL	1	0	1	1	0	0	0	0	0	0	0	0	0	0	1	0
Total			3	2	1	2	1	0	0	0	0	0	0	0	0	0	2	1

Rank among batters: 3,735 • *Total ballparks homered in*: 3 • *First HR*: 06/06/1954 off Bob Feller

Mark Portugal

MARK STEVEN PORTUGAL
B: 10/30/1962
BR

Year	Tm	Lg	Tot	H	A	Men-On 0	1	2	3	One-Game 2	3	4	LO	XN	IP	PH	RHP	LHP
1989	HOU	NL	1	1	0	1	0	0	0	0	0	0	0	0	0	0	1	0
1993	HOU	NL	1	1	0	1	0	0	0	0	0	0	0	0	0	0	1	0
Total			2	2	0	2	0	0	0	0	0	0	0	0	0	0	2	0

Rank among batters: 4,129 • *Total ballparks homered in*: 1 • *First HR*: 09/08/1989 off Don Robinson

Leo Posada

LEOPOLDO JESUS (HERNANDEZ) POSADA
B: 04/15/1936
BR

Year	Tm	Lg	Tot	H	A	Men-On 0	1	2	3	One-Game 2	3	4	LO	XN	IP	PH	RHP	LHP
1960	KC	AL	1	1	0	1	0	0	0	0	0	0	0	0	0	0	1	0
1961	KC	AL	7	2	5	3	2	2	0	0	0	0	0	1	0	1	5	2
Total			8	3	5	4	2	2	0	0	0	0	0	1	0	1	6	2

Rank among batters: 2,703 • *Top target (2 home runs)*: Jim Perry • *Number of pitchers victimized*: 7 • *Total ballparks homered in*: 5 • *First HR*: 09/28/1960 off Jim Perry

Wally Post

WALTER CHARLES POST
B: 07/09/1929 D: 01/06/1982
BR

Year	Tm	Lg	Tot	H	A	Men-On 0	1	2	3	One-Game 2	3	4	LO	XN	IP	PH	RHP	LHP
1951	CIN	NL	1	1	0	0	0	1	0	0	0	0	0	0	0	0	0	1
1952	CIN	NL	2	2	0	2	0	0	0	0	0	0	0	0	0	0	1	1
1953	CIN	NL	1	0	1	0	1	0	0	0	0	0	0	0	0	0	0	1
1954	CIN	NL	18	8	10	10	5	3	0	2	0	0	0	0	1	0	12	6
1955	CIN	NL	40	25	15	21	13	6	0	4	0	0	0	0	0	0	23	17
1956	CIN	NL	36	23	13	24	6	5	1	5	0	0	0	0	0	0	25	11
1957	CIN	NL	20	13	7	9	7	2	2	0	0	0	0	1	0	0	17	3
1958	PHI	NL	12	5	7	5	6	0	1	0	0	0	0	1	1	3	7	5
1959	PHI	NL	22	11	11	11	10	1	0	2	0	0	0	0	0	1	10	12
1960	PHI	NL	2	0	2	1	1	0	0	0	0	0	0	0	0	0	1	1
	CIN	NL	17	11	6	12	3	2	0	1	0	0	0	0	0	2	5	12
	Total		19	11	8	13	4	2	0	1	0	0	0	0	0	2	6	13
1961	CIN	NL	20	9	11	9	7	4	0	0	0	0	0	0	0	1	4	16
1962	CIN	NL	17	10	7	10	3	4	0	0	0	0	0	0	0	3	4	13
1963	MIN	AL	2	1	1	1	1	0	0	0	0	0	0	0	0	0	0	2
Total			210	119	91	115	63	28	4	14	0	0	0	2	2	10	109	101

Rank among batters: 166 • *Top target (10 home runs)*: Warren Spahn • *Number of pitchers victimized*: 106 • *Total ballparks homered in*: 14 • *First HR*: 09/25/1951 off Max Lanier • *World Series HR*—1

John Potts

JOHN FREDERICK POTTS
B: 02/06/1887 D: 09/05/1962
BL

Year	Tm	Lg	Tot	H	A	Men-On 0	1	2	3	One-Game 2	3	4	LO	XN	IP	PH	RHP	LHP
1914	KC	FL	1	0	1	0	1	0	0	0	0	0	0	0	0	0	1	0

Rank among batters: 4,707 • *Total ballparks homered in*: 1 • *First HR*: 04/26/1914 off Tom McGuire

Alonzo Powell

ALONZO SIDNEY POWELL
B: 12/12/1964
BR

Year	Tm	Lg	Tot	H	A	Men-On 0	1	2	3	One-Game 2	3	4	LO	XN	IP	PH	RHP	LHP
1991	SEA	AL	3	1	2	2	1	0	0	0	0	0	0	0	0	0	0	3

Rank among batters: 3,735 • *Total ballparks homered in*: 3 • *First HR*: 07/01/1991 off Dave Wells

Boog Powell

JOHN WESLEY POWELL
B: 08/17/1941
BL

Year	Tm	Lg	Tot	H	A	Men-On 0	1	2	3	One-Game 2	3	4	LO	XN	IP	PH	RHP	LHP
1962	BAL	AL	15	12	3	4	9	1	1	2	0	0	0	0	0	0	12	3
1963	BAL	AL	25	9	16	14	11	0	0	2	1	0	0	0	0	0	21	4
1964	BAL	AL	39	16	23	21	16	2	0	4	1	0	0	1	0	0	35	4
1965	BAL	AL	17	10	7	8	6	3	0	1	0	0	0	0	0	1	14	3
1966	BAL	AL	34	11	23	15	16	2	1	3	1	0	0	1	0	1	25	9

Boog Powell *continued*

Year	Tm	Lg	Tot	H	A	Men-On 0	Men-On 1	Men-On 2	Men-On 3	One-Game 2	One-Game 3	One-Game 4	LO	XN	IP	PH	RHP	LHP
1967	BAL	AL	13	5	8	6	1	6	0	0	0	0	0	0	0	1	9	4
1968	BAL	AL	22	10	12	11	6	5	0	0	0	0	0	1	0	0	18	4
1969	BAL	AL	37	16	21	17	17	3	0	2	0	0	0	1	1	0	25	12
1970	BAL	AL	35	18	17	18	11	5	1	1	0	0	0	0	0	0	25	10
1971	BAL	AL	22	6	16	9	10	2	1	2	0	0	0	0	0	0	18	4
1972	BAL	AL	21	9	12	6	9	4	2	0	0	0	0	0	0	0	18	3
1973	BAL	AL	11	5	6	4	5	2	0	0	0	0	0	0	0	0	10	1
1974	BAL	AL	12	6	6	8	1	2	1	0	0	0	0	1	0	0	12	0
1975	CLE	AL	27	12	15	15	9	3	0	2	0	0	0	0	0	0	21	6
1976	CLE	AL	9	5	4	4	4	1	0	1	0	0	0	0	0	0	7	2
Total			339	150	189	160	131	41	7	20	3	0	0	5	1	3	270	69

Rank among batters: 48 • *Top target (9 home runs)*: Denny McLain, Luis Tiant • *Number of pitchers victimized*: 185 • *Total ballparks homered in*: 16 • *First HR*: 05/02/1962 off Jim Kaat • *World Series HR*—2; *LCS HR*—4

Hosken Powell

HOSKEN POWELL
B: 05/14/1955
BL

Year	Tm	Lg	Tot	H	A	Men-On 0	Men-On 1	Men-On 2	Men-On 3	One-Game 2	One-Game 3	One-Game 4	LO	XN	IP	PH	RHP	LHP
1978	MIN	AL	3	2	1	2	0	1	0	0	0	0	1	0	0	0	3	0
1979	MIN	AL	2	1	1	2	0	0	0	0	0	0	0	0	0	0	2	0
1980	MIN	AL	6	4	2	4	1	1	0	0	0	0	0	0	0	0	5	1
1981	MIN	AL	2	1	1	1	0	1	0	0	0	0	0	0	0	0	2	0
1982	TOR	AL	3	2	1	2	1	0	0	0	0	0	0	0	0	0	3	0
1983	TOR	AL	1	1	0	0	1	0	0	0	0	0	0	0	0	0	1	0
Total			17	11	6	11	3	3	0	0	0	0	1	0	0	0	16	1

Rank among batters: 1,969 • *Top target (2 home runs)*: Jim Palmer • *Number of pitchers victimized*: 16 • *Total ballparks homered in*: 7 • *First HR*: 05/16/1978 off Jim Palmer

Jack Powell

JOHN JOSEPH POWELL
B: 07/09/1874 D: 10/17/1944
BR

Year	Tm	Lg	Tot	H	A	Men-On 0	Men-On 1	Men-On 2	Men-On 3	One-Game 2	One-Game 3	One-Game 4	LO	XN	IP	PH	RHP	LHP
1899	STL	NL	1	1	0	1	0	0	0	0	0	0	0	1	0	0	1	0
1900	STL	NL	1	1	0	0	1	0	0	0	0	0	0	0	0	0	1	0
1901	STL	NL	2	2	0	2	0	0	0	0	0	0	0	0	2	0	2	0
1902	STL	AL	1	1	0	0	0	1	0	0	0	0	0	0	0	0	1	0
1905	NY	AL	1	1	0	1	0	0	0	0	0	0	0	0	0	0	0	1
1906	STL	AL	1	0	1	0	0	1	0	0	0	0	0	0	0	0	1	0
1912	STL	AL	1	1	0	0	1	0	0	0	0	0	0	0	0	0	1	0
Total			8	7	1	4	2	2	0	0	0	0	0	1	2	0	7	1

Rank among batters: 2,703 • *Total ballparks homered in*: 5 • *First HR*: 08/01/1899 off Kid Nichols

Jake Powell

ALVIN JACOB POWELL
B: 07/15/1908 D: 11/04/1948
BR

Year	Tm	Lg	Tot	H	A	Men-On 0	Men-On 1	Men-On 2	Men-On 3	One-Game 2	One-Game 3	One-Game 4	LO	XN	IP	PH	RHP	LHP
1935	WAS	AL	6	1	5	1	3	1	1	0	0	0	0	0	0	0	2	4
1936	WAS	AL	1	1	0	1	0	0	0	0	0	0	0	0	1	0	1	0
	NY	AL	7	3	4	2	3	1	1	0	0	0	0	0	0	0	3	4
	Total		8	4	4	3	3	1	1	0	0	0	0	0	1	0	4	4
1937	NY	AL	3	1	2	2	1	0	0	0	0	0	0	0	0	0	3	0
1938	NY	AL	2	0	2	2	0	0	0	0	0	0	0	0	0	0	1	1
1939	NY	AL	1	0	1	1	0	0	0	0	0	0	0	0	0	0	0	1
1944	WAS	AL	1	0	1	1	0	0	0	0	0	0	0	0	0	0	1	0
1945	PHI	NL	1	1	0	0	1	0	0	0	0	0	0	0	0	0	0	1
Total			22	7	15	10	8	2	2	0	0	0	0	0	1	0	11	11

Rank among batters: 1,719 • *Top target (2 home runs)*: Thornton Lee, Earl Whitehill • *Number of pitchers victimized*: 20 • *Total ballparks homered in*: 7 • *First HR*: 04/30/1935 off Johnny Broaca • *World Series HR*—1

Martin Powell

MARTIN J. POWELL
B: 03/25/1856 D: 02/05/1888
BL

Year	Tm	Lg	Tot	H	A	Men-On 0	Men-On 1	Men-On 2	Men-On 3	One-Game 2	One-Game 3	One-Game 4	LO	XN	IP	PH	RHP	LHP
1881	DET	NL	1	0	1	1	0	0	0	0	0	0	0	0	0	0	1	0

Martin Powell *continued*

Year	Tm	Lg	Tot	H	A	Men-On 0	1	2	3	One-Game 2	3	4	LO	XN	IP	PH	RHP	LHP
1883	DET	NL	1	1	0	1	0	0	0	0	0	0	0	0	1	0	1	0
1884	CIN	UA	1	1	0	1	0	0	0	0	0	0	0	0	0	0	0	0
Total			3	2	1	3	0	0	0	0	0	0	0	0	1	0	2	0

Rank among batters: 3,735 • *Total ballparks homered in*: 3 • *First HR*: 08/25/1881 off Larry Corcoran

Paul Powell

PAUL RAY POWELL
B: 03/19/1948
BR

Year	Tm	Lg	Tot	H	A	Men-On 0	1	2	3	One-Game 2	3	4	LO	XN	IP	PH	RHP	LHP
1971	MIN	AL	1	0	1	1	0	0	0	0	0	0	0	0	0	0	0	1

Rank among batters: 4,707 • *Total ballparks homered in*: 1 • *First HR*: 04/10/1971 off Don Eddy

Ray Powell

RAYMOND RAETH POWELL
B: 11/20/1888 D: 10/16/1962
BL

Year	Tm	Lg	Tot	H	A	Men-On 0	1	2	3	One-Game 2	3	4	LO	XN	IP	PH	RHP	LHP
1917	BOS	NL	4	3	1	2	1	1	0	0	0	0	0	0	3	0	3	1
1919	BOS	NL	2	2	0	2	0	0	0	0	0	0	0	0	2	0	1	1
1920	BOS	NL	6	0	6	5	0	1	0	0	0	0	2	0	1	0	5	1
1921	BOS	NL	12	5	7	5	3	4	0	0	0	0	1	0	5	0	9	3
1922	BOS	NL	6	2	4	6	0	0	0	0	0	0	0	0	2	0	6	0
1923	BOS	NL	4	0	4	1	1	2	0	0	0	0	0	0	0	0	4	0
1924	BOS	NL	1	1	0	0	1	0	0	0	0	0	0	0	0	1	1	0
Total			35	13	22	21	6	8	0	0	0	0	3	0	13	1	29	6

Rank among batters: 1,291 • *Top target (4 home runs)*: Jesse Haines • *Number of pitchers victimized*: 29 • *Total ballparks homered in*: 7 • *First HR*: 07/14/1917 off Gene Packard

Ted Power

TED HENRY POWER
B: 01/31/1955
BR

Year	Tm	Lg	Tot	H	A	Men-On 0	1	2	3	One-Game 2	3	4	LO	XN	IP	PH	RHP	LHP
1987	CIN	NL	1	1	0	1	0	0	0	0	0	0	0	0	0	0	1	0

Rank among batters: 4,707 • *Total ballparks homered in*: 1 • *First HR*: 07/11/1987 off Dennis Martinez

Vic Power

VICTOR PELLOT POWER
B: 11/01/1927
BR

Year	Tm	Lg	Tot	H	A	Men-On 0	1	2	3	One-Game 2	3	4	LO	XN	IP	PH	RHP	LHP
1954	PHI	AL	8	5	3	7	1	0	0	0	0	0	0	0	0	0	8	0
1955	KC	AL	19	12	7	14	5	0	0	1	0	0	2	1	0	0	14	5
1956	KC	AL	14	8	6	8	4	2	0	1	0	0	0	0	0	0	8	6
1957	KC	AL	14	7	7	9	4	1	0	1	0	0	2	1	0	0	12	2
1958	KC	AL	4	3	1	2	0	2	0	0	0	0	0	0	0	0	3	1
	CLE	AL	12	8	4	6	4	2	0	0	0	0	0	0	0	0	10	2
	Total		16	11	5	8	4	4	0	0	0	0	0	0	0	0	13	3
1959	CLE	AL	10	6	4	7	2	1	0	0	0	0	1	1	1	0	7	3
1960	CLE	AL	10	7	3	3	4	2	1	0	0	0	0	0	0	0	7	3
1961	CLE	AL	5	2	3	3	1	1	0	0	0	0	0	0	0	0	4	1
1962	MIN	AL	16	9	7	11	3	0	2	1	0	0	0	1	0	0	14	2
1963	MIN	AL	10	4	6	8	0	1	1	1	0	0	0	0	1	0	6	4
1964	LA	AL	3	0	3	2	1	0	0	0	0	0	0	0	0	0	2	1
1965	CAL	AL	1	0	1	1	0	0	0	0	0	0	0	0	0	0	0	1
Total			126	71	55	81	29	12	4	5	0	0	5	4	2	0	95	31

Rank among batters: 360 • *Top target (6 home runs)*: Tom Brewer • *Number of pitchers victimized*: 81 • *Total ballparks homered in*: 11 • *First HR*: 05/05/1954 off Bob Lemon

John Powers

JOHN CALVIN POWERS
B: 07/08/1929
BL

Year	Tm	Lg	Tot	H	A	Men-On 0	1	2	3	One-Game 2	3	4	LO	XN	IP	PH	RHP	LHP
1957	PIT	NL	2	1	1	1	0	1	0	0	0	0	0	0	0	1	2	0
1958	PIT	NL	2	2	0	2	0	0	0	0	0	0	0	0	0	1	2	0

John Powers *continued*

						Men-On				One-Game								
Year	Tm	Lg	Tot	H	A	0	1	2	3	2	3	4	LO	XN	IP	PH	RHP	LHP
1959	CIN	NL	2	2	0	2	0	0	0	0	0	0	0	0	0	2	2	0
Total			6	5	1	5	0	1	0	0	0	0	0	0	0	4	6	0

Rank among batters: 2,988 • *Total ballparks homered in*: 3 • *First HR*: 05/02/1957 off Lew Burdette

Mike Powers

MICHAEL RILEY POWERS
B: 09/22/1870 D: 04/26/1909
BR

Year	Tm	Lg	Tot	H	A	0	1	2	3	2	3	4	LO	XN	IP	PH	RHP	LHP
1898	LOU	NL	1	1	0	0	0	1	0	0	0	0	0	0	0	0	0	0
1901	PHI	AL	1	0	1	0	1	0	0	0	0	0	0	0	0	0	1	0
1902	PHI	AL	2	0	2	1	1	0	0	0	0	0	0	0	0	0	2	0
Total			4	1	3	1	2	1	0	0	0	0	0	0	0	0	3	0

Rank among batters: 3,427 • *Total ballparks homered in*: 3 • *First HR*: 09/04/1898 off Jim Callahan

Johnny Pramesa

JOHN STEVEN PRAMESA
B: 08/28/1925
BR

Year	Tm	Lg	Tot	H	A	0	1	2	3	2	3	4	LO	XN	IP	PH	RHP	LHP
1949	CIN	NL	1	1	0	1	0	0	0	0	0	0	0	0	0	0	0	1
1950	CIN	NL	5	1	4	1	4	0	0	0	0	0	0	0	1	0	4	1
1951	CIN	NL	6	4	2	3	2	0	1	0	0	0	0	1	0	0	4	2
1952	CHI	NL	1	0	1	1	0	0	0	0	0	0	0	0	0	0	0	1
Total			13	6	7	6	6	0	1	0	0	0	0	1	1	0	8	5

Rank among batters: 2,248 • *Top target (2 home runs)*: Sal Maglie, Dave Koslo • *Number of pitchers victimized*: 11 • *Total ballparks homered in*: 4 • *First HR*: 09/21/1949 off Dave Koslo

Del Pratt

DERRILL BURNHAM PRATT
B: 01/10/1888 D: 09/30/1977
BR

Year	Tm	Lg	Tot	H	A	0	1	2	3	2	3	4	LO	XN	IP	PH	RHP	LHP
1912	STL	AL	5	2	3	4	1	0	0	0	0	0	0	0	1	0	4	1
1913	STL	AL	2	0	2	1	0	1	0	0	0	0	0	0	0	0	2	0
1914	STL	AL	5	3	2	3	2	0	0	0	0	0	0	0	1	0	3	2
1915	STL	AL	3	1	2	2	1	0	0	0	0	0	0	0	1	0	2	1
1916	STL	AL	5	3	2	4	1	0	0	0	0	0	0	0	0	0	4	1
1917	STL	AL	1	0	1	0	1	0	0	0	0	0	0	0	0	0	1	0
1918	NY	AL	2	1	1	0	2	0	0	0	0	0	0	0	0	0	0	2
1919	NY	AL	4	3	1	3	1	0	0	0	0	0	0	0	2	0	3	1
1920	NY	AL	4	3	1	1	0	2	1	0	0	0	0	0	0	0	2	2
1921	BOS	AL	5	0	5	2	2	1	0	0	0	0	0	1	0	0	5	0
1922	BOS	AL	6	1	5	2	3	1	0	0	0	0	0	1	0	0	6	0
1924	DET	AL	1	1	0	1	0	0	0	0	0	0	0	0	0	0	1	0
Total			43	18	25	23	14	5	1	0	0	0	0	2	5	0	33	10

Rank among batters: 1,116 • *Top target (3 home runs)*: Rollie Naylor • *Number of pitchers victimized*: 37 • *Total ballparks homered in*: 7 • *First HR*: 05/05/1912 off Ed Willett

Larry Pratt

LESTER JOHN PRATT
B: 10/08/1886 D: 01/08/1969
BR

Year	Tm	Lg	Tot	H	A	0	1	2	3	2	3	4	LO	XN	IP	PH	RHP	LHP
1915	BRO	FL	1	0	1	1	0	0	0	0	0	0	0	0	0	0	1	0

Rank among batters: 4,707 • *Total ballparks homered in*: 1 • *First HR*: 05/22/1915 off Mordecai Brown

Todd Pratt

TODD ALAN PRATT
B: 02/09/1967
BR

Year	Tm	Lg	Tot	H	A	0	1	2	3	2	3	4	LO	XN	IP	PH	RHP	LHP
1992	PHI	NL	2	2	0	1	0	1	0	0	0	0	0	0	0	0	2	0
1993	PHI	NL	5	4	1	3	2	0	0	1	0	0	0	0	0	0	1	4
1994	PHI	NL	2	1	1	1	1	0	0	0	0	0	0	0	0	0	2	0
Total			9	7	2	5	3	1	0	1	0	0	0	0	0	0	5	4

Rank among batters: 2,587 • *Total ballparks homered in*: 3 • *First HR*: 08/09/1992 off Mark Gardner

Jim Presley

JAMES ARTHUR PRESLEY
B: 10/23/1961
BR

Year	Tm	Lg	Tot	H	A	Men-On 0	Men-On 1	Men-On 2	Men-On 3	One-Game 2	One-Game 3	One-Game 4	LO	XN	IP	PH	RHP	LHP
1984	SEA	AL	10	5	5	6	3	0	1	1	0	0	0	0	0	0	6	4
1985	SEA	AL	28	12	16	16	9	3	0	1	0	0	0	0	0	0	20	8
1986	SEA	AL	27	16	11	14	9	2	2	1	1	0	0	2	0	0	21	6
1987	SEA	AL	24	11	13	11	10	3	0	3	0	0	0	1	0	1	19	5
1988	SEA	AL	14	7	7	7	5	2	0	0	0	0	0	0	0	0	12	2
1989	SEA	AL	12	7	5	8	4	0	0	0	0	0	0	1	0	1	8	4
1990	ATL	NL	19	10	9	16	2	1	0	2	0	0	0	0	0	0	13	6
1991	SD	NL	1	0	1	1	0	0	0	0	0	0	0	0	0	0	0	1
Total			135	68	67	79	42	11	3	8	1	0	0	4	0	2	99	36

Rank among batters: 326 • *Top target (5 home runs)*: Doyle Alexander • *Number of pitchers victimized*: 107 • *Total ballparks homered in*: 21 • *First HR*: 06/29/1984 off Bobby Ojeda

Walt Preston

WALTER B. PRESTON
B: 1870 BL

Year	Tm	Lg	Tot	H	A	Men-On 0	Men-On 1	Men-On 2	Men-On 3	One-Game 2	One-Game 3	One-Game 4	LO	XN	IP	PH	RHP	LHP
1895	LOU	NL	1	0	1	1	0	0	0	0	0	0	0	0	0	0	1	0

Rank among batters: 4,707 • *Total ballparks homered in*: 1 • *First HR*: 06/18/1895 off Ed Stein

Jim Price

JIMMIE WILLIAM PRICE
B: 10/13/1941
BR

Year	Tm	Lg	Tot	H	A	Men-On 0	Men-On 1	Men-On 2	Men-On 3	One-Game 2	One-Game 3	One-Game 4	LO	XN	IP	PH	RHP	LHP
1968	DET	AL	3	1	2	3	0	0	0	0	0	0	0	1	0	1	1	2
1969	DET	AL	9	8	1	6	2	1	0	0	0	0	0	0	0	1	2	7
1970	DET	AL	5	2	3	3	1	0	1	0	0	0	0	0	0	0	2	3
1971	DET	AL	1	0	1	0	1	0	0	0	0	0	0	0	0	0	1	0
Total			18	11	7	12	4	1	1	0	0	0	0	1	0	2	6	12

Rank among batters: 1,914 • *Top target (2 home runs)*: Mike Paul • *Number of pitchers victimized*: 17 • *Total ballparks homered in*: 5 • *First HR*: 06/24/1968 off Mike Paul

Bob Priddy

ROBERT SIMPSON PRIDDY
B: 12/10/1939
BR

Year	Tm	Lg	Tot	H	A	Men-On 0	Men-On 1	Men-On 2	Men-On 3	One-Game 2	One-Game 3	One-Game 4	LO	XN	IP	PH	RHP	LHP
1968	CHI	AL	1	1	0	1	0	0	0	0	0	0	0	0	0	0	1	0

Rank among batters: 4,707 • *Total ballparks homered in*: 1 • *First HR*: 06/19/1968 off Luis Tiant

Jerry Priddy

GERALD EDWARD PRIDDY
B: 11/09/1919 D: 03/03/1980
BR

Year	Tm	Lg	Tot	H	A	Men-On 0	Men-On 1	Men-On 2	Men-On 3	One-Game 2	One-Game 3	One-Game 4	LO	XN	IP	PH	RHP	LHP
1941	NY	AL	1	0	1	0	0	1	0	0	0	0	0	0	0	0	1	0
1942	NY	AL	2	0	2	2	0	0	0	0	0	0	0	0	0	1	2	0
1943	WAS	AL	4	2	2	2	2	0	0	0	0	0	0	0	0	0	3	1
1946	WAS	AL	6	1	5	4	1	1	0	1	0	0	0	1	1	0	2	4
1947	WAS	AL	3	0	3	2	0	1	0	0	0	0	0	0	0	0	1	2
1948	STL	AL	8	5	3	4	4	0	0	1	0	0	0	0	0	0	5	3
1949	STL	AL	11	7	4	7	4	0	0	0	0	0	0	0	0	0	8	3
1950	DET	AL	13	8	5	8	4	1	0	0	0	0	1	0	0	0	9	4
1951	DET	AL	8	4	4	6	2	0	0	0	0	0	2	0	0	0	3	5
1952	DET	AL	4	2	2	3	1	0	0	0	0	0	1	0	0	0	3	1
1953	DET	AL	1	1	0	1	0	0	0	0	0	0	0	0	0	0	1	0
Total			61	30	31	39	18	4	0	2	0	0	4	1	1	1	38	23

Rank among batters: 844 • *Top target (3 home runs)*: Chuck Stobbs, Early Wynn • *Number of pitchers victimized*: 51 • *Total ballparks homered in*: 8 • *First HR*: 05/06/1941 off Johnny Gorsica

Curtis Pride

CURTIS JOHN PRIDE
B: 12/17/1968
BL

Year	Tm	Lg	Tot	H	A	Men-On 0	Men-On 1	Men-On 2	Men-On 3	One-Game 2	One-Game 3	One-Game 4	LO	XN	IP	PH	RHP	LHP
1993	MON	NL	1	0	1	0	1	0	0	0	0	0	0	0	0	1	1	0

Rank among batters: 4,707 • *Total ballparks homered in*: 1 • *First HR*: 09/30/1993 off Richie Lewis

Tom Prince

THOMAS ALBERT PRINCE
B: 08/13/1964
BR

Year	Tm	Lg	Tot	H	A	Men-On 0	Men-On 1	Men-On 2	Men-On 3	One-Game 2	One-Game 3	One-Game 4	LO	XN	IP	PH	RHP	LHP
1987	PIT	NL	1	0	1	0	1	0	0	0	0	0	0	0	0	0	0	1
1991	PIT	NL	1	0	1	1	0	0	0	0	0	0	0	0	0	0	0	1
1993	PIT	NL	2	2	0	0	0	2	0	0	0	0	0	0	1	0	2	0
1995	LA	NL	1	0	1	1	0	0	0	0	0	0	0	0	0	0	1	0
Total			5	2	3	2	1	2	0	0	0	0	0	0	1	0	3	2

Rank among batters: 3,191 • *Total ballparks homered in*: 3 • *First HR*: 09/27/1987 off Bobby Ojeda

Walter Prince

WALTER FARR PRINCE
B: 05/09/1861 D: 03/02/1938
BL

Year	Tm	Lg	Tot	H	A	Men-On 0	Men-On 1	Men-On 2	Men-On 3	One-Game 2	One-Game 3	One-Game 4	LO	XN	IP	PH	RHP	LHP
1884	WAS	AA	1	1	0	0	1	0	0	0	0	0	0	0	0	0	0	0

Rank among batters: 4,707 • *Total ballparks homered in*: 1 • *First HR*: 07/21/1884 off Fleury Sullivan

George Proeser

GEORGE PROESER
B: 05/30/1864 D: 10/13/1941
BL

Year	Tm	Lg	Tot	H	A	Men-On 0	Men-On 1	Men-On 2	Men-On 3	One-Game 2	One-Game 3	One-Game 4	LO	XN	IP	PH	RHP	LHP
1890	SYR	AA	1	0	1	0	0	1	0	0	0	0	0	0	0	0	1	0

Rank among batters: 4,707 • *Total ballparks homered in*: 1 • *First HR*: 07/04/1890 off Fred Smith

Ron Pruitt

RONALD RALPH PRUITT
B: 10/21/1951
BR

Year	Tm	Lg	Tot	H	A	Men-On 0	Men-On 1	Men-On 2	Men-On 3	One-Game 2	One-Game 3	One-Game 4	LO	XN	IP	PH	RHP	LHP
1977	CLE	AL	2	1	1	1	0	1	0	0	0	0	0	0	0	0	1	1
1978	CLE	AL	6	6	0	5	0	1	0	0	0	0	0	0	0	0	3	3
1979	CLE	AL	2	0	2	0	2	0	0	0	0	0	0	0	0	0	0	2
1980	CHI	AL	2	1	1	2	0	0	0	0	0	0	0	0	0	0	0	2
Total			12	8	4	8	2	2	0	0	0	0	0	0	0	0	4	8

Rank among batters: 2,325 • *Total ballparks homered in*: 5 • *First HR*: 08/06/1977 off Tom Burgmeier

Greg Pryor

GREGORY RUSSELL PRYOR
B: 10/02/1949
BR

Year	Tm	Lg	Tot	H	A	Men-On 0	Men-On 1	Men-On 2	Men-On 3	One-Game 2	One-Game 3	One-Game 4	LO	XN	IP	PH	RHP	LHP
1978	CHI	AL	2	2	0	1	1	0	0	1	0	0	0	0	0	0	2	0
1979	CHI	AL	3	1	2	3	0	0	0	0	0	0	0	0	0	0	3	0
1980	CHI	AL	1	1	0	0	1	0	0	0	0	0	0	0	0	1	0	1
1982	KC	AL	2	0	2	2	0	0	0	0	0	0	0	0	0	0	0	2
1983	KC	AL	1	0	1	0	0	1	0	0	0	0	0	0	0	0	1	0
1984	KC	AL	4	4	0	3	0	1	0	0	0	0	0	1	0	0	1	3
1985	KC	AL	1	0	1	1	0	0	0	0	0	0	0	0	0	0	1	0
Total			14	8	6	10	2	2	0	1	0	0	0	1	0	1	8	6

Rank among batters: 2,169 • *Top target (2 home runs)*: Jim Colborn • *Number of pitchers victimized*: 13 • *Total ballparks homered in*: 6 • *First HR*: 09/08/1978 off Jim Colborn

George Puccinelli

GEORGE LAWRENCE PUCCINELLI
B: 06/22/1907 D: 04/16/1956
BR

Year	Tm	Lg	Tot	H	A	Men-On 0	Men-On 1	Men-On 2	Men-On 3	One-Game 2	One-Game 3	One-Game 4	LO	XN	IP	PH	RHP	LHP
1930	STL	NL	3	0	3	0	2	1	0	0	0	0	0	0	0	2	0	3
1932	STL	NL	3	2	1	1	2	0	0	0	0	0	0	0	0	0	2	1
1934	STL	AL	2	0	2	1	1	0	0	1	0	0	0	0	0	0	2	0
1936	PHI	AL	11	7	4	7	4	0	0	1	0	0	0	0	0	0	11	0
Total			19	9	10	9	9	1	0	2	0	0	0	0	0	2	15	4

Rank among batters: 1,861 • *Top target (2 home runs)*: Ted Lyons, Red Ruffing • *Number of pitchers victimized*: 17 • *Total ballparks homered in*: 10 • *First HR*: 07/21/1930 off Watty Clark

Kirby Puckett

KIRBY PUCKETT
B: 03/14/1961
BR

Year	Tm	Lg	Tot	H	A	Men-On 0	1	2	3	One-Game 2	3	4	LO	XN	IP	PH	RHP	LHP
1985	MIN	AL	4	2	2	1	1	2	0	0	0	0	0	0	0	0	0	4
1986	MIN	AL	31	14	17	18	9	4	0	1	0	0	4	0	0	0	25	6
1987	MIN	AL	28	18	10	20	7	1	0	2	0	0	0	0	0	0	17	11
1988	MIN	AL	24	13	11	16	8	0	0	2	0	0	0	0	0	0	16	8
1989	MIN	AL	9	7	2	5	3	1	0	0	0	0	0	1	0	0	8	1
1990	MIN	AL	12	6	6	5	4	3	0	2	0	0	0	0	0	0	8	4
1991	MIN	AL	15	7	8	10	5	0	0	0	0	0	0	0	0	0	8	7
1992	MIN	AL	19	9	10	9	6	1	3	1	0	0	0	0	0	0	16	3
1993	MIN	AL	22	12	10	10	8	2	2	2	0	0	0	0	0	0	15	7
1994	MIN	AL	20	12	8	7	9	3	1	2	0	0	0	0	0	0	12	8
1995	MIN	AL	23	13	10	10	6	6	1	1	0	0	0	0	0	0	17	6
Total			207	113	94	111	66	23	7	13	0	0	4	1	0	0	142	65

Rank among batters: 169 • *Top target (4 home runs)*: Doyle Alexander, Frank Tanana, Bobby Witt • *Number of pitchers victimized*: 147 • *Total ballparks homered in*: 19 • *First HR*: 04/22/1985 off Matt Young • *Hit for Cycle*—vs OAK: 08/01/1986 • *World Series HR*—2; *LCS HR*—3; *All-Star HR*—1

Terry Puhl

TERRY STEPHEN PUHL
B: 07/08/1956
BL

Year	Tm	Lg	Tot	H	A	Men-On 0	1	2	3	One-Game 2	3	4	LO	XN	IP	PH	RHP	LHP
1978	HOU	NL	3	1	2	3	0	0	0	0	0	0	2	0	0	0	1	2
1979	HOU	NL	8	2	6	7	1	0	0	0	0	0	4	0	0	0	6	2
1980	HOU	NL	13	4	9	12	1	0	0	1	0	0	5	0	0	0	10	3
1981	HOU	NL	3	1	2	2	0	1	0	0	0	0	1	0	0	0	3	0
1982	HOU	NL	8	5	3	5	2	0	1	1	0	0	1	0	0	0	6	2
1983	HOU	NL	8	1	7	6	2	0	0	0	0	0	0	0	1	0	8	0
1984	HOU	NL	9	2	7	7	2	0	0	0	0	0	0	0	0	0	8	1
1985	HOU	NL	2	1	1	2	0	0	0	0	0	0	0	0	0	0	2	0
1986	HOU	NL	3	1	2	1	1	0	1	0	0	0	0	0	0	0	3	0
1987	HOU	NL	2	1	1	0	0	1	1	0	0	0	0	0	0	0	2	0
1988	HOU	NL	3	2	1	3	0	0	0	0	0	0	0	0	0	0	3	0
Total			62	21	41	48	9	2	3	2	0	0	13	0	1	0	52	10

Rank among batters: 835 • *Top target (3 home runs)*: Phil Niekro, Larry McWilliams • *Number of pitchers victimized*: 51 • *Total ballparks homered in*: 12 • *First HR*: 04/06/1978 off Tom Seaver

Luis Pujols

LUIS BIENVENIDO (TORIBIO) PUJOLS
B: 11/18/1955
BR

Year	Tm	Lg	Tot	H	A	Men-On 0	1	2	3	One-Game 2	3	4	LO	XN	IP	PH	RHP	LHP
1978	HOU	NL	1	0	1	0	1	0	0	0	0	0	0	0	0	0	1	0
1981	HOU	NL	1	1	0	1	0	0	0	0	0	0	0	0	0	0	0	1
1982	HOU	NL	4	1	3	4	0	0	0	0	0	0	0	0	0	0	3	1
Total			6	2	4	5	1	0	0	0	0	0	0	0	0	0	4	2

Rank among batters: 2,988 • *Total ballparks homered in*: 4 • *First HR*: 07/14/1978 off Hal Dues

Charlie Puleo

CHARLES MICHAEL PULEO
B: 02/07/1955
BR

Year	Tm	Lg	Tot	H	A	Men-On 0	1	2	3	One-Game 2	3	4	LO	XN	IP	PH	RHP	LHP
1987	ATL	NL	1	0	1	1	0	0	0	0	0	0	0	0	0	0	1	0

Rank among batters: 4,707 • *Total ballparks homered in*: 1 • *First HR*: 05/24/1987 off Rick Sutcliffe

Harvey Pulliam

HARVEY JEROME PULLIAM
B: 10/20/1967
BR

Year	Tm	Lg	Tot	H	A	Men-On 0	1	2	3	One-Game 2	3	4	LO	XN	IP	PH	RHP	LHP
1991	KC	AL	3	2	1	2	1	0	0	1	0	0	0	0	1	0	0	3
1993	KC	AL	1	0	1	0	1	0	0	0	0	0	0	0	0	0	0	1
1995	COL	NL	1	1	0	1	0	0	0	0	0	0	0	0	0	1	0	1
Total			5	3	2	3	2	0	0	1	0	0	0	0	1	1	0	5

Rank among batters: 3,191 • *Top target (2 home runs)*: Wilson Alvarez • *Number of pitchers victimized*: 4 • *Total ballparks homered in*: 4 • *First HR*: 08/13/1991 off Jeff Johnson

Blondie Purcell

WILLIAM ALOYSIUS PURCELL
B: 03/16/1854 D: 02/20/1912
BR

Year	Tm	Lg	Tot	H	A	Men-On 0	Men-On 1	Men-On 2	Men-On 3	One-Game 2	One-Game 3	One-Game 4	LO	XN	IP	PH	RHP	LHP
1880	CIN	NL	1	0	1	1	0	0	0	0	0	0	0	0	0	0	1	0
1882	BUF	NL	2	1	1	2	0	0	0	0	0	0	1	0	0	0	2	0
1883	PHI	NL	1	0	1	0	0	1	0	0	0	0	0	0	0	0	1	0
1884	PHI	NL	1	0	1	1	0	0	0	0	0	0	0	0	0	0	1	0
1887	BAL	AA	4	2	2	2	1	1	0	0	0	0	0	0	1	0	1	2
1888	BAL	AA	2	1	1	2	0	0	0	0	0	0	1	0	0	0	2	0
1890	PHI	AA	2	2	0	0	2	0	0	0	0	0	0	0	0	0	2	0
Total			13	6	7	8	3	2	0	0	0	0	2	0	1	0	10	1

Rank among batters: 2,248 • *Total ballparks homered in*: 8 • *First HR*: 07/24/1880 off Monte Ward

Pid Purdy

EVERETT VIRGIL PURDY
B: 06/15/1904 D: 01/16/1951
BL

Year	Tm	Lg	Tot	H	A	Men-On 0	Men-On 1	Men-On 2	Men-On 3	One-Game 2	One-Game 3	One-Game 4	LO	XN	IP	PH	RHP	LHP
1927	CIN	NL	1	0	1	0	1	0	0	0	0	0	0	0	0	0	1	0
1929	CIN	NL	1	0	1	1	0	0	0	0	0	0	0	0	0	0	1	0
Total			2	0	2	1	1	0	0	0	0	0	0	0	0	0	2	0

Rank among batters: 4,129 • *Total ballparks homered in*: 2 • *First HR*: 09/05/1927 off Lee Meadows

Bob Purkey

ROBERT THOMAS PURKEY
B: 07/14/1929
BR

Year	Tm	Lg	Tot	H	A	Men-On 0	Men-On 1	Men-On 2	Men-On 3	One-Game 2	One-Game 3	One-Game 4	LO	XN	IP	PH	RHP	LHP
1955	PIT	NL	1	1	0	1	0	0	0	0	0	0	0	0	0	0	0	1
1958	CIN	NL	1	0	1	1	0	0	0	0	0	0	0	0	0	0	1	0
1959	CIN	NL	1	1	0	0	0	0	1	0	0	0	0	0	0	0	1	0
1961	CIN	NL	1	0	1	1	0	0	0	0	0	0	0	0	0	0	1	0
1962	CIN	NL	2	1	1	2	0	0	0	0	0	0	0	0	0	0	1	1
Total			6	3	3	5	0	0	1	0	0	0	0	0	0	0	4	2

Rank among batters: 2,988 • *Total ballparks homered in*: 4 • *First HR*: 06/05/1955 off Jackie Collum

Billy Purtell

WILLIAM PATRICK PURTELL
B: 01/06/1886 D: 03/17/1962
BR

Year	Tm	Lg	Tot	H	A	Men-On 0	Men-On 1	Men-On 2	Men-On 3	One-Game 2	One-Game 3	One-Game 4	LO	XN	IP	PH	RHP	LHP
1910	CHI	AL	1	0	1	0	1	0	0	0	0	0	0	0	0	0	1	0
	BOS	AL	1	1	0	0	0	0	1	0	0	0	0	0	0	0	1	0
	Total		2	1	1	0	1	1	0	0	0	0	0	0	0	0	2	0
Total			2	1	1	0	1	1	0	0	0	0	0	0	0	0	2	0

Rank among batters: 4,129 • *Total ballparks homered in*: 2 • *First HR*: 07/25/1910 off Doc Reisling

Ed Putman

EDDY WILLIAM PUTMAN
B: 09/25/1953
BR

Year	Tm	Lg	Tot	H	A	Men-On 0	Men-On 1	Men-On 2	Men-On 3	One-Game 2	One-Game 3	One-Game 4	LO	XN	IP	PH	RHP	LHP
1979	DET	AL	2	0	2	1	1	0	0	0	0	0	0	0	0	0	2	0

Rank among batters: 4,129 • *Total ballparks homered in*: 2 • *First HR*: 07/31/1979 off Doc Medich

Pat Putnam

PATRICK EDWARD PUTNAM
B: 12/03/1953
BL

Year	Tm	Lg	Tot	H	A	Men-On 0	Men-On 1	Men-On 2	Men-On 3	One-Game 2	One-Game 3	One-Game 4	LO	XN	IP	PH	RHP	LHP
1978	TEX	AL	1	1	0	1	0	0	0	0	0	0	0	0	0	0	1	0
1979	TEX	AL	18	7	11	11	5	2	0	1	0	0	0	0	0	2	17	1
1980	TEX	AL	13	7	6	8	4	1	0	1	0	0	0	1	0	2	12	1
1981	TEX	AL	8	3	5	5	1	2	0	1	0	0	0	1	0	0	7	1
1982	TEX	AL	2	1	1	2	0	0	0	0	0	0	0	0	0	0	2	0
1983	SEA	AL	19	11	8	9	8	2	0	1	0	0	0	0	0	1	17	2
1984	SEA	AL	2	1	1	0	1	1	0	0	0	0	0	0	0	0	2	0
Total			63	31	32	36	19	8	0	4	0	0	0	2	0	5	58	5

Rank among batters: 826 • *Top target (3 home runs)*: Dennis Leonard, Pete Redfern, Dave Stieb • *Number of pitchers victimized*: 47 • *Total ballparks homered in*: 14 • *First HR*: 09/24/1978 off Jim Colborn

Year	Tm	Lg	Tot	H	A	Men-On				One-Game			LO	XN	IP	PH	RHP	LHP
						0	1	2	3	2	3	4						

Jim Pyburn

JAMES EDWARD PYBURN
B: 11/01/1932
BR

Year	Tm	Lg	Tot	H	A	0	1	2	3	2	3	4	LO	XN	IP	PH	RHP	LHP
1956	BAL	AL	2	0	2	1	1	0	0	0	0	0	0	0	0	0	2	0
1957	BAL	AL	1	0	1	0	1	0	0	0	0	0	0	0	0	0	0	1
Total			3	0	3	1	2	0	0	0	0	0	0	0	0	0	2	1

Rank among batters: 3,735 • *Total ballparks homered in*: 3 • *First HR*: 04/27/1956 off Dick Brodowski

Shadow Pyle

HARRY THOMAS PYLE
B: 11/29/1861 D: 12/26/1908

Year	Tm	Lg	Tot	H	A	0	1	2	3	2	3	4	LO	XN	IP	PH	RHP	LHP
1887	CHI	NL	1	1	0	0	1	0	0	0	0	0	0	0	0	0	1	0

Rank among batters: 4,707 • *Total ballparks homered in*: 1 • *First HR*: 05/10/1887 off Egyptian Healy

Frankie Pytlak

FRANK ANTHONY PYTLAK
B: 07/30/1908 D: 05/08/1977
BR

Year	Tm	Lg	Tot	H	A	0	1	2	3	2	3	4	LO	XN	IP	PH	RHP	LHP
1933	CLE	AL	2	1	1	1	0	1	0	0	0	0	0	0	0	0	2	0
1935	CLE	AL	1	0	1	1	0	0	0	0	0	0	0	0	0	0	0	1
1937	CLE	AL	1	0	1	0	1	0	0	0	0	0	0	0	1	0	1	0
1938	CLE	AL	1	0	1	1	0	0	0	0	0	0	0	0	1	0	1	0
1941	BOS	AL	2	0	2	2	0	0	0	0	0	0	0	0	0	0	2	0
Total			7	1	6	5	1	1	0	0	0	0	0	0	2	0	6	1

Rank among batters: 2,834 • *Top target (2 home runs)*: Bump Hadley • *Number of pitchers victimized*: 6 • *Total ballparks homered in*: 6 • *First HR*: 04/25/1933 off Bump Hadley

Mel Queen

MELVIN DOUGLAS QUEEN
B: 03/26/1942
BL

Year	Tm	Lg	Tot	H	A	0	1	2	3	2	3	4	LO	XN	IP	PH	RHP	LHP
1964	CIN	NL	2	1	1	0	1	1	0	0	0	0	0	0	0	1	2	0

Rank among batters: 4,129 • *Total ballparks homered in*: 2 • *First HR*: 07/14/1964 off Gordon Jones

George Quellich

GEORGE WILLIAM QUELLICH
B: 02/10/1903 D: 08/21/1958
BR

Year	Tm	Lg	Tot	H	A	0	1	2	3	2	3	4	LO	XN	IP	PH	RHP	LHP
1931	DET	AL	1	1	0	0	1	0	0	0	0	0	0	0	0	0	1	0

Rank among batters: 4,707 • *Total ballparks homered in*: 1 • *First HR*: 08/03/1931 off Red Faber

Joe Quest

JOSEPH L. QUEST
B: 11/16/1852 D: 11/14/1924
BR

Year	Tm	Lg	Tot	H	A	0	1	2	3	2	3	4	LO	XN	IP	PH	RHP	LHP
1881	CHI	NL	1	1	0	0	1	0	0	0	0	0	0	0	0	0	1	0

Rank among batters: 4,707 • *Total ballparks homered in*: 1 • *First HR*: 06/27/1881 off Monte Ward

Frank Quilici

FRANCIS RALPH QUILICI
B: 05/11/1939
BR

Year	Tm	Lg	Tot	H	A	0	1	2	3	2	3	4	LO	XN	IP	PH	RHP	LHP
1968	MIN	AL	1	0	1	1	0	0	0	0	0	0	0	0	0	0	1	0
1969	MIN	AL	2	1	1	2	0	0	0	0	0	0	0	0	0	0	1	1
1970	MIN	AL	2	1	1	0	1	1	0	0	0	0	0	0	0	0	0	2
Total			5	2	3	3	1	1	0	0	0	0	0	0	0	0	2	3

Rank among batters: 3,191 • *Top target (2 home runs)*: Jim Nash • *Number of pitchers victimized*: 4 • *Total ballparks homered in*: 3 • *First HR*: 09/29/1968 off Jim Nash

Tom Quinlan

THOMAS RAYMOND QUINLAN
B: 03/27/1968
BR

Year	Tm	Lg	Tot	H	A	0	1	2	3	2	3	4	LO	XN	IP	PH	RHP	LHP
1994	PHI	NL	1	1	0	0	1	0	0	0	0	0	0	0	0	0	1	0

Tom Quinlan *continued*

Rank among batters: 4,707 • *Total ballparks homered in*: 1 • *First HR*: 05/29/1994 off Doug Drabek

Jack Quinn

JOHN PICUS QUINN
B: 07/05/1883 D: 04/17/1946
BR

Year	Tm	Lg	Tot	H	A	Men-On				One-Game			LO	XN	IP	PH	RHP	LHP
						0	1	2	3	2	3	4						
1911	NY	AL	1	1	0	1	0	0	0	0	0	0	0	0	0	0	1	0
1914	BAL	FL	2	2	0	1	1	0	0	0	0	0	0	1	0	0	2	0
1920	NY	AL	2	2	0	0	2	0	0	0	0	0	0	0	0	0	2	0
1921	NY	AL	1	1	0	0	1	0	0	0	0	0	0	0	0	0	1	0
1922	BOS	AL	1	0	1	0	0	1	0	0	0	0	0	0	0	0	1	0
1930	PHI	AL	1	1	0	1	0	0	0	0	0	0	0	0	0	0	1	0
Total			8	7	1	3	4	1	0	0	0	0	0	1	0	0	8	0

Rank among batters: 2,703 • *Total ballparks homered in*: 5 • *First HR*: 09/11/1911 off Chief Bender

Joe Quinn

JOSEPH J. QUINN
B: 12/25/1864 D: 11/12/1940
BR

Year	Tm	Lg	Tot	H	A	Men-On				One-Game			LO	XN	IP	PH	RHP	LHP
						0	1	2	3	2	3	4						
1886	STL	NL	1	0	1	1	0	0	0	0	0	0	0	0	0	0	1	0
1888	BOS	NL	4	1	3	2	1	1	0	0	0	0	0	0	1	0	4	0
1889	BOS	NL	2	1	1	0	2	0	0	0	0	0	0	0	0	0	2	0
1890	BOS	PL	7	6	1	5	2	0	0	1	0	0	0	0	0	0	6	1
1891	BOS	NL	3	3	0	0	1	1	1	0	0	0	0	1	0	0	2	1
1892	BOS	NL	1	1	0	0	1	0	0	0	0	0	0	0	0	0	1	0
1894	STL	NL	4	3	1	0	2	2	0	0	0	0	0	0	1	0	3	1
1895	STL	NL	2	0	2	0	1	1	0	0	0	0	0	0	1	0	2	0
1896	STL	NL	1	1	0	0	0	1	0	0	0	0	0	0	0	0	1	0
1897	BAL	NL	1	1	0	1	0	0	0	0	0	0	0	0	1	0	1	0
1900	STL	NL	1	0	1	1	0	0	0	0	0	0	0	0	0	0	1	0
1901	WAS	AL	2	2	0	0	2	0	0	0	0	0	0	0	0	0	1	1
Total			29	19	10	10	12	6	1	1	0	0	0	1	4	0	25	3

Rank among batters: 1,465 • *Top target (3 home runs)*: Jersey Bakely • *Number of pitchers victimized*: 25 • *Total ballparks homered in*: 12 • *First HR*: 06/17/1886 off John Clarkson

Tom Quinn

THOMAS OSCAR QUINN
B: 04/25/1864 D: 07/24/1932
BR

Year	Tm	Lg	Tot	H	A	Men-On				One-Game			LO	XN	IP	PH	RHP	LHP
						0	1	2	3	2	3	4						
1889	BAL	AA	1	1	0	0	0	1	0	0	0	0	0	0	0	0	1	0
1890	PIT	PL	1	0	1	1	0	0	0	0	0	0	0	0	0	0	1	0
Total			2	1	1	1	0	1	0	0	0	0	0	0	0	0	2	0

Rank among batters: 4,129 • *Total ballparks homered in*: 2 • *First HR*: 08/30/1889 off Red Ehret

Luis Quinones

LUIS RAUL (TORRUELLAS) QUINONES
B: 04/28/1962
BB

Year	Tm	Lg	Tot	H	A	Men-On				One-Game			LO	XN	IP	PH	RHP	LHP
						0	1	2	3	2	3	4						
1988	CIN	NL	1	0	1	0	0	1	0	0	0	0	0	0	0	0	0	1
1989	CIN	NL	12	5	7	10	1	1	0	1	0	0	0	0	0	0	3	9
1990	CIN	NL	2	1	1	1	1	0	0	0	0	0	0	0	0	1	0	2
1991	CIN	NL	4	2	2	3	1	0	0	0	0	0	0	0	0	1	3	1
Total			19	8	11	14	3	2	0	1	0	0	0	0	0	2	6	13

Rank among batters: 1,861 • *Top target (2 home runs)*: David West, Neal Heaton • *Number of pitchers victimized*: 17 • *Total ballparks homered in*: 7 • *First HR*: 09/04/1988 off Frank DiPino

Rey Quinones

REY FRANCISCO (SANTIAGO) QUINONES
B: 11/11/1963
BR

Year	Tm	Lg	Tot	H	A	Men-On				One-Game			LO	XN	IP	PH	RHP	LHP
						0	1	2	3	2	3	4						
1986	BOS	AL	2	2	0	1	1	0	0	0	0	0	0	0	0	0	2	0
1987	SEA	AL	12	7	5	8	3	1	0	0	0	0	0	1	0	0	8	4

Year	Tm	Lg	Tot	H	A	Men-On 0	1	2	3	One-Game 2	3	4	LO	XN	IP	PH	RHP	LHP

Rey Quinones *continued*

Year	Tm	Lg	Tot	H	A	0	1	2	3	2	3	4	LO	XN	IP	PH	RHP	LHP
1988	SEA	AL	12	9	3	10	1	1	0	1	0	0	0	0	0	0	6	6
1989	PIT	NL	3	1	2	1	1	1	0	0	0	0	0	0	0	0	1	2
Total			29	19	10	20	6	3	0	1	0	0	0	1	0	0	17	12

Rank among batters: 1,465 • Top target (2 home runs): Phil Niekro, Jeff Ballard, Charlie Leibrandt, Bobby Witt • *Number of pitchers victimized*: 25 • *Total ballparks homered in*: 11 • *First HR*: 06/04/1986 off Phil Niekro

Carlos Quintana

CARLOS NARCIS (HERNANDEZ) QUINTANA
B: 08/26/1965
BR

Year	Tm	Lg	Tot	H	A	0	1	2	3	2	3	4	LO	XN	IP	PH	RHP	LHP
1990	BOS	AL	7	3	4	3	3	1	0	0	0	0	0	0	0	0	4	3
1991	BOS	AL	11	2	9	5	4	1	1	2	0	0	0	0	0	0	6	5
1993	BOS	AL	1	0	1	1	0	0	0	0	0	0	0	0	0	0	1	0
Total			19	5	14	9	7	2	1	2	0	0	0	0	0	0	11	8

Rank among batters: 1,861 • *Top target (2 home runs)*: Dave Wells • *Number of pitchers victimized*: 18 • *Total ballparks homered in*: 11 • *First HR*: 05/09/1990 off Gary Eave

Jamie Quirk

JAMES PATRICK QUIRK
B: 10/22/1954
BL

Year	Tm	Lg	Tot	H	A	0	1	2	3	2	3	4	LO	XN	IP	PH	RHP	LHP
1975	KC	AL	1	1	0	1	0	0	0	0	0	0	0	0	0	1	1	0
1976	KC	AL	1	1	0	1	0	0	0	0	0	0	0	0	0	0	1	0
1977	MIL	AL	3	2	1	2	1	0	0	0	0	0	0	0	0	0	3	0
1979	KC	AL	1	1	0	0	1	0	0	0	0	0	0	0	0	0	1	0
1980	KC	AL	5	3	2	3	2	0	0	1	0	0	0	0	0	0	5	0
1982	KC	AL	1	1	0	1	0	0	0	0	0	0	0	0	0	0	1	0
1983	STL	NL	2	0	2	0	0	2	0	0	0	0	0	0	0	0	2	0
1984	CLE	AL	1	1	0	1	0	0	0	0	0	0	0	0	0	0	1	0
1986	KC	AL	8	5	3	3	4	1	0	0	0	0	0	0	0	0	8	0
1987	KC	AL	5	0	5	3	0	1	1	0	0	0	0	0	0	0	5	0
1988	KC	AL	8	2	6	8	0	0	0	0	0	0	0	0	0	0	8	0
1989	OAK	AL	1	0	1	1	0	0	0	0	0	0	0	0	0	0	1	0
1990	OAK	AL	3	1	2	0	3	0	0	0	0	0	0	0	0	1	3	0
1991	OAK	AL	1	0	1	1	0	0	0	0	0	0	0	0	0	0	1	0
1992	OAK	AL	2	2	0	2	0	0	0	0	0	0	0	0	0	0	2	0
Total			43	20	23	27	11	4	1	1	0	0	0	0	0	2	43	0

Rank among batters: 1,116 • *Top target (3 home runs)*: Jim Clancy • *Number of pitchers victimized*: 37 • *Total ballparks homered in*: 14 • *First HR*: 09/20/1975 off Rollie Fingers

John Rabb

JOHN ANDREW RABB
B: 06/23/1960
BR

Year	Tm	Lg	Tot	H	A	0	1	2	3	2	3	4	LO	XN	IP	PH	RHP	LHP
1983	SF	NL	1	0	1	0	0	1	0	0	0	0	0	0	0	0	0	1
1984	SF	NL	3	0	3	1	2	0	0	0	0	0	0	0	0	0	1	2
Total			4	0	4	1	2	1	0	0	0	0	0	0	0	0	1	3

Rank among batters: 3,427 • *Total ballparks homered in*: 4 • *First HR*: 07/25/1983 off Dave LaPoint

Marv Rackley

MARVIN EUGENE RACKLEY
B: 07/25/1921
BL

Year	Tm	Lg	Tot	H	A	0	1	2	3	2	3	4	LO	XN	IP	PH	RHP	LHP
1949	BRO	NL	1	0	1	0	1	0	0	0	0	0	0	0	0	0	1	0

Rank among batters: 4,707 • *Total ballparks homered in*: 1 • *First HR*: 06/23/1949 off Eddie Erautt

Dick Radatz

RICHARD RAYMOND RADATZ
B: 04/02/1937
BR

Year	Tm	Lg	Tot	H	A	0	1	2	3	2	3	4	LO	XN	IP	PH	RHP	LHP
1965	BOS	AL	1	0	1	1	0	0	0	0	0	0	0	1	0	0	1	0

Dick Radatz *continued*

Rank among batters: 4,707 • *Total ballparks homered in*: 1 • *First HR*: 06/05/1965 off Jesse Hickman

Charley Radbourn

CHARLES GARDNER RADBOURN
B: 12/11/1854 D: 02/05/1897
BR HOF

Year	Tm	Lg	Tot	H	A	Men-On 0	1	2	3	One-Game 2	3	4	LO	XN	IP	PH	RHP	LHP
1882	PRO	NL	1	1	0	1	0	0	0	0	0	0	0	1	0	0	1	0
1883	PRO	NL	3	2	1	2	1	0	0	0	0	0	0	0	0	0	3	0
1884	PRO	NL	1	0	1	1	0	0	0	0	0	0	0	0	0	0	1	0
1886	BOS	NL	2	1	1	1	1	0	0	0	0	0	0	0	0	0	2	0
1887	BOS	NL	1	1	0	1	0	0	0	0	0	0	0	0	0	0	1	0
1889	BOS	NL	1	1	0	1	0	0	0	0	0	0	0	0	0	0	1	0
Total			9	6	3	7	2	0	0	0	0	0	0	1	0	0	9	0

Rank among batters: 2,587 • *Top target (2 home runs)*: Larry Corcoran • *Number of pitchers victimized*: 8 • *Total ballparks homered in*: 6 • *First HR*: 08/17/1882 off Stump Wiedman

Rip Radcliff

RAYMOND ALLEN RADCLIFF
B: 01/19/1906 D: 05/23/1962
BL

Year	Tm	Lg	Tot	H	A	Men-On 0	1	2	3	One-Game 2	3	4	LO	XN	IP	PH	RHP	LHP
1935	CHI	AL	10	8	2	5	3	2	0	0	0	0	0	0	0	0	10	0
1936	CHI	AL	8	1	7	4	2	2	0	1	0	0	0	0	0	0	7	1
1937	CHI	AL	4	1	3	2	1	1	0	0	0	0	1	0	0	0	4	0
1938	CHI	AL	5	2	3	1	3	1	0	0	0	0	0	0	0	0	5	0
1939	CHI	AL	2	2	0	0	2	0	0	0	0	0	0	0	0	0	2	0
1940	STL	AL	7	5	2	5	2	0	0	0	0	0	0	0	0	0	4	3
1941	STL	AL	2	1	1	1	0	1	0	0	0	0	0	0	0	0	2	0
	DET	AL	3	3	0	2	0	1	0	0	0	0	0	0	0	0	3	0
	Total		5	4	1	3	0	2	0	0	0	0	0	0	0	0	5	0
1942	DET	AL	1	1	0	0	0	1	0	0	0	0	0	0	0	0	0	1
Total			42	24	18	20	13	9	0	1	0	0	1	0	0	0	37	5

Rank among batters: 1,138 • *Top target (3 home runs)*: Johnny Broaca • *Number of pitchers victimized*: 34 • *Total ballparks homered in*: 7 • *First HR*: 04/18/1935 off Tommy Bridges

Dave Rader

DAVID MARTIN RADER
B: 12/26/1948
BL

Year	Tm	Lg	Tot	H	A	Men-On 0	1	2	3	One-Game 2	3	4	LO	XN	IP	PH	RHP	LHP
1972	SF	NL	6	3	3	4	2	0	0	0	0	0	0	0	0	0	4	2
1973	SF	NL	9	4	5	8	1	0	0	1	0	0	0	1	1	0	4	5
1974	SF	NL	1	1	0	1	0	0	0	0	0	0	0	0	0	0	1	0
1975	SF	NL	5	1	4	3	1	1	0	0	0	0	0	0	0	0	5	0
1976	SF	NL	1	0	1	1	0	0	0	0	0	0	0	0	0	0	1	0
1977	STL	NL	1	0	1	1	0	0	0	0	0	0	0	0	0	0	1	0
1978	CHI	NL	3	3	0	1	1	0	1	0	0	0	0	0	0	1	2	1
1979	PHI	NL	1	1	0	1	0	0	0	0	0	0	0	0	0	0	1	0
1980	BOS	AL	3	2	1	1	2	0	0	0	0	0	0	0	0	0	2	1
Total			30	15	15	21	7	1	1	1	0	0	0	1	1	1	21	9

Rank among batters: 1,437 • *Total ballparks homered in*: 13 • *First HR*: 05/01/1972 off Tom Seaver

Doug Rader

DOUGLAS LEE RADER
B: 07/30/1944
BR

Year	Tm	Lg	Tot	H	A	Men-On 0	1	2	3	One-Game 2	3	4	LO	XN	IP	PH	RHP	LHP
1967	HOU	NL	2	1	1	1	1	0	0	0	0	0	0	0	0	0	2	0
1968	HOU	NL	6	1	5	3	2	1	0	0	0	0	0	0	0	0	6	0
1969	HOU	NL	11	7	4	7	2	1	1	0	0	0	0	0	1	0	9	2
1970	HOU	NL	25	11	14	15	6	3	1	1	0	0	0	0	0	0	17	8
1971	HOU	NL	12	4	8	8	2	1	1	0	0	0	0	0	0	0	5	7
1972	HOU	NL	22	10	12	9	7	6	0	1	0	0	0	0	0	0	13	9
1973	HOU	NL	21	11	10	14	6	1	0	2	0	0	0	0	0	0	12	9
1974	HOU	NL	17	8	9	9	5	3	0	0	0	0	0	1	1	0	12	5
1975	HOU	NL	12	10	2	4	6	2	0	2	0	0	0	0	0	0	8	4
1976	SD	NL	9	5	4	4	1	3	1	0	0	0	0	0	0	0	7	2
1977	SD	NL	5	3	2	2	0	3	0	0	0	0	0	1	0	0	3	2

Doug Rader *continued*

Year	Tm	Lg	Tot	H	A	Men-On 0	1	2	3	One-Game 2	3	4	LO	XN	IP	PH	RHP	LHP
1977	TOR	AL	13	4	9	8	4	1	0	0	0	0	0	1	1	1	8	5
	Total		18	7	11	10	4	4	0	0	0	0	0	2	1	1	11	7
Total			155	75	80	84	42	25	4	6	0	0	0	3	3	1	102	53

Rank among batters: 274 • *Top target (5 home runs)*: Jerry Koosman • *Number of pitchers victimized*: 113 • *Total ballparks homered in*: 22 • *First HR*: 08/19/1967 off Dick Hughes

Paul Radford

PAUL REVERE RADFORD
B: 10/14/1861 D: 02/21/1945
BR

Year	Tm	Lg	Tot	H	A	Men-On 0	1	2	3	One-Game 2	3	4	LO	XN	IP	PH	RHP	LHP
1884	PRO	NL	1	0	1	0	1	0	0	0	0	0	0	0	0	0	1	0
1887	NY	AA	4	3	1	3	1	0	0	1	0	0	0	0	1	0	3	1
1888	BRO	AA	2	2	0	0	1	1	0	0	0	0	0	0	0	0	2	0
1889	CLE	NL	1	0	1	0	1	0	0	0	0	0	0	0	0	0	1	0
1890	CLE	PL	2	2	0	0	0	1	1	0	0	0	0	0	0	0	1	0
1892	WAS	NL	1	1	0	0	1	0	0	0	0	0	0	0	0	0	2	0
1893	WAS	NL	2	1	1	2	0	0	0	0	0	0	0	0	0	0	1	0
Total			13	9	4	5	5	2	1	1	0	0	0	0	1	0	12	1

Rank among batters: 2,248 • *Top target (2 home runs)*: Billy Serad, Ed Crane • *Number of pitchers victimized*: 11 • *Total ballparks homered in*: 8 • *First HR*: 09/25/1884 off Larry Corcoran

Ken Raffensberger

KENNETH DAVID RAFFENSBERGER
B: 08/08/1917
BR

Year	Tm	Lg	Tot	H	A	Men-On 0	1	2	3	One-Game 2	3	4	LO	XN	IP	PH	RHP	LHP
1949	CIN	NL	1	0	1	1	0	0	0	0	0	0	0	0	0	0	1	0
1950	CIN	NL	1	1	0	0	1	0	0	0	0	0	0	0	0	0	1	0
1952	CIN	NL	1	1	0	1	0	0	0	0	0	0	0	0	0	0	1	0
1953	CIN	NL	1	0	1	0	0	1	0	0	0	0	0	0	0	0	1	0
Total			4	2	2	2	1	1	0	0	0	0	0	0	0	0	4	0

Rank among batters: 3,427 • *Total ballparks homered in*: 2 • *First HR*: 09/07/1949 off Murry Dickson

Pat Ragan

DON CARLOS PATRICK RAGAN
B: 11/15/1888 D: 09/04/1956
BR

Year	Tm	Lg	Tot	H	A	Men-On 0	1	2	3	One-Game 2	3	4	LO	XN	IP	PH	RHP	LHP
1917	BOS	NL	1	0	1	1	0	0	0	0	0	0	0	0	0	0	1	0

Rank among batters: 4,707 • *Total ballparks homered in*: 1 • *First HR*: 04/20/1917 off Jeff Tesreau

Larry Raines

LAWRENCE GLENN HOPE RAINES
B: 03/09/1930 D: 01/28/1978
BR

Year	Tm	Lg	Tot	H	A	Men-On 0	1	2	3	One-Game 2	3	4	LO	XN	IP	PH	RHP	LHP
1957	CLE	AL	2	1	1	1	1	0	0	0	0	0	0	0	0	0	1	1

Rank among batters: 4,129 • *Total ballparks homered in*: 2 • *First HR*: 05/29/1957 off Jack Harshman

Tim Raines

TIMOTHY RAINES
B: 09/16/1959
BB

Year	Tm	Lg	Tot	H	A	Men-On 0	1	2	3	One-Game 2	3	4	LO	XN	IP	PH	RHP	LHP
1981	MON	NL	5	3	2	4	1	0	0	0	0	0	1	1	1	0	4	1
1982	MON	NL	4	1	3	3	1	0	0	0	0	0	0	1	0	0	2	2
1983	MON	NL	11	5	6	7	1	1	2	0	0	0	0	0	0	0	4	7
1984	MON	NL	8	2	6	2	4	2	0	0	0	0	1	0	0	0	5	3
1985	MON	NL	11	4	7	9	2	0	0	1	0	0	0	0	0	0	5	6
1986	MON	NL	9	4	5	6	1	1	1	0	0	0	1	0	0	0	5	4
1987	MON	NL	18	9	9	11	5	1	1	0	0	0	0	1	0	0	13	5
1988	MON	NL	12	5	7	6	5	1	0	1	0	0	1	0	0	0	8	4
1989	MON	NL	9	6	3	7	1	1	0	0	0	0	0	0	0	0	6	3
1990	MON	NL	9	6	3	5	2	1	1	0	0	0	0	0	0	0	6	3
1991	CHI	AL	5	1	4	3	2	0	0	0	0	0	1	0	0	0	3	2
1992	CHI	AL	7	4	3	6	0	1	0	0	0	0	1	0	0	0	7	0
1993	CHI	AL	16	7	9	11	3	2	0	1	0	0	5	0	0	0	13	3

Tim Raines *continued*

Year	Tm	Lg	Tot	H	A	Men-On 0	Men-On 1	Men-On 2	Men-On 3	One-Game 2	One-Game 3	One-Game 4	LO	XN	IP	PH	RHP	LHP
1994	CHI	AL	10	5	5	5	4	1	0	1	1	0	1	0	0	0	9	1
1995	CHI	AL	12	6	6	10	2	0	0	0	0	0	1	0	0	0	9	3
Total			146	68	78	95	34	12	5	4	1	0	13	3	1	0	99	47

Rank among batters: 302 • *Top target (5 home runs)*: Bill Gullickson • *Number of pitchers victimized*: 112 • *Total ballparks homered in*: 24 • *First HR*: 05/01/1981 off Robert Castillo • *Switch hit HR in 1 game*—2 times • *Hit for Cycle*—vs PIT: 08/16/1987

John Rainey

JOHN PAUL RAINEY
B: 07/26/1864 D: 11/11/1912
BL

Year	Tm	Lg	Tot	H	A	Men-On 0	Men-On 1	Men-On 2	Men-On 3	One-Game 2	One-Game 3	One-Game 4	LO	XN	IP	PH	RHP	LHP
1890	BUF	PL	1	1	0	0	0	1	0	0	0	0	0	0	0	0	1	0

Rank among batters: 4,707 • *Total ballparks homered in*: 1 • *First HR*: 04/19/1890 off Henry Gruber

Gary Rajsich

GARY LOUIS RAJSICH
B: 10/28/1954
BL

Year	Tm	Lg	Tot	H	A	Men-On 0	Men-On 1	Men-On 2	Men-On 3	One-Game 2	One-Game 3	One-Game 4	LO	XN	IP	PH	RHP	LHP
1982	NY	NL	2	2	0	1	0	1	0	0	0	0	0	0	0	1	2	0
1983	NY	NL	1	0	1	1	0	0	0	0	0	0	0	0	0	0	1	0
Total			3	2	1	2	0	1	0	0	0	0	0	0	0	1	3	0

Rank among batters: 3,735 • *Total ballparks homered in*: 2 • *First HR*: 05/18/1982 off Bruce Berenyi

Bob Ramazzotti

ROBERT LOUIS RAMAZZOTTI
B: 01/16/1917
BR

Year	Tm	Lg	Tot	H	A	Men-On 0	Men-On 1	Men-On 2	Men-On 3	One-Game 2	One-Game 3	One-Game 4	LO	XN	IP	PH	RHP	LHP
1949	BRO	NL	1	1	0	0	1	0	0	0	0	0	0	0	0	0	0	1
1950	CHI	NL	1	0	1	1	0	0	0	0	0	0	0	0	0	0	1	0
1951	CHI	NL	1	0	1	0	1	0	0	0	0	0	0	0	0	0	1	0
1952	CHI	NL	1	0	1	1	0	0	0	0	0	0	0	0	0	0	1	0
Total			4	1	3	2	2	0	0	0	0	0	0	0	0	0	3	1

Rank among batters: 3,427 • *Total ballparks homered in*: 2 • *First HR*: 05/11/1949 off Bill Werle

Manny Ramirez

MANUEL ARISTIDES (ONELCIDA) RAMIREZ
B: 05/30/1972
BR

Year	Tm	Lg	Tot	H	A	Men-On 0	Men-On 1	Men-On 2	Men-On 3	One-Game 2	One-Game 3	One-Game 4	LO	XN	IP	PH	RHP	LHP
1993	CLE	AL	2	0	2	1	1	0	0	1	0	0	0	0	0	0	1	1
1994	CLE	AL	17	9	8	6	7	4	0	1	0	0	0	1	0	0	10	7
1995	CLE	AL	31	12	19	17	8	5	1	2	0	0	0	2	0	0	24	7
Total			50	21	29	24	16	9	1	4	0	0	0	3	0	0	35	15

Rank among batters: 991 • *Top target (3 home runs)*: Tim Belcher • *Number of pitchers victimized*: 45 • *Total ballparks homered in*: 13 • *First HR*: 09/03/1993 off Melido Perez • *World Series HR*—1; *LCS HR*—2

Mario Ramirez

MARIO (TORRES) RAMIREZ
B: 09/12/1957
BR

Year	Tm	Lg	Tot	H	A	Men-On 0	Men-On 1	Men-On 2	Men-On 3	One-Game 2	One-Game 3	One-Game 4	LO	XN	IP	PH	RHP	LHP
1984	SD	NL	2	1	1	0	1	1	0	0	0	0	0	0	0	0	1	1
1985	SD	NL	2	2	0	1	1	0	0	0	0	0	0	0	0	1	0	2
Total			4	3	1	1	2	1	0	0	0	0	0	0	0	1	1	3

Rank among batters: 3,427 • *Total ballparks homered in*: 2 • *First HR*: 04/22/1984 off Burt Hooton

Rafael Ramirez

RAFAEL EMILIO (PEGUERO) RAMIREZ
B: 02/18/1958
BR

Year	Tm	Lg	Tot	H	A	Men-On 0	Men-On 1	Men-On 2	Men-On 3	One-Game 2	One-Game 3	One-Game 4	LO	XN	IP	PH	RHP	LHP
1980	ATL	NL	2	2	0	1	1	0	0	0	0	0	0	0	0	0	2	0
1981	ATL	NL	2	1	1	2	0	0	0	0	0	0	0	0	0	0	2	0
1982	ATL	NL	10	7	3	8	1	1	0	1	0	0	0	0	0	0	6	4
1983	ATL	NL	7	2	5	6	0	1	0	0	0	0	0	0	0	0	4	3

Rafael Ramirez *continued*

Year	Tm	Lg	Tot	H	A	Men-On 0	1	2	3	One-Game 2	3	4	LO	XN	IP	PH	RHP	LHP
1984	ATL	NL	2	1	1	2	0	0	0	0	0	0	0	0	0	0	1	1
1985	ATL	NL	5	4	1	3	1	1	0	0	0	0	0	1	0	0	5	0
1986	ATL	NL	8	1	7	6	2	0	0	0	0	0	0	0	0	0	6	2
1987	ATL	NL	1	0	1	1	0	0	0	0	0	0	0	0	0	0	1	0
1988	HOU	NL	6	2	4	3	2	0	1	0	0	0	0	0	0	0	4	2
1989	HOU	NL	6	3	3	2	3	0	1	0	0	0	0	0	0	0	4	2
1990	HOU	NL	2	1	1	1	1	0	0	0	0	0	0	0	0	0	1	1
1991	HOU	NL	1	0	1	1	0	0	0	0	0	0	0	0	0	0	0	1
1992	HOU	NL	1	0	1	0	1	0	0	0	0	0	0	0	0	0	0	1
Total			53	24	29	36	12	3	2	1	0	0	0	1	0	0	36	17

Rank among batters: 953 • *Top target (3 home runs)*: Don Robinson • *Number of pitchers victimized*: 48 • *Total ballparks homered in*: 10 • *First HR*: 08/19/1980 off Dennis Lamp

Bobby Ramos

ROBERTO RAMOS
B: 11/05/1955
BR

Year	Tm	Lg	Tot	H	A	Men-On 0	1	2	3	One-Game 2	3	4	LO	XN	IP	PH	RHP	LHP
1981	MON	NL	1	0	1	1	0	0	0	0	0	0	0	0	0	0	1	0
1982	NY	AL	1	1	0	0	1	0	0	0	0	0	0	0	0	0	0	1
1984	MON	NL	2	2	0	1	1	0	0	0	0	0	0	0	0	0	0	2
Total			4	3	1	2	2	0	0	0	0	0	0	0	0	0	1	3

Rank among batters: 3,427 • *Total ballparks homered in*: 3 • *First HR*: 04/19/1981 off Pat Zachry

Domingo Ramos

DOMINGO ANTONIO (DERAMOS) RAMOS
B: 03/29/1958
BR

Year	Tm	Lg	Tot	H	A	Men-On 0	1	2	3	One-Game 2	3	4	LO	XN	IP	PH	RHP	LHP
1983	SEA	AL	2	2	0	2	0	0	0	0	0	0	0	0	0	0	2	0
1985	SEA	AL	1	0	1	1	0	0	0	0	0	0	0	0	0	0	1	0
1987	SEA	AL	2	1	1	0	1	1	0	0	0	0	0	0	1	0	2	0
1989	CHI	NL	1	1	0	0	1	0	0	0	0	0	0	0	0	0	0	1
1990	CHI	NL	2	2	0	1	1	0	0	0	0	0	0	0	0	0	2	0
Total			8	6	2	4	3	1	0	0	0	0	0	0	1	0	7	1

Rank among batters: 2,703 • *Total ballparks homered in*: 4 • *First HR*: 04/17/1983 off Mike Norris

Pedro Ramos

PEDRO (GUERRA) RAMOS
B: 04/28/1935
BB

Year	Tm	Lg	Tot	H	A	Men-On 0	1	2	3	One-Game 2	3	4	LO	XN	IP	PH	RHP	LHP
1957	WAS	AL	1	1	0	0	0	1	0	0	0	0	0	0	0	0	1	0
1959	WAS	AL	1	1	0	1	0	0	0	0	0	0	0	0	0	0	1	0
1960	WAS	AL	2	1	1	2	0	0	0	0	0	0	0	0	0	0	2	0
1961	MIN	AL	3	2	1	3	0	0	0	0	0	0	0	0	0	0	3	0
1962	CLE	AL	3	1	2	2	0	0	1	1	0	0	0	0	0	0	3	0
1963	CLE	AL	3	2	1	2	1	0	0	1	0	0	0	0	0	0	3	0
1964	CLE	AL	2	2	0	2	0	0	0	0	0	0	0	0	0	0	2	0
Total			15	10	5	12	1	1	1	2	0	0	0	0	0	0	15	0

Rank among batters: 2,096 • Top target (2 home runs): Mudcat Grant, Chuck Estrada, Eli Grba, Paul Foytack • *Number of pitchers victimized*: 11 • *Total ballparks homered in*: 6 • *First HR*: 08/04/1957 off Frank Lary

Bill Ramsey

WILLIAM THRACE RAMSEY
B: 02/20/1920
BR

Year	Tm	Lg	Tot	H	A	Men-On 0	1	2	3	One-Game 2	3	4	LO	XN	IP	PH	RHP	LHP
1945	BOS	NL	1	0	1	1	0	0	0	0	0	0	0	0	0	0	1	0

Rank among batters: 4,707 • *Total ballparks homered in*: 1 • *First HR*: 09/22/1945 off Jack Brewer

Mike Ramsey

MICHAEL JEFFREY RAMSEY
B: 03/29/1954
BB

Year	Tm	Lg	Tot	H	A	Men-On 0	1	2	3	One-Game 2	3	4	LO	XN	IP	PH	RHP	LHP
1982	STL	NL	1	1	0	0	0	1	0	0	0	0	0	0	0	0	1	0

Mike Ramsey *continued*

Year	Tm	Lg	Tot	H	A	Men-On 0	Men-On 1	Men-On 2	Men-On 3	One-Game 2	One-Game 3	One-Game 4	LO	XN	IP	PH	RHP	LHP
1983	STL	NL	1	0	1	1	0	0	0	0	0	0	0	0	0	0	1	0
Total			2	1	1	1	0	1	0	0	0	0	0	0	0	0	2	0

Rank among batters: 4,129 • *Total ballparks homered in*: 2 • *First HR*: 07/25/1982 off Don Sutton

Dick Rand

RICHARD HILTON RAND
B: 03/07/1931
BR

Year	Tm	Lg	Tot	H	A	Men-On 0	Men-On 1	Men-On 2	Men-On 3	One-Game 2	One-Game 3	One-Game 4	LO	XN	IP	PH	RHP	LHP
1955	STL	NL	1	1	0	0	1	0	0	0	0	0	0	0	0	0	0	1
1957	PIT	NL	1	0	1	1	0	0	0	0	0	0	0	0	0	0	1	0
Total			2	1	1	1	1	0	0	0	0	0	0	0	0	0	1	1

Rank among batters: 4,129 • *Total ballparks homered in*: 2 • *First HR*: 09/23/1955 off Warren Spahn

Joe Randa

JOSEPH GREGORY RANDA
B: 12/18/1969
BR

Year	Tm	Lg	Tot	H	A	Men-On 0	Men-On 1	Men-On 2	Men-On 3	One-Game 2	One-Game 3	One-Game 4	LO	XN	IP	PH	RHP	LHP
1995	KC	AL	1	1	0	1	0	0	0	0	0	0	0	0	0	0	0	1

Rank among batters: 4,707 • *Total ballparks homered in*: 1 • *First HR*: 05/16/1995 off Dave Fleming

Bob Randall

ROBERT LEE RANDALL
B: 06/06/1948
BR

Year	Tm	Lg	Tot	H	A	Men-On 0	Men-On 1	Men-On 2	Men-On 3	One-Game 2	One-Game 3	One-Game 4	LO	XN	IP	PH	RHP	LHP
1976	MIN	AL	1	1	0	1	0	0	0	0	0	0	0	0	0	0	1	0

Rank among batters: 4,707 • *Total ballparks homered in*: 1 • *First HR*: 06/23/1976 off Chris Knapp

Len Randle

LEONARD SHENOFF RANDLE
B: 02/12/1949
BB

Year	Tm	Lg	Tot	H	A	Men-On 0	Men-On 1	Men-On 2	Men-On 3	One-Game 2	One-Game 3	One-Game 4	LO	XN	IP	PH	RHP	LHP
1971	WAS	AL	2	0	2	2	0	0	0	0	0	0	0	0	0	0	2	0
1972	TEX	AL	2	0	2	0	1	1	0	0	0	0	0	0	0	0	2	0
1973	TEX	AL	1	0	1	1	0	0	0	0	0	0	0	0	0	0	0	1
1974	TEX	AL	1	1	0	1	0	0	0	0	0	0	0	0	0	0	0	1
1975	TEX	AL	4	1	3	3	1	0	0	0	0	0	0	0	0	0	0	4
1976	TEX	AL	1	1	0	0	1	0	0	0	0	0	0	0	0	0	1	0
1977	NY	NL	5	4	1	4	1	0	0	0	0	0	1	1	0	0	3	2
1978	NY	NL	2	2	0	1	0	1	0	0	0	0	1	0	0	0	2	0
1980	CHI	NL	5	0	5	2	2	1	0	0	0	0	1	1	0	0	3	2
1981	SEA	AL	4	1	3	2	1	0	1	0	0	0	0	1	0	0	3	1
Total			27	10	17	16	7	3	1	0	0	0	3	3	0	0	16	11

Rank among batters: 1,532 • *Top target (2 home runs)*: John Montefusco • *Number of pitchers victimized*: 26 • *Total ballparks homered in*: 12 • *First HR*: 07/04/1971 off Steve Dunning

Willie Randolph

WILLIE LARRY RANDOLPH
B: 07/06/1954
BR

Year	Tm	Lg	Tot	H	A	Men-On 0	Men-On 1	Men-On 2	Men-On 3	One-Game 2	One-Game 3	One-Game 4	LO	XN	IP	PH	RHP	LHP
1976	NY	AL	1	0	1	1	0	0	0	0	0	0	0	0	0	0	1	0
1977	NY	AL	4	2	2	2	2	0	0	0	0	0	0	0	0	0	2	2
1978	NY	AL	3	2	1	2	0	1	0	0	0	0	0	1	0	0	1	2
1979	NY	AL	5	2	3	2	1	1	1	0	0	0	0	0	0	0	2	3
1980	NY	AL	7	2	5	5	2	0	0	0	0	0	3	0	0	0	1	6
1981	NY	AL	2	1	1	1	0	1	0	0	0	0	0	0	0	0	1	1
1982	NY	AL	3	1	2	2	0	1	0	0	0	0	1	0	0	0	1	2
1983	NY	AL	2	1	1	0	2	0	0	0	0	0	0	0	0	0	2	0
1984	NY	AL	2	1	1	1	1	0	0	0	0	0	0	1	0	0	1	1
1985	NY	AL	5	3	2	3	2	0	0	1	0	0	0	0	0	0	3	2
1986	NY	AL	5	2	3	5	0	0	0	0	0	0	0	0	0	0	1	4
1987	NY	AL	7	3	4	2	3	2	0	0	0	0	0	0	0	0	4	3

Willie Randolph *continued*

Year	Tm	Lg	Tot	H	A	Men-On 0	1	2	3	One-Game 2	3	4	LO	XN	IP	PH	RHP	LHP
1988	NY	AL	2	1	1	0	0	2	0	0	0	0	0	0	0	0	1	1
1989	LA	NL	2	0	2	1	0	1	0	0	0	0	0	0	0	0	1	1
1990	LA	NL	1	0	1	1	0	0	0	0	0	0	0	0	0	0	1	0
	OAK	AL	1	1	0	1	0	0	0	0	0	0	0	0	0	0	1	0
	Total		2	1	1	2	0	0	0	0	0	0	0	0	0	0	2	0
1992	NY	NL	2	2	0	2	0	0	0	0	0	0	0	0	0	0	0	2
Total			54	24	30	31	13	9	1	1	0	0	4	2	0	0	24	30

Rank among batters: 938 • *Top target (3 home runs)*: Scott McGregor • *Number of pitchers victimized*: 45 • *Total ballparks homered in*: 14 • *First HR*: 04/13/1976 off Jim Palmer • *World Series HR*—3; *LCS HR*—1

Merritt Ranew

MERRITT THOMAS RANEW
B: 05/10/1938
BL

Year	Tm	Lg	Tot	H	A	Men-On 0	1	2	3	One-Game 2	3	4	LO	XN	IP	PH	RHP	LHP
1962	HOU	NL	4	2	2	2	2	0	0	0	0	0	0	0	0	0	4	0
1963	CHI	NL	3	1	2	2	1	0	0	0	0	0	0	0	0	1	3	0
1965	CAL	AL	1	0	1	1	0	0	0	0	0	0	0	0	0	0	1	0
Total			8	3	5	5	3	0	0	0	0	0	0	0	0	1	8	0

Rank among batters: 2,703 • *Total ballparks homered in*: 6 • *First HR*: 04/25/1962 off Ray Washburn

Jeff Ransom

JEFFREY DEAN RANSOM
B: 11/11/1960
BR

Year	Tm	Lg	Tot	H	A	Men-On 0	1	2	3	One-Game 2	3	4	LO	XN	IP	PH	RHP	LHP
1983	SF	NL	1	0	1	1	0	0	0	0	0	0	0	0	0	0	1	0

Rank among batters: 4,707 • *Total ballparks homered in*: 1 • *First HR*: 09/29/1983 off Bruce Berenyi

Earl Rapp

EARL WELLINGTON RAPP
B: 05/20/1921 D: 02/13/1992
BL

Year	Tm	Lg	Tot	H	A	Men-On 0	1	2	3	One-Game 2	3	4	LO	XN	IP	PH	RHP	LHP
1951	STL	AL	2	0	2	1	1	0	0	0	0	0	0	0	0	0	2	0

Rank among batters: 4,129 • *Total ballparks homered in*: 2 • *First HR*: 09/11/1951 off Tom Morgan

Goldie Rapp

JOSEPH ALOYSIUS RAPP
B: 02/06/1892 D: 07/01/1966
BB

Year	Tm	Lg	Tot	H	A	Men-On 0	1	2	3	One-Game 2	3	4	LO	XN	IP	PH	RHP	LHP
1921	PHI	NL	1	0	1	1	0	0	0	0	0	0	1	0	0	0	0	1
1923	PHI	NL	1	0	1	1	0	0	0	0	0	0	0	0	1	0	1	0
Total			2	0	2	2	0	0	0	0	0	0	1	0	1	0	1	1

Rank among batters: 4,129 • *Total ballparks homered in*: 2 • *First HR*: 07/29/1921 off Lefty York

Bill Rariden

WILLIAM ANGEL RARIDEN
B: 02/04/1888 D: 08/28/1942
BR

Year	Tm	Lg	Tot	H	A	Men-On 0	1	2	3	One-Game 2	3	4	LO	XN	IP	PH	RHP	LHP
1910	BOS	NL	1	1	0	0	0	1	0	0	0	0	0	0	0	0	1	0
1912	BOS	NL	1	1	0	1	0	0	0	0	0	0	0	0	0	0	0	1
1913	BOS	NL	3	0	3	1	1	0	1	0	0	0	0	0	0	0	2	1
1916	NY	NL	1	1	0	1	0	0	0	0	0	0	0	0	0	0	1	0
1919	CIN	NL	1	0	1	0	1	0	0	0	0	0	0	0	0	0	0	1
Total			7	3	4	3	2	1	1	0	0	0	0	0	0	0	4	3

Rank among batters: 2,834 • *Total ballparks homered in*: 4 • *First HR*: 10/06/1910 off Bob Ewing

Vic Raschi

VICTOR JOHN ANGELO RASCHI
B: 03/28/1919 D: 10/14/1988
BR

Year	Tm	Lg	Tot	H	A	Men-On 0	1	2	3	One-Game 2	3	4	LO	XN	IP	PH	RHP	LHP
1950	NY	AL	1	1	0	0	0	1	0	0	0	0	0	0	0	0	1	0

Rank among batters: 4,707 • *Total ballparks homered in*: 1 • *First HR*: 08/29/1950 off Early Wynn

Morris Rath

MORRIS CHARLES RATH
B: 12/25/1886 D: 11/18/1945
BL

Year	Tm	Lg	Tot	H	A	Men-On 0	1	2	3	One-Game 2	3	4	LO	XN	IP	PH	RHP	LHP
1912	CHI	AL	1	0	1	0	1	0	0	0	0	0	0	0	1	0	1	0
1919	CIN	NL	1	1	0	1	0	0	0	0	0	0	1	0	1	0	0	1
1920	CIN	NL	2	0	2	1	1	0	0	1	0	0	0	0	2	0	0	2
Total			4	1	3	2	2	0	0	1	0	0	1	0	4	0	1	3

Rank among batters: 3,427 • *Top target (2 home runs)*: Rube Benton • *Number of pitchers victimized*: 3 • *Total ballparks homered in*: 3 • *First HR*: 05/10/1912 off Bob Groom

Paul Ratliff

PAUL HAWTHORNE RATLIFF
B: 01/23/1944
BL

Year	Tm	Lg	Tot	H	A	Men-On 0	1	2	3	One-Game 2	3	4	LO	XN	IP	PH	RHP	LHP
1963	MIN	AL	1	1	0	1	0	0	0	0	0	0	0	0	0	0	1	0
1970	MIN	AL	5	1	4	3	1	1	0	0	0	0	0	0	0	1	5	0
1971	MIN	AL	2	0	2	0	1	1	0	0	0	0	0	0	0	0	2	0
	MIL	AL	3	0	3	1	2	0	0	0	0	0	0	0	0	0	3	0
	Total		5	0	5	1	3	1	0	0	0	0	0	0	0	0	5	0
1972	MIL	AL	1	1	0	0	0	1	0	0	0	0	0	0	0	0	1	0
Total			12	3	9	5	4	3	0	0	0	0	0	0	0	1	12	0

Rank among batters: 2,325 • *Total ballparks homered in*: 8 • *First HR*: 09/19/1963 off Jim Bunning

Johnny Rawlings

JOHN WILLIAM RAWLINGS
B: 08/17/1892 D: 10/16/1972
BR

Year	Tm	Lg	Tot	H	A	Men-On 0	1	2	3	One-Game 2	3	4	LO	XN	IP	PH	RHP	LHP
1915	KC	FL	2	1	1	2	0	0	0	0	0	0	0	0	1	0	1	1
1917	BOS	NL	2	2	0	2	0	0	0	0	0	0	0	0	2	0	2	0
1919	BOS	NL	1	0	1	1	0	0	0	0	0	0	0	0	1	0	0	1
1920	PHI	NL	3	2	1	1	2	0	0	0	0	0	0	0	0	0	2	1
1921	PHI	NL	1	1	0	0	0	1	0	0	0	0	0	0	0	0	1	0
	NY	NL	1	1	0	1	0	0	0	0	0	0	0	0	0	0	1	0
	Total		2	2	0	1	0	1	0	0	0	0	0	0	0	0	2	0
1922	NY	NL	1	1	0	0	0	1	0	0	0	0	0	0	0	0	1	0
1923	PIT	NL	1	0	1	1	0	0	0	0	0	0	0	0	0	0	1	0
1925	PIT	NL	2	0	2	1	1	0	0	0	0	0	0	0	1	0	2	0
Total			14	8	6	9	3	2	0	0	0	0	0	0	5	0	11	3

Rank among batters: 2,169 • *Total ballparks homered in*: 7 • *First HR*: 04/19/1915 off Bunny Hearn

Irv Ray

IRVING BURTON RAY
B: 01/22/1864 D: 02/21/1948
BL

Year	Tm	Lg	Tot	H	A	Men-On 0	1	2	3	One-Game 2	3	4	LO	XN	IP	PH	RHP	LHP
1888	BOS	NL	2	1	1	1	1	0	0	0	0	0	0	0	1	0	2	0
1890	BAL	AA	1	1	0	1	0	0	0	0	0	0	0	0	0	0	0	1
Total			3	2	1	2	1	0	0	0	0	0	0	0	1	0	2	1

Rank among batters: 3,735 • *Total ballparks homered in*: 3 • *First HR*: 08/18/1888 off Mark Baldwin

Johnny Ray

JOHN CORNELIUS RAY
B: 03/01/1957
BB

Year	Tm	Lg	Tot	H	A	Men-On 0	1	2	3	One-Game 2	3	4	LO	XN	IP	PH	RHP	LHP
1982	PIT	NL	7	6	1	5	0	2	0	0	0	0	0	1	0	0	7	0
1983	PIT	NL	5	3	2	3	2	0	0	1	0	0	0	0	0	1	5	0
1984	PIT	NL	6	3	3	4	1	1	0	0	0	0	0	1	0	0	6	0
1985	PIT	NL	7	3	4	4	1	2	0	0	0	0	1	0	0	0	6	1
1986	PIT	NL	7	2	5	5	1	1	0	0	0	0	0	0	0	0	6	1
1987	PIT	NL	5	5	0	2	2	1	0	0	0	0	0	0	0	0	3	2
1988	CAL	AL	6	4	2	4	0	2	0	0	0	0	0	0	0	1	4	2
1989	CAL	AL	5	3	2	2	3	0	0	0	0	0	0	0	0	0	4	1
1990	CAL	AL	5	5	0	4	0	1	0	0	0	0	0	0	0	0	5	0
Total			53	34	19	33	10	10	0	1	0	0	1	2	0	2	46	7

Rank among batters: 953 • *Top target (2 home runs)*: Charles Hudson, Rick Aguilera • *Number of pitchers victimized*: 51 • *Total ballparks homered in*: 12 • *First HR*: 04/10/1982 off Steve Mura

Year	Tm	Lg	Tot	H	A	Men-On 0	1	2	3	One-Game 2	3	4	LO	XN	IP	PH	RHP	LHP

Floyd Rayford

FLOYD KINNARD RAYFORD
B: 07/27/1957
BR

Year	Tm	Lg	Tot	H	A	Men-On 0	1	2	3	One-Game 2	3	4	LO	XN	IP	PH	RHP	LHP
1982	BAL	AL	3	1	2	1	2	0	0	0	0	0	0	1	0	0	2	1
1983	STL	NL	3	1	2	1	1	1	0	0	0	0	0	0	0	2	0	3
1984	BAL	AL	4	4	0	2	1	1	0	0	0	0	0	0	0	0	1	3
1985	BAL	AL	18	6	12	10	7	1	0	0	0	0	0	0	0	1	6	12
1986	BAL	AL	8	5	3	5	2	1	0	0	0	0	0	0	0	0	4	4
1987	BAL	AL	2	1	1	1	1	0	0	0	0	0	0	0	0	1	0	2
Total			38	18	20	20	14	4	0	0	0	0	0	1	0	4	13	25

Rank among batters: 1,225 • Top target (2 home runs): Jimmy Key, Frank Tanana, Charlie Leibrandt, Mark Langston, Al Nipper, Oil Can Boyd, Steve Carlton • *Number of pitchers victimized*: 31 • *Total ballparks homered in*: 13 • *First HR*: 07/03/1982 off Aurelio Lopez

Fred Raymer

FREDERICK CHARLES RAYMER
B: 11/12/1875 D: 06/11/1957
BR

Year	Tm	Lg	Tot	H	A	Men-On 0	1	2	3	One-Game 2	3	4	LO	XN	IP	PH	RHP	LHP
1904	BOS	NL	1	1	0	1	0	0	0	0	0	0	0	0	0	0	1	0

Rank among batters: 4,707 • *Total ballparks homered in*: 1 • *First HR*: 06/17/1904 off Fred Mitchell

Harry Raymond

HARRY H. RAYMOND
B: 02/20/1862 D: 03/21/1925

Year	Tm	Lg	Tot	H	A	Men-On 0	1	2	3	One-Game 2	3	4	LO	XN	IP	PH	RHP	LHP
1890	LOU	AA	2	2	0	1	1	0	0	0	0	0	0	0	0	0	0	1

Rank among batters: 4,129 • *Total ballparks homered in*: 1 • *First HR*: 06/29/1890 off Charlie McCullough

Randy Ready

RANDY MAX READY
B: 01/08/1960
BR

Year	Tm	Lg	Tot	H	A	Men-On 0	1	2	3	One-Game 2	3	4	LO	XN	IP	PH	RHP	LHP
1983	MIL	AL	1	0	1	1	0	0	0	0	0	0	0	0	0	0	1	0
1984	MIL	AL	3	3	0	2	0	1	0	0	0	0	1	0	0	0	1	2
1985	MIL	AL	1	0	1	0	1	0	0	0	0	0	0	1	0	0	0	1
1986	MIL	AL	1	0	1	1	0	0	0	0	0	0	0	0	0	0	1	0
1987	SD	NL	12	7	5	8	4	0	0	0	0	0	0	1	0	0	6	6
1988	SD	NL	7	3	4	4	3	0	0	0	0	0	0	0	0	0	2	5
1989	PHI	NL	8	3	5	6	2	0	0	0	0	0	2	0	0	1	3	5
1990	PHI	NL	1	0	1	0	1	0	0	0	0	0	0	0	0	0	0	1
1991	PHI	NL	1	1	0	1	0	0	0	0	0	0	0	0	0	0	0	1
1992	OAK	AL	3	1	2	1	1	0	1	0	0	0	0	0	0	1	0	3
1993	MON	NL	1	0	1	1	0	0	0	0	0	0	1	0	0	0	1	0
1994	PHI	NL	1	0	1	1	0	0	0	0	0	0	0	0	0	0	0	1
Total			40	18	22	26	12	1	1	0	0	0	4	2	0	2	15	25

Rank among batters: 1,181 • *Top target (2 home runs)*: Fernando Valenzuela, Doug Drabek, Steve Avery • *Number of pitchers victimized*: 37 • *Total ballparks homered in*: 16 • *First HR*: 09/22/1983 off Lary Sorensen

Jeff Reboulet

JEFFREY ALLEN REBOULET
B: 04/30/1964
BR

Year	Tm	Lg	Tot	H	A	Men-On 0	1	2	3	One-Game 2	3	4	LO	XN	IP	PH	RHP	LHP
1992	MIN	AL	1	1	0	1	0	0	0	0	0	0	0	0	0	0	1	0
1993	MIN	AL	1	0	1	0	1	0	0	0	0	0	0	0	0	0	1	0
1994	MIN	AL	3	2	1	1	2	0	0	0	0	0	0	0	0	0	1	2
1995	MIN	AL	4	1	3	4	0	0	0	0	0	0	0	0	0	0	0	4
Total			9	4	5	6	3	0	0	0	0	0	0	0	0	0	3	6

Rank among batters: 2,587 • *Total ballparks homered in*: 4 • *First HR*: 08/02/1992 off Ricky Bones

John Reccius

JOHN RECCIUS
B: 10/29/1859 D: 09/01/1930

Year	Tm	Lg	Tot	H	A	Men-On 0	1	2	3	One-Game 2	3	4	LO	XN	IP	PH	RHP	LHP
1882	LOU	AA	1	0	1	0	1	0	0	0	0	0	0	0	0	0	1	0

Rank among batters: 4,707 • *Total ballparks homered in*: 1 • *First HR*: 07/21/1882 off Emil Geis

Philip Reccius

PHILIP RECCIUS
B: 06/07/1862 D: 02/15/1903

Year	Tm	Lg	Tot	H	A	Men-On 0	Men-On 1	Men-On 2	Men-On 3	One-Game 2	One-Game 3	One-Game 4	LO	XN	IP	PH	RHP	LHP
1884	LOU	AA	3	0	3	1	2	0	0	0	0	0	0	0	0	0	2	0
1885	LOU	AA	1	1	0	0	1	0	0	0	0	0	0	0	0	0	1	0
Total			4	1	3	1	3	0	0	0	0	0	0	0	0	0	3	0

Rank among batters: 3,427 • *Total ballparks homered in*: 4 • *First HR*: 08/13/1884 off Bill Mountjoy

Jack Redmond

JOHN MCKITTRICK REDMOND
B: 09/03/1910 D: 07/27/1968
BL

Year	Tm	Lg	Tot	H	A	Men-On 0	Men-On 1	Men-On 2	Men-On 3	One-Game 2	One-Game 3	One-Game 4	LO	XN	IP	PH	RHP	LHP
1935	WAS	AL	1	0	1	0	1	0	0	0	0	0	0	0	0	0	1	0

Rank among batters: 4,707 • *Total ballparks homered in*: 1 • *First HR*: 07/28/1935 off Jumbo Brown

Gary Redus

GARY EUGENE REDUS
B: 11/01/1956
BR

Year	Tm	Lg	Tot	H	A	Men-On 0	Men-On 1	Men-On 2	Men-On 3	One-Game 2	One-Game 3	One-Game 4	LO	XN	IP	PH	RHP	LHP
1982	CIN	NL	1	1	0	1	0	0	0	0	0	0	1	0	0	0	1	0
1983	CIN	NL	17	6	11	14	1	2	0	1	0	0	2	0	0	0	14	3
1984	CIN	NL	7	4	3	5	2	0	0	0	0	0	1	0	0	0	5	2
1985	CIN	NL	6	4	2	3	1	2	0	0	0	0	1	0	0	0	4	2
1986	PHI	NL	11	8	3	8	3	0	0	2	0	0	2	0	0	0	9	2
1987	CHI	AL	12	4	8	9	3	0	0	0	0	0	3	0	0	0	5	7
1988	CHI	AL	6	1	5	3	0	1	2	0	0	0	0	0	0	0	3	3
	PIT	NL	2	2	0	2	0	0	0	0	0	0	0	0	0	1	1	1
	Total		8	3	5	5	0	1	2	0	0	0	0	0	0	1	4	4
1989	PIT	NL	6	3	3	3	0	3	0	0	0	0	0	0	0	0	3	3
1990	PIT	NL	6	2	4	4	1	0	1	0	0	0	2	0	0	0	0	6
1991	PIT	NL	7	3	4	6	0	0	1	0	0	0	1	0	0	1	2	5
1992	PIT	NL	3	1	2	2	1	0	0	0	0	0	1	1	0	0	1	2
1993	TEX	AL	6	2	4	3	0	3	0	1	0	0	0	0	0	1	4	2
Total			90	41	49	63	12	11	4	4	0	0	14	1	0	3	52	38

Rank among batters: 573 • *Top target (4 home runs)*: Rick Mahler, Sid Fernandez • *Number of pitchers victimized*: 71 • *Total ballparks homered in*: 23 • *First HR*: 09/19/1982 off Rick Mahler • *Hit for Cycle*—@CIN: 08/25/1989

Darren Reed

DARREN A DOUGLASS REED
B: 10/16/1965
BR

Year	Tm	Lg	Tot	H	A	Men-On 0	Men-On 1	Men-On 2	Men-On 3	One-Game 2	One-Game 3	One-Game 4	LO	XN	IP	PH	RHP	LHP
1990	NY	NL	1	1	0	1	0	0	0	0	0	0	0	0	0	0	0	1
1992	MON	NL	5	1	4	3	1	1	0	0	0	0	0	0	0	0	2	3
Total			6	2	4	4	1	1	0	0	0	0	0	0	0	0	2	4

Rank among batters: 2,988 • *Total ballparks homered in*: 4 • *First HR*: 09/30/1990 off Steve Wilson

Howie Reed

HOWARD DEAN REED
B: 12/21/1936 D: 12/07/1984
BR

Year	Tm	Lg	Tot	H	A	Men-On 0	Men-On 1	Men-On 2	Men-On 3	One-Game 2	One-Game 3	One-Game 4	LO	XN	IP	PH	RHP	LHP
1969	MON	NL	1	1	0	1	0	0	0	0	0	0	0	0	0	0	1	0

Rank among batters: 4,707 • *Total ballparks homered in*: 1 • *First HR*: 06/26/1969 off Nelson Briles

Jack Reed

JOHN BURWELL REED
B: 02/02/1933
BR

Year	Tm	Lg	Tot	H	A	Men-On 0	Men-On 1	Men-On 2	Men-On 3	One-Game 2	One-Game 3	One-Game 4	LO	XN	IP	PH	RHP	LHP
1962	NY	AL	1	0	1	0	1	0	0	0	0	0	0	1	0	0	1	0

Rank among batters: 4,707 • *Total ballparks homered in*: 1 • *First HR*: 06/24/1962 off Phil Regan

Jeff Reed

JEFFREY SCOTT REED
B: 11/12/1962
BL

Year	Tm	Lg	Tot	H	A	Men-On 0	Men-On 1	Men-On 2	Men-On 3	One-Game 2	One-Game 3	One-Game 4	LO	XN	IP	PH	RHP	LHP
1986	MIN	AL	2	1	1	1	1	0	0	0	0	0	0	0	0	0	2	0
1987	MON	NL	1	1	0	0	0	1	0	0	0	0	0	0	0	0	1	0

Jeff Reed *continued*

Year	Tm	Lg	Tot	H	A	Men-On 0	1	2	3	One-Game 2	3	4	LO	XN	IP	PH	RHP	LHP
1988	CIN	NL	1	1	0	1	0	0	0	0	0	0	0	0	0	0	1	0
1989	CIN	NL	3	1	2	1	2	0	0	0	0	0	0	0	0	0	3	0
1990	CIN	NL	3	2	1	2	1	0	0	0	0	0	0	0	0	0	1	2
1991	CIN	NL	3	1	2	1	1	0	1	0	0	0	0	0	0	0	3	0
1993	SF	NL	6	5	1	5	1	0	0	0	0	0	0	0	0	2	4	2
1994	SF	NL	1	0	1	0	0	1	0	0	0	0	0	0	0	0	1	0
Total			20	12	8	11	6	2	1	0	0	0	0	0	0	2	16	4

Rank among batters: 1,810 • *Top target (2 home runs)*: Andy Benes • *Number of pitchers victimized*: 19 • *Total ballparks homered in*: 9 • *First HR*: 06/04/1986 off Jim Acker

Jody Reed

JODY ERIC REED
B: 07/26/1962
BR

Year	Tm	Lg	Tot	H	A	Men-On 0	1	2	3	One-Game 2	3	4	LO	XN	IP	PH	RHP	LHP
1988	BOS	AL	1	1	0	0	1	0	0	0	0	0	0	0	0	0	1	0
1989	BOS	AL	3	2	1	2	1	0	0	0	0	0	0	0	0	1	2	1
1990	BOS	AL	5	3	2	4	1	0	0	0	0	0	0	0	0	0	5	0
1991	BOS	AL	5	3	2	2	3	0	0	0	0	0	0	0	0	0	5	0
1992	BOS	AL	3	2	1	3	0	0	0	0	0	0	0	0	0	0	2	1
1993	LA	NL	2	0	2	1	1	0	0	0	0	0	0	0	0	0	2	0
1994	MIL	AL	2	1	1	1	0	1	0	0	0	0	0	0	0	0	2	0
1995	SD	NL	4	4	0	3	0	1	0	0	0	0	0	0	3	0	4	0
Total			25	16	9	16	7	2	0	0	0	0	0	0	3	1	23	2

Rank among batters: 1,608 • *Top target (2 home runs)*: John Farrell, Scott Sanderson, Willie Blair • *Number of pitchers victimized*: 22 • *Total ballparks homered in*: 9 • *First HR*: 06/27/1988 off John Farrell

Jimmie Reese

JAMES HERMAN REESE
B: 10/01/1901 D: 07/13/1994
BL

Year	Tm	Lg	Tot	H	A	Men-On 0	1	2	3	One-Game 2	3	4	LO	XN	IP	PH	RHP	LHP
1930	NY	AL	3	3	0	1	1	0	1	0	0	0	0	0	0	0	3	0
1931	NY	AL	3	2	1	2	1	0	0	0	0	0	0	0	2	0	3	0
1932	STL	NL	2	1	1	0	2	0	0	0	0	0	0	0	0	0	2	0
Total			8	6	2	3	4	0	1	0	0	0	0	0	2	0	8	0

Rank among batters: 2,703 • *Total ballparks homered in*: 4 • *First HR*: 05/30/1930 off Hod Lisenbee

Pee Wee Reese

HAROLD HENRY REESE
B: 07/23/1918
BR HOF

Year	Tm	Lg	Tot	H	A	Men-On 0	1	2	3	One-Game 2	3	4	LO	XN	IP	PH	RHP	LHP
1940	BRO	NL	5	2	3	3	1	0	1	0	0	0	0	1	0	0	4	1
1941	BRO	NL	2	0	2	2	0	0	0	0	0	0	0	0	0	0	1	1
1942	BRO	NL	3	1	2	1	2	0	0	0	0	0	0	0	0	0	1	2
1946	BRO	NL	5	1	4	3	0	2	0	0	0	0	0	0	0	0	4	1
1947	BRO	NL	12	6	6	6	4	1	1	0	0	0	0	0	0	0	9	3
1948	BRO	NL	9	4	5	3	4	1	1	0	0	0	0	0	0	0	5	4
1949	BRO	NL	16	8	8	9	4	3	0	2	0	0	4	0	0	0	11	5
1950	BRO	NL	11	6	5	8	2	1	0	0	0	0	0	0	1	0	8	3
1951	BRO	NL	10	6	4	3	2	4	1	0	0	0	0	0	0	0	9	1
1952	BRO	NL	6	3	3	3	2	0	1	0	0	0	0	0	0	0	5	1
1953	BRO	NL	13	8	5	6	5	1	1	1	0	0	0	1	0	0	12	1
1954	BRO	NL	10	3	7	4	6	0	0	0	0	0	0	0	0	0	8	2
1955	BRO	NL	10	7	3	6	3	1	0	0	0	0	0	0	0	0	6	4
1956	BRO	NL	9	5	4	6	2	1	0	0	0	0	0	0	0	0	8	1
1957	BRO	NL	1	0	1	0	1	0	0	0	0	0	0	0	0	0	1	0
1958	LA	NL	4	3	1	3	1	0	0	1	0	0	0	0	0	0	4	0
Total			126	63	63	66	39	15	6	4	0	0	4	2	1	0	96	30

Rank among batters: 360 • *Top target (6 home runs)*: Robin Roberts • *Number of pitchers victimized*: 86 • *Total ballparks homered in*: 10 • *First HR*: 05/26/1940 off Kirby Higbe • *World Series HR*—2

Randy Reese

ANDREW JACKSON REESE
B: 02/07/1904 D: 01/10/1966
BR

Year	Tm	Lg	Tot	H	A	Men-On 0	1	2	3	One-Game 2	3	4	LO	XN	IP	PH	RHP	LHP
1927	NY	NL	4	3	1	3	1	0	0	0	0	0	0	0	0	0	2	2

Randy Reese *continued*

Year	Tm	Lg	Tot	H	A	Men-On 0	Men-On 1	Men-On 2	Men-On 3	One-Game 2	One-Game 3	One-Game 4	LO	XN	IP	PH	RHP	LHP
1928	NY	NL	6	4	2	0	5	1	0	0	0	0	0	0	1	0	3	3
1930	NY	NL	4	0	4	2	1	0	1	0	0	0	0	0	1	0	2	2
Total			14	7	7	5	7	1	1	0	0	0	0	0	2	0	7	7

Rank among batters: 2,169 • *Top target (2 home runs)*: Bill Sherdel, Ray Kremer • *Number of pitchers victimized*: 12 • *Total ballparks homered in*: 5 • *First HR*: 06/19/1927 off Bill Sherdel

Rich Reese

RICHARD BENJAMIN REESE
B: 09/29/1941
BL

Year	Tm	Lg	Tot	H	A	Men-On 0	Men-On 1	Men-On 2	Men-On 3	One-Game 2	One-Game 3	One-Game 4	LO	XN	IP	PH	RHP	LHP
1967	MIN	AL	4	3	1	1	2	1	0	0	0	0	0	0	0	2	4	0
1968	MIN	AL	4	2	2	2	1	1	0	0	0	0	0	0	0	0	2	2
1969	MIN	AL	16	8	8	7	4	4	1	3	0	0	0	0	0	1	10	6
1970	MIN	AL	10	5	5	5	3	1	1	0	0	0	0	0	0	1	9	1
1971	MIN	AL	10	4	6	5	5	0	0	2	0	0	0	0	0	0	10	0
1972	MIN	AL	5	2	3	3	0	1	1	0	0	0	0	0	0	1	5	0
1973	DET	AL	2	1	1	1	1	0	0	0	0	0	1	0	0	0	2	0
	MIN	AL	1	0	1	1	0	0	0	0	0	0	0	0	0	0	1	0
	Total		3	1	2	2	1	0	0	0	0	0	1	0	0	0	3	0
Total			52	25	27	25	16	8	3	5	0	0	1	0	0	5	43	9

Rank among batters: 965 • *Top target (6 home runs)*: Catfish Hunter • *Number of pitchers victimized*: 40 • *Total ballparks homered in*: 10 • *First HR*: 05/11/1967 off Catfish Hunter

Bobby Reeves

ROBERT EDWIN REEVES
B: 06/24/1904 D: 06/04/1993
BR

Year	Tm	Lg	Tot	H	A	Men-On 0	Men-On 1	Men-On 2	Men-On 3	One-Game 2	One-Game 3	One-Game 4	LO	XN	IP	PH	RHP	LHP
1927	WAS	AL	1	0	1	0	1	0	0	0	0	0	0	0	0	0	1	0
1928	WAS	AL	3	0	3	1	1	1	0	0	0	0	0	0	1	0	2	1
1929	BOS	AL	2	0	2	2	0	0	0	0	0	0	1	0	0	0	1	1
1930	BOS	AL	2	0	2	1	0	1	0	0	0	0	0	1	0	0	0	2
Total			8	0	8	4	2	2	0	0	0	0	1	1	1	0	4	4

Rank among batters: 2,703 • *Total ballparks homered in*: 5 • *First HR*: 09/29/1927 off Urban Shocker

Rudy Regalado

RUDOLPH VALENTINO REGALADO
B: 05/21/1930
BR

Year	Tm	Lg	Tot	H	A	Men-On 0	Men-On 1	Men-On 2	Men-On 3	One-Game 2	One-Game 3	One-Game 4	LO	XN	IP	PH	RHP	LHP
1954	CLE	AL	2	2	0	2	0	0	0	0	0	0	0	0	0	0	1	1

Rank among batters: 4,129 • *Total ballparks homered in*: 1 • *First HR*: 05/13/1954 off Mickey McDermott

Bill Regan

WILLIAM WRIGHT REGAN
B: 01/23/1899 D: 06/11/1968
BR

Year	Tm	Lg	Tot	H	A	Men-On 0	Men-On 1	Men-On 2	Men-On 3	One-Game 2	One-Game 3	One-Game 4	LO	XN	IP	PH	RHP	LHP
1926	BOS	AL	4	0	4	3	0	1	0	0	0	0	0	0	0	0	2	2
1927	BOS	AL	2	1	1	1	1	0	0	0	0	0	0	0	0	0	2	0
1928	BOS	AL	7	1	6	3	2	1	1	1	0	0	0	0	2	0	6	1
1929	BOS	AL	1	1	0	1	0	0	0	0	0	0	0	0	0	0	0	1
1930	BOS	AL	3	1	2	1	1	1	0	0	0	0	0	0	0	0	1	2
1931	PIT	NL	1	0	1	1	0	0	0	0	0	0	0	0	0	0	0	1
Total			18	4	14	10	4	3	1	1	0	0	0	0	2	0	11	7

Rank among batters: 1,914 • *Top target (2 home runs)*: Rip Collins • *Number of pitchers victimized*: 17 • *Total ballparks homered in*: 7 • *First HR*: 07/07/1926 off Jack Quinn • *2 HR in 1 inning—@CHI*: 06/16/1928

Phil Regan

PHILIP RAYMOND REGAN
B: 04/06/1937
BR

Year	Tm	Lg	Tot	H	A	Men-On 0	Men-On 1	Men-On 2	Men-On 3	One-Game 2	One-Game 3	One-Game 4	LO	XN	IP	PH	RHP	LHP
1963	DET	AL	1	1	0	1	0	0	0	0	0	0	0	0	0	0	1	0

Rank among batters: 4,707 • *Total ballparks homered in*: 1 • *First HR*: 05/10/1963 off Gary Bell

Walter Rehg

WALTER PHILLIP REHG
B: 08/31/1888 D: 04/05/1946
BR

Year	Tm	Lg	Tot	H	A	Men-On 0	1	2	3	One-Game 2	3	4	LO	XN	IP	PH	RHP	LHP
1917	BOS	NL	1	0	1	1	0	0	0	0	0	0	0	0	0	0	1	0
1918	BOS	NL	1	1	0	0	1	0	0	0	0	0	0	0	1	0	0	1
Total			2	1	1	1	1	0	0	0	0	0	0	0	1	0	1	1

Rank among batters: 4,129 • *Total ballparks homered in*: 2 • *First HR*: 09/04/1917 off Al Demaree

Frank Reiber

FRANK BERNARD REIBER
B: 09/19/1909
BR

Year	Tm	Lg	Tot	H	A	Men-On 0	1	2	3	One-Game 2	3	4	LO	XN	IP	PH	RHP	LHP
1933	DET	AL	1	0	1	1	0	0	0	0	0	0	0	0	0	0	1	0
1936	DET	AL	1	0	1	1	0	0	0	0	0	0	0	0	0	0	1	0
Total			2	0	2	2	0	0	0	0	0	0	0	0	0	0	2	0

Rank among batters: 4,129 • *Total ballparks homered in*: 2 • *First HR*: 04/28/1933 off Dick Coffman

Herman Reich

HERMAN CHARLES REICH
B: 11/23/1917
BR

Year	Tm	Lg	Tot	H	A	Men-On 0	1	2	3	One-Game 2	3	4	LO	XN	IP	PH	RHP	LHP
1949	CHI	NL	3	2	1	1	1	1	0	0	0	0	0	0	0	0	2	1

Rank among batters: 3,735 • *Total ballparks homered in*: 2 • *First HR*: 06/22/1949 off Bob Hall

Rick Reichardt

FREDERIC CARL REICHARDT
B: 03/16/1943
BR

Year	Tm	Lg	Tot	H	A	Men-On 0	1	2	3	One-Game 2	3	4	LO	XN	IP	PH	RHP	LHP
1965	CAL	AL	1	1	0	1	0	0	0	0	0	0	0	0	0	0	1	0
1966	CAL	AL	16	6	10	7	8	1	0	1	0	0	0	0	0	0	10	6
1967	CAL	AL	17	8	9	7	7	1	2	1	0	0	0	0	1	0	9	8
1968	CAL	AL	21	15	6	14	5	2	0	1	0	0	0	1	0	0	13	8
1969	CAL	AL	13	10	3	8	4	1	0	2	0	0	0	0	1	0	10	3
1970	WAS	AL	15	6	9	9	5	0	1	1	0	0	0	1	0	3	5	10
1971	CHI	AL	19	8	11	12	5	1	1	2	0	0	0	0	0	0	12	7
1972	CHI	AL	8	2	6	2	4	2	0	1	0	0	0	0	0	0	4	4
1973	CHI	AL	3	1	2	2	0	1	0	0	0	0	0	0	0	1	3	0
	KC	AL	3	3	0	0	3	0	0	0	0	0	0	1	0	0	2	1
	Total		6	4	2	2	3	1	0	0	0	0	0	1	0	1	5	1
Total			116	60	56	62	41	9	4	9	0	0	0	3	2	4	69	47

Rank among batters: 411 • *Top target (4 home runs)*: Paul Lindblad, Dave McNally • *Number of pitchers victimized*: 82 • *Total ballparks homered in*: 13 • *First HR*: 09/15/1965 off Joe Horlen • *2 HR in 1 inning*—@BOS: 04/30/1966

Dick Reichle

RICHARD WENDELL REICHLE
B: 11/23/1896 D: 06/13/1967
BL

Year	Tm	Lg	Tot	H	A	Men-On 0	1	2	3	One-Game 2	3	4	LO	XN	IP	PH	RHP	LHP
1923	BOS	AL	1	0	1	0	1	0	0	0	0	0	0	0	0	0	1	0

Rank among batters: 4,707 • *Total ballparks homered in*: 1 • *First HR*: 04/20/1923 off Waite Hoyt

Jessie Reid

JESSIE THOMAS REID
B: 06/01/1962
BL

Year	Tm	Lg	Tot	H	A	Men-On 0	1	2	3	One-Game 2	3	4	LO	XN	IP	PH	RHP	LHP
1987	SF	NL	1	0	1	1	0	0	0	0	0	0	0	0	0	0	1	0

Rank among batters: 4,707 • *Total ballparks homered in*: 1 • *First HR*: 09/29/1987 off Jimmy Jones

Charlie Reilly

CHARLES THOMAS REILLY
B: 02/15/1867 D: 12/16/1937
BB

Year	Tm	Lg	Tot	H	A	Men-On 0	1	2	3	One-Game 2	3	4	LO	XN	IP	PH	RHP	LHP
1889	COL	AA	3	3	0	2	1	0	0	1	0	0	0	0	0	0	3	0
1890	COL	AA	4	3	1	2	2	0	0	0	0	0	0	0	0	0	2	0
1891	PIT	NL	3	2	1	1	1	1	0	0	0	0	0	0	0	0	3	0
1892	PHI	NL	1	0	1	0	1	0	0	0	0	0	0	0	0	0	1	0

Year	Tm	Lg	Tot	H	A	Men-On 0	1	2	3	One-Game 2	3	4	LO	XN	IP	PH	RHP	LHP

Charlie Reilly *continued*

Year	Tm	Lg	Tot	H	A	Men-On 0	1	2	3	One-Game 2	3	4	LO	XN	IP	PH	RHP	LHP
1893	PHI	NL	4	1	3	4	0	0	0	0	0	0	0	0	0	0	4	0
1897	WAS	NL	2	1	1	1	0	0	1	0	0	0	0	0	0	0	0	2
Total			17	10	7	10	5	1	1	1	0	0	0	0	0	0	13	2

Rank among batters: 1,969 • *Top target (2 home runs)*: Sadie McMahon, Bill Hutchison • *Number of pitchers victimized*: 15 • *Total ballparks homered in*: 10 • *First HR*: 10/09/1889 off Gus Weyhing

John Reilly

JOHN GOOD REILLY
B: 10/05/1858 D: 05/31/1937
BR

Year	Tm	Lg	Tot	H	A	Men-On 0	1	2	3	One-Game 2	3	4	LO	XN	IP	PH	RHP	LHP
1883	CIN	AA	9	9	0	2	6	1	0	1	0	0	0	0	0	0	6	3
1884	CIN	AA	11	8	3	6	3	2	0	0	0	0	0	0	2	0	6	1
1885	CIN	AA	5	4	1	1	4	0	0	0	0	0	0	0	0	0	4	0
1886	CIN	AA	6	5	1	0	3	3	0	0	0	0	0	0	1	0	2	2
1887	CIN	AA	10	5	5	7	1	2	0	0	0	0	0	0	1	0	9	1
1888	CIN	AA	13	10	3	7	3	3	0	1	0	0	0	1	8	0	11	2
1889	CIN	AA	5	2	3	4	1	0	0	0	0	0	0	0	0	0	4	0
1890	CIN	NL	6	4	2	4	2	0	0	0	0	0	0	1	2	0	5	0
1891	CIN	NL	4	0	4	2	0	2	0	0	0	0	0	0	0	0	4	0
Total			69	47	22	33	23	13	0	2	0	0	0	2	14	0	51	7

Rank among batters: 756 • *Top target (4 home runs)*: Adonis Terry, Henry Porter • *Number of pitchers victimized*: 47 • *Total ballparks homered in*: 14 • *First HR*: 07/06/1883 off Dave Rowe • *Hit for Cycle*—vs PIT: 09/12/1883; vs PHI: 09/19/1883; vs PIT: 08/06/1890

Tom Reilly

THOMAS HENRY REILLY
B: 08/03/1884 D: 10/18/1918
BR

Year	Tm	Lg	Tot	H	A	Men-On 0	1	2	3	One-Game 2	3	4	LO	XN	IP	PH	RHP	LHP
1908	STL	NL	1	0	1	1	0	0	0	0	0	0	0	0	0	0	1	0

Rank among batters: 4,707 • *Total ballparks homered in*: 1 • *First HR*: 08/10/1908 off Jake Boultes

Kevin Reimer

KEVIN MICHAEL REIMER
B: 06/28/1964
BL

Year	Tm	Lg	Tot	H	A	Men-On 0	1	2	3	One-Game 2	3	4	LO	XN	IP	PH	RHP	LHP
1988	TEX	AL	1	0	1	1	0	0	0	0	0	0	0	0	0	0	1	0
1990	TEX	AL	2	0	2	1	1	0	0	0	0	0	0	0	0	0	2	0
1991	TEX	AL	20	13	7	8	6	6	0	0	0	0	0	1	0	2	19	1
1992	TEX	AL	16	10	6	10	5	1	0	0	0	0	0	0	0	0	14	2
1993	MIL	AL	13	8	5	8	3	1	1	0	0	0	0	0	0	0	12	1
Total			52	31	21	28	15	8	1	0	0	0	0	1	0	2	48	4

Rank among batters: 965 • *Top target (3 home runs)*: Jose Mesa, Jack Morris • *Number of pitchers victimized*: 43 • *Total ballparks homered in*: 13 • *First HR*: 09/27/1988 off Shawn Hillegas

Pete Reiser

HAROLD PATRICK REISER
B: 03/17/1919 D: 10/25/1981
BL

Year	Tm	Lg	Tot	H	A	Men-On 0	1	2	3	One-Game 2	3	4	LO	XN	IP	PH	RHP	LHP
1940	BRO	NL	3	1	2	3	0	0	0	0	0	0	0	0	0	0	3	0
1941	BRO	NL	14	9	5	7	5	1	1	0	0	0	0	1	1	0	12	2
1942	BRO	NL	10	5	5	5	3	2	0	0	0	0	0	0	0	0	7	3
1946	BRO	NL	11	5	6	6	3	2	0	0	0	0	0	0	3	0	9	2
1947	BRO	NL	5	1	4	2	2	1	0	0	0	0	0	0	0	0	5	0
1948	BRO	NL	1	1	0	0	0	1	0	0	0	0	0	0	0	0	0	1
1949	BOS	NL	8	5	3	5	2	0	1	0	0	0	0	0	0	2	8	0
1950	BOS	NL	1	0	1	1	0	0	0	0	0	0	0	0	0	0	1	0
1951	PIT	NL	2	0	2	1	0	1	0	0	0	0	0	0	0	0	2	0
1952	CLE	AL	3	2	1	2	0	1	0	0	0	0	0	0	0	1	3	0
Total			58	29	29	32	15	9	2	0	0	0	0	1	4	3	50	8

Rank among batters: 886 • *Top target (3 home runs)*: Bucky Walters • *Number of pitchers victimized*: 51 • *Total ballparks homered in*: 9 • *First HR*: 08/21/1940 off Bill McGee • *World Series HR*—1

Heinie Reitz

HENRY P. REITZ
B: 06/29/1867 D: 11/10/1914
BL

Year	Tm	Lg	Tot	H	A	Men-On 0	1	2	3	One-Game 2	3	4	LO	XN	IP	PH	RHP	LHP
1893	BAL	NL	1	0	1	1	0	0	0	0	0	0	0	0	0	0	1	0

Heinie Reitz *continued*

Year	Tm	Lg	Tot	H	A	Men-On 0	1	2	3	One-Game 2	3	4	LO	XN	IP	PH	RHP	LHP
1894	BAL	NL	2	1	1	1	0	0	1	0	0	0	0	0	2	0	2	0
1896	BAL	NL	4	2	2	1	2	1	0	0	0	0	0	0	2	0	3	0
1897	BAL	NL	2	0	2	0	1	1	0	0	0	0	0	0	0	0	2	0
1898	WAS	NL	2	2	0	1	1	0	0	0	0	0	0	0	0	0	1	1
Total			11	5	6	4	4	2	1	0	0	0	0	0	4	0	9	1

Rank among batters: 2,419 • *Top target (2 home runs)*: Adonis Terry, Jack Stivetts • *Number of pitchers victimized*: 9 • *Total ballparks homered in*: 7 • *First HR*: 07/28/1893 off Jack Stivetts • *World Series HR*—1

Ken Reitz

KENNETH JOHN REITZ
B: 06/24/1951
BR

Year	Tm	Lg	Tot	H	A	Men-On 0	1	2	3	One-Game 2	3	4	LO	XN	IP	PH	RHP	LHP
1973	STL	NL	6	1	5	3	1	2	0	0	0	0	0	0	0	0	1	5
1974	STL	NL	7	2	5	4	3	0	0	0	0	0	0	0	0	0	5	2
1975	STL	NL	5	3	2	2	2	1	0	0	0	0	0	1	0	0	5	0
1976	SF	NL	5	4	1	1	2	2	0	0	0	0	0	0	0	0	2	3
1977	STL	NL	17	11	6	5	6	4	2	1	0	0	0	0	0	0	12	5
1978	STL	NL	10	3	7	7	2	1	0	0	0	0	0	0	0	0	3	7
1979	STL	NL	8	4	4	6	1	1	0	0	0	0	0	0	0	0	3	5
1980	STL	NL	8	3	5	5	2	1	0	1	0	0	0	1	0	0	6	2
1981	CHI	NL	2	1	1	1	1	0	0	0	0	0	0	0	0	0	1	1
Total			68	32	36	34	20	12	2	2	0	0	0	2	0	0	38	30

Rank among batters: 767 • *Top target (3 home runs)*: Larry Dierker, Steve Carlton • *Number of pitchers victimized*: 56 • *Total ballparks homered in*: 13 • *First HR*: 05/09/1973 off Ron Bryant

Jack Remsen

JOHN JAY REMSEN
B: 1851 BR

Year	Tm	Lg	Tot	H	A	Men-On 0	1	2	3	One-Game 2	3	4	LO	XN	IP	PH	RHP	LHP
1876	HAR	NL	1	0	1	1	0	0	0	0	0	0	1	0	0	0	1	0
1878	CHI	NL	1	1	0	1	0	0	0	0	0	0	0	0	0	0	1	0
1884	BRO	AA	3	1	2	2	0	1	0	0	0	0	0	0	1	0	3	0
Total			5	2	3	4	0	1	0	0	0	0	1	0	1	0	5	0

Rank among batters: 3,191 • *Total ballparks homered in*: 5 • *First HR*: 07/06/1876 off Al Spalding

Jerry Remy

GERALD PETER REMY
B: 11/08/1952
BL

Year	Tm	Lg	Tot	H	A	Men-On 0	1	2	3	One-Game 2	3	4	LO	XN	IP	PH	RHP	LHP
1975	CAL	AL	1	0	1	0	0	1	0	0	0	0	0	0	0	0	1	0
1977	CAL	AL	4	2	2	3	1	0	0	0	0	0	0	0	0	0	4	0
1978	BOS	AL	2	0	2	0	1	1	0	0	0	0	0	0	0	0	2	0
Total			7	2	5	3	2	2	0	0	0	0	0	0	0	0	7	0

Rank among batters: 2,834 • *Total ballparks homered in*: 6 • *First HR*: 05/19/1975 off Jim Perry

Rick Renick

WARREN RICHARD RENICK
B: 03/16/1944
BR

Year	Tm	Lg	Tot	H	A	Men-On 0	1	2	3	One-Game 2	3	4	LO	XN	IP	PH	RHP	LHP
1968	MIN	AL	3	3	0	3	0	0	0	0	0	0	0	0	0	0	2	1
1969	MIN	AL	5	2	3	4	1	0	0	0	0	0	0	0	0	0	1	4
1970	MIN	AL	7	6	1	5	0	0	2	1	0	0	0	0	0	1	1	6
1971	MIN	AL	1	1	0	1	0	0	0	0	0	0	0	0	0	0	0	1
1972	MIN	AL	4	3	1	4	0	0	0	0	0	0	0	0	0	1	1	3
Total			20	15	5	17	1	0	2	1	0	0	0	0	0	2	5	15

Rank among batters: 1,810 • *Top target (2 home runs)*: Mike Kekich, Mike Cuellar • *Number of pitchers victimized*: 18 • *Total ballparks homered in*: 6 • *First HR*: 07/11/1968 off Mickey Lolich • *Hit HR in first major league AB*—vs DET: 07/11/1968

Steve Renko

STEVEN RENKO
B: 12/10/1944
BR

Year	Tm	Lg	Tot	H	A	Men-On 0	1	2	3	One-Game 2	3	4	LO	XN	IP	PH	RHP	LHP
1969	MON	NL	1	1	0	1	0	0	0	0	0	0	0	0	0	0	1	0
1970	MON	NL	1	1	0	1	0	0	0	0	0	0	0	0	0	0	1	0
1971	MON	NL	2	0	2	1	1	0	0	0	0	0	0	0	0	0	2	0

Year	Tm	Lg	Tot	H	A	Men-On 0	1	2	3	One-Game 2	3	4	LO	XN	IP	PH	RHP	LHP

Steve Renko *continued*

Year	Tm	Lg	Tot	H	A	0	1	2	3	2	3	4	LO	XN	IP	PH	RHP	LHP
1974	MON	NL	1	1	0	1	0	0	0	0	0	0	0	0	0	0	1	0
1975	MON	NL	1	1	0	1	0	0	0	0	0	0	0	0	0	0	1	0
Total			6	4	2	5	1	0	0	0	0	0	0	0	0	0	6	0

Rank among batters: 2,988 • *Top target (2 home runs)*: Larry Dierker • *Number of pitchers victimized*: 5 • *Total ballparks homered in*: 3 • *First HR*: 08/12/1969 off Tony Cloninger

Bill Renna

WILLIAM BENEDITTO RENNA
B: 10/14/1924
BR

Year	Tm	Lg	Tot	H	A	0	1	2	3	2	3	4	LO	XN	IP	PH	RHP	LHP
1953	NY	AL	2	0	2	2	0	0	0	0	0	0	0	0	0	0	0	2
1954	PHI	AL	13	5	8	7	5	1	0	0	0	0	0	0	0	0	8	5
1955	KC	AL	7	5	2	5	0	2	0	0	0	0	0	0	0	0	4	3
1956	KC	AL	2	1	1	2	0	0	0	0	0	0	0	0	0	1	1	1
1958	BOS	AL	4	0	4	1	2	1	0	0	0	0	0	0	0	1	3	1
Total			28	11	17	17	7	4	0	0	0	0	0	0	0	2	16	12

Rank among batters: 1,500 • Top target (2 home runs): Steve Gromek, Don Johnson, Jack Harshman, Frank Sullivan, Art Houtteman, Billy Pierce • *Number of pitchers victimized*: 22 • *Total ballparks homered in*: 8 • *First HR*: 04/30/1953 off Gene Bearden

Tony Rensa

GEORGE ANTHONY RENSA
B: 09/29/1901 D: 01/04/1987
BR

Year	Tm	Lg	Tot	H	A	0	1	2	3	2	3	4	LO	XN	IP	PH	RHP	LHP
1930	DET	AL	1	0	1	1	0	0	0	0	0	0	0	0	0	0	1	0
	PHI	NL	3	2	1	0	2	0	0	1	0	0	0	0	0	0	2	1
	Total		4	2	2	3	0	0	1	0	0	0	0	0	0	0	3	1
1938	CHI	AL	3	1	2	1	1	1	0	0	0	0	0	0	0	0	3	0
Total			7	3	4	4	1	1	1	0	0	0	0	0	0	0	6	1

Rank among batters: 2,834 • *Total ballparks homered in*: 6 • *First HR*: 06/26/1930 off Firpo Marberry

Rich Renteria

RICHARD AVINA RENTERIA
B: 12/25/1961
BR

Year	Tm	Lg	Tot	H	A	0	1	2	3	2	3	4	LO	XN	IP	PH	RHP	LHP
1993	FLO	NL	2	2	0	1	0	1	0	0	0	0	0	0	0	0	1	1
1994	FLO	NL	2	2	0	2	0	0	0	0	0	0	0	0	0	0	0	2
Total			4	4	0	3	0	1	0	0	0	0	0	0	0	0	1	3

Rank among batters: 3,427 • *Total ballparks homered in*: 1 • *First HR*: 06/01/1993 off Bud Black

Bob Repass

ROBERT WILLIS REPASS
B: 11/06/1917
BR

Year	Tm	Lg	Tot	H	A	0	1	2	3	2	3	4	LO	XN	IP	PH	RHP	LHP
1942	WAS	AL	2	0	2	1	1	0	0	0	0	0	0	0	0	0	2	0

Rank among batters: 4,129 • *Total ballparks homered in*: 2 • *First HR*: 04/20/1942 off Mike Ryba

Roger Repoz

ROGER ALLEN REPOZ
B: 08/03/1940
BL

Year	Tm	Lg	Tot	H	A	0	1	2	3	2	3	4	LO	XN	IP	PH	RHP	LHP
1965	NY	AL	12	6	6	7	3	2	0	0	0	0	0	0	1	0	11	1
1966	KC	AL	11	1	10	7	3	1	0	1	0	0	0	1	0	0	10	1
1967	KC	AL	2	2	0	2	0	0	0	0	0	0	0	0	0	0	2	0
	CAL	AL	5	4	1	3	2	0	0	0	0	0	0	0	0	0	5	0
	Total		7	6	1	5	2	0	0	0	0	0	0	0	0	0	7	0
1968	CAL	AL	13	6	7	7	3	3	0	1	0	0	1	0	0	1	11	2
1969	CAL	AL	8	3	5	6	1	1	0	1	0	0	0	1	0	0	7	1
1970	CAL	AL	18	3	15	12	6	0	0	0	0	0	0	0	0	0	16	2
1971	CAL	AL	13	5	8	8	2	2	1	0	0	0	0	0	0	0	11	2
Total			82	30	52	52	20	9	1	3	0	0	1	2	1	1	73	9

Rank among batters: 637 • Top target (3 home runs): Fred Talbot, Earl Wilson, Dave Boswell, Denny McLain, Dick Bosman, Marty Pattin • *Number of pitchers victimized*: 59 • *Total ballparks homered in*: 12 • *First HR*: 07/01/1965 off Steve Barber

Rip Repulski

ELDON JOHN REPULSKI
B: 10/04/1927 D: 02/10/1993
BR

Year	Tm	Lg	Tot	H	A	Men-On 0	1	2	3	One-Game 2	3	4	LO	XN	IP	PH	RHP	LHP
1953	STL	NL	15	2	13	10	1	4	0	1	0	0	0	0	0	0	8	7
1954	STL	NL	19	3	16	13	4	2	0	1	0	0	2	0	1	0	13	6
1955	STL	NL	23	7	16	16	5	2	0	2	0	0	0	1	0	0	10	13
1956	STL	NL	11	5	6	7	3	1	0	0	0	0	0	1	0	1	8	3
1957	PHI	NL	20	11	9	11	6	3	0	0	0	0	0	0	0	0	15	5
1958	PHI	NL	13	6	7	5	3	4	1	0	0	0	0	0	0	4	9	4
1959	LA	NL	2	0	2	2	0	0	0	0	0	0	0	0	0	0	0	2
1960	BOS	AL	3	1	2	1	1	0	1	0	0	0	0	0	0	2	1	2
Total			106	35	71	65	23	16	2	4	0	0	2	2	1	7	64	42

Rank among batters: 451 • *Top target (4 home runs)*: Robin Roberts • *Number of pitchers victimized*: 68 • *Total ballparks homered in*: 12 • *First HR*: 06/03/1953 off Curt Simmons

Dino Restelli

DINO PAUL RESTELLI
B: 09/23/1924
BR

Year	Tm	Lg	Tot	H	A	Men-On 0	1	2	3	One-Game 2	3	4	LO	XN	IP	PH	RHP	LHP
1949	PIT	NL	12	11	1	5	6	1	0	2	0	0	0	0	0	0	7	5
1951	PIT	NL	1	1	0	1	0	0	0	0	0	0	0	0	0	0	0	1
Total			13	12	1	6	6	1	0	2	0	0	0	0	0	0	7	6

Rank among batters: 2,248 • *Top target (2 home runs)*: Warren Spahn, Robin Roberts • *Number of pitchers victimized*: 11 • *Total ballparks homered in*: 2 • *First HR*: 06/15/1949 off Warren Spahn

Merv Rettenmund

MERVIN WELDON RETTENMUND
B: 06/06/1943
BR

Year	Tm	Lg	Tot	H	A	Men-On 0	1	2	3	One-Game 2	3	4	LO	XN	IP	PH	RHP	LHP
1968	BAL	AL	2	2	0	0	2	0	0	0	0	0	0	0	0	1	0	2
1969	BAL	AL	4	3	1	2	1	1	0	0	0	0	0	0	0	0	3	1
1970	BAL	AL	18	7	11	13	3	1	1	0	0	0	0	0	0	0	8	10
1971	BAL	AL	11	3	8	7	2	2	0	0	0	0	0	1	0	0	6	5
1972	BAL	AL	6	1	5	3	2	1	0	0	0	0	0	0	0	0	1	5
1973	BAL	AL	9	5	4	2	6	1	0	1	0	0	2	0	0	0	2	7
1974	CIN	NL	6	3	3	4	0	1	1	0	0	0	0	0	1	0	4	2
1975	CIN	NL	2	2	0	2	0	0	0	0	0	0	0	0	0	0	1	1
1976	SD	NL	2	1	1	1	1	0	0	0	0	0	0	0	0	2	1	1
1977	SD	NL	4	1	3	2	1	1	0	0	0	0	1	1	0	1	2	2
1978	CAL	AL	1	1	0	0	0	0	1	0	0	0	0	0	0	1	0	1
1979	CAL	AL	1	1	0	1	0	0	0	0	0	0	0	0	0	0	1	0
Total			66	30	36	37	18	8	3	1	0	0	3	2	1	5	29	37

Rank among batters: 786 • *Top target (3 home runs)*: Les Cain, Ken Holtzman • *Number of pitchers victimized*: 54 • *Total ballparks homered in*: 20 • *First HR*: 08/27/1968 off Warren Bogle • *World Series HR—2*

George Rettger

GEORGE EDWARD RETTGER
B: 07/29/1868 D: 06/05/1921
BR

Year	Tm	Lg	Tot	H	A	Men-On 0	1	2	3	One-Game 2	3	4	LO	XN	IP	PH	RHP	LHP
1891	STL	AA	1	1	0	1	0	0	0	0	0	0	0	0	0	0	1	0
Total			1	1	0	1	0	0	0	0	0	0	0	0	0	0	1	0

Rank among batters: 4,707 • *Total ballparks homered in*: 1 • *First HR*: 09/22/1891 off Kid Carsey

Ken Retzer

KENNETH LEO RETZER
B: 04/30/1934
BL

Year	Tm	Lg	Tot	H	A	Men-On 0	1	2	3	One-Game 2	3	4	LO	XN	IP	PH	RHP	LHP
1961	WAS	AL	1	1	0	1	0	0	0	0	0	0	0	0	0	0	1	0
1962	WAS	AL	8	2	6	4	2	2	0	1	0	0	0	0	0	0	8	0
1963	WAS	AL	5	3	2	2	2	1	0	0	0	0	0	0	0	0	5	0
Total			14	6	8	7	4	3	0	1	0	0	0	0	0	0	14	0

Rank among batters: 2,169 • *Top target (4 home runs)*: Milt Pappas • *Number of pitchers victimized*: 11 • *Total ballparks homered in*: 6 • *First HR*: 09/16/1961 off Jerry Walker

Year	Tm	Lg	Tot	H	A	Men-On 0	Men-On 1	Men-On 2	Men-On 3	One-Game 2	One-Game 3	One-Game 4	LO	XN	IP	PH	RHP	LHP

Ed Reulbach

EDWARD MARVIN REULBACH
B: 12/01/1882 D: 07/17/1961
BR

Year	Tm	Lg	Tot	H	A	Men-On 0	Men-On 1	Men-On 2	Men-On 3	One-Game 2	One-Game 3	One-Game 4	LO	XN	IP	PH	RHP	LHP
1907	CHI	NL	1	0	1	1	0	0	0	0	0	0	0	0	0	0	1	0

Rank among batters: 4,707 • *Total ballparks homered in*: 1 • *First HR*: 07/17/1907 off Gus Dorner

Rick Reuschel

RICKEY EUGENE REUSCHEL
B: 05/16/1949
BR

Year	Tm	Lg	Tot	H	A	Men-On 0	Men-On 1	Men-On 2	Men-On 3	One-Game 2	One-Game 3	One-Game 4	LO	XN	IP	PH	RHP	LHP
1975	CHI	NL	1	1	0	1	0	0	0	0	0	0	0	0	0	0	1	0
1977	CHI	NL	1	1	0	0	1	0	0	0	0	0	0	0	0	0	1	0
1985	PIT	NL	1	1	0	1	0	0	0	0	0	0	0	0	0	0	0	1
1987	PIT	NL	1	0	1	1	0	0	0	0	0	0	0	0	0	0	1	0
Total			4	3	1	3	1	0	0	0	0	0	0	0	0	0	3	1

Rank among batters: 3,427 • *Total ballparks homered in*: 3 • *First HR*: 05/27/1975 off Phil Niekro

Jerry Reuss

JERRY REUSS
B: 06/19/1949
BL

Year	Tm	Lg	Tot	H	A	Men-On 0	Men-On 1	Men-On 2	Men-On 3	One-Game 2	One-Game 3	One-Game 4	LO	XN	IP	PH	RHP	LHP
1980	LA	NL	1	0	1	0	1	0	0	0	0	0	0	0	0	0	1	0

Rank among batters: 4,707 • *Total ballparks homered in*: 1 • *First HR*: 08/25/1980 off Nino Espinosa

Dave Revering

DAVID ALLEN REVERING
B: 02/12/1953
BL

Year	Tm	Lg	Tot	H	A	Men-On 0	Men-On 1	Men-On 2	Men-On 3	One-Game 2	One-Game 3	One-Game 4	LO	XN	IP	PH	RHP	LHP
1978	OAK	AL	16	10	6	12	3	1	0	0	0	0	0	0	0	2	9	7
1979	OAK	AL	19	8	11	14	4	1	0	3	0	0	0	0	0	0	15	4
1980	OAK	AL	15	3	12	10	3	2	0	1	0	0	0	1	0	1	13	2
1981	OAK	AL	2	1	1	2	0	0	0	0	0	0	0	0	0	0	2	0
	NY	AL	2	2	0	0	2	0	0	0	0	0	0	1	0	0	2	0
	Total		4	3	1	2	2	0	0	0	0	0	0	1	0	0	4	0
1982	TOR	AL	5	2	3	2	2	1	0	0	0	0	0	0	0	0	4	1
	SEA	AL	3	2	1	0	2	1	0	0	0	0	0	0	0	0	3	0
	Total		8	4	4	2	4	2	0	0	0	0	0	0	0	0	7	1
Total			62	28	34	40	16	6	0	4	0	0	0	2	0	3	48	14

Rank among batters: 835 • Top target (2 home runs): Wilbur Wood, Dennis Eckersley, Dennis Leonard, Steve Stone, Dave LaRoche, Byron McLaughlin, Rob Dressler, Mike Parrott, Rollie Fingers, Jack Morris • *Number of pitchers victimized*: 52 • *Total ballparks homered in*: 13 • *First HR*: 04/16/1978 off Don Aase

Nap Reyes

NAPOLEON AGUILERA REYES
B: 11/24/1919 D: 09/15/1995
BR

Year	Tm	Lg	Tot	H	A	Men-On 0	Men-On 1	Men-On 2	Men-On 3	One-Game 2	One-Game 3	One-Game 4	LO	XN	IP	PH	RHP	LHP
1944	NY	NL	8	7	1	3	3	2	0	1	0	0	0	0	1	0	8	0
1945	NY	NL	5	4	1	3	1	1	0	1	0	0	0	1	0	0	4	1
Total			13	11	2	6	4	3	0	2	0	0	0	1	1	0	12	1

Rank among batters: 2,248 • *Top target (2 home runs)*: Hy Vandenberg • *Number of pitchers victimized*: 12 • *Total ballparks homered in*: 3 • *First HR*: 05/12/1944 off Ed Heusser

Allie Reynolds

ALLIE PIERCE REYNOLDS
B: 02/10/1915 D: 12/26/1994
BR

Year	Tm	Lg	Tot	H	A	Men-On 0	Men-On 1	Men-On 2	Men-On 3	One-Game 2	One-Game 3	One-Game 4	LO	XN	IP	PH	RHP	LHP
1948	NY	AL	1	0	1	0	0	1	0	0	0	0	0	0	0	0	1	0

Rank among batters: 4,707 • *Total ballparks homered in*: 1 • *First HR*: 04/19/1948 off Early Wynn

Carl Reynolds

CARL NETTLES REYNOLDS
B: 02/01/1903 D: 05/29/1978
BR

Year	Tm	Lg	Tot	H	A	Men-On 0	Men-On 1	Men-On 2	Men-On 3	One-Game 2	One-Game 3	One-Game 4	LO	XN	IP	PH	RHP	LHP
1927	CHI	AL	1	0	1	0	1	0	0	0	0	0	0	0	1	0	1	0

Carl Reynolds *continued*

Year	Tm	Lg	Tot	H	A	Men-On 0	1	2	3	One-Game 2	3	4	LO	XN	IP	PH	RHP	LHP
1928	CHI	AL	2	2	0	0	2	0	0	0	0	0	0	0	0	0	2	0
1929	CHI	AL	11	7	4	2	7	2	0	0	0	0	0	0	0	0	6	5
1930	CHI	AL	22	9	13	9	10	3	0	2	1	0	0	0	4	0	20	2
1931	CHI	AL	6	5	1	3	2	1	0	0	0	0	0	0	0	0	5	1
1932	WAS	AL	9	2	7	4	4	1	0	1	0	0	0	0	0	0	6	3
1933	STL	AL	8	4	4	4	3	1	0	0	0	0	0	0	0	0	4	4
1934	BOS	AL	4	2	2	3	0	1	0	0	0	0	0	0	0	2	4	0
1935	BOS	AL	6	0	6	4	1	1	0	0	0	0	0	0	0	0	4	2
1936	WAS	AL	4	1	3	2	1	1	0	0	0	0	0	1	1	1	1	3
1938	CHI	NL	3	1	2	2	1	0	0	0	0	0	0	0	0	0	2	1
1939	CHI	NL	4	2	2	2	1	1	0	0	0	0	0	0	0	1	4	0
Total			80	35	45	35	33	12	0	3	1	0	0	1	6	4	59	21

Rank among batters: 650 • Top target (3 home runs): Vic Sorrell, George Uhle, Earl Whitehill, George Blaeholder, Gordon Rhodes • *Number of pitchers victimized*: 56 • *Total ballparks homered in*: 12 • *First HR*: 09/08/1927 off Sloppy Thurston

Craig Reynolds

GORDON CRAIG REYNOLDS
B: 12/27/1952
BL

Year	Tm	Lg	Tot	H	A	Men-On 0	1	2	3	One-Game 2	3	4	LO	XN	IP	PH	RHP	LHP
1976	PIT	NL	1	0	1	1	0	0	0	0	0	0	0	0	0	0	1	0
1977	SEA	AL	4	2	2	3	1	0	0	0	0	0	0	0	0	0	4	0
1978	SEA	AL	5	2	3	2	2	0	1	0	0	0	0	0	0	0	4	1
1980	HOU	NL	3	2	1	3	0	0	0	0	0	0	0	0	0	0	3	0
1981	HOU	NL	4	0	4	3	1	0	0	0	0	0	0	0	0	0	4	0
1982	HOU	NL	1	0	1	0	1	0	0	0	0	0	0	0	0	0	1	0
1983	HOU	NL	1	1	0	1	0	0	0	0	0	0	0	0	0	0	1	0
1984	HOU	NL	6	0	6	3	2	0	1	0	0	0	0	0	0	0	4	2
1985	HOU	NL	4	1	3	3	1	0	0	0	0	0	0	0	0	0	4	0
1986	HOU	NL	6	4	2	4	1	0	1	0	0	0	0	0	0	1	6	0
1987	HOU	NL	4	0	4	2	1	1	0	1	0	0	0	0	0	0	4	0
1988	HOU	NL	1	0	1	0	1	0	0	0	0	0	0	0	0	0	1	0
1989	HOU	NL	2	0	2	1	1	0	0	0	0	0	0	0	0	1	2	0
Total			42	12	30	26	12	1	3	1	0	0	0	0	0	2	39	3

Rank among batters: 1,138 • *Top target (3 home runs)*: Pascual Perez, Mike LaCoss • *Number of pitchers victimized*: 36 • *Total ballparks homered in*: 16 • *First HR*: 09/24/1976 off Bob Forsch

Harold Reynolds

HAROLD CRAIG REYNOLDS
B: 11/26/1960
BB

Year	Tm	Lg	Tot	H	A	Men-On 0	1	2	3	One-Game 2	3	4	LO	XN	IP	PH	RHP	LHP
1986	SEA	AL	1	1	0	1	0	0	0	0	0	0	0	0	0	0	0	1
1987	SEA	AL	1	1	0	1	0	0	0	0	0	0	0	0	0	0	0	1
1988	SEA	AL	4	4	0	2	2	0	0	0	0	0	0	0	0	0	2	2
1990	SEA	AL	5	0	5	2	2	0	1	0	0	0	0	0	0	0	4	1
1991	SEA	AL	3	1	2	1	1	1	0	0	0	0	0	0	0	0	2	1
1992	SEA	AL	3	2	1	2	1	0	0	0	0	0	0	0	0	0	3	0
1993	BAL	AL	4	2	2	3	0	1	0	0	0	0	0	0	0	0	4	0
Total			21	11	10	12	6	2	1	0	0	0	0	0	0	0	15	6

Rank among batters: 1,768 • *Total ballparks homered in*: 8 • *First HR*: 09/16/1986 off Pete Filson

R. J. Reynolds

ROBERT JAMES REYNOLDS
B: 04/19/1959
BB

Year	Tm	Lg	Tot	H	A	Men-On 0	1	2	3	One-Game 2	3	4	LO	XN	IP	PH	RHP	LHP
1983	LA	NL	2	1	1	1	0	1	0	0	0	0	0	0	0	2	2	0
1984	LA	NL	2	1	1	1	1	0	0	0	0	0	0	0	0	0	1	1
1985	PIT	NL	3	1	2	2	0	1	0	0	0	0	0	1	0	0	3	0
1986	PIT	NL	9	6	3	5	2	1	1	0	0	0	1	0	0	0	9	0
1987	PIT	NL	7	2	5	3	4	0	0	0	0	0	0	0	0	0	7	0
1988	PIT	NL	6	4	2	4	1	1	0	0	0	0	1	0	0	1	3	3
1989	PIT	NL	6	3	3	1	4	1	0	0	0	0	0	0	0	0	5	1
Total			35	18	17	17	12	5	1	0	0	0	2	1	0	3	30	5

Rank among batters: 1,291 • Top target (2 home runs): Joe Johnson, Scott Sanderson, Mike Krukow, Eddie Whitson, Ron Darling, Greg Maddux • *Number of pitchers victimized*: 29 • *Total ballparks homered in*: 9 • *First HR*: 09/06/1983 off Eddie Whitson

Year	Tm	Lg	Tot	H	A	Men-On 0	1	2	3	One-Game 2	3	4	LO	XN	IP	PH	RHP	LHP

Ronn Reynolds

RONN DWAYNE REYNOLDS
B: 09/28/1958
BR

Year	Tm	Lg	Tot	H	A	0	1	2	3	2	3	4	LO	XN	IP	PH	RHP	LHP
1986	PHI	NL	3	1	2	2	1	0	0	0	0	0	0	0	0	1	0	3
1987	HOU	NL	1	0	1	1	0	0	0	0	0	0	0	0	0	0	1	0
Total			4	1	3	3	1	0	0	0	0	0	0	0	0	1	1	3

Rank among batters: 3,427 • *Total ballparks homered in*: 3 • *First HR*: 06/25/1986 off Ray Fontenot

Tommie Reynolds

TOMMIE D REYNOLDS
B: 08/15/1941
BB

Year	Tm	Lg	Tot	H	A	0	1	2	3	2	3	4	LO	XN	IP	PH	RHP	LHP
1964	KC	AL	2	2	0	0	0	2	0	0	0	0	0	0	0	0	0	2
1965	KC	AL	1	1	0	1	0	0	0	0	0	0	0	0	0	0	1	0
1967	NY	NL	2	1	1	2	0	0	0	0	0	0	0	1	0	0	1	1
1969	OAK	AL	2	2	0	2	0	0	0	0	0	0	0	0	0	1	2	0
1970	CAL	AL	1	1	0	0	1	0	0	0	0	0	0	0	0	0	0	1
1971	CAL	AL	2	1	1	1	1	0	0	0	0	0	0	0	0	1	0	2
1972	MIL	AL	2	2	0	1	0	1	0	0	0	0	0	0	0	0	1	1
Total			12	10	2	7	2	3	0	0	0	0	0	1	0	2	5	7

Rank among batters: 2,325 • *Top target (2 home runs)*: Mickey Lolich • *Number of pitchers victimized*: 11 • *Total ballparks homered in*: 7 • *First HR*: 04/30/1964 off Mickey Lolich

Armando Reynoso

ARMANDO MARTIN (GUTIERREZ) REYNOSO
B: 05/01/1966
BR

Year	Tm	Lg	Tot	H	A	0	1	2	3	2	3	4	LO	XN	IP	PH	RHP	LHP
1993	COL	NL	2	1	1	1	0	1	0	0	0	0	0	0	0	0	1	1

Rank among batters: 4,129 • *Total ballparks homered in*: 2 • *First HR*: 05/10/1993 off Trevor Wilson

Rocky Rhawn

ROBERT JOHN RHAWN
B: 02/13/1919 D: 06/09/1984
BR

Year	Tm	Lg	Tot	H	A	0	1	2	3	2	3	4	LO	XN	IP	PH	RHP	LHP
1947	NY	NL	1	1	0	0	1	0	0	0	0	0	0	0	1	0	1	0
1948	NY	NL	1	1	0	0	1	0	0	0	0	0	0	0	0	0	1	0
Total			2	2	0	0	2	0	0	0	0	0	0	0	1	0	2	0

Rank among batters: 4,129 • *Total ballparks homered in*: 1 • *First HR*: 09/21/1947 off Schoolboy Rowe

Cy Rheam

KENNETH JOHNSTON RHEAM
B: 09/28/1893 D: 10/23/1947
BR

Year	Tm	Lg	Tot	H	A	0	1	2	3	2	3	4	LO	XN	IP	PH	RHP	LHP
1915	PIT	FL	1	1	0	1	0	0	0	0	0	0	1	0	0	0	1	0

Rank among batters: 4,707 • *Total ballparks homered in*: 1 • *First HR*: 05/28/1915 off Russ Ford

Flint Rhem

CHARLES FLINT RHEM
B: 01/24/1901 D: 07/30/1969
BR

Year	Tm	Lg	Tot	H	A	0	1	2	3	2	3	4	LO	XN	IP	PH	RHP	LHP
1925	STL	NL	1	1	0	1	0	0	0	0	0	0	0	0	0	0	1	0
1926	STL	NL	1	1	0	0	1	0	0	0	0	0	0	0	0	0	1	0
1928	STL	NL	1	0	1	0	1	0	0	0	0	0	0	0	0	0	1	0
Total			3	2	1	1	2	0	0	0	0	0	0	0	0	0	3	0

Rank among batters: 3,735 • *Total ballparks homered in*: 2 • *First HR*: 06/10/1925 off Rube Ehrhardt

Billy Rhiel

WILLIAM JOSEPH RHIEL
B: 08/16/1900 D: 08/16/1946
BR

Year	Tm	Lg	Tot	H	A	0	1	2	3	2	3	4	LO	XN	IP	PH	RHP	LHP
1929	BRO	NL	4	2	2	3	0	0	1	0	0	0	0	0	0	0	3	1
1932	DET	AL	3	1	2	2	1	0	0	0	0	0	0	0	0	0	2	1
Total			7	3	4	5	1	0	1	0	0	0	0	0	0	0	5	2

Year	Tm	Lg	Tot	H	A	Men-On				One-Game			LO	XN	IP	PH	RHP	LHP
						0	1	2	3	2	3	4						

Billy Rhiel *continued*

Rank among batters: 2,834 • *Total ballparks homered in*: 5 • *First HR*: 05/16/1929 off Claude Willoughby

Billy Rhines

WILLIAM PEARL RHINES
B: 03/14/1869 D: 01/30/1922
BR

Year	Tm	Lg	Tot	H	A	0	1	2	3	2	3	4	LO	XN	IP	PH	RHP	LHP
1892	CIN	NL	1	0	1	1	0	0	0	0	0	0	0	0	1	0	1	0

Rank among batters: 4,707 • *Total ballparks homered in*: 1 • *First HR*: 07/20/1892 off Jesse Duryea

Bob Rhoads

ROBERT BARTON RHOADS
B: 10/04/1879 D: 02/12/1967
BR

Year	Tm	Lg	Tot	H	A	0	1	2	3	2	3	4	LO	XN	IP	PH	RHP	LHP
1903	STL	NL	1	1	0	0	1	0	0	0	0	0	0	0	0	0	1	0
1905	CLE	AL	1	0	1	1	0	0	0	0	0	0	0	0	1	0	1	0
Total			2	1	1	1	1	0	0	0	0	0	0	0	1	0	2	0

Rank among batters: 4,129 • *Total ballparks homered in*: 2 • *First HR*: 04/30/1903 off Deacon Phillippe

Rick Rhoden

RICHARD ALAN RHODEN
B: 05/16/1953
BR

Year	Tm	Lg	Tot	H	A	0	1	2	3	2	3	4	LO	XN	IP	PH	RHP	LHP
1976	LA	NL	1	1	0	1	0	0	0	0	0	0	0	0	0	0	0	1
1977	LA	NL	3	1	2	2	0	1	0	0	0	0	0	0	0	0	3	0
1980	PIT	NL	1	1	0	0	1	0	0	0	0	0	0	0	0	0	1	0
1982	PIT	NL	3	2	1	1	2	0	0	0	0	0	0	0	0	0	1	2
1986	PIT	NL	1	0	1	1	0	0	0	0	0	0	0	0	0	0	1	0
Total			9	5	4	5	3	1	0	0	0	0	0	0	0	0	6	3

Rank among batters: 2,587 • *Total ballparks homered in*: 5 • *First HR*: 06/12/1976 off Dan Warthen

Dusty Rhodes

JAMES LAMAR RHODES
B: 05/13/1927
BL

Year	Tm	Lg	Tot	H	A	0	1	2	3	2	3	4	LO	XN	IP	PH	RHP	LHP
1952	NY	NL	10	9	1	6	2	1	1	0	0	0	0	0	0	0	9	1
1953	NY	NL	11	9	2	7	2	2	0	0	1	0	0	0	0	0	9	2
1954	NY	NL	15	11	4	7	6	2	0	2	1	0	0	0	0	2	11	4
1955	NY	NL	6	3	3	4	1	0	1	1	0	0	0	0	0	0	3	3
1956	NY	NL	8	5	3	5	3	0	0	0	0	0	0	0	0	1	7	1
1957	NY	NL	4	3	1	2	2	0	0	0	0	0	0	0	0	0	3	1
Total			54	40	14	31	16	5	2	3	2	0	0	0	0	3	42	12

Rank among batters: 938 • *Top target (3 home runs)*: Joe Nuxhall • *Number of pitchers victimized*: 42 • *Total ballparks homered in*: 9 • *First HR*: 07/22/1952 off Gerry Staley • *World Series HR—2*

Gordon Rhodes

JOHN GORDON RHODES
B: 08/11/1907 D: 03/24/1960
BR

Year	Tm	Lg	Tot	H	A	0	1	2	3	2	3	4	LO	XN	IP	PH	RHP	LHP
1933	BOS	AL	1	0	1	1	0	0	0	0	0	0	0	0	0	0	1	0
1934	BOS	AL	1	1	0	0	1	0	0	0	0	0	0	0	0	0	0	1
Total			2	1	1	1	1	0	0	0	0	0	0	0	0	0	1	1

Rank among batters: 4,129 • *Total ballparks homered in*: 2 • *First HR*: 08/25/1933 off Hal Haid

Karl Rhodes

KARL DERRICK RHODES
B: 08/21/1968
BL

Year	Tm	Lg	Tot	H	A	0	1	2	3	2	3	4	LO	XN	IP	PH	RHP	LHP
1990	HOU	NL	1	0	1	1	0	0	0	0	0	0	0	0	0	0	1	0
1991	HOU	NL	1	0	1	1	0	0	0	0	0	0	0	0	0	0	1	0
1993	CHI	NL	3	0	3	2	1	0	0	0	0	0	1	0	0	0	1	2
1994	CHI	NL	8	4	4	8	0	0	0	1	1	0	4	0	0	0	7	1
Total			13	4	9	12	1	0	0	1	1	0	5	0	0	0	10	3

Rank among batters: 2,248 • *Top target (3 home runs)*: Dwight Gooden • *Number of pitchers victimized*: 8 • *Total ballparks homered in*: 5 • *First HR*: 08/15/1990 off Mike Bielecki

Year	Tm	Lg	Tot	H	A	Men-On 0	1	2	3	One-Game 2	3	4	LO	XN	IP	PH	RHP	LHP

Kevin Rhomberg

KEVIN JAY RHOMBERG
B: 11/22/1955
BR

Year	Tm	Lg	Tot	H	A	0	1	2	3	2	3	4	LO	XN	IP	PH	RHP	LHP
1982	CLE	AL	1	1	0	1	0	0	0	0	0	0	0	0	0	0	0	1

Rank among batters: 4,707 • *Total ballparks homered in*: 1 • *First HR*: 09/08/1982 off John Tudor

Hal Rhyne

HAROLD J. RHYNE
B: 03/30/1899 D: 01/07/1971
BR

Year	Tm	Lg	Tot	H	A	0	1	2	3	2	3	4	LO	XN	IP	PH	RHP	LHP
1926	PIT	NL	2	1	1	0	1	1	0	0	0	0	0	1	2	0	2	0

Rank among batters: 4,129 • *Total ballparks homered in*: 2 • *First HR*: 06/17/1926 off Freddie Fitzsimmons

Del Rice

DELBERT W. RICE
B: 10/27/1922 D: 01/26/1983
BR

Year	Tm	Lg	Tot	H	A	0	1	2	3	2	3	4	LO	XN	IP	PH	RHP	LHP
1945	STL	NL	1	1	0	1	0	0	0	0	0	0	0	1	0	0	1	0
1946	STL	NL	1	1	0	1	0	0	0	0	0	0	0	0	0	0	0	1
1947	STL	NL	12	5	7	6	3	2	1	0	0	0	0	0	0	0	5	7
1948	STL	NL	4	1	3	1	2	0	1	0	0	0	0	0	0	0	2	2
1949	STL	NL	4	2	2	2	2	0	0	0	0	0	0	0	0	0	0	4
1950	STL	NL	9	5	4	3	4	2	0	0	0	0	0	1	0	0	5	4
1951	STL	NL	9	2	7	5	2	2	0	0	0	0	0	0	0	0	3	6
1952	STL	NL	11	4	7	7	4	0	0	0	0	0	0	0	0	0	6	5
1953	STL	NL	6	4	2	4	1	0	1	0	0	0	0	0	0	0	4	2
1954	STL	NL	2	1	1	0	2	0	0	0	0	0	0	0	0	0	1	1
1955	STL	NL	1	0	1	1	0	0	0	0	0	0	0	0	0	0	0	1
	MIL	NL	2	0	2	1	1	0	0	0	0	0	0	0	0	0	2	0
	Total		3	0	3	2	1	0	0	0	0	0	0	0	0	0	2	1
1956	MIL	NL	3	1	2	2	1	0	0	0	0	0	0	0	0	1	0	3
1957	MIL	NL	9	3	6	4	3	2	0	0	0	0	0	0	0	0	6	3
1958	MIL	NL	1	0	1	1	0	0	0	0	0	0	0	0	0	0	0	1
1961	LA	AL	4	1	3	2	2	0	0	1	0	0	0	1	0	1	3	1
Total			79	31	48	41	27	8	3	1	0	0	0	3	0	2	38	41

Rank among batters: 661 • *Top target (5 home runs)*: Preacher Roe • *Number of pitchers victimized*: 58 • *Total ballparks homered in*: 12 • *First HR*: 09/30/1945 off Johnny Hetki

Hal Rice

HAROLD HOUSTEN RICE
B: 02/11/1924
BL

Year	Tm	Lg	Tot	H	A	0	1	2	3	2	3	4	LO	XN	IP	PH	RHP	LHP
1949	STL	NL	1	1	0	0	1	0	0	0	0	0	0	0	0	1	1	0
1950	STL	NL	2	2	0	1	1	0	0	0	0	0	0	0	0	0	2	0
1951	STL	NL	4	1	3	0	2	2	0	0	0	0	0	0	0	0	4	0
1952	STL	NL	7	2	5	2	3	0	2	0	0	0	0	0	0	0	7	0
1953	PIT	NL	4	0	4	2	2	0	0	0	0	0	0	1	0	0	3	1
1954	PIT	NL	1	1	0	0	0	1	0	0	0	0	0	0	0	0	1	0
Total			19	7	12	5	9	3	2	0	0	0	0	1	0	1	18	1

Rank among batters: 1,861 • *Top target (2 home runs)*: Bob Rush, Cal McLish, Hoyt Wilhelm • *Number of pitchers victimized*: 16 • *Total ballparks homered in*: 7 • *First HR*: 05/30/1949 off Harry Gumbert

Harry Rice

HARRY FRANCIS RICE
B: 11/22/1901 D: 01/01/1971
BL

Year	Tm	Lg	Tot	H	A	0	1	2	3	2	3	4	LO	XN	IP	PH	RHP	LHP
1925	STL	AL	11	8	3	9	2	0	0	0	0	0	1	0	2	0	7	4
1926	STL	AL	9	8	1	4	4	1	0	0	0	0	0	0	0	0	6	3
1927	STL	AL	7	6	1	2	5	0	0	0	0	0	0	0	0	0	4	3
1928	DET	AL	6	3	3	3	1	1	1	0	0	0	0	0	0	0	3	3
1929	DET	AL	6	2	4	4	1	1	0	1	0	0	0	0	0	0	5	1
1930	DET	AL	2	0	2	0	2	0	0	0	0	0	0	0	1	0	2	0
	NY	AL	7	2	5	4	2	0	1	0	0	0	0	1	0	0	4	3
	Total		9	2	7	4	4	0	1	0	0	0	0	1	1	0	6	3
Total			48	29	19	26	17	3	2	1	0	0	1	1	3	0	31	17

Rank among batters: 1,024 • Top target (3 home runs): Waite Hoyt, Ted Blankenship, Herb Pennock, Lefty Grove • *Number of pitchers victimized*: 36 • *Total ballparks homered in*: 7 • *First HR*: 05/31/1925 off Ted Blankenship

Jim Rice

JAMES EDWARD RICE
B: 03/08/1953
BR

Year	Tm	Lg	Tot	H	A	Men-On 0	Men-On 1	Men-On 2	Men-On 3	One-Game 2	One-Game 3	One-Game 4	LO	XN	IP	PH	RHP	LHP
1974	BOS	AL	1	1	0	1	0	0	0	0	0	0	0	0	0	0	1	0
1975	BOS	AL	22	12	10	14	4	4	0	2	0	0	0	0	0	0	13	9
1976	BOS	AL	25	12	13	17	6	2	0	3	0	0	0	1	0	1	16	9
1977	BOS	AL	39	27	12	23	12	3	1	6	1	0	0	0	0	0	34	5
1978	BOS	AL	46	28	18	18	24	4	0	4	0	0	0	1	0	0	36	10
1979	BOS	AL	39	27	12	20	13	6	0	5	0	0	0	0	0	0	25	14
1980	BOS	AL	24	11	13	15	6	3	0	2	0	0	0	1	0	0	13	11
1981	BOS	AL	17	10	7	11	3	2	1	1	0	0	0	1	0	0	13	4
1982	BOS	AL	24	9	15	13	7	4	0	1	0	0	0	0	0	0	22	2
1983	BOS	AL	39	16	23	14	23	1	1	5	1	0	0	0	0	0	29	10
1984	BOS	AL	28	17	11	9	15	3	1	2	0	0	0	1	0	0	20	8
1985	BOS	AL	27	11	16	17	7	3	0	1	0	0	0	1	0	0	20	7
1986	BOS	AL	20	10	10	9	8	1	2	0	0	0	0	1	0	0	13	7
1987	BOS	AL	13	7	6	9	2	1	1	0	0	0	0	0	0	0	9	4
1988	BOS	AL	15	9	6	6	7	1	1	1	0	0	0	0	0	0	9	6
1989	BOS	AL	3	1	2	1	2	0	0	0	0	0	0	0	0	0	2	1
Total			382	208	174	197	139	38	8	33	2	0	0	7	0	1	275	107

Rank among batters: 31 • *Top target (9 home runs)*: Jim Palmer • *Number of pitchers victimized*: 227 • *Total ballparks homered in*: 15 • *First HR*: 10/01/1974 off Steve Kline • *LCS HR*—2; *All-Star HR*—1

Sam Rice

EDGAR CHARLES RICE
B: 02/20/1890 D: 10/13/1974
BL HOF

Year	Tm	Lg	Tot	H	A	Men-On 0	Men-On 1	Men-On 2	Men-On 3	One-Game 2	One-Game 3	One-Game 4	LO	XN	IP	PH	RHP	LHP
1916	WAS	AL	1	0	1	1	0	0	0	0	0	0	0	0	1	0	1	0
1919	WAS	AL	3	0	3	1	1	1	0	0	0	0	0	0	2	0	1	2
1920	WAS	AL	3	1	2	1	1	1	0	0	0	0	0	1	2	0	0	3
1921	WAS	AL	4	3	1	2	1	1	0	0	0	0	0	0	3	0	3	1
1922	WAS	AL	6	1	5	4	2	0	0	0	0	0	0	0	4	0	5	1
1923	WAS	AL	3	0	3	2	1	0	0	0	0	0	0	0	2	0	2	1
1924	WAS	AL	1	0	1	0	1	0	0	0	0	0	0	0	0	0	0	1
1925	WAS	AL	1	1	0	1	0	0	0	0	0	0	0	0	1	0	1	0
1926	WAS	AL	3	0	3	2	1	0	0	0	0	0	0	0	0	0	3	0
1927	WAS	AL	2	0	2	2	0	0	0	0	0	0	1	0	2	0	2	0
1928	WAS	AL	2	2	0	1	1	0	0	0	0	0	0	0	2	0	1	1
1929	WAS	AL	1	0	1	1	0	0	0	0	0	0	0	0	1	0	0	1
1930	WAS	AL	1	1	0	0	0	1	0	0	0	0	0	0	1	0	0	1
1932	WAS	AL	1	0	1	0	1	0	0	0	0	0	0	0	0	0	1	0
1933	WAS	AL	1	0	1	1	0	0	0	0	0	0	0	0	0	1	1	0
1934	CLE	AL	1	0	1	1	0	0	0	0	0	0	1	0	0	0	1	0
Total			34	9	25	20	10	4	0	0	0	0	2	1	21	1	22	12

Rank among batters: 1,315 • Top target (2 home runs): Sam Jones, Stan Coveleski, Herb Pennock, Urban Shocker, Jacob Miller • *Number of pitchers victimized*: 29 • *Total ballparks homered in*: 9 • *First HR*: 10/04/1916 off Allen Russell

J. R. Richard

JAMES RODNEY RICHARD
B: 03/07/1950
BR

Year	Tm	Lg	Tot	H	A	Men-On 0	Men-On 1	Men-On 2	Men-On 3	One-Game 2	One-Game 3	One-Game 4	LO	XN	IP	PH	RHP	LHP
1974	HOU	NL	1	0	1	1	0	0	0	0	0	0	0	0	0	0	0	1
1975	HOU	NL	1	0	1	1	0	0	0	0	0	0	0	0	0	0	1	0
1976	HOU	NL	2	1	1	1	1	0	0	0	0	0	0	0	0	0	2	0
1977	HOU	NL	2	0	2	2	0	0	0	0	0	0	0	0	0	0	2	0
1978	HOU	NL	1	0	1	1	0	0	0	0	0	0	0	0	0	0	0	1
1979	HOU	NL	2	1	1	2	0	0	0	0	0	0	0	0	0	0	1	1
1980	HOU	NL	1	0	1	1	0	0	0	0	0	0	0	0	0	0	1	0
Total			10	2	8	9	1	0	0	0	0	0	0	0	0	0	7	3

Rank among batters: 2,500 • *Total ballparks homered in*: 6 • *First HR*: 09/13/1974 off Ron Bryant

Lee Richard

LEE EDWARD RICHARD
B: 09/18/1948
BR

Year	Tm	Lg	Tot	H	A	Men-On 0	Men-On 1	Men-On 2	Men-On 3	One-Game 2	One-Game 3	One-Game 4	LO	XN	IP	PH	RHP	LHP
1971	CHI	AL	2	1	1	1	0	1	0	0	0	0	0	0	0	0	2	0

Rank among batters: 4,129 • *Total ballparks homered in*: 2 • *First HR*: 06/27/1971 off Rickey Clark

Gene Richards

EUGENE RICHARDS
B: 09/29/1953
BL

Year	Tm	Lg	Tot	H	A	Men-On 0	1	2	3	One-Game 2	3	4	LO	XN	IP	PH	RHP	LHP
1977	SD	NL	5	2	3	3	2	0	0	0	0	0	1	0	0	0	4	1
1978	SD	NL	4	1	3	2	2	0	0	0	0	0	1	0	0	0	4	0
1979	SD	NL	4	0	4	3	1	0	0	0	0	0	0	0	0	0	2	2
1980	SD	NL	4	1	3	2	1	1	0	0	0	0	0	0	0	0	4	0
1981	SD	NL	3	0	3	0	1	2	0	0	0	0	0	0	0	0	2	1
1982	SD	NL	3	0	3	3	0	0	0	0	0	0	0	0	2	0	2	1
1983	SD	NL	3	2	1	1	2	0	0	0	0	0	1	0	0	0	3	0
Total			26	6	20	14	9	3	0	0	0	0	3	0	2	0	21	5

Rank among batters: 1,576 • *Top target (2 home runs)*: Rick Camp, Burt Hooton • *Number of pitchers victimized*: 24 • *Total ballparks homered in*: 10 • *First HR*: 05/04/1977 off Jim Kaat

Paul Richards

PAUL RAPIER RICHARDS
B: 11/21/1908 D: 05/04/1986
BR

Year	Tm	Lg	Tot	H	A	Men-On 0	1	2	3	One-Game 2	3	4	LO	XN	IP	PH	RHP	LHP
1935	PHI	AL	4	3	1	1	3	0	0	0	0	0	0	0	0	0	4	0
1943	DET	AL	5	2	3	3	2	0	0	0	0	0	0	0	0	0	4	1
1944	DET	AL	3	1	2	1	2	0	0	0	0	0	0	0	0	0	2	1
1945	DET	AL	3	1	2	2	0	0	1	0	0	0	0	0	0	0	3	0
Total			15	7	8	7	7	0	1	0	0	0	0	0	0	0	13	2

Rank among batters: 2,096 • *Total ballparks homered in*: 6 • *First HR*: 07/06/1935 off Wes Ferrell

Bill Richardson

WILLIAM HENRY RICHARDSON
B: 09/24/1878 D: 11/06/1949
BR

Year	Tm	Lg	Tot	H	A	Men-On 0	1	2	3	One-Game 2	3	4	LO	XN	IP	PH	RHP	LHP
1901	STL	NL	2	2	0	2	0	0	0	0	0	0	0	1	1	0	2	0

Rank among batters: 4,129 • *Total ballparks homered in*: 1 • *First HR*: 09/25/1901 off Vic Willis

Bobby Richardson

ROBERT CLINTON RICHARDSON
B: 08/19/1935
BR

Year	Tm	Lg	Tot	H	A	Men-On 0	1	2	3	One-Game 2	3	4	LO	XN	IP	PH	RHP	LHP
1959	NY	AL	2	1	1	1	1	0	0	0	0	0	1	0	0	0	2	0
1960	NY	AL	1	0	1	1	0	0	0	0	0	0	0	0	0	0	1	0
1961	NY	AL	3	2	1	1	0	2	0	0	0	0	1	0	0	0	2	1
1962	NY	AL	8	3	5	3	3	1	1	0	0	0	0	0	0	0	4	4
1963	NY	AL	3	1	2	2	1	0	0	0	0	0	0	0	0	0	1	2
1964	NY	AL	4	2	2	3	1	0	0	0	0	0	0	0	0	0	4	0
1965	NY	AL	6	4	2	5	1	0	0	0	0	0	2	0	0	0	5	1
1966	NY	AL	7	2	5	6	1	0	0	0	0	0	0	2	0	0	4	3
Total			34	15	19	22	8	3	1	0	0	0	4	2	0	0	23	11

Rank among batters: 1,315 • Top target (2 home runs): Paul Foytack, Earl Wilson, Rollie Sheldon, Jim Kaat • *Number of pitchers victimized*: 30 • *Total ballparks homered in*: 9 • *First HR*: 07/25/1959 off Paul Foytack • *World Series HR*—1

Danny Richardson

DANIEL RICHARDSON
B: 01/25/1863 D: 09/12/1926
BR

Year	Tm	Lg	Tot	H	A	Men-On 0	1	2	3	One-Game 2	3	4	LO	XN	IP	PH	RHP	LHP
1884	NY	NL	1	0	1	1	0	0	0	0	0	0	0	0	1	0	1	0
1886	NY	NL	1	1	0	0	1	0	0	0	0	0	0	0	0	0	0	1
1887	NY	NL	3	2	1	3	0	0	0	0	0	0	0	0	1	0	3	0
1888	NY	NL	8	4	4	3	3	2	0	0	0	0	0	0	0	0	6	1
1889	NY	NL	7	1	6	4	1	2	0	0	0	0	0	0	1	0	5	2
1890	NY	PL	4	0	4	2	2	0	0	0	0	0	0	0	0	0	3	1
1891	NY	NL	4	0	4	3	1	0	0	0	0	0	0	0	0	0	3	1
1892	WAS	NL	3	1	2	1	2	0	0	0	0	0	0	0	1	0	1	0
1894	LOU	NL	1	0	1	1	0	0	0	0	0	0	0	0	0	0	1	0
Total			32	9	23	18	10	4	0	0	0	0	0	0	4	0	23	6

Rank among batters: 1,360 • *Top target (5 home runs)*: Egyptian Healy • *Number of pitchers victimized*: 25 • *Total ballparks homered in*: 15 • *First HR*: 07/01/1884 off Frank Brill • *World Series HR*—3

Hardy Richardson

ABRAM HARDING RICHARDSON
B: 04/21/1855 D: 01/14/1931
BR

Year	Tm	Lg	Tot	H	A	Men-On 0	1	2	3	One-Game 2	3	4	LO	XN	IP	PH	RHP	LHP
1881	BUF	NL	2	0	2	1	1	0	0	0	0	0	0	0	0	0	1	1
1882	BUF	NL	2	0	2	0	0	2	0	0	0	0	0	0	0	0	2	0
1883	BUF	NL	1	1	0	0	0	1	0	0	0	0	0	0	0	0	1	0
1884	BUF	NL	6	3	3	4	2	0	0	1	0	0	1	0	0	0	5	0
1885	BUF	NL	6	2	4	4	2	0	0	0	0	0	2	0	0	0	6	0
1886	DET	NL	11	7	4	6	5	0	0	2	0	0	2	0	3	0	8	3
1887	DET	NL	8	3	5	6	1	1	0	1	0	0	3	0	0	0	7	1
1888	DET	NL	6	2	4	2	3	1	0	0	0	0	1	0	1	0	5	1
1889	BOS	NL	6	3	3	4	2	0	0	0	0	0	2	0	0	0	6	0
1890	BOS	PL	13	10	3	3	6	3	1	1	0	0	0	0	1	0	11	1
1891	BOS	AA	7	6	1	2	4	0	1	0	0	0	0	0	1	0	4	0
1892	NY	NL	2	1	1	0	1	1	0	0	0	0	0	0	0	0	1	1
Total			70	38	32	32	27	9	2	5	0	0	11	0	6	0	57	8

Rank among batters: 742 • Top target (4 home runs): Charley Radbourn, John Clarkson, Egyptian Healy • *Number of pitchers victimized*: 43 • *Total ballparks homered in*: 23 • *First HR*: 06/21/1881 off Mickey Welch • *World Series HR*—1

Jeff Richardson

JEFFREY SCOTT RICHARDSON
B: 08/26/1965
BR

Year	Tm	Lg	Tot	H	A	Men-On 0	1	2	3	One-Game 2	3	4	LO	XN	IP	PH	RHP	LHP
1989	CIN	NL	2	1	1	1	1	0	0	0	0	0	0	0	0	1	0	2

Rank among batters: 4,129 • *Total ballparks homered in*: 2 • *First HR*: 08/29/1989 off Joe Magrane

Mike Richardt

MICHAEL ANTHONY RICHARDT
B: 05/24/1958
BR

Year	Tm	Lg	Tot	H	A	Men-On 0	1	2	3	One-Game 2	3	4	LO	XN	IP	PH	RHP	LHP
1982	TEX	AL	3	0	3	1	0	2	0	0	0	0	0	0	0	0	3	0
1983	TEX	AL	1	1	0	1	0	0	0	0	0	0	0	0	0	0	1	0
Total			4	1	3	2	0	2	0	0	0	0	0	0	0	0	4	0

Rank among batters: 3,427 • *Total ballparks homered in*: 3 • *First HR*: 04/27/1982 off Mark Bomback

Lance Richbourg

LANCE CLAYTON RICHBOURG
B: 12/18/1897 D: 09/10/1975
BL

Year	Tm	Lg	Tot	H	A	Men-On 0	1	2	3	One-Game 2	3	4	LO	XN	IP	PH	RHP	LHP
1927	BOS	NL	2	1	1	2	0	0	0	0	0	0	0	0	1	0	2	0
1928	BOS	NL	2	0	2	1	0	1	0	0	0	0	1	0	0	0	2	0
1929	BOS	NL	3	0	3	0	3	0	0	0	0	0	0	0	0	0	2	1
1930	BOS	NL	3	1	2	1	1	0	1	0	0	0	0	0	1	0	3	0
1931	BOS	NL	2	1	1	2	0	0	0	0	0	0	0	0	0	1	2	0
1932	CHI	NL	1	1	0	0	1	0	0	0	0	0	0	0	0	0	1	0
Total			13	4	9	6	5	1	1	0	0	0	1	0	2	1	12	1

Rank among batters: 2,248 • *Top target (2 home runs)*: Steve Swetonic • *Number of pitchers victimized*: 12 • *Total ballparks homered in*: 6 • *First HR*: 05/18/1927 off Carlisle Littlejohn

Pete Richert

PETER GERARD RICHERT
B: 10/29/1939
BL

Year	Tm	Lg	Tot	H	A	Men-On 0	1	2	3	One-Game 2	3	4	LO	XN	IP	PH	RHP	LHP
1966	WAS	AL	1	0	1	1	0	0	0	0	0	0	0	0	0	0	1	0

Rank among batters: 4,707 • *Total ballparks homered in*: 1 • *First HR*: 08/17/1966 off Steve Hargan

Rob Richie

ROBERT EUGENE RICHIE
B: 09/05/1965
BL

Year	Tm	Lg	Tot	H	A	Men-On 0	1	2	3	One-Game 2	3	4	LO	XN	IP	PH	RHP	LHP
1989	DET	AL	1	1	0	0	1	0	0	0	0	0	0	0	0	0	1	0

Rank among batters: 4,707 • *Total ballparks homered in*: 1 • *First HR*: 09/22/1989 off John Dopson

Don Richmond

DONALD LESTER RICHMOND
B: 10/27/1919 D: 05/24/1981
BL

Year	Tm	Lg	Tot	H	A	Men-On 0	Men-On 1	Men-On 2	Men-On 3	One-Game 2	One-Game 3	One-Game 4	LO	XN	IP	PH	RHP	LHP
1946	PHI	AL	1	0	1	1	0	0	0	0	0	0	0	0	0	0	1	0
1951	STL	NL	1	0	1	1	0	0	0	0	0	0	0	0	0	0	1	0
Total			2	0	2	2	0	0	0	0	0	0	0	0	0	0	2	0

Rank among batters: 4,129 • *Total ballparks homered in*: 2 • *First HR*: 09/19/1946 off Virgil Trucks

Lee Richmond

J LEE RICHMOND
B: 05/05/1857 D: 10/01/1929

Year	Tm	Lg	Tot	H	A	Men-On 0	Men-On 1	Men-On 2	Men-On 3	One-Game 2	One-Game 3	One-Game 4	LO	XN	IP	PH	RHP	LHP
1882	WOR	NL	2	2	0	1	0	1	0	0	0	0	0	0	1	0	2	0
1883	PRO	NL	1	0	1	0	1	0	0	0	0	0	0	0	0	0	1	0
Total			3	2	1	1	1	1	0	0	0	0	0	0	1	0	3	0

Rank among batters: 3,735 • *Total ballparks homered in*: 2 • *First HR*: 06/09/1882 off George Derby

John Richmond

JOHN H. RICHMOND
B: 1854

Year	Tm	Lg	Tot	H	A	Men-On 0	Men-On 1	Men-On 2	Men-On 3	One-Game 2	One-Game 3	One-Game 4	LO	XN	IP	PH	RHP	LHP
1879	SYR	NL	1	0	1	1	0	0	0	0	0	0	0	0	0	0	1	0
1881	BOS	NL	1	0	1	0	1	0	0	0	0	0	0	0	0	0	1	0
1884	COL	AA	3	2	1	0	2	1	0	0	0	0	0	0	0	0	3	0
Total			5	2	3	1	3	1	0	0	0	0	0	0	0	0	5	0

Rank among batters: 3,191 • *Top target (2 home runs)*: Bobby Mathews • *Number of pitchers victimized*: 4 • *Total ballparks homered in*: 3 • *First HR*: 08/20/1879 off Bobby Mathews

Marv Rickert

MARVIN AUGUST RICKERT
B: 01/08/1921 D: 06/03/1978
BL

Year	Tm	Lg	Tot	H	A	Men-On 0	Men-On 1	Men-On 2	Men-On 3	One-Game 2	One-Game 3	One-Game 4	LO	XN	IP	PH	RHP	LHP
1946	CHI	NL	7	4	3	5	1	1	0	0	0	0	0	0	1	0	7	0
1947	CHI	NL	2	1	1	1	1	0	0	0	0	0	0	0	0	1	2	0
1949	BOS	NL	6	2	4	4	1	1	0	0	0	0	0	1	0	0	6	0
1950	CHI	AL	4	2	2	3	1	0	0	0	0	0	0	1	0	0	4	0
Total			19	9	10	13	4	2	0	0	0	0	0	2	1	1	19	0

Rank among batters: 1,861 • *Total ballparks homered in*: 8 • *First HR*: 06/01/1946 off Bill Lee • *World Series HR*—1

Dave Ricketts

DAVID WILLIAM RICKETTS
B: 07/12/1935
BB

Year	Tm	Lg	Tot	H	A	Men-On 0	Men-On 1	Men-On 2	Men-On 3	One-Game 2	One-Game 3	One-Game 4	LO	XN	IP	PH	RHP	LHP
1967	STL	NL	1	1	0	1	0	0	0	0	0	0	0	0	0	0	1	0

Rank among batters: 4,707 • *Total ballparks homered in*: 1 • *First HR*: 09/04/1967 off Dennis Ribant

Branch Rickey

WESLEY BRANCH RICKEY
B: 12/20/1881 D: 12/09/1965
BL HOF

Year	Tm	Lg	Tot	H	A	Men-On 0	Men-On 1	Men-On 2	Men-On 3	One-Game 2	One-Game 3	One-Game 4	LO	XN	IP	PH	RHP	LHP
1906	STL	AL	3	3	0	1	2	0	0	1	0	0	0	0	1	0	3	0

Rank among batters: 3,735 • *Top target (2 home runs)*: Walter Clarkson • *Number of pitchers victimized*: 2 • *Total ballparks homered in*: 1 • *First HR*: 08/02/1906 off Charlie Smith

Harry Riconda

HENRY PAUL RICONDA
B: 05/17/1897 D: 11/15/1958
BR

Year	Tm	Lg	Tot	H	A	Men-On 0	Men-On 1	Men-On 2	Men-On 3	One-Game 2	One-Game 3	One-Game 4	LO	XN	IP	PH	RHP	LHP
1924	PHI	AL	1	1	0	1	0	0	0	0	0	0	0	0	0	0	1	0
1928	BRO	NL	3	1	2	2	1	0	0	0	0	0	0	0	0	0	3	0
Total			4	2	2	3	1	0	0	0	0	0	0	0	0	0	4	0

Rank among batters: 3,427 • *Total ballparks homered in*: 4 • *First HR*: 05/24/1924 off Urban Shocker

Elmer Riddle

ELMER RAY RIDDLE
B: 07/31/1914 D: 05/14/1984
BR

Year	Tm	Lg	Tot	H	A	Men-On 0	Men-On 1	Men-On 2	Men-On 3	One-Game 2	One-Game 3	One-Game 4	LO	XN	IP	PH	RHP	LHP
1948	PIT	NL	1	1	0	1	0	0	0	0	0	0	0	0	0	0	1	0

Rank among batters: 4,707 • *Total ballparks homered in*: 1 • *First HR*: 07/21/1948 off Monk Dubiel

Steve Ridzik

STEPHEN GEORGE RIDZIK
B: 04/29/1929
BR

Year	Tm	Lg	Tot	H	A	Men-On 0	Men-On 1	Men-On 2	Men-On 3	One-Game 2	One-Game 3	One-Game 4	LO	XN	IP	PH	RHP	LHP
1953	PHI	NL	1	0	1	1	0	0	0	0	0	0	0	0	0	0	0	1

Rank among batters: 4,707 • *Total ballparks homered in*: 1 • *First HR*: 06/30/1953 off Preacher Roe

Joe Riggert

JOSEPH ALOYSIUS RIGGERT
B: 12/11/1886 D: 12/10/1973
BR

Year	Tm	Lg	Tot	H	A	Men-On 0	Men-On 1	Men-On 2	Men-On 3	One-Game 2	One-Game 3	One-Game 4	LO	XN	IP	PH	RHP	LHP
1911	BOS	AL	2	1	1	1	1	0	0	0	0	0	0	0	0	0	1	1
1914	BRO	NL	2	1	1	1	1	0	0	0	0	0	0	0	0	0	1	1
1919	BOS	NL	4	1	3	2	2	0	0	0	0	0	0	1	1	0	3	1
Total			8	3	5	4	4	0	0	0	0	0	0	1	1	0	5	3

Rank among batters: 2,703 • *Total ballparks homered in*: 6 • *First HR*: 08/11/1911 off Chief Bender

Lew Riggs

LEWIS SIDNEY RIGGS
B: 04/22/1910 D: 08/12/1975
BL

Year	Tm	Lg	Tot	H	A	Men-On 0	Men-On 1	Men-On 2	Men-On 3	One-Game 2	One-Game 3	One-Game 4	LO	XN	IP	PH	RHP	LHP
1935	CIN	NL	5	1	4	2	2	1	0	0	0	0	0	0	0	0	5	0
1936	CIN	NL	6	0	6	1	5	0	0	0	0	0	0	0	0	0	6	0
1937	CIN	NL	6	0	6	3	2	1	0	2	0	0	0	0	0	0	5	1
1938	CIN	NL	2	0	2	2	0	0	0	0	0	0	0	0	0	0	2	0
1940	CIN	NL	1	1	0	1	0	0	0	0	0	0	0	0	0	0	1	0
1941	BRO	NL	5	2	3	3	1	1	0	0	0	0	0	0	0	1	5	0
1942	BRO	NL	3	1	2	2	0	1	0	0	0	0	0	0	0	2	2	1
Total			28	5	23	14	10	4	0	2	0	0	0	0	0	3	26	2

Rank among batters: 1,500 • *Top target (4 home runs)*: Harry Gumbert • *Number of pitchers victimized*: 20 • *Total ballparks homered in*: 6 • *First HR*: 04/20/1935 off Tex Carleton

Bill Rigney

WILLIAM JOSEPH RIGNEY
B: 01/29/1918
BR

Year	Tm	Lg	Tot	H	A	Men-On 0	Men-On 1	Men-On 2	Men-On 3	One-Game 2	One-Game 3	One-Game 4	LO	XN	IP	PH	RHP	LHP
1946	NY	NL	3	3	0	1	1	1	0	0	0	0	0	0	0	0	2	1
1947	NY	NL	17	14	3	9	6	1	1	2	0	0	1	0	0	0	10	7
1948	NY	NL	10	3	7	7	1	2	0	0	0	0	1	0	0	0	5	5
1949	NY	NL	6	5	1	4	2	0	0	0	0	0	1	0	0	0	2	4
1951	NY	NL	4	3	1	4	0	0	0	0	0	0	0	1	0	2	4	0
1952	NY	NL	1	1	0	0	1	0	0	0	0	0	0	0	0	0	0	1
Total			41	29	12	25	11	4	1	2	0	0	3	1	0	2	23	18

Rank among batters: 1,163 • Top target (3 home runs): Preacher Roe, Ralph Branca, Harry Brecheen, Vic Lombardi, Murry Dickson • *Number of pitchers victimized*: 26 • *Total ballparks homered in*: 8 • *First HR*: 04/28/1946 off Hank Behrman

Topper Rigney

EMORY ELMO RIGNEY
B: 01/07/1897 D: 06/06/1972
BR

Year	Tm	Lg	Tot	H	A	Men-On 0	Men-On 1	Men-On 2	Men-On 3	One-Game 2	One-Game 3	One-Game 4	LO	XN	IP	PH	RHP	LHP
1922	DET	AL	2	0	2	1	1	0	0	0	0	0	0	0	1	0	1	1
1923	DET	AL	1	1	0	1	0	0	0	0	0	0	0	0	0	0	1	0
1924	DET	AL	4	3	1	2	1	0	1	0	0	0	0	0	0	0	4	0
1925	DET	AL	2	0	2	0	2	0	0	0	0	0	0	0	0	0	2	0
1926	BOS	AL	4	1	3	2	1	1	0	0	0	0	0	0	2	0	2	2
Total			13	5	8	6	5	1	1	0	0	0	0	0	3	0	10	3

Rank among batters: 2,248 • *Top target (2 home runs)*: Howard Ehmke, Dixie Davis, Eddie Rommel • *Number of pitchers victimized*: 10 • *Total ballparks homered in*: 4 • *First HR*: 05/30/1922 off Bill Bayne

Jose Rijo

JOSE ANTONIO (ABREU) RIJO
B: 05/13/1965
BR

Year	Tm	Lg	Tot	H	A	Men-On 0	Men-On 1	Men-On 2	Men-On 3	One-Game 2	One-Game 3	One-Game 4	LO	XN	IP	PH	RHP	LHP
1988	CIN	NL	1	1	0	1	0	0	0	0	0	0	0	0	0	0	1	0
1993	CIN	NL	1	1	0	1	0	0	0	0	0	0	0	0	0	0	1	0
Total			2	2	0	2	0	0	0	0	0	0	0	0	0	0	2	0

Rank among batters: 4,129 • *Total ballparks homered in*: 1 • *First HR*: 07/19/1988 off Terry Leach

Cully Rikard

CULLY RIKARD
B: 05/09/1914
BL

Year	Tm	Lg	Tot	H	A	Men-On 0	Men-On 1	Men-On 2	Men-On 3	One-Game 2	One-Game 3	One-Game 4	LO	XN	IP	PH	RHP	LHP
1947	PIT	NL	4	1	3	2	2	0	0	0	0	0	0	0	0	1	4	0

Rank among batters: 3,427 • *Total ballparks homered in*: 4 • *First HR*: 05/26/1947 off Johnny Hetki

Ernest Riles

ERNEST RILES
B: 10/02/1960
BL

Year	Tm	Lg	Tot	H	A	Men-On 0	Men-On 1	Men-On 2	Men-On 3	One-Game 2	One-Game 3	One-Game 4	LO	XN	IP	PH	RHP	LHP
1985	MIL	AL	5	2	3	3	1	1	0	0	0	0	0	0	0	0	5	0
1986	MIL	AL	9	2	7	1	5	3	0	0	0	0	0	0	0	0	6	3
1987	MIL	AL	4	1	3	3	1	0	0	0	0	0	0	0	0	0	4	0
1988	MIL	AL	1	1	0	1	0	0	0	0	0	0	0	0	0	0	1	0
	SF	NL	3	3	0	1	0	2	0	0	0	0	0	0	0	1	2	1
	Total		4	4	0	2	0	2	0	0	0	0	0	0	0	1	3	1
1989	SF	NL	7	5	2	2	3	1	1	0	0	0	0	0	0	0	7	0
1990	SF	NL	8	7	1	6	0	1	1	0	0	0	0	0	0	4	7	1
1991	OAK	AL	5	3	2	1	2	1	1	0	0	0	0	0	0	0	5	0
1992	HOU	NL	1	0	1	1	0	0	0	0	0	0	0	1	0	0	1	0
1993	BOS	AL	5	2	3	4	0	1	0	0	0	0	0	0	0	1	4	1
Total			48	26	22	23	12	10	3	0	0	0	0	1	0	6	42	6

Rank among batters: 1,024 • *Top target (3 home runs)*: Bill Gullickson • *Number of pitchers victimized*: 42 • *Total ballparks homered in*: 15 • *First HR*: 05/29/1985 off Don Schulze

Jimmy Ring

JAMES JOSEPH RING
B: 02/15/1895 D: 07/06/1965
BR

Year	Tm	Lg	Tot	H	A	Men-On 0	Men-On 1	Men-On 2	Men-On 3	One-Game 2	One-Game 3	One-Game 4	LO	XN	IP	PH	RHP	LHP
1922	PHI	NL	1	0	1	1	0	0	0	0	0	0	0	0	0	0	0	1
1923	PHI	NL	1	1	0	0	1	0	0	0	0	0	0	0	0	0	1	0
1925	PHI	NL	2	2	0	1	0	0	1	0	0	0	0	0	0	0	2	0
Total			4	3	1	2	1	0	1	0	0	0	0	0	0	0	3	1

Rank among batters: 3,427 • *Total ballparks homered in*: 2 • *First HR*: 07/12/1922 off Bill Sherdel

Juan Rios

JUAN ONOFRE VELEZ RIOS
B: 07/14/1942
BR

Year	Tm	Lg	Tot	H	A	Men-On 0	Men-On 1	Men-On 2	Men-On 3	One-Game 2	One-Game 3	One-Game 4	LO	XN	IP	PH	RHP	LHP
1969	KC	AL	1	1	0	1	0	0	0	0	0	0	1	0	0	0	0	1

Rank among batters: 4,707 • *Total ballparks homered in*: 1 • *First HR*: 06/02/1969 off Frank Bertaina

Billy Ripken

WILLIAM OLIVER RIPKEN
B: 12/16/1964
BR

Year	Tm	Lg	Tot	H	A	Men-On 0	Men-On 1	Men-On 2	Men-On 3	One-Game 2	One-Game 3	One-Game 4	LO	XN	IP	PH	RHP	LHP
1987	BAL	AL	2	0	2	0	0	2	0	0	0	0	0	0	0	0	1	1
1988	BAL	AL	2	0	2	1	1	0	0	0	0	0	0	0	0	0	2	0
1989	BAL	AL	2	0	2	1	1	0	0	0	0	0	0	0	0	0	2	0
1990	BAL	AL	3	2	1	2	1	0	0	0	0	0	0	0	0	0	1	2
1992	BAL	AL	4	3	1	3	1	0	0	0	0	0	0	0	0	0	4	0
1995	CLE	AL	2	1	1	2	0	0	0	0	0	0	0	0	0	0	1	1
Total			15	6	9	9	4	2	0	0	0	0	0	0	0	0	11	4

Rank among batters: 2,096 • *Total ballparks homered in*: 11 • *First HR*: 07/19/1987 off Bud Black

Cal Ripken

CALVIN EDWIN RIPKEN, JR.
B: 08/24/1960
BR

Year	Tm	Lg	Tot	H	A	Men-On 0	1	2	3	One-Game 2	3	4	LO	XN	IP	PH	RHP	LHP
1982	BAL	AL	28	11	17	17	8	2	1	0	0	0	0	0	0	0	16	12
1983	BAL	AL	27	12	15	15	9	2	1	2	0	0	0	1	0	0	19	8
1984	BAL	AL	27	16	11	16	8	3	0	3	0	0	0	1	0	0	20	7
1985	BAL	AL	26	15	11	15	6	5	0	2	0	0	0	0	0	0	20	6
1986	BAL	AL	25	10	15	16	7	2	0	0	0	0	0	1	0	0	13	12
1987	BAL	AL	27	17	10	10	11	6	0	0	0	0	0	0	0	0	20	7
1988	BAL	AL	23	11	12	14	8	1	0	0	0	0	0	0	0	0	14	9
1989	BAL	AL	21	13	8	8	9	4	0	0	0	0	0	0	0	0	16	5
1990	BAL	AL	21	8	13	17	2	2	0	2	0	0	0	1	0	0	12	9
1991	BAL	AL	34	16	18	21	11	2	0	2	0	0	0	0	0	0	22	12
1992	BAL	AL	14	5	9	6	7	1	0	1	0	0	0	0	0	0	12	2
1993	BAL	AL	24	14	10	14	2	8	0	2	0	0	0	0	0	0	17	7
1994	BAL	AL	13	5	8	5	4	3	1	0	0	0	0	0	0	0	11	2
1995	BAL	AL	17	10	7	10	4	2	1	1	0	0	0	0	0	0	10	7
Total			327	163	164	184	96	43	4	15	0	0	0	4	0	0	222	105

Rank among batters: 54 • Top target (5 home runs): Bret Saberhagen, Richard Dotson, Greg Swindell, Mike Moore, Frank Viola, Charlie Leibrandt • *Number of pitchers victimized*: 220 • *Total ballparks homered in*: 18 • *First HR*: 04/05/1982 off Dennis Leonard • *Hit for Cycle*—@TEX: 05/06/1984 • *All-Star HR*—1

Ray Rippelmeyer

RAYMOND ROY RIPPELMEYER
B: 07/09/1933
BR

Year	Tm	Lg	Tot	H	A	Men-On 0	1	2	3	One-Game 2	3	4	LO	XN	IP	PH	RHP	LHP
1962	WAS	AL	1	1	0	1	0	0	0	0	0	0	0	0	0	0	1	0

Rank among batters: 4,707 • *Total ballparks homered in*: 1 • *First HR*: 05/03/1962 off Bill Monbouquette

Jimmy Ripple

JAMES ALBERT RIPPLE
B: 10/14/1909 D: 07/16/1959
BL

Year	Tm	Lg	Tot	H	A	Men-On 0	1	2	3	One-Game 2	3	4	LO	XN	IP	PH	RHP	LHP
1936	NY	NL	7	7	0	7	0	0	0	0	0	0	0	0	0	2	7	0
1937	NY	NL	5	3	2	1	1	2	1	0	0	0	0	0	0	1	4	1
1938	NY	NL	10	7	3	6	4	0	0	0	0	0	0	0	1	0	8	2
1939	NY	NL	1	1	0	0	0	1	0	0	0	0	0	0	0	0	1	0
1940	CIN	NL	4	1	3	1	2	1	0	0	0	0	0	0	0	0	4	0
1941	CIN	NL	1	0	1	1	0	0	0	0	0	0	0	0	0	0	1	0
Total			28	19	9	16	7	4	1	0	0	0	0	0	1	3	25	3

Rank among batters: 1,500 • *Top target (3 home runs)*: Tiny Chaplin • *Number of pitchers victimized*: 22 • *Total ballparks homered in*: 7 • *First HR*: 05/28/1936 off Tiny Chaplin • *World Series HR*—2

Swede Risberg

CHARLES AUGUST RISBERG
B: 10/13/1894 D: 10/13/1975
BR

Year	Tm	Lg	Tot	H	A	Men-On 0	1	2	3	One-Game 2	3	4	LO	XN	IP	PH	RHP	LHP
1917	CHI	AL	1	0	1	1	0	0	0	0	0	0	0	0	0	0	1	0
1918	CHI	AL	1	1	0	1	0	0	0	0	0	0	0	0	0	0	1	0
1919	CHI	AL	2	1	1	2	0	0	0	0	0	0	0	0	0	0	1	1
1920	CHI	AL	2	1	1	1	1	0	0	0	0	0	0	0	1	0	1	1
Total			6	3	3	5	1	0	0	0	0	0	0	0	1	0	4	2

Rank among batters: 2,988 • *Total ballparks homered in*: 4 • *First HR*: 06/09/1917 off Bert Gallia

Claude Ritchey

CLAUDE CASSIUS RITCHEY
B: 10/05/1873 D: 11/08/1951
BB

Year	Tm	Lg	Tot	H	A	Men-On 0	1	2	3	One-Game 2	3	4	LO	XN	IP	PH	RHP	LHP
1898	LOU	NL	5	4	1	1	4	0	0	0	0	0	0	0	0	0	2	1
1899	LOU	NL	4	2	2	3	1	0	0	0	0	0	0	0	1	0	3	1
1900	PIT	NL	1	0	1	0	1	0	0	0	0	0	0	0	0	0	1	0
1901	PIT	NL	1	1	0	0	1	0	0	0	0	0	0	0	0	0	1	0
1902	PIT	NL	2	1	1	0	2	0	0	0	0	0	0	0	2	0	1	1
1906	PIT	NL	1	0	1	1	0	0	0	0	0	0	0	0	1	0	1	0
1907	BOS	NL	2	1	1	1	1	0	0	0	0	0	0	0	0	0	2	0

Claude Ritchey *continued*

Year	Tm	Lg	Tot	H	A	Men-On 0	1	2	3	One-Game 2	3	4	LO	XN	IP	PH	RHP	LHP
1908	BOS	NL	2	1	1	0	1	1	0	0	0	0	0	0	0	0	2	0
Total			18	10	8	6	11	1	0	0	0	0	0	0	4	0	13	3

Rank among batters: 1,914 • *Total ballparks homered in*: 7 • *First HR*: 05/25/1898 off Amos Rusie

Lew Ritter

LEWIS ELMER RITTER
B: 09/07/1875 D: 05/27/1952
BR

Year	Tm	Lg	Tot	H	A	Men-On 0	1	2	3	One-Game 2	3	4	LO	XN	IP	PH	RHP	LHP
1905	BRO	NL	1	1	0	1	0	0	0	0	0	0	0	0	0	0	0	1

Rank among batters: 4,707 • *Total ballparks homered in*: 1 • *First HR*: 10/07/1905 off Patrick Dolan

Bombo Rivera

JESUS MANUEL (TORRES) RIVERA
B: 08/02/1952
BR

Year	Tm	Lg	Tot	H	A	Men-On 0	1	2	3	One-Game 2	3	4	LO	XN	IP	PH	RHP	LHP
1976	MON	NL	2	1	1	0	1	0	1	0	0	0	0	0	1	0	0	2
1978	MIN	AL	3	2	1	2	0	1	0	0	0	0	0	0	0	0	1	2
1979	MIN	AL	2	2	0	1	1	0	0	0	0	0	0	0	0	0	0	2
1980	MIN	AL	3	2	1	2	1	0	0	0	0	0	0	0	0	0	1	2
Total			10	7	3	5	3	1	1	0	0	0	0	0	1	0	2	8

Rank among batters: 2,500 • *Total ballparks homered in*: 5 • *First HR*: 06/26/1976 off Jerry Reuss

German Rivera

GERMAN (DIAZ) RIVERA
B: 07/06/1960
BR

Year	Tm	Lg	Tot	H	A	Men-On 0	1	2	3	One-Game 2	3	4	LO	XN	IP	PH	RHP	LHP
1984	LA	NL	2	1	1	1	1	0	0	0	0	0	0	0	0	0	2	0

Rank among batters: 4,129 • *Total ballparks homered in*: 2 • *First HR*: 07/14/1984 off Scott Sanderson

Jim Rivera

MANUEL JOSEPH RIVERA
B: 07/22/1922
BL

Year	Tm	Lg	Tot	H	A	Men-On 0	1	2	3	One-Game 2	3	4	LO	XN	IP	PH	RHP	LHP
1952	STL	AL	4	2	2	4	0	0	0	0	0	0	0	0	1	0	4	0
	CHI	AL	3	3	0	0	1	2	0	0	0	0	0	0	0	0	2	1
	Total		7	5	2	5	2	0	0	0	0	0	0	0	1	0	6	1
1953	CHI	AL	11	5	6	9	2	0	0	0	0	0	0	0	1	0	10	1
1954	CHI	AL	13	5	8	11	0	2	0	2	0	0	0	0	1	0	10	3
1955	CHI	AL	10	3	7	4	5	0	1	1	0	0	0	0	0	0	9	1
1956	CHI	AL	12	9	3	9	1	2	0	1	0	0	0	0	0	0	11	1
1957	CHI	AL	14	6	8	7	6	1	0	1	0	0	1	0	0	0	14	0
1958	CHI	AL	9	3	6	3	6	0	0	0	0	0	0	0	0	0	8	1
1959	CHI	AL	4	2	2	3	1	0	0	0	0	0	0	0	0	0	2	2
1960	CHI	AL	1	1	0	1	0	0	0	0	0	0	0	0	0	0	1	0
1961	KC	AL	2	0	2	1	1	0	0	0	0	0	0	0	0	1	2	0
Total			83	39	44	53	24	5	1	5	0	0	1	0	3	1	73	10

Rank among batters: 628 • *Top target (5 home runs)*: Tom Brewer • *Number of pitchers victimized*: 56 • *Total ballparks homered in*: 11 • *First HR*: 04/20/1952 off Hal Brown

Luis Rivera

LUIS ANTONIO (PEDRAZA) RIVERA
B: 01/03/1964
BR

Year	Tm	Lg	Tot	H	A	Men-On 0	1	2	3	One-Game 2	3	4	LO	XN	IP	PH	RHP	LHP
1988	MON	NL	4	2	2	3	1	0	0	0	0	0	0	0	0	0	2	2
1989	BOS	AL	5	4	1	2	3	0	0	0	0	0	0	0	0	0	3	2
1990	BOS	AL	7	4	3	4	1	1	1	0	0	0	0	0	0	0	5	2
1991	BOS	AL	8	4	4	6	1	1	0	0	0	0	0	0	1	0	4	4
1993	BOS	AL	1	1	0	0	1	0	0	0	0	0	0	0	0	0	1	0
1994	NY	NL	3	2	1	2	1	0	0	0	0	0	0	0	0	1	2	1
Total			28	17	11	17	8	2	1	0	0	0	0	0	1	1	17	11

Rank among batters: 1,500 • *Top target (2 home runs)*: Jeff Robinson, Tom Glavine • *Number of pitchers victimized*: 26 • *Total ballparks homered in*: 11 • *First HR*: 04/15/1988 off Todd Frohwirth

Mickey Rivers

JOHN MILTON RIVERS
B: 10/31/1948
BL

Year	Tm	Lg	Tot	H	A	Men-On 0	1	2	3	One-Game 2	3	4	LO	XN	IP	PH	RHP	LHP
1971	CAL	AL	1	0	1	0	1	0	0	0	0	0	0	0	0	0	1	0
1974	CAL	AL	3	2	1	2	1	0	0	0	0	0	1	0	0	0	2	1
1975	CAL	AL	1	1	0	1	0	0	0	0	0	0	0	0	0	0	1	0
1976	NY	AL	8	5	3	5	2	1	0	0	0	0	0	0	1	0	4	4
1977	NY	AL	12	8	4	7	3	2	0	1	0	0	3	1	0	0	11	1
1978	NY	AL	11	9	2	7	4	0	0	1	0	0	3	0	1	0	8	3
1979	NY	AL	3	2	1	2	1	0	0	0	0	0	1	1	0	1	2	1
	TEX	AL	6	4	2	5	1	0	0	1	0	0	2	0	0	0	4	2
	Total		9	6	3	7	2	0	0	1	0	0	3	1	0	1	6	3
1980	TEX	AL	7	0	7	6	1	0	0	0	0	0	1	0	0	0	4	3
1981	TEX	AL	3	0	3	2	1	0	0	0	0	0	0	0	0	0	3	0
1982	TEX	AL	1	0	1	1	0	0	0	0	0	0	0	0	0	0	1	0
1983	TEX	AL	1	0	1	1	0	0	0	0	0	0	0	0	0	0	1	0
1984	TEX	AL	4	3	1	2	2	0	0	0	0	0	0	0	0	1	4	0
Total			61	34	27	41	17	3	0	3	0	0	11	2	2	2	46	15

Rank among batters: 844 • *Top target (3 home runs)*: Bill Travers • *Number of pitchers victimized*: 54 • *Total ballparks homered in*: 14 • *First HR*: 08/15/1971 off Dick Bosman

Eppa Rixey

EPPA RIXEY
B: 05/03/1891 D: 02/28/1963
BR HOF

Year	Tm	Lg	Tot	H	A	Men-On 0	1	2	3	One-Game 2	3	4	LO	XN	IP	PH	RHP	LHP
1920	PHI	NL	1	1	0	1	0	0	0	0	0	0	0	0	0	0	1	0
1924	CIN	NL	1	0	1	1	0	0	0	0	0	0	0	0	0	0	1	0
1928	CIN	NL	1	0	1	1	0	0	0	0	0	0	0	0	0	0	1	0
Total			3	1	2	3	0	0	0	0	0	0	0	0	0	0	3	0

Rank among batters: 3,735 • *Total ballparks homered in*: 3 • *First HR*: 09/13/1920 off Hod Eller

Johnny Rizzo

JOHN COSTA RIZZO
B: 07/30/1912 D: 12/04/1977
BR

Year	Tm	Lg	Tot	H	A	Men-On 0	1	2	3	One-Game 2	3	4	LO	XN	IP	PH	RHP	LHP
1938	PIT	NL	23	6	17	10	7	5	1	2	0	0	0	1	1	0	12	11
1939	PIT	NL	6	3	3	3	1	2	0	1	0	0	0	0	0	0	4	2
1940	CIN	NL	4	3	1	0	3	1	0	1	0	0	0	0	0	0	3	1
	PHI	NL	20	7	13	10	8	2	0	3	0	0	0	0	0	0	18	2
	Total		24	10	14	10	11	3	0	4	0	0	0	0	0	0	21	3
1941	PHI	NL	4	1	3	3	1	0	0	0	0	0	0	0	0	0	4	0
1942	BRO	NL	4	2	2	3	1	0	0	0	0	0	0	0	0	0	1	3
Total			61	22	39	29	21	10	1	7	0	0	0	1	1	0	42	19

Rank among batters: 844 • Top target (3 home runs): Johnny Vander Meer, Paul Dean, Jake Mooty, Curt Davis, Bucky Walters, Nick Strincevich • *Number of pitchers victimized*: 43 • *Total ballparks homered in*: 9 • *First HR*: 05/15/1938 off Bill Lee

Phil Rizzuto

PHILIP FRANCIS RIZZUTO
B: 09/25/1917
BR HOF

Year	Tm	Lg	Tot	H	A	Men-On 0	1	2	3	One-Game 2	3	4	LO	XN	IP	PH	RHP	LHP
1941	NY	AL	3	3	0	2	1	0	0	0	0	0	0	1	0	0	3	0
1942	NY	AL	4	2	2	0	3	0	1	0	0	0	0	0	0	0	2	2
1946	NY	AL	2	1	1	0	1	1	0	0	0	0	0	0	0	0	1	1
1947	NY	AL	2	1	1	1	0	0	1	0	0	0	0	0	0	0	2	0
1948	NY	AL	6	4	2	4	2	0	0	0	0	0	0	0	1	0	4	2
1949	NY	AL	5	3	2	3	2	0	0	1	0	0	0	0	0	0	2	3
1950	NY	AL	7	4	3	6	0	1	0	0	0	0	0	0	1	0	5	2
1951	NY	AL	2	2	0	0	1	1	0	0	0	0	0	0	0	0	0	2
1952	NY	AL	2	0	2	2	0	0	0	0	0	0	0	0	0	0	1	1
1953	NY	AL	2	0	2	0	1	1	0	0	0	0	0	0	0	0	0	2
1954	NY	AL	2	1	1	1	1	0	0	0	0	0	0	0	0	0	1	1
1955	NY	AL	1	0	1	1	0	0	0	0	0	0	0	0	0	0	1	0
Total			38	21	17	20	12	4	2	1	0	0	0	1	2	0	22	16

Rank among batters: 1,225 • *Top target (3 home runs)*: Bob Lemon • *Number of pitchers victimized*: 30 • *Total ballparks homered in*: 7 • *First HR*: 04/23/1941 off Charlie Wagner • *World Series HR*—2

Year	Tm	Lg	Tot	H	A	Men-On 0	1	2	3	One-Game 2	3	4	LO	XN	IP	PH	RHP	LHP

Mel Roach

MELVIN EARL ROACH
B: 01/25/1933
BR

Year	Tm	Lg	Tot	H	A	0	1	2	3	2	3	4	LO	XN	IP	PH	RHP	LHP
1958	MIL	NL	3	2	1	2	1	0	0	0	0	0	0	0	0	0	1	2
1960	MIL	NL	3	1	2	2	1	0	0	0	0	0	0	0	0	0	1	2
1961	MIL	NL	1	0	1	0	0	1	0	0	0	0	0	0	0	1	1	0
Total			7	3	4	4	2	1	0	0	0	0	0	0	0	1	3	4

Rank among batters: 2,834 • *Top target (2 home runs)*: Mike McCormick • *Number of pitchers victimized*: 6 • *Total ballparks homered in*: 3 • *First HR*: 04/19/1958 off Curt Simmons

Roxey Roach

WILBUR CHARLES ROACH
B: 11/28/1882 D: 12/26/1947
BR

Year	Tm	Lg	Tot	H	A	0	1	2	3	2	3	4	LO	XN	IP	PH	RHP	LHP
1912	WAS	AL	1	1	0	1	0	0	0	0	0	0	0	0	1	0	1	0
1915	BUF	FL	2	0	2	2	0	0	0	0	0	0	0	1	0	0	1	1
Total			3	1	2	3	0	0	0	0	0	0	0	1	1	0	2	1

Rank among batters: 3,735 • *Total ballparks homered in*: 2 • *First HR*: 07/04/1912 off Jack Quinn

Mike Roarke

MICHAEL THOMAS ROARKE
B: 11/08/1930
BR

Year	Tm	Lg	Tot	H	A	0	1	2	3	2	3	4	LO	XN	IP	PH	RHP	LHP
1961	DET	AL	2	2	0	1	1	0	0	0	0	0	0	0	0	0	2	0
1962	DET	AL	4	1	3	2	2	0	0	0	0	0	0	0	0	0	2	2
Total			6	3	3	3	3	0	0	0	0	0	0	0	0	0	4	2

Rank among batters: 2,988 • *Top target (2 home runs)*: Jack Fisher • *Number of pitchers victimized*: 5 • *Total ballparks homered in*: 3 • *First HR*: 06/04/1961 off Ted Sadowski

Fred Roat

FREDERICK R. ROAT
B: 11/10/1867 D: 09/24/1913

Year	Tm	Lg	Tot	H	A	0	1	2	3	2	3	4	LO	XN	IP	PH	RHP	LHP
1890	PIT	NL	2	0	2	1	1	0	0	0	0	0	0	0	0	0	2	0

Rank among batters: 4,129 • *Total ballparks homered in*: 1 • *First HR*: 06/16/1890 off Bill Hutchison

Skippy Roberge

JOSEPH ALBERT ARMAND ROBERGE
B: 05/19/1917 D: 06/07/1993
BR

Year	Tm	Lg	Tot	H	A	0	1	2	3	2	3	4	LO	XN	IP	PH	RHP	LHP
1942	BOS	NL	1	0	1	0	1	0	0	0	0	0	0	0	0	0	0	1
1946	BOS	NL	2	0	2	1	0	1	0	0	0	0	0	0	0	0	2	0
Total			3	0	3	1	1	1	0	0	0	0	0	0	0	0	2	1

Rank among batters: 3,735 • *Total ballparks homered in*: 2 • *First HR*: 07/04/1942 off Cliff Melton

Kevin Roberson

KEVIN LYNN ROBERSON
B: 01/29/1968
BB

Year	Tm	Lg	Tot	H	A	0	1	2	3	2	3	4	LO	XN	IP	PH	RHP	LHP
1993	CHI	NL	9	4	5	3	4	2	0	0	0	0	0	0	0	1	7	2
1994	CHI	NL	4	2	2	3	1	0	0	0	0	0	0	0	0	3	3	1
1995	CHI	NL	4	2	2	2	2	0	0	0	0	0	0	0	0	2	3	1
Total			17	8	9	8	7	2	0	0	0	0	0	0	0	6	13	4

Rank among batters: 1,969 • *Total ballparks homered in*: 7 • *First HR*: 07/18/1993 off Bruce Ruffin

Bip Roberts

LEON JOSEPH ROBERTS
B: 10/27/1963
BB

Year	Tm	Lg	Tot	H	A	0	1	2	3	2	3	4	LO	XN	IP	PH	RHP	LHP
1986	SD	NL	1	0	1	1	0	0	0	0	0	0	0	0	0	0	0	1
1989	SD	NL	3	2	1	1	2	0	0	0	0	0	0	0	0	0	0	3
1990	SD	NL	9	4	5	3	5	1	0	0	0	0	1	1	1	0	5	4
1991	SD	NL	3	3	0	2	1	0	0	1	0	0	1	0	0	0	3	0
1992	CIN	NL	4	3	1	2	1	1	0	0	0	0	0	0	0	0	1	3

Year	Tm	Lg	Tot	H	A	Men-On				One-Game			LO	XN	IP	PH	RHP	LHP
						0	1	2	3	2	3	4						

Bip Roberts *continued*

Year	Tm	Lg	Tot	H	A	0	1	2	3	2	3	4	LO	XN	IP	PH	RHP	LHP
1993	CIN	NL	1	0	1	0	1	0	0	0	0	0	0	0	0	0	1	0
1994	SD	NL	2	1	1	1	0	1	0	0	0	0	0	0	0	0	0	2
1995	SD	NL	2	2	0	1	0	0	1	0	0	0	1	0	0	0	2	0
Total			25	15	10	11	10	3	1	1	0	0	3	1	1	0	12	13

Rank among batters: 1,608 • *Top target (2 home runs)*: Kip Gross, Steve Avery • *Number of pitchers victimized*: 23 • *Total ballparks homered in*: 9 • *First HR*: 08/15/1986 off Tom Browning

Curt Roberts

CURTIS BENJAMIN ROBERTS
B: 08/16/1929 D: 11/14/1969
BR

Year	Tm	Lg	Tot	H	A	0	1	2	3	2	3	4	LO	XN	IP	PH	RHP	LHP
1954	PIT	NL	1	0	1	0	1	0	0	0	0	0	0	0	0	0	1	0

Rank among batters: 4,707 • *Total ballparks homered in*: 1 • *First HR*: 06/11/1954 off Joe Presko

Dave Roberts

DAVID LEONARD ROBERTS
B: 06/30/1933
BL

Year	Tm	Lg	Tot	H	A	0	1	2	3	2	3	4	LO	XN	IP	PH	RHP	LHP
1962	HOU	NL	1	0	1	1	0	0	0	0	0	0	0	0	0	0	1	0
1964	HOU	NL	1	0	1	1	0	0	0	0	0	0	0	0	0	0	1	0
Total			2	0	2	2	0	0	0	0	0	0	0	0	0	0	2	0

Rank among batters: 4,129 • *Total ballparks homered in*: 2 • *First HR*: 09/18/1962 off Larry Foss

Dave Roberts

DAVID ARTHUR ROBERTS
B: 09/11/1944
BL

Year	Tm	Lg	Tot	H	A	0	1	2	3	2	3	4	LO	XN	IP	PH	RHP	LHP
1970	SD	NL	2	0	2	1	1	0	0	0	0	0	0	0	0	0	2	0
1972	HOU	NL	2	1	1	0	2	0	0	0	0	0	0	0	0	0	1	1
1974	HOU	NL	1	0	1	0	1	0	0	0	0	0	0	0	0	0	1	0
1978	CHI	NL	2	1	1	2	0	0	0	0	0	0	0	0	0	0	1	1
Total			7	2	5	3	4	0	0	0	0	0	0	0	0	0	5	2

Rank among batters: 2,834 • *Total ballparks homered in*: 6 • *First HR*: 05/08/1970 off John Strohmayer

Dave Roberts

DAVID WAYNE ROBERTS
B: 02/17/1951
BR

Year	Tm	Lg	Tot	H	A	0	1	2	3	2	3	4	LO	XN	IP	PH	RHP	LHP
1972	SD	NL	5	2	3	3	1	1	0	0	0	0	0	0	0	0	4	1
1973	SD	NL	21	10	11	16	4	1	0	1	0	0	0	1	1	0	14	7
1974	SD	NL	5	2	3	4	1	0	0	0	0	0	0	0	0	0	1	4
1975	SD	NL	2	1	1	0	2	0	0	0	0	0	0	0	0	0	0	2
1977	SD	NL	1	0	1	0	0	1	0	0	0	0	0	0	0	0	1	0
1978	SD	NL	1	1	0	1	0	0	0	0	0	0	0	0	0	0	1	0
1979	TEX	AL	3	0	3	0	2	1	0	0	0	0	0	1	0	1	0	3
1980	TEX	AL	10	5	5	4	4	1	1	1	0	0	0	0	0	1	5	5
1981	HOU	NL	1	0	1	1	0	0	0	0	0	0	0	0	0	0	0	1
Total			49	21	28	29	14	5	1	2	0	0	0	2	1	2	26	23

Rank among batters: 1,008 • Top target (2 home runs): Ferguson Jenkins, Jim Lonborg, Floyd Bannister • *Number of pitchers victimized*: 46 • *Total ballparks homered in*: 18 • *First HR*: 06/29/1972 off Mike McQueen

Leon Roberts

LEON KAUFFMAN ROBERTS
B: 01/22/1951
BR

Year	Tm	Lg	Tot	H	A	0	1	2	3	2	3	4	LO	XN	IP	PH	RHP	LHP
1975	DET	AL	10	7	3	6	3	1	0	0	0	0	0	0	0	0	7	3
1976	HOU	NL	7	2	5	3	2	2	0	0	0	0	0	0	0	1	3	4
1978	SEA	AL	22	9	13	11	5	4	2	1	0	0	0	2	0	2	8	14
1979	SEA	AL	15	10	5	6	6	2	1	0	0	0	0	0	0	0	9	6
1980	SEA	AL	10	8	2	8	2	0	0	1	0	0	0	1	0	0	2	8
1981	TEX	AL	4	2	2	1	1	2	0	0	0	0	0	0	0	0	2	2
1982	TEX	AL	1	0	1	0	0	1	0	0	0	0	0	0	0	1	1	0

Year	Tm	Lg	Tot	H	A	Men-On 0	1	2	3	One-Game 2	3	4	LO	XN	IP	PH	RHP	LHP

Leon Roberts *continued*

Year	Tm	Lg	Tot	H	A	Men-On 0	1	2	3	One-Game 2	3	4	LO	XN	IP	PH	RHP	LHP
1982	TOR	AL	1	1	0	1	0	0	0	0	0	0	0	0	0	0	0	1
	Total		2	1	1	1	0	1	0	0	0	0	0	0	0	1	1	1
1983	KC	AL	8	2	6	7	1	0	0	0	0	0	0	0	0	0	1	7
Total			78	41	37	43	20	12	3	2	0	0	0	3	0	4	33	45

Rank among batters: 672 • *Top target (3 home runs)*: Mike Flanagan, Ferguson Jenkins, Frank Tanana • *Number of pitchers victimized*: 64 • *Total ballparks homered in*: 17 • *First HR*: 05/03/1975 off Rick Wise

Red Roberts

CHARLES EMORY ROBERTS
B: 08/08/1918
BR

Year	Tm	Lg	Tot	H	A	Men-On 0	1	2	3	One-Game 2	3	4	LO	XN	IP	PH	RHP	LHP
1943	WAS	AL	1	0	1	1	0	0	0	0	0	0	0	0	1	0	1	0

Rank among batters: 4,707 • *Total ballparks homered in*: 1 • *First HR*: 09/05/1943 off Butch Wensloff

Robin Roberts

ROBIN EVAN ROBERTS
B: 09/30/1926
BB HOF

Year	Tm	Lg	Tot	H	A	Men-On 0	1	2	3	One-Game 2	3	4	LO	XN	IP	PH	RHP	LHP
1948	PHI	NL	1	1	0	1	0	0	0	0	0	0	0	0	0	0	1	0
1953	PHI	NL	1	0	1	1	0	0	0	0	0	0	0	0	0	0	0	1
1955	PHI	NL	2	0	2	2	0	0	0	0	0	0	0	0	0	0	2	0
1956	PHI	NL	1	0	1	1	0	0	0	0	0	0	0	0	0	0	1	0
Total			5	1	4	5	0	0	0	0	0	0	0	0	0	0	4	1

Rank among batters: 3,191 • *Total ballparks homered in*: 5 • *First HR*: 08/07/1948 off Gerry Staley

Skipper Roberts

CLARENCE ASHLEY ROBERTS
B: 01/11/1888 D: 12/24/1963
BL

Year	Tm	Lg	Tot	H	A	Men-On 0	1	2	3	One-Game 2	3	4	LO	XN	IP	PH	RHP	LHP
1914	PIT	FL	1	1	0	0	1	0	0	0	0	0	0	0	0	0	1	0

Rank among batters: 4,707 • *Total ballparks homered in*: 1 • *First HR*: 09/12/1914 off Dwight Stone

Andre Robertson

ANDRE LEVETT ROBERTSON
B: 10/02/1957
BR

Year	Tm	Lg	Tot	H	A	Men-On 0	1	2	3	One-Game 2	3	4	LO	XN	IP	PH	RHP	LHP
1982	NY	AL	2	0	2	2	0	0	0	0	0	0	0	0	0	0	2	0
1983	NY	AL	1	1	0	1	0	0	0	0	0	0	0	0	0	0	0	1
1985	NY	AL	2	2	0	2	0	0	0	0	0	0	0	0	0	0	1	1
Total			5	3	2	5	0	0	0	0	0	0	0	0	0	0	3	2

Rank among batters: 3,191 • *Total ballparks homered in*: 3 • *First HR*: 05/16/1982 off Steve McCatty

Bob Robertson

ROBERT EUGENE ROBERTSON
B: 10/02/1946
BR

Year	Tm	Lg	Tot	H	A	Men-On 0	1	2	3	One-Game 2	3	4	LO	XN	IP	PH	RHP	LHP
1967	PIT	NL	2	1	1	1	1	0	0	0	0	0	0	0	0	0	1	1
1969	PIT	NL	1	1	0	1	0	0	0	0	0	0	0	0	0	0	0	1
1970	PIT	NL	27	7	20	13	11	2	1	2	0	0	0	1	0	1	20	7
1971	PIT	NL	26	10	16	18	6	2	0	1	0	0	0	0	0	0	16	10
1972	PIT	NL	12	6	6	5	6	1	0	0	0	0	0	0	0	0	7	5
1973	PIT	NL	14	6	8	10	2	2	0	1	0	0	0	1	0	0	10	4
1974	PIT	NL	16	9	7	5	11	0	0	2	0	0	0	1	0	2	10	6
1975	PIT	NL	6	1	5	4	2	0	0	0	0	0	0	0	0	1	2	4
1976	PIT	NL	2	1	1	0	1	1	0	0	0	0	0	0	0	0	1	1
1978	SEA	AL	8	4	4	4	2	2	0	0	0	0	0	0	0	1	2	6
1979	TOR	AL	1	1	0	1	0	0	0	0	0	0	0	0	0	0	0	1
Total			115	47	68	62	42	10	1	6	0	0	0	3	0	5	69	46

Rank among batters: 415 • *Top target (4 home runs)*: Milt Pappas, Carl Morton, Jerry Koosman • *Number of pitchers victimized*: 85 • *Total ballparks homered in*: 20 • *First HR*: 09/19/1967 off Bruce Von Hoff • *World Series HR—2; LCS HR—4*

Year	Tm	Lg	Tot	H	A	Men-On 0	1	2	3	One-Game 2	3	4	LO	XN	IP	PH	RHP	LHP

Dave Robertson

DAVIS AYDELOTTE ROBERTSON
B: 09/25/1889 D: 11/05/1970
BL

Year	Tm	Lg	Tot	H	A	0	1	2	3	2	3	4	LO	XN	IP	PH	RHP	LHP
1914	NY	NL	2	1	1	2	0	0	0	0	0	0	0	0	0	0	2	0
1915	NY	NL	3	2	1	1	2	0	0	0	0	0	0	0	0	0	3	0
1916	NY	NL	12	4	8	5	4	3	0	0	0	0	0	0	1	0	8	4
1917	NY	NL	12	7	5	5	6	0	1	0	0	0	0	0	2	0	9	3
1919	CHI	NL	1	1	0	0	1	0	0	0	0	0	0	0	0	0	0	1
1920	CHI	NL	10	6	4	5	3	2	0	0	0	0	0	0	1	0	10	0
1921	PIT	NL	6	2	4	1	2	2	1	1	0	0	0	0	0	0	6	0
1922	NY	NL	1	0	1	0	1	0	0	0	0	0	0	0	0	1	1	0
Total			47	23	24	19	19	7	2	1	0	0	0	0	4	1	39	8

Rank among batters: 1,040 • *Top target (4 home runs)*: Bill Doak • *Number of pitchers victimized*: 37 • *Total ballparks homered in*: 9 • *First HR*: 06/16/1914 off Bob Harmon • *Hit for Cycle*—@BRO: 08/30/1921

Gene Robertson

EUGENE EDWARD ROBERTSON
B: 12/25/1898 D: 10/21/1981
BL

Year	Tm	Lg	Tot	H	A	0	1	2	3	2	3	4	LO	XN	IP	PH	RHP	LHP
1924	STL	AL	4	3	1	2	2	0	0	0	0	0	0	0	1	0	4	0
1925	STL	AL	14	11	3	5	7	2	0	1	0	0	2	1	0	0	9	5
1926	STL	AL	1	1	0	1	0	0	0	0	0	0	0	0	0	0	1	0
1928	NY	AL	1	1	0	0	1	0	0	0	0	0	0	0	0	0	1	0
Total			20	16	4	8	10	2	0	1	0	0	2	1	1	0	15	5

Rank among batters: 1,810 • *Top target (2 home runs)*: Waite Hoyt, Sam Jones • *Number of pitchers victimized*: 18 • *Total ballparks homered in*: 3 • *First HR*: 04/27/1924 off George Uhle

Rich Robertson

RICHARD PAUL ROBERTSON
B: 10/14/1944
BR

Year	Tm	Lg	Tot	H	A	0	1	2	3	2	3	4	LO	XN	IP	PH	RHP	LHP
1970	SF	NL	2	0	2	2	0	0	0	0	0	0	0	0	0	0	2	0

Rank among batters: 4,129 • *Total ballparks homered in*: 2 • *First HR*: 06/22/1970 off Ray Washburn

Sherry Robertson

SHERRARD ALEXANDER ROBERTSON
B: 01/01/1919 D: 10/23/1970
BL

Year	Tm	Lg	Tot	H	A	0	1	2	3	2	3	4	LO	XN	IP	PH	RHP	LHP
1943	WAS	AL	3	0	3	2	0	1	0	0	0	0	0	0	0	0	3	0
1946	WAS	AL	6	2	4	6	0	0	0	0	0	0	3	0	0	0	5	1
1947	WAS	AL	1	0	1	1	0	0	0	0	0	0	0	0	0	0	1	0
1948	WAS	AL	2	1	1	2	0	0	0	0	0	0	0	0	0	0	2	0
1949	WAS	AL	11	4	7	6	3	1	1	1	0	0	0	0	0	0	10	1
1950	WAS	AL	2	0	2	0	1	1	0	1	0	0	0	0	0	0	2	0
1951	WAS	AL	1	0	1	0	1	0	0	0	0	0	0	0	0	1	1	0
Total			26	7	19	17	5	3	1	2	0	0	3	0	0	1	24	2

Rank among batters: 1,576 • Top target (2 home runs): Phil Marchildon, Al Benton, Carl Scheib, Cliff Fannin, Joe Dobson • *Number of pitchers victimized*: 21 • *Total ballparks homered in*: 9 • *First HR*: 08/19/1943 off Orval Grove

Billy Jo Robidoux

WILLIAM JOSEPH ROBIDOUX
B: 01/13/1964
BL

Year	Tm	Lg	Tot	H	A	0	1	2	3	2	3	4	LO	XN	IP	PH	RHP	LHP
1985	MIL	AL	3	0	3	1	2	0	0	1	0	0	0	0	0	0	1	2
1986	MIL	AL	1	0	1	0	0	1	0	0	0	0	0	0	0	0	0	1
1990	BOS	AL	1	1	0	1	0	0	0	0	0	0	0	0	0	0	1	0
Total			5	1	4	2	2	1	0	1	0	0	0	0	0	0	2	3

Rank among batters: 3,191 • *Top target (2 home runs)*: Bruce Hurst • *Number of pitchers victimized*: 4 • *Total ballparks homered in*: 3 • *First HR*: 09/19/1985 off Mike Boddicker

Aaron Robinson

AARON ANDREW ROBINSON
B: 06/23/1915 D: 03/09/1966
BL

Year	Tm	Lg	Tot	H	A	0	1	2	3	2	3	4	LO	XN	IP	PH	RHP	LHP
1945	NY	AL	8	8	0	4	2	2	0	2	0	0	0	0	0	0	8	0

Aaron Robinson *continued*

Year	Tm	Lg	Tot	H	A	Men-On 0	1	2	3	One-Game 2	3	4	LO	XN	IP	PH	RHP	LHP
1946	NY	AL	16	10	6	7	6	2	1	2	0	0	0	1	0	0	14	2
1947	NY	AL	5	1	4	3	2	0	0	0	0	0	0	0	0	0	5	0
1948	CHI	AL	8	3	5	2	6	0	0	0	0	0	0	0	0	0	8	0
1949	DET	AL	13	8	5	5	5	3	0	0	0	0	0	1	0	0	13	0
1950	DET	AL	9	4	5	7	1	1	0	0	0	0	0	0	0	1	7	2
1951	BOS	AL	2	1	1	2	0	0	0	0	0	0	0	0	0	0	2	0
Total			61	35	26	30	22	8	1	4	0	0	0	2	0	1	57	4

Rank among batters: 844 • *Top target (4 home runs)*: Bob Feller • *Number of pitchers victimized*: 50 • *Total ballparks homered in*: 8 • *First HR*: 07/29/1945 off Bobo Newsom

Bill Robinson

WILLIAM HENRY ROBINSON
B: 06/26/1943
BR

Year	Tm	Lg	Tot	H	A	Men-On 0	1	2	3	One-Game 2	3	4	LO	XN	IP	PH	RHP	LHP
1967	NY	AL	7	3	4	4	3	0	0	0	0	0	0	0	1	0	2	5
1968	NY	AL	6	4	2	5	0	1	0	0	0	0	0	0	0	0	4	2
1969	NY	AL	3	1	2	3	0	0	0	0	0	0	0	0	0	0	2	1
1972	PHI	NL	8	2	6	5	3	0	0	0	0	0	0	0	0	0	5	3
1973	PHI	NL	25	12	13	16	8	0	1	3	0	0	1	0	0	0	13	12
1974	PHI	NL	5	3	2	2	1	2	0	0	0	0	0	0	0	1	2	3
1975	PIT	NL	6	3	3	5	1	0	0	0	0	0	0	0	0	0	1	5
1976	PIT	NL	21	14	7	12	7	2	0	1	1	0	0	2	0	1	11	10
1977	PIT	NL	26	12	14	10	10	4	2	1	0	0	0	2	0	0	21	5
1978	PIT	NL	14	7	7	4	7	2	1	2	0	0	0	0	0	0	9	5
1979	PIT	NL	24	16	8	14	8	2	0	4	0	0	0	0	0	1	9	15
1980	PIT	NL	12	6	6	6	5	1	0	0	0	0	0	1	0	0	3	9
1981	PIT	NL	2	2	0	1	1	0	0	0	0	0	0	0	0	0	0	2
1982	PIT	NL	4	3	1	2	1	1	0	0	0	0	0	0	0	1	0	4
	PHI	NL	3	0	3	0	2	0	1	0	0	0	0	0	0	0	2	1
	Total		7	3	4	2	3	1	1	0	0	0	0	0	0	1	2	5
Total			166	88	78	89	57	15	5	11	1	0	1	5	1	4	84	82

Rank among batters: 245 • *Top target (6 home runs)*: Phil Niekro • *Number of pitchers victimized*: 113 • *Total ballparks homered in*: 20 • *First HR*: 04/10/1967 off Pete Richert

Brooks Robinson

BROOKS CALBERT ROBINSON
B: 05/18/1937
BR HOF

Year	Tm	Lg	Tot	H	A	Men-On 0	1	2	3	One-Game 2	3	4	LO	XN	IP	PH	RHP	LHP
1956	BAL	AL	1	0	1	1	0	0	0	0	0	0	0	0	0	0	1	0
1957	BAL	AL	2	0	2	1	1	0	0	0	0	0	0	0	0	0	1	1
1958	BAL	AL	3	2	1	3	0	0	0	0	0	0	0	0	0	0	2	1
1959	BAL	AL	4	3	1	2	1	1	0	0	0	0	0	0	0	0	1	3
1960	BAL	AL	14	7	7	5	5	3	1	0	0	0	0	0	0	0	8	6
1961	BAL	AL	7	5	2	7	0	0	0	1	0	0	1	0	0	0	5	2
1962	BAL	AL	23	13	10	16	4	1	2	0	0	0	0	1	0	0	17	6
1963	BAL	AL	11	5	6	6	4	1	0	0	0	0	0	0	0	0	4	7
1964	BAL	AL	28	12	16	18	6	4	0	0	0	0	0	0	0	0	20	8
1965	BAL	AL	18	10	8	7	9	2	0	1	0	0	0	0	0	0	12	6
1966	BAL	AL	23	13	10	11	8	4	0	1	0	0	0	0	0	0	18	5
1967	BAL	AL	22	10	12	16	6	0	0	0	0	0	0	0	0	0	15	7
1968	BAL	AL	17	8	9	11	6	0	0	1	0	0	0	1	0	0	15	2
1969	BAL	AL	23	10	13	13	6	4	0	2	0	0	0	1	0	0	16	7
1970	BAL	AL	18	9	9	8	5	4	1	1	0	0	0	2	0	0	14	4
1971	BAL	AL	20	16	4	9	7	2	2	0	0	0	0	0	0	0	16	4
1972	BAL	AL	8	3	5	6	2	0	0	0	0	0	0	1	0	0	5	3
1973	BAL	AL	9	5	4	4	1	4	0	1	0	0	0	0	0	0	7	2
1974	BAL	AL	7	2	5	6	0	1	0	0	0	0	0	0	0	0	4	3
1975	BAL	AL	6	1	5	3	1	2	0	0	0	0	0	0	0	0	5	1
1976	BAL	AL	3	2	1	1	2	0	0	0	0	0	0	0	0	0	2	1
1977	BAL	AL	1	1	0	0	0	1	0	0	0	0	0	1	0	1	0	1
Total			268	137	131	154	74	34	6	8	0	0	1	7	0	1	188	80

Rank among batters: 91 • *Top target (6 home runs)*: Bill Monbouquette, Dean Chance • *Number of pitchers victimized*: 166 • *Total ballparks homered in*: 16 • *First HR*: 09/29/1956 off Evelio Hernandez • *Hit for Cycle*—@CHI: 07/15/1960 • *World Series HR*—3; *LCS HR*—2; *All-Star HR*—1

Dave Robinson

DAVID TANNER ROBINSON
B: 05/22/1946
BB

Year	Tm	Lg	Tot	H	A	Men-On 0	1	2	3	One-Game 2	3	4	LO	XN	IP	PH	RHP	LHP
1970	SD	NL	2	0	2	1	1	0	0	0	0	0	0	0	0	0	1	1

Rank among batters: 4,129 • *Total ballparks homered in*: 1 • *First HR*: 09/25/1970 off Skip Pitlock

Don Robinson

DON ALLEN ROBINSON
B: 06/08/1957
BR

Year	Tm	Lg	Tot	H	A	Men-On 0	1	2	3	One-Game 2	3	4	LO	XN	IP	PH	RHP	LHP
1980	PIT	NL	1	0	1	0	1	0	0	0	0	0	0	0	0	0	1	0
1982	PIT	NL	2	1	1	0	2	0	0	0	0	0	0	0	0	0	2	0
1983	PIT	NL	1	0	1	1	0	0	0	0	0	0	0	0	0	0	1	0
1984	PIT	NL	1	0	1	1	0	0	0	0	0	0	0	0	0	0	0	1
1985	PIT	NL	1	1	0	0	0	0	1	0	0	0	0	0	0	0	1	0
1987	SF	NL	1	0	1	1	0	0	0	0	0	0	0	0	0	0	1	0
1988	SF	NL	1	0	1	0	1	0	0	0	0	0	0	0	0	0	1	0
1989	SF	NL	3	2	1	0	3	0	0	0	0	0	0	0	0	0	2	1
1990	SF	NL	2	1	1	2	0	0	0	0	0	0	0	0	0	1	1	1
Total			13	5	8	5	7	0	1	0	0	0	0	0	0	1	10	3

Rank among batters: 2,248 • *Total ballparks homered in*: 7 • *First HR*: 07/13/1980 off Nino Espinosa

Earl Robinson

EARL JOHN ROBINSON
B: 11/03/1936
BR

Year	Tm	Lg	Tot	H	A	Men-On 0	1	2	3	One-Game 2	3	4	LO	XN	IP	PH	RHP	LHP
1961	BAL	AL	8	3	5	4	2	2	0	0	0	0	0	0	0	1	4	4
1962	BAL	AL	1	1	0	1	0	0	0	0	0	0	0	0	0	0	1	0
1964	BAL	AL	3	1	2	1	2	0	0	0	0	0	0	0	0	0	1	2
Total			12	5	7	6	4	2	0	0	0	0	0	0	0	1	6	6

Rank among batters: 2,325 • *Total ballparks homered in*: 5 • *First HR*: 06/20/1961 off Jack Kralick

Eddie Robinson

WILLIAM EDWARD ROBINSON
B: 12/15/1920
BL

Year	Tm	Lg	Tot	H	A	Men-On 0	1	2	3	One-Game 2	3	4	LO	XN	IP	PH	RHP	LHP
1946	CLE	AL	3	1	2	3	0	0	0	1	0	0	0	0	0	0	3	0
1947	CLE	AL	14	8	6	7	5	2	0	2	0	0	0	0	0	0	14	0
1948	CLE	AL	16	8	8	12	3	1	0	2	0	0	0	1	0	0	14	2
1949	WAS	AL	18	4	14	7	7	4	0	2	0	0	0	0	0	0	15	3
1950	WAS	AL	1	0	1	0	1	0	0	0	0	0	0	0	0	0	0	1
	CHI	AL	20	13	7	11	5	3	1	1	0	0	0	0	0	0	16	4
	Total		21	13	8	11	6	3	1	1	0	0	0	0	0	0	16	5
1951	CHI	AL	29	9	20	16	10	3	0	1	0	0	0	0	0	0	21	8
1952	CHI	AL	22	14	8	9	9	4	0	2	0	0	0	1	0	0	16	6
1953	PHI	AL	22	8	14	9	11	2	0	2	0	0	0	0	0	0	18	4
1954	NY	AL	3	2	1	2	0	1	0	0	0	0	0	0	0	1	3	0
1955	NY	AL	16	7	9	6	4	6	0	3	0	0	0	1	0	0	11	5
1956	NY	AL	5	4	1	4	0	0	1	0	0	0	0	0	0	1	5	0
	KC	AL	2	1	1	1	1	0	0	0	0	0	0	0	0	0	1	1
	Total		7	5	2	5	1	0	1	0	0	0	0	0	0	1	6	1
1957	CLE	AL	1	0	1	0	1	0	0	0	0	0	0	0	0	1	0	1
Total			172	79	93	87	57	26	2	14	0	0	0	3	0	3	137	35

Rank among batters: 233 • *Top target (7 home runs)*: Steve Gromek • *Number of pitchers victimized*: 99 • *Total ballparks homered in*: 11 • *First HR*: 09/20/1946 off Fred Hutchinson

Floyd Robinson

FLOYD ANDREW ROBINSON
B: 05/09/1936
BL

Year	Tm	Lg	Tot	H	A	Men-On 0	1	2	3	One-Game 2	3	4	LO	XN	IP	PH	RHP	LHP
1961	CHI	AL	11	8	3	4	4	2	1	0	0	0	1	0	0	1	11	0
1962	CHI	AL	11	2	9	3	7	1	0	0	0	0	0	0	0	0	10	1
1963	CHI	AL	13	5	8	8	3	2	0	1	0	0	0	0	0	0	8	5
1964	CHI	AL	11	5	6	6	4	1	0	0	0	0	0	0	0	0	9	2
1965	CHI	AL	14	4	10	8	4	2	0	0	0	0	0	1	0	0	12	2

Year	Tm	Lg	Tot	H	A	Men-On				One-Game			LO	XN	IP	PH	RHP	LHP
						0	1	2	3	2	3	4						

Floyd Robinson *continued*

Year	Tm	Lg	Tot	H	A	0	1	2	3	2	3	4	LO	XN	IP	PH	RHP	LHP
1966	CHI	AL	5	1	4	2	3	0	0	0	0	0	0	0	0	0	4	1
1967	CIN	NL	1	1	0	1	0	0	0	0	0	0	0	0	0	0	1	0
1968	OAK	AL	1	0	1	0	1	0	0	0	0	0	0	0	0	1	1	0
Total			67	26	41	32	26	8	1	1	0	0	1	1	0	2	56	11

Rank among batters: 777 • *Top target (4 home runs)*: Ralph Terry • *Number of pitchers victimized*: 51 • *Total ballparks homered in*: 10 • *First HR*: 05/13/1961 off Jerry Walker

Frank Robinson

FRANK ROBINSON
B: 08/31/1935
BR HOF

Year	Tm	Lg	Tot	H	A	0	1	2	3	2	3	4	LO	XN	IP	PH	RHP	LHP
1956	CIN	NL	38	22	16	24	9	5	0	2	0	0	0	1	0	0	30	8
1957	CIN	NL	29	14	15	21	5	3	0	2	0	0	0	1	0	0	21	8
1958	CIN	NL	31	18	13	22	8	1	0	2	0	0	0	2	0	0	24	7
1959	CIN	NL	36	26	10	14	16	5	1	3	1	0	0	0	0	0	23	13
1960	CIN	NL	31	16	15	19	11	1	0	2	0	0	0	1	0	0	22	9
1961	CIN	NL	37	17	20	19	16	2	0	3	0	0	0	0	0	0	27	10
1962	CIN	NL	39	24	15	23	8	5	3	7	0	0	0	3	0	0	26	13
1963	CIN	NL	21	10	11	7	10	3	1	3	0	0	0	0	0	0	15	6
1964	CIN	NL	29	11	18	17	9	3	0	4	0	0	0	0	0	0	21	8
1965	CIN	NL	33	18	15	19	6	8	0	3	0	0	0	0	0	0	19	14
1966	BAL	AL	49	27	22	27	16	6	0	7	0	0	0	0	0	0	39	10
1967	BAL	AL	30	19	11	11	16	3	0	2	0	0	0	1	0	0	20	10
1968	BAL	AL	15	7	8	9	4	2	0	0	0	0	0	1	0	0	9	6
1969	BAL	AL	32	20	12	19	8	5	0	1	0	0	0	3	0	0	20	12
1970	BAL	AL	25	12	13	16	6	1	2	3	0	0	0	1	0	0	15	10
1971	BAL	AL	28	17	11	12	8	8	0	3	0	0	0	0	0	0	18	10
1972	LA	NL	19	10	9	12	6	1	0	1	0	0	0	1	0	0	9	10
1973	CAL	AL	30	16	14	13	11	6	0	2	0	0	0	0	0	1	18	12
1974	CAL	AL	20	8	12	11	8	1	0	1	0	0	0	0	0	0	11	9
	CLE	AL	2	0	2	1	1	0	0	0	0	0	0	0	0	0	1	1
	Total		22	8	14	12	9	1	0	1	0	0	0	0	0	0	12	10
1975	CLE	AL	9	8	1	6	1	2	0	2	0	0	0	0	0	0	4	5
1976	CLE	AL	3	1	2	2	1	0	0	0	0	0	0	1	0	1	0	3
Total			586	321	265	324	184	71	7	53	1	0	0	16	0	2	392	194

Rank among batters: 4 • *Top target (10 home runs)*: Larry Jackson • *Number of pitchers victimized*: 275 • *Total ballparks homered in*: 32 • *First HR*: 04/28/1956 off Paul Minner • *Hit for Cycle*—vs LA: 05/02/1959 • *World Series HR*—8; *LCS HR*—2; *All-Star HR*—2

Jackie Robinson

JOHN ROOSEVELT ROBINSON
B: 01/31/1919 D: 10/24/1972
BR HOF

Year	Tm	Lg	Tot	H	A	0	1	2	3	2	3	4	LO	XN	IP	PH	RHP	LHP
1947	BRO	NL	12	6	6	6	5	1	0	0	0	0	0	0	0	0	4	8
1948	BRO	NL	12	7	5	5	2	4	1	0	0	0	0	1	1	0	8	4
1949	BRO	NL	16	8	8	8	7	1	0	1	0	0	0	2	0	0	11	5
1950	BRO	NL	14	7	7	9	3	1	1	1	0	0	0	0	0	0	8	6
1951	BRO	NL	19	8	11	11	6	2	0	0	0	0	0	3	0	0	17	2
1952	BRO	NL	19	10	9	9	7	3	0	1	0	0	0	0	0	0	18	1
1953	BRO	NL	12	7	5	6	2	4	0	2	0	0	0	0	0	0	12	0
1954	BRO	NL	15	12	3	8	6	1	0	2	0	0	0	0	0	0	12	3
1955	BRO	NL	8	6	2	3	5	0	0	0	0	0	0	0	0	0	6	2
1956	BRO	NL	10	7	3	9	1	0	0	1	0	0	0	0	0	0	8	2
Total			137	78	59	74	44	17	2	8	0	0	0	6	1	0	104	33

Rank among batters: 319 • *Top target (9 home runs)*: Robin Roberts • *Number of pitchers victimized*: 76 • *Total ballparks homered in*: 10 • *First HR*: 04/18/1947 off Dave Koslo • *Hit for Cycle*—@STL: 08/29/1948 (1) • *World Series HR*—2; *All-Star HR*—1

Jeff Robinson

JEFFREY DANIEL ROBINSON
B: 12/13/1960
BR

Year	Tm	Lg	Tot	H	A	0	1	2	3	2	3	4	LO	XN	IP	PH	RHP	LHP
1987	PIT	NL	1	0	1	1	0	0	0	0	0	0	0	0	0	0	1	0
1989	PIT	NL	1	0	1	0	1	0	0	0	0	0	0	0	0	0	1	0
Total			2	0	2	1	1	0	0	0	0	0	0	0	0	0	2	0

Rank among batters: 4,129 • *Total ballparks homered in*: 2 • *First HR*: 09/09/1987 off Lee Smith

Wilbert Robinson

WILBERT ROBINSON
B: 06/29/1863 D: 08/08/1934
BR HOF

Year	Tm	Lg	Tot	H	A	Men-On 0	1	2	3	One-Game 2	3	4	LO	XN	IP	PH	RHP	LHP
1886	PHI	AA	1	0	1	0	1	0	0	0	0	0	0	0	0	0	1	0
1887	PHI	AA	1	0	1	0	1	0	0	0	0	0	0	0	1	0	1	0
1888	PHI	AA	1	0	1	1	0	0	0	0	0	0	0	0	0	0	1	0
1890	PHI	AA	4	4	0	1	2	1	0	0	0	0	0	0	0	0	1	0
1891	BAL	AA	2	0	2	0	1	1	0	1	0	0	0	0	0	0	0	2
1892	BAL	NL	2	1	1	0	2	0	0	0	0	0	0	0	0	0	1	1
1893	BAL	NL	3	3	0	2	1	0	0	0	0	0	0	0	0	0	2	0
1894	BAL	NL	1	0	1	0	0	1	0	0	0	0	0	0	1	0	0	0
1896	BAL	NL	2	2	0	1	0	1	0	0	0	0	0	0	0	0	0	2
1902	BAL	AL	1	0	1	1	0	0	0	0	0	0	0	0	0	0	1	0
Total			18	10	8	6	8	4	0	1	0	0	0	0	2	0	8	5

Rank among batters: 1,914 • *Top target (2 home runs)*: Kid Madden, Mike Sullivan • *Number of pitchers victimized*: 16 • *Total ballparks homered in*: 9 • *First HR*: 07/05/1886 off Will White

William Robinson

WILLIAM CLYDE ROBINSON
B: 03/05/1882 D: 04/09/1915
BR

Year	Tm	Lg	Tot	H	A	Men-On 0	1	2	3	One-Game 2	3	4	LO	XN	IP	PH	RHP	LHP
1903	WAS	AL	1	1	0	1	0	0	0	0	0	0	0	0	0	0	1	0

Rank among batters: 4,707 • *Total ballparks homered in*: 1 • *First HR*: 07/09/1903 off John Deering

Yank Robinson

WILLIAM H. ROBINSON
B: 09/19/1859 D: 08/25/1894
BR

Year	Tm	Lg	Tot	H	A	Men-On 0	1	2	3	One-Game 2	3	4	LO	XN	IP	PH	RHP	LHP
1884	BAL	UA	3	3	0	1	2	0	0	0	0	0	0	0	0	0	1	0
1886	STL	AA	3	1	2	1	1	1	0	0	0	0	0	0	1	0	0	2
1887	STL	AA	1	0	1	0	1	0	0	0	0	0	0	0	0	0	1	0
1888	STL	AA	3	1	2	1	1	1	0	0	0	0	0	0	1	0	1	2
1889	STL	AA	5	4	1	1	3	1	0	0	0	0	0	0	0	0	2	2
1891	CIN	AA	1	0	1	1	0	0	0	0	0	0	0	0	0	0	0	1
Total			16	9	7	5	8	3	0	0	0	0	0	0	2	0	5	5

Rank among batters: 2,029 • *Top target (2 home runs)*: Milo Lockwood, Tony Mullane, Frank Foreman • *Number of pitchers victimized*: 13 • *Total ballparks homered in*: 8 • *First HR*: 04/17/1884 off Milo Lockwood

Mike Rocco

MICHAEL DOMINICK ROCCO
B: 03/02/1916
BL

Year	Tm	Lg	Tot	H	A	Men-On 0	1	2	3	One-Game 2	3	4	LO	XN	IP	PH	RHP	LHP
1943	CLE	AL	5	1	4	1	2	2	0	0	0	0	0	0	0	0	5	0
1944	CLE	AL	13	4	9	10	2	1	0	1	0	0	1	2	0	0	13	0
1945	CLE	AL	10	4	6	8	1	1	0	1	0	0	0	0	0	0	9	1
1946	CLE	AL	2	2	0	1	1	0	0	0	0	0	0	0	0	0	2	0
Total			30	11	19	20	6	4	0	2	0	0	1	2	0	0	29	1

Rank among batters: 1,437 • *Top target (2 home runs)*: Bobo Newsom, Bob Muncrief, Tiny Bonham • *Number of pitchers victimized*: 27 • *Total ballparks homered in*: 8 • *First HR*: 06/20/1943 off Bill Dietrich

Pat Rockett

PATRICK EDWARD ROCKETT
B: 01/09/1955
BR

Year	Tm	Lg	Tot	H	A	Men-On 0	1	2	3	One-Game 2	3	4	LO	XN	IP	PH	RHP	LHP
1977	ATL	NL	1	1	0	1	0	0	0	0	0	0	0	0	0	0	1	0

Rank among batters: 4,707 • *Total ballparks homered in*: 1 • *First HR*: 09/28/1977 off Mark Lemongello

Andre Rodgers

KENNETH ANDRE IAN RODGERS
B: 12/02/1934
BR

Year	Tm	Lg	Tot	H	A	Men-On 0	1	2	3	One-Game 2	3	4	LO	XN	IP	PH	RHP	LHP
1957	NY	NL	3	2	1	2	0	0	1	0	0	0	0	0	0	0	1	2
1958	SF	NL	2	0	2	1	1	0	0	0	0	0	0	0	0	0	1	1
1959	SF	NL	6	5	1	5	1	0	0	1	0	0	1	0	0	0	5	1
1960	SF	NL	2	0	2	1	0	1	0	0	0	0	0	0	0	0	2	0

Andre Rodgers *continued*

Year	Tm	Lg	Tot	H	A	Men-On 0	Men-On 1	Men-On 2	Men-On 3	One-Game 2	One-Game 3	One-Game 4	LO	XN	IP	PH	RHP	LHP
1961	CHI	NL	6	3	3	3	2	1	0	0	0	0	0	0	0	0	2	4
1962	CHI	NL	5	4	1	3	1	1	0	0	0	0	0	0	0	0	3	2
1963	CHI	NL	5	2	3	4	1	0	0	0	0	0	0	0	0	0	4	1
1964	CHI	NL	12	7	5	8	2	2	0	0	0	0	0	0	0	0	6	6
1965	PIT	NL	2	0	2	1	0	0	1	0	0	0	0	0	0	0	2	0
1967	PIT	NL	2	0	2	2	0	0	0	0	0	0	0	0	0	0	2	0
Total			45	23	22	30	8	5	2	1	0	0	1	0	0	0	28	17

Rank among batters: 1,082 • *Top target (3 home runs)*: Lew Burdette • *Number of pitchers victimized*: 37 • *Total ballparks homered in*: 12 • *First HR*: 04/20/1957 off Harvey Haddix

Bob Rodgers

ROBERT LEROY RODGERS
B: 08/16/1938
BB

Year	Tm	Lg	Tot	H	A	Men-On 0	Men-On 1	Men-On 2	Men-On 3	One-Game 2	One-Game 3	One-Game 4	LO	XN	IP	PH	RHP	LHP
1961	LA	AL	2	2	0	0	1	0	1	0	0	0	0	0	0	0	2	0
1962	LA	AL	6	0	6	5	1	0	0	0	0	0	0	0	0	0	4	2
1963	LA	AL	4	1	3	4	0	0	0	0	0	0	0	0	0	0	2	2
1964	LA	AL	4	1	3	3	1	0	0	0	0	0	0	0	1	0	2	2
1965	CAL	AL	1	0	1	1	0	0	0	0	0	0	0	0	0	0	1	0
1966	CAL	AL	7	4	3	4	3	0	0	0	0	0	0	0	0	0	6	1
1967	CAL	AL	6	3	3	4	1	1	0	0	0	0	0	0	0	0	5	1
1968	CAL	AL	1	0	1	0	0	1	0	0	0	0	0	1	0	0	1	0
Total			31	11	20	21	7	2	1	0	0	0	0	1	1	0	23	8

Rank among batters: 1,400 • *Top target (3 home runs)*: Moe Drabowsky • *Number of pitchers victimized*: 28 • *Total ballparks homered in*: 11 • *First HR*: 09/29/1961 off Barry Latman

Alex Rodriguez

ALEXANDER EMMANUEL RODRIGUEZ
B: 07/27/1975
BR

Year	Tm	Lg	Tot	H	A	Men-On 0	Men-On 1	Men-On 2	Men-On 3	One-Game 2	One-Game 3	One-Game 4	LO	XN	IP	PH	RHP	LHP
1995	SEA	AL	5	1	4	5	0	0	0	0	0	0	0	0	0	0	3	2

Rank among batters: 3,191 • *Total ballparks homered in*: 5 • *First HR*: 06/12/1995 off Tom Gordon

Aurelio Rodriguez

AURELIO (ITUARTE) RODRIGUEZ
B: 12/28/1947
BR

Year	Tm	Lg	Tot	H	A	Men-On 0	Men-On 1	Men-On 2	Men-On 3	One-Game 2	One-Game 3	One-Game 4	LO	XN	IP	PH	RHP	LHP
1967	CAL	AL	1	1	0	1	0	0	0	0	0	0	0	0	0	0	1	0
1968	CAL	AL	1	1	0	0	1	0	0	0	0	0	0	0	0	0	0	1
1969	CAL	AL	7	3	4	6	1	0	0	0	0	0	0	0	0	0	2	5
1970	WAS	AL	19	10	9	12	4	3	0	0	0	0	0	0	0	0	15	4
1971	DET	AL	15	5	10	14	1	0	0	0	0	0	3	0	0	0	12	3
1972	DET	AL	13	7	6	7	5	1	0	0	0	0	0	2	0	0	7	6
1973	DET	AL	9	6	3	6	3	0	0	0	0	0	0	0	0	0	5	4
1974	DET	AL	5	5	0	4	0	1	0	1	0	0	0	0	0	0	2	3
1975	DET	AL	13	7	6	7	4	1	1	1	0	0	0	2	0	0	8	5
1976	DET	AL	8	5	3	3	3	2	0	0	0	0	0	0	0	0	4	4
1977	DET	AL	10	3	7	7	3	0	0	1	0	0	0	0	0	0	5	5
1978	DET	AL	7	4	3	4	3	0	0	0	0	0	0	0	0	1	0	7
1979	DET	AL	5	3	2	2	3	0	0	0	0	0	0	0	0	0	1	4
1980	SD	NL	2	1	1	0	2	0	0	0	0	0	0	0	0	0	0	2
	NY	AL	3	1	2	0	3	0	0	0	0	0	0	0	0	0	2	1
	Total		5	2	3	0	5	0	0	0	0	0	0	0	0	0	2	3
1981	NY	AL	2	0	2	1	1	0	0	1	0	0	0	0	0	0	0	2
1982	CHI	AL	3	0	3	2	1	0	0	0	0	0	0	0	0	0	1	2
1983	CHI	AL	1	0	1	1	0	0	0	0	0	0	0	0	0	0	0	1
Total			124	62	62	77	38	8	1	4	0	0	3	4	0	1	65	59

Rank among batters: 370 • *Top target (4 home runs)*: Dave McNally • *Number of pitchers victimized*: 90 • *Total ballparks homered in*: 16 • *First HR*: 09/05/1967 off Eddie Fisher

Carlos Rodriguez

CARLOS (MARQUEZ) RODRIGUEZ
B: 11/01/1967
BB

Year	Tm	Lg	Tot	H	A	Men-On 0	Men-On 1	Men-On 2	Men-On 3	One-Game 2	One-Game 3	One-Game 4	LO	XN	IP	PH	RHP	LHP
1994	BOS	AL	1	0	1	1	0	0	0	0	0	0	0	0	0	0	1	0

Rank among batters: 4,707 • *Total ballparks homered in*: 1 • *First HR*: 05/07/1994 off Melido Perez

Ellie Rodriguez

ELISEO (DELGADO) RODRIGUEZ
B: 05/24/1946
BR

Year	Tm	Lg	Tot	H	A	Men-On 0	1	2	3	One-Game 2	3	4	LO	XN	IP	PH	RHP	LHP
1969	KC	AL	2	0	2	1	0	1	0	0	0	0	0	0	0	0	1	1
1970	KC	AL	1	0	1	1	0	0	0	0	0	0	0	0	0	0	0	1
1971	MIL	AL	1	0	1	0	1	0	0	0	0	0	0	0	0	0	1	0
1972	MIL	AL	2	1	1	0	2	0	0	0	0	0	0	0	0	0	1	1
1974	CAL	AL	7	6	1	5	1	1	0	1	0	0	0	0	0	0	1	6
1975	CAL	AL	3	0	3	1	2	0	0	0	0	0	0	1	0	0	2	1
Total			16	7	9	8	6	2	0	1	0	0	0	1	0	0	6	10

Rank among batters: 2,029 • *Top target (3 home runs)*: Mickey Lolich • *Number of pitchers victimized*: 14 • *Total ballparks homered in*: 8 • *First HR*: 06/08/1969 off Jim Lonborg

Hector Rodriguez

HECTOR ANTONIO (ORDENANA) RODRIGUEZ
B: 06/13/1920
BR

Year	Tm	Lg	Tot	H	A	Men-On 0	1	2	3	One-Game 2	3	4	LO	XN	IP	PH	RHP	LHP
1952	CHI	AL	1	0	1	0	0	1	0	0	0	0	0	0	1	0	1	0

Rank among batters: 4,707 • *Total ballparks homered in*: 1 • *First HR*: 06/10/1952 off Johnny Kucab

Henry Rodriguez

HENRY ANDERSON (LORENZO) RODRIGUEZ
B: 11/08/1967
BL

Year	Tm	Lg	Tot	H	A	Men-On 0	1	2	3	One-Game 2	3	4	LO	XN	IP	PH	RHP	LHP
1992	LA	NL	3	2	1	1	2	0	0	0	0	0	0	0	0	0	3	0
1993	LA	NL	8	5	3	2	3	3	0	0	0	0	0	0	0	1	8	0
1994	LA	NL	8	5	3	4	4	0	0	1	0	0	0	0	0	0	6	2
1995	LA	NL	1	0	1	1	0	0	0	0	0	0	0	0	0	0	1	0
	MON	NL	1	1	0	0	1	0	0	0	0	0	0	0	0	0	1	0
	Total		2	1	1	1	1	0	0	0	0	0	0	0	0	0	2	0
Total			21	13	8	8	10	3	0	1	0	0	0	0	0	1	19	2

Rank among batters: 1,768 • *Top target (2 home runs)*: Jack Armstrong, Ryan Bowen • *Number of pitchers victimized*: 19 • *Total ballparks homered in*: 7 • *First HR*: 08/13/1992 off Jose Rijo

Ivan Rodriguez

IVAN (TORRES) RODRIGUEZ
B: 11/27/1971
BR

Year	Tm	Lg	Tot	H	A	Men-On 0	1	2	3	One-Game 2	3	4	LO	XN	IP	PH	RHP	LHP
1991	TEX	AL	3	3	0	2	0	1	0	0	0	0	0	0	0	0	2	1
1992	TEX	AL	8	4	4	4	4	0	0	0	0	0	0	0	0	0	6	2
1993	TEX	AL	10	7	3	4	4	2	0	0	0	0	0	0	0	0	8	2
1994	TEX	AL	16	7	9	11	5	0	0	0	0	0	0	0	0	0	12	4
1995	TEX	AL	12	5	7	9	2	1	0	1	0	0	0	0	0	0	8	4
Total			49	26	23	30	15	4	0	1	0	0	0	0	0	0	36	13

Rank among batters: 1,008 • Top target (2 home runs): Jose Mesa, Rick Aguilera, Wilson Alvarez, Roger Clemens • *Number of pitchers victimized*: 45 • *Total ballparks homered in*: 12 • *First HR*: 08/30/1991 off Storm Davis

Roberto Rodriguez

ROBERTO (MUNOZ) RODRIGUEZ
B: 11/29/1941
BR

Year	Tm	Lg	Tot	H	A	Men-On 0	1	2	3	One-Game 2	3	4	LO	XN	IP	PH	RHP	LHP
1970	CHI	NL	1	1	0	1	0	0	0	0	0	0	0	0	0	0	1	0

Rank among batters: 4,707 • *Total ballparks homered in*: 1 • *First HR*: 07/26/1970 off Pat Jarvis

Preacher Roe

ELWIN CHARLES ROE
B: 02/26/1915
BR

Year	Tm	Lg	Tot	H	A	Men-On 0	1	2	3	One-Game 2	3	4	LO	XN	IP	PH	RHP	LHP
1953	BRO	NL	1	0	1	1	0	0	0	0	0	0	0	0	0	0	1	0

Rank among batters: 4,707 • *Total ballparks homered in*: 1 • *First HR*: 07/07/1953 off Bob Hall

Ed Roebuck

EDWARD JACK ROEBUCK
B: 07/03/1931
BR

Year	Tm	Lg	Tot	H	A	Men-On 0	1	2	3	One-Game 2	3	4	LO	XN	IP	PH	RHP	LHP
1957	BRO	NL	2	2	0	2	0	0	0	0	0	0	0	0	0	0	2	0

Year	Tm	Lg	Tot	H	A	Men-On 0	1	2	3	One-Game 2	3	4	LO	XN	IP	PH	RHP	LHP

Ed Roebuck *continued*

Rank among batters: 4,129 • *Total ballparks homered in*: 1 • *First HR*: 08/20/1957 off Raul Sanchez

Gary Roenicke

GARY STEVEN ROENICKE
B: 12/05/1954
BR

Year	Tm	Lg	Tot	H	A	Men-On 0	1	2	3	One-Game 2	3	4	LO	XN	IP	PH	RHP	LHP
1976	MON	NL	2	0	2	2	0	0	0	0	0	0	0	0	0	0	2	0
1978	BAL	AL	3	1	2	2	0	0	1	0	0	0	0	0	0	0	0	3
1979	BAL	AL	25	8	17	19	4	2	0	1	0	0	0	1	0	0	17	8
1980	BAL	AL	10	4	6	8	2	0	0	0	0	0	0	1	0	0	7	3
1981	BAL	AL	3	0	3	2	1	0	0	0	0	0	0	0	0	0	1	2
1982	BAL	AL	21	6	15	8	5	7	1	1	0	0	0	0	0	2	13	8
1983	BAL	AL	19	10	9	9	7	2	1	1	0	0	0	0	0	1	1	18
1984	BAL	AL	10	7	3	6	0	3	1	0	0	0	0	0	0	0	5	5
1985	BAL	AL	15	9	6	6	8	0	1	1	0	0	0	0	0	0	3	12
1986	NY	AL	3	3	0	1	2	0	0	0	0	0	0	0	0	1	0	3
1987	ATL	NL	9	8	1	5	2	2	0	1	0	0	0	0	0	1	1	8
1988	ATL	NL	1	0	1	1	0	0	0	0	0	0	0	0	0	0	0	1
Total			121	56	65	69	31	16	5	5	0	0	0	2	0	5	50	71

Rank among batters: 382 • Top target (4 home runs): Paul Splittorff, Larry Gura, Floyd Bannister, Britt Burns • *Number of pitchers victimized*: 84 • *Total ballparks homered in*: 18 • *First HR*: 06/15/1976 off Alan Foster • *LCS HR*—1

Ron Roenicke

RONALD JON ROENICKE
B: 08/19/1956
BB

Year	Tm	Lg	Tot	H	A	Men-On 0	1	2	3	One-Game 2	3	4	LO	XN	IP	PH	RHP	LHP
1982	LA	NL	1	0	1	1	0	0	0	0	0	0	0	0	0	0	1	0
1983	LA	NL	2	2	0	1	0	1	0	1	0	0	0	0	0	0	0	2
	SEA	AL	4	2	2	2	1	1	0	0	0	0	1	0	0	0	1	3
	Total		6	4	2	3	1	2	0	1	0	0	1	0	0	0	1	5
1984	SD	NL	1	1	0	1	0	0	0	0	0	0	0	0	0	0	1	0
1985	SF	NL	3	1	2	2	1	0	0	0	0	0	0	0	0	1	3	0
1986	PHI	NL	5	4	1	4	1	0	0	0	0	0	0	0	0	0	2	3
1987	PHI	NL	1	0	1	1	0	0	0	0	0	0	0	0	0	1	0	1
Total			17	10	7	12	3	2	0	1	0	0	1	0	0	2	8	9

Rank among batters: 1,969 • *Top target (2 home runs)*: Dave Dravecky • *Number of pitchers victimized*: 16 • *Total ballparks homered in*: 10 • *First HR*: 06/20/1982 off Tom Seaver

Wally Roettger

WALTER HENRY ROETTGER
B: 08/28/1902 D: 09/14/1951
BR

Year	Tm	Lg	Tot	H	A	Men-On 0	1	2	3	One-Game 2	3	4	LO	XN	IP	PH	RHP	LHP
1928	STL	NL	6	3	3	3	3	0	0	0	0	0	0	0	0	0	4	2
1929	STL	NL	3	2	1	0	1	1	1	0	0	0	0	0	0	0	1	2
1930	NY	NL	5	3	2	3	0	1	1	0	0	0	0	0	0	0	5	0
1931	CIN	NL	1	0	1	1	0	0	0	0	0	0	0	0	0	0	1	0
1932	CIN	NL	3	0	3	2	0	1	0	0	0	0	0	0	0	0	3	0
1933	CIN	NL	1	0	1	1	0	0	0	0	0	0	0	0	0	0	1	0
Total			19	8	11	10	4	3	2	0	0	0	0	0	0	0	15	4

Rank among batters: 1,861 • *Top target (3 home runs)*: Leo Sweetland • *Number of pitchers victimized*: 17 • *Total ballparks homered in*: 6 • *First HR*: 05/06/1928 off Dazzy Vance

Billy Rogell

WILLIAM GEORGE ROGELL
B: 11/24/1904
BB

Year	Tm	Lg	Tot	H	A	Men-On 0	1	2	3	One-Game 2	3	4	LO	XN	IP	PH	RHP	LHP
1927	BOS	AL	2	0	2	1	1	0	0	0	0	0	0	0	0	0	2	0
1931	DET	AL	2	2	0	2	0	0	0	0	0	0	0	1	0	0	0	2
1932	DET	AL	9	3	6	6	1	2	0	1	0	0	0	0	0	0	4	5
1934	DET	AL	3	0	3	1	2	0	0	0	0	0	0	0	0	0	2	1
1935	DET	AL	6	0	6	2	2	2	0	1	0	0	0	0	1	0	3	3
1936	DET	AL	6	2	4	3	1	2	0	0	0	0	0	0	0	0	4	2
1937	DET	AL	8	5	3	6	2	0	0	0	0	0	0	0	0	0	7	1
1938	DET	AL	3	1	2	2	1	0	0	0	0	0	1	0	0	0	3	0

Billy Rogell *continued*

Year	Tm	Lg	Tot	H	A	Men-On 0	Men-On 1	Men-On 2	Men-On 3	One-Game 2	One-Game 3	One-Game 4	LO	XN	IP	PH	RHP	LHP
1939	DET	AL	2	2	0	2	0	0	0	0	0	0	0	0	0	0	2	0
1940	CHI	NL	1	0	1	0	1	0	0	0	0	0	0	0	0	1	1	0
Total			42	15	27	25	11	6	0	2	0	0	1	1	1	1	28	14

Rank among batters: 1,138 • *Top target (5 home runs)*: Lefty Gomez • *Number of pitchers victimized*: 32 • *Total ballparks homered in*: 8 • *First HR*: 07/13/1927 off Milt Gaston

Jim Rogers

JAMES F. ROGERS
B: 04/09/1872 D: 01/21/1900

Year	Tm	Lg	Tot	H	A	Men-On 0	Men-On 1	Men-On 2	Men-On 3	One-Game 2	One-Game 3	One-Game 4	LO	XN	IP	PH	RHP	LHP
1896	WAS	NL	1	1	0	0	1	0	0	0	0	0	0	0	1	0	0	1
1897	LOU	NL	2	0	2	0	2	0	0	0	0	0	0	0	0	0	1	0
Total			3	1	2	0	3	0	0	0	0	0	0	0	1	0	1	1

Rank among batters: 3,735 • *Total ballparks homered in*: 3 • *First HR*: 04/18/1896 off George Van Haltren

Tom Rogers

THOMAS ANDREW ROGERS
B: 02/12/1892 D: 03/07/1936
BR

Year	Tm	Lg	Tot	H	A	Men-On 0	Men-On 1	Men-On 2	Men-On 3	One-Game 2	One-Game 3	One-Game 4	LO	XN	IP	PH	RHP	LHP
1919	PHI	AL	1	1	0	1	0	0	0	0	0	0	0	0	0	0	0	1

Rank among batters: 4,707 • *Total ballparks homered in*: 1 • *First HR*: 06/02/1919 off Hank Thormahlen

Mike Rogodzinski

MICHAEL GEORGE ROGODZINSKI
B: 02/22/1948
BL

Year	Tm	Lg	Tot	H	A	Men-On 0	Men-On 1	Men-On 2	Men-On 3	One-Game 2	One-Game 3	One-Game 4	LO	XN	IP	PH	RHP	LHP
1973	PHI	NL	2	2	0	1	1	0	0	0	0	0	0	0	0	2	2	0

Rank among batters: 4,129 • *Total ballparks homered in*: 1 • *First HR*: 05/18/1973 off Ferguson Jenkins

Saul Rogovin

SAUL WALTER ROGOVIN
B: 10/10/1923 D: 01/23/1995
BR

Year	Tm	Lg	Tot	H	A	Men-On 0	Men-On 1	Men-On 2	Men-On 3	One-Game 2	One-Game 3	One-Game 4	LO	XN	IP	PH	RHP	LHP
1950	DET	AL	1	0	1	0	0	0	1	0	0	0	0	0	0	0	0	1
1952	CHI	AL	1	1	0	0	1	0	0	0	0	0	0	0	0	0	0	1
1955	PHI	NL	1	1	0	1	0	0	0	0	0	0	0	0	0	0	0	1
Total			3	2	1	1	1	0	1	0	0	0	0	0	0	0	0	3

Rank among batters: 3,735 • *Total ballparks homered in*: 3 • *First HR*: 07/23/1950 off Eddie Lopat

George Rohe

GEORGE ANTHONY ROHE
B: 09/15/1875 D: 06/10/1957
BR

Year	Tm	Lg	Tot	H	A	Men-On 0	Men-On 1	Men-On 2	Men-On 3	One-Game 2	One-Game 3	One-Game 4	LO	XN	IP	PH	RHP	LHP
1905	CHI	AL	1	1	0	1	0	0	0	0	0	0	0	0	0	0	1	0
1907	CHI	AL	2	0	2	0	1	1	0	0	0	0	0	0	1	0	1	1
Total			3	1	2	1	1	1	0	0	0	0	0	0	1	0	2	1

Rank among batters: 3,735 • *Total ballparks homered in*: 3 • *First HR*: 09/14/1905 off Harry Howell

Dan Rohn

DANIEL JAY ROHN
B: 01/10/1956
BL

Year	Tm	Lg	Tot	H	A	Men-On 0	Men-On 1	Men-On 2	Men-On 3	One-Game 2	One-Game 3	One-Game 4	LO	XN	IP	PH	RHP	LHP
1984	CHI	NL	1	0	1	1	0	0	0	0	0	0	0	0	0	1	1	0

Rank among batters: 4,707 • *Total ballparks homered in*: 1 • *First HR*: 07/07/1984 off Mike Krukow

Ray Rohwer

RAY ROHWER
B: 06/05/1895 D: 01/24/1988
BL

Year	Tm	Lg	Tot	H	A	Men-On 0	Men-On 1	Men-On 2	Men-On 3	One-Game 2	One-Game 3	One-Game 4	LO	XN	IP	PH	RHP	LHP
1922	PIT	NL	3	1	2	2	1	0	0	0	0	0	0	1	0	0	3	0

Rank among batters: 3,735 • *Total ballparks homered in*: 3 • *First HR*: 04/22/1922 off Jesse Haines

Year	Tm	Lg	Tot	H	A	Men-On 0	1	2	3	One-Game 2	3	4	LO	XN	IP	PH	RHP	LHP

Cookie Rojas

OCTAVIO VICTOR (RIVAS) ROJAS
B: 03/06/1939
BR

Year	Tm	Lg	Tot	H	A	Men-On 0	1	2	3	One-Game 2	3	4	LO	XN	IP	PH	RHP	LHP
1963	PHI	NL	1	0	1	1	0	0	0	0	0	0	0	0	0	0	1	0
1964	PHI	NL	2	0	2	0	2	0	0	0	0	0	0	0	1	0	2	0
1965	PHI	NL	3	2	1	2	0	1	0	0	0	0	0	0	0	0	2	1
1966	PHI	NL	6	3	3	4	1	1	0	1	0	0	0	0	0	0	5	1
1967	PHI	NL	4	1	3	2	1	0	1	0	0	0	1	0	0	0	3	1
1968	PHI	NL	9	7	2	5	2	2	0	0	0	0	0	0	0	0	5	4
1969	PHI	NL	4	3	1	4	0	0	0	0	0	0	0	0	0	0	2	2
1970	KC	AL	2	0	2	1	1	0	0	0	0	0	0	0	0	0	1	1
1971	KC	AL	6	0	6	3	2	1	0	0	0	0	0	0	0	0	3	3
1972	KC	AL	3	1	2	0	1	1	1	0	0	0	0	1	0	0	1	2
1973	KC	AL	6	3	3	4	1	1	0	1	0	0	0	0	0	0	4	2
1974	KC	AL	6	3	3	1	3	1	1	0	0	0	0	1	1	0	3	3
1975	KC	AL	2	1	1	1	0	1	0	0	0	0	0	0	0	0	2	0
Total			54	24	30	28	14	9	3	2	0	0	1	2	2	0	34	20

Rank among batters: 938 • Top target (2 home runs): Bobby Bolin, Mike McCormick, Rich Nye, Wilbur Wood, Doc Medich, Catfish Hunter, Ray Corbin • *Number of pitchers victimized*: 47 • *Total ballparks homered in*: 18 • *First HR*: 09/17/1963 off Tracy Stallard • *All-Star HR*—1

Stan Rojek

STANLEY ANDREW ROJEK
B: 04/21/1919
BR

Year	Tm	Lg	Tot	H	A	Men-On 0	1	2	3	One-Game 2	3	4	LO	XN	IP	PH	RHP	LHP
1948	PIT	NL	4	3	1	3	1	0	0	0	0	0	1	0	0	0	4	0

Rank among batters: 3,427 • *Total ballparks homered in*: 2 • *First HR*: 07/05/1948 off Herm Wehmeier

Red Rolfe

ROBERT ABIAL ROLFE
B: 10/17/1908 D: 07/08/1969
BL

Year	Tm	Lg	Tot	H	A	Men-On 0	1	2	3	One-Game 2	3	4	LO	XN	IP	PH	RHP	LHP
1935	NY	AL	5	5	0	1	2	2	0	0	0	0	0	0	1	0	2	3
1936	NY	AL	10	4	6	6	3	1	0	0	0	0	0	1	0	0	9	1
1937	NY	AL	4	3	1	1	3	0	0	0	0	0	0	1	0	0	4	0
1938	NY	AL	10	9	1	4	5	1	0	0	0	0	0	0	0	0	9	1
1939	NY	AL	14	11	3	11	3	0	0	0	0	0	0	0	0	0	12	2
1940	NY	AL	10	9	1	5	4	1	0	1	0	0	0	0	0	0	7	3
1941	NY	AL	8	6	2	5	3	0	0	0	0	0	0	0	0	0	5	3
1942	NY	AL	8	8	0	6	2	0	0	0	0	0	0	1	0	0	7	1
Total			69	55	14	39	25	5	0	1	0	0	0	3	1	0	55	14

Rank among batters: 756 • *Top target (3 home runs)*: Johnny Marcum, Dutch Leonard, Mel Harder • *Number of pitchers victimized*: 53 • *Total ballparks homered in*: 7 • *First HR*: 06/02/1935 off Gordon Rhodes

Rich Rollins

RICHARD JOHN ROLLINS
B: 04/16/1938
BR

Year	Tm	Lg	Tot	H	A	Men-On 0	1	2	3	One-Game 2	3	4	LO	XN	IP	PH	RHP	LHP
1962	MIN	AL	16	9	7	8	7	1	0	1	0	0	0	1	0	0	16	0
1963	MIN	AL	16	9	7	12	4	0	0	0	0	0	1	0	0	0	14	2
1964	MIN	AL	12	7	5	6	3	2	1	0	0	0	0	0	1	0	11	1
1965	MIN	AL	5	0	5	3	2	0	0	0	0	0	0	0	1	0	5	0
1966	MIN	AL	10	4	6	5	2	2	1	0	0	0	0	0	0	2	5	5
1967	MIN	AL	6	5	1	5	0	0	1	1	0	0	0	0	0	0	4	2
1968	MIN	AL	6	4	2	3	2	1	0	0	0	0	0	0	0	0	4	2
1969	SEA	AL	4	2	2	1	1	1	1	0	0	0	0	0	0	0	3	1
1970	CLE	AL	2	1	1	2	0	0	0	0	0	0	0	0	0	1	1	1
Total			77	41	36	45	21	7	4	2	0	0	1	1	2	3	63	14

Rank among batters: 682 • *Top target (3 home runs)*: Orlando Pena, Bennie Daniels • *Number of pitchers victimized*: 61 • *Total ballparks homered in*: 12 • *First HR*: 04/11/1962 off Bill Kunkel

Bill Roman

WILLIAM ANTHONY ROMAN
B: 10/11/1938
BL

Year	Tm	Lg	Tot	H	A	Men-On 0	1	2	3	One-Game 2	3	4	LO	XN	IP	PH	RHP	LHP
1964	DET	AL	1	0	1	1	0	0	0	0	0	0	0	0	0	1	1	0

Rank among batters: 4,707 • *Total ballparks homered in*: 1 • *First HR*: 09/30/1964 off Jim Bouton • *Hit HR in first major league AB*—@NY: 09/30/1964 (2)

John Romano

JOHN ANTHONY ROMANO
B: 08/23/1934
BR

Year	Tm	Lg	Tot	H	A	Men-On 0	1	2	3	One-Game 2	3	4	LO	XN	IP	PH	RHP	LHP
1959	CHI	AL	5	2	3	4	1	0	0	0	0	0	0	0	0	3	1	4
1960	CLE	AL	16	10	6	7	7	2	0	2	0	0	0	0	0	0	12	4
1961	CLE	AL	21	12	9	11	10	0	0	1	0	0	0	0	0	0	14	7
1962	CLE	AL	25	10	15	13	8	4	0	2	0	0	0	0	0	0	19	6
1963	CLE	AL	10	6	4	7	2	0	1	0	0	0	0	0	0	1	8	2
1964	CLE	AL	19	9	10	12	7	0	0	2	0	0	0	0	0	0	10	9
1965	CHI	AL	18	6	12	12	2	3	1	1	0	0	0	0	0	0	9	9
1966	CHI	AL	15	5	10	11	3	1	0	1	0	0	0	0	0	0	8	7
Total			129	60	69	77	40	10	2	9	0	0	0	0	0	4	81	48

Rank among batters: 354 • *Top target (5 home runs)*: Steve Barber • *Number of pitchers victimized*: 88 • *Total ballparks homered in*: 12 • *First HR*: 05/03/1959 off Billy O'Dell

Ed Romero

EDGARDO RALPH (RIVERA) ROMERO
B: 12/09/1957
BR

Year	Tm	Lg	Tot	H	A	Men-On 0	1	2	3	One-Game 2	3	4	LO	XN	IP	PH	RHP	LHP
1980	MIL	AL	1	1	0	1	0	0	0	0	0	0	0	0	0	0	1	0
1981	MIL	AL	1	0	1	0	0	1	0	0	0	0	0	0	0	0	0	1
1982	MIL	AL	1	1	0	1	0	0	0	0	0	0	0	0	0	0	0	1
1983	MIL	AL	1	0	1	1	0	0	0	0	0	0	0	0	0	0	0	1
1984	MIL	AL	1	1	0	1	0	0	0	0	0	0	0	0	0	0	0	1
1986	BOS	AL	2	2	0	1	0	1	0	0	0	0	0	0	0	0	2	0
1989	ATL	NL	1	0	1	1	0	0	0	0	0	0	0	0	0	0	0	1
Total			8	5	3	6	0	2	0	0	0	0	0	0	0	0	3	5

Rank among batters: 2,703 • *Total ballparks homered in*: 4 • *First HR*: 10/05/1980 off Rick Langford

Kevin Romine

KEVIN ANDREW ROMINE
B: 05/23/1961
BR

Year	Tm	Lg	Tot	H	A	Men-On 0	1	2	3	One-Game 2	3	4	LO	XN	IP	PH	RHP	LHP
1988	BOS	AL	1	1	0	1	0	0	0	0	0	0	0	0	0	0	1	0
1989	BOS	AL	1	1	0	1	0	0	0	0	0	0	0	0	0	0	1	0
1990	BOS	AL	2	2	0	2	0	0	0	0	0	0	0	0	0	0	1	1
1991	BOS	AL	1	0	1	0	0	0	1	0	0	0	0	0	0	0	1	0
Total			5	4	1	4	0	0	1	0	0	0	0	0	0	0	4	1

Rank among batters: 3,191 • *Total ballparks homered in*: 2 • *First HR*: 07/16/1988 off Steve Farr

Eddie Rommel

EDWIN AMERICUS ROMMEL
B: 09/13/1897 D: 08/26/1970
BR

Year	Tm	Lg	Tot	H	A	Men-On 0	1	2	3	One-Game 2	3	4	LO	XN	IP	PH	RHP	LHP
1925	PHI	AL	1	1	0	0	0	1	0	0	0	0	0	0	0	0	0	1

Rank among batters: 4,707 • *Total ballparks homered in*: 1 • *First HR*: 04/16/1925 off Buster Ross

Enrique Romo

ENRIQUE (NAVARRO) ROMO
B: 07/15/1947
BR

Year	Tm	Lg	Tot	H	A	Men-On 0	1	2	3	One-Game 2	3	4	LO	XN	IP	PH	RHP	LHP
1980	PIT	NL	1	0	1	0	0	0	1	0	0	0	0	0	0	0	1	0

Rank among batters: 4,707 • *Total ballparks homered in*: 1 • *First HR*: 10/01/1980 off Roy Lee Jackson

Vicente Romo

VICENTE (NAVARRO) ROMO
B: 04/12/1943
BR

Year	Tm	Lg	Tot	H	A	Men-On 0	1	2	3	One-Game 2	3	4	LO	XN	IP	PH	RHP	LHP
1970	BOS	AL	1	1	0	1	0	0	0	0	0	0	0	0	0	0	1	0

Rank among batters: 4,707 • *Total ballparks homered in*: 1 • *First HR*: 05/30/1970 off Jerry Crider

John Romonosky

JOHN ROMONOSKY
B: 07/07/1929
BR

Year	Tm	Lg	Tot	H	A	Men-On 0	1	2	3	One-Game 2	3	4	LO	XN	IP	PH	RHP	LHP
1958	WAS	AL	1	0	1	1	0	0	0	0	0	0	0	0	0	0	0	1

Year	Tm	Lg	Tot	H	A	Men-On 0	Men-On 1	Men-On 2	Men-On 3	One-Game 2	One-Game 3	One-Game 4	LO	XN	IP	PH	RHP	LHP

John Romonosky *continued*

Rank among batters: 4,707 • *Total ballparks homered in*: 1 • *First HR*: 07/22/1958 off Hal Woodeshick

Henri Rondeau

HENRI JOSEPH RONDEAU
B: 05/05/1887 D: 05/28/1943
BR

Year	Tm	Lg	Tot	H	A	Men-On 0	Men-On 1	Men-On 2	Men-On 3	One-Game 2	One-Game 3	One-Game 4	LO	XN	IP	PH	RHP	LHP
1916	WAS	AL	1	1	0	0	0	1	0	0	0	0	0	0	1	0	1	0

Rank among batters: 4,707 • *Total ballparks homered in*: 1 • *First HR*: 04/21/1916 off Ray Caldwell

Phil Roof

PHILLIP ANTHONY ROOF
B: 03/05/1941
BR

Year	Tm	Lg	Tot	H	A	Men-On 0	Men-On 1	Men-On 2	Men-On 3	One-Game 2	One-Game 3	One-Game 4	LO	XN	IP	PH	RHP	LHP
1966	KC	AL	7	3	4	5	1	1	0	0	0	0	0	1	0	0	6	1
1967	KC	AL	6	0	6	4	2	0	0	0	0	0	0	0	0	0	4	2
1968	OAK	AL	1	0	1	1	0	0	0	0	0	0	0	0	0	0	0	1
1969	OAK	AL	2	1	1	0	1	1	0	0	0	0	0	0	0	0	0	2
1970	MIL	AL	13	9	4	7	3	3	0	0	0	0	0	0	0	1	7	6
1971	MIL	AL	1	1	0	0	1	0	0	0	0	0	0	0	0	0	0	1
1972	MIN	AL	3	3	0	3	0	0	0	1	0	0	0	0	0	0	1	2
1973	MIN	AL	1	0	1	0	0	1	0	0	0	0	0	0	0	0	1	0
1974	MIN	AL	2	1	1	0	0	1	1	0	0	0	0	0	0	0	1	1
1975	MIN	AL	7	5	2	3	3	1	0	0	0	0	0	0	0	0	6	1
Total			43	23	20	23	11	8	1	1	0	0	0	1	0	1	26	17

Rank among batters: 1,116 • *Top target (3 home runs)*: Tom Murphy • *Number of pitchers victimized*: 37 • *Total ballparks homered in*: 14 • *First HR*: 05/23/1966 off Casey Cox

Jim Rooker

JAMES PHILLIP ROOKER
B: 09/23/1942
BR

Year	Tm	Lg	Tot	H	A	Men-On 0	Men-On 1	Men-On 2	Men-On 3	One-Game 2	One-Game 3	One-Game 4	LO	XN	IP	PH	RHP	LHP
1969	KC	AL	4	1	3	2	2	0	0	1	0	0	0	0	0	0	1	3
1970	KC	AL	1	0	1	0	1	0	0	0	0	0	0	0	0	0	1	0
1976	PIT	NL	1	0	1	0	1	0	0	0	0	0	0	0	0	0	1	0
1980	PIT	NL	1	0	1	0	1	0	0	0	0	0	0	0	0	0	1	0
Total			7	1	6	2	5	0	0	1	0	0	0	0	0	0	4	3

Rank among batters: 2,834 • *Top target (2 home runs)*: Jim Kaat • *Number of pitchers victimized*: 6 • *Total ballparks homered in*: 6 • *First HR*: 07/07/1969 off Jim Kaat

Rolando Roomes

ROLANDO AUDLEY ROOMES
B: 02/15/1962
BR

Year	Tm	Lg	Tot	H	A	Men-On 0	Men-On 1	Men-On 2	Men-On 3	One-Game 2	One-Game 3	One-Game 4	LO	XN	IP	PH	RHP	LHP
1989	CIN	NL	7	5	2	3	4	0	0	0	0	0	0	1	0	0	5	2
1990	CIN	NL	2	2	0	1	0	1	0	0	0	0	0	0	0	0	0	2
Total			9	7	2	4	4	1	0	0	0	0	0	1	0	0	5	4

Rank among batters: 2,587 • *Total ballparks homered in*: 3 • *First HR*: 05/17/1989 off John Smiley

Frank Rooney

FRANK ROONEY
B: 10/12/1884 D: 04/06/1977

Year	Tm	Lg	Tot	H	A	Men-On 0	Men-On 1	Men-On 2	Men-On 3	One-Game 2	One-Game 3	One-Game 4	LO	XN	IP	PH	RHP	LHP
1914	IND	FL	1	0	1	0	1	0	0	0	0	0	0	0	0	0	0	1

Rank among batters: 4,707 • *Total ballparks homered in*: 1 • *First HR*: 05/30/1914 off Ad Brennan

Charlie Root

CHARLES HENRY ROOT
B: 03/17/1899 D: 11/05/1970
BR

Year	Tm	Lg	Tot	H	A	Men-On 0	Men-On 1	Men-On 2	Men-On 3	One-Game 2	One-Game 3	One-Game 4	LO	XN	IP	PH	RHP	LHP
1926	CHI	NL	1	1	0	0	1	0	0	0	0	0	0	0	0	0	1	0
1929	CHI	NL	1	0	1	0	0	1	0	0	0	0	0	0	0	0	0	1
1930	CHI	NL	1	1	0	1	0	0	0	0	0	0	0	0	0	0	1	0
1932	CHI	NL	1	0	1	1	0	0	0	0	0	0	0	0	0	0	1	0

Charlie Root *continued*

Year	Tm	Lg	Tot	H	A	Men-On 0	Men-On 1	Men-On 2	Men-On 3	One-Game 2	One-Game 3	One-Game 4	LO	XN	IP	PH	RHP	LHP
1934	CHI	NL	2	1	1	1	1	0	0	0	0	0	0	0	0	0	1	1
1935	CHI	NL	1	1	0	1	0	0	0	0	0	0	0	0	0	0	1	0
1937	CHI	NL	1	0	1	1	0	0	0	0	0	0	0	0	0	0	1	0
1939	CHI	NL	2	1	1	1	1	0	0	0	0	0	0	0	0	0	2	0
1941	CHI	NL	1	0	1	1	0	0	0	0	0	0	0	0	0	0	1	0
Total			11	5	6	7	3	1	0	0	0	0	0	0	0	0	9	2

Rank among batters: 2,419 • *Total ballparks homered in*: 6 • *First HR*: 08/29/1926 off Carl Mays

Jorge Roque

JORGE (VARGAS) ROQUE
B: 04/28/1950
BR

Year	Tm	Lg	Tot	H	A	Men-On 0	Men-On 1	Men-On 2	Men-On 3	One-Game 2	One-Game 3	One-Game 4	LO	XN	IP	PH	RHP	LHP
1972	STL	NL	1	0	1	1	0	0	0	0	0	0	0	1	0	1	1	0
1973	MON	NL	1	0	1	0	0	0	1	0	0	0	0	0	0	0	1	0
Total			2	0	2	1	0	0	1	0	0	0	0	1	0	1	2	0

Rank among batters: 4,129 • *Total ballparks homered in*: 2 • *First HR*: 09/13/1972 off John Strohmayer

Buddy Rosar

WARREN VINCENT ROSAR
B: 07/03/1914 D: 03/13/1994
BR

Year	Tm	Lg	Tot	H	A	Men-On 0	Men-On 1	Men-On 2	Men-On 3	One-Game 2	One-Game 3	One-Game 4	LO	XN	IP	PH	RHP	LHP
1940	NY	AL	4	2	2	2	1	0	1	1	0	0	0	0	0	0	3	1
1941	NY	AL	1	0	1	1	0	0	0	0	0	0	0	1	0	0	1	0
1942	NY	AL	2	1	1	1	0	1	0	0	0	0	0	0	0	0	0	2
1943	CLE	AL	1	0	1	1	0	0	0	0	0	0	0	0	0	0	1	0
1945	PHI	AL	1	0	1	1	0	0	0	0	0	0	0	0	0	0	0	1
1946	PHI	AL	2	2	0	2	0	0	0	0	0	0	0	0	0	0	1	1
1947	PHI	AL	1	1	0	1	0	0	0	0	0	0	0	0	0	0	1	0
1948	PHI	AL	4	2	2	3	1	0	0	0	0	0	0	0	0	0	2	2
1950	BOS	AL	1	1	0	0	1	0	0	0	0	0	0	0	0	0	0	1
1951	BOS	AL	1	1	0	1	0	0	0	0	0	0	0	0	0	0	1	0
Total			18	10	8	13	3	1	1	1	0	0	0	1	0	0	10	8

Rank among batters: 1,914 • *Top target (2 home runs)*: Emerson Dickman • *Number of pitchers victimized*: 17 • *Total ballparks homered in*: 6 • *First HR*: 07/04/1940 off Emerson Dickman • *Hit for Cycle*—vs CLE: 07/19/1940

Jimmy Rosario

ANGEL RAMON (FERRER) ROSARIO
B: 05/05/1945
BB

Year	Tm	Lg	Tot	H	A	Men-On 0	Men-On 1	Men-On 2	Men-On 3	One-Game 2	One-Game 3	One-Game 4	LO	XN	IP	PH	RHP	LHP
1976	MIL	AL	1	1	0	1	0	0	0	0	0	0	0	0	0	0	1	0

Rank among batters: 4,707 • *Total ballparks homered in*: 1 • *First HR*: 06/10/1976 off Francisco Barrios

Santiago Rosario

SANTIAGO ROSARIO
B: 07/25/1939
BL

Year	Tm	Lg	Tot	H	A	Men-On 0	Men-On 1	Men-On 2	Men-On 3	One-Game 2	One-Game 3	One-Game 4	LO	XN	IP	PH	RHP	LHP
1965	KC	AL	2	2	0	2	0	0	0	0	0	0	0	0	0	1	2	0

Rank among batters: 4,129 • *Total ballparks homered in*: 1 • *First HR*: 07/08/1965 off Dick Hall

Bobby Rose

ROBERT RICHARD ROSE
B: 03/15/1967
BR

Year	Tm	Lg	Tot	H	A	Men-On 0	Men-On 1	Men-On 2	Men-On 3	One-Game 2	One-Game 3	One-Game 4	LO	XN	IP	PH	RHP	LHP
1989	CAL	AL	1	1	0	1	0	0	0	0	0	0	0	0	0	0	0	1
1990	CAL	AL	1	1	0	1	0	0	0	0	0	0	0	0	0	0	0	1
1991	CAL	AL	1	0	1	0	0	1	0	0	0	0	0	0	0	1	0	1
1992	CAL	AL	2	1	1	0	2	0	0	0	0	0	0	0	0	1	1	1
Total			5	3	2	2	2	1	0	0	0	0	0	0	0	2	1	4

Rank among batters: 3,191 • *Top target (2 home runs)*: Steve Howe • *Number of pitchers victimized*: 4 • *Total ballparks homered in*: 2 • *First HR*: 08/16/1989 off Shane Rawley

Year	Tm	Lg	Tot	H	A	Men-On				One-Game			LO	XN	IP	PH	RHP	LHP
						0	1	2	3	2	3	4						

Don Rose

DONALD GARY ROSE
B: 03/19/1947
BR

Year	Tm	Lg	Tot	H	A	0	1	2	3	2	3	4	LO	XN	IP	PH	RHP	LHP
1972	CAL	AL	1	0	1	1	0	0	0	0	0	0	0	0	0	0	1	0

Rank among batters: 4,707 • *Total ballparks homered in*: 1 • *First HR*: 05/24/1972 off Diego Segui • *Hit HR on first major league pitch*—@OAK: 05/24/1972

Pete Rose

PETER EDWARD ROSE
B: 04/14/1941
BB

Year	Tm	Lg	Tot	H	A	0	1	2	3	2	3	4	LO	XN	IP	PH	RHP	LHP
1963	CIN	NL	6	2	4	4	2	0	0	0	0	0	1	0	1	0	6	0
1964	CIN	NL	4	3	1	2	0	1	1	0	0	0	1	1	0	0	1	3
1965	CIN	NL	11	7	4	5	6	0	0	0	0	0	0	0	0	0	3	8
1966	CIN	NL	16	11	5	9	6	1	0	2	0	0	0	0	0	0	9	7
1967	CIN	NL	12	7	5	5	5	2	0	1	0	0	1	0	0	0	11	1
1968	CIN	NL	10	6	4	8	2	0	0	0	0	0	1	0	0	0	7	3
1969	CIN	NL	16	10	6	10	4	2	0	0	0	0	3	1	0	0	16	0
1970	CIN	NL	15	7	8	10	4	1	0	1	0	0	1	0	0	0	12	3
1971	CIN	NL	13	8	5	12	1	0	0	0	0	0	3	0	0	0	10	3
1972	CIN	NL	6	1	5	6	0	0	0	0	0	0	0	0	0	0	5	1
1973	CIN	NL	5	3	2	3	2	0	0	0	0	0	1	0	1	0	5	0
1974	CIN	NL	3	2	1	2	0	1	0	0	0	0	0	0	0	0	2	1
1975	CIN	NL	7	3	4	4	2	1	0	0	0	0	1	0	0	0	5	2
1976	CIN	NL	10	7	3	7	3	0	0	0	0	0	3	0	0	0	6	4
1977	CIN	NL	9	3	6	6	3	0	0	0	0	0	1	0	0	0	6	3
1978	CIN	NL	7	2	5	3	3	1	0	0	1	0	0	0	1	0	6	1
1979	PHI	NL	4	1	3	3	1	0	0	0	0	0	0	0	0	0	3	1
1980	PHI	NL	1	0	1	0	1	0	0	0	0	0	0	0	0	0	1	0
1982	PHI	NL	3	2	1	1	2	0	0	0	0	0	0	0	0	0	3	0
1985	CIN	NL	2	0	2	1	1	0	0	0	0	0	0	0	0	0	2	0
Total			160	85	75	101	48	10	1	4	1	0	17	2	3	0	119	41

Rank among batters: 263 • *Top target (4 home runs)*: Juan Marichal, Don Sutton, Ferguson Jenkins • *Number of pitchers victimized*: 120 • *Total ballparks homered in*: 19 • *First HR*: 05/03/1963 off Ernie Broglio • *Switch hit HR in 1 game*—2 times • *World Series HR*—2; *LCS HR*—3

John Roseboro

JOHN JUNIOR ROSEBORO
B: 05/13/1933
BL

Year	Tm	Lg	Tot	H	A	0	1	2	3	2	3	4	LO	XN	IP	PH	RHP	LHP
1957	BRO	NL	2	2	0	0	1	1	0	0	0	0	0	1	0	0	2	0
1958	LA	NL	14	2	12	12	2	0	0	1	0	0	0	0	0	0	14	0
1959	LA	NL	10	3	7	7	3	0	0	1	0	0	0	0	0	0	9	1
1960	LA	NL	8	3	5	3	4	0	1	0	0	0	0	0	0	1	8	0
1961	LA	NL	18	12	6	13	4	1	0	0	0	0	0	0	0	1	17	1
1962	LA	NL	7	4	3	5	2	0	0	0	0	0	0	0	0	0	7	0
1963	LA	NL	9	4	5	7	1	0	1	0	0	0	0	0	0	0	9	0
1964	LA	NL	3	0	3	3	0	0	0	0	0	0	0	0	0	0	3	0
1965	LA	NL	8	2	6	6	1	1	0	0	0	0	0	0	0	0	6	2
1966	LA	NL	9	2	7	2	6	1	0	0	0	0	0	0	0	0	8	1
1967	LA	NL	4	1	3	4	0	0	0	0	0	0	0	0	0	0	3	1
1968	MIN	AL	8	4	4	5	3	0	0	0	0	0	0	1	0	0	6	2
1969	MIN	AL	3	3	0	2	1	0	0	0	0	0	0	0	0	0	3	0
1970	WAS	AL	1	0	1	1	0	0	0	0	0	0	0	0	0	1	1	0
Total			104	42	62	70	28	4	2	2	0	0	0	2	0	3	96	8

Rank among batters: 469 • *Top target (3 home runs)*: Bob Purkey, Joey Jay, Carl Willey • *Number of pitchers victimized*: 78 • *Total ballparks homered in*: 20 • *First HR*: 07/19/1957 off Turk Lown • *World Series HR*—1; *All-Star HR*—1

Bob Roselli

ROBERT EDWARD ROSELLI
B: 12/10/1931
BR

Year	Tm	Lg	Tot	H	A	0	1	2	3	2	3	4	LO	XN	IP	PH	RHP	LHP
1956	MIL	NL	1	1	0	1	0	0	0	0	0	0	0	0	0	1	0	1
1962	CHI	AL	1	0	1	1	0	0	0	0	0	0	0	0	0	0	1	0
Total			2	1	1	2	0	0	0	0	0	0	0	0	0	1	1	1

Rank among batters: 4,129 • *Total ballparks homered in*: 2 • *First HR*: 07/21/1956 off Harvey Haddix

Dave Rosello

DAVID (RODRIGUEZ) ROSELLO
B: 06/26/1950
BR

Year	Tm	Lg	Tot	H	A	Men-On 0	1	2	3	One-Game 2	3	4	LO	XN	IP	PH	RHP	LHP
1972	CHI	NL	1	1	0	0	0	1	0	0	0	0	0	0	0	0	1	0
1975	CHI	NL	1	1	0	0	1	0	0	0	0	0	0	0	0	0	1	0
1976	CHI	NL	1	1	0	0	1	0	0	0	0	0	0	0	0	0	0	1
1977	CHI	NL	1	1	0	1	0	0	0	0	0	0	0	0	0	0	1	0
1979	CLE	AL	3	2	1	1	2	0	0	0	0	0	0	0	0	0	1	2
1980	CLE	AL	2	2	0	1	1	0	0	0	0	0	0	0	0	0	2	0
1981	CLE	AL	1	0	1	1	0	0	0	0	0	0	0	0	0	0	0	1
Total			10	8	2	4	5	1	0	0	0	0	0	0	0	0	6	4

Rank among batters: 2,500 • *Total ballparks homered in*: 4 • *First HR*: 09/16/1972 off Bob Rauch

Chief Roseman

JAMES JOHN ROSEMAN
B: 07/04/1856 D: 07/04/1938
BR

Year	Tm	Lg	Tot	H	A	Men-On 0	1	2	3	One-Game 2	3	4	LO	XN	IP	PH	RHP	LHP
1882	TRO	NL	1	0	1	1	0	0	0	0	0	0	0	0	0	0	1	0
1884	NY	AA	4	2	2	0	1	3	0	0	0	0	0	0	0	0	2	1
1885	NY	AA	4	3	1	1	3	0	0	0	0	0	0	0	2	0	2	1
1886	NY	AA	5	4	1	3	1	1	0	0	0	0	1	0	1	0	1	1
1887	NY	AA	1	1	0	0	0	1	0	0	0	0	0	0	0	0	1	0
1890	STL	AA	2	1	1	1	0	1	0	0	0	0	0	0	0	0	1	1
Total			17	11	6	6	5	6	0	0	0	0	1	0	3	0	8	2

Rank among batters: 1,969 • *Top target (3 home runs)*: Larry McKeon • *Number of pitchers victimized*: 13 • *Total ballparks homered in*: 9 • *First HR*: 07/04/1882 off Larry Corcoran

Al Rosen

ALBERT LEONARD ROSEN
B: 02/29/1924
BR

Year	Tm	Lg	Tot	H	A	Men-On 0	1	2	3	One-Game 2	3	4	LO	XN	IP	PH	RHP	LHP
1950	CLE	AL	37	21	16	18	12	5	2	3	0	0	0	1	1	0	23	14
1951	CLE	AL	24	13	11	11	6	3	4	0	0	0	0	0	0	0	17	7
1952	CLE	AL	28	11	17	13	6	8	1	1	1	0	0	0	1	0	17	11
1953	CLE	AL	43	24	19	15	17	9	2	3	0	0	0	1	0	0	27	16
1954	CLE	AL	24	14	10	15	8	1	0	1	0	0	0	0	1	0	18	6
1955	CLE	AL	21	13	8	12	7	2	0	1	0	0	0	1	0	0	10	11
1956	CLE	AL	15	6	9	8	4	3	0	0	0	0	0	0	0	0	8	7
Total			192	102	90	92	60	31	9	9	1	0	0	3	3	0	120	72

Rank among batters: 198 • Top target (5 home runs): Alex Kellner, Art Houtteman, Ned Garver, Bobby Shantz • *Number of pitchers victimized*: 100 • *Total ballparks homered in*: 10 • *First HR*: 04/18/1950 off Fred Hutchinson • *All-Star HR—2*

Goody Rosen

GOODWIN GEORGE ROSEN
B: 08/28/1912 D: 04/06/1994
BL

Year	Tm	Lg	Tot	H	A	Men-On 0	1	2	3	One-Game 2	3	4	LO	XN	IP	PH	RHP	LHP
1938	BRO	NL	4	2	2	3	1	0	0	0	0	0	0	0	0	0	2	2
1939	BRO	NL	1	1	0	1	0	0	0	0	0	0	1	0	0	0	1	0
1945	BRO	NL	12	8	4	3	7	2	0	0	0	0	0	2	0	0	10	2
1946	NY	NL	5	3	2	3	0	2	0	0	0	0	0	0	0	0	5	0
Total			22	14	8	10	8	4	0	0	0	0	1	2	0	0	18	4

Rank among batters: 1,719 • *Top target (2 home runs)*: Ace Adams, Andy Karl • *Number of pitchers victimized*: 20 • *Total ballparks homered in*: 6 • *First HR*: 06/29/1938 off Lou Fette

Max Rosenfeld

MAX ROSENFELD
B: 12/23/1902 D: 03/10/1969
BR

Year	Tm	Lg	Tot	H	A	Men-On 0	1	2	3	One-Game 2	3	4	LO	XN	IP	PH	RHP	LHP
1932	BRO	NL	2	1	1	1	0	1	0	0	0	0	0	0	0	0	1	1

Rank among batters: 4,129 • *Total ballparks homered in*: 2 • *First HR*: 04/28/1932 off Jumbo Elliott

Larry Rosenthal

LAWRENCE JOHN ROSENTHAL
B: 05/21/1910 D: 03/04/1992
BL

Year	Tm	Lg	Tot	H	A	Men-On 0	1	2	3	One-Game 2	3	4	LO	XN	IP	PH	RHP	LHP
1936	CHI	AL	3	2	1	1	2	0	0	0	0	0	0	0	0	0	3	0

Larry Rosenthal *continued*

Year	Tm	Lg	Tot	H	A	Men-On 0	1	2	3	One-Game 2	3	4	LO	XN	IP	PH	RHP	LHP
1938	CHI	AL	1	1	0	0	1	0	0	0	0	0	0	0	0	1	1	0
1939	CHI	AL	10	4	6	3	6	1	0	0	0	0	0	0	1	0	9	1
1940	CHI	AL	6	2	4	4	2	0	0	0	0	0	0	0	0	1	6	0
1941	CLE	AL	1	1	0	1	0	0	0	0	0	0	0	0	0	0	1	0
1944	PHI	AL	1	0	1	0	1	0	0	0	0	0	0	0	0	1	1	0
Total			22	10	12	9	12	1	0	0	0	0	0	0	1	3	21	1

Rank among batters: 1,719 • *Top target (3 home runs)*: Vern Kennedy • *Number of pitchers victimized*: 19 • *Total ballparks homered in*: 7 • *First HR*: 06/27/1936 off Jimmie DeShong

Si Rosenthal

SIMON ROSENTHAL
B: 11/13/1903 D: 04/07/1969
BL

Year	Tm	Lg	Tot	H	A	Men-On 0	1	2	3	One-Game 2	3	4	LO	XN	IP	PH	RHP	LHP
1926	BOS	AL	4	2	2	1	3	0	0	0	0	0	0	0	0	0	3	1

Rank among batters: 3,427 • *Total ballparks homered in*: 3 • *First HR*: 04/25/1926 off Firpo Marberry

Buck Ross

LEE RAVON ROSS
B: 02/02/1915 D: 11/23/1978
BR

Year	Tm	Lg	Tot	H	A	Men-On 0	1	2	3	One-Game 2	3	4	LO	XN	IP	PH	RHP	LHP
1938	PHI	AL	1	1	0	1	0	0	0	0	0	0	0	0	0	0	1	0
1940	PHI	AL	1	1	0	0	1	0	0	0	0	0	0	0	0	0	1	0
1943	CHI	AL	1	1	0	1	0	0	0	0	0	0	0	0	0	0	1	0
Total			3	3	0	2	1	0	0	0	0	0	0	0	0	0	3	0

Rank among batters: 3,735 • *Total ballparks homered in*: 2 • *First HR*: 07/15/1938 off Willis Hudlin

Chet Ross

CHESTER JAMES ROSS
B: 04/01/1917 D: 02/21/1989
BR

Year	Tm	Lg	Tot	H	A	Men-On 0	1	2	3	One-Game 2	3	4	LO	XN	IP	PH	RHP	LHP
1940	BOS	NL	17	10	7	10	4	2	1	0	0	0	0	0	0	0	13	4
1942	BOS	NL	5	3	2	4	1	0	0	0	0	0	0	0	0	0	1	4
1943	BOS	NL	7	6	1	3	2	2	0	0	0	0	0	0	0	1	6	1
1944	BOS	NL	5	2	3	3	1	1	0	0	0	0	0	0	0	0	0	5
Total			34	21	13	20	8	5	1	0	0	0	0	0	0	1	20	14

Rank among batters: 1,315 • Top target (2 home runs): Max Butcher, Vern Olsen, Ernie White, Whit Wyatt, Johnnie Wittig, Clyde Shoun • *Number of pitchers victimized*: 28 • *Total ballparks homered in*: 7 • *First HR*: 05/18/1940 off Max Butcher

Don Ross

DONALD RAYMOND ROSS
B: 07/16/1914
BR

Year	Tm	Lg	Tot	H	A	Men-On 0	1	2	3	One-Game 2	3	4	LO	XN	IP	PH	RHP	LHP
1938	DET	AL	1	1	0	0	1	0	0	0	0	0	0	0	0	0	0	1
1940	BRO	NL	1	1	0	0	1	0	0	0	0	0	0	0	0	0	1	0
1942	DET	AL	3	2	1	2	0	1	0	0	0	0	0	0	0	1	3	0
1944	DET	AL	2	2	0	1	1	0	0	0	0	0	0	0	0	1	1	1
1945	CLE	AL	2	1	1	1	1	0	0	0	0	0	0	0	0	0	1	1
1946	CLE	AL	3	2	1	2	1	0	0	0	0	0	0	0	0	0	3	0
Total			12	9	3	6	5	1	0	0	0	0	0	0	0	2	9	3

Rank among batters: 2,325 • *Total ballparks homered in*: 6 • *First HR*: 06/19/1938 off Ken Chase

Joe Rossi

JOSEPH ANTHONY ROSSI
B: 03/13/1923
BR

Year	Tm	Lg	Tot	H	A	Men-On 0	1	2	3	One-Game 2	3	4	LO	XN	IP	PH	RHP	LHP
1952	CIN	NL	1	1	0	1	0	0	0	0	0	0	0	0	0	0	1	0

Rank among batters: 4,707 • *Total ballparks homered in*: 1 • *First HR*: 07/04/1952 off Harry Fisher

Claude Rossman

CLAUDE R. ROSSMAN
B: 06/17/1881 D: 01/16/1928
BL

Year	Tm	Lg	Tot	H	A	Men-On 0	1	2	3	One-Game 2	3	4	LO	XN	IP	PH	RHP	LHP
1906	CLE	AL	1	0	1	1	0	0	0	0	0	0	0	0	0	0	0	1

Year	Tm	Lg	Tot	H	A	Men-On 0	Men-On 1	Men-On 2	Men-On 3	One-Game 2	One-Game 3	One-Game 4	LO	XN	IP	PH	RHP	LHP

Claude Rossman *continued*

Year	Tm	Lg	Tot	H	A	0	1	2	3	2	3	4	LO	XN	IP	PH	RHP	LHP
1908	DET	AL	2	1	1	2	0	0	0	0	0	0	0	1	0	0	2	0
Total			3	1	2	3	0	0	0	0	0	0	0	1	0	0	2	1

Rank among batters: 3,735 • *Total ballparks homered in*: 3 • *First HR*: 08/21/1906 off Case Patten

Rico Rossy

ELAM JOSE (RAMOS) ROSSY
B: 02/16/1964
BR

Year	Tm	Lg	Tot	H	A	0	1	2	3	2	3	4	LO	XN	IP	PH	RHP	LHP
1992	KC	AL	1	0	1	1	0	0	0	0	0	0	0	0	0	0	1	0
1993	KC	AL	2	2	0	2	0	0	0	0	0	0	0	0	0	0	0	2
Total			3	2	1	3	0	0	0	0	0	0	0	0	0	0	1	2

Rank among batters: 3,735 • *Total ballparks homered in*: 2 • *First HR*: 05/05/1992 off Jack Armstrong

Braggo Roth

ROBERT FRANK ROTH
B: 08/28/1892 D: 09/11/1936
BR

Year	Tm	Lg	Tot	H	A	0	1	2	3	2	3	4	LO	XN	IP	PH	RHP	LHP
1914	CHI	AL	1	1	0	1	0	0	0	0	0	0	0	0	0	0	0	1
1915	CHI	AL	3	0	3	1	2	0	0	0	0	0	0	0	0	0	2	1
	CLE	AL	4	0	4	4	0	0	0	0	0	0	0	0	0	0	4	0
	Total		7	0	7	5	2	0	0	0	0	0	0	0	0	0	6	1
1916	CLE	AL	4	1	3	2	2	0	0	1	0	0	0	0	1	1	3	1
1917	CLE	AL	1	0	1	0	1	0	0	0	0	0	0	0	0	0	1	0
1918	CLE	AL	1	0	1	1	0	0	0	0	0	0	0	0	0	0	0	1
1919	PHI	AL	5	4	1	4	1	0	0	1	0	0	0	0	0	0	5	0
1920	WAS	AL	9	3	6	5	2	2	0	0	0	0	0	0	3	0	4	5
1921	NY	AL	2	0	2	2	0	0	0	0	0	0	0	0	0	0	2	0
Total			30	9	21	20	8	2	0	2	0	0	0	0	4	1	21	9

Rank among batters: 1,437 • *Top target (3 home runs)*: Jing Johnson, Bernie Boland • *Number of pitchers victimized*: 25 • *Total ballparks homered in*: 8 • *First HR*: 09/13/1914 off Red Oldham

Frank Roth

FRANCIS CHARLES ROTH
B: 10/11/1878 D: 03/27/1955
BR

Year	Tm	Lg	Tot	H	A	0	1	2	3	2	3	4	LO	XN	IP	PH	RHP	LHP
1904	PHI	NL	1	0	1	1	0	0	0	0	0	0	0	0	0	0	1	0

Rank among batters: 4,707 • *Total ballparks homered in*: 1 • *First HR*: 06/17/1904 off Kaiser Wilhelm

Jack Rothfuss

JOHN ALBERT ROTHFUSS
B: 04/18/1872 D: 04/20/1947
BR

Year	Tm	Lg	Tot	H	A	0	1	2	3	2	3	4	LO	XN	IP	PH	RHP	LHP
1897	PIT	NL	2	0	2	0	0	2	0	0	0	0	0	0	1	0	1	1

Rank among batters: 4,129 • *Total ballparks homered in*: 1 • *First HR*: 09/14/1897 off Bill Hill

Jack Rothrock

JOHN HOUSTON ROTHROCK
B: 03/14/1905 D: 02/02/1980
BB

Year	Tm	Lg	Tot	H	A	0	1	2	3	2	3	4	LO	XN	IP	PH	RHP	LHP
1927	BOS	AL	1	0	1	0	1	0	0	0	0	0	0	0	1	0	1	0
1928	BOS	AL	3	1	2	2	0	0	1	0	0	0	0	0	0	0	2	1
1929	BOS	AL	6	2	4	3	2	0	1	0	0	0	0	0	0	0	5	1
1931	BOS	AL	4	2	2	3	1	0	0	0	0	0	1	0	0	0	3	1
1934	STL	NL	11	8	3	4	4	3	0	0	0	0	0	0	0	0	9	2
1935	STL	NL	3	0	3	2	1	0	0	0	0	0	0	0	0	0	2	1
Total			28	13	15	14	9	3	2	0	0	0	1	0	1	0	22	6

Rank among batters: 1,500 • *Top target (3 home runs)*: Carl Hubbell • *Number of pitchers victimized*: 23 • *Total ballparks homered in*: 8 • *First HR*: 08/31/1927 off George Pipgras

Edd Roush

EDD J. ROUSH
B: 05/08/1893 D: 03/21/1988
BL HOF

Year	Tm	Lg	Tot	H	A	0	1	2	3	2	3	4	LO	XN	IP	PH	RHP	LHP
1914	IND	FL	1	1	0	0	1	0	0	0	0	0	0	0	1	1	1	0

Year	Tm	Lg	Tot	H	A	Men-On 0	1	2	3	One-Game 2	3	4	LO	XN	IP	PH	RHP	LHP

Edd Roush *continued*

Year	Tm	Lg	Tot	H	A	Men-On 0	1	2	3	One-Game 2	3	4	LO	XN	IP	PH	RHP	LHP
1915	NWK	FL	3	2	1	2	1	0	0	0	0	0	0	1	3	0	2	1
1917	CIN	NL	4	2	2	3	0	1	0	0	0	0	0	1	3	0	2	2
1918	CIN	NL	5	4	1	1	1	2	1	0	0	0	0	1	5	0	4	1
1919	CIN	NL	4	2	2	1	3	0	0	0	0	0	0	0	4	0	4	0
1920	CIN	NL	4	3	1	1	2	1	0	0	0	0	0	0	3	0	3	1
1921	CIN	NL	4	0	4	3	0	1	0	0	0	0	0	0	0	0	4	0
1922	CIN	NL	1	0	1	1	0	0	0	0	0	0	0	0	1	0	1	0
1923	CIN	NL	6	1	5	2	2	2	0	0	0	0	0	1	1	0	5	1
1924	CIN	NL	3	1	2	1	0	2	0	0	0	0	0	0	1	0	2	1
1925	CIN	NL	8	2	6	3	4	1	0	0	0	0	0	2	1	0	5	3
1926	CIN	NL	7	1	6	3	3	1	0	0	0	0	0	0	2	0	5	2
1927	NY	NL	7	3	4	5	2	0	0	0	0	0	0	0	2	0	6	1
1928	NY	NL	2	1	1	1	1	0	0	0	0	0	0	0	0	0	2	0
1929	NY	NL	8	5	3	6	2	0	0	0	0	0	3	0	3	0	5	3
1931	CIN	NL	1	0	1	1	0	0	0	0	0	0	0	0	0	0	1	0
Total			68	28	40	34	22	11	1	0	0	0	3	6	30	1	52	16

Rank among batters: 767 • *Top target (3 home runs)*: Bill Sherdel, Jesse Haines • *Number of pitchers victimized*: 56 • *Total ballparks homered in*: 12 • *First HR*: 08/17/1914 off Elmer Knetzer

Wade Rowdon

WADE LEE ROWDON
B: 09/07/1960
BR

Year	Tm	Lg	Tot	H	A	Men-On 0	1	2	3	One-Game 2	3	4	LO	XN	IP	PH	RHP	LHP
1987	CHI	NL	1	0	1	0	1	0	0	0	0	0	0	0	0	0	0	1

Rank among batters: 4,707 • *Total ballparks homered in*: 1 • *First HR*: 09/17/1987 off Don Carman

Dave Rowe

DAVID ELWOOD ROWE
B: 10/09/1854 D: 12/09/1930
BR

Year	Tm	Lg	Tot	H	A	Men-On 0	1	2	3	One-Game 2	3	4	LO	XN	IP	PH	RHP	LHP
1882	CLE	NL	1	0	1	0	0	0	0	0	0	0	0	0	0	0	0	1
1884	STL	UA	4	1	3	3	1	0	0	0	0	0	0	0	0	0	3	0
1886	KC	NL	3	2	1	1	2	0	0	0	0	0	0	0	0	0	3	0
Total			8	3	5	4	3	0	0	0	0	0	0	0	0	0	6	1

Rank among batters: 2,703 • *Top target (2 home runs)*: George Bradley, Bill Stemmeyer • *Number of pitchers victimized*: 6 • *Total ballparks homered in*: 6 • *First HR*: 08/18/1882 off J Richmond

Jack Rowe

JOHN CHARLES ROWE
B: 12/08/1857 D: 04/26/1911
BL

Year	Tm	Lg	Tot	H	A	Men-On 0	1	2	3	One-Game 2	3	4	LO	XN	IP	PH	RHP	LHP
1880	BUF	NL	1	1	0	0	1	0	0	0	0	0	0	0	0	0	0	0
1881	BUF	NL	1	0	1	1	0	0	0	0	0	0	0	0	0	0	1	0
1882	BUF	NL	1	1	0	1	0	0	0	0	0	0	0	0	0	0	1	0
1883	BUF	NL	1	0	1	0	0	1	0	0	0	0	0	0	0	0	1	0
1884	BUF	NL	4	1	3	2	1	1	0	0	0	0	0	0	0	0	3	0
1885	BUF	NL	2	2	0	0	1	1	0	0	0	0	0	0	0	0	2	0
1886	DET	NL	6	4	2	3	1	2	0	1	0	0	0	0	0	0	6	0
1887	DET	NL	6	5	1	3	3	0	0	1	0	0	0	0	0	0	6	0
1888	DET	NL	2	0	2	0	0	2	0	0	0	0	0	0	0	0	2	0
1889	PIT	NL	2	0	2	2	0	0	0	0	0	0	0	0	0	0	2	0
1890	BUF	PL	2	1	1	0	1	1	0	0	0	0	0	0	0	0	1	1
Total			28	15	13	12	8	8	0	2	0	0	0	0	0	0	25	1

Rank among batters: 1,500 • *Top target (4 home runs)*: Charlie Sweeney, Charlie Buffinton • *Number of pitchers victimized*: 19 • *Total ballparks homered in*: 12 • *First HR*: 09/15/1880 off Franklin Gardner • *Hit for Cycle*—vs CHI: 08/21/1886

Schoolboy Rowe

LYNWOOD THOMAS ROWE
B: 01/11/1910 D: 01/08/1961
BR

Year	Tm	Lg	Tot	H	A	Men-On 0	1	2	3	One-Game 2	3	4	LO	XN	IP	PH	RHP	LHP
1934	DET	AL	2	0	2	0	2	0	0	0	0	0	0	1	0	0	2	0
1935	DET	AL	3	3	0	1	2	0	0	0	0	0	0	0	0	0	3	0
1936	DET	AL	1	1	0	0	1	0	0	0	0	0	0	0	0	0	0	1

Schoolboy Rowe *continued*

Year	Tm	Lg	Tot	H	A	Men-On 0	Men-On 1	Men-On 2	Men-On 3	One-Game 2	One-Game 3	One-Game 4	LO	XN	IP	PH	RHP	LHP
1939	DET	AL	1	1	0	0	0	0	1	0	0	0	0	0	0	0	1	0
1940	DET	AL	1	1	0	0	1	0	0	0	0	0	0	0	0	0	1	0
1941	DET	AL	1	0	1	1	0	0	0	0	0	0	0	0	0	0	0	1
1943	PHI	NL	4	2	2	2	0	1	1	0	0	0	0	0	0	2	4	0
1946	PHI	NL	1	1	0	1	0	0	0	0	0	0	0	0	0	0	1	0
1947	PHI	NL	2	2	0	2	0	0	0	0	0	0	0	0	0	0	1	1
1948	PHI	NL	1	1	0	1	0	0	0	0	0	0	0	0	0	0	1	0
1949	PHI	NL	1	1	0	1	0	0	0	0	0	0	0	0	0	0	1	0
Total			18	13	5	9	6	1	2	0	0	0	0	1	0	2	15	3

Rank among batters: 1,914 • *Top target (2 home runs)*: Nels Potter • *Number of pitchers victimized*: 17 • *Total ballparks homered in*: 7 • *First HR*: 05/07/1934 off Johnny Welch

Bama Rowell

CARVEL WILLIAM ROWELL
B: 01/13/1916 D: 08/16/1993
BL

Year	Tm	Lg	Tot	H	A	Men-On 0	Men-On 1	Men-On 2	Men-On 3	One-Game 2	One-Game 3	One-Game 4	LO	XN	IP	PH	RHP	LHP
1940	BOS	NL	3	2	1	1	1	1	0	0	0	0	0	0	0	0	3	0
1941	BOS	NL	7	3	4	4	2	1	0	0	0	0	0	0	1	0	5	2
1946	BOS	NL	3	0	3	1	2	0	0	0	0	0	0	0	0	1	3	0
1947	BOS	NL	5	3	2	3	0	2	0	0	0	0	0	0	0	0	5	0
1948	PHI	NL	1	0	1	1	0	0	0	0	0	0	0	0	0	0	1	0
Total			19	8	11	10	5	4	0	0	0	0	0	0	1	1	17	2

Rank among batters: 1,861 • *Top target (2 home runs)*: Kirby Higbe, Hank Wyse • *Number of pitchers victimized*: 17 • *Total ballparks homered in*: 7 • *First HR*: 05/20/1940 off Johnny Hutchings

Ed Rowen

W. EDWARD ROWEN
B: 10/22/1857 D: 02/22/1892

Year	Tm	Lg	Tot	H	A	Men-On 0	Men-On 1	Men-On 2	Men-On 3	One-Game 2	One-Game 3	One-Game 4	LO	XN	IP	PH	RHP	LHP
1882	BOS	NL	1	0	1	1	0	0	0	0	0	0	0	0	0	0	1	0

Rank among batters: 4,707 • *Total ballparks homered in*: 1 • *First HR*: 06/21/1882 off George Bradley

Rich Rowland

RICHARD GARNET ROWLAND
B: 02/25/1964
BR

Year	Tm	Lg	Tot	H	A	Men-On 0	Men-On 1	Men-On 2	Men-On 3	One-Game 2	One-Game 3	One-Game 4	LO	XN	IP	PH	RHP	LHP
1994	BOS	AL	9	3	6	5	4	0	0	1	0	0	0	0	0	0	5	4

Rank among batters: 2,587 • *Total ballparks homered in*: 4 • *First HR*: 05/08/1994 off Terry Mulholland

Stan Royer

STANLEY DEAN ROYER
B: 08/31/1967
BR

Year	Tm	Lg	Tot	H	A	Men-On 0	Men-On 1	Men-On 2	Men-On 3	One-Game 2	One-Game 3	One-Game 4	LO	XN	IP	PH	RHP	LHP
1992	STL	NL	2	1	1	0	2	0	0	0	0	0	0	0	0	0	2	0
1993	STL	NL	1	0	1	1	0	0	0	0	0	0	0	0	0	0	1	0
1994	STL	NL	1	0	1	1	0	0	0	0	0	0	0	0	0	0	0	1
Total			4	1	3	2	2	0	0	0	0	0	0	0	0	0	3	1

Rank among batters: 3,427 • *Total ballparks homered in*: 3 • *First HR*: 09/20/1992 off Jeff Hartsock

Jerry Royster

JERON KENNIS ROYSTER
B: 10/18/1952
BR

Year	Tm	Lg	Tot	H	A	Men-On 0	Men-On 1	Men-On 2	Men-On 3	One-Game 2	One-Game 3	One-Game 4	LO	XN	IP	PH	RHP	LHP
1976	ATL	NL	5	2	3	3	1	1	0	0	0	0	0	0	0	0	4	1
1977	ATL	NL	6	5	1	4	1	1	0	0	0	0	0	0	0	0	4	2
1978	ATL	NL	2	2	0	1	1	0	0	0	0	0	0	0	0	0	1	1
1979	ATL	NL	3	2	1	1	1	1	0	0	0	0	0	0	0	0	2	1
1980	ATL	NL	1	0	1	1	0	0	0	0	0	0	0	0	0	0	1	0
1982	ATL	NL	2	1	1	2	0	0	0	0	0	0	1	0	0	0	1	1
1983	ATL	NL	3	2	1	3	0	0	0	0	0	0	0	0	0	0	2	1
1984	ATL	NL	1	0	1	1	0	0	0	0	0	0	0	0	0	0	0	1
1985	SD	NL	5	4	1	4	0	0	1	0	0	0	1	0	0	0	2	3
1986	SD	NL	5	2	3	3	2	0	0	0	0	0	0	0	0	0	2	3

Jerry Royster *continued*

Year	Tm	Lg	Tot	H	A	Men-On 0	1	2	3	One-Game 2	3	4	LO	XN	IP	PH	RHP	LHP
1987	CHI	AL	7	3	4	6	1	0	0	0	0	0	2	0	0	0	2	5
Total			40	23	17	29	7	3	1	0	0	0	4	0	0	0	21	19

Rank among batters: 1,181 • *Top target (2 home runs)*: Tom Seaver, Bob Knepper, Tommy John • *Number of pitchers victimized*: 37 • *Total ballparks homered in*: 12 • *First HR*: 05/30/1976 off Mike Cosgrove

Vic Roznovsky

VICTOR JOSEPH ROZNOVSKY
B: 10/19/1938
BL

Year	Tm	Lg	Tot	H	A	Men-On 0	1	2	3	One-Game 2	3	4	LO	XN	IP	PH	RHP	LHP
1965	CHI	NL	3	2	1	1	1	1	0	0	0	0	0	0	0	0	3	0
1966	BAL	AL	1	1	0	1	0	0	0	0	0	0	0	0	0	1	1	0
Total			4	3	1	2	1	1	0	0	0	0	0	0	0	1	4	0

Rank among batters: 3,427 • *Total ballparks homered in*: 3 • *First HR*: 05/09/1965 off Ken Johnson

Al Rubeling

ALBERT WILLIAM RUBELING
B: 05/10/1913 D: 01/28/1988
BR

Year	Tm	Lg	Tot	H	A	Men-On 0	1	2	3	One-Game 2	3	4	LO	XN	IP	PH	RHP	LHP
1940	PHI	AL	4	4	0	4	0	0	0	0	0	0	1	0	0	0	2	2
1944	PIT	NL	4	1	3	2	1	1	0	0	0	0	0	1	0	3	4	0
Total			8	5	3	6	1	1	0	0	0	0	1	1	0	3	6	2

Rank among batters: 2,703 • *Total ballparks homered in*: 5 • *First HR*: 04/27/1940 off Jim Bagby

Johnny Rucker

JOHN JOEL RUCKER
B: 01/15/1917 D: 08/07/1985
BL

Year	Tm	Lg	Tot	H	A	Men-On 0	1	2	3	One-Game 2	3	4	LO	XN	IP	PH	RHP	LHP
1940	NY	NL	4	4	0	1	1	1	1	1	0	0	0	0	1	0	4	0
1941	NY	NL	1	1	0	0	1	0	0	0	0	0	0	0	0	0	0	1
1943	NY	NL	2	1	1	1	1	0	0	0	0	0	0	1	0	0	2	0
1944	NY	NL	6	6	0	4	2	0	0	1	0	0	1	0	1	0	5	1
1945	NY	NL	7	5	2	5	2	0	0	0	0	0	1	0	2	0	7	0
1946	NY	NL	1	1	0	0	1	0	0	0	0	0	0	0	0	0	1	0
Total			21	18	3	11	8	1	1	2	0	0	2	1	4	0	19	2

Rank among batters: 1,768 • *Total ballparks homered in*: 4 • *First HR*: 09/26/1940 off Kirby Higbe

Nap Rucker

GEORGE RUCKER
B: 09/30/1884 D: 12/19/1970
BR

Year	Tm	Lg	Tot	H	A	Men-On 0	1	2	3	One-Game 2	3	4	LO	XN	IP	PH	RHP	LHP
1911	BRO	NL	1	0	1	1	0	0	0	0	0	0	0	1	0	0	1	0

Rank among batters: 4,707 • *Total ballparks homered in*: 1 • *First HR*: 07/01/1911 off George Chalmers

Joe Rudi

JOSEPH ODEN RUDI
B: 09/07/1946
BR

Year	Tm	Lg	Tot	H	A	Men-On 0	1	2	3	One-Game 2	3	4	LO	XN	IP	PH	RHP	LHP
1968	OAK	AL	1	1	0	1	0	0	0	0	0	0	0	0	0	0	0	1
1969	OAK	AL	2	2	0	1	1	0	0	1	0	0	0	0	0	0	2	0
1970	OAK	AL	11	5	6	7	3	1	0	0	0	0	0	0	0	1	3	8
1971	OAK	AL	10	5	5	7	3	0	0	1	0	0	0	0	0	0	6	4
1972	OAK	AL	19	7	12	9	7	3	0	0	0	0	0	2	0	0	13	6
1973	OAK	AL	12	6	6	4	5	2	1	0	0	0	0	0	0	0	8	4
1974	OAK	AL	22	11	11	12	5	3	2	0	0	0	0	0	0	0	12	10
1975	OAK	AL	21	12	9	15	4	0	2	2	0	0	0	1	0	0	15	6
1976	OAK	AL	13	4	9	6	6	1	0	0	0	0	0	0	0	0	9	4
1977	CAL	AL	13	6	7	5	4	3	1	2	0	0	0	0	0	0	10	3
1978	CAL	AL	17	7	10	12	1	1	3	0	0	0	0	1	0	1	13	4
1979	CAL	AL	11	5	6	4	1	3	3	0	0	0	0	0	0	0	10	1
1980	CAL	AL	16	11	5	11	4	1	0	2	0	0	0	0	0	0	11	5
1981	BOS	AL	6	4	2	2	3	1	0	1	0	0	0	1	0	1	5	1

Joe Rudi *continued*

Year	Tm	Lg	Tot	H	A	Men-On 0	1	2	3	One-Game 2	3	4	LO	XN	IP	PH	RHP	LHP
1982	OAK	AL	5	2	3	2	2	1	0	0	0	0	0	0	0	0	1	4
Total			179	88	91	98	49	20	12	9	0	0	0	5	0	3	118	61

Rank among batters: 221 • *Top target (5 home runs)*: Mickey Lolich • *Number of pitchers victimized*: 123 • *Total ballparks homered in*: 16 • *First HR*: 07/15/1968 off Dick Ellsworth • *World Series HR—2; LCS HR—1*

Dick Rudolph

RICHARD RUDOLPH
B: 08/25/1887 D: 10/20/1949
BR

Year	Tm	Lg	Tot	H	A	Men-On 0	1	2	3	One-Game 2	3	4	LO	XN	IP	PH	RHP	LHP
1915	BOS	NL	1	0	1	0	0	1	0	0	0	0	0	0	0	0	1	0
1919	BOS	NL	1	1	0	1	0	0	0	0	0	0	0	0	1	0	1	0
Total			2	1	1	1	0	1	0	0	0	0	0	0	1	0	2	0

Rank among batters: 4,129 • *Total ballparks homered in*: 2 • *First HR*: 09/14/1915 off Jimmy Lavender

Don Rudolph

FREDERICK DONALD RUDOLPH
B: 08/16/1931 D: 09/12/1968
BL

Year	Tm	Lg	Tot	H	A	Men-On 0	1	2	3	One-Game 2	3	4	LO	XN	IP	PH	RHP	LHP
1963	WAS	AL	1	0	1	1	0	0	0	0	0	0	0	0	0	0	0	1

Rank among batters: 4,707 • *Total ballparks homered in*: 1 • *First HR*: 09/02/1963 off Jack Kralick

Ken Rudolph

KENNETH VICTOR RUDOLPH
B: 12/29/1946
BR

Year	Tm	Lg	Tot	H	A	Men-On 0	1	2	3	One-Game 2	3	4	LO	XN	IP	PH	RHP	LHP
1969	CHI	NL	1	1	0	0	1	0	0	0	0	0	0	0	0	0	1	0
1972	CHI	NL	2	0	2	1	1	0	0	0	0	0	0	0	0	0	2	0
1973	CHI	NL	2	2	0	2	0	0	0	0	0	0	0	0	0	0	1	1
1975	STL	NL	1	1	0	0	1	0	0	0	0	0	0	0	0	0	0	1
Total			6	4	2	3	3	0	0	0	0	0	0	0	0	0	4	2

Rank among batters: 2,988 • *Total ballparks homered in*: 3 • *First HR*: 06/26/1969 off Dock Ellis

Muddy Ruel

HEROLD DOMINIC RUEL
B: 02/20/1896 D: 11/13/1963
BR

Year	Tm	Lg	Tot	H	A	Men-On 0	1	2	3	One-Game 2	3	4	LO	XN	IP	PH	RHP	LHP
1920	NY	AL	1	1	0	0	1	0	0	0	0	0	0	0	1	0	1	0
1921	BOS	AL	1	0	1	1	0	0	0	0	0	0	0	0	0	0	1	0
1926	WAS	AL	1	0	1	0	1	0	0	0	0	0	0	0	1	0	1	0
1927	WAS	AL	1	0	1	1	0	0	0	0	0	0	0	0	0	0	1	0
Total			4	1	3	2	2	0	0	0	0	0	0	0	2	0	4	0

Rank among batters: 3,427 • *Total ballparks homered in*: 4 • *First HR*: 06/02/1920 off Jim Shaw

Dutch Ruether

WALTER HENRY RUETHER
B: 09/13/1893 D: 05/16/1970
BL

Year	Tm	Lg	Tot	H	A	Men-On 0	1	2	3	One-Game 2	3	4	LO	XN	IP	PH	RHP	LHP
1921	BRO	NL	2	0	2	2	0	0	0	0	0	0	0	0	0	0	2	0
1922	BRO	NL	2	0	2	2	0	0	0	0	0	0	0	0	0	0	2	0
1925	WAS	AL	1	0	1	0	1	0	0	0	0	0	0	0	0	0	1	0
1926	WAS	AL	1	0	1	1	0	0	0	0	0	0	0	0	0	0	1	0
1927	NY	AL	1	1	0	0	1	0	0	0	0	0	0	0	0	0	1	0
Total			7	1	6	5	2	0	0	0	0	0	0	0	0	0	7	0

Rank among batters: 2,834 • *Total ballparks homered in*: 5 • *First HR*: 07/31/1921 off Bill Pertica

Red Ruffing

CHARLES HERBERT RUFFING
B: 05/03/1904 D: 02/17/1986
BR HOF

Year	Tm	Lg	Tot	H	A	Men-On 0	1	2	3	One-Game 2	3	4	LO	XN	IP	PH	RHP	LHP
1926	BOS	AL	1	0	1	0	0	1	0	0	0	0	0	0	0	0	1	0

Red Ruffing *continued*

Year	Tm	Lg	Tot	H	A	Men-On 0	Men-On 1	Men-On 2	Men-On 3	One-Game 2	One-Game 3	One-Game 4	LO	XN	IP	PH	RHP	LHP
1928	BOS	AL	2	0	2	0	1	1	0	0	0	0	0	0	0	0	2	0
1929	BOS	AL	2	1	1	1	1	0	0	0	0	0	0	0	0	1	1	1
1930	NY	AL	4	1	3	2	2	0	0	1	0	0	0	0	0	0	0	4
1931	NY	AL	3	1	2	1	2	0	0	0	0	0	0	0	0	0	2	1
1932	NY	AL	3	1	2	2	1	0	0	0	0	0	0	1	0	0	2	1
1933	NY	AL	2	2	0	0	1	0	1	0	0	0	0	0	0	0	1	1
1934	NY	AL	2	0	2	0	1	1	0	0	0	0	0	0	0	0	2	0
1935	NY	AL	2	1	1	1	1	0	0	0	0	0	0	0	0	0	1	1
1936	NY	AL	5	2	3	4	1	0	0	1	0	0	0	0	0	0	5	0
1937	NY	AL	1	0	1	0	1	0	0	0	0	0	0	0	0	1	1	0
1938	NY	AL	3	1	2	0	2	1	0	0	0	0	0	0	0	0	3	0
1939	NY	AL	1	1	0	1	0	0	0	0	0	0	0	0	0	0	0	1
1940	NY	AL	1	0	1	0	0	1	0	0	0	0	0	0	0	0	0	1
1941	NY	AL	2	1	1	1	1	0	0	0	0	0	0	0	0	0	0	2
1942	NY	AL	1	1	0	0	0	1	0	0	0	0	0	0	0	0	0	1
1945	NY	AL	1	1	0	0	0	1	0	0	0	0	0	0	0	0	1	0
Total			36	14	22	13	15	7	1	2	0	0	0	1	0	2	22	14

Rank among batters: 1,274 • *Top target (2 home runs)*: Fred Stiely, George Blaeholder, Tommy Thomas • *Number of pitchers victimized*: 33 • *Total ballparks homered in*: 8 • *First HR*: 06/14/1926 off Hooks Dauss

Chico Ruiz

HIRALDO (SABLON) RUIZ
B: 12/05/1938 D: 02/09/1972
BB

Year	Tm	Lg	Tot	H	A	Men-On 0	Men-On 1	Men-On 2	Men-On 3	One-Game 2	One-Game 3	One-Game 4	LO	XN	IP	PH	RHP	LHP
1964	CIN	NL	2	0	2	1	1	0	0	0	0	0	0	0	1	0	1	1

Rank among batters: 4,129 • *Total ballparks homered in*: 2 • *First HR*: 04/21/1964 off Larry Yellen

William Rumler

WILLIAM GEORGE RUMLER
B: 03/27/1891 D: 05/26/1966
BR

Year	Tm	Lg	Tot	H	A	Men-On 0	Men-On 1	Men-On 2	Men-On 3	One-Game 2	One-Game 3	One-Game 4	LO	XN	IP	PH	RHP	LHP
1917	STL	AL	1	0	1	0	1	0	0	0	0	0	0	0	0	1	0	1

Rank among batters: 4,707 • *Total ballparks homered in*: 1 • *First HR*: 09/21/1917 off George Mogridge

Paul Runge

PAUL WILLIAM RUNGE
B: 05/21/1958
BR

Year	Tm	Lg	Tot	H	A	Men-On 0	Men-On 1	Men-On 2	Men-On 3	One-Game 2	One-Game 3	One-Game 4	LO	XN	IP	PH	RHP	LHP
1985	ATL	NL	1	0	1	1	0	0	0	0	0	0	0	0	1	0	0	1
1987	ATL	NL	3	1	2	2	1	0	0	0	0	0	0	0	0	0	1	2
Total			4	1	3	3	1	0	0	0	0	0	0	0	1	0	1	3

Rank among batters: 3,427 • *Total ballparks homered in*: 4 • *First HR*: 07/28/1985 off Jerry Koosman

Pete Runnels

JAMES EDWARD RUNNELS
B: 01/28/1928 D: 05/20/1991
BL

Year	Tm	Lg	Tot	H	A	Men-On 0	Men-On 1	Men-On 2	Men-On 3	One-Game 2	One-Game 3	One-Game 4	LO	XN	IP	PH	RHP	LHP
1952	WAS	AL	1	0	1	1	0	0	0	0	0	0	0	0	0	0	1	0
1953	WAS	AL	2	0	2	1	1	0	0	0	0	0	0	0	0	0	2	0
1954	WAS	AL	3	2	1	2	0	1	0	0	0	0	0	0	0	0	3	0
1955	WAS	AL	2	0	2	1	1	0	0	0	0	0	0	0	0	0	2	0
1956	WAS	AL	8	2	6	3	4	1	0	0	0	0	0	0	0	0	6	2
1957	WAS	AL	2	0	2	0	2	0	0	0	0	0	0	0	0	0	2	0
1958	BOS	AL	8	1	7	3	5	0	0	0	0	0	0	0	0	0	8	0
1959	BOS	AL	6	2	4	3	3	0	0	0	0	0	0	1	0	0	2	4
1960	BOS	AL	2	1	1	2	0	0	0	0	0	0	0	0	0	0	2	0
1961	BOS	AL	3	1	2	0	2	1	0	0	0	0	0	0	0	0	2	1
1962	BOS	AL	10	3	7	8	1	1	0	1	0	0	0	0	0	0	9	1
1963	HOU	NL	2	0	2	0	2	0	0	0	0	0	0	0	0	0	2	0
Total			49	12	37	24	21	4	0	1	0	0	0	1	0	0	41	8

Rank among batters: 1,008 • Top target (2 home runs): Steve Gromek, Bob Lemon, Duke Maas, Herb Score, Jim Bunning, Jim Perry, Early Wynn, Joe McClain • *Number of pitchers victimized*: 41 • *Total ballparks homered in*: 12 • *First HR*: 06/19/1952 off Early Wynn • *All-Star HR*—1

Bob Rush

ROBERT RANSOM RUSH
B: 12/21/1925
BR

Year	Tm	Lg	Tot	H	A	Men-On 0	Men-On 1	Men-On 2	Men-On 3	One-Game 2	One-Game 3	One-Game 4	LO	XN	IP	PH	RHP	LHP
1950	CHI	NL	1	0	1	0	1	0	0	0	0	0	0	0	0	0	1	0
1954	CHI	NL	2	1	1	2	0	0	0	0	0	0	0	0	0	0	2	0
1955	CHI	NL	1	0	1	0	1	0	0	0	0	0	0	0	0	0	1	0
Total			4	1	3	2	2	0	0	0	0	0	0	0	0	0	4	0

Rank among batters: 3,427 • *Total ballparks homered in*: 4 • *First HR*: 08/12/1950 off Bill Macdonald

Amos Rusie

AMOS WILSON RUSIE
B: 05/30/1871 D: 12/06/1942
BR HOF

Year	Tm	Lg	Tot	H	A	Men-On 0	Men-On 1	Men-On 2	Men-On 3	One-Game 2	One-Game 3	One-Game 4	LO	XN	IP	PH	RHP	LHP
1892	NY	NL	1	1	0	1	0	0	0	0	0	0	0	0	0	0	0	1
1893	NY	NL	3	3	0	1	1	1	0	0	0	0	0	0	0	0	3	0
1894	NY	NL	3	2	1	2	0	1	0	0	0	0	0	0	0	0	2	1
1895	NY	NL	1	1	0	0	1	0	0	0	0	0	0	0	0	0	1	0
Total			8	7	1	4	2	2	0	0	0	0	0	0	0	0	6	2

Rank among batters: 2,703 • *Total ballparks homered in*: 2 • *First HR*: 10/04/1892 off Frank Killen

Bill Russell

WILLIAM ELLIS RUSSELL
B: 10/21/1948
BR

Year	Tm	Lg	Tot	H	A	Men-On 0	Men-On 1	Men-On 2	Men-On 3	One-Game 2	One-Game 3	One-Game 4	LO	XN	IP	PH	RHP	LHP
1969	LA	NL	5	1	4	5	0	0	0	0	0	0	0	0	0	0	1	4
1971	LA	NL	2	1	1	2	0	0	0	0	0	0	1	0	0	0	0	2
1972	LA	NL	4	3	1	3	0	1	0	0	0	0	0	0	0	0	3	1
1973	LA	NL	4	2	2	4	0	0	0	0	0	0	0	0	0	0	2	2
1974	LA	NL	5	3	2	3	1	1	0	0	0	0	0	0	0	0	3	2
1976	LA	NL	5	1	4	5	0	0	0	0	0	0	0	0	0	0	4	1
1977	LA	NL	4	2	2	2	1	1	0	0	0	0	0	0	0	0	3	1
1978	LA	NL	3	0	3	3	0	0	0	0	0	0	0	0	0	0	3	0
1979	LA	NL	7	4	3	3	4	0	0	0	0	0	0	1	0	0	4	3
1980	LA	NL	3	2	1	1	1	1	0	0	0	0	0	0	0	0	1	2
1982	LA	NL	3	2	1	1	2	0	0	0	0	0	0	0	0	0	3	0
1983	LA	NL	1	0	1	0	1	0	0	0	0	0	0	0	0	0	1	0
Total			46	21	25	32	10	4	0	0	0	0	1	1	0	0	28	18

Rank among batters: 1,060 • *Top target (3 home runs)*: Ken Reynolds • *Number of pitchers victimized*: 38 • *Total ballparks homered in*: 13 • *First HR*: 04/11/1969 off Jim Ray

Jack Russell

JACK ERWIN RUSSELL
B: 10/24/1905 D: 11/03/1990
BR

Year	Tm	Lg	Tot	H	A	Men-On 0	Men-On 1	Men-On 2	Men-On 3	One-Game 2	One-Game 3	One-Game 4	LO	XN	IP	PH	RHP	LHP
1930	BOS	AL	1	0	1	1	0	0	0	0	0	0	0	0	0	0	0	1

Rank among batters: 4,707 • *Total ballparks homered in*: 1 • *First HR*: 08/03/1930 off Bobby Burke

Jeff Russell

JEFFREY LEE RUSSELL
B: 09/02/1961
BR

Year	Tm	Lg	Tot	H	A	Men-On 0	Men-On 1	Men-On 2	Men-On 3	One-Game 2	One-Game 3	One-Game 4	LO	XN	IP	PH	RHP	LHP
1983	CIN	NL	1	0	1	0	1	0	0	0	0	0	0	0	0	0	1	0

Rank among batters: 4,707 • *Total ballparks homered in*: 1 • *First HR*: 08/23/1983 off Ferguson Jenkins

Jim Russell

JAMES WILLIAM RUSSELL
B: 10/01/1918 D: 11/24/1987
BB

Year	Tm	Lg	Tot	H	A	Men-On 0	Men-On 1	Men-On 2	Men-On 3	One-Game 2	One-Game 3	One-Game 4	LO	XN	IP	PH	RHP	LHP
1943	PIT	NL	4	0	4	1	2	1	0	1	0	0	0	0	1	0	3	1
1944	PIT	NL	8	4	4	5	1	1	1	1	0	0	0	0	0	1	7	1
1945	PIT	NL	12	4	8	7	4	1	0	0	0	0	0	1	0	0	11	1
1946	PIT	NL	8	6	2	4	4	0	0	0	0	0	0	0	0	0	7	1
1947	PIT	NL	8	4	4	4	4	0	0	0	0	0	0	0	0	0	7	1
1948	BOS	NL	9	2	7	2	4	2	1	1	0	0	0	0	0	0	4	5

Jim Russell *continued*

Year	Tm	Lg	Tot	H	A	Men-On 0	1	2	3	One-Game 2	3	4	LO	XN	IP	PH	RHP	LHP
1949	BOS	NL	8	3	5	5	2	0	1	0	0	0	0	0	0	0	2	6
1950	BRO	NL	10	7	3	5	5	0	0	1	0	0	0	1	0	0	3	7
Total			67	30	37	33	26	5	3	4	0	0	0	2	1	1	44	23

Rank among batters: 777 • Top target (2 home runs): Bill Voiselle, Rube Fischer, Ted Wilks, Art Herring, Ed Wright, Bucky Walters, Murry Dickson, Fritz Ostermueller, Ken Heintzelman, Woody Main, Harry Brecheen, Bill Werle • *Number of pitchers victimized*: 55 • *Total ballparks homered in*: 8 • *First HR*: 08/16/1943 off Al Javery • *Switch hit HR in 1 game*—2 times

John Russell

JOHN WILLIAM RUSSELL
B: 01/05/1961
BR

Year	Tm	Lg	Tot	H	A	Men-On 0	1	2	3	One-Game 2	3	4	LO	XN	IP	PH	RHP	LHP
1984	PHI	NL	2	1	1	2	0	0	0	0	0	0	0	0	0	1	2	0
1985	PHI	NL	9	6	3	4	2	2	1	0	0	0	0	0	0	1	5	4
1986	PHI	NL	13	8	5	6	6	1	0	0	0	0	0	2	0	0	9	4
1987	PHI	NL	3	1	2	3	0	0	0	0	0	0	0	0	0	1	2	1
1988	PHI	NL	2	1	1	2	0	0	0	0	0	0	0	0	0	0	1	1
1989	ATL	NL	2	1	1	1	1	0	0	0	0	0	0	0	0	0	1	1
1990	TEX	AL	2	0	2	2	0	0	0	0	0	0	0	0	0	0	1	1
1993	TEX	AL	1	1	0	1	0	0	0	0	0	0	0	0	0	0	1	0
Total			34	19	15	21	9	3	1	0	0	0	0	2	0	3	22	12

Rank among batters: 1,315 • Top target (2 home runs): Mark Thurmond, Jerry Reuss, Tom Browning, Scott Sanderson • *Number of pitchers victimized*: 30 • *Total ballparks homered in*: 13 • *First HR*: 06/25/1984 off Ron Darling

Reb Russell

EWELL ALBERT RUSSELL
B: 04/12/1889 D: 09/30/1973
BL

Year	Tm	Lg	Tot	H	A	Men-On 0	1	2	3	One-Game 2	3	4	LO	XN	IP	PH	RHP	LHP
1913	CHI	AL	1	0	1	1	0	0	0	0	0	0	0	0	0	0	1	0
1922	PIT	NL	12	6	6	6	4	2	0	2	0	0	0	0	3	0	12	0
1923	PIT	NL	9	4	5	4	4	1	0	0	0	0	0	0	1	0	9	0
Total			22	10	12	11	8	3	0	2	0	0	0	0	4	0	22	0

Rank among batters: 1,719 • *Top target (3 home runs)*: Joe Genewich • *Number of pitchers victimized*: 17 • *Total ballparks homered in*: 7 • *First HR*: 06/16/1913 off Bob Groom

Rip Russell

GLEN DAVID RUSSELL
B: 01/26/1915 D: 09/26/1976
BR

Year	Tm	Lg	Tot	H	A	Men-On 0	1	2	3	One-Game 2	3	4	LO	XN	IP	PH	RHP	LHP
1939	CHI	NL	9	5	4	7	2	0	0	0	0	0	0	0	0	0	8	1
1940	CHI	NL	5	2	3	2	2	0	1	0	0	0	0	1	0	0	3	2
1942	CHI	NL	8	5	3	6	1	0	1	0	0	0	0	0	0	0	5	3
1946	BOS	AL	6	3	3	4	1	1	0	0	0	0	0	0	0	0	6	0
1947	BOS	AL	1	0	1	0	0	1	0	0	0	0	0	0	0	0	1	0
Total			29	15	14	19	6	2	2	0	0	0	0	1	0	0	23	6

Rank among batters: 1,465 • Top target (2 home runs): Tot Pressnell, Johnny Podgajny, Phil Marchildon • *Number of pitchers victimized*: 26 • *Total ballparks homered in*: 8 • *First HR*: 06/03/1939 off Tot Pressnell

Hank Ruszkowski

HENRY ALEXANDER RUSZKOWSKI
B: 11/10/1925
BR

Year	Tm	Lg	Tot	H	A	Men-On 0	1	2	3	One-Game 2	3	4	LO	XN	IP	PH	RHP	LHP
1947	CLE	AL	3	1	2	3	0	0	0	1	0	0	0	0	0	1	2	1

Rank among batters: 3,735 • *Total ballparks homered in*: 2 • *First HR*: 08/06/1947 off Fred Hutchinson

Babe Ruth

GEORGE HERMAN RUTH
B: 02/06/1895 D: 08/16/1948
BL HOF

Year	Tm	Lg	Tot	H	A	Men-On 0	1	2	3	One-Game 2	3	4	LO	XN	IP	PH	RHP	LHP
1915	BOS	AL	4	1	3	2	1	1	0	0	0	0	0	0	0	0	4	0
1916	BOS	AL	3	0	3	2	0	1	0	0	0	0	0	0	0	1	3	0
1917	BOS	AL	2	1	1	1	1	0	0	0	0	0	0	0	0	0	2	0
1918	BOS	AL	11	0	11	3	7	1	0	0	0	0	0	1	0	0	9	2

Year	Tm	Lg	Tot	H	A	Men-On				One-Game			LO	XN	IP	PH	RHP	LHP
						0	1	2	3	2	3	4						

Babe Ruth *continued*

Year	Tm	Lg	Tot	H	A	0	1	2	3	2	3	4	LO	XN	IP	PH	RHP	LHP
1919	BOS	AL	29	9	20	10	13	2	4	3	0	0	0	1	1	0	20	9
1920	NY	AL	54	29	25	32	18	4	0	7	0	0	0	1	0	0	38	16
1921	NY	AL	59	32	27	22	26	11	0	5	0	0	0	1	0	0	46	13
1922	NY	AL	35	14	21	19	11	4	1	4	0	0	0	1	0	0	20	15
1923	NY	AL	41	19	22	19	14	8	0	2	0	0	0	2	4	0	30	11
1924	NY	AL	46	24	22	24	12	10	0	4	0	0	0	2	2	0	34	12
1925	NY	AL	25	11	14	17	6	1	1	1	0	0	0	1	0	0	12	13
1926	NY	AL	47	23	24	20	20	6	1	5	0	0	0	1	1	0	27	20
1927	NY	AL	60	28	32	30	22	6	2	8	0	0	0	2	1	0	41	19
1928	NY	AL	54	29	25	32	15	7	0	7	0	0	0	0	0	0	38	16
1929	NY	AL	46	21	25	20	13	10	3	5	0	0	0	1	1	0	29	17
1930	NY	AL	49	26	23	28	14	6	1	5	1	0	0	0	0	0	37	12
1931	NY	AL	46	24	22	21	19	5	1	5	0	0	0	1	0	0	33	13
1932	NY	AL	41	19	22	19	16	5	1	4	0	0	0	1	0	0	26	15
1933	NY	AL	34	22	12	15	16	3	0	4	0	0	0	0	0	0	25	9
1934	NY	AL	22	13	9	9	5	7	1	1	0	0	0	0	0	0	16	6
1935	BOS	NL	6	2	4	3	3	0	0	0	1	0	0	0	0	0	5	1
Total			714	347	367	348	252	98	16	70	2	0	0	16	10	1	495	219

Rank among batters: 2 • *Top target (17 home runs)*: Rube Walberg • *Number of pitchers victimized*: 216 • *Total ballparks homered in*: 12 • *First HR*: 05/06/1915 off Jack Warhop • *World Series HR*—15; *All-Star HR*—1

Dick Ruthven

RICHARD DAVID RUTHVEN
B: 03/27/1951
BR

Year	Tm	Lg	Tot	H	A	0	1	2	3	2	3	4	LO	XN	IP	PH	RHP	LHP
1977	ATL	NL	1	1	0	1	0	0	0	0	0	0	0	0	0	0	1	0

Rank among batters: 4,707 • *Total ballparks homered in*: 1 • *First HR*: 08/16/1977 off Mark Lemongello

Mickey Rutner

MILTON RUTNER
B: 03/18/1920
BR

Year	Tm	Lg	Tot	H	A	0	1	2	3	2	3	4	LO	XN	IP	PH	RHP	LHP
1947	PHI	AL	1	1	0	1	0	0	0	0	0	0	0	0	0	0	1	0

Rank among batters: 4,707 • *Total ballparks homered in*: 1 • *First HR*: 09/13/1947 off Earl Caldwell

Mark Ryal

MARK DWAYNE RYAL
B: 08/28/1960
BL

Year	Tm	Lg	Tot	H	A	0	1	2	3	2	3	4	LO	XN	IP	PH	RHP	LHP
1986	CAL	AL	2	1	1	1	1	0	0	0	0	0	0	0	0	1	2	0
1987	CAL	AL	5	3	2	1	3	0	1	1	0	0	0	0	0	2	5	0
Total			7	4	3	2	4	0	1	1	0	0	0	0	0	3	7	0

Rank among batters: 2,834 • *Total ballparks homered in*: 3 • *First HR*: 09/02/1986 off Rich Bordi

Blondy Ryan

JOHN COLLINS RYAN
B: 01/04/1906 D: 11/28/1959
BR

Year	Tm	Lg	Tot	H	A	0	1	2	3	2	3	4	LO	XN	IP	PH	RHP	LHP
1930	CHI	AL	1	1	0	0	1	0	0	0	0	0	0	0	0	0	0	1
1933	NY	NL	3	2	1	2	0	1	0	0	0	0	0	0	0	0	3	0
1934	NY	NL	2	1	1	1	1	0	0	0	0	0	0	0	0	0	2	0
1935	PHI	NL	1	0	1	0	1	0	0	0	0	0	0	0	0	0	1	0
1937	NY	NL	1	0	1	1	0	0	0	0	0	0	0	0	0	0	1	0
Total			8	4	4	4	3	1	0	0	0	0	0	0	0	0	7	1

Rank among batters: 2,703 • *Total ballparks homered in*: 4 • *First HR*: 07/15/1930 off Herb Pennock

Buddy Ryan

JOHN BUDD RYAN
B: 10/06/1885 D: 07/09/1956
BL

Year	Tm	Lg	Tot	H	A	0	1	2	3	2	3	4	LO	XN	IP	PH	RHP	LHP
1912	CLE	AL	1	1	0	0	0	0	1	0	0	0	0	0	0	0	1	0

Rank among batters: 4,707 • *Total ballparks homered in*: 1 • *First HR*: 05/12/1912 off Jerry Akers

Year	Tm	Lg	Tot	H	A	Men-On 0	1	2	3	One-Game 2	3	4	LO	XN	IP	PH	RHP	LHP

Connie Ryan

CORNELIUS JOSEPH RYAN
B: 02/27/1920
BR

Year	Tm	Lg	Tot	H	A	0	1	2	3	2	3	4	LO	XN	IP	PH	RHP	LHP
1943	BOS	NL	1	0	1	0	0	1	0	0	0	0	0	0	0	0	1	0
1944	BOS	NL	4	4	0	3	1	0	0	0	0	0	0	0	0	0	2	2
1946	BOS	NL	1	0	1	1	0	0	0	0	0	0	1	0	0	0	0	1
1947	BOS	NL	5	1	4	1	3	0	1	0	0	0	0	0	0	0	3	2
1949	BOS	NL	6	2	4	5	1	0	0	0	0	0	0	0	0	0	2	4
1950	BOS	NL	3	0	3	2	1	0	0	0	0	0	0	0	0	0	2	1
	CIN	NL	3	0	3	3	0	0	0	0	0	0	0	0	0	0	1	2
	Total		6	0	6	5	1	0	0	0	0	0	0	0	0	0	3	3
1951	CIN	NL	16	6	10	8	5	2	1	1	0	0	0	1	0	1	5	11
1952	PHI	NL	12	3	9	10	1	0	1	0	0	0	0	1	0	0	6	6
1953	PHI	NL	5	3	2	4	1	0	0	0	0	0	2	0	0	1	4	1
Total			56	19	37	37	13	3	3	1	0	0	3	2	0	2	26	30

Rank among batters: 913 • *Top target (3 home runs)*: Preacher Roe, Al Brazle, Bob Rush • *Number of pitchers victimized*: 44 • *Total ballparks homered in*: 8 • *First HR*: 04/28/1943 off Johnnie Wittig

Jack Ryan

JOHN BERNARD RYAN
B: 11/12/1868 D: 08/21/1952
BR

Year	Tm	Lg	Tot	H	A	0	1	2	3	2	3	4	LO	XN	IP	PH	RHP	LHP
1891	LOU	AA	2	0	2	1	1	0	0	0	0	0	0	0	1	0	1	1
1894	BOS	NL	1	1	0	1	0	0	0	0	0	0	0	0	0	0	1	0
1903	STL	NL	1	1	0	1	0	0	0	0	0	0	0	0	0	0	0	1
Total			4	2	2	3	1	0	0	0	0	0	0	0	1	0	2	2

Rank among batters: 3,427 • *Total ballparks homered in*: 3 • *First HR*: 05/14/1891 off George Meakim

Jimmy Ryan

JAMES EDWARD RYAN
B: 02/11/1863 D: 10/26/1923
BR

Year	Tm	Lg	Tot	H	A	0	1	2	3	2	3	4	LO	XN	IP	PH	RHP	LHP
1886	CHI	NL	4	4	0	1	1	1	1	0	0	0	0	0	0	0	3	0
1887	CHI	NL	11	9	2	5	5	1	0	0	0	0	0	0	2	0	10	1
1888	CHI	NL	16	9	7	9	7	0	0	0	0	0	4	0	4	0	13	2
1889	CHI	NL	17	11	6	11	4	1	1	0	0	0	6	1	2	0	15	0
1890	CHI	PL	6	4	2	3	2	1	0	0	0	0	0	0	0	0	6	0
1891	CHI	NL	9	8	1	6	0	3	0	1	0	0	2	0	0	0	8	0
1892	CHI	NL	10	4	6	4	6	0	0	0	0	0	1	0	3	0	7	2
1893	CHI	NL	3	2	1	3	0	0	0	0	0	0	2	0	0	0	1	2
1894	CHI	NL	3	3	0	0	1	2	0	0	0	0	0	0	0	0	3	0
1895	CHI	NL	6	2	4	3	1	1	1	0	0	0	1	0	1	0	4	2
1896	CHI	NL	3	0	3	1	2	0	0	1	0	0	0	0	0	0	3	0
1897	CHI	NL	5	1	4	1	2	1	1	0	0	0	0	0	0	0	4	1
1898	CHI	NL	4	1	3	3	1	0	0	0	0	0	1	0	0	0	4	0
1899	CHI	NL	3	1	2	2	0	1	0	1	0	0	2	0	0	0	3	0
1900	CHI	NL	5	2	3	3	1	1	0	0	0	0	1	0	0	0	4	1
1902	WAS	AL	6	6	0	4	2	0	0	0	0	0	2	0	1	0	5	1
1903	WAS	AL	7	7	0	5	1	1	0	0	0	0	0	0	0	0	5	2
Total			118	74	44	64	36	14	4	3	0	0	22	1	13	0	98	13

Rank among batters: 396 • *Top target (7 home runs)*: Pretzels Getzien • *Number of pitchers victimized*: 73 • *Total ballparks homered in*: 24 • *First HR*: 07/20/1886 off Joe Murphy • *Hit for Cycle*—vs DET: 07/28/1888; vs CLE: 07/01/1891

Johnny Ryan

JOHN JOSEPH RYAN
B: 10/ /1853 D: 03/22/1902

Year	Tm	Lg	Tot	H	A	0	1	2	3	2	3	4	LO	XN	IP	PH	RHP	LHP
1876	LOU	NL	1	1	0	0	0	1	0	0	0	0	0	0	1	0	1	0

Rank among batters: 4,707 • *Total ballparks homered in*: 1 • *First HR*: 07/15/1876 off George Zettlein

Mike Ryan

MICHAEL JAMES RYAN
B: 11/25/1941
BR

Year	Tm	Lg	Tot	H	A	0	1	2	3	2	3	4	LO	XN	IP	PH	RHP	LHP
1965	BOS	AL	3	1	2	2	1	0	0	1	0	0	0	0	0	0	2	1
1966	BOS	AL	2	2	0	1	1	0	0	0	0	0	0	0	0	0	1	1

Mike Ryan *continued*

Year	Tm	Lg	Tot	H	A	Men-On 0	1	2	3	One-Game 2	3	4	LO	XN	IP	PH	RHP	LHP
1967	BOS	AL	2	1	1	1	0	1	0	0	0	0	0	0	0	0	2	0
1968	PHI	NL	1	1	0	1	0	0	0	0	0	0	0	0	0	0	0	1
1969	PHI	NL	12	8	4	8	3	0	1	0	0	0	0	0	0	0	10	2
1970	PHI	NL	2	1	1	1	1	0	0	0	0	0	0	0	0	0	2	0
1971	PHI	NL	3	2	1	3	0	0	0	0	0	0	0	0	0	0	0	3
1972	PHI	NL	2	1	1	1	1	0	0	0	0	0	0	1	0	0	1	1
1973	PHI	NL	1	1	0	1	0	0	0	0	0	0	0	0	0	0	1	0
Total			28	18	10	19	7	1	1	1	0	0	0	1	0	0	19	9

Rank among batters: 1,500 • *Top target (2 home runs)*: Jim Merritt • *Number of pitchers victimized*: 27 • *Total ballparks homered in*: 10 • *First HR*: 05/02/1965 off Julio Navarro

Nolan Ryan

LYNN NOLAN RYAN
B: 01/31/1947
BR

Year	Tm	Lg	Tot	H	A	Men-On 0	1	2	3	One-Game 2	3	4	LO	XN	IP	PH	RHP	LHP
1980	HOU	NL	1	1	0	0	0	1	0	0	0	0	0	0	0	0	1	0
1987	HOU	NL	1	0	1	0	0	1	0	0	0	0	0	0	0	0	1	0
Total			2	1	1	0	0	2	0	0	0	0	0	0	0	0	2	0

Rank among batters: 4,129 • *Total ballparks homered in*: 2 • *First HR*: 04/12/1980 off Don Sutton

Rosy Ryan

WILFRED PATRICK DOLAN RYAN
B: 03/15/1898 D: 12/10/1980
BL

Year	Tm	Lg	Tot	H	A	Men-On 0	1	2	3	One-Game 2	3	4	LO	XN	IP	PH	RHP	LHP
1925	BOS	NL	1	1	0	1	0	0	0	0	0	0	0	0	1	0	1	0

Rank among batters: 4,707 • *Total ballparks homered in*: 1 • *First HR*: 05/29/1925 off Rube Ehrhardt • *World Series HR*—1

Chris Sabo

CHRISTOPHER ANDREW SABO
B: 01/19/1962
BR

Year	Tm	Lg	Tot	H	A	Men-On 0	1	2	3	One-Game 2	3	4	LO	XN	IP	PH	RHP	LHP
1988	CIN	NL	11	8	3	9	0	2	0	0	0	0	0	1	0	0	7	4
1989	CIN	NL	6	3	3	5	1	0	0	0	0	0	1	0	0	0	6	0
1990	CIN	NL	25	15	10	17	6	2	0	1	0	0	3	1	0	0	11	14
1991	CIN	NL	26	15	11	14	9	3	0	2	0	0	2	0	0	0	17	9
1992	CIN	NL	12	8	4	7	1	4	0	1	0	0	0	0	0	0	6	6
1993	CIN	NL	21	12	9	11	5	2	3	0	0	0	0	0	0	0	17	4
1994	BAL	AL	11	3	8	5	6	0	0	0	0	0	0	0	0	0	7	4
1995	CHI	AL	1	1	0	0	1	0	0	0	0	0	0	0	0	1	1	0
Total			113	65	48	68	29	13	3	4	0	0	6	2	0	1	72	41

Rank among batters: 421 • *Top target (3 home runs)*: Bruce Hurst, Ramon Martinez • *Number of pitchers victimized*: 94 • *Total ballparks homered in*: 21 • *First HR*: 04/18/1988 off Mike Krukow • *World Series HR*—2; *LCS HR*—1

Ray Sadecki

RAYMOND MICHAEL SADECKI
B: 12/26/1940
BL

Year	Tm	Lg	Tot	H	A	Men-On 0	1	2	3	One-Game 2	3	4	LO	XN	IP	PH	RHP	LHP
1962	STL	NL	1	1	0	1	0	0	0	0	0	0	0	0	0	0	1	0
1966	STL	NL	1	1	0	0	1	0	0	0	0	0	0	0	0	0	1	0
	SF	NL	2	2	0	1	1	0	0	0	0	0	0	0	0	0	2	0
	Total		3	3	0	1	2	0	0	0	0	0	0	0	0	0	3	0
1969	SF	NL	1	1	0	1	0	0	0	0	0	0	0	0	0	0	0	1
Total			5	5	0	3	2	0	0	0	0	0	0	0	0	0	4	1

Rank among batters: 3,191 • *Total ballparks homered in*: 2 • *First HR*: 06/09/1962 off Gaylord Perry

Mike Sadek

MICHAEL GEORGE SADEK
B: 05/30/1946
BR

Year	Tm	Lg	Tot	H	A	Men-On 0	1	2	3	One-Game 2	3	4	LO	XN	IP	PH	RHP	LHP
1977	SF	NL	1	1	0	1	0	0	0	0	0	0	0	0	0	0	0	1
1978	SF	NL	2	1	1	2	0	0	0	0	0	0	0	0	0	0	0	2
1979	SF	NL	1	1	0	0	1	0	0	0	0	0	0	0	0	0	1	0

Mike Sadek *continued*

Year	Tm	Lg	Tot	H	A	Men-On 0	1	2	3	One-Game 2	3	4	LO	XN	IP	PH	RHP	LHP
1980	SF	NL	1	0	1	1	0	0	0	0	0	0	0	0	0	0	0	1
Total			5	3	2	4	1	0	0	0	0	0	0	0	0	0	1	4

Rank among batters: 3,191 • *Total ballparks homered in*: 3 • *First HR*: 06/19/1977 off Grant Jackson

Bob Sadowski

ROBERT FRANK SADOWSKI
B: 01/15/1937
BL

Year	Tm	Lg	Tot	H	A	Men-On 0	1	2	3	One-Game 2	3	4	LO	XN	IP	PH	RHP	LHP
1962	CHI	AL	6	4	2	2	2	2	0	0	0	0	0	0	0	2	6	0
1963	LA	AL	1	1	0	0	1	0	0	0	0	0	0	0	0	0	1	0
Total			7	5	2	2	3	2	0	0	0	0	0	0	0	2	7	0

Rank among batters: 2,834 • *Total ballparks homered in*: 4 • *First HR*: 04/27/1962 off Bill Monbouquette

Ed Sadowski

EDWARD ROMAN SADOWSKI
B: 01/19/1931 D: 11/06/1993
BR

Year	Tm	Lg	Tot	H	A	Men-On 0	1	2	3	One-Game 2	3	4	LO	XN	IP	PH	RHP	LHP
1960	BOS	AL	3	1	2	2	1	0	0	0	0	0	0	0	0	0	3	0
1961	LA	AL	4	1	3	3	1	0	0	0	0	0	0	1	0	0	4	0
1962	LA	AL	1	1	0	1	0	0	0	0	0	0	0	1	0	1	0	1
1963	LA	AL	4	0	4	2	2	0	0	0	0	0	0	0	0	0	2	2
Total			12	3	9	8	4	0	0	0	0	0	0	2	0	1	9	3

Rank among batters: 2,325 • *Total ballparks homered in*: 9 • *First HR*: 04/26/1960 off Art Ditmar

Tom Saffell

THOMAS JUDSON SAFFELL
B: 07/26/1921
BL

Year	Tm	Lg	Tot	H	A	Men-On 0	1	2	3	One-Game 2	3	4	LO	XN	IP	PH	RHP	LHP
1949	PIT	NL	2	1	1	0	1	0	1	0	0	0	0	0	0	0	2	0
1950	PIT	NL	2	0	2	2	0	0	0	0	0	0	0	0	0	0	2	0
1951	PIT	NL	1	0	1	1	0	0	0	0	0	0	0	0	0	0	1	0
1955	PIT	NL	1	0	1	1	0	0	0	0	0	0	0	0	0	0	1	0
Total			6	1	5	4	1	0	1	0	0	0	0	0	0	0	6	0

Rank among batters: 2,988 • *Total ballparks homered in*: 4 • *First HR*: 08/12/1949 off Gerry Staley

Harry Sage

HARRY SAGE
B: 03/16/1864 D: 05/27/1947
BR

Year	Tm	Lg	Tot	H	A	Men-On 0	1	2	3	One-Game 2	3	4	LO	XN	IP	PH	RHP	LHP
1890	TOL	AA	2	2	0	1	1	0	0	0	0	0	0	0	0	0	2	0

Rank among batters: 4,129 • *Total ballparks homered in*: 1 • *First HR*: 07/16/1890 off Bob Barr

Vic Saier

VICTOR SYLVESTER SAIER
B: 05/04/1891 D: 05/14/1967
BL

Year	Tm	Lg	Tot	H	A	Men-On 0	1	2	3	One-Game 2	3	4	LO	XN	IP	PH	RHP	LHP
1911	CHI	NL	1	1	0	0	0	0	1	0	0	0	0	0	0	0	1	0
1912	CHI	NL	2	2	0	1	1	0	0	0	0	0	0	0	0	0	2	0
1913	CHI	NL	14	11	3	6	5	2	1	0	0	0	0	0	3	0	13	1
1914	CHI	NL	18	12	6	10	3	5	0	1	0	0	0	0	1	0	15	3
1915	CHI	NL	11	6	5	6	5	0	0	0	0	0	0	1	0	0	5	6
1916	CHI	NL	7	4	3	2	3	2	0	0	0	0	0	0	1	0	6	1
1919	PIT	NL	2	1	1	2	0	0	0	0	0	0	0	0	1	1	1	1
Total			55	37	18	27	17	9	2	1	0	0	0	1	6	1	43	12

Rank among batters: 926 • *Top target (5 home runs)*: Christy Mathewson • *Number of pitchers victimized*: 34 • *Total ballparks homered in*: 9 • *First HR*: 09/21/1911 off George Chalmers

Johnny Sain

JOHN FRANKLIN SAIN
B: 09/25/1917
BR

Year	Tm	Lg	Tot	H	A	Men-On 0	1	2	3	One-Game 2	3	4	LO	XN	IP	PH	RHP	LHP
1950	BOS	NL	1	1	0	1	0	0	0	0	0	0	0	0	0	0	1	0
1951	BOS	NL	1	0	1	0	1	0	0	0	0	0	0	0	0	0	0	1

Johnny Sain *continued*

Year	Tm	Lg	Tot	H	A	Men-On 0	1	2	3	One-Game 2	3	4	LO	XN	IP	PH	RHP	LHP
1952	NY	AL	1	1	0	0	1	0	0	0	0	0	0	0	0	0	0	1
Total			3	2	1	1	2	0	0	0	0	0	0	0	0	0	1	2

Rank among batters: 3,735 • *Total ballparks homered in*: 3 • *First HR*: 09/23/1950 off Larry Jansen

Lenn Sakata

LENN HARUKI SAKATA
B: 06/08/1954
BR

Year	Tm	Lg	Tot	H	A	Men-On 0	1	2	3	One-Game 2	3	4	LO	XN	IP	PH	RHP	LHP
1977	MIL	AL	2	0	2	1	1	0	0	0	0	0	0	0	0	0	2	0
1980	BAL	AL	1	1	0	1	0	0	0	0	0	0	0	1	0	1	0	1
1981	BAL	AL	5	3	2	3	0	1	1	2	0	0	1	0	0	0	4	1
1982	BAL	AL	6	3	3	5	1	0	0	0	0	0	1	0	0	0	3	3
1983	BAL	AL	3	2	1	2	0	1	0	0	0	0	0	1	0	0	2	1
1984	BAL	AL	3	1	2	0	3	0	0	0	0	0	0	0	0	0	2	1
1985	BAL	AL	3	2	1	3	0	0	0	0	0	0	0	0	0	0	0	3
1987	NY	AL	2	1	1	2	0	0	0	0	0	0	0	0	0	0	0	2
Total			25	13	12	17	5	2	1	2	0	0	2	2	0	1	13	12

Rank among batters: 1,608 • Top target (2 home runs): Dave Tobik, Bob McClure, Mike Caldwell, Frank Tanana, Floyd Bannister • *Number of pitchers victimized*: 20 • *Total ballparks homered in*: 8 • *First HR*: 07/25/1977 off Dennis Martinez

Mark Salas

MARK BRUCE SALAS
B: 03/08/1961
BL

Year	Tm	Lg	Tot	H	A	Men-On 0	1	2	3	One-Game 2	3	4	LO	XN	IP	PH	RHP	LHP
1985	MIN	AL	9	6	3	5	3	1	0	0	0	0	0	0	0	1	9	0
1986	MIN	AL	8	5	3	4	2	2	0	1	0	0	0	0	0	0	8	0
1987	MIN	AL	3	1	2	1	1	1	0	1	0	0	0	0	0	1	3	0
	NY	AL	3	2	1	0	1	2	0	0	0	0	0	0	0	1	3	0
	Total		6	3	3	1	2	3	0	1	0	0	0	0	0	2	6	0
1988	CHI	AL	3	2	1	2	0	1	0	0	0	0	0	0	0	0	3	0
1989	CLE	AL	2	1	1	1	1	0	0	0	0	0	0	0	0	0	2	0
1990	DET	AL	9	8	1	5	3	1	0	1	0	0	0	0	0	0	8	1
1991	DET	AL	1	0	1	0	0	1	0	0	0	0	0	1	0	1	1	0
Total			38	25	13	18	11	9	0	3	0	0	0	1	0	4	37	1

Rank among batters: 1,225 • *Top target (3 home runs)*: Charlie Hough • *Number of pitchers victimized*: 33 • *Total ballparks homered in*: 10 • *First HR*: 04/27/1985 off Don Sutton

Angel Salazar

ARGENIS ANTONIO (YEPEZ) SALAZAR
B: 11/04/1961
BR

Year	Tm	Lg	Tot	H	A	Men-On 0	1	2	3	One-Game 2	3	4	LO	XN	IP	PH	RHP	LHP
1987	KC	AL	2	1	1	1	1	0	0	0	0	0	0	0	0	0	0	2

Rank among batters: 4,129 • *Total ballparks homered in*: 2 • *First HR*: 05/14/1987 off Jeff Ballard

Luis Salazar

LUIS ERNESTO (GARCIA) SALAZAR
B: 05/19/1956
BR

Year	Tm	Lg	Tot	H	A	Men-On 0	1	2	3	One-Game 2	3	4	LO	XN	IP	PH	RHP	LHP
1980	SD	NL	1	0	1	0	0	1	0	0	0	0	0	0	0	0	1	0
1981	SD	NL	3	2	1	2	1	0	0	0	0	0	0	0	0	0	3	0
1982	SD	NL	8	6	2	5	2	1	0	0	0	0	0	0	1	0	5	3
1983	SD	NL	14	10	4	7	5	2	0	0	0	0	0	0	0	0	6	8
1984	SD	NL	3	1	2	2	1	0	0	0	0	0	0	0	0	0	0	3
1985	CHI	AL	10	4	6	4	4	2	0	0	0	0	0	1	0	1	6	4
1987	SD	NL	3	1	2	1	1	1	0	0	0	0	0	0	0	0	1	2
1988	DET	AL	12	5	7	7	3	2	0	0	0	0	0	0	0	0	4	8
1989	SD	NL	8	5	3	5	3	0	0	0	0	0	0	0	0	3	4	4
	CHI	NL	1	1	0	0	1	0	0	0	0	0	0	0	0	0	0	1
	Total		9	6	3	5	4	0	0	0	0	0	0	0	0	3	4	5
1990	CHI	NL	12	7	5	7	2	3	0	0	0	0	0	1	0	0	6	6
1991	CHI	NL	14	8	6	9	2	3	0	1	0	0	0	0	0	0	4	10
1992	CHI	NL	5	3	2	4	1	0	0	0	0	0	0	0	0	0	1	4
Total			94	53	41	53	26	15	0	1	0	0	0	2	1	4	41	53

Rank among batters: 535 • *Top target (3 home runs)*: Bud Black • *Number of pitchers victimized*: 82 • *Total ballparks homered in*: 24 • *First HR*: 10/03/1980 off Allen Ripley • *LCS HR*—1

Ed Sales

EDWARD A. SALES
B: 1861 D: 08/10/1912
BL

Year	Tm	Lg	Tot	H	A	Men-On 0	1	2	3	One-Game 2	3	4	LO	XN	IP	PH	RHP	LHP
1890	PIT	NL	1	0	1	0	1	0	0	0	0	0	0	0	0	0	0	1

Rank among batters: 4,707 • *Total ballparks homered in*: 1 • *First HR*: 08/07/1890 off Frank Foreman

Bill Salkeld

WILLIAM FRANKLIN SALKELD
B: 03/08/1917 D: 04/22/1967
BL

Year	Tm	Lg	Tot	H	A	Men-On 0	1	2	3	One-Game 2	3	4	LO	XN	IP	PH	RHP	LHP
1945	PIT	NL	15	11	4	9	1	5	0	1	0	0	0	0	0	0	13	2
1946	PIT	NL	3	1	2	2	1	0	0	0	0	0	0	0	0	1	2	1
1948	BOS	NL	8	3	5	5	3	0	0	0	0	0	0	0	0	0	8	0
1949	BOS	NL	5	4	1	2	3	0	0	0	0	0	0	0	0	0	5	0
Total			31	19	12	18	8	5	0	1	0	0	0	0	0	1	28	3

Rank among batters: 1,400 • Top target (2 home runs): Jack Brewer, Ace Adams, Johnny Hutchings, Ted Wilks, Herm Wehmeier, Gerry Staley • *Number of pitchers victimized*: 25 • *Total ballparks homered in*: 5 • *First HR*: 05/27/1945 off Jack Brewer • *Hit for Cycle*—vs STL: 08/04/1945 • *World Series HR*—1

Slim Sallee

HARRY FRANKLIN SALLEE
B: 02/03/1885 D: 03/22/1950
BL

Year	Tm	Lg	Tot	H	A	Men-On 0	1	2	3	One-Game 2	3	4	LO	XN	IP	PH	RHP	LHP
1913	STL	NL	2	2	0	2	0	0	0	0	0	0	0	0	0	0	1	1

Rank among batters: 4,129 • *Total ballparks homered in*: 1 • *First HR*: 04/18/1913 off Charlie Smith

Chico Salmon

RUTHFORD EDUARDO SALMON
B: 12/03/1940
BR

Year	Tm	Lg	Tot	H	A	Men-On 0	1	2	3	One-Game 2	3	4	LO	XN	IP	PH	RHP	LHP
1964	CLE	AL	4	3	1	3	1	0	0	0	0	0	0	0	0	0	3	1
1965	CLE	AL	3	2	1	1	1	0	1	1	0	0	0	0	0	0	1	2
1966	CLE	AL	7	4	3	3	3	1	0	0	0	0	0	0	0	0	2	5
1967	CLE	AL	2	0	2	1	1	0	0	0	0	0	0	0	0	0	1	1
1968	CLE	AL	3	3	0	1	1	1	0	0	0	0	0	0	0	0	1	2
1969	BAL	AL	3	0	3	0	2	1	0	1	0	0	0	0	0	1	3	0
1970	BAL	AL	7	3	4	2	5	0	0	0	0	0	0	0	0	0	6	1
1971	BAL	AL	2	0	2	1	1	0	0	0	0	0	0	0	0	0	1	1
Total			31	15	16	12	15	3	1	2	0	0	0	0	0	1	18	13

Rank among batters: 1,400 • Top target (2 home runs): Gary Peters, Dick Stigman, Bob Humphreys, Sonny Siebert • *Number of pitchers victimized*: 27 • *Total ballparks homered in*: 12 • *First HR*: 08/05/1964 off Alan Koch

Tim Salmon

TIMOTHY JAMES SALMON
B: 08/24/1968
BR

Year	Tm	Lg	Tot	H	A	Men-On 0	1	2	3	One-Game 2	3	4	LO	XN	IP	PH	RHP	LHP
1992	CAL	AL	2	1	1	2	0	0	0	0	0	0	0	1	0	0	1	1
1993	CAL	AL	31	23	8	17	7	6	1	2	0	0	0	0	0	0	24	7
1994	CAL	AL	23	12	11	15	6	2	0	4	0	0	0	0	0	0	18	5
1995	CAL	AL	34	15	19	20	8	5	1	3	0	0	0	2	1	0	23	11
Total			90	51	39	54	21	13	2	9	0	0	0	3	1	0	66	24

Rank among batters: 573 • *Top target (5 home runs)*: Mike Mussina • *Number of pitchers victimized*: 70 • *Total ballparks homered in*: 14 • *First HR*: 08/23/1992 off Scott Sanderson

Jack Saltzgaver

OTTO HAMLIN SALTZGAVER
B: 01/23/1903 D: 02/01/1978
BL

Year	Tm	Lg	Tot	H	A	Men-On 0	1	2	3	One-Game 2	3	4	LO	XN	IP	PH	RHP	LHP
1934	NY	AL	6	3	3	1	5	0	0	0	0	0	0	0	0	0	6	0
1935	NY	AL	3	2	1	1	1	1	0	0	0	0	0	0	0	0	3	0
1936	NY	AL	1	1	0	1	0	0	0	0	0	0	0	0	0	0	1	0
Total			10	6	4	3	6	1	0	0	0	0	0	0	0	0	10	0

Rank among batters: 2,500 • *Total ballparks homered in*: 4 • *First HR*: 05/28/1934 off Ivy Andrews

Jack Salveson

JOHN THEODORE SALVESON
B: 01/05/1914 D: 12/28/1974
BR

Year	Tm	Lg	Tot	H	A	Men-On 0	Men-On 1	Men-On 2	Men-On 3	One-Game 2	One-Game 3	One-Game 4	LO	XN	IP	PH	RHP	LHP
1935	CHI	AL	1	1	0	0	1	0	0	0	0	0	0	0	0	0	1	0
1943	CLE	AL	1	0	1	1	0	0	0	0	0	0	0	0	0	0	1	0
1945	CLE	AL	1	0	1	1	0	0	0	0	0	0	0	0	0	0	0	1
Total			3	1	2	2	1	0	0	0	0	0	0	0	0	0	2	1

Rank among batters: 3,735 • *Total ballparks homered in*: 3 • *First HR*: 06/14/1935 off Jack Russell

Manny Salvo

MANUEL SALVO
B: 06/30/1913
BR

Year	Tm	Lg	Tot	H	A	Men-On 0	Men-On 1	Men-On 2	Men-On 3	One-Game 2	One-Game 3	One-Game 4	LO	XN	IP	PH	RHP	LHP
1939	NY	NL	1	1	0	1	0	0	0	0	0	0	0	0	1	0	1	0

Rank among batters: 4,707 • *Total ballparks homered in*: 1 • *First HR*: 06/06/1939 off Wes Livengood

Ron Samford

RONALD EDWARD SAMFORD
B: 02/28/1930
BR

Year	Tm	Lg	Tot	H	A	Men-On 0	Men-On 1	Men-On 2	Men-On 3	One-Game 2	One-Game 3	One-Game 4	LO	XN	IP	PH	RHP	LHP
1959	WAS	AL	5	0	5	3	1	1	0	0	0	0	0	2	0	0	4	1

Rank among batters: 3,191 • *Total ballparks homered in*: 4 • *First HR*: 04/28/1959 off Ray Herbert

Billy Sample

WILLIAM AMOS SAMPLE
B: 04/02/1955
BR

Year	Tm	Lg	Tot	H	A	Men-On 0	Men-On 1	Men-On 2	Men-On 3	One-Game 2	One-Game 3	One-Game 4	LO	XN	IP	PH	RHP	LHP
1979	TEX	AL	5	4	1	4	1	0	0	0	0	0	0	0	0	0	2	3
1980	TEX	AL	4	2	2	3	1	0	0	0	0	0	1	0	0	0	0	4
1981	TEX	AL	3	2	1	1	1	1	0	0	0	0	0	0	0	0	2	1
1982	TEX	AL	10	7	3	7	2	1	0	1	0	0	2	0	0	0	8	2
1983	TEX	AL	12	6	6	10	1	1	0	0	0	0	1	0	0	0	9	3
1984	TEX	AL	5	2	3	4	1	0	0	0	0	0	2	0	0	0	2	3
1985	NY	AL	1	1	0	1	0	0	0	0	0	0	0	0	0	0	0	1
1986	ATL	NL	6	1	5	4	1	1	0	0	0	0	1	0	0	1	2	4
Total			46	25	21	34	8	4	0	1	0	0	7	0	0	1	25	21

Rank among batters: 1,060 • Top target (2 home runs): Bill Travers, Don Aase, Dennis Martinez, Dennis Eckersley, Dan Petry, Matt Keough • *Number of pitchers victimized*: 40 • *Total ballparks homered in*: 17 • *First HR*: 06/12/1979 off Lary Sorensen

Amado Samuel

AMADO RUPERTO SAMUEL
B: 12/06/1938
BR

Year	Tm	Lg	Tot	H	A	Men-On 0	Men-On 1	Men-On 2	Men-On 3	One-Game 2	One-Game 3	One-Game 4	LO	XN	IP	PH	RHP	LHP
1962	MIL	NL	3	0	3	1	0	2	0	0	0	0	0	0	0	0	3	0

Rank among batters: 3,735 • *Total ballparks homered in*: 2 • *First HR*: 05/29/1962 off Bob Buhl

Juan Samuel

JUAN MILTON SAMUEL
B: 12/09/1960
BR

Year	Tm	Lg	Tot	H	A	Men-On 0	Men-On 1	Men-On 2	Men-On 3	One-Game 2	One-Game 3	One-Game 4	LO	XN	IP	PH	RHP	LHP
1983	PHI	NL	2	1	1	2	0	0	0	0	0	0	0	0	0	0	1	1
1984	PHI	NL	15	8	7	9	4	2	0	0	0	0	2	0	1	0	14	1
1985	PHI	NL	19	8	11	9	6	4	0	0	0	0	3	0	1	0	14	5
1986	PHI	NL	16	10	6	7	4	4	1	1	0	0	0	1	0	1	11	5
1987	PHI	NL	28	15	13	17	9	1	1	3	0	0	3	0	0	0	19	9
1988	PHI	NL	12	7	5	6	6	0	0	0	0	0	2	0	0	1	10	2
1989	PHI	NL	8	3	5	7	1	0	0	0	0	0	4	0	0	0	4	4
	NY	NL	3	2	1	1	2	0	0	0	0	0	0	0	0	0	1	2
	Total		11	5	6	8	3	0	0	0	0	0	4	0	0	0	5	6
1990	LA	NL	13	6	7	7	5	1	0	1	0	0	0	0	0	0	4	9
1991	LA	NL	12	4	8	7	4	1	0	0	0	0	0	0	0	0	5	7
1993	CIN	NL	4	1	3	2	0	2	0	0	0	0	0	0	0	1	3	1

Year	Tm	Lg	Tot	H	A	Men-On 0	1	2	3	One-Game 2	3	4	LO	XN	IP	PH	RHP	LHP

Juan Samuel *continued*

Year	Tm	Lg	Tot	H	A	Men-On 0	1	2	3	One-Game 2	3	4	LO	XN	IP	PH	RHP	LHP
1994	DET	AL	5	4	1	4	1	0	0	0	0	0	0	0	0	0	4	1
1995	DET	AL	10	6	4	5	3	2	0	0	0	0	0	0	0	0	4	6
	KC	AL	2	0	2	0	2	0	0	0	0	0	0	0	0	0	0	2
	Total		12	6	6	5	5	2	0	0	0	0	0	0	0	0	4	8
Total			149	75	74	83	47	17	2	5	0	0	14	1	2	3	94	55

Rank among batters: 289 • *Top target (5 home runs)*: Eddie Whitson • *Number of pitchers victimized*: 115 • *Total ballparks homered in*: 20 • *First HR*: 09/04/1983 off Andy McGaffigan

Alejandro Sanchez

ALEJANDRO (PIMENTEL) SANCHEZ
B: 02/14/1959
BR

Year	Tm	Lg	Tot	H	A	Men-On 0	1	2	3	One-Game 2	3	4	LO	XN	IP	PH	RHP	LHP
1982	PHI	NL	2	2	0	2	0	0	0	0	0	0	0	0	0	0	2	0
1985	DET	AL	6	2	4	3	3	0	0	1	0	0	0	0	0	2	1	5
Total			8	4	4	5	3	0	0	1	0	0	0	0	0	2	3	5

Rank among batters: 2,703 • *Top target (3 home runs)*: Mike Mason • *Number of pitchers victimized*: 6 • *Total ballparks homered in*: 5 • *First HR*: 09/28/1982 off Doug Bird

Celerino Sanchez

CELERINO (PEREZ) SANCHEZ
B: 02/03/1944 D: 05/01/1992
BR

Year	Tm	Lg	Tot	H	A	Men-On 0	1	2	3	One-Game 2	3	4	LO	XN	IP	PH	RHP	LHP
1973	NY	AL	1	1	0	0	1	0	0	0	0	0	0	0	0	1	0	1

Rank among batters: 4,707 • *Total ballparks homered in*: 1 • *First HR*: 05/12/1973 off Mickey Scott

Rey Sanchez

REY FRANCISCO (GUADALUPE) SANCHEZ
B: 10/05/1967
BR

Year	Tm	Lg	Tot	H	A	Men-On 0	1	2	3	One-Game 2	3	4	LO	XN	IP	PH	RHP	LHP
1992	CHI	NL	1	1	0	1	0	0	0	0	0	0	0	0	0	0	1	0
1995	CHI	NL	3	0	3	1	2	0	0	0	0	0	0	0	0	0	2	1
Total			4	1	3	2	2	0	0	0	0	0	0	0	0	0	3	1

Rank among batters: 3,427 • *Total ballparks homered in*: 4 • *First HR*: 08/29/1992 off Francisco Oliveras

Heinie Sand

JOHN HENRY SAND
B: 07/03/1897 D: 11/03/1958
BR

Year	Tm	Lg	Tot	H	A	Men-On 0	1	2	3	One-Game 2	3	4	LO	XN	IP	PH	RHP	LHP
1923	PHI	NL	4	2	2	3	1	0	0	0	0	0	0	0	0	0	3	1
1924	PHI	NL	6	2	4	4	2	0	0	0	0	0	2	0	0	0	6	0
1925	PHI	NL	3	2	1	2	1	0	0	0	0	0	0	0	0	0	2	1
1926	PHI	NL	4	4	0	4	0	0	0	0	0	0	1	0	0	0	3	1
1927	PHI	NL	1	0	1	0	1	0	0	0	0	0	0	0	0	0	1	0
Total			18	10	8	13	5	0	0	0	0	0	3	0	0	0	15	3

Rank among batters: 1,914 • *Top target (3 home runs)*: Vic Keen • *Number of pitchers victimized*: 14 • *Total ballparks homered in*: 5 • *First HR*: 04/18/1923 off Burleigh Grimes

Ryne Sandberg

RYNE DEE SANDBERG
B: 09/18/1959
BR

Year	Tm	Lg	Tot	H	A	Men-On 0	1	2	3	One-Game 2	3	4	LO	XN	IP	PH	RHP	LHP
1982	CHI	NL	7	5	2	4	2	1	0	1	0	0	1	0	0	0	7	0
1983	CHI	NL	8	4	4	5	2	0	1	0	0	0	0	0	0	0	6	2
1984	CHI	NL	19	11	8	15	3	1	0	2	0	0	0	2	0	0	16	3
1985	CHI	NL	26	17	9	14	11	1	0	3	0	0	0	0	0	0	21	5
1986	CHI	NL	14	8	6	8	4	2	0	1	0	0	0	0	1	0	10	4
1987	CHI	NL	16	8	8	12	2	2	0	0	0	0	0	0	0	0	14	2
1988	CHI	NL	19	10	9	12	5	2	0	1	0	0	0	0	0	0	12	7
1989	CHI	NL	30	16	14	22	8	0	0	5	0	0	0	0	0	0	23	7
1990	CHI	NL	40	25	15	24	11	5	0	4	0	0	0	0	0	0	30	10
1991	CHI	NL	26	15	11	12	10	3	1	1	0	0	0	1	1	0	18	8
1992	CHI	NL	26	16	10	12	11	2	1	2	0	0	0	0	0	0	22	4

Ryne Sandberg *continued*

Year	Tm	Lg	Tot	H	A	Men-On 0	1	2	3	One-Game 2	3	4	LO	XN	IP	PH	RHP	LHP
1993	CHI	NL	9	5	4	8	1	0	0	0	0	0	0	0	0	0	8	1
1994	CHI	NL	5	3	2	2	2	1	0	0	0	0	0	0	0	0	3	2
Total			245	143	102	150	72	20	3	20	0	0	1	3	2	0	190	55

Rank among batters: 117 • *Top target (6 home runs)*: Terry Mulholland, John Smoltz • *Number of pitchers victimized*: 150 • *Total ballparks homered in*: 12 • *First HR*: 04/23/1982 off Eddie Solomon • *LCS HR*—1

Ben Sanders

ALEXANDER BENNETT SANDERS
B: 02/16/1865 D: 08/29/1930
BR

Year	Tm	Lg	Tot	H	A	Men-On 0	1	2	3	One-Game 2	3	4	LO	XN	IP	PH	RHP	LHP
1888	PHI	NL	1	0	1	0	1	0	0	0	0	0	0	0	1	0	0	1
1891	PHI	AA	1	1	0	0	1	0	0	0	0	0	0	0	1	0	0	0
1892	LOU	NL	3	1	2	3	0	0	0	0	0	0	0	0	0	0	3	0
Total			5	2	3	3	2	0	0	0	0	0	0	0	2	0	3	1

Rank among batters: 3,191 • *Total ballparks homered in*: 4 • *First HR*: 09/18/1888 off Gus Krock

Deion Sanders

DEION LUWYNN SANDERS
B: 08/09/1967
BL

Year	Tm	Lg	Tot	H	A	Men-On 0	1	2	3	One-Game 2	3	4	LO	XN	IP	PH	RHP	LHP
1989	NY	AL	2	0	2	1	1	0	0	0	0	0	0	0	0	0	2	0
1990	NY	AL	3	1	2	1	1	1	0	0	0	0	0	0	1	0	3	0
1991	ATL	NL	4	2	2	3	0	1	0	0	0	0	1	0	0	0	4	0
1992	ATL	NL	8	5	3	7	1	0	0	0	0	0	2	0	0	1	6	2
1993	ATL	NL	6	1	5	5	0	1	0	0	0	0	0	0	1	1	6	0
1994	ATL	NL	4	2	2	2	2	0	0	0	0	0	0	0	0	0	3	1
1995	CIN	NL	1	1	0	1	0	0	0	0	0	0	0	0	0	0	1	0
	SF	NL	5	2	3	5	0	0	0	0	0	0	3	0	0	0	5	0
	Total		6	3	3	6	0	0	0	0	0	0	3	0	0	0	6	0
Total			33	14	19	25	5	3	0	0	0	0	6	0	2	2	30	3

Rank among batters: 1,336 • *Top target (2 home runs)*: Jeff Brantley, Orel Hershiser • *Number of pitchers victimized*: 31 • *Total ballparks homered in*: 16 • *First HR*: 06/04/1989 off Bryan Clutterbuck

Ray Sanders

RAYMOND FLOYD SANDERS
B: 12/04/1916 D: 10/28/1983
BL

Year	Tm	Lg	Tot	H	A	Men-On 0	1	2	3	One-Game 2	3	4	LO	XN	IP	PH	RHP	LHP
1942	STL	NL	5	2	3	3	1	1	0	0	0	0	0	0	0	0	4	1
1943	STL	NL	11	7	4	6	5	0	0	1	0	0	0	0	0	0	9	2
1944	STL	NL	12	6	6	6	3	3	0	0	0	0	0	0	0	0	8	4
1945	STL	NL	8	5	3	2	4	2	0	0	0	0	0	1	0	1	7	1
1946	BOS	NL	6	2	4	4	2	0	0	0	0	0	0	0	0	0	4	2
Total			42	22	20	21	15	6	0	1	0	0	0	1	0	1	32	10

Rank among batters: 1,138 • *Top target (3 home runs)*: Ace Adams, Red Barrett • *Number of pitchers victimized*: 32 • *Total ballparks homered in*: 6 • *First HR*: 04/26/1942 off Rip Sewell • *World Series HR*—2

Reggie Sanders

REGINALD JEROME SANDERS
B: 09/09/1949
BR

Year	Tm	Lg	Tot	H	A	Men-On 0	1	2	3	One-Game 2	3	4	LO	XN	IP	PH	RHP	LHP
1974	DET	AL	3	1	2	1	2	0	0	0	0	0	0	0	0	0	1	2

Rank among batters: 3,735 • *Total ballparks homered in*: 3 • *First HR*: 09/01/1974 off Catfish Hunter • *Hit HR in first major league AB*—vs OAK: 09/01/1974

Reggie Sanders

REGINALD LAVERNE SANDERS
B: 12/01/1967
BR

Year	Tm	Lg	Tot	H	A	Men-On 0	1	2	3	One-Game 2	3	4	LO	XN	IP	PH	RHP	LHP
1991	CIN	NL	1	0	1	0	1	0	0	0	0	0	0	0	0	0	1	0
1992	CIN	NL	12	6	6	9	3	0	0	1	0	0	0	0	0	1	5	7
1993	CIN	NL	20	8	12	13	5	2	0	0	0	0	0	0	0	0	14	6
1994	CIN	NL	17	10	7	9	6	2	0	1	0	0	0	1	0	0	11	6

Reggie Sanders *continued*

Year	Tm	Lg	Tot	H	A	Men-On 0	1	2	3	One-Game 2	3	4	LO	XN	IP	PH	RHP	LHP
1995	CIN	NL	28	9	19	14	12	2	0	1	1	0	0	0	1	0	20	8
Total			78	33	45	45	27	6	0	3	1	0	0	1	1	1	51	27

Rank among batters: 672 • *Top target (3 home runs)*: Armando Reynoso, Butch Henry • *Number of pitchers victimized*: 63 • *Total ballparks homered in*: 15 • *First HR*: 09/26/1991 off Armando Reynoso • *LCS HR*—1

Scott Sanderson

SCOTT DOUGLAS SANDERSON
B: 07/22/1956
BR

Year	Tm	Lg	Tot	H	A	Men-On 0	1	2	3	One-Game 2	3	4	LO	XN	IP	PH	RHP	LHP
1982	MON	NL	1	0	1	0	0	0	1	0	0	0	0	0	0	0	1	0
1987	CHI	NL	1	1	0	1	0	0	0	0	0	0	0	0	0	0	1	0
Total			2	1	1	1	0	0	1	0	0	0	0	0	0	0	2	0

Rank among batters: 4,129 • *Total ballparks homered in*: 1 • *First HR*: 09/11/1982 off Randy Martz

Mike Sandlock

MICHAEL JOSEPH SANDLOCK
B: 10/17/1915
BB

Year	Tm	Lg	Tot	H	A	Men-On 0	1	2	3	One-Game 2	3	4	LO	XN	IP	PH	RHP	LHP
1945	BRO	NL	2	1	1	0	1	1	0	0	0	0	0	0	0	0	2	0

Rank among batters: 4,129 • *Top target (2 home runs)*: Harry Feldman • *Number of pitchers victimized*: 1 • *Total ballparks homered in*: 2 • *First HR*: 04/20/1945 off Harry Feldman

Charlie Sands

CHARLES DUANE SANDS
B: 12/17/1947
BL

Year	Tm	Lg	Tot	H	A	Men-On 0	1	2	3	One-Game 2	3	4	LO	XN	IP	PH	RHP	LHP
1971	PIT	NL	1	1	0	0	1	0	0	0	0	0	0	0	0	1	0	1
1973	CAL	AL	1	1	0	0	1	0	0	0	0	0	0	0	0	0	1	0
1974	CAL	AL	4	2	2	2	1	1	0	0	0	0	0	0	0	1	4	0
Total			6	4	2	2	3	1	0	0	0	0	0	0	0	2	5	1

Rank among batters: 2,988 • *Total ballparks homered in*: 3 • *First HR*: 05/25/1971 off Ross Grimsley

Fred Sanford

JOHN FREDERICK SANFORD
B: 08/09/1919
BB

Year	Tm	Lg	Tot	H	A	Men-On 0	1	2	3	One-Game 2	3	4	LO	XN	IP	PH	RHP	LHP
1948	STL	AL	1	0	1	1	0	0	0	0	0	0	0	0	0	0	1	0

Rank among batters: 4,707 • *Total ballparks homered in*: 1 • *First HR*: 07/09/1948 off Bob Lemon

Jack Sanford

JOHN STANLEY SANFORD
B: 05/18/1929
BR

Year	Tm	Lg	Tot	H	A	Men-On 0	1	2	3	One-Game 2	3	4	LO	XN	IP	PH	RHP	LHP
1961	SF	NL	3	2	1	2	1	0	0	0	0	0	0	0	0	0	3	0

Rank among batters: 3,735 • *Total ballparks homered in*: 2 • *First HR*: 06/02/1961 off Roger Craig

Manny Sanguillen

MANUEL DE JESUS (MAGAN) SANGUILLEN
B: 03/21/1944
BR

Year	Tm	Lg	Tot	H	A	Men-On 0	1	2	3	One-Game 2	3	4	LO	XN	IP	PH	RHP	LHP
1969	PIT	NL	5	0	5	3	2	0	0	0	0	0	0	0	0	0	4	1
1970	PIT	NL	7	4	3	5	2	0	0	1	0	0	0	0	0	0	4	3
1971	PIT	NL	7	3	4	4	2	1	0	0	0	0	0	0	0	0	3	4
1972	PIT	NL	7	2	5	5	0	1	1	0	0	0	0	0	0	0	6	1
1973	PIT	NL	12	6	6	8	4	0	0	0	0	0	0	0	0	0	7	5
1974	PIT	NL	7	1	6	3	3	1	0	0	0	0	0	0	0	0	7	0
1975	PIT	NL	9	3	6	2	7	0	0	0	0	0	0	0	0	0	3	6
1976	PIT	NL	2	0	2	0	2	0	0	0	0	0	0	0	0	0	2	0
1977	OAK	AL	6	1	5	4	2	0	0	0	0	0	0	0	0	0	4	2
1978	PIT	NL	3	2	1	1	2	0	0	0	0	0	0	0	0	0	1	2
Total			65	22	43	35	26	3	1	1	0	0	0	0	0	0	41	24

Rank among batters: 799 • *Top target (5 home runs)*: Steve Carlton • *Number of pitchers victimized*: 50 • *Total ballparks homered in*: 20 • *First HR*: 06/07/1969 off Pat Jarvis • *LCS HR*—1

Year	Tm	Lg	Tot	H	A	Men-On 0	1	2	3	One-Game 2	3	4	LO	XN	IP	PH	RHP	LHP

Ed Sanicki

EDWARD ROBERT SANICKI
B: 07/07/1923
BR

Year	Tm	Lg	Tot	H	A	0	1	2	3	2	3	4	LO	XN	IP	PH	RHP	LHP
1949	PHI	NL	3	1	2	1	1	1	0	0	0	0	0	0	0	0	2	1

Rank among batters: 3,735 • *Total ballparks homered in*: 3 • *First HR*: 09/14/1949 off Rip Sewell • *Hit HR in first major league AB—*@PIT: 09/14/1949

Rafael Santana

RAFAEL FRANCISCO (DE LA CRUZ) SANTANA
B: 01/31/1958
BR

Year	Tm	Lg	Tot	H	A	0	1	2	3	2	3	4	LO	XN	IP	PH	RHP	LHP
1984	NY	NL	1	1	0	1	0	0	0	0	0	0	0	0	0	0	0	1
1985	NY	NL	1	0	1	0	1	0	0	0	0	0	0	0	0	0	1	0
1986	NY	NL	1	0	1	0	1	0	0	0	0	0	0	0	0	0	0	1
1987	NY	NL	5	2	3	3	1	1	0	0	0	0	0	0	0	0	2	3
1988	NY	AL	4	2	2	2	0	2	0	0	0	0	0	0	0	0	3	1
1990	CLE	AL	1	0	1	0	1	0	0	0	0	0	0	0	0	0	0	1
Total			13	5	8	6	4	3	0	0	0	0	0	0	0	0	6	7

Rank among batters: 2,248 • *Top target (2 home runs)*: Don Carman • *Number of pitchers victimized*: 12 • *Total ballparks homered in*: 8 • *First HR*: 09/26/1984 off Jerry Koosman

F. P. Santangelo

FRANK-PAUL SANTANGELO
B: 10/24/1967
BB

Year	Tm	Lg	Tot	H	A	0	1	2	3	2	3	4	LO	XN	IP	PH	RHP	LHP
1995	MON	NL	1	1	0	1	0	0	0	0	0	0	1	0	0	0	1	0

Rank among batters: 4,707 • *Total ballparks homered in*: 1 • *First HR*: 08/24/1995 off Sergio Valdez

Benito Santiago

BENITO (RIVERA) SANTIAGO
B: 03/09/1965
BR

Year	Tm	Lg	Tot	H	A	0	1	2	3	2	3	4	LO	XN	IP	PH	RHP	LHP
1986	SD	NL	3	2	1	3	0	0	0	0	0	0	0	1	0	0	1	2
1987	SD	NL	18	11	7	7	7	4	0	1	0	0	0	2	0	0	10	8
1988	SD	NL	10	3	7	7	2	0	1	1	0	0	0	1	0	0	5	5
1989	SD	NL	16	8	8	8	6	1	1	0	0	0	0	0	0	0	14	2
1990	SD	NL	11	5	6	3	4	3	1	0	0	0	0	0	0	0	10	1
1991	SD	NL	17	6	11	10	4	3	0	0	0	0	0	0	0	0	9	8
1992	SD	NL	10	8	2	7	2	1	0	1	0	0	0	0	0	0	3	7
1993	FLO	NL	13	6	7	8	5	0	0	0	0	0	0	0	0	0	9	4
1994	FLO	NL	11	4	7	5	5	1	0	0	0	0	0	0	0	0	8	3
1995	CIN	NL	11	7	4	7	3	1	0	2	0	0	0	0	0	0	8	3
Total			120	60	60	65	38	14	3	5	0	0	0	4	0	0	77	43

Rank among batters: 388 • *Top target (5 home runs)*: Zane Smith • *Number of pitchers victimized*: 93 • *Total ballparks homered in*: 14 • *First HR*: 09/17/1986 off Mark Davis • *LCS HR*—1

Jose Santiago

JOSE RAFAEL (ALFONSO) SANTIAGO
B: 08/15/1940
BR

Year	Tm	Lg	Tot	H	A	0	1	2	3	2	3	4	LO	XN	IP	PH	RHP	LHP
1967	BOS	AL	1	1	0	1	0	0	0	0	0	0	0	0	0	0	0	1

Rank among batters: 4,707 • *Total ballparks homered in*: 1 • *First HR*: 05/14/1967 off Mickey Lolich • *World Series HR*—1

Ron Santo

RONALD EDWARD SANTO
B: 02/25/1940
BR

Year	Tm	Lg	Tot	H	A	0	1	2	3	2	3	4	LO	XN	IP	PH	RHP	LHP
1960	CHI	NL	9	7	2	6	1	1	1	1	0	0	0	0	0	0	6	3
1961	CHI	NL	23	15	8	16	5	2	0	2	0	0	0	0	0	0	12	11
1962	CHI	NL	17	12	5	7	7	3	0	0	0	0	0	0	0	0	11	6
1963	CHI	NL	25	13	12	15	6	3	1	2	0	0	0	2	0	0	18	7
1964	CHI	NL	30	16	14	16	8	6	0	2	0	0	0	0	0	0	20	10
1965	CHI	NL	33	20	13	17	9	7	0	3	0	0	0	1	0	0	27	6
1966	CHI	NL	30	17	13	19	8	3	0	4	0	0	0	3	0	0	24	6
1967	CHI	NL	31	21	10	21	9	1	0	1	0	0	0	0	0	0	19	12
1968	CHI	NL	26	21	5	13	9	3	1	2	0	0	0	0	0	0	18	8

Year	Tm	Lg	Tot	H	A	Men-On 0	1	2	3	One-Game 2	3	4	LO	XN	IP	PH	RHP	LHP

Ron Santo *continued*

Year	Tm	Lg	Tot	H	A	0	1	2	3	2	3	4	LO	XN	IP	PH	RHP	LHP
1969	CHI	NL	29	18	11	14	13	2	0	2	0	0	0	0	0	0	24	5
1970	CHI	NL	26	16	10	10	11	3	2	2	0	0	0	0	0	0	22	4
1971	CHI	NL	21	13	8	8	7	6	0	1	0	0	0	0	0	0	15	6
1972	CHI	NL	17	10	7	6	8	3	0	1	0	0	0	0	0	0	11	6
1973	CHI	NL	20	13	7	11	8	1	0	2	0	0	0	2	0	0	14	6
1974	CHI	AL	5	4	1	1	3	0	1	1	0	0	0	0	1	0	3	2
Total			342	216	126	180	112	44	6	26	0	0	0	8	1	0	244	98

Rank among batters: 46 • *Top target (8 home runs)*: Dave Giusti, Ray Sadecki • *Number of pitchers victimized*: 171 • *Total ballparks homered in*: 22 • *First HR*: 07/03/1960 off Jim O'Toole

Al Santorini

ALAN JOEL SANTORINI
B: 05/19/1948
BR

Year	Tm	Lg	Tot	H	A	0	1	2	3	2	3	4	LO	XN	IP	PH	RHP	LHP
1969	SD	NL	1	0	1	1	0	0	0	0	0	0	0	0	0	0	1	0

Rank among batters: 4,707 • *Total ballparks homered in*: 1 • *First HR*: 08/19/1969 off Steve Renko

Nelson Santovenia

NELSON GIL (MAYOL) SANTOVENIA
B: 07/27/1961
BR

Year	Tm	Lg	Tot	H	A	0	1	2	3	2	3	4	LO	XN	IP	PH	RHP	LHP
1988	MON	NL	8	6	2	5	3	0	0	1	0	0	0	1	0	0	5	3
1989	MON	NL	5	4	1	3	2	0	0	0	0	0	0	0	0	0	3	2
1990	MON	NL	6	4	2	3	2	1	0	0	0	0	0	0	0	1	5	1
1991	MON	NL	2	1	1	1	1	0	0	0	0	0	0	0	0	1	0	2
1992	CHI	AL	1	0	1	0	1	0	0	0	0	0	0	0	0	0	1	0
Total			22	15	7	12	9	1	0	1	0	0	0	1	0	2	14	8

Rank among batters: 1,719 • *Top target (2 home runs)*: John Smiley, Ron Darling • *Number of pitchers victimized*: 20 • *Total ballparks homered in*: 6 • *First HR*: 05/26/1988 off Lance McCullers

Joe Sargent

JOSEPH ALEXANDER SARGENT
B: 09/24/1893 D: 07/05/1950
BR

Year	Tm	Lg	Tot	H	A	0	1	2	3	2	3	4	LO	XN	IP	PH	RHP	LHP
1921	DET	AL	2	1	1	1	1	0	0	0	0	0	0	0	0	0	1	1

Rank among batters: 4,129 • *Total ballparks homered in*: 2 • *First HR*: 07/23/1921 off George Mogridge

Bill Sarni

WILLIAM FLORINE SARNI
B: 09/19/1927 D: 04/15/1983
BR

Year	Tm	Lg	Tot	H	A	0	1	2	3	2	3	4	LO	XN	IP	PH	RHP	LHP
1954	STL	NL	9	6	3	4	3	2	0	0	0	0	0	0	0	1	5	4
1955	STL	NL	3	2	1	3	0	0	0	0	0	0	0	0	0	0	2	1
1956	STL	NL	5	2	3	4	0	1	0	1	0	0	0	0	0	0	3	2
	NY	NL	5	3	2	3	2	0	0	0	0	0	0	0	0	0	3	2
	Total		10	5	5	7	2	1	0	1	0	0	0	0	0	0	6	4
Total			22	13	9	14	5	3	0	1	0	0	0	0	0	1	13	9

Rank among batters: 1,719 • *Top target (4 home runs)*: Robin Roberts • *Number of pitchers victimized*: 17 • *Total ballparks homered in*: 5 • *First HR*: 06/06/1954 off Bob Miller

Mackey Sasser

MACK DANIEL SASSER
B: 08/03/1962
BL

Year	Tm	Lg	Tot	H	A	0	1	2	3	2	3	4	LO	XN	IP	PH	RHP	LHP
1988	NY	NL	1	0	1	1	0	0	0	0	0	0	0	0	0	0	1	0
1989	NY	NL	1	1	0	1	0	0	0	0	0	0	0	0	0	0	1	0
1990	NY	NL	6	3	3	0	3	2	1	1	0	0	0	0	0	0	5	1
1991	NY	NL	5	3	2	2	1	2	0	0	0	0	0	0	0	2	5	0
1992	NY	NL	2	1	1	2	0	0	0	0	0	0	0	0	0	0	2	0
1993	SEA	AL	1	0	1	0	1	0	0	0	0	0	0	0	0	0	1	0
Total			16	8	8	6	5	4	1	1	0	0	0	0	0	2	15	1

Rank among batters: 2,029 • *Total ballparks homered in*: 8 • *First HR*: 05/14/1988 off Mike Krukow

Tom Satriano

THOMAS VICTOR NICHOLAS SATRIANO
B: 08/28/1940
BL

Year	Tm	Lg	Tot	H	A	Men-On 0	1	2	3	One-Game 2	3	4	LO	XN	IP	PH	RHP	LHP
1961	LA	AL	1	0	1	0	1	0	0	0	0	0	0	0	0	0	1	0
1962	LA	AL	2	0	2	2	0	0	0	0	0	0	0	0	0	1	1	1
1964	LA	AL	1	0	1	0	1	0	0	0	0	0	0	0	0	1	1	0
1965	CAL	AL	1	0	1	0	1	0	0	0	0	0	0	0	0	1	1	0
1967	CAL	AL	4	0	4	3	1	0	0	0	0	0	0	0	0	0	2	2
1968	CAL	AL	8	5	3	5	2	1	0	0	0	0	0	0	0	0	6	2
1969	CAL	AL	1	1	0	0	1	0	0	0	0	0	0	0	0	0	1	0
1970	BOS	AL	3	0	3	2	1	0	0	0	0	0	0	0	0	0	3	0
Total			21	6	15	12	8	1	0	0	0	0	0	0	0	2	16	5

Rank among batters: 1,768 • *Top target (2 home runs)*: Mudcat Grant, Jim Bouton, Jim Hardin, Jim Perry • *Number of pitchers victimized*: 17 • *Total ballparks homered in*: 6 • *First HR*: 08/12/1961 off Mudcat Grant

Eddie Sauer

EDWARD SAUER
B: 01/03/1919 D: 07/01/1988
BR

Year	Tm	Lg	Tot	H	A	Men-On 0	1	2	3	One-Game 2	3	4	LO	XN	IP	PH	RHP	LHP
1945	CHI	NL	2	1	1	2	0	0	0	0	0	0	0	0	0	0	0	2
1949	BOS	NL	3	0	3	1	0	2	0	0	0	0	0	0	0	0	0	3
Total			5	1	4	3	0	2	0	0	0	0	0	0	0	0	0	5

Rank among batters: 3,191 • *Top target (3 home runs)*: Harry Brecheen • *Number of pitchers victimized*: 3 • *Total ballparks homered in*: 4 • *First HR*: 04/19/1945 off Harry Brecheen

Hank Sauer

HENRY JOHN SAUER
B: 03/17/1917
BR

Year	Tm	Lg	Tot	H	A	Men-On 0	1	2	3	One-Game 2	3	4	LO	XN	IP	PH	RHP	LHP
1942	CIN	NL	2	1	1	2	0	0	0	0	0	0	0	0	0	1	2	0
1945	CIN	NL	5	5	0	4	1	0	0	1	0	0	0	0	0	0	4	1
1948	CIN	NL	35	22	13	21	7	5	2	4	0	0	0	0	0	0	19	16
1949	CIN	NL	4	2	2	2	2	0	0	0	0	0	0	0	0	0	1	3
	CHI	NL	27	20	7	12	10	5	0	2	0	0	0	0	0	0	15	12
	Total		31	22	9	14	12	5	0	2	0	0	0	0	0	0	16	15
1950	CHI	NL	32	18	14	19	8	5	0	4	1	0	0	0	0	0	21	11
1951	CHI	NL	30	13	17	14	14	2	0	3	0	0	0	1	0	0	23	7
1952	CHI	NL	37	23	14	16	16	4	1	2	1	0	0	0	0	0	29	8
1953	CHI	NL	19	13	6	11	6	2	0	0	0	0	0	0	0	0	11	8
1954	CHI	NL	41	21	20	20	14	6	1	4	0	0	0	0	0	0	35	6
1955	CHI	NL	12	5	7	9	3	0	0	1	0	0	0	0	0	0	5	7
1956	STL	NL	5	4	1	3	0	2	0	0	0	0	0	0	0	1	2	3
1957	NY	NL	26	15	11	12	8	6	0	5	0	0	0	0	0	2	21	5
1958	SF	NL	12	6	6	8	3	1	0	3	0	0	0	1	0	1	5	7
1959	SF	NL	1	1	0	1	0	0	0	0	0	0	0	0	0	1	0	1
Total			288	169	119	154	92	38	4	29	2	0	0	2	0	6	193	95

Rank among batters: 77 • *Top target (12 home runs)*: Robin Roberts • *Number of pitchers victimized*: 135 • *Total ballparks homered in*: 12 • *First HR*: 05/03/1942 off Bob Carpenter • *All-Star HR*—1

Don Savage

DONALD ANTHONY SAVAGE
B: 03/05/1919 D: 12/25/1961
BR

Year	Tm	Lg	Tot	H	A	Men-On 0	1	2	3	One-Game 2	3	4	LO	XN	IP	PH	RHP	LHP
1944	NY	AL	4	3	1	1	2	1	0	0	0	0	0	0	0	0	3	1

Rank among batters: 3,427 • *Total ballparks homered in*: 2 • *First HR*: 05/14/1944 off Ray Poat

Jimmie Savage

JAMES HAROLD SAVAGE
B: 08/29/1883 D: 06/26/1940
BB

Year	Tm	Lg	Tot	H	A	Men-On 0	1	2	3	One-Game 2	3	4	LO	XN	IP	PH	RHP	LHP
1914	PIT	FL	1	0	1	0	0	1	0	0	0	0	0	0	0	0	1	0

Rank among batters: 4,707 • *Total ballparks homered in*: 1 • *First HR*: 09/04/1914 off Happy Finneran

Ted Savage

THEODORE EDMUND SAVAGE
B: 02/21/1937
BR

Year	Tm	Lg	Tot	H	A	Men-On 0	Men-On 1	Men-On 2	Men-On 3	One-Game 2	One-Game 3	One-Game 4	LO	XN	IP	PH	RHP	LHP
1962	PHI	NL	7	4	3	3	4	0	0	0	0	0	0	0	0	0	2	5
1963	PIT	NL	5	3	2	2	1	2	0	0	0	0	0	0	0	1	0	5
1965	STL	NL	1	1	0	0	1	0	0	0	0	0	0	0	0	0	0	1
1967	CHI	NL	5	2	3	3	1	1	0	0	0	0	0	0	0	1	2	3
1968	LA	NL	2	1	1	2	0	0	0	0	0	0	0	0	0	1	1	1
1969	CIN	NL	2	2	0	2	0	0	0	0	0	0	0	0	0	0	1	1
1970	MIL	AL	12	7	5	8	3	1	0	0	0	0	0	1	0	1	4	8
Total			34	20	14	20	10	4	0	0	0	0	0	1	0	4	10	24

Rank among batters: 1,315 • *Top target (2 home runs)*: Ray Sadecki, Steve Carlton, Jim Shellenback • *Number of pitchers victimized*: 31 • *Total ballparks homered in*: 14 • *First HR*: 05/04/1962 off Roger Craig

Bob Saverine

ROBERT PAUL SAVERINE
B: 06/02/1941
BB

Year	Tm	Lg	Tot	H	A	Men-On 0	Men-On 1	Men-On 2	Men-On 3	One-Game 2	One-Game 3	One-Game 4	LO	XN	IP	PH	RHP	LHP
1963	BAL	AL	1	0	1	0	1	0	0	0	0	0	0	0	0	1	1	0
1966	WAS	AL	5	2	3	2	3	0	0	0	0	0	0	0	0	0	4	1
Total			6	2	4	2	4	0	0	0	0	0	0	0	0	1	5	1

Rank among batters: 2,988 • *Total ballparks homered in*: 4 • *First HR*: 06/19/1963 off Ted Abernathy

Carl Sawatski

CARL ERNEST SAWATSKI
B: 11/04/1927 D: 11/24/1991
BL

Year	Tm	Lg	Tot	H	A	Men-On 0	Men-On 1	Men-On 2	Men-On 3	One-Game 2	One-Game 3	One-Game 4	LO	XN	IP	PH	RHP	LHP
1950	CHI	NL	1	1	0	1	0	0	0	0	0	0	0	0	0	0	1	0
1953	CHI	NL	1	1	0	0	0	1	0	0	0	0	0	0	0	1	1	0
1954	CHI	AL	1	1	0	0	1	0	0	0	0	0	0	0	0	0	1	0
1957	MIL	NL	6	2	4	5	0	1	0	0	0	0	0	0	0	1	6	0
1958	PHI	NL	5	2	3	5	0	0	0	1	0	0	0	0	0	0	5	0
1959	PHI	NL	9	3	6	3	5	1	0	0	0	0	0	0	0	1	9	0
1960	STL	NL	6	6	0	4	2	0	0	0	0	0	0	0	0	1	6	0
1961	STL	NL	10	6	4	5	4	1	0	0	0	0	0	0	0	4	10	0
1962	STL	NL	13	8	5	10	2	0	1	1	0	0	0	0	0	1	13	0
1963	STL	NL	6	5	1	4	2	0	0	0	0	0	0	0	0	0	6	0
Total			58	35	23	37	16	4	1	2	0	0	0	0	0	9	58	0

Rank among batters: 886 • *Top target (4 home runs)*: Bob Buhl, Don Drysdale • *Number of pitchers victimized*: 39 • *Total ballparks homered in*: 12 • *First HR*: 09/27/1950 off Bob Chesnes

Dave Sax

DAVID JOHN SAX
B: 09/22/1958
BR

Year	Tm	Lg	Tot	H	A	Men-On 0	Men-On 1	Men-On 2	Men-On 3	One-Game 2	One-Game 3	One-Game 4	LO	XN	IP	PH	RHP	LHP
1986	BOS	AL	1	0	1	1	0	0	0	0	0	0	0	0	0	0	0	1

Rank among batters: 4,707 • *Total ballparks homered in*: 1 • *First HR*: 09/21/1986 off Jimmy Key

Steve Sax

STEPHEN LOUIS SAX
B: 01/29/1960
BR

Year	Tm	Lg	Tot	H	A	Men-On 0	Men-On 1	Men-On 2	Men-On 3	One-Game 2	One-Game 3	One-Game 4	LO	XN	IP	PH	RHP	LHP
1981	LA	NL	2	0	2	2	0	0	0	0	0	0	0	0	0	0	1	1
1982	LA	NL	4	2	2	2	1	1	0	0	0	0	1	0	0	0	4	0
1983	LA	NL	5	3	2	5	0	0	0	0	0	0	1	0	0	0	4	1
1984	LA	NL	1	1	0	1	0	0	0	0	0	0	0	0	0	0	1	0
1985	LA	NL	1	1	0	0	1	0	0	0	0	0	0	0	0	0	0	1
1986	LA	NL	6	1	5	4	1	0	1	0	0	0	0	0	0	0	3	3
1987	LA	NL	6	2	4	5	1	0	0	0	0	0	2	0	0	0	4	2
1988	LA	NL	5	2	3	3	1	1	0	1	0	0	3	0	1	0	2	3
1989	NY	AL	5	2	3	3	0	2	0	0	0	0	1	0	0	0	3	2
1990	NY	AL	4	3	1	3	0	1	0	0	0	0	2	0	0	0	4	0
1991	NY	AL	10	6	4	7	3	0	0	0	0	0	1	0	0	0	5	5
1992	CHI	AL	4	1	3	2	1	0	1	0	0	0	0	0	0	0	3	1
1993	CHI	AL	1	1	0	1	0	0	0	0	0	0	1	0	0	0	1	0
Total			54	25	29	38	9	5	2	1	0	0	12	0	1	0	35	19

Rank among batters: 938 • *Top target (2 home runs)*: Eddie Whitson, Shane Rawley, Mike Flanagan • *Number of pitchers victimized*: 51 • *Total ballparks homered in*: 21 • *First HR*: 08/23/1981 off Bob Shirley

Jimmy Say

JAMES I. SAY
B: 1862 D: 06/23/1894

Year	Tm	Lg	Tot	H	A	Men-On 0	1	2	3	One-Game 2	3	4	LO	XN	IP	PH	RHP	LHP
1882	PHI	AA	1	0	1	1	0	0	0	0	0	0	0	0	0	0	0	1

Rank among batters: 4,707 • *Total ballparks homered in*: 1 • *First HR*: 09/29/1882 off Jack Leary

Lou Say

LOUIS I. SAY
B: 02/04/1854 D: 06/05/1930
BR

Year	Tm	Lg	Tot	H	A	Men-On 0	1	2	3	One-Game 2	3	4	LO	XN	IP	PH	RHP	LHP
1882	PHI	AA	1	1	0	0	1	0	0	0	0	0	0	0	0	0	0	0
1883	BAL	AA	1	1	0	0	0	1	0	0	0	0	0	0	0	0	1	0
1884	BAL	UA	2	1	1	1	1	0	0	0	0	0	0	0	0	0	0	0
	KC	UA	1	1	0	0	0	1	0	0	0	0	0	0	0	0	0	1
	Total		3	2	1	1	1	1	0	0	0	0	0	0	0	0	0	1
Total			5	4	1	1	2	2	0	0	0	0	0	0	0	0	1	1

Rank among batters: 3,191 • *Total ballparks homered in*: 5 • *First HR*: 05/23/1882 off Jumbo McGinnis

Gerald Scala

GERALD MICHAEL SCALA
B: 09/27/1924 D: 12/14/1993
BL

Year	Tm	Lg	Tot	H	A	Men-On 0	1	2	3	One-Game 2	3	4	LO	XN	IP	PH	RHP	LHP
1949	CHI	AL	1	0	1	1	0	0	0	0	0	0	0	0	0	0	1	0

Rank among batters: 4,707 • *Total ballparks homered in*: 1 • *First HR*: 05/01/1949 off Red Embree

Pat Scanlon

JAMES PATRICK SCANLON
B: 09/23/1952
BL

Year	Tm	Lg	Tot	H	A	Men-On 0	1	2	3	One-Game 2	3	4	LO	XN	IP	PH	RHP	LHP
1975	MON	NL	2	2	0	1	0	1	0	0	0	0	0	0	0	0	2	0
1976	MON	NL	1	0	1	1	0	0	0	0	0	0	0	0	0	0	1	0
1977	SD	NL	1	0	1	1	0	0	0	0	0	0	0	0	0	0	1	0
Total			4	2	2	3	0	1	0	0	0	0	0	0	0	0	4	0

Rank among batters: 3,427 • *Total ballparks homered in*: 3 • *First HR*: 05/12/1975 off Carl Morton

Ray Scarborough

RAE WILSON SCARBOROUGH
B: 07/23/1917 D: 07/01/1982
BR

Year	Tm	Lg	Tot	H	A	Men-On 0	1	2	3	One-Game 2	3	4	LO	XN	IP	PH	RHP	LHP
1953	NY	AL	1	0	1	0	0	1	0	0	0	0	0	0	0	0	1	0

Rank among batters: 4,707 • *Total ballparks homered in*: 1 • *First HR*: 05/29/1953 off Harry Byrd

Russ Scarritt

STEPHEN RUSSELL MALLORY SCARRITT
B: 01/14/1903 D: 12/04/1994
BL

Year	Tm	Lg	Tot	H	A	Men-On 0	1	2	3	One-Game 2	3	4	LO	XN	IP	PH	RHP	LHP
1929	BOS	AL	1	1	0	1	0	0	0	0	0	0	0	0	1	0	1	0
1930	BOS	AL	2	0	2	1	0	1	0	0	0	0	0	0	1	0	2	0
Total			3	1	2	2	0	1	0	0	0	0	0	0	2	0	3	0

Rank among batters: 3,735 • *Total ballparks homered in*: 3 • *First HR*: 06/02/1929 off Wes Ferrell

Les Scarsella

LESLIE GEORGE SCARSELLA
B: 11/23/1913 D: 12/17/1958
BL

Year	Tm	Lg	Tot	H	A	Men-On 0	1	2	3	One-Game 2	3	4	LO	XN	IP	PH	RHP	LHP
1936	CIN	NL	3	3	0	1	2	0	0	0	0	0	0	0	0	0	3	0
1937	CIN	NL	3	2	1	1	1	1	0	0	0	0	0	0	0	0	3	0
Total			6	5	1	2	3	1	0	0	0	0	0	0	0	0	6	0

Rank among batters: 2,988 • *Total ballparks homered in*: 2 • *First HR*: 06/02/1936 off Claude Passeau

Steve Scarsone

STEVEN WAYNE SCARSONE
B: 04/11/1966
BR

Year	Tm	Lg	Tot	H	A	Men-On 0	1	2	3	One-Game 2	3	4	LO	XN	IP	PH	RHP	LHP
1993	SF	NL	2	1	1	0	1	1	0	0	0	0	0	0	0	0	2	0

Steve Scarsone *continued*

Year	Tm	Lg	Tot	H	A	Men-On 0	Men-On 1	Men-On 2	Men-On 3	One-Game 2	One-Game 3	One-Game 4	LO	XN	IP	PH	RHP	LHP
1994	SF	NL	2	0	2	0	2	0	0	0	0	0	0	0	0	1	1	1
1995	SF	NL	11	7	4	7	3	1	0	0	0	0	0	0	0	0	8	3
Total			15	8	7	7	6	2	0	0	0	0	0	0	0	1	11	4

Rank among batters: 2,096 • *Total ballparks homered in*: 7 • *First HR*: 07/09/1993 off Ben Rivera

Paul Schaal

PAUL SCHAAL
B: 03/03/1943
BR

Year	Tm	Lg	Tot	H	A	Men-On 0	Men-On 1	Men-On 2	Men-On 3	One-Game 2	One-Game 3	One-Game 4	LO	XN	IP	PH	RHP	LHP
1965	CAL	AL	9	5	4	8	1	0	0	1	0	0	0	0	0	0	8	1
1966	CAL	AL	6	3	3	5	1	0	0	0	0	0	0	1	1	0	4	2
1967	CAL	AL	6	4	2	5	1	0	0	0	0	0	0	0	0	0	2	4
1968	CAL	AL	2	2	0	2	0	0	0	0	0	0	0	0	0	0	2	0
1969	KC	AL	1	1	0	1	0	0	0	0	0	0	0	0	0	0	0	1
1970	KC	AL	5	1	4	5	0	0	0	0	0	0	0	1	0	0	4	1
1971	KC	AL	11	2	9	9	1	1	0	0	0	0	0	0	0	0	9	2
1972	KC	AL	6	2	4	4	0	1	1	0	0	0	0	0	0	0	4	2
1973	KC	AL	8	6	2	6	2	0	0	1	0	0	0	0	1	0	6	2
1974	KC	AL	1	0	1	0	1	0	0	0	0	0	0	0	0	0	1	0
	CAL	AL	2	0	2	1	1	0	0	0	0	0	0	0	0	0	1	1
	Total		3	0	3	1	2	0	0	0	0	0	0	0	0	0	2	1
Total			57	26	31	46	8	2	1	2	0	0	0	2	2	0	41	16

Rank among batters: 902 • *Top target (3 home runs)*: Sam McDowell • *Number of pitchers victimized*: 48 • *Total ballparks homered in*: 14 • *First HR*: 04/18/1965 off Denny McLain

Germany Schaefer

HERMAN A. SCHAEFER
B: 02/04/1877 D: 05/16/1919
BR

Year	Tm	Lg	Tot	H	A	Men-On 0	Men-On 1	Men-On 2	Men-On 3	One-Game 2	One-Game 3	One-Game 4	LO	XN	IP	PH	RHP	LHP
1905	DET	AL	2	0	2	1	1	0	0	0	0	0	0	0	0	0	1	1
1906	DET	AL	2	0	2	0	2	0	0	0	0	0	0	0	1	1	0	2
1907	DET	AL	1	1	0	1	0	0	0	0	0	0	0	0	0	0	0	1
1908	DET	AL	3	1	2	2	0	0	1	0	0	0	0	0	1	0	2	1
1909	WAS	AL	1	0	1	1	0	0	0	0	0	0	0	0	1	0	1	0
Total			9	2	7	5	3	0	1	0	0	0	0	0	3	1	4	5

Rank among batters: 2,587 • *Top target (2 home runs)*: Jesse Tannehill • *Number of pitchers victimized*: 8 • *Total ballparks homered in*: 6 • *First HR*: 06/03/1905 off Willie Sudhoff

Jeff Schaefer

JEFFREY SCOTT SCHAEFER
B: 05/31/1960
BR

Year	Tm	Lg	Tot	H	A	Men-On 0	Men-On 1	Men-On 2	Men-On 3	One-Game 2	One-Game 3	One-Game 4	LO	XN	IP	PH	RHP	LHP
1991	SEA	AL	1	0	1	1	0	0	0	0	0	0	0	0	0	0	0	1
1992	SEA	AL	1	0	1	0	1	0	0	0	0	0	0	0	0	0	1	0
Total			2	0	2	1	1	0	0	0	0	0	0	0	0	0	1	1

Rank among batters: 4,129 • *Total ballparks homered in*: 1 • *First HR*: 06/24/1991 off Greg Hibbard

Jimmie Schaffer

JIMMIE RONALD SCHAFFER
B: 04/05/1936
BR

Year	Tm	Lg	Tot	H	A	Men-On 0	Men-On 1	Men-On 2	Men-On 3	One-Game 2	One-Game 3	One-Game 4	LO	XN	IP	PH	RHP	LHP
1961	STL	NL	1	0	1	0	0	0	1	0	0	0	0	0	0	0	0	1
1963	CHI	NL	7	3	4	3	2	2	0	0	0	0	0	0	0	0	6	1
1964	CHI	NL	2	1	1	1	1	0	0	0	0	0	0	0	0	0	1	1
1966	PHI	NL	1	1	0	0	0	1	0	0	0	0	0	0	0	0	0	1
Total			11	5	6	4	3	3	1	0	0	0	0	0	0	0	7	4

Rank among batters: 2,419 • *Total ballparks homered in*: 7 • *First HR*: 06/30/1961 off Jim Brewer

Johnny Schaive

JOHN EDWARD SCHAIVE
B: 02/25/1934
BR

Year	Tm	Lg	Tot	H	A	Men-On 0	Men-On 1	Men-On 2	Men-On 3	One-Game 2	One-Game 3	One-Game 4	LO	XN	IP	PH	RHP	LHP
1962	WAS	AL	6	4	2	4	2	0	0	1	0	0	0	0	0	0	3	3

Rank among batters: 2,988 • *Total ballparks homered in*: 2 • *First HR*: 04/27/1962 off Bill Stafford

Leroy Schalk

LEROY JOHN SCHALK
B: 11/09/1908 D: 03/11/1990
BR

Year	Tm	Lg	Tot	H	A	Men-On 0	Men-On 1	Men-On 2	Men-On 3	One-Game 2	One-Game 3	One-Game 4	LO	XN	IP	PH	RHP	LHP
1944	CHI	AL	1	0	1	1	0	0	0	0	0	0	0	0	0	0	1	0
1945	CHI	AL	1	0	1	0	0	1	0	0	0	0	0	0	0	0	1	0
Total			2	0	2	1	0	1	0	0	0	0	0	0	0	0	2	0

Rank among batters: 4,129 • *Total ballparks homered in*: 1 • *First HR*: 07/07/1944 off Lum Harris

Ray Schalk

RAYMOND WILLIAM SCHALK
B: 08/12/1892 D: 05/19/1970
BR HOF

Year	Tm	Lg	Tot	H	A	Men-On 0	Men-On 1	Men-On 2	Men-On 3	One-Game 2	One-Game 3	One-Game 4	LO	XN	IP	PH	RHP	LHP
1913	CHI	AL	1	0	1	1	0	0	0	0	0	0	0	0	1	0	1	0
1915	CHI	AL	1	1	0	0	0	1	0	0	0	0	0	0	0	0	0	1
1917	CHI	AL	2	1	1	0	1	1	0	0	0	0	0	0	0	0	1	1
1920	CHI	AL	1	1	0	1	0	0	0	0	0	0	0	0	0	0	0	1
1922	CHI	AL	4	0	4	2	2	0	0	0	0	0	0	0	1	0	3	1
1923	CHI	AL	1	0	1	1	0	0	0	0	0	0	0	0	0	0	1	0
1924	CHI	AL	1	1	0	1	0	0	0	0	0	0	0	0	0	0	1	0
Total			11	4	7	6	3	2	0	0	0	0	0	0	2	0	7	4

Rank among batters: 2,419 • *Total ballparks homered in*: 7 • *First HR*: 06/14/1913 off Walter Johnson • *Hit for Cycle*—@DET: 06/27/1922

Biff Schaller

WALTER SCHALLER
B: 09/23/1889 D: 10/09/1939
BL

Year	Tm	Lg	Tot	H	A	Men-On 0	Men-On 1	Men-On 2	Men-On 3	One-Game 2	One-Game 3	One-Game 4	LO	XN	IP	PH	RHP	LHP
1911	DET	AL	1	0	1	1	0	0	0	0	0	0	0	0	0	0	0	1

Rank among batters: 4,707 • *Total ballparks homered in*: 1 • *First HR*: 05/08/1911 off Jesse Baker

Wally Schang

WALTER HENRY SCHANG
B: 08/22/1889 D: 03/06/1965
BB

Year	Tm	Lg	Tot	H	A	Men-On 0	Men-On 1	Men-On 2	Men-On 3	One-Game 2	One-Game 3	One-Game 4	LO	XN	IP	PH	RHP	LHP
1913	PHI	AL	3	0	3	2	0	1	0	0	0	0	0	0	0	0	2	1
1914	PHI	AL	3	3	0	3	0	0	0	1	0	0	0	0	1	0	2	1
1915	PHI	AL	1	0	1	1	0	0	0	0	0	0	0	0	0	0	1	0
1916	PHI	AL	7	6	1	5	1	0	1	1	0	0	0	0	1	0	4	3
1917	PHI	AL	3	1	2	0	2	1	0	0	0	0	0	1	0	0	3	0
1920	BOS	AL	4	0	4	4	0	0	0	0	0	0	0	0	1	0	3	1
1921	NY	AL	6	5	1	4	1	1	0	0	0	0	0	0	2	0	5	1
1922	NY	AL	1	0	1	1	0	0	0	0	0	0	0	1	0	0	1	0
1923	NY	AL	2	1	1	2	0	0	0	0	0	0	0	0	0	0	2	0
1924	NY	AL	5	2	3	3	2	0	0	0	0	0	0	0	0	0	5	0
1925	NY	AL	2	0	2	0	1	1	0	0	0	0	0	0	0	0	2	0
1926	STL	AL	8	7	1	6	1	0	1	0	0	0	0	0	0	1	7	1
1927	STL	AL	5	3	2	0	3	1	1	0	0	0	0	0	0	0	4	1
1928	STL	AL	3	2	1	2	1	0	0	0	0	0	0	0	0	0	3	0
1929	STL	AL	5	5	0	1	4	0	0	0	0	0	0	0	0	0	5	0
1930	PHI	AL	1	0	1	0	1	0	0	0	0	0	0	0	0	0	1	0
Total			59	35	24	34	17	5	3	2	0	0	0	2	5	1	50	9

Rank among batters: 873 • *Top target (4 home runs)*: Red Faber • *Number of pitchers victimized*: 48 • *Total ballparks homered in*: 8 • *First HR*: 06/27/1913 off Tom Hughes • *Switch hit HR in 1 game*—1 time • *World Series HR*—1

Charley Schanz

CHARLES MURRELL SCHANZ
B: 06/08/1919 D: 05/28/1992
BR

Year	Tm	Lg	Tot	H	A	Men-On 0	Men-On 1	Men-On 2	Men-On 3	One-Game 2	One-Game 3	One-Game 4	LO	XN	IP	PH	RHP	LHP
1944	PHI	NL	1	0	1	1	0	0	0	0	0	0	0	0	0	0	1	0

Rank among batters: 4,707 • *Total ballparks homered in*: 1 • *First HR*: 08/25/1944 off Nate Andrews

George Scharein

GEORGE ALBERT SCHAREIN
B: 11/21/1914 D: 12/23/1981
BR

Year	Tm	Lg	Tot	H	A	Men-On 0	Men-On 1	Men-On 2	Men-On 3	One-Game 2	One-Game 3	One-Game 4	LO	XN	IP	PH	RHP	LHP
1938	PHI	NL	1	1	0	1	0	0	0	0	0	0	0	0	0	0	1	0

George Scharein *continued*

Year	Tm	Lg	Tot	H	A	Men-On 0	Men-On 1	Men-On 2	Men-On 3	One-Game 2	One-Game 3	One-Game 4	LO	XN	IP	PH	RHP	LHP
1939	PHI	NL	1	0	1	0	1	0	0	0	0	0	0	0	0	0	1	0
Total			2	1	1	1	1	0	0	0	0	0	0	0	0	0	2	0

Rank among batters: 4,129 • *Total ballparks homered in*: 2 • *First HR*: 05/19/1938 off Peaches Davis

Nick Scharf

EDWARD T. SCHARF
B: 07/ /1858 D: 03/12/1937

Year	Tm	Lg	Tot	H	A	Men-On 0	Men-On 1	Men-On 2	Men-On 3	One-Game 2	One-Game 3	One-Game 4	LO	XN	IP	PH	RHP	LHP
1882	BAL	AA	1	1	0	1	0	0	0	0	0	0	0	0	0	0	1	0

Rank among batters: 4,707 • *Total ballparks homered in*: 1 • *First HR*: 05/20/1882 off John Schappert

Dan Schatzeder

DANIEL ERNEST SCHATZEDER
B: 12/01/1954
BL

Year	Tm	Lg	Tot	H	A	Men-On 0	Men-On 1	Men-On 2	Men-On 3	One-Game 2	One-Game 3	One-Game 4	LO	XN	IP	PH	RHP	LHP
1978	MON	NL	1	0	1	0	1	0	0	0	0	0	0	0	0	0	1	0
1979	MON	NL	1	0	1	1	0	0	0	0	0	0	0	0	0	0	1	0
1985	MON	NL	2	1	1	0	2	0	0	0	0	0	0	0	0	0	1	1
1986	MON	NL	1	1	0	0	1	0	0	0	0	0	0	0	0	0	1	0
Total			5	2	3	1	4	0	0	0	0	0	0	0	0	0	4	1

Rank among batters: 3,191 • *Total ballparks homered in*: 4 • *First HR*: 08/25/1978 off John Montefusco

Allen Scheer

ALLEN G. SCHEER
B: 10/21/1888 D: 05/06/1959
BL

Year	Tm	Lg	Tot	H	A	Men-On 0	Men-On 1	Men-On 2	Men-On 3	One-Game 2	One-Game 3	One-Game 4	LO	XN	IP	PH	RHP	LHP
1914	IND	FL	3	2	1	2	1	0	0	0	0	0	0	0	0	0	2	1
1915	NWK	FL	2	0	2	1	1	0	0	0	0	0	0	0	0	0	2	0
Total			5	2	3	3	2	0	0	0	0	0	0	0	0	0	4	1

Rank among batters: 3,191 • *Total ballparks homered in*: 4 • *First HR*: 04/29/1914 off Ed Henderson

Heinie Scheer

HENRY WILLIAM SCHEER
B: 07/31/1900 D: 03/21/1976
BR

Year	Tm	Lg	Tot	H	A	Men-On 0	Men-On 1	Men-On 2	Men-On 3	One-Game 2	One-Game 3	One-Game 4	LO	XN	IP	PH	RHP	LHP
1922	PHI	AL	4	4	0	1	2	1	0	0	0	0	0	0	0	0	2	2
1923	PHI	AL	2	2	0	0	2	0	0	0	0	0	0	0	0	0	1	1
Total			6	6	0	1	4	1	0	0	0	0	0	0	0	0	3	3

Rank among batters: 2,988 • *Total ballparks homered in*: 1 • *First HR*: 08/28/1922 off Frank Mack

Fritz Scheeren

FREDERICK SCHEEREN
B: 09/08/1891 D: 06/17/1973
BR

Year	Tm	Lg	Tot	H	A	Men-On 0	Men-On 1	Men-On 2	Men-On 3	One-Game 2	One-Game 3	One-Game 4	LO	XN	IP	PH	RHP	LHP
1914	PIT	NL	1	0	1	1	0	0	0	0	0	0	0	0	1	0	1	0

Rank among batters: 4,707 • *Total ballparks homered in*: 1 • *First HR*: 09/23/1914 off Jeff Pfeffer

Bob Scheffing

ROBERT BODEN SCHEFFING
B: 08/11/1913 D: 10/26/1985
BR

Year	Tm	Lg	Tot	H	A	Men-On 0	Men-On 1	Men-On 2	Men-On 3	One-Game 2	One-Game 3	One-Game 4	LO	XN	IP	PH	RHP	LHP
1941	CHI	NL	1	0	1	0	0	0	1	0	0	0	0	0	0	1	1	0
1942	CHI	NL	2	2	0	0	2	0	0	0	0	0	0	0	0	0	2	0
1947	CHI	NL	5	3	2	1	1	3	0	0	0	0	0	0	0	0	2	3
1948	CHI	NL	5	3	2	3	2	0	0	0	0	0	0	0	0	0	3	2
1949	CHI	NL	3	1	2	0	2	1	0	0	0	0	0	0	0	0	2	1
1950	CIN	NL	2	0	2	1	0	1	0	0	0	0	0	0	0	0	0	2
1951	CIN	NL	2	1	1	1	0	1	0	0	0	0	0	0	0	0	0	2
Total			20	10	10	6	7	6	1	0	0	0	0	0	0	1	10	10

Rank among batters: 1,810 • *Top target (2 home runs)*: Warren Spahn, Joe Hatten • *Number of pitchers victimized*: 18 • *Total ballparks homered in*: 7 • *First HR*: 09/20/1941 off Howie Krist

Year	Tm	Lg	Tot	H	A	Men-On 0	Men-On 1	Men-On 2	Men-On 3	One-Game 2	One-Game 3	One-Game 4	LO	XN	IP	PH	RHP	LHP

Ted Scheffler

THEODORE J. SCHEFFLER
B: 04/05/1864 D: 02/24/1949
BR

Year	Tm	Lg	Tot	H	A	Men-On 0	Men-On 1	Men-On 2	Men-On 3	One-Game 2	One-Game 3	One-Game 4	LO	XN	IP	PH	RHP	LHP
1890	ROC	AA	3	2	1	3	0	0	0	0	0	0	1	0	0	0	2	1

Rank among batters: 3,735 • *Total ballparks homered in*: 2 • *First HR*: 04/18/1890 off Ed Seward

Carl Scheib

CARL ALVIN SCHEIB
B: 01/01/1927
BR

Year	Tm	Lg	Tot	H	A	Men-On 0	Men-On 1	Men-On 2	Men-On 3	One-Game 2	One-Game 3	One-Game 4	LO	XN	IP	PH	RHP	LHP
1948	PHI	AL	2	2	0	1	0	0	1	0	0	0	0	0	0	1	2	0
1950	PHI	AL	1	0	1	1	0	0	0	0	0	0	0	0	0	0	0	1
1951	PHI	AL	2	1	1	2	0	0	0	0	0	0	0	0	0	0	0	2
Total			5	3	2	4	0	0	1	0	0	0	0	0	0	1	2	3

Rank among batters: 3,191 • *Total ballparks homered in*: 3 • *First HR*: 05/08/1948 off Bob Gillespie

Frank Scheibeck

FRANK S. SCHEIBECK
B: 06/28/1865 D: 10/22/1956
BR

Year	Tm	Lg	Tot	H	A	Men-On 0	Men-On 1	Men-On 2	Men-On 3	One-Game 2	One-Game 3	One-Game 4	LO	XN	IP	PH	RHP	LHP
1890	TOL	AA	1	1	0	1	0	0	0	0	0	0	0	0	0	0	0	0
1894	PIT	NL	1	0	1	0	0	1	0	0	0	0	0	0	0	0	1	0
Total			2	1	1	1	0	1	0	0	0	0	0	0	0	0	1	0

Rank among batters: 4,129 • *Total ballparks homered in*: 2 • *First HR*: 08/14/1890 off Tom Ford

Richie Scheinblum

RICHARD ALAN SCHEINBLUM
B: 11/05/1942
BB

Year	Tm	Lg	Tot	H	A	Men-On 0	Men-On 1	Men-On 2	Men-On 3	One-Game 2	One-Game 3	One-Game 4	LO	XN	IP	PH	RHP	LHP
1969	CLE	AL	1	1	0	1	0	0	0	0	0	0	0	0	0	1	1	0
1972	KC	AL	8	4	4	6	1	1	0	0	0	0	0	0	0	1	4	4
1973	CIN	NL	1	0	1	0	1	0	0	0	0	0	0	0	0	1	0	1
	CAL	AL	3	1	2	2	1	0	0	0	0	0	0	1	0	0	3	0
	Total		4	1	3	2	2	0	0	0	0	0	0	1	0	1	3	1
Total			13	6	7	9	3	1	0	0	0	0	0	1	0	3	8	5

Rank among batters: 2,248 • *Total ballparks homered in*: 9 • *First HR*: 07/20/1969 off Tom Timmermann

Danny Schell

CLYDE DANIEL SCHELL
B: 12/26/1927 D: 05/11/1972
BR

Year	Tm	Lg	Tot	H	A	Men-On 0	Men-On 1	Men-On 2	Men-On 3	One-Game 2	One-Game 3	One-Game 4	LO	XN	IP	PH	RHP	LHP
1954	PHI	NL	7	4	3	3	4	0	0	0	0	0	0	0	0	0	4	3

Rank among batters: 2,834 • *Total ballparks homered in*: 4 • *First HR*: 06/26/1954 off Ray Crone

Mike Schemer

MICHAEL SCHEMER
B: 11/20/1917 D: 04/22/1983
BL

Year	Tm	Lg	Tot	H	A	Men-On 0	Men-On 1	Men-On 2	Men-On 3	One-Game 2	One-Game 3	One-Game 4	LO	XN	IP	PH	RHP	LHP
1945	NY	NL	1	1	0	0	0	1	0	0	0	0	0	0	0	0	1	0

Rank among batters: 4,707 • *Total ballparks homered in*: 1 • *First HR*: 08/20/1945 off Hank Wyse

Bill Schenck

WILLIAM G. SCHENCK

Year	Tm	Lg	Tot	H	A	Men-On 0	Men-On 1	Men-On 2	Men-On 3	One-Game 2	One-Game 3	One-Game 4	LO	XN	IP	PH	RHP	LHP
1884	RIC	AA	3	1	2	0	2	1	0	1	0	0	0	0	0	0	0	1

Rank among batters: 3,735 • *Top target (2 home runs)*: Larry McKeon • *Number of pitchers victimized*: 2 • *Total ballparks homered in*: 2 • *First HR*: 08/27/1884 off Charlie Eden

Hank Schenz

HENRY LEONARD SCHENZ
B: 04/11/1919 D: 05/12/1988
BR

Year	Tm	Lg	Tot	H	A	Men-On 0	Men-On 1	Men-On 2	Men-On 3	One-Game 2	One-Game 3	One-Game 4	LO	XN	IP	PH	RHP	LHP
1948	CHI	NL	1	0	1	0	1	0	0	0	0	0	0	0	0	0	0	1

Hank Schenz *continued*

Year	Tm	Lg	Tot	H	A	Men-On 0	1	2	3	One-Game 2	3	4	LO	XN	IP	PH	RHP	LHP
1950	PIT	NL	1	1	0	1	0	0	0	0	0	0	1	0	0	0	1	0
Total			2	1	1	1	1	0	0	0	0	0	1	0	0	0	1	1

Rank among batters: 4,129 • *Total ballparks homered in*: 2 • *First HR*: 08/13/1948 off Kent Peterson

Chuck Schilling

CHARLES THOMAS SCHILLING
B: 10/25/1937
BR

Year	Tm	Lg	Tot	H	A	Men-On 0	1	2	3	One-Game 2	3	4	LO	XN	IP	PH	RHP	LHP
1961	BOS	AL	5	4	1	4	0	0	1	0	0	0	2	0	0	0	3	2
1962	BOS	AL	7	3	4	5	1	1	0	0	0	0	0	0	0	0	5	2
1963	BOS	AL	8	5	3	6	2	0	0	0	0	0	0	0	0	0	8	0
1965	BOS	AL	3	1	2	3	0	0	0	0	0	0	0	0	0	2	0	3
Total			23	13	10	18	3	1	1	0	0	0	2	0	0	2	16	7

Rank among batters: 1,686 • Top target (2 home runs): Frank Baumann, Phil Regan, Jim Bunning, Mickey Lolich • *Number of pitchers victimized*: 19 • *Total ballparks homered in*: 6 • *First HR*: 05/07/1961 off Camilo Pascual

Calvin Schiraldi

CALVIN DREW SCHIRALDI
B: 06/16/1962
BR

Year	Tm	Lg	Tot	H	A	Men-On 0	1	2	3	One-Game 2	3	4	LO	XN	IP	PH	RHP	LHP
1989	SD	NL	1	0	1	0	0	1	0	0	0	0	0	0	0	0	0	1
1990	SD	NL	1	1	0	1	0	0	0	0	0	0	0	0	0	0	0	1
Total			2	1	1	1	0	1	0	0	0	0	0	0	0	0	0	2

Rank among batters: 4,129 • *Total ballparks homered in*: 2 • *First HR*: 09/23/1989 off Fernando Valenzuela

Larry Schlafly

HARRY LINTON SCHLAFLY
B: 09/20/1878 D: 06/27/1919
BR

Year	Tm	Lg	Tot	H	A	Men-On 0	1	2	3	One-Game 2	3	4	LO	XN	IP	PH	RHP	LHP
1906	WAS	AL	2	0	2	1	0	1	0	0	0	0	0	0	1	0	1	1
1907	WAS	AL	1	0	1	0	0	1	0	0	0	0	0	0	0	0	1	0
1914	BUF	FL	2	1	1	1	1	0	0	0	0	0	0	0	0	0	1	1
Total			5	1	4	2	1	2	0	0	0	0	0	0	1	0	3	2

Rank among batters: 3,191 • *Total ballparks homered in*: 5 • *First HR*: 05/04/1906 off Bill Dinneen

Admiral Schlei

GEORGE HENRY SCHLEI
B: 01/12/1878 D: 01/24/1958
BR

Year	Tm	Lg	Tot	H	A	Men-On 0	1	2	3	One-Game 2	3	4	LO	XN	IP	PH	RHP	LHP
1905	CIN	NL	1	0	1	0	1	0	0	0	0	0	0	0	1	0	1	0
1906	CIN	NL	4	2	2	2	2	0	0	0	0	0	0	1	1	0	4	0
1908	CIN	NL	1	1	0	1	0	0	0	0	0	0	0	0	1	0	1	0
Total			6	3	3	3	3	0	0	0	0	0	0	1	3	0	6	0

Rank among batters: 2,988 • *Total ballparks homered in*: 3 • *First HR*: 09/05/1905 off Chappie McFarland

Dutch Schliebner

FREDERICK PAUL SCHLIEBNER
B: 05/19/1891 D: 04/15/1975
BR

Year	Tm	Lg	Tot	H	A	Men-On 0	1	2	3	One-Game 2	3	4	LO	XN	IP	PH	RHP	LHP
1923	STL	AL	4	2	2	2	1	1	0	0	0	0	0	0	1	0	3	1

Rank among batters: 3,427 • *Total ballparks homered in*: 3 • *First HR*: 06/19/1923 off Lefty O'Doul

Ray Schmandt

RAYMOND HENRY SCHMANDT
B: 01/25/1896 D: 02/02/1969
BR

Year	Tm	Lg	Tot	H	A	Men-On 0	1	2	3	One-Game 2	3	4	LO	XN	IP	PH	RHP	LHP
1921	BRO	NL	1	0	1	1	0	0	0	0	0	0	0	1	1	0	1	0
1922	BRO	NL	2	1	1	2	0	0	0	0	0	0	0	0	1	0	1	1
Total			3	1	2	3	0	0	0	0	0	0	0	1	2	0	2	1

Rank among batters: 3,735 • *Total ballparks homered in*: 3 • *First HR*: 07/07/1921 off Rosy Ryan

Bob Schmidt

ROBERT BENJAMIN SCHMIDT
B: 04/22/1933
BR

Year	Tm	Lg	Tot	H	A	Men-On 0	1	2	3	One-Game 2	3	4	LO	XN	IP	PH	RHP	LHP
1958	SF	NL	14	8	6	9	3	1	1	0	0	0	0	1	0	1	10	4
1959	SF	NL	5	1	4	3	1	1	0	0	0	0	0	0	0	0	5	0
1960	SF	NL	8	2	6	3	2	2	1	0	0	0	0	0	0	0	3	5
1961	CIN	NL	1	0	1	0	1	0	0	0	0	0	0	0	0	0	1	0
1962	WAS	AL	10	6	4	8	2	0	0	0	0	0	0	1	0	1	5	5
1965	NY	AL	1	1	0	1	0	0	0	0	0	0	0	0	0	0	0	1
Total			39	18	21	24	9	4	2	0	0	0	0	2	0	2	24	15

Rank among batters: 1,204 • *Top target (3 home runs)*: Warren Spahn • *Number of pitchers victimized*: 34 • *Total ballparks homered in*: 14 • *First HR*: 04/17/1958 off Don Newcombe

Boss Schmidt

CHARLES SCHMIDT
B: 09/12/1880 D: 11/14/1932
BB

Year	Tm	Lg	Tot	H	A	Men-On 0	1	2	3	One-Game 2	3	4	LO	XN	IP	PH	RHP	LHP
1908	DET	AL	1	1	0	0	1	0	0	0	0	0	0	0	0	0	0	1
1909	DET	AL	1	0	1	0	0	1	0	0	0	0	0	0	0	0	0	1
1910	DET	AL	1	1	0	1	0	0	0	0	0	0	0	0	0	0	1	0
Total			3	2	1	1	1	1	0	0	0	0	0	0	0	0	1	2

Rank among batters: 3,735 • *Total ballparks homered in*: 2 • *First HR*: 09/25/1908 off Al Kellogg

Butch Schmidt

CHARLES JOHN SCHMIDT
B: 07/19/1886 D: 09/04/1952
BL

Year	Tm	Lg	Tot	H	A	Men-On 0	1	2	3	One-Game 2	3	4	LO	XN	IP	PH	RHP	LHP
1913	BOS	NL	1	1	0	0	0	1	0	0	0	0	0	0	0	0	1	0
1914	BOS	NL	1	0	1	0	0	1	0	0	0	0	0	0	0	0	1	0
1915	BOS	NL	2	0	2	1	0	1	0	0	0	0	0	0	0	0	2	0
Total			4	1	3	1	0	3	0	0	0	0	0	0	0	0	4	0

Rank among batters: 3,427 • *Top target (2 home runs)*: Pol Perritt • *Number of pitchers victimized*: 3 • *Total ballparks homered in*: 2 • *First HR*: 10/03/1913 off Ed Reulbach

Dave Schmidt

DAVID FREDERICK SCHMIDT
B: 12/22/1956
BR

Year	Tm	Lg	Tot	H	A	Men-On 0	1	2	3	One-Game 2	3	4	LO	XN	IP	PH	RHP	LHP
1981	BOS	AL	2	0	2	2	0	0	0	0	0	0	0	1	0	0	1	1

Rank among batters: 4,129 • *Total ballparks homered in*: 2 • *First HR*: 05/14/1981 off Don Cooper

Henry Schmidt

HENRY MARTIN SCHMIDT
B: 06/26/1873 D: 04/23/1926
BR

Year	Tm	Lg	Tot	H	A	Men-On 0	1	2	3	One-Game 2	3	4	LO	XN	IP	PH	RHP	LHP
1903	BRO	NL	1	0	1	0	1	0	0	0	0	0	0	0	0	0	0	1

Rank among batters: 4,707 • *Total ballparks homered in*: 1 • *First HR*: 06/17/1903 off Wiley Piatt

Mike Schmidt

MICHAEL JACK SCHMIDT
B: 09/27/1949
BR HOF

Year	Tm	Lg	Tot	H	A	Men-On 0	1	2	3	One-Game 2	3	4	LO	XN	IP	PH	RHP	LHP
1972	PHI	NL	1	1	0	0	0	1	0	0	0	0	0	0	0	0	0	1
1973	PHI	NL	18	9	9	8	3	5	2	2	0	0	0	0	0	0	10	8
1974	PHI	NL	36	19	17	17	12	7	0	6	0	0	0	0	1	0	21	15
1975	PHI	NL	38	22	16	22	12	4	0	4	0	0	0	0	0	0	33	5
1976	PHI	NL	38	17	21	19	14	5	0	3	0	1	0	1	0	0	30	8
1977	PHI	NL	38	17	21	21	10	7	0	3	0	0	0	1	1	0	26	12
1978	PHI	NL	21	13	8	11	4	6	0	0	0	0	1	1	0	0	13	8
1979	PHI	NL	45	16	29	26	12	6	1	2	1	0	0	1	0	0	36	9
1980	PHI	NL	48	25	23	27	18	2	1	5	0	0	0	1	0	0	38	10
1981	PHI	NL	31	17	14	14	9	7	1	2	0	0	0	0	0	1	23	8
1982	PHI	NL	35	17	18	17	14	4	0	0	0	0	0	0	1	0	25	10
1983	PHI	NL	40	19	21	18	16	4	2	5	0	0	0	1	0	0	33	7
1984	PHI	NL	36	16	20	23	10	3	0	3	0	0	0	0	0	1	28	8

Mike Schmidt *continued*

						Men-On				One-Game								
Year	Tm	Lg	Tot	H	A	0	1	2	3	2	3	4	LO	XN	IP	PH	RHP	LHP
1985	PHI	NL	33	14	19	25	3	5	0	1	0	0	0	1	0	0	27	6
1986	PHI	NL	37	20	17	16	14	7	0	3	0	0	0	2	0	0	22	15
1987	PHI	NL	35	15	20	18	11	6	0	2	1	0	0	0	0	0	29	6
1988	PHI	NL	12	6	6	7	4	1	0	0	0	0	0	0	0	0	9	3
1989	PHI	NL	6	2	4	2	2	2	0	0	0	0	0	0	0	0	4	2
Total			548	265	283	291	168	82	7	41	2	1	1	9	3	2	407	141

Rank among batters: 7 • *Top target (11 home runs)*: Bob Forsch • *Number of pitchers victimized*: 269 • *Total ballparks homered in*: 13 • *First HR*: 09/16/1972 off Balor Moore • *World Series HR—2; LCS HR—2; All-Star HR—1*

Walter Schmidt

WALTER JOSEPH SCHMIDT
B: 03/20/1887 D: 07/04/1973
BR

Year	Tm	Lg	Tot	H	A	Men-On 0	1	2	3	One-Game 2	3	4	LO	XN	IP	PH	RHP	LHP
1916	PIT	NL	2	2	0	1	0	1	0	0	0	0	0	0	1	1	1	1
1924	PIT	NL	1	0	1	0	0	0	1	0	0	0	0	0	0	0	1	0
Total			3	2	1	1	0	1	1	0	0	0	0	0	1	1	2	1

Rank among batters: 3,735 • *Total ballparks homered in*: 2 • *First HR*: 05/09/1916 off Christy Mathewson

Johnny Schmitz

JOHN ALBERT SCHMITZ
B: 11/27/1920
BR

Year	Tm	Lg	Tot	H	A	Men-On 0	1	2	3	One-Game 2	3	4	LO	XN	IP	PH	RHP	LHP
1946	CHI	NL	1	0	1	1	0	0	0	0	0	0	0	0	0	0	0	1
1951	BRO	NL	1	0	1	1	0	0	0	0	0	0	0	0	0	0	0	1
Total			2	0	2	2	0	0	0	0	0	0	0	0	0	0	0	2

Rank among batters: 4,129 • *Total ballparks homered in*: 2 • *First HR*: 05/18/1946 off Jack Kraus

Dave Schneck

DAVID LEE SCHNECK
B: 06/18/1949
BL

Year	Tm	Lg	Tot	H	A	Men-On 0	1	2	3	One-Game 2	3	4	LO	XN	IP	PH	RHP	LHP
1972	NY	NL	3	0	3	1	1	1	0	0	0	0	0	0	0	0	3	0
1974	NY	NL	5	0	5	1	3	1	0	2	0	0	0	0	0	0	5	0
Total			8	0	8	2	4	2	0	2	0	0	0	0	0	0	8	0

Rank among batters: 2,703 • *Top target (2 home runs)*: Steve Rogers, Tom Bradley • *Number of pitchers victimized*: 6 • *Total ballparks homered in*: 4 • *First HR*: 07/14/1972 off Steve Arlin

Pete Schneider

PETER JOSEPH SCHNEIDER
B: 08/20/1895 D: 06/01/1957
BR

Year	Tm	Lg	Tot	H	A	Men-On 0	1	2	3	One-Game 2	3	4	LO	XN	IP	PH	RHP	LHP
1914	CIN	NL	1	0	1	1	0	0	0	0	0	0	0	0	1	0	1	0
1915	CIN	NL	2	1	1	2	0	0	0	0	0	0	0	0	2	0	2	0
1917	CIN	NL	1	0	1	1	0	0	0	0	0	0	0	0	0	0	1	0
1918	CIN	NL	1	0	1	0	0	1	0	0	0	0	0	0	0	0	1	0
Total			5	1	4	4	0	1	0	0	0	0	0	0	3	0	5	0

Rank among batters: 3,191 • *Total ballparks homered in*: 4 • *First HR*: 09/18/1914 off Art Fromme

Red Schoendienst

ALBERT FRED SCHOENDIENST
B: 02/02/1923
BB HOF

Year	Tm	Lg	Tot	H	A	Men-On 0	1	2	3	One-Game 2	3	4	LO	XN	IP	PH	RHP	LHP
1945	STL	NL	1	0	1	1	0	0	0	0	0	0	0	0	0	0	1	0
1947	STL	NL	3	0	3	3	0	0	0	0	0	0	1	0	0	0	2	1
1948	STL	NL	4	2	2	2	1	1	0	0	0	0	0	0	0	0	4	0
1949	STL	NL	3	1	2	3	0	0	0	0	0	0	0	0	0	0	2	1
1950	STL	NL	7	4	3	3	3	1	0	0	0	0	0	0	0	0	6	1
1951	STL	NL	6	1	5	3	2	1	0	1	0	0	0	0	0	0	3	3
1952	STL	NL	7	6	1	3	2	1	1	0	0	0	0	0	0	0	4	3
1953	STL	NL	15	9	6	9	5	1	0	1	0	0	0	0	0	1	10	5
1954	STL	NL	5	1	4	3	2	0	0	0	0	0	0	0	0	0	2	3
1955	STL	NL	11	9	2	9	2	0	0	0	0	0	0	0	0	0	11	0

Red Schoendienst *continued*

Year	Tm	Lg	Tot	H	A	Men-On 0	1	2	3	One-Game 2	3	4	LO	XN	IP	PH	RHP	LHP
1956	NY	NL	2	2	0	1	1	0	0	0	0	0	0	0	0	1	2	0
1957	NY	NL	9	8	1	7	1	0	1	1	0	0	1	0	0	0	9	0
	MIL	NL	6	2	4	5	1	0	0	0	0	0	2	0	0	0	6	0
	Total		15	10	5	12	2	0	1	1	0	0	3	0	0	0	15	0
1958	MIL	NL	1	1	0	0	1	0	0	0	0	0	0	0	0	0	1	0
1960	MIL	NL	1	1	0	1	0	0	0	0	0	0	0	0	0	0	1	0
1961	STL	NL	1	0	1	1	0	0	0	0	0	0	1	0	0	0	1	0
1962	STL	NL	2	0	2	1	1	0	0	0	0	0	0	0	0	1	1	1
Total			84	47	37	55	22	5	2	3	0	0	5	0	0	3	66	18

Rank among batters: 617 • *Top target (4 home runs)*: Warren Spahn • *Number of pitchers victimized*: 66 • *Total ballparks homered in*: 10 • *First HR*: 08/10/1945 off Bill Voiselle • *Switch hit HR in 1 game*—1 time • *All-Star HR*—1

Jumbo Schoeneck

LEWIS W. SCHOENECK
B: 03/03/1862 D: 01/20/1930
BR

Year	Tm	Lg	Tot	H	A	Men-On 0	1	2	3	One-Game 2	3	4	LO	XN	IP	PH	RHP	LHP
1884	CHI	UA	2	0	2	1	1	0	0	0	0	0	0	0	1	0	1	1

Rank among batters: 4,129 • *Total ballparks homered in*: 2 • *First HR*: 04/28/1884 off Dick Burns

Dick Schofield

JOHN RICHARD SCHOFIELD
B: 01/07/1935
BB

Year	Tm	Lg	Tot	H	A	Men-On 0	1	2	3	One-Game 2	3	4	LO	XN	IP	PH	RHP	LHP
1953	STL	NL	2	0	2	2	0	0	0	0	0	0	0	0	0	0	2	0
1958	STL	NL	1	0	1	1	0	0	0	0	0	0	0	0	0	1	1	0
1959	PIT	NL	1	1	0	1	0	0	0	0	0	0	0	0	0	0	1	0
1962	PIT	NL	2	1	1	0	2	0	0	0	0	0	0	0	0	1	2	0
1963	PIT	NL	3	2	1	2	1	0	0	0	0	0	0	0	0	0	2	1
1964	PIT	NL	3	0	3	2	0	1	0	0	0	0	0	0	0	0	2	1
1965	SF	NL	2	2	0	2	0	0	0	0	0	0	1	0	0	0	2	0
1967	LA	NL	2	1	1	2	0	0	0	0	0	0	1	0	0	0	1	1
1968	STL	NL	1	0	1	1	0	0	0	0	0	0	0	1	0	0	1	0
1969	BOS	AL	2	2	0	2	0	0	0	0	0	0	0	0	0	1	2	0
1970	BOS	AL	1	0	1	1	0	0	0	0	0	0	0	0	0	0	1	0
1971	STL	NL	1	0	1	0	1	0	0	0	0	0	0	0	0	0	1	0
Total			21	9	12	16	4	1	0	0	0	0	2	1	0	3	18	3

Rank among batters: 1,768 • *Total ballparks homered in*: 13 • *First HR*: 08/16/1953 off Frank Smith

Dick Schofield

RICHARD CRAIG SCHOFIELD
B: 11/21/1962
BR

Year	Tm	Lg	Tot	H	A	Men-On 0	1	2	3	One-Game 2	3	4	LO	XN	IP	PH	RHP	LHP
1983	CAL	AL	3	2	1	3	0	0	0	0	0	0	0	0	0	0	3	0
1984	CAL	AL	4	0	4	1	2	1	0	0	0	0	0	0	0	0	3	1
1985	CAL	AL	8	5	3	5	2	0	1	0	0	0	0	0	0	0	6	2
1986	CAL	AL	13	7	6	9	0	2	2	0	0	0	0	0	0	0	9	4
1987	CAL	AL	9	4	5	5	2	1	1	0	0	0	0	0	0	0	7	2
1988	CAL	AL	6	3	3	4	2	0	0	0	0	0	1	0	0	0	2	4
1989	CAL	AL	4	1	3	3	0	1	0	0	0	0	1	0	0	0	3	1
1990	CAL	AL	1	1	0	1	0	0	0	0	0	0	0	0	0	0	0	1
1992	NY	NL	4	3	1	3	0	1	0	0	0	0	0	0	0	0	2	2
1994	TOR	AL	4	2	2	2	1	0	1	0	0	0	0	0	0	0	3	1
Total			56	28	28	36	9	6	5	0	0	0	2	0	0	0	38	18

Rank among batters: 913 • Top target (2 home runs): Lamarr Hoyt, Salome Barojas, Neal Heaton, Rick Rhoden, Dave Stewart • *Number of pitchers victimized*: 51 • *Total ballparks homered in*: 16 • *First HR*: 09/10/1983 off Salome Barojas • *LCS HR*—1

Otto Schomberg

OTTO H. SCHOMBERG
B: 11/14/1864 D: 05/03/1927
BL

Year	Tm	Lg	Tot	H	A	Men-On 0	1	2	3	One-Game 2	3	4	LO	XN	IP	PH	RHP	LHP
1886	PIT	AA	1	1	0	1	0	0	0	0	0	0	0	0	0	0	0	1
1887	IND	NL	5	3	2	2	1	2	0	0	0	0	0	0	0	0	3	2

Year	Tm	Lg	Tot	H	A	Men-On 0	1	2	3	One-Game 2	3	4	LO	XN	IP	PH	RHP	LHP

Otto Schomberg *continued*

Year	Tm	Lg	Tot	H	A	0	1	2	3	2	3	4	LO	XN	IP	PH	RHP	LHP
1888	IND	NL	1	1	0	0	1	0	0	0	0	0	0	0	0	0	1	0
Total			7	5	2	3	2	2	0	0	0	0	0	0	0	0	4	3

Rank among batters: 2,834 • *Total ballparks homered in*: 5 • *First HR*: 07/13/1886 off Ed Cushman

Jerry Schoonmaker

JERALD LEE SCHOONMAKER
B: 12/14/1933
BR

Year	Tm	Lg	Tot	H	A	0	1	2	3	2	3	4	LO	XN	IP	PH	RHP	LHP
1955	WAS	AL	1	0	1	0	1	0	0	0	0	0	0	0	0	0	1	0

Rank among batters: 4,707 • *Total ballparks homered in*: 1 • *First HR*: 07/23/1955 off Steve Gromek

Gene Schott

ARTHUR EUGENE SCHOTT
B: 07/14/1913 D: 11/16/1992
BR

Year	Tm	Lg	Tot	H	A	0	1	2	3	2	3	4	LO	XN	IP	PH	RHP	LHP
1936	CIN	NL	1	0	1	0	1	0	0	0	0	0	0	0	0	0	1	0

Rank among batters: 4,707 • *Total ballparks homered in*: 1 • *First HR*: 06/19/1936 off Tiny Chaplin

Pete Schourek

PETER ALAN SCHOUREK
B: 05/10/1969
BL

Year	Tm	Lg	Tot	H	A	0	1	2	3	2	3	4	LO	XN	IP	PH	RHP	LHP
1994	CIN	NL	1	0	1	1	0	0	0	0	0	0	0	0	0	0	1	0

Rank among batters: 4,707 • *Total ballparks homered in*: 1 • *First HR*: 06/13/1994 off Ramon Martinez

Ossee Schreckengost

OSSEE FREEMAN SCHRECKENGOST
B: 04/11/1875 D: 07/09/1914
BR

Year	Tm	Lg	Tot	H	A	0	1	2	3	2	3	4	LO	XN	IP	PH	RHP	LHP
1899	STL	NL	2	1	1	1	0	1	0	0	0	0	0	0	1	0	2	0
1902	PHI	AL	2	1	1	1	1	0	0	0	0	0	0	0	0	0	1	1
1903	PHI	AL	3	1	2	3	0	0	0	0	0	0	0	0	0	0	2	1
1904	PHI	AL	1	0	1	1	0	0	0	0	0	0	0	0	1	0	1	0
1906	PHI	AL	1	1	0	1	0	0	0	0	0	0	0	0	0	0	1	0
Total			9	4	5	7	1	1	0	0	0	0	0	0	2	0	7	2

Rank among batters: 2,587 • *Total ballparks homered in*: 6 • *First HR*: 08/09/1899 off Joe McGinnity

Pop Schriver

WILLIAM FREDERICK SCHRIVER
B: 07/11/1865 D: 12/27/1932
BR

Year	Tm	Lg	Tot	H	A	0	1	2	3	2	3	4	LO	XN	IP	PH	RHP	LHP
1888	PHI	NL	1	0	1	1	0	0	0	0	0	0	0	0	0	0	0	0
1889	PHI	NL	1	1	0	0	1	0	0	0	0	0	0	0	1	0	0	1
1891	CHI	NL	1	0	1	0	0	1	0	0	0	0	0	0	0	0	0	0
1892	CHI	NL	1	0	1	0	1	0	0	0	0	0	0	0	0	0	1	0
1893	CHI	NL	4	3	1	4	0	0	0	0	0	0	0	0	0	0	3	0
1894	CHI	NL	3	0	3	1	1	1	0	0	0	0	0	0	0	0	2	0
1895	NY	NL	1	1	0	1	0	0	0	0	0	0	0	0	0	0	1	0
1897	CIN	NL	1	0	1	0	0	1	0	0	0	0	0	0	0	0	1	0
1899	PIT	NL	1	0	1	1	0	0	0	0	0	0	0	0	0	0	1	0
1900	PIT	NL	1	1	0	0	1	0	0	0	0	0	0	0	0	0	1	0
1901	STL	NL	1	1	0	0	1	0	0	0	0	0	0	0	1	0	0	1
Total			16	7	9	8	5	3	0	0	0	0	0	0	2	0	10	2

Rank among batters: 2,029 • *Total ballparks homered in*: 10 • *First HR*: 06/19/1888 off Frank Gilmore

Bill Schroeder

ALFRED WILLIAM SCHROEDER
B: 09/07/1958
BR

Year	Tm	Lg	Tot	H	A	0	1	2	3	2	3	4	LO	XN	IP	PH	RHP	LHP
1983	MIL	AL	3	2	1	2	1	0	0	0	0	0	0	0	0	0	1	2
1984	MIL	AL	14	7	7	13	1	0	0	2	0	0	0	0	0	0	9	5
1985	MIL	AL	8	2	6	4	3	0	1	1	0	0	0	0	0	0	3	5
1986	MIL	AL	7	2	5	2	4	1	0	0	0	0	0	0	0	0	4	3

Bill Schroeder *continued*

Year	Tm	Lg	Tot	H	A	Men-On 0	1	2	3	One-Game 2	3	4	LO	XN	IP	PH	RHP	LHP
1987	MIL	AL	14	5	9	6	5	3	0	1	0	0	0	0	0	0	6	8
1988	MIL	AL	5	2	3	2	2	1	0	0	0	0	0	0	0	0	2	3
1989	CAL	AL	6	2	4	4	0	1	1	1	0	0	0	0	0	0	2	4
1990	CAL	AL	4	0	4	2	2	0	0	1	0	0	0	0	0	0	1	3
Total			61	22	39	35	18	6	2	6	0	0	0	0	0	0	28	33

Rank among batters: 844 • *Top target (3 home runs)*: Oil Can Boyd, Floyd Bannister, Frank Viola • *Number of pitchers victimized*: 47 • *Total ballparks homered in*: 13 • *First HR*: 07/14/1983 off Albert Williams

Al Schroll

ALBERT BRINGHURST SCHROLL
B: 03/22/1932
BR

Year	Tm	Lg	Tot	H	A	Men-On 0	1	2	3	One-Game 2	3	4	LO	XN	IP	PH	RHP	LHP
1961	MIN	AL	1	0	1	1	0	0	0	0	0	0	0	0	0	0	1	0

Rank among batters: 4,707 • *Total ballparks homered in*: 1 • *First HR*: 08/20/1961 off Art Fowler

Rick Schu

RICHARD SPENCER SCHU
B: 01/26/1962
BR

Year	Tm	Lg	Tot	H	A	Men-On 0	1	2	3	One-Game 2	3	4	LO	XN	IP	PH	RHP	LHP
1984	PHI	NL	2	1	1	1	1	0	0	0	0	0	0	0	0	0	1	1
1985	PHI	NL	7	2	5	6	1	0	0	0	0	0	0	0	0	0	3	4
1986	PHI	NL	8	1	7	4	4	0	0	1	0	0	0	0	0	2	4	4
1987	PHI	NL	7	5	2	4	2	1	0	0	0	0	0	0	0	0	2	5
1988	BAL	AL	4	2	2	2	1	0	1	0	0	0	0	0	0	0	1	3
1989	DET	AL	7	3	4	7	0	0	0	0	0	0	0	0	0	0	2	5
1990	CAL	AL	6	3	3	5	1	0	0	0	0	0	0	0	0	0	1	5
Total			41	17	24	29	10	1	1	1	0	0	0	0	0	2	14	27

Rank among batters: 1,163 • *Top target (2 home runs)*: Dwight Gooden, Ricky Horton, Mike Jeffcoat • *Number of pitchers victimized*: 38 • *Total ballparks homered in*: 17 • *First HR*: 09/02/1984 off Mark Davis

Heinie Schuble

HENRY GEORGE SCHUBLE
B: 11/01/1906 D: 10/02/1990
BR

Year	Tm	Lg	Tot	H	A	Men-On 0	1	2	3	One-Game 2	3	4	LO	XN	IP	PH	RHP	LHP
1927	STL	NL	4	1	3	0	2	2	0	0	0	0	0	0	1	0	4	0
1929	DET	AL	2	2	0	1	1	0	0	0	0	0	0	0	0	0	2	0
1932	DET	AL	5	4	1	3	1	1	0	1	0	0	0	0	0	0	2	3
Total			11	7	4	4	4	3	0	1	0	0	0	0	1	0	8	3

Rank among batters: 2,419 • *Top target (3 home runs)*: Herb Pennock • *Number of pitchers victimized*: 9 • *Total ballparks homered in*: 5 • *First HR*: 07/10/1927 off Burleigh Grimes

Wes Schulmerich

EDWARD WESLEY SCHULMERICH
B: 04/21/1901 D: 06/26/1985
BR

Year	Tm	Lg	Tot	H	A	Men-On 0	1	2	3	One-Game 2	3	4	LO	XN	IP	PH	RHP	LHP
1931	BOS	NL	2	1	1	1	1	0	0	0	0	0	0	0	0	0	1	1
1932	BOS	NL	11	5	6	9	1	1	0	1	0	0	0	0	0	1	9	2
1933	BOS	NL	1	1	0	1	0	0	0	0	0	0	0	0	0	0	1	0
	PHI	NL	8	8	0	4	1	3	0	0	0	0	0	0	0	0	7	1
	Total		9	9	0	5	1	3	0	0	0	0	0	0	0	0	8	1
1934	CIN	NL	5	0	5	3	0	2	0	0	0	0	0	0	0	0	5	0
Total			27	15	12	18	3	6	0	1	0	0	0	0	0	1	23	4

Rank among batters: 1,532 • Top target (2 home runs): Phil Collins, Larry French, Fred Frankhouse, Jim Lindsey • *Number of pitchers victimized*: 23 • *Total ballparks homered in*: 7 • *First HR*: 05/05/1931 off Clise Dudley

Art Schult

ARTHUR WILLIAM SCHULT
B: 06/20/1928
BR

Year	Tm	Lg	Tot	H	A	Men-On 0	1	2	3	One-Game 2	3	4	LO	XN	IP	PH	RHP	LHP
1957	WAS	AL	4	3	1	3	1	0	0	0	0	0	0	0	0	0	2	2
1959	CHI	NL	2	1	1	2	0	0	0	0	0	0	0	0	0	0	2	0
Total			6	4	2	5	1	0	0	0	0	0	0	0	0	0	4	2

Rank among batters: 2,988 • *Total ballparks homered in*: 4 • *First HR*: 06/21/1957 off Don Mossi

Wildfire Schulte

FRANK M. SCHULTE
B: 09/17/1882 D: 10/02/1949
BL

Year	Tm	Lg	Tot	H	A	Men-On 0	1	2	3	One-Game 2	3	4	LO	XN	IP	PH	RHP	LHP
1904	CHI	NL	2	0	2	0	0	2	0	0	0	0	0	0	1	0	2	0
1905	CHI	NL	1	0	1	0	1	0	0	0	0	0	0	0	0	0	1	0
1906	CHI	NL	7	3	4	3	2	2	0	0	0	0	0	0	4	0	5	2
1907	CHI	NL	2	0	2	1	1	0	0	0	0	0	0	0	1	0	2	0
1908	CHI	NL	1	1	0	1	0	0	0	0	0	0	0	0	1	0	1	0
1909	CHI	NL	4	2	2	1	2	1	0	0	0	0	0	0	2	0	3	1
1910	CHI	NL	10	6	4	5	3	2	0	2	0	0	0	0	2	0	8	2
1911	CHI	NL	21	11	10	9	5	3	4	1	0	0	0	0	2	0	15	6
1912	CHI	NL	12	7	5	9	2	1	0	0	0	0	0	1	3	0	9	3
1913	CHI	NL	9	6	3	6	2	1	0	1	0	0	0	0	1	0	8	1
1914	CHI	NL	5	3	2	2	3	0	0	0	0	0	0	0	1	0	5	0
1915	CHI	NL	12	8	4	5	6	1	0	0	0	0	0	0	0	0	8	4
1916	CHI	NL	5	3	2	3	1	1	0	0	0	0	0	0	0	0	5	0
1917	PHI	NL	1	1	0	1	0	0	0	0	0	0	0	0	0	0	1	0
Total			92	51	41	46	28	14	4	4	0	0	0	1	18	0	73	19

Rank among batters: 554 • *Top target (4 home runs)*: Hub Perdue • *Number of pitchers victimized*: 62 • *Total ballparks homered in*: 11 • *First HR*: 09/24/1904 off Jack Cronin

Fred Schulte

FRED WILLIAM SCHULTE
B: 01/13/1901 D: 05/20/1983
BR

Year	Tm	Lg	Tot	H	A	Men-On 0	1	2	3	One-Game 2	3	4	LO	XN	IP	PH	RHP	LHP
1927	STL	AL	3	1	2	2	1	0	0	0	0	0	0	0	0	0	3	0
1928	STL	AL	7	4	3	2	4	1	0	0	0	0	0	1	1	0	5	2
1929	STL	AL	3	2	1	2	1	0	0	0	0	0	0	0	0	0	3	0
1930	STL	AL	5	3	2	3	2	0	0	0	0	0	0	0	0	0	3	2
1931	STL	AL	9	5	4	6	2	1	0	1	0	0	2	0	0	0	6	3
1932	STL	AL	9	6	3	6	3	0	0	0	0	0	3	0	0	0	7	2
1933	WAS	AL	5	1	4	3	1	1	0	0	0	0	0	0	1	0	2	3
1934	WAS	AL	3	0	3	2	0	1	0	0	0	0	0	0	0	0	3	0
1935	WAS	AL	2	0	2	1	1	0	0	0	0	0	0	0	0	0	1	1
1936	PIT	NL	1	0	1	1	0	0	0	0	0	0	0	0	0	0	0	1
Total			47	22	25	28	15	4	0	1	0	0	5	1	2	0	33	14

Rank among batters: 1,040 • *Top target (4 home runs)*: Rube Walberg • *Number of pitchers victimized*: 38 • *Total ballparks homered in*: 8 • *First HR*: 06/04/1927 off Walter Johnson • *World Series HR*—1

Ham Schulte

HERMAN JOSEPH SCHULTE
B: 09/01/1912 D: 12/21/1993
BR

Year	Tm	Lg	Tot	H	A	Men-On 0	1	2	3	One-Game 2	3	4	LO	XN	IP	PH	RHP	LHP
1940	PHI	NL	1	0	1	0	1	0	0	0	0	0	0	0	0	0	1	0

Rank among batters: 4,707 • *Total ballparks homered in*: 1 • *First HR*: 08/16/1940 off Hal Schumacher

Johnny Schulte

JOHN CLEMENT SCHULTE
B: 09/08/1896 D: 06/28/1978
BL

Year	Tm	Lg	Tot	H	A	Men-On 0	1	2	3	One-Game 2	3	4	LO	XN	IP	PH	RHP	LHP
1927	STL	NL	9	6	3	5	4	0	0	0	0	0	0	1	0	0	9	0
1928	PHI	NL	4	3	1	1	3	0	0	0	0	0	0	0	0	2	4	0
1932	BOS	NL	1	0	1	1	0	0	0	0	0	0	0	0	0	0	1	0
Total			14	9	5	7	7	0	0	0	0	0	0	1	0	2	14	0

Rank among batters: 2,169 • *Top target (2 home runs)*: Charlie Root • *Number of pitchers victimized*: 13 • *Total ballparks homered in*: 4 • *First HR*: 06/08/1927 off Hal Goldsmith

Howie Schultz

HOWARD HENRY SCHULTZ
B: 07/03/1922
BR

Year	Tm	Lg	Tot	H	A	Men-On 0	1	2	3	One-Game 2	3	4	LO	XN	IP	PH	RHP	LHP
1943	BRO	NL	1	1	0	0	1	0	0	0	0	0	0	0	0	0	1	0
1944	BRO	NL	11	3	8	5	4	1	1	1	0	0	0	0	0	1	9	2
1945	BRO	NL	1	1	0	1	0	0	0	0	0	0	0	0	0	0	0	1
1946	BRO	NL	3	1	2	3	0	0	0	0	0	0	0	0	0	0	0	3

Howie Schultz *continued*

Year	Tm	Lg	Tot	H	A	Men-On				One-Game			LO	XN	IP	PH	RHP	LHP
						0	1	2	3	2	3	4						
1947	PHI	NL	6	1	5	3	1	1	1	0	0	0	0	0	0	0	4	2
1948	CIN	NL	2	2	0	0	1	1	0	0	0	0	0	0	0	0	0	2
Total			24	9	15	12	7	3	2	1	0	0	0	0	0	1	14	10

Rank among batters: 1,643 • *Top target (3 home runs)*: Bill Voiselle • *Number of pitchers victimized*: 21 • *Total ballparks homered in*: 7 • *First HR*: 08/22/1943 off Xavier Rescigno

Joe Schultz

JOSEPH CHARLES SCHULTZ, SR.
B: 07/24/1893 D: 04/13/1941
BR

Year	Tm	Lg	Tot	H	A	Men-On				One-Game			LO	XN	IP	PH	RHP	LHP
						0	1	2	3	2	3	4						
1919	STL	NL	2	1	1	2	0	0	0	0	0	0	0	0	0	1	2	0
1921	STL	NL	6	3	3	3	2	0	1	0	0	0	0	1	0	2	2	4
1922	STL	NL	2	1	1	2	0	0	0	0	0	0	0	0	0	0	2	0
1924	PHI	NL	5	2	3	3	1	0	1	1	0	0	0	0	0	0	4	1
Total			15	7	8	10	3	0	2	1	0	0	0	1	0	3	10	5

Rank among batters: 2,096 • *Top target (3 home runs)*: Art Nehf • *Number of pitchers victimized*: 13 • *Total ballparks homered in*: 6 • *First HR*: 05/19/1919 off Elmer Jacobs

Joe Schultz

JOSEPH CHARLES SCHULTZ, JR.
B: 08/29/1918
BL

Year	Tm	Lg	Tot	H	A	Men-On				One-Game			LO	XN	IP	PH	RHP	LHP
						0	1	2	3	2	3	4						
1947	STL	AL	1	0	1	1	0	0	0	0	0	0	0	0	0	1	1	0

Rank among batters: 4,707 • *Total ballparks homered in*: 1 • *First HR*: 08/11/1947 off Pete Gebrian

Al Schulz

ALBERT CHRISTOPHER SCHULZ
B: 05/12/1889 D: 12/13/1931
BR

Year	Tm	Lg	Tot	H	A	Men-On				One-Game			LO	XN	IP	PH	RHP	LHP
						0	1	2	3	2	3	4						
1914	BUF	FL	1	1	0	0	1	0	0	0	0	0	0	0	0	0	1	0

Rank among batters: 4,707 • *Total ballparks homered in*: 1 • *First HR*: 09/11/1914 off Dave Black

Hal Schumacher

HAROLD HENRY SCHUMACHER
B: 11/23/1910 D: 04/21/1993
BR

Year	Tm	Lg	Tot	H	A	Men-On				One-Game			LO	XN	IP	PH	RHP	LHP
						0	1	2	3	2	3	4						
1934	NY	NL	6	1	5	4	1	1	0	1	0	0	0	0	0	0	5	1
1935	NY	NL	2	1	1	1	0	1	0	0	0	0	0	0	0	0	1	1
1936	NY	NL	1	1	0	1	0	0	0	0	0	0	0	0	0	0	1	0
1937	NY	NL	2	1	1	1	0	1	0	0	0	0	0	0	0	0	2	0
1938	NY	NL	2	2	0	2	0	0	0	0	0	0	0	0	0	0	0	2
1940	NY	NL	1	1	0	1	0	0	0	0	0	0	0	0	0	0	1	0
1942	NY	NL	1	1	0	0	1	0	0	0	0	0	0	0	0	0	1	0
Total			15	8	7	10	2	3	0	1	0	0	0	0	0	0	11	4

Rank among batters: 2,096 • *Top target (2 home runs)*: Cy Moore • *Number of pitchers victimized*: 14 • *Total ballparks homered in*: 6 • *First HR*: 04/24/1934 off Cy Moore

Ferdie Schupp

FERDINAND MAURICE SCHUPP
B: 01/16/1891 D: 12/16/1971
BR

Year	Tm	Lg	Tot	H	A	Men-On				One-Game			LO	XN	IP	PH	RHP	LHP
						0	1	2	3	2	3	4						
1919	STL	NL	1	1	0	1	0	0	0	0	0	0	0	0	1	0	1	0

Rank among batters: 4,707 • *Total ballparks homered in*: 1 • *First HR*: 09/11/1919 off Leon Cadore

Bill Schuster

WILLIAM CHARLES SCHUSTER
B: 08/04/1912 D: 06/28/1987
BR

Year	Tm	Lg	Tot	H	A	Men-On				One-Game			LO	XN	IP	PH	RHP	LHP
						0	1	2	3	2	3	4						
1944	CHI	NL	1	0	1	0	0	1	0	0	0	0	0	0	0	0	1	0

Rank among batters: 4,707 • *Total ballparks homered in*: 1 • *First HR*: 04/30/1944 off Ted Wilks

Bill Schwartz

WILLIAM AUGUST SCHWARTZ
B: 04/03/1864 D: 12/22/1940
BR

Year	Tm	Lg	Tot	H	A	Men-On 0	Men-On 1	Men-On 2	Men-On 3	One-Game 2	One-Game 3	One-Game 4	LO	XN	IP	PH	RHP	LHP
1884	CIN	UA	1	1	0	1	0	0	0	0	0	0	0	0	1	0	1	0

Rank among batters: 4,707 • *Total ballparks homered in*: 1 • *First HR*: 05/08/1884 off Bill Sweeney

Al Schweitzer

ALBERT CASPER SCHWEITZER
B: 12/23/1882 D: 01/27/1969
BR

Year	Tm	Lg	Tot	H	A	Men-On 0	Men-On 1	Men-On 2	Men-On 3	One-Game 2	One-Game 3	One-Game 4	LO	XN	IP	PH	RHP	LHP
1908	STL	AL	1	1	0	1	0	0	0	0	0	0	0	0	0	0	1	0
1910	STL	AL	2	0	2	2	0	0	0	0	0	0	0	0	0	0	2	0
Total			3	1	2	3	0	0	0	0	0	0	0	0	0	0	3	0

Rank among batters: 3,735 • *Total ballparks homered in*: 3 • *First HR*: 10/05/1908 off Edward Foster

Mike Scioscia

MICHAEL LORRI SCIOSCIA
B: 11/27/1958
BL

Year	Tm	Lg	Tot	H	A	Men-On 0	Men-On 1	Men-On 2	Men-On 3	One-Game 2	One-Game 3	One-Game 4	LO	XN	IP	PH	RHP	LHP
1980	LA	NL	1	1	0	1	0	0	0	0	0	0	0	0	0	0	1	0
1981	LA	NL	2	0	2	1	0	1	0	0	0	0	0	0	0	0	2	0
1982	LA	NL	5	2	3	3	1	1	0	0	0	0	0	0	0	0	4	1
1983	LA	NL	1	0	1	0	1	0	0	0	0	0	0	0	0	0	1	0
1984	LA	NL	5	0	5	3	0	2	0	0	0	0	0	0	0	0	5	0
1985	LA	NL	7	1	6	6	1	0	0	0	0	0	0	0	0	0	6	1
1986	LA	NL	5	2	3	4	1	0	0	0	0	0	0	0	0	0	3	2
1987	LA	NL	6	2	4	6	0	0	0	0	0	0	0	0	0	0	6	0
1988	LA	NL	3	1	2	1	2	0	0	0	0	0	0	0	0	0	3	0
1989	LA	NL	10	4	6	6	1	1	2	0	0	0	0	0	0	0	7	3
1990	LA	NL	12	5	7	10	2	0	0	0	0	0	0	0	0	0	10	2
1991	LA	NL	8	3	5	8	0	0	0	0	0	0	0	0	0	0	5	3
1992	LA	NL	3	1	2	1	2	0	0	0	0	0	0	0	0	0	2	1
Total			68	22	46	50	11	5	2	0	0	0	0	0	0	0	55	13

Rank among batters: 767 • *Top target (4 home runs)*: Don Robinson • *Number of pitchers victimized*: 54 • *Total ballparks homered in*: 12 • *First HR*: 07/06/1980 off John Montefusco • *LCS HR—2*

Daryl Sconiers

DARYL ANTHONY SCONIERS
B: 10/03/1958
BL

Year	Tm	Lg	Tot	H	A	Men-On 0	Men-On 1	Men-On 2	Men-On 3	One-Game 2	One-Game 3	One-Game 4	LO	XN	IP	PH	RHP	LHP
1981	CAL	AL	1	1	0	0	1	0	0	0	0	0	0	0	0	0	1	0
1983	CAL	AL	8	5	3	2	1	3	2	0	0	0	0	1	0	2	7	1
1984	CAL	AL	4	4	0	4	0	0	0	0	0	0	0	0	0	1	4	0
1985	CAL	AL	2	1	1	1	1	0	0	0	0	0	0	0	0	0	2	0
Total			15	11	4	7	3	3	2	0	0	0	0	1	0	3	14	1

Rank among batters: 2,096 • *Top target (2 home runs)*: Len Barker, Richard Dotson • *Number of pitchers victimized*: 13 • *Total ballparks homered in*: 5 • *First HR*: 09/27/1981 off Dave Stieb

Herb Score

HERBERT JUDE SCORE
B: 06/07/1933
BL

Year	Tm	Lg	Tot	H	A	Men-On 0	Men-On 1	Men-On 2	Men-On 3	One-Game 2	One-Game 3	One-Game 4	LO	XN	IP	PH	RHP	LHP
1956	CLE	AL	1	0	1	1	0	0	0	0	0	0	0	0	0	0	0	1

Rank among batters: 4,707 • *Total ballparks homered in*: 1 • *First HR*: 08/21/1956 off Mickey McDermott

Scott

SCOTT

Year	Tm	Lg	Tot	H	A	Men-On 0	Men-On 1	Men-On 2	Men-On 3	One-Game 2	One-Game 3	One-Game 4	LO	XN	IP	PH	RHP	LHP
1884	BAL	UA	1	1	0	0	0	1	0	0	0	0	0	0	0	0	1	0

Rank among batters: 4,707 • *Total ballparks homered in*: 1 • *First HR*: 07/19/1884 off Bernard McLaughlin

Donnie Scott

DONALD MALCOLM SCOTT
B: 08/16/1961
BB

Year	Tm	Lg	Tot	H	A	Men-On 0	Men-On 1	Men-On 2	Men-On 3	One-Game 2	One-Game 3	One-Game 4	LO	XN	IP	PH	RHP	LHP
1984	TEX	AL	3	0	3	2	0	1	0	0	0	0	0	0	0	0	3	0

Donnie Scott *continued*

Year	Tm	Lg	Tot	H	A	Men-On 0	1	2	3	One-Game 2	3	4	LO	XN	IP	PH	RHP	LHP
1985	SEA	AL	4	3	1	1	2	1	0	1	0	0	0	1	0	0	3	1
Total			7	3	4	3	2	2	0	1	0	0	0	1	0	0	6	1

Rank among batters: 2,834 • *Total ballparks homered in*: 4 • *First HR*: 07/17/1984 off Mike Armstrong • *Switch hit HR in 1 game*—1 time

Ed Scott

EDWARD SCOTT
B: 08/12/1870 D: 11/01/1933
BR

Year	Tm	Lg	Tot	H	A	Men-On 0	1	2	3	One-Game 2	3	4	LO	XN	IP	PH	RHP	LHP
1900	CIN	NL	1	0	1	0	1	0	0	0	0	0	0	0	0	0	0	1
1901	CLE	AL	1	0	1	1	0	0	0	0	0	0	0	1	0	0	1	0
Total			2	0	2	1	1	0	0	0	0	0	0	1	0	0	1	1

Rank among batters: 4,129 • *Total ballparks homered in*: 2 • *First HR*: 06/17/1900 off Cowboy Jones

Everett Scott

LEWIS EVERETT SCOTT
B: 11/19/1892 D: 11/02/1960
BR

Year	Tm	Lg	Tot	H	A	Men-On 0	1	2	3	One-Game 2	3	4	LO	XN	IP	PH	RHP	LHP
1914	BOS	AL	2	0	2	2	0	0	0	0	0	0	0	0	2	0	2	0
1920	BOS	AL	4	0	4	3	1	0	0	0	0	0	0	0	0	0	3	1
1921	BOS	AL	1	1	0	0	1	0	0	0	0	0	0	0	1	0	0	1
1922	NY	AL	3	2	1	2	0	1	0	0	0	0	0	0	0	0	3	0
1923	NY	AL	6	5	1	4	1	0	1	1	0	0	0	0	2	0	6	0
1924	NY	AL	4	3	1	2	1	1	0	0	0	0	0	0	1	0	2	2
Total			20	11	9	13	4	2	1	1	0	0	0	0	6	0	16	4

Rank among batters: 1,810 • *Top target (2 home runs)*: Scott Perry • *Number of pitchers victimized*: 19 • *Total ballparks homered in*: 6 • *First HR*: 06/10/1914 off Alex Main

Gary Scott

GARY THOMAS SCOTT
B: 08/22/1968
BR

Year	Tm	Lg	Tot	H	A	Men-On 0	1	2	3	One-Game 2	3	4	LO	XN	IP	PH	RHP	LHP
1991	CHI	NL	1	1	0	1	0	0	0	0	0	0	0	0	0	0	1	0
1992	CHI	NL	2	1	1	0	1	0	1	0	0	0	0	0	0	0	1	1
Total			3	2	1	1	1	0	1	0	0	0	0	0	0	0	2	1

Rank among batters: 3,735 • *Total ballparks homered in*: 2 • *First HR*: 04/30/1991 off Darryl Kile

George Scott

GEORGE CHARLES SCOTT
B: 03/23/1944
BR

Year	Tm	Lg	Tot	H	A	Men-On 0	1	2	3	One-Game 2	3	4	LO	XN	IP	PH	RHP	LHP
1966	BOS	AL	27	11	16	13	10	4	0	3	0	0	0	0	0	0	21	6
1967	BOS	AL	19	13	6	11	7	1	0	1	0	0	0	0	1	0	17	2
1968	BOS	AL	3	0	3	3	0	0	0	0	0	0	0	0	0	0	0	3
1969	BOS	AL	16	11	5	11	4	1	0	2	0	0	0	1	0	0	9	7
1970	BOS	AL	16	8	8	11	4	1	0	1	0	0	0	0	0	0	9	7
1971	BOS	AL	24	17	7	10	11	3	0	2	0	0	0	0	0	0	21	3
1972	MIL	AL	20	7	13	13	5	2	0	1	0	0	0	0	0	0	12	8
1973	MIL	AL	24	14	10	11	9	3	1	2	0	0	0	0	0	1	13	11
1974	MIL	AL	17	8	9	10	5	2	0	1	0	0	0	0	0	0	14	3
1975	MIL	AL	36	18	18	19	15	2	0	4	0	0	0	0	0	0	30	6
1976	MIL	AL	18	12	6	11	4	3	0	0	0	0	0	0	0	0	14	4
1977	BOS	AL	33	19	14	24	7	1	1	3	0	0	0	0	0	0	23	10
1978	BOS	AL	12	9	3	6	4	1	1	0	0	0	0	0	0	0	8	4
1979	BOS	AL	4	2	2	1	2	1	0	0	0	0	0	0	0	0	1	3
	KC	AL	1	1	0	0	1	0	0	0	0	0	0	0	0	0	1	0
	NY	AL	1	0	1	0	0	1	0	0	0	0	0	0	0	0	0	1
	Total		6	3	3	1	3	2	0	0	0	0	0	0	0	0	2	4
Total			271	150	121	154	88	26	3	20	0	0	0	1	1	1	193	78

Rank among batters: 88 • *Top target (5 home runs)*: Luis Tiant, Joe Coleman, Vida Blue, Dick Pole • *Number of pitchers victimized*: 172 • *Total ballparks homered in*: 16 • *First HR*: 04/19/1966 off Joe Sparma • *All-Star HR*—1

Jack Scott

JOHN WILLIAM SCOTT
B: 04/18/1892 D: 11/30/1959
BL

Year	Tm	Lg	Tot	H	A	Men-On 0	1	2	3	One-Game 2	3	4	LO	XN	IP	PH	RHP	LHP
1921	BOS	NL	1	1	0	1	0	0	0	0	0	0	0	0	1	0	1	0

Jack Scott *continued*

Year	Tm	Lg	Tot	H	A	Men-On 0	1	2	3	One-Game 2	3	4	LO	XN	IP	PH	RHP	LHP
1923	NY	NL	1	0	1	0	1	0	0	0	0	0	0	0	1	0	1	0
1925	NY	NL	1	1	0	1	0	0	0	0	0	0	0	0	0	0	1	0
1926	NY	NL	1	1	0	1	0	0	0	0	0	0	0	0	0	0	1	0
1927	PHI	NL	1	1	0	1	0	0	0	0	0	0	0	0	0	0	1	0
Total			5	4	1	4	1	0	0	0	0	0	0	0	2	0	5	0

Rank among batters: 3,191 • *Total ballparks homered in*: 3 • *First HR*: 08/17/1921 off Elmer Ponder

Jim Scott

JAMES SCOTT
B: 04/23/1888 D: 04/07/1957
BR

Year	Tm	Lg	Tot	H	A	Men-On 0	1	2	3	One-Game 2	3	4	LO	XN	IP	PH	RHP	LHP
1913	CHI	AL	1	0	1	0	1	0	0	0	0	0	0	0	0	0	1	0

Rank among batters: 4,707 • *Total ballparks homered in*: 1 • *First HR*: 06/10/1913 off George McConnell

John Scott

JOHN HENRY SCOTT
B: 01/24/1952
BR

Year	Tm	Lg	Tot	H	A	Men-On 0	1	2	3	One-Game 2	3	4	LO	XN	IP	PH	RHP	LHP
1977	TOR	AL	2	0	2	1	1	0	0	0	0	0	0	0	0	0	1	1

Rank among batters: 4,129 • *Total ballparks homered in*: 2 • *First HR*: 06/05/1977 off Vida Blue

LeGrant Scott

LEGRANT EDWARD SCOTT
B: 07/25/1910 D: 11/12/1993
BL

Year	Tm	Lg	Tot	H	A	Men-On 0	1	2	3	One-Game 2	3	4	LO	XN	IP	PH	RHP	LHP
1939	PHI	NL	1	0	1	0	1	0	0	0	0	0	0	0	0	0	1	0

Rank among batters: 4,707 • *Total ballparks homered in*: 1 • *First HR*: 06/14/1939 off Junior Thompson

Mike Scott

MICHAEL WARREN SCOTT
B: 04/26/1955
BR

Year	Tm	Lg	Tot	H	A	Men-On 0	1	2	3	One-Game 2	3	4	LO	XN	IP	PH	RHP	LHP
1985	HOU	NL	1	0	1	1	0	0	0	0	0	0	0	0	0	0	0	1
1989	HOU	NL	1	0	1	1	0	0	0	0	0	0	0	0	0	0	1	0
Total			2	0	2	2	0	0	0	0	0	0	0	0	0	0	1	1

Rank among batters: 4,129 • *Total ballparks homered in*: 2 • *First HR*: 07/31/1985 off Tom Browning

Milt Scott

MILTON PARKER SCOTT
B: 01/17/1866 D: 11/03/1938
BR

Year	Tm	Lg	Tot	H	A	Men-On 0	1	2	3	One-Game 2	3	4	LO	XN	IP	PH	RHP	LHP
1884	DET	NL	3	1	2	0	1	1	0	0	0	0	0	0	0	0	3	0
1886	BAL	AA	2	0	2	0	1	1	0	0	0	0	0	0	0	0	1	1
Total			5	1	4	0	2	2	0	0	0	0	0	0	0	0	4	0

Rank among batters: 3,191 • *Top target (2 home runs)*: Larry Corcoran • *Number of pitchers victimized*: 4 • *Total ballparks homered in*: 4 • *First HR*: 05/31/1884 off Larry Corcoran

Pete Scott

FLOYD JOHN SCOTT
B: 12/21/1898 D: 05/03/1953
BR

Year	Tm	Lg	Tot	H	A	Men-On 0	1	2	3	One-Game 2	3	4	LO	XN	IP	PH	RHP	LHP
1926	CHI	NL	3	0	3	2	0	0	1	0	0	0	0	0	0	0	2	1
1928	PIT	NL	5	0	5	3	2	0	0	2	0	0	0	1	0	0	3	2
Total			8	0	8	5	2	0	1	2	0	0	0	1	0	0	5	3

Rank among batters: 2,703 • *Top target (2 home runs)*: Ed Brandt • *Number of pitchers victimized*: 7 • *Total ballparks homered in*: 4 • *First HR*: 05/28/1926 off Emil Yde

Rodney Scott

RODNEY DARRELL SCOTT
B: 10/16/1953
BB

Year	Tm	Lg	Tot	H	A	Men-On 0	1	2	3	One-Game 2	3	4	LO	XN	IP	PH	RHP	LHP
1979	MON	NL	3	1	2	0	3	0	0	0	0	0	0	1	0	0	0	3

Year	Tm	Lg	Tot	H	A	Men-On 0	Men-On 1	Men-On 2	Men-On 3	One-Game 2	One-Game 3	One-Game 4	LO	XN	IP	PH	RHP	LHP

Rodney Scott *continued*

Rank among batters: 3,735 • *Total ballparks homered in*: 3 • *First HR*: 05/10/1979 off Phil Nastu

Tony Scott

ANTHONY SCOTT
B: 09/18/1951
BB

Year	Tm	Lg	Tot	H	A	Men-On 0	Men-On 1	Men-On 2	Men-On 3	One-Game 2	One-Game 3	One-Game 4	LO	XN	IP	PH	RHP	LHP
1977	STL	NL	3	1	2	2	0	1	0	0	0	0	0	0	0	0	1	2
1978	STL	NL	1	0	1	1	0	0	0	0	0	0	0	0	0	1	0	1
1979	STL	NL	6	1	5	4	1	0	1	0	0	0	0	0	0	0	3	3
1981	STL	NL	2	2	0	1	1	0	0	0	0	0	0	0	0	0	2	0
	HOU	NL	2	1	1	2	0	0	0	0	0	0	1	0	0	0	1	1
	Total		4	3	1	3	1	0	0	0	0	0	1	0	0	0	3	1
1982	HOU	NL	1	0	1	1	0	0	0	0	0	0	0	0	0	0	0	1
1983	HOU	NL	2	1	1	2	0	0	0	0	0	0	1	0	0	0	1	1
Total			17	6	11	13	2	1	1	0	0	0	2	0	0	1	8	9

Rank among batters: 1,969 • *Top target (2 home runs)*: John Candelaria • *Number of pitchers victimized*: 16 • *Total ballparks homered in*: 8 • *First HR*: 05/04/1977 off Woodie Fryman

Chuck Scrivener

WAYNE ALLISON SCRIVENER
B: 10/03/1947
BR

Year	Tm	Lg	Tot	H	A	Men-On 0	Men-On 1	Men-On 2	Men-On 3	One-Game 2	One-Game 3	One-Game 4	LO	XN	IP	PH	RHP	LHP
1976	DET	AL	2	2	0	1	0	1	0	0	0	0	0	0	0	0	2	0

Rank among batters: 4,129 • *Total ballparks homered in*: 1 • *First HR*: 08/08/1976 off Tom Buskey

Scott Scudder

WILLIAM SCOTT SCUDDER
B: 02/14/1968
BR

Year	Tm	Lg	Tot	H	A	Men-On 0	Men-On 1	Men-On 2	Men-On 3	One-Game 2	One-Game 3	One-Game 4	LO	XN	IP	PH	RHP	LHP
1991	CIN	NL	1	1	0	1	0	0	0	0	0	0	0	0	0	0	0	1

Rank among batters: 4,707 • *Total ballparks homered in*: 1 • *First HR*: 06/26/1991 off Dennis Rasmussen

Ken Sears

KENNETH EUGENE SEARS
B: 07/06/1917 D: 07/17/1968
BL

Year	Tm	Lg	Tot	H	A	Men-On 0	Men-On 1	Men-On 2	Men-On 3	One-Game 2	One-Game 3	One-Game 4	LO	XN	IP	PH	RHP	LHP
1943	NY	AL	2	1	1	1	0	1	0	0	0	0	0	0	0	0	2	0

Rank among batters: 4,129 • *Total ballparks homered in*: 2 • *First HR*: 08/13/1943 off Johnny Niggeling

Thomas Seaton

THOMAS GORDON SEATON
B: 08/30/1887 D: 04/10/1940
BB

Year	Tm	Lg	Tot	H	A	Men-On 0	Men-On 1	Men-On 2	Men-On 3	One-Game 2	One-Game 3	One-Game 4	LO	XN	IP	PH	RHP	LHP
1913	PHI	NL	1	1	0	0	1	0	0	0	0	0	0	0	0	0	1	0
1914	BRO	FL	1	0	1	0	1	0	0	0	0	0	0	1	0	0	1	0
1915	BRO	FL	1	0	1	0	1	0	0	0	0	0	0	0	0	0	1	0
	NWK	FL	1	0	1	1	0	0	0	0	0	0	0	0	0	0	1	0
	Total		2	0	2	1	1	0	0	0	0	0	0	0	0	0	2	0
Total			4	1	3	1	3	0	0	0	0	0	0	1	0	0	4	0

Rank among batters: 3,427 • *Total ballparks homered in*: 4 • *First HR*: 05/21/1913 off Frank Harter

Tom Seaver

GEORGE THOMAS SEAVER
B: 11/17/1944
BR HOF

Year	Tm	Lg	Tot	H	A	Men-On 0	Men-On 1	Men-On 2	Men-On 3	One-Game 2	One-Game 3	One-Game 4	LO	XN	IP	PH	RHP	LHP
1970	NY	NL	1	1	0	1	0	0	0	0	0	0	0	0	0	0	0	1
1971	NY	NL	1	0	1	1	0	0	0	0	0	0	0	0	0	0	1	0
1972	NY	NL	3	0	3	2	1	0	0	0	0	0	0	0	0	0	2	1
1973	NY	NL	1	0	1	1	0	0	0	0	0	0	0	0	0	0	1	0
1977	CIN	NL	3	2	1	3	0	0	0	0	0	0	0	0	0	0	2	1
1979	CIN	NL	2	1	1	2	0	0	0	0	0	0	0	0	0	0	2	0
1981	CIN	NL	1	1	0	0	1	0	0	0	0	0	0	0	0	0	1	0
Total			12	5	7	10	2	0	0	0	0	0	0	0	0	0	9	3

Rank among batters: 2,325 • *Total ballparks homered in*: 6 • *First HR*: 07/09/1970 off Rich Nye

Year	Tm	Lg	Tot	H	A	Men-On 0	1	2	3	One-Game 2	3	4	LO	XN	IP	PH	RHP	LHP

Jimmy Sebring

JAMES DENNISON SEBRING
B: 03/22/1882 D: 12/22/1909
BL

Year	Tm	Lg	Tot	H	A	0	1	2	3	2	3	4	LO	XN	IP	PH	RHP	LHP
1903	PIT	NL	4	2	2	3	0	0	1	1	0	0	0	0	2	0	3	1
1905	CIN	NL	2	1	1	0	2	0	0	0	0	0	0	0	2	0	1	1
Total			6	3	3	3	2	0	1	1	0	0	0	0	4	0	4	2

Rank among batters: 2,988 • *Top target (3 home runs)*: Clarence Currie • *Number of pitchers victimized*: 4 • *Total ballparks homered in*: 5 • *First HR*: 04/23/1903 off Clarence Currie • *World Series HR*—1

Frank Secory

FRANK EDWARD SECORY
B: 08/24/1912 D: 04/07/1995
BR

Year	Tm	Lg	Tot	H	A	0	1	2	3	2	3	4	LO	XN	IP	PH	RHP	LHP
1944	CHI	NL	4	2	2	2	0	2	0	1	0	0	0	0	0	0	2	2
1946	CHI	NL	3	2	1	1	1	0	1	0	0	0	0	2	0	2	1	2
Total			7	4	3	3	1	2	1	1	0	0	0	2	0	2	3	4

Rank among batters: 2,834 • *Top target (2 home runs)*: Bill Trotter • *Number of pitchers victimized*: 6 • *Total ballparks homered in*: 3 • *First HR*: 09/13/1944 off Clyde Shoun

Charlie See

CHARLES HENRY SEE
B: 10/13/1896 D: 07/19/1948
BL

Year	Tm	Lg	Tot	H	A	0	1	2	3	2	3	4	LO	XN	IP	PH	RHP	LHP
1921	CIN	NL	1	0	1	1	0	0	0	0	0	0	0	0	0	0	1	0

Rank among batters: 4,707 • *Total ballparks homered in*: 1 • *First HR*: 05/16/1921 off Fred Toney

Bob Seeds

IRA ROBERT SEEDS
B: 02/24/1907 D: 10/28/1993
BR

Year	Tm	Lg	Tot	H	A	0	1	2	3	2	3	4	LO	XN	IP	PH	RHP	LHP
1930	CLE	AL	3	0	3	2	1	0	0	0	0	0	0	0	1	0	1	2
1931	CLE	AL	1	0	1	0	1	0	0	0	0	0	0	0	0	0	1	0
1932	CHI	AL	2	1	1	2	0	0	0	0	0	0	0	0	1	0	2	0
1936	NY	AL	4	2	2	3	1	0	0	1	0	0	0	0	0	0	3	1
1938	NY	NL	9	5	4	3	5	1	0	0	0	0	1	0	1	0	6	3
1939	NY	NL	5	5	0	4	0	1	0	1	0	0	0	0	0	0	3	2
1940	NY	NL	4	1	3	3	1	0	0	1	0	0	0	0	0	0	1	3
Total			28	14	14	17	9	2	0	3	0	0	1	0	3	0	17	11

Rank among batters: 1,500 • *Top target (2 home runs)*: Bill Dietrich, Curt Davis, Lefty Smoll • *Number of pitchers victimized*: 25 • *Total ballparks homered in*: 9 • *First HR*: 05/06/1930 off Hank Johnson

Pat Seerey

JAMES PATRICK SEEREY
B: 03/17/1923 D: 04/28/1986
BR

Year	Tm	Lg	Tot	H	A	0	1	2	3	2	3	4	LO	XN	IP	PH	RHP	LHP
1943	CLE	AL	1	0	1	1	0	0	0	0	0	0	0	0	0	0	1	0
1944	CLE	AL	15	4	11	10	4	1	0	0	0	0	0	1	0	0	10	5
1945	CLE	AL	14	7	7	4	7	1	2	1	1	0	0	0	0	0	10	4
1946	CLE	AL	26	8	18	15	6	4	1	2	0	0	0	0	0	0	17	9
1947	CLE	AL	11	6	5	6	3	2	0	0	0	0	0	0	0	0	8	3
1948	CLE	AL	1	1	0	0	1	0	0	0	0	0	0	0	0	0	0	1
	CHI	AL	18	6	12	9	5	4	0	0	0	1	0	1	0	0	11	7
	Total		19	7	12	9	6	4	0	0	0	1	0	1	0	0	11	8
Total			86	32	54	45	26	12	3	3	1	1	0	2	0	0	57	29

Rank among batters: 602 • *Top target (5 home runs)*: Stubby Overmire • *Number of pitchers victimized*: 59 • *Total ballparks homered in*: 9 • *First HR*: 06/20/1943 off Orval Grove

Emmett Seery

JOHN EMMETT SEERY
B: 02/13/1861 D: 08/07/1930
BL

Year	Tm	Lg	Tot	H	A	0	1	2	3	2	3	4	LO	XN	IP	PH	RHP	LHP
1884	BAL	UA	2	1	1	0	1	1	0	0	0	0	0	0	0	0	1	0
1885	STL	NL	1	1	0	1	0	0	0	0	0	0	0	0	0	0	1	0
1886	STL	NL	2	0	2	1	1	0	0	0	0	0	0	0	0	0	2	0

Emmett Seery *continued*

Year	Tm	Lg	Tot	H	A	Men-On 0	1	2	3	One-Game 2	3	4	LO	XN	IP	PH	RHP	LHP
1887	IND	NL	4	1	3	3	1	0	0	0	0	0	0	0	0	0	2	2
1888	IND	NL	5	3	2	4	1	0	0	0	0	0	1	0	1	0	4	1
1889	IND	NL	8	5	3	2	3	3	0	0	0	0	2	0	0	0	8	0
1890	BRO	PL	1	1	0	0	1	0	0	0	0	0	0	0	0	0	1	0
1891	CIN	AA	4	4	0	2	2	0	0	1	0	0	1	0	1	0	1	3
Total			27	16	11	13	10	4	0	1	0	0	4	0	2	0	20	6

Rank among batters: 1,532 • Top target (2 home runs): Charlie Ferguson, Charley Radbourn, Ben Sanders, John Clarkson, Willie McGill • *Number of pitchers victimized*: 22 • *Total ballparks homered in*: 11 • *First HR*: 05/05/1884 off Milo Lockwood

David Segui

DAVID VINCENT SEGUI
B: 07/19/1966
BB

Year	Tm	Lg	Tot	H	A	Men-On 0	1	2	3	One-Game 2	3	4	LO	XN	IP	PH	RHP	LHP
1990	BAL	AL	2	1	1	0	1	1	0	0	0	0	0	0	0	0	1	1
1991	BAL	AL	2	1	1	1	0	1	0	0	0	0	0	0	0	0	1	1
1992	BAL	AL	1	1	0	1	0	0	0	0	0	0	0	0	0	0	1	0
1993	BAL	AL	10	6	4	8	2	0	0	0	0	0	0	1	0	0	5	5
1994	NY	NL	10	5	5	8	2	0	0	0	0	0	0	0	0	0	5	5
1995	NY	NL	2	2	0	2	0	0	0	0	0	0	0	0	0	0	1	1
	MON	NL	10	4	6	5	2	2	1	0	0	0	0	0	0	0	9	1
	Total		12	6	6	7	2	2	1	0	0	0	0	0	0	0	10	2
Total			37	20	17	25	7	4	1	0	0	0	0	1	0	0	23	14

Rank among batters: 1,252 • *Total ballparks homered in*: 18 • *First HR*: 09/16/1990 off Tom Henke

Diego Segui

DIEGO PABLO (GONZALEZ) SEGUI
B: 08/17/1937
BR

Year	Tm	Lg	Tot	H	A	Men-On 0	1	2	3	One-Game 2	3	4	LO	XN	IP	PH	RHP	LHP
1962	KC	AL	1	0	1	1	0	0	0	0	0	0	0	0	0	0	1	0
1964	KC	AL	1	1	0	1	0	0	0	0	0	0	0	0	0	0	1	0
1965	KC	AL	1	1	0	1	0	0	0	0	0	0	0	0	0	0	1	0
1971	OAK	AL	1	0	1	0	0	1	0	0	0	0	0	0	0	0	0	1
Total			4	2	2	3	0	1	0	0	0	0	0	0	0	0	3	1

Rank among batters: 3,427 • *Total ballparks homered in*: 3 • *First HR*: 08/04/1962 off Jim Perry

Socks Seibold

HARRY SEIBOLD
B: 04/03/1896 D: 09/21/1965
BR

Year	Tm	Lg	Tot	H	A	Men-On 0	1	2	3	One-Game 2	3	4	LO	XN	IP	PH	RHP	LHP
1930	BOS	NL	1	0	1	1	0	0	0	0	0	0	0	0	0	0	1	0

Rank among batters: 4,707 • *Total ballparks homered in*: 1 • *First HR*: 05/11/1930 off Jesse Haines

Ricky Seilheimer

RICKY ALLEN SEILHEIMER
B: 08/30/1960
BL

Year	Tm	Lg	Tot	H	A	Men-On 0	1	2	3	One-Game 2	3	4	LO	XN	IP	PH	RHP	LHP
1980	CHI	AL	1	1	0	1	0	0	0	0	0	0	0	0	0	0	1	0

Rank among batters: 4,707 • *Total ballparks homered in*: 1 • *First HR*: 07/26/1980 off Ferguson Jenkins

Kevin Seitzer

KEVIN LEE SEITZER
B: 03/26/1962
BR

Year	Tm	Lg	Tot	H	A	Men-On 0	1	2	3	One-Game 2	3	4	LO	XN	IP	PH	RHP	LHP
1986	KC	AL	2	1	1	1	1	0	0	0	0	0	0	0	0	0	1	1
1987	KC	AL	15	7	8	8	5	1	1	1	0	0	0	0	0	0	13	2
1988	KC	AL	5	4	1	4	1	0	0	0	0	0	0	0	0	0	4	1
1989	KC	AL	4	2	2	4	0	0	0	0	0	0	0	0	1	0	1	3
1990	KC	AL	6	5	1	4	2	0	0	0	0	0	1	0	0	0	4	2
1991	KC	AL	1	0	1	1	0	0	0	0	0	0	0	0	0	0	0	1
1992	MIL	AL	5	2	3	4	1	0	0	1	0	0	0	0	0	0	3	2
1993	OAK	AL	4	2	2	4	0	0	0	1	0	0	0	0	0	0	4	0
	MIL	AL	7	4	3	3	0	3	1	0	0	0	0	0	0	0	3	4

Kevin Seitzer *continued*

Year	Tm	Lg	Tot	H	A	Men-On 0	1	2	3	One-Game 2	3	4	LO	XN	IP	PH	RHP	LHP
1993	Total		11	6	5	7	0	3	1	1	0	0	0	0	0	0	7	4
1994	MIL	AL	5	4	1	3	1	1	0	0	0	0	0	0	0	1	4	1
1995	MIL	AL	5	1	4	3	1	0	1	0	0	0	0	0	0	0	5	0
Total			59	32	27	39	12	5	3	3	0	0	1	0	1	1	42	17

Rank among batters: 873 • *Top target (2 home runs)*: Mark Guthrie, Alex Fernandez, Bill Wegman • *Number of pitchers victimized*: 56 • *Total ballparks homered in*: 14 • *First HR*: 09/21/1986 off Mike Brown

Kip Selbach

ALBERT KARL SELBACH
B: 03/24/1872 D: 02/17/1956
BR

Year	Tm	Lg	Tot	H	A	Men-On 0	1	2	3	One-Game 2	3	4	LO	XN	IP	PH	RHP	LHP
1894	WAS	NL	7	4	3	2	3	2	0	0	0	0	0	0	1	0	6	1
1895	WAS	NL	6	4	2	4	2	0	0	0	0	0	0	0	0	0	4	2
1896	WAS	NL	5	5	0	2	3	0	0	0	0	0	0	0	1	0	5	0
1897	WAS	NL	5	3	2	3	2	0	0	0	0	0	3	0	1	0	3	1
1898	WAS	NL	3	3	0	0	2	0	1	0	0	0	0	0	0	0	2	1
1899	CIN	NL	3	0	3	1	0	2	0	0	0	0	0	0	0	0	2	1
1900	NY	NL	4	2	2	1	3	0	0	0	0	0	0	0	0	0	3	1
1901	NY	NL	1	0	1	0	0	1	0	0	0	0	0	0	0	0	1	0
1902	BAL	AL	3	2	1	1	2	0	0	0	0	0	0	0	1	0	2	1
1903	WAS	AL	3	3	0	0	3	0	0	0	0	0	0	0	0	0	3	0
1905	BOS	AL	4	4	0	2	2	0	0	0	0	0	0	0	0	0	3	1
Total			44	30	14	16	22	5	1	0	0	0	3	0	4	0	34	9

Rank among batters: 1,095 • Top target (2 home runs): Ed Stein, Chick Fraser, Gus Weyhing, Kid Nichols, Rube Waddell • *Number of pitchers victimized*: 39 • *Total ballparks homered in*: 13 • *First HR*: 07/20/1894 off Stub Brown

George Selkirk

GEORGE ALEXANDER SELKIRK
B: 01/04/1908 D: 01/19/1987
BL

Year	Tm	Lg	Tot	H	A	Men-On 0	1	2	3	One-Game 2	3	4	LO	XN	IP	PH	RHP	LHP
1934	NY	AL	5	1	4	4	1	0	0	0	0	0	0	1	0	0	4	1
1935	NY	AL	11	8	3	8	0	2	1	1	0	0	0	0	1	0	11	0
1936	NY	AL	18	8	10	5	10	3	0	0	0	0	0	1	1	0	17	1
1937	NY	AL	18	13	5	7	9	2	0	2	0	0	0	0	1	0	14	4
1938	NY	AL	10	9	1	7	1	1	1	1	0	0	0	0	0	0	9	1
1939	NY	AL	21	15	6	10	8	3	0	3	0	0	0	0	0	0	20	1
1940	NY	AL	19	13	6	8	6	4	1	1	0	0	0	0	0	2	11	8
1941	NY	AL	6	2	4	2	2	1	1	0	0	0	0	0	0	2	5	1
Total			108	69	39	51	37	16	4	8	0	0	0	2	3	4	91	17

Rank among batters: 443 • *Top target (8 home runs)*: Ted Lyons • *Number of pitchers victimized*: 68 • *Total ballparks homered in*: 9 • *First HR*: 09/08/1934 off George Earnshaw • *World Series HR*—2

Andy Seminick

ANDREW WASIL SEMINICK
B: 09/12/1920
BR

Year	Tm	Lg	Tot	H	A	Men-On 0	1	2	3	One-Game 2	3	4	LO	XN	IP	PH	RHP	LHP
1943	PHI	NL	2	1	1	1	1	0	0	0	0	0	0	0	0	0	2	0
1945	PHI	NL	6	5	1	2	3	1	0	0	0	0	0	0	0	1	4	2
1946	PHI	NL	12	7	5	6	3	2	1	2	0	0	0	1	0	0	6	6
1947	PHI	NL	13	7	6	9	4	0	0	0	0	0	0	0	1	0	9	4
1948	PHI	NL	13	6	7	8	4	1	0	1	0	0	0	0	0	0	8	5
1949	PHI	NL	24	17	7	17	2	4	1	2	1	0	0	0	0	1	14	10
1950	PHI	NL	24	10	14	16	6	0	2	1	0	0	0	1	1	0	19	5
1951	PHI	NL	11	3	8	8	3	0	0	0	0	0	0	0	0	0	7	4
1952	CIN	NL	14	7	7	8	1	3	2	1	0	0	0	0	0	1	8	6
1953	CIN	NL	19	12	7	8	9	1	1	1	0	0	0	0	0	0	5	14
1954	CIN	NL	7	3	4	7	0	0	0	0	0	0	0	0	0	0	3	4
1955	CIN	NL	1	1	0	1	0	0	0	0	0	0	0	0	0	0	1	0
	PHI	NL	11	7	4	7	2	1	1	0	0	0	0	0	0	0	8	3
	Total		12	8	4	8	2	1	1	0	0	0	0	0	0	0	9	3
1956	PHI	NL	7	4	3	3	3	1	0	0	0	0	0	0	0	0	4	3
Total			164	90	74	101	41	14	8	8	1	0	0	2	2	3	98	66

Rank among batters: 250 • *Top target (9 home runs)*: Ken Raffensberger • *Number of pitchers victimized*: 105 • *Total ballparks homered in*: 9 • *First HR*: 09/15/1943 off Hugh East • *2 HR in 1 inning*—vs CIN: 06/02/1949

Sonny Senerchia

EMANUEL ROBERT SENERCHIA
B: 04/06/1931
BR

Year	Tm	Lg	Tot	H	A	Men-On 0	1	2	3	One-Game 2	3	4	LO	XN	IP	PH	RHP	LHP
1952	PIT	NL	3	1	2	2	1	0	0	0	0	0	0	0	0	0	3	0

Rank among batters: 3,735 • *Total ballparks homered in*: 2 • *First HR*: 08/24/1952 off Ernie Johnson

Paul Sentell

LEOPOLD THEODORE SENTELL
B: 08/27/1879 D: 04/27/1923
BR

Year	Tm	Lg	Tot	H	A	Men-On 0	1	2	3	One-Game 2	3	4	LO	XN	IP	PH	RHP	LHP
1906	PHI	NL	1	1	0	0	0	1	0	0	0	0	0	0	1	0	1	0

Rank among batters: 4,707 • *Total ballparks homered in*: 1 • *First HR*: 10/01/1906 off Ed Reulbach

Bill Serena

WILLIAM ROBERT SERENA
B: 10/02/1924
BR

Year	Tm	Lg	Tot	H	A	Men-On 0	1	2	3	One-Game 2	3	4	LO	XN	IP	PH	RHP	LHP
1949	CHI	NL	1	0	1	1	0	0	0	0	0	0	0	0	0	0	0	1
1950	CHI	NL	17	12	5	9	4	4	0	2	0	0	0	0	0	0	15	2
1951	CHI	NL	1	1	0	1	0	0	0	0	0	0	0	0	0	0	1	0
1952	CHI	NL	15	8	7	7	8	0	0	1	0	0	0	0	0	0	11	4
1953	CHI	NL	10	5	5	5	2	2	1	0	0	0	0	0	0	1	7	3
1954	CHI	NL	4	2	2	2	2	0	0	0	0	0	0	0	0	1	4	0
Total			48	28	20	25	16	6	1	3	0	0	0	0	0	2	38	10

Rank among batters: 1,024 • *Top target (2 home runs)*: Dan Bankhead, Robin Roberts, Gerry Staley • *Number of pitchers victimized*: 45 • *Total ballparks homered in*: 9 • *First HR*: 09/25/1949 off Harry Brecheen

Paul Serna

PAUL DAVID SERNA
B: 11/16/1958
BR

Year	Tm	Lg	Tot	H	A	Men-On 0	1	2	3	One-Game 2	3	4	LO	XN	IP	PH	RHP	LHP
1981	SEA	AL	4	2	2	4	0	0	0	0	0	0	0	0	0	0	0	4
1982	SEA	AL	3	3	0	2	1	0	0	1	0	0	0	1	0	0	0	3
Total			7	5	2	6	1	0	0	1	0	0	0	1	0	0	0	7

Rank among batters: 2,834 • *Total ballparks homered in*: 3 • *First HR*: 09/07/1981 off Juan Agosto

Scott Servais

SCOTT DANIEL SERVAIS
B: 06/04/1967
BR

Year	Tm	Lg	Tot	H	A	Men-On 0	1	2	3	One-Game 2	3	4	LO	XN	IP	PH	RHP	LHP
1993	HOU	NL	11	5	6	8	1	2	0	0	0	0	0	0	0	0	4	7
1994	HOU	NL	9	3	6	5	3	1	0	0	0	0	0	0	0	0	7	2
1995	HOU	NL	1	1	0	1	0	0	0	0	0	0	0	0	0	0	1	0
	CHI	NL	12	7	5	9	2	1	0	1	0	0	0	0	0	0	10	2
	Total		13	8	5	10	2	1	0	1	0	0	0	0	0	0	11	2
Total			33	16	17	23	6	4	0	1	0	0	0	0	0	0	22	11

Rank among batters: 1,336 • *Top target (2 home runs)*: Greg Harris • *Number of pitchers victimized*: 32 • *Total ballparks homered in*: 12 • *First HR*: 04/25/1993 off Randy Tomlin

Walter Sessi

WALTER ANTHONY SESSI
B: 07/23/1918
BL

Year	Tm	Lg	Tot	H	A	Men-On 0	1	2	3	One-Game 2	3	4	LO	XN	IP	PH	RHP	LHP
1946	STL	NL	1	1	0	0	1	0	0	0	0	0	0	0	0	1	1	0

Rank among batters: 4,707 • *Total ballparks homered in*: 1 • *First HR*: 08/28/1946 off Bill Voiselle

Hank Severeid

HENRY LEVAI SEVEREID
B: 06/01/1891 D: 12/17/1968
BR

Year	Tm	Lg	Tot	H	A	Men-On 0	1	2	3	One-Game 2	3	4	LO	XN	IP	PH	RHP	LHP
1915	STL	AL	1	1	0	0	0	1	0	0	0	0	0	0	0	0	1	0
1917	STL	AL	1	0	1	1	0	0	0	0	0	0	0	0	0	0	1	0
1920	STL	AL	2	0	2	2	0	0	0	0	0	0	0	0	0	0	2	0

Year	Tm	Lg	Tot	H	A	Men-On 0	1	2	3	One-Game 2	3	4	LO	XN	IP	PH	RHP	LHP

Hank Severeid *continued*

Year	Tm	Lg	Tot	H	A	0	1	2	3	2	3	4	LO	XN	IP	PH	RHP	LHP
1921	STL	AL	2	1	1	1	0	1	0	0	0	0	0	0	0	0	2	0
1922	STL	AL	3	1	2	3	0	0	0	0	0	0	0	0	0	0	3	0
1923	STL	AL	3	2	1	2	0	0	1	0	0	0	0	0	0	0	3	0
1924	STL	AL	4	2	2	3	1	0	0	0	0	0	0	0	0	0	4	0
1925	STL	AL	1	0	1	0	0	1	0	0	0	0	0	0	0	1	1	0
Total			17	7	10	12	1	3	1	0	0	0	0	0	0	1	17	0

Rank among batters: 1,969 • *Top target (2 home runs)*: Hooks Dauss, Rip Collins, Slim Harriss • *Number of pitchers victimized*: 14 • *Total ballparks homered in*: 4 • *First HR*: 04/17/1915 off Hi Jasper

Rich Severson

RICHARD ALLEN SEVERSON
B: 01/18/1945
BR

Year	Tm	Lg	Tot	H	A	0	1	2	3	2	3	4	LO	XN	IP	PH	RHP	LHP
1970	KC	AL	1	1	0	0	0	1	0	0	0	0	0	0	0	0	1	0

Rank among batters: 4,707 • *Total ballparks homered in*: 1 • *First HR*: 08/07/1970 off Skip Lockwood

Ed Seward

EDWARD WILLIAM SEWARD
B: 06/29/1867 D: 07/30/1947

Year	Tm	Lg	Tot	H	A	0	1	2	3	2	3	4	LO	XN	IP	PH	RHP	LHP
1887	PHI	AA	5	5	0	0	2	3	0	0	0	0	0	0	0	0	3	2
1888	PHI	AA	2	2	0	0	2	0	0	0	0	0	0	0	1	0	1	1
1889	PHI	AA	2	0	2	0	2	0	0	0	0	0	0	0	0	0	2	0
Total			9	7	2	0	6	3	0	0	0	0	0	0	1	0	6	3

Rank among batters: 2,587 • *Top target (2 home runs)*: Billy Crowell, Matt Kilroy • *Number of pitchers victimized*: 7 • *Total ballparks homered in*: 3 • *First HR*: 06/14/1887 off Billy Crowell

Joe Sewell

JOSEPH WHEELER SEWELL
B: 10/09/1898 D: 03/06/1990
BL HOF

Year	Tm	Lg	Tot	H	A	0	1	2	3	2	3	4	LO	XN	IP	PH	RHP	LHP
1921	CLE	AL	4	1	3	1	2	1	0	0	0	0	0	0	0	0	4	0
1922	CLE	AL	2	1	1	1	0	1	0	0	0	0	0	0	0	0	2	0
1923	CLE	AL	3	1	2	2	0	1	0	0	0	0	0	0	0	0	2	1
1924	CLE	AL	4	3	1	3	0	1	0	0	0	0	0	0	1	0	2	2
1925	CLE	AL	1	0	1	1	0	0	0	0	0	0	0	0	1	0	0	1
1926	CLE	AL	4	1	3	1	2	1	0	0	0	0	0	0	0	0	2	2
1927	CLE	AL	1	0	1	0	0	1	0	0	0	0	0	0	0	0	1	0
1928	CLE	AL	4	1	3	2	2	0	0	1	0	0	0	0	0	0	4	0
1929	CLE	AL	7	2	5	4	1	2	0	0	0	0	0	0	0	0	5	2
1931	NY	AL	6	4	2	1	3	2	0	0	0	0	0	1	0	0	5	1
1932	NY	AL	11	11	0	7	3	1	0	1	0	0	0	0	0	0	8	3
1933	NY	AL	2	2	0	1	0	1	0	0	0	0	0	0	0	0	2	0
Total			49	27	22	24	13	12	0	2	0	0	0	1	2	0	37	12

Rank among batters: 1,008 • *Top target (4 home runs)*: Sam Gray • *Number of pitchers victimized*: 34 • *Total ballparks homered in*: 6 • *First HR*: 04/14/1921 off Bill Burwell

Luke Sewell

JAMES LUTHER SEWELL
B: 01/05/1901 D: 05/14/1987
BR

Year	Tm	Lg	Tot	H	A	0	1	2	3	2	3	4	LO	XN	IP	PH	RHP	LHP
1928	CLE	AL	3	1	2	1	2	0	0	0	0	0	0	0	1	0	2	1
1929	CLE	AL	1	0	1	0	0	1	0	0	0	0	0	0	0	0	0	1
1930	CLE	AL	1	0	1	1	0	0	0	0	0	0	0	0	0	0	0	1
1931	CLE	AL	1	0	1	1	0	0	0	0	0	0	0	0	0	0	1	0
1932	CLE	AL	2	1	1	1	0	1	0	0	0	0	0	0	1	0	1	1
1933	WAS	AL	2	0	2	1	1	0	0	0	0	0	0	0	0	0	1	1
1934	WAS	AL	2	0	2	2	0	0	0	0	0	0	0	0	0	0	1	1
1935	CHI	AL	2	2	0	1	0	0	1	0	0	0	0	0	0	0	1	1
1936	CHI	AL	5	3	2	2	2	1	0	0	0	0	0	0	0	0	4	1
1937	CHI	AL	1	1	0	0	1	0	0	0	0	0	0	0	0	0	1	0
Total			20	8	12	10	6	3	1	0	0	0	0	0	2	0	12	8

Luke Sewell *continued*

Rank among batters: 1,810 • *Top target (2 home runs)*: Herb Pennock, Lefty Gomez • *Number of pitchers victimized*: 18 • *Total ballparks homered in*: 6 • *First HR*: 05/11/1928 off Waite Hoyt

Rip Sewell

TRUETT BANKS SEWELL
B: 05/11/1907 D: 09/03/1989
BL

Year	Tm	Lg	Tot	H	A	Men-On 0	1	2	3	One-Game 2	3	4	LO	XN	IP	PH	RHP	LHP
1939	PIT	NL	1	0	1	1	0	0	0	0	0	0	0	0	0	0	1	0
1940	PIT	NL	1	1	0	0	1	0	0	0	0	0	0	0	0	0	1	0
1941	PIT	NL	1	0	1	1	0	0	0	0	0	0	0	0	0	0	1	0
1944	PIT	NL	1	1	0	1	0	0	0	0	0	0	0	0	0	0	1	0
1947	PIT	NL	1	0	1	0	1	0	0	0	0	0	0	0	0	0	1	0
1948	PIT	NL	1	1	0	1	0	0	0	0	0	0	0	0	0	0	1	0
Total			6	3	3	4	2	0	0	0	0	0	0	0	0	0	6	0

Rank among batters: 2,988 • *Total ballparks homered in*: 4 • *First HR*: 05/10/1939 off Harry Gumbert

Jimmy Sexton

JIMMY DALE SEXTON
B: 12/15/1951
BR

Year	Tm	Lg	Tot	H	A	Men-On 0	1	2	3	One-Game 2	3	4	LO	XN	IP	PH	RHP	LHP
1977	SEA	AL	1	0	1	1	0	0	0	0	0	0	0	0	0	0	0	1
1978	HOU	NL	2	1	1	2	0	0	0	0	0	0	0	0	0	0	1	1
1982	OAK	AL	2	1	1	2	0	0	0	0	0	0	0	0	0	0	1	1
Total			5	2	3	5	0	0	0	0	0	0	0	0	0	0	2	3

Rank among batters: 3,191 • *Total ballparks homered in*: 5 • *First HR*: 09/04/1977 off Jerry Garvin

Socks Seybold

RALPH ORLANDO SEYBOLD
B: 11/23/1870 D: 12/22/1921
BR

Year	Tm	Lg	Tot	H	A	Men-On 0	1	2	3	One-Game 2	3	4	LO	XN	IP	PH	RHP	LHP
1901	PHI	AL	8	4	4	2	4	2	0	0	0	0	0	0	0	0	6	2
1902	PHI	AL	16	8	8	6	5	4	1	0	0	0	0	0	0	0	14	2
1903	PHI	AL	8	4	4	4	2	2	0	0	0	0	0	0	0	0	4	4
1904	PHI	AL	3	1	2	3	0	0	0	0	0	0	0	0	0	0	3	0
1905	PHI	AL	6	1	5	1	5	0	0	0	0	0	0	0	0	0	6	0
1906	PHI	AL	5	5	0	4	1	0	0	0	0	0	0	0	0	0	5	0
1907	PHI	AL	5	2	3	0	3	2	0	0	0	0	0	0	0	0	4	1
Total			51	25	26	20	20	10	1	0	0	0	0	0	0	0	42	9

Rank among batters: 979 • *Top target (5 home runs)*: Case Patten • *Number of pitchers victimized*: 33 • *Total ballparks homered in*: 8 • *First HR*: 06/24/1901 off Nixey Callahan

Cy Seymour

JAMES BENTLEY SEYMOUR
B: 12/09/1872 D: 09/20/1919
BL

Year	Tm	Lg	Tot	H	A	Men-On 0	1	2	3	One-Game 2	3	4	LO	XN	IP	PH	RHP	LHP
1897	NY	NL	2	1	1	1	1	0	0	0	0	0	0	0	0	0	2	0
1898	NY	NL	4	1	3	3	0	1	0	0	0	0	0	0	0	0	3	1
1899	NY	NL	2	1	1	1	0	1	0	0	0	0	0	0	0	0	2	0
1901	BAL	AL	1	0	1	0	1	0	0	0	0	0	0	0	0	0	1	0
1902	BAL	AL	3	3	0	1	2	0	0	0	0	0	0	0	1	0	3	0
	CIN	NL	2	2	0	0	1	1	0	0	0	0	0	0	2	0	2	0
	Total		5	5	0	1	3	1	0	0	0	0	0	0	3	0	5	0
1903	CIN	NL	7	2	5	4	3	0	0	0	0	0	0	0	2	0	5	2
1904	CIN	NL	5	2	3	4	1	0	0	0	0	0	0	0	3	0	4	1
1905	CIN	NL	8	5	3	2	4	2	0	1	0	0	0	1	7	0	7	1
1906	CIN	NL	4	2	2	3	1	0	0	1	0	0	0	0	4	0	4	0
	NY	NL	4	4	0	4	0	0	0	1	0	0	0	1	0	0	4	0
	Total		8	6	2	7	1	0	0	1	0	0	0	1	4	0	8	0
1907	NY	NL	3	2	1	1	2	0	0	0	0	0	0	0	0	0	1	2
1908	NY	NL	5	3	2	5	0	0	0	1	0	0	0	0	2	0	5	0
1909	NY	NL	1	0	1	1	0	0	0	0	0	0	0	0	0	0	1	0
1910	NY	NL	1	0	1	1	0	0	0	0	0	0	0	0	0	0	1	0
Total			52	28	24	31	16	5	0	3	0	0	0	2	21	0	45	7

Cy Seymour *continued*

Rank among batters: 965 • Top target (2 home runs): Jack Dunn, Jack Powell, Deacon Phillippe, Christy Mathewson, Chick Fraser, Fred Mitchell, Mal Eason, Mordecai Brown, Sam Leever, Irv Young, Andy Coakley, Earl Moore • *Number of pitchers victimized*: 40 • *Total ballparks homered in*: 11 • *First HR*: 04/30/1897 off Bill Hoffer

Tillie Shafer

ARTHUR JOSEPH SHAFER
B: 03/22/1889 D: 01/10/1962
BB

						Men-On				One-Game								
Year	Tm	Lg	Tot	H	A	0	1	2	3	2	3	4	LO	XN	IP	PH	RHP	LHP
1913	NY	NL	5	5	0	1	2	2	0	0	0	0	0	0	0	0	5	0

Rank among batters: 3,191 • *Total ballparks homered in*: 1 • *First HR*: 04/24/1913 off Earl Moore

Orator Shaffer

GEORGE SHAFFER
B: 1852 BL

						Men-On				One-Game								
Year	Tm	Lg	Tot	H	A	0	1	2	3	2	3	4	LO	XN	IP	PH	RHP	LHP
1877	LOU	NL	3	3	0	1	0	2	0	0	0	0	0	0	1	0	3	0
1881	CLE	NL	1	1	0	1	0	0	0	0	0	0	0	0	1	0	1	0
1882	CLE	NL	3	0	3	0	2	1	0	0	0	0	0	0	0	0	2	1
1884	STL	UA	2	0	2	1	1	0	0	0	0	0	0	0	0	0	2	0
1890	PHI	AA	1	1	0	0	1	0	0	0	0	0	0	0	0	0	1	0
Total			10	5	5	3	4	3	0	0	0	0	0	0	2	0	9	1

Rank among batters: 2,500 • *Top target (2 home runs)*: Tommy Bond, Jim Galvin • *Number of pitchers victimized*: 8 • *Total ballparks homered in*: 7 • *First HR*: 05/22/1877 off Tommy Bond

Art Shamsky

ARTHUR LOUIS SHAMSKY
B: 10/14/1941
BL

						Men-On				One-Game								
Year	Tm	Lg	Tot	H	A	0	1	2	3	2	3	4	LO	XN	IP	PH	RHP	LHP
1965	CIN	NL	2	1	1	1	1	0	0	0	0	0	0	0	0	2	2	0
1966	CIN	NL	21	15	6	10	8	3	0	0	1	0	0	3	0	2	19	2
1967	CIN	NL	3	1	2	2	0	1	0	0	0	0	0	0	0	1	3	0
1968	NY	NL	12	7	5	8	3	0	1	0	0	0	0	0	0	1	12	0
1969	NY	NL	14	7	7	11	2	1	0	1	0	0	0	0	0	0	13	1
1970	NY	NL	11	6	5	7	3	1	0	1	0	0	0	0	0	0	11	0
1971	NY	NL	5	2	3	3	1	1	0	0	0	0	0	0	0	0	5	0
Total			68	39	29	42	18	7	1	2	1	0	0	3	0	6	65	3

Rank among batters: 767 • *Top target (4 home runs)*: Nelson Briles • *Number of pitchers victimized*: 50 • *Total ballparks homered in*: 13 • *First HR*: 05/02/1965 off Tom Parsons

Wally Shaner

WALTER DEDAKER SHANER
B: 05/24/1900 D: 11/13/1992
BR

						Men-On				One-Game								
Year	Tm	Lg	Tot	H	A	0	1	2	3	2	3	4	LO	XN	IP	PH	RHP	LHP
1927	BOS	AL	3	1	2	2	1	0	0	0	0	0	0	0	1	0	2	1
1929	CIN	NL	1	0	1	1	0	0	0	0	0	0	0	0	0	1	0	1
Total			4	1	3	3	1	0	0	0	0	0	0	0	1	1	2	2

Rank among batters: 3,427 • *Total ballparks homered in*: 4 • *First HR*: 06/25/1927 off Garland Braxton

Howie Shanks

HOWARD SAMUEL SHANKS
B: 07/21/1890 D: 07/30/1941
BR

						Men-On				One-Game								
Year	Tm	Lg	Tot	H	A	0	1	2	3	2	3	4	LO	XN	IP	PH	RHP	LHP
1912	WAS	AL	1	1	0	1	0	0	0	0	0	0	0	0	0	0	1	0
1913	WAS	AL	1	0	1	0	0	1	0	0	0	0	0	0	0	0	1	0
1914	WAS	AL	4	3	1	2	2	0	0	0	0	0	0	0	1	0	3	1
1916	WAS	AL	1	1	0	1	0	0	0	0	0	0	0	0	0	0	0	1
1918	WAS	AL	1	0	1	1	0	0	0	0	0	0	0	0	0	0	1	0
1919	WAS	AL	1	0	1	0	1	0	0	0	0	0	0	0	1	0	0	1
1920	WAS	AL	4	0	4	2	2	0	0	0	0	0	0	0	3	0	3	1
1921	WAS	AL	7	1	6	4	1	1	1	1	0	0	0	0	1	0	6	1
1922	WAS	AL	1	0	1	0	1	0	0	0	0	0	0	0	0	0	0	1
1923	BOS	AL	3	0	3	1	1	1	0	0	0	0	0	0	0	0	3	0

Year	Tm	Lg	Tot	H	A	Men-On				One-Game			LO	XN	IP	PH	RHP	LHP
						0	1	2	3	2	3	4						

Howie Shanks *continued*

Year	Tm	Lg	Tot	H	A	0	1	2	3	2	3	4	LO	XN	IP	PH	RHP	LHP
1925	NY	AL	1	1	0	1	0	0	0	0	0	0	0	0	0	0	0	1
Total			25	7	18	13	8	3	1	1	0	0	0	0	6	0	18	7

Rank among batters: 1,608 • *Top target (3 home runs)*: Carl Mays • *Number of pitchers victimized*: 22 • *Total ballparks homered in*: 8 • *First HR*: 07/04/1912 off George McConnell

Dan Shannon

DANIEL WEBSTER SHANNON
B: 03/23/1865 D: 10/25/1913

Year	Tm	Lg	Tot	H	A	0	1	2	3	2	3	4	LO	XN	IP	PH	RHP	LHP
1889	LOU	AA	4	0	4	1	2	1	0	0	0	0	1	0	2	0	4	0
1890	PHI	PL	1	1	0	0	0	1	0	0	0	0	0	0	1	0	0	1
	NY	PL	3	2	1	1	1	1	0	0	0	0	0	0	0	0	3	0
	Total		4	3	1	1	1	2	0	0	0	0	0	0	1	0	3	1
Total			8	3	5	2	3	3	0	0	0	0	1	0	3	0	7	1

Rank among batters: 2,703 • *Total ballparks homered in*: 6 • *First HR*: 06/06/1889 off John Coleman

Frank Shannon

JOHN FRANCIS SHANNON
B: 12/03/1873 D: 02/27/1934

Year	Tm	Lg	Tot	H	A	0	1	2	3	2	3	4	LO	XN	IP	PH	RHP	LHP
1896	LOU	NL	1	1	0	0	0	1	0	0	0	0	0	0	0	0	1	0

Rank among batters: 4,707 • *Total ballparks homered in*: 1 • *First HR*: 05/12/1896 off Bert Abbey

Mike Shannon

THOMAS MICHAEL SHANNON
B: 07/15/1939
BR

Year	Tm	Lg	Tot	H	A	0	1	2	3	2	3	4	LO	XN	IP	PH	RHP	LHP
1963	STL	NL	1	1	0	0	1	0	0	0	0	0	0	0	0	0	0	1
1964	STL	NL	9	3	6	5	2	2	0	0	0	0	0	1	0	0	5	4
1965	STL	NL	3	2	1	3	0	0	0	0	0	0	0	0	0	0	1	2
1966	STL	NL	16	5	11	5	8	3	0	0	0	0	0	0	0	0	7	9
1967	STL	NL	12	4	8	6	5	1	0	0	0	0	0	0	0	0	6	6
1968	STL	NL	15	7	8	8	5	1	1	0	0	0	0	1	0	0	11	4
1969	STL	NL	12	4	8	6	3	3	0	0	0	0	0	0	0	0	9	3
Total			68	26	42	33	24	10	1	0	0	0	0	2	0	0	39	29

Rank among batters: 767 • *Top target (4 home runs)*: Bob Hendley • *Number of pitchers victimized*: 55 • *Total ballparks homered in*: 13 • *First HR*: 09/11/1963 off Dick Ellsworth • *World Series HR—3*

Spike Shannon

WILLIAM PORTER SHANNON
B: 02/07/1878 D: 05/16/1940
BB

Year	Tm	Lg	Tot	H	A	0	1	2	3	2	3	4	LO	XN	IP	PH	RHP	LHP
1904	STL	NL	1	1	0	0	1	0	0	0	0	0	0	0	0	0	1	0
1907	NY	NL	1	1	0	0	1	0	0	0	0	0	0	0	0	0	1	0
1908	NY	NL	1	1	0	0	0	1	0	0	0	0	0	0	0	0	1	0
Total			3	3	0	0	2	1	0	0	0	0	0	0	0	0	3	0

Rank among batters: 3,735 • *Total ballparks homered in*: 2 • *First HR*: 07/16/1904 off Vic Willis

Billy Shantz

WILMER EBERT SHANTZ
B: 07/31/1927 D: 12/13/1993
BR

Year	Tm	Lg	Tot	H	A	0	1	2	3	2	3	4	LO	XN	IP	PH	RHP	LHP
1954	PHI	AL	1	0	1	0	0	0	1	0	0	0	0	0	0	0	1	0
1955	KC	AL	1	1	0	0	1	0	0	0	0	0	0	0	0	0	1	0
Total			2	1	1	0	1	0	1	0	0	0	0	0	0	0	2	0

Rank among batters: 4,129 • *Total ballparks homered in*: 2 • *First HR*: 05/09/1954 off Harry Byrd

Bobby Shantz

ROBERT CLAYTON SHANTZ
B: 09/26/1925
BR

Year	Tm	Lg	Tot	H	A	0	1	2	3	2	3	4	LO	XN	IP	PH	RHP	LHP
1950	PHI	AL	1	0	1	1	0	0	0	0	0	0	0	0	0	0	1	0

Rank among batters: 4,707 • *Total ballparks homered in*: 1 • *First HR*: 08/12/1950 off Allie Reynolds

Year	Tm	Lg	Tot	H	A	Men-On 0	1	2	3	One-Game 2	3	4	LO	XN	IP	PH	RHP	LHP

Dick Sharon

RICHARD LOUIS SHARON
B: 04/15/1950
BR

Year	Tm	Lg	Tot	H	A	0	1	2	3	2	3	4	LO	XN	IP	PH	RHP	LHP
1973	DET	AL	7	3	4	6	1	0	0	1	0	0	0	0	0	0	1	6
1974	DET	AL	2	1	1	0	2	0	0	0	0	0	0	0	0	0	1	1
1975	SD	NL	4	2	2	1	1	2	0	0	0	0	0	0	0	0	1	3
Total			13	6	7	7	4	2	0	1	0	0	0	0	0	0	3	10

Rank among batters: 2,248 • *Top target (2 home runs)*: Jim Merritt • *Number of pitchers victimized*: 12 • *Total ballparks homered in*: 8 • *First HR*: 05/31/1973 off Eddie Fisher

Bill Sharp

WILLIAM HOWARD SHARP
B: 01/18/1950
BL

Year	Tm	Lg	Tot	H	A	0	1	2	3	2	3	4	LO	XN	IP	PH	RHP	LHP
1973	CHI	AL	4	0	4	2	1	1	0	0	0	0	0	0	0	1	4	0
1974	CHI	AL	4	2	2	4	0	0	0	0	0	0	0	0	0	0	4	0
1975	MIL	AL	1	1	0	1	0	0	0	0	0	0	0	0	0	0	1	0
Total			9	3	6	7	1	1	0	0	0	0	0	0	0	1	9	0

Rank among batters: 2,587 • *Top target (2 home runs)*: Ray Corbin, Dick Tidrow • *Number of pitchers victimized*: 7 • *Total ballparks homered in*: 7 • *First HR*: 06/10/1973 off Dick Tidrow

Mike Sharperson

MICHAEL TYRONE SHARPERSON
B: 10/04/1961
BR

Year	Tm	Lg	Tot	H	A	0	1	2	3	2	3	4	LO	XN	IP	PH	RHP	LHP
1990	LA	NL	3	1	2	2	1	0	0	0	0	0	0	0	0	0	2	1
1991	LA	NL	2	1	1	2	0	0	0	0	0	0	0	0	0	0	0	2
1992	LA	NL	3	2	1	1	2	0	0	0	0	0	0	0	0	0	0	3
1993	LA	NL	2	1	1	1	1	0	0	0	0	0	0	0	0	1	0	2
Total			10	5	5	6	4	0	0	0	0	0	0	0	0	1	2	8

Rank among batters: 2,500 • *Top target (2 home runs)*: Craig Lefferts, Terry Mulholland • *Number of pitchers victimized*: 8 • *Total ballparks homered in*: 5 • *First HR*: 08/16/1990 off Ron Darling

George Sharrott

GEORGE OSCAR SHARROTT
B: 11/02/1869 D: 01/06/1932
BL

Year	Tm	Lg	Tot	H	A	0	1	2	3	2	3	4	LO	XN	IP	PH	RHP	LHP
1893	BRO	NL	1	1	0	0	1	0	0	0	0	0	0	0	0	0	1	0

Rank among batters: 4,707 • *Total ballparks homered in*: 1 • *First HR*: 08/07/1893 off Amos Rusie

Jack Sharrott

JOHN HENRY SHARROTT
B: 08/13/1869 D: 12/31/1927
BR

Year	Tm	Lg	Tot	H	A	0	1	2	3	2	3	4	LO	XN	IP	PH	RHP	LHP
1891	NY	NL	1	1	0	1	0	0	0	0	0	0	0	0	0	0	1	0
1893	PHI	NL	1	1	0	0	1	0	0	0	0	0	0	0	1	0	1	0
Total			2	2	0	1	1	0	0	0	0	0	0	0	1	0	2	0

Rank among batters: 4,129 • *Total ballparks homered in*: 2 • *First HR*: 04/25/1891 off John Clarkson

Joe Shaute

JOSEPH BENJAMIN SHAUTE
B: 08/01/1899 D: 02/21/1970
BL

Year	Tm	Lg	Tot	H	A	0	1	2	3	2	3	4	LO	XN	IP	PH	RHP	LHP
1924	CLE	AL	1	1	0	1	0	0	0	0	0	0	0	0	0	0	1	0

Rank among batters: 4,707 • *Total ballparks homered in*: 1 • *First HR*: 08/10/1924 off Al Mamaux

Al Shaw

ALFRED SHAW
B: 10/03/1874 D: 03/25/1958
BR

Year	Tm	Lg	Tot	H	A	0	1	2	3	2	3	4	LO	XN	IP	PH	RHP	LHP
1901	DET	AL	1	0	1	1	0	0	0	0	0	0	0	0	0	0	1	0

Rank among batters: 4,707 • *Total ballparks homered in*: 1 • *First HR*: 06/18/1901 off Bill Carrick

Al Shaw

ALBERT SIMPSON SHAW
B: 03/01/1881 D: 12/30/1974
BL

Year	Tm	Lg	Tot	H	A	Men-On 0	1	2	3	One-Game 2	3	4	LO	XN	IP	PH	RHP	LHP
1908	STL	NL	1	1	0	0	0	1	0	0	0	0	0	0	1	0	0	1
1909	STL	NL	2	2	0	1	0	1	0	0	0	0	0	1	0	0	1	1
1914	BRO	FL	5	4	1	4	0	1	0	0	0	0	0	0	0	0	5	0
1915	KC	FL	6	3	3	2	2	2	0	0	0	0	0	0	0	0	6	0
Total			14	10	4	7	2	5	0	0	0	0	0	1	1	0	12	2

Rank among batters: 2,169 • *Top target (2 home runs)*: Kaiser Wilhelm, Russ Ford • *Number of pitchers victimized*: 12 • *Total ballparks homered in*: 5 • *First HR*: 08/23/1908 off Patsy Flaherty

Dupee Shaw

FREDERICK LANDER SHAW
B: 05/31/1859 D: 06/11/1938
BL

Year	Tm	Lg	Tot	H	A	Men-On 0	1	2	3	One-Game 2	3	4	LO	XN	IP	PH	RHP	LHP
1884	DET	NL	1	0	1	1	0	0	0	0	0	0	0	0	0	0	1	0

Rank among batters: 4,707 • *Total ballparks homered in*: 1 • *First HR*: 05/29/1884 off Larry Corcoran

Jim Shaw

JAMES ALOYSIUS SHAW
B: 08/19/1893 D: 01/27/1962
BR

Year	Tm	Lg	Tot	H	A	Men-On 0	1	2	3	One-Game 2	3	4	LO	XN	IP	PH	RHP	LHP
1914	WAS	AL	1	0	1	1	0	0	0	0	0	0	0	0	0	0	1	0
1919	WAS	AL	3	0	3	2	0	0	1	1	0	0	0	0	0	0	1	2
Total			4	0	4	3	0	0	1	1	0	0	0	0	0	0	2	2

Rank among batters: 3,427 • *Top target (2 home runs)*: Walt Kinney • *Number of pitchers victimized*: 3 • *Total ballparks homered in*: 2 • *First HR*: 06/03/1914 off Ray Caldwell

Bob Shawkey

JAMES ROBERT SHAWKEY
B: 12/04/1890 D: 12/31/1980
BR

Year	Tm	Lg	Tot	H	A	Men-On 0	1	2	3	One-Game 2	3	4	LO	XN	IP	PH	RHP	LHP
1921	NY	AL	1	1	0	0	1	0	0	0	0	0	0	0	0	0	1	0
1922	NY	AL	1	0	1	1	0	0	0	0	0	0	0	0	0	0	1	0
1924	NY	AL	1	1	0	1	0	0	0	0	0	0	0	0	0	0	1	0
Total			3	2	1	2	1	0	0	0	0	0	0	0	0	0	3	0

Rank among batters: 3,735 • *Total ballparks homered in*: 3 • *First HR*: 06/02/1921 off Urban Shocker

Danny Shay

DANIEL C. SHAY
B: 11/08/1876 D: 12/01/1927

Year	Tm	Lg	Tot	H	A	Men-On 0	1	2	3	One-Game 2	3	4	LO	XN	IP	PH	RHP	LHP
1904	STL	NL	1	1	0	1	0	0	0	0	0	0	0	0	1	0	0	1
1907	NY	NL	1	1	0	0	1	0	0	0	0	0	0	0	1	0	1	0
Total			2	2	0	1	1	0	0	0	0	0	0	0	2	0	1	1

Rank among batters: 4,129 • *Total ballparks homered in*: 2 • *First HR*: 06/20/1904 off Patsy Flaherty

Merv Shea

MERVYN DAVID JOHN SHEA
B: 09/05/1900 D: 01/27/1953
BR

Year	Tm	Lg	Tot	H	A	Men-On 0	1	2	3	One-Game 2	3	4	LO	XN	IP	PH	RHP	LHP
1929	DET	AL	3	0	3	1	1	1	0	0	0	0	0	0	0	0	2	1
1933	STL	AL	1	1	0	1	0	0	0	0	0	0	0	0	0	0	0	1
1944	PHI	NL	1	0	1	1	0	0	0	0	0	0	0	0	0	0	1	0
Total			5	1	4	3	1	1	0	0	0	0	0	0	0	0	3	2

Rank among batters: 3,191 • *Total ballparks homered in*: 4 • *First HR*: 05/27/1929 off Ed Walsh

Spec Shea

FRANCIS JOSEPH SHEA
B: 10/02/1920
BR

Year	Tm	Lg	Tot	H	A	Men-On 0	1	2	3	One-Game 2	3	4	LO	XN	IP	PH	RHP	LHP
1951	NY	AL	1	1	0	0	0	1	0	0	0	0	0	0	0	0	0	1

Rank among batters: 4,707 • *Total ballparks homered in*: 1 • *First HR*: 05/27/1951 off Morrie Martin

Danny Sheaffer

DANNY TODD SHEAFFER
B: 08/02/1961
BR

Year	Tm	Lg	Tot	H	A	Men-On 0	Men-On 1	Men-On 2	Men-On 3	One-Game 2	One-Game 3	One-Game 4	LO	XN	IP	PH	RHP	LHP
1987	BOS	AL	1	0	1	1	0	0	0	0	0	0	0	0	0	0	1	0
1993	COL	NL	4	2	2	3	0	1	0	0	0	0	0	0	0	0	3	1
1994	COL	NL	1	0	1	1	0	0	0	0	0	0	0	0	0	0	1	0
1995	STL	NL	5	2	3	3	0	1	1	0	0	0	0	0	0	1	4	1
Total			11	4	7	8	0	2	1	0	0	0	0	0	0	1	9	2

Rank among batters: 2,419 • *Total ballparks homered in*: 6 • *First HR*: 04/09/1987 off Chris Bosio

Al Shealy

ALBERT BERLY SHEALY
B: 03/20/1900 D: 03/07/1967
BR

Year	Tm	Lg	Tot	H	A	Men-On 0	Men-On 1	Men-On 2	Men-On 3	One-Game 2	One-Game 3	One-Game 4	LO	XN	IP	PH	RHP	LHP
1928	NY	AL	1	1	0	1	0	0	0	0	0	0	0	0	0	0	1	0

Rank among batters: 4,707 • *Total ballparks homered in*: 1 • *First HR*: 07/17/1928 off George Uhle

Dave Shean

DAVID WILLIAM SHEAN
B: 07/09/1883 D: 05/22/1963
BR

Year	Tm	Lg	Tot	H	A	Men-On 0	Men-On 1	Men-On 2	Men-On 3	One-Game 2	One-Game 3	One-Game 4	LO	XN	IP	PH	RHP	LHP
1909	BOS	NL	1	1	0	0	1	0	0	0	0	0	0	0	0	0	0	1
1910	BOS	NL	3	3	0	2	1	0	0	0	0	0	0	0	0	0	2	1
1917	CIN	NL	2	1	1	1	1	0	0	0	0	0	0	0	2	0	1	1
Total			6	5	1	3	3	0	0	0	0	0	0	0	2	0	3	3

Rank among batters: 2,988 • *Total ballparks homered in*: 3 • *First HR*: 07/24/1909 off Lefty Leifield

Jimmy Sheckard

SAMUEL JAMES TILDEN SHECKARD
B: 11/23/1878 D: 01/15/1947
BL

Year	Tm	Lg	Tot	H	A	Men-On 0	Men-On 1	Men-On 2	Men-On 3	One-Game 2	One-Game 3	One-Game 4	LO	XN	IP	PH	RHP	LHP
1897	BRO	NL	3	3	0	2	1	0	0	1	0	0	0	0	0	0	2	0
1898	BRO	NL	4	3	1	1	2	1	0	0	0	0	0	0	0	0	4	0
1899	BAL	NL	3	0	3	2	1	0	0	0	0	0	0	0	0	0	3	0
1900	BRO	NL	1	0	1	0	1	0	0	0	0	0	0	0	1	0	1	0
1901	BRO	NL	11	4	7	4	4	1	2	0	0	0	0	0	5	0	11	0
1902	BRO	NL	4	1	3	4	0	0	0	0	0	0	1	0	2	0	4	0
1903	BRO	NL	9	6	3	3	2	3	1	1	0	0	0	0	2	0	9	0
1904	BRO	NL	1	0	1	0	0	1	0	0	0	0	0	0	0	0	1	0
1905	BRO	NL	3	1	2	1	1	1	0	0	0	0	0	0	0	0	3	0
1906	CHI	NL	1	0	1	1	0	0	0	0	0	0	0	0	0	0	1	0
1907	CHI	NL	1	0	1	0	0	1	0	0	0	0	0	0	0	0	1	0
1908	CHI	NL	2	2	0	1	1	0	0	0	0	0	0	0	0	0	1	1
1909	CHI	NL	1	0	1	1	0	0	0	0	0	0	0	0	0	0	1	0
1910	CHI	NL	5	3	2	3	0	2	0	1	0	0	0	0	2	0	4	1
1911	CHI	NL	4	2	2	2	2	0	0	0	0	0	0	0	1	0	4	0
1912	CHI	NL	3	3	0	1	2	0	0	0	0	0	0	1	0	0	2	1
Total			56	28	28	26	17	10	3	3	0	0	1	1	13	0	51	3

Rank among batters: 913 • *Top target (4 home runs)*: Bill Duggleby, Dummy Taylor • *Number of pitchers victimized*: 40 • *Total ballparks homered in*: 11 • *First HR*: 09/17/1897 off Cy Swaim

Biff Sheehan

TIMOTHY JAMES SHEEHAN
B: 02/13/1868 D: 10/21/1923

Year	Tm	Lg	Tot	H	A	Men-On 0	Men-On 1	Men-On 2	Men-On 3	One-Game 2	One-Game 3	One-Game 4	LO	XN	IP	PH	RHP	LHP
1895	STL	NL	1	1	0	0	1	0	0	0	0	0	0	0	0	0	0	1

Rank among batters: 4,707 • *Total ballparks homered in*: 1 • *First HR*: 09/25/1895 off Frank Foreman

Tommy Sheehan

THOMAS H. SHEEHAN
B: 11/06/1877 D: 05/22/1959
BR

Year	Tm	Lg	Tot	H	A	Men-On 0	Men-On 1	Men-On 2	Men-On 3	One-Game 2	One-Game 3	One-Game 4	LO	XN	IP	PH	RHP	LHP
1906	PIT	NL	1	0	1	0	1	0	0	0	0	0	0	0	1	0	1	0

Rank among batters: 4,707 • *Total ballparks homered in*: 1 • *First HR*: 07/01/1906 off Jack Taylor

Earl Sheely

EARL HOMER SHEELY
B: 02/12/1893 D: 09/16/1952
BR

Year	Tm	Lg	Tot	H	A	Men-On				One-Game			LO	XN	IP	PH	RHP	LHP
						0	1	2	3	2	3	4						
1921	CHI	AL	11	3	8	4	5	2	0	1	0	0	0	0	0	0	5	6
1922	CHI	AL	6	1	5	4	1	1	0	1	0	0	0	1	0	0	2	4
1923	CHI	AL	4	2	2	2	2	0	0	0	0	0	0	0	2	0	3	1
1924	CHI	AL	3	3	0	1	1	1	0	0	0	0	0	0	0	0	2	1
1925	CHI	AL	9	3	6	7	2	0	0	0	0	0	0	0	0	0	4	5
1926	CHI	AL	6	1	5	4	1	1	0	0	0	0	0	0	0	0	4	2
1927	CHI	AL	2	0	2	2	0	0	0	0	0	0	0	0	0	0	1	1
1929	PIT	NL	6	4	2	3	2	1	0	0	0	0	0	0	0	0	6	0
1931	BOS	NL	1	1	0	0	1	0	0	0	0	0	0	0	0	0	0	1
Total			48	18	30	27	15	6	0	2	0	0	0	1	2	0	27	21

Rank among batters: 1,024 • *Top target (3 home runs)*: Eddie Rommel, Lefty Grove • *Number of pitchers victimized*: 35 • *Total ballparks homered in*: 11 • *First HR*: 05/26/1921 off Red Oldham

Larry Sheets

LARRY KENT SHEETS
B: 12/06/1959
BL

Year	Tm	Lg	Tot	H	A	Men-On				One-Game			LO	XN	IP	PH	RHP	LHP
						0	1	2	3	2	3	4						
1984	BAL	AL	1	0	1	0	1	0	0	0	0	0	0	0	0	0	1	0
1985	BAL	AL	17	5	12	9	6	2	0	0	0	0	0	0	0	2	17	0
1986	BAL	AL	18	10	8	4	13	0	1	1	0	0	0	1	0	0	17	1
1987	BAL	AL	31	21	10	18	10	3	0	5	0	0	0	1	0	1	21	10
1988	BAL	AL	10	6	4	5	5	0	0	0	0	0	0	0	0	1	9	1
1989	BAL	AL	7	1	6	4	2	1	0	1	0	0	0	0	0	0	7	0
1990	DET	AL	10	7	3	5	1	4	0	0	0	0	0	0	0	1	10	0
Total			94	50	44	45	38	10	1	7	0	0	0	2	0	5	82	12

Rank among batters: 535 • *Top target (3 home runs)*: Jack Morris, Kirk McCaskill • *Number of pitchers victimized*: 74 • *Total ballparks homered in*: 15 • *First HR*: 09/28/1984 off Rich Gale

Gary Sheffield

GARY ANTONIAN SHEFFIELD
B: 11/18/1968
BR

Year	Tm	Lg	Tot	H	A	Men-On				One-Game			LO	XN	IP	PH	RHP	LHP
						0	1	2	3	2	3	4						
1988	MIL	AL	4	1	3	1	2	1	0	0	0	0	0	0	0	0	3	1
1989	MIL	AL	5	2	3	4	1	0	0	0	0	0	0	0	0	0	2	3
1990	MIL	AL	10	3	7	6	4	0	0	0	0	0	0	0	0	0	7	3
1991	MIL	AL	2	2	0	1	0	1	0	0	0	0	0	0	0	0	2	0
1992	SD	NL	33	23	10	16	8	7	2	3	0	0	0	1	0	0	20	13
1993	SD	NL	10	6	4	4	5	1	0	1	0	0	0	0	0	0	8	2
	FLO	NL	10	4	6	3	7	0	0	1	0	0	0	0	0	0	8	2
	Total		20	10	10	7	12	1	0	2	0	0	0	0	0	0	16	4
1994	FLO	NL	27	15	12	9	15	3	0	1	0	0	0	0	0	1	19	8
1995	FLO	NL	16	4	12	8	5	2	1	1	0	0	0	0	1	0	13	3
Total			117	60	57	52	47	15	3	7	0	0	0	1	1	1	82	35

Rank among batters: 402 • *Top target (5 home runs)*: Bob Walk • *Number of pitchers victimized*: 89 • *Total ballparks homered in*: 24 • *First HR*: 09/09/1988 off Mark Langston • *All-Star HR—1*

John Shelby

JOHN T. SHELBY
B: 02/23/1958
BB

Year	Tm	Lg	Tot	H	A	Men-On				One-Game			LO	XN	IP	PH	RHP	LHP
						0	1	2	3	2	3	4						
1982	BAL	AL	1	1	0	1	0	0	0	0	0	0	0	0	0	0	0	1
1983	BAL	AL	5	0	5	3	0	1	1	0	0	0	1	0	0	0	1	4
1984	BAL	AL	6	2	4	4	1	1	0	0	0	0	0	0	0	1	2	4
1985	BAL	AL	7	4	3	3	4	0	0	0	0	0	1	0	0	1	5	2
1986	BAL	AL	11	5	6	9	2	0	0	2	0	0	2	0	0	1	6	5
1987	BAL	AL	1	0	1	0	1	0	0	0	0	0	0	0	0	0	0	1
	LA	NL	21	8	13	13	7	1	0	2	0	0	0	0	1	0	11	10
	Total		22	8	14	13	8	1	0	2	0	0	0	0	1	0	11	11
1988	LA	NL	10	5	5	6	2	2	0	0	0	0	0	0	0	0	8	2
1989	LA	NL	1	0	1	0	1	0	0	0	0	0	0	0	0	0	1	0
1990	DET	AL	4	3	1	1	1	2	0	0	0	0	0	0	0	1	2	2
1991	DET	AL	3	2	1	1	2	0	0	0	0	0	0	1	0	1	1	2
Total			70	30	40	41	21	7	1	4	0	0	4	1	1	5	37	33

John Shelby *continued*

Rank among batters: 742 • *Top target (3 home runs)*: Mark Langston • *Number of pitchers victimized*: 60 • *Total ballparks homered in*: 21 • *First HR*: 10/01/1982 off Mike Caldwell

Ben Shelton

BENJAMIN DAVIS SHELTON
B: 09/21/1969
BR

Year	Tm	Lg	Tot	H	A	Men-On 0	1	2	3	One-Game 2	3	4	LO	XN	IP	PH	RHP	LHP
1993	PIT	NL	2	2	0	2	0	0	0	0	0	0	0	0	0	1	2	0

Rank among batters: 4,129 • *Total ballparks homered in*: 1 • *First HR*: 06/21/1993 off Jose Bautista

Jack Shepard

JACK LEROY SHEPARD
B: 05/13/1931 D: 12/13/1994
BR

Year	Tm	Lg	Tot	H	A	Men-On 0	1	2	3	One-Game 2	3	4	LO	XN	IP	PH	RHP	LHP
1954	PIT	NL	3	0	3	2	1	0	0	0	0	0	0	0	0	0	1	2
1955	PIT	NL	2	0	2	1	1	0	0	0	0	0	0	0	0	0	0	2
1956	PIT	NL	7	3	4	2	3	2	0	1	0	0	0	0	0	1	3	4
Total			12	3	9	5	5	2	0	1	0	0	0	0	0	1	4	8

Rank among batters: 2,325 • *Top target (2 home runs)*: Joe Nuxhall • *Number of pitchers victimized*: 11 • *Total ballparks homered in*: 6 • *First HR*: 08/14/1954 off Jim Konstanty

Ron Shepherd

RONALD WAYNE SHEPHERD
B: 10/27/1960
BR

Year	Tm	Lg	Tot	H	A	Men-On 0	1	2	3	One-Game 2	3	4	LO	XN	IP	PH	RHP	LHP
1986	TOR	AL	2	1	1	1	1	0	0	0	0	0	0	0	0	0	1	1

Rank among batters: 4,129 • *Total ballparks homered in*: 2 • *First HR*: 07/12/1986 off Steve Ontiveros

Bill Sherdel

WILLIAM HENRY SHERDEL
B: 08/15/1896 D: 11/14/1968
BL

Year	Tm	Lg	Tot	H	A	Men-On 0	1	2	3	One-Game 2	3	4	LO	XN	IP	PH	RHP	LHP
1918	STL	NL	1	0	1	0	1	0	0	0	0	0	0	0	0	0	1	0
1920	STL	NL	1	1	0	1	0	0	0	0	0	0	0	0	0	1	1	0
1922	STL	NL	1	1	0	1	0	0	0	0	0	0	0	0	0	0	1	0
1923	STL	NL	1	0	1	0	1	0	0	0	0	0	0	0	0	0	1	0
1925	STL	NL	1	1	0	1	0	0	0	0	0	0	0	0	0	0	1	0
1926	STL	NL	1	0	1	1	0	0	0	0	0	0	0	0	0	0	1	0
1927	STL	NL	1	0	1	1	0	0	0	0	0	0	0	0	0	0	1	0
1928	STL	NL	1	1	0	1	0	0	0	0	0	0	0	0	0	0	1	0
1929	STL	NL	1	1	0	0	1	0	0	0	0	0	0	0	0	0	1	0
Total			9	5	4	6	3	0	0	0	0	0	0	0	0	1	9	0

Rank among batters: 2,587 • *Total ballparks homered in*: 4 • *First HR*: 07/27/1918 off Burleigh Grimes

Pat Sheridan

PATRICK ARTHUR SHERIDAN
B: 12/04/1957
BL

Year	Tm	Lg	Tot	H	A	Men-On 0	1	2	3	One-Game 2	3	4	LO	XN	IP	PH	RHP	LHP
1983	KC	AL	7	4	3	6	1	0	0	0	0	0	0	0	0	0	7	0
1984	KC	AL	8	3	5	4	3	0	1	0	0	0	0	0	0	0	7	1
1985	KC	AL	3	2	1	2	1	0	0	1	0	0	0	0	1	0	3	0
1986	DET	AL	6	3	3	5	1	0	0	0	0	0	0	0	0	0	6	0
1987	DET	AL	6	3	3	4	2	0	0	0	0	0	0	0	0	0	6	0
1988	DET	AL	11	7	4	6	2	1	2	1	0	0	0	0	0	1	10	1
1989	DET	AL	3	2	1	2	1	0	0	0	0	0	1	0	0	0	3	0
	SF	NL	3	0	3	3	0	0	0	0	0	0	0	0	0	0	3	0
	Total		6	2	4	5	1	0	0	0	0	0	1	0	0	0	6	0
1991	NY	AL	4	2	2	3	1	0	0	0	0	0	0	0	0	2	4	0
Total			51	26	25	35	12	1	3	2	0	0	1	0	1	3	49	2

Rank among batters: 979 • *Top target (2 home runs)*: Juan Berenguer, Phil Niekro, Keith Atherton • *Number of pitchers victimized*: 48 • *Total ballparks homered in*: 16 • *First HR*: 05/15/1983 off Milt Wilcox • *LCS HR*—3

Larry Sherry

LAWRENCE SHERRY
B: 07/25/1935
BR

Year	Tm	Lg	Tot	H	A	Men-On 0	Men-On 1	Men-On 2	Men-On 3	One-Game 2	One-Game 3	One-Game 4	LO	XN	IP	PH	RHP	LHP
1959	LA	NL	2	1	1	1	1	0	0	0	0	0	0	0	0	0	2	0
1960	LA	NL	1	0	1	1	0	0	0	0	0	0	0	0	0	0	1	0
Total			3	1	2	2	1	0	0	0	0	0	0	0	0	0	3	0

Rank among batters: 3,735 • *Total ballparks homered in*: 3 • *First HR*: 08/15/1959 off Ernie Broglio

Norm Sherry

NORMAN BURT SHERRY
B: 07/16/1931
BR

Year	Tm	Lg	Tot	H	A	Men-On 0	Men-On 1	Men-On 2	Men-On 3	One-Game 2	One-Game 3	One-Game 4	LO	XN	IP	PH	RHP	LHP
1960	LA	NL	8	7	1	4	3	0	1	1	0	0	0	1	0	0	6	2
1961	LA	NL	5	4	1	2	1	2	0	0	0	0	0	0	0	0	1	4
1962	LA	NL	3	2	1	0	2	1	0	0	0	0	0	0	0	1	1	2
1963	NY	NL	2	2	0	1	0	1	0	0	0	0	0	0	0	0	0	2
Total			18	15	3	7	6	4	1	1	0	0	0	1	0	1	8	10

Rank among batters: 1,914 • Top target (2 home runs): Dick Ellsworth, Ray Sadecki, Bill Henry, Warren Spahn • *Number of pitchers victimized*: 14 • *Total ballparks homered in*: 6 • *First HR*: 05/07/1960 off Ruben Gomez

Barry Shetrone

BARRY STEVEN SHETRONE
B: 07/06/1938
BL

Year	Tm	Lg	Tot	H	A	Men-On 0	Men-On 1	Men-On 2	Men-On 3	One-Game 2	One-Game 3	One-Game 4	LO	XN	IP	PH	RHP	LHP
1962	BAL	AL	1	0	1	1	0	0	0	0	0	0	0	0	0	0	1	0

Rank among batters: 4,707 • *Total ballparks homered in*: 1 • *First HR*: 09/01/1962 off Dave Tyriver

Billy Shindle

WILLIAM SHINDLE
B: 12/05/1863 D: 06/03/1936
BR

Year	Tm	Lg	Tot	H	A	Men-On 0	Men-On 1	Men-On 2	Men-On 3	One-Game 2	One-Game 3	One-Game 4	LO	XN	IP	PH	RHP	LHP
1888	BAL	AA	1	0	1	0	1	0	0	0	0	0	0	0	0	0	1	0
1889	BAL	AA	3	2	1	2	1	0	0	0	0	0	0	0	0	0	1	2
1890	PHI	PL	10	3	7	3	3	3	1	1	0	0	0	0	2	0	6	4
1892	BAL	NL	3	0	3	2	1	0	0	0	0	0	0	0	0	0	3	0
1893	BAL	NL	1	0	1	0	1	0	0	0	0	0	0	0	0	0	0	0
1894	BRO	NL	4	1	3	0	2	1	1	0	0	0	0	0	0	0	4	0
1895	BRO	NL	3	2	1	1	2	0	0	0	0	0	0	0	0	0	2	0
1896	BRO	NL	1	0	1	0	0	1	0	0	0	0	0	0	0	0	1	0
1897	BRO	NL	4	2	2	1	3	0	0	0	0	0	0	0	1	0	3	1
1898	BRO	NL	1	0	1	1	0	0	0	0	0	0	0	0	1	0	1	0
Total			31	10	21	10	14	5	2	1	0	0	0	0	4	0	22	7

Rank among batters: 1,400 • Top target (2 home runs): John Ewing, Matt Kilroy, Bob Caruthers, Ad Gumbert • *Number of pitchers victimized*: 27 • *Total ballparks homered in*: 16 • *First HR*: 07/07/1888 off Red Ehret

Ralph Shinners

RALPH PETER SHINNERS
B: 10/04/1895 D: 07/23/1962
BR

Year	Tm	Lg	Tot	H	A	Men-On 0	Men-On 1	Men-On 2	Men-On 3	One-Game 2	One-Game 3	One-Game 4	LO	XN	IP	PH	RHP	LHP
1925	STL	NL	7	4	3	3	2	2	0	0	0	0	1	0	0	0	3	4

Rank among batters: 2,834 • *Total ballparks homered in*: 4 • *First HR*: 06/04/1925 off Jack Bentley

Tim Shinnick

TIMOTHY JAMES SHINNICK
B: 11/06/1867 D: 05/18/1944
BB

Year	Tm	Lg	Tot	H	A	Men-On 0	Men-On 1	Men-On 2	Men-On 3	One-Game 2	One-Game 3	One-Game 4	LO	XN	IP	PH	RHP	LHP
1890	LOU	AA	1	0	1	0	1	0	0	0	0	0	0	0	0	0	0	1
1891	LOU	AA	1	1	0	0	0	0	1	0	0	0	0	0	1	0	0	0
Total			2	1	1	0	1	0	1	0	0	0	0	0	1	0	0	1

Rank among batters: 4,129 • *Total ballparks homered in*: 2 • *First HR*: 06/27/1890 off Toad Ramsey

Bill Shipke

WILLIAM MARTIN SHIPKE
B: 11/18/1882 D: 09/10/1940
BR

Year	Tm	Lg	Tot	H	A	Men-On 0	Men-On 1	Men-On 2	Men-On 3	One-Game 2	One-Game 3	One-Game 4	LO	XN	IP	PH	RHP	LHP
1907	WAS	AL	1	1	0	0	0	1	0	0	0	0	0	0	0	0	1	0

Year	Tm	Lg	Tot	H	A	Men-On 0	Men-On 1	Men-On 2	Men-On 3	One-Game 2	One-Game 3	One-Game 4	LO	XN	IP	PH	RHP	LHP

Bill Shipke *continued*

Rank among batters: 4,707 • *Total ballparks homered in*: 1 • *First HR*: 09/17/1907 off Ralph Glaze

Craig Shipley

CRAIG BARRY SHIPLEY
B: 01/07/1963
BR

Year	Tm	Lg	Tot	H	A	Men-On 0	Men-On 1	Men-On 2	Men-On 3	One-Game 2	One-Game 3	One-Game 4	LO	XN	IP	PH	RHP	LHP
1991	SD	NL	1	0	1	1	0	0	0	0	0	0	0	0	0	0	0	1
1993	SD	NL	4	2	2	2	1	1	0	0	0	0	0	0	0	0	3	1
1994	SD	NL	4	2	2	3	0	0	1	0	0	0	0	0	0	1	4	0
1995	HOU	NL	3	1	2	2	1	0	0	0	0	0	0	0	0	1	2	1
Total			12	5	7	8	2	1	1	0	0	0	0	0	0	2	9	3

Rank among batters: 2,325 • *Total ballparks homered in*: 7 • *First HR*: 09/28/1991 off Tom Browning

Art Shires

CHARLES ARTHUR SHIRES
B: 08/13/1907 D: 07/13/1967
BL

Year	Tm	Lg	Tot	H	A	Men-On 0	Men-On 1	Men-On 2	Men-On 3	One-Game 2	One-Game 3	One-Game 4	LO	XN	IP	PH	RHP	LHP
1928	CHI	AL	1	1	0	1	0	0	0	0	0	0	0	0	1	0	1	0
1929	CHI	AL	3	0	3	2	1	0	0	0	0	0	0	0	0	0	3	0
1930	CHI	AL	1	0	1	1	0	0	0	0	0	0	0	0	0	0	1	0
	WAS	AL	1	0	1	1	0	0	0	0	0	0	0	0	0	0	1	0
	Total		2	0	2	2	0	0	0	0	0	0	0	0	0	0	2	0
1932	BOS	NL	5	1	4	3	1	1	0	0	0	0	0	0	0	0	4	1
Total			11	2	9	8	2	1	0	0	0	0	0	0	1	0	10	1

Rank among batters: 2,419 • *Total ballparks homered in*: 7 • *First HR*: 09/23/1928 off Firpo Marberry

Ivey Shiver

IVEY MERWIN SHIVER
B: 01/22/1907 D: 08/31/1972
BR

Year	Tm	Lg	Tot	H	A	Men-On 0	Men-On 1	Men-On 2	Men-On 3	One-Game 2	One-Game 3	One-Game 4	LO	XN	IP	PH	RHP	LHP
1934	CIN	NL	2	0	2	2	0	0	0	0	0	0	0	0	0	0	2	0

Rank among batters: 4,129 • *Total ballparks homered in*: 2 • *First HR*: 04/24/1934 off Guy Bush

George Shoch

GEORGE QUINTUS SHOCH
B: 01/06/1859 D: 09/30/1937
BR

Year	Tm	Lg	Tot	H	A	Men-On 0	Men-On 1	Men-On 2	Men-On 3	One-Game 2	One-Game 3	One-Game 4	LO	XN	IP	PH	RHP	LHP
1886	WAS	NL	1	1	0	1	0	0	0	0	0	0	0	0	0	0	1	0
1887	WAS	NL	1	1	0	0	1	0	0	0	0	0	0	0	0	0	1	0
1888	WAS	NL	2	1	1	0	1	0	1	0	0	0	0	0	1	0	1	1
1891	MIL	AA	1	1	0	0	1	0	0	0	0	0	0	0	0	0	1	0
1892	BAL	NL	1	1	0	0	1	0	0	0	0	0	0	0	0	0	0	1
1893	BRO	NL	2	2	0	0	2	0	0	0	0	0	0	0	0	0	2	0
1894	BRO	NL	1	0	1	0	0	1	0	0	0	0	0	0	0	0	1	0
1896	BRO	NL	1	1	0	0	0	1	0	0	0	0	0	0	0	0	1	0
Total			10	8	2	1	6	2	1	0	0	0	0	0	1	0	8	2

Rank among batters: 2,500 • *Top target (2 home runs)*: John Clarkson • *Number of pitchers victimized*: 9 • *Total ballparks homered in*: 6 • *First HR*: 10/01/1886 off John Clarkson

Urban Shocker

URBAN JAMES SHOCKER
B: 08/22/1890 D: 09/09/1928
BR

Year	Tm	Lg	Tot	H	A	Men-On 0	Men-On 1	Men-On 2	Men-On 3	One-Game 2	One-Game 3	One-Game 4	LO	XN	IP	PH	RHP	LHP
1922	STL	AL	1	1	0	1	0	0	0	0	0	0	0	0	0	0	0	1

Rank among batters: 4,707 • *Total ballparks homered in*: 1 • *First HR*: 04/28/1922 off Walter Mails

Costen Shockley

JOHN COSTEN SHOCKLEY
B: 02/08/1942
BL

Year	Tm	Lg	Tot	H	A	Men-On 0	Men-On 1	Men-On 2	Men-On 3	One-Game 2	One-Game 3	One-Game 4	LO	XN	IP	PH	RHP	LHP
1964	PHI	NL	1	0	1	1	0	0	0	0	0	0	0	0	0	0	1	0
1965	CAL	AL	2	1	1	0	1	0	1	0	0	0	0	0	0	0	2	0
Total			3	1	2	1	1	0	1	0	0	0	0	0	0	0	3	0

Rank among batters: 3,735 • *Total ballparks homered in*: 3 • *First HR*: 07/18/1964 off John Tsitouris

Milt Shoffner

MILBURN JAMES SHOFFNER
B: 11/13/1905 D: 01/19/1978
BL

Year	Tm	Lg	Tot	H	A	Men-On 0	1	2	3	One-Game 2	3	4	LO	XN	IP	PH	RHP	LHP
1930	CLE	AL	1	1	0	1	0	0	0	0	0	0	0	0	0	0	1	0
1937	BOS	NL	1	0	1	0	1	0	0	0	0	0	0	0	0	0	1	0
Total			2	1	1	1	1	0	0	0	0	0	0	0	0	0	2	0

Rank among batters: 4,129 • *Total ballparks homered in*: 2 • *First HR*: 09/28/1930 off Rollie Stiles

Tom Shopay

THOMAS MICHAEL SHOPAY
B: 02/21/1945
BL

Year	Tm	Lg	Tot	H	A	Men-On 0	1	2	3	One-Game 2	3	4	LO	XN	IP	PH	RHP	LHP
1967	NY	AL	2	1	1	1	0	1	0	0	0	0	0	0	0	0	1	1
1977	BAL	AL	1	0	1	1	0	0	0	0	0	0	0	0	0	0	0	1
Total			3	1	2	2	0	1	0	0	0	0	0	0	0	0	1	2

Rank among batters: 3,735 • *Total ballparks homered in*: 3 • *First HR*: 09/23/1967 off Dave Boswell

Chick Shorten

CHARLES HENRY SHORTEN
B: 04/19/1892 D: 10/23/1965
BL

Year	Tm	Lg	Tot	H	A	Men-On 0	1	2	3	One-Game 2	3	4	LO	XN	IP	PH	RHP	LHP
1920	DET	AL	1	1	0	0	1	0	0	0	0	0	0	0	0	0	1	0
1922	STL	AL	2	1	1	2	0	0	0	0	0	0	0	0	0	1	2	0
Total			3	2	1	2	1	0	0	0	0	0	0	0	0	1	3	0

Rank among batters: 3,735 • *Total ballparks homered in*: 3 • *First HR*: 06/15/1920 off Rollie Naylor

Burt Shotton

BURTON EDWIN SHOTTON
B: 10/18/1884 D: 07/29/1962
BL

Year	Tm	Lg	Tot	H	A	Men-On 0	1	2	3	One-Game 2	3	4	LO	XN	IP	PH	RHP	LHP
1912	STL	AL	2	0	2	2	0	0	0	0	0	0	1	0	2	0	2	0
1913	STL	AL	1	1	0	1	0	0	0	0	0	0	0	0	1	0	1	0
1915	STL	AL	1	1	0	1	0	0	0	0	0	0	0	0	0	0	1	0
1916	STL	AL	1	0	1	1	0	0	0	0	0	0	0	0	1	0	1	0
1917	STL	AL	1	0	1	1	0	0	0	0	0	0	1	0	1	0	1	0
1919	STL	NL	1	0	1	1	0	0	0	0	0	0	0	0	0	0	0	1
1920	STL	NL	1	1	0	0	1	0	0	0	0	0	0	0	1	0	1	0
1921	STL	NL	1	0	1	1	0	0	0	0	0	0	0	0	1	0	1	0
Total			9	3	6	8	1	0	0	0	0	0	2	0	7	0	8	1

Rank among batters: 2,587 • *Total ballparks homered in*: 6 • *First HR*: 06/22/1912 off Joe Benz

Eric Show

ERIC VAUGHN SHOW
B: 05/19/1956 D: 03/16/1994
BR

Year	Tm	Lg	Tot	H	A	Men-On 0	1	2	3	One-Game 2	3	4	LO	XN	IP	PH	RHP	LHP
1984	SD	NL	3	1	2	2	1	0	0	0	0	0	0	0	0	0	0	3
1985	SD	NL	1	0	1	0	0	1	0	0	0	0	0	0	0	0	1	0
Total			4	1	3	2	1	1	0	0	0	0	0	0	0	0	1	3

Rank among batters: 3,427 • *Top target (2 home runs)*: Joe Price • *Number of pitchers victimized*: 3 • *Total ballparks homered in*: 4 • *First HR*: 06/24/1984 off Joe Price

George Shuba

GEORGE THOMAS SHUBA
B: 12/13/1924
BL

Year	Tm	Lg	Tot	H	A	Men-On 0	1	2	3	One-Game 2	3	4	LO	XN	IP	PH	RHP	LHP
1948	BRO	NL	4	0	4	4	0	0	0	0	0	0	0	0	0	0	3	1
1950	BRO	NL	3	2	1	2	1	0	0	0	0	0	0	0	0	0	3	0
1952	BRO	NL	9	3	6	4	4	1	0	0	0	0	0	0	0	1	8	1
1953	BRO	NL	5	2	3	3	2	0	0	0	0	0	1	0	0	0	4	1
1954	BRO	NL	2	0	2	1	0	1	0	0	0	0	0	0	0	2	2	0
1955	BRO	NL	1	1	0	0	1	0	0	0	0	0	0	0	0	0	1	0
Total			24	8	16	14	8	2	0	0	0	0	1	0	0	3	21	3

Rank among batters: 1,643 • *Top target (3 home runs)*: Murry Dickson • *Number of pitchers victimized*: 21 • *Total ballparks homered in*: 9 • *First HR*: 07/06/1948 off Ken Heintzelman • *World Series HR*—1

Frank Shugart

FRANK HARRY SHUGART
B: 12/10/1866 D: 09/09/1944
BB

Year	Tm	Lg	Tot	H	A	Men-On 0	Men-On 1	Men-On 2	Men-On 3	One-Game 2	One-Game 3	One-Game 4	LO	XN	IP	PH	RHP	LHP
1891	PIT	NL	3	2	1	0	3	0	0	0	0	0	0	0	1	0	2	1
1893	PIT	NL	1	0	1	0	1	0	0	0	0	0	0	0	0	0	1	0
1894	STL	NL	7	2	5	2	4	1	0	0	1	0	0	0	1	0	6	1
1895	LOU	NL	4	2	2	0	4	0	0	0	0	0	0	0	1	0	3	1
1897	PHI	NL	5	3	2	1	3	1	0	0	0	0	0	0	0	0	2	1
1901	CHI	AL	2	1	1	2	0	0	0	0	0	0	0	0	0	0	1	1
Total			22	10	12	5	15	2	0	0	1	0	0	0	3	0	15	5

Rank among batters: 1,719 • *Top target (3 home runs)*: Tom Parrott • *Number of pitchers victimized*: 18 • *Total ballparks homered in*: 13 • *First HR*: 07/11/1891 off Phil Saylor

Terry Shumpert

TERRANCE DARNELL SHUMPERT
B: 08/16/1966
BR

Year	Tm	Lg	Tot	H	A	Men-On 0	Men-On 1	Men-On 2	Men-On 3	One-Game 2	One-Game 3	One-Game 4	LO	XN	IP	PH	RHP	LHP
1991	KC	AL	5	1	4	4	1	0	0	0	0	0	0	0	0	0	3	2
1992	KC	AL	1	0	1	0	0	1	0	0	0	0	0	0	0	0	0	1
1994	KC	AL	8	2	6	5	2	0	1	1	0	0	0	0	0	0	3	5
Total			14	3	11	9	3	1	1	1	0	0	0	0	0	0	6	8

Rank among batters: 2,169 • *Top target (2 home runs)*: Terry Mulholland • *Number of pitchers victimized*: 13 • *Total ballparks homered in*: 9 • *First HR*: 06/01/1991 off Allan Anderson

Norm Siebern

NORMAN LEROY SIEBERN
B: 07/26/1933
BL

Year	Tm	Lg	Tot	H	A	Men-On 0	Men-On 1	Men-On 2	Men-On 3	One-Game 2	One-Game 3	One-Game 4	LO	XN	IP	PH	RHP	LHP
1956	NY	AL	4	1	3	1	3	0	0	1	0	0	0	0	0	0	3	1
1958	NY	AL	14	7	7	7	6	1	0	1	0	0	0	0	1	0	10	4
1959	NY	AL	11	4	7	9	1	1	0	0	0	0	1	0	0	1	10	1
1960	KC	AL	19	6	13	16	2	1	0	2	0	0	0	0	0	0	17	2
1961	KC	AL	18	5	13	8	7	3	0	1	0	0	0	0	1	0	16	2
1962	KC	AL	25	14	11	8	14	3	0	5	0	0	0	0	0	0	19	6
1963	KC	AL	16	10	6	8	6	2	0	1	0	0	0	0	0	0	8	8
1964	BAL	AL	12	8	4	8	4	0	0	0	0	0	0	1	0	0	9	3
1965	BAL	AL	8	3	5	3	5	0	0	0	0	0	0	0	0	0	7	1
1966	CAL	AL	5	2	3	4	1	0	0	0	0	0	0	0	0	0	5	0
Total			132	60	72	72	49	11	0	11	0	0	1	1	2	1	104	28

Rank among batters: 339 • *Top target (5 home runs)*: Hal Brown • *Number of pitchers victimized*: 88 • *Total ballparks homered in*: 11 • *First HR*: 06/17/1956 off Early Wynn

Dick Siebert

RICHARD WALTHER SIEBERT
B: 02/19/1912 D: 12/09/1978
BL

Year	Tm	Lg	Tot	H	A	Men-On 0	Men-On 1	Men-On 2	Men-On 3	One-Game 2	One-Game 3	One-Game 4	LO	XN	IP	PH	RHP	LHP
1939	PHI	AL	6	1	5	4	2	0	0	0	0	0	0	1	0	0	5	1
1940	PHI	AL	5	0	5	2	2	1	0	0	0	0	0	0	0	0	5	0
1941	PHI	AL	5	1	4	3	2	0	0	2	0	0	0	0	0	0	5	0
1942	PHI	AL	2	0	2	2	0	0	0	0	0	0	0	0	0	0	2	0
1943	PHI	AL	1	0	1	1	0	0	0	0	0	0	0	0	0	0	1	0
1944	PHI	AL	6	4	2	4	2	0	0	0	0	0	0	0	1	0	6	0
1945	PHI	AL	8	5	3	6	2	0	0	0	0	0	0	1	0	0	7	1
Total			33	11	22	22	10	1	0	2	0	0	0	2	1	0	31	2

Rank among batters: 1,336 • Top target (2 home runs): Bobo Newsom, Red Ruffing, Yank Terry, Johnny Humphries • *Number of pitchers victimized*: 29 • *Total ballparks homered in*: 7 • *First HR*: 07/17/1939 off Bob Harris

Sonny Siebert

WILFRED CHARLES SIEBERT
B: 01/14/1937
BR

Year	Tm	Lg	Tot	H	A	Men-On 0	Men-On 1	Men-On 2	Men-On 3	One-Game 2	One-Game 3	One-Game 4	LO	XN	IP	PH	RHP	LHP
1964	CLE	AL	2	1	1	1	1	0	0	0	0	0	0	0	0	0	2	0
1965	CLE	AL	1	0	1	1	0	0	0	0	0	0	0	0	0	0	1	0
1967	CLE	AL	1	1	0	0	1	0	0	0	0	0	0	0	0	0	0	1
1969	BOS	AL	1	1	0	1	0	0	0	0	0	0	0	0	0	0	1	0
1971	BOS	AL	6	4	2	3	3	0	0	1	0	0	0	0	0	0	3	3

Sonny Siebert *continued*

Year	Tm	Lg	Tot	H	A	Men-On 0	1	2	3	One-Game 2	3	4	LO	XN	IP	PH	RHP	LHP
1972	BOS	AL	1	1	0	1	0	0	0	0	0	0	0	0	0	0	1	0
Total			12	8	4	7	5	0	0	1	0	0	0	0	0	0	8	4

Rank among batters: 2,325 • *Top target (2 home runs)*: Dave McNally, Pat Dobson • *Number of pitchers victimized*: 10 • *Total ballparks homered in*: 4 • *First HR*: 08/28/1964 off Wes Stock

Johnny Siegle

JOHN HERBERT SIEGLE
B: 07/08/1874 D: 02/12/1968
BR

Year	Tm	Lg	Tot	H	A	Men-On 0	1	2	3	One-Game 2	3	4	LO	XN	IP	PH	RHP	LHP
1905	CIN	NL	1	1	0	0	1	0	0	0	0	0	0	0	1	0	1	0

Rank among batters: 4,707 • *Total ballparks homered in*: 1 • *First HR*: 09/23/1905 off Harry McIntire

Oscar Siemer

OSCAR SYLVESTER SIEMER
B: 08/14/1901 D: 12/05/1959
BR

Year	Tm	Lg	Tot	H	A	Men-On 0	1	2	3	One-Game 2	3	4	LO	XN	IP	PH	RHP	LHP
1925	BOS	NL	1	1	0	1	0	0	0	0	0	0	0	0	1	0	1	0

Rank among batters: 4,707 • *Total ballparks homered in*: 1 • *First HR*: 05/22/1925 off Clyde Day

Ruben Sierra

RUBEN ANGEL (GARCIA) SIERRA
B: 10/06/1965
BB

Year	Tm	Lg	Tot	H	A	Men-On 0	1	2	3	One-Game 2	3	4	LO	XN	IP	PH	RHP	LHP
1986	TEX	AL	16	8	8	10	3	3	0	1	0	0	0	0	0	0	12	4
1987	TEX	AL	30	15	15	15	11	4	0	3	0	0	0	0	3	0	18	12
1988	TEX	AL	23	15	8	10	10	3	0	1	0	0	0	0	0	0	15	8
1989	TEX	AL	29	21	8	14	12	3	0	1	0	0	0	0	0	0	19	10
1990	TEX	AL	16	10	6	8	5	2	1	0	0	0	0	0	0	0	13	3
1991	TEX	AL	25	12	13	11	10	4	0	1	0	0	0	0	0	0	18	7
1992	TEX	AL	14	8	6	6	5	3	0	0	0	0	0	0	0	0	11	3
	OAK	AL	3	2	1	0	1	2	0	0	0	0	0	0	0	0	1	2
	Total		17	10	7	6	6	5	0	0	0	0	0	0	0	0	12	5
1993	OAK	AL	22	9	13	6	6	9	1	0	0	0	0	1	0	0	14	8
1994	OAK	AL	23	11	12	9	11	3	0	1	0	0	0	0	0	0	13	10
1995	OAK	AL	12	3	9	7	5	0	0	1	0	0	0	0	0	0	10	2
	NY	AL	7	5	2	2	2	2	1	0	0	0	0	0	0	0	4	3
	Total		19	8	11	9	7	2	1	1	0	0	0	0	0	0	14	5
Total			220	119	101	98	81	38	3	9	0	0	0	1	3	0	148	72

Rank among batters: 149 • *Top target (5 home runs)*: Storm Davis, Jimmy Key, Jack Morris • *Number of pitchers victimized*: 164 • *Total ballparks homered in*: 18 • *First HR*: 06/01/1986 off Charlie Leibrandt • *Switch hit HR in 1 game*—4 times • *LCS HR*—3; *All-Star HR*—1

Roy Sievers

ROY EDWARD SIEVERS
B: 11/18/1926
BR

Year	Tm	Lg	Tot	H	A	Men-On 0	1	2	3	One-Game 2	3	4	LO	XN	IP	PH	RHP	LHP
1949	STL	AL	16	6	10	7	6	2	1	0	0	0	0	0	0	1	10	6
1950	STL	AL	10	3	7	7	2	0	1	0	0	0	0	0	0	0	3	7
1951	STL	AL	1	1	0	1	0	0	0	0	0	0	0	0	0	0	0	1
1953	STL	AL	8	4	4	5	2	1	0	0	0	0	0	0	0	0	1	7
1954	WAS	AL	24	10	14	13	7	3	1	2	0	0	0	0	0	0	16	8
1955	WAS	AL	25	7	18	11	7	6	1	5	0	0	0	0	0	0	19	6
1956	WAS	AL	29	11	18	11	12	6	0	2	0	0	0	0	0	0	24	5
1957	WAS	AL	42	26	16	20	18	2	2	3	0	0	0	3	0	1	29	13
1958	WAS	AL	39	18	21	24	7	8	0	5	0	0	0	1	0	1	33	6
1959	WAS	AL	21	8	13	15	5	1	0	1	0	0	0	1	0	1	18	3
1960	CHI	AL	28	13	15	15	9	4	0	2	0	0	0	0	0	0	22	6
1961	CHI	AL	27	13	14	13	11	1	2	5	0	0	0	2	0	2	21	6
1962	PHI	NL	21	16	5	12	5	3	1	1	0	0	0	1	0	0	16	5
1963	PHI	NL	19	12	7	7	7	4	1	1	0	0	0	0	0	2	13	6
1964	PHI	NL	4	1	3	1	1	2	0	0	0	0	0	0	0	0	2	2
	WAS	AL	4	1	3	1	0	3	0	0	0	0	0	0	0	2	2	2
	Total		8	2	6	2	1	5	0	0	0	0	0	0	0	2	4	4
Total			318	150	168	163	99	46	10	27	0	0	0	8	0	10	229	89

Rank among batters: 59 • *Top target (11 home runs)*: Art Ditmar • *Number of pitchers victimized*: 157 • *Total ballparks homered in*: 21 • *First HR*: 05/14/1949 off Fred Hutchinson

Tripp Sigman

WESLEY TRIPLETT SIGMAN
B: 01/17/1899 D: 03/08/1971
BL

Year	Tm	Lg	Tot	H	A	Men-On 0	1	2	3	One-Game 2	3	4	LO	XN	IP	PH	RHP	LHP
1929	PHI	NL	2	2	0	1	1	0	0	0	0	0	0	0	0	0	2	0
1930	PHI	NL	4	1	3	3	1	0	0	0	0	0	0	0	0	1	4	0
Total			6	3	3	4	2	0	0	0	0	0	0	0	0	1	6	0

Rank among batters: 2,988 • *Total ballparks homered in*: 4 • *First HR*: 09/25/1929 off Ray Moss

Charlie Silvera

CHARLES ANTHONY RYAN SILVERA
B: 10/13/1924
BR

Year	Tm	Lg	Tot	H	A	Men-On 0	1	2	3	One-Game 2	3	4	LO	XN	IP	PH	RHP	LHP
1951	NY	AL	1	1	0	1	0	0	0	0	0	0	0	0	0	0	1	0

Rank among batters: 4,707 • *Total ballparks homered in*: 1 • *First HR*: 07/04/1951 off Fred Sanford

Dave Silvestri

DAVID JOSEPH SILVESTRI
B: 09/29/1967
BR

Year	Tm	Lg	Tot	H	A	Men-On 0	1	2	3	One-Game 2	3	4	LO	XN	IP	PH	RHP	LHP
1993	NY	AL	1	0	1	0	1	0	0	0	0	0	0	0	0	0	0	1
1994	NY	AL	1	1	0	1	0	0	0	0	0	0	0	0	0	0	0	1
1995	NY	AL	1	0	1	0	0	1	0	0	0	0	0	0	0	1	0	1
	MON	NL	2	0	2	2	0	0	0	0	0	0	0	0	0	0	2	0
	Total		3	0	3	2	0	1	0	0	0	0	0	0	0	1	2	1
Total			5	1	4	3	1	1	0	0	0	0	0	0	0	1	2	3

Rank among batters: 3,191 • *Total ballparks homered in*: 5 • *First HR*: 06/25/1993 off Fernando Valenzuela

Ken Silvestri

KENNETH JOSEPH SILVESTRI
B: 05/03/1916 D: 03/31/1992
BB

Year	Tm	Lg	Tot	H	A	Men-On 0	1	2	3	One-Game 2	3	4	LO	XN	IP	PH	RHP	LHP
1939	CHI	AL	2	1	1	1	1	0	0	0	0	0	0	0	0	0	1	1
1940	CHI	AL	2	1	1	0	2	0	0	0	0	0	0	0	0	2	2	0
1941	NY	AL	1	1	0	1	0	0	0	0	0	0	0	0	0	0	1	0
Total			5	3	2	2	3	0	0	0	0	0	0	0	0	2	4	1

Rank among batters: 3,191 • *Total ballparks homered in*: 2 • *First HR*: 05/04/1939 off Ken Chase

Al Sima

ALBERT SIMA
B: 10/07/1921 D: 08/17/1993
BR

Year	Tm	Lg	Tot	H	A	Men-On 0	1	2	3	One-Game 2	3	4	LO	XN	IP	PH	RHP	LHP
1951	WAS	AL	1	0	1	1	0	0	0	0	0	0	0	0	0	0	1	0

Rank among batters: 4,707 • *Total ballparks homered in*: 1 • *First HR*: 06/03/1951 off Dizzy Trout

Al Simmons

ALOYSIUS HARRY SIMMONS
B: 05/22/1902 D: 05/26/1956
BR HOF

Year	Tm	Lg	Tot	H	A	Men-On 0	1	2	3	One-Game 2	3	4	LO	XN	IP	PH	RHP	LHP
1924	PHI	AL	8	6	2	3	0	5	0	0	0	0	0	0	0	0	8	0
1925	PHI	AL	24	11	13	14	7	3	0	0	0	0	0	1	0	0	17	7
1926	PHI	AL	19	9	10	9	8	2	0	0	0	0	0	1	0	0	13	6
1927	PHI	AL	15	6	9	8	4	2	1	2	0	0	0	0	1	0	10	5
1928	PHI	AL	15	9	6	6	5	2	2	1	0	0	0	0	0	0	13	2
1929	PHI	AL	34	16	18	11	14	8	1	3	0	0	0	0	0	0	24	10
1930	PHI	AL	36	25	11	13	17	5	1	2	0	0	0	2	0	1	27	9
1931	PHI	AL	22	10	12	14	5	3	0	1	0	0	0	0	0	0	12	10
1932	PHI	AL	35	22	13	15	14	6	0	4	1	0	0	0	0	0	29	6
1933	CHI	AL	14	7	7	8	4	2	0	1	0	0	0	0	0	0	9	5
1934	CHI	AL	18	8	10	11	6	0	1	0	0	0	0	0	0	0	17	1
1935	CHI	AL	16	11	5	6	6	2	2	0	0	0	0	0	0	0	8	8
1936	DET	AL	13	10	3	7	2	4	0	2	0	0	0	0	0	0	8	5
1937	WAS	AL	8	3	5	4	4	0	0	0	0	0	0	0	0	0	4	4
1938	WAS	AL	21	7	14	10	9	0	2	2	0	0	0	0	0	0	12	9
1939	BOS	NL	7	2	5	4	3	0	0	0	0	0	0	0	0	0	2	5
1940	PHI	AL	1	0	1	0	1	0	0	0	0	0	0	0	0	0	0	1

Al Simmons *continued*

Year	Tm	Lg	Tot	H	A	Men-On 0	1	2	3	One-Game 2	3	4	LO	XN	IP	PH	RHP	LHP
1943	BOS	AL	1	0	1	1	0	0	0	0	0	0	0	0	0	0	1	0
Total			307	162	145	144	109	44	10	18	1	0	0	4	1	1	214	93

Rank among batters: 63 • Top target (8 home runs): General Crowder, Hank Johnson, George Blaeholder, Earl Whitehill • *Number of pitchers victimized*: 144 • *Total ballparks homered in*: 12 • *First HR*: 04/25/1924 off Walter Johnson • *World Series HR*—6

Curt Simmons

CURTIS THOMAS SIMMONS
B: 05/19/1929
BL

Year	Tm	Lg	Tot	H	A	Men-On 0	1	2	3	One-Game 2	3	4	LO	XN	IP	PH	RHP	LHP
1952	PHI	NL	1	1	0	0	0	1	0	0	0	0	0	0	1	0	1	0

Rank among batters: 4,707 • *Total ballparks homered in*: 1 • *First HR*: 05/22/1952 off Red Munger

Hack Simmons

GEORGE WASHINGTON SIMMONS
B: 01/29/1885 D: 04/26/1942
BR

Year	Tm	Lg	Tot	H	A	Men-On 0	1	2	3	One-Game 2	3	4	LO	XN	IP	PH	RHP	LHP
1914	BAL	FL	1	1	0	1	0	0	0	0	0	0	0	0	0	0	1	0
1915	BAL	FL	1	1	0	0	0	1	0	0	0	0	0	0	0	1	1	0
Total			2	2	0	1	0	1	0	0	0	0	0	0	0	1	2	0

Rank among batters: 4,129 • *Total ballparks homered in*: 1 • *First HR*: 04/18/1914 off Gene Krapp

Nelson Simmons

NELSON BERNARD SIMMONS
B: 06/27/1963
BB

Year	Tm	Lg	Tot	H	A	Men-On 0	1	2	3	One-Game 2	3	4	LO	XN	IP	PH	RHP	LHP
1985	DET	AL	10	7	3	4	5	1	0	2	0	0	0	0	0	1	7	3
1987	BAL	AL	1	0	1	1	0	0	0	0	0	0	0	0	0	0	1	0
Total			11	7	4	5	5	1	0	2	0	0	0	0	0	1	8	3

Rank among batters: 2,419 • *Top target (2 home runs)*: Roy Smith • *Number of pitchers victimized*: 10 • *Total ballparks homered in*: 4 • *First HR*: 05/04/1985 off Gene Nelson • *Switch hit HR in 1 game*—1 time

Ted Simmons

TED LYLE SIMMONS
B: 08/09/1949
BB

Year	Tm	Lg	Tot	H	A	Men-On 0	1	2	3	One-Game 2	3	4	LO	XN	IP	PH	RHP	LHP
1970	STL	NL	3	2	1	1	2	0	0	0	0	0	0	0	0	0	2	1
1971	STL	NL	7	2	5	3	3	1	0	0	0	0	0	0	0	0	5	2
1972	STL	NL	16	6	10	7	5	2	2	0	0	0	0	1	0	0	11	5
1973	STL	NL	13	4	9	7	1	5	0	0	0	0	0	1	0	0	8	5
1974	STL	NL	20	13	7	7	6	6	1	1	0	0	0	0	0	0	15	5
1975	STL	NL	18	10	8	9	6	1	2	1	0	0	0	1	0	1	6	12
1976	STL	NL	5	1	4	3	2	0	0	0	0	0	0	0	0	0	1	4
1977	STL	NL	21	9	12	10	8	3	0	0	0	0	0	2	0	0	11	10
1978	STL	NL	22	9	13	14	7	1	0	0	0	0	0	0	0	0	17	5
1979	STL	NL	26	17	9	18	5	2	1	2	0	0	0	1	0	0	11	15
1980	STL	NL	21	8	13	13	4	3	1	2	0	0	0	0	0	1	14	7
1981	MIL	AL	14	8	6	4	7	3	0	0	0	0	0	0	0	0	10	4
1982	MIL	AL	23	7	16	9	10	4	0	1	0	0	0	1	0	0	13	10
1983	MIL	AL	13	8	5	7	5	1	0	0	0	0	0	0	0	0	10	3
1984	MIL	AL	4	0	4	0	3	1	0	0	0	0	0	0	0	0	3	1
1985	MIL	AL	12	8	4	8	1	2	1	1	0	0	0	1	0	0	5	7
1986	ATL	NL	4	3	1	2	0	1	1	0	0	0	0	0	0	2	2	2
1987	ATL	NL	4	1	3	1	2	1	0	0	0	0	0	0	0	2	1	3
1988	ATL	NL	2	0	2	0	1	1	0	0	0	0	0	0	0	0	1	1
Total			248	116	132	123	78	38	9	8	0	0	0	8	0	6	146	102

Rank among batters: 112 • *Top target (7 home runs)*: Steve Carlton • *Number of pitchers victimized*: 172 • *Total ballparks homered in*: 26 • *First HR*: 06/07/1970 off Roberto Rodriguez • *Switch hit HR in 1 game*—3 times • *World Series HR*—2; *LCS HR*—1

Mike Simms

MICHAEL HOWARD SIMMS
B: 01/12/1967
BR

Year	Tm	Lg	Tot	H	A	Men-On 0	1	2	3	One-Game 2	3	4	LO	XN	IP	PH	RHP	LHP
1990	HOU	NL	1	0	1	1	0	0	0	0	0	0	0	1	0	0	0	1

Year	Tm	Lg	Tot	H	A	Men-On				One-Game			LO	XN	IP	PH	RHP	LHP
						0	1	2	3	2	3	4						

Mike Simms *continued*

Year	Tm	Lg	Tot	H	A	0	1	2	3	2	3	4	LO	XN	IP	PH	RHP	LHP
1991	HOU	NL	3	1	2	2	1	0	0	0	0	0	0	0	0	1	1	2
1992	HOU	NL	1	0	1	1	0	0	0	0	0	0	0	0	0	0	0	1
1995	HOU	NL	9	5	4	3	4	2	0	0	0	0	0	0	0	1	3	6
Total			14	6	8	7	5	2	0	0	0	0	0	1	0	2	4	10

Rank among batters: 2,169 • *Top target (2 home runs)*: Kent Mercker • *Number of pitchers victimized*: 13 • *Total ballparks homered in*: 7 • *First HR*: 09/21/1990 off Kent Mercker

Hank Simon

HENRY JOSEPH SIMON
B: 08/25/1862 D: 01/01/1925
BR

Year	Tm	Lg	Tot	H	A	0	1	2	3	2	3	4	LO	XN	IP	PH	RHP	LHP
1890	SYR	AA	2	0	2	1	0	1	0	0	0	0	0	0	0	0	0	0

Rank among batters: 4,129 • *Total ballparks homered in*: 2 • *First HR*: 10/01/1890 off Billy Hart

Mike Simon

MICHAEL EDWARD SIMON
B: 04/13/1883 D: 06/10/1963
BR

Year	Tm	Lg	Tot	H	A	0	1	2	3	2	3	4	LO	XN	IP	PH	RHP	LHP
1913	PIT	NL	1	1	0	1	0	0	0	0	0	0	0	0	0	0	1	0

Rank among batters: 4,707 • *Total ballparks homered in*: 1 • *First HR*: 09/15/1913 off Jack Quinn

Dick Simpson

RICHARD CHARLES SIMPSON
B: 07/28/1943
BR

Year	Tm	Lg	Tot	H	A	0	1	2	3	2	3	4	LO	XN	IP	PH	RHP	LHP
1964	LA	AL	2	1	1	2	0	0	0	0	0	0	0	0	0	0	1	1
1966	CIN	NL	4	1	3	1	2	1	0	0	0	0	0	0	1	0	1	3
1967	CIN	NL	1	1	0	1	0	0	0	0	0	0	0	0	0	1	0	1
1968	STL	NL	3	1	2	1	2	0	0	0	0	0	0	0	0	0	0	3
	HOU	NL	3	2	1	2	1	0	0	0	0	0	1	0	0	0	1	2
	Total		6	3	3	3	3	0	0	0	0	0	1	0	0	0	1	5
1969	SEA	AL	2	0	2	2	0	0	0	0	0	0	1	0	0	0	1	1
Total			15	6	9	9	5	1	0	0	0	0	2	0	1	1	4	11

Rank among batters: 2,096 • *Top target (2 home runs)*: Rich Nye, Woodie Fryman • *Number of pitchers victimized*: 13 • *Total ballparks homered in*: 10 • *First HR*: 05/10/1964 off Gary Peters

Harry Simpson

HARRY LEON SIMPSON
B: 12/03/1925 D: 04/03/1979
BL

Year	Tm	Lg	Tot	H	A	0	1	2	3	2	3	4	LO	XN	IP	PH	RHP	LHP
1951	CLE	AL	7	6	1	5	2	0	0	0	0	0	0	0	2	0	7	0
1952	CLE	AL	10	5	5	7	1	1	1	0	0	0	1	0	3	0	6	4
1953	CLE	AL	7	5	2	4	2	1	0	0	0	0	0	0	0	0	4	3
1955	KC	AL	5	2	3	0	5	0	0	0	0	0	0	0	0	0	5	0
1956	KC	AL	21	15	6	11	6	2	2	2	0	0	0	1	0	0	16	5
1957	KC	AL	6	4	2	3	3	0	0	0	0	0	0	0	0	0	6	0
	NY	AL	7	2	5	1	4	1	1	0	0	0	0	0	0	0	5	2
	Total		13	6	7	4	7	1	1	0	0	0	0	0	0	0	11	2
1958	KC	AL	7	2	5	5	1	1	0	1	0	0	0	1	0	0	7	0
1959	KC	AL	1	1	0	1	0	0	0	0	0	0	0	0	0	1	1	0
	CHI	AL	2	1	1	1	0	0	1	0	0	0	0	0	0	0	1	1
	Total		3	2	1	2	0	0	1	0	0	0	0	0	0	1	2	1
Total			73	43	30	38	24	6	5	3	0	0	1	2	5	1	58	15

Rank among batters: 715 • *Top target (4 home runs)*: Dave Sisler • *Number of pitchers victimized*: 57 • *Total ballparks homered in*: 8 • *First HR*: 06/07/1951 off Bob Hooper

Joe Simpson

JOE ALLEN SIMPSON
B: 12/31/1951
BL

Year	Tm	Lg	Tot	H	A	0	1	2	3	2	3	4	LO	XN	IP	PH	RHP	LHP
1979	SEA	AL	2	2	0	1	1	0	0	0	0	0	0	0	0	1	1	1
1980	SEA	AL	3	2	1	2	1	0	0	0	0	0	0	0	0	0	3	0

Joe Simpson *continued*

Year	Tm	Lg	Tot	H	A	Men-On 0	1	2	3	One-Game 2	3	4	LO	XN	IP	PH	RHP	LHP
1981	SEA	AL	2	0	2	1	1	0	0	0	0	0	0	0	0	0	2	0
1982	SEA	AL	2	1	1	2	0	0	0	0	0	0	0	0	0	0	2	0
Total			9	5	4	6	3	0	0	0	0	0	0	0	0	1	8	1

Rank among batters: 2,587 • *Total ballparks homered in*: 5 • *First HR*: 04/25/1979 off Tom Burgmeier

Duke Sims

DUANE B. SIMS
B: 06/05/1941
BL

Year	Tm	Lg	Tot	H	A	Men-On 0	1	2	3	One-Game 2	3	4	LO	XN	IP	PH	RHP	LHP
1965	CLE	AL	6	3	3	3	3	0	0	0	0	0	0	0	0	1	5	1
1966	CLE	AL	6	4	2	3	2	1	0	0	0	0	0	0	0	0	6	0
1967	CLE	AL	12	9	3	6	3	3	0	0	0	0	0	0	0	0	10	2
1968	CLE	AL	11	4	7	6	2	3	0	1	0	0	0	1	0	0	10	1
1969	CLE	AL	18	8	10	8	5	5	0	0	0	0	0	1	0	1	16	2
1970	CLE	AL	23	15	8	12	8	3	0	6	0	0	0	1	0	0	22	1
1971	LA	NL	6	2	4	3	2	1	0	0	0	0	0	0	0	0	5	1
1972	LA	NL	2	0	2	2	0	0	0	0	0	0	0	0	0	1	1	1
	DET	AL	4	2	2	2	2	0	0	0	0	0	0	0	0	0	4	0
	Total		6	2	4	4	2	0	0	0	0	0	0	0	0	1	5	1
1973	DET	AL	8	6	2	4	4	0	0	0	0	0	0	0	0	0	5	3
	NY	AL	1	1	0	1	0	0	0	0	0	0	0	0	0	0	1	0
	Total		9	7	2	5	4	0	0	0	0	0	0	0	0	0	6	3
1974	TEX	AL	3	1	2	2	1	0	0	0	0	0	0	0	0	0	2	1
Total			100	55	45	52	32	16	0	7	0	0	0	3	0	3	87	13

Rank among batters: 499 • *Top target (5 home runs)*: Joe Coleman • *Number of pitchers victimized*: 75 • *Total ballparks homered in*: 20 • *First HR*: 06/22/1965 off Al Worthington

Matt Sinatro

MATTHEW STEPHEN SINATRO
B: 03/22/1960
BR

Year	Tm	Lg	Tot	H	A	Men-On 0	1	2	3	One-Game 2	3	4	LO	XN	IP	PH	RHP	LHP
1982	ATL	NL	1	0	1	0	1	0	0	0	0	0	0	0	0	0	0	1

Rank among batters: 4,707 • *Total ballparks homered in*: 1 • *First HR*: 08/27/1982 off Pete Falcone

Ken Singleton

KENNETH WAYNE SINGLETON
B: 06/10/1947
BB

Year	Tm	Lg	Tot	H	A	Men-On 0	1	2	3	One-Game 2	3	4	LO	XN	IP	PH	RHP	LHP
1970	NY	NL	5	3	2	3	1	1	0	0	0	0	0	0	0	0	4	1
1971	NY	NL	13	9	4	6	5	2	0	1	0	0	0	1	0	0	11	2
1972	MON	NL	14	7	7	12	2	0	0	1	0	0	0	0	0	0	12	2
1973	MON	NL	23	10	13	8	9	6	0	0	0	0	0	0	0	0	14	9
1974	MON	NL	9	3	6	6	0	2	1	0	0	0	0	0	0	0	8	1
1975	BAL	AL	15	6	9	15	0	0	0	0	0	0	4	0	0	0	14	1
1976	BAL	AL	13	7	6	8	2	2	1	0	0	0	0	0	0	0	8	5
1977	BAL	AL	24	11	13	13	6	4	1	0	0	0	0	0	0	0	15	9
1978	BAL	AL	20	12	8	12	6	2	0	1	0	0	0	0	0	0	16	4
1979	BAL	AL	35	13	22	24	7	4	0	1	0	0	0	0	0	0	25	10
1980	BAL	AL	24	12	12	14	10	0	0	1	0	0	0	0	0	0	16	8
1981	BAL	AL	13	5	8	8	4	1	0	1	0	0	0	0	0	0	11	2
1982	BAL	AL	14	9	5	8	3	3	0	0	0	0	0	0	0	0	14	0
1983	BAL	AL	18	8	10	8	7	2	1	1	0	0	0	0	0	1	13	5
1984	BAL	AL	6	2	4	2	1	1	2	0	0	0	0	0	0	1	5	1
Total			246	117	129	147	63	30	6	7	0	0	4	1	0	2	186	60

Rank among batters: 116 • *Top target (5 home runs)*: Dave Roberts, Glenn Abbott • *Number of pitchers victimized*: 165 • *Total ballparks homered in*: 27 • *First HR*: 06/26/1970 off Bill Stoneman • *All-Star HR*—1

Frederic Sington

FREDERIC WILLIAM SINGTON
B: 02/24/1910
BR

Year	Tm	Lg	Tot	H	A	Men-On 0	1	2	3	One-Game 2	3	4	LO	XN	IP	PH	RHP	LHP
1936	WAS	AL	1	0	1	1	0	0	0	0	0	0	0	0	0	0	0	1
1937	WAS	AL	3	0	3	3	0	0	0	0	0	0	0	0	0	0	2	1

Frederic Sington *continued*

Year	Tm	Lg	Tot	H	A	Men-On 0	Men-On 1	Men-On 2	Men-On 3	One-Game 2	One-Game 3	One-Game 4	LO	XN	IP	PH	RHP	LHP
1938	BRO	NL	2	2	0	1	1	0	0	0	0	0	0	0	0	0	1	1
1939	BRO	NL	1	1	0	1	0	0	0	0	0	0	0	0	0	0	1	0
Total			7	3	4	6	1	0	0	0	0	0	0	0	0	0	4	3

Rank among batters: 2,834 • *Total ballparks homered in*: 5 • *First HR*: 09/09/1936 off Jake Wade

John Sipin

JOHN WHITE SIPIN
B: 08/29/1946
BR

Year	Tm	Lg	Tot	H	A	Men-On 0	Men-On 1	Men-On 2	Men-On 3	One-Game 2	One-Game 3	One-Game 4	LO	XN	IP	PH	RHP	LHP
1969	SD	NL	2	1	1	2	0	0	0	0	0	0	0	1	0	0	1	1

Rank among batters: 4,129 • *Total ballparks homered in*: 2 • *First HR*: 05/30/1969 off Dan McGinn

Dick Sisler

RICHARD ALLAN SISLER
B: 11/02/1920
BL

Year	Tm	Lg	Tot	H	A	Men-On 0	Men-On 1	Men-On 2	Men-On 3	One-Game 2	One-Game 3	One-Game 4	LO	XN	IP	PH	RHP	LHP
1946	STL	NL	3	0	3	1	1	0	1	0	0	0	0	0	0	0	2	1
1948	PHI	NL	11	0	11	5	4	2	0	2	0	0	0	0	0	0	11	0
1949	PHI	NL	7	3	4	2	4	1	0	0	0	0	0	0	0	1	5	2
1950	PHI	NL	13	2	11	5	5	3	0	0	0	0	0	1	0	0	9	4
1951	PHI	NL	8	3	5	3	4	1	0	0	0	0	0	1	0	0	5	3
1952	STL	NL	13	7	6	6	6	1	0	0	0	0	0	0	1	0	10	3
Total			55	15	40	22	24	8	1	2	0	0	0	2	1	1	42	13

Rank among batters: 926 • *Top target (3 home runs)*: Warren Spahn • *Number of pitchers victimized*: 44 • *Total ballparks homered in*: 8 • *First HR*: 05/28/1946 off Bob Chipman

George Sisler

GEORGE HAROLD SISLER
B: 03/24/1893 D: 03/26/1973
BL HOF

Year	Tm	Lg	Tot	H	A	Men-On 0	Men-On 1	Men-On 2	Men-On 3	One-Game 2	One-Game 3	One-Game 4	LO	XN	IP	PH	RHP	LHP
1915	STL	AL	3	2	1	2	1	0	0	0	0	0	0	0	1	0	3	0
1916	STL	AL	4	2	2	3	0	1	0	0	0	0	0	0	2	0	2	2
1917	STL	AL	2	1	1	1	1	0	0	0	0	0	0	0	1	0	2	0
1918	STL	AL	2	1	1	0	1	1	0	0	0	0	0	0	1	0	2	0
1919	STL	AL	10	7	3	3	4	3	0	1	0	0	0	1	2	0	8	2
1920	STL	AL	19	15	4	12	5	2	0	0	0	0	0	0	5	0	17	2
1921	STL	AL	12	7	5	5	4	2	1	0	0	0	0	0	2	0	10	2
1922	STL	AL	8	4	4	5	2	0	1	0	0	0	0	0	0	0	8	0
1924	STL	AL	9	3	6	5	3	1	0	0	0	0	0	0	3	0	5	4
1925	STL	AL	12	10	2	4	5	2	1	0	0	0	0	0	2	0	10	2
1926	STL	AL	7	4	3	2	5	0	0	0	0	0	0	0	1	0	7	0
1927	STL	AL	5	5	0	0	2	2	1	0	0	0	0	0	0	0	4	1
1928	BOS	NL	4	1	3	1	2	1	0	0	0	0	0	1	0	0	4	0
1929	BOS	NL	2	1	1	1	0	1	0	0	0	0	0	0	0	0	2	0
1930	BOS	NL	3	0	3	3	0	0	0	0	0	0	0	0	0	0	2	1
Total			102	63	39	47	35	16	4	1	0	0	0	2	20	0	86	16

Rank among batters: 483 • *Top target (5 home runs)*: Hooks Dauss, Eddie Rommel • *Number of pitchers victimized*: 69 • *Total ballparks homered in*: 11 • *First HR*: 07/24/1915 off Ernie Shore • *Hit for Cycle*—vs WAS: 08/08/1920 (2); @DET: 08/13/1921

Sibby Sisti

SEBASTIAN DANIEL SISTI
B: 07/26/1920
BR

Year	Tm	Lg	Tot	H	A	Men-On 0	Men-On 1	Men-On 2	Men-On 3	One-Game 2	One-Game 3	One-Game 4	LO	XN	IP	PH	RHP	LHP
1939	BOS	NL	1	0	1	1	0	0	0	0	0	0	0	0	0	0	1	0
1940	BOS	NL	6	2	4	4	0	2	0	0	0	0	1	0	0	0	5	1
1941	BOS	NL	1	1	0	0	0	1	0	0	0	0	0	1	0	0	1	0
1942	BOS	NL	4	3	1	4	0	0	0	0	0	0	0	0	0	0	3	1
1947	BOS	NL	2	0	2	2	0	0	0	0	0	0	0	0	0	0	2	0
1949	BOS	NL	5	2	3	4	1	0	0	0	0	0	0	0	0	0	1	4
1950	BOS	NL	2	0	2	1	0	0	1	0	0	0	0	0	0	1	1	1
1951	BOS	NL	2	0	2	1	1	0	0	0	0	0	1	0	0	0	0	2
1952	BOS	NL	4	1	3	2	1	1	0	0	0	0	0	0	0	0	2	2
Total			27	9	18	19	3	4	1	0	0	0	2	1	0	1	16	11

Rank among batters: 1,532 • *Top target (2 home runs)*: Luke Hamlin, Al Brazle • *Number of pitchers victimized*: 25 • *Total ballparks homered in*: 8 • *First HR*: 09/04/1939 off Luke Hamlin

Year	Tm	Lg	Tot	H	A	Men-On 0	1	2	3	One-Game 2	3	4	LO	XN	IP	PH	RHP	LHP

Ted Sizemore

THEODORE CRAWFORD SIZEMORE
B: 04/15/1945
BR

Year	Tm	Lg	Tot	H	A	Men-On 0	1	2	3	One-Game 2	3	4	LO	XN	IP	PH	RHP	LHP
1969	LA	NL	4	1	3	2	2	0	0	0	0	0	0	0	0	0	3	1
1970	LA	NL	1	0	1	1	0	0	0	0	0	0	0	0	0	0	1	0
1971	STL	NL	3	2	1	3	0	0	0	0	0	0	0	0	0	0	2	1
1972	STL	NL	2	2	0	2	0	0	0	0	0	0	0	1	1	0	1	1
1973	STL	NL	1	0	1	1	0	0	0	0	0	0	0	0	0	0	1	0
1974	STL	NL	2	1	1	1	1	0	0	0	0	0	0	0	0	0	1	1
1975	STL	NL	3	0	3	1	2	0	0	0	0	0	0	0	0	0	1	2
1977	PHI	NL	4	4	0	3	1	0	0	0	0	0	0	0	0	0	1	3
1979	CHI	NL	2	2	0	2	0	0	0	0	0	0	0	0	0	0	1	1
	BOS	AL	1	0	1	1	0	0	0	0	0	0	0	0	0	0	0	1
	Total		3	2	1	3	0	0	0	0	0	0	0	0	0	0	1	2
Total			23	12	11	17	6	0	0	0	0	0	0	1	1	0	12	11

Rank among batters: 1,686 • *Top target (2 home runs)*: John Candelaria • *Number of pitchers victimized*: 22 • *Total ballparks homered in*: 8 • *First HR*: 05/04/1969 off Milt Pappas

Frank Skaff

FRANCIS MICHAEL SKAFF
B: 09/30/1913 D: 04/12/1988
BR

Year	Tm	Lg	Tot	H	A	Men-On 0	1	2	3	One-Game 2	3	4	LO	XN	IP	PH	RHP	LHP
1943	PHI	AL	1	1	0	0	0	0	1	0	0	0	0	0	0	0	0	1

Rank among batters: 4,707 • *Total ballparks homered in*: 1 • *First HR*: 09/27/1943 off Al Hollingsworth

Dave Skaggs

DAVID LINDSEY SKAGGS
B: 06/12/1951
BR

Year	Tm	Lg	Tot	H	A	Men-On 0	1	2	3	One-Game 2	3	4	LO	XN	IP	PH	RHP	LHP
1977	BAL	AL	1	0	1	1	0	0	0	0	0	0	0	0	0	0	1	0
1979	BAL	AL	1	0	1	0	1	0	0	0	0	0	0	0	0	0	1	0
1980	CAL	AL	1	0	1	0	1	0	0	0	0	0	0	0	0	0	1	0
Total			3	0	3	1	2	0	0	0	0	0	0	0	0	0	3	0

Rank among batters: 3,735 • *Top target (2 home runs)*: Rick Wise • *Number of pitchers victimized*: 2 • *Total ballparks homered in*: 2 • *First HR*: 10/01/1977 off Rick Wise

Bob Skinner

ROBERT RALPH SKINNER
B: 10/03/1931
BL

Year	Tm	Lg	Tot	H	A	Men-On 0	1	2	3	One-Game 2	3	4	LO	XN	IP	PH	RHP	LHP
1954	PIT	NL	8	1	7	5	1	1	1	0	0	0	0	0	0	0	5	3
1956	PIT	NL	5	2	3	2	2	1	0	0	0	0	0	1	0	3	5	0
1957	PIT	NL	13	3	10	8	5	0	0	1	0	0	0	1	1	0	10	3
1958	PIT	NL	13	6	7	8	5	0	0	0	0	0	0	0	0	0	11	2
1959	PIT	NL	13	4	9	5	5	2	1	3	0	0	0	0	0	0	10	3
1960	PIT	NL	15	8	7	4	7	2	2	0	0	0	1	0	2	0	13	2
1961	PIT	NL	3	1	2	2	1	0	0	0	0	0	0	0	1	0	3	0
1962	PIT	NL	20	7	13	11	8	1	0	1	0	0	0	1	1	0	18	2
1963	CIN	NL	3	3	0	2	1	0	0	0	0	0	0	0	0	0	3	0
1964	CIN	NL	3	1	2	2	1	0	0	0	0	0	0	0	0	0	3	0
	STL	NL	1	1	0	0	0	1	0	0	0	0	0	0	0	1	1	0
	Total		4	2	2	2	1	1	0	0	0	0	0	0	0	1	4	0
1965	STL	NL	5	2	3	2	3	0	0	0	0	0	0	0	0	2	5	0
1966	STL	NL	1	1	0	0	1	0	0	0	0	0	0	0	0	1	1	0
Total			103	40	63	51	40	8	4	5	0	0	1	3	5	7	88	15

Rank among batters: 477 • *Top target (4 home runs)*: Warren Spahn • *Number of pitchers victimized*: 74 • *Total ballparks homered in*: 11 • *First HR*: 05/01/1954 off Stu Miller

Joel Skinner

JOEL PATRICK SKINNER
B: 02/21/1961
BR

Year	Tm	Lg	Tot	H	A	Men-On 0	1	2	3	One-Game 2	3	4	LO	XN	IP	PH	RHP	LHP
1985	CHI	AL	1	1	0	1	0	0	0	0	0	0	0	0	0	0	1	0
1986	CHI	AL	4	1	3	0	2	2	0	0	0	0	0	0	0	0	3	1
	NY	AL	1	0	1	1	0	0	0	0	0	0	0	0	0	0	1	0
	Total		5	1	4	1	2	2	0	0	0	0	0	0	0	0	4	1
1987	NY	AL	3	1	2	2	0	0	1	0	0	0	0	0	0	0	2	1

Joel Skinner *continued*

Year	Tm	Lg	Tot	H	A	Men-On 0	Men-On 1	Men-On 2	Men-On 3	One-Game 2	One-Game 3	One-Game 4	LO	XN	IP	PH	RHP	LHP
1988	NY	AL	4	1	3	3	1	0	0	0	0	0	0	0	0	0	3	1
1989	CLE	AL	1	0	1	1	0	0	0	0	0	0	0	0	0	0	1	0
1990	CLE	AL	2	1	1	1	0	1	0	0	0	0	0	0	0	0	2	0
1991	CLE	AL	1	0	1	1	0	0	0	0	0	0	0	0	0	0	1	0
Total			17	5	12	10	3	3	1	0	0	0	0	0	0	0	14	3

Rank among batters: 1,969 • *Top target (2 home runs)*: Scott Bankhead • *Number of pitchers victimized*: 16 • *Total ballparks homered in*: 9 • *First HR*: 09/18/1985 off Don Sutton

Lou Skizas

LOUIS PETER SKIZAS
B: 06/02/1932
BR

Year	Tm	Lg	Tot	H	A	Men-On 0	Men-On 1	Men-On 2	Men-On 3	One-Game 2	One-Game 3	One-Game 4	LO	XN	IP	PH	RHP	LHP
1956	KC	AL	11	6	5	5	6	0	0	1	0	0	0	0	0	0	9	2
1957	KC	AL	18	10	8	14	1	3	0	0	0	0	0	0	0	0	15	3
1958	DET	AL	1	1	0	0	1	0	0	0	0	0	0	0	0	0	0	1
Total			30	17	13	19	8	3	0	1	0	0	0	0	0	0	24	6

Rank among batters: 1,437 • *Top target (3 home runs)*: Tom Sturdivant, Paul Foytack • *Number of pitchers victimized*: 22 • *Total ballparks homered in*: 7 • *First HR*: 07/13/1956 off Connie Johnson

John Skopec

JOHN S. SKOPEC
B: 05/08/1880 D: 10/20/1912
BR

Year	Tm	Lg	Tot	H	A	Men-On 0	Men-On 1	Men-On 2	Men-On 3	One-Game 2	One-Game 3	One-Game 4	LO	XN	IP	PH	RHP	LHP
1901	CHI	AL	1	1	0	1	0	0	0	0	0	0	0	0	0	0	1	0

Rank among batters: 4,707 • *Total ballparks homered in*: 1 • *First HR*: 04/30/1901 off Jack Cronin

Bill Skowron

WILLIAM JOSEPH SKOWRON
B: 12/18/1930
BR

Year	Tm	Lg	Tot	H	A	Men-On 0	Men-On 1	Men-On 2	Men-On 3	One-Game 2	One-Game 3	One-Game 4	LO	XN	IP	PH	RHP	LHP
1954	NY	AL	7	3	4	4	2	0	1	0	0	0	0	0	0	1	2	5
1955	NY	AL	12	4	8	9	0	3	0	0	0	0	0	0	0	1	8	4
1956	NY	AL	23	6	17	13	5	5	0	3	0	0	0	0	0	0	14	9
1957	NY	AL	17	3	14	11	4	1	1	2	0	0	0	0	0	1	13	4
1958	NY	AL	14	9	5	8	5	1	0	1	0	0	0	0	0	1	11	3
1959	NY	AL	15	7	8	8	4	2	1	1	0	0	0	1	0	0	11	4
1960	NY	AL	26	12	14	17	8	1	0	3	0	0	0	1	0	1	19	7
1961	NY	AL	28	7	21	16	8	3	1	2	0	0	0	0	0	0	22	6
1962	NY	AL	23	9	14	11	9	2	1	0	0	0	0	0	1	0	8	15
1963	LA	NL	4	3	1	2	2	0	0	0	0	0	0	0	0	3	3	1
1964	WAS	AL	13	9	4	7	5	1	0	1	0	0	0	0	0	0	10	3
	CHI	AL	4	3	1	4	0	0	0	0	0	0	0	1	0	0	4	0
	Total		17	12	5	11	5	1	0	1	0	0	0	1	0	0	14	3
1965	CHI	AL	18	8	10	16	2	0	0	1	0	0	0	1	0	0	15	3
1966	CHI	AL	6	3	3	4	1	1	0	0	0	0	0	0	0	1	4	2
1967	CAL	AL	1	0	1	1	0	0	0	0	0	0	0	0	0	0	0	1
Total			211	86	125	131	55	20	5	14	0	0	0	4	1	9	144	67

Rank among batters: 162 • *Top target (6 home runs)*: Bill Monbouquette • *Number of pitchers victimized*: 135 • *Total ballparks homered in*: 15 • *First HR*: 04/15/1954 off Alex Kellner • *World Series HR*—8

Gordon Slade

GORDON LEIGH SLADE
B: 10/09/1904 D: 01/02/1974
BR

Year	Tm	Lg	Tot	H	A	Men-On 0	Men-On 1	Men-On 2	Men-On 3	One-Game 2	One-Game 3	One-Game 4	LO	XN	IP	PH	RHP	LHP
1930	BRO	NL	1	0	1	1	0	0	0	0	0	0	0	0	0	0	1	0
1931	BRO	NL	1	0	1	0	0	0	1	0	0	0	0	0	0	0	1	0
1932	BRO	NL	1	1	0	0	1	0	0	0	0	0	0	0	0	0	0	1
1934	CIN	NL	4	0	4	4	0	0	0	0	0	0	0	0	0	0	4	0
1935	CIN	NL	1	0	1	1	0	0	0	0	0	0	0	0	0	0	1	0
Total			8	1	7	6	1	0	1	0	0	0	0	0	0	0	7	1

Rank among batters: 2,703 • *Top target (2 home runs)*: Bob Smith • *Number of pitchers victimized*: 7 • *Total ballparks homered in*: 4 • *First HR*: 05/24/1930 off Bob Smith • *Hit HR in first major league AB*—@BOS: 05/24/1930

						Men-On				One-Game								
Year	Tm	Lg	Tot	H	A	0	1	2	3	2	3	4	LO	XN	IP	PH	RHP	LHP

Jimmy Slagle

JAMES FRANKLIN SLAGLE
B: 07/11/1873 D: 05/10/1956
BL

Year	Tm	Lg	Tot	H	A	0	1	2	3	2	3	4	LO	XN	IP	PH	RHP	LHP
1901	PHI	NL	1	0	1	0	0	1	0	0	0	0	0	0	0	0	1	0
1904	CHI	NL	1	0	1	0	1	0	0	0	0	0	0	0	0	0	1	0
Total			2	0	2	0	1	1	0	0	0	0	0	0	0	0	2	0

Rank among batters: 4,129 • *Total ballparks homered in*: 2 • *First HR*: 05/12/1901 off Kid Nichols

Mike Slattery

MICHAEL J. SLATTERY
B: 11/26/1866 D: 10/16/1904
BL

Year	Tm	Lg	Tot	H	A	0	1	2	3	2	3	4	LO	XN	IP	PH	RHP	LHP
1888	NY	NL	1	0	1	1	0	0	0	0	0	0	0	0	0	0	0	1
1889	NY	NL	1	1	0	1	0	0	0	0	0	0	0	0	0	0	1	0
1890	NY	PL	5	3	2	1	3	1	0	0	0	0	0	0	1	0	5	0
1891	CIN	NL	1	0	1	0	1	0	0	0	0	0	0	0	0	0	1	0
Total			8	4	4	3	4	1	0	0	0	0	0	0	1	0	7	1

Rank among batters: 2,703 • *Top target (2 home runs)*: Ad Gumbert • *Number of pitchers victimized*: 7 • *Total ballparks homered in*: 5 • *First HR*: 09/14/1888 off Gus Krock

Don Slaught

DONALD MARTIN SLAUGHT
B: 09/11/1958
BR

Year	Tm	Lg	Tot	H	A	0	1	2	3	2	3	4	LO	XN	IP	PH	RHP	LHP
1982	KC	AL	3	0	3	2	1	0	0	0	0	0	0	0	0	0	1	2
1984	KC	AL	4	1	3	1	1	1	1	0	0	0	0	0	0	0	1	3
1985	TEX	AL	8	4	4	6	2	0	0	0	0	0	0	0	0	0	5	3
1986	TEX	AL	13	5	8	8	5	0	0	0	0	0	0	2	0	0	8	5
1987	TEX	AL	8	5	3	7	1	0	0	1	0	0	0	0	0	0	2	6
1988	NY	AL	9	7	2	8	1	0	0	0	0	0	0	2	0	0	6	3
1989	NY	AL	5	3	2	5	0	0	0	0	0	0	0	0	0	0	3	2
1990	PIT	NL	4	1	3	3	1	0	0	0	0	0	0	0	0	1	2	2
1991	PIT	NL	1	0	1	1	0	0	0	0	0	0	0	1	0	0	1	0
1992	PIT	NL	4	2	2	3	1	0	0	0	0	0	0	0	0	0	1	3
1993	PIT	NL	10	1	9	4	4	2	0	1	0	0	0	1	0	1	8	2
1994	PIT	NL	2	1	1	1	1	0	0	0	0	0	0	0	0	0	2	0
Total			71	30	41	49	18	3	1	2	0	0	0	6	0	2	40	31

Rank among batters: 731 • Top target (2 home runs): Teddy Higuera, Tommy John, Frank Tanana, Curt Young, Charlie Leibrandt, Bud Black, Pete Harnisch, Mike Morgan • *Number of pitchers victimized*: 63 • *Total ballparks homered in*: 21 • *First HR*: 07/09/1982 off Mike Caldwell • *LCS HR*—1

Enos Slaughter

ENOS BRADSHER SLAUGHTER
B: 04/27/1916
BL HOF

Year	Tm	Lg	Tot	H	A	0	1	2	3	2	3	4	LO	XN	IP	PH	RHP	LHP
1938	STL	NL	8	5	3	3	4	1	0	0	0	0	0	1	0	0	8	0
1939	STL	NL	12	11	1	6	5	1	0	0	0	0	0	0	1	0	10	2
1940	STL	NL	17	11	6	11	3	2	1	3	0	0	0	0	0	0	17	0
1941	STL	NL	13	7	6	7	6	0	0	0	0	0	0	0	1	0	10	3
1942	STL	NL	13	4	9	10	1	2	0	0	0	0	0	2	1	0	9	4
1946	STL	NL	18	9	9	7	8	3	0	2	0	0	0	0	1	0	11	7
1947	STL	NL	10	5	5	4	2	4	0	0	0	0	0	0	0	0	7	3
1948	STL	NL	11	8	3	5	5	0	1	0	0	0	0	0	0	0	7	4
1949	STL	NL	13	9	4	5	6	1	1	1	0	0	0	0	0	0	5	8
1950	STL	NL	10	4	6	3	7	0	0	1	0	0	0	0	0	0	8	2
1951	STL	NL	4	3	1	3	1	0	0	0	0	0	0	0	0	0	1	3
1952	STL	NL	11	5	6	3	3	5	0	1	0	0	0	1	0	0	9	2
1953	STL	NL	6	4	2	3	2	1	0	0	0	0	0	0	0	0	5	1
1954	NY	AL	1	1	0	1	0	0	0	0	0	0	0	0	0	0	1	0
1955	KC	AL	5	3	2	5	0	0	0	0	0	0	0	0	0	1	3	2
1956	KC	AL	2	2	0	1	1	0	0	0	0	0	0	0	0	0	0	2
1957	NY	AL	5	3	2	3	1	1	0	0	0	0	0	1	0	0	4	1
1958	NY	AL	4	1	3	1	2	1	0	0	0	0	0	1	0	0	2	2
1959	NY	AL	6	4	2	1	3	2	0	1	0	0	0	0	0	1	4	2
Total			169	99	70	82	60	24	3	9	0	0	0	6	4	2	121	48

Rank among batters: 238 • *Top target (5 home runs)*: Bill Posedel • *Number of pitchers victimized*: 120 • *Total ballparks homered in*: 14 • *First HR*: 04/20/1938 off Jim Tobin • *World Series HR*—3

Lou Sleater

LOUIS MORTIMER SLEATER
B: 09/08/1926
BL

Year	Tm	Lg	Tot	H	A	Men-On				One-Game			LO	XN	IP	PH	RHP	LHP
						0	1	2	3	2	3	4						
1957	DET	AL	3	3	0	1	0	2	0	0	0	0	0	1	0	0	2	1
1958	DET	AL	1	1	0	1	0	0	0	0	0	0	0	0	0	0	1	0
Total			4	4	0	2	0	2	0	0	0	0	0	1	0	0	3	1

Rank among batters: 3,427 • *Total ballparks homered in*: 1 • *First HR*: 05/30/1957 off Wally Burnette

Bruce Sloan

BRUCE ADAMS SLOAN
B: 10/04/1914 D: 09/24/1973
BL

Year	Tm	Lg	Tot	H	A	Men-On				One-Game			LO	XN	IP	PH	RHP	LHP
						0	1	2	3	2	3	4						
1944	NY	NL	1	1	0	1	0	0	0	0	0	0	0	0	0	0	1	0

Rank among batters: 4,707 • *Total ballparks homered in*: 1 • *First HR*: 09/22/1944 off Hank Wyse

Tod Sloan

YALE YEASTMAN SLOAN
B: 12/24/1890 D: 09/12/1956
BL

Year	Tm	Lg	Tot	H	A	Men-On				One-Game			LO	XN	IP	PH	RHP	LHP
						0	1	2	3	2	3	4						
1917	STL	AL	2	1	1	0	2	0	0	0	0	0	0	0	0	0	2	0

Rank among batters: 4,129 • *Total ballparks homered in*: 2 • *First HR*: 06/26/1917 off Jim Bagby

Ron Slocum

RONALD REECE SLOCUM
B: 07/02/1945
BR

Year	Tm	Lg	Tot	H	A	Men-On				One-Game			LO	XN	IP	PH	RHP	LHP
						0	1	2	3	2	3	4						
1969	SD	NL	1	1	0	0	1	0	0	0	0	0	0	0	0	0	1	0
1970	SD	NL	1	0	1	0	0	1	0	0	0	0	0	0	0	0	0	1
Total			2	1	1	0	1	1	0	0	0	0	0	0	0	0	1	1

Rank among batters: 4,129 • *Total ballparks homered in*: 2 • *First HR*: 09/16/1969 off Jack Billingham

Roy Smalley

ROY FREDERICK SMALLEY, JR.
B: 06/09/1926
BR

Year	Tm	Lg	Tot	H	A	Men-On				One-Game			LO	XN	IP	PH	RHP	LHP
						0	1	2	3	2	3	4						
1948	CHI	NL	4	2	2	2	1	1	0	0	0	0	0	0	0	0	3	1
1949	CHI	NL	8	3	5	7	1	0	0	0	0	0	0	0	0	0	5	3
1950	CHI	NL	21	11	10	10	8	2	1	0	0	0	0	1	0	0	17	4
1951	CHI	NL	8	3	5	4	3	1	0	0	0	0	0	0	0	0	6	2
1952	CHI	NL	5	2	3	3	0	2	0	0	0	0	0	0	0	0	4	1
1953	CHI	NL	6	2	4	4	2	0	0	0	0	0	0	0	0	0	5	1
1954	MIL	NL	1	0	1	1	0	0	0	0	0	0	0	0	0	1	0	1
1955	PHI	NL	7	4	3	2	3	2	0	0	0	0	0	0	0	0	7	0
1957	PHI	NL	1	1	0	1	0	0	0	0	0	0	0	0	0	0	0	1
Total			61	28	33	34	18	8	1	0	0	0	0	1	0	1	47	14

Rank among batters: 844 • Top target (2 home runs): Ken Burkhart, Bob Chesnes, Howie Pollet, Mel Queen, Johnny Sain, Cliff Chambers, Bud Podbielan, Clyde King, Larry Jansen, Bob Miller, Warren Hacker • *Number of pitchers victimized*: 50 • *Total ballparks homered in*: 8 • *First HR*: 05/20/1948 off Monk Dubiel • *Hit for Cycle*—vs STL: 06/28/1950

Roy Smalley

ROY FREDERICK SMALLEY, III
B: 10/25/1952
BB

Year	Tm	Lg	Tot	H	A	Men-On				One-Game			LO	XN	IP	PH	RHP	LHP
						0	1	2	3	2	3	4						
1975	TEX	AL	3	2	1	2	0	0	1	0	0	0	0	0	0	0	2	1
1976	TEX	AL	1	1	0	1	0	0	0	0	0	0	0	0	0	0	0	1
	MIN	AL	2	1	1	1	1	0	0	0	0	0	0	0	0	0	1	1
	Total		3	2	1	2	1	0	0	0	0	0	0	0	0	0	1	2
1977	MIN	AL	6	2	4	6	0	0	0	0	0	0	1	1	0	0	3	3
1978	MIN	AL	19	8	11	13	4	1	1	1	0	0	0	0	0	0	12	7
1979	MIN	AL	24	19	5	10	12	2	0	1	0	0	0	0	0	0	11	13
1980	MIN	AL	12	5	7	4	7	1	0	0	0	0	0	1	0	0	9	3
1981	MIN	AL	7	2	5	3	3	0	1	0	0	0	0	1	0	0	3	4
1982	NY	AL	20	8	12	10	5	3	2	3	0	0	0	0	0	0	16	4
1983	NY	AL	18	7	11	12	2	4	0	1	0	0	0	1	0	1	12	6

Roy Smalley *continued*

Year	Tm	Lg	Tot	H	A	Men-On 0	1	2	3	One-Game 2	3	4	LO	XN	IP	PH	RHP	LHP
1984	NY	AL	7	4	3	7	0	0	0	0	0	0	0	2	0	1	5	2
	CHI	AL	4	4	0	2	2	0	0	0	0	0	0	0	0	0	4	0
	Total		11	8	3	9	2	0	0	0	0	0	0	2	0	1	9	2
1985	MIN	AL	12	7	5	10	2	0	0	0	0	0	0	0	0	0	12	0
1986	MIN	AL	20	9	11	15	3	2	0	3	0	0	2	0	0	0	18	2
1987	MIN	AL	8	5	3	5	1	2	0	0	0	0	0	0	0	1	7	1
Total			163	84	79	101	42	15	5	9	0	0	3	6	0	3	115	48

Rank among batters: 257 • *Top target (4 home runs)*: Mike Flanagan, Danny Darwin • *Number of pitchers victimized*: 121 • *Total ballparks homered in*: 15 • *First HR*: 05/11/1975 off John Hiller • *Switch hit HR in 1 game*—2 times

John Smiley

JOHN PATRICK SMILEY
B: 03/17/1965
BL

Year	Tm	Lg	Tot	H	A	Men-On 0	1	2	3	One-Game 2	3	4	LO	XN	IP	PH	RHP	LHP
1995	CIN	NL	2	1	1	1	1	0	0	0	0	0	0	0	0	0	1	1

Rank among batters: 4,129 • *Total ballparks homered in*: 2 • *First HR*: 04/27/1995 off Steve Trachsel

Al Smith

ALFRED JOHN SMITH
B: 10/12/1907 D: 04/28/1977
BL

Year	Tm	Lg	Tot	H	A	Men-On 0	1	2	3	One-Game 2	3	4	LO	XN	IP	PH	RHP	LHP
1935	NY	NL	1	1	0	1	0	0	0	0	0	0	0	0	0	0	1	0
1941	CLE	AL	1	0	1	1	0	0	0	0	0	0	0	0	0	0	1	0
Total			2	1	1	2	0	0	0	0	0	0	0	0	0	0	2	0

Rank among batters: 4,129 • *Total ballparks homered in*: 2 • *First HR*: 09/24/1935 off Curt Davis

Al Smith

ALPHONSE EUGENE SMITH
B: 02/07/1928
BR

Year	Tm	Lg	Tot	H	A	Men-On 0	1	2	3	One-Game 2	3	4	LO	XN	IP	PH	RHP	LHP
1953	CLE	AL	3	2	1	3	0	0	0	0	0	0	0	0	0	0	0	3
1954	CLE	AL	11	4	7	7	0	4	0	0	0	0	2	1	0	0	6	5
1955	CLE	AL	22	14	8	11	11	0	0	1	0	0	4	0	0	0	15	7
1956	CLE	AL	16	7	9	9	3	4	0	1	0	0	3	0	0	0	15	1
1957	CLE	AL	11	6	5	9	2	0	0	2	0	0	2	0	0	0	6	5
1958	CHI	AL	12	3	9	7	3	1	1	1	0	0	0	0	0	0	9	3
1959	CHI	AL	17	8	9	8	7	1	1	0	0	0	0	2	1	0	11	6
1960	CHI	AL	12	6	6	7	5	0	0	0	0	0	1	0	0	0	11	1
1961	CHI	AL	28	17	11	15	9	2	2	2	0	0	0	0	0	1	24	4
1962	CHI	AL	16	9	7	10	6	0	0	1	0	0	0	0	0	0	13	3
1963	BAL	AL	10	5	5	6	3	1	0	0	0	0	0	0	0	0	5	5
1964	CLE	AL	4	0	4	2	2	0	0	0	0	0	0	0	0	0	2	2
	BOS	AL	2	0	2	1	0	1	0	0	0	0	0	0	0	0	1	1
	Total		6	0	6	3	2	1	0	0	0	0	0	0	0	0	3	3
Total			164	81	83	95	51	14	4	8	0	0	12	3	1	1	118	46

Rank among batters: 250 • *Top target (5 home runs)*: Pedro Ramos • *Number of pitchers victimized*: 105 • *Total ballparks homered in*: 13 • *First HR*: 07/25/1953 off Johnny Schmitz • *World Series HR*—1

Aleck Smith

ALEXANDER BENJAMIN SMITH
B: 1871 D: 07/09/1919

Year	Tm	Lg	Tot	H	A	Men-On 0	1	2	3	One-Game 2	3	4	LO	XN	IP	PH	RHP	LHP
1897	BRO	NL	1	1	0	1	0	0	0	0	0	0	0	0	1	0	1	0

Rank among batters: 4,707 • *Total ballparks homered in*: 1 • *First HR*: 08/20/1897 off Willie Sudhoff

Bernie Smith

CALVIN BERNARD SMITH
B: 09/04/1941
BR

Year	Tm	Lg	Tot	H	A	Men-On 0	1	2	3	One-Game 2	3	4	LO	XN	IP	PH	RHP	LHP
1970	MIL	AL	1	0	1	0	1	0	0	0	0	0	0	1	0	0	1	0
1971	MIL	AL	1	1	0	1	0	0	0	0	0	0	0	0	0	0	1	0
Total			2	1	1	1	1	0	0	0	0	0	0	1	0	0	2	0

Rank among batters: 4,129 • *Total ballparks homered in*: 2 • *First HR*: 08/25/1970 off Dennis Higgins

Billy Smith

BILLY EDWARD SMITH
B: 07/14/1953
BB

Year	Tm	Lg	Tot	H	A	Men-On 0	Men-On 1	Men-On 2	Men-On 3	One-Game 2	One-Game 3	One-Game 4	LO	XN	IP	PH	RHP	LHP
1977	BAL	AL	5	0	5	3	2	0	0	0	0	0	1	0	0	1	5	0
1978	BAL	AL	5	2	3	2	1	1	1	0	0	0	0	0	0	0	4	1
1979	BAL	AL	6	2	4	3	1	1	1	0	0	0	0	0	0	0	6	0
1981	SF	NL	1	0	1	0	1	0	0	0	0	0	0	0	0	0	1	0
Total			17	4	13	8	5	2	2	0	0	0	1	0	0	1	16	1

Rank among batters: 1,969 • *Total ballparks homered in*: 10 • *First HR*: 04/17/1977 off Bert Blyleven

Bob Smith

ROBERT ELDRIDGE SMITH
B: 04/22/1895 D: 07/19/1987
BR

Year	Tm	Lg	Tot	H	A	Men-On 0	Men-On 1	Men-On 2	Men-On 3	One-Game 2	One-Game 3	One-Game 4	LO	XN	IP	PH	RHP	LHP
1924	BOS	NL	2	2	0	1	1	0	0	0	0	0	0	0	2	0	2	0
1927	BOS	NL	1	0	1	1	0	0	0	0	0	0	0	0	1	0	1	0
1928	BOS	NL	1	0	1	0	1	0	0	0	0	0	0	0	0	0	1	0
1929	BOS	NL	1	1	0	1	0	0	0	0	0	0	0	0	0	0	1	0
Total			5	3	2	3	2	0	0	0	0	0	0	0	3	0	5	0

Rank among batters: 3,191 • *Top target (2 home runs)*: Larry Benton • *Number of pitchers victimized*: 4 • *Total ballparks homered in*: 2 • *First HR*: 06/07/1924 off Jeff Pfeffer

Bobby Gene Smith

BOBBY GENE SMITH
B: 05/28/1934
BR

Year	Tm	Lg	Tot	H	A	Men-On 0	Men-On 1	Men-On 2	Men-On 3	One-Game 2	One-Game 3	One-Game 4	LO	XN	IP	PH	RHP	LHP
1957	STL	NL	3	2	1	1	1	1	0	0	0	0	0	0	0	0	3	0
1958	STL	NL	2	1	1	2	0	0	0	0	0	0	0	0	0	0	2	0
1959	STL	NL	1	1	0	0	1	0	0	0	0	0	0	0	0	0	0	1
1960	PHI	NL	4	4	0	2	2	0	0	0	0	0	0	0	0	1	2	2
1961	PHI	NL	2	2	0	1	1	0	0	0	0	0	0	0	0	0	0	2
1962	CHI	NL	1	0	1	1	0	0	0	0	0	0	1	0	0	0	0	1
Total			13	10	3	7	5	1	0	0	0	0	1	0	0	1	7	6

Rank among batters: 2,248 • *Total ballparks homered in*: 5 • *First HR*: 04/16/1957 off Art Fowler

Bryn Smith

BRYN NELSON SMITH
B: 08/11/1955
BR

Year	Tm	Lg	Tot	H	A	Men-On 0	Men-On 1	Men-On 2	Men-On 3	One-Game 2	One-Game 3	One-Game 4	LO	XN	IP	PH	RHP	LHP
1985	MON	NL	1	0	1	1	0	0	0	0	0	0	0	0	0	0	0	1
1986	MON	NL	1	0	1	0	0	1	0	0	0	0	0	0	0	0	1	0
1990	STL	NL	1	0	1	0	1	0	0	0	0	0	0	0	0	0	1	0
Total			3	0	3	1	1	1	0	0	0	0	0	0	0	0	2	1

Rank among batters: 3,735 • *Total ballparks homered in*: 3 • *First HR*: 08/14/1985 off Ray Fontenot

Charley Smith

CHARLES WILLIAM SMITH
B: 09/15/1937 D: 11/29/1994
BR

Year	Tm	Lg	Tot	H	A	Men-On 0	Men-On 1	Men-On 2	Men-On 3	One-Game 2	One-Game 3	One-Game 4	LO	XN	IP	PH	RHP	LHP
1961	LA	NL	2	1	1	1	1	0	0	0	0	0	0	0	0	0	0	2
	PHI	NL	9	3	6	0	4	3	1	1	0	0	0	0	0	0	7	2
	Total		11	4	7	5	4	1	1	0	0	0	0	0	0	0	7	4
1962	CHI	AL	2	1	1	1	0	1	0	0	0	0	0	0	0	0	2	0
1964	NY	NL	20	11	9	11	4	5	0	1	0	0	1	0	0	0	14	6
1965	NY	NL	16	9	7	8	7	1	0	0	0	0	0	0	0	1	10	6
1966	STL	NL	10	5	5	8	1	1	0	0	0	0	0	0	0	0	7	3
1967	NY	AL	9	3	6	5	4	0	0	1	0	0	0	0	0	0	6	3
1968	NY	AL	1	1	0	1	0	0	0	0	0	0	0	0	0	0	0	1
Total			69	34	35	39	20	9	1	2	0	0	1	0	0	1	46	23

Rank among batters: 756 • Top target (3 home runs): Lew Burdette, Don Drysdale, Roger Craig, Curt Simmons • *Number of pitchers victimized*: 55 • *Total ballparks homered in*: 15 • *First HR*: 04/20/1961 off Curt Simmons

Charlie Smith

CHARLES EDWIN SMITH
B: 04/20/1880 D: 01/03/1929
BR

Year	Tm	Lg	Tot	H	A	Men-On 0	Men-On 1	Men-On 2	Men-On 3	One-Game 2	One-Game 3	One-Game 4	LO	XN	IP	PH	RHP	LHP
1906	WAS	AL	1	1	0	0	1	0	0	0	0	0	0	0	0	0	1	0

Year	Tm	Lg	Tot	H	A	Men-On				One-Game			LO	XN	IP	PH	RHP	LHP
						0	1	2	3	2	3	4						

Charlie Smith *continued*

Rank among batters: 4,707 • *Total ballparks homered in*: 1 • *First HR*: 05/17/1906 off Roy Patterson

Chris Smith

CHRISTOPHER WILLIAM SMITH
B: 07/18/1957
BB

Year	Tm	Lg	Tot	H	A	Men-On 0	Men-On 1	Men-On 2	Men-On 3	One-Game 2	One-Game 3	One-Game 4	LO	XN	IP	PH	RHP	LHP
1983	SF	NL	1	0	1	0	1	0	0	0	0	0	0	0	0	0	1	0

Rank among batters: 4,707 • *Total ballparks homered in*: 1 • *First HR*: 09/29/1983 off Ben Hayes

Dwight Smith

JOHN DWIGHT SMITH
B: 11/08/1963
BL

Year	Tm	Lg	Tot	H	A	Men-On 0	Men-On 1	Men-On 2	Men-On 3	One-Game 2	One-Game 3	One-Game 4	LO	XN	IP	PH	RHP	LHP
1989	CHI	NL	9	5	4	4	3	1	1	0	0	0	0	0	0	1	8	1
1990	CHI	NL	6	3	3	6	0	0	0	0	0	0	0	0	0	0	5	1
1991	CHI	NL	3	2	1	1	1	1	0	0	0	0	0	0	0	0	3	0
1992	CHI	NL	3	3	0	3	0	0	0	0	0	0	0	0	0	1	2	1
1993	CHI	NL	11	6	5	8	3	0	0	1	0	0	3	0	0	0	11	0
1994	CAL	AL	5	2	3	4	1	0	0	0	0	0	0	0	0	1	5	0
	BAL	AL	3	0	3	1	2	0	0	0	0	0	0	0	0	0	3	0
	Total		8	2	6	5	3	0	0	0	0	0	0	0	0	1	8	0
1995	ATL	NL	3	1	2	1	0	1	1	0	0	0	0	0	0	2	3	0
Total			43	22	21	28	10	3	2	1	0	0	3	0	0	5	40	3

Rank among batters: 1,116 • *Top target (2 home runs)*: Danny Cox, Jack Armstrong, Ken Hill • *Number of pitchers victimized*: 40 • *Total ballparks homered in*: 17 • *First HR*: 06/05/1989 off David Cone

Earl Smith

EARL LEONARD SMITH
B: 01/20/1891 D: 03/14/1943
BB

Year	Tm	Lg	Tot	H	A	Men-On 0	Men-On 1	Men-On 2	Men-On 3	One-Game 2	One-Game 3	One-Game 4	LO	XN	IP	PH	RHP	LHP
1919	STL	AL	1	1	0	1	0	0	0	0	0	0	0	0	0	0	1	0
1920	STL	AL	3	2	1	2	1	0	0	0	0	0	0	1	0	0	3	0
1921	STL	AL	2	2	0	2	0	0	0	0	0	0	0	0	0	0	1	1
	WAS	AL	2	0	2	2	0	0	0	0	0	0	1	0	0	0	2	0
	Total		4	2	2	4	0	0	0	0	0	0	1	0	0	0	3	1
1922	WAS	AL	1	0	1	1	0	0	0	0	0	0	0	0	1	0	1	0
Total			9	5	4	8	1	0	0	0	0	0	1	1	1	0	8	1

Rank among batters: 2,587 • *Top target (2 home runs)*: Dixie Davis • *Number of pitchers victimized*: 8 • *Total ballparks homered in*: 2 • *First HR*: 08/23/1919 off Eric Erickson

Earl Smith

EARL SUTTON SMITH
B: 02/14/1897 D: 06/08/1963
BL

Year	Tm	Lg	Tot	H	A	Men-On 0	Men-On 1	Men-On 2	Men-On 3	One-Game 2	One-Game 3	One-Game 4	LO	XN	IP	PH	RHP	LHP
1920	NY	NL	1	0	1	0	1	0	0	0	0	0	0	0	0	0	1	0
1921	NY	NL	10	8	2	5	4	0	1	0	0	0	0	0	0	0	10	0
1922	NY	NL	9	4	5	5	3	1	0	0	0	0	0	0	0	0	9	0
1923	NY	NL	1	1	0	1	0	0	0	0	0	0	0	0	0	0	1	0
	BOS	NL	3	0	3	2	1	0	0	0	0	0	0	1	0	0	3	0
	Total		4	1	3	3	1	0	0	0	0	0	0	1	0	0	4	0
1924	PIT	NL	4	1	3	3	1	0	0	1	0	0	0	0	1	0	4	0
1925	PIT	NL	8	4	4	5	3	0	0	0	0	0	0	0	0	1	7	1
1926	PIT	NL	2	1	1	2	0	0	0	0	0	0	0	0	0	0	2	0
1927	PIT	NL	5	3	2	5	0	0	0	1	0	0	0	0	0	0	5	0
1928	PIT	NL	2	2	0	1	1	0	0	0	0	0	0	0	0	0	2	0
1929	STL	NL	1	1	0	0	1	0	0	0	0	0	0	0	0	0	1	0
Total			46	25	21	29	15	1	1	2	0	0	0	1	1	1	45	1

Rank among batters: 1,060 • *Top target (3 home runs)*: Virgil Barnes, Jesse Haines • *Number of pitchers victimized*: 36 • *Total ballparks homered in*: 7 • *First HR*: 08/23/1920 off Jesse Haines

Eddie Smith

EDGAR SMITH
B: 12/14/1913 D: 01/02/1994
BB

Year	Tm	Lg	Tot	H	A	Men-On 0	Men-On 1	Men-On 2	Men-On 3	One-Game 2	One-Game 3	One-Game 4	LO	XN	IP	PH	RHP	LHP
1943	CHI	AL	1	0	1	0	1	0	0	0	0	0	0	0	0	0	0	1

Year	Tm	Lg	Tot	H	A	Men-On 0	1	2	3	One-Game 2	3	4	LO	XN	IP	PH	RHP	LHP

Eddie Smith *continued*

Rank among batters: 4,707 • *Total ballparks homered in*: 1 • *First HR*: 09/26/1943 off Bill LeFebvre

Elmer Smith

ELMER JOHN SMITH
B: 09/21/1892 D: 08/03/1984
BL

Year	Tm	Lg	Tot	H	A	0	1	2	3	2	3	4	LO	XN	IP	PH	RHP	LHP
1915	CLE	AL	3	2	1	3	0	0	0	0	0	0	0	0	0	0	2	1
1916	CLE	AL	3	2	1	2	1	0	0	0	0	0	0	0	0	2	3	0
	WAS	AL	2	1	1	0	1	0	1	0	0	0	0	0	0	0	2	0
	Total		5	3	2	2	2	0	1	0	0	0	0	0	0	2	5	0
1917	CLE	AL	3	0	3	3	0	0	0	0	0	0	0	1	0	0	3	0
1919	CLE	AL	9	4	5	5	4	0	0	0	0	0	0	0	3	0	8	1
1920	CLE	AL	12	7	5	6	2	2	2	0	0	0	0	0	1	0	11	1
1921	CLE	AL	16	8	8	8	6	2	0	1	0	0	0	0	0	0	16	0
1922	BOS	AL	6	0	6	4	1	0	1	0	0	0	0	0	0	0	6	0
	NY	AL	1	1	0	1	0	0	0	0	0	0	0	1	0	0	0	1
	Total		7	1	6	5	1	0	1	0	0	0	0	1	0	0	6	1
1923	NY	AL	7	4	3	6	1	0	0	0	0	0	0	0	1	1	6	1
1925	CIN	NL	8	0	8	4	3	1	0	0	0	0	0	0	0	0	8	0
Total			70	29	41	42	19	5	4	1	0	0	0	2	5	3	65	5

Rank among batters: 742 • *Top target (6 home runs)*: Bob Shawkey • *Number of pitchers victimized*: 52 • *Total ballparks homered in*: 12 • *First HR*: 05/31/1915 off Parson Perryman • *World Series HR*—1

Frank Smith

FRANK ELMER SMITH
B: 10/28/1879 D: 11/03/1952
BR

Year	Tm	Lg	Tot	H	A	0	1	2	3	2	3	4	LO	XN	IP	PH	RHP	LHP
1905	CHI	AL	1	1	0	1	0	0	0	0	0	0	0	0	0	0	1	0
1915	BAL	FL	1	1	0	0	1	0	0	0	0	0	0	0	0	0	0	1
Total			2	2	0	1	1	0	0	0	0	0	0	0	0	0	1	1

Rank among batters: 4,129 • *Total ballparks homered in*: 2 • *First HR*: 04/29/1905 off Bill Donovan

Fred Smith

FRED VINCENT SMITH
B: 07/29/1891 D: 05/28/1961
BR

Year	Tm	Lg	Tot	H	A	0	1	2	3	2	3	4	LO	XN	IP	PH	RHP	LHP
1914	BUF	FL	2	1	1	1	0	1	0	0	0	0	0	1	0	0	2	0
1915	BRO	FL	5	3	2	3	1	0	1	0	0	0	0	0	1	0	3	2
1917	STL	NL	1	0	1	1	0	0	0	0	0	0	0	0	1	0	0	1
Total			8	4	4	5	1	1	1	0	0	0	0	1	2	0	5	3

Rank among batters: 2,703 • *Total ballparks homered in*: 5 • *First HR*: 06/10/1914 off Ben Harris

George Smith

GEORGE SHELBY SMITH
B: 10/27/1901 D: 05/26/1981
BR

Year	Tm	Lg	Tot	H	A	0	1	2	3	2	3	4	LO	XN	IP	PH	RHP	LHP
1927	DET	AL	2	2	0	1	0	1	0	0	0	0	0	0	0	0	1	1

Rank among batters: 4,129 • *Total ballparks homered in*: 1 • *First HR*: 05/09/1927 off Rudy Sommers

George Smith

GEORGE CORNELIUS SMITH
B: 07/07/1937 D: 06/15/1987
BR

Year	Tm	Lg	Tot	H	A	0	1	2	3	2	3	4	LO	XN	IP	PH	RHP	LHP
1965	DET	AL	1	0	1	1	0	0	0	0	0	0	0	0	0	0	1	0
1966	BOS	AL	8	5	3	4	1	2	1	1	0	0	0	1	1	0	5	3
Total			9	5	4	5	1	2	1	1	0	0	0	1	1	0	6	3

Rank among batters: 2,587 • *Total ballparks homered in*: 5 • *First HR*: 09/14/1965 off Milt Pappas

Germany Smith

GEORGE J. SMITH
B: 04/21/1863 D: 12/01/1927
BR

Year	Tm	Lg	Tot	H	A	0	1	2	3	2	3	4	LO	XN	IP	PH	RHP	LHP
1884	CLE	NL	4	1	3	1	1	2	0	1	0	0	0	0	0	0	3	0
1885	BRO	AA	4	4	0	1	3	0	0	0	0	0	0	0	0	0	3	1

Year	Tm	Lg	Tot	H	A	Men-On				One-Game			LO	XN	IP	PH	RHP	LHP
						0	1	2	3	2	3	4						

Germany Smith *continued*

Year	Tm	Lg	Tot	H	A	0	1	2	3	2	3	4	LO	XN	IP	PH	RHP	LHP
1886	BRO	AA	2	0	2	0	0	2	0	0	0	0	0	0	0	0	0	2
1887	BRO	AA	4	1	3	0	3	1	0	0	0	0	0	0	0	0	3	1
1888	BRO	AA	3	1	2	1	2	0	0	0	0	0	0	0	0	0	2	1
1889	BRO	AA	3	1	2	2	1	0	0	0	0	0	0	0	2	0	3	0
1890	BRO	NL	1	0	1	0	1	0	0	0	0	0	0	0	0	0	1	0
1891	CIN	NL	3	1	2	0	2	1	0	0	0	0	0	0	0	0	3	0
1892	CIN	NL	8	5	3	3	3	1	1	0	0	0	0	0	0	0	7	1
1893	CIN	NL	4	2	2	1	2	1	0	0	0	0	0	0	1	0	2	1
1894	CIN	NL	3	3	0	2	1	0	0	0	0	0	0	1	0	0	2	0
1895	CIN	NL	4	1	3	3	0	1	0	0	0	0	0	0	2	0	4	0
1896	CIN	NL	3	1	2	1	2	0	0	0	0	0	0	0	1	0	3	0
1898	STL	NL	1	1	0	0	1	0	0	0	0	0	0	0	0	0	1	0
Total			47	22	25	15	22	9	1	1	0	0	0	1	6	0	37	7

Rank among batters: 1,040 • *Top target (3 home runs)*: Bob Caruthers • *Number of pitchers victimized*: 41 • *Total ballparks homered in*: 21 • *First HR*: 07/07/1884 off Charlie Buffinton

Hal Smith

HAROLD WAYNE SMITH
B: 12/07/1930
BR

Year	Tm	Lg	Tot	H	A	0	1	2	3	2	3	4	LO	XN	IP	PH	RHP	LHP
1955	BAL	AL	4	0	4	1	2	1	0	0	0	0	0	0	0	0	1	3
1956	BAL	AL	3	1	2	3	0	0	0	0	0	0	0	0	0	0	2	1
	KC	AL	2	1	1	2	0	0	0	0	0	0	0	0	0	0	2	0
	Total		5	2	3	5	0	0	0	0	0	0	0	0	0	0	4	1
1957	KC	AL	13	8	5	11	1	0	1	0	0	0	0	0	0	0	12	1
1958	KC	AL	5	3	2	3	1	1	0	0	0	0	0	0	0	0	3	2
1959	KC	AL	5	1	4	3	2	0	0	0	0	0	0	1	0	0	4	1
1960	PIT	NL	11	3	8	5	2	4	0	2	0	0	0	0	0	1	4	7
1961	PIT	NL	3	1	2	2	0	1	0	0	0	0	0	0	0	0	1	2
1962	HOU	NL	12	5	7	8	4	0	0	0	0	0	0	0	0	0	9	3
Total			58	23	35	38	12	7	1	2	0	0	0	1	0	1	38	20

Rank among batters: 886 • *Top target (4 home runs)*: Johnny Podres • *Number of pitchers victimized*: 50 • *Total ballparks homered in*: 18 • *First HR*: 04/20/1955 off Art Schallock • *World Series HR*—1

Hal Smith

HAROLD RAYMOND SMITH
B: 06/01/1931
BR

Year	Tm	Lg	Tot	H	A	0	1	2	3	2	3	4	LO	XN	IP	PH	RHP	LHP
1956	STL	NL	5	3	2	4	1	0	0	0	0	0	0	0	0	0	2	3
1957	STL	NL	2	0	2	1	1	0	0	0	0	0	0	0	0	0	0	2
1958	STL	NL	1	1	0	0	0	1	0	0	0	0	0	0	0	0	0	1
1959	STL	NL	13	6	7	6	5	1	1	1	0	0	0	0	0	0	7	6
1960	STL	NL	2	0	2	0	1	1	0	0	0	0	0	0	0	0	1	1
Total			23	10	13	11	8	3	1	1	0	0	0	0	0	0	10	13

Rank among batters: 1,686 • *Top target (2 home runs)*: Curt Simmons, Johnny Antonelli • *Number of pitchers victimized*: 21 • *Total ballparks homered in*: 8 • *First HR*: 05/08/1956 off Bob Ross

Harry Smith

HARRY THOMAS SMITH
B: 10/31/1874 D: 02/17/1933
BR

Year	Tm	Lg	Tot	H	A	0	1	2	3	2	3	4	LO	XN	IP	PH	RHP	LHP
1908	BOS	NL	1	0	1	1	0	0	0	0	0	0	0	0	0	0	1	0
1910	BOS	NL	1	1	0	1	0	0	0	0	0	0	0	0	0	0	1	0
Total			2	1	1	2	0	0	0	0	0	0	0	0	0	0	2	0

Rank among batters: 4,129 • *Total ballparks homered in*: 2 • *First HR*: 06/25/1908 off Dummy Taylor

Harry Smith

JAMES HARRY SMITH
B: 05/15/1890 D: 04/01/1922
BR

Year	Tm	Lg	Tot	H	A	0	1	2	3	2	3	4	LO	XN	IP	PH	RHP	LHP
1915	BRO	FL	1	1	0	0	1	0	0	0	0	0	0	0	0	0	1	0

Rank among batters: 4,707 • *Total ballparks homered in*: 1 • *First HR*: 08/07/1915 off Dave Black

Heinie Smith

GEORGE HENRY SMITH
B: 10/24/1871 D: 06/25/1939
BR

Year	Tm	Lg	Tot	H	A	Men-On 0	1	2	3	One-Game 2	3	4	LO	XN	IP	PH	RHP	LHP
1897	LOU	NL	1	1	0	0	1	0	0	0	0	0	0	0	0	0	1	0
1901	NY	NL	1	0	1	0	1	0	0	0	0	0	0	0	0	0	1	0
1903	DET	AL	1	1	0	0	0	1	0	0	0	0	0	0	1	0	1	0
Total			3	2	1	0	2	1	0	0	0	0	0	0	1	0	3	0

Rank among batters: 3,735 • *Total ballparks homered in*: 3 • *First HR*: 09/13/1897 off Jim Hughey

Jack Smith

JACK SMITH
B: 06/23/1895 D: 05/02/1972
BL

Year	Tm	Lg	Tot	H	A	Men-On 0	1	2	3	One-Game 2	3	4	LO	XN	IP	PH	RHP	LHP
1916	STL	NL	6	2	4	4	2	0	0	0	0	0	0	0	0	0	6	0
1917	STL	NL	3	2	1	2	0	1	0	0	0	0	1	0	0	0	3	0
1920	STL	NL	1	1	0	0	1	0	0	0	0	0	0	0	0	0	1	0
1921	STL	NL	7	5	2	5	1	1	0	0	0	0	3	0	0	0	7	0
1922	STL	NL	8	6	2	4	3	1	0	0	0	0	0	0	0	0	8	0
1923	STL	NL	5	1	4	3	0	2	0	0	0	0	0	0	1	0	5	0
1924	STL	NL	2	1	1	2	0	0	0	0	0	0	0	0	1	0	2	0
1925	STL	NL	4	4	0	2	2	0	0	0	0	0	1	0	0	0	4	0
1926	BOS	NL	2	0	2	0	1	1	0	0	0	0	0	0	0	0	2	0
1927	BOS	NL	1	0	1	1	0	0	0	0	0	0	0	0	0	0	1	0
1928	BOS	NL	1	1	0	1	0	0	0	0	0	0	0	0	0	0	1	0
Total			40	23	17	24	10	6	0	0	0	0	5	0	2	0	40	0

Rank among batters: 1,181 • *Top target (3 home runs)*: Phil Douglas • *Number of pitchers victimized*: 29 • *Total ballparks homered in*: 7 • *First HR*: 05/11/1916 off George Chalmers

Jimmy Smith

JAMES LAWRENCE SMITH
B: 05/15/1895 D: 01/01/1974
BB

Year	Tm	Lg	Tot	H	A	Men-On 0	1	2	3	One-Game 2	3	4	LO	XN	IP	PH	RHP	LHP
1915	CHI	FL	4	1	3	2	1	0	1	1	0	0	0	0	0	0	3	0
	BAL	FL	1	0	1	0	0	1	0	0	0	0	0	0	0	0	0	1
	Total		5	1	4	2	2	0	1	1	0	0	0	0	0	0	3	1
1918	BOS	NL	1	1	0	0	0	1	0	0	0	0	0	0	1	0	0	1
1919	CIN	NL	1	1	0	0	1	0	0	0	0	0	0	0	1	0	0	1
1921	PHI	NL	4	2	2	2	1	1	0	0	0	0	0	0	0	0	3	1
1922	PHI	NL	1	1	0	1	0	0	0	0	0	0	0	0	0	0	0	1
Total			12	6	6	5	4	2	1	1	0	0	0	0	2	0	6	5

Rank among batters: 2,325 • *Top target (2 home runs)*: Gene Packard • *Number of pitchers victimized*: 11 • *Total ballparks homered in*: 8 • *First HR*: 04/17/1915 off Bob Groom

Jud Smith

GRANT JUDSON SMITH
B: 01/13/1869 D: 12/07/1947
BR

Year	Tm	Lg	Tot	H	A	Men-On 0	1	2	3	One-Game 2	3	4	LO	XN	IP	PH	RHP	LHP
1893	CIN	NL	1	1	0	1	0	0	0	0	0	0	0	0	1	0	1	0
1898	WAS	NL	3	2	1	0	2	0	1	0	0	0	0	0	0	0	2	1
Total			4	3	1	1	2	0	1	0	0	0	0	0	1	0	3	1

Rank among batters: 3,427 • *Total ballparks homered in*: 3 • *First HR*: 07/15/1893 off Jack Stivetts

Keith Smith

KEITH LAVARNE SMITH
B: 05/03/1953
BR

Year	Tm	Lg	Tot	H	A	Men-On 0	1	2	3	One-Game 2	3	4	LO	XN	IP	PH	RHP	LHP
1977	TEX	AL	2	1	1	1	0	1	0	0	0	0	0	1	0	0	1	1

Rank among batters: 4,129 • *Total ballparks homered in*: 2 • *First HR*: 08/12/1977 off Lerrin LaGrow

Ken Smith

KENNETH EARL SMITH
B: 02/12/1958
BL

Year	Tm	Lg	Tot	H	A	Men-On 0	1	2	3	One-Game 2	3	4	LO	XN	IP	PH	RHP	LHP
1983	ATL	NL	1	0	1	0	1	0	0	0	0	0	0	0	0	0	1	0

Rank among batters: 4,707 • *Total ballparks homered in*: 1 • *First HR*: 04/19/1983 off Mike Couchee

Lee Smith

LEE ARTHUR SMITH
B: 12/04/1957
BR

Year	Tm	Lg	Tot	H	A	Men-On 0	1	2	3	One-Game 2	3	4	LO	XN	IP	PH	RHP	LHP
1982	CHI	NL	1	0	1	1	0	0	0	0	0	0	0	0	0	0	1	0

Rank among batters: 4,707 • *Total ballparks homered in*: 1 • *First HR*: 07/05/1982 off Phil Niekro

Lonnie Smith

LONNIE SMITH
B: 12/22/1955
BR

Year	Tm	Lg	Tot	H	A	Men-On 0	1	2	3	One-Game 2	3	4	LO	XN	IP	PH	RHP	LHP
1980	PHI	NL	3	2	1	3	0	0	0	0	0	0	1	0	0	0	2	1
1981	PHI	NL	2	1	1	1	1	0	0	0	0	0	0	0	0	0	2	0
1982	STL	NL	8	3	5	4	2	1	1	0	0	0	1	1	1	0	6	2
1983	STL	NL	8	4	4	8	0	0	0	1	0	0	1	0	0	0	6	2
1984	STL	NL	6	3	3	5	0	0	1	0	0	0	3	0	1	0	4	2
1985	KC	AL	6	2	4	3	3	0	0	0	0	0	0	0	0	0	4	2
1986	KC	AL	8	2	6	6	2	0	0	0	0	0	1	0	0	0	6	2
1987	KC	AL	3	1	2	3	0	0	0	0	0	0	0	0	0	0	3	0
1988	ATL	NL	3	2	1	2	1	0	0	0	0	0	0	0	0	0	0	3
1989	ATL	NL	21	10	11	15	5	1	0	0	0	0	0	0	0	0	14	7
1990	ATL	NL	9	2	7	8	1	0	0	0	0	0	0	0	0	0	3	6
1991	ATL	NL	7	6	1	4	3	0	0	1	0	0	0	0	0	0	7	0
1992	ATL	NL	6	3	3	2	0	3	1	0	0	0	0	0	0	2	3	3
1993	PIT	NL	6	4	2	5	1	0	0	1	0	0	1	1	0	0	3	3
	BAL	AL	2	2	0	2	0	0	0	0	0	0	0	0	0	0	0	2
	Total		8	6	2	7	1	0	0	1	0	0	1	1	0	0	3	5
Total			98	47	51	71	19	5	3	3	0	0	8	2	2	2	63	35

Rank among batters: 506 • Top target (3 home runs): Rick Rhoden, Dennis Cook, Mark Thurmond, Bob Walk • *Number of pitchers victimized*: 82 • *Total ballparks homered in*: 21 • *First HR*: 07/25/1980 off Larry McWilliams • *World Series HR*—4

Mark Smith

MARK EDWARD SMITH
B: 05/07/1970
BR

Year	Tm	Lg	Tot	H	A	Men-On 0	1	2	3	One-Game 2	3	4	LO	XN	IP	PH	RHP	LHP
1995	BAL	AL	3	1	2	1	0	2	0	0	0	0	0	0	0	0	2	1

Rank among batters: 3,735 • *Total ballparks homered in*: 3 • *First HR*: 08/25/1995 off Mike Butcher

Mike Smith

ELMER ELLSWORTH SMITH
B: 03/23/1868 D: 11/05/1945
BL

Year	Tm	Lg	Tot	H	A	Men-On 0	1	2	3	One-Game 2	3	4	LO	XN	IP	PH	RHP	LHP
1889	CIN	AA	2	1	1	0	1	1	0	0	0	0	0	0	0	0	2	0
1892	PIT	NL	4	2	2	0	3	1	0	0	0	0	0	0	0	0	4	0
1893	PIT	NL	7	6	1	3	2	2	0	1	0	0	1	0	1	0	7	0
1894	PIT	NL	6	4	2	4	2	0	0	0	0	0	0	0	1	0	6	0
1895	PIT	NL	1	1	0	1	0	0	0	0	0	0	0	1	0	0	1	0
1896	PIT	NL	6	2	4	1	3	2	0	0	0	0	0	0	0	0	3	3
1897	PIT	NL	6	2	4	3	3	0	0	0	0	0	0	0	1	0	4	2
1898	CIN	NL	1	0	1	1	0	0	0	0	0	0	1	0	0	0	0	1
1899	CIN	NL	1	1	0	0	0	1	0	0	0	0	0	0	1	0	1	0
1900	CIN	NL	1	0	1	1	0	0	0	0	0	0	0	0	1	0	1	0
	NY	NL	2	2	0	1	1	0	0	0	0	0	0	0	0	0	2	0
	Total		3	2	1	2	1	0	0	0	0	0	0	0	1	0	3	0
Total			37	21	16	15	15	7	0	1	0	0	2	1	5	0	30	6

Rank among batters: 1,252 • *Top target (2 home runs)*: Kid Nichols, Al Maul, Chick Fraser, Cy Young • *Number of pitchers victimized*: 33 • *Total ballparks homered in*: 14 • *First HR*: 06/22/1889 off Parke Swartzel

Milt Smith

MILTON SMITH
B: 03/27/1929
BR

Year	Tm	Lg	Tot	H	A	Men-On 0	1	2	3	One-Game 2	3	4	LO	XN	IP	PH	RHP	LHP
1955	CIN	NL	3	2	1	3	0	0	0	0	0	0	0	0	0	0	3	0

Rank among batters: 3,735 • *Total ballparks homered in*: 2 • *First HR*: 07/24/1955 off Hoyt Wilhelm

Ollie Smith

OLIVER H. SMITH
B: 1868 BL

Year	Tm	Lg	Tot	H	A	Men-On 0	1	2	3	One-Game 2	3	4	LO	XN	IP	PH	RHP	LHP
1894	LOU	NL	3	2	1	3	0	0	0	0	0	0	0	0	0	0	3	0

Rank among batters: 3,735 • *Total ballparks homered in*: 2 • *First HR*: 07/14/1894 off Al Maul

Ozzie Smith

OSBORNE EARL SMITH
B: 12/26/1954
BB

Year	Tm	Lg	Tot	H	A	Men-On 0	1	2	3	One-Game 2	3	4	LO	XN	IP	PH	RHP	LHP
1978	SD	NL	1	0	1	1	0	0	0	0	0	0	0	0	0	0	0	1
1982	STL	NL	2	0	2	2	0	0	0	0	0	0	0	0	0	0	0	2
1983	STL	NL	3	1	2	2	1	0	0	0	0	0	0	0	0	0	0	3
1984	STL	NL	1	1	0	0	0	1	0	0	0	0	0	0	0	0	0	1
1985	STL	NL	6	2	4	4	1	1	0	0	0	0	0	0	0	0	0	6
1988	STL	NL	3	2	1	1	1	1	0	0	0	0	0	0	0	0	1	2
1989	STL	NL	2	1	1	2	0	0	0	0	0	0	0	0	0	0	1	1
1990	STL	NL	1	0	1	1	0	0	0	0	0	0	0	0	0	0	0	1
1991	STL	NL	3	2	1	1	2	0	0	0	0	0	0	0	0	0	1	2
1993	STL	NL	1	1	0	0	1	0	0	0	0	0	0	0	0	0	0	1
1994	STL	NL	3	1	2	3	0	0	0	0	0	0	0	0	0	0	1	2
Total			26	11	15	17	6	3	0	0	0	0	0	0	0	0	4	22

Rank among batters: 1,576 • *Top target (2 home runs)*: Dan Schatzeder • *Number of pitchers victimized*: 25 • *Total ballparks homered in*: 8 • *First HR*: 09/04/1978 off Larry McWilliams • *LCS HR*—1

Paul Smith

PAUL LESLIE SMITH
B: 03/19/1931
BL

Year	Tm	Lg	Tot	H	A	Men-On 0	1	2	3	One-Game 2	3	4	LO	XN	IP	PH	RHP	LHP
1953	PIT	NL	4	2	2	3	1	0	0	0	0	0	0	0	0	0	4	0
1957	PIT	NL	3	1	2	3	0	0	0	0	0	0	0	0	0	0	3	0
Total			7	3	4	6	1	0	0	0	0	0	0	0	0	0	7	0

Rank among batters: 2,834 • *Top target (2 home runs)*: Max Surkont • *Number of pitchers victimized*: 6 • *Total ballparks homered in*: 4 • *First HR*: 06/12/1953 off Max Surkont

Phenomenal Smith

JOHN FRANCIS SMITH
B: 12/12/1864 D: 04/03/1952
BL

Year	Tm	Lg	Tot	H	A	Men-On 0	1	2	3	One-Game 2	3	4	LO	XN	IP	PH	RHP	LHP
1887	BAL	AA	1	0	1	1	0	0	0	0	0	0	0	0	0	0	1	0
1888	BAL	AA	1	0	1	0	0	1	0	0	0	0	0	0	0	0	1	0
Total			2	0	2	1	0	1	0	0	0	0	0	0	0	0	2	0

Rank among batters: 4,129 • *Total ballparks homered in*: 2 • *First HR*: 07/09/1887 off Dave Foutz

Pop Smith

CHARLES MARVIN SMITH
B: 10/12/1856 D: 04/18/1927
BR

Year	Tm	Lg	Tot	H	A	Men-On 0	1	2	3	One-Game 2	3	4	LO	XN	IP	PH	RHP	LHP
1883	COL	AA	4	2	2	2	1	1	0	0	0	0	0	0	1	0	4	0
1884	COL	AA	6	5	1	4	2	0	0	0	0	0	0	0	0	0	5	0
1886	PIT	AA	2	0	2	1	1	0	0	0	0	0	0	0	0	0	1	0
1887	PIT	NL	2	0	2	0	2	0	0	0	0	0	0	0	0	0	0	1
1888	PIT	NL	4	0	4	1	3	0	0	0	0	0	0	0	1	0	2	2
1889	PIT	NL	5	0	5	1	2	2	0	0	0	0	0	0	0	0	4	1
1890	BOS	NL	1	0	1	0	1	0	0	0	0	0	0	0	0	0	1	0
Total			24	7	17	9	12	3	0	0	0	0	0	0	2	0	17	4

Rank among batters: 1,643 • *Top target (2 home runs)*: Bobby Mathews, Jack Neagle, Gus Krock • *Number of pitchers victimized*: 21 • *Total ballparks homered in*: 13 • *First HR*: 06/23/1883 off Bobby Mathews

Ray Smith

RAYMOND EDWARD SMITH
B: 09/18/1955
BR

Year	Tm	Lg	Tot	H	A	Men-On 0	1	2	3	One-Game 2	3	4	LO	XN	IP	PH	RHP	LHP
1981	MIN	AL	1	0	1	1	0	0	0	0	0	0	0	0	0	0	0	1

Rank among batters: 4,707 • *Total ballparks homered in*: 1 • *First HR*: 04/15/1981 off Jerry Gleaton

						Men-On				One-Game								
Year	Tm	Lg	Tot	H	A	0	1	2	3	2	3	4	LO	XN	IP	PH	RHP	LHP

Red Smith

JAMES CARLISLE SMITH
B: 04/06/1890 D: 10/11/1966
BR

Year	Tm	Lg	Tot	H	A	0	1	2	3	2	3	4	LO	XN	IP	PH	RHP	LHP
1912	BRO	NL	4	3	1	3	1	0	0	0	0	0	0	0	2	0	3	1
1913	BRO	NL	6	3	3	3	2	1	0	0	0	0	0	0	2	0	5	1
1914	BRO	NL	4	3	1	2	2	0	0	0	0	0	0	0	2	0	1	3
	BOS	NL	3	2	1	1	1	1	0	0	0	0	0	0	1	0	3	0
	Total		7	5	2	3	3	1	0	0	0	0	0	0	3	0	4	3
1915	BOS	NL	2	0	2	1	1	0	0	0	0	0	0	0	0	0	2	0
1916	BOS	NL	3	1	2	1	1	0	1	0	0	0	0	0	1	0	1	2
1917	BOS	NL	2	1	1	2	0	0	0	0	0	0	0	0	1	0	2	0
1918	BOS	NL	2	0	2	1	1	0	0	0	0	0	0	0	0	0	1	1
1919	BOS	NL	1	0	1	1	0	0	0	0	0	0	0	0	0	0	1	0
Total			27	13	14	15	9	2	1	0	0	0	0	0	9	0	19	8

Rank among batters: 1,532 • Top target (2 home runs): Thomas Seaton, Hank Robinson, Jeff Tesreau, Wilbur Cooper, Red Ames, Erskine Mayer, Al Demaree • *Number of pitchers victimized*: 20 • *Total ballparks homered in*: 7 • *First HR*: 05/31/1912 off Ed Donnelly

Reggie Smith

CARL REGINALD SMITH
B: 04/02/1945
BB

Year	Tm	Lg	Tot	H	A	0	1	2	3	2	3	4	LO	XN	IP	PH	RHP	LHP
1967	BOS	AL	15	9	6	12	2	1	0	1	0	0	3	0	0	0	11	4
1968	BOS	AL	15	7	8	5	8	1	1	2	0	0	0	1	0	0	12	3
1969	BOS	AL	25	9	16	13	6	6	0	2	0	0	1	0	0	0	18	7
1970	BOS	AL	22	14	8	16	6	0	0	0	0	0	0	0	0	0	20	2
1971	BOS	AL	30	15	15	16	8	6	0	1	0	0	0	0	0	0	26	4
1972	BOS	AL	21	10	11	6	9	5	1	3	0	0	0	0	0	0	16	5
1973	BOS	AL	21	12	9	10	9	2	0	3	0	0	0	1	0	0	17	4
1974	STL	NL	23	14	9	15	6	2	0	3	0	0	0	0	0	0	17	6
1975	STL	NL	19	14	5	15	4	0	0	1	0	0	0	0	0	0	12	7
1976	STL	NL	8	2	6	5	1	2	0	0	1	0	0	1	0	0	4	4
	LA	NL	10	4	6	7	2	1	0	1	0	0	0	0	0	0	9	1
	Total		18	6	12	12	3	3	0	1	1	0	0	1	0	0	13	5
1977	LA	NL	32	15	17	18	13	1	0	3	0	0	0	0	0	0	27	5
1978	LA	NL	29	11	18	13	13	2	1	2	0	0	0	0	0	0	22	7
1979	LA	NL	10	4	6	6	2	2	0	0	0	0	0	1	0	0	9	1
1980	LA	NL	15	8	7	13	2	0	0	0	0	0	0	0	0	0	14	1
1981	LA	NL	1	0	1	0	1	0	0	0	0	0	0	0	0	1	1	0
1982	SF	NL	18	10	8	11	6	1	0	1	0	0	0	1	0	1	16	2
Total			314	158	156	181	98	32	3	23	1	0	4	5	0	2	251	63

Rank among batters: 62 • *Top target (6 home runs)*: Bill Parsons, Phil Niekro, John Montefusco • *Number of pitchers victimized*: 203 • *Total ballparks homered in*: 27 • *First HR*: 04/14/1967 off Whitey Ford • *Switch hit HR in 1 game*—6 times • *World Series HR*—6; *All-Star HR*—1

Sherry Smith

SHERROD MALONE SMITH
B: 02/18/1891 D: 09/12/1949
BR

Year	Tm	Lg	Tot	H	A	0	1	2	3	2	3	4	LO	XN	IP	PH	RHP	LHP
1921	BRO	NL	1	1	0	1	0	0	0	0	0	0	0	0	0	0	1	0
1922	BRO	NL	1	1	0	0	0	1	0	0	0	0	0	0	0	0	0	1
1923	CLE	AL	1	0	1	0	1	0	0	0	0	0	0	0	0	0	1	0
1924	CLE	AL	1	0	1	1	0	0	0	0	0	0	0	0	0	0	1	0
1925	CLE	AL	1	0	1	1	0	0	0	0	0	0	0	0	0	0	1	0
1926	CLE	AL	1	0	1	1	0	0	0	0	0	0	0	1	0	0	1	0
Total			6	2	4	4	1	1	0	0	0	0	0	1	0	0	5	1

Rank among batters: 2,988 • *Top target (2 home runs)*: Elam Vangilder • *Number of pitchers victimized*: 5 • *Total ballparks homered in*: 3 • *First HR*: 05/24/1921 off Speed Martin

Skyrocket Smith

SAMUEL J. SMITH
B: 03/19/1868 D: 04/26/1916
BR

Year	Tm	Lg	Tot	H	A	0	1	2	3	2	3	4	LO	XN	IP	PH	RHP	LHP
1888	LOU	AA	1	0	1	0	0	1	0	0	0	0	0	0	0	0	0	1

Rank among batters: 4,707 • *Total ballparks homered in*: 1 • *First HR*: 04/25/1888 off Steve Toole

Syd Smith

SYDNEY E. SMITH
B: 08/31/1883 D: 06/05/1961
BR

Year	Tm	Lg	Tot	H	A	0	1	2	3	2	3	4	LO	XN	IP	PH	RHP	LHP
1908	PHI	AL	1	0	1	0	0	1	0	0	0	0	0	0	0	0	0	1

Syd Smith *continued*

Year	Tm	Lg	Tot	H	A	Men-On 0	Men-On 1	Men-On 2	Men-On 3	One-Game 2	One-Game 3	One-Game 4	LO	XN	IP	PH	RHP	LHP
1911	CLE	AL	1	0	1	1	0	0	0	0	0	0	0	0	1	0	0	1
Total			2	0	2	1	0	1	0	0	0	0	0	0	1	0	0	2

Rank among batters: 4,129 • *Total ballparks homered in*: 2 • *First HR*: 06/14/1908 off Ed Killian

Tommy Smith

TOMMY ALEXANDER SMITH
B: 08/01/1948
BL

Year	Tm	Lg	Tot	H	A	Men-On 0	Men-On 1	Men-On 2	Men-On 3	One-Game 2	One-Game 3	One-Game 4	LO	XN	IP	PH	RHP	LHP
1973	CLE	AL	2	0	2	1	1	0	0	0	0	0	0	0	0	0	2	0
1976	CLE	AL	2	2	0	2	0	0	0	0	0	0	0	0	0	0	2	0
Total			4	2	2	3	1	0	0	0	0	0	0	0	0	0	4	0

Rank among batters: 3,427 • *Total ballparks homered in*: 3 • *First HR*: 09/11/1973 off Pat Dobson

Tony Smith

ANTHONY SMITH
B: 05/14/1884 D: 02/27/1964
BR

Year	Tm	Lg	Tot	H	A	Men-On 0	Men-On 1	Men-On 2	Men-On 3	One-Game 2	One-Game 3	One-Game 4	LO	XN	IP	PH	RHP	LHP
1910	BRO	NL	1	0	1	1	0	0	0	0	0	0	0	0	0	0	1	0

Rank among batters: 4,707 • *Total ballparks homered in*: 1 • *First HR*: 04/27/1910 off Kirby White

Wally Smith

WALLACE H. SMITH
B: 03/13/1889 D: 06/10/1930
BR

Year	Tm	Lg	Tot	H	A	Men-On 0	Men-On 1	Men-On 2	Men-On 3	One-Game 2	One-Game 3	One-Game 4	LO	XN	IP	PH	RHP	LHP
1911	STL	NL	2	2	0	0	1	1	0	0	0	0	0	0	1	0	2	0

Rank among batters: 4,129 • *Total ballparks homered in*: 1 • *First HR*: 07/24/1911 off Grover Alexander

Willie Smith

WILLIE SMITH
B: 02/11/1939
BL

Year	Tm	Lg	Tot	H	A	Men-On 0	Men-On 1	Men-On 2	Men-On 3	One-Game 2	One-Game 3	One-Game 4	LO	XN	IP	PH	RHP	LHP
1964	LA	AL	11	6	5	6	3	1	1	0	0	0	0	0	0	0	11	0
1965	CAL	AL	14	7	7	8	6	0	0	1	0	0	0	0	0	0	13	1
1966	CAL	AL	1	0	1	0	1	0	0	0	0	0	0	0	0	0	1	0
1968	CHI	NL	5	3	2	3	1	1	0	1	0	0	0	1	0	0	5	0
1969	CHI	NL	9	6	3	6	2	1	0	0	0	0	0	1	0	3	9	0
1970	CHI	NL	5	2	3	3	2	0	0	0	0	0	0	0	0	1	5	0
1971	CIN	NL	1	0	1	1	0	0	0	0	0	0	0	0	0	0	1	0
Total			46	24	22	27	15	3	1	2	0	0	0	2	0	4	45	1

Rank among batters: 1,060 • *Top target (3 home runs)*: Earl Wilson • *Number of pitchers victimized*: 35 • *Total ballparks homered in*: 15 • *First HR*: 06/14/1964 off Denny McLain

John Smoltz

JOHN ANDREW SMOLTZ
B: 05/15/1967
BR

Year	Tm	Lg	Tot	H	A	Men-On 0	Men-On 1	Men-On 2	Men-On 3	One-Game 2	One-Game 3	One-Game 4	LO	XN	IP	PH	RHP	LHP
1989	ATL	NL	1	1	0	0	1	0	0	0	0	0	0	0	0	0	0	1
1992	ATL	NL	1	0	1	1	0	0	0	0	0	0	0	0	0	0	1	0
1994	ATL	NL	1	0	1	1	0	0	0	0	0	0	0	0	0	0	0	1
Total			3	1	2	2	1	0	0	0	0	0	0	0	0	0	1	2

Rank among batters: 3,735 • *Total ballparks homered in*: 3 • *First HR*: 05/03/1989 off Don Carman

Homer Smoot

HOMER VERNON SMOOT
B: 03/23/1878 D: 03/25/1928
BL

Year	Tm	Lg	Tot	H	A	Men-On 0	Men-On 1	Men-On 2	Men-On 3	One-Game 2	One-Game 3	One-Game 4	LO	XN	IP	PH	RHP	LHP
1902	STL	NL	3	0	3	1	2	0	0	1	0	0	0	1	3	0	3	0
1903	STL	NL	4	3	1	1	1	2	0	0	0	0	0	0	2	0	2	1
1904	STL	NL	3	2	1	3	0	0	0	0	0	0	0	0	1	0	3	0
1905	STL	NL	4	2	2	3	1	0	0	0	0	0	0	0	1	0	4	0
1906	CIN	NL	1	1	0	1	0	0	0	0	0	0	0	0	0	0	1	0
Total			15	8	7	9	4	2	0	1	0	0	0	1	7	0	13	1

Year	Tm	Lg	Tot	H	A	Men-On 0	1	2	3	One-Game 2	3	4	LO	XN	IP	PH	RHP	LHP

Homer Smoot *continued*

Rank among batters: 2,096 • *Total ballparks homered in*: 5 • *First HR*: 04/25/1902 off Bill Phillips

Jonathan Sneed

JONATHAN L. SNEED
D: 01/04/1899

Year	Tm	Lg	Tot	H	A	0	1	2	3	2	3	4	LO	XN	IP	PH	RHP	LHP
1884	IND	AA	1	0	1	1	0	0	0	0	0	0	0	0	0	0	1	0
1890	COL	AA	2	1	1	0	1	1	0	0	0	0	0	0	0	0	2	0
1891	COL	AA	1	0	1	0	0	1	0	0	0	0	0	0	0	0	1	0
Total			4	1	3	1	1	2	0	0	0	0	0	0	0	0	4	0

Rank among batters: 3,427 • *Total ballparks homered in*: 4 • *First HR*: 06/10/1884 off Hardie Henderson

Duke Snider

EDWIN DONALD SNIDER
B: 09/19/1926
BL HOF

Year	Tm	Lg	Tot	H	A	0	1	2	3	2	3	4	LO	XN	IP	PH	RHP	LHP
1948	BRO	NL	5	1	4	1	4	0	0	1	0	0	0	0	1	1	3	2
1949	BRO	NL	23	8	15	10	5	8	0	0	0	0	0	0	0	0	20	3
1950	BRO	NL	31	18	13	14	15	2	0	1	1	0	0	0	0	0	25	6
1951	BRO	NL	29	21	8	17	7	4	1	2	0	0	0	0	0	0	21	8
1952	BRO	NL	21	12	9	15	6	0	0	2	0	0	0	1	0	0	21	0
1953	BRO	NL	42	23	19	23	17	0	2	4	0	0	0	0	0	1	39	3
1954	BRO	NL	40	23	17	22	11	7	0	2	0	0	0	0	0	0	38	2
1955	BRO	NL	42	23	19	18	14	9	1	5	1	0	0	0	0	0	39	3
1956	BRO	NL	43	25	18	23	15	4	1	7	0	0	0	1	1	1	42	1
1957	BRO	NL	40	23	17	23	14	3	0	4	0	0	0	2	0	0	40	0
1958	LA	NL	15	6	9	8	7	0	0	0	0	0	0	0	0	0	15	0
1959	LA	NL	23	13	10	13	8	2	0	2	0	0	0	0	1	0	23	0
1960	LA	NL	14	11	3	9	4	1	0	1	0	0	0	0	0	2	13	1
1961	LA	NL	16	8	8	9	5	2	0	0	0	0	0	0	0	2	15	1
1962	LA	NL	5	1	4	3	2	0	0	0	0	0	0	0	0	0	5	0
1963	NY	NL	14	7	7	9	3	2	0	1	0	0	0	0	0	0	11	3
1964	SF	NL	4	1	3	1	3	0	0	0	0	0	0	0	0	0	4	0
Total			407	224	183	218	140	44	5	32	2	0	0	4	3	7	374	33

Rank among batters: 25 • *Top target (19 home runs)*: Robin Roberts • *Number of pitchers victimized*: 169 • *Total ballparks homered in*: 14 • *First HR*: 05/02/1948 off Curt Simmons • *World Series HR*—11

Van Snider

VAN VOORHEES SNIDER
B: 08/11/1963
BL

Year	Tm	Lg	Tot	H	A	0	1	2	3	2	3	4	LO	XN	IP	PH	RHP	LHP
1988	CIN	NL	1	1	0	0	0	1	0	0	0	0	0	0	0	0	1	0

Rank among batters: 4,707 • *Total ballparks homered in*: 1 • *First HR*: 09/21/1988 off Rick Reuschel

Fred Snodgrass

FREDERICK CHARLES SNODGRASS
B: 10/19/1887 D: 04/05/1974
BR

Year	Tm	Lg	Tot	H	A	0	1	2	3	2	3	4	LO	XN	IP	PH	RHP	LHP
1909	NY	NL	1	1	0	0	1	0	0	0	0	0	0	0	0	0	1	0
1910	NY	NL	2	2	0	1	1	0	0	0	0	0	0	0	0	0	2	0
1911	NY	NL	1	0	1	0	1	0	0	0	0	0	0	0	0	0	1	0
1912	NY	NL	3	2	1	2	0	1	0	0	0	0	0	0	0	0	2	1
1913	NY	NL	3	2	1	2	1	0	0	0	0	0	0	0	0	0	2	1
1916	BOS	NL	1	0	1	0	1	0	0	0	0	0	0	0	1	0	0	1
Total			11	7	4	5	5	1	0	0	0	0	0	0	1	0	8	3

Rank among batters: 2,419 • *Total ballparks homered in*: 6 • *First HR*: 06/24/1909 off Jake Boultes

Chris Snopek

CHRISTOPHER CHARLES SNOPEK
B: 09/20/1970
BR

Year	Tm	Lg	Tot	H	A	0	1	2	3	2	3	4	LO	XN	IP	PH	RHP	LHP
1995	CHI	AL	1	1	0	1	0	0	0	0	0	0	0	0	0	0	1	0

Rank among batters: 4,707 • *Total ballparks homered in*: 1 • *First HR*: 09/20/1995 off Joe Roa

J. T. Snow

JACK THOMAS SNOW
B: 02/26/1968
BB

Year	Tm	Lg	Tot	H	A	Men-On 0	Men-On 1	Men-On 2	Men-On 3	One-Game 2	One-Game 3	One-Game 4	LO	XN	IP	PH	RHP	LHP
1993	CAL	AL	16	10	6	10	4	2	0	1	0	0	0	0	0	0	14	2
1994	CAL	AL	8	7	1	3	2	2	1	1	0	0	0	0	0	0	6	2
1995	CAL	AL	24	14	10	11	8	4	1	0	0	0	0	0	0	0	19	5
Total			48	31	17	24	14	8	2	2	0	0	0	0	0	0	39	9

Rank among batters: 1,024 • *Top target (2 home runs)*: Jason Bere, Tim VanEgmond • *Number of pitchers victimized*: 46 • *Total ballparks homered in*: 10 • *First HR*: 04/06/1993 off Bill Wegman

Cory Snyder

JAMES CORY SNYDER
B: 11/11/1962
BR

Year	Tm	Lg	Tot	H	A	Men-On 0	Men-On 1	Men-On 2	Men-On 3	One-Game 2	One-Game 3	One-Game 4	LO	XN	IP	PH	RHP	LHP
1986	CLE	AL	24	12	12	13	8	3	0	3	0	0	0	0	0	0	16	8
1987	CLE	AL	33	17	16	23	7	1	2	2	1	0	0	1	0	0	28	5
1988	CLE	AL	26	11	15	14	9	2	1	0	0	0	0	0	0	0	17	9
1989	CLE	AL	18	6	12	10	6	2	0	1	0	0	0	0	0	0	8	10
1990	CLE	AL	14	3	11	7	5	1	1	1	0	0	0	1	0	0	10	4
1991	CHI	AL	3	2	1	3	0	0	0	0	0	0	0	0	0	0	0	3
1992	SF	NL	14	8	6	9	3	2	0	1	0	0	0	0	0	0	8	6
1993	LA	NL	11	5	6	7	3	1	0	1	0	0	0	1	0	0	8	3
1994	LA	NL	6	1	5	1	4	1	0	0	1	0	0	0	0	0	1	5
Total			149	65	84	87	45	13	4	9	2	0	0	3	0	0	96	53

Rank among batters: 289 • *Top target (4 home runs)*: Bert Blyleven • *Number of pitchers victimized*: 111 • *Total ballparks homered in*: 26 • *First HR*: 06/15/1986 off Frank Viola

Frank Snyder

FRANK ELTON SNYDER
B: 05/27/1893 D: 01/05/1962
BR

Year	Tm	Lg	Tot	H	A	Men-On 0	Men-On 1	Men-On 2	Men-On 3	One-Game 2	One-Game 3	One-Game 4	LO	XN	IP	PH	RHP	LHP
1914	STL	NL	1	0	1	1	0	0	0	0	0	0	0	0	0	0	0	1
1915	STL	NL	2	1	1	0	1	1	0	0	0	0	0	0	1	0	1	1
1917	STL	NL	1	1	0	1	0	0	0	0	0	0	0	0	0	0	1	0
1920	NY	NL	3	2	1	1	1	1	0	0	0	0	0	0	1	0	0	3
1921	NY	NL	8	3	5	5	0	2	1	2	0	0	0	0	0	0	3	5
1922	NY	NL	5	5	0	3	1	1	0	1	0	0	0	0	0	0	2	3
1923	NY	NL	5	3	2	2	2	0	1	0	0	0	0	0	0	0	4	1
1924	NY	NL	5	1	4	2	2	1	0	1	0	0	0	0	1	0	5	0
1925	NY	NL	11	5	6	6	2	3	0	1	0	0	0	0	0	0	7	4
1926	NY	NL	5	3	2	3	0	2	0	0	0	0	0	0	1	0	3	2
1927	STL	NL	1	1	0	0	0	1	0	0	0	0	0	0	0	0	0	1
Total			47	25	22	24	9	12	2	5	0	0	0	0	4	0	26	21

Rank among batters: 1,040 • *Top target (3 home runs)*: Bill Hubbell • *Number of pitchers victimized*: 35 • *Total ballparks homered in*: 10 • *First HR*: 07/30/1914 off Lefty Tyler • *World Series HR*—2

Jerry Snyder

GERALD GEORGE SNYDER
B: 07/21/1929
BR

Year	Tm	Lg	Tot	H	A	Men-On 0	Men-On 1	Men-On 2	Men-On 3	One-Game 2	One-Game 3	One-Game 4	LO	XN	IP	PH	RHP	LHP
1956	WAS	AL	2	1	1	1	0	1	0	0	0	0	0	0	1	0	1	1
1957	WAS	AL	1	0	1	1	0	0	0	0	0	0	0	0	0	0	1	0
Total			3	1	2	2	0	1	0	0	0	0	0	0	1	0	2	1

Rank among batters: 3,735 • *Total ballparks homered in*: 3 • *First HR*: 05/12/1956 off Frank Baumann

Jim Snyder

JAMES ROBERT SNYDER
B: 08/15/1932
BR

Year	Tm	Lg	Tot	H	A	Men-On 0	Men-On 1	Men-On 2	Men-On 3	One-Game 2	One-Game 3	One-Game 4	LO	XN	IP	PH	RHP	LHP
1964	MIN	AL	1	1	0	1	0	0	0	0	0	0	0	0	0	0	0	1

Rank among batters: 4,707 • *Total ballparks homered in*: 1 • *First HR*: 07/15/1964 off Don Rudolph

Pop Snyder

CHARLES N. SNYDER
B: 10/06/1854 D: 10/29/1924
BR

Year	Tm	Lg	Tot	H	A	Men-On 0	Men-On 1	Men-On 2	Men-On 3	One-Game 2	One-Game 3	One-Game 4	LO	XN	IP	PH	RHP	LHP
1876	LOU	NL	1	1	0	1	0	0	0	0	0	0	0	1	1	0	1	0
1877	LOU	NL	2	1	1	0	1	1	0	0	0	0	0	0	0	0	2	0

Pop Snyder *continued*

Year	Tm	Lg	Tot	H	A	Men-On 0	Men-On 1	Men-On 2	Men-On 3	One-Game 2	One-Game 3	One-Game 4	LO	XN	IP	PH	RHP	LHP
1879	BOS	NL	2	2	0	1	1	0	0	0	0	0	0	0	0	0	2	0
1882	CIN	AA	1	0	1	0	1	0	0	0	0	0	0	0	0	0	0	0
1885	CIN	AA	1	1	0	1	0	0	0	0	0	0	0	0	0	0	1	0
Total			7	5	2	3	3	1	0	0	0	0	0	1	1	0	6	0

Rank among batters: 2,834 • *Total ballparks homered in*: 5 • *First HR*: 06/29/1876 off Joe Borden

Russ Snyder

RUSSELL HENRY SNYDER
B: 06/22/1934
BL

Year	Tm	Lg	Tot	H	A	Men-On 0	Men-On 1	Men-On 2	Men-On 3	One-Game 2	One-Game 3	One-Game 4	LO	XN	IP	PH	RHP	LHP
1959	KC	AL	3	1	2	2	1	0	0	0	0	0	0	0	0	0	3	0
1960	KC	AL	4	1	3	4	0	0	0	0	0	0	0	0	0	0	3	1
1961	BAL	AL	1	1	0	0	1	0	0	0	0	0	0	0	0	0	1	0
1962	BAL	AL	9	2	7	9	0	0	0	0	0	0	0	1	0	1	9	0
1963	BAL	AL	7	4	3	5	1	1	0	1	0	0	0	0	0	0	7	0
1964	BAL	AL	1	0	1	1	0	0	0	0	0	0	0	0	0	0	1	0
1965	BAL	AL	1	0	1	0	1	0	0	0	0	0	0	0	0	0	1	0
1966	BAL	AL	3	3	0	2	1	0	0	0	0	0	0	0	0	0	3	0
1967	BAL	AL	4	3	1	1	2	1	0	0	0	0	0	0	0	1	3	1
1968	CHI	AL	1	0	1	0	0	0	1	0	0	0	0	0	0	0	1	0
	CLE	AL	2	0	2	1	1	0	0	0	0	0	0	0	0	0	2	0
	Total		3	0	3	1	1	0	1	0	0	0	0	0	0	0	3	0
1969	CLE	AL	2	1	1	1	0	1	0	0	0	0	0	0	0	1	2	0
1970	MIL	AL	4	2	2	2	0	1	1	0	0	0	0	0	0	0	4	0
Total			42	18	24	28	8	4	2	1	0	0	0	1	0	3	40	2

Rank among batters: 1,138 • *Top target (3 home runs)*: Jim Bunning, Jim Perry, Catfish Hunter • *Number of pitchers victimized*: 32 • *Total ballparks homered in*: 12 • *First HR*: 08/09/1959 off Eli Grba

Chief Sockalexis

LOUIS M. SOCKALEXIS
B: 10/24/1871 D: 12/24/1913
BL

Year	Tm	Lg	Tot	H	A	Men-On 0	Men-On 1	Men-On 2	Men-On 3	One-Game 2	One-Game 3	One-Game 4	LO	XN	IP	PH	RHP	LHP
1897	CLE	NL	3	1	2	2	1	0	0	0	0	0	0	0	0	0	2	1

Rank among batters: 3,735 • *Total ballparks homered in*: 3 • *First HR*: 04/30/1897 off Bill Hutchison

Eric Soderholm

ERIC THANE SODERHOLM
B: 09/24/1948
BR

Year	Tm	Lg	Tot	H	A	Men-On 0	Men-On 1	Men-On 2	Men-On 3	One-Game 2	One-Game 3	One-Game 4	LO	XN	IP	PH	RHP	LHP
1971	MIN	AL	1	1	0	1	0	0	0	0	0	0	0	0	0	0	1	0
1972	MIN	AL	13	11	2	5	4	3	1	0	0	0	0	1	1	2	7	6
1973	MIN	AL	1	1	0	1	0	0	0	0	0	0	0	0	0	0	0	1
1974	MIN	AL	10	5	5	5	3	1	1	1	0	0	0	0	0	0	7	3
1975	MIN	AL	11	10	1	5	3	3	0	2	0	0	0	0	0	0	4	7
1977	CHI	AL	25	9	16	15	8	2	0	2	0	0	0	1	0	0	15	10
1978	CHI	AL	20	9	11	12	8	0	0	3	0	0	0	0	0	0	11	9
1979	CHI	AL	6	1	5	4	1	1	0	0	0	0	0	0	0	0	3	3
	TEX	AL	4	0	4	2	1	1	0	1	0	0	0	0	0	0	1	3
	Total		10	1	9	6	2	2	0	1	0	0	0	0	0	0	4	6
1980	NY	AL	11	3	8	7	3	0	1	0	0	0	0	0	0	1	2	9
Total			102	50	52	57	31	11	3	9	0	0	0	2	1	3	51	51

Rank among batters: 483 • *Top target (4 home runs)*: Paul Splittorff • *Number of pitchers victimized*: 73 • *Total ballparks homered in*: 14 • *First HR*: 09/03/1971 off Diego Segui

Rick Sofield

RICHARD MICHAEL SOFIELD
B: 12/16/1956
BL

Year	Tm	Lg	Tot	H	A	Men-On 0	Men-On 1	Men-On 2	Men-On 3	One-Game 2	One-Game 3	One-Game 4	LO	XN	IP	PH	RHP	LHP
1980	MIN	AL	9	5	4	5	1	3	0	0	0	0	0	1	1	0	8	1

Rank among batters: 2,587 • *Total ballparks homered in*: 5 • *First HR*: 04/10/1980 off Steve McCatty

Luis Sojo

LUIS BELTRAN (SOJO) SOJO
B: 01/03/1966
BR

Year	Tm	Lg	Tot	H	A	Men-On 0	Men-On 1	Men-On 2	Men-On 3	One-Game 2	One-Game 3	One-Game 4	LO	XN	IP	PH	RHP	LHP
1990	TOR	AL	1	0	1	0	0	1	0	0	0	0	0	0	0	0	1	0

Luis Sojo *continued*

Year	Tm	Lg	Tot	H	A	Men-On 0	1	2	3	One-Game 2	3	4	LO	XN	IP	PH	RHP	LHP
1991	CAL	AL	3	1	2	3	0	0	0	0	0	0	0	0	0	0	3	0
1992	CAL	AL	7	2	5	5	1	1	0	0	0	0	0	1	0	0	7	0
1994	SEA	AL	6	4	2	4	1	0	1	0	0	0	1	0	0	0	4	2
1995	SEA	AL	7	4	3	3	4	0	0	0	0	0	0	0	0	0	2	5
Total			24	11	13	15	6	2	1	0	0	0	1	1	0	0	17	7

Rank among batters: 1,643 • *Top target (2 home runs)*: Ricky Bones • *Number of pitchers victimized*: 23 • *Total ballparks homered in*: 9 • *First HR*: 08/31/1990 off Colby Ward

Tony Solaita

TOLIA SOLAITA
B: 01/15/1947 D: 02/10/1990
BL

Year	Tm	Lg	Tot	H	A	Men-On 0	1	2	3	One-Game 2	3	4	LO	XN	IP	PH	RHP	LHP
1974	KC	AL	7	1	6	3	3	1	0	0	0	0	0	0	0	0	6	1
1975	KC	AL	16	6	10	11	4	1	0	2	1	0	0	0	0	1	12	4
1976	CAL	AL	9	3	6	4	4	1	0	0	0	0	0	0	0	0	9	0
1977	CAL	AL	14	7	7	8	5	1	0	0	0	0	0	0	0	2	14	0
1978	CAL	AL	1	0	1	0	1	0	0	0	0	0	0	0	0	0	1	0
1979	MON	NL	1	0	1	1	0	0	0	0	0	0	0	0	0	0	1	0
	TOR	AL	2	1	1	1	1	0	0	0	0	0	0	0	0	0	2	0
	Total		3	1	2	2	1	0	0	0	0	0	0	0	0	0	3	0
Total			50	18	32	28	18	4	0	2	1	0	0	0	0	3	45	5

Rank among batters: 991 • *Top target (3 home runs)*: Mickey Scott, Stan Bahnsen • *Number of pitchers victimized*: 40 • *Total ballparks homered in*: 14 • *First HR*: 04/21/1974 off Stan Bahnsen

Moose Solters

JULIUS JOSEPH SOLTERS
B: 03/22/1906 D: 09/28/1975
BR

Year	Tm	Lg	Tot	H	A	Men-On 0	1	2	3	One-Game 2	3	4	LO	XN	IP	PH	RHP	LHP
1934	BOS	AL	7	5	2	5	0	2	0	0	0	0	0	0	0	1	7	0
1935	STL	AL	18	12	6	7	7	4	0	2	1	0	0	1	0	0	13	5
1936	STL	AL	17	10	7	9	5	2	1	0	0	0	0	0	0	0	17	0
1937	CLE	AL	20	5	15	11	5	3	1	1	0	0	0	1	0	0	14	6
1938	CLE	AL	2	0	2	1	0	1	0	0	0	0	0	0	0	0	1	1
1939	CLE	AL	2	0	2	1	0	1	0	0	0	0	0	0	0	0	1	1
1940	CHI	AL	12	8	4	6	4	2	0	0	0	0	0	1	0	1	8	4
1941	CHI	AL	4	4	0	3	1	0	0	0	0	0	0	0	0	0	3	1
1943	CHI	AL	1	0	1	0	1	0	0	0	0	0	0	0	0	0	0	1
Total			83	44	39	43	23	15	2	3	1	0	0	3	0	2	64	19

Rank among batters: 628 • *Top target (5 home runs)*: Elden Auker • *Number of pitchers victimized*: 55 • *Total ballparks homered in*: 9 • *First HR*: 04/19/1934 off General Crowder • *Hit for Cycle*—vs DET: 08/19/1934 (1)

Joe Sommer

JOSEPH JOHN SOMMER
B: 11/20/1858 D: 01/16/1938
BR

Year	Tm	Lg	Tot	H	A	Men-On 0	1	2	3	One-Game 2	3	4	LO	XN	IP	PH	RHP	LHP
1882	CIN	AA	1	0	1	0	1	0	0	0	0	0	0	0	0	0	1	0
1883	CIN	AA	3	2	1	1	2	0	0	0	0	0	0	0	0	0	2	0
1884	BAL	AA	4	3	1	1	2	1	0	0	0	0	1	0	0	0	0	0
1885	BAL	AA	1	0	1	0	1	0	0	0	0	0	0	0	0	0	1	0
1886	BAL	AA	1	0	1	1	0	0	0	0	0	0	0	0	1	0	1	0
1889	BAL	AA	1	0	1	0	0	1	0	0	0	0	0	0	0	0	1	0
Total			11	5	6	3	6	2	0	0	0	0	1	0	1	0	6	0

Rank among batters: 2,419 • *Top target (2 home runs)*: Larry McKeon, Guy Hecker • *Number of pitchers victimized*: 9 • *Total ballparks homered in*: 7 • *First HR*: 07/07/1882 off Sam Weaver

Pete Sommers

JOSEPH ANDREWS SOMMERS
B: 10/26/1866 D: 07/22/1908
BR

Year	Tm	Lg	Tot	H	A	Men-On 0	1	2	3	One-Game 2	3	4	LO	XN	IP	PH	RHP	LHP
1887	NY	AA	1	0	1	0	1	0	0	0	0	0	0	0	1	0	1	0
1889	IND	NL	2	2	0	1	1	0	0	0	0	0	0	1	0	0	2	0
Total			3	2	1	1	2	0	0	0	0	0	0	1	1	0	3	0

Rank among batters: 3,735 • *Total ballparks homered in*: 2 • *First HR*: 07/31/1887 off Henry Porter

Year	Tm	Lg	Tot	H	A	Men-On 0	1	2	3	One-Game 2	3	4	LO	XN	IP	PH	RHP	LHP

Bill Sorrell

WILLIAM SORRELL
B: 10/14/1940
BL

Year	Tm	Lg	Tot	H	A	0	1	2	3	2	3	4	LO	XN	IP	PH	RHP	LHP
1965	PHI	NL	1	0	1	1	0	0	0	0	0	0	0	1	0	0	1	0
1970	KC	AL	4	2	2	3	1	0	0	0	0	0	0	0	0	0	4	0
Total			5	2	3	4	1	0	0	0	0	0	0	1	0	0	5	0

Rank among batters: 3,191 • *Total ballparks homered in*: 4 • *First HR*: 10/03/1965 off Jack Fisher

Paul Sorrento

PAUL ANTHONY SORRENTO
B: 11/17/1965
BL

Year	Tm	Lg	Tot	H	A	0	1	2	3	2	3	4	LO	XN	IP	PH	RHP	LHP
1990	MIN	AL	5	2	3	3	2	0	0	0	0	0	0	1	0	1	5	0
1991	MIN	AL	4	2	2	2	1	1	0	0	0	0	0	0	0	2	3	1
1992	CLE	AL	18	11	7	13	3	2	0	2	0	0	0	0	0	1	18	0
1993	CLE	AL	18	8	10	9	8	0	1	1	0	0	0	0	0	0	16	2
1994	CLE	AL	14	8	6	8	4	2	0	2	0	0	0	0	0	0	11	3
1995	CLE	AL	25	12	13	12	8	3	2	3	0	0	0	0	0	0	23	2
Total			84	43	41	47	26	8	3	8	0	0	0	1	0	4	76	8

Rank among batters: 617 • *Top target (4 home runs)*: Todd Stottlemyre, Jack McDowell • *Number of pitchers victimized*: 69 • *Total ballparks homered in*: 17 • *First HR*: 06/24/1990 off Storm Davis

Jose Sosa

JOSE YNOCENCIO SOSA
B: 12/28/1952
BR

Year	Tm	Lg	Tot	H	A	0	1	2	3	2	3	4	LO	XN	IP	PH	RHP	LHP
1975	HOU	NL	1	1	0	0	0	1	0	0	0	0	0	0	0	0	1	0

Rank among batters: 4,707 • *Total ballparks homered in*: 1 • *First HR*: 07/30/1975 off Danny Frisella • *Hit HR in first major league AB*—vs SD: 07/30/1975

Sammy Sosa

SAMUEL PERALTA SOSA
B: 11/12/1968
BR

Year	Tm	Lg	Tot	H	A	0	1	2	3	2	3	4	LO	XN	IP	PH	RHP	LHP
1989	TEX	AL	1	0	1	1	0	0	0	0	0	0	0	0	0	0	1	0
	CHI	AL	3	1	2	0	2	1	0	0	0	0	0	0	0	0	1	2
	Total		4	1	3	3	1	0	0	0	0	0	0	0	0	0	2	2
1990	CHI	AL	15	10	5	9	4	2	0	0	0	0	4	0	0	0	3	12
1991	CHI	AL	10	3	7	4	3	3	0	1	0	0	0	2	0	1	5	5
1992	CHI	NL	8	4	4	4	2	2	0	1	0	0	2	1	0	0	8	0
1993	CHI	NL	33	23	10	18	13	2	0	5	0	0	0	1	0	0	23	10
1994	CHI	NL	25	11	14	16	6	3	0	4	0	0	2	0	0	0	16	9
1995	CHI	NL	36	19	17	15	13	8	0	5	0	0	0	1	2	0	27	9
Total			131	71	60	69	42	20	0	16	0	0	8	5	2	1	84	47

Rank among batters: 342 • *Top target (4 home runs)*: Rheal Cormier • *Number of pitchers victimized*: 97 • *Total ballparks homered in*: 26 • *First HR*: 06/21/1989 off Roger Clemens

Denny Sothern

DENNIS ELWOOD SOTHERN
B: 01/20/1904 D: 12/07/1977
BR

Year	Tm	Lg	Tot	H	A	0	1	2	3	2	3	4	LO	XN	IP	PH	RHP	LHP
1926	PHI	NL	3	3	0	1	0	2	0	0	0	0	0	0	0	0	1	2
1928	PHI	NL	5	1	4	3	2	0	0	0	0	0	0	0	1	0	3	2
1929	PHI	NL	5	2	3	3	1	0	1	0	0	0	1	0	0	0	1	4
1930	PHI	NL	5	3	2	2	1	2	0	1	0	0	1	0	0	0	4	1
	PIT	NL	1	1	0	1	0	0	0	0	0	0	1	0	0	0	0	1
	Total		6	4	2	3	1	2	0	1	0	0	2	0	0	0	4	2
Total			19	10	9	10	4	4	1	1	0	0	3	0	1	0	9	10

Rank among batters: 1,861 • *Top target (3 home runs)*: Dolf Luque • *Number of pitchers victimized*: 15 • *Total ballparks homered in*: 7 • *First HR*: 09/10/1926 off Sheriff Blake

Mario Soto

MARIO MELVIN SOTO
B: 07/12/1956
BR

Year	Tm	Lg	Tot	H	A	0	1	2	3	2	3	4	LO	XN	IP	PH	RHP	LHP
1984	CIN	NL	1	1	0	1	0	0	0	0	0	0	0	0	0	0	1	0

Year	Tm	Lg	Tot	H	A	Men-On 0	1	2	3	One-Game 2	3	4	LO	XN	IP	PH	RHP	LHP

Mario Soto *continued*

Rank among batters: 4,707 • *Total ballparks homered in*: 1 • *First HR*: 06/30/1984 off Bryn Smith

Bud Souchock

STEPHEN SOUCHOCK
B: 03/03/1919
BR

Year	Tm	Lg	Tot	H	A	Men-On 0	1	2	3	One-Game 2	3	4	LO	XN	IP	PH	RHP	LHP
1946	NY	AL	2	1	1	1	1	0	0	0	0	0	0	0	0	0	1	1
1948	NY	AL	3	1	2	2	1	0	0	1	0	0	0	0	0	0	0	3
1949	CHI	AL	7	3	4	5	2	0	0	1	0	0	0	0	0	0	2	5
1951	DET	AL	11	4	7	6	4	1	0	0	0	0	0	0	0	0	2	9
1952	DET	AL	13	10	3	6	6	0	1	0	0	0	0	2	0	1	6	7
1953	DET	AL	11	5	6	4	6	1	0	1	0	0	0	0	0	0	9	2
1954	DET	AL	3	2	1	1	0	2	0	1	0	0	0	0	0	0	1	2
Total			50	26	24	25	20	4	1	4	0	0	0	2	0	1	21	29

Rank among batters: 991 • *Top target (5 home runs)*: Alex Kellner • *Number of pitchers victimized*: 35 • *Total ballparks homered in*: 8 • *First HR*: 07/20/1946 off Eddie Smith

Bill Southworth

WILLIAM FREDERICK SOUTHWORTH
B: 11/10/1945
BR

Year	Tm	Lg	Tot	H	A	Men-On 0	1	2	3	One-Game 2	3	4	LO	XN	IP	PH	RHP	LHP
1964	MIL	NL	1	1	0	0	1	0	0	0	0	0	0	0	0	0	1	0

Rank among batters: 4,707 • *Total ballparks homered in*: 1 • *First HR*: 10/04/1964 off Earl Francis

Billy Southworth

WILLIAM HARRISON SOUTHWORTH
B: 03/09/1893 D: 11/15/1969
BL

Year	Tm	Lg	Tot	H	A	Men-On 0	1	2	3	One-Game 2	3	4	LO	XN	IP	PH	RHP	LHP
1918	PIT	NL	2	2	0	1	1	0	0	0	0	0	0	0	2	0	1	1
1919	PIT	NL	4	3	1	2	2	0	0	0	0	0	0	1	3	0	3	1
1920	PIT	NL	2	1	1	0	2	0	0	0	0	0	0	0	1	0	2	0
1921	BOS	NL	7	2	5	5	1	1	0	1	0	0	0	0	2	0	5	2
1922	BOS	NL	4	0	4	0	4	0	0	0	0	0	0	0	1	0	3	1
1923	BOS	NL	6	4	2	4	2	0	0	0	0	0	0	2	4	0	5	1
1924	NY	NL	3	1	2	3	0	0	0	0	0	0	0	0	1	0	2	1
1925	NY	NL	6	2	4	3	2	0	1	0	0	0	0	0	1	0	6	0
1926	NY	NL	5	0	5	1	3	1	0	0	0	0	0	0	1	0	4	1
	STL	NL	11	8	3	5	4	2	0	1	0	0	0	1	0	0	10	1
	Total		16	8	8	6	7	3	0	1	0	0	0	1	1	0	14	2
1927	STL	NL	2	2	0	0	1	1	0	0	0	0	0	0	0	0	2	0
Total			52	25	27	24	22	5	1	2	0	0	0	4	16	0	43	9

Rank among batters: 965 • *Top target (3 home runs)*: Bill Sherdel, Doug McWeeny • *Number of pitchers victimized*: 41 • *Total ballparks homered in*: 8 • *First HR*: 07/15/1918 off Rube Marquard • *World Series HR*—1

John Sowders

JOHN SOWDERS
B: 12/10/1866 D: 07/29/1939
BR

Year	Tm	Lg	Tot	H	A	Men-On 0	1	2	3	One-Game 2	3	4	LO	XN	IP	PH	RHP	LHP
1890	BRO	PL	1	0	1	0	1	0	0	0	0	0	0	0	0	0	1	0

Rank among batters: 4,707 • *Total ballparks homered in*: 1 • *First HR*: 07/23/1890 off Jersey Bakely

Warren Spahn

WARREN EDWARD SPAHN
B: 04/23/1921
BL HOF

Year	Tm	Lg	Tot	H	A	Men-On 0	1	2	3	One-Game 2	3	4	LO	XN	IP	PH	RHP	LHP
1948	BOS	NL	1	0	1	0	1	0	0	0	0	0	0	0	0	0	1	0
1949	BOS	NL	2	1	1	1	1	0	0	0	0	0	0	0	0	0	2	0
1950	BOS	NL	1	0	1	0	1	0	0	0	0	0	0	0	0	0	1	0
1951	BOS	NL	1	0	1	0	0	1	0	0	0	0	0	0	0	0	1	0
1952	BOS	NL	2	2	0	2	0	0	0	0	0	0	0	0	0	0	1	1
1953	MIL	NL	2	0	2	2	0	0	0	0	0	0	0	0	0	0	2	0
1954	MIL	NL	1	0	1	1	0	0	0	0	0	0	0	0	0	0	1	0
1955	MIL	NL	4	1	3	2	1	1	0	0	0	0	0	0	0	0	3	1

Warren Spahn *continued*

Year	Tm	Lg	Tot	H	A	Men-On				One-Game			LO	XN	IP	PH	RHP	LHP
						0	1	2	3	2	3	4						
1956	MIL	NL	3	1	2	3	0	0	0	0	0	0	0	0	0	0	3	0
1957	MIL	NL	2	1	1	2	0	0	0	0	0	0	0	0	0	0	2	0
1958	MIL	NL	2	2	0	0	2	0	0	0	0	0	0	0	0	0	2	0
1959	MIL	NL	2	2	0	2	0	0	0	0	0	0	0	0	0	0	1	1
1960	MIL	NL	3	2	1	3	0	0	0	0	0	0	0	0	0	0	3	0
1961	MIL	NL	4	1	3	3	0	1	0	0	0	0	0	0	0	0	4	0
1962	MIL	NL	2	1	1	2	0	0	0	0	0	0	0	0	0	0	2	0
1963	MIL	NL	2	2	0	2	0	0	0	0	0	0	0	0	0	0	2	0
1964	MIL	NL	1	1	0	1	0	0	0	0	0	0	0	0	0	0	1	0
Total			35	17	18	26	6	3	0	0	0	0	0	0	0	0	32	3

Rank among batters: 1,291 • Top target (2 home runs): Larry Jansen, Ruben Gomez, Bob Friend, Jack Sanford • *Number of pitchers victimized*: 31 • *Total ballparks homered in*: 10 • *First HR*: 09/11/1948 off Charlie Bicknell

Al Spangler

ALBERT DONALD SPANGLER
B: 07/08/1933
BL

Year	Tm	Lg	Tot	H	A	Men-On 0	Men-On 1	Men-On 2	Men-On 3	One-Game 2	One-Game 3	One-Game 4	LO	XN	IP	PH	RHP	LHP
1962	HOU	NL	5	2	3	4	1	0	0	0	0	0	2	1	0	0	5	0
1963	HOU	NL	4	0	4	4	0	0	0	0	0	0	2	0	0	0	4	0
1964	HOU	NL	4	0	4	4	0	0	0	0	0	0	2	0	0	0	3	1
1965	HOU	NL	1	1	0	1	0	0	0	0	0	0	0	0	0	0	1	0
1968	CHI	NL	2	0	2	2	0	0	0	0	0	0	0	0	0	0	2	0
1969	CHI	NL	4	2	2	1	2	1	0	1	0	0	0	0	0	0	4	0
1970	CHI	NL	1	1	0	1	0	0	0	0	0	0	0	0	0	1	1	0
Total			21	6	15	17	3	1	0	1	0	0	6	1	0	1	20	1

Rank among batters: 1,768 • *Total ballparks homered in*: 11 • *First HR*: 06/02/1962 off Vern Law

Bob Speake

ROBERT CHARLES SPEAKE
B: 08/22/1930
BL

Year	Tm	Lg	Tot	H	A	Men-On 0	Men-On 1	Men-On 2	Men-On 3	One-Game 2	One-Game 3	One-Game 4	LO	XN	IP	PH	RHP	LHP
1955	CHI	NL	12	5	7	3	9	0	0	0	0	0	0	2	0	0	11	1
1957	CHI	NL	16	6	10	9	5	2	0	0	0	0	0	0	0	1	11	5
1958	SF	NL	3	1	2	2	1	0	0	0	0	0	0	0	0	1	3	0
Total			31	12	19	14	15	2	0	0	0	0	0	2	0	2	25	6

Rank among batters: 1,400 • Top target (2 home runs): Gene Conley, Sal Maglie, Sandy Koufax, Sam Jones, Lew Burdette • *Number of pitchers victimized*: 26 • *Total ballparks homered in*: 9 • *First HR*: 05/05/1955 off Sal Maglie

Tris Speaker

TRISTRAM E. SPEAKER
B: 04/04/1888 D: 12/08/1958
BL HOF

Year	Tm	Lg	Tot	H	A	Men-On 0	Men-On 1	Men-On 2	Men-On 3	One-Game 2	One-Game 3	One-Game 4	LO	XN	IP	PH	RHP	LHP
1909	BOS	AL	7	6	1	1	4	2	0	0	0	0	0	0	5	0	2	5
1910	BOS	AL	7	4	3	4	3	0	0	0	0	0	0	0	5	0	6	1
1911	BOS	AL	8	5	3	5	3	0	0	0	0	0	0	0	4	0	6	2
1912	BOS	AL	10	4	6	4	4	2	0	0	0	0	0	1	8	0	8	2
1913	BOS	AL	3	0	3	2	1	0	0	0	0	0	0	0	1	0	2	1
1914	BOS	AL	4	0	4	0	4	0	0	0	0	0	0	0	2	0	3	1
1916	CLE	AL	2	0	2	2	0	0	0	0	0	0	0	0	0	0	2	0
1917	CLE	AL	2	1	1	1	0	1	0	0	0	0	0	0	0	0	1	1
1919	CLE	AL	2	1	1	1	1	0	0	0	0	0	0	0	1	0	1	1
1920	CLE	AL	8	6	2	3	3	2	0	0	0	0	0	0	4	0	5	3
1921	CLE	AL	3	2	1	3	0	0	0	0	0	0	0	0	0	0	3	0
1922	CLE	AL	11	5	6	7	3	0	1	2	0	0	0	0	2	0	10	1
1923	CLE	AL	17	10	7	6	5	3	3	0	0	0	0	1	1	0	15	2
1924	CLE	AL	9	3	6	4	5	0	0	0	0	0	0	0	1	0	6	3
1925	CLE	AL	12	6	6	5	5	2	0	0	0	0	0	0	2	0	8	4
1926	CLE	AL	7	3	4	2	3	2	0	0	0	0	0	0	1	0	5	2
1927	WAS	AL	2	0	2	1	1	0	0	0	0	0	0	0	0	0	1	1
1928	PHI	AL	3	3	0	1	2	0	0	0	0	0	0	0	0	0	3	0
Total			117	59	58	52	47	14	4	2	0	0	0	2	37	0	87	30

Rank among batters: 402 • *Top target (5 home runs)*: Tom Zachary • *Number of pitchers victimized*: 82 • *Total ballparks homered in*: 12 • *First HR*: 05/03/1909 off Dolly Gray • *Hit for Cycle*—@STL: 06/09/1912

Tim Spehr

TIMOTHY JOSEPH SPEHR
B: 07/02/1966
BR

Year	Tm	Lg	Tot	H	A	Men-On 0	1	2	3	One-Game 2	3	4	LO	XN	IP	PH	RHP	LHP
1991	KC	AL	3	1	2	2	0	0	1	0	0	0	0	0	0	0	0	3
1993	MON	NL	2	0	2	1	1	0	0	0	0	0	0	0	0	0	1	1
1995	MON	NL	1	0	1	0	1	0	0	0	0	0	0	0	0	1	0	1
Total			6	1	5	3	2	0	1	0	0	0	0	0	0	1	1	5

Rank among batters: 2,988 • *Total ballparks homered in*: 6 • *First HR*: 09/19/1991 off Bill Krueger

Chris Speier

CHRIS EDWARD SPEIER
B: 06/28/1950
BR

Year	Tm	Lg	Tot	H	A	Men-On 0	1	2	3	One-Game 2	3	4	LO	XN	IP	PH	RHP	LHP
1971	SF	NL	8	4	4	5	2	1	0	0	0	0	0	0	0	0	4	4
1972	SF	NL	15	11	4	9	5	0	1	0	0	0	0	0	1	0	8	7
1973	SF	NL	11	3	8	7	4	0	0	0	0	0	0	0	0	0	7	4
1974	SF	NL	9	3	6	8	1	0	0	0	0	0	0	0	0	0	8	1
1975	SF	NL	10	4	6	8	1	1	0	0	0	0	0	0	0	0	8	2
1976	SF	NL	3	0	3	3	0	0	0	0	0	0	0	0	0	1	1	2
1977	MON	NL	5	4	1	3	2	0	0	0	0	0	0	0	0	0	5	0
1978	MON	NL	5	2	3	2	2	1	0	0	0	0	0	0	0	0	2	3
1979	MON	NL	7	1	6	4	3	0	0	0	0	0	0	0	0	0	7	0
1980	MON	NL	1	0	1	1	0	0	0	0	0	0	0	0	0	0	1	0
1981	MON	NL	2	1	1	1	1	0	0	0	0	0	0	0	0	0	1	1
1982	MON	NL	7	2	5	5	0	2	0	0	0	0	0	0	0	0	6	1
1983	MON	NL	2	1	1	1	1	0	0	0	0	0	0	0	0	0	1	1
1984	STL	NL	3	2	1	2	0	1	0	0	0	0	0	1	0	0	2	1
1985	CHI	NL	4	1	3	1	3	0	0	0	0	0	0	0	0	1	1	3
1986	CHI	NL	6	2	4	3	2	1	0	1	0	0	0	0	0	0	4	2
1987	SF	NL	11	6	5	8	1	0	2	1	0	0	1	1	0	0	7	4
1988	SF	NL	3	3	0	2	0	0	1	0	0	0	0	0	0	0	3	0
Total			112	50	62	73	28	7	4	2	0	0	1	2	1	2	76	36

Rank among batters: 429 • Top target (3 home runs): Ross Grimsley, Steve Carlton, Larry Dierker, Phil Niekro, Ron Reed • *Number of pitchers victimized*: 92 • *Total ballparks homered in*: 13 • *First HR*: 05/14/1971 off Al Downing • *Hit for Cycle*—vs ATL: 07/20/1978; vs STL: 07/09/1988 • *LCS HR*—1

Bob Spence

JOHN ROBERT SPENCE
B: 02/10/1946
BL

Year	Tm	Lg	Tot	H	A	Men-On 0	1	2	3	One-Game 2	3	4	LO	XN	IP	PH	RHP	LHP
1970	CHI	AL	4	3	1	2	2	0	0	0	0	0	0	0	0	0	4	0

Rank among batters: 3,427 • *Total ballparks homered in*: 2 • *First HR*: 06/27/1970 off Bert Blyleven

Stan Spence

STANLEY ORVILLE SPENCE
B: 03/20/1915 D: 01/09/1983
BL

Year	Tm	Lg	Tot	H	A	Men-On 0	1	2	3	One-Game 2	3	4	LO	XN	IP	PH	RHP	LHP
1940	BOS	AL	2	1	1	2	0	0	0	0	0	0	0	0	0	2	2	0
1941	BOS	AL	2	1	1	1	1	0	0	0	0	0	0	0	0	1	2	0
1942	WAS	AL	4	1	3	2	1	1	0	0	0	0	0	0	1	0	4	0
1943	WAS	AL	12	2	10	7	4	1	0	2	0	0	0	0	0	0	11	1
1944	WAS	AL	18	2	16	12	2	4	0	1	0	0	0	0	1	0	16	2
1946	WAS	AL	16	2	14	11	3	2	0	2	0	0	0	1	0	0	12	4
1947	WAS	AL	16	5	11	5	10	1	0	4	0	0	0	0	0	0	14	2
1948	BOS	AL	12	7	5	6	2	4	0	0	0	0	0	0	0	0	12	0
1949	STL	AL	13	9	4	8	3	2	0	3	0	0	0	0	0	0	10	3
Total			95	30	65	54	26	15	0	12	0	0	0	1	2	3	83	12

Rank among batters: 529 • *Top target (5 home runs)*: Bobo Newsom • *Number of pitchers victimized*: 60 • *Total ballparks homered in*: 9 • *First HR*: 08/20/1940 off Johnny Allen

Daryl Spencer

DARYL DEAN SPENCER
B: 07/13/1929
BR

Year	Tm	Lg	Tot	H	A	Men-On 0	1	2	3	One-Game 2	3	4	LO	XN	IP	PH	RHP	LHP
1953	NY	NL	20	14	6	12	6	0	2	3	0	0	0	0	1	0	14	6
1956	NY	NL	14	13	1	9	5	0	0	1	0	0	0	0	1	0	11	3
1957	NY	NL	11	9	2	8	3	0	0	2	0	0	0	0	0	0	9	2

						Men-On				One-Game								
Year	Tm	Lg	Tot	H	A	0	1	2	3	2	3	4	LO	XN	IP	PH	RHP	LHP

Daryl Spencer *continued*

Year	Tm	Lg	Tot	H	A	0	1	2	3	2	3	4	LO	XN	IP	PH	RHP	LHP
1958	SF	NL	17	6	11	10	5	2	0	2	0	0	0	0	0	0	13	4
1959	SF	NL	12	5	7	10	0	2	0	1	0	0	0	0	0	0	7	5
1960	STL	NL	16	12	4	11	3	2	0	0	0	0	0	0	0	0	9	7
1961	STL	NL	4	0	4	3	0	0	1	1	0	0	0	1	0	0	3	1
	LA	NL	8	4	4	3	3	2	0	0	0	0	0	0	0	0	6	2
	Total		12	4	8	6	3	2	1	1	0	0	0	1	0	0	9	3
1962	LA	NL	2	0	2	2	0	0	0	0	0	0	0	0	0	0	1	1
1963	CIN	NL	1	1	0	1	0	0	0	0	0	0	0	0	0	0	1	0
Total			105	64	41	69	25	8	3	10	0	0	0	1	2	0	74	31

Rank among batters: 462 • *Top target (4 home runs)*: Moe Drabowsky, Joe Nuxhall • *Number of pitchers victimized*: 73 • *Total ballparks homered in*: 10 • *First HR*: 04/24/1953 off Carl Erskine

Jim Spencer

JAMES LLOYD SPENCER
B: 07/30/1946
BL

Year	Tm	Lg	Tot	H	A	0	1	2	3	2	3	4	LO	XN	IP	PH	RHP	LHP
1969	CAL	AL	10	7	3	7	3	0	0	0	0	0	0	0	0	0	5	5
1970	CAL	AL	12	5	7	7	5	0	0	2	0	0	0	0	0	0	8	4
1971	CAL	AL	18	8	10	13	4	1	0	0	0	0	0	0	0	0	13	5
1972	CAL	AL	1	0	1	1	0	0	0	0	0	0	0	0	0	0	1	0
1973	CAL	AL	2	2	0	1	1	0	0	0	0	0	0	0	0	0	2	0
	TEX	AL	4	2	2	3	1	0	0	0	0	0	0	0	0	0	4	0
	Total		6	4	2	4	2	0	0	0	0	0	0	0	0	0	6	0
1974	TEX	AL	7	3	4	4	3	0	0	1	0	0	0	0	0	0	6	1
1975	TEX	AL	11	4	7	4	5	2	0	0	0	0	0	0	0	0	11	0
1976	CHI	AL	14	5	9	6	5	3	0	0	0	0	0	0	0	0	11	3
1977	CHI	AL	18	8	10	10	4	2	2	3	0	0	0	0	0	0	10	8
1978	NY	AL	7	4	3	5	1	0	1	0	0	0	0	0	0	1	7	0
1979	NY	AL	23	16	7	9	11	3	0	3	0	0	0	0	0	0	19	4
1980	NY	AL	13	8	5	6	3	3	1	0	0	0	0	0	0	1	12	1
1981	NY	AL	2	1	1	1	1	0	0	0	0	0	0	0	0	0	2	0
	OAK	AL	2	0	2	2	0	0	0	0	0	0	0	0	0	0	1	1
	Total		4	1	3	3	1	0	0	0	0	0	0	0	0	0	3	1
1982	OAK	AL	2	0	2	2	0	0	0	0	0	0	0	0	0	0	2	0
Total			146	73	73	81	47	14	4	9	0	0	0	0	0	2	114	32

Rank among batters: 302 • Top target (4 home runs): Catfish Hunter, Pat Dobson, Jim Palmer, Mike Norris • *Number of pitchers victimized*: 105 • *Total ballparks homered in*: 16 • *First HR*: 07/15/1969 off Bill Butler

Roy Spencer

ROY HAMPTON SPENCER
B: 02/22/1900 D: 02/08/1973
BR

Year	Tm	Lg	Tot	H	A	0	1	2	3	2	3	4	LO	XN	IP	PH	RHP	LHP
1929	WAS	AL	1	0	1	1	0	0	0	0	0	0	0	0	0	0	0	1
1931	WAS	AL	1	0	1	1	0	0	0	0	0	0	0	0	0	0	0	1
1932	WAS	AL	1	1	0	0	0	1	0	0	0	0	0	0	0	0	1	0
Total			3	1	2	2	0	1	0	0	0	0	0	0	0	0	1	2

Rank among batters: 3,735 • *Total ballparks homered in*: 2 • *First HR*: 08/17/1929 off Bob Weiland

Tubby Spencer

EDWARD RUSSELL SPENCER
B: 01/26/1884 D: 02/01/1945
BR

Year	Tm	Lg	Tot	H	A	0	1	2	3	2	3	4	LO	XN	IP	PH	RHP	LHP
1907	STL	AL	1	1	0	1	0	0	0	0	0	0	0	0	0	0	1	0
1911	PHI	NL	1	0	1	0	1	0	0	0	0	0	0	0	0	0	0	1
1916	DET	AL	1	0	1	0	1	0	0	0	0	0	0	0	0	0	0	1
Total			3	1	2	1	2	0	0	0	0	0	0	0	0	0	1	2

Rank among batters: 3,735 • *Total ballparks homered in*: 2 • *First HR*: 05/26/1907 off Bill Dinneen

Ed Sperber

EDWIN GEORGE SPERBER
B: 01/21/1895 D: 01/05/1976
BL

Year	Tm	Lg	Tot	H	A	0	1	2	3	2	3	4	LO	XN	IP	PH	RHP	LHP
1924	BOS	NL	1	1	0	0	1	0	0	0	0	0	0	0	1	0	0	1

Rank among batters: 4,707 • *Total ballparks homered in*: 1 • *First HR*: 06/07/1924 off Bill Sherdel

						Men-On				One-Game								
Year	Tm	Lg	Tot	H	A	0	1	2	3	2	3	4	LO	XN	IP	PH	RHP	LHP

Rob Sperring

ROBERT WALTER SPERRING
B: 10/10/1949
BR

Year	Tm	Lg	Tot	H	A	0	1	2	3	2	3	4	LO	XN	IP	PH	RHP	LHP
1974	CHI	NL	1	1	0	1	0	0	0	0	0	0	0	0	0	0	0	1
1975	CHI	NL	1	0	1	1	0	0	0	0	0	0	0	0	0	0	0	1
1977	HOU	NL	1	0	1	0	1	0	0	0	0	0	0	0	0	0	1	0
Total			3	1	2	2	1	0	0	0	0	0	0	0	0	0	1	2

Rank among batters: 3,735 • *Total ballparks homered in*: 3 • *First HR*: 08/11/1974 off Mike Caldwell

Billy Spiers

WILLIAM JAMES SPIERS
B: 06/05/1966
BL

Year	Tm	Lg	Tot	H	A	0	1	2	3	2	3	4	LO	XN	IP	PH	RHP	LHP
1989	MIL	AL	4	1	3	3	0	0	1	0	0	0	0	0	0	0	3	1
1990	MIL	AL	2	2	0	1	1	0	0	0	0	0	0	0	0	0	2	0
1991	MIL	AL	8	1	7	3	2	2	1	1	0	0	0	0	0	0	6	2
1993	MIL	AL	2	2	0	2	0	0	0	0	0	0	0	0	0	0	2	0
Total			16	6	10	9	3	2	2	1	0	0	0	0	0	0	13	3

Rank among batters: 2,029 • *Total ballparks homered in*: 8 • *First HR*: 04/17/1989 off Brad Arnsberg

Harry Spies

HENRY SPIES
B: 06/12/1866 D: 07/08/1942
BR

Year	Tm	Lg	Tot	H	A	0	1	2	3	2	3	4	LO	XN	IP	PH	RHP	LHP
1895	LOU	NL	2	1	1	2	0	0	0	0	0	0	0	0	1	0	1	1

Rank among batters: 4,129 • *Total ballparks homered in*: 2 • *First HR*: 07/31/1895 off Ted Breitenstein

Ed Spiezio

EDWARD WAYNE SPIEZIO
B: 10/31/1941
BR

Year	Tm	Lg	Tot	H	A	0	1	2	3	2	3	4	LO	XN	IP	PH	RHP	LHP
1966	STL	NL	2	1	1	1	1	0	0	0	0	0	0	0	0	0	1	1
1967	STL	NL	3	1	2	2	1	0	0	0	0	0	0	0	0	0	0	3
1969	SD	NL	13	10	3	8	4	1	0	1	0	0	0	0	0	0	9	4
1970	SD	NL	12	5	7	7	3	1	1	0	0	0	0	0	0	1	11	1
1971	SD	NL	7	2	5	4	3	0	0	0	0	0	0	0	0	0	4	3
1972	CHI	AL	2	0	2	1	1	0	0	0	0	0	0	1	0	0	2	0
Total			39	19	20	23	13	2	1	1	0	0	0	1	0	1	27	12

Rank among batters: 1,204 • *Top target (3 home runs)*: Tom Seaver • *Number of pitchers victimized*: 33 • *Total ballparks homered in*: 15 • *First HR*: 09/11/1966 off Bob Veale

Charlie Spikes

LESLIE CHARLES SPIKES
B: 01/23/1951
BR

Year	Tm	Lg	Tot	H	A	0	1	2	3	2	3	4	LO	XN	IP	PH	RHP	LHP
1973	CLE	AL	23	13	10	15	5	3	0	2	0	0	0	0	0	0	15	8
1974	CLE	AL	22	12	10	11	9	2	0	0	0	0	0	0	0	0	13	9
1975	CLE	AL	11	5	6	9	2	0	0	0	0	0	0	0	0	1	2	9
1976	CLE	AL	3	1	2	2	0	0	1	0	0	0	0	0	0	0	2	1
1977	CLE	AL	3	3	0	1	2	0	0	0	0	0	0	0	0	0	2	1
1979	ATL	NL	3	2	1	1	0	2	0	0	0	0	0	0	0	2	1	2
Total			65	36	29	39	18	7	1	2	0	0	0	0	0	3	35	30

Rank among batters: 799 • Top target (3 home runs): Mike Cuellar, Jim Kaat, Ross Grimsley, Bill Lee, Reggie Cleveland • *Number of pitchers victimized*: 52 • *Total ballparks homered in*: 13 • *First HR*: 04/15/1973 off Tom Timmermann

Harry Spilman

WILLIAM HARRY SPILMAN
B: 07/18/1954
BL

Year	Tm	Lg	Tot	H	A	0	1	2	3	2	3	4	LO	XN	IP	PH	RHP	LHP
1980	CIN	NL	4	2	2	2	1	1	0	0	0	0	0	0	0	2	4	0
1982	HOU	NL	3	1	2	2	1	0	0	1	0	0	0	1	0	1	3	0
1983	HOU	NL	1	1	0	0	0	1	0	0	0	0	0	0	0	1	1	0
1984	HOU	NL	2	0	2	0	1	1	0	0	0	0	0	0	0	0	2	0
1985	HOU	NL	1	0	1	0	0	1	0	0	0	0	0	0	0	1	1	0
1986	DET	AL	3	0	3	1	1	0	1	0	0	0	0	0	0	0	3	0

Harry Spilman *continued*

Year	Tm	Lg	Tot	H	A	Men-On 0	Men-On 1	Men-On 2	Men-On 3	One-Game 2	One-Game 3	One-Game 4	LO	XN	IP	PH	RHP	LHP
	SF	NL	2	1	1	0	1	1	0	0	0	0	0	0	0	0	2	0
	Total		5	1	4	1	2	1	1	0	0	0	0	0	0	0	5	0
1987	SF	NL	1	1	0	0	0	1	0	0	0	0	0	0	0	1	1	0
1988	SF	NL	1	1	0	1	0	0	0	0	0	0	0	0	0	1	1	0
Total			18	7	11	6	5	6	1	1	0	0	0	1	0	7	18	0

Rank among batters: 1,914 • *Total ballparks homered in*: 10 • *First HR*: 05/11/1980 off Dick Ruthven • *LCS HR*—1

Scipio Spinks

SCIPIO RONALD SPINKS
B: 07/12/1947
BR

Year	Tm	Lg	Tot	H	A	Men-On 0	Men-On 1	Men-On 2	Men-On 3	One-Game 2	One-Game 3	One-Game 4	LO	XN	IP	PH	RHP	LHP
1973	STL	NL	1	1	0	1	0	0	0	0	0	0	0	0	0	0	0	1

Rank among batters: 4,707 • *Total ballparks homered in*: 1 • *First HR*: 04/25/1973 off Al Downing

Al Spohrer

ALFRED RAY SPOHRER
B: 12/03/1902 D: 07/17/1972
BR

Year	Tm	Lg	Tot	H	A	Men-On 0	Men-On 1	Men-On 2	Men-On 3	One-Game 2	One-Game 3	One-Game 4	LO	XN	IP	PH	RHP	LHP
1929	BOS	NL	2	1	1	1	1	0	0	0	0	0	0	0	0	0	2	0
1930	BOS	NL	2	1	1	1	1	0	0	0	0	0	0	0	0	0	1	1
1933	BOS	NL	1	1	0	1	0	0	0	0	0	0	0	0	0	0	0	1
1935	BOS	NL	1	1	0	1	0	0	0	0	0	0	0	0	0	0	0	1
Total			6	4	2	4	2	0	0	0	0	0	0	0	0	0	3	3

Rank among batters: 2,988 • *Total ballparks homered in*: 3 • *First HR*: 06/10/1929 off Hal Carlson

Charlie Sprague

CHARLES WELLINGTON SPRAGUE
B: 10/10/1864 D: 12/31/1912
BL

Year	Tm	Lg	Tot	H	A	Men-On 0	Men-On 1	Men-On 2	Men-On 3	One-Game 2	One-Game 3	One-Game 4	LO	XN	IP	PH	RHP	LHP
1890	TOL	AA	1	1	0	0	0	1	0	0	0	0	0	0	0	0	1	0

Rank among batters: 4,707 • *Total ballparks homered in*: 1 • *First HR*: 06/20/1890 off Red Ehret

Ed Sprague

EDWARD NELSON SPRAGUE, JR.
B: 07/25/1967
BR

Year	Tm	Lg	Tot	H	A	Men-On 0	Men-On 1	Men-On 2	Men-On 3	One-Game 2	One-Game 3	One-Game 4	LO	XN	IP	PH	RHP	LHP
1991	TOR	AL	4	3	1	1	3	0	0	0	0	0	0	0	0	0	1	3
1992	TOR	AL	1	1	0	0	0	1	0	0	0	0	0	0	0	0	1	0
1993	TOR	AL	12	8	4	9	2	1	0	0	0	0	0	0	0	0	10	2
1994	TOR	AL	11	6	5	7	3	1	0	0	0	0	0	1	0	0	8	3
1995	TOR	AL	18	12	6	11	5	0	2	1	0	0	0	1	0	0	13	5
Total			46	30	16	28	13	3	2	1	0	0	0	2	0	0	33	13

Rank among batters: 1,060 • Top target (2 home runs): Tom Gordon, Melido Perez, Todd Van Poppel, Mark Clark • *Number of pitchers victimized*: 42 • *Total ballparks homered in*: 11 • *First HR*: 05/18/1991 off Greg Hibbard • *World Series HR*—1

Harry Spratt

HENRY LEE SPRATT
B: 07/10/1888 D: 07/03/1969
BL

Year	Tm	Lg	Tot	H	A	Men-On 0	Men-On 1	Men-On 2	Men-On 3	One-Game 2	One-Game 3	One-Game 4	LO	XN	IP	PH	RHP	LHP
1911	BOS	NL	2	1	1	2	0	0	0	0	0	0	0	0	0	0	1	1
1912	BOS	NL	3	1	2	1	2	0	0	0	0	0	0	0	0	0	3	0
Total			5	2	3	3	2	0	0	0	0	0	0	0	0	0	4	1

Rank among batters: 3,191 • *Top target (3 home runs)*: Grover Alexander • *Number of pitchers victimized*: 3 • *Total ballparks homered in*: 3 • *First HR*: 07/26/1911 off Ed Reulbach

George Spriggs

GEORGE HERMAN SPRIGGS
B: 05/22/1941
BL

Year	Tm	Lg	Tot	H	A	Men-On 0	Men-On 1	Men-On 2	Men-On 3	One-Game 2	One-Game 3	One-Game 4	LO	XN	IP	PH	RHP	LHP
1970	KC	AL	1	0	1	0	1	0	0	0	0	0	0	0	0	0	1	0

Rank among batters: 4,707 • *Total ballparks homered in*: 1 • *First HR*: 09/21/1970 off Joe Horlen

Freddy Spurgeon

FRED SPURGEON
B: 10/09/1900 D: 11/05/1970
BR

Year	Tm	Lg	Tot	H	A	Men-On				One-Game			LO	XN	IP	PH	RHP	LHP
						0	1	2	3	2	3	4						
1927	CLE	AL	1	1	0	1	0	0	0	0	0	0	0	0	0	0	0	1

Rank among batters: 4,707 • *Total ballparks homered in*: 1 • *First HR*: 07/13/1927 off Dutch Ruether

Mike Squires

MICHAEL LYNN SQUIRES
B: 03/05/1952
BL

Year	Tm	Lg	Tot	H	A	Men-On				One-Game			LO	XN	IP	PH	RHP	LHP
						0	1	2	3	2	3	4						
1979	CHI	AL	2	1	1	2	0	0	0	0	0	0	0	0	0	0	2	0
1980	CHI	AL	2	2	0	1	1	0	0	0	0	0	0	0	0	0	1	1
1982	CHI	AL	1	1	0	1	0	0	0	0	0	0	0	0	0	0	1	0
1983	CHI	AL	1	0	1	1	0	0	0	0	0	0	0	0	0	0	1	0
Total			6	4	2	5	1	0	0	0	0	0	0	0	0	0	5	1

Rank among batters: 2,988 • *Top target (2 home runs)*: Matt Keough • *Number of pitchers victimized*: 5 • *Total ballparks homered in*: 3 • *First HR*: 08/18/1979 off Steve Renko

Ebba St. Claire

EDWARD JOSEPH ST. CLAIRE
B: 08/05/1921 D: 08/22/1982
BB

Year	Tm	Lg	Tot	H	A	Men-On				One-Game			LO	XN	IP	PH	RHP	LHP
						0	1	2	3	2	3	4						
1951	BOS	NL	1	1	0	1	0	0	0	0	0	0	0	0	0	0	1	0
1952	BOS	NL	2	0	2	1	1	0	0	0	0	0	0	0	0	0	2	0
1953	MIL	NL	2	0	2	1	1	0	0	0	0	0	0	0	0	0	2	0
1954	NY	NL	2	2	0	0	2	0	0	0	0	0	0	0	0	0	2	0
Total			7	3	4	3	4	0	0	0	0	0	0	0	0	0	7	0

Rank among batters: 2,834 • *Total ballparks homered in*: 5 • *First HR*: 08/14/1951 off Robin Roberts

Marv Staehle

MARVIN GUSTAVE STAEHLE
B: 03/13/1942
BL

Year	Tm	Lg	Tot	H	A	Men-On				One-Game			LO	XN	IP	PH	RHP	LHP
						0	1	2	3	2	3	4						
1969	MON	NL	1	1	0	1	0	0	0	0	0	0	0	0	0	0	1	0

Rank among batters: 4,707 • *Total ballparks homered in*: 1 • *First HR*: 09/21/1969 off Lowell Palmer

General Stafford

JAMES JOSEPH STAFFORD
B: 07/09/1868 D: 09/18/1923
BR

Year	Tm	Lg	Tot	H	A	Men-On				One-Game			LO	XN	IP	PH	RHP	LHP
						0	1	2	3	2	3	4						
1893	NY	NL	5	3	2	4	1	0	0	0	0	0	1	0	1	0	1	4
1895	NY	NL	3	3	0	2	1	0	0	0	0	0	0	0	0	0	2	1
1897	LOU	NL	7	6	1	3	4	0	0	0	0	0	0	0	1	0	6	1
1898	LOU	NL	1	1	0	0	1	0	0	0	0	0	0	0	0	0	1	0
	BOS	NL	1	1	0	1	0	0	0	0	0	0	0	0	0	0	1	0
	Total		2	2	0	1	1	0	0	0	0	0	0	0	0	0	2	0
1899	BOS	NL	3	3	0	1	0	2	0	0	0	0	0	0	0	0	3	0
	WAS	NL	1	1	0	1	0	0	0	0	0	0	0	0	0	0	1	0
	Total		4	4	0	2	0	2	0	0	0	0	0	0	0	0	4	0
Total			21	18	3	12	7	2	0	0	0	0	1	0	2	0	15	6

Rank among batters: 1,768 • *Top target (2 home runs)*: Frank Killen, Jouett Meekin • *Number of pitchers victimized*: 19 • *Total ballparks homered in*: 6 • *First HR*: 07/10/1893 off Frank Killen

Steve Staggs

STEPHEN ROBERT STAGGS
B: 05/06/1951
BR

Year	Tm	Lg	Tot	H	A	Men-On				One-Game			LO	XN	IP	PH	RHP	LHP
						0	1	2	3	2	3	4						
1977	TOR	AL	2	1	1	1	0	1	0	0	0	0	0	0	0	0	2	0

Rank among batters: 4,129 • *Total ballparks homered in*: 2 • *First HR*: 07/01/1977 off Doyle Alexander

Chick Stahl

CHARLES SYLVESTER STAHL
B: 01/10/1873 D: 03/28/1907
BL

Year	Tm	Lg	Tot	H	A	Men-On				One-Game			LO	XN	IP	PH	RHP	LHP
						0	1	2	3	2	3	4						
1897	BOS	NL	4	1	3	1	2	0	1	0	0	0	0	0	0	0	3	1
1898	BOS	NL	3	3	0	2	1	0	0	0	0	0	0	0	0	0	3	0

Chick Stahl *continued*

						Men-On				One-Game								
Year	Tm	Lg	Tot	H	A	0	1	2	3	2	3	4	LO	XN	IP	PH	RHP	LHP
1899	BOS	NL	7	5	2	3	3	1	0	0	0	0	0	0	1	0	5	1
1900	BOS	NL	5	3	2	3	1	1	0	0	0	0	0	1	1	0	5	0
1901	BOS	AL	6	5	1	3	1	2	0	0	0	0	0	0	0	0	5	1
1902	BOS	AL	2	1	1	1	0	1	0	0	0	0	0	0	0	0	2	0
1903	BOS	AL	2	2	0	0	2	0	0	0	0	0	0	0	0	0	1	1
1904	BOS	AL	3	2	1	1	0	2	0	0	0	0	0	0	1	0	3	0
1906	BOS	AL	4	4	0	2	1	1	0	0	0	0	0	0	3	0	4	0
Total			36	26	10	16	11	8	1	0	0	0	0	1	6	0	31	4

Rank among batters: 1,274 • *Top target (2 home runs)*: Bill Hart, Pink Hawley, Bill Carrick • *Number of pitchers victimized*: 33 • *Total ballparks homered in*: 10 • *First HR*: 05/17/1897 off Roger Denzer

Jake Stahl

GARLAND STAHL
B: 04/13/1879 D: 09/18/1922
BR

Year	Tm	Lg	Tot	H	A	0	1	2	3	2	3	4	LO	XN	IP	PH	RHP	LHP
1903	BOS	AL	2	1	1	1	1	0	0	0	0	0	0	0	0	0	1	1
1904	WAS	AL	3	0	3	0	3	0	0	0	0	0	0	0	0	0	3	0
1905	WAS	AL	5	1	4	5	0	0	0	0	0	0	0	0	0	0	5	0
1908	NY	AL	2	1	1	1	0	1	0	0	0	0	0	0	2	0	2	0
1909	BOS	AL	6	5	1	4	1	1	0	0	0	0	0	0	1	0	3	3
1910	BOS	AL	10	9	1	3	5	1	1	0	0	0	0	0	2	0	7	3
1912	BOS	AL	3	1	2	2	0	0	1	0	0	0	0	0	0	0	2	1
Total			31	18	13	16	10	3	2	0	0	0	0	0	5	0	23	8

Rank among batters: 1,400 • Top target (2 home runs): Fred Glade, Bob Groom, Willie Mitchell, Ed Walsh • *Number of pitchers victimized*: 27 • *Total ballparks homered in*: 11 • *First HR*: 08/23/1903 off Ed Siever

Larry Stahl

LARRY FLOYD STAHL
B: 06/29/1941
BL

Year	Tm	Lg	Tot	H	A	0	1	2	3	2	3	4	LO	XN	IP	PH	RHP	LHP
1964	KC	AL	3	0	3	1	2	0	0	1	0	0	0	1	0	0	3	0
1965	KC	AL	4	1	3	2	2	0	0	0	0	0	0	0	0	0	4	0
1966	KC	AL	5	3	2	4	1	0	0	0	0	0	0	0	0	1	5	0
1967	NY	NL	1	0	1	0	0	1	0	0	0	0	0	0	0	0	1	0
1968	NY	NL	3	3	0	3	0	0	0	0	0	0	0	0	0	0	3	0
1969	SD	NL	3	0	3	2	1	0	0	0	0	0	0	0	0	0	3	0
1971	SD	NL	8	4	4	5	1	2	0	0	0	0	0	0	0	0	8	0
1972	SD	NL	7	3	4	6	1	0	0	0	0	0	0	0	0	1	7	0
1973	CIN	NL	2	0	2	1	0	1	0	0	0	0	0	0	0	1	2	0
Total			36	14	22	24	8	4	0	1	0	0	0	1	0	3	36	0

Rank among batters: 1,274 • *Top target (2 home runs)*: Dave Boswell, Ron Reed, Ferguson Jenkins • *Number of pitchers victimized*: 33 • *Total ballparks homered in*: 11 • *First HR*: 09/29/1964 off Dave Boswell

Scott Stahoviak

SCOTT EDMUND STAHOVIAK
B: 03/06/1970
BL

Year	Tm	Lg	Tot	H	A	0	1	2	3	2	3	4	LO	XN	IP	PH	RHP	LHP
1995	MIN	AL	3	1	2	2	0	1	0	0	0	0	0	0	0	0	3	0

Rank among batters: 3,735 • *Total ballparks homered in*: 3 • *First HR*: 06/02/1995 off Matt Whiteside

Roy Staiger

ROY JOSEPH STAIGER
B: 01/06/1950
BR

Year	Tm	Lg	Tot	H	A	0	1	2	3	2	3	4	LO	XN	IP	PH	RHP	LHP
1976	NY	NL	2	1	1	1	1	0	0	0	0	0	0	0	0	0	1	1
1977	NY	NL	2	0	2	1	1	0	0	0	0	0	0	0	0	0	2	0
Total			4	1	3	2	2	0	0	0	0	0	0	0	0	0	3	1

Rank among batters: 3,427 • *Total ballparks homered in*: 4 • *First HR*: 08/02/1976 off Woodie Fryman

Tuck Stainback

GEORGE TUCKER STAINBACK
B: 08/04/1911 D: 11/29/1992
BR

Year	Tm	Lg	Tot	H	A	0	1	2	3	2	3	4	LO	XN	IP	PH	RHP	LHP
1934	CHI	NL	2	0	2	0	1	0	1	0	0	0	0	0	0	0	2	0

Tuck Stainback *continued*

Year	Tm	Lg	Tot	H	A	Men-On 0	1	2	3	One-Game 2	3	4	LO	XN	IP	PH	RHP	LHP
1935	CHI	NL	3	2	1	2	0	1	0	0	0	0	0	0	0	0	0	3
1936	CHI	NL	1	0	1	0	1	0	0	0	0	0	0	0	0	0	0	1
1938	PHI	NL	1	0	1	0	0	1	0	0	0	0	0	0	0	0	0	1
1939	BRO	NL	3	0	3	2	1	0	0	0	0	0	0	0	0	0	0	3
1941	DET	AL	2	2	0	2	0	0	0	0	0	0	0	0	0	0	2	0
1945	NY	AL	5	3	2	1	2	2	0	0	0	0	0	0	0	0	3	2
Total			17	7	10	7	5	4	1	0	0	0	0	0	0	0	7	10

Rank among batters: 1,969 • *Top target (2 home runs)*: Ed Brandt, Johnny Vander Meer • *Number of pitchers victimized*: 15 • *Total ballparks homered in*: 10 • *First HR*: 05/18/1934 off Ed Holley

Matt Stairs

MATTHEW WADE STAIRS
B: 02/27/1968
BL

Year	Tm	Lg	Tot	H	A	Men-On 0	1	2	3	One-Game 2	3	4	LO	XN	IP	PH	RHP	LHP
1995	BOS	AL	1	0	1	1	0	0	0	0	0	0	0	0	0	0	1	0

Rank among batters: 4,707 • *Total ballparks homered in*: 1 • *First HR*: 07/05/1995 off Tom Gordon

Gerry Staley

GERALD LEE STALEY
B: 08/21/1920
BR

Year	Tm	Lg	Tot	H	A	Men-On 0	1	2	3	One-Game 2	3	4	LO	XN	IP	PH	RHP	LHP
1948	STL	NL	1	0	1	1	0	0	0	0	0	0	0	0	0	0	1	0

Rank among batters: 4,707 • *Total ballparks homered in*: 1 • *First HR*: 05/30/1948 off Woody Main

Harry Staley

HENRY ELI STALEY
B: 11/03/1866 D: 01/12/1910
BR

Year	Tm	Lg	Tot	H	A	Men-On 0	1	2	3	One-Game 2	3	4	LO	XN	IP	PH	RHP	LHP
1890	PIT	PL	1	0	1	0	1	0	0	0	0	0	0	0	0	0	1	0
1891	BOS	NL	1	1	0	0	1	0	0	0	0	0	0	0	0	0	0	1
1892	BOS	NL	1	1	0	0	1	0	0	0	0	0	0	0	0	0	1	0
1893	BOS	NL	2	2	0	0	0	2	0	1	0	0	0	0	0	0	2	0
1894	BOS	NL	2	2	0	0	0	1	1	0	0	0	0	0	0	0	2	0
Total			7	6	1	0	3	3	1	1	0	0	0	0	0	0	6	1

Rank among batters: 2,834 • *Top target (2 home runs)*: Billy Rhines • *Number of pitchers victimized*: 6 • *Total ballparks homered in*: 4 • *First HR*: 08/25/1890 off Ed Crane

Virgil Stallcup

THOMAS VIRGIL STALLCUP
B: 01/03/1922 D: 05/02/1989
BR

Year	Tm	Lg	Tot	H	A	Men-On 0	1	2	3	One-Game 2	3	4	LO	XN	IP	PH	RHP	LHP
1948	CIN	NL	3	1	2	2	1	0	0	0	0	0	0	0	0	0	1	2
1949	CIN	NL	3	0	3	1	1	1	0	0	0	0	0	0	0	0	0	3
1950	CIN	NL	8	5	3	6	2	0	0	0	0	0	0	0	0	0	1	7
1951	CIN	NL	8	2	6	4	2	2	0	0	0	0	0	1	0	0	6	2
Total			22	8	14	13	6	3	0	0	0	0	0	1	0	0	8	14

Rank among batters: 1,719 • Top target (2 home runs): Preacher Roe, Monita Kennedy, Sheldon Jones, Cliff Chambers • *Number of pitchers victimized*: 18 • *Total ballparks homered in*: 6 • *First HR*: 05/29/1948 off Dutch McCall

George Staller

GEORGE WALBORN STALLER
B: 04/01/1916 D: 07/03/1992
BL

Year	Tm	Lg	Tot	H	A	Men-On 0	1	2	3	One-Game 2	3	4	LO	XN	IP	PH	RHP	LHP
1943	PHI	AL	3	2	1	2	0	1	0	0	0	0	0	0	1	0	3	0

Rank among batters: 3,735 • *Total ballparks homered in*: 2 • *First HR*: 09/15/1943 off Hank Borowy

Oscar Stanage

OSCAR HARLAND STANAGE
B: 03/17/1883 D: 11/11/1964
BR

Year	Tm	Lg	Tot	H	A	Men-On 0	1	2	3	One-Game 2	3	4	LO	XN	IP	PH	RHP	LHP
1910	DET	AL	2	2	0	0	1	1	0	0	0	0	0	0	0	0	1	1

Year	Tm	Lg	Tot	H	A	Men-On 0	Men-On 1	Men-On 2	Men-On 3	One-Game 2	One-Game 3	One-Game 4	LO	XN	IP	PH	RHP	LHP

Oscar Stanage *continued*

Year	Tm	Lg	Tot	H	A	0	1	2	3	2	3	4	LO	XN	IP	PH	RHP	LHP
1911	DET	AL	3	3	0	2	0	1	0	0	0	0	0	0	0	0	1	2
1915	DET	AL	1	0	1	1	0	0	0	0	0	0	0	0	0	0	0	1
1918	DET	AL	1	0	1	0	1	0	0	0	0	0	0	0	0	0	0	1
1919	DET	AL	1	1	0	1	0	0	0	0	0	0	0	0	0	0	0	1
Total			8	6	2	4	2	2	0	0	0	0	0	0	0	0	2	6

Rank among batters: 2,703 • *Top target (2 home runs)*: Ed Karger • *Number of pitchers victimized*: 7 • *Total ballparks homered in*: 4 • *First HR*: 06/15/1910 off Ed Karger

Don Stanhouse

DONALD JOSEPH STANHOUSE
B: 02/12/1951
BR

Year	Tm	Lg	Tot	H	A	0	1	2	3	2	3	4	LO	XN	IP	PH	RHP	LHP
1977	MON	NL	1	0	1	0	0	0	1	0	0	0	0	0	0	0	1	0

Rank among batters: 4,707 • *Total ballparks homered in*: 1 • *First HR*: 07/06/1977 off Bill Bonham

Pete Stanicek

PETER LOUIS STANICEK
B: 04/18/1963
BB

Year	Tm	Lg	Tot	H	A	0	1	2	3	2	3	4	LO	XN	IP	PH	RHP	LHP
1988	BAL	AL	4	2	2	4	0	0	0	0	0	0	2	0	0	0	0	4

Rank among batters: 3,427 • *Top target (2 home runs)*: Frank Tanana • *Number of pitchers victimized*: 3 • *Total ballparks homered in*: 3 • *First HR*: 06/22/1988 off John Cerutti

Andy Stankewicz

ANDREW NEAL STANKEWICZ
B: 08/10/1964
BR

Year	Tm	Lg	Tot	H	A	0	1	2	3	2	3	4	LO	XN	IP	PH	RHP	LHP
1992	NY	AL	2	2	0	2	0	0	0	0	0	0	0	0	0	0	2	0
1994	HOU	NL	1	1	0	0	0	1	0	0	0	0	0	0	0	0	0	1
Total			3	3	0	2	0	1	0	0	0	0	0	0	0	0	2	1

Rank among batters: 3,735 • *Total ballparks homered in*: 2 • *First HR*: 04/24/1992 off Alan Milis

Eddie Stanky

EDWARD RAYMOND STANKY
B: 09/03/1916
BR

Year	Tm	Lg	Tot	H	A	0	1	2	3	2	3	4	LO	XN	IP	PH	RHP	LHP
1945	BRO	NL	1	0	1	1	0	0	0	0	0	0	0	0	0	0	1	0
1947	BRO	NL	3	0	3	1	2	0	0	0	0	0	1	0	0	0	2	1
1948	BOS	NL	2	0	2	1	1	0	0	0	0	0	0	0	0	0	1	1
1949	BOS	NL	1	1	0	1	0	0	0	0	0	0	0	0	0	0	1	0
1950	NY	NL	8	6	2	7	1	0	0	2	0	0	3	0	0	0	5	3
1951	NY	NL	14	12	2	11	3	0	0	0	0	0	0	0	1	0	9	5
Total			29	19	10	22	7	0	0	2	0	0	4	0	1	0	19	10

Rank among batters: 1,465 • *Top target (4 home runs)*: Mel Queen • *Number of pitchers victimized*: 23 • *Total ballparks homered in*: 6 • *First HR*: 04/20/1945 off Harry Feldman

Fred Stanley

FREDERICK BLAIR STANLEY
B: 08/13/1947
BR

Year	Tm	Lg	Tot	H	A	0	1	2	3	2	3	4	LO	XN	IP	PH	RHP	LHP
1971	CLE	AL	2	1	1	1	1	0	0	0	0	0	0	0	0	0	2	0
1973	NY	AL	1	1	0	0	0	0	1	0	0	0	0	0	0	0	0	1
1976	NY	AL	1	1	0	1	0	0	0	0	0	0	0	0	0	0	1	0
1977	NY	AL	1	1	0	0	1	0	0	0	0	0	0	0	0	0	0	1
1978	NY	AL	1	0	1	0	0	0	1	0	0	0	0	0	0	0	1	0
1979	NY	AL	2	1	1	1	0	1	0	0	0	0	0	0	0	0	0	2
1982	OAK	AL	2	1	1	1	1	0	0	0	0	0	0	0	0	0	1	1
Total			10	6	4	4	3	1	2	0	0	0	0	0	0	0	5	5

Rank among batters: 2,500 • *Top target (2 home runs)*: Paul Splittorff • *Number of pitchers victimized*: 9 • *Total ballparks homered in*: 6 • *First HR*: 08/29/1971 off Jim Perry

Year	Tm	Lg	Tot	H	A	Men-On 0	Men-On 1	Men-On 2	Men-On 3	One-Game 2	One-Game 3	One-Game 4	LO	XN	IP	PH	RHP	LHP

Joe Stanley

JOSEPH BERNARD STANLEY
B: 04/02/1881 D: 09/13/1967
BB

Year	Tm	Lg	Tot	H	A	0	1	2	3	2	3	4	LO	XN	IP	PH	RHP	LHP
1903	BOS	NL	1	1	0	0	0	0	1	0	0	0	0	0	0	0	1	0
1905	WAS	AL	1	1	0	0	0	0	1	0	0	0	0	0	1	0	1	0
Total			2	2	0	0	0	0	2	0	0	0	0	0	1	0	2	0

Rank among batters: 4,129 • *Total ballparks homered in*: 2 • *First HR*: 08/12/1903 off Jock Menefee

Mickey Stanley

MITCHELL JACK STANLEY
B: 07/20/1942
BR

Year	Tm	Lg	Tot	H	A	0	1	2	3	2	3	4	LO	XN	IP	PH	RHP	LHP
1965	DET	AL	3	2	1	3	0	0	0	0	0	0	0	0	0	0	1	2
1966	DET	AL	3	1	2	3	0	0	0	0	0	0	0	0	0	0	0	3
1967	DET	AL	7	5	2	5	2	0	0	0	0	0	0	1	0	0	3	4
1968	DET	AL	11	7	4	4	4	2	1	0	0	0	0	0	0	0	5	6
1969	DET	AL	16	10	6	12	1	2	1	1	0	0	2	0	0	1	9	7
1970	DET	AL	13	6	7	11	2	0	0	1	0	0	3	1	0	0	7	6
1971	DET	AL	7	2	5	5	0	2	0	1	0	0	0	0	0	0	2	5
1972	DET	AL	14	6	8	8	5	1	0	1	0	0	0	1	0	0	7	7
1973	DET	AL	17	9	8	12	4	1	0	0	0	0	1	1	0	0	10	7
1974	DET	AL	8	4	4	3	2	3	0	0	0	0	1	0	0	0	3	5
1975	DET	AL	3	2	1	0	1	2	0	0	0	0	0	0	0	0	3	0
1976	DET	AL	4	2	2	2	2	0	0	1	0	0	0	0	0	0	0	4
1977	DET	AL	8	5	3	4	4	0	0	0	0	0	0	0	0	1	2	6
1978	DET	AL	3	1	2	3	0	0	0	0	0	0	0	0	0	0	0	3
Total			117	62	55	75	27	13	2	5	0	0	7	4	0	2	52	65

Rank among batters: 402 • *Top target (6 home runs)*: Dave McNally • *Number of pitchers victimized*: 88 • *Total ballparks homered in*: 15 • *First HR*: 09/03/1965 off Marshall Bridges

Mike Stanley

ROBERT MICHAEL STANLEY
B: 06/25/1963
BR

Year	Tm	Lg	Tot	H	A	0	1	2	3	2	3	4	LO	XN	IP	PH	RHP	LHP
1986	TEX	AL	1	0	1	1	0	0	0	0	0	0	0	0	0	0	0	1
1987	TEX	AL	6	3	3	3	1	0	2	0	0	0	0	0	0	1	4	2
1988	TEX	AL	3	1	2	2	1	0	0	0	0	0	0	0	0	0	1	2
1989	TEX	AL	1	1	0	1	0	0	0	0	0	0	0	0	0	0	0	1
1990	TEX	AL	2	1	1	0	1	1	0	0	0	0	0	0	0	1	0	2
1991	TEX	AL	3	1	2	3	0	0	0	0	0	0	0	0	0	0	0	3
1992	NY	AL	8	5	3	5	1	1	1	0	0	0	0	0	0	0	3	5
1993	NY	AL	26	17	9	13	6	4	3	0	0	0	0	0	0	0	12	14
1994	NY	AL	17	8	9	9	8	0	0	3	0	0	0	0	0	0	8	9
1995	NY	AL	18	13	5	11	4	1	2	0	1	0	0	0	0	0	10	8
Total			85	50	35	48	22	7	8	3	1	0	0	0	0	2	38	47

Rank among batters: 612 • *Top target (4 home runs)*: Wilson Alvarez • *Number of pitchers victimized*: 66 • *Total ballparks homered in*: 16 • *First HR*: 09/11/1986 off Frank Viola • *LCS HR*—1

Leroy Stanton

LEROY BOBBY STANTON
B: 04/10/1946
BR

Year	Tm	Lg	Tot	H	A	0	1	2	3	2	3	4	LO	XN	IP	PH	RHP	LHP
1972	CAL	AL	12	5	7	6	6	0	0	2	0	0	0	0	0	0	6	6
1973	CAL	AL	8	3	5	5	3	0	0	0	1	0	0	2	0	0	4	4
1974	CAL	AL	11	6	5	5	3	3	0	0	0	0	0	0	0	0	8	3
1975	CAL	AL	14	9	5	7	4	1	2	0	0	0	0	1	0	0	8	6
1976	CAL	AL	2	1	1	0	1	0	1	0	0	0	0	1	0	0	2	0
1977	SEA	AL	27	14	13	11	11	5	0	1	0	0	0	0	0	0	16	11
1978	SEA	AL	3	2	1	3	0	0	0	0	0	0	0	0	0	0	1	2
Total			77	40	37	37	28	9	3	3	1	0	0	4	0	0	45	32

Rank among batters: 682 • *Top target (4 home runs)*: Wilbur Wood • *Number of pitchers victimized*: 56 • *Total ballparks homered in*: 12 • *First HR*: 05/14/1972 off Fred Beene

Dave Stapleton

DAVID LESLIE STAPLETON
B: 01/16/1954
BR

Year	Tm	Lg	Tot	H	A	0	1	2	3	2	3	4	LO	XN	IP	PH	RHP	LHP
1980	BOS	AL	7	5	2	6	0	1	0	1	0	0	0	1	0	1	4	3

Year	Tm	Lg	Tot	H	A	Men-On				One-Game			LO	XN	IP	PH	RHP	LHP
						0	1	2	3	2	3	4						

Dave Stapleton *continued*

Year	Tm	Lg	Tot	H	A	0	1	2	3	2	3	4	LO	XN	IP	PH	RHP	LHP
1981	BOS	AL	10	4	6	8	1	1	0	1	0	0	0	0	0	0	8	2
1982	BOS	AL	14	7	7	10	3	1	0	0	0	0	0	0	1	0	10	4
1983	BOS	AL	10	5	5	5	2	3	0	0	0	0	0	0	0	0	8	2
Total			41	21	20	29	6	6	0	2	0	0	0	1	1	1	30	11

Rank among batters: 1,163 • *Top target (3 home runs)*: Bob McClure • *Number of pitchers victimized*: 33 • *Total ballparks homered in*: 11 • *First HR*: 05/31/1980 off Mike Caldwell

Willie Stargell

WILVER DORNEL STARGELL
B: 03/06/1940
BL HOF

Year	Tm	Lg	Tot	H	A	0	1	2	3	2	3	4	LO	XN	IP	PH	RHP	LHP
1963	PIT	NL	11	3	8	4	3	4	0	1	0	0	0	0	1	1	10	1
1964	PIT	NL	21	12	9	13	4	4	0	0	0	0	0	0	1	0	18	3
1965	PIT	NL	27	8	19	10	10	5	2	3	1	0	0	0	0	0	25	2
1966	PIT	NL	33	11	22	12	14	7	0	2	0	0	0	3	1	1	30	3
1967	PIT	NL	20	11	9	10	9	1	0	0	0	0	0	0	0	0	18	2
1968	PIT	NL	24	11	13	13	7	4	0	0	1	0	0	0	0	0	21	3
1969	PIT	NL	29	14	15	18	10	0	1	1	0	0	0	1	0	0	23	6
1970	PIT	NL	31	13	18	18	9	3	1	3	0	0	0	1	0	0	25	6
1971	PIT	NL	48	21	27	28	13	5	2	3	2	0	0	2	0	0	36	12
1972	PIT	NL	33	16	17	16	10	6	1	4	0	0	0	0	0	0	23	10
1973	PIT	NL	44	24	20	21	14	8	1	4	0	0	0	2	0	1	32	12
1974	PIT	NL	25	8	17	11	8	5	1	2	0	0	0	1	0	0	17	8
1975	PIT	NL	22	12	10	11	8	3	0	1	0	0	0	0	0	0	14	8
1976	PIT	NL	20	11	9	11	7	1	1	0	0	0	0	0	0	0	13	7
1977	PIT	NL	13	7	6	8	3	2	0	2	0	0	0	1	0	0	11	2
1978	PIT	NL	28	15	13	11	11	5	1	1	0	0	0	0	0	1	21	7
1979	PIT	NL	32	16	16	20	12	0	0	4	0	0	0	1	0	1	23	9
1980	PIT	NL	11	7	4	2	8	1	0	1	0	0	0	0	0	0	9	2
1982	PIT	NL	3	1	2	1	1	1	0	0	0	0	0	0	0	3	3	0
Total			475	221	254	238	161	65	11	32	4	0	0	12	3	8	372	103

Rank among batters: 17 • *Top target (8 home runs)*: Tom Seaver, Phil Niekro • *Number of pitchers victimized*: 243 • *Total ballparks homered in*: 20 • *First HR*: 05/08/1963 off Lindy McDaniel • *Hit for Cycle—@STL*: 07/22/1964 • *World Series HR—3; LCS HR—4; All-Star HR—1*

Joe Start

JOSEPH START
B: 10/14/1842 D: 03/27/1927
BL

Year	Tm	Lg	Tot	H	A	0	1	2	3	2	3	4	LO	XN	IP	PH	RHP	LHP
1877	HAR	NL	1	1	0	1	0	0	0	0	0	0	0	0	0	0	1	0
1878	CHI	NL	1	0	1	0	1	0	0	0	0	0	0	0	0	0	1	0
1879	PRO	NL	2	2	0	0	1	1	0	0	0	0	0	1	1	0	2	0
1883	PRO	NL	1	0	1	1	0	0	0	0	0	0	0	0	0	0	1	0
1884	PRO	NL	2	0	2	1	0	1	0	0	0	0	0	0	0	0	0	0
Total			7	3	4	3	2	2	0	0	0	0	0	1	1	0	5	0

Rank among batters: 2,834 • *Total ballparks homered in*: 5 • *First HR*: 08/27/1877 off Amos Booth

Dave Staton

DAVID ALAN STATON
B: 04/12/1968
BR

Year	Tm	Lg	Tot	H	A	0	1	2	3	2	3	4	LO	XN	IP	PH	RHP	LHP
1993	SD	NL	5	3	2	4	1	0	0	0	0	0	0	0	0	1	5	0
1994	SD	NL	4	2	2	2	2	0	0	0	0	0	0	0	0	0	1	3
Total			9	5	4	6	3	0	0	0	0	0	0	0	0	1	6	3

Rank among batters: 2,587 • *Total ballparks homered in*: 4 • *First HR*: 09/15/1993 off Kevin Gross

Jigger Statz

ARNOLD JOHN STATZ
B: 10/20/1897 D: 03/16/1988
BR

Year	Tm	Lg	Tot	H	A	0	1	2	3	2	3	4	LO	XN	IP	PH	RHP	LHP
1922	CHI	NL	1	0	1	1	0	0	0	0	0	0	1	0	0	0	1	0
1923	CHI	NL	10	9	1	4	6	0	0	0	0	0	1	0	1	0	7	3
1924	CHI	NL	3	0	3	2	0	0	1	0	0	0	0	1	1	0	3	0
1925	CHI	NL	2	1	1	1	1	0	0	0	0	0	0	0	0	0	1	1
1927	BRO	NL	1	1	0	1	0	0	0	0	0	0	0	0	1	0	1	0
Total			17	11	6	9	7	0	1	0	0	0	2	1	3	0	13	4

Year	Tm	Lg	Tot	H	A	Men-On 0	1	2	3	One-Game 2	3	4	LO	XN	IP	PH	RHP	LHP

Jigger Statz *continued*

Rank among batters: 1,969 • *Top target (2 home runs)*: Virgil Barnes • *Number of pitchers victimized*: 16 • *Total ballparks homered in*: 5 • *First HR*: 09/20/1922 off Petie Behan

Rusty Staub

DANIEL JOSEPH STAUB
B: 04/01/1944
BL

Year	Tm	Lg	Tot	H	A	0	1	2	3	2	3	4	LO	XN	IP	PH	RHP	LHP
1963	HOU	NL	6	4	2	3	3	0	0	0	0	0	0	0	0	0	4	2
1964	HOU	NL	8	4	4	6	2	0	0	1	0	0	0	0	0	0	3	5
1965	HOU	NL	14	2	12	6	2	6	0	0	0	0	0	0	0	0	9	5
1966	HOU	NL	13	1	12	6	7	0	0	1	0	0	0	0	1	0	7	6
1967	HOU	NL	10	4	6	5	4	1	0	1	0	0	0	0	0	0	8	2
1968	HOU	NL	6	3	3	4	2	0	0	0	0	0	0	0	0	0	5	1
1969	MON	NL	29	12	17	18	9	2	0	0	0	0	0	0	0	0	23	6
1970	MON	NL	30	13	17	19	10	0	1	4	0	0	0	0	0	0	19	11
1971	MON	NL	19	15	4	7	7	4	1	1	0	0	0	0	0	0	15	4
1972	NY	NL	9	5	4	5	2	1	1	0	0	0	0	0	0	0	6	3
1973	NY	NL	15	6	9	7	4	2	2	3	0	0	0	0	0	0	14	1
1974	NY	NL	19	10	9	13	5	1	0	0	0	0	0	0	0	0	13	6
1975	NY	NL	19	11	8	11	6	1	1	0	0	0	0	1	0	0	15	4
1976	DET	AL	15	9	6	8	3	3	1	0	0	0	0	1	0	0	8	7
1977	DET	AL	22	10	12	12	6	4	0	0	0	0	0	1	0	0	15	7
1978	DET	AL	24	16	8	9	9	5	1	0	0	0	0	2	0	0	14	10
1979	DET	AL	9	5	4	5	3	1	0	0	0	0	0	1	0	0	6	3
	MON	NL	3	2	1	2	1	0	0	0	0	0	0	0	0	0	3	0
	Total		12	7	5	7	4	1	0	0	0	0	0	1	0	0	9	3
1980	TEX	AL	9	3	6	3	3	2	1	0	0	0	0	0	0	3	8	1
1981	NY	NL	5	3	2	4	1	0	0	1	0	0	0	0	0	0	5	0
1982	NY	NL	3	2	1	2	1	0	0	0	0	0	0	0	0	1	2	1
1983	NY	NL	3	2	1	1	2	0	0	0	0	0	0	0	0	3	3	0
1984	NY	NL	1	1	0	0	1	0	0	0	0	0	0	0	0	1	1	0
1985	NY	NL	1	1	0	0	0	1	0	0	0	0	0	0	0	1	1	0
Total			292	144	148	156	93	34	9	12	0	0	0	6	1	9	207	85

Rank among batters: 72 • *Top target (5 home runs)*: Phil Niekro • *Number of pitchers victimized*: 195 • *Total ballparks homered in*: 32 • *First HR*: 06/03/1963 off Don Drysdale • *World Series HR*—1; *LCS HR*—3

Dan Stearns

DANIEL ECKFORD STEARNS
B: 10/17/1861 D: 06/28/1944
BL

Year	Tm	Lg	Tot	H	A	0	1	2	3	2	3	4	LO	XN	IP	PH	RHP	LHP
1883	BAL	AA	1	1	0	1	0	0	0	0	0	0	0	0	1	0	1	0
1884	BAL	AA	3	3	0	0	2	1	0	0	0	0	0	0	0	0	1	0
1885	BAL	AA	1	1	0	0	1	0	0	0	0	0	0	0	1	0	1	0
1889	KC	AA	3	3	0	0	2	1	0	1	0	0	0	0	0	0	3	0
Total			8	8	0	1	5	2	0	1	0	0	0	0	2	0	6	0

Rank among batters: 2,703 • *Top target (2 home runs)*: Gus Weyhing • *Number of pitchers victimized*: 7 • *Total ballparks homered in*: 2 • *First HR*: 07/13/1883 off Jack Lynch

John Stearns

JOHN HARDIN STEARNS
B: 08/21/1951
BR

Year	Tm	Lg	Tot	H	A	0	1	2	3	2	3	4	LO	XN	IP	PH	RHP	LHP
1975	NY	NL	3	1	2	2	1	0	0	0	0	0	0	0	0	0	3	0
1976	NY	NL	2	1	1	1	1	0	0	0	0	0	0	0	0	0	2	0
1977	NY	NL	12	4	8	9	0	2	1	0	0	0	0	0	0	0	9	3
1978	NY	NL	15	4	11	10	3	2	0	0	0	0	0	0	0	0	6	9
1979	NY	NL	9	3	6	5	4	0	0	0	0	0	0	0	0	0	5	4
1981	NY	NL	1	1	0	0	1	0	0	0	0	0	0	0	0	0	0	1
1982	NY	NL	4	0	4	3	1	0	0	0	0	0	0	0	0	0	4	0
Total			46	14	32	30	11	4	1	0	0	0	0	0	0	0	29	17

Rank among batters: 1,060 • *Top target (3 home runs)*: Steve Carlton • *Number of pitchers victimized*: 38 • *Total ballparks homered in*: 11 • *First HR*: 04/30/1975 off Ray Burris

John Stefero

JOHN ROBERT STEFERO
B: 09/22/1959
BL

Year	Tm	Lg	Tot	H	A	0	1	2	3	2	3	4	LO	XN	IP	PH	RHP	LHP
1986	BAL	AL	2	2	0	0	0	2	0	0	0	0	0	0	0	0	2	0

Year	Tm	Lg	Tot	H	A	Men-On 0	Men-On 1	Men-On 2	Men-On 3	One-Game 2	One-Game 3	One-Game 4	LO	XN	IP	PH	RHP	LHP

John Stefero *continued*

Year	Tm	Lg	Tot	H	A	0	1	2	3	2	3	4	LO	XN	IP	PH	RHP	LHP
1987	MON	NL	1	0	1	0	1	0	0	0	0	0	0	0	0	0	1	0
Total			3	2	1	0	1	2	0	0	0	0	0	0	0	0	3	0

Rank among batters: 3,735 • *Total ballparks homered in*: 2 • *First HR*: 04/26/1986 off Tom Henke

Dave Stegman

DAVID WILLIAM STEGMAN
B: 01/30/1954
BR

Year	Tm	Lg	Tot	H	A	0	1	2	3	2	3	4	LO	XN	IP	PH	RHP	LHP
1978	DET	AL	1	1	0	1	0	0	0	0	0	0	0	0	0	0	0	1
1979	DET	AL	3	1	2	3	0	0	0	0	0	0	0	0	0	0	0	3
1980	DET	AL	2	0	2	1	1	0	0	0	0	0	0	0	0	0	0	2
1984	CHI	AL	2	2	0	1	1	0	0	1	0	0	0	0	0	0	0	2
Total			8	4	4	6	2	0	0	1	0	0	0	0	0	0	0	8

Rank among batters: 2,703 • *Top target (2 home runs)*: Ron Guidry, Larry Gura • *Number of pitchers victimized*: 6 • *Total ballparks homered in*: 5 • *First HR*: 09/30/1978 off Mike Flanagan

Bill Stein

WILLIAM ALLEN STEIN
B: 01/21/1947
BR

Year	Tm	Lg	Tot	H	A	0	1	2	3	2	3	4	LO	XN	IP	PH	RHP	LHP
1972	STL	NL	2	0	2	2	0	0	0	0	0	0	0	0	0	0	0	2
1975	CHI	AL	3	2	1	2	0	0	1	0	0	0	0	0	0	0	2	1
1976	CHI	AL	4	3	1	0	2	2	0	0	0	0	0	0	0	0	3	1
1977	SEA	AL	13	6	7	8	3	2	0	2	0	0	0	0	0	0	6	7
1978	SEA	AL	4	3	1	2	2	0	0	0	0	0	0	0	0	0	1	3
1979	SEA	AL	7	4	3	5	0	2	0	0	0	0	0	0	0	0	1	6
1980	SEA	AL	5	2	3	1	3	1	0	0	0	0	0	0	0	0	2	3
1981	TEX	AL	2	1	1	1	0	1	0	0	0	0	0	0	0	0	1	1
1982	TEX	AL	1	1	0	1	0	0	0	0	0	0	0	0	0	1	1	0
1983	TEX	AL	2	2	0	1	1	0	0	0	0	0	0	0	0	1	2	0
1985	TEX	AL	1	0	1	1	0	0	0	0	0	0	0	0	0	0	0	1
Total			44	24	20	24	11	8	1	2	0	0	0	0	0	2	19	25

Rank among batters: 1,095 • *Top target (2 home runs)*: Pete Broberg, Catfish Hunter, Jerry Koosman • *Number of pitchers victimized*: 41 • *Total ballparks homered in*: 13 • *First HR*: 09/06/1972 off Ken Reynolds

Ed Stein

EDWARD F. STEIN
B: 09/05/1869 D: 05/10/1928
BR

Year	Tm	Lg	Tot	H	A	0	1	2	3	2	3	4	LO	XN	IP	PH	RHP	LHP
1894	BRO	NL	2	2	0	1	0	1	0	0	0	0	0	0	1	0	2	0

Rank among batters: 4,129 • *Total ballparks homered in*: 1 • *First HR*: 05/15/1894 off Charlie Petty

Terry Steinbach

TERRY LEE STEINBACH
B: 03/02/1962
BR

Year	Tm	Lg	Tot	H	A	0	1	2	3	2	3	4	LO	XN	IP	PH	RHP	LHP
1986	OAK	AL	2	0	2	1	0	1	0	0	0	0	0	0	0	1	0	2
1987	OAK	AL	16	6	10	10	4	2	0	1	0	0	0	0	0	2	11	5
1988	OAK	AL	9	6	3	5	2	1	1	0	0	0	0	0	0	0	7	2
1989	OAK	AL	7	5	2	4	2	0	1	0	0	0	0	0	0	1	4	3
1990	OAK	AL	9	3	6	4	3	1	1	0	0	0	0	0	0	0	6	3
1991	OAK	AL	6	1	5	3	1	2	0	0	0	0	0	0	0	0	4	2
1992	OAK	AL	12	3	9	8	1	3	0	0	0	0	0	0	0	0	7	5
1993	OAK	AL	10	5	5	5	2	3	0	0	0	0	0	1	0	0	4	6
1994	OAK	AL	11	5	6	6	1	3	1	1	0	0	0	0	0	0	6	5
1995	OAK	AL	15	9	6	4	7	2	2	0	0	0	0	0	0	0	10	5
Total			97	43	54	50	23	18	6	2	0	0	0	1	0	4	59	38

Rank among batters: 515 • *Top target (5 home runs)*: Chuck Finley • *Number of pitchers victimized*: 79 • *Total ballparks homered in*: 17 • *First HR*: 09/12/1986 off Greg Swindell • *Hit HR in first major league AB*—@CLE: 09/12/1986 • *World Series HR*—1; *LCS HR*—1; *All-Star HR*—1

Hank Steinbacher

HENRY JOHN STEINBACHER
B: 03/22/1913 D: 04/03/1977
BL

Year	Tm	Lg	Tot	H	A	0	1	2	3	2	3	4	LO	XN	IP	PH	RHP	LHP
1937	CHI	AL	1	1	0	0	1	0	0	0	0	0	0	0	0	0	1	0

Year	Tm	Lg	Tot	H	A	Men-On 0	1	2	3	One-Game 2	3	4	LO	XN	IP	PH	RHP	LHP

Hank Steinbacher *continued*

Year	Tm	Lg	Tot	H	A	Men-On 0	1	2	3	One-Game 2	3	4	LO	XN	IP	PH	RHP	LHP
1938	CHI	AL	4	2	2	1	2	1	0	0	0	0	0	0	1	0	2	2
1939	CHI	AL	1	0	1	0	1	0	0	0	0	0	0	0	0	0	1	0
Total			6	3	3	1	4	1	0	0	0	0	0	0	1	0	4	2

Rank among batters: 2,988 • *Total ballparks homered in*: 3 • *First HR*: 05/08/1937 off Wes Ferrell

Benjamin Steiner

BENJAMIN SAUNDERS STEINER
B: 07/28/1921 D: 10/27/1988
BL

Year	Tm	Lg	Tot	H	A	Men-On 0	1	2	3	One-Game 2	3	4	LO	XN	IP	PH	RHP	LHP
1945	BOS	AL	3	1	2	2	1	0	0	0	0	0	0	0	0	0	3	0

Rank among batters: 3,735 • *Total ballparks homered in*: 3 • *First HR*: 04/17/1945 off Atley Donald

Harry Steinfeldt

HARRY M. STEINFELDT
B: 09/29/1877 D: 08/17/1914
BR

Year	Tm	Lg	Tot	H	A	Men-On 0	1	2	3	One-Game 2	3	4	LO	XN	IP	PH	RHP	LHP
1900	CIN	NL	2	0	2	1	1	0	0	1	0	0	0	0	0	0	2	0
1901	CIN	NL	6	4	2	5	1	0	0	0	0	0	0	0	4	0	6	0
1902	CIN	NL	1	1	0	0	1	0	0	0	0	0	0	0	0	0	1	0
1903	CIN	NL	6	1	5	3	0	3	0	0	0	0	0	1	3	0	6	0
1904	CIN	NL	1	1	0	0	1	0	0	0	0	0	0	0	0	0	1	0
1905	CIN	NL	1	0	1	0	1	0	0	0	0	0	0	0	0	0	0	1
1906	CHI	NL	3	0	3	2	1	0	0	0	0	0	0	0	0	0	1	2
1907	CHI	NL	1	1	0	0	1	0	0	0	0	0	0	0	0	0	1	0
1908	CHI	NL	1	0	1	0	1	0	0	0	0	0	0	0	0	0	1	0
1909	CHI	NL	2	1	1	1	0	1	0	0	0	0	0	0	1	0	2	0
1910	CHI	NL	2	1	1	2	0	0	0	0	0	0	0	0	0	0	1	1
1911	BOS	NL	1	1	0	1	0	0	0	0	0	0	0	0	0	0	0	1
Total			27	11	16	15	8	4	0	1	0	0	0	1	8	0	22	5

Rank among batters: 1,532 • *Top target (3 home runs)*: Jack Harper • *Number of pitchers victimized*: 21 • *Total ballparks homered in*: 6 • *First HR*: 07/31/1900 off Nig Cuppy

Rick Stelmaszek

RICHARD FRANCIS STELMASZEK
B: 10/08/1948
BL

Year	Tm	Lg	Tot	H	A	Men-On 0	1	2	3	One-Game 2	3	4	LO	XN	IP	PH	RHP	LHP
1974	CHI	NL	1	1	0	0	1	0	0	0	0	0	0	0	0	0	1	0

Rank among batters: 4,707 • *Total ballparks homered in*: 1 • *First HR*: 08/20/1974 off Don Sutton

Bill Stemmeyer

WILLIAM STEMMEYER
B: 05/06/1865 D: 05/03/1945
BR

Year	Tm	Lg	Tot	H	A	Men-On 0	1	2	3	One-Game 2	3	4	LO	XN	IP	PH	RHP	LHP
1887	BOS	NL	1	1	0	0	0	1	0	0	0	0	0	0	0	0	1	0

Rank among batters: 4,707 • *Total ballparks homered in*: 1 • *First HR*: 05/20/1887 off Henry Boyle

Casey Stengel

CHARLES DILLON STENGEL
B: 07/30/1890 D: 09/29/1975
BL HOF

Year	Tm	Lg	Tot	H	A	Men-On 0	1	2	3	One-Game 2	3	4	LO	XN	IP	PH	RHP	LHP
1912	BRO	NL	1	1	0	1	0	0	0	0	0	0	0	0	0	0	1	0
1913	BRO	NL	7	4	3	5	2	0	0	1	0	0	1	0	3	0	4	3
1914	BRO	NL	4	2	2	3	0	1	0	0	0	0	0	0	3	0	3	1
1915	BRO	NL	3	1	2	1	1	1	0	0	0	0	0	0	1	0	3	0
1916	BRO	NL	8	4	4	3	3	2	0	0	0	0	0	0	3	0	6	2
1917	BRO	NL	6	5	1	4	1	1	0	0	0	0	0	1	3	0	5	1
1918	PIT	NL	1	1	0	1	0	0	0	0	0	0	0	0	1	0	1	0
1919	PIT	NL	4	2	2	2	1	1	0	0	0	0	0	0	2	0	4	0
1920	PHI	NL	9	7	2	6	3	0	0	1	0	0	0	0	1	0	9	0
1922	NY	NL	7	7	0	5	1	1	0	0	0	0	0	1	0	0	7	0
1923	NY	NL	5	4	1	3	1	1	0	0	0	0	0	0	0	0	5	0
1924	BOS	NL	5	1	4	3	1	1	0	0	0	0	0	1	0	0	5	0
Total			60	39	21	37	14	9	0	2	0	0	1	3	17	0	53	7

Year	Tm	Lg	Tot	H	A	Men-On 0	Men-On 1	Men-On 2	Men-On 3	One-Game 2	One-Game 3	One-Game 4	LO	XN	IP	PH	RHP	LHP

Casey Stengel *continued*

Rank among batters: 863 • Top target (2 home runs): Otto Hess, Rube Geyer, Pete Schneider, Lee Meadows, Dana Fillingim, George Smith, Fred Toney • *Number of pitchers victimized*: 53 • *Total ballparks homered in*: 10 • *First HR*: 09/21/1912 off Rube Geyer • *World Series HR*—2

Mike Stenhouse

MICHAEL STEVEN STENHOUSE
B: 05/29/1958
BL

Year	Tm	Lg	Tot	H	A	0	1	2	3	2	3	4	LO	XN	IP	PH	RHP	LHP
1984	MON	NL	4	4	0	2	2	0	0	0	0	0	0	0	0	0	4	0
1985	MIN	AL	5	2	3	1	4	0	0	0	0	0	0	0	0	0	5	0
Total			9	6	3	3	6	0	0	0	0	0	0	0	0	0	9	0

Rank among batters: 2,587 • *Total ballparks homered in*: 5 • *First HR*: 05/23/1984 off Andy Hawkins

Rennie Stennett

RENALDO ANTONIO (PORTE) STENNETT
B: 04/05/1951
BR

Year	Tm	Lg	Tot	H	A	0	1	2	3	2	3	4	LO	XN	IP	PH	RHP	LHP
1971	PIT	NL	1	1	0	0	1	0	0	0	0	0	0	0	0	0	1	0
1972	PIT	NL	3	2	1	2	1	0	0	0	0	0	1	0	1	0	1	2
1973	PIT	NL	10	4	6	7	3	0	0	1	0	0	1	1	0	0	2	8
1974	PIT	NL	7	5	2	5	1	1	0	0	0	0	1	0	0	0	3	4
1975	PIT	NL	7	3	4	5	0	2	0	0	0	0	0	0	1	0	3	4
1976	PIT	NL	2	1	1	2	0	0	0	0	0	0	0	0	0	0	2	0
1977	PIT	NL	5	4	1	3	2	0	0	0	0	0	0	0	1	0	3	2
1978	PIT	NL	3	1	2	1	1	0	1	0	0	0	0	0	0	0	2	1
1980	SF	NL	2	0	2	1	0	1	0	0	0	0	0	0	0	0	1	1
1981	SF	NL	1	1	0	1	0	0	0	0	0	0	0	0	0	0	0	1
Total			41	22	19	27	9	4	1	1	0	0	3	1	3	0	18	23

Rank among batters: 1,163 • *Top target (3 home runs)*: Pete Falcone • *Number of pitchers victimized*: 33 • *Total ballparks homered in*: 9 • *First HR*: 09/05/1971 off Bill Stoneman

Jake Stenzel

JACOB CHARLES STENZEL
B: 06/24/1867 D: 01/06/1919
BR

Year	Tm	Lg	Tot	H	A	0	1	2	3	2	3	4	LO	XN	IP	PH	RHP	LHP
1893	PIT	NL	4	4	0	3	0	1	0	0	0	0	0	0	2	0	3	0
1894	PIT	NL	13	5	8	5	5	3	0	2	0	0	0	0	0	0	8	5
1895	PIT	NL	7	4	3	4	2	1	0	0	0	0	0	0	1	0	4	2
1896	PIT	NL	2	0	2	0	0	1	1	0	0	0	0	0	1	0	1	1
1897	BAL	NL	4	1	3	2	2	0	0	0	0	0	0	0	1	0	4	0
1898	STL	NL	1	0	1	1	0	0	0	0	0	0	0	0	0	0	0	1
1899	STL	NL	1	1	0	0	1	0	0	0	0	0	0	0	0	0	1	0
Total			32	15	17	15	10	6	1	2	0	0	0	0	5	0	21	9

Rank among batters: 1,360 • *Top target (3 home runs)*: Kid Nichols, Brickyard Kennedy • *Number of pitchers victimized*: 26 • *Total ballparks homered in*: 9 • *First HR*: 07/11/1893 off George Davies • *2 HR in 1 inning*—@BOS: 06/06/1894

Gene Stephens

GLEN EUGENE STEPHENS
B: 01/20/1933
BL

Year	Tm	Lg	Tot	H	A	0	1	2	3	2	3	4	LO	XN	IP	PH	RHP	LHP
1953	BOS	AL	3	0	3	3	0	0	0	0	0	0	0	0	0	0	3	0
1955	BOS	AL	3	2	1	1	0	2	0	0	0	0	0	0	0	0	3	0
1956	BOS	AL	1	1	0	1	0	0	0	0	0	0	0	0	1	1	1	0
1957	BOS	AL	3	2	1	3	0	0	0	0	0	0	0	0	0	0	2	1
1958	BOS	AL	9	5	4	5	4	0	0	0	0	0	1	1	0	1	9	0
1959	BOS	AL	3	3	0	1	1	0	1	0	0	0	0	0	0	0	3	0
1960	BOS	AL	2	0	2	1	1	0	0	0	0	0	0	0	0	0	2	0
	BAL	AL	5	3	2	3	1	1	0	0	0	0	0	0	0	1	5	0
	Total		7	3	4	4	2	1	0	0	0	0	0	0	0	1	7	0
1961	KC	AL	4	2	2	1	3	0	0	0	0	0	0	0	0	0	4	0
1963	CHI	AL	1	1	0	1	0	0	0	0	0	0	0	0	0	0	1	0
1964	CHI	AL	3	0	3	2	1	0	0	0	0	0	0	0	0	0	3	0
Total			37	19	18	22	11	3	1	0	0	0	1	1	1	3	36	1

Rank among batters: 1,252 • *Top target (3 home runs)*: Frank Lary • *Number of pitchers victimized*: 31 • *Total ballparks homered in*: 10 • *First HR*: 05/24/1953 off Johnny Sain

Jim Stephens

JAMES WALTER STEPHENS
B: 12/10/1883 D: 01/02/1965
BR

Year	Tm	Lg	Tot	H	A	Men-On 0	Men-On 1	Men-On 2	Men-On 3	One-Game 2	One-Game 3	One-Game 4	LO	XN	IP	PH	RHP	LHP
1909	STL	AL	3	2	1	0	2	1	0	0	0	0	0	0	2	0	3	0

Rank among batters: 3,735 • *Total ballparks homered in*: 2 • *First HR*: 04/16/1909 off Heinie Berger

Ray Stephens

CARL RAY STEPHENS
B: 09/22/1962
BR

Year	Tm	Lg	Tot	H	A	Men-On 0	Men-On 1	Men-On 2	Men-On 3	One-Game 2	One-Game 3	One-Game 4	LO	XN	IP	PH	RHP	LHP
1990	STL	NL	1	1	0	1	0	0	0	0	0	0	0	0	0	0	0	1

Rank among batters: 4,707 • *Total ballparks homered in*: 1 • *First HR*: 09/20/1990 off Terry Mulholland

Vern Stephens

VERNON DECATUR STEPHENS
B: 10/23/1920 D: 11/03/1968
BR

Year	Tm	Lg	Tot	H	A	Men-On 0	Men-On 1	Men-On 2	Men-On 3	One-Game 2	One-Game 3	One-Game 4	LO	XN	IP	PH	RHP	LHP
1942	STL	AL	14	8	6	7	4	3	0	0	0	0	0	0	0	0	10	4
1943	STL	AL	22	13	9	11	8	3	0	5	0	0	0	2	0	0	20	2
1944	STL	AL	20	9	11	10	7	1	2	1	0	0	0	0	0	0	16	4
1945	STL	AL	24	13	11	12	10	1	1	1	0	0	0	0	0	0	15	9
1946	STL	AL	14	6	8	7	6	0	1	0	0	0	0	0	0	0	10	4
1947	STL	AL	15	11	4	7	4	3	1	1	0	0	0	0	1	0	13	2
1948	BOS	AL	29	16	13	11	10	7	1	2	0	0	0	1	0	0	25	4
1949	BOS	AL	39	21	18	16	16	5	2	4	0	0	0	2	0	0	30	9
1950	BOS	AL	30	17	13	10	11	7	2	3	0	0	0	1	0	0	21	9
1951	BOS	AL	17	12	5	7	8	2	0	3	0	0	0	1	0	0	10	7
1952	BOS	AL	7	4	3	3	1	3	0	1	0	0	0	0	0	0	5	2
1953	CHI	AL	1	0	1	1	0	0	0	0	0	0	0	0	0	0	1	0
	STL	AL	4	2	2	2	1	1	0	0	0	0	0	0	0	0	3	1
	Total		5	2	3	3	1	1	0	0	0	0	0	0	0	0	4	1
1954	BAL	AL	8	5	3	7	1	0	0	0	0	0	0	0	1	0	5	3
1955	CHI	AL	3	0	3	2	0	1	0	1	0	0	0	0	0	1	3	0
Total			247	137	110	113	87	37	10	22	0	0	0	7	2	1	187	60

Rank among batters: 115 • *Top target (7 home runs)*: Fred Hutchinson, Dizzy Trout • *Number of pitchers victimized*: 122 • *Total ballparks homered in*: 10 • *First HR*: 04/15/1942 off Buck Ross

John Stephenson

JOHN HERMAN STEPHENSON
B: 04/13/1941
BL

Year	Tm	Lg	Tot	H	A	Men-On 0	Men-On 1	Men-On 2	Men-On 3	One-Game 2	One-Game 3	One-Game 4	LO	XN	IP	PH	RHP	LHP
1964	NY	NL	1	0	1	1	0	0	0	0	0	0	1	0	0	0	1	0
1965	NY	NL	4	2	2	1	2	1	0	1	0	0	0	0	0	0	3	1
1966	NY	NL	1	1	0	0	1	0	0	0	0	0	0	0	0	1	1	0
1971	CAL	AL	3	3	0	2	0	1	0	0	0	0	0	0	0	0	3	0
1972	CAL	AL	2	1	1	1	1	0	0	0	0	0	0	0	0	1	2	0
1973	CAL	AL	1	0	1	1	0	0	0	0	0	0	0	0	0	0	1	0
Total			12	7	5	6	4	2	0	1	0	0	1	0	0	2	11	1

Rank among batters: 2,325 • *Total ballparks homered in*: 6 • *First HR*: 06/29/1964 off Bobby Bolin

Phil Stephenson

PHILLIP RAYMOND STEPHENSON
B: 09/19/1960
BL

Year	Tm	Lg	Tot	H	A	Men-On 0	Men-On 1	Men-On 2	Men-On 3	One-Game 2	One-Game 3	One-Game 4	LO	XN	IP	PH	RHP	LHP
1989	SD	NL	2	2	0	2	0	0	0	0	0	0	0	0	0	0	2	0
1990	SD	NL	4	2	2	3	1	0	0	0	0	0	0	0	0	0	4	0
Total			6	4	2	5	1	0	0	0	0	0	0	0	0	0	6	0

Rank among batters: 2,988 • *Total ballparks homered in*: 3 • *First HR*: 09/30/1989 off Rick Reuschel

Riggs Stephenson

JACKSON RIGGS STEPHENSON
B: 01/05/1898 D: 11/15/1985
BR

Year	Tm	Lg	Tot	H	A	Men-On 0	Men-On 1	Men-On 2	Men-On 3	One-Game 2	One-Game 3	One-Game 4	LO	XN	IP	PH	RHP	LHP
1921	CLE	AL	2	1	1	0	2	0	0	0	0	0	0	0	1	0	1	1

Riggs Stephenson *continued*

Year	Tm	Lg	Tot	H	A	Men-On 0	Men-On 1	Men-On 2	Men-On 3	One-Game 2	One-Game 3	One-Game 4	LO	XN	IP	PH	RHP	LHP
1922	CLE	AL	2	0	2	0	1	1	0	0	0	0	0	0	0	0	2	0
1923	CLE	AL	5	1	4	2	2	1	0	0	0	0	0	0	0	0	4	1
1924	CLE	AL	4	0	4	1	1	2	0	1	0	0	0	0	0	0	2	2
1925	CLE	AL	1	0	1	1	0	0	0	0	0	0	0	0	0	0	0	1
1926	CHI	NL	3	0	3	2	1	0	0	1	0	0	0	0	0	0	2	1
1927	CHI	NL	7	3	4	3	1	3	0	0	0	0	0	0	0	0	7	0
1928	CHI	NL	8	3	5	4	3	0	1	0	0	0	0	0	0	0	7	1
1929	CHI	NL	17	7	10	7	5	4	1	1	0	0	0	0	0	0	13	4
1930	CHI	NL	5	2	3	4	1	0	0	0	0	0	0	0	0	0	3	2
1931	CHI	NL	1	0	1	1	0	0	0	0	0	0	0	0	0	0	0	1
1932	CHI	NL	4	3	1	2	1	1	0	0	0	0	0	0	0	0	4	0
1933	CHI	NL	4	2	2	2	1	1	0	0	0	0	0	0	0	0	3	1
Total			63	22	41	29	19	13	2	3	0	0	0	0	1	0	48	15

Rank among batters: 826 • *Top target (3 home runs)*: Larry Benton, Jesse Haines • *Number of pitchers victimized*: 56 • *Total ballparks homered in*: 13 • *First HR*: 05/20/1921 off Rollie Naylor

Dutch Sterrett

CHARLES HURLBUT STERRETT
B: 10/01/1889 D: 12/08/1965
BR

Year	Tm	Lg	Tot	H	A	Men-On 0	Men-On 1	Men-On 2	Men-On 3	One-Game 2	One-Game 3	One-Game 4	LO	XN	IP	PH	RHP	LHP
1912	NY	AL	1	0	1	0	0	1	0	0	0	0	0	0	1	0	0	1

Rank among batters: 4,707 • *Total ballparks homered in*: 1 • *First HR*: 06/28/1912 off Ray Collins

Chuck Stevens

CHARLES AUGUSTUS STEVENS
B: 07/20/1918
BB

Year	Tm	Lg	Tot	H	A	Men-On 0	Men-On 1	Men-On 2	Men-On 3	One-Game 2	One-Game 3	One-Game 4	LO	XN	IP	PH	RHP	LHP
1946	STL	AL	3	2	1	2	1	0	0	0	0	0	1	0	0	0	3	0
1948	STL	AL	1	1	0	0	1	0	0	0	0	0	0	0	0	0	1	0
Total			4	3	1	2	2	0	0	0	0	0	1	0	0	0	4	0

Rank among batters: 3,427 • *Total ballparks homered in*: 2 • *First HR*: 05/09/1946 off Al Gettel

Ed Stevens

EDWARD LEE STEVENS
B: 01/12/1925
BL

Year	Tm	Lg	Tot	H	A	Men-On 0	Men-On 1	Men-On 2	Men-On 3	One-Game 2	One-Game 3	One-Game 4	LO	XN	IP	PH	RHP	LHP
1945	BRO	NL	4	2	2	3	1	0	0	0	0	0	0	0	1	0	2	2
1946	BRO	NL	10	3	7	6	3	1	0	0	0	0	0	0	0	0	10	0
1948	PIT	NL	10	4	6	6	3	1	0	0	0	0	0	0	0	3	9	1
1949	PIT	NL	4	3	1	4	0	0	0	0	0	0	0	0	0	0	3	1
Total			28	12	16	19	7	2	0	0	0	0	0	0	1	3	24	4

Rank among batters: 1,500 • *Top target (2 home runs)*: Bill Voiselle, Ray Poat, Larry Jansen • *Number of pitchers victimized*: 25 • *Total ballparks homered in*: 7 • *First HR*: 08/19/1945 off Fritz Ostermueller

Lee Stevens

DEWAIN LEE STEVENS
B: 07/10/1967
BL

Year	Tm	Lg	Tot	H	A	Men-On 0	Men-On 1	Men-On 2	Men-On 3	One-Game 2	One-Game 3	One-Game 4	LO	XN	IP	PH	RHP	LHP
1990	CAL	AL	7	4	3	3	2	2	0	0	0	0	0	0	0	0	6	1
1992	CAL	AL	7	2	5	4	2	0	1	0	0	0	0	0	0	0	7	0
Total			14	6	8	7	4	2	1	0	0	0	0	0	0	0	13	1

Rank among batters: 2,169 • *Top target (2 home runs)*: Rick Sutcliffe • *Number of pitchers victimized*: 13 • *Total ballparks homered in*: 8 • *First HR*: 07/20/1990 off Bud Black

R. C. Stevens

R. C. STEVENS
B: 07/22/1934
BR

Year	Tm	Lg	Tot	H	A	Men-On 0	Men-On 1	Men-On 2	Men-On 3	One-Game 2	One-Game 3	One-Game 4	LO	XN	IP	PH	RHP	LHP
1958	PIT	NL	7	2	5	4	2	1	0	0	0	0	0	0	0	1	4	3
1959	PIT	NL	1	0	1	1	0	0	0	0	0	0	0	0	0	0	1	0
Total			8	2	6	5	2	1	0	0	0	0	0	0	0	1	5	3

Rank among batters: 2,703 • *Top target (2 home runs)*: Willard Schmidt • *Number of pitchers victimized*: 7 • *Total ballparks homered in*: 6 • *First HR*: 04/19/1958 off Harvey Haddix

Todd Steverson

TODD ANTHONY STEVERSON
B: 11/15/1971
BR

Year	Tm	Lg	Tot	H	A	Men-On 0	1	2	3	One-Game 2	3	4	LO	XN	IP	PH	RHP	LHP
1995	DET	AL	2	0	2	2	0	0	0	0	0	0	0	0	0	0	1	1

Rank among batters: 4,129 • *Total ballparks homered in*: 1 • *First HR*: 06/10/1995 off Eddie Guardado

Ace Stewart

ASA STEWART
B: 02/14/1869 D: 04/17/1912
BR

Year	Tm	Lg	Tot	H	A	Men-On 0	1	2	3	One-Game 2	3	4	LO	XN	IP	PH	RHP	LHP
1895	CHI	NL	8	5	3	3	0	4	1	0	0	0	0	0	2	0	7	1

Rank among batters: 2,703 • *Total ballparks homered in*: 3 • *First HR*: 04/18/1895 off Ted Breitenstein

Bud Stewart

EDWARD PERRY STEWART
B: 06/15/1916
BL

Year	Tm	Lg	Tot	H	A	Men-On 0	1	2	3	One-Game 2	3	4	LO	XN	IP	PH	RHP	LHP
1948	WAS	AL	7	3	4	3	3	1	0	0	0	0	0	0	1	0	5	2
1949	WAS	AL	8	3	5	7	1	0	0	0	0	0	0	0	1	0	8	0
1950	WAS	AL	4	1	3	3	1	0	0	0	0	0	0	0	1	0	4	0
1951	CHI	AL	6	0	6	4	0	1	1	0	0	0	0	1	0	0	6	0
1952	CHI	AL	5	1	4	2	3	0	0	0	0	0	0	0	0	2	5	0
1953	CHI	AL	2	1	1	0	2	0	0	0	0	0	0	0	0	2	2	0
Total			32	9	23	19	10	2	1	0	0	0	0	1	3	4	30	2

Rank among batters: 1,360 • *Top target (3 home runs)*: Vic Raschi • *Number of pitchers victimized*: 28 • *Total ballparks homered in*: 8 • *First HR*: 05/30/1948 off Denny Galehouse

Glen Stewart

GLEN WELDON STEWART
B: 09/29/1912
BR

Year	Tm	Lg	Tot	H	A	Men-On 0	1	2	3	One-Game 2	3	4	LO	XN	IP	PH	RHP	LHP
1943	PHI	NL	2	0	2	1	0	1	0	1	0	0	0	0	0	0	2	0

Rank among batters: 4,129 • *Total ballparks homered in*: 1 • *First HR*: 08/07/1943 off Johnnie Wittig

Jimmy Stewart

JAMES FRANKLIN STEWART
B: 06/11/1939
BB

Year	Tm	Lg	Tot	H	A	Men-On 0	1	2	3	One-Game 2	3	4	LO	XN	IP	PH	RHP	LHP
1964	CHI	NL	3	2	1	2	1	0	0	0	0	0	2	0	0	0	1	2
1969	CIN	NL	4	3	1	0	2	2	0	1	0	0	0	0	0	1	4	0
1970	CIN	NL	1	0	1	0	0	1	0	0	0	0	0	0	0	1	1	0
Total			8	5	3	2	3	3	0	1	0	0	2	0	0	2	6	2

Rank among batters: 2,703 • *Top target (2 home runs)*: Pat Jarvis • *Number of pitchers victimized*: 7 • *Total ballparks homered in*: 5 • *First HR*: 04/21/1964 off Vern Law

Stuffy Stewart

JOHN FRANKLIN STEWART
B: 01/31/1894 D: 09/30/1980
BR

Year	Tm	Lg	Tot	H	A	Men-On 0	1	2	3	One-Game 2	3	4	LO	XN	IP	PH	RHP	LHP
1923	BRO	NL	1	0	1	1	0	0	0	0	0	0	0	0	0	0	1	0

Rank among batters: 4,707 • *Total ballparks homered in*: 1 • *First HR*: 05/01/1923 off Fred Johnson

Royle Stillman

ROYLE ELDON STILLMAN
B: 01/02/1951
BL

Year	Tm	Lg	Tot	H	A	Men-On 0	1	2	3	One-Game 2	3	4	LO	XN	IP	PH	RHP	LHP
1977	CHI	AL	3	1	2	1	2	0	0	0	0	0	0	0	0	0	3	0

Rank among batters: 3,735 • *Total ballparks homered in*: 3 • *First HR*: 04/24/1977 off Mike Torrez

Kurt Stillwell

KURT ANDREW STILLWELL
B: 06/04/1965
BB

Year	Tm	Lg	Tot	H	A	Men-On 0	1	2	3	One-Game 2	3	4	LO	XN	IP	PH	RHP	LHP
1987	CIN	NL	4	3	1	1	2	0	1	0	0	0	0	0	0	0	4	0

Kurt Stillwell *continued*

Year	Tm	Lg	Tot	H	A	Men-On 0	1	2	3	One-Game 2	3	4	LO	XN	IP	PH	RHP	LHP
1988	KC	AL	10	4	6	5	3	2	0	0	0	0	0	0	1	0	8	2
1989	KC	AL	7	2	5	4	3	0	0	1	0	0	2	0	0	0	6	1
1990	KC	AL	3	3	0	1	1	1	0	0	0	0	0	0	1	0	3	0
1991	KC	AL	6	1	5	2	2	1	1	0	0	0	0	0	0	1	5	1
1992	SD	NL	2	1	1	1	1	0	0	0	0	0	0	0	0	0	1	1
1993	SD	NL	1	1	0	1	0	0	0	0	0	0	0	0	0	0	1	0
Total			33	15	18	15	12	4	2	1	0	0	2	0	2	1	28	5

Rank among batters: 1,336 • *Top target (2 home runs)*: Charlie Hough • *Number of pitchers victimized*: 32 • *Total ballparks homered in*: 13 • *First HR*: 04/17/1987 off Aurelio Lopez

Kelly Stinnett

KELLY LEE STINNETT
B: 02/14/1970
BR

Year	Tm	Lg	Tot	H	A	Men-On 0	1	2	3	One-Game 2	3	4	LO	XN	IP	PH	RHP	LHP
1994	NY	NL	2	0	2	1	1	0	0	0	0	0	0	0	0	0	0	2
1995	NY	NL	4	1	3	3	1	0	0	0	0	0	0	0	0	0	1	3
Total			6	1	5	4	2	0	0	0	0	0	0	0	0	0	1	5

Rank among batters: 2,988 • *Total ballparks homered in*: 6 • *First HR*: 05/05/1994 off Allen Watson

Bob Stinson

GORRELL ROBERT STINSON
B: 10/11/1945
BB

Year	Tm	Lg	Tot	H	A	Men-On 0	1	2	3	One-Game 2	3	4	LO	XN	IP	PH	RHP	LHP
1973	MON	NL	3	2	1	3	0	0	0	0	0	0	0	0	0	0	2	1
1974	MON	NL	1	1	0	0	0	1	0	0	0	0	0	0	0	1	1	0
1975	KC	AL	1	0	1	1	0	0	0	0	0	0	0	0	0	0	1	0
1976	KC	AL	2	0	2	0	0	2	0	0	0	0	0	0	0	0	1	1
1977	SEA	AL	8	2	6	4	4	0	0	0	0	0	0	0	0	0	8	0
1978	SEA	AL	11	7	4	2	4	3	2	1	0	0	0	0	0	0	8	3
1979	SEA	AL	6	4	2	4	2	0	0	0	0	0	0	0	0	1	6	0
1980	SEA	AL	1	1	0	0	0	1	0	0	0	0	0	0	0	0	1	0
Total			33	17	16	14	10	7	2	1	0	0	0	0	0	2	28	5

Rank among batters: 1,336 • *Top target (3 home runs)*: Rick Wise • *Number of pitchers victimized*: 29 • *Total ballparks homered in*: 13 • *First HR*: 07/19/1973 off Ross Grimsley

Snuffy Stirnweiss

GEORGE HENRY STIRNWEISS
B: 10/26/1918 D: 09/15/1958
BR

Year	Tm	Lg	Tot	H	A	Men-On 0	1	2	3	One-Game 2	3	4	LO	XN	IP	PH	RHP	LHP
1943	NY	AL	1	0	1	0	1	0	0	0	0	0	0	0	0	0	1	0
1944	NY	AL	8	3	5	5	2	1	0	0	0	0	2	0	2	0	7	1
1945	NY	AL	10	7	3	8	2	0	0	0	0	0	3	0	0	0	7	3
1947	NY	AL	5	3	2	4	0	1	0	1	0	0	1	1	0	0	5	0
1948	NY	AL	3	2	1	2	1	0	0	0	0	0	0	0	0	0	2	1
1950	STL	AL	1	1	0	1	0	0	0	0	0	0	0	0	0	0	0	1
1951	CLE	AL	1	0	1	1	0	0	0	0	0	0	0	0	0	0	0	1
Total			29	16	13	21	6	2	0	1	0	0	6	1	2	0	22	7

Rank among batters: 1,465 • Top target (2 home runs): Jesse Flores, Al Benton, Walt Masterson, Eddie Lopat • *Number of pitchers victimized*: 25 • *Total ballparks homered in*: 7 • *First HR*: 08/25/1943 off Dizzy Trout

Jack Stivetts

JOHN ELMER STIVETTS
B: 03/31/1868 D: 04/18/1930
BR

Year	Tm	Lg	Tot	H	A	Men-On 0	1	2	3	One-Game 2	3	4	LO	XN	IP	PH	RHP	LHP
1890	STL	AA	7	6	1	2	3	1	1	1	0	0	0	0	0	0	7	0
1891	STL	AA	7	7	0	3	3	1	0	1	0	0	0	0	0	0	7	0
1892	BOS	NL	3	0	3	0	2	1	0	0	0	0	0	1	0	0	3	0
1893	BOS	NL	3	3	0	2	0	1	0	0	0	0	0	0	0	0	1	1
1894	BOS	NL	8	2	6	2	5	1	0	0	0	0	0	0	0	1	5	2
1896	BOS	NL	3	3	0	1	2	0	0	1	0	0	0	0	0	0	3	0
1897	BOS	NL	2	1	1	1	1	0	0	0	0	0	0	0	0	1	2	0
1898	BOS	NL	2	2	0	1	1	0	0	0	0	0	0	0	0	1	1	1
Total			35	24	11	12	17	5	1	3	0	0	0	1	0	3	29	3

Rank among batters: 1,291 • *Top target (3 home runs)*: Hank Gastright, Gus Weyhing, Chauncey Fisher • *Number of pitchers victimized*: 26 • *Total ballparks homered in*: 11 • *First HR*: 04/27/1890 off Hank Gastright

Year	Tm	Lg	Tot	H	A	Men-On				One-Game			LO	XN	IP	PH	RHP	LHP
						0	1	2	3	2	3	4						

Milt Stock

MILTON JOSEPH STOCK
B: 07/11/1893 D: 07/16/1977
BR

Year	Tm	Lg	Tot	H	A	0	1	2	3	2	3	4	LO	XN	IP	PH	RHP	LHP
1914	NY	NL	3	2	1	2	1	0	0	0	0	0	0	0	0	0	1	2
1915	PHI	NL	1	0	1	0	1	0	0	0	0	0	0	0	1	0	1	0
1916	PHI	NL	1	1	0	1	0	0	0	0	0	0	0	0	0	0	1	0
1917	PHI	NL	3	1	2	2	0	1	0	0	0	0	0	0	0	0	1	2
1918	PHI	NL	1	1	0	0	1	0	0	0	0	0	0	0	0	0	1	0
1921	STL	NL	3	0	3	2	1	0	0	0	0	0	0	0	1	0	2	1
1922	STL	NL	5	1	4	2	1	2	0	1	0	0	0	0	3	0	5	0
1923	STL	NL	2	0	2	2	0	0	0	0	0	0	0	0	0	0	2	0
1924	BRO	NL	2	0	2	1	0	1	0	0	0	0	0	0	0	0	1	1
1925	BRO	NL	1	0	1	0	0	1	0	0	0	0	0	0	0	0	1	0
Total			22	6	16	12	5	5	0	1	0	0	0	0	5	0	16	6

Rank among batters: 1,719 • *Top target (2 home runs)*: Rube Marquard, Jess Barnes • *Number of pitchers victimized*: 20 • *Total ballparks homered in*: 7 • *First HR*: 04/21/1914 off Frank Allen

Kevin Stocker

KEVIN DOUGLAS STOCKER
B: 02/13/1970
BB

Year	Tm	Lg	Tot	H	A	0	1	2	3	2	3	4	LO	XN	IP	PH	RHP	LHP
1993	PHI	NL	2	1	1	1	0	1	0	0	0	0	0	0	0	0	2	0
1994	PHI	NL	2	2	0	2	0	0	0	0	0	0	0	0	0	0	1	1
1995	PHI	NL	1	1	0	1	0	0	0	0	0	0	0	0	0	0	1	0
Total			5	4	1	4	0	1	0	0	0	0	0	0	0	0	4	1

Rank among batters: 3,191 • *Total ballparks homered in*: 2 • *First HR*: 07/08/1993 off Rod Beck

Tim Stoddard

TIMOTHY PAUL STODDARD
B: 01/24/1953
BR

Year	Tm	Lg	Tot	H	A	0	1	2	3	2	3	4	LO	XN	IP	PH	RHP	LHP
1986	SD	NL	1	1	0	1	0	0	0	0	0	0	0	0	0	0	1	0

Rank among batters: 4,707 • *Total ballparks homered in*: 1 • *First HR*: 06/18/1986 off Mike LaCoss

Darragh Stone

DARRAGH DEAN STONE
B: 09/01/1930
BL

Year	Tm	Lg	Tot	H	A	0	1	2	3	2	3	4	LO	XN	IP	PH	RHP	LHP
1954	WAS	AL	1	1	0	0	0	1	0	0	0	0	0	0	0	0	1	0

Rank among batters: 4,707 • *Total ballparks homered in*: 1 • *First HR*: 09/17/1954 off Frank Sullivan

Dwight Stone

DWIGHT ELY STONE
B: 08/02/1886 D: 06/03/1976
BR

Year	Tm	Lg	Tot	H	A	0	1	2	3	2	3	4	LO	XN	IP	PH	RHP	LHP
1914	KC	FL	1	0	1	0	0	1	0	0	0	0	0	0	0	0	1	0

Rank among batters: 4,707 • *Total ballparks homered in*: 1 • *First HR*: 07/24/1914 off Russ Ford

George Stone

GEORGE ROBERT STONE
B: 09/03/1877 D: 01/03/1945
BL

Year	Tm	Lg	Tot	H	A	0	1	2	3	2	3	4	LO	XN	IP	PH	RHP	LHP
1905	STL	AL	7	1	6	2	4	1	0	0	0	0	0	0	5	0	5	2
1906	STL	AL	6	3	3	3	2	1	0	0	0	0	0	0	5	0	2	4
1907	STL	AL	4	3	1	1	1	2	0	0	0	0	0	0	4	0	4	0
1908	STL	AL	5	3	2	4	1	0	0	0	0	0	2	0	4	0	5	0
1909	STL	AL	1	0	1	1	0	0	0	0	0	0	1	0	0	0	1	0
Total			23	10	13	11	8	4	0	0	0	0	3	0	18	0	17	6

Rank among batters: 1,686 • *Top target (2 home runs)*: Jack Powell, Doc Newton, Judd Doyle • *Number of pitchers victimized*: 20 • *Total ballparks homered in*: 6 • *First HR*: 06/10/1905 off Jack Powell

George Stone

GEORGE HEARD STONE
B: 07/09/1946
BL

Year	Tm	Lg	Tot	H	A	0	1	2	3	2	3	4	LO	XN	IP	PH	RHP	LHP
1969	ATL	NL	1	1	0	0	1	0	0	0	0	0	0	0	0	0	1	0

George Stone *continued*

Rank among batters: 4,707 • *Total ballparks homered in*: 1 • *First HR*: 09/12/1969 off Tom Griffin

Jeff Stone

JEFFREY GLEN STONE
B: 12/26/1960
BL

Year	Tm	Lg	Tot	H	A	Men-On 0	1	2	3	One-Game 2	3	4	LO	XN	IP	PH	RHP	LHP
1984	PHI	NL	1	1	0	1	0	0	0	0	0	0	1	0	0	0	1	0
1985	PHI	NL	3	2	1	1	1	1	0	1	0	0	0	0	0	1	3	0
1986	PHI	NL	6	4	2	4	2	0	0	0	0	0	1	1	0	1	4	2
1987	PHI	NL	1	1	0	0	1	0	0	0	0	0	0	0	0	0	1	0
Total			11	8	3	6	4	1	0	1	0	0	2	1	0	2	9	2

Rank among batters: 2,419 • *Top target (2 home runs)*: Ed Lynch • *Number of pitchers victimized*: 10 • *Total ballparks homered in*: 4 • *First HR*: 08/11/1984 off Joaquin Andujar

John Stone

JOHN THOMAS STONE
B: 10/10/1905 D: 11/30/1955
BL

Year	Tm	Lg	Tot	H	A	Men-On 0	1	2	3	One-Game 2	3	4	LO	XN	IP	PH	RHP	LHP
1928	DET	AL	2	2	0	0	0	2	0	0	0	0	0	0	1	0	1	1
1929	DET	AL	2	1	1	1	1	0	0	0	0	0	0	0	0	0	2	0
1930	DET	AL	3	2	1	2	1	0	0	0	0	0	0	0	0	0	2	1
1931	DET	AL	10	2	8	7	2	1	0	0	0	0	0	1	1	0	7	3
1932	DET	AL	17	5	12	5	8	3	1	1	0	0	0	1	1	0	12	5
1933	DET	AL	11	4	7	6	1	4	0	1	0	0	0	0	0	0	7	4
1934	WAS	AL	7	3	4	4	2	1	0	1	0	0	0	0	0	0	7	0
1935	WAS	AL	1	1	0	0	1	0	0	0	0	0	0	0	0	0	1	0
1936	WAS	AL	15	6	9	8	6	1	0	0	0	0	0	2	2	0	15	0
1937	WAS	AL	6	2	4	2	3	1	0	0	0	0	0	0	3	0	4	2
1938	WAS	AL	3	1	2	2	0	0	1	0	0	0	0	0	0	0	3	0
Total			77	29	48	37	25	13	2	3	0	0	0	4	8	0	61	16

Rank among batters: 682 • *Top target (4 home runs)*: Red Ruffing • *Number of pitchers victimized*: 47 • *Total ballparks homered in*: 8 • *First HR*: 09/11/1928 off Tommy Thomas

Ron Stone

HARRY RONALD STONE
B: 09/09/1942
BL

Year	Tm	Lg	Tot	H	A	Men-On 0	1	2	3	One-Game 2	3	4	LO	XN	IP	PH	RHP	LHP
1969	PHI	NL	1	0	1	1	0	0	0	0	0	0	0	0	0	0	1	0
1970	PHI	NL	3	2	1	3	0	0	0	0	0	0	0	0	0	0	3	0
1971	PHI	NL	2	1	1	1	1	0	0	0	0	0	0	0	0	0	2	0
Total			6	3	3	5	1	0	0	0	0	0	0	0	0	0	6	0

Rank among batters: 2,988 • *Total ballparks homered in*: 5 • *First HR*: 07/11/1969 off Ted Abernathy

John Stoneham

JOHN ANDREW STONEHAM
B: 11/08/1908
BL

Year	Tm	Lg	Tot	H	A	Men-On 0	1	2	3	One-Game 2	3	4	LO	XN	IP	PH	RHP	LHP
1933	CHI	AL	1	0	1	1	0	0	0	0	0	0	1	0	1	0	1	0

Rank among batters: 4,707 • *Total ballparks homered in*: 1 • *First HR*: 09/19/1933 off George Uhle

Lil Stoner

ULYSSES SIMPSON GRANT STONER
B: 02/28/1899 D: 06/26/1966
BR

Year	Tm	Lg	Tot	H	A	Men-On 0	1	2	3	One-Game 2	3	4	LO	XN	IP	PH	RHP	LHP
1924	DET	AL	2	1	1	1	0	1	0	0	0	0	0	0	0	0	0	2

Rank among batters: 4,129 • *Total ballparks homered in*: 2 • *First HR*: 04/24/1924 off James Edwards

Alan Storke

ALAN MARSHALL STORKE
B: 09/27/1884 D: 03/18/1910
BR

Year	Tm	Lg	Tot	H	A	Men-On 0	1	2	3	One-Game 2	3	4	LO	XN	IP	PH	RHP	LHP
1907	PIT	NL	1	0	1	1	0	0	0	0	0	0	0	0	0	0	1	0

Alan Storke *continued*

Year	Tm	Lg	Tot	H	A	Men-On 0	1	2	3	One-Game 2	3	4	LO	XN	IP	PH	RHP	LHP
1908	PIT	NL	1	1	0	1	0	0	0	0	0	0	0	0	0	0	1	0
Total			2	1	1	2	0	0	0	0	0	0	0	0	0	0	2	0

Rank among batters: 4,129 • *Total ballparks homered in*: 2 • *First HR*: 06/30/1907 off Orval Overall

Lin Storti

LINDO IVAN STORTI
B: 12/05/1906 D: 07/24/1982
BB

Year	Tm	Lg	Tot	H	A	Men-On 0	1	2	3	One-Game 2	3	4	LO	XN	IP	PH	RHP	LHP
1931	STL	AL	3	1	2	1	2	0	0	0	0	0	0	0	0	0	3	0
1932	STL	AL	3	2	1	1	1	1	0	0	0	0	0	0	0	0	3	0
1933	STL	AL	3	2	1	0	3	0	0	0	0	0	0	0	0	0	3	0
Total			9	5	4	2	6	1	0	0	0	0	0	0	0	0	9	0

Rank among batters: 2,587 • *Top target (2 home runs)*: Danny MacFayden • *Number of pitchers victimized*: 8 • *Total ballparks homered in*: 4 • *First HR*: 07/15/1931 off Danny MacFayden

Mel Stottlemyre

MELVIN LEON STOTTLEMYRE
B: 11/13/1941
BR

Year	Tm	Lg	Tot	H	A	Men-On 0	1	2	3	One-Game 2	3	4	LO	XN	IP	PH	RHP	LHP
1965	NY	AL	2	2	0	1	0	0	1	0	0	0	0	0	1	0	1	1
1966	NY	AL	1	0	1	1	0	0	0	0	0	0	0	0	0	0	1	0
1969	NY	AL	1	0	1	0	1	0	0	0	0	0	0	0	0	0	0	1
1970	NY	AL	2	1	1	2	0	0	0	0	0	0	0	0	0	0	0	2
1971	NY	AL	1	1	0	1	0	0	0	0	0	0	0	0	0	0	0	1
Total			7	4	3	5	1	0	1	0	0	0	0	0	1	0	2	5

Rank among batters: 2,834 • *Top target (2 home runs)*: Wilbur Wood, Gary Peters • *Number of pitchers victimized*: 5 • *Total ballparks homered in*: 4 • *First HR*: 06/05/1965 off Gary Peters

Allyn Stout

ALLYN MCCLELLAND STOUT
B: 10/31/1904 D: 12/22/1974
BR

Year	Tm	Lg	Tot	H	A	Men-On 0	1	2	3	One-Game 2	3	4	LO	XN	IP	PH	RHP	LHP
1935	NY	NL	1	1	0	1	0	0	0	0	0	0	0	0	0	0	1	0

Rank among batters: 4,707 • *Total ballparks homered in*: 1 • *First HR*: 07/30/1935 off Joe Bowman

George Stovall

GEORGE THOMAS STOVALL
B: 11/23/1878 D: 11/05/1951
BR

Year	Tm	Lg	Tot	H	A	Men-On 0	1	2	3	One-Game 2	3	4	LO	XN	IP	PH	RHP	LHP
1904	CLE	AL	1	0	1	0	0	1	0	0	0	0	0	0	0	0	1	0
1905	CLE	AL	1	0	1	1	0	0	0	0	0	0	0	0	0	0	1	0
1907	CLE	AL	1	1	0	0	1	0	0	0	0	0	0	0	0	0	0	1
1908	CLE	AL	2	1	1	1	1	0	0	0	0	0	0	0	0	0	2	0
1909	CLE	AL	2	0	2	0	2	0	0	0	0	0	0	0	0	0	2	0
1913	STL	AL	1	0	1	0	1	0	0	0	0	0	0	0	0	0	1	0
1914	KC	FL	7	5	2	4	2	1	0	0	0	0	0	0	0	1	7	0
Total			15	7	8	6	7	2	0	0	0	0	0	0	0	1	14	1

Rank among batters: 2,096 • *Top target (3 home runs)*: Russ Ford • *Number of pitchers victimized*: 13 • *Total ballparks homered in*: 7 • *First HR*: 10/07/1904 off Jesse Stovall

Harry Stovey

HARRY DUFFIELD STOVEY
B: 12/20/1856 D: 09/20/1937
BR

Year	Tm	Lg	Tot	H	A	Men-On 0	1	2	3	One-Game 2	3	4	LO	XN	IP	PH	RHP	LHP
1880	WOR	NL	6	4	2	4	2	0	0	1	0	0	2	0	2	0	6	0
1881	WOR	NL	2	2	0	1	0	0	1	0	0	0	0	0	0	0	2	0
1882	WOR	NL	5	3	2	4	1	0	0	1	0	0	1	0	0	0	5	0
1883	PHI	AA	14	7	7	5	9	0	0	0	0	0	0	0	4	0	12	2
1884	PHI	AA	10	3	7	4	2	4	0	1	0	0	2	0	0	0	6	1
1885	PHI	AA	13	8	5	4	6	3	0	0	0	0	0	0	1	0	7	0
1886	PHI	AA	7	4	3	4	1	1	1	0	0	0	1	0	1	0	5	1
1887	PHI	AA	4	1	3	1	0	3	0	0	0	0	1	0	2	0	4	0
1888	PHI	AA	9	8	1	3	4	2	0	0	0	0	0	0	1	0	5	4

Harry Stovey *continued*

Year	Tm	Lg	Tot	H	A	Men-On 0	1	2	3	One-Game 2	3	4	LO	XN	IP	PH	RHP	LHP
1889	PHI	AA	19	7	12	12	4	3	0	1	0	0	0	0	1	0	13	4
1890	BOS	PL	12	9	3	7	4	1	0	0	0	0	0	0	1	0	9	2
1891	BOS	NL	16	8	8	10	4	2	0	1	0	0	0	1	1	0	13	3
1892	BAL	NL	4	1	3	2	1	0	1	0	0	0	0	0	0	0	4	0
1893	BRO	NL	1	1	0	0	1	0	0	0	0	0	0	0	0	0	1	0
Total			122	66	56	61	39	19	3	5	0	0	7	1	14	0	92	14

Rank among batters: 377 • *Top target (5 home runs)*: Guy Hecker, Silver King • *Number of pitchers victimized*: 70 • *Total ballparks homered in*: 32 • *First HR*: 07/17/1880 off Jim McCormick • *Hit for Cycle*—vs BAL: 05/15/1888

Joe Strain

JOSEPH ALLAN STRAIN
B: 04/30/1954
BR

Year	Tm	Lg	Tot	H	A	Men-On 0	1	2	3	One-Game 2	3	4	LO	XN	IP	PH	RHP	LHP
1979	SF	NL	1	0	1	0	1	0	0	0	0	0	0	0	0	0	0	1

Rank among batters: 4,707 • *Total ballparks homered in*: 1 • *First HR*: 07/10/1979 off Rudy May

Larry Strands

JOHN LAWRENCE STRANDS
B: 12/05/1885 D: 01/19/1957
BR

Year	Tm	Lg	Tot	H	A	Men-On 0	1	2	3	One-Game 2	3	4	LO	XN	IP	PH	RHP	LHP
1915	NWK	FL	1	0	1	1	0	0	0	0	0	0	0	0	0	0	0	1

Rank among batters: 4,707 • *Total ballparks homered in*: 1 • *First HR*: 07/17/1915 off Gene Packard

Sammy Strang

SAMUEL NICKLIN STRANG
B: 12/16/1876 D: 03/13/1932
BB

Year	Tm	Lg	Tot	H	A	Men-On 0	1	2	3	One-Game 2	3	4	LO	XN	IP	PH	RHP	LHP
1901	NY	NL	1	1	0	1	0	0	0	0	0	0	0	0	0	0	1	0
1902	CHI	AL	3	1	2	1	1	1	0	0	0	0	0	0	0	0	1	2
1904	BRO	NL	1	0	1	1	0	0	0	0	0	0	0	0	1	0	0	1
1905	NY	NL	3	2	1	2	1	0	0	0	0	0	0	0	0	0	3	0
1906	NY	NL	4	3	1	2	1	0	1	0	0	0	0	0	1	0	2	2
1907	NY	NL	4	4	0	2	1	1	0	0	0	0	0	0	1	1	4	0
Total			16	11	5	9	4	2	1	0	0	0	0	0	3	1	11	5

Rank among batters: 2,029 • *Top target (2 home runs)*: Togie Pittinger • *Number of pitchers victimized*: 15 • *Total ballparks homered in*: 7 • *First HR*: 09/02/1901 off Mal Eason

Alan Strange

ALAN COCHRANE STRANGE
B: 11/07/1906 D: 06/27/1994
BR

Year	Tm	Lg	Tot	H	A	Men-On 0	1	2	3	One-Game 2	3	4	LO	XN	IP	PH	RHP	LHP
1934	STL	AL	1	1	0	0	1	0	0	0	0	0	0	0	0	0	1	0

Rank among batters: 4,707 • *Total ballparks homered in*: 1 • *First HR*: 09/02/1934 off Bill Gallivan

Doug Strange

JOSEPH DOUGLAS STRANGE
B: 04/13/1964
BB

Year	Tm	Lg	Tot	H	A	Men-On 0	1	2	3	One-Game 2	3	4	LO	XN	IP	PH	RHP	LHP
1989	DET	AL	1	1	0	1	0	0	0	0	0	0	0	0	0	0	1	0
1992	CHI	NL	1	0	1	1	0	0	0	0	0	0	0	0	0	0	1	0
1993	TEX	AL	7	4	3	3	3	1	0	0	0	0	0	1	0	1	7	0
1994	TEX	AL	5	3	2	3	2	0	0	0	0	0	0	0	0	0	5	0
1995	SEA	AL	2	1	1	0	2	0	0	0	0	0	0	0	0	1	2	0
Total			16	9	7	8	7	1	0	0	0	0	0	1	0	2	16	0

Rank among batters: 2,029 • *Total ballparks homered in*: 9 • *First HR*: 09/04/1989 off Bret Saberhagen

Monty Stratton

MONTY FRANKLIN PIERCE STRATTON
B: 05/21/1912 D: 09/29/1982
BR

Year	Tm	Lg	Tot	H	A	Men-On 0	1	2	3	One-Game 2	3	4	LO	XN	IP	PH	RHP	LHP
1936	CHI	AL	1	1	0	1	0	0	0	0	0	0	0	0	0	0	1	0
1937	CHI	AL	1	1	0	1	0	0	0	0	0	0	0	0	0	0	1	0

Monty Stratton *continued*

Year	Tm	Lg	Tot	H	A	Men-On 0	1	2	3	One-Game 2	3	4	LO	XN	IP	PH	RHP	LHP
1938	CHI	AL	2	0	2	1	0	0	1	0	0	0	0	0	0	0	2	0
Total			4	2	2	3	0	0	1	0	0	0	0	0	0	0	4	0

Rank among batters: 3,427 • *Total ballparks homered in*: 3 • *First HR*: 09/11/1936 off Hod Lisenbee

Scott Stratton

C. SCOTT STRATTON
B: 10/02/1869 D: 03/08/1939
BL

Year	Tm	Lg	Tot	H	A	Men-On 0	1	2	3	One-Game 2	3	4	LO	XN	IP	PH	RHP	LHP
1888	LOU	AA	1	0	1	0	1	0	0	0	0	0	0	0	0	0	1	0
1889	LOU	AA	4	1	3	1	2	0	1	0	0	0	0	0	1	0	4	0
1894	CHI	NL	3	1	2	0	2	1	0	1	0	0	0	0	0	0	3	0
Total			8	2	6	1	5	1	1	1	0	0	0	0	1	0	8	0

Rank among batters: 2,703 • *Top target (2 home runs)*: Frank Dwyer • *Number of pitchers victimized*: 7 • *Total ballparks homered in*: 6 • *First HR*: 04/21/1888 off Silver King

Joe Strauss

JOSEPH STRAUSS
B: 11/16/1858 D: 06/24/1906
BR

Year	Tm	Lg	Tot	H	A	Men-On 0	1	2	3	One-Game 2	3	4	LO	XN	IP	PH	RHP	LHP
1886	LOU	AA	1	1	0	0	0	1	0	0	0	0	0	0	0	0	0	0

Rank among batters: 4,707 • *Total ballparks homered in*: 1 • *First HR*: 07/08/1886 off Ted Kennedy

Darryl Strawberry

DARRYL EUGENE STRAWBERRY
B: 03/12/1962
BL

Year	Tm	Lg	Tot	H	A	Men-On 0	1	2	3	One-Game 2	3	4	LO	XN	IP	PH	RHP	LHP
1983	NY	NL	26	10	16	12	10	4	0	4	0	0	0	0	0	0	22	4
1984	NY	NL	26	8	18	12	9	5	0	2	0	0	0	0	1	0	20	6
1985	NY	NL	29	14	15	18	7	2	2	2	1	0	0	1	0	0	18	11
1986	NY	NL	27	11	16	13	11	2	1	2	0	0	0	2	0	0	22	5
1987	NY	NL	39	20	19	16	17	6	0	4	0	0	0	0	0	1	24	15
1988	NY	NL	39	21	18	19	17	3	0	3	0	0	0	1	0	0	19	20
1989	NY	NL	29	15	14	18	8	3	0	2	0	0	0	0	1	0	20	9
1990	NY	NL	37	24	13	19	10	7	1	2	0	0	0	0	0	0	28	9
1991	LA	NL	28	14	14	13	9	5	1	2	0	0	0	2	0	0	18	10
1992	LA	NL	5	3	2	0	3	2	0	1	0	0	0	0	0	0	3	2
1993	LA	NL	5	3	2	3	2	0	0	0	0	0	0	0	0	0	5	0
1994	SF	NL	4	2	2	3	0	0	1	0	0	0	0	0	0	0	3	1
1995	NY	AL	3	3	0	1	1	1	0	0	0	0	0	0	0	0	3	0
Total			297	148	149	147	104	40	6	24	1	0	0	6	2	1	205	92

Rank among batters: 70 • Top target (5 home runs): Mario Soto, Bob Forsch, Rick Mahler, Don Carman, Jose DeLeon, Doug Drabek • *Number of pitchers victimized*: 175 • *Total ballparks homered in*: 13 • *First HR*: 05/16/1983 off Lee Tunnell • *World Series HR*—1; *LCS HR*—3

Gabby Street

CHARLES EVARD STREET
B: 09/30/1882 D: 02/06/1951
BR

Year	Tm	Lg	Tot	H	A	Men-On 0	1	2	3	One-Game 2	3	4	LO	XN	IP	PH	RHP	LHP
1908	WAS	AL	1	0	1	1	0	0	0	0	0	0	0	0	0	0	1	0
1910	WAS	AL	1	0	1	1	0	0	0	0	0	0	0	0	0	0	1	0
Total			2	0	2	2	0	0	0	0	0	0	0	0	0	0	2	0

Rank among batters: 4,129 • *Total ballparks homered in*: 2 • *First HR*: 04/30/1908 off Nick Carter

Cub Stricker

JOHN A. STRICKER
B: 06/08/1859 D: 11/19/1937
BR

Year	Tm	Lg	Tot	H	A	Men-On 0	1	2	3	One-Game 2	3	4	LO	XN	IP	PH	RHP	LHP
1883	PHI	AA	1	0	1	0	1	0	0	0	0	0	0	0	0	0	1	0
1884	PHI	AA	1	0	1	0	1	0	0	0	0	0	0	0	0	0	1	0
1885	PHI	AA	1	1	0	1	0	0	0	0	0	0	0	0	0	0	1	0
1887	CLE	AA	2	0	2	0	2	0	0	0	0	0	0	0	0	0	1	1
1888	CLE	AA	1	0	1	1	0	0	0	0	0	0	0	0	0	0	0	1
1889	CLE	NL	1	1	0	0	1	0	0	0	0	0	0	0	1	0	0	1
1890	CLE	PL	2	0	2	0	0	2	0	0	0	0	0	0	0	0	1	1

Cub Stricker *continued*

Year	Tm	Lg	Tot	H	A	Men-On 0	Men-On 1	Men-On 2	Men-On 3	One-Game 2	One-Game 3	One-Game 4	LO	XN	IP	PH	RHP	LHP
1892	BAL	NL	3	1	2	1	1	1	0	0	0	0	0	0	0	0	1	2
Total			12	3	9	3	6	3	0	0	0	0	0	0	1	0	6	4

Rank among batters: 2,325 • *Top target (2 home runs)*: Tony Mullane • *Number of pitchers victimized*: 11 • *Total ballparks homered in*: 10 • *First HR*: 09/18/1883 off Will White

George Strickland

GEORGE BEVAN STRICKLAND
B: 01/10/1926
BR

Year	Tm	Lg	Tot	H	A	Men-On 0	Men-On 1	Men-On 2	Men-On 3	One-Game 2	One-Game 3	One-Game 4	LO	XN	IP	PH	RHP	LHP
1951	PIT	NL	9	8	1	6	2	1	0	1	0	0	0	0	0	0	8	1
1952	PIT	NL	5	3	2	3	2	0	0	0	0	0	0	0	0	0	3	2
	CLE	AL	1	0	1	0	1	0	0	0	0	0	0	0	0	0	0	1
	Total		6	3	3	3	3	0	0	0	0	0	0	0	0	0	3	3
1953	CLE	AL	5	4	1	3	1	1	0	0	0	0	0	0	0	0	1	4
1954	CLE	AL	6	2	4	4	0	1	1	0	0	0	0	0	0	0	2	4
1955	CLE	AL	2	1	1	1	1	0	0	0	0	0	0	0	0	0	1	1
1956	CLE	AL	3	1	2	0	1	2	0	0	0	0	0	0	0	0	3	0
1957	CLE	AL	1	1	0	0	0	1	0	0	0	0	0	0	0	0	0	1
1959	CLE	AL	3	1	2	2	1	0	0	0	0	0	0	0	0	0	3	0
1960	CLE	AL	1	0	1	1	0	0	0	0	0	0	0	0	0	0	1	0
Total			36	21	15	20	9	6	1	1	0	0	0	0	0	0	22	14

Rank among batters: 1,274 • *Top target (2 home runs)*: Ralph Branca, Billy Pierce, Chuck Stobbs • *Number of pitchers victimized*: 33 • *Total ballparks homered in*: 10 • *First HR*: 04/29/1951 off Ken Raffensberger

George Strief

GEORGE ANDREW STRIEF
B: 10/16/1856 D: 04/01/1946
BR

Year	Tm	Lg	Tot	H	A	Men-On 0	Men-On 1	Men-On 2	Men-On 3	One-Game 2	One-Game 3	One-Game 4	LO	XN	IP	PH	RHP	LHP
1882	PIT	AA	2	1	1	1	1	0	0	0	0	0	0	0	0	0	1	0
1883	STL	AA	1	1	0	0	0	1	0	0	0	0	0	0	0	0	1	0
1884	STL	AA	2	2	0	1	1	0	0	0	0	0	0	0	0	0	2	0
Total			5	4	1	2	2	1	0	0	0	0	0	0	0	0	4	0

Rank among batters: 3,191 • *Total ballparks homered in*: 3 • *First HR*: 05/03/1882 off Will White

Lou Stringer

LOUIS BERNARD STRINGER
B: 05/13/1917
BR

Year	Tm	Lg	Tot	H	A	Men-On 0	Men-On 1	Men-On 2	Men-On 3	One-Game 2	One-Game 3	One-Game 4	LO	XN	IP	PH	RHP	LHP
1941	CHI	NL	5	1	4	3	2	0	0	0	0	0	1	0	0	0	4	1
1942	CHI	NL	9	4	5	6	2	1	0	0	0	0	0	0	1	0	6	3
1946	CHI	NL	3	0	3	0	3	0	0	0	0	0	0	0	0	0	2	1
1948	BOS	AL	1	0	1	1	0	0	0	0	0	0	0	0	0	0	0	1
1949	BOS	AL	1	1	0	0	1	0	0	0	0	0	0	0	0	0	0	1
Total			19	6	13	10	8	1	0	0	0	0	1	0	1	0	12	7

Rank among batters: 1,861 • *Top target (2 home runs)*: Johnny Vander Meer • *Number of pitchers victimized*: 18 • *Total ballparks homered in*: 8 • *First HR*: 07/06/1941 off Max Butcher

Joe Stripp

JOSEPH VALENTINE STRIPP
B: 02/03/1903 D: 06/10/1989
BR

Year	Tm	Lg	Tot	H	A	Men-On 0	Men-On 1	Men-On 2	Men-On 3	One-Game 2	One-Game 3	One-Game 4	LO	XN	IP	PH	RHP	LHP
1928	CIN	NL	1	0	1	1	0	0	0	0	0	0	0	0	0	0	1	0
1929	CIN	NL	3	0	3	1	1	1	0	1	0	0	0	0	0	0	3	0
1930	CIN	NL	3	1	2	1	2	0	0	0	0	0	0	0	0	0	3	0
1931	CIN	NL	3	1	2	1	2	0	0	0	0	0	0	0	0	0	3	0
1932	BRO	NL	6	2	4	4	1	0	1	0	0	0	0	0	0	0	6	0
1933	BRO	NL	1	1	0	1	0	0	0	0	0	0	0	0	0	0	1	0
1934	BRO	NL	1	1	0	0	0	1	0	0	0	0	0	0	0	0	1	0
1935	BRO	NL	3	3	0	3	0	0	0	0	0	0	0	0	0	0	3	0
1936	BRO	NL	1	0	1	0	1	0	0	0	0	0	0	0	0	0	1	0
1937	BRO	NL	1	0	1	1	0	0	0	0	0	0	0	0	0	0	1	0
1938	BOS	NL	1	0	1	1	0	0	0	0	0	0	0	0	0	0	1	0
Total			24	9	15	14	7	2	1	1	0	0	0	0	0	0	24	0

Rank among batters: 1,643 • *Top target (3 home runs)*: Freddie Fitzsimmons • *Number of pitchers victimized*: 22 • *Total ballparks homered in*: 7 • *First HR*: 09/23/1928 off Joe Genewich

Year	Tm	Lg	Tot	H	A	Men-On 0	1	2	3	One-Game 2	3	4	LO	XN	IP	PH	RHP	LHP

Allie Strobel

ALBERT IRVING STROBEL
B: 06/11/1884 D: 02/10/1955
BR

Year	Tm	Lg	Tot	H	A	Men-On 0	1	2	3	One-Game 2	3	4	LO	XN	IP	PH	RHP	LHP
1906	BOS	NL	1	0	1	1	0	0	0	0	0	0	0	0	1	0	0	1

Rank among batters: 4,707 • *Total ballparks homered in*: 1 • *First HR*: 05/25/1906 off Jack Pfiester

Ed Stroud

EDWIN MARVIN STROUD
B: 10/31/1939
BL

Year	Tm	Lg	Tot	H	A	Men-On 0	1	2	3	One-Game 2	3	4	LO	XN	IP	PH	RHP	LHP
1967	WAS	AL	1	0	1	0	1	0	0	0	0	0	0	0	0	0	1	0
1968	WAS	AL	4	1	3	3	1	0	0	0	0	0	0	0	0	0	4	0
1969	WAS	AL	4	0	4	2	1	1	0	0	0	0	0	0	0	1	4	0
1970	WAS	AL	5	5	0	2	2	1	0	0	0	0	1	0	0	0	4	1
Total			14	6	8	7	5	2	0	0	0	0	1	0	0	1	13	1

Rank among batters: 2,169 • *Top target (2 home runs)*: Jose Santiago • *Number of pitchers victimized*: 13 • *Total ballparks homered in*: 6 • *First HR*: 08/23/1967 off Jose Santiago

Steve Stroughter

STEPHEN LEWIS STROUGHTER
B: 03/15/1952
BL

Year	Tm	Lg	Tot	H	A	Men-On 0	1	2	3	One-Game 2	3	4	LO	XN	IP	PH	RHP	LHP
1982	SEA	AL	1	0	1	1	0	0	0	0	0	0	0	0	0	0	1	0

Rank among batters: 4,707 • *Total ballparks homered in*: 1 • *First HR*: 05/04/1982 off Dennis Martinez

Amos Strunk

AMOS AARON STRUNK
B: 01/22/1889 D: 07/22/1979
BL

Year	Tm	Lg	Tot	H	A	Men-On 0	1	2	3	One-Game 2	3	4	LO	XN	IP	PH	RHP	LHP
1911	PHI	AL	1	0	1	1	0	0	0	0	0	0	0	0	0	0	1	0
1912	PHI	AL	3	0	3	0	3	0	0	0	0	0	0	0	1	0	2	1
1914	PHI	AL	2	0	2	1	0	1	0	0	0	0	0	0	0	0	1	1
1915	PHI	AL	1	1	0	1	0	0	0	0	0	0	0	0	1	0	1	0
1916	PHI	AL	3	3	0	1	2	0	0	0	0	0	0	0	0	0	3	0
1917	PHI	AL	1	0	1	1	0	0	0	0	0	0	0	0	0	0	0	1
1920	CHI	AL	1	1	0	1	0	0	0	0	0	0	0	0	1	0	1	0
1921	CHI	AL	3	1	2	1	2	0	0	0	0	0	0	0	0	0	3	0
Total			15	6	9	7	7	1	0	0	0	0	0	0	3	0	12	3

Rank among batters: 2,096 • *Top target (2 home runs)*: Allen Russell, Dave Keefe • *Number of pitchers victimized*: 13 • *Total ballparks homered in*: 6 • *First HR*: 05/11/1911 off Jack Powell

Dick Stuart

RICHARD LEE STUART
B: 11/07/1932
BR

Year	Tm	Lg	Tot	H	A	Men-On 0	1	2	3	One-Game 2	3	4	LO	XN	IP	PH	RHP	LHP
1958	PIT	NL	16	3	13	8	7	0	1	1	0	0	0	1	0	0	11	5
1959	PIT	NL	27	12	15	12	12	3	0	1	0	0	0	1	0	3	17	10
1960	PIT	NL	23	8	15	9	9	4	1	2	1	0	0	0	0	2	18	5
1961	PIT	NL	35	16	19	16	15	3	1	3	0	0	0	0	0	1	24	11
1962	PIT	NL	16	9	7	6	8	2	0	1	0	0	0	0	1	0	13	3
1963	BOS	AL	42	25	17	20	16	5	1	4	0	0	0	2	1	0	37	5
1964	BOS	AL	33	18	15	16	9	5	3	4	0	0	0	1	0	0	25	8
1965	PHI	NL	28	17	11	14	11	1	2	1	0	0	0	0	0	0	15	13
1966	NY	NL	4	4	0	2	2	0	0	0	0	0	0	0	0	0	1	3
	LA	NL	3	2	1	3	0	0	0	0	0	0	0	0	0	0	1	2
	Total		7	6	1	5	2	0	0	0	0	0	0	0	0	0	2	5
1969	CAL	AL	1	1	0	1	0	0	0	0	0	0	0	0	0	0	0	1
Total			228	115	113	107	89	23	9	17	1	0	0	5	2	6	162	66

Rank among batters: 140 • Top target (5 home runs): Stan Williams, Sandy Koufax, Johnny Podres, Don Cardwell • *Number of pitchers victimized*: 132 • *Total ballparks homered in*: 25 • *First HR*: 07/10/1958 off Don Elston

Luke Stuart

LUTHER LANE STUART
B: 05/23/1892 D: 06/15/1947
BR

Year	Tm	Lg	Tot	H	A	Men-On 0	1	2	3	One-Game 2	3	4	LO	XN	IP	PH	RHP	LHP
1921	STL	AL	1	0	1	0	1	0	0	0	0	0	0	0	1	0	1	0

Luke Stuart *continued*

Rank among batters: 4,707 • *Total ballparks homered in*: 1 • *First HR*: 08/08/1921 off Walter Johnson • *Hit HR in first major league AB*—@WAS: 08/08/1921

Marlin Stuart

MARLIN HENRY STUART
B: 08/08/1918 D: 06/16/1994
BL

Year	Tm	Lg	Tot	H	A	Men-On 0	1	2	3	One-Game 2	3	4	LO	XN	IP	PH	RHP	LHP
1951	DET	AL	1	0	1	1	0	0	0	0	0	0	0	0	0	0	1	0

Rank among batters: 4,707 • *Total ballparks homered in*: 1 • *First HR*: 09/15/1951 off Johnny Sain

Franklin Stubbs

FRANKLIN LEE STUBBS
B: 10/21/1960
BL

Year	Tm	Lg	Tot	H	A	Men-On 0	1	2	3	One-Game 2	3	4	LO	XN	IP	PH	RHP	LHP
1984	LA	NL	8	4	4	4	4	0	0	0	0	0	0	0	0	0	7	1
1986	LA	NL	23	12	11	15	7	1	0	2	0	0	0	0	0	0	19	4
1987	LA	NL	16	6	10	8	5	3	0	1	0	0	0	1	0	0	16	0
1988	LA	NL	8	3	5	5	1	1	1	0	0	0	0	0	0	2	8	0
1989	LA	NL	4	1	3	0	3	1	0	0	0	0	0	0	0	1	3	1
1990	HOU	NL	23	9	14	11	9	3	0	1	0	0	0	0	1	0	16	7
1991	MIL	AL	11	8	3	7	1	2	1	0	0	0	0	0	0	0	9	2
1992	MIL	AL	9	3	6	5	3	0	1	0	0	0	0	1	0	0	8	1
1995	DET	AL	2	1	1	0	2	0	0	0	0	0	0	0	0	0	2	0
Total			104	47	57	55	35	11	3	4	0	0	0	2	1	3	88	16

Rank among batters: 469 • *Top target (4 home runs)*: Bryn Smith • *Number of pitchers victimized*: 89 • *Total ballparks homered in*: 21 • *First HR*: 05/14/1984 off Charles Hudson

George Stumpf

GEORGE FREDERICK STUMPF
B: 12/15/1910 D: 03/06/1993
BL

Year	Tm	Lg	Tot	H	A	Men-On 0	1	2	3	One-Game 2	3	4	LO	XN	IP	PH	RHP	LHP
1932	BOS	AL	1	1	0	0	1	0	0	0	0	0	0	0	0	0	1	0

Rank among batters: 4,707 • *Total ballparks homered in*: 1 • *First HR*: 08/24/1932 off Ted Lyons

Guy Sturdy

GUY R. STURDY
B: 08/07/1899 D: 05/04/1965
BL

Year	Tm	Lg	Tot	H	A	Men-On 0	1	2	3	One-Game 2	3	4	LO	XN	IP	PH	RHP	LHP
1928	STL	AL	1	1	0	0	1	0	0	0	0	0	0	0	0	1	1	0

Rank among batters: 4,707 • *Total ballparks homered in*: 1 • *First HR*: 04/19/1928 off Ken Holloway

Bobby Sturgeon

ROBERT HOWARD STURGEON
B: 08/06/1919
BR

Year	Tm	Lg	Tot	H	A	Men-On 0	1	2	3	One-Game 2	3	4	LO	XN	IP	PH	RHP	LHP
1946	CHI	NL	1	1	0	1	0	0	0	0	0	0	0	0	0	0	0	1

Rank among batters: 4,707 • *Total ballparks homered in*: 1 • *First HR*: 09/22/1946 off Howie Pollet

Johnny Sturm

JOHN PETER JOSEPH STURM
B: 01/23/1916
BL

Year	Tm	Lg	Tot	H	A	Men-On 0	1	2	3	One-Game 2	3	4	LO	XN	IP	PH	RHP	LHP
1941	NY	AL	3	2	1	1	2	0	0	0	0	0	0	0	0	0	3	0

Rank among batters: 3,735 • *Total ballparks homered in*: 2 • *First HR*: 06/01/1941 off Mel Harder

Ken Suarez

KENNETH RAYMOND SUAREZ
B: 04/12/1943
BR

Year	Tm	Lg	Tot	H	A	Men-On 0	1	2	3	One-Game 2	3	4	LO	XN	IP	PH	RHP	LHP
1967	KC	AL	2	1	1	1	1	0	0	0	0	0	0	0	0	0	1	1
1969	CLE	AL	1	0	1	1	0	0	0	0	0	0	0	0	0	0	1	0

Ken Suarez *continued*

Year	Tm	Lg	Tot	H	A	Men-On 0	1	2	3	One-Game 2	3	4	LO	XN	IP	PH	RHP	LHP
1971	CLE	AL	1	0	1	1	0	0	0	0	0	0	0	0	0	0	0	1
1973	TEX	AL	1	0	1	1	0	0	0	0	0	0	0	0	0	0	1	0
Total			5	1	4	4	1	0	0	0	0	0	0	0	0	0	3	2

Rank among batters: 3,191 • *Total ballparks homered in*: 5 • *First HR*: 04/16/1967 off Mickey Lolich

Bill Sudakis

WILLIAM PAUL SUDAKIS
B: 03/27/1946
BB

Year	Tm	Lg	Tot	H	A	Men-On 0	1	2	3	One-Game 2	3	4	LO	XN	IP	PH	RHP	LHP
1968	LA	NL	3	1	2	2	0	0	1	0	0	0	0	0	0	0	2	1
1969	LA	NL	14	4	10	10	3	1	0	0	0	0	0	1	0	0	8	6
1970	LA	NL	14	7	7	9	3	2	0	0	0	0	0	1	0	1	8	6
1971	LA	NL	3	3	0	3	0	0	0	1	0	0	0	0	0	0	0	3
1972	NY	NL	1	1	0	0	0	1	0	0	0	0	0	0	0	0	0	1
1973	TEX	AL	15	6	9	6	6	3	0	0	0	0	0	0	0	1	4	11
1974	NY	AL	7	4	3	2	4	0	1	0	0	0	0	0	0	0	1	6
1975	CAL	AL	1	0	1	1	0	0	0	0	0	0	0	0	0	0	1	0
	CLE	AL	1	0	1	1	0	0	0	0	0	0	0	0	0	0	0	1
	Total		2	0	2	2	0	0	0	0	0	0	0	0	0	0	1	1
Total			59	26	33	34	16	7	2	1	0	0	0	2	0	2	24	35

Rank among batters: 873 • *Top target (3 home runs)*: Dave Roberts • *Number of pitchers victimized*: 49 • *Total ballparks homered in*: 20 • *First HR*: 09/03/1968 off Dick Hall

Pete Suder

PETER SUDER
B: 04/16/1916
BR

Year	Tm	Lg	Tot	H	A	Men-On 0	1	2	3	One-Game 2	3	4	LO	XN	IP	PH	RHP	LHP
1941	PHI	AL	4	1	3	2	0	2	0	0	0	0	0	0	0	0	4	0
1942	PHI	AL	4	1	3	4	0	0	0	0	0	0	0	0	0	0	3	1
1943	PHI	AL	3	1	2	3	0	0	0	0	0	0	0	0	0	0	2	1
1946	PHI	AL	2	1	1	1	0	0	1	0	0	0	0	0	0	0	2	0
1947	PHI	AL	5	3	2	4	1	0	0	0	0	0	0	0	0	0	3	2
1948	PHI	AL	7	5	2	4	2	1	0	0	0	0	0	0	0	0	4	3
1949	PHI	AL	10	6	4	5	3	1	1	0	0	0	0	0	0	0	7	3
1950	PHI	AL	8	2	6	5	2	1	0	0	0	0	0	0	0	0	5	3
1951	PHI	AL	1	1	0	0	1	0	0	0	0	0	0	0	0	0	1	0
1952	PHI	AL	1	1	0	0	1	0	0	0	0	0	0	0	0	0	0	1
1953	PHI	AL	4	3	1	3	1	0	0	0	0	0	0	1	0	0	4	0
Total			49	25	24	31	11	5	2	0	0	0	0	1	0	0	35	14

Rank among batters: 1,008 • *Top target (5 home runs)*: Joe Dobson • *Number of pitchers victimized*: 36 • *Total ballparks homered in*: 8 • *First HR*: 05/08/1941 off Jack Kramer

Willie Sudhoff

JOHN WILLIAM SUDHOFF
B: 09/17/1874 D: 05/25/1917
BR

Year	Tm	Lg	Tot	H	A	Men-On 0	1	2	3	One-Game 2	3	4	LO	XN	IP	PH	RHP	LHP
1901	STL	NL	1	0	1	0	1	0	0	0	0	0	0	0	0	0	1	0

Rank among batters: 4,707 • *Total ballparks homered in*: 1 • *First HR*: 06/24/1901 off Christy Mathewson

Joe Sugden

JOSEPH SUGDEN
B: 07/31/1870 D: 06/28/1959
BB

Year	Tm	Lg	Tot	H	A	Men-On 0	1	2	3	One-Game 2	3	4	LO	XN	IP	PH	RHP	LHP
1894	PIT	NL	2	2	0	0	2	0	0	0	0	0	0	0	2	0	2	0
1895	PIT	NL	1	0	1	0	1	0	0	0	0	0	0	0	0	0	1	0
Total			3	2	1	0	3	0	0	0	0	0	0	0	2	0	3	0

Rank among batters: 3,735 • *Total ballparks homered in*: 2 • *First HR*: 07/28/1894 off Cy Young

George Suggs

GEORGE FRANKLIN SUGGS
B: 07/07/1882 D: 04/04/1949
BR

Year	Tm	Lg	Tot	H	A	Men-On 0	1	2	3	One-Game 2	3	4	LO	XN	IP	PH	RHP	LHP
1912	CIN	NL	1	0	1	0	0	1	0	0	0	0	0	0	1	0	1	0

Rank among batters: 4,707 • *Total ballparks homered in*: 1 • *First HR*: 09/27/1912 off Ed Reulbach

Gus Suhr

AUGUST RICHARD SUHR
B: 01/03/1906
BL

Year	Tm	Lg	Tot	H	A	Men-On 0	Men-On 1	Men-On 2	Men-On 3	One-Game 2	One-Game 3	One-Game 4	LO	XN	IP	PH	RHP	LHP
1930	PIT	NL	17	7	10	9	5	3	0	0	0	0	0	0	1	0	14	3
1931	PIT	NL	4	2	2	2	2	0	0	0	0	0	0	1	0	1	2	2
1932	PIT	NL	5	2	3	2	2	1	0	0	0	0	0	0	0	0	3	2
1933	PIT	NL	10	3	7	7	3	0	0	0	0	0	0	0	0	0	9	1
1934	PIT	NL	13	3	10	9	4	0	0	1	0	0	0	2	0	0	10	3
1935	PIT	NL	10	3	7	3	5	2	0	1	0	0	0	1	0	0	5	5
1936	PIT	NL	11	7	4	6	3	2	0	0	0	0	0	0	0	0	8	3
1937	PIT	NL	5	2	3	2	1	2	0	0	0	0	0	0	0	0	2	3
1938	PIT	NL	3	2	1	1	1	1	0	0	0	0	0	0	0	0	3	0
1939	PIT	NL	1	0	1	1	0	0	0	0	0	0	0	1	0	0	1	0
	PHI	NL	3	1	2	2	1	0	0	0	0	0	0	0	0	0	2	1
	Total		4	1	3	3	1	0	0	0	0	0	0	1	0	0	3	1
1940	PHI	NL	2	0	2	1	0	1	0	0	0	0	0	0	0	1	1	1
Total			84	32	52	45	27	12	0	2	0	0	0	5	1	2	60	24

Rank among batters: 617 • *Top target (4 home runs)*: Lon Warneke • *Number of pitchers victimized*: 56 • *Total ballparks homered in*: 8 • *First HR*: 05/12/1930 off Johnny Morrison

Clyde Sukeforth

CLYDE LEROY SUKEFORTH
B: 11/30/1901
BL

Year	Tm	Lg	Tot	H	A	Men-On 0	Men-On 1	Men-On 2	Men-On 3	One-Game 2	One-Game 3	One-Game 4	LO	XN	IP	PH	RHP	LHP
1929	CIN	NL	1	0	1	0	0	1	0	0	0	0	0	0	0	0	1	0
1930	CIN	NL	1	0	1	1	0	0	0	0	0	0	0	0	0	0	1	0
Total			2	0	2	1	0	1	0	0	0	0	0	0	0	0	2	0

Rank among batters: 4,129 • *Total ballparks homered in*: 2 • *First HR*: 07/17/1929 off Doug McWeeny

Guy Sularz

GUY PATRICK SULARZ
B: 11/07/1955
BR

Year	Tm	Lg	Tot	H	A	Men-On 0	Men-On 1	Men-On 2	Men-On 3	One-Game 2	One-Game 3	One-Game 4	LO	XN	IP	PH	RHP	LHP
1982	SF	NL	1	0	1	1	0	0	0	0	0	0	0	0	0	0	1	0

Rank among batters: 4,707 • *Total ballparks homered in*: 1 • *First HR*: 08/24/1982 off Ferguson Jenkins

Ernie Sulik

ERNEST RICHARD SULIK
B: 07/07/1910 D: 05/31/1963
BL

Year	Tm	Lg	Tot	H	A	Men-On 0	Men-On 1	Men-On 2	Men-On 3	One-Game 2	One-Game 3	One-Game 4	LO	XN	IP	PH	RHP	LHP
1936	PHI	NL	6	2	4	3	2	1	0	0	0	0	0	0	0	0	4	2

Rank among batters: 2,988 • *Total ballparks homered in*: 4 • *First HR*: 05/22/1936 off Dick Coffman

Billy Sullivan

WILLIAM JOSEPH, SR. SULLIVAN
B: 02/01/1875 D: 01/28/1965
BR

Year	Tm	Lg	Tot	H	A	Men-On 0	Men-On 1	Men-On 2	Men-On 3	One-Game 2	One-Game 3	One-Game 4	LO	XN	IP	PH	RHP	LHP
1899	BOS	NL	2	2	0	1	0	1	0	0	0	0	0	0	0	0	1	1
1900	BOS	NL	8	7	1	4	3	1	0	0	0	0	0	1	0	1	6	2
1901	CHI	AL	4	1	3	1	3	0	0	0	0	0	0	0	1	0	4	0
1902	CHI	AL	1	0	1	0	1	0	0	0	0	0	0	0	0	0	0	1
1903	CHI	AL	1	0	1	1	0	0	0	0	0	0	0	0	0	0	0	1
1904	CHI	AL	1	0	1	1	0	0	0	0	0	0	0	0	0	0	1	0
1905	CHI	AL	2	0	2	1	1	0	0	0	0	0	0	0	1	0	1	1
1906	CHI	AL	2	0	2	1	1	0	0	0	0	0	0	0	1	0	1	1
Total			21	10	11	10	9	2	0	0	0	0	0	1	3	1	14	7

Rank among batters: 1,768 • *Top target (2 home runs)*: Cy Young, Rube Waddell, Jack Chesbro • *Number of pitchers victimized*: 18 • *Total ballparks homered in*: 9 • *First HR*: 09/27/1899 off Bill Magee

Billy Sullivan

WILLIAM JOSEPH, JR. SULLIVAN
B: 10/23/1910 D: 01/04/1994
BL

Year	Tm	Lg	Tot	H	A	Men-On 0	Men-On 1	Men-On 2	Men-On 3	One-Game 2	One-Game 3	One-Game 4	LO	XN	IP	PH	RHP	LHP
1931	CHI	AL	2	0	2	1	0	1	0	0	0	0	0	0	0	0	1	1
1932	CHI	AL	1	0	1	1	0	0	0	0	0	0	0	0	0	0	1	0
1935	CIN	NL	2	0	2	1	0	1	0	0	0	0	0	0	0	0	1	1

Billy Sullivan *continued*

Year	Tm	Lg	Tot	H	A	Men-On 0	Men-On 1	Men-On 2	Men-On 3	One-Game 2	One-Game 3	One-Game 4	LO	XN	IP	PH	RHP	LHP
1936	CLE	AL	2	1	1	1	1	0	0	0	0	0	0	0	1	0	2	0
1937	CLE	AL	3	1	2	1	0	2	0	0	0	0	0	0	0	1	2	1
1938	STL	AL	7	5	2	3	4	0	0	0	0	0	0	0	0	0	7	0
1939	STL	AL	5	3	2	4	1	0	0	0	0	0	0	0	0	1	5	0
1940	DET	AL	3	2	1	1	2	0	0	0	0	0	0	0	0	2	3	0
1941	DET	AL	3	3	0	2	1	0	0	0	0	0	0	0	0	0	3	0
1942	BRO	NL	1	1	0	0	1	0	0	0	0	0	0	0	0	0	1	0
Total			29	16	13	15	10	4	0	0	0	0	0	0	1	4	26	3

Rank among batters: 1,465 • *Top target (3 home runs)*: Johnny Allen • *Number of pitchers victimized*: 25 • *Total ballparks homered in*: 9 • *First HR*: 07/27/1931 off Gordon Rhodes

Denny Sullivan

DENNIS WILLIAM SULLIVAN
B: 09/28/1882 D: 06/02/1956
BL

Year	Tm	Lg	Tot	H	A	Men-On 0	Men-On 1	Men-On 2	Men-On 3	One-Game 2	One-Game 3	One-Game 4	LO	XN	IP	PH	RHP	LHP
1907	BOS	AL	1	1	0	1	0	0	0	0	0	0	1	0	1	0	1	0

Rank among batters: 4,707 • *Total ballparks homered in*: 1 • *First HR*: 05/02/1907 off Bill Hogg

Haywood Sullivan

HAYWOOD COOPER SULLIVAN
B: 12/15/1930
BR

Year	Tm	Lg	Tot	H	A	Men-On 0	Men-On 1	Men-On 2	Men-On 3	One-Game 2	One-Game 3	One-Game 4	LO	XN	IP	PH	RHP	LHP
1960	BOS	AL	3	1	2	0	3	0	0	0	0	0	0	0	0	0	2	1
1961	KC	AL	6	3	3	3	2	1	0	0	0	0	0	0	0	1	3	3
1962	KC	AL	4	2	2	1	2	1	0	0	0	0	0	0	0	0	2	2
Total			13	6	7	4	7	2	0	0	0	0	0	0	0	1	7	6

Rank among batters: 2,248 • *Total ballparks homered in*: 7 • *First HR*: 05/17/1960 off Bob Shaw

Jim Sullivan

JAMES E. SULLIVAN
B: 04/25/1869 D: 11/30/1901
BR

Year	Tm	Lg	Tot	H	A	Men-On 0	Men-On 1	Men-On 2	Men-On 3	One-Game 2	One-Game 3	One-Game 4	LO	XN	IP	PH	RHP	LHP
1896	BOS	NL	1	1	0	1	0	0	0	0	0	0	0	0	0	0	0	1

Rank among batters: 4,707 • *Total ballparks homered in*: 1 • *First HR*: 08/17/1896 off Harley Payne

Joe Sullivan

JOSEPH DANIEL SULLIVAN
B: 01/06/1870 D: 11/02/1897

Year	Tm	Lg	Tot	H	A	Men-On 0	Men-On 1	Men-On 2	Men-On 3	One-Game 2	One-Game 3	One-Game 4	LO	XN	IP	PH	RHP	LHP
1893	WAS	NL	2	0	2	0	2	0	0	0	0	0	0	0	0	0	2	0
1894	PHI	NL	3	1	2	2	0	1	0	0	0	0	0	0	0	0	2	1
1895	PHI	NL	2	0	2	0	1	1	0	0	0	0	0	0	0	0	1	1
1896	PHI	NL	2	1	1	0	2	0	0	0	0	0	0	0	0	0	1	1
	STL	NL	2	1	1	1	0	1	0	0	0	0	0	0	0	0	1	1
	Total		4	2	2	1	2	1	0	0	0	0	0	0	0	0	2	2
Total			11	3	8	3	5	3	0	0	0	0	0	0	0	0	7	4

Rank among batters: 2,419 • *Top target (2 home runs)*: Dad Clarkson • *Number of pitchers victimized*: 10 • *Total ballparks homered in*: 9 • *First HR*: 05/27/1893 off Kid Nichols

John Sullivan

JOHN LAWRENCE SULLIVAN
B: 03/21/1890 D: 04/01/1966
BR

Year	Tm	Lg	Tot	H	A	Men-On 0	Men-On 1	Men-On 2	Men-On 3	One-Game 2	One-Game 3	One-Game 4	LO	XN	IP	PH	RHP	LHP
1920	BOS	NL	1	0	1	1	0	0	0	0	0	0	0	0	0	0	1	0
1921	CHI	NL	4	2	2	1	1	2	0	0	0	0	0	0	0	0	4	0
Total			5	2	3	2	1	2	0	0	0	0	0	0	0	0	5	0

Rank among batters: 3,191 • *Top target (2 home runs)*: Ferdie Schupp • *Number of pitchers victimized*: 4 • *Total ballparks homered in*: 4 • *First HR*: 09/25/1920 off George Smith

John Sullivan

JOHN PAUL SULLIVAN
B: 11/02/1920
BR

Year	Tm	Lg	Tot	H	A	Men-On 0	Men-On 1	Men-On 2	Men-On 3	One-Game 2	One-Game 3	One-Game 4	LO	XN	IP	PH	RHP	LHP
1943	WAS	AL	1	0	1	1	0	0	0	0	0	0	0	0	0	0	1	0

Rank among batters: 4,707 • *Total ballparks homered in*: 1 • *First HR*: 07/04/1943 off Steve Sundra

John Sullivan

JOHN PETER SULLIVAN
B: 01/03/1941
BL

Year	Tm	Lg	Tot	H	A	Men-On 0	Men-On 1	Men-On 2	Men-On 3	One-Game 2	One-Game 3	One-Game 4	LO	XN	IP	PH	RHP	LHP
1965	DET	AL	2	0	2	0	2	0	0	0	0	0	0	0	0	0	2	0

Rank among batters: 4,129 • *Total ballparks homered in*: 2 • *First HR*: 04/12/1965 off Wes Stock

Marc Sullivan

MARC COOPER SULLIVAN
B: 07/25/1958
BR

Year	Tm	Lg	Tot	H	A	Men-On 0	Men-On 1	Men-On 2	Men-On 3	One-Game 2	One-Game 3	One-Game 4	LO	XN	IP	PH	RHP	LHP
1985	BOS	AL	2	2	0	1	1	0	0	0	0	0	0	0	0	0	0	2
1986	BOS	AL	1	1	0	0	0	1	0	0	0	0	0	0	0	0	0	1
1987	BOS	AL	2	1	1	1	1	0	0	0	0	0	0	0	0	0	2	0
Total			5	4	1	2	2	1	0	0	0	0	0	0	0	0	2	3

Rank among batters: 3,191 • *Top target (2 home runs)*: Mark Langston • *Number of pitchers victimized*: 4 • *Total ballparks homered in*: 2 • *First HR*: 05/15/1985 off Mark Langston

Marty Sullivan

MARTIN C. SULLIVAN
B: 10/20/1862 D: 01/06/1894
BR

Year	Tm	Lg	Tot	H	A	Men-On 0	Men-On 1	Men-On 2	Men-On 3	One-Game 2	One-Game 3	One-Game 4	LO	XN	IP	PH	RHP	LHP
1887	CHI	NL	6	5	1	1	4	1	0	0	0	0	0	0	0	0	4	2
1888	CHI	NL	7	4	3	6	1	0	0	0	0	0	0	0	1	0	5	1
1889	IND	NL	4	4	0	1	2	1	0	1	0	0	0	0	0	0	4	0
1890	BOS	NL	6	4	2	6	0	0	0	0	0	0	0	0	1	0	5	1
1891	BOS	NL	2	1	1	2	0	0	0	0	0	0	0	0	0	0	2	0
Total			25	18	7	16	7	2	0	1	0	0	0	0	2	0	20	4

Rank among batters: 1,608 • Top target (2 home runs): Pretzels Getzien, Al Maul, Charley Radbourn, Jesse Duryea • *Number of pitchers victimized*: 21 • *Total ballparks homered in*: 8 • *First HR*: 05/14/1887 off Pretzels Getzien

Mike Sullivan

MICHAEL JOSEPH SULLIVAN
B: 06/10/1860 D: 06/16/1929
BR

Year	Tm	Lg	Tot	H	A	Men-On 0	Men-On 1	Men-On 2	Men-On 3	One-Game 2	One-Game 3	One-Game 4	LO	XN	IP	PH	RHP	LHP
1888	PHI	AA	1	0	1	0	1	0	0	0	0	0	0	0	0	0	1	0

Rank among batters: 4,707 • *Total ballparks homered in*: 1 • *First HR*: 05/05/1888 off Jersey Bakely

Mike Sullivan

MICHAEL JOSEPH SULLIVAN
B: 10/23/1866 D: 06/14/1906
BL

Year	Tm	Lg	Tot	H	A	Men-On 0	Men-On 1	Men-On 2	Men-On 3	One-Game 2	One-Game 3	One-Game 4	LO	XN	IP	PH	RHP	LHP
1893	CIN	NL	1	1	0	0	1	0	0	0	0	0	0	0	0	0	1	0
1894	WAS	NL	1	0	1	0	1	0	0	0	0	0	0	0	1	0	1	0
Total			2	1	1	0	2	0	0	0	0	0	0	0	1	0	2	0

Rank among batters: 4,129 • *Total ballparks homered in*: 2 • *First HR*: 06/27/1893 off Mark Baldwin

Russ Sullivan

RUSSELL GUY SULLIVAN
B: 02/19/1923
BL

Year	Tm	Lg	Tot	H	A	Men-On 0	Men-On 1	Men-On 2	Men-On 3	One-Game 2	One-Game 3	One-Game 4	LO	XN	IP	PH	RHP	LHP
1951	DET	AL	1	0	1	1	0	0	0	0	0	0	0	0	0	0	1	0
1952	DET	AL	3	3	0	2	1	0	0	0	0	0	0	0	0	0	2	1
1953	DET	AL	1	1	0	0	0	1	0	0	0	0	0	0	0	0	1	0
Total			5	4	1	3	1	1	0	0	0	0	0	0	0	0	4	1

Rank among batters: 3,191 • *Total ballparks homered in*: 2 • *First HR*: 09/16/1951 off Dick Starr

Tom Sullivan

THOMAS AUGUSTIN SULLIVAN
B: 10/18/1895 D: 09/23/1962
BL

Year	Tm	Lg	Tot	H	A	Men-On 0	Men-On 1	Men-On 2	Men-On 3	One-Game 2	One-Game 3	One-Game 4	LO	XN	IP	PH	RHP	LHP
1922	PHI	NL	1	0	1	0	1	0	0	0	0	0	0	0	0	0	1	0

Rank among batters: 4,707 • *Total ballparks homered in*: 1 • *First HR*: 05/15/1922 off Clyde Barfoot

Homer Summa

HOMER WAYNE SUMMA
B: 11/03/1898 D: 01/29/1966
BL

Year	Tm	Lg	Tot	H	A	Men-On 0	1	2	3	One-Game 2	3	4	LO	XN	IP	PH	RHP	LHP
1922	CLE	AL	1	1	0	0	1	0	0	0	0	0	0	0	1	0	1	0
1923	CLE	AL	3	1	2	1	1	0	1	0	0	0	0	0	1	0	3	0
1924	CLE	AL	2	2	0	0	2	0	0	0	0	0	0	0	0	0	1	1
1926	CLE	AL	4	1	3	0	1	3	0	0	0	0	0	0	0	0	2	2
1927	CLE	AL	4	1	3	2	2	0	0	0	0	0	0	0	0	0	3	1
1928	CLE	AL	3	1	2	3	0	0	0	0	0	0	0	0	0	0	3	0
1930	PHI	AL	1	0	1	1	0	0	0	0	0	0	0	0	0	1	1	0
Total			18	7	11	7	7	3	1	0	0	0	0	0	2	1	14	4

Rank among batters: 1,914 • *Top target (2 home runs)*: Howard Ehmke • *Number of pitchers victimized*: 17 • *Total ballparks homered in*: 7 • *First HR*: 09/23/1922 off Sam Jones

Champ Summers

JOHN JUNIOR SUMMERS
B: 06/15/1946
BL

Year	Tm	Lg	Tot	H	A	Men-On 0	1	2	3	One-Game 2	3	4	LO	XN	IP	PH	RHP	LHP
1975	CHI	NL	1	1	0	0	0	0	1	0	0	0	0	0	0	1	1	0
1976	CHI	NL	3	0	3	2	0	1	0	0	0	0	0	1	0	1	3	0
1977	CIN	NL	3	3	0	3	0	0	0	0	0	0	0	0	1	2	3	0
1978	CIN	NL	1	1	0	1	0	0	0	0	0	0	0	0	0	0	1	0
1979	CIN	NL	1	1	0	0	0	1	0	0	0	0	0	0	0	0	1	0
	DET	AL	20	17	3	14	3	3	0	1	0	0	0	0	0	2	19	1
	Total		21	18	3	14	3	4	0	1	0	0	0	0	0	2	20	1
1980	DET	AL	17	9	8	10	6	0	1	1	0	0	0	0	0	1	15	2
1981	DET	AL	3	1	2	1	1	1	0	0	0	0	0	0	0	0	3	0
1982	SF	NL	4	2	2	1	2	1	0	0	0	0	0	0	0	2	4	0
1984	SD	NL	1	1	0	0	0	0	1	0	0	0	0	0	0	1	1	0
Total			54	36	18	32	12	7	3	2	0	0	0	1	1	10	51	3

Rank among batters: 938 • *Top target (3 home runs)*: Steve Renko • *Number of pitchers victimized*: 47 • *Total ballparks homered in*: 14 • *First HR*: 08/23/1975 off Jim York

Ed Summers

ORON EDGAR SUMMERS
B: 12/05/1884 D: 05/12/1953
BB

Year	Tm	Lg	Tot	H	A	Men-On 0	1	2	3	One-Game 2	3	4	LO	XN	IP	PH	RHP	LHP
1910	DET	AL	2	2	0	0	2	0	0	1	0	0	0	0	0	0	0	2

Rank among batters: 4,129 • *Top target (2 home runs)*: Harry Krause • *Number of pitchers victimized*: 1 • *Total ballparks homered in*: 1 • *First HR*: 09/17/1910 off Harry Krause

Billy Sunday

WILLIAM ASHLEY SUNDAY
B: 11/09/1862 D: 11/06/1935
BL

Year	Tm	Lg	Tot	H	A	Men-On 0	1	2	3	One-Game 2	3	4	LO	XN	IP	PH	RHP	LHP
1884	CHI	NL	4	4	0	3	0	0	0	0	0	0	0	0	0	0	4	0
1885	CHI	NL	2	2	0	2	0	0	0	0	0	0	0	0	0	0	2	0
1887	CHI	NL	3	3	0	2	1	0	0	0	0	0	0	0	0	0	3	0
1889	PIT	NL	2	0	2	1	1	0	0	0	0	0	0	0	0	0	2	0
1890	PIT	NL	1	0	1	1	0	0	0	0	0	0	0	0	0	0	1	0
Total			12	9	3	9	2	0	0	0	0	0	0	0	0	0	12	0

Rank among batters: 2,325 • *Top target (2 home runs)*: Jim McCormick, Pretzels Getzien • *Number of pitchers victimized*: 10 • *Total ballparks homered in*: 3 • *First HR*: 06/06/1884 off Jim McCormick

Jim Sundberg

JAMES HOWARD SUNDBERG
B: 05/18/1951
BR

Year	Tm	Lg	Tot	H	A	Men-On 0	1	2	3	One-Game 2	3	4	LO	XN	IP	PH	RHP	LHP
1974	TEX	AL	3	1	2	2	1	0	0	0	0	0	0	0	0	0	1	2
1975	TEX	AL	6	1	5	2	1	2	1	0	0	0	0	0	0	0	3	3
1976	TEX	AL	3	2	1	2	1	0	0	0	0	0	0	0	0	0	2	1
1977	TEX	AL	6	3	3	4	1	1	0	0	0	0	0	1	0	0	3	3
1978	TEX	AL	6	0	6	3	1	2	0	0	0	0	0	1	0	0	5	1
1979	TEX	AL	5	3	2	3	1	1	0	0	0	0	0	0	0	0	3	2
1980	TEX	AL	10	5	5	6	2	1	1	0	0	0	0	0	0	0	6	4
1981	TEX	AL	3	1	2	1	1	1	0	0	0	0	0	0	0	0	1	2

Jim Sundberg *continued*

Year	Tm	Lg	Tot	H	A	Men-On 0	1	2	3	One-Game 2	3	4	LO	XN	IP	PH	RHP	LHP
1982	TEX	AL	10	3	7	8	1	1	0	0	0	0	0	0	0	0	8	2
1983	TEX	AL	2	0	2	0	2	0	0	0	0	0	0	0	0	0	2	0
1984	MIL	AL	7	4	3	3	3	1	0	1	0	0	0	0	0	0	5	2
1985	KC	AL	10	2	8	8	1	1	0	0	0	0	0	1	0	0	3	7
1986	KC	AL	12	5	7	6	2	3	1	1	0	0	0	0	0	1	6	6
1987	CHI	NL	4	2	2	2	1	0	1	0	0	0	0	0	0	2	3	1
1988	CHI	NL	2	1	1	2	0	0	0	0	0	0	0	0	0	0	1	1
	TEX	AL	4	1	3	4	0	0	0	0	0	0	0	0	1	0	2	2
	Total		6	2	4	6	0	0	0	0	0	0	0	0	1	0	3	3
1989	TEX	AL	2	2	0	2	0	0	0	0	0	0	0	0	0	0	1	1
Total			95	36	59	58	19	14	4	2	0	0	0	3	1	3	55	40

Rank among batters: 529 • *Top target (3 home runs)*: Mike Torrez • *Number of pitchers victimized*: 85 • *Total ballparks homered in*: 19 • *First HR*: 07/01/1974 off Joe Decker • *LCS HR*—1

Steve Sundra

STEPHEN RICHARD SUNDRA
B: 03/27/1910 D: 03/23/1952
BB

Year	Tm	Lg	Tot	H	A	Men-On 0	1	2	3	One-Game 2	3	4	LO	XN	IP	PH	RHP	LHP
1938	NY	AL	1	0	1	1	0	0	0	0	0	0	0	0	0	0	1	0
1942	STL	AL	1	0	1	1	0	0	0	0	0	0	0	0	0	0	0	1
Total			2	0	2	2	0	0	0	0	0	0	0	0	0	0	1	1

Rank among batters: 4,129 • *Total ballparks homered in*: 2 • *First HR*: 07/27/1938 off Fred Johnson

B. J. Surhoff

WILLIAM JAMES SURHOFF
B: 08/04/1964
BL

Year	Tm	Lg	Tot	H	A	Men-On 0	1	2	3	One-Game 2	3	4	LO	XN	IP	PH	RHP	LHP
1987	MIL	AL	7	5	2	3	1	3	0	0	0	0	0	1	0	0	5	2
1988	MIL	AL	5	2	3	3	1	1	0	0	0	0	0	0	0	0	3	2
1989	MIL	AL	5	3	2	3	0	1	1	0	0	0	0	0	0	0	3	2
1990	MIL	AL	6	4	2	4	0	2	0	0	0	0	0	0	0	0	4	2
1991	MIL	AL	5	3	2	5	0	0	0	0	0	0	0	0	0	0	5	0
1992	MIL	AL	4	3	1	2	0	1	1	0	0	0	0	1	0	0	2	2
1993	MIL	AL	7	4	3	6	0	1	0	0	0	0	0	0	0	0	4	3
1994	MIL	AL	5	2	3	3	0	2	0	0	0	0	0	0	0	0	3	2
1995	MIL	AL	13	7	6	5	4	4	0	2	0	0	0	0	0	0	10	3
Total			57	33	24	34	6	15	2	2	0	0	0	2	0	0	39	18

Rank among batters: 902 • *Top target (3 home runs)*: Bobby Witt • *Number of pitchers victimized*: 47 • *Total ballparks homered in*: 13 • *First HR*: 04/09/1987 off Steve Crawford

Max Surkont

MATTHEW CONSTANTINE SURKONT
B: 06/16/1922 D: 10/08/1986
BR

Year	Tm	Lg	Tot	H	A	Men-On 0	1	2	3	One-Game 2	3	4	LO	XN	IP	PH	RHP	LHP
1950	BOS	NL	1	1	0	0	0	1	0	0	0	0	0	0	0	0	1	0

Rank among batters: 4,707 • *Total ballparks homered in*: 1 • *First HR*: 09/15/1950 off Mel Queen

George Susce

GEORGE CYRIL METHODIUS SUSCE
B: 08/13/1908 D: 02/25/1986
BR

Year	Tm	Lg	Tot	H	A	Men-On 0	1	2	3	One-Game 2	3	4	LO	XN	IP	PH	RHP	LHP
1929	PHI	NL	1	0	1	1	0	0	0	0	0	0	0	0	0	0	0	1
1939	PIT	NL	1	0	1	1	0	0	0	0	0	0	0	0	0	0	1	0
Total			2	0	2	2	0	0	0	0	0	0	0	0	0	0	1	1

Rank among batters: 4,129 • *Total ballparks homered in*: 2 • *First HR*: 06/25/1929 off Bunny Hearn

Pete Susko

PETER JONATHAN SUSKO
B: 07/02/1904 D: 05/22/1978
BL

Year	Tm	Lg	Tot	H	A	Men-On 0	1	2	3	One-Game 2	3	4	LO	XN	IP	PH	RHP	LHP
1934	WAS	AL	2	0	2	1	1	0	0	0	0	0	0	0	0	0	1	1

Rank among batters: 4,129 • *Total ballparks homered in*: 1 • *First HR*: 08/01/1934 off Mort Flohr

Rick Sutcliffe

RICHARD LEE SUTCLIFFE
B: 06/21/1956
BL

Year	Tm	Lg	Tot	H	A	Men-On				One-Game			LO	XN	IP	PH	RHP	LHP
						0	1	2	3	2	3	4						
1979	LA	NL	1	1	0	1	0	0	0	0	0	0	0	0	0	0	1	0
1985	CHI	NL	1	0	1	1	0	0	0	0	0	0	0	0	0	0	1	0
1986	CHI	NL	1	1	0	0	0	1	0	0	0	0	0	0	0	0	1	0
1988	CHI	NL	1	0	1	0	1	0	0	0	0	0	0	0	0	0	0	1
Total			4	2	2	2	1	1	0	0	0	0	0	0	0	0	3	1

Rank among batters: 3,427 • *Total ballparks homered in*: 4 • *First HR*: 05/25/1979 off Tom Seaver • *LCS HR*—1

Sy Sutcliffe

ELMER ELLSWORTH SUTCLIFFE
B: 04/15/1862 D: 02/13/1893
BL

Year	Tm	Lg	Tot	H	A	Men-On				One-Game			LO	XN	IP	PH	RHP	LHP
						0	1	2	3	2	3	4						
1889	CLE	NL	1	1	0	1	0	0	0	0	0	0	0	0	0	0	1	0
1890	CLE	PL	2	1	1	1	1	0	0	0	0	0	0	0	0	0	2	0
1891	WAS	AA	2	1	1	1	1	0	0	0	0	0	0	0	1	0	2	0
1892	BAL	NL	1	0	1	0	1	0	0	0	0	0	0	0	0	0	0	0
Total			6	3	3	3	3	0	0	0	0	0	0	0	1	0	5	0

Rank among batters: 2,988 • *Total ballparks homered in*: 6 • *First HR*: 08/30/1889 off Amos Rusie

Gary Sutherland

GARY LYNN SUTHERLAND
B: 09/27/1944
BR

Year	Tm	Lg	Tot	H	A	Men-On				One-Game			LO	XN	IP	PH	RHP	LHP
						0	1	2	3	2	3	4						
1967	PHI	NL	1	1	0	1	0	0	0	0	0	0	0	0	0	0	0	1
1969	MON	NL	3	1	2	2	1	0	0	0	0	0	0	0	0	0	1	2
1970	MON	NL	3	3	0	2	1	0	0	0	0	0	0	0	0	1	1	2
1971	MON	NL	4	2	2	4	0	0	0	0	0	0	0	0	0	0	3	1
1974	DET	AL	5	2	3	3	2	0	0	1	0	0	0	0	0	0	4	1
1975	DET	AL	6	3	3	6	0	0	0	1	0	0	0	0	0	0	5	1
1976	MIL	AL	1	1	0	0	1	0	0	0	0	0	0	0	0	0	0	1
1977	SD	NL	1	1	0	1	0	0	0	0	0	0	0	0	0	1	1	0
Total			24	14	10	19	5	0	0	2	0	0	0	0	0	2	15	9

Rank among batters: 1,643 • Top target (2 home runs): Denny Lemaster, Jim Nash, Steve Carlton, Catfish Hunter, Al Fitzmorris, Bill Campbell • *Number of pitchers victimized*: 18 • *Total ballparks homered in*: 11 • *First HR*: 08/19/1967 off Rich Nye

Ezra Sutton

EZRA BALLOU SUTTON
B: 09/17/1850 D: 06/20/1907
BR

Year	Tm	Lg	Tot	H	A	Men-On				One-Game			LO	XN	IP	PH	RHP	LHP
						0	1	2	3	2	3	4						
1876	PHI	NL	1	0	1	0	1	0	0	0	0	0	0	0	1	0	1	0
1878	BOS	NL	1	0	1	1	0	0	0	0	0	0	0	1	0	0	1	0
1882	BOS	NL	2	0	2	1	0	1	0	0	0	0	0	0	0	0	2	0
1883	BOS	NL	3	1	2	0	2	1	0	0	0	0	0	0	1	0	3	0
1884	BOS	NL	3	2	1	2	0	1	0	0	0	0	0	0	0	0	3	0
1885	BOS	NL	4	1	3	3	1	0	0	1	0	0	0	1	0	0	4	0
1886	BOS	NL	3	1	2	2	1	0	0	0	0	0	0	0	0	0	3	0
1887	BOS	NL	3	1	2	0	2	1	0	0	0	0	0	0	1	0	3	0
1888	BOS	NL	1	0	1	0	0	1	0	0	0	0	0	0	0	0	1	0
Total			21	6	15	9	7	5	0	1	0	0	0	2	3	0	21	0

Rank among batters: 1,768 • *Top target (4 home runs)*: Jim McCormick • *Number of pitchers victimized*: 13 • *Total ballparks homered in*: 10 • *First HR*: 07/15/1876 off Jim Devlin

Dale Sveum

DALE CURTIS SVEUM
B: 11/23/1963
BB

Year	Tm	Lg	Tot	H	A	Men-On				One-Game			LO	XN	IP	PH	RHP	LHP
						0	1	2	3	2	3	4						
1986	MIL	AL	7	4	3	6	1	0	0	0	0	0	0	0	0	0	5	2
1987	MIL	AL	25	9	16	11	9	5	0	1	1	0	0	0	0	0	14	11
1988	MIL	AL	9	2	7	4	4	1	0	1	0	0	0	0	0	0	5	4
1990	MIL	AL	1	1	0	0	1	0	0	0	0	0	0	0	0	0	0	1
1991	MIL	AL	4	3	1	3	0	1	0	0	0	0	0	0	0	0	2	2
1992	PHI	NL	2	0	2	0	2	0	0	0	0	0	0	0	0	0	2	0
	CHI	AL	2	1	1	2	0	0	0	0	0	0	0	0	0	0	2	0
	Total		4	1	3	2	2	0	0	0	0	0	0	0	0	0	4	0

Dale Sveum *continued*

Year	Tm	Lg	Tot	H	A	Men-On 0	1	2	3	One-Game 2	3	4	LO	XN	IP	PH	RHP	LHP
1993	OAK	AL	2	0	2	2	0	0	0	0	0	0	0	0	0	1	2	0
1994	SEA	AL	1	0	1	1	0	0	0	0	0	0	0	0	0	0	1	0
Total			53	20	33	29	17	7	0	2	1	0	0	0	0	1	33	20

Rank among batters: 953 • Top target (2 home runs): Greg Swindell, Dave Stewart, Mike Witt, Eric Bell, Bill Gullickson • *Number of pitchers victimized*: 48 • *Total ballparks homered in*: 16 • *First HR*: 05/20/1986 off Ken Schrom • *Switch hit HR in 1 game*—2 times

Harry Swacina

HARRY JOSEPH SWACINA
B: 08/22/1881 D: 06/21/1944
BR

Year	Tm	Lg	Tot	H	A	Men-On 0	1	2	3	One-Game 2	3	4	LO	XN	IP	PH	RHP	LHP
1915	BAL	FL	1	0	1	1	0	0	0	0	0	0	0	0	0	0	1	0

Rank among batters: 4,707 • *Total ballparks homered in*: 1 • *First HR*: 05/17/1915 off George McConnell

Craig Swan

CRAIG STEVEN SWAN
B: 11/30/1950
BR

Year	Tm	Lg	Tot	H	A	Men-On 0	1	2	3	One-Game 2	3	4	LO	XN	IP	PH	RHP	LHP
1982	NY	NL	1	0	1	0	1	0	0	0	0	0	0	0	0	0	1	0

Rank among batters: 4,707 • *Total ballparks homered in*: 1 • *First HR*: 08/04/1982 off Ferguson Jenkins

Evar Swanson

ERNEST EVAR SWANSON
B: 10/15/1902 D: 07/17/1973
BR

Year	Tm	Lg	Tot	H	A	Men-On 0	1	2	3	One-Game 2	3	4	LO	XN	IP	PH	RHP	LHP
1929	CIN	NL	4	0	4	2	2	0	0	0	0	0	2	0	0	0	2	2
1930	CIN	NL	2	0	2	2	0	0	0	0	0	0	0	0	0	0	2	0
1933	CHI	AL	1	0	1	1	0	0	0	0	0	0	0	0	0	0	0	1
Total			7	0	7	5	2	0	0	0	0	0	2	0	0	0	4	3

Rank among batters: 2,834 • *Total ballparks homered in*: 4 • *First HR*: 05/13/1929 off Bill Walker

Stan Swanson

STANLEY LAWRENCE SWANSON
B: 05/19/1944
BR

Year	Tm	Lg	Tot	H	A	Men-On 0	1	2	3	One-Game 2	3	4	LO	XN	IP	PH	RHP	LHP
1971	MON	NL	2	0	2	0	2	0	0	0	0	0	0	0	0	1	0	2

Rank among batters: 4,129 • *Total ballparks homered in*: 1 • *First HR*: 07/15/1971 off Steve Carlton

Ed Swartwood

CYRUS EDWARD SWARTWOOD
B: 01/12/1859 D: 05/15/1924
BL

Year	Tm	Lg	Tot	H	A	Men-On 0	1	2	3	One-Game 2	3	4	LO	XN	IP	PH	RHP	LHP
1882	PIT	AA	4	3	1	3	0	1	0	0	0	0	0	0	1	0	3	0
1883	PIT	AA	3	2	1	2	0	1	0	0	0	0	0	0	0	0	3	0
1886	BRO	AA	3	1	2	1	2	0	0	0	0	0	0	1	1	0	3	0
1887	BRO	AA	1	1	0	0	0	1	0	0	0	0	0	0	0	0	1	0
1890	TOL	AA	3	3	0	1	2	0	0	0	0	0	0	0	0	0	0	1
Total			14	10	4	7	4	3	0	0	0	0	0	1	2	0	9	1

Rank among batters: 2,169 • *Top target (2 home runs)*: Bill Sweeney • *Number of pitchers victimized*: 13 • *Total ballparks homered in*: 9 • *First HR*: 05/30/1882 off Tony Mullane

Bill Sweeney

WILLIAM JOHN SWEENEY
B: 03/06/1886 D: 05/26/1948
BR

Year	Tm	Lg	Tot	H	A	Men-On 0	1	2	3	One-Game 2	3	4	LO	XN	IP	PH	RHP	LHP
1909	BOS	NL	1	0	1	1	0	0	0	0	0	0	0	0	0	0	0	1
1910	BOS	NL	5	4	1	5	0	0	0	0	0	0	0	1	0	0	4	1
1911	BOS	NL	3	3	0	2	1	0	0	0	0	0	1	0	0	0	2	1
1912	BOS	NL	1	1	0	1	0	0	0	0	0	0	0	0	0	0	1	0
1914	CHI	NL	1	0	1	1	0	0	0	0	0	0	0	0	1	0	0	1
Total			11	8	3	10	1	0	0	0	0	0	1	1	1	0	7	4

Rank among batters: 2,419 • *Total ballparks homered in*: 4 • *First HR*: 06/23/1909 off Rube Marquard

Bill Sweeney

WILLIAM JOSEPH SWEENEY
B: 12/29/1904 D: 04/18/1957
BR

Year	Tm	Lg	Tot	H	A	Men-On 0	Men-On 1	Men-On 2	Men-On 3	One-Game 2	One-Game 3	One-Game 4	LO	XN	IP	PH	RHP	LHP
1930	BOS	AL	4	3	1	0	3	1	0	0	0	0	0	0	0	1	3	1
1931	BOS	AL	1	0	1	0	1	0	0	0	0	0	0	0	0	0	1	0
Total			5	3	2	0	4	1	0	0	0	0	0	0	0	1	4	1

Rank among batters: 3,191 • *Total ballparks homered in*: 3 • *First HR*: 05/09/1930 off General Crowder

Charlie Sweeney

CHARLES J. SWEENEY
B: 04/13/1863 D: 04/04/1902
BR

Year	Tm	Lg	Tot	H	A	Men-On 0	Men-On 1	Men-On 2	Men-On 3	One-Game 2	One-Game 3	One-Game 4	LO	XN	IP	PH	RHP	LHP
1884	PRO	NL	1	0	1	0	1	0	0	0	0	0	0	0	0	0	1	0
	STL	UA	1	0	1	0	0	1	0	0	0	0	0	0	0	0	0	0
	Total		2	0	2	0	2	0	0	0	0	0	0	0	0	0	1	0
Total			2	0	2	0	2	0	0	0	0	0	0	0	0	0	1	0

Rank among batters: 4,129 • *Total ballparks homered in*: 2 • *First HR*: 06/26/1884 off Fred Goldsmith

Dan Sweeney

DANIEL J. SWEENEY
B: 01/28/1868 D: 07/13/1913

Year	Tm	Lg	Tot	H	A	Men-On 0	Men-On 1	Men-On 2	Men-On 3	One-Game 2	One-Game 3	One-Game 4	LO	XN	IP	PH	RHP	LHP
1895	LOU	NL	1	0	1	0	1	0	0	0	0	0	0	0	0	0	1	0

Rank among batters: 4,707 • *Total ballparks homered in*: 1 • *First HR*: 06/01/1895 off John Malarkey

Jeff Sweeney

EDWARD FRANCIS SWEENEY
B: 07/19/1888 D: 07/04/1947
BR

Year	Tm	Lg	Tot	H	A	Men-On 0	Men-On 1	Men-On 2	Men-On 3	One-Game 2	One-Game 3	One-Game 4	LO	XN	IP	PH	RHP	LHP
1913	NY	AL	2	2	0	1	1	0	0	0	0	0	0	0	0	0	1	1
1914	NY	AL	1	1	0	1	0	0	0	0	0	0	0	0	0	0	1	0
Total			3	3	0	2	1	0	0	0	0	0	0	0	0	0	2	1

Rank among batters: 3,735 • *Total ballparks homered in*: 1 • *First HR*: 05/05/1913 off Eddie Plank

Mark Sweeney

MARK PATRICK SWEENEY
B: 10/26/1969
BL

Year	Tm	Lg	Tot	H	A	Men-On 0	Men-On 1	Men-On 2	Men-On 3	One-Game 2	One-Game 3	One-Game 4	LO	XN	IP	PH	RHP	LHP
1995	STL	NL	2	0	2	2	0	0	0	0	0	0	0	0	0	0	1	1

Rank among batters: 4,129 • *Total ballparks homered in*: 2 • *First HR*: 08/10/1995 off Hideo Nomo

Pete Sweeney

PETER JAY SWEENEY
B: 12/31/1863 D: 08/22/1901
BR

Year	Tm	Lg	Tot	H	A	Men-On 0	Men-On 1	Men-On 2	Men-On 3	One-Game 2	One-Game 3	One-Game 4	LO	XN	IP	PH	RHP	LHP
1889	WAS	NL	1	1	0	0	1	0	0	0	0	0	0	0	0	0	1	0

Rank among batters: 4,707 • *Total ballparks homered in*: 1 • *First HR*: 06/04/1889 off Tim Keefe

Rick Sweet

RICKY JOE SWEET
B: 09/07/1952
BB

Year	Tm	Lg	Tot	H	A	Men-On 0	Men-On 1	Men-On 2	Men-On 3	One-Game 2	One-Game 3	One-Game 4	LO	XN	IP	PH	RHP	LHP
1978	SD	NL	1	1	0	1	0	0	0	0	0	0	0	0	0	0	0	1
1982	SEA	AL	4	3	1	4	0	0	0	0	0	0	0	0	0	0	4	0
1983	SEA	AL	1	1	0	1	0	0	0	0	0	0	0	0	0	0	1	0
Total			6	5	1	6	0	0	0	0	0	0	0	0	0	0	5	1

Rank among batters: 2,988 • *Total ballparks homered in*: 3 • *First HR*: 05/15/1978 off Dave Hamilton

Charles Swett

WILLIAM E. SWETT
B: 04/16/1870 D: 11/22/1934

Year	Tm	Lg	Tot	H	A	Men-On 0	Men-On 1	Men-On 2	Men-On 3	One-Game 2	One-Game 3	One-Game 4	LO	XN	IP	PH	RHP	LHP
1890	BOS	PL	1	0	1	0	0	1	0	0	0	0	0	0	0	0	1	0

Rank among batters: 4,707 • *Total ballparks homered in*: 1 • *First HR*: 06/07/1890 off Ben Sanders

Bill Swift

WILLIAM VINCENT SWIFT
B: 01/10/1908 D: 02/23/1969
BR

Year	Tm	Lg	Tot	H	A	Men-On 0	1	2	3	One-Game 2	3	4	LO	XN	IP	PH	RHP	LHP
1936	PIT	NL	2	0	2	0	2	0	0	0	0	0	0	0	0	0	2	0
1938	PIT	NL	1	1	0	0	0	1	0	0	0	0	0	0	0	0	1	0
Total			3	1	2	0	2	1	0	0	0	0	0	0	0	0	3	0

Rank among batters: 3,735 • *Total ballparks homered in*: 2 • *First HR*: 06/17/1936 off Max Butcher

Bill Swift

WILLIAM CHARLES SWIFT
B: 10/27/1961
BR

Year	Tm	Lg	Tot	H	A	Men-On 0	1	2	3	One-Game 2	3	4	LO	XN	IP	PH	RHP	LHP
1995	COL	NL	1	1	0	0	0	1	0	0	0	0	0	0	0	0	1	0

Rank among batters: 4,707 • *Total ballparks homered in*: 1 • *First HR*: 05/07/1995 off Hideo Nomo

Bob Swift

ROBERT VIRGIL SWIFT
B: 03/06/1915 D: 10/17/1966
BR

Year	Tm	Lg	Tot	H	A	Men-On 0	1	2	3	One-Game 2	3	4	LO	XN	IP	PH	RHP	LHP
1942	STL	AL	1	1	0	1	0	0	0	0	0	0	0	0	0	0	0	1
1943	PHI	AL	1	1	0	1	0	0	0	0	0	0	0	0	0	0	0	1
1944	DET	AL	1	1	0	1	0	0	0	0	0	0	0	0	0	0	1	0
1946	DET	AL	2	2	0	1	1	0	0	0	0	0	0	0	0	0	2	0
1947	DET	AL	1	1	0	1	0	0	0	0	0	0	0	0	0	0	0	1
1948	DET	AL	4	2	2	3	0	1	0	0	0	0	0	0	0	0	4	0
1949	DET	AL	2	1	1	1	1	0	0	0	0	0	0	0	0	0	0	2
1950	DET	AL	2	0	2	2	0	0	0	0	0	0	0	0	0	0	0	2
Total			14	9	5	11	2	1	0	0	0	0	0	0	0	0	7	7

Rank among batters: 2,169 • *Total ballparks homered in*: 4 • *First HR*: 05/10/1942 off Eddie Smith

Steve Swisher

STEVEN EUGENE SWISHER
B: 08/09/1951
BR

Year	Tm	Lg	Tot	H	A	Men-On 0	1	2	3	One-Game 2	3	4	LO	XN	IP	PH	RHP	LHP
1974	CHI	NL	5	3	2	2	2	0	1	0	0	0	0	0	0	0	4	1
1975	CHI	NL	1	1	0	0	1	0	0	0	0	0	0	0	0	0	1	0
1976	CHI	NL	5	4	1	3	1	1	0	0	0	0	0	0	0	0	3	2
1977	CHI	NL	5	1	4	4	1	0	0	0	0	0	0	0	0	0	2	3
1978	STL	NL	1	1	0	0	1	0	0	0	0	0	0	0	0	0	0	1
1979	STL	NL	1	1	0	1	0	0	0	0	0	0	0	0	0	0	0	1
1982	SD	NL	2	0	2	2	0	0	0	0	0	0	0	0	0	0	2	0
Total			20	11	9	12	6	1	1	0	0	0	0	0	0	0	12	8

Rank among batters: 1,810 • *Total ballparks homered in*: 8 • *First HR*: 06/28/1974 off John Montague

Ron Swoboda

RONALD ALAN SWOBODA
B: 06/30/1944
BR

Year	Tm	Lg	Tot	H	A	Men-On 0	1	2	3	One-Game 2	3	4	LO	XN	IP	PH	RHP	LHP
1965	NY	NL	19	10	9	12	5	2	0	1	0	0	0	1	0	2	14	5
1966	NY	NL	8	2	6	2	2	4	0	0	0	0	0	1	0	2	1	7
1967	NY	NL	13	6	7	6	5	2	0	0	0	0	0	1	0	0	8	5
1968	NY	NL	11	6	5	5	2	4	0	0	0	0	0	0	0	0	8	3
1969	NY	NL	9	3	6	4	4	0	1	1	0	0	0	0	0	0	5	4
1970	NY	NL	9	6	3	4	4	0	1	1	0	0	0	0	0	1	2	7
1971	NY	AL	2	1	1	2	0	0	0	0	0	0	0	0	0	0	0	2
1972	NY	AL	1	0	1	1	0	0	0	0	0	0	0	0	0	1	0	1
1973	NY	AL	1	1	0	1	0	0	0	0	0	0	0	0	0	0	0	1
Total			73	35	38	37	22	12	2	3	0	0	0	3	0	6	38	35

Rank among batters: 715 • *Top target (4 home runs)*: Ferguson Jenkins • *Number of pitchers victimized*: 53 • *Total ballparks homered in*: 17 • *First HR*: 04/14/1965 off Turk Farrell

Lou Sylvester

LOUIS J. SYLVESTER
B: 02/14/1855
BR

Year	Tm	Lg	Tot	H	A	Men-On 0	1	2	3	One-Game 2	3	4	LO	XN	IP	PH	RHP	LHP
1884	CIN	UA	2	1	1	2	0	0	0	0	0	0	0	0	0	0	0	0

Lou Sylvester *continued*

Year	Tm	Lg	Tot	H	A	Men-On 0	1	2	3	One-Game 2	3	4	LO	XN	IP	PH	RHP	LHP
1886	CIN	AA	3	1	2	1	2	0	0	0	0	0	0	0	1	0	2	1
1887	STL	AA	1	1	0	0	1	0	0	0	0	0	0	0	0	0	0	0
Total			6	3	3	3	3	0	0	0	0	0	0	0	1	0	2	1

Rank among batters: 2,988 • *Total ballparks homered in*: 6 • *First HR*: 05/28/1884 off Bill Wise

Ken Szotkiewicz

KENNETH JOHN SZOTKIEWICZ
B: 02/25/1947
BL

Year	Tm	Lg	Tot	H	A	Men-On 0	1	2	3	One-Game 2	3	4	LO	XN	IP	PH	RHP	LHP
1970	DET	AL	3	3	0	2	0	1	0	0	0	0	0	0	0	0	3	0

Rank among batters: 3,735 • *Total ballparks homered in*: 1 • *First HR*: 05/06/1970 off Dave Boswell

Jerry Tabb

JERRY LYNN TABB
B: 03/17/1952
BL

Year	Tm	Lg	Tot	H	A	Men-On 0	1	2	3	One-Game 2	3	4	LO	XN	IP	PH	RHP	LHP
1977	OAK	AL	6	2	4	5	1	0	0	1	0	0	0	1	0	0	6	0

Rank among batters: 2,988 • *Top target (2 home runs)*: Dennis Eckersley, Dave Rozema • *Number of pitchers victimized*: 4 • *Total ballparks homered in*: 4 • *First HR*: 08/08/1977 off Bert Blyleven

Pat Tabler

PATRICK SEAN TABLER
B: 02/02/1958
BR

Year	Tm	Lg	Tot	H	A	Men-On 0	1	2	3	One-Game 2	3	4	LO	XN	IP	PH	RHP	LHP
1981	CHI	NL	1	1	0	0	0	1	0	0	0	0	0	0	0	0	1	0
1982	CHI	NL	1	0	1	1	0	0	0	0	0	0	0	0	0	0	1	0
1983	CLE	AL	6	3	3	4	2	0	0	0	0	0	0	0	0	0	3	3
1984	CLE	AL	10	5	5	4	3	2	1	0	0	0	0	0	0	0	7	3
1985	CLE	AL	5	5	0	2	2	0	1	0	0	0	0	0	0	0	2	3
1986	CLE	AL	6	5	1	3	3	0	0	0	0	0	0	1	0	0	4	2
1987	CLE	AL	11	5	6	6	4	1	0	0	0	0	0	0	0	0	5	6
1988	CLE	AL	1	0	1	0	1	0	0	0	0	0	0	0	0	0	0	1
	KC	AL	1	0	1	0	1	0	0	0	0	0	0	0	0	0	1	0
	Total		2	0	2	0	2	0	0	0	0	0	0	0	0	0	1	1
1989	KC	AL	2	2	0	0	2	0	0	0	0	0	0	0	0	1	0	2
1990	KC	AL	1	0	1	1	0	0	0	0	0	0	0	0	0	0	0	1
	NY	NL	1	1	0	0	0	1	0	0	0	0	0	0	0	0	1	0
	Total		2	1	1	1	0	1	0	0	0	0	0	0	0	0	1	1
1991	TOR	AL	1	1	0	0	0	1	0	0	0	0	0	0	0	0	1	0
Total			47	28	19	21	18	6	2	0	0	0	0	1	0	1	26	21

Rank among batters: 1,040 • *Top target (3 home runs)*: Jimmy Key, Guillermo Hernandez • *Number of pitchers victimized*: 39 • *Total ballparks homered in*: 16 • *First HR*: 09/27/1981 off Dick Ruthven

Jim Tabor

JAMES REUBIN TABOR
B: 11/05/1916 D: 08/22/1953
BR

Year	Tm	Lg	Tot	H	A	Men-On 0	1	2	3	One-Game 2	3	4	LO	XN	IP	PH	RHP	LHP
1938	BOS	AL	1	0	1	0	0	0	1	0	0	0	0	0	0	0	1	0
1939	BOS	AL	14	3	11	7	3	2	2	0	1	0	0	0	1	0	13	1
1940	BOS	AL	21	6	15	13	6	1	1	3	0	0	0	1	0	0	16	5
1941	BOS	AL	16	12	4	6	5	3	2	1	0	0	0	0	0	0	14	2
1942	BOS	AL	12	8	4	6	4	2	0	1	0	0	0	0	0	0	11	1
1943	BOS	AL	13	8	5	7	4	2	0	1	0	0	0	2	0	0	13	0
1944	BOS	AL	13	11	2	7	6	0	0	0	0	0	0	0	0	0	11	2
1946	PHI	NL	10	6	4	6	2	1	1	0	0	0	0	2	0	0	8	2
1947	PHI	NL	4	2	2	2	2	0	0	0	0	0	0	0	0	0	3	1
Total			104	56	48	54	32	11	7	6	1	0	0	5	1	0	90	14

Rank among batters: 469 • *Top target (6 home runs)*: Mel Harder • *Number of pitchers victimized*: 73 • *Total ballparks homered in*: 11 • *First HR*: 08/09/1938 off Nels Potter

Jeff Tackett

JEFFREY WILSON TACKETT
B: 12/01/1965
BR

Year	Tm	Lg	Tot	H	A	Men-On 0	1	2	3	One-Game 2	3	4	LO	XN	IP	PH	RHP	LHP
1992	BAL	AL	5	4	1	4	0	1	0	0	0	0	0	0	0	0	1	4

Jeff Tackett *continued*

Year	Tm	Lg	Tot	H	A	Men-On 0	1	2	3	One-Game 2	3	4	LO	XN	IP	PH	RHP	LHP
1994	BAL	AL	2	0	2	2	0	0	0	0	0	0	0	0	0	0	2	0
Total			7	4	3	6	0	1	0	0	0	0	0	0	0	0	3	4

Rank among batters: 2,834 • *Top target (2 home runs)*: Mark Langston • *Number of pitchers victimized*: 6 • *Total ballparks homered in*: 4 • *First HR*: 04/18/1992 off Frank Tanana

Doug Taitt

DOUGLAS JOHN TAITT
B: 08/03/1902 D: 12/12/1970
BL

Year	Tm	Lg	Tot	H	A	Men-On 0	1	2	3	One-Game 2	3	4	LO	XN	IP	PH	RHP	LHP
1928	BOS	AL	3	0	3	3	0	0	0	0	0	0	0	0	0	0	3	0
1931	PHI	NL	1	1	0	1	0	0	0	0	0	0	0	0	0	0	0	1
Total			4	1	3	4	0	0	0	0	0	0	0	0	0	0	3	1

Rank among batters: 3,427 • *Total ballparks homered in*: 3 • *First HR*: 05/21/1928 off Waite Hoyt

Bob Talbot

ROBERT DALE TALBOT
B: 06/06/1927
BR

Year	Tm	Lg	Tot	H	A	Men-On 0	1	2	3	One-Game 2	3	4	LO	XN	IP	PH	RHP	LHP
1954	CHI	NL	1	1	0	1	0	0	0	0	0	0	0	0	0	0	1	0

Rank among batters: 4,707 • *Total ballparks homered in*: 1 • *First HR*: 05/02/1954 off Bob Friend

Fred Talbot

FREDERICK LEALAND TALBOT
B: 06/28/1941
BR

Year	Tm	Lg	Tot	H	A	Men-On 0	1	2	3	One-Game 2	3	4	LO	XN	IP	PH	RHP	LHP
1967	NY	AL	1	0	1	1	0	0	0	0	0	0	0	0	0	0	0	1
1968	NY	AL	1	0	1	1	0	0	0	0	0	0	0	0	0	0	1	0
1969	SEA	AL	2	1	1	1	0	0	1	0	0	0	0	0	0	0	2	0
Total			4	1	3	3	0	0	1	0	0	0	0	0	0	0	3	1

Rank among batters: 3,427 • *Total ballparks homered in*: 4 • *First HR*: 05/08/1967 off Nick Willhite

Tim Talton

MARION LEE TALTON
B: 01/14/1939
BL

Year	Tm	Lg	Tot	H	A	Men-On 0	1	2	3	One-Game 2	3	4	LO	XN	IP	PH	RHP	LHP
1966	KC	AL	2	0	2	1	1	0	0	0	0	0	0	0	0	1	2	0

Rank among batters: 4,129 • *Total ballparks homered in*: 2 • *First HR*: 08/20/1966 off Mel Stottlemyre

John Tamargo

JOHN FELIX TAMARGO
B: 11/07/1951
BB

Year	Tm	Lg	Tot	H	A	Men-On 0	1	2	3	One-Game 2	3	4	LO	XN	IP	PH	RHP	LHP
1978	SF	NL	1	0	1	1	0	0	0	0	0	0	0	0	0	0	1	0
1979	SF	NL	2	1	1	1	1	0	0	0	0	0	0	0	0	1	2	0
1980	MON	NL	1	1	0	0	0	1	0	0	0	0	0	0	0	1	1	0
Total			4	2	2	2	1	1	0	0	0	0	0	0	0	2	4	0

Rank among batters: 3,427 • *Total ballparks homered in*: 4 • *First HR*: 08/22/1978 off Nino Espinosa

Vito Tamulis

VITAUTRIS CASIMIRUS TAMULIS
B: 07/11/1911 D: 05/05/1974
BL

Year	Tm	Lg	Tot	H	A	Men-On 0	1	2	3	One-Game 2	3	4	LO	XN	IP	PH	RHP	LHP
1935	NY	AL	1	0	1	0	1	0	0	0	0	0	0	0	0	0	0	1

Rank among batters: 4,707 • *Total ballparks homered in*: 1 • *First HR*: 06/11/1935 off Russ Van Atta

Jesse Tannehill

JESSE NILES TANNEHILL
B: 07/14/1874 D: 09/22/1956
BB

Year	Tm	Lg	Tot	H	A	Men-On 0	1	2	3	One-Game 2	3	4	LO	XN	IP	PH	RHP	LHP
1898	PIT	NL	1	0	1	1	0	0	0	0	0	0	0	0	0	0	0	0
1901	PIT	NL	1	1	0	0	1	0	0	0	0	0	0	0	0	0	1	0

Jesse Tannehill *continued*

Year	Tm	Lg	Tot	H	A	Men-On 0	1	2	3	One-Game 2	3	4	LO	XN	IP	PH	RHP	LHP
1902	PIT	NL	1	0	1	0	0	1	0	0	0	0	0	0	1	0	0	1
1903	NY	AL	1	0	1	1	0	0	0	0	0	0	0	0	0	0	0	1
1905	BOS	AL	1	0	1	0	0	1	0	0	0	0	0	0	0	0	1	0
Total			5	1	4	2	1	2	0	0	0	0	0	0	1	0	2	2

Rank among batters: 3,191 • *Total ballparks homered in*: 5 • *First HR*: 06/07/1898 off Cy Swaim

Lee Tannehill

LEE FORD TANNEHILL
B: 10/26/1880 D: 02/16/1938
BR

Year	Tm	Lg	Tot	H	A	Men-On 0	1	2	3	One-Game 2	3	4	LO	XN	IP	PH	RHP	LHP
1903	CHI	AL	2	1	1	2	0	0	0	0	0	0	0	0	0	0	2	0
1910	CHI	AL	1	1	0	0	0	0	1	0	0	0	0	0	0	0	1	0
Total			3	2	1	2	0	0	1	0	0	0	0	0	0	0	3	0

Rank among batters: 3,735 • *Total ballparks homered in*: 2 • *First HR*: 07/21/1903 off Al Orth

Chuck Tanner

CHARLES WILLIAM TANNER
B: 07/04/1929
BL

Year	Tm	Lg	Tot	H	A	Men-On 0	1	2	3	One-Game 2	3	4	LO	XN	IP	PH	RHP	LHP
1955	MIL	NL	6	5	1	4	1	1	0	0	0	0	0	0	0	1	6	0
1956	MIL	NL	1	0	1	0	1	0	0	0	0	0	0	0	0	0	0	1
1957	MIL	NL	2	1	1	2	0	0	0	0	0	0	0	1	0	0	2	0
	CHI	NL	7	4	3	5	0	2	0	0	0	0	0	0	1	0	6	1
	Total		9	5	4	7	0	2	0	0	0	0	0	1	1	0	8	1
1958	CHI	NL	4	1	3	2	0	2	0	0	0	0	0	0	0	3	4	0
1959	CLE	AL	1	1	0	1	0	0	0	0	0	0	0	0	0	0	1	0
Total			21	12	9	14	2	5	0	0	0	0	0	1	1	4	19	2

Rank among batters: 1,768 • *Top target (2 home runs)*: Robin Roberts, Carl Erskine • *Number of pitchers victimized*: 19 • *Total ballparks homered in*: 8 • *First HR*: 04/12/1955 off Gerry Staley • *Hit HR on first major league pitch*—vs CIN: 04/12/1955

Walter Tappan

WALTER VAN DORN TAPPAN
B: 10/08/1890 D: 12/19/1967
BR

Year	Tm	Lg	Tot	H	A	Men-On 0	1	2	3	One-Game 2	3	4	LO	XN	IP	PH	RHP	LHP
1914	KC	FL	1	1	0	0	1	0	0	0	0	0	0	0	0	0	1	0

Rank among batters: 4,707 • *Total ballparks homered in*: 1 • *First HR*: 05/04/1914 off Elmer Knetzer

Ted Tappe

THEODORE NASH TAPPE
B: 02/02/1931
BL

Year	Tm	Lg	Tot	H	A	Men-On 0	1	2	3	One-Game 2	3	4	LO	XN	IP	PH	RHP	LHP
1950	CIN	NL	1	0	1	1	0	0	0	0	0	0	0	0	0	1	1	0
1955	CHI	NL	4	2	2	3	1	0	0	0	0	0	0	0	0	1	4	0
Total			5	2	3	4	1	0	0	0	0	0	0	0	0	2	5	0

Rank among batters: 3,191 • *Total ballparks homered in*: 4 • *First HR*: 09/14/1950 off Erv Palica • *Hit HR in first major league AB*—@BRO: 09/14/1950 (1)

Tony Tarasco

ANTHONY GIACINTO TARASCO
B: 12/09/1970
BL

Year	Tm	Lg	Tot	H	A	Men-On 0	1	2	3	One-Game 2	3	4	LO	XN	IP	PH	RHP	LHP
1994	ATL	NL	5	2	3	2	3	0	0	0	0	0	0	0	0	1	4	1
1995	MON	NL	14	7	7	11	2	1	0	0	0	0	3	0	0	0	13	1
Total			19	9	10	13	5	1	0	0	0	0	3	0	0	1	17	2

Rank among batters: 1,861 • *Total ballparks homered in*: 9 • *First HR*: 04/10/1994 off Gary Wayne

Danny Tartabull

DANILO (MORA) TARTABULL
B: 10/30/1962
BR

Year	Tm	Lg	Tot	H	A	Men-On 0	1	2	3	One-Game 2	3	4	LO	XN	IP	PH	RHP	LHP
1984	SEA	AL	2	1	1	1	0	1	0	0	0	0	0	0	0	0	2	0
1985	SEA	AL	1	0	1	0	1	0	0	0	0	0	0	0	0	0	0	1

Danny Tartabull *continued*

Year	Tm	Lg	Tot	H	A	Men-On 0	1	2	3	One-Game 2	3	4	LO	XN	IP	PH	RHP	LHP
1986	SEA	AL	25	13	12	9	10	4	2	1	0	0	0	0	0	0	22	3
1987	KC	AL	34	15	19	18	12	3	1	2	0	0	0	1	1	0	27	7
1988	KC	AL	26	15	11	13	8	2	3	1	0	0	0	0	1	0	18	8
1989	KC	AL	18	9	9	13	4	1	0	0	0	0	0	1	0	0	11	7
1990	KC	AL	15	5	10	7	6	2	0	1	0	0	0	0	1	0	11	4
1991	KC	AL	31	13	18	17	11	2	1	2	1	0	0	2	0	0	23	8
1992	NY	AL	25	11	14	10	6	7	2	1	0	0	0	0	0	0	14	11
1993	NY	AL	31	11	20	19	6	6	0	1	0	0	0	0	0	0	24	7
1994	NY	AL	19	10	9	12	5	1	1	0	0	0	0	1	0	1	10	9
1995	NY	AL	6	2	4	5	1	0	0	0	0	0	0	0	0	0	2	4
	OAK	AL	2	1	1	1	1	0	0	0	0	0	0	0	0	0	0	2
	Total		8	3	5	6	2	0	0	0	0	0	0	0	0	0	2	6
Total			235	106	129	125	71	29	10	9	1	0	0	5	3	1	164	71

Rank among batters: 135 • *Top target (6 home runs)*: Bert Blyleven, Dave Stewart • *Number of pitchers victimized*: 163 • *Total ballparks homered in*: 18 • *First HR*: 09/22/1984 off Lamarr Hoyt

Jose Tartabull

JOSE MILAGES (GUZMAN) TARTABULL
B: 11/27/1938
BL

Year	Tm	Lg	Tot	H	A	Men-On 0	1	2	3	One-Game 2	3	4	LO	XN	IP	PH	RHP	LHP
1963	KC	AL	1	0	1	1	0	0	0	0	0	0	0	0	0	0	1	0
1965	KC	AL	1	1	0	1	0	0	0	0	0	0	0	0	0	0	1	0
Total			2	1	1	2	0	0	0	0	0	0	0	0	0	0	2	0

Rank among batters: 4,129 • *Total ballparks homered in*: 2 • *First HR*: 08/11/1963 off Barry Latman

Willie Tasby

WILLIE TASBY
B: 01/08/1933
BR

Year	Tm	Lg	Tot	H	A	Men-On 0	1	2	3	One-Game 2	3	4	LO	XN	IP	PH	RHP	LHP
1958	BAL	AL	1	0	1	1	0	0	0	0	0	0	0	0	0	0	1	0
1959	BAL	AL	13	8	5	8	5	0	0	1	0	0	1	0	0	0	8	5
1960	BOS	AL	7	6	1	5	0	1	1	0	0	0	1	0	0	0	5	2
1961	WAS	AL	17	5	12	13	3	0	1	0	0	0	0	0	0	0	12	5
1962	CLE	AL	4	1	3	3	0	1	0	0	0	0	0	0	0	0	0	4
1963	CLE	AL	4	3	1	4	0	0	0	0	0	0	0	0	0	0	0	4
Total			46	23	23	34	8	2	2	1	0	0	2	0	0	0	26	20

Rank among batters: 1,060 • *Top target (3 home runs)*: Don Mossi • *Number of pitchers victimized*: 39 • *Total ballparks homered in*: 11 • *First HR*: 09/10/1958 off Bob Grim

Bennie Tate

HENRY BENNETT TATE
B: 12/03/1901 D: 10/27/1973
BL

Year	Tm	Lg	Tot	H	A	Men-On 0	1	2	3	One-Game 2	3	4	LO	XN	IP	PH	RHP	LHP
1926	WAS	AL	1	1	0	1	0	0	0	0	0	0	0	0	0	0	1	0
1927	WAS	AL	1	0	1	0	1	0	0	0	0	0	0	0	0	0	0	1
1932	BOS	AL	2	2	0	1	1	0	0	0	0	0	0	1	0	0	2	0
Total			4	3	1	2	2	0	0	0	0	0	0	1	0	0	3	1

Rank among batters: 3,427 • *Total ballparks homered in*: 3 • *First HR*: 08/11/1926 off Myles Thomas

Lee Tate

LEE WILLIE TATE
B: 03/18/1932
BR

Year	Tm	Lg	Tot	H	A	Men-On 0	1	2	3	One-Game 2	3	4	LO	XN	IP	PH	RHP	LHP
1959	STL	NL	1	0	1	1	0	0	0	0	0	0	0	0	0	0	0	1

Rank among batters: 4,707 • *Total ballparks homered in*: 1 • *First HR*: 05/27/1959 off Johnny Antonelli

Pop Tate

EDWARD CHRISTOPHER TATE
B: 12/22/1860 D: 06/25/1932
BR

Year	Tm	Lg	Tot	H	A	Men-On 0	1	2	3	One-Game 2	3	4	LO	XN	IP	PH	RHP	LHP
1888	BOS	NL	1	0	1	0	1	0	0	0	0	0	0	0	0	0	0	1
1889	BAL	AA	1	0	1	0	1	0	0	0	0	0	0	0	0	0	1	0
Total			2	0	2	0	2	0	0	0	0	0	0	0	0	0	1	1

Rank among batters: 4,129 • *Total ballparks homered in*: 2 • *First HR*: 07/17/1888 off Ed Beatin

Jim Tatum

JAMES RAY TATUM
B: 10/09/1967
BR

Year	Tm	Lg	Tot	H	A	Men-On 0	1	2	3	One-Game 2	3	4	LO	XN	IP	PH	RHP	LHP
1993	COL	NL	1	0	1	0	0	0	1	0	0	0	0	0	0	1	0	1

Rank among batters: 4,707 • *Total ballparks homered in*: 1 • *First HR*: 05/04/1993 off Dan Plesac

Ken Tatum

KENNETH RAY TATUM
B: 04/25/1944
BR

Year	Tm	Lg	Tot	H	A	Men-On 0	1	2	3	One-Game 2	3	4	LO	XN	IP	PH	RHP	LHP
1969	CAL	AL	2	0	2	2	0	0	0	0	0	0	0	0	0	0	2	0
1970	CAL	AL	1	0	1	0	0	1	0	0	0	0	0	0	0	0	1	0
1971	BOS	AL	1	1	0	1	0	0	0	0	0	0	0	0	0	0	1	0
Total			4	1	3	3	0	1	0	0	0	0	0	0	0	0	4	0

Rank among batters: 3,427 • *Total ballparks homered in*: 3 • *First HR*: 07/04/1969 off Gary Bell

Tommy Tatum

V T TATUM
B: 07/16/1919 D: 11/07/1989
BR

Year	Tm	Lg	Tot	H	A	Men-On 0	1	2	3	One-Game 2	3	4	LO	XN	IP	PH	RHP	LHP
1947	CIN	NL	1	1	0	1	0	0	0	0	0	0	0	0	0	0	0	1

Rank among batters: 4,707 • *Total ballparks homered in*: 1 • *First HR*: 05/14/1947 off Joe Hatten

Ed Taubensee

EDWARD KENNETH TAUBENSEE
B: 10/31/1968
BL

Year	Tm	Lg	Tot	H	A	Men-On 0	1	2	3	One-Game 2	3	4	LO	XN	IP	PH	RHP	LHP
1992	HOU	NL	5	2	3	3	2	0	0	0	0	0	0	0	0	0	3	2
1993	HOU	NL	9	4	5	4	5	0	0	1	0	0	0	0	0	0	8	1
1994	CIN	NL	8	2	6	5	3	0	0	2	0	0	0	0	0	0	7	1
1995	CIN	NL	9	4	5	5	4	0	0	0	0	0	0	0	1	1	7	2
Total			31	12	19	17	14	0	0	3	0	0	0	0	1	1	25	6

Rank among batters: 1,400 • *Top target (2 home runs)*: Rene Arocha • *Number of pitchers victimized*: 30 • *Total ballparks homered in*: 12 • *First HR*: 07/20/1992 off Jeff Robinson

Don Taussig

DONALD FRANKLIN TAUSSIG
B: 02/19/1932
BR

Year	Tm	Lg	Tot	H	A	Men-On 0	1	2	3	One-Game 2	3	4	LO	XN	IP	PH	RHP	LHP
1958	SF	NL	1	1	0	1	0	0	0	0	0	0	0	0	0	0	0	1
1961	STL	NL	2	1	1	1	1	0	0	0	0	0	0	0	0	0	0	2
1962	HOU	NL	1	1	0	1	0	0	0	0	0	0	0	0	0	0	1	0
Total			4	3	1	3	1	0	0	0	0	0	0	0	0	0	1	3

Rank among batters: 3,427 • *Total ballparks homered in*: 4 • *First HR*: 06/06/1958 off Harvey Haddix

Jesus Tavarez

JESUS RAFAEL (ALCANTARAS) TAVAREZ
B: 03/26/1971
BB

Year	Tm	Lg	Tot	H	A	Men-On 0	1	2	3	One-Game 2	3	4	LO	XN	IP	PH	RHP	LHP
1995	FLO	NL	2	1	1	1	0	1	0	0	0	0	0	0	0	0	2	0

Rank among batters: 4,129 • *Total ballparks homered in*: 2 • *First HR*: 08/26/1995 off Todd Jones

Jackie Tavener

JOHN ADAM TAVENER
B: 12/27/1897 D: 09/14/1969
BL

Year	Tm	Lg	Tot	H	A	Men-On 0	1	2	3	One-Game 2	3	4	LO	XN	IP	PH	RHP	LHP
1926	DET	AL	1	0	1	1	0	0	0	0	0	0	0	0	0	0	1	0
1927	DET	AL	5	0	5	1	3	1	0	0	0	0	0	0	1	0	4	1
1928	DET	AL	5	2	3	3	1	0	1	0	0	0	0	0	0	0	4	1
1929	CLE	AL	2	1	1	0	1	1	0	0	0	0	0	0	1	0	2	0
Total			13	3	10	5	5	2	1	0	0	0	0	0	2	0	11	2

Rank among batters: 2,248 • *Total ballparks homered in*: 7 • *First HR*: 08/29/1926 off Urban Shocker

Year	Tm	Lg	Tot	H	A	Men-On 0	Men-On 1	Men-On 2	Men-On 3	One-Game 2	One-Game 3	One-Game 4	LO	XN	IP	PH	RHP	LHP

Frank Taveras

FRANKLIN CRISOSTOMO (FABIAN) TAVERAS
B: 12/24/1949
BR

Year	Tm	Lg	Tot	H	A	Men-On 0	Men-On 1	Men-On 2	Men-On 3	One-Game 2	One-Game 3	One-Game 4	LO	XN	IP	PH	RHP	LHP
1977	PIT	NL	1	0	1	0	0	0	1	0	0	0	0	0	1	0	0	1
1979	NY	NL	1	0	1	1	0	0	0	0	0	0	0	0	0	0	1	0
Total			2	0	2	1	0	0	1	0	0	0	0	0	1	0	1	1

Rank among batters: 4,129 • *Total ballparks homered in*: 1 • *First HR*: 08/05/1977 off Doug Capilla

Ben Taylor

BENJAMIN EUGENE TAYLOR
B: 09/30/1927
BL

Year	Tm	Lg	Tot	H	A	Men-On 0	Men-On 1	Men-On 2	Men-On 3	One-Game 2	One-Game 3	One-Game 4	LO	XN	IP	PH	RHP	LHP
1951	STL	AL	3	0	3	3	0	0	0	0	0	0	0	0	0	0	3	0

Rank among batters: 3,735 • *Total ballparks homered in*: 3 • *First HR*: 07/29/1951 off Sandy Consuegra

Bill Taylor

WILLIAM MICHAEL TAYLOR
B: 12/30/1929
BL

Year	Tm	Lg	Tot	H	A	Men-On 0	Men-On 1	Men-On 2	Men-On 3	One-Game 2	One-Game 3	One-Game 4	LO	XN	IP	PH	RHP	LHP
1954	NY	NL	2	1	1	1	1	0	0	0	0	0	0	1	0	2	2	0
1955	NY	NL	4	0	4	2	1	1	0	0	0	0	0	0	0	4	3	1
1957	DET	AL	1	1	0	1	0	0	0	0	0	0	0	0	0	0	1	0
Total			7	2	5	4	2	1	0	0	0	0	0	1	0	6	6	1

Rank among batters: 2,834 • *Top target (2 home runs)*: Warren Hacker • *Number of pitchers victimized*: 6 • *Total ballparks homered in*: 6 • *First HR*: 06/10/1954 off Gene Conley

Billy Taylor

WILLIAM HENRY TAYLOR
B: 1855 D: 05/14/1900
BR

Year	Tm	Lg	Tot	H	A	Men-On 0	Men-On 1	Men-On 2	Men-On 3	One-Game 2	One-Game 3	One-Game 4	LO	XN	IP	PH	RHP	LHP
1882	PIT	AA	3	2	1	2	0	1	0	0	0	0	0	0	0	0	2	0
1883	PIT	AA	2	1	1	1	0	1	0	0	0	0	0	0	0	0	2	0
1884	STL	UA	3	2	1	2	1	0	0	0	0	0	0	0	0	0	2	0
Total			8	5	3	5	1	2	0	0	0	0	0	0	0	0	6	0

Rank among batters: 2,703 • *Top target (2 home runs)*: George Bradley • *Number of pitchers victimized*: 7 • *Total ballparks homered in*: 5 • *First HR*: 07/10/1882 off Doc Landis

Bob Taylor

ROBERT LEE TAYLOR
B: 03/20/1944
BL

Year	Tm	Lg	Tot	H	A	Men-On 0	Men-On 1	Men-On 2	Men-On 3	One-Game 2	One-Game 3	One-Game 4	LO	XN	IP	PH	RHP	LHP
1970	SF	NL	2	2	0	0	1	1	0	0	0	0	0	0	0	1	2	0

Rank among batters: 4,129 • *Total ballparks homered in*: 1 • *First HR*: 05/27/1970 off Jose Pena

Carl Taylor

CARL MEANS TAYLOR
B: 01/20/1944
BR

Year	Tm	Lg	Tot	H	A	Men-On 0	Men-On 1	Men-On 2	Men-On 3	One-Game 2	One-Game 3	One-Game 4	LO	XN	IP	PH	RHP	LHP
1969	PIT	NL	4	1	3	2	2	0	0	0	0	0	0	0	0	0	3	1
1970	STL	NL	6	1	5	4	1	0	1	0	0	0	0	0	0	1	2	4
Total			10	2	8	6	3	0	1	0	0	0	0	0	0	1	5	5

Rank among batters: 2,500 • *Top target (2 home runs)*: Ron Herbel • *Number of pitchers victimized*: 9 • *Total ballparks homered in*: 6 • *First HR*: 05/25/1969 off Ron Herbel

Danny Taylor

DANIEL TURNEY TAYLOR
B: 12/23/1900 D: 10/11/1972
BR

Year	Tm	Lg	Tot	H	A	Men-On 0	Men-On 1	Men-On 2	Men-On 3	One-Game 2	One-Game 3	One-Game 4	LO	XN	IP	PH	RHP	LHP
1926	WAS	AL	1	0	1	1	0	0	0	0	0	0	0	0	0	0	1	0
1930	CHI	NL	2	1	1	1	1	0	0	0	0	0	0	0	1	0	2	0
1931	CHI	NL	5	5	0	3	1	1	0	0	0	0	0	0	0	0	4	1
1932	BRO	NL	11	7	4	8	1	1	1	1	0	0	2	0	1	0	11	0
1933	BRO	NL	9	6	3	7	2	0	0	1	0	0	0	1	0	0	3	6

Danny Taylor *continued*

Year	Tm	Lg	Tot	H	A	Men-On 0	1	2	3	One-Game 2	3	4	LO	XN	IP	PH	RHP	LHP
1934	BRO	NL	7	4	3	4	2	1	0	0	0	0	0	0	0	0	6	1
1935	BRO	NL	7	3	4	1	4	0	2	0	0	0	0	0	0	0	6	1
1936	BRO	NL	2	1	1	1	1	0	0	0	0	0	0	0	0	0	2	0
Total			44	27	17	26	12	3	3	2	0	0	2	1	2	0	35	9

Rank among batters: 1,095 • *Top target (3 home runs)*: Red Lucas • *Number of pitchers victimized*: 37 • *Total ballparks homered in*: 9 • *First HR*: 06/30/1926 off Ted Wingfield

Harry Taylor

HARRY LEONARD TAYLOR
B: 04/04/1866 D: 07/12/1955
BL

Year	Tm	Lg	Tot	H	A	Men-On 0	1	2	3	One-Game 2	3	4	LO	XN	IP	PH	RHP	LHP
1891	LOU	AA	2	0	2	1	1	0	0	0	0	0	0	0	1	0	1	0
1893	BAL	NL	1	1	0	1	0	0	0	0	0	0	0	0	0	0	1	0
Total			3	1	2	2	1	0	0	0	0	0	0	0	1	0	2	0

Rank among batters: 3,735 • *Total ballparks homered in*: 3 • *First HR*: 05/08/1891 off Bert Cunningham

Hawk Taylor

ROBERT DALE TAYLOR
B: 04/03/1939
BR

Year	Tm	Lg	Tot	H	A	Men-On 0	1	2	3	One-Game 2	3	4	LO	XN	IP	PH	RHP	LHP
1961	MIL	NL	1	1	0	1	0	0	0	0	0	0	0	0	0	1	0	1
1964	NY	NL	4	4	0	0	3	1	0	1	0	0	0	0	0	0	2	2
1965	NY	NL	4	1	3	1	2	1	0	1	0	0	0	0	0	0	1	3
1966	NY	NL	3	3	0	1	0	1	1	0	0	0	0	0	0	1	1	2
1967	CAL	AL	1	0	1	1	0	0	0	0	0	0	0	0	0	0	0	1
1969	KC	AL	3	1	2	0	0	3	0	0	0	0	0	0	0	1	2	1
Total			16	10	6	4	5	6	1	2	0	0	0	0	0	3	6	10

Rank among batters: 2,029 • *Total ballparks homered in*: 8 • *First HR*: 10/01/1961 off Mike McCormick

Jack Taylor

JOHN BUDD TAYLOR
B: 05/23/1873 D: 02/07/1900
BR

Year	Tm	Lg	Tot	H	A	Men-On 0	1	2	3	One-Game 2	3	4	LO	XN	IP	PH	RHP	LHP
1895	PHI	NL	3	3	0	2	1	0	0	0	0	0	0	0	0	0	3	0
1897	PHI	NL	1	0	1	0	1	0	0	0	0	0	0	0	0	0	1	0
1898	STL	NL	1	1	0	1	0	0	0	0	0	0	0	0	0	0	1	0
Total			5	4	1	3	2	0	0	0	0	0	0	0	0	0	5	0

Rank among batters: 3,191 • *Top target (2 home runs)*: Kid Nichols • *Number of pitchers victimized*: 4 • *Total ballparks homered in*: 3 • *First HR*: 08/19/1895 off Kid Nichols

Jack Taylor

JOHN W. TAYLOR
B: 01/14/1874 D: 03/04/1938
BR

Year	Tm	Lg	Tot	H	A	Men-On 0	1	2	3	One-Game 2	3	4	LO	XN	IP	PH	RHP	LHP
1900	CHI	NL	1	1	0	1	0	0	0	0	0	0	0	0	0	0	1	0
1904	STL	NL	1	0	1	1	0	0	0	0	0	0	0	0	1	0	1	0
Total			2	1	1	2	0	0	0	0	0	0	0	0	1	0	2	0

Rank among batters: 4,129 • *Total ballparks homered in*: 1 • *First HR*: 05/19/1900 off Bill Dinneen

Joe Taylor

JOE CEPHUS TAYLOR
B: 03/02/1926
BR

Year	Tm	Lg	Tot	H	A	Men-On 0	1	2	3	One-Game 2	3	4	LO	XN	IP	PH	RHP	LHP
1954	PHI	AL	1	1	0	1	0	0	0	0	0	0	0	0	0	0	1	0
1957	CIN	NL	4	4	0	3	1	0	0	1	0	0	0	0	0	0	1	3
1958	STL	NL	1	0	1	1	0	0	0	0	0	0	0	0	0	1	1	0
	BAL	AL	2	0	2	2	0	0	0	0	0	0	0	0	1	0	1	1
	Total		3	0	3	3	0	0	0	0	0	0	0	0	1	1	2	1
1959	BAL	AL	1	0	1	1	0	0	0	0	0	0	0	0	0	0	1	0
Total			9	5	4	8	1	0	0	1	0	0	0	0	1	1	5	4

Rank among batters: 2,587 • *Top target (2 home runs)*: Johnny Podres, Russ Kemmerer • *Number of pitchers victimized*: 7 • *Total ballparks homered in*: 4 • *First HR*: 09/05/1954 off Russ Kemmerer

Sammy Taylor

SAMUEL DOUGLAS TAYLOR
B: 02/27/1933
BL

Year	Tm	Lg	Tot	H	A	Men-On 0	Men-On 1	Men-On 2	Men-On 3	One-Game 2	One-Game 3	One-Game 4	LO	XN	IP	PH	RHP	LHP
1958	CHI	NL	6	2	4	2	3	1	0	0	0	0	0	0	0	0	6	0
1959	CHI	NL	13	10	3	10	3	0	0	0	0	0	0	0	0	0	13	0
1960	CHI	NL	3	0	3	1	2	0	0	0	0	0	0	0	0	1	3	0
1961	CHI	NL	8	6	2	4	4	0	0	2	0	0	0	0	0	0	8	0
1962	NY	NL	3	2	1	3	0	0	0	0	0	0	0	0	0	0	3	0
Total			33	20	13	20	12	1	0	2	0	0	0	0	0	1	33	0

Rank among batters: 1,336 • *Top target (4 home runs)*: Don Drysdale • *Number of pitchers victimized*: 24 • *Total ballparks homered in*: 9 • *First HR*: 04/30/1958 off Bob Buhl

Tony Taylor

ANTONIO NEMESIO (SANCHEZ) TAYLOR
B: 12/19/1935
BR

Year	Tm	Lg	Tot	H	A	Men-On 0	Men-On 1	Men-On 2	Men-On 3	One-Game 2	One-Game 3	One-Game 4	LO	XN	IP	PH	RHP	LHP
1958	CHI	NL	6	3	3	5	1	0	0	1	0	0	2	0	1	0	3	3
1959	CHI	NL	8	3	5	8	0	0	0	0	0	0	1	1	0	0	5	3
1960	CHI	NL	1	1	0	0	1	0	0	0	0	0	0	0	0	0	1	0
	PHI	NL	4	3	1	4	0	0	0	0	0	0	0	0	0	0	2	2
	Total		5	4	1	4	1	0	0	0	0	0	0	0	0	0	3	2
1961	PHI	NL	2	1	1	1	1	0	0	0	0	0	0	0	0	0	2	0
1962	PHI	NL	7	4	3	6	1	0	0	0	0	0	1	0	0	0	4	3
1963	PHI	NL	5	3	2	3	2	0	0	0	0	0	0	0	0	0	2	3
1964	PHI	NL	4	1	3	4	0	0	0	0	0	0	1	0	0	0	2	2
1965	PHI	NL	3	1	2	2	0	1	0	0	0	0	0	0	0	0	0	3
1966	PHI	NL	5	2	3	3	0	2	0	0	0	0	0	0	0	0	4	1
1967	PHI	NL	2	1	1	2	0	0	0	0	0	0	0	0	0	0	2	0
1968	PHI	NL	3	1	2	2	1	0	0	0	0	0	0	0	0	0	3	0
1969	PHI	NL	3	1	2	1	1	0	1	0	0	0	1	0	0	0	2	1
1970	PHI	NL	9	4	5	5	2	1	1	1	0	0	3	1	1	0	5	4
1971	PHI	NL	1	1	0	0	1	0	0	0	0	0	0	0	0	0	0	1
	DET	AL	3	3	0	2	1	0	0	0	0	0	0	0	1	0	0	3
	Total		4	4	0	2	2	0	0	0	0	0	0	0	1	0	0	4
1972	DET	AL	1	1	0	1	0	0	0	0	0	0	0	0	0	0	1	0
1973	DET	AL	5	2	3	5	0	0	0	0	0	0	1	0	0	0	0	5
1974	PHI	NL	2	1	1	0	2	0	0	0	0	0	0	0	0	2	0	2
1975	PHI	NL	1	0	1	0	0	1	0	0	0	0	0	0	0	1	0	1
Total			75	37	38	54	14	5	2	2	0	0	10	2	3	3	38	37

Rank among batters: 699 • *Top target (3 home runs)*: Bobby Bolin, Jack Curtis • *Number of pitchers victimized*: 61 • *Total ballparks homered in*: 16 • *First HR*: 06/19/1958 off Warren Spahn

Zack Taylor

JAMES WREN TAYLOR
B: 07/27/1898 D: 09/19/1974
BR

Year	Tm	Lg	Tot	H	A	Men-On 0	Men-On 1	Men-On 2	Men-On 3	One-Game 2	One-Game 3	One-Game 4	LO	XN	IP	PH	RHP	LHP
1924	BRO	NL	1	1	0	1	0	0	0	0	0	0	0	0	0	0	1	0
1925	BRO	NL	3	2	1	1	0	1	1	0	0	0	0	0	0	0	2	1
1927	BOS	NL	1	1	0	0	0	1	0	0	0	0	0	0	1	0	1	0
1928	BOS	NL	2	1	1	2	0	0	0	0	0	0	0	0	0	0	2	0
1929	CHI	NL	1	0	1	1	0	0	0	0	0	0	0	0	0	0	1	0
1930	CHI	NL	1	1	0	0	0	1	0	0	0	0	0	0	0	0	0	1
Total			9	6	3	5	0	3	1	0	0	0	0	0	1	0	7	2

Rank among batters: 2,587 • *Top target (2 home runs)*: Jimmy Ring • *Number of pitchers victimized*: 8 • *Total ballparks homered in*: 4 • *First HR*: 06/01/1924 off Jimmy Ring

Birdie Tebbetts

GEORGE ROBERT TEBBETTS
B: 11/10/1912
BR

Year	Tm	Lg	Tot	H	A	Men-On 0	Men-On 1	Men-On 2	Men-On 3	One-Game 2	One-Game 3	One-Game 4	LO	XN	IP	PH	RHP	LHP
1936	DET	AL	1	1	0	1	0	0	0	0	0	0	0	0	0	0	1	0
1937	DET	AL	2	1	1	1	0	1	0	0	0	0	0	2	0	0	2	0
1938	DET	AL	1	1	0	0	0	0	1	0	0	0	0	0	0	0	0	1
1939	DET	AL	4	3	1	1	2	0	1	0	0	0	0	0	0	0	4	0
1940	DET	AL	4	4	0	4	0	0	0	0	0	0	0	0	0	0	3	1
1941	DET	AL	2	1	1	0	2	0	0	0	0	0	0	0	0	0	2	0
1942	DET	AL	1	1	0	0	1	0	0	0	0	0	0	0	0	0	1	0

Birdie Tebbetts *continued*

Year	Tm	Lg	Tot	H	A	Men-On 0	1	2	3	One-Game 2	3	4	LO	XN	IP	PH	RHP	LHP
1946	DET	AL	1	1	0	1	0	0	0	0	0	0	0	0	0	0	0	1
1947	BOS	AL	1	1	0	1	0	0	0	0	0	0	0	0	0	0	1	0
1948	BOS	AL	5	3	2	2	1	1	1	0	0	0	0	0	0	0	4	1
1949	BOS	AL	5	3	2	2	2	1	0	0	0	0	0	0	0	0	5	0
1950	BOS	AL	8	6	2	6	1	1	0	1	0	0	0	0	0	0	7	1
1951	CLE	AL	2	1	1	0	2	0	0	0	0	0	0	0	0	0	0	2
1952	CLE	AL	1	0	1	0	0	1	0	0	0	0	0	0	0	0	1	0
Total			38	27	11	19	11	5	3	1	0	0	0	2	0	0	31	7

Rank among batters: 1,225 • *Top target (3 home runs)*: Joe Hеving • *Number of pitchers victimized*: 34 • *Total ballparks homered in*: 6 • *First HR*: 09/22/1936 off Earl Caldwell

George Tebeau

GEORGE E. TEBEAU
B: 12/26/1861 D: 02/04/1923
BR

Year	Tm	Lg	Tot	H	A	Men-On 0	1	2	3	One-Game 2	3	4	LO	XN	IP	PH	RHP	LHP
1887	CIN	AA	4	3	1	0	2	2	0	0	0	0	0	0	0	0	4	0
1888	CIN	AA	3	1	2	2	1	0	0	0	0	0	0	0	0	0	2	1
1889	CIN	AA	7	7	0	4	2	1	0	0	0	0	0	0	2	0	5	2
1890	TOL	AA	1	1	0	1	0	0	0	0	0	0	0	0	0	0	0	1
Total			15	12	3	7	5	3	0	0	0	0	0	0	2	0	11	4

Rank among batters: 2,096 • *Top target (2 home runs)*: Henry Porter • *Number of pitchers victimized*: 14 • *Total ballparks homered in*: 5 • *First HR*: 04/16/1887 off George Pechiney • *Hit HR in first major league AB*—vs CLE: 04/16/1887

Patsy Tebeau

OLIVER WENDELL TEBEAU
B: 12/05/1864 D: 05/15/1918
BR

Year	Tm	Lg	Tot	H	A	Men-On 0	1	2	3	One-Game 2	3	4	LO	XN	IP	PH	RHP	LHP
1889	CLE	NL	8	2	6	2	4	2	0	0	0	0	0	1	1	0	6	1
1890	CLE	PL	5	2	3	1	2	2	0	1	0	0	0	0	0	0	3	2
1891	CLE	NL	1	1	0	0	0	1	0	0	0	0	0	0	0	0	0	1
1892	CLE	NL	2	0	2	0	0	2	0	0	0	0	0	0	1	0	1	1
1893	CLE	NL	2	2	0	1	0	1	0	0	0	0	0	0	1	0	1	1
1894	CLE	NL	3	0	3	1	2	0	0	0	0	0	0	0	0	0	2	1
1895	CLE	NL	2	0	2	2	0	0	0	0	0	0	0	0	0	0	2	0
1896	CLE	NL	2	1	1	0	1	1	0	0	0	0	0	0	0	0	1	1
1898	CLE	NL	1	0	1	1	0	0	0	0	0	0	0	0	1	0	1	0
1899	STL	NL	1	0	1	0	0	1	0	0	0	0	0	0	0	0	0	1
Total			27	8	19	8	9	10	0	1	0	0	0	1	4	0	17	8

Rank among batters: 1,532 • *Top target (3 home runs)*: Ad Gumbert • *Number of pitchers victimized*: 24 • *Total ballparks homered in*: 16 • *First HR*: 07/13/1889 off Mickey Welch

Johnny Temple

JOHN ELLIS TEMPLE
B: 08/08/1927 D: 01/09/1994
BR

Year	Tm	Lg	Tot	H	A	Men-On 0	1	2	3	One-Game 2	3	4	LO	XN	IP	PH	RHP	LHP
1952	CIN	NL	1	0	1	0	0	0	1	0	0	0	0	0	0	0	1	0
1953	CIN	NL	1	0	1	0	1	0	0	0	0	0	0	0	0	0	0	1
1956	CIN	NL	2	0	2	1	0	1	0	0	0	0	0	0	0	0	0	2
1958	CIN	NL	3	1	2	2	0	0	1	0	0	0	0	0	1	0	1	2
1959	CIN	NL	8	5	3	5	0	3	0	0	0	0	1	0	0	0	3	5
1960	CLE	AL	2	0	2	1	1	0	0	0	0	0	0	1	0	0	1	1
1961	CLE	AL	3	2	1	1	2	0	0	0	0	0	0	0	0	0	1	2
1962	BAL	AL	1	0	1	1	0	0	0	0	0	0	0	0	0	0	0	1
1963	HOU	NL	1	0	1	1	0	0	0	0	0	0	0	0	0	0	1	0
Total			22	8	14	12	4	4	2	0	0	0	1	1	1	0	8	14

Rank among batters: 1,719 • *Top target (2 home runs)*: Wilmer Mizell, Johnny Antonelli, Whitey Ford • *Number of pitchers victimized*: 19 • *Total ballparks homered in*: 11 • *First HR*: 09/12/1952 off Jim Hearn

Garry Templeton

GARRY LEWIS TEMPLETON
B: 03/24/1956
BB

Year	Tm	Lg	Tot	H	A	Men-On 0	1	2	3	One-Game 2	3	4	LO	XN	IP	PH	RHP	LHP
1976	STL	NL	1	1	0	1	0	0	0	0	0	0	0	0	0	0	1	0

Garry Templeton *continued*

Year	Tm	Lg	Tot	H	A	Men-On 0	Men-On 1	Men-On 2	Men-On 3	One-Game 2	One-Game 3	One-Game 4	LO	XN	IP	PH	RHP	LHP
1977	STL	NL	8	2	6	4	3	1	0	0	0	0	0	0	1	0	5	3
1978	STL	NL	2	1	1	2	0	0	0	0	0	0	2	0	0	0	0	2
1979	STL	NL	9	2	7	5	3	1	0	1	0	0	0	1	0	0	5	4
1980	STL	NL	4	1	3	1	3	0	0	0	0	0	0	0	0	0	2	2
1981	STL	NL	1	1	0	1	0	0	0	0	0	0	0	0	0	0	0	1
1982	SD	NL	6	2	4	1	4	1	0	0	0	0	0	0	0	1	5	1
1983	SD	NL	3	1	2	2	1	0	0	0	0	0	0	0	0	0	2	1
1984	SD	NL	2	2	0	0	0	1	1	0	0	0	0	0	0	0	2	0
1985	SD	NL	6	4	2	4	2	0	0	0	0	0	0	0	0	0	5	1
1986	SD	NL	2	1	1	1	0	1	0	0	0	0	0	0	0	0	0	2
1987	SD	NL	5	2	3	2	1	2	0	0	0	0	0	1	1	0	3	2
1988	SD	NL	3	3	0	0	3	0	0	0	0	0	0	0	0	0	3	0
1989	SD	NL	6	5	1	5	0	0	1	0	0	0	0	0	0	0	5	1
1990	SD	NL	9	6	3	3	5	0	1	0	0	0	0	0	0	0	5	4
1991	SD	NL	1	1	0	0	0	1	0	0	0	0	0	0	0	1	0	1
	NY	NL	2	1	1	1	1	0	0	0	0	0	0	0	0	0	2	0
	Total		3	2	1	1	1	1	0	0	0	0	0	0	0	1	2	1
Total			70	36	34	33	26	8	3	1	0	0	2	2	2	2	45	25

Rank among batters: 742 • *Top target (3 home runs)*: Danny Darwin • *Number of pitchers victimized*: 60 • *Total ballparks homered in*: 12 • *First HR*: 09/09/1976 off Don Carrithers

Gene Tenace

FURY GENE TENACE
B: 10/10/1946
BR

Year	Tm	Lg	Tot	H	A	Men-On 0	Men-On 1	Men-On 2	Men-On 3	One-Game 2	One-Game 3	One-Game 4	LO	XN	IP	PH	RHP	LHP
1969	OAK	AL	1	0	1	1	0	0	0	0	0	0	0	0	0	0	1	0
1970	OAK	AL	7	3	4	4	2	1	0	0	0	0	0	0	1	0	5	2
1971	OAK	AL	7	2	5	4	2	1	0	0	0	0	0	0	0	0	4	3
1972	OAK	AL	5	2	3	1	2	2	0	0	0	0	0	0	0	1	4	1
1973	OAK	AL	24	12	12	13	6	3	2	1	0	0	0	3	0	0	16	8
1974	OAK	AL	26	19	7	14	7	2	3	3	0	0	0	0	0	0	21	5
1975	OAK	AL	29	15	14	16	8	4	1	1	0	0	0	0	0	0	15	14
1976	OAK	AL	22	9	13	17	4	1	0	3	0	0	0	0	0	0	17	5
1977	SD	NL	15	4	11	8	6	0	1	3	0	0	0	0	0	0	11	4
1978	SD	NL	16	9	7	8	4	4	0	3	0	0	0	0	0	0	7	9
1979	SD	NL	20	2	18	11	9	0	0	0	0	0	0	2	0	1	12	8
1980	SD	NL	17	11	6	8	4	5	0	1	0	0	0	1	0	1	10	7
1981	STL	NL	5	3	2	2	1	2	0	1	0	0	0	0	0	0	1	4
1982	STL	NL	7	3	4	5	1	1	0	0	0	0	0	0	0	0	3	4
Total			201	94	107	112	56	26	7	16	0	0	0	6	1	3	127	74

Rank among batters: 181 • *Top target (6 home runs)*: Luis Tiant • *Number of pitchers victimized*: 144 • *Total ballparks homered in*: 26 • *First HR*: 06/06/1969 off Earl Wilson • *World Series HR*—4

John Tener

JOHN KINLEY TENER
B: 07/25/1863 D: 05/19/1946
BR

Year	Tm	Lg	Tot	H	A	Men-On 0	Men-On 1	Men-On 2	Men-On 3	One-Game 2	One-Game 3	One-Game 4	LO	XN	IP	PH	RHP	LHP
1889	CHI	NL	1	0	1	1	0	0	0	0	0	0	0	0	0	0	0	1
1890	PIT	PL	2	0	2	2	0	0	0	0	0	0	0	0	0	0	2	0
Total			3	0	3	3	0	0	0	0	0	0	0	0	0	0	2	1

Rank among batters: 3,735 • *Total ballparks homered in*: 3 • *First HR*: 07/27/1889 off Gus Krock

Fred Tenney

FREDERICK TENNEY
B: 11/26/1871 D: 07/03/1952
BL

Year	Tm	Lg	Tot	H	A	Men-On 0	Men-On 1	Men-On 2	Men-On 3	One-Game 2	One-Game 3	One-Game 4	LO	XN	IP	PH	RHP	LHP
1894	BOS	NL	2	1	1	0	2	0	0	0	0	0	0	0	0	0	1	0
1895	BOS	NL	1	1	0	0	1	0	0	0	0	0	0	0	0	0	1	0
1896	BOS	NL	2	1	1	1	0	1	0	0	0	0	0	0	0	0	2	0
1897	BOS	NL	1	0	1	1	0	0	0	0	0	0	0	0	1	0	0	1
1899	BOS	NL	1	1	0	0	1	0	0	0	0	0	0	0	0	0	1	0
1900	BOS	NL	1	0	1	1	0	0	0	0	0	0	0	0	0	0	1	0
1901	BOS	NL	1	0	1	1	0	0	0	0	0	0	0	0	0	0	1	0
1902	BOS	NL	2	2	0	1	1	0	0	0	0	0	0	0	0	0	2	0

Fred Tenney *continued*

Year	Tm	Lg	Tot	H	A	Men-On 0	1	2	3	One-Game 2	3	4	LO	XN	IP	PH	RHP	LHP
1903	BOS	NL	3	0	3	0	1	2	0	0	0	0	0	0	0	0	3	0
1904	BOS	NL	1	1	0	1	0	0	0	0	0	0	0	0	0	0	1	0
1906	BOS	NL	1	1	0	0	0	1	0	0	0	0	0	0	0	0	1	0
1908	NY	NL	2	1	1	2	0	0	0	0	0	0	0	0	1	0	2	0
1909	NY	NL	3	3	0	2	0	1	0	0	0	0	1	0	0	0	3	0
1911	BOS	NL	1	1	0	1	0	0	0	0	0	0	0	0	0	0	1	0
Total			22	13	9	11	6	5	0	0	0	0	1	0	2	0	20	1

Rank among batters: 1,719 • *Total ballparks homered in*: 8 • *First HR*: 07/21/1894 off Jouett Meekin

Frank Tepedino

FRANK RONALD TEPEDINO
B: 11/23/1947
BL

Year	Tm	Lg	Tot	H	A	Men-On 0	1	2	3	One-Game 2	3	4	LO	XN	IP	PH	RHP	LHP
1971	MIL	AL	2	1	1	2	0	0	0	0	0	0	0	0	0	0	2	0
1973	ATL	NL	4	2	2	3	1	0	0	0	0	0	0	0	0	0	4	0
Total			6	3	3	5	1	0	0	0	0	0	0	0	0	0	6	0

Rank among batters: 2,988 • *Total ballparks homered in*: 4 • *First HR*: 06/18/1971 off Catfish Hunter

Jerry Terrell

JERRY WAYNE TERRELL
B: 07/13/1946
BR

Year	Tm	Lg	Tot	H	A	Men-On 0	1	2	3	One-Game 2	3	4	LO	XN	IP	PH	RHP	LHP
1973	MIN	AL	1	0	1	1	0	0	0	0	0	0	1	0	0	0	1	0
1975	MIN	AL	1	1	0	1	0	0	0	0	0	0	0	0	0	0	0	1
1977	MIN	AL	1	0	1	0	1	0	0	0	0	0	0	0	0	0	1	0
1979	KC	AL	1	0	1	1	0	0	0	0	0	0	0	0	0	0	0	1
Total			4	1	3	3	1	0	0	0	0	0	1	0	0	0	2	2

Rank among batters: 3,427 • *Total ballparks homered in*: 4 • *First HR*: 08/17/1973 off Dick Bosman

Walt Terrell

CHARLES WALTER TERRELL
B: 05/11/1958
BL

Year	Tm	Lg	Tot	H	A	Men-On 0	1	2	3	One-Game 2	3	4	LO	XN	IP	PH	RHP	LHP
1983	NY	NL	3	0	3	0	2	1	0	1	0	0	0	0	0	0	2	1

Rank among batters: 3,735 • *Top target (2 home runs)*: Ferguson Jenkins • *Number of pitchers victimized*: 2 • *Total ballparks homered in*: 2 • *First HR*: 08/06/1983 off Ferguson Jenkins

Adonis Terry

WILLIAM H. TERRY
B: 08/07/1864 D: 02/24/1915
BR

Year	Tm	Lg	Tot	H	A	Men-On 0	1	2	3	One-Game 2	3	4	LO	XN	IP	PH	RHP	LHP
1885	BRO	AA	1	1	0	0	0	1	0	0	0	0	0	0	0	0	0	1
1886	BRO	AA	2	1	1	0	1	1	0	0	0	0	0	0	0	0	1	0
1887	BRO	AA	3	3	0	2	0	1	0	0	0	0	0	0	0	0	3	0
1889	BRO	AA	2	1	1	2	0	0	0	0	0	0	0	0	0	0	2	0
1890	BRO	NL	4	1	3	1	2	1	0	0	0	0	0	0	0	0	4	0
1892	PIT	NL	2	2	0	2	0	0	0	0	0	0	0	0	1	0	2	0
1895	CHI	NL	1	1	0	0	1	0	0	0	0	0	0	0	0	0	1	0
Total			15	10	5	7	4	4	0	0	0	0	0	0	1	0	13	1

Rank among batters: 2,096 • *Total ballparks homered in*: 9 • *First HR*: 06/24/1885 off Ed Cushman

Bill Terry

WILLIAM HAROLD TERRY
B: 10/30/1896 D: 01/09/1989
BL HOF

Year	Tm	Lg	Tot	H	A	Men-On 0	1	2	3	One-Game 2	3	4	LO	XN	IP	PH	RHP	LHP
1924	NY	NL	5	2	3	2	1	2	0	1	0	0	0	0	0	1	4	1
1925	NY	NL	11	3	8	4	6	1	0	0	0	0	0	1	0	0	10	1
1926	NY	NL	5	3	2	1	2	2	0	0	0	0	0	0	1	1	4	1
1927	NY	NL	20	6	14	9	9	1	1	2	0	0	0	0	2	0	16	4
1928	NY	NL	17	8	9	7	6	3	1	0	0	0	0	1	2	0	13	4
1929	NY	NL	14	5	9	5	4	4	1	0	0	0	0	0	1	0	9	5
1930	NY	NL	23	11	12	17	2	4	0	1	0	0	0	0	3	0	16	7

Bill Terry *continued*

Year	Tm	Lg	Tot	H	A	Men-On 0	Men-On 1	Men-On 2	Men-On 3	One-Game 2	One-Game 3	One-Game 4	LO	XN	IP	PH	RHP	LHP
1931	NY	NL	9	8	1	6	1	2	0	0	0	0	0	0	1	0	8	1
1932	NY	NL	28	16	12	16	8	4	0	2	1	0	0	0	3	0	21	7
1933	NY	NL	6	5	1	4	1	1	0	0	0	0	0	1	0	1	5	1
1934	NY	NL	8	4	4	6	2	0	0	0	0	0	0	0	0	0	7	1
1935	NY	NL	6	3	3	3	3	0	0	0	0	0	0	0	2	0	5	1
1936	NY	NL	2	2	0	2	0	0	0	0	0	0	0	0	0	0	2	0
Total			154	76	78	82	45	24	3	6	1	0	0	3	15	3	120	34

Rank among batters: 278 • Top target (5 home runs): Grover Alexander, Larry Benton, Phil Collins, Guy Bush, Larry French • *Number of pitchers victimized*: 87 • *Total ballparks homered in*: 8 • *First HR*: 05/16/1924 off Rip Wheeler • *Hit for Cycle*—@BRO: 05/29/1928 • *World Series HR*—2

Ralph Terry

RALPH WILLARD TERRY
B: 01/09/1936
BR

Year	Tm	Lg	Tot	H	A	Men-On 0	Men-On 1	Men-On 2	Men-On 3	One-Game 2	One-Game 3	One-Game 4	LO	XN	IP	PH	RHP	LHP
1965	CLE	AL	1	0	1	1	0	0	0	0	0	0	0	0	0	0	1	0

Rank among batters: 4,707 • *Total ballparks homered in*: 1 • *First HR*: 08/06/1965 off Joe Horlen

Scott Terry

SCOTT RAY TERRY
B: 11/21/1959
BR

Year	Tm	Lg	Tot	H	A	Men-On 0	Men-On 1	Men-On 2	Men-On 3	One-Game 2	One-Game 3	One-Game 4	LO	XN	IP	PH	RHP	LHP
1989	STL	NL	2	2	0	1	0	1	0	0	0	0	0	0	0	0	1	1

Rank among batters: 4,129 • *Total ballparks homered in*: 1 • *First HR*: 04/27/1989 off Joe Price

Zeb Terry

ZEBULON ALEXANDER TERRY
B: 06/17/1891 D: 03/14/1988
BR

Year	Tm	Lg	Tot	H	A	Men-On 0	Men-On 1	Men-On 2	Men-On 3	One-Game 2	One-Game 3	One-Game 4	LO	XN	IP	PH	RHP	LHP
1921	CHI	NL	2	0	2	0	1	1	0	0	0	0	0	0	0	0	2	0

Rank among batters: 4,129 • *Total ballparks homered in*: 1 • *First HR*: 05/20/1921 off Fred Toney

Wayne Terwilliger

WILLARD WAYNE TERWILLIGER
B: 06/27/1925
BR

Year	Tm	Lg	Tot	H	A	Men-On 0	Men-On 1	Men-On 2	Men-On 3	One-Game 2	One-Game 3	One-Game 4	LO	XN	IP	PH	RHP	LHP
1949	CHI	NL	2	1	1	0	0	2	0	0	0	0	0	0	0	0	1	1
1950	CHI	NL	10	5	5	7	2	1	0	0	0	0	0	0	0	0	6	4
1953	WAS	AL	4	0	4	2	1	0	1	0	0	0	0	0	0	0	3	1
1954	WAS	AL	3	0	3	1	1	1	0	0	0	0	0	0	0	0	2	1
1955	NY	NL	1	1	0	1	0	0	0	0	0	0	0	0	0	0	1	0
1959	KC	AL	2	0	2	2	0	0	0	0	0	0	0	0	0	0	2	0
Total			22	7	15	13	4	4	1	0	0	0	0	0	0	0	15	7

Rank among batters: 1,719 • *Top target (2 home runs)*: Dave Koslo • *Number of pitchers victimized*: 21 • *Total ballparks homered in*: 8 • *First HR*: 08/23/1949 off Dave Koslo

Jeff Tesreau

CHARLES MONROE TESREAU
B: 03/05/1889 D: 09/24/1946
BR

Year	Tm	Lg	Tot	H	A	Men-On 0	Men-On 1	Men-On 2	Men-On 3	One-Game 2	One-Game 3	One-Game 4	LO	XN	IP	PH	RHP	LHP
1915	NY	NL	1	0	1	1	0	0	0	0	0	0	0	0	0	0	1	0
1916	NY	NL	1	1	0	1	0	0	0	0	0	0	0	0	0	0	1	0
Total			2	1	1	2	0	0	0	0	0	0	0	0	0	0	2	0

Rank among batters: 4,129 • *Total ballparks homered in*: 2 • *First HR*: 09/10/1915 off George McQuillan

Dick Tettelbach

RICHARD MORLEY TETTELBACH
B: 06/26/1929 D: 01/26/1995
BR

Year	Tm	Lg	Tot	H	A	Men-On 0	Men-On 1	Men-On 2	Men-On 3	One-Game 2	One-Game 3	One-Game 4	LO	XN	IP	PH	RHP	LHP
1956	WAS	AL	1	1	0	1	0	0	0	0	0	0	0	0	0	0	1	0

Rank among batters: 4,707 • *Total ballparks homered in*: 1 • *First HR*: 04/17/1956 off Don Larsen

Mickey Tettleton

MICKEY LEE TETTLETON
B: 09/16/1960
BB

Year	Tm	Lg	Tot	H	A	Men-On 0	Men-On 1	Men-On 2	Men-On 3	One-Game 2	One-Game 3	One-Game 4	LO	XN	IP	PH	RHP	LHP
1984	OAK	AL	1	1	0	1	0	0	0	0	0	0	0	0	0	0	0	1
1985	OAK	AL	3	1	2	3	0	0	0	0	0	0	0	0	0	0	2	1
1986	OAK	AL	10	4	6	8	1	1	0	0	0	0	0	0	1	0	4	6
1987	OAK	AL	8	5	3	4	2	2	0	0	0	0	0	0	0	0	6	2
1988	BAL	AL	11	7	4	6	4	1	0	1	0	0	0	0	0	0	2	9
1989	BAL	AL	26	15	11	17	4	5	0	1	0	0	0	0	0	0	16	10
1990	BAL	AL	15	8	7	9	3	3	0	0	0	0	0	1	0	0	10	5
1991	DET	AL	31	15	16	14	12	4	1	2	0	0	0	2	0	1	22	9
1992	DET	AL	32	18	14	19	5	7	1	0	0	0	0	1	0	0	24	8
1993	DET	AL	32	16	16	17	7	6	2	1	0	0	0	1	0	0	26	6
1994	DET	AL	17	9	8	8	5	3	1	0	0	0	0	2	0	0	14	3
1995	TEX	AL	32	22	10	17	8	6	1	4	0	0	0	0	0	0	25	7
Total			218	121	97	123	51	38	6	9	0	0	0	7	1	1	151	67

Rank among batters: 155 • *Top target (5 home runs)*: Jimmy Key, Charles Nagy • *Number of pitchers victimized*: 157 • *Total ballparks homered in*: 19 • *First HR*: 09/18/1984 off Frank Tanana • *Switch hit HR in 1 game*—3 times

Tim Teufel

TIMOTHY SHAWN TEUFEL
B: 07/07/1958
BR

Year	Tm	Lg	Tot	H	A	Men-On 0	Men-On 1	Men-On 2	Men-On 3	One-Game 2	One-Game 3	One-Game 4	LO	XN	IP	PH	RHP	LHP
1983	MIN	AL	3	3	0	3	0	0	0	1	0	0	2	0	0	0	2	1
1984	MIN	AL	14	9	5	10	3	1	0	1	0	0	0	1	1	0	9	5
1985	MIN	AL	10	6	4	7	2	1	0	0	0	0	0	0	0	1	9	1
1986	NY	NL	4	2	2	2	1	0	1	0	0	0	0	1	0	2	1	3
1987	NY	NL	14	4	10	6	4	3	1	1	0	0	0	0	0	1	6	8
1988	NY	NL	4	1	3	1	3	0	0	0	0	0	0	0	0	0	1	3
1989	NY	NL	2	1	1	2	0	0	0	0	0	0	0	0	0	0	1	1
1990	NY	NL	10	4	6	7	2	1	0	0	0	0	0	0	0	2	5	5
1991	NY	NL	1	1	0	1	0	0	0	0	0	0	0	0	0	0	1	0
	SD	NL	11	5	6	3	4	3	1	0	0	0	0	1	0	0	4	7
	Total		12	6	6	4	4	3	1	0	0	0	0	1	0	0	5	7
1992	SD	NL	6	2	4	4	2	0	0	1	0	0	0	1	0	0	3	3
1993	SD	NL	7	5	2	3	4	0	0	0	0	0	0	0	0	1	1	6
Total			86	43	43	49	25	9	3	4	0	0	2	4	1	7	43	43

Rank among batters: 602 • *Top target (5 home runs)*: Tom Browning • *Number of pitchers victimized*: 73 • *Total ballparks homered in*: 17 • *First HR*: 09/16/1983 off Jim Gott • *World Series HR*—1

Moe Thacker

MORRIS BENTON THACKER
B: 05/21/1934
BR

Year	Tm	Lg	Tot	H	A	Men-On 0	Men-On 1	Men-On 2	Men-On 3	One-Game 2	One-Game 3	One-Game 4	LO	XN	IP	PH	RHP	LHP
1958	CHI	NL	2	1	1	2	0	0	0	0	0	0	0	0	0	0	1	1

Rank among batters: 4,129 • *Total ballparks homered in*: 2 • *First HR*: 08/03/1958 off Seth Morehead

Ron Theobald

RONALD MERRILL THEOBALD
B: 07/28/1943
BR

Year	Tm	Lg	Tot	H	A	Men-On 0	Men-On 1	Men-On 2	Men-On 3	One-Game 2	One-Game 3	One-Game 4	LO	XN	IP	PH	RHP	LHP
1971	MIL	AL	1	0	1	1	0	0	0	0	0	0	1	0	0	0	0	1
1972	MIL	AL	1	0	1	1	0	0	0	0	0	0	0	0	0	0	0	1
Total			2	0	2	2	0	0	0	0	0	0	1	0	0	0	0	2

Rank among batters: 4,129 • *Total ballparks homered in*: 2 • *First HR*: 06/08/1971 off Mickey Lolich

George Theodore

GEORGE BASIL THEODORE
B: 11/13/1947
BR

Year	Tm	Lg	Tot	H	A	Men-On 0	Men-On 1	Men-On 2	Men-On 3	One-Game 2	One-Game 3	One-Game 4	LO	XN	IP	PH	RHP	LHP
1973	NY	NL	1	0	1	0	0	1	0	0	0	0	0	0	0	0	0	1
1974	NY	NL	1	0	1	1	0	0	0	0	0	0	0	0	0	0	1	0
Total			2	0	2	1	0	1	0	0	0	0	0	0	0	0	1	1

Rank among batters: 4,129 • *Total ballparks homered in*: 2 • *First HR*: 07/04/1973 off Balor Moore

Tommy Thevenow

THOMAS JOSEPH THEVENOW
B: 09/06/1903 D: 07/29/1957
BR

Year	Tm	Lg	Tot	H	A	Men-On 0	Men-On 1	Men-On 2	Men-On 3	One-Game 2	One-Game 3	One-Game 4	LO	XN	IP	PH	RHP	LHP
1926	STL	NL	2	0	2	1	1	0	0	0	0	0	0	0	2	0	2	0

Rank among batters: 4,129 • *Total ballparks homered in*: 2 • *First HR*: 09/17/1926 off Jack Knight • *World Series HR*—1

Henry Thielman

HENRY JOSEPH THIELMAN
B: 10/03/1880 D: 09/02/1942
BR

Year	Tm	Lg	Tot	H	A	Men-On 0	Men-On 1	Men-On 2	Men-On 3	One-Game 2	One-Game 3	One-Game 4	LO	XN	IP	PH	RHP	LHP
1903	BRO	NL	1	1	0	1	0	0	0	0	0	0	0	0	1	0	1	0

Rank among batters: 4,707 • *Total ballparks homered in*: 1 • *First HR*: 05/06/1903 off Joe McGinnity

Andres Thomas

ANDRES PEREZ THOMAS
B: 11/10/1963
BR

Year	Tm	Lg	Tot	H	A	Men-On 0	Men-On 1	Men-On 2	Men-On 3	One-Game 2	One-Game 3	One-Game 4	LO	XN	IP	PH	RHP	LHP
1986	ATL	NL	6	1	5	4	1	1	0	1	0	0	0	0	0	0	4	2
1987	ATL	NL	5	4	1	2	2	1	0	0	0	0	0	0	0	0	4	1
1988	ATL	NL	13	6	7	11	1	1	0	1	0	0	0	0	0	0	6	7
1989	ATL	NL	13	5	8	7	6	0	0	0	0	0	0	0	0	0	9	4
1990	ATL	NL	5	1	4	4	0	0	1	0	0	0	0	1	0	0	1	4
Total			42	17	25	28	10	3	1	2	0	0	0	1	0	0	24	18

Rank among batters: 1,138 • *Top target (3 home runs)*: Rick Reuschel, Craig Lefferts • *Number of pitchers victimized*: 36 • *Total ballparks homered in*: 12 • *First HR*: 05/28/1986 off Larry McWilliams

Bud Thomas

LUTHER BAXTER THOMAS
B: 09/09/1910
BR

Year	Tm	Lg	Tot	H	A	Men-On 0	Men-On 1	Men-On 2	Men-On 3	One-Game 2	One-Game 3	One-Game 4	LO	XN	IP	PH	RHP	LHP
1937	PHI	AL	1	1	0	0	0	1	0	0	0	0	0	0	0	0	0	1

Rank among batters: 4,707 • *Total ballparks homered in*: 1 • *First HR*: 08/14/1937 off Kemp Wicker

Bud Thomas

JOHN TILLMAN THOMAS
B: 03/10/1929
BR

Year	Tm	Lg	Tot	H	A	Men-On 0	Men-On 1	Men-On 2	Men-On 3	One-Game 2	One-Game 3	One-Game 4	LO	XN	IP	PH	RHP	LHP
1951	STL	AL	1	0	1	1	0	0	0	0	0	0	0	0	0	0	0	1

Rank among batters: 4,707 • *Total ballparks homered in*: 1 • *First HR*: 09/16/1951 off Alex Kellner

Dan Thomas

DANNY LEE THOMAS
B: 05/09/1951 D: 07/03/1980
BR

Year	Tm	Lg	Tot	H	A	Men-On 0	Men-On 1	Men-On 2	Men-On 3	One-Game 2	One-Game 3	One-Game 4	LO	XN	IP	PH	RHP	LHP
1976	MIL	AL	4	2	2	3	1	0	0	0	0	0	0	0	0	0	1	3
1977	MIL	AL	2	0	2	1	1	0	0	0	0	0	0	0	0	0	2	0
Total			6	2	4	4	2	0	0	0	0	0	0	0	0	0	3	3

Rank among batters: 2,988 • *Total ballparks homered in*: 5 • *First HR*: 09/10/1976 off Catfish Hunter

Derrel Thomas

DERREL OSBORN THOMAS
B: 01/14/1951
BR

Year	Tm	Lg	Tot	H	A	Men-On 0	Men-On 1	Men-On 2	Men-On 3	One-Game 2	One-Game 3	One-Game 4	LO	XN	IP	PH	RHP	LHP
1972	SD	NL	5	2	3	2	2	1	0	0	0	0	0	0	0	0	5	0
1974	SD	NL	3	1	2	1	1	1	0	0	0	0	0	0	1	0	3	0
1975	SF	NL	6	3	3	5	0	1	0	0	0	0	0	0	0	0	5	1
1976	SF	NL	2	2	0	2	0	0	0	0	0	0	0	0	0	0	1	1
1977	SF	NL	8	4	4	7	1	0	0	0	0	0	2	0	1	0	4	4
1978	SD	NL	3	0	3	2	1	0	0	0	0	0	0	0	0	0	2	1
1979	LA	NL	5	3	2	4	0	0	1	1	0	0	0	0	0	0	4	1
1980	LA	NL	1	1	0	1	0	0	0	0	0	0	0	0	0	0	1	0
1981	LA	NL	4	2	2	4	0	0	0	0	0	0	0	0	0	0	3	1
1983	LA	NL	2	0	2	2	0	0	0	0	0	0	0	1	0	1	2	0

Year	Tm	Lg	Tot	H	A	Men-On 0	1	2	3	One-Game 2	3	4	LO	XN	IP	PH	RHP	LHP

Derrel Thomas *continued*

Year	Tm	Lg	Tot	H	A	0	1	2	3	2	3	4	LO	XN	IP	PH	RHP	LHP
1985	PHI	NL	4	3	1	2	1	1	0	0	0	0	0	1	0	0	3	1
Total			43	21	22	32	6	4	1	1	0	0	2	2	2	1	33	10

Rank among batters: 1,116 • *Top target (2 home runs)*: Gary Gentry, Oscar Zamora, Bill Caudill • *Number of pitchers victimized*: 40 • *Total ballparks homered in*: 12 • *First HR*: 05/07/1972 off Gary Gentry

Frank Thomas

FRANK JOSEPH THOMAS
B: 06/11/1929
BR

Year	Tm	Lg	Tot	H	A	0	1	2	3	2	3	4	LO	XN	IP	PH	RHP	LHP
1951	PIT	NL	2	1	1	1	1	0	0	0	0	0	0	0	0	0	2	0
1953	PIT	NL	30	18	12	11	12	6	1	1	0	0	0	1	0	0	21	9
1954	PIT	NL	23	7	16	12	8	3	0	0	0	0	0	0	0	0	16	7
1955	PIT	NL	25	8	17	17	6	2	0	0	0	0	0	1	0	0	13	12
1956	PIT	NL	25	10	15	12	9	4	0	1	0	0	0	0	0	0	21	4
1957	PIT	NL	23	8	15	14	9	0	0	1	0	0	0	1	0	0	18	5
1958	PIT	NL	35	9	26	19	14	1	1	4	1	0	0	0	0	0	22	13
1959	CIN	NL	12	6	6	9	2	1	0	0	0	0	0	0	0	1	5	7
1960	CHI	NL	21	11	10	9	7	5	0	2	0	0	0	0	1	0	13	8
1961	CHI	NL	2	1	1	2	0	0	0	0	0	0	0	0	0	0	1	1
	MIL	NL	25	13	12	18	4	2	1	1	0	0	0	0	0	0	18	7
	Total		27	14	13	20	4	2	1	1	0	0	0	0	0	0	19	8
1962	NY	NL	34	18	16	26	5	2	1	5	0	0	0	1	0	0	28	6
1963	NY	NL	15	8	7	4	8	3	0	0	0	0	0	0	0	1	13	2
1964	NY	NL	3	2	1	2	1	0	0	0	0	0	0	0	0	1	2	1
	PHI	NL	7	5	2	2	5	0	0	0	0	0	0	0	0	0	6	1
	Total		10	7	3	4	6	0	0	0	0	0	0	0	0	1	8	2
1965	PHI	NL	1	1	0	1	0	0	0	0	0	0	0	0	0	1	0	1
	HOU	NL	3	0	3	1	1	1	0	1	0	0	0	0	0	0	1	2
	Total		4	1	3	2	1	1	0	1	0	0	0	0	0	1	1	3
Total			286	126	160	160	92	30	4	16	1	0	0	4	1	4	200	86

Rank among batters: 80 • *Top target (8 home runs)*: Don Newcombe • *Number of pitchers victimized*: 149 • *Total ballparks homered in*: 13 • *First HR*: 08/30/1951 off George Spencer

Frank Thomas

FRANK EDWARD THOMAS
B: 05/27/1968
BR

Year	Tm	Lg	Tot	H	A	0	1	2	3	2	3	4	LO	XN	IP	PH	RHP	LHP
1990	CHI	AL	7	2	5	5	1	1	0	0	0	0	0	0	0	0	2	5
1991	CHI	AL	32	24	8	18	10	3	1	2	0	0	0	0	0	0	21	11
1992	CHI	AL	24	10	14	16	7	1	0	1	0	0	0	1	0	0	18	6
1993	CHI	AL	41	26	15	19	15	6	1	3	0	0	0	1	0	0	27	14
1994	CHI	AL	38	22	16	25	10	2	1	2	0	0	0	0	0	0	26	12
1995	CHI	AL	40	15	25	24	15	1	0	3	0	0	0	1	0	0	24	16
Total			182	99	83	107	58	14	3	11	0	0	0	3	0	0	118	64

Rank among batters: 216 • *Top target (5 home runs)*: Mike Mussina, Mark Langston • *Number of pitchers victimized*: 133 • *Total ballparks homered in*: 18 • *First HR*: 08/28/1990 off Gary Wayne • *LCS HR*—1; *All-Star HR*—1

Fred Thomas

FREDERICK HARVEY THOMAS
B: 12/19/1892 D: 01/15/1986
BR

Year	Tm	Lg	Tot	H	A	0	1	2	3	2	3	4	LO	XN	IP	PH	RHP	LHP
1918	BOS	AL	1	0	1	1	0	0	0	0	0	0	0	0	0	0	1	0
1919	PHI	AL	2	1	1	0	2	0	0	0	0	0	0	0	1	0	1	1
1920	PHI	AL	1	0	1	1	0	0	0	0	0	0	0	0	1	0	0	1
Total			4	1	3	2	2	0	0	0	0	0	0	0	2	0	2	2

Rank among batters: 3,427 • *Total ballparks homered in*: 3 • *First HR*: 06/25/1918 off Happy Finneran

George Thomas

GEORGE EDWARD THOMAS
B: 11/29/1937
BR

Year	Tm	Lg	Tot	H	A	0	1	2	3	2	3	4	LO	XN	IP	PH	RHP	LHP
1961	LA	AL	13	10	3	6	5	1	1	1	0	0	0	0	0	0	8	5
1962	LA	AL	4	1	3	2	2	0	0	0	0	0	0	0	0	0	2	2

Year	Tm	Lg	Tot	H	A	Men-On 0	1	2	3	One-Game 2	3	4	LO	XN	IP	PH	RHP	LHP

George Thomas *continued*

Year	Tm	Lg	Tot	H	A	0	1	2	3	2	3	4	LO	XN	IP	PH	RHP	LHP
1963	LA	AL	4	2	2	2	1	0	1	0	0	0	0	0	0	0	2	2
	DET	AL	1	1	0	1	0	0	0	0	0	0	0	0	0	0	0	1
	Total		5	3	2	3	1	0	1	0	0	0	0	0	0	0	2	3
1964	DET	AL	12	6	6	10	2	0	0	1	0	0	0	0	0	1	6	6
1965	DET	AL	3	3	0	3	0	0	0	0	0	0	0	0	0	1	1	2
1966	BOS	AL	5	3	2	5	0	0	0	0	0	0	0	0	0	0	1	4
1967	BOS	AL	1	0	1	0	1	0	0	0	0	0	0	0	0	0	0	1
1968	BOS	AL	1	0	1	1	0	0	0	0	0	0	0	0	0	0	1	0
1970	BOS	AL	2	1	1	1	1	0	0	0	0	0	0	0	0	0	1	1
Total			46	27	19	31	12	1	2	2	0	0	0	0	0	2	22	24

Rank among batters: 1,060 • *Top target (3 home runs)*: Gary Bell • *Number of pitchers victimized*: 40 • *Total ballparks homered in*: 12 • *First HR*: 07/02/1961 off Warren Hacker

Gorman Thomas

JAMES GORMAN THOMAS
B: 12/12/1950
BR

Year	Tm	Lg	Tot	H	A	0	1	2	3	2	3	4	LO	XN	IP	PH	RHP	LHP
1973	MIL	AL	2	2	0	2	0	0	0	0	0	0	0	0	0	1	1	1
1974	MIL	AL	2	1	1	0	1	0	1	0	0	0	0	0	0	0	2	0
1975	MIL	AL	10	5	5	6	3	0	1	0	0	0	0	0	0	0	5	5
1976	MIL	AL	8	4	4	2	5	1	0	0	0	0	0	0	0	0	5	3
1978	MIL	AL	32	19	13	10	18	3	1	2	0	0	0	0	0	0	22	10
1979	MIL	AL	45	22	23	23	17	5	0	4	0	0	0	0	0	0	33	12
1980	MIL	AL	38	18	20	22	15	0	1	3	0	0	0	1	0	0	24	14
1981	MIL	AL	21	8	13	11	6	4	0	4	0	0	0	0	0	0	18	3
1982	MIL	AL	39	19	20	19	14	6	0	6	0	0	0	2	0	0	24	15
1983	MIL	AL	5	2	3	3	0	2	0	0	0	0	0	0	0	0	4	1
	CLE	AL	17	8	9	8	7	2	0	0	0	0	0	0	0	0	14	3
	Total		22	10	12	11	7	4	0	0	0	0	0	0	0	0	18	4
1984	SEA	AL	1	0	1	1	0	0	0	0	0	0	0	0	0	0	1	0
1985	SEA	AL	32	16	16	12	15	4	1	4	1	0	0	0	0	0	19	13
1986	SEA	AL	10	5	5	6	2	2	0	0	0	0	0	0	0	0	8	2
	MIL	AL	6	2	4	6	0	0	0	0	0	0	0	1	0	0	3	3
	Total		16	7	9	12	2	2	0	0	0	0	0	1	0	0	11	5
Total			268	131	137	131	103	29	5	23	1	0	0	4	0	1	183	85

Rank among batters: 91 • *Top target (6 home runs)*: Dennis Leonard, Jim Clancy • *Number of pitchers victimized*: 164 • *Total ballparks homered in*: 15 • *First HR*: 04/15/1973 off Jim Palmer • *LCS HR*—2

Herb Thomas

HERBERT MARK THOMAS
B: 05/26/1902 D: 12/04/1991
BR

Year	Tm	Lg	Tot	H	A	0	1	2	3	2	3	4	LO	XN	IP	PH	RHP	LHP
1924	BOS	NL	1	0	1	1	0	0	0	0	0	0	0	0	1	0	1	0

Rank among batters: 4,707 • *Total ballparks homered in*: 1 • *First HR*: 09/28/1924 off Dazzy Vance

Ira Thomas

IRA FELIX THOMAS
B: 01/22/1881 D: 10/11/1958
BR

Year	Tm	Lg	Tot	H	A	0	1	2	3	2	3	4	LO	XN	IP	PH	RHP	LHP
1907	NY	AL	1	1	0	0	1	0	0	0	0	0	0	0	0	0	1	0
1910	PHI	AL	1	0	1	0	0	1	0	0	0	0	0	0	0	0	1	0
1912	PHI	AL	1	0	1	1	0	0	0	0	0	0	0	0	0	0	0	1
Total			3	1	2	1	1	1	0	0	0	0	0	0	0	0	2	1

Rank among batters: 3,735 • *Total ballparks homered in*: 3 • *First HR*: 08/03/1907 off Frank Smith

Kite Thomas

KEITH MARSHALL THOMAS
B: 04/27/1923 D: 01/07/1995
BR

Year	Tm	Lg	Tot	H	A	0	1	2	3	2	3	4	LO	XN	IP	PH	RHP	LHP
1952	PHI	AL	6	3	3	5	0	1	0	0	0	0	0	0	0	3	4	2
1953	WAS	AL	1	0	1	1	0	0	0	0	0	0	0	0	0	1	0	1
Total			7	3	4	6	0	1	0	0	0	0	0	0	0	4	4	3

Rank among batters: 2,834 • *Total ballparks homered in*: 5 • *First HR*: 05/30/1952 off Bobby Hogue

Lee Thomas

JAMES LEROY THOMAS
B: 02/05/1936
BL

Year	Tm	Lg	Tot	H	A	Men-On 0	Men-On 1	Men-On 2	Men-On 3	One-Game 2	One-Game 3	One-Game 4	LO	XN	IP	PH	RHP	LHP
1961	LA	AL	24	12	12	12	6	4	2	1	1	0	0	0	0	1	23	1
1962	LA	AL	26	12	14	16	6	4	0	3	0	0	0	0	0	0	21	5
1963	LA	AL	9	2	7	5	3	1	0	0	0	0	0	0	0	0	8	1
1964	LA	AL	2	1	1	2	0	0	0	0	0	0	0	0	0	0	2	0
	BOS	AL	13	3	10	7	5	0	1	2	0	0	0	0	0	0	11	2
	Total		15	4	11	9	5	0	1	2	0	0	0	0	0	0	13	2
1965	BOS	AL	22	9	13	15	5	2	0	0	0	0	0	1	0	0	22	0
1966	ATL	NL	6	3	3	3	2	1	0	0	0	0	0	0	0	0	6	0
	CHI	NL	1	1	0	1	0	0	0	0	0	0	0	0	0	0	1	0
	Total		7	4	3	4	2	1	0	0	0	0	0	0	0	0	7	0
1967	CHI	NL	2	0	2	1	1	0	0	0	0	0	0	0	0	0	2	0
1968	HOU	NL	1	0	1	1	0	0	0	0	0	0	0	0	0	0	0	1
Total			106	43	63	63	28	12	3	6	1	0	0	1	0	1	96	10

Rank among batters: 451 • *Top target (4 home runs)*: Ralph Terry, Orlando Pena • *Number of pitchers victimized*: 75 • *Total ballparks homered in*: 17 • *First HR*: 05/25/1961 off Mudcat Grant

Leo Thomas

LEO RAYMOND THOMAS
B: 07/26/1923
BR

Year	Tm	Lg	Tot	H	A	Men-On 0	Men-On 1	Men-On 2	Men-On 3	One-Game 2	One-Game 3	One-Game 4	LO	XN	IP	PH	RHP	LHP
1950	STL	AL	1	0	1	1	0	0	0	0	0	0	0	0	0	0	1	0

Rank among batters: 4,707 • *Total ballparks homered in*: 1 • *First HR*: 06/07/1950 off Joe Dobson

Pinch Thomas

CHESTER DAVID THOMAS
B: 01/24/1888 D: 12/24/1953
BL

Year	Tm	Lg	Tot	H	A	Men-On 0	Men-On 1	Men-On 2	Men-On 3	One-Game 2	One-Game 3	One-Game 4	LO	XN	IP	PH	RHP	LHP
1913	BOS	AL	1	0	1	1	0	0	0	0	0	0	0	0	0	0	1	0
1916	BOS	AL	1	0	1	1	0	0	0	0	0	0	0	0	0	0	1	0
Total			2	0	2	2	0	0	0	0	0	0	0	0	0	0	2	0

Rank among batters: 4,129 • *Total ballparks homered in*: 1 • *First HR*: 09/29/1913 off Ray Fisher

Red Thomas

ROBERT WILLIAM THOMAS
B: 04/25/1898 D: 03/29/1962
BR

Year	Tm	Lg	Tot	H	A	Men-On 0	Men-On 1	Men-On 2	Men-On 3	One-Game 2	One-Game 3	One-Game 4	LO	XN	IP	PH	RHP	LHP
1921	CHI	NL	1	1	0	1	0	0	0	0	0	0	0	0	0	0	0	1

Rank among batters: 4,707 • *Total ballparks homered in*: 1 • *First HR*: 09/23/1921 off Johnny Cooney

Roy Thomas

ROY ALLEN THOMAS
B: 03/24/1874 D: 11/20/1959
BL

Year	Tm	Lg	Tot	H	A	Men-On 0	Men-On 1	Men-On 2	Men-On 3	One-Game 2	One-Game 3	One-Game 4	LO	XN	IP	PH	RHP	LHP
1901	PHI	NL	1	0	1	1	0	0	0	0	0	0	1	0	1	0	1	0
1903	PHI	NL	1	1	0	1	0	0	0	0	0	0	0	0	0	0	1	0
1904	PHI	NL	3	2	1	2	1	0	0	0	0	0	1	0	1	0	2	1
1907	PHI	NL	1	1	0	0	1	0	0	0	0	0	0	0	1	0	1	0
1908	PIT	NL	1	1	0	1	0	0	0	0	0	0	0	0	1	0	0	1
Total			7	5	2	5	2	0	0	0	0	0	2	0	4	0	5	2

Rank among batters: 2,834 • *Total ballparks homered in*: 4 • *First HR*: 10/01/1901 off Len Swormstedt

Tommy Thomas

ALPHONSE THOMAS
B: 12/23/1899 D: 04/27/1988
BR

Year	Tm	Lg	Tot	H	A	Men-On 0	Men-On 1	Men-On 2	Men-On 3	One-Game 2	One-Game 3	One-Game 4	LO	XN	IP	PH	RHP	LHP
1927	CHI	AL	1	0	1	0	1	0	0	0	0	0	0	0	0	0	1	0
1928	CHI	AL	2	2	0	0	2	0	0	0	0	0	0	0	0	0	2	0
Total			3	2	1	0	3	0	0	0	0	0	0	0	0	0	3	0

Rank among batters: 3,735 • *Total ballparks homered in*: 2 • *First HR*: 06/03/1927 off Tony Welzer

						Men-On				One-Game								
Year	Tm	Lg	Tot	H	A	0	1	2	3	2	3	4	LO	XN	IP	PH	RHP	LHP

Valmy Thomas

VALMY THOMAS
B: 10/21/1928
BR

Year	Tm	Lg	Tot	H	A	0	1	2	3	2	3	4	LO	XN	IP	PH	RHP	LHP
1957	NY	NL	6	5	1	4	1	1	0	0	0	0	0	1	0	0	4	2
1958	SF	NL	3	2	1	1	1	1	0	0	0	0	0	0	0	0	1	2
1959	PHI	NL	1	0	1	0	0	1	0	0	0	0	0	0	0	0	1	0
1961	CLE	AL	2	1	1	2	0	0	0	0	0	0	0	0	0	0	1	1
Total			12	8	4	7	2	3	0	0	0	0	0	1	0	0	7	5

Rank among batters: 2,325 • *Top target (2 home runs)*: Joe Nuxhall • *Number of pitchers victimized*: 11 • *Total ballparks homered in*: 7 • *First HR*: 05/11/1957 off Don Bessent

Gary Thomasson

GARY LEAH THOMASSON
B: 07/29/1951
BL

Year	Tm	Lg	Tot	H	A	0	1	2	3	2	3	4	LO	XN	IP	PH	RHP	LHP
1973	SF	NL	4	2	2	2	2	0	0	0	0	0	0	0	0	0	4	0
1974	SF	NL	2	2	0	1	0	1	0	0	0	0	0	0	0	0	1	1
1975	SF	NL	7	5	2	6	0	1	0	0	0	0	1	0	0	1	3	4
1976	SF	NL	8	3	5	5	2	1	0	0	0	0	1	1	0	2	5	3
1977	SF	NL	17	7	10	9	4	3	1	0	0	0	1	1	0	0	15	2
1978	OAK	AL	5	4	1	3	1	1	0	0	0	0	0	0	0	1	4	1
	NY	AL	3	2	1	1	1	1	0	0	0	0	0	0	0	0	3	0
	Total		8	6	2	4	2	2	0	0	0	0	0	0	0	1	7	1
1979	LA	NL	14	6	8	6	7	1	0	0	0	0	0	0	0	0	14	0
1980	LA	NL	1	0	1	1	0	0	0	0	0	0	0	0	0	0	1	0
Total			61	31	30	34	17	9	1	0	0	0	3	2	0	4	50	11

Rank among batters: 844 • Top target (2 home runs): Ken Forsch, Bob Moose, Fred Norman, Larry Dierker, Jim Lonborg, Jack Billingham, John Denny, Bert Blyleven • *Number of pitchers victimized*: 53 • *Total ballparks homered in*: 14 • *First HR*: 04/12/1973 off Ken Forsch

Jim Thome

JAMES HOWARD THOME
B: 08/27/1970
BL

Year	Tm	Lg	Tot	H	A	0	1	2	3	2	3	4	LO	XN	IP	PH	RHP	LHP
1991	CLE	AL	1	0	1	0	1	0	0	0	0	0	0	0	0	0	1	0
1992	CLE	AL	2	1	1	2	0	0	0	0	0	0	0	0	0	0	2	0
1993	CLE	AL	7	5	2	6	1	0	0	0	0	0	0	0	0	0	5	2
1994	CLE	AL	20	10	10	13	5	2	0	1	1	0	0	1	0	0	18	2
1995	CLE	AL	25	13	12	14	5	6	0	0	0	0	0	1	0	0	22	3
Total			55	29	26	35	12	8	0	1	1	0	0	2	0	0	48	7

Rank among batters: 926 • *Top target (3 home runs)*: John Doherty • *Number of pitchers victimized*: 46 • *Total ballparks homered in*: 14 • *First HR*: 10/04/1991 off Steve Farr • *World Series HR—1; LCS HR—3*

Bobby Thompson

BOBBY LARUE THOMPSON
B: 11/03/1953
BB

Year	Tm	Lg	Tot	H	A	0	1	2	3	2	3	4	LO	XN	IP	PH	RHP	LHP
1978	TEX	AL	2	1	1	2	0	0	0	0	0	0	0	0	0	0	1	1

Rank among batters: 4,129 • *Total ballparks homered in*: 2 • *First HR*: 06/24/1978 off Dave LaRoche

Danny Thompson

DANNY LEON THOMPSON
B: 02/01/1947 D: 12/10/1976
BR

Year	Tm	Lg	Tot	H	A	0	1	2	3	2	3	4	LO	XN	IP	PH	RHP	LHP
1972	MIN	AL	4	2	2	3	1	0	0	0	0	0	0	0	0	0	1	3
1973	MIN	AL	1	0	1	1	0	0	0	0	0	0	0	0	0	0	0	1
1974	MIN	AL	4	2	2	3	1	0	0	0	0	0	0	0	1	0	1	3
1975	MIN	AL	5	4	1	2	1	2	0	0	0	0	0	0	0	0	4	1
1976	TEX	AL	1	1	0	0	0	1	0	0	0	0	0	0	0	0	0	1
Total			15	9	6	9	3	3	0	0	0	0	0	0	1	0	6	9

Rank among batters: 2,096 • *Total ballparks homered in*: 5 • *First HR*: 04/15/1972 off Ken Holtzman

Don Thompson

DONALD NEWLIN THOMPSON
B: 12/28/1923
BL

Year	Tm	Lg	Tot	H	A	0	1	2	3	2	3	4	LO	XN	IP	PH	RHP	LHP
1953	BRO	NL	1	0	1	1	0	0	0	0	0	0	0	0	0	0	1	0

						Men-On				One-Game								
Year	Tm	Lg	Tot	H	A	0	1	2	3	2	3	4	LO	XN	IP	PH	RHP	LHP

Don Thompson *continued*

Rank among batters: 4,707 • *Total ballparks homered in*: 1 • *First HR*: 09/15/1953 off Stu Miller

Fresco Thompson

LAFAYETTE FRESCO THOMPSON
B: 06/06/1902 D: 11/20/1968
BR

Year	Tm	Lg	Tot	H	A	0	1	2	3	2	3	4	LO	XN	IP	PH	RHP	LHP
1927	PHI	NL	1	1	0	1	0	0	0	0	0	0	0	0	0	0	0	1
1928	PHI	NL	3	3	0	2	1	0	0	0	0	0	0	0	0	0	3	0
1929	PHI	NL	4	2	2	3	1	0	0	0	0	0	0	0	0	0	1	3
1930	PHI	NL	4	2	2	3	1	0	0	0	0	0	1	0	0	0	2	2
1931	BRO	NL	1	1	0	0	1	0	0	0	0	0	0	0	0	0	0	1
Total			13	9	4	9	4	0	0	0	0	0	1	0	0	0	6	7

Rank among batters: 2,248 • *Top target (2 home runs)*: Frank Henry • *Number of pitchers victimized*: 12 • *Total ballparks homered in*: 5 • *First HR*: 06/24/1927 off Frank Henry

Hank Thompson

HENRY CURTIS THOMPSON
B: 12/08/1925 D: 09/30/1969
BL

Year	Tm	Lg	Tot	H	A	0	1	2	3	2	3	4	LO	XN	IP	PH	RHP	LHP
1949	NY	NL	9	6	3	5	3	1	0	0	0	0	1	0	0	0	5	4
1950	NY	NL	20	15	5	14	3	2	1	1	0	0	0	0	3	0	14	6
1951	NY	NL	8	8	0	4	2	2	0	0	0	0	0	0	0	0	6	2
1952	NY	NL	17	11	6	8	6	2	1	1	0	0	0	0	1	0	14	3
1953	NY	NL	24	14	10	12	9	2	1	2	0	0	0	0	0	1	22	2
1954	NY	NL	26	14	12	10	11	4	1	1	1	0	0	0	0	0	17	9
1955	NY	NL	17	8	9	9	5	3	0	0	0	0	0	0	0	1	14	3
1956	NY	NL	8	6	2	3	3	2	0	0	0	0	0	0	0	2	7	1
Total			129	82	47	65	42	18	4	5	1	0	1	0	4	4	99	30

Rank among batters: 354 • *Top target (6 home runs)*: Gerry Staley • *Number of pitchers victimized*: 75 • *Total ballparks homered in*: 9 • *First HR*: 07/16/1949 off Tiny Bonham

Jason Thompson

JASON DOLPH THOMPSON
B: 07/06/1954
BL

Year	Tm	Lg	Tot	H	A	0	1	2	3	2	3	4	LO	XN	IP	PH	RHP	LHP
1976	DET	AL	17	7	10	10	5	2	0	1	0	0	0	0	0	0	16	1
1977	DET	AL	31	15	16	21	5	4	1	0	0	0	0	1	0	0	22	9
1978	DET	AL	26	13	13	18	6	1	1	0	0	0	0	0	0	0	16	10
1979	DET	AL	20	13	7	11	7	1	1	1	0	0	0	0	0	0	17	3
1980	DET	AL	4	2	2	1	2	1	0	0	0	0	0	1	0	0	4	0
	CAL	AL	17	9	8	10	4	3	0	1	0	0	0	0	0	1	15	2
	Total		21	11	10	11	6	4	0	1	0	0	0	1	0	1	19	2
1981	PIT	NL	15	8	7	10	4	1	0	0	0	0	0	0	0	1	13	2
1982	PIT	NL	31	17	14	17	13	1	0	2	0	0	0	0	0	0	30	1
1983	PIT	NL	18	10	8	8	7	2	1	0	0	0	0	0	0	0	16	2
1984	PIT	NL	17	6	11	10	6	1	0	2	0	0	0	0	0	0	16	1
1985	PIT	NL	12	9	3	4	5	3	0	0	0	0	0	0	0	0	9	3
Total			208	109	99	120	64	20	4	7	0	0	0	2	0	2	174	34

Rank among batters: 168 • *Top target (5 home runs)*: Moose Haas • *Number of pitchers victimized*: 158 • *Total ballparks homered in*: 26 • *First HR*: 05/01/1976 off Jack Kucek

Milt Thompson

MILTON BERNARD THOMPSON
B: 01/05/1959
BL

Year	Tm	Lg	Tot	H	A	0	1	2	3	2	3	4	LO	XN	IP	PH	RHP	LHP
1984	ATL	NL	2	0	2	2	0	0	0	0	0	0	1	0	0	0	2	0
1986	PHI	NL	6	4	2	5	1	0	0	0	0	0	0	0	0	0	6	0
1987	PHI	NL	7	3	4	5	2	0	0	0	0	0	0	0	0	0	7	0
1988	PHI	NL	2	1	1	2	0	0	0	0	0	0	0	0	0	0	2	0
1989	STL	NL	4	2	2	1	1	2	0	0	0	0	0	0	0	0	3	1
1990	STL	NL	6	3	3	3	3	0	0	1	0	0	0	0	0	0	6	0
1991	STL	NL	6	4	2	5	1	0	0	0	0	0	0	0	0	1	5	1
1992	STL	NL	4	1	3	4	0	0	0	0	0	0	0	0	0	1	4	0
1993	PHI	NL	4	2	2	2	2	0	0	0	0	0	0	0	0	0	4	0
1994	PHI	NL	3	3	0	1	0	2	0	0	0	0	0	0	0	0	3	0

Milt Thompson *continued*

Year	Tm	Lg	Tot	H	A	Men-On				One-Game			LO	XN	IP	PH	RHP	LHP
						0	1	2	3	2	3	4						
	HOU	NL	1	1	0	0	1	0	0	0	0	0	0	0	0	1	1	0
	Total		4	4	0	1	1	2	0	0	0	0	0	0	0	1	4	0
1995	HOU	NL	2	0	2	1	0	1	0	0	0	0	0	0	0	2	2	0
Total			47	24	23	31	11	5	0	1	0	0	1	0	0	5	45	2

Rank among batters: 1,040 • Top target (2 home runs): Doyle Alexander, Bryn Smith, Danny Cox, Mark Portugal, John Burkett • *Number of pitchers victimized*: 42 • *Total ballparks homered in*: 12 • *First HR*: 09/22/1984 off Luis DeLeon • *World Series HR*—1

Robby Thompson

ROBERT RANDALL THOMPSON
B: 05/10/1962
BR

Year	Tm	Lg	Tot	H	A	Men-On 0	1	2	3	One-Game 2	3	4	LO	XN	IP	PH	RHP	LHP
1986	SF	NL	7	4	3	5	1	0	1	0	0	0	0	1	0	0	4	3
1987	SF	NL	10	7	3	6	2	1	1	0	0	0	0	0	0	0	7	3
1988	SF	NL	7	3	4	4	2	1	0	0	0	0	0	0	0	0	6	1
1989	SF	NL	13	7	6	7	4	2	0	0	0	0	0	0	0	0	8	5
1990	SF	NL	15	8	7	10	3	2	0	0	0	0	0	1	0	0	7	8
1991	SF	NL	19	11	8	15	2	2	0	0	0	0	0	0	0	0	12	7
1992	SF	NL	14	8	6	8	5	1	0	0	0	0	0	0	0	0	13	1
1993	SF	NL	19	13	6	15	4	0	0	3	0	0	0	0	0	0	14	5
1994	SF	NL	2	1	1	2	0	0	0	0	0	0	0	0	0	0	0	2
1995	SF	NL	8	4	4	5	2	1	0	1	0	0	0	1	0	0	7	1
Total			114	66	48	77	25	10	2	4	0	0	0	3	0	0	78	36

Rank among batters: 419 • *Top target (4 home runs)*: Jose Rijo • *Number of pitchers victimized*: 86 • *Total ballparks homered in*: 13 • *First HR*: 05/17/1986 off Shane Rawley • *Hit for Cycle*—vs SD: 04/22/1991 • *LCS HR*—3

Ryan Thompson

RYAN ORLANDO THOMPSON
B: 11/04/1967
BR

Year	Tm	Lg	Tot	H	A	Men-On 0	1	2	3	One-Game 2	3	4	LO	XN	IP	PH	RHP	LHP
1992	NY	NL	3	3	0	2	0	1	0	1	0	0	0	0	0	0	3	0
1993	NY	NL	11	5	6	9	0	2	0	1	0	0	0	0	0	0	10	1
1994	NY	NL	18	5	13	8	9	0	1	0	0	0	0	0	0	0	13	5
1995	NY	NL	7	3	4	5	2	0	0	0	0	0	1	0	0	0	5	2
Total			39	16	23	24	11	3	1	2	0	0	1	0	0	0	31	8

Rank among batters: 1,204 • *Top target (2 home runs)*: Mike Morgan, John Smoltz • *Number of pitchers victimized*: 37 • *Total ballparks homered in*: 12 • *First HR*: 09/22/1992 off Mike Morgan

Sam Thompson

SAMUEL LUTHER THOMPSON
B: 03/05/1860 D: 11/07/1922
BL HOF

Year	Tm	Lg	Tot	H	A	Men-On 0	1	2	3	One-Game 2	3	4	LO	XN	IP	PH	RHP	LHP
1885	DET	NL	7	5	2	2	3	2	0	0	0	0	0	0	1	0	6	1
1886	DET	NL	8	6	2	2	4	2	0	1	0	0	0	0	3	0	7	1
1887	DET	NL	10	6	4	2	4	4	0	0	0	0	0	0	1	0	8	2
1888	DET	NL	6	1	5	4	1	1	0	1	0	0	0	0	1	0	6	0
1889	PHI	NL	20	14	6	10	5	4	1	2	0	0	0	0	0	0	18	2
1890	PHI	NL	4	4	0	0	2	1	1	0	0	0	0	0	0	0	4	0
1891	PHI	NL	7	2	5	3	2	2	0	1	0	0	0	0	2	0	6	0
1892	PHI	NL	9	7	2	3	4	2	0	1	0	0	0	0	0	0	7	0
1893	PHI	NL	11	8	3	4	6	1	0	0	0	0	0	0	1	0	10	1
1894	PHI	NL	13	7	6	4	5	3	1	1	0	0	0	0	0	0	13	0
1895	PHI	NL	18	13	5	4	8	6	0	1	0	0	0	0	0	0	12	3
1896	PHI	NL	12	11	1	4	5	3	0	0	0	0	0	0	0	0	10	1
1898	PHI	NL	1	0	1	1	0	0	0	0	0	0	0	0	0	0	1	0
Total			126	84	42	43	49	31	3	8	0	0	0	0	9	0	106	11

Rank among batters: 360 • *Top target (6 home runs)*: John Clarkson • *Number of pitchers victimized*: 76 • *Total ballparks homered in*: 23 • *First HR*: 07/28/1885 off Tim Keefe • *Hit for Cycle*—vs LOU: 08/17/1894 • *World Series HR*—2

Scot Thompson

VERNON SCOT THOMPSON
B: 12/07/1955
BL

Year	Tm	Lg	Tot	H	A	Men-On 0	1	2	3	One-Game 2	3	4	LO	XN	IP	PH	RHP	LHP
1979	CHI	NL	2	0	2	2	0	0	0	0	0	0	0	0	0	0	2	0
1980	CHI	NL	2	0	2	2	0	0	0	0	0	0	0	0	0	0	2	0

Scot Thompson *continued*

Year	Tm	Lg	Tot	H	A	Men-On 0	Men-On 1	Men-On 2	Men-On 3	One-Game 2	One-Game 3	One-Game 4	LO	XN	IP	PH	RHP	LHP
1984	SF	NL	1	1	0	1	0	0	0	0	0	0	0	0	0	0	1	0
Total			5	1	4	5	0	0	0	0	0	0	0	0	0	0	5	0

Rank among batters: 3,191 • *Total ballparks homered in*: 5 • *First HR*: 07/26/1979 off Tom Hausman

Tim Thompson

CHARLES LEMOINE THOMPSON
B: 03/01/1924
BL

Year	Tm	Lg	Tot	H	A	Men-On 0	Men-On 1	Men-On 2	Men-On 3	One-Game 2	One-Game 3	One-Game 4	LO	XN	IP	PH	RHP	LHP
1956	KC	AL	1	0	1	1	0	0	0	0	0	0	0	0	0	0	1	0
1957	KC	AL	7	3	4	4	2	1	0	0	0	0	0	0	0	0	7	0
Total			8	3	5	5	2	1	0	0	0	0	0	0	0	0	8	0

Rank among batters: 2,703 • *Total ballparks homered in*: 3 • *First HR*: 05/27/1956 off Duke Maas

Tommy Thompson

RUPERT LOCKHART THOMPSON
B: 05/19/1910 D: 05/24/1971
BL

Year	Tm	Lg	Tot	H	A	Men-On 0	Men-On 1	Men-On 2	Men-On 3	One-Game 2	One-Game 3	One-Game 4	LO	XN	IP	PH	RHP	LHP
1935	BOS	NL	4	1	3	1	2	0	1	0	0	0	0	0	0	1	4	0
1936	BOS	NL	4	0	4	2	1	1	0	0	0	0	0	0	0	1	4	0
1939	STL	AL	1	0	1	1	0	0	0	0	0	0	1	0	0	0	1	0
Total			9	1	8	4	3	1	1	0	0	0	1	0	0	2	9	0

Rank among batters: 2,587 • *Top target (2 home runs)*: Leroy Parmelee • *Number of pitchers victimized*: 8 • *Total ballparks homered in*: 6 • *First HR*: 05/24/1935 off Jim Weaver

Bobby Thomson

ROBERT BROWN THOMSON
B: 10/25/1923
BR

Year	Tm	Lg	Tot	H	A	Men-On 0	Men-On 1	Men-On 2	Men-On 3	One-Game 2	One-Game 3	One-Game 4	LO	XN	IP	PH	RHP	LHP
1946	NY	NL	2	2	0	2	0	0	0	0	0	0	0	0	0	0	0	2
1947	NY	NL	29	15	14	16	11	2	0	3	0	0	0	0	0	0	19	10
1948	NY	NL	16	6	10	11	3	2	0	1	0	0	0	0	0	1	10	6
1949	NY	NL	27	19	8	12	9	6	0	2	0	0	0	1	1	0	20	7
1950	NY	NL	25	13	12	12	8	3	2	2	0	0	0	0	0	0	18	7
1951	NY	NL	32	13	19	14	14	4	0	1	0	0	0	1	0	0	17	15
1952	NY	NL	24	15	9	10	10	3	1	1	0	0	0	0	1	0	15	9
1953	NY	NL	26	15	11	13	10	2	1	1	0	0	0	1	0	0	18	8
1954	MIL	NL	2	1	1	0	1	1	0	0	0	0	0	0	0	0	2	0
1955	MIL	NL	12	3	9	6	5	0	1	0	0	0	0	0	0	0	10	2
1956	MIL	NL	20	7	13	10	7	1	2	3	0	0	0	0	0	0	16	4
1957	MIL	NL	4	1	3	3	0	0	1	0	0	0	0	1	0	0	3	1
	NY	NL	8	5	3	5	3	0	0	0	0	0	0	1	0	1	7	1
	Total		12	6	6	8	3	0	1	0	0	0	0	2	0	1	10	2
1958	CHI	NL	21	11	10	15	4	2	0	2	0	0	0	1	0	0	14	7
1959	CHI	NL	11	3	8	7	2	2	0	1	0	0	0	0	0	1	3	8
1960	BOS	AL	5	1	4	3	2	0	0	0	0	0	0	0	0	0	2	3
Total			264	130	134	139	89	28	8	17	0	0	0	6	2	3	174	90

Rank among batters: 97 • *Top target (10 home runs)*: Herm Wehmeier • *Number of pitchers victimized*: 136 • *Total ballparks homered in*: 15 • *First HR*: 09/18/1946 off Bob Chipman

Dickie Thon

RICHARD WILLIAM THON
B: 06/20/1958
BR

Year	Tm	Lg	Tot	H	A	Men-On 0	Men-On 1	Men-On 2	Men-On 3	One-Game 2	One-Game 3	One-Game 4	LO	XN	IP	PH	RHP	LHP
1982	HOU	NL	3	1	2	3	0	0	0	0	0	0	1	0	0	0	3	0
1983	HOU	NL	20	4	16	16	3	1	0	3	0	0	0	1	0	0	17	3
1985	HOU	NL	6	3	3	3	2	1	0	0	0	0	0	0	0	1	2	4
1986	HOU	NL	3	0	3	2	0	1	0	0	0	0	0	0	0	1	2	1
1987	HOU	NL	1	0	1	0	1	0	0	0	0	0	0	0	0	0	0	1
1988	SD	NL	1	0	1	1	0	0	0	0	0	0	0	0	0	1	0	1
1989	PHI	NL	15	8	7	7	4	4	0	1	0	0	0	0	0	0	9	6
1990	PHI	NL	8	3	5	5	2	0	1	1	0	0	0	0	0	0	4	4
1991	PHI	NL	9	4	5	6	3	0	0	1	0	0	0	1	0	0	7	2
1992	TEX	AL	4	2	2	2	2	0	0	0	0	0	0	0	0	0	1	3

Year	Tm	Lg	Tot	H	A	Men-On				One-Game			LO	XN	IP	PH	RHP	LHP
						0	1	2	3	2	3	4						

Dickie Thon *continued*

Year	Tm	Lg	Tot	H	A	0	1	2	3	2	3	4	LO	XN	IP	PH	RHP	LHP
1993	MIL	AL	1	0	1	1	0	0	0	0	0	0	0	0	0	0	0	1
Total			71	25	46	46	17	7	1	6	0	0	1	2	0	3	45	26

Rank among batters: 731 • *Top target (3 home runs)*: Eric Show • *Number of pitchers victimized*: 58 • *Total ballparks homered in*: 16 • *First HR*: 06/29/1982 off Bob Walk • *LCS HR*—1

Jack Thoney

JOHN THONEY
B: 12/08/1879 D: 10/24/1948
BR

Year	Tm	Lg	Tot	H	A	0	1	2	3	2	3	4	LO	XN	IP	PH	RHP	LHP
1903	CLE	AL	1	1	0	0	1	0	0	0	0	0	0	0	0	0	1	0
1908	BOS	AL	2	1	1	1	1	0	0	0	0	0	0	0	0	0	2	0
Total			3	2	1	1	2	0	0	0	0	0	0	0	0	0	3	0

Rank among batters: 3,735 • *Total ballparks homered in*: 2 • *First HR*: 05/08/1903 off Frank Kitson

Andre Thornton

ANDRE THORNTON
B: 08/13/1949
BR

Year	Tm	Lg	Tot	H	A	0	1	2	3	2	3	4	LO	XN	IP	PH	RHP	LHP
1974	CHI	NL	10	6	4	4	4	2	0	0	0	0	0	0	0	1	7	3
1975	CHI	NL	18	8	10	12	4	2	0	1	0	0	0	0	1	0	15	3
1976	CHI	NL	2	1	1	2	0	0	0	0	0	0	0	0	0	0	2	0
	MON	NL	9	4	5	6	3	0	0	0	0	0	0	0	0	1	6	3
	Total		11	5	6	8	3	0	0	0	0	0	0	0	0	1	8	3
1977	CLE	AL	28	19	9	17	10	1	0	3	0	0	0	2	1	1	23	5
1978	CLE	AL	33	16	17	18	9	6	0	1	0	0	0	1	0	0	21	12
1979	CLE	AL	26	17	9	15	5	3	3	0	0	0	0	0	0	0	21	5
1981	CLE	AL	6	2	4	3	2	1	0	0	0	0	0	0	0	1	2	4
1982	CLE	AL	32	16	16	12	14	5	1	2	0	0	0	1	0	0	21	11
1983	CLE	AL	17	6	11	11	4	2	0	1	0	0	0	0	0	0	13	4
1984	CLE	AL	33	19	14	21	9	2	1	3	0	0	0	0	0	0	23	10
1985	CLE	AL	22	12	10	7	13	2	0	2	0	0	0	0	0	1	14	8
1986	CLE	AL	17	12	5	10	4	2	1	1	0	0	0	0	0	1	11	6
Total			253	138	115	138	81	28	6	14	0	0	0	4	2	6	179	74

Rank among batters: 103 • *Top target (6 home runs)*: Dennis Leonard • *Number of pitchers victimized*: 172 • *Total ballparks homered in*: 27 • *First HR*: 05/11/1974 off Ray Sadecki • *Hit for Cycle*—@BOS: 04/22/1978

Lou Thornton

LOUIS THORNTON
B: 04/26/1963
BL

Year	Tm	Lg	Tot	H	A	0	1	2	3	2	3	4	LO	XN	IP	PH	RHP	LHP
1985	TOR	AL	1	1	0	0	0	1	0	0	0	0	0	0	0	0	1	0

Rank among batters: 4,707 • *Total ballparks homered in*: 1 • *First HR*: 07/27/1985 off Luis Sanchez

Walter Thornton

WALTER MILLER THORNTON
B: 02/18/1875 D: 07/14/1960
BL

Year	Tm	Lg	Tot	H	A	0	1	2	3	2	3	4	LO	XN	IP	PH	RHP	LHP
1895	CHI	NL	1	1	0	1	0	0	0	0	0	0	0	0	0	0	1	0

Rank among batters: 4,707 • *Total ballparks homered in*: 1 • *First HR*: 08/09/1895 off Nig Cuppy

Bob Thorpe

BENJAMIN ROBERT THORPE
B: 11/19/1926
BR

Year	Tm	Lg	Tot	H	A	0	1	2	3	2	3	4	LO	XN	IP	PH	RHP	LHP
1952	BOS	NL	3	1	2	2	1	0	0	0	0	0	0	0	0	0	2	1

Rank among batters: 3,735 • *Total ballparks homered in*: 3 • *First HR*: 05/22/1952 off Johnny Klippstein

Jim Thorpe

JAMES FRANCIS THORPE
B: 05/28/1887 D: 03/28/1953
BR

Year	Tm	Lg	Tot	H	A	0	1	2	3	2	3	4	LO	XN	IP	PH	RHP	LHP
1913	NY	NL	1	0	1	1	0	0	0	0	0	0	0	0	0	0	0	1

Jim Thorpe *continued*

Year	Tm	Lg	Tot	H	A	Men-On 0	Men-On 1	Men-On 2	Men-On 3	One-Game 2	One-Game 3	One-Game 4	LO	XN	IP	PH	RHP	LHP
1917	CIN	NL	4	0	4	2	0	2	0	0	0	0	0	0	1	0	2	2
1918	NY	NL	1	0	1	1	0	0	0	0	0	0	0	1	0	0	1	0
1919	BOS	NL	1	0	1	1	0	0	0	0	0	0	0	0	1	0	0	1
Total			7	0	7	5	0	2	0	0	0	0	0	1	2	0	3	4

Rank among batters: 2,834 • *Total ballparks homered in*: 5 • *First HR*: 09/29/1913 off Otto Hess

Faye Throneberry

MAYNARD FAYE THRONEBERRY
B: 06/22/1931
BL

Year	Tm	Lg	Tot	H	A	Men-On 0	Men-On 1	Men-On 2	Men-On 3	One-Game 2	One-Game 3	One-Game 4	LO	XN	IP	PH	RHP	LHP
1952	BOS	AL	5	1	4	2	1	0	2	0	0	0	0	0	1	0	5	0
1955	BOS	AL	6	4	2	3	3	0	0	1	0	0	0	0	0	0	5	1
1956	BOS	AL	1	0	1	0	1	0	0	0	0	0	0	0	0	0	1	0
1957	WAS	AL	2	1	1	1	1	0	0	0	0	0	0	0	0	0	2	0
1958	WAS	AL	4	0	4	3	1	0	0	1	0	0	1	0	0	0	4	0
1959	WAS	AL	10	4	6	8	1	0	1	0	0	0	2	0	0	0	8	2
1960	WAS	AL	1	1	0	0	1	0	0	0	0	0	0	0	0	0	1	0
Total			29	11	18	17	9	0	3	2	0	0	3	0	1	0	26	3

Rank among batters: 1,465 • *Top target (3 home runs)*: Bob Turley, Ned Garver • *Number of pitchers victimized*: 20 • *Total ballparks homered in*: 8 • *First HR*: 04/17/1952 off Don Johnson

Marv Throneberry

MARVIN EUGENE THRONEBERRY
B: 09/02/1933 D: 06/23/1994
BL

Year	Tm	Lg	Tot	H	A	Men-On 0	Men-On 1	Men-On 2	Men-On 3	One-Game 2	One-Game 3	One-Game 4	LO	XN	IP	PH	RHP	LHP
1958	NY	AL	7	3	4	6	0	1	0	0	0	0	0	1	0	0	5	2
1959	NY	AL	8	5	3	5	2	1	0	0	0	0	0	0	0	0	8	0
1960	KC	AL	11	6	5	5	4	0	2	0	0	0	0	0	0	1	10	1
1961	KC	AL	6	4	2	0	2	3	1	0	0	0	0	0	0	0	3	3
	BAL	AL	5	1	4	3	2	0	0	1	0	0	0	0	0	1	5	0
	Total		11	5	6	3	4	3	1	1	0	0	0	0	0	1	8	3
1962	NY	NL	16	12	4	12	2	2	0	1	0	0	0	0	0	2	16	0
Total			53	31	22	31	12	7	3	2	0	0	0	1	0	4	47	6

Rank among batters: 953 • *Top target (4 home runs)*: Cal McLish • *Number of pitchers victimized*: 41 • *Total ballparks homered in*: 11 • *First HR*: 05/20/1958 off Bill Fischer

Bob Thurman

ROBERT BURNS THURMAN
B: 05/14/1917
BL

Year	Tm	Lg	Tot	H	A	Men-On 0	Men-On 1	Men-On 2	Men-On 3	One-Game 2	One-Game 3	One-Game 4	LO	XN	IP	PH	RHP	LHP
1955	CIN	NL	7	6	1	2	3	1	1	0	0	0	0	0	0	2	6	1
1956	CIN	NL	8	6	2	5	3	0	0	0	1	0	0	0	0	0	7	1
1957	CIN	NL	16	12	4	6	6	3	1	0	0	0	0	1	0	4	16	0
1958	CIN	NL	4	4	0	2	1	1	0	0	0	0	0	0	0	0	4	0
Total			35	28	7	15	13	5	2	0	1	0	0	1	0	6	33	2

Rank among batters: 1,291 • *Top target (3 home runs)*: Gene Conley, Don Drysdale • *Number of pitchers victimized*: 27 • *Total ballparks homered in*: 6 • *First HR*: 04/16/1955 off Lew Burdette

Gary Thurman

GARY MONTEZ THURMAN
B: 11/12/1964
BR

Year	Tm	Lg	Tot	H	A	Men-On 0	Men-On 1	Men-On 2	Men-On 3	One-Game 2	One-Game 3	One-Game 4	LO	XN	IP	PH	RHP	LHP
1991	KC	AL	2	1	1	2	0	0	0	0	0	0	0	0	1	0	1	1

Rank among batters: 4,129 • *Total ballparks homered in*: 2 • *First HR*: 05/15/1991 off Denis Boucher

Sloppy Thurston

HOLLIS JOHN THURSTON
B: 06/02/1899 D: 09/14/1973
BR

Year	Tm	Lg	Tot	H	A	Men-On 0	Men-On 1	Men-On 2	Men-On 3	One-Game 2	One-Game 3	One-Game 4	LO	XN	IP	PH	RHP	LHP
1924	CHI	AL	1	0	1	1	0	0	0	0	0	0	0	0	0	0	1	0
1927	WAS	AL	2	1	1	0	1	1	0	0	0	0	0	0	0	0	1	1
1930	BRO	NL	1	1	0	0	1	0	0	0	0	0	0	0	0	0	0	1

Sloppy Thurston *continued*

Year	Tm	Lg	Tot	H	A	Men-On 0	1	2	3	One-Game 2	3	4	LO	XN	IP	PH	RHP	LHP
1931	BRO	NL	1	1	0	1	0	0	0	0	0	0	0	0	0	0	1	0
Total			5	3	2	2	2	1	0	0	0	0	0	0	0	0	3	2

Rank among batters: 3,191 • *Total ballparks homered in*: 4 • *First HR*: 04/29/1924 off Syl Johnson

Luis Tiant

LUIS CLEMENTE (VEGA) TIANT
B: 11/23/1940
BR

Year	Tm	Lg	Tot	H	A	Men-On 0	1	2	3	One-Game 2	3	4	LO	XN	IP	PH	RHP	LHP
1964	CLE	AL	1	0	1	1	0	0	0	0	0	0	0	0	0	0	1	0
1965	CLE	AL	1	1	0	1	0	0	0	0	0	0	0	0	0	0	1	0
1967	CLE	AL	1	1	0	1	0	0	0	0	0	0	0	0	0	0	1	0
1969	CLE	AL	2	1	1	0	2	0	0	0	0	0	0	0	0	0	1	1
Total			5	3	2	3	2	0	0	0	0	0	0	0	0	0	4	1

Rank among batters: 3,191 • *Top target (2 home runs)*: Jim Bouton • *Number of pitchers victimized*: 4 • *Total ballparks homered in*: 3 • *First HR*: 10/04/1964 off Jim Bouton

Mike Tiernan

MICHAEL JOSEPH TIERNAN
B: 01/21/1867 D: 11/09/1918
BL

Year	Tm	Lg	Tot	H	A	Men-On 0	1	2	3	One-Game 2	3	4	LO	XN	IP	PH	RHP	LHP
1887	NY	NL	10	2	8	3	7	0	0	0	0	0	0	0	1	0	6	4
1888	NY	NL	9	4	5	5	3	1	0	0	0	0	1	0	1	0	5	4
1889	NY	NL	10	4	6	2	7	1	0	2	0	0	0	0	1	0	6	4
1890	NY	NL	13	6	7	6	6	1	0	0	0	0	3	1	2	0	11	1
1891	NY	NL	16	7	9	9	5	2	0	0	0	0	1	0	3	0	13	1
1892	NY	NL	5	3	2	1	2	1	1	0	0	0	0	0	0	0	5	0
1893	NY	NL	14	12	2	8	6	0	0	2	0	0	0	1	1	0	12	2
1894	NY	NL	5	3	2	2	3	0	0	0	0	0	0	0	1	0	3	2
1895	NY	NL	7	2	5	3	2	2	0	0	0	0	0	0	1	0	7	0
1896	NY	NL	7	3	4	4	3	0	0	0	0	0	0	0	0	0	6	1
1897	NY	NL	5	2	3	3	2	0	0	0	0	0	0	0	0	0	4	1
1898	NY	NL	5	2	3	2	2	1	0	0	0	0	1	0	0	0	4	1
Total			106	50	56	48	48	9	1	4	0	0	6	2	11	0	81	21

Rank among batters: 451 • *Top target (6 home runs)*: Kid Nichols • *Number of pitchers victimized*: 67 • *Total ballparks homered in*: 26 • *First HR*: 05/16/1887 off Egyptian Healy • *Hit for Cycle*—@PHI: 08/25/1888; @CIN: 06/28/1890 • *World Series HR*—2

Cotton Tierney

JAMES ARTHUR TIERNEY
B: 02/10/1894 D: 04/18/1953
BR

Year	Tm	Lg	Tot	H	A	Men-On 0	1	2	3	One-Game 2	3	4	LO	XN	IP	PH	RHP	LHP
1921	PIT	NL	3	1	2	1	2	0	0	0	0	0	0	1	1	0	2	1
1922	PIT	NL	7	3	4	4	3	0	0	1	0	0	0	0	1	0	5	2
1923	PIT	NL	2	0	2	1	1	0	0	0	0	0	0	0	0	0	1	1
	PHI	NL	11	4	7	6	5	0	0	0	0	0	0	0	0	0	6	5
	Total		13	4	9	7	6	0	0	0	0	0	0	0	0	0	7	6
1924	BOS	NL	6	1	5	3	3	0	0	0	0	0	0	0	1	0	4	2
1925	BRO	NL	2	0	2	2	0	0	0	0	0	0	0	0	0	1	1	1
Total			31	9	22	17	14	0	0	1	0	0	0	1	3	1	19	12

Rank among batters: 1,400 • *Top target (3 home runs)*: Art Nehf, Vic Aldridge • *Number of pitchers victimized*: 23 • *Total ballparks homered in*: 6 • *First HR*: 04/22/1921 off Dolf Luque

Bob Tillman

JOHN ROBERT TILLMAN
B: 03/24/1937
BR

Year	Tm	Lg	Tot	H	A	Men-On 0	1	2	3	One-Game 2	3	4	LO	XN	IP	PH	RHP	LHP
1962	BOS	AL	14	8	6	9	5	0	0	1	0	0	0	2	0	2	11	3
1963	BOS	AL	8	4	4	4	2	2	0	0	0	0	0	1	0	0	5	3
1964	BOS	AL	17	13	4	8	4	3	2	1	0	0	0	0	0	0	13	4
1965	BOS	AL	6	2	4	5	1	0	0	0	0	0	0	0	0	0	4	2
1966	BOS	AL	3	3	0	3	0	0	0	0	0	0	0	0	0	1	2	1
1967	BOS	AL	1	1	0	1	0	0	0	0	0	0	0	0	0	0	1	0
	NY	AL	2	0	2	1	0	1	0	0	0	0	0	0	0	0	0	2
	Total		3	1	2	2	0	1	0	0	0	0	0	0	0	0	1	2

Bob Tillman *continued*

Year	Tm	Lg	Tot	H	A	Men-On 0	1	2	3	One-Game 2	3	4	LO	XN	IP	PH	RHP	LHP
1968	ATL	NL	5	3	2	4	1	0	0	0	0	0	0	0	0	0	3	2
1969	ATL	NL	12	5	7	7	4	0	1	0	1	0	0	2	0	0	6	6
1970	ATL	NL	11	5	6	7	3	1	0	1	0	0	0	1	0	0	8	3
Total			79	44	35	49	20	7	3	3	1	0	0	6	0	3	53	26

Rank among batters: 661 • *Top target (3 home runs)*: Mudcat Grant, Grant Jackson • *Number of pitchers victimized*: 67 • *Total ballparks homered in*: 15 • *First HR*: 05/19/1962 off Ted Bowsfield • *Hit HR in first major league AB*—vs LA: 05/19/1962

Rusty Tillman

KERRY JEROME TILLMAN
B: 08/29/1960
BR

Year	Tm	Lg	Tot	H	A	Men-On 0	1	2	3	One-Game 2	3	4	LO	XN	IP	PH	RHP	LHP
1986	OAK	AL	1	1	0	1	0	0	0	0	0	0	0	0	0	0	0	1
1988	SF	NL	1	1	0	0	0	1	0	0	0	0	0	0	0	0	0	1
Total			2	2	0	1	0	1	0	0	0	0	0	0	0	0	0	2

Rank among batters: 4,129 • *Total ballparks homered in*: 2 • *First HR*: 09/23/1986 off Steve Carlton

Ozzie Timmons

OSBORNE LLEWELLYN TIMMONS
B: 09/18/1970
BR

Year	Tm	Lg	Tot	H	A	Men-On 0	1	2	3	One-Game 2	3	4	LO	XN	IP	PH	RHP	LHP
1995	CHI	NL	8	5	3	5	3	0	0	0	0	0	0	0	1	1	5	3

Rank among batters: 2,703 • *Total ballparks homered in*: 4 • *First HR*: 05/27/1995 off John Burkett

Ron Tingley

RONALD IRVIN TINGLEY
B: 05/27/1959
BR

Year	Tm	Lg	Tot	H	A	Men-On 0	1	2	3	One-Game 2	3	4	LO	XN	IP	PH	RHP	LHP
1988	CLE	AL	1	0	1	0	1	0	0	0	0	0	0	0	0	0	0	1
1991	CAL	AL	1	1	0	1	0	0	0	0	0	0	0	0	0	0	1	0
1992	CAL	AL	3	2	1	2	1	0	0	0	0	0	0	0	0	0	2	1
1994	FLO	NL	1	0	1	0	1	0	0	0	0	0	0	0	0	0	1	0
1995	DET	AL	4	3	1	2	1	0	1	0	0	0	0	0	0	0	2	2
Total			10	6	4	5	4	0	1	0	0	0	0	0	0	0	6	4

Rank among batters: 2,500 • *Total ballparks homered in*: 5 • *First HR*: 08/03/1988 off Jeff Ballard

Joe Tinker

JOSEPH BERT TINKER
B: 07/27/1880 D: 07/27/1948
BR HOF

Year	Tm	Lg	Tot	H	A	Men-On 0	1	2	3	One-Game 2	3	4	LO	XN	IP	PH	RHP	LHP
1902	CHI	NL	2	0	2	0	2	0	0	0	0	0	0	0	0	0	2	0
1903	CHI	NL	2	1	1	0	1	1	0	0	0	0	0	0	0	0	2	0
1904	CHI	NL	3	1	2	1	1	1	0	0	0	0	0	0	0	0	1	2
1905	CHI	NL	2	2	0	1	0	1	0	0	0	0	0	0	1	0	2	0
1906	CHI	NL	1	1	0	0	1	0	0	0	0	0	0	0	1	0	1	0
1907	CHI	NL	1	0	1	0	0	1	0	0	0	0	0	0	0	0	1	0
1908	CHI	NL	6	4	2	3	3	0	0	0	0	0	0	0	0	0	5	1
1909	CHI	NL	4	1	3	3	1	0	0	0	0	0	0	0	0	0	3	1
1910	CHI	NL	3	1	2	1	2	0	0	0	0	0	0	0	0	0	3	0
1911	CHI	NL	4	3	1	1	1	1	1	0	0	0	0	0	0	0	2	2
1913	CIN	NL	1	0	1	0	1	0	0	0	0	0	0	0	0	0	1	0
1914	CHI	FL	2	2	0	1	0	1	0	0	0	0	0	0	0	0	2	0
Total			31	16	15	11	13	6	1	0	0	0	0	0	2	0	25	6

Rank among batters: 1,400 • *Top target (3 home runs)*: Christy Mathewson • *Number of pitchers victimized*: 26 • *Total ballparks homered in*: 10 • *First HR*: 05/27/1902 off Ed Murphy • *World Series HR*—1

Lee Tinsley

LEE OWEN TINSLEY
B: 03/04/1969
BB

Year	Tm	Lg	Tot	H	A	Men-On 0	1	2	3	One-Game 2	3	4	LO	XN	IP	PH	RHP	LHP
1993	SEA	AL	1	0	1	0	1	0	0	0	0	0	0	0	0	0	1	0
1994	BOS	AL	2	1	1	1	1	0	0	0	0	0	0	0	0	0	2	0
1995	BOS	AL	7	4	3	5	2	0	0	0	0	0	1	0	0	0	5	2
Total			10	5	5	6	4	0	0	0	0	0	1	0	0	0	8	2

Rank among batters: 2,500 • *Total ballparks homered in*: 6 • *First HR*: 07/21/1993 off Steve Farr

Eric Tipton

ERIC GORDON TIPTON
B: 04/20/1915
BR

Year	Tm	Lg	Tot	H	A	Men-On 0	1	2	3	One-Game 2	3	4	LO	XN	IP	PH	RHP	LHP
1939	PHI	AL	1	1	0	0	1	0	0	0	0	0	0	0	0	0	1	0
1942	CIN	NL	4	1	3	3	1	0	0	0	0	0	0	0	0	1	4	0
1943	CIN	NL	9	3	6	7	2	0	0	1	0	0	0	0	0	0	8	1
1944	CIN	NL	3	1	2	3	0	0	0	0	0	0	0	0	0	0	3	0
1945	CIN	NL	5	1	4	2	1	2	0	0	0	0	0	0	0	0	4	1
Total			22	7	15	15	5	2	0	1	0	0	0	0	0	1	20	2

Rank among batters: 1,719 • *Top target (2 home runs)*: Lon Warneke • *Number of pitchers victimized*: 21 • *Total ballparks homered in*: 6 • *First HR*: 08/06/1939 off John Whitehead

Joe Tipton

JOE HICKS TIPTON
B: 02/18/1922 D: 03/01/1994
BR

Year	Tm	Lg	Tot	H	A	Men-On 0	1	2	3	One-Game 2	3	4	LO	XN	IP	PH	RHP	LHP
1948	CLE	AL	1	0	1	0	0	1	0	0	0	0	0	0	0	0	1	0
1949	CHI	AL	3	1	2	2	1	0	0	1	0	0	0	0	0	0	1	2
1950	PHI	AL	6	3	3	4	1	1	0	0	0	0	0	0	0	0	5	1
1951	PHI	AL	3	1	2	2	1	0	0	0	0	0	0	0	0	0	2	1
1952	PHI	AL	3	2	1	2	1	0	0	0	0	0	0	0	0	0	3	0
	CLE	AL	6	2	4	2	2	1	1	1	0	0	0	0	0	0	4	2
	Total		9	4	5	4	3	1	1	1	0	0	0	0	0	0	7	2
1953	CLE	AL	6	3	3	5	1	0	0	0	0	0	0	0	0	0	2	4
1954	WAS	AL	1	0	1	1	0	0	0	0	0	0	0	0	0	0	0	1
Total			29	12	17	18	7	3	1	2	0	0	0	0	0	0	18	11

Rank among batters: 1,465 • *Top target (3 home runs)*: Ray Scarborough • *Number of pitchers victimized*: 25 • *Total ballparks homered in*: 7 • *First HR*: 05/09/1948 off Fritz Dorish

Tom Tischinski

THOMAS ARTHUR TISCHINSKI
B: 07/12/1944
BR

Year	Tm	Lg	Tot	H	A	Men-On 0	1	2	3	One-Game 2	3	4	LO	XN	IP	PH	RHP	LHP
1970	MIN	AL	1	1	0	1	0	0	0	0	0	0	0	0	0	0	1	0

Rank among batters: 4,707 • *Total ballparks homered in*: 1 • *First HR*: 08/21/1970 off Casey Cox

John Titus

JOHN FRANKLIN TITUS
B: 02/21/1876 D: 01/08/1943
BL

Year	Tm	Lg	Tot	H	A	Men-On 0	1	2	3	One-Game 2	3	4	LO	XN	IP	PH	RHP	LHP
1903	PHI	NL	2	2	0	1	0	1	0	0	0	0	0	0	0	0	2	0
1904	PHI	NL	4	1	3	3	0	1	0	0	0	0	0	0	1	0	4	0
1905	PHI	NL	2	2	0	0	2	0	0	0	0	0	0	0	0	0	2	0
1906	PHI	NL	1	0	1	0	1	0	0	0	0	0	0	0	1	0	1	0
1907	PHI	NL	3	0	3	0	3	0	0	0	0	0	0	0	2	0	2	1
1908	PHI	NL	2	0	2	2	0	0	0	0	0	0	0	0	0	0	2	0
1909	PHI	NL	3	2	1	2	1	0	0	0	0	0	0	0	2	0	3	0
1910	PHI	NL	3	1	2	2	0	1	0	0	0	0	1	0	0	0	3	0
1911	PHI	NL	8	6	2	5	3	0	0	0	0	0	0	0	1	0	5	3
1912	PHI	NL	3	1	2	1	2	0	0	0	0	0	0	0	0	0	3	0
	BOS	NL	2	0	2	0	1	1	0	0	0	0	0	0	0	0	2	0
	Total		5	1	4	1	3	1	0	0	0	0	0	0	0	0	5	0
1913	BOS	NL	5	3	2	2	1	2	0	0	0	0	0	0	0	0	4	1
Total			38	18	20	18	14	6	0	0	0	0	1	0	7	0	33	5

Rank among batters: 1,225 • Top target (2 home runs): Dummy Taylor, Vive Lindaman, Christy Mathewson, Bob Ewing, Lefty Tyler, Doc Crandall • *Number of pitchers victimized*: 32 • *Total ballparks homered in*: 8 • *First HR*: 06/25/1903 off Bucky Veil

Jack Tobin

JOHN THOMAS TOBIN
B: 05/04/1892 D: 12/10/1969
BL

Year	Tm	Lg	Tot	H	A	Men-On 0	1	2	3	One-Game 2	3	4	LO	XN	IP	PH	RHP	LHP
1914	STL	FL	7	4	3	5	1	1	0	0	0	0	0	1	0	0	6	1
1915	STL	FL	6	3	3	3	2	1	0	0	0	0	1	0	0	0	4	2
1919	STL	AL	6	2	4	2	3	1	0	0	0	0	0	0	0	0	2	4
1920	STL	AL	4	3	1	2	1	0	1	0	0	0	1	0	1	0	3	1
1921	STL	AL	8	6	2	4	2	2	0	0	0	0	1	0	1	0	6	2
1922	STL	AL	13	11	2	8	3	1	1	2	0	0	1	1	1	0	12	1

Jack Tobin *continued*

Year	Tm	Lg	Tot	H	A	Men-On 0	1	2	3	One-Game 2	3	4	LO	XN	IP	PH	RHP	LHP
1923	STL	AL	13	11	2	8	4	1	0	2	0	0	2	0	0	0	12	1
1924	STL	AL	2	2	0	1	0	1	0	0	0	0	0	0	0	0	2	0
1925	STL	AL	2	2	0	0	1	1	0	0	0	0	0	0	0	1	2	0
1926	BOS	AL	1	0	1	0	0	0	1	0	0	0	0	0	0	0	1	0
1927	BOS	AL	2	1	1	1	0	0	1	0	0	0	0	0	0	0	2	0
Total			64	45	19	34	17	9	4	4	0	0	6	2	3	1	52	12

Rank among batters: 815 • *Top target (5 home runs)*: Red Faber • *Number of pitchers victimized*: 47 • *Total ballparks homered in*: 13 • *First HR*: 05/29/1914 off Dan Adams

Jim Tobin

JAMES ANTHONY TOBIN
B: 12/27/1912 D: 05/19/1969
BR

Year	Tm	Lg	Tot	H	A	Men-On 0	1	2	3	One-Game 2	3	4	LO	XN	IP	PH	RHP	LHP
1939	PIT	NL	2	1	1	1	0	1	0	0	0	0	0	0	0	0	1	1
1942	BOS	NL	6	4	2	2	4	0	0	0	1	0	0	0	0	1	5	1
1943	BOS	NL	2	1	1	1	1	0	0	0	0	0	0	0	0	0	1	1
1944	BOS	NL	2	1	1	2	0	0	0	0	0	0	0	0	0	0	1	1
1945	BOS	NL	3	2	1	1	2	0	0	0	0	0	0	0	0	0	3	0
	DET	AL	2	2	0	0	1	1	0	0	0	0	0	1	0	0	2	0
	Total		5	4	1	1	3	1	0	0	0	0	0	1	0	0	5	0
Total			17	11	6	7	8	2	0	0	1	0	0	1	0	1	13	4

Rank among batters: 1,969 • *Top target (2 home runs)*: Jake Mooty • *Number of pitchers victimized*: 16 • *Total ballparks homered in*: 7 • *First HR*: 04/24/1939 off Earl Whitehill

Al Todd

ALFRED CHESTER TODD
B: 01/07/1902 D: 03/08/1985
BR

Year	Tm	Lg	Tot	H	A	Men-On 0	1	2	3	One-Game 2	3	4	LO	XN	IP	PH	RHP	LHP
1934	PHI	NL	4	2	2	1	3	0	0	0	0	0	0	0	1	0	3	1
1935	PHI	NL	3	3	0	0	2	1	0	0	0	0	0	0	0	0	1	2
1936	PIT	NL	2	0	2	0	1	1	0	0	0	0	0	0	0	0	2	0
1937	PIT	NL	8	3	5	4	3	0	1	0	0	0	0	0	1	0	4	4
1938	PIT	NL	7	1	6	6	1	0	0	0	0	0	0	1	0	0	5	2
1939	BRO	NL	5	3	2	5	0	0	0	0	0	0	0	0	0	0	2	3
1940	CHI	NL	6	4	2	5	1	0	0	0	0	0	0	2	0	0	4	2
Total			35	16	19	21	11	2	1	0	0	0	0	3	2	0	21	14

Rank among batters: 1,291 • *Top target (4 home runs)*: Carl Hubbell • *Number of pitchers victimized*: 28 • *Total ballparks homered in*: 8 • *First HR*: 05/22/1934 off Ralph Birkofer

Phil Todt

PHILIP JULIUS TODT
B: 08/09/1901 D: 11/15/1973
BL

Year	Tm	Lg	Tot	H	A	Men-On 0	1	2	3	One-Game 2	3	4	LO	XN	IP	PH	RHP	LHP
1924	BOS	AL	1	0	1	1	0	0	0	0	0	0	0	0	0	0	1	0
1925	BOS	AL	11	3	8	4	6	1	0	0	0	0	0	0	0	0	10	1
1926	BOS	AL	7	0	7	6	1	0	0	1	0	0	0	1	0	0	6	1
1927	BOS	AL	6	1	5	5	1	0	0	1	0	0	0	1	0	0	6	0
1928	BOS	AL	12	4	8	5	5	2	0	2	0	0	0	0	1	0	10	2
1929	BOS	AL	4	2	2	2	2	0	0	0	0	0	0	0	1	0	4	0
1930	BOS	AL	11	3	8	6	4	1	0	1	0	0	0	0	0	0	11	0
1931	PHI	AL	5	3	2	2	1	2	0	1	0	0	0	0	0	0	4	1
Total			57	16	41	31	20	6	0	6	0	0	0	2	2	0	52	5

Rank among batters: 902 • *Top target (3 home runs)*: Joe Bush, Tom Zachary, Sam Gray, Clint Brown • *Number of pitchers victimized*: 43 • *Total ballparks homered in*: 7 • *First HR*: 06/22/1924 off Joe Bush

Bobby Tolan

ROBERT TOLAN
B: 11/19/1945
BL

Year	Tm	Lg	Tot	H	A	Men-On 0	1	2	3	One-Game 2	3	4	LO	XN	IP	PH	RHP	LHP
1966	STL	NL	1	1	0	1	0	0	0	0	0	0	0	0	0	1	1	0
1967	STL	NL	6	3	3	4	2	0	0	0	0	0	0	0	0	0	5	1
1968	STL	NL	5	4	1	4	1	0	0	0	0	0	0	0	1	0	5	0
1969	CIN	NL	21	15	6	9	8	4	0	0	0	0	0	0	0	0	17	4
1970	CIN	NL	16	8	8	8	7	0	1	0	0	0	1	0	0	0	12	4

Bobby Tolan *continued*

Year	Tm	Lg	Tot	H	A	Men-On				One-Game			LO	XN	IP	PH	RHP	LHP
						0	1	2	3	2	3	4						
1972	CIN	NL	8	4	4	3	2	3	0	0	0	0	0	0	0	0	5	3
1973	CIN	NL	9	3	6	5	2	2	0	0	0	0	0	0	0	1	8	1
1974	SD	NL	8	6	2	4	1	3	0	2	0	0	2	0	0	0	8	0
1975	SD	NL	5	2	3	2	1	2	0	0	0	0	0	0	0	0	5	0
1976	PHI	NL	5	4	1	2	2	0	1	0	0	0	0	0	0	0	5	0
1977	PIT	NL	2	0	2	2	0	0	0	0	0	0	0	0	0	0	2	0
Total			86	50	36	44	26	14	2	2	0	0	3	0	1	2	73	13

Rank among batters: 602 • *Top target (4 home runs)*: Steve Blass • *Number of pitchers victimized*: 70 • *Total ballparks homered in*: 14 • *First HR*: 06/17/1966 off Larry Jackson • *World Series HR*—1; *LCS HR*—1

Jose Tolentino

JOSE (FRANCO) TOLENTINO
B: 06/03/1961
BL

Year	Tm	Lg	Tot	H	A	Men-On 0	1	2	3	One-Game 2	3	4	LO	XN	IP	PH	RHP	LHP
1991	HOU	NL	1	1	0	0	1	0	0	0	0	0	0	0	0	1	1	0

Rank among batters: 4,707 • *Total ballparks homered in*: 1 • *First HR*: 08/26/1991 off Alejandro Pena

Wayne Tolleson

JIMMY WAYNE TOLLESON
B: 11/22/1955
BB

Year	Tm	Lg	Tot	H	A	Men-On 0	1	2	3	One-Game 2	3	4	LO	XN	IP	PH	RHP	LHP
1983	TEX	AL	3	2	1	2	1	0	0	0	0	0	1	0	0	0	0	3
1985	TEX	AL	1	0	1	0	1	0	0	0	0	0	0	0	0	0	1	0
1986	CHI	AL	3	1	2	1	1	1	0	0	0	0	0	0	0	0	0	3
1987	NY	AL	1	0	1	1	0	0	0	0	0	0	0	0	0	0	1	0
1989	NY	AL	1	0	1	1	0	0	0	0	0	0	0	0	0	0	0	1
Total			9	3	6	5	3	1	0	0	0	0	1	0	0	0	2	7

Rank among batters: 2,587 • *Top target (2 home runs)*: Scott McGregor • *Number of pitchers victimized*: 8 • *Total ballparks homered in*: 7 • *First HR*: 06/11/1983 off Jack O'Connor

Tim Tolman

TIMOTHY LEE TOLMAN
B: 04/20/1956
BR

Year	Tm	Lg	Tot	H	A	Men-On 0	1	2	3	One-Game 2	3	4	LO	XN	IP	PH	RHP	LHP
1982	HOU	NL	1	1	0	1	0	0	0	0	0	0	0	0	0	0	0	1
1983	HOU	NL	2	0	2	1	1	0	0	0	0	0	0	0	0	2	0	2
1985	HOU	NL	2	1	1	0	0	2	0	0	0	0	0	0	0	1	0	2
Total			5	2	3	2	1	2	0	0	0	0	0	0	0	3	0	5

Rank among batters: 3,191 • *Total ballparks homered in*: 3 • *First HR*: 10/01/1982 off Bob Shirley

Chick Tolson

CHARLES JULIUS TOLSON
B: 05/03/1895 D: 04/16/1965
BR

Year	Tm	Lg	Tot	H	A	Men-On 0	1	2	3	One-Game 2	3	4	LO	XN	IP	PH	RHP	LHP
1926	CHI	NL	1	0	1	0	1	0	0	0	0	0	0	1	1	1	0	1
1927	CHI	NL	2	1	1	0	1	0	1	0	0	0	0	0	0	1	1	1
1929	CHI	NL	1	1	0	1	0	0	0	0	0	0	0	0	0	0	1	0
Total			4	2	2	1	2	0	1	0	0	0	0	1	1	2	2	2

Rank among batters: 3,427 • *Total ballparks homered in*: 3 • *First HR*: 06/23/1926 off Eppa Rixey

Dick Tomanek

RICHARD CARL TOMANEK
B: 01/06/1931
BL

Year	Tm	Lg	Tot	H	A	Men-On 0	1	2	3	One-Game 2	3	4	LO	XN	IP	PH	RHP	LHP
1958	CLE	AL	1	0	1	0	1	0	0	0	0	0	0	0	0	0	1	0

Rank among batters: 4,707 • *Total ballparks homered in*: 1 • *First HR*: 06/06/1958 off Bob Turley

Andy Tomberlin

ANDY LEE TOMBERLIN
B: 11/07/1966
BL

Year	Tm	Lg	Tot	H	A	Men-On 0	1	2	3	One-Game 2	3	4	LO	XN	IP	PH	RHP	LHP
1993	PIT	NL	1	0	1	1	0	0	0	0	0	0	0	0	0	0	1	0

Year	Tm	Lg	Tot	H	A	Men-On 0	1	2	3	One-Game 2	3	4	LO	XN	IP	PH	RHP	LHP

Andy Tomberlin *continued*

Year	Tm	Lg	Tot	H	A	Men-On 0	1	2	3	One-Game 2	3	4	LO	XN	IP	PH	RHP	LHP
1994	BOS	AL	1	1	0	1	0	0	0	0	0	0	0	0	0	1	1	0
1995	OAK	AL	4	3	1	3	0	1	0	0	0	0	0	0	0	2	4	0
Total			6	4	2	5	0	1	0	0	0	0	0	0	0	3	6	0

Rank among batters: 2,988 • *Total ballparks homered in*: 4 • *First HR*: 08/24/1993 off Kevin Gross

Phil Tomney

PHILIP H. TOMNEY
B: 06/17/1863 D: 03/18/1892
BR

Year	Tm	Lg	Tot	H	A	Men-On 0	1	2	3	One-Game 2	3	4	LO	XN	IP	PH	RHP	LHP
1889	LOU	AA	4	1	3	0	2	2	0	0	0	0	0	0	0	0	4	0
1890	LOU	AA	1	1	0	0	0	1	0	0	0	0	0	0	0	0	1	0
Total			5	2	3	0	2	3	0	0	0	0	0	0	0	0	5	0

Rank among batters: 3,191 • *Total ballparks homered in*: 4 • *First HR*: 04/22/1889 off Elton Chamberlin

Fred Toney

FRED ALEXANDRA TONEY
B: 12/11/1888 D: 03/11/1953
BR

Year	Tm	Lg	Tot	H	A	Men-On 0	1	2	3	One-Game 2	3	4	LO	XN	IP	PH	RHP	LHP
1921	NY	NL	3	3	0	2	0	1	0	0	0	0	0	0	0	0	3	0

Rank among batters: 3,735 • *Total ballparks homered in*: 1 • *First HR*: 05/30/1921 off Bill Hubbell

Steve Toole

STEPHEN JOHN TOOLE
B: 04/09/1859 D: 03/28/1919
BR

Year	Tm	Lg	Tot	H	A	Men-On 0	1	2	3	One-Game 2	3	4	LO	XN	IP	PH	RHP	LHP
1887	BRO	AA	1	1	0	1	0	0	0	0	0	0	0	0	0	0	0	1

Rank among batters: 4,707 • *Total ballparks homered in*: 1 • *First HR*: 08/07/1887 off Phenomenal Smith

Bert Tooley

ALBERT R. TOOLEY
B: 08/30/1886 D: 08/17/1976
BR

Year	Tm	Lg	Tot	H	A	Men-On 0	1	2	3	One-Game 2	3	4	LO	XN	IP	PH	RHP	LHP
1911	BRO	NL	1	0	1	1	0	0	0	0	0	0	0	0	0	0	1	0
1912	BRO	NL	2	1	1	1	0	1	0	0	0	0	0	0	0	0	1	1
Total			3	1	2	2	0	1	0	0	0	0	0	0	0	0	2	1

Rank among batters: 3,735 • *Total ballparks homered in*: 3 • *First HR*: 06/06/1911 off Lew Richie

Specs Toporcer

GEORGE TOPORCER
B: 02/09/1899 D: 05/17/1989
BL

Year	Tm	Lg	Tot	H	A	Men-On 0	1	2	3	One-Game 2	3	4	LO	XN	IP	PH	RHP	LHP
1922	STL	NL	3	2	1	0	3	0	0	0	0	0	0	0	0	0	3	0
1923	STL	NL	3	2	1	1	2	0	0	0	0	0	0	0	0	0	3	0
1924	STL	NL	1	1	0	0	1	0	0	0	0	0	0	0	0	0	1	0
1925	STL	NL	2	1	1	0	2	0	0	0	0	0	0	0	0	0	2	0
Total			9	6	3	1	8	0	0	0	0	0	0	0	0	0	9	0

Rank among batters: 2,587 • *Total ballparks homered in*: 4 • *First HR*: 05/15/1922 off Huck Betts

Jeff Torborg

JEFFREY ALLEN TORBORG
B: 11/26/1941
BR

Year	Tm	Lg	Tot	H	A	Men-On 0	1	2	3	One-Game 2	3	4	LO	XN	IP	PH	RHP	LHP
1965	LA	NL	3	0	3	3	0	0	0	0	0	0	0	0	0	0	0	3
1966	LA	NL	1	1	0	0	1	0	0	0	0	0	0	0	0	0	0	1
1967	LA	NL	2	0	2	1	0	1	0	0	0	0	0	0	0	0	0	2
1970	LA	NL	1	0	1	0	0	1	0	0	0	0	0	0	0	0	0	1
1973	CAL	AL	1	1	0	1	0	0	0	0	0	0	0	0	0	0	0	1
Total			8	2	6	5	1	2	0	0	0	0	0	0	0	0	0	8

Rank among batters: 2,703 • *Total ballparks homered in*: 6 • *First HR*: 05/08/1965 off Bob Hendley

Earl Torgeson

CLIFFORD EARL TORGESON
B: 01/01/1924 D: 11/08/1990
BL

Year	Tm	Lg	Tot	H	A	Men-On 0	1	2	3	One-Game 2	3	4	LO	XN	IP	PH	RHP	LHP
1947	BOS	NL	16	9	7	8	6	2	0	0	0	0	0	0	0	0	14	2
1948	BOS	NL	10	4	6	3	6	1	0	0	0	0	0	0	0	0	10	0
1949	BOS	NL	4	1	3	3	1	0	0	0	0	0	0	0	0	0	0	4
1950	BOS	NL	23	15	8	8	14	1	0	2	0	0	0	0	0	0	15	8
1951	BOS	NL	24	17	7	12	5	6	1	1	0	0	0	0	0	0	17	7
1952	BOS	NL	5	1	4	4	0	0	1	0	0	0	0	0	0	0	3	2
1953	PHI	NL	11	6	5	7	2	2	0	0	0	0	0	0	0	1	7	4
1954	PHI	NL	5	1	4	4	0	1	0	0	0	0	0	0	0	0	4	1
1955	PHI	NL	1	1	0	1	0	0	0	0	0	0	0	0	0	0	1	0
	DET	AL	9	7	2	3	2	4	0	1	0	0	0	1	0	1	8	1
	Total		10	8	2	4	2	4	0	1	0	0	0	1	0	1	9	1
1956	DET	AL	12	8	4	8	4	0	0	0	0	0	0	1	0	1	11	1
1957	DET	AL	1	1	0	1	0	0	0	0	0	0	0	0	0	0	1	0
	CHI	AL	7	6	1	3	2	2	0	1	0	0	0	0	0	0	3	4
	Total		8	7	1	4	2	2	0	1	0	0	0	0	0	0	4	4
1958	CHI	AL	10	3	7	6	4	0	0	2	0	0	0	0	0	2	10	0
1959	CHI	AL	9	5	4	6	2	1	0	0	0	0	0	1	0	1	9	0
1960	CHI	AL	2	1	1	2	0	0	0	0	0	0	0	0	0	1	2	0
Total			149	86	63	79	48	20	2	7	0	0	0	3	0	7	115	34

Rank among batters: 289 • *Top target (4 home runs)*: Johnny Hetki, Ewell Blackwell, Murry Dickson • *Number of pitchers victimized*: 107 • *Total ballparks homered in*: 16 • *First HR*: 04/18/1947 off Al Jurisich

Frank Torre

FRANK JOSEPH TORRE
B: 12/30/1931
BL

Year	Tm	Lg	Tot	H	A	Men-On 0	1	2	3	One-Game 2	3	4	LO	XN	IP	PH	RHP	LHP
1957	MIL	NL	5	0	5	3	2	0	0	0	0	0	0	1	0	1	3	2
1958	MIL	NL	6	6	0	3	0	2	1	0	0	0	0	0	0	0	5	1
1959	MIL	NL	1	1	0	1	0	0	0	0	0	0	0	0	0	0	1	0
1963	PHI	NL	1	0	1	0	1	0	0	0	0	0	0	0	0	0	1	0
Total			13	7	6	7	3	2	1	0	0	0	0	1	0	1	10	3

Rank among batters: 2,248 • *Total ballparks homered in*: 5 • *First HR*: 05/01/1957 off Windy McCall • *World Series HR—2*

Joe Torre

JOSEPH PAUL TORRE
B: 07/18/1940
BR

Year	Tm	Lg	Tot	H	A	Men-On 0	1	2	3	One-Game 2	3	4	LO	XN	IP	PH	RHP	LHP
1961	MIL	NL	10	6	4	6	4	0	0	0	0	0	0	0	0	0	9	1
1962	MIL	NL	5	2	3	4	1	0	0	0	0	0	0	0	0	1	4	1
1963	MIL	NL	14	6	8	10	3	0	1	0	0	0	0	1	0	0	10	4
1964	MIL	NL	20	10	10	11	6	2	1	2	0	0	0	1	0	0	18	2
1965	MIL	NL	27	13	14	18	5	4	0	3	0	0	0	1	0	1	21	6
1966	ATL	NL	36	18	18	20	11	4	1	5	0	0	0	2	0	0	26	10
1967	ATL	NL	20	9	11	12	8	0	0	2	0	0	0	1	0	0	16	4
1968	ATL	NL	10	5	5	7	1	2	0	1	0	0	0	0	0	0	8	2
1969	STL	NL	18	10	8	11	6	1	0	0	0	0	0	0	0	0	12	6
1970	STL	NL	21	7	14	15	4	2	0	0	0	0	0	1	0	0	16	5
1971	STL	NL	24	9	15	9	12	3	0	1	0	0	0	0	0	0	19	5
1972	STL	NL	11	6	5	5	2	4	0	0	0	0	0	0	0	0	7	4
1973	STL	NL	13	3	10	5	6	2	0	1	0	0	0	0	0	0	7	6
1974	STL	NL	11	4	7	5	5	1	0	0	0	0	0	1	0	0	11	0
1975	NY	NL	6	4	2	2	4	0	0	0	0	0	0	0	0	0	1	5
1976	NY	NL	5	3	2	3	2	0	0	1	0	0	0	0	0	0	1	4
1977	NY	NL	1	1	0	1	0	0	0	0	0	0	0	0	0	1	1	0
Total			252	116	136	144	80	25	3	16	0	0	0	8	0	3	187	65

Rank among batters: 106 • *Top target (8 home runs)*: Juan Marichal • *Number of pitchers victimized*: 143 • *Total ballparks homered in*: 19 • *First HR*: 05/21/1961 off Joey Jay • *Hit for Cycle—@PIT*: 06/27/1973 • *All-Star HR—1*

Felix Torres

FELIX (SANCHEZ) TORRES
B: 05/01/1932
BR

Year	Tm	Lg	Tot	H	A	Men-On 0	1	2	3	One-Game 2	3	4	LO	XN	IP	PH	RHP	LHP
1962	LA	AL	11	3	8	5	4	2	0	0	0	0	0	0	0	0	6	5

Felix Torres *continued*

Year	Tm	Lg	Tot	H	A	Men-On 0	1	2	3	One-Game 2	3	4	LO	XN	IP	PH	RHP	LHP
1963	LA	AL	4	0	4	2	0	1	1	0	0	0	0	0	0	0	2	2
1964	LA	AL	12	3	9	10	1	1	0	0	0	0	0	0	0	0	6	6
Total			27	6	21	17	5	4	1	0	0	0	0	0	0	0	14	13

Rank among batters: 1,532 • *Top target (3 home runs)*: Dick Stigman • *Number of pitchers victimized*: 23 • *Total ballparks homered in*: 9 • *First HR*: 06/15/1962 off Early Wynn

Hector Torres

HECTOR EPITACIO (MARROQUIN) TORRES
B: 09/16/1945
BR

Year	Tm	Lg	Tot	H	A	Men-On 0	1	2	3	One-Game 2	3	4	LO	XN	IP	PH	RHP	LHP
1968	HOU	NL	1	0	1	1	0	0	0	0	0	0	0	0	0	0	1	0
1969	HOU	NL	1	0	1	0	0	0	1	0	0	0	0	0	0	0	0	1
1972	MON	NL	2	1	1	2	0	0	0	0	0	0	0	0	0	0	0	2
1975	SD	NL	5	3	2	4	1	0	0	0	0	0	0	1	0	0	4	1
1976	SD	NL	4	2	2	3	1	0	0	0	0	0	0	0	0	0	3	1
1977	TOR	AL	5	4	1	3	0	1	1	0	0	0	0	0	0	0	3	2
Total			18	10	8	13	2	1	2	0	0	0	0	1	0	0	11	7

Rank among batters: 1,914 • *Total ballparks homered in*: 9 • *First HR*: 08/13/1968 off Jeff James

Rusty Torres

ROSENDO (HERNANDEZ) TORRES
B: 09/30/1948
BB

Year	Tm	Lg	Tot	H	A	Men-On 0	1	2	3	One-Game 2	3	4	LO	XN	IP	PH	RHP	LHP
1971	NY	AL	2	0	2	1	1	0	0	0	0	0	0	0	0	0	1	1
1972	NY	AL	3	0	3	2	1	0	0	0	0	0	0	0	0	0	1	2
1973	CLE	AL	7	5	2	3	3	1	0	0	0	0	0	0	0	1	3	4
1974	CLE	AL	3	0	3	2	1	0	0	0	0	0	0	0	0	0	3	0
1976	CAL	AL	6	2	4	4	1	1	0	0	0	0	0	2	0	0	3	3
1977	CAL	AL	3	1	2	2	1	0	0	0	0	0	0	0	0	0	2	1
1978	CHI	AL	3	1	2	2	1	0	0	0	0	0	0	0	0	0	1	2
1979	CHI	AL	8	3	5	4	4	0	0	0	0	0	0	0	0	0	7	1
Total			35	12	23	20	13	2	0	0	0	0	0	2	0	1	21	14

Rank among batters: 1,291 • *Top target (2 home runs)*: Jackie Brown, Jim Umbarger, Vida Blue • *Number of pitchers victimized*: 32 • *Total ballparks homered in*: 13 • *First HR*: 09/26/1971 off Mickey Lolich

Kelvin Torve

KELVIN CURTIS TORVE
B: 01/10/1960
BL

Year	Tm	Lg	Tot	H	A	Men-On 0	1	2	3	One-Game 2	3	4	LO	XN	IP	PH	RHP	LHP
1988	MIN	AL	1	0	1	1	0	0	0	0	0	0	0	0	0	0	1	0

Rank among batters: 4,707 • *Total ballparks homered in*: 1 • *First HR*: 06/27/1988 off Stew Cliburn

Cesar Tovar

CESAR LEONARDO TOVAR
B: 07/03/1940 D: 07/14/1994
BR

Year	Tm	Lg	Tot	H	A	Men-On 0	1	2	3	One-Game 2	3	4	LO	XN	IP	PH	RHP	LHP
1966	MIN	AL	2	1	1	0	2	0	0	0	0	0	0	0	0	0	1	1
1967	MIN	AL	6	3	3	5	1	0	0	2	0	0	1	0	0	0	6	0
1968	MIN	AL	6	4	2	4	2	0	0	0	0	0	1	0	0	0	3	3
1969	MIN	AL	11	6	5	5	4	1	1	0	0	0	2	2	0	0	6	5
1970	MIN	AL	10	5	5	6	2	2	0	0	0	0	0	0	0	0	7	3
1971	MIN	AL	1	0	1	0	0	1	0	0	0	0	0	0	0	0	1	0
1972	MIN	AL	2	2	0	1	1	0	0	0	0	0	0	0	0	0	1	1
1973	PHI	NL	1	0	1	1	0	0	0	0	0	0	0	0	0	0	0	1
1974	TEX	AL	4	2	2	1	1	2	0	0	0	0	0	0	0	0	3	1
1975	TEX	AL	3	3	0	3	0	0	0	0	0	0	3	0	0	0	3	0
Total			46	26	20	26	13	6	1	2	0	0	7	2	0	0	31	15

Rank among batters: 1,060 • Top target (2 home runs): Dick Ellsworth, George Lauzerique, Rickey Clark • *Number of pitchers victimized*: 43 • *Total ballparks homered in*: 13 • *First HR*: 05/06/1966 off Dick Stigman • *Hit for Cycle*—vs TEX: 09/19/1972

Happy Townsend

JOHN TOWNSEND
B: 04/09/1879 D: 12/21/1963
BR

Year	Tm	Lg	Tot	H	A	Men-On 0	1	2	3	One-Game 2	3	4	LO	XN	IP	PH	RHP	LHP
1904	WAS	AL	1	1	0	1	0	0	0	0	0	0	0	0	0	0	1	0

Happy Townsend *continued*

Rank among batters: 4,707 • *Total ballparks homered in*: 1 • *First HR*: 08/30/1904 off Barney Pelty

Jim Toy

JAMES MADISON TOY
B: 02/20/1858 D: 03/13/1919
BR

Year	Tm	Lg	Tot	H	A	Men-On 0	Men-On 1	Men-On 2	Men-On 3	One-Game 2	One-Game 3	One-Game 4	LO	XN	IP	PH	RHP	LHP
1887	CLE	AA	1	0	1	0	1	0	0	0	0	0	0	0	0	0	1	0

Rank among batters: 4,707 • *Total ballparks homered in*: 1 • *First HR*: 07/02/1887 off Billy Serad

Jim Traber

JAMES JOSEPH TRABER
B: 12/26/1961
BL

Year	Tm	Lg	Tot	H	A	Men-On 0	Men-On 1	Men-On 2	Men-On 3	One-Game 2	One-Game 3	One-Game 4	LO	XN	IP	PH	RHP	LHP
1986	BAL	AL	13	9	4	5	6	1	1	1	0	0	0	0	0	0	11	2
1988	BAL	AL	10	4	6	3	6	1	0	0	0	0	0	0	0	0	8	2
1989	BAL	AL	4	0	4	2	1	1	0	0	0	0	0	0	0	1	3	1
Total			27	13	14	10	13	3	1	1	0	0	0	0	0	1	22	5

Rank among batters: 1,532 • *Top target (2 home runs)*: Bret Saberhagen, Willie Fraser • *Number of pitchers victimized*: 25 • *Total ballparks homered in*: 8 • *First HR*: 07/20/1986 off Mike Smithson

Dick Tracewski

RICHARD JOSEPH TRACEWSKI
B: 02/03/1935
BR

Year	Tm	Lg	Tot	H	A	Men-On 0	Men-On 1	Men-On 2	Men-On 3	One-Game 2	One-Game 3	One-Game 4	LO	XN	IP	PH	RHP	LHP
1963	LA	NL	1	1	0	1	0	0	0	0	0	0	0	0	0	0	1	0
1964	LA	NL	1	1	0	1	0	0	0	0	0	0	0	0	0	0	0	1
1965	LA	NL	1	0	1	0	1	0	0	0	0	0	0	0	0	0	0	1
1967	DET	AL	1	1	0	1	0	0	0	0	0	0	0	0	0	0	0	1
1968	DET	AL	4	3	1	3	0	1	0	0	0	0	0	0	0	0	1	3
Total			8	6	2	6	1	1	0	0	0	0	0	0	0	0	2	6

Rank among batters: 2,703 • *Total ballparks homered in*: 4 • *First HR*: 06/12/1963 off Don Nottebart

Jim Tracy

JAMES EDWIN TRACY
B: 12/31/1955
BL

Year	Tm	Lg	Tot	H	A	Men-On 0	Men-On 1	Men-On 2	Men-On 3	One-Game 2	One-Game 3	One-Game 4	LO	XN	IP	PH	RHP	LHP
1980	CHI	NL	3	3	0	3	0	0	0	0	0	0	0	0	0	0	3	0

Rank among batters: 3,735 • *Total ballparks homered in*: 1 • *First HR*: 09/21/1980 off Dick Ruthven

Bill Traffley

WILLIAM FRANKLIN TRAFFLEY
B: 12/21/1859 D: 06/23/1908
BR

Year	Tm	Lg	Tot	H	A	Men-On 0	Men-On 1	Men-On 2	Men-On 3	One-Game 2	One-Game 3	One-Game 4	LO	XN	IP	PH	RHP	LHP
1885	BAL	AA	1	1	0	1	0	0	0	0	0	0	0	0	0	0	1	0

Rank among batters: 4,707 • *Total ballparks homered in*: 1 • *First HR*: 04/21/1885 off Henry Porter

Walt Tragesser

WALTER JOSEPH TRAGESSER
B: 06/14/1887 D: 12/14/1970
BR

Year	Tm	Lg	Tot	H	A	Men-On 0	Men-On 1	Men-On 2	Men-On 3	One-Game 2	One-Game 3	One-Game 4	LO	XN	IP	PH	RHP	LHP
1920	PHI	NL	6	6	0	4	1	1	0	0	0	0	0	0	0	0	6	0

Rank among batters: 2,988 • *Total ballparks homered in*: 1 • *First HR*: 06/10/1920 off Speed Martin

Alan Trammell

ALAN STUART TRAMMELL
B: 02/21/1958
BR

Year	Tm	Lg	Tot	H	A	Men-On 0	Men-On 1	Men-On 2	Men-On 3	One-Game 2	One-Game 3	One-Game 4	LO	XN	IP	PH	RHP	LHP
1978	DET	AL	2	0	2	2	0	0	0	0	0	0	0	0	0	0	2	0
1979	DET	AL	6	4	2	1	4	1	0	0	0	0	0	0	0	0	4	2
1980	DET	AL	9	5	4	6	2	1	0	1	0	0	0	0	0	0	6	3
1981	DET	AL	2	2	0	2	0	0	0	0	0	0	1	0	0	0	0	2
1982	DET	AL	9	5	4	2	5	0	2	0	0	0	0	0	0	0	6	3

Year	Tm	Lg	Tot	H	A	Men-On				One-Game			LO	XN	IP	PH	RHP	LHP
						0	1	2	3	2	3	4						

Alan Trammell *continued*

Year	Tm	Lg	Tot	H	A	Men-On 0	1	2	3	One-Game 2	3	4	LO	XN	IP	PH	RHP	LHP
1983	DET	AL	14	8	6	10	2	2	0	1	0	0	1	1	0	0	11	3
1984	DET	AL	14	7	7	7	6	0	1	0	0	0	0	0	0	0	5	9
1985	DET	AL	13	7	6	9	3	1	0	0	0	0	0	0	0	0	9	4
1986	DET	AL	21	8	13	15	6	0	0	1	0	0	0	0	0	0	13	8
1987	DET	AL	28	13	15	18	6	4	0	0	0	0	0	0	0	0	17	11
1988	DET	AL	15	7	8	9	4	1	1	0	0	0	0	1	0	0	10	5
1989	DET	AL	5	2	3	4	1	0	0	0	0	0	0	0	0	0	4	1
1990	DET	AL	14	9	5	7	4	3	0	0	0	0	0	0	0	0	7	7
1991	DET	AL	9	6	3	4	4	1	0	0	0	0	0	0	0	0	5	4
1992	DET	AL	1	0	1	1	0	0	0	0	0	0	0	0	0	0	1	0
1993	DET	AL	12	6	6	6	4	2	0	0	0	0	0	0	0	0	5	7
1994	DET	AL	8	6	2	5	3	0	0	0	0	0	0	0	0	1	6	2
1995	DET	AL	2	1	1	1	0	0	1	0	0	0	0	0	0	0	1	1
Total			184	96	88	109	54	16	5	3	0	0	2	2	0	1	112	72

Rank among batters: 210 • *Top target (5 home runs)*: Frank Viola • *Number of pitchers victimized*: 139 • *Total ballparks homered in*: 17 • *First HR*: 05/07/1978 off Matt Keough • *World Series HR*—2; *LCS HR*—1

Cecil Travis

CECIL HOWELL TRAVIS
B: 08/08/1913
BL

Year	Tm	Lg	Tot	H	A	Men-On 0	1	2	3	One-Game 2	3	4	LO	XN	IP	PH	RHP	LHP
1934	WAS	AL	1	1	0	0	1	0	0	0	0	0	0	0	0	0	1	0
1936	WAS	AL	2	1	1	0	2	0	0	0	0	0	0	0	1	0	2	0
1937	WAS	AL	3	2	1	3	0	0	0	0	0	0	0	0	2	0	2	1
1938	WAS	AL	5	3	2	4	0	1	0	0	0	0	0	0	1	0	3	2
1939	WAS	AL	5	1	4	2	3	0	0	0	0	0	0	0	1	0	5	0
1940	WAS	AL	2	1	1	1	0	1	0	0	0	0	0	0	0	0	2	0
1941	WAS	AL	7	1	6	5	2	0	0	1	0	0	0	0	1	0	5	2
1946	WAS	AL	1	0	1	1	0	0	0	0	0	0	0	0	0	0	1	0
1947	WAS	AL	1	0	1	1	0	0	0	0	0	0	0	0	0	0	1	0
Total			27	10	17	17	8	2	0	1	0	0	0	0	6	0	22	5

Rank among batters: 1,532 • *Top target (2 home runs)*: Russ Van Atta, Vern Kennedy, Atley Donald • *Number of pitchers victimized*: 24 • *Total ballparks homered in*: 8 • *First HR*: 06/23/1934 off Vic Sorrell

Pie Traynor

HAROLD JOSEPH TRAYNOR
B: 11/11/1899 D: 03/16/1972
BR HOF

Year	Tm	Lg	Tot	H	A	Men-On 0	1	2	3	One-Game 2	3	4	LO	XN	IP	PH	RHP	LHP
1922	PIT	NL	4	3	1	2	1	1	0	0	0	0	0	1	1	0	2	2
1923	PIT	NL	12	4	8	6	4	2	0	0	0	0	0	1	5	0	10	2
1924	PIT	NL	5	3	2	5	0	0	0	0	0	0	0	1	1	0	4	1
1925	PIT	NL	6	2	4	2	2	1	1	1	0	0	0	0	3	0	5	1
1926	PIT	NL	3	2	1	1	0	2	0	0	0	0	0	0	1	0	3	0
1927	PIT	NL	5	0	5	3	1	0	1	0	0	0	0	1	0	0	4	1
1928	PIT	NL	3	2	1	2	1	0	0	0	0	0	0	0	1	0	2	1
1929	PIT	NL	4	2	2	3	1	0	0	0	0	0	0	1	0	0	4	0
1930	PIT	NL	9	2	7	6	2	1	0	0	0	0	0	1	2	0	6	3
1931	PIT	NL	2	2	0	0	1	1	0	0	0	0	0	0	1	0	1	1
1932	PIT	NL	2	1	1	0	1	1	0	0	0	0	0	0	2	0	2	0
1933	PIT	NL	1	0	1	1	0	0	0	0	0	0	0	0	1	0	0	1
1934	PIT	NL	1	0	1	0	1	0	0	0	0	0	0	0	0	0	1	0
1935	PIT	NL	1	0	1	0	0	0	1	0	0	0	0	0	0	0	0	1
Total			58	23	35	31	15	9	3	1	0	0	0	6	18	0	44	14

Rank among batters: 886 • *Top target (3 home runs)*: Hugh McQuillan • *Number of pitchers victimized*: 52 • *Total ballparks homered in*: 8 • *First HR*: 04/29/1922 off Eppa Rixey • *Hit for Cycle*—@PHI: 07/07/1923 • *World Series HR*—1

George Treadway

GEORGE B. TREADWAY
BL

Year	Tm	Lg	Tot	H	A	Men-On 0	1	2	3	One-Game 2	3	4	LO	XN	IP	PH	RHP	LHP
1893	BAL	NL	1	0	1	1	0	0	0	0	0	0	0	0	0	0	1	0
1894	BRO	NL	4	2	2	2	1	1	0	0	0	0	0	0	0	0	4	0
1895	BRO	NL	7	2	5	3	3	1	0	0	0	0	0	0	0	0	5	2
Total			12	4	8	6	4	2	0	0	0	0	0	0	0	0	10	2

Rank among batters: 2,325 • *Total ballparks homered in*: 8 • *First HR*: 07/27/1893 off Harry Staley

Jeff Treadway

HUGH JEFFERY TREADWAY
B: 01/22/1963
BL

Year	Tm	Lg	Tot	H	A	Men-On				One-Game			LO	XN	IP	PH	RHP	LHP
						0	1	2	3	2	3	4						
1987	CIN	NL	2	2	0	2	0	0	0	0	0	0	0	0	0	0	2	0
1988	CIN	NL	2	2	0	2	0	0	0	0	0	0	0	0	0	0	2	0
1989	ATL	NL	8	2	6	5	3	0	0	0	0	0	1	0	1	0	8	0
1990	ATL	NL	11	5	6	6	3	2	0	0	1	0	0	0	0	0	7	4
1991	ATL	NL	3	1	2	1	2	0	0	0	0	0	0	0	0	0	3	0
1993	CLE	AL	2	0	2	1	1	0	0	0	0	0	0	0	0	1	2	0
Total			28	12	16	17	9	2	0	0	1	0	1	0	1	1	24	4

Rank among batters: 1,500 • *Top target (2 home runs)*: Tim Leary, David Cone, Eric Show, Doug Drabek • *Number of pitchers victimized*: 24 • *Total ballparks homered in*: 11 • *First HR*: 09/23/1987 off Eric Show

Red Treadway

THADFORD LEON TREADWAY
B: 04/28/1920 D: 05/26/1994
BL

Year	Tm	Lg	Tot	H	A	Men-On				One-Game			LO	XN	IP	PH	RHP	LHP
						0	1	2	3	2	3	4						
1945	NY	NL	4	4	0	2	1	1	0	0	0	0	0	0	0	0	4	0

Rank among batters: 3,427 • *Total ballparks homered in*: 1 • *First HR*: 06/15/1945 off Dick Mauney

Mike Tresh

MICHAEL TRESH
B: 02/23/1914 D: 10/04/1966
BR

Year	Tm	Lg	Tot	H	A	Men-On				One-Game			LO	XN	IP	PH	RHP	LHP
						0	1	2	3	2	3	4						
1940	CHI	AL	1	1	0	0	0	1	0	0	0	0	0	0	0	0	1	0
1948	CHI	AL	1	1	0	1	0	0	0	0	0	0	0	0	0	0	0	1
Total			2	2	0	1	0	1	0	0	0	0	0	0	0	0	1	1

Rank among batters: 4,129 • *Total ballparks homered in*: 1 • *First HR*: 05/19/1940 off Dutch Leonard

Tom Tresh

THOMAS MICHAEL TRESH
B: 09/20/1937
BB

Year	Tm	Lg	Tot	H	A	Men-On				One-Game			LO	XN	IP	PH	RHP	LHP
						0	1	2	3	2	3	4						
1962	NY	AL	20	10	10	11	6	3	0	1	0	0	1	1	0	0	13	7
1963	NY	AL	25	9	16	13	11	1	0	3	0	0	0	0	0	0	14	11
1964	NY	AL	16	10	6	5	8	2	1	2	0	0	0	0	0	0	13	3
1965	NY	AL	26	14	12	14	11	1	0	0	1	0	0	2	0	0	16	10
1966	NY	AL	27	13	14	16	9	1	1	1	0	0	2	0	0	1	12	15
1967	NY	AL	14	9	5	9	4	1	0	0	0	0	0	0	0	0	10	4
1968	NY	AL	11	7	4	5	4	1	1	0	0	0	0	0	0	0	7	4
1969	NY	AL	1	0	1	0	1	0	0	0	0	0	0	0	0	0	1	0
	DET	AL	13	9	4	9	3	1	0	1	0	0	1	1	0	0	12	1
	Total		14	9	5	9	4	1	0	1	0	0	1	1	0	0	13	1
Total			153	81	72	82	57	11	3	8	1	0	4	4	0	1	98	55

Rank among batters: 280 • *Top target (5 home runs)*: Dean Chance, Earl Wilson • *Number of pitchers victimized*: 97 • *Total ballparks homered in*: 13 • *First HR*: 04/22/1962 off Dick Donovan • *Switch hit HR in 1 game*—3 times • *World Series HR*—4

Alex Trevino

ALEJANDRO (CASTRO) TREVINO
B: 08/26/1957
BR

Year	Tm	Lg	Tot	H	A	Men-On				One-Game			LO	XN	IP	PH	RHP	LHP
						0	1	2	3	2	3	4						
1982	CIN	NL	1	0	1	1	0	0	0	0	0	0	0	0	0	0	0	1
1983	CIN	NL	1	0	1	1	0	0	0	0	0	0	0	0	0	0	0	1
1984	ATL	NL	3	1	2	2	1	0	0	0	0	0	0	0	0	0	2	1
1985	SF	NL	6	3	3	2	2	2	0	0	0	0	0	0	0	0	5	1
1986	LA	NL	4	2	2	4	0	0	0	0	0	0	0	0	0	0	2	2
1987	LA	NL	3	2	1	3	0	0	0	0	0	0	0	0	0	1	1	2
1988	HOU	NL	2	0	2	1	1	0	0	0	0	0	0	0	0	0	0	2
1989	HOU	NL	2	1	1	1	0	1	0	0	0	0	0	1	0	0	2	0
1990	HOU	NL	1	1	0	0	1	0	0	0	0	0	0	0	0	1	0	1
Total			23	10	13	15	5	3	0	0	0	0	0	1	0	2	12	11

Rank among batters: 1,686 • *Total ballparks homered in*: 7 • *First HR*: 09/14/1982 off Atlee Hammaker

Gus Triandos

GUS CONSTANTINE TRIANDOS
B: 07/30/1930
BR

Year	Tm	Lg	Tot	H	A	Men-On 0	1	2	3	One-Game 2	3	4	LO	XN	IP	PH	RHP	LHP
1953	NY	AL	1	1	0	1	0	0	0	0	0	0	0	0	0	0	0	1
1955	BAL	AL	12	3	9	7	4	1	0	2	0	0	0	0	0	0	9	3
1956	BAL	AL	21	10	11	13	6	2	0	2	0	0	0	0	0	0	15	6
1957	BAL	AL	19	9	10	11	4	4	0	2	0	0	0	0	1	1	11	8
1958	BAL	AL	30	13	17	15	12	2	1	1	0	0	0	0	0	0	24	6
1959	BAL	AL	25	11	14	11	9	3	2	2	0	0	0	0	0	0	19	6
1960	BAL	AL	12	5	7	7	2	1	2	0	0	0	0	0	0	0	10	2
1961	BAL	AL	17	10	7	8	7	2	0	2	0	0	0	1	0	0	14	3
1962	BAL	AL	6	4	2	5	1	0	0	0	0	0	0	0	0	0	4	2
1963	DET	AL	14	9	5	13	0	0	1	0	0	0	0	1	0	0	9	5
1964	PHI	NL	8	5	3	5	1	1	1	1	0	0	0	0	0	0	1	7
1965	HOU	NL	2	0	2	0	2	0	0	0	0	0	0	0	0	0	0	2
Total			167	80	87	96	48	16	7	12	0	0	0	2	1	1	116	51

Rank among batters: 242 • *Top target (6 home runs)*: Ike Delock • *Number of pitchers victimized*: 99 • *Total ballparks homered in*: 16 • *First HR*: 08/05/1953 off Billy Hoeft

Bob Trice

ROBERT LEE TRICE
B: 08/28/1926 D: 09/16/1988
BR

Year	Tm	Lg	Tot	H	A	Men-On 0	1	2	3	One-Game 2	3	4	LO	XN	IP	PH	RHP	LHP
1954	PHI	AL	1	0	1	0	1	0	0	0	0	0	0	0	0	0	0	1

Rank among batters: 4,707 • *Total ballparks homered in*: 1 • *First HR*: 06/01/1954 off Bill Werle

Manny Trillo

JESUS MANUEL MARCANO TRILLO
B: 12/25/1950
BR

Year	Tm	Lg	Tot	H	A	Men-On 0	1	2	3	One-Game 2	3	4	LO	XN	IP	PH	RHP	LHP
1975	CHI	NL	7	3	4	4	1	2	0	0	0	0	0	0	0	0	3	4
1976	CHI	NL	4	2	2	1	1	2	0	0	0	0	0	1	0	0	3	1
1977	CHI	NL	7	6	1	4	1	2	0	0	0	0	0	0	0	0	3	4
1978	CHI	NL	4	4	0	3	1	0	0	0	0	0	0	1	0	0	2	2
1979	PHI	NL	6	5	1	3	2	1	0	0	0	0	0	0	0	0	4	2
1980	PHI	NL	7	4	3	6	1	0	0	0	0	0	0	0	0	0	6	1
1981	PHI	NL	6	5	1	4	2	0	0	0	0	0	0	2	0	0	5	1
1983	CLE	AL	1	1	0	1	0	0	0	0	0	0	0	0	0	0	0	1
	MON	NL	2	2	0	2	0	0	0	0	0	0	0	0	0	0	2	0
	Total		3	3	0	3	0	0	0	0	0	0	0	0	0	0	2	1
1984	SF	NL	4	3	1	3	1	0	0	0	0	0	0	0	0	0	3	1
1985	SF	NL	3	1	2	3	0	0	0	0	0	0	0	0	0	0	2	1
1986	CHI	NL	1	1	0	1	0	0	0	0	0	0	0	0	0	0	1	0
1987	CHI	NL	8	6	2	4	4	0	0	0	0	0	0	0	0	1	4	4
1988	CHI	NL	1	0	1	1	0	0	0	0	0	0	0	0	0	0	0	1
Total			61	43	18	40	14	7	0	0	0	0	0	4	0	1	38	23

Rank among batters: 844 • *Top target (3 home runs)*: Steve Carlton, Bob Shirley • *Number of pitchers victimized*: 53 • *Total ballparks homered in*: 12 • *First HR*: 04/16/1975 off Steve Carlton

Coaker Triplett

HERMAN COAKER TRIPLETT
B: 12/18/1911 D: 01/30/1992
BR

Year	Tm	Lg	Tot	H	A	Men-On 0	1	2	3	One-Game 2	3	4	LO	XN	IP	PH	RHP	LHP
1941	STL	NL	3	1	2	1	1	1	0	0	0	0	0	1	1	0	1	2
1942	STL	NL	1	0	1	1	0	0	0	0	0	0	0	0	0	0	0	1
1943	STL	NL	1	0	1	0	1	0	0	0	0	0	0	0	0	0	0	1
	PHI	NL	14	5	9	7	4	3	0	2	0	0	0	0	0	0	11	3
	Total		15	5	10	7	5	3	0	2	0	0	0	0	0	0	11	4
1944	PHI	NL	1	0	1	1	0	0	0	0	0	0	0	0	0	0	1	0
1945	PHI	NL	7	3	4	2	4	1	0	0	0	0	0	0	0	1	7	0
Total			27	9	18	12	10	5	0	2	0	0	0	1	1	1	20	7

Rank among batters: 1,532 • *Top target (2 home runs)*: Ernie White, Rip Sewell • *Number of pitchers victimized*: 25 • *Total ballparks homered in*: 8 • *First HR*: 05/21/1941 off Kemp Wicker

Hal Trosky

HAROLD ARTHUR TROSKY, SR.
B: 11/11/1912 D: 06/18/1979
BL

						Men-On				One-Game								
Year	Tm	Lg	Tot	H	A	0	1	2	3	2	3	4	LO	XN	IP	PH	RHP	LHP
1933	CLE	AL	1	0	1	0	0	1	0	0	0	0	0	0	0	0	1	0
1934	CLE	AL	35	17	18	16	10	7	2	3	1	0	0	0	0	0	32	3
1935	CLE	AL	26	19	7	8	10	7	1	2	0	0	0	0	0	0	21	5
1936	CLE	AL	42	30	12	20	12	10	0	5	0	0	0	0	1	0	34	8
1937	CLE	AL	32	17	15	15	10	6	1	6	1	0	0	1	1	0	27	5
1938	CLE	AL	19	11	8	8	8	3	0	2	0	0	0	0	0	0	13	6
1939	CLE	AL	25	11	14	13	10	2	0	1	0	0	0	0	0	0	19	6
1940	CLE	AL	25	8	17	17	5	3	0	3	0	0	0	1	0	0	17	8
1941	CLE	AL	11	4	7	6	2	3	0	1	0	0	0	0	0	0	7	4
1944	CHI	AL	10	5	5	3	6	1	0	0	0	0	0	0	0	0	9	1
1946	CHI	AL	2	0	2	2	0	0	0	0	0	0	0	0	0	0	2	0
Total			228	122	106	108	73	43	4	23	2	0	0	2	2	0	182	46

Rank among batters: 140 • *Top target (10 home runs)*: Tommy Bridges, Bump Hadley • *Number of pitchers victimized*: 112 • *Total ballparks homered in*: 9 • *First HR*: 09/18/1933 off Gordon Rhodes

Mike Trost

MICHAEL J. TROST
B: 1866 D: 03/24/1901

						Men-On				One-Game								
Year	Tm	Lg	Tot	H	A	0	1	2	3	2	3	4	LO	XN	IP	PH	RHP	LHP
1890	STL	AA	1	1	0	0	1	0	0	0	0	0	0	0	0	0	1	0

Rank among batters: 4,707 • *Total ballparks homered in*: 1 • *First HR*: 10/05/1890 off Egyptian Healy

Sam Trott

SAMUEL W. TROTT
B: 03/ /1859 D: 06/05/1925
BL

						Men-On				One-Game								
Year	Tm	Lg	Tot	H	A	0	1	2	3	2	3	4	LO	XN	IP	PH	RHP	LHP
1884	BAL	AA	3	1	2	0	2	1	0	0	0	0	0	0	0	0	1	0

Rank among batters: 3,735 • *Total ballparks homered in*: 3 • *First HR*: 07/01/1884 off Jumbo McGinnis

Dizzy Trout

PAUL HOWARD TROUT
B: 06/29/1915 D: 02/28/1972
BR

						Men-On				One-Game								
Year	Tm	Lg	Tot	H	A	0	1	2	3	2	3	4	LO	XN	IP	PH	RHP	LHP
1942	DET	AL	1	1	0	0	0	1	0	0	0	0	0	0	0	0	1	0
1943	DET	AL	1	0	1	1	0	0	0	0	0	0	0	0	0	0	1	0
1944	DET	AL	5	3	2	3	2	0	0	0	0	0	0	0	0	0	5	0
1945	DET	AL	2	1	1	2	0	0	0	0	0	0	0	0	0	0	2	0
1946	DET	AL	3	3	0	0	2	1	0	0	0	0	0	0	0	0	3	0
1947	DET	AL	3	1	2	3	0	0	0	0	0	0	0	1	0	0	3	0
1948	DET	AL	1	0	1	1	0	0	0	0	0	0	0	0	0	0	1	0
1949	DET	AL	1	0	1	0	0	0	1	0	0	0	0	0	0	0	1	0
1950	DET	AL	1	1	0	0	0	0	1	0	0	0	0	0	0	0	0	1
1951	DET	AL	1	0	1	1	0	0	0	0	0	0	0	0	0	0	1	0
1952	BOS	AL	1	0	1	1	0	0	0	0	0	0	0	0	0	0	0	1
Total			20	10	10	12	4	2	2	0	0	0	0	1	0	0	18	2

Rank among batters: 1,810 • *Top target (2 home runs)*: Red Embree, Bob Muncrief • *Number of pitchers victimized*: 18 • *Total ballparks homered in*: 6 • *First HR*: 08/02/1942 off Dick Newsome

Dasher Troy

JOHN JOSEPH TROY
B: 05/08/1856 D: 03/30/1938
BR

						Men-On				One-Game								
Year	Tm	Lg	Tot	H	A	0	1	2	3	2	3	4	LO	XN	IP	PH	RHP	LHP
1884	NY	AA	2	0	2	1	1	0	0	0	0	0	0	0	0	0	2	0
1885	NY	AA	2	1	1	1	1	0	0	0	0	0	0	0	0	0	2	0
Total			4	1	3	2	2	0	0	0	0	0	0	0	0	0	4	0

Rank among batters: 3,427 • *Total ballparks homered in*: 4 • *First HR*: 07/24/1884 off Bobby Mathews

Harry Truby

HARRY GARVIN TRUBY
B: 05/12/1870 D: 03/21/1953

						Men-On				One-Game								
Year	Tm	Lg	Tot	H	A	0	1	2	3	2	3	4	LO	XN	IP	PH	RHP	LHP
1896	CHI	NL	2	2	0	0	2	0	0	0	0	0	0	0	1	0	2	0

Rank among batters: 4,129 • *Total ballparks homered in*: 1 • *First HR*: 05/02/1896 off Tom Parrott

Virgil Trucks

VIRGIL OLIVER TRUCKS
B: 04/26/1917
BR

Year	Tm	Lg	Tot	H	A	Men-On 0	1	2	3	One-Game 2	3	4	LO	XN	IP	PH	RHP	LHP
1952	DET	AL	1	1	0	1	0	0	0	0	0	0	0	0	0	0	0	1
1953	CHI	AL	1	0	1	0	1	0	0	0	0	0	0	0	0	0	0	1
Total			2	1	1	1	1	0	0	0	0	0	0	0	0	0	0	2

Rank among batters: 4,129 • *Total ballparks homered in*: 2 • *First HR*: 07/31/1952 off Alex Kellner

Frank Truesdale

FRANK DAY TRUESDALE
B: 03/31/1884 D: 08/27/1943
BB

Year	Tm	Lg	Tot	H	A	Men-On 0	1	2	3	One-Game 2	3	4	LO	XN	IP	PH	RHP	LHP
1910	STL	AL	1	0	1	0	0	1	0	0	0	0	0	0	0	0	0	1

Rank among batters: 4,707 • *Total ballparks homered in*: 1 • *First HR*: 08/23/1910 off Ed Karger

Greg Tubbs

GREGORY ALAN TUBBS
B: 08/31/1962
BR

Year	Tm	Lg	Tot	H	A	Men-On 0	1	2	3	One-Game 2	3	4	LO	XN	IP	PH	RHP	LHP
1993	CIN	NL	1	1	0	1	0	0	0	0	0	0	0	0	0	0	1	0

Rank among batters: 4,707 • *Total ballparks homered in*: 1 • *First HR*: 08/17/1993 off Dave Telgheder

Eddie Tucker

EDDIE JACK TUCKER
B: 11/18/1966
BR

Year	Tm	Lg	Tot	H	A	Men-On 0	1	2	3	One-Game 2	3	4	LO	XN	IP	PH	RHP	LHP
1995	HOU	NL	1	0	1	1	0	0	0	0	0	0	0	0	0	0	1	0

Rank among batters: 4,707 • *Total ballparks homered in*: 1 • *First HR*: 05/06/1995 off Ken Hill

Michael Tucker

MICHAEL ANTHONY TUCKER
B: 06/25/1971
BL

Year	Tm	Lg	Tot	H	A	Men-On 0	1	2	3	One-Game 2	3	4	LO	XN	IP	PH	RHP	LHP
1995	KC	AL	4	1	3	3	0	1	0	0	0	0	0	0	0	0	4	0

Rank among batters: 3,427 • *Total ballparks homered in*: 4 • *First HR*: 08/13/1995 off Bob Wells

Ollie Tucker

OLIVER DINWIDDIE TUCKER
B: 01/27/1902 D: 07/13/1940
BL

Year	Tm	Lg	Tot	H	A	Men-On 0	1	2	3	One-Game 2	3	4	LO	XN	IP	PH	RHP	LHP
1928	CLE	AL	1	1	0	1	0	0	0	0	0	0	0	0	0	0	0	1

Rank among batters: 4,707 • *Total ballparks homered in*: 1 • *First HR*: 09/18/1928 off Rube Walberg

Thurman Tucker

THURMAN LOWELL TUCKER
B: 09/26/1917 D: 05/07/1993
BL

Year	Tm	Lg	Tot	H	A	Men-On 0	1	2	3	One-Game 2	3	4	LO	XN	IP	PH	RHP	LHP
1943	CHI	AL	3	2	1	3	0	0	0	0	0	0	0	0	1	0	3	0
1944	CHI	AL	2	1	1	1	1	0	0	0	0	0	0	0	1	0	2	0
1946	CHI	AL	1	1	0	1	0	0	0	0	0	0	1	0	0	0	1	0
1947	CHI	AL	1	1	0	1	0	0	0	0	0	0	0	0	0	1	1	0
1948	CLE	AL	1	1	0	1	0	0	0	0	0	0	0	0	0	0	1	0
1950	CLE	AL	1	1	0	1	0	0	0	0	0	0	0	0	0	0	0	1
Total			9	7	2	8	1	0	0	0	0	0	1	0	2	1	8	1

Rank among batters: 2,587 • *Top target (2 home runs)*: Bob Muncrief • *Number of pitchers victimized*: 8 • *Total ballparks homered in*: 4 • *First HR*: 07/25/1943 off Tiny Bonham

Tommy Tucker

THOMAS JOSEPH TUCKER
B: 10/28/1863 D: 10/22/1935
BB

Year	Tm	Lg	Tot	H	A	Men-On 0	1	2	3	One-Game 2	3	4	LO	XN	IP	PH	RHP	LHP
1887	BAL	AA	6	3	3	3	2	1	0	0	0	0	0	0	1	0	3	3

Tommy Tucker *continued*

Year	Tm	Lg	Tot	H	A	Men-On 0	1	2	3	One-Game 2	3	4	LO	XN	IP	PH	RHP	LHP
1888	BAL	AA	6	3	3	2	4	0	0	0	0	0	0	0	0	0	3	2
1889	BAL	AA	5	4	1	2	0	3	0	0	0	0	0	0	0	0	4	1
1890	BOS	NL	1	0	1	0	1	0	0	0	0	0	0	0	0	0	1	0
1891	BOS	NL	2	1	1	0	0	1	1	0	0	0	0	0	1	0	1	0
1892	BOS	NL	1	0	1	1	0	0	0	0	0	0	0	0	0	0	0	1
1893	BOS	NL	7	5	2	3	1	3	0	0	0	0	0	0	1	0	6	1
1894	BOS	NL	3	1	2	0	1	2	0	0	0	0	0	0	0	0	1	2
1895	BOS	NL	3	3	0	0	2	1	0	0	0	0	0	0	0	0	2	1
1896	BOS	NL	2	1	1	0	2	0	0	0	0	0	0	0	0	0	2	0
1897	WAS	NL	5	5	0	2	3	0	0	0	0	0	0	1	0	0	5	0
1898	BRO	NL	1	0	1	1	0	0	0	0	0	0	0	0	0	0	0	1
Total			42	26	16	14	16	11	1	0	0	0	0	1	3	0	28	11

Rank among batters: 1,138 • *Top target (4 home runs)*: Adonis Terry • *Number of pitchers victimized*: 36 • *Total ballparks homered in*: 14 • *First HR*: 05/15/1887 off Toad Ramsey • *World Series HR*—1

Brian Turang

BRIAN CRAIG TURANG
B: 06/14/1967
BR

Year	Tm	Lg	Tot	H	A	Men-On 0	1	2	3	One-Game 2	3	4	LO	XN	IP	PH	RHP	LHP
1994	SEA	AL	1	0	1	0	1	0	0	0	0	0	0	0	0	0	0	1

Rank among batters: 4,707 • *Total ballparks homered in*: 1 • *First HR*: 04/20/1994 off Jimmy Key

Bob Turley

ROBERT LEE TURLEY
B: 09/19/1930
BR

Year	Tm	Lg	Tot	H	A	Men-On 0	1	2	3	One-Game 2	3	4	LO	XN	IP	PH	RHP	LHP
1953	STL	AL	1	1	0	1	0	0	0	0	0	0	0	0	0	0	1	0
1958	NY	AL	2	1	1	2	0	0	0	0	0	0	0	0	0	0	2	0
1963	LA	AL	1	0	1	0	1	0	0	0	0	0	0	0	0	0	0	1
Total			4	2	2	3	1	0	0	0	0	0	0	0	0	0	3	1

Rank among batters: 3,427 • *Total ballparks homered in*: 4 • *First HR*: 08/31/1953 off Sonny Dixon

Chris Turner

CHRISTOPHER WAN TURNER
B: 03/23/1969
BR

Year	Tm	Lg	Tot	H	A	Men-On 0	1	2	3	One-Game 2	3	4	LO	XN	IP	PH	RHP	LHP
1993	CAL	AL	1	0	1	0	0	1	0	0	0	0	0	0	0	0	1	0
1994	CAL	AL	1	1	0	1	0	0	0	0	0	0	0	0	0	0	0	1
Total			2	1	1	1	0	1	0	0	0	0	0	0	0	0	1	1

Rank among batters: 4,129 • *Total ballparks homered in*: 2 • *First HR*: 09/11/1993 off Pat Hentgen

Earl Turner

EARL EDWIN TURNER
B: 05/06/1923
BR

Year	Tm	Lg	Tot	H	A	Men-On 0	1	2	3	One-Game 2	3	4	LO	XN	IP	PH	RHP	LHP
1950	PIT	NL	3	2	1	3	0	0	0	0	0	0	0	0	0	0	3	0

Rank among batters: 3,735 • *Total ballparks homered in*: 2 • *First HR*: 06/24/1950 off Ralph Branca

Jerry Turner

JOHN WEBBER TURNER
B: 01/17/1954
BL

Year	Tm	Lg	Tot	H	A	Men-On 0	1	2	3	One-Game 2	3	4	LO	XN	IP	PH	RHP	LHP
1976	SD	NL	5	2	3	3	2	0	0	0	0	0	0	0	0	0	5	0
1977	SD	NL	10	5	5	4	5	1	0	0	0	0	0	0	0	1	10	0
1978	SD	NL	8	3	5	2	3	3	0	0	0	0	0	0	0	5	7	1
1979	SD	NL	9	5	4	4	4	1	0	0	0	0	0	0	0	0	7	2
1980	SD	NL	3	1	2	1	2	0	0	0	0	0	0	0	0	1	3	0
1981	SD	NL	2	0	2	1	0	1	0	0	0	0	0	0	0	2	2	0
1982	DET	AL	8	7	1	5	3	0	0	0	0	0	0	0	0	1	8	0
Total			45	23	22	20	19	6	0	0	0	0	0	0	0	10	42	3

Rank among batters: 1,082 • Top target (2 home runs): Jim Barr, Ed Halicki, Randy Lerch, Mike Krukow • *Number of pitchers victimized*: 41 • *Total ballparks homered in*: 13 • *First HR*: 06/26/1976 off Mike Marshall

Jim Turner

JAMES RILEY TURNER
B: 08/06/1903
BL

Year	Tm	Lg	Tot	H	A	Men-On 0	1	2	3	One-Game 2	3	4	LO	XN	IP	PH	RHP	LHP
1939	BOS	NL	1	0	1	1	0	0	0	0	0	0	0	0	0	0	1	0

Rank among batters: 4,707 • *Total ballparks homered in*: 1 • *First HR*: 05/30/1939 off Hugh Mulcahy

Terrance Turner

TERRANCE LAMONT TURNER
B: 02/28/1881 D: 07/18/1960
BR

Year	Tm	Lg	Tot	H	A	Men-On 0	1	2	3	One-Game 2	3	4	LO	XN	IP	PH	RHP	LHP
1904	CLE	AL	1	0	1	0	1	0	0	0	0	0	0	0	0	0	1	0
1905	CLE	AL	4	1	3	3	1	0	0	0	0	0	0	0	0	0	2	2
1906	CLE	AL	2	0	2	0	2	0	0	0	0	0	0	0	1	0	1	1
1914	CLE	AL	1	1	0	0	0	1	0	0	0	0	0	0	1	0	0	1
Total			8	2	6	3	4	1	0	0	0	0	0	0	2	0	4	4

Rank among batters: 2,703 • *Total ballparks homered in*: 6 • *First HR*: 09/03/1904 off Cy Young

Tom Turner

THOMAS RICHARD TURNER
B: 09/08/1916 D: 05/14/1986
BR

Year	Tm	Lg	Tot	H	A	Men-On 0	1	2	3	One-Game 2	3	4	LO	XN	IP	PH	RHP	LHP
1942	CHI	AL	3	3	0	1	1	0	1	0	0	0	0	0	0	0	3	0
1943	CHI	AL	2	2	0	1	1	0	0	0	0	0	0	0	0	0	2	0
1944	CHI	AL	2	1	1	2	0	0	0	0	0	0	0	0	0	0	1	1
Total			7	6	1	4	2	0	1	0	0	0	0	0	0	0	6	1

Rank among batters: 2,834 • *Top target (2 home runs)*: Tiny Bonham • *Number of pitchers victimized*: 6 • *Total ballparks homered in*: 2 • *First HR*: 06/24/1942 off Early Wynn

Tuck Turner

GEORGE A. TURNER
B: 02/13/1873 D: 07/16/1945
BB

Year	Tm	Lg	Tot	H	A	Men-On 0	1	2	3	One-Game 2	3	4	LO	XN	IP	PH	RHP	LHP
1893	PHI	NL	1	1	0	0	1	0	0	0	0	0	0	0	0	0	1	0
1894	PHI	NL	1	1	0	1	0	0	0	0	0	0	0	0	0	0	1	0
1895	PHI	NL	2	2	0	1	1	0	0	0	0	0	0	0	0	0	1	1
1896	STL	NL	1	1	0	1	0	0	0	0	0	0	0	0	0	0	1	0
1897	STL	NL	2	2	0	0	1	0	1	0	0	0	0	0	2	0	1	1
Total			7	7	0	3	3	0	1	0	0	0	0	0	2	0	5	2

Rank among batters: 2,834 • *Total ballparks homered in*: 3 • *First HR*: 08/22/1893 off Cy Young

Bill Tuttle

WILLIAM ROBERT TUTTLE
B: 07/04/1929
BR

Year	Tm	Lg	Tot	H	A	Men-On 0	1	2	3	One-Game 2	3	4	LO	XN	IP	PH	RHP	LHP
1954	DET	AL	7	3	4	4	3	0	0	0	0	0	0	0	0	0	6	1
1955	DET	AL	14	9	5	8	5	1	0	0	0	0	0	0	1	0	8	6
1956	DET	AL	9	4	5	5	3	0	1	0	0	0	0	1	0	0	5	4
1957	DET	AL	5	3	2	2	2	1	0	0	0	0	0	0	0	0	2	3
1958	KC	AL	11	8	3	6	2	3	0	0	0	0	3	1	0	0	9	2
1959	KC	AL	7	3	4	6	1	0	0	0	0	0	0	0	0	0	5	2
1960	KC	AL	8	5	3	7	1	0	0	1	0	0	1	0	0	0	5	3
1961	MIN	AL	5	3	2	4	0	0	1	0	0	0	0	1	0	0	2	3
1962	MIN	AL	1	0	1	1	0	0	0	0	0	0	0	0	0	0	1	0
Total			67	38	29	43	17	5	2	1	0	0	4	3	1	0	43	24

Rank among batters: 777 • *Top target (5 home runs)*: Arnie Portocarrero • *Number of pitchers victimized*: 50 • *Total ballparks homered in*: 11 • *First HR*: 04/14/1954 off Duane Pillette

Art Twineham

ARTHUR W. TWINEHAM
B: 11/26/1866
BL

Year	Tm	Lg	Tot	H	A	Men-On 0	1	2	3	One-Game 2	3	4	LO	XN	IP	PH	RHP	LHP
1894	STL	NL	1	0	1	1	0	0	0	0	0	0	0	0	0	0	1	0

Rank among batters: 4,707 • *Total ballparks homered in*: 1 • *First HR*: 08/12/1894 off Tom Parrott

Year	Tm	Lg	Tot	H	A	Men-On				One-Game			LO	XN	IP	PH	RHP	LHP
						0	1	2	3	2	3	4						

Larry Twitchell

LAWRENCE GRANT TWITCHELL
B: 02/18/1864 D: 04/23/1930
BR

Year	Tm	Lg	Tot	H	A	0	1	2	3	2	3	4	LO	XN	IP	PH	RHP	LHP
1888	DET	NL	5	2	3	2	2	1	0	0	0	0	0	0	2	0	3	2
1889	CLE	NL	4	1	3	1	3	0	0	0	0	0	0	1	2	0	2	2
1890	CLE	PL	2	1	1	0	1	1	0	0	0	0	0	0	1	0	2	0
	BUF	PL	2	1	1	1	1	0	0	0	0	0	0	0	0	0	0	2
	Total		4	2	2	1	2	1	0	0	0	0	0	0	1	0	2	2
1891	COL	AA	2	0	2	0	2	0	0	0	0	0	0	0	1	0	1	1
1893	LOU	NL	2	0	2	1	1	0	0	0	0	0	0	0	0	0	2	0
1894	LOU	NL	2	0	2	1	1	0	0	0	0	0	0	0	0	0	2	0
Total			19	5	14	6	11	2	0	0	0	0	0	1	6	0	12	7

Rank among batters: 1,861 • *Top target (2 home runs)*: Kid Madden, Frank Dwyer, Harry Staley • *Number of pitchers victimized*: 16 • *Total ballparks homered in*: 17 • *First HR*: 05/02/1888 off Ed Morris • *Hit for Cycle*—vs BOS: 08/15/1889 • *World Series HR*—1

Babe Twombly

CLARENCE EDWARD TWOMBLY
B: 01/18/1896 D: 11/23/1974
BL

Year	Tm	Lg	Tot	H	A	0	1	2	3	2	3	4	LO	XN	IP	PH	RHP	LHP
1920	CHI	NL	2	2	0	1	0	1	0	0	0	0	0	0	0	0	2	0
1921	CHI	NL	1	0	1	1	0	0	0	0	0	0	0	0	0	0	1	0
Total			3	2	1	2	0	1	0	0	0	0	0	0	0	0	3	0

Rank among batters: 3,735 • *Total ballparks homered in*: 2 • *First HR*: 06/02/1920 off Dolf Luque

Johnnie Tyler

JOHN ANTHONY TYLER
B: 07/30/1906 D: 07/11/1972
BB

Year	Tm	Lg	Tot	H	A	0	1	2	3	2	3	4	LO	XN	IP	PH	RHP	LHP
1935	BOS	NL	2	0	2	0	2	0	0	0	0	0	0	0	0	0	2	0

Rank among batters: 4,129 • *Total ballparks homered in*: 2 • *First HR*: 09/21/1935 off Jim Bivin

Lefty Tyler

GEORGE ALBERT TYLER
B: 12/14/1889 D: 09/29/1953
BL

Year	Tm	Lg	Tot	H	A	0	1	2	3	2	3	4	LO	XN	IP	PH	RHP	LHP
1915	BOS	NL	1	0	1	1	0	0	0	0	0	0	0	0	0	0	1	0
1916	BOS	NL	3	0	3	2	1	0	0	0	0	0	0	0	0	0	3	0
Total			4	0	4	3	1	0	0	0	0	0	0	0	0	0	4	0

Rank among batters: 3,427 • *Total ballparks homered in*: 4 • *First HR*: 08/05/1915 off Bert Humphries

Jim Tyrone

JAMES VERNON TYRONE
B: 01/29/1949
BR

Year	Tm	Lg	Tot	H	A	0	1	2	3	2	3	4	LO	XN	IP	PH	RHP	LHP
1974	CHI	NL	3	2	1	3	0	0	0	0	0	0	0	0	0	1	1	2
1977	OAK	AL	5	3	2	4	1	0	0	0	0	0	0	0	0	0	2	3
Total			8	5	3	7	1	0	0	0	0	0	0	0	0	1	3	5

Rank among batters: 2,703 • *Total ballparks homered in*: 5 • *First HR*: 08/21/1974 off Andy Messersmith

Wayne Tyrone

OSCAR WAYNE TYRONE
B: 08/01/1950
BR

Year	Tm	Lg	Tot	H	A	0	1	2	3	2	3	4	LO	XN	IP	PH	RHP	LHP
1976	CHI	NL	1	1	0	1	0	0	0	0	0	0	0	0	0	0	0	1

Rank among batters: 4,707 • *Total ballparks homered in*: 1 • *First HR*: 08/03/1976 off Jim Kaat

Mike Tyson

MICHAEL RAY TYSON
B: 01/13/1950
BR

Year	Tm	Lg	Tot	H	A	0	1	2	3	2	3	4	LO	XN	IP	PH	RHP	LHP
1973	STL	NL	1	1	0	1	0	0	0	0	0	0	0	0	0	0	0	1
1974	STL	NL	1	0	1	1	0	0	0	0	0	0	0	0	0	0	1	0

Year	Tm	Lg	Tot	H	A	Men-On 0	1	2	3	One-Game 2	3	4	LO	XN	IP	PH	RHP	LHP

Mike Tyson *continued*

Year	Tm	Lg	Tot	H	A	Men-On 0	1	2	3	One-Game 2	3	4	LO	XN	IP	PH	RHP	LHP
1975	STL	NL	2	1	1	0	1	1	0	0	0	0	0	0	0	0	1	1
1976	STL	NL	3	2	1	1	1	1	0	0	0	0	0	0	1	0	1	2
1977	STL	NL	7	4	3	1	5	0	1	0	0	0	0	0	0	0	4	3
1978	STL	NL	3	1	2	2	0	1	0	0	0	0	0	0	0	0	0	3
1979	STL	NL	5	1	4	3	1	1	0	0	0	0	0	0	0	0	1	4
1980	CHI	NL	3	2	1	3	0	0	0	0	0	0	0	0	0	0	2	1
1981	CHI	NL	2	1	1	1	0	1	0	0	0	0	0	0	0	1	1	1
Total			27	13	14	13	8	5	1	0	0	0	0	0	1	1	11	16

Rank among batters: 1,532 • *Top target (3 home runs)*: John Candelaria • *Number of pitchers victimized*: 24 • *Total ballparks homered in*: 9 • *First HR*: 06/18/1973 off Balor Moore

Ty Tyson

ALBERT THOMAS TYSON
B: 06/01/1892 D: 08/16/1953
BR

Year	Tm	Lg	Tot	H	A	Men-On 0	1	2	3	One-Game 2	3	4	LO	XN	IP	PH	RHP	LHP
1926	NY	NL	3	3	0	1	2	0	0	0	0	0	0	0	0	0	1	2
1927	NY	NL	1	1	0	1	0	0	0	0	0	0	0	0	0	0	0	1
1928	BRO	NL	1	1	0	1	0	0	0	0	0	0	0	0	0	0	0	1
Total			5	5	0	3	2	0	0	0	0	0	0	0	0	0	1	4

Rank among batters: 3,191 • *Total ballparks homered in*: 2 • *First HR*: 06/09/1926 off Bill Sherdel

Bob Uecker

ROBERT GEORGE UECKER
B: 01/26/1935
BR

Year	Tm	Lg	Tot	H	A	Men-On 0	1	2	3	One-Game 2	3	4	LO	XN	IP	PH	RHP	LHP
1962	MIL	NL	1	1	0	0	1	0	0	0	0	0	0	0	0	0	0	1
1964	STL	NL	1	1	0	1	0	0	0	0	0	0	0	0	0	0	0	1
1965	STL	NL	2	1	1	2	0	0	0	0	0	0	0	0	0	0	1	1
1966	PHI	NL	7	3	4	3	3	1	0	0	0	0	0	0	0	1	2	5
1967	ATL	NL	3	1	2	2	0	0	1	0	0	0	0	0	0	0	1	2
Total			14	7	7	8	4	1	1	0	0	0	0	0	0	1	4	10

Rank among batters: 2,169 • *Top target (2 home runs)*: Ray Sadecki • *Number of pitchers victimized*: 13 • *Total ballparks homered in*: 9 • *First HR*: 09/30/1962 off Diomedes Olivo

Ted Uhlaender

THEODORE OTTO UHLAENDER
B: 10/21/1940
BL

Year	Tm	Lg	Tot	H	A	Men-On 0	1	2	3	One-Game 2	3	4	LO	XN	IP	PH	RHP	LHP
1966	MIN	AL	2	1	1	2	0	0	0	0	0	0	0	0	0	0	1	1
1967	MIN	AL	6	3	3	2	3	1	0	0	0	0	0	0	1	0	5	1
1968	MIN	AL	7	6	1	4	2	1	0	0	0	0	0	0	0	0	5	2
1969	MIN	AL	8	2	6	5	1	2	0	0	0	0	1	0	0	0	7	1
1970	CLE	AL	11	11	0	8	1	2	0	0	0	0	1	0	0	3	11	0
1971	CLE	AL	2	1	1	2	0	0	0	0	0	0	1	0	0	0	1	1
Total			36	24	12	23	7	6	0	0	0	0	3	0	1	3	30	6

Rank among batters: 1,274 • *Top target (3 home runs)*: Phil Ortega • *Number of pitchers victimized*: 31 • *Total ballparks homered in*: 7 • *First HR*: 07/18/1966 off Al Downing

George Uhle

GEORGE ERNEST UHLE
B: 09/18/1898 D: 02/26/1985
BR

Year	Tm	Lg	Tot	H	A	Men-On 0	1	2	3	One-Game 2	3	4	LO	XN	IP	PH	RHP	LHP
1921	CLE	AL	1	1	0	0	0	0	1	0	0	0	0	0	0	0	0	1
1924	CLE	AL	1	0	1	1	0	0	0	0	0	0	0	0	0	1	0	1
1926	CLE	AL	[illegible]	1	0	0	1	0	0	0	0	0	0	1	0	0	0	1
1928	CLE	AL	[illegible]	0	1	0	1	0	0	0	0	0	0	0	0	0	1	0
1930	DET	AL	[illegible]	1	1	0	1	1	0	0	0	0	0	0	0	0	2	0
1931	DET	AL	2	1	1	1	1	0	0	0	0	0	0	0	0	0	2	0
1936	CLE	AL	[illegible]	1	0	0	1	0	0	0	0	0	0	0	0	0	1	0
Total			9	5	4	2	5	1	1	0	0	0	0	1	0	1	6	3

Rank among batters: 2,587 • *Total ballparks homered in*: 6 • *First HR*: 04/28/1921 off Dutch Leonard

Mike Ulisney

MICHAEL EDWARD ULISNEY
B: 09/28/1917
BR

Year	Tm	Lg	Tot	H	A	Men-On 0	1	2	3	One-Game 2	3	4	LO	XN	IP	PH	RHP	LHP
1945	BOS	NL	1	1	0	0	1	0	0	0	0	0	0	0	0	0	1	0

Rank among batters: 4,707 • *Total ballparks homered in*: 1 • *First HR*: 05/20/1945 off Bucky Walters

Tom Umphlett

THOMAS MULLEN UMPHLETT
B: 05/12/1930
BR

Year	Tm	Lg	Tot	H	A	Men-On 0	1	2	3	One-Game 2	3	4	LO	XN	IP	PH	RHP	LHP
1953	BOS	AL	3	1	2	2	0	1	0	0	0	0	0	0	0	0	2	1
1954	WAS	AL	1	0	1	1	0	0	0	0	0	0	0	0	0	0	1	0
1955	WAS	AL	2	2	0	1	1	0	0	0	0	0	0	0	0	0	1	1
Total			6	3	3	4	1	1	0	0	0	0	0	0	0	0	4	2

Rank among batters: 2,988 • *Top target (2 home runs)*: Marion Fricano • *Number of pitchers victimized*: 5 • *Total ballparks homered in*: 5 • *First HR*: 05/28/1953 off Marion Fricano

Bob Unglaub

ROBERT ALEXANDER UNGLAUB
B: 07/31/1881 D: 11/29/1916
BR

Year	Tm	Lg	Tot	H	A	Men-On 0	1	2	3	One-Game 2	3	4	LO	XN	IP	PH	RHP	LHP
1907	BOS	AL	1	1	0	1	0	0	0	0	0	0	0	0	0	0	1	0
1908	BOS	AL	1	1	0	1	0	0	0	0	0	0	0	0	0	0	1	0
1909	WAS	AL	3	1	2	2	1	0	0	0	0	0	0	0	2	0	3	0
Total			5	3	2	4	1	0	0	0	0	0	0	0	2	0	5	0

Rank among batters: 3,191 • *Total ballparks homered in*: 3 • *First HR*: 06/17/1907 off Cy Morgan

Al Unser

ALBERT BERNARD UNSER
B: 10/12/1912 D: 07/07/1995
BR

Year	Tm	Lg	Tot	H	A	Men-On 0	1	2	3	One-Game 2	3	4	LO	XN	IP	PH	RHP	LHP
1944	DET	AL	1	1	0	0	0	0	1	0	0	0	0	0	0	1	1	0
1945	CIN	NL	3	0	3	1	2	0	0	0	0	0	0	0	0	0	3	0
Total			4	1	3	1	2	0	1	0	0	0	0	0	0	1	4	0

Rank among batters: 3,427 • *Total ballparks homered in*: 4 • *First HR*: 05/31/1944 off Monk Dubiel

Del Unser

DELBERT BERNARD UNSER
B: 12/09/1944
BL

Year	Tm	Lg	Tot	H	A	Men-On 0	1	2	3	One-Game 2	3	4	LO	XN	IP	PH	RHP	LHP
1968	WAS	AL	1	0	1	1	0	0	0	0	0	0	1	0	0	0	1	0
1969	WAS	AL	7	2	5	5	1	1	0	0	0	0	0	3	0	1	4	3
1970	WAS	AL	5	0	5	3	1	1	0	0	0	0	1	0	0	0	5	0
1971	WAS	AL	9	1	8	6	2	1	0	0	0	0	2	0	0	0	7	2
1972	CLE	AL	1	1	0	0	1	0	0	0	0	0	0	0	0	0	0	1
1973	PHI	NL	11	7	4	6	3	2	0	0	0	0	0	0	0	1	11	0
1974	PHI	NL	11	5	6	3	4	4	0	0	0	0	0	0	0	1	11	0
1975	NY	NL	10	4	6	9	1	0	0	0	0	0	2	0	0	0	8	2
1976	NY	NL	5	1	4	2	3	0	0	0	0	0	0	1	0	0	3	2
	MON	NL	7	7	0	6	1	0	0	0	0	0	1	1	0	0	7	0
	Total		12	8	4	8	4	0	0	0	0	0	1	2	0	0	10	2
1977	MON	NL	12	2	10	6	5	1	0	0	0	0	0	0	0	1	12	0
1978	MON	NL	2	1	1	2	0	0	0	0	0	0	0	0	0	0	2	0
1979	PHI	NL	6	3	3	2	3	1	0	0	0	0	0	0	0	4	6	0
Total			87	34	53	51	25	11	0	0	0	0	7	5	0	8	77	10

Rank among batters: 594 • *Top target (4 home runs)*: Lynn McGlothen • *Number of pitchers victimized*: 76 • *Total ballparks homered in*: 22 • *First HR*: 08/20/1968 off Jim Nash

Roy Upright

ROY T. UPRIGHT
B: 05/30/1926 D: 11/13/1986
BL

Year	Tm	Lg	Tot	H	A	Men-On 0	1	2	3	One-Game 2	3	4	LO	XN	IP	PH	RHP	LHP
1953	STL	AL	1	0	1	1	0	0	0	0	0	0	0	0	0	1	1	0

Rank among batters: 4,707 • *Total ballparks homered in*: 1 • *First HR*: 04/21/1953 off Bob Lemon

Cecil Upshaw

CECIL LEE UPSHAW
B: 10/22/1942 D: 02/07/1995
BR

Year	Tm	Lg	Tot	H	A	Men-On 0	1	2	3	One-Game 2	3	4	LO	XN	IP	PH	RHP	LHP
1969	ATL	NL	1	1	0	1	0	0	0	0	0	0	0	0	0	0	1	0

Rank among batters: 4,707 • *Total ballparks homered in*: 1 • *First HR*: 05/25/1969 off Turk Farrell

Willie Upshaw

WILLIE CLAY UPSHAW
B: 04/27/1957
BL

Year	Tm	Lg	Tot	H	A	Men-On 0	1	2	3	One-Game 2	3	4	LO	XN	IP	PH	RHP	LHP
1978	TOR	AL	1	0	1	1	0	0	0	0	0	0	0	0	0	0	1	0
1980	TOR	AL	1	0	1	1	0	0	0	0	0	0	0	0	0	0	1	0
1981	TOR	AL	4	1	3	3	1	0	0	0	0	0	0	0	0	1	4	0
1982	TOR	AL	21	11	10	16	5	0	0	2	0	0	0	0	1	0	15	6
1983	TOR	AL	27	16	11	19	3	4	1	0	0	0	0	0	1	0	20	7
1984	TOR	AL	19	6	13	13	6	0	0	1	0	0	0	1	0	0	15	4
1985	TOR	AL	15	6	9	10	5	0	0	1	0	0	0	0	0	0	10	5
1986	TOR	AL	9	3	6	5	2	2	0	0	0	0	0	0	0	0	5	4
1987	TOR	AL	15	7	8	8	4	2	1	0	0	0	0	0	0	0	13	2
1988	CLE	AL	11	3	8	8	1	2	0	0	0	0	0	0	0	0	11	0
Total			123	53	70	84	27	10	2	4	0	0	0	1	2	1	95	28

Rank among batters: 372 • *Top target (5 home runs)*: Ken Schrom • *Number of pitchers victimized*: 94 • *Total ballparks homered in*: 14 • *First HR*: 05/28/1978 off Rich Gossage

Tom Upton

THOMAS HERBERT UPTON
B: 12/29/1926
BR

Year	Tm	Lg	Tot	H	A	Men-On 0	1	2	3	One-Game 2	3	4	LO	XN	IP	PH	RHP	LHP
1950	STL	AL	2	0	2	2	0	0	0	0	0	0	0	1	0	0	2	0

Rank among batters: 4,129 • *Total ballparks homered in*: 2 • *First HR*: 07/15/1950 off Dick Fowler

Tom Urbani

THOMAS JAMES URBANI
B: 01/21/1968
BL

Year	Tm	Lg	Tot	H	A	Men-On 0	1	2	3	One-Game 2	3	4	LO	XN	IP	PH	RHP	LHP
1995	STL	NL	1	0	1	1	0	0	0	0	0	0	0	0	0	0	1	0

Rank among batters: 4,707 • *Total ballparks homered in*: 1 • *First HR*: 06/30/1995 off Frank Castillo

Billy Urbanski

WILLIAM MICHAEL URBANSKI
B: 06/05/1903 D: 07/12/1973
BR

Year	Tm	Lg	Tot	H	A	Men-On 0	1	2	3	One-Game 2	3	4	LO	XN	IP	PH	RHP	LHP
1932	BOS	NL	8	3	5	3	3	2	0	0	0	0	0	0	0	0	7	1
1934	BOS	NL	7	5	2	5	0	2	0	0	0	0	2	0	0	0	7	0
1935	BOS	NL	4	4	0	3	1	0	0	0	0	0	1	0	0	0	3	1
Total			19	12	7	11	4	4	0	0	0	0	3	0	0	0	17	2

Rank among batters: 1,861 • Top target (2 home runs): Freddie Fitzsimmons, Phil Collins, Paul Derringer • *Number of pitchers victimized*: 16 • *Total ballparks homered in*: 5 • *First HR*: 05/14/1932 off Charlie Root

Jose Uribe

JOSE ALTAGARCIA URIBE
B: 01/21/1959
BB

Year	Tm	Lg	Tot	H	A	Men-On 0	1	2	3	One-Game 2	3	4	LO	XN	IP	PH	RHP	LHP
1985	SF	NL	3	2	1	3	0	0	0	0	0	0	0	1	0	0	2	1
1986	SF	NL	3	1	2	2	1	0	0	0	0	0	0	0	0	0	0	3
1987	SF	NL	5	4	1	2	3	0	0	0	0	0	0	0	0	0	2	3
1988	SF	NL	3	1	2	2	1	0	0	0	0	0	0	0	0	0	1	2
1989	SF	NL	1	0	1	0	1	0	0	0	0	0	0	0	0	0	1	0
1990	SF	NL	1	0	1	0	1	0	0	0	0	0	0	0	0	0	1	0
1991	SF	NL	1	0	1	1	0	0	0	0	0	0	0	0	0	0	1	0
1992	SF	NL	2	0	2	2	0	0	0	0	0	0	0	0	0	0	1	1
Total			19	8	11	12	7	0	0	0	0	0	0	1	0	0	9	10

Rank among batters: 1,861 • *Total ballparks homered in*: 8 • *First HR*: 05/21/1985 off Larry Andersen

Bob Usher

ROBERT ROYCE USHER
B: 03/01/1925
BR

Year	Tm	Lg	Tot	H	A	Men-On 0	1	2	3	One-Game 2	3	4	LO	XN	IP	PH	RHP	LHP
1946	CIN	NL	1	0	1	0	1	0	0	0	0	0	0	0	0	0	0	1
1947	CIN	NL	1	0	1	1	0	0	0	0	0	0	0	0	0	0	0	1
1950	CIN	NL	6	3	3	2	3	1	0	0	0	0	0	0	0	2	0	6
1951	CIN	NL	5	3	2	3	1	1	0	0	0	0	0	1	0	0	1	4
1957	WAS	AL	5	2	3	3	2	0	0	0	0	0	0	0	0	0	2	3
Total			18	8	10	9	7	2	0	0	0	0	0	1	0	2	3	15

Rank among batters: 1,914 • *Top target (2 home runs)*: Dave Koslo, Bobby Shantz • *Number of pitchers victimized*: 16 • *Total ballparks homered in*: 6 • *First HR*: 07/28/1946 off Woody Abernathy

Tex Vache

ERNEST LEWIS VACHE
B: 11/17/1895 D: 06/11/1953
BR

Year	Tm	Lg	Tot	H	A	Men-On 0	1	2	3	One-Game 2	3	4	LO	XN	IP	PH	RHP	LHP
1925	BOS	AL	3	1	2	2	0	1	0	0	0	0	0	0	0	0	2	1

Rank among batters: 3,735 • *Total ballparks homered in*: 2 • *First HR*: 04/22/1925 off Eddie Rommel

Mike Vail

MICHAEL LEWIS VAIL
B: 11/10/1951
BR

Year	Tm	Lg	Tot	H	A	Men-On 0	1	2	3	One-Game 2	3	4	LO	XN	IP	PH	RHP	LHP
1975	NY	NL	3	2	1	2	1	0	0	0	0	0	0	0	0	0	1	2
1977	NY	NL	8	3	5	5	2	1	0	0	0	0	0	0	0	0	3	5
1978	CHI	NL	4	1	3	2	1	1	0	0	0	0	0	0	0	1	4	0
1979	CHI	NL	7	7	0	0	6	0	1	1	0	0	0	1	0	2	2	5
1980	CHI	NL	6	2	4	3	2	1	0	0	0	0	0	1	0	0	5	1
1982	CIN	NL	4	0	4	0	3	1	0	0	0	0	0	0	0	0	3	1
1983	MON	NL	2	0	2	1	1	0	0	0	0	0	0	0	0	0	0	2
Total			34	15	19	13	16	4	1	1	0	0	0	2	0	3	18	16

Rank among batters: 1,315 • *Top target (2 home runs)*: Jim Kaat, Steve Carlton • *Number of pitchers victimized*: 32 • *Total ballparks homered in*: 9 • *First HR*: 09/01/1975 off John Candelaria

Sandy Valdespino

HILARIO (BORROTO) VALDESPINO
B: 01/24/1939
BL

Year	Tm	Lg	Tot	H	A	Men-On 0	1	2	3	One-Game 2	3	4	LO	XN	IP	PH	RHP	LHP
1965	MIN	AL	1	0	1	0	1	0	0	0	0	0	0	0	0	0	1	0
1966	MIN	AL	2	2	0	1	1	0	0	0	0	0	0	0	0	0	2	0
1967	MIN	AL	1	1	0	1	0	0	0	0	0	0	0	0	0	1	1	0
1968	ATL	NL	1	0	1	1	0	0	0	0	0	0	0	0	0	0	1	0
1971	KC	AL	2	2	0	1	0	1	0	0	0	0	0	0	0	0	2	0
Total			7	5	2	4	2	1	0	0	0	0	0	0	0	1	7	0

Rank among batters: 2,834 • *Total ballparks homered in*: 4 • *First HR*: 06/23/1965 off Floyd Weaver

Julio Valdez

JULIO JULIAN CASTILLO VALDEZ
B: 06/03/1956
BB

Year	Tm	Lg	Tot	H	A	Men-On 0	1	2	3	One-Game 2	3	4	LO	XN	IP	PH	RHP	LHP
1980	BOS	AL	1	1	0	1	0	0	0	0	0	0	0	0	0	0	0	1

Rank among batters: 4,707 • *Total ballparks homered in*: 1 • *First HR*: 10/04/1980 off Paul Mirabella

Jose Valdivielso

JOSE LOPEZ VALDIVIELSO
B: 05/22/1934
BR

Year	Tm	Lg	Tot	H	A	Men-On 0	1	2	3	One-Game 2	3	4	LO	XN	IP	PH	RHP	LHP
1955	WAS	AL	2	0	2	2	0	0	0	0	0	0	0	0	0	0	1	1
1956	WAS	AL	4	3	1	1	2	1	0	0	0	0	0	0	0	0	3	1
1960	WAS	AL	2	2	0	1	1	0	0	0	0	0	0	0	0	0	1	1
1961	MIN	AL	1	0	1	1	0	0	0	0	0	0	0	0	0	0	1	0
Total			9	5	4	5	3	1	0	0	0	0	0	0	0	0	6	3

Rank among batters: 2,587 • *Total ballparks homered in*: 4 • *First HR*: 07/21/1955 off Art Houtteman

John Valentin

JOHN WILLIAM VALENTIN
B: 02/18/1967
BR

Year	Tm	Lg	Tot	H	A	Men-On				One-Game			LO	XN	IP	PH	RHP	LHP
						0	1	2	3	2	3	4						
1992	BOS	AL	5	1	4	4	0	0	1	0	0	0	0	0	0	0	4	1
1993	BOS	AL	11	7	4	7	3	1	0	1	0	0	0	0	0	0	8	3
1994	BOS	AL	9	6	3	4	4	1	0	0	0	0	0	0	0	0	6	3
1995	BOS	AL	27	11	16	15	8	3	1	1	1	0	0	0	0	0	21	6
Total			52	25	27	30	15	5	2	2	1	0	0	0	0	0	39	13

Rank among batters: 965 • *Top target (3 home runs)*: Todd Stottlemyre • *Number of pitchers victimized*: 46 • *Total ballparks homered in*: 14 • *First HR*: 08/22/1992 off Mike Schooler • *LCS HR*—1

Jose Valentin

JOSE ANTONIO (ROSARIO) VALENTIN
B: 10/12/1969
BB

Year	Tm	Lg	Tot	H	A	Men-On				One-Game			LO	XN	IP	PH	RHP	LHP
						0	1	2	3	2	3	4						
1993	MIL	AL	1	1	0	0	0	1	0	0	0	0	0	0	0	0	1	0
1994	MIL	AL	11	8	3	5	3	2	1	0	0	0	0	0	0	0	11	0
1995	MIL	AL	11	3	8	7	2	1	1	1	0	0	0	0	0	0	11	0
Total			23	12	11	12	5	4	2	1	0	0	0	0	0	0	23	0

Rank among batters: 1,686 • *Top target (2 home runs)*: Orel Hershiser, Chris Bosio, Dennis Martinez • *Number of pitchers victimized*: 20 • *Total ballparks homered in*: 8 • *First HR*: 09/15/1993 off Rich Monteleone

Bobby Valentine

ROBERT JOHN VALENTINE
B: 05/13/1950
BR

Year	Tm	Lg	Tot	H	A	Men-On				One-Game			LO	XN	IP	PH	RHP	LHP
						0	1	2	3	2	3	4						
1971	LA	NL	1	0	1	0	0	1	0	0	0	0	0	0	0	0	1	0
1972	LA	NL	3	1	2	2	1	0	0	0	0	0	1	0	0	0	1	2
1973	CAL	AL	1	0	1	1	0	0	0	0	0	0	0	0	0	0	1	0
1974	CAL	AL	3	2	1	1	1	1	0	0	0	0	0	0	0	0	1	2
1975	SD	NL	1	0	1	1	0	0	0	0	0	0	0	0	0	0	0	1
1977	SD	NL	1	0	1	0	1	0	0	0	0	0	0	0	0	0	0	1
	NY	NL	1	1	0	1	0	0	0	0	0	0	0	0	0	0	1	0
	Total		2	1	1	1	1	0	0	0	0	0	0	0	0	0	1	1
1978	NY	NL	1	0	1	0	1	0	0	0	0	0	0	0	0	0	1	0
Total			12	4	8	6	4	2	0	0	0	0	1	0	0	0	6	6

Rank among batters: 2,325 • *Total ballparks homered in*: 9 • *First HR*: 06/13/1971 off Steve Renko

Ellis Valentine

ELLIS CLARENCE VALENTINE
B: 07/30/1954
BR

Year	Tm	Lg	Tot	H	A	Men-On				One-Game			LO	XN	IP	PH	RHP	LHP
						0	1	2	3	2	3	4						
1975	MON	NL	1	1	0	1	0	0	0	0	0	0	0	0	0	0	0	1
1976	MON	NL	7	3	4	4	3	0	0	0	0	0	1	0	0	0	4	3
1977	MON	NL	25	12	13	16	6	3	0	2	0	0	0	0	2	0	13	12
1978	MON	NL	25	9	16	17	7	1	0	0	0	0	0	0	0	1	20	5
1979	MON	NL	21	12	9	13	4	4	0	2	0	0	0	0	0	1	14	7
1980	MON	NL	13	4	9	9	4	0	0	1	0	0	0	1	0	0	8	5
1981	MON	NL	3	3	0	2	1	0	0	0	0	0	0	0	0	0	3	0
	NY	NL	5	2	3	4	0	1	0	1	0	0	0	0	0	0	5	0
	Total		8	5	3	6	1	1	0	1	0	0	0	0	0	0	8	0
1982	NY	NL	8	4	4	0	6	2	0	0	0	0	0	0	0	0	3	5
1983	CAL	AL	13	6	7	7	3	2	1	1	0	0	0	0	0	0	5	8
1985	TEX	AL	2	2	0	1	1	0	0	0	0	0	0	0	0	0	2	0
Total			123	58	65	74	35	13	1	7	0	0	1	1	2	2	77	46

Rank among batters: 372 • *Top target (5 home runs)*: Jerry Koosman • *Number of pitchers victimized*: 86 • *Total ballparks homered in*: 20 • *First HR*: 09/05/1975 off Jim Rooker

Fred Valentine

FRED LEE VALENTINE
B: 01/19/1935
BB

Year	Tm	Lg	Tot	H	A	Men-On				One-Game			LO	XN	IP	PH	RHP	LHP
						0	1	2	3	2	3	4						
1964	WAS	AL	4	2	2	2	1	1	0	0	0	0	0	0	0	1	4	0
1966	WAS	AL	16	6	10	9	5	1	1	0	0	0	2	0	0	0	7	9
1967	WAS	AL	11	6	5	7	3	1	0	0	0	0	0	0	0	1	7	4

						Men-On				One-Game								
Year	**Tm**	**Lg**	**Tot**	**H**	**A**	**0**	**1**	**2**	**3**	**2**	**3**	**4**	**LO**	**XN**	**IP**	**PH**	**RHP**	**LHP**

Fred Valentine *continued*

Year	Tm	Lg	Tot	H	A	0	1	2	3	2	3	4	LO	XN	IP	PH	RHP	LHP
1968	WAS	AL	3	1	2	3	0	0	0	0	0	0	0	0	0	0	3	0
	BAL	AL	2	0	2	2	0	0	0	0	0	0	0	0	0	0	2	0
	Total		5	1	4	5	0	0	0	0	0	0	0	0	0	0	5	0
Total			36	15	21	23	9	3	1	0	0	0	2	0	0	2	23	13

Rank among batters: 1,274 • *Top target (2 home runs)*: Mickey Lolich, Jim Merritt, Sonny Siebert • *Number of pitchers victimized*: 33 • *Total ballparks homered in*: 12 • *First HR*: 04/27/1964 off Ken McBride

Fernando Valenzuela

FERNANDO (ANGUAMEA) VALENZUELA
B: 11/01/1960
BL

Year	Tm	Lg	Tot	H	A	0	1	2	3	2	3	4	LO	XN	IP	PH	RHP	LHP
1982	LA	NL	1	0	1	1	0	0	0	0	0	0	0	0	0	0	1	0
1983	LA	NL	1	0	1	1	0	0	0	0	0	0	0	0	0	0	1	0
1984	LA	NL	3	1	2	2	1	0	0	0	0	0	0	0	0	0	2	1
1985	LA	NL	1	0	1	1	0	0	0	0	0	0	0	0	0	0	1	0
1987	LA	NL	1	1	0	1	0	0	0	0	0	0	0	0	0	0	1	0
1990	LA	NL	1	1	0	1	0	0	0	0	0	0	0	0	0	0	1	0
1995	SD	NL	2	1	1	1	0	1	0	0	0	0	0	0	0	0	2	0
Total			10	4	6	8	1	1	0	0	0	0	0	0	0	0	9	1

Rank among batters: 2,500 • *Total ballparks homered in*: 6 • *First HR*: 08/25/1982 off Steve Mura

Dave Valle

DAVID VALLE
B: 10/30/1960
BR

Year	Tm	Lg	Tot	H	A	0	1	2	3	2	3	4	LO	XN	IP	PH	RHP	LHP
1984	SEA	AL	1	1	0	0	0	1	0	0	0	0	0	0	0	0	1	0
1986	SEA	AL	5	4	1	2	1	2	0	0	0	0	0	0	0	1	3	2
1987	SEA	AL	12	8	4	7	5	0	0	1	0	0	0	0	0	0	5	7
1988	SEA	AL	10	5	5	5	3	2	0	0	0	0	0	0	0	0	6	4
1989	SEA	AL	7	1	6	5	2	0	0	0	0	0	0	0	0	0	4	3
1990	SEA	AL	7	1	6	5	1	1	0	0	0	0	0	0	0	0	5	2
1991	SEA	AL	8	0	8	4	3	0	1	0	0	0	0	0	0	0	2	6
1992	SEA	AL	9	7	2	8	1	0	0	0	0	0	0	0	0	0	5	4
1993	SEA	AL	13	4	9	8	5	0	0	0	0	0	0	0	0	0	8	5
1994	BOS	AL	1	0	1	1	0	0	0	0	0	0	0	0	0	0	1	0
	MIL	AL	1	1	0	1	0	0	0	0	0	0	0	0	0	0	0	1
	Total		2	1	1	2	0	0	0	0	0	0	0	0	0	0	1	1
Total			74	32	42	46	21	6	1	1	0	0	0	0	0	1	40	34

Rank among batters: 707 • *Top target (3 home runs)*: Jeff Ballard • *Number of pitchers victimized*: 64 • *Total ballparks homered in*: 15 • *First HR*: 09/27/1984 off Lamarr Hoyt

Elmer Valo

ELMER WILLIAM VALO
B: 03/05/1921
BL

Year	Tm	Lg	Tot	H	A	0	1	2	3	2	3	4	LO	XN	IP	PH	RHP	LHP
1941	PHI	AL	2	1	1	1	0	1	0	0	0	0	0	0	0	0	2	0
1942	PHI	AL	2	1	1	1	1	0	0	0	0	0	0	0	0	0	1	1
1943	PHI	AL	3	2	1	3	0	0	0	0	0	0	1	0	1	0	3	0
1946	PHI	AL	1	1	0	0	1	0	0	0	0	0	0	0	0	0	1	0
1947	PHI	AL	5	1	4	3	2	0	0	0	0	0	0	0	0	0	5	0
1948	PHI	AL	3	1	2	3	0	0	0	0	0	0	0	0	0	0	2	1
1949	PHI	AL	5	4	1	3	0	1	1	0	0	0	0	0	1	0	3	2
1950	PHI	AL	10	2	8	7	2	1	0	1	0	0	0	0	0	0	8	2
1951	PHI	AL	7	3	4	3	4	0	0	2	0	0	0	0	0	0	5	2
1952	PHI	AL	5	3	2	2	0	3	0	0	0	0	0	0	0	0	4	1
1954	PHI	AL	1	0	1	0	0	1	0	0	0	0	0	0	0	0	1	0
1955	KC	AL	3	0	3	2	1	0	0	0	0	0	0	0	0	0	3	0
1956	PHI	NL	5	3	2	4	0	1	0	1	0	0	0	0	0	1	5	0
1957	BRO	NL	4	0	4	2	2	0	0	0	0	0	0	0	0	1	4	0
1958	LA	NL	1	0	1	0	0	1	0	0	0	0	0	0	0	0	1	0
1961	PHI	NL	1	1	0	1	0	0	0	0	0	0	0	0	0	1	1	0
Total			58	23	35	35	13	9	1	4	0	0	1	0	2	3	49	9

Rank among batters: 886 • *Top target (4 home runs)*: Art Houtteman, Early Wynn • *Number of pitchers victimized*: 44 • *Total ballparks homered in*: 11 • *First HR*: 09/16/1941 off Johnny Niggeling • *Hit for Cycle*—@CHI: 08/02/1950

						Men-On				One-Game								
Year	Tm	Lg	Tot	H	A	0	1	2	3	2	3	4	LO	XN	IP	PH	RHP	LHP

Clay Van Alstyne

CLAYTON EMORY VAN ALSTYNE
B: 05/24/1900 D: 01/05/1960
BR

Year	Tm	Lg	Tot	H	A	0	1	2	3	2	3	4	LO	XN	IP	PH	RHP	LHP
1928	WAS	AL	1	1	0	1	0	0	0	0	0	0	0	0	0	0	0	1

Rank among batters: 4,707 • *Total ballparks homered in*: 1 • *First HR*: 05/07/1928 off Lefty Stewart

Russ Van Atta

RUSSELL VAN ATTA
B: 06/21/1906 D: 10/10/1986
BL

Year	Tm	Lg	Tot	H	A	0	1	2	3	2	3	4	LO	XN	IP	PH	RHP	LHP
1934	NY	AL	1	1	0	1	0	0	0	0	0	0	0	0	0	0	1	0
1937	STL	AL	1	1	0	1	0	0	0	0	0	0	0	0	0	0	1	0
Total			2	2	0	2	0	0	0	0	0	0	0	0	0	0	2	0

Rank among batters: 4,129 • *Total ballparks homered in*: 2 • *First HR*: 07/03/1934 off Hank Johnson

Ty Van Burkleo

TYLER LEE VAN BURKLEO
B: 10/07/1963
BL

Year	Tm	Lg	Tot	H	A	0	1	2	3	2	3	4	LO	XN	IP	PH	RHP	LHP
1993	CAL	AL	1	1	0	1	0	0	0	0	0	0	0	0	0	0	1	0

Rank among batters: 4,707 • *Total ballparks homered in*: 1 • *First HR*: 08/16/1993 off Bill Gullickson

Bill Van Dyke

WILLIAM JENNINGS VAN DYKE
B: 12/15/1863 D: 05/05/1933
BR

Year	Tm	Lg	Tot	H	A	0	1	2	3	2	3	4	LO	XN	IP	PH	RHP	LHP
1890	TOL	AA	2	2	0	2	0	0	0	0	0	0	0	0	0	0	1	1

Rank among batters: 4,129 • *Total ballparks homered in*: 1 • *First HR*: 07/05/1890 off Dan Casey • *Hit for Cycle*—vs SYR: 07/05/1890

Dave Van Gorder

DAVID THOMAS VAN GORDER
B: 03/27/1957
BR

Year	Tm	Lg	Tot	H	A	0	1	2	3	2	3	4	LO	XN	IP	PH	RHP	LHP
1985	CIN	NL	2	0	2	1	0	1	0	0	0	0	0	0	0	0	2	0
1987	BAL	AL	1	1	0	1	0	0	0	0	0	0	0	0	0	0	0	1
Total			3	1	2	2	0	1	0	0	0	0	0	0	0	0	2	1

Rank among batters: 3,735 • *Total ballparks homered in*: 3 • *First HR*: 05/08/1985 off John Denny

George Van Haltren

GEORGE EDWARD MARTIN VAN HALTREN
B: 03/30/1866 D: 09/29/1945
BL

Year	Tm	Lg	Tot	H	A	0	1	2	3	2	3	4	LO	XN	IP	PH	RHP	LHP
1887	CHI	NL	3	3	0	2	1	0	0	0	0	0	1	0	0	0	3	0
1888	CHI	NL	4	2	2	3	1	0	0	0	0	0	0	0	1	0	3	1
1889	CHI	NL	9	6	3	2	4	3	0	0	0	0	0	0	0	0	7	2
1890	BRO	PL	5	3	2	1	1	3	0	0	0	0	0	0	1	0	4	0
1891	BAL	AA	9	5	4	3	2	4	0	0	0	0	0	0	2	0	8	1
1892	BAL	NL	7	4	3	3	3	1	0	0	0	0	0	0	1	0	6	1
1893	PIT	NL	3	3	0	1	0	1	1	0	0	0	0	0	2	0	2	0
1894	NY	NL	7	5	2	4	1	1	1	1	0	0	0	0	0	0	6	1
1895	NY	NL	8	4	4	2	3	3	0	0	0	0	0	0	1	0	6	2
1896	NY	NL	5	2	3	2	2	0	1	0	0	0	0	1	0	0	2	3
1897	NY	NL	3	3	0	1	1	1	0	0	0	0	0	0	1	0	3	0
1898	NY	NL	2	2	0	1	0	1	0	0	0	0	1	0	0	0	2	0
1899	NY	NL	2	1	1	2	0	0	0	0	0	0	0	0	0	0	2	0
1900	NY	NL	1	1	0	1	0	0	0	0	0	0	1	0	0	0	1	0
1901	NY	NL	1	0	1	0	1	0	0	0	0	0	0	0	0	0	1	0
Total			69	44	25	28	20	18	3	1	0	0	3	1	9	0	56	11

Rank among batters: 756 • *Top target (4 home runs)*: Gus Weyhing • *Number of pitchers victimized*: 55 • *Total ballparks homered in*: 22 • *First HR*: 07/02/1887 off Jim Whitney

Maurice Van Robays

MAURICE RENE VAN ROBAYS
B: 11/15/1914 D: 03/01/1965
BR

Year	Tm	Lg	Tot	H	A	0	1	2	3	2	3	4	LO	XN	IP	PH	RHP	LHP
1939	PIT	NL	2	1	1	1	1	0	0	0	0	0	0	0	0	0	2	0

Maurice Van Robays *continued*

Year	Tm	Lg	Tot	H	A	Men-On 0	1	2	3	One-Game 2	3	4	LO	XN	IP	PH	RHP	LHP
1940	PIT	NL	11	3	8	4	4	3	0	0	0	0	0	0	1	0	9	2
1941	PIT	NL	4	1	3	3	1	0	0	0	0	0	0	0	0	0	3	1
1942	PIT	NL	1	0	1	1	0	0	0	0	0	0	0	0	0	0	1	0
1943	PIT	NL	1	1	0	0	1	0	0	0	0	0	0	0	0	0	0	1
1946	PIT	NL	1	0	1	0	0	1	0	0	0	0	0	0	0	0	0	1
Total			20	6	14	9	7	4	0	0	0	0	0	0	1	0	15	5

Rank among batters: 1,810 • *Top target (2 home runs)*: Bob Bowman, Cliff Melton • *Number of pitchers victimized*: 18 • *Total ballparks homered in*: 6 • *First HR*: 09/18/1939 off Roy Bruner

Andy Van Slyke

ANDREW JAMES VAN SLYKE
B: 12/21/1960
BL

Year	Tm	Lg	Tot	H	A	Men-On 0	1	2	3	One-Game 2	3	4	LO	XN	IP	PH	RHP	LHP
1983	STL	NL	8	3	5	5	2	1	0	0	0	0	0	1	0	0	6	2
1984	STL	NL	7	3	4	3	3	1	0	0	0	0	0	0	0	0	7	0
1985	STL	NL	13	5	8	7	4	2	0	0	0	0	0	0	0	0	13	0
1986	STL	NL	13	6	7	7	5	1	0	0	0	0	0	0	1	0	12	1
1987	PIT	NL	21	11	10	11	8	1	1	1	0	0	0	1	0	1	18	3
1988	PIT	NL	25	16	9	15	9	1	0	1	0	0	0	0	0	0	22	3
1989	PIT	NL	9	4	5	7	2	0	0	0	0	0	0	0	0	0	8	1
1990	PIT	NL	17	6	11	8	8	1	0	2	0	0	0	0	0	0	12	5
1991	PIT	NL	17	9	8	8	9	0	0	0	0	0	0	0	0	0	13	4
1992	PIT	NL	14	6	8	9	5	0	0	0	0	0	0	0	0	0	10	4
1993	PIT	NL	8	5	3	2	5	1	0	0	0	0	0	0	1	0	7	1
1994	PIT	NL	6	4	2	5	1	0	0	0	0	0	0	0	0	0	5	1
1995	BAL	AL	3	1	2	1	2	0	0	0	0	0	0	0	0	0	3	0
	PHI	NL	3	0	3	2	1	0	0	0	0	0	0	0	0	0	3	0
	Total		6	1	5	3	3	0	0	0	0	0	0	0	0	0	6	0
Total			164	79	85	90	64	9	1	4	0	0	0	2	2	1	139	25

Rank among batters: 250 • *Top target (4 home runs)*: Pascual Perez, Greg Maddux • *Number of pitchers victimized*: 129 • *Total ballparks homered in*: 16 • *First HR*: 06/21/1983 off Scott Holman • *LCS HR*—1

Ike Van Zandt

CHARLES ISAAC VAN ZANDT
B: 1877 D: 09/14/1908
BL

Year	Tm	Lg	Tot	H	A	Men-On 0	1	2	3	One-Game 2	3	4	LO	XN	IP	PH	RHP	LHP
1905	STL	AL	1	1	0	1	0	0	0	0	0	0	0	0	0	0	0	1

Rank among batters: 4,707 • *Total ballparks homered in*: 1 • *First HR*: 07/11/1905 off Beany Jacobson

Dazzy Vance

CLARENCE ARTHUR VANCE
B: 03/04/1891 D: 02/16/1961
BR HOF

Year	Tm	Lg	Tot	H	A	Men-On 0	1	2	3	One-Game 2	3	4	LO	XN	IP	PH	RHP	LHP
1923	BRO	NL	1	0	1	1	0	0	0	0	0	0	0	0	0	0	0	1
1924	BRO	NL	2	0	2	0	2	0	0	0	0	0	0	0	0	0	1	1
1925	BRO	NL	3	2	1	1	2	0	0	0	0	0	0	0	0	0	1	2
1934	STL	NL	1	0	1	1	0	0	0	0	0	0	0	0	0	0	0	1
Total			7	2	5	3	4	0	0	0	0	0	0	0	0	0	2	5

Rank among batters: 2,834 • *Total ballparks homered in*: 5 • *First HR*: 05/30/1923 off Art Nehf

Johnny Vander Meer

JOHN SAMUEL VANDER MEER
B: 11/02/1914
BB

Year	Tm	Lg	Tot	H	A	Men-On 0	1	2	3	One-Game 2	3	4	LO	XN	IP	PH	RHP	LHP
1948	CIN	NL	1	1	0	1	0	0	0	0	0	0	0	0	0	0	1	0

Rank among batters: 4,707 • *Total ballparks homered in*: 1 • *First HR*: 06/12/1948 off Red Barrett

John Vander Wal

JOHN HENRY VANDER WAL
B: 04/29/1966
BL

Year	Tm	Lg	Tot	H	A	Men-On 0	1	2	3	One-Game 2	3	4	LO	XN	IP	PH	RHP	LHP
1991	MON	NL	1	0	1	1	0	0	0	0	0	0	0	0	0	0	1	0
1992	MON	NL	4	2	2	3	1	0	0	0	0	0	0	0	0	1	4	0
1993	MON	NL	5	1	4	3	1	1	0	0	0	0	0	0	0	0	5	0

John Vander Wal *continued*

Year	Tm	Lg	Tot	H	A	Men-On 0	1	2	3	One-Game 2	3	4	LO	XN	IP	PH	RHP	LHP
1994	COL	NL	5	1	4	2	3	0	0	0	0	0	0	0	0	1	5	0
1995	COL	NL	5	2	3	3	1	1	0	0	0	0	0	0	0	4	5	0
Total			20	6	14	12	6	2	0	0	0	0	0	0	0	6	20	0

Rank among batters: 1,810 • *Top target (2 home runs)*: Orel Hershiser • *Number of pitchers victimized*: 19 • *Total ballparks homered in*: 10 • *First HR*: 09/14/1991 off Shawn Boskie

Elam Vangilder

ELAM RUSSELL VANGILDER
B: 04/23/1896 D: 04/30/1977
BR

Year	Tm	Lg	Tot	H	A	Men-On 0	1	2	3	One-Game 2	3	4	LO	XN	IP	PH	RHP	LHP
1921	STL	AL	1	1	0	1	0	0	0	0	0	0	0	0	0	0	1	0
1922	STL	AL	2	1	1	1	1	0	0	0	0	0	0	0	0	0	0	2
1923	STL	AL	1	1	0	0	1	0	0	0	0	0	0	0	0	0	0	1
1924	STL	AL	1	1	0	0	1	0	0	0	0	0	0	0	0	0	0	1
1927	STL	AL	1	0	1	1	0	0	0	0	0	0	0	0	0	0	1	0
1928	DET	AL	2	2	0	1	1	0	0	0	0	0	0	0	0	0	2	0
Total			8	6	2	4	4	0	0	0	0	0	0	0	0	0	4	4

Rank among batters: 2,703 • *Total ballparks homered in*: 4 • *First HR*: 09/11/1921 off Ray Caldwell

Bill VanLandingham

WILLIAM JOSEPH VANLANDINGHAM
B: 07/16/1970
BR

Year	Tm	Lg	Tot	H	A	Men-On 0	1	2	3	One-Game 2	3	4	LO	XN	IP	PH	RHP	LHP
1995	SF	NL	1	1	0	1	0	0	0	0	0	0	0	0	0	0	1	0

Rank among batters: 4,707 • *Total ballparks homered in*: 1 • *First HR*: 08/04/1995 off Tom Candiotti

Pete Varney

RICHARD FRED VARNEY
B: 04/10/1949
BR

Year	Tm	Lg	Tot	H	A	Men-On 0	1	2	3	One-Game 2	3	4	LO	XN	IP	PH	RHP	LHP
1975	CHI	AL	2	0	2	2	0	0	0	0	0	0	0	0	0	0	1	1
1976	CHI	AL	3	2	1	2	1	0	0	0	0	0	0	0	0	0	2	1
Total			5	2	3	4	1	0	0	0	0	0	0	0	0	0	3	2

Rank among batters: 3,191 • *Total ballparks homered in*: 3 • *First HR*: 08/19/1975 off Larry Gura

Gary Varsho

GARY ANDREW VARSHO
B: 06/20/1961
BL

Year	Tm	Lg	Tot	H	A	Men-On 0	1	2	3	One-Game 2	3	4	LO	XN	IP	PH	RHP	LHP
1991	PIT	NL	4	1	3	0	4	0	0	1	0	0	0	0	0	1	4	0
1992	PIT	NL	4	3	1	1	2	1	0	0	0	0	1	0	1	1	3	1
1993	CIN	NL	2	1	1	1	1	0	0	0	0	0	0	0	0	2	2	0
Total			10	5	5	2	7	1	0	1	0	0	1	0	1	4	9	1

Rank among batters: 2,500 • *Top target (2 home runs)*: Heathcliff Slocumb • *Number of pitchers victimized*: 9 • *Total ballparks homered in*: 4 • *First HR*: 07/02/1991 off Shawn Boskie

Jim Vatcher

JAMES ERNEST VATCHER
B: 05/27/1966
BR

Year	Tm	Lg	Tot	H	A	Men-On 0	1	2	3	One-Game 2	3	4	LO	XN	IP	PH	RHP	LHP
1990	PHI	NL	1	1	0	0	1	0	0	0	0	0	0	0	0	0	0	1

Rank among batters: 4,707 • *Total ballparks homered in*: 1 • *First HR*: 07/02/1990 off Juan Agosto

Arky Vaughan

JOSEPH FLOYD VAUGHAN
B: 03/09/1912 D: 08/30/1952
BL HOF

Year	Tm	Lg	Tot	H	A	Men-On 0	1	2	3	One-Game 2	3	4	LO	XN	IP	PH	RHP	LHP
1932	PIT	NL	4	2	2	1	2	1	0	0	0	0	0	0	1	0	0	4
1933	PIT	NL	9	3	6	4	2	2	1	0	0	0	0	0	2	0	7	2
1934	PIT	NL	12	5	7	6	5	1	0	0	0	0	0	0	1	0	12	0
1935	PIT	NL	19	12	7	12	4	2	1	1	0	0	0	0	1	0	16	3

Arky Vaughan *continued*

Year	Tm	Lg	Tot	H	A	Men-On 0	Men-On 1	Men-On 2	Men-On 3	One-Game 2	One-Game 3	One-Game 4	LO	XN	IP	PH	RHP	LHP
1936	PIT	NL	9	4	5	4	5	0	0	1	0	0	0	0	0	0	7	2
1937	PIT	NL	5	1	4	4	1	0	0	1	0	0	0	0	0	0	2	3
1938	PIT	NL	7	5	2	4	2	0	1	0	0	0	0	0	1	0	2	5
1939	PIT	NL	6	3	3	3	3	0	0	0	0	0	0	0	0	0	4	2
1940	PIT	NL	7	4	3	3	2	2	0	0	0	0	0	0	1	0	6	1
1941	PIT	NL	6	2	4	3	2	1	0	0	0	0	0	0	0	0	5	1
1942	BRO	NL	2	1	1	1	1	0	0	0	0	0	0	0	0	0	2	0
1943	BRO	NL	5	1	4	3	0	1	1	0	0	0	0	1	1	0	4	1
1947	BRO	NL	2	1	1	1	1	0	0	0	0	0	0	0	0	0	2	0
1948	BRO	NL	3	1	2	3	0	0	0	1	0	0	0	0	1	0	3	0
Total			96	45	51	52	30	10	4	4	0	0	0	1	9	0	72	24

Rank among batters: 520 • *Top target (5 home runs)*: Lon Warneke • *Number of pitchers victimized*: 65 • *Total ballparks homered in*: 9 • *First HR*: 07/26/1932 off Jim Mooney • *Hit for Cycle*—@BRO: 06/24/1933; @NY: 07/19/1939 • *All-Star HR*—2

Fred Vaughn

FREDERICK THOMAS VAUGHN
B: 10/18/1918 D: 03/02/1964
BR

Year	Tm	Lg	Tot	H	A	Men-On 0	Men-On 1	Men-On 2	Men-On 3	One-Game 2	One-Game 3	One-Game 4	LO	XN	IP	PH	RHP	LHP
1944	WAS	AL	1	1	0	1	0	0	0	0	0	0	0	0	0	0	1	0
1945	WAS	AL	1	0	1	1	0	0	0	0	0	0	0	0	0	0	0	1
Total			2	1	1	2	0	0	0	0	0	0	0	0	0	0	1	1

Rank among batters: 4,129 • *Total ballparks homered in*: 2 • *First HR*: 08/21/1944 off Sig Jakucki

Greg Vaughn

GREGORY LAMONT VAUGHN
B: 07/03/1965
BR

Year	Tm	Lg	Tot	H	A	Men-On 0	Men-On 1	Men-On 2	Men-On 3	One-Game 2	One-Game 3	One-Game 4	LO	XN	IP	PH	RHP	LHP
1989	MIL	AL	5	1	4	1	3	1	0	1	0	0	0	0	0	0	5	0
1990	MIL	AL	17	9	8	10	4	3	0	1	0	0	0	0	0	0	13	4
1991	MIL	AL	27	16	11	14	7	5	1	3	0	0	0	1	0	1	22	5
1992	MIL	AL	23	11	12	11	7	5	0	0	0	0	0	1	0	0	17	6
1993	MIL	AL	30	12	18	20	6	4	0	4	0	0	0	1	0	0	24	6
1994	MIL	AL	19	9	10	12	6	1	0	2	0	0	0	0	0	0	12	7
1995	MIL	AL	17	8	9	7	8	2	0	0	0	0	0	0	0	0	12	5
Total			138	66	72	75	41	21	1	11	0	0	0	3	0	1	105	33

Rank among batters: 314 • *Top target (8 home runs)*: Dave Stewart • *Number of pitchers victimized*: 105 • *Total ballparks homered in*: 15 • *First HR*: 08/17/1989 off Wes Gardner

Henry Vaughn

HENRY FRANCIS VAUGHN
B: 03/01/1864 D: 02/21/1914
BR

Year	Tm	Lg	Tot	H	A	Men-On 0	Men-On 1	Men-On 2	Men-On 3	One-Game 2	One-Game 3	One-Game 4	LO	XN	IP	PH	RHP	LHP
1888	LOU	AA	1	0	1	0	0	1	0	0	0	0	0	0	0	0	1	0
1889	LOU	AA	3	2	1	2	1	0	0	0	0	0	0	0	0	0	1	1
1890	NY	PL	1	1	0	1	0	0	0	0	0	0	0	0	0	0	1	0
1891	CIN	AA	1	1	0	0	1	0	0	0	0	0	0	0	0	0	1	0
1892	CIN	NL	2	1	1	0	0	2	0	0	0	0	0	0	0	0	1	0
1893	CIN	NL	1	1	0	1	0	0	0	0	0	0	0	0	0	0	1	0
1894	CIN	NL	8	5	3	3	1	3	1	1	0	0	0	1	1	0	5	2
1895	CIN	NL	1	0	1	0	1	0	0	0	0	0	0	0	0	0	0	1
1896	CIN	NL	2	0	2	2	0	0	0	0	0	0	0	0	2	0	2	0
1898	CIN	NL	1	0	1	1	0	0	0	0	0	0	0	0	0	0	1	0
Total			21	11	10	10	4	6	1	1	0	0	0	1	3	0	14	4

Rank among batters: 1,768 • *Top target (2 home runs)*: Nat Hudson, Hank Gastright, Kid Nichols • *Number of pitchers victimized*: 18 • *Total ballparks homered in*: 14 • *First HR*: 09/11/1888 off Nat Hudson

Hippo Vaughn

JAMES LESLIE VAUGHN
B: 04/09/1888 D: 05/29/1966
BB

Year	Tm	Lg	Tot	H	A	Men-On 0	Men-On 1	Men-On 2	Men-On 3	One-Game 2	One-Game 3	One-Game 4	LO	XN	IP	PH	RHP	LHP
1914	CHI	NL	1	0	1	1	0	0	0	0	0	0	0	0	0	0	1	0
1920	CHI	NL	1	1	0	1	0	0	0	0	0	0	0	0	0	0	1	0

Year	Tm	Lg	Tot	H	A	Men-On 0	Men-On 1	Men-On 2	Men-On 3	One-Game 2	One-Game 3	One-Game 4	LO	XN	IP	PH	RHP	LHP

Hippo Vaughn *continued*

Year	Tm	Lg	Tot	H	A	0	1	2	3	2	3	4	LO	XN	IP	PH	RHP	LHP
1921	CHI	NL	1	0	1	1	0	0	0	0	0	0	0	0	0	0	1	0
Total			3	1	2	3	0	0	0	0	0	0	0	0	0	0	3	0

Rank among batters: 3,735 • *Total ballparks homered in*: 3 • *First HR*: 06/26/1914 off Phil Douglas

Mo Vaughn

MAURICE SAMUEL VAUGHN
B: 12/15/1967
BL

Year	Tm	Lg	Tot	H	A	0	1	2	3	2	3	4	LO	XN	IP	PH	RHP	LHP
1991	BOS	AL	4	1	3	3	1	0	0	0	0	0	0	0	0	0	4	0
1992	BOS	AL	13	8	5	7	3	3	0	0	0	0	0	0	0	1	8	5
1993	BOS	AL	29	13	16	15	9	3	2	1	0	0	0	0	0	0	17	12
1994	BOS	AL	26	15	11	12	13	1	0	4	0	0	0	1	0	0	15	11
1995	BOS	AL	39	15	24	23	10	3	3	4	0	0	0	0	1	0	33	6
Total			111	52	59	60	36	10	5	9	0	0	0	1	1	1	77	34

Rank among batters: 434 • *Top target (4 home runs)*: Jaime Navarro • *Number of pitchers victimized*: 88 • *Total ballparks homered in*: 17 • *First HR*: 06/30/1991 off Jeff Robinson

Bobby Veach

ROBERT HAYES VEACH
B: 06/29/1888 D: 08/07/1945
BL

Year	Tm	Lg	Tot	H	A	0	1	2	3	2	3	4	LO	XN	IP	PH	RHP	LHP
1914	DET	AL	1	0	1	0	1	0	0	0	0	0	0	0	0	0	1	0
1915	DET	AL	3	1	2	2	1	0	0	0	0	0	0	0	0	0	2	1
1916	DET	AL	3	2	1	3	0	0	0	0	0	0	0	0	1	0	2	1
1917	DET	AL	8	1	7	3	4	1	0	0	0	0	0	0	1	0	7	1
1918	DET	AL	3	0	3	2	1	0	0	0	0	0	0	0	0	0	1	2
1919	DET	AL	3	1	2	3	0	0	0	0	0	0	0	0	0	0	2	1
1920	DET	AL	11	5	6	5	5	1	0	0	0	0	0	0	0	0	6	5
1921	DET	AL	16	6	10	9	3	4	0	1	0	0	0	0	1	0	11	5
1922	DET	AL	9	1	8	4	2	1	2	1	0	0	0	0	0	0	9	0
1923	DET	AL	2	2	0	1	0	1	0	0	0	0	0	0	0	0	2	0
1924	BOS	AL	5	1	4	3	2	0	0	0	0	0	0	1	0	0	4	1
Total			64	20	44	35	19	8	2	2	0	0	0	1	3	0	47	17

Rank among batters: 815 • Top target (3 home runs): Carl Weilman, Stan Coveleski, Elam Vangilder, Bob Hasty, Urban Shocker • *Number of pitchers victimized*: 44 • *Total ballparks homered in*: 9 • *First HR*: 08/29/1914 off Jack Warhop • *Hit for Cycle*—vs BOS: 09/17/1920

Peak-A-Boo Veach

WILLIAM WALTER VEACH
B: 06/15/1862 D: 11/12/1937

Year	Tm	Lg	Tot	H	A	0	1	2	3	2	3	4	LO	XN	IP	PH	RHP	LHP
1884	KC	UA	1	1	0	1	0	0	0	0	0	0	0	0	0	0	1	0
1890	PIT	NL	2	0	2	2	0	0	0	0	0	0	0	0	1	0	1	1
Total			3	1	2	3	0	0	0	0	0	0	0	0	1	0	2	1

Rank among batters: 3,735 • *Total ballparks homered in*: 3 • *First HR*: 10/02/1884 off Al Atkinson

Coot Veal

ORVILLE INMAN VEAL
B: 07/09/1932
BR

Year	Tm	Lg	Tot	H	A	0	1	2	3	2	3	4	LO	XN	IP	PH	RHP	LHP
1959	DET	AL	1	1	0	1	0	0	0	0	0	0	0	0	0	0	0	1

Rank among batters: 4,707 • *Total ballparks homered in*: 1 • *First HR*: 08/11/1959 off Billy Pierce

Jesus Vega

JESUS ANTHONY (MORALES) VEGA
B: 10/14/1955
BR

Year	Tm	Lg	Tot	H	A	0	1	2	3	2	3	4	LO	XN	IP	PH	RHP	LHP
1982	MIN	AL	5	3	2	2	1	2	0	0	0	0	0	0	0	0	2	3

Rank among batters: 3,191 • *Total ballparks homered in*: 3 • *First HR*: 04/09/1982 off Angel Moreno

Randy Velarde

RANDY LEE VELARDE
B: 11/24/1962
BR

Year	Tm	Lg	Tot	H	A	0	1	2	3	2	3	4	LO	XN	IP	PH	RHP	LHP
1988	NY	AL	5	2	3	3	1	1	0	0	0	0	0	0	0	0	4	1

Randy Velarde *continued*

Year	Tm	Lg	Tot	H	A	Men-On 0	1	2	3	One-Game 2	3	4	LO	XN	IP	PH	RHP	LHP
1989	NY	AL	2	1	1	2	0	0	0	0	0	0	0	0	0	0	2	0
1990	NY	AL	5	1	4	1	2	2	0	0	0	0	0	0	0	0	4	1
1991	NY	AL	1	0	1	1	0	0	0	0	0	0	0	0	0	0	1	0
1992	NY	AL	7	2	5	4	1	2	0	0	0	0	0	1	0	0	3	4
1993	NY	AL	7	4	3	5	2	0	0	0	0	0	0	0	0	1	1	6
1994	NY	AL	9	3	6	5	2	2	0	0	0	0	0	0	0	0	4	5
1995	NY	AL	7	2	5	4	3	0	0	0	0	0	0	0	0	0	6	1
Total			43	15	28	25	11	7	0	0	0	0	0	1	0	1	25	18

Rank among batters: 1,116 • *Top target (2 home runs)*: Bill Gullickson, Wilson Alvarez • *Number of pitchers victimized*: 41 • *Total ballparks homered in*: 14 • *First HR*: 06/21/1988 off Jack Morris

Guillermo Velasquez

GUILLERMO (BURGARA) VELASQUEZ
B: 04/23/1968
BL

Year	Tm	Lg	Tot	H	A	Men-On 0	1	2	3	One-Game 2	3	4	LO	XN	IP	PH	RHP	LHP
1992	SD	NL	1	1	0	0	1	0	0	0	0	0	0	0	0	1	1	0
1993	SD	NL	3	1	2	2	1	0	0	0	0	0	0	0	0	1	2	1
Total			4	2	2	2	2	0	0	0	0	0	0	0	0	2	3	1

Rank among batters: 3,427 • *Total ballparks homered in*: 3 • *First HR*: 09/23/1992 off Pete Harnisch

Otto Velez

OTONIEL (FRANCESCHI) VELEZ
B: 11/29/1950
BR

Year	Tm	Lg	Tot	H	A	Men-On 0	1	2	3	One-Game 2	3	4	LO	XN	IP	PH	RHP	LHP
1973	NY	AL	2	0	2	2	0	0	0	1	0	0	0	0	0	0	2	0
1974	NY	AL	2	1	1	1	1	0	0	0	0	0	0	0	0	0	0	2
1976	NY	AL	2	1	1	1	1	0	0	0	0	0	0	0	0	0	0	2
1977	TOR	AL	16	7	9	11	4	1	0	2	0	0	0	0	0	1	9	7
1978	TOR	AL	9	4	5	5	4	0	0	0	0	0	0	1	0	0	0	9
1979	TOR	AL	15	7	8	6	5	4	0	1	0	0	0	1	0	2	8	7
1980	TOR	AL	20	12	8	8	7	4	1	0	1	0	0	1	0	0	11	9
1981	TOR	AL	11	7	4	8	2	1	0	1	0	0	0	0	0	0	2	9
1982	TOR	AL	1	0	1	1	0	0	0	0	0	0	0	0	0	0	0	1
Total			78	39	39	43	24	10	1	5	1	0	0	3	0	3	32	46

Rank among batters: 672 • *Top target (4 home runs)*: Rick Waits • *Number of pitchers victimized*: 61 • *Total ballparks homered in*: 14 • *First HR*: 09/23/1973 off Dick Tidrow

Max Venable

WILLIAM MCKINLEY VENABLE
B: 06/06/1957
BL

Year	Tm	Lg	Tot	H	A	Men-On 0	1	2	3	One-Game 2	3	4	LO	XN	IP	PH	RHP	LHP
1982	SF	NL	1	1	0	1	0	0	0	0	0	0	0	0	0	0	1	0
1983	SF	NL	6	3	3	3	3	0	0	0	0	0	0	0	0	1	6	0
1984	MON	NL	2	0	2	2	0	0	0	0	0	0	0	0	0	1	2	0
1986	CIN	NL	2	1	1	1	0	1	0	0	0	0	0	0	0	0	2	0
1990	CAL	AL	4	3	1	4	0	0	0	0	0	0	1	0	0	0	4	0
1991	CAL	AL	3	2	1	2	0	0	1	0	0	0	1	0	0	1	3	0
Total			18	10	8	13	3	1	1	0	0	0	2	0	0	3	18	0

Rank among batters: 1,914 • *Top target (2 home runs)*: Dick Ruthven • *Number of pitchers victimized*: 17 • *Total ballparks homered in*: 8 • *First HR*: 06/25/1982 off Juan Eichelberger

Robin Ventura

ROBIN MARK VENTURA
B: 07/14/1967
BL

Year	Tm	Lg	Tot	H	A	Men-On 0	1	2	3	One-Game 2	3	4	LO	XN	IP	PH	RHP	LHP
1990	CHI	AL	5	2	3	2	3	0	0	0	0	0	0	0	0	0	5	0
1991	CHI	AL	23	16	7	11	7	3	2	4	0	0	0	1	0	0	18	5
1992	CHI	AL	16	7	9	10	4	2	0	0	0	0	0	0	0	0	14	2
1993	CHI	AL	22	12	10	12	7	1	2	1	0	0	0	0	0	0	17	5
1994	CHI	AL	18	8	10	10	4	3	1	2	0	0	0	0	0	0	14	4
1995	CHI	AL	26	8	18	16	3	5	2	4	0	0	0	0	0	0	21	5
Total			110	53	57	61	28	14	7	11	0	0	0	1	0	0	89	21

Rank among batters: 436 • *Top target (4 home runs)*: Kevin Tapani • *Number of pitchers victimized*: 88 • *Total ballparks homered in*: 18 • *First HR*: 04/18/1990 off Roger Clemens • *LCS HR*—1

Quilvio Veras

QUILVIO ALBERTO (PEREZ) VERAS
B: 04/03/1971
BB

Year	Tm	Lg	Tot	H	A	Men-On 0	1	2	3	One-Game 2	3	4	LO	XN	IP	PH	RHP	LHP
1995	FLO	NL	5	2	3	1	3	0	1	0	0	0	0	0	0	0	2	3

Rank among batters: 3,191 • *Total ballparks homered in*: 4 • *First HR*: 05/05/1995 off Curt Schmidt

Emil Verban

EMIL MATTHEW VERBAN
B: 08/27/1915 D: 06/08/1989
BR

Year	Tm	Lg	Tot	H	A	Men-On 0	1	2	3	One-Game 2	3	4	LO	XN	IP	PH	RHP	LHP
1948	CHI	NL	1	0	1	1	0	0	0	0	0	0	0	0	0	0	0	1

Rank among batters: 4,707 • *Total ballparks homered in*: 1 • *First HR*: 09/06/1948 off Johnny Vander Meer

Johnny Vergez

JOHN LOUIS VERGEZ
B: 07/09/1906 D: 07/15/1991
BR

Year	Tm	Lg	Tot	H	A	Men-On 0	1	2	3	One-Game 2	3	4	LO	XN	IP	PH	RHP	LHP
1931	NY	NL	13	13	0	8	3	2	0	0	0	0	0	0	0	0	11	2
1932	NY	NL	6	6	0	5	0	0	1	0	0	0	0	0	0	0	5	1
1933	NY	NL	16	12	4	12	1	2	1	1	0	0	0	0	0	0	13	3
1934	NY	NL	7	5	2	4	3	0	0	0	0	0	0	0	0	0	5	2
1935	PHI	NL	9	2	7	3	4	1	1	1	0	0	0	0	0	0	7	2
1936	PHI	NL	1	0	1	1	0	0	0	0	0	0	0	0	0	0	1	0
Total			52	38	14	33	11	5	3	2	0	0	0	0	0	0	42	10

Rank among batters: 965 • *Top target (3 home runs)*: Burleigh Grimes • *Number of pitchers victimized*: 39 • *Total ballparks homered in*: 6 • *First HR*: 04/25/1931 off Clise Dudley

Mickey Vernon

JAMES BARTON VERNON
B: 04/22/1918
BL

Year	Tm	Lg	Tot	H	A	Men-On 0	1	2	3	One-Game 2	3	4	LO	XN	IP	PH	RHP	LHP
1939	WAS	AL	1	0	1	0	1	0	0	0	0	0	0	0	0	0	1	0
1941	WAS	AL	9	2	7	4	4	1	0	0	0	0	0	0	0	0	8	1
1942	WAS	AL	9	4	5	6	3	0	0	0	0	0	0	0	0	0	5	4
1943	WAS	AL	7	1	6	3	3	1	0	0	0	0	0	0	1	0	7	0
1946	WAS	AL	8	2	6	4	4	0	0	0	0	0	0	0	2	0	7	1
1947	WAS	AL	7	1	6	5	1	1	0	0	0	0	0	0	0	0	7	0
1948	WAS	AL	3	0	3	1	2	0	0	0	0	0	0	0	0	0	3	0
1949	CLE	AL	18	11	7	8	9	1	0	1	0	0	0	1	0	0	12	6
1950	WAS	AL	9	1	8	4	3	2	0	1	0	0	0	1	0	0	5	4
1951	WAS	AL	9	2	7	4	4	1	0	1	0	0	0	1	0	0	8	1
1952	WAS	AL	10	5	5	5	4	1	0	0	0	0	0	1	1	0	5	5
1953	WAS	AL	15	3	12	7	5	3	0	0	0	0	0	0	0	0	13	2
1954	WAS	AL	20	8	12	10	9	1	0	0	0	0	0	1	0	0	18	2
1955	WAS	AL	14	3	11	6	4	3	1	0	0	0	0	0	0	0	11	3
1956	BOS	AL	15	7	8	5	6	4	0	0	0	0	0	0	0	0	15	0
1957	BOS	AL	7	2	5	5	2	0	0	0	0	0	0	0	0	1	7	0
1958	CLE	AL	8	3	5	2	4	1	1	0	0	0	0	0	0	0	6	2
1959	MIL	NL	3	2	1	2	0	1	0	0	0	0	0	0	0	2	3	0
Total			172	57	115	81	68	21	2	3	0	0	0	5	4	3	141	31

Rank among batters: 233 • *Top target (5 home runs)*: Allie Reynolds, Steve Gromek • *Number of pitchers victimized*: 110 • *Total ballparks homered in*: 13 • *First HR*: 07/22/1939 off Johnny Broaca • *Hit for Cycle*—@CHI: 05/19/1946 (2)

Zoilo Versalles

ZOILO CASANOVA (RODRIGUEZ) VERSALLES
B: 12/18/1939 D: 06/09/1995
BR

Year	Tm	Lg	Tot	H	A	Men-On 0	1	2	3	One-Game 2	3	4	LO	XN	IP	PH	RHP	LHP
1959	WAS	AL	1	1	0	1	0	0	0	0	0	0	0	0	0	0	1	0
1961	MIN	AL	7	3	4	4	2	1	0	0	0	0	0	1	0	0	3	4
1962	MIN	AL	17	13	4	8	6	3	0	0	0	0	0	0	1	0	16	1
1963	MIN	AL	10	7	3	8	1	1	0	1	0	0	1	0	0	0	7	3
1964	MIN	AL	20	14	6	13	6	1	0	2	0	0	3	1	0	0	13	7
1965	MIN	AL	19	11	8	9	7	2	1	0	0	0	2	0	1	0	11	8
1966	MIN	AL	7	4	3	3	2	2	0	0	0	0	0	0	0	0	5	2
1967	MIN	AL	6	5	1	4	1	1	0	0	0	0	0	0	0	0	4	2
1968	LA	NL	2	0	2	2	0	0	0	0	0	0	0	1	0	0	1	1
1969	CLE	AL	1	1	0	0	1	0	0	0	0	0	0	0	0	0	0	1

Zoilo Versalles *continued*

Year	Tm	Lg	Tot	H	A	Men-On 0	1	2	3	One-Game 2	3	4	LO	XN	IP	PH	RHP	LHP
1971	ATL	NL	5	3	2	4	0	1	0	1	0	0	0	0	0	1	3	2
Total			95	62	33	56	26	12	1	4	0	0	6	3	2	1	64	31

Rank among batters: 529 • *Top target (4 home runs)*: Mike McCormick, Whitey Ford • *Number of pitchers victimized*: 69 • *Total ballparks homered in*: 15 • *First HR*: 08/05/1959 off Mudcat Grant • *World Series HR*—1

Tom Veryzer

THOMAS MARTIN VERYZER
B: 02/11/1953
BR

Year	Tm	Lg	Tot	H	A	Men-On 0	1	2	3	One-Game 2	3	4	LO	XN	IP	PH	RHP	LHP
1974	DET	AL	2	1	1	0	2	0	0	0	0	0	0	1	0	0	2	0
1975	DET	AL	5	3	2	3	2	0	0	0	0	0	0	0	0	0	5	0
1976	DET	AL	1	0	1	0	1	0	0	0	0	0	0	0	0	0	1	0
1977	DET	AL	2	1	1	1	0	1	0	0	0	0	0	0	0	0	2	0
1978	CLE	AL	1	1	0	1	0	0	0	0	0	0	0	0	0	0	1	0
1980	CLE	AL	2	1	1	1	1	0	0	0	0	0	0	0	0	0	1	1
1983	CHI	NL	1	1	0	1	0	0	0	0	0	0	0	0	0	0	0	1
Total			14	8	6	7	6	1	0	0	0	0	0	1	0	0	12	2

Rank among batters: 2,169 • *Total ballparks homered in*: 7 • *First HR*: 09/12/1974 off Tom Murphy

Sammy Vick

SAMUEL BRUCE VICK
B: 04/12/1895 D: 08/17/1986
BR

Year	Tm	Lg	Tot	H	A	Men-On 0	1	2	3	One-Game 2	3	4	LO	XN	IP	PH	RHP	LHP
1919	NY	AL	2	2	0	1	0	0	1	0	0	0	1	0	0	0	2	0

Rank among batters: 4,129 • *Total ballparks homered in*: 1 • *First HR*: 04/30/1919 off Mule Watson

Sam Vico

GEORGE STEVE VICO
B: 08/09/1923 D: 01/13/1994
BL

Year	Tm	Lg	Tot	H	A	Men-On 0	1	2	3	One-Game 2	3	4	LO	XN	IP	PH	RHP	LHP
1948	DET	AL	8	4	4	6	1	1	0	1	0	0	0	0	0	0	5	3
1949	DET	AL	4	3	1	1	2	1	0	0	0	0	0	0	0	0	4	0
Total			12	7	5	7	3	2	0	1	0	0	0	0	0	0	9	3

Rank among batters: 2,325 • *Top target (2 home runs)*: Clem Dreisewerd, Joe Haynes, Fred Sanford • *Number of pitchers victimized*: 9 • *Total ballparks homered in*: 4 • *First HR*: 04/20/1948 off Joe Haynes • *Hit HR on first major league pitch*—@CHI: 04/20/1948

Jose Vidal

JOSE (NICOLAS) VIDAL
B: 04/03/1940
BR

Year	Tm	Lg	Tot	H	A	Men-On 0	1	2	3	One-Game 2	3	4	LO	XN	IP	PH	RHP	LHP
1968	CLE	AL	2	1	1	1	1	0	0	0	0	0	0	1	0	0	1	1
1969	SEA	AL	1	1	0	1	0	0	0	0	0	0	0	0	0	0	0	1
Total			3	2	1	2	1	0	0	0	0	0	0	1	0	0	1	2

Rank among batters: 3,735 • *Total ballparks homered in*: 3 • *First HR*: 05/23/1968 off Clyde Wright

Hector Villanueva

HECTOR (BALASQUIDE) VILLANUEVA
B: 10/02/1964
BR

Year	Tm	Lg	Tot	H	A	Men-On 0	1	2	3	One-Game 2	3	4	LO	XN	IP	PH	RHP	LHP
1990	CHI	NL	7	2	5	1	5	1	0	0	0	0	0	0	0	1	2	5
1991	CHI	NL	13	11	2	7	5	1	0	1	0	0	0	1	0	0	7	6
1992	CHI	NL	2	2	0	0	0	2	0	0	0	0	0	0	0	0	2	0
1993	STL	NL	3	2	1	1	2	0	0	0	0	0	0	0	0	0	1	2
Total			25	17	8	9	12	4	0	1	0	0	0	1	0	1	12	13

Rank among batters: 1,608 • *Top target (2 home runs)*: Jim Deshaies, Dennis Rasmussen, Omar Olivares • *Number of pitchers victimized*: 22 • *Total ballparks homered in*: 8 • *First HR*: 06/01/1990 off Ken Dayley

Fernando Vina

FERNANDO VINA
B: 04/16/1969
BL

Year	Tm	Lg	Tot	H	A	Men-On 0	1	2	3	One-Game 2	3	4	LO	XN	IP	PH	RHP	LHP
1995	MIL	AL	3	1	2	2	1	0	0	0	0	0	1	0	1	0	3	0

Rank among batters: 3,735 • *Total ballparks homered in*: 2 • *First HR*: 05/29/1995 off Scott Erickson

Charlie Vinson

CHARLES ANTHONY VINSON
B: 01/05/1944
BL

Year	Tm	Lg	Tot	H	A	Men-On 0	1	2	3	One-Game 2	3	4	LO	XN	IP	PH	RHP	LHP
1966	CAL	AL	1	1	0	0	0	1	0	0	0	0	0	0	0	0	1	0

Rank among batters: 4,707 • *Total ballparks homered in*: 1 • *First HR*: 09/25/1966 off Eddie Fisher

Jim Viox

JAMES HARRY VIOX
B: 12/30/1890 D: 01/06/1969
BR

Year	Tm	Lg	Tot	H	A	Men-On 0	1	2	3	One-Game 2	3	4	LO	XN	IP	PH	RHP	LHP
1912	PIT	NL	1	1	0	1	0	0	0	0	0	0	0	0	0	0	1	0
1913	PIT	NL	2	2	0	2	0	0	0	0	0	0	0	0	1	0	1	1
1914	PIT	NL	1	0	1	0	0	1	0	0	0	0	0	0	1	0	1	0
1915	PIT	NL	2	1	1	1	1	0	0	0	0	0	0	0	1	0	2	0
1916	PIT	NL	1	1	0	0	0	1	0	0	0	0	0	0	1	0	1	0
Total			7	5	2	4	1	2	0	0	0	0	0	0	4	0	6	1

Rank among batters: 2,834 • *Total ballparks homered in*: 3 • *First HR*: 05/30/1912 off Gene Dale

Bill Virdon

WILLIAM CHARLES VIRDON
B: 06/09/1931
BL

Year	Tm	Lg	Tot	H	A	Men-On 0	1	2	3	One-Game 2	3	4	LO	XN	IP	PH	RHP	LHP
1955	STL	NL	17	13	4	11	6	0	0	1	0	0	0	2	0	0	10	7
1956	STL	NL	2	0	2	1	0	1	0	0	0	0	0	0	0	0	2	0
	PIT	NL	8	2	6	7	1	0	0	0	0	0	1	0	0	0	6	2
	Total		10	2	8	8	1	1	0	0	0	0	1	0	0	0	8	2
1957	PIT	NL	8	0	8	4	2	2	0	1	0	0	0	0	0	0	8	0
1958	PIT	NL	9	4	5	9	0	0	0	0	0	0	1	1	0	0	8	1
1959	PIT	NL	8	5	3	3	2	3	0	0	0	0	0	0	1	0	7	1
1960	PIT	NL	8	2	6	6	2	0	0	0	0	0	1	0	0	1	8	0
1961	PIT	NL	9	3	6	5	2	2	0	1	0	0	2	0	0	0	7	2
1962	PIT	NL	6	4	2	3	2	1	0	0	0	0	0	0	0	0	6	0
1963	PIT	NL	8	5	3	3	3	1	1	0	0	0	0	0	0	0	6	2
1964	PIT	NL	3	1	2	1	2	0	0	0	0	0	0	0	0	0	1	2
1965	PIT	NL	4	1	3	3	1	0	0	0	0	0	0	0	0	0	4	0
1968	PIT	NL	1	1	0	0	1	0	0	0	0	0	0	0	0	1	1	0
Total			91	41	50	56	24	10	1	3	0	0	5	3	1	2	74	17

Rank among batters: 559 • *Top target (6 home runs)*: Larry Jackson • *Number of pitchers victimized*: 67 • *Total ballparks homered in*: 11 • *First HR*: 04/14/1955 off Dave Koslo

Ozzie Virgil

OSVALDO JOSE (PICHARDO) VIRGIL
B: 05/17/1933
BR

Year	Tm	Lg	Tot	H	A	Men-On 0	1	2	3	One-Game 2	3	4	LO	XN	IP	PH	RHP	LHP
1957	NY	NL	4	3	1	1	2	1	0	0	0	0	0	0	1	0	1	3
1958	DET	AL	3	0	3	3	0	0	0	0	0	0	0	0	0	0	3	0
1960	DET	AL	3	2	1	2	1	0	0	0	0	0	1	0	0	0	2	1
1961	DET	AL	1	1	0	1	0	0	0	0	0	0	0	0	0	1	1	0
1965	PIT	NL	1	0	1	1	0	0	0	0	0	0	0	0	0	1	1	0
1966	SF	NL	2	1	1	2	0	0	0	0	0	0	0	0	0	0	1	1
Total			14	7	7	10	3	1	0	0	0	0	1	0	1	2	9	5

Rank among batters: 2,169 • *Top target (2 home runs)*: Dave Sisler • *Number of pitchers victimized*: 13 • *Total ballparks homered in*: 9 • *First HR*: 04/27/1957 off Robin Roberts

Ozzie Virgil

OSVALDO JOSE (LOPEZ) VIRGIL
B: 12/07/1956
BR

Year	Tm	Lg	Tot	H	A	Men-On 0	1	2	3	One-Game 2	3	4	LO	XN	IP	PH	RHP	LHP
1982	PHI	NL	3	1	2	3	0	0	0	0	0	0	0	0	0	0	3	0
1983	PHI	NL	6	2	4	3	1	1	1	0	0	0	0	0	0	1	5	1
1984	PHI	NL	18	10	8	7	10	1	0	1	0	0	0	0	0	1	12	6
1985	PHI	NL	19	7	12	12	6	1	0	3	0	0	0	1	0	0	15	4
1986	ATL	NL	15	6	9	9	5	1	0	0	0	0	0	1	0	0	13	2
1987	ATL	NL	27	15	12	20	5	2	0	3	0	0	0	1	0	0	20	7
1988	ATL	NL	9	5	4	8	0	1	0	0	0	0	0	0	0	0	6	3

Ozzie Virgil *continued*

Year	Tm	Lg	Tot	H	A	Men-On 0	Men-On 1	Men-On 2	Men-On 3	One-Game 2	One-Game 3	One-Game 4	LO	XN	IP	PH	RHP	LHP
1989	TOR	AL	1	1	0	0	1	0	0	0	0	0	0	0	0	0	0	1
Total			98	47	51	62	28	7	1	7	0	0	0	3	0	2	74	24

Rank among batters: 506 • *Top target (4 home runs)*: Ted Power • *Number of pitchers victimized*: 73 • *Total ballparks homered in*: 13 • *First HR*: 06/21/1982 off Doug Bair

Jake Virtue

JACOB KITCHLINE VIRTUE
B: 03/02/1865 D: 02/03/1943
BB

Year	Tm	Lg	Tot	H	A	Men-On 0	Men-On 1	Men-On 2	Men-On 3	One-Game 2	One-Game 3	One-Game 4	LO	XN	IP	PH	RHP	LHP
1890	CLE	NL	2	1	1	0	2	0	0	0	0	0	0	0	0	0	2	0
1891	CLE	NL	2	0	2	0	1	1	0	0	0	0	0	0	0	0	2	0
1892	CLE	NL	2	1	1	1	0	1	0	0	0	0	0	0	0	0	1	1
1893	CLE	NL	1	0	1	1	0	0	0	0	0	0	0	0	1	0	0	1
Total			7	2	5	2	3	2	0	0	0	0	0	0	1	0	5	2

Rank among batters: 2,834 • *Top target (2 home runs)*: Frank Killen • *Number of pitchers victimized*: 6 • *Total ballparks homered in*: 7 • *First HR*: 08/06/1890 off Bill Hutchison

Joe Visner

JOSEPH PAUL VISNER
B: 09/27/1859 D: 06/17/1945
BL

Year	Tm	Lg	Tot	H	A	Men-On 0	Men-On 1	Men-On 2	Men-On 3	One-Game 2	One-Game 3	One-Game 4	LO	XN	IP	PH	RHP	LHP
1889	BRO	AA	8	5	3	4	2	2	0	0	0	0	0	0	1	0	7	1
1890	PIT	PL	3	3	0	2	1	0	0	0	0	0	0	0	3	0	0	3
1891	WAS	AA	1	0	1	0	1	0	0	0	0	0	0	0	0	0	1	0
Total			12	8	4	6	4	2	0	0	0	0	0	0	4	0	8	4

Rank among batters: 2,325 • *Top target (2 home runs)*: Gus Weyhing • *Number of pitchers victimized*: 11 • *Total ballparks homered in*: 8 • *First HR*: 04/25/1889 off William Widner

Joe Vitiello

JOSEPH DAVID VITIELLO
B: 04/11/1970
BR

Year	Tm	Lg	Tot	H	A	Men-On 0	Men-On 1	Men-On 2	Men-On 3	One-Game 2	One-Game 3	One-Game 4	LO	XN	IP	PH	RHP	LHP
1995	KC	AL	7	3	4	3	2	2	0	1	0	0	0	0	1	1	1	6

Rank among batters: 2,834 • *Top target (2 home runs)*: Mark Langston • *Number of pitchers victimized*: 6 • *Total ballparks homered in*: 3 • *First HR*: 08/01/1995 off Dave Righetti

Ossie Vitt

OSCAR JOSEPH VITT
B: 01/04/1890 D: 01/31/1963
BR

Year	Tm	Lg	Tot	H	A	Men-On 0	Men-On 1	Men-On 2	Men-On 3	One-Game 2	One-Game 3	One-Game 4	LO	XN	IP	PH	RHP	LHP
1913	DET	AL	2	1	1	0	2	0	0	0	0	0	0	0	0	0	2	0
1915	DET	AL	1	0	1	0	1	0	0	0	0	0	0	0	0	0	1	0
1920	BOS	AL	1	0	1	0	0	1	0	0	0	0	0	0	0	0	1	0
Total			4	1	3	0	3	1	0	0	0	0	0	0	0	0	4	0

Rank among batters: 3,427 • *Total ballparks homered in*: 4 • *First HR*: 05/19/1913 off John Wyckoff

Jose Vizcaino

JOSE LUIS (PIMENTAL) VIZCAINO
B: 03/26/1968
BB

Year	Tm	Lg	Tot	H	A	Men-On 0	Men-On 1	Men-On 2	Men-On 3	One-Game 2	One-Game 3	One-Game 4	LO	XN	IP	PH	RHP	LHP
1992	CHI	NL	1	0	1	1	0	0	0	0	0	0	0	0	0	0	1	0
1993	CHI	NL	4	1	3	1	1	2	0	0	0	0	0	1	0	0	4	0
1994	NY	NL	3	1	2	1	2	0	0	0	0	0	0	0	0	0	3	0
1995	NY	NL	3	2	1	2	0	1	0	0	0	0	0	0	0	0	3	0
Total			11	4	7	5	3	3	0	0	0	0	0	1	0	0	11	0

Rank among batters: 2,419 • *Total ballparks homered in*: 7 • *First HR*: 08/01/1992 off Tom Filer

Omar Vizquel

OMAR ENRIQUE (GONZALEZ) VIZQUEL
B: 04/24/1967
BB

Year	Tm	Lg	Tot	H	A	Men-On 0	Men-On 1	Men-On 2	Men-On 3	One-Game 2	One-Game 3	One-Game 4	LO	XN	IP	PH	RHP	LHP
1989	SEA	AL	1	1	0	1	0	0	0	0	0	0	0	0	0	0	0	1

Year	Tm	Lg	Tot	H	A	Men-On				One-Game			LO	XN	IP	PH	RHP	LHP
						0	1	2	3	2	3	4						

Omar Vizquel *continued*

Year	Tm	Lg	Tot	H	A	0	1	2	3	2	3	4	LO	XN	IP	PH	RHP	LHP
1990	SEA	AL	2	0	2	1	0	1	0	0	0	0	0	0	0	0	1	1
1991	SEA	AL	1	1	0	1	0	0	0	0	0	0	0	0	0	0	1	0
1993	SEA	AL	2	1	1	1	0	0	1	0	0	0	1	0	0	0	2	0
1994	CLE	AL	1	0	1	1	0	0	0	0	0	0	0	0	0	0	0	1
1995	CLE	AL	6	3	3	5	1	0	0	0	0	0	0	0	0	0	4	2
Total			13	6	7	10	1	1	1	0	0	0	1	0	0	0	8	5

Rank among batters: 2,248 • *Total ballparks homered in*: 6 • *First HR*: 07/23/1989 off Jimmy Key

Otto Vogel

OTTO HENRY VOGEL
B: 10/26/1899 D: 07/19/1969
BR

Year	Tm	Lg	Tot	H	A	0	1	2	3	2	3	4	LO	XN	IP	PH	RHP	LHP
1923	CHI	NL	1	1	0	0	1	0	0	0	0	0	0	0	0	0	0	1
1924	CHI	NL	1	0	1	1	0	0	0	0	0	0	0	0	0	0	1	0
Total			2	1	1	1	1	0	0	0	0	0	0	0	0	0	1	1

Rank among batters: 4,129 • *Total ballparks homered in*: 2 • *First HR*: 07/01/1923 off Bill Sherdel

Jack Voigt

JOHN DAVID VOIGT
B: 05/17/1966
BR

Year	Tm	Lg	Tot	H	A	0	1	2	3	2	3	4	LO	XN	IP	PH	RHP	LHP
1993	BAL	AL	6	5	1	4	2	0	0	0	0	0	0	0	0	0	0	6
1994	BAL	AL	3	1	2	3	0	0	0	0	0	0	0	0	0	0	1	2
1995	TEX	AL	2	2	0	1	0	1	0	0	0	0	0	0	0	0	0	2
Total			11	8	3	8	2	1	0	0	0	0	0	0	0	0	1	10

Rank among batters: 2,419 • *Top target (2 home runs)*: Kenny Rogers, Angel Miranda • *Number of pitchers victimized*: 9 • *Total ballparks homered in*: 4 • *First HR*: 06/04/1993 off Randy Johnson

Clyde Vollmer

CLYDE FREDERICK VOLLMER
B: 09/24/1921
BR

Year	Tm	Lg	Tot	H	A	0	1	2	3	2	3	4	LO	XN	IP	PH	RHP	LHP
1942	CIN	NL	1	1	0	1	0	0	0	0	0	0	0	0	0	0	1	0
1947	CIN	NL	1	1	0	0	1	0	0	0	0	0	0	0	0	0	1	0
1949	WAS	AL	14	3	11	7	7	0	0	2	0	0	0	0	0	0	10	4
1950	BOS	AL	7	6	1	2	3	1	1	1	0	0	1	0	0	2	5	2
1951	BOS	AL	22	14	8	8	7	5	2	1	1	0	0	2	0	0	16	6
1952	BOS	AL	11	10	1	3	3	5	0	1	0	0	0	1	0	1	9	2
1953	WAS	AL	11	4	7	6	2	3	0	1	0	0	0	0	0	1	6	5
1954	WAS	AL	2	0	2	0	2	0	0	0	0	0	0	0	0	0	2	0
Total			69	39	30	27	25	14	3	6	1	0	1	3	0	4	50	19

Rank among batters: 756 • *Top target (4 home runs)*: Early Wynn • *Number of pitchers victimized*: 47 • *Total ballparks homered in*: 9 • *First HR*: 05/31/1942 off Max Butcher • *Hit HR on first major league pitch*—vs PIT: 05/31/1942 (2)

Joe Vosmik

JOSEPH FRANKLIN VOSMIK
B: 04/04/1910 D: 01/27/1962
BR

Year	Tm	Lg	Tot	H	A	0	1	2	3	2	3	4	LO	XN	IP	PH	RHP	LHP
1931	CLE	AL	7	2	5	4	1	2	0	0	0	0	0	1	0	0	4	3
1932	CLE	AL	10	4	6	5	4	1	0	0	0	0	0	0	0	0	6	4
1933	CLE	AL	4	3	1	2	2	0	0	0	0	0	0	0	1	0	1	3
1934	CLE	AL	6	3	3	0	5	1	0	0	0	0	0	0	0	0	3	3
1935	CLE	AL	10	3	7	5	3	2	0	0	0	0	0	0	0	0	7	3
1936	CLE	AL	7	1	6	4	2	1	0	1	0	0	0	1	0	0	5	2
1937	STL	AL	4	3	1	2	1	1	0	0	0	0	0	0	0	0	2	2
1938	BOS	AL	9	7	2	4	3	2	0	0	0	0	0	0	0	0	8	1
1939	BOS	AL	7	3	4	3	3	1	0	0	0	0	0	0	0	0	7	0
1940	BRO	NL	1	0	1	1	0	0	0	0	0	0	0	0	0	0	1	0
Total			65	29	36	30	24	11	0	1	0	0	0	2	1	0	44	21

Rank among batters: 799 • *Top target (6 home runs)*: Earl Whitehill • *Number of pitchers victimized*: 50 • *Total ballparks homered in*: 10 • *First HR*: 04/19/1931 off Earl Whitehill

Bill Voss

WILLIAM EDWARD VOSS
B: 10/31/1943
BL

Year	Tm	Lg	Tot	H	A	Men-On 0	Men-On 1	Men-On 2	Men-On 3	One-Game 2	One-Game 3	One-Game 4	LO	XN	IP	PH	RHP	LHP
1965	CHI	AL	1	0	1	1	0	0	0	0	0	0	0	0	0	0	1	0
1968	CHI	AL	2	0	2	0	1	0	1	0	0	0	0	0	0	0	2	0
1969	CAL	AL	2	0	2	1	0	1	0	0	0	0	0	0	0	0	1	1
1970	CAL	AL	3	1	2	2	0	0	1	0	0	0	0	0	0	0	3	0
1971	MIL	AL	10	7	3	8	2	0	0	0	0	0	0	0	0	0	9	1
1972	OAK	AL	1	0	1	1	0	0	0	0	0	0	0	0	0	0	1	0
Total			19	8	11	13	3	1	2	0	0	0	0	0	0	0	17	2

Rank among batters: 1,861 • *Top target (3 home runs)*: Denny McLain • *Number of pitchers victimized*: 16 • *Total ballparks homered in*: 6 • *First HR*: 09/21/1965 off Denny McLain

George Vukovich

GEORGE STEPHEN VUKOVICH
B: 06/24/1956
BL

Year	Tm	Lg	Tot	H	A	Men-On 0	Men-On 1	Men-On 2	Men-On 3	One-Game 2	One-Game 3	One-Game 4	LO	XN	IP	PH	RHP	LHP
1981	PHI	NL	1	0	1	0	1	0	0	0	0	0	0	0	0	1	1	0
1982	PHI	NL	6	3	3	2	2	2	0	0	0	0	0	0	0	0	6	0
1983	CLE	AL	3	3	0	1	1	0	1	0	0	0	0	0	0	0	2	1
1984	CLE	AL	9	4	5	4	3	2	0	1	0	0	0	0	0	0	9	0
1985	CLE	AL	8	4	4	2	4	1	1	0	0	0	0	0	0	0	8	0
Total			27	14	13	9	11	5	2	1	0	0	0	0	0	1	26	1

Rank among batters: 1,532 • *Top target (4 home runs)*: Dan Petry • *Number of pitchers victimized*: 24 • *Total ballparks homered in*: 11 • *First HR*: 06/06/1981 off John Montefusco • *LCS HR*—1

John Vukovich

JOHN CHRISTOPHER VUKOVICH
B: 07/31/1947
BR

Year	Tm	Lg	Tot	H	A	Men-On 0	Men-On 1	Men-On 2	Men-On 3	One-Game 2	One-Game 3	One-Game 4	LO	XN	IP	PH	RHP	LHP
1973	MIL	AL	2	2	0	0	1	1	0	0	0	0	0	0	0	0	1	1
1974	MIL	AL	3	2	1	1	2	0	0	0	0	0	0	0	0	0	1	2
1976	PHI	NL	1	1	0	1	0	0	0	0	0	0	0	0	0	0	0	1
Total			6	5	1	2	3	1	0	0	0	0	0	0	0	0	2	4

Rank among batters: 2,988 • *Total ballparks homered in*: 3 • *First HR*: 04/22/1973 off Sparky Lyle

Rube Waddell

GEORGE EDWARD WADDELL
B: 10/13/1876 D: 04/01/1914
BR HOF

Year	Tm	Lg	Tot	H	A	Men-On 0	Men-On 1	Men-On 2	Men-On 3	One-Game 2	One-Game 3	One-Game 4	LO	XN	IP	PH	RHP	LHP
1901	CHI	NL	2	1	1	0	1	1	0	0	0	0	0	0	0	0	1	1
1902	PHI	AL	1	1	0	1	0	0	0	0	0	0	0	0	0	0	0	1
1908	STL	AL	1	1	0	0	0	1	0	0	0	0	0	0	0	0	1	0
Total			4	3	1	1	1	2	0	0	0	0	0	0	0	0	2	2

Rank among batters: 3,427 • *Total ballparks homered in*: 4 • *First HR*: 05/10/1901 off Cowboy Jones

Ben Wade

BENJAMIN STYRON WADE
B: 11/26/1922
BR

Year	Tm	Lg	Tot	H	A	Men-On 0	Men-On 1	Men-On 2	Men-On 3	One-Game 2	One-Game 3	One-Game 4	LO	XN	IP	PH	RHP	LHP
1952	BRO	NL	3	1	2	2	1	0	0	1	0	0	0	0	0	0	1	2
1953	BRO	NL	1	0	1	0	1	0	0	0	0	0	0	0	0	0	1	0
Total			4	1	3	2	2	0	0	1	0	0	0	0	0	0	2	2

Rank among batters: 3,427 • *Top target (2 home runs)*: Warren Spahn • *Number of pitchers victimized*: 3 • *Total ballparks homered in*: 3 • *First HR*: 05/13/1952 off Cloyd Boyer

Gale Wade

GALEARD LEE WADE
B: 01/20/1929
BL

Year	Tm	Lg	Tot	H	A	Men-On 0	Men-On 1	Men-On 2	Men-On 3	One-Game 2	One-Game 3	One-Game 4	LO	XN	IP	PH	RHP	LHP
1955	CHI	NL	1	0	1	1	0	0	0	0	0	0	0	0	0	0	1	0

Rank among batters: 4,707 • *Total ballparks homered in*: 1 • *First HR*: 09/21/1955 off Willard Schmidt

Rip Wade

RICHARD FRANK WADE
B: 01/12/1898 D: 06/16/1957
BL

Year	Tm	Lg	Tot	H	A	Men-On 0	Men-On 1	Men-On 2	Men-On 3	One-Game 2	One-Game 3	One-Game 4	LO	XN	IP	PH	RHP	LHP
1923	WAS	AL	2	1	1	1	0	1	0	0	0	0	0	0	0	0	2	0

Rank among batters: 4,129 • *Total ballparks homered in*: 2 • *First HR*: 05/04/1923 off Alex Ferguson

Bill Wagner

WILLIAM JOSEPH WAGNER
B: 01/02/1894 D: 01/11/1951
BR

Year	Tm	Lg	Tot	H	A	Men-On 0	Men-On 1	Men-On 2	Men-On 3	One-Game 2	One-Game 3	One-Game 4	LO	XN	IP	PH	RHP	LHP
1918	BOS	NL	1	0	1	1	0	0	0	0	0	0	0	0	0	0	1	0

Rank among batters: 4,707 • *Total ballparks homered in*: 1 • *First HR*: 08/31/1918 off Mike Prendergast

Butts Wagner

ALBERT WAGNER
B: 09/17/1869 D: 11/26/1928
BR

Year	Tm	Lg	Tot	H	A	Men-On 0	Men-On 1	Men-On 2	Men-On 3	One-Game 2	One-Game 3	One-Game 4	LO	XN	IP	PH	RHP	LHP
1898	WAS	NL	1	1	0	0	1	0	0	0	0	0	0	0	0	0	1	0

Rank among batters: 4,707 • *Total ballparks homered in*: 1 • *First HR*: 07/04/1898 off Joe Yeager

Hal Wagner

HAROLD EDWARD WAGNER
B: 07/02/1915 D: 08/04/1979
BL

Year	Tm	Lg	Tot	H	A	Men-On 0	Men-On 1	Men-On 2	Men-On 3	One-Game 2	One-Game 3	One-Game 4	LO	XN	IP	PH	RHP	LHP
1941	PHI	AL	1	1	0	1	0	0	0	0	0	0	0	0	0	0	0	1
1942	PHI	AL	1	0	1	1	0	0	0	0	0	0	0	0	0	0	1	0
1943	PHI	AL	1	1	0	0	1	0	0	0	0	0	0	0	0	1	1	0
1944	BOS	AL	1	0	1	0	1	0	0	0	0	0	0	0	0	0	1	0
1946	BOS	AL	6	4	2	4	0	2	0	1	0	0	0	0	1	0	6	0
1947	DET	AL	5	4	1	2	3	0	0	0	0	0	0	0	0	0	5	0
Total			15	10	5	8	5	2	0	1	0	0	0	0	1	1	14	1

Rank among batters: 2,096 • *Total ballparks homered in*: 7 • *First HR*: 09/28/1941 off Earl Johnson

Heinie Wagner

CHARLES F. WAGNER
B: 09/23/1880 D: 03/20/1943
BR

Year	Tm	Lg	Tot	H	A	Men-On 0	Men-On 1	Men-On 2	Men-On 3	One-Game 2	One-Game 3	One-Game 4	LO	XN	IP	PH	RHP	LHP
1907	BOS	AL	2	0	2	2	0	0	0	1	0	0	0	0	2	0	2	0
1908	BOS	AL	1	0	1	0	0	1	0	0	0	0	0	0	1	0	0	1
1909	BOS	AL	1	1	0	0	0	1	0	0	0	0	0	0	0	0	1	0
1910	BOS	AL	1	1	0	1	0	0	0	0	0	0	0	0	1	0	0	1
1911	BOS	AL	1	0	1	0	0	1	0	0	0	0	0	0	0	0	0	1
1912	BOS	AL	2	1	1	1	0	1	0	0	0	0	0	0	2	0	2	0
1913	BOS	AL	2	1	1	2	0	0	0	0	0	0	0	0	2	0	2	0
Total			10	4	6	6	0	4	0	1	0	0	0	0	8	0	7	3

Rank among batters: 2,500 • *Top target (2 home runs)*: Bill Donovan • *Number of pitchers victimized*: 9 • *Total ballparks homered in*: 5 • *First HR*: 08/22/1907 off Bill Donovan

Honus Wagner

JOHN PETER WAGNER
B: 02/24/1874 D: 12/06/1955
BR HOF

Year	Tm	Lg	Tot	H	A	Men-On 0	Men-On 1	Men-On 2	Men-On 3	One-Game 2	One-Game 3	One-Game 4	LO	XN	IP	PH	RHP	LHP
1897	LOU	NL	2	1	1	0	2	0	0	0	0	0	0	0	1	0	2	0
1898	LOU	NL	10	7	3	3	4	2	1	0	0	0	0	0	6	0	8	2
1899	LOU	NL	7	5	2	5	2	0	0	2	0	0	0	0	3	0	4	3
1900	PIT	NL	4	2	2	2	0	2	0	0	0	0	0	0	3	0	3	1
1901	PIT	NL	6	4	2	1	4	0	1	0	0	0	0	0	5	0	3	3
1902	PIT	NL	3	0	3	1	2	0	0	0	0	0	0	1	3	0	0	3
1903	PIT	NL	5	0	5	3	1	1	0	0	0	0	0	0	0	0	4	1
1904	PIT	NL	4	3	1	2	2	0	0	0	0	0	0	0	3	0	3	1
1905	PIT	NL	6	1	5	2	3	1	0	0	0	0	0	0	1	0	5	1
1906	PIT	NL	2	1	1	1	0	1	0	0	0	0	0	0	1	0	1	1
1907	PIT	NL	6	0	6	2	4	0	0	0	0	0	0	0	1	0	3	3
1908	PIT	NL	10	4	6	4	5	1	0	0	0	0	0	1	2	0	8	2

Honus Wagner *continued*

Year	Tm	Lg	Tot	H	A	Men-On 0	Men-On 1	Men-On 2	Men-On 3	One-Game 2	One-Game 3	One-Game 4	LO	XN	IP	PH	RHP	LHP
1909	PIT	NL	5	3	2	2	2	0	1	0	0	0	0	0	1	0	4	1
1910	PIT	NL	4	2	2	2	2	0	0	0	0	0	0	0	0	0	4	0
1911	PIT	NL	9	3	6	3	2	3	1	0	0	0	0	0	3	0	7	2
1912	PIT	NL	7	4	3	3	3	1	0	0	0	0	0	0	3	0	1	6
1913	PIT	NL	3	0	3	1	1	1	0	0	0	0	0	0	1	0	1	2
1914	PIT	NL	1	0	1	0	1	0	0	0	0	0	0	0	0	0	1	0
1915	PIT	NL	6	2	4	3	1	1	1	0	0	0	0	0	3	0	4	2
1916	PIT	NL	1	0	1	1	0	0	0	0	0	0	0	0	1	0	1	0
Total			101	42	59	41	41	14	5	2	0	0	0	2	41	0	67	34

Rank among batters: 491 • *Top target (4 home runs)*: Rube Marquard • *Number of pitchers victimized*: 78 • *Total ballparks homered in*: 15 • *First HR*: 08/27/1897 off Jack Dunn • *Hit for Cycle*—vs NY: 08/22/1912 (2)

Leon Wagner

LEON LAMAR WAGNER
B: 05/13/1934
BL

Year	Tm	Lg	Tot	H	A	Men-On 0	Men-On 1	Men-On 2	Men-On 3	One-Game 2	One-Game 3	One-Game 4	LO	XN	IP	PH	RHP	LHP
1958	SF	NL	13	9	4	8	5	0	0	1	0	0	0	0	0	0	13	0
1959	SF	NL	5	4	1	2	1	1	1	0	0	0	0	0	0	1	5	0
1960	STL	NL	4	2	2	4	0	0	0	1	0	0	0	0	0	0	3	1
1961	LA	AL	28	19	9	16	9	2	1	3	0	0	0	0	0	1	27	1
1962	LA	AL	37	13	24	20	15	2	0	4	0	0	0	2	0	1	32	5
1963	LA	AL	26	2	24	13	9	4	0	5	0	0	0	0	0	0	16	10
1964	CLE	AL	31	15	16	17	8	5	1	1	0	0	0	0	0	0	19	12
1965	CLE	AL	28	14	14	17	9	2	0	1	0	0	0	2	0	2	23	5
1966	CLE	AL	23	13	10	18	3	2	0	1	0	0	0	2	0	0	16	7
1967	CLE	AL	15	8	7	7	6	1	1	0	0	0	0	0	0	0	13	2
1968	CHI	AL	1	1	0	0	1	0	0	0	0	0	0	0	0	0	0	1
Total			211	100	111	122	66	19	4	17	0	0	0	6	0	5	167	44

Rank among batters: 162 • *Top target (6 home runs)*: Bill Monbouquette, Ralph Terry, Mudcat Grant • *Number of pitchers victimized*: 130 • *Total ballparks homered in*: 17 • *First HR*: 07/06/1958 off Jim Brosnan • *All-Star HR*—1

Mark Wagner

MARK DUANE WAGNER
B: 03/04/1954
BR

Year	Tm	Lg	Tot	H	A	Men-On 0	Men-On 1	Men-On 2	Men-On 3	One-Game 2	One-Game 3	One-Game 4	LO	XN	IP	PH	RHP	LHP
1977	DET	AL	1	1	0	1	0	0	0	0	0	0	0	0	0	0	0	1
1979	DET	AL	1	1	0	0	0	1	0	0	0	0	0	0	0	0	1	0
1981	TEX	AL	1	1	0	0	1	0	0	0	0	0	0	1	0	0	0	1
Total			3	3	0	1	1	1	0	0	0	0	0	1	0	0	1	2

Rank among batters: 3,735 • *Total ballparks homered in*: 2 • *First HR*: 05/11/1977 off Geoff Zahn

Kermit Wahl

KERMIT EMERSON WAHL
B: 11/18/1922 D: 09/16/1987
BR

Year	Tm	Lg	Tot	H	A	Men-On 0	Men-On 1	Men-On 2	Men-On 3	One-Game 2	One-Game 3	One-Game 4	LO	XN	IP	PH	RHP	LHP
1947	CIN	NL	1	0	1	0	1	0	0	0	0	0	0	0	0	0	0	1
1950	PHI	AL	2	2	0	1	1	0	0	0	0	0	0	0	0	0	1	1
Total			3	2	1	1	2	0	0	0	0	0	0	0	0	0	1	2

Rank among batters: 3,735 • *Total ballparks homered in*: 2 • *First HR*: 06/27/1947 off Howie Pollet

Eddie Waitkus

EDWARD STEPHEN WAITKUS
B: 09/04/1919 D: 09/15/1972
BL

Year	Tm	Lg	Tot	H	A	Men-On 0	Men-On 1	Men-On 2	Men-On 3	One-Game 2	One-Game 3	One-Game 4	LO	XN	IP	PH	RHP	LHP
1946	CHI	NL	4	1	3	2	2	0	0	0	0	0	0	0	3	0	3	1
1947	CHI	NL	2	1	1	0	1	0	1	0	0	0	0	0	1	0	1	1
1948	CHI	NL	7	2	5	1	4	2	0	0	0	0	0	0	1	0	7	0
1949	PHI	NL	1	0	1	1	0	0	0	0	0	0	0	0	0	0	1	0
1950	PHI	NL	2	0	2	1	1	0	0	0	0	0	1	0	0	0	2	0
1951	PHI	NL	1	0	1	1	0	0	0	0	0	0	0	0	0	0	1	0
1952	PHI	NL	2	0	2	2	0	0	0	0	0	0	0	0	0	0	2	0
1953	PHI	NL	1	1	0	0	1	0	0	0	0	0	0	0	0	0	1	0

Eddie Waitkus *continued*

Year	Tm	Lg	Tot	H	A	Men-On 0	Men-On 1	Men-On 2	Men-On 3	One-Game 2	One-Game 3	One-Game 4	LO	XN	IP	PH	RHP	LHP
1954	BAL	AL	2	1	1	2	0	0	0	0	0	0	0	0	0	0	1	1
1955	PHI	NL	2	0	2	1	0	1	0	0	0	0	0	0	0	0	2	0
Total			24	6	18	11	9	3	1	0	0	0	1	0	5	0	21	3

Rank among batters: 1,643 • *Top target (2 home runs)*: Bill Voiselle, Larry Jansen • *Number of pitchers victimized*: 22 • *Total ballparks homered in*: 10 • *First HR*: 06/22/1946 off Bill Voiselle

Dick Wakefield

RICHARD CUMMINGS WAKEFIELD
B: 05/06/1921 D: 08/26/1985
BL

Year	Tm	Lg	Tot	H	A	Men-On 0	Men-On 1	Men-On 2	Men-On 3	One-Game 2	One-Game 3	One-Game 4	LO	XN	IP	PH	RHP	LHP
1943	DET	AL	7	4	3	3	2	2	0	0	0	0	0	0	0	0	7	0
1944	DET	AL	12	9	3	7	3	1	1	0	0	0	0	0	2	0	11	1
1946	DET	AL	12	6	6	9	1	2	0	0	0	0	0	0	0	0	9	3
1947	DET	AL	8	5	3	5	3	0	0	0	0	0	0	0	0	0	6	2
1948	DET	AL	11	5	6	6	3	2	0	0	0	0	0	0	0	3	10	1
1949	DET	AL	6	5	1	4	1	1	0	0	0	0	0	0	0	1	5	1
Total			56	34	22	34	13	8	1	0	0	0	0	0	2	4	48	8

Rank among batters: 913 • *Top target (3 home runs)*: Mel Queen, Eddie Lopat, Bob Lemon • *Number of pitchers victimized*: 42 • *Total ballparks homered in*: 9 • *First HR*: 06/23/1943 off Vern Kennedy

Howard Wakefield

HOWARD JOHN WAKEFIELD
B: 04/02/1884 D: 04/16/1941
BR

Year	Tm	Lg	Tot	H	A	Men-On 0	Men-On 1	Men-On 2	Men-On 3	One-Game 2	One-Game 3	One-Game 4	LO	XN	IP	PH	RHP	LHP
1906	WAS	AL	1	0	1	0	0	1	0	0	0	0	0	0	0	0	1	0

Rank among batters: 4,707 • *Total ballparks homered in*: 1 • *First HR*: 09/08/1906 off Ralph Glaze

Tim Wakefield

TIMOTHY STEPHEN WAKEFIELD
B: 08/02/1966
BR

Year	Tm	Lg	Tot	H	A	Men-On 0	Men-On 1	Men-On 2	Men-On 3	One-Game 2	One-Game 3	One-Game 4	LO	XN	IP	PH	RHP	LHP
1993	PIT	NL	1	0	1	1	0	0	0	0	0	0	0	0	0	0	1	0

Rank among batters: 4,707 • *Total ballparks homered in*: 1 • *First HR*: 07/07/1993 off Mark Portugal

Matt Walbeck

MATTHEW LOVICK WALBECK
B: 10/02/1969
BB

Year	Tm	Lg	Tot	H	A	Men-On 0	Men-On 1	Men-On 2	Men-On 3	One-Game 2	One-Game 3	One-Game 4	LO	XN	IP	PH	RHP	LHP
1993	CHI	NL	1	1	0	0	1	0	0	0	0	0	0	1	0	0	1	0
1994	MIN	AL	5	0	5	3	1	0	1	0	0	0	0	0	0	0	4	1
1995	MIN	AL	1	1	0	1	0	0	0	0	0	0	0	0	0	0	1	0
Total			7	2	5	4	2	0	1	0	0	0	0	1	0	0	6	1

Rank among batters: 2,834 • *Total ballparks homered in*: 6 • *First HR*: 04/18/1993 off Jose DeLeon

Rube Walberg

GEORGE ELVIN WALBERG
B: 07/27/1896 D: 10/27/1978
BL

Year	Tm	Lg	Tot	H	A	Men-On 0	Men-On 1	Men-On 2	Men-On 3	One-Game 2	One-Game 3	One-Game 4	LO	XN	IP	PH	RHP	LHP
1927	PHI	AL	2	0	2	1	1	0	0	0	0	0	0	0	0	0	1	1
1928	PHI	AL	1	0	1	1	0	0	0	0	0	0	0	0	0	0	1	0
1929	PHI	AL	1	0	1	1	0	0	0	0	0	0	0	0	0	0	1	0
Total			4	0	4	3	1	0	0	0	0	0	0	0	0	0	3	1

Rank among batters: 3,427 • *Total ballparks homered in*: 4 • *First HR*: 05/21/1927 off Ted Lyons

Jim Walewander

JAMES WALEWANDER
B: 05/02/1962
BB

Year	Tm	Lg	Tot	H	A	Men-On 0	Men-On 1	Men-On 2	Men-On 3	One-Game 2	One-Game 3	One-Game 4	LO	XN	IP	PH	RHP	LHP
1987	DET	AL	1	1	0	0	1	0	0	0	0	0	0	0	0	0	1	0

Rank among batters: 4,707 • *Total ballparks homered in*: 1 • *First HR*: 07/26/1987 off Willie Fraser

Bob Walk

ROBERT VERNON WALK
B: 11/26/1956
BR

Year	Tm	Lg	Tot	H	A	Men-On 0	Men-On 1	Men-On 2	Men-On 3	One-Game 2	One-Game 3	One-Game 4	LO	XN	IP	PH	RHP	LHP
1991	PIT	NL	1	0	1	1	0	0	0	0	0	0	0	0	0	0	0	1

Rank among batters: 4,707 • *Total ballparks homered in*: 1 • *First HR*: 04/14/1991 off Danny Jackson

Bill Walker

WILLIAM HENRY WALKER
B: 10/07/1903 D: 06/14/1966
BR

Year	Tm	Lg	Tot	H	A	Men-On 0	Men-On 1	Men-On 2	Men-On 3	One-Game 2	One-Game 3	One-Game 4	LO	XN	IP	PH	RHP	LHP
1929	NY	NL	1	1	0	1	0	0	0	0	0	0	0	0	0	0	1	0
1930	NY	NL	2	0	2	0	1	0	1	0	0	0	0	0	0	0	1	1
1933	STL	NL	1	0	1	1	0	0	0	0	0	0	0	0	0	0	1	0
Total			4	1	3	2	1	0	1	0	0	0	0	0	0	0	3	1

Rank among batters: 3,427 • *Total ballparks homered in*: 3 • *First HR*: 07/14/1929 off Jesse Haines

Chico Walker

CLEOTHA WALKER
B: 11/25/1957
BB

Year	Tm	Lg	Tot	H	A	Men-On 0	Men-On 1	Men-On 2	Men-On 3	One-Game 2	One-Game 3	One-Game 4	LO	XN	IP	PH	RHP	LHP
1980	BOS	AL	1	1	0	1	0	0	0	0	0	0	0	0	0	0	1	0
1986	CHI	NL	1	0	1	1	0	0	0	0	0	0	0	0	0	0	1	0
1991	CHI	NL	6	4	2	2	3	0	1	1	0	0	1	0	1	1	3	3
1992	NY	NL	4	0	4	2	0	2	0	0	0	0	1	0	0	0	4	0
1993	NY	NL	5	1	4	2	1	2	0	0	0	0	0	0	0	1	3	2
Total			17	6	11	8	4	4	1	1	0	0	2	0	1	2	12	5

Rank among batters: 1,969 • *Top target (2 home runs)*: Mark Gardner, Matt Turner • *Number of pitchers victimized*: 15 • *Total ballparks homered in*: 10 • *First HR*: 09/07/1980 off Manny Sarmiento

Curt Walker

WILLIAM CURTIS WALKER
B: 07/03/1896 D: 12/09/1955
BL

Year	Tm	Lg	Tot	H	A	Men-On 0	Men-On 1	Men-On 2	Men-On 3	One-Game 2	One-Game 3	One-Game 4	LO	XN	IP	PH	RHP	LHP
1921	NY	NL	3	2	1	2	1	0	0	0	0	0	0	1	0	0	3	0
1922	PHI	NL	12	10	2	7	2	3	0	0	0	0	0	0	0	0	10	2
1923	PHI	NL	5	4	1	3	1	1	0	0	0	0	0	0	0	0	3	2
1924	PHI	NL	1	0	1	0	1	0	0	0	0	0	0	0	0	0	1	0
	CIN	NL	4	0	4	2	2	0	0	1	0	0	0	0	0	0	4	0
	Total		5	0	5	2	3	0	0	1	0	0	0	0	0	0	5	0
1925	CIN	NL	6	3	3	3	3	0	0	0	0	0	0	1	2	0	4	2
1926	CIN	NL	6	1	5	3	1	2	0	1	0	0	0	0	1	0	6	0
1927	CIN	NL	6	0	6	5	1	0	0	0	0	0	0	0	1	0	6	0
1928	CIN	NL	6	0	6	3	2	1	0	1	0	0	0	1	0	0	6	0
1929	CIN	NL	7	2	5	3	2	1	1	0	0	0	0	0	1	0	7	0
1930	CIN	NL	8	2	6	4	3	1	0	0	0	0	1	0	0	1	8	0
Total			64	24	40	35	19	9	1	3	0	0	1	3	5	1	58	6

Rank among batters: 815 • *Top target (4 home runs)*: Grover Alexander, Flint Rhem • *Number of pitchers victimized*: 47 • *Total ballparks homered in*: 8 • *First HR*: 05/01/1921 off Hugh McQuillan

Dixie Walker

FRED WALKER
B: 09/24/1910 D: 05/17/1982
BL

Year	Tm	Lg	Tot	H	A	Men-On 0	Men-On 1	Men-On 2	Men-On 3	One-Game 2	One-Game 3	One-Game 4	LO	XN	IP	PH	RHP	LHP
1933	NY	AL	15	10	5	8	4	3	0	0	0	0	2	0	0	1	13	2
1936	NY	AL	1	1	0	0	0	1	0	0	0	0	0	0	0	0	1	0
1937	CHI	AL	9	5	4	3	2	4	0	0	0	0	0	1	0	0	9	0
1938	DET	AL	6	4	2	4	2	0	0	0	0	0	0	0	0	0	5	1
1939	DET	AL	4	2	2	1	3	0	0	0	0	0	0	0	0	0	4	0
	BRO	NL	2	1	1	1	1	0	0	0	0	0	0	0	0	0	2	0
	Total		6	3	3	2	4	0	0	0	0	0	0	0	0	0	6	0
1940	BRO	NL	6	3	3	4	1	0	1	0	0	0	0	0	0	0	5	1
1941	BRO	NL	9	7	2	7	0	1	1	1	0	0	1	0	0	0	7	2
1942	BRO	NL	6	2	4	2	2	1	1	1	0	0	0	0	1	0	6	0
1943	BRO	NL	5	3	2	2	3	0	0	1	0	0	0	0	0	0	4	1
1944	BRO	NL	13	7	6	7	3	3	0	0	0	0	0	0	0	0	11	2

Dixie Walker *continued*

Year	Tm	Lg	Tot	H	A	Men-On 0	1	2	3	One-Game 2	3	4	LO	XN	IP	PH	RHP	LHP
1945	BRO	NL	8	6	2	2	1	4	1	0	0	0	0	0	0	0	8	0
1946	BRO	NL	9	3	6	4	4	1	0	0	0	0	0	0	0	1	8	1
1947	BRO	NL	9	3	6	3	5	1	0	0	0	0	0	1	0	0	6	3
1948	PIT	NL	2	1	1	1	1	0	0	0	0	0	0	0	0	0	2	0
1949	PIT	NL	1	0	1	0	1	0	0	0	0	0	0	0	0	1	1	0
Total			105	58	47	49	33	19	4	3	0	0	3	2	1	3	92	13

Rank among batters: 462 • *Top target (5 home runs)*: Rip Sewell • *Number of pitchers victimized*: 81 • *Total ballparks homered in*: 12 • *First HR*: 06/11/1933 off Johnny Welch • *Hit for Cycle*—vs NY: 09/02/1944 • *World Series HR*—1

Duane Walker

DUANE ALLEN WALKER
B: 03/13/1957
BL

Year	Tm	Lg	Tot	H	A	Men-On 0	1	2	3	One-Game 2	3	4	LO	XN	IP	PH	RHP	LHP
1982	CIN	NL	5	3	2	3	2	0	0	1	0	0	0	0	0	0	5	0
1983	CIN	NL	2	1	1	2	0	0	0	0	0	0	0	0	0	0	2	0
1984	CIN	NL	10	6	4	6	3	1	0	0	0	0	0	0	0	1	10	0
1985	CIN	NL	2	1	1	0	2	0	0	0	0	0	0	0	0	1	2	0
	TEX	AL	5	3	2	4	1	0	0	0	0	0	0	0	0	0	5	0
	Total		7	4	3	4	3	0	0	0	0	0	0	0	0	1	7	0
Total			24	14	10	15	8	1	0	1	0	0	0	0	0	2	24	0

Rank among batters: 1,643 • *Top target (3 home runs)*: Nolan Ryan • *Number of pitchers victimized*: 18 • *Total ballparks homered in*: 10 • *First HR*: 07/05/1982 off Bob Forsch

Ernie Walker

ERNEST ROBERT WALKER
B: 09/17/1890 D: 04/01/1965
BL

Year	Tm	Lg	Tot	H	A	Men-On 0	1	2	3	One-Game 2	3	4	LO	XN	IP	PH	RHP	LHP
1914	STL	AL	1	1	0	1	0	0	0	0	0	0	0	0	0	0	0	1

Rank among batters: 4,707 • *Total ballparks homered in*: 1 • *First HR*: 06/09/1914 off Joe Engel

Frank Walker

CHARLES FRANKLIN WALKER
B: 09/22/1894 D: 09/16/1974
BR

Year	Tm	Lg	Tot	H	A	Men-On 0	1	2	3	One-Game 2	3	4	LO	XN	IP	PH	RHP	LHP
1918	DET	AL	1	0	1	0	0	1	0	0	0	0	0	0	0	0	0	1
1921	PHI	AL	1	0	1	1	0	0	0	0	0	0	0	0	0	0	1	0
1925	NY	NL	1	1	0	1	0	0	0	0	0	0	0	0	0	0	1	0
Total			3	1	2	2	0	1	0	0	0	0	0	0	0	0	2	1

Rank among batters: 3,735 • *Total ballparks homered in*: 2 • *First HR*: 07/18/1918 off Hank Thormahlen

Gee Walker

GERALD HOLMES WALKER
B: 03/19/1908 D: 03/20/1981
BR

Year	Tm	Lg	Tot	H	A	Men-On 0	1	2	3	One-Game 2	3	4	LO	XN	IP	PH	RHP	LHP
1931	DET	AL	1	0	1	0	0	1	0	0	0	0	0	0	0	0	1	0
1932	DET	AL	8	3	5	5	3	0	0	0	0	0	0	0	0	1	5	3
1933	DET	AL	9	2	7	4	4	1	0	1	0	0	0	1	0	0	6	3
1934	DET	AL	6	2	4	3	2	1	0	0	0	0	0	0	0	0	4	2
1935	DET	AL	7	4	3	6	1	0	0	1	0	0	0	0	0	0	3	4
1936	DET	AL	12	5	7	4	3	5	0	1	0	0	0	0	0	0	12	0
1937	DET	AL	18	15	3	8	7	2	1	2	0	0	1	0	0	0	15	3
1938	CHI	AL	16	5	11	7	7	2	0	0	0	0	0	0	0	0	14	2
1939	CHI	AL	13	9	4	4	7	2	0	0	0	0	0	0	0	0	12	1
1940	WAS	AL	13	5	8	5	6	2	0	1	0	0	0	0	0	0	8	5
1941	CLE	AL	6	2	4	5	1	0	0	0	0	0	0	0	1	0	2	4
1942	CIN	NL	5	1	4	3	0	1	1	0	0	0	0	0	0	0	4	1
1943	CIN	NL	3	3	0	1	2	0	0	0	0	0	0	0	0	0	3	0
1944	CIN	NL	5	3	2	2	1	1	1	0	0	0	0	0	0	0	5	0
1945	CIN	NL	2	2	0	1	1	0	0	0	0	0	0	0	0	0	2	0
Total			124	61	63	58	45	18	3	6	0	0	1	1	1	1	96	28

Rank among batters: 370 • *Top target (5 home runs)*: Lefty Gomez • *Number of pitchers victimized*: 81 • *Total ballparks homered in*: 13 • *First HR*: 09/04/1931 off Ted Lyons • *Hit for Cycle*—vs CLE: 04/20/1937

Year	Tm	Lg	Tot	H	A	Men-On 0	1	2	3	One-Game 2	3	4	LO	XN	IP	PH	RHP	LHP

Greg Walker

GREGORY LEE WALKER
B: 10/06/1959
BL

Year	Tm	Lg	Tot	H	A	Men-On 0	1	2	3	One-Game 2	3	4	LO	XN	IP	PH	RHP	LHP
1982	CHI	AL	2	1	1	2	0	0	0	0	0	0	0	0	0	0	2	0
1983	CHI	AL	10	4	6	6	3	1	0	0	0	0	0	1	0	1	10	0
1984	CHI	AL	24	16	8	10	6	8	0	3	0	0	0	0	0	0	22	2
1985	CHI	AL	24	11	13	12	9	3	0	0	0	0	0	1	0	0	20	4
1986	CHI	AL	13	6	7	6	3	3	1	1	0	0	0	0	0	1	11	2
1987	CHI	AL	27	12	15	14	11	1	1	1	0	0	0	1	0	0	14	13
1988	CHI	AL	8	2	6	6	1	1	0	0	0	0	0	1	0	0	7	1
1989	CHI	AL	5	4	1	5	0	0	0	0	0	0	0	0	0	0	5	0
Total			113	56	57	61	33	17	2	5	0	0	0	3	0	2	91	22

Rank among batters: 421 • *Top target (6 home runs)*: Dan Petry • *Number of pitchers victimized*: 76 • *Total ballparks homered in*: 14 • *First HR*: 09/27/1982 off Bob Stoddard

Harry Walker

HARRY WILLIAM WALKER
B: 10/22/1916
BL

Year	Tm	Lg	Tot	H	A	Men-On 0	1	2	3	One-Game 2	3	4	LO	XN	IP	PH	RHP	LHP
1943	STL	NL	2	1	1	0	2	0	0	0	0	0	0	1	1	0	2	0
1946	STL	NL	3	2	1	1	2	0	0	0	0	0	0	0	0	0	2	1
1947	PHI	NL	1	0	1	0	0	1	0	0	0	0	0	0	0	0	1	0
1948	PHI	NL	2	0	2	0	1	1	0	0	0	0	0	0	1	0	2	0
1949	CHI	NL	1	0	1	0	1	0	0	0	0	0	0	0	0	0	1	0
	CIN	NL	1	1	0	0	1	0	0	0	0	0	0	0	0	0	1	0
	Total		2	1	1	0	2	0	0	0	0	0	0	0	0	0	2	0
Total			10	4	6	1	7	2	0	0	0	0	0	1	2	0	9	1

Rank among batters: 2,500 • *Total ballparks homered in*: 5 • *First HR*: 06/01/1943 off Rube Melton

Hub Walker

HARVEY WILLOS WALKER
B: 08/17/1906 D: 11/26/1982
BL

Year	Tm	Lg	Tot	H	A	Men-On 0	1	2	3	One-Game 2	3	4	LO	XN	IP	PH	RHP	LHP
1936	CIN	NL	4	0	4	1	3	0	0	0	0	0	1	0	0	0	4	0
1937	CIN	NL	1	0	1	0	0	1	0	0	0	0	0	0	0	0	1	0
Total			5	0	5	1	3	1	0	0	0	0	1	0	0	0	5	0

Rank among batters: 3,191 • *Total ballparks homered in*: 4 • *First HR*: 07/26/1936 off Frank Gabler

Jerry Walker

JERRY ALLEN WALKER
B: 02/12/1939
BB

Year	Tm	Lg	Tot	H	A	Men-On 0	1	2	3	One-Game 2	3	4	LO	XN	IP	PH	RHP	LHP
1959	BAL	AL	1	1	0	1	0	0	0	0	0	0	0	0	0	0	0	1
1962	KC	AL	3	1	2	2	1	0	0	0	0	0	0	0	0	0	2	1
Total			4	2	2	3	1	0	0	0	0	0	0	0	0	0	2	2

Rank among batters: 3,427 • *Total ballparks homered in*: 4 • *First HR*: 06/18/1959 off Don Mossi

Johnny Walker

JOHN MILES WALKER
B: 12/11/1896 D: 08/19/1976
BR

Year	Tm	Lg	Tot	H	A	Men-On 0	1	2	3	One-Game 2	3	4	LO	XN	IP	PH	RHP	LHP
1921	PHI	AL	2	2	0	2	0	0	0	0	0	0	0	0	0	0	2	0

Rank among batters: 4,129 • *Total ballparks homered in*: 1 • *First HR*: 06/16/1921 off George Uhle

Larry Walker

LARRY KENNETH ROBERT WALKER
B: 12/01/1966
BL

Year	Tm	Lg	Tot	H	A	Men-On 0	1	2	3	One-Game 2	3	4	LO	XN	IP	PH	RHP	LHP
1990	MON	NL	19	9	10	12	5	2	0	0	0	0	0	0	0	0	13	6
1991	MON	NL	16	5	11	7	8	1	0	1	0	0	0	1	0	1	12	4
1992	MON	NL	23	13	10	13	8	2	0	2	0	0	0	1	1	0	13	10
1993	MON	NL	22	13	9	15	6	0	1	0	0	0	0	0	0	0	15	7
1994	MON	NL	19	7	12	9	6	4	0	1	0	0	0	1	0	0	15	4

Larry Walker *continued*

Year	Tm	Lg	Tot	H	A	Men-On 0	1	2	3	One-Game 2	3	4	LO	XN	IP	PH	RHP	LHP
1995	COL	NL	36	24	12	23	9	4	0	3	0	0	0	0	0	1	29	7
Total			135	71	64	79	42	13	1	7	0	0	0	3	1	2	97	38

Rank among batters: 326 • *Top target (4 home runs)*: John Burkett, Bob Tewksbury, Tom Candiotti • *Number of pitchers victimized*: 108 • *Total ballparks homered in*: 15 • *First HR*: 04/20/1990 off Ron Darling • *LCS HR*—1

Oscar Walker

OSCAR WALKER
B: 03/18/1854 D: 05/20/1889
BL

Year	Tm	Lg	Tot	H	A	Men-On 0	1	2	3	One-Game 2	3	4	LO	XN	IP	PH	RHP	LHP
1879	BUF	NL	1	0	1	1	0	0	0	0	0	0	0	0	0	0	1	0
1880	BUF	NL	1	0	1	0	1	0	0	0	0	0	0	0	0	0	1	0
1882	STL	AA	7	5	2	3	3	1	0	0	0	0	0	0	1	0	3	0
1884	BRO	AA	2	1	1	1	0	1	0	0	0	0	0	0	0	0	2	0
Total			11	6	5	5	4	2	0	0	0	0	0	0	1	0	6	0

Rank among batters: 2,419 • *Top target (2 home runs)*: Doc Landis, Tricky Nichols • *Number of pitchers victimized*: 9 • *Total ballparks homered in*: 6 • *First HR*: 08/11/1879 off Jim McCormick

Rube Walker

ALBERT BLUFORD WALKER
B: 05/16/1926 D: 12/12/1992
BL

Year	Tm	Lg	Tot	H	A	Men-On 0	1	2	3	One-Game 2	3	4	LO	XN	IP	PH	RHP	LHP
1948	CHI	NL	5	0	5	3	0	2	0	0	0	0	0	0	0	1	5	0
1949	CHI	NL	3	1	2	1	1	1	0	0	0	0	0	0	0	0	3	0
1950	CHI	NL	6	2	4	5	0	0	1	0	0	0	0	0	0	0	6	0
1951	CHI	NL	2	1	1	1	1	0	0	0	0	0	0	0	0	0	0	2
	BRO	NL	2	0	2	1	1	0	0	0	0	0	0	0	0	0	2	0
	Total		4	1	3	2	2	0	0	0	0	0	0	0	0	0	2	2
1952	BRO	NL	1	1	0	0	1	0	0	0	0	0	0	0	0	0	1	0
1953	BRO	NL	3	3	0	2	1	0	0	0	0	0	0	0	0	0	2	1
1954	BRO	NL	5	1	4	1	3	1	0	1	0	0	0	0	0	0	3	2
1955	BRO	NL	2	1	1	2	0	0	0	0	0	0	0	0	0	0	2	0
1956	BRO	NL	3	1	2	2	1	0	0	0	0	0	0	0	0	0	2	1
1957	BRO	NL	2	2	0	1	0	1	0	0	0	0	0	0	0	0	2	0
1958	LA	NL	1	0	1	0	0	1	0	0	0	0	0	0	0	1	1	0
Total			35	13	22	19	9	6	1	1	0	0	0	0	0	2	29	6

Rank among batters: 1,291 • *Top target (2 home runs)*: Murry Dickson, Warren Hacker • *Number of pitchers victimized*: 33 • *Total ballparks homered in*: 9 • *First HR*: 07/28/1948 off Blix Donnelly

Tilly Walker

CLARENCE WILLIAM WALKER
B: 09/04/1887 D: 09/21/1959
BR

Year	Tm	Lg	Tot	H	A	Men-On 0	1	2	3	One-Game 2	3	4	LO	XN	IP	PH	RHP	LHP
1911	WAS	AL	2	2	0	1	0	1	0	0	0	0	0	0	2	0	1	1
1914	STL	AL	6	3	3	3	2	1	0	1	0	0	0	1	0	0	4	2
1915	STL	AL	5	0	5	2	3	0	0	0	0	0	0	0	0	0	2	3
1916	BOS	AL	3	1	2	2	1	0	0	0	0	0	0	0	1	0	1	2
1917	BOS	AL	2	0	2	2	0	0	0	0	0	0	0	0	0	0	1	1
1918	PHI	AL	11	6	5	8	3	0	0	0	0	0	0	0	0	1	9	2
1919	PHI	AL	10	10	0	6	4	0	0	0	0	0	0	0	0	1	8	2
1920	PHI	AL	17	12	5	11	5	1	0	2	0	0	0	0	0	0	12	5
1921	PHI	AL	23	18	5	12	5	5	1	1	0	0	0	2	1	0	18	5
1922	PHI	AL	37	26	11	21	13	3	0	4	0	0	0	1	0	0	33	4
1923	PHI	AL	2	1	1	2	0	0	0	0	0	0	0	0	0	1	1	1
Total			118	79	39	70	36	11	1	8	0	0	0	4	4	3	90	28

Rank among batters: 396 • *Top target (11 home runs)*: Bob Shawkey • *Number of pitchers victimized*: 64 • *Total ballparks homered in*: 8 • *First HR*: 07/29/1911 off Cy Young

Tony Walker

ANTHONY BRUCE WALKER
B: 07/01/1959
BR

Year	Tm	Lg	Tot	H	A	Men-On 0	1	2	3	One-Game 2	3	4	LO	XN	IP	PH	RHP	LHP
1986	HOU	NL	2	2	0	1	1	0	0	0	0	0	0	0	0	0	0	2

Rank among batters: 4,129 • *Top target (2 home runs)*: Shane Rawley • *Number of pitchers victimized*: 1 • *Total ballparks homered in*: 1 • *First HR*: 05/12/1986 off Shane Rawley

Rhoderick Wallace

RHODERICK JOHN WALLACE
B: 11/04/1873 D: 11/03/1960
BR HOF

Year	Tm	Lg	Tot	H	A	Men-On 0	1	2	3	One-Game 2	3	4	LO	XN	IP	PH	RHP	LHP
1896	CLE	NL	1	0	1	0	0	1	0	0	0	0	0	0	0	0	1	0
1897	CLE	NL	4	2	2	2	1	0	1	0	0	0	0	0	3	0	2	2
1898	CLE	NL	3	1	2	0	1	2	0	0	0	0	0	0	2	0	3	0
1899	STL	NL	12	10	2	6	4	2	0	0	0	0	0	0	3	0	8	3
1900	STL	NL	4	3	1	2	2	0	0	0	0	0	0	0	0	0	2	2
1901	STL	NL	2	1	1	1	1	0	0	0	0	0	0	0	0	0	2	0
1902	STL	AL	1	1	0	0	1	0	0	0	0	0	0	0	1	0	1	0
1903	STL	AL	1	1	0	1	0	0	0	0	0	0	0	0	0	0	0	1
1904	STL	AL	2	0	2	0	1	1	0	0	0	0	0	0	2	0	1	1
1905	STL	AL	1	0	1	1	0	0	0	0	0	0	0	0	1	0	1	0
1906	STL	AL	2	0	2	1	1	0	0	0	0	0	0	0	2	0	2	0
1908	STL	AL	1	0	1	1	0	0	0	0	0	0	0	0	1	0	1	0
Total			34	19	15	15	12	6	1	0	0	0	0	0	15	0	24	9

Rank among batters: 1,315 • *Top target (2 home runs)*: Gus Weyhing, Sam Leever • *Number of pitchers victimized*: 32 • *Total ballparks homered in*: 14 • *First HR*: 09/04/1896 off George Harper

Tim Wallach

TIMOTHY CHARLES WALLACH
B: 09/14/1957
BR

Year	Tm	Lg	Tot	H	A	Men-On 0	1	2	3	One-Game 2	3	4	LO	XN	IP	PH	RHP	LHP
1980	MON	NL	1	0	1	1	0	0	0	0	0	0	0	0	0	0	0	1
1981	MON	NL	4	1	3	4	0	0	0	0	0	0	0	0	0	0	4	0
1982	MON	NL	28	11	17	11	9	6	2	3	0	0	0	2	0	1	15	13
1983	MON	NL	19	9	10	12	4	3	0	0	0	0	0	0	0	0	14	5
1984	MON	NL	18	4	14	8	6	4	0	0	0	0	0	0	0	0	11	7
1985	MON	NL	22	9	13	11	7	3	1	2	0	0	0	1	0	0	17	5
1986	MON	NL	18	6	12	11	4	3	0	2	0	0	0	2	0	0	15	3
1987	MON	NL	26	13	13	16	6	4	0	0	1	0	0	2	2	0	25	1
1988	MON	NL	12	3	9	10	1	1	0	0	0	0	0	1	0	0	8	4
1989	MON	NL	13	6	7	5	7	0	1	0	0	0	0	0	0	0	5	8
1990	MON	NL	21	9	12	10	5	5	1	2	0	0	0	0	0	0	15	6
1991	MON	NL	13	5	8	8	4	1	0	0	0	0	0	0	0	0	8	5
1992	MON	NL	9	5	4	5	3	1	0	0	0	0	0	0	0	0	2	7
1993	LA	NL	12	4	8	10	2	0	0	0	0	0	0	0	0	0	7	5
1994	LA	NL	23	7	16	6	13	4	0	2	0	0	0	0	0	0	15	8
1995	LA	NL	9	4	5	4	5	0	0	0	0	0	0	0	0	0	5	4
Total			248	96	152	132	76	35	5	11	1	0	0	8	2	1	166	82

Rank among batters: 112 • *Top target (5 home runs)*: Tom Glavine • *Number of pitchers victimized*: 183 • *Total ballparks homered in*: 14 • *First HR*: 09/06/1980 off Phil Nastu • *Hit HR in first major league AB—@SF*: 09/06/1980

Jack Wallaesa

JOHN WALLAESA
B: 08/31/1919 D: 12/27/1986
BB

Year	Tm	Lg	Tot	H	A	Men-On 0	1	2	3	One-Game 2	3	4	LO	XN	IP	PH	RHP	LHP
1942	PHI	AL	2	1	1	1	0	1	0	0	0	0	0	0	0	0	2	0
1946	PHI	AL	5	2	3	3	2	0	0	0	0	0	0	0	0	1	5	0
1947	CHI	AL	7	1	6	2	2	1	2	1	0	0	0	0	0	1	7	0
1948	CHI	AL	1	0	1	1	0	0	0	0	0	0	0	0	0	0	1	0
Total			15	4	11	7	4	2	2	1	0	0	0	0	0	2	15	0

Rank among batters: 2,096 • *Top target (2 home runs)*: Hal White, Don Black • *Number of pitchers victimized*: 13 • *Total ballparks homered in*: 8 • *First HR*: 05/04/1942 off Charlie Fuchs

Ty Waller

ELLIOTT TYRONE WALLER
B: 03/14/1957
BR

Year	Tm	Lg	Tot	H	A	Men-On 0	1	2	3	One-Game 2	3	4	LO	XN	IP	PH	RHP	LHP
1981	CHI	NL	3	3	0	1	1	1	0	0	0	0	0	0	0	0	2	1

Rank among batters: 3,735 • *Total ballparks homered in*: 1 • *First HR*: 09/22/1981 off Bob Forsch

Dennis Walling

DENNIS MARTIN WALLING
B: 04/17/1954
BL

Year	Tm	Lg	Tot	H	A	Men-On 0	1	2	3	One-Game 2	3	4	LO	XN	IP	PH	RHP	LHP
1978	HOU	NL	3	2	1	1	1	1	0	0	0	0	0	0	0	0	3	0

Dennis Walling *continued*

Year	Tm	Lg	Tot	H	A	Men-On 0	1	2	3	One-Game 2	3	4	LO	XN	IP	PH	RHP	LHP
1979	HOU	NL	3	3	0	1	0	2	0	0	0	0	0	0	1	1	3	0
1980	HOU	NL	3	1	2	2	1	0	0	0	0	0	0	0	0	1	3	0
1981	HOU	NL	5	2	3	2	3	0	0	0	0	0	1	0	0	1	5	0
1982	HOU	NL	1	1	0	0	1	0	0	0	0	0	0	0	0	0	0	1
1983	HOU	NL	3	1	2	0	2	1	0	0	0	0	0	0	0	1	1	2
1984	HOU	NL	3	0	3	1	1	1	0	0	0	0	0	0	0	0	3	0
1985	HOU	NL	7	2	5	3	3	1	0	0	0	0	0	0	0	1	7	0
1986	HOU	NL	13	5	8	6	4	3	0	2	0	0	0	0	0	1	13	0
1987	HOU	NL	5	2	3	1	4	0	0	0	0	0	0	0	0	0	4	1
1988	HOU	NL	1	0	1	1	0	0	0	0	0	0	0	0	0	0	1	0
1989	STL	NL	1	0	1	0	1	0	0	0	0	0	0	0	0	0	1	0
1990	STL	NL	1	1	0	0	1	0	0	0	0	0	0	0	0	0	1	0
Total			49	20	29	18	22	9	0	2	0	0	1	0	1	6	45	4

Rank among batters: 1,008 • *Top target (4 home runs)*: Andy Hawkins • *Number of pitchers victimized*: 41 • *Total ballparks homered in*: 12 • *First HR*: 05/20/1978 off Dave Campbell

Joe Wallis

HAROLD JOSEPH WALLIS
B: 01/09/1952
BB

Year	Tm	Lg	Tot	H	A	Men-On 0	1	2	3	One-Game 2	3	4	LO	XN	IP	PH	RHP	LHP
1975	CHI	NL	1	0	1	1	0	0	0	0	0	0	0	0	0	0	1	0
1976	CHI	NL	5	4	1	4	1	0	0	0	0	0	1	0	1	0	4	1
1977	CHI	NL	2	1	1	2	0	0	0	0	0	0	0	0	0	0	1	1
1978	CHI	NL	1	0	1	1	0	0	0	0	0	0	0	0	0	0	1	0
	OAK	AL	6	2	4	3	2	1	0	1	0	0	1	0	0	0	4	2
	Total		7	2	5	4	2	1	0	1	0	0	1	0	0	0	5	2
1979	OAK	AL	1	0	1	0	1	0	0	0	0	0	0	0	0	0	0	1
Total			16	7	9	11	4	1	0	1	0	0	2	0	1	0	11	5

Rank among batters: 2,029 • *Total ballparks homered in*: 9 • *First HR*: 09/09/1975 off Bruce Kison

Lee Walls

RAY LEE WALLS
B: 01/06/1933 D: 10/11/1993
BR

Year	Tm	Lg	Tot	H	A	Men-On 0	1	2	3	One-Game 2	3	4	LO	XN	IP	PH	RHP	LHP
1952	PIT	NL	2	1	1	1	1	0	0	0	0	0	0	0	0	0	1	1
1956	PIT	NL	11	6	5	7	3	1	0	0	0	0	0	0	0	0	7	4
1957	CHI	NL	6	3	3	5	1	0	0	1	0	0	0	1	0	0	4	2
1958	CHI	NL	24	15	9	16	5	3	0	2	1	0	0	0	0	0	18	6
1959	CHI	NL	8	6	2	5	2	1	0	0	0	0	0	0	0	0	2	6
1960	CIN	NL	1	0	1	0	0	1	0	0	0	0	0	0	0	0	1	0
	PHI	NL	3	1	2	2	0	1	0	0	0	0	0	0	1	0	3	0
	Total		4	1	3	2	0	2	0	0	0	0	0	0	1	0	4	0
1961	PHI	NL	8	4	4	4	2	2	0	1	0	0	0	0	0	0	4	4
1963	LA	NL	3	2	1	2	0	1	0	0	0	0	0	0	0	1	1	2
Total			66	38	28	42	14	10	0	4	1	0	0	1	1	1	41	25

Rank among batters: 786 • Top target (3 home runs): Warren Spahn, Carl Erskine, Johnny Antonelli, Johnny Podres, Harvey Haddix • *Number of pitchers victimized*: 50 • *Total ballparks homered in*: 11 • *First HR*: 08/10/1952 off Paul Minner • *Hit for Cycle*—vs CIN: 07/02/1957

Augie Walsh

AUGUST SOTHLEY WALSH
B: 08/17/1904 D: 11/12/1985
BR

Year	Tm	Lg	Tot	H	A	Men-On 0	1	2	3	One-Game 2	3	4	LO	XN	IP	PH	RHP	LHP
1928	PHI	NL	1	0	1	1	0	0	0	0	0	0	0	0	0	0	1	0

Rank among batters: 4,707 • *Total ballparks homered in*: 1 • *First HR*: 08/20/1928 off Guy Bush

Austin Walsh

AUSTIN EDWARD WALSH
B: 09/01/1891 D: 01/26/1955
BL

Year	Tm	Lg	Tot	H	A	Men-On 0	1	2	3	One-Game 2	3	4	LO	XN	IP	PH	RHP	LHP
1914	CHI	FL	1	0	1	1	0	0	0	0	0	0	0	0	0	0	1	0

Rank among batters: 4,707 • *Total ballparks homered in*: 1 • *First HR*: 08/06/1914 off George Suggs

Ed Walsh

EDWARD AUGUSTINE WALSH
B: 05/14/1881 D: 05/26/1959
BR HOF

Year	Tm	Lg	Tot	H	A	Men-On 0	Men-On 1	Men-On 2	Men-On 3	One-Game 2	One-Game 3	One-Game 4	LO	XN	IP	PH	RHP	LHP
1904	CHI	AL	1	0	1	1	0	0	0	0	0	0	0	0	0	0	1	0
1907	CHI	AL	1	0	1	0	1	0	0	0	0	0	0	0	0	0	0	1
1908	CHI	AL	1	1	0	0	1	0	0	0	0	0	0	0	1	0	1	0
Total			3	1	2	1	2	0	0	0	0	0	0	0	1	0	2	1

Rank among batters: 3,735 • *Total ballparks homered in*: 3 • *First HR*: 05/24/1904 off Bill Dinneen

Jimmy Walsh

MICHAEL TIMOTHY WALSH
B: 03/25/1886 D: 01/21/1947
BR

Year	Tm	Lg	Tot	H	A	Men-On 0	Men-On 1	Men-On 2	Men-On 3	One-Game 2	One-Game 3	One-Game 4	LO	XN	IP	PH	RHP	LHP
1910	PHI	NL	3	3	0	1	1	1	0	0	0	0	0	0	0	0	3	0
1911	PHI	NL	1	1	0	1	0	0	0	0	0	0	0	0	0	0	1	0
1912	PHI	NL	2	2	0	1	1	0	0	0	0	0	0	0	0	0	1	1
1914	BAL	FL	10	7	3	9	1	0	0	0	0	0	0	0	0	0	7	2
1915	BAL	FL	9	9	0	5	1	1	2	0	0	0	0	0	0	0	7	2
Total			25	22	3	17	4	2	2	0	0	0	0	0	0	0	19	5

Rank among batters: 1,608 • *Top target (2 home runs)*: Bob Groom, Walt Dickson • *Number of pitchers victimized*: 23 • *Total ballparks homered in*: 5 • *First HR*: 06/23/1910 off Buster Brown

Jimmy Walsh

JAMES CHARLES WALSH
B: 09/22/1885 D: 07/03/1962
BL

Year	Tm	Lg	Tot	H	A	Men-On 0	Men-On 1	Men-On 2	Men-On 3	One-Game 2	One-Game 3	One-Game 4	LO	XN	IP	PH	RHP	LHP
1914	NY	AL	1	1	0	1	0	0	0	0	0	0	0	0	0	0	0	1
	PHI	AL	3	2	1	0	0	2	1	0	0	0	0	0	0	0	1	2
	Total		4	3	1	1	2	1	0	0	0	0	0	0	0	0	1	3
1915	PHI	AL	1	0	1	1	0	0	0	0	0	0	0	0	0	0	1	0
1916	PHI	AL	1	1	0	0	0	1	0	0	0	0	0	0	0	0	0	1
Total			6	4	2	2	2	2	0	0	0	0	0	0	0	0	2	4

Rank among batters: 2,988 • *Total ballparks homered in*: 3 • *First HR*: 04/29/1914 off Dutch Leonard

Joe Walsh

JOSEPH R. WALSH
B: 11/05/1864 D: 08/08/1911

Year	Tm	Lg	Tot	H	A	Men-On 0	Men-On 1	Men-On 2	Men-On 3	One-Game 2	One-Game 3	One-Game 4	LO	XN	IP	PH	RHP	LHP
1891	BAL	AA	1	0	1	1	0	0	0	0	0	0	0	0	1	0	1	0

Rank among batters: 4,707 • *Total ballparks homered in*: 1 • *First HR*: 09/16/1891 off Frank Dwyer

Bucky Walters

WILLIAM HENRY WALTERS
B: 04/19/1909 D: 04/20/1991
BR

Year	Tm	Lg	Tot	H	A	Men-On 0	Men-On 1	Men-On 2	Men-On 3	One-Game 2	One-Game 3	One-Game 4	LO	XN	IP	PH	RHP	LHP
1933	BOS	AL	4	2	2	1	2	1	0	0	0	0	0	0	0	0	4	0
1934	BOS	AL	4	4	0	0	3	0	1	1	0	0	0	0	0	0	4	0
	PHI	NL	4	2	2	2	0	2	0	0	0	0	0	1	0	0	2	2
	Total		8	6	2	2	3	2	1	1	0	0	0	1	0	0	6	2
1936	PHI	NL	1	0	1	0	1	0	0	0	0	0	0	0	0	0	1	0
1937	PHI	NL	1	1	0	0	0	0	1	0	0	0	0	0	0	0	1	0
1938	PHI	NL	1	0	1	0	1	0	0	0	0	0	0	0	0	0	1	0
1939	CIN	NL	1	0	1	1	0	0	0	0	0	0	0	0	0	0	1	0
1940	CIN	NL	1	1	0	1	0	0	0	0	0	0	0	0	0	0	0	1
1942	CIN	NL	2	1	1	0	2	0	0	0	0	0	0	0	0	0	2	0
1943	CIN	NL	1	0	1	1	0	0	0	0	0	0	0	0	0	0	1	0
1945	CIN	NL	3	0	3	2	1	0	0	1	0	0	0	0	0	0	2	1
Total			23	11	12	8	10	3	2	2	0	0	0	1	0	0	19	4

Rank among batters: 1,686 • *Top target (2 home runs)*: Sugar Cain, Harry Gumbert, Jim Tobin • *Number of pitchers victimized*: 20 • *Total ballparks homered in*: 8 • *First HR*: 07/23/1933 off Chad Kimsey • *World Series HR*—1

Dan Walters

DANIEL GENE WALTERS
B: 08/15/1966
BR

Year	Tm	Lg	Tot	H	A	Men-On 0	Men-On 1	Men-On 2	Men-On 3	One-Game 2	One-Game 3	One-Game 4	LO	XN	IP	PH	RHP	LHP
1992	SD	NL	4	3	1	4	0	0	0	0	0	0	0	0	0	0	3	1

Dan Walters *continued*

Year	Tm	Lg	Tot	H	A	Men-On 0	Men-On 1	Men-On 2	Men-On 3	One-Game 2	One-Game 3	One-Game 4	LO	XN	IP	PH	RHP	LHP
1993	SD	NL	1	1	0	1	0	0	0	0	0	0	0	0	0	0	1	0
Total			5	4	1	5	0	0	0	0	0	0	0	0	0	0	4	1

Rank among batters: 3,191 • *Total ballparks homered in*: 2 • *First HR*: 06/09/1992 off Jimmy Jones

Ken Walters

KENNETH ROGERS WALTERS
B: 11/11/1933
BR

Year	Tm	Lg	Tot	H	A	Men-On 0	Men-On 1	Men-On 2	Men-On 3	One-Game 2	One-Game 3	One-Game 4	LO	XN	IP	PH	RHP	LHP
1960	PHI	NL	8	4	4	6	2	0	0	1	0	0	0	0	0	0	3	5
1961	PHI	NL	2	2	0	1	1	0	0	0	0	0	0	0	0	0	1	1
1963	CIN	NL	1	0	1	1	0	0	0	0	0	0	0	0	0	0	0	1
Total			11	6	5	8	3	0	0	1	0	0	0	0	0	0	4	7

Rank among batters: 2,419 • *Top target (2 home runs)*: Seth Morehead • *Number of pitchers victimized*: 10 • *Total ballparks homered in*: 6 • *First HR*: 05/03/1960 off Seth Morehead

Danny Walton

DANIEL JAMES WALTON
B: 07/14/1947
BR

Year	Tm	Lg	Tot	H	A	Men-On 0	Men-On 1	Men-On 2	Men-On 3	One-Game 2	One-Game 3	One-Game 4	LO	XN	IP	PH	RHP	LHP
1969	SEA	AL	3	1	2	2	1	0	0	0	0	0	0	0	0	0	1	2
1970	MIL	AL	17	6	11	9	8	0	0	2	0	0	0	0	0	0	10	7
1971	MIL	AL	2	2	0	1	1	0	0	0	0	0	0	0	0	0	1	1
	NY	AL	1	0	1	1	0	0	0	0	0	0	0	0	0	0	0	1
	Total		3	2	1	2	1	0	0	0	0	0	0	0	0	0	1	2
1973	MIN	AL	4	2	2	3	0	0	1	0	0	0	0	0	0	1	1	3
1975	MIN	AL	1	0	1	1	0	0	0	0	0	0	0	0	0	1	1	0
Total			28	11	17	17	10	0	1	2	0	0	0	0	0	2	14	14

Rank among batters: 1,500 • *Top target (3 home runs)*: Rudy May • *Number of pitchers victimized*: 22 • *Total ballparks homered in*: 11 • *First HR*: 09/02/1969 off Al Downing

Jerome Walton

JEROME O'TERRELL WALTON
B: 07/08/1965
BR

Year	Tm	Lg	Tot	H	A	Men-On 0	Men-On 1	Men-On 2	Men-On 3	One-Game 2	One-Game 3	One-Game 4	LO	XN	IP	PH	RHP	LHP
1989	CHI	NL	5	3	2	5	0	0	0	0	0	0	2	0	0	0	3	2
1990	CHI	NL	2	2	0	2	0	0	0	0	0	0	1	0	0	0	1	1
1991	CHI	NL	5	3	2	5	0	0	0	0	0	0	1	0	0	0	5	0
1994	CIN	NL	1	1	0	0	0	1	0	0	0	0	0	1	0	0	1	0
1995	CIN	NL	8	4	4	6	1	1	0	0	0	0	4	0	0	1	2	6
Total			21	13	8	18	1	2	0	0	0	0	8	1	0	1	12	9

Rank among batters: 1,768 • *Top target (2 home runs)*: John Smiley, Bill Landrum • *Number of pitchers victimized*: 19 • *Total ballparks homered in*: 8 • *First HR*: 04/06/1989 off Steve Ontiveros

Reggie Walton

REGINALD SHERARD WALTON
B: 10/24/1952
BR

Year	Tm	Lg	Tot	H	A	Men-On 0	Men-On 1	Men-On 2	Men-On 3	One-Game 2	One-Game 3	One-Game 4	LO	XN	IP	PH	RHP	LHP
1980	SEA	AL	2	1	1	1	1	0	0	0	0	0	0	0	0	1	1	1

Rank among batters: 4,129 • *Total ballparks homered in*: 2 • *First HR*: 08/25/1980 off Tippy Martinez

Bill Wambsganss

WILLIAM ADOLPH WAMBSGANSS
B: 03/19/1894 D: 12/08/1985
BR

Year	Tm	Lg	Tot	H	A	Men-On 0	Men-On 1	Men-On 2	Men-On 3	One-Game 2	One-Game 3	One-Game 4	LO	XN	IP	PH	RHP	LHP
1919	CLE	AL	2	2	0	1	0	1	0	0	0	0	0	0	1	0	1	1
1920	CLE	AL	1	1	0	0	1	0	0	0	0	0	0	0	1	0	0	1
1921	CLE	AL	2	0	2	2	0	0	0	0	0	0	0	0	0	0	2	0
1923	CLE	AL	1	0	1	0	1	0	0	0	0	0	0	0	1	0	1	0
1925	BOS	AL	1	0	1	1	0	0	0	0	0	0	0	0	0	0	1	0
Total			7	3	4	4	2	1	0	0	0	0	0	0	3	0	5	2

Rank among batters: 2,834 • *Total ballparks homered in*: 3 • *First HR*: 05/18/1919 off George Mogridge

Lloyd Waner

LLOYD JAMES WANER
B: 03/16/1906 D: 07/22/1982
BL HOF

Year	Tm	Lg	Tot	H	A	Men-On 0	1	2	3	One-Game 2	3	4	LO	XN	IP	PH	RHP	LHP
1927	PIT	NL	2	0	2	2	0	0	0	0	0	0	0	0	0	0	2	0
1928	PIT	NL	5	2	3	1	3	1	0	0	0	0	0	0	3	0	3	2
1929	PIT	NL	5	2	3	2	2	1	0	0	0	0	0	0	1	0	4	1
1930	PIT	NL	1	0	1	1	0	0	0	0	0	0	0	0	1	0	1	0
1931	PIT	NL	4	3	1	2	1	1	0	0	0	0	0	0	4	0	1	3
1932	PIT	NL	2	2	0	1	1	0	0	0	0	0	0	0	2	0	1	1
1934	PIT	NL	1	1	0	1	0	0	0	0	0	0	0	0	1	0	1	0
1936	PIT	NL	1	0	1	0	0	1	0	0	0	0	0	0	0	0	1	0
1937	PIT	NL	1	0	1	1	0	0	0	0	0	0	1	0	0	0	1	0
1938	PIT	NL	5	3	2	1	3	1	0	0	0	0	0	0	1	0	3	2
Total			27	13	14	12	10	5	0	0	0	0	1	0	13	0	18	9

Rank among batters: 1,532 • *Top target (2 home runs)*: Jim Faulkner, Eppa Rixey • *Number of pitchers victimized*: 25 • *Total ballparks homered in*: 8 • *First HR*: 08/11/1927 off Grover Alexander

Paul Waner

PAUL GLEE WANER
B: 04/16/1903 D: 08/29/1965
BL HOF

Year	Tm	Lg	Tot	H	A	Men-On 0	1	2	3	One-Game 2	3	4	LO	XN	IP	PH	RHP	LHP
1926	PIT	NL	8	4	4	4	4	0	0	0	0	0	0	0	2	0	8	0
1927	PIT	NL	9	6	3	3	4	2	0	0	0	0	0	0	1	0	7	2
1928	PIT	NL	6	2	4	2	3	0	1	0	0	0	0	0	0	0	4	2
1929	PIT	NL	15	8	7	8	6	1	0	0	0	0	0	0	1	0	14	1
1930	PIT	NL	8	4	4	5	3	0	0	0	0	0	0	0	1	0	8	0
1931	PIT	NL	6	5	1	3	3	0	0	1	0	0	0	0	0	0	6	0
1932	PIT	NL	8	4	4	1	6	1	0	1	0	0	0	0	0	0	6	2
1933	PIT	NL	7	4	3	5	1	1	0	1	0	0	0	0	1	0	7	0
1934	PIT	NL	14	10	4	9	4	1	0	0	0	0	0	0	0	0	13	1
1935	PIT	NL	11	5	6	7	1	2	1	0	0	0	0	0	0	0	11	0
1936	PIT	NL	5	0	5	1	4	0	0	0	0	0	0	0	0	0	4	1
1937	PIT	NL	2	0	2	1	0	1	0	0	0	0	0	0	0	0	2	0
1938	PIT	NL	6	2	4	4	0	2	0	1	0	0	0	0	0	0	5	1
1939	PIT	NL	3	2	1	1	2	0	0	0	0	0	0	0	0	0	3	0
1940	PIT	NL	1	0	1	0	1	0	0	0	0	0	0	0	0	0	1	0
1941	BOS	NL	2	0	2	0	0	1	1	0	0	0	0	0	0	0	2	0
1942	BOS	NL	1	1	0	0	1	0	0	0	0	0	0	0	0	0	1	0
1943	BRO	NL	1	1	0	0	1	0	0	0	0	0	0	0	0	0	1	0
Total			113	58	55	54	44	12	3	4	0	0	0	0	6	0	103	10

Rank among batters: 421 • *Top target (5 home runs)*: Clarence Mitchell • *Number of pitchers victimized*: 73 • *Total ballparks homered in*: 8 • *First HR*: 05/08/1926 off Skinny Graham

Pee-Wee Wanninger

PAUL LOUIS WANNINGER
B: 12/12/1902 D: 03/07/1981
BL

Year	Tm	Lg	Tot	H	A	Men-On 0	1	2	3	One-Game 2	3	4	LO	XN	IP	PH	RHP	LHP
1925	NY	AL	1	1	0	0	0	1	0	0	0	0	0	0	1	0	0	1

Rank among batters: 4,707 • *Total ballparks homered in*: 1 • *First HR*: 06/05/1925 off Joe Giard

Aaron Ward

AARON LEE WARD
B: 08/28/1896 D: 01/30/1961
BR

Year	Tm	Lg	Tot	H	A	Men-On 0	1	2	3	One-Game 2	3	4	LO	XN	IP	PH	RHP	LHP
1920	NY	AL	11	8	3	6	3	2	0	1	0	0	1	0	3	0	4	7
1921	NY	AL	5	4	1	4	1	0	0	0	0	0	0	0	0	0	4	1
1922	NY	AL	7	4	3	4	2	1	0	0	0	0	0	0	0	0	5	2
1923	NY	AL	10	5	5	8	1	1	0	0	0	0	0	0	1	0	8	2
1924	NY	AL	8	4	4	2	2	3	1	0	0	0	0	0	1	0	5	3
1925	NY	AL	4	2	2	2	0	2	0	0	0	0	0	0	0	0	2	2
1927	CHI	AL	5	2	3	4	0	1	0	0	0	0	0	0	0	0	5	0
Total			50	29	21	30	9	10	1	1	0	0	1	0	5	0	33	17

Rank among batters: 991 • *Top target (4 home runs)*: Urban Shocker • *Number of pitchers victimized*: 35 • *Total ballparks homered in*: 7 • *First HR*: 05/12/1920 off Lefty Williams • *World Series HR*—3

Chris Ward

CHRIS GILBERT WARD
B: 05/18/1949
BL

Year	Tm	Lg	Tot	H	A	Men-On 0	1	2	3	One-Game 2	3	4	LO	XN	IP	PH	RHP	LHP
1974	CHI	NL	1	1	0	0	1	0	0	0	0	0	0	0	0	0	1	0

Rank among batters: 4,707 • *Total ballparks homered in*: 1 • *First HR*: 06/18/1974 off Dave Freisleben

Gary Ward

GARY LAMELL WARD
B: 12/06/1953
BR

Year	Tm	Lg	Tot	H	A	Men-On 0	1	2	3	One-Game 2	3	4	LO	XN	IP	PH	RHP	LHP
1980	MIN	AL	1	0	1	1	0	0	0	0	0	0	0	0	0	0	0	1
1981	MIN	AL	3	2	1	2	1	0	0	0	0	0	1	0	0	0	2	1
1982	MIN	AL	28	16	12	16	7	4	1	0	0	0	0	0	1	1	18	10
1983	MIN	AL	19	7	12	9	8	2	0	1	0	0	0	0	0	0	8	11
1984	TEX	AL	21	7	14	11	8	2	0	2	0	0	0	0	1	0	16	5
1985	TEX	AL	15	10	5	9	2	3	1	0	0	0	0	0	0	0	8	7
1986	TEX	AL	5	3	2	2	2	1	0	0	0	0	0	0	1	0	2	3
1987	NY	AL	16	7	9	10	5	1	0	1	0	0	0	0	0	0	12	4
1988	NY	AL	4	3	1	1	1	2	0	0	0	0	0	1	0	1	0	4
1989	DET	AL	9	6	3	7	1	1	0	0	0	0	0	0	0	0	0	9
1990	DET	AL	9	2	7	5	2	1	1	0	0	0	0	0	0	0	4	5
Total			130	63	67	73	37	17	3	4	0	0	1	1	3	2	70	60

Rank among batters: 348 • *Top target (5 home runs)*: Bruce Hurst • *Number of pitchers victimized*: 96 • *Total ballparks homered in*: 16 • *First HR*: 09/18/1980 off Mike Caldwell • *Hit for Cycle*—@MIL: 09/18/1980 (1)

Kevin Ward

KEVIN MICHAEL WARD
B: 09/28/1961
BR

Year	Tm	Lg	Tot	H	A	Men-On 0	1	2	3	One-Game 2	3	4	LO	XN	IP	PH	RHP	LHP
1991	SD	NL	2	0	2	2	0	0	0	0	0	0	0	0	0	0	0	2
1992	SD	NL	3	0	3	1	2	0	0	0	0	0	0	0	0	1	0	3
Total			5	0	5	3	2	0	0	0	0	0	0	0	0	1	0	5

Rank among batters: 3,191 • *Top target (2 home runs)*: Randy Tomlin • *Number of pitchers victimized*: 4 • *Total ballparks homered in*: 3 • *First HR*: 08/26/1991 off Randy Tomlin

Monte Ward

JOHN MONTGOMERY WARD
B: 03/03/1860 D: 03/04/1925
BL HOF

Year	Tm	Lg	Tot	H	A	Men-On 0	1	2	3	One-Game 2	3	4	LO	XN	IP	PH	RHP	LHP
1878	PRO	NL	1	1	0	1	0	0	0	0	0	0	0	0	0	0	1	0
1879	PRO	NL	2	1	1	1	0	1	0	0	0	0	0	0	0	0	2	0
1882	PRO	NL	1	0	1	0	1	0	0	0	0	0	0	0	0	0	1	0
1883	NY	NL	7	7	0	4	2	0	0	2	0	0	0	0	1	0	7	0
1884	NY	NL	2	1	1	2	0	0	0	0	0	0	0	0	1	0	1	1
1886	NY	NL	2	1	1	0	1	1	0	0	0	0	0	0	0	0	1	1
1887	NY	NL	1	1	0	1	0	0	0	0	0	0	0	0	0	0	0	1
1888	NY	NL	2	2	0	1	1	0	0	0	0	0	0	0	0	0	1	1
1889	NY	NL	1	0	1	0	0	0	1	0	0	0	0	0	1	0	1	0
1890	BRO	PL	4	2	2	2	2	0	0	1	0	0	1	0	0	0	0	4
1892	BRO	NL	1	1	0	1	0	0	0	0	0	0	1	0	0	0	0	1
1893	NY	NL	2	2	0	1	1	0	0	0	0	0	0	0	1	0	2	0
Total			26	19	7	14	8	2	1	3	0	0	2	0	4	0	17	9

Rank among batters: 1,576 • *Top target (3 home runs)*: Jim Whitney, John Coleman • *Number of pitchers victimized*: 21 • *Total ballparks homered in*: 10 • *First HR*: 09/27/1878 off Tommy Bond

Pete Ward

PETER THOMAS WARD
B: 07/26/1939
BL

Year	Tm	Lg	Tot	H	A	Men-On 0	1	2	3	One-Game 2	3	4	LO	XN	IP	PH	RHP	LHP
1963	CHI	AL	22	13	9	15	4	3	0	0	0	0	0	0	0	0	16	6
1964	CHI	AL	23	9	14	14	5	1	3	1	0	0	0	1	0	0	15	8
1965	CHI	AL	10	3	7	6	4	0	0	0	0	0	0	1	0	0	8	2
1966	CHI	AL	3	2	1	2	1	0	0	0	0	0	0	0	0	0	2	1
1967	CHI	AL	18	9	9	11	6	1	0	1	0	0	0	0	0	0	15	3
1968	CHI	AL	15	7	8	9	4	1	1	1	0	0	0	0	0	0	15	0
1969	CHI	AL	6	4	2	2	2	2	0	0	0	0	0	0	0	2	5	1

Pete Ward *continued*

Year	Tm	Lg	Tot	H	A	Men-On				One-Game			LO	XN	IP	PH	RHP	LHP
						0	1	2	3	2	3	4						
1970	NY	AL	1	0	1	1	0	0	0	0	0	0	0	0	0	1	1	0
Total			98	47	51	60	26	8	4	3	0	0	0	2	0	3	77	21

Rank among batters: 506 • *Top target (5 home runs)*: Earl Wilson • *Number of pitchers victimized*: 68 • *Total ballparks homered in*: 12 • *First HR*: 04/09/1963 off Jim Bunning

Piggy Ward

FRANK GRAY WARD
B: 04/16/1867 D: 10/24/1912
BB

Year	Tm	Lg	Tot	H	A	Men-On				One-Game			LO	XN	IP	PH	RHP	LHP
						0	1	2	3	2	3	4						
1892	BAL	NL	1	1	0	0	1	0	0	0	0	0	0	0	0	0	1	0

Rank among batters: 4,707 • *Total ballparks homered in*: 1 • *First HR*: 08/09/1892 off Brickyard Kennedy

Preston Ward

PRESTON MEYER WARD
B: 07/24/1927
BL

Year	Tm	Lg	Tot	H	A	Men-On				One-Game			LO	XN	IP	PH	RHP	LHP
						0	1	2	3	2	3	4						
1948	BRO	NL	1	1	0	0	0	0	1	0	0	0	0	0	0	0	0	1
1950	CHI	NL	6	2	4	4	1	1	0	0	0	0	0	0	0	0	3	3
1953	CHI	NL	4	2	2	2	2	0	0	0	0	0	0	0	0	0	3	1
	PIT	NL	8	3	5	3	3	0	2	1	0	0	0	0	0	0	6	2
	Total		12	5	7	5	5	0	2	1	0	0	0	0	0	0	9	3
1954	PIT	NL	7	4	3	3	1	3	0	0	0	0	0	0	0	2	7	0
1955	PIT	NL	5	5	0	2	0	3	0	0	0	0	0	0	0	1	3	2
1956	PIT	NL	1	0	1	0	1	0	0	0	0	0	0	0	0	0	1	0
	CLE	AL	6	4	2	5	0	1	0	0	0	0	0	0	0	1	5	1
	Total		7	4	3	5	1	1	0	0	0	0	0	0	0	1	6	1
1958	CLE	AL	4	0	4	3	1	0	0	0	0	0	0	0	0	0	3	1
	KC	AL	6	6	0	5	1	0	0	0	1	0	0	0	0	0	6	0
	Total		10	6	4	8	2	0	0	0	1	0	0	0	0	0	9	1
1959	KC	AL	2	1	1	1	0	0	1	0	0	0	0	0	0	0	2	0
Total			50	28	22	28	10	8	4	1	1	0	0	0	0	4	39	11

Rank among batters: 991 • Top target (2 home runs): Max Surkont, Stu Miller, Lew Burdette, Tom Poholsky, Herm Wehmeier, Robin Roberts, Hal Griggs • *Number of pitchers victimized*: 43 • *Total ballparks homered in*: 14 • *First HR*: 04/29/1948 off Thornton Lee

Turner Ward

TURNER MAX WARD
B: 04/11/1965
BB

Year	Tm	Lg	Tot	H	A	Men-On				One-Game			LO	XN	IP	PH	RHP	LHP
						0	1	2	3	2	3	4						
1990	CLE	AL	1	0	1	0	0	1	0	0	0	0	0	0	0	0	1	0
1992	TOR	AL	1	0	1	1	0	0	0	0	0	0	0	0	0	0	1	0
1993	TOR	AL	4	2	2	1	2	1	0	0	0	0	0	0	0	0	3	1
1994	MIL	AL	9	3	6	6	3	0	0	0	0	0	0	0	0	0	7	2
1995	MIL	AL	4	3	1	2	1	1	0	0	0	0	0	0	0	0	4	0
Total			19	8	11	10	6	3	0	0	0	0	0	0	0	0	16	3

Rank among batters: 1,861 • *Total ballparks homered in*: 10 • *First HR*: 09/15/1990 off Andy McGaffigan

Lon Warneke

LONNIE WARNEKE
B: 03/28/1909 D: 06/23/1976
BR

Year	Tm	Lg	Tot	H	A	Men-On				One-Game			LO	XN	IP	PH	RHP	LHP
						0	1	2	3	2	3	4						
1933	CHI	NL	2	1	1	2	0	0	0	0	0	0	0	0	0	0	2	0
1936	CHI	NL	1	0	1	1	0	0	0	0	0	0	0	0	0	0	1	0
1940	STL	NL	1	0	1	0	0	1	0	0	0	0	0	0	0	0	0	1
Total			4	1	3	3	0	1	0	0	0	0	0	0	0	0	3	1

Rank among batters: 3,427 • *Total ballparks homered in*: 3 • *First HR*: 05/07/1933 off Ben Cantwell

Fred Warner

FREDERICK JOHN RODNEY WARNER
B: 1855 D: 02/13/1886

Year	Tm	Lg	Tot	H	A	Men-On				One-Game			LO	XN	IP	PH	RHP	LHP
						0	1	2	3	2	3	4						
1884	BRO	AA	1	1	0	1	0	0	0	0	0	0	0	0	0	0	0	0

Rank among batters: 4,707 • *Total ballparks homered in*: 1 • *First HR*: 05/19/1884 off John Fox

						Men-On				One-Game								
Year	Tm	Lg	Tot	H	A	0	1	2	3	2	3	4	LO	XN	IP	PH	RHP	LHP

Hooks Warner

HOKE HAYDEN WARNER
B: 05/22/1894 D: 02/19/1947
BL

Year	Tm	Lg	Tot	H	A	0	1	2	3	2	3	4	LO	XN	IP	PH	RHP	LHP
1916	PIT	NL	2	2	0	2	0	0	0	0	0	0	0	0	2	0	2	0

Rank among batters: 4,129 • *Total ballparks homered in*: 1 • *First HR*: 08/24/1916 off Jeff Tesreau

Jack Warner

JOHN RALPH WARNER
B: 08/29/1903 D: 03/13/1986
BR

Year	Tm	Lg	Tot	H	A	0	1	2	3	2	3	4	LO	XN	IP	PH	RHP	LHP
1927	DET	AL	1	1	0	1	0	0	0	0	0	0	0	0	0	0	0	1

Rank among batters: 4,707 • *Total ballparks homered in*: 1 • *First HR*: 07/10/1927 off Herb Pennock

Jackie Warner

JOHN JOSEPH WARNER
B: 08/01/1943
BR

Year	Tm	Lg	Tot	H	A	0	1	2	3	2	3	4	LO	XN	IP	PH	RHP	LHP
1966	CAL	AL	7	2	5	2	5	0	0	0	0	0	0	0	0	0	4	3

Rank among batters: 2,834 • *Total ballparks homered in*: 6 • *First HR*: 04/14/1966 off Joe Horlen

John Warner

JOHN JOSEPH WARNER
B: 08/15/1872 D: 12/21/1943
BL

Year	Tm	Lg	Tot	H	A	0	1	2	3	2	3	4	LO	XN	IP	PH	RHP	LHP
1895	LOU	NL	1	0	1	0	1	0	0	0	0	0	0	0	0	0	0	0
1897	NY	NL	2	1	1	0	1	1	0	0	0	0	0	0	0	0	2	0
1904	NY	NL	1	1	0	0	1	0	0	0	0	0	0	1	0	0	1	0
1905	STL	NL	1	1	0	0	0	1	0	0	0	0	0	0	1	0	1	0
1906	WAS	AL	1	0	1	1	0	0	0	0	0	0	0	0	1	0	0	1
Total			6	3	3	1	3	2	0	0	0	0	0	1	2	0	4	1

Rank among batters: 2,988 • *Total ballparks homered in*: 4 • *First HR*: 09/02/1895 off Oscar Purner

Bennie Warren

BENNIE LOUIS WARREN
B: 03/02/1912 D: 05/11/1994
BR

Year	Tm	Lg	Tot	H	A	0	1	2	3	2	3	4	LO	XN	IP	PH	RHP	LHP
1939	PHI	NL	1	0	1	1	0	0	0	0	0	0	0	0	0	0	1	0
1940	PHI	NL	12	2	10	6	4	2	0	2	0	0	0	0	0	0	10	2
1941	PHI	NL	9	6	3	5	2	2	0	0	0	0	0	1	0	0	9	0
1942	PHI	NL	7	4	3	3	4	0	0	0	0	0	0	0	0	0	7	0
1946	NY	NL	4	1	3	4	0	0	0	0	0	0	0	0	0	0	2	2
Total			33	13	20	19	10	4	0	2	0	0	0	1	0	0	29	4

Rank among batters: 1,336 • Top target (2 home runs): Jake Mooty, Manny Salvo, Vance Page, Bob Carpenter, Johnny Allen, Claude Passeau • *Number of pitchers victimized*: 27 • *Total ballparks homered in*: 8 • *First HR*: 09/15/1939 off Vance Page

Rabbit Warstler

HAROLD BURTON WARSTLER
B: 09/13/1903 D: 05/31/1964
BR

Year	Tm	Lg	Tot	H	A	0	1	2	3	2	3	4	LO	XN	IP	PH	RHP	LHP
1930	BOS	AL	1	1	0	0	1	0	0	0	0	0	0	0	1	0	0	1
1933	BOS	AL	1	0	1	0	0	1	0	0	0	0	0	0	1	0	1	0
1934	PHI	AL	1	1	0	1	0	0	0	0	0	0	1	0	0	0	1	0
1935	PHI	AL	3	3	0	2	1	0	0	0	0	0	0	0	0	0	3	0
1936	PHI	AL	1	1	0	0	0	1	0	0	0	0	0	0	0	0	1	0
1937	BOS	NL	3	0	3	3	0	0	0	0	0	0	0	0	0	0	2	1
1940	CHI	NL	1	0	1	1	0	0	0	0	0	0	0	0	0	0	0	1
Total			11	6	5	7	2	2	0	0	0	0	1	0	2	0	8	3

Rank among batters: 2,419 • *Top target (2 home runs)*: Carl Hubbell • *Number of pitchers victimized*: 10 • *Total ballparks homered in*: 5 • *First HR*: 07/31/1930 off Ed Wells

Bill Warwick

FIRMIN NEWTON WARWICK
B: 11/26/1897 D: 12/19/1984
BR

Year	Tm	Lg	Tot	H	A	0	1	2	3	2	3	4	LO	XN	IP	PH	RHP	LHP
1925	STL	NL	1	1	0	1	0	0	0	0	0	0	0	0	0	0	1	0

Bill Warwick *continued*

Rank among batters: 4,707 • *Total ballparks homered in*: 1 • *First HR*: 09/13/1925 off Johnny Morrison

Carl Warwick

CARL WAYNE WARWICK
B: 02/27/1937
BR

Year	Tm	Lg	Tot	H	A	Men-On 0	1	2	3	One-Game 2	3	4	LO	XN	IP	PH	RHP	LHP
1961	STL	NL	4	2	2	4	0	0	0	0	0	0	0	0	0	2	2	2
1962	STL	NL	1	0	1	0	0	1	0	0	0	0	0	0	0	0	1	0
	HOU	NL	16	6	10	8	6	2	0	0	0	0	2	0	0	0	11	5
	Total		17	6	11	8	6	3	0	0	0	0	2	0	0	0	12	5
1963	HOU	NL	7	4	3	4	2	1	0	0	0	0	0	0	0	0	3	4
1964	STL	NL	3	2	1	0	2	1	0	0	0	0	0	0	0	1	3	0
Total			31	14	17	16	10	5	0	0	0	0	2	0	0	3	20	11

Rank among batters: 1,400 • *Top target (2 home runs)*: Bob Buhl, Bob Hendley, Jack Hamilton • *Number of pitchers victimized*: 28 • *Total ballparks homered in*: 10 • *First HR*: 06/03/1961 off Bob Buhl

Jimmy Wasdell

JAMES CHARLES WASDELL
B: 05/15/1914 D: 08/06/1983
BL

Year	Tm	Lg	Tot	H	A	Men-On 0	1	2	3	One-Game 2	3	4	LO	XN	IP	PH	RHP	LHP
1937	WAS	AL	2	1	1	1	1	0	0	0	0	0	0	0	1	0	1	1
1938	WAS	AL	2	2	0	1	0	0	1	0	0	0	0	0	0	0	2	0
1940	BRO	NL	3	0	3	3	0	0	0	0	0	0	0	0	0	0	3	0
1941	BRO	NL	4	0	4	0	2	2	0	0	0	0	0	1	0	0	3	1
1942	PIT	NL	3	1	2	2	1	0	0	0	0	0	0	0	0	0	1	2
1943	PHI	NL	4	2	2	1	2	1	0	0	0	0	0	0	0	0	3	1
1944	PHI	NL	3	0	3	3	0	0	0	0	0	0	0	0	0	0	2	1
1945	PHI	NL	7	0	7	4	2	1	0	0	0	0	0	0	0	0	7	0
1946	PHI	NL	1	0	1	1	0	0	0	0	0	0	0	0	0	0	1	0
Total			29	6	23	16	8	4	1	0	0	0	0	1	1	0	23	6

Rank among batters: 1,465 • *Top target (3 home runs)*: Thomas Earley • *Number of pitchers victimized*: 26 • *Total ballparks homered in*: 8 • *First HR*: 09/16/1937 off Roxie Lawson

Ray Washburn

RAY CLARK WASHBURN
B: 05/31/1938
BR

Year	Tm	Lg	Tot	H	A	Men-On 0	1	2	3	One-Game 2	3	4	LO	XN	IP	PH	RHP	LHP
1966	STL	NL	1	0	1	0	1	0	0	0	0	0	0	0	0	0	1	0

Rank among batters: 4,707 • *Total ballparks homered in*: 1 • *First HR*: 07/27/1966 off Joey Jay

Claudell Washington

CLAUDELL WASHINGTON
B: 08/31/1954
BL

Year	Tm	Lg	Tot	H	A	Men-On 0	1	2	3	One-Game 2	3	4	LO	XN	IP	PH	RHP	LHP
1975	OAK	AL	10	7	3	7	1	2	0	1	0	0	0	0	0	0	8	2
1976	OAK	AL	5	1	4	2	1	2	0	0	0	0	0	0	0	0	5	0
1977	TEX	AL	12	6	6	6	4	2	0	0	0	0	0	0	0	0	11	1
1978	CHI	AL	6	3	3	2	4	0	0	0	0	0	0	0	0	0	4	2
1979	CHI	AL	13	10	3	8	3	2	0	0	1	0	0	0	0	0	12	1
1980	CHI	AL	1	0	1	1	0	0	0	0	0	0	0	0	0	0	1	0
	NY	NL	10	5	5	5	4	1	0	1	1	0	0	0	0	0	10	0
	Total		11	5	6	6	4	1	0	1	1	0	0	0	0	0	11	0
1981	ATL	NL	5	3	2	1	3	1	0	0	0	0	0	0	0	0	5	0
1982	ATL	NL	16	8	8	9	4	3	0	1	0	0	0	1	0	0	13	3
1983	ATL	NL	9	4	5	6	2	1	0	0	0	0	1	0	0	1	9	0
1984	ATL	NL	17	12	5	12	3	2	0	1	0	0	5	0	0	0	14	3
1985	ATL	NL	15	4	11	11	4	0	0	0	0	0	3	1	0	1	14	1
1986	ATL	NL	5	3	2	4	1	0	0	0	0	0	1	0	0	0	5	0
	NY	AL	6	4	2	5	1	0	0	0	0	0	0	0	0	1	6	0
	Total		11	7	4	9	2	0	0	0	0	0	1	0	0	1	11	0
1987	NY	AL	9	5	4	4	3	2	0	0	0	0	0	0	0	1	8	1
1988	NY	AL	11	6	5	7	2	2	0	0	0	0	0	1	0	2	10	1
1989	CAL	AL	13	9	4	11	2	0	0	1	0	0	1	0	0	1	13	0

Year	Tm	Lg	Tot	H	A	Men-On				One-Game			LO	XN	IP	PH	RHP	LHP
						0	1	2	3	2	3	4						

Claudell Washington *continued*

Year	Tm	Lg	Tot	H	A	0	1	2	3	2	3	4	LO	XN	IP	PH	RHP	LHP
1990	CAL	AL	1	0	1	1	0	0	0	0	0	0	0	0	0	0	1	0
Total			164	90	74	102	42	20	0	5	2	0	11	3	0	7	149	15

Rank among batters: 250 • *Top target (6 home runs)*: Mario Soto • *Number of pitchers victimized*: 121 • *Total ballparks homered in*: 26 • *First HR*: 04/16/1975 off Nelson Briles

George Washington

SLOAN VERNON WASHINGTON
B: 06/04/1907 D: 02/17/1985
BL

Year	Tm	Lg	Tot	H	A	0	1	2	3	2	3	4	LO	XN	IP	PH	RHP	LHP
1935	CHI	AL	8	5	3	3	5	0	0	0	0	0	0	0	0	0	7	1
1936	CHI	AL	1	1	0	1	0	0	0	0	0	0	0	0	0	0	0	1
Total			9	6	3	4	5	0	0	0	0	0	0	0	0	0	7	2

Rank among batters: 2,587 • *Top target (2 home runs)*: Dick Coffman • *Number of pitchers victimized*: 8 • *Total ballparks homered in*: 4 • *First HR*: 04/24/1935 off Chief Hogsett

Ron Washington

RONALD WASHINGTON
B: 04/29/1952
BR

Year	Tm	Lg	Tot	H	A	0	1	2	3	2	3	4	LO	XN	IP	PH	RHP	LHP
1982	MIN	AL	5	4	1	3	1	1	0	0	0	0	0	0	0	0	4	1
1983	MIN	AL	4	1	3	1	2	1	0	0	0	0	0	1	0	0	4	0
1984	MIN	AL	3	2	1	3	0	0	0	0	0	0	0	1	0	0	2	1
1985	MIN	AL	1	1	0	1	0	0	0	0	0	0	0	0	0	0	0	1
1986	MIN	AL	4	4	0	3	0	1	0	0	0	0	0	0	1	1	2	2
1987	BAL	AL	1	0	1	1	0	0	0	0	0	0	1	0	0	0	0	1
1988	CLE	AL	2	0	2	1	0	1	0	0	0	0	0	0	0	0	1	1
Total			20	12	8	13	3	4	0	0	0	0	1	2	1	1	13	7

Rank among batters: 1,810 • *Total ballparks homered in*: 7 • *First HR*: 04/30/1982 off Dwight Bernard

U. L. Washington

U. L. WASHINGTON
B: 10/27/1953
BB

Year	Tm	Lg	Tot	H	A	0	1	2	3	2	3	4	LO	XN	IP	PH	RHP	LHP
1979	KC	AL	2	0	2	0	0	2	0	1	0	0	0	0	0	0	1	1
1980	KC	AL	6	3	3	3	3	0	0	0	0	0	0	0	0	0	1	5
1981	KC	AL	2	0	2	2	0	0	0	0	0	0	0	0	0	0	1	1
1982	KC	AL	10	2	8	7	3	0	0	1	0	0	0	0	0	0	1	9
1983	KC	AL	5	1	4	3	1	1	0	0	0	0	0	0	1	0	0	5
1984	KC	AL	1	0	1	1	0	0	0	0	0	0	0	0	0	0	0	1
1985	MON	NL	1	1	0	1	0	0	0	0	0	0	0	0	0	0	0	1
Total			27	7	20	17	7	3	0	2	0	0	0	0	1	0	4	23

Rank among batters: 1,532 • *Top target (4 home runs)*: Scott McGregor • *Number of pitchers victimized*: 20 • *Total ballparks homered in*: 11 • *First HR*: 09/21/1979 off Rick Langford • *Switch hit HR in 1 game*—1 time

Mark Wasinger

MARK THOMAS WASINGER
B: 08/04/1961
BR

Year	Tm	Lg	Tot	H	A	0	1	2	3	2	3	4	LO	XN	IP	PH	RHP	LHP
1987	SF	NL	1	1	0	1	0	0	0	0	0	0	1	0	0	0	1	0

Rank among batters: 4,707 • *Total ballparks homered in*: 1 • *First HR*: 05/09/1987 off Bob Patterson

John Wathan

JOHN DAVID WATHAN
B: 10/04/1949
BR

Year	Tm	Lg	Tot	H	A	0	1	2	3	2	3	4	LO	XN	IP	PH	RHP	LHP
1977	KC	AL	2	0	2	0	1	1	0	0	0	0	0	0	0	0	1	1
1978	KC	AL	2	2	0	2	0	0	0	0	0	0	0	0	1	0	1	1
1979	KC	AL	2	0	2	1	1	0	0	0	0	0	0	0	0	0	1	1
1980	KC	AL	6	5	1	3	0	3	0	0	0	0	0	0	1	0	5	1
1981	KC	AL	1	0	1	1	0	0	0	0	0	0	0	0	0	0	1	0
1982	KC	AL	3	2	1	0	2	1	0	0	0	0	0	0	0	0	2	1
1983	KC	AL	2	2	0	2	0	0	0	0	0	0	0	0	1	0	2	0
1984	KC	AL	2	1	1	2	0	0	0	0	0	0	0	0	0	0	0	2

						Men-On				One-Game								
Year	Tm	Lg	Tot	H	A	0	1	2	3	2	3	4	LO	XN	IP	PH	RHP	LHP

John Wathan *continued*

Year	Tm	Lg	Tot	H	A	0	1	2	3	2	3	4	LO	XN	IP	PH	RHP	LHP
1985	KC	AL	1	1	0	1	0	0	0	0	0	0	0	0	0	0	0	1
Total			21	13	8	12	4	5	0	0	0	0	0	0	3	0	13	8

Rank among batters: 1,768 • *Top target (2 home runs)*: Floyd Bannister • *Number of pitchers victimized*: 20 • *Total ballparks homered in*: 8 • *First HR*: 08/25/1977 off Sam Hinds

Dave Watkins

DAVID ROGER WATKINS
B: 03/15/1944
BR

Year	Tm	Lg	Tot	H	A	0	1	2	3	2	3	4	LO	XN	IP	PH	RHP	LHP
1969	PHI	NL	4	2	2	4	0	0	0	0	0	0	0	0	0	0	3	1

Rank among batters: 3,427 • *Total ballparks homered in*: 3 • *First HR*: 06/25/1969 off Cal Koonce

George Watkins

GEORGE ARCHIBALD WATKINS
B: 06/04/1900 D: 06/01/1970
BL

Year	Tm	Lg	Tot	H	A	0	1	2	3	2	3	4	LO	XN	IP	PH	RHP	LHP
1930	STL	NL	17	9	8	9	6	2	0	1	0	0	0	0	1	1	17	0
1931	STL	NL	13	7	6	10	2	1	0	2	1	0	0	0	0	0	11	2
1932	STL	NL	9	5	4	3	5	1	0	0	0	0	0	0	1	0	9	0
1933	STL	NL	5	2	3	2	3	0	0	0	0	0	0	0	0	0	5	0
1934	NY	NL	6	6	0	2	2	2	0	1	0	0	0	0	1	0	3	3
1935	PHI	NL	17	10	7	8	5	4	0	2	0	0	0	1	0	1	16	1
1936	PHI	NL	2	0	2	0	2	0	0	0	0	0	0	0	0	0	2	0
	BRO	NL	4	3	1	1	2	1	0	0	0	0	0	0	0	0	4	0
	Total		6	3	3	1	4	1	0	0	0	0	0	0	0	0	6	0
Total			73	42	31	35	27	11	0	6	1	0	0	1	3	2	67	6

Rank among batters: 715 • *Top target (5 home runs)*: Phil Collins • *Number of pitchers victimized*: 50 • *Total ballparks homered in*: 7 • *First HR*: 04/26/1930 off Erv Brame • *World Series HR*—2

Art Watson

ARTHUR STANHOPE WATSON
B: 01/11/1884 D: 05/09/1950
BL

Year	Tm	Lg	Tot	H	A	0	1	2	3	2	3	4	LO	XN	IP	PH	RHP	LHP
1914	BRO	FL	1	1	0	1	0	0	0	0	0	0	0	0	0	0	1	0
1915	BUF	FL	1	1	0	0	0	1	0	0	0	0	0	0	0	1	1	0
Total			2	2	0	1	0	1	0	0	0	0	0	0	0	1	2	0

Rank among batters: 4,129 • *Total ballparks homered in*: 2 • *First HR*: 09/28/1914 off Claude Hendrix

Bob Watson

ROBERT JOSE WATSON
B: 04/10/1946
BR

Year	Tm	Lg	Tot	H	A	0	1	2	3	2	3	4	LO	XN	IP	PH	RHP	LHP
1967	HOU	NL	1	0	1	0	1	0	0	0	0	0	0	0	0	0	0	1
1968	HOU	NL	2	1	1	2	0	0	0	0	0	0	0	0	0	0	0	2
1970	HOU	NL	11	1	10	4	4	1	2	0	0	0	0	0	0	0	6	5
1971	HOU	NL	9	1	8	4	4	1	0	1	0	0	0	0	0	0	9	0
1972	HOU	NL	16	6	10	11	3	2	0	0	0	0	0	1	0	0	12	4
1973	HOU	NL	16	10	6	10	4	1	1	1	0	0	0	0	0	0	12	4
1974	HOU	NL	11	4	7	7	3	1	0	0	0	0	0	0	0	0	8	3
1975	HOU	NL	18	6	12	11	6	1	0	0	0	0	0	0	0	0	14	4
1976	HOU	NL	16	9	7	9	2	4	1	2	0	0	0	0	0	0	9	7
1977	HOU	NL	22	4	18	6	9	6	1	0	0	0	0	0	0	0	14	8
1978	HOU	NL	14	6	8	7	4	3	0	0	0	0	0	0	0	0	8	6
1979	HOU	NL	3	1	2	2	0	1	0	0	0	0	0	0	0	0	2	1
	BOS	AL	13	7	6	5	6	2	0	2	0	0	0	1	0	0	12	1
	Total		16	8	8	7	6	3	0	2	0	0	0	1	0	0	14	2
1980	NY	AL	13	3	10	8	2	2	1	1	0	0	0	0	0	0	9	4
1981	NY	AL	6	1	5	6	0	0	0	1	0	0	0	0	0	0	1	5
1982	ATL	NL	5	3	2	1	3	1	0	1	0	0	0	1	0	1	0	5
1983	ATL	NL	6	3	3	3	3	0	0	0	0	0	0	0	0	2	0	6
1984	ATL	NL	2	1	1	2	0	0	0	0	0	0	0	0	0	0	0	2
Total			184	67	117	98	54	26	6	9	0	0	0	3	0	3	116	68

Rank among batters: 210 • *Top target (7 home runs)*: Fred Norman • *Number of pitchers victimized*: 138 • *Total ballparks homered in*: 26 • *First HR*: 09/30/1967 off Jim Shellenback • *Hit for Cycle*—vs SF: 06/24/1977; @BAL: 09/15/1979 • *World Series HR*—2

Mule Watson

JOHN REEVES WATSON
B: 10/15/1896 D: 08/25/1949
BR

Year	Tm	Lg	Tot	H	A	Men-On 0	1	2	3	One-Game 2	3	4	LO	XN	IP	PH	RHP	LHP
1924	NY	NL	2	2	0	0	0	1	1	0	0	0	0	0	0	0	2	0

Rank among batters: 4,129 • *Total ballparks homered in*: 1 • *First HR*: 06/08/1924 off Johnny Morrison

Eddie Watt

EDWARD DEAN WATT
B: 04/04/1941
BR

Year	Tm	Lg	Tot	H	A	Men-On 0	1	2	3	One-Game 2	3	4	LO	XN	IP	PH	RHP	LHP
1966	BAL	AL	2	1	1	2	0	0	0	0	0	0	0	0	0	0	0	2
1967	BAL	AL	1	1	0	1	0	0	0	0	0	0	0	0	0	0	0	1
Total			3	2	1	3	0	0	0	0	0	0	0	0	0	0	0	3

Rank among batters: 3,735 • *Total ballparks homered in*: 2 • *First HR*: 07/19/1966 off Johnny Podres

Johnny Watwood

JOHN CLIFFORD WATWOOD
B: 08/17/1905 D: 03/01/1980
BL

Year	Tm	Lg	Tot	H	A	Men-On 0	1	2	3	One-Game 2	3	4	LO	XN	IP	PH	RHP	LHP
1929	CHI	AL	2	0	2	2	0	0	0	0	0	0	0	0	1	0	2	0
1930	CHI	AL	2	2	0	0	1	1	0	0	0	0	0	0	1	0	1	1
1931	CHI	AL	1	0	1	0	1	0	0	0	0	0	0	0	0	0	1	0
Total			5	2	3	2	2	1	0	0	0	0	0	0	2	0	4	1

Rank among batters: 3,191 • *Top target (2 home runs)*: Roy Mahaffey • *Number of pitchers victimized*: 4 • *Total ballparks homered in*: 4 • *First HR*: 06/16/1929 off Firpo Marberry

Roy Weatherly

CYRIL ROY WEATHERLY
B: 02/25/1915 D: 01/19/1991
BL

Year	Tm	Lg	Tot	H	A	Men-On 0	1	2	3	One-Game 2	3	4	LO	XN	IP	PH	RHP	LHP
1936	CLE	AL	8	6	2	6	1	1	0	2	0	0	0	0	0	0	7	1
1937	CLE	AL	5	2	3	4	1	0	0	0	0	0	0	0	0	1	3	2
1938	CLE	AL	2	2	0	2	0	0	0	0	0	0	0	1	0	0	2	0
1939	CLE	AL	1	0	1	1	0	0	0	0	0	0	0	0	0	0	1	0
1940	CLE	AL	12	7	5	7	5	0	0	0	0	0	0	0	0	0	9	3
1941	CLE	AL	3	2	1	1	2	0	0	0	0	0	0	0	0	0	1	2
1942	CLE	AL	5	1	4	4	1	0	0	0	0	0	1	0	0	0	5	0
1943	NY	AL	7	6	1	4	2	1	0	0	0	0	1	1	0	0	7	0
Total			43	26	17	29	12	2	0	2	0	0	2	2	0	1	35	8

Rank among batters: 1,116 • *Top target (3 home runs)*: Schoolboy Rowe, Eddie Smith • *Number of pitchers victimized*: 34 • *Total ballparks homered in*: 7 • *First HR*: 07/09/1936 off Monte Pearson

Buck Weaver

GEORGE DANIEL WEAVER
B: 08/18/1890 D: 01/31/1956
BR

Year	Tm	Lg	Tot	H	A	Men-On 0	1	2	3	One-Game 2	3	4	LO	XN	IP	PH	RHP	LHP
1912	CHI	AL	1	1	0	0	1	0	0	0	0	0	0	0	0	0	0	1
1913	CHI	AL	4	0	4	2	2	0	0	0	0	0	0	0	1	0	1	3
1914	CHI	AL	2	1	1	2	0	0	0	0	0	0	2	0	0	0	0	2
1915	CHI	AL	3	1	2	0	2	1	0	0	0	0	0	0	1	0	2	1
1916	CHI	AL	3	2	1	3	0	0	0	0	0	0	0	0	0	0	1	2
1917	CHI	AL	3	1	2	1	2	0	0	0	0	0	0	0	1	0	1	2
1919	CHI	AL	3	0	3	2	1	0	0	0	0	0	0	0	1	0	1	2
1920	CHI	AL	2	1	1	2	0	0	0	0	0	0	0	0	0	0	1	1
Total			21	7	14	12	8	1	0	0	0	0	2	0	4	0	7	14

Rank among batters: 1,768 • Top target (2 home runs): Willie Mitchell, Bob Shawkey, Dutch Leonard, Harry Harper, Herb Pennock • *Number of pitchers victimized*: 16 • *Total ballparks homered in*: 7 • *First HR*: 07/06/1912 off Harry Moran

Farmer Weaver

WILLIAM B. WEAVER
B: 03/23/1865 D: 01/23/1943
BL

Year	Tm	Lg	Tot	H	A	Men-On 0	1	2	3	One-Game 2	3	4	LO	XN	IP	PH	RHP	LHP
1890	LOU	AA	3	2	1	1	1	1	0	0	0	0	0	0	0	0	1	1
1891	LOU	AA	1	1	0	0	1	0	0	0	0	0	0	0	1	0	0	1

						Men-On				One-Game							
Year	Tm	Lg	Tot	H	A	0	1	2	3	2	3	4	LO	XN	IP	PH	RHP	LHP

Farmer Weaver *continued*

Year	Tm	Lg	Tot	H	A	0	1	2	3	2	3	4	LO	XN	IP	PH	RHP	LHP
1893	LOU	NL	2	0	2	1	1	0	0	0	0	0	0	0	0	0	2	0
1894	LOU	NL	3	0	3	0	2	1	0	0	0	0	0	0	1	0	2	0
Total			9	3	6	2	5	2	0	0	0	0	0	0	2	0	5	2

Rank among batters: 2,587 • *Top target (3 home runs)*: Frank Dwyer • *Number of pitchers victimized*: 7 • *Total ballparks homered in*: 6 • *First HR*: 08/08/1890 off Ed Daily • *Hit for Cycle*—vs SYR: 08/12/1890

Earl Webb

WILLIAM EARL WEBB
B: 09/17/1897 D: 05/23/1965
BL

Year	Tm	Lg	Tot	H	A	0	1	2	3	2	3	4	LO	XN	IP	PH	RHP	LHP
1927	CHI	NL	14	9	5	9	3	2	0	1	0	0	0	1	0	1	11	3
1928	CHI	NL	3	1	2	2	0	1	0	0	0	0	0	0	0	1	3	0
1930	BOS	AL	16	4	12	9	6	1	0	0	0	0	0	0	1	0	15	1
1931	BOS	AL	14	5	9	7	7	0	0	1	0	0	0	0	0	0	10	4
1932	BOS	AL	5	0	5	4	1	0	0	0	0	0	0	0	0	0	5	0
	DET	AL	3	1	2	2	1	0	0	0	0	0	0	0	0	0	3	0
	Total		8	1	7	6	2	0	0	0	0	0	0	0	0	0	8	0
1933	CHI	AL	1	0	1	1	0	0	0	0	0	0	0	0	0	1	1	0
Total			56	20	36	34	18	4	0	2	0	0	0	1	1	3	48	8

Rank among batters: 913 • Top target (3 home runs): Virgil Barnes, Grover Alexander, George Earnshaw, George Pipgras • *Number of pitchers victimized*: 41 • *Total ballparks homered in*: 13 • *First HR*: 04/12/1927 off Grover Alexander

Skeeter Webb

JAMES LAVERNE WEBB
B: 11/04/1909 D: 07/08/1986
BR

Year	Tm	Lg	Tot	H	A	0	1	2	3	2	3	4	LO	XN	IP	PH	RHP	LHP
1939	CLE	AL	2	0	2	2	0	0	0	0	0	0	0	0	0	0	2	0
1940	CHI	AL	1	1	0	0	1	0	0	0	0	0	0	0	0	0	0	1
Total			3	1	2	2	1	0	0	0	0	0	0	0	0	0	2	1

Rank among batters: 3,735 • *Total ballparks homered in*: 3 • *First HR*: 06/16/1939 off Atley Donald

Les Webber

LESTER ELMER WEBBER
B: 05/06/1915 D: 11/13/1986
BR

Year	Tm	Lg	Tot	H	A	0	1	2	3	2	3	4	LO	XN	IP	PH	RHP	LHP
1944	BRO	NL	1	0	1	1	0	0	0	0	0	0	0	0	0	0	1	0

Rank among batters: 4,707 • *Total ballparks homered in*: 1 • *First HR*: 04/28/1944 off Bill Voiselle

Lenny Webster

LEONARD IRELL WEBSTER
B: 02/10/1965
BR

Year	Tm	Lg	Tot	H	A	0	1	2	3	2	3	4	LO	XN	IP	PH	RHP	LHP
1991	MIN	AL	3	1	2	1	2	0	0	0	0	0	0	0	0	0	3	0
1992	MIN	AL	1	1	0	1	0	0	0	0	0	0	0	0	0	0	0	1
1993	MIN	AL	1	1	0	1	0	0	0	0	0	0	0	0	0	0	1	0
1994	MON	NL	5	2	3	3	1	1	0	0	0	0	0	1	0	0	3	2
1995	PHI	NL	4	1	3	4	0	0	0	0	0	0	0	0	0	0	3	1
Total			14	6	8	10	3	1	0	0	0	0	0	1	0	0	10	4

Rank among batters: 2,169 • *Total ballparks homered in*: 8 • *First HR*: 06/02/1991 off Tom Gordon

Mitch Webster

MITCHELL DEAN WEBSTER
B: 05/16/1959
BB

Year	Tm	Lg	Tot	H	A	0	1	2	3	2	3	4	LO	XN	IP	PH	RHP	LHP
1985	MON	NL	11	3	8	8	3	0	0	1	0	0	1	0	0	0	5	6
1986	MON	NL	8	2	6	6	2	0	0	0	0	0	0	0	0	0	3	5
1987	MON	NL	15	9	6	9	3	1	2	1	0	0	0	0	0	0	8	7
1988	MON	NL	2	0	2	2	0	0	0	0	0	0	0	0	0	0	2	0
	CHI	NL	4	3	1	1	3	0	0	0	0	0	0	0	0	0	4	0
	Total		6	3	3	3	3	0	0	0	0	0	0	0	0	0	6	0
1989	CHI	NL	3	1	2	1	2	0	0	0	0	0	0	0	0	0	2	1
1990	CLE	AL	12	6	6	5	5	1	1	0	0	0	1	0	0	1	4	8

Mitch Webster *continued*

Year	Tm	Lg	Tot	H	A	Men-On 0	Men-On 1	Men-On 2	Men-On 3	One-Game 2	One-Game 3	One-Game 4	LO	XN	IP	PH	RHP	LHP
1991	PIT	NL	1	1	0	1	0	0	0	0	0	0	0	0	0	0	0	1
	LA	NL	1	1	0	1	0	0	0	0	0	0	0	0	0	0	0	1
	Total		2	2	0	2	0	0	0	0	0	0	0	0	0	0	0	2
1992	LA	NL	6	1	5	4	1	1	0	0	0	0	0	0	0	2	3	3
1993	LA	NL	2	1	1	1	1	0	0	0	0	0	0	1	0	0	2	0
1994	LA	NL	4	1	3	3	1	0	0	0	0	0	0	1	1	1	1	3
1995	LA	NL	1	0	1	0	1	0	0	0	0	0	0	0	0	1	0	1
Total			70	29	41	42	22	3	3	2	0	0	2	2	1	5	34	36

Rank among batters: 742 • *Top target (3 home runs)*: Mike Dunne • *Number of pitchers victimized*: 62 • *Total ballparks homered in*: 18 • *First HR*: 06/30/1985 off Jerry Koosman

Ray Webster

RAYMOND GEORGE WEBSTER
B: 11/15/1937
BR

Year	Tm	Lg	Tot	H	A	Men-On 0	Men-On 1	Men-On 2	Men-On 3	One-Game 2	One-Game 3	One-Game 4	LO	XN	IP	PH	RHP	LHP
1959	CLE	AL	2	1	1	1	0	1	0	0	0	0	0	0	0	0	2	0

Rank among batters: 4,129 • *Total ballparks homered in*: 2 • *First HR*: 05/06/1959 off Billy Loes

Ray Webster

RAMON ALBERTO WEBSTER
B: 08/31/1942
BL

Year	Tm	Lg	Tot	H	A	Men-On 0	Men-On 1	Men-On 2	Men-On 3	One-Game 2	One-Game 3	One-Game 4	LO	XN	IP	PH	RHP	LHP
1967	KC	AL	11	4	7	4	7	0	0	0	0	0	0	0	0	1	11	0
1968	OAK	AL	3	0	3	1	1	1	0	0	0	0	0	0	0	0	3	0
1969	OAK	AL	1	1	0	1	0	0	0	0	0	0	0	0	0	0	1	0
1970	SD	NL	2	1	1	1	0	0	1	0	0	0	0	0	0	1	2	0
Total			17	6	11	7	8	1	1	0	0	0	0	0	0	2	17	0

Rank among batters: 1,969 • *Top target (2 home runs)*: Earl Wilson • *Number of pitchers victimized*: 16 • *Total ballparks homered in*: 10 • *First HR*: 04/23/1967 off Moe Drabowsky

Eric Wedge

ERIC MICHAEL WEDGE
B: 01/27/1968
BR

Year	Tm	Lg	Tot	H	A	Men-On 0	Men-On 1	Men-On 2	Men-On 3	One-Game 2	One-Game 3	One-Game 4	LO	XN	IP	PH	RHP	LHP
1992	BOS	AL	5	3	2	2	3	0	0	0	0	0	0	0	0	0	1	4

Rank among batters: 3,191 • *Total ballparks homered in*: 3 • *First HR*: 08/21/1992 off Shawn Barton

John Weekly

JOHN WEEKLY
B: 06/14/1937 D: 11/24/1974
BR

Year	Tm	Lg	Tot	H	A	Men-On 0	Men-On 1	Men-On 2	Men-On 3	One-Game 2	One-Game 3	One-Game 4	LO	XN	IP	PH	RHP	LHP
1962	HOU	NL	2	1	1	2	0	0	0	0	0	0	0	0	0	0	1	1
1963	HOU	NL	3	0	3	1	2	0	0	0	0	0	0	0	0	1	3	0
Total			5	1	4	3	2	0	0	0	0	0	0	0	0	1	4	1

Rank among batters: 3,191 • *Total ballparks homered in*: 4 • *First HR*: 04/19/1962 off Don Cardwell

Herm Wehmeier

HERMAN RALPH WEHMEIER
B: 02/18/1927 D: 05/21/1973
BR

Year	Tm	Lg	Tot	H	A	Men-On 0	Men-On 1	Men-On 2	Men-On 3	One-Game 2	One-Game 3	One-Game 4	LO	XN	IP	PH	RHP	LHP
1952	CIN	NL	1	0	1	1	0	0	0	0	0	0	0	0	0	0	1	0
1956	STL	NL	2	0	2	1	1	0	0	0	0	0	0	0	0	0	2	0
Total			3	0	3	2	1	0	0	0	0	0	0	0	0	0	3	0

Rank among batters: 3,735 • *Total ballparks homered in*: 3 • *First HR*: 08/11/1952 off Woody Main

Podge Weihe

JOHN GARIBALDI WEIHE
B: 11/13/1862 D: 04/15/1914
BR

Year	Tm	Lg	Tot	H	A	Men-On 0	Men-On 1	Men-On 2	Men-On 3	One-Game 2	One-Game 3	One-Game 4	LO	XN	IP	PH	RHP	LHP
1884	IND	AA	4	4	0	1	2	1	0	1	0	0	0	0	1	0	2	0

Rank among batters: 3,427 • *Top target (2 home runs)*: Pete Meegan • *Number of pitchers victimized*: 3 • *Total ballparks homered in*: 2 • *First HR*: 07/06/1884 off John Hamill

Year	Tm	Lg	Tot	H	A	Men-On				One-Game			LO	XN	IP	PH	RHP	LHP
						0	1	2	3	2	3	4						

Bob Weiland

ROBERT GEORGE WEILAND
B: 12/14/1905 D: 11/09/1988
BL

Year	Tm	Lg	Tot	H	A	0	1	2	3	2	3	4	LO	XN	IP	PH	RHP	LHP
1934	CLE	AL	1	1	0	1	0	0	0	0	0	0	0	0	0	0	1	0
1937	STL	NL	2	1	1	1	0	1	0	0	0	0	0	0	0	0	2	0
Total			3	2	1	2	0	1	0	0	0	0	0	0	0	0	3	0

Rank among batters: 3,735 • *Total ballparks homered in*: 3 • *First HR*: 09/17/1934 off Reese Diggs

Jake Weimer

JACOB WEIMER
B: 11/29/1873 D: 06/19/1928
BR

Year	Tm	Lg	Tot	H	A	0	1	2	3	2	3	4	LO	XN	IP	PH	RHP	LHP
1907	CIN	NL	1	0	1	1	0	0	0	0	0	0	0	0	0	0	1	0

Rank among batters: 4,707 • *Total ballparks homered in*: 1 • *First HR*: 07/06/1907 off Gus Dorner

Phil Weintraub

PHILIP WEINTRAUB
B: 10/12/1907 D: 06/21/1987
BL

Year	Tm	Lg	Tot	H	A	0	1	2	3	2	3	4	LO	XN	IP	PH	RHP	LHP
1933	NY	NL	1	0	1	1	0	0	0	0	0	0	0	0	0	0	1	0
1935	NY	NL	1	0	1	1	0	0	0	0	0	0	0	0	0	0	1	0
1937	CIN	NL	3	1	2	2	0	1	0	0	0	0	0	0	0	0	3	0
1938	PHI	NL	4	2	2	4	0	0	0	0	0	0	0	0	0	0	3	1
1944	NY	NL	13	10	3	6	4	2	1	1	0	0	0	0	0	0	9	4
1945	NY	NL	10	8	2	5	3	2	0	1	0	0	0	0	0	0	8	2
Total			32	21	11	19	7	5	1	2	0	0	0	0	0	0	25	7

Rank among batters: 1,360 • *Top target (2 home runs)*: Fritz Ostermueller, Frank Dasso • *Number of pitchers victimized*: 30 • *Total ballparks homered in*: 7 • *First HR*: 09/07/1933 off Heinie Meine

Al Weis

ALBERT JOHN WEIS
B: 04/02/1938
BB

Year	Tm	Lg	Tot	H	A	0	1	2	3	2	3	4	LO	XN	IP	PH	RHP	LHP
1964	CHI	AL	2	0	2	2	0	0	0	0	0	0	0	0	0	0	0	2
1965	CHI	AL	1	0	1	1	0	0	0	0	0	0	0	0	0	0	0	1
1968	NY	NL	1	0	1	1	0	0	0	0	0	0	0	0	0	0	1	0
1969	NY	NL	2	0	2	1	0	1	0	0	0	0	0	0	0	0	1	1
1970	NY	NL	1	0	1	0	1	0	0	0	0	0	0	0	0	0	0	1
Total			7	0	7	5	1	1	0	0	0	0	0	0	0	0	2	5

Rank among batters: 2,834 • *Total ballparks homered in*: 6 • *First HR*: 06/03/1964 off Tommy John • *World Series HR*—1

Butch Weis

ARTHUR JOHN WEIS
B: 03/02/1901
BL

Year	Tm	Lg	Tot	H	A	0	1	2	3	2	3	4	LO	XN	IP	PH	RHP	LHP
1925	CHI	NL	2	1	1	1	0	1	0	0	0	0	0	0	1	0	1	1

Rank among batters: 4,129 • *Total ballparks homered in*: 2 • *First HR*: 06/12/1925 off Johnny Cooney

Walt Weiss

WALTER WILLIAM WEISS
B: 11/28/1963
BB

Year	Tm	Lg	Tot	H	A	0	1	2	3	2	3	4	LO	XN	IP	PH	RHP	LHP
1988	OAK	AL	3	0	3	2	0	0	1	0	0	0	0	0	0	0	3	0
1989	OAK	AL	3	2	1	0	3	0	0	1	0	0	0	0	0	0	3	0
1990	OAK	AL	2	1	1	2	0	0	0	0	0	0	0	0	0	0	2	0
1993	FLO	NL	1	0	1	1	0	0	0	0	0	0	0	0	0	0	1	0
1994	COL	NL	1	1	0	1	0	0	0	0	0	0	0	0	0	0	0	1
1995	COL	NL	1	0	1	1	0	0	0	0	0	0	0	0	0	0	1	0
Total			11	4	7	7	3	0	1	1	0	0	0	0	0	0	10	1

Rank among batters: 2,419 • *Total ballparks homered in*: 8 • *First HR*: 05/15/1988 off Mark Williamson • *World Series HR*—1

Johnny Welaj

JOHN LUDWIG WELAJ
B: 05/27/1914
BR

Year	Tm	Lg	Tot	H	A	0	1	2	3	2	3	4	LO	XN	IP	PH	RHP	LHP
1939	WAS	AL	1	0	1	0	1	0	0	0	0	0	0	0	0	0	0	1

Johnny Welaj *continued*

Year	Tm	Lg	Tot	H	A	Men-On 0	Men-On 1	Men-On 2	Men-On 3	One-Game 2	One-Game 3	One-Game 4	LO	XN	IP	PH	RHP	LHP
1940	WAS	AL	3	1	2	3	0	0	0	0	0	0	0	1	1	1	2	1
Total			4	1	3	3	1	0	0	0	0	0	0	1	1	1	2	2

Rank among batters: 3,427 • *Total ballparks homered in*: 4 • *First HR*: 09/10/1939 off Marius Russo

Bob Welch

ROBERT LYNN WELCH
B: 11/03/1956
BR

Year	Tm	Lg	Tot	H	A	Men-On 0	Men-On 1	Men-On 2	Men-On 3	One-Game 2	One-Game 3	One-Game 4	LO	XN	IP	PH	RHP	LHP
1983	LA	NL	1	1	0	1	0	0	0	0	0	0	0	0	0	0	1	0
1986	LA	NL	1	0	1	0	0	1	0	0	0	0	0	0	0	0	0	1
Total			2	1	1	1	0	1	0	0	0	0	0	0	0	0	1	1

Rank among batters: 4,129 • *Total ballparks homered in*: 2 • *First HR*: 06/17/1983 off Mario Soto

Curt Welch

CURTIS BENTON WELCH
B: 02/11/1862 D: 08/29/1896
BR

Year	Tm	Lg	Tot	H	A	Men-On 0	Men-On 1	Men-On 2	Men-On 3	One-Game 2	One-Game 3	One-Game 4	LO	XN	IP	PH	RHP	LHP
1885	STL	AA	3	0	3	1	2	0	0	0	0	0	0	0	1	0	3	0
1886	STL	AA	2	2	0	0	0	1	1	0	0	0	0	0	1	0	1	1
1887	STL	AA	3	1	2	1	0	2	0	0	0	0	0	0	0	0	2	0
1888	PHI	AA	1	1	0	1	0	0	0	0	0	0	0	0	0	0	1	0
1890	PHI	AA	2	1	1	1	0	1	0	0	0	0	1	0	0	0	0	1
1891	BAL	AA	3	1	2	2	1	0	0	0	0	0	1	0	0	0	1	2
1892	BAL	NL	1	0	1	1	0	0	0	0	0	0	0	0	0	0	1	0
	CIN	NL	1	1	0	0	1	0	0	0	0	0	0	0	0	0	1	0
	Total		2	1	1	1	1	0	0	0	0	0	0	0	0	0	2	0
Total			16	7	9	7	4	4	1	0	0	0	2	0	2	0	10	4

Rank among batters: 2,029 • *Top target (2 home runs)*: Bobby Mathews • *Number of pitchers victimized*: 15 • *Total ballparks homered in*: 9 • *First HR*: 04/29/1885 off Will White • *World Series HR*—1

Frank Welch

FRANK TIGUER WELCH
B: 08/10/1897 D: 07/25/1957
BR

Year	Tm	Lg	Tot	H	A	Men-On 0	Men-On 1	Men-On 2	Men-On 3	One-Game 2	One-Game 3	One-Game 4	LO	XN	IP	PH	RHP	LHP
1919	PHI	AL	2	2	0	1	1	0	0	0	0	0	0	0	0	0	1	1
1920	PHI	AL	4	4	0	1	1	2	0	0	0	0	0	0	0	0	1	3
1921	PHI	AL	7	5	2	1	6	0	0	1	0	0	0	0	1	0	3	4
1922	PHI	AL	11	7	4	6	4	1	0	0	0	0	1	0	0	0	10	1
1923	PHI	AL	4	2	2	4	0	0	0	0	0	0	0	0	1	0	2	2
1924	PHI	AL	5	2	3	2	2	1	0	0	0	0	0	0	0	0	5	0
1925	PHI	AL	4	3	1	1	2	1	0	0	0	0	0	0	0	1	3	1
1926	PHI	AL	4	3	1	2	2	0	0	0	0	0	0	0	0	0	1	3
Total			41	28	13	18	18	5	0	1	0	0	1	0	2	1	26	15

Rank among batters: 1,163 • *Top target (3 home runs)*: Bob Shawkey • *Number of pitchers victimized*: 34 • *Total ballparks homered in*: 8 • *First HR*: 09/09/1919 off Dutch Leonard

Johnny Welch

JOHN VERNON WELCH
B: 12/02/1906 D: 09/02/1940
BL

Year	Tm	Lg	Tot	H	A	Men-On 0	Men-On 1	Men-On 2	Men-On 3	One-Game 2	One-Game 3	One-Game 4	LO	XN	IP	PH	RHP	LHP
1932	BOS	AL	1	0	1	1	0	0	0	0	0	0	0	0	0	0	1	0

Rank among batters: 4,707 • *Total ballparks homered in*: 1 • *First HR*: 08/09/1932 off Buck Marrow

Mickey Welch

MICHAEL FRANCIS WELCH
B: 07/04/1859 D: 07/30/1941
BR HOF

Year	Tm	Lg	Tot	H	A	Men-On 0	Men-On 1	Men-On 2	Men-On 3	One-Game 2	One-Game 3	One-Game 4	LO	XN	IP	PH	RHP	LHP
1882	TRO	NL	1	0	1	1	0	0	0	0	0	0	0	0	0	0	1	0
1883	NY	NL	2	2	0	0	1	1	0	0	0	0	0	0	0	0	2	0
1884	NY	NL	3	2	1	2	0	1	0	0	0	0	0	0	0	0	2	1
1885	NY	NL	2	1	1	0	2	0	0	0	0	0	0	0	0	0	2	0
1887	NY	NL	2	1	1	1	1	0	0	0	0	0	0	0	0	0	2	0

Mickey Welch *continued*

Year	Tm	Lg	Tot	H	A	Men-On 0	1	2	3	One-Game 2	3	4	LO	XN	IP	PH	RHP	LHP
1888	NY	NL	2	1	1	1	1	0	0	0	0	0	0	0	0	0	1	1
Total			12	7	5	5	5	2	0	0	0	0	0	0	0	0	10	2

Rank among batters: 2,325 • *Top target (2 home runs)*: Larry Corcoran • *Number of pitchers victimized*: 11 • *Total ballparks homered in*: 6 • *First HR*: 06/22/1882 off Hugh Daily

Tub Welch

JAMES T. WELCH
B: 07/03/1866

Year	Tm	Lg	Tot	H	A	Men-On 0	1	2	3	One-Game 2	3	4	LO	XN	IP	PH	RHP	LHP
1890	TOL	AA	1	1	0	1	0	0	0	0	0	0	1	0	0	0	1	0
1895	LOU	NL	1	0	1	1	0	0	0	0	0	0	0	0	0	0	1	0
Total			2	1	1	2	0	0	0	0	0	0	1	0	0	0	2	0

Rank among batters: 4,129 • *Total ballparks homered in*: 2 • *First HR*: 08/18/1890 off Con Murphy

Bob Wellman

ROBERT JOSEPH WELLMAN
B: 07/15/1925 D: 12/20/1994
BR

Year	Tm	Lg	Tot	H	A	Men-On 0	1	2	3	One-Game 2	3	4	LO	XN	IP	PH	RHP	LHP
1950	PHI	AL	1	1	0	1	0	0	0	0	0	0	0	0	0	0	0	1

Rank among batters: 4,707 • *Total ballparks homered in*: 1 • *First HR*: 04/23/1950 off Mel Parnell

Brad Wellman

BRAD EUGENE WELLMAN
B: 08/17/1959
BR

Year	Tm	Lg	Tot	H	A	Men-On 0	1	2	3	One-Game 2	3	4	LO	XN	IP	PH	RHP	LHP
1983	SF	NL	1	1	0	0	1	0	0	0	0	0	0	0	0	0	1	0
1984	SF	NL	2	2	0	0	2	0	0	0	0	0	0	0	0	0	1	1
1988	KC	AL	1	1	0	1	0	0	0	0	0	0	0	0	1	0	1	0
1989	KC	AL	2	0	2	2	0	0	0	0	0	0	0	0	0	0	1	1
Total			6	4	2	3	3	0	0	0	0	0	0	0	1	0	4	2

Rank among batters: 2,988 • *Total ballparks homered in*: 4 • *First HR*: 06/03/1983 off Bill Gullickson

Leo Wells

LEO DONALD WELLS
B: 07/18/1917
BR

Year	Tm	Lg	Tot	H	A	Men-On 0	1	2	3	One-Game 2	3	4	LO	XN	IP	PH	RHP	LHP
1942	CHI	AL	1	0	1	1	0	0	0	0	0	0	0	0	0	0	1	0
1946	CHI	AL	1	0	1	0	1	0	0	0	0	0	0	0	1	0	0	1
Total			2	0	2	1	1	0	0	0	0	0	0	0	1	0	1	1

Rank among batters: 4,129 • *Total ballparks homered in*: 2 • *First HR*: 05/06/1942 off Joe Dobson

Chris Welsh

CHRISTOPHER CHARLES WELSH
B: 04/14/1955
BL

Year	Tm	Lg	Tot	H	A	Men-On 0	1	2	3	One-Game 2	3	4	LO	XN	IP	PH	RHP	LHP
1986	CIN	NL	1	0	1	1	0	0	0	0	0	0	0	0	0	0	0	1

Rank among batters: 4,707 • *Total ballparks homered in*: 1 • *First HR*: 07/05/1986 off Don Carman

Jimmy Welsh

JAMES DANIEL WELSH
B: 10/09/1902 D: 10/30/1970
BL

Year	Tm	Lg	Tot	H	A	Men-On 0	1	2	3	One-Game 2	3	4	LO	XN	IP	PH	RHP	LHP
1925	BOS	NL	7	0	7	4	2	1	0	1	0	0	0	0	1	0	6	1
1926	BOS	NL	3	1	2	1	2	0	0	0	0	0	0	0	1	0	3	0
1927	BOS	NL	9	0	9	6	2	1	0	0	0	0	0	0	0	0	7	2
1928	NY	NL	9	4	5	8	0	1	0	0	0	0	2	0	0	0	9	0
1929	NY	NL	2	1	1	2	0	0	0	0	0	0	1	0	0	0	2	0
	BOS	NL	2	1	1	2	0	0	0	0	0	0	0	0	0	0	2	0
	Total		4	2	2	4	0	0	0	0	0	0	1	0	0	0	4	0
1930	BOS	NL	3	1	2	2	1	0	0	0	0	0	0	0	0	0	3	0
Total			35	8	27	25	7	3	0	1	0	0	3	0	2	0	32	3

Rank among batters: 1,291 • *Top target (2 home runs)*: Huck Betts, Wayland Dean, Jesse Petty, Charlie Root, Ray Kremer, Hal Carlson • *Number of pitchers victimized*: 29 • *Total ballparks homered in*: 8 • *First HR*: 05/01/1925 off Skinny O'Neal

Julie Wera

JULIAN VALENTINE WERA
B: 02/09/1902 D: 12/12/1975
BR

Year	Tm	Lg	Tot	H	A	Men-On 0	Men-On 1	Men-On 2	Men-On 3	One-Game 2	One-Game 3	One-Game 4	LO	XN	IP	PH	RHP	LHP
1927	NY	AL	1	1	0	0	1	0	0	0	0	0	0	0	0	0	0	1

Rank among batters: 4,707 • *Total ballparks homered in*: 1 • *First HR*: 07/04/1927 off Bobby Burke

Billy Werber

WILLIAM MURRAY WERBER
B: 06/20/1908
BR

Year	Tm	Lg	Tot	H	A	Men-On 0	Men-On 1	Men-On 2	Men-On 3	One-Game 2	One-Game 3	One-Game 4	LO	XN	IP	PH	RHP	LHP
1933	BOS	AL	3	0	3	2	1	0	0	0	0	0	1	0	0	0	3	0
1934	BOS	AL	11	2	9	9	2	0	0	1	0	0	0	0	3	0	11	0
1935	BOS	AL	14	6	8	8	4	2	0	2	0	0	0	0	0	0	13	1
1936	BOS	AL	10	2	8	2	3	5	0	0	0	0	0	0	0	0	9	1
1937	PHI	AL	7	6	1	5	0	2	0	0	0	0	0	0	0	0	7	0
1938	PHI	AL	11	7	4	4	6	1	0	0	0	0	0	0	0	0	10	1
1939	CIN	NL	5	3	2	3	2	0	0	0	0	0	1	0	0	0	4	1
1940	CIN	NL	12	5	7	9	2	1	0	0	0	0	1	0	1	0	11	1
1941	CIN	NL	4	2	2	2	1	1	0	0	0	0	0	0	0	0	3	1
1942	NY	NL	1	1	0	0	1	0	0	0	0	0	0	0	0	0	1	0
Total			78	34	44	44	22	12	0	3	0	0	3	0	4	0	72	6

Rank among batters: 672 • *Top target (3 home runs)*: Max Butcher • *Number of pitchers victimized*: 55 • *Total ballparks homered in*: 13 • *First HR*: 07/01/1933 off Sam Jones

Perry Werden

PERCIVAL WHERITT WERDEN
B: 07/21/1865 D: 01/09/1934
BR

Year	Tm	Lg	Tot	H	A	Men-On 0	Men-On 1	Men-On 2	Men-On 3	One-Game 2	One-Game 3	One-Game 4	LO	XN	IP	PH	RHP	LHP
1890	TOL	AA	6	3	3	3	2	1	0	0	0	0	1	0	0	0	2	2
1891	BAL	AA	6	1	5	1	1	4	0	0	0	0	0	0	0	0	1	3
1892	STL	NL	8	5	3	2	3	2	1	0	0	0	0	0	0	0	6	1
1893	STL	NL	1	0	1	1	0	0	0	0	0	0	0	0	0	0	1	0
1897	LOU	NL	5	4	1	3	2	0	0	0	0	0	0	0	2	0	4	1
Total			26	13	13	10	8	7	1	0	0	0	1	0	2	0	14	6

Rank among batters: 1,576 • *Top target (2 home runs)*: Tim Keefe, Kid Carsey • *Number of pitchers victimized*: 24 • *Total ballparks homered in*: 10 • *First HR*: 04/22/1890 off Elton Chamberlin

Johnny Werhas

JOHN CHARLES WERHAS
B: 02/07/1938
BR

Year	Tm	Lg	Tot	H	A	Men-On 0	Men-On 1	Men-On 2	Men-On 3	One-Game 2	One-Game 3	One-Game 4	LO	XN	IP	PH	RHP	LHP
1967	CAL	AL	2	0	2	1	1	0	0	0	0	0	0	0	0	1	0	2

Rank among batters: 4,129 • *Total ballparks homered in*: 2 • *First HR*: 06/04/1967 off Jim Merritt

Don Werner

DONALD PAUL WERNER
B: 03/08/1953
BR

Year	Tm	Lg	Tot	H	A	Men-On 0	Men-On 1	Men-On 2	Men-On 3	One-Game 2	One-Game 3	One-Game 4	LO	XN	IP	PH	RHP	LHP
1977	CIN	NL	2	0	2	2	0	0	0	0	0	0	0	0	0	0	0	2

Rank among batters: 4,129 • *Total ballparks homered in*: 2 • *First HR*: 09/18/1977 off Bob Knepper

Joe Werrick

JOSEPH ABRAHAM WERRICK
B: 10/25/1861 D: 05/10/1943
BR

Year	Tm	Lg	Tot	H	A	Men-On 0	Men-On 1	Men-On 2	Men-On 3	One-Game 2	One-Game 3	One-Game 4	LO	XN	IP	PH	RHP	LHP
1886	LOU	AA	3	3	0	0	1	1	1	0	0	0	0	0	0	0	2	1
1887	LOU	AA	7	4	3	3	3	1	0	0	0	0	0	0	0	0	3	3
Total			10	7	3	3	4	2	1	0	0	0	0	0	0	0	5	4

Rank among batters: 2,500 • *Top target (2 home runs)*: Matt Kilroy • *Number of pitchers victimized*: 9 • *Total ballparks homered in*: 4 • *First HR*: 08/12/1886 off John Harkins

Don Wert

DONALD RALPH WERT
B: 07/29/1938
BR

Year	Tm	Lg	Tot	H	A	Men-On 0	Men-On 1	Men-On 2	Men-On 3	One-Game 2	One-Game 3	One-Game 4	LO	XN	IP	PH	RHP	LHP
1963	DET	AL	7	5	2	6	0	1	0	0	0	0	1	0	0	0	2	5

Don Wert *continued*

Year	Tm	Lg	Tot	H	A	Men-On 0	1	2	3	One-Game 2	3	4	LO	XN	IP	PH	RHP	LHP
1964	DET	AL	9	5	4	4	1	4	0	0	0	0	0	0	0	0	4	5
1965	DET	AL	12	9	3	8	2	2	0	0	0	0	0	0	0	0	5	7
1966	DET	AL	11	8	3	6	4	0	1	0	0	0	1	1	0	0	6	5
1967	DET	AL	6	4	2	6	0	0	0	1	0	0	0	0	0	0	4	2
1968	DET	AL	12	3	9	11	1	0	0	1	0	0	0	1	0	0	10	2
1969	DET	AL	14	9	5	11	1	2	0	1	0	0	0	1	0	0	9	5
1970	DET	AL	6	4	2	2	2	2	0	0	0	0	0	0	0	0	3	3
Total			77	47	30	54	11	11	1	3	0	0	2	3	0	0	43	34

Rank among batters: 682 • Top target (3 home runs): Claude Osteen, Tommy John, Jim Perry, Wally Bunker • *Number of pitchers victimized*: 58 • *Total ballparks homered in*: 14 • *First HR*: 07/25/1963 off Joe Horlen

Dennis Werth

DENNIS DEAN WERTH
B: 12/29/1952
BR

Year	Tm	Lg	Tot	H	A	Men-On 0	1	2	3	One-Game 2	3	4	LO	XN	IP	PH	RHP	LHP
1980	NY	AL	3	1	2	1	1	1	0	0	0	0	0	0	0	1	0	3

Rank among batters: 3,735 • *Total ballparks homered in*: 3 • *First HR*: 05/23/1980 off Paul Mirabella

Johnny Wertz

HENRY LEVI WERTZ
B: 04/20/1898 D: 09/24/1990
BR

Year	Tm	Lg	Tot	H	A	Men-On 0	1	2	3	One-Game 2	3	4	LO	XN	IP	PH	RHP	LHP
1926	BOS	NL	1	0	1	1	0	0	0	0	0	0	0	0	0	0	1	0

Rank among batters: 4,707 • *Total ballparks homered in*: 1 • *First HR*: 08/26/1926 off Guy Bush

Vic Wertz

VICTOR WOODROW WERTZ
B: 02/09/1925 D: 07/07/1983
BL

Year	Tm	Lg	Tot	H	A	Men-On 0	1	2	3	One-Game 2	3	4	LO	XN	IP	PH	RHP	LHP
1947	DET	AL	6	3	3	3	1	2	0	0	0	0	0	0	0	0	5	1
1948	DET	AL	7	5	2	4	0	3	0	0	0	0	0	0	0	0	6	1
1949	DET	AL	20	12	8	7	8	3	2	2	0	0	0	0	0	0	12	8
1950	DET	AL	27	16	11	13	7	7	0	2	0	0	0	1	0	0	19	8
1951	DET	AL	27	13	14	16	4	7	0	2	0	0	0	0	0	0	24	3
1952	DET	AL	17	9	8	5	8	4	0	1	0	0	0	0	0	1	15	2
	STL	AL	6	2	4	4	1	1	0	2	0	0	0	0	0	0	4	2
	Total		23	11	12	9	9	5	0	3	0	0	0	0	0	1	19	4
1953	STL	AL	19	10	9	12	4	2	1	1	0	0	0	0	0	0	13	6
1954	BAL	AL	1	0	1	1	0	0	0	0	0	0	0	0	0	0	1	0
	CLE	AL	14	8	6	10	4	0	0	1	0	0	0	0	0	0	12	2
	Total		15	8	7	11	4	0	0	1	0	0	0	0	0	0	13	2
1955	CLE	AL	14	6	8	5	7	1	1	1	0	0	0	0	0	0	7	7
1956	CLE	AL	32	13	19	15	12	5	0	3	0	0	0	1	0	0	26	6
1957	CLE	AL	28	9	19	14	9	4	1	5	0	0	0	0	0	0	24	4
1958	CLE	AL	3	1	2	1	2	0	0	0	0	0	0	0	0	1	3	0
1959	BOS	AL	7	3	4	3	2	1	1	0	0	0	0	0	0	1	6	1
1960	BOS	AL	19	16	3	4	4	8	3	1	0	0	0	1	0	1	17	2
1961	BOS	AL	11	5	6	3	7	0	1	0	0	0	0	0	0	0	9	2
1962	DET	AL	5	3	2	4	1	0	0	0	0	0	0	0	0	3	5	0
1963	MIN	AL	3	0	3	1	2	0	0	0	0	0	0	0	0	2	3	0
Total			266	134	132	125	83	48	10	21	0	0	0	3	0	9	211	55

Rank among batters: 95 • *Top target (8 home runs)*: Frank Sullivan • *Number of pitchers victimized*: 134 • *Total ballparks homered in*: 12 • *First HR*: 08/13/1947 off Bob Muncrief • *Hit for Cycle*—@WAS: 09/14/1947 (1) • *World Series HR*—1; *All-Star HR*—1

Buck West

MILTON DOUGLAS WEST
B: 08/29/1860 D: 01/13/1929
BL

Year	Tm	Lg	Tot	H	A	Men-On 0	1	2	3	One-Game 2	3	4	LO	XN	IP	PH	RHP	LHP
1884	CIN	AA	1	1	0	0	0	1	0	0	0	0	0	0	0	0	1	0
1890	CLE	NL	2	2	0	0	0	2	0	0	0	0	0	0	0	0	1	1
Total			3	3	0	0	0	3	0	0	0	0	0	0	0	0	2	1

Rank among batters: 3,735 • *Total ballparks homered in*: 3 • *First HR*: 09/11/1884 off Jack Neagle

Year	Tm	Lg	Tot	H	A	Men-On				One-Game			LO	XN	IP	PH	RHP	LHP
						0	1	2	3	2	3	4						

David West

DAVID LEE WEST
B: 09/01/1964
BL

Year	Tm	Lg	Tot	H	A	0	1	2	3	2	3	4	LO	XN	IP	PH	RHP	LHP
1995	PHI	NL	1	0	1	0	0	1	0	0	0	0	0	0	0	0	1	0

Rank among batters: 4,707 • *Total ballparks homered in*: 1 • *First HR*: 07/06/1995 off Steve Parris

Dick West

RICHARD THOMAS WEST
B: 11/24/1915
BR

Year	Tm	Lg	Tot	H	A	0	1	2	3	2	3	4	LO	XN	IP	PH	RHP	LHP
1940	CIN	NL	1	1	0	1	0	0	0	0	0	0	0	0	0	0	0	1
1941	CIN	NL	1	0	1	1	0	0	0	0	0	0	0	0	0	0	1	0
1942	CIN	NL	1	0	1	0	1	0	0	0	0	0	0	0	0	0	1	0
Total			3	1	2	2	1	0	0	0	0	0	0	0	0	0	2	1

Rank among batters: 3,735 • *Total ballparks homered in*: 3 • *First HR*: 09/29/1940 off Ken Heintzelman

Max West

MAX EDWARD WEST
B: 11/28/1916
BL

Year	Tm	Lg	Tot	H	A	0	1	2	3	2	3	4	LO	XN	IP	PH	RHP	LHP
1938	BOS	NL	10	2	8	5	4	1	0	1	0	0	0	0	0	0	8	2
1939	BOS	NL	19	2	17	6	9	4	0	1	0	0	0	2	0	0	18	1
1940	BOS	NL	7	2	5	2	2	3	0	0	0	0	0	0	0	0	7	0
1941	BOS	NL	12	6	6	9	3	0	0	0	0	0	0	0	0	2	10	2
1942	BOS	NL	16	12	4	7	6	2	1	2	0	0	0	2	0	0	16	0
1946	CIN	NL	5	3	2	3	2	0	0	0	0	0	0	0	0	0	5	0
1948	PIT	NL	8	1	7	3	2	3	0	0	0	0	0	0	0	1	7	1
Total			77	28	49	35	28	13	1	4	0	0	0	4	0	3	71	6

Rank among batters: 682 • *Top target (6 home runs)*: Curt Davis • *Number of pitchers victimized*: 58 • *Total ballparks homered in*: 8 • *First HR*: 04/20/1938 off Hal Schumacher • *All-Star HR*—1

Sam West

SAMUEL FILMORE WEST
B: 10/05/1904 D: 11/23/1985
BL

Year	Tm	Lg	Tot	H	A	0	1	2	3	2	3	4	LO	XN	IP	PH	RHP	LHP
1928	WAS	AL	3	3	0	2	1	0	0	0	0	0	0	0	1	0	3	0
1929	WAS	AL	3	0	3	1	2	0	0	0	0	0	0	0	0	1	2	1
1930	WAS	AL	6	4	2	3	2	1	0	0	0	0	1	0	1	0	6	0
1931	WAS	AL	3	2	1	2	0	1	0	0	0	0	0	0	0	0	2	1
1932	WAS	AL	6	0	6	3	2	1	0	0	0	0	0	0	0	0	4	2
1933	STL	AL	11	8	3	7	3	1	0	0	0	0	0	0	0	0	8	3
1934	STL	AL	9	6	3	6	3	0	0	0	0	0	0	0	0	0	8	1
1935	STL	AL	10	6	4	7	1	1	1	1	0	0	0	0	1	0	9	1
1936	STL	AL	7	6	1	4	2	1	0	0	0	0	0	0	0	0	6	1
1937	STL	AL	7	4	3	3	1	2	1	0	0	0	0	1	0	0	7	0
1938	STL	AL	1	0	1	0	0	1	0	0	0	0	0	0	0	0	1	0
	WAS	AL	5	0	5	1	4	0	0	0	0	0	0	0	0	0	4	1
	Total		6	0	6	1	4	1	0	0	0	0	0	0	0	0	5	1
1939	WAS	AL	3	0	3	1	1	1	0	0	0	0	0	0	0	0	3	0
1940	WAS	AL	1	1	0	0	0	1	0	0	0	0	0	0	0	0	1	0
Total			75	40	35	40	22	11	2	1	0	0	1	1	3	1	64	11

Rank among batters: 699 • *Top target (4 home runs)*: Ted Lyons • *Number of pitchers victimized*: 56 • *Total ballparks homered in*: 8 • *First HR*: 04/22/1928 off Red Ruffing

Wally Westlake

WALDON THOMAS WESTLAKE
B: 11/08/1920
BR

Year	Tm	Lg	Tot	H	A	0	1	2	3	2	3	4	LO	XN	IP	PH	RHP	LHP
1947	PIT	NL	17	11	6	11	1	3	2	2	0	0	0	1	0	0	16	1
1948	PIT	NL	17	12	5	11	2	2	2	2	0	0	0	0	2	0	12	5
1949	PIT	NL	23	14	9	10	10	2	1	2	0	0	0	0	0	0	19	4
1950	PIT	NL	24	13	11	12	6	4	2	2	0	0	0	0	0	0	22	2
1951	PIT	NL	16	11	5	7	7	2	0	1	0	0	0	0	0	1	14	2
	STL	NL	6	3	3	3	2	1	0	0	0	0	0	0	0	0	4	2
	Total		22	14	8	10	9	3	0	1	0	0	0	0	0	1	18	4
1952	CIN	NL	3	2	1	2	1	0	0	0	0	0	0	0	0	0	2	1

Year	Tm	Lg	Tot	H	A	Men-On 0	1	2	3	One-Game 2	3	4	LO	XN	IP	PH	RHP	LHP

Wally Westlake *continued*

Year	Tm	Lg	Tot	H	A	0	1	2	3	2	3	4	LO	XN	IP	PH	RHP	LHP
1952	CLE	AL	1	0	1	0	1	0	0	0	0	0	0	0	0	0	0	1
	Total		4	2	2	2	2	0	0	0	0	0	0	0	0	0	2	2
1953	CLE	AL	9	6	3	4	5	0	0	1	0	0	0	1	0	0	4	5
1954	CLE	AL	11	3	8	8	2	1	0	1	0	0	0	0	0	0	7	4
Total			127	75	52	68	37	15	7	11	0	0	0	2	2	1	100	27

Rank among batters: 358 • *Top target (4 home runs)*: Warren Spahn, Howie Fox, Russ Meyer • *Number of pitchers victimized*: 82 • *Total ballparks homered in*: 12 • *First HR*: 04/18/1947 off Joe Beggs • *Hit for Cycle*—@BRO: 07/30/1948; vs BOS: 06/14/1949

Wes Westrum

WESLEY NOREEN WESTRUM
B: 11/28/1922
BR

Year	Tm	Lg	Tot	H	A	0	1	2	3	2	3	4	LO	XN	IP	PH	RHP	LHP
1948	NY	NL	4	0	4	1	3	0	0	0	0	0	0	0	0	0	3	1
1949	NY	NL	7	4	3	2	2	3	0	1	0	0	0	0	0	0	6	1
1950	NY	NL	23	12	11	12	6	4	1	1	1	0	0	0	1	0	12	11
1951	NY	NL	20	14	6	8	6	3	3	3	0	0	0	0	0	0	13	7
1952	NY	NL	14	8	6	7	4	3	0	0	0	0	0	0	0	0	9	5
1953	NY	NL	12	8	4	6	6	0	0	0	0	0	0	0	0	0	11	1
1954	NY	NL	8	5	3	5	2	0	1	0	0	0	0	0	0	0	5	3
1955	NY	NL	4	4	0	2	1	1	0	0	0	0	0	0	0	0	3	1
1956	NY	NL	3	3	0	2	1	0	0	1	0	0	0	0	0	0	3	0
1957	NY	NL	1	0	1	1	0	0	0	0	0	0	0	0	0	0	0	1
Total			96	58	38	46	31	14	5	6	1	0	0	0	1	0	65	31

Rank among batters: 520 • *Top target (5 home runs)*: Ken Raffensberger • *Number of pitchers victimized*: 63 • *Total ballparks homered in*: 9 • *First HR*: 06/07/1948 off Elmer Singleton

Jeff Wetherby

JEFFREY BARRET WETHERBY
B: 10/18/1963
BL

Year	Tm	Lg	Tot	H	A	0	1	2	3	2	3	4	LO	XN	IP	PH	RHP	LHP
1989	ATL	NL	1	1	0	1	0	0	0	0	0	0	0	0	0	1	1	0

Rank among batters: 4,707 • *Total ballparks homered in*: 1 • *First HR*: 09/02/1989 off Greg Maddux

John Wetteland

JOHN KARL WETTELAND
B: 08/21/1966
BR

Year	Tm	Lg	Tot	H	A	0	1	2	3	2	3	4	LO	XN	IP	PH	RHP	LHP
1990	LA	NL	1	0	1	0	1	0	0	0	0	0	0	0	0	0	0	1

Rank among batters: 4,707 • *Total ballparks homered in*: 1 • *First HR*: 05/27/1990 off Frank DiPino

Dutch Wetzel

FRANKLIN BURTON WETZEL
B: 07/07/1893 D: 03/05/1942
BR

Year	Tm	Lg	Tot	H	A	0	1	2	3	2	3	4	LO	XN	IP	PH	RHP	LHP
1921	STL	AL	2	0	2	1	0	1	0	0	0	0	0	0	0	0	1	1

Rank among batters: 4,129 • *Total ballparks homered in*: 2 • *First HR*: 04/26/1921 off Dickie Kerr

Gus Weyhing

AUGUST WEYHING
B: 09/29/1866 D: 09/04/1955
BR

Year	Tm	Lg	Tot	H	A	0	1	2	3	2	3	4	LO	XN	IP	PH	RHP	LHP
1888	PHI	AA	1	1	0	0	1	0	0	0	0	0	0	0	0	0	0	1
1890	BRO	PL	1	1	0	0	1	0	0	0	0	0	0	0	0	0	0	1
1895	LOU	NL	1	0	1	1	0	0	0	0	0	0	0	0	0	0	1	0
Total			3	2	1	1	2	0	0	0	0	0	0	0	0	0	1	2

Rank among batters: 3,735 • *Total ballparks homered in*: 2 • *First HR*: 10/17/1888 off George Proeser

McKinley Wheat

MCKINLEY DAVIS WHEAT
B: 06/09/1893 D: 08/14/1979
BR

Year	Tm	Lg	Tot	H	A	0	1	2	3	2	3	4	LO	XN	IP	PH	RHP	LHP
1918	BRO	NL	1	1	0	0	0	1	0	0	0	0	0	0	1	0	1	0

McKinley Wheat *continued*

Year	Tm	Lg	Tot	H	A	Men-On 0	1	2	3	One-Game 2	3	4	LO	XN	IP	PH	RHP	LHP
1920	PHI	NL	3	3	0	2	1	0	0	0	0	0	0	0	0	0	3	0
Total			4	4	0	2	1	1	0	0	0	0	0	0	1	0	4	0

Rank among batters: 3,427 • *Top target (2 home runs)*: Phil Douglas • *Number of pitchers victimized*: 3 • *Total ballparks homered in*: 2 • *First HR*: 08/07/1918 off Phil Douglas

Zach Wheat

ZACHARY DAVIS WHEAT
B: 05/23/1888 D: 03/11/1972
BL HOF

Year	Tm	Lg	Tot	H	A	Men-On 0	1	2	3	One-Game 2	3	4	LO	XN	IP	PH	RHP	LHP
1910	BRO	NL	2	1	1	1	1	0	0	0	0	0	0	0	2	0	1	1
1911	BRO	NL	5	1	4	2	2	1	0	0	0	0	0	0	4	0	5	0
1912	BRO	NL	8	6	2	5	2	1	0	0	0	0	0	0	1	0	7	1
1913	BRO	NL	7	5	2	2	3	2	0	0	0	0	0	1	2	0	5	2
1914	BRO	NL	9	6	3	4	4	1	0	0	0	0	0	0	2	0	8	1
1915	BRO	NL	5	4	1	2	2	1	0	0	0	0	0	0	3	0	3	2
1916	BRO	NL	9	6	3	5	3	0	1	0	0	0	0	0	3	0	7	2
1917	BRO	NL	1	1	0	0	1	0	0	0	0	0	0	0	0	0	1	0
1919	BRO	NL	5	4	1	3	2	0	0	0	0	0	0	0	2	0	5	0
1920	BRO	NL	9	5	4	5	1	3	0	0	0	0	0	1	1	0	9	0
1921	BRO	NL	14	12	2	9	4	1	0	0	0	0	0	0	1	0	13	1
1922	BRO	NL	16	10	6	7	7	2	0	1	0	0	0	0	1	0	16	0
1923	BRO	NL	8	4	4	4	4	0	0	0	0	0	0	0	2	1	8	0
1924	BRO	NL	14	7	7	2	10	2	0	2	0	0	0	1	1	0	14	0
1925	BRO	NL	14	6	8	4	4	5	1	1	0	0	0	0	0	0	8	6
1926	BRO	NL	5	3	2	4	1	0	0	0	0	0	0	1	0	0	5	0
1927	PHI	AL	1	0	1	0	1	0	0	0	0	0	0	0	0	0	1	0
Total			132	81	51	59	52	19	2	4	0	0	0	4	25	1	116	16

Rank among batters: 339 • *Top target (5 home runs)*: Joe Oeschger • *Number of pitchers victimized*: 86 • *Total ballparks homered in*: 12 • *First HR*: 08/25/1910 off Lefty Leifield

Don Wheeler

DONALD WESLEY WHEELER
B: 09/29/1922
BR

Year	Tm	Lg	Tot	H	A	Men-On 0	1	2	3	One-Game 2	3	4	LO	XN	IP	PH	RHP	LHP
1949	CHI	AL	1	1	0	1	0	0	0	0	0	0	0	0	0	0	1	0

Rank among batters: 4,707 • *Total ballparks homered in*: 1 • *First HR*: 06/12/1949 off Ellis Kinder

George Wheeler

GEORGE L. WHEELER
B: 08/03/1869 D: 03/23/1946
BB

Year	Tm	Lg	Tot	H	A	Men-On 0	1	2	3	One-Game 2	3	4	LO	XN	IP	PH	RHP	LHP
1899	PHI	NL	1	0	1	0	1	0	0	0	0	0	0	0	0	0	1	0

Rank among batters: 4,707 • *Total ballparks homered in*: 1 • *First HR*: 04/19/1899 off Davey Dunkle

Harry Wheeler

HARRY EUGENE WHEELER
B: 03/03/1858 D: 10/09/1900
BR

Year	Tm	Lg	Tot	H	A	Men-On 0	1	2	3	One-Game 2	3	4	LO	XN	IP	PH	RHP	LHP
1882	CIN	AA	1	0	1	0	0	1	0	0	0	0	0	0	0	0	1	0
1884	CHI	UA	1	0	1	1	0	0	0	0	0	0	0	0	0	0	1	0
Total			2	0	2	1	0	1	0	0	0	0	0	0	0	0	2	0

Rank among batters: 4,129 • *Total ballparks homered in*: 2 • *First HR*: 05/30/1882 off Frank Mountain

Bobby Wheelock

WARREN H. WHEELOCK
B: 08/06/1864 D: 03/13/1928
BR

Year	Tm	Lg	Tot	H	A	Men-On 0	1	2	3	One-Game 2	3	4	LO	XN	IP	PH	RHP	LHP
1887	BOS	NL	2	1	1	1	0	1	0	0	0	0	0	1	1	0	1	1
1890	COL	AA	1	0	1	0	1	0	0	0	0	0	0	0	0	0	1	0
Total			3	1	2	1	1	1	0	0	0	0	0	1	1	0	2	1

Rank among batters: 3,735 • *Total ballparks homered in*: 3 • *First HR*: 06/04/1887 off Charlie Ferguson

Pete Whisenant

THOMAS PETER WHISENANT
B: 12/14/1929
BR

Year	Tm	Lg	Tot	H	A	Men-On 0	1	2	3	One-Game 2	3	4	LO	XN	IP	PH	RHP	LHP
1955	STL	NL	2	0	2	1	1	0	0	0	0	0	0	0	0	1	0	2
1956	CHI	NL	11	10	1	4	4	3	0	1	0	0	0	0	0	0	8	3
1957	CIN	NL	5	2	3	2	2	1	0	1	0	0	0	0	0	1	0	5
1958	CIN	NL	11	3	8	5	3	2	1	1	0	0	0	0	0	1	2	9
1959	CIN	NL	5	3	2	4	1	0	0	1	0	0	0	0	0	0	0	5
1960	WAS	AL	3	3	0	1	2	0	0	0	0	0	0	0	0	1	1	2
Total			37	21	16	17	13	6	1	4	0	0	0	0	0	4	11	26

Rank among batters: 1,252 • *Top target (6 home runs)*: Wilmer Mizell • *Number of pitchers victimized*: 24 • *Total ballparks homered in*: 9 • *First HR*: 06/12/1955 off Johnny Antonelli

Larry Whisenton

LARRY WHISENTON
B: 07/03/1956
BL

Year	Tm	Lg	Tot	H	A	Men-On 0	1	2	3	One-Game 2	3	4	LO	XN	IP	PH	RHP	LHP
1982	ATL	NL	4	2	2	4	0	0	0	0	0	0	0	0	0	1	4	0

Rank among batters: 3,427 • *Total ballparks homered in*: 3 • *First HR*: 07/10/1982 off Don Robinson

Lew Whistler

LEWIS W. WHISTLER
B: 03/10/1868 D: 12/30/1959

Year	Tm	Lg	Tot	H	A	Men-On 0	1	2	3	One-Game 2	3	4	LO	XN	IP	PH	RHP	LHP
1890	NY	NL	2	1	1	0	2	0	0	0	0	0	0	0	0	0	0	1
1891	NY	NL	3	2	1	2	1	0	0	0	0	0	0	0	1	0	1	1
1892	BAL	NL	2	1	1	1	0	1	0	0	0	0	0	0	0	0	2	0
	LOU	NL	5	3	2	2	1	2	0	0	0	0	0	0	2	0	2	2
	Total		7	4	3	3	1	3	0	0	0	0	0	0	2	0	4	2
Total			12	7	5	5	4	3	0	0	0	0	0	0	3	0	5	2

Rank among batters: 2,325 • *Top target (2 home runs)*: Tony Mullane, Tom Lovett • *Number of pitchers victimized*: 10 • *Total ballparks homered in*: 9 • *First HR*: 08/22/1890 off Tony Mullane

Lou Whitaker

LOUIS RODMAN WHITAKER
B: 05/12/1957
BL

Year	Tm	Lg	Tot	H	A	Men-On 0	1	2	3	One-Game 2	3	4	LO	XN	IP	PH	RHP	LHP
1978	DET	AL	3	2	1	0	1	2	0	0	0	0	0	0	1	0	1	2
1979	DET	AL	3	3	0	3	0	0	0	0	0	0	0	0	0	0	2	1
1980	DET	AL	1	1	0	0	1	0	0	0	0	0	0	0	0	0	1	0
1981	DET	AL	5	4	1	2	2	1	0	0	0	0	0	0	0	0	3	2
1982	DET	AL	15	9	6	9	5	1	0	3	0	0	4	0	0	0	12	3
1983	DET	AL	12	7	5	7	3	2	0	0	0	0	4	0	1	0	8	4
1984	DET	AL	13	8	5	6	6	0	1	0	0	0	3	2	1	0	11	2
1985	DET	AL	21	11	10	12	7	2	0	1	0	0	4	1	0	0	19	2
1986	DET	AL	20	8	12	10	10	0	0	2	0	0	3	0	0	0	17	3
1987	DET	AL	16	10	6	9	4	3	0	1	0	0	4	1	0	0	12	4
1988	DET	AL	12	8	4	5	6	1	0	0	0	0	1	0	0	0	12	0
1989	DET	AL	28	17	11	16	9	3	0	0	0	0	0	2	0	0	23	5
1990	DET	AL	18	8	10	5	9	4	0	0	0	0	0	0	0	0	17	1
1991	DET	AL	23	15	8	11	9	3	0	1	0	0	0	0	1	1	21	2
1992	DET	AL	19	11	8	10	6	2	1	0	0	0	0	0	0	0	17	2
1993	DET	AL	9	5	4	3	4	2	0	0	0	0	0	0	0	0	9	0
1994	DET	AL	12	8	4	6	3	1	2	1	0	0	0	0	0	0	11	1
1995	DET	AL	14	11	3	8	2	4	0	0	0	0	0	0	0	1	13	1
Total			244	146	98	122	87	31	4	9	0	0	23	6	4	2	209	35

Rank among batters: 119 • *Top target (5 home runs)*: Scott Sanderson • *Number of pitchers victimized*: 186 • *Total ballparks homered in*: 18 • *First HR*: 07/28/1978 off Enrique Romo • *LCS HR*—1; *All-Star HR*—1

Steve Whitaker

STEPHEN EDWARD WHITAKER
B: 05/07/1943
BL

Year	Tm	Lg	Tot	H	A	Men-On 0	1	2	3	One-Game 2	3	4	LO	XN	IP	PH	RHP	LHP
1966	NY	AL	7	4	3	5	1	0	1	0	0	0	0	0	1	0	4	3
1967	NY	AL	11	9	2	6	4	1	0	0	0	0	0	1	0	0	8	3

Year	Tm	Lg	Tot	H	A	Men-On 0	1	2	3	One-Game 2	3	4	LO	XN	IP	PH	RHP	LHP

Steve Whitaker *continued*

Year	Tm	Lg	Tot	H	A	0	1	2	3	2	3	4	LO	XN	IP	PH	RHP	LHP
1969	SEA	AL	6	6	0	4	2	0	0	0	0	0	0	0	0	0	4	2
Total			24	19	5	15	7	1	1	0	0	0	0	1	1	0	16	8

Rank among batters: 1,643 • *Top target (3 home runs)*: Earl Wilson • *Number of pitchers victimized*: 22 • *Total ballparks homered in*: 6 • *First HR*: 08/26/1966 off Earl Wilson

Bill White

WILLIAM DIGHTON WHITE
B: 05/01/1860 D: 12/29/1924

Year	Tm	Lg	Tot	H	A	0	1	2	3	2	3	4	LO	XN	IP	PH	RHP	LHP
1886	LOU	AA	1	1	0	1	0	0	0	0	0	0	0	0	0	0	1	0
1887	LOU	AA	2	2	0	1	1	0	0	0	0	0	0	0	0	0	1	1
1888	LOU	AA	1	0	1	0	1	0	0	0	0	0	0	0	0	0	1	0
	STL	AA	2	2	0	1	1	0	0	0	0	0	0	0	0	0	1	1
	Total		3	2	1	1	2	0	0	0	0	0	0	0	0	0	2	1
Total			6	5	1	3	3	0	0	0	0	0	0	0	0	0	4	2

Rank among batters: 2,988 • *Total ballparks homered in*: 2 • *First HR*: 10/09/1886 off Bill Hart

Bill White

WILLIAM DEKOVA WHITE
B: 01/28/1934
BL

Year	Tm	Lg	Tot	H	A	0	1	2	3	2	3	4	LO	XN	IP	PH	RHP	LHP
1956	NY	NL	22	10	12	14	7	1	0	1	0	0	0	0	0	0	17	5
1958	SF	NL	1	0	1	1	0	0	0	0	0	0	0	0	0	0	1	0
1959	STL	NL	12	9	3	7	4	0	1	0	0	0	0	0	0	0	9	3
1960	STL	NL	16	8	8	8	4	3	1	1	0	0	0	0	0	0	14	2
1961	STL	NL	20	14	6	9	8	1	2	2	1	0	0	0	0	0	17	3
1962	STL	NL	20	12	8	12	6	2	0	0	0	0	0	0	1	0	15	5
1963	STL	NL	27	16	11	13	12	0	2	0	0	0	0	2	1	0	18	9
1964	STL	NL	21	15	6	12	6	3	0	0	0	0	0	1	0	0	19	2
1965	STL	NL	24	15	9	14	8	2	0	2	0	0	0	1	0	0	16	8
1966	PHI	NL	22	11	11	10	9	2	1	0	0	0	0	0	2	0	16	6
1967	PHI	NL	8	5	3	6	1	1	0	0	0	0	0	1	0	0	7	1
1968	PHI	NL	9	5	4	5	3	1	0	1	0	0	0	0	0	0	8	1
Total			202	120	82	111	68	16	7	7	1	0	0	5	4	0	157	45

Rank among batters: 178 • *Top target (7 home runs)*: Don Drysdale • *Number of pitchers victimized*: 130 • *Total ballparks homered in*: 16 • *First HR*: 05/07/1956 off Ben Flowers • *Hit for Cycle—@PIT*: 08/14/1960 (1) • *Hit HR in first major league AB—@STL*: 05/07/1956

Charlie White

CHARLES WHITE
B: 08/12/1928
BL

Year	Tm	Lg	Tot	H	A	0	1	2	3	2	3	4	LO	XN	IP	PH	RHP	LHP
1954	MIL	NL	1	0	1	1	0	0	0	0	0	0	0	1	0	0	1	0

Rank among batters: 4,707 • *Total ballparks homered in*: 1 • *First HR*: 04/23/1954 off Cot Deal

Deacon White

JAMES LAURIE WHITE
B: 12/07/1847 D: 07/07/1939
BL

Year	Tm	Lg	Tot	H	A	0	1	2	3	2	3	4	LO	XN	IP	PH	RHP	LHP
1876	CHI	NL	1	1	0	0	1	0	0	0	0	0	0	0	1	0	1	0
1877	BOS	NL	2	0	2	0	1	1	0	0	0	0	0	0	0	0	2	0
1879	CIN	NL	1	1	0	1	0	0	0	0	0	0	0	0	0	0	1	0
1882	BUF	NL	1	0	1	0	0	1	0	0	0	0	0	0	0	0	0	1
1884	BUF	NL	5	4	1	3	0	2	0	0	0	0	0	0	2	0	4	0
1886	DET	NL	1	1	0	1	0	0	0	0	0	0	0	0	0	0	1	0
1887	DET	NL	3	0	3	1	1	1	0	0	0	0	0	0	0	0	3	0
1888	DET	NL	4	3	1	3	0	1	0	0	0	0	0	0	1	0	3	1
Total			18	10	8	9	3	6	0	0	0	0	0	0	4	0	15	2

Rank among batters: 1,914 • Top target (2 home runs): George Bradley, Fred Goldsmith, Charlie Ferguson, John Clarkson • *Number of pitchers victimized*: 14 • *Total ballparks homered in*: 8 • *First HR*: 07/15/1876 off Joe Borden

Derrick White

DERRICK RAMON WHITE
B: 10/12/1969
BR

Year	Tm	Lg	Tot	H	A	0	1	2	3	2	3	4	LO	XN	IP	PH	RHP	LHP
1993	MON	NL	2	1	1	2	0	0	0	0	0	0	0	0	0	0	0	2

Rank among batters: 4,129 • *Total ballparks homered in*: 2 • *First HR*: 07/25/1993 off Mark Davis

Year	Tm	Lg	Tot	H	A	Men-On 0	Men-On 1	Men-On 2	Men-On 3	One-Game 2	One-Game 3	One-Game 4	LO	XN	IP	PH	RHP	LHP

Devon White

DEVON MARKES WHITE
B: 12/29/1962
BB

Year	Tm	Lg	Tot	H	A	0	1	2	3	2	3	4	LO	XN	IP	PH	RHP	LHP
1986	CAL	AL	1	0	1	1	0	0	0	0	0	0	0	0	0	0	1	0
1987	CAL	AL	24	11	13	15	6	2	1	1	0	0	0	2	0	0	13	11
1988	CAL	AL	11	3	8	7	3	0	1	0	0	0	3	0	0	0	5	6
1989	CAL	AL	12	9	3	8	3	1	0	0	0	0	1	0	0	0	10	2
1990	CAL	AL	11	5	6	6	3	2	0	1	0	0	0	0	0	0	8	3
1991	TOR	AL	17	9	8	14	3	0	0	0	0	0	6	0	0	0	9	8
1992	TOR	AL	17	7	10	10	7	0	0	1	0	0	5	1	1	0	12	5
1993	TOR	AL	15	10	5	11	3	1	0	1	0	0	5	0	0	0	12	3
1994	TOR	AL	13	5	8	9	4	0	0	0	0	0	4	0	0	0	9	4
1995	TOR	AL	10	4	6	6	1	2	1	0	0	0	2	0	0	0	9	1
Total			131	63	68	87	33	8	3	4	0	0	26	3	1	0	88	43

Rank among batters: 342 • *Top target (3 home runs)*: Scott Bailes, Mike Boddicker, Jack Morris • *Number of pitchers victimized*: 104 • *Total ballparks homered in*: 18 • *First HR*: 10/02/1986 off Jeff Russell • *Switch hit HR in 1 game*—3 times • *World Series HR*—1; *LCS HR*—1

Doc White

GUY HARRIS WHITE
B: 04/09/1879 D: 02/19/1969
BL

Year	Tm	Lg	Tot	H	A	0	1	2	3	2	3	4	LO	XN	IP	PH	RHP	LHP
1901	PHI	NL	1	1	0	0	0	1	0	0	0	0	0	0	0	0	1	0
1902	PHI	NL	1	0	1	0	0	1	0	0	0	0	0	0	0	1	1	0
Total			2	1	1	0	0	2	0	0	0	0	0	0	0	1	2	0

Rank among batters: 4,129 • *Total ballparks homered in*: 2 • *First HR*: 06/24/1901 off Bill Phillips

Don White

DONALD WILLIAM WHITE
B: 01/08/1919 D: 06/15/1987
BR

Year	Tm	Lg	Tot	H	A	0	1	2	3	2	3	4	LO	XN	IP	PH	RHP	LHP
1948	PHI	AL	1	0	1	0	0	0	1	0	0	0	0	0	0	0	0	1

Rank among batters: 4,707 • *Total ballparks homered in*: 1 • *First HR*: 08/05/1948 off Frank Papish

Frank White

FRANK WHITE
B: 09/04/1950
BR

Year	Tm	Lg	Tot	H	A	0	1	2	3	2	3	4	LO	XN	IP	PH	RHP	LHP
1974	KC	AL	1	1	0	1	0	0	0	0	0	0	0	0	0	0	0	1
1975	KC	AL	7	4	3	5	0	1	1	0	0	0	0	1	2	0	3	4
1976	KC	AL	2	0	2	2	0	0	0	0	0	0	0	0	0	0	1	1
1977	KC	AL	5	3	2	3	0	2	0	0	0	0	0	0	0	0	3	2
1978	KC	AL	7	3	4	5	1	1	0	0	0	0	0	0	0	0	5	2
1979	KC	AL	10	5	5	7	3	0	0	0	0	0	3	0	1	0	6	4
1980	KC	AL	7	1	6	5	1	1	0	0	0	0	0	0	0	0	1	6
1981	KC	AL	9	4	5	4	2	2	1	0	0	0	0	0	0	0	2	7
1982	KC	AL	11	7	4	7	3	1	0	0	0	0	0	0	0	0	6	5
1983	KC	AL	11	8	3	5	3	3	0	1	0	0	0	0	0	0	6	5
1984	KC	AL	17	6	11	12	3	1	1	1	0	0	0	0	0	0	10	7
1985	KC	AL	22	9	13	18	3	0	1	2	0	0	0	0	0	0	13	9
1986	KC	AL	22	12	10	14	5	2	1	1	0	0	0	1	0	0	21	1
1987	KC	AL	17	6	11	11	2	3	1	0	0	0	0	0	0	0	12	5
1988	KC	AL	8	3	5	5	3	0	0	0	0	0	0	0	0	0	6	2
1989	KC	AL	2	1	1	2	0	0	0	0	0	0	0	0	0	0	2	0
1990	KC	AL	2	2	0	0	2	0	0	0	0	0	0	0	0	0	1	1
Total			160	75	85	106	31	17	6	5	0	0	3	2	3	0	98	62

Rank among batters: 263 • *Top target (5 home runs)*: Frank Tanana • *Number of pitchers victimized*: 124 • *Total ballparks homered in*: 15 • *First HR*: 04/06/1974 off Tom Burgmeier • *Hit for Cycle*—@CAL: 09/26/1979; vs DET: 08/03/1982 • *World Series HR*—1; *LCS HR*—1; *All-Star HR*—1

Jerry White

JEROME CARDELL WHITE
B: 08/23/1952
BB

Year	Tm	Lg	Tot	H	A	0	1	2	3	2	3	4	LO	XN	IP	PH	RHP	LHP
1975	MON	NL	2	2	0	2	0	0	0	0	0	0	1	0	0	0	2	0
1976	MON	NL	2	1	1	1	1	0	0	0	0	0	0	0	0	0	2	0
1978	CHI	NL	1	1	0	1	0	0	0	0	0	0	0	0	0	0	1	0
1979	MON	NL	3	1	2	2	0	1	0	0	0	0	0	0	0	0	2	1

Jerry White *continued*

Year	Tm	Lg	Tot	H	A	Men-On 0	1	2	3	One-Game 2	3	4	LO	XN	IP	PH	RHP	LHP
1980	MON	NL	7	5	2	4	2	1	0	0	0	0	1	1	1	1	5	2
1981	MON	NL	3	3	0	1	1	1	0	0	0	0	0	0	0	2	1	2
1982	MON	NL	2	1	1	1	0	1	0	0	0	0	0	0	0	1	2	0
1986	STL	NL	1	1	0	1	0	0	0	0	0	0	0	1	0	1	1	0
Total			21	15	6	13	4	4	0	0	0	0	2	2	1	5	16	5

Rank among batters: 1,768 • *Total ballparks homered in*: 7 • *First HR*: 09/08/1975 off Hank Webb • *LCS HR*—1

Jo-Jo White

JOYNER CLIFFORD WHITE
B: 06/01/1909 D: 10/09/1986
BL

Year	Tm	Lg	Tot	H	A	Men-On 0	1	2	3	One-Game 2	3	4	LO	XN	IP	PH	RHP	LHP
1932	DET	AL	2	1	1	2	0	0	0	0	0	0	0	0	0	0	1	1
1933	DET	AL	2	1	1	1	1	0	0	0	0	0	1	0	0	0	2	0
1935	DET	AL	2	0	2	1	1	0	0	0	0	0	1	0	0	0	2	0
1943	PHI	AL	1	0	1	1	0	0	0	0	0	0	0	0	0	0	1	0
1944	PHI	AL	1	0	1	0	1	0	0	0	0	0	0	0	0	0	1	0
Total			8	2	6	5	3	0	0	0	0	0	2	0	0	0	7	1

Rank among batters: 2,703 • *Top target (2 home runs)*: Hank Borowy • *Number of pitchers victimized*: 7 • *Total ballparks homered in*: 4 • *First HR*: 05/18/1932 off Lefty Grove

Rondell White

RONDELL BERNARD WHITE
B: 02/23/1972
BR

Year	Tm	Lg	Tot	H	A	Men-On 0	1	2	3	One-Game 2	3	4	LO	XN	IP	PH	RHP	LHP
1993	MON	NL	2	1	1	1	1	0	0	0	0	0	0	0	0	0	0	2
1994	MON	NL	2	1	1	0	1	1	0	0	0	0	0	0	0	0	2	0
1995	MON	NL	13	6	7	10	1	1	1	0	0	0	2	0	0	0	11	2
Total			17	8	9	11	3	2	1	0	0	0	2	0	0	0	13	4

Rank among batters: 1,969 • *Top target (2 home runs)*: Kevin Foster • *Number of pitchers victimized*: 16 • *Total ballparks homered in*: 8 • *First HR*: 09/04/1993 off Greg Swindell • *Hit for Cycle*—@SF: 06/11/1995

Roy White

ROY HILTON WHITE
B: 12/27/1943
BB

Year	Tm	Lg	Tot	H	A	Men-On 0	1	2	3	One-Game 2	3	4	LO	XN	IP	PH	RHP	LHP
1966	NY	AL	7	4	3	5	2	0	0	0	0	0	0	0	1	0	4	3
1967	NY	AL	2	2	0	1	1	0	0	0	0	0	0	0	0	1	2	0
1968	NY	AL	17	10	7	5	12	0	0	0	0	0	0	0	0	0	16	1
1969	NY	AL	7	2	5	3	3	1	0	0	0	0	0	0	0	0	7	0
1970	NY	AL	22	12	10	11	6	4	1	1	0	0	0	1	0	0	16	6
1971	NY	AL	19	9	10	12	7	0	0	0	0	0	0	1	1	0	14	5
1972	NY	AL	10	6	4	6	3	1	0	0	0	0	0	1	0	0	7	3
1973	NY	AL	18	11	7	10	6	0	2	2	0	0	0	0	0	0	10	8
1974	NY	AL	7	4	3	2	4	1	0	0	0	0	0	0	0	0	5	2
1975	NY	AL	12	4	8	9	2	1	0	1	0	0	0	0	0	0	7	5
1976	NY	AL	14	8	6	8	4	2	0	1	0	0	0	0	0	0	10	4
1977	NY	AL	14	9	5	8	4	2	0	0	0	0	0	0	0	0	11	3
1978	NY	AL	8	3	5	4	2	2	0	1	0	0	0	0	0	0	6	2
1979	NY	AL	3	2	1	1	2	0	0	0	0	0	0	0	0	1	3	0
Total			160	86	74	85	58	14	3	6	0	0	0	3	2	2	118	42

Rank among batters: 263 • *Top target (7 home runs)*: Mickey Lolich • *Number of pitchers victimized*: 120 • *Total ballparks homered in*: 16 • *First HR*: 04/19/1966 off Sam McDowell • *Switch hit HR in 1 game*—5 times • *World Series HR*—1; *LCS HR*—1

Sammy White

SAMUEL CHARLES WHITE
B: 07/07/1928 D: 08/05/1991
BR

Year	Tm	Lg	Tot	H	A	Men-On 0	1	2	3	One-Game 2	3	4	LO	XN	IP	PH	RHP	LHP
1952	BOS	AL	10	6	4	6	1	2	1	0	0	0	0	1	0	0	7	3
1953	BOS	AL	13	5	8	9	4	0	0	0	0	0	0	0	0	0	10	3
1954	BOS	AL	14	9	5	6	5	3	0	1	0	0	0	1	0	0	7	7
1955	BOS	AL	11	6	5	7	4	0	0	0	0	0	0	0	0	0	8	3
1956	BOS	AL	5	1	4	2	3	0	0	0	0	0	0	0	0	0	1	4
1957	BOS	AL	3	3	0	3	0	0	0	0	0	0	0	0	0	0	3	0
1958	BOS	AL	6	2	4	5	1	0	0	0	0	0	0	0	0	0	5	1

Year	Tm	Lg	Tot	H	A	Men-On				One-Game			LO	XN	IP	PH	RHP	LHP
						0	1	2	3	2	3	4						

Sammy White *continued*

Year	Tm	Lg	Tot	H	A	0	1	2	3	2	3	4	LO	XN	IP	PH	RHP	LHP
1959	BOS	AL	1	1	0	1	0	0	0	0	0	0	0	0	0	0	0	1
1961	MIL	NL	1	1	0	1	0	0	0	0	0	0	0	0	0	0	0	1
1962	PHI	NL	2	2	0	0	2	0	0	0	0	0	0	0	0	0	0	2
Total			66	36	30	40	20	5	1	1	0	0	0	2	0	0	41	25

Rank among batters: 786 • *Top target (5 home runs)*: Billy Hoeft • *Number of pitchers victimized*: 55 • *Total ballparks homered in*: 11 • *First HR*: 04/24/1952 off Eddie Lopat

Will White

WILLIAM HENRY WHITE
B: 10/11/1854 D: 08/31/1911
BB

Year	Tm	Lg	Tot	H	A	0	1	2	3	2	3	4	LO	XN	IP	PH	RHP	LHP
1884	CIN	AA	1	1	0	1	0	0	0	0	0	0	0	0	0	0	1	0

Rank among batters: 4,707 • *Total ballparks homered in*: 1 • *First HR*: 06/28/1884 off Jack Lynch

Ed Whited

EDWARD MORRIS WHITED
B: 02/09/1964
BR

Year	Tm	Lg	Tot	H	A	0	1	2	3	2	3	4	LO	XN	IP	PH	RHP	LHP
1989	ATL	NL	1	1	0	0	1	0	0	0	0	0	0	0	0	0	0	1

Rank among batters: 4,707 • *Total ballparks homered in*: 1 • *First HR*: 07/25/1989 off Craig Lefferts

Burgess Whitehead

BURGESS URQUHART WHITEHEAD
B: 06/29/1910 D: 11/25/1993
BR

Year	Tm	Lg	Tot	H	A	0	1	2	3	2	3	4	LO	XN	IP	PH	RHP	LHP
1934	STL	NL	1	0	1	1	0	0	0	0	0	0	1	0	0	0	1	0
1936	NY	NL	4	4	0	3	0	1	0	0	0	0	0	0	1	0	4	0
1937	NY	NL	5	5	0	2	2	1	0	1	0	0	0	0	1	0	2	3
1939	NY	NL	2	2	0	1	1	0	0	0	0	0	1	0	0	0	2	0
1940	NY	NL	4	4	0	1	2	1	0	0	0	0	0	0	1	0	4	0
1941	NY	NL	1	1	0	0	1	0	0	0	0	0	0	0	0	0	0	1
Total			17	16	1	8	6	3	0	1	0	0	2	0	3	0	13	4

Rank among batters: 1,969 • *Top target (2 home runs)*: Roy Henshaw • *Number of pitchers victimized*: 16 • *Total ballparks homered in*: 1 • *First HR*: 05/21/1934 off Joe Bowman

Milt Whitehead

MILTON P. WHITEHEAD
B: 1862 D: 08/15/1901
BB

Year	Tm	Lg	Tot	H	A	0	1	2	3	2	3	4	LO	XN	IP	PH	RHP	LHP
1884	STL	UA	1	0	1	0	1	0	0	0	0	0	0	0	0	0	1	0

Rank among batters: 4,707 • *Total ballparks homered in*: 1 • *First HR*: 07/30/1884 off Jim Cudworth

Earl Whitehill

EARL OLIVER WHITEHILL
B: 02/07/1900 D: 10/22/1954
BL

Year	Tm	Lg	Tot	H	A	0	1	2	3	2	3	4	LO	XN	IP	PH	RHP	LHP
1929	DET	AL	3	0	3	1	1	1	0	0	0	0	0	0	0	0	2	1
1934	WAS	AL	1	0	1	1	0	0	0	0	0	0	0	0	0	0	1	0
Total			4	0	4	2	1	1	0	0	0	0	0	0	0	0	3	1

Rank among batters: 3,427 • *Total ballparks homered in*: 3 • *First HR*: 04/21/1929 off Herb Cobb

Gurdon Whiteley

GURDON W. WHITELEY
B: 10/05/1859 D: 11/24/1924

Year	Tm	Lg	Tot	H	A	0	1	2	3	2	3	4	LO	XN	IP	PH	RHP	LHP
1885	BOS	NL	1	1	0	1	0	0	0	0	0	0	0	0	0	0	1	0

Rank among batters: 4,707 • *Total ballparks homered in*: 1 • *First HR*: 05/28/1885 off John Clarkson

George Whiteman

GEORGE WHITEMAN
B: 12/23/1882 D: 02/10/1947
BR

Year	Tm	Lg	Tot	H	A	0	1	2	3	2	3	4	LO	XN	IP	PH	RHP	LHP
1918	BOS	AL	1	0	1	1	0	0	0	0	0	0	0	0	0	0	0	1

Rank among batters: 4,707 • *Total ballparks homered in*: 1 • *First HR*: 09/02/1918 off George Mogridge

Year	Tm	Lg	Tot	H	A	Men-On				One-Game			LO	XN	IP	PH	RHP	LHP
						0	1	2	3	2	3	4						

Mark Whiten

MARK ANTHONY WHITEN
B: 11/25/1966
BB

Year	Tm	Lg	Tot	H	A	0	1	2	3	2	3	4	LO	XN	IP	PH	RHP	LHP
1990	TOR	AL	2	1	1	1	1	0	0	0	0	0	0	0	0	0	1	1
1991	TOR	AL	2	2	0	2	0	0	0	0	0	0	0	1	0	0	1	1
	CLE	AL	7	2	5	6	1	0	0	1	0	0	0	0	0	0	6	1
	Total		9	4	5	8	1	0	0	1	0	0	0	1	0	0	7	2
1992	CLE	AL	9	6	3	5	1	2	1	0	0	0	0	0	0	0	7	2
1993	STL	NL	25	12	13	10	8	6	1	1	0	1	0	0	0	0	17	8
1994	STL	NL	14	6	8	8	3	3	0	0	0	0	0	0	0	0	10	4
1995	BOS	AL	1	0	1	0	1	0	0	0	0	0	0	0	0	0	1	0
	PHI	NL	11	5	6	6	3	2	0	1	0	0	0	1	0	0	5	6
	Total		12	5	7	6	4	2	0	1	0	0	0	1	0	0	6	6
Total			71	34	37	38	18	13	2	3	0	1	0	2	0	0	48	23

Rank among batters: 731 • *Top target (3 home runs)*: Butch Henry • *Number of pitchers victimized*: 57 • *Total ballparks homered in*: 22 • *First HR*: 07/26/1990 off Kevin Appier • *Switch hit HR in 1 game*—1 time

Fred Whitfield

FRED DWIGHT WHITFIELD
B: 01/07/1938
BL

Year	Tm	Lg	Tot	H	A	0	1	2	3	2	3	4	LO	XN	IP	PH	RHP	LHP
1962	STL	NL	8	5	3	2	1	4	1	0	0	0	0	1	0	3	6	2
1963	CLE	AL	21	10	11	15	4	1	1	3	0	0	0	0	0	2	20	1
1964	CLE	AL	10	7	3	7	2	0	1	0	0	0	0	2	0	1	10	0
1965	CLE	AL	26	14	12	10	7	8	1	0	0	0	0	0	0	3	21	5
1966	CLE	AL	27	15	12	15	7	5	0	2	0	0	0	0	0	0	19	8
1967	CLE	AL	9	3	6	4	3	2	0	0	0	0	0	2	0	2	7	2
1968	CIN	NL	6	4	2	2	3	1	0	1	0	0	0	0	0	0	4	2
1969	CIN	NL	1	0	1	0	1	0	0	0	0	0	0	0	0	0	1	0
Total			108	58	50	55	28	21	4	6	0	0	0	5	0	11	88	20

Rank among batters: 443 • *Top target (5 home runs)*: Jim Bouton • *Number of pitchers victimized*: 75 • *Total ballparks homered in*: 16 • *First HR*: 06/10/1962 off Billy Pierce

Terry Whitfield

TERRY BERTLAND WHITFIELD
B: 01/12/1953
BL

Year	Tm	Lg	Tot	H	A	0	1	2	3	2	3	4	LO	XN	IP	PH	RHP	LHP
1977	SF	NL	7	2	5	4	2	1	0	0	0	0	1	0	0	0	7	0
1978	SF	NL	10	5	5	7	2	1	0	0	0	0	0	1	0	0	9	1
1979	SF	NL	5	3	2	2	3	0	0	0	0	0	0	0	1	0	5	0
1980	SF	NL	4	1	3	4	0	0	0	0	0	0	0	0	0	0	4	0
1984	LA	NL	4	4	0	1	1	2	0	0	0	0	0	0	0	0	4	0
1985	LA	NL	3	2	1	2	1	0	0	0	0	0	0	0	0	2	3	0
Total			33	17	16	20	9	4	0	0	0	0	1	1	1	2	32	1

Rank among batters: 1,336 • Top target (2 home runs): John Denny, Phil Niekro, Neil Allen, Joaquin Andujar • *Number of pitchers victimized*: 29 • *Total ballparks homered in*: 9 • *First HR*: 05/15/1977 off Gary Nolan

Ed Whiting

EDWARD C. WHITING
B: 1860 BL

Year	Tm	Lg	Tot	H	A	0	1	2	3	2	3	4	LO	XN	IP	PH	RHP	LHP
1883	LOU	AA	2	2	0	1	1	0	0	0	0	0	0	0	0	0	2	0

Rank among batters: 4,129 • *Total ballparks homered in*: 1 • *First HR*: 07/01/1883 off Bob Barr

Dick Whitman

DICK CORWIN WHITMAN
B: 11/09/1920
BL

Year	Tm	Lg	Tot	H	A	0	1	2	3	2	3	4	LO	XN	IP	PH	RHP	LHP
1946	BRO	NL	2	1	1	1	1	0	0	0	0	0	0	0	0	0	2	0

Rank among batters: 4,129 • *Total ballparks homered in*: 2 • *First HR*: 06/29/1946 off Ed Wright

Darrell Whitmore

DARRELL LAMONT WHITMORE
B: 11/18/1968
BL

Year	Tm	Lg	Tot	H	A	0	1	2	3	2	3	4	LO	XN	IP	PH	RHP	LHP
1993	FLO	NL	4	3	1	3	1	0	0	0	0	0	0	0	0	0	4	0

Darrell Whitmore *continued*

Year	Tm	Lg	Tot	H	A	Men-On 0	1	2	3	One-Game 2	3	4	LO	XN	IP	PH	RHP	LHP
1995	FLO	NL	1	1	0	1	0	0	0	0	0	0	0	0	0	0	1	0
Total			5	4	1	4	1	0	0	0	0	0	0	0	0	0	5	0

Rank among batters: 3,191 • *Total ballparks homered in*: 2 • *First HR*: 07/15/1993 off Tim Belcher

Art Whitney

ARTHUR WILSON WHITNEY
B: 01/16/1858 D: 08/15/1943
BR

Year	Tm	Lg	Tot	H	A	Men-On 0	1	2	3	One-Game 2	3	4	LO	XN	IP	PH	RHP	LHP
1880	WOR	NL	1	0	1	0	0	1	0	0	0	0	0	0	0	0	1	0
1888	NY	NL	1	0	1	0	1	0	0	0	0	0	0	0	0	0	0	1
1889	NY	NL	1	1	0	1	0	0	0	0	0	0	0	0	0	0	1	0
1891	CIN	AA	3	2	1	1	1	1	0	0	0	0	0	0	0	0	2	0
Total			6	3	3	2	2	2	0	0	0	0	0	0	0	0	4	1

Rank among batters: 2,988 • *Total ballparks homered in*: 5 • *First HR*: 06/23/1880 off Will White

Jim Whitney

JAMES EVANS WHITNEY
B: 11/10/1857 D: 05/21/1891
BL

Year	Tm	Lg	Tot	H	A	Men-On 0	1	2	3	One-Game 2	3	4	LO	XN	IP	PH	RHP	LHP
1882	BOS	NL	5	4	1	3	1	1	0	0	0	0	0	0	0	0	5	0
1883	BOS	NL	5	3	2	1	2	2	0	0	0	0	0	0	0	0	4	1
1884	BOS	NL	3	1	2	2	1	0	0	0	0	0	0	0	0	0	3	0
1886	KC	NL	2	2	0	0	1	1	0	0	0	0	0	0	0	0	2	0
1887	WAS	NL	2	1	1	2	0	0	0	0	0	0	0	0	0	0	2	0
1888	WAS	NL	1	0	1	0	1	0	0	0	0	0	0	0	0	0	1	0
Total			18	11	7	8	6	4	0	0	0	0	0	0	0	0	17	1

Rank among batters: 1,914 • Top target (2 home runs): Jim McCormick, John Coleman, John Clarkson, Charley Radbourn • *Number of pitchers victimized*: 14 • *Total ballparks homered in*: 8 • *First HR*: 05/03/1882 off Fred Corey

Pinky Whitney

ARTHUR CARTER WHITNEY
B: 01/02/1905 D: 09/01/1987
BR

Year	Tm	Lg	Tot	H	A	Men-On 0	1	2	3	One-Game 2	3	4	LO	XN	IP	PH	RHP	LHP
1928	PHI	NL	10	5	5	5	5	0	0	0	0	0	0	0	0	0	6	4
1929	PHI	NL	8	4	4	4	4	0	0	0	0	0	0	0	1	0	6	2
1930	PHI	NL	8	4	4	4	4	0	0	0	0	0	0	0	1	0	5	3
1931	PHI	NL	9	3	6	5	3	1	0	0	0	0	0	0	0	0	6	3
1932	PHI	NL	13	7	6	7	4	1	1	0	0	0	0	0	0	0	10	3
1933	PHI	NL	3	1	2	2	1	0	0	0	0	0	0	0	0	0	3	0
	BOS	NL	8	5	3	2	3	3	0	0	0	0	0	0	0	0	7	1
	Total		11	6	5	4	4	3	0	0	0	0	0	0	0	0	10	1
1934	BOS	NL	12	7	5	4	7	1	0	0	0	0	0	0	0	0	10	2
1935	BOS	NL	4	2	2	2	2	0	0	0	0	0	0	0	0	0	4	0
1936	PHI	NL	6	5	1	1	3	1	1	1	0	0	0	0	0	0	4	2
1937	PHI	NL	8	6	2	4	2	2	0	0	0	0	0	0	0	0	5	3
1938	PHI	NL	3	2	1	0	2	1	0	0	0	0	0	0	0	0	3	0
1939	PHI	NL	1	0	1	1	0	0	0	0	0	0	0	0	0	0	0	1
Total			93	51	42	41	40	10	2	1	0	0	0	0	2	0	69	24

Rank among batters: 545 • *Top target (4 home runs)*: Ray Kremer, Guy Bush, Freddie Fitzsimmons • *Number of pitchers victimized*: 61 • *Total ballparks homered in*: 8 • *First HR*: 05/26/1928 off Bill Walker

Eddie Whitson

EDDIE LEE WHITSON
B: 05/19/1955
BR

Year	Tm	Lg	Tot	H	A	Men-On 0	1	2	3	One-Game 2	3	4	LO	XN	IP	PH	RHP	LHP
1990	SD	NL	1	1	0	1	0	0	0	0	0	0	0	0	0	0	1	0

Rank among batters: 4,707 • *Total ballparks homered in*: 1 • *First HR*: 04/25/1990 off Mike Bielecki

Ernie Whitt

LEO ERNEST WHITT
B: 06/13/1952
BL

Year	Tm	Lg	Tot	H	A	Men-On 0	1	2	3	One-Game 2	3	4	LO	XN	IP	PH	RHP	LHP
1976	BOS	AL	1	1	0	1	0	0	0	0	0	0	0	0	0	0	1	0

Ernie Whitt *continued*

Year	Tm	Lg	Tot	H	A	Men-On 0	1	2	3	One-Game 2	3	4	LO	XN	IP	PH	RHP	LHP
1980	TOR	AL	6	2	4	4	0	2	0	0	0	0	0	0	0	0	6	0
1981	TOR	AL	1	0	1	1	0	0	0	0	0	0	0	0	0	0	1	0
1982	TOR	AL	11	8	3	8	3	0	0	0	0	0	0	0	0	2	10	1
1983	TOR	AL	17	11	6	11	3	3	0	2	0	0	0	2	0	1	17	0
1984	TOR	AL	15	5	10	8	5	2	0	0	0	0	0	0	0	1	15	0
1985	TOR	AL	19	7	12	11	4	3	1	0	0	0	0	0	0	0	17	2
1986	TOR	AL	16	7	9	10	4	1	1	0	0	0	0	2	0	0	13	3
1987	TOR	AL	19	11	8	9	7	3	0	1	1	0	0	0	0	0	19	0
1988	TOR	AL	16	9	7	9	5	2	0	2	0	0	0	1	0	0	14	2
1989	TOR	AL	11	8	3	4	2	4	1	0	0	0	0	0	0	0	10	1
1990	ATL	NL	2	2	0	2	0	0	0	0	0	0	0	0	0	0	2	0
Total			134	71	63	78	33	20	3	5	1	0	0	5	0	4	125	9

Rank among batters: 331 • *Top target (6 home runs)*: Jack Morris • *Number of pitchers victimized*: 98 • *Total ballparks homered in*: 16 • *First HR*: 09/21/1976 off Jim Colborn • *LCS HR*—1

Possum Whitted

GEORGE BOSTIC WHITTED
B: 02/04/1890 D: 10/16/1962
BR

Year	Tm	Lg	Tot	H	A	Men-On 0	1	2	3	One-Game 2	3	4	LO	XN	IP	PH	RHP	LHP
1914	BOS	NL	2	0	2	0	1	0	1	0	0	0	0	0	2	0	1	1
1915	PHI	NL	1	1	0	1	0	0	0	0	0	0	0	1	0	0	1	0
1916	PHI	NL	6	4	2	3	2	1	0	0	0	0	0	1	2	0	4	2
1917	PHI	NL	3	2	1	2	0	1	0	0	0	0	0	0	1	0	3	0
1919	PHI	NL	3	1	2	1	1	1	0	0	0	0	0	0	2	0	3	0
1920	PIT	NL	1	1	0	0	1	0	0	0	0	0	0	0	1	0	1	0
1921	PIT	NL	7	3	4	3	2	2	0	1	0	0	0	0	0	0	4	3
Total			23	12	11	10	7	5	1	1	0	0	0	2	8	0	17	6

Rank among batters: 1,686 • *Top target (2 home runs)*: Fred Toney, Jess Barnes, Stan Baumgartner • *Number of pitchers victimized*: 20 • *Total ballparks homered in*: 7 • *First HR*: 10/05/1914 off Raleigh Aitchison

Floyd Wicker

FLOYD EULISS WICKER
B: 09/12/1943
BL

Year	Tm	Lg	Tot	H	A	Men-On 0	1	2	3	One-Game 2	3	4	LO	XN	IP	PH	RHP	LHP
1970	MIL	AL	1	0	1	0	1	0	0	0	0	0	0	0	0	0	1	0

Rank among batters: 4,707 • *Total ballparks homered in*: 1 • *First HR*: 09/26/1970 off Floyd Weaver

Al Wickland

ALBERT WICKLAND
B: 01/27/1888 D: 03/14/1980
BL

Year	Tm	Lg	Tot	H	A	Men-On 0	1	2	3	One-Game 2	3	4	LO	XN	IP	PH	RHP	LHP
1914	CHI	FL	6	3	3	3	0	3	0	0	0	0	0	0	0	0	5	1
1915	CHI	FL	1	0	1	1	0	0	0	0	0	0	1	0	1	0	1	0
	PIT	FL	1	1	0	0	1	0	0	0	0	0	0	0	1	0	0	1
	Total		2	1	1	1	1	0	0	0	0	0	1	0	2	0	1	1
1918	BOS	NL	4	2	2	3	1	0	0	0	0	0	0	0	2	0	3	1
Total			12	6	6	7	2	3	0	0	0	0	1	0	4	0	9	3

Rank among batters: 2,325 • *Total ballparks homered in*: 7 • *First HR*: 05/06/1914 off Harry Moran

Chris Widger

CHRISTOPHER JON WIDGER
B: 05/21/1971
BR

Year	Tm	Lg	Tot	H	A	Men-On 0	1	2	3	One-Game 2	3	4	LO	XN	IP	PH	RHP	LHP
1995	SEA	AL	1	1	0	1	0	0	0	0	0	0	0	0	0	0	0	1

Rank among batters: 4,707 • *Total ballparks homered in*: 1 • *First HR*: 07/26/1995 off Brian Givens

William Widner

WILLIAM WATERFIELD WIDNER
B: 06/03/1867 D: 12/10/1908
BR

Year	Tm	Lg	Tot	H	A	Men-On 0	1	2	3	One-Game 2	3	4	LO	XN	IP	PH	RHP	LHP
1889	COL	AA	2	0	2	1	0	1	0	0	0	0	0	0	1	0	2	0

Rank among batters: 4,129 • *Total ballparks homered in*: 2 • *First HR*: 07/04/1889 off John McCarty

Stump Wiedman

GEORGE EDWARD WIEDMAN
B: 02/17/1861 D: 03/03/1905
BR

Year	Tm	Lg	Tot	H	A	Men-On 0	1	2	3	One-Game 2	3	4	LO	XN	IP	PH	RHP	LHP
1883	DET	NL	1	1	0	1	0	0	0	0	0	0	0	0	0	0	1	0
1885	DET	NL	1	0	1	1	0	0	0	0	0	0	0	0	0	0	0	0
1887	DET	NL	1	0	1	0	1	0	0	0	0	0	0	0	0	0	0	1
Total			3	1	2	2	1	0	0	0	0	0	0	0	0	0	1	1

Rank among batters: 3,735 • *Total ballparks homered in*: 2 • *First HR*: 08/23/1883 off Jim McCormick

Whitey Wietelmann

WILLIAM FREDERICK WIETELMANN
B: 03/15/1919
BB

Year	Tm	Lg	Tot	H	A	Men-On 0	1	2	3	One-Game 2	3	4	LO	XN	IP	PH	RHP	LHP
1944	BOS	NL	2	1	1	2	0	0	0	0	0	0	0	0	0	0	2	0
1945	BOS	NL	4	3	1	0	3	1	0	0	0	0	0	0	0	0	4	0
1947	PIT	NL	1	1	0	1	0	0	0	0	0	0	0	0	0	0	1	0
Total			7	5	2	3	3	1	0	0	0	0	0	0	0	0	7	0

Rank among batters: 2,834 • *Total ballparks homered in*: 3 • *First HR*: 08/15/1944 off Xavier Rescigno

Al Wiggins

ALAN ANTHONY WIGGINS
B: 02/17/1958 D: 01/06/1991
BB

Year	Tm	Lg	Tot	H	A	Men-On 0	1	2	3	One-Game 2	3	4	LO	XN	IP	PH	RHP	LHP
1982	SD	NL	1	1	0	1	0	0	0	0	0	0	0	0	0	0	0	1
1984	SD	NL	3	3	0	3	0	0	0	0	0	0	1	0	0	0	0	3
1987	BAL	AL	1	0	1	1	0	0	0	0	0	0	0	0	0	0	1	0
Total			5	4	1	5	0	0	0	0	0	0	1	0	0	0	1	4

Rank among batters: 3,191 • *Total ballparks homered in*: 2 • *First HR*: 05/20/1982 off Dave LaPoint

Del Wilber

DELBERT QUENTIN WILBER
B: 02/24/1919
BR

Year	Tm	Lg	Tot	H	A	Men-On 0	1	2	3	One-Game 2	3	4	LO	XN	IP	PH	RHP	LHP
1951	PHI	NL	8	5	3	6	2	0	0	0	1	0	0	0	1	0	3	5
1952	BOS	AL	3	0	3	1	2	0	0	0	0	0	0	0	0	0	2	1
1953	BOS	AL	7	6	1	3	2	2	0	0	0	0	0	1	0	4	5	2
1954	BOS	AL	1	1	0	1	0	0	0	0	0	0	0	0	0	0	1	0
Total			19	12	7	11	6	2	0	0	1	0	0	1	1	4	11	8

Rank among batters: 1,861 • *Top target (3 home runs)*: Ken Raffensberger • *Number of pitchers victimized*: 17 • *Total ballparks homered in*: 6 • *First HR*: 05/05/1951 off Red Munger

Rob Wilfong

ROBERT DANIEL WILFONG
B: 09/01/1953
BL

Year	Tm	Lg	Tot	H	A	Men-On 0	1	2	3	One-Game 2	3	4	LO	XN	IP	PH	RHP	LHP
1977	MIN	AL	1	1	0	1	0	0	0	0	0	0	0	0	0	0	1	0
1978	MIN	AL	1	1	0	0	1	0	0	0	0	0	0	0	0	0	1	0
1979	MIN	AL	9	4	5	6	2	1	0	0	0	0	0	0	0	0	9	0
1980	MIN	AL	8	3	5	6	1	0	1	0	0	0	0	0	0	0	6	2
1981	MIN	AL	3	3	0	2	1	0	0	0	0	0	0	0	0	0	2	1
1982	CAL	AL	1	0	1	1	0	0	0	0	0	0	0	0	0	0	1	0
1983	CAL	AL	2	1	1	1	1	0	0	0	0	0	0	0	0	1	2	0
1984	CAL	AL	6	3	3	5	0	1	0	0	0	0	0	0	0	0	6	0
1985	CAL	AL	4	2	2	3	1	0	0	0	0	0	0	0	0	0	2	2
1986	CAL	AL	3	3	0	3	0	0	0	0	0	0	0	0	0	0	3	0
1987	SF	NL	1	1	0	0	1	0	0	0	0	0	0	0	0	0	1	0
Total			39	22	17	28	8	2	1	0	0	0	0	0	0	1	34	5

Rank among batters: 1,204 • *Top target (2 home runs)*: Danny Darwin • *Number of pitchers victimized*: 38 • *Total ballparks homered in*: 14 • *First HR*: 05/01/1977 off Dave Rozema

Harry Wilhelm

HARRY LESTER WILHELM
B: 04/07/1874 D: 02/20/1944
BR

Year	Tm	Lg	Tot	H	A	Men-On 0	1	2	3	One-Game 2	3	4	LO	XN	IP	PH	RHP	LHP
1899	LOU	NL	1	1	0	1	0	0	0	0	0	0	0	0	1	0	0	1

Rank among batters: 4,707 • *Total ballparks homered in*: 1 • *First HR*: 08/23/1899 off Harry Colliflower

Year	Tm	Lg	Tot	H	A	Men-On 0	Men-On 1	Men-On 2	Men-On 3	One-Game 2	One-Game 3	One-Game 4	LO	XN	IP	PH	RHP	LHP

Hoyt Wilhelm

JAMES HOYT WILHELM
B: 07/26/1923
BR HOF

Year	Tm	Lg	Tot	H	A	0	1	2	3	2	3	4	LO	XN	IP	PH	RHP	LHP
1952	NY	NL	1	1	0	1	0	0	0	0	0	0	0	0	0	0	0	1

Rank among batters: 4,707 • *Total ballparks homered in*: 1 • *First HR*: 04/23/1952 off Dick Hoover • *Hit HR in first major league AB*—vs BOS: 04/23/1952

Joe Wilhoit

JOSEPH WILLIAM WILHOIT
B: 12/20/1885 D: 09/25/1930
BL

Year	Tm	Lg	Tot	H	A	0	1	2	3	2	3	4	LO	XN	IP	PH	RHP	LHP
1916	BOS	NL	2	0	2	1	0	1	0	0	0	0	0	0	2	0	1	1
1917	BOS	NL	1	0	1	0	0	1	0	0	0	0	0	0	0	0	1	0
Total			3	0	3	1	0	2	0	0	0	0	0	0	2	0	2	1

Rank among batters: 3,735 • *Total ballparks homered in*: 3 • *First HR*: 05/10/1916 off Thomas Seaton

Denney Wilie

DENNIS ERNEST WILIE
B: 09/22/1890 D: 06/20/1966
BL

Year	Tm	Lg	Tot	H	A	0	1	2	3	2	3	4	LO	XN	IP	PH	RHP	LHP
1915	CLE	AL	2	0	2	1	1	0	0	0	0	0	0	0	0	0	2	0

Rank among batters: 4,129 • *Total ballparks homered in*: 1 • *First HR*: 08/10/1915 off King Cole

Curt Wilkerson

CURTIS VERNON WILKERSON
B: 04/26/1961
BB

Year	Tm	Lg	Tot	H	A	0	1	2	3	2	3	4	LO	XN	IP	PH	RHP	LHP
1984	TEX	AL	1	0	1	1	0	0	0	0	0	0	0	0	0	0	1	0
1987	TEX	AL	2	1	1	2	0	0	0	0	0	0	0	0	0	0	1	1
1989	CHI	NL	1	1	0	1	0	0	0	0	0	0	0	0	0	0	0	1
1991	PIT	NL	2	2	0	1	0	0	1	0	0	0	0	0	0	1	2	0
1992	KC	AL	2	2	0	1	0	1	0	0	0	0	0	0	0	0	1	1
Total			8	6	2	6	0	1	1	0	0	0	0	0	0	1	5	3

Rank among batters: 2,703 • *Total ballparks homered in*: 6 • *First HR*: 09/08/1984 off John Butcher

Rick Wilkins

RICHARD DAVID WILKINS
B: 06/04/1967
BL

Year	Tm	Lg	Tot	H	A	0	1	2	3	2	3	4	LO	XN	IP	PH	RHP	LHP
1991	CHI	NL	6	2	4	4	0	2	0	0	0	0	0	0	0	1	5	1
1992	CHI	NL	8	3	5	6	1	1	0	0	0	0	0	0	0	0	8	0
1993	CHI	NL	30	10	20	21	4	4	1	2	0	0	0	2	0	2	27	3
1994	CHI	NL	7	4	3	5	2	0	0	0	0	0	0	0	0	0	6	1
1995	CHI	NL	6	3	3	5	1	0	0	0	0	0	0	0	0	0	5	1
	HOU	NL	1	0	1	1	0	0	0	0	0	0	0	0	0	0	1	0
	Total		7	3	4	6	1	0	0	0	0	0	0	0	0	0	6	1
Total			58	22	36	42	8	7	1	2	0	0	0	2	0	3	52	6

Rank among batters: 886 • *Top target (4 home runs)*: John Smoltz • *Number of pitchers victimized*: 45 • *Total ballparks homered in*: 15 • *First HR*: 06/25/1991 off Bob Kipper

Bob Will

ROBERT LEE WILL
B: 07/15/1931
BL

Year	Tm	Lg	Tot	H	A	0	1	2	3	2	3	4	LO	XN	IP	PH	RHP	LHP
1957	CHI	NL	1	1	0	0	1	0	0	0	0	0	0	0	0	1	1	0
1960	CHI	NL	6	1	5	5	1	0	0	0	0	0	0	1	0	0	6	0
1962	CHI	NL	2	1	1	2	0	0	0	0	0	0	0	0	0	2	2	0
Total			9	3	6	7	2	0	0	0	0	0	0	1	0	3	9	0

Rank among batters: 2,587 • *Top target (2 home runs)*: Don Newcombe, Lew Burdette • *Number of pitchers victimized*: 7 • *Total ballparks homered in*: 5 • *First HR*: 07/04/1957 off Lindy McDaniel

Jerry Willard

GERALD DUANE WILLARD
B: 03/14/1960
BL

Year	Tm	Lg	Tot	H	A	0	1	2	3	2	3	4	LO	XN	IP	PH	RHP	LHP
1984	CLE	AL	10	5	5	6	4	0	0	1	0	0	0	0	0	0	9	1

Jerry Willard *continued*

Year	Tm	Lg	Tot	H	A	Men-On 0	1	2	3	One-Game 2	3	4	LO	XN	IP	PH	RHP	LHP
1985	CLE	AL	7	4	3	3	4	0	0	0	0	0	0	0	0	0	7	0
1986	OAK	AL	4	2	2	2	0	2	0	0	0	0	0	0	0	0	4	0
1991	ATL	NL	1	1	0	0	1	0	0	0	0	0	0	0	0	0	1	0
1992	ATL	NL	2	1	1	1	1	0	0	0	0	0	0	0	0	1	2	0
1994	SEA	AL	1	1	0	0	0	1	0	0	0	0	0	0	0	1	1	0
Total			25	14	11	12	10	3	0	1	0	0	0	0	0	2	24	1

Rank among batters: 1,608 • *Top target (2 home runs)*: Dennis Eckersley, John Butcher • *Number of pitchers victimized*: 23 • *Total ballparks homered in*: 10 • *First HR*: 05/21/1984 off Dennis Eckersley

Ed Willett

ROBERT EDGAR WILLETT
B: 03/07/1884 D: 05/10/1934
BR

Year	Tm	Lg	Tot	H	A	Men-On 0	1	2	3	One-Game 2	3	4	LO	XN	IP	PH	RHP	LHP
1911	DET	AL	1	1	0	0	1	0	0	0	0	0	0	0	0	0	0	1
1912	DET	AL	2	2	0	1	1	0	0	1	0	0	0	0	0	0	1	1
1913	DET	AL	1	0	1	1	0	0	0	0	0	0	0	0	0	0	1	0
1914	STL	FL	1	0	1	0	1	0	0	0	0	0	0	0	0	0	1	0
Total			5	3	2	2	3	0	0	1	0	0	0	0	0	0	3	2

Rank among batters: 3,191 • *Total ballparks homered in*: 4 • *First HR*: 04/26/1911 off Eral Yingling

Carl Willey

CARLTON FRANCIS WILLEY
B: 06/06/1931
BR

Year	Tm	Lg	Tot	H	A	Men-On 0	1	2	3	One-Game 2	3	4	LO	XN	IP	PH	RHP	LHP
1960	MIL	NL	1	1	0	1	0	0	0	0	0	0	0	0	0	0	1	0
1963	NY	NL	1	1	0	0	0	0	1	0	0	0	0	0	0	0	1	0
Total			2	2	0	1	0	0	1	0	0	0	0	0	0	0	2	0

Rank among batters: 4,129 • *Total ballparks homered in*: 2 • *First HR*: 09/10/1960 off Ed Palmquist

Bernie Williams

BERNARD WILLIAMS
B: 10/08/1948
BR

Year	Tm	Lg	Tot	H	A	Men-On 0	1	2	3	One-Game 2	3	4	LO	XN	IP	PH	RHP	LHP
1971	SF	NL	1	1	0	1	0	0	0	0	0	0	0	0	0	0	0	1
1972	SF	NL	3	0	3	1	2	0	0	0	0	0	0	0	0	2	1	2
Total			4	1	3	2	2	0	0	0	0	0	0	0	0	2	1	3

Rank among batters: 3,427 • *Total ballparks homered in*: 3 • *First HR*: 06/20/1971 off Fred Norman

Bernie Williams

BERNABE (FIGUEROA) WILLIAMS
B: 09/13/1968
BB

Year	Tm	Lg	Tot	H	A	Men-On 0	1	2	3	One-Game 2	3	4	LO	XN	IP	PH	RHP	LHP
1991	NY	AL	3	1	2	3	0	0	0	0	0	0	0	0	0	0	1	2
1992	NY	AL	5	3	2	3	2	0	0	0	0	0	0	0	0	0	4	1
1993	NY	AL	12	5	7	7	3	1	1	0	0	0	1	0	0	0	6	6
1994	NY	AL	12	4	8	6	4	1	1	1	0	0	2	0	0	0	6	6
1995	NY	AL	18	7	11	11	6	1	0	0	0	0	1	1	0	0	5	13
Total			50	20	30	30	15	3	2	1	0	0	4	1	0	0	22	28

Rank among batters: 991 • Top target (2 home runs): Chuck Finley, Dennis Cook, Dave Fleming, Brian Bohanon, Jamie Moyer • *Number of pitchers victimized*: 45 • *Total ballparks homered in*: 15 • *First HR*: 07/14/1991 off Chuck Finley • *Switch hit HR in 1 game*—1 time • *LCS HR*—2

Billy Williams

BILLY LEO WILLIAMS
B: 06/15/1938
BL HOF

Year	Tm	Lg	Tot	H	A	Men-On 0	1	2	3	One-Game 2	3	4	LO	XN	IP	PH	RHP	LHP
1960	CHI	NL	2	0	2	1	1	0	0	0	0	0	0	0	0	0	2	0
1961	CHI	NL	25	17	8	17	5	1	2	2	0	0	0	0	1	0	19	6
1962	CHI	NL	22	12	10	16	6	0	0	1	0	0	0	1	0	0	17	5
1963	CHI	NL	25	16	9	10	13	2	0	2	0	0	0	1	2	0	22	3
1964	CHI	NL	33	20	13	17	12	3	1	2	0	0	0	2	1	0	23	10
1965	CHI	NL	34	20	14	17	12	4	1	1	0	0	0	0	0	0	24	10
1966	CHI	NL	29	16	13	19	8	2	0	1	0	0	0	0	0	0	18	11

Billy Williams *continued*

Year	Tm	Lg	Tot	H	A	Men-On				One-Game			LO	XN	IP	PH	RHP	LHP
						0	1	2	3	2	3	4						
1967	CHI	NL	28	12	16	16	10	2	0	4	0	0	0	0	0	0	19	9
1968	CHI	NL	30	16	14	12	13	4	1	4	1	0	0	1	1	0	22	8
1969	CHI	NL	21	14	7	12	5	4	0	1	0	0	0	0	0	0	18	3
1970	CHI	NL	42	28	14	26	10	5	1	3	0	0	0	1	0	0	36	6
1971	CHI	NL	28	16	12	10	15	3	0	4	0	0	0	1	0	1	22	6
1972	CHI	NL	37	24	13	15	17	4	1	2	0	0	0	1	0	0	30	7
1973	CHI	NL	20	10	10	6	13	1	0	1	0	0	0	0	0	0	11	9
1974	CHI	NL	16	10	6	9	5	1	1	0	0	0	0	1	0	0	14	2
1975	OAK	AL	23	8	15	9	9	5	0	3	0	0	0	0	1	0	19	4
1976	OAK	AL	11	6	5	6	4	1	0	0	0	0	0	0	0	0	9	2
Total			426	245	181	218	158	42	8	31	1	0	0	9	6	1	325	101

Rank among batters: 23 • *Top target (10 home runs)*: Bob Gibson • *Number of pitchers victimized*: 230 • *Total ballparks homered in*: 29 • *First HR*: 10/01/1960 off Stan Williams • *Hit for Cycle—*@STL: 07/17/1966 (2) • *All-Star HR*—1

Bob Williams

ROBERT ELIAS WILLIAMS
B: 04/27/1884 D: 08/06/1962
BR

Year	Tm	Lg	Tot	H	A	Men-On 0	1	2	3	One-Game 2	3	4	LO	XN	IP	PH	RHP	LHP
1914	NY	AL	1	0	1	1	0	0	0	0	0	0	0	0	0	0	1	0

Rank among batters: 4,707 • *Total ballparks homered in*: 1 • *First HR*: 05/04/1914 off Doc Ayers

Cy Williams

FRED WILLIAMS
B: 12/21/1887 D: 04/23/1974
BL

Year	Tm	Lg	Tot	H	A	Men-On 0	1	2	3	One-Game 2	3	4	LO	XN	IP	PH	RHP	LHP
1913	CHI	NL	4	3	1	0	3	0	1	0	0	0	0	0	3	1	3	1
1915	CHI	NL	13	6	7	7	4	2	0	1	0	0	0	0	6	0	11	2
1916	CHI	NL	12	8	4	7	3	2	0	1	0	0	0	0	2	1	10	2
1917	CHI	NL	5	5	0	2	2	1	0	0	0	0	0	0	0	0	2	3
1918	PHI	NL	6	2	4	2	3	1	0	0	0	0	0	0	0	0	3	3
1919	PHI	NL	9	4	5	5	3	1	0	0	0	0	0	0	0	0	9	0
1920	PHI	NL	15	12	3	12	3	0	0	0	0	0	0	0	1	0	11	4
1921	PHI	NL	18	15	3	11	6	1	0	0	0	0	0	1	0	0	14	4
1922	PHI	NL	26	17	9	12	10	4	0	2	0	0	0	0	0	0	23	3
1923	PHI	NL	41	26	15	18	20	3	0	5	1	0	0	1	1	0	29	12
1924	PHI	NL	24	14	10	12	6	5	1	2	0	0	0	1	1	0	17	7
1925	PHI	NL	13	12	1	5	4	2	2	1	0	0	0	1	0	2	12	1
1926	PHI	NL	18	11	7	8	5	3	2	1	0	0	0	1	0	1	17	1
1927	PHI	NL	30	15	15	16	6	7	1	2	0	0	0	0	0	1	27	3
1928	PHI	NL	12	8	4	2	8	2	0	0	0	0	0	0	0	3	12	0
1929	PHI	NL	5	3	2	2	2	1	0	0	0	0	0	0	0	2	4	1
Total			251	161	90	121	88	35	7	15	1	0	0	5	14	11	204	47

Rank among batters: 108 • *Top target (8 home runs)*: Dazzy Vance, Grover Alexander • *Number of pitchers victimized*: 115 • *Total ballparks homered in*: 11 • *First HR*: 08/03/1913 off Bull Wagner • *Hit for Cycle—*@PIT: 08/05/1927

Davey Williams

DAVID CARLOUS WILLIAMS
B: 11/02/1927
BR

Year	Tm	Lg	Tot	H	A	Men-On 0	1	2	3	One-Game 2	3	4	LO	XN	IP	PH	RHP	LHP
1949	NY	NL	1	0	1	0	1	0	0	0	0	0	0	1	0	0	1	0
1951	NY	NL	2	1	1	0	1	0	1	0	0	0	0	0	0	0	2	0
1952	NY	NL	13	6	7	8	2	3	0	0	0	0	4	0	0	0	9	4
1953	NY	NL	3	2	1	0	2	1	0	0	0	0	0	0	0	0	3	0
1954	NY	NL	9	9	0	7	1	1	0	0	0	0	1	0	0	0	9	0
1955	NY	NL	4	4	0	3	0	0	1	1	0	0	2	0	0	0	3	1
Total			32	22	10	18	7	5	2	1	0	0	7	1	0	0	27	5

Rank among batters: 1,360 • *Top target (3 home runs)*: Harry Brecheen, Murry Dickson • *Number of pitchers victimized*: 25 • *Total ballparks homered in*: 6 • *First HR*: 09/19/1949 off Harry Gumbert

Dewey Williams

DEWEY EDGAR WILLIAMS
B: 02/05/1916
BR

Year	Tm	Lg	Tot	H	A	Men-On 0	1	2	3	One-Game 2	3	4	LO	XN	IP	PH	RHP	LHP
1945	CHI	NL	2	1	1	1	0	1	0	0	0	0	0	0	0	0	2	0

Dewey Williams *continued*

Year	Tm	Lg	Tot	H	A	Men-On 0	Men-On 1	Men-On 2	Men-On 3	One-Game 2	One-Game 3	One-Game 4	LO	XN	IP	PH	RHP	LHP
1948	CIN	NL	1	1	0	0	1	0	0	0	0	0	0	0	0	0	0	1
Total			3	2	1	1	1	1	0	0	0	0	0	0	0	0	2	1

Rank among batters: 3,735 • *Total ballparks homered in*: 3 • *First HR*: 05/14/1945 off Bill Voiselle

Dib Williams

EDWIN DIBRELL WILLIAMS
B: 01/19/1910 D: 04/02/1992
BR

Year	Tm	Lg	Tot	H	A	Men-On 0	Men-On 1	Men-On 2	Men-On 3	One-Game 2	One-Game 3	One-Game 4	LO	XN	IP	PH	RHP	LHP
1930	PHI	AL	3	1	2	1	0	2	0	0	0	0	0	0	0	1	2	1
1931	PHI	AL	6	3	3	1	1	3	1	0	0	0	0	0	0	1	5	1
1932	PHI	AL	4	4	0	2	2	0	0	0	0	0	0	0	0	0	2	2
1933	PHI	AL	11	5	6	3	5	2	1	0	0	0	0	0	0	0	7	4
1934	PHI	AL	2	2	0	2	0	0	0	0	0	0	0	0	0	0	2	0
1935	BOS	AL	3	1	2	3	0	0	0	0	0	0	0	0	0	0	3	0
Total			29	16	13	12	8	7	2	0	0	0	0	0	0	2	21	8

Rank among batters: 1,465 • *Top target (2 home runs)*: George Uhle, Sam Jones, Sam Gray, Bob Weiland • *Number of pitchers victimized*: 25 • *Total ballparks homered in*: 9 • *First HR*: 06/01/1930 off Myles Thomas

Dick Williams

RICHARD HIRSCHFELD WILLIAMS
B: 05/07/1929
BR

Year	Tm	Lg	Tot	H	A	Men-On 0	Men-On 1	Men-On 2	Men-On 3	One-Game 2	One-Game 3	One-Game 4	LO	XN	IP	PH	RHP	LHP
1951	BRO	NL	1	1	0	0	0	1	0	0	0	0	0	0	0	0	0	1
1953	BRO	NL	2	0	2	2	0	0	0	0	0	0	0	0	0	0	0	2
1954	BRO	NL	1	0	1	1	0	0	0	0	0	0	0	0	0	0	0	1
1956	BAL	AL	11	7	4	7	3	0	1	0	0	0	1	0	0	0	5	6
1957	BAL	AL	1	1	0	1	0	0	0	0	0	0	0	0	0	0	0	1
	CLE	AL	6	3	3	5	1	0	0	0	0	0	0	0	0	0	1	5
	Total		7	4	3	6	1	0	0	0	0	0	0	0	0	0	1	6
1958	BAL	AL	4	3	1	2	1	1	0	0	0	0	0	0	0	0	4	0
1959	KC	AL	16	11	5	8	7	1	0	0	0	0	0	0	0	0	13	3
1960	KC	AL	12	5	7	8	1	2	1	0	0	0	0	1	0	0	8	4
1961	BAL	AL	8	4	4	6	1	1	0	0	0	0	1	0	0	1	4	4
1962	BAL	AL	1	0	1	0	0	1	0	0	0	0	0	0	0	1	0	1
1963	BOS	AL	2	1	1	1	0	1	0	0	0	0	0	0	0	1	1	1
1964	BOS	AL	5	2	3	4	1	0	0	1	0	0	0	1	0	0	3	2
Total			70	38	32	45	15	8	2	1	0	0	2	2	0	3	39	31

Rank among batters: 742 • Top target (3 home runs): Chuck Stobbs, Jack Fisher, Whitey Ford, Billy Pierce • *Number of pitchers victimized*: 55 • *Total ballparks homered in*: 13 • *First HR*: 07/13/1951 off Bob Schultz

Earl Williams

EARL CRAIG WILLIAMS
B: 07/14/1948
BR

Year	Tm	Lg	Tot	H	A	Men-On 0	Men-On 1	Men-On 2	Men-On 3	One-Game 2	One-Game 3	One-Game 4	LO	XN	IP	PH	RHP	LHP
1971	ATL	NL	33	14	19	22	5	5	1	5	0	0	0	0	0	0	29	4
1972	ATL	NL	28	15	13	18	8	2	0	2	0	0	0	0	0	0	17	11
1973	BAL	AL	22	13	9	8	9	4	1	2	0	0	0	1	0	0	17	5
1974	BAL	AL	14	6	8	9	4	1	0	1	0	0	0	0	0	0	7	7
1975	ATL	NL	11	7	4	6	3	2	0	0	0	0	0	0	0	0	5	6
1976	ATL	NL	9	4	5	6	1	2	0	0	0	0	0	0	0	0	7	2
	MON	NL	8	3	5	5	2	1	0	0	0	0	0	0	0	0	3	5
	Total		17	7	10	11	3	3	0	0	0	0	0	0	0	0	10	7
1977	OAK	AL	13	8	5	8	4	1	0	0	0	0	0	0	0	0	10	3
Total			138	70	68	82	36	18	2	10	0	0	0	1	0	0	95	43

Rank among batters: 314 • *Top target (4 home runs)*: Bill Singer • *Number of pitchers victimized*: 101 • *Total ballparks homered in*: 23 • *First HR*: 04/17/1971 off Barry Lersch • *LCS HR*—1

Eddie Williams

EDWARD LAQUAN WILLIAMS
B: 11/01/1964
BR

Year	Tm	Lg	Tot	H	A	Men-On 0	Men-On 1	Men-On 2	Men-On 3	One-Game 2	One-Game 3	One-Game 4	LO	XN	IP	PH	RHP	LHP
1987	CLE	AL	1	0	1	1	0	0	0	0	0	0	0	0	0	0	1	0
1989	CHI	AL	3	2	1	2	1	0	0	0	0	0	0	0	0	0	2	1
1990	SD	NL	3	1	2	3	0	0	0	0	0	0	0	0	0	0	1	2

Eddie Williams *continued*

Year	Tm	Lg	Tot	H	A	Men-On 0	Men-On 1	Men-On 2	Men-On 3	One-Game 2	One-Game 3	One-Game 4	LO	XN	IP	PH	RHP	LHP
1994	SD	NL	11	5	6	5	3	2	1	1	0	0	0	0	0	0	8	3
1995	SD	NL	12	4	8	8	2	1	1	0	0	0	0	0	0	1	5	7
Total			30	12	18	19	6	3	2	1	0	0	0	0	0	1	17	13

Rank among batters: 1,437 • *Top target (3 home runs)*: Pete Smith • *Number of pitchers victimized*: 27 • *Total ballparks homered in*: 14 • *First HR*: 09/30/1987 off Eric Plunk

George Williams

GEORGE ERIK WILLIAMS
B: 04/22/1969
BB

Year	Tm	Lg	Tot	H	A	Men-On 0	Men-On 1	Men-On 2	Men-On 3	One-Game 2	One-Game 3	One-Game 4	LO	XN	IP	PH	RHP	LHP
1995	OAK	AL	3	1	2	2	0	0	1	0	0	0	0	0	0	0	2	1

Rank among batters: 3,735 • *Total ballparks homered in*: 3 • *First HR*: 08/05/1995 off Jeff Nelson

Gerald Williams

GERALD FLOYD WILLIAMS
B: 08/10/1966
BR

Year	Tm	Lg	Tot	H	A	Men-On 0	Men-On 1	Men-On 2	Men-On 3	One-Game 2	One-Game 3	One-Game 4	LO	XN	IP	PH	RHP	LHP
1992	NY	AL	3	2	1	2	1	0	0	0	0	0	0	0	0	0	1	2
1994	NY	AL	4	2	2	4	0	0	0	1	0	0	0	0	0	1	1	3
1995	NY	AL	6	4	2	2	2	1	1	0	0	0	0	0	0	0	2	4
Total			13	8	5	8	3	1	1	1	0	0	0	0	0	1	4	9

Rank among batters: 2,248 • *Top target (2 home runs)*: Randy Johnson • *Number of pitchers victimized*: 12 • *Total ballparks homered in*: 5 • *First HR*: 09/24/1992 off Frank Tanana

Gus Williams

AUGUST JOSEPH WILLIAMS
B: 05/07/1888 D: 04/16/1964
BL

Year	Tm	Lg	Tot	H	A	Men-On 0	Men-On 1	Men-On 2	Men-On 3	One-Game 2	One-Game 3	One-Game 4	LO	XN	IP	PH	RHP	LHP
1912	STL	AL	2	2	0	1	1	0	0	0	0	0	0	0	0	0	2	0
1913	STL	AL	5	4	1	1	3	1	0	0	0	0	0	0	1	0	4	1
1914	STL	AL	4	3	1	2	2	0	0	0	0	0	0	0	0	0	4	0
1915	STL	AL	1	0	1	0	0	1	0	0	0	0	0	0	0	0	1	0
Total			12	9	3	4	6	2	0	0	0	0	0	0	1	0	11	1

Rank among batters: 2,325 • *Top target (2 home runs)*: Frank Lange • *Number of pitchers victimized*: 11 • *Total ballparks homered in*: 3 • *First HR*: 09/27/1912 off Frank Lange

Harry Williams

HARRY PETER WILLIAMS
B: 06/23/1890 D: 12/21/1963
BR

Year	Tm	Lg	Tot	H	A	Men-On 0	Men-On 1	Men-On 2	Men-On 3	One-Game 2	One-Game 3	One-Game 4	LO	XN	IP	PH	RHP	LHP
1913	NY	AL	1	1	0	1	0	0	0	0	0	0	0	0	0	0	1	0

Rank among batters: 4,707 • *Total ballparks homered in*: 1 • *First HR*: 08/07/1913 off Joe Lake

Jimmy Williams

JAMES THOMAS WILLIAMS
B: 12/20/1876 D: 01/16/1965
BR

Year	Tm	Lg	Tot	H	A	Men-On 0	Men-On 1	Men-On 2	Men-On 3	One-Game 2	One-Game 3	One-Game 4	LO	XN	IP	PH	RHP	LHP
1899	PIT	NL	9	4	5	3	3	2	1	0	0	0	0	0	1	0	9	0
1900	PIT	NL	5	0	5	2	2	1	0	0	0	0	0	0	0	0	4	1
1901	BAL	AL	7	3	4	2	2	2	1	0	0	0	0	0	1	0	7	0
1902	BAL	AL	8	3	5	3	5	0	0	0	0	0	0	0	0	0	7	1
1903	NY	AL	3	1	2	1	2	0	0	0	0	0	0	0	0	0	3	0
1904	NY	AL	2	0	2	2	0	0	0	0	0	0	0	0	1	0	1	1
1905	NY	AL	6	3	3	3	0	3	0	0	0	0	0	0	4	0	4	2
1906	NY	AL	3	2	1	2	1	0	0	0	0	0	0	1	2	0	3	0
1907	NY	AL	2	1	1	2	0	0	0	0	0	0	0	0	2	0	1	1
1908	STL	AL	4	2	2	4	0	0	0	0	0	0	0	0	0	0	4	0
Total			49	19	30	24	15	8	2	0	0	0	0	1	11	0	43	6

Rank among batters: 1,008 • *Top target (4 home runs)*: Bill Bernhard • *Number of pitchers victimized*: 34 • *Total ballparks homered in*: 15 • *First HR*: 06/29/1899 off Jack Dunn

Ken Williams

KENNETH ROY WILLIAMS
B: 06/28/1890 D: 01/22/1959
BL

Year	Tm	Lg	Tot	H	A	Men-On 0	1	2	3	One-Game 2	3	4	LO	XN	IP	PH	RHP	LHP
1919	STL	AL	6	5	1	4	2	0	0	0	0	0	0	0	1	0	4	2
1920	STL	AL	10	9	1	8	1	0	1	0	0	0	0	0	1	0	8	2
1921	STL	AL	24	15	9	13	8	3	0	2	0	0	0	1	1	0	22	2
1922	STL	AL	39	32	7	13	19	5	2	2	1	0	0	0	0	0	28	11
1923	STL	AL	29	18	11	18	7	4	0	0	0	0	0	1	0	0	24	5
1924	STL	AL	18	14	4	6	9	3	0	0	0	0	0	0	0	0	13	5
1925	STL	AL	25	17	8	13	6	5	1	2	0	0	0	0	0	0	20	5
1926	STL	AL	17	13	4	7	7	2	1	1	0	0	0	0	0	1	9	8
1927	STL	AL	17	14	3	11	5	1	0	1	0	0	0	1	0	0	16	1
1928	BOS	AL	8	4	4	5	3	0	0	0	0	0	0	0	0	0	6	2
1929	BOS	AL	3	1	2	2	1	0	0	0	0	0	0	0	0	0	3	0
Total			196	142	54	100	68	23	5	8	1	0	0	3	3	1	153	43

Rank among batters: 191 • *Top target (8 home runs)*: Jack Quinn • *Number of pitchers victimized*: 98 • *Total ballparks homered in*: 10 • *First HR*: 07/07/1919 off Guy Morton • *2 HR in 1 inning*—vs WAS: 08/07/1922

Kenny Williams

KENNETH ROYAL WILLIAMS
B: 04/06/1964
BR

Year	Tm	Lg	Tot	H	A	Men-On 0	1	2	3	One-Game 2	3	4	LO	XN	IP	PH	RHP	LHP
1986	CHI	AL	1	1	0	1	0	0	0	0	0	0	0	0	0	0	0	1
1987	CHI	AL	11	4	7	6	4	1	0	0	0	0	0	0	0	0	3	8
1988	CHI	AL	8	3	5	3	3	2	0	0	0	0	0	0	0	0	5	3
1989	DET	AL	6	3	3	4	2	0	0	0	0	0	0	0	0	0	3	3
1991	TOR	AL	1	0	1	1	0	0	0	0	0	0	0	0	0	0	0	1
Total			27	11	16	15	9	3	0	0	0	0	0	0	0	0	11	16

Rank among batters: 1,532 • *Top target (2 home runs)*: Charlie Hough, Mark Langston • *Number of pitchers victimized*: 25 • *Total ballparks homered in*: 11 • *First HR*: 09/27/1986 off Neal Heaton

Matt Williams

MATTHEW DERRICK WILLIAMS
B: 11/28/1965
BR

Year	Tm	Lg	Tot	H	A	Men-On 0	1	2	3	One-Game 2	3	4	LO	XN	IP	PH	RHP	LHP
1987	SF	NL	8	5	3	6	2	0	0	1	0	0	0	0	0	0	4	4
1988	SF	NL	8	7	1	7	0	0	1	1	0	0	0	0	0	0	3	5
1989	SF	NL	18	10	8	8	6	2	2	1	0	0	0	0	0	0	9	9
1990	SF	NL	33	20	13	17	7	8	1	3	0	0	0	1	0	0	21	12
1991	SF	NL	34	17	17	19	13	2	0	2	0	0	0	0	0	0	27	7
1992	SF	NL	20	9	11	10	5	5	0	1	0	0	0	1	0	0	10	10
1993	SF	NL	38	19	19	21	12	5	0	4	0	0	0	2	0	0	21	17
1994	SF	NL	43	20	23	27	12	4	0	5	0	0	0	1	0	0	27	16
1995	SF	NL	23	9	14	11	8	3	1	3	0	0	0	0	0	0	17	6
Total			225	116	109	126	65	29	5	21	0	0	0	5	0	0	139	86

Rank among batters: 145 • *Top target (7 home runs)*: John Smiley, Ramon Martinez • *Number of pitchers victimized*: 144 • *Total ballparks homered in*: 15 • *First HR*: 04/19/1987 off Jeff Dedmon • *World Series HR*—1; *LCS HR*—2

Mitch Williams

MITCHELL STEVEN WILLIAMS
B: 11/17/1964
BL

Year	Tm	Lg	Tot	H	A	Men-On 0	1	2	3	One-Game 2	3	4	LO	XN	IP	PH	RHP	LHP
1989	CHI	NL	1	1	0	0	0	1	0	0	0	0	0	0	0	0	1	0

Rank among batters: 4,707 • *Total ballparks homered in*: 1 • *First HR*: 09/18/1989 off Don Aase

Reggie Williams

REGINALD DEWAYNE WILLIAMS
B: 08/29/1960
BR

Year	Tm	Lg	Tot	H	A	Men-On 0	1	2	3	One-Game 2	3	4	LO	XN	IP	PH	RHP	LHP
1986	LA	NL	4	1	3	1	2	1	0	0	0	0	0	0	0	0	3	1
1988	CLE	AL	1	1	0	1	0	0	0	0	0	0	0	0	0	0	0	1
Total			5	2	3	2	2	1	0	0	0	0	0	0	0	0	3	2

Rank among batters: 3,191 • *Total ballparks homered in*: 5 • *First HR*: 07/18/1986 off Danny Cox

Rip Williams

ALVA MITCHELL WILLIAMS
B: 01/31/1882 D: 07/23/1933
BR

Year	Tm	Lg	Tot	H	A	Men-On 0	Men-On 1	Men-On 2	Men-On 3	One-Game 2	One-Game 3	One-Game 4	LO	XN	IP	PH	RHP	LHP
1913	WAS	AL	1	0	1	0	1	0	0	0	0	0	0	0	0	1	1	0
1914	WAS	AL	1	1	0	0	0	1	0	0	0	0	0	0	1	0	1	0
Total			2	1	1	0	1	1	0	0	0	0	0	0	1	1	2	0

Rank among batters: 4,129 • *Total ballparks homered in*: 2 • *First HR*: 05/21/1913 off George Kahler

Stan Williams

STANLEY WILSON WILLIAMS
B: 09/14/1936
BR

Year	Tm	Lg	Tot	H	A	Men-On 0	Men-On 1	Men-On 2	Men-On 3	One-Game 2	One-Game 3	One-Game 4	LO	XN	IP	PH	RHP	LHP
1958	LA	NL	1	1	0	1	0	0	0	0	0	0	0	0	0	0	1	0
1960	LA	NL	2	2	0	0	1	1	0	0	0	0	0	0	0	0	1	1
1962	LA	NL	2	1	1	1	1	0	0	0	0	0	0	0	0	0	0	2
Total			5	4	1	2	2	1	0	0	0	0	0	0	0	0	2	3

Rank among batters: 3,191 • *Total ballparks homered in*: 3 • *First HR*: 08/15/1958 off Sal Maglie

Ted Williams

THEODORE SAMUEL WILLIAMS
B: 08/30/1918
BL HOF

Year	Tm	Lg	Tot	H	A	Men-On 0	Men-On 1	Men-On 2	Men-On 3	One-Game 2	One-Game 3	One-Game 4	LO	XN	IP	PH	RHP	LHP
1939	BOS	AL	31	14	17	8	12	9	2	2	0	0	0	1	0	0	26	5
1940	BOS	AL	23	9	14	13	5	4	1	2	0	0	0	1	0	0	18	5
1941	BOS	AL	37	19	18	15	17	4	1	3	0	0	0	1	0	1	35	2
1942	BOS	AL	36	16	20	16	17	2	1	1	0	0	0	0	0	0	32	4
1946	BOS	AL	38	18	20	21	12	3	2	1	1	0	0	3	1	0	36	2
1947	BOS	AL	32	16	16	10	16	5	1	4	0	0	0	1	0	0	31	1
1948	BOS	AL	25	9	16	12	9	4	0	1	0	0	0	0	0	0	20	5
1949	BOS	AL	43	23	20	19	14	9	1	4	0	0	0	0	0	0	38	5
1950	BOS	AL	28	16	12	10	12	5	1	4	0	0	0	0	0	0	24	4
1951	BOS	AL	30	18	12	11	15	3	1	1	0	0	0	2	0	0	25	5
1952	BOS	AL	1	1	0	0	1	0	0	0	0	0	0	0	0	0	1	0
1953	BOS	AL	13	8	5	6	4	3	0	1	0	0	0	0	0	2	13	0
1954	BOS	AL	29	16	13	11	13	5	0	2	0	0	0	1	0	1	27	2
1955	BOS	AL	28	15	13	14	8	3	3	2	0	0	0	0	0	0	20	8
1956	BOS	AL	24	10	14	11	8	5	0	1	0	0	0	1	0	0	18	6
1957	BOS	AL	38	12	26	25	6	6	1	1	2	0	0	0	0	3	33	5
1958	BOS	AL	26	10	16	11	9	4	2	1	0	0	0	2	0	0	25	1
1959	BOS	AL	10	3	7	7	3	0	0	0	0	0	0	0	0	0	9	1
1960	BOS	AL	29	15	14	15	11	3	0	3	0	0	0	0	0	0	26	3
Total			521	248	273	235	192	77	17	34	3	0	0	13	1	7	457	64

Rank among batters: 10 • *Top target (12 home runs)*: Virgil Trucks • *Number of pitchers victimized*: 224 • *Total ballparks homered in*: 11 • *First HR*: 04/23/1939 off Bud Thomas • *Hit for Cycle*—vs STL: 07/21/1946 (2) • *All-Star HR*—4

Walt Williams

WALTER ALLEN WILLIAMS
B: 12/19/1943
BR

Year	Tm	Lg	Tot	H	A	Men-On 0	Men-On 1	Men-On 2	Men-On 3	One-Game 2	One-Game 3	One-Game 4	LO	XN	IP	PH	RHP	LHP
1967	CHI	AL	3	1	2	1	1	1	0	0	0	0	0	0	0	0	2	1
1968	CHI	AL	1	0	1	1	0	0	0	0	0	0	0	0	0	0	1	0
1969	CHI	AL	3	3	0	3	0	0	0	0	0	0	0	1	0	0	3	0
1970	CHI	AL	3	1	2	2	0	1	0	0	0	0	1	0	0	0	2	1
1971	CHI	AL	8	3	5	4	2	2	0	0	0	0	1	0	0	0	6	2
1972	CHI	AL	2	1	1	2	0	0	0	0	0	0	1	0	0	0	0	2
1973	CLE	AL	8	2	6	5	2	1	0	0	0	0	0	0	0	1	4	4
1975	NY	AL	5	2	3	4	0	1	0	0	0	0	0	0	0	0	3	2
Total			33	13	20	22	5	6	0	0	0	0	3	1	0	1	21	12

Rank among batters: 1,336 • *Top target (3 home runs)*: Dick Bosman • *Number of pitchers victimized*: 26 • *Total ballparks homered in*: 12 • *First HR*: 06/14/1967 off Dennis Bennett

Woody Williams

WOODROW WILSON WILLIAMS
B: 08/21/1912 D: 02/24/1995
BR

Year	Tm	Lg	Tot	H	A	Men-On 0	Men-On 1	Men-On 2	Men-On 3	One-Game 2	One-Game 3	One-Game 4	LO	XN	IP	PH	RHP	LHP
1944	CIN	NL	1	0	1	1	0	0	0	0	0	0	0	0	0	0	1	0

Rank among batters: 4,707 • *Total ballparks homered in*: 1 • *First HR*: 09/25/1944 off Harry Feldman

Ned Williamson

EDWARD NAGLE WILLIAMSON
B: 10/24/1857 D: 03/03/1894
BR

Year	Tm	Lg	Tot	H	A	Men-On 0	1	2	3	One-Game 2	3	4	LO	XN	IP	PH	RHP	LHP
1878	IND	NL	1	1	0	0	1	0	0	0	0	0	0	0	0	0	1	0
1879	CHI	NL	1	1	0	1	0	0	0	0	0	0	0	0	0	0	0	1
1881	CHI	NL	1	1	0	1	0	0	0	0	0	0	0	0	1	0	0	1
1882	CHI	NL	3	2	1	0	2	1	0	0	0	0	0	0	0	0	3	0
1883	CHI	NL	2	2	0	1	1	0	0	0	0	0	0	0	0	0	2	0
1884	CHI	NL	27	25	2	12	6	4	1	2	1	0	0	0	0	0	24	0
1885	CHI	NL	3	2	1	2	0	1	0	0	0	0	0	0	0	0	2	1
1886	CHI	NL	6	6	0	4	1	1	0	0	0	0	0	0	0	0	5	1
1887	CHI	NL	9	8	1	4	2	3	0	0	0	0	0	0	0	0	8	1
1888	CHI	NL	8	7	1	3	4	1	0	0	0	0	0	0	1	0	7	1
1889	CHI	NL	1	0	1	0	0	1	0	0	0	0	0	0	0	0	1	0
1890	CHI	PL	2	2	0	0	2	0	0	0	0	0	0	0	1	0	2	0
Total			64	57	7	28	19	12	1	2	1	0	0	0	3	0	55	6

Rank among batters: 815 • *Top target (10 home runs)*: Mickey Welch • *Number of pitchers victimized*: 35 • *Total ballparks homered in*: 11 • *First HR*: 09/07/1878 off Sam Weaver

Hugh Willingham

THOMAS HUGH WILLINGHAM
B: 05/30/1906 D: 06/15/1988
BR

Year	Tm	Lg	Tot	H	A	Men-On 0	1	2	3	One-Game 2	3	4	LO	XN	IP	PH	RHP	LHP
1931	PHI	NL	1	0	1	1	0	0	0	0	0	0	0	0	0	0	0	1

Rank among batters: 4,707 • *Total ballparks homered in*: 1 • *First HR*: 09/27/1931 off Tom Zachary

Vic Willis

VICTOR GAZAWAY WILLIS
B: 04/12/1876 D: 08/03/1947
BR

Year	Tm	Lg	Tot	H	A	Men-On 0	1	2	3	One-Game 2	3	4	LO	XN	IP	PH	RHP	LHP
1901	BOS	NL	1	0	1	0	1	0	0	0	0	0	0	0	1	0	0	1

Rank among batters: 4,707 • *Total ballparks homered in*: 1 • *First HR*: 06/10/1901 off Doc Newton

Jim Willoughby

JAMES ARTHUR WILLOUGHBY
B: 01/31/1949
BR

Year	Tm	Lg	Tot	H	A	Men-On 0	1	2	3	One-Game 2	3	4	LO	XN	IP	PH	RHP	LHP
1973	SF	NL	1	0	1	1	0	0	0	0	0	0	0	0	0	0	0	1

Rank among batters: 4,707 • *Total ballparks homered in*: 1 • *First HR*: 04/07/1973 off Tom Hall

Bump Wills

ELLIOTT TAYLOR WILLS
B: 07/27/1952
BB

Year	Tm	Lg	Tot	H	A	Men-On 0	1	2	3	One-Game 2	3	4	LO	XN	IP	PH	RHP	LHP
1977	TEX	AL	9	4	5	6	3	0	0	1	0	0	0	1	1	0	6	3
1978	TEX	AL	9	4	5	7	2	0	0	0	0	0	0	0	0	0	8	1
1979	TEX	AL	5	2	3	4	1	0	0	0	0	0	1	0	1	0	0	5
1980	TEX	AL	5	2	3	1	3	0	1	0	0	0	0	1	1	0	4	1
1981	TEX	AL	2	2	0	0	1	1	0	0	0	0	0	0	0	0	1	1
1982	CHI	NL	6	3	3	4	0	2	0	0	0	0	1	0	0	1	3	3
Total			36	17	19	22	10	3	1	1	0	0	2	2	3	1	22	14

Rank among batters: 1,274 • *Top target (2 home runs)*: Dave Rozema, Rich Wortham • *Number of pitchers victimized*: 34 • *Total ballparks homered in*: 14 • *First HR*: 05/03/1977 off Bob Sykes

Maury Wills

MAURICE MORNING WILLS
B: 10/02/1932
BB

Year	Tm	Lg	Tot	H	A	Men-On 0	1	2	3	One-Game 2	3	4	LO	XN	IP	PH	RHP	LHP
1961	LA	NL	1	1	0	1	0	0	0	0	0	0	0	0	0	0	0	1
1962	LA	NL	6	0	6	5	0	1	0	1	0	0	0	0	1	0	1	5
1964	LA	NL	2	0	2	0	2	0	0	0	0	0	0	0	0	0	1	1
1966	LA	NL	1	0	1	1	0	0	0	0	0	0	1	0	0	0	1	0
1967	PIT	NL	3	2	1	2	0	1	0	0	0	0	0	0	1	0	0	3
1969	LA	NL	4	1	3	3	0	0	1	0	0	0	1	0	0	0	1	3

Maury Wills *continued*

Year	Tm	Lg	Tot	H	A	Men-On 0	1	2	3	One-Game 2	3	4	LO	XN	IP	PH	RHP	LHP
1971	LA	NL	3	2	1	2	0	1	0	0	0	0	0	0	0	0	1	2
Total			20	6	14	14	2	3	1	1	0	0	2	0	2	0	5	15

Rank among batters: 1,810 • *Top target (2 home runs)*: Ray Sadecki, Denny Lemaster • *Number of pitchers victimized*: 18 • *Total ballparks homered in*: 9 • *First HR*: 08/06/1961 off Jack Curtis • *Switch hit HR in 1 game*—1 time

Walt Wilmot

WALTER ROBERT WILMOT
B: 10/18/1863 D: 02/01/1929
BB

Year	Tm	Lg	Tot	H	A	Men-On 0	1	2	3	One-Game 2	3	4	LO	XN	IP	PH	RHP	LHP
1888	WAS	NL	4	0	4	1	3	0	0	0	0	0	0	1	0	0	4	0
1889	WAS	NL	9	2	7	5	3	1	0	1	0	0	0	0	1	0	7	1
1890	CHI	NL	13	10	3	8	4	1	0	2	0	0	0	0	0	0	10	2
1891	CHI	NL	11	9	2	5	4	2	0	2	0	0	0	1	0	0	9	1
1892	CHI	NL	2	0	2	2	0	0	0	0	0	0	1	0	1	0	2	0
1893	CHI	NL	3	2	1	0	3	0	0	0	0	0	0	0	0	0	3	0
1894	CHI	NL	5	2	3	0	2	2	1	0	0	0	0	0	0	0	4	1
1895	CHI	NL	8	3	5	3	5	0	0	1	0	0	0	0	1	0	5	3
1897	NY	NL	1	0	1	1	0	0	0	0	0	0	0	0	0	0	0	1
1898	NY	NL	2	1	1	1	1	0	0	0	0	0	0	0	0	0	2	0
Total			58	29	29	26	25	6	1	6	0	0	1	2	3	0	46	9

Rank among batters: 886 • *Top target (6 home runs)*: John Clarkson • *Number of pitchers victimized*: 39 • *Total ballparks homered in*: 20 • *First HR*: 06/25/1888 off John Clarkson

Art Wilson

ARTHUR EARL WILSON
B: 12/11/1885 D: 06/12/1960
BR

Year	Tm	Lg	Tot	H	A	Men-On 0	1	2	3	One-Game 2	3	4	LO	XN	IP	PH	RHP	LHP
1911	NY	NL	1	1	0	1	0	0	0	0	0	0	0	0	0	0	0	1
1912	NY	NL	3	3	0	0	1	1	1	0	0	0	0	0	0	0	1	2
1914	CHI	FL	10	5	5	8	2	0	0	2	0	0	0	0	0	0	9	1
1915	CHI	FL	7	2	5	2	4	1	0	0	0	0	0	0	0	0	5	2
1916	PIT	NL	1	0	1	1	0	0	0	0	0	0	0	1	0	0	1	0
1917	CHI	NL	2	1	1	1	1	0	0	0	0	0	0	0	0	0	1	1
Total			24	12	12	13	8	2	1	2	0	0	0	1	0	0	17	7

Rank among batters: 1,643 • *Top target (2 home runs)*: Ben Harris, Russ Ford, Pete Henning • *Number of pitchers victimized*: 21 • *Total ballparks homered in*: 8 • *First HR*: 08/11/1911 off Bill Burns

Bill Wilson

WILLIAM G. WILSON
B: 10/28/1867 D: 05/09/1924

Year	Tm	Lg	Tot	H	A	Men-On 0	1	2	3	One-Game 2	3	4	LO	XN	IP	PH	RHP	LHP
1897	LOU	NL	1	1	0	1	0	0	0	0	0	0	0	0	1	0	0	1
1898	LOU	NL	1	1	0	0	1	0	0	0	0	0	0	0	1	0	0	1
Total			2	2	0	1	1	0	0	0	0	0	0	0	2	0	0	2

Rank among batters: 4,129 • *Total ballparks homered in*: 1 • *First HR*: 08/04/1897 off Charlie Brown

Bill Wilson

WILLIAM DONALD WILSON
B: 11/06/1928
BR

Year	Tm	Lg	Tot	H	A	Men-On 0	1	2	3	One-Game 2	3	4	LO	XN	IP	PH	RHP	LHP
1954	CHI	AL	2	1	1	0	2	0	0	0	0	0	0	0	0	0	1	1
	PHI	AL	15	7	8	0	9	5	1	0	1	0	0	0	1	0	13	2
	Total		17	8	9	9	7	1	0	1	0	0	0	0	1	0	14	3
1955	KC	AL	15	9	6	10	3	2	0	0	0	0	0	0	0	0	8	7
Total			32	17	15	19	10	3	0	1	0	0	0	0	1	0	22	10

Rank among batters: 1,360 • *Top target (2 home runs)*: Sandy Consuegra, Tommy Byrne • *Number of pitchers victimized*: 30 • *Total ballparks homered in*: 8 • *First HR*: 04/24/1954 off Marlin Stuart

Charlie Wilson

CHARLES WOODROW WILSON
B: 01/13/1905 D: 12/19/1970
BB

Year	Tm	Lg	Tot	H	A	Men-On 0	1	2	3	One-Game 2	3	4	LO	XN	IP	PH	RHP	LHP
1931	BOS	NL	1	1	0	0	0	1	0	0	0	0	0	0	0	0	1	0

Charlie Wilson *continued*

Year	Tm	Lg	Tot	H	A	Men-On 0	1	2	3	One-Game 2	3	4	LO	XN	IP	PH	RHP	LHP
1932	STL	NL	1	1	0	1	0	0	0	0	0	0	0	0	0	0	1	0
Total			2	2	0	1	0	1	0	0	0	0	0	0	0	0	2	0

Rank among batters: 4,129 • *Total ballparks homered in*: 2 • *First HR*: 04/16/1931 off Dazzy Vance

Chief Wilson

JOHN OWEN WILSON
B: 08/21/1883 D: 02/22/1954
BL

Year	Tm	Lg	Tot	H	A	Men-On 0	1	2	3	One-Game 2	3	4	LO	XN	IP	PH	RHP	LHP
1908	PIT	NL	3	2	1	2	1	0	0	0	0	0	0	0	3	0	2	1
1909	PIT	NL	4	1	3	3	1	0	0	0	0	0	0	0	3	0	3	1
1910	PIT	NL	4	0	4	1	2	0	1	0	0	0	0	0	4	0	3	1
1911	PIT	NL	12	7	5	5	4	3	0	1	0	0	0	0	8	0	12	0
1912	PIT	NL	11	2	9	3	4	3	1	0	0	0	0	0	3	0	10	1
1913	PIT	NL	10	5	5	6	4	0	0	1	0	0	0	0	3	0	8	2
1914	STL	NL	9	6	3	3	5	1	0	0	0	0	0	0	6	0	8	1
1915	STL	NL	3	2	1	2	0	1	0	0	0	0	0	0	1	0	3	0
1916	STL	NL	3	2	1	2	0	1	0	0	0	0	0	0	0	0	3	0
Total			59	27	32	27	21	9	2	2	0	0	0	0	31	0	52	7

Rank among batters: 873 • *Top target (4 home runs)*: Christy Mathewson • *Number of pitchers victimized*: 44 • *Total ballparks homered in*: 10 • *First HR*: 04/23/1908 off Johnny Lush • *Hit for Cycle—@CIN*: 07/03/1910

Craig Wilson

CRAIG WILSON
B: 11/28/1964
BR

Year	Tm	Lg	Tot	H	A	Men-On 0	1	2	3	One-Game 2	3	4	LO	XN	IP	PH	RHP	LHP
1993	KC	AL	1	1	0	0	1	0	0	0	0	0	0	0	0	0	0	1

Rank among batters: 4,707 • *Total ballparks homered in*: 1 • *First HR*: 09/24/1993 off Joe Magrane

Dan Wilson

DANIEL ALLEN WILSON
B: 03/25/1969
BR

Year	Tm	Lg	Tot	H	A	Men-On 0	1	2	3	One-Game 2	3	4	LO	XN	IP	PH	RHP	LHP
1994	SEA	AL	3	1	2	3	0	0	0	0	0	0	0	0	0	0	1	2
1995	SEA	AL	9	5	4	7	1	1	0	0	0	0	0	0	0	0	6	3
Total			12	6	6	10	1	1	0	0	0	0	0	0	0	0	7	5

Rank among batters: 2,325 • *Top target (2 home runs)*: Jim Abbott • *Number of pitchers victimized*: 11 • *Total ballparks homered in*: 5 • *First HR*: 06/11/1994 off Ron Darling

Don Wilson

DONALD EDWARD WILSON
B: 02/12/1945 D: 01/05/1975
BR

Year	Tm	Lg	Tot	H	A	Men-On 0	1	2	3	One-Game 2	3	4	LO	XN	IP	PH	RHP	LHP
1968	HOU	NL	1	0	1	1	0	0	0	0	0	0	0	0	0	0	1	0

Rank among batters: 4,707 • *Total ballparks homered in*: 1 • *First HR*: 08/31/1968 off Jack Lamabe

Earl Wilson

EARL LAWRENCE WILSON
B: 10/02/1934
BR

Year	Tm	Lg	Tot	H	A	Men-On 0	1	2	3	One-Game 2	3	4	LO	XN	IP	PH	RHP	LHP
1962	BOS	AL	3	2	1	2	0	1	0	0	0	0	0	0	0	0	2	1
1963	BOS	AL	1	0	1	0	0	1	0	0	0	0	0	0	0	0	1	0
1964	BOS	AL	5	3	2	3	2	0	0	0	0	0	0	0	0	0	4	1
1965	BOS	AL	6	3	3	3	2	1	0	1	0	0	0	0	0	0	5	1
1966	BOS	AL	2	0	2	2	0	0	0	0	0	0	0	1	0	0	2	0
	DET	AL	5	2	3	1	2	1	1	0	0	0	0	1	0	1	4	1
	Total		7	2	5	3	2	1	1	0	0	0	0	2	0	1	6	1
1967	DET	AL	4	2	2	2	2	0	0	0	0	0	0	0	0	1	3	1
1968	DET	AL	7	4	3	5	0	2	0	0	0	0	0	0	0	0	5	2
1970	DET	AL	1	0	1	1	0	0	0	0	0	0	0	0	0	0	1	0
	SD	NL	1	1	0	0	1	0	0	0	0	0	0	0	0	0	1	0
	Total		2	1	1	1	1	0	0	0	0	0	0	0	0	0	2	0
Total			35	17	18	19	9	6	1	1	0	0	0	2	0	2	28	7

Rank among batters: 1,291 • Top target (2 home runs): Bennie Daniels, Buster Narum, Joe Horlen, Al Downing • *Number of pitchers victimized*: 31 • *Total ballparks homered in*: 11 • *First HR*: 06/07/1962 off Frank Lary

Eddie Wilson

EDWARD FRANCIS WILSON
B: 09/07/1909 D: 04/11/1979
BL

Year	Tm	Lg	Tot	H	A	Men-On 0	1	2	3	One-Game 2	3	4	LO	XN	IP	PH	RHP	LHP
1936	BRO	NL	3	0	3	1	1	1	0	0	0	0	0	0	0	0	3	0
1937	BRO	NL	1	1	0	0	0	0	1	0	0	0	0	0	0	0	1	0
Total			4	1	3	1	1	1	1	0	0	0	0	0	0	0	4	0

Rank among batters: 3,427 • *Total ballparks homered in*: 3 • *First HR*: 07/08/1936 off Bill Lee

Frank Wilson

FRANCIS EDWARD WILSON
B: 04/20/1901 D: 11/25/1974
BL

Year	Tm	Lg	Tot	H	A	Men-On 0	1	2	3	One-Game 2	3	4	LO	XN	IP	PH	RHP	LHP
1924	BOS	NL	1	1	0	0	1	0	0	0	0	0	0	0	1	0	1	0

Rank among batters: 4,707 • *Total ballparks homered in*: 1 • *First HR*: 08/09/1924 off Guy Bush

George Wilson

GEORGE WASHINGTON WILSON
B: 08/30/1925 D: 10/29/1974
BL

Year	Tm	Lg	Tot	H	A	Men-On 0	1	2	3	One-Game 2	3	4	LO	XN	IP	PH	RHP	LHP
1952	NY	NL	2	2	0	2	0	0	0	0	0	0	0	0	0	1	2	0
1956	NY	NL	1	1	0	1	0	0	0	0	0	0	0	0	0	1	1	0
Total			3	3	0	3	0	0	0	0	0	0	0	0	0	2	3	0

Rank among batters: 3,735 • *Total ballparks homered in*: 1 • *First HR*: 08/05/1952 off Billy Loes

Glenn Wilson

GLENN DWIGHT WILSON
B: 12/22/1958
BR

Year	Tm	Lg	Tot	H	A	Men-On 0	1	2	3	One-Game 2	3	4	LO	XN	IP	PH	RHP	LHP
1982	DET	AL	12	9	3	6	6	0	0	0	0	0	0	0	0	0	12	0
1983	DET	AL	11	9	2	5	4	2	0	1	0	0	0	0	0	0	9	2
1984	PHI	NL	6	5	1	3	1	2	0	0	0	0	0	0	0	0	3	3
1985	PHI	NL	14	7	7	4	4	5	1	1	0	0	0	0	1	1	8	6
1986	PHI	NL	15	7	8	7	3	5	0	0	0	0	0	0	0	0	11	4
1987	PHI	NL	14	5	9	11	3	0	0	0	0	0	0	0	0	0	12	2
1988	SEA	AL	3	2	1	1	1	1	0	0	0	0	0	0	0	0	2	1
	PIT	NL	2	0	2	2	0	0	0	1	0	0	0	0	0	0	0	2
	Total		5	2	3	3	1	1	0	1	0	0	0	0	0	0	2	3
1989	PIT	NL	9	2	7	6	3	0	0	1	0	0	0	0	0	0	6	3
	HOU	NL	2	2	0	1	0	1	0	0	0	0	0	0	0	0	1	1
	Total		11	4	7	7	3	1	0	1	0	0	0	0	0	0	7	4
1990	HOU	NL	10	5	5	6	2	2	0	0	0	0	0	1	0	1	8	2
Total			98	53	45	52	27	18	1	4	0	0	0	1	1	2	72	26

Rank among batters: 506 • *Top target (3 home runs)*: Ron Darling, Randy Johnson • *Number of pitchers victimized*: 80 • *Total ballparks homered in*: 19 • *First HR*: 04/19/1982 off Dave Frost

Hack Wilson

LEWIS ROBERT WILSON
B: 04/26/1900 D: 11/23/1948
BR HOF

Year	Tm	Lg	Tot	H	A	Men-On 0	1	2	3	One-Game 2	3	4	LO	XN	IP	PH	RHP	LHP
1924	NY	NL	10	4	6	10	0	0	0	0	0	0	0	0	1	0	7	3
1925	NY	NL	6	2	4	1	3	2	0	1	0	0	0	0	0	1	5	1
1926	CHI	NL	21	12	9	9	11	1	0	1	0	0	0	2	0	0	17	4
1927	CHI	NL	30	15	15	16	11	3	0	2	0	0	0	0	0	0	25	5
1928	CHI	NL	31	14	17	18	10	2	1	6	0	0	0	0	0	0	23	8
1929	CHI	NL	39	25	14	20	10	7	2	7	0	0	0	0	0	0	30	9
1930	CHI	NL	56	33	23	23	24	9	0	7	1	0	0	0	0	0	42	14
1931	CHI	NL	13	6	7	8	1	4	0	0	0	0	0	0	0	1	9	4
1932	BRO	NL	23	16	7	5	10	7	1	2	0	0	0	0	0	0	13	10
1933	BRO	NL	9	5	4	4	3	1	1	0	0	0	0	0	1	1	5	4
1934	BRO	NL	6	5	1	2	3	1	0	0	0	0	0	0	0	1	3	3
Total			244	137	107	116	86	37	5	26	1	0	0	2	2	4	179	65

Rank among batters: 119 • *Top target (8 home runs)*: Bob Smith, Dazzy Vance • *Number of pitchers victimized*: 99 • *Total ballparks homered in*: 8 • *First HR*: 06/25/1924 off Burleigh Grimes • *2 HR in 1 inning*—@PHI: 07/01/1925 (2) • *Hit for Cycle*—vs PHI: 06/23/1930

Year	Tm	Lg	Tot	H	A	Men-On 0	1	2	3	One-Game 2	3	4	LO	XN	IP	PH	RHP	LHP

Jack Wilson

JOHN FRANCIS WILSON
B: 04/12/1912 D: 04/19/1995
BR

Year	Tm	Lg	Tot	H	A	0	1	2	3	2	3	4	LO	XN	IP	PH	RHP	LHP
1935	BOS	AL	1	1	0	1	0	0	0	0	0	0	0	1	0	0	1	0
1940	BOS	AL	2	0	2	2	0	0	0	1	0	0	0	0	0	0	2	0
Total			3	1	2	3	0	0	0	1	0	0	0	1	0	0	3	0

Rank among batters: 3,735 • *Total ballparks homered in*: 2 • *First HR*: 09/02/1935 off Phil Hensiek

Jim Wilson

JAMES ALGER WILSON
B: 02/20/1922 D: 09/02/1986
BR

Year	Tm	Lg	Tot	H	A	0	1	2	3	2	3	4	LO	XN	IP	PH	RHP	LHP
1953	MIL	NL	1	0	1	1	0	0	0	0	0	0	0	0	0	0	1	0
1956	CHI	AL	1	0	1	1	0	0	0	0	0	0	0	0	0	0	1	0
Total			2	0	2	2	0	0	0	0	0	0	0	0	0	0	2	0

Rank among batters: 4,129 • *Total ballparks homered in*: 2 • *First HR*: 05/01/1953 off Karl Drews

Jimmy Wilson

JAMES WILSON
B: 07/23/1900 D: 05/31/1947
BR

Year	Tm	Lg	Tot	H	A	0	1	2	3	2	3	4	LO	XN	IP	PH	RHP	LHP
1923	PHI	NL	1	1	0	0	0	1	0	0	0	0	0	0	0	0	0	1
1924	PHI	NL	6	5	1	2	3	1	0	0	0	0	0	0	1	0	5	1
1925	PHI	NL	3	2	1	1	1	0	1	0	0	0	0	0	0	1	2	1
1926	PHI	NL	4	2	2	3	1	0	0	0	0	0	0	0	0	0	4	0
1927	PHI	NL	2	2	0	1	1	0	0	0	0	0	0	0	0	0	2	0
1928	STL	NL	2	1	1	2	0	0	0	0	0	0	0	0	0	0	1	1
1929	STL	NL	4	2	2	1	2	1	0	0	0	0	0	0	0	0	1	3
1930	STL	NL	1	1	0	1	0	0	0	0	0	0	0	0	0	0	0	1
1932	STL	NL	2	0	2	2	0	0	0	0	0	0	0	1	0	0	1	1
1933	STL	NL	1	0	1	0	1	0	0	0	0	0	0	0	0	0	1	0
1934	PHI	NL	3	1	2	2	0	1	0	0	0	0	0	0	0	0	2	1
1935	PHI	NL	1	1	0	1	0	0	0	0	0	0	0	0	0	0	0	1
1936	PHI	NL	1	0	1	1	0	0	0	0	0	0	0	0	0	0	0	1
1937	PHI	NL	1	1	0	0	1	0	0	0	0	0	0	0	0	0	1	0
Total			32	19	13	17	10	4	1	0	0	0	0	1	1	1	20	12

Rank among batters: 1,360 • *Top target (3 home runs)*: Ed Brandt • *Number of pitchers victimized*: 27 • *Total ballparks homered in*: 5 • *First HR*: 07/21/1923 off Fred Fussell

Mookie Wilson

WILLIAM HAYWARD WILSON
B: 02/09/1956
BB

Year	Tm	Lg	Tot	H	A	0	1	2	3	2	3	4	LO	XN	IP	PH	RHP	LHP
1981	NY	NL	3	2	1	2	1	0	0	0	0	0	1	0	0	0	2	1
1982	NY	NL	5	2	3	3	2	0	0	0	0	0	1	0	0	0	4	1
1983	NY	NL	7	4	3	4	1	2	0	0	0	0	1	1	0	0	4	3
1984	NY	NL	10	7	3	5	5	0	0	0	0	0	0	0	0	0	6	4
1985	NY	NL	6	2	4	6	0	0	0	0	0	0	0	1	0	0	2	4
1986	NY	NL	9	4	5	5	3	1	0	0	0	0	3	0	0	0	6	3
1987	NY	NL	9	5	4	7	1	1	0	0	0	0	0	0	0	0	6	3
1988	NY	NL	8	1	7	4	3	1	0	1	0	0	0	0	0	0	4	4
1989	NY	NL	3	1	2	3	0	0	0	0	0	0	0	0	0	0	2	1
	TOR	AL	2	1	1	2	0	0	0	0	0	0	0	0	0	0	2	0
	Total		5	2	3	5	0	0	0	0	0	0	0	0	0	0	4	1
1990	TOR	AL	3	0	3	3	0	0	0	0	0	0	0	0	0	0	1	2
1991	TOR	AL	2	1	1	1	0	1	0	0	0	0	0	0	0	0	2	0
Total			67	30	37	45	16	6	0	1	0	0	6	2	0	0	41	26

Rank among batters: 777 • *Top target (3 home runs)*: Gary Lucas • *Number of pitchers victimized*: 55 • *Total ballparks homered in*: 16 • *First HR*: 06/02/1981 off Nino Espinosa

Parke Wilson

PARKE ASEL WILSON
B: 10/26/1867 D: 12/20/1934
BR

Year	Tm	Lg	Tot	H	A	0	1	2	3	2	3	4	LO	XN	IP	PH	RHP	LHP
1893	NY	NL	2	2	0	0	1	0	1	0	0	0	0	0	1	0	2	0

Parke Wilson *continued*

Year	Tm	Lg	Tot	H	A	Men-On 0	1	2	3	One-Game 2	3	4	LO	XN	IP	PH	RHP	LHP
1894	NY	NL	1	1	0	0	1	0	0	0	0	0	0	0	0	0	1	0
Total			3	3	0	0	2	0	1	0	0	0	0	0	1	0	3	0

Rank among batters: 3,735 • *Total ballparks homered in*: 1 • *First HR*: 08/31/1893 off Pink Hawley

Red Wilson

ROBERT JAMES WILSON
B: 03/07/1929
BR

Year	Tm	Lg	Tot	H	A	Men-On 0	1	2	3	One-Game 2	3	4	LO	XN	IP	PH	RHP	LHP
1954	CHI	AL	1	0	1	1	0	0	0	0	0	0	0	0	0	0	1	0
	DET	AL	2	0	2	0	1	0	0	1	1	0	0	0	0	0	2	0
	Total		3	0	3	2	0	0	1	1	0	0	0	0	0	0	3	0
1955	DET	AL	2	1	1	1	1	0	0	0	0	0	0	0	0	0	1	1
1956	DET	AL	7	3	4	2	3	2	0	0	0	0	0	0	0	0	4	3
1957	DET	AL	3	1	2	3	0	0	0	0	0	0	0	0	0	0	2	1
1958	DET	AL	3	3	0	2	1	0	0	0	0	0	0	0	0	0	3	0
1959	DET	AL	4	2	2	3	1	0	0	0	0	0	0	0	0	0	3	1
1960	DET	AL	1	0	1	1	0	0	0	0	0	0	0	0	0	0	1	0
	CLE	AL	1	1	0	0	1	0	0	0	0	0	0	0	0	0	1	0
	Total		2	1	1	1	1	0	0	0	0	0	0	0	0	0	2	0
Total			24	11	13	14	7	2	1	1	0	0	0	0	0	0	18	6

Rank among batters: 1,643 • *Top target (2 home runs)*: Charlie Bishop, Art Ditmar • *Number of pitchers victimized*: 22 • *Total ballparks homered in*: 7 • *First HR*: 05/02/1954 off Arnie Portocarrero

Trevor Wilson

TREVOR KIRK WILSON
B: 06/07/1966
BL

Year	Tm	Lg	Tot	H	A	Men-On 0	1	2	3	One-Game 2	3	4	LO	XN	IP	PH	RHP	LHP
1991	SF	NL	1	1	0	1	0	0	0	0	0	0	0	0	0	0	1	0
1993	SF	NL	1	1	0	1	0	0	0	0	0	0	0	0	0	0	1	0
Total			2	2	0	2	0	0	0	0	0	0	0	0	0	0	2	0

Rank among batters: 4,129 • *Total ballparks homered in*: 1 • *First HR*: 07/25/1991 off Wally Whitehurst

Willie Wilson

WILLIE JAMES WILSON
B: 07/09/1955
BB

Year	Tm	Lg	Tot	H	A	Men-On 0	1	2	3	One-Game 2	3	4	LO	XN	IP	PH	RHP	LHP
1979	KC	AL	6	3	3	3	1	2	0	1	0	0	1	1	5	0	4	2
1980	KC	AL	3	2	1	3	0	0	0	0	0	0	1	0	2	0	1	2
1981	KC	AL	1	0	1	1	0	0	0	0	0	0	1	0	0	0	0	1
1982	KC	AL	3	2	1	1	1	1	0	0	0	0	0	0	3	0	3	0
1983	KC	AL	2	2	0	2	0	0	0	0	0	0	1	0	2	0	1	1
1984	KC	AL	2	1	1	0	1	1	0	0	0	0	0	0	1	0	1	1
1985	KC	AL	4	1	3	3	0	1	0	0	0	0	1	0	0	0	3	1
1986	KC	AL	9	5	4	7	2	0	0	0	0	0	4	1	0	0	5	4
1987	KC	AL	4	0	4	4	0	0	0	0	0	0	1	0	0	0	3	1
1988	KC	AL	1	0	1	1	0	0	0	0	0	0	1	0	0	0	1	0
1989	KC	AL	3	1	2	2	1	0	0	0	0	0	0	0	0	0	2	1
1990	KC	AL	2	1	1	1	0	1	0	0	0	0	0	0	0	0	2	0
1993	CHI	NL	1	0	1	1	0	0	0	0	0	0	0	0	0	0	1	0
Total			41	18	23	29	6	6	0	1	0	0	11	2	13	0	27	14

Rank among batters: 1,163 • *Top target (2 home runs)*: Ron Guidry, Floyd Bannister • *Number of pitchers victimized*: 39 • *Total ballparks homered in*: 12 • *First HR*: 05/13/1979 off Steve Trout • *Switch hit HR in 1 game*—1 time • *LCS HR*—1

Zeke Wilson

FRANK EALTON WILSON
B: 12/24/1869 D: 04/26/1928
BR

Year	Tm	Lg	Tot	H	A	Men-On 0	1	2	3	One-Game 2	3	4	LO	XN	IP	PH	RHP	LHP
1895	BOS	NL	1	1	0	0	1	0	0	0	0	0	0	0	0	0	1	0

Rank among batters: 4,707 • *Total ballparks homered in*: 1 • *First HR*: 05/28/1895 off Harry Staley

Hooks Wiltse

GEORGE LEROY WILTSE
B: 09/07/1880 D: 01/21/1959
BR

Year	Tm	Lg	Tot	H	A	Men-On 0	1	2	3	One-Game 2	3	4	LO	XN	IP	PH	RHP	LHP
1904	NY	NL	1	1	0	0	1	0	0	0	0	0	0	0	0	0	0	0

Hooks Wiltse *continued*

Year	Tm	Lg	Tot	H	A	Men-On				One-Game								
						0	1	2	3	2	3	4	LO	XN	IP	PH	RHP	LHP
1909	NY	NL	1	1	0	0	1	0	0	0	0	0	0	0	0	0	1	0
Total			2	2	0	0	2	0	0	0	0	0	0	0	0	0	1	0

Rank among batters: 4,129 • *Total ballparks homered in*: 1 • *First HR*: 06/26/1904 off John McPherson

Snake Wiltse

LEWIS DEWITT WILTSE
B: 12/05/1871 D: 08/25/1928
BR

Year	Tm	Lg	Tot	H	A	Men-On				One-Game								
						0	1	2	3	2	3	4	LO	XN	IP	PH	RHP	LHP
1902	BAL	AL	2	1	1	0	0	1	1	0	0	0	0	0	0	0	2	0

Rank among batters: 4,129 • *Total ballparks homered in*: 2 • *First HR*: 08/23/1902 off Roy Patterson

Ed Winceniak

EDWARD JOSEPH WINCENIAK
B: 04/16/1929
BR

Year	Tm	Lg	Tot	H	A	Men-On				One-Game								
						0	1	2	3	2	3	4	LO	XN	IP	PH	RHP	LHP
1957	CHI	NL	1	1	0	1	0	0	0	0	0	0	0	0	0	0	1	0

Rank among batters: 4,707 • *Total ballparks homered in*: 1 • *First HR*: 05/12/1957 off Hal Jeffcoat

Gordie Windhorn

GORDON RAY WINDHORN
B: 12/19/1933
BR

Year	Tm	Lg	Tot	H	A	Men-On				One-Game								
						0	1	2	3	2	3	4	LO	XN	IP	PH	RHP	LHP
1961	LA	NL	2	2	0	2	0	0	0	0	0	0	0	1	0	1	0	2

Rank among batters: 4,129 • *Total ballparks homered in*: 1 • *First HR*: 09/11/1961 off Don Ferrarese

Bobby Wine

ROBERT PAUL, SR. WINE
B: 09/17/1938
BR

Year	Tm	Lg	Tot	H	A	Men-On				One-Game								
						0	1	2	3	2	3	4	LO	XN	IP	PH	RHP	LHP
1962	PHI	NL	4	2	2	2	2	0	0	0	0	0	0	0	0	0	3	1
1963	PHI	NL	6	3	3	3	2	1	0	0	0	0	0	0	0	0	2	4
1964	PHI	NL	4	1	3	2	0	2	0	0	0	0	0	0	0	0	1	3
1965	PHI	NL	5	5	0	2	3	0	0	0	0	0	0	0	0	0	1	4
1967	PHI	NL	2	1	1	0	1	1	0	0	0	0	0	0	0	0	1	1
1968	PHI	NL	2	1	1	1	0	1	0	0	0	0	0	0	0	0	1	1
1969	MON	NL	3	1	2	2	1	0	0	0	0	0	0	0	0	0	2	1
1970	MON	NL	3	0	3	2	1	0	0	0	0	0	0	0	1	0	3	0
1971	MON	NL	1	0	1	1	0	0	0	0	0	0	0	0	0	0	1	0
Total			30	14	16	15	10	5	0	0	0	0	0	0	1	0	15	15

Rank among batters: 1,437 • Top target (2 home runs): Pete Richert, Al Jackson, Warren Spahn, Juan Marichal • *Number of pitchers victimized*: 26 • *Total ballparks homered in*: 11 • *First HR*: 06/01/1962 off Stan Williams

Ralph Winegarner

RALPH LEE WINEGARNER
B: 10/29/1909 D: 04/14/1988
BR

Year	Tm	Lg	Tot	H	A	Men-On				One-Game								
						0	1	2	3	2	3	4	LO	XN	IP	PH	RHP	LHP
1934	CLE	AL	1	1	0	1	0	0	0	0	0	0	0	0	0	0	1	0
1935	CLE	AL	3	1	2	3	0	0	0	0	0	0	0	0	0	1	2	1
1949	STL	AL	1	1	0	0	1	0	0	0	0	0	0	0	0	0	0	1
Total			5	3	2	4	1	0	0	0	0	0	0	0	0	1	3	2

Rank among batters: 3,191 • *Total ballparks homered in*: 3 • *First HR*: 09/10/1934 off George Caster

Dave Winfield

DAVID MARK WINFIELD
B: 10/03/1951
BR

Year	Tm	Lg	Tot	H	A	Men-On				One-Game								
						0	1	2	3	2	3	4	LO	XN	IP	PH	RHP	LHP
1973	SD	NL	3	2	1	2	0	1	0	0	0	0	0	0	0	1	3	0
1974	SD	NL	20	12	8	18	2	0	0	1	0	0	0	1	0	0	9	11
1975	SD	NL	15	7	8	10	4	1	0	0	0	0	0	0	0	0	10	5
1976	SD	NL	13	4	9	6	1	4	2	0	0	0	0	0	0	0	8	5
1977	SD	NL	25	12	13	12	13	0	0	1	0	0	0	2	0	0	18	7
1978	SD	NL	24	11	13	16	4	3	1	1	0	0	0	0	0	0	14	10

Year	Tm	Lg	Tot	H	A	Men-On 0	Men-On 1	Men-On 2	Men-On 3	One-Game 2	One-Game 3	One-Game 4	LO	XN	IP	PH	RHP	LHP

Dave Winfield *continued*

Year	Tm	Lg	Tot	H	A	0	1	2	3	2	3	4	LO	XN	IP	PH	RHP	LHP
1979	SD	NL	34	16	18	17	9	8	0	2	0	0	0	1	0	0	22	12
1980	SD	NL	20	7	13	13	5	2	0	0	0	0	0	0	0	1	12	8
1981	NY	AL	13	4	9	6	5	2	0	1	0	0	0	0	1	0	6	7
1982	NY	AL	37	14	23	21	6	9	1	4	0	0	0	0	0	0	18	19
1983	NY	AL	32	13	19	19	10	3	0	3	0	0	0	1	0	0	18	14
1984	NY	AL	19	9	10	9	6	3	1	0	0	0	0	1	0	0	14	5
1985	NY	AL	26	15	11	12	10	4	0	2	0	0	0	2	0	0	16	10
1986	NY	AL	24	12	12	10	10	3	1	1	0	0	0	0	0	0	12	12
1987	NY	AL	27	11	16	17	7	2	1	4	0	0	0	0	0	0	14	13
1988	NY	AL	25	12	13	12	9	3	1	3	0	0	0	1	0	0	14	11
1990	NY	AL	2	0	2	2	0	0	0	1	0	0	0	0	0	0	2	0
	CAL	AL	19	13	6	10	6	3	0	2	0	0	0	0	0	1	14	5
	Total		21	13	8	12	6	3	0	3	0	0	0	0	0	1	16	5
1991	CAL	AL	28	13	15	17	9	1	1	0	1	0	0	0	0	0	19	9
1992	TOR	AL	26	13	13	13	7	5	1	1	0	0	0	0	0	0	18	8
1993	MIN	AL	21	12	9	8	9	3	1	1	0	0	0	0	0	0	17	4
1994	MIN	AL	10	5	5	6	2	2	0	1	0	0	0	0	0	0	5	5
1995	CLE	AL	2	1	1	1	0	1	0	0	0	0	0	0	0	0	1	1
Total			465	218	247	257	134	63	11	29	1	0	0	9	1	3	284	181

Rank among batters: 19 • *Top target (8 home runs)*: Floyd Bannister • *Number of pitchers victimized*: 281 • *Total ballparks homered in*: 32 • *First HR*: 06/21/1973 off Ken Forsch • *Hit for Cycle—@KC*: 06/24/1991 • *LCS HR—2*

Ernie Wingard

ERNEST JAMES WINGARD
B: 10/17/1900 D: 01/17/1977
BL

Year	Tm	Lg	Tot	H	A	0	1	2	3	2	3	4	LO	XN	IP	PH	RHP	LHP
1924	STL	AL	3	2	1	1	1	1	0	0	0	0	0	0	0	0	2	1
1925	STL	AL	1	0	1	1	0	0	0	0	0	0	0	0	0	0	1	0
1927	STL	AL	3	1	2	1	1	1	0	0	0	0	0	0	0	0	3	0
Total			7	3	4	3	2	2	0	0	0	0	0	0	0	0	6	1

Rank among batters: 2,834 • *Total ballparks homered in*: 5 • *First HR*: 07/11/1924 off Alex Ferguson

Ted Wingfield

FREDERICK DAVIS WINGFIELD
B: 08/07/1899 D: 07/18/1975
BR

Year	Tm	Lg	Tot	H	A	0	1	2	3	2	3	4	LO	XN	IP	PH	RHP	LHP
1925	BOS	AL	1	0	1	0	1	0	0	0	0	0	0	0	0	0	0	1

Rank among batters: 4,707 • *Total ballparks homered in*: 1 • *First HR*: 09/05/1925 off Dutch Ruether

Al Wingo

ABSALOM HOLBROOK WINGO
B: 05/06/1898 D: 10/09/1964
BL

Year	Tm	Lg	Tot	H	A	0	1	2	3	2	3	4	LO	XN	IP	PH	RHP	LHP
1924	DET	AL	1	1	0	1	0	0	0	0	0	0	0	0	0	1	1	0
1925	DET	AL	5	1	4	2	2	1	0	0	0	0	0	0	1	0	4	1
1926	DET	AL	1	0	1	0	0	0	1	0	0	0	0	0	0	0	1	0
1928	DET	AL	2	1	1	0	2	0	0	0	0	0	0	0	0	0	2	0
Total			9	3	6	3	4	1	1	0	0	0	0	0	1	1	8	1

Rank among batters: 2,587 • *Total ballparks homered in*: 5 • *First HR*: 04/29/1924 off Sloppy Thurston

Ivey Wingo

IVEY BROWN WINGO
B: 07/08/1890 D: 03/01/1941
BL

Year	Tm	Lg	Tot	H	A	0	1	2	3	2	3	4	LO	XN	IP	PH	RHP	LHP
1912	STL	NL	2	2	0	0	1	1	0	0	0	0	0	0	0	0	2	0
1913	STL	NL	2	1	1	2	0	0	0	0	0	0	0	0	1	0	2	0
1914	STL	NL	4	1	3	1	3	0	0	0	0	0	0	0	1	0	4	0
1915	CIN	NL	3	1	2	2	1	0	0	0	0	0	0	0	1	0	3	0
1916	CIN	NL	2	0	2	2	0	0	0	0	0	0	0	0	1	0	2	0
1917	CIN	NL	2	1	1	0	2	0	0	0	0	0	0	0	1	0	1	1
1920	CIN	NL	2	0	2	1	1	0	0	0	0	0	0	0	0	0	2	0
1921	CIN	NL	3	1	2	1	2	0	0	0	0	0	0	0	1	0	3	0

Ivey Wingo *continued*

Year	Tm	Lg	Tot	H	A	Men-On 0	1	2	3	One-Game 2	3	4	LO	XN	IP	PH	RHP	LHP
1922	CIN	NL	3	0	3	0	3	0	0	0	0	0	0	1	1	0	3	0
1923	CIN	NL	1	0	1	1	0	0	0	0	0	0	0	0	0	0	1	0
1924	CIN	NL	1	0	1	1	0	0	0	0	0	0	0	1	0	0	1	0
Total			25	7	18	11	13	1	0	0	0	0	0	2	7	0	24	1

Rank among batters: 1,608 • *Top target (3 home runs)*: Christy Mathewson • *Number of pitchers victimized*: 21 • *Total ballparks homered in*: 9 • *First HR*: 05/23/1912 off Frank Smith

Herm Winningham

HERMAN SON WINNINGHAM
B: 12/01/1961
BL

Year	Tm	Lg	Tot	H	A	Men-On 0	1	2	3	One-Game 2	3	4	LO	XN	IP	PH	RHP	LHP
1985	MON	NL	3	0	3	3	0	0	0	0	0	0	0	0	0	0	2	1
1986	MON	NL	4	1	3	3	1	0	0	0	0	0	0	0	0	0	3	1
1987	MON	NL	4	2	2	0	3	1	0	0	0	0	0	0	0	0	4	0
1989	CIN	NL	3	1	2	2	1	0	0	0	0	0	0	0	0	1	2	1
1990	CIN	NL	3	0	3	3	0	0	0	0	0	0	0	0	0	0	2	1
1991	CIN	NL	1	1	0	1	0	0	0	0	0	0	0	0	0	0	1	0
1992	BOS	AL	1	1	0	0	1	0	0	0	0	0	0	0	0	0	1	0
Total			19	6	13	12	6	1	0	0	0	0	0	0	0	1	15	4

Rank among batters: 1,861 • *Total ballparks homered in*: 11 • *First HR*: 04/12/1985 off Dennis Eckersley

Tom Winsett

JOHN THOMAS WINSETT
B: 11/24/1909 D: 07/20/1987
BL

Year	Tm	Lg	Tot	H	A	Men-On 0	1	2	3	One-Game 2	3	4	LO	XN	IP	PH	RHP	LHP
1931	BOS	AL	1	0	1	0	1	0	0	0	0	0	0	0	0	1	1	0
1936	BRO	NL	1	1	0	0	0	1	0	0	0	0	0	0	0	0	1	0
1937	BRO	NL	5	2	3	3	1	1	0	0	0	0	0	1	2	0	5	0
1938	BRO	NL	1	0	1	1	0	0	0	0	0	0	0	0	0	0	1	0
Total			8	3	5	4	2	2	0	0	0	0	0	1	2	1	8	0

Rank among batters: 2,703 • *Top target (3 home runs)*: Si Johnson • *Number of pitchers victimized*: 6 • *Total ballparks homered in*: 5 • *First HR*: 04/14/1931 off Red Ruffing

George Winter

GEORGE LOVINGTON WINTER
B: 04/27/1878 D: 05/26/1951

Year	Tm	Lg	Tot	H	A	Men-On 0	1	2	3	One-Game 2	3	4	LO	XN	IP	PH	RHP	LHP
1901	BOS	AL	1	0	1	0	1	0	0	0	0	0	0	0	0	0	1	0

Rank among batters: 4,707 • *Total ballparks homered in*: 1 • *First HR*: 07/18/1901 off Bill Hart

Matt Winters

MATTHEW LITTLETON WINTERS
B: 03/18/1960
BL

Year	Tm	Lg	Tot	H	A	Men-On 0	1	2	3	One-Game 2	3	4	LO	XN	IP	PH	RHP	LHP
1989	KC	AL	2	2	0	2	0	0	0	0	0	0	0	0	0	0	1	1

Rank among batters: 4,129 • *Total ballparks homered in*: 1 • *First HR*: 07/07/1989 off Richard Dotson

Kettle Wirts

ELWOOD VERNON WIRTS
B: 10/31/1897 D: 07/12/1968
BR

Year	Tm	Lg	Tot	H	A	Men-On 0	1	2	3	One-Game 2	3	4	LO	XN	IP	PH	RHP	LHP
1922	CHI	NL	1	1	0	0	0	0	1	0	0	0	0	0	0	0	1	0

Rank among batters: 4,707 • *Total ballparks homered in*: 1 • *First HR*: 06/27/1922 off Whitey Glazner

Bill Wise

WILLIAM E. WISE
B: 03/15/1861 D: 05/05/1940

Year	Tm	Lg	Tot	H	A	Men-On 0	1	2	3	One-Game 2	3	4	LO	XN	IP	PH	RHP	LHP
1884	WAS	UA	2	2	0	1	0	1	0	0	0	0	0	0	0	0	1	0

Rank among batters: 4,129 • *Total ballparks homered in*: 1 • *First HR*: 04/19/1884 off Chris McFarland

Casey Wise

KENDALL COLE WISE
B: 09/08/1932
BB

Year	Tm	Lg	Tot	H	A	Men-On 0	1	2	3	One-Game 2	3	4	LO	XN	IP	PH	RHP	LHP
1959	MIL	NL	1	0	1	0	1	0	0	0	0	0	0	0	0	0	0	1
1960	DET	AL	2	2	0	1	1	0	0	1	0	0	0	0	0	0	0	2
Total			3	2	1	1	2	0	0	1	0	0	0	0	0	0	0	3

Rank among batters: 3,735 • *Total ballparks homered in*: 2 • *First HR*: 06/11/1959 off Wilmer Mizell

Rick Wise

RICHARD CHARLES WISE
B: 09/13/1945
BR

Year	Tm	Lg	Tot	H	A	Men-On 0	1	2	3	One-Game 2	3	4	LO	XN	IP	PH	RHP	LHP
1968	PHI	NL	2	2	0	1	0	1	0	0	0	0	0	0	0	0	1	1
1969	PHI	NL	1	1	0	1	0	0	0	0	0	0	0	0	0	0	1	0
1970	PHI	NL	2	0	2	2	0	0	0	0	0	0	0	0	0	0	1	1
1971	PHI	NL	6	3	3	3	1	1	1	2	0	0	0	0	0	0	4	2
1972	STL	NL	1	0	1	0	1	0	0	0	0	0	0	0	0	0	0	1
1973	STL	NL	3	0	3	1	0	1	1	0	0	0	0	0	0	0	3	0
Total			15	6	9	8	2	3	2	2	0	0	0	0	0	0	10	5

Rank among batters: 2,096 • *Total ballparks homered in*: 7 • *First HR*: 06/16/1968 off Claude Osteen

Sam Wise

SAMUEL WASHINGTON WISE
B: 08/18/1857 D: 01/22/1910
BL

Year	Tm	Lg	Tot	H	A	Men-On 0	1	2	3	One-Game 2	3	4	LO	XN	IP	PH	RHP	LHP
1882	BOS	NL	4	3	1	2	2	0	0	0	0	0	0	0	1	0	4	0
1883	BOS	NL	4	4	0	2	1	1	0	0	0	0	0	0	0	0	4	0
1884	BOS	NL	4	0	4	2	1	1	0	0	0	0	0	0	1	0	3	0
1885	BOS	NL	4	3	1	1	2	1	0	0	0	0	0	0	0	0	4	0
1886	BOS	NL	4	1	3	2	2	0	0	1	0	0	0	0	1	0	4	0
1887	BOS	NL	9	3	6	4	5	0	0	2	0	0	0	0	0	0	7	2
1888	BOS	NL	4	2	2	3	0	1	0	0	0	0	0	0	1	0	3	1
1889	WAS	NL	4	3	1	1	1	2	0	0	0	0	0	0	0	0	4	0
1890	BUF	PL	5	1	4	2	0	3	0	0	0	0	0	1	1	0	2	2
1891	BAL	AA	1	1	0	1	0	0	0	0	0	0	0	0	0	0	0	1
1893	WAS	NL	5	0	5	2	2	1	0	0	0	0	0	0	0	0	5	0
Total			48	21	27	22	16	10	0	3	0	0	0	1	5	0	40	6

Rank among batters: 1,024 • *Top target (5 home runs)*: Jim Galvin • *Number of pitchers victimized*: 35 • *Total ballparks homered in*: 16 • *First HR*: 05/08/1882 off Tim Keefe

Mickey Witek

NICHOLAS JOSEPH WITEK
B: 12/19/1915 D: 08/24/1990
BR

Year	Tm	Lg	Tot	H	A	Men-On 0	1	2	3	One-Game 2	3	4	LO	XN	IP	PH	RHP	LHP
1940	NY	NL	3	2	1	2	1	0	0	0	0	0	0	0	1	0	2	1
1941	NY	NL	1	1	0	0	0	1	0	0	0	0	0	0	0	0	1	0
1942	NY	NL	5	5	0	3	2	0	0	0	0	0	0	0	0	0	5	0
1943	NY	NL	6	6	0	5	0	1	0	1	0	0	0	2	0	0	4	2
1946	NY	NL	4	3	1	0	2	1	1	0	0	0	0	0	1	0	3	1
1947	NY	NL	3	3	0	2	1	0	0	0	0	0	0	0	2	0	3	0
Total			22	20	2	12	6	3	1	1	0	0	0	2	4	0	18	4

Rank among batters: 1,719 • *Top target (2 home runs)*: Bill Fleming • *Number of pitchers victimized*: 21 • *Total ballparks homered in*: 3 • *First HR*: 05/02/1940 off Clyde Shoun

Whitey Witt

LAWTON WALTER WITT
B: 09/28/1895 D: 07/14/1988
BL

Year	Tm	Lg	Tot	H	A	Men-On 0	1	2	3	One-Game 2	3	4	LO	XN	IP	PH	RHP	LHP
1916	PHI	AL	2	0	2	1	1	0	0	0	0	0	1	0	1	0	1	1
1920	PHI	AL	1	0	1	1	0	0	0	0	0	0	0	0	1	0	1	0
1921	PHI	AL	4	4	0	4	0	0	0	0	0	0	1	0	0	0	3	1
1922	NY	AL	4	3	1	2	1	1	0	0	0	0	0	1	2	0	4	0
1923	NY	AL	6	5	1	4	2	0	0	0	0	0	3	0	3	0	5	1

Whitey Witt *continued*

Year	Tm	Lg	Tot	H	A	Men-On 0	1	2	3	One-Game 2	3	4	LO	XN	IP	PH	RHP	LHP
1924	NY	AL	1	0	1	1	0	0	0	0	0	0	1	0	0	0	1	0
Total			18	12	6	13	4	1	0	0	0	0	6	1	7	0	15	3

Rank among batters: 1,914 • *Top target (2 home runs)*: Curt Fullerton • *Number of pitchers victimized*: 17 • *Total ballparks homered in*: 7 • *First HR*: 08/05/1916 off Stan Coveleski

Jerry Witte

JEROME CHARLES WITTE
B: 07/30/1915
BR

Year	Tm	Lg	Tot	H	A	Men-On 0	1	2	3	One-Game 2	3	4	LO	XN	IP	PH	RHP	LHP
1946	STL	AL	2	2	0	1	1	0	0	0	0	0	0	0	0	0	1	1
1947	STL	AL	2	0	2	1	0	1	0	0	0	0	0	0	0	0	2	0
Total			4	2	2	2	1	1	0	0	0	0	0	0	0	0	3	1

Rank among batters: 3,427 • *Total ballparks homered in*: 3 • *First HR*: 09/21/1946 off Earl Caldwell

John Wockenfuss

JOHNNY BILTON WOCKENFUSS
B: 02/27/1949
BR

Year	Tm	Lg	Tot	H	A	Men-On 0	1	2	3	One-Game 2	3	4	LO	XN	IP	PH	RHP	LHP
1975	DET	AL	4	3	1	4	0	0	0	0	0	0	0	0	0	0	1	3
1976	DET	AL	3	2	1	3	0	0	0	0	0	0	0	0	0	0	2	1
1977	DET	AL	9	2	7	4	4	1	0	2	0	0	0	0	0	0	1	8
1978	DET	AL	7	5	2	4	3	0	0	0	0	0	0	0	0	0	0	7
1979	DET	AL	15	7	8	8	3	3	1	1	0	0	0	0	0	2	1	14
1980	DET	AL	16	8	8	9	2	5	0	0	0	0	0	0	0	1	0	16
1981	DET	AL	9	4	5	8	1	0	0	1	0	0	0	0	0	0	3	6
1982	DET	AL	8	3	5	4	2	2	0	0	0	0	0	0	0	2	1	7
1983	DET	AL	9	8	1	3	3	2	1	0	0	0	0	0	0	1	2	7
1984	PHI	NL	6	5	1	4	1	1	0	1	0	0	0	0	0	0	0	6
Total			86	47	39	51	19	14	2	5	0	0	0	0	0	6	11	75

Rank among batters: 602 • *Top target (4 home runs)*: Mike Flanagan, Geoff Zahn, John Tudor • *Number of pitchers victimized*: 57 • *Total ballparks homered in*: 16 • *First HR*: 06/11/1975 off Frank Tanana

Jim Wohlford

JAMES EUGENE WOHLFORD
B: 02/28/1951
BR

Year	Tm	Lg	Tot	H	A	Men-On 0	1	2	3	One-Game 2	3	4	LO	XN	IP	PH	RHP	LHP
1973	KC	AL	2	0	2	1	1	0	0	0	0	0	0	0	0	0	0	2
1974	KC	AL	2	1	1	2	0	0	0	0	0	0	0	0	1	0	1	1
1976	KC	AL	1	1	0	1	0	0	0	0	0	0	1	0	1	0	1	0
1977	MIL	AL	2	1	1	1	1	0	0	0	0	0	0	0	0	0	1	1
1978	MIL	AL	1	0	1	1	0	0	0	0	0	0	0	0	0	0	0	1
1979	MIL	AL	1	0	1	1	0	0	0	0	0	0	0	0	0	0	0	1
1980	SF	NL	1	0	1	1	0	0	0	0	0	0	0	0	0	0	1	0
1981	SF	NL	1	0	1	1	0	0	0	0	0	0	0	0	0	0	1	0
1982	SF	NL	2	1	1	1	1	0	0	0	0	0	0	0	0	0	1	1
1983	MON	NL	1	0	1	1	0	0	0	0	0	0	0	0	0	0	0	1
1984	MON	NL	5	3	2	3	1	1	0	1	0	0	0	0	0	0	2	3
1985	MON	NL	1	1	0	0	0	1	0	0	0	0	0	0	0	1	0	1
1986	MON	NL	1	0	1	0	1	0	0	0	0	0	0	0	0	0	0	1
Total			21	8	13	14	5	2	0	1	0	0	1	0	2	1	8	13

Rank among batters: 1,768 • *Top target (2 home runs)*: Bill Lee, Shane Rawley • *Number of pitchers victimized*: 19 • *Total ballparks homered in*: 13 • *First HR*: 05/18/1973 off Ken Holtzman

Chicken Wolf

WILLIAM VAN WINKLE WOLF
B: 05/12/1862 D: 05/16/1903
BR

Year	Tm	Lg	Tot	H	A	Men-On 0	1	2	3	One-Game 2	3	4	LO	XN	IP	PH	RHP	LHP
1883	LOU	AA	1	0	1	0	1	0	0	0	0	0	0	0	0	0	1	0
1884	LOU	AA	3	2	1	1	1	1	0	0	0	0	0	0	0	0	2	0
1885	LOU	AA	1	1	0	0	1	0	0	0	0	0	0	0	0	0	1	0
1886	LOU	AA	3	3	0	2	0	1	0	1	0	0	0	1	1	0	2	1
1887	LOU	AA	2	1	1	0	1	1	0	0	0	0	0	0	0	0	2	0

Chicken Wolf *continued*

Year	Tm	Lg	Tot	H	A	Men-On 0	Men-On 1	Men-On 2	Men-On 3	One-Game 2	One-Game 3	One-Game 4	LO	XN	IP	PH	RHP	LHP
1889	LOU	AA	3	3	0	1	2	0	0	0	0	0	0	0	0	0	3	0
1890	LOU	AA	4	2	2	1	2	1	0	0	0	0	0	0	0	0	0	3
1891	LOU	AA	1	1	0	1	0	0	0	0	0	0	0	0	0	0	0	0
Total			18	13	5	6	8	4	0	1	0	0	0	1	1	0	11	4

Rank among batters: 1,914 • *Top target (2 home runs)*: Frank Mountain, George Pechiney, Ed Seward • *Number of pitchers victimized*: 15 • *Total ballparks homered in*: 6 • *First HR*: 08/07/1883 off Frank Mountain

Barney Wolfe

WILBERT OTTO WOLFE
B: 06/07/1876 D: 02/27/1953
BR

Year	Tm	Lg	Tot	H	A	Men-On 0	Men-On 1	Men-On 2	Men-On 3	One-Game 2	One-Game 3	One-Game 4	LO	XN	IP	PH	RHP	LHP
1905	WAS	AL	1	0	1	1	0	0	0	0	0	0	0	0	0	0	1	0

Rank among batters: 4,707 • *Total ballparks homered in*: 1 • *First HR*: 07/26/1905 off Bill Bernhard

Larry Wolfe

LAURENCE MARCY WOLFE
B: 03/02/1953
BR

Year	Tm	Lg	Tot	H	A	Men-On 0	Men-On 1	Men-On 2	Men-On 3	One-Game 2	One-Game 3	One-Game 4	LO	XN	IP	PH	RHP	LHP
1978	MIN	AL	3	1	2	1	0	2	0	1	0	0	0	0	0	1	1	2
1979	BOS	AL	3	1	2	2	1	0	0	1	0	0	0	0	0	0	0	3
1980	BOS	AL	1	1	0	1	0	0	0	0	0	0	0	0	0	1	0	1
Total			7	3	4	4	1	2	0	2	0	0	0	0	0	2	1	6

Rank among batters: 2,834 • *Top target (2 home runs)*: Larry Gura • *Number of pitchers victimized*: 6 • *Total ballparks homered in*: 4 • *First HR*: 06/03/1978 off Bob Sykes

Harry Wolter

HARRY MEIGS WOLTER
B: 07/11/1884 D: 07/07/1970
BL

Year	Tm	Lg	Tot	H	A	Men-On 0	Men-On 1	Men-On 2	Men-On 3	One-Game 2	One-Game 3	One-Game 4	LO	XN	IP	PH	RHP	LHP
1909	BOS	AL	2	2	0	1	0	1	0	0	0	0	0	0	1	0	0	2
1910	NY	AL	4	3	1	1	1	2	0	0	0	0	0	0	0	0	3	1
1911	NY	AL	4	1	3	4	0	0	0	0	0	0	0	0	0	0	4	0
1913	NY	AL	2	2	0	1	1	0	0	1	0	0	0	0	1	0	2	0
Total			12	8	4	7	2	3	0	1	0	0	0	0	2	0	9	3

Rank among batters: 2,325 • *Top target (2 home runs)*: Bill Steen • *Number of pitchers victimized*: 11 • *Total ballparks homered in*: 5 • *First HR*: 06/02/1909 off Ed Killian

Harry Wolverton

HARRY STERLING WOLVERTON
B: 12/06/1873 D: 02/04/1937
BL

Year	Tm	Lg	Tot	H	A	Men-On 0	Men-On 1	Men-On 2	Men-On 3	One-Game 2	One-Game 3	One-Game 4	LO	XN	IP	PH	RHP	LHP
1899	CHI	NL	1	1	0	0	0	1	0	0	0	0	0	0	0	0	1	0
1900	PHI	NL	3	2	1	1	2	0	0	0	0	0	0	0	0	0	2	1
1902	WAS	AL	1	0	1	1	0	0	0	0	0	0	0	0	1	0	0	1
1905	BOS	NL	2	1	1	1	0	1	0	0	0	0	0	0	0	0	2	0
Total			7	4	3	3	2	2	0	0	0	0	0	0	1	0	5	2

Rank among batters: 2,834 • *Total ballparks homered in*: 6 • *First HR*: 05/08/1899 off Willie Sudhoff

Bob Wood

ROBERT LYNN WOOD
B: 07/28/1865 D: 05/22/1943
BR

Year	Tm	Lg	Tot	H	A	Men-On 0	Men-On 1	Men-On 2	Men-On 3	One-Game 2	One-Game 3	One-Game 4	LO	XN	IP	PH	RHP	LHP
1901	CLE	AL	1	0	1	1	0	0	0	0	0	0	0	0	1	0	1	0
1904	DET	AL	1	0	1	0	1	0	0	0	0	0	0	0	0	0	1	0
Total			2	0	2	1	1	0	0	0	0	0	0	0	1	0	2	0

Rank among batters: 4,129 • *Total ballparks homered in*: 2 • *First HR*: 06/15/1901 off Dale Gear

George Wood

GEORGE A. WOOD
B: 11/09/1858 D: 04/04/1924
BL

Year	Tm	Lg	Tot	H	A	Men-On 0	Men-On 1	Men-On 2	Men-On 3	One-Game 2	One-Game 3	One-Game 4	LO	XN	IP	PH	RHP	LHP
1881	DET	NL	2	2	0	2	0	0	0	0	0	0	1	0	1	0	2	0
1882	DET	NL	7	6	1	4	3	0	0	1	0	0	3	0	1	0	7	0
1883	DET	NL	5	5	0	4	0	1	0	0	0	0	1	0	0	0	5	0
1884	DET	NL	8	4	4	5	1	0	0	1	0	0	3	0	0	0	7	0

George Wood *continued*

Year	Tm	Lg	Tot	H	A	Men-On 0	1	2	3	One-Game 2	3	4	LO	XN	IP	PH	RHP	LHP
1885	DET	NL	5	1	4	4	0	1	0	0	0	0	0	0	1	0	5	0
1886	PHI	NL	4	1	3	2	2	0	0	0	0	0	0	0	0	0	3	1
1887	PHI	NL	14	8	6	8	2	4	0	1	0	0	1	0	0	0	13	1
1888	PHI	NL	6	5	1	1	4	1	0	1	0	0	0	0	0	0	5	1
1889	PHI	NL	5	4	1	3	1	1	0	1	0	0	2	1	0	0	5	0
1890	PHI	PL	9	6	3	5	1	3	0	1	0	0	0	0	3	0	7	1
1891	PHI	AA	3	2	1	1	1	1	0	0	0	0	0	0	2	0	3	0
Total			68	44	24	39	15	12	0	6	0	0	11	1	8	0	62	4

Rank among batters: 767 • *Top target (6 home runs)*: Larry Corcoran • *Number of pitchers victimized*: 37 • *Total ballparks homered in*: 13 • *First HR*: 08/02/1881 off Jim McCormick • *Hit for Cycle*—@CHI: 06/13/1885

Jake Wood

JACOB WOOD
B: 06/22/1937
BR

Year	Tm	Lg	Tot	H	A	Men-On 0	1	2	3	One-Game 2	3	4	LO	XN	IP	PH	RHP	LHP
1961	DET	AL	11	8	3	3	5	2	1	0	0	0	0	0	0	0	9	2
1962	DET	AL	8	5	3	4	1	3	0	1	0	0	3	0	1	0	8	0
1963	DET	AL	11	5	6	10	1	0	0	1	0	0	4	0	1	0	7	4
1964	DET	AL	1	1	0	1	0	0	0	0	0	0	0	0	0	0	0	1
1965	DET	AL	2	1	1	2	0	0	0	0	0	0	1	0	0	0	0	2
1966	DET	AL	2	2	0	1	0	1	0	0	0	0	0	0	0	0	2	0
Total			35	22	13	21	7	6	1	2	0	0	8	0	2	0	26	9

Rank among batters: 1,291 • *Top target (3 home runs)*: Jim Bouton • *Number of pitchers victimized*: 30 • *Total ballparks homered in*: 8 • *First HR*: 04/11/1961 off Jim Perry

Joe Wood

JOE WOOD
B: 10/25/1889 D: 07/27/1985
BR

Year	Tm	Lg	Tot	H	A	Men-On 0	1	2	3	One-Game 2	3	4	LO	XN	IP	PH	RHP	LHP
1910	BOS	AL	1	1	0	0	1	0	0	0	0	0	0	0	0	0	1	0
1911	BOS	AL	2	2	0	1	0	1	0	0	0	0	0	0	0	0	2	0
1912	BOS	AL	1	0	1	0	1	0	0	0	0	0	0	0	0	0	1	0
1915	BOS	AL	1	1	0	1	0	0	0	0	0	0	0	0	0	0	1	0
1918	CLE	AL	5	0	5	4	1	0	0	1	0	0	0	1	0	0	3	2
1920	CLE	AL	1	0	1	0	1	0	0	0	0	0	0	0	0	0	0	1
1921	CLE	AL	4	1	3	2	1	1	0	0	0	0	0	0	0	0	0	4
1922	CLE	AL	8	1	7	2	5	1	0	0	0	0	0	0	0	0	7	1
Total			23	6	17	10	10	3	0	1	0	0	0	1	0	0	15	8

Rank among batters: 1,686 • *Top target (2 home runs)*: Allen Russell, George Mogridge • *Number of pitchers victimized*: 21 • *Total ballparks homered in*: 8 • *First HR*: 08/23/1910 off Barney Pelty

Joe Wood

JOSEPH PERRY WOOD
B: 10/03/1919 D: 03/25/1985
BR

Year	Tm	Lg	Tot	H	A	Men-On 0	1	2	3	One-Game 2	3	4	LO	XN	IP	PH	RHP	LHP
1943	DET	AL	1	0	1	0	0	1	0	0	0	0	0	0	0	0	1	0

Rank among batters: 4,707 • *Total ballparks homered in*: 1 • *First HR*: 08/29/1943 off Ox Miller

Ken Wood

KENNETH LANIER WOOD
B: 07/01/1924
BR

Year	Tm	Lg	Tot	H	A	Men-On 0	1	2	3	One-Game 2	3	4	LO	XN	IP	PH	RHP	LHP
1950	STL	AL	13	9	4	5	4	3	1	1	0	0	1	0	0	1	10	3
1951	STL	AL	15	8	7	6	9	0	0	0	0	0	0	0	0	0	11	4
1952	WAS	AL	6	2	4	2	3	1	0	1	0	0	0	0	0	0	3	3
Total			34	19	15	13	16	4	1	2	0	0	1	0	0	1	24	10

Rank among batters: 1,315 • *Top target (3 home runs)*: Bob Lemon, Alex Kellner • *Number of pitchers victimized*: 26 • *Total ballparks homered in*: 7 • *First HR*: 04/23/1950 off Bob Lemon

Roy Wood

ROY WINTON WOOD
B: 08/29/1892 D: 04/06/1974
BR

Year	Tm	Lg	Tot	H	A	Men-On 0	1	2	3	One-Game 2	3	4	LO	XN	IP	PH	RHP	LHP
1914	CLE	AL	1	1	0	0	1	0	0	0	0	0	0	0	1	0	0	1

Rank among batters: 4,707 • *Total ballparks homered in*: 1 • *First HR*: 06/15/1914 off Joe Boehling

Ted Wood

EDWARD ROBERT WOOD
B: 01/04/1967
BL

Year	Tm	Lg	Tot	H	A	Men-On 0	Men-On 1	Men-On 2	Men-On 3	One-Game 2	One-Game 3	One-Game 4	LO	XN	IP	PH	RHP	LHP
1992	SF	NL	1	0	1	1	0	0	0	0	0	0	0	0	0	1	1	0

Rank among batters: 4,707 • *Total ballparks homered in*: 1 • *First HR*: 09/21/1992 off Tim Scott

Larry Woodall

CHARLES LAWRENCE WOODALL
B: 07/26/1894 D: 05/06/1963
BR

Year	Tm	Lg	Tot	H	A	Men-On 0	Men-On 1	Men-On 2	Men-On 3	One-Game 2	One-Game 3	One-Game 4	LO	XN	IP	PH	RHP	LHP
1923	DET	AL	1	0	1	0	1	0	0	0	0	0	0	0	0	0	0	1

Rank among batters: 4,707 • *Total ballparks homered in*: 1 • *First HR*: 06/20/1923 off Herb Pennock

Mike Woodard

MICHAEL CARY WOODARD
B: 03/02/1960
BL

Year	Tm	Lg	Tot	H	A	Men-On 0	Men-On 1	Men-On 2	Men-On 3	One-Game 2	One-Game 3	One-Game 4	LO	XN	IP	PH	RHP	LHP
1986	SF	NL	1	1	0	1	0	0	0	0	0	0	0	0	0	0	1	0

Rank among batters: 4,707 • *Total ballparks homered in*: 1 • *First HR*: 06/23/1986 off Dane Iorg

Gene Woodling

EUGENE RICHARD WOODLING
B: 08/16/1922
BL

Year	Tm	Lg	Tot	H	A	Men-On 0	Men-On 1	Men-On 2	Men-On 3	One-Game 2	One-Game 3	One-Game 4	LO	XN	IP	PH	RHP	LHP
1943	CLE	AL	1	0	1	1	0	0	0	0	0	0	0	0	0	0	1	0
1949	NY	AL	5	3	2	3	0	2	0	1	0	0	0	0	1	0	5	0
1950	NY	AL	6	5	1	3	2	1	0	0	0	0	0	0	2	0	4	2
1951	NY	AL	15	9	6	11	4	0	0	1	0	0	0	0	0	0	13	2
1952	NY	AL	12	7	5	5	7	0	0	0	0	0	0	0	0	0	9	3
1953	NY	AL	10	6	4	7	2	1	0	0	0	0	0	0	0	0	7	3
1954	NY	AL	3	1	2	0	2	1	0	0	0	0	0	0	0	0	3	0
1955	BAL	AL	3	1	2	3	0	0	0	0	0	0	0	0	0	0	3	0
	CLE	AL	5	2	3	3	2	0	0	0	0	0	0	0	0	0	5	0
	Total		8	3	5	6	2	0	0	0	0	0	0	0	0	0	8	0
1956	CLE	AL	8	6	2	5	2	1	0	0	0	0	0	1	0	0	7	1
1957	CLE	AL	19	11	8	12	4	3	0	0	0	0	0	0	1	0	13	6
1958	BAL	AL	15	9	6	5	10	0	0	0	0	0	0	0	0	0	15	0
1959	BAL	AL	14	5	9	6	4	3	1	0	0	0	0	0	0	1	10	4
1960	BAL	AL	11	6	5	6	3	1	1	0	0	0	0	0	0	0	8	3
1961	WAS	AL	10	1	9	6	1	3	0	1	0	0	0	0	0	0	8	2
1962	WAS	AL	5	2	3	3	1	0	1	1	0	0	0	0	0	1	4	1
	NY	NL	5	2	3	3	2	0	0	0	0	0	0	0	0	1	3	2
	Total		10	4	6	6	3	0	1	1	0	0	0	0	0	2	7	3
Total			147	76	71	82	46	16	3	4	0	0	0	1	4	3	118	29

Rank among batters: 299 • *Top target (7 home runs)*: Early Wynn • *Number of pitchers victimized*: 87 • *Total ballparks homered in*: 12 • *First HR*: 09/27/1943 off Hank Borowy • *World Series HR*—3

Pete Woodruff

PETER FRANK WOODRUFF
B: 06/ /1873
BR

Year	Tm	Lg	Tot	H	A	Men-On 0	Men-On 1	Men-On 2	Men-On 3	One-Game 2	One-Game 3	One-Game 4	LO	XN	IP	PH	RHP	LHP
1899	NY	NL	2	0	2	1	1	0	0	0	0	0	0	0	1	0	2	0

Rank among batters: 4,129 • *Total ballparks homered in*: 2 • *First HR*: 10/10/1899 off Doc McJames

Al Woods

ALVIS WOODS
B: 08/08/1953
BL

Year	Tm	Lg	Tot	H	A	Men-On 0	Men-On 1	Men-On 2	Men-On 3	One-Game 2	One-Game 3	One-Game 4	LO	XN	IP	PH	RHP	LHP
1977	TOR	AL	6	2	4	4	2	0	0	0	0	0	0	0	0	2	5	1
1978	TOR	AL	3	2	1	1	0	2	0	0	0	0	0	0	0	0	2	1
1979	TOR	AL	5	2	3	3	1	1	0	0	0	0	0	0	1	0	5	0
1980	TOR	AL	15	9	6	9	5	1	0	0	0	0	0	0	0	0	10	5
1981	TOR	AL	1	1	0	1	0	0	0	0	0	0	0	0	0	0	1	0

Year	Tm	Lg	Tot	H	A	Men-On 0	1	2	3	One-Game 2	3	4	LO	XN	IP	PH	RHP	LHP

Al Woods *continued*

Year	Tm	Lg	Tot	H	A	Men-On 0	1	2	3	One-Game 2	3	4	LO	XN	IP	PH	RHP	LHP
1982	TOR	AL	3	3	0	1	2	0	0	0	0	0	0	0	0	0	2	1
1986	MIN	AL	2	2	0	1	0	1	0	0	0	0	0	0	0	2	2	0
Total			35	21	14	20	10	5	0	0	0	0	0	0	1	4	27	8

Rank among batters: 1,291 • *Top target (2 home runs)*: Dennis Eckersley, Chris Knapp • *Number of pitchers victimized*: 33 • *Total ballparks homered in*: 10 • *First HR*: 04/07/1977 off Francisco Barrios • *Hit HR on first major league pitch*—vs CHI: 04/07/1977

Gary Woods

GARY LEE WOODS
B: 07/20/1954
BR

Year	Tm	Lg	Tot	H	A	Men-On 0	1	2	3	One-Game 2	3	4	LO	XN	IP	PH	RHP	LHP
1980	HOU	NL	2	2	0	2	0	0	0	0	0	0	0	0	0	0	0	2
1982	CHI	NL	4	2	2	3	1	0	0	0	0	0	0	0	0	0	1	3
1983	CHI	NL	4	2	2	3	1	0	0	0	0	0	2	0	0	1	3	1
1984	CHI	NL	3	2	1	1	2	0	0	0	0	0	0	0	0	0	0	3
Total			13	8	5	9	4	0	0	0	0	0	2	0	0	1	4	9

Rank among batters: 2,248 • *Top target (3 home runs)*: Bob Shirley, Larry McWilliams • *Number of pitchers victimized*: 9 • *Total ballparks homered in*: 6 • *First HR*: 09/15/1980 off Bob Shirley

Jim Woods

JAMES JEROME WOODS
B: 09/17/1939
BR

Year	Tm	Lg	Tot	H	A	Men-On 0	1	2	3	One-Game 2	3	4	LO	XN	IP	PH	RHP	LHP
1960	PHI	NL	1	1	0	1	0	0	0	0	0	0	0	0	0	0	1	0
1961	PHI	NL	2	1	1	2	0	0	0	0	0	0	0	0	0	0	2	0
Total			3	2	1	3	0	0	0	0	0	0	0	0	0	0	3	0

Rank among batters: 3,735 • *Top target (2 home runs)*: Bob Friend • *Number of pitchers victimized*: 2 • *Total ballparks homered in*: 2 • *First HR*: 09/20/1960 off Bob Friend

Ron Woods

RONALD LAWRENCE WOODS
B: 02/01/1943
BR

Year	Tm	Lg	Tot	H	A	Men-On 0	1	2	3	One-Game 2	3	4	LO	XN	IP	PH	RHP	LHP
1969	DET	AL	1	0	1	1	0	0	0	0	0	0	0	0	0	0	1	0
	NY	AL	1	0	1	0	1	0	0	0	0	0	0	0	0	0	0	1
	Total		2	0	2	2	0	0	0	0	0	0	0	0	0	0	1	1
1970	NY	AL	8	2	6	3	4	1	0	0	0	0	0	0	0	0	1	7
1971	NY	AL	1	1	0	1	0	0	0	0	0	0	0	0	0	1	0	1
	MON	NL	1	0	1	0	1	0	0	0	0	0	0	0	0	0	0	1
	Total		2	1	1	1	1	0	0	0	0	0	0	0	0	1	0	2
1972	MON	NL	10	7	3	5	2	3	0	1	0	0	0	0	0	0	4	6
1973	MON	NL	3	3	0	1	0	2	0	0	0	0	0	1	0	1	1	2
1974	MON	NL	1	0	1	1	0	0	0	0	0	0	0	0	0	1	0	1
Total			26	13	13	13	7	6	0	1	0	0	0	1	0	3	7	19

Rank among batters: 1,576 • *Top target (2 home runs)*: Clyde Wright, Ed Sprague • *Number of pitchers victimized*: 24 • *Total ballparks homered in*: 12 • *First HR*: 05/29/1969 off Ed Sprague

Walt Woods

WALTER SYDNEY WOODS
B: 04/28/1875 D: 10/30/1951
BR

Year	Tm	Lg	Tot	H	A	Men-On 0	1	2	3	One-Game 2	3	4	LO	XN	IP	PH	RHP	LHP
1899	LOU	NL	1	1	0	1	0	0	0	0	0	0	0	0	0	0	1	0

Rank among batters: 4,707 • *Total ballparks homered in*: 1 • *First HR*: 07/06/1899 off Frank Dwyer

Tracy Woodson

TRACY MICHAEL WOODSON
B: 10/05/1962
BR

Year	Tm	Lg	Tot	H	A	Men-On 0	1	2	3	One-Game 2	3	4	LO	XN	IP	PH	RHP	LHP
1987	LA	NL	1	1	0	0	1	0	0	0	0	0	0	0	0	0	1	0
1988	LA	NL	3	2	1	3	0	0	0	0	0	0	0	0	0	0	1	2
1992	STL	NL	1	0	1	0	1	0	0	0	0	0	0	0	0	0	0	1
Total			5	3	2	3	2	0	0	0	0	0	0	0	0	0	2	3

Rank among batters: 3,191 • *Total ballparks homered in*: 3 • *First HR*: 04/13/1987 off Nolan Ryan

Woody Woodward

WILLIAM FREDERICK WOODWARD
B: 09/23/1942
BR

Year	Tm	Lg	Tot	H	A	Men-On 0	1	2	3	One-Game 2	3	4	LO	XN	IP	PH	RHP	LHP
1970	CIN	NL	1	0	1	0	1	0	0	0	0	0	0	0	0	0	1	0

Rank among batters: 4,707 • *Total ballparks homered in*: 1 • *First HR*: 07/10/1970 off Ron Reed

Junior Wooten

EARL HAZWELL WOOTEN
B: 01/16/1924
BR

Year	Tm	Lg	Tot	H	A	Men-On 0	1	2	3	One-Game 2	3	4	LO	XN	IP	PH	RHP	LHP
1948	WAS	AL	1	0	1	1	0	0	0	0	0	0	0	0	0	0	1	0

Rank among batters: 4,707 • *Total ballparks homered in*: 1 • *First HR*: 06/22/1948 off Fred Hutchinson

Chuck Workman

CHARLES THOMAS WORKMAN
B: 01/06/1915 D: 01/03/1953
BL

Year	Tm	Lg	Tot	H	A	Men-On 0	1	2	3	One-Game 2	3	4	LO	XN	IP	PH	RHP	LHP
1943	BOS	NL	10	5	5	4	4	2	0	0	0	0	0	1	0	0	8	2
1944	BOS	NL	11	6	5	8	1	2	0	0	0	0	0	0	0	0	9	2
1945	BOS	NL	25	19	6	13	9	3	0	2	0	0	0	1	0	0	20	5
1946	BOS	NL	2	0	2	1	1	0	0	0	0	0	0	0	0	1	2	0
	PIT	NL	2	0	2	1	1	0	0	0	0	0	0	1	0	0	2	0
	Total		4	0	4	2	2	0	0	0	0	0	0	1	0	1	4	0
Total			50	30	20	27	16	7	0	2	0	0	0	3	0	1	41	9

Rank among batters: 991 • *Top target (5 home runs)*: Bill Voiselle • *Number of pitchers victimized*: 39 • *Total ballparks homered in*: 7 • *First HR*: 05/04/1943 off Bill Lohrman

Al Worthington

ALLAN FULTON WORTHINGTON
B: 02/05/1929
BR

Year	Tm	Lg	Tot	H	A	Men-On 0	1	2	3	One-Game 2	3	4	LO	XN	IP	PH	RHP	LHP
1956	NY	NL	1	0	1	1	0	0	0	0	0	0	0	0	0	0	1	0

Rank among batters: 4,707 • *Total ballparks homered in*: 1 • *First HR*: 09/30/1956 off Robin Roberts

Craig Worthington

CRAIG RICHARD WORTHINGTON
B: 04/17/1965
BR

Year	Tm	Lg	Tot	H	A	Men-On 0	1	2	3	One-Game 2	3	4	LO	XN	IP	PH	RHP	LHP
1988	BAL	AL	2	0	2	2	0	0	0	0	0	0	0	0	0	0	2	0
1989	BAL	AL	15	12	3	9	5	1	0	0	0	0	0	1	0	0	11	4
1990	BAL	AL	8	3	5	7	1	0	0	0	0	0	0	0	0	0	6	2
1991	BAL	AL	4	1	3	2	2	0	0	0	0	0	0	0	0	0	3	1
1995	CIN	NL	1	0	1	1	0	0	0	0	0	0	0	0	0	0	0	1
	TEX	AL	2	1	1	2	0	0	0	0	0	0	0	1	0	0	1	1
	Total		3	1	2	3	0	0	0	0	0	0	0	1	0	0	1	2
Total			32	17	15	23	8	1	0	0	0	0	0	2	0	0	23	9

Rank among batters: 1,360 • *Top target (2 home runs)*: Jack Morris • *Number of pitchers victimized*: 31 • *Total ballparks homered in*: 13 • *First HR*: 04/27/1988 off Bert Blyleven

Red Worthington

ROBERT LEE WORTHINGTON
B: 04/24/1906 D: 12/08/1963
BR

Year	Tm	Lg	Tot	H	A	Men-On 0	1	2	3	One-Game 2	3	4	LO	XN	IP	PH	RHP	LHP
1931	BOS	NL	4	3	1	2	2	0	0	0	0	0	0	0	1	0	3	1
1932	BOS	NL	8	3	5	5	3	0	0	1	0	0	0	0	0	0	5	3
Total			12	6	6	7	5	0	0	1	0	0	0	0	1	0	8	4

Rank among batters: 2,325 • *Top target (3 home runs)*: Phil Collins • *Number of pitchers victimized*: 10 • *Total ballparks homered in*: 5 • *First HR*: 05/05/1931 off Clise Dudley

Chuck Wortman

WILLIAM LEWIS WORTMAN
B: 01/05/1892 D: 08/19/1977
BR

Year	Tm	Lg	Tot	H	A	Men-On 0	1	2	3	One-Game 2	3	4	LO	XN	IP	PH	RHP	LHP
1916	CHI	NL	2	0	2	2	0	0	0	0	0	0	0	1	1	0	2	0

Chuck Wortman *continued*

Year	Tm	Lg	Tot	H	A	Men-On 0	1	2	3	One-Game 2	3	4	LO	XN	IP	PH	RHP	LHP
1918	CHI	NL	1	1	0	0	0	1	0	0	0	0	0	0	0	0	1	0
Total			3	1	2	2	0	1	0	0	0	0	0	1	1	0	3	0

Rank among batters: 3,735 • *Total ballparks homered in*: 3 • *First HR*: 09/12/1916 off Dick Rudolph

Ab Wright

ALBERT OWEN WRIGHT
B: 11/16/1905
BR

Year	Tm	Lg	Tot	H	A	Men-On 0	1	2	3	One-Game 2	3	4	LO	XN	IP	PH	RHP	LHP
1935	CLE	AL	2	1	1	1	1	0	0	0	0	0	0	0	0	0	0	2
1944	BOS	NL	7	3	4	1	3	3	0	0	0	0	0	0	0	1	5	2
Total			9	4	5	2	4	3	0	0	0	0	0	0	0	1	5	4

Rank among batters: 2,587 • *Total ballparks homered in*: 5 • *First HR*: 05/15/1935 off Bobby Burke

Clyde Wright

CLYDE WRIGHT
B: 02/20/1941
BR

Year	Tm	Lg	Tot	H	A	Men-On 0	1	2	3	One-Game 2	3	4	LO	XN	IP	PH	RHP	LHP
1970	CAL	AL	2	1	1	1	0	1	0	0	0	0	0	0	0	0	1	1
1972	CAL	AL	2	1	1	1	0	1	0	0	0	0	0	0	0	0	1	1
Total			4	2	2	2	0	2	0	0	0	0	0	0	0	0	2	2

Rank among batters: 3,427 • *Total ballparks homered in*: 3 • *First HR*: 07/17/1970 off Jackie Brown

Gene Wright

CLARENCE EUGENE WRIGHT
B: 12/11/1878 D: 10/29/1930
BR

Year	Tm	Lg	Tot	H	A	Men-On 0	1	2	3	One-Game 2	3	4	LO	XN	IP	PH	RHP	LHP
1902	CLE	AL	1	0	1	1	0	0	0	0	0	0	0	0	0	0	1	0

Rank among batters: 4,707 • *Total ballparks homered in*: 1 • *First HR*: 05/26/1902 off Al Orth

George Wright

GEORGE WRIGHT
B: 01/28/1847 D: 08/21/1937
BR HOF

Year	Tm	Lg	Tot	H	A	Men-On 0	1	2	3	One-Game 2	3	4	LO	XN	IP	PH	RHP	LHP
1876	BOS	NL	1	1	0	1	0	0	0	0	0	0	1	0	0	0	1	0
1879	PRO	NL	1	1	0	0	1	0	0	0	0	0	0	0	0	0	1	0
Total			2	2	0	1	1	0	0	0	0	0	1	0	0	0	2	0

Rank among batters: 4,129 • *Total ballparks homered in*: 2 • *First HR*: 09/16/1876 off Al Spalding

George Wright

GEORGE DEWITT WRIGHT
B: 12/22/1958
BB

Year	Tm	Lg	Tot	H	A	Men-On 0	1	2	3	One-Game 2	3	4	LO	XN	IP	PH	RHP	LHP
1982	TEX	AL	11	3	8	6	3	2	0	0	0	0	2	0	1	0	4	7
1983	TEX	AL	18	7	11	11	4	3	0	0	0	0	0	1	0	0	9	9
1984	TEX	AL	9	6	3	4	4	1	0	0	0	0	0	0	0	0	6	3
1985	TEX	AL	2	2	0	2	0	0	0	0	0	0	0	0	0	0	2	0
1986	TEX	AL	2	1	1	2	0	0	0	0	0	0	0	0	0	0	2	0
Total			42	19	23	25	11	6	0	0	0	0	2	1	1	0	23	19

Rank among batters: 1,138 • Top target (2 home runs): Rick Waits, Mike Caldwell, Luis Leal, John Tudor, Tim Conroy, Mark Huismann • *Number of pitchers victimized*: 36 • *Total ballparks homered in*: 13 • *First HR*: 04/10/1982 off Rick Waits

Glenn Wright

FOREST GLENN WRIGHT
B: 02/06/1901 D: 04/06/1984
BR

Year	Tm	Lg	Tot	H	A	Men-On 0	1	2	3	One-Game 2	3	4	LO	XN	IP	PH	RHP	LHP
1924	PIT	NL	7	2	5	4	1	2	0	0	0	0	0	0	2	0	7	0
1925	PIT	NL	18	6	12	8	7	2	1	0	0	0	0	1	2	0	12	6
1926	PIT	NL	8	4	4	5	2	1	0	2	0	0	0	0	1	0	7	1
1927	PIT	NL	9	6	3	4	3	2	0	0	0	0	0	0	2	0	7	2
1928	PIT	NL	8	1	7	3	3	2	0	1	0	0	0	0	0	0	5	3
1929	BRO	NL	1	1	0	0	1	0	0	0	0	0	0	0	0	0	1	0
1930	BRO	NL	22	14	8	8	11	3	0	1	0	0	0	0	0	0	14	8

Glenn Wright *continued*

Year	Tm	Lg	Tot	H	A	Men-On 0	1	2	3	One-Game 2	3	4	LO	XN	IP	PH	RHP	LHP
1931	BRO	NL	9	5	4	6	3	0	0	1	0	0	0	0	0	0	4	5
1932	BRO	NL	11	5	6	6	5	0	0	0	0	0	0	0	1	0	9	2
1933	BRO	NL	1	1	0	1	0	0	0	0	0	0	0	0	0	0	1	0
Total			94	45	49	45	36	12	1	5	0	0	0	1	8	0	67	27

Rank among batters: 535 • Top target (4 home runs): Vic Keen, Bill Sherdel, Leo Sweetland, Ray Benge • *Number of pitchers victimized*: 58 • *Total ballparks homered in*: 8 • *First HR*: 04/28/1924 off Vic Keen • *World Series HR*—1

Joe Wright

JOSEPH S. WRIGHT
B: 1873 BL

Year	Tm	Lg	Tot	H	A	Men-On 0	1	2	3	One-Game 2	3	4	LO	XN	IP	PH	RHP	LHP
1895	LOU	NL	1	0	1	1	0	0	0	0	0	0	0	0	0	0	1	0

Rank among batters: 4,707 • *Total ballparks homered in*: 1 • *First HR*: 08/23/1895 off Kid Carsey

Taffy Wright

TAFT SHEDRON WRIGHT
B: 08/10/1911 D: 10/22/1981
BL

Year	Tm	Lg	Tot	H	A	Men-On 0	1	2	3	One-Game 2	3	4	LO	XN	IP	PH	RHP	LHP
1938	WAS	AL	2	1	1	1	0	0	1	0	0	0	0	0	0	0	2	0
1939	WAS	AL	4	0	4	2	1	1	0	0	0	0	0	0	0	1	4	0
1940	CHI	AL	5	2	3	2	1	1	1	0	0	0	0	0	0	1	4	1
1941	CHI	AL	10	1	9	7	1	2	0	1	0	0	0	1	0	0	10	0
1946	CHI	AL	7	4	3	4	3	0	0	0	0	0	0	0	0	0	7	0
1947	CHI	AL	4	4	0	2	2	0	0	0	0	0	0	0	0	0	4	0
1948	CHI	AL	4	3	1	2	1	0	1	0	0	0	0	0	0	0	4	0
1949	PHI	AL	2	0	2	1	0	1	0	0	0	0	0	0	0	0	2	0
Total			38	15	23	21	9	5	3	1	0	0	0	1	0	2	37	1

Rank among batters: 1,225 • Top target (2 home runs): George Caster, Bob Muncrief, Bobo Newsom, Dutch Leonard, Dick Fowler, Red Embree, Fred Hutchinson • *Number of pitchers victimized*: 31 • *Total ballparks homered in*: 8 • *First HR*: 05/26/1938 off Bobo Newsom

Tom Wright

THOMAS EVERETTE WRIGHT
B: 09/22/1923
BL

Year	Tm	Lg	Tot	H	A	Men-On 0	1	2	3	One-Game 2	3	4	LO	XN	IP	PH	RHP	LHP
1951	BOS	AL	1	0	1	1	0	0	0	0	0	0	0	1	0	0	1	0
1952	STL	AL	1	1	0	1	0	0	0	0	0	0	0	0	0	0	1	0
	CHI	AL	1	1	0	0	1	0	0	0	0	0	0	0	0	0	1	0
	Total		2	2	0	1	1	0	0	0	0	0	0	0	0	0	2	0
1953	CHI	AL	2	1	1	1	0	1	0	0	0	0	0	0	0	1	2	0
1954	WAS	AL	1	0	1	1	0	0	0	0	0	0	0	0	0	1	1	0
Total			6	3	3	4	1	1	0	0	0	0	0	1	0	2	6	0

Rank among batters: 2,988 • *Total ballparks homered in*: 4 • *First HR*: 04/29/1951 off Johnny Kucab

Russ Wrightstone

RUSSELL GUY WRIGHTSTONE
B: 03/18/1893 D: 02/25/1969
BL

Year	Tm	Lg	Tot	H	A	Men-On 0	1	2	3	One-Game 2	3	4	LO	XN	IP	PH	RHP	LHP
1920	PHI	NL	3	2	1	1	2	0	0	0	0	0	0	0	1	0	3	0
1921	PHI	NL	9	8	1	6	3	0	0	0	0	0	0	0	0	0	8	1
1922	PHI	NL	5	4	1	3	2	0	0	0	0	0	1	1	0	0	5	0
1923	PHI	NL	7	5	2	0	4	2	1	0	0	0	0	0	0	1	7	0
1924	PHI	NL	7	4	3	5	2	0	0	0	0	0	0	0	0	0	7	0
1925	PHI	NL	14	11	3	7	5	2	0	1	0	0	0	0	0	1	14	0
1926	PHI	NL	7	6	1	4	1	1	1	0	0	0	0	0	0	0	6	1
1927	PHI	NL	6	3	3	2	2	0	2	0	0	0	0	0	0	0	5	1
1928	PHI	NL	1	0	1	0	1	0	0	0	0	0	0	0	0	0	1	0
	NY	NL	1	1	0	0	0	1	0	0	0	0	0	0	0	1	1	0
	Total		2	1	1	0	1	1	0	0	0	0	0	0	0	1	2	0
Total			60	44	16	28	22	6	4	1	0	0	1	1	1	3	57	3

Rank among batters: 863 • *Top target (4 home runs)*: Burleigh Grimes • *Number of pitchers victimized*: 40 • *Total ballparks homered in*: 7 • *First HR*: 07/09/1920 off Hal Carlson

Year	Tm	Lg	Tot	H	A	Men-On 0	1	2	3	One-Game 2	3	4	LO	XN	IP	PH	RHP	LHP

Zeke Wrigley

GEORGE WATSON WRIGLEY
B: 01/18/1874 D: 09/28/1952

Year	Tm	Lg	Tot	H	A	0	1	2	3	2	3	4	LO	XN	IP	PH	RHP	LHP
1897	WAS	NL	3	1	2	1	2	0	0	0	0	0	0	0	0	0	3	0
1898	WAS	NL	2	1	1	0	2	0	0	0	0	0	0	0	0	0	1	0
Total			5	2	3	1	4	0	0	0	0	0	0	0	0	0	4	0

Rank among batters: 3,191 • *Top target (2 home runs)*: Red Donahue • *Number of pitchers victimized*: 4 • *Total ballparks homered in*: 3 • *First HR*: 05/25/1897 off Red Donahue

Rick Wrona

RICHARD JAMES WRONA
B: 12/10/1963
BR

Year	Tm	Lg	Tot	H	A	0	1	2	3	2	3	4	LO	XN	IP	PH	RHP	LHP
1989	CHI	NL	2	0	2	1	0	1	0	0	0	0	0	0	0	0	2	0
1994	MIL	AL	1	0	1	1	0	0	0	0	0	0	0	0	0	0	1	0
Total			3	0	3	2	0	1	0	0	0	0	0	0	0	0	3	0

Rank among batters: 3,735 • *Total ballparks homered in*: 3 • *First HR*: 09/02/1989 off Marty Clary

Whit Wyatt

JOHN WHITLOW WYATT
B: 09/27/1907
BR

Year	Tm	Lg	Tot	H	A	0	1	2	3	2	3	4	LO	XN	IP	PH	RHP	LHP
1930	DET	AL	1	0	1	0	1	0	0	0	0	0	0	0	0	0	1	0
1932	DET	AL	2	1	1	2	0	0	0	0	0	0	0	0	0	0	2	0
1940	BRO	NL	1	0	1	1	0	0	0	0	0	0	0	0	0	0	1	0
1941	BRO	NL	3	1	2	3	0	0	0	0	0	0	0	1	0	0	3	0
Total			7	2	5	6	1	0	0	0	0	0	0	1	0	0	7	0

Rank among batters: 2,834 • *Total ballparks homered in*: 7 • *First HR*: 08/29/1930 off Dick Coffman

John Wyckoff

JOHN WELDON WYCKOFF
B: 02/19/1892 D: 05/08/1961
BR

Year	Tm	Lg	Tot	H	A	0	1	2	3	2	3	4	LO	XN	IP	PH	RHP	LHP
1914	PHI	AL	1	0	1	1	0	0	0	0	0	0	0	0	1	0	0	1

Rank among batters: 4,707 • *Total ballparks homered in*: 1 • *First HR*: 09/18/1914 off Harry Coveleski

Butch Wynegar

HAROLD DELANO WYNEGAR
B: 03/14/1956
BB

Year	Tm	Lg	Tot	H	A	0	1	2	3	2	3	4	LO	XN	IP	PH	RHP	LHP
1976	MIN	AL	10	4	6	5	2	2	1	1	0	0	0	1	0	0	8	2
1977	MIN	AL	10	4	6	7	2	1	0	0	0	0	0	1	0	0	4	6
1978	MIN	AL	4	4	0	2	2	0	0	0	0	0	0	0	0	0	4	0
1979	MIN	AL	7	3	4	6	1	0	0	0	0	0	0	0	0	0	5	2
1980	MIN	AL	5	3	2	4	1	0	0	0	0	0	1	0	0	0	4	1
1982	MIN	AL	1	1	0	1	0	0	0	0	0	0	0	0	0	0	1	0
	NY	AL	3	1	2	2	1	0	0	0	0	0	0	0	0	0	1	2
	Total		4	2	2	3	1	0	0	0	0	0	0	0	0	0	2	2
1983	NY	AL	6	4	2	3	3	0	0	0	0	0	0	1	0	0	4	2
1984	NY	AL	6	3	3	2	2	2	0	0	0	0	0	0	0	0	5	1
1985	NY	AL	5	2	3	1	3	1	0	0	0	0	0	0	0	1	3	2
1986	NY	AL	7	3	4	3	0	4	0	0	0	0	0	0	0	0	1	6
1988	CAL	AL	1	0	1	1	0	0	0	0	0	0	0	0	0	0	1	0
Total			65	32	33	37	17	10	1	1	0	0	1	3	0	1	41	24

Rank among batters: 799 • *Top target (3 home runs)*: Rick Langford • *Number of pitchers victimized*: 57 • *Total ballparks homered in*: 14 • *First HR*: 04/18/1976 off Catfish Hunter

Early Wynn

EARLY WYNN
B: 01/06/1920
BB HOF

Year	Tm	Lg	Tot	H	A	0	1	2	3	2	3	4	LO	XN	IP	PH	RHP	LHP
1943	WAS	AL	1	0	1	1	0	0	0	0	0	0	0	0	0	0	1	0
1944	WAS	AL	1	0	1	0	1	0	0	0	0	0	0	0	0	0	1	0
1946	WAS	AL	1	0	1	0	0	0	1	0	0	0	0	0	0	1	1	0

Year	Tm	Lg	Tot	H	A	Men-On 0	Men-On 1	Men-On 2	Men-On 3	One-Game 2	One-Game 3	One-Game 4	LO	XN	IP	PH	RHP	LHP

Early Wynn *continued*

Year	Tm	Lg	Tot	H	A	0	1	2	3	2	3	4	LO	XN	IP	PH	RHP	LHP
1947	WAS	AL	2	1	1	2	0	0	0	0	0	0	0	0	0	1	2	0
1949	CLE	AL	1	1	0	1	0	0	0	0	0	0	0	0	0	0	1	0
1950	CLE	AL	2	2	0	2	0	0	0	0	0	0	0	0	0	0	2	0
1951	CLE	AL	1	1	0	1	0	0	0	0	0	0	0	0	0	0	1	0
1953	CLE	AL	3	1	2	3	0	0	0	0	0	0	0	0	0	0	2	1
1955	CLE	AL	1	1	0	0	1	0	0	0	0	0	0	0	0	0	1	0
1956	CLE	AL	1	1	0	1	0	0	0	0	0	0	0	0	0	0	1	0
1959	CHI	AL	2	1	1	2	0	0	0	0	0	0	0	0	0	0	2	0
1960	CHI	AL	1	1	0	1	0	0	0	0	0	0	0	0	0	0	1	0
Total			17	10	7	14	2	0	1	0	0	0	0	0	0	2	16	1

Rank among batters: 1,969 • *Top target (2 home runs)*: Joe Dobson, Connie Marrero • *Number of pitchers victimized*: 15 • *Total ballparks homered in*: 7 • *First HR*: 08/22/1943 off Bob Muncrief

Jim Wynn

JAMES SHERMAN WYNN
B: 03/12/1942
BR

Year	Tm	Lg	Tot	H	A	0	1	2	3	2	3	4	LO	XN	IP	PH	RHP	LHP
1963	HOU	NL	4	2	2	1	3	0	0	0	0	0	0	0	0	0	3	1
1964	HOU	NL	5	2	3	1	4	0	0	0	0	0	0	0	0	0	3	2
1965	HOU	NL	22	7	15	15	5	2	0	0	0	0	0	0	0	0	18	4
1966	HOU	NL	18	10	8	9	5	4	0	1	0	0	0	1	0	0	10	8
1967	HOU	NL	37	15	22	22	9	6	0	3	1	0	0	2	1	0	27	10
1968	HOU	NL	26	9	17	18	4	4	0	1	0	0	0	0	0	0	16	10
1969	HOU	NL	33	16	17	17	13	2	1	4	0	0	0	1	0	0	26	7
1970	HOU	NL	27	13	14	15	10	2	0	2	0	0	0	1	0	1	20	7
1971	HOU	NL	7	2	5	3	3	1	0	0	0	0	0	0	0	0	6	1
1972	HOU	NL	24	13	11	17	5	1	1	1	0	0	0	2	0	0	20	4
1973	HOU	NL	20	8	12	15	4	1	0	2	0	0	1	0	0	1	14	6
1974	LA	NL	32	18	14	17	11	3	1	2	1	0	0	1	0	0	26	6
1975	LA	NL	18	9	9	10	4	3	1	1	0	0	0	0	0	0	16	2
1976	ATL	NL	17	12	5	9	4	4	0	2	0	0	0	0	0	3	11	6
1977	NY	AL	1	1	0	1	0	0	0	0	0	0	0	0	0	0	0	1
Total			291	137	154	170	84	33	4	19	2	0	1	8	1	5	216	75

Rank among batters: 75 • *Top target (6 home runs)*: Gary Nolan • *Number of pitchers victimized*: 172 • *Total ballparks homered in*: 20 • *First HR*: 07/14/1963 off Don Rowe • *World Series HR*—1; *All-Star HR*—1

Marvell Wynne

MARVELL WYNNE
B: 12/17/1959
BL

Year	Tm	Lg	Tot	H	A	0	1	2	3	2	3	4	LO	XN	IP	PH	RHP	LHP
1983	PIT	NL	7	3	4	6	0	0	1	0	0	0	0	0	0	0	7	0
1985	PIT	NL	2	1	1	2	0	0	0	0	0	0	0	0	1	0	1	1
1986	SD	NL	7	5	2	7	0	0	0	1	0	0	1	0	0	1	5	2
1987	SD	NL	2	2	0	1	1	0	0	0	0	0	1	0	0	0	2	0
1988	SD	NL	11	6	5	5	4	1	1	1	0	0	0	1	0	1	10	1
1989	SD	NL	6	3	3	3	1	2	0	0	0	0	0	0	0	0	5	1
	CHI	NL	1	0	1	1	0	0	0	0	0	0	0	0	0	0	1	0
	Total		7	3	4	4	1	2	0	0	0	0	0	0	0	0	6	1
1990	CHI	NL	4	2	2	3	1	0	0	0	0	0	0	0	0	0	3	1
Total			40	22	18	28	7	3	2	2	0	0	2	1	1	2	34	6

Rank among batters: 1,181 • Top target (2 home runs): Charles Hudson, Bill Laskey, Jose Rijo, Charlie Puleo, Joe Price, Scott Sanderson, Ron Darling • *Number of pitchers victimized*: 33 • *Total ballparks homered in*: 9 • *First HR*: 06/19/1983 off Charles Hudson

Johnny Wyrostek

JOHN BARNEY WYROSTEK
B: 07/12/1919 D: 12/12/1986
BL

Year	Tm	Lg	Tot	H	A	0	1	2	3	2	3	4	LO	XN	IP	PH	RHP	LHP
1946	PHI	NL	6	3	3	3	3	0	0	0	0	0	0	0	0	0	5	1
1947	PHI	NL	5	2	3	2	1	2	0	0	0	0	0	0	0	0	5	0
1948	CIN	NL	17	13	4	11	5	1	0	2	0	0	0	0	0	0	11	6
1949	CIN	NL	9	5	4	6	2	1	0	0	0	0	0	0	0	0	7	2
1950	CIN	NL	8	3	5	3	5	0	0	0	0	0	0	0	0	0	4	4
1951	CIN	NL	2	0	2	1	1	0	0	0	0	0	0	0	0	0	0	2
1952	CIN	NL	1	0	1	0	1	0	0	0	0	0	0	0	0	0	1	0
	PHI	NL	1	1	0	1	0	0	0	0	0	0	0	0	0	0	1	0
	Total		2	1	1	1	1	0	0	0	0	0	0	0	0	0	2	0

Johnny Wyrostek *continued*

Year	Tm	Lg	Tot	H	A	Men-On 0	Men-On 1	Men-On 2	Men-On 3	One-Game 2	One-Game 3	One-Game 4	LO	XN	IP	PH	RHP	LHP
1953	PHI	NL	6	1	5	3	2	1	0	0	0	0	0	0	0	0	5	1
1954	PHI	NL	3	1	2	0	3	0	0	0	0	0	0	0	0	0	3	0
Total			58	29	29	30	23	5	0	2	0	0	0	0	0	0	42	16

Rank among batters: 886 • Top target (2 home runs): Mike Budnick, Kirby Higbe, Red Munger, Elmer Riddle, Ralph Branca, Preacher Roe, Hank Borowy, Howie Pollet, Ken Heintzelman, Murry Dickson, Larry Jansen, Roy Face • *Number of pitchers victimized*: 46 • *Total ballparks homered in*: 7 • *First HR*: 05/04/1946 off Nate Andrews

Yam Yaryan

CLARENCE EVERETT YARYAN
B: 11/05/1892 D: 11/16/1964
BR

Year	Tm	Lg	Tot	H	A	Men-On 0	Men-On 1	Men-On 2	Men-On 3	One-Game 2	One-Game 3	One-Game 4	LO	XN	IP	PH	RHP	LHP
1922	CHI	AL	2	1	1	2	0	0	0	0	0	0	0	1	0	0	1	1

Rank among batters: 4,129 • *Total ballparks homered in*: 2 • *First HR*: 07/16/1922 off Joe Bush

Carl Yastrzemski

CARL MICHAEL YASTRZEMSKI
B: 08/22/1939
BL HOF

Year	Tm	Lg	Tot	H	A	Men-On 0	Men-On 1	Men-On 2	Men-On 3	One-Game 2	One-Game 3	One-Game 4	LO	XN	IP	PH	RHP	LHP
1961	BOS	AL	11	6	5	5	5	1	0	0	0	0	0	1	0	0	7	4
1962	BOS	AL	19	11	8	14	3	2	0	1	0	0	0	0	1	0	16	3
1963	BOS	AL	14	6	8	9	5	0	0	1	0	0	0	1	0	0	13	1
1964	BOS	AL	15	6	9	8	5	1	1	0	0	0	0	1	0	0	15	0
1965	BOS	AL	20	16	4	13	5	2	0	2	0	0	0	1	0	0	16	4
1966	BOS	AL	16	11	5	9	5	2	0	1	0	0	0	0	1	1	14	2
1967	BOS	AL	44	27	17	25	12	7	0	5	0	0	0	1	0	0	38	6
1968	BOS	AL	23	11	12	17	5	1	0	1	0	0	0	0	1	0	17	6
1969	BOS	AL	40	21	19	20	14	3	3	4	0	0	0	0	0	0	33	7
1970	BOS	AL	40	22	18	20	14	6	0	3	0	0	0	0	0	0	32	8
1971	BOS	AL	15	7	8	7	6	2	0	1	0	0	0	0	0	0	12	3
1972	BOS	AL	12	5	7	5	7	0	0	0	0	0	0	1	0	0	9	3
1973	BOS	AL	19	8	11	8	3	7	1	2	0	0	0	0	0	0	16	3
1974	BOS	AL	15	5	10	13	2	0	0	1	0	0	0	0	0	0	11	4
1975	BOS	AL	14	8	6	6	6	1	1	1	0	0	0	2	0	0	11	3
1976	BOS	AL	21	10	11	11	6	4	0	1	1	0	0	0	0	0	15	6
1977	BOS	AL	28	14	14	17	10	1	0	2	0	0	0	0	0	0	24	4
1978	BOS	AL	17	7	10	7	5	5	0	0	0	0	0	0	0	0	11	6
1979	BOS	AL	21	15	6	8	10	2	1	0	0	0	0	0	0	0	20	1
1980	BOS	AL	15	5	10	7	7	1	0	0	0	0	0	0	0	0	13	2
1981	BOS	AL	7	3	4	2	4	1	0	0	0	0	0	0	0	0	7	0
1982	BOS	AL	16	7	9	7	6	3	0	0	0	0	0	0	0	0	14	2
1983	BOS	AL	10	6	4	2	7	1	0	0	0	0	0	0	0	0	10	0
Total			452	237	215	240	152	53	7	26	1	0	0	8	3	1	374	78

Rank among batters: 20 • *Top target (7 home runs)*: Joe Coleman, Mickey Lolich, Pat Dobson • *Number of pitchers victimized*: 259 • *Total ballparks homered in*: 18 • *First HR*: 05/09/1961 off Jerry Casale • *Hit for Cycle*—vs DET: 05/14/1965 • *World Series HR*—3; *LCS HR*—1; *All-Star HR*—1

Al Yates

ALBERT ARTHUR YATES
B: 05/26/1945
BR

Year	Tm	Lg	Tot	H	A	Men-On 0	Men-On 1	Men-On 2	Men-On 3	One-Game 2	One-Game 3	One-Game 4	LO	XN	IP	PH	RHP	LHP
1971	MIL	AL	1	1	0	1	0	0	0	0	0	0	0	0	0	0	0	1

Rank among batters: 4,707 • *Total ballparks homered in*: 1 • *First HR*: 06/06/1971 off Dave McNally

Emil Yde

EMIL OGDEN YDE
B: 01/28/1900 D: 12/04/1968
BB

Year	Tm	Lg	Tot	H	A	Men-On 0	Men-On 1	Men-On 2	Men-On 3	One-Game 2	One-Game 3	One-Game 4	LO	XN	IP	PH	RHP	LHP
1924	PIT	NL	1	0	1	0	1	0	0	0	0	0	0	0	0	0	1	0

Rank among batters: 4,707 • *Total ballparks homered in*: 1 • *First HR*: 05/28/1924 off Vic Aldridge

George Yeager

GEORGE J. YEAGER
B: 06/04/1873 D: 06/05/1940
BR

Year	Tm	Lg	Tot	H	A	Men-On 0	Men-On 1	Men-On 2	Men-On 3	One-Game 2	One-Game 3	One-Game 4	LO	XN	IP	PH	RHP	LHP
1897	BOS	NL	2	2	0	1	1	0	0	0	0	0	0	0	0	0	2	0

George Yeager *continued*

Year	Tm	Lg	Tot	H	A	Men-On 0	Men-On 1	Men-On 2	Men-On 3	One-Game 2	One-Game 3	One-Game 4	LO	XN	IP	PH	RHP	LHP
1898	BOS	NL	3	1	2	1	1	1	0	0	0	0	0	0	0	0	3	0
Total			5	3	2	2	2	1	0	0	0	0	0	0	0	0	5	0

Rank among batters: 3,191 • *Total ballparks homered in*: 3 • *First HR*: 06/01/1897 off Bill Kissinger

Joe Yeager

JOSEPH F. YEAGER
B: 08/28/1875 D: 07/02/1937
BR

Year	Tm	Lg	Tot	H	A	Men-On 0	Men-On 1	Men-On 2	Men-On 3	One-Game 2	One-Game 3	One-Game 4	LO	XN	IP	PH	RHP	LHP
1901	DET	AL	2	0	2	1	0	0	1	0	0	0	0	0	0	0	1	1
1902	DET	AL	1	1	0	1	0	0	0	0	0	0	0	0	0	0	0	1
1907	STL	AL	1	0	1	0	1	0	0	0	0	0	0	0	0	0	1	0
Total			4	1	3	2	1	0	1	0	0	0	0	0	0	0	2	2

Rank among batters: 3,427 • *Total ballparks homered in*: 4 • *First HR*: 06/14/1901 off Win Kellum

Steve Yeager

STEPHEN WAYNE YEAGER
B: 11/24/1948
BR

Year	Tm	Lg	Tot	H	A	Men-On 0	Men-On 1	Men-On 2	Men-On 3	One-Game 2	One-Game 3	One-Game 4	LO	XN	IP	PH	RHP	LHP
1972	LA	NL	4	2	2	1	2	1	0	1	0	0	0	0	0	0	2	2
1973	LA	NL	2	0	2	1	0	1	0	0	0	0	0	0	0	0	0	2
1974	LA	NL	12	6	6	7	2	2	1	0	0	0	0	0	0	0	10	2
1975	LA	NL	12	6	6	9	1	1	1	0	0	0	0	1	0	0	10	2
1976	LA	NL	11	5	6	6	5	0	0	0	0	0	0	0	0	0	7	4
1977	LA	NL	16	10	6	10	3	2	1	0	0	0	0	0	0	0	13	3
1978	LA	NL	4	2	2	2	2	0	0	0	0	0	0	0	0	0	3	1
1979	LA	NL	13	6	7	5	4	4	0	2	0	0	0	1	0	0	6	7
1980	LA	NL	2	0	2	1	0	1	0	0	0	0	0	0	0	0	1	1
1981	LA	NL	3	1	2	3	0	0	0	0	0	0	0	0	0	0	1	2
1982	LA	NL	2	2	0	1	1	0	0	0	0	0	0	0	0	0	0	2
1983	LA	NL	15	7	8	10	5	0	0	2	0	0	0	1	0	0	9	6
1984	LA	NL	4	1	3	3	0	0	1	0	0	0	0	0	0	2	0	4
1986	SEA	AL	2	1	1	1	0	1	0	0	0	0	0	0	0	0	1	1
Total			102	49	53	60	25	13	4	5	0	0	0	3	0	2	63	39

Rank among batters: 483 • *Top target (5 home runs)*: Ken Forsch • *Number of pitchers victimized*: 82 • *Total ballparks homered in*: 14 • *First HR*: 09/04/1972 off Jim McGlothlin • *World Series HR*—4; *LCS HR*—1

Eric Yelding

ERIC GIRARD YELDING
B: 02/22/1965
BR

Year	Tm	Lg	Tot	H	A	Men-On 0	Men-On 1	Men-On 2	Men-On 3	One-Game 2	One-Game 3	One-Game 4	LO	XN	IP	PH	RHP	LHP
1990	HOU	NL	1	0	1	1	0	0	0	0	0	0	1	0	0	0	1	0
1991	HOU	NL	1	0	1	1	0	0	0	0	0	0	0	0	0	0	1	0
1993	CHI	NL	1	1	0	1	0	0	0	0	0	0	0	0	0	0	1	0
Total			3	1	2	3	0	0	0	0	0	0	1	0	0	0	3	0

Rank among batters: 3,735 • *Total ballparks homered in*: 3 • *First HR*: 09/13/1990 off Rick Mahler

Steve Yerkes

STEPHEN DOUGLAS YERKES
B: 05/15/1888 D: 01/31/1971
BR

Year	Tm	Lg	Tot	H	A	Men-On 0	Men-On 1	Men-On 2	Men-On 3	One-Game 2	One-Game 3	One-Game 4	LO	XN	IP	PH	RHP	LHP
1911	BOS	AL	1	1	0	0	1	0	0	0	0	0	0	0	0	0	1	0
1913	BOS	AL	1	0	1	0	0	1	0	0	0	0	0	0	0	0	1	0
1914	BOS	AL	1	0	1	0	1	0	0	0	0	0	0	0	0	0	1	0
	PIT	FL	1	1	0	1	0	0	0	0	0	0	0	0	0	0	1	0
	Total		2	1	1	1	1	0	0	0	0	0	0	0	0	0	2	0
1915	PIT	FL	1	0	1	1	0	0	0	0	0	0	0	0	0	0	0	1
1916	CHI	NL	1	1	0	1	0	0	0	0	0	0	0	0	0	0	1	0
Total			6	3	3	3	2	1	0	0	0	0	0	0	0	0	5	1

Rank among batters: 2,988 • *Total ballparks homered in*: 6 • *First HR*: 06/30/1911 off Ray Caldwell

Earl Yingling

EARL HERSHEY YINGLING
B: 10/29/1888 D: 10/02/1962
BL

Year	Tm	Lg	Tot	H	A	Men-On 0	Men-On 1	Men-On 2	Men-On 3	One-Game 2	One-Game 3	One-Game 4	LO	XN	IP	PH	RHP	LHP
1914	CIN	NL	1	1	0	0	1	0	0	0	0	0	0	0	1	0	1	0

Year	Tm	Lg	Tot	H	A	Men-On 0	1	2	3	One-Game 2	3	4	LO	XN	IP	PH	RHP	LHP

Earl Yingling *continued*

Rank among batters: 4,707 • *Total ballparks homered in*: 1 • *First HR*: 10/04/1914 off Al Mamaux

Jim York

JAMES HARLAN YORK
B: 08/27/1947
BR

Year	Tm	Lg	Tot	H	A	Men-On 0	1	2	3	One-Game 2	3	4	LO	XN	IP	PH	RHP	LHP
1971	KC	AL	1	0	1	0	0	1	0	0	0	0	0	0	0	0	1	0

Rank among batters: 4,707 • *Total ballparks homered in*: 1 • *First HR*: 07/24/1971 off Alan Foster

Rudy York

RUDOLPH PRESTON YORK
B: 08/17/1913 D: 02/05/1970
BR

Year	Tm	Lg	Tot	H	A	Men-On 0	1	2	3	One-Game 2	3	4	LO	XN	IP	PH	RHP	LHP
1937	DET	AL	35	17	18	15	7	11	2	3	0	0	0	1	0	1	29	6
1938	DET	AL	33	19	14	12	8	9	4	5	0	0	0	0	0	0	24	9
1939	DET	AL	20	11	9	9	7	3	1	1	0	0	0	0	0	1	14	6
1940	DET	AL	33	19	14	15	13	5	0	1	0	0	0	0	0	0	26	7
1941	DET	AL	27	18	9	15	5	5	2	0	1	0	0	0	0	0	18	9
1942	DET	AL	21	14	7	15	4	2	0	3	0	0	0	0	0	0	15	6
1943	DET	AL	34	19	15	18	10	5	1	4	0	0	0	3	0	0	27	7
1944	DET	AL	18	13	5	9	7	2	0	1	0	0	0	0	0	0	17	1
1945	DET	AL	18	9	9	11	4	3	0	1	0	0	0	0	0	0	16	2
1946	BOS	AL	17	11	6	7	6	2	2	1	0	0	0	0	0	0	15	2
1947	BOS	AL	6	3	3	2	3	1	0	0	0	0	0	0	0	0	6	0
	CHI	AL	15	5	10	6	6	3	0	0	0	0	0	1	0	0	12	3
	Total		21	8	13	8	9	4	0	0	0	0	0	1	0	0	18	3
Total			277	158	119	134	80	51	12	20	1	0	0	5	0	2	219	58

Rank among batters: 83 • *Top target (7 home runs)*: Nels Potter • *Number of pitchers victimized*: 135 • *Total ballparks homered in*: 9 • *First HR*: 04/29/1937 off Earl Whitehill • *World Series HR*—3; *All-Star HR*—1

Tom York

THOMAS JEFFERSON YORK
B: 07/13/1851 D: 02/17/1936
BL

Year	Tm	Lg	Tot	H	A	Men-On 0	1	2	3	One-Game 2	3	4	LO	XN	IP	PH	RHP	LHP
1876	HAR	NL	1	0	1	0	1	0	0	0	0	0	0	0	0	0	1	0
1877	HAR	NL	1	1	0	0	1	0	0	0	0	0	0	0	0	0	1	0
1878	PRO	NL	1	1	0	1	0	0	0	0	0	0	0	0	0	0	1	0
1879	PRO	NL	1	0	1	0	1	0	0	0	0	0	0	0	0	0	1	0
1881	PRO	NL	2	0	2	2	0	0	0	0	0	0	0	0	0	0	2	0
1882	PRO	NL	1	0	1	1	0	0	0	0	0	0	0	0	0	0	1	0
1883	CLE	NL	2	0	2	2	0	0	0	0	0	0	0	0	0	0	2	0
1884	BAL	AA	1	1	0	1	0	0	0	0	0	0	0	0	0	0	1	0
Total			10	3	7	7	3	0	0	0	0	0	0	0	0	0	10	0

Rank among batters: 2,500 • *Total ballparks homered in*: 9 • *First HR*: 07/22/1876 off Bobby Mathews

Eddie Yost

EDWARD FREDERICK YOST
B: 10/13/1926
BR

Year	Tm	Lg	Tot	H	A	Men-On 0	1	2	3	One-Game 2	3	4	LO	XN	IP	PH	RHP	LHP
1948	WAS	AL	2	0	2	2	0	0	0	0	0	0	0	0	0	0	2	0
1949	WAS	AL	9	0	9	6	2	1	0	0	0	0	0	0	0	0	6	3
1950	WAS	AL	11	1	10	7	3	1	0	0	0	0	3	0	0	0	6	5
1951	WAS	AL	12	1	11	7	3	2	0	0	0	0	1	0	0	0	7	5
1952	WAS	AL	12	0	12	9	2	1	0	0	0	0	1	0	0	0	7	5
1953	WAS	AL	9	1	8	6	3	0	0	0	0	0	2	0	0	0	4	5
1954	WAS	AL	11	4	7	10	0	1	0	0	0	0	2	0	0	0	10	1
1955	WAS	AL	7	0	7	4	3	0	0	0	0	0	2	0	0	0	7	0
1956	WAS	AL	11	9	2	7	2	1	1	1	0	0	3	0	0	0	7	4
1957	WAS	AL	9	2	7	6	3	0	0	0	0	0	2	0	0	0	7	2
1958	WAS	AL	8	5	3	5	2	0	1	1	0	0	3	0	0	0	8	0
1959	DET	AL	21	12	9	14	5	0	2	3	0	0	6	1	0	0	18	3
1960	DET	AL	14	7	7	11	3	0	0	1	0	0	3	0	0	0	12	2
1961	LA	AL	3	2	1	2	0	1	0	0	0	0	0	0	0	0	1	2
Total			139	44	95	96	31	8	4	6	0	0	28	1	0	0	102	37

Rank among batters: 311 • *Top target (6 home runs)*: Art Ditmar • *Number of pitchers victimized*: 91 • *Total ballparks homered in*: 11 • *First HR*: 09/19/1948 off Randy Gumpert

Ned Yost

EDGAR FREDERICK YOST
B: 08/19/1955
BR

Year	Tm	Lg	Tot	H	A	Men-On 0	1	2	3	One-Game 2	3	4	LO	XN	IP	PH	RHP	LHP
1981	MIL	AL	3	1	2	3	0	0	0	0	0	0	0	0	0	0	3	0
1982	MIL	AL	1	0	1	0	0	1	0	0	0	0	0	0	0	0	1	0
1983	MIL	AL	6	2	4	3	2	1	0	0	0	0	0	0	0	0	1	5
1984	TEX	AL	6	4	2	3	2	1	0	0	0	0	0	0	0	0	1	5
Total			16	7	9	9	4	3	0	0	0	0	0	0	0	0	6	10

Rank among batters: 2,029 • *Top target (2 home runs)*: Ron Guidry, Tommy John • *Number of pitchers victimized*: 14 • *Total ballparks homered in*: 8 • *First HR*: 04/20/1981 off Jackson Todd

Floyd Youmans

FLOYD EVERETT YOUMANS
B: 05/11/1964
BR

Year	Tm	Lg	Tot	H	A	Men-On 0	1	2	3	One-Game 2	3	4	LO	XN	IP	PH	RHP	LHP
1986	MON	NL	1	1	0	0	1	0	0	0	0	0	0	0	0	0	1	0
1987	MON	NL	1	0	1	1	0	0	0	0	0	0	0	0	0	0	1	0
Total			2	1	1	1	1	0	0	0	0	0	0	0	0	0	2	0

Rank among batters: 4,129 • *Total ballparks homered in*: 2 • *First HR*: 06/08/1986 off Mike Maddux

Babe Young

NORMAN ROBERT YOUNG
B: 07/01/1915 D: 12/25/1983
BL

Year	Tm	Lg	Tot	H	A	Men-On 0	1	2	3	One-Game 2	3	4	LO	XN	IP	PH	RHP	LHP
1939	NY	NL	3	2	1	1	1	1	0	1	0	0	0	0	0	0	3	0
1940	NY	NL	17	10	7	12	1	2	2	2	0	0	0	0	0	0	14	3
1941	NY	NL	25	14	11	12	8	4	1	1	0	0	0	3	1	0	20	5
1942	NY	NL	11	11	0	6	2	2	1	0	0	0	0	1	0	0	9	2
1946	NY	NL	7	5	2	4	2	1	0	0	0	0	0	0	1	1	5	2
1947	CIN	NL	14	8	6	5	6	3	0	1	0	0	0	0	1	0	11	3
1948	CIN	NL	1	0	1	1	0	0	0	0	0	0	0	0	0	0	1	0
	STL	NL	1	0	1	1	0	0	0	0	0	0	0	0	0	0	1	0
	Total		2	0	2	2	0	0	0	0	0	0	0	0	0	0	2	0
Total			79	50	29	42	20	13	4	5	0	0	0	4	3	1	64	15

Rank among batters: 661 • *Top target (4 home runs)*: Rip Sewell, Si Johnson • *Number of pitchers victimized*: 57 • *Total ballparks homered in*: 8 • *First HR*: 09/23/1939 off Danny MacFayden

Bobby Young

ROBERT GEORGE YOUNG
B: 01/22/1925 D: 01/28/1985
BL

Year	Tm	Lg	Tot	H	A	Men-On 0	1	2	3	One-Game 2	3	4	LO	XN	IP	PH	RHP	LHP
1951	STL	AL	1	1	0	1	0	0	0	0	0	0	0	0	0	0	1	0
1952	STL	AL	4	1	3	3	0	1	0	0	0	0	0	0	0	0	3	1
1953	STL	AL	4	2	2	2	2	0	0	0	0	0	0	1	0	0	3	1
1954	BAL	AL	4	0	4	4	0	0	0	0	0	0	0	0	0	0	3	1
1955	BAL	AL	1	0	1	1	0	0	0	0	0	0	0	0	0	0	1	0
1958	PHI	NL	1	1	0	1	0	0	0	0	0	0	0	0	0	0	1	0
Total			15	5	10	12	2	1	0	0	0	0	0	1	0	0	12	3

Rank among batters: 2,096 • *Total ballparks homered in*: 7 • *First HR*: 05/05/1951 off Vic Raschi

Cy Young

DENTON TRUE YOUNG
B: 03/29/1867 D: 11/04/1955
BR HOF

Year	Tm	Lg	Tot	H	A	Men-On 0	1	2	3	One-Game 2	3	4	LO	XN	IP	PH	RHP	LHP
1891	CLE	NL	1	1	0	1	0	0	0	0	0	0	0	0	0	0	0	1
1892	CLE	NL	1	0	1	0	1	0	0	0	0	0	0	0	0	0	0	1
1893	CLE	NL	1	1	0	0	0	1	0	0	0	0	0	0	0	0	0	1
1894	CLE	NL	2	0	2	1	1	0	0	0	0	0	0	0	0	0	2	0
1896	CLE	NL	3	2	1	1	2	0	0	0	0	0	0	0	0	0	3	0
1898	CLE	NL	2	0	2	2	0	0	0	1	0	0	0	0	0	0	2	0
1899	STL	NL	1	0	1	1	0	0	0	0	0	0	0	0	0	0	1	0
1900	STL	NL	1	1	0	0	0	1	0	0	0	0	0	0	0	0	1	0
1902	BOS	AL	1	0	1	0	1	0	0	0	0	0	0	0	1	0	1	0
1903	BOS	AL	1	1	0	0	1	0	0	0	0	0	0	0	1	0	0	1
1904	BOS	AL	1	1	0	1	0	0	0	0	0	0	0	0	0	0	1	0
1905	BOS	AL	2	2	0	0	1	1	0	0	0	0	0	0	0	0	1	1

Year	Tm	Lg	Tot	H	A	Men-On 0	Men-On 1	Men-On 2	Men-On 3	One-Game 2	One-Game 3	One-Game 4	LO	XN	IP	PH	RHP	LHP

Cy Young *continued*

Year	Tm	Lg	Tot	H	A	0	1	2	3	2	3	4	LO	XN	IP	PH	RHP	LHP
1907	BOS	AL	1	1	0	1	0	0	0	0	0	0	0	0	0	0	1	0
Total			18	10	8	8	7	3	0	1	0	0	0	0	2	0	13	4

Rank among batters: 1,914 • *Top target (2 home runs)*: Jack Stivetts, Willie Sudhoff • *Number of pitchers victimized*: 16 • *Total ballparks homered in*: 8 • *First HR*: 07/17/1891 off Tony Mullane

Del Young

DELMER JOHN YOUNG
B: 10/24/1885 D: 12/17/1959
BL

Year	Tm	Lg	Tot	H	A	0	1	2	3	2	3	4	LO	XN	IP	PH	RHP	LHP
1914	BUF	FL	4	1	3	2	2	0	0	0	0	0	0	0	0	1	3	1

Rank among batters: 3,427 • *Total ballparks homered in*: 3 • *First HR*: 06/12/1914 off Mordecai Brown

Del Young

DELMER EDWARD YOUNG
B: 03/11/1912 D: 12/08/1979
BB

Year	Tm	Lg	Tot	H	A	0	1	2	3	2	3	4	LO	XN	IP	PH	RHP	LHP
1939	PHI	NL	3	1	2	1	2	0	0	0	0	0	0	0	0	0	3	0

Rank among batters: 3,735 • *Total ballparks homered in*: 3 • *First HR*: 05/20/1939 off Whitey Moore

Don Young

DONALD WAYNE YOUNG
B: 10/18/1945
BR

Year	Tm	Lg	Tot	H	A	0	1	2	3	2	3	4	LO	XN	IP	PH	RHP	LHP
1965	CHI	NL	1	0	1	1	0	0	0	0	0	0	0	0	0	0	1	0
1969	CHI	NL	6	6	0	3	2	1	0	0	0	0	0	0	0	0	4	2
Total			7	6	1	4	2	1	0	0	0	0	0	0	0	0	5	2

Rank among batters: 2,834 • *Total ballparks homered in*: 2 • *First HR*: 09/10/1965 off Ron Herbel

Eric Young

ERIC ORLANDO YOUNG
B: 05/18/1967
BR

Year	Tm	Lg	Tot	H	A	0	1	2	3	2	3	4	LO	XN	IP	PH	RHP	LHP
1992	LA	NL	1	0	1	1	0	0	0	0	0	0	0	0	0	0	0	1
1993	COL	NL	3	3	0	3	0	0	0	1	0	0	1	0	0	0	3	0
1994	COL	NL	7	6	1	5	2	0	0	0	0	0	1	0	1	0	6	1
1995	COL	NL	6	5	1	4	2	0	0	0	0	0	2	0	0	0	2	4
Total			17	14	3	13	4	0	0	1	0	0	4	0	1	0	11	6

Rank among batters: 1,969 • *Top target (2 home runs)*: Jim Bullinger • *Number of pitchers victimized*: 16 • *Total ballparks homered in*: 4 • *First HR*: 09/18/1992 off Bud Black • *LCS HR*—1

Ernie Young

ERNEST WESLEY YOUNG
B: 07/08/1969
BR

Year	Tm	Lg	Tot	H	A	0	1	2	3	2	3	4	LO	XN	IP	PH	RHP	LHP
1995	OAK	AL	2	2	0	1	1	0	0	0	0	0	0	0	0	0	1	1

Rank among batters: 4,129 • *Total ballparks homered in*: 1 • *First HR*: 07/06/1995 off Scott Karl

Gerald Young

GERALD ANTHONY YOUNG
B: 10/22/1964
BB

Year	Tm	Lg	Tot	H	A	0	1	2	3	2	3	4	LO	XN	IP	PH	RHP	LHP
1987	HOU	NL	1	0	1	1	0	0	0	0	0	0	0	0	0	0	0	1
1990	HOU	NL	1	1	0	1	0	0	0	0	0	0	0	0	0	0	0	1
1991	HOU	NL	1	0	1	1	0	0	0	0	0	0	0	0	0	0	0	1
Total			3	1	2	3	0	0	0	0	0	0	0	0	0	0	0	3

Rank among batters: 3,735 • *Total ballparks homered in*: 3 • *First HR*: 09/16/1987 off Dave Dravecky

Kevin Young

KEVIN STACEY YOUNG
B: 06/16/1969
BR

Year	Tm	Lg	Tot	H	A	0	1	2	3	2	3	4	LO	XN	IP	PH	RHP	LHP
1993	PIT	NL	6	6	0	4	2	0	0	0	0	0	0	0	0	0	3	3

Kevin Young *continued*

Year	Tm	Lg	Tot	H	A	Men-On 0	1	2	3	One-Game 2	3	4	LO	XN	IP	PH	RHP	LHP
1994	PIT	NL	1	1	0	1	0	0	0	0	0	0	0	0	0	0	1	0
1995	PIT	NL	6	5	1	2	4	0	0	0	0	0	0	0	0	0	3	3
Total			13	12	1	7	6	0	0	0	0	0	0	0	0	0	7	6

Rank among batters: 2,248 • *Top target (2 home runs)*: Chris Hammond • *Number of pitchers victimized*: 12 • *Total ballparks homered in*: 2 • *First HR*: 04/09/1993 off Rod Beck

Mike Young

MICHAEL DARREN YOUNG
B: 03/20/1960
BB

Year	Tm	Lg	Tot	H	A	Men-On 0	1	2	3	One-Game 2	3	4	LO	XN	IP	PH	RHP	LHP
1984	BAL	AL	17	9	8	11	4	1	1	1	0	0	1	0	0	1	14	3
1985	BAL	AL	28	15	13	15	8	5	0	2	0	0	0	1	0	0	16	12
1986	BAL	AL	9	5	4	7	1	1	0	0	0	0	0	0	0	0	6	3
1987	BAL	AL	16	11	5	8	7	1	0	2	0	0	0	2	0	0	11	5
1988	PHI	NL	1	1	0	1	0	0	0	0	0	0	0	0	0	0	0	1
1989	CLE	AL	1	0	1	1	0	0	0	0	0	0	0	0	0	1	1	0
Total			72	41	31	43	20	8	1	5	0	0	1	3	0	2	48	24

Rank among batters: 723 • *Top target (3 home runs)*: Bruce Hurst, Guillermo Hernandez, Curt Young • *Number of pitchers victimized*: 58 • *Total ballparks homered in*: 13 • *First HR*: 05/19/1984 off Ed Vande Berg • *Switch hit HR in 1 game*—1 time

Pep Young

LEMUEL FLOYD YOUNG
B: 08/29/1907 D: 01/14/1962
BR

Year	Tm	Lg	Tot	H	A	Men-On 0	1	2	3	One-Game 2	3	4	LO	XN	IP	PH	RHP	LHP
1935	PIT	NL	7	3	4	4	2	1	0	0	0	0	0	0	2	0	5	2
1936	PIT	NL	6	3	3	1	4	1	0	1	0	0	0	0	0	0	2	4
1937	PIT	NL	9	2	7	2	5	2	0	0	0	0	0	0	1	0	8	1
1938	PIT	NL	4	0	4	2	2	0	0	0	0	0	0	0	0	0	1	3
1939	PIT	NL	3	1	2	1	1	1	0	0	0	0	0	0	0	0	3	0
1940	PIT	NL	2	0	2	1	1	0	0	0	0	0	0	0	0	0	2	0
1945	STL	NL	1	0	1	1	0	0	0	0	0	0	0	0	0	0	1	0
Total			32	9	23	12	15	5	0	1	0	0	0	0	3	0	22	10

Rank among batters: 1,360 • Top target (2 home runs): Tom Zachary, Bill Hallahan, Carl Hubbell, Cliff Melton • *Number of pitchers victimized*: 28 • *Total ballparks homered in*: 9 • *First HR*: 05/25/1935 off Huck Betts

Ralph Young

RALPH STUART YOUNG
B: 09/19/1889 D: 01/24/1965
BB

Year	Tm	Lg	Tot	H	A	Men-On 0	1	2	3	One-Game 2	3	4	LO	XN	IP	PH	RHP	LHP
1916	DET	AL	1	1	0	0	1	0	0	0	0	0	0	0	0	0	0	1
1917	DET	AL	1	0	1	0	0	1	0	0	0	0	0	0	0	0	1	0
1919	DET	AL	1	0	1	1	0	0	0	0	0	0	0	0	0	0	1	0
1922	PHI	AL	1	0	1	1	0	0	0	0	0	0	1	0	1	0	1	0
Total			4	1	3	2	1	1	0	0	0	0	1	0	1	0	3	1

Rank among batters: 3,427 • *Total ballparks homered in*: 3 • *First HR*: 09/22/1916 off Claude Thomas

Russ Young

RUSSELL CHARLES YOUNG
B: 09/15/1902 D: 05/13/1984
BB

Year	Tm	Lg	Tot	H	A	Men-On 0	1	2	3	One-Game 2	3	4	LO	XN	IP	PH	RHP	LHP
1931	STL	AL	1	1	0	1	0	0	0	0	0	0	0	0	0	0	0	1

Rank among batters: 4,707 • *Total ballparks homered in*: 1 • *First HR*: 07/04/1931 off Pat Caraway

Joel Youngblood

JOEL RANDOLPH YOUNGBLOOD
B: 08/28/1951
BR

Year	Tm	Lg	Tot	H	A	Men-On 0	1	2	3	One-Game 2	3	4	LO	XN	IP	PH	RHP	LHP
1978	NY	NL	7	3	4	6	1	0	0	0	0	0	0	0	0	0	5	2
1979	NY	NL	16	8	8	10	5	1	0	0	0	0	1	1	0	0	9	7
1980	NY	NL	8	6	2	2	6	0	0	0	0	0	0	1	0	0	3	5
1981	NY	NL	4	2	2	2	0	2	0	0	0	0	0	0	0	0	2	2
1982	NY	NL	3	2	1	2	0	1	0	0	0	0	0	0	0	0	2	1
1983	SF	NL	17	6	11	8	7	2	0	1	0	0	0	0	0	0	9	8
1984	SF	NL	10	6	4	8	1	1	0	0	0	0	0	0	0	0	7	3

Year	Tm	Lg	Tot	H	A	Men-On				One-Game			LO	XN	IP	PH	RHP	LHP
						0	1	2	3	2	3	4						

Joel Youngblood *continued*

Year	Tm	Lg	Tot	H	A	0	1	2	3	2	3	4	LO	XN	IP	PH	RHP	LHP
1985	SF	NL	4	1	3	2	1	1	0	0	0	0	0	0	0	1	3	1
1986	SF	NL	5	0	5	3	2	0	0	0	0	0	0	0	0	1	5	0
1987	SF	NL	3	2	1	3	0	0	0	0	0	0	0	0	0	3	1	2
1989	CIN	NL	3	1	2	2	0	1	0	0	0	0	0	0	0	1	1	2
Total			80	37	43	48	23	9	0	1	0	0	1	2	0	6	47	33

Rank among batters: 650 • *Top target (5 home runs)*: Steve Carlton • *Number of pitchers victimized*: 62 • *Total ballparks homered in*: 12 • *First HR*: 06/07/1978 off Burt Hooton

Royce Youngs

ROYCE MIDDLEBROOK YOUNGS
B: 04/10/1897 D: 10/22/1927
BL HOF

Year	Tm	Lg	Tot	H	A	0	1	2	3	2	3	4	LO	XN	IP	PH	RHP	LHP
1918	NY	NL	1	1	0	0	1	0	0	0	0	0	0	0	1	0	0	1
1919	NY	NL	2	2	0	2	0	0	0	0	0	0	0	0	0	0	0	2
1920	NY	NL	6	5	1	4	2	0	0	0	0	0	0	0	1	0	5	1
1921	NY	NL	3	2	1	1	1	1	0	0	0	0	0	0	1	0	2	1
1922	NY	NL	7	2	5	3	4	0	0	0	0	0	0	0	2	0	6	1
1923	NY	NL	3	2	1	1	1	1	0	0	0	0	0	2	2	0	2	1
1924	NY	NL	10	7	3	8	1	1	0	0	0	0	2	0	0	0	9	1
1925	NY	NL	6	5	1	2	2	2	0	0	0	0	1	0	1	0	2	4
1926	NY	NL	4	4	0	1	1	2	0	0	0	0	0	0	0	0	3	1
Total			42	30	12	22	13	7	0	0	0	0	3	2	8	0	29	13

Rank among batters: 1,138 • *Top target (3 home runs)*: Wilbur Cooper • *Number of pitchers victimized*: 33 • *Total ballparks homered in*: 6 • *First HR*: 06/14/1918 off Hippo Vaughn • *Hit for Cycle*—@BOS: 04/29/1922 • *World Series HR*—1

Robin Yount

ROBIN R. YOUNT
B: 09/16/1955
BR

Year	Tm	Lg	Tot	H	A	0	1	2	3	2	3	4	LO	XN	IP	PH	RHP	LHP
1974	MIL	AL	3	3	0	1	2	0	0	0	0	0	0	0	0	0	1	2
1975	MIL	AL	8	4	4	5	2	1	0	0	0	0	0	0	0	0	5	3
1976	MIL	AL	2	1	1	1	1	0	0	0	0	0	0	0	0	0	2	0
1977	MIL	AL	4	2	2	1	1	2	0	0	0	0	0	0	0	0	4	0
1978	MIL	AL	9	5	4	4	4	1	0	1	0	0	1	0	0	0	7	2
1979	MIL	AL	8	4	4	5	1	2	0	0	0	0	0	0	2	0	7	1
1980	MIL	AL	23	13	10	15	5	1	2	1	0	0	0	0	1	0	16	7
1981	MIL	AL	10	1	9	6	2	2	0	1	0	0	0	0	0	0	6	4
1982	MIL	AL	29	9	20	16	10	3	0	7	0	0	0	1	1	0	22	7
1983	MIL	AL	17	6	11	10	5	2	0	0	0	0	0	1	0	0	13	4
1984	MIL	AL	16	8	8	6	9	0	1	2	0	0	0	0	0	0	11	5
1985	MIL	AL	15	11	4	8	7	0	0	1	0	0	0	0	0	0	11	4
1986	MIL	AL	9	4	5	7	2	0	0	0	0	0	1	0	0	0	6	3
1987	MIL	AL	21	12	9	9	10	2	0	0	0	0	0	0	0	0	19	2
1988	MIL	AL	13	7	6	9	4	0	0	0	0	0	0	0	1	0	6	7
1989	MIL	AL	21	14	7	14	4	3	0	1	0	0	0	0	0	0	15	6
1990	MIL	AL	17	8	9	7	6	4	0	0	0	0	0	0	1	0	12	5
1991	MIL	AL	10	8	2	4	3	3	0	0	0	0	0	2	0	0	8	2
1992	MIL	AL	8	3	5	4	4	0	0	0	0	0	0	1	0	0	6	2
1993	MIL	AL	8	1	7	8	0	0	0	0	0	0	0	0	0	0	6	2
Total			251	124	127	140	82	26	3	14	0	0	2	5	6	0	183	68

Rank among batters: 108 • *Top target (6 home runs)*: Larry Gura • *Number of pitchers victimized*: 183 • *Total ballparks homered in*: 16 • *First HR*: 04/13/1974 off Ross Grimsley • *Hit for Cycle*—@CHI: 06/12/1988 • *World Series HR*—1

Sal Yvars

SALVADOR ANTHONY YVARS
B: 02/20/1924
BR

Year	Tm	Lg	Tot	H	A	0	1	2	3	2	3	4	LO	XN	IP	PH	RHP	LHP
1948	NY	NL	1	1	0	1	0	0	0	0	0	0	0	0	0	0	1	0
1951	NY	NL	2	2	0	1	1	0	0	0	0	0	0	1	0	0	1	1
1952	NY	NL	4	3	1	2	2	0	0	0	0	0	0	0	0	0	1	3
1953	STL	NL	1	0	1	1	0	0	0	0	0	0	0	0	0	0	1	0
1954	STL	NL	2	0	2	1	1	0	0	0	0	0	0	0	0	1	1	1
Total			10	6	4	6	4	0	0	0	0	0	0	1	0	1	5	5

Rank among batters: 2,500 • *Top target (2 home runs)*: Warren Spahn • *Number of pitchers victimized*: 9 • *Total ballparks homered in*: 3 • *First HR*: 09/28/1948 off Lou Possehl

Tom Zachary

JONATHAN THOMPSON WALTON ZACHARY
B: 05/07/1896 D: 01/24/1969
BL

Year	Tm	Lg	Tot	H	A	Men-On 0	1	2	3	One-Game 2	3	4	LO	XN	IP	PH	RHP	LHP
1922	WAS	AL	1	0	1	1	0	0	0	0	0	0	0	0	0	0	1	0
1925	WAS	AL	1	1	0	1	0	0	0	0	0	0	0	0	0	0	1	0
1926	STL	AL	1	1	0	0	1	0	0	0	0	0	0	0	0	0	1	0
1928	NY	AL	1	0	1	0	1	0	0	0	0	0	0	0	0	0	1	0
1930	BOS	NL	2	2	0	2	0	0	0	0	0	0	0	0	0	0	1	1
Total			6	4	2	4	2	0	0	0	0	0	0	0	0	0	5	1

Rank among batters: 2,988 • *Total ballparks homered in*: 5 • *First HR*: 09/30/1922 off Slim Harriss

Eddie Zambrano

EDUARDO JOSE (GUERRA) ZAMBRANO
B: 02/01/1966
BR

Year	Tm	Lg	Tot	H	A	Men-On 0	1	2	3	One-Game 2	3	4	LO	XN	IP	PH	RHP	LHP
1994	CHI	NL	6	1	5	4	2	0	0	1	0	0	0	0	0	0	2	4

Rank among batters: 2,988 • *Total ballparks homered in*: 5 • *First HR*: 04/09/1994 off Jeff Fassero

Al Zarilla

ALLEN LEE ZARILLA
B: 05/01/1919
BL

Year	Tm	Lg	Tot	H	A	Men-On 0	1	2	3	One-Game 2	3	4	LO	XN	IP	PH	RHP	LHP
1943	STL	AL	2	2	0	1	0	1	0	0	0	0	0	0	0	0	2	0
1944	STL	AL	6	4	2	4	2	0	0	0	0	0	0	0	0	0	6	0
1946	STL	AL	4	1	3	2	1	1	0	0	0	0	0	0	0	0	4	0
1947	STL	AL	3	2	1	3	0	0	0	0	0	0	0	0	0	0	2	1
1948	STL	AL	12	6	6	7	4	1	0	0	0	0	0	0	0	0	11	1
1949	STL	AL	1	0	1	0	1	0	0	0	0	0	0	0	0	0	1	0
	BOS	AL	9	7	2	3	2	3	1	0	0	0	0	0	1	0	8	1
	Total		10	7	3	3	3	3	1	0	0	0	0	0	1	0	9	1
1950	BOS	AL	9	2	7	6	3	0	0	0	0	0	0	0	0	0	5	4
1951	CHI	AL	10	3	7	2	7	1	0	0	0	0	0	0	0	0	10	0
1952	CHI	AL	2	1	1	0	2	0	0	0	0	0	0	0	0	0	2	0
	STL	AL	1	1	0	0	1	0	0	0	0	0	0	0	0	0	1	0
	BOS	AL	2	0	2	1	1	0	0	0	0	0	0	0	0	0	2	0
	Total		5	2	3	1	4	0	0	0	0	0	0	0	0	0	5	0
Total			61	29	32	29	24	7	1	0	0	0	0	0	1	0	54	7

Rank among batters: 844 • *Top target (3 home runs)*: Al Widmar, Steve Gromek • *Number of pitchers victimized*: 49 • *Total ballparks homered in*: 8 • *First HR*: 08/29/1943 off Tommy Bridges

Norm Zauchin

NORBERT HENRY ZAUCHIN
B: 11/17/1929
BR

Year	Tm	Lg	Tot	H	A	Men-On 0	1	2	3	One-Game 2	3	4	LO	XN	IP	PH	RHP	LHP
1955	BOS	AL	27	17	10	10	9	7	1	1	1	0	0	1	0	0	23	4
1956	BOS	AL	2	2	0	2	0	0	0	0	0	0	0	0	0	0	2	0
1957	BOS	AL	3	1	2	1	0	2	0	0	0	0	0	0	0	0	2	1
1958	WAS	AL	15	6	9	10	4	1	0	0	0	0	0	1	0	0	14	1
1959	WAS	AL	3	0	3	2	1	0	0	0	0	0	0	0	0	0	3	0
Total			50	26	24	25	14	10	1	1	1	0	0	2	0	0	44	6

Rank among batters: 991 • *Top target (4 home runs)*: Art Ditmar • *Number of pitchers victimized*: 36 • *Total ballparks homered in*: 8 • *First HR*: 04/26/1955 off Arnie Portocarrero

Greg Zaun

GREGORY OWEN ZAUN
B: 04/14/1971
BB

Year	Tm	Lg	Tot	H	A	Men-On 0	1	2	3	One-Game 2	3	4	LO	XN	IP	PH	RHP	LHP
1995	BAL	AL	3	1	2	2	1	0	0	0	0	0	0	0	0	0	2	1

Rank among batters: 3,735 • *Total ballparks homered in*: 3 • *First HR*: 07/02/1995 off Woody Williams

Joe Zdeb

JOSEPH EDMUND ZDEB
B: 06/27/1953
BR

Year	Tm	Lg	Tot	H	A	Men-On 0	1	2	3	One-Game 2	3	4	LO	XN	IP	PH	RHP	LHP
1977	KC	AL	2	0	2	0	1	1	0	0	0	0	0	0	0	1	1	1

Rank among batters: 4,129 • *Total ballparks homered in*: 2 • *First HR*: 06/25/1977 off Bob Lacey

George Zeber

GEORGE WILLIAM ZEBER
B: 08/29/1950
BB

Year	Tm	Lg	Tot	H	A	Men-On 0	Men-On 1	Men-On 2	Men-On 3	One-Game 2	One-Game 3	One-Game 4	LO	XN	IP	PH	RHP	LHP
1977	NY	AL	3	0	3	1	2	0	0	0	0	0	0	0	0	0	1	2

Rank among batters: 3,735 • *Total ballparks homered in*: 3 • *First HR*: 06/05/1977 off Dave Hamilton

Rollie Zeider

ROLLIE HUBERT ZEIDER
B: 11/16/1883 D: 09/12/1967
BR

Year	Tm	Lg	Tot	H	A	Men-On 0	Men-On 1	Men-On 2	Men-On 3	One-Game 2	One-Game 3	One-Game 4	LO	XN	IP	PH	RHP	LHP
1911	CHI	AL	2	1	1	1	1	0	0	0	0	0	0	0	0	1	2	0
1912	CHI	AL	1	1	0	1	0	0	0	0	0	0	0	0	0	0	1	0
1914	CHI	FL	1	1	0	0	0	0	1	0	0	0	0	0	0	0	0	1
1916	CHI	NL	1	1	0	0	1	0	0	0	0	0	0	0	0	0	0	1
Total			5	4	1	2	2	0	1	0	0	0	0	0	0	1	3	2

Rank among batters: 3,191 • *Total ballparks homered in*: 3 • *First HR*: 07/04/1911 off Ed Summers

Todd Zeile

TODD EDWARD ZEILE
B: 09/09/1965
BR

Year	Tm	Lg	Tot	H	A	Men-On 0	Men-On 1	Men-On 2	Men-On 3	One-Game 2	One-Game 3	One-Game 4	LO	XN	IP	PH	RHP	LHP
1989	STL	NL	1	0	1	1	0	0	0	0	0	0	0	0	0	0	1	0
1990	STL	NL	15	8	7	10	4	1	0	0	0	0	0	0	0	0	9	6
1991	STL	NL	11	7	4	9	1	1	0	0	0	0	0	1	0	0	7	4
1992	STL	NL	7	4	3	5	2	0	0	0	0	0	0	0	0	0	6	1
1993	STL	NL	17	8	9	7	3	5	2	0	0	0	0	0	0	0	13	4
1994	STL	NL	19	9	10	6	7	5	1	2	0	0	0	0	0	0	12	7
1995	STL	NL	5	2	3	3	2	0	0	1	0	0	0	0	0	0	5	0
	CHI	NL	9	6	3	4	5	0	0	0	0	0	0	0	0	0	6	3
	Total		14	8	6	7	7	0	0	1	0	0	0	0	0	0	11	3
Total			84	44	40	45	24	12	3	3	0	0	0	1	0	0	59	25

Rank among batters: 617 • *Top target (3 home runs)*: Brian Williams, John Smiley • *Number of pitchers victimized*: 72 • *Total ballparks homered in*: 15 • *First HR*: 08/20/1989 off Tim Leary

Gus Zernial

GUS EDWARD ZERNIAL
B: 06/27/1923
BR

Year	Tm	Lg	Tot	H	A	Men-On 0	Men-On 1	Men-On 2	Men-On 3	One-Game 2	One-Game 3	One-Game 4	LO	XN	IP	PH	RHP	LHP
1949	CHI	AL	5	2	3	3	0	2	0	0	0	0	0	0	0	1	3	2
1950	CHI	AL	29	19	10	13	13	3	0	2	1	0	0	1	0	0	18	11
1951	PHI	AL	33	21	12	8	18	5	2	6	0	0	0	0	0	0	29	4
1952	PHI	AL	29	18	11	12	11	3	3	4	0	0	0	0	0	0	23	6
1953	PHI	AL	42	20	22	26	9	6	1	6	0	0	0	0	1	1	33	9
1954	PHI	AL	14	5	9	6	3	4	1	3	0	0	0	0	0	1	8	6
1955	KC	AL	30	14	16	16	8	4	2	4	0	0	0	0	0	1	21	9
1956	KC	AL	16	7	9	8	7	1	0	2	0	0	0	0	0	1	11	5
1957	KC	AL	27	12	15	14	10	3	0	3	0	0	0	1	0	1	22	5
1958	DET	AL	5	2	3	4	1	0	0	0	0	0	0	0	0	3	5	0
1959	DET	AL	7	5	2	4	1	2	0	1	0	0	0	0	0	1	4	3
Total			237	125	112	114	81	33	9	31	1	0	0	2	1	10	177	60

Rank among batters: 132 • *Top target (10 home runs)*: Ned Garver • *Number of pitchers victimized*: 116 • *Total ballparks homered in*: 10 • *First HR*: 04/22/1949 off Red Embree

Benny Zientara

BENEDICT JOSEPH ZIENTARA
B: 02/14/1920 D: 04/16/1985
BR

Year	Tm	Lg	Tot	H	A	Men-On 0	Men-On 1	Men-On 2	Men-On 3	One-Game 2	One-Game 3	One-Game 4	LO	XN	IP	PH	RHP	LHP
1947	CIN	NL	2	0	2	0	1	1	0	0	0	0	0	0	0	0	2	0

Rank among batters: 4,129 • *Total ballparks homered in*: 2 • *First HR*: 06/09/1947 off Hugh Casey

Chief Zimmer

CHARLES LOUIS ZIMMER
B: 11/23/1860 D: 08/22/1949
BR

Year	Tm	Lg	Tot	H	A	Men-On 0	Men-On 1	Men-On 2	Men-On 3	One-Game 2	One-Game 3	One-Game 4	LO	XN	IP	PH	RHP	LHP
1889	CLE	NL	1	0	1	0	0	1	0	0	0	0	0	0	0	0	1	0

Chief Zimmer *continued*

Year	Tm	Lg	Tot	H	A	Men-On 0	Men-On 1	Men-On 2	Men-On 3	One-Game 2	One-Game 3	One-Game 4	LO	XN	IP	PH	RHP	LHP
1890	CLE	NL	2	2	0	0	0	1	1	0	0	0	0	0	0	0	2	0
1891	CLE	NL	3	0	3	1	1	1	0	0	0	0	0	0	0	0	2	1
1892	CLE	NL	1	0	1	0	0	1	0	0	0	0	0	0	0	0	1	0
1893	CLE	NL	2	1	1	0	0	2	0	0	0	0	0	0	0	0	2	0
1894	CLE	NL	4	0	4	2	2	0	0	0	0	0	0	0	0	0	4	0
1895	CLE	NL	5	1	4	2	0	1	2	1	0	0	0	0	0	0	3	2
1896	CLE	NL	3	3	0	2	1	0	0	0	0	0	0	0	0	0	3	0
1899	CLE	NL	2	1	1	1	0	1	0	0	0	0	0	0	0	0	0	2
	LOU	NL	2	1	1	0	1	1	0	0	0	0	0	0	1	0	1	1
	Total		4	2	2	1	1	2	0	0	0	0	0	0	1	0	1	3
1903	PHI	NL	1	0	1	0	0	1	0	0	0	0	0	0	0	0	1	0
Total			26	9	17	8	5	10	3	1	0	0	0	0	1	0	20	6

Rank among batters: 1,576 • *Top target (3 home runs)*: Kid Nichols • *Number of pitchers victimized*: 22 • *Total ballparks homered in*: 14 • *First HR*: 09/09/1889 off Tim Keefe

Don Zimmer

DONALD WILLIAM ZIMMER
B: 01/17/1931
BR

Year	Tm	Lg	Tot	H	A	Men-On 0	Men-On 1	Men-On 2	Men-On 3	One-Game 2	One-Game 3	One-Game 4	LO	XN	IP	PH	RHP	LHP
1955	BRO	NL	15	6	9	6	7	1	1	3	0	0	0	0	0	0	13	2
1957	BRO	NL	6	3	3	5	1	0	0	0	0	0	0	2	0	0	6	0
1958	LA	NL	17	11	6	10	3	4	0	1	0	0	0	0	0	0	15	2
1959	LA	NL	4	1	3	1	1	2	0	0	0	0	0	0	0	0	4	0
1960	CHI	NL	6	2	4	4	2	0	0	0	0	0	0	0	0	0	5	1
1961	CHI	NL	13	3	10	6	7	0	0	1	0	0	0	2	0	1	11	2
1962	CIN	NL	2	1	1	2	0	0	0	0	0	0	0	0	0	0	1	1
1963	LA	NL	1	0	1	1	0	0	0	0	0	0	0	0	0	1	1	0
	WAS	AL	13	3	10	6	5	0	2	1	0	0	0	0	0	1	10	3
	Total		14	3	11	7	5	0	2	1	0	0	0	0	0	2	11	3
1964	WAS	AL	12	6	6	10	1	0	1	1	0	0	1	0	0	1	12	0
1965	WAS	AL	2	1	1	2	0	0	0	0	0	0	0	0	0	1	0	2
Total			91	37	54	53	27	7	4	7	0	0	1	4	0	5	78	13

Rank among batters: 559 • *Top target (4 home runs)*: Lew Burdette, Robin Roberts • *Number of pitchers victimized*: 72 • *Total ballparks homered in*: 18 • *First HR*: 04/19/1955 off Curt Simmons

Eddie Zimmerman

EDWARD DESMOND ZIMMERMAN
B: 01/04/1883 D: 05/06/1945
BR

Year	Tm	Lg	Tot	H	A	Men-On 0	Men-On 1	Men-On 2	Men-On 3	One-Game 2	One-Game 3	One-Game 4	LO	XN	IP	PH	RHP	LHP
1911	BRO	NL	3	1	2	1	0	2	0	0	0	0	0	0	2	0	3	0

Rank among batters: 3,735 • *Total ballparks homered in*: 3 • *First HR*: 05/05/1911 off Toots Shultz

Heinie Zimmerman

HENRY ZIMMERMAN
B: 02/09/1887 D: 03/14/1969
BR

Year	Tm	Lg	Tot	H	A	Men-On 0	Men-On 1	Men-On 2	Men-On 3	One-Game 2	One-Game 3	One-Game 4	LO	XN	IP	PH	RHP	LHP
1910	CHI	NL	3	1	2	2	1	0	0	1	0	0	1	0	0	0	3	0
1911	CHI	NL	9	3	6	2	3	4	0	1	0	0	0	0	1	0	5	4
1912	CHI	NL	14	7	7	6	8	0	0	1	0	0	0	1	0	0	7	7
1913	CHI	NL	9	4	5	3	4	2	0	1	0	0	0	0	1	0	5	4
1914	CHI	NL	4	1	3	1	1	1	1	0	0	0	0	0	1	0	3	1
1915	CHI	NL	3	2	1	2	1	0	0	0	0	0	0	0	0	0	2	1
1916	CHI	NL	6	5	1	4	1	1	0	1	0	0	0	0	0	0	3	3
1917	NY	NL	5	4	1	2	2	1	0	0	0	0	0	0	1	0	2	3
1918	NY	NL	1	1	0	1	0	0	0	0	0	0	0	0	0	0	0	1
1919	NY	NL	4	3	1	2	1	1	0	0	0	0	0	0	0	0	4	0
Total			58	31	27	25	22	10	1	5	0	0	1	1	4	0	34	24

Rank among batters: 886 • *Top target (6 home runs)*: Lefty Tyler • *Number of pitchers victimized*: 45 • *Total ballparks homered in*: 11 • *First HR*: 06/23/1910 off Babe Adams

Jerry Zimmerman

GERALD ROBERT ZIMMERMAN
B: 09/21/1934
BR

Year	Tm	Lg	Tot	H	A	Men-On 0	Men-On 1	Men-On 2	Men-On 3	One-Game 2	One-Game 3	One-Game 4	LO	XN	IP	PH	RHP	LHP
1965	MIN	AL	1	1	0	0	1	0	0	0	0	0	0	0	0	0	1	0

Jerry Zimmerman *continued*

Year	Tm	Lg	Tot	H	A	Men-On 0	1	2	3	One-Game 2	3	4	LO	XN	IP	PH	RHP	LHP
1966	MIN	AL	1	1	0	0	1	0	0	0	0	0	0	0	0	0	1	0
1967	MIN	AL	1	1	0	0	1	0	0	0	0	0	0	0	0	0	1	0
Total			3	3	0	0	3	0	0	0	0	0	0	0	0	0	3	0

Rank among batters: 3,735 • *Total ballparks homered in*: 1 • *First HR*: 06/06/1965 off Phil Ortega

Roy Zimmerman

ROY FRANKLIN ZIMMERMAN
B: 09/13/1916
BL

Year	Tm	Lg	Tot	H	A	Men-On 0	1	2	3	One-Game 2	3	4	LO	XN	IP	PH	RHP	LHP
1945	NY	NL	5	1	4	2	3	0	0	0	0	0	0	0	1	0	3	2

Rank among batters: 3,191 • *Total ballparks homered in*: 4 • *First HR*: 09/03/1945 off Charlie Sproull

Guy Zinn

GUY ZINN
B: 02/13/1887 D: 10/06/1949
BL

Year	Tm	Lg	Tot	H	A	Men-On 0	1	2	3	One-Game 2	3	4	LO	XN	IP	PH	RHP	LHP
1912	NY	AL	6	4	2	3	0	3	0	0	0	0	0	1	0	0	5	1
1913	BOS	NL	1	0	1	0	1	0	0	0	0	0	0	0	0	0	1	0
1914	BAL	FL	3	2	1	0	2	1	0	0	0	0	0	0	0	1	3	0
1915	BAL	FL	5	5	0	3	1	0	1	0	0	0	0	0	0	0	5	0
Total			15	11	4	6	4	4	1	0	0	0	0	1	0	1	14	1

Rank among batters: 2,096 • *Top target (2 home runs)*: Mike Prendergast • *Number of pitchers victimized*: 14 • *Total ballparks homered in*: 6 • *First HR*: 05/21/1912 off George Mogridge

Jimmy Zinn

JAMES EDWARD ZINN
B: 01/21/1895 D: 02/26/1991
BL

Year	Tm	Lg	Tot	H	A	Men-On 0	1	2	3	One-Game 2	3	4	LO	XN	IP	PH	RHP	LHP
1919	PHI	AL	1	1	0	0	0	1	0	0	0	0	0	0	0	1	1	0
1929	CLE	AL	1	0	1	1	0	0	0	0	0	0	0	0	0	0	1	0
Total			2	1	1	1	0	1	0	0	0	0	0	0	0	1	2	0

Rank among batters: 4,129 • *Total ballparks homered in*: 2 • *First HR*: 09/15/1919 off Red Faber

Bud Zipfel

MARION SYLVESTER ZIPFEL
B: 11/18/1938
BL

Year	Tm	Lg	Tot	H	A	Men-On 0	1	2	3	One-Game 2	3	4	LO	XN	IP	PH	RHP	LHP
1961	WAS	AL	4	1	3	3	1	0	0	0	0	0	0	1	0	0	4	0
1962	WAS	AL	6	1	5	5	1	0	0	0	0	0	0	2	0	0	5	1
Total			10	2	8	8	2	0	0	0	0	0	0	3	0	0	9	1

Rank among batters: 2,500 • *Top target (2 home runs)*: Phil Regan • *Number of pitchers victimized*: 9 • *Total ballparks homered in*: 8 • *First HR*: 08/02/1961 off Phil Regan

Richie Zisk

RICHARD WALTER ZISK
B: 02/06/1949
BR

Year	Tm	Lg	Tot	H	A	Men-On 0	1	2	3	One-Game 2	3	4	LO	XN	IP	PH	RHP	LHP
1971	PIT	NL	1	1	0	0	1	0	0	0	0	0	0	0	0	0	0	1
1973	PIT	NL	10	4	6	6	3	0	1	0	0	0	0	0	0	0	5	5
1974	PIT	NL	17	8	9	9	5	2	1	1	0	0	0	0	0	1	5	12
1975	PIT	NL	20	8	12	15	4	1	0	2	0	0	0	0	0	0	16	4
1976	PIT	NL	21	8	13	12	8	1	0	0	0	0	0	1	0	1	8	13
1977	CHI	AL	30	12	18	16	10	4	0	4	0	0	0	0	0	0	21	9
1978	TEX	AL	22	13	9	12	8	1	1	0	0	0	0	2	0	0	14	8
1979	TEX	AL	18	10	8	14	2	2	0	0	0	0	0	0	0	1	8	10
1980	TEX	AL	19	11	8	10	6	3	0	1	0	0	0	1	0	1	8	11
1981	SEA	AL	16	10	6	14	1	1	0	0	0	0	0	0	0	0	13	3
1982	SEA	AL	21	8	13	13	7	1	0	1	0	0	0	0	0	0	14	7
1983	SEA	AL	12	8	4	8	4	0	0	2	0	0	0	0	0	0	1	11
Total			207	101	106	129	59	16	3	11	0	0	0	4	0	4	113	94

Rank among batters: 169 • *Top target (5 home runs)*: Geoff Zahn • *Number of pitchers victimized*: 146 • *Total ballparks homered in*: 27 • *First HR*: 09/18/1971 off Ray Sadecki • *Hit for Cycle*—@SF: 06/09/1974

Year	Tm	Lg	Tot	H	A	Men-On 0	Men-On 1	Men-On 2	Men-On 3	One-Game 2	One-Game 3	One-Game 4	LO	XN	IP	PH	RHP	LHP

William Zitzmann

WILLIAM ARTHUR ZITZMANN
B: 11/19/1895 D: 05/29/1985
BR

Year	Tm	Lg	Tot	H	A	0	1	2	3	2	3	4	LO	XN	IP	PH	RHP	LHP
1928	CIN	NL	3	1	2	1	2	0	0	0	0	0	0	0	1	0	2	1

Rank among batters: 3,735 • *Total ballparks homered in*: 3 • *First HR*: 06/09/1928 off Jesse Petty

Bob Zupcic

ROBERT ZUPCIC
B: 08/18/1966
BR

Year	Tm	Lg	Tot	H	A	0	1	2	3	2	3	4	LO	XN	IP	PH	RHP	LHP
1991	BOS	AL	1	1	0	1	0	0	0	0	0	0	0	0	0	0	1	0
1992	BOS	AL	3	3	0	1	0	0	2	0	0	0	0	0	0	0	3	0
1993	BOS	AL	2	1	1	2	0	0	0	0	0	0	0	0	0	0	0	2
1994	CHI	AL	1	0	1	1	0	0	0	0	0	0	0	0	0	0	0	1
Total			7	5	2	5	0	0	2	0	0	0	0	0	0	0	4	3

Rank among batters: 2,834 • *Total ballparks homered in*: 3 • *First HR*: 09/21/1991 off Dave Eiland

Paul Zuvella

PAUL ZUVELLA
B: 10/31/1958
BR

Year	Tm	Lg	Tot	H	A	0	1	2	3	2	3	4	LO	XN	IP	PH	RHP	LHP
1989	CLE	AL	2	2	0	2	0	0	0	0	0	0	0	0	0	0	2	0

Rank among batters: 4,129 • *Total ballparks homered in*: 1 • *First HR*: 07/14/1989 off Charlie Hough

Edward Zwilling

EDWARD HARRISON ZWILLING
B: 11/02/1888 D: 03/27/1978
BL

Year	Tm	Lg	Tot	H	A	0	1	2	3	2	3	4	LO	XN	IP	PH	RHP	LHP
1914	CHI	FL	16	9	7	8	7	1	0	1	0	0	0	0	1	0	16	0
1915	CHI	FL	13	11	2	8	4	1	0	1	0	0	0	0	0	0	10	3
1916	CHI	NL	1	1	0	1	0	0	0	0	0	0	0	0	0	0	1	0
Total			30	21	9	17	11	2	0	2	0	0	0	0	1	0	27	3

Rank among batters: 1,437 • *Top target (3 home runs)*: Happy Finneran, Thomas Seaton • *Number of pitchers victimized*: 20 • *Total ballparks homered in*: 5 • *First HR*: 04/28/1914 off Frank Smith

SABR: It's A Blast

The Society for American Baseball Research (SABR) was founded in Cooperstown, New York, in 1971 and has been thriving and contributing to the understanding of the game ever since. SABR's objectives are to foster the study of baseball as a significant American institution, to establish an accurate historical account of baseball through the years, to facilitate the dissemination of baseball research information, and to stimulate the best interests of baseball as our national pastime.

Membership in SABR is open to anyone who loves to read about, talk about, write about, learn more about, or simply derive greater pleasure from the game. The society sponsors seventeen research committees, ranging alphabetically from Ballparks to Women in Baseball, has regional groups around the world, and holds a national convention each summer. Members come from all walks of life, united by a love for baseball and interest in learning more about the game.

Every year, SABR members receive *The Baseball Research Journal, The National Pastime,* and one or more special publications such as *Minor League Baseball Stars, The Negro Leagues Book,* or *Nineteenth Century Stars*. They also receive *The SABR Bulletin* and a membership directory that helps them tap into this network of baseball interest that currently numbers over 6,300 members.

Whether you're a researcher yourself, would like to receive SABR's quality publications, or simply enjoy SABR's camaraderie, you can join by sending your name, address, phone number and $35 ($45 Canada/Mexico, $50 overseas) to SABR, Dept. HR, P.O. Box 93183, Cleveland, OH, 44101, or call (216) 575–0500.